Comprehensive Concordance

of the

NEW WORLD TRANSLATION OF THE HOLY SCRIPTURES

"The understanding heart is one
that searches for knowledge."
—Proverbs 15:14.

200,000 copies

PUBLISHERS
WATCHTOWER BIBLE AND TRACT SOCIETY
OF NEW YORK, INC.
INTERNATIONAL BIBLE STUDENTS ASSOCIATION
Brooklyn, New York, U.S.A.

Printed in the United States of America

FOREWORD

This *Comprehensive Concordance* is designed to aid you in locating words and Scripture passages in the *New World Translation of the Holy Scriptures.*

A number of fine concordances have been produced in the past two centuries, the majority of which have been for use with the King James Version of the Bible. However, since 1950, millions of copies of the *New World Translation* have been printed and distributed world wide. Many of these are in the hands of persons who are diligent students of the Bible and who would therefore make good use of a concordance designed for this translation, since it is the one they most often use.

In this *Comprehensive Concordance* you will find listed every occurrence of all the principal words in the *New World Translation* (1971 edition). This has required some 14,700 word headings and a total of about 333,200 entries.

Use of a concordance can save much time in searching out desired Bible verses. Also, a complete listing of the occurrences of Bible words, such as is found in this *Comprehensive Concordance,* can assist one to ascertain what the Bible really teaches on any subject. It enables one to get a balanced, Biblical view of the topics that one studies. By showing all the various settings in which a term is used it also helps one to resolve any seeming discrepancies.

HOW TO USE THIS CONCORDANCE

When you look up a word in this *Comprehensive Concordance,* you will find the occurrences of the word listed in the order in which they appear in the Bible. In each case the location of the text is shown. This is followed by a brief excerpt showing the immediate context of the word, to enable you to determine whether it is the reference that you are seeking. Where there is more than one listing for the same Bible book, the abbreviation for the name of the book appears in the first entry but not in entries below it, as shown here. The key word itself is represented simply by the first letter, in italics. To illustrate, under WORD you will find entries such as the following:

Ac 17:11 for they received the *w* with
17:13 *w* of God was published also

A basic rule to remember in using this concordance is this: *Everything is listed as it is spelled.* This includes numbers, such as "two" and "forty."

All words that are spelled the same are put under the same heading. This is true even if some of the words are capitalized and others are not. Thus all occurrences of "God" and "god" are in one listing, and the same is true of "Put" (the name of an individual and of a people) and "put." Similarly, all parts of speech that are spelled the same appear under the same heading. So, the verb "bear" (often meaning "to carry") and the noun "bear" (the animal), as an example, are found under just one heading.

Two or more words joined by a hyphen are treated as one word. For example, "only-begotten" is listed, not under "begotten," but with the words beginning with "O." As for words that are frequently used together but are not joined by a hyphen, these are listed separately. That is the case with the expression "active force." It is found under both "active" and "force."

Singular, plural and possessive forms of words are listed separately. This is because they are spelled differently. Thus "son" (singular), "sons" (plural), "son's" (singular possessive) and "sons'" (plural possessive) are found in separate listings.

To simplify the use of this concordance, some words have been omitted entirely. These include only words that experience has shown would seldom, if ever, be consulted and which would therefore make the volume needlessly cumbersome if they were included. The omitted words are: a, accordingly, ah, along, also, although, an, and, another, another's, any, are, as, at, be, because, been, begin, besides, both, but, by, can, cannot, concerning, consequently, could, did, do, does, done, during, each, either, ever, everybody, fairly, for, forth, from, further, furthermore, had, having, he, hence, henceforth, her, here, hers, herself, him, himself, his, however, I, if, in, including, indeed, instead, into, is, it, its, itself, likewise, may, me, meantime, meanwhile, moreover, my, myself, neither, nevertheless, next, nor, not, O, of, off, onto, or, other, other's, others, otherwise, our, ours, ourselves, quite, rather, shall, she, should,

simply, since, some, something, subsequently, than, that, the, their, theirs, them, themselves, then, there, thereby, therefore, therefrom, thereof, thereupon, these, they, this, those, thus, to, too, up, upon, us, very, was, we, were, when, where, whereas, wherefore, wherever, whether, which, while, who, whoever, whom, whomever, with, would, yet, you, your, yours, yourself, yourselves.

To facilitate research, certain listings are only partial. There are words that appear hundreds or even thousands of times in the Bible and that would rarely be consulted. Yet certain occurrences of the word may be valuable. An exhaustive listing would make it difficult to locate the desired texts. To illustrate: the verb "will" could fill many pages if the list of references were complete, and these would probably never be used. Yet the noun "will" (as in the expression "the will of God") can be used in locating valuable information. The compilers of this *Comprehensive Concordance* have eliminated those occurrences of the word that would only hinder you in locating the information that you really want. The words treated in this manner are limited in number and each of them is clearly marked by an asterisk (*) so that you will realize that the listing is only partial.

Abbreviations that are used for the names of Bible books are as follows:

Ac	– Acts	Isa	– Isaiah	Na	– Nahum
Am	– Amos	Jas	– James	Ne	– Nehemiah
Ca	– Song of Solomon (Canticles)	Jer	– Jeremiah	Nu	– Numbers
		Jg	– Judges	Ob	– Obadiah
1Ch	– 1 Chronicles	1Jo	– 1 John	1Pe	– 1 Peter
2Ch	– 2 Chronicles	2Jo	– 2 John	2Pe	– 2 Peter
1Co	– 1 Corinthians	3Jo	– 3 John	Phm	– Philemon
2Co	– 2 Corinthians	Job	– Job	Php	– Philippians
Col	– Colossians	Joe	– Joel	Pr	– Proverbs
Da	– Daniel	Joh	– John	Ps	– Psalms
De	– Deuteronomy	Jon	– Jonah	Re	– Revelation
Ec	– Ecclesiastes	Jos	– Joshua	Ro	– Romans
Eph	– Ephesians	Jude	– Jude	Ru	– Ruth
Es	– Esther	1Ki	– 1 Kings	1Sa	– 1 Samuel
Ex	– Exodus	2Ki	– 2 Kings	2Sa	– 2 Samuel
Eze	– Ezekiel	La	– Lamentations	1Th	– 1 Thessalonians
Ezr	– Ezra	Le	– Leviticus	2Th	– 2 Thessalonians
Ga	– Galatians	Lu	– Luke	1Ti	– 1 Timothy
Ge	– Genesis	Mal	– Malachi	2Ti	– 2 Timothy
Hab	– Habakkuk	Mic	– Micah	Tit	– Titus
Hag	– Haggai	Mr	– Mark	Zec	– Zechariah
Heb	– Hebrews	Mt	– Matthew	Zep	– Zephaniah
Ho	– Hosea				

The abbreviation *super* used in connection with certain Psalms refers to the superscription.

IF YOU HAVE DIFFICULTY IN LOCATING A PARTICULAR VERSE

These suggestions may help you:

1. Are you sure that you have the correct spelling?

2. May it be that the text you are seeking is listed under another form of the word that you have in mind (possibly plural or possessive)?

3. Is the word for which you are looking part of a hyphenated expression? If so, look under the letter representing the first part of the word combination.

4. It may be that the word you have in mind does not appear in the *New World Translation.* Perhaps it is in some other Bible version or is simply the way that you personally have paraphrased what is in the text. Why not try looking up another word that you believe is in the Scripture?

Comprehensive Concordance

Aaron
Ex 4:14 *A* the Levite your brother
4:27 Then Jehovah said to *A*: Go to
4:28 Moses proceeded to tell *A* all
4:29 Moses and *A* went and gathered
4:30 *A* spoke all the words that
5:1 afterward Moses and *A* went in
5:4 Why is it, Moses and *A*, that
5:20 they encountered Moses and *A*
6:13 to speak to Moses and *A* and
6:20 she bore him *A* and Moses
6:23 *A* took Elisheba . . . his wife
6:26 *A* and Moses to whom Jehovah
6:27 This is the Moses and *A*
7:1 *A* . . . will become your prophet
7:2 *A* . . . will do the speaking to
7:6 Moses and *A* went ahead doing
7:7 *A* was eighty-three years old
7:8 now said to Moses and *A*
7:9 must say to *A*, Take your rod
7:10 and *A* went on in to Pharaoh
7:10 *A* threw his rod down before
7:19 Say to *A*, Take your rod and
7:20 Moses and *A* did so, just as
8:5 *A*, Stretch your hand with your
8:6 *A* stretched his hand out over
8:8 Pharaoh called Moses and *A* and
8:12 Moses and *A* went out from
8:16 Say to *A*, Stretch your rod out
8:17 *A* stretched out his hand with
8:25 Pharaoh called Moses and *A*
9:8 Jehovah said to Moses and *A*
9:27 Pharaoh sent and called . . . *A*
10:3 and *A* went in to Pharaoh and
10:8 Moses and *A* were brought back
10:16 called Moses and *A* and said
11:10 Moses and *A* performed all
12:1 Moses and *A* in the land of
12:28 Moses and *A*. They did just
12:31 called Moses and *A* by night
12:43 say to Moses and *A*: This is
12:50 had commanded Moses and *A*
16:2 murmur against Moses and *A*
16:6 Moses and *A* said to all the
16:9 Moses went on to say to *A*
16:10 as soon as *A* had spoken to
16:33 Moses said to *A*: Take a jar
16:34 *A* proceeded to deposit it
17:10 Moses, *A* and Hur went up to
17:12 *A* and Hur supported his hands
18:12 *A* and all the older men of
19:24 come up, you and *A* with you
24:1 you and *A*, Nadab and Abihu
24:9 Moses and *A*, Nadab and Abihu
24:14 *A* and Hur are with you
27:21 *A* and his sons will set it
28:1 bring near to yourself *A* your
28:1 priest to me, *A*, Nadab and
28:1 and Ithamar, the sons of *A*
28:2 make holy garments for *A* your
28:4 make the holy garments for *A*
28:12 and *A* must carry their names
28:29 *A* must carry the names of
28:30 *A* must carry the judgments
28:35 upon *A* that he may minister
28:38 *A* must answer for the error
28:41 with them you must clothe *A*
28:43 they must be upon *A* and his
29:4 present *A* and his sons at the
29:5 clothe *A* with the robe and
29:9 sashes, *A* as well as his sons
29:9 you must fill the hand of *A*
29:10 *A* and his sons must lay
29:15 *A* and his sons must lay
29:19 take the other ram, and *A*
29:21 spatter it upon *A* and his
29:24 upon the palms of *A* and upon
29:26 breast of the ram . . . for *A*
29:27 from what was for *A* and
29:32 *A* and his sons must eat the
29:35 you must do this way to *A*
Ex 29:44 sanctify *A* and his sons for
30:7 *A* must make perfumed
30:8 when *A* lights up the lamps
30:10 *A* must make atonement upon
30:19 *A* and his sons must wash
30:30 anoint *A* and his sons, and
31:10 garments for *A* the priest
32:1 congregated . . . about *A*
32:2 At this *A* said to them: Tear
32:3 gold earrings . . . to *A*
32:5 When *A* got to see this, he
32:5 Finally *A* called out and
32:21 Moses said to *A*: What did
32:22 To this *A* said: Do not let
32:25 *A* had let them go
32:35 the calf, which *A* had made
34:30 *A* and all the sons of Israel
34:31 So *A* and all the chieftains
35:19 holy garments for *A* the
38:21 Ithamar the son of *A* the
39:1 holy garments that were for *A*
39:27 worker, for *A* and his sons
39:41 holy garments for *A* the
40:12 bring *A* and his sons near to
40:13 must clothe *A* with the holy
40:31 *A* and his sons washed their
Le 1:5 sons of *A*, the priests, must
1:7 And the sons of *A*, the priests
1:8 And the sons of *A*, the priests
1:11 and the sons of *A*, the priests
2:2 the sons of *A*, the priests
2:3 belongs to *A* and his sons, as
2:10 belongs to *A* and his sons, as
6:9 Command *A* and his sons, saying
6:14 sons of *A*, present it before
6:16 of it *A* and his sons will eat
6:18 male among the sons of *A*
6:20 offering of *A* and his sons
6:25 Speak to *A* and his sons
7:34 give them to *A* the priest and
7:35 the priestly share of *A* and
8:2 Take *A* and his sons with him
8:6 *A* and his sons near and washed
8:14 *A* and his sons laid their
8:18 *A* and his sons then laid their
8:22 *A* and his sons laid their
8:27 palms of *A* and the palms of
8:30 spattered it upon *A* and his
8:30 sanctified *A* and his garments
8:31 Moses said to *A* and his sons
8:31 *A* and his sons will eat it
8:36 *A* and his sons proceeded to
9:1 Moses called *A* and his sons
9:2 said to *A*: Take for yourself a
9:7 Then Moses said to *A*: Go near
9:8 *A* immediately went near to
9:21 right leg *A* waved to and fro
9:22 *A* raised his hands toward
9:23 Moses and *A* went into the
10:3 Then Moses said to *A*: This
10:3 And *A* kept silent
10:6 Moses said to *A* and to
10:8 to speak to *A*, saying
10:12 to *A* and to Eleazar and
10:19 At this *A* spoke to Moses
11:1 to speak to Moses and *A*
13:1 to speak to Moses and *A*
13:2 brought to *A* the priest or to
14:33 speak to Moses and *A*, saying
15:1 speak to Moses and *A*, saying
16:2 to *A* your brother, that he
16:3 *A* should come into the holy
16:6 *A* must present the bull of
16:8 *A* must draw lots over the two
16:9 And *A* must present the goat
16:11 *A* must present the bull of
16:21 *A* must lay both his hands
16:23 *A* must come into the tent
17:2 Speak to *A* and his sons and
21:17 to *A*, saying, No man of your
21:21 *A* the priest in whom there
Le 21:24 Moses spoke to *A* and his
22:2 *A* and his sons, that they may
22:18 *A* and his sons and all the
24:3 *A* should set it in order from
Nu 1:3 register them . . . you and *A*
1:17 Moses and *A* took these men
1:44 with *A* and the chieftains of
2:1 now spoke to Moses and *A*
3:1 generations of *A* and Moses in
3:4 along with *A* their father
3:6 stand them before *A* the priest
3:9 give the Levites to *A* and his
3:10 appoint *A* and his sons, and
3:32 was Eleazar the son of *A* the
3:38 Moses and *A* and his sons
3:39 Moses and *A* registered at the
3:48 money to *A* and his sons as
3:51 ransom price to *A* and his
4:1 now spoke to Moses and *A*
4:5 *A* and his sons must come in
4:15 *A* and his sons must finish
4:16 Eleazar the son of *A* the
4:17 spoke further to Moses and *A*
4:19 *A* and his sons will come in
4:27 order of *A* and his sons all
4:28 Ithamar the son of *A* the
4:33 Ithamar the son of *A* the
4:34 Moses and *A* and the
4:37 Moses and *A* registered at the
4:41 Moses and *A* registered at the
4:45 Moses and *A* registered at the
4:46 whom Moses and *A* and the
6:23 Speak to *A* and his sons
7:8 Ithamar the son of *A* the
8:2 Speak to *A*, and you must say
8:3 And *A* began to do so
8:11 *A* must cause the Levites to
8:13 Levites stand before *A* and his
8:19 Levites as given ones to *A* and
8:20 Moses and *A* and all the
8:21 *A* caused them to move to and
8:21 *A* made an atonement for them
8:22 tent of meeting before *A* and
9:6 before Moses and *A* on that day
12:1 Miriam and *A* began to speak
12:4 said to Moses and *A* and
12:5 and called *A* and Miriam
12:10 *A* turned toward Miriam, and
12:11 *A* said to Moses: Excuse me
13:26 came to Moses and *A* and all
14:2 murmur against Moses and *A*
14:5 Moses and *A* fell upon their
14:26 to speak to Moses and *A*
15:33 up to Moses and *A* and the
16:3 against Moses and *A* and said
16:11 As for *A*, what is he that
16:16 you and they and *A*, tomorrow
16:17 and *A* each his fire holder
16:18 together with Moses and *A*
16:20 now spoke to Moses and *A*
16:37 to Eleazar the son of *A* the
16:40 is not of the offspring of *A*
16:41 murmur against Moses and *A*
16:42 together against Moses and *A*
16:43 And Moses and *A* proceeded to
16:46 Moses said to *A*: Take the
16:47 *A* at once took it, just as
16:50 *A* returned to Moses at the
18:1 to say to *A*: You and your sons
18:8 Jehovah spoke further to *A*: As
18:20 went on to say to *A*: In
18:28 give the contribution . . . to *A*
19:1 to speak to Moses and *A*
20:2 against Moses and *A*
20:6 Moses and *A* came from before
20:8 you and *A* your brother, and
20:10 and *A* called the congregation
20:12 Jehovah said to Moses and *A*
20:23 Moses and *A* in Mount Hor by
20:24 *A* will be gathered to his
20:25 Take *A* and Eleazar his son

Nu 20:26 strip *A* of his garments, and
20:26 *A* will be gathered and must
20:28 Then Moses stripped *A* of his
20:28 *A* died there on the top of
20:29 got to see that *A* had expired
20:29 weeping for *A* thirty days
25:7 Eleazar the son of *A* the
25:11 Eleazar the son of *A* the
26:1 the son of *A* the priest
26:9 struggle against Moses and *A*
26:59 bore to Amram *A* and Moses
26:60 born to *A* Nadab and Abihu
26:64 registered by Moses and *A*
27:13 *A* your brother was gathered
33:1 by the hand of Moses and *A*
33:38 *A* the priest proceeded to go
33:39 And *A* was a hundred and
De 9:20 At *A*, too, Jehovah got very
9:20 also in behalf of *A* at that
10:6 There *A* died, and he got to
32:50 as *A* your brother died on
Jos 21:4 to belong to the sons of *A*
21:10 belong to the sons of *A*
21:13 to the sons of *A* the priest
21:19 the cities of the sons of *A*
24:5 I sent Moses and *A*, and I
24:33 Eleazar the son of *A* died
Jg 20:28 son of Eleazar, the son of *A*
1Sa 12:6 who used Moses and *A* and
12:8 send Moses and *A*, that they
1Ch 6:3 the sons of Amram were *A* and
6:3 the sons of *A* were Nadab and
6:49 *A* and his sons were making
6:50 sons of *A*: Eleazar his son
6:54 the sons of *A* belonging to
6:57 to the sons of *A* they gave
12:27 the leader of the sons of *A*
15:4 gather the sons of *A* and the
23:13 sons of Amram were *A* and
23:13 But *A* was separated that he
23:28 sons of *A* for the service
23:32 guarding of the sons of *A*
24:1 sons of *A* had their divisions
24:1 The sons of *A* were Nadab and
24:19 due right by the hand of *A*
24:31 their brothers the sons of *A*
27:17 of *A*, Zadok
2Ch 13:9 priests, the sons of *A*
13:10 sons of *A*, and also the
26:18 priests the sons of *A*, the
29:21 sons of *A* the priests to
31:19 sons of *A*, the priests, in
35:14 the priests the sons of *A*
35:14 the priests the sons of *A*
Ezr 7:5 the son of *A* the chief priest
Ne 10:38 the priest, the son of *A*
12:47 to the sons of *A*
Ps 77:20 By the hand of Moses and *A*
99:6 and *A* were among his priests
105:26 *A* whom he had chosen
106:16 *A* the holy one of Jehovah
115:10 house of *A*, put your trust
115:12 will bless the house of *A*
118:3 of the house of *A* now say
135:19 *A*, do you men bless Jehovah
Mic 6:4 send before you Moses, *A* and
Lu 1:5 wife from the daughters of *A*
Ac 7:40 saying to *A*, Make gods for
Heb 5:4 called by God, just as *A* also
7:11 according to the manner of *A*
9:4 the rod of *A* that budded and

Aaron's
Ex 6:25 Eleazar, *A* son, took for
7:12 *A* rod swallowed up their rods
15:20 *A* sister, proceeded to take
28:3 *A* garments for sanctifying
28:30 prove to be over *A* heart
28:38 come to be upon *A* forehead
28:40 And for *A* sons you will make
29:20 upon the lobe of *A* right ear
29:28 must become *A* and his sons'
29:29 garments that are *A* will
Le 3:2 and *A* sons, the priests, must
3:5 And *A* sons must make it smoke
3:8 *A* sons must sprinkle its blood
3:13 and *A* sons must sprinkle its
7:10 come to be for all of *A* sons
7:31 must become *A* and his sons'
7:33 one of *A* sons who presents
8:12 the anointing oil upon *A* head
8:13 *A* sons near and clothed them
8:23 the lobe of *A* right ear and
8:24 Moses brought *A* sons near and
Le 9:9 *A* sons presented the blood to
9:12 *A* sons handed him the blood
9:18 *A* sons handed him the blood
10:1 *A* sons Nadab and Abihu took
10:4 the sons of Uzziel, *A* uncle
10:16 *A* sons that were left
16:1 death of *A* two sons for their
21:1 *A* sons, and you must say to
22:4 *A* offspring when he is
24:9 *A* and his sons', and they
Nu 3:2 *A* sons: the firstborn Nadab and
3:3 *A* sons, the anointed priests
10:8 *A* sons, the priests, should
17:3 *A* name you will write upon
17:6 *A* rod was in among their rods
17:8 *A* rod . . . had budded, and it
17:10 Put *A* rod back before the
Ps 133:2 down upon the beard, *A* beard

Abaddon
Re 9:11 In Hebrew his name is *A*

Abagtha
Es 1:10 Bigtha and *A*, Zethar and

Abanah
2Ki 5:12 *A* and the Pharpar, the rivers

Abandon
De 2:31 I have started to *a* Sihon and
7:2 God will certainly *a* them to
7:23 God will indeed *a* them to you
12:19 you may not *a* the Levite all
14:27 you must not *a* him, for he
23:14 and to *a* your enemies to you
Jg 11:9 Jehovah does *a* them to me
Ru 1:16 Do not plead with me to *a* you
1Ki 8:46 and *a* them to the enemy
2Ch 6:36 *a* them to an enemy, and
Ps 119:121 *a* me to those defrauding
Jer 23:33 I shall certainly *a* you
Eze 29:5 will *a* you to the wilderness
31:12 *a* it upon the mountains
31:12 will come down and *a* it
32:4 must *a* you on the land
Joh 8:29 he did not *a* me to myself

Abandoned
Le 26:43 land was left *a* by them and
De 1:21 your God has *a* the land to you
2:33 Jehovah our God *a* him to us
2:36 Jehovah our God *a* them all to
29:25 *a* the covenant of Jehovah
31:5 Jehovah has *a* them to you
Jg 2:12 they *a* Jehovah the God of
2:13 they *a* Jehovah and took up
10:13 you *a* me and took up serving
Job 18:4 will the earth be *a*, Or a
Isa 27:10 and *a* like a wilderness
32:14 hubbub of the city has been *a*
Jer 49:25 praise has not been *a*
Eze 36:4 *a* cities that have come to
Zep 2:4 Gaza, an *a* city is what
Mt 23:38 Look! Your house is *a* to you
24:40 and the other be *a*
24:41 and the other be *a*
26:56 the disciples *a* him and fled
Mr 1:18 *a* their nets and followed
14:50 And they all *a* him and fled
Lu 5:11 *a* everything and followed him
13:35 Your house is *a* to you
17:34 but the other will be *a*
17:35 but the other will be *a*

Abandoning
Jos 10:12 *a* the Amorites to the sons
11:6 I am *a* all of them slain to
Mt 4:20 *a* the nets, they followed
2Pe 2:15 *A* the straight path, they

Abandons
Joh 10:12 and *a* the sheep and flees

Abarim
Nu 27:12 into this mountain of *A* and
33:47 mountains of *A* before Nebo
33:48 from the mountains of *A*
De 32:49 mountain of *A*, Mount Nebo
Jer 22:20 And cry out from *A*

Abase
Ps 18:27 the haughty eyes you will *a*
Pr 25:7 than to *a* you before a noble
Isa 13:11 of the tyrants I shall *a*
25:11 *a* its haughtiness with the
25:12 *a* it, bring it into contact

Abased
Isa 32:19 becomes low in an *a* state
Eze 17:24 *a* the high tree, have put

Abaser
1Sa 2:7 Jehovah is . . . An *A*

Abases
Ps 75:7 This one he *a*, and that
Isa 26:5, 5 he *a* it, he *a* it to the

Abashed
Ps 35:4 *a* who are scheming calamity
35:26 ashamed and *a* all together
40:14 ashamed and *a* all together
70:2 May those be ashamed and *a*
71:24 for they have become *a*
83:17 they become *a* and perish
Isa 1:29 *a* because of the gardens that
24:23 full moon has become *a*
33:9 Lebanon has become *a*; it has
Jer 15:9 become ashamed and felt *a*

Abasing
Ps 147:6 *a* the wicked ones to the

Abated
Ge 8:8 see whether the waters had *a*
8:11 waters had *a* from the earth
Mt 14:32 the windstorm *a*
Mr 4:39 Be quiet! And the wind *a*, and
6:51 the wind *a*. At this they

Abba
Mr 14:36 *A*, Father, all things are
Ro 8:15 spirit we cry out: *A*, Father!
Ga 4:6 and it cries out: *A*, Father!

Abda
1Ki 4:6 Adoniram the son of *A*, over
Ne 11:17 and *A* the son of Shammua the

Abdeel
Jer 36:26 Shelemiah the son of *A* to

Abdi
1Ch 6:44 son of *A*, the son of Malluch
2Ch 29:12 Kish the son of *A* and
Ezr 10:26 of the sons of Elam . . . *A*

Abdiel
1Ch 5:15 Ahi the son of *A*, the son of

Abdomen
2Sa 2:23 strike him in the *a* with the
3:27 struck him in the *a*, so that
4:6 then struck him in the *a*
20:10 struck him with it in the *a*
Ca 5:14 His *a* is an ivory plate
Jer 51:34 has filled his *a* with my

Abdon
Jos 21:30 *A* and its pasture ground
Jg 12:13 *A* the son of Hillel the
12:15 Then *A* the son of Hillel the
1Ch 6:74 *A* with its pasture grounds
8:23 and *A* and Zichri and Hanan
8:30 son, the firstborn, was *A*
9:36 son, the firstborn, was *A*
2Ch 34:20 *A* the son of Micah and

Abednego
Da 1:7 and to Azariah, *A*
2:49 appointed . . . Meshach and *A*
3:12 whom you appointed . . . and *A*
3:13 said to bring in . . . *A*
3:14 Is it really so, O . . . *A*
3:16 *A* . . . saying to the king
3:19 Shadrach, Meshach and *A*
3:20 bind Shadrach, Meshach and *A*
3:22 men that took up . . . *A* were
3:23 *A*, fell down bound in the
3:26 *A* . . . step out and come here
3:26 Shadrach, Meshach and *A* were
3:28 God of . . . Meshach and *A*
3:29 the God of . . . *A*
3:30 *A* to prosper in the

Abel
Ge 4:2 gave birth, to his brother *A*
4:2 *A* came to be a herder of sheep
4:4 as for *A*, he too brought some
4:4 with favor upon *A* and his
4:8 Cain said to *A* his brother
4:8 Cain proceeded to assault *A*
4:9 Where is *A* your brother?
4:25 another seed in place of *A*
2Sa 20:14 to *A* of Beth-maacah
20:15 in *A* of Beth-maacah and
20:18 Let them but inquire in *A*
Mt 23:35 the blood of righteous *A* to
Lu 11:51 from the blood of *A* down to
Heb 11:4 *A* offered God a sacrifice

Abel-beth-maacah
1Ki 15:20 *A* and all Chinnereth, as
2Ki 15:29 and *A* and Janoah and Kedesh

Abel-keramim
Jg 11:33 far as *A* with a very great

Abel-maim
2Ch 16:4 struck Ijon and Dan and *A*

Abel-meholah
Jg 7:22 the outskirts of *A* by Tabbath
1Ki 4:12 from Beth-shean to *A* to the
19:16 Elisha . . . from *A*

Abel-mizraim
Ge 50:11 why its name was called *A*

Abel's
Heb 12:24 a better way than *A* blood

Abel-shittim
Nu 33:49 from Beth-jeshimoth to *A* on

Abhor
Ge 27:46 I have come to *a* this life
Le 20:23 these things and I *a* them
26:11 my soul will not *a* you
26:15 souls will *a* my judicial
26:30 my soul will simply *a* you
26:44 *a* them so as to exterminate
Nu 21:5 to *a* the contemptible bread
Pr 3:11 and do not *a* his reproof
Ro 12:9 *A* what is wicked, cling to

Abhorred
Le 26:43 souls had *a* my statutes
Jer 14:19 has your soul *a* even Zion?
Eze 16:45 *a* their husbands and their

Abhorrence
1Ki 11:25 he had an *a* of Israel while
Da 12:2 and to indefinitely lasting *a*
Ro 2:22 one expressing *a* of the idols

Abhorrent
Le 20:21 *a*. It is the nakedness of his
La 1:8 she has become a mere *a* thing
1:17 Jerusalem has become an *a*
Eze 7:19 *a* thing their own gold will
7:20 make it to them an *a* thing
Zec 13:1 for sin and for an *a* thing
Tit 3:3 *a*, hating one another

Abhorring
Eze 16:5 was an *a* of your soul in the
16:45 *a* her husband and her sons

Abi
2Ki 18:2 *A* the daughter of Zechariah

Abi-albon
2Sa 23:31 *A* the Arbathite, Azmaveth

Abiasaph
Ex 6:24 the sons of Korah were . . . *A*

Abiathar
1Sa 22:20 name was *A*, made his escape
22:21 *A* told David: Saul has
22:22 David said to *A*: I well
23:6 *A* the son of Ahimelech ran
23:9 said to *A* the priest: Do
30:7 David said to *A* the priest
30:7 *A* came bringing the ephod
2Sa 8:17 Ahimelech the son of *A* were
15:24 set the ark . . . down by *A*
15:27 and Jonathan the son of *A*
15:29 Zadok and *A* took the ark of
15:35 Zadok and *A* the priests
15:35 tell to Zadok and *A* the
15:36 Jonathan belonging to *A*
17:15 Hushai said to Zadok and *A*
19:11 he sent to Zadok and *A* the
20:25 Zadok and *A* were priests
1Ki 1:7 with *A* the priest, and they
1:19 *A* the priest and Joab the
1:25 the army and *A* the priest
1:42 Jonathan the son of *A* the
2:22 for *A* the priest and for
2:26 to *A* the priest the king said
2:27 Solomon drove out *A* from
2:35 king put in the place of *A*
4:4 Zadok and *A* were priests
1Ch 15:11 Zadok and *A* the priests, and
18:16 and Ahimelech the son of *A*
24:6 and Ahimelech the son of *A*
27:34 the son of Benaiah and *A*
Mr 2:26 about *A* the chief priest, and

Abib
Ex 13:4 are going out in the month of *A*
23:15 in the month of *A*, because
34:18 time in the month of *A*
34:18 month of *A* that you came out
De 16:1 observing of the month of *A*
16:1 in the month of *A* Jehovah your

Abida
Ge 25:4 sons of Midian were . . . *A* and
1Ch 1:33 sons of Midian . . . *A*

Abidan
Nu 1:11 *A* the son of Gideoni
2:22 is *A* the son of Gideoni
7:60 *A* the son of Gideoni
7:65 of *A* the son of Gideoni
10:24 *A* the son of Gideoni

Abide
Lu 24:49 *a* in the city until you
Php 1:25 shall *a* with all of you for
1Jo 2:24 *a* in union with the Son and

Abides
Ps 68:12 *a* at home, she shares in the

Abiding
Ex 15:13 them to your holy *a* place
2Sa 15:25 see it and its *a* place
Job 5:3 began to execrate his *a* place
8:6 restore your righteous *a* place
18:15 upon his own *a* place
Ps 79:7 own *a* place to be desolated
83:12 *a* places of God for ourselves
Pr 3:33 *a* place of the righteous ones
24:15 *a* place of the righteous one
Isa 32:18 dwell in a peaceful *a* place
33:20 undisturbed *a* place, a
34:13 an *a* place of jackals
35:7 In the *a* place of jackals
Jer 10:25 his *a* place they have
25:30 will roar upon his *a* place
25:37 the peaceful *a* places have
49:19 to the durable *a* place
50:7 Jehovah the *a* place of
50:44 to the durable *a* place
50:45 *a* place to be desolated
La 2:2 upon any *a* places of Jacob
Eze 34:14 *a* place will come to be
34:14 lie down in a good *a* place
Heb 10:34 better and an *a* possession

Abiel
1Sa 9:1 Kish, the son of *A*, the son
14:51 was the son of *A*
1Ch 11:32 *A* the Arbathite

Abi-ezer
Jos 17:2 for the sons of *A* and the
Jg 8:2 the grape gathering of *A*
2Sa 23:27 *A* the Anathothite, Mebunnai
1Ch 7:18 gave birth to Ishhod and *A*
11:28 *A* the Anathothite
27:12 *A* the Anathothite of the

Abi-ezrite
Jg 6:11 which belonged to Joash the *A*

Abi-ezrites
Jg 6:24 It is yet in Ophrah of the *A*
6:34 *A* got to be called together
8:32 in Ophrah of the *A*

Abigail
1Sa 25:3 and his wife's name was *A*
25:14 to *A*, Nabal's wife, one of
25:18 *A* hastened and took two
25:23 *A* caught sight of David
25:32 David said to *A*: Blessed
25:36 *A* came in to Nabal, and
25:39 propose to *A* to take her
25:40 servants came to *A* at
25:42 *A* hastened and rose up and
27:3 *A*, Nabal's wife, the
30:5 *A* the wife of Nabal the
2Sa 2:2 *A* the wife of Nabal the
3:3 second was Chileab by *A* the
17:25 *A* the daughter of Nahash
1Ch 2:16 sisters were Zeruiah and *A*
2:17 *A*, she gave birth to Amasa
3:1 *A* the Carmelitess

Abihail
Nu 3:35 Zuriel the son of *A*
1Ch 2:29 Abishur's wife was *A*
5:14 the sons of *A* the son of Huri
2Ch 11:18 *A* the daughter of Eliab the
Es 2:15 of *A* the uncle of Mordecai
9:29 Esther . . . the daughter of *A*

Abihu
Ex 6:23 she bore him Nadab and *A*
24:1 you and Aaron, Nadab and *A*
24:9 Moses and Aaron, Nadab and *A*
28:1 Aaron, Nadab and *A*, Eleazar
Le 10:1 Aaron's sons Nadab and *A* took
Nu 3:2 Aaron's sons . . . Nadab and *A*
3:4 Nadab and *A* died before Jehovah
26:60 born to Aaron Nadab and *A*
26:61 Nadab and *A* died for their
1Ch 6:3 sons of Aaron . . . *A*, Eleazar
24:1 of Aaron were Nadab and *A*
24:2 Nadab and *A* died before their

Abihud
1Ch 8:3 And Bela came to have . . . *A*

Abijah
1Sa 8:2 and the name of his second *A*
1Ki 14:1 *A* the son of Jeroboam fell
1Ch 2:24 *A* being the wife of Hezron
3:10 *A* his son, Asa his son
6:28 sons of Samuel . . . second *A*
7:8 the sons of Becher were . . . *A*
24:10 for *A* the eighth
2Ch 11:20 she bore him *A* and Attai
11:22 *A* the son of Maacah in
12:16 *A* his son began to reign
13:1 *A* began to reign over Judah
13:2 between *A* and Jeroboam
13:3 *A* engaged in the war with
13:4 *A* now rose up upon Mount
13:15 Israel before *A* and Judah
13:17 *A* and his people went
13:19 *A* kept chasing after
13:20 power in the days of *A*
13:21 *A* continued to strengthen
14:1 *A* lay down with his
29:1 mother's name was *A* the
Ne 10:7 Meshullam, *A*, Mijamin
12:4 Iddo, Ginnethoi, *A*
12:17 for *A*, Zichri; for Miniamin
Mt 1:7 Rehoboam became father to *A*
1:7 *A* became father to Asa
Lu 1:5 Zechariah of the division of *A*

Abijah's
2Ch 13:22 *A* affairs, even his ways

Abijam
1Ki 14:31 *A* his son began to reign in
15:1 *A* became king over Judah
15:7 affairs of *A* and all that he
15:7 between *A* and Jeroboam
15:8 Finally *A* lay down with his

Abilene
Lu 3:1 was district ruler of *A*

Abilities
Pr 5:2 so as to guard thinking *a*
8:12 the knowledge of thinking *a*
14:17 man of thinking *a* is hated
1Co 12:28 *a* to direct, different

Ability
Ex 15:6 proving itself powerful in *a*
Le 26:37 prove to be no *a* to stand
Jos 8:20 to be no *a* in them to flee
1Ch 9:13 mighty men of *a* for the
29:12 *a* to make great and to give
Pr 1:4 man knowledge and thinking *a*
2:11 thinking *a* itself will keep
3:21 wisdom and thinking *a*
Da 1:4 *a* to stand in the palace of
Mt 25:15 according to his own *a*, and
Ro 7:18 *a* to wish is present with me
7:18 *a* to work out what is fine
1Co 1:5 full *a* to speak and in full
2Co 8:3 according to their actual *a*
8:3 beyond their actual *a* this
Eph 6:19 *a* to speak may be given me

Abimael
Ge 10:28 Obal and *A* and Sheba
1Ch 1:22 and Obal and *A* and Sheba

Abimelech
Ge 20:2 *A* king of Gerar sent and took
20:3 God came to *A* in a dream by
20:4 *A* had not gone near her
20:8 *A* got up early in the morning
20:9 *A* called Abraham and said to
20:10 *A* went on to say to Abraham
20:14 *A* took sheep and cattle and
20:15 *A* said: Here my land is
20:17 heal *A* and his wife and his
20:18 house of *A* because of Sarah

Ge 21:22 *A* together with Phicol the
21:25 When Abraham criticized *A*
21:25 servants of *A* had seized by
21:26 *A* said: I do not know who
21:27 gave them to *A*, and both of
21:29 *A* went on to say to Abraham
21:32 *A* got up together with
26:1 Isaac directed himself to *A*
26:8 *A*, king of the Philistines
26:9 *A* called Isaac and said: Why
26:10 *A* continued: What is this
26:11 *A* commanded all the people
26:16 *A* said to Isaac: Move from
26:26 *A* came to him from Gerar
Jg 8:31 a son. So he named him *A*
9:1 *A* the son of Jerubbaal went to
9:3 heart inclined toward *A*, for
9:4 *A* proceeded to hire idle and
9:6 made *A* reign as king, close by
9:16 you went making *A* king, and
9:18 *A*, the son of his slave girl
9:19 rejoice over *A* and let him
9:20 let fire come out of *A* and
9:20 house of Millo and consume *A*
9:21 dwelling there because of *A*
9:22 *A* kept playing the prince over
9:23 bad spirit between *A* and the
9:23 to deal treacherously with *A*
9:24 blood upon *A* their brother
9:25 In time it was reported to *A*
9:27 and called down evil upon *A*
9:28 Who is *A*, and who is Shechem
9:29 Then I would remove *A*. And he
9:29 to say to *A*: Make your army
9:31 to *A*, saying: Look! Gaal the
9:34 *A* and all the people that
9:35 *A* and the people that were
9:38 Who is *A* that we should serve
9:39 took up the fight against *A*
9:40 *A* set out after him, and he
9:41 *A* continued to dwell in
9:42 So they told *A*
9:44 *A* and the bands that were
9:45 *A* fought against the city all
9:47 it was reported to *A* that all
9:48 *A* went up Mount Zalmon, he
9:48 *A* now took an ax in his hand
9:49 and went following *A*
9:50 *A* proceeded to go to Thebez
9:52 *A* made his way to the tower
9:55 *A* had died, they now went
9:56 the evil of *A* that he had done
10:1 after *A* there rose up to save
2Sa 11:21 *A* the son of Jerubbesheth
Ps 34:*super* Of David . . . before *A*

Abimelech's
Jg 9:53 *A* head and broke his skull in

Abinadab
1Sa 7:1 into the house of *A* on the
16:8 Jesse called *A* and had him
17:13 and his second son *A* and the
31:2 struck down Jonathan and *A*
2Sa 6:3 from the house of *A*
6:3 Uzzah and Ahio, the sons of *A*
1Ki 4:11 the son of *A*, all the
1Ch 2:13 father to . . . *A* the second
8:33 father to Jonathan . . . and *A*
9:39 father to Jonathan and . . . *A*
10:2 strike down Jonathan and *A*
13:7 from the house of *A*, and

Abinadab's
2Sa 6:4 carried it from *A* house

Abinoam
Jg 4:6 call Barak the son of *A* out of
4:12 Barak the son of *A* had gone
5:1 Barak the son of *A* broke out in
5:12 Barak . . . you son of *A*

Abiram
Nu 16:1 Dathan and *A* the sons of Eliab
16:12 Dathan and *A* the sons of
16:24 of Korah, Dathan and *A*
16:25 went to Dathan and *A*, and
16:27 Korah, Dathan and *A*, from
16:27 and Dathan and *A* came out
26:9 sons of Eliab . . . Dathan and *A*
26:9 Dathan and *A* were summoned
De 11:6 what he did to Dathan and *A*
1Ki 16:34 forfeit of *A* his firstborn
Ps 106:17 over the assembly of *A*

Abishag
1Ki 1:3 found *A* the Shunammite and
1Ki 1:15 *A* the Shunammite was waiting
2:17 give me *A* the Shunammite as
2:21 *A* the Shunammite be given
2:22 why are you requesting *A* the

Abishai
1Sa 26:6 *A* the son of Zeruiah, the
26:6 *A* said: I myself shall go
26:7 David made his way with *A*
26:8 *A* now said to David: God
26:9 David said to *A*: Do not bring
2Sa 2:18 Joab and *A* and Asahel; and
2:24 Joab and *A* went chasing
3:30 Joab and *A* his brother, they
10:10 hand of *A* his brother, that
10:14 flight from before *A* and
16:9 *A* the son of Zeruiah said to
16:11 David went on to say to *A*
18:2 one third under the hand of *A*
18:5 to command Joab and *A* and
18:12 king commanded you and *A*
19:21 *A* the son of Zeruiah
20:6 David said to *A*: Now Sheba
20:10 Joab and *A* his brother, for
21:17 *A* the son of Zeruiah came
23:18 *A* the brother of Joab the
1Ch 2:16 sons of Zeruiah were *A* and
11:20 As for *A* the brother of Joab
18:12 As for *A* the son of Zeruiah
19:11 gave into the hand of *A* his
19:15 to flight from before *A* his

Abishalom
1Ki 15:2 the granddaughter of *A*
15:10 the granddaughter of *A*

Abishua
1Ch 6:4 Phinehas . . . father to *A*
6:5 *A* . . . became father to Bukki
6:50 Phinehas his son, *A* his son
8:4 and *A* and Naaman and Ahoah
Ezr 7:5 *A* the son of Phinehas the son

Abishur
1Ch 2:28 sons of Shammai . . . *A*

Abishur's
1Ch 2:29 name of *A* wife was Abihail

Abital
2Sa 3:4 was Shephatiah the son of *A*
1Ch 3:3 the fifth, Shephatiah, of *A*

Abitub
1Ch 8:11 father to *A* and Elpaal

Abiud
Mt 1:13 Zerubbabel became father to *A*
1:13 *A* became father to Eliakim

Ablaze
De 32:22 set *a* the foundations of
2Sa 14:30 Go and set it *a* with fire
14:30 set the tract of land *a*
14:31 land that is mine *a* with
Job 41:21 Its soul itself sets coals *a*
Isa 33:12 be set *a* even with fire
50:11 sparks that you have set *a*
Jer 17:27 set a fire *a* in her gates
21:14 set a fire *a* in her forest
43:12 set a fire *a* in the houses
49:27 set a fire *a* on the wall of
50:32 set a fire *a* in its cities
La 4:11 he sets a fire *a* in Zion
Eze 20:47 a fire *a* against you, and
Ob 18 set them *a* and devour them

Able
Ge 13:6 they were not *a* to dwell all
13:16 man could be *a* to count the
15:5 if you are possibly *a* to count
19:19 I am not *a* to escape to the
19:22 I am not *a* to do a thing
31:35 not *a* to get up before you
36:7 land . . . not *a* to sustain
37:4 not *a* to speak peacefully to
43:32 Egyptians were not *a* to eat
44:1 extent they are *a* to carry it
44:22 The boy is not *a* to leave
44:26 We are not *a* to go down
44:26 not *a* to see the man's face
45:1 no longer *a* to control
Ex 2:3 no longer *a* to conceal him
12:39 and had not been *a* to linger
15:23 not *a* to drink the water
18:23 certainly be *a* to stand it
19:23 The people are not *a* to come
33:20 are not *a* to see my face
40:35 Moses was not *a* to go into
Nu 9:6 not *a* to prepare the passover
11:14 I am not *a*, I by myself, to
13:31 We are not *a* to go up against
14:16 not being *a* to bring this
22:6 I may be *a* to strike them and
22:11 I may be *a* to fight against
22:18 not be *a* to pass beyond the
22:37 and truly *a* to honor you
22:38 Shall I be *a* at all to speak
24:13 not be *a* to pass beyond the
De 1:9 not *a* by myself to carry you
7:17 be *a* to drive them away
14:24 you will not be *a* to carry
28:27 will not be *a* to be healed
28:35 will not be *a* to be healed
Jos 7:12 not be *a* to rise up against
7:13 not be *a* to rise up against
15:63 not *a* to drive them away
17:12 did not prove *a* to take
24:19 You are not *a* to serve
Jg 2:14 no longer *a* to stand before
8:3 I been *a* to do in comparison
Ru 4:6 not *a* to do the repurchasing
1Sa 3:2 he was not *a* to see
6:20 be *a* to stand before Jehovah
17:9 If he is *a* to fight with me
17:33 You are not *a* to go against
2Sa 3:11 *a* to say one word more in
12:23 Am I *a* to bring him back
17:17 not *a* to appear entering the
1Ki 3:9 *a* to judge this . . . people
5:3 not *a* to build a house to the
13:4 was not *a* to draw it back to
13:16 I am not *a* to go back with
20:9 this thing I am not *a* to do
2Ki 3:26 but they were not *a* to
4:40 And they were not *a* to eat
16:5 they were not *a* to fight
18:23 to see whether you are *a*
18:29 not *a* to deliver you out of
1Ch 21:30 David had not been *a* to go
2Ch 5:14 priests were not *a* to stand
7:7 not *a* to contain the burnt
29:34 not *a* to skin all the burnt
30:3 *a* to hold it at that time
32:13 *a* to deliver their land out
32:14 *a* to deliver his people out
32:14 *a* to deliver you out of my
32:15 *a* to deliver his people out
Ne 4:10 not *a* to build on the wall
6:3 and I am not *a* to go down
7:61 not *a* to tell the house of
Job 4:2 restraint on words who is *a*
33:5 If you are *a*, make reply to
42:2 you are *a* to do all things
Ps 18:38 will not be *a* to rise up
40:12 than I was *a* to see
78:19 God *a* to arrange a table in
78:20 *a* also to give bread itself
Pr 30:21 four it is not *a* to endure
Ec 1:8 no one is *a* to speak of it
6:10 not *a* to plead his cause with
7:13 for who is *a* to make straight
8:17 mankind are not *a* to find out
Ca 8:7 are not *a* to extinguish love
Isa 10:19 boy will be *a* to write
36:8 see whether you are *a*, on
36:14 he is not *a* to deliver you
47:11 will not be *a* to avert it
47:12 you might be *a* to benefit
56:10 dogs; they are not *a* to bark
Jer 11:11 will not be *a* to get out of
13:23 would also be *a* to do good
18:6 *a* to do just like this potter
19:11 no more *a* to be repaired
44:22 longer *a* to put up with it
49:10 not be *a* to hide oneself
49:23 not *a* to keep undisturbed
La 4:14 So that none are *a* to touch
Eze 7:19 will be *a* to deliver them in
33:12 be *a* to keep living
46:5 offering as he is *a* to give
46:7 to what he is *a* to afford
46:11 lambs as he is *a* to give
47:5 I was not *a* to pass through
Da 2:10 *a* to show the matter of the
2:47 were *a* to reveal this secret
3:17 our God . . . is *a* to rescue us
3:29 god that is *a* to deliver like
4:37 pride he is *a* to humiliate
5:16 *a* to furnish interpretations
5:16 *a* to read the writing and to
6:4 all that they were *a* to find
6:20 *a* to rescue you from the

Da 10:17 *a* to speak with this my lord
Am 7:10 The land is not *a* to put up
Hab 1:13 look on trouble you are not *a*
Zep 1:18 *a* to deliver them in the
Mt 3:9 God is *a* to raise up children
22:46 nobody was *a* to say a word
26:61 *a* to throw down the temple
Mr 1:45 no longer *a* to enter openly
2:4 not being *a* to bring him right
3:20 not *a* even to eat a meal
3:25 house will not be *a* to stand
3:27 is *a* to plunder his movable
4:32 birds . . . *a* to find lodging
4:33 far as they were *a* to listen
5:3 nobody was *a* to bind him fast
6:5 was *a* to do no powerful work
8:4 be *a* to satisfy these people
9:39 quickly be *a* to revile me
10:38 Are you *a* to drink the cup
10:39 They said to him: We are *a*
Lu 1:20 not *a* to speak until the day
1:22 he was not *a* to speak to them
8:43 not been *a* to get a cure
12:4 are not *a* to do anything more
13:24 to get in but will not be *a*
14:6 not *a* to answer back on these
14:29 but not be *a* to finish it
14:30 but was not *a* to finish
14:31 is *a* with ten thousand
20:26 not *a* to catch him in this
21:15 not be *a* to resist or dispute
Joh 2:6 each *a* to hold two or three
11:37 *a* to prevent this one from
12:39 they were not *a* to believe
16:12 you are not *a* to bear them
21:6 no longer *a* to draw it in
Ac 5:39 will not be *a* to overthrow
11:17 I should be *a* to hinder God
27:15 *a* to keep its head against
27:16 *a* to get possession of the
27:43 those *a* to swim to cast
Ro 4:21 promised he was also *a* to do
8:39 *a* to separate us from God's
11:23 God is *a* to graft them in
1Co 3:1 I was not *a* to speak to you
6:5 be *a* to judge between his
10:13 for you to be *a* to endure it
2Co 1:4 we may be *a* to comfort those
9:8 God, moreover, is *a* to make
Ga 3:21 that was *a* to give life
Eph 3:18 *a* to grasp mentally with
6:11 you may be *a* to stand firm
6:13 may be *a* to resist in the
6:16 *a* to quench all the wicked
2Ti 1:12 confident he is *a* to guard
3:7 learning and yet never *a* to
3:15 are *a* to make you wise for
Tit 1:9 be *a* both to exhort by the
Heb 2:18 is *a* to come to the aid of
4:12 *a* to discern thoughts and
5:2 He is *a* to deal moderately
5:7 *a* to save him out of death
7:25 *a* also to save completely
9:9 not *a* to make the man doing
10:11 *a* to take sins away
11:19 God was *a* to raise him up
Jas 1:21 is *a* to save your souls
3:2 *a* to bridle also his whole
4:2 yet you are not *a* to obtain
4:12 is *a* to save and to destroy
2Pe 1:15 *a* to make mention of these
Jude 24 *a* to guard you from stumbling
Re 5:3 one *a* to open the scroll or to
6:17 come, and who is *a* to stand?
7:9 no man was *a* to number, out
13:17 *a* to buy or sell except a
14:3 *a* to master that song but
15:8 *a* to enter into the sanctuary

Able-bodied
Ex 10:11 you who are *a* men, and serve
12:37 six hundred thousand *a* men
Nu 24:3 *a* man with the eye unsealed
De 22:5 No garb of an *a* man should be
22:5 neither should an *a* man wear
Jos 7:14, 14 near, *a* man by *a* man
7:17, 17 *a* man by *a* man, and
7:18, 18 *a* man by *a* man, and
Jg 5:30 two wombs to every *a* man
2Sa 23:1 the utterance of the *a* man
1Ki 12:21 choice men *a* for war
1Ch 23:3, 3 *a* man by *a* man, came to
2Ch 11:1 choice men *a* for war, to
Ezr 4:21 for these *a* men to stop
Ezr 5:4 names of the *a* men that are
5:10 the names of the *a* men that
6:8 *a* men without cessation
Job 3:3 An *a* man has been conceived
3:23 Why does he give light to *a*
4:17 Or can *a* man be cleaner than
10:5 like the days of an *a* man
14:10 But an *a* man dies and lies
14:14 If an *a* man dies can he
16:21 between an *a* man and God
22:2 an *a* man be of use to God
33:17 pride itself from an *a* man
33:29 in the case of an *a* man
34:7 What *a* man is like Job
34:9 An *a* man does not profit
34:34 *a* man that is listening
38:3 please, like an *a* man
40:7 please, like an *a* man
Ps 18:25 With the faultless, *a* man
34:8 the *a* man that takes refuge
37:23 steps of an *a* man have been
40:4 Happy is the *a* man that has
52:7 the *a* man that does not put
88:4 an *a* man without strength
89:48 What *a* man is there alive
94:12 Happy is the *a* man whom you
127:5 *a* man that has filled his
128:4 the *a* man will be blessed
Pr 6:34 rage of an *a* man is jealousy
20:24 the steppings of an *a* man
24:5 wise in strength is an *a* man
28:3 *a* man that is of little means
28:21 nor that an *a* man should
29:5 *a* man that is flattering his
30:1 The utterance of the *a* man to
30:19 of an *a* man with a maiden
Isa 22:17 violent hurling, O *a* man
Jer 17:5 Cursed is the *a* man who puts
17:7 Blessed is the *a* man who
22:30 an *a* man who will not have
23:9 like an *a* man whom wine has
30:6 *a* man with his hands upon
31:22 press around an *a* man
41:16 *a* men, men of war, and
43:6 *a* men and the wives and the
44:20 to the *a* men and to the
La 3:1 I am the *a* man that has seen
3:27 Good it is for an *a* man that
3:35 judgment of an *a* man before
3:39 *a* man on account of his sin
Da 2:25 *a* man of the exiles of Judah
3:12 *a* men have paid no regard to
3:13 *a* men were brought in before
3:20 *a* men of vital energy who
3:21 *a* men were bound in their
3:22 *a* men that took up Shadrach
3:23 *a* men, the three of them
3:24 *a* men that we threw bound
3:25 I am beholding four *a* men
3:27 beholding these *a* men, that
6:5 *a* men were saying: We shall
6:11 *a* men themselves crowded in
6:15 *a* men themselves entered as
6:24 *a* men who had accused Daniel
8:15 appearance like an *a* man
Joe 2:8 As an *a* man in his course
Mic 2:2 defrauded an *a* man and his
Hab 2:5 an *a* man is self-assuming
Zec 13:7 *a* man who is my associate

Abloom
Ca 2:13 vines are *a*, they have given
2:15 as our vineyards are *a*

Abner
1Sa 14:50 the chief of his army was *A*
14:51 Ner the father of *A* was the
17:55 to *A* the chief of the army
17:55 Whose son is the boy, *A*?
17:55 *A* said: By the life of your
17:57 *A* proceeded to take him and
20:25 *A* was sitting at Saul's
26:5 *A* the son of Ner the chief
26:7 *A* and the people were lying
26:14 to *A* the son of Ner, saying
26:14 Will you not answer, *A*?
26:14 *A* began to answer and say
26:15 David went on to say to *A*
2Sa 2:8 *A* the son of Ner the chief of
2:12 *A* the son of Ner and the
2:14 *A* said to Joab: Let the
2:17 *A* and the men of Israel were
2:19 Asahel went chasing after *A*
2:19 the left from following *A*
2:20 *A* looked behind him and said
2Sa 2:21 *A* said to him: Veer to your
2:22 *A* said to Asahel yet again
2:23 *A* got to strike him in the
2:24 went chasing after *A*
2:25 together behind *A*, and they
2:26 *A* began to call to Joab and
2:29 *A* and his men, they marched
2:30 back from following *A* and
2:31 men of *A*—there were three
3:6 *A* himself was continually
3:7 Ish-bosheth said to *A*: Why was
3:8 *A* got very angry at the words
3:9 So may God do to *A* and so may
3:11 one word more in reply to *A*
3:12 *A* sent messengers to David
3:16 *A* said to him: Go, return
3:17 communication by *A* with the
3:19 *A* also spoke in the ears of
3:19 *A* also went to speak in the
3:20 *A* came to David at Hebron
3:20 make a feast for *A* and for
3:21 *A* said to David: Let me rise
3:21 David sent *A* off, and he got
3:22 *A*, he was not with David in
3:23 *A* the son of Ner came to the
3:24 *A* has come to you. Why was
3:25 know *A* the son of Ner, that
3:26 sent messengers after *A*, and
3:27 *A* returned to Hebron, Joab
3:28 of bloodguilt for *A* the son
3:30 killed *A* over the fact that
3:31 sackcloth and wail before *A*
3:32 burial of *A* in Hebron
3:33 king went on to chant over *A*
3:33 should *A* die
3:37 *A* the son of Ner put to death
4:1 that *A* had died in Hebron
4:12 burial place of *A* in Hebron
1Ki 2:5 to *A* the son of Ner and Amasa
2:32 *A* the son of Ner the chief
1Ch 26:28 *A* the son of Ner and Joab
27:21 Jaasiel the son of *A*

Abner's
2Sa 3:32 weep at *A* burial place, and

Abnormal
Le 13:30 is an *a* falling off of hair
13:31 plague of *a* falling off of
13:31 of *a* falling off of hair
13:32 *a* falling off of hair has not
13:32 the *a* falling off of hair is
13:33 *a* falling off of hair shaved
13:33 *a* falling off of hair seven
13:34 the *a* falling off of hair on
13:34 *a* falling off of hair has not
13:35 if the *a* falling off of hair
13:36 *a* falling off of hair has
13:37 *a* falling off of hair has
13:37 *a* falling off of hair has
14:54 the *a* falling off of hair

Aboard
Mt 8:23 when he got *a* a boat, his
13:2 went *a* a boat and sat down
Mr 4:1 he went *a* a boat and sat out
8:13 got *a* again, and went off to
Lu 5:3 Going *a* one of the boats
8:37 he went *a* the boat and turned
Joh 21:3 and got *a* the boat, but
Ac 20:13 intending to take Paul *a*
20:14 we took him *a* and went to
21:2 we went *a* and sailed away
27:2 Going *a* a boat from
27:17 hoisting it *a* they began

Abode
Nu 24:21 and set on the crag is your *a*
1Ki 8:13 a house of lofty *a* for you
2Ch 6:2 built a house of lofty *a* for
Ps 49:14 Sheol rather than a lofty *a*
Pr 21:20 are in the *a* of the wise one
Isa 63:15 lofty *a* of holiness and
Hab 3:11 stood still, in the lofty *a*
Joh 14:23 and make our *a* with him

Abodes
Ps 74:20 full of the *a* of violence
Joh 14:2 there are many *a*

Abolish
Ro 3:31 *a* law by means of our faith
Ga 3:17 so as to *a* the promise

Abolished
Ro 4:14 and the promise has been *a*
Ga 5:11 torture stake has been *a*

Eph 2:15 he *a* the enmity, the Law of
2Ti 1:10 Jesus, who has *a* death but

Abortion
Ex 23:26 woman suffering an *a* nor a
Job 21:10 His cows . . . suffer no *a*
Ps 144:14 Our cattle . . . with no *a*

Abortions
Ge 31:38 she-goats did not suffer *a*

Abound
Isa 2:6 children of foreigners they *a*
40:29 he makes full might *a*
La 2:5 mourning and lamentation *a*
Eze 16:26 prostitution *a* in order to
16:29 making your prostitution *a*
16:51 detestable things *a* more
28:5 you have made your wealth *a*
36:29 the grain and make it *a*
36:30 the fruitage of the tree *a*
Da 11:39 make *a* with glory, and he
Ho 2:8 I had made silver itself *a* for
Mt 5:20 does not *a* more than that of
13:12 and he will be made to *a*
Ro 5:20 that trespassing might *a*
6:1 that undeserved kindness may *a*
15:13 may *a* in hope with power
1Co 14:12 seek to *a* in them for the
2Co 1:5 sufferings for the Christ *a* in
3:9 of righteousness *a* with glory
4:15 *a* because of the thanksgiving
8:2 riches of their generosity *a*
8:7 you also *a* in this kind giving
9:8 undeserved kindness *a* toward
10:15 Then we will *a* still more
Eph 1:8 *a* toward us in all wisdom
Php 1:9 your love may *a* yet more and
1Th 3:12 *a*, in love to one another

Abounded
Ps 4:7 and their new wine have *a*
Ac 9:36 She *a* in good deeds and gifts
Ro 5:15 *a* much more to many
5:20 where sin *a*, undeserved
5:20 kindness *a* still more
1Ti 1:14 kindness of our Lord *a*

Abounding
De 33:19 the *a* wealth of the seas
Ne 9:37 produce is *a* for the kings
Isa 63:1 the One *a* in power to save
Jer 51:13 woman residing on *a* waters
Eze 22:5 *a* in confusion
Lu 15:17 are *a* with bread, while I
2Co 8:7 you are *a* in everything, in

Abounds
Pr 29:16 become many, transgression *a*
2Co 1:5 comfort we get also *a* through

About*
Ge 3:8 *a* the breezy part of the day
6:1 Now it came *a* that when men
11:2 it came *a* . . . journeying
Da 12:4 Many will rove *a*, and the
Lu 3:23 Jesus . . . *a* thirty years old
Ac 1:15 *a* one hundred and twenty
13:20 *a* four hundred and fifty
Ro 4:19 was *a* one hundred years old
Jas 1:6 by the wind and blown *a*

About-face
Jg 20:41 the men of Israel made an *a*

Above*
Ps 148:13 dignity is *a* earth and
Isa 14:13 *A* the stars of God I shall
40:22 dwelling *a* the circle of
Mic 5:9 be high *a* your adversaries
Mt 21:9 we pray, in the heights *a*
Joh 8:23 I am from the realms *a*
Eph 6:16 *A* all things, take up the
Jas 3:17 wisdom from *a* is first of
1Pe 4:8 *A* all things, have intense

Abraham
Ge 17:5 and your name must become *A*
17:9 God said further to *A*: As for
17:15 say to *A*: As for Sarai your
17:17 *A* fell upon his face and
17:18 *A* said to the true God: O
17:22 with him and went up from *A*
17:23 *A* then proceeded to take
17:23 men of the household of *A*
17:24 *A* was ninety-nine years old
17:26 *A* got circumcised, and also
18:6 *A* went hurrying to the tent
18:7 Next *A* ran to the herd and
Ge 18:11 *A* and Sarah were old, being
18:13 Jehovah said to *A*: Why was
18:16 *A* was walking with them to
18:17 Am I keeping covered from *A*
18:18 Why, *A* is surely going to
18:19 bring upon *A* what he has
18:22 was still standing before *A*
18:23 *A* approached and began to
18:27 *A* went on to answer and say
18:33 finished speaking to *A*
18:33 and *A* returned to his place
19:27 *A* made his way early in the
19:29 God kept *A* in mind in that
20:1 *A* moved camp from there to
20:2 *A* repeated concerning Sarah
20:9 Abimelech called *A* and said
20:10 went on to say to *A*: What
20:11 *A* said: It was because I
20:14 gave them to *A* and returned
20:17 *A* began to make supplication
21:2 bore a son to *A* in his old age
21:3 *A* called the name of his son
21:4 *A* proceeded to circumcise
21:5 *A* was a hundred years old
21:7 have uttered to *A*, Sarah will
21:8 *A* then prepared a big feast
21:9 she had borne to *A*, poking fun
21:10 say to *A*: Drive out this
21:11 displeasing to *A* as regards
21:12 God said to *A*: Do not let
21:14 So *A* got up early in the
21:22 said to *A*: God is with you
21:24 So *A* said: I shall swear
21:25 When *A* criticized Abimelech
21:27 *A* took sheep and cattle and
21:28 *A* set seven female lambs of
21:29 say to *A*: What is the
21:34 *A* extended his residence as
22:1 true God put *A* to the test
22:1 *A*! to which he said: Here I
22:3 *A* got up early in the morning
22:4 *A* raised his eyes and began
22:5 *A* now said to his attendants
22:6 *A* took the wood of the burnt
22:7 Isaac began to say to *A* his
22:8 *A* said: God will provide
22:9 *A* built an altar there and set
22:10 *A* put out his hand and took
22:11, 11 saying: *A*, *A*! to which
22:13 *A* raised his eyes and looked
22:13 *A* went and took the ram and
22:14 *A* began to call the name of
22:15 call to *A* the second time
22:19 *A* returned to his attendants
22:19 *A* continued to dwell at
22:20 report got through to *A*: Here
22:23 to Nahor the brother of *A*
23:2 *A* came in to bewail Sarah and
23:3 *A* got up from before his dead
23:5 the sons of Heth answered *A*
23:7 *A* got up and bowed down to
23:10 answered *A* in the hearing of
23:12 *A* bowed down before the
23:14 Ephron answered *A*, saying to
23:16 *A* listened to Ephron, and
23:16 *A* weighed out to Ephron the
23:18 *A* as his purchased property
23:19 *A* buried Sarah his wife in
23:20 became confirmed to *A* for the
24:1 *A* was old, advanced in years
24:1 and Jehovah had blessed *A* in
24:2 *A* said to his servant, the
24:6 *A* said to him: Be on your
24:9 hand under the thigh of *A* his
24:12 God of my master *A*, cause it
24:12 loving-kindness with . . . *A*
24:27 the God of my master *A*
24:42 God of my master *A*, if you
24:48 God of my master *A*, who had
25:1 *A* again took a wife, and her
25:5 *A* gave everything he had to
25:6 the concubines that *A* had
25:6 *A* gave gifts. Then he sent
25:8 *A* expired and died in a good
25:10 *A* had purchased from the
25:10 *A* was buried, and also Sarah
25:12 Ishmael the son of *A* whom
25:12 Hagar . . . bore to *A*
25:19 history of Isaac the son of *A*
25:19 *A* became father to Isaac
26:1 famine . . . in the days of *A*
26:3 statement that I swore to *A*
26:5 *A* listened to my voice and
26:15 dug in the days of *A* his
Ge 26:18 had dug in the days of *A* his
26:24 the God of *A* your father
26:24 on account of *A* my servant
28:4 give to you the blessing of *A*
28:4 which God has given to *A*
28:9 Ishmael the son of *A*
28:13 I am Jehovah the God of *A*
31:42 God of *A* and the Dread of
31:53 Let the god of *A* and the god
32:9 O God of my father *A* and God
35:12 land that I have given to *A*
35:27 Hebron, where *A* and also
48:15 before whom my fathers *A*
48:16 my fathers, *A* and Isaac
49:30 the field that *A* purchased
49:31 buried *A* and Sarah his wife
50:13 field that *A* had purchased
50:24 he swore to *A*, to Isaac and
Ex 2:24 his covenant with *A*, Isaac and
3:6 the God of *A*, the God of Isaac
3:15 Jehovah . . . the God of *A*, the
3:16 the God of *A*, Isaac and Jacob
4:5 the God of *A*, the God of Isaac
6:3 used to appear to *A*, Isaac and
6:8 give to *A*, Isaac and Jacob
32:13 Remember *A*, Isaac and Israel
33:1 I swore to *A*, Isaac and Jacob
Le 26:42 my covenant with *A* I shall
Nu 32:11 sworn to *A*, Isaac and Jacob
De 1:8 to *A*, Isaac and Jacob, to give
6:10 your forefathers *A*, Isaac and
9:5 swore to . . . *A*, Isaac and
9:27 Remember your servants *A*
29:13 forefathers *A*, Isaac and
30:20 *A*, Isaac and Jacob to give
34:4 sworn to *A*, Isaac and Jacob
Jos 24:2 Terah the father of *A* and
24:3 I took your forefather *A*
1Ki 18:36 God of *A*, Isaac and Israel
2Ki 13:23 covenant with *A*, Isaac and
1Ch 1:27 Abram, that is to say, *A*
1:28 sons of *A* were Isaac and
1:34 *A* came to be father to Isaac
16:16 he concluded with *A*
29:18 God of *A*, Isaac and Israel
2Ch 20:7 give it to the seed of *A*
30:6 God of *A*, Isaac and Israel
Ne 9:7 and constituted his name *A*
Ps 47:9 the people of the God of *A*
105:6 you seed of *A* his servant
105:9 covenant he concluded with *A*
105:42 word with *A* his servant
Isa 29:22 he that redeemed *A*
41:8 the seed of *A* my friend
51:2 Look to *A* your father and to
63:16 *A* himself may not have
Jer 33:26 rulers over the seed of *A*
Eze 33:24 *A* happened to be just one
Mic 7:20 loving-kindness given to *A*
Mt 1:1 son of David, son of *A*
1:2 *A* became father to Isaac
1:17 from *A* until David were
3:9 As a father we have *A*. For I
3:9 children to *A* from these
8:11 recline at the table with *A*
22:32 I am the God of *A* and the
Mr 12:26 I am the God of *A* and God of
Lu 1:55 to *A* and to his seed, forever
1:73 the oath that he swore to *A*
3:8 As a father we have *A*. For I
3:8 raise up children to *A* from
3:34 son of *A*, son of Terah
13:16 woman who is a daughter of *A*
13:28 when you see *A* and Isaac and
16:22 to the bosom position of *A*
16:23 saw *A* afar off and Lazarus
16:24 Father *A*, have mercy on me
16:25 *A* said, Child, remember that
16:29 *A* said, They have Moses and
16:30 father *A*, but if someone
19:9 because he also is a son of *A*
20:37 calls Jehovah the God of *A*
Joh 8:39 said to him: Our father is *A*
8:39 do the works of *A*
8:40 *A* did not do this
8:52 *A* died, also the prophets
8:53 greater than our father *A*
8:56 *A* your father rejoiced
8:57 and still you have seen *A*
8:58 Before *A* came into existence
Ac 3:13 God of *A* and of Isaac and of
3:25 to *A*, And in your seed all
7:2 appeared to our forefather *A*
7:16 tomb that *A* had bought for a

Ac 7:17 had openly declared to *A*
7:32 God of *A* and of Isaac and of
13:26 sons of the stock of *A* and
Ro 4:1 *A* our forefather according to
4:2 *A* were declared righteous as
4:3 *A* exercised faith in Jehovah
4:9 counted to *A* as righteousness
4:12 state which our father *A* had
4:13 *A* or his seed had the promise
4:16 adheres to the faith of *A*
11:1 of the seed of *A*, of the tribe
Ga 3:6 *A* put faith in Jehovah, and it
3:7 the ones who are sons of *A*
3:8 the good news beforehand to *A*
3:9 together with faithful *A*
3:14 blessing of *A* might come to
3:16 promises were spoken to *A*
3:18 it to *A* through a promise
4:22 *A* acquired two sons, one by
Heb 6:13 God made his promise to *A*
6:15 after *A* had shown patience
7:1 met *A* returning from the
7:2 *A* apportioned a tenth from
7:4 *A*, the family head, gave a
7:5 issued from the loins of *A*
7:6 took tithes from *A* and
7:9 through *A* even Levi who
11:8 *A*, when he was called
11:17 *A*, when he was tested, as
Jas 2:21 not *A* our father declared
2:23 *A* put faith in Jehovah, and
1Pe 3:6 as Sarah used to obey *A*

Abraham's
Ge 20:18 because of Sarah, *A* wife
24:15 wife of Nahor, *A* brother, and
24:34 to say: I am *A* servant
24:52 *A* servant had heard their
24:59 and *A* servant and his men
25:7 *A* life which he lived, a
25:11 after *A* death God continued
26:18 stopping up after *A* death
1Ch 1:32 Keturah, *A* concubine, she
Joh 8:33 We are *A* offspring and never
8:37 that you are *A* offspring
8:39 If you are *A* children, do
Ro 9:7 *A* seed are they all children
2Co 11:22 Are they *A* seed? I am also
Ga 3:29 *A* seed, heirs with
Heb 2:16 he is assisting *A* seed

Abram
Ge 11:26 Terah . . . father to *A*, Nahor
11:27 Terah became father to *A*
11:29 *A* and Nahor proceeded to
11:31 Terah took *A* his son and Lot
11:31 Sarai . . . wife of *A* his son
12:1 say to *A*: Go your way out of
12:4 *A* went just as Jehovah had
12:4 *A* was seventy-five years old
12:5 *A* took Sarai his wife and Lot
12:6 *A* went on through the land as
12:7 Jehovah now appeared to *A* and
12:9 *A* broke camp, going then from
12:10 *A* made his way down toward
12:14 as soon as *A* entered Egypt
12:16 treated *A* well on her account
12:18 Pharaoh called *A* and said
13:1 *A* went up out of Egypt, he
13:2 *A* was heavily stocked with
13:4 *A* proceeded to call there on
13:5 Lot . . . going along with *A*
13:8 *A* said to Lot: Please, do not
13:12 *A* dwelt in the land of
13:14 Jehovah said to *A* after Lot
13:18 *A* continued to live in tents
14:13 escaped came and told *A* the
14:13 they were confederates of *A*
14:14 *A* got to hear that his
14:19 Blessed be *A* of the Most
14:20 At that *A* gave him a tenth
14:21 king of Sodom said to *A*
14:22 *A* said to the king of Sodom
14:23 It was I who made *A* rich
15:1 word of Jehovah came to *A* in
15:1 Do not fear, *A*. I am a shield
15:2 *A* said: Sovereign Lord Jehovah
15:3 *A* added: Look! You have given
15:11 but *A* kept driving them away
15:12 a deep sleep fell upon *A*
15:13 say to *A*: You may know for
15:18 Jehovah concluded with *A* a
16:2 Sarai said to *A*: Please now!
16:2 *A* listened to the voice of
16:3 gave her to *A* her husband as
Ge 16:5 Sarai said to *A*: The violence
16:6 *A* said to Sarai: Look! Your
16:15 Hagar bore to *A* a son and
16:15 *A* called the name of his son
16:16 *A* was eighty-six years old
16:16 Hagar's bearing Ishmael to *A*
17:1 *A* got to be ninety-nine years
17:1 Jehovah appeared to *A* and said
17:3 *A* fell upon his face, and God
17:5 name will not be called *A*
1Ch 1:27 *A*, that is to say, Abraham
Ne 9:7 chose *A* and brought him out of

Abram's
Ge 11:29 The name of *A* wife was Sarai
12:17 plagues because of Sarai, *A*
13:7 the herders of *A* livestock
14:12 Lot the son of *A* brother
16:1 Sarai, *A* wife, had borne him
16:3 Sarai, *A* wife, took Hagar
16:3 *A* dwelling in the land of

Abreast
2Sa 16:13 walking *a* of him that he
16:13 throwing stones while *a* of

Abroad
Ge 9:19 earth's population spread *a*
28:14 spread *a* to the west and to
Ex 1:12 they kept spreading *a*, so that
1Sa 3:1 was no vision being spread *a*
Job 1:10 has spread *a* in the earth
Ps 68:14 scattered *a* the kings in it
Pr 13:16 will spread *a* foolishness
Eze 17:21 spread *a* even to every wind
34:12 that have been spread *a*
Zec 2:6 I have spread you people *a*
Mt 21:33 householder . . . traveled *a*
25:14 a man, about to travel *a*
25:15 and he went *a*
28:15 saying has been spread *a*
Mr 1:45 and to spread the account *a*
12:1 let it out . . . and traveled *a*
13:34 like a man traveling *a* that
Lu 1:51 has scattered *a* those who are
9:60 declare *a* the kingdom of God
15:13 and traveled *a* into a distant
20:9 *a* for considerable time
Ac 4:17 spread *a* further among the
5:37 obeying him were scattered *a*
1Th 1:8 faith toward God has spread *a*
1Pe 2:9 declare *a* the excellencies

Abronah
Nu 33:34 and went camping in *A*
33:35 pulled away from *A* and went

Absalom
2Sa 3:3 third was *A* the son of Maacah
13:1 *A* the son of David had a
13:4 With Tamar the sister of *A*
13:20 *A* her brother said to her
13:20 house of *A* her brother
13:22 *A* did not speak with Amnon
13:22 *A* hated Amnon over the fact
13:23 *A* came to have
13:23 *A* proceeded to invite all
13:24 *A* came in to the king and
13:25 king said to *A*: No, my son
13:26 *A* said: If not you, let
13:27 *A* began to urge him, so
13:28 *A* commanded his attendants
13:29 just as *A* had commanded
13:30 *A* has struck down all the
13:32 at the order of *A* it has
13:34 *A* went running away
13:37 *A*, he ran off that he might
13:38 *A*, he ran off and made his
13:39 longed to go out to *A*
14:1 king's heart was toward *A*
14:21 bring the young man *A* back
14:23 and brought *A* to Jerusalem
14:24 *A* turned toward his own
14:25 compared with *A* there
14:27 born to *A* three sons and
14:28 *A* continued dwelling in
14:29 *A* sent for Joab to send him
14:30 servants of *A* set the tract
14:31 came to *A* at the house
14:32 *A* said to Joab: Look! I sent
14:33 Then he called *A*, who now
14:33 the king kissed *A*
15:1 *A* proceeded to have a chariot
15:2 *A* rose up early and stood at
15:2 *A* would call him and say
15:3 And *A* would say to him
2Sa 15:4 *A* would go on to say: O that
15:6 *A* kept doing a thing like
15:6 *A* kept stealing the hearts
15:7 *A* proceeded to say to the
15:10 *A* now sent spies through
15:10 *A* has become king in Hebron
15:11 with *A* two hundred men
15:12 *A* sent for Ahithophel the
15:12 growing in number with *A*
15:13 has come to be behind *A*
15:14 no escaping . . . because of *A*
15:31 those conspiring with *A*
15:34 say to *A*, I am your servant
15:37 As for *A*, he proceeded to
16:8 kingship into the hand of *A*
16:15 As for *A* and all the people
16:16 Hushai . . . came in to *A*
16:16 say to *A*: Let the king live
16:17 At this *A* said to Hushai
16:18 So Hushai said to *A*
16:20 Later *A* said to Ahithophel
16:21 Then Ahithophel said to *A*
16:22 they pitched a tent for *A*
16:22 *A* began to have relations
16:23 was both to David and to *A*
17:1 say to *A*: Let me choose
17:4 just right in the eyes of *A*
17:5 *A* said: Call, please, Hushai
17:6 So Hushai came in to *A*
17:6 *A* said to him: According to
17:7 At this Hushai said to *A*
17:9 people that are following *A*
17:14 *A* and all the men of Israel
17:14 might bring calamity upon *A*
17:15 Ahithophel counseled *A* and
17:18 got to see them and told *A*
17:20 The servants of *A* now came
17:24 and *A* himself crossed the
17:25 *A* put in the place of Joab
17:26 *A* took up camping in the
18:5 with the young man *A*
18:5 chiefs over the matter of *A*
18:9 *A* found himself before the
18:9 *A* was riding upon a mule
18:10 seen *A* hung in a big tree
18:12 over the young man, over *A*
18:14 through the heart of *A*
18:15 came around and struck *A*
18:17 took *A* and pitched him in
18:18 *A* himself, while he was
18:29 well with the young man *A*
18:32 well with the young man *A*
18:33, 33 *A*, my son, my son *A*!
18:33 *A* my son, my son!
19:1 carries on mourning over *A*
19:4, 4 My son *A*! *A* my son
19:6 if only *A* were alive and all
19:9 away out of the land from *A*
19:10 *A*, whom we anointed over
20:6 will be worse for us than *A*
1Ki 1:6 mother had borne him after *A*
2:7 I ran away from before *A*
2:28 *A* he had not inclined to
1Ch 3:2 *A* the son of Maacah the
2Ch 11:20 the granddaughter of *A*
11:21 the granddaughter of *A*
Ps 3:*super* on account of *A* his son

Absalom's
2Sa 13:29 *A* attendants proceeded to
18:18 to be called *A* Monument

Absence
1Sa 20:6 asked leave of *a* of me to
20:28 asked leave of *a* from me
Ne 13:6 leave of *a* from the king
Zep 3:18 in *a* from your festal season
Php 2:12 more readily during my *a*

Absent
Zep 3:18 *a* from you they happened to
1Co 5:3 although *a* in body but present
2Co 5:6 we are *a* from the Lord
5:8 become *a* from the body and
5:9 or being *a* from him, we may
10:1 when *a* I am bold toward you
10:11 our word by letters when *a*
13:2 and yet *a* now, I say in
13:10 write these things while *a*
Php 1:27 I come and see you or be *a*
Col 2:5 though I am *a* in the flesh

Absolutely
Ge 39:23 looking after *a* nothing that
Nu 30:14 if her husband *a* keeps silent
De 7:26 loathe it and *a* detest it

De 8:19 you people will *a* perish
12:2 You should *a* destroy all the
31:18 I shall *a* conceal my face in
Jg 11:34 Now she was *a* the only child
1Ki 19:10 been *a* jealous for Jehovah
19:14 been *a* jealous for Jehovah
Job 13:5 only you would *a* keep silent
Isa 24:19 land has *a* burst apart, the
24:19 land has *a* been shaken up
24:19 land has *a* been sent
24:20 land *a* moves unsteadily
Jer 4:10 you have *a* deceived this
14:19 Have you *a* rejected Judah
46:28 *a* not leave you unpunished
49:12 you be *a* left unpunished
La 1:20 for I have been *a* rebellious
Am 3:5 when it has *a* caught nothing
Mr 5:3 *a* nobody was able to bind him
Joh 12:19 you are getting *a* nowhere
2Co 4:8 but not *a* with no way out

Absorbed
1Ti 4:15 be *a* in them, that your

Abstain
Ac 15:20 *a* from things polluted by
2Co 12:6 I *a*, in order that no one
1Th 4:3 that you *a* from fornication
5:22 *A* from . . . wickedness
1Ti 4:3 commanding to *a* from foods

Abstaining
Ac 15:29 *a* from things sacrificed to
1Pe 2:11 keep *a* from fleshly desires

Abstinence
Nu 30:2 bind a vow of *a* upon his soul
30:3 bind herself with a vow of *a*
30:4 hears her vow or her *a* vow
30:4 every *a* vow . . . will stand
30:5 her *a* vows that she has bound
30:7 her *a* vows . . . will stand
30:10 bound an *a* vow upon her soul
30:11 any *a* vow that she has bound
30:12 or as an *a* vow of her soul
30:13 *a* vow to afflict the soul
30:14 established . . . her *a* vows
Zec 7:3 practicing an *a*, the way I
Ac 27:21 long *a* from food, then Paul
2Co 11:27 in *a* from food many times

Abundance
Ge 27:28 an *a* of grain and new wine
Ex 15:7 in the *a* of your superiority
De 28:47 for the *a* of everything
1Sa 1:16 out of the *a* of my concern
1Ch 29:16 *a* that we have prepared
2Ch 9:6 half of the *a* of your wisdom
9:27 are in the Shephelah for *a*
11:23 gave them food in *a* and
17:5 have riches and glory in *a*
18:1 have riches and glory in *a*
18:2 sheep and cattle in *a* for
20:25 in *a* both goods and clothing
24:11 they gathered money in *a*
24:27 *a* of the pronouncement
31:10 and having a surplus in *a*
32:5 made missiles in *a* and
32:29 flock and of the herd in *a*
Ne 5:18 every sort of wine in *a*
9:25 groves and trees for food in *a*
13:22 the *a* of your loving-kindness
Job 23:6 with an *a* of power contend
30:18 the *a* of power my garment
36:31 He gives food in *a*
37:23 *a* of righteousness he will
Ps 5:7 the *a* of your loving-kindness
33:16 saved by the *a* of military
33:16 delivered by the *a* of power
33:17 the *a* of its vital energy it
37:11 delight in the *a* of peace
37:16 the *a* of the many wicked
49:6 about the *a* of their riches
51:1 the *a* of your mercies wipe
52:7 trusts in the *a* of his riches
65:9 earth, that you may give it *a*
66:3 the *a* of your strength your
69:13 the *a* of your loving-kindness
72:7 *a* of peace until the moon
78:15 cause them to drink an *a*
106:7 the *a* of your grand
106:45 to the *a* of his grand
123:3 For to an *a* we have been
145:7 *a* of your goodness they
150:2 to the *a* of his greatness
Pr 5:23 *a* of his foolishness he goes
Pr 7:21 by the *a* of her persuasiveness
10:19 *a* of words there does not
16:8 *a* of products without justice
20:15 gold, also an *a* of corals
Ec 1:18 in the *a* of wisdom there is
1:18 there is an *a* of vexation
5:3 because of *a* of occupation
5:3 because of the *a* of words
5:7 because of *a* of occupation
5:7 are vanities and words in *a*
Isa 7:22 *a* of the producing of milk
9:7 *a* of the princely rule and to
24:22 after an *a* of days they
30:33 Fire and wood are in *a*
33:23 spoil in *a* will have to be
40:26 the *a* of dynamic energy
47:9 for the *a* of your sorceries
47:12 the *a* of your sorceries
63:1 in the *a* of his power
63:7 *a* of his loving-kindnesses
Jer 13:22 the *a* of your error your
30:14 the *a* of your error
30:15 the *a* of your error
33:6 an *a* of peace and truth
48:36 *a* that he has produced will
La 1:3 because of the *a* of servitude
1:5 of the *a* of her transgressions
3:32 the *a* of his loving-kindness
Eze 19:11 of the *a* of its foliage
27:12 *a* of all sorts of valuable
27:16 the *a* of your works
27:18 in the *a* of your works
27:18 the *a* of all your valuable
27:33 the *a* of your valuable
28:5 By the *a* of your wisdom
28:16 the *a* of your sales goods
28:18 the *a* of your errors
31:9 in the *a* of its foliage, and
Ho 9:7 the *a* of your error, even
10:1 the *a* of his fruit he has
Na 3:4 *a* of the acts of prostitution
Zec 8:4 of the *a* of his days
14:14 garments in excessive *a*
Mt 12:34 out of the *a* of the heart
25:29 be given and he will have *a*
Lu 6:45 out of the heart's *a* his
12:15 even when a person has an *a*
Joh 10:10 life and might have it in *a*
Ro 5:17 *a* of the undeserved kindness
2Co 8:2 their *a* of joy and their deep
Php 4:12 know indeed how to have an *a*
4:12 how to have an *a* and how to
4:18 things in full and have an *a*

Abundant
Ge 6:5 badness of man was *a* in the
Ex 34:6 and *a* in loving-kindness and
Nu 14:18 and *a* in loving-kindness
1Sa 2:5 she that was *a* in sons has
12:17 your evil is *a* that you have
2Sa 3:22 spoil . . . with them was *a*
2Ch 20:25 the spoil, for it was *a*
28:13 *a* is the guilt we have, and
Ne 9:17 and *a* in loving-kindness
9:19 your *a* mercy did not leave
9:27 in accord with your *a* mercy
9:28 in accord with your *a* mercy
9:31 your *a* mercy you did not
9:35 and amid your *a* good things
Job 32:9 not those merely *a* in days
39:11 because its power is *a*
Ps 31:19 How *a* your goodness is
86:5 And the loving-kindness . . . is *a*
86:15 *a* in loving-kindness and
103:8 and *a* in loving-kindness
119:165 *A* peace belongs to those
147:5 great and is *a* in power
Pr 14:4 crop is *a* because of the
14:29 is *a* in discernment, but one
15:6 there is an *a* store, but in
15:16 an *a* supply and confusion
22:1 name . . . rather than *a* riches
28:12 exulting, there is *a* beauty
28:16 *a* in fraudulent practices
Ec 8:6 calamity of mankind is *a* upon
Isa 54:13 the peace . . . will be *a*
57:9 making your ointments *a*
63:7 *a* goodness to the house of
Jer 13:9 and the *a* pride of Jerusalem
32:19 and *a* in acts, you whose
41:12 *a* waters that were in
51:13 waters, *a* in treasures
La 1:1 city that was *a* with people
3:23 Your faithfulness is *a*
Eze 19:10 became because of *a* water
Da 4:12 and its fruit was *a*, and
4:21 the fruit of which was *a*
12:4 true knowledge will become *a*
Ho 9:7 even animosity being *a*
Joe 2:13 and *a* in loving-kindness
3:13 their badness has become *a*
Jon 4:2 *a* in loving-kindness, and
1Co 12:23 surround with more *a* honor
12:23 have the more *a* comeliness
12:24 giving honor more *a* to the
2Co 7:15 affections are more *a* toward

Abundantly
2Sa 10:5 until your beards grow *a*
1Ch 19:5 until your beards grow *a*
2Ch 31:5 everything they brought in *a*
Job 36:28 They drip upon mankind *a*
Ps 123:4 *A* our soul has been glutted
130:7 *a* so is there redemption
2Co 7:13 we rejoiced still more *a*
9:10 he that *a* supplies seed to the
9:12 to supply *a* the wants of the
11:9 *a* supplied my deficiency
12:15 If I love you the more *a*
Heb 6:17 demonstrate more *a* to the
7:15 still more *a* clear that

Abuse
Le 24:11 *a* the Name and to call down
Isa 43:28 Israel over to words of *a*
1Co 9:18 not *a* my authority in the

Abused
Ac 7:24 for the one being *a* by

Abuser
Le 24:16 *a* of Jehovah's name should

Abusing
Le 24:16 to death for his *a* the Name
Jg 19:25 kept on *a* her all night long

Abusive
Isa 51:7 because of their *a* words
Zep 2:8 *a* words of the sons of Ammon
Eph 4:31 *a* speech be taken away from
Col 3:8 *a* speech, and obscene talk
1Ti 6:4 envy, strife, *a* speeches
2Pe 2:11 an accusation in *a* terms
Jude 9 against him in *a* terms, but

Abusively
Nu 15:30 he speaking *a* of Jehovah, in
1Sa 31:4 and deal *a* with me
2Ki 19:6 king of Assyria spoke *a* of
19:22 you taunted and spoken of *a*
1Ch 10:4 and certainly deal *a* with me
Ps 44:16 reproaching and speaking *a*
Isa 37:6 Assyria spoke *a* of me
37:23 taunted and spoken of *a*
Jer 38:19 actually deal *a* with me
Eze 20:27 forefathers spoke *a* of me
Mt 27:39 passersby began speaking *a*
Mr 15:29 would speak *a* to him
Lu 23:39 began to say *a* to him
Ac 18:6 opposing and speaking *a*, he
1Co 10:30 am I to be spoken of *a* over
Tit 2:5 may not be spoken of *a*
1Pe 4:4 go on speaking *a* of you
2Pe 2:2 the truth will be spoken of *a*
2:10 not tremble . . . but speak *a*
2:12 are ignorant and speak *a*
Jude 8 speaking *a* of glorious ones
10 are speaking *a* of all the

Abyss
Ps 88:6 In dark places, in a large *a*
Lu 8:31 to go away into the *a*
Ro 10:7 Who will descend into the *a*?
Re 9:1 key of the pit of the *a* was
9:2 he opened the pit of the *a*
9:11 a king, the angel of the *a*
11:7 that ascends out of the *a*
17:8 about to ascend out of the *a*
20:1 key of the *a* and a great
20:3 he hurled him into the *a*

Acacia
Ex 25:5 and sealskins, and *a* wood
25:10 make an Ark of *a* wood, two
25:13 make poles of *a* wood and
25:23 must make a table of *a* wood
25:28 make the poles of *a* wood and
26:15 of *a* wood, standing on end
26:26 must make bars of *a* wood
26:32 put it upon four pillars of *a*
26:37 five pillars of *a* and overlay

Ex 27:1 make the altar of *a* wood
27:6 its poles being of *a* wood
30:1 of *a* wood you will make
30:5 make the poles of *a* wood
35:7 and sealskins and *a* wood
35:24 *a* wood for all the work of
36:20 tabernacle out of *a* wood
36:31 make bars of *a* wood, five
36:36 made for it four *a* pillars
37:1 now made the Ark of *a* wood
37:4 next made poles of *a* wood
37:10 make the table of *a* wood
37:15 he made the poles of *a* wood
37:25 altar of incense . . . *a* wood
37:28 he made the poles of *a* wood
38:1 the altar . . . out of *a* wood
38:6 he made the poles of *a* wood
De 10:3 I made an ark of *a* wood and
Isa 41:19 the *a* and the myrtle and
Joe 3:18 torrent valley of the *A* Trees

Accad
Ge 10:10 Babel and Erech and *A* and

Accede
De 13:8 you must not *a* to his wish

Accept
Ge 21:30 *a* the seven female lambs at
Ex 22:11 and their owner must *a* it
23:8 You are not to *a* a bribe, for
Nu 7:5 *A* them from them, as they must
De 16:19 not be partial or *a* a bribe
1Sa 8:3 would *a* a bribe and pervert
10:4 must *a* them from their hand
2Sa 18:31 my lord the king *a* news
2Ki 5:15 *a*, please, a blessing gift
5:16 I will not *a* it
5:16 he began to urge him to *a* it
5:26 Is it a time to *a* silver or
5:26 or to *a* garments or olive
Ezr 9:12 do you *a* for your sons
Ne 13:25 not *a* any of their daughters
Es 4:4 And he did not *a* them
Job 2:10 *a* merely what is good from
2:10 and not *a* also what is bad
42:8 His face only I shall *a* so as
Ps 6:9 will *a* my own prayer
20:3 *a* your burnt offering as
Pr 4:10 my son, and *a* my sayings
10:8 one wise in heart will *a*
19:20 to counsel and *a* discipline
Ho 14:2 *a* what is good, and we will
Zep 3:2 she did not *a* discipline
3:7 will *a* discipline; so that
Mt 10:38 not *a* his torture stake and
11:14 and if you want to *a* it, He
Mr 4:16 the word, they *a* it with joy
Joh 5:34 not *a* the witness from man
5:41 I do not *a* glory from men
2Co 6:1 *a* the undeserved kindness of
11:16 *a* me even if as
Eph 6:17 *a* the helmet of salvation
2Th 2:10 not *a* the love of the truth
Heb 11:35 would not *a* release by some
Jas 1:21 and *a* with mildness the

Acceptable
1Ch 13:2 is *a* with Jehovah our God
Ps 69:13 At an *a* time, O God
Isa 58:5 and a day *a* to Jehovah
Lu 4:19 to preach Jehovah's *a* year
Ac 10:35 righteousness is *a* to him
Ro 12:1 living, holy, *a* to God
12:2 *a* and perfect will of God
14:18 slaves for Christ is *a* to
15:16 nations, might prove to be *a*
15:31 prove to be *a* to the holy
2Co 5:9 we may be *a* to him
6:2 In an *a* time I heard you
6:2 Now is the especially *a* time
8:12 *a* according to what a person
Eph 5:10 of what is *a* to the Lord
Php 4:18 received . . . an *a* sacrifice
1Ti 2:3 *a* in the sight of our Savior
5:4 for this is *a* in God's sight
1Pe 2:5 spiritual sacrifices *a* to God

Acceptably
Heb 12:28 *a* render God sacred service

Acceptance
Isa 56:7 will be for *a* upon my altar
1Ti 1:15 deserving of full *a* is the
4:9 and deserving of full *a* is

Accepted
Le 1:4 graciously *a* for him to make
Le 7:18 not be *a* with approval
19:7 will not be *a* with approval
22:23 vow it will not be *a* with
22:25 not be *a* with approval of
22:27 will be *a* with approval as an
Nu 7:6 Moses *a* the wagons and the
31:51 priest *a* the gold from them
31:54 priest *a* the gold from the
Jg 13:23 not have *a* a burnt offering
1Sa 12:3 have I *a* hush money that I
12:4 nor have you *a* anything at
25:35 David *a* from her hand what
Ezr 9:2 *a* some of their daughters for
10:44 had *a* foreign wives, and
Es 9:23 Jews *a* what they had started
9:27 the Jews imposed and *a* upon
Job 42:9 and so Jehovah *a* Job's face
Pr 1:25 my reproof you have not *a*
Lu 4:24 no prophet is *a* in his home
Joh 3:33 He that has *a* his witness
Ac 8:14 Samaria had *a* the word of
2Co 11:4 news other than what you *a*
Ga 1:9 something beyond what you *a*
Php 4:9 you learned as well as *a* and
Col 2:6 as you have *a* Christ Jesus
4:17 the ministry which you *a* in
1Th 1:6 you *a* the word under much
2:13 *a* it, not as the word of men

Accepting
2Ki 5:20 not *a* from his hand what he
Mt 13:20 and at once *a* it with joy
Lu 22:17 *a* a cup, he gave thanks and
Joh 3:32 but no man is *a* his witness
5:44 are *a* glory from one another
2Co 11:8 I robbed by *a* provisions in

Accepts
De 10:17 nor *a* a bribe
27:25 *a* a bribe to strike a soul

Access
2Ki 25:19 those having *a* to the king
Es 1:14 having *a* to the king, and who
Jer 52:25 those having *a* to the king
Da 7:13 Ancient of Days he gained *a*
Zec 3:7 give you free *a* among these

Accident
Ge 42:4 a fatal *a* may befall him
42:38 If a fatal *a* should befall
44:29 a fatal *a* were to befall him
Ex 21:22 but no fatal *a* occurs, he is
21:23 if a fatal *a* should occur
1Sa 6:9 *a* it was that happened to us

Acco
Jg 1:31 of *A* and the inhabitants of

Accompanied
Jg 13:11 Manoah got up and *a* his wife
Mt 27:55 had *a* Jesus from Galilee to
Heb 6:9 and things *a* with salvation

Accompany
Jg 9:4 men, that they might *a* him
Ec 8:15 *a* them in their hard work for
Mr 15:41 *a* him and minister to him
Re 14:2 singers who *a* themselves on
18:22 singers who *a* themselves on

Accompanying
De 23:14 turn away from *a* you
Ru 1:16 to turn back from *a* you; for
1Sa 25:42 *a* the messengers of David
Mr 9:38 because he was not *a* us
Ac 20:4 were *a* him Sopater the son of
Eph 5:19 singing and *a* yourselves

Accomplish
Job 7:20 what can I *a* against you
11:8 What can you *a*? It is deeper
22:17 And what can the Almighty *a*
35:6 what do you *a* against him?
Ec 2:11 that I had worked hard to *a*
Isa 16:12 he could not *a* anything
26:18 real salvation do we *a* as
Joh 5:36 Father assigned me to *a*
2Ti 4:5 fully *a* your ministry

Accomplished
2Ch 36:22 of Jeremiah might be *a*
Ezr 1:1 of Jeremiah might be *a*
La 2:17 Jehovah . . . has *a* his saying
4:11 Jehovah has *a* his rage. He has
Lu 22:37 is written must be *a* in me
Joh 19:28 now all things had been *a*
19:28 scripture might be *a* he
19:30 Jesus said: It has been *a*
Ac 13:29 *a* all the things written
2Ti 4:17 preaching might be fully *a*
Jas 1:15 sin, when it has been *a*
1Pe 5:9 *a* in the entire association
Re 17:17 words of God . . . have been *a*

Accomplishing
Ps 148:8 wind, *a* his word
Lu 13:32 and *a* healing today and

Accomplishment
Pr 15:22 of counselors there is *a*
Lu 22:37 concerns me is having an *a*

Accord
Nu 8:20 *a* with all that Jehovah had
8:26 *a* with this you will do to
De 1:41 fight in *a* with all that
26:13 *a* with all your commandment
26:14 I have done in *a* with all
29:21 *a* with all the oath of the
Jos 9:4 of their own *a*, acted with
18:4 in *a* with their inheritance
22:29 to rebel of our own *a*
24:22 of your own *a* have chosen
1Sa 8:8 In *a* with all their doings
14:7 in *a* with your heart
25:9 *a* with all these words in
25:12 in *a* with all these words
2Sa 9:11 In *a* with all that my lord
13:35 *a* with the word of your
24:19 in *a* with the word of Gad
1Ki 20:33 as a decision of his own *a*
Ne 9:27 in *a* with your abundant mercy
9:28 in *a* with your abundant mercy
Ps 119:85 are not in *a* with your law
Ec 8:16 In *a* with this I applied my
Jer 13:2 *a* with the word of Jehovah
17:4 loose, even of your own *a*
26:20 *a* with all the words of
29:10 In *a* with the fulfilling of
Eze 24:24 In *a* with all that he has
Da 6:9 In *a* with this, King Darius
Ho 10:12 in *a* with loving-kindness
Jon 3:3 in *a* with the word of Jehovah
Lu 1:6 *a* with all the commandments
Ac 1:14 With one *a* all these were
2:46 at the temple with one *a*
4:24 one *a* raised their voices
5:12 all with one *a* in Solomon's
7:57 rushed upon him with one *a*
8:6 one *a* the crowds were paying
12:10 opened to them of its own *a*
12:20 one *a* they came to him and
15:25 have come to a unanimous *a*
18:12 the Jews rose up with one *a*
19:29 with one *a* they rushed into
23:3 judge me in *a* with the Law
Ro 2:2 in *a* with truth, against
4:18 in *a* with what had been said
7:5 we were in *a* with the flesh
8:4 walk, not in *a* with the flesh
8:4 but in *a* with the spirit
8:5 who are in *a* with the flesh
8:5 those in *a* with the spirit on
8:12 to live in *a* with the flesh
8:13 you live in *a* with the flesh
8:27 pleading in *a* with God for
14:15 no longer walking in *a* with
14:22 have it in *a* with yourself
15:6 with one *a* you may with one
16:25 in *a* with the good news I
16:26 in *a* with the command of
2Co 8:4 of their own *a* kept begging
8:17 is going forth of his own *a*
2Th 1:12 in *a* with the undeserved
1Ti 1:18 in *a* with the predictions
2Ti 4:3 in *a* with their own desires
Heb 5:4 this honor, not of his own *a*
1Pe 1:15 in *a* with the Holy One who

Accordance
Ex 34:27 in *a* with these words that I
De 17:10 you must do in *a* with the
17:11 In *a* with the law that they
2Ch 31:2 *a* with its service for the
Isa 59:18 In *a* with the dealings he
Col 1:25 in *a* with the stewardship
1:29 in *a* with the operation of
2:22 in *a* with the commands and

According*
Ge 1:11 fruit *a* to their kinds
1:12 vegetation bearing seed *a* to
1:12 which is in it *a* to its kind
1:21 waters swarmed forth *a* to

Ge 1:21 flying creature *a* to its kind
1:24 living souls *a* to their kinds
1:24 wild beast . . . *a* to its kind
1:25 of the earth *a* to its kind
1:25 domestic animal *a* to its kind
1:25 animal . . . *a* to its kind
1:26 *a* to our likeness, and let
6:20 creatures *a* to their kinds
6:20 domestic animals *a* to their
6:20 animals of the ground *a* to
7:14 wild beast *a* to its kind
7:14 domestic animal *a* to its kind
7:14 animal . . . *a* to its kind
7:14 flying creature . . . *a* to its
8:19 *a* to their families they went
10:20 sons of Ham *a* to their
10:20 *a* to their tongues, in their
10:31 *a* to their families
10:31 *a* to their tongues, in their
10:31 *a* to their nations
10:32 *a* to their family descents
Le 11:14 the black kite *a* to its kind
11:15 and every raven *a* to its kind
11:16 and the falcon *a* to its kind
11:19 the heron *a* to its kind, and
11:22 migratory locust *a* to its
11:22 the cricket *a* to its kind
11:22 the grasshopper *a* to its kind
11:29 the lizard *a* to its kind
De 14:13 the glede *a* to its kind
14:14 every raven *a* to its kind
14:15 the falcon *a* to its kind
14:18 the heron *a* to its kind, and
Ps 110:4 *A* to the manner of
Mt 25:15 *a* to his own ability, and he
1Co 3:8 reward *a* to his own labor
2Co 11:15 shall be *a* to their works
11:18 are boasting *a* to the flesh
2Ti 4:14 repay him *a* to his deeds
Heb 5:6 *a* . . . manner of Melchizedek
5:10 *a* . . . manner of Melchizedek
6:20 *a* . . . manner of Melchizedek
7:11 *a* . . . manner of Melchizedek
7:17 *a* . . . manner of Melchizedek
1Pe 1:17 *a* to each one's work
Re 20:12 the scrolls *a* to their deeds
20:13 individually *a* to their deeds

Accords
Php 3:17 that *a* with the example you
1Ti 6:3 that *a* with godly devotion
Tit 1:1 which *a* with godly devotion

Account
Ge 3:17 cursed is the ground on your *a*
8:21 upon the ground on man's *a*
12:13 go well with me on your *a*
12:16 treated Abram well on her *a*
18:26 the whole place on their *a*
18:29 not do it on *a* of the forty
18:31 to ruin on *a* of the twenty
18:32 not bring it to ruin on *a* of
26:9 for fear I should die on her *a*
26:24 on *a* of Abraham my servant
27:41 on *a* of the blessing with
Ex 6:1 on *a* of a strong hand he will
6:1 on *a* of a strong hand he will
18:8 on *a* of Israel, and all the
Le 7:18 It will not be put to his *a*
Nu 12:1 Moses on *a* of the Cushite
13:24 on *a* of the cluster that the
16:49 those dead on *a* of Korah
De 1:37 Jehovah got incensed on your *a*
3:26 furious against me on your *a*
4:21 got incensed at me on your *a*
11:23 all these nations on *a* of you
15:10 on this *a* Jehovah your God
18:12 on *a* of these detestable
18:19 I shall myself require an *a*
21:8 to the *a* of your people Israel
21:8 bloodguilt . . . set to their *a*
24:16 put to death on *a* of children
24:16 put to death on *a* of fathers
Jos 23:3 all these nations on your *a*
23:5 dispossessed them on your *a*
23:13 these nations on your *a*
Jg 6:7 Jehovah for aid on *a* of Midian
1Sa 2:30 will be of little *a*
7:7 afraid on *a* of the Philistines
15:2 call to *a* what Amalek did to
17:24 went fleeing on *a* of him
21:10 running away on *a* of Saul
21:12 afraid on *a* of Achish the
23:10 the city in ruin on my *a*
30:16 on *a* of all the great spoil
2Sa 3:8 *a* for an error concerning a
6:12 *a* of the ark of the true God
7:15 whom I removed on *a* of you
13:2 felt sick on *a* of Tamar his
21:7 on *a* of the oath of Jehovah
1Ki 9:15 *a* of those conscripted for
11:39 shall humiliate . . . on *a* of
12:2 run off on *a* of King Solomon
14:16 *a* of the sins of Jeroboam
15:4 on *a* of David, Jehovah his
15:30 on *a* of the sins of
16:13 on *a* of all the sins of
21:29 humbled himself on my *a*
2Ki 19:4 call him to *a* for the words
24:20 on *a* of the anger of Jehovah
1Ch 14:2 on *a* of his people Israel
16:21 on their *a* he reproved kings
16:30 in severe pains on *a* of him
16:33 joyfully on *a* of Jehovah
27:24 the *a* of the affairs of the
29:12 the glory are on *a* of you
2Ch 10:2 run away on *a* of Solomon the
24:6 required an *a* of the Levites
28:19 humbled Judah on *a* of Ahaz
32:7 *a* of all the crowd that is
36:12 *a* of Jeremiah the prophet
Ezr 4:14 on this *a* we have sent and
6:11 a public privy on this *a*
9:15 stand before you on *a* of this
10:9 on *a* of the showers of rain
10:14 on *a* of this matter
Ne 4:9 day and night on *a* of them
4:14 Do not be afraid on their *a*
5:7 a great assembly on their *a*
5:15 on *a* of the fear of God
13:22 do remember to my *a*
13:29 on *a* of the defilement of
Es 5:9 not quake on *a* of him, Haman
Job 13:20 not conceal . . . on your *a*
17:12 is near on *a* of darkness
20:2 *a* of my inward excitement
23:2 is heavy on *a* of my sighing
30:11 they left loose on my *a*
36:23 Who has called his way to *a*
39:22 turn back on *a* of a sword
40:4 I have become of little *a*
Ps 3:*super* on *a* of Absalom his son
8:2 *a* of those showing hostility
27:11 on *a* of my foes
32:2 whose *a* Jehovah does not put
32:6 On this *a* every loyal one
38:3 no peace . . . on *a* of my sin
40:17 Jehovah himself takes *a* of
48:11 *a* of your judicial decisions
56:7 On *a* of their hurtfulness
57:2 to an end on my *a*
60:4 flee zigzag on *a* of the bow
69:7 For on your *a* I have borne
69:18 On *a* of my enemies redeem
79:9 our sins on *a* of your name
97:5 like wax on *a* of Jehovah
97:5 *a* of the Lord of the whole
105:14 their *a* he reproved kings
132:10 On *a* of David your servant
144:3 you should take *a* of him
Ec 3:14 may be afraid on *a* of him
5:6 indignant on *a* of your voice
10:5 on *a* of the one in power
11:9 know that on *a* of all these
Isa 2:22 himself to be taken into *a*
13:17 Medes, who *a* silver itself
17:9 on *a* of the sons of Israel
26:21 call to *a* the error of
30:11 to cease just on *a* of us
30:17 on *a* of the rebuke of one
30:17 *a* of the rebuke of five
33:8 taken no *a* of mortal man
37:4 *a* for the words that Jehovah
38:16 on that *a* they keep living
43:26 tell your own *a* of it in
51:13 on *a* of the rage of the one
53:3 and we held him as of no *a*
54:15 will fall even on *a* of you
64:1 on *a* of you the very
64:2 on *a* of you the nations
64:3 On *a* of you the mountains
Jer 2:35 on *a* of your saying, I have
4:1 disgusting things on my *a*
4:4 on *a* of the badness of your
4:8 On this *a* gird on sackcloth
4:28 On this *a* the land will
9:7 on *a* of the daughter of my
9:12 On what *a* should the land
9:13 On *a* of their leaving my law
Jer 10:19 on *a* of my breakdown
11:17 on *a* of the badness of the
14:4 On *a* of the soil that has
15:4 on *a* of Manasseh the son
15:15 on *a* of your own self
16:7 on *a* of mourning to comfort
16:7 on *a* of one's father and
16:7 and on *a* of one's mother
16:10 On what *a* has Jehovah
16:11 On *a* of the fact that your
16:18 on *a* of their profaning my
22:8 On what *a* did Jehovah do
22:9 On *a* of the fact that they
25:12 call to *a* against the king
30:14 on *a* of the abundance of
30:15 on *a* of your breakdown
30:15 pain is incurable on *a* of
31:37 Israel on *a* of all that they
32:32 *a* of all the badness of the
33:4 *a* of the siege ramparts and
33:4 and on *a* of the sword
33:5 *a* of all whose badness I
33:9 *a* of all the goodness and
33:9 *a* of all the peace that I am
36:31 call to *a* against him and
47:4 *a* of the day that is coming
49:17 on *a* of all her plagues
49:20 on *a* of them he will make
50:13 on *a* of all her plagues
50:45 on *a* of them he will cause
52:3 *a* of the anger of Jehovah
La 1:5 on *a* of the abundance of her
1:22 on *a* of all my transgressions
2:11 on *a* of the crash of the
2:19 *a* of the soul of your children
3:39 man on *a* of his sin
3:48 on *a* of the breakdown of the
5:17 On this *a* our heart has
5:17 On *a* of these things our eyes
5:18 On *a* of Zion's mountain that
Eze 6:11 *a* of all the bad detestable
14:15 on *a* of the wild beasts
16:15 on *a* of your name and to
16:27 humiliated on *a* of your way
18:26 does injustice and dies on *a*
21:7 On *a* of what are you sighing?
23:30 on *a* of the fact that you
28:17 *a* of your beaming splendor
31:15 On its *a* I will cover the
31:15 on its *a* I shall darken
31:15 on its *a* the trees of the
32:8 shall darken them on your *a*
33:19 it will be on *a* of them
33:29 on *a* of all their detestable
36:18 on *a* of the blood that they
36:31 on *a* of your errors and
36:31 *a* of your detestable things
39:23 on *a* of the fact that they
44:7 *a* of all your detestable
Da 7:1 complete *a* of the matters he
7:15 distressed within on *a* of it
8:27 numbed on *a* of the thing seen
11:22 flooded over on *a* of him
Ho 7:14 On *a* of their grain and sweet
9:7 *a* of the abundance of your
9:15 On *a* of the evil of their
10:5 on *a* of its glory
Joe 1:3 give an *a* to your own sons
1:5 on *a* of sweet wine, for it
1:11 have howled, on *a* of wheat
1:11 and on *a* of barley
2:13 regret on *a* of the calamity
3:2 on *a* of my people and my
Am 1:3 *a* of three revolts of Damascus
1:3 and on *a* of four, I shall not
1:3 on *a* of their threshing Gilead
1:6 On *a* of three revolts of Gaza
1:6 on *a* of four, I shall not turn
1:6 on *a* of their taking into
1:9 On *a* of three revolts of Tyre
1:9 on *a* of four, I shall not turn
1:9 on *a* of their handing over a
1:11 On *a* of three revolts of Edom
1:11 and on *a* of four, I shall not
1:11 on *a* of his pursuing his own
1:13 On *a* of three revolts of the
1:13 and on *a* of four, I shall not
1:13 on *a* of their slitting open
2:1 On *a* of three revolts of Moab
2:1 on *a* of four, I shall not turn
2:1 on *a* of his burning the bones
2:4 On *a* of three revolts of Judah
2:4 on *a* of four, I shall not
2:4 on *a* of their rejecting the

Am 2:6 On *a* of three revolts of Israel
2:6 *a* of four, I shall not turn it
2:6 on *a* of their selling someone
2:9 the Amorite on *a* of them
8:8 on this *a* that the land will
Jon 1:7 whose *a* we have this calamity
1:8 on whose *a* it is that we
1:12 on my *a* that this great
Mic 1:8 On this *a* I will wail and
1:16 shear your hair off on *a* of
3:12 on *a* of you men Zion will
6:13 on *a* of your sins
7:13 desolate waste on *a* of its
Na 1:14 because you have been of no *a*
Zep 3:7 I must call to *a* against her
3:18 bearing reproach on her *a*
Mal 2:3 I am rebuking on your *a* the
2:14, 14 On what *a*? On this *a*
3:14 dejectedly on *a* of Jehovah
Mt 5:32 except on *a* of fornication
6:25 On this *a* I say to you: Stop
10:22 hatred . . . on *a* of my name
12:31 On this *a* I say to you
12:36 render an *a* concerning it on
13:21 has arisen on *a* of the word
13:58 on *a* of their lack of faith
14:3 on *a* of Herodias the wife of
19:12 eunuchs on *a* of the kingdom
24:9 hatred . . . on *a* of my name
24:22 but on *a* of the chosen ones
24:44 On this *a* you too prove
Mr 1:45 and to spread the *a* abroad
2:4 to Jesus on *a* of the crowd
2:26 *a* about Abiathar the chief
6:14 on that *a* the powerful works
6:17 on *a* of Herodias the wife of
9:12 and be treated as of no *a*
10:7 On this *a* a man will leave
12:26 in the *a* about the thornbush
13:13 hatred . . . on *a* of my name
13:20 on *a* of the chosen ones
Lu 5:19 on *a* of the crowd, they
11:49 On this *a* the wisdom of God
12:22 On this *a* I say to you
16:2 Hand in the *a* of your
20:37 in the *a* about the thornbush
Joh 3:29 on *a* of the voice of the
4:39 put faith in him on *a* of the
4:41 on *a* of what he said
4:42 not believe any longer on *a*
5:16 on this *a* the Jews went
5:18 On this *a*, indeed, the Jews
11:15 I rejoice on your *a* that I
11:42 on *a* of the crowd standing
12:9 not on *a* of Jesus only, but
12:11 *a* of him many of the Jews
12:18 *a* the crowd, because they
14:11 believe on *a* of the works
15:19 this *a* the world hates you
15:21 against you on *a* of my name
17:11 on *a* of your own name
17:12 on *a* of your own name
19:42 *a* of the preparation of the
Ac 1:1 The first *a*, O Theophilus, I
2:26 On this *a* my heart became
4:11 as of no *a* that has become
4:21 and on *a* of the people
11:22 *a* about them got to the ears
18:3 *a* of being of the same trade
18:27 on *a* of God's undeserved
20:24 do not make my soul of any *a*
21:19 an *a* of the things God did
24:26 On that *a* he sent for him
26:21 On *a* of these things Jews
28:20 on this *a* I entreated to
Ro 2:24 blasphemed on *a* of you people
4:8 will by no means take into *a*
4:16 On this *a* it was as a result
8:10 is dead on *a* of sin, but the
8:10 is life on *a* of righteousness
13:5 *a* of that wrath but also on
13:5 also on *a* of your conscience
14:12 render an *a* for himself
1Co 10:25 on *a* of your conscience
10:27 making no inquiry on *a* of
10:28 Do not eat on *a* of the one
10:28 and on *a* of conscience
13:5 does not keep *a* of the injury
2Co 2:13 on *a* of not finding Titus my
10:7 this fact into *a* for himself
10:11 such a man take this into *a*
Eph 3:1 On *a* of this I, Paul, the
3:13 on *a* of these tribulations
3:14 On *a* of this I bend my knees
Eph 5:17 On this *a* cease becoming
6:13 On this *a* take up the
Php 1:7 on *a* of my having you in my
1:24 is more necessary on your *a*
2:30 on *a* of the Lord's work he
3:7 loss on *a* of the Christ
3:8 on *a* of the excelling value
3:8 On *a* of him I have taken the
4:17 brings more credit to your *a*
Col 3:6 On *a* of those things the
1Th 3:9 we are rejoicing on your *a*
2Th 1:6 This takes into *a* that it is
2Ti 2:10 On this *a* I go on enduring
4:16 may it not be put to their *a*
Phm 15 on this *a* he broke away for an
18 keep this charged to my *a*
Heb 5:3 on its *a* he is obliged to
7:18 on *a* of its weakness and
13:17 those who will render an *a*
1Pe 4:5 render an *a* to the one ready
5:12 faithful brother, as I *a* him
2Pe 2:2 on *a* of these the way of the
Re 12:12 this *a* be glad, you heavens

Accountable
Mt 5:21 *a* to the court of justice
5:22 *a* to the court of justice
5:22 be *a* to the Supreme Court

Accounted
Le 25:31 *a* as part of the field of
Ps 44:22 *a* as sheep for slaughtering
Pr 27:14 a malediction it will be *a*
Isa 5:28 to be *a* as flint itself
29:16 potter himself be *a* just
29:17 will be *a* just as a forest
32:15 itself is *a* as a real forest
40:15 scales they have been *a*
40:17 unreality they have been *a*
53:4 *a* him as plagued, stricken
Ho 8:12 they have been *a*
Ro 8:36 *a* as sheep for slaughtering

Accounting
2Ki 12:15 not call for an *a* with the
22:7 no *a* should be taken of the
Job 31:14 And when he calls for an *a*
35:15 has not called for an *a*
Ps 10:13 You will not require an *a*
Isa 10:12 *a* for the fruitage of the
Jer 5:9 Should I not take an *a*
5:29 an *a* because of these very
6:6 with which an *a* must be held
6:15 I must hold an *a* with them
9:9 should I not hold an *a* with
9:25 *a* with everyone circumcised
21:14 hold an *a* against you
44:13 *a* against those dwelling in
44:13 an *a* against Jerusalem
Ho 1:4 hold an *a* for the acts of
2:13 hold an *a* against her for all
4:9 hold an *a* against them for
4:14 an *a* against your daughters
8:13 hold an *a* for their sins
12:2 to hold an *a* against Jacob
Am 3:2 hold an *a* against you for all
3:14 *a* for the revolts of Israel
3:14 *a* against the altars of
Zec 10:3 I shall hold an *a*
Ro 9:28 Jehovah will make an *a* on
Heb 4:13 him with whom we have an *a*

Accounts
Mt 18:23 to settle *a* with his slaves
25:19 and settled *a* with them

Accredited
1Sa 3:20 *a* for the position of prophet

Accumulate
2Ti 4:3 *a* teachers for themselves to

Accumulated
Ge 12:5 all the goods that they had *a*
31:18 all the goods that he had *a*
31:18 he had *a* in Paddan-aram
36:6 wealth, which he had *a* in
46:6 *a* in the land of Canaan
Ec 2:8 I *a* also silver and gold for

Accumulating
Eze 38:12 one that is *a* wealth and

Accuracy
Lu 1:3 things from the start with *a*

Accurate
Le 19:36 should prove to have *a* scales
19:36, 36 *a* weights, an *a* ephah
Le 19:36 prove to have . . . an *a* hin
De 25:15 A weight *a* and just
25:15 An ephah *a* and just
Job 31:6 will weigh me in *a* scales
Eze 45:10, 10 *A* scales and an *a* ephah
45:10 *a* bath measure you men
Ac 23:20 something more *a* about him
Ro 1:28 holding God in *a* knowledge
3:20 is the *a* knowledge of sin
10:2 not according to *a* knowledge
Eph 1:17 in the *a* knowledge of him
4:13 the *a* knowledge of the Son
Php 1:9 with *a* knowledge and full
Col 1:9 the *a* knowledge of his will
1:10 in the *a* knowledge of God
2:2 a view to an *a* knowledge
3:10 through *a* knowledge is being
1Ti 2:4 to an *a* knowledge of truth
2Ti 2:25 to an *a* knowledge of truth
3:7 to an *a* knowledge of truth
Tit 1:1 the *a* knowledge of the truth
Heb 10:26 *a* knowledge of the truth
2Pe 1:2 by an *a* knowledge of God
1:3 *a* knowledge of the one who
1:8 *a* knowledge of our Lord Jesus
2:20 an *a* knowledge of the Lord

Accurately
Ac 23:15 to determine more *a* the
24:22 Felix, knowing quite *a* the
1Co 13:12 I shall know *a* even as I
13:12 even as I am *a* known
Col 1:6 and *a* knew the undeserved
1Ti 4:3 faith and *a* know the truth
2Pe 2:21 to have *a* known the path of
2:21 after knowing it *a* to turn

Accursed
De 21:23 *a* of God is the one hung up
2Ki 9:34 take care of this *a* one
Joh 7:49 does not know the Law are *a*
1Co 12:3 nobody . . . says: Jesus is *a!*
16:22 let him be *a*. O our Lord
Ga 1:8 let him be *a*
1:9 you accepted, let him be *a*
3:13 *A* is every man hanged upon a
2Pe 2:14 They are *a* children

Accusation
Ezr 4:6 wrote an *a* against the
Mt 12:10 might get an *a* against him
Lu 19:8 extorted . . . by false *a*
Joh 18:29 What *a* do you bring against
Ro 8:33 *a* against God's chosen ones
1Co 1:8 be open to no *a* in the day of
Col 1:22 and open to no *a* before him
1Ti 3:10 as they are free from *a*
5:19 an *a* against an older man
Tit 1:6 there is any man free from *a*
1:7 overseer must be free from *a*
2Pe 2:11 bring against them an *a* in

Accuse
Mr 3:2 order that they might *a* him
15:3 to *a* him of many things
Lu 3:14 or *a* anybody falsely, but be
6:7 to find some way to *a* him
23:2 they started to *a* him, saying
Joh 5:45 will *a* you to the Father
Ac 24:19 *a* me if they might have
25:5 come down with me and *a* him
25:11 of which these men *a* me
28:19 of which to *a* my nation

Accused
Da 3:8 Chaldeans approached and *a* the
6:24 men who had *a* Daniel, and
Mt 27:12 being *a* by the chief priests
Lu 16:1 *a* to him as handling his
Ac 22:30 he was being *a* by the Jews
23:29 *a* about questions of . . . Law
25:16 before the *a* man meets his
26:2 of which I am *a* by Jews
26:7 Concerning this hope I am *a*
Ro 2:15 they are being *a* or even

Accuser
Re 12:10 *a* of our brothers has been

Accusers
Ac 23:30 the *a* to speak against him
23:35 when your *a* arrive also
25:16 meets his *a* face to face and
25:18 the *a* produced no charge of

Accuses
Joh 5:45 one that *a* you, Moses, in
Re 12:10 *a* them day and night before

Accusing
Lu 23:10 and vehemently *a* him
Ac 23:28 for which they were *a* him
24:2 Tertullus started *a* him
24:8 of which we are *a* him
24:13 they are *a* me right now

Accustomed
Ge 24:11 women . . . were *a* to go out
29:2 *a* to water the droves
32:32 not *a* to eat the sinew of
Jg 17:6 he was *a* to do
21:25 what each one was *a* to do
Isa 47:11 that you are not *a* to know
Jer 2:24 a zebra *a* to the wilderness
Eze 16:33 all prostitutes they are *a*
Mt 16:2 are *a* to say, It will be fair
Mr 10:1 as he was *a* to do he again
Lu 2:41 his parents were *a* to go
1Co 8:7 being *a* until now to the idol
1Th 5:7 are *a* to sleep at night, and

Achaia
Ac 18:12 Gallio was proconsul of *A*
18:27 desiring to go across into *A*
19:21 through Macedonia and *A*, he
Ro 15:26 those in Macedonia and *A*
1Co 16:15 the firstfruits of *A* and
2Co 1:1 holy ones who are in all of *A*
9:2 that *A* has stood ready now
11:10 in the regions of *A*
1Th 1:7 in Macedonia and in *A*
1:8 from you in Macedonia and *A*

Achaicus
1Co 16:17 and Fortunatus and *A*

Achan
Jos 7:1 *A* the son of Carmi, the son
7:18 and *A* the son of Carmi the
7:19 Joshua said to *A*: My son
7:20 *A* answered Joshua and said
7:24 took *A* the son of Zerah and
22:20 *A* the son of Zerah that

Achar
1Ch 2:7 the sons of Carmi were *A*

Achbor
Ge 36:38 Baal-hanan son of *A* began to
36:39 Baal-hanan son of *A* died
2Ki 22:12 *A* the son of Micaiah
22:14 Ahikam and *A* and Shaphan
1Ch 1:49 Baal-hanan the son of *A*
Jer 26:22 Elnathan the son of *A* and
36:12 Elnathan the son of *A* and

Achievement
Isa 41:24 and your *a* is nothing
45:9 And your *a* say: He has no

Achievements
1Ch 17:19 all the great *a* known
17:21 a name of great *a* and
Pr 8:22 earliest of his *a* of long ago

Achim
Mt 1:14 Zadok became father to *A*
1:14 *A* became father to Eliud

Aching
Ge 34:25 when they got to be *a*, the
Job 14:22 own flesh . . . will keep *a*
Ps 69:29 But I am afflicted and *a*

Achish
1Sa 21:10 came to *A* the king of Gath
21:11 servants of *A* began to say
21:12 afraid on account of *A* the
21:14 *A* said to his servants
27:2 *A* the son of Maoch, the king
27:3 dwell with *A* in Gath, he
27:5 David said to *A*: If, now I
27:6 *A* gave him Ziklag on that
27:9 he returned and came to *A*
27:10 *A* said: Where did you men
27:12 *A* believed David, saying to
28:1 *A* said to David
28:2 David said to *A*: That is
28:2 *A* said to David: That is
29:2 passing along . . . with *A*
29:3 *A* said to the princes of the
29:6 *A* called David and said to
29:8 David said to *A*: Why, what
29:9 *A* answered and said to David
1Ki 2:39 away to *A* the son of Maacah
2:40 to *A* to look for his slaves

Achor
Jos 7:24 up to the low plain of *A*
Jos 7:26 been called Low Plain of *A*
15:7 Debir at the low plain of *A*
Isa 65:10 plain of *A* a resting-place
Ho 2:15 *A* as an entrance to hope

Achsah
Jos 15:16 give him *A* my daughter
15:17 gave him *A* his daughter as
Jg 1:12 why, I will give him *A* my
1:13 he gave him *A* his daughter
1Ch 2:49 And Caleb's daughter was *A*

Achshaph
Jos 11:1 and the king of *A*
12:20 the king of *A*, one
19:25 and Hali and Beten and *A*

Achzib
Ge 38:5 in *A* at the time she bore
Jos 15:44 Keilah and *A* and Mareshah
19:29 the sea in the region of *A*
Jg 1:31 *A* and Helbah and Aphik and
Mic 1:14 The houses of *A* were as

Acknowledge
De 33:9 his brothers he did not *a*
1Sa 2:12 they did not *a* Jehovah
Job 7:10 And his place will not *a* him
Ps 103:16 place will *a* it no further
Jer 14:20 We do *a*, O Jehovah, our
Ro 15:9 I will openly *a* you among
1Co 14:37 let him *a* the things I am
Php 2:11 *a* that Jesus Christ is Lord

Acknowledged
Nu 1:18 descent *a* as regards their
Ho 5:4 Jehovah . . . they have not *a*

Acknowledging
Phm 6 *a* of every good thing among

Acknowledgment
Ro 14:11 will make open *a* to God
Re 3:5 *a* of his name before my Father

Acquaint
Job 22:21 *A* yourself, please, with

Acquaintance
Ex 32:27 each one his intimate *a*
2Ki 12:5 take . . . each one from his *a*
Ps 15:3 against his intimate *a*
55:13 One familiar to me and my *a*
Isa 53:3 for having *a* with sickness

Acquaintances
2Ki 10:11 his *a* and his priests
12:7 any more money from your *a*
Job 19:14 intimate *a* have ceased to
Ps 31:11 And a dread to my *a*
38:11 *a* . . . stood off at a distance
88:8 put my *a* far away from me
88:18 My *a* are a dark place
Lu 2:44 among the relatives and *a*

Acquainted
Ge 18:19 I have become *a* with him in
De 32:17 your forefathers were not *a*
2Ki 4:39 they were not *a* with them
Da 1:4 being *a* with knowledge, and
Lu 23:49 all those *a* with him were
Ac 18:25 *a* with only the baptism of
19:15 I am *a* with Paul; but who
26:5 *a* with me from the first
1Co 13:2 and am *a* with all the sacred
2Pe 1:16 *a* you with the power and

Acquiesced
Ac 11:18 they *a*, and they glorified
21:14 we *a* with the words: Let

Acquire
Ne 5:16 and not a field did we *a*
Pr 4:5, 5 *A* wisdom, *a* understanding
4:7 *A* wisdom; and with all that
4:7 and with all that you *a*
4:7 *a* understanding
17:16 the price to *a* wisdom, when
Isa 11:11 *a* the remnant of his people
Lu 18:12 tenth of all things I *a*
21:19 you will *a* your souls
Ro 1:13 *a* some fruitage also among

Acquired
Ge 12:5 the souls whom they had *a* in
33:19 he *a* a tract of the field
Jos 24:32 field that Jacob had *a*
2Ch 32:29 And cities he *a* for himself
Ne 5:13 from his *a* property every
Job 20:18 giving back his *a* property
Ps 74:2 assembly that you *a* long ago
Ps 78:54 region that his right hand *a*
Ec 2:7 *a* menservants and maidservants
Zec 13:5 *a* me from my youth on
1Co 8:2 thinks he has *a* knowledge of
Ga 4:22 Abraham *a* two sons, one by
Re 3:17 have *a* riches and do not need

Acquires
Pr 1:5 one who *a* skillful direction
18:15 the understanding one *a*

Acquiring
Pr 15:32 to reproof is *a* heart
19:8 is *a* heart is loving his own
Ac 9:22 Saul kept on *a* power all the
Eph 6:10 go on *a* power in the Lord
1Th 5:9 *a* of salvation through our
2Th 2:14 *a* the glory of our Lord Jesus
1Ti 3:13 are *a* for themselves a fine
2Ti 2:1 keep on *a* power in the

Acquisition
Ge 31:18 herd of his *a* that he had
Job 15:29 he spread out the *a* of them

Acquitted
Ro 6:7 died has been *a* from his sin

Acre
1Sa 14:14 plowing line in an *a* of

Acres
Isa 5:10 ten *a* of vineyard will

Across
Ge 28:11 In time he came *a* a place
Nu 22:1 *a* the Jordan from Jericho
De 2:13 *a* the torrent valley of Zered
3:20 giving them *a* the Jordan
3:25 land that is *a* the Jordan
Jos 7:7 all the way *a* the Jordan
22:19 make your way *a* to the
1Sa 14:1 Philistines who are *a* over
15:12 went *a* and descended to
2Sa 2:8 bring him *a* to Mahanaim
2:15 went *a* by number, twelve
15:33 actually went *a* with me
19:15 the king *a* the Jordan
19:18 the household of the king *a*
19:38 With me Chimham will go *a*
19:40 the king went *a* to Gilgal
19:40 they might bring the king *a*
1Ki 6:21 chainwork of gold pass *a*
7:30 with wreaths *a* from each
2Ki 2:8 went *a* on the dry ground
2:9 as soon as they had gone *a*
2:14 so that Elisha went *a*
1Ch 12:37 And from *a* the Jordan of
Ezr 4:9 lesser governors *a* the River
Isa 34:10 one will be passing *a* her
51:10 repurchased ones to go *a*
Eze 40:13 entrance was *a* from
Mic 1:11 Make your way *a*, O
Mt 9:1 proceeded *a* and went into his
13:53 went *a* country from there
14:34 they got *a* and came to land
19:1 of Judea *a* the Jordan
Mr 3:8 from *a* the Jordan and around
6:53 when they got *a* to land, they
10:1 Judea and *a* the Jordan, and
Joh 1:28 in Bethany *a* the Jordan
3:26 was with you *a* the Jordan
6:1 *a* the sea of Galilee, or
6:17 *a* the sea for Capernaum
6:25 they found him *a* the sea
10:40 *a* the Jordan to the place
18:1 *a* the winter torrent of
Ac 18:27 desiring to go *a* into Achaia
1Th 2:18 but Satan cut *a* our path

Act
Ge 6:3 My spirit shall not *a* toward
18:21 they *a* altogether according
19:7 my brothers, do not *a* badly
41:34 Let Pharaoh *a* and appoint
42:11 servants do not *a* as spies
42:31 We do not *a* as spies
Ex 22:2 found in the *a* of breaking in
28:1 may *a* as priest to me, Aaron
28:3 that he may *a* as priest to me
28:4 that he may *a* as priest to me
28:41 they must *a* as priests to me
29:44 for them to *a* as priests to
40:13 he must *a* as priest to me
40:15 so they must *a* as priests to
Le 7:35 to *a* as priests to Jehovah
16:32 *a* as priest as successor of
Nu 3:3 with power to *a* as priests

Nu 3:4 *a* as priests along with Aaron
5:6 *a* of unfaithfulness against
5:12 commit an *a* of unfaithfulness
5:27 *a* of unfaithfulness toward her
11:25 proceeded to *a* as prophets
11:26 *a* as prophets in the camp
31:18 the *a* of lying with a male
31:35 the *a* of lying with a male
De 4:16 that you may not *a* ruinously
4:25 *a* ruinously and do make a
10:6 his son began to *a* as priest
17:13 not *a* presumptuously anymore
31:29 without fail *a* ruinously
Jos 1:7 order that you may *a* wisely
1:8 and then you will *a* wisely
7:1 an *a* of unfaithfulness
22:16 this *a* of unfaithfulness
22:20 an *a* of unfaithfulness in
22:31 this *a* of unfaithfulness
Jg 2:19 *a* more ruinously than their
Ru 2:12 Jehovah reward the way you *a*
1Sa 2:28 to *a* as priest and go up upon
18:5 he would *a* prudently, so
20:38 *A* quickly! Do not stand
2Sa 3:18 *a*, for Jehovah himself said
5:24 *a* with decision, because at
6:7 for the irreverent *a*
14:15 king will *a* on the word of
17:6 Shall we *a* upon his word?
22:26 you will *a* in loyalty
22:27 you will *a* as silly
1Ki 2:3 *a* prudently in everything that
2:6 *a* according to your wisdom
8:32 *a* and judge your servants
8:39 forgive and *a* and give to
14:9 you began to *a* worse than
2Ki 18:7 go out, he would *a* prudently
1Ch 2:7 an *a* of unfaithfulness
5:25 they began to *a* unfaithfully
15:21 to *a* as directors
22:16 Rise and *a*, and may Jehovah
24:2 continued to *a* as priests
28:10 Be courageous and *a*
28:20 courageous and strong and *a*
2Ch 6:23 *a* and judge your servants so
19:7 *a*, for with Jehovah our God
19:11 Be strong and *a*, and let
24:5 *a* quickly in the matter
24:5 Levites did not *a* quickly
25:8 *a*, be courageous for the war
34:12 to *a* as overseers
Ezr 3:8 to *a* as supervisors over the
3:9 *a* as supervisors over the
10:4 Be strong and *a*
10:14 princes *a* representatively
Ne 1:8 for your part, *a* unfaithfully
Es 5:5 have Haman *a* quickly on the
5:8 and to *a* on my request, let
Job 21:27 *a* violently against me
34:10 the true God to *a* wickedly
34:10 the Almighty to *a* unjustly
34:12 God himself does not *a*
34:31 I do not *a* corruptly
36:9 about the way they *a*
Ps 18:25 you will *a* in loyalty
37:5 and he himself will *a*
70:5 O God, do *a* quickly for me
89:5 will laud your marvelous *a*
101:2 I will *a* with discretion in
119:17 *A* appropriately toward your
119:122 *A* as a surety for your
119:126 time for Jehovah to *a*
Pr 13:5 wicked ones *a* shamefully and
13:16 shrewd will *a* with
Ec 7:7 may make a wise one *a* crazy
Isa 10:13 hand I shall certainly *a*
26:10 he will *a* unjustly and
29:14 *a* wonderfully again with
44:25 diviners . . . *a* crazily
46:4 I myself shall certainly *a*
48:11 for my own sake I shall *a*
52:13 servant will *a* with insight
Jer 2:34 Not in the *a* of breaking in
9:7 *a* on account of the daughter
12:5 *a* among the proud thickets
14:7 *a* for the sake of your name
23:5 reign and *a* with discretion
25:16 *a* like crazed men because
50:36 will certainly *a* foolishly
Eze 7:27 I shall *a* toward them, and
8:18 myself also shall *a* in rage
16:47 *a* more ruinously than they
24:14 It must come, and I will *a*
31:11 he will *a* against it
Eze 35:11 *a* also according to your
36:27 I will *a* so that in my
44:13 to me to *a* as priest to me
Da 5:20 so as to *a* presumptuously, he
6:22 king, no hurtful *a* have I done
8:23 the transgressors *a* to a
9:19 do pay attention and *a*
11:7 *a* against them and prevail
11:17 and he will *a* effectively
11:28 *a* effectively and certainly
11:30 covenant and *a* effectively
11:32 prevail and *a* effectively
11:39 *a* effectively against the
12:10 will certainly *a* wickedly
Ho 9:1 not *a* joyful like the peoples
Mt 4:9 and do an *a* of worship to me
Lu 4:7 if you do an *a* of worship
Ac 17:7 these men *a* in opposition to
18:14 or a wicked *a* of villainy
19:36 keep calm and not *a* rashly
Ro 5:18 one *a* of justification the
2Co 13:10 I may not *a* with severity
Php 2:13 you both to will and to *a*
Phm 14 so that your good *a* may be
Heb 2:2 disobedient *a* received a
Re 13:5 authority to *a* forty-two

Acted

Ge 30:6 God has *a* as my judge and
31:28 Now you have *a* foolishly
40:13 when you *a* as his cupbearer
Ex 18:11 *a* presumptuously against
32:7 people . . . have *a* ruinously
Nu 12:11 in which we have *a* foolishly
32:15 *a* ruinously toward all this
De 9:12 your people . . . *a* ruinously
32:5 *a* ruinously on their own part
32:51 you men *a* undutifully toward
Jos 9:4 *a* with shrewdness and went
Jg 9:16 you have *a* and that you went
9:19 faultlessness that you have *a*
20:37 *a* quickly and went dashing
1Sa 13:13 You have *a* foolishly
18:30 David *a* most prudently of
26:21 I have *a* foolishly and am
2Sa 12:12 you yourself *a* in secret
14:22 king has *a* on the word of
17:23 counsel had not been *a* upon
24:10 I have *a* very foolishly
1Ki 8:47 erred, we have *a* wickedly
14:24 They *a* according to all the
16:27 mightiness with which he *a*
22:45 mightiness with which he *a*
2Ki 10:19 As for Jehu, he *a* slyly
10:30 *a* well in doing what is
21:11 *a* more wickedly than all
1Ch 6:10 *a* as priest in the house that
10:13 he had *a* faithlessly against
21:8 for I have *a* very foolishly
2Ch 6:37 and we have *a* wickedly
11:23 he *a* understandingly and
16:9 *a* foolishly respecting this
20:35 Ahaziah . . . who *a* wickedly
26:16 *a* unfaithfully against
26:18 for you have *a* unfaithfully
28:22 he *a* unfaithfully still
29:6 fathers have *a* unfaithfully
30:7 brothers that *a* unfaithfully
31:21 all his heart that he *a*
Ezr 10:2 *a* unfaithfully against our
10:10 have *a* unfaithfully in that
Ne 1:7 *a* corruptly against you and
9:10 *a* presumptuously against them
9:16 forefathers, *a* presumptuously
9:29 *a* presumptuously and did not
9:33 faithfully is how you have *a*
Ps 14:1 They have *a* ruinously, they
14:1 they have *a* detestably in
36:2 *a* too smoothly to himself in
39:9 For you yourself *a*
44:17 *a* falsely in your covenant
53:1 They have *a* ruinously and have
53:1 and have *a* detestably
68:28 God, you who have *a* for us
73:15 I should have *a* treacherously
106:6 we have *a* wickedly
116:7 *a* appropriately toward you
Pr 30:32 *a* senselessly by lifting
Ec 8:10 city where they *a* that way
Isa 19:13 of Zoan have *a* foolishly
26:13 have *a* as owners of us
38:15 He himself has also *a*
48:3 Suddenly I *a*, and the things
Jer 5:4 They *a* foolishly, for they
Jer 7:26 They *a* worse than their
10:21 have not *a* with insight
16:12 *a* worse in your doing than
23:13 *a* as prophets incited by
50:29 she has *a* presumptuously
Eze 15:8 that they have *a* unfaithfully
16:52 you *a* more detestably than
17:20 with which he *a* against me
20:14 I *a* for the sake of my own
22:7 have *a* with defrauding in
25:12 has *a* in taking vengeance
25:15 have *a* with vengeance and
29:20 because they *a* for me
39:26 they have *a* toward me
Da 8:12 and it *a* and had success
9:5 and *a* wickedly and rebelled
9:7 with which they *a* against you
9:15 sinned, we have *a* wickedly
Ho 2:5 with them has *a* shamefully
Am 3:6 not also Jehovah who has *a*
Zep 3:7 *a* promptly in making all
Lu 10:37 The one that *a* mercifully
16:8 he *a* with practical wisdom
Ac 3:17 know that you *a* in ignorance
Php 4:14 you *a* well in becoming
1Ti 1:13 *a* with a lack of faith
Heb 3:18 to those who *a* disobediently
11:31 those who *a* disobediently

Acting

Ge 18:25 you are *a* in this manner to
50:20 *a* as at this day to preserve
Ex 29:1 for *a* as priests to me: Take
30:30 for *a* as priests to me
31:10 of his sons for *a* as priests
35:19 his sons for *a* as priests
39:41 of his sons for *a* as priests
Le 26:13 *a* as slaves to them, and I
Nu 11:27 and Medad are *a* as prophets
De 17:9 the judge who will be *a* in
19:17 judges . . . *a* in those days
26:3 the priest who will be *a* in
1Sa 14:48 he went on *a* valiantly and
18:14 *a* prudently in all his ways
18:15 he was *a* very prudently
21:13 *a* insane in their hand and
28:9 *a* like a trapper against my
1Ki 21:26 went *a* very detestably by
22:10 *a* as prophets before them
1Ch 23:4 for *a* as supervisors over the
2Ch 11:14 them from *a* as priests to
18:9 prophets were *a* as prophets
27:2 people were yet *a* ruinously
28:19 *a* with great unfaithfulness
30:22 *a* with fine discretion
34:12 men were *a* in faithfulness
Ezr 4:22 no negligence about *a* in
Ne 13:27 badness in *a* unfaithfully
Es 1:22 *a* as prince in his own house
Ps 28:4 to them according to their *a*
41:1 *a* with consideration toward
47:7 melody, *a* with discretion
71:4 palm of the one *a* unjustly
78:57 *a* treacherously like their
Pr 10:5 son *a* with insight is
10:5 son *a* shamefully is fast
10:19 lips in check is *a* discreetly
12:22 *a* in faithfulness are a
14:35 servant . . . is *a* with insight
14:35 toward one *a* shamefully
15:24 upward to one *a* with insight
17:2 the son who is *a* shamefully
19:26 is a son *a* shamefully and
21:24 one who is *a* in a fury of
24:29 each one according to his *a*
Jer 6:13 each one is *a* falsely
8:10 each one is *a* falsely
50:38 visions they keep *a* crazy
51:7 the nations keep *a* crazed
Eze 13:17 *a* as prophetesses out of
14:13 sin . . . in *a* unfaithfully
20:9 *a* for the sake of my own
20:22 *a* for the sake of my own
20:27 in their *a* against me with
35:13 *a* in great style against me
Da 11:32 are *a* wickedly against the
Ho 9:15 their princes are *a* stubborn
Zep 3:19 *a* against all those
Mal 1:14 cursed is the one *a* cunningly
3:5 against those *a* fraudulently
4:3 in the day on which I am *a*
Lu 1:8 he was *a* as priest in the
22:26 the one *a* as chief as the
Ac 13:27 *a* as judges, they fulfilled

2Co 11:21 I too am *a* bold in it
Eph 6:20 *a* as an ambassador in chains
Php 2:13 is *a* within you in order for
2Th 2:7 is right now *a* as a restraint

Action
Ex 14:31 hand that Jehovah put in *a*
Jos 22:12 military *a* against them
22:26 Let us take *a* in our behalf
Jg 20:10 *a* by going against Gibeah
Ps 52:9 for you have taken *a*
Pr 6:3 take this *a* then, my son
Isa 44:23 for Jehovah has taken *a*
Jer 18:23 take *a* against them
23:10 course of *a* proves to be bad
Eze 20:44 when I take *a* with you
22:14 I am taking *a* toward you
22:14 and I will take *a*
23:25 take *a* against you in rage
23:29 take *a* against you in hatred
Lu 23:51 support of their design and *a*
Ac 13:18 up with their manner of *a*
2Co 10:11 also be in *a* when present
Phm 6 faith may go into *a* by your

Active
Ge 1:2 God's *a* force was moving to
6:17 which the force of life is *a*
7:15 which the force of life was *a*
7:22 force of life was *a* in its
1Ki 5:16 who were *a* in the work
9:23 who were *a* in the work
20:40 your servant was *a* here and
2Ch 34:10 *a* in the house of Jehovah
Ne 4:16 young men were *a* in the work
4:17 each one was *a* in the work
4:21 we were *a* in the work
Isa 41:4 has been *a* and has done this
43:13 I shall get *a*, and who can

Activities
Ps 17:4 As for the *a* of men, By the
28:5 regard for the *a* of Jehovah
46:8 behold the *a* of Jehovah
66:5 and see the *a* of God

Activity
De 32:4 The Rock, perfect is his *a*
33:11 in the *a* of his hands
2Ch 15:7 exists a reward for your *a*
Job 24:5 have gone forth in their *a*
36:24 you should magnify his *a*
Ps 9:16 By the *a* of his own hands
44:1 The *a* that you performed in
64:9 will tell of the *a* of God
77:12 meditate on all your *a*
90:16 *a* appear to your own
92:4 Jehovah, because of your *a*
95:9 they also saw my *a*
104:23 Man goes forth to his *a*
111:3 *a* is dignity and splendor
143:5 have meditated on all your *a*
Pr 10:16 *a* of the righteous one
20:11 his *a* is pure and upright
21:8 pure one is upright in his *a*
24:12 pay . . . according to his *a*
Isa 1:31 the product of his *a* a spark
5:12 *a* of Jehovah they do not
45:11 *a* of my hands you people
59:6 *a* of violence is in their
Jer 25:14 according to their *a* and
31:16 reward for your *a*, is the
50:29 to her according to her *a*
Hab 1:5 *a* that one is carrying on in
3:2 afraid, O Jehovah, of your *a*
Lu 19:15 had gained by business *a*
1Co 16:9 large door that leads to *a*
1Pe 1:13 brace up your minds for *a*

Acts
Ge 49:7 fury, because it *a* harshly
Ex 3:20 wonderful *a* that I shall do
Nu 14:33 for your *a* of fornication
Jg 5:11 to recount the righteous *a* of
5:11 righteous *a* of his dwellers
6:13 *a* that our fathers related to
11:36 *a* of vengeance for you upon
1Sa 12:7 the righteous *a* of Jehovah
2Sa 22:48 Giver of *a* of vengeance to
22:51 *a* of salvation for his king
1Ch 16:9 with all his wonderful *a*
16:12 Remember his wonderful *a*
16:24 Relate . . . his wonderful *a*
2Ch 24:24 they executed *a* of judgment
32:32 his *a* of loving-kindness
35:26 and his *a* of loving-kindness
Ne 9:17 *a* that you performed with
9:17 are a God of *a* of forgiveness
9:18 commit great *a* of disrespect
9:26 *a* of great disrespect
13:14 my *a* of loving-kindness that
Job 10:16 if it *a* haughtily, like a
34:11 the way earthling man *a*
36:22 God himself *a* exaltedly
40:23 If the river *a* violently
Ps 11:7 he does love righteous *a*
17:7 your *a* of loving-kindnesses
18:47 Giver of *a* of vengeance to
18:50 *a* of salvation for his king
19:13 from presumptuous *a* hold
20:6 mighty *a* of his right hand
68:20 is for us a God of saving *a*
89:49 former *a* of loving-kindness
94:1 O God of *a* of vengeance
94:1 God of *a* of vengeance, beam
103:6 executing *a* of righteousness
107:43 toward Jehovah's *a* of
145:4 mighty *a* they will tell
145:12 sons of men his mighty *a*
Pr 4:17 wine of *a* of violence is
12:4 is she that *a* shamefully
28:20 man of faithful *a* will get
Ec 4:1 see all the *a* of oppression
Isa 32:7 for *a* of loose conduct
64:4 *a* for the one that keeps in
64:6 all our *a* of righteousness
Jer 2:19 your own *a* of unfaithfulness
3:2 with your *a* of prostitution
5:6 their *a* of unfaithfulness have
13:27 your *a* of adultery and your
14:7 our *a* of unfaithfulness have
32:19 and abundant in *a*, you
La 3:22 It is the *a* of loving-kindness
Eze 3:20 righteous *a* that he did will
5:10 execute in you *a* of judgment
5:15 *a* of judgment in anger and
11:9 upon you *a* of judgment
14:21 injurious *a* of judgment
16:15 your *a* of prostitution on
16:20 of your *a* of prostitution
16:22 your *a* of prostitution you
16:25 your *a* of prostitution
16:33 in your *a* of prostitution
16:34 in your *a* of prostitution
16:36 in your *a* of prostitution
16:41 in you *a* of judgment before
18:24 none of all his righteous *a*
22:13 over your *a* of bloodshed
23:10 *a* of judgment were what
23:14 to her *a* of prostitution
23:18 her *a* of prostitution
23:19 her *a* of prostitution to
23:29 of your *a* of fornication
23:29 your *a* of prostitution must
23:35 and your *a* of prostitution
25:11 shall execute *a* of judgment
25:17 great *a* of vengeance, with
28:22 execute *a* of judgment in
28:26 execute *a* of judgment upon
30:14 execute *a* of judgment in No
30:19 *a* of judgment in Egypt
33:13 own righteous *a* will not be
Da 9:9 and the *a* of forgiveness, for
9:16 to all your *a* of righteousness
9:18 according to our righteous *a*
Ho 1:4 for the *a* of bloodshed
2:2 *a* of adultery from between her
4:2 *a* of bloodshed have touched
4:2 touched other *a* of bloodshed
Mic 3:10 with *a* of bloodshed and
6:5 the righteous *a* of Jehovah
Na 3:4 the *a* of prostitution of the
3:4 by her *a* of prostitution and
Mr 7:22 *a* of wickedness, deceit
Ac 26:9 commit many *a* of opposition
2Co 11:21 if anyone else *a* bold in
Col 3:22 not with *a* of eyeservice, as
2Th 2:6 thing that *a* as a restraint
Jas 2:1 with *a* of favoritism, are
2Pe 2:2 their *a* of loose conduct
3:11 holy *a* of conduct and deeds
Re 18:5 her *a* of injustice to mind
19:8 righteous *a* of the holy ones

Actual
Jer 5:10 make an *a* extermination
Lu 9:28 In *a* fact, about eight days
2Co 8:3 according to their *a* ability
8:3 beyond their *a* ability this

Actuality
Ac 4:27 in *a* gathered together in this

Actually*
Ge 3:22 not put his hand out and *a*
4:14 Here you are *a* driving me this
16:13 *a* looked upon him who sees
39:9 and *a* sin against God
Ex 4:21 *a* perform all the miracles
12:48 *a* celebrate the passover to
1Ki 8:35 *a* pray toward this place and
8:38 *a* spread out their palms to
8:41 *a* comes from a distant land
8:42 *a* comes and prays toward
8:46 captors *a* carry them off
8:47 *a* return and make request
9:6 *a* go and serve other gods and
2Ki 5:11 *a* give the leper recovery
20:17 *a* be carried to Babylon
Job 34:31 will anyone *a* say to God
35:6 If you *a* sin, what do you
Isa 44:17 *a* makes into a god itself
Ga 4:23 *a* born in the manner of flesh

Actuating
Eph 4:23 new in the force *a* your mind

Adadah
Jos 15:22 Kinah and Dimonah and *A*

Adah
Ge 4:19 The name of the first was *A*
4:20 In time *A* gave birth to Jabal
4:23 words for his wives *A* and
36:2 Esau took his wives . . . *A*
36:4 *A* proceeded to bear Eliphaz
36:10 the son of *A*, Esau's wife
36:12 the sons of *A*, Esau's wife
36:16 These are the sons by *A*

Adaiah
2Ki 22:1 Jedidah the daughter of *A*
1Ch 6:41 son of Zerah, the son of *A*
8:21 and *A* . . . the sons of Shimei
9:12 and *A* the son of Jeroham the
2Ch 23:1 Maaseiah the son of *A* and
Ezr 10:29 the sons of Bani . . . *A*
10:39 Shelemiah and Nathan and *A*
Ne 11:5 *A* the son of Joiarib the
11:12 and *A* the son of Jeroham the

Adalia
Es 9:8 and Poratha and *A* and Aridatha

Adam
Ge 3:17 to *A* he said: Because you
3:20 *A* called his wife's name Eve
3:21 long garments of skin for *A*
4:1 *A* had intercourse with Eve
4:25 And *A* . . . to have intercourse
5:1 In the day of God's creating *A*
5:3 *A* lived on for a hundred and
5:4 days of *A* after his fathering
5:5 all the days of *A* that he lived
De 32:8 parted the sons of *A* from one
Jos 3:16 *A*, the city at the side of
2Sa 7:14 the strokes of the sons of *A*
1Ch 1:1 *A*, Seth, Enosh
Lu 3:38 Seth, son of *A*, son of God
Ro 5:14 death ruled as king from *A*
5:14 of the transgression by *A*
1Co 15:22 just as in *A* all are dying
15:45 *A* became a living soul
15:45 last *A* became a life-giving
1Ti 2:13 *A* was formed first, then Eve
2:14 *A* was not deceived, but the
Jude 14 seventh one in line from *A*

Adamah
Jos 19:36 and *A* and Ramah and Hazor

Adami-nekeb
Jos 19:33 and *A* and Jabneel as far as

Adam's
Ge 5:1 This is the book of *A* history

Adar
Ezr 6:15 day of the lunar month *A*
Es 3:7 twelfth, that is, the month *A*
3:13 the month *A*, and to plunder
8:12 twelfth month . . . month of *A*
9:1 twelfth month . . . month of *A*
9:15 fourteenth day of the month *A*
9:17 thirteenth day of the month *A*
9:19 fourteenth day of the month *A*
9:21 fourteenth day of the month *A*

Adbeel
Ge 25:13 Kedar and *A* and Mibsam
1Ch 1:29 Kedar and *A* and Mibsam

Add
Le 5:16 he will *a* to it a fifth of
6:5 he will *a* to it a fifth of it
19:25 in order to *a* its produce
22:14 *a* the fifth of it to it and
Nu 32:14 to *a* further to the burning
De 4:2 You must not *a* to the word
12:32 You must not *a* to it nor
19:9 then *a* three other cities for
25:3 He should *a* none, for fear he
Ru 1:17 May Jehovah do so to me and *a*
1Sa 3:17 may he *a* to it if you should
14:44 and thus may he *a* to it, if
20:13 to Jonathan and so may he *a*
25:22 and so may he *a* to it if I
2Sa 3:9 so may he *a* to it, if, just
3:35 so may he *a* to it, if before
7:20 David *a* and speak to you
12:8 *a* to you things like these
19:13 and so may he *a* to it if
24:3 *a* to the people a hundred
1Ki 2:23 and so may he *a* to it, if it
12:11 shall *a* to your yoke
12:14 shall *a* to your yoke
19:2 and so may they *a* to it
20:10 and so may they *a* to it
2Ki 6:31 and so may he *a* to it
20:6 *a* fifteen years to your days
1Ch 21:3 May Jehovah *a* to his people
2Ch 10:11 shall *a* to your yoke
10:14 for my part, shall *a* to it
Ezr 10:10 to *a* to the guiltiness of
Job 40:5 twice, and I will *a* nothing
Ps 61:6 *a* to the days of the king
71:14 I will *a* to all your praise
120:3 what will one *a* to you
Pr 10:27 fear of Jehovah will *a* days
30:6 *A* nothing to his words, that
Ec 3:14 To it there is nothing to *a*
Isa 1:5 in that you *a* more revolt
29:1 *A* year upon year, you people
30:1 in order to *a* sin to sin
Jer 7:21 *A* those whole burnt
Mt 6:27 can *a* one cubit to his
Lu 12:25 *a* a cubit to his life-span
Re 22:18 God will *a* to him the

Addar
Jos 15:3 went up to *A* and went around
1Ch 8:3 Bela came to have sons, *A* and

Added
Ge 9:12 God *a:* This is the sign of the
9:26 And he *a:* Blessed be Jehovah
15:3 Abram *a:* Look! You have given
15:7 he *a* to him: I am Jehovah
16:11 angel *a* to her: Here you are
19:9 they *a:* This lone man came
21:7 she *a:* Who would have uttered
25:33 Jacob *a:* Swear to me first
27:36 he *a:* Have you not reserved a
28:17 And he grew fearful and *a*
30:28 he *a:* Stipulate your wages
38:25 she *a:* Examine, please, to
41:41 Pharaoh *a* to Joseph: See, I
42:2 he *a:* Here I have heard that
43:29 he *a:* May God show you his
Ex 1:10 *a* to those who hate us and
3:7 Jehovah *a:* Unquestionably I
3:14 *a:* This is what you are to
33:20 he *a:* You are not able to
Nu 36:3 *a* to the inheritance of the
36:4 *a* to the inheritance of the
De 5:22 and he *a* nothing; after which
1Sa 12:19 *a* to all our sins an evil
17:37 Then David *a:* Jehovah, who
26:18 he *a:* Why is this that my
1Ki 22:28 *a:* Hear, all you peoples
2Ch 18:27 he *a:* Hear, all you peoples
Pr 3:2 and peace will be *a* to you
9:11 years of life will be *a*
Isa 26:15 You have *a* to the nation
26:15 you have *a* to the nation
Jer 36:32 *a* to them many more words
45:3 Jehovah has *a* grief to my
Da 4:36 greatness extraordinary was *a*
Mt 6:33 other things will be *a* to you
Mr 4:9 he *a* the word: Let him that
4:24 you will have more *a* to you
Lu 3:20 *a* also this to all those deeds
12:31 these things will be *a* to
Ac 2:41 three thousand souls were *a*
5:14 *a,* multitudes both of men and
11:24 crowd was *a* to the Lord
Ga 3:19 *a* to make transgressions
Heb 12:19 no word should be *a* to them

Addi
Lu 3:28 son of Melchi, son of *A*

Adding
Ge 30:24 Jehovah is *a* another son to
Nu 5:7 also *a* a fifth of it to it
2Sa 3:12 *a:* Do conclude your covenant
2Ch 28:13 thinking of *a* to our sins
Ne 13:18 *a* to the burning anger
Isa 38:5 *a* onto your days fifteen
Eze 23:14 she kept *a* to her acts of
Ac 15:28 favored *a* no further burden

Addition
Ge 31:50 wives in *a* to my daughters
Le 18:18 woman in *a* to her sister as
27:13 in *a* to the estimated value
27:15 a fifth . . . in *a* to it
27:19 fifth . . . in *a* to it
27:27 give a fifth of it in *a* to it
27:31 give a fifth of it in *a* to it
Nu 28:15 sin offering to Jehovah in *a*
De 25:3 many strokes in *a* to these
Jos 22:19 an altar in *a* to the altar
1Sa 20:3 David swore in *a* and said
Job 42:10 in *a* all that had been Job's
Eze 23:40 in *a* to that, when they
Am 3:15 in *a* to the summer house
Lu 19:11 he spoke in *a* an illustration
2Co 7:13 in *a* to our comfort we
1Jo 4:14 In *a,* we ourselves have
Re 22:18 makes an *a* to these things

Additional
Isa 15:9 Dimon I shall place *a* things
Ho 13:2 they commit *a* sin and make
Mt 25:20 and brought five *a* talents

Additionally
Ex 37:29 made *a* the holy anointing oil

Additions
1Ch 22:14 to them you will make *a*
Ga 3:15 aside or attaches *a* to it

Addon
Ezr 2:59 *A* and Immer, and they proved
Ne 7:61 Cherub, *A* and Immer, and they

Address
De 11:2 I do not *a* your sons who have
Ps 5:3 I shall *a* myself to you and be
Joh 13:13 You *a* me, Teacher, and
Ac 12:21 giving them a public *a*

Addressed
Da 2:14 *a* himself with counsel and
Lu 13:12 Jesus *a* her and said to her
Ac 21:40 he *a* them in the Hebrew
2Co 1:18 speech *a* to you is not Yes

Addresses
Mt 5:22 whoever *a* his brother with
Ro 3:19 *a* to those under the Law, so
Heb 12:5 exhortation which *a* you as

Addressing
Ac 22:2 *a* them in the Hebrew language

Adds
Job 34:37 top of his sin he *a* revolt
Pr 10:22 and he *a* no pain with it
16:21 in his lips *a* persuasiveness
16:23 his lips it *a* persuasiveness
19:4 Wealth . . . *a* many companions

Adequate
Nu 11:22 for it to be *a* for them
11:22 for it to be *a* for them

Adequately
2Co 2:16 who is *a* qualified for these
3:5 *a* qualified to reckon anything
3:5 being *a* qualified issues from
3:6 has indeed *a* qualified us to
2Ti 2:2 *a* qualified to teach others

Adhere
2Ch 31:4 *a* strictly to the law of
Ro 4:12 those who *a* to circumcision
4:14 those who *a* to law are heirs
Ga 3:7 those who *a* to faith are the
3:9 those who *a* to faith are being
3:12 Law does not *a* to faith, but
Tit 1:10 who *a* to the circumcision

Adheres
Ro 4:16 to that which *a* to the Law
4:16 *a* to the faith of Abraham

Adhering
Ne 10:29 were *a* to their brothers

Adiel
1Ch 4:36 *A* and Jesimiel and Benaiah
9:12 *A* the son of Jahzerah the son
27:25 was Azmaveth the son of *A*

Adin
Ezr 2:15 sons of *A,* four hundred and
8:6 the sons of *A,* Ebed the son of
Ne 7:20 sons of *A,* six hundred and
10:16 Adonijah, Bigvai, *A*

Adina
1Ch 11:42 *A* the son of Shiza the

Adithaim
Jos 15:36 *A* and Gederah and

Adjacent
Jos 15:47 Great Sea and the *a* region

Adjoining
1Ki 7:20 belly that was *a* the network
Ac 18:7 house was *a* the synagogue

Adjudge
Isa 26:12 Jehovah, you will *a* peace

Adjusted
Ps 75:3 It was I that *a* its pillars
Eze 18:25 The way of Jehovah is not *a*
18:25 Is not my own way *a* right?
18:25 ways of you people not *a*
18:29 The way of Jehovah is not *a*
18:29 ways, are they not *a* right
18:29 ones that are not *a* right
33:17 way of Jehovah is not *a*
33:17 way that is not *a* right
33:20 way of Jehovah is not *a*

Adjutant
2Ki 7:2 *a* upon whose hand the king
7:17 the *a* upon whose hand he was
7:19 the *a* answered the man of
9:25 He now said to Bidkar his *a*
15:25 his *a* conspired against him

Adjutants
1Ki 9:22 his princes and his *a* and
2Ki 10:25 to the runners and the *a*
10:25 and the *a* began to strike
2Ch 8:9 warriors and chiefs of his *a*

Adlai
1Ch 27:29 was Shaphat the son of *A*

Admah
Ge 10:19 Sodom and Gomorrah and *A*
14:2 Shinab king of *A,* and
14:8 on the march . . . king of *A*
De 29:23 *A* and Zeboiim, which Jehovah
Ho 11:8 How can I set you as *A?*

Admatha
Es 1:14 *A* . . . seven princes of Persia

Administered
Ru 1:1 days when the judges *a* justice
1Sa 14:47 he *a* condemnation
2Co 8:19 gift to be *a* by us for the
8:20 contribution to be *a* by us
Eph 3:9 how the sacred secret is *a*

Administering
Eze 3:26 a man *a* reproof, because
2Co 3:8 why should not the *a* of the
3:9 the code *a* condemnation was
3:9 *a* of righteousness abound

Administers
2Co 3:7 code which *a* death and which

Administration
1Ch 26:30 over the *a* of Israel in the
Da 2:49 *a* of the jurisdictional
3:12 the *a* of the . . . district
Eph 1:10 *a* at the full limit of the

Administrators
Da 3:2 all the *a* of the jurisdictional
3:3 the *a* of the jurisdictional

Admiration
Re 13:3 the wild beast with *a*

Admiring
Jude 16 *a* personalities for the sake

Admiringly
Re 17:8 earth will wonder *a,* but

Admissible
Ex 8:26 Moses said: It is not *a* to do

Lu 13:33 it is not *a* for a prophet

Admit
Ac 24:14 But I do *a* this to you, that
1Ti 5:19 not *a* an accusation against

Admittance
Isa 1:23 a widow does not get *a*

Admittedly
1Ti 3:16 godly devotion is *a* great

Admonish
Ro 15:14 you can also *a* one another
1Co 4:14 *a* you as my beloved children
1Th 5:14 brothers, *a* the disorderly

Admonished
Jer 11:7 solemnly *a* your forefathers

Admonishing
Jer 11:7 rising up early and *a*
Ac 20:31 *a* each one with tears
Col 1:28 *a* every man and teaching
3:16 Keep on teaching and *a* one
1Th 5:12 presiding over you . . . *a* you
2Th 3:15 continue *a* him as a brother

Admonition
Tit 3:10 after a first and a second *a*

Adna
Ezr 10:30 the sons of Pahath-moab, *A*
Ne 12:15 for Harim, *A*; for Meraioth

Adnah
1Ch 12:20 from Manasseh *A* and Jozabad
2Ch 17:14 of thousands, *A* the chief

Adoni-bezek
Jg 1:5 When they found *A* in Bezek
1:6 When *A* took to flight, then
1:7 At this *A* said: There have

Adonijah
2Sa 3:4 was *A* the son of Haggith
1Ki 1:5 *A* the son of Haggith was
1:7 help as followers of *A*
1:8 not become involved with *A*
1:9 *A* held a sacrifice of sheep
1:11 *A* the son of Haggith has
1:13 So why has *A* become king?
1:18 *A* himself has become king
1:24 *A* is the one that will
1:25 saying, Let King *A* live
1:41 *A* and all the ones invited
1:42 *A* said: Come on in, for you
1:43 answered and said to *A*: No
1:49 those . . . with *A* began to
1:50 *A* himself was afraid because
1:51 *A* himself has become afraid
2:13 *A* the son of Haggith came to
2:19 to speak to him for *A*
2:21 the Shunammite be given to *A*
2:22 Abishag the Shunammite for *A*
2:23 *A* spoke this thing
2:24 today *A* will be put to death
2:28 had inclined to follow *A*
1Ch 3:2 *A* the son of Haggith
2Ch 17:8 *A* and Tobijah and
Ne 10:16 *A*, Bigvai, Adin

Adonikam
Ezr 2:13 sons of *A*, six hundred and
8:13 and of the sons of *A*, those
Ne 7:18 sons of *A*, six hundred and

Adoniram
1Ki 4:6 *A* the son of Abda, over those
5:14 *A* was over those conscripted

Adoni-zedek
Jos 10:1 *A* the king of Jerusalem
10:3 *A* the king of Jerusalem sent

Adoption
Ro 8:15 spirit of *a* as sons, by which
8:23 waiting for *a* as sons, the
9:4 belong the *a* as sons and the
Ga 4:5 might receive the *a* as sons
Eph 1:5 *a* through Jesus Christ as

Adoraim
2Ch 11:9 and *A* and Lachish and Azekah

Adoram
2Sa 20:24 *A* was over . . . conscripted
1Ki 12:18 King Rehoboam sent *A*

Adorn
1Ti 2:9 *a* themselves in well-arranged
Tit 2:10 *a* the teaching of our Savior
1Pe 3:5 used to *a* themselves

Adorned
Mt 12:44 but swept clean and *a*
Lu 11:25 finds it swept clean and *a*
21:5 *a* with fine stones and
Re 17:4 *a* with gold and precious
18:16 richly *a* with gold ornament
21:2 as a bride *a* for her husband
21:19 wall were *a* with every sort

Adornment
1Ch 16:29 to Jehovah in holy *a*
2Ch 20:21 praise in holy *a* as they
Ps 29:2 Bow down to Jehovah in holy *a*
96:9 down to Jehovah in holy *a*
Pr 14:28 there is an *a* of a king, but
1Pe 3:3 do not let your *a* be that of

Adrammelech
2Ki 17:31 their sons in the fire to *A*
19:37 *A* and Sharezer, his sons
Isa 37:38 *A* and Sharezer, his own

Adramyttium
Ac 27:2 aboard a boat from *A* that

Adria
Ac 27:27 to and fro on the sea of *A*

Adriel
1Sa 18:19 given to *A* the Meholathite
2Sa 21:8 *A* the son of Barzillai

Adroitly
Mr 7:9 *A* you set aside the

Adullam
Jos 12:15 the king of *A*, one
15:35 Jarmuth and *A*, Socoh and
1Sa 22:1 escape to the cave of *A*; and
2Sa 23:13 to David at the cave of *A*
1Ch 11:15 to David at the cave of *A*
2Ch 11:7 and Beth-zur and Soco and *A*
Ne 11:30 *A* and their settlements
Mic 1:15 As far as *A* the glory of

Adullamite
Ge 38:1 an *A*, and his name was Hirah
38:12 Hirah his companion the *A*
38:20 hand of his companion the *A*

Adulterating
2Co 4:2 neither *a* the word of God

Adulterer
Le 20:10 death without fail, the *a*
Job 24:15 As for the eye of the *a*, it

Adulterers
Ps 50:18 And your sharing was with *a*
Jer 9:2 for all of them are *a*
23:10 it is with *a* that the land
Ho 7:4 All of them are *a*, like a
Mal 3:5 and against the *a*, and
Lu 18:11 unrighteous, *a*, or even as
1Co 6:9 nor idolaters, nor *a*, nor men
Heb 13:4 will judge fornicators and *a*

Adulteress
Le 20:10 death without fail . . . *a* as
Ro 7:3 *a* if she became another man's
7:3 an *a* if she becomes another

Adulteresses
Eze 16:38 with the judgments of *a* and
23:45 the judgment for *a* and
23:45 for *a* are what they are
Jas 4:4 *A*, do you not know that the

Adulteries
Mt 15:19 out of the heart come . . . *a*
Mr 7:22 *a*, covetings, acts of

Adulterous
Pr 30:20 is the way of an *a* woman
Isa 57:3 the seed of an *a* person and
Mt 12:39 A wicked and *a* generation
16:4 A wicked and *a* generation
Mr 8:38 *a* and sinful generation

Adultery
Ex 20:14 You must not commit *a*
Le 20:10 a man who commits *a* with
20:10 *a* with the wife of his
De 5:18 Neither must you commit *a*
Pr 6:32 *a* with a woman is in want of
Jer 3:8 Israel had committed *a*
3:9 committing *a* with stones and
5:7 they continued committing *a*
7:9 murdering and committing *a*
13:27 your acts of *a* and your
23:14 committing *a* and walking in
29:23 committing *a* with the wives
Eze 16:32 of the wife that commits *a*
23:37 they have committed *a* and
23:37 they have committed *a*
23:43 who was worn out with *a*
Ho 2:2 *a* from between her breasts
3:1 committing *a*, as in the case
4:2 stealing and committing of *a*
4:13 daughters-in-law commit *a*
4:14 because they commit *a*
Mt 5:27 you must not commit *a*
5:28 committed *a* with her in his
5:32 makes her a subject for *a*
5:32 divorced woman commits *a*
19:9 marries another commits *a*
19:18 You must not commit *a*, You
Mr 10:11 marries another commits *a*
10:12 marries . . . she commits *a*
10:19 Do not commit *a*, Do not
Lu 16:18 marries another commits *a*
16:18 from a husband commits *a*
18:20 Do not commit *a*, Do not
Ro 2:22 saying Do not commit *a*, do
2:22 do you commit *a*?
13:9 You must not commit *a*, You
Jas 2:11 You must not commit *a*
2:11 not commit *a* but you do
2Pe 2:14 They have eyes full of *a*
Re 2:22 those committing *a* with her

Adummim
Jos 15:7 in front of the ascent of *A*
18:17 in front of the ascent of *A*

Advance
Ge 33:12 and let me go in *a* of you
46:28 sent Judah in *a* of him to
Lu 1:76 will go in *a* before Jehovah
9:52 he sent forth messengers in *a*
10:1 by twos in *a* of him into
18:39 those going in *a* began to
19:4 ran ahead to an *a* position
Joh 3:28 sent forth in *a* of that one
Ac 7:52 who made announcement in *a*
13:24 *a* of the entry of that One
2Co 9:5 to come to you in *a* and to
9:5 and to get ready in *a* your
13:2 I say in *a* to those who
Ga 3:8 seeing in *a* that God would
Eph 1:14 is a token in *a* of our
2:10 which God prepared in *a* for
2Ti 2:16 will *a* to more and more
3:13 will *a* from bad to worse
2Pe 3:17 having this *a* knowledge, be

Advanced
Ge 18:11 were old, being *a* in years
24:1 Abraham was old, *a* in years
Jos 13:1 Joshua was . . . *a* in years
13:1 old and have *a* in years
23:1 Joshua was old and *a* in
23:2 grown old, I have *a* in days
2Sa 10:13 *a* to the battle against the
1Ki 1:1 David was old, *a* in days
1Ch 19:14 *a* before the Syrians to the
Mt 14:15 the hour is already far *a*
Joh 1:15 behind me has *a* in front of
1:30 man who has *a* in front of
Ac 12:10 they *a* down one street, and
Re 20:9 *a* over the breadth of the

Advancement
Php 1:12 for the *a* of the good news
1:25 for your *a* and the joy that
1Ti 4:15 *a* may be manifest to all

Advancing
Ge 26:13 and went on *a* more and more
2Ch 17:12 Jehoshaphat continued *a*
24:13 repair work kept *a* by their
Mr 10:32 they were *a* on the road up
10:33 we are, *a* up to Jerusalem

Advantage
Pr 14:23 toil there comes to be an *a*
21:5 surely make for *a*, but
Ec 2:11 nothing of *a* under the sun
2:13 exists more *a* for wisdom
2:13 *a* for light than for darkness
3:9 What *a* is there for the doer
5:11 what *a* is there to the grand
6:8 what *a* does the wise have over
6:11 what *a* does a man have?
7:12 the *a* of knowledge is that
10:10 wisdom to success means *a*
10:11 no *a* to the one indulging in
Lu 17:2 more *a* to him if a millstone
1Co 7:35 saying for your personal *a*

1Co 10:24 not his own *a*, but that of
10:33 not seeking my own *a* but
2Co 7:2 we have taken *a* of no one
12:17 I did not take *a* of you
12:18 Titus did not take *a* of you

Advantageous
Ec 7:11 is *a* for those seeing the sun
1Co 6:12 but not all things are *a*
10:23 but not all things are *a*

Adversaries
De 32:27 their *a* might misconstrue
32:41 pay back vengeance to my *a*
32:43 pay back vengeance to his *a*
33:7 a helper from his *a*
Jos 5:13 Are you for us or for our *a*?
2Sa 24:13 your fleeing before your *a*
1Ch 12:17 is to betray me to my *a*
21:12 away from before your *a*
Ezr 4:1 the *a* of Judah and Benjamin
Ne 4:11 our *a* kept saying: They will
9:27 into the hand of their *a*
9:27 out of the hand of their *a*
Ps 3:1 why have my *a* become many?
13:4 my *a* themselves may not be
27:2 being my *a* and my enemies
27:12 over to the soul of my *a*
44:5 By you we shall push our *a*
44:7 For you saved us from our *a*
60:12 will tread down our *a*
78:66 striking down his *a* from
81:14 against their *a* I would turn
89:23 I crushed his *a* to pieces
89:42 the right hand of his *a*
97:3 consumes his *a* all around
105:24 mightier than their *a*
106:11 came covering their *a*
108:13 will tread down our *a*
112:8 Until he looks on his *a*
119:139 *a* have forgotten your
119:157 persecutors and my *a* are
136:24 tore us away from our *a*
139:20 in a worthless way—your *a*
Isa 1:24 shall relieve myself of my *a*
9:11 And Jehovah will set the *a*
26:11 fire for your own *a* will
59:18 rage to his *a*, due
63:18 *a* have stamped down your
64:2 your name known to your *a*
Jer 30:16 your *a*, into captivity they
46:10 avenging himself upon his *a*
50:7 *a* have said, We shall not
La 1:5 Her *a* have become the head
1:7 The *a* saw her. They laughed
1:17 who are around him as his *a*
2:17 made the horn of your *a* high
Eze 30:16 be *a* during the daytime
39:23 into the hand of their *a*
Da 4:19 its interpretation to your *a*
Mic 5:9 will be high above your *a*
Na 1:2 taking vengeance against his *a*

Adversary
1Sa 2:32 upon an *a* in my dwelling
28:16 and proves to be your *a*
Es 7:6 *a* and enemy, is this bad Haman
Job 6:23 out of the hand of an *a*, And
16:9 My *a* himself sharpens his
19:11 reckoning me as an *a* of his
Ps 44:10 turn back from the *a*
74:10 will the *a* keep reproaching
78:42 redeemed them from the *a*
78:61 into the hand of the *a*
107:2 from the hand of the *a*
La 1:5 walked captive before the *a*
1:7 fell into the hand of the *a*
1:10 *a* has spread out his own hand
2:4 taken its position Like an *a*
4:12 the *a* and the enemy would
Ho 5:11 to walk after his *a*
Am 3:11 There is an *a* even round
Zec 8:10 no peace because of the *a*
Lu 12:58 going with your *a* at law to
18:3 justice from my *a* at law
1Pe 5:8 Your *a*, the Devil, walks

Adverse
2Ch 20:9 sword, *a* judgment, or

Adversities
Ps 38:12 spoken of *a*, And deceptions
52:2 *A* your tongue schemes up
52:7 takes shelter in *a* by him
55:11 *A* are within it; And from
57:1 refuge until the *a* pass over
Ps 91:3 From the pestilence causing *a*
94:20 throne causing *a* be allied
Pr 17:4 ear to the tongue causing *a*
19:13 A stupid son means *a* to his

Adversity
Job 6:2 my *a* they would put on scales
6:30 my own palate not discern *a*
30:13 beneficial only for *a* to me
Ps 5:9 Their inward part is *a* indeed
Isa 47:11 And upon you *a* will fall
Eze 7:26, 26 There will come *a* upon *a*

Advice
Ps 16:7 Jehovah, who has given me *a*
32:8 I will give *a* with my eye
62:4 they give *a* so as to allure
Ac 27:21 taken my *a* and not have put

Advices
1Ti 4:6 giving these *a* to the brothers

Advisable
Mt 19:10 it is not *a* to marry

Advise
Ex 18:19 I shall *a* you, and God will
Nu 24:14 *a* you what this people will
Jer 38:15 And in case I *a* you, you
Re 3:18 I *a* you to buy from me gold

Advised
1Ki 12:8 with which they had *a* him
2Ch 10:8 which they had *a* him, and
Job 26:3 How much you have *a* one that
Isa 7:5 *a* what is bad against you
Ac 27:12 majority *a* setting sail

Advising
1Ki 12:6 How are you *a* to reply to
2Ch 10:6 are you *a* to reply to this
Eze 11:2 *a* bad counsel against this

Aeneas
Ac 9:33 man named *A*, who had been
9:34 *A*, Jesus Christ heals you

Aenon
Joh 3:23 baptizing in *A* near Salim

Afar
Ps 10:1 do you keep standing *a* off
Isa 26:15 extended *a* all the borders
Lu 16:23 he saw Abraham *a* off and
17:12 but they stood up *a* off
Ac 2:39 all those *a* off, just as
Heb 11:13 they saw them *a* off and

Affair
Ex 18:11 by reason of this *a* in which
Nu 25:18 cunningly in the *a* of Peor
25:18 Peor and in the *a* of Cozbi
25:18 scourge over the *a* of Peor
31:16 over the *a* of Peor, so that
Es 1:17 *a* of the queen will go out to
1:18 have heard the *a* of the queen
Ec 3:1 a time for every *a* under the
3:17 there is a time for every *a*
5:8 do not be amazed over the *a*
8:6 and judgment even for every *a*
Jon 4:2 was not this an *a* of mine
Mt 8:33 *a* of the demon-possessed men
Ac 15:6 together to see about this *a*
19:40 with sedition over today's *a*

Affairs
1Ki 11:41 the *a* of Solomon and all
11:41 book of the *a* of Solomon
12:15 turn of *a* took place at the
14:19 rest of the *a* of Jeroboam
14:19 *a* of the days of the kings
14:29 rest of the *a* of Rehoboam
14:29 *a* of the times of the kings
15:7 the *a* of Abijam and all that
15:7 *a* of the days of the kings
15:23 all the *a* of Asa and all
15:23 *a* of the days of the kings
15:31 the rest of the *a* of Nadab
15:31 book of the *a* of the days of
16:5 the rest of the *a* of Baasha
16:5 book of the *a* of the days of
16:14 the rest of the *a* of Elah
16:14 book of the *a* of the days of
16:20 the rest of the *a* of Zimri
16:20 book of the *a* of the days of
16:27 the rest of the *a* of Omri
16:27 *a* of the days of the kings
22:39 the rest of the *a* of Ahab
22:39 book of the *a* of the days of
22:45 the *a* of Jehoshaphat and the
1Ki 22:45 *a* of the days of the kings
2Ki 1:18 *a* of the days of the kings of
8:23 the *a* of Jehoram and all
8:23 *a* of the days of the kings
10:34 *a* of Jehu and all that he
10:34 *a* of the days of the kings
12:19 *a* of Jehoash and all that
12:19 *a* of the days of the kings
13:8 the *a* of Jehoahaz and all
13:8 *a* of the days of the kings
13:12 the *a* of Jehoash and all
13:12 *a* of the days of the kings
14:15 the *a* of Jehoash, what he
14:15 *a* of the days of the kings
14:18 rest of the *a* of Amaziah
14:18 *a* of the days of the kings
14:28 the *a* of Jeroboam and all
14:28 *a* of the days of the kings
15:6 rest of the *a* of Azariah
15:6 *a* of the days of the kings
15:11 rest of the *a* of Zechariah
15:11 *a* of the days of the kings
15:15 the *a* of Shallum and his
15:15 *a* of the days of the kings
15:21 the *a* of Menahem and all
15:21 *a* of the days of the kings
15:26 the *a* of Pekahiah and all
15:26 *a* of the days of the kings
15:31 the *a* of Pekah and all
15:31 *a* of the days of the kings
15:36 the rest of the *a* of Jotham
15:36 *a* of the days of the kings
16:19 the rest of the *a* of Ahaz
16:19 *a* of the days of the kings
20:20 the *a* of Hezekiah and all
20:20 *a* of the days of the kings
21:17 rest of the *a* of Manasseh
21:17 *a* of the days of the kings
21:25 *a* of Amon, what he did
21:25 *a* of the days of the kings
23:28 the rest of the *a* of Josiah
23:28 *a* of the days of the kings
24:5 rest of the *a* of Jehoiakim
24:5 *a* of the days of the kings
1Ch 27:24 *a* of the days of King David
29:29 for the *a* of David the king
2Ch 9:29 *a* of Solomon, the first and
10:15 turn of *a* from the true God
12:15 Rehoboam's *a*, the first and
13:22 Abijah's *a*, even his ways
16:11 *a* of Asa, the first and the
20:34 *a* of Jehoshaphat, the first
25:26 *a* of Amaziah, the first and
26:22 *a* of Uzziah, the first and
27:7 *a* of Jotham and all his
28:26 rest of his *a* and all his
32:32 *a* of Hezekiah and his acts
33:18 of the *a* of Manasseh and his
33:18 *a* of the kings of Israel
35:26 the rest of the *a* of Josiah
35:27 his *a*, the first and the
36:8 rest of the *a* of Jehoiakim
Ne 12:23 book of the *a* of the times
Es 2:23 the book of the *a* of the days
3:4 Mordecai's *a* would stand
6:1 records of the *a* of the times
10:2 Book of the *a* of the times of
Ps 56:5 keep hurting my personal *a*
112:5 sustains his *a* with justice
1Co 16:14 your *a* take place with love
Eph 6:21 also know about my *a*, as
Php 1:12 my *a* have turned out for the
Col 4:7 All my *a* Tychicus, my beloved
1Ti 5:13 meddlers in other people's *a*

Affection
De 7:7 Jehovah showed *a* for you so
Ps 18:1 *a* for you, O Jehovah my
91:14 on me he has set his *a*
Mt 10:37 has greater *a* for father or
10:37 has greater *a* for son or
Joh 5:20 Father has *a* for the Son
11:3 for whom you have *a* is sick
11:36 *a* he used to have for him
16:27 Father himself has *a* for
16:27 you have had *a* for me and
20:2 for whom Jesus had *a*, and
21:15 you know I have *a* for you
21:16 you know I have *a* for you
21:17 do you have *a* for me?
21:17 Do you have *a* for me?
21:17 aware that I have *a* for you
Ro 1:31 having no natural *a*
12:10 tender *a* for one another

1Co 16:22 has no *a* for the Lord, let
Php 1:8 in such tender *a* as Christ
1Th 2:8 having a tender *a* for you
2Ti 3:3 having no natural *a*, not open
Tit 3:15 have *a* for us in the faith
Jas 5:11 Jehovah is very tender in *a*
1Pe 3:8 having brotherly *a*, tenderly
2Pe 1:7 godly devotion brotherly *a*
1:7 to your brotherly *a* love
Re 3:19 for whom I have *a* I reprove

Affections
2Co 6:12 room in your own tender *a*
7:15 tender *a* are more abundant
Php 2:1 any tender *a* and compassions
Col 3:12 the tender *a* of compassion
Phm 7 tender *a* of the holy ones have
12 my own tender *a*
20 tender *a* in connection with

Affirm
1Co 15:31 This I *a* by the exultation

Affixed
De 32:34 With a seal *a* to it in my
Jer 32:10 deed and *a* the seal and

Afflict
Ge 15:13 certainly *a* them for four
Ex 22:22 must not *a* any widow or
22:23 If you should *a* him at all
Le 16:29 you should *a* your souls, and
16:31 you must *a* your souls. It is
23:27 *a* your souls and present an
23:32 *a* your souls on the ninth of
Nu 24:24 will certainly *a* Assyria
24:24 And they will indeed *a* Eber
29:7 and you must *a* your souls
30:13 abstinence vow to *a* the soul
2Sa 7:10 unrighteousness will not *a*
Ps 89:22 son of unrighteousness *a* him
Isa 58:3 did we *a* our soul and you
58:5 earthling man to *a* his soul
Na 1:12 I shall certainly *a* you, so
1:12 I shall not *a* you anymore
Ac 7:6 *a* them for four hundred years

Afflicted
Ex 22:25 to the *a* alongside you, you
Le 19:10 For the *a* one and the alien
23:22 leave them for the *a* one and
23:29 soul that will not be *a* on
De 15:11 open up your hand to your *a*
Job 24:4 the *a* of the earth have kept
24:9 what is on the *a* one they
24:14 to slay the *a* and the poor
29:12 rescue the *a* one crying for
34:28 hears the outcry of the *a*
36:6 the judgment of the *a* ones
36:15 He will rescue the *a* one in
Ps 9:12 the outcry of the *a* ones
10:2 hotly pursues the *a* one
10:9 carry off some *a* one by force
10:9 carries off the *a* one by force
10:12 Do not forget the *a* ones
12:5 the despoiling of the *a* ones
14:6 The counsel of the *a* one you
18:27 *a* people you yourself will
22:24 the affliction of the *a* one
25:16 For I am solitary and *a*
34:6 This *a* one called, and Jehovah
35:10 Delivering the *a* one from
35:10 the *a* and poor one from the
35:13 With fasting I *a* my soul
37:14 the *a* and poor one to fall
40:17 But I am *a* and poor
68:10 make it ready for the *a* one
69:29 But I am *a* and aching
70:5 But I am *a* and poor. O God
72:2 *a* ones with judicial decision
72:4 Let him judge the *a* ones of
72:12 *a* one and whoever has no
74:19 life of your *a* ones forever
74:21 *a* one and the poor one praise
82:3 To the *a* one and the one of
86:1 For I am *a* and poor
88:7 breaking waves you have *a* me
88:15 *a* and about to expire from
90:15 the days that you have *a* us
102:*super* A prayer of the *a* in case
102:23 On the way he *a* my power
105:18 fetters they *a* his feet
109:16 pursuing the *a* and poor man
109:22 For I am *a* and poor
116:10 I myself was very much *a*
119:71 for me that I have been *a*
Ps 119:75 faithfulness you have *a* me
119:107 been *a* to a great extent
140:12 legal claim of the *a* one
Pr 14:21 showing favor to the *a* ones
15:15 the days of the *a* one are bad
22:22 Do not crush the *a* one in the
30:14 eat up the *a* ones off the
31:9 plead the cause of the *a* one
31:20 stretched out to the *a* one
Ec 6:8 What does the *a* one have in
Isa 3:14 robbery from the *a* one
3:15 very faces of the *a* ones
10:2 away justice from the *a*
10:30 O you *a* one, Anathoth!
14:32 *a* ones of his people will
26:6 feet of the *a* one, the steps
32:7 wreck the *a* ones with false
41:17 *a* ones and the poor ones
49:13 pity upon his own *a* ones
51:21 O woman *a* and drunk, but
53:4 stricken by God and *a*
53:7 was letting himself be *a*
54:11 O woman *a*, tempest-tossed
58:7 the *a*, homeless people
58:10 the soul that is being *a*
64:12 let us be *a* to the extreme
66:2 *a* and contrite in spirit
Jer 22:16 legal claim of the *a* one
La 3:33 has he *a* or does he grieve the
Eze 16:49 hand of the *a* one and the
18:12 the *a* and poor one he has
18:17 from the *a* one he has drawn
22:29 the *a* one and the poor one
Hab 3:14 bent on devouring an *a* one
Zec 7:10 no alien resident or *a* one
10:2 will become *a*, because there
11:7 O *a* ones of the flock
11:11 the *a* ones of the flock who
2Co 7:5 we continued to be *a* in every

Afflicting
Ge 31:50 If you go to *a* my daughters
De 26:6 *a* us and putting hard slavery
1Ki 8:35 because you kept *a* them
2Ki 17:20 *a* them and giving them into
2Ch 6:26 because you kept *a* them
Ps 94:5 your inheritance they keep *a*
Isa 60:14 sons of those *a* you must go
Zep 3:19 against all those *a* you, at

Affliction
Ge 16:11 Jehovah has heard your *a*
Ex 3:7 I have seen the *a* of my people
3:17 up out of *a* by the Egyptians
4:31 Jehovah . . . had seen their *a*
De 16:3 the bread of *a*, because it
26:7 look on our *a* and our trouble
1Sa 1:11 upon the *a* of your slave girl
9:16 have seen the *a* of my people
1Ki 2:26 *a* during all the time that
2:26 my father suffered *a*
2Ki 14:26 the very bitter *a* of Israel
1Ch 22:14 during my *a* I have prepared
Ne 9:9 *a* of our forefathers in Egypt
Job 10:15 and saturated with *a*
30:16 Days of *a* take hold upon me
30:27 Days of *a* confronted me
36:8 captured with ropes of *a*
36:15 the afflicted one in his *a*
36:21 have chosen rather than *a*
Ps 9:13 see my *a* by those hating me
22:24 the *a* of the afflicted one
25:18 See my *a* and my trouble
31:7 In that you have seen my *a*
44:24 Why do you forget our *a* and
88:9 languished because of my *a*
107:10 Prisoners in *a* and irons
107:17 finally caused themselves *a*
107:41 the poor one from *a*
119:50 This is my comfort in my *a*
119:67 under *a* I was sinning by
119:92 have perished in my *a*
119:153 see my *a*, and rescue me
Pr 31:5 cause of any of the sons of *a*
Isa 48:10 the smelting furnace of *a*
La 1:3 into exile because of the *a*
1:7 in the days of her *a* and of her
1:9 O Jehovah, see my *a*, for the
3:1 seen *a* because of the staff of
3:19 Remember my *a* and my
2Co 7:4 with joy in all our *a*
8:2 during a great test under *a*

Afford
Le 5:7 he cannot *a* enough for a sheep
Le 12:8 cannot *a* enough for a sheep
27:8 to what the vower can *a*, the
Nu 6:21 besides that which he can *a*
Ps 33:17 it does not *a* escape
Eze 46:7 to what he is able to *a*
Ac 11:29 as anyone could *a* it, to

Afire
2Ki 22:13 set *a* against us over the
22:17 set *a* against this place and
Isa 9:19 the land has been set *a*, and
Jer 2:15 cities have been set *a*, so
46:19 actually be set *a*, so as
Eze 20:48 Jehovah, have set it *a*

Aflame
Job 41:20 set *a* even with rushes
Isa 9:18 wickedness has become *a* just
Jer 32:29 city *a* with fire and must
49:2 be set *a* in the very fire
51:58 will be set *a* with fire
Heb 12:18 has been set *a* with fire
Jas 3:6 the wheel of natural life *a*
3:6 and it is set *a* by Gehenna

Aforesaid
Eph 5:6 because of the *a* things the

Aforetime
Ro 1:2 he promised *a* through his
9:29 just as Isaiah had said *a*
15:4 written *a* were written for

Afraid
Ge 3:10 I was *a* because I was naked
18:15 did not laugh! For she was *a*
19:30 he got *a* of dwelling in Zoar
20:8 And the men got very much *a*
21:17 Do not be *a*, because God has
26:7 *a* to say My wife for fear
26:24 Do not be *a*, because I am
31:31 It was because I was *a*
32:7 Jacob became very much *a* and
32:11 I am *a* of him that he may
35:17 Do not be *a*, for you will
42:35 and they became *a*
43:18 the men got *a* because they
43:23 Do not be *a*. Your God and the
46:3 *a* to go down to Egypt
50:19 Do not be *a*, for am I in the
50:21 do not be *a*. I myself shall
Ex 2:14 Moses now got *a* and said
3:6 *a* to look at the true God
14:10 sons of Israel got quite *a*
14:13 Do not be *a*. Stand firm and
20:20 Do not be *a*, because for the
34:30 grew *a* of coming near to
Nu 16:34 We are *a* that the earth may
21:34 Do not be *a* of him, for into
De 1:21 Do not be *a*, nor be terrified
1:29 not suffer a shock or be *a*
2:4 they will be *a* because of you
3:2 Do not be *a* of him, for I
3:22 men must not be *a* of them
5:5 you were *a* because of the fire
7:18 you must not be *a* of them
7:19 peoples before whom you are *a*
13:11 will hear and become *a*
17:13 hear and become *a*, and they
19:20 hear and be *a*, and they will
20:1 you must not be *a* of them
20:3 Do not be *a* and run in panic
21:21 hear and indeed become *a*
28:10 they will indeed be *a* of you
31:6 not be *a* or suffer a shock
31:8 Do not be *a* or be terrified
32:27 *a* of vexation from the enemy
Jos 8:1 Do not be *a* or be terrified
9:24 *a* for our souls because of
10:2 he became very much *a*
10:8 Do not be *a* of them, for
10:25 Do not be *a* or be terrified
11:6 Do not be *a* because of them
Jg 4:18 Do not be *a*. So he turned
7:3 Who is there *a* and trembling?
7:10 But if you are *a* to descend
8:20 he was *a*, for he was yet a
Ru 3:11 my daughter, do not be *a*
1Sa 3:15 Samuel was *a* to tell Eli of
4:7 Philistines became *a*, because
4:20 Do not be *a*, because it is a
7:7 Israel . . . *a* on account of
12:20 Samuel said . . . Do not be *a*
14:26 people were *a* of the oath
17:11 and were greatly *a*
17:24 and were very much *a*

1Sa 18:12 And Saul grew *a* of David
21:12 *a* on account of Achish the
22:23 Do not be *a*, for whoever
23:3 We are *a* while here in Judah
23:17 Do not be *a*; for the hand of
28:5 Saul . . . became *a*, and
28:13 Do not be *a*, but what did
28:20 became very much *a* because
31:4 because he was very much *a*
2Sa 3:11 Abner because of being *a* of
6:9 David became *a* of Jehovah on
9:7 not be *a*, for without fail I
10:19 Syrians were *a* to try saving
12:18 servants of David were *a*
13:28 him to death. Do not be *a*
14:15 the people made me *a*
1Ki 1:50 was *a* because of Solomon
1:51 has become *a* of King Solomon
17:13 said to her: Do not be *a*
19:3 he became *a*. Consequently he
2Ki 1:15 Do not be *a* because of him
6:16 Do not be *a*, for there are
10:4 became very greatly *a* and
19:6 Do not be *a* because of the
25:24 not be *a* of being servants
25:26 *a* because of the Chaldeans
1Ch 10:4 because he was very much *a*
13:12 David became *a* of the true
22:13 Do not be *a* nor be terrified
28:20 Do not be *a* nor be terrified
2Ch 20:3 Jehoshaphat became *a* and set
20:15 not you be *a* or be terrified
20:17 Jerusalem, do not be *a* or
32:7 *a* nor be terrified because of
32:18 make them *a* and to disturb
Ne 2:2 At this I became very much *a*
4:14 Do not be *a* on their account
6:9 trying to make us *a*, saying
6:13 in order that I might be *a*
6:14 trying to make me *a*
6:19 that Tobiah sent to make me *a*
Job 5:21 not be *a* of despoiling when
5:22 you need not be *a*
6:21 see terror, and you become *a*
9:35 Let me speak and not be *a* of
32:6 *a* To declare my knowledge
Ps 3:6 *a* of ten thousands of people
49:5 be *a* in the days of evil
49:16 Do not be *a* because some man
52:6 will see it and will be *a*
56:3 Whatever day I get *a*, I, for
56:4 my trust; I shall not be *a*
56:11 my trust. I shall not be *a*
64:9 earthling men will become *a*
65:8 will be *a* of your signs
91:5 *a* of anything dreadful by
112:7 not be *a* even of bad news
112:8 he will not be *a*
119:120 decisions I have been *a*
Pr 3:25 *a* of any sudden dreadful
Ec 3:14 may be *a* on account of him
9:2 has been *a* of a sworn oath
12:5 *a* merely at what is high, and
Isa 7:4 Do not be *a*, and do not let
10:24 not be *a*, O my people who
35:4 Be strong. Do not be *a*
37:6 Do not be *a* because of the
40:9 Raise it. Do not be *a*
41:10 Do not be *a*, for I am with
41:13 Do not be *a*. I myself will
41:14 Do not be *a*, you worm Jacob
43:1 Do not be *a*, for I have
43:5 Do not be *a*, for I am with
44:2 not be *a*, O my servant Jacob
51:7 not be *a* of the reproach of
51:12 *a* of a mortal man that
54:4 Do not be *a*, for you will
Jer 1:8 Do not be *a* because of their
3:8 her sister did not become *a*
10:5 Do not be *a* because of them
23:4 and they will be *a* no more
26:21 became *a* and ran away and
30:10 do not be *a*, O my servant
40:9 *a* of serving the Chaldeans
41:18 become *a* because of them
42:11 *a* because of the king of
42:11 Do not be *a* because of him
42:16 sword of which you are *a*
44:10 and they did not become *a*
46:27 do not be *a*, O my servant
46:28 do not be *a*, O my servant
51:46 *a* because of the report
La 3:57 You said: Do not be *a*
Eze 2:6 do not be *a* of them
Eze 2:6 of their words do not be *a*
2:6 their words do not you be *a*
3:9 You must not be *a* of them
Da 4:5 and it began to make me *a*
10:12 Do not be *a*, O Daniel, for
10:19 Do not be *a*, O very desirable
Am 3:8 Who will not be *a*?
Mic 7:17 and they will be *a* of you
Hab 3:2 I have become *a*, O Jehovah
Zep 3:16 Do not be *a*, O Zion
Hag 2:5 in among you. Do not be *a*
Zec 8:13 Do not be *a*. May your hands
8:15 house of Judah. Do not be *a*
9:5 Ashkelon will see and get *a*
Mt 1:20 not be *a* to take Mary your
2:22 became *a* to depart for there
14:30 he got *a* and, after starting
17:6 and became very much *a*
25:25 I grew *a* and went off and
27:54 grew very much *a*, saying
Mr 9:32 they were *a* to question him
Lu 5:10 Stop being *a*. From now on
9:45 they were *a* to question him
Ac 5:26 *a* of being stoned by the
9:26 they were all *a* of him
22:29 became *a* on ascertaining
23:10 *a* that Paul would be pulled
2Co 11:3 But I am *a* that somehow, as
12:20 I am *a* that somehow, when
Heb 13:6 I will not be *a*. What can
Re 2:10 *a* of the things you are about

Afresh
Heb 6:6 they impale the Son of God *a*

After*
Job 31:7 has walked merely *a* my eyes
Mt 27:63 *A* three days I am to be
Mr 13:8 earthquakes in one place *a*

Afterbirth
De 28:57 even toward her *a* that comes

Afterdays
De 8:16 to do you good in your *a*

Aftereffect
Pr 5:4 *a* from her is as bitter as

Afternoon
Mt 27:57 Now as it was late in the *a*
Mr 15:42 it was already late in the *a*

Afterward*
Pr 14:12 death are the end of it *a*
16:25 death are the end of it *a*
20:17 *a* his mouth will be filled
24:27 *A* . . . build up your household
28:23 will *a* find more favor than
Ec 4:16 will people *a* rejoice in him
7:8 Better is the end *a* of a
10:13 end *a* of his mouth is
Isa 41:23 things that are to come *a*
1Co 15:23 *a* those who belong to the
Heb 4:8 God would not *a* have spoken
12:11 yet *a* to those who have
12:17 *a* also when he wanted to

Afterwards*
Joh 13:36 but you will follow *a*
Heb 3:5 that were to be spoken *a*
Jude 5 *a* destroyed those not showing

Agabus
Ac 11:28 *A* rose and proceeded to
21:10 prophet named *A* came down

Agag
Nu 24:7 also will be higher than *A*
1Sa 15:8 catch *A* the king of Amalek
15:9 people had compassion upon *A*
15:20 *A* the king of Amalek
15:32 Bring *A* the king of Amalek
15:32 *A* went to him reluctantly
15:32 *A* began to say to himself
15:33 Samuel went hacking *A* to

Agagite
Es 3:1 the son of Hammedatha the *A*
3:10 the son of Hammedatha the *A*
8:3 the badness of Haman the *A* and
8:5 the son of Hammedatha the *A*
9:24 the son of Hammedatha, the *A*

Again*
Ge 24:20, 20 ran yet *a* and *a* to the
29:34 she became pregnant yet *a*
Ex 8:29 let not Pharaoh trifle *a* in
Nu 11:4 Israel too began to weep *a*
De 17:16 never go back *a* by this way
De 18:16 hear *a* the voice of Jehovah
24:4 allowed to take her back *a*
1Ki 13:17 not go back *a* by the way by
2Ki 21:3 built *a* the high places that
2Ch 36:15, 15 sending *a* and *a*
Job 34:32 I shall not do it *a*
Jer 36:28 Take *a* for yourself a roll
Joh 3:3 Unless anyone is born *a*, he
3:7 You people must be born *a*
Ac 22:13 brother, have your sight *a*!
Heb 2:13 And *a*: I will have my trust
2:13 And *a*: Look! I and the young

Against
Ge 13:13 were gross sinners *a* Jehovah
14:8 drew up in battle order *a*
14:9 *a* Chedorlaomer king of Elam
14:9 four kings *a* the five
14:15 he and his slaves, *a* them
16:12 His hand will be *a* everyone
16:12 everyone will be *a* him
19:13 outcry *a* them has grown loud
20:6 you back from sinning *a* me
20:9 sin have I committed *a* you
22:12 hand *a* the boy and do not do
30:2 Jacob's anger burned *a* Rachel
31:29 Watch yourself *a* speaking
31:43 What can I do *a* these today
31:43 *a* their children whom they
31:52 not pass this heap *a* you
31:52 this pillar *a* me for harm
34:7 a disgraceful folly *a* Israel
34:30 gather together *a* me and
37:18 plotting cunningly *a* him
39:9 and actually sin *a* God
40:1 the baker sinned *a* their lord
42:22 Do not sin *a* the child
43:9 I shall have sinned *a* you
44:18 anger grow hot *a* your slave
44:32 sinned *a* my father forever
49:23 harboring animosity *a* him
50:15 harboring animosity *a* us
50:20 you had evil in mind *a* me
Ex 1:10 hate us and will fight *a* us
4:14 anger grew hot *a* Moses
7:5 stretch out my hand *a* Egypt
9:14 sending all my blows *a* your
9:17 behaving haughtily *a* my people
10:16 I have sinned *a* Jehovah your
10:16 I have sinned . . . *a* you
11:7 *a* any of the sons of Israel
14:25 for them *a* the Egyptians
14:31 in action *a* the Egyptians
15:7 those who rise up *a* you
15:24 began to murmur *a* Moses
16:2 murmur *a* Moses and Aaron in
16:7 your murmurings *a* Jehovah
16:7 that you should murmur *a* us
16:8 you are murmuring *a* him
16:8, 8 are not *a* us, but *a* Jehovah
17:3 kept murmuring *a* Moses and
17:8 fight *a* Israel in Rephidim
17:9 fight *a* the Amalekites
17:10 to fight *a* the Amalekites
17:16 hand is *a* the throne of Jah
18:11 acted presumptuously *a* them
19:12 Guard yourselves *a* going up
20:3 have any other gods *a* my face
20:16 a witness *a* your fellowman
21:6 must bring him up *a* the door
21:14 becomes heated *a* his fellow
23:21 behave rebelliously *a* him
23:29 beasts . . . multiply *a* you
23:33 not cause you to sin *a* me
24:11 hand *a* the distinguished men
28:38 error committed *a* the holy
32:10 my anger may blaze *a* them
32:11 anger blaze *a* your people
32:12 over the evil *a* your people
32:29 *a* his own son and his own
32:33 Whoever has sinned *a* me
Le 4:14 committed *a* it has become
4:23 sin that he has committed *a*
5:15 sins by mistake *a* the holy
5:16 sin he has committed *a* the
5:19 become guilty *a* Jehovah
10:6 indignant *a* all the assembly
17:10 set my face *a* the soul that
19:16 up *a* your fellow's blood
19:18 a grudge *a* the sons of your
20:3 set my face *a* that man
20:5 my face *a* that man and his
20:6 face *a* that soul and cut him
26:17 set my face *a* you, and you

Le 26:37 stumble *a* one another as if
Nu 1:53 *a* the assembly of the sons
5:6 unfaithfulness *a* Jehovah
5:7 one *a* whom he did wrong
5:12 act of unfaithfulness *a* him
5:13 no witness *a* her, and she
10:9 *a* the oppressor who is
11:1 blaze *a* them and to consume
11:3 fire of Jehovah had blazed *a*
11:33 Jehovah's anger blazed *a*
12:1 speak *a* Moses on account of
12:8, 8 *a* my servant, *a* Moses
12:9 anger got to be hot *a* them
13:31 able to go up *a* the people
14:2 to murmur *a* Moses and Aaron
14:2 to say *a* them: If only we had
14:9 Only *a* Jehovah do not rebel
14:27 they are carrying on *a* me
14:27 they are murmuring *a* me
14:29 you who have murmured *a* me
14:35 have gathered together *a* me
14:36 whole assembly murmur *a* him
14:36 a bad report *a* the land
16:3 *a* Moses and Aaron and said to
16:11 together are *a* Jehovah
16:11 men should murmur *a* him
16:19 assembly together *a* them at
16:22 *a* the entire assembly
16:38 who sinned *a* their own souls
16:41 to murmur *a* Moses and Aaron
16:42 together *a* Moses and Aaron
17:5 make subside from *a* me the
17:5 they are murmuring *a* you
17:10 murmurings . . . *a* me, that
18:1 for error *a* the sanctuary
18:1 for error *a* your priesthood
18:5 occur *a* the sons of Israel
20:2 congregate themselves *a* Moses
20:24 you men rebelled *a* my order
21:5 kept speaking *a* God and Moses
21:7 we have spoken *a* Jehovah and
21:7 we have spoken . . . *a* you
21:15 leaned *a* the border of Moab
22:11 may be able to fight *a* them
22:25 squeeze herself *a* the wall
22:25 Balaam's foot *a* the wall
22:32 has been headlong *a* my will
23:21 any uncanny power *a* Jacob
23:21 trouble has he seen *a* Israel
23:23 is no unlucky spell *a* Jacob
23:23 Nor any divination *a* Israel
24:10 anger blazed *a* Balaam and
25:3 began to blaze *a* Israel
25:18 committed *a* you cunningly
26:9 a struggle *a* Moses and Aaron
26:9 in a struggle *a* Jehovah
27:3 ranged themselves *a* Jehovah
27:14 you men rebelled *a* my order
30:9 will stand *a* her
31:3 that they may serve *a* Midian
31:7 went waging war *a* Midian
32:13 So Jehovah's anger blazed *a*
32:14 anger of Jehovah *a* Israel
32:22 free from guilt *a* Jehovah
32:22 free from guilt . . . *a* Israel
32:23 also certainly sin *a* Jehovah
35:30 testify *a* a soul for him to
De 1:26 *a* the order of Jehovah your
1:37 *a* me Jehovah got incensed on
1:41 We have sinned *a* Jehovah
1:43 rebelliously *a* Jehovah's order
3:26 furious *a* me on your account
4:26 take as witnesses *a* you today
5:7 any other gods *a* my face
5:20 a falsehood *a* your fellowman
6:15 anger of . . . God may blaze *a*
7:4 anger will indeed blaze *a* you
7:22 beasts . . . may multiply *a* you
7:24 will take a firm stand *a* you
8:19 I do bear witness *a* you
9:16 you had sinned *a* Jehovah your
9:23 you behaved rebelliously *a* the
11:4 *a* the faces of which he made
11:17 anger does blaze *a* you, and
11:25 make a firm stand *a* you
12:27 poured out *a* the altar of
13:5 spoken of revolt *a* Jehovah
15:9 call out to Jehovah *a* you
19:11 risen up *a* him and struck
19:15 rise up *a* a man respecting
19:16 rise up *a* a man to bring a
19:16 a charge of revolt *a* him
19:18 a false charge *a* his brother
20:1 battle *a* your enemies and
De 20:3 the battle *a* your enemies
20:4 fight for you *a* your enemies
20:10 near to a city to fight *a* it
20:18 sin *a* Jehovah your God
20:19 by fighting *a* it so as to
20:19 by wielding an ax *a* them
20:20 build siegeworks *a* the city
21:10 to the battle *a* your enemies
22:26 rises up *a* his fellowman
23:4 they hired *a* you Balaam the
23:9 into camp *a* your enemies
24:15 cry out to Jehovah *a* you
28:7 enemies who rise up *a* you
28:7 they will come out *a* you
28:25 you will go out *a* them
28:48 Jehovah will send *a* you
28:49 Jehovah will raise up *a* you
29:20 will smoke *a* that man, and
29:27 anger blazed *a* that land by
30:19 as witnesses *a* you today
31:17 blaze *a* them in that day
31:19 witness *a* the sons of Israel
31:26 as a witness there *a* you
31:28 earth as witnesses *a* them
33:11 those who rise up *a* him
Jos 1:18 behaves rebelliously *a* your
7:1 *a* the sons of Israel
7:12 to rise up *a* their enemies
7:13 to rise up *a* your enemies
7:20 I have sinned *a* Jehovah the
8:2 an ambush of yours *a* the city
8:4 lying in ambush *a* the city to
8:14 an ambush *a* him to the rear
9:2 make war *a* Joshua and Israel
9:18 to murmur *a* the chieftains
10:5 to camp *a* Gibeon and to war
10:5 Gibeon and to war *a* it
10:6 have collected together *a* us
10:8 Not a man . . . stand *a* you
10:9 come *a* them by surprise
10:21 eagerly *a* the sons of Israel
10:25 *a* whom you are warring
10:29 and warred *a* Libnah
10:31 went camping *a* it and
10:34 camping *a* it and warring
10:34 and warring *a* it
10:36 and began to war *a* it
10:38 Debir and began to war *a* it
11:5 to fight *a* Israel
11:7 come *a* them along the waters
11:20 to declare war *a* Israel
19:47 to go up and war *a* Leshem
22:12 for military action *a* them
22:16 perpetrated *a* the God of
22:16 rebel today *a* Jehovah
22:18 rebel today *a* Jehovah, then
22:18 *a* the entire assembly of
22:19 *a* Jehovah do not you rebel
22:20 *a* all the assembly of
22:22 in unfaithfulness *a* Jehovah
22:29 to rebel . . . *a* Jehovah and
22:31 not perpetrated *a* Jehovah
22:33 for army service *a* them to
23:16 blaze *a* you, and you will
24:8 they went fighting *a* you
24:9 and went fighting *a* Israel
24:11 began fighting *a* you; but
24:22 You are witnesses *a*
24:27 serve as a witness *a* us
24:27 must serve as a witness *a*
Jg 1:1 Canaanites to fight *a* them
1:3 let us fight *a* the Canaanites
1:5 then they fought *a* him and
1:8 war *a* Jerusalem and got to
1:9 to fight *a* the Canaanites
1:10 So Judah marched *a* the
1:11 *a* the inhabitants of Debir
1:22 also went up *a* Bethel, and
2:14 anger blazed *a* Israel, so
2:15 Jehovah proved to be *a* them
2:20 anger blazed *a* Israel and he
3:8 anger blazed *a* Israel, so
3:12 Moab grow strong *a* Israel
3:13 he gathered *a* them the sons
3:28 Jordan *a* the Moabites, and
4:24 and harder *a* Jabin the king of
5:13 down to me *a* the mighty ones
5:20 they fought *a* Sisera
6:3 yes, they came up *a* them
6:4 And they would camp *a* them and
6:31 those who stood *a* him: Will
6:39 your anger blaze *a* me, but
7:2 brag about itself *a* me, saying
7:22 sword of each one *a* the other
Jg 8:1 to fight *a* Midian? And they
9:18 *a* the household of my father
9:31 are massing the city *a* you
9:33 make a dash *a* the city; and
9:33 are going out *a* you, you must
9:34 to lie in wait *a* Shechem in
9:38 Go . . . and fight *a* them
9:39 the fight *a* Abimelech
9:43 rose up *a* them and struck
9:44 made a dash *a* all who were
9:45 fought *a* the city all that day
9:49 put them *a* the vault, and
9:50 camp *a* Thebez and capture it
9:52 fighting *a* it, and he went on
10:7 anger blazed *a* Israel, so that
10:9 to fight even *a* Judah and
10:10 saying: We have sinned *a* you
10:18 in fighting *a* the sons of
11:4 Ammon began to fight *a* Israel
11:5 did fight *a* Israel, the older
11:6 let us fight *a* the sons of
11:8 and fight *a* the sons of Ammon
11:9 to fight *a* the sons of Ammon
11:12 you have come *a* me to fight
11:20 and fighting *a* Israel
11:25 or did he ever fight *a* them?
11:27 I have not sinned *a* you, but
11:27 fighting *a* me. Let Jehovah
11:32 Ammon to fight *a* them, and
12:1 to fight *a* the sons of Ammon
12:3 go over *a* the sons of Ammon
12:3 up *a* me this day to fight
12:3 this day to fight *a* me
14:4 opportunity *a* the Philistines
15:3 guilt *a* the Philistines
15:10 Why have you come up *a* us?
16:26 and let me lean *a* them
16:29 braced himself *a* the two
18:9 let us go up *a* them
18:27 *a* a people quiet and
19:2 to commit fornication *a* him
19:22 one another *a* the door
20:5 rise up *a* me and to surround
20:5 surround the house *a* me by
20:9 Let us go up by lot *a* it
20:10 going *a* Gibeah of Benjamin
20:11 gathered *a* the city as one
20:14 battle *a* the sons of Israel
20:18 *a* the sons of Benjamin
20:19 and camped *a* Gibeah
20:20 out to battle *a* Benjamin
20:20 in battle formation *a* them
20:23 *a* the sons of Benjamin my
20:23 Jehovah said: Go up *a* him
20:28 *a* the sons of Benjamin
20:29 set men in ambush *a* Gibeah
20:30 go up *a* the sons of Benjamin
20:30 in formation *a* Gibeah the
20:36 that they had set *a* Gibeah
20:48 back *a* the sons of Benjamin
21:22 to conduct a legal case *a* us
Ru 1:13 hand of Jehovah has gone out *a*
1Sa 2:1 My mouth is widened *a* my
2:10 those contending *a* him will
2:10 *A* them he will thunder in
2:25 If a man should sin *a* a man
2:25 if it is *a* Jehovah that a
5:7 his hand has been hard *a* us
5:7 and *a* Dagon our god
7:6 We have sinned *a* Jehovah
7:7 got on their way up *a* Israel
7:10 near for battle *a* Israel
7:10 that day *a* the Philistines
7:13 *a* the Philistines all the
11:1 and camp *a* Jabesh in Gilead
12:3 Answer *a* me in front of
12:5 Jehovah is a witness *a* you
12:9 they kept fighting *a* them
12:12 sons of Ammon had come *a*
12:14 rebel *a* the order of Jehovah
12:15 rebel *a* the order of Jehovah
12:15 to be *a* you and your fathers
12:23 sin *a* Jehovah by ceasing to
13:5 to fight *a* Israel, thirty
13:12 come down *a* me at Gilgal
14:4 to cross over *a* the outpost
14:10 should say, Come up *a* us
14:20 come to be *a* his fellowman
14:33 are sinning *a* Jehovah by
14:34 not sin *a* Jehovah by eating
14:47 about *a* all his enemies
14:47 all his enemies, *a* Moab and
14:47 and *a* the sons of Ammon and
14:47 sons of Ammon and *a* Edom

1Sa 14:47 and *a* the kings of Zobah and
14:47 and *a* the Philistines
14:52 heavy *a* the Philistines all
15:2 he set himself *a* him in the
15:18 and you must fight *a* them
17:19 fighting *a* the Philistines
17:28 anger grew hot *a* David
17:33 to go *a* this Philistine
17:35 When it began rising *a* me
19:4 king sin *a* his servant David
19:5 sin *a* innocent blood in
19:8 fighting *a* the Philistines
20:13 my father to do evil *a* you
20:30 anger grew hot *a* Jonathan
22:8 conspired, all of you, *a* me
22:8 servant *a* me as a lier in
22:13 men conspired *a* me, you and
22:13 rise up *a* me as a lier in
22:15 anything *a* his servant and
22:15 *a* the entire house of my
23:1 warring *a* Keilah, and they
23:3 to Keilah *a* the battle lines
23:5 fought *a* the Philistines and
23:9 fabricating mischief *a* him
24:6 my hand *a* him, for he is
24:7 allow them to rise up *a* Saul
24:10 not thrust out my hand *a*
24:11 I have not sinned *a* you
25:17 determined *a* our master
25:17 *a* all his house, as he is
25:22 urinates *a* the wall remain
25:34 anyone urinating *a* a wall
26:9 *a* the anointed of Jehovah and
26:11 *a* the anointed of Jehovah
26:19 that has incited you *a* me
26:23 *a* the anointed of Jehovah
28:1 army to make war *a* Israel
28:9 like a trapper *a* my soul
28:15 are fighting *a* me, and God
28:18 his burning anger *a* Amalek
29:8 fight *a* the enemies of my
30:23 marauder band that came *a*
31:1 fighting *a* Israel, and the
31:3 fighting became heavy *a* Saul
2Sa 1:16 mouth has testified *a* you
5:6 *a* the Jebusites inhabiting
5:19 I go up *a* the Philistines
5:23 come *a* them in front of the
6:7 anger blazed *a* Uzzah and
6:8 in a rupture *a* Uzzah
8:10 fought *a* Hadadezer so that
8:10 trained in warfare *a* Toi
10:9 charges had come to be *a* him
10:13 battle *a* the Syrians, and
10:17 David and began to fight *a*
11:17 and went fighting *a* Joab
11:23 *a* us into the field; but
11:25 your battle *a* the city and
12:5 grew very hot *a* the man
12:11 raising up *a* you calamity
12:13 I have sinned *a* Jehovah
12:26 fight *a* Rabbah of the sons
12:27 I have fought *a* Rabbah
12:28 encamp *a* the city, and
12:29 Rabbah and fought *a* it and
14:7 risen up *a* your maidservant
14:13 reasoned like this *a* the
17:12 *a* him in one of the places
17:21 Ahithophel counseled *a* you
18:12 hand out *a* the king's son
18:13 treacherously *a* his soul
18:28 hand *a* my lord the king
18:31 all those rising up *a* you
18:32 rose up *a* you for evil
20:10 not on guard *a* the sword
20:15 lay siege *a* him in Abel of
20:15 a siege rampart *a* the city
20:21 his hand *a* King David
22:28 your eyes are *a* the haughty
22:30 I can run *a* a marauder band
22:40 those rising *a* me collapse
22:49 those who rise up *a* me
24:1 came to be hot *a* Israel
24:1 incited David *a* them, saying
1Ki 2:23 *a* his own soul that Adonijah
2:27 spoken *a* the house of Eli
6:5 built *a* the wall of the house
6:5 *a* the walls of the house all
6:10 side chambers *a* the whole
8:31 a man sins *a* his fellowman
8:33 they kept sinning *a* you
8:35 they kept sinning *a* you, and
8:44 out to the war *a* their enemy
8:46 In case they sin *a* you (for

1Ki 8:50 who had sinned *a* you and all
8:50 they transgressed *a* you
11:26 lift up his hand *a* the king
11:27 his hand *a* the king
12:19 revolt *a* the house of David
12:21 fight *a* the house of Israel
12:24 *a* your brothers the sons of
13:2 he called out *a* the altar by
13:4 *a* the altar in Bethel
13:4 hand that he thrust out *a*
13:21 *a* the order of Jehovah and
13:26 *a* the order of Jehovah
13:32 *a* the altar . . . in Bethel
13:32 *a* all the houses of the high
14:10 anyone urinating *a* a wall
14:25 Egypt came up *a* Jerusalem
15:17 came up *a* Judah and began
15:20 *a* the cities of Israel and
15:27 conspire *a* him; and Baasha
16:1 *a* Baasha, saying
16:7 come *a* Baasha and his house
16:9 began to conspire *a* him
16:11 that urinates *a* a wall or
16:12 spoken *a* Baasha by means of
16:15 were encamping *a* Gibbethon
20:1 Samaria and fight *a* it
20:12 to get set *a* the city
20:22 Syria is coming up *a* you
20:23 fight *a* them on the level
20:25 fight *a* them on the level
20:26 to Aphek for battle *a* Israel
21:10 them bear witness *a* him
21:13 began to bear witness *a* him
21:21 urinating *a* a wall and the
22:6 Shall I go *a* Ramoth-gilead
22:32 turned aside *a* him to fight
2Ki 1:1 revolt *a* Israel after the
3:5 revolt *a* the king of Israel
3:7 Moab himself has revolted *a*
3:21 had come up to fight *a* them
3:27 great indignation *a* Israel
3:27 pulled away from *a* him and
6:8 involved in war *a* Israel
6:9 Guard yourself *a* passing by
7:6 *a* us the kings of the Hittites
7:6 kings of Egypt to come *a* us
8:28 *a* Hazael the king of Syria
9:8 urinating *a* a wall and any
9:14 to conspire *a* Jehoram
9:25 this pronouncement *a* him
10:9 conspired *a* my lord, and I
10:10 spoken *a* the house of Ahab
12:17 go up and fight *a* Gath
12:17 to go up *a* Jerusalem
12:18 withdrew from *a* Jerusalem
13:3 anger became hot *a* Israel
13:12 fought *a* Amaziah the king
13:17 arrow of salvation *a* Syria
14:15 fought *a* Amaziah the king
14:19 *a* him in a conspiracy
15:10 conspired *a* him and struck
15:25 adjutant conspired *a* him
15:30 conspiracy *a* Pekah the son
15:37 started to send *a* Judah
16:5 *a* Jerusalem in war and laid
16:5 and laid siege *a* Ahaz
16:7 who are rising up *a* me
17:3 *a* him that Shalmaneser the
17:5 come up *a* all the land and
17:5 Samaria and lay siege *a* it
17:7 Israel had sinned *a* Jehovah
17:18 got very incensed *a* Israel
18:7 rebel *a* the king of Assyria
18:9 Assyria came up *a* Samaria
18:13 *a* all the fortified cities
18:14 Turn back from *a* me
18:20 you have rebelled *a* me
18:25 *a* this place to bring it to
18:25 Go up *a* this land, and you
19:8 Assyria fighting *a* Libnah
19:9 has come out to fight *a* you
19:21 Jehovah has spoken *a* him
19:22 *a* whom have you lifted up
19:22 is *a* the Holy One of Israel
19:27 your exciting yourself *a* me
19:28 your exciting yourself *a* me
19:32 cast up a siege rampart *a*
21:23 conspired *a* him and put the
21:24 conspirators *a* King Amon
22:13 been set afire *a* us over
22:17 set afire *a* this place and
22:19 I have spoken *a* this place
23:17 done *a* the altar of Bethel
23:26 his anger burned *a* Judah

2Ki 24:1 turned back and rebelled *a*
24:2 send *a* him marauder bands
24:2 kept sending them *a* Judah
24:3 it took place *a* Judah
24:11 to come *a* the city
24:11 were laying siege *a* it
24:20 rebel *a* the king of Babylon
25:1 military force, *a* Jerusalem
25:1 began camping *a* it and
25:1 building *a* it a siege wall
25:4 Chaldeans were all around *a*
1Ch 5:20 came to be helped *a* them
10:3 fighting became heavy *a* Saul
10:13 acted faithlessly *a* Jehovah
12:19 with the Philistines *a* Saul
12:21 David *a* the marauder band
13:10 anger blazed *a* Uzzah, so
13:11 in a rupture *a* Uzzah
14:8 then he went out *a* them
14:10 I go up *a* the Philistines
14:14 Go around from directly *a*
15:13 our God broke through *a* us
18:10 he had fought *a* Hadadezer
18:10 trained in warfare *a* Tou
19:10 *a* him from the front and
19:17 up in formation *a* them
19:17 they began to fight *a* him
21:1 to stand up *a* Israel and to
21:10 that I am directing *a* you
22:8 But Jehovah's word came *a*
27:24 indignation *a* Israel, and
2Ch 6:22 man sins *a* his fellowman
6:24 they kept sinning *a* you, and
6:26 they kept sinning *a* you, and
6:34 war *a* their enemies in the
6:36 In case they sin *a* you
6:39 people who have sinned *a* you
10:19 revolt *a* the house of David
11:1 to fight *a* Israel so as to
11:4 and fight *a* your brothers
11:4 from going *a* Jeroboam
12:2 Egypt came up *a* Jerusalem
12:9 *a* Jerusalem and took the
13:3 *a* him with eight hundred
13:6 and rebel *a* his lord
13:7 did not hold his own *a* them
13:8 *a* the kingdom of Jehovah in
13:12 the battle alarm *a* you
13:12 fight *a* Jehovah the God of
14:6 no war *a* him during these
14:9 *a* them with a military
14:10 Asa went out *a* him and
14:11 we have come *a* this crowd
14:11 man retain strength *a* you
15:6 nation *a* nation and city
15:6 and city *a* city, because
16:1 of Israel came up *a* Judah
16:4 *a* the cities of Israel, so
16:9 there will exist wars *a* you
17:10 did not fight *a* Jehoshaphat
18:2 to go up *a* Ramoth-gilead
18:5 *a* Ramoth-gilead in war, or
18:31 around *a* him to fight
19:2 indignation *a* you from the
19:10 not do wrong *a* Jehovah and
19:10 to take place *a* you and
19:10 you and *a* your brothers
20:1 Ammonim came *a* Jehoshaphat
20:2 *a* you a large crowd from the
20:6 hold his ground *a* you
20:12 crowd that is coming *a* us
20:16 Tomorrow go down *a* them
20:17 go out *a* them, and Jehovah
20:22 ambush *a* the sons of Ammon
20:23 *a* the inhabitants of the
20:29 Jehovah had fought *a* the
20:37 prophetically *a* Jehoshaphat
21:16 Jehovah aroused *a* Jehoram
22:5 war *a* Hazael the king of
24:18 be indignation *a* Judah and
24:19 bearing witness *a* them, but
24:21 conspired *a* him and pelted
24:23 of Syria came up *a* him
24:25 servants conspired *a* him
24:26 conspirators *a* him: Zabad
24:27 pronouncement *a* him and
25:10 anger got very hot *a* Judah
25:15 became hot *a* Amaziah
25:27 conspiracy *a* him in
26:6 fight *a* the Philistines and
26:7 help him *a* the Philistines
26:7 *a* the Arabians that were
26:13 help the king *a* the enemy
26:16 unfaithfully *a* Jehovah his

2Ch 26:18 stood up *a* Uzziah the king
26:19 his rage *a* the priests
27:5 warred *a* the king of the
28:9 *a* Judah that he gave them
28:10 cases of guilt *a* Jehovah
28:11 burning anger is *a* you
28:12 *a* those coming in from the
28:13 guilt *a* Jehovah on our
28:13 is burning anger *a* Israel
28:20 king of Assyria came *a* him
29:8 indignation came to be *a*
32:1 *a* the fortified cities, and
32:2 face set for war *a* Jerusalem
32:16 *a* Jehovah the true God and
32:16 and *a* Hezekiah his servant
32:17 and to talk *a* him, saying
32:19 speaking *a* the God of
32:19 *a* the gods of the peoples
32:25 to be indignation *a* him
32:25 and *a* Judah and Jerusalem
33:11 Jehovah brought *a* them the
33:24 servants conspired *a* him
33:25 conspirators *a* King Amon
34:21 poured out *a* us because of
35:21 not *a* you that I am coming
35:21 it is *a* another house that
35:22 but to fight *a* him he
36:6 *A* him Nebuchadnezzar the
36:8 was to be found *a* him
36:13 even *a* King Nebuchadnezzar
36:15 *a* them by means of his
36:16 came up *a* his people
36:17 brought up *a* them the king
Ezr 4:5 hiring counselors *a* them to
4:6 *a* the inhabitants of Judah
4:8 wrote a letter *a* Jerusalem to
4:19 one rising up *a* kings and
7:23 no wrath *a* the king's realm
8:22 help us *a* the enemy in the
8:22 *a* all those leaving him
9:4 *a* the unfaithfulness of the
10:2 unfaithfully *a* our God
10:15 stood up *a* this, and
Ne 1:6 we have sinned *a* you
1:7 acted corruptly *a* you and have
2:19 Is it *a* the king that you are
4:3 if a fox went up *a* it, he
4:5 offense *a* the builders
4:8 come and fight *a* Jerusalem
4:9 kept a guard posted *a* them
5:1 *a* their Jewish brothers
6:12 spoken this prophecy *a* me as
9:10 signs and miracles *a* Pharaoh
9:10 acted presumptuously *a* them
9:26 and rebelled *a* you and kept
9:26 who bore witness *a* them to
9:29 bear witness *a* them to bring
9:29 *a* your own judicial decisions
9:30 kept bearing witness *a* them
9:34 you bore witness *a* them
13:2 went hiring *a* them Balaam
13:15 bear witness *a* them on the
13:18 the burning anger *a* Israel
13:21 bear witness *a* them and say
13:27 unfaithfully *a* our God by
Es 1:16 It is not *a* the king alone
1:16 but *a* all the princes and
1:16 *a* all the peoples that are in
2:1 what had been decided *a* her
4:7 *a* the Jews, to destroy them
5:9 filled with rage *a* Mordecai
6:13 you will not prevail *a* him
7:7 bad had been determined *a* him
8:3 that he had schemed *a* the Jews
8:7 thrust out his hand *a* the Jews
9:24 schemed *a* the Jews to destroy
9:25 he has schemed *a* the Jews
Job 1:12 Only *a* him himself do not
1:17 dashing *a* the camels and
2:3 although you incite me *a* him
6:4 terrors from God . . . *a* me
7:20 what can I accomplish *a* you
8:4 own sons have sinned *a* him
13:26 writing *a* me bitter things
15:6 your own lips answer *a* you
15:13 you turn your spirit *a* God
15:25 stretches out his hand *a* God
15:26 runs *a* him stiff-neckedly
16:4 be brilliant in words *a* you
16:4 would I wag my head *a* you?
16:8 my leanness rises up *a* me
16:9 he harbors animosity *a* me
16:9 grinds his teeth *a* me
16:9 sharpens his eyes *a* me
Job 16:10 opened their mouth wide *a*
16:10 they mass themselves *a* me
16:20 are spokesmen *a* me
19:5 *a* me you men do put on great
19:5 reproach to be proper *a* me
19:11 anger also grows hot *a* me
19:12 and cast up their way *a* me
19:18 they begin to speak *a* me
19:19 whom I loved have turned *a*
19:29 means a raging *a* errors
20:22 misfortune . . . come *a* him
20:25 Frightful objects will go *a*
20:27 earth will be in revolt *a*
21:27 would act violently *a* me
22:17 Almighty accomplish *a* us
24:13 among the rebels *a* light
27:7 the one revolting *a* me
30:12 cast up *a* me . . . barriers
30:24 *a* a mere heap of ruins
31:21 *a* the fatherless boy
31:23 *a* his dignity I could not
31:30 for an oath *a* his soul
31:38 *a* me my own ground would
32:2 *A* Job his anger blazed over
32:3 *a* his three companions his
32:14 has not arrayed words *a* me
33:13 *a* him that you contended
34:6 *A* my own judgment do I tell
34:37 his sayings *a* the true God
35:6 you accomplish *a* him
35:8 wickedness may be *a* a man
36:23 his way to account *a* him
36:32 upon it *a* an assailant
39:23 *A* it a quiver rattles
40:23 burst forth *a* its mouth
42:7 My anger has grown hot *a* you
Ps 2:2, 2 *A* Jehovah and *a* his anointed
3:1 Why are many rising up *a* me?
3:6 in array *a* me round about
5:10 they have rebelled *a* you
7:7 And *a* it do you return on high
15:3 *a* his intimate acquaintance
15:5 a bribe *a* the innocent one he
17:4 watched *a* the paths of the
17:7 revolters *a* your right hand
17:9 The enemies *a* my soul
18:29 I can run *a* a marauder band
18:39 those rising *a* me collapse
18:48 Above those who rise up *a* me
21:11 directed *a* you what is bad
21:12 you make ready *a* their face
22:13 opened *a* me their mouth
27:2 *a* me to eat up my flesh
27:3 *a* me an encampment should
27:3 Though *a* me war should rise
27:12 For *a* me false witnesses
31:13 mass together as one *a* me
31:18 speaking *a* the righteous one
34:13 your tongue *a* what is bad
34:13 lips *a* speaking deception
34:16 Jehovah is *a* those doing
35:1 conduct my case, O Jehovah, *a*
35:1, 1 War *a* those warring *a* me
35:15 They gathered together *a* me
35:16 their teeth even *a* me
35:20 *a* the quiet ones of the earth
35:21 their mouth even *a* me
35:26 assuming great airs *a* me
36:11 haughtiness come *a* me
37:12 plotting *a* the righteous one
38:16 assume great airs *a* me
39:11 *a* error you have corrected
41:4 for I have sinned *a* you
41:7 *a* me all those hating me
41:7 *A* me they keep scheming
41:9 has magnified his heel *a* me
42:10 With murder *a* my bones
43:1 case *a* a nation not loyal
44:5 tread down those rising up *a*
50:7 I will bear witness *a* you
50:20 and speak *a* your own brother
50:20 *A* the son of your mother you
51:4 *A* you . . . I have sinned
53:5 bones of anyone camping *a* you
54:3 strangers that have risen up *a*
55:3 they harbor animosity *a* me
55:12 that assumed great airs *a* me
55:18 from the fight that is *a* me
55:18 they have come to be *a* me
55:20 *a* those at peace with him
56:2 there are many warring *a* me
56:5 thoughts are *a* me for bad
59:1 From those rising up *a* me
62:3 *a* the man whom you would
Ps 64:8 tongue is *a* their own selves
73:15 *a* the generation of your sons
74:1 *a* the flock of your pasturage
74:5 on high *a* a thicket of trees
74:23 those rising up *a* you is
78:17 sinning still more *a* him
78:17 rebelling *a* the Most High
78:19 So they began to speak *a* God
78:21 fire . . . was kindled *a* Jacob
78:21 anger also ascended *a* Israel
78:31 wrath itself ascended *a* them
78:40 would rebel *a* him in the
78:56 rebel *a* God the Most High
78:62 *a* his inheritance he became
79:8 remember *a* us the errors of
80:4 fume *a* the prayer of your
81:8 and I will bear witness *a* you
81:14 *a* their adversaries I would
83:3 *A* your people they cunningly
83:3 conspire *a* your concealed ones
83:5 *A* you they proceeded to
86:14 have risen up *a* me
91:12 strike your foot *a* any stone
92:11 ones who rise up *a* me, the
94:16 up for me *a* the evildoers
94:16 for me *a* the practicers of
99:8 vengeance *a* their notorious
105:25 cunningly *a* his servants
105:28 did not rebel *a* his words
106:40 began to blaze *a* his people
107:11 *a* the sayings of God
109:2 deception have opened *a* me
109:3 fighting *a* me without cause
109:20 speaking evil *a* my soul
119:11 that I may not sin *a* you
119:23 *a* me they have spoken with
119:84 *a* those persecuting me
121:7 guard you *a* all calamity
124:2 When men rose up *a* us
124:3 anger was burning *a* us
137:9 Your children *a* the crag
139:21 for those revolting *a* you
Pr 3:23 will not strike *a* anything
3:26 keep your foot *a* capture
3:29 fabricate *a* your fellowman
6:24 guard you *a* the bad woman
6:24 *a* the smoothness of the
7:5 guard you *a* the woman stranger
7:5 *a* the foreigner who has made
17:11 messenger that is sent *a* him
17:26 To strike nobles is *a* what
18:1 *a* all practical wisdom he
18:19 who is transgressed *a* is
19:3 becomes enraged *a* Jehovah
20:2 drawing his fury *a* himself is
20:2 is sinning *a* his own soul
24:18 turn back his anger from *a*
24:28 a witness *a* your fellowman
25:18 testifying *a* his fellowman
28:4 excite themselves *a* them
Ec 4:12 together could make a stand *a*
8:11 sentence *a* a bad work has not
9:14 built *a* it great strongholds
10:4 a ruler should mount up *a* you
Isa 1:2 they . . . have revolted *a* me
2:4 not lift up sword *a* nation
3:5 the boy *a* the old man, and
3:5 esteemed one *a* the one to be
3:8 dealings are *a* Jehovah
3:9 actually testifies *a* them
5:25 grown hot *a* his people
5:25 out his hand *a* them and
7:1 to Jerusalem for war *a* it
7:1 proved unable to war *a* it
7:5 advised what is bad *a* you
7:6 *a* Judah and tear it apart and
7:17 Jehovah will bring *a* you
7:17 you and *a* your people and
7:17 *a* the house of your father
8:7 *a* them the mighty and the
8:14 stone to strike *a* and as a
9:8 that Jehovah sent *a* Jacob
9:11 of Rezin on high *a* him
9:21 they will be *a* Judah
10:6 *A* an apostate nation I shall
10:6 *a* the people of my fury I
10:24 *a* you in the way that Egypt
10:26 brandish *a* him a whip as at
13:1 pronouncement *a* Babylon that
13:17 arousing *a* them the Medes
14:4 proverbial saying *a* the king
14:8 no woodcutter comes up *a* us
14:22 And I will rise up *a* them
14:26 counseled *a* all the earth

Isa 14:26 stretched out *a* all the
15:1 The pronouncement *a* Moab
17:1 The pronouncement *a* Damascus
19:1 The pronouncement *a* Egypt
19:2 goad Egyptians *a* Egyptians
19:2 war each one *a* his brother
19:2 each one *a* his companion
19:2 his companion, city *a* city
19:2 city, kingdom *a* kingdom
19:16 which he is waving *a* it
19:17 he is counseling *a* him
20:1 war *a* Ashdod and to capture
20:3 sign and a portent *a* Egypt
20:3 Egypt and *a* Ethiopia
21:1 *a* the wilderness of the sea
21:11 pronouncement *a* Dumah
21:13 pronouncement *a* the desert
23:8 given this counsel *a* Tyre
23:11 a command *a* Phoenicia, to
25:4 like a rainstorm *a* a wall
26:21 of the land *a* him, and
27:3 may turn his attention *a* her
29:3 encamp on all sides *a* you
29:3 raise up *a* you siegeworks
29:7 that are waging war *a* Ariel
29:7 all those waging war *a* her
29:7 siege towers *a* her and those
29:8 waging war *a* Mount Zion
30:6 *a* the beasts of the south
30:32 actually fight *a* them
30:33 sulphur, is burning *a* it
31:2 *a* the house of evildoers
31:2 *a* the assistance of those
31:4 *a* it a full number of
31:6 *a* whom the sons of Israel
32:6 speak *a* Jehovah what is
33:4 that is rushing *a* one
34:2 Jehovah has indignation *a* all
34:2 and rage *a* all their army
36:1 *a* all the fortified cities
36:5 you have rebelled *a* me
36:10 *a* this land to bring it to
36:10 Go up *a* this land, and
37:8 Assyria fighting *a* Libnah
37:9 has come out to fight *a* you
37:22 Jehovah has spoken *a* him
37:23 *a* whom have you lifted up
37:23 *a* the Holy One of Israel
37:28 your exciting yourself *a* me
37:29 exciting yourself *a* me and
37:33 a siege rampart *a* it
41:11 getting heated up *a* you
42:24 One *a* whom we have sinned
42:25 it kept blazing up *a* him
43:27 have transgressed *a* me
45:24 getting heated up *a* him
47:11 know no charming *a* it
49:25 And *a* anyone contending
49:25 anyone contending *a* you I
54:17 that will be formed *a* you
54:17 *a* you in the judgment
57:4 *A* whom do you keep opening
59:12 each one has testified *a* us
63:10 he himself warred *a* them
63:17 heart hard *a* the fear of you
66:16 his sword, *a* all flesh
66:24 were transgressing *a* me
Jer 1:14 *a* all the inhabitants of the
1:15 *a* all her walls round about
1:15 *a* all the cities of Judah
1:18 walls *a* all the land
1:19 be certain to fight *a* you
1:19 they will not prevail *a* you
2:8 transgressed *a* me, and even
2:15 *A* him maned young lions roar
2:29 people keep contending *a* me
2:29 transgressed, all of you, *a*
3:13 for it is *a* Jehovah your God
4:16 Publish it *a* Jerusalem
4:16 *a* the very cities of Judah
4:17 become *a* her on all sides
4:17 she has rebelled even *a* me
5:10 Come up *a* her vine rows and
6:3 *A* her they pitched their tents
6:4 *A* her they have sanctified
6:6 *a* Jerusalem a siege rampart
6:12 *a* the inhabitants of the land
6:23 like a man of war *a* you
8:14 we have sinned *a* Jehovah
9:4 each one *a* his own companion
10:1 Jehovah has spoken *a* you
11:16 has set a fire blazing *a* her
11:17 spoken *a* you a calamity
11:19 *a* me that they thought out

Jer 11:21 said *a* the men of Anathoth
12:8 her voice even *a* me
12:14 said *a* all my bad neighbors
13:14 dash them one *a* another
13:16 your feet strike up *a* each
14:7 errors do testify *a* us
14:7 *a* you that we have sinned
14:20 for we have sinned *a* you
15:6 stretch out my hand *a* you
15:11 distress, *a* the enemy
15:14 *A* you people it is kindled
15:20 certainly fight *a* you
16:10 has Jehovah spoken *a* us all
16:10 sinned *a* Jehovah our God
18:7 I may speak *a* a nation and
18:7 *a* a kingdom to uproot it and
18:8 its badness *a* which I spoke
18:11 forming *a* you a calamity
18:11 thinking *a* you a thought
18:18 think out *a* Jeremiah some
18:23 counsel *a* me for my death
18:23 take action *a* them
19:15 that I have spoken *a* it
20:7 You used your strength *a* me
20:10 that we may prevail *a* him
21:2 Babylon is making war *a* us
21:4 who are laying siege *a* you
21:5 will fight *a* you with a
21:9 who are laying siege *a* you
21:10 set my face *a* this city
21:13 I am *a* you, O inhabitress
21:13 Who will descend *a* us?
21:14 hold an accounting *a* you
22:7 I will sanctify *a* you those
23:2 has said *a* the shepherds who
23:15 has said *a* the prophets
23:30 here I am *a* the prophets
23:31 Here I am *a* the prophets
23:32 *a* the prophets of false
24:10 send *a* them the sword
25:9 will bring them *a* this land
25:9 land and *a* its inhabitants
25:9 *a* all these nations round
25:12 *a* the king of Babylon
25:12 *a* that nation, is the
25:12 *a* the land of the Chaldeans
25:13 words that I have spoken *a*
25:13 prophesied *a* all the nations
25:29 *a* all the inhabitants of
25:30 he will sing out *a* all the
26:13 that he has spoken *a* you
26:19 that he had spoken *a* them
26:19 great calamity *a* our souls
26:20 prophesying *a* this city
26:20 this city and *a* this land
28:16 outright revolt *a* Jehovah
29:17 sending *a* them the sword
29:32 outright revolt *a* Jehovah
31:20 extent of my speaking *a* him
32:5 warring *a* the Chaldeans
32:24 who are fighting *a* it
32:29 fighting *a* this city must
33:5 to fight *a* the Chaldeans
33:8 they have sinned *a* me, and
33:8 they have sinned *a* me and
33:8 they have transgressed *a* me
34:1 fighting *a* Jerusalem and
34:1 *a* all her cities, saying
34:7 fighting *a* Jerusalem and
34:7 *a* all the cities of Judah
34:7, 7 *a* Lachish and *a* Azekah
34:21 withdrawing from *a* you men
34:22 fight *a* it and capture it
35:11 came up *a* the land that
35:17 I have spoken *a* them, for
36:2 spoken to you *a* Israel and
36:2 Israel and *a* Judah and
36:2 and *a* all the nations, since
36:7 has spoken *a* this people
36:29 *a* Jehoiakim the king of
36:30 Jehovah has said *a*
36:31 call to account *a* him and
36:31 and *a* his offspring and
36:31 and *a* his servants their
36:31 that I have spoken *a* them
37:5 withdrew from *a* Jerusalem
37:8 fight *a* this city and capture
37:9 go away from *a* us, because
37:11 from *a* Jerusalem because of
37:18 have I sinned *a* you and
37:18 you and *a* your servants and
37:18 and *a* this people, so that
37:19 Babylon will not come *a* you
37:19 you men and *a* this land

Jer 38:5 himself can prevail *a* you
40:2 this calamity *a* this place
40:3 people have sinned *a* Jehovah
41:12 fight *a* Ishmael the son
42:5 faithful witness *a* us if
42:19 Jehovah has spoken *a* you
42:19 I have borne witness *a* you
42:20 error *a* your souls
43:3 instigating you *a* us for the
44:11 setting my face *a* you
44:13 accounting *a* those dwelling
44:13 accounting *a* Jerusalem
44:23 sinned *a* Jehovah and did
46:12 mighty man *a* mighty man
46:20 will certainly come *a* her
48:2 thought out *a* her a calamity
48:15 gone up *a* her own cities
48:18 of Moab has come up *a* you
48:21 to Jahaz and *a* Mephaath
48:22, 22 *a* Dibon and *a* Nebo
48:22 and *a* Beth-diblathaim
48:23 and *a* Kiriathaim and
48:23 Kiriathaim and *a* Beth-gamul
48:23 Beth-gamul and *a* Beth-meon
48:24, 24 *a* Kerioth and *a* Bozrah
48:24 *a* all the cities of the
48:26 put on great airs *a* Jehovah
48:27 as often as you spoke *a* him
48:42 *a* Jehovah that he has put
49:2 *a* Rabbah of the sons of
49:14 come *a* her, and rise up
49:20 he has formulated *a* Edom
49:20 *a* the inhabitants of Teman
49:30 counsel even *a* you and
49:30 has thought out *a* you a
49:31 *a* the nation that is at ease
50:3 *a* her a nation has come up
50:7 they have sinned *a* Jehovah
50:9 bringing up *a* Babylon a
50:9 array themselves *a* her
50:14 Array yourselves *a* Babylon
50:14 *a* Jehovah that she has
50:15 Shout a war cry *a* her on
50:21 *A* the land of Merathaim
50:21 Merathaim—come up *a* her
50:21 *a* the inhabitants of Pekod
50:24 *a* Jehovah that you excited
50:29 Summon *a* Babylon archers
50:29 Encamp *a* her all around
50:29 *a* Jehovah that she has acted
50:29 *a* the Holy One of Israel
50:31 *a* you, O Presumptuousness
50:35 sword *a* the Chaldeans, is
50:35 *a* the inhabitants of Babylon
50:35 Babylon and *a* her princes
50:35 and *a* her wise ones
50:36 sword *a* the empty talkers
50:36 sword *a* her mighty men
50:37 sword *a* their horses and
50:37 *a* their war chariots and
50:37 *a* all the mixed company
50:37 is a sword *a* her treasures
50:42 as one man for war *a* you
50:45 he has formulated *a* Babylon
50:45 thought out *a* the land of
51:1 rousing up *a* Babylon and
51:1 *a* the inhabitants of
51:2 *a* her on all sides in the
51:11 *a* Babylon that his idea is
51:12 *A* the walls of Babylon lift
51:12 *a* the inhabitants of
51:25 *a* you, O ruinous mountain
51:25 stretch out my hand *a* you
51:27 Sanctify *a* her the nations
51:27 Summon *a* her the kingdoms
51:27 *a* her a recruiting officer
51:28 Sanctify *a* her the nations
51:29 *a* Babylon the thoughts of
51:46 the earth and ruler *a* ruler
51:51 come *a* the holy places of
51:60 words written *a* Babylon
51:62 have spoken *a* this place
52:3 rebel *a* the king of Babylon
52:4 military force, *a* Jerusalem
52:4 camp *a* her and to build
52:4 build *a* her a siege wall
52:7 were all around *a* the city
La 1:10 *a* all her desirable things
1:14 alert *a* my transgressions
1:14 *a* whom I am unable to rise up
1:15 He has called *a* me a meeting
1:18 it is *a* his mouth that I have
3:3 *a* me that he repeatedly turns
3:5 He has built *a* me, that he may

La 3:14 laughter to all people *a* me
3:46 *A* us all our enemies have
3:60 all their thoughts *a* me
3:61 all their thoughts *a* me
3:62 lips of those rising up *a* me
3:62 whispering *a* me all day long
4:2 were weighed *a* refined gold
Eze 2:3 that have rebelled *a* me
2:3 transgressed *a* me down to
4:2 lay siege *a* it and build a
4:2 build a siege wall *a* it and
4:2 throw up a siege rampart *a* it
4:2 set encampments *a* it and put
4:2 battering rams all around *a*
4:3 you must fix your face *a* it
4:7 and you must prophesy *a* it
5:6 *a* my judicial decisions in
5:6 *a* my statutes more than the
5:8 I am *a* you, O city, even I
6:12 to its finish my rage *a* them
6:14 stretch out my hand *a* them
7:3 I must send my anger *a* you
7:8 my anger *a* you to its finish
7:12 hot feeling *a* all its crowd
7:14 my hot feeling is *a* all its
11:2 bad counsel *a* this city
11:4 prophesy *a* them. Prophesy, O
12:10 pronouncement *a* Jerusalem
13:8 therefore here I am *a* you, is
13:9 come to be *a* the prophets
13:17 your face *a* the daughters
13:17 and prophesy *a* them
13:20 *a* the bands of you women
14:8 set my face *a* that man and
14:9 stretch out my hand *a* him
14:13 commits sin *a* me in acting
14:13 stretch out my hand *a* it
14:23 all that I must do *a* her
15:7 I have set my face *a* them
15:7 I direct my face *a* them
16:27 stretch out my hand *a* you
16:30 filled up with rage *a* you
16:37 collect them together *a* you
16:40 *a* you a congregation and
16:44 using a proverb *a* you will
17:15 rebelled *a* him in sending
17:20 with which he acted *a* me
18:22 not be remembered *a* him
19:8 began to set *a* him and got
20:8 And they began to rebel *a* me
20:13 Israel, rebelled *a* me in
20:21 sons began to rebel *a* me
20:27 in their acting *a* me with
20:47 setting a fire ablaze *a* you
21:2 prophesy *a* the soil of Israel
21:3 Here I am *a* you, and I will
21:4 *a* all flesh from south to
21:12 has come to be *a* my people
21:12 is *a* all the chieftains of
21:14 and strike palm *a* palm
21:17 one palm *a* my other palm
21:20 sword to enter *a* Rabbah
21:20, 20 *a* Judah, *a* Jerusalem
21:22 set battering-rams *a* gates
23:22 passionate lovers *a* you
23:22 *a* you on all sides
23:24 they must come in *a* you
23:24 set themselves *a* you all
23:25 express my ardor *a* you
23:25 take action *a* you in rage
23:29 take action *a* you in hatred
23:46 a congregation *a* them and
24:2 thrown himself *a* Jerusalem
25:2 Ammon and prophesy *a* them
25:3 *a* my sanctuary, because it
25:3 *a* the soil of Israel
25:3 *a* the house of Judah, because
25:6 soul *a* the soil of Israel
25:7 stretched out my hand *a* you
25:13 stretch out my hand *a* Edom
25:16 my hand *a* the Philistines
26:2 Tyre has said *a* Jerusalem
26:3 I am *a* you, O Tyre, and
26:3 bring up *a* you many nations
26:7 *a* Tyre Nebuchadrezzar the
26:8 make *a* you a siege wall
26:8 throw up *a* you a siege
26:8 raise up *a* you a large shield
26:9 he will direct *a* your walls
28:7 *a* the beauty of your wisdom
28:21 Sidon, and prophesy *a* her
28:22 Here I am *a* you, O Sidon
28:23 sword *a* her on every side
29:2 set your face *a* Pharaoh the
Eze 29:2 Pharaoh . . . prophesy *a* him
29:2 prophesy . . . *a* Egypt in its
29:3 *a* you, O Pharaoh, king of
29:10 here I am *a* you and
29:10 and *a* your Nile canals, and
29:18 a great service *a* Tyre
29:18 that he had performed *a* her
29:20 service that he did *a* her
30:11 draw their swords *a* Egypt
30:22 *a* Pharaoh the king of Egypt
30:25 out *a* the land of Egypt
31:11 Without fail he will act *a*
31:14 stand up *a* them in their
33:16 will be remembered *a* him
34:2 prophesy *a* the shepherds of
34:10 I am *a* the shepherds, and
35:2 *a* the mountainous region of
35:2 Seir and prophesy *a* it
35:3 *a* you, O mountainous region
35:3 stretch out my hand *a* you
35:13 acting in great style *a* me
35:13 multiplied *a* me your words
36:2 enemy has said *a* you, Aha!
36:5 speak *a* the remaining ones
36:5 and *a* Edom, all of it
38:2 *a* Gog of the land of Magog
38:2 Tubal, and prophesy *a* him
38:3 I am *a* you, O Gog, you head
38:11 I shall go up *a* the land
38:16 come up *a* my people Israel
38:16 bring you *a* my land
38:21 *a* him throughout all my
38:21 *A* his own brother the sword
39:1 prophesy *a* Gog, and you
39:1 I am *a* you, O Gog, you head
44:12 have raised my hand *a* them
Da 3:29 wrong *a* the God of Shadrach
5:23 *a* the Lord of the heavens you
6:4 to find some pretext *a* Daniel
6:5 *a* him in the law of his God
7:21 and it was prevailing *a* them
7:25 even words *a* the Most High
8:25 *a* the Prince of princes he
9:7 with which they acted *a* you
9:8 because we have sinned *a* you
9:9 for we have rebelled *a* him
9:11 for we have sinned *a* Him
9:12 that he had spoken *a* us and
9:12 *a* our judges who judged us
11:2 *a* the kingdom of Greece
11:5 he will prevail *a* him and
11:7 *a* the fortress of the king of
11:7 act *a* them and prevail
11:14 up *a* the king of the south
11:16 one coming *a* him will do
11:24 *a* fortified places he will
11:25 his heart *a* the king of the
11:25 they will scheme out *a* him
11:28 will be *a* the holy covenant
11:29 come *a* the south; but it
11:30 come *a* him the ships of
11:30 denunciations *a* the holy
11:32 wickedly *a* the covenant, he
11:36 and *a* the God of gods he
11:39 *a* the most fortified
11:40 *a* him the king of the north
11:42 out his hand *a* the lands
Ho 1:4 Jezreel *a* the house of Jehu
2:6 heap up a stone wall *a* her
2:13 hold an accounting *a* her for
4:4 who are contending *a* a priest
4:7 so they have sinned *a* me
4:9 hold an accounting *a* them for
4:14 an accounting *a* your daughters
4:14 *a* your daughters-in-law
7:13 they have transgressed *a* me
7:13 have spoken lies even *a* me
7:14 they kept turning *a* me
7:15 but *a* me they kept scheming
8:1 an eagle *a* the house of Jehovah
8:1 and *a* my law they have
8:5 My anger has grown hot *a* them
10:9 In Gibeah war *a* the sons of
10:10 and *a* them peoples will
12:2 hold an accounting *a* Jacob
13:9, 9 it was *a* me, *a* your helper
13:16 actually rebellious *a* her God
Am 3:2 hold an accounting *a* you for
3:9 *a* the mountains of Samaria
3:14 the revolts of Israel *a* him
3:14 *a* the altars of Bethel
5:19 his hand *a* the wall
6:14 up *a* you, O house of Israel
7:9 up *a* the house of Jeroboam
Am 7:10 Amos has conspired *a* you
7:16 must not prophesy *a* Israel
7:16 no word drop *a* the house of
Ob 1 let us rise up *a* her in battle
7 have prevailed *a* you
15 day of Jehovah *a* all the nations
Jon 1:2 proclaim *a* her that their
1:13 growing more tempestuous *a*
Mic 1:2 serve *a* you as a witness
2:3 thinking up *a* this family
3:5 *a* the prophets that are
3:5 actually sanctify war *a* him
4:3 sword, nation *a* nation
4:11 gathered *a* you many nations
5:1 a siege he has laid *a* us
5:5 up *a* him seven shepherds
6:3 tired you out? Testify *a* me
7:6 is rising up *a* her mother
7:6 *a* her mother-in-law; a man's
7:9 for I have sinned *a* him
Na 1:1 The pronouncement *a* Nineveh
1:2 vengeance *a* his adversaries
1:6 rise up *a* the heat of his anger
1:9 you men think up *a* Jehovah
1:11 thinking up *a* Jehovah what is
2:13 I am *a* you, is the utterance
3:5 I am *a* you, is the utterance
Hab 2:6 *a* him a proverbial saying
2:6 making debt heavy *a* himself
3:8 Is it *a* the rivers, O Jehovah
3:8 Jehovah, is it *a* the rivers
3:8 or is your fury *a* the sea?
Zep 1:4 stretch out my hand *a* Judah
1:4 *a* all the inhabitants of
1:16 *a* the fortified cities and
1:16 and *a* the high corner towers
1:17 *a* Jehovah that they have
2:5 The word of Jehovah is *a* you
2:8 great airs *a* their territory
2:10 *a* the people of Jehovah of
2:11 be fear-inspiring *a* them
3:7 I must call to account *a* her
3:11 you transgressed *a* me, for
3:19 *a* all those afflicting you
Zec 1:15 indignant *a* the nations that
1:21 a horn *a* the land of Judah
2:9 I am waving my hand *a* them
7:10 nothing bad *a* one another in
8:10 all mankind *a* one another
9:1 *a* the land of Hadrach, and
9:13 *a* your sons, O Greece
10:3 *A* the shepherds my anger has
10:3 *a* the goatlike leaders I
12:2 and also *a* Judah he will come
12:2 siege, even *a* Jerusalem
12:3 *a* her all the nations of the
12:9 that are coming *a* Jerusalem
13:7 sword, awake *a* my shepherd
13:7 even *a* the able-bodied man
14:2 all the nations *a* Jerusalem
14:3 and war *a* those nations as
14:12 service *a* Jerusalem
14:13 come up *a* the hand of his
14:16 are coming *a* Jerusalem
Mal 3:5 witness *a* the sorcerers
3:5 and *a* the adulterers, and
3:5 and *a* those swearing falsely
3:5 *a* those acting fraudulently
3:13 have been your words *a* me
3:13 with one another *a* you
Mt 4:6 strike your foot *a* a stone
5:11 *a* you for my sake
5:23 brother has something *a* you
5:25 the one complaining *a* you
7:25 and lashed *a* that house, but
7:27 and struck *a* that house and
10:17 Be on your guard *a* men; for
10:21 will rise up *a* parents and
10:35 with a man *a* his father
10:35 and a daughter *a* her mother
10:35 wife *a* her mother-in-law
12:10 get an accusation *a* him
12:14 took counsel *a* him that they
12:25 kingdom divided *a* itself
12:25 house divided *a* itself will
12:26 Satan . . . divided *a* himself
12:30 is not on my side is *a* me
12:31 blasphemy *a* the spirit will
12:32 word *a* the Son of man, it
12:32 speaks *a* the holy spirit, it
14:24 because the wind was *a* them
18:21 is my brother to sin *a* me
20:11 to murmur *a* the householder
23:31 bearing witness *a* yourselves

Mt 24:7 For nation will rise *a* nation
24:7 and kingdom *a* kingdom, and
26:55 and clubs as *a* a robber to
26:59 for false witness *a* Jesus in
26:62 these are testifying *a* you
27:1 held a consultation *a* Jesus
27:13 they are testifying *a* you
27:37 charge *a* him, in writing
Mr 3:6 *a* him, in order to destroy
3:24 kingdom . . . divided *a* itself
3:25 a house . . . divided *a* itself
3:26 Satan has risen up *a* himself
3:29 blasphemes *a* the holy spirit
5:24 crowd was . . . pressing *a* him
6:19 was nursing a grudge *a* him
6:48 for the wind was *a* them
9:40 he that is not *a* us is for us
10:11 commits adultery *a* her
11:25 whatever you have *a* anyone
13:8 nation will rise *a* nation
13:8 and kingdom *a* kingdom, there
13:12 will rise up *a* parents
14:48 as *a* a robber to arrest me
14:55 testimony *a* Jesus to put
14:56 giving false witness *a* him
14:57 bearing false witness *a* him
14:60 these are testifying *a* you
15:4 charges they are bringing *a*
15:26 charge *a* him was written
Lu 2:34 for a sign to be talked *a*
4:11 strike your foot *a* a stone
6:48 the river dashed *a* that house
6:49 *A* it the river dashed, and
9:5 for a witness *a* them
9:50 he that is not *a* you is for
10:11 dust . . . we wipe off *a* you
11:17 kingdom divided *a* itself
11:17 house divided *a* itself falls
11:18 if Satan is also divided *a*
11:22 comes *a* him and conquers
11:23 is not on my side is *a* me
12:10 says a word *a* the Son of man
12:10 blasphemes *a* the holy spirit
12:15 and guard *a* . . . covetousness
12:52 divided, three *a* two and two
12:52 divided . . . two *a* three
12:53 divided, father *a* son and
12:53 divided . . . son *a* father
12:53 mother *a* daughter and
12:53 and daughter *a* her mother
12:53 mother-in-law *a* her
12:53 daughter-in-law *a* her
14:31 the one that comes *a* him
15:18, 18 sinned *a* heaven and *a* you
15:21, 21 sinned *a* heaven and *a* you
17:4 sins seven times a day *a* you
21:10 Nation will rise *a* nation
21:10 and kingdom *a* kingdom
22:52 and clubs as *a* a robber
22:53 stretch out your hands *a* me
22:65 things in blasphemy *a* him
23:14 charges you are bringing *a*
Joh 10:35 *a* whom the word of God
11:9 he does not bump *a* anything
11:10 he bumps *a* something
11:38 and a stone was lying *a* it
13:18 lifted up his heel *a* me
15:21 *a* you on account of my name
18:29 do you bring *a* this man
19:11 no authority at all *a* me
19:12 a king speaks *a* Caesar
Ac 4:26 together as one *a* Jehovah
4:26 and *a* his anointed one
4:27 *a* your holy servant Jesus
5:39 fighters actually *a* God
6:1 *a* the Hebrew-speaking Jews
6:10 *a* the wisdom and the spirit
6:11 blasphemous sayings *a* Moses
6:13 things *a* this holy place and
6:13 holy place and *a* the Law
7:19 statecraft *a* our race and
7:60 do not charge this sin *a* them
8:1 *a* the congregation that was
9:1 murder *a* the disciples of the
9:23 plot *a* him became known to
12:20 fighting mood *a* the people
13:50 a persecution *a* Paul and
13:51 dust off their feet *a* them
14:2 influenced . . . *a* the brothers
16:22 the crowd rose up together *a*
18:12 with one accord *a* Paul and
19:16 prevailed *a* them, so that
19:38 have a case *a* someone, court
19:38 bring charges *a* one another

Ac 20:3 a plot was hatched *a* him by
21:28 *a* the people and the Law and
22:24 shouting *a* him this way
23:30 plot . . . *a* the man has been
23:30 the accusers to speak *a* him
24:1 to the governor *a* Paul
24:16 no offense *a* God and men
24:19 might have anything *a* me
25:2 gave him information *a* Paul
25:3 as a favor *a* the man that
25:7 leveling *a* him many and
25:8 Neither *a* the Law of the Jews
25:8 nor *a* the temple nor
25:8 nor *a* Caesar have I committed
25:15 a judgment of condemnation *a*
25:27 signify the charges *a* him
26:9 *a* the name of Jesus the
26:10 I cast my vote *a* them
26:11 I was extremely mad *a* them
26:14 kicking *a* the goads makes
27:15 keep its head *a* the wind
28:19 Jews kept speaking *a* it, I
28:22 everywhere it is spoken *a*
Ro 1:18 *a* all ungodliness and
2:2 *a* those who practice such
3:8 judgment *a* those men is in
5:13 sin is not charged *a* anyone
7:23 warring *a* the law of my mind
8:31 is for us, who will be *a* us
8:33 accusation *a* God's chosen
11:2 he pleads with God *a* Israel
13:2 *a* the arrangement of God
13:2 who have taken a stand *a* it
1Co 4:4 not conscious of anything *a*
4:6 in favor of the one *a* the
6:1 a case *a* the other dare to go
6:18 is sinning *a* his own body
8:12 thus sin *a* your brothers and
8:12 you are sinning *a* Christ
9:17 if I do it *a* my will, all
11:29 drinks judgment *a* himself
15:15 borne witness *a* God that he
2Co 1:23 call upon God as a witness *a*
10:2 taking bold measures *a* some
10:5 raised up *a* the knowledge of
13:8 can do nothing *a* the truth
Ga 3:21 *a* the promises of God
5:17 flesh is *a* the spirit in its
5:17 and the spirit *a* the flesh
5:23 *A* such things there is no
Eph 6:11 firm *a* the machinations of
6:12 not *a* blood and flesh, but
6:12 but *a* the governments
6:12 *a* the authorities
6:12 *a* the world rulers of this
6:12 *a* the wicked spirit forces
Col 2:14 handwritten document *a* us
3:13 has a cause for complaint *a*
1Th 2:15 *a* the interests of all men
1Ti 5:19 an accusation *a* an older man
2Ti 4:15 you too be on guard *a* him
Heb 12:3 talk by sinners *a* their own
12:4 your contest *a* that sin you
Jas 2:10 an offender *a* them all
3:14 and lying *a* the truth
4:11 Quit speaking *a* one another
4:11 He who speaks *a* a brother
4:11 speaks *a* law and judges law
5:3 will be as a witness *a* you
5:9 heave sighs *a* one another
1Pe 2:11 a conflict *a* the soul
2:12 speaking *a* you as evildoers
3:12 Jehovah is *a* those doing bad
3:16 in which you are spoken *a*
5:9 *a* him, solid in the faith
2Pe 2:11 bring *a* them an accusation
Jude 9 judgment *a* him in abusive
15 to execute judgment *a* all
15 ungodly sinners spoke *a* him
Re 2:4 I hold this *a* you, that you
2:14 I have a few things *a* you
2:20 I do hold this *a* you, that
13:6 mouth in blasphemies *a* God

Agate
Ex 28:19 *lesh'em* stone, *a* and
39:12 was *lesh'em* stone, *a* and

Age
Ge 15:15 be buried at a good old *a*
21:2 son to Abraham in his old *a*
21:7 birth to a son in his old *a*
25:8 good old *a*, old and satisfied
37:3 he was the son of his old *a*
44:20 and a child of his old *a*
Ge 48:10 eyes . . . dull from old *a*
50:26 *a* of a hundred and ten years
Ex 38:26 from twenty years of *a* and
Le 27:5 *a* is from five years old up
27:6 *a* is from a month old up to
27:7 *a* is from sixty years old
Nu 8:25 after the *a* of fifty years he
26:2 twenty years of *a* and upward
26:4 *a* of twenty years and upward
Jos 24:29 Joshua . . . died at the *a* of
Jg 2:8 died at the *a* of a hundred and
8:32 died at a good old *a* and was
Ru 4:15 and one to nourish your old *a*
2Sa 19:32 being eighty years of *a*
1Ki 14:4 eyes had set because of his *a*
1Ch 23:3 the *a* of thirty years upward
23:24 *a* of twenty years upward
23:27 *a* of twenty years upward
27:23 twenty years of *a* and under
29:28 he died in a good old *a*
2Ch 25:1 *a* of twenty-five years
25:5 twenty years of *a* upward
29:1 king at the *a* of twenty-five
31:16 three years of *a* upward
31:17 *a* of twenty years upward
Ezr 3:8 twenty years of *a* upward to
Ps 71:9 away in the time of old *a*
71:18 And even until old *a* and
Isa 46:4 Even to one's old *a* I am the
65:20 a hundred years of *a*
65:20 a hundred years of *a* he
Da 1:10 are of the same *a* as yours
Mt 2:16 two years of *a* and under
Lu 1:36 conceived a son, in her old *a*
Joh 9:21 Ask him. He is of *a*
9:23 He is of *a*. Question him
Ga 1:14 many of my own *a* in my race
Heb 11:11 she was past the *a* limit

Aged
Ge 43:27 Is your father, the *a* man
44:20 We do have an *a* father and a
Job 12:12 wisdom among the *a* And
15:10 and the *a* one are with us
29:8 And even the *a* ones rose up
32:6 you men are *a*. That is why
Isa 9:15 *a* and highly respected one
Lu 1:18 I am *a* and my wife is well
Tit 2:2 Let the *a* men be moderate in
2:3 let the *a* women be reverent
Phm 9 Paul an *a* man, yes, now also

Agee
2Sa 23:11 the son of *A* the Hararite

Agent
Ac 3:15 killed the Chief *A* of life
5:31 exalted this one as Chief *A*
Heb 2:10 Chief *A* of their salvation
12:2 look intently at the Chief *A*

Agents
Jg 3:4 they kept serving as *a* to test

Agitate
Ac 17:13 to incite and *a* the masses

Agitated
Ge 41:8 that his spirit became *a*
Ex 15:14 they will be *a*; Birth pangs
De 2:25 be *a* and have pains like those
2Sa 22:8 heavens themselves became *a*
Ps 4:4 Be *a*, but do not sin
18:7 the mountains . . . became *a*
77:4 I have become *a*, and I cannot
77:16 watery deeps began to be *a*
77:18 earth became *a* and began
99:1 Let the peoples be *a*
Pr 30:21 the earth has been *a*, and
Isa 5:25 mountains will be *a*, and
13:13 heaven itself to become *a*
14:9 has become *a* at you in order
23:11 caused kingdoms to be *a*
28:21 *a* just as in the low plain
32:10 you careless ones will be *a*
32:11 Be *a*, you careless ones!
64:2 the nations might be *a*
Jer 33:9 *a* on account of all the
Da 2:1 spirit began to feel *a*
2:3 spirit is *a* to know the dream
Joe 2:1 the inhabitants . . . get *a*
2:10 the land has become *a*, the
Am 8:8 that the land will be *a*
Hab 3:7 land of Midian began to be *a*
3:16 my belly began to be *a*
3:16 and in my situation I was *a*
Mt 2:3 hearing this King Herod was *a*

Ac 17:8 *a* the crowd and the city
1Pe 3:14 you fear, neither become *a*

Agitating
Isa 14:16 man that was *a* the earth

Agitation
Job 3:17 have ceased from *a*, And
3:26 at rest, and yet *a* comes
14:1 Man . . . glutted with *a*
Isa 14:3 pain and from your *a* and
Jer 50:34 *a* to the inhabitants of
Eze 12:18 *a* and with anxious care
16:43 and you would cause me *a*
Mic 7:17 come in *a* out of their
Hab 3:2 During the *a*, to show mercy
Mt 8:24 a great *a* arose in the sea
Lu 21:25 roaring of the sea and its *a*

Aglow
Ac 18:25 as he was *a* with the spirit
Ro 12:11 Be *a* with the spirit

Ago
Jos 24:2 a long time *a*, Terah the
1Sa 9:20 lost to you three days *a*
30:13 I took sick three days *a*
Job 22:15 to the very way of long *a*
29:2 the lunar months of long *a*
Ps 44:1 In the days of long *a*
74:2 that you acquired long *a*
74:12 God is my King from long *a*
77:5 upon the days of long *a*
77:11 marvelous doing of long *a*
78:2 riddles of long *a* to bubble
93:2 established from long *a*
102:25 Long *a* you laid the
119:152 Long *a* I have known some
143:5 remembered days of long *a*
Pr 8:22 his achievements of long *a*
22:28 a boundary of long *a*, which
23:10 back the boundary of long *a*
Isa 22:11 one forming it long *a* you
23:7 exultant from days of long *a*
44:7 the people of long *a*
45:21 be heard from a long time *a*
46:9 things of a long time *a*
46:10 from long *a* the things that
51:9 as in the days of long *a*
63:9 all the days of long *a*
63:11 remember the days of long *a*
63:16 Repurchaser of long *a* is
64:4 from time long *a* none have
Jer 2:20 long *a* I broke your yoke
5:15 It is a nation of long *a*, a
6:16 for the roadways of long *a*
18:15 the paths of long *a*, to
25:5 your forefathers from long *a*
28:8 prior to you from long *a*
La 1:7 to be from days of long *a*
2:17 from the days of long *a*
5:21 days for us as in the long *a*
Eze 26:20 to the people of long *a*
Am 9:11 as in the days of long *a*
Mic 7:14 in the days of a long time *a*
7:20 from the days of long *a*
Hab 1:12 Are you not from long *a*, O
3:6 walkings of long *a* are his
Mal 3:4 as in the days of long *a* and
Mt 11:21 would long *a* have repented
Lu 10:13 long *a* have repented sitting
Ac 10:30 Cornelius said: Four days *a*
2Co 8:10 a year *a* you initiated not
12:2 fourteen years *a*—whether
Heb 1:1 God, who long *a* spoke on many
2Pe 1:9 from his sins of long *a*
Jude 4 long *a* been appointed by the

Agony
Lu 22:44 getting into an *a* he
Re 12:2 and in her *a* to give birth

Agree
Ge 23:8 your souls *a* to bury my dead
Mt 18:19 If two of you on earth *a*
Ac 15:15 the words of the Prophets *a*
22:18 will not *a* to your witness
Ro 7:16 I *a* that the Law is fine

Agreeable
1Sa 13:14 a man *a* to his heart
Ps 16:6 own possession has proved *a*
Ca 4:3 and your speaking is *a*
Ac 13:22 a man *a* to my heart, who
1Co 7:12 is *a* to dwelling with him
7:13 he is *a* to dwelling with her
1Pe 2:19 unjustly, this is an *a* thing
2:20 this is a thing *a* with God

Agreeably
De 21:14 send her away, *a* to her own
Ps 105:22 his princes *a* to his soul
Jer 34:16 let go free *a* to their soul

Agreed
Da 2:9 that you have *a* to say before
Mt 20:2 he had *a* with the workers for
20:13 *a* with me for a denarius
Mr 14:44 had given them an *a* sign
Lu 22:5 *a* to give him silver money
Ac 5:9 *a* upon between you two to
23:20 *a* to request you to bring

Agreement
2Sa 7:21 *a* with your own heart you
1Ch 17:19 in *a* with your own heart
Ps 119:154 in *a* with your saying
Pr 14:9 upright ones there is *a*
Jer 3:15 in *a* with my heart, and they
Ho 7:12 discipline them in *a* with the
Mr 14:56 testimonies were not in *a*
14:59 was their testimony in *a*
Lu 16:6 Take your written *a* back and
16:7 Take your written *a* back and
Joh 9:22 had already come to an *a*
1Co 1:10 all speak in *a*, and that
2Co 6:16 *a* does God's temple have
13:11 to think in *a*, to live
2Ti 3:3 not open to any *a*, slanderers
1Jo 5:8 and the three are in *a*

Agreements
Ro 1:31 false to *a*, having no natural

Agrees
2Ki 9:15 If your soul *a*, do not let

Agricultural
Ne 10:37 tenth in all our *a* cities

Agriculture
2Ch 26:10 lover of *a* he proved to be

Agrippa
Ac 25:13 *A* the king and Bernice
25:22 *A* said to Festus: I myself
25:23 *A* and Bernice came with
25:24 King *A* and all you men who
25:26 before you, King *A*, in order
26:1 *A* said to Paul: You are
26:2 King *A*, I count myself happy
26:19 King *A*, I did not become
26:27 Do you, King *A*, believe
26:28 *A* said to Paul: In a short
26:32 *A* said to Festus: This man

Aground
Ac 27:17 running *a* on the Syrtis
27:41 they ran the ship *a* and

Agur
Pr 30:1 words of *A* the son of Jakeh

Aha
Job 39:25 as the horn blows it says *A!*
Ps 35:21, 21 *A! A!* our eye has seen it
35:25 in their heart: *A*, our soul!
40:15, 15 are saying to me: *A! A!*
70:3, 3 shame who are saying: *A, a!*
Isa 1:24 *A!* I shall relieve myself of
10:5 *A*, the Assyrian, the rod for
44:16 *A!* I have warmed myself
Jer 47:6 *A*, the sword of Jehovah!
Eze 25:3 said *A!* against my sanctuary
26:2 said against Jerusalem, *A!*
36:2 *A!* Even the high places of

Ahab
1Ki 16:28 *A* his son began to reign in
16:29 *A* the son of Omri
16:29 *A* . . . twenty-two years
16:30 *A* the son of Omri
16:33 *A* went on to make the
16:33 *A* came to do more to offend
17:1 to say to *A*: As Jehovah the
18:1 Go, show yourself to *A*, as I
18:2 went to show himself to *A*
18:3 *A* called Obadiah, who was
18:5 *A* went on to say to Obadiah
18:6 *A* himself went alone by one
18:9 hand of *A* to put me to death
18:12 tell *A*, and he will not
18:16 Obadiah went off to meet *A*
18:16 so *A* went to meet Elijah
18:17 as soon as *A* saw Elijah
18:17 *A* immediately said to him
18:20 *A* proceeded to send among
18:41 Elijah now said to *A*: Go up
1Ki 18:42 *A* proceeded to go up to eat
18:44 Go up, say to *A*, Hitch up!
18:45 *A* kept riding and made his
18:46 running ahead of *A* all the
19:1 *A* told Jezebel all that
20:2 messengers to *A* the king of
20:13 prophet approached *A* the
20:14 *A* said: By whom? to which
21:1 the palace of *A* the king of
21:2 *A* spoke to Naboth, saying
21:3 But Naboth said to *A*: It is
21:4 *A* came into his house
21:15 said to *A*: Rise up, take
21:16 *A* heard that Naboth was
21:16 *A* at once rose up to go
21:18 go down to meet *A* the king
21:20 *A* proceeded to say to Elijah
21:21 and cut off from *A* anyone
21:25 *A*, who sold himself to do
21:27 soon as *A* heard these words
21:29 how *A* has humbled himself
22:20 Who will fool *A*, that he
22:39 the rest of the affairs of *A*
22:40 Finally *A* lay down with his
22:41 fourth year of *A* the king
22:49 Ahaziah the son of *A* said
22:51 Ahaziah the son of *A*
2Ki 1:1 Israel after the death of *A*
3:1 Jehoram the son of *A*, he
3:5 as soon as *A* died, the king
8:16 Jehoram the son of *A* the
8:18 those of the house of *A* had
8:25 son of *A* the king of Israel
8:27 in the way of the house of *A*
8:27 like the house of *A*
8:27 a relative of the house of *A*
8:28 with Jehoram the son of *A*
8:29 the son of *A* in Jezreel
9:7 strike down the house of *A*
9:8 whole house of *A* must perish
9:8 cut off from *A* anyone
9:9 constitute the house of *A* like
9:25 riding teams behind *A* his
9:29 Jehoram the son of *A* that
10:1 Now *A* had seventy sons in
10:1 and the caretakers of *A*
10:10 against the house of *A*
10:11 of the house of *A* in Jezreel
10:18 *A*, on the one hand
10:30 have done to the house of *A*
21:3 just as *A* the king of Israel
21:13 applied to the house of *A*
2Ch 18:1 a marriage alliance with *A*
18:2 he went down to *A* at Samaria
18:2 *A* proceeded to sacrifice
18:3 *A* the king of Israel went on
18:19 fool *A* the king of Israel
21:6 those of the house of *A* had
21:13 house of *A* caused the having
22:3 ways of the house of *A*, for
22:4 same as the house of *A*, for
22:5 *A* the king of Israel to the
22:6 see Jehoram the son of *A* in
22:7 to cut off the house of *A*
22:8 with the house of *A*, he got
Jer 29:21 *A* the son of Kolaiah and to
29:22 like Zedekiah and like *A*
Mic 6:16 the work of the house of *A*

Ahab's
1Ki 21:8 she wrote letters in *A* name
21:24 of *A* that is dying in the
2Ki 8:18 *A* daughter that became his
10:17 left over of *A* in Samaria
2Ch 21:6 *A* own daughter had become

Aharah
1Ch 8:1 the second and *A* the third

Aharhel
1Ch 4:8 *A* the son of Harum

Ahasbai
2Sa 23:34 *A* the son of the Maacathite

Ahasuerus
Ezr 4:6 And in the reign of *A*, at the
Es 1:1 came about in the days of *A*
1:1 *A* who was ruling as king from
1:2 as King *A* was sitting upon his
1:9 house that belonged to King *A*
1:10 to the person of King *A*
1:15 the saying of King *A* by means
1:16 districts of King *A*
1:17 King *A* himself said to bring
1:19 may not come in before King *A*

Es 2:1 the rage of King *A* had subsided
2:12 go in to King *A* after it had
2:16 Esther was taken to King *A* at
2:21 seeking to lay hand on King *A*
3:1 King *A* magnified Haman the son
3:6 were in all the realm of *A*
3:7 in the twelfth year of King *A*
3:8 to say to King *A*: There is one
3:12 in the name of King *A* it was
6:2 sought to lay hand on King *A*
7:5 King *A* now said, yes, he went
8:1 King *A* gave to Esther the queen
8:7 King *A* said to Esther the queen
8:10 write in the name of King *A*
8:12 districts of King *A*, on the
9:2 districts of King *A* to lay hand
9:20 districts of King *A*, the
9:30 the realm of *A*, in words of
10:1 King *A* proceeded to lay forced
10:3 was second to King *A* and was
Da 9:1 Darius the son of *A* of the seed

Ahava
Ezr 8:15 the river that comes to *A*
8:21 a fast there at the river *A*
8:31 from the river *A* on the

Ahaz
2Ki 15:38 *A* his son began to reign
16:1 *A* the son of Jotham the
16:2 *A* when he began to reign
16:5 and laid siege against *A*
16:7 *A* sent messengers to
16:8 *A* took the silver and the
16:10 Then King *A* went to meet
16:10 King *A* sent Urijah the
16:11 that King *A* had sent from
16:11 the time that King *A* came
16:15 King *A* went on to command
16:16 that King *A* had commanded
16:17 King *A* cut the sidewalls of
16:19 the rest of the affairs of *A*
16:20 *A* lay down with his
17:1 twelfth year of *A* the king
18:1 Hezekiah the son of *A* the
20:11 steps of the stairs of *A*
23:12 the roof chamber of *A* that
1Ch 3:13 *A* his son, Hezekiah his son
8:35 the sons of Micah . . . *A*
8:36 *A* . . . father to Jehoaddah
9:41 the sons of Micah . . . *A*
9:42 *A*, he became father to Jarah
2Ch 27:9 *A* his son began to reign in
28:1 Twenty years old was *A*
28:16 King *A* sent to the kings
28:19 on account of *A* the king of
28:21 *A* stripped the house of
28:22 that is, King *A* did
28:24 *A* gathered together the
28:27 *A* lay down with his
29:19 utensils that King *A*
Isa 1:1 *A* and Hezekiah, kings of Judah
7:1 days of *A* the son of Jotham
7:3 Go out, please, to meet *A*
7:10 speaking some more to *A*
7:12 *A* said: I shall not ask
14:28 year that King *A* died this
38:8 steps of the stairs of *A* by
Ho 1:1 *A* and Hezekiah, kings of Judah
Mic 1:1 in the days of Jotham, *A*
Mt 1:9 Jotham became father to *A*
1:9 *A* became father to Hezekiah

Ahaziah
1Ki 22:40 *A* his son began to reign in
22:49 *A* the son of Ahab said to
22:51 As for *A* the son of Ahab
2Ki 1:2 *A* fell down through the
8:24 *A* his son began to reign in
8:25 *A* the son of Jehoram the
8:26 Twenty-two years old was *A*
8:29 *A* the son of Jehoram the
9:16 *A* the king of Judah
9:21 and *A* the king of Judah
9:23 said to *A*: There is trickery
9:23 There is trickery, *A*
9:27 And *A* the king of Judah
9:29 *A* had become king over Judah
10:13 *A* the king of Judah
10:13 We are the brothers of *A*
11:1 Athaliah the mother of *A*
11:2 the sister of *A*, took Jehoash
11:2 took Jehoash the son of *A*
12:18 and *A* his forefathers
13:1 *A* the king of Judah
2Ki 14:13 Jehoash the son of *A* that
1Ch 3:11 *A* his son, Jehoash his son
2Ch 20:35 *A* the king of Israel, who
20:37 have had partnership with *A*
22:1 *A* his youngest son king in
22:1 *A* the son of Jehoram began
22:2 *A* when he began to reign
22:7 downfall of *A* occurred by
22:8 sons of the brothers of *A*
22:8 ministers of *A*, and he
22:9 looking for *A*, and they
22:9 no one of the house of *A* to
22:10 Athaliah the mother of *A*
22:11 Jehoash the son of *A* and
22:11 to be the sister of *A*

Ahaziah's
2Ki 1:18 rest of *A* things that he did

Ahban
1Ch 2:29 bore him *A* and Molid

Ahead*
Ge 32:3 Jacob sent messengers *a* of
Ex 14:19 *a* of the camp of Israel
Le 26:10 the old *a* of the new
De 1:22 Do let us send men *a* of us
1Sa 15:23 pushing *a* presumptuously
Ps 119:148 *a* of the night watches
Pr 4:25 your eyes, straight *a* they
8:25 *a* of the hills, I was brought
Am 4:3 go forth, each one straight *a*
Jon 4:2 I went *a* and ran away to
Lu 7:27 prepare your way *a* of you
19:4 ran *a* to an advance position
Joh 5:7 another steps down *a* of me
Ac 7:40 gods for us to go *a* of us
20:13 We now went *a* to the boat
Ro 13:14 planning *a* for the desires
Php 3:13 forward to the things *a*
2Jo 9 Everyone that pushes *a* and does

Aher
1Ch 7:12 Hushim were the sons of *A*

Ahi
1Ch 5:15 *A* the son of Abdiel, the son
7:34 the sons of Shemer were *A*

Ahiam
2Sa 23:33 *A* the son of Sharar the
1Ch 11:35 *A* the son of Sacar the

Ahian
1Ch 7:19 sons of Shemida came to be *A*

Ahiezer
Nu 1:12 *A* the son of Ammishaddai
2:25 is *A* the son of Ammishaddai
7:66 *A* the son of Ammishaddai
7:71 of *A* the son of Ammishaddai
10:25 *A* the son of Ammishaddai

Ahi-ezer
1Ch 12:3 the head *A* and Joash the sons

Ahihud
Nu 34:27 of Asher a chieftain, *A* the
1Ch 8:7 became father to Uzza and *A*

Ahijah
1Sa 14:3 And *A* the son of Ahitub, the
14:18 Saul now said to *A*
1Ki 4:3 and *A*, the sons of Shisha
11:29 *A* the Shilonite the prophet
11:29 *A* was covering himself
11:30 *A* now took . . . new garment
12:15 *A* the Shilonite to Jeroboam
14:2 is where *A* the prophet is
14:4 and came to the house of *A*
14:4 *A* himself was unable to see
14:5 said to *A*: Here is the wife
14:6 *A* heard the sound of her feet
14:18 his servant *A* the prophet
15:27 *A* of the house of Issachar
15:29 his servant *A* the Shilonite
15:33 Baasha the son of *A* became
21:22 Baasha the son of *A*, for
2Ki 9:9 Baasha the son of *A*
1Ch 2:25 sons of Jerahmeel . . . *A*
8:7 And Naaman and *A*; and Gera
11:36 *A* the Pelonite
26:20 *A* was over the treasures of
2Ch 9:29 prophecy of *A* the Shilonite
10:15 *A* the Shilonite to Jeroboam
Ne 10:26 and *A*, Hanan, Anan

Ahikam
2Ki 22:12 *A* the son of Shaphan
22:14 *A* and Achbor and Shaphan
2Ki 25:22 Gedaliah the son of *A*
2Ch 34:20 *A* the son of Shaphan
Jer 26:24 *A* the son of Shaphan that
39:14 Gedaliah the son of *A* the
40:5 Gedaliah the son of *A* the
40:6 Gedaliah the son of *A* at
40:7 Gedaliah the son of *A* over
40:9 Gedaliah the son of *A* the
40:11 Gedaliah the son of *A* the
40:14 Gedaliah the son of *A* did
40:16 Gedaliah the son of *A* said
41:1 Gedaliah the son of *A* at
41:2 Gedaliah the son of *A* the
41:6 to Gedaliah the son of *A*
41:10 Gedaliah the son of *A*
41:16 Gedaliah the son of *A*
41:18 Gedaliah the son of *A*
43:6 Gedaliah the son of *A* the

Ahilud
2Sa 8:16 Jehoshaphat the son of *A*
20:24 Jehoshaphat the son of *A*
1Ki 4:3 Jehoshaphat the son of *A*
4:12 Baana the son of *A*, in
1Ch 18:15 Jehoshaphat the son of *A*

Ahimaaz
1Sa 14:50 Ahinoam the daughter of *A*
2Sa 15:27 *A* your son and Jonathan the
15:36 *A* belonging to Zadok and
17:17 As Jonathan and *A* were
17:20 Where are *A* and Jonathan?
18:19 *A* the son of Zadok, he said
18:22 *A* the son of Zadok now said
18:23 *A* began to run by the way
18:27 like the running style of *A*
18:28 *A* called and said to the
18:29 *A* said: I saw the great
1Ki 4:15 *A*, in Naphtali (he, too, took
1Ch 6:8 Zadok . . . became father to *A*
6:9 *A* . . . father to Azariah
6:53 Zadok his son, *A* his son

Ahiman
Nu 13:22 *A*, Sheshai and Talmai, those
Jos 15:14 Sheshai and *A* and Talmai
Jg 1:10 went striking down . . . *A*
1Ch 9:17 and Akkub and Talmon and *A*

Ahimelech
1Sa 21:1 David came into Nob to *A*
21:1 *A* began to tremble at
21:2 David said to *A* the priest
21:8 David went on to say to *A*
22:9 to Nob to *A* the son of Ahitub
22:11 king sent to call *A* the son
22:14 *A* answered the king and
22:16 You will positively die, *A*
22:20 *A* the son of Ahitub, whose
23:6 Abiathar the son of *A* ran
26:6 said to *A* the Hittite and
30:7 Abiathar . . . son of *A*
2Sa 8:17 *A* the son of Abiathar were
1Ch 18:16 and *A* the son of Abiathar
24:3 *A* from the sons of Ithamar
24:6 and *A* the son of Abiathar
24:31 and *A* and the heads of the
Ps 52:*super* come to the house of *A*

Ahimoth
1Ch 6:25 of Elkanah were Amasai and *A*

Ahinadab
1Ki 4:14 *A* the son of Iddo, in

Ahinoam
1Sa 14:50 name of Saul's wife was *A*
25:43 David had also taken *A* from
27:3 wives, *A* the Jezreelitess
30:5 *A* the Jezreelitess and
2Sa 2:2 *A* the Jezreelitess and
3:2 Amnon by *A* the Jezreelitess
1Ch 3:1 *A* the Jezreelitess

Ahio
2Sa 6:3 Uzzah and *A*, the sons of
6:4 *A* was walking ahead of the
1Ch 8:14 there were *A*, Shashak and
8:31 and Gedor and *A* and Zecher
9:37 Gedor and *A* and Zechariah and
13:7 Uzzah and *A* were leading the

Ahira
Nu 1:15 of Naphtali, *A* the son of Enan
2:29 is *A* the son of Enan
7:78 *A* the son of Enan
7:83 offering of *A* the son of Enan
10:27 *A* the son of Enan

Ahiram
Nu 26:38 of *A* the family of the
Ahiramites
Nu 26:38 Ahiram the family of the *A*
Ahisamach
Ex 31:6 *A* of the tribe of Dan, and
35:34 *A* of the tribe of Dan
38:23 Oholiab the son of *A* of
Ahishahar
1Ch 7:10 sons of Bilhan were . . . *A*
Ahishar
1Ki 4:6 *A* was over the household
Ahithophel
2Sa 15:12 Absalom sent for *A* the
15:31 *A* himself is among those
15:31 the counsel of *A* into
15:34 frustrate the counsel of *A*
16:15 and *A* was with him
16:20 Later Absalom said to *A*
16:21 Then *A* said to Absalom
16:23 And the counsel of *A*, with
16:23 the counsel of *A* was both
17:1 And *A* proceeded to say to
17:6 this word is the way *A* spoke
17:7 The counsel with which *A* has
17:14 better than the counsel of *A*
17:14 frustrate the counsel of *A*
17:15 *A* counseled Absalom and the
17:21 the way that *A* counseled
17:23 As for *A*, he saw that his
23:34 Eliam the son of *A* the
1Ch 27:33 *A* was a counselor of the
27:34 after *A* there were Jehoiada
Ahitub
1Sa 14:3 And Ahijah the son of *A*, the
22:9 to Ahimelech the son of *A*
22:11 Ahimelech the son of *A*
22:12 you son of *A!* to which he
22:20 Ahimelech the son of *A*
2Sa 8:17 Zadok the son of *A* and
1Ch 6:7 Amariah . . . father to *A*
6:8 *A* . . . became father to Zadok
6:11 Amariah . . . father to *A*
6:12 *A* . . . became father to Zadok
6:52 Amariah his son, *A* his son
9:11 son of Meraioth the son of *A*
18:16 And Zadok the son of *A* and
Ezr 7:2 Zadok the son of *A*
Ne 11:11 Meraioth the son of *A*
Ahlab
Jg 1:31 *A* and Achzib and Helbah and
Ahlai
1Ch 2:31 the sons of Sheshan, *A*
11:41 Zabad the son of *A*
Ahoah
1Ch 8:4 and Abishua and Naaman and *A*
Ahohi
2Sa 23:9 Dodo the son of *A* was among
Ahohite
2Sa 23:28 Zalmon the *A*, Maharai the
1Ch 11:12 the son of Dodo the *A*
11:29 Ilai the *A*
27:4 was Dodai the *A* with his
Ahold
Ps 137:9 grabs *a* and does dash to
Ahumai
1Ch 4:2 Jahath . . . became father to *A*
Ahuzzam
1Ch 4:6 Naarah bore to him *A* and
Ahuzzath
Ge 26:26 *A* his confidential friend and
Ahzai
Ne 11:13 *A* the son of Meshillemoth
Ai
Ge 12:8 Bethel on the west and *A* on
13:3 at first between Bethel and *A*
Jos 7:2 men out from Jericho to *A*
7:2 men went up and spied on *A*
7:3 go up and strike *A*
7:4 flight before the men of *A*
7:5 men of *A* got to strike down
8:1 go up to *A*. See, I have given
8:1 the king of *A* and his people
8:2 do to *A* and to its king just
8:3 rose to go up to *A*, and Joshua
Jos 8:9, 9 and *A* to the west of *A*
8:10 before the people to *A*
8:11 camp to the north of *A*, with
8:11 valley between them and *A*
8:12 ambush between Bethel and *A*
8:14 as soon as the king of *A* saw
8:17 not a man remaining in *A* and
8:18 is in your hand toward *A*
8:20 men of *A* began to turn back
8:21 striking the men of *A* down
8:23 king of *A* they caught alive
8:24 inhabitants of *A* in the
8:24 returned to *A* and struck it
8:25 all the people of *A*
8:26 of *A* to destruction
8:28 Joshua burned *A* and reduced
8:29 hanged the king of *A* upon a
9:3 had done to Jericho and *A*
10:1 Joshua had captured *A* and
10:1 had done to *A* and its king
10:2 it was greater than *A*, and
12:9 the king of *A*, which was
Ezr 2:28 the men of Bethel and *A*
Ne 7:32 the men of Bethel and *A*
Jer 49:3 for *A* has been despoiled
Aiah
Ge 36:24 sons of Zibeon: *A* and Anah
2Sa 3:7 was Rizpah the daughter of *A*
21:8 Rizpah the daughter of *A*
21:10 Rizpah the daughter of *A*
21:11 *A*, Saul's concubine, had
1Ch 1:40 sons of Zibeon were *A* and
Aiath
Isa 10:28 He has come upon *A*
Aid
Ge 4:1 a man with the *a* of Jehovah
De 23:4 to your *a* with bread and
Jg 3:9 began to call to Jehovah for *a*
3:15 to call to Jehovah for *a*
6:6 began to call to Jehovah for *a*
6:7 called to Jehovah for *a* on
10:10 call to Jehovah for *a*, saying
10:14 call for *a* to the gods whom
12:2 to call to you for *a*, and you
1Sa 7:8 to Jehovah our God for *a*
7:9 calling to Jehovah for *a* in
12:8 calling to Jehovah for *a*
12:10 to call to Jehovah for *a*
1Ki 22:32 began to cry for *a*
1Ch 5:20 to God that they called for *a*
2Ch 18:31 began to cry for *a*, and
20:9 call to you for *a* out of our
32:20 crying to the heavens for *a*
Ezr 5:2 God's prophets giving them *a*
Ne 9:28 return and call to you for *a*
Es 9:31 the fasts and their cry for *a*
Job 31:38 own ground would cry for *a*
35:9 they keep calling for *a*
Ps 142:1 I proceeded to call for *a*
142:5 to you, O Jehovah, for *a*
Isa 57:13 When you cry for *a* your
Jer 11:11 certainly call to me for *a*
11:12 and call for *a* to the gods
La 3:8 I call for *a* and cry for help
Ho 7:14 they did not call to me for *a*
Joe 1:14 and cry to Jehovah for *a*
3:11 Lend your *a* and come, all
Jon 1:5 for *a*, each one to his god
Mic 3:4 will call to Jehovah for *a*
Hab 1:2 to you for *a* from violence
Lu 1:54 come to the *a* of Israel his
Ac 9:27 Barnabas came to his *a* and
Col 4:11 a strengthening *a* to me
Heb 2:18 come to the *a* of those who
Aija
Ne 11:31 Michmash and *A* and Bethel
Aijalon
Jos 10:12 over the low plain of *A*
19:42 and *A* and Ithlah
21:24 *A* and its pasture ground
Jg 1:35 and in *A* and Shaalbim
12:12 in *A* in the land of Zebulun
1Sa 14:31 from Michmash to *A*, and
1Ch 6:69 *A* with its pasture grounds
8:13 to the inhabitants of *A*
2Ch 11:10 *A* and Hebron, fortified
28:18 capture Beth-shemesh and *A*
Ailing
Isa 10:18 away of one that is *a*
Eze 34:4 *a* one you have not healed
34:16 *a* one I shall strengthen
Mt 9:12 a physician, but the *a* do
Mr 6:55 on cots those who were *a*
Lu 5:31 but those who are *a* do
7:2 was *a* and was about to pass
Ac 4:9 of a good deed to an *a* man
19:12 to the *a* people, and the
Ailment
2Ch 16:12 *a* in his feet until he was
Aim
Ex 10:10 something evil is your *a*
Ro 15:20 made it my *a* not to declare
2Co 5:9 we are also making it our *a*
1Th 4:11 to make it your *a* to live
1Ti 4:7 with godly devotion as your *a*
Aimed
Ps 64:3 *a* their arrow, bitter speech
Aimlessly
Jer 2:23 *a* running to and fro in her
Ain
Nu 34:11 to Riblah on the east of *A*
Jos 15:32 Shilhim and *A* and Rimmon
19:7 *A*, Rimmon and Ether and
21:16 and *A* and its pasture ground
1Ch 4:32 settlements were Etam and *A*
Air
Job 36:9 they take a superior *a*
41:16 not even *a* can come in
Ac 22:23 and tossing dust into the *a*
1Co 9:26 as not to be striking the *a*
14:9 be speaking into the *a*
Eph 2:2 of the authority of the *a*
1Th 4:17 to meet the Lord in the *a*
Re 9:2 sun was darkened, also the *a*
16:17 out his bowl upon the *a*
Airhole
Jg 3:23 to go out through the *a*, but
Airs
Job 19:5 you men do put on great *a*
Ps 35:26 assuming great *a* against me
38:16 assume great *a* against me
55:12 assumed great *a* against me
Jer 48:26 on great *a* against Jehovah
48:42 that he has put on great *a*
La 1:9 the enemy has put on great *a*
1:16 the enemy has put on great *a*
Da 8:4 and it put on great *a*
8:8 put on great *a* to an extreme
8:11 it put on great *a*, and from
8:25 heart he will put on great *a*
Zep 2:8 putting on great *a* against
2:10 putting on great *a* against
Akan
Ge 36:27 sons of Ezer . . . *A*
1Ch 1:42 sons of Ezer were . . . *A*
Akeldama
Ac 1:19 *A*, that is, Field of Blood
Akkub
1Ch 3:24 sons of Elioenai were . . . *A*
9:17 were Shallum and *A* and
Ezr 2:42 the sons of *A*
2:45 the sons of *A*
Ne 7:45 the sons of *A*, the sons of
8:7 Jamin, *A*, Shabbethai, Hodiah
11:19 gatekeepers were *A*, Talmon
12:25 Meshullam, Talmon, *A*
Akrabbim
Nu 34:4 the south of the ascent of *A*
Jos 15:3 southward to the ascent of *A*
Jg 1:36 from the ascent of *A*, from
Alabaster
1Ch 29:2 *a* stones in great quantity
Mt 26:7 *a* case of costly perfumed oil
Mr 14:3 an *a* case of perfumed oil
14:3 Breaking open the *a* case she
Lu 7:37 an *a* case of perfumed oil
Alamoth
1Ch 15:20 instruments tuned to *A*
Alarm
2Ch 13:12 for sounding the battle *a*
Jer 4:19 the *a* signal of war
20:16 an *a* signal at the time of
49:2 *a* signal of war to be heard
Eze 21:22 the sound in an *a* signal
Am 1:14 *a* signal in the day of battle
2:2 an *a* signal, with the sound
Zep 1:16 day of horn and of *a* signal

Alarmed
Ca 6:5 your eyes . . . have *a* me
Alas
Jos 7:7 *A*, Sovereign Lord Jehovah
Jg 6:22 *A*, Sovereign Lord Jehovah, for
11:35 *A*, my daughter! You have
2Ki 6:5 *A*, my master, for it was
6:15 *A*, my master! What shall we
Jer 1:6 *A*, O Sovereign Lord Jehovah!
4:10 *A*, O Sovereign Lord Jehovah!
14:13 *A*, O Sovereign Lord Jehovah!
22:18 wail for him: *A*, my brother!
22:18 brother! And *a*, my sister!
22:18, 18 *A*, O master! And *a*, his
30:7 *A!* For that day is a great
32:17 *A*, O Sovereign Lord Jehovah!
34:5 *A*, O master! is what they
Eze 4:14 *A*, O Sovereign Lord Jehovah
6:11 *A!* on account of all the bad
9:8 *A*, O Sovereign Lord Jehovah!
11:13 *A*, O Sovereign Lord Jehovah!
20:49 *A*, O Sovereign Lord Jehovah!
21:15 *A*, it is made for a
30:2 Howl . . . *A* for the day!
Joe 1:15 *A* for the day; because the
Alemeth
1Ch 6:60 *A* with its pasture grounds
7:8 the sons of Becher were . . . *A*
8:36 Jehoaddah . . . father to *A*
9:42 Jarah . . . became father to *A*
Alert
Isa 29:20 those keeping *a* to do harm
Jer 31:28 *a* toward them to uproot
31:28 *a* toward them to build up
44:27 *a* toward them for calamity
La 1:14 *a* against my transgressions
Da 9:14 Jehovah kept *a* to the
Lu 11:35 Be *a*, therefore. Perhaps the
Alexander
Mr 15:21 the father of *A* and Rufus
Ac 4:6 John and *A* and as many as
19:33 brought *A* out of the crowd
19:33 *A* motioned with his hand and
1Ti 1:20 Hymenaeus and *A* belong to
2Ti 4:14 *A* the coppersmith did me
Alexandria
Ac 18:24 named Apollos, a native of *A*
27:6 boat from *A* that was sailing
28:11 in a boat from *A* that had
Alexandrians
Ac 6:9 Cyrenians and *A* and of those
Alien
Ge 12:10 Egypt to reside there as an *a*
15:13 your seed will become an *a*
17:8 land of your *a* residences
19:9 came here to reside as an *a*
20:1 and residing as an *a* at Gerar
21:23 have been residing as an *a*
21:34 *a* in the land of the
23:4 An *a* resident and settler I
26:3 Reside as an *a* in this land
28:4 the land of your *a* residences
32:4 I have resided as an *a* and I
36:7 land of their *a* residences
37:1 the land of the *a* residences
47:9 the years of my *a* residences
47:9 days of their *a* residences
Ex 2:22 An *a* resident I have come to
3:22 residing as an *a* in her house
6:4 Canaan, the land of their *a*
12:19 whether he is an *a* resident
12:48 in case an *a* resident resides
12:48 resides as an *a* with you
12:49 for the native and for the *a*
12:49 as an *a* in your midst
18:3 an *a* resident I have come to
20:10 nor your *a* resident who is
22:21 not maltreat an *a* resident
22:21 people became *a* residents in
23:9 not oppress an *a* resident
23:9 the soul of the *a* resident
23:9 you became *a* residents in the
23:12 the *a* resident may refresh
Le 16:29 *a* resident who is residing
16:29 as an *a* in your midst
17:8 some *a* resident who may be
17:8 residing as an *a* in your
17:10 some *a* resident who is
17:10 *a* in their midst who eats
17:12 *a* resident who is residing
Le 17:12 *a* in your midst should eat
17:13 *a* resident who is residing
17:13 *a* in your midst who in
17:15 *a* resident, he must in that
18:26 *a* resident who is residing
18:26 residing as an *a* in your
19:10 *a* resident you should leave
19:33 *a* resident resides with you
19:33 *a* in your land, you must not
19:34 *a* resident who resides as
19:34 an *a* . . . like a native
19:34 you became *a* residents in
20:2 *a* resident who resides as an
20:2 *a* in Israel, who gives any of
22:18 *a* resident in Israel who
23:22 afflicted one and the *a*
24:16 *a* resident the same as the
24:22 *a* resident should prove to
25:23 you are *a* residents and
25:35 *a* resident and a settler, he
25:47 *a* resident or the settler
25:47 must sell himself to the *a*
25:47 family of the *a* resident
Nu 9:14 *a* resident should be residing
9:14 residing with you as an *a*, he
9:14 both for the *a* resident and
15:14, 14 *a* with you an *a* resident
15:15 and the *a* resident who is
15:15 who is residing as an *a* will
15:15 *a* resident should prove to be
15:16 and for the *a* resident who
15:16 is residing as an *a* with you
15:26 and the *a* resident who is
15:26 residing as an *a* in their
15:29 and the *a* resident who is
15:29 residing as an *a* in their
15:30 is a native or an *a* resident
19:10 *a* resident who is residing
19:10 as an *a* in their midst as a
35:15 for the *a* resident and for
De 1:16 his brother or his *a* resident
5:14 your *a* resident who is inside
10:18 loving the *a* resident so as
10:19 must love the *a* resident
10:19 *a* residents in the land of
14:21 To the *a* resident who is
14:29 the *a* resident and the
16:11 the *a* resident and the
16:14 the Levite and the *a* resident
23:7 you became an *a* resident in
24:14 *a* residents who are in your
24:17 judgment of the *a* resident
24:19 It should stay for the *a*
24:20 It should stay for the *a*
24:21 They should stay for the *a*
26:5 an *a* with very few in number
26:11 the Levite and the *a* resident
26:12 to the Levite, the *a* resident
26:13 the Levite and the *a* resident
27:19 judgment of an *a* resident
28:43 *a* resident who is in your
29:11 your *a* resident who is in
31:12 *a* resident who is within
Jos 8:33 the *a* resident as well as
8:35 the *a* residents who walked
20:9 the *a* resident who resides
20:9 who resides as an *a* in their
Ru 1:1 as an *a* in the fields of Moab
2Sa 1:13 *a* resident, an Amalekite
4:3 *a* residents there down to
1Ki 17:20 I am residing as an *a* that
2Ki 8:1 and reside as an *a* wherever
8:1 you can reside as an *a*
8:2 took up residence as an *a* in
1Ch 16:19 and *a* residents in it
22:2 said to bring together the *a*
29:15 are *a* residents before you
2Ch 2:17 men that were *a* residents
15:9 *a* residents with them from
30:25 *a* residents that came from
Ezr 1:4 where he is residing as an *a*
Job 18:19 in his place of *a* residence
31:32 Outside no *a* resident would
Ps 39:12 but an *a* resident with you
55:15 during their *a* residence bad
94:6 and the *a* resident they kill
105:12 few, and *a* residents in it
105:23 as an *a* in the land of Ham
119:19 an *a* resident in the land
119:54 house of my *a* residences
120:5 resided as an *a* in Meshech
146:9 is guarding the *a* residents
Isa 5:17 *a* residents will eat
14:1 *a* resident must be joined to
Isa 23:7 far away to reside as an *a*
Jer 7:6 no *a* resident, no fatherless
14:8 become like an *a* resident in
22:3 not maltreat any *a* resident
49:18 reside in her as an *a*
49:33 mankind will reside as an *a*
50:40 reside in her as an *a*
La 2:22 my places of *a* residence all
Eze 14:7 from the *a* residents that
20:38 land of their *a* residence
22:7 Toward the *a* resident they
22:29 the *a* resident they have
47:22 to the *a* residents who are
47:23 *a* resident has taken up
47:23 taken up residence as an *a*
Zec 7:10 no *a* resident or afflicted
Mal 3:5 turning away the *a* resident
Lu 24:18 Are you dwelling as an *a* by
Ac 7:6 his seed would be *a* residents
7:29 *a* resident in the land of
13:17 *a* residence in the land of
Eph 2:19 strangers and *a* residents
Heb 11:9 By faith he resided as an *a*
1Pe 1:17 the time of your *a* residence
Alienated
Eph 2:12 *a* from the state of Israel
4:18 *a* from the life that belongs
Col 1:21 were once *a* and enemies
Aliens
Ge 35:27 also Isaac had resided as *a*
47:4 reside as *a* in the land
Ex 6:4 in which they resided as *a*
Le 25:6 who are residing as *a* with
25:45 *a* with you, from them you
Job 19:15 residing as *a* in my house
28:4 where people reside as *a*
Isa 16:4 dispersed ones reside as *a*
52:4 to reside there as *a*
Jer 35:7 you are residing as *a*
42:15 in to reside there as *a*
42:17 Egypt to reside there as *a*
42:22 to enter to reside as *a*
43:2 Egypt to reside there as *a*
44:8 entering to reside as *a*
44:12 Egypt to reside there as *a*
44:14 reside there as *a*, in the
44:28 Egypt to reside there as *a*
La 4:15 will not reside again as *a*
Eze 14:7 that reside as *a* in Israel
47:22 residing as *a* in your midst
1Pe 2:11 I exhort you as *a* and
Alike
Ps 14:3 they are all *a* corrupt
53:3 they are all *a* corrupt
Ec 11:6 both of them will *a* be good
Isa 46:2 they must each *a* bend down
Eze 42:11 and all their exits were *a*
42:11 and their plans *a* and their
42:11 and their entrances *a*
Alive
Ge 6:19 the ark to preserve them *a*
6:20 to you to preserve them *a*
7:3 preserve offspring *a* on the
9:3 animal that is *a* may serve as
12:12 but you they will preserve *a*
19:19 to preserve my soul *a*
25:6 his son, while he was still *a*
25:22 just why am I *a?* With that
42:2 that we may keep *a* and not
42:18 Do this and keep *a*. I fear
43:7 Is your father yet *a?* Do you
43:8 we may keep *a* and not die off
43:27 Is he still *a?*
43:28 He is still *a*. Then they
45:3 Is my father still *a?*
45:7 keep you *a* by a great escape
45:26 Joseph is still *a*, and he is
45:28 Joseph my son is still *a*
46:30 since you are still *a*
50:20 to preserve many people *a*
Ex 1:17 preserve the male children *a*
1:18 preserved the . . . children *a*
1:22 you are to preserve *a*
4:18 whether they are still *a*
22:4 bull to ass and to sheep, *a*, he is
22:18 not preserve a sorceress *a*
Le 16:10 *a* before Jehovah to make
25:35 he must keep *a* with you
25:36 brother must keep *a* with you
Nu 4:19 that they may indeed keep *a*
16:30 have to go down *a* into Sheol
16:33 *a* into Sheol, and the earth

Nu 21:8 look at it and so must keep *a*
21:9 he then kept *a*
22:33 her I should have preserved *a*
31:15 preserved *a* every female
31:18 preserve *a* for yourselves all
De 4:4 all of you *a* today
4:10 all the days that they are *a*
5:3 all those of us *a* here today
6:24 might keep *a* as at this day
12:1 all the days that you are *a*
16:20 in order that you may keep *a*
20:16 any breathing thing *a*
30:16 to keep *a* and to multiply
30:19 in order that you may keep *a*
31:27 I am yet *a* with you today
32:39 put to death, and I make *a*
32:40 As I am *a* to time indefinite
Jos 2:13 preserve *a* my father and my
6:25 Rahab . . . Joshua preserved *a*
8:23 the king of Ai they caught *a*
14:10 Jehovah has preserved me *a*
Jg 8:19 if you had preserved them *a*
21:14 preserved *a* from the women
1Sa 14:39 Deliverer of Israel, is *a*
14:45 As Jehovah is *a*, not as
15:8 Agag the king of Amalek *a*
20:14 if I shall be still *a*
20:31 son of Jesse is *a* on the
27:9 neither man nor woman *a*
27:11 not preserving any *a* to
28:10 As Jehovah is *a*, guilt for
2Sa 8:2 full line to preserve them *a*
12:3 he was preserving it *a*, and
12:18 child continued *a* we did
12:21 sake of the child while *a*
12:22 child was yet *a* I did fast
18:14 while he was yet *a*
18:18 Absalom . . . while he was *a*
19:6 if only Absalom were *a* and
1Ki 8:40 the days that they are *a*
12:6 while he continued *a*, saying
17:23 said: See, your son is *a*
18:5 the horses and mules *a* and
20:18 you should seize them *a*
20:18 *a* is how you should seize
20:31 will preserve your soul *a*
20:32 he said: Is he still *a*?
21:15 Naboth is no longer *a*, but
2Ki 5:7 put to death and to preserve *a*
7:4 If they preserve us *a*
7:12 and we shall catch them *a*
10:14 Seize them *a*, you men!
10:14 So they seized them *a* and
2Ch 6:31 *a* upon the surface of the
10:6 father while he continued *a*
14:13 there was no one *a* of them
25:12 sons of Judah captured *a*
Ne 5:2 get grain and eat and keep *a*
9:6 are preserving all of them *a*
Es 4:11 he will also certainly stay *a*
Job 12:10 is the soul of everyone *a*
19:25 know that my redeemer is *a*
28:21 from the eyes of everyone *a*
36:6 not preserve anyone wicked *a*
Ps 22:29 preserve his own soul *a*
27:13 in the land of those *a*
30:3 You have kept me *a*, that I
33:19 to preserve them *a* in famine
38:19 enemies who are *a* became
41:2 guard him and preserve him *a*
55:15 go down into Sheol *a*
56:13 in the light of those *a*
69:32 let your heart also keep *a*
80:18 May you preserve us *a*, that
89:48 man is there *a* who will not
119:25 Preserve me *a* according to
119:37 Preserve me *a* in your own
119:40 righteousness preserve me *a*
119:50 saying has preserved me *a*
119:88 preserve me *a*
119:93 you have preserved me *a*
119:107 O Jehovah, preserve me *a*
119:149 decision preserve me *a*
119:154 Preserve me *a* in agreement
119:156 O preserve me *a*
119:159 preserve me *a*
124:3 swallowed us up even *a*
138:7 you will preserve me *a*
143:2 no one *a* can be righteous
143:11 may you preserve me *a*
Pr 1:12 swallow them down *a* just
Ec 4:2 the living who were still *a*
4:15 have seen all those *a* who are
7:2 *a* should take it to his heart
Ec 7:12 wisdom itself preserves *a* its
Isa 7:21 preserve *a* a young cow of
38:16 certainly preserve me *a*
55:3 and your soul will keep *a*
Jer 4:2 As Jehovah is *a* in truth
5:2 As Jehovah is *a*! they would
12:16 As Jehovah is *a*! just as
16:14 As Jehovah is *a* who brought
16:15 As Jehovah is *a* who brought
22:24 As I am *a*, is the utterance
23:7 Jehovah is *a* who brought the
23:8 Jehovah is *a* who brought up
38:2 his soul as a spoil and *a*
38:16 As Jehovah is *a*, who has
44:26 Sovereign Lord Jehovah is *a*
46:18 As I am *a*, is the utterance
49:11 shall preserve them *a*
Eze 3:18 to preserve him *a*, he being
5:11 as I am *a*, is the utterance
13:18 the ones that you preserve *a*
13:19 to preserve *a* the souls that
13:22 in order to preserve him *a*
14:16 as I am *a*, is the utterance
14:18 as I am *a*, is the utterance
14:20 as I am *a*, is the utterance
16:48 As I am *a*, is the utterance
17:16 As I am *a*, is the utterance
17:19 As I am *a*, surely my oath
18:3 As I am *a*, is the utterance
18:27 preserve his own soul *a*
20:3 As I am *a*, I will not be
20:31 As I am *a*, is the utterance
20:33 As I am *a*, is the utterance
26:20 in the land of those *a*
32:23 in the land of those *a*
32:24 in the land of those *a*
32:25 in the land of those *a*
32:26 in the land of those *a*
32:27 in the land of those *a*
32:32 in the land of those *a*
33:11 As I am *a*, is the utterance
33:27 As I am *a*, surely the ones
34:8 As I am *a*, is the utterance
35:6 as I am *a*, is the utterance
35:11 I am *a*, is the utterance
47:9 be *a* where the torrent comes
Da 2:30 me more than in any others *a*
12:7 who is *a* for time indefinite
Ho 4:15 nor swear As Jehovah is *a*!
6:2 will make us *a* after two days
Am 8:14 As your god is *a*, O Dan!
8:14 As the way of Beer-sheba is *a*!
Jon 4:3 is better than my being *a*
4:8 is better than my being *a*
Zep 2:9 as I am *a*, is the utterance
Mt 27:63 impostor said while yet *a*
Lu 5:10 you will be catching men *a*
17:33 loses it will preserve it *a*
24:23 angels, who said he is *a*
Joh 5:21 dead up and makes them *a*
5:21 Son also makes those *a* whom
Ac 1:3 he showed himself *a* after he
7:19 they might not be preserved *a*
9:41 widows and presented her *a*
20:12 they took the boy away *a* and
25:19 Paul kept asserting was *a*
Ro 4:17 God, who makes the dead *a*
6:13 God as those *a* from the dead
7:2 to her husband while he is *a*
7:9 I was once *a* apart from law
8:11 make your mortal bodies *a*
1Co 7:39 the time her husband is *a*
15:22 all will be made *a*
15:36 not made *a* unless first it
2Co 3:6 but the spirit makes *a*
13:4 is *a* owing to God's power
Ga 2:19 I might become *a* toward God
Eph 2:1 it is you God made *a* though
2:5 made us *a* together with the
Col 2:13 God made you *a* together with
1Ti 6:13 who preserves all things *a*
2Ti 2:26 caught *a* by him for the will
Heb 4:12 word of God is *a* and exerts
7:24 continuing *a* forever has
7:25 always *a* to plead for them
10:39 the preserving *a* of the soul
1Pe 3:18 being made *a* in the spirit
Re 3:1 have the name that you are *a*
19:20 still *a*, they both were

Alkali

Pr 25:20 is as vinegar upon *a* and as a
Jer 2:22 do the washing with *a* and

All*

Ge 7:21 *a* flesh . . . expired
Job 34:15 *A* flesh will expire
42:2 you are able to do *a* things
Ps 125:2 mountains are *a* around it
125:2 Jehovah is *a* around his
Mt 12:15 Jesus . . . cured them *a*
19:26 with God *a* things are
19:27 left *a* things and followed
22:4 *a* things are ready. Come to
23:5 *A* the works they do they do
23:36 *A* these things will come
24:14 preached in *a* the inhabited
24:14 a witness to *a* the nations
24:39 came and swept them *a* away
26:70 he denied it before them *a*
Mr 9:12 Elijah . . . restore *a* things
9:23 *a* things can be to one if
10:27 *a* things are possible with
10:44 must be the slave of *a*
11:24 *A* the things you pray and
12:44 dropped in *a* of what she had
13:23 told you *a* things beforehand
13:30 until *a* these things happen
Lu 6:19 out of him and healing them *a*
15:31 *a* the things that are mine
21:3 dropped in more than they *a*
Joh 3:31 comes from heaven is over *a*
4:25 declare *a* things to us openly
4:29 told me *a* the things I did
Ro 5:12 thus death spread to *a* men
5:12 because they had *a* sinned
5:18 the result to men of *a* sorts
6:10 to sin once for *a* time
8:32 but delivered him up for us *a*
1Co 3:22 *a* things belong to you
6:12 *A* things are lawful for me
6:12 not *a* things are advantageous
6:12 *A* things are lawful for me
7:17 ordain in *a* the congregations
8:6 out of whom *a* things are, and
8:6 through whom *a* things are
8:7 this knowledge in *a* persons
10:1 were *a* under the cloud
10:1 and *a* passed through the sea
10:2 *a* got baptized into Moses
10:3 and *a* ate the same spiritual
10:4 *a* drank the same spiritual
10:23 *A* things are lawful; but
10:23 not *a* things are advantageous
10:23 but not *a* things build up
10:33, 33 *a* people in *a* things
11:12 *a* things are out of God
12:6 performs *a* the operations in
12:13 *a* made to drink one spirit
13:2 with *a* the sacred secrets
13:2 if I have *a* the faith so as
13:3 if I give *a* my belongings to
13:3 I am not profited at *a*
13:7 It bears *a* things, believes
13:7 believes *a* things, hopes
13:7 hopes *a* things, endures
13:7 endures *a* things
14:24 he is reproved by them *a*
14:24 he is closely examined by *a*
14:26 Let *a* things take place for
14:33 in *a* the congregations of
14:40 But let *a* things take place
15:22 just as in Adam *a* are dying
15:22 *a* will be made alive
15:24 to nothing *a* government
15:24 and *a* authority and power
15:25 *a* enemies under his feet
15:27 God subjected *a* things under
15:27 *a* things have been subjected
15:27 subjected *a* things to him
15:28 *a* things will have been
15:28 One who subjected *a* things
15:28 may be *a* things to everyone
15:51 not *a* fall asleep in death
15:51 but we shall *a* be changed
2Co 5:14 so, then, *a* had died
5:15 he died for *a* that those
6:10 and yet possessing *a* things
12:19 *a* things are for your
Ga 3:28 *a* one person in union with
4:1 lord of *a* things though he is
6:6 share in *a* good things with
6:10 work what is good toward *a*
Eph 1:22 made him head over *a* things
1:23, 23 fills up *a* things in *a*
3:9 God, who created *a* things
3:20 beyond *a* the things we ask
4:6 God and Father of *a* persons

Eph 4:6 one God . . . who is over *a*
4:6, 6 and through *a* and in *a*
4:10 give fullness to *a* things
4:15 by love grow up in *a* things
4:16 From him *a* the body, by
5:13 *a* the things that are being
5:20 thanks always for *a* things
6:16 Above *a* things, take up the
Php 3:8 *a* things to be loss on account
3:8 taken the loss of *a* things and
3:21 subject *a* things to himself
4:5 become known to *a* men
4:7 that excels *a* thought will
4:12 in *a* circumstances I have
4:13 For *a* things I have the
4:18 I have *a* things in full and
Col 1:9 *a* wisdom and spiritual
1:18 one who is first in *a* things
1:19 *a* fullness to dwell in him
2:2 with a view to *a* the riches
2:10 is the head of *a* government
3:11 Christ is *a* things and in
3:11 but Christ is . . . in *a*
1Th 1:2 *a* of you in our prayers
3:12 love to one another and to *a*
5:21 Make sure of *a* things; hold
2Th 3:2 faith is not a possession of *a*
1Ti 2:1 concerning *a* sorts of men
2:2 *a* those who are in high
2:4 that *a* sorts of men should be
4:8 is beneficial for *a* things
4:10 a Savior of *a* sorts of men
4:15 may be manifest to *a* persons
5:2 as sisters with *a* chasteness
5:20 Reprove before *a* onlookers
6:10 root of *a* sorts of injurious
6:13 who preserves *a* things alive
6:17 furnishes us *a* things richly
2Ti 2:10 enduring *a* things for the
3:16 *A* Scripture is inspired of
4:2 with *a* long-suffering and art
4:5 keep your senses in *a* things
4:8 *a* those who have loved his
Tit 1:15 *A* things are clean to clean
2:9 subjection . . . in *a* things
2:10 Savior, God, in *a* things
2:11 salvation to *a* sorts of men
Heb 1:2 appointed heir of *a* things
1:3 sustains *a* things by the
2:8 *A* things you subjected under
2:8 he subjected *a* things to him
2:8 see *a* things in subjection
2:10 *a* things are and through
2:10 through whom *a* things are
8:11 they will *a* know me, from
9:12 once for *a* time into the
9:22 nearly *a* things are cleansed
9:26 once for *a* time at the
9:27 men to die once for *a* time
9:28 was offered once for *a* time
10:2 cleansed once for *a* time
10:10 Christ once for *a* time
12:14 Pursue peace with *a* people
12:23 and God the Judge of *a*, and
13:18 honestly in *a* things
Jas 1:4 and sound in *a* respects, not
1:8 unsteady in *a* his ways
2:10 whoever observes *a* the Law
3:2 For we *a* stumble many times
4:16 *A* such taking of pride is
5:12 Above *a* things, though, my
1Pe 4:7 end of *a* things has drawn
1Jo 1:7 cleanses us from *a* sin
2:27 teaching you about *a* things
3:20 God . . . knows *a* things
5:17 *A* unrighteousness is sin
3Jo 2 I pray that in *a* things you may
12 borne to him by them *a*
Jude 5 things once for *a* time, that
10 *a* the things they really do
15 execute judgment against *a*
15 convict *a* the ungodly
15 *a* their ungodly deeds that
25 authority for *a* past eternity
Re 1:7 *a* the tribes of the earth
3:19 *A* those for whom I have
4:11 because you created *a* things
7:11 *a* the angels were standing
8:3 prayers of *a* the holy ones
8:7 and *a* the green vegetation was
19:21 *a* the birds were filled from

Allammelech
Jos 19:26 and *A* and Amad and Mishal

Allays
Ec 10:4 calmness itself *a* great sins

Alliance
De 7:3 form no marriage *a* with them
1Sa 18:21 a marriage *a* with me today
18:22 a marriage *a* with the king
18:23 a marriage *a* with the king
18:26 a marriage *a* with the king
18:27 a marriage *a* with the king
1Ki 3:1 marriage *a* with Pharaoh the
2Ch 18:1 a marriage *a* with Ahab

Alliances
Ge 34:9 and form marriage *a* with us
Jos 23:12 you do form marriage *a*
Ezr 9:14 forming marriage *a* with the

Allied
Ps 94:20 adversities be *a* with you

Allies
Ge 14:3 these marched as *a* to the Low
Jg 20:11 as one man, as *a*

Allon
1Ch 4:37 *A* the son of Jedaiah

Allon-bacuth
Ge 35:8 Hence he called its name *A*

Allot
Eze 45:1 *a* the land as an inheritance
47:22 *a* it for inheritance to

Allotment
De 32:9 Jacob is the *a* that he
33:21 the *a* of a statute-giver is
Jos 17:14 one lot and one *a*
19:9 *a* of the sons of Judah
1Ch 16:18 As the *a* of your inheritance
Ps 105:11 the *a* of your inheritance

Allotments
Jos 17:5 ten *a* falling to Manasseh

Allotted
Ps 16:5 the portion of my *a* share

Allotting
Ps 78:55 went *a* them an inheritance

Allow
Ge 13:6 land did not *a* for them to
20:6 I did not *a* you to touch her
38:16 *A* me, please, to have
Ex 12:23 not *a* the ruination to enter
Le 2:13 you must not *a* the salt of the
18:21 not *a* the devoting of any of
Nu 21:23 Sihon did not *a* Israel to
De 12:1 *a* you to take possession of
Jos 10:19 Do not *a* them to enter into
Jg 1:34 they did not *a* them to come
3:28 they did not *a* anybody to
15:1 father did not *a* him to go in
1Sa 18:2 he did not *a* him to return
24:7 *a* them to rise up against
2Sa 21:10 did not *a* the fowls of the
1Ki 15:17 to *a* no one to go out or
1Ch 16:21 did not *a* anyone to defraud
2Ch 16:1 *a* anyone to go out or come
20:10 not *a* Israel to invade when
Job 31:30 did not *a* my palate to sin
Ps 16:10 not *a* your loyal one to see
55:22 Never will he *a* the
105:14 *a* any human to defraud them
121:3 *a* your foot to totter
Ec 5:6 not *a* your mouth to cause your
Mt 7:4 *A* me to extract the straw
Lu 6:42 *a* me to extract the straw
Ac 2:27 you *a* your loyal one to see
13:35 not *a* your loyal one to see
2Co 7:2 *A* room for us. We have
Eph 4:27 neither *a* place for the Devil

Allowable
Ac 2:29 *a* to speak with freeness of

Allowance
Le 6:18 It is an *a* to time indefinite
10:13 because it is your *a* and the
10:13 and the *a* of your sons
10:14 have been given as your *a*
10:14 and the *a* of your sons from
10:15 an *a* to time indefinite for
Nu 18:8 as an *a* to time indefinite
18:11 as an *a* to time indefinite
18:19 as an *a* to time indefinite
1Ki 22:27 a reduced *a* of bread and a
22:27 a reduced *a* of water until
2Ki 25:30 As for his *a*, an
2Ki 25:30 an *a* was constantly given
2Ch 18:26 reduced *a* of bread and a
18:26 reduced *a* of water until I
30:18 Jehovah himself make *a* for
Jer 40:5 gave him a food *a* and a
52:34 And as for his *a*, there was
52:34 constant *a* given him from
Eze 16:27 I shall diminish your *a* and
45:14 *a* of the oil, there is the
Da 1:5 king appointed a daily *a* from
1Th 4:7 not with *a* for uncleanness

Allowed
Ge 29:8 not *a* to do so until all the
31:7 not *a* him to do me harm
Ex 10:26 Not a hoof will be *a* to
De 7:22 *a* to finish them off quickly
12:17 not be *a* to eat inside your
16:5 not be *a* to sacrifice the
17:15 You will not be *a* to put
21:16 *a* to constitute the son of
22:3 not be *a* to withdraw yourself
22:19 will not be *a* to divorce her
22:29 He will not be *a* to divorce
24:4 not be *a* to take her back
31:2 no more be *a* to go out and
Jos 9:19 we are not *a* to hurt them
Jg 21:18 are not *a* to give them wives
2Ch 30:9 be *a* to return to this land
Ezr 7:24 is *a* to be imposed upon them
Ps 66:9 not *a* our foot to totter
Mt 24:43 not *a* his house to be broken
Mr 10:4 Moses *a* the writing of a
Ac 21:37 Am I *a* to say something to

Allows
Job 11:6 God *a* some of your error to

Alloyed
1Ki 10:16 large shields of *a* gold
10:17 bucklers of *a* gold
2Ch 9:15 large shields of *a* gold
9:15 hundred shekels of *a* gold
9:16 hundred bucklers of *a* gold

Alluding
Hab 2:6 *a* remark, insinuations at him

Allure
De 13:6 should try to *a* you in secrecy
2Ch 18:2 *a* him to go up against
32:15 Hezekiah deceive you or *a*
Job 36:16 will also certainly *a* you
36:18 rage does not *a* you into
Ps 62:4 *a* from one's own dignity
Isa 36:18 that Hezekiah may not *a* you

Allured
2Ch 18:31 God at once *a* them away
Jer 38:22 have *a* you and prevailed

Allures
2Ki 18:32 Hezekiah, for he *a* you

Alluring
2Ch 32:11 Hezekiah *a* you so as to give

Ally
Da 11:6 *a* themselves with each other

Allying
Da 11:23 *a* themselves with him he

Almighty
Ge 17:1 I am God *A*. Walk before me
28:3 God *A* will bless you and make
35:11 I am God *A*. Be fruitful and
43:14 may God *A* give you pity
48:3 God *A* appeared to me at Luz
49:25 and he is with the *A*, and he
Ex 6:3 used to appear . . . as God *A*
Nu 24:4 got to see a vision of the *A*
24:16 vision of the *A* he got to see
Ru 1:20 the *A* has made it very bitter
1:21 *A* that has caused me calamity
Job 5:17 discipline of the *A* do not
6:4 arrows of the *A* are with me
6:14 leave . . . the fear of the *A*
8:3 will the *A* himself pervert
8:5 of the *A* . . . implore favor
11:7 to the very limit of the *A*
13:3 would speak to the *A* himself
15:25 over the *A* he tries to show
21:15 What does the *A* amount to
21:20 rage of the *A* he will drink
22:3 Does the *A* have any delight
22:17 what can the *A* accomplish
22:23 If you return to the *A*, you
22:25 *A* also will indeed become

Job 22:26 in the *A* you will find your
23:16 *A* himself has disturbed me
24:1 not been stored up by the *A*
27:2 as the *A* lives, who has made
27:10 in the *A* will he find
27:11 That which is with the *A*
27:13 will receive from the *A*
29:5 When the *A* was yet with me
31:2 inheritance from the *A* from
31:35 *A* himself would answer me
32:8 breath of the *A* that gives
34:10 And the *A* to act unjustly
34:12 the *A* himself does not
35:13 *A* himself does not behold
37:23 As for the *A*, we have not
40:2 a faultfinder with the *A*
Ps 68:14 the *A* One scattered abroad
91:1 the very shadow of the *A* One
Isa 13:6 despoiling from the *A* it
Eze 1:24 like the sound of the *A* One
10:5 like the sound of God *A* when
Joe 1:15 a despoiling from the *A* One
2Co 6:18 to me, says Jehovah the *A*
Re 1:8 was and who is coming, the *A*
4:8 holy is Jehovah God, the *A*
11:17 Jehovah God, the *A*, the One
15:3 works, Jehovah God, the *A*
16:7 Jehovah God, the *A*, true and
16:14 of the great day of God the *A*
19:6 Jehovah our God, the *A*, has
19:15 of the wrath of God the *A*
21:22 God the *A* is its temple

Almighty's
Job 33:4 the *A* own breath proceeded

Almodad
Ge 10:26 Joktan became father to *A*
1Ch 1:20 Joktan . . . father to *A* and

Almon
Jos 21:18 *A* and its pasture ground

Almond
Ge 30:37 and of the *a* tree and of
Ex 25:33 shaped like flowers of *a*
25:33 shaped like flowers of *a*
25:34 shaped like flowers of *a*
37:19 shaped like flowers of *a*
37:19 shaped like flowers of *a*
37:20 shaped like flowers of *a*
Ec 12:5 the *a* tree carries blossoms
Jer 1:11 An offshoot of an *a* tree is

Almon-diblathaim
Nu 33:46 and went camping in *A*
33:47 pulled away from *A* and went

Almonds
Ge 43:11 bark, pistachio nuts and *a*
Nu 17:8 and was bearing ripe *a*

Almost
Ps 73:2 my feet had *a* turned aside

Almug
1Ki 10:11 timbers of *a* trees
10:12 the timbers of the *a* trees
10:12 Timbers of *a* trees like
2Ch 2:8 juniper and *a* from Lebanon
9:10 brought timbers of *a* trees
9:11 timbers of the *a* trees

Aloe
Nu 24:6 Like *a* plants that Jehovah has

Aloes
Pr 7:17 bed with myrrh, *a*, and
Ca 4:14 frankincense, myrrh and *a*
Joh 19:39 a roll of myrrh and *a*

Aloeswood
Ps 45:8 your garments are myrrh and *a*

Aloft
Isa 9:18 *a* as the billowing of smoke

Alone
Ge 44:20 he *a* is left of his mother
Ex 12:16 that *a* may be done for you
14:12 Let us *a*, that we may serve
18:14 do you *a* continue sitting
22:20 to any gods but Jehovah *a* is
Nu 11:17 not carry it, just you *a*
12:2 by Moses *a* that Jehovah has
De 8:3 not by bread *a* does man live
9:14 Let me *a* that I may
29:14 it is not with you *a* that I
32:12 Jehovah *a* kept leading him
Jg 6:37 on the fleece *a* but on all the
6:39 dryness occur to the fleece *a*
Jg 6:40 on the fleece *a*, and upon all
11:37 Let me *a* for two months
1Sa 7:3 to Jehovah and serve him *a*
7:4 and began serving Jehovah *a*
2Sa 13:32 Amnon *a* that has died
13:33 it is Amnon *a* that has died
16:11 Let him *a* that he may call
1Ki 8:39 *a* well know the heart of all
14:13 this one *a* of Jeroboam's
18:6 Ahab himself went *a* by one
18:6 Obadiah himself went *a* by
18:22 as a prophet of Jehovah, I *a*
22:31 with the king of Israel *a*
2Ki 4:27 Let her *a*, for her soul is
17:18 but the tribe of Judah *a*
19:15 you *a* are the true God of
19:19 you, O Jehovah, are God *a*
23:18 they let his bones *a* along
2Ch 6:30 *a* well know the heart of the
18:30 with the king of Israel *a*
Ezr 6:7 work on that house of God *a*
Ne 9:6 are Jehovah *a*; you yourself
Es 1:16 It is not against the king *a*
3:6 to lay hand upon Mordecai *a*
3:8 not appropriate to let them *a*
Job 7:19 let me *a* until I swallow
15:19 them *a* the land was given
Ps 4:8 For you yourself *a*, O Jehovah
37:8 Let anger *a* and leave rage
51:4 Against you, you *a*, I have
71:16 righteousness, yours *a*
72:18 *a* is doing wonderful works
83:18 You *a* are the Most High over
86:10 You are God, you *a*
148:13 name *a* is unreachably high
Pr 5:17 prove to be for you *a*, and
9:12 you will bear it, just you *a*
Ec 4:12 could overpower one *a*, two
Isa 2:11 Jehovah *a* . . . put on high in
2:17 Jehovah *a* must be put on
37:16 *a* are the true God of all
37:20 you, O Jehovah, are God *a*
49:21 had been left behind *a*
Mic 7:14 residing *a* in a forest—in
Mt 4:4 Man must live, not on bread *a*
4:10 is to him *a* you must render
14:23 became late, he was there *a*
18:15 fault between you and him *a*
19:14 Let the young children *a*
Mr 4:10 when he got to be *a*, those
6:8 except a staff *a*, no bread, no
6:47 but he was *a* on the land
9:2 mountain to themselves *a*
9:8 no one . . . except Jesus *a*
14:6 But Jesus said: Let her *a*
Lu 4:4 Man must not live by bread *a*
4:8 it is to him *a* you must render
5:21 can forgive sins except God *a*
9:18 Later, while he was praying *a*
9:36 Jesus was found *a*
10:40 left me *a* to attend to
13:8 let it *a* also this year, until
24:12 he beheld the bandages *a*
Joh 5:31 If I *a* bear witness about
6:15 into the mountain all *a*
8:16 I am not *a*, but the Father
11:48 let him *a* this way, they
12:7 Jesus said: Let her *a*, that
16:32 and you will leave me *a*
16:32 and yet I am not *a*, because
Ac 5:38 these men, but let them *a*
Ro 9:10 not that case *a*, but also
11:3 I *a* am left, and they are
16:27 to God, wise *a*, be the glory
2Co 7:7 yet not *a* by his presence
Ga 3:2 This *a* I want to learn from
6:4 in regard to himself *a*, and
Php 4:15 and receiving, except you *a*
1Th 1:5 with speech *a* but also with
3:1 to be left *a* in Athens
1Ti 6:16 the one *a* having immortality
2Ti 4:11 Luke *a* is with me
Heb 9:7 priest *a* enters once a year
Jas 2:24 by works, and not by faith *a*
2Jo 1 I truly love, and not I *a*
Re 15:4 because you *a* are loyal

Alongside*
Pr 5:8 your way far off from *a* her
Isa 40:18 likeness can you put *a* him
Mt 13:4 some seeds fell *a* the road
13:19 is the one sown *a* the road
Mr 4:4 some seed fell *a* the road, and
4:15 *a* the road where the word is
Lu 8:5 some of it fell *a* the road and
8:12 Those *a* the road are the ones
Joh 17:5 glorify me *a* yourself with
17:5 glory that I had *a* you

Aloud
Jos 8:34 read *a* all the words of the
8:35 read *a* in front of all the
1Ch 15:16 playing *a* to cause a sound
15:19 copper cymbals to play *a*
15:28 playing *a* on stringed
16:5 with the cymbals playing *a*
Ne 8:3 to read *a* from it before the
8:8 reading *a* from the book
8:18 reading *a* of the book of the
9:3 read *a* from the book of the
Ps 26:7 thanksgiving to be heard *a*
Pr 1:20 wisdom itself keeps crying *a*
Isa 42:11 let people cry *a*
Jer 36:6 read *a* from the roll that
36:6 you should read them *a*
36:8 read *a* from the book the
36:10 Baruch began to read *a*
36:13 Baruch read *a* from the book
36:14 roll from which you read *a*
36:15 and read it *a* in our ears
36:15 Baruch read *a* in their ears
36:21 Jehudi began to read it *a*
51:61 read *a* all these words
Hab 2:2 one reading *a* from it may do
Mt 12:19 will not wrangle, nor cry *a*
15:22 cried *a*, saying: Have mercy
Mr 6:49 apparition! and they cried *a*
Lu 8:28 he cried *a* and fell down
Ac 8:28 reading *a* the prophet Isaiah
8:30 reading *a* Isaiah the prophet
8:32 that he was reading *a*
13:27 are read *a* every Sabbath
15:21 is read *a* in the synagogues
Ga 4:27 cry *a*, you woman who does
Re 1:3 Happy is he who reads *a* and

Alpha
Re 1:8 I am the *A* and the Omega
21:6 I am the *A* and the Omega
22:13 I am the *A* and the Omega

Alphaeus
Mt 10:3 James the son of *A*, and
Mr 2:14 Levi the son of *A* sitting at
3:18 and James the son of *A* and
Lu 6:15 James the son of *A*, and Simon
Ac 1:13 James the son of *A* and

Already*
Ex 19:23 you yourself *a* warned us
Le 7:24 fat of a body *a* dead and the
17:15 body *a* dead or something
22:8 *a* dead or anything torn by
De 14:21 must not eat any body *a* dead
Ps 139:4 Jehovah, you *a* know it all
Ec 1:10 It has *a* had existence for
2:12 thing that people have *a* done
2:16 the days that are *a* coming in
3:15 happened to be, it had *a* been
3:15 to be has *a* proved to be
9:7 *a* the true God has found
Isa 48:7 Look! I have *a* known them
Eze 4:14 neither a body *a* dead nor a
17:8 it was *a* transplanted, in
Mt 3:10 *A* the ax is lying at the root
5:28 has *a* committed adultery
14:15 the hour is *a* far advanced
15:32 *a* three days that they have
17:12 Elijah has *a* come and they
Mr 8:2 *a* three days that they have
11:11 as the hour was *a* late, he
Lu 3:9 the ax is *a* in position at the
21:30 When they are *a* in the bud
Joh 3:18 has been judged *a*, because
4:35 are white for harvesting. *A*
Ac 4:3 for it was *a* evening
Ro 4:19 his own body, now *a* deadened
13:11 *a* the hour for you to awake
1Co 4:8 You men *a* have your fill, do
4:8 You are rich *a*, are you? You
Php 3:12 Not that I have *a* received it
3:12 or am *a* made perfect, but
2Th 2:7 this lawlessness is *a* at work
1Ti 5:15 *A*, in fact, some have been
2Ti 2:18 resurrection has *a* occurred

Altar
Ge 8:20 Noah began to build an *a* to
8:20 burnt offerings upon the *a*
12:7 he built an *a* there to Jehovah

Ge 12:8 he built an *a* there to Jehovah
13:4 *a* that he had made there
13:18 to build an *a* to Jehovah
22:9 Abraham built an *a* there and
22:9 put him upon the *a* on top of
26:25 built an *a* there and called
33:20 he set up there an *a* and
35:1 make an *a* there to the true
35:3 make an *a* to the true God
35:7 he built an *a* there and began
Ex 17:15 to build an *a* and to call its
20:24 *a* of ground you are to make
20:25 make an *a* of stones for me
20:26 not go up by steps to my *a*
21:14 from being at my *a* to die
24:4 an *a* and twelve pillars
24:6 blood he sprinkled upon the *a*
27:1 make the *a* of acacia wood
27:1 The *a* should be foursquare
27:5 be toward the center of the *a*
27:6 you must make poles for the *a*
27:7 upon the two sides of the *a*
28:43 near to the *a* to minister in
29:12 upon the horns of the *a*, and
29:12 pour out at the base of the *a*
29:13 make them smoke upon the *a*
29:16 sprinkle it . . . upon the *a*
29:18 entire ram smoke upon the *a*
29:20 blood round about upon the *a*
29:21 the blood that is upon the *a*
29:25 make them smoke upon the *a*
29:36 purify the *a* from sin by
29:37 make atonement over the *a*
29:37 become a most holy *a*
29:37 touches the *a* is to be holy
29:38 offer upon the *a*: young rams
29:44 I will sanctify . . . the *a*
30:1 an *a* as a place for burning
30:18 tent of meeting and the *a*
30:20 go near the *a* to minister
30:27 utensils and the *a* of incense
30:28 the *a* of burnt offering and
31:8 and the *a* of incense
31:9 and the *a* of burnt offering
32:5 he went to building an *a*
35:15 *a* of incense and its poles
35:16 *a* of burnt offering and the
37:25 *a* of incense out of acacia
38:1 make the *a* of burnt offering
38:3 all the utensils of the *a*
38:4 made for the *a* a grating, a
38:7 rings on the sides of the *a*
38:30 and the copper *a* and the
38:30 and all the utensils of the *a*
39:38 *a* of gold and the anointing
39:39 the *a* of copper and the
40:5 put the golden *a* for incense
40:6 *a* of burnt offering before the
40:7 and the *a* and put water in it
40:10 the *a* of burnt offering and
40:10 and sanctify the *a*, and so
40:10 must become a most holy *a*
40:26 the golden *a* in the tent of
40:29 the *a* of burnt offering at
40:30 tent of meeting and the *a*
40:32 they went near to the *a* they
40:33 the tabernacle and the *a* and
Le 1:5 blood round about upon the *a*
1:7 must put fire on the *a* and set
1:8 on the fire that is on the *a*
1:9 on the *a* as a burnt offering
1:11 the side of the *a* to the north
1:11 blood round about upon the *a*
1:12 on the fire that is on the *a*
1:13 and make it smoke on the *a*
1:15 must present it at the *a* and
1:15 and make it smoke upon the *a*
1:15 out upon the side of the *a*
1:16 beside the *a*, to the east
1:17 smoke on the *a* over the wood
2:2 remembrancer of it upon the *a*
2:8 he must bring it near to the *a*
2:9 must make it smoke on the *a*
2:12 must not come up onto the *a*
3:2 blood round about upon the *a*
3:5 must make it smoke on the *a*
3:8 blood round about upon the *a*
3:11 it smoke on the *a* as food, an
3:13 blood round about upon the *a*
3:16 smoke upon the *a* as food, an
4:7 the horns of the *a* of perfumed
4:7 of the *a* of burnt offering
4:10 make them smoke upon the *a*
4:18 the *a* that is before Jehovah
Le 4:18 of the *a* of burnt offering
4:19 must make it smoke on the *a*
4:25 the horns of the *a* of burnt
4:25 of the *a* of burnt offering
4:26 all its fat smoke on the *a*
4:30 put it upon the horns of the *a*
4:30 blood at the base of the *a*
4:31 smoke on the *a* as a restful
4:34 of the *a* of burnt offering
4:34 blood at the base of the *a*
4:35 make them smoke on the *a* upon
5:9 offering upon the side of the *a*
5:9 out at the base of the *a*
5:12 make it smoke on the *a* upon
6:9 upon the *a* all night long until
6:9 fire of the *a* will be kindled
6:10 regularly consumes upon the *a*
6:10 must place them beside the *a*
6:12 fire on the *a* will be kept
6:13 constantly burning on the *a*
6:14 Jehovah in front of the *a*
6:15 make it smoke upon the *a* as
7:2 round about upon the *a*
7:5 make them smoke on the *a* as
7:31 the fat smoke upon the *a*
8:11 seven times upon the *a* and
8:11 anointed the *a* and all its
8:15 horns of the *a* round about
8:15 and purify the *a* from sin
8:15 poured at the base of the *a*
8:16 made them smoke upon the *a*
8:19 blood round about upon the *a*
8:21 entire ram smoke upon the *a*
8:24 blood round about upon the *a*
8:28 made them smoke upon the *a*
8:30 blood that was upon the *a* and
9:7 to the *a* and render up your
9:8 the *a* and slaughtered the calf
9:9 put it upon the horns of the *a*
9:9 he poured at the base of the *a*
9:10 offering smoke upon the *a*
9:12 it round about upon the *a*
9:13 make them smoke upon the *a*
9:14 the burnt offering on the *a*
9:17 and made it smoke upon the *a*
9:18 round about upon the *a*
9:20 fatty pieces smoke upon the *a*
9:24 the fatty pieces upon the *a*
10:12 it unfermented near the *a*
14:20 the grain offering upon the *a*
16:12 fire from off the *a* before
16:18 come out to the *a*, which is
16:18 the horns of the *a* round about
16:20 the *a*, he must also present
16:25 smoke upon the *a*
16:33 *a* he will make atonement
17:6 blood upon Jehovah's *a* at the
17:11 put it upon the *a* for you to
21:23 he may not approach the *a*
22:22 put upon the *a* for Jehovah
Nu 3:26 tabernacle and the *a*, and its
4:11 over the golden *a* they will
4:13 fatty ashes of the *a* and
4:14 all the utensils of the *a*; and
4:26 about the tabernacle and the *a*
5:25 he must bring it near the *a*
5:26 must make it smoke upon the *a*
7:1 and the *a* and all its utensils
7:10 inauguration of the *a* on the
7:10 their offering before the *a*
7:11 for the inauguration of the *a*
7:84 offering of the *a* on the day
7:88 offering of the *a* after its
16:38 as an overlaying for the *a*
16:39 into an overlaying for the *a*
16:46 put fire from upon the *a* in
18:3 the *a* they must not come near
18:5 your obligation to the *a*, that
18:7 regards every concern of the *a*
18:17 should sprinkle upon the *a*
23:2 a bull and a ram on each *a*
23:4 a bull and a ram on each *a*
23:14 a bull and a ram on each *a*
23:30 a bull and a ram on each *a*
De 12:27 upon the *a* of Jehovah your
12:27 against the *a* of Jehovah
16:21 sacred pole near the *a* of
26:4 deposit it before the *a* of
27:5 build an *a* there to Jehovah
27:5 build . . . an *a* of stones
27:6 the *a* of Jehovah your God
33:10 a whole offering on your *a*
Jos 8:30 build an *a* to Jehovah the God
8:31 An *a* of whole stones, upon
Jos 9:27 and for Jehovah's *a*, down
22:10 built . . . an *a* by the Jordan
22:10 *a* great in conspicuousness
22:11 built an *a* on the frontier
22:16 an *a*, that you may rebel
22:19, 19 *a* in addition to the *a*
22:23 *a* so as to turn back from
22:26 building the *a*, not for
22:28 of Jehovah's *a* that our
22:29 building an *a* for burnt
22:29 besides the *a* of Jehovah
22:34 of Gad began to name the *a*
Jg 6:24 built an *a* there to Jehovah
6:25 tear down the *a* of Baal that
6:26 build an *a* to Jehovah your God
6:28 the *a* of Baal had been pulled
6:28 offered up on the *a* that had
6:30 has pulled down the *a* of Baal
6:31 someone has pulled down his *a*
6:32 someone has pulled down his *a*
13:20 from off the *a* heavenward
13:20 in the flame of the *a* while
21:4 get up early and to build an *a*
1Sa 2:28 and go up upon my *a* to make
2:33 cut off from being at my *a*
7:17 build an *a* there to Jehovah
14:35 Saul proceeded to build an *a*
14:35 *a* building to Jehovah
2Sa 24:18 *a* on the threshing floor of
24:21 for building an *a* to Jehovah
24:25 build there an *a* to Jehovah
1Ki 1:50 hold of the horns of the *a*
1:51 hold on the horns of the *a*
1:53 down from off the *a*
2:28 fast to the horns of the *a*
2:29 there he is beside the *a*
3:4 proceeded to offer upon that *a*
6:20 overlay the *a* with cedarwood
6:22 the *a* that was toward the
7:48 the *a* of gold and the table
8:22 before the *a* of Jehovah in
8:31 before your *a* in this house
8:54 rose up from before the *a*
8:64 the copper *a* that is before
9:25 sacrifices upon the *a* that he
9:25 sacrificial smoke on the *a*
12:32 *a* that he had made in Bethel
12:33 *a* that he had made in
12:33 make offerings upon the *a*
13:1 Jeroboam was . . . by the *a*
13:2 he called out against the *a*
13:2, 2 *a*, *a*, this is what Jehovah
13:3 The *a* is ripped apart
13:4 against the *a* in Bethel
13:4 his hand from off the *a*
13:5 *a* itself was ripped apart
13:5 were spilled out from the *a*
13:32 the *a* that is in Bethel
16:32 he set up an *a* to Baal
18:26 kept limping around the *a*
18:30 to mend the *a* of Jehovah
18:32 build the stones into an *a*
18:32 all around the *a*
18:35 water went all around the *a*
2Ki 11:11 by the *a* and by the house
12:9 beside the *a* on the right
16:10 *a* that was in Damascus
16:10 design of the *a* and its
16:11 to build the *a*
16:12 the king got to see the *a*
16:12 to go near to the *a* and
16:13 that were his upon the *a*
16:14 copper *a* that was before
16:14 between his *a* and the house
16:14 at the north side of his *a*
16:15 Upon the great *a* make the
16:15 copper *a*, it will become
18:22 this *a* you should bow down
23:9 to the *a* of Jehovah in
23:15 the *a* that was in Bethel
23:15 that *a* and the high place
23:16 burned them upon the *a*
23:17 done against the *a* of Bethel
1Ch 6:49 upon the *a* of burnt offering
6:49 and upon the *a* of incense
16:40 on the *a* of burnt offering
21:18 erect an *a* to Jehovah on the
21:22 build in it an *a* to Jehovah
21:26 David built there an *a* to
21:26 upon the *a* of burnt offering
21:29 and the *a* of burnt offering
22:1 an *a* for burnt offering for
28:18 the incense *a* refined gold
2Ch 1:5 copper *a* that Bezalel the son

2Ch 1:6 copper *a* that belonged to the
4:1 copper *a*, twenty cubits being
4:19 the golden *a* and the tables
5:12 standing to the east of the *a*
6:12 before the *a* of Jehovah in
6:22 before your *a* in this house
7:7 copper *a* that Solomon had
7:9 inauguration of the *a* they had
8:12 *a* of Jehovah that he had
15:8 renew Jehovah's *a* that was
23:10 by the *a* and by the house
26:16 upon the *a* of incense
26:19 beside the *a* of incense
29:18 *a* of burnt offering and all
29:19 before the *a* of Jehovah
29:21 up upon the *a* of Jehovah
29:22 and sprinkled it upon the *a*
29:22 the blood upon the *a*
29:22 the blood upon the *a*
29:24 with their blood upon the *a*
29:27 burnt sacrifice on the *a*
32:12 Before one *a* you should bow
33:16 prepared the *a* of Jehovah
35:16 burnt offerings upon the *a*
Ezr 3:2 the *a* of the God of Israel
3:3 established the *a* firmly upon
7:17 *a* of the house of your God
Ne 10:34 burn upon the *a* of Jehovah
Ps 26:6 I will march around your *a*
43:4 I will come to the *a* of God
51:19 up on your very own *a*
84:3 Your grand *a*, O Jehovah of
118:27 far as the horns of the *a*
Isa 6:6 taken with tongs off the *a*
19:19 *a* to Jehovah in the midst
27:9 stones of the *a* like
29:2 to me as the *a* hearth of God
36:7 this *a* you should bow down
56:7 for acceptance upon my *a*
60:7 they will come up upon my *a*
La 2:7 Jehovah has cast off his *a*
Eze 8:5 the north of the gate of the *a*
8:16 between the porch and the *a*
9:2 and stand beside the copper *a*
40:46 the obligation of the *a*
40:47 the *a* was before the house
41:22 wooden *a* was three cubits
43:13 measurements of the *a* in
43:13 this is the base of the *a*
43:15 *a* hearth is four cubits
43:15 *a* hearth and upward there
43:16 *a* hearth is twelve cubits
43:18 statutes of the *a* on the
43:22 purify the *a* from sin the
43:26 make atonement for the *a*
43:27 render upon the *a* the whole
45:19 ledge belonging to the *a*
47:1 House, south of the *a*
Joe 1:13 you ministers of the *a*
2:17 Between the porch and the *a*
Am 2:8 stretch . . . out beside every *a*
3:14 the horns of the *a* will
9:1 Jehovah stationed above the *a*
Zec 9:15 like the corners of the *a*
14:20 like the bowls before the *a*
Mal 1:7 upon my *a* polluted bread
1:10 you men will not light my *a*
2:13 with tears the *a* of Jehovah
Mt 5:23 bringing your gift to the *a*
5:24 gift there in front of the *a*
23:18 If anyone swears by the *a*
23:19 greater, the gift or the *a*
23:20 he that swears by the *a* is
23:35 the sanctuary and the *a*
Lu 1:11 right side of the incense *a*
11:51 between the *a* and the house
Ac 17:23 an *a* . . . To an Unknown God
1Co 9:13 attending at the *a* have a
9:13 for themselves with the *a*
10:18 sharers with the *a*
Heb 7:13 one has officiated at the *a*
13:10 *a* from which those who do
Jas 2:21 up Isaac his son upon the *a*
Re 6:9 underneath the *a* the souls of
8:3 stood at the *a*, having a golden
8:3 upon the golden *a* that was
8:5 some of the fire of the *a* and
9:13 golden *a* that is before God
11:1 *a* and those worshiping in it
14:18 angel emerged from the *a*
16:7 *a* say: Yes, Jehovah God, the

Altar's
Ex 27:5 put it under the *a* rim down

Altars
Ex 34:13 *a* you people are to pull
Nu 3:31 lampstand and the *a* and the
23:1 for me on this spot seven *a*
23:4 I set the seven *a* in rows
23:14 build seven *a* and to offer up
23:29 for me on this spot seven *a*
De 7:5 Their *a* you should pull down
12:3 must pull down their *a* and
Jg 2:2 Their *a* you should pull down
1Ki 19:10 your *a* they have torn down
19:14 your *a* they have torn down
2Ki 11:18 Baal and pulled down his *a*
11:18 they killed before the *a*
18:22 *a* Hezekiah has removed
21:3 and set up *a* to Baal and
21:4 *a* in the house of Jehovah
21:5 build *a* to all the army of
23:12 *a* that were upon the roof
23:12 *a* that Manasseh had made
23:20 that were there upon the *a*
2Ch 14:3 removed the foreign *a* and
23:17 *a* and his images they broke
23:17 they killed before the *a*
28:24 *a* for himself at every
30:14 removed the *a* that were in
30:14 incense *a* they removed and
31:1 *a* out of all Judah and
32:12 high places and his *a* and
33:3 set up *a* to the Baals and
33:4 *a* in the house of Jehovah
33:5 *a* to all the army of the
33:15 *a* that he had built in the
34:4 the *a* of the Baals
34:5 he burned upon their *a*
34:7 pulling down the *a* and the
Isa 17:8 he will not look to the *a*
36:7 *a* Hezekiah has removed
Jer 11:13 as many *a* as the streets
11:13 *a* to make sacrificial smoke
17:1 on the horns of their *a*
17:2 their sons remember their *a*
Eze 6:4 your *a* must be made desolate
6:5 your bones all around your *a*
6:6 your *a* may lie desolated and
6:13 all around their *a*, upon
Ho 8:11 For Ephraim has multiplied *a*
8:11 have *a* in order to sin
10:1 he has multiplied his *a*
10:2 one who will break their *a*
10:8 will come up upon their *a*
12:11 *a* are like piles of stones
Am 3:14 against the *a* of Bethel
Ro 11:3 they have dug up your *a*, and

Alter
Job 9:27 Let me *a* my countenance and
Ps 15:4 and yet he does not *a*
Joe 2:7 they do not *a* their paths

Altering
2Sa 14:20 *a* the face of the matter

Alternating
Ex 25:33 with knobs and blossoms *a*
25:33 with knobs and blossoms *a*
25:34 its knobs and its blossoms *a*
37:19 with knobs and blossoms *a*
37:19 with knobs and blossoms *a*
37:20 its knobs and its blossoms *a*

Alters
Mic 2:4 portion of my people he *a*

Altogether
Ge 18:21 they act *a* according to the
Ex 11:1 the time he sends you away *a*
Nu 11:15 kill me off *a*, if I have
1Sa 25:21 *a* for disappointment that I
2Sa 20:20 *a* unthinkable on my part
Es 4:14 if you are *a* silent at this
Job 6:2 my vexation were *a* weighed
21:23 When he is *a* carefree and
Ps 19:9 they have proved *a* righteous
Ca 4:7 You are *a* beautiful, O girl
5:16 about him is *a* desirable
Joh 9:34 You were *a* born in sins, and
1Co 6:7 means *a* a defeat for you that
9:9 is it *a* for our sakes he says
Php 1:7 It is *a* right for me to think

Alush
Nu 33:13 and went camping at *A*
33:14 pulled away from *A* and went

Alvah
Ge 36:40 sheiks of Esau . . . sheik *A*
1Ch 1:51 sheiks of Edom . . . *A*

Alvan
Ge 36:23 sons of Shobal: *A* and
1Ch 1:40 sons of Shobal were *A*

Always
Ge 30:41 *a* occurred that whenever the
30:42 feeble ones *a* came to be
De 4:40 God is giving you, *a*
5:29 keep all my commandments *a*
6:24 for our good *a*, that we might
11:1 keep . . . his commandments *a*
14:23 fear Jehovah your God *a*
18:5 he and his sons, *a*
19:9 to walk in his ways *a*, you
28:29 one who is *a* defrauded and
28:32 and yearning for them *a*
28:33 defrauded and crushed *a*
Jos 4:24 fear Jehovah your God *a*
1Sa 2:35 before my anointed one *a*
18:29 to be an enemy of David *a*
23:14 kept looking for him *a*
28:2 I shall appoint you *a*
2Sa 19:13 chief before me *a* instead
1Ki 5:1 Hiram had *a* proved to be
9:3 certainly prove to be there *a*
11:36 lamp *a* before me in
11:39 shall humiliate . . . not *a*
12:7 to become your servants *a*
14:30 Rehoboam and Jeroboam *a*
2Ki 8:19 to him and to his sons *a*
17:37 should take care to do *a*
2Ch 7:16 certainly prove to be there *a*
10:7 become your servants *a*
21:7 him and his sons a lamp *a*
Job 1:5 is the way Job would do *a*
Ps 9:18 not *a* will the poor one be
Jer 31:36 be a nation before me *a*
32:39 in order to fear me *a*, for
33:18 and to render sacrifice *a*
35:19 man to stand before me *a*
Mt 18:10 angels in heaven *a* behold
26:11 you *a* have the poor with you
26:11 but you will not *a* have me
Mr 14:7 you *a* have the poor with you
14:7 you can *a* do them good, but
14:7 but me you do not have *a*
Lu 15:31 Child, you have *a* been with
18:1 *a* to pray and not to give up
Joh 6:34 Lord, *a* give us this bread
7:6 your due time is *a* at hand
8:29 I *a* do the things pleasing
11:42 I knew that you *a* hear me
12:8 have the poor *a* with you
12:8 me you will not have *a*
18:20 I *a* taught in a synagogue
Ac 7:51 *a* resisting the holy spirit
Ro 1:9 I *a* make mention of you in my
11:10 and *a* bow down their back
1Co 1:4 I *a* thank God for you in view
15:58 *a* having plenty to do in
2Co 2:14 to God who *a* leads us in a
4:10 *A* we endure everywhere in
5:6 *a* of good courage and know
9:8 *a* have full self-sufficiency
Eph 5:20 giving thanks *a* for all
Php 1:3 I thank my God *a* upon every
1:20 Christ will, as *a* before
2:12 way that you have *a* obeyed
4:4 *A* rejoice in the Lord
Col 1:3 *a* when we pray for you
4:6 *a* with graciousness, seasoned
4:12 *a* exerting himself in your
1Th 1:2 We *a* thank God when we make
2:16 *a* fill up the measure of
3:6 good remembrance of us *a*
4:17 we shall *a* be with the Lord
5:15 *a* pursue what is good toward
5:16 *A* be rejoicing
2Th 1:3 give God thanks *a* for you
1:11 we *a* pray for you, that our
2:13 obligated to thank God *a* for
2Ti 3:7 *a* learning and yet never able
Tit 1:12 Cretans are *a* liars
Phm 4 I *a* thank my God when I make
Heb 3:10 *a* go astray in their hearts
7:25 is *a* alive to plead for them
13:15 *a* offer to God a sacrifice
1Pe 3:15 *a* ready to make a defense
2Pe 1:12 disposed *a* to remind you of

Am*
Nu 10:10 I *a* Jehovah your God
15:41 I *a* Jehovah your God
Ps 81:10 I, Jehovah, *a* your God
Isa 6:8 say: Here I *a*! Send me

Isa 44:6 Jehovah . . . I *a* the first
44:6 Jehovah . . . I *a* the last
47:10 I *a*, and there is nobody
48:12 the same One. I *a* the first
48:12 Moreover, I *a* the last
48:17 I, Jehovah, *a* your God, the
49:26 I, Jehovah, *a* your Savior
60:16 I, Jehovah, *a* your Savior
61:8 I, Jehovah, *a* loving justice
65:1, 1 Here I *a*, here I *a*! to a
Jer 9:24 that I *a* Jehovah, the One
23:23 *A* I a God nearby, is the
32:27 Here I *a*, Jehovah, the God
Eze 36:11 to know that I *a* Jehovah
37:6 to know that I *a* Jehovah
37:28 I, Jehovah, *a* sanctifying
Zep 2:15 I *a*, and there is nobody else

Amad
Jos 19:26 and *A* and Mishal

Amal
1Ch 7:35 the sons of Helem . . . *A*

Amalek
Ge 36:12 she bore to Eliphaz *A*
36:16 sheik *A* . . . of Edom
Ex 17:13 Joshua vanquished *A* and his
17:14 the remembrance of *A* from
17:16 war with *A* from generation
Nu 24:20 When he got to see *A*, he
24:20 *A* was the first one of the
De 25:17 what *A* did to you in the way
25:19 wipe out the mention of *A*
Jg 3:13 the sons of Ammon and *A*
6:3 *A* and the Easterners came up
6:33 *A* and the Easterners gathered
7:12 *A* and all the Easterners were
10:12 and *A* and Midian, when they
1Sa 14:48 to strike down *A* and to
15:2 call to account what *A* did
15:3 and you must strike down *A*
15:5 come as far as the city of *A*
15:6 Kenites departed from . . . *A*
15:7 Saul went striking down *A*
15:8 to catch Agag the king of *A*
15:20 I brought Agag the king of *A*
15:20 but *A* I have devoted to
15:32 Bring Agag the king of *A*
28:18 his burning anger against *A*
2Sa 8:12 Philistines and from *A* and
1Ch 1:36 sons of Eliphaz were . . . *A*
4:43 that had escaped of *A*
18:11 the Philistines and from *A*
Ps 83:7 Gebal and Ammon and *A*

Amalekite
Jg 12:15 in the mountain of the *A*
1Sa 30:13 slave of an *A* man, but my
2Sa 1:8 I said to him, I am an *A*
1:13 an alien resident, an *A*

Amalekites
Ge 14:7 the whole field of the *A*
Ex 17:8 *A* proceeded to come and fight
17:9 go out, fight against the *A*
17:10 to fight against the *A*; and
17:11 the *A* proved superior
Nu 13:29 *A* are dwelling in the land
14:25 the *A* and the Canaanites are
14:43 the *A* and the Canaanites are
14:45 the *A* and the Canaanites who
1Sa 15:6 from the midst of the *A*
15:15 Saul said: From the *A* they
15:18 the *A*, to destruction
27:8 they might raid the . . . *A*
30:1 *A* made a raid on the south
30:18 all that the *A* had taken
2Sa 1:1 striking down the *A*, that

Amam
Jos 15:26 *A* and Shema and Moladah

Amariah
1Ch 6:7 Meraioth . . . father to *A*
6:7 *A* . . . became father to Ahitub
6:11 Azariah . . . father to *A*
6:11 *A* . . . father to Ahitub
6:52 *A* his son, Ahitub his son
23:19 of Hebron . . . *A* the second
24:23 of Hebron . . . *A* the second
2Ch 19:11 *A* the chief priest over you
31:15 *A* . . . in office of trust
Ezr 7:3 *A* the son of Azariah the son
10:42 Shallum, *A*, Joseph
Ne 10:3 Pashhur, *A*, Malchijah
11:4 Zechariah the son of *A*
Ne 12:2 *A*, Malluch, Hattush
12:13 Meshullam; for *A*, Jehohanan
Zep 1:1 *A* the son of Hezekiah in the

Amasa
2Sa 17:25 *A* was the one whom Absalom
17:25 *A* was the son of . . . Ithra
19:13 to *A* you should say, Are you
20:4 The king now said to *A*
20:5 So *A* went to call Judah
20:8 *A* himself came to meet them
20:9 Joab proceeded to say to *A*
20:10 As for *A*, he was not on
20:12 *A* was wallowing in the
20:12 moved *A* from the highway
1Ki 2:5 *A* the son of Jether, when he
2:32 *A* the son of Jether the chief
1Ch 2:17 Abigail, she gave birth to *A*
2:17 the father of *A* was Jether
2Ch 28:12 *A* the son of Hadlai, rose

Amasai
1Ch 6:25 sons of Elkanah were *A* and
6:35 son of Mahath, the son of *A*
12:18 spirit itself enveloped *A*
15:24 *A* and Zechariah and Benaiah
2Ch 29:12 Mahath the son of *A* and

Amasa's
2Sa 20:9 took hold of *A* beard so as to

Amashsai
Ne 11:13 *A* the son of Azarel the

Amasiah
2Ch 17:16 *A* the son of Zichri the

Amass
Da 11:2 one will *a* greater riches

Amassed
Ge 31:1 he has *a* all this wealth

Amazed
Job 26:11 are *a* because of his rebuke
Ps 48:5 and so they were *a*
Ec 5:8 do not be *a* over the affair
Isa 29:9 Linger, you men, and be *a*
Jer 4:9 prophets themselves will be *a*
Hab 1:5 Be *a*; for there is an activity
Mt 8:10 Jesus became *a* and said to
8:27 the men became *a* and said
Mr 6:51 they were very much *a*
Ac 8:11 *a* them for quite a while by
8:13 *a* at beholding great signs
10:45 *a*, because the free gift of

Amazement
Ge 43:33 looking at one another in *a*
Le 26:32 simply stare in *a* over it
1Ki 9:8 stare in *a* and will certainly
2Ch 7:21 stare in *a* and be certain
Job 17:8 Upright people stare in *a* at
18:20 West will indeed stare in *a*
21:5 faces to me and stare in *a*
Ps 40:15 stare in *a* in consequence of
Isa 13:8 look at each other in *a*
52:14 have stared at him in *a*
Jer 2:12 Stare in *a*, O you heavens
Eze 26:16 and stare in *a* at you
27:35 in *a* they will certainly
28:19 certainly stare in *a* at you
Hab 1:5 stare in *a* at one another
Mt 9:33 the crowds felt *a* and said
15:31 crowd felt *a* as they saw
Mr 10:32 they felt *a*; but those who
Lu 2:47 were in constant *a* at his
20:26 in *a* at his answer, they

Amaziah
2Ki 12:21 *A* his son began to reign
13:12 against *A* the king of Judah
14:1 *A* the son of Jehoash the
14:8 *A* sent messengers to Jehoash
14:9 sent to *A* the king of Judah
14:11 And *A* did not listen
14:11 he and *A* the king of Judah
14:13 was *A* the king of Judah
14:15 against *A* the king of Judah
14:17 *A* the son of Jehoash the
14:18 rest of the affairs of *A*
14:21 in place of his father *A*
14:23 *A* the son of Jehoash the
15:1 *A* the king of Judah
15:3 that *A* his father had done
1Ch 3:12 *A* his son, Azariah his son
4:34 and Joshah the son of *A*
6:45 son of *A*, the son of Hilkiah
2Ch 24:27 *A* his son began to reign
2Ch 25:1 *A* became king, and for
25:5 *A* proceeded to collect Judah
25:9 *A* said to the man of the
25:10 *A* separated them, namely
25:11 *A*, for his part, took
25:13 *A* had sent back from going
25:14 *A* came from striking down
25:15 anger became hot against *A*
25:17 *A* the king of Judah took
25:18 sent to *A* the king of Judah
25:20 *A* did not listen
25:21 he and *A* the king of Judah
25:23 *A* the king of Judah, the
25:25 *A* the son of Jehoash the
25:26 affairs of *A*, the first and
25:27 *A* turned aside from
26:1 in place of his father *A*
26:4 that *A* his father had done
Am 7:10 *A* the priest of Bethel
7:12 *A* proceeded to say to Amos
7:14 Amos answered and said to *A*

Amazing
Ac 8:9 and *a* the nation of Samaria

Ambassador
Eph 6:20 am acting as an *a* in chains

Ambassadors
Lu 14:32 he sends out a body of *a* and
19:14 sent out a body of *a* after
2Co 5:20 *a* substituting for Christ

Ambiguous
Da 8:23 and understanding *a* sayings

Ambush
Jos 8:2 an *a* of yours against the city
8:4 lying in *a* against the city to
8:7 you will rise up from the *a*
8:9 marched to the place of *a*
8:12 an *a* between Bethel and Ai
8:14 an *a* against him to the rear
8:19 the *a* rose up quickly from
8:21 the *a* had captured the city
Jg 9:25 set *a* men for him upon the
9:35 rose up from the place of *a*
16:9 Now the *a* was sitting in the
16:12 the *a* was sitting in the
20:29 set men in *a* against Gibeah
20:33 those of Israel in *a* were
20:36 they trusted in the *a* that
20:37 As for the *a*, they acted
20:37 *a* spread out and struck all
20:38 arrangement with the *a* for
1Sa 15:5 lie in *a* by the torrent
22:8 lier in *a* the way it is
22:13 lier in *a* the way it is
2Ch 13:13 *a* around to come behind
13:13 and the *a* behind them
20:22 Jehovah set men in *a*
Ezr 8:31 enemy and the *a* by the way
Job 37:8 wild beast comes into the *a*
38:40 lying in the covert for an *a*
Ps 10:8 sits in an *a* of settlements
Pr 1:11 Do let us lie in *a* for blood
1:18 *a* for the very blood of
Jer 9:8 within himself he sets his *a*
51:12 ready those lying in *a*
Ac 25:3 they were laying an *a* to do

Amen
Nu 5:22, 22 the woman must say: *A! A!*
De 27:15 must answer and say, *A!*
27:16 all the people must say, *A!*
27:17 all the people must say, *A!*
27:18 all the people must say, *A!*
27:19 all the people must say, *A!*
27:20 all the people must say, *A!*
27:21 all the people must say, *A!*
27:22 all the people must say, *A!*
27:23 all the people must say, *A!*
27:24 all the people must say, *A!*
27:25 all the people must say, *A!*
27:26 all the people must say, *A!*
1Ki 1:36 *A!* Thus may Jehovah the God
1Ch 16:36 people proceeded to say, *A!*
Ne 5:13 all the congregation said: *A!*
8:6, 6 the people answered, *A! A!*
Ps 41:13, 13 time indefinite. *A* and *A*
72:19, 19 the whole earth. *A* and *A*
89:52, 52 time indefinite. *A* and *A*
106:48 all the people must say *A*
Jer 11:5 answer and say: *A*, O Jehovah
28:6 *A!* Thus may Jehovah do
Ro 1:25 who is blessed forever. *A*
9:5 over all, be blessed forever. *A*

Ro 11:36 him be the glory forever. *A*
15:33 peace be with all of you. *A*
16:27 Jesus Christ forever. *A*
1Co 14:16 say *A* to your giving of
2Co 1:20 through him is the *A* said to
Ga 1:5 glory forever and ever. *A*
6:18 spirit you show, brothers. *A*
Eph 3:21 forever and ever. *A*
Php 4:20 the glory forever and ever. *A*
1Ti 1:17 glory forever and ever. *A*
6:16 and might everlasting. *A*
2Ti 4:18 glory forever and ever. *A*
Heb 13:21 glory forever and ever. *A*
1Pe 4:11 are his forever and ever. *A*
5:11 him be the might forever. *A*
Jude 25 and into all eternity. *A*
Re 1:6 and the might forever. *A*
1:7 grief because of him. Yes, *A*
3:14 things that the *A* says, the
5:14 creatures went saying: *A!* and
7:12 saying: *A!* The blessing and
7:12 to our God forever and ever. *A*
19:4 *A!* Praise Jah, you people!
22:20 *A!* Come, Lord Jesus

Amends
Ex 32:30 can make *a* for your sin

Amethyst
Ex 28:19 *lesh'em* stone, agate and *a*
39:12 *lesh'em* stone, agate and *a*
Re 21:20 hyacinth, the twelfth *a*

Ami
Ezr 2:57 the sons of *A*

Amid
1Sa 2:32 *a* all the good that is done
Ne 9:35 *a* your abundant good things
Job 17:2 *a* their rebellious behavior
Isa 50:11 *a* the sparks that you have
Ac 26:12 *A* these efforts as I was
Tit 2:12 *a* this present system of

Amidst
Mt 10:16 you forth as sheep *a* wolves

Amittai
2Ki 14:25 Jonah the son of *A*
Jon 1:1 occur to Jonah the son of *A*

Ammah
2Sa 2:24 hill of *A*, which is in front

Ammiel
Nu 13:12 of Dan, *A* the son of Gemalli
2Sa 9:4 Machir the son of *A* at
9:5 Machir the son of *A* at
17:27 the son of *A* from Lo-debar
1Ch 3:5 Bath-sheba the daughter of *A*
26:5 *A* the sixth, Issachar the

Ammihud
Nu 1:10 Elishama the son of *A*
2:18 is Elishama the son of *A*
7:48 Elishama the son of *A*
7:53 of Elishama the son of *A*
10:22 Elishama the son of *A* was
34:20 Shemuel the son of *A*
34:28 Pedahel the son of *A*
2Sa 13:37 *A* the king of Geshur
1Ch 7:26 *A* his son, Elishama his son
9:4 the son of *A* the son of Omri

Amminadab
Nu 1:7 of Judah, Nahshon the son of *A*
2:3 is Nahshon the son of *A*
7:12 Nahshon the son of *A* of the
7:17 of Nahshon the son of *A*
10:14 Nahshon the son of *A*
Ru 4:19 and Ram became father to *A*
4:20 *A* became father to Nahshon
1Ch 2:10 Ram, he became father to *A*
2:10 *A*, in turn, became father to
6:22 sons of Kohath were *A* his
15:10 of the sons of Uzziel, *A* the
15:11 Levites . . . Eliel and *A*
Mt 1:4 Ram became father to *A*
1:4 *A* became father to Nahshon
Lu 3:33 son of *A*, son of Arni, son of

Amminadab's
Ex 6:23 took Elisheba, *A* daughter

Ammishaddai
Nu 1:12 Ahiezer the son of *A*
2:25 Ahiezer the son of *A*
7:66 Ahiezer the son of *A*
7:71 Ahiezer the son of *A*
10:25 Ahiezer the son of *A*

Ammizabad
1Ch 27:6 there was *A* his son

Ammon
Ge 19:38 father of the sons of *A*, to
Nu 21:24 Jabbok, near the sons of *A*
21:24 the border of the sons of *A*
De 2:19 in front of the sons of *A*
2:19 the land of the sons of *A* as
2:37 the land of the sons of *A*
3:11 in Rabbah of the sons of *A*
3:16 boundary of the sons of *A*
Jos 12:2 boundary of the sons of *A*
13:10 the border of the sons of *A*
13:25 the land of the sons of *A*
Jg 3:13 against them the sons of *A*
10:6 the gods of the sons of *A* and
10:7 into the hand of the sons of *A*
10:9 the sons of *A* would cross the
10:11 from the sons of *A* and from
10:17 the sons of *A* were called
10:18 against the sons of *A*? Let
11:4 the sons of *A* began to fight
11:5 *A* did fight against Israel
11:6 fight against the sons of *A*
11:8 fight against the sons of *A*
11:9 to fight against the sons of *A*
11:12 the king of the sons of *A*
11:13 the king of the sons of *A*
11:14 to the king of the sons of *A*
11:15 and the land of the sons of *A*
11:27 Israel and the sons of *A*
11:28 king of the sons of *A* did not
11:29 passed along to the sons of *A*
11:30 give the sons of *A* into my
11:31 in peace from the sons of *A*
11:32 sons of *A* to fight against
11:33 the sons of *A* were subdued
11:36 your enemies, the sons of *A*
12:1 to fight against the sons of *A*
12:2 with the sons of *A*
12:3 go over against the sons of *A*
1Sa 12:12 the king of the sons of *A*
14:47 and against the sons of *A*
2Sa 8:12 from the sons of *A* and
10:1 king of the sons of *A* came
10:2 the land of the sons of *A*
10:3 princes of the sons of *A*
10:6 sons of *A* saw that they had
10:6 sons of *A* proceeded to send
10:8 sons of *A* began to go out
10:10 to meet the sons of *A*
10:11 sons of *A* themselves become
10:14 sons of *A*, they saw that
10:14 returned from the sons of *A*
10:19 try saving the sons of *A*
11:1 sons of *A* to ruin and lay
12:9 the sword of the sons of *A*
12:26 Rabbah of the sons of *A* and
12:31 cities of the sons of *A*
17:27 Rabbah of the sons of *A*
1Ki 11:7 disgusting thing of . . . *A*
11:33 the god of the sons of *A*
2Ki 23:13 thing of the sons of *A*
24:2 bands of the sons of *A*
1Ch 18:11 from the sons of *A* and from
19:1 the king of the sons of *A*
19:2 the land of the sons of *A*
19:3 princes of the sons of *A* said
19:6 sons of *A* saw that they had
19:6 and Hanun and the sons of *A*
19:7 and as for the sons of *A*
19:9 sons of *A* began to go out
19:11 to meet the sons of *A*
19:12 if the sons of *A* themselves
19:15 sons of *A*, they saw that
19:19 to try saving the sons of *A*
20:1 the land of the sons of *A*
20:3 the cities of the sons of *A*
2Ch 20:1 sons of *A* and with them
20:10 sons of *A*, and Moab and the
20:22 against the sons of *A*
20:23 *A* and Moab proceeded to
27:5 king of the sons of *A* and
27:5 sons of *A* gave him in that
27:5 sons of *A* paid to him, also
Ps 83:7 Gebal and *A* and Amalek
Isa 11:14 *A* will be their subjects
Jer 9:26 and upon the sons of *A*
25:21 Moab and the sons of *A*
27:3 to the king of the sons of *A*
40:11 sons of *A* and in Edom
40:14 king of the sons of *A*
41:10 cross over to the sons of *A*
Jer 41:15 go to the sons of *A*
49:1 For the sons of *A* this is
49:2 Rabbah of the sons of *A*
49:6 captive ones of the sons of *A*
Eze 21:20 Rabbah of the sons of *A*
21:28 concerning the sons of *A*
25:2 face toward the sons of *A*
25:3 sons of *A*, Hear the word of
25:5 the sons of *A* a resting-place
25:10 alongside the sons of *A*
25:10 the sons of *A*, among the
Da 11:41 main part of the sons of *A*
Am 1:13 three revolts of . . . *A*
Zep 2:8 words of the sons of *A*
2:9 the sons of *A* like Gomorrah

Ammonim
2Ch 20:1 some of the *A* came against

Ammonite
De 23:3 No *A* or Moabite may come
1Sa 11:1 Nahash the *A* proceeded to go
11:2 Nahash the *A* said to them
2Sa 23:37 Zelek the *A*, Naharai the
1Ki 11:1 foreign wives . . . *A*
1Ch 11:39 Zelek the *A*, Naharai the
Ne 2:10 and Tobiah the servant, the *A*
2:19 Tobiah the servant, the *A*
4:3 Tobiah the *A* was alongside
13:1 the *A* and the Moabite should
13:23 *A* and Moabite wives

Ammonites
De 2:20 the *A* used to call them
1Sa 11:11 striking down the *A* till
1Ki 11:5 disgusting thing of the *A*
2Ch 26:8 *A* began to give tribute to
Ezr 9:1 the *A*, the Moabites, the
Ne 4:7 the Arabians and the *A* and

Ammonitess
1Ki 14:21 name was Naamah the *A*
14:31 name was Naamah the *A*
2Ch 12:13 name was Naamah the *A*
24:26 son of Shimeath the *A* and

Amnesty
Es 2:18 an *a* for the jurisdictional

Amnon
2Sa 3:2 firstborn came to be *A* by
13:1 *A* the son of David fell in
13:2 so distressing to *A* that he
13:2 difficult in the eyes of *A*
13:3 *A* had a companion whose
13:4 *A* said to him: With Tamar
13:6 *A* lay down and played sick
13:6 *A* said to the king: Please
13:7 house of *A* your brother and
13:8 the house of *A* her brother
13:9 *A* refused to eat and said
13:10 *A* now said to Tamar: Bring
13:10 them in to *A* her brother
13:15 *A* began hating her with a
13:15 *A* said to her: Get up, go
13:20 Was it *A* your brother that
13:22 did not speak with *A*
13:22 Absalom hated *A* over the
13:26 let *A* my brother go with
13:27 sent *A* and all the sons of
13:28 Strike down *A!* you must
13:29 do to *A* just as Absalom had
13:32 *A* alone that has died
13:33 it is *A* alone that has died
13:39 comforted . . . concerning *A*
1Ch 3:1 firstborn *A*, of Ahinoam the
4:20 the sons of Shimon were *A*

Amnon's
2Sa 13:28 *A* heart is in a merry mood

Amok
Ne 12:7 Sallu, *A*, Hilkiah, Jedaiah
12:20 Kallai; for *A*, Eber

Amon
1Ki 22:26 *A* the chief of the city and
2Ki 21:18 *A* his son began to reign
21:19 Twenty-two years old was *A*
21:23 servants of *A* conspired
21:24 conspirators against King *A*
21:25 the rest of the affairs of *A*
1Ch 3:14 *A* his son, Josiah his son
2Ch 18:25 *A* the chief of the city and
33:20 *A* his son began to reign in
33:21 Twenty-two years old was *A*
33:22 *A* sacrificed, and he
33:23 *A* was one that made

2Ch 33:25 conspirators against King *A*
Ne 7:59 the sons of *A*
Jer 1:2 days of Josiah the son of *A*
25:3 Josiah the son of *A*, the king
46:25 my attention upon *A* from
Zep 1:1 Josiah the son of *A* the king
Mt 1:10 Manasseh became father to *A*
1:10 *A* became father to Josiah

Among*
Ex 15:11 Who *a* the gods is like you
2Ch 32:14 *a* all the gods of these
Ne 6:6 *A* the nations it has been
Ps 9:11 Tell *a* the peoples his deeds
22:18 They apportion my garments *a*
Mr 6:4 *a* his relatives and in his own
Joh 1:14 flesh and resided *a* us
Ac 20:30 from *a* you yourselves men
Jas 4:1 are there fights *a* you? Are
1Pe 4:12 puzzled at the burning *a* you

Amorite
Ge 10:16 Jebusite and the *A* and the
14:13 big trees of Mamre the *A*
De 2:24 the king of Heshbon, the *A*
1Ch 1:14 the Jebusite and the *A* and
Eze 16:3 Your father was the *A*, and
16:45 and your father was an *A*
Am 2:9 I had annihilated the *A* on
2:10 of the land of the *A*

Amorites
Ge 14:7 *A* who were dwelling in
15:16 error of the *A* has not yet
15:21 the *A* and the Canaanites and
48:22 took from the hand of the *A*
Ex 3:8 to the locality of . . . the *A*
3:17 to the land of . . . the *A*
13:5 into the land of the . . . *A*
23:23 bring you to the *A* and the
33:2 and drive out the . . . *A* and
34:11 driving out . . . the *A*
Nu 13:29 the *A* are dwelling in the
21:13 from the border of the *A*
21:13 between Moab and the *A*
21:21 to Sihon the king of the *A*
21:25 in all the cities of the *A*
21:26 He was the king of the *A*
21:29 to the king of the *A*, Sihon
21:31 dwell in the land of the *A*
21:32 dispossessed the *A* who were
21:34 Sihon, the king of the *A*
22:2 that Israel had done to the *A*
32:33 of Sihon the king of the *A*
32:39 drive away the *A* who were
De 1:4 Sihon the king of the *A*, who
1:7 mountainous region of the *A*
1:19 mountainous region of the *A*
1:20 mountainous region of the *A*
1:27 give us into the hand of the *A*
1:44 the *A* who were dwelling in
3:2 Sihon the king of the *A*, who
3:8 the two kings of the *A* who
3:9 the *A* used to call it Senir
4:46 Sihon the king of the *A*, who
4:47 the two kings of the *A* who
7:1 the *A* and the Canaanites and
20:17 the *A*, the Canaanites and the
31:4 the kings of the *A*, and to
Jos 2:10 the two kings of the *A* who
3:10 and the *A* and the Jebusites
5:1 kings of the *A*, who were on
7:7 into the hand of the *A* for
9:1 the Hittites and the *A*, the
9:10 to the two kings of the *A*
10:5 five kings of the *A*, the king
10:6 all the kings of the *A*
10:12 abandoning the *A* to the sons
11:3 the *A* and the Hittites and
12:2 Sihon the king of the *A*
12:8 the Hittites, the *A* and the
13:4 far as the border of the *A*
13:10 Sihon the king of the *A*
13:21 Sihon the king of the *A*
24:8 the land of the *A* who were
24:11 of Jericho, the *A* and the
24:12 two kings of the *A*—not
24:15 the gods of the *A* in whose
24:18 *A*, dwelling in the land
Jg 1:34 the *A* kept pressing the sons
1:35 the *A* persisted in dwelling
1:36 the territory of the *A* was
3:5 dwelt in among . . . the *A* and
6:10 the gods of the *A* in whose
10:8 the land of the *A* that was in
10:11 and from the *A* and from the
11:19 Sihon the king of the *A*, the
11:21 land of the *A* inhabiting that
11:22 territory of the *A* from the
11:23 that dispossessed the *A* from
1Sa 7:14 between Israel and the *A*
2Sa 21:2 of the remainder of the *A*
1Ki 4:19 Sihon the king of the *A*, and
9:20 remaining over from the *A*
21:26 as all that the *A* had done
2Ki 21:11 the *A* did that were prior
2Ch 8:7 left over of the . . . *A* and
Ezr 9:1 the Egyptians and the *A*
Ne 9:8 the *A* and the Perizzites and
Ps 135:11 Sihon the king of the *A*
136:19 Even Sihon the king of the *A*

Amos
Am 1:1 The words of *A*, who happened
7:8 What are you seeing, *A?*
7:10 *A* has conspired against you
7:11 this is what *A* has said
7:12 Amaziah proceeded to say to *A*
7:14 Then *A* answered and said to
8:2 What are you seeing, *A?*
Lu 3:25 son of *A*, son of Nahum, son

Amount
Ge 6:3 his days shall *a* to a hundred
23:9 full *a* of silver let him give
23:13 give you the *a* of silver for
23:16 the *a* of silver that he had
47:26 to have to the *a* of a fifth
Ex 5:8 *a* of bricks that they were
5:18 give the fixed *a* of bricks
16:4 pick up each his *a* day for day
30:23 cinnamon in half that *a*
38:24 the *a* of the gold of the wave
Le 6:5 for it in its full *a*, and he
25:8 *a* to forty-nine years for you
27:23 *a* of the valuation up till
27:25 should *a* to twenty gerahs
Nu 5:7 return the *a* of his guilt in
5:8 return the *a* of the guilt, the
5:8 *a* of the guilt that is being
1Ki 10:11 almug trees in very great *a*
2Ch 3:8 the *a* of six hundred talents
32:27 and glory to a very great *a*
Job 21:15 What does the Almighty *a* to
42:10 had been Job's, in double *a*
Ps 139:17 grand sum of them *a* to
Isa 40:2 full *a* for all her sins
Jer 16:18 I will repay the full *a*
Eze 24:12 the great *a* of its rust
45:11 come to be but one fixed *a*
45:11 required *a* should prove to
Da 11:28 with a great *a* of goods
Na 2:9 a heavy *a* of all sorts of
Ro 8:18 do not *a* to anything in

Amounted
Ge 5:5 days of Adam . . . *a* to nine
5:8 So all the days of Seth *a* to
5:11 all the days of Enosh *a* to
5:14 all the days of Kenan *a* to
5:17 all the days of Mahalalel *a*
5:20 days of Jared *a* to nine
5:23 all the days of Enoch *a* to
5:27 days of Methuselah *a* to
5:31 all the days of Lamech *a* to
9:29 days of Noah *a* to nine hundred
Ex 36:30 *a* to eight panel frames and
Nu 16:49 dead from the scourge *a* to
25:9 died from the scourge *a* to
26:7 their registered ones *a* to
26:62 their registered ones *a* to
31:32 plunder, *a* to six hundred and
31:36 *a* in number to three hundred
31:37 tax for Jehovah . . . *a* to
31:43 flock *a* to three hundred and
31:52 contributed to Jehovah *a* to
Jos 8:25 *a* to twelve thousand, all
Jg 8:26 gold that he had requested *a*
20:46 that fell on that day *a* at
1Sa 7:2 that they *a* to twenty years
11:8 *a* to three hundred thousand
14:14 *a* to about twenty men
2Sa 24:9 *a* to eight hundred thousand
1Ki 5:13 *a* to thirty thousand men
10:14 *a* up to six hundred and
1Ch 21:5 all Israel *a* to a million
2Ch 9:13 *a* to six hundred and
Job 6:21 you men have *a* to nothing

Amounting
Ex 38:26 *a* to six hundred and three

Amounts
Zec 2:2 to see what her breadth *a* to
2:2 and what her length *a* to

Amoz
2Ki 19:2 Isaiah . . . the son of *A*
19:20 And Isaiah the son of *A*
20:1 Isaiah the son of *A* the
2Ch 26:22 Isaiah the son of *A* the
32:20 Isaiah the son of *A*, the
32:32 prophet, the son of *A*, in
Isa 1:1 vision of Isaiah the son of *A*
2:1 Isaiah the son of *A* visioned
13:1 Isaiah the son of *A* saw in
20:2 Isaiah the son of *A*, saying
37:2 Isaiah the son of *A* the
37:21 Isaiah the son of *A*
38:1 the son of *A* the prophet

Amphipolis
Ac 17:1 They now journeyed through *A*

Ample
Ge 9:27 Let God grant *a* space to
26:22 Jehovah has given us *a* room

Ampliatus
Ro 16:8 to *A* my beloved in the Lord

Amputate
De 25:12 you must then *a* her hand

Amram
Ex 6:18 sons of Kohath were *A* and
6:20 *A* took Jochebed his father's
Nu 3:19 sons of Kohath . . . *A* and Izhar
26:58 Kohath became father to *A*
26:59 bore to *A* Aaron and Moses
1Ch 6:2 sons of Kohath were *A*, Izhar
6:3 the sons of *A* were Aaron and
6:18 the sons of Kohath were *A* and
23:12 The sons of Kohath were *A*
23:13 sons of *A* were Aaron and
24:20 of the sons of *A* there was
Ezr 10:34 sons of Bani, Maadai, *A*

Amramites
Nu 3:27 family of the *A* and the
1Ch 26:23 For the *A*, for the Izharites

Amram's
Ex 6:20 the years of *A* life were a
Nu 26:59 name of *A* wife was Jochebed

Amraphel
Ge 14:1 days of *A* king of Shinar
14:9 *A* king of Shinar and

Amusement
Jg 16:25 that he may offer us some *a*
16:27 while Samson offered some *a*

Amzi
1Ch 6:46 the son of *A*, the son of Bani
Ne 11:12 *A* the son of Zechariah

Anab
Jos 11:21 from *A* and from all the
15:50 *A* and Eshtemoh and Anim

Anah
Ge 36:2 Oholibamah the daughter of *A*
36:14 Oholibamah the daughter of *A*
36:18 Oholibamah the daughter of *A*
36:20 sons of Seir . . . *A*
36:24 sons of Zibeon: Aiah and *A*
36:24 *A* who found the hot springs
36:25 children of *A:* Dishon and
36:25 Oholibamah the daughter of *A*
36:29 sheiks of the Horite . . . *A*
1Ch 1:38 sons of Seir were . . . *A*
1:40 sons of Zibeon were . . . *A*
1:41 sons of *A* were Dishon

Anaharath
Jos 19:19 Hapharaim and Shion and *A*

Anak
Nu 13:22 those born of *A*, were there
13:28 those born of *A* we saw there
13:33 the Nephilim, the sons of *A*
De 9:2 stand before the sons of *A*
Jos 15:13 Arba being the father of *A*
15:14 the three sons of *A*, namely
15:14 and Talmai, those born of *A*
21:11 Arba being the father of *A*
Jg 1:20 the three sons of *A*

Anakim
De 1:28 sons of the *A* we saw there
2:10 numerous and tall like the *A*
2:11 were considered like the *A*

De 2:21 tall people like the *A;* and
9:2 the sons of *A*, about whom
Jos 11:21 went and cut off the *A*
11:22 No *A* were left in the land
14:12 that there were *A* there and
14:15 the great man among the *A*

Anamim
Ge 10:13 Mizraim became father . . . *A*
1Ch 1:11 Ludim and *A* and Lehabim

Anammelech
2Ki 17:31 *A* the gods of Sepharvaim

Anan
Ne 10:26 and Ahijah, Hanan, *A*

Anani
1Ch 3:24 sons of Elioenai were . . . *A*

Ananiah
Ne 3:23 Maaseiah the son of *A* did
8:4 and *A* and Uriah and Hilkiah
10:22 Pelatiah, Hanan, *A*
11:32 Anathoth, Nob, *A*

Ananias
Ac 5:1 man, *A* by name, together
5:3 *A*, why has Satan emboldened
5:5 *A* fell down and expired
9:10 disciple named *A*, and the
9:10 said to him in a vision: *A!*
9:12 man named *A* come in and lay
9:13 *A* answered: Lord, I have
9:17 *A* went off and entered into
22:12 *A*, a certain man reverent
23:2 high priest *A* ordered those
24:1 the high priest *A* came down

Anath
Jg 3:31 Shamgar the son of *A*, and he
5:6 days of Shamgar the son of *A*

Anathoth
Jos 21:18 *A* and its pasture ground
1Ki 2:26 Go to *A* to your fields
1Ch 6:60 *A* with its pasture grounds
7:8 the sons of Becher were . . . *A*
Ezr 2:23 the men of *A*, a hundred and
Ne 7:27 men of *A*, a hundred and
10:19 Hariph, *A*, Nebai
11:32 *A*, Nob, Ananiah
Isa 10:30 O you afflicted one, *A!*
Jer 1:1 *A* in the land of Benjamin
11:21 against the men of *A*
11:23 calamity upon the men of *A*
29:27 rebuked Jeremiah of *A*, who
32:7 field of mine that is in *A*
32:8 field of mine that is in *A*
32:9 the field that was in *A*

Anathothite
2Sa 23:27 Abi-ezer the *A*, Mebunnai
1Ch 11:28 Abi-ezer the *A*
12:3 Beracah and Jehu the *A*
27:12 was Abi-ezer the *A* of the

Ancestors
Le 26:45 *a* whom I brought forth out
De 19:14 the *a* will have set the
Ezr 4:15 the book of records of your *a*
Ps 79:8 not remember . . . errors of *a*

Ancestral
Ex 12:3 a sheep for the *a* house, a
De 18:8 things he sells of his *a* goods
Ac 22:3 the strictness of the *a* Law

Anchor
Ac 27:13 lifted *a* and began coasting
Heb 6:19 This hope we have as an *a*

Anchored
Ge 49:13 where the ships lie *a;* and
Mr 6:53 came into Gennesaret and *a*

Anchors
Ac 27:29 cast out four *a* from the
27:30 let down *a* from the prow
27:40 cutting away the *a*, they

Ancient
De 33:27 is the God of *a* time
Jg 5:21 The torrent of *a* days, the
Ps 68:33 One riding on the *a* heaven
Isa 19:11 son of kings of *a* time
Da 7:9 and the *A* of Days sat down
7:13 *A* of Days he gained access
7:22 *A* of Days came and judgment
Mt 5:21 said to those of *a* times
5:33 said to those of *a* times, You
Lu 9:8 one of the *a* prophets had risen
Lu 9:19 that one of the *a* prophets has
Ac 15:21 from *a* times Moses has had
2Pe 2:5 punishing an *a* world, but

Ancients
1Sa 24:13 the proverb of the *a* says

Andrew
Mt 4:18 Peter and *A* his brother
10:2 Peter, and *A* his brother; and
Mr 1:16 and *A* the brother of Simon
1:29 into the home of Simon and *A*
3:18 *A* and Philip and Bartholomew
13:3 *A* began to ask him privately
Lu 6:14 Peter, and *A* his brother, and
Joh 1:40 *A* the brother of Simon Peter
1:44 the city of *A* and Peter
6:8 *A* the brother of Simon Peter
12:22 Philip came and told *A*
12:22 *A* and Philip came and told
Ac 1:13 and *A*, Philip and Thomas

Andronicus
Ro 16:7 Greet *A* and Junias my

Anem
1Ch 6:73 *A* with its pasture grounds

Aner
Ge 14:13 Mamre . . . brother of *A*
14:24 men who went with me, *A*
1Ch 6:70 *A* with its pasture grounds

Anew
1Sa 11:14 there make the kingship *a*
Isa 61:4 make *a* the devastated cities

Angel
Ge 16:7 Later Jehovah's *a* found her
16:9 Jehovah's *a* went on to say to
16:10 Jehovah's *a* said to her: I
16:11 *a* added to her: Here you are
21:17 God's *a* called to Hagar out
22:11 Jehovah's *a* began calling to
22:15 Jehovah's *a* proceeded to call
24:7 he will send his *a* ahead of
24:40 send his *a* with you and will
31:11 *a* of the true God said to
48:16 *a* who has been recovering me
Ex 3:2 Jehovah's *a* appeared to him in
14:19 *a* of the true God who was
23:20 sending an *a* ahead of you to
23:23 my *a* will go ahead of you
32:34 My *a* will go ahead of you
33:2 I will send an *a* ahead of you
Nu 20:16 sent an *a* and brought us out
22:22 and Jehovah's *a* proceeded to
22:23 ass got to see Jehovah's *a*
22:24 Jehovah's *a* kept standing in
22:25 kept seeing Jehovah's *a* and
22:26 Jehovah's *a* now passed by
22:27 ass got to see Jehovah's *a*
22:31 Jehovah's *a* stationed in the
22:32 Jehovah's *a* said to him: Why
22:34 Balaam said to Jehovah's *a*
22:35 Jehovah's *a* said to Balaam
Jg 2:1 Then Jehovah's *a* went up from
2:4 *a* had spoken these words to
5:23 Curse Meroz, said the *a* of
6:11 *a* came and sat under the big
6:12 *a* appeared to him and said to
6:20 The *a* of the true God now
6:21 *a* thrust out the tip of the
6:21 *a*, he vanished from his sight
6:22 that it was Jehovah's *a*
6:22 seen Jehovah's *a* face to face
13:3 *a* appeared to the woman
13:6 appearance of the *a* of the
13:9 the *a* of the true God came
13:13 Jehovah's *a* said to Manoah
13:15 said to Jehovah's *a:* Let us
13:16 Jehovah's *a* said to Manoah
13:16 know that he was Jehovah's *a*
13:17 Manoah said to Jehovah's *a*
13:18 Jehovah's *a* said to him
13:20 Jehovah's *a* ascended in the
13:21 *a* did not repeat appearing to
13:21 he had been Jehovah's *a*
1Sa 29:9 like an *a* of God
2Sa 14:17 like an *a* of the true God
14:20 *a* of the true God so as to
19:27 my lord the king is as an *a*
24:16 the *a* kept his hand thrust
24:16 *a* that was bringing ruin
24:16 *a* himself happened to be
24:17 *a* that was striking the
1Ki 13:18 an *a* himself spoke to me by
1Ki 19:5 now an *a* was touching him
19:7 the *a* of Jehovah came back a
2Ki 1:3 *a* of Jehovah, he spoke to
1:15 *a* of Jehovah spoke to Elijah
19:35 night that the *a* of Jehovah
1Ch 21:12 Jehovah's *a* bringing ruin in
21:15 God sent an *a* to Jerusalem
21:15 the *a* that was bringing the
21:15 Jehovah's *a* was standing
21:16 to see Jehovah's *a* standing
21:18 Jehovah's *a*, for his part
21:20 turned back and saw the *a*
21:27 said the word to the *a*
21:30 the sword of Jehovah's *a*
2Ch 32:21 send an *a* and efface every
Ps 34:7 The *a* of Jehovah is camping
35:5 Jehovah's *a* be pushing them
35:6 let Jehovah's *a* be pursuing
Ec 5:6 neither say before the *a* that
Isa 37:36 *a* of Jehovah proceeded to
Da 3:28 God . . . sent his *a* and rescued
6:22 My own God sent his *a* and
Ho 12:4 he kept contending with an *a*
Zec 1:9 *a* who was speaking with me
1:11 answer the *a* of Jehovah who
1:12 *a* of Jehovah answered and
1:13 the *a* who was speaking with
1:14 the *a* who was speaking with
1:19 *a* who was speaking with me
2:3 *a* who was speaking with me
2:3 *a* going forth to meet him
3:1 before the *a* of Jehovah
3:2 *a* of Jehovah said to Satan
3:3 and standing before the *a*
3:5 *a* of Jehovah was standing by
3:6 *a* of Jehovah began to bear
4:1 the *a* who was speaking with
4:4 *a* who was speaking with me
4:5 *a* who was speaking with me
5:5 *a* who was speaking with me
5:10 *a* who was speaking with me
6:4 *a* who was speaking with me
6:5 *a* answered and said to me
12:8 like Jehovah's *a* before them
Mt 1:20 Jehovah's *a* appeared to him
1:24 *a* of Jehovah had directed
2:13 *a* appeared in a dream to
2:19 *a* appeared in a dream to
28:2 for Jehovah's *a* had descended
28:5 the *a* in answer said to the
Lu 1:11 To him Jehovah's *a* appeared
1:13 the *a* said to him: Have no
1:18 Zechariah said to the *a*
1:19 In reply the *a* said to him
1:26 the *a* Gabriel was sent forth
1:30 the *a* said to her: Have no
1:34 But Mary said to the *a*
1:35 In answer the *a* said to her
1:38 the *a* departed from her
2:9 Jehovah's *a* stood by them
2:10 the *a* said to them: Have no
2:13 there came to be with the *a*
2:21 name called by the *a* before
22:43 an *a* from heaven appeared to
Joh 12:29 An *a* has spoken to him
Ac 5:19 Jehovah's *a* opened the doors
7:30 *a* in the fiery flame of a
7:35 *a* that appeared to him in the
7:38 *a* that spoke to him on Mount
8:26 Jehovah's *a* spoke to Philip
10:3 *a* of God come in to him and
10:7 *a* that spoke to him had left
10:22 instructions by a holy *a* to
11:13 *a* stand in his house and say
12:7 Jehovah's *a* stood by, and a
12:8 *a* said to him: Gird yourself
12:9 happening through the *a* was
12:10 the *a* departed from him
12:11 Jehovah sent his *a* forth
12:15 began to say: It is his *a*
12:23 *a* of Jehovah struck him
23:8 Sadducees say . . . nor *a* nor
23:9 a spirit or an *a* spoke to him
27:23 *a* of the God to whom I
2Co 11:14 Satan . . . into an *a* of light
12:7 *a* of Satan, to keep slapping
Ga 1:8 *a* out of heaven were to
4:14 received me like an *a* of God
Re 1:1 he sent forth his *a* and
2:1 To the *a* of the congregation
2:8 *a* of the congregation in
2:12 *a* of the congregation in
2:18 to the *a* of the congregation
3:1 *a* of the congregation in

Re 3:7 *a* of the congregation in
3:14 *a* of the congregation in
5:2 *a* proclaiming with a loud
7:2 another *a* ascending from the
8:3 another *a* arrived and stood at
8:4 from the hand of the *a* with
8:5 the *a* took the incense vessel
8:8 the second *a* blew his trumpet
8:10 the third *a* blew his trumpet
8:12 fourth *a* blew his trumpet
9:1 the fifth *a* blew his trumpet
9:11 a king, the *a* of the abyss
9:13 the sixth *a* blew his trumpet
9:14 say to the sixth *a*, who had
10:1 I saw another strong *a*
10:5 the *a* that I saw standing on
10:7 sounding of the seventh *a*
10:8 in the hand of the *a* who is
10:9 I went away to the *a* and told
10:10 out of the hand of the *a* and
11:15 seventh *a* blew his trumpet
14:6 *a* flying in midheaven, and
14:8 second *a*, followed, saying
14:9 *a*, a third, followed them
14:15 *a* emerged from the temple
14:17 *a* emerged from the temple
14:18 *a* emerged from the altar
14:19 *a* thrust his sickle into the
16:5 the *a* over the waters say
17:7 *a* said to me: Why is it you
18:1 *a* descending from heaven
18:21 strong *a* lifted up a stone
19:17 an *a* standing in the sun
20:1 *a* coming down out of heaven
22:6 sent his *a* forth to show
22:8 *a* that had been showing me
22:16 I, Jesus, sent my *a* to bear

Angel's
Ac 6:15 his face was as an *a* face
Re 21:17 at the same time an *a*

Angels
Ge 19:1 the two *a* arrived at Sodom by
19:15 the *a* became urgent with Lot
28:12 there were God's *a* ascending
32:1 the *a* of God now met up with
Ps 78:49 Deputations of *a* bringing
91:11 own *a* a command concerning
103:20 Bless Jehovah, O you *a* of
104:4 Making his *a* spirits, His
148:2 Praise him, all you his *a*
Mt 4:6 He will give his *a* a charge
4:11 *a* came and began to minister
13:39 and the reapers are *a*
13:41 will send forth his *a*, and
13:49 *a* will go out and separate
16:27 Son of man . . . with his *a*
18:10 their *a* in heaven always
22:30 but are as *a* in heaven
24:31 And he will send forth his *a*
24:36 neither the *a* of the heavens
25:31 all the *a* with him, then
25:41 for the Devil and his *a*
26:53 than twelve legions of *a*
Mr 1:13 *a* were ministering to him
8:38 his Father with the holy *a*
12:25 but are as *a* in the heavens
13:27 he will send forth the *a* and
13:32 the *a* in heaven nor the Son
Lu 2:15 when the *a* had departed from
4:10 He will give his *a* a charge
9:26 the Father and of the holy *a*
12:8 with him before the *a* of God
12:9 disowned before the *a* of God
15:10 joy arises among the *a* of
16:22 carried off by the *a* to the
20:36 for they are like the *a*, and
24:23 a supernatural sight of *a*
Joh 1:51 *a* of God ascending and
20:12 two *a* in white sitting one
Ac 7:53 Law as transmitted by *a* but
Ro 8:38 nor *a* nor governments nor
1Co 4:9 to the world, and to *a*, and
6:3 know that we shall judge *a*
11:10 because of the *a*
13:1 tongues of men and of *a* but
Ga 3:19 transmitted through *a* by
Col 2:18 a form of worship of the *a*
2Th 1:7 Jesus . . . with his powerful *a*
1Ti 3:16 appeared to *a*, was preached
5:21 Christ Jesus and the chosen *a*
Heb 1:4 has become better than the *a*
1:5 to which one of the *a* did he
1:6 all God's *a* do obeisance to
Heb 1:7 with reference to the *a* he
1:7 he makes his *a* spirits, and
1:13 to which one of the *a* has
2:2 the word spoken through *a*
2:5 it is not to *a* that he has
2:7 him a little lower than *a*
2:9 made a little lower than *a*
2:16 he is really not assisting *a*
12:22 Jerusalem, and myriads of *a*
13:2 some . . . entertained *a*
1Pe 1:12 *a* are desiring to peer
3:22 and *a* and authorities and
2Pe 2:4 punishing the *a* that sinned
2:11 *a*, although they are greater
Jude 6 *a* that did not keep their
Re 1:20 stars mean the *a* of the
3:5 my Father and before his *a*
5:11 I heard a voice of many *a*
7:1 I saw four *a* standing upon the
7:2 four *a* to whom it was granted
7:11 And all the *a* were standing
8:2 I saw the seven *a* that stand
8:6 And the seven *a* with the seven
8:13 trumpet blasts of the three *a*
9:14 Untie the four *a* that are
9:15 And the four *a* were untied
12:7 Michael and his *a* battled
12:7 the dragon and its *a* battled
12:9 *a* were hurled down with him
14:10 the sight of the holy *a* and
15:1 seven *a* with seven plagues
15:6 seven *a* . . . the seven plagues
15:7 creatures gave the seven *a*
15:8 plagues of the seven *a* were
16:1 say to the seven *a*: Go and
17:1 one of the seven *a* that had
21:9 one of the seven *a* who had
21:12 and at the gates twelve *a*

Anger
Ge 4:5 Cain grew hot with great *a*
4:6 Why are you hot with *a* and
18:30 please, not grow hot with *a*
18:32 not grow hot with *a*, but
27:45 *a* of your brother turns away
30:2 Jacob's *a* burned against Rachel
31:35 Do not let *a* gleam in the
39:19 did to me, his *a* blazed
44:18 do not let your *a* grow hot
49:6 in their *a* they killed men
49:7 Cursed be their *a*, because it
Ex 4:14 Jehovah's *a* grew hot against
11:8 from Pharaoh in the heat of *a*
15:7 You send out your burning *a*
22:24 my *a* will indeed blaze, and
32:10 my *a* may blaze against them
32:11 O Jehovah, should your *a*
32:12 Turn from your burning *a* and
32:19 Moses' *a* began to blaze, and
32:22 the *a* of my lord blaze
34:6 slow to *a* and abundant in
Nu 11:1 *a* grew hot, and a fire of
11:10 Jehovah's *a* began growing
11:33 Jehovah's *a* blazed against
12:9 And Jehovah's *a* got to be hot
14:18 Jehovah, slow to *a* and
22:22 the *a* of God began to blaze
22:27 Balaam's *a* blazed, and he
24:10 Balak's *a* blazed against
25:3 *a* of Jehovah began to blaze
25:4 that the burning *a* of Jehovah
32:10 Jehovah's *a* blazed on that
32:13 Jehovah's *a* blazed against
32:14 *a* of Jehovah against Israel
De 6:15 for fear the *a* of Jehovah your
7:4 Jehovah's *a* will indeed blaze
9:8 you provoked Jehovah to *a* so
9:19 hot *a* with which Jehovah
9:22 provokers of Jehovah to *a*
11:17 Jehovah's *a* does blaze
13:17 turn from his burning *a*
29:20 Jehovah's *a* and his ardor
29:23 in his *a* and in his wrath
29:24 the heat of this great *a*
29:27 Jehovah's *a* blazed against
29:28 in *a* and rage and great
31:17 *a* will indeed blaze against
32:22 has been ignited in my *a*
Jos 7:1 Jehovah's *a* grew hot against
7:26 turned away from his hot *a*
23:16 Jehovah's *a* will certainly
Jg 2:14 Jehovah's *a* blazed against
2:20 Jehovah's *a* blazed against
3:8 Jehovah's *a* blazed against
Jg 6:39 your *a* blazed against me, but
9:30 Then his *a* blazed
10:7 *a* blazed against Israel, so
14:19 his *a* continued hot, and he
1Sa 11:6 and his *a* got very hot
17:28 Eliab's *a* grew hot against
20:30 Saul's *a* grew hot against
20:34 in the heat of *a*, and he
28:18 execute his burning *a*
2Sa 6:7 Jehovah's *a* blazed against
12:5 David's *a* grew very hot
24:1 *a* of Jehovah came to be hot
2Ki 13:3 Jehovah's *a* became hot
23:26 the great burning of his *a*
23:26 his *a* burned against Judah
24:20 account of the *a* of Jehovah
1Ch 13:10 Jehovah's *a* blazed against
2Ch 12:12 Jehovah's *a* turned back
25:10 *a* got very hot against Judah
25:10 in the heat of *a*
25:15 Jehovah's *a* became hot
28:11 Jehovah's burning *a* is
28:13 is burning *a* against Israel
29:10 burning *a* may turn back
30:8 his burning *a* may turn back
Ezr 8:22 his strength and his *a* are
10:14 burning *a* of our God from
Ne 9:17 slow to *a* and abundant in
13:18 the burning *a* against Israel
Job 4:9 through the spirit of his *a*
9:5 has overthrown them in his *a*
9:13 will not turn back his *a*
14:13 until your *a* turns back
16:9 His very *a* has torn me to
18:4 tearing his soul . . . in his *a*
19:11 *a* also grows hot against me
20:23 send his burning *a* upon him
20:28 on the day of his *a*
21:17 How many times in his *a*
32:2 the *a* of Elihu the son of
32:2 Against Job his *a* blazed over
32:3 his *a* blazed over the fact
32:5 his *a* kept getting hotter
35:15 his *a* has not called for an
36:13 will themselves lay up *a*
40:11 furious outburst of your *a*
42:7 My *a* has grown hot against
Ps 2:5 will speak to them in his *a*
2:12 For his *a* flares up easily
6:1 do not in your *a* reprove me
7:6 Do arise, O Jehovah, in your *a*
21:9 in his *a* will swallow them
27:9 Do not in *a* turn your servant
30:5 under his *a* is for a moment
37:8 Let *a* alone and leave rage
55:3 in *a* they harbor animosity
56:7 In *a* bring down even the
69:24 own burning *a* overtake them
74:1 *a* keep smoking against the
76:7 of the strength of your *a*
77:9 he shut off his mercies in *a*
78:21 *a* . . . ascended against Israel
78:38 he made his *a* turn back
78:49 sending . . . his burning *a*
78:50 prepare a pathway for his *a*
85:3 back from the heat of your *a*
85:5 draw out your *a* to generation
86:15 Slow to *a* and abundant in
88:16 flashes of burning *a* have
90:7 have come to an end in your *a*
90:11 the strength of your *a*
95:11 I swore in my *a*: They shall
103:8 Slow to *a* and abundant in
106:40 *a* of Jehovah began to blaze
110:5 pieces on the day of his *a*
124:3 *a* was burning against us
138:7 of the *a* of my enemies
145:8 Slow to *a* and great in
Pr 14:17 He that is quick to *a* will
14:29 is slow to *a* is abundant in
15:1 word causing pain makes *a* to
15:18 one that is slow to *a* quiets
16:32 slow to *a* is better than a
19:11 insight . . . slows down his *a*
21:14 made in secrecy subdues *a*
22:24 with anyone given to *a*
24:18 certainly turn back his *a*
27:4 also the flood of *a*, but who
29:8 who are wise turn back *a*
29:22 *a* stirs up contention, and
30:33 squeezing out of *a* is what
Isa 5:25 *a* of Jehovah has grown hot
5:25 his *a* has not turned back
7:4 hot *a* of Rezin and Syria

Isa 9:12 his *a* has not turned back
9:17 his *a* has not turned back
9:21 his *a* has not turned back
10:4 his *a* has not turned back
10:5 Assyrian, the rod for my *a*
10:25 my *a*, in their wearing
12:1 *a* gradually turned back, and
13:3 ones for expressing my *a*
13:9 fury and with burning *a*
13:13 the day of his burning *a*
14:6 subduing nations in sheer *a*
30:27 burning with his *a* and
30:30 in the raging of *a* and the
42:25 *a*, and the strength of war
48:9 I shall check my *a*, and for
63:3 I kept treading them in my *a*
63:6 down peoples in my *a*
66:15 pay back his *a* with sheer
Jer 2:35 Surely his *a* has turned back
4:8 *a* of Jehovah has not turned
4:26 because of his burning *a*
7:20 My *a* and my rage are being
10:24 judgment; not in your *a*
12:13 the burning *a* of Jehovah
15:14 has been ignited in my *a*
15:15 In your slowness to *a* do
17:4 have been ignited in my *a*
18:23 In the time of your *a* take
21:5 with *a* and with rage and
23:20 The *a* of Jehovah will not
25:37 the burning *a* of Jehovah
25:38 because of his burning *a*
30:24 burning *a* of Jehovah will
32:31 cause of *a* in me and a
32:37 dispersed them in my *a* and
33:5 struck down in my *a* and in
36:7 *a* and the rage that Jehovah
42:18 my *a* and my rage have been
44:6 my *a*, was poured out and it
49:37 calamity, my burning *a*
51:45 the burning *a* of Jehovah
52:3 account of the *a* of Jehovah
La 1:12 in the day of his burning *a*
2:1 Jehovah in his *a* beclouds the
2:1 footstool in the day of his *a*
2:3 In the heat of *a* he has cut
2:21 killed in the day of your *a*
3:43 have blocked approach with *a*
3:66 pursue in *a* and annihilate
4:11 has poured out his burning *a*
Eze 5:13 my *a* will certainly come to
5:15 in you acts of judgment in *a*
7:3 I must send my *a* against you
7:8 bring my *a* against you to its
13:13 in my *a* there will occur a
20:8 my *a* to its finish upon them
20:21 to bring my *a* to its finish
22:20 in my *a* and in my rage
25:14 in Edom according to my *a*
35:11 according to your *a* and
43:8 exterminating them in my *a*
Da 9:16 *a* and your rage turn back
11:20 broken, but not in *a* nor in
Ho 8:5 My *a* has grown hot against
11:9 not express my burning *a*
13:11 to give you a king in my *a*
14:4 *a* has turned back from him
Joe 2:13 slow to *a* and abundant in
Am 1:11 *a* keeps tearing away forever
Jon 3:9 turn back from his burning *a*
4:1 and he got to be hot with *a*
4:2 slow to *a* and abundant in
4:4 you rightly become hot with *a*
4:9 *a* over the bottle-gourd plant
4:9 *a*, to the point of death
Mic 5:15 in *a* and in rage I will
7:18 not hold onto his *a* forever
Na 1:3 Jehovah is slow to *a* and great
1:6 up against the heat of his *a*
Hab 2:15 your rage and *a*, in order to
3:8 that your *a* has become hot
3:12 In *a* you went threshing the
Zep 2:2 the burning *a* of Jehovah
2:2 the day of Jehovah's *a*
2:3 in the day of Jehovah's *a*
3:8 pour out . . . all my burning *a*
Zec 10:3 my *a* has grown hot, and
Lu 4:28 became filled with *a*
Ac 15:39 occurred a sharp burst of *a*
19:28 becoming full of *a*, the men
Ro 2:8 there will be wrath and *a*
10:19 incite you to violent *a*
2Co 12:20 cases of *a*, contentions
Ga 5:20 fits of *a*, contentions
Eph 4:31 *a* and wrath and screaming
Col 3:8 *a*, badness, abusive speech
Heb 3:8 occasion of causing bitter *a*
3:11 I swore in my *a*, They shall
3:15 occasion of causing bitter *a*
3:16 and yet provoked to bitter *a*
4:3 I swore in my *a*, They shall
11:27 fearing the *a* of the king
Re 12:12 having great *a*, knowing he
14:8 of the *a* of her fornication
14:10 the wine of the *a* of God
14:19 winepress of the *a* of God
15:1 *a* of God is brought to a
15:7 were full of the *a* of God
16:1 seven bowls of the *a* of God
16:19 wine of the *a* of his wrath
18:3 the wine of the *a* of her
19:15 winepress of the *a* of the

Angered
2Sa 22:8 because he had been *a*
Ps 18:7 because he had been *a*

Angrily
Jer 3:12 *a* upon you people, for I am

Angry
Ge 31:36 Jacob became *a* and began to
34:7 and they grew very *a*, because
45:5 do not be *a* with yourselves
Nu 16:15 Moses became very *a* and said
1Sa 18:8 And Saul began to be very *a*
20:7 he should at all become *a*
2Sa 3:8 Abner got very *a* at the words
6:8 David became *a* over the fact
13:21 and he became very *a*
19:42 become *a* over this thing
1Ch 13:11 And David became *a* because
Ne 4:1 became *a* and highly offended
4:7 they became very *a*
5:6 *a* as soon as I heard their
Ps 18:48 from my *a* enemies; Above
Ca 1:6 sons of my own mother grew *a*
La 2:6 in his *a* denunciation he shows
Da 2:12 king himself became *a* and got
Joh 7:23 violently *a* at me because I
Col 3:19 not be bitterly *a* with them

Anguish
Job 15:24 and *a* keep terrifying him
Eze 7:25 There will come *a*, and they
Zep 1:15 a day of distress and of *a*
Lu 16:24 am in *a* in this blazing fire
16:25 here but you are in *a*
21:25 on the earth *a* of nations
2Co 2:4 *a* of heart I wrote you with

Aniam
1Ch 7:19 sons of Shemida . . . *A*

Anim
Jos 15:50 Anab and Eshtemoh and *A*

Animal
Ge 1:24, 24 domestic *a* and moving *a*
1:25 domestic *a* according to its
1:25 every moving *a* of the ground
1:26 moving *a* . . . upon the earth
6:7 from man to domestic *a*, to
6:7 to moving *a* and to flying
7:14 every domestic *a* according
7:14 every moving *a* that moves on
7:23 wiped out . . . moving *a* and
8:1 every domestic *a* that was with
8:19 every moving *a* . . . went out
9:3 moving *a* that is alive may
31:39 Any *a* torn to pieces I did
49:27 he will eat the *a* seized
Ex 20:10 nor your domestic *a* nor your
21:34 dead *a* will become his own
22:10 any domestic *a* to keep, and
Le 5:2 body of an unclean domestic *a*
7:24 fat of an *a* torn to pieces
24:18 of the soul of a domestic *a*
25:7 domestic *a* and for the wild
Nu 31:30 of every sort of domestic *a*
De 5:14 nor any domestic *a* of yours
Jg 20:48 from men to domestic *a* up
Ne 2:12 no domestic *a* with me except
2:12 *a* on which I was riding
2:14 no place for the domestic *a*
Ps 50:10 every wild *a* of the forest
50:11 the *a* throngs of the open
80:13 *a* throngs of the open field
Pr 12:10 the soul of his domestic *a*
Isa 11:6 well-fed *a* all together
Jer 7:20 upon domestic *a*, and upon
Jer 31:27 with the seed of domestic *a*
32:43 without man and domestic *a*
33:10 man and without domestic *a*
33:10 without domestic *a*, there
33:12 man and even domestic *a* and
50:3 domestic *a* have taken flight
51:62 or even domestic *a*, but
Eze 4:14 nor a torn *a* have I eaten
14:13 man and domestic *a*
14:17 man and domestic *a*
14:19 man and domestic *a*
14:21 man and domestic *a*
25:13 man and domestic *a*, and
29:8 earthling man and domestic *a*
29:11 the foot of domestic *a*
32:13 a domestic *a* muddy them
34:3 *a* is what you slaughter
Joe 1:18 the domestic *a* has sighed
Jon 3:7 No man and no domestic *a*, no
3:8 sackcloth, man and domestic *a*
Hag 1:11 and upon domestic *a*, and
Zec 9:9 *a* the son of a she-ass
14:15 every sort of domestic *a*
Mal 1:8 a blind *a* for sacrificing
1:8 present a lame *a* or a sick
1:14 in his drove a male *a*, and
Jas 3:15 is the earthly, *a*, demonic

Animalistic
Jude 19 *a* men, not having

Animalkind
Eze 36:11 multiply upon you . . . *a*

Animals
Ge 1:26 domestic *a* and all the earth
2:20 names of all the domestic *a*
3:14 out of all the domestic *a*
6:20 domestic *a* according to their
6:20 all moving *a* of the ground
7:21 among the domestic *a* and
8:17 all the moving *a* that move
43:16 slaughter *a* and make
47:18 the stock of domestic *a* have
Ex 12:38 a very numerous stock of *a*
Le 1:2 offering . . . the domestic *a*
19:19 interbreed your domestic *a*
26:22 cut off your domestic *a* and
Nu 3:41 domestic *a* of the Levites in
3:41 among the domestic *a* of
3:45 domestic *a* of the Levites in
3:45 in place of their domestic *a*
31:9 all their domestic *a* and all
31:11 way of humans and domestic *a*
31:26 captives . . . of domestic *a*
31:47 humankind and of domestic *a*
32:26 domestic *a* will stay there
35:3 serve for their domestic *a*
De 2:35 *a* did we take as plunder for
3:7 the domestic *a* and the spoil
7:14 nor among your domestic *a*
11:15 for your domestic *a*
13:15 domestic *a*, to destruction
20:14 domestic *a* and everything
28:11 the fruit of your domestic *a*
28:51 fruit of your domestic *a*
30:9 fruit of your domestic *a* and
Jos 8:2 its spoil and its domestic *a*
8:27 the domestic *a* and the spoil
11:14 and the domestic *a* the
21:2 grounds for our domestic *a*
2Ki 3:9 camp and for the domestic *a*
3:17 and your domestic *a*
Ezr 1:4 goods and with domestic *a*
1:6 domestic *a* and with choice
Ne 9:37 and over our domestic *a*
10:36 sons and of our domestic *a*
Job 12:7 domestic *a* . . . will instruct
Ps 104:20 wild *a* of the forest move
148:10 You wild *a* and all you
148:10 and all you domestic *a*
Pr 12:27 start up one's game *a*, but
Isa 1:11 and the fat of well-fed *a*
5:17 places of well-fed *a*
34:14 meet up with howling *a*
40:16 wild *a* are not sufficient
46:1 and for the domestic *a*
46:1 a burden for the tired *a*
56:9 wild *a* of the open field
56:9 you wild *a* in the forest
Jer 10:21 *a* have been scattered
50:8 leading *a* before the flock
50:39 dwell with the howling *a*
51:23 his span of *a* to pieces
Eze 32:13 destroy all her domestic *a*

Jon 4:11 besides many domestic *a*
Na 2:12 with *a* torn to pieces
Zep 2:14 all the wild *a* of a nation
2:15 wild *a* to lie stretched out
Zec 2:4 domestic *a* in the midst of
8:10 the wages of domestic *a*
Mt 22:4 fattened *a* are slaughtered
Heb 13:11 *a* whose blood is taken into
2Pe 2:12 *a* born naturally to be
Jude 10 like the unreasoning *a*, in

Animosity
Ge 27:41 Esau harbored *a* for Jacob
49:23 kept harboring *a* against him
50:15 Joseph is harboring *a*
Job 16:9 and he harbors *a* against me
30:21 you harbor *a* toward me
Ps 55:3 they harbor *a* against me
Ho 9:7 even *a* being abundant
9:8 *a* in the house of his God

Ankle
Nu 31:50 gold, *a* chainlets, and
Ac 3:7 his *a* bones were made firm

Ankles
2Sa 22:37 *a* will certainly not wobble
Ps 18:36 *a* will certainly not wobble
Eze 47:3 water up to the *a*

Anna
Lu 2:36 Now there was *A* a prophetess

Annas
Lu 3:2 in the days of chief priest *A*
Joh 18:13 they led him first to *A*
18:24 *A* sent him away bound to
Ac 4:6 *A* the chief priest and

Annex
Isa 5:8 those who *a* field to field

Annihilate
Le 26:30 *a* your sacred high places and
Nu 33:52 high places you should *a*
De 1:27 he brought us out . . . to *a* us
2:12 dispossess them and to *a* them
6:15 *a* you from off the surface of
7:4 certainly *a* you in a hurry
9:3 will *a* them, and he himself
9:14 *a* them and wipe out their
28:63 to destroy you and to *a* you
31:3 will *a* these nations from
33:27 And he will say, *A* them!
Jos 7:12 you *a* the thing devoted to
9:24 to *a* all the inhabitants of
11:20 order that he might *a* them
1Sa 24:21 not *a* my name out of the
2Sa 14:7 and let us even *a* the heir
14:11 that they may not *a* my son
14:16 man seeking to *a* me and
21:5 schemed to *a* us from
22:38 enemies, that I may *a* them
2Ch 20:10 and did not *a* them
20:23 to destruction and *a* them
Es 3:6 seeking to *a* all the Jews
3:13 to *a*, to kill and to destroy
8:11 to *a* and kill and destroy all
Ps 106:23 about to say to *a* them
106:34 They did not *a* the peoples
145:20 wicked ones he will *a*
Isa 10:7 to *a* is in his heart, and
13:9 *a* the land's sinners out of
23:11 Phoenicia, to *a* her
26:14 you might *a* them and
La 3:66 *a* them from under the heavens
Eze 14:9 *a* him from the midst of my
25:7 I shall *a* you, and you will
34:16 and the strong one I shall *a*
Da 7:26 *a* him and to destroy him
11:44 rage in order to *a* and to
Am 9:8 *a* it from upon the surface
9:8 *a* the house of Jacob
Mic 5:14 and *a* your cities
Hag 2:22 *a* the strength of the
Zec 12:9 seek to *a* all the nations
Lu 9:54 fire . . . from heaven and *a*

Annihilated
Ge 34:30 I must be *a*, I and my house
De 2:22 he *a* the Horites from before
2:23 *a* them, that they might dwell
4:3 your God *a* from your midst
4:26 you will positively be *a*
7:23 rout, until they are *a*
12:30 been *a* from before you, and
28:20 until you have been *a* and
28:24 until you have been *a*
28:45 until you have been *a*
28:48 until he has *a* you
28:51 until you have been *a*, and
28:61 until you have been *a*
31:4 to their land, when he *a* them
Jos 11:14 until they had *a* them
23:15 until he has *a* you from
24:8 I *a* them from before you
Jg 21:16 womankind has been *a* out of
1Ki 15:29 until he had *a* them
16:12 *a* the whole house of Baasha
2Ki 10:17 until he had *a* them
10:28 Jehu *a* Baal out of Israel
21:9 nations whom Jehovah had *a*
1Ch 5:25 whom God had *a* from before
2Ch 33:9 nations that Jehovah had *a*
Es 4:8 in Shushan to have them *a*
7:4 to be *a*, killed and destroyed
Ps 37:38 will certainly be *a* together
83:10 They were *a* at En-dor; They
92:7 is that they may be *a* forever
Pr 14:11 house of wicked people . . . *a*
Isa 48:19 cut off or be *a* from before
Jer 48:8 and the level land be *a*
48:42 Moab will certainly be *a*
Eze 32:12 all her crowd must be *a*
Ho 10:8 Israel, will actually be *a*
Am 2:9 I had *a* the Amorite on account
Ga 5:15 do not get *a* by one another

Annihilating
De 2:21 Jehovah went *a* them from
9:8 to the point of *a* you
9:19 to the point of *a* you
9:20 incensed to the point of *a*
9:25 Jehovah talked of *a* you
1Ki 13:34 *a* them off the surface of
Am 2:9 I went *a* his fruitage above

Annihilation
Isa 14:23 her with the broom of *a*

Announce
Ge 41:16 God will *a* welfare to
De 20:10 *a* to it terms of peace
2Sa 1:20 not *a* it in the streets of
1Ch 16:23 *A* from day to day the
Isa 60:6 praises of Jehovah . . . *a*

Announced
Ac 3:18 he *a* beforehand through the
1Pe 1:12 have now been *a* to you

Announcement
Ex 36:6 *a* to pass through the camp
Ac 7:52 those who made *a* in advance
Ro 15:21 no *a* has been made about him

Announcing
1Jo 1:5 *a* to you, that God is light

Annoy
Ru 2:22 not *a* you in another field

Annoyed
Ac 4:2 *a* because they were teaching

Annul
Nu 30:13 or her husband should *a* it

Annulled
Nu 30:8 he has also *a* her vow that
30:12 if her husband has totally *a*
30:12 Her husband has *a* them, and
Da 6:8 law of the Medes . . . not *a*
6:12 law of the Medes . . . not *a*

Annuls
Nu 30:15 if he totally *a* them after

Anoint
Ex 28:41 *a* them and fill their hand
29:7 pour it upon his head and *a*
29:29 sons after him to *a* them
29:36 must *a* it to sanctify it
30:26 must *a* with it the tent of
30:30 will *a* Aaron and his sons
40:9 *a* the tabernacle and all that
40:10 *a* the altar of burnt offering
40:11 *a* the basin and its stand
40:13 and *a* him and sanctify him
40:15 *a* them just as you anointed
Nu 7:1 *a* it and to sanctify it and all
Jg 9:8 trees went to *a* a king over
1Sa 9:16 *a* him as leader over my
15:1 I whom Jehovah sent to *a* you
15:17 to *a* you as king over Israel
16:3 you must *a* for me the one
16:12 *a* him, for this is he
1Ki 1:34 Nathan the prophet must *a*
1Ki 19:15 *a* Hazael as king over Syria
19:16 should *a* as king over Israel
19:16 *a* as prophet in place of you
2Ki 9:3 I do *a* you as king over Israel
9:6 *a* you as king over Jehovah's
9:12 *a* you as king over Israel
1Ch 29:22 *a* him to Jehovah as leader
Isa 21:5 you princes, *a* the shield
Da 9:24 and to *a* the Holy of Holies

Anointed
Ge 31:13 where you *a* a pillar and
Ex 40:15 just as you *a* their father
Le 4:3 If the priest, the *a* one, sins
4:5 the priest, the *a* one, must
4:16 the priest, the *a* one, must
6:20 on the day of his being *a*
6:22 the one *a* in place of him
8:10 and *a* the tabernacle and all
8:11 and *a* the altar and all its
8:12 *a* him so as to sanctify him
16:32 priest who will be *a* and
Nu 3:3 *a* priests whose hands had been
7:1 he *a* them and sanctified them
7:10 on the day of its being *a*
7:84 day of its being *a*, on the
7:88 the altar after its being *a*
35:25 who was *a* with the holy oil
1Sa 2:10 exalt the horn of his *a* one
2:35 walk before my *a* one always
10:1 Jehovah has *a* you as a leader
12:3 and in front of his *a* one
12:5 and his *a* one is a witness
16:6 his *a* one is before Jehovah
16:13 *a* him in the midst of his
24:6 my lord, the *a* of Jehovah
24:6 for he is the *a* of Jehovah
24:10 for he is the *a* of Jehovah
26:9 against the *a* of Jehovah and
26:11 against the *a* of Jehovah
26:16 over the *a* of Jehovah
26:23 against the *a* of Jehovah
2Sa 1:14 the *a* of Jehovah to ruin
1:16 the *a* of Jehovah to death
1:21 there was none *a* with oil
2:4 men of Judah came and *a* David
2:7 house of Judah have *a* as king
3:39 weak although *a* as king, and
5:3 *a* David as king over Israel
5:17 *a* David as king over Israel
12:7 *a* you as king over Israel
19:10 Absalom, whom we *a* over us
19:21 called evil down upon the *a*
22:51 loving-kindness to his *a* one
23:1 The *a* of the God of Jacob
1Ki 1:39 horn of oil . . . *a* Solomon
1:45 *a* him as king in Gihon
5:1 *a* as king in place of his
2Ki 11:12 made him king and *a* him
23:30 *a* him and made him king in
1Ch 11:3 they *a* David as king over
14:8 David had been *a* as king over
16:22 not you men touch my *a* ones
2Ch 6:42 back the face of your *a* one
22:7 Jehovah had *a* to cut off the
23:11 Jehoiada and his sons *a* him
Ps 2:2 Jehovah and against his *a* one
18:50 loving-kindness to his *a* one
20:6 Jehovah certainly saves his *a*
28:8 grand salvation of his *a* one
45:7 God, has *a* you with the oil
84:9 upon the face of your *a* one
89:20 With my holy oil I have *a*
89:38 furious toward your *a* one
89:51 footprints of your *a* one
105:15 not you men touch my *a* ones
132:10 back the face of your *a* one
132:17 a lamp for my *a* one
Isa 45:1 said to his *a* one, to Cyrus
61:1 *a* me to tell good news to
La 4:20 the *a* one of Jehovah, has been
Eze 28:14 *a* cherub that is covering
Hab 3:13 to save your *a* one
Zec 4:14 two *a* ones who are standing
Lu 4:18 *a* me to declare good news to
Ac 4:26 and against his *a* one
4:27 servant Jesus, whom you *a*
10:38 God *a* him with holy spirit
2Co 1:21 and he who has *a* us is God
Heb 1:9 God, *a* you with the oil of

Anointing
Ex 25:6 balsam oil for the *a* oil
29:7 take the *a* oil and pour it
29:21 *a* oil, and you must spatter

Ex 30:25 a holy *a* oil, an ointment
30:25 It is to be a holy *a* oil
30:31 to continue as a holy *a* oil
31:11 the *a* oil and the perfumed
35:8 balsam oil for the *a* oil
35:15 the *a* oil and the perfumed
35:28 *a* oil and for the perfumed
37:29 the holy *a* oil and the pure
39:38 altar of gold and the *a* oil
40:9 take the *a* oil and anoint the
40:15 *a* must serve continually
Le 7:36 day of his *a* them from among
8:2 the garments and the *a* oil and
8:10 took the *a* oil and anointed
8:12 the *a* oil upon Aaron's head
8:30 some of the *a* oil and some of
10:7 Jehovah's *a* oil is upon you
21:10 *a* oil would be poured and
21:12 sign of dedication, the *a* oil
Nu 4:16 *a* oil, the oversight of all
Jg 9:15 you are *a* me as king over you
Am 6:6 the choicest oils do their *a*
1Jo 2:20 have an *a* from the holy one
2:27 the *a* that you received from
2:27 *a* from him is teaching you

Answer

Ge 18:27 Abraham went on to *a* and
27:37 in *a* to Esau Isaac continued
27:39 in *a* Isaac his father said
30:33 right-doing must *a* for me
31:31 In *a* Jacob proceeded to say
31:36 in *a* Jacob went on to say to
31:43 Laban in *a* said to Jacob
34:13 Jacob's sons began to *a*
45:3 his brothers were unable to *a*
Ex 19:19 God began to *a* him with a
28:38 Aaron must *a* for the error
Le 5:1 then he must *a* for his error
5:17 and must *a* for his error
7:18 soul that eats . . . will *a* for
10:17 that you may *a* for the error
17:16 he must then *a* for his error
19:8 one eating it will *a* for his
20:17 He should *a* for his error
20:19 They should *a* for their error
20:20 They should *a* for their sin
24:15 he must then *a* for his sin
Nu 5:31 wife will *a* for her error
9:13 For his sin that man will *a*
14:33 will have to *a* for your acts
14:34 *a* for your errors forty years
18:1 *a* for error against the
18:1 will *a* for error against your
18:23 who should *a* for their error
De 20:11 if it gives a peaceful *a*
21:7 *a* and say, Our hands did not
25:9 spit in his face and *a* and say
26:5 *a* and say before Jehovah your
27:14 the Levites must *a* and say
27:15 the people must *a* and say
31:21 *a* before them as a witness
Jg 5:29 her noble ladies would *a* her
1Sa 4:20 she did not *a* and did not set
7:9 Jehovah proceeded to *a* him
8:18 Jehovah will not *a* you in
9:19 Samuel proceeded to *a* Saul
12:3 *A* against me in front of
14:37 did not *a* him on that day
16:18 proceeded to *a* and say: Look!
20:10 father may *a* you is harsh
26:14 Will you not *a*, Abner?
26:14 Abner began to *a* and say
2Sa 22:42 he actually does not *a* them
1Ki 12:7 *a* them and speak to them
12:13 to *a* the people harshly
18:21 not say a word in *a* to him
18:26 saying: O Baal, *a* us!
18:37, 37 *A* me, O Jehovah, *a* me
2Ki 4:29 you must not *a* him. And you
18:36 did not *a* him a word
18:36 saying: You must not *a* him
2Ch 10:13 began to *a* them harshly
Job 6:1 And Job proceeded to *a* and say
8:1 the Shuhite proceeded to *a* and
9:1 And Job proceeded to *a* and say
9:3 *a* him once out of a thousand
9:14 in case I myself *a* him
9:15 I would not *a*, even though
9:16 If I called him, would he *a*
9:32 like me that I should *a* him
11:1 Zophar . . . proceeded to *a* and
12:1 Job proceeded to *a* and say
12:4 to God that he should *a* him

Job 13:22 call that I myself may *a*
13:22 may I speak, and you . . . *a*
14:15 call, and I myself shall *a*
15:1 Eliphaz . . . proceeded to *a*
15:2 *a* with windy knowledge
15:6 your own lips *a* against you
16:1 Job proceeded to *a* and say
16:3 what galls you, that you *a*?
18:1 the Shuhite proceeded to *a*
19:1 Job proceeded to *a* and say
19:7 but I get no *a*; I keep crying
19:16 my servant . . . does not *a*
20:2 thoughts themselves *a* me
21:1 Job proceeded to *a* and say
22:1 the Temanite proceeded to *a*
23:1 Job proceeded to *a* and say
25:1 the Shuhite proceeded to *a*
26:1 Job proceeded to *a* and say
30:20 but you do not *a* me
31:14 what can I *a* him
31:35 Almighty himself would *a*
32:3 they had not found an *a* but
32:5 no *a* in the mouth of the
32:6 the Buzite proceeded to *a* and
32:17 I shall give in *a* my part
32:20 open my lips that I may *a*
33:12 been in the right, I *a* you
33:13 your words he does not *a*
34:1 Elihu continued to *a* and
35:12 but he does not *a*, Because
38:1 Jehovah proceeded to *a* Job
40:1 Jehovah proceeded to *a* Job
40:2 reprover of God himself *a* it
40:3 Job went on to *a* Jehovah and
40:5 spoken, and I will not *a*
40:6 Jehovah went on to *a* Job
42:1 Job proceeded to *a* Jehovah
Ps 3:4 *a* me from his holy mountain
4:1 *a* me, O my righteous God
13:3 *a* me, O Jehovah my God
17:6 because you will *a* me, O God
18:41 he actually does not *a* them
20:1 *a* you in the day of distress
20:9 *a* us in the day that we call
22:2 calling . . . and you do not *a*
22:21 you must *a* and save me
27:7 And show me favor and *a* me
38:15 You yourself proceeded to *a*
55:2 pay attention to me and *a* me
55:19 God will hear and *a* them
60:5 right hand and *a* us
65:5 you will *a* us, O God of our
69:13 *a* me with the truth of
69:16 *A* me, O Jehovah, for your
69:17 sore straits, *a* me quickly
81:7 *a* you in the concealed place
86:1 Jehovah, your ear. *A* me
86:7 For you will *a* me
91:15 upon me, and I shall *a* him
102:2 that I call, hurry, *a* me
108:6 your right hand and *a* me
119:26 that you may *a* me
119:42 *a* the one reproaching me
119:145 *A* me, O Jehovah
120:1 And he proceeded to *a* me
138:3 you also proceeded to *a* me
143:1 In your faithfulness *a* me
143:7 O hurry, *a* me, O Jehovah
Pr 1:28 calling me, but I shall not *a*
15:1 An *a*, when mild, turns away
15:23 has rejoicing in the *a* of his
15:28 meditates so as to *a*, but
16:1 from Jehovah is the *a* of the
26:4 not *a* anyone stupid according
26:5 *A* someone stupid according to
Ca 5:6 I called him, but he did not *a*
Isa 14:32 *a* to the messengers of the
30:19 he will actually *a* you
36:21 did not *a* him a word, for
36:21 You must not *a* him
41:17 Jehovah, shall *a* them
46:7 to it, but it does not *a*
50:4 know how to *a* the tired one
58:9 and Jehovah himself would *a*
65:12 called, but you did not *a*
65:24 call out I myself shall *a*
Jer 7:13 but you did not *a*
7:27 but they will not *a* you
11:5 I proceeded to *a* and say
23:37 What *a* has Jehovah given
33:3 I shall *a* you and readily
35:17 to them but they did not *a*
42:4 Jehovah gives in *a* to you
44:15 to *a* Jeremiah, saying

Eze 14:4 myself be brought to *a* him
14:7 brought to *a* him by myself
Ho 2:15 *a* there as in the days of
2:21 in that day that I shall *a*
2:21 I shall *a* the heavens, and
2:21 their part, will *a* the earth
2:22 earth, for its part, will *a*
2:22 their part, will *a* Jezreel
14:8 give an *a* and I shall keep
Joe 2:19 Jehovah will *a* and say to
Jon 2:2 and he proceeded to *a* me
Mic 3:4 but he will not *a* them
3:7 for there is no *a* from God
Hab 2:2 Jehovah proceeded to *a* me
2:11 a rafter itself will *a* it
Hag 2:12 proceeded to *a* and say: No!
Zec 1:11 *a* the angel of Jehovah who
1:13 to *a* the angel who was
4:11 to *a* and say to him: What do
6:4 to *a* and say to the angel who
10:6 God, and I shall *a* them
13:9 I, for my part, will *a* it
Mt 12:38 as an *a* to him some of the
12:48 As an *a* he said to the one
15:23 he did not say a word in *a*
15:24 In *a* he said: I was not sent
15:26 *a* he said: It is not right
16:16 In *a* Simon Peter said: You
20:22 Jesus said in *a*: You men do
21:21 In *a* Jesus said to them
21:27 in *a* to Jesus they said: We
21:29 In *a* this one said, I will
24:4 And in *a* Jesus said to them
25:12 In *a* he said, I tell you the
25:37 righteous ones will *a* him
25:44 will *a* with the words, Lord
25:45 Then he will *a* them with
26:33 But Peter, in *a*, said to him
26:62 said to him: Have you no *a*?
26:66 *a*: He is liable to death
27:12 he made no *a*
27:14 he did not *a* him, no, not a
27:25 people said in *a*: His blood
28:5 angel in *a* said to the women
Mr 8:29 In *a* Peter said to him
10:3 In *a* he said to them
10:51 And in *a* to him Jesus said
11:29 You *a* me, and I will also
11:30 heaven or from men? *A* me
14:40 they did not know what to *a*
15:2 In *a* to him he said
15:5 Jesus made no further *a*, so
Lu 1:35 In *a* the angel said to her
3:16 John gave the *a*, saying to
4:12 In *a* Jesus said to him: It is
5:22 said in *a* to them: What are
7:22 in *a* he said to the two
7:43 In *a* Simon said: I suppose
10:27 In *a* he said: You must love
10:41 In *a* the Lord said to her
11:45 In *a* a certain one of those
13:25 But in *a* he will say to you
14:6 not able to *a* back on these
20:26 in amazement at his *a*, they
22:68 you would not *a* at all
23:3 In *a* he said: You yourself
23:9 but he made him no *a*
24:18 In *a* the one named Cleopas
Joh 1:22 an *a* to those who sent us
1:48 Jesus in *a* said to him
1:50 Jesus in *a* said to him
2:18 in *a*, the Jews said to him
2:19 In *a* Jesus said to them
3:3 In *a* Jesus said to him
3:9 In *a* Nicodemus said to him
3:10 In *a* Jesus said to him
3:27 In *a* John said: A man cannot
4:10 In *a* Jesus said to her
4:13 In *a* Jesus said to her
4:17 In *a* the woman said: I do
5:19 In *a*, Jesus went on to say
6:29 In *a* Jesus said to them
6:43 In *a* Jesus said to them
7:21 In *a* Jesus said to them
7:52 In *a* they said to him
8:14 In *a* Jesus said to them
8:39 In *a* they said to him
8:48 In *a* the Jews said to him
9:20 Then in *a* his parents said
9:30 In *a* the man said to them
9:34 In *a* they said to him: You
12:30 In *a* Jesus said: This voice
13:7 In *a* Jesus said to him
14:23 *a* Jesus said to him: If

Joh 18:22 way you *a* the chief priest
18:30 In *a* they said to him
19:9 But Jesus gave him no *a*
20:28 In *a* Thomas said to him
Ac 5:29 In *a* Peter and the other
8:24 In *a* Simon said: You men
8:34 In *a* the eunuch said to
19:15 in *a* the wicked spirit said
2Co 5:12 *a* for those who boast over
Col 4:6 ought to give an *a* to each one

Answered
Ge 22:11 to which he *a:* Here I am!
23:5 Heth *a* Abraham, saying to him
23:10 So Ephron the Hittite *a*
23:14 Ephron *a* Abraham, saying to
24:50 Laban and Bethuel *a* and said
30:17 God heard and *a* Leah
30:22 God heard and *a* her in that
31:14 Rachel and Leah *a* and said
35:3 God who *a* me in the day of
40:18 Joseph *a* and said: This is
41:16 Joseph *a* Pharaoh, saying
42:22 Then Reuben *a* them, saying
Ex 19:8 all the people *a* unanimously
24:3 all the people *a* with one
Nu 22:18 But Balaam *a* and said to the
23:12 In turn he *a* and said: Is it
23:26 Balaam *a* and said to Balak
32:31 and the sons of Reuben *a*
De 1:14 At that you *a* me and said
1:41 you *a* and said to me, We have
Jos 1:16 they *a* Joshua, saying: All
7:20 Achan *a* Joshua and said: For
9:24 Then they *a* Joshua and said
22:21 half tribe of Manasseh *a*
24:16 the people *a* and said
Jg 7:14 companion *a* and said: This
8:8 Penuel *a* him just as the men
8:8 as the men of Succoth had *a*
18:14 *a* and said to their brothers
20:4 *a* and said: It was to Gibeah
Ru 2:6 *a* and said: The young woman is
2:11 Then Boaz *a* and said to her
1Sa 1:15 At this Hannah *a* and said
1:17 Eli *a* and said: Go in peace
4:17 the news bearer *a* and said
9:8 attendant *a* Saul once more
9:12 Then they *a* them and said
9:17 Jehovah, for his part, *a* him
9:21 At this Saul *a* and said
10:12 a man from there *a* and said
14:12 So the men . . . *a* Jonathan
14:28 one of the people *a* and said
20:28 Jonathan *a* Saul: David
20:32 Jonathan *a* Saul his father
21:4 priest *a* David and said
21:5 David *a* the priest and said
22:9 *a* and said: I saw the son of
22:14 Ahimelech *a* the king and
23:4 Jehovah now *a* him and said
25:10 Nabal *a* David's servants
26:6 David *a* and said to
26:22 David *a* and said: Here is
28:6 Jehovah never *a* him, either
28:15 and has *a* me no more
29:9 Achish *a* and said to David
30:22 *a* and kept saying
2Sa 4:9 David *a* Rechab and Baanah his
13:32 David's brother, *a* and said
14:18 king now *a* and said to the
14:19 woman *a* and said: As your
15:21 Ittai *a* the king and said
19:21 *a* and said: In return for
19:42 all the men of Judah *a* the
19:43 *a* the men of Judah and said
20:20 To this Joab *a* and said
1Ki 1:28 King David now *a* and said
1:36 Benaiah . . . *a* the king and
1:43 Jonathan *a* and said to
2:22 Solomon *a* and said to his
2:30 and this is what he *a* me
3:27 the king *a* and said: You men
13:6 The king now *a* and said to
18:24 all the people *a* and said
20:4 the king of Israel *a* and said
20:11 the king of Israel *a* and
2Ki 1:10 Elijah *a* and spoke to the
1:11 he *a* and spoke to him: Man
1:12 Elijah *a* and spoke to them
3:11 *a* and said: There is here
7:2 *a* the man of the true God
7:13 one of his servants *a* and
7:19 adjutant *a* the man of the
1Ch 12:17 and *a* and said to them
1Ch 21:26 *a* him with fire from the
21:28 Jehovah had *a* him at the
2Ch 29:31 Hezekiah *a* and said: Now
34:15 Hilkiah *a* and said to
Ezr 10:2 sons of Elam *a* and said to
10:12 all the congregation *a* and
Ne 8:6 all the people *a*, Amen! Amen!
Es 5:7 To this Esther *a* and said
7:3 Esther the queen *a* and said
Job 1:7 Satan *a* Jehovah and said
1:9 Satan *a* Jehovah and said
2:2 Satan *a* Jehovah and said
2:4 But Satan *a* Jehovah and said
3:2 Job now *a* and said
32:15 they have *a* no more
32:16 stood still, they *a* no more
Ps 34:4 inquired of Jehovah, and he *a*
99:8 God, you yourself *a* them
118:5 Jah *a* and put me into a
118:21 I shall laud you, for you *a*
Pr 21:13 will call and not be *a*
Ca 2:10 My dear one has *a* and said to
Isa 49:8 time of goodwill I have *a*
Jer 23:35 What has Jehovah *a?*
Da 2:7 *a* a second time and were
2:10 Chaldeans *a* before the king
3:9 They *a*, and they were saying
3:16 and Abednego *a* and they were
5:10 queen *a* and said: O king
6:13 Immediately they *a*, and they
Am 7:14 Amos *a* and said to Amaziah
Mic 6:5 Balaam the son of Beor *a*
Hag 2:13 priests *a* and said: It will
2:14 Haggai *a* and said: That is
Zec 1:10 *a* and said: These are the
1:12 angel of Jehovah *a* and said
3:4 he *a* and said to those
4:4 *a* and said to the angel who
4:5 *a* and said to me: Do you not
4:6 he *a* and said to me: This is
4:12 *a* the second time and said
6:5 the angel *a* and said to me
Mt 9:28 They *a* him: Yes, Lord
25:9 discreet *a* with the words
Mr 8:4 But his disciples *a* him
9:17 one of the crowd *a* him
12:28 had *a* them in a fine way
12:29 Jesus *a:* The first is, Hear
12:34 he had *a* intelligently, said
Lu 1:60 But its mother *a* and said
8:50 Jesus *a* him: Have no fear
10:28 You *a* correctly; keep on
13:15 the Lord *a* him and said
17:20 he *a* them and said: The
Joh 1:21 The Prophet? And he *a:* No!
1:26 *a* them, saying: I baptize
1:49 Nathanael *a* him: Rabbi, you
3:5 Jesus *a:* Most truly I say to
5:7 sick man *a* him: Sir, I do not
5:11 he *a* them: The very one that
5:17 he *a* them: My Father has
6:7 Philip *a* him: Two hundred
6:26 Jesus *a* them and said
6:68 Peter *a* him: Lord, whom
6:70 Jesus *a* them: I chose you
7:16 Jesus, in turn, *a* them and
7:20 crowd *a:* You have a demon
7:47 Pharisees *a:* You have not
8:19 Jesus *a:* You know neither
8:34 Jesus *a* them: Most truly
8:49 Jesus *a:* I do not have a
8:54 Jesus *a:* If I glorify myself
9:3 Jesus *a:* Neither this man
9:11 He *a:* The man called Jesus
9:25 he *a:* Whether he is a sinner
9:27 He *a* them: I told you
9:36 man *a:* And who is he, sir
10:25 Jesus *a* them: I told you
10:33 The Jews *a* him: We are
10:34 Jesus *a* them: Is it not
11:9 Jesus *a:* There are twelve
12:23 But Jesus *a* them, saying
12:34 crowd *a* him: We heard from
13:8 Jesus *a* him: Unless I wash
13:26 Jesus *a:* It is that one to
13:36 Jesus *a:* Where I am going
13:38 Jesus *a:* Will you surrender
16:31 Jesus *a* them: Do you
18:5 *a* him: Jesus the Nazarene
18:8 Jesus *a:* I told you I am he
18:20 Jesus *a* him: I have spoken
18:23 Jesus *a* him: If I spoke
18:34 Jesus *a:* Is it of your own
18:35 Pilate *a:* I am not a Jew
Joh 18:36 Jesus *a:* My kingdom is no
18:37 Jesus *a:* You yourself are
19:7 Jews *a* him: We have a law
19:11 Jesus *a* him: You would
19:15 *a:* We have no king but
19:22 Pilate *a:* What I have
21:5 They *a* No! to him
Ac 9:13 Ananias *a:* Lord, I have heard
11:9 voice from heaven *a*, You
15:13 James *a*, saying: Men
21:13 Paul *a:* What are you doing
22:8 I *a*, Who are you, Lord?
24:10 *a:* Knowing well that this
24:25 *a:* For the present go your
25:4 Festus *a* that Paul was to be

Answering
Ex 4:1 However, Moses in *a* said
Jg 19:28 But there was no one *a*
1Sa 14:39 no one *a* him out of all the
1Ki 18:26 and there was no one *a*
18:29 and there was no one *a*, and
Job 5:1 Is there anyone *a* you? And to
32:1 three men ceased from *a* Job
32:12 None of you *a* his sayings
35:1 Elihu continued *a* and saying
Ps 99:6 and he himself kept *a* them
Isa 50:2 called, there was nobody *a*
66:4 but there was no one *a*
Jer 44:20 *a* him with a word, saying
Da 2:5 *a* and saying to the Chaldeans
2:8 The king was *a* and saying
2:15 *a* and saying to Arioch the
2:20 Daniel was *a* and saying
2:26 was *a* and saying to Daniel
2:27 Daniel was *a* before the king
2:47 king was *a* Daniel and saying
3:14 Nebuchadnezzar was *a* and
3:19 *a* and saying to heat up the
3:24 He was *a* and saying to his
3:24 *a* and saying to the king
3:25 *a* and saying: Look! I am
3:26 He was *a* and saying: Shadrach
3:28 Nebuchadnezzar was *a* and
4:19 The king was *a* and saying
4:19 Belteshazzar was *a* and saying
4:30 The king was *a* and saying
5:7 king was *a* and saying to the
5:17 Daniel was *a* and saying
6:12 The king was *a* and saying
6:16 king was *a* and saying to
Mal 2:12 *a*, from the tents of Jacob
Ro 9:20 are you to be *a* back to God

Answers
1Ki 18:24 the true God that *a* by fire
Job 23:5 words with which he *a* me
Ps 20:6 *a* him from his holy heavens
Pr 18:23 rich *a* in a strong way
Lu 2:47 at his understanding and his *a*

Ant
Pr 6:6 Go to the *a*, you lazy one

Antagonist
Isa 50:8 Who is my judicial *a?*

Antagonists
Job 22:20 our *a* have been effaced

Antelope
De 14:5 *a* and wild sheep and chamois

Anthothijah
1Ch 8:24 and Hananiah and Elam and *A*

Antichrist
1Jo 2:18 have heard that *a* is coming
2:22 This is the *a*, the one that
2Jo 7 This is the deceiver and the *a*

Antichrist's
1Jo 4:3 is the *a* inspired expression

Antichrists
1Jo 2:18 have come to be many *a*

Anti-Lebanon
Ca 4:8 you descend from the top of *A*

Antioch
Ac 6:5 Nicolaus, a proselyte of *A*
11:19 Phoenicia and Cyprus and *A*
11:20 that came to *A* and began
11:22 out Barnabas as far as *A*
11:26 he brought him to *A*
11:26 was first in *A* that the
11:27 down from Jerusalem to *A*
13:1 in *A* there were prophets and
13:14 and came to *A* in Pisidia

Ac 14:19 But Jews arrived from *A* and
14:21 and to Iconium and to *A*
14:26 they sailed off for *A*
15:22 men from among them to *A*
15:23 to those brothers in *A* and
15:30 they went down to *A*, and
15:35 in *A* teaching and declaring
18:22 and went down to *A*
Ga 2:11 when Cephas came to *A*, I
2Ti 3:11 happened to me in *A*, in

Antipas
Re 2:13 *A*, my witness, the faithful

Antipatris
Ac 23:31 brought him by night to *A*

Antiquity
Mal 3:4 and as in the years of *a*

Ants
Pr 30:25 the *a* are a people not strong

Anub
1Ch 4:8 Koz, he became father to *A*

Anvil
Isa 41:7 is hammering away at the *a*

Anxieties
Mt 6:34 next day will have its own *a*
Mr 4:19 *a* of this system of things
Lu 8:14 carried away by *a* and riches
21:34 and *a* of life, and suddenly

Anxiety
Mt 13:22 *a* of this system of things
1Co 7:32 I want you to be free from *a*
2Co 11:28 *a* for all the congregations
1Pe 5:7 you throw all your *a* upon

Anxious
Ge 32:7 very much afraid and grew *a*
Jos 22:24 rather out of *a* care for
1Sa 9:5 actually become *a* about us
10:2 has become *a* about you men
Job 20:22 he will be feeling *a*
Ps 38:18 I began to be *a* over my sin
Pr 12:25 *A* care in the heart of a man
Isa 35:4 those who are *a* at heart
Jer 17:8 he will not become *a*, nor will
49:23 sea there is *a* care
Eze 4:16 by weight and in *a* care
12:18 with *a* care your water you
12:19 With *a* care . . . will eat
Mt 6:25 Stop being *a* about your souls
6:27 Who of you by being *a* can add
6:28 why are you *a*? Take a lesson
6:31 never be *a* and say, What are
6:34 never be *a* about the next day
10:19 do not become *a* about how
Mr 13:11 do not be *a* beforehand about
Lu 10:41 Martha, Martha, you are *a*
12:11 do not become *a* about how
12:22 Quit being *a* about your souls
12:25 by being *a* can add a cubit to
12:26 why be *a* about the remaining
12:29 quit being in *a* suspense
1Co 7:32 unmarried man is *a* for the
7:33 married man is *a* for the
7:34 is *a* for the things of the
7:34 is *a* for the things of
Php 4:6 Do not be *a* over anything

Anxiously
Job 35:14 you should wait *a* for him

Anybody
Ge 26:11 *A* touching this man and his
Ex 19:12 *A* touching the mountain will
22:14 But in case *a* should ask for
35:2 *A* doing work on it will be
De 22:5 *a* doing these things is
Jos 2:11 spirit has arisen yet in *a*
Jg 3:28 did not allow *a* to pass over
4:20 if *a* comes and does ask you
Ezr 6:11 *a* that violates this decree
Eze 14:15 without *a* passing through
Mt 16:20 not to say to *a* that he was
22:16 you do not care for *a*, for
Mr 2:26 it is not lawful for *a* to eat
8:4 *a* here in an isolated place
9:9 not to relate to *a* what they
12:14 and you do not care for *a*
Lu 3:14 Do not harass *a* or accuse
3:14 or accuse *a* falsely, but be
9:21 not to be telling this to *a*
10:4 do not embrace *a* in greeting
Joh 8:33 have we been slaves to *a*
Ro 13:8 owing *a* a single thing
1Co 1:16 whether I baptized *a* else

Anymore
Ge 8:12 not come back again to him *a*
17:5 will not be called Abram *a*
31:14 inheritance for us *a* in the
44:23 you may not see my face *a*
Ex 10:29 not try to see your face *a*
De 17:13 not act presumptuously *a*
18:16 fire do not let me see *a*
Jos 5:1 no spiritedness in them *a*
5:12 manna did not occur *a* for
Jg 8:28 did not lift up their head *a*
13:21 to Manoah and his wife *a*
18:24 and what do I have *a*?
1Sa 7:13 they did not come *a* into the
30:4 in them no power to weep *a*
2Sa 2:28 chasing after Israel *a*, and
2:28 not renew the fighting *a*
9:3 nobody of the house of Saul *a*
10:19 saving the sons of Ammon *a*
19:35 listen *a* to the voice of
19:35 a burden *a* to my lord the
21:17 out with us to the battle *a*
1Ki 10:10 *a* the like of that balsam
18:5 not have *a* of the beasts cut
2Ki 2:12 And he did not see him *a*
1Ch 19:19 saving the sons of Ammon *a*
Es 2:14 not come in *a* to the king
Job 7:10 not return *a* to his house
7:10 will not acknowledge him *a*
Ps 74:9 there is no prophet *a*, And
Ec 9:5 neither do they *a* have wages
9:6 they have no portion *a* to time
Isa 2:4 neither will they learn war *a*
51:22 repeat the drinking of it *a*
Jer 3:1 should he return to her *a*?
10:20 stretching out my tent *a*
22:30 David and ruling *a* in Judah
31:40 torn down *a* to time
38:9 is no bread *a* in the city
Eze 5:9 of which I shall not do *a*
12:25 will be no postponement *a*
12:28 will be no postponement *a*
Joe 2:19 *a* a reproach among the
Mic 4:3 neither . . . learn war *a*
Na 1:12 I shall not afflict you *a*
1:14 Nothing . . . will be sown *a*
Zec 13:3 case a man should prophesy *a*
Mt 21:19 no fruit come from you *a*
Mr 11:14 no one eat fruit from you *a*
12:34 courage *a* to question him
Lu 20:36 neither can they die *a*, for
Joh 5:14 Do not sin *a*, in order that
14:30 not speak much with you *a*
Ac 4:17 speak *a* upon the basis of this
8:39 eunuch did not see him *a*, for
Heb 8:12 call their sins to mind *a*
10:2 no consciousness of sins *a*
10:17 lawless deeds to mind *a*
Re 3:12 by no means go out from it *a*
7:16 hunger no more nor thirst *a*
18:11 to buy their full stock *a*
20:3 mislead the nations *a* until
21:4 nor outcry nor pain be *a*

Anyone*
Ge 4:14 *a* finding me will kill me
4:15 *a* killing Cain must suffer
Ex 12:15 *a* eating what is leavened
1Ki 15:29 not let *a* breathing remain
Ps 14:2 there exists *a* having insight
24:4 *A* innocent in his hands and
Pr 11:29 *a* bringing ostracism upon
15:5 *A* foolish disrespects the
15:5 *a* regarding reproof is shrewd
15:10 *a* hating reproof will die
15:32 *A* shunning discipline is
17:15 *A* pronouncing the wicked one
17:15 *a* pronouncing the righteous
Ec 10:20 call down evil upon *a* rich
Mt 23:18 If *a* swears by the altar, it
Mr 8:30 charged them not to tell *a*
8:34 If *a* wants to come after me
Lu 9:23 If *a* wants to come after me
Joh 3:3 Unless *a* is born again, he
3:5 Unless *a* is born from water
6:50 *a* may eat of it and not die
6:51 if *a* eats of this bread he
8:51 If *a* observes my word, he
8:52 If *a* observes my word, he
14:23 If *a* loves me, he will
1Co 5:11 *a* called a brother that is a
2Co 2:10 Anything you kindly forgive *a*
5:17 if *a* is in union with Christ
1Jo 5:16 If *a* catches sight of his
Re 22:17 let *a* hearing say: Come!
22:17 And let *a* thirsting come
22:17 *a* that wishes take life's

Anyone's*
Isa 22:22 open without *a* shutting
22:22 shut without *a* opening
1Co 3:14 If *a* work that he has built
3:15 if *a* work is burned up, he

Anything*
Ex 20:4 *a* that is in the heavens above
20:17 nor *a* that belongs to your
Ps 49:17 he cannot take along *a* at all
Ec 1:10 Does *a* exist of which one may
Lu 22:35 did not want for *a*, did you?
Joh 1:46 *a* good come out of Nazareth
11:49 You do not know *a* at all
16:23 Father for *a* he will give
Ac 10:14 never have I eaten *a* defiled
25:5 if there is *a* out of the way
Ro 14:21 drink wine or do *a* over
1Co 6:12 brought under authority by *a*
10:19 sacrificed to an idol is *a*
10:19 or that an idol is *a*
2Co 2:10 *A* you kindly forgive anyone
2:10 if I have kindly forgiven *a*
1Ti 6:7 neither can we carry *a* out
Re 22:19 takes *a* away from the words

Anywhere
2Ki 5:15 no God *a* in the earth but in
5:25 servant did not go *a* at all
Re 18:17 every man that voyages *a*

Apart
Ge 37:29 he ripped his garments *a*
37:34 Jacob ripped his mantles *a*
44:13 they ripped their mantles *a*
Ex 14:16 over the sea and split it *a*
14:21 waters were being split *a*
Le 9:17 *a* from the burnt offering of
Nu 14:6 ripped their garments *a*
16:31 the ground . . . split *a*
24:17 break *a* the temples of
De 4:41 set *a* three cities on the side
19:2 set *a* three cities for
19:7 Three cities you will set *a*
Jos 17:5 *a* from the land of Gilead
Jg 5:26 she broke *a* and cut up his
20:15 *a* from the inhabitants of
20:17 mustered *a* from Benjamin
1Sa 4:12 his garments ripped *a* and
2Sa 1:2 garments ripped *a* and dirt
1:11 garments and ripped them *a*
3:31 Rip your garments *a* and tie
13:19 robe . . . she ripped *a*
13:31 ripped his clothes *a* and
13:31 their garments ripped *a*
15:32 his robe ripped *a* and dirt
1Ki 10:13 *a* from what he gave her
10:15 *a* from the men of travel
13:3 The altar is ripped *a*
13:5 altar itself was ripped *a*
21:27 to rip his garments *a* and
2Ki 5:7 ripped his garments *a* and
5:8 had ripped his garments *a*
5:8 did you rip your garments *a*
6:30 ripped his garments *a*
11:14 ripped her garments *a*
18:37 their garments ripped *a* and
19:1 ripped his garments *a* and
22:11 ripped his garments *a*
22:19 you ripped your garments *a*
2Ch 17:19 *a* from those whom the king
23:13 ripped her garments *a* and
25:12 they, one and all, burst *a*
31:16 *a* from their genealogical
34:19 ripped his garments *a*
34:27 ripped your garments *a* and
Ezr 2:65 *a* from their men slaves and
9:3 ripped *a* my garment and my
9:5 my sleeveless coat torn *a*
Ne 4:19 far *a* from one another
7:67 *a* from their men slaves and
Es 4:1 rip his garments *a* and put on
Job 1:20 rip his sleeveless coat *a* and
2:12 his sleeveless coat *a* and
17:11 own plans have been torn *a*
Ps 2:3 Let us tear their bands *a*
46:9 The bow he breaks *a* and does
107:14 tearing even their bands *a*
Pr 3:20 deeps themselves were split *a*
Ec 3:7 a time to rip *a* and a time to
Isa 7:6 Judah and tear it *a* and by

Isa 24:19 land has absolutely burst *a*
36:22 their garments ripped *a*
37:1 ripped his garments *a* and
57:8 For *a* from me you uncovered
64:1 had ripped the heavens *a*
Jer 2:20 I tore your bands *a*
5:5 must have torn *a* the bands
12:3 set them *a* for the day of
36:23 to tear it *a* with the
36:24 rip their garments *a*
41:5 their garments ripped *a* and
Eze 19:3 to learn how to tear *a* prey
19:6 learned how to tear *a* prey
Ho 13:8 rip *a* the enclosure of their
Joe 2:13 rip *a* your hearts, and not
Mic 1:4 split *a*, like wax because of
Mt 19:6 let no man put *a*
Mr 5:4 chains were snapped *a* by him
10:9 let no man put *a*
Lu 5:6 their nets began ripping *a*
Joh 1:3 *a* from him not even one thing
15:5 *a* from me you can do nothing
Ac 13:2 set Barnabas and Saul *a* for
Ro 3:21 now *a* from law God's
3:28 faith *a* from works of law
4:6 righteousness *a* from works
7:8 for *a* from law sin was dead
7:9 I was once alive *a* from law
2Co 12:3 or *a* from the body, I do not
1Ti 2:8 *a* from wrath and debates
Heb 9:28 it will be *a* from sin and
11:40 not be made perfect *a* from
Jas 2:18 faith *a* from the works, and
2:20 that faith *a* from works is

Apelles
Ro 16:10 Greet *A*, the approved one in

Aperture
Isa 11:8 light *a* of a poisonous snake

Apes
1Ki 10:22 carrying . . . ivory, and *a*
2Ch 9:21 silver, ivory, and *a* and

Aphek
Jos 12:18 the king of *A*, one
13:4 to the Sidonians, as far as *A*
19:30 and Ummah and *A* and Rehob
1Sa 4:1 Philistines . . . encamped in *A*
29:1 their camps together at *A*
1Ki 20:26 to *A* for battle against
20:30 fleeing to *A*, to the city
2Ki 13:17 strike down Syria at *A* to

Aphekah
Jos 15:53 and Beth-tappuah and *A*

Aphiah
1Sa 9:1 son of Becorath, the son of *A*

Aphik
Jg 1:31 and Helbah and *A* and Rehob

Aphrah
Mic 1:10 In the house of *A* wallow in

Apollonia
Ac 17:1 through Amphipolis and *A* and

Apollos
Ac 18:24 Jew named *A*, a native of
19:1 while *A* was in Corinth, Paul
1Co 1:12 I belong to Paul, But I to *A*
3:4 but another says: I to *A*, are
3:5 What, then, is *A*? Yes, what
3:6 I planted, *A* watered, but God
3:22 whether Paul or *A* or Cephas
4:6 to apply to myself and *A* for
16:12 concerning *A* our brother
Tit 3:13 and *A* for their trip, that

Apollyon
Re 9:11 in Greek he has the name *A*

Apostasy
Isa 32:6 work at *a* and to speak
Jer 23:15 *a* has gone forth to all the
Da 11:32 lead into *a* by means of
Ac 21:21 an *a* from Moses, telling
2Th 2:3 unless the *a* comes first and

Apostate
Job 8:13 hope of an *a* will perish
13:16 before him no *a* will come
17:8 one gets excited over the *a*
20:5 rejoicing of an *a* is for a
27:8 what is the hope of an *a*
34:30 an *a* man may not reign
36:13 And those *a* in heart will
Ps 35:16 Among the *a* mockers for a
Pr 11:9 *a* brings his fellowman to
Isa 10:6 Against an *a* nation I shall

Apostates
Job 15:34 assembly of *a* is sterile
Isa 9:17 all of them are *a* and
33:14 has grabbed hold of the *a*

Apostatizing
Jer 17:13 Those *a* from me will be

Apostle
Ro 1:1 and called to be an *a*
11:13 an *a* to the nations, I
1Co 1:1 Paul, called to be an *a* of
9:1 Am I not an *a*? Have I not
9:2 If I am not an *a* to others, I
15:9 am not fit to be called an *a*
2Co 1:1 Paul, an *a* of Christ Jesus
12:12 the signs of an *a* were
Ga 1:1 Paul, an *a*, neither from men
Eph 1:1 Paul, an *a* of Christ Jesus
Col 1:1 Paul, an *a* of Christ Jesus
1Ti 1:1 Paul, an *a* of Christ Jesus
2:7 appointed a preacher and an *a*
2Ti 1:1 Paul, an *a* of Christ Jesus
1:11 a preacher and *a* and teacher
Tit 1:1 Paul . . . an *a* of Jesus Christ
Heb 3:1 the *a* and high priest whom
1Pe 1:1 Peter, an *a* of Jesus Christ
2Pe 1:1 Simon Peter, a slave and *a*

Apostles
Mt 10:2 names of the twelve *a* are
Mr 3:14 twelve, whom he also named *a*
6:30 the *a* gathered together
Lu 6:13 twelve, whom he also named *a*
9:10 when the *a* returned they
11:49 and *a*, and they will kill
17:5 the *a* said to the Lord
22:14 reclined . . . the *a* with him
24:10 telling the *a* these things
Ac 1:2 spirit to the *a* whom he chose
1:26 along with the eleven *a*
2:37 Peter and the rest of the *a*
2:42 to the teaching of the *a* and
2:43 began to occur through the *a*
4:33 *a* continued giving forth the
4:35 them at the feet of the *a*
4:36 surnamed Barnabas by the *a*
4:37 it at the feet of the *a*
5:2 it at the feet of the *a*
5:12 hands of the *a* many signs
5:18 laid hands upon the *a* and
5:29 *a* said: We must obey God as
5:40 they summoned the *a*, flogged
6:6 placed them before the *a*, and
8:1 except the *a* were scattered
8:14 *a* in Jerusalem heard that
8:18 on of the hands of the *a*
9:27 led him to the *a*, and he
11:1 *a* and the brothers that were
14:4 but others for the *a*
14:14 *a* Barnabas and Paul heard of
15:2 *a* and older men in Jerusalem
15:4 and the *a* and the older men
15:6 *a* and the older men gathered
15:22 *a* and the older men together
15:23 The *a* and the older men
16:4 been decided upon by the *a* and
Ro 16:7 are men of note among the *a*
1Co 4:9 God has put us the *a* last on
9:5 even as the rest of the *a* and
12:28 first, *a*; second, prophets
12:29 Not all are *a*, are they?
15:7 to James, then to all the *a*
15:9 I am the least of the *a*, and
2Co 8:23 are *a* of congregations and a
11:5 inferior to your superfine *a*
11:13 For such men are false *a*
11:13 into *a* of Christ
12:11 inferior to your superfine *a*
Ga 1:17 those who were *a* previous to
1:19 I saw no one else of the *a*
Eph 2:20 upon the foundation of the *a*
3:5 revealed to his holy *a* and
4:11 he gave some as *a*, some as
1Th 2:6 an expensive burden as *a* of
2Pe 3:2 and Savior through your *a*
Jude 17 spoken by the *a* of our Lord
Re 2:2 test who say they are *a*, but
18:20 you holy ones and you *a* and
21:14 the twelve *a* of the Lamb

Apostleship
Ac 1:25 place of this ministry and *a*
Ro 1:5 kindness and an *a* in order
1Co 9:2 are the seal confirming my *a*
Ga 2:8 powers necessary for an *a* to

Appaim
1Ch 2:30 the sons of Nadab . . . *A*
2:31 the sons of *A* were Ishi

Apparel
Es 6:8 let them bring royal *a* with
6:9 *a* and the horse into the charge
6:10 take the *a* and the horse, just
6:11 Haman proceeded to take the *a*
8:15 in royal *a* of blue and linen
Ps 45:14 In woven *a* she will be
Lu 9:29 *a* became glitteringly white
Joh 19:24 upon my *a* they cast lots
Ac 20:33 no man's silver or gold or *a*
1Pe 3:4 incorruptible *a* of the quiet

Apparently
Ge 40:10 it was *a* sprouting shoots

Apparition
Mt 14:26 troubled, saying: It is an *a*!
Mr 6:49 they thought: It is an *a*

Appeal
Mt 26:53 *a* to my Father to supply me
Ac 7:59 Stephen as he made *a* and
25:11 I *a* to Caesar!
28:19 compelled to *a* to Caesar

Appealed
Ac 25:12 To Caesar you have *a*; to
25:21 when Paul *a* to be kept for
25:25 himself *a* to the August One
26:32 if he had not *a* to Caesar

Appear
Ge 1:9 and let the dry land *a*
9:14 rainbow will certainly *a* in
26:24 Jehovah proceeded to *a* to
Ex 4:1 say, Jehovah did not *a* to you
6:3 I used to *a* to Abraham, Isaac
23:15 not *a* before me empty-handed
23:17 every male of yours will *a*
34:20 not *a* before me empty-handed
34:23 *a* before the true Lord
Le 9:4 Jehovah will certainly *a* to
9:6 glory of Jehovah may *a* to you
13:7 *a* the second time before the
16:2 cloud I shall *a* over the cover
Nu 16:42 Jehovah's glory began to *a*
20:6 Jehovah's glory began to *a* to
De 16:16 every male of yours should *a*
16:16 none should *a* before Jehovah
1Sa 1:22 he must *a* before Jehovah and
3:21 Jehovah proceeded to *a* again
2Sa 11:25 not let this matter *a* bad
17:17 able to *a* entering the city
Ps 42:2 shall I come and *a* before God
90:16 activity *a* to your own
102:16 He must *a* in his glory
Isa 66:5 must also *a* with rejoicing
Eze 16:51 your sisters *a* righteous
16:52 you make your sisters *a*
Da 1:13 of the king *a* before you
Mt 6:16 may *a* to men to be fasting
6:18 *a* to be fasting, not to men
23:27 outwardly indeed *a* beautiful
23:28 indeed, *a* righteous to men
24:30 will *a* in heaven, and then
Mr 10:42 those who *a* to be ruling the
2Co 13:7 ourselves may *a* approved
13:7 ourselves may *a* disapproved
Heb 9:24 *a* before the person of God
11:3 out of things that do not *a*

Appearance
Ge 12:11 are a woman beautiful in *a*
24:16 attractive in *a*, a virgin
26:7 she was attractive in *a*
39:6 in form and beautiful in *a*
41:2 seven cows beautiful in *a*
41:3 ugly in *a* and thin-fleshed
41:4 the cows that were ugly in *a*
41:4 cows that were beautiful in *a*
41:21 their *a* was bad just as at
Le 13:3 the *a* of the plague is deeper
13:4 its *a* is not deeper than the
13:20 its *a* is lower than the skin
13:25 its *a* is deeper than the skin
13:30 its *a* is deeper than the skin
13:31 its *a* is not deeper than the
13:32 *a* of the abnormal falling
13:34 *a* is not deeper than the skin
13:43 *a* of leprosy in the skin

Le 14:37 *a* is lower than the wall
Nu 9:16 and the *a* of fire by night
12:8 *a* of Jehovah is what he
Jg 13:6 came to me, and his *a* was
13:6 like the *a* of the angel of the
1Sa 16:7 Do not look at his *a* and at
16:12 and handsome in *a*
17:42 and ruddy, of beautiful *a*
2Sa 11:2 woman was very good in *a*
14:27 woman most beautiful in *a*
2Ki 1:7 the *a* of the man that came up
Es 1:11 for she was beautiful in *a*
2:2 virgins, beautiful in *a*, for
2:3 women, virgins, beautiful in *a*
2:7 and beautiful in *a*, and at the
Job 4:16 But I did not recognize its *a*
Ps 46:5 help it at the *a* of morning
Pr 27:23 the *a* of your flock
Ca 5:15 His *a* is like Lebanon, choice
Isa 11:3 judge by any mere *a* to his
52:14 as respects his *a* more than
53:2 not the *a* so that we should
Eze 1:13 *a* was like burning coals of
1:13 *a* of torches was moving back
1:14 with the *a* of the lightning
1:16 *a* of the wheels and their
1:16 their *a* and their structure
1:26 in *a* like sapphire stone, the
1:26 *a* like an earthling man upon
1:27 *a* of fire all around inside
1:27 the *a* of his hips and upward
1:27 *a* of his hips and downward
1:27 something like the *a* of fire
1:28 *a* of the bow that occurs in
1:28 the *a* was of the brightness
1:28 the *a* of the likeness of the
8:2 similar to the *a* of fire
8:2 *a* of his hips even downward
8:2 *a* of a shining, like the glow
8:4 the *a* that I had seen in the
10:1 *a* of the likeness of a throne
10:9 *a* of the wheels was like the
10:10 as for their *a*, the four of
10:22 faces the *a* of which I had
23:15 having the *a* of warriors
40:3 a man. His *a* was like the
40:3 was like the *a* of copper
41:21, 21 *a* like the following *a*
42:11 the *a* of the dining rooms
43:3 *a* of the vision that I had
43:3 *a* that I saw by the river
Da 1:4 good in *a* and having insight
2:31 and its *a* was dreadful
3:25 the *a* of the fourth one is
7:20 *a* of which was bigger than
8:15 *a* like an able-bodied man
10:6 face like the *a* of lightning
10:7 I Daniel by myself, the *a*
10:7 they did not see the *a*
10:8 so that I saw this great *a*
10:16 my lord, because of the *a*
10:18 the *a* of an earthling man
Joe 2:4, 4 Its *a* is like the *a* of
Mt 16:3 to interpret the *a* of the sky
22:16 look upon men's outward *a*
28:3 outward *a* was as lightning
Mr 12:14 look upon men's outward *a*
Lu 9:29 the *a* of his face became
12:56 outward *a* of earth and sky
Joh 7:24 judging from the outward *a*
2Co 5:12 boast over the outward *a*
10:1 lowly though I am in *a*
Ga 2:6 not go by a man's outward *a*
6:12 make a pleasing *a* in the flesh
Col 2:23 of an *a* of wisdom in a
Jas 1:11 beauty of its outward *a*
Re 4:3 in *a*, like a jasper stone and
4:3 a rainbow like an emerald in *a*

Appearances
Eze 43:3 and there were *a* like the
Na 2:4 Their *a* are like torches

Appeared
Ge 8:5 the tops of the mountains *a*
12:7 Jehovah now *a* to Abram and
12:7 Jehovah, who had *a* to him
17:1 Jehovah *a* to Abram and said
18:1 Jehovah *a* to him among the
26:2 Jehovah *a* to him and said
35:1 the true God who *a* to you
35:9 God now *a* to Jacob once again
46:29 When he *a* to him he at once
48:3 God Almighty *a* to me at Luz
Ex 3:2 Jehovah's angel *a* to him in a
3:16 God of your forefathers has *a*
4:5 the God of Jacob, has *a* to you
16:10 Jehovah's glory *a* in the
34:1 that *a* on the first tablets
Le 9:23 Jehovah's glory *a* to all the
14:35 a plague has *a* to me in the
Nu 9:15 what *a* to be fire continued
14:10 Jehovah's glory *a* on the tent
14:14 who has *a* face to face
16:19 Jehovah's glory *a* to all the
De 10:2 the words that *a* on the first
31:15 Jehovah *a* at the tent in the
Jg 6:12 angel *a* to him and said to
13:3 angel *a* to the woman and said
13:10 The man . . . has *a* to me
2Sa 11:27 David had done *a* bad in the
1Ki 3:5 Jehovah *a* to Solomon in a
9:2 Jehovah *a* to Solomon the
9:2 he had *a* to him in Gibeon
2Ki 23:24 disgusting things that had *a*
2Ch 1:7 God *a* to Solomon and then
3:1 where Jehovah had *a* to David
7:12 Jehovah now *a* to Solomon
Pr 27:25 and the new grass has *a*, and
Ca 2:12 Blossoms themselves have *a* in
Jer 31:3 Jehovah himself *a* to me
Da 1:15 countenances *a* better and
8:1 vision that *a* to me, even me
Mt 1:20 angel *a* to him in a dream
2:13 angel *a* in a dream to Joseph
2:19 angel *a* in a dream to Joseph
13:26 then the weeds *a* also
17:3 *a* to them Moses and Elijah
Mr 9:4 Elijah with Moses *a* to them
Lu 1:11 To him Jehovah's angel *a*
9:8 that Elijah had *a*, but by still
9:31 These *a* with glory and began
22:43 angel from heaven *a* to him
24:11 sayings *a* as nonsense to
24:34 raised up and he *a* to Simon
Joh 21:14 third time that Jesus *a*
Ac 7:2 *a* to our forefather Abraham
7:26 *a* to them as they were
7:30 *a* to him in the wilderness
7:35 angel that *a* to him in the
9:17 Jesus that *a* to you on the
16:9 a vision *a* to Paul: a certain
27:20 nor stars *a* for many days
1Co 15:5 he *a* to Cephas, then to the
15:6 *a* to upward of five hundred
15:7 he *a* to James, then to all
15:8 last of all he *a* also to me
1Ti 3:16 *a* to angels, was preached

Appearing
Le 13:7 his *a* before the priest for
Jg 13:21 *a* to Manoah and his wife
1Sa 3:15 afraid to tell Eli of the *a*
1Ki 11:9 the one *a* to him twice
Eze 10:1 likeness of a throne, *a* above
Da 8:1 the one *a* to me at the start
Mt 2:7 the time of the star's *a*
Jas 4:14 you are a mist *a* for a little

Appears
Le 13:14 the living flesh *a* in it, he
13:57 it still *a* in the garment or
1Sa 16:7 man sees what *a* to the eyes
Ps 84:7 Each one *a* to God in Zion
Mal 3:2 the one standing when he *a*
Heb 9:28 he *a* it will be apart from

Appease
Ge 32:20 I may *a* him by the gift
Eze 5:13 I will *a* my rage on them

Appendage
Ex 29:13 and the *a* upon the liver, and
29:22 the *a* of the liver, and the
Le 3:4 as for the *a* upon the liver
3:10 as for the *a* upon the liver
3:15 as for the *a* upon the liver
4:9 as for the *a* upon the liver
7:4 as for the *a* upon the liver
8:16 the *a* of the liver and the
8:25 the *a* of the liver and the
9:10 the *a* of the liver from the
9:19 kidneys and the *a* of the liver

Appendages
1Ki 22:34 between the *a* and the coat
2Ch 18:33 between the *a* and the coat

Appetite
Job 38:39 the lively *a* of young lions
Col 3:5 sexual *a*, hurtful desire, and
1Th 4:5 not in covetous sexual *a* such

Appetites
Ro 1:26 disgraceful sexual *a*, for

Apphia
Phm 2 to *A*, our sister, and to

Appius
Ac 28:15 Marketplace of *A* and Three

Applause
Job 38:7 sons of God . . . shouting in *a*

Apple
Ca 2:3 Like an *a* tree among the trees
8:5 Under the *a* tree I aroused you
Joe 1:12 the *a* tree, all the trees of

Apples
Pr 25:11 *a* of gold in silver carvings
Ca 2:5 sustain me with *a*; for I am
7:8 fragrance of your nose like *a*

Application
Isa 8:19 *a* to dead persons in behalf

Applied
2Ki 21:13 *a* to Samaria and also the
21:13 leveling instrument *a* to
2Ch 1:5 congregation *a* as usual to it
34:10 *a* it to mending and
Ec 8:16 I *a* my heart to know wisdom
Isa 40:21 not *a* understanding from
Ac 12:1 *a* his hands to mistreating
25:24 Jews together have *a* to me

Applies
Nu 8:24 This is what *a* to the Levites

Apply
De 11:18 *a* these words of mine to
32:46 *A* your hearts to all the
1Ki 14:5 coming to *a* for a word from
Job 5:8 I myself would *a* to God, And
14:17 you *a* glue over my error
Pr 22:17 may *a* your very heart to my
Isa 8:19 *A* to the spiritistic mediums
8:19 God that any people should *a*
41:22 *a* our heart and know the
Da 4:19 dream *a* to those hating you
Lu 4:23 *a* this illustration to me
1Co 4:6 to *a* to myself and Apollos

Applying
Ec 8:9 an *a* of my heart to every work
1Ti 4:13 *a* yourself to public reading

Appoint
Ge 41:34 *a* overseers over the land
45:8 *a* me a father to Pharaoh and
47:6 *a* them cattle chiefs over
Nu 1:50 *a* the Levites over the
3:10 *a* Aaron and his sons, and they
14:4 *a* a head, and let us return
27:16 *a* over the assembly a man
De 20:9 *a* chiefs of the armies at the
1Sa 2:20 Jehovah *a* to you an offspring
8:5 do *a* for us a king to judge us
8:12 *a* for himself chiefs over
22:7 *a* all of you chiefs of
28:2 guardian . . . I shall *a* you
2Sa 7:10 *a* a place for my people
1Ch 17:9 *a* a place for my people
Ezr 7:25 *a* magistrates and judges
Es 2:3 let the king *a* commissioners
Ps 18:43 *a* me the head of the nations
45:16 *a* as princes in all the earth
109:6 *A* over him someone wicked
Isa 60:17 *a* peace as your overseers
Jer 49:19 I shall *a* over her
50:44 I shall *a* over her
Jon 4:8 *a* a parching east wind, and
Mt 24:47 He will *a* him over all his
25:21 will *a* you over many things
25:23 will *a* you over many things
Lu 12:42 his master will *a* over his
12:44 He will *a* him over all his
Ac 6:3 *a* them over this necessary

Appointed
Ge 4:25 God has *a* another seed in
17:21 bear to you at this *a* time
18:14 *a* time I shall return to you
21:2 *a* time of which God had
27:37 have *a* him master over you
39:4 he *a* him over his house, and
39:5 *a* him over his house and in
45:9 *a* me lord for all Egypt
Ex 2:14 Who *a* you as a prince and
4:11 Who *a* a mouth for man or
9:5 Jehovah set an *a* time, saying

Ex 13:10 at its *a* time from year to
23:15 *a* time in the month of Abib
34:18 *a* time in the month of Abib
Le 23:4 proclaim at their *a* times
Nu 9:2 sacrifice at its *a* time
9:3 prepare it at its *a* time
9:7 to Jehovah at its *a* time in
9:13 not present at its *a* time
28:2 at their *a* times
31:14 *a* men of the combat forces
31:48 the *a* men who were of the
De 11:14 at its *a* time, autumn rain
16:6 at the *a* time of your coming
31:10 in the *a* time of the year of
32:35 the *a* time their foot will
Jos 4:4 he had *a* from the sons of
8:14 at the *a* time, before the
20:9 *a* for all the sons of Israel
Jg 8:33 *a* Baal-berith as their god
1Sa 9:24 Eat, because to the *a* time
13:8 *a* time that Samuel had said
13:11 not come within the *a* days
18:13 and *a* him as chief of a
20:35 field of David's *a* place
2Sa 13:32 *a* from the day that he
15:4 O that I were *a* judge in the
20:5 time that he had *a* for him
23:23 *a* him to his own bodyguard
24:15 morning until the time *a*
1Ki 10:9 he *a* you as king to render
2Ki 4:16 At this *a* time next year you
4:17 at this *a* time the next year
7:17 *a* the adjutant upon whose
11:15 *a* ones of the military
12:11 *a* to the house of Jehovah
22:5 the *a* ones, in the house of
22:9 of the work, the ones *a*
25:22 now *a* over them Gedaliah
25:23 king . . . had *a* Gedaliah
1Ch 9:29 men *a* over the utensils and
26:10 his father *a* him as head
2Ch 8:13 the *a* festivals three times
23:14 *a* ones of the military
30:22 eat the *a* feast for seven
34:10 *a* over the house of Jehovah
34:12 over them . . . were *a* Jahath
34:17 in the hand of the *a* men
Ezr 6:18 *a* the priests in their
7:9 *a* the going up from Babylon
10:14 come at the times *a* and
Ne 2:6 when I gave him the *a* time
6:7 prophets that you have *a* to
7:1 *a* the gatekeepers and the
9:17 *a* a head to return to their
10:33 the *a* feasts and for the holy
10:34 the *a* times, year by year
12:31 *a* two large thanksgiving
12:44 *a* on that day men over the
13:31 the wood at *a* times and for
Es 9:27 *a* time in each and every year
9:31 of Purim at their *a* times
Job 34:13 who has *a* to him the . . . land
34:23 sets no *a* time for any man
38:32 constellation in its *a* time
39:1 *a* time for the mountain
39:2 *a* time that they give birth
39:6 house I have *a* the desert
Ps 21:9 the *a* time for your attention
49:14 they have been *a* to Sheol
79:11 preserve those *a* to death
102:13 For the *a* time has come
102:20 To loosen those *a* to death
104:19 made the moon for *a* times
Ec 3:1 everything there is an *a* time
Ca 1:6 they *a* me the keeper of the
Isa 28:25 and barley in the *a* place
44:7 I *a* the people of long ago
Jer 8:7 it well knows its *a* times
33:25 *a* my own covenant of the
Eze 30:3 an *a* time of nations it
43:21 burn it in the *a* place of
Da 1:5 king *a* a daily allowance from
1:10 *a* your food and your drink
1:11 official had *a* over Daniel
2:24 *a* to destroy the wise men of
2:49 *a* over the administration of
3:12 Jews whom you *a* over the
8:19 for the *a* time of the end
11:27 end is yet for the time *a*
11:29 time *a* he will go back, and
11:35 it is yet for the time *a*
12:7 It will be for an *a* time
12:7 *a* times and a half
Ho 12:9 as in the days of an *a* time
Jon 1:17 Jehovah *a* a great fish to
4:6 God *a* a bottle-gourd plant
4:7 But the true God *a* a worm at
Hab 2:3 the vision is yet for the *a*
Mt 8:4 offer the gift that Moses *a*
8:29 torment us before the *a* time
24:45 master *a* over his domestics
26:18 My *a* time is near; I will
Mr 1:15 The *a* time has been fulfilled
13:33 not know when the *a* time is
Lu 1:20 be fulfilled in their *a* time
12:14 *a* me judge or apportioner
21:24 *a* times of the nations are
Joh 15:16 I *a* you to go on and keep
Ac 3:20 the Christ *a* for you, Jesus
7:10 *a* him to govern Egypt and
7:27 Who *a* you ruler and judge
7:35 Who *a* you ruler and judge?
10:41 witnesses *a* beforehand by
13:47 *a* you as a light of nations
14:23 they *a* older men for them
17:26 he decreed the *a* times and
17:31 by a man whom he has *a*, and
20:28 spirit has *a* you overseers
22:10 it is *a* for you to do
Ro 4:17 I have *a* you a father of
5:6 ungodly men at the *a* time
1Co 4:9 as men *a* to death, because we
7:5 for an *a* time, that you may
2Co 8:19 also *a* by the congregations
Ga 4:2 day his father *a* beforehand
Eph 1:10 full limit of the *a* times
1Th 3:3 we are *a* to this very thing
1Ti 2:7 *a* a preacher and an apostle
6:15 show in its own *a* times
2Ti 1:11 *a* a preacher and apostle and
Heb 1:2 he *a* heir of all things, and
2:7 *a* him over the works of your
5:1 is *a* in behalf of men over
8:3 high priest is *a* to offer both
9:9 illustration for the *a* time
9:10 *a* time to set things
1Pe 2:8 this very end they were also *a*
4:17 *a* time for the judgment to
Jude 4 *a* by the Scriptures to this
Re 1:3 for the *a* time is near
11:18 *a* time for the dead to be
22:10 for the *a* time is near

Appointment
Nu 10:3 *a* with you at the entrance
10:4 Israel must also keep their *a*
Jos 11:5 kings met together by *a*
1Sa 21:2 *a* with the young men for
1Ki 8:5 keeping their *a* with him
2Ch 5:6 *a* with him before the Ark
Ne 6:2 let us meet together by *a*
6:10 meet by *a* at the house of the
Job 2:11 they met together by *a* to
37:15 God laid an *a* upon them
Ps 48:4 kings . . . have met by *a*
Am 3:3 unless they have met by *a*

Appointments
1Sa 8:1 *a* of his sons as judges for
Tit 1:5 make *a* of older men in city

Appoints
Ex 4:11 who *a* the speechless or the
Heb 7:28 Law *a* men high priests
7:28 oath . . . *a* a Son, who is

Apportion
Nu 33:54 *a* the land to yourselves as a
34:13 the land that you will *a* to
Jos 13:7 *a* this land as an inheritance
14:5 proceeded to *a* the land
18:5 *a* it among themselves into
Ne 9:22 and to *a* them piece by piece
Job 21:17 does he *a* destruction
Ps 22:18 They *a* my garments among
Isa 53:12 *a* the spoil, due to the
Eze 47:21 *a* this land to yourselves
Da 11:39 he will *a* out for a price

Apportioned
Nu 26:53 To these the land should be *a*
26:55 by the lot . . . land be *a*
26:56 *a* between the many and the
De 4:19 God has *a* to all the peoples
29:26 and he had not *a* to them
Jos 18:2 inheritance they had not *a*
18:10 *a* the land to the sons of
2Sa 6:19 *a* to all the people, to the
1Ch 16:3 he *a* to all the Israelites
Isa 34:17 *a* the place to them by
Joe 3:2 they *a* out my own land
Am 7:17 your ground . . . will be *a* out
Zec 14:1 spoil . . . be *a* out in the
Joh 19:24 They *a* my outer garments
2Co 10:13 territory that God *a* to us
Heb 7:2 Abraham *a* a tenth from all

Apportioner
Lu 12:14 judge or *a* over you persons

Apportioning
Jos 19:51 left off from *a* the land

Apportions
Mic 2:4 he *a* out our own fields

Appraise
1Co 4:1 *a* us as being subordinates of
2Co 10:2 who *a* us as if we walked

Appreciating
Heb 12:16 anyone not *a* sacred things

Appreciation
Ps 27:4 look with *a* upon his temple

Approach
Ex 24:2 And Moses . . . must *a* Jehovah
24:2 but they should not *a*, and the
24:14 case at law, let him *a* them
36:2 *a* the work in order to do it
40:3 shut off *a* to the Ark with
40:21 shut off *a* to the ark of the
Le 21:21 defect may not *a* to present
21:21 *a* to present the bread of his
21:23 may not *a* the altar, because
Nu 8:19 Israel *a* the holy place
31:48 proceeded to *a* Moses
De 20:2 *a* and speak to the people
21:5 the sons of Levi must *a*
25:9 brother's widow must *a* him
Jos 3:9 *A* here and listen to the
8:11 *a* and get in front of the
Jg 6:2 and the places difficult to *a*
19:13 *a* one of the places, and we
20:23 again *a* for battle against
Ru 2:14 *A* here, and you must eat some
1Sa 14:36 us *a* here to the true God
23:14 places difficult to *a*, and
23:19 places difficult to *a* at
23:29 places difficult to *a* at
24:22 to the place difficult to *a*
2Sa 5:17 down to the place hard to *a*
23:14 in the place hard to *a*
1Ki 18:30 to all the people: *A* me
18:36 prophet began to *a* and say
1Ch 11:7 in the place difficult to *a*
11:16 then in the place hard to *a*
12:8 at the place difficult to *a*
12:16 to the place difficult to *a*
2Ch 29:31 *A*, and bring sacrifices and
Job 31:37 Like a leader I would *a* him
Ps 5:11 you will block *a* to them
65:4 you choose and cause to *a*
91:4 pinions he will block *a* to
Pr 7:9 *a* of the night and the gloom
20:20 at the *a* of darkness
Isa 33:16 places difficult to *a*
41:1 Let them *a*. At that time
50:8 antagonist? Let him *a* me
65:5 Do not *a* me, for I shall
Jer 30:21 and he must *a* to me
30:21 pledge in order to *a* to me
46:3 large shield, and *a* to battle
La 3:43 You have blocked *a* with anger
3:44 blocked *a* to yourself with a
Eze 37:7 and bones began to *a*
37:17 cause them to *a* each other
42:14 *a* to what has to do with
44:13 *a* to me to act as priest
44:13 *a* to any holy things of
Ac 8:29 said to Philip: *A* and join
10:28 *a* a man of another race
27:33 close to the *a* of day Paul
Ro 5:2 gained our *a* by faith into
Eph 2:18 have the *a* to the Father by
3:12 an *a* with confidence through
Heb 4:16 *a* with freeness of speech to
10:1 make those who *a* perfect
10:22 *a* with true hearts in the full

Approached
Ge 18:23 Abraham *a* and began to say
29:10 *a* and rolled away the stone
31:25 Laban *a* Jacob, as Jacob had
43:19 they *a* the man who was over
47:29 the days *a* for Israel to die
Nu 32:16 Later they *a* him and said

Jos 14:6 sons of Judah *a* Joshua in
21:1 now *a* Eleazar the priest and
1Sa 9:18 Saul *a* Samuel in the middle
1Ki 18:21 Elijah *a* all the people and
18:30 So all the people *a* him
20:13 prophet *a* Ahab the king
20:22 prophet *a* the king of Israel
20:28 *a* and said to the king of
22:24 *a* and struck Micaiah upon
2Ki 2:5 *a* Elisha and said to him
5:13 servants now *a* and spoke to
2Ch 18:23 *a* and struck Micaiah on the
Ezr 4:2 *a* Zerubbabel and the heads of
9:1 the princes *a* me, saying
Ps 27:2 *a* against me to eat up my
Jer 42:1 even to the greatest one, *a*
Da 3:8 Chaldeans *a* and accused the
3:26 *a* the door of the burning
6:12 *a* and were saying before the
Mt 9:18 ruler who had *a* began to do
15:30 great crowds *a* him, having
16:1 Pharisees and Sadducees *a* him
17:14 a man *a* him, kneeling down
17:24 *a* Peter and said: Does your
20:20 *a* him with her sons, doing
24:1 his disciples *a* to show him
24:3 the disciples *a* him privately
26:7 *a* him, and she began pouring
28:2 *a* and rolled away the stone
28:9 They *a* and caught him by his
28:18 Jesus *a* and spoke to them
Mr 10:2 Pharisees now *a* and, to put
14:45 and *a* him and said: Rabbi!
Lu 7:14 he *a* and touched the bier, and
8:44 *a* from behind and touched
10:34 he *a* him and bound up his
21:8 The due time has *a*. Do not go
22:47 he *a* Jesus to kiss him
24:15 *a* and began walking with
Joh 12:21 *a* Philip who was from
Ac 9:3 he *a* Damascus, when suddenly
22:27 military commander *a* and
Heb 12:18 you have not *a* that which
12:22 you have *a* a Mount Zion and

Approaches
Le 20:16 woman *a* any beast to have a
Heb 11:6 he that *a* God must believe

Approaching
Ex 14:27 at the *a* of morning
Le 16:1 *a* before Jehovah so that they
Nu 4:19 their *a* the most holy things
17:13 Anyone *a* . . . will die
1Sa 17:40 he began *a* the Philistine
1Ki 4:27 everyone *a* the table of King
Eze 40:46 *a* Jehovah to minister to
42:13 priests who are *a* Jehovah
43:19 of Zadok, the ones *a* me
45:4 *a* to minister to Jehovah
Mt 21:30 *A* the second, he said the
Lu 9:42 even as he was *a*, the demon
23:54 light of the sabbath was *a*
Ac 7:17 time was *a* for fulfillment
7:31 as he was *a* to investigate
10:9 *a* the city, Peter went up
Heb 7:25 who are *a* God through him

Appropriate
Es 2:9 her massages and her *a* food
3:8 it is not *a* to let them alone
7:4 But the distress is not *a* when
Ps 119:30 I have considered *a*

Appropriately
Ps 116:7 Jehovah himself has acted *a*
119:17 Act *a* toward your servant
142:7 Because you deal *a* with me

Approval
Ex 28:38 *a* for them before Jehovah
Le 7:18 will not be accepted with *a*
19:5 sacrifice it to gain *a* for
19:7 will not be accepted with *a*
22:19 gain *a* for you it must be
22:20 not serve to gain *a* for you
22:21 in order to gain *a*. No defect
22:23 will not be accepted with *a*
22:25 not be accepted with *a* of
22:27 will be accepted with *a* as
22:29 sacrifice it to gain *a* for
23:11 before Jehovah to gain *a* for
De 33:16 the *a* of the One residing in
33:23 satisfied with the *a* And
Ps 5:12 with *a* you will surround
Pr 12:2 One that is good gets *a* from
Isa 60:7 With *a* they will come up
Joh 6:27 has put his seal of *a*
Ro 14:18 acceptable to God and has *a*
1Co 7:32 how he may gain the Lord's *a*
7:33 may gain the *a* of his wife
7:34 gain the *a* of her husband
10:5 God did not express his *a*
2Ti 2:4 gain the *a* of the one who

Approve
Ro 1:28 *a* of holding God in accurate
2:18 *a* of things that are excellent
1Co 11:28 let a man *a* himself after
16:3 men you *a* of by letters
Heb 10:6 *a* of whole burnt offerings
10:8 you *a* of sacrifices and

Approved
De 33:24 become one *a* by his brothers
1Ch 28:4 he *a*, to make me king over
Es 10:3 and *a* by the multitude of his
Isa 42:1 one, whom my soul has *a*
Mt 3:17 the beloved, whom I have *a*
11:26 came to be the way *a* by you
12:18 my beloved, whom my soul *a*
17:5 the beloved, whom I have *a*
Mr 1:11 the beloved; I have *a* you
Lu 3:22 Son, the beloved; I have *a* you
10:21 came to be the way *a* by you
12:32 *a* of giving you the kingdom
Ro 5:4 in turn, an *a* condition; the
5:4 the *a* condition, in turn, hope
16:10 Apelles, the *a* one in Christ
1Co 11:19 persons *a* may also become
2Co 10:18 recommends himself is *a*
13:7 ourselves may appear *a*, but
2Ti 2:15 present yourself *a* to God
Tit 1:16 not *a* for good work of any
Jas 1:12 *a* he will receive the crown
2Pe 1:17 whom I myself have *a*

Approves
Ro 14:22 on judgment by what he *a*

Approving
Ac 8:1 Saul, for his part, was *a* of
22:20 was also standing by and *a*

Apron
Lu 17:8 put on an *a* and minister to

Aprons
Ac 19:12 *a* were borne from his body

Aptly
Mt 15:7 Isaiah *a* prophesied about you
Mr 7:6 Isaiah *a* prophesied about you
Ac 28:25 holy spirit *a* spoke through

Aquila
Ac 18:2 *A*, a native of Pontus who had
18:18 and with him Priscilla and *A*
18:26 Priscilla and *A* heard him
Ro 16:3 Prisca and *A* my fellow
1Co 16:19 *A* and Prisca together with
2Ti 4:19 greetings to Prisca and *A*

Ar
Nu 21:15 toward the seat of *A* and has
21:28 It has consumed *A* of Moab
De 2:9 I have given *A* as a holding
2:18 territory of Moab, that is, *A*
2:29 the Moabites dwelling in *A*
Isa 15:1 *A* of Moab itself has been

Ara
1Ch 7:38 And the sons of Jether . . . *A*
7:39 the sons of Ulla were *A* and

Arab
Jos 15:52 *A* and Dumah and Eshan
Isa 13:20 *A* will not pitch his tent

Arabah
De 1:7 all their neighbors in the *A*
2:8 from the way of the *A*, from
3:17 the *A* and the Jordan and the
3:17 the sea of the *A*, the Salt Sea
4:49 *A* in the region of the Jordan
4:49 as far as the sea of the *A*
11:30 in the *A*, in front of Gilgal
Jos 3:16 the *A*, the Salt Sea, were
11:16 the Shephelah and the *A*
12:1 Mount Hermon and all the *A*
12:3 the *A* as far as the sea of
12:3 as far as the sea of the *A*
12:8 the Shephelah and in the *A*
18:18 slope in front of the *A*
18:18 and went down to the *A*
1Sa 23:24 Maon in the *A* to the south
2Sa 2:29 marched through the *A* all
4:7 walked on the road to the *A*
2Ki 14:25 clear to the sea of the *A*
25:4 go in the direction of the *A*
Jer 39:4 out by the way of the *A*
52:7 going by the way of the *A*
Eze 47:8 must go down through the *A*
Am 6:14 the torrent valley of the *A*
Zec 14:10 will be changed like the *A*

Arabia
Ga 1:17 went off into *A*, and I came
4:25 Sinai, a mountain in *A*, and

Arabian
Ne 2:19 and Geshem the *A* heard of it
6:1 and to Geshem the *A* and to the
Jer 3:2 like an *A* in the wilderness

Arabians
2Ch 26:7 against the *A* that were
Ne 4:7 the *A* and the Ammonites and
Ac 2:11 Cretans and *A*, we hear them

Arable
Jer 4:3 Plow for yourselves *a* land
Ho 10:12 Till for yourselves *a* land

Arabs
1Ki 10:15 and all the kings of the *A*
2Ch 9:14 all the kings of the *A* and
17:11 *A* also were bringing to
21:16 *A* that were by the side of
22:1 band that came with the *A* to
Jer 25:24 all the kings of the *A* and
Eze 27:21 The *A* and all the chieftains

Arad
Nu 21:1 the Canaanite the king of *A*
33:40 the Canaanite, the king of *A*
Jos 12:14 the king of *A*, one
Jg 1:16 to the south of *A*. Then they
1Ch 8:15 and Zebadiah and *A* and Eder

Arah
Ezr 2:5 sons of *A*, seven hundred and
Ne 6:18 to Shecaniah the son of *A*
7:10 sons of *A*, six hundred and

Aram
Ge 10:22 The sons of Shem . . . *A*
10:23 sons of *A* were Uz and Hul
22:21 and Kemuel the father of *A*
Nu 23:7 From *A* Balak the king of Moab
1Ch 1:17 sons of Shem were . . . *A*
7:34 sons of Shemer were . . . *A*

Aramaic
Ezr 4:7 was written in *A* characters
4:7 translated into the *A* language
Da 2:4 spoke to the king in the *A*

Aram-maacah
1Ch 19:6 and from *A* and from Zobah

Aram-naharaim
Ps 60:*super* in a struggle with *A* and

Aram-Zobah
Ps 60:*super* with Aram-naharaim and *A*

Aran
Ge 36:28 sons of Dishan: Uz and *A*
1Ch 1:42 sons of Dishan were Uz and *A*

Ararat
Ge 8:4 rest on the mountains of *A*
2Ki 19:37 escaped to the land of *A*
Isa 37:38 escaped to the land of *A*
Jer 51:27 kingdoms of *A*, Minni and

Araunah
2Sa 24:16 floor of *A* the Jebusite
24:18 threshing floor of *A* the
24:20 *A* looked down and saw the
24:20 *A* at once went out and
24:21 *A* said: Why has my lord
24:22 *A* said to David: Let my
24:23 Everything *A*, O king, does
24:23 *A* went on to say to the
24:24 the king said to *A*: No, but

Arba
Jos 14:15 said *A* was the great man
15:13 *A* being the father of Anak
21:11 *A* being the father of Anak

Arbathite
2Sa 23:31 Abi-albon the *A*, Azmaveth
1Ch 11:32 Abiel the *A*

Arbel
Ho 10:14 Shalman of the house of *A*

Arbite
2Sa 23:35 the Carmelite, Paarai the *A*

Arbitrariness
Ge 49:6 in their *a* they hamstrung

Arbitrary
Isa 3:4 mere *a* power will rule over

Arbitrate
1Sa 2:25 God will *a* for him; but if

Archangel
Jude 9 when Michael the *a* had a

Archangel's
1Th 4:16 call, with an *a* voice and

Archelaus
Mt 2:22 *A* ruled as king of Judea

Archer
Ge 21:20 and he became an *a*
Pr 26:10 As an *a* piercing everything

Archers
Ge 49:23 the *a* kept harassing him and
Job 16:13 His *a* encircle me
Jer 50:29 against Babylon *a*, all who

Archippus
Col 4:17 tell *A*: Keep watching the
Phm 2 and to *A*, our fellow soldier

Archite
2Sa 15:32 Hushai the *A*, with his robe
16:16 Hushai the *A*, David's
17:5 Call, please, Hushai the *A*
17:14 The counsel of Hushai the *A*
1Ch 27:33 Hushai the *A* was the king's

Architectural
1Ch 28:11 Solomon his son the *a* plan
28:12 the *a* plan of everything
28:19 all the works of the *a* plan

Archites
Jos 16:2 boundary of the *A* at Ataroth

Ard
Ge 46:21 sons of Benjamin were . . . *A*
Nu 26:40 sons of Bela came to be *A*
26:40 *A* the family of the Ardites

Ardites
Nu 26:40 Of Ard the family of the *A*

Ardon
1Ch 2:18 Jesher and Shobab and *A*

Ardor
De 29:20 his *a* will smoke against
Ps 79:5 How long will your *a* burn
119:139 *a* has made an end of me
Eze 23:25 express my *a* against you
38:19 in my *a*, in the fire of my

Area
Ex 25:37 shine upon the *a* in front of
Nu 8:2 *a* in front of the lampstand
8:3 *a* in front of the lampstand
1Ki 18:32 the *a* sowed with two seah
Eze 40:12 *a* in front of the guard
40:12 fenced *a* of one cubit on
41:11 width of the *a* of the space
41:12 the separated *a*, the side of
41:13 separated *a* and the building
41:14 separated *a* to the east was
41:15 separated *a* that was behind
42:1 in front of the separated *a*
42:10 before the separated *a* and
42:13 are before the separated *a*

Areli
Ge 46:16 the sons of Gad were . . . *A*
Nu 26:17 *A* the family of the Arelites

Arelites
Nu 26:17 of Areli the family of the *A*

Areopagus
Ac 17:19 and led him to the *A*, saying
17:22 stood in the midst of the *A*
17:34 judge of the court of the *A*

Aretas
2Co 11:32 under *A* the king was

Argob
De 3:4 the region of *A*, the kingdom
3:13 the region of *A* of all Bashan
3:14 the region of *A* as far as the
1Ki 4:13 *A*, which is in Bashan
2Ki 15:25 house with *A* and Arieh

Argue
Job 13:15 *a* to his face for my own
Eze 16:52 *a* in favor of your sisters
Mic 6:2 with Israel that he will *a*
Mr 8:17 *a* over your having no loaves

Argued
Mr 9:34 they had *a* . . . who is greater

Arguing
Job 13:3 *a* with God . . . find delight
Mr 8:16 they went *a* with one another
9:33 What were you *a* over on the
Ac 24:12 in the temple *a* with anyone

Arguments
Isa 29:21 righteous one with empty *a*
41:21 Produce your *a*, says the
Php 2:14 free from murmurings and *a*
Col 2:4 delude you with persuasive *a*

Aridai
Es 9:9 and Arisai and *A* and Vaizatha

Aridatha
Es 9:8 and Poratha and Adalia and *A*

Arieh
2Ki 15:25 house with Argob and *A*

Ariel
2Sa 23:20 two sons of *A* of Moab; and
1Ch 11:22 the two sons of *A* of Moab
Ezr 8:16 sent for Eliezer, *A*
Isa 29:1, 1 *A*, to *A*, the town where
29:2 to make things tight for *A*
29:7 are waging war against *A*

Aright
2Ti 2:15 the word of the truth *a*

Arimathea
Mt 27:57 there came a rich man of *A*
Mr 15:43 there came Joseph of *A*, a
Lu 23:51 *A*, a city of the Judeans
Joh 19:38 Joseph from *A*, who was a

Arioch
Ge 14:1 days of . . . *A* king of Ellasar
14:9 and *A* king of Ellasar
Da 2:14 *A* the chief of the king's
2:15 to *A* the officer of the king
2:15 *A* made known the matter
2:24 Daniel himself went in to *A*
2:25 *A*, in a hurry, took Daniel

Arisai
Es 9:9 and *A* and Aridai and Vaizatha

Arise
Ge 41:30 famine will certainly *a*
Ex 18:16 they have a case *a*, it must
Nu 1:53 indignation may *a* against the
10:35 *a*, O Jehovah, and let your
1Ch 15:16 a sound of rejoicing to *a*
Job 6:29 let no unrighteousness *a*
11:17 will your life's duration *a*
Ps 3:7 Do *a*, O Jehovah! Save me, O my
7:6 Do *a*, O Jehovah, in your anger
9:19 *a*, O Jehovah! Let not mortal
10:12 Do *a*, O Jehovah. O God, lift
12:5 I shall at this time *a*, says
44:26 Do *a* in assistance to us
68:1 Let God *a*, let his enemies be
74:22 Do *a*, O God, do conduct your
88:10 in death themselves *a*
102:13 *a*, you will have mercy on
107:25 a tempestuous wind to *a*
132:8 Do *a*, O Jehovah, to your
Pr 24:22 disaster will *a* so suddenly
Isa 60:1 *A*, O woman, shed forth light
Mt 24:11 many false prophets will *a*
24:24 and false prophets will *a*
26:5 in order that no uproar may *a*
Mr 13:22 and false prophets will *a*
Eph 5:14 and *a* from the dead, and the
1Th 2:3 does not *a* from error or
2Ti 3:6 from these *a* those men who
Heb 7:11 priest to *a* according to the

Arisen
Jos 2:11 and no spirit has *a* yet in
Mt 13:21 persecution has *a* on account

Arises
De 13:1 dreamer of a dream *a* in your
25:1 a dispute *a* between men, and
Mr 4:17 persecution *a* because of the
Lu 15:10 joy *a* among the angels of the
Heb 7:15 there *a* another priest

Arising
Ex 12:30 there began *a* a great outcry
Isa 33:3 At your *a* nations have been
Mt 27:24 but, rather, an uproar was *a*
Ro 15:12 will be one *a* to rule

Aristarchus
Ac 19:29 Gaius and *A*, Macedonians
20:4 *A* . . . of the Thessalonians
27:2 with us *A* a Macedonian from
Col 4:10 *A* my fellow captive sends
Phm 24 also Mark, *A*, Demas, Luke

Aristobulus
Ro 16:10 from the household of *A*

Ark
Ge 6:14 Make for yourself an *a* out of
6:14 make compartments in the *a*
6:15 cubits the length of the *a*
6:16 [roof; or, window] for the *a*
6:16 entrance of the *a* you will
6:18 and you must go into the *a*
6:19 you will bring into the *a* to
7:1 all your household, into the *a*
7:7 into the *a* ahead of the waters
7:9 by twos to Noah inside the *a*
7:13 Noah . . . with him, into the *a*
7:15 going to Noah inside the *a*
7:17 waters . . . carrying the *a*
7:18 *a* kept going on the surface
7:23 with him in the *a* kept on
8:1 that was with him in the *a*
8:4 *a* came to rest on the
8:6 of the *a* that he had made
8:9 it returned to him into the *a*
8:9 it to himself inside the *a*
8:10 sent out the dove from the *a*
8:13 remove the covering of the *a*
8:16 Go out of the *a*, you and your
8:19 they went out of the *a*
9:10 those going out of the *a* to
9:18 sons who came out of the *a*
Ex 2:3 took for him an *a* of papyrus
2:5 she caught sight of the *a* in
25:10 make an *A* of acacia wood
25:14 rings upon the sides of the *A*
25:14 in order to carry the *A* with
25:15 In the rings of the *A* the
25:16 place in the *A* the testimony
25:21 the cover above upon the *A*
25:21 in the *A* you will place the
25:22 upon the *a* of the testimony
26:33 bring the *a* of the testimony
26:34 put the cover upon the *a* of
30:6 near the *a* of the testimony
30:26 tent of meeting and the *a* of
31:7 tent of meeting and the *A* for
35:12 the *A* and its poles, the
37:1 now made the *A* of acacia wood
37:5 rings on the sides of the *A*
37:5 for carrying the *A*
39:35 the *a* of the testimony and
40:3 place the *a* of the testimony
40:3 shut off approach to the *A*
40:5 before the *a* of the testimony
40:20 into the *A* and placed the
40:20 placed the poles on the *A* and
40:20 the cover above upon the *A*
40:21 the *A* into the tabernacle and
40:21 to the *a* of the testimony
Le 16:2 the cover which is upon the *A*
16:13 overspread the *A* cover
Nu 3:31 obligation was the *A* and the
4:5 cover the *a* of the testimony
7:89 upon the *a* of the testimony
10:33 *a* of Jehovah's covenant was
10:35 *A* would set out, Moses would
14:44 *a* of Jehovah's covenant and
De 10:1 you must make an *a* of wood
10:2 you must place them in the *a*
10:3 I made an *a* of acacia wood
10:5 placed the tablets in the *a*
10:8 tribe of Levi to carry the *a*
31:9 carriers of the *a* of Jehovah's
31:25 the *a* of Jehovah's covenant
31:26 *a* of the covenant of Jehovah
Jos 3:3 *a* of the covenant of Jehovah
3:6 Take up the *a* of the covenant
3:6 took up the *a* of the covenant
3:8 carrying the *a* of the covenant
3:11 The *a* of the covenant of the
3:13 carrying the *a* of Jehovah
3:14 the *a* of the covenant
3:15 carriers of the *A* came as

Jos 3:15 the priests carrying the *A*
3:17 the *a* of Jehovah's covenant
4:5 ahead of the *a* of Jehovah your
4:7 cut off from before the *a*
4:9 carrying the *a* of the covenant
4:10 the priests carrying the *A*
4:11 the *a* of Jehovah passed over
4:16 the *a* of the testimony that
4:18 *a* of the covenant of Jehovah
6:4 rams' horns, before the *A*
6:6 Take up the *a* of the covenant
6:6 horns before the *a* of Jehovah
6:7 on ahead of the *a* of Jehovah
6:8 *a* of the covenant of Jehovah
6:9 guard was following the *A*
6:11 *a* of Jehovah go marching
6:12 carrying the *a* of Jehovah
6:13 before the *a* of Jehovah
6:13 guard was following the *a*
7:6 before the *a* of Jehovah until
8:33 that side of the *A* in front
8:33 *a* of the covenant of Jehovah
Jg 20:27 *a* of the covenant of the true
1Sa 3:3 where the *a* of God was
4:3 the *a* of Jehovah's covenant
4:4 the *a* of the covenant of
4:4 with the *a* of the covenant
4:5 *a* of the covenant of Jehovah
4:6 *a* of Jehovah itself had come
4:11 *a* of God itself was captured
4:13 atremble over the *a* of the
4:17 *a* of the true God has been
4:18 the *a* of the true God
4:19 the *a* of the true God was
4:21 *a* of the true God's being
4:22 *a* of the true God has been
5:1 took the *a* of the true God and
5:2 take the *a* of the true God and
5:3 before the *a* of Jehovah
5:4 before the *a* of Jehovah
5:7 not let the *a* of the God of
5:8 What shall we do to the *a* of
5:8 Toward Gath let the *a* of the
5:8 the *a* of the God of Israel
5:10 *a* of the true God to Ekron
5:10 the *a* . . . came to Ekron
5:10 the *a* of the God of Israel
5:11 *a* of the God of Israel away
6:1 *a* of Jehovah proved to be in
6:2 we do with the *a* of Jehovah
6:3 *a* of the God of Israel away
6:8 take the *a* of Jehovah and
6:11 *a* of Jehovah upon the wagon
6:13 saw the *A*, they gave way to
6:15 took the *a* of Jehovah down
6:18 they rested the *a* of Jehovah
6:19 looked upon the *a* of Jehovah
6:21 returned the *a* of Jehovah
7:1 brought the *a* of Jehovah up
7:1 to guard the *a* of Jehovah
14:18 bring the *a* of the true God
14:18 *a* of the true God proved to
2Sa 6:2 *a* of the true God, where a
6:3 *a* of the true God ride upon
6:4 with the *a* of the true God
6:4 was walking ahead of the *A*
6:6 *a* of the true God and grabbed
6:7 by the *a* of the true God
6:9 *a* of Jehovah come to me
6:10 remove the *a* of Jehovah to
6:11 *a* of Jehovah kept dwelling
6:12 of the *a* of the true God
6:12 bring the *a* of the true God
6:13 carriers of the *a* of Jehovah
6:15 bringing up the *a* of Jehovah
6:16 *a* of Jehovah came into the
6:17 *a* of Jehovah in and set it
7:2 *a* of the true God is dwelling
11:11 *A* and Israel and Judah are
15:24 the Levites carrying the *a*
15:24 to set the *a* of the true God
15:25 Take the *a* of the true God
15:29 Abiathar took the *a* of the
1Ki 2:26 you carried the *a* of the
3:15 *a* of the covenant of Jehovah
6:19 the *a* of the covenant
8:1 the *a* of the covenant of
8:3 priests began to carry the *A*
8:4 bringing up the *a* of Jehovah
8:5 before the *A*, sacrificing
8:6 the priests brought in the *a*
8:7 wings over the place of the *A*
8:7 cherubs kept the *A* and its
8:9 nothing in the *A* but the two
1Ki 8:21 a place there for the *A*
1Ch 6:31 the *A* had a resting-place
13:3 let us bring the *a* of our God
13:5 bring the *a* of the true God
13:6 *a* of the true God, Jehovah
13:7 *a* of the true God ride upon
13:9 to grab hold of the *A*, for
13:10 his hand out upon the *A*, and
13:12 How shall I bring the *a* of
13:13 David did not remove the *A*
13:14 the *a* of the true God kept
15:1 to prepare a place for the *a*
15:2 No one is to carry the *a* of
15:2 to carry the *a* of Jehovah and
15:3 bring the *a* of Jehovah up to
15:12 must bring the *a* of Jehovah
15:14 to bring up the *a* of Jehovah
15:15 Levites began to carry the *a*
15:23 the gatekeepers for the *A*
15:24 before the *a* of the true God
15:24 the gatekeepers for the *A*
15:25 *a* of the covenant of Jehovah
15:26 *a* of the covenant of Jehovah
15:27 the Levites carrying the *A*
15:28 *a* of the covenant of Jehovah
15:29 *a* of the covenant of Jehovah
16:1 brought the *a* of the true God
16:4 put before the *a* of Jehovah
16:6 constantly before the *a* of
16:37 he left there before the *a*
16:37 to minister before the *A*
17:1 *a* . . . is under tent cloths
22:19 bring the *a* of the covenant
28:2 resting house for the *a* of
28:18 screening over the *a* of the
2Ch 1:4 *a* of the true God David had
5:2 bring the *a* of the covenant
5:4 Levites began to carry the *A*
5:5 bringing up the *A* and the tent
5:6 with him before the *A* were
5:7 the priests brought the *a* of
5:8 wings over the place of the *A*
5:8 cherubs covered over the *A* and
5:10 nothing in the *A* but the two
6:11 the *a* where the covenant of
6:41 and the *A* of your strength
8:11 to which the *a* of Jehovah
35:3 Put the holy *A* in the house
Ps 132:8 and the *a* of your strength
Jer 3:16 The *a* of the covenant of
Mt 24:38 that Noah entered into the *a*
Lu 17:27 Noah entered into the *a*, and
Heb 9:4 the *a* of the covenant overlaid
11:7 *a* for the saving of his
1Pe 3:20 the *a* was being constructed
Re 11:19 *a* of his covenant was seen

Arkite
Ge 10:17 and the *A* and the Sinite
1Ch 1:15 Hivite and the *A* and the

Ark's
1Sa 7:2 *A* dwelling in Kiriath-jearim

Arm
Ex 6:6 with an outstretched *a* and
15:16 the greatness of your *a* they
De 3:24 greatness and your strong *a*
4:34 with an outstretched *a* and
5:15 and an outstretched *a*
7:19 the outstretched *a* with which
9:29 power and your outstretched *a*
11:2 and his outstretched *a*
26:8 an outstretched *a* and with
33:20 tear the *a*, yes, the crown
1Sa 2:31 certainly chop off your *a*
2:31 the *a* of the house of your
2Sa 1:10 bracelet that was upon his *a*
1Ki 8:42 and of your stretched-out *a*
2Ki 17:36 power and a stretched-out *a*
2Ch 6:32 hand and your stretched-out *a*
32:8 there is an *a* of flesh
Job 26:2 *a* that is without strength
31:22 let my own *a* be broken
35:9 the *a* of the great ones
38:15 high *a* itself gets broken
40:9 *a* like that of the true God
Ps 10:15 Break the *a* of the wicked
44:3 *a* was not what brought them
44:3 your right hand and your *a*
71:18 I may tell about your *a*
77:15 your *a* you have recovered
79:11 greatness of your *a* preserve
83:8 an *a* to the sons of Lot
89:10 *a* of your strength you have
89:13 *a* with mightiness is yours
Ps 89:21 own *a* also will strengthen
98:1 right hand, even his holy *a*
136:12 and by an *a* stretched out
Ca 8:6 as a seal upon your *a*
Isa 9:20 eat the flesh of his own *a*
17:5 own *a* harvests the ears of
30:30 descending of his *a* to be
33:2 Become our *a* every morning
40:10 *a* will be ruling for him
40:11 With his *a* he will collect
44:12 at it with his powerful *a*
48:14 his own *a* will be upon the
51:5 for my *a* they will wait
51:9 strength, O *a* of Jehovah
52:10 bared his holy *a* before the
53:1 And as for the *a* of Jehovah
59:16 his *a* proceeded to save
62:8 hand and with his strong *a*
63:5 my *a* furnished me salvation
63:12 *a* go at the right hand of
Jer 17:5 actually makes flesh his *a*
21:5 a strong *a* and with anger
27:5 and by my stretched-out *a*
32:17 and by your outstretched *a*
32:21 and with a stretched-out *a*
48:25 own *a* has been broken, is
Eze 4:7 with your *a* bared, and you
17:9 Neither by a great *a* nor by
20:33 with a stretched-out *a* and
20:34 with a stretched-out *a* and
22:6 each one given over to his *a*
30:21 the *a* of Pharaoh the king
Da 11:6 retain the power of her *a*
11:6 not stand, neither his *a*
Zec 11:17 A sword will be upon his *a*
11:17 *a* will without fail dry up
Lu 1:51 mightily with his *a*, he has
Joh 12:38 *a* of Jehovah, to whom has
Ac 13:17 out of it with an uplifted *a*
1Pe 4:1 *a* yourselves with the same

Armament
Lu 11:22 he takes away his full *a*

Armed
2Sa 23:7 *a* with iron and the shaft of
1Ch 12:2 *a* with the bow, using the
2Ch 20:21 out ahead of the *a* men
28:14 *a* men left the captives
Ps 78:9 Ephraim, though *a* shooters
140:7 in the day of the *a* force
Pr 6:11 and your want like an *a* man
24:34 your neediness as an *a* man
Isa 15:4 *a* men of Moab themselves
Lu 11:21 When a strong man, well *a*

Armies
Ex 6:26 of Egypt according to their *a*
7:4 hand upon Egypt and bring my *a*
12:17 *a* out from the land of Egypt
12:41 *a* of Jehovah went out of the
12:51 Israel together with their *a*
Nu 1:3 them according to their *a*
1:52 division by their *a*
2:3 the camp of Judah in their *a*
2:9 camp of Judah . . . in their *a*
2:10 toward the south in their *a*
2:16 camp of Reuben . . . in their *a*
2:18 Ephraim in their *a* will be
2:24 Ephraim . . . in their *a*
2:25 toward the north in their *a*
2:32 in their *a* were six hundred
10:14 first of all in their *a*, and
10:18 pulled away in their *a*
10:22 pulled away in their *a*, and
10:25 all the camps in their *a*
10:28 Israel in their *a* when they
33:1 their *a* by the hand of Moses
De 20:9 appoint chiefs of the *a* at
1Sa 1:3 sacrifice to Jehovah of *a* in
1:11 O Jehovah of *a*, if you will
4:4 Jehovah of *a*, who is sitting
15:2 what Jehovah of *a* has said
17:45 the name of Jehovah of *a*
2Sa 5:10 Jehovah the God of *a* was
6:2 name of Jehovah of *a*
6:18 in the name of Jehovah of *a*
7:8 Jehovah of *a* has said: I
7:26 Jehovah of *a* is God over
7:27 Jehovah of *a* the God of
1Ki 2:5 two chiefs of the *a* of Israel
18:15 Jehovah of *a* before whom I
19:10 for Jehovah the God of *a*
19:14 jealous for . . . the God of *a*
2Ki 3:14 Jehovah of *a* before whom I
19:31 very zeal of Jehovah of *a*

1Ch 11:9 Jehovah of *a* was with him
17:7 what Jehovah of *a* has said
17:24 Jehovah of *a*, the God of
Ps 24:10 Jehovah of *a*—he is the
44:9 do not go forth with our *a*
46:7 Jehovah of *a* is with us
46:11 Jehovah of *a* is with us
48:8 In the city of Jehovah of *a*
59:5 Jehovah God of *a*, are the God
60:10 go forth with our *a* as God
68:12 Even the kings of *a* flee
69:6 Sovereign Lord, Jehovah of *a*
80:4 God of *a*, how long must you
80:7 O God of *a*, bring us back
80:14 O God of *a*, return, please
80:19 God of *a*, bring us back
84:1 O Jehovah of *a*
84:3 Jehovah of *a*, my King and
84:8 God of *a*, do hear my prayer
84:12 Jehovah of *a*, happy is the
89:8 God of *a*, Who is vigorous
103:21 Bless Jehovah, all you *a* of
108:11 go forth with our *a* as God
Isa 1:9 Unless Jehovah of *a* himself
1:24 Jehovah of *a*, the Powerful
2:12 day belonging to Jehovah of *a*
3:1 Jehovah of *a*, is removing
3:15 Sovereign Lord, Jehovah of *a*
5:7 vineyard of Jehovah of *a* is
5:9 Jehovah of *a* has sworn that
5:16 Jehovah of *a* will become
5:24 the law of Jehovah of *a*
6:3 holy is Jehovah of *a*
6:5 seen the King, Jehovah of *a*
8:13 Jehovah of *a*—he is the One
8:18 Jehovah of *a*, who is
9:7 zeal of Jehovah of *a* will do
9:13 Jehovah of *a* they have not
9:19 fury of Jehovah of *a* the
10:16 Jehovah of *a*, will keep
10:23 Sovereign Lord, Jehovah of *a*
10:24 Jehovah of *a*, has said
10:26 Jehovah of *a* will certainly
10:33 Jehovah of *a*, is lopping off
13:4 Jehovah of *a* is mustering
13:13 fury of Jehovah of *a* and
14:22 utterance of Jehovah of *a*
14:23 utterance of Jehovah of *a*
14:24 Jehovah of *a* has sworn
14:27 Jehovah of *a* himself has
17:3 utterance of Jehovah of *a*
18:7 brought to Jehovah of *a*
18:7 the name of Jehovah of *a*
19:4 true Lord, Jehovah of *a*
19:12 Jehovah of *a* has counseled
19:16 hand of Jehovah of *a* which
19:17 counsel of Jehovah of *a*
19:18 swearing to Jehovah of *a*
19:20 witness to Jehovah of *a* in
19:25 Jehovah of *a* will have
21:10 heard from Jehovah of *a*
22:5 Jehovah of *a*, has in the
22:12 Jehovah of *a*, will call in
22:14 Jehovah of *a* has revealed
22:14 Jehovah of *a*, has said
22:15 Jehovah of *a*, has said: Go
22:25 utterance of Jehovah of *a*
23:9 Jehovah of *a* himself has
24:23 Jehovah of *a* has become
25:6 Jehovah of *a* will certainly
28:5 Jehovah of *a* will become as
28:22 Sovereign Lord, Jehovah of *a*
28:29 forth from Jehovah of *a*
29:6 From Jehovah of *a* you will
31:4 Jehovah of *a* will come down
31:5 Jehovah of *a* will in the
37:16 Jehovah of *a*, the God of
37:32 zeal of Jehovah of *a* will
39:5 the word of Jehovah of *a*
44:6 Jehovah of *a*, I am the first
45:13 Jehovah of *a* has said
47:4 Jehovah of *a* is his name
48:2 Jehovah of *a* being his name
51:15 Jehovah of *a* is his name
54:5 Jehovah of *a* being his name
Jer 2:19 Lord, Jehovah of *a*
3:19 of the *a* of the nations
5:14 Jehovah, the God of *a*, has
6:6 what Jehovah of *a* has said
6:9 what Jehovah of *a* has said
7:3 This is what Jehovah of *a*
7:21 This is what Jehovah of *a*
8:3 utterance of Jehovah of *a*
9:7 what Jehovah of *a* has said
Jer 9:15 Jehovah of *a*, the God of
9:17 what Jehovah of *a* has said
10:16 Jehovah of *a* is his name
11:17 And Jehovah of *a* himself
11:20 Jehovah of *a* is judging
11:22 what Jehovah of *a* has said
15:16 O Jehovah God of *a*
16:9 this is what Jehovah of *a*
19:3 This is what Jehovah of *a*
19:11 what Jehovah of *a* has said
19:15 Jehovah of *a*, the God of
20:12 you, O Jehovah of *a*, are
23:15 what Jehovah of *a* has said
23:16 what Jehovah of *a* has said
23:36 Jehovah of *a*, our God
25:8 what Jehovah of *a* has said
25:27 Jehovah of *a*, the God of
25:28 what Jehovah of *a* has said
25:29 utterance of Jehovah of *a*
25:32 This is what Jehovah of *a*
26:18 Jehovah of *a* has said
27:4 This is what Jehovah of *a*
27:18 please, beseech Jehovah of *a*
27:19 what Jehovah of *a* has said
27:21 this is what Jehovah of *a*
28:2 This is what Jehovah of *a*
28:14 this is what Jehovah of *a*
29:4 This is what Jehovah of *a*
29:8 this is what Jehovah of *a*
29:17 what Jehovah of *a* has said
29:21 This is what Jehovah of *a*
29:25 This is what Jehovah of *a*
30:8 utterance of Jehovah of *a*
31:23 Jehovah of *a*, the God of
31:35 whose name is Jehovah of *a*
32:14 Jehovah of *a*, the God of
32:15 Jehovah of *a*, the God of
32:18 Jehovah of *a* being his name
33:11 Laud Jehovah of *a*, for
33:12 Jehovah of *a* has said, In
35:13 Jehovah of *a*, the God of
35:17 Jehovah the God of *a*, the
35:18 Jehovah of *a*, the God of
35:19 Jehovah of *a*, the God of
38:17 Jehovah, the God of *a*, the
39:16 Jehovah of *a*, the God of
42:15 Jehovah of *a*, the God of
42:18 Jehovah of *a*, the God of
43:10 what Jehovah of *a*, the God
44:2 what Jehovah of *a*, the God
44:7 Jehovah, the God of *a*, the
44:11 this is what Jehovah of *a*
44:25 is what Jehovah of *a*, the
46:10 Jehovah of *a*, the day of
46:10 Jehovah of *a*, has a
46:18 whose name is Jehovah of *a*
46:25 Jehovah of *a*, the God of
48:1 Jehovah of *a*, the God of
48:15 whose name is Jehovah of *a*
49:5 Sovereign Lord, Jehovah of *a*
49:7 what Jehovah of *a* has said
49:26 utterance of Jehovah of *a*
49:35 Jehovah of *a* has said, Here
50:18 Jehovah of *a*, the God of
50:25 Jehovah of *a*, has in the
50:31 Jehovah of *a*, for your day
50:33 Jehovah of *a* has said
50:34 Jehovah of *a* being his name
51:5 their God, from Jehovah of *a*
51:14 Jehovah of *a* has sworn by
51:19 Jehovah of *a* is his name
51:33 Jehovah of *a*, the God of
51:57 whose name is Jehovah of *a*
51:58 Jehovah of *a* has said
Ho 12:5 Jehovah the God of the *a*
Am 3:13 Jehovah, the God of the *a*
4:13 the God of *a* is his name
5:14 the God of *a* may come to be
5:15 the God of *a* will show favor
5:16 Jehovah the God of *a*, Jehovah
5:27 the God of *a* has said
6:8 of Jehovah the God of *a*
6:14 Jehovah the God of the *a*
9:5 Lord, Jehovah of the *a*
Mic 4:4 Jehovah of *a* has spoken it
Na 2:13 the utterance of Jehovah of *a*
3:5 the utterance of Jehovah of *a*
Hab 2:13 Is it not from Jehovah of *a*
Zep 2:9 Jehovah of *a*, the God of
2:10 the people of Jehovah of *a*
Hag 1:2 what Jehovah of *a* has said
1:5 what Jehovah of *a* has said
1:7 what Jehovah of *a* has said
1:9 the utterance of Jehovah of *a*
Hag 1:14 the house of Jehovah of *a*
2:4 the utterance of Jehovah of *a*
2:6 what Jehovah of *a* has said
2:7 Jehovah of *a* has said
2:8 the utterance of Jehovah of *a*
2:9 Jehovah of *a* has said
2:9 the utterance of Jehovah of *a*
2:11 what Jehovah of *a* has said
2:23 the utterance of Jehovah of *a*
2:23 the utterance of Jehovah of *a*
Zec 1:3 what Jehovah of *a* has said
1:3 the utterance of Jehovah of *a*
1:3 Jehovah of *a* has said
1:4 Jehovah of *a* has said, Return
1:6 what Jehovah of *a* had in mind
1:12 Jehovah of *a*, how long will
1:14 what Jehovah of *a* has said
1:16 the utterance of Jehovah of *a*
1:17 what Jehovah of *a* has said
2:8 what Jehovah of *a* has said
2:9 know that Jehovah of *a*
2:11 to know that Jehovah of *a*
3:7 what Jehovah of *a* has said
3:9 the utterance of Jehovah of *a*
3:10 the utterance of Jehovah of *a*
4:6 Jehovah of *a* has said
4:9 to know that Jehovah of *a*
5:4 the utterance of Jehovah of *a*
6:12 what Jehovah of *a* has said
6:15 to know that Jehovah of *a*
7:3 the house of Jehovah of *a*
7:4 the word of Jehovah of *a*
7:9 what Jehovah of *a* has said
7:12 words that Jehovah of *a* sent
7:12 on the part of Jehovah of *a*
7:13 Jehovah of *a* has said
8:1 the word of Jehovah of *a*
8:2 what Jehovah of *a* has said
8:3 the mountain of Jehovah of *a*
8:4 what Jehovah of *a* has said
8:6 what Jehovah of *a* has said
8:6 the utterance of Jehovah of *a*
8:7 what Jehovah of *a* has said
8:9 what Jehovah of *a* has said
8:9 house of Jehovah of *a* was
8:11 the utterance of Jehovah of *a*
8:14 what Jehovah of *a* has said
8:14 Jehovah of *a* has said, and I
8:18 the word of Jehovah of *a*
8:19 what Jehovah of *a* has said
8:20 what Jehovah of *a* has said
8:21 and to seek Jehovah of *a*
8:22 come to seek Jehovah of *a* in
8:23 what Jehovah of *a* has said
9:15 Jehovah of *a* himself will
10:3 Jehovah of *a* has turned his
12:5 Jehovah of *a* their God
13:2 the utterance of Jehovah of *a*
13:7 the utterance of Jehovah of *a*
14:16 the King, Jehovah of *a*
14:17 to the King, Jehovah of *a*
14:21 belonging to Jehovah of *a*
14:21 the house of Jehovah of *a*
Mal 1:4 what Jehovah of *a* has said
1:6 Jehovah of *a* has said to you
1:8 Jehovah of *a* has said
1:9 Jehovah of *a* has said
1:10 Jehovah of *a* has said, and
1:11 Jehovah of *a* has said
1:13 Jehovah of *a* has said
1:14 a great King, Jehovah of *a*
2:2 Jehovah of *a* has said
2:4 Jehovah of *a* has said
2:7 messenger of Jehovah of *a*
2:8 Jehovah of *a* has said
2:12 offering to Jehovah of *a*
2:16 Jehovah of *a* has said
3:1 Jehovah of *a* has said
3:5 Jehovah of *a* has said
3:7 Jehovah of *a* has said
3:10 Jehovah of *a* has said
3:11 Jehovah of *a* has said
3:12 Jehovah of *a* has said
3:14 on account of Jehovah of *a*
3:17 Jehovah of *a* has said
4:1 Jehovah of *a* has said
4:3 Jehovah of *a* has said
Mt 22:7 and sent his *a* and destroyed
Lu 21:20 surrounded by encamped *a*
Ro 9:29 Jehovah of *a* had left a seed
Heb 11:34 routed the *a* of foreigners
Jas 5:4 into the ears of Jehovah of *a*
Re 9:16 number of the *a* of cavalry
19:14 *a* that were in heaven were

Re 19:19 *a* gathered together to wage

Armoni

2Sa 21:8 *A* and Mephibosheth, and the

Armor

1Sa 31:9 strip off his *a* and send
31:10 put his *a* in the house of
1Ki 10:25 garments and *a* and balsam
2Ki 10:2 a fortified city and the *a*
1Ch 10:9 take off his head and his *a*
10:10 *a* in the house of their god
2Ch 9:24 *a* and balsam oil, horses
Job 20:24 run away from *a* of iron
39:21 It goes forth to meet *a*
Eze 39:9 build fires with the *a* and
39:10 the *a* they will light fires
Eph 6:11 complete suit of *a* from God
6:13 complete suit of *a* from God

Armor-bearer

1Sa 14:6 said to the attendant, his *a*
14:7 *a* said to him: Do whatever
14:12 answered Jonathan and his *a*
14:12 Jonathan said to his *a*
14:13 and his *a* after him
14:13 his *a* was putting them to
14:14 and his *a* struck them down
14:17 Jonathan and his *a* were not
16:21 David . . . came to be his *a*
31:4 Saul said to his *a:* Draw
31:4 his *a* was unwilling, because
31:5 *a* saw that Saul had died
31:6 his *a*, even all his men
1Ch 10:4 Saul said to his *a:* Draw
10:4 his *a* was unwilling, because
10:5 his *a* saw that Saul had died
11:39 *a* of Joab the son of Zeruiah

Armor-bearers

2Sa 23:37 *a* of Joab the son of Zeruiah

Armory

2Ki 20:13 his *a* and all that was to
Ne 3:19 to the *A* at the Buttress
Isa 22:8 *a* of the house of the forest
39:2 all his *a* and all that was

Armpits

Jer 38:12 cloth under your *a* beneath

Armrests

1Ki 10:19 *a* on this side and on that
10:19 were standing beside the *a*
2Ch 9:18 *a* on this side and on that
9:18 were standing beside the *a*

Arms

De 33:7 His *a* have contended for what
33:27 the indefinitely lasting *a*
Jg 15:14 ropes that were upon his *a*
16:12 from off his *a* like a thread
2Sa 22:35 *a* have pressed down a bow
2Ki 9:24 shoot Jehoram between the *a*
Ezr 4:23 stopped them by force of *a*
Job 22:9 the *a* of fatherless boys are
Ps 18:34 my *a* have pressed down a bow
37:17 *a* of the wicked ones will be
Pr 31:17 and she invigorates her *a*
Isa 51:5 my own *a* will judge even
Eze 13:20 rip them from off your *a*
30:22 and I will break his *a*
30:24 *a* of the king of Babylon
30:24 will break the *a* of Pharaoh
30:25 the *a* of the king of Babylon
30:25 very *a* of Pharaoh will fall
Da 2:32 and its *a* were of silver
10:6 his *a* and the place of his
11:15 *a* of the south, they will
11:22 regards the *a* of the flood
11:31 be *a* that will stand up
Ho 7:15 I strengthened their *a*, but
11:3 taking them upon my *a*
Mr 9:36 put his *a* around it and said
10:16 took the children into his *a*
Lu 2:28 received it into his *a* and

Army

Ge 2:1 *a* came to their completion
21:22 Phicol the chief of his *a*
21:32 Phicol the chief of his *a* and
26:26 Phicol the chief of his *a*
Nu 1:3 going out to the *a* in Israel
1:20 everyone going out to the *a*
1:22 everyone going out to the *a*
1:24 everyone going out to the *a*
1:26 everyone going out to the *a*
1:28 everyone going out to the *a*
1:30 everyone going out to the *a*
Nu 1:32 everyone going out to the *a*
1:34 everyone going out to the *a*
1:36 everyone going out to the *a*
1:38 everyone going out to the *a*
1:40 everyone going out to the *a*
1:42 everyone going out to the *a*
1:45 everyone going out to the *a* in
2:4 his *a* and the ones registered
2:6 his *a* and his registered ones
2:8 his *a* and his registered ones
2:11 his *a* and his registered ones
2:13 his *a* and the ones registered
2:15 his *a* and the ones registered
2:19 his *a* and the ones registered
2:21 his *a* and the ones registered
2:23 his *a* and the ones registered
2:26 his *a* and the ones registered
2:28 his *a* and the ones registered
2:30 his *a* and the ones registered
10:14 Nahshon . . . over its *a*
10:15 over the *a* of . . . Issachar
10:16 over the *a* of . . . Zebulun
10:18 camp of Reuben . . . its *a*
10:19 over the *a* of . . . Simeon
10:20 over the *a* of . . . Gad
10:22 sons of Ephraim . . . its *a*
10:23 over the *a* of . . . Manasseh
10:24 over the *a* of . . . Benjamin
10:25 Ahiezer . . . was over its *a*
10:26 over the *a* of . . . Asher
10:27 over the *a* of . . . Naphtali
26:2 going out to the *a* in Israel
31:3 men from among you for the *a*
31:4 you will send into the *a*
31:5 thousand equipped for the *a*
31:6 Moses sent them . . . to the *a*
31:6 and Phinehas . . . to the *a*
31:21 said to the men of the *a*
31:48 of the thousands of the *a*
31:53 The men of the *a* had taken
32:27 everyone equipped for the *a*
De 4:19 all the *a* of the heavens, and
17:3 or all the *a* of the heavens
24:5 should not go out into the *a*
Jos 4:13 thousand equipped for the *a*
5:14 as prince of the *a* of Jehovah
5:15 prince of the *a* of Jehovah
22:33 going up for *a* service
Jg 4:2 the chief of his *a* was Sisera
4:7 Sisera the chief of Jabin's *a*
8:6 has to be given to your *a*
9:29 Make your *a* numerous and
1Sa 12:9 the chief of the *a* of Hazor
14:50 chief of his *a* was Abner
17:55 to Abner the chief of the *a*
26:5 the chief of his *a;* and Saul
28:1 *a* to make war against Israel
2Sa 2:8 chief of the *a* that had
3:23 Joab and all the *a* that was
8:16 Joab . . . was over the *a*
10:7 Joab and all the *a* and the
10:16 chief of the *a* of Hadadezer
10:18 Shobach the chief of their *a*
17:25 Amasa . . . over the *a*
19:13 *a* chief before me always
20:23 Joab was over all the *a* of
1Ki 1:19 Joab the chief of the *a*
1:25 the chiefs of the *a* and
2:32 the chief of the *a* of Israel
2:32 the chief of the *a* of Judah
2:35 in place of him over the *a*
4:4 Benaiah . . . was over the *a*
11:15 Joab the chief of the *a*
11:21 Joab the chief of the *a* had
16:16 Omri, the chief of the *a*
22:19 *a* of the heavens standing by
2Ki 4:13 to the chief of the *a* for you
5:1 Naaman, the chief of the *a* of
17:16 to all the *a* of the heavens
21:3 to bow down to all the *a* of
21:5 all the *a* of the heavens in
23:4 for all the *a* of the heavens
23:5 to all the *a* of the heavens
25:19 the chief of the *a*, the one
1Ch 5:18 and sixty going out to the *a*
7:4 were troops of the *a* for war
7:11 going out to the *a* for war
7:40 was in the *a* in the war
12:8 *a* men for the war, keeping
12:14 sons of Gad, heads of the *a*
12:21 came to be chiefs in the *a*
12:23 those equipped for the *a*
12:24 hundred, equipped for the *a*
12:25 men of valor of the *a* were
1Ch 12:33 those going out to the *a*
12:36 those going out to the *a* for
12:37 weapons of the military *a*
18:15 And Joab . . . was over the *a*
19:8 sent Joab and all the *a* and
19:16 chief of the *a* of Hadadezer
19:18 Shophach the chief of the *a*
20:1 the combat force of the *a*
26:26 chiefs of the *a* had made
27:34 chief of the *a* of the king
2Ch 17:18 men outfitted for the *a*
18:18 *a* of the heavens standing
25:5 men going out to the *a*
25:7 let the *a* of Israel come
26:13 *a* forces were three hundred
26:14 for the entire *a*, shields
28:9 *a* that was coming to
33:3 *a* of the heavens and serve
33:5 to all the *a* of the heavens
33:11 *a* that belonged to the king
Ne 9:6 the heavens, and all their *a*
9:6 *a* of the heavens are bowing
Ps 10:10 the *a* of dejected ones has to
33:6 by the spirit . . . all their *a*
68:11 The women . . . are a large *a*
148:2 Praise him, all you his *a*
Isa 13:4 is mustering the *a* of war
24:21 *a* of the height in the
34:2 rage against all their *a*
34:4 *a* of the heavens must rot
34:4 *a* will all shrivel away
40:26 *a* of them even by number
45:12 *a* of them I have commanded
Jer 8:2 to all the *a* of the heavens
19:13 to all the *a* of the heavens
33:22 *a* of the heavens cannot be
51:3 to destruction all her *a*
52:25 of the chief of the *a*, the
Da 4:35 among the *a* of the heavens
8:10 to the *a* of the heavens, so
8:10 caused some of the *a* and some
8:11 to the Prince of the *a* it put
8:12 *a* itself was gradually given
8:13 the *a* things to trample on
Zep 1:5 to the *a* of the heavens
Mt 8:5 an *a* officer came to him
8:8 In reply the *a* officer said
8:13 Jesus said to the *a* officer
27:54 the *a* officer and those with
Mr 15:39 when the *a* officer that was
15:44 summoning the *a* officer, he
15:45 certain from the *a* officer
Lu 2:13 a multitude of the heavenly *a*
7:2 a certain *a* officer's slave
7:6 the *a* officer had already
23:47 *a* officer began to glorify
Ac 7:42 service to the *a* of heaven
10:1 Cornelius, an *a* officer of
10:22 Cornelius, an *a* officer
21:32 took soldiers and *a* officers
22:25 Paul said to the *a* officer
22:26 when the *a* officer heard
23:17 called one of the *a* officers
23:23 two of the *a* officers and
24:23 he ordered the *a* officer
27:1 *a* officer named Julius of
27:6 *a* officer found a boat from
27:11 *a* officer went heeding the
27:31 Paul said to the *a* officer
27:43 *a* officer desired to bring
Re 19:19 on the horse and with his *a*

Arnan

1Ch 3:21 the sons of Rephaiah *A*
3:21 the sons of *A* Obadiah

Arni

Lu 3:33 son of *A*, son of Hezron, son

Arnon

Nu 21:13 the region of the *A*, which
21:13 *A* is the boundary of Moab
21:14 and the torrent valleys of *A*
21:24 from the *A* to the Jabbok
21:26 as far as the *A*
21:28 of the high places of the *A*
22:36 is on the bank of the *A*
De 2:24 cross the torrent valley of *A*
2:36 the torrent valley of *A*, and
3:8 torrent valley of *A* as far as
3:12 by the torrent valley of *A*
3:16 to the torrent valley of *A*
4:48 the torrent valley of *A*, up to
Jos 12:1 from the torrent valley of *A*
12:2 of the torrent valley of *A*

Lu 18:8 when the Son of man *a*, will
22:18 until the kingdom of God *a*
Joh 4:25 Whenever that one *a*, he
7:31 When the Christ *a*, he will
15:26 helper *a* that I will send
16:4 hour for them *a*, you may
16:8 one *a* he will give the world
16:13 one *a*, the spirit of the
Ac 1:8 the holy spirit *a* upon you
2:20 illustrious day of Jehovah *a*
1Co 11:26 of the Lord, until he *a*
13:10 that which is complete *a*
16:10 if Timothy *a*, see that he

Arriving
Ge 19:22 to do a thing until your *a*
Ex 10:26 to Jehovah until our *a* there
1Ki 14:17 she was *a* at the threshold
Ps 107:18 *a* at the gates of death
Da 9:21 *a* by me at the time of the
Mt 12:44 on *a* it finds it unoccupied
24:46 master on *a* finds him doing
Lu 11:25 on *a* it finds it swept clean
12:36 at his *a* and knocking they
12:37 master on *a* finds watching
12:43 if his master on *a* finds him
Ac 9:26 *a* in Jerusalem he made
15:4 On *a* in Jerusalem they were
17:10 *a*, went into the synagogue

Arrogant
Ps 75:5 Do not speak with an *a* neck
101:5 haughty eyes and of *a* heart
123:4 on the part of the *a* ones
Pr 21:4 an *a* heart, the lamp of the
28:25 *a* in soul stirs up contention

Arrogantly
Job 22:29 when you speak *a*

Arrow
1Sa 20:36 shot the *a* to make it pass
20:37 *a* that Jonathan had shot
20:37 the *a* farther away from you
2Ki 9:24 the *a* came out at his heart
13:17 Jehovah's *a* of salvation
13:17 *a* of salvation against Syria
19:32 nor will he shoot an *a*
Job 41:28 An *a* does not chase it away
Ps 11:2 make ready their *a* upon the
64:3 aimed their *a*, bitter speech
64:7 shoot at them with an *a*
91:5 of the *a* that flies by day
Pr 7:23 *a* cleaves open his liver
25:18 *a* is a man testifying
Isa 34:15 *a* snake has made its nest
37:33 nor will he shoot an *a*
49:2 made me a polished *a*
Jer 9:8 tongue is a slaughtering *a*
50:14 Spare no *a*, for it is
La 3:12 as the target for the *a*
Zec 9:14 *a* will certainly go forth

Arrowhead
Job 41:26 Nor spear, dart or *a*

Arrows
Nu 24:8 them to pieces with his *a*
De 32:23 My *a* I shall spend upon them
32:42 intoxicate my *a* with blood
1Sa 20:20 shoot three *a* to one side
20:21 saying, Go, find the *a*
20:21 *a* are on this side of you
20:22 *a* are farther away from you
20:36 the *a* that I am shooting
20:38 picking up the *a* and then
2Sa 22:15 he kept sending out *a*, that
2Ki 13:15 Take a bow and *a*. So he
13:15 to himself a bow and *a*
13:18 Take the *a*. At that he took
1Ch 12:2 stones or with *a* in the bow
2Ch 26:15 shoot *a* and great stones
Job 6:4 *a* of the Almighty are with
Ps 7:13 *a* he will make flaming ones
18:14 he kept sending out his *a*
38:2 *a* have sunk themselves deep
45:5 Your *a* are sharp—under you
57:4 Whose teeth are spears and *a*
58:7 bend the bow for his *a* as
77:17 own *a* proceeded to go here
120:4 Sharpened *a* of a mighty man
127:4 *a* in the hand of a mighty
144:6 Send out your *a* that you
Pr 26:18 fiery missiles, *a* and death
Isa 5:28 *a* are sharpened and all
7:24 With *a* and the bow he will
Jer 50:9 *a* are like those of a mighty
Jer 51:11 Polish the *a*. Fill the
Eze 5:16 injurious *a* of the famine
5:16 *a* I shall send to bring you
21:21 He has shaken the *a*
39:3 *a* I shall cause to fall out
39:9 the bows and with the *a*
Hab 3:11 your own *a* kept going

Art
Ac 16:16 the *a* of prediction
17:29 the *a* and contrivance of man
2Ti 4:2 and *a* of teaching
Tit 1:9 as respects his *a* of teaching

Artaxerxes
Ezr 4:7 in the days of *A*, Bishlam
4:7 to *A* the king of Persia
4:8 to *A* the king, as follows
4:11 To *A* the king your servants
4:23 document of *A* the king had
6:14 and *A* the king of Persia
7:1 reign of *A* the king of Persia
7:7 seventh year of *A* the king
7:11 letter that King *A* gave Ezra
7:12 *A*, the king of kings, to
7:21 *A* the king, an order has been
8:1 *A* the king out of Babylon
Ne 2:1 twentieth year of *A* the king
5:14 the thirty-second year of *A*
13:6 the thirty-second year of *A*

Artemas
Tit 3:12 I send *A* or Tychicus to you

Artemis
Ac 19:24 making silver shrines of *A*
19:27 temple . . . great goddess *A*
19:28 Great is *A* of the Ephesians!
19:34 Great is *A* of the Ephesians!
19:35 temple keeper of the great *A*

Artfully
2Pe 1:16 *a* contrived false stories

Article
Le 13:49 in any *a* of skin, it is the
13:52 any *a* of skin in which the
13:53 the woof or in any *a* of skin
13:57 *a* of skin, it is breaking out
13:58 any *a* of skin that you may
13:59 in any *a* of skin, in order to
15:4 any *a* upon which he may sit
15:6 sits upon the *a* upon which
15:22 *a* upon which she was sitting
15:23 upon another *a* that she was
15:26 any *a* upon which she may sit
Nu 31:20 and every *a* of skin and
31:20 every *a* of wood you should
35:22 him or has thrown any *a*
2Ki 12:13 any sort of gold *a* and
12:13 *a* of silver from the money

Articles
Ge 24:53, 53 *a* of silver and *a* of gold
Ex 3:22, 22 *a* of silver and *a* of gold
11:2, 2 *a* of silver and *a* of gold
12:35, 35 *a* of silver and *a* of gold
22:7 give his fellow money or *a* to
35:22 all sorts of *a* of gold
Nu 31:50 *a* of gold, ankle chainlets
Jos 6:19 the *a* of copper and iron are
6:24 and the *a* of copper and iron
7:11 put it among their own *a*
1Sa 6:8 golden *a* that you must return
6:15 in which the golden *a* were
2Sa 8:10, 10 *a* of silver and *a* of gold
8:10 and *a* of copper
1Ki 7:51 *a* he put in the treasures of
10:25, 25 *a* of silver and *a* of gold
15:15 silver and gold and *a*
2Ki 14:14 *a* to be found at the house
1Ch 18:10 *a* of gold and silver and
2Ch 9:24, 24 *a* of silver and *a* of gold
20:25 clothing and desirable *a*
25:24 *a* that were to be found in
32:27 for all the desirable *a*
36:10 *a* of the house of Jehovah
36:19 and also all its desirable *a*
Isa 10:28 Michmash he deposits his *a*
Jer 49:29 tent cloths and all their *a*
52:20 copper of them—all these *a*
Eze 16:17 beautiful *a* from my gold
16:39 and take your beautiful *a*
23:26 take away your beautiful *a*
27:9 to exchange *a* of merchandise
27:13 mankind and *a* of copper
27:13 *a* of exchange were given
27:17 *a* of exchange were given
Eze 27:19 *a* of exchange they proved
27:25 caravans for your *a* of
27:27 your *a* of exchange, your
27:27 those exchanging your *a* of
27:33 your *a* of exchange you made
27:34 As for your *a* of exchange
Da 11:8 desirable *a* of silver and of
Ho 13:15 pillage . . . all desirable *a*
Jon 1:5 the *a* that were in the ship
Na 2:9 of all sorts of desirable *a*

Artisan's
Ca 7:1 the work of an *a* hands

Artistic
Isa 3:24 of an *a* hair arrangement

Arts
Ex 7:11 same thing with . . . magic *a*
7:22 same thing with . . . secret *a*
8:7 same thing by their secret *a*
8:18 do the same by their secret *a*
Isa 3:3 and expert in magical *a*, and
Ac 8:9 been practicing magical *a* and
8:11 amazed . . . by his magical *a*
19:19 who practiced magical *a*

Arubboth
1Ki 4:10 the son of Hesed, in *A*

Arumah
Jg 9:41 continued to dwell in *A*, and

Arvad
Eze 27:8 inhabitants of Sidon and of *A*
27:11 The sons of *A*, even your

Arvadite
Ge 10:18 and the *A* and the Zemarite
1Ch 1:16 the *A* and the Zemarite and

Arzah
1Ki 16:9 drunk at the house of *A*

Asa
1Ki 15:8 *A* his son began to reign in
15:9 *A* reigned as king of Judah
15:11 *A* proceeded to do what was
15:13 *A* cut down her horrible
15:16 between *A* and Baasha the
15:17 to *A* the king of Judah
15:18 *A* took all the silver and
15:18 King *A* now sent them to
15:20 Ben-hadad listened to King *A*
15:22 And King *A*, for his part
15:22 and King *A* began to build
15:23 all the affairs of *A*
15:24 *A* lay down with his
15:25 *A* the king of Judah
15:28 the third year of *A* the king
15:32 between *A* and Baasha the
15:33 third year of *A* the king of
16:8 year of *A* the king of Judah
16:10 twenty-seventh year of *A*
16:15 *A* the king of Judah
16:23 thirty-first year of *A*
16:29 thirty-eighth year of *A*
22:41 Jehoshaphat the son of *A*
22:43 walking in all the way of *A*
22:46 in the days of *A* his father
1Ch 3:10 *A* his son, Jehoshaphat his
9:16 son of *A* the son of Elkanah
2Ch 14:1 *A* his son began to reign in
14:2 *A* proceeded to do what was
14:8 *A* came to have a military
14:10 *A* went out against him and
14:11 *A* began to call to Jehovah
14:12 the Ethiopians before *A*
14:13 *A* and the people that were
15:2 before *A* and said to him
15:2 Hear me, O *A* and all Judah
15:8 *A* heard these words and the
15:16 *A* the king himself removed
15:16 *A* cut down her horrible
16:1 year of the reign of *A*
16:1 in to *A* the king of Judah
16:2 *A* now brought out silver and
16:4 Ben-hadad listened to King *A*
16:6 *A* the king, he took all Judah
16:7 Hanani the seer came to *A*
16:10 *A* became offended at the
16:10 *A* began to crush some
16:11 affairs of *A*, the first and
16:12 *A* in the thirty-ninth year
16:13 *A* lay down with his
17:2 *A* his father had captured
20:32 way of his father *A*, and
21:12 ways of *A* the king of Judah
Jer 41:9 one that King *A* had made

Mt 1:7 Abijah became father to *A*
1:8 *A* became father to Jehoshaphat

Asahel
2Sa 2:18 Joab and Abishai and *A*
2:18 *A* was swift on his feet
2:19 *A* went chasing after Abner
2:20 Is this you, *A?* to which he
2:21 *A* did not want to turn aside
2:22 Abner said to *A* yet again
2:23 *A* fell and then died
2:30 nineteen men and *A*
2:32 *A* and bury him in the burial
3:27 because of the blood of *A*
3:30 *A* their brother to death at
23:24 *A* the brother of Joab was
1Ch 2:16 sons of Zeruiah were . . . *A*
11:26 were *A* the brother of Joab
27:7 was *A*, Joab's brother, and
2Ch 17:8 *A* and Shemiramoth and
31:13 and *A* . . . commissioners at
Ezr 10:15 Jonathan the son of *A* and

Asaiah
2Ki 22:12 and *A* the king's servant
22:14 *A* went to Huldah the
1Ch 4:36 *A* and Adiel and Jesimiel
6:30 Haggiah his son, *A* his son
9:5 Shilonites, *A* the firstborn
15:6 of the sons of Merari, *A* the
15:11 Levites Uriel, *A* and Joel
2Ch 34:20 *A* the king's servant

Asaph
2Ki 18:18 the son of *A* the recorder
18:37 *A* the recorder came to
1Ch 6:39 *A*, who was attending at his
6:39 *A* was the son of Berechiah
9:15 son of Zichri the son of *A*
15:17 *A* the son of Berechiah
15:19 singers Heman, *A* and Ethan
16:5 *A* the head, and second to
16:5 *A* with the cymbals playing
16:7 thank Jehovah by means of *A*
16:37 *A* and his brothers to
25:1 the sons of *A*, Heman and
25:2 Of the sons of *A*, Zaccur and
25:2 sons of *A* under the control
25:2 under the control of *A* the
25:6 control of the king were *A*
25:9 belonging to *A* for Joseph
26:1 of Kore of the sons of *A*
2Ch 5:12 singers belonging to . . . *A*
20:14 Levite of the sons of *A*
29:13 sons of *A*, Zechariah and
29:30 and of *A* the visionary
35:15 the singers the sons of *A*
35:15 *A* and of Heman and of
Ezr 2:41 The singers, the sons of *A*
3:10 the Levites the sons of *A*
Ne 2:8 to *A* the keeper of the park
7:44 The singers, the sons of *A*
11:17 Zabdi the son of *A*, the
11:22 Mica of the sons of *A*, the
12:35 Zaccur the son of *A*
12:46 in the days of David and *A*
Ps 50:*super* A melody of *A*
73:*super* A melody of *A*
74:*super* A maskil. Of *A*
75:*super* A melody. Of *A*. A song
76:*super* A melody. Of *A*. A song
77:*super* Of *A*. A melody
78:*super* Maskil. Of *A*
79:*super* A melody of *A*
80:*super* A reminder. Of *A*
81:*super* upon the Gittith. Of *A*
82:*super* A melody of *A*
83:*super* A song. A melody of *A*
Isa 36:3 Joah the son of *A* the
36:22 Joah the son of *A* the

Asarel
1Ch 4:16 sons of Jehallelel . . . *A*

Asa's
1Ki 15:14 *A* heart itself proved to be
2Ch 15:10 fifteenth year of *A* reign
15:17 *A* heart itself proved to
15:19 year of *A* reign

Ascend
De 30:12 *a* for us into the heavens
Jg 6:21 and fire began to *a* out of the
2Ki 19:23 *a* the height of mountainous
Ps 24:3 may *a* into the mountain of
104:8 Mountains proceeded to *a*
135:7 causing vapors to *a* from the
137:6 not to make Jerusalem *a*
139:8 *a* to heaven, there you would
Isa 34:3 their stink will *a;* and the
37:24 *a* the height of mountainous
Jer 10:13 he causes vapors to *a* from
49:22 will *a* and pounce down
51:16 causes vapors to *a* from the
51:53 Babylon should *a* to the
Joe 2:20 stink from him will . . . *a*
Am 4:10 the stink of your camps *a*
Ac 2:34 David did not *a* to the
Ro 10:6 Who will *a* into heaven?
Re 17:8 about to *a* out of the abyss

Ascendancy
1Ch 17:17 the man in the *a*, O Jehovah

Ascended
Ge 19:15 the dawn *a*, then the angels
19:28 smoke *a* from the land like
32:24 grapple . . . until the dawn *a*
32:26 the dawn has *a*. To this he
Jos 6:15 early, as soon as the dawn *a*
8:20 smoke of the city *a* to the
8:21 that the smoke of the city *a*
Jg 13:20 as the flame *a* from off the
13:20 angel *a* in the flame of the
1Sa 9:26 as soon as the dawn *a* Samuel
Ps 47:5 has *a* with joyful shouting
68:18 You have *a* on high; You have
78:21 anger also *a* against Israel
78:31 God's wrath itself *a*
Pr 30:4 Who has *a* to heaven that he
31:29 you have *a* above them all
Mr 3:13 he *a* a mountain and summoned
Joh 3:13 no man has *a* into heaven
20:17 not yet *a* to the Father
Ac 10:4 gifts of mercy have *a* as a
Eph 4:8 When he *a* on high he carried
4:9 he *a*, what does it mean
4:10 *a* far above all the heavens
Re 8:4 smoke of the incense *a* from
9:2 smoke *a* out of the pit as the

Ascending
Ge 28:12 God's angels *a* and descending
41:2 *a* out of the river Nile were
41:3 seven other cows *a* after them
41:18 *a* out of the river Nile were
41:19 seven other cows *a* after
Ex 19:18 *a* like the smoke of a kiln
De 28:43 keep *a* higher and higher
Jg 19:25 off at the *a* of the dawn
1Sa 5:12 kept *a* to the heavens
1Ki 18:44 cloud . . . *a* out of the sea
2Ki 2:11 went *a* in the windstorm to
Ne 2:15 *a* in the torrent valley by
4:21 the *a* of the dawn until the
Ps 74:23 against you is *a* constantly
Ec 3:21 spirit . . . whether it is *a*
Isa 34:10 its smoke will keep *a*
Eze 8:11 cloud of the incense was *a*
11:23 the glory of Jehovah went *a*
11:24 vision . . . went *a* from upon
Joe 2:20 stench from him will keep *a*
Jon 4:7 at the *a* of the dawn on the
Joh 1:51 *a* and descending to the Son
6:62 the Son of man *a* to where
20:17 I am *a* to my Father and
Re 7:2 angel *a* from the sunrising
13:1 wild beast *a* out of the sea
13:11 beast *a* out of the earth
19:3 smoke from her goes on *a*

Ascends
Job 20:6 excellency *a* to heaven itself
Re 11:7 beast that *a* out of the abyss
14:11 smoke of their torment *a*

Ascent
Nu 34:4 south of the *a* of Akrabbim
Jos 10:10 way of the *a* of Beth-horon
15:3 to the *a* of Akrabbim and
15:7 front of the *a* of Adummim
18:17 front of the *a* of Adummim
Jg 1:36 was from the *a* of Akrabbim
1Sa 9:11 going up on the *a* to the city
2Sa 15:30 up by the *a* of the Olives
2Ch 32:33 *a* to the burial places of
Ne 12:37 *a* of the wall above the
Ps 47:9 He is very high in his *a*
97:9 your *a* over all other gods
Isa 15:5 on the *a* of Luhith—with
Eze 40:31 and its *a* was eight steps
40:34 And its *a* was eight steps
40:37 And its *a* was eight steps

Ascents
Ps 120:*super* A Song of the *A*
121:*super* A Song for the *A*
122:*super* A Song of the *A*. Of David
123:*super* A Song of the *A*
124:*super* A Song of the *A*
125:*super* A Song of the *A*
126:*super* A Song of the *A*
127:*super* A Song of the *A*
128:*super* A Song of the *A*
129:*super* A Song of the *A*
130:*super* A Song of the *A*
131:*super* A Song of the *A*. Of David
132:*super* A Song of the *A*
133:*super* A Song of the *A*. Of David
134:*super* A Song of the *A*

Ascertain
1Sa 14:38 *a* and see in what way this
23:22 *a* and see his place where
23:23 *a* about all the hiding
Lu 19:15 in order to *a* what they had
Ac 23:28 wishing to *a* the cause for
2Co 2:9 write to *a* the proof of you

Ascertained
1Ki 7:47 the copper was not *a*
2Ch 4:18 of the copper was not *a*
Mt 2:7 and carefully *a* from them the
2:16 *a* from the astrologers
Ac 23:34 *a* that he was from Cilicia

Ascertaining
Mr 6:38 After *a* it, they said: Five
Lu 23:7 after *a* that he was from the
Ac 22:29 on *a* that he was a Roman and

Ascribe
Job 1:22 *a* anything improper to God
36:3 I shall *a* righteousness
Ps 29:1 *A* to Jehovah, O you sons of
29:1 *A* to Jehovah glory and
29:2 *A* to Jehovah the glory of his
68:34 *A* strength to God. Over
96:7 *A* to Jehovah, O you families
96:7 *A* to Jehovah glory and
96:8 *A* to Jehovah the glory

Asenappar
Ezr 4:10 *A* took into exile and settled

Asenath
Ge 41:45 gave him *A* the daughter of
41:50 *A* the daughter of Potiphera
46:20 *A* the daughter of Potiphera

Ash
Job 9:9 Making the *A* constellation
38:32 as for the *A* constellation
Ps 68:13 between the camp *a* heaps
Isa 41:19 the *a* and the cypress at
60:13 juniper tree, the *a* tree
La 4:5 have had to embrace *a* heaps

Ashamed
Ge 2:25 and yet they did not become *a*
Jg 3:25 waiting until they were *a*
2Ki 19:26 be terrified and will be *a*
Ezr 8:22 felt *a* to ask a military
9:6 my God, I do feel *a* and
Job 6:20 *a* because they had trusted
19:3 not *a* that you deal so hard
Ps 6:10 very much *a* and disturbed
6:10 they will be *a* instantly
25:2 O may I not be *a*. May my
25:3 hoping in you will be *a*
25:3 will be *a* who are dealing
25:20 May I not be *a*, for I have
31:1 O may I never be *a*
31:17 O Jehovah, may I not be *a*
31:17 May the wicked ones be *a*
34:5 faces could not possibly be *a*
35:26 Let those be *a* and abashed
37:19 *a* in the time of calamity
40:14 be *a* and abashed all together
69:6 those hoping in you not be *a*
70:2 May those be *a* and abashed
71:1 O may I never be *a*
71:13 May those be *a*, may those
71:24 For they have become *a*, for
83:17 be *a* and be disturbed for
86:17 may see it and be *a*
97:7 serving any carved image be *a*
109:28 but let them be *a*
119:6 that case I should not be *a*
119:46 And I shall not be *a*
119:78 presumptuous ones be *a*, for
119:80 order that I may not be *a*

Ps 127:5 They will not be *a*
129:5 They will be *a* and turn
Isa 1:29 *a* of the mighty trees that
19:9 must become *a*; also the
20:5 and be *a* of Ethiopia their
23:4 Be *a*, O Sidon; because the
24:23 glowing sun has become *a*
26:11 *a* at the zeal for your
29:22 Jacob will not now be *a*
30:5 *a* of a people that bring no
37:27 simply be terrified and *a*
41:11 become *a* and be humiliated
42:17 they will be very much *a*
44:9 in order that they may be *a*
44:11 be *a*, and the craftsmen
44:11 will be *a* at the same time
45:16 certainly be *a* and even be
45:17 You people will not be *a*
45:24 straight to him and be *a*
49:23 hoping in me will not be *a*
50:7 I know that I shall not be *a*
Jer 2:36 you will become *a*, just as
2:36 as you became *a* of Assyria
8:9 The wise ones have become *a*
8:12 positively could not feel *a*
12:13 *a* of the products of you
14:4 the farmers have become *a*
15:9 become *a* and felt abashed
22:22 you will be *a* and certainly
31:19 I became *a*, and I also felt
48:13 have to be *a* of Chemosh
48:13 Israel have become *a* of
48:39 He has become *a*. And Moab
49:23 and Arpad have become *a*
50:12 has become very much *a*
51:17 *a* because of the carved
51:47 own land will become *a*
Eze 16:52 *a* and bear your humiliation
16:63 remember and actually be *a*
32:30 their mightiness, *a*
36:32 Be *a* and feel humiliation
Ho 4:19 be *a* of their sacrifices
10:6 Israel will be *a* of its
Joe 1:12 exultation has gone *a* away
2:26 my people will not be *a*
2:27 my people will not be *a* to
Mic 3:7 visionaries will have to be *a*
7:16 *a* of all their mightiness
Zep 3:11 that day you will not be *a*
Zec 13:4 prophets will become *a*
Mr 8:38 For whoever becomes *a* of me
8:38 be *a* of him when he arrives
Lu 9:26 *a* of me and of my words
9:26 *a* of this one when he arrives
16:3 I am *a* to beg
Ro 1:16 I am not *a* of the good news
6:21 Things of which you are now *a*
1Co 11:22 those who have nothing *a*
2Co 4:2 things of which to be *a*
Php 1:20 shall not be *a* in any respect
2Th 3:14 that he may become *a*
2Ti 1:8 not become *a* of the witness
1:12 but I am not *a*. For I know
1:16 not become *a* of my chains
2:15 with nothing to be *a* of
Tit 2:8 may get *a*, having nothing
Heb 2:11 not *a* to call them brothers
11:16 God is not *a* of them, to
1Pe 3:16 they may get *a* who are

Ashan
Jos 15:42 Libnah and Ether and *A*
19:7 Ain, Rimmon and Ether and *A*
1Ch 4:32 Tochen and *A*, five cities
6:59 *A* with its pasture grounds

Asharelah
1Ch 25:2 Of the sons of Asaph . . . *A*

Ashbea
1Ch 4:21 fine fabric of the house of *A*

Ashbel
Ge 46:21 sons of Benjamin were . . . *A*
Nu 26:38 of *A* the family of the
1Ch 8:1 *A* the second and Aharah the

Ashbelites
Nu 26:38 Ashbel the family of the *A*

Ashdod
Jos 11:22 and in *A* that they remained
15:46 *A* and their settlements
15:47 *A*, its dependent towns and
1Sa 5:1 brought it from Ebenezer to *A*
5:5 the threshold of Dagon in *A*
5:6 namely, *A* and its territories
1Sa 5:7 men of *A* came to see that it
6:17 golden piles . . . for *A* one
2Ch 26:6 and the wall of *A*, after
26:6 built cities in *A* territory
Isa 20:1 year that Tartan came to *A*
20:1 war against *A* and to capture
Jer 25:20 and the remnant of *A*
Am 1:8 cut off the inhabitant from *A*
3:9 on the dwelling towers in *A*
Zep 2:4 *A*, at high noon they will
Zec 9:6 actually seat himself in *A*
Ac 8:40 Philip was found to be in *A*

Ashdodite
Ne 13:23 had given a dwelling to *A*
13:24 sons, half were speaking *A*

Ashdodites
Jos 13:3 the *A*, the Ashkelonites, the
1Sa 5:3 *A* got up early the very next
5:6 came to be heavy upon the *A*
Ne 4:7 the *A* heard that the repairing

Asher
Ge 30:13 So she called his name *A*
35:26 sons by Zilpah . . . *A*
46:17 sons of *A* were Imnah and
49:20 Out of *A* his bread will be
Ex 1:4 Dan and Naphtali, Gad and *A*
Nu 1:13 of *A*, Pagiel the son of Ochran
1:40 the sons of *A*, their births
1:41 registered . . . tribe of *A*
2:27 tribe of *A*, and the chieftain
2:27 for the sons of *A* is Pagiel
7:72 chieftain for the sons of *A*
10:26 the tribe of the sons of *A*
13:13 of the tribe of *A*, Sethur the
26:44 sons of *A* by their families
26:47 families of the sons of *A*
34:27 of *A* a chieftain, Ahihud the
De 27:13 Gad and *A* and Zebulun, Dan
33:24 And as to *A* he said: Blessed
33:24 Blessed with sons is *A*
Jos 17:7 from *A* to Michmethath
17:10 the north they reach to *A*
17:11 and in *A* Beth-shean and its
19:24 the tribe of the sons of *A*
19:31 the tribe of the sons of *A*
19:34 to *A* it reached on the west
21:6 and out of the tribe of *A* and
21:30 And out of the tribe of *A*
Jg 1:31 *A* did not drive out the
5:17 *A* sat idle at the seashore
6:35 messengers through *A* and
7:23 and *A* and all of Manasseh, and
1Ki 4:16 the son of Hushai, in *A* and
1Ch 2:2 Benjamin, Naphtali, Gad and *A*
6:62 from the tribe of *A* and from
6:74 from the tribe of *A*, Mashal
7:30 The sons of *A* were Imnah and
7:40 All these were the sons of *A*
12:36 of *A* those going out to the
2Ch 30:11 individuals from *A* and
Eze 48:2 the western border, *A* one
48:3 on the boundary of *A*, from
48:34 the gate of *A*, one
Re 7:6 out of the tribe of *A* twelve

Asherites
Jg 1:32 the *A* continued to dwell in

Asher's
Nu 26:46 name of *A* daughter was Serah
Lu 2:36 of *A* tribe (this woman was

Ashes
Ge 18:27 whereas I am dust and *a*
Ex 27:3 for clearing away its fatty *a*
Le 1:16 to the place for the fatty *a*
4:12 the fatty *a* are poured out
4:12 the fatty *a* are poured out
6:10 lift up the fatty *a* of the
6:11 fatty *a* out to a clean place
Nu 4:13 clear away the fatty *a* of the
19:9 gather up the *a* of the cow
19:10 one gathering the *a* of the
2Sa 13:19 Tamar placed *a* upon her
1Ki 13:3 the fatty *a* that are upon it
13:5 the fatty *a* were spilled out
Es 4:1 put on sackcloth and *a* and go
4:3 Sackcloth and *a* themselves
Job 2:8 he was sitting in among the *a*
13:12 sayings are proverbs of *a*
30:19 show myself like dust and *a*
42:6 I do repent in dust and *a*
Ps 102:9 I have eaten *a* themselves
147:16 he scatters just like *a*
Isa 44:20 He is feeding on *a*
58:5 sackcloth and *a* as his couch
61:3 a headdress instead of *a*
Jer 6:26 and wallow in the *a*
31:40 carcasses and of the fatty *a*
La 3:16 has made me cower in the *a*
Eze 27:30 In the *a* they will wallow
28:18 make you *a* upon the earth
Da 9:3 fasting and sackcloth and *a*
Jon 3:6 and sat down in the *a*
Mt 11:21 repented in sackcloth and *a*
Lu 10:13 sitting in sackcloth and *a*
Heb 9:13 the *a* of a heifer sprinkled
2Pe 2:6 Sodom and Gomorrah to *a*

Ash-heaps
Ne 2:13 and to the Gate of the *A*
3:13 as far as the Gate of the *A*
3:14 the Gate of the *A* was what
12:31 wall to the Gate of the *A*

Ashhur
1Ch 2:24 *A* the father of Tekoa
4:5 *A* the father of Tekoa came

Ashima
2Ki 17:30 men of Hamath . . . made *A*

Ashkelon
Jg 1:18 *A* and its territory and Ekron
14:19 he went down to *A* and struck
1Sa 6:17 golden piles . . . for *A* one
2Sa 1:20 in the streets of *A*
Jer 25:20 kings of the land of . . . *A*
47:5 *A* has been put to silence
47:7 *A* and for the coast of the
Am 1:8 holder of the scepter from *A*
Zep 2:4 *A* is to be a desolate waste
2:7 In the houses of *A*, in the
Zec 9:5 *A* will see and get afraid
9:5 *A* . . . will not be inhabited

Ashkelonites
Jos 13:3 the *A*, the Gittites and the

Ashkenaz
Ge 10:3 sons of Gomer were *A* and
1Ch 1:6 sons of Gomer were *A* and
Jer 51:27 of Ararat, Minni and *A*

Ashnah
Jos 15:33 Eshtaol and Zorah and *A*
15:43 Iphtah and *A* and Nezib

Ashore
Ac 27:26 cast *a* on a certain island

Ashpenaz
Da 1:3 to *A* his chief court official

Ashpit
1Sa 2:8 From the *a* he lifts up a poor
Ps 113:7 poor one from the *a* itself

Ashtaroth
De 1:4 was dwelling in *A*, in Edrei
Jos 9:10 king of Bashan, who was in *A*
12:4 who dwelt in *A* and Edrei
13:12 reigned in *A* and in Edrei
13:31 half of Gilead, and *A* and
1Ch 6:71 *A* with its pasture grounds

Ashterathite
1Ch 11:44 Uzzia the *A*

Ashteroth-karnaim
Ge 14:5 defeats on the Rephaim in *A*

Ashtoreth
Jg 2:13 serving Baal and the *A* images
10:6 the *A* images and the gods of
1Sa 7:3 put away . . . the *A* images
7:4 the Baals and the *A* images
12:10 the Baals and the *A* images
31:10 the house of the *A* images
1Ki 11:5 *A* the goddess of the
11:33 bow down to *A* the goddess
2Ki 23:13 *A* the disgusting thing of

Ashurites
2Sa 2:9 king over Gilead and the *A*

Ashvath
1Ch 7:33 sons of Japhlet . . . *A*

Asia
Ac 2:9 Pontus and the district of *A*
6:9 and *A*, to dispute with Stephen
16:6 the word in the district of *A*
19:10 inhabiting the district of *A*
19:22 time in the district of *A*
19:26 nearly all the district of *A*
19:27 the whole district of *A* and

Ac 20:4 the district of *A* Tychicus and
20:16 time in the district of *A*
20:18 into the district of *A* I was
21:27 the Jews from *A* on beholding
24:18 Jews from the district of *A*
27:2 coast of the district of *A*
Ro 16:5 a firstfruits of *A* for Christ
1Co 16:19 congregations of *A* send you
2Co 1:8 to us in the district of *A*
2Ti 1:15 the men in the district of *A*
1Pe 1:1 Galatia, Cappadocia, *A*, and
Re 1:4 congregations . . . district of *A*

Aside

Ge 19:2 turn *a*, please, into the house
19:3 they turned *a* to him and came
30:32 set *a* . . . sheep speckled
30:35 he set *a* on that day the
38:16 turned *a* to her by the road
46:26 *a* from the wives of Jacob's
49:10 will not turn *a* from Judah
Ex 3:3 Let me just turn *a* that I may
3:4 that he turned *a* to inspect
23:2 to turn *a* with the crowd in
32:8 turned *a* in a hurry from the
Nu 5:12 man's wife turns *a* in that
5:19 turned *a* in any uncleanness
5:20 turned *a* while under your
5:29 turn *a* while under her
16:26 Turn *a*, please, from before
16:49 *a* from those dead on account
22:23 the ass tried to turn *a* from
22:23 to turn her *a* to the road
22:26 was no way to turn *a* to the
22:33 tried to turn *a* before me
22:33 not turned *a* from before me
28:23 *A* from the morning burnt
28:31 *A* from the constant burnt
29:6 *a* from the monthly burnt
29:11 *a* from the sin offering of
29:16 *a* from the constant burnt
29:19 *a* from the constant burnt
29:22 *a* from the constant burnt
29:25 *a* from the constant burnt
29:28 *a* from the constant burnt
29:31 *a* from the constant burnt
29:34 *a* from the constant burnt
29:38 *a* from the constant burnt
De 3:5 *a* from very many rural towns
9:12 turned *a* quickly from the way
9:16 turned *a* quickly from the way
11:16 turn *a* and worship other
11:28 turn *a* from the way about
17:11 not turn *a* from the word
17:17 his heart may not turn *a*
17:20 turn *a* from the commandment
28:14 turn *a* from all the words
29:1 *a* from the covenant that he
31:29 turn *a* from the way about
Jos 1:7 Do not turn *a* from it to the
Jg 2:17 They quickly turned *a* from
4:18 So he turned *a* to her into
14:8 he turned *a* to look at the
18:3 so that they turned *a* there
18:15 they turned *a* there and came
19:11 let us turn *a* to this city
19:12 Let us not turn *a* to a city
19:15 they turned *a* there to go in
20:8 nor shall we turn *a* any of us
Ru 4:1 Do turn *a*, do sit down here
4:1 Hence he turned *a* and sat down
1Sa 6:12 did not turn *a* to the right
12:20 not turn *a* from following
12:21 must not turn *a* to follow
18:11 David turned *a* from before
2Sa 2:21 did not want to turn *a*
2:22 Turn your course *a* from
2:23 he kept refusing to turn *a*
3:27 Joab now led him *a* inside
6:10 David had it carried *a* to the
18:30 Step *a*, take your position
18:30 stepped *a* and kept standing
22:23 shall not turn *a* from them
1Ki 15:5 and he did not turn *a* from
22:32 they turned *a* against him
22:43 He did not turn *a* from it
2Ki 4:4 full ones you should set *a*
4:8 turn *a* there to eat bread
4:10 he can turn *a* there
4:11 turned *a* to the roof chamber
10:27 kept it set *a* for privies
10:29 Jehu did not turn *a* from
10:31 not turn *a* from the sins
13:2 He did not turn *a* from it
2Ki 18:6 not turn *a* from following
22:2 not turn *a* to the right or
1Ch 13:13 *a* to the house of Obed-edom
2Ch 8:15 not turn *a* from the king's
9:14 *a* from the men of travel and
20:32 he did not turn *a* from it
25:27 Amaziah turned *a* from
34:2 not turn *a* to the right or to
34:33 not turn *a* from following
35:15 turn *a* from their service
Job 1:1 and turning *a* from bad
1:8 and turning *a* from bad
2:3 and turning *a* from bad
6:18 The paths . . . are turned *a*
15:30 turn *a* by a blast of His
19:13 have even turned *a* from me
23:9 He turns *a* to the right, but
24:4 turn *a* the poor ones from
33:17 turn *a* a man from his deed
34:5 turned *a* the judgment of me
34:27 turned *a* from following
Ps 14:3 They have all turned *a*, they
66:20 has not turned *a* my prayer
73:2 my feet had almost turned *a*
78:30 turned *a* from their desire
81:6 turned *a* his shoulder even
119:102 I have not turned *a*
125:5 turning *a* to their crooked
Pr 4:5 not turn *a* from the sayings
4:15 turn *a* from it, and pass
7:25 heart not turn *a* to her ways
9:4 let him turn *a* here
9:16 let him turn *a* here
18:5 turning *a* of the righteous one
22:6 grows old he will not turn *a*
Isa 8:11 turn *a* from walking in the
29:21 push *a* the righteous one
30:11 Turn *a* from the way
Jer 5:23 turned *a* and keep walking
14:8 turned *a* to spend the night
15:5 turn *a* to ask about your
32:40 order not to turn *a* from me
La 1:15 tossed *a* from the midst of
3:35 turning *a* the judgment of an
Eze 6:9 heart that has turned *a* from
Da 9:5 been a turning *a* from your
9:11 turning *a* by not obeying your
Am 2:7 meek people they turn *a*
5:12 who have turned *a* poor people
Mal 2:8 have turned *a* from the way
3:7 turned *a* from my regulations
Mt 16:22 At this Peter took him *a* and
Mr 6:43 *a* from the fishes
7:9 you set *a* the commandment of
8:32 But Peter took him *a* and
10:32 he took the twelve *a* and
Lu 18:31 took the twelve *a* and said
Joh 5:13 for Jesus had turned *a*
13:4 laid *a* his outer garments
Ac 7:39 they thrust him *a* and in
1Co 1:19 men I will shove *a*
16:2 set something *a* in store as
Ga 2:21 do not shove *a* the undeserved
3:15 no one sets *a* or attaches
1Ti 1:6 been turned *a* into idle talk
1:19 which some have thrust *a*
5:15 turned *a* to follow Satan
2Ti 4:4 be turned *a* to false stories
Heb 7:18 setting *a* of the preceding

Asiel

1Ch 4:35 Seraiah the son of *A*

Asinine

Job 11:12 as an *a* zebra be born a man

Ask

Ge 9:5 blood of your souls shall I *a*
9:5 shall I *a* it back
9:5 shall I *a* back the soul of man
32:17 Esau . . . *a* you, saying, To
Ex 3:22 must *a* from her neighbor and
11:2 *a* every man of his companion
22:14 *a* for something of his
De 4:32 *a*, please, concerning the
6:20 In case your son should *a* you
14:26 your soul may *a* of you
32:7 *A* your father, and he can tell
Jos 4:6 sons should *a* in time to come
4:21 sons *a* their fathers in time
15:18 *a* a field from her father
Jg 1:14 she kept inciting him to *a* a
4:20 anybody comes and does *a* you
13:6 And I did not *a* him from just
13:18 should you *a* about my name
18:15 *a* how he was getting along
1Sa 10:4 *a* about your welfare and
25:5 *a* him in my name about his
25:8 *A* your own young men, and
30:21 to *a* them how they were
2Sa 8:10 to King David to *a* him about
11:7 David began to *a* how Joab
1Ki 1:16 What do you have to *a?*
19:4 *a* that his soul might die
2Ki 2:9 *A* what I should do for you
4:3 *a* for vessels for yourself
4:28 Did I *a* for a son through
10:13 to *a* if all is well with
1Ch 18:10 to *a* him about his welfare
2Ch 1:7 *A!* What shall I give you?
1:11 *a* for wisdom and knowledge
24:22 see to it and *a* it back
Ezr 8:22 to *a* a military force and
Ne 1:2 to *a* about the Jews, those
5:12 we shall *a* nothing back
Job 8:8 *a* . . . the former generation
12:7 *a*, please, the domestic
Ps 2:8 *A* of me, that I may give
35:11 What I have not known they *a*
40:6 sin offering you did not *a* for
122:6 *A*, O you people, for the
Isa 7:11 *A* for yourself a sign from
7:12 I shall not *a*, neither shall
45:11 *A* me even about the things
Jer 6:16 *a* for the roadways of long
15:5 to *a* about your welfare
18:13 *A* . . . among the nations
30:6 *A*, please, O men, and see
48:19 *A* him that is fleeing and
Eze 3:18 but his blood I shall *a* back
3:20 but his blood I shall *a* back
33:6 its blood I shall *a* back
33:8 his blood I shall *a* back at
34:10 *a* back my sheep from their
Da 2:18 *a* for mercies on the part of
Hag 2:11 *A*, please, the priests as to
Mt 6:8 before ever you *a* him
7:10 perhaps, he will *a* for a fish
19:17 you *a* me about what is good
21:22 the things you *a* in prayer
21:24 also, will *a* you one thing
27:20 the crowds to *a* for Barabbas
Mr 5:9 to *a* him: What is your name?
6:22 *A* me for whatever you want
6:23 Whatever you *a* me for, I
6:24 What should I *a* for? She said
8:5 *a* them: How many loaves have
8:23 began to *a* him: Do you see
9:28 proceeded to *a* him privately
10:35 whatever it is we *a* you for
11:24 things you pray and *a* for
11:29 I will *a* you one question
13:3 began to *a* him privately
Lu 3:10 And the crowds would *a* him
3:14 in military service would *a*
6:9 I *a* you men, Is it lawful on
6:30 do not *a* them back
7:3 to *a* him to come and bring his
8:9 *a* him what this illustration
14:18 I *a* you, Have me excused
14:19 I *a* you, Have me excused
16:27 I *a* you, father, to send him
20:3 I will also *a* you a question
20:40 to *a* him a single question
22:64 would *a* and say: Prophesy
Joh 1:19 to *a* him: Who are you?
4:9 *a* me for a drink, when I am
9:21 *A* him. He is of age
11:22 things as you *a* God for
14:13 is that you *a* in my name
14:14 *a* anything in my name, I
15:7 *a* whatever you wish and it
15:16 *a* the Father in my name he
16:23 you will *a* me no question
16:23 *a* the Father for anything
16:24 *A* and you will receive
16:26 *a* in my name, and I do not
Ac 3:2 in order to *a* gifts of mercy
25:20 *a* if he would like to go to
Ro 10:18 I *a*, They did not fail to
10:19 I *a*, Israel did not fail to
11:1 I *a*, then, God did not reject
11:11 I *a*, Did they stumble so
1Co 1:22 the Jews *a* for signs and the
Eph 3:13 I *a* you not to give up on
3:20 beyond all the things we *a*
Jas 4:3 *a*, and yet you do not receive
1Jo 3:22 whatever we *a* we receive
5:14 we *a* according to his will
5:16 he will *a*, and he will give

Asked
Ge 24:47 I *a* her and said, Whose
42:22 here it is certainly *a* back
44:19 My master *a* his slaves
Ex 12:36 these granted what was *a*
De 18:16 all that you *a* of Jehovah
Jos 19:50 the city for which he *a*
Jg 5:25 Water he *a*, milk she gave; In
1Sa 1:17 that you have *a* of him
1:20 from Jehovah that I have *a*
1:27 my petition that I *a* of him
12:13 the king . . . for whom you *a*
20:6 David earnestly *a* leave of
20:28 David earnestly *a* leave of
2Sa 12:20 *a*, and they promptly set
1Ki 10:13 delight for which she *a*
2Ki 2:10 You have *a* a difficult thing
8:6 king *a* the woman, and she
1Ch 4:10 to pass what he had *a*
2Ch 1:11 you have not *a* for wealth
1:11 many days that you have *a*
9:12 delight for which she had *a*
Ezr 5:9 Then we *a* these older men
5:10 also *a* them their names
Ne 13:6 later I *a* leave of absence
Job 21:29 you not *a* those traveling
Ps 21:4 Life he *a* of you. You gave it
27:4 I have *a* from Jehovah
105:40 *a*, and he proceeded to bring
137:3 *a* us for the words of a song
Pr 30:7 Two things I have *a* of you
Ec 2:10 anything that my eyes *a* for
7:10 that you have *a* about this
Isa 65:1 those who had not *a* for me
Jer 36:17 And Baruch they *a*, saying
La 4:4 Children . . . have *a* for bread
Eze 21:21 *a* by means of the teraphim
Da 2:10 governor has *a* such a thing
2:16 Daniel himself went in and *a*
Mt 9:14 *a*: Why is it that we and the
9:28 Jesus *a* them: Do you have
12:10 *a* him, Is it lawful to cure
14:7 to give her whatever she *a*
16:1 *a* him to display to them a
22:23 came up to him and *a* him
22:35 *a*, testing him
22:41 the Pharisees . . . Jesus *a*
27:58 and *a* for the body of Jesus
Mr 7:5 Pharisees and scribes *a* him
9:16 he *a* them: What are you
9:21 he *a* his father: How long has
12:28 *a* him: Which commandment
15:43 and *a* for the body of Jesus
15:44 he *a* him whether he had
Lu 1:63 he *a* for a tablet and wrote
5:3 *a* him to pull away a bit from
8:30 Jesus *a* him: What is your
8:37 *a* him to get away from them
17:20 on being *a* by the Pharisees
18:40 he got near, Jesus *a* him
23:3 Pilate *a* him the question
23:6 Pilate *a* whether the man was
23:52 and *a* for the body of Jesus
Joh 1:21 they *a* him: What, then?
4:10 you would have *a* him, and
5:12 *a* him: Who is the man that
9:2 his disciples *a* him: Rabbi
9:19 *a* them: Is this your son
16:24 *a* a single thing in my name
18:7 he *a* them again: Whom are
Ac 3:14 you *a* for a man, a murderer
7:46 and *a* for the privilege of
9:2 and *a* him for letters to the
16:29 he *a* for lights and leaped in
1Jo 5:15 we are to have the things *a*
5:15 since we have *a* them of him

Asking
Ge 26:7 *a* with respect to his wife
Ex 12:35 went *a* from the Egyptians
18:7 began *a* how the other was
De 10:12 Jehovah your God *a* of you
1Sa 8:10 the people who were *a* a king
12:17 in *a* for yourselves a king
12:19 in *a* for ourselves a king
17:22 *a* about the welfare of his
2Sa 3:13 there is that I am *a* of you
14:18 thing about which I am *a*
1Ch 10:13 *a* of a spirit medium to
Job 31:30 *a* for an oath against his
Ps 78:18 *a* for something to eat for
Isa 41:28 I kept *a* them, that they
58:2 *a* me for righteous judgments
Jer 37:17 king began *a* him questions
Jer 38:14 I am *a* something of you
44:19 without *a* our husbands
50:5 they will keep *a* the way
Da 2:11 king himself is *a* is
2:27 that the king himself is *a*
Jon 4:8 *a* that his soul might die
Mic 6:8 what is Jehovah *a* back from
7:3 the prince is *a* for something
Mt 5:42 Give to the one *a* you, and
7:7 Keep on *a*, and it will be
7:8 For everyone *a* receives, and
7:11 give good things to those *a*
16:13 Jesus went *a* his disciples
20:20 *a* for something from him
20:22 not know what you are *a* for
Mr 7:26 *a* him to expel the demon
10:38 not know what you are *a* for
Lu 1:62 *a* its father by signs what he
6:30 Give to everyone *a* you, and
7:36 kept *a* him to dine with him
11:9 Keep on *a*, and it will be
11:10 For everyone *a* receives, and
11:13 give holy spirit to those *a*
Joh 4:40 began *a* him to stay with
4:47 *a* him to come down and heal
9:15 Pharisees also took up *a* him
Ac 1:6 *a* him: Lord, are you restoring
25:3 *a* for themselves as a favor
25:15 *a* a judgment of condemnation
Ro 10:20 those who were not *a* for me
Col 1:9 and *a* that you may be filled
Jas 1:5 let him keep on *a* God, for
1:6 him keep on *a* in faith, not
4:2 because of your not *a*
4:3 you are *a* for a wrong purpose
1Jo 5:15 whatever we are *a*, we know

Asks
Jer 23:33 prophet or priest *a* you
Da 6:12 man that *a* a petition from
Mt 7:9 his son *a* for bread—he will
Lu 11:11 his son *a* for a fish, will
11:12 Or if he also *a* for an egg
19:31 anyone *a* you, Why is it you
Joh 16:5 *a* me, Where are you going?

Asleep
Jg 4:21 he was fast *a* and weary
1Sa 26:7 Saul was lying *a* in the
26:12 for all of them were *a*
1Ki 3:20 slave girl herself was *a*
18:27 is *a* and ought to wake up
19:5 fell *a* under the broom tree
Ps 13:3 that I may not fall *a* in death
76:6 the horse have fallen fast *a*
Pr 10:5 acting shamefully is fast *a*
Ca 5:2 I am *a*, but my heart is awake
Da 8:18 fast *a* on my face on the
10:9 fast *a* upon my face, with my
12:2 those *a* in the ground of dust
Jon 1:5 to lie down and go fast *a*
Mt 27:52 holy ones that had fallen *a*
Lu 8:23 they were sailing he fell *a*
Ac 7:60 saying this he fell *a* in death
13:36 fell *a* in death and was
1Co 7:39 should fall *a* in death, she
15:6 some have fallen *a* in death
15:18 fell *a* in death in union
15:20 have fallen *a* in death
15:51 not all fall *a* in death, but
1Th 4:14 who have fallen *a* in death
4:15 who have fallen *a* in death
5:10 we stay awake or are *a*
2Pe 3:4 forefathers fell *a* in death

Asnah
Ezr 2:50 the sons of *A*

Aspatha
Es 9:7 Parshandatha and Dalphon and *A*

Aspect
La 4:8 Their *a* has become darker than
Zec 5:6 is their *a* in all the earth

Aspires
Pr 15:14 stupid . . . *a* to foolishness

Asps
Ro 3:13 Poison of *a* is behind their

Asriel
Nu 26:31 of *A* the family of the
Jos 17:2 and the sons of *A* and the
1Ch 7:14 The sons of Manasseh were *A*

Asrielites
Nu 26:31 Asriel the family of the *A*

Ass
Ge 22:3 saddled his *a* and took two of
22:5 You stay here with the *a*, but
42:27 to give fodder to his *a*
44:13 back onto his *a* and returned
49:11 Tying his full-grown *a* to a
49:14 Issachar is a strong-boned *a*
Ex 4:20 and made them ride on an *a*
13:13 every firstling *a* you are to
20:17 must not desire . . . his *a*
21:33 or an *a* does fall into it
22:4 stolen, from bull to *a* and to
22:9 concerning a bull, an *a*, a
22:10 give his fellow an *a* or bull
23:4 your enemy's bull or his *a*
23:5 *a* of someone who hates you
23:12 bull and your *a* may rest
34:20 firstling of an *a* . . . redeem
Nu 16:15 Not one male *a* have I taken
22:23 *a* got to see Jehovah's angel
22:23 the *a* tried to turn aside
22:23 Balaam began to strike the *a*
22:27 *a* got to see Jehovah's angel
22:27 beating the *a* with his staff
22:28 opened the mouth of the *a*
22:29 At this Balaam said to the *a*
De 5:14 nor your *a* nor any domestic
5:21 his bull or his *a* or anything
22:3 that you will do with his *a*
22:4 the *a* of your brother or his
22:10 a bull and an *a* together
28:31 Your *a* taken in robbery
Jos 6:21 to bull and sheep and *a*, to
7:24 and his *a* and his flock and
15:18 her hands while upon the *a*
Jg 1:14 while upon the *a*. At this
6:4 or bull or *a* remain in Israel
15:15 a moist jawbone of a male *a*
15:16 the jawbone of a male *a*
15:16 jawbone of a male *a* I have
19:28 the man took her upon the *a*
1Sa 12:3 or whose *a* have I taken or
15:3 camel as well as *a*
16:20 Jesse took an *a*, bread and a
22:19 *a* and sheep with the edge
25:20 riding on the *a* and secretly
25:23 down off the *a* and fell
25:42 went riding on the *a* with
2Sa 17:23 saddle an *a* and rise up and
19:26 saddle the female *a* for me
1Ki 2:40 saddled his *a* and went to
13:13 Saddle the *a* for me
13:13 they saddled the *a* for him
13:23 saddled for him the *a*
13:24 the *a* was standing beside
13:27 saying: Saddle the *a* for me
13:28 the *a* and the lion standing
13:28 nor had it crushed the *a*
13:29 to deposit him upon the *a*
Job 24:3 male *a* of fatherless boys
39:5 very bands of the wild *a*
Pr 26:3 a bridle is for the *a*, and the
Isa 1:3 the *a* the manger of its owner
32:20 of the bull and of the *a*
Zec 9:9 humble, and riding upon an *a*
14:15 the camel, and the male *a*
Mt 18:6 millstone . . . turned by an *a*
21:2 will at once find an *a* tied
21:5 mounted upon an *a*, yes, upon
21:7 brought the *a* and its colt
Mr 9:42 such as is turned by an *a*
Lu 13:15 untie his bull or his *a* from
Joh 12:14 Jesus had found a young *a*

Assail
Pr 30:9 and *a* the name of my God

Assailant
Job 36:32 upon it against an *a*

Assault
Ge 4:8 Cain proceeded to *a* Abel his
32:8 come to the one camp and *a* it
32:11 may come and certainly *a* me
34:30 and they will . . . *a* me and I
Jg 8:21 Get up yourself and *a* us, for
15:12 you yourselves will not *a* me
18:25 men . . . may *a* you people
1Sa 22:17 to *a* the priests of Jehovah
22:18 You turn and *a* the priests
Job 15:24 king in readiness for the *a*
Ac 18:10 no man will *a* you so as to

Assaulted
1Sa 22:18 *a* the priests and put to
Ac 17:5 they *a* the house of Jason and

Assemble
Ge 49:2 *A* yourselves and listen, you
Jos 9:2 to *a* themselves all together
24:1 Joshua proceeded to *a* all
Da 3:2 king sent to *a* the satraps
Ac 22:30 and all the Sanhedrin to *a*

Assembled
Da 3:27 that were *a* were beholding
Mr 14:53 older men and the scribes *a*
Lu 24:33 those with them *a* together
Ac 1:6 *a*, they went asking him: Lord
1:21 men that *a* with us during
10:27 and found many people *a*
12:22 the *a* people began shouting
16:13 to the women that had *a*
28:17 Jews. When they had *a*, he

Assemblies
Am 5:21 the smell of your solemn *a*
Lu 12:11 bring you in before public *a*

Assembling
Job 16:7 all those *a* with me desolate
Da 3:3 were *a* themselves for the
Hab 1:9 The *a* of their faces is as

Assembly
Ex 12:3 to the entire *a* of Israel
12:6 *a* of Israel must slaughter it
12:19 cut off from the *a* of Israel
12:47 *a* of Israel are to celebrate
16:1 entire *a* of the sons of Israel
16:2 entire *a* of the sons of Israel
16:9 entire *a* of the sons of Israel
16:10 *a* of the sons of Israel
16:22 chieftains of the *a* came and
17:1 entire *a* of the sons of Israel
34:31 chieftains among the *a* came
35:1 Moses called the entire *a* of
35:4 entire *a* of the sons of Israel
35:20 *a* of the sons of Israel went
38:25 the ones registered of the *a*
Le 4:13 entire *a* of Israel makes a
4:15 the older men of the *a* must
8:3 all the *a* congregate at the
8:4 *a* congregated at the entrance
8:5 Moses now said to the *a*: This
9:5 whole *a* came near and stood
10:6 indignant against all the *a*
10:17 for the error of the *a*
16:5 the *a* of the sons of Israel
19:2 to the entire *a* of the sons of
23:36 It is a solemn *a*. No sort of
24:14 the entire *a* must pelt him
24:16 entire *a* should without fail
Nu 1:2 whole *a* of the sons of Israel
1:16 ones called of the *a*, the
1:18 *a* on the first day of the
1:53 against the *a* of the sons of
3:7 obligation to all the *a* before
4:34 chieftains of the *a* proceeded
8:9 all the *a* of the sons of Israel
8:20 *a* of the sons of Israel
10:2 service for convening the *a*
10:3 whole *a* must keep their
13:26 the *a* of the sons of Israel
13:26 word to them and all the *a*
14:1 all the *a* raised their voice
14:2 the *a* began to say against
14:5 the *a* of the sons of Israel
14:7 the *a* of the sons of Israel
14:10 *a* talked of pelting them
14:27 evil *a* have this murmuring
14:35 shall do to all this evil *a*
14:36 making the whole *a* murmur
15:24 far from the eyes of the *a*
15:24 whole *a* must then render up
15:25 atonement for the whole *a* of
15:26 must be forgiven the whole *a*
15:33 and Aaron and the whole *a*
15:35 *a* pelting him with stones
15:36 whole *a* brought him forth
16:2 chieftains of the *a*, summoned
16:3 whole *a* are all of them holy
16:5 to Korah and to his entire *a*
16:6 Korah and his entire *a*
16:9 separated you men from the *a*
16:9 before the *a* to minister to
16:11 you and all your *a* who are
16:16 You and all your *a*, be
16:19 Korah got all the *a* together
16:19 glory appeared to all the *a*
16:21 from the midst of this *a*
16:22 against the entire *a*
Nu 16:24 Speak to the *a*, saying, Get
16:26 spoke to the *a*, saying: Turn
16:40 become like Korah and his *a*
16:41 *a* of the sons of Israel
16:42 *a* had congregated themselves
16:45 up from the midst of this *a*
16:46 go to the *a* in a hurry and
19:9 the *a* of the sons of Israel
20:1 sons of Israel, the entire *a*
20:2 no water for the *a*
20:8 and call the *a* together, you
20:8 give the *a* and their beasts of
20:11 and the *a* and their beasts of
20:22 sons of Israel, the entire *a*
20:27 before the eyes of all the *a*
20:29 the *a* got to see that Aaron
25:6 before the eyes of all the *a*
25:7 up from the midst of the *a*
26:2 sum of the whole *a* of the
26:9 were summoned ones of the *a*
26:9 in the *a* of Korah, when they
26:10 death of the *a* when the fire
27:2 chieftains and all the *a* at
27:3 prove to be in among the *a*
27:3 in the *a* of Korah, but for his
27:14 at the quarreling of the *a*
27:16 appoint over the *a* a man
27:17 *a* may not become like sheep
27:19 before all the *a*, and you
27:20 *a* of the sons of Israel may
27:21 with him and all the *a*
27:22 stood him before . . . the *a*
29:35 you should hold a solemn *a*
31:12 the *a* of the sons of Israel
31:13 the chieftains of the *a* went
31:16 the scourge came upon the *a*
31:26 heads of the fathers of the *a*
31:27 and all the rest of the *a*
31:43 half of the *a* from the flock
32:2 and to the chieftains of the *a*
32:4 Jehovah defeated before the *a*
35:12 before the *a* for judgment
35:24 *a* must then judge between
35:25 *a* must deliver the manslayer
35:25 the *a* must return him to his
De 16:8 a solemn *a* to Jehovah your
Jos 9:15 chieftains of the *a* swore to
9:18 chieftains of the *a* had
9:18 *a* began to murmur against
9:19 chieftains said to all the *a*
9:21 of water for all the *a*
9:27 the *a* and for Jehovah's altar
18:1 *a* of the sons of Israel
20:6 before the *a* for judgment
20:9 his standing before the *a*
22:12 the whole *a* of the sons of
22:16 the *a* of Jehovah have said
22:17 upon the *a* of Jehovah
22:18 against the entire *a* of
22:20 against all the *a* of Israel
22:30 the chieftains of the *a* and
Jg 20:1 *a* congregated themselves as
21:10 *a* proceeded to send twelve
21:13 *a* now sent and spoke to the
21:16 the older men of the *a* said
1Ki 8:5 with him all the *a* of Israel
12:20 called him to the *a* and
2Ki 10:20 a solemn *a* for Baal
2Ch 5:6 all the *a* of Israelites that
7:9 held a solemn *a*, because the
Ne 5:7 a great *a* on their account
8:18 a solemn *a*, according to the
Job 15:34 *a* of apostates is sterile
Ps 1:5 sinners in the *a* of righteous
7:7 *a* of national groups surround
22:16 The *a* of evildoers themselves
68:30 the reeds, the *a* of bulls
74:2 *a* that you acquired long ago
82:1 in the *a* of the Divine One
86:14 *a* of tyrannical ones have
106:17 over the *a* of Abiram
106:18 went burning among their *a*
111:1 of upright ones and the *a*
Pr 5:14 congregation and of the *a*
Isa 1:13 along with the solemn *a*
Jer 6:18 know, O you *a*, what will be
9:2 *a* of treacherous dealers
30:20 own *a* will be firmly
Ho 7:12 the report to their *a*
Joe 1:14 Call together a solemn *a*
2:15 Call together a solemn *a*
Lu 22:66 *a* of older men of the people
Joh 6:59 in public *a* at Capernaum
Ac 5:21 and the *a* of older men of the
Ac 13:43 synagogue *a* was dissolved
19:32 for the *a* was in confusion
19:39 be decided in a regular *a*
19:41 he dismissed the *a*
22:5 all the *a* of older men can
25:12 with the *a* of counselors
Heb 12:23 in general *a*, and the

Assent
1Ti 6:3 does not *a* to healthful words

Asserting
Ac 12:15 kept on strongly *a* it was so
24:9 *a* that these things were so
25:19 who Paul kept *a* was alive
Ro 1:22 *a* they were wise, they

Assertions
1Ti 1:7 they are making strong *a*
Tit 3:8 to make firm *a* constantly

Asses
Ge 12:16 have sheep and cattle and *a*
24:35 giving him . . . camels and *a*
30:43 camels and *a* came to be his
32:5 have bulls and *a*, sheep, and
32:15 and ten full-grown *a*
34:28 their herds and their *a* and
36:24 tending the *a* for Zibeon
42:26 their cereals upon their *a*
43:18 us for slaves and also our *a*
43:24 he gave fodder for their *a*
44:3 both they and their *a*
45:23 ten *a* carrying good things
47:17 the herd and the *a*, and he
Ex 9:3 the *a*, the camels, the herd
Nu 31:28 of the herd and of the *a* and
31:30 of the herd, of the *a* and of
31:34 and sixty-one thousand *a*
31:39 *a* were thirty thousand five
31:45 the *a*, thirty thousand five
Jos 9:4 worn-out sacks for their *a*
Jg 10:4 rode on thirty full-grown *a*
12:14 rode on seventy full-grown *a*
1Sa 8:16 and your *a* he will take, and
25:18 and put them upon the *a*
27:9 took flocks and herds and *a*
2Sa 16:1 meet him with a couple of *a*
16:2 The *a* are for the household
2Ki 7:7 and their horses and their *a*
7:10 horses tied and the *a* tied
1Ch 5:21 *a* two thousand, and human
12:40 bringing food upon *a* and
2Ch 28:15 transportation on the *a* and
Ezr 2:67 their *a* six thousand seven
Ne 7:69 The *a* were six thousand seven
13:15 and loading them upon *a*
Isa 21:7 a war chariot of *a*
30:6 shoulders of full-grown *a*
30:24 full-grown *a* cultivating
Eze 23:20 fleshly member of male *a*
Da 5:21 the wild *a* his dwelling was

Assessed
2Ki 12:4 each one is *a*, the money

Asshur
Ge 10:22 sons of Shem . . . *A* and
1Ch 1:17 sons of Shem were . . . *A*
Eze 27:23 *A* and Chilmad were your

Asshurim
Ge 25:3 sons of Dedan became *A* and

Assign
Ge 24:14 *a* to your servant, to Isaac
Nu 4:19 *a* them each one to his
4:27 *a* all their loads to them by
4:32 *a* the equipment for which
6:26 Jehovah . . . *a* peace to you
Jos 10:18 *a* men over it to guard them
2Sa 7:23 *a* himself a name and to do
14:7 *a* to my husband neither a
1Ki 20:34 *a* to yourself in Damascus
1Ch 17:21 to *a* to yourself a name of
Ne 13:30 *a* duties to the priests and
Ps 61:7 *a* loving-kindness and trueness
Isa 61:3 *a* to those mourning over
Eze 47:13 territory that you will *a*
Mt 24:51 *a* him his part with the
Lu 12:46 and *a* him a part with the

Assigned
Ge 24:44 woman whom Jehovah has *a*
40:4 *a* Joseph to be with them that
Nu 31:5 a thousand were *a* of a tribe
Jos 23:4 I *a* to you by lot these
1Sa 29:4 place where you *a* him; and

2Sa 23:5 covenant that he has *a* to me
1Ki 11:18 bread he *a* to him, and land
20:34 as my father *a* in Samaria
1Ch 26:32 David the king *a* them over
2Ch 33:8 ground that I *a* to their
Job 34:13 Who has *a* to him the earth
Da 1:7 he *a* to Daniel the name of
Lu 17:9 because he did the things *a*
17:10 have done all the things *a*
Joh 5:36 works that my Father *a* me
2Co 10:13 not outside our *a* boundaries
10:15 outside our *a* boundaries in
Eph 1:11 we were also *a* as heirs, in
1Th 5:9 God *a* us, not to wrath, but

Assigners
Isa 3:12 task *a* are dealing severely
60:17 righteousness as your task *a*

Assigning
Da 1:7 court official went *a* names
1Ti 1:12 by *a* me to a ministry
1Pe 3:7 *a* them honor as to a weaker

Assignment
Lu 1:8 *a* of his division before God

Assir
Ex 6:24 sons of Korah were *A* and
1Ch 6:22 Korah his son, *A* his son
6:23 his son and *A* his son
6:37 son of *A*, the son of Ebiasaph

Assist
Ezr 1:4 *a* him with silver and with
Lu 5:7 to come and *a* them; and they
Ac 20:35 must *a* those who are weak
Ro 16:2 *a* her in any matter where she

Assistance
Jg 5:23 not come to the *a* of Jehovah
5:23 *a* of Jehovah with the mighty
2Ch 28:21 it was of no *a* to him
Job 31:21 need of my *a* in the gate
Ps 22:19 do make haste to my *a*
27:9 My *a* you must become
35:2 And do rise up in *a* of me
38:22 Do make haste to my *a*
40:13 to my *a* do make haste
40:17 are my *a* and the Provider
44:26 Do arise in *a* to us
60:11 Do give us *a* from distress
63:7 have proved to be of *a* to me
70:1 to my *a* do make haste
71:12 O my God, do hurry to my *a*
94:17 Jehovah had been of *a* to me
108:12 give us *a* from distress
Isa 10:3 whom will you flee for *a*
20:6 to which we fled for *a*
31:1 going down to Egypt for *a*
31:2 *a* of those practicing what
Jer 37:7 for the purpose of *a* will
La 4:17 pining away in vain for *a* to
Na 3:9 proved to be of *a* to you

Assisted
1Ki 9:11 *a* Solomon with timbers of
Ezr 8:36 *a* the people and the house

Assisting
Es 9:3 were *a* the Jews, for the dread
Php 4:3 keep *a* these women who have
Heb 2:16 he is really not *a* angels
2:16 he is *a* Abraham's seed

Associate
Le 6:2 and does deceive his *a* about
6:2 or he does defraud his *a*
18:20 wife of your *a* to become
19:11 falsely anyone with his *a*
19:15 you should judge your *a*
19:17 by all means reprove your *a*
24:19 cause a defect in his *a*, then
25:14 to your *a* or be buying from
25:15 should buy from your *a*
25:17 not wrong anyone his *a*, and
Zec 13:7 able-bodied man who is my *a*

Associated
Jg 14:20 who had *a* with him
Ac 17:4 *a* themselves with Paul and
1Co 7:24 him remain in it *a* with God

Associate's
Le 25:14 buying from your *a* hand, do

Associating
2Th 3:14 stop *a* with him, that he

Association
2Sa 13:20 kept from *a* with others, at
Ho 6:9 the *a* of priests are marauding
Php 1:13 in *a* with Christ among all
2Ti 3:12 in *a* with Christ Jesus
1Pe 2:17 have love for the whole *a* of
5:9 entire *a* of your brothers

Associations
1Co 15:33 Bad *a* spoil useful habits

Assos
Ac 20:13 and set sail to *A*, where we
20:14 he caught up with us in *A*

Ass's
2Ki 6:25 an *a* head got to be worth
Joh 12:15 seated upon an *a* colt

Assume
Ps 38:16 *a* great airs against me

Assumed
Ps 55:12 that *a* great airs against me

Assuming
Ps 35:26 are *a* great airs against me
Lu 2:44 *A* that he was in the company

Assurance
2Co 9:4 put to shame in this *a* of
Col 2:2 full *a* of their understanding
Heb 6:11 the full *a* of the hope down
10:22 in the full *a* of faith

Assure
1Jo 3:19 *a* our hearts before him

Assured
Ac 21:13 Rest *a*, I am ready not only
Heb 11:1 Faith is the *a* expectation

Assuredly
Jer 22:6 *A* I shall make you a
22:17 *A* your eyes and your heart
Heb 6:14 *A* in blessing I will bless

Assyria
Ge 2:14 one going to the east of *A*
10:11 he went forth into *A* and
25:18 tabernacling . . . as far as *A*
Nu 24:22 till *A* will carry you away
24:24 will certainly afflict *A*
2Ki 15:19 Pul the king of *A* came into
15:20 to give to the king of *A*
15:20 the king of *A* turned back
15:29 the king of *A* came in and
15:29 carry them into exile in *A*
16:7 Tiglath-pileser the king of *A*
16:8 sent the king of *A* a bribe
16:9 king of *A* listened to him
16:9 the king of *A* went up to
16:10 the king of *A* at Damascus
16:18 because of the king of *A*
17:3 Shalmaneser the king of *A*
17:4 the king of *A* got to find
17:4 tribute up to the king of *A*
17:4 the king of *A* shut him up
17:5 king of *A* proceeded to come
17:6 king of *A* captured Samaria
17:6 led Israel into exile in *A*
17:23 into exile in *A* down to
17:24 king of *A* brought people
17:26 to the king of *A*, saying
17:27 king of *A* commanded, saying
18:7 rebel against the king of *A*
18:9 Shalmaneser the king of *A*
18:11 king of *A* took Israel into
18:11 took Israel into exile in *A*
18:13 Sennacherib the king of *A*
18:14 the king of *A* at Lachish
18:14 the king of *A* laid upon
18:16 gave them to the king of *A*
18:17 king of *A* proceeded to send
18:19 great king, the king of *A*
18:23 with my lord the king of *A*
18:28 great king, the king of *A*
18:30 the hand of the king of *A*
18:31 the king of *A* has said
18:33 the hand of the king of *A*
19:4 the king of *A* his lord sent
19:6 king of *A* spoke abusively
19:8 king of *A* fighting against
19:10 the hand of the king of *A*
19:11 what the kings of *A* did to
19:17 kings of *A* have devastated
19:20 Sennacherib the king of *A*
19:32 concerning the king of *A*
19:36 Sennacherib the king of *A*
20:6 the palm of the king of *A*
23:29 came up to the king of *A* by
1Ch 5:6 Tilgath-pilneser the king of *A*
5:26 spirit of Pul the king of *A*
5:26 king of *A*, so that he took
2Ch 28:16 sent to the kings of *A* for
28:20 king of *A* came against him
28:21 gift to the king of *A*
30:6 palm of the kings of *A*
32:1 Sennacherib the king of *A*
32:4 kings of *A* come and actually
32:7 because of the king of *A*
32:9 Sennacherib the king of *A*
32:10 the king of *A* has said
32:11 the palm of the king of *A*
32:21 camp of the king of *A*, so
32:22 Sennacherib the king of *A*
33:11 belonged to the king of *A*
Ezr 4:2 Esar-haddon the king of *A*
6:22 the heart of the king of *A*
Ne 9:32 the days of the kings of *A*
Ps 83:8 *A* itself has become joined
Isa 7:17 namely, the king of *A*
7:18 that are in the land of *A*
7:20 by means of the king of *A*
8:4 before the king of *A*
8:7 king of *A* and all his glory
10:12 heart of the king of *A*
11:11 remain over from *A* and
11:16 highway out of *A* for the
19:23 highway out of Egypt to *A*
19:23 *A* will actually come into
19:23 and Egypt into *A*; and they
19:23 service, Egypt with *A*
19:24 with Egypt and with *A*
19:25 work of my hands, *A*, and
20:1 Sargon the king of *A* sent
20:4 king of *A* will lead the body
20:6 because of the king of *A*
23:13 *A* did not prove to be the
27:13 perishing in the land of *A*
30:31 *A* will be struck with
30:32 to settle down upon *A*
36:1 Sennacherib the king of *A*
36:2 king of *A* finally sent
36:4 the king of *A*, has said
36:8 my lord the king of *A*, and
36:13 great king, the king of *A*
36:15 the hand of the king of *A*
36:16 the king of *A* has said
36:18 the hand of the king of *A*
37:4 king of *A* his lord sent to
37:6 attendants of the king of *A*
37:8 king of *A* fighting against
37:10 the hand of the king of *A*
37:11 *A* did to all the lands by
37:18 *A* have devastated all the
37:21 Sennacherib the king of *A*
37:33 king of *A*: He will not come
37:37 Sennacherib the king of *A*
38:6 the king of *A* I shall deliver
52:4 *A*, for its part, oppressed
Jer 2:18 for the way of *A* in order to
2:36 as you became ashamed of *A*
50:17 king of *A* has devoured
50:18 attention upon the king of *A*
La 5:6 we have given the hand; to *A*
Eze 16:28 yourself to the sons of *A*
23:7 the choicest sons of *A*
23:9 the hand of the sons of *A*
23:12 For the sons of *A* she lusted
23:23 all the sons of *A* with them
32:22 *A* and all her congregation
Ho 5:13 Ephraim proceeded to go to *A*
7:11 to *A* they have gone
8:9 have gone up to *A*, as a zebra
9:3 in *A* they will eat what is
10:6 bring to *A* itself as a gift
11:5 but *A* will be his king
11:11 a dove out of the land of *A*
12:1 covenant with *A* they conclude
14:3 *A* itself will not save us
Mic 5:6 shepherd the land of *A* with
7:12 they will come from *A* and
Na 3:18 become drowsy, O king of *A*
Zep 2:13 and he will destroy *A*
Zec 10:10 from *A* I shall collect them
10:11 pride of *A* must be brought

Assyrian
Isa 10:5 *A*, the rod for my anger, and
10:24 *A*, who with the rod used to
14:25 break the *A* in my land and
31:8 *A* must fall by the sword
Eze 31:3 An *A*, a cedar in Lebanon
Mic 5:5 the *A* . . . comes into our land
5:6 deliverance from the *A*

Assyrians
2Ki 19:35 in the camp of the *A*
Isa 37:36 in the camp of the *A*
Eze 23:5 after the *A*, who were near

Astir
Ps 45:1 *a* with a goodly matter

Astonished
Isa 59:16 *a* that there was no one
63:5 I began to show myself *a*
Eze 4:17 may look *a* at one another
Da 4:19 Belteshazzar, was *a* for a
Mr 1:27 the people were all so *a* that
Lu 24:22 *a* us, because they had been
Ac 2:7 *a* and began to wonder and say
2:12 they were all *a* and were in
12:16 they saw him and were *a*

Astonishing
Ps 46:8 set *a* events on the earth
Isa 24:12 *a* condition has been left
Jer 5:30 *a* situation, even a horrible

Astonishment
De 28:37 must become an object of *a*
2Ki 22:19 to become an object of *a*
2Ch 29:8 an object of *a* and a cause
30:7 object of *a*, just as you are
Ps 73:19 object of *a* as in a moment
Isa 5:9 outright object of *a*
13:9 the land an object of *a*
Jer 2:15 his land an object of *a*
4:7 your land as an object of *a*
4:9 the priests . . . driven to *a*
8:21 *a* has seized hold of me
18:16 their land an object of *a*
18:16 stare in *a* and shake his
19:8 this city an object of *a*
19:8 stare in *a* and whistle over
25:9 make them an object of *a*
25:11 an object of *a*, and these
25:18 an object of *a*, something
25:38 land . . . an object of *a*
29:18 an object of *a* and for a
42:18 curse and an object of *a* and
44:12 an object of *a* and a
44:22 and an object of *a* and a
46:19 become a mere object of *a*
48:9 become a mere object of *a*
49:13 nothing but an object of *a*
49:17 become an object of *a*
49:17 stare in *a* and whistle on
50:3 her land an object of *a*
50:13 he will stare in *a* and
50:23 become a mere object of *a*
51:29 Babylon an object of *a*
51:37 an object of *a* and
51:41 mere object of *a* among the
51:43 become an object of *a*
La 4:5 struck with *a* in the streets
Eze 23:33 cup of *a* and of desolation
Ho 5:9 Ephraim, a mere object of *a*
Joe 1:7 my vine as an object of *a*
Mic 6:16 make you an object of *a*
Zep 2:15 has become an object of *a*
Zec 7:14 desirable land an object of *a*
Lu 4:36 *a* fell upon all, and they
5:9 *a* overwhelmed him and all
Ac 3:10 they became filled with *a*
9:21 gave way to *a* and would say

Astounded
Jer 14:9 become like a man *a*, like a
Mt 7:28 *a* at his way of teaching
13:54 were *a* and said: Where did
22:33 were *a* at his teaching
Mr 1:22 *a* at his way of teaching, for
6:2 those listening were *a* and
7:37 they were being *a* in a most
10:26 They became still more *a*
11:18 being *a* at his teaching
Lu 2:48 they saw him they were *a*
4:32 were *a* at his way of teaching
9:43 *a* at the majestic power of
Ac 13:12 *a* at the teaching of Jehovah

Astray
Ex 23:4 bull or his ass going *a*, you
De 27:18 causes the blind to go *a*
Job 12:16 and the one leading *a*
15:31 being led *a*, For mere
36:18 ransom itself lead you *a*
Ps 119:10 *a* from your commandments
Pr 5:23 of his foolishness he goes *a*
20:1 going *a* by it is not wise
28:10 to go *a* into the bad way
Isa 28:7 of wine they have gone *a* and
28:7 *a* because of intoxicating
28:7 gone *a* in their seeing
44:20 has led him *a*. And he does
Eze 13:10 they have led my people *a*
Mr 13:22 signs and wonders to lead *a*
1Ti 6:10 been led *a* from the faith
Heb 3:10 always go *a* in their hearts
1Pe 2:25 were like sheep, going *a*

Astrologers
Da 2:27 *a* themselves are unable to
4:7 and the *a* were entering; and
5:7 the Chaldeans and the *a*
5:11 the Chaldeans and the *a*, even
Mt 2:1 *a* from eastern parts came to
2:7 Herod secretly summoned the *a*
2:16 had been outwitted by the *a*
2:16 ascertained from the *a*

Astute
Job 5:13 counsel of *a* ones is carried

Asunder
Heb 11:37 they were sawn *a*, they

Asyncritus
Ro 16:14 Greet *A*, Phlegon, Hermes

Atad
Ge 50:10 the threshing floor of *A*
50:11 the threshing floor of *A*, and

Atarah
1Ch 2:26 wife, whose name was *A*

Ataroth
Nu 32:3 *A* and Dibon and Jazer and
32:34 build Dibon and *A* and Aroer
Jos 16:2 boundary of the Archites at *A*
16:7 went down from Janoah to *A*

Ataroth-addar
Jos 16:5 came to be *A*, as far as
18:13 boundary went down to *A*

Ate
Ge 3:12 she gave me fruit . . . so I *a*
3:13 it deceived me and so I *a*
24:54 *a* and drank, he and the men
26:30 feast for them and they *a*
27:33 I *a* of everything before you
31:38 rams of your flock I never *a*
31:46 they *a* there on the heap
31:54 *a* bread and passed the night
47:22 *a* their rations that Pharaoh
Ex 16:35 *a* the manna forty years
16:35 manna was what they *a* until
24:11 of the true God and *a* and
34:28 He *a* no bread and he drank no
De 9:9 I neither *a* bread nor drank
9:18 I neither *a* bread nor drank
32:13 he *a* the produce of the field
Jg 9:27 and *a* and drank and called
Ru 3:7 Meantime Boaz *a* and drank, and
1Sa 9:24 Saul *a* with Samuel on that
28:25 his servants, and they *a*
30:12 *a* and his spirit returned
2Sa 19:35 what I *a* and what I drank
1Ki 19:8 he rose up and *a* and drank
2Ki 4:40 soon as they *a* from the stew
6:29 we boiled my son and *a* him
9:34 came on in and *a* and drank
23:9 they *a* unfermented cakes in
25:29 he *a* bread constantly before
Ezr 6:21 returned from the Exile *a*
10:6 he *a* no bread and drank no
Ps 78:25 Men *a* the very bread of
78:63 His young men a fire *a* up
Jer 31:29 ones that *a* the unripe grape
52:33 he *a* bread before him
Eze 16:13 and oil were what you *a*
Am 7:4 and *a* up the tract of land
Mt 12:4 *a* the loaves of presentation
13:4 the birds came and *a* them up
14:20 So all *a* and were satisfied
15:37 And all *a* and were satisfied
Mr 2:26 *a* the loaves of presentation
4:4 and the birds came and *a* it up
6:42 they all *a* and were satisfied
6:44 those who *a* of the loaves
8:8 they *a* and were satisfied
Lu 4:2 he *a* nothing in those days
6:4 *a* and gave some to the men
8:5 the birds of heaven *a* it up
9:17 they all *a* and were satisfied
13:26 We *a* and drank in front of
15:30 son who *a* up your means of
Lu 24:43 and *a* it before their eyes
Joh 6:23 *a* the bread after the Lord
6:26 *a* from the loaves and were
6:31 forefathers *a* the manna in
6:49 forefathers *a* the manna in
6:58 forefathers *a* and yet died
Ac 9:9 and he neither *a* nor drank
10:41 *a* and drank with him after
1Co 10:3 *a* the same spiritual food
Re 10:10 *a* it up, and in my mouth it

Ater
Ezr 2:16 sons of *A*, of Hezekiah
2:42 the sons of *A*
Ne 7:21 the sons of *A*, of Hezekiah
7:45 the sons of *A*, the sons of
10:17 *A*, Hezekiah, Azzur

Athach
1Sa 30:30 and to those in *A*

Athaiah
Ne 11:4 sons of Judah there were *A*

Athaliah
2Ki 8:26 *A* the granddaughter of Omri
11:1 *A* the mother of Ahaziah
11:2 concealed from the face of *A*
11:3 *A* was reigning over the land
11:13 *A* heard the sound of the
11:14 *A* ripped her garments apart
11:20 *A* herself they had put to
1Ch 8:26 and Shehariah and *A*
2Ch 22:2 *A* the granddaughter of Omri
22:10 *A* the mother of Ahaziah
22:11 concealed because of *A*, and
22:12 *A* was ruling as queen over
23:12 *A* heard the sound of the
23:13 *A* ripped her garments apart
23:21 *A* they had put to death
24:7 *A* the wicked woman, her
Ezr 8:7 Jeshaiah the son of *A*

Atharim
Nu 21:1 had come by the way of *A*, and

Athenians
Ac 17:21 all *A* and the foreigners

Athens
Ac 17:15 brought him as far as *A* and
17:16 Paul was waiting . . . in *A*
17:22 Men of *A*, I behold that in
18:1 he departed from *A* and came
1Th 3:1 to be left alone in *A*

Athlai
Ezr 10:28 the sons of Bebai . . . *A*

Atoned
Pr 16:6 and trueness error is *a* for
Isa 6:7 your sin itself is *a* for
22:14 error will not be *a* for in
27:9 error of Jacob will be *a* for

Atonement
Ex 29:33 eat the things with which *a*
29:36 sin offering daily for an *a*
29:36 from sin by your making *a*
29:37 seven days to make *a* over
30:10 *a* upon its horns once a year
30:10 the sin offering of the *a* he
30:10 make *a* for it once a year
30:15 to make *a* for your souls
30:16 silver money of the *a* from
30:16 to make *a* for your souls
Le 1:4 accepted for him to make *a*
4:20 must make an *a* for them
4:26 the priest must make an *a* for
4:31 priest must make an *a* for him
4:35 priest must make an *a* for
5:6 an *a* for him for his sin
5:10 the priest must make an *a* for
5:13 an *a* for him for his sin that
5:16 an *a* for him with the ram of
5:18 priest must make an *a* for
6:7 priest must make an *a* for
6:30 to make *a* in the holy place
7:7 priest who will make *a* with
8:15 sanctify it to make *a* upon it
8:34 so as to make *a* for you
9:7 make *a* in your own behalf and
9:7 make *a* in their behalf, just
10:17 *a* for them before Jehovah
12:7 make *a* for her, and she must
12:8 priest must make *a* for her
14:18 *a* for him before Jehovah
14:19 *a* for the one cleansing
14:20 make *a* for him; and he must

Le 14:21 in order to make *a* for him
14:29 *a* for him before Jehovah
14:31 make *a* for the one cleansing
14:53 must make *a* for the house
15:15 *a* for him before Jehovah
15:30 *a* for her before Jehovah
16:6 *a* in behalf of himself and
16:10 to make *a* for it, so as to
16:11 an *a* in behalf of himself
16:16 make *a* for the holy place
16:17 make *a* in the holy place
16:17 *a* in behalf of himself and
16:18 make *a* for it, and he must
16:20 making *a* for the holy place
16:24 *a* in his own behalf and in
16:27 *a* in the holy place, taken
16:30 on this day *a* will be made
16:32 make an *a* and must put on
16:33 *a* for the holy sanctuary
16:33 for the altar he will make *a*
16:33 congregation he will make *a*
16:34 *a* for the sons of Israel
17:11 *a* for your souls, because it
17:11 blood that makes *a* by the
19:22 priest must make *a* for him
23:27 month is the day of *a*
23:28, 28 day of *a* to make *a* for
25:9 day of *a* you people should
Nu 5:8 except the ram of *a* with which
5:8 which he will make *a* for him
6:11 make *a* for him, since he has
8:12 to make *a* for the Levites
8:19 make *a* for the sons of Israel
8:21 Aaron made an *a* for them to
15:25 *a* for the whole assembly of
15:28 *a* for the soul who made a
15:28 so as to make *a* for it, and
16:46 in a hurry and make *a* for
16:47 making *a* for the people
25:13 *a* for the sons of Israel
28:22 sin offering to make *a* for
28:30 kid of the goats to make *a*
29:5 sin offering to make *a* for
29:11 the sin offering of *a* and the
31:50 make *a* for our souls before
35:33 and for the land . . . no *a*
De 32:43 make *a* for the ground of his
2Sa 21:3 with what shall I make *a*
1Ch 6:49 and to make *a* for Israel
2Ch 29:24 to make *a* for all Israel
Ne 10:33 to make *a* for Israel and all
Eze 16:63 when I make an *a* for you
43:20 and make *a* for it
43:26 will make *a* for the altar
45:15 order to make *a* for them
45:17 *a* in behalf of the house of
45:20 must make *a* for the House
Da 9:24 and to make *a* for error, and
Ac 27:9 fast of *a* day had already

Atremble
1Sa 4:13 heart had become *a* over the

Atroth-beth-joab
1Ch 2:54 sons of Salma were . . . *A*

Atroth-shophan
Nu 32:35 and *A* and Jazer and Jogbehah

Attach
Ex 28:14 must *a* the ropelike chains
1Sa 2:36 *A* me, please, to one of the
Ps 106:28 *a* themselves to Baal of
Isa 14:1 *a* themselves to the house of
Mic 1:13 *A* the chariot to the team

Attached
Ge 34:8 his soul is *a* to your daughter
Nu 25:3 Israel *a* itself to the Baal
De 10:15 get *a* so as to love them
21:11 and you have got *a* to her
1Sa 26:19 *a* to the inheritance of
2Sa 20:8 girded a sword *a* to his hip
2Ch 9:18 (they were *a*)
Ps 50:19 your tongue you keep *a* to
Isa 38:17 *a* to my soul and kept it
Lu 15:15 and *a* himself to one of the

Attaches
Ga 3:15 aside or *a* additions to it

Attaching
Hab 2:15 *a* to it your rage and anger

Attachment
Nu 25:5 an *a* with the Baal of Peor
Isa 21:4 for which I had an *a*

Attack
Ge 43:18 *a* us and to take us for
Ps 56:6 They *a*, they conceal
59:3 Strong ones make an *a* upon me
Isa 54:15 should at all make an *a*
54:15 is making an *a* upon you
Eze 26:9 the strike of his *a* engine
Ac 24:9 the Jews also joined in the *a*

Attacked
Ge 34:27 *a* the fatally wounded men

Attacking
Ps 140:2 day long keep *a* as in wars

Attacks
Ps 94:21 make sharp *a* on the soul of

Attai
1Ch 2:35 who in time bore him *A*
2:36 *A*, in turn, became father to
12:11 *A* the sixth, Eliel the
2Ch 11:20 she bore him Abijah and *A*

Attain
Ps 139:6 so high up that I cannot *a* to
Isa 35:10 rejoicing they will *a*, and
51:11 and rejoicing they will *a*
Ac 26:7 *a* to the fulfillment of this
Ro 9:31 did not *a* to the law
1Co 9:24 in such a way that you may *a*
Eph 4:13 all *a* to the oneness in the
Php 3:11 *a* to the earlier resurrection
Heb 11:35 *a* a better resurrection
2Pe 3:9 desires all to *a* to repentance

Attained
Es 4:14 you have *a* to royal dignity

Attalia
Ac 14:25 they went down to *A*

Attempt
De 4:34 did God *a* to come to take a
Ac 14:5 violent *a* took place on the

Attempted
Ex 2:15 Pharaoh . . . *a* to kill Moses
De 28:56 *a* to set the sole of her foot
Ac 26:21 Jews . . . *a* to slay me
Heb 11:17 *a* to offer up his

Attempts
Ac 9:29 made *a* to do away with him

Attend
De 21:12 and *a* to her nails
1Ki 1:2 will have to *a* upon the king
Es 4:5 he had made to *a* upon her
Isa 41:1 *A* to me in silence, you
Lu 10:40 left me alone to *a* to things
Ac 12:13 Rhoda came to *a* to the call

Attendance
1Ki 12:32 in *a* at Bethel the priests
1Ch 6:33 those in *a* and also their
Ne 12:44 Levites who were in *a*
Ac 2:46 constant *a* at the temple
8:13 in constant *a* upon Philip
10:7 were in constant *a* upon him
1Co 7:35 constant *a* upon the Lord

Attendant
Ge 18:7 bull and to give it to the *a*
Ex 33:11 Joshua, the son of Nun, as *a*
Jg 7:10 with Purah your *a*, to the
7:11 his *a* made their descent to
9:54 the *a* bearing his weapons and
9:54 *a* ran him through, so that he
19:3 his *a* and a couple of he-asses
19:9 he and his concubine and his *a*
19:10 and his concubine and his *a*
19:11 the *a* now said to his master
19:13 say to his *a*: Come and let
19:19 for the *a* with your servant
1Sa 2:13 *a* of the priest came with
2:15 an *a* of the priest came and
9:5 Saul . . . said to his *a* that
9:7 At this Saul said to his *a*
9:8 *a* answered Saul once more and
9:10 Then Saul said to his *a*
9:22 Samuel took Saul and his *a*
9:27 Say to the *a* that he should
10:14 said to him and to his *a*
14:1 the *a* carrying his weapons
14:6 to the *a*, his armor-bearer
20:21 I shall send the *a*, saying
20:21 say to the *a*, Look! The
20:35 and a young *a* was with him
20:36 say to his *a*: Run, please
1Sa 20:36 *a* ran, and he himself shot
20:37 *a* came as far as the place
20:37 call from behind the *a* and
20:38 calling from behind the *a*
20:38 *a* of Jonathan went picking
20:39 As for the *a*, he did not
20:40 his weapons to the *a* that
20:41 *a* went. As for David, he
30:13 I am an Egyptian *a*, a slave
2Sa 9:9 called Ziba, Saul's *a*, and
13:17 called his *a* who waited
16:1 Ziba the *a* of Mephibosheth
19:17 Ziba the *a* of the house of
1Ki 18:43 said to his *a*: Go up, please
19:3 he left his *a* behind there
2Ki 4:12 So he said to Gehazi his *a*
4:19 to the *a*: Carry him to his
4:24 said to her *a*: Drive and go
4:25 said to Gehazi his *a*: Look!
4:38 he in time said to his *a*
5:20 Then Gehazi the *a* of Elisha
6:15 At once his *a* said to him
8:4 Gehazi the *a* of the man of
9:4, 4 the *a*, the prophet's *a*, got
Ne 4:22 each one with his *a*, in the
6:5 Sanballat sent his *a* to me
Mt 5:25 judge to the court *a*, and
Lu 4:20 handed it back to the *a* and
Joh 4:46 *a* of the king whose son
4:49 The *a* of the king said to
Ac 13:5 They had John also as an *a*
26:16 to choose you as an *a* and
Heb 3:5 Moses as an *a* was faithful

Attendant's
2Ki 6:17 Jehovah opened the *a* eyes

Attendants
Ge 22:3 his *a* with him and Isaac his
22:5 said to his *a*: You stay here
22:19 Abraham returned to his *a*
24:61 Rebekah and her lady *a* rose
Ex 2:5 her female *a* were walking by
Nu 22:22 two *a* of his were with him
1Sa 2:17 sin of the *a* came to be very
9:3 with you one of the *a* and get
16:18 one of the *a* proceeded to
2Sa 13:28 Absalom commanded his *a*
13:29 Absalom's *a* proceeded to
18:15 *a* carrying Joab's weapons
2Ki 4:22 one of the *a* and one of the
5:23 gave them to two of his *a*
19:6 the *a* of the king of Assyria
Ne 4:23 my brothers and my *a* and the
5:10 my brothers and my *a* are
5:15 *a* themselves domineered
5:16 *a* were collected together
13:19 *a* I stationed at the gates
Es 2:2 king's *a*, his ministers, said
6:3 king's *a*, his ministers, said
6:5 king's *a* said to him: Here is
Job 1:15 *a* they struck down with the
1:16 among the sheep and the *a*
1:17 *a* they struck down with the
29:5 my *a* were all around me
Pr 9:3 It has sent forth its lady *a*
Isa 37:6 *a* of the king of Assyria
Mt 26:58 sitting with the house *a* to
Mr 14:54 together with the house *a*
14:65 the court *a* took him
Lu 1:2 *a* of the message delivered
12:42 appoint over his body of *a* to
Joh 18:36 *a* would have fought that I

Attended
1Sa 16:21 David came to Saul and *a*
2Sa 19:24 he had not *a* to his feet
19:24 had he *a* to his mustache
Ac 17:25 *a* to by human hands as if he
20:34 have *a* to the needs of me

Attending
1Sa 9:5 not quit *a* to the she-asses
16:22 David, please, keep *a* upon
1Ki 12:6 *a* upon Solomon his father
12:8 were the ones *a* upon him
1Ch 6:32 kept *a* upon their service
6:39 was *a* at his right, Asaph
2Ch 10:6 *a* upon Solomon his father
10:8 were the ones *a* upon him
Lu 10:40 distracted with *a* to many
1Co 9:13 those constantly *a* at the

Attention
Ge 21:1 Jehovah turned his *a* to Sarah
50:24 turn his *a* to you, and he

Ge 50:25 without fail turn his *a* to
Ex 3:16 without fail give *a* to you
4:31 Jehovah had turned his *a* to
5:9 them not pay *a* to false words
13:19 God will . . . turn his *a* to
Ru 1:6 Jehovah had turned his *a* to his
1Sa 2:21 turned his *a* to Hannah, so
15:22 pay *a* than the fat of rams
1Ki 18:29 there was no paying of *a*
2Ki 4:31 no voice nor paying of *a*
2Ch 20:15 Pay *a*, all Judah and you
33:10 people, but they paid no *a*
Ne 9:34 paid *a* to your commandments
Job 6:28 pay *a* to me, And see whether
7:18 pay *a* to him every morning
8:8 *a* to the things searched out
13:6 pleadings of my lips pay *a*
31:11 error for *a* by the justices
31:28 error for *a* by the justices
32:12 to you I kept my *a* turned
33:31 Pay *a*, O Job! Listen to me
Ps 5:2 pay *a* to the sound of my cry
10:17 will pay *a* with your ear
17:1 pay *a* to my entreating cry
21:9 the appointed time for your *a*
37:10 give *a* to his place, and he
55:2 pay *a* to me and answer me
59:5 turn your *a* to all the nations
61:1 Do pay *a* to my prayer
65:9 turned your *a* to the earth
66:19 *a* to the voice of my prayer
86:6 pay *a* to the voice of my
89:32 turn my *a* to their
142:6 pay *a* to my entreating cry
Pr 1:24 there is no one paying *a*
2:2 pay *a* to wisdom with your
4:1 and pay *a*, so as to know
4:20 son, to my words do pay *a*
5:1 to my wisdom O do pay *a*
7:24 pay *a* to the sayings of my
17:4 The evildoer is paying *a* to
29:12 is paying *a* to false speech
Ca 8:13 partners are paying *a* to your
Isa 10:3 day of being given *a* and
10:30 Pay *a*, O Laishah
21:7 he paid strict *a*, with
23:17 Jehovah will turn his *a* to
24:21 Jehovah will turn his *a*
24:22 they will be given *a*
26:14 turned your *a* that you
26:16 have turned their *a* to you
27:1 turn his *a* to Leviathan
27:3 may turn his *a* against her
28:23 pay *a* and listen to my
29:6 you will have *a* with thunder
32:3 those hearing will pay *a*
34:1 national groups, pay *a*
42:23 Who will pay *a* and listen
48:18 pay *a* to my commandments
49:1 pay *a*, you national groups
51:4 Pay *a* to me, O my people
Jer 6:10 they are unable to pay *a*
6:17 *a* to the sound of the horn
6:17 We are not going to pay *a*
6:19 no *a* to my very own words
8:6 I have paid *a*, and I kept
8:12 time of their being given *a*
10:15 given *a* they will perish
11:22 turning my *a* upon them
11:23 year of their being given *a*
13:21 one turns his *a* upon you
14:10 will give *a* to their sins
15:15 turn your *a* to me and
18:18 *a* to any of his words
18:19 Do pay *a* to me, O Jehovah
23:2 not turned your *a* to them
23:2 I am turning my *a* upon you
23:12 year of their being given *a*
23:18 Who has given *a* to his word
23:34 turn my *a* upon that man
27:8 turn my *a* upon that nation
27:22 my turning my *a* to them
29:10 turn my *a* to you people
29:32 turning my *a* upon Shemaiah
30:20 turn my *a* upon all his
32:5 until I turn my *a* to him
44:29 turning my *a* upon you in
46:21 of their being given *a*
46:25 turning my *a* upon Amon
48:44 of their being given *a*
49:8 I must turn my *a* to him
50:18 I am turning my *a* upon the
50:18 turned my *a* upon the king
50:27 for their being given *a*
Jer 50:31 time that I must give you *a*
51:18 given *a* they will perish
51:44 turn my *a* upon Bel in
51:47 *a* upon the graven images of
51:52 turn my *a* upon her graven
La 4:22 has turned his *a* to your error
Eze 9:1 giving their *a* to the city
23:21 *a* to the loose conduct of
38:8 you will be given *a*
Da 9:19 Jehovah, do pay *a* and act
Ho 5:1 pay *a*, O house of Israel, and
9:7 The days of being given *a*
9:9 he will give *a* to their sins
Mic 1:2 pay *a*, O earth and what fills
7:4 your being given *a*, must
Zep 1:8 give *a* to the princes, and
1:9 give *a* to everyone that is
1:12 give *a* to the men who are
2:7 God will turn his *a* to them
Zec 1:4 and they paid no *a* to me, is
7:11 they kept refusing to pay *a*
10:3 has turned his *a* to his drove
11:16 he will give no *a*
Mal 3:16 Jehovah kept paying *a* and
Mr 4:24 Pay *a* to what you are hearing
Lu 1:25 he has given me his *a* to take
1:68 turned his *a* and performed
7:16 has turned his *a* to his people
8:18 pay *a* to how you listen; for
17:3 Pay *a* to yourselves. If your
21:34 pay *a* to yourselves that
Ac 3:5 he fixed his *a* upon them
4:29 Jehovah, give *a* to their
5:35 pay *a* to yourselves as to
8:6 paying *a* to the things said by
8:10 would pay *a* to him and say
8:11 pay *a* to him because of his
15:14 turned his *a* to the nations
16:14 her heart wide to pay *a* to
20:28 Pay *a* to yourselves and to
1Ti 1:4 nor to pay *a* to false stories
4:1 paying *a* to misleading
4:16 Pay constant *a* to yourself
Tit 1:14 paying no *a* to Jewish fables
Heb 2:1 pay more than the usual *a*
2Pe 1:19 doing well in paying *a* to it

Attentive
2Ch 6:40 ears *a* to the prayer
7:15 my ears *a* to prayer at this
Ne 1:6 let your ear become *a* and your
1:11 become *a* to the prayer of
8:3 people were *a* to the book of
Job 11:11 also show himself *a*
23:15 I show myself *a* and am in
30:20 might show yourself *a* to me
31:1 show myself *a* to a virgin
37:14 *a* to the wonderful works of
Ps 107:43 *a* toward Jehovah's acts of
119:95 I keep showing myself *a*
130:2 to be *a* to the voice of my

Attentively
Job 21:2 Listen, you men, *a* to my
37:2 Listen *a*, you men, to the
1Jo 1:1 which we have viewed *a* and

Attentiveness
Isa 21:7 attention, with much *a*

Attestation
Ru 4:7 and this was the *a* in Israel
Isa 8:2 *a* for myself by faithful
8:16 Wrap up the *a*, put a seal
8:20 To the law and to the *a!*

Attested
Ne 9:38 in writing and *a* by the seal

Attesting
Ne 10:1 *a* it by seal there were

Attire
1Ki 10:5 his waiters and their *a* and
2Ki 10:22 brought the *a* out for them
2Ch 9:4 waiters and their *a* and his
9:4 drinking service and their *a*
Job 27:16 prepare *a* just as if clay
Eze 16:13 your *a* was fine linen and
Zep 1:8 all those wearing foreign *a*

Attitude
La 3:21 why I shall show a waiting *a*
3:24 show a waiting *a* for him
Mic 7:7 show a waiting *a* for the God
Ro 15:5 the same mental *a* that Christ
Php 2:5 Keep this mental *a* in you
3:15 mature, be of this mental *a*
Php 3:15 reveal the above *a* to you

Attractive
Ge 24:16 *a* in appearance, a virgin
26:7 she was *a* in appearance
Na 3:4 prostitute, *a* with charm, a

Attractiveness
Pr 1:9 wreath of *a* to your head and

Attribute
Nu 12:11 *a* to us the sin in which we
De 32:3 Do you *a* greatness to our God
2Sa 19:19 Do not let my lord *a* error
1Ch 16:28 *A* to Jehovah, O families of
16:28 *A* to Jehovah glory and
16:29 *A* to Jehovah the glory of
Isa 42:12 *a* to Jehovah glory, and in

Audacious
Job 41:10 None is so *a* that he should

Audience
Ac 25:23 entered into the *a* chamber

Auditorium
Ac 19:9 in the school *a* of Tyrannus

August
Ac 25:21 the decision by the *A* One
25:25 appealed to the *A* One

Augustus
Lu 2:1 went forth from Caesar *A* for
Ac 27:1 Julius of the band of *A*

Aunt
Le 18:14 She is your *a*

Authoritatively
Mr 1:27 He *a* orders even the unclean

Authorities
Lu 12:11 government officials and *a*
Ro 13:1 subjection to the superior *a*
13:1 *a* stand placed in their
Eph 3:10 *a* in the heavenly places
6:12 against the *a*, against the
Col 1:16 governments or *a*. All other
2:15 the governments and the *a*
Tit 3:1 obedient to governments and *a*
1Pe 3:22 and *a* and powers were made

Authority
Job 38:33 you put its *a* in the earth
Mt 5:41 if someone under *a* impresses
7:29 as a person having *a*, and not
8:9 a man placed under *a*, having
9:6 Son of man has *a* on earth to
9:8 God, who gave such *a* to men
10:1 *a* over unclean spirits, in
20:25 great men wield *a* over them
21:23 By what *a* do you do these
21:23 And who gave you this *a?*
21:24 by what *a* I do these things
21:27 by what *a* I do these things
28:18 All *a* has been given me in
Mr 1:22 teaching them as one having *a*
2:10 has *a* to forgive sins upon
3:15 to have *a* to expel the demons
6:7 *a* over the unclean spirits
10:42 great ones wield *a* over
11:28 By what *a* do you do these
11:28 this *a* to do these things
11:29 by what *a* I do these things
11:33 by what *a* I do these things
13:34 gave the *a* to his slaves
Lu 4:6 I will give you all this *a* and
4:32 his speech was with *a*
4:36 with *a* and power he orders
5:24 *a* on the earth to forgive sins
7:8 I too am a man placed under *a*
9:1 *a* over all the demons and to
10:19 *a* to trample underfoot
12:5 has *a* to throw into Gehenna
19:17 hold *a* over ten cities
20:2 by what *a* you do these things
20:2 who . . . gave you this *a*
20:8 by what *a* I do these things
20:20 and to the *a* of the governor
22:25 those having *a* over them are
22:53 hour and the *a* of darkness
Joh 1:12 *a* to become God's children
5:27 given him *a* to do judging
10:18 I have *a* to surrender it
10:18 I have *a* to receive it again
17:2 given him *a* over all flesh
19:10 I have *a* to release you
19:10 I have *a* to impale you
19:11 have no *a* at all against me

Ac 8:19 Give me also this *a*, that
9:14 *a* from the chief priests to
14:3 boldness by the *a* of Jehovah
26:10 *a* from the chief priests
26:12 with *a* and a commission
26:18 from the *a* of Satan to God
Ro 9:21 potter have *a* over the clay
13:1 there is no *a* except by God
13:2 he who opposes the *a* has
13:3 want to have no fear of the *a*
1Co 6:12 brought under *a* by anything
7:4 exercise *a* over her own body
7:4 exercise *a* over his own body
7:37 has *a* over his own will and
8:9 that this *a* of yours does not
9:4 We have *a* to eat and drink, do
9:5 have *a* to lead about a sister
9:6 do not have *a* to refrain from
9:12 partake of this *a* over you
9:12 have not made use of this *a*
9:18 not abuse my *a* in the good
11:10 a sign of *a* upon her head
15:24 and all *a* and power
2Co 10:8 the *a* that the Lord gave us
13:10 *a* that the Lord gave me
Eph 1:21 above every government and *a*
2:2 the ruler of the *a* of the air
Col 1:13 from the *a* of the darkness
2:10 head of all government and *a*
2Th 3:9 Not that we do not have *a*
1Ti 2:12 or to exercise *a* over a man
Tit 2:15 and reproving with full *a*
Heb 13:10 the tent have no *a* to eat
Jude 25 *a* for all past eternity and
Re 2:26 will give *a* over the nations
6:8 *a* was given them over the
9:3 *a* was given them, the same
9:3 the same *a* as the scorpions
9:10 *a* to hurt the men five months
9:19 the *a* of the horses is in
11:6 *a* to shut up heaven that no
11:6 *a* over the waters to turn
12:10 God and the *a* of his Christ
13:2 and its throne and great *a*
13:4 gave the *a* to the wild beast
13:5 *a* to act forty-two months
13:7 *a* was given it over every
13:12 *a* of the first wild beast
14:18 and he had *a* over the fire
16:9 has the *a* over these plagues
17:12 *a* as kings one hour with
17:13 and *a* to the wild beast
18:1 from heaven, with great *a*
20:6 the second death has no *a*
22:14 *a* to go to the trees of life

Authorization
Ge 41:44 without your *a* no man may
2Ki 18:25 without *a* from Jehovah
Isa 36:10 without *a* from Jehovah that

Autumn
De 11:14 *a* rain and spring rain, and
Jer 5:24 the downpour and the *a* rain
Joe 2:23 give you the *a* rain in
2:23 *a* rain and spring rain, as
Jude 12 trees in late *a*, but

Avail
Ps 127:1 to no *a* that its builders
127:1 to no *a* that the guard has
127:2 no *a* it is for you men that

Available
Ge 13:9 Is not the whole land *a* to
20:15 Here my land is *a* to you
34:10 land will become *a* for you
Ex 5:13 just as when straw was *a*
2Ch 14:7 land is yet *a*, because we
19:11 the Levites are *a* for you
Ne 9:35 land that you made *a* for them

Avenge
De 32:43 *a* the blood of his servants
Jg 15:7 for me to *a* myself upon you
16:28 let me *a* myself upon the
1Sa 18:25 to *a* himself on the enemies
2Ki 9:7 *a* the blood of my servants
Es 8:13 to *a* themselves upon their
Isa 1:24 will *a* myself on my enemies
Jer 5:9 should not my soul *a* itself?
5:29 should not my soul *a* itself?
9:9 should not my soul *a* itself?
15:15 *a* me upon my persecutors
Ro 12:19 Do not *a* yourselves, beloved

Avenged
Ge 4:24 seven times Cain is to be *a*
Ex 21:20 one is to be *a* without fail
21:21 he is not to be *a*, because
Eze 25:12 and *a* themselves on them
Re 19:2 *a* the blood of his slaves at

Avenger
Nu 35:12 as a refuge from the blood *a*
35:19 *a* of blood is the one who
35:21 *a* of blood will put the
35:24 striker and the *a* of blood
35:25 out of the hand of the *a* of
35:27 the *a* of blood does find him
35:27 the *a* of blood does slay the
De 19:6 Otherwise, the *a* of blood may
19:12 the hand of the *a* of blood
Jos 20:3 a refuge from the *a* of blood
20:5 the *a* of blood chases after
20:9 the hand of the *a* of blood
2Sa 14:11 *a* of blood may not be
Ps 78:35 the Most High was their *A*
Ro 13:4 *a* to express wrath upon the

Avengers
1Ki 16:11 *a* of blood or his friends

Avenging
Es 9:16 an *a* of themselves upon their
Ps 79:10 *a* . . . blood of your servants
Jer 46:10 for *a* himself upon his
Eze 25:15 and they kept *a* themselves
Re 6:10 from judging and *a* our blood

Avert
Isa 47:11 will not be able to *a* it

Averts
Pr 16:14 wise man is one that *a* it

Avith
Ge 36:35 the name of his city was *A*
1Ch 1:46 name of his city was *A*

Avoid
Ro 16:17 keep your eye . . . and *a* them

Avoided
Isa 53:3 despised and was *a* by men

Avoiding
2Co 8:20 *a* having any man find fault

Avrekh
Ge 41:43 call out ahead of him, *A!*

Avva
2Ki 17:24 Babylon and Cuthah and *A*

Avvim
De 2:23 the *A*, who were dwelling in
Jos 13:3 and the Ekronites; and the *A*
18:23 and *A* and Parah and Ophrah

Avvites
2Ki 17:31 the *A*, they made Nibhaz and

Awaiting
Job 30:26 I kept *a* the light, but
Heb 10:13 *a* until his enemies should
11:10 *a* the city having real
2Pe 3:12 *a* and keeping close in mind
3:13 a new earth that we are *a*
3:14 since you are *a* these things

Awake
Jg 5:12, 12, 12 *A*, *a*, O Deborah; *A*
5:12 *a*, utter a song! Rise up
Ezr 8:29 Keep *a* and be on guard until
Job 8:6 By now he would *a* for you And
Ps 3:5 I shall certainly *a*, for
7:6 do *a* for me, since you have
35:23 and *a* to my judgment
44:23 Do *a*. Do not keep casting
57:8 Do *a*, O my glory
57:8 Do *a*, O stringed instrument
78:65 Jehovah began to *a* as from
108:2 *a*, O stringed instrument
127:1 that the guard has kept *a*
Pr 8:34 keeping *a* at my doors day by
Ca 4:16 *A*, O north wind, and come in
5:2 I am asleep, but my heart is *a*
Isa 26:19 *A* and cry out joyfully, you
51:9, 9 *A*, *a*, clothe yourself
51:9 *A* as in the days of long ago
Jer 1:12 I am keeping *a* concerning
5:6 a leopard is keeping *a* at
Hab 2:19 the piece of wood: O do *a!*
Zec 13:7 sword, *a* against my shepherd
Mal 2:12 one who is *a* and one who
Mt 24:43 he would have kept *a* and not
Mr 13:33 Keep looking, keep *a*, for
Lu 9:32 when they got fully *a* they
21:36 Keep *a*, then, all the time
Ac 20:31 keep *a*, and bear in mind
Ro 13:11 hour for you to *a* from sleep
1Co 16:13 Stay *a*, stand firm in the
Eph 5:14 *A*, O sleeper, and arise from
6:18 keep *a* with all constancy
Col 4:2 prayer, remaining *a* in it
1Th 5:6 stay *a* and keep our senses
5:10 we stay *a* or are asleep
Re 16:15 one that stays *a* and keeps

Awaked
Ps 139:18 I have *a*, and yet I am

Awaken
Job 3:8 Those ready to *a* Leviathan
Ps 57:8 I will *a* the dawn
108:2 I will *a* the dawn
Ca 2:7 try not to *a* or arouse love in
3:5 not to *a* or arouse love in me
8:4 try not to *a* or arouse love in
Isa 42:13 a warrior he will *a* a zeal
Eze 7:6 end must come; it must *a* for
Zec 9:13 I will *a* your sons, O Zion
Joh 11:11 there to *a* him from sleep

Awakened
Isa 14:9 *a* those impotent in death
Jer 6:22 nation that will be *a* from
Zec 4:1 man that is *a* from his sleep
Ac 16:27 jailer, being *a* out of sleep

Awakening
Ps 17:15 when *a* to see your form

Awakens
Isa 50:4 He *a* morning by morning
50:4 he *a* my ear to hear like

Awakes
Isa 29:8 *a* and his soul is empty
29:8 *a* and here he is tired and

Awaking
Ps 73:20 Like a dream after *a*

Award
2Co 5:10 his *a* for the things done

Aware
Ge 16:4 she became *a* that she was
16:5 *a* that she was pregnant
33:13 My lord is *a* that the
Ru 3:11 *a* that you are an excellent
1Sa 3:20 became *a* that Samuel was
2Sa 17:10 Israel is *a* that your father
Es 4:11 *a* that, as regards any man or
Ps 37:18 Jehovah is *a* of the days of
44:21 *a* of the secrets of the heart
139:14 As my soul is very well *a*
Pr 14:10 heart is *a* of the bitterness
24:22 who is *a* of the extinction
Ec 5:1 are not *a* of doing what is bad
8:12 *a* that it will turn out well
9:1 Mankind are not *a* of either
11:5 not *a* of what is the way of
Da 2:8 I am *a* that time is what you
Jon 1:12 *a* that it is on my account
Mt 15:17 *a* that everything entering
26:10 *A* of this, Jesus said to
27:18 he was *a* that out of envy
Mr 7:18 *a* that nothing from outside
15:10 *a* that because of envy the
Joh 4:1 the Lord became *a* that the
5:6 *a* that he had already been
21:17 *a* that I have affection for
Ga 6:1 false step before he is *a* of

Away*
Ge 4:16 Cain went *a* from the face of
Ex 4:23 Send my son *a* that he may
7:2 must send the sons of Israel *a*
7:16 Send my people *a* that they
Nu 6:3 he should keep *a* from wine and
16:24 Get *a* from . . . Korah, Dathan
De 4:2 neither must you take *a* from
Jer 23:23 Jehovah, and not a God far *a*
2Co 3:14 is done *a* with by means of
4:16 we are outside is wasting *a*
5:17 the old things passed *a*
1Ti 4:1 will fall *a* from the faith
2Ti 1:15 Asia have turned *a* from me
Heb 6:6 but who have fallen *a*, to
9:26 sin *a* through the sacrifice
10:4 and of goats to take sins *a*
Jas 1:11 rich man will fade *a* in his
1Pe 3:21 the putting *a* of the filth

2Pe 3:10 the heavens will pass *a* with

Awe
Le 19:30 stand in *a* of my sanctuary
26:2 stand in *a* of my sanctuary
Ps 89:7 God is to be held in *a* among
Isa 29:23 they will regard with *a*
47:12 might strike people with *a*
Heb 12:28 with godly fear and *a*

Awesome
Ca 6:4 *a* as companies gathered around
6:10 *a* as companies gathered
Eze 1:22 like the sparkle of *a* ice

Awesomeness
De 34:12 all the great *a* that Moses

Awestruck
Eze 32:10 cause many peoples to be *a*

Awl
Ex 21:6 pierce his ear . . . with an *a*
De 15:17 take an *a* and put it through

Awoke
Ge 9:24 Noah *a* from his wine and got
28:16 Jacob *a* from his sleep and
Jg 16:14 So he *a* from his sleep and
1Ki 3:15 When Solomon *a*, why, here
Jer 31:26 I *a* and began to see

Ax
De 19:5 strike with the *a* to cut the
20:19 wielding an *a* against them
Jg 9:48 took an *a* in his hand and cut
1Sa 13:20 or his mattock or his *a* or
Ps 35:3 draw spear and double *a* to
Isa 10:15 *a* enhance itself over the
Mt 3:10 *a* is lying at the root of the
Lu 3:9 the *a* is already in position
Re 20:4 those executed with the *a* for

Axes
1Sa 13:21 for the *a* and for fixing
2Sa 12:31 *a* of iron, and he made
1Ki 6:7 hammers and *a* or any tools of
1Ch 20:3 instruments of iron and at *a*
Ps 74:5 *a* on high against a thicket
Jer 46:22 with *a* they will actually

Axhead
2Ki 6:5 *a* itself fell into the water
6:6 and made the *a* float

Axis
Jos 13:3 five *a* lords of the
Jg 3:3 *a* lords of the Philistines
16:5 the *a* lords of the Philistines
16:8 the *a* lords of the Philistines
16:18 called the Philistine *a* lords
16:18 Philistine *a* lords came up
16:23 Philistine *a* lords, they
16:27 the Philistine *a* lords were
16:30 falling upon the *a* lords and
1Sa 5:8 the *a* lords of the Philistines
5:11 *a* lords of the Philistines
6:4 the *a* lords of the Philistines
6:4 *a* lords have the same scourge
6:12 *a* lords of the Philistines
6:16 *a* lords of the Philistines
6:18 belonging to the five *a* lords
7:7 *a* lords of the Philistines got
29:2 *a* lords of the Philistines
29:6 eyes of the *a* lords you are
29:7 *a* lords of the Philistines
1Ch 12:19 *a* lords of the Philistines

Axles
1Ki 7:30 carriage, with *a* of copper

Azaliah
2Ki 22:3 *A* the son of Meshullam
2Ch 34:8 sent Shaphan the son of *A*

Azaniah
Ne 10:9 Jeshua the son of *A*

Azarel
1Ch 12:6 and Isshiah and *A* and Joezer
25:18 the eleventh for *A*, his sons
27:22 of Dan, *A* the son of
Ezr 10:41 *A* and Shelemiah, Shemariah
Ne 11:13 *A* the son of Ahzai the son of
12:36 his brothers Shemaiah and *A*

Azariah
1Ki 4:2 *A* the son of Zadok, the priest
4:5 *A* the son of Nathan was over
2Ki 14:21 the people of Judah took *A*
15:1 *A* the son of Amaziah the
15:6 the rest of the affairs of *A*
2Ki 15:7 *A* lay down with his
15:8 *A* the king of Judah
15:17 *A* the king of Judah
15:23 *A* the king of Judah
15:27 *A* the king of Judah
1Ch 2:8 the sons of Ethan were *A*
2:38 in turn, became father to *A*
2:39 *A*, in turn, became father to
3:12 Amaziah his son, *A* his son
6:9 Ahimaaz . . . father to *A*
6:9 *A* . . . father to Johanan
6:10 Johanan . . . father to *A*
6:11 *A* . . . father to Amariah
6:13 Hilkiah . . . father to *A*
6:14 *A* . . . father to Seraiah
6:36 son of Joel, the son of *A*
9:11 and *A* the son of Hilkiah the
2Ch 15:1 *A* the son of Oded, the spirit
21:2 Jehoshaphat's sons, *A* and
21:2 Jehoshaphat's sons . . . *A* and
22:6 *A* the son of Jehoram the
23:1 *A* the son of Jeroham and
23:1 *A* the son of Obed and
26:17 *A* the priest and with him
26:20 *A* the chief priest and all
28:12 *A* the son of Jehohanan
29:12 Joel the son of *A* of the
29:12 *A* the son of Jehallelel
31:10 *A* the chief priest of the
31:13 *A* was the leading one of
Ezr 7:1 *A* the son of Hilkiah
7:3 *A* the son of Meraioth
Ne 3:23 *A* the son of Maaseiah the
3:24 the house of *A* as far as the
7:7 *A*, Raamiah, Nahamani
8:7 *A*, Jozabad, Hanan, Pelaiah
10:2 Seraiah, *A*, Jeremiah
12:33 *A*, Ezra and Meshullam
Jer 43:2 *A* the son of Hoshaiah and
Da 1:6 Hananiah, Mishael and *A*
1:7 and to *A*, Abednego
1:11 Hananiah, Mishael and *A*
1:19 Hananiah, Mishael and *A*
2:17 Hananiah, Mishael and *A* his

Azaz
1Ch 5:8 the son of *A* the son of Shema

Azazel
Le 16:8 and the other lot for *A*
16:10 lot came up for *A* should be
16:10 for *A* into the wilderness
16:26 who sent the goat away for *A*

Azaziah
1Ch 15:21 and Jeiel and *A* with harps
27:20 Hoshea the son of *A*; of the
2Ch 31:13 and *A* . . . commissioners at

Azbuk
Ne 3:16 Nehemiah the son of *A*

Azekah
Jos 10:10 slaying them as far as *A*
10:11 as far as *A*, so that they
1Sa 17:1 camping between Socoh and *A*
2Ch 11:9 Adoraim and Lachish and *A*
Ne 11:30 *A* and its dependent towns
Jer 34:7 Lachish and against *A*

Azekkah
Jos 15:35 Adullam, Socoh and *A*

Azel
1Ch 8:37 Eleasah his son, *A* his son
8:38 And *A* had six sons, and these
8:38 All these were the sons of *A*
9:43 Eleasah his son, *A* his son
9:44 *A* had six sons, and these
9:44 These were the sons of *A*
Zec 14:5 will reach all the way to *A*

Azgad
Ezr 2:12 sons of *A*, a thousand two
8:12 of the sons of *A*, Johanan
Ne 7:17 the sons of *A*, two thousand
10:15 Bunni, *A*, Bebai

Aziel
1Ch 15:20 and Zechariah and *A* and

Aziza
Ezr 10:27 the sons of Zattu . . . *A*

Azmaveth
2Sa 23:31 Arbathite, *A* the Bar-humite
1Ch 8:36 father to Alemeth and *A* and
9:42 father to Alemeth and *A* and
11:33 *A* the Baharumite
12:3 and Pelet the sons of *A*
1Ch 27:25 was *A* the son of Adiel
Ezr 2:24 the sons of *A*, forty-two
Ne 12:29 the fields of Geba and *A*

Azmon
Nu 34:4 and pass over to *A*
34:5 change direction at *A* to the
Jos 15:4 passed on to *A* and went

Aznoth-tabor
Jos 19:34 went back westward to *A*

Azor
Mt 1:13 Eliakim became father to *A*
1:14 *A* became father to Zadok

Azriel
1Ch 5:24 Eliel and *A* and Jeremiah and
27:19 Jerimoth the son of *A*
Jer 36:26 Seraiah the son of *A* and

Azrikam
1Ch 3:23 sons of Neariah were . . . *A*
8:38 *A* . . . the sons of Azel
9:14 *A* the son of Hashabiah from
9:44 *A* . . . the sons of Azel
2Ch 28:7 and *A* the leader of the
Ne 11:15 *A* the son of Hashabiah the

Azubah
1Ki 22:42 *A* the daughter of Shilhi
1Ch 2:18 sons by *A* his wife and by
2:19 *A* died. So Caleb took to
2Ch 20:31 *A* the daughter of Shilhi

Azzan
Nu 34:26 Paltiel the son of *A*

Azzur
Ne 10:17 Ater, Hezekiah, *A*
Jer 28:1 Hananiah the son of *A*
Eze 11:1 Jaazaniah the son of *A* and

Baal
Nu 25:3 to the *B* of Peor; and the
25:5 attachment with the *B* of Peor
De 4:3 in the case of the *B* of Peor
4:3 *B* of Peor was the one whom
Jg 2:13 and took up serving *B* and the
6:25 tear down the altar of *B* that
6:28 the altar of *B* had been pulled
6:30 pulled down the altar of *B*
6:31 defense for *B* to see whether
6:32 Let *B* make a legal defense in
1Ki 16:31 serve *B* and to bow down to
16:32 he set up an altar to *B*
16:32 house of *B* that he built in
18:19 prophets of *B* and the
18:21 if *B* is, go following him
18:22 prophets of *B* are four
18:25 said to the prophets of *B*
18:26 calling upon the name of *B*
18:26 saying: O *B* answer us!
18:40 Seize the prophets of *B*!
19:18 have not bent down to *B*
22:53 serving *B* and bowing down
2Ki 3:2 the sacred pillar of *B* that
10:18 worshiped *B* a little
10:19 call all the prophets of *B*
10:19 a great sacrifice for *B*
10:19 the worshipers of *B*
10:20 a solemn assembly for *B*
10:21 worshipers of *B* came in
10:21 coming into the house of *B*
10:21 house of *B* came to be full
10:22 for all the worshipers of *B*
10:23 into the house of *B*
10:23 said to the worshipers of *B*
10:23 only the worshipers of *B*
10:25 the city of the house of *B*
10:26 pillars of the house of *B*
10:27 down the sacred pillar of *B*
10:27 pulled down the house of *B*
10:28 annihilated *B* out of Israel
11:18 house of *B* and pulled down
11:18 priest of *B* they killed
17:16 the heavens and to serve *B*
21:3 and set up altars to *B* and
23:4 all the utensils made for *B*
23:5 sacrificial smoke to *B*
1Ch 4:33 cities were as far as *B*
5:5 Reaiah his son, *B* his son
8:30 Zur and Kish and *B* and Nadab
9:36 Kish and *B* and Ner and Nadab
2Ch 23:17 house of *B* and pulled it
23:17 Mattan the priest of *B* they
Ps 106:28 attach themselves to *B* of
Jer 2:8 the prophets prophesied by *B*
7:9 making sacrificial smoke to *B*

Jer 9:14 and after the *B* images
11:13 make sacrificial smoke to *B*
11:17 sacrificial smoke to *B*
12:16 my people to swear by *B*
19:5 the high places of the *B*
19:5 burnt offerings to the *B*
23:13 as prophets incited by *B*
23:27 my name by means of *B*
32:29 sacrificial smoke to *B* and
32:35 built the high places of *B*
Ho 2:8 which they made use of for *B*
2:13 days of the *B* images to which
2:17 names of the *B* images from
9:10 went in to *B* of Peor, and
11:2 To the *B* images they took up
13:1 guilty in regard to *B* and die
Zep 1:4 the remaining ones of the *B*
Ro 11:4 have not bent the knee to *B*

Baalah
Jos 15:9 boundary was marked out to *B*
15:10 *B* westward to Mount Seir
15:11 passed over to Mount *B* and
15:29 *B* and Iim and Ezem
1Ch 13:6 up to *B*, to Kiriath-jearim

Baalath
Jos 19:44 Eltekeh and Gibbethon and *B*
1Ki 9:18 and *B* and Tamar in the
2Ch 8:6 *B* and all the storage cities

Baalath-beer
Jos 19:8 these cities as far as *B*

Baal-berith
Jg 8:33 they appointed *B* as their god
9:4 silver from the house of *B*

Baale-judah
2Sa 6:2 went to *B* to bring up from

Baal-gad
Jos 11:17 as far as *B* in the valley
12:7 from *B* in the valley plain
13:5 from *B* at the base of Mount

Baal-hamon
Ca 8:11 Solomon happened to have in *B*

Baal-hanan
Ge 36:38 *B* son of Achbor began to
36:39 When *B* son of Achbor died
1Ch 1:49 *B* the son of Achbor began to
1:50 *B* died, and Hadad began to
27:28 there was *B* the Gederite

Baal-hazor
2Sa 13:23 sheepshearers at *B*, which

Baal-hermon
Jg 3:3 from Mount *B* as far as to the
1Ch 5:23 from Bashan to *B* and Senir

Baalis
Jer 40:14 *B*, the king of the sons of

Baal-meon
Nu 32:38 and Nebo and *B*—their names
1Ch 5:8 and as far as Nebo and *B*
Eze 25:9 *B*, even to Kiriathaim

Baal-perazim
2Sa 5:20 So David came to *B*, and
5:20 the name of that place *B*
1Ch 14:11 So David went up to *B* and
14:11 the name of that place *B*

Baals
Jg 2:11 of Jehovah and serving the *B*
3:7 went serving the *B* and the
8:33 intercourse with the *B*, so
10:6 they began to serve the *B* and
10:10 and we serve the *B*
1Sa 7:4 Israel put away the *B* and the
12:10 that we might serve the *B*
1Ki 18:18 you went following the *B*
2Ch 17:3 and did not search for the *B*
24:7 they had rendered up to the *B*
28:2 statues he made of the *B*
33:3 set up altars to the *B* and
34:4 the altars of the *B*
Jer 2:23 After the *B* I have not

Baal-shalishah
2Ki 4:42 was a man that came from *B*

Baal-tamar
Jg 20:33 up in formation at *B*

Baal-zebub
2Ki 1:2 inquire of *B* the god of Ekron
1:3 inquire of *B* the god of Ekron
1:6 inquire of *B* the god of Ekron
2Ki 1:16 inquire of *B* the god of Ekron

Baal-zephon
Ex 14:2 in view of *B*. In front of it
14:9 by Pihahiroth in view of *B*
Nu 33:7 which is in view of *B*; and

Baana
1Ki 4:12 *B* the son of Ahilud, in
4:16 *B* the son of Hushai, in Asher
Ne 3:4 Zadok the son of *B* did repair

Baanah
2Sa 4:2 name of the one being *B*
4:5 Rechab and *B*, proceeded to go
4:6 Rechab and *B* his brother
4:9 David answered Rechab and *B*
23:29 Heleb the son of *B* the
1Ch 11:30 Heled the son of *B* the
Ezr 2:2 Mispar, Bigvai, Rehum, *B*
Ne 7:7 Mispereth, Bigvai, Nehum, *B*
10:27 Malluch, Harim, *B*

Baara
1Ch 8:8 Hushim and *B* were his wives

Baaseiah
1Ch 6:40 of *B*, the son of Malchijah

Baasha
1Ki 15:16 Asa and *B* the king of Israel
15:17 *B* the king of Israel came
15:19 break your covenant with *B*
15:21 as soon as *B* heard of it
15:22 which *B* had been building
15:27 *B* the son of Ahijah of the
15:27 *B* got to strike him down
15:28 *B* put him to death in the
15:32 *B* the king of Israel all
15:33 *B* . . . became king
16:1 against *B*, saying
16:3 a clean sweep after *B* and
16:4 Anyone of *B* that is dying in
16:5 the rest of the affairs of *B*
16:6 Finally *B* lay down with his
16:7 come against *B* and his house
16:8 Elah the son of *B* became
16:11 all the house of *B*
16:12 the whole house of *B*
16:12 spoken against *B* by means
16:13 all the sins of *B* and the
21:22 house of *B* the son of Ahijah
2Ki 9:9 *B* the son of Ahijah
2Ch 16:1 *B* the king of Israel came up
16:3 break your covenant with *B*
16:5 soon as *B* heard of it, he
16:6 with which *B* had built
Jer 41:9 of *B* the king of Israel

Babe
1Co 13:11 When I was a *b*, I used to
13:11 I used to speak as a *b*
13:11 to think as a *b*, to reason
13:11 to reason as a *b*; but now
13:11 with the traits of a *b*
Ga 4:1 as long as the heir is a *b* he
Heb 5:13 partakes of milk . . . is a *b*

Babel
Ge 10:10 kingdom came to be *B* and
11:9 why its name was called *B*

Babes
Mt 11:25 and have revealed them to *b*
21:16 Out of the mouth of *b* and
Lu 10:21 and have revealed them to *b*
Ro 2:20 a teacher of *b*, and having
1Co 3:1 fleshly men, as to *b* in
14:20 *b* as to badness; yet become
Ga 4:3 when we were *b*, continued
Eph 4:14 we should no longer be *b*

Baby
Mt 24:19 Woe . . . those suckling a *b*
Mr 13:17 suckling a *b* in those days
Lu 21:23 ones suckling a *b* in those

Babylon
2Ki 17:24 people from *B* and Cuthah
17:30 men of *B*, for their part
20:12 king of *B* sent letters and
20:14 land they came, from *B*
20:17 actually be carried to *B*
20:18 the palace of the king of *B*
24:1 Nebuchadnezzar the king of *B*
24:7 king of *B* had taken all that
24:10 Nebuchadnezzar the king of *B*
24:11 Nebuchadnezzar the king of *B*
24:12 went out to the king of *B*
2Ki 24:12 the king of *B* got to take
24:15 Jehoiachin into exile to *B*
24:15 people from Jerusalem to *B*
24:16 the king of *B* proceeded to
24:16 as exiled people to *B*
24:17 king of *B* made Mattaniah
24:20 rebel against the king of *B*
25:1 Nebuchadnezzar the king of *B*
25:6 the king of *B* at Riblah
25:7 fetters and brought him to *B*
25:8 Nebuchadnezzar the king of *B*
25:8 the servant of the king of *B*
25:11 gone over to the king of *B*
25:13 the copper of them to *B*
25:20 the king of *B* at Riblah
25:21 king of *B* proceeded to
25:22 Nebuchadnezzar the king of *B*
25:23 heard that the king of *B*
25:24 and serve the king of *B*
25:27 Evil-merodach the king of *B*
25:28 that were with him in *B*
1Ch 9:1 was taken into exile at *B* for
2Ch 32:31 princes of *B* that were sent
33:11 and took him to *B*
36:6 Nebuchadnezzar the king of *B*
36:6 to carry him off to *B*
36:7 brought to *B* and then put
36:7 put them in his palace in *B*
36:10 to bring him to *B* with
36:18 everything he brought to *B*
36:20 captive to *B*, and they came
Ezr 1:11 people out of *B* to Jerusalem
2:1 Nebuchadnezzar the king of *B*
2:1 had taken into exile at *B*
5:12 Nebuchadnezzar the king of *B*
5:12 the people into exile at *B*
5:13 Cyrus the king of *B*
5:14 brought to the temple of *B*
5:14 took out of the temple of *B*
5:17 that is there in *B*, whether
6:1 treasures deposited there in *B*
6:5 and brought to *B* be returned
7:6 Ezra himself went up from *B*
7:9 appointed the going up from *B*
7:16 jurisdictional district of *B*
8:1 Artaxerxes the king out of *B*
Ne 7:6 Nebuchadnezzar the king of *B*
13:6 Artaxerxes the king of *B*
Es 2:6 Nebuchadnezzar the king of *B*
Ps 87:4 *B* as among those knowing me
137:1 By the rivers of *B*—there
137:8 O daughter of *B*, who are to
Isa 13:1 against *B* that Isaiah the
13:19 *B*, the decoration of
14:4 saying against the king of *B*
14:22 cut off from *B* name and
21:9 *B* has fallen, and all the
39:1 Baladan the king of *B* sent
39:3 they came to me, from *B*
39:6 actually be carried to *B*
39:7 the palace of the king of *B*
43:14 I will send to *B* and cause
47:1 O virgin daughter of *B*
48:14 what is his delight upon *B*
48:20 you people, out of *B*! Run
Jer 20:4 the hand of the king of *B*
20:4 take them into exile in *B*
20:5 and bring them to *B*
20:6 to *B* you will come and there
21:2 the king of *B* is making war
21:4 fighting the king of *B*
21:7 Nebuchadrezzar the king of *B*
21:10 the hand of the king of *B*
22:25 Nebuchadrezzar the king of *B*
24:1 Nebuchadrezzar the king of *B*
24:1 he might bring them to *B*
25:1 Nebuchadrezzar the king of *B*
25:9 Nebuchadrezzar the king of *B*
25:11 have to serve the king of *B*
25:12 against the king of *B*
27:6 Nebuchadnezzar the king of *B*
27:8 Nebuchadnezzar the king of *B*
27:8 the yoke of the king of *B*
27:9 not serve the king of *B*
27:11 the yoke of the king of *B*
27:12 the yoke of the king of *B*
27:13 does not serve the king of *B*
27:14 not serve the king of *B*
27:16 brought back from *B* soon
27:17 Serve the king of *B* and
27:18 may not come into *B*
27:20 Nebuchadnezzar the king of *B*
27:20 exile from Jerusalem to *B*
27:22 To *B* is where they will be

Jer 28:2 the yoke of the king of *B*
28:3 the king of *B* took from
28:3 he might bring them to *B*
28:4 of Judah who have come to *B*
28:4 the yoke of the king of *B*
28:6 the exiled people from *B*
28:11 Nebuchadnezzar the king of *B*
28:14 Nebuchadnezzar the king of *B*
29:1 exile from Jerusalem to *B*
29:3 sent to *B* to Nebuchadnezzar
29:3 Nebuchadnezzar the king of *B*
29:4 exile from Jerusalem to *B*
29:10 seventy years at *B*
29:15 for us prophets in *B*
29:20 away from Jerusalem to *B*
29:21 Nebuchadrezzar the king of *B*
29:22 body of exiles . . . in *B*
29:22 whom the king of *B* roasted
29:28 sent to us at *B*, saying
32:2 forces of the king of *B*
32:3 the hand of the king of *B*
32:4 hand of the king of *B*, and
32:5 to *B* he will take Zedekiah
32:28 Nebuchadrezzar the king of *B*
32:36 hand of the king of *B* by
34:1 king of *B* and all his
34:2 hand of the king of *B*, and
34:3 the eyes of the king of *B*
34:3 and to *B* you will come
34:7 forces of the king of *B*
34:21 forces of the king of *B*
35:11 Nebuchadrezzar the king of *B*
36:29 The king of *B* will come
37:1 Nebuchadrezzar the king of *B*
37:17 king of *B* you will be given
37:19 king of *B* will not come
38:3 force of the king of *B*
38:17 princes of the king of *B*
38:18 princes of the king of *B*
38:22 princes of the king of *B*
38:23 hand of the king of *B* you
39:1 Nebuchadrezzar the king of *B*
39:3 princes of the king of *B*
39:3 princes of the king of *B*
39:5 king of *B* at Riblah in the
39:6 king of *B* proceeded to
39:6 king of *B* slaughtered
39:7 in order to bring him to *B*
39:9 took into exile to *B*
39:11 Nebuchadrezzar the king of *B*
39:13 men of the king of *B* sent
40:1 taken into exile in *B*
40:4 to come with me to *B*
40:4 come with me to *B*, refrain
40:5 king of *B* has commissioned
40:7 king of *B* had commissioned
40:7 been taken into exile in *B*
40:9 serve the king of *B*, and
40:11 king of *B* had given a
41:2 king of *B* had commissioned
41:18 king of *B* had commissioned
42:11 because of the king of *B*
43:3 to take us into exile in *B*
43:10 king of *B*, my servant, and
44:30 Nebuchadrezzar the king of *B*
46:2 king of *B* defeated in the
46:13 Nebuchadrezzar the king of *B*
46:26 Nebuchadrezzar the king of *B*
49:28 Nebuchadrezzar the king of *B*
49:30 Nebuchadrezzar the king of *B*
50:1 Jehovah spoke concerning *B*
50:2 *B* has been captured
50:8 out of the midst of *B*
50:9 bringing up against *B* a
50:13 anyone passing along by *B*
50:14 Array yourselves against *B*
50:16 Cut off the sower from *B*
50:17 Nebuchadrezzar the king of *B*
50:18 king of *B* and upon his land
50:23 *B* has become a mere object
50:24 also been caught, O *B*
50:28 escaping from the land of *B*
50:29 Summon against *B* archers
50:34 to the inhabitants of *B*
50:35 against the inhabitants of *B*
50:42 against you, O daughter of *B*
50:43 *B* has heard the report about
50:45 he has formulated against *B*
50:46 when *B* has been seized
51:1 rousing up against *B* and
51:2 send to *B* winnowers who
51:6 Flee out of the midst of *B*
51:7 *B* has been a golden cup in
51:8 *B* has fallen, so that she
Jer 51:9 We would have healed *B*, but
51:11 against *B* that his idea is
51:12 Against the walls of *B*
51:12 the inhabitants of *B*
51:24 I will pay back to *B* and
51:29 against *B* the thoughts of
51:29 *B* an object of astonishment
51:30 of *B* have ceased to fight
51:31 report to the king of *B* that
51:33 *B* is like a threshing floor
51:34 Nebuchadrezzar the king of *B*
51:35 violence . . . be upon *B*
51:37 *B* must become piles of
51:41 *B* has become a mere object
51:42 has come up even over *B*
51:44 attention upon Bel in *B*
51:44 wall itself of *B* must fall
51:47 upon the graven images of *B*
51:48 over *B* the heavens and the
51:49 *B* the cause for the slain
51:49 at *B* the slain ones of all
51:53 *B* should ascend to the
51:54 is an outcry from *B*, and
51:55 for Jehovah is despoiling *B*
51:56 upon *B*, the despoiler, and
51:58 wall of *B*, although broad
51:59 to *B* in the fourth year of
51:60 that would come upon *B*
51:60 words written against *B*
51:61 to *B* and actually see her
51:64 *B* will sink down and never
52:3 rebel against the king of *B*
52:4 Nebuchadrezzar the king of *B*
52:9 up to the king of *B* at
52:10 king of *B* proceeded to
52:11 king of *B* bound him with
52:11 brought him to *B* and put
52:12 the king of *B*
52:12 before the king of *B*
52:15 away to the king of *B* and
52:17 the copper of them to *B*
52:26 to the king of *B* at Riblah
52:27 And these the king of *B*
52:31 Evil-merodach the king of *B*
52:32 that were with him in *B*
52:34 from the king of *B*
Eze 12:13 and I will bring him to *B*
17:12 Look! The king of *B* came to
17:12 bring them to himself at *B*
17:16 the midst of *B* he will die
17:20 I will bring him to *B* and
19:9 brought him to the king of *B*
21:19 sword of the king of *B* to
21:21 the king of *B* stood still
23:15 likeness of the sons of *B*
23:17 sons of *B* kept coming in to
23:23 *B* and all the Chaldeans
24:2 The king of *B* has thrown
26:7 Nebuchadrezzar the king of *B*
29:18 Nebuchadrezzar . . . king of *B*
29:19 Nebuchadrezzar the king of *B*
30:10 Nebuchadrezzar the king of *B*
30:24 the arms of the king of *B*
30:25 the arms of the king of *B*
30:25 the hand of the king of *B*
32:11 sword of the king of *B* will
Da 1:1 Nebuchadnezzar the king of *B*
2:12 all the wise men of *B*
2:14 to kill the wise men of *B*
2:18 of the wise men of *B*
2:24 destroy the wise men of *B*
2:24 destroy any wise men of *B*
2:48 jurisdictional district of *B*
2:48 over all the wise men of *B*
2:49 jurisdictional district of *B*
3:1 jurisdictional district of *B*
3:12 jurisdictional district of *B*
3:30 jurisdictional district of *B*
4:6 bring . . . all the wise men of *B*
4:29 upon the royal palace of *B*
4:30 *B* the Great, that I myself
5:7 saying to the wise men of *B*
7:1 Belshazzar the king of *B*
Mic 4:10 have to come as far as to *B*
Zec 2:7 with the daughter of *B*
6:10 these who have come from *B*
Mt 1:11 time of the deportation to *B*
1:12 After the deportation to *B*
1:17 until the deportation to *B*
1:17 from the deportation to *B*
Ac 7:43 I will deport you beyond *B*
1Pe 5:13 She who is in *B*, a chosen
Re 14:8 *B* the great has fallen, she
16:19 *B* the Great was remembered
Re 17:5 *B* the Great, the mother of
18:2 *B* the Great has fallen, and
18:10 *B* you strong city, because
18:21 *B* the great city be hurled

Babylonians
Ezr 4:9 the *B*, the inhabitants of Susa

Baca
2Sa 5:23 in front of the *b* bushes
5:24 in the tops of the *b* bushes
1Ch 14:14 in front of the *b* bushes
14:15 in the tops of the *b* bushes
Ps 84:6 low plain of the *b* bushes

Back
Ge 4:12 will not give you *b* its power
8:12 dove . . . did not come *b* again
9:5 of your souls shall I ask *b*
9:5 creature shall I ask it *b*
9:5 shall I ask *b* the soul of man
19:9 Stand *b* there! And they added
20:6 holding you *b* from sinning
23:6 hold *b* his burial place from
27:30 Esau his brother came *b* from
30:2 held *b* the fruit of the belly
33:16 Esau turned *b* on his way to
37:14 and bring me *b* word
38:20 get *b* the security from the
38:29 soon as he drew *b* his hand
41:5 went *b* to sleep and dreamed a
42:22 here it is certainly asked *b*
42:34 Your brother I shall give *b*
42:37 if I do not bring him *b*
43:10 there and *b* these two times
43:12 you will take *b* in your hand
43:18 money that went *b* with us
44:8 *b* to you from the land of
44:13 lifted each one his load *b*
44:32 If I fail to bring him *b*
49:8 *b* of the neck of your enemies
Ex 10:8 were brought *b* to Pharaoh
14:2 they should turn *b* and encamp
14:21 sea go *b* by a strong east
14:26 waters may come *b* over the
14:27 *b* to its normal condition
14:28 And the waters kept coming *b*
15:19 Jehovah brought *b* the waters
19:8 Moses took *b* the words of the
23:27 give the *b* of the neck of all
26:12 over the *b* of the tabernacle
33:23 you will indeed see my *b*
34:31 So Aaron . . . came *b* to him
34:35 Moses put the veil *b* over
Le 13:16 goes *b* and it does change
25:24 grant . . . right of buying *b*
25:25 buy *b* what his brother sold
25:28 find enough to give *b* to him
25:30 bought *b* before the complete
25:33 property . . . not bought *b*
25:48 brothers may buy him *b*
25:49 his uncle may buy him *b*
25:49 his family, may buy him *b*
25:49 he must also buy himself *b*
25:54 buy himself *b* on these terms
26:26 give *b* your bread by weight
27:13 buy it *b* at all, he must
27:15 buy his house *b*, he must
27:19 buy the field *b*, he must
27:20 not buy the field *b* but if
27:20 it may not be bought *b* again
27:27 not be bought *b*, it must
27:28 thing may be bought *b*
27:31 buy any of his tenth part *b*
27:33 It may not be bought *b*
Nu 13:26 came bringing *b* word to
14:43 you turned *b* from following
17:10 Put Aaron's rod *b* before the
22:34 let me go my way *b*
24:11 has held you *b* from honor
25:4 anger of Jehovah may turn *b*
25:11 turned *b* my wrath from upon
32:15 turn *b* from following him
33:7 turned *b* toward Pihahiroth
De 1:22 bring us *b* word concerning
1:25 they came bringing us *b* word
3:20 you must come *b*, each one to
4:39 call *b* to your heart that
17:16 nor make the people go *b*
17:16 never go *b* again by this way
19:14 not move *b* the boundary
22:1 lead them *b* to your brother
24:4 not be allowed to take her *b*
24:19 you must not go *b* to get it
27:17 moves *b* the boundary mark of

Pr 22:28 Do not move *b* a boundary of
23:10 not move *b* the boundary of
23:13 not hold *b* discipline from
24:11 O may you hold them *b*
24:12 pay *b* to earthling man
24:18 certainly turn *b* his anger
26:3 the rod is for the *b* of stupid
26:15 too weary to bring it *b* to
26:27 *b* to him it will return
29:8 who are wise turn *b* anger
30:30 turn *b* from before anyone
Ec 1:6 *b* to its circlings the wind is
2:10 I did not hold *b* my heart
Ca 5:3 robe. How can I put it *b* on?
5:4 My dear one himself pulled *b*
6:13, 13 Come *b*, come *b*, O
6:13 O Shulammite! Come *b*
6:13 come *b*, that we may behold
Isa 1:25 will turn *b* my hand upon you
1:26 bring *b* again judges for you
5:25 his anger has not turned *b*
6:10 turn *b* and get healing for
9:12 his anger has not turned *b*
9:17 his anger has not turned *b*
9:21 his anger has not turned *b*
10:4 his anger has not turned *b*
10:15 one moving it *b* and forth
10:15 staff moved *b* and forth
12:1 anger gradually turned *b*
14:27 and who can turn it *b*?
30:15 coming *b* and resting you
31:2 not called *b* his own words
36:9 turn *b* the face of one
37:29 *b* by the way by which you
38:8 went *b* ten steps on the
38:17 behind your *b* all my sins
42:17 They must be turned *b*, they
42:22 anyone to say: Bring *b*!
43:6 to the south, Do not keep *b*
43:13 and who can turn it *b*
49:5 to bring *b* Jacob to him
49:6 bring *b* even the safeguarded
50:6 My *b* I gave to the strikers
51:23 your *b* just like the earth
52:8 when Jehovah gathers *b* Zion
54:2 Do not hold *b*. Lengthen out
58:1 do not hold *b*. Raise your
58:13 turn *b* your foot as regards
59:13 a moving *b* from our God
59:14 was forced to move *b*
63:17 Come *b* for the sake of your
66:15 pay *b* his anger with sheer
Jer 2:24 who can turn her *b*?
2:25 *b* from becoming barefoot
2:27 turned the *b* of the neck and
2:35 anger has turned *b* from me
3:19 you people will not turn *b*
4:8 Jehovah has not turned *b*
4:28 nor shall I turn *b* from it
5:3 They refused to turn *b*
5:25 held *b* what is good from you
6:9 Put your hand *b* like one
8:4 If one would turn *b*, will the
8:4 the other not also turn *b*
8:5 they have refused to turn *b*
8:6 *b* into the popular course
12:15 bring them *b*, each one to
15:7 *b* from their own ways
15:19 If you will come *b*, then I
15:19 then I shall bring you *b*
15:19 will come *b* to you, but you
15:19 will not come *b* to them
16:15 bring them *b* to their soil
18:4 he turned *b* and went making
18:8 turns *b* from its badness
18:11 Turn *b*, please, each one
18:17 The *b*, and not the face
18:20 turn *b* your rage from them
23:3 *b* to their pasture ground
23:20 will not turn *b* until he
23:22 turn *b* from their bad way
25:5 Turn *b*, please, every one
25:16 drink and shake *b* and forth
27:16 brought *b* from Babylon soon
28:3 bringing *b* to this place
28:4 bringing *b* to this place
28:6 bringing *b* the utensils of
29:10 bringing you *b* to this place
29:14 *b* to the place from which
30:3 bring them *b* to the land
30:24 turn *b* until he will have
31:16 Hold *b* your voice from
31:18 Cause me to turn *b*, and
31:18 I shall readily turn *b*, for
Jer 31:19 after my turning *b* I felt
31:21 Come *b*, O virgin of Israel
31:21 Come *b* to these cities of
32:33 kept turning to me the *b*
32:37 bring them *b* to this place
32:40 not turn *b* from behind them
32:44 bring *b* their captives
33:7 bring *b* the captives of Judah
33:11 bring *b* the captives of the
34:11 bring *b* the menservants
34:16 turn *b* and profane my name
34:16 *b* each one his manservant
34:22 bring them *b* to this city
35:15 Turn *b*, please, each one
37:7 go *b* to their land, Egypt
37:8 come *b* and fight against
37:20 send me *b* to the house of
38:26 *b* to the house of Jehonathan
41:16 brought *b* from Ishmael the
41:16 he brought *b* from Gibeon
42:4 not hold *b* from you a word
44:5 turn *b* from their badness
46:5 They are turning *b*, and
48:10 holding *b* his sword from
48:39 how Moab has turned the *b*!
50:9 not come *b* without results
50:19 I will bring Israel *b* to
50:29 Pay *b* to her according to
51:6 that he is paying *b* to her
51:24 I will pay *b* to Babylon and
La 1:8 is also sighing and turns her *b*
2:3 turned his right hand *b* from
2:8 has not turned *b* his hand from
2:14 order to turn *b* your captivity
3:21 I shall bring *b* to my heart
3:64 give *b* to them a treatment
5:21 Bring us *b*, O Jehovah, to
5:21 and we shall readily come *b*
Eze 1:13 moving *b* and forth between
2:10 upon in front and on the *b*
3:18 his blood I shall ask *b* from
3:19 turn *b* from his wickedness
3:20 someone righteous turns *b*
3:20 his blood I shall ask *b* from
9:11 was bringing *b* word, saying
13:22 not turn *b* from his bad way
14:6 Come *b* and turn yourselves
14:6 *b* from your dungy idols and
14:6 turn your faces *b* even from
18:8 he would draw *b* his hand
18:17 he has drawn *b* his hand
18:21 turn *b* from all his sins
18:23 should turn *b* from his ways
18:24 someone righteous turns *b*
18:26 someone righteous turns *b*
18:27 someone wicked turns *b*
18:28 When he sees and he turns *b*
18:30 Turn *b*, yes, cause a turning
18:30 cause a turning *b* from all
18:32 cause a turning *b* and keep
20:22 I drew *b* my hand and went
21:5 No more will it go *b*
23:35 to cast me behind your *b*
27:15 have paid *b* as gift to you
29:14 bring *b* the captive group
29:14 *b* to the land of Pathros
31:15 hold *b* its streams and
33:6 its blood I shall ask *b*
33:8 his blood I shall ask *b* at
33:9 for him to turn *b* from it
33:9 not turn *b* from his way
33:11 wicked turns *b* from his
33:11, 11 Turn *b*, turn *b* from
33:12 *b* from his wickedness
33:14 turns *b* from his sin and
33:15 pays *b* the very things taken
33:18 someone righteous turns *b*
33:19 turns *b* from his wickedness
34:4 one you have not brought *b*
34:10 ask *b* my sheep from their
34:16 one I shall bring *b*
38:8 brought *b* from the sword
38:12 in order to turn your hand *b*
39:25 bring *b* the captive ones
39:27 I bring them *b* from the
44:1 *b* by way of the gate of
46:9 go *b* by the way of the gate
47:1 brought me *b* to the entrance
Da 3:16 to say *b* a word to you
5:5 *b* of the hand that was writing
5:24 being sent the *b* of a hand
7:6 four wings . . . on its *b*
9:13 turning *b* from our error and
9:16 rage turn *b* from your city
Da 10:20 *b* to fight with the prince
11:9 and go *b* to his own soil
11:10 But he will go *b*, and he
11:18 turn his face *b* to the
11:18 make it turn *b* upon that one
11:19 his face *b* to the fortresses
11:28 go *b* to his land with a
11:28 certainly go *b* to his land
11:29 time appointed he will go *b*
11:30 go *b* and hurl denunciations
11:30 have to go *b* and will give
Ho 2:9 turn *b* and certainly take away
3:5 the sons of Israel will come *b*
4:9 I shall bring *b* upon them
5:10 those moving *b* a boundary
6:11 gather *b* the captive ones of
14:1 come *b*, O Israel, to Jehovah
14:2 words and come *b* to Jehovah
14:4 anger has turned *b* from him
Joe 2:12 come *b* to me with all your
2:13 come *b* to Jehovah your God
2:14 whether he will turn *b* and
3:1 bring *b* the captive ones of
3:4 I shall pay *b* your treatment
3:7 I will pay *b* your treatment
Am 1:3 I shall not turn it *b*
1:6 I shall not turn it *b*
1:8 turn my hand *b* upon Ekron
1:9 I shall not turn it *b*
1:11 I shall not turn it *b*
1:13 I shall not turn it *b*
2:1 I shall not turn it *b*
2:4 I shall not turn it *b*
2:6 I shall not turn it *b*
4:6 you did not come *b* to me
4:8 you did not come *b* to me
4:9 yet you did not come *b* to me
4:10 you did not come *b* to me
4:11 you did not come *b* to me
9:14 gather *b* the captive ones of
Jon 1:13 the ship *b* to the dry land
3:8 come *b*, each one from his bad
3:9 turn *b* and actually feel
3:9 turn *b* from his burning anger
3:10 turned *b* from their bad way
Mic 4:10 buy you *b* out of the palm
6:8 Jehovah asking *b* from you but
Na 1:3 Jehovah hold *b* from punishing
2:8 But there is no one turning *b*
Zep 1:6 drawing *b* from following
2:7 gather *b* the captive ones of
3:20 gather *b* your captive ones
Hag 1:10 heavens kept *b* their dew
1:10 earth itself kept *b* its yield
Zec 4:1 to come *b* and wake me up
5:8 throw her *b* into the midst of
10:10 *b* from the land of Egypt
13:7 turn my hand *b* upon those
Mal 2:6 whom he turned *b* from error
4:6 of fathers *b* toward sons
4:6 heart of sons *b* toward
Mt 2:8 found it report *b* to me, that
5:24 come *b*, offer up your gift
12:44 I will go *b* to my house out
13:15 and turn *b*, and I heal them
16:23 But, turning his *b*, he said
18:25 have the means to pay it *b*
18:26 I will pay *b* everything to
18:28 Pay *b* whatever you owe
18:29 and I will pay you *b*
18:30 should pay *b* what was owing
18:34 until he should pay *b* all
22:21 Pay *b*, therefore, Caesar's
27:3 the thirty silver pieces *b* to
Mr 4:12 ever turn *b* and forgiveness
5:21 Jesus had crossed *b* again in
7:4 when *b* from market, they do
7:31 *b* out of the regions of Tyre
11:3 at once send it off *b* here
12:17 Pay *b* Caesar's things to
Lu 1:16 turn *b* to Jehovah their God
1:17 turn *b* the hearts of fathers
2:20 shepherds went *b*, glorifying
2:39 they went *b* into Galilee to
4:20 handed it *b* to the attendant
5:11 brought the boats *b* to land
6:30 do not ask them *b*
6:34 that they may get *b* as much
6:35 not hoping for anything *b*
7:10 on getting *b* to the house
7:42 anything with which to pay *b*
8:39 Be on your way *b* home, and
8:40 When Jesus got *b*, the crowd
10:6 it will turn *b* to you

Lu 10:35 repay you when I come *b* here
14:6 not able to answer *b* on these
15:27 he got him *b* in good health
16:6 Take your written agreement *b*
16:7 Take your written agreement *b*
17:4 and he comes *b* to you seven
17:15 turned *b*, glorifying God
17:18 turned *b* to give glory to God
19:15 when he got *b* after having
20:25 pay *b* Caesar's things to
23:11 and sent him *b* to Pilate
23:15 for he sent him *b* to us
23:56 went *b* to prepare spices and
Joh 7:45 officers went *b* to the chief
9:7 washed, and came *b* seeing
13:25 leaned *b* upon the breast of
14:26 bring *b* to your minds all
14:28 and I am coming *b* to you
18:6 they drew *b* and fell to the
20:10 went *b* to their homes
20:14 turned *b* and viewed Jesus
21:20 leaned *b* upon his breast
Ac 5:2 secretly held *b* some of the
5:3 hold *b* secretly some of the
7:39 they turned *b* to Egypt
8:25 they turned *b* to Jerusalem
20:20 did not hold *b* from telling
20:27 not held *b* from telling you
28:27 turn *b*, and I should heal
Ro 9:20 to be answering *b* to God
10:21 is disobedient and talks *b*
11:10 always bow down their *b*
2Co 1:16 come *b* from Macedonia to
Ga 1:17 I came *b* again to Damascus
4:9 turning *b* again to the weak
Eph 6:8 receive this *b* from Jehovah
Col 3:25 receive *b* what he wrongly
2Ti 2:26 *b* to their proper senses
Tit 2:9 them well, not talking *b*
Phm 12 one I am sending *b* to you
13 like to hold him *b* for myself
15 you may have him *b* forever
19 I will pay it *b*—not to be
Heb 10:38 if he shrinks *b*, my soul
10:39 shrink *b* to destruction
Jas 5:19 and another turns him *b*
5:20 a sinner *b* from the error of
1Pe 3:9 not paying *b* injury for injury
2Pe 2:4 did not hold *b* from punishing
2:5 not hold *b* from punishing an

Backbiters
Ro 1:30 *b*, haters of God, insolent

Backbiting
1Pe 2:1 envies and all sorts of *b*

Backbitings
2Co 12:20 contentions, *b*, whisperings

Backbone
Le 3:9 he will remove near the *b*

Backs
Ps 21:12 turn their *b* in flight
Eze 8:16 with their *b* to the temple
10:12 their *b* . . . full of eyes

Backward
Ge 49:17 so that its rider falls *b*
1Sa 4:18 to fall from the seat *b*
2Ki 20:10 should go *b* ten steps
20:11 ten steps *b*
Isa 38:8 retrace *b* ten steps
Jer 7:24 they became *b* in direction
La 1:13 He has turned me *b*. He has

Backwards
Ge 9:23 walked in *b*. Thus they
Isa 1:4 disrespect, they have turned *b*
28:13 stumble *b* and actually
44:25 the One turning wise men *b*
Jer 15:6 *B* is the way you keep

Bad
Ge 2:9 of the knowledge of good and *b*
2:17 the knowledge of good and *b*
3:5 like God, knowing good and *b*
3:22 of us in knowing good and *b*
6:5 heart was only *b* all the time
8:21 heart of man is *b* from his
13:13 men of Sodom were *b* and
24:50 unable to speak *b* or good to
26:29 do nothing *b* toward us just
31:24 speaking either good or *b*
31:29 speaking either good or *b*
37:2 Joseph brought a *b* report
38:7 proved to be *b* in the eyes
Ge 38:10 was *b* in the eyes of Jehovah
41:19 poor and very *b* in form and
41:20 *b* cows began to eat up the
41:21 their appearance was *b* just
41:27 the seven skinny and *b* cows
44:4 have you repaid *b* for good
44:5 a *b* deed you have committed
Le 27:10 exchange it with good for *b*
27:10 or with *b* for good
27:12 whether it is good or *b*
27:14 whether it is good or *b*
27:33 whether it is good or *b*
Nu 11:10 in the eyes of Moses . . . *b*
13:19 whether it is good or *b*
13:32 a *b* report of the land that
14:36 a *b* report against the land
14:37 bringing forth the *b* report
22:34 if it is *b* in your eyes, let
24:13 or *b* out of my own heart
De 1:39 do not know good or *b*, these
13:11 do anything like this *b* thing
15:21 lame or blind, any *b* defect
17:1 anything *b*; because it is a
17:2 *b* in the eyes of Jehovah
17:5 woman who has done this *b*
17:7 clear out what is *b* from your
17:12 clear out what is *b* from
19:19 clear away what is *b* from
19:20 never again do anything *b*
21:21 clear away what is *b* from
22:14 a *b* name upon her and has
22:19 a *b* name upon a virgin of
22:21 what is *b* from your midst
22:22 clear away what is *b* out of
23:9 keep yourself from every *b*
24:7 clear away what is *b* from
30:15 and good, and death and *b*
31:29 do what is *b* in the eyes of
Jos 24:15 if it is *b* in your eyes to
Jg 2:11 doing what was *b* in the eyes
3:7 what was *b* in Jehovah's eyes
3:12 went doing what was *b* in
3:12 they did what was *b* in
4:1 what was *b* in Jehovah's eyes
6:1 do what was *b* in the eyes of
9:23 a *b* spirit between Abimelech
10:6 do what was *b* in the eyes of
13:1 what was *b* in Jehovah's eyes
20:3 How has this *b* thing been
20:12 What is this *b* thing that
20:13 let us clear out what is *b*
1Sa 1:8 why does your heart feel *b*?
2:23 from all the people are *b*
8:6 was *b* in the eyes of Samuel
12:25 you flagrantly do what is *b*
15:19 *b* in the eyes of Jehovah
16:14 and a *b* spirit from Jehovah
16:15 *b* spirit is terrorizing
16:16 when God's *b* spirit comes
16:23 *b* spirit departed from upon
18:8 was *b* from his viewpoint
18:10 *b* spirit became operative
19:9 Jehovah's *b* spirit came to
20:7 know that what is *b* has been
25:3 husband was harsh and *b* in
29:7 not do anything *b* in the
30:22 every *b* and good-for-nothing
2Sa 3:39 repay the doer of what is *b*
11:25 let this matter appear *b*
11:27 appeared *b* in the eyes of
12:9 doing what is *b* in his eyes
12:18 certainly do something *b*
13:22 speak with Amnon either *b*
14:17 what is good and what is *b*
15:14 down upon us what is *b*
19:35 discern between good and *b*
1Ki 1:52 if what is *b* should be found
3:9 discern between good and *b*
5:4 there is nothing *b* happening
11:6 was *b* in the eyes of Jehovah
13:30 Too *b*, my brother!
13:33 turn back from his *b* way
14:22 *b* in the eyes of Jehovah
15:26 *b* in the eyes of Jehovah
15:34 *b* in the eyes of Jehovah
16:19 *b* in the eyes of Jehovah
16:25 *b* in the eyes of Jehovah
21:20 is *b* in the eyes of Jehovah
21:25 *b* in the eyes of Jehovah
22:8 not prophesy good . . . but *b*
22:18 not good things, but *b*
22:52 *b* in Jehovah's eyes and
2Ki 2:19 water is *b*, and the land is
3:2 doing . . . *b* in Jehovah's eyes
2Ki 8:18 what was *b* in Jehovah's eyes
8:27 what was *b* in Jehovah's eyes
13:2 what was *b* in Jehovah's eyes
13:11 was *b* in Jehovah's eyes
14:24 was *b* in Jehovah's eyes
15:9 was *b* in Jehovah's eyes
15:18 was *b* in Jehovah's eyes
15:24 was *b* in Jehovah's eyes
15:28 was *b* in Jehovah's eyes
17:2 what was *b* in Jehovah's eyes
17:11 *b* things to offend Jehovah
17:13 Turn back from your *b* ways
17:17 *b* in the eyes of Jehovah
21:2 what was *b* in Jehovah's eyes
21:6 what was *b* in Jehovah's eyes
21:9 to do what was *b* more than
21:15 did what was *b* in my eyes
21:16 *b* in the eyes of Jehovah
21:20 was *b* in Jehovah's eyes
23:32 was *b* in Jehovah's eyes
23:37 was *b* in Jehovah's eyes
24:9 what was *b* in Jehovah's eyes
24:19 was *b* in Jehovah's eyes
1Ch 2:3 to be *b* in the eyes of Jehovah
16:22 to my prophets do nothing *b*
21:7 *b* in the eyes of the true God
21:17 have unquestionably done *b*
2Ch 7:14 turn back from their *b* ways
12:14 he did what was *b*, for he
18:7 but, all his days, for *b*
18:17 not good things, but *b*
21:6 what was *b* in Jehovah's eyes
21:19 died in his *b* maladies
22:4 *b* in Jehovah's eyes, the
25:19 *b* position and have to fall
29:6 *b* in the eyes of Jehovah our
33:2 what was *b* in Jehovah's eyes
33:6 *b* in the eyes of Jehovah
33:22 was *b* in Jehovah's eyes
36:5 *b* in the eyes of Jehovah his
36:9 was *b* in Jehovah's eyes
36:12 *b* in the eyes of Jehovah
Ezr 4:12 the rebellious and *b* city
9:13 upon us for our *b* deeds and
Ne 1:3 are in a very *b* plight and
2:10 very *b* that a man had come to
2:17 You are seeing the *b* plight
6:13 possession a *b* reputation
9:28 again do what is *b* before you
9:35 not turn back from their *b*
13:8 And it seemed very *b* to me
13:17 *b* thing that you are doing
Es 7:6 and enemy, is this *b* Haman
7:7 *b* had been determined against
9:25 Let his *b* scheme that he has
Job 1:1 and turning aside from *b*
1:8 and turning aside from *b*
2:3 and turning aside from *b*
2:10 not accept also what is *b*
10:15 If . . . wrong, too *b* for me
20:12 If what is *b* tastes sweet
28:28 to turn away from *b* is
30:26 good I waited, yet *b* came
35:12 the pride of the *b* ones
Ps 5:4 No one *b* may reside for any
7:4 rewarding me with what is *b*
10:15 arm of the wicked and *b* one
15:3 he has done nothing *b*
15:4 He has sworn to what is *b* for
21:11 against you what is *b*
23:4 I fear nothing *b*, For you are
28:3 in whose hearts is what is *b*
31:13 heard the *b* report by many
34:13 tongue against what is *b*
34:14 Turn away from what is *b*
34:16 those doing what is *b*
35:12 reward me with *b* for good
36:4 What is *b* he does not reject
37:27 Turn away from what is *b*
38:20 rewarding me with *b* for good
41:5 say what is *b* concerning me
41:7 scheming something *b* for me
50:19 have let loose to what is *b*
51:4 *b* in your eyes I have done
52:1 your boast over what is *b*
52:3 loved what is *b* more than
54:5 will repay the *b* to my foes
55:15 *b* things have been within
56:5 thoughts are against me for *b*
64:5 *b* speech; They make
73:8 and speak about what is *b*
97:10 hate what is *b*
101:4 Nothing *b* do I know
105:15 to my prophets do nothing *b*

Ps 109:5 they render to me *b* for good
112:7 not be afraid even of *b* news
119:101 From every *b* path I have
140:1 Rescue me . . . from *b* men
140:2 schemed *b* things in their
141:4 my heart to anything *b*
Pr 2:12 deliver you from the *b* way
2:14 are rejoicing in doing *b*
3:7 and turn away from *b*
3:29 your fellowman anything *b*
3:30 he has rendered no *b* to you
4:14 into the way of the *b* ones
4:27 your foot from what is *b*
6:14 fabricating something *b* all
6:24 guard you against the *b* woman
8:13 Jehovah means the hating of *b*
8:13 pride and the *b* way and the
10:18 forth a *b* report is stupid
11:19 one chasing after what is *b*
11:21 *b* person will not go
11:27 one searching for *b*, it will
12:12 the netted prey of *b* men
12:13 the *b* person is ensnared
13:17 is wicked will fall into *b*
13:19 ones to turn away from *b*
14:19 *B* people will have to bow
15:3 keeping watch upon the *b* ones
15:10 Discipline is *b* to the one
15:15 days of the afflicted . . . *b*
15:26 The schemes of the *b* one are
15:28 bubbles forth with *b* things
16:6 one turns away from *b*
16:17 is to turn away from *b*
16:27 man is digging up what is *b*
17:11 rebellion is what the *b* one
17:13 anyone repaying *b* for good
17:13 *b* will not move away from
19:23 be visited with what is *b*
20:14, 14 It is *b*, *b!* says the
20:30 are what scours away the *b*
21:10 wicked . . . craved what is *b*
24:1 Do not be envious of *b* men
24:8 for anyone scheming to do *b*
24:18 and it be *b* in his eyes and
24:20 to be no future for anyone *b*
25:10 *b* report by you can have no
26:23 lips along with a *b* heart
28:10 to go astray into the *b* way
29:6 the transgression of a *b* man
31:12 not *b*, all the days of her
Ec 5:1 not aware of doing what is *b*
6:2 vanity and it is a *b* sickness
8:3 Do not stand in a *b* thing
8:11 sentence against a *b* work has
8:11 fully set in them to do *b*
8:12 a sinner may be doing *b* a
9:3 sons of men is also full of *b*
12:14 to whether it is good or *b*
Isa 1:16 cease to do *b*
5:20, 20 good is *b* and *b* is good
7:5 advised what is *b* against you
7:15 reject the *b* and choose the
7:16 reject the *b* and choose the
32:7 his instruments are *b*
33:15 so as not to see what is *b*
41:23 ought to do good or do *b*
59:15 and it was *b* in his eyes
65:12 what was *b* in my eyes
66:4 doing what was *b* in my eyes
Jer 2:13 two *b* things that my people
2:19 is something *b* and bitter
2:33 in *b* things that you have
3:5 to do *b* things and prevail
3:17 stubbornness of their *b* heart
4:22 Wise they are for doing *b*
5:28 overflowed with *b* things
6:29 *b* have not been separated
7:24 stubbornness of their *b* heart
7:30 done what is *b* in my eyes
8:3 out of this *b* family
11:8 stubbornness of their *b* heart
12:14 against all my *b* neighbors
13:10 *b* people who are refusing
13:23 are persons taught to do *b*
15:21 the hand of the *b* ones, and
16:12 the stubbornness of his *b*
18:10 it actually does what is *b*
18:11 each one from his *b* way
18:12 stubbornness of his *b* heart
18:20 Should *b* be repaid for good?
20:10 heard the *b* report of many
23:10 action proves to be *b*, and
23:22 turn back from their *b* way
24:2 the figs were very *b*, so
Jer 24:3, 3 the *b* ones being very *b*
24:8 like the *b* figs that cannot
25:5 from his *b* way and from the
26:3 each one from his *b* way
32:30 of what was *b* in my eyes
35:15 each one from his *b* way
36:3 each one from his *b* way
36:7 each one from his *b* way
38:9 men have done *b* in all that
39:12 do to him anything *b* at all
40:4 *b* in your eyes to come with
41:11 all the *b* that Ishmael the
42:6 Whether good or *b*, it is
44:9 forgotten the *b* deeds of your
44:9 *b* deeds of the kings of Judah
44:9 *b* deeds of their wives and
44:9 your own *b* deeds and the
44:9 the *b* deeds of your wives
49:23 *b* report that they have
52:2 *b* in the eyes of Jehovah
La 3:38 *b* things and what is good do
Eze 6:9 *b* things that they have done
6:11 *b* detestable things of the
8:9 see the *b* detestable things
11:2 *b* counsel against this city
13:22 turn back from his *b* way in
20:43 your *b* things that you did
20:44 according to your *b* ways
30:12 into the hand of *b* men
33:11 turn back from your *b* ways
36:3 is a *b* report among people
36:31 remember your *b* ways and
Da 11:27 inclined to doing what is *b*
Ho 7:1 the *b* things of Samaria
7:15 kept scheming what was *b*
Am 5:14 is good, and not what is *b*
5:15 Hate what is *b*, and love
9:4 my eyes upon them for *b*
Jon 3:8 each one from his *b* way and
3:10 turned back from their *b* way
Mic 1:12 what is *b* has come down
2:1 what is *b*, upon their beds
7:1 Too *b* for me, for I have
7:3 hands are upon what is *b*
Na 1:11 against Jehovah what is *b*
Hab 1:13 too pure in eyes to see . . . *b*
Zep 1:12 and he will not do *b*
Zec 1:4 from your *b* ways and from
1:4 and from your *b* dealings
7:10 scheme out nothing *b* against
Mal 1:8 It is nothing *b*. And when you
1:8 a sick one: It is nothing *b*
2:17 doing *b* is good in the eyes
Mt 27:23 what *b* thing did he do?
Mr 3:4 or to do a *b* deed, to save or
15:14 Why, what *b* thing did he do?
Lu 23:22 what *b* thing did this man do?
Ro 3:8 Let us do the *b* things that
7:19 *b* that I do not wish is what
7:21 what is *b* is present with me
13:3 the good deed, but to the *b*
13:4 doing what is *b*, be in fear
13:4 the one practicing what is *b*
1Co 15:33 *B* associations spoil useful
2Co 6:8 through *b* report and good
2Ti 3:13 advance from *b* to worse
1Pe 3:10 his tongue from what is *b*
3:11 turn away from what is *b*
3:12 against those doing *b* things
3Jo 11 imitator, not of what is *b*
11 that does *b* has not seen God
Jude 11 Too *b* for them, because they
Re 2:2 that you cannot bear *b* men
18:10, 10 Too *b*, too *b*, you great
18:16, 16 Too *b*, too *b*—the great
18:19, 19 Too *b*, too *b*—the great

Badger
Le 11:5 the rock *b*, because it is a
De 14:7 the hare and the rock *b*

Badgers
Ps 104:18 a refuge for the rock *b*
Pr 30:26 the rock *b* are a people not

Badly
Ge 19:7 my brothers, do not act *b*
De 26:6 Egyptians went treating us *b*
1Sa 4:2 battle went *b*, so that Israel
1Ki 22:34 I have been *b* wounded
2Ch 18:33 I have been *b* wounded
Job 20:26 go *b* with a survivor in his
Ps 74:3 enemy has treated *b* in the
106:32 *b* with Moses by reason of
Pr 11:15 fare *b* because he has gone
Pr 13:20 stupid ones will fare *b*
Mic 4:6 her whom I have treated *b*
Mt 4:24 those faring *b*, distressed
8:16 cured all who were faring *b*
15:22 My daughter is *b* demonized

Badness
Ge 6:5 Jehovah saw that the *b* of man
39:9 could I commit this great *b*
41:19 For *b* I have not seen the
De 28:20 the *b* of your practices in
31:18 all the *b* that they have done
1Sa 17:28 and the *b* of your heart
24:11 no *b* or revolt in my hand
25:28 *b*, it will not be found in
25:39 his servant back from *b*
25:39 of Nabal Jehovah has
26:18 what *b* is there in my hand
29:6 not found *b* in you from the
2Sa 3:39 according to his own *b*
13:16 *b* in sending me away is
1Ki 16:7 the *b* that he committed in
Ne 13:7 *b* that Eliashib had committed
13:27 *b* in acting unfaithfully
Es 8:3 to turn away the *b* of Haman
Job 22:5 your own *b* too much already
Ps 7:9 *b* of wicked ones come to an
28:4 to the *b* of their practices
107:34 Owing to the *b* of those
Pr 1:16 those that run to sheer *b*
2:14 in the perverse things of *b*
4:16 not sleep unless they do *b*
5:14 to be in every sort of *b*
6:18 are in a hurry to run to *b*
14:16 and is turning away from *b*
14:32 Because of his *b* the wicked
20:8 scattering all *b* with his own
26:26 *b* will be uncovered in the
28:5 Men given to *b* cannot
Ec 7:15 one continuing long in his *b*
Isa 1:16 the *b* of your dealings from
13:11 own *b* upon the productive
47:10 you kept trusting in your *b*
56:2 not to do any kind of *b*
59:7 feet keep running to sheer *b*
59:15 turning away from *b* is
Jer 1:16 judgments over all their *b*
2:19 Your *b* should correct you
3:2 prostitution and with your *b*
4:4 the *b* of your dealings
4:14 your heart clean of sheer *b*
6:7 she has kept her *b* cool
7:12 the *b* of my people Israel
8:6 man repenting over his *b*
9:3, 3 from *b* to *b* they went
11:17 the *b* of the house of Israel
12:4 the *b* of those dwelling in
18:8 turns back from its *b*
21:12 the *b* of your dealings
23:2 for the *b* of your dealings
23:11 I have found their *b*
23:14 each one from his own *b*
23:22 the *b* of their dealings
24:2 they could not be eaten for *b*
24:3 they cannot be eaten for *b*
24:8 that cannot be eaten for *b*
25:5 from the *b* of your dealings
26:3 the *b* of their dealings
29:17 that cannot be eaten for *b*
32:32 *b* of the sons of Israel
33:5 all whose *b* I have concealed
44:3 because of their *b* that they
44:5 turn back from their *b* by
44:22 *b* of your dealings, because
51:24 *b* that they have committed
La 1:22 all their *b* come before you
Eze 16:23 came about after all your *b*
16:57 own *b* got to be exposed
Ho 7:2 all their *b* I will remember
7:3 By their *b* they make the king
9:15 All their *b* was in Gilgal
10:15 because of your extreme *b*
Joe 3:13 their *b* has become abundant
Jon 1:2 their *b* has come up before me
Mic 3:2 lovers of *b*, tearing off
3:4 *b* in their dealings
Na 3:19 your *b* did not pass over
Mt 6:34 for each day is its own *b*
Ac 8:22 Repent, therefore, of this *b*
Ro 1:29 *b*, being full of envy, murder
1Co 5:8 neither with leaven of *b* and
14:20 but be babes as to *b*; yet
Eph 4:31 from you along with all *b*
Col 3:8 anger, *b*, abusive speech

Tit 3:3 carrying on in *b* and envy
Jas 1:21 that superfluous thing, *b*
1Pe 2:1 put away all *b* and all
2:16 not as a blind for *b*, but as

Bag
Ge 42:27 it was in the mouth of his *b*
42:28 and now here it is in my *b*
43:21 in the mouth of his *b*, our
44:1 in the mouth of his *b*
44:2 the *b* of the youngest and the
44:11 let down each one his *b* to
44:11 opened each one his own *b*
44:12 was found in Benjamin's *b*
De 25:13 have in your *b* two sorts of
1Sa 17:40 shepherds' *b* that served
17:49 thrust his hand into his *b*
25:29 wrapped up in the *b* of life
2Ki 4:42 and new grain in his bread *b*
Job 14:17 in a *b* is my revolt, And
Pr 1:14 one *b* belonging to all of us
7:20 *b* of money he has taken in
16:11 stone weights of the *b* are
Ca 1:13 As a *b* of myrrh my dear one
Mic 6:11 *b* of deceptive stone weights
Hag 1:6 for a *b* having holes

Bagful
Job 28:18 *b* of wisdom is worth more
Ps 126:6 Carrying along a *b* of seed

Baggage
1Sa 17:22 David left the *b* from off
17:22 care of the keeper of the *b*
25:13 two hundred sat by the *b*
30:24 one that sat by the *b* be
Jer 46:19 Make for yourself mere *b*

Bagpipe
Da 3:5 *b* and all sorts of musical
3:10 *b* and all sorts of musical
3:15 *b* and all sorts of musical

Bags
Ge 43:12 in the mouth of your *b*
43:18 went back with us in our *b*
43:21 began opening our *b*, why
43:22 placed our money in our *b*
43:23 gave you treasure in your *b*
44:1 Fill the *b* of the men with
44:8 found in the mouth of our *b*
2Ki 5:23 talents of silver in two *b*

Bah
Mr 15:29 *B!* You would-be thrower-down

Baharumite
1Ch 11:33 Azmaveth the *B*

Bahurim
2Sa 3:16 walked after her as far as *B*
16:5 King David came as far as *B*
17:18 to the house of a man in *B*
19:16 who was from *B*, hurried
1Ki 2:8 Gera the Benjaminite from *B*

Bait
Isa 29:21 and those who lay *b* even

Baiters
Ps 124:7 escaped From the trap of *b*

Bakbakkar
1Ch 9:15 and *B*, Heresh and Galal, and

Bakbuk
Ezr 2:51 the sons of *B*
Ne 7:53 the sons of *B*, the sons of

Bakbukiah
Ne 11:17 *B* was second of his brothers
12:9 *B* and Unni their brothers
12:25 Mattaniah and *B*, Obadiah

Bake
Ge 11:3 make bricks and *b* them with
Ex 12:39 began to *b* the flour dough
16:23, 23 What you can *b*, *b*, and
Le 24:5 and *b* it up into twelve
26:26 *b* your bread in but one oven
2Sa 13:6 *b* two heart-shaped cakes
Ne 3:11 also the Tower of the *B* Ovens
12:38 Tower of the *B* Ovens and on
Eze 4:12 will *b* it before their eyes
46:20 *b* the grain offering, in

Baked
Ge 19:3 he *b* unfermented cakes, and
Le 2:4 way of something *b* in the oven
6:17 should not be *b* with anything
7:9 that may be *b* in the oven and
23:17 *b* leavened, as first ripe
1Sa 28:24 *b* it into unfermented cakes
1Ch 9:31 over the things *b* in pans
Isa 44:19 coals I have also *b* bread

Baker
Ge 40:1 the *b* sinned against their
40:5 the cupbearer and the *b* who
40:17 the product of a *b*, and there
Ho 7:4 a furnace set burning by a *b*
7:6 their *b* is sleeping

Bakers
Ge 40:2 and at the chief of the *b*
40:16 the chief of the *b* saw that
40:20 head of the chief of the *b*
40:22 chief of the *b* he hung up
41:10 me and the chief of the *b*
1Sa 8:13 mixers and cooks and *b*
Jer 37:21 from the street of the *b*

Bakes
Isa 44:15 fire and actually *b* bread

Balaam
Nu 22:5 sent messengers to *B* the son
22:7 to *B* and spoke to him Balak's
22:8 princes of Moab stayed with *B*
22:9 Then God came to *B* and said
22:10 *B* said to the true God: Balak
22:12 God said to *B:* You must not
22:13 *B* got up in the morning and
22:14 *B* has refused to come with
22:16 they came to *B* and said to
22:18 *B* answered and said to the
22:20 God came to *B* by night and
22:21 *B* got up in the morning and
22:23 *B* began to strike the ass in
22:27 she now lay down under *B;* so
22:28 of the ass and she said to *B*
22:29 At this *B* said to the ass: It
22:30 she-ass said to *B:* Am I not
22:34 *B* said to Jehovah's angel: I
22:35 Jehovah's angel said to *B:* Go
22:35 *B* continued going with the
22:36 Balak got to hear that *B* had
22:37 Balak said to *B:* Have I not
22:38 *B* said to Balak: Here I have
22:39 *B* went with Balak and they
22:40 and to send some to *B* and
22:41 that Balak went taking *B* and
23:1 *B* said to Balak: Build for me
23:2 did just as *B* had spoken
23:2 Balak and *B* offered up a bull
23:3 And *B* went on to say to Balak
23:4 When God got in touch with *B*
23:5 put a word in the mouth of *B*
23:11 Balak said to *B:* What have
23:16 Jehovah got in touch with *B*
23:25 Balak said to *B:* If, on the
23:26 *B* answered and said to Balak
23:27 Then Balak said to *B:* O come
23:28 Balak took *B* to the top of
23:29 *B* said to Balak: Build for
23:30 Balak did just as *B* had said
24:1 *B* got to see that it was good
24:2 *B* raised his eyes and saw
24:3 utterance of *B* the son of Beor
24:10 anger blazed against *B* and
24:10 Balak went on to say to *B*
24:12 *B* said to Balak: Was it not
24:15 The utterance of *B* the son of
24:25 *B* got up and went and
31:8 killed *B* the son of Beor with
De 23:4 *B* the son of Beor from Pethor
23:5 did not want to listen to *B*
Jos 13:22 *B* the son of Beor, the
24:9 he sent and summoned *B* the
24:10 not want to listen to *B*
Ne 13:2 went hiring against them *B*
Mic 6:5 *B* the son of Beor answered
2Pe 2:15 followed the path of *B*
Jude 11 course of *B* for reward, and
Re 2:14 *B*, who went teaching Balak

Balaam's
Nu 22:25 squeeze *B* foot against the
22:27 *B* anger blazed, and he kept
22:31 to uncover *B* eyes, so that he
31:16 are the ones who, by *B* word

Baladan
2Ki 20:12 the son of *B*
Isa 39:1 *B* the king of Babylon sent

Balah
Jos 19:3 Hazar-shual and *B* and Ezem

Balak
Nu 22:2 *B* the son of Zippor got to see
22:4 *B* the son of Zippor was king
22:10 *B* the son of Zippor, the king
22:13 and said to the princes of *B*
22:14 got up and came to *B* and
22:15 *B* sent again other princes in
22:16 *B* the son of Zippor has said
22:18 and said to the servants of *B*
22:18 If *B* were to give me his
22:35 going with the princes of *B*
22:36 *B* got to hear that Balaam
22:37 *B* said to Balaam: Have I not
22:38 Balaam said to *B:* Here I
22:39 Balaam went with *B* and they
22:40 And *B* proceeded to sacrifice
22:41 *B* went taking Balaam and
23:1 Balaam said to *B:* Build for
23:2 *B* immediately did just as
23:2 *B* and Balaam offered up a
23:3 Balaam went on to say to *B*
23:5 Return to *B*, and this is what
23:7 *B* the king of Moab tried to
23:11 *B* said to Balaam: What have
23:13 Then *B* said to him: Do come
23:15 said to *B:* Station yourself
23:16 Return to *B*, and this is
23:17 *B* said to him: What has
23:18 said: Get up, *B*, and listen
23:25 *B* said to Balaam: If, on the
23:26 said to *B:* Did I not speak to
23:27 *B* said to Balaam: O come
23:28 *B* took Balaam to the top of
23:29 Balaam said to *B:* Build for
23:30 So *B* did just as Balaam had
24:10 *B* went on to say to Balaam
24:12 Balaam said to *B:* Was it not
24:13 If *B* were to give me his
24:25 And *B* also went his own way
Jos 24:9 *B* the son of Zippor, the
Jg 11:25 *B* the son of Zippor, the king
Mic 6:5 *B* the king of Moab counseled
Re 2:14 Balaam, who went teaching *B*

Balak's
Nu 22:7 and spoke to him *B* words
24:10 *B* anger blazed against

Balances
Da 5:27 have been weighed in the *b*

Bald
Le 13:40 in case his head grows *b*
13:41 his head grows *b* up in front
Jer 16:6 or make himself *b* for them
Eze 27:31 *b* with a baldness for you
29:18 Every head was one made *b*

Baldhead
2Ki 2:23, 23 up, you *b!* Go up, you *b!*

Baldness
Le 13:40 head grows bald, it is *b*
13:41 up in front, it is forehead *b*
13:42 plague develops in the *b* of
13:42 leprosy breaking out in the *b*
13:43 plague in the *b* of his crown
21:5 not produce *b* upon their heads
De 14:1 impose *b* on your foreheads
Isa 3:24 hair arrangement, *b*
15:2 all heads in it there is *b*
22:12 and for mourning and for *b*
Jer 47:5 *B* must come to Gaza
48:37 upon every head there is *b*
Eze 7:18 on all their heads there is *b*
27:31 bald with a *b* for you
Am 8:10 and upon every head *b*
Mic 1:16 Cause *b*, and shear your hair
1:16 *b* like that of the eagle

Ball
Isa 22:18 like a *b* for a wide land

Balsam
Ge 37:25 labdanum and *b* and resinous
43:11 little *b*, and a little honey
Ex 25:6 *b* oil for the anointing oil
35:8 *b* oil for the anointing oil
35:28 and the *b* oil and the oil for
1Ki 10:2 camels carrying *b* oil and
10:10 a very great deal of *b* oil
10:10 the like of that *b* oil for
10:25 armor and *b* oil, horses and
2Ki 20:13 the *b* oil and the good oil
1Ch 9:29 frankincense and the *b* oil
9:30 ointment mixture of *b* oil
2Ch 9:1 camels carrying *b* oil, and

2Ch 9:9 *b* oil in very great quantity
9:9 like of that *b* oil which
9:24 armor and *b* oil, horses and
16:14 filled with *b* oil and
32:27 *b* oil and for shields and
Es 2:12 and six months with *b* oil and
Isa 3:24 instead of *b* oil there will
39:2 the *b* oil and the good oil
Jer 8:22 Is there no *b* in Gilead?
46:11 to Gilead and get some *b*
51:8 Take *b* for her pain
Eze 27:17 and honey and oil and *b*

Bamoth
Nu 21:19 and from Nahaliel on to *B*
21:20 from *B* on to the valley that

Bamoth-baal
Nu 22:41 bringing him up to *B*, that
Jos 13:17 and *B* and Beth-baal-meon

Ban
De 13:17 the thing made sacred by *b*
Ezr 10:8 goods would be put under a *b*
Mic 4:13 by a *b* you will actually

Band
Ge 49:19 Gad, a marauder *b* will raid
Ex 13:16 frontlet *b* between your eyes
De 6:8 a frontlet *b* between your eyes
11:18 frontlet *b* between your eyes
Jg 9:37 one *b* is coming by the way of
1Sa 13:17 The one *b* would turn to the
13:18 the other *b* would turn to
13:18 the third *b* would turn to
30:8 chase after this marauder *b*
30:15 down to this marauder *b*
30:15 Lead . . . to this marauder *b*
30:23 marauder *b* that came
2Sa 22:30 run against a marauder *b*
1Ki 11:24 be chief of a marauder *b*
2Ki 13:21 they saw the marauding *b*
1Ch 12:21 against the marauder *b*
2Ch 22:1 marauder *b* that came with
Job 38:9 gloom as its swaddling *b*
Ps 18:29 run against a marauder *b*
Pr 30:31 king of a *b* of soldiers of
Jer 18:22 suddenly a marauder *b*
Ho 7:1 a marauder *b* actually makes a
Joh 18:3 Judas took the soldier *b* and
18:12 soldier *b* and the military
Ac 10:1 army officer of the Italian *b*
21:31 up to the commander of the *b*
27:1 Julius of the *b* of Augustus

Bandage
1Ki 20:38 disguised with a *b* over his
20:41 the *b* from over his eyes
Eze 30:21 putting a *b* on for binding
34:16 the broken one I shall *b*

Bandaged
Eze 34:4 broken one you have not *b*

Bandages
Lu 24:12 he beheld the *b* alone
Joh 19:40 bound it up with *b* with
20:5 he beheld the *b* lying, yet
20:6 And he viewed the *b* lying
20:7 not lying with the *b* but

Banding
Ps 31:20 From the *b* together of men
Da 4:15 a *b* of iron and of copper
4:23 a *b* of iron and of copper

Bands
Jg 7:16 men up into three *b* and put
7:20 the three *b* blew the horns
9:34 against Shechem in four *b*
9:43 divided them up into three *b*
9:44 Abimelech and the *b* that were
9:44 two *b* made a dash against all
1Sa 11:11 put the people into three *b*
13:17 the Philistines in three *b*
2Sa 4:2 chiefs of the marauding *b*
2Ki 5:2 had gone out as marauder *b*
6:23 marauding *b* of the Syrians
13:20 marauding *b* of the Moabites
24:2 marauder *b* of Chaldeans and
24:2 and marauder *b* of Syrians
24:2 and marauder *b* of Moabites
24:2 marauder *b* of the sons of
Job 1:17 Chaldeans made up three *b*
39:5 the very *b* of the wild ass
Ps 2:3 Let us tear their *b* apart
107:14 tearing even their *b* apart
116:16 You have loosened my *b*
Isa 28:22 *b* may not grow strong
52:2 Loosen for yourself the *b*
58:6 release the *b* of the yoke bar
Jer 2:20 I tore your *b* apart
5:5 must have torn apart the *b*
27:2 make . . . *b* and yoke bars
30:8 your *b* I shall tear in two
Eze 12:14 all his military *b*, I shall
13:18 sewing *b* together upon all
13:20 against the *b* of you women
17:21 in all his *b*, by the sword
38:6 Gomer and all its *b*, the
38:6 all its *b*, many peoples with
38:9 your *b* and many peoples with
38:22 upon his *b* and upon the
39:4 your *b* and the peoples that
Ho 6:9 priests are marauding *b*
Na 1:13 the *b* upon you I shall tear
Lu 2:7 she bound him with cloth *b* and
2:12 an infant bound in cloth *b*

Bangles
Isa 3:18 beauty of the *b* and the

Bani
2Sa 23:36 of Zobah, *B* the Gadite
1Ch 6:46 son of *B*, the son of Shemer
9:4 *B*, of the sons of Perez the
Ezr 2:10 sons of *B*, six hundred and
8:10 of the sons of *B*, Shelomith
10:29 of the sons of *B*, Meshullam
10:34 sons of *B*, Maadai, Amram
Ne 3:17 Rehum the son of *B*
8:7 and *B* and Sherebiah, Jamin
9:4 and *B*, Kadmiel, Shebaniah
9:4 Sherebiah, *B* and Chenani
9:5 Levites Jeshua and Kadmiel, *B*
10:13 Hodiah, *B* and Beninu
10:14 heads of the people . . . *B*
11:22 *B* the son of Hashabiah the

Banished
2Sa 14:13 bring back his own *b* one
14:14 reasons why the one *b*
14:14 should not be *b* from him

Banishment
Ge 4:11 And now you are cursed in *b*
Ezr 7:26 for death or for *b*, or for

Bank
Ge 41:3 cows by the *b* of the river
41:17 on the *b* of the river Nile
Ex 2:3 reeds by the *b* of the river
Nu 22:36 is on the *b* of the Arnon
De 2:36 the *b* of the torrent valley of
2:37 *b* of the torrent valley of
4:48 on the *b* of the torrent valley
Jos 12:2 the *b* of the torrent valley
13:9 *b* of the torrent valley of
13:16 *b* of the torrent valley of
Isa 57:14, 14 *B* up, you people, *b* up!
62:10, 10 *B* up, *b* up the highway
Jer 46:6 *b* of the river Euphrates
50:26 *B* her up, just like those
Eze 47:6 to the *b* of the torrent
47:7 on the *b* of the torrent there
47:12 along its *b* on this side
Da 10:4 on the *b* of the great river
12:5 on the *b* here of the stream
12:5 on the *b* there of the stream
Lu 19:23 put my silver money in a *b*

Banked
Jer 18:15 roadways, a way not *b* up

Bankers
Mt 25:27 my silver monies with the *b*

Banks
Jos 3:15 Jordan overflows all its *b*
4:18 overflowing all its *b* as
Jg 11:26 are by the *b* of Arnon for
1Ch 12:15 was overflowing all its *b*
Isa 8:7 and go over all his *b*

Banner
Ca 2:4 and his *b* over me was love

Banners
Ps 20:5 we shall lift our *b*
Ca 6:4 as companies gathered around *b*
6:10 companies gathered around *b*

Banning
Zec 14:11 any *b* to destruction

Banquet
Jg 5:25 large *b* bowl of majestic ones
6:38 to fill a large *b* bowl with
14:10 to hold a *b* there; for that
14:12 the seven days of the *b* and
14:17 the *b* continued for them
2Ch 35:13 pots and in *b* bowls
Es 1:3 he held a *b* for all his princes
1:5 king held a *b* for seven days
1:9 held a *b* for the women at the
2:18 a great *b* for all his princes
2:18 the *b* of Esther
5:4 the *b* that I have made for him
5:5 king and Haman came to the *b*
5:6 to Esther during the *b* of wine
5:8 king and Haman come to the *b*
5:12 to the *b* that she had made
5:14 with the king to the *b* joyful
6:14 the *b* that Esther had made
7:1 in to *b* with Esther the queen
7:2 day during the *b* of wine
7:7 from the *b* of wine to go to
7:8 to the house of the wine *b*
8:17 for the Jews, a *b* and a good
Job 1:4 his son went and held a *b* at
1:5 the *b* days had gone round the
Pr 19:24 his hand in the *b* bowl
26:15 his hand in the *b* bowl
Ec 7:2 than to go to the *b* house
Isa 25:6 *b* of well-oiled dishes
25:6 *b* of wine kept on the dregs

Banqueting
Ge 43:34 they continued *b* and drinking
Es 9:17 a day of *b* and of rejoicing
9:18 a day of *b* and of rejoicing
9:19 and a *b* and a good day and a
9:22 hold them as days of *b* and
Jer 16:8 enter no house of *b* at all
Da 5:10 entered right into the *b* hall

Banquets
Jer 51:39 I shall set their *b* and

Baptism
Mt 3:7 and Sadducees coming to the *b*
21:25 *b* by John, from what source
Mr 1:4 *b* in symbol of repentance for
10:38 *b* with which I am being
10:39 the *b* with which I am being
11:30 *b* by John from heaven or
Lu 3:3 *b* in symbol of repentance for
7:29 baptized with the *b* of John
12:50 *b* with which to be baptized
20:4 Was the *b* of John from heaven
Ac 1:22 starting with his *b* by John
10:37 the *b* that John preached
13:24 *b* in symbol of repentance
18:25 with only the *b* of John
19:3 They said: In John's *b*
19:4 the *b* in symbol of repentance
Ro 6:4 buried with him through our *b*
Eph 4:5 one Lord, one faith, one *b*
Col 2:12 buried with him in his *b*
1Pe 3:21 now saving you, namely, *b*

Baptisms
Mr 7:4 *b* of cups and pitchers and
Heb 6:2 teaching on *b* and the laying
9:10 and drinks and various *b*

Baptist
Mt 3:1 John the *B* came preaching in
11:11 a greater than John the *B*
11:12 days of John the *B* until now
14:2 is John the *B*. He was raised
14:8 the head of John the *B*
16:14 Some say John the *B*, others
17:13 to them about John the *B*
Mr 6:25 the head of John the *B*
8:28 John the *B*, and others
Lu 7:20 John the *B* dispatched us to
7:33 John the *B* has come neither
9:19 John the *B*; but others, Elijah

Baptize
Mt 3:11 *b* you with water because of
3:11 That one will *b* you people
Mr 1:8 will *b* you with holy spirit
Lu 3:16 *b* you with water; but the one
3:16 He will *b* you people with
Joh 1:25 Why, then, do you *b* if you
1:26 I *b* in water. In the midst
1:33 who sent me to *b* in water

Baptized
Mt 3:6 *b* by him in the Jordan River
3:13 to John, in order to be *b*
3:14 one needing to be *b* by you
3:16 being *b* Jesus immediately
Mr 1:5 *b* by him in the Jordan River

Mr 1:8 I b you with water, but he
1:9 was b in the Jordan by John
10:38 be b with the baptism with
10:38 with which I am being b
10:39 with which I am being b
10:39 you will be b
Lu 3:7 crowds coming out to be b by
3:12 tax collectors came to be b
3:21 when all the people were b
3:21 Jesus also was b and, as he
7:29 b with the baptism of John
7:30 they not having been b by him
12:50 baptism with which to be b
Joh 3:23 kept coming and being b
Ac 1:5 John, indeed, b with water
1:5 b in holy spirit not many
2:38 b in the name of Jesus Christ
2:41 his word heartily were b
8:12 to be b, both men and women
8:13 after being b, he was in
8:16 b in the name of the Lord
8:36 prevents me from getting b
8:38 and the eunuch; and he b him
9:18 and he rose and was b
10:47 b who have received the holy
10:48 be b in the name of Jesus
11:16 b with water, but you will
11:16 you will be b in holy spirit
16:15 she and her household got b
16:33 and his were b without delay
18:8 began to believe and be b
19:3 In what, then, were you b?
19:4 John b with the baptism in
19:5 got b in the name of the Lord
22:16 get b and wash your sins
Ro 6:3 of us who were b into Christ
6:3 Jesus were b into his death
1Co 1:13 you b in the name of Paul
1:14 am thankful I b none of you
1:15 that you were b in my name
1:16 b the household of Stephanas
1:16 whether I b anybody else
10:2 and all got b into Moses by
12:13 we were all b into one body
15:29 b . . . purpose of being dead
15:29 b for the purpose of being
Ga 3:27 b into Christ have put on

Baptizer
Mr 1:4 John the b turned up in the
6:14 John the b has been raised
6:24 The head of John the b

Baptizes
Joh 1:33 one that b in holy spirit

Baptizing
Mt 28:19 b them in the name of the
Joh 1:28 Jordan, where John was b
1:31 why I came b in water was
3:22 with them and did b
3:23 John also was b in Aenon
3:26 this one is b and all are
4:1 b more disciples than John
4:2 Jesus himself did no b but
10:40 where John was b at first
1Co 1:17 not to go b, but to go

Bar
Ex 26:28 middle b at the center of
36:33 middle b to run through at
Nu 4:10 and put it upon a b
4:12 and put them upon a b
13:23 carrying it with a b on two
De 3:5 with a high wall, doors and b
Jos 7:21 one gold b, fifty shekels
7:24 the b of gold and his sons
Jg 16:3 the b and put them upon his
1Sa 23:7 into a city with doors and b
1Ki 4:13 with wall and copper b
2Ch 8:5 with walls, doors and b
Job 38:10 And to set a b and doors
Pr 18:19 the b of a dwelling tower
Isa 58:6 the bands of the yoke b
58:6 tear in two every yoke b
58:9 the yoke b, the poking out
Jer 28:10 yoke b from off the neck
28:12 broken the yoke b from off
49:31 doors and no b does it have
Eze 38:11 not have even b and doors
Am 1:5 will break the b of Damascus
Na 1:13 I shall break his carrying b

Barabbas
Mt 27:16 notorious prisoner called B
27:17 release to you, B or Jesus
27:20 the crowds to ask for B, but
27:21 release to you? They said: B
27:26 Then he released B to them
Mr 15:7 so-called B in bonds with the
15:11 release B to them, instead
15:15 released B to them, and
Lu 23:18 but release B to us!
Joh 18:40 Not this man, but B!
18:40 Now B was a robber

Barachel
Job 32:2 Elihu the son of B the
32:6 Elihu the son of B the Buzite

Barachiah
Mt 23:35 blood of Zechariah son of B

Barak
Jg 4:6 to send and call B the son of
4:8 B said to her: If you will go
4:9 went with B to Kedesh
4:10 B began to call Zebulun and
4:12 B the son of Abinoam had
4:14 Deborah now said to B: Get up
4:14 And B went descending from
4:15 edge of the sword before B
4:16 And B chased after the war
4:22 there was B pursuing Sisera
5:1 B the son of Abinoam broke out
5:12 Rise up, B, and lead your
5:15 And as Issachar, so was B
Heb 11:32 go on to relate about . . . B

Barbarians
Ro 1:14 to Greeks and to B, both to

Barbers'
Eze 5:1 As a b razor you will take it

Bare
Ge 30:37 laying b white places which
Le 18:6 relative of his to lay b
18:7 mother you must not lay b
18:7 You must not lay b her
18:8 wife you must not lay b
18:9 not lay b their nakedness
18:10 not lay b their nakedness
18:11 not lay b her nakedness
18:12 sister you must not lay b
18:13 sister you must not lay b
18:14 brother you must not lay b
18:15 you must not lay b. She is
18:15 not lay her nakedness b
18:16 wife you must not lay b
18:17 daughter you must not lay b
18:17 to lay her nakedness b
18:19 to lay her nakedness b
20:11 laid b the nakedness of his
20:17 sister that he has laid b
20:18 lay b her nakedness, he has
20:18 has laid b the source of her
20:19 nakedness . . . not lay b
20:20 b the nakedness of his uncle
20:21 brother that he has laid b
Nu 23:3 So he went to a b hill
1Sa 24:2 b rocks of the mountain
2Ki 9:13 under him upon the b steps
Job 33:21 And his bones . . . grow b
Ps 29:9 And strips b the forests
137:7, 7 Lay it b! Lay it b to the
Isa 3:17 lay their very forehead b
13:2 mountain of b rocks raise up
19:7 b places by the Nile River
23:13 stripped b her dwelling
32:14 have become b fields, for
41:18 Upon b hills I shall open
Jer 7:29 upon the b hills raise a
14:6 stood still upon the b hills
49:10 I will strip Esau b
Eze 24:7 Upon the shining, b surface
24:8 shining, b surface of a crag
26:4 shining, b surface of a crag
26:14 shining, b surface of a crag
29:18 shoulder was one rubbed b
Joe 1:7 stripped it b and thrown it
Mic 1:6 her foundations I shall lay b
Hab 3:13 a laying of the foundation b
Zep 2:14 lay b the very wainscoting
Mt 18:15 go lay b his fault between
1Co 15:37 but a b grain, it may be
Col 2:15 and the authorities b, he

Bared
Isa 52:10 Jehovah has b his holy arm
Eze 4:7 with your arm b, and you

Barefoot
2Sa 15:30 he was walking b, and all
Job 12:17 is making counselors go b
12:19 He is making priests walk b
Isa 20:2 walking about naked and b
20:3 naked and b three years as
20:4 old men, naked and b, and
Jer 2:25 foot back from becoming b
Mic 1:8 I will walk b and naked

Barely
Ge 27:30 Jacob had b come out from

Bar-humite
2Sa 23:31 Azmaveth the B

Bariah
1Ch 3:22 Hattush and Igal and B

Bar-Jesus
Ac 13:6 a Jew whose name was B

Bark
Ge 37:25 balsam and resinous b
43:11 resinous b, pistachio nuts
Ps 59:14 Let them b like a dog and go
Isa 56:10 dogs; they are not able to b

Barking
Ps 59:6 They keep b like a dog and

Barkos
Ezr 2:53 the sons of B
Ne 7:55 the sons of B, the sons of

Barley
Ex 9:31 flax and the b had been struck
9:31 b was in the ear and the flax
Le 27:16 homer of b seed, then at
Nu 5:15 tenth of an ephah of b flour
De 8:8 a land of wheat and b and
Jg 7:13 cake of b bread turning over
Ru 1:22 commencement of b harvest
2:17 to be about an ephah of b
2:23 until the harvest of the b and
3:2 He is winnowing b at the
3:15 measure out six measures of b
3:17 six measures of b he gave me
2Sa 14:30 and there he has b
17:28 wheat and b and flour and
21:9 the start of the b harvest
1Ki 4:28 the b and the straw for the
2Ki 4:42 twenty b loaves, and new
7:1 two seah measures of b worth
7:16 two seah measures of b
7:18 Two seah measures of b
1Ch 11:13 tract of the field full of b
2Ch 2:10 and b twenty thousand cors
2:15 And now the wheat and the b
27:5 wheat and ten thousand of b
Job 31:40 instead of b stinking weeds
Isa 28:25 b in the appointed place
Jer 41:8 and b and oil and honey
Eze 4:9 wheat and b and broad beans
4:12 round cake of b you will eat
13:19 for the handfuls of b and
45:13 ephah from the homer of b
Ho 3:2 and a homer measure of b and
3:2 and a half-homer of b
Joe 1:11 of wheat and on account of b
Joh 6:9 boy that has five b loaves
6:13 from the five b loaves
Re 6:6 and three quarts of b for a

Barn
Lu 12:24 have neither b nor storehouse

Barnabas
Ac 4:36 Joseph, who was surnamed B
9:27 B came to his aid and led
11:22 they sent out B as far as
11:30 by the hand of B and Saul
12:25 B and Saul, after having
13:1 B as well as Symeon who was
13:2 set B and Saul apart for me
13:7 Calling B and Saul to him
13:43 followed Paul and B, who in
13:46 with boldness, Paul and B
13:50 against Paul and B and threw
14:12 And they went calling B Zeus
14:14 apostles B and Paul heard of
14:20 he left with B for Derbe
15:2 disputing by Paul and B with
15:2 arranged for Paul and B and
15:12 listen to B and Paul relate
15:22 along with Paul and B
15:25 our loved ones, B and Paul
15:35 Paul and B continued spending
15:36 Paul said to B: Above all
15:37 B was determined to take
15:39 B took Mark along and sailed

1Co 9:6 only *B* and I that do not have
Ga 2:1 up to Jerusalem with *B*, taking
2:9 gave me and *B* the right hand
2:13 *B* was led along with them
Col 4:10 so does Mark the cousin of *B*

Barns
Joe 1:17 *B* have been torn down, for

Barred
Ezr 2:62 *b* as polluted from the
Ne 7:64 *b* as polluted from the
Ca 4:12 A garden *b* in is my sister
4:12 my bride, a garden *b* in, a

Barren
Ge 11:30 Sarai continued to be *b*
25:21 because she was *b*; so Jehovah
29:31 but Rachel was *b*
Ex 23:26 nor a *b* woman will exist in
Jg 13:2 his wife was *b* and had borne
13:3 you are *b* and have borne no
1Sa 2:5 the *b* has given birth to seven
Job 24:21 dealings with a *b* woman
Ps 113:9 the *b* woman to dwell in a
Isa 54:1 you *b* woman that did not
Lu 1:7 Elizabeth was *b*, and they both
1:36 the so-called *b* woman
23:29 Happy are the *b* women, and
Ga 4:27 Be glad, you *b* woman who

Barricade
Na 2:5 the *b* will have to be firmly

Barricaded
Job 38:8 And who *b* the sea with doors

Barriers
Job 30:12 their disastrous *b*

Bars
Ex 26:26 must make *b* of acacia wood
26:27 five *b* for the panel frames
26:27 five *b* for the panel frames
26:29 as supports for the *b*; and
26:29 must overlay the *b* with gold
35:11 its *b*, its pillars and its
36:31 make *b* of acacia wood, five
36:32 five *b* for the panel frames
36:32 five *b* for the panel frames
36:34 of gold as supports for the *b*
36:34 to overlay the *b* with gold
39:33 its panel frames, its *b* and
40:18 its *b* in and setting up its
Le 26:13 break the *b* of your yoke and
Nu 3:36 its *b* and its pillars and its
4:31 tabernacle and its *b* and its
2Ch 14:7 towers, double doors and *b*
Ne 3:3 its doors, its bolts and its *b*
3:6 doors and its bolts and its *b*
3:13 doors, its bolts and its *b*
3:14 its doors, its bolts and its *b*
3:15 its doors, its bolts and its *b*
Job 17:16 the *b* of Sheol they will go
Ps 107:16 cut down even the *b* of iron
147:13 *b* of your gates strong
Isa 43:14 *b* of the prisons to come
45:2 the iron *b* I shall cut down
Jer 27:2 make . . . bands and yoke *b*
28:13 Yoke *b* of wood you have
28:13 have to make yoke *b* of iron
51:30 Her *b* have been broken
La 2:9 and broken her *b* in pieces
Eze 30:18 the yoke *b* of Egypt
34:27 break the *b* of their yoke
Ho 11:6 make an end of his *b* and
Jon 2:6 its *b* were upon me for
Na 3:13 will certainly devour your *b*

Barsabbas
Ac 1:23 Joseph called *B*, who was
15:22 Judas who was called *B* and

Barter
Job 6:27 And *b* over your companion
41:6 Will partners *b* for it?

Bartholomew
Mt 10:3 Philip and *B*; Thomas and
Mr 3:18 Philip and *B* and Matthew and
Lu 6:14 and John, and Philip and *B*
Ac 1:13 *B* and Matthew, James the son

Bartimaeus
Mr 10:46 *B* (the son of Timaeus), a

Baruch
Ne 3:20 *B* the son of Zabbai worked
10:6 Daniel, Ginnethon, *B*
11:5 *B* the son of Colhozeh the
Jer 32:12 *B* the son of Neriah the
32:13 commanded *B* before their
32:16 *B* the son of Neriah, saying
36:4 *B* the son of Neriah that
36:4 *B* might write at the mouth
36:5 Jeremiah commanded *B*
36:8 *B* the son of Neriah proceeded
36:10 *B* began to read aloud from
36:13 *B* read aloud from the book
36:14 princes sent out to *B*
36:14 *B* the son of Neriah took
36:15 *B* read aloud in their ears
36:16 say to *B*: We shall without
36:17 And *B* they asked, saying
36:18 *B* said to them: Out of his
36:19 the princes said to *B*
36:26 to get *B* the secretary and
36:27 *B* had written at the mouth
36:32 *B* the son of Neriah the
43:3 *B* the son of Neriah is
43:6 and *B* the son of Neriah
45:1 *B* the son of Neriah when he
45:2 concerning you, O *B*

Barzillai
2Sa 17:27 *B* the Gileadite from
19:31 *B* the Gileadite himself
19:32 And *B* was very old, being
19:33 So the king said to *B*
19:34 But *B* said to the king
19:39 king kissed *B* and blessed
21:8 bore to Adriel the son of *B*
1Ki 2:7 the sons of *B* the Gileadite
Ezr 2:61 the sons of *B*
2:61 daughters of *B* the Gileadite
Ne 7:63 the sons of *B*, who took a
7:63 *B* the Gileadite and came to

Base
Ex 19:17 at the *b* of the mountain
25:31 Its *b*, its branches, its cups
29:12 out at the *b* of the altar
Le 4:7 the *b* of the altar of burnt
4:18 *b* of the altar of burnt
4:25 the *b* of the altar of burnt
4:30 blood at the *b* of the altar
4:34 blood at the *b* of the altar
5:9 drained out at the *b* of the
8:15 poured at the *b* of the altar
9:9 he poured at the *b* of the altar
De 3:17 the *b* of the slopes of Pisgah
4:11 and stood at the *b* of the
4:49 the *b* of the slopes of Pisgah
15:9 for fear a *b* word should come
Jos 11:3 Hivites at the *b* of Hermon
11:17 at the *b* of Mount Hermon
13:5 at the *b* of Mount Hermon as
Eze 43:13 this is the *b* of the altar

Based
Pr 11:7 expectation *b* on powerfulness
Ca 5:15 pillars of marble *b* on socket
Ro 4:18 yet *b* on hope he had faith
5:2 *b* on hope of the glory of God

Basemath
Ge 26:34 *B* the daughter of Elon the
36:3 *B*, Ishmael's daughter, the
36:4 and *B* bore Reuel
36:10 Reuel the son of *B*, Esau's
36:13 sons of *B*, Esau's wife
36:17 sons by *B*, Esau's wife
1Ki 4:15 took *B*, Solomon's daughter

Bashan
Nu 21:33 and went up by the way of *B*
21:33 Og the king of *B* came out to
32:33 kingdom of Og the king of *B*
De 1:4 and Og the king of *B*, who was
3:1 and went up by the way of *B*
3:1 Og the king of *B* came on out
3:3 Og the king of *B* and all his
3:4 the kingdom of Og in *B*
3:10 *B* as far as Salecah and Edrei
3:10 the kingdom of Og in *B*
3:11 Og the king of *B* remained
3:13 *B* of the kingdom of Og I have
3:13 the region of Argob of all *B*
3:14 call those villages of *B* by
4:43 Golan in *B* for the Manassites
4:47 the land of Og the king of *B*
29:7 Og the king of *B* proceeded to
32:14 male sheep, the breed of *B*
33:22 He will leap out from *B*
Jos 9:10 Og the king of *B*, who was in
12:4 territory of Og the king of *B*
12:5 and in Salecah and in all *B*
13:11 all *B* as far as Salecah
13:12 the royal realm of Og in *B*
13:30 *B*, all the royal realm of
13:30 realm of Og the king of *B*
13:30 that are in *B*, sixty towns
13:31 the royal realm of Og in *B*
17:1 and *B* came to belong to him
17:5 the land of Gilead and *B*
20:8 and Golan in *B* out of the
21:6 half tribe of Manasseh in *B*
21:27 Golan, in *B*, and its pasture
22:7 Moses had made a gift in *B*
1Ki 4:13 Argob, which is in *B*
4:19 Og the king of *B*, and there
2Ki 10:33 even Gilead and *B*
1Ch 5:11 dwelt in the land of *B* as
5:12 and Janai and Shaphat in *B*
5:16 *B* and in its dependent towns
5:23 from *B* to Baal-hermon and
6:62 the tribe of Manasseh in *B*
6:71 Golan in *B* with its pasture
Ne 9:22 the land of Og the king of *B*
Ps 22:12 The powerful ones of *B*
68:15 The mountainous region of *B*
68:15 The mountainous region of *B*
68:22 From *B* I shall bring back
135:11 And Og the king of *B*
136:20 And Og the king of *B*
Isa 2:13 all the massive trees of *B*
33:9 *B* and Carmel are shaking off
Jer 22:20 on *B* let your voice out
50:19 graze on Carmel and on *B*
Eze 27:6 Out of massive trees from *B*
39:18 fatlings of *B* all of them
Am 4:1 you cows of *B*, who are on
Mic 7:14 feed on *B* and Gilead as in
Na 1:4 *B* and Carmel have withered
Zec 11:2 Howl, you massive trees of *B*

Basin
Ex 12:22 into the blood in a *b* and
12:22 the blood that is in the *b*
14:21 the sea *b* into dry ground
30:18 make a *b* of copper and its
30:28 and the *b* and its stand
31:9 and the *b* and its stand
35:16 the *b* and its stand
38:8 he made the *b* of copper and
39:39 utensils, the *b* and its stand
40:7 put the *b* between the tent of
40:11 anoint the *b* and its stand
40:30 the *b* between the tent of
Le 8:11 and the *b* and its stand so
1Sa 2:14 made a thrust into the *b* or
1Ki 7:30 Beneath the *b* were the
7:38 what each *b* would contain
7:38 Each *b* was four cubits
7:38 one *b* upon each carriage
Isa 22:11 collecting *b* that you must
Joh 13:5 he put water into a *b* and

Basins
Ge 1:22 fill the waters in the sea *b*
2Sa 17:28 *b* and potter's vessels, and
1Ki 7:38 to make ten *b* of copper
7:40 Hiram gradually made the *b*
7:43 the ten *b* upon the carriages
7:50 the *b* and the extinguishers
2Ki 12:13 were not made *b* of silver
16:17 removed . . . the *b*
2Ch 4:6 made ten *b*, and put five to
4:14 the ten *b* upon the carriages
Jer 52:19 *b* and the fire holders and

Basis
Job 4:6 Is not your reverence the *b* of
Isa 2:22 on what *b* is he himself to
Mt 18:5 on the *b* of my name receives
24:5 come on the *b* of my name
Mr 9:37 children on the *b* of my name
9:39 work on the *b* of my name
13:6 Many . . . on the *b* of my name
Lu 9:48 child on the *b* of my name
21:8 come on the *b* of my name
24:47 *b* of his name repentance for
Joh 3:19 this is the *b* for judgment
Ac 4:9 *b* of a good deed to an ailing
4:17 upon the *b* of this name to
4:18 the *b* of the name of Jesus
5:28 teaching upon the *b* of this
5:40 upon the *b* of Jesus' name
Ro 8:20 subjected it, on the *b* of hope
Php 3:9 from God on the *b* of faith
Tit 1:2 upon the *b* of a hope of the

Phm 9 on the *b* of love, seeing that

Basket

Ge 31:34 in the woman's saddle *b*
40:17 in the topmost *b* there were
40:17 the *b* on top of my head
Ex 29:3 put them upon a *b* and present
29:3 and present them in the *b*
29:23 *b* of unfermented cakes that
29:32 bread that is in the *b* at
Le 8:2 and the *b* of unfermented cakes
8:26 the *b* of unfermented cakes
8:31 that is in the installation *b*
Nu 6:15 *b* of unfermented ring-shaped
6:17 the *b* of unfermented cakes
6:19 ring-shaped cake out of the *b*
De 26:2 put them in a *b* and go to the
26:4 the priest must take the *b*
28:5 Blessed will be your *b* and
28:17 Cursed will be your *b* and
Jg 6:19 The meat he put in the *b*, and
Ps 81:6 to be free even from the *b*
Jer 24:2 As for the one *b*, the figs
24:2 as for the other *b*, the figs
Am 8:1 there was a *b* of summer fruit
8:2 I said: A *b* of summer fruit
Mt 5:15 not under the measuring *b*
Mr 4:21 to be put under a measuring *b*
Lu 11:33 nor under a measuring *b*, but
Ac 9:25 wall, lowering him in a *b*
2Co 11:33 lowered in a wicker *b* and

Baskets

Ge 40:16 three *b* of white bread upon
40:18 The three *b* are three days
2Ki 10:7 put their heads in *b* and
Jer 24:1 two *b* of figs set before the
Mt 14:20 of fragments, twelve *b* full
15:37 seven provision *b* full
16:9 and how many *b* you took up
16:10 provision *b* you took up
Mr 6:43 fragments, twelve *b* full
8:8 seven provision *b* full
8:19 *b* full of fragments you took
8:20 provision *b* full of fragments
Lu 9:17 twelve *b* of fragments
Joh 6:13 twelve *b* with fragments

Basket-shaped

Ezr 1:9 thirty *b* vessels of gold
1:9 a thousand *b* vessels of silver

Bat

Le 11:19 and the hoopoe and the *b*
De 14:18 the hoopoe and the *b*

Bath

1Ki 7:26 Two thousand *b* measures were
7:38 Forty *b* measures were what
2Ch 4:5 three thousand *b* measures
Ezr 7:22 hundred *b* measures of wine
7:22 a hundred *b* measures of oil
Isa 5:10 produce but one *b* measure
Eze 45:10 accurate *b* measure you men
45:11 *b* measure, there should
45:11 *b* to carry a tenth of a
45:14 the *b* measure of the oil
45:14 *b* is a tenth of the cor
Lu 16:6 A hundred *b* measures of olive
Eph 5:26 *b* of water by means of the
Tit 3:5 the *b* that brought us to life

Bathe

Ex 2:5 came down to *b* in the Nile
Le 14:8 *b* in water and must be clean
14:9 and *b* his flesh in water; and
15:5 *b* in water and be unclean
15:6 *b* in water and be unclean
15:7 *b* in water and be unclean
15:8 wash his garments and *b* in
15:10 he must *b* in water and be
15:11 *b* in water and be unclean
15:13 *b* his flesh in running water
15:16 *b* all his flesh in water
15:18 they must *b* in water and be
15:21 *b* in water and be unclean
15:22 *b* in water and be unclean
15:27 *b* in water and be unclean
16:4 *b* his flesh in water and put
16:24 he must *b* his flesh in water
16:26 he must *b* his flesh in water
16:28 he must *b* his flesh in water
17:15 *b* in water and be unclean
17:16 not *b* his flesh, he must then
22:6 must *b* his flesh in water
Nu 19:7 and *b* his flesh in water, and
19:8 must *b* his flesh in water
Nu 19:19 *b* in water, and he must be
2Sa 11:8 to your house and *b* your feet
2Ki 5:10 *b* seven times in the Jordan
5:12 Can I not *b* in them and
5:13 said to you, *B* and be clean
Ps 58:10 steps he will *b* in the blood

Bathed

1Ki 22:38 prostitutes themselves *b*
Joh 13:10 He that has *b* does not need
Ac 9:37 they *b* her and laid her in an
16:33 *b* their stripes; and, one and
Heb 10:22 bodies *b* with clean water
2Pe 2:22 the sow that was *b* to

Bathing

2Sa 11:2 sight of a woman *b* herself
Ca 5:12 are *b* themselves in milk

Bath-rabbim

Ca 7:4 in Heshbon, by the gate of *B*

Baths

2Ch 2:10 and wine twenty thousand *b*
2:10 and oil twenty thousand *b*
Eze 45:14 Ten *b* are a homer; because
45:14 because ten *b* are a homer

Bath-sheba

2Sa 11:3 *B* the daughter of Eliam the
12:24 David began to comfort *B*
1Ki 1:11 Nathan now said to *B*
1:15 *B* went in to the king in the
1:16 *B* bowed low and prostrated
1:28 You men, call *B* for me
1:31 *B* bowed low with her face
2:13 Adonijah . . . came to *B*
2:18 *B* said: Good! I myself
2:19 *B* came in to King Solomon to
1Ch 3:5 *B* the daughter of Ammiel
Ps 51:*super* had had relations with *B*

Bats

Isa 2:20 the shrewmice and to the *b*

Battering

Eze 4:2 put *b* rams all around against
21:22 set *b* rams, to open one's
21:22 to set *b* rams against gates

Battle

Ge 14:8 they drew up in *b* order
Ex 13:18 it was in *b* formation that
32:17 is a noise of *b* in the camp
Nu 21:33 to the *b* of Edrei
31:21 who had gone into the *b*
31:27 those taking part in the *b*
32:17 go equipped in *b* formation
De 2:32 to meet us in *b* at Jahaz
3:1 to meet us in *b* at Edrei
20:1 *b* against your enemies and
20:2 you have drawn near to the *b*
20:3 drawing near today to the *b*
20:5 for fear he may die in the *b*
20:6 for fear he may die in the *b*
20:7 for fear he may die in the *b*
21:10 go out to the *b* against your
29:7 come out to meet us in *b*
Jos 1:14 pass over in *b* formation
4:12 pass over in *b* formation in
8:14 went out to meet Israel in *b*
Jg 3:10 When he went out to *b*, then
7:11 of those in *b* formation who
20:14 *b* against the sons of Israel
20:18 go up in the lead to the *b*
20:20 out to *b* against Benjamin
20:20 to draw up in *b* formation
20:22 drawing up in *b* formation in
20:23 again approach for *b* against
20:28 to *b* against the sons of
20:39 Israel turned around in the *b*
20:39 just as in the first *b*
20:42 *b* followed them up closely
1Sa 4:1 to meet the Philistines in *b*
4:2 *b* went badly, so that Israel
4:2 in closed *b* line in the field
4:12 went running from the *b* line
4:16 one coming from the *b* line
4:16 from the *b* line that I have
7:10 near for *b* against Israel
13:22 it happened on the day of *b*
14:20 they came as far as the *b*
14:22 after them into the *b*
14:23 *b* itself passed over to
17:2 drawing up in *b* formation to
17:8 call to the *b* lines of Israel
17:8 to draw up in *b* formation
17:10 taunt the *b* lines of Israel
1Sa 17:20 going out to the *b* line
17:20 raised a shout for the *b*
17:21, 21 *b* line to meet *b* line
17:22 went running to the *b* line
17:23 *b* lines of the Philistines
17:26 *b* lines of the living God
17:28 the purpose of seeing the *b*
17:36 he has taunted the *b* lines
17:45 God of the *b* lines of Israel
17:47 to Jehovah belongs the *b*
17:48 running toward the *b* line
23:3 *b* lines of the Philistines
26:10 or down into *b* he will go
29:4 go down with us into the *b*
29:4 a resister of us in the *b*
29:9 go up with us into the *b*
30:24 that went down into the *b*
2Sa 1:4 people have fled from the *b*
1:25 fallen in the midst of *b*
3:30 to death at Gibeon in the *b*
10:8 *b* formation at the entrance
10:9 Joab saw that the *b* charges
10:13 *b* against the Syrians, and
11:15 of the heaviest *b* charges
11:25 Intensify your *b* against
18:6 *b* came to be in the forest
18:8 the *b* there got to be spread
19:3 because they fled in the *b*
19:10 he had died in the *b*
21:17 not go out with us to the *b*
22:40 with vital energy for the *b*
23:9 there for the *b*, and so the
1Ki 20:14 will open the *b* engagement
20:18 for *b* that they have come
20:26 Aphek for *b* against Israel
20:29 the engagement in *b* began
20:39 into the thick of the *b*
22:30 entering into the *b* for me
22:30 entered into the *b*
22:35 *b* kept rising in intensity
2Ki 3:26 the *b* had proved too strong
1Ch 12:19 against Saul for *b*
12:33 drawing up in *b* formation
12:35 drawing up in *b* formation
12:36 drawing up in *b* formation
12:38 flocking together in *b* line
19:9 and draw up in *b* formation
19:10 the *b* charges had come to
19:14 before the Syrians to the *b*
19:17 drew up in *b* formation to
2Ch 13:3 drew up in *b* formation
13:12 for sounding the *b* alarm
13:14 the *b* in front and behind
14:10 *b* formation in the valley
18:29 entering into the *b* for me
18:29 they entered into the *b*
18:34 *b* kept rising in intensity
20:15 *b* is not yours, but God's
Job 39:25 far off it smells the *b*
41:8 Remember the *b*. Do not do it
Ps 24:8 Jehovah mighty in *b*
76:3 and the sword and the *b*
89:43 not to gain ground in the *b*
Pr 21:31 prepared for the day of *b*
Ec 9:11 nor the mighty ones the *b*
Isa 22:2 nor those dead in *b*
27:4 and weeds in the *b*
28:6 away the *b* from the gate
Jer 6:23 *b* order like a man of war
8:6 horse . . . dashing into the *b*
18:21 with the sword in the *b*
46:3 shield, and approach to *b*
49:14 and rise up to *b*
Eze 7:14 is no one going to the *b*
13:5 the *b* in the day of Jehovah
Ho 10:14 in the day of *b* when a
Joe 2:5 people, drawn up in *b* order
Am 1:14 alarm signal in the day of *b*
Ob 1 let us rise up against her in *b*
Zec 9:10 the *b* bow must be cut off
10:3 his horse of dignity in the *b*
10:4 out of him is the *b* bow
10:5 mire of the streets in the *b*
10:5 engaged in *b*, for Jehovah
1Co 14:8 who will get ready for *b*?
Re 9:7 horses prepared for *b*
9:9 many horses running into *b*
13:4 and who can do *b* with it?
17:14 will *b* with the Lamb, but

Battled

Re 12:7 Michael and his angels *b* with
12:7 the dragon and its angels *b*

Battlement
Ca 8:9 build upon her a *b* of silver
Mt 4:5 upon the *b* of the temple
Lu 4:9 stationed him upon the *b* of

Battlements
Isa 54:12 make your *b* of rubies, and

Battles
1Sa 8:20 out before us and fight our *b*
2Ch 32:8 help us and to fight our *b*
Isa 30:32 with *b* of brandishing he

Bavvai
Ne 3:18 *B* the son of Henadad, a prince

Bay
Jos 15:2 *b* that faces southward
15:5 was at the *b* of the sea, at the
18:19 northern *b* of the Salt Sea
Ac 27:39 certain *b* with a beach, and

Bazlith
Ne 7:54 the sons of *B*, the sons of

Bazluth
Ezr 2:52 the sons of *B*

Bdellium
Ge 2:12 There also are the *b* gum and
Nu 11:7 was like the look of *b* gum

Beach
Mt 13:2 crowd was standing on the *b*
13:48 they hauled it up onto the *b*
Joh 21:4 Jesus stood on the *b*, but
Ac 21:5 down on the *b* we had prayer
27:39 certain bay with a *b*, and
27:39 if they could, to *b* the boat
27:40 they made for the *b*

Beads
Ca 1:10 your neck in a string of *b*

Bealiah
1Ch 12:5 Jerimoth and *B* and Shemariah

Bealoth
Jos 15:24 Ziph and Telem and *B*
1Ki 4:16 son of Hushai, in Asher and *B*

Beam
1Sa 14:27 and his eyes began to *b*
17:7 like the *b* of loom workers
2Sa 21:19 like the *b* of loom workers
2Ki 6:2 each one a *b* and make for
6:5 certain one was felling his *b*
1Ch 11:23 a spear like the *b* of loom
20:5 like the *b* of loom workers
Ezr 5:3 to finish this *b* structure
5:9 to finish this *b* structure
Job 3:4 Nor let daylight *b* upon it
10:3 you should actually *b*
37:15 the light of his cloud to *b*
Ps 80:1 sitting upon the cherubs, do *b*
94:1 God of acts of vengeance, *b*
Isa 46:6 with the scale *b* they weigh

Beamed
De 33:2 *b* forth from the mountainous
1Sa 14:29 my eyes have *b* because I
Ps 50:2 God himself has *b* forth

Beaming
Ps 11:4 *b* eyes examine the sons of
132:4 slumber to my own *b* eyes
Pr 4:25 *b* eyes should gaze straight
6:4 any slumber to your *b* eyes
30:13 whose *b* eyes are lifted up
Jer 9:18 *b* eyes trickle with waters
Eze 28:7 profane your *b* splendor
28:17 account of your *b* splendor

Beams
1Ki 6:9 with *b* and rows in cedarwood
6:36 and a row of *b* of cedarwood
7:2 there were *b* of cedarwood
7:12 and a row of *b* of cedarwood
2Ch 34:11 to build with *b* the houses
Job 3:9 let it not see the *b* of dawn
10:22 *b* no more than gloom does
41:18 eyes are like the *b* of dawn
Ps 74:6 hatchet and iron-tipped *b*
104:3 with *b* in the very waters
Ca 1:17 The *b* of our grand house are

Beamwork
Ec 10:18 great laziness the *b* sinks in

Beans
2Sa 17:28 broad *b* and lentils and
Eze 4:9 barley and broad *b* and lentils

Bear
Ge 17:21 Sarah will *b* to you at this
36:4 Adah proceeded to *b* Eliphaz
38:5 she went on to *b* a son and
49:15 his shoulder to *b* burdens and
Ex 21:4 does *b* him sons or daughters
Le 12:2 seed and does *b* a male, she
12:5 Now if she should *b* a female
19:17 you may not *b* sin along with
22:16 to *b* the punishment of
De 8:19 I do *b* witness against you
25:6 the firstborn whom she will *b*
28:57 sons whom she proceeded to *b*
Ru 1:12 also should certainly *b* sons
1Sa 2:28 to *b* an ephod before me
17:34 came a lion, and also a *b*
17:36 Both the lion and the *b* your
17:37 and from the paw of the *b*
2Sa 17:8 *b* that has lost her cubs in
1Ki 21:10 let them *b* witness against
21:13 men began to *b* witness
Ne 9:29 *b* witness against them to
13:15 *b* witness against them on
13:21 *b* witness against them and
Es 8:6 how can I *b* it when I must
8:6 how can I *b* it when I must
Job 24:21 woman who does not *b*
29:11 to *b* witness for me
40:20 mountains themselves *b*
Ps 50:7 I will *b* witness against you
50:16 *b* my covenant in your mouth
81:8 I will *b* witness against you
Pr 9:12 you will *b* it, just you alone
14:18 *b* knowledge as a headdress
17:12 of a *b* bereaved of its cubs
18:14 stricken spirit, who can *b*
28:15 an onrushing *b* is a wicked
Isa 11:7 cow and the *b* themselves
46:4 may *b* up and furnish escape
46:7 they *b* it and deposit it in
53:11 errors he himself will *b*
Jer 3:16 *b* fruit in the land in those
La 3:10 a *b* lying in wait he is to me
5:7 is their errors that we . . . *b*
Eze 3:12 a spirit proceeded to *b* me
14:10 will have to *b* their error
16:52 *b* your humiliation when you
16:52 *b* your humiliation in that
16:54 you may *b* your humiliation
16:58 you yourself must *b* them
17:8 produce boughs and to *b* fruit
17:23 *b* boughs and produce fruit
18:19 the son does not have to *b*
18:20 son himself will *b* nothing
18:20 father . . . will *b* nothing
23:35 also *b* your loose conduct
23:49 your dungy idols you will *b*
32:24 *b* their humiliation with
32:25 will *b* their humiliation
32:30 will *b* their humiliation
34:29 no longer *b* the humiliation
36:7 *b* their own humiliation
36:8 and *b* your own fruitage
36:15 reproach . . . *b* no more
44:10 must also *b* their error
44:12 and they must *b* their error
44:13 must *b* their humiliation
47:12 they will *b* new fruit
Da 7:5 second one, it being like a *b*
Ho 5:15 until they *b* their guilt
13:8 a *b* that has lost its cubs
Joe 1:18 the ones made to *b* guilt
Am 5:19 and the *b* actually meets him
Mic 6:16 reproach . . . you men will *b*
7:9 raging of Jehovah I shall *b*
Zec 3:6 began to *b* witness to Joshua
Mt 7:18 good tree cannot *b* worthless
13:23 who really does *b* fruit and
19:18 must not *b* false witness
Mr 4:20 *b* fruit thirtyfold and sixty
10:19 Do not *b* false witness, Do
Lu 8:15 and *b* fruit with endurance
18:20 Do not *b* false witness
23:26 torture stake upon him to *b*
Joh 1:7 *b* witness about the light
1:8 *b* witness about that light
2:25 to have anyone *b* witness
3:11 we have seen we *b* witness
3:28 *b* me witness that I said
5:31 If I alone *b* witness about
5:36 *b* witness about me that the
5:39 ones that *b* witness about me
7:7 I *b* witness concerning it
8:13 You *b* witness about yourself
Joh 8:14 Even if I do *b* witness about
10:25 these *b* witness about me
15:2 that it may *b* more fruit
15:4 branch cannot *b* fruit of
15:20 *B* in mind the word I said
15:26 will *b* witness about me
15:27 *b* witness, because you have
16:12 you are not able to *b* them
18:23 *b* witness concerning the
18:37 *b* witness to the truth
21:18 *b* you where you do not
Ac 9:15 *b* my name to the nations as
10:43 all the prophets *b* witness
20:24 to *b* thorough witness to the
20:31 and *b* in mind that for three
20:35 *b* in mind the words of the
22:5 older men can *b* me witness
23:11 must also *b* witness in Rome
26:5 they but wish to *b* witness
Ro 7:4 that we should *b* fruit to God
10:2 I *b* them witness that they
11:18 not you that *b* the root, but
15:1 *b* the weaknesses of those
1Co 4:12 being persecuted, we *b* up
10:13 beyond what you can *b*, but
15:49 *b* also the image of the
Ga 4:15 I *b* you witness that, if it
5:3 I *b* witness again to every man
5:10 *b* his judgment, no matter
Eph 4:17 I say and *b* witness to in
Col 4:13 I indeed *b* him witness that
1Th 1:3 we *b* incessantly in mind your
2:9 *b* in mind, brothers, our
3:1 when we could *b* it no longer
3:5 when I could *b* it no longer
1Ti 5:14 to marry, to *b* children, to
Phm 13 prison bonds I *b* for the sake
Heb 9:28 to *b* the sins of many; and
13:22 *b* with this word of
Re 2:2 and that you cannot *b* bad men
13:2 feet were as those of a *b*
22:16 my angel to *b* witness to

Bearable
Heb 12:20 command was not *b* to them

Beard
Le 19:27 the extremity of your *b*
21:5 *b* they should not shave, and
1Sa 17:35 I grabbed hold of its *b* and
21:13 saliva run down upon his *b*
2Sa 20:9 took hold of Amasa's *b* so as
Ezr 9:3 hair of my head and of my *b*
Ps 133:2, 2 upon the *b*, Aaron's *b*
Isa 7:20 sweep away even the *b* itself
15:2 every *b* is clipped
Jer 48:37 and every *b* is clipped
Eze 5:1 upon your head and upon your *b*

Beards
2Sa 10:4 shaved off half their *b* and
10:5 until your *b* grow abundantly
1Ch 19:5 until your *b* grow abundantly
Jer 41:5 with their *b* shaved off

Bearer
1Sa 4:17 the news *b* answered and said
17:7 *b* of the large shield was
2Sa 18:26 This one also is a news *b*
Ne 4:10 power of the burden *b* has
Eze 19:10 A *b* of fruit and full of

Bearers
Jg 3:18 the *b* of the tribute
1Ki 5:15 seventy thousand burden *b*
2Ch 2:2 men as burden *b* and eighty
2:18 thousand of them burden *b*
34:13 were over the burden *b*, and
Ne 4:17 carrying the burden of load *b*
Lu 7:14 the *b* stood still, and he said
1Jo 5:7 there are three witness *b*

Bearing
Ge 1:11 vegetation *b* seed, fruit trees
1:12 vegetation *b* seed according to
1:29 to you all vegetation *b* seed
1:29 the fruit of a tree *b* seed
16:2 shut me off from *b* children
16:16 Hagar's *b* Ishmael to Abram
17:19 Sarah your wife is indeed *b*
20:17 and they began *b* children
Ex 2:11 at the burdens they were *b*
5:4 Go *b* your burdens
5:5 desist from their *b* of burdens
Nu 17:8 and was *b* ripe almonds
De 29:18 *b* the fruit of a poisonous
Jg 9:54 the attendant *b* his weapons

Jg 11:2 Gilead's wife kept *b* sons to
1Sa 22:18 eighty-five men *b* an ephod
1Ch 18:2 David's servants *b* tribute
18:6 David's servants *b* tribute
2Ch 14:8 force *b* the large shield and
14:8 *b* the buckler and bending
24:19 *b* witness against them, but
Ne 9:30 kept *b* witness against them
Job 30:15 My noble *b* is chased like
Pr 19:19 rage will be *b* the fine
Ca 4:2 all of which are *b* twins
6:6 all of which are *b* twins, none
Isa 1:14 have become tired of *b* them
46:4 I myself shall keep *b* up
Jer 15:15 Take note of my *b* reproach
Zep 3:18 *b* reproach on her account
Mt 23:31 *b* witness against yourselves
Mr 4:8 they were *b* thirtyfold, and
14:57 *b* false witness against him
Lu 24:1 *b* the spices they had prepared
Joh 12:17 crowd . . . kept *b* witness
15:2 branch in me not *b* fruit he
15:2 one *b* fruit he cleans
15:8 you keep *b* much fruit and
15:16 and keep *b* fruit and that
19:17 *b* the torture stake for
Ac 5:16 *b* sick people and those
15:10 nor we were capable of *b*
26:22 *b* witness to both small and
28:23 by *b* thorough witness
Ro 2:15 conscience is *b* witness with
1Co 9:12 are *b* all things, in order
Eph 2:11 keep *b* in mind that formerly
Col 1:6 is *b* fruit and increasing in
1:10 *b* fruit in every good work
4:18 *b* my prison bonds in mind
1Th 2:11 consoling and *b* witness to
2Th 1:4 tribulations that you are *b*
Heb 2:4 God joined in *b* witness with
11:4 God *b* witness respecting
13:13 *b* the reproach he bore
1Pe 1:11 *b* witness beforehand about
1Jo 1:2 have seen and are *b* witness
4:14 *b* witness that the Father
5:6 *b* witness, because the spirit
3Jo 12 we, also, are *b* witness, and
Re 1:9 God and *b* witness to Jesus
12:17 work of *b* witness to Jesus
19:10 *b* witness to Jesus is what
22:18 I am *b* witness to everyone

Bears

Ge 31:52 pillar is something that *b*
Le 12:7 *b* either a male or a female
Nu 30:15 he also actually *b* her error
Ps 144:4 Man himself *b* resemblance
Pr 10:31 it *b* the fruit of wisdom
29:2 wicked *b* rule . . . people sigh
Isa 59:11 groaning . . . just like *b*
Mr 4:28 Of its own self the ground *b*
Joh 3:32 of this he *b* witness, but
5:32 another that *b* witness about
5:32 witness which he *b* about me
8:18 one that *b* witness about
8:18 Father . . . *b* witness about
12:24 it then *b* much fruit
15:5 this one *b* much fruit
21:24 disciple that *b* witness
Ac 20:23 spirit repeatedly *b* witness
Ro 5:14 Adam, who *b* a resemblance
8:16 spirit itself *b* witness with
9:1 my conscience *b* witness with
11:18 but the root *b* you
13:4 purpose that it *b* the sword
1Co 13:7 *b* all things, believes all
2Co 1:12 our conscience *b* witness
Heb 10:15 holy spirit also *b* witness
1Pe 2:19 *b* up under grievous things
Re 22:20 *b* witness of these things

Beast

Ge 1:24 and wild *b* of the earth
1:25 make the wild *b* of the earth
1:30 to every wild *b* of the earth
2:19 from the ground every wild *b*
2:20 every wild *b* of the field
7:2 Of every clean *b* you must take
7:2 every *b* that is not clean just
7:8 Of every clean *b* and of every
7:8 of every *b* that is not clean
7:14 every wild *b* according to
7:23 of the ground, from man to *b*
8:1 Noah and every wild *b* and
37:20 vicious wild *b* devoured him
37:33 wild *b* must have devoured
Ex 8:17 the gnats came to be on . . . *b*
8:18 gnats came to be on man and *b*
9:9 blisters upon man and *b* in all
9:10 breaking out on man and *b*
9:19 *b* that will be found in the
9:22 hail . . . upon man and *b* and
9:25 from man to *b*, and all sorts
11:5 and every firstborn of *b*
11:7 from man to *b*; in order that
12:12 firstborn . . . from man to *b*
12:29 struck . . . firstborn of *b*
13:12 firstling, the young of a *b*
13:15 to the firstborn of *b*
19:13 *b* or man, he will not live
22:13 be torn by a wild *b*, he is
22:13 something torn by a wild *b*
22:19 Anyone lying down with a *b*
22:31 something torn by a wild *b*
Le 5:2 dead body of an unclean wild *b*
7:21 a man or an unclean *b* or any
7:25 anyone eating fat from the *b*
7:26 that of fowl or that of *b*
11:26 any *b* that is a splitter of
11:39 *b* that is yours for food
11:46 the law about the *b* and the
17:13 *b* or a fowl that may be
17:15 something torn by a wild *b*
18:23 emission to any *b* to become
18:23 a *b* to have connection with
20:15 seminal emission to a *b*, he
20:15 and you should kill the *b*
20:16 woman approaches any *b* to
20:16 kill the woman and the *b*
20:25 between the clean *b* and the
20:25 *b* and the fowl and anything
24:21 striker of a *b* should make
25:7 wild *b* that is in your land
26:6 the injurious wild *b* cease
27:9 *b* such as one presents in
27:10, 10 exchange . . . *b* for *b*
27:11 unclean *b* such as one may
27:11 stand the *b* before the priest
Nu 3:13 in Israel from man to *b*
8:17 mine, among man and among *b*
18:15 among man and among *b*
18:15 firstborn of the unclean *b*
De 4:17 the representation of any *b*
14:4 sort of *b* that you may eat
14:6 every *b* that splits the hoof
27:21 who lies down with any *b*
28:4 the fruit of your domestic *b*
28:26 and to the *b* of the field
2Ki 14:9 wild *b* of the field that was
2Ch 25:18 wild *b* of the field that
Job 5:22 of the wild *b* of the earth
5:23 And the wild *b* of the field
37:8 *b* comes into the ambush
39:15 *b* of the field may tread on
Ps 36:6 Man and *b* you save, O Jehovah
68:30 Rebuke the wild *b* of the
74:19 give to the wild *b* the soul
135:8 of Egypt, Both man and *b*
Ec 3:19 eventuality as respects the *b*
3:19 no superiority . . . over the *b*
3:21 spirit of the *b*, whether
Isa 18:6 for the *b* of the earth
18:6 *b* of the earth will pass the
43:20 wild *b* of the field will
63:14 Just as when a *b* itself
Jer 9:10 and the *b* will have fled
21:6 this city, both man and *b*
36:29 cause man and *b* to cease
Eze 14:21 famine and injurious wild *b*
33:27 to the wild *b* I shall
34:5 became food for every wild *b*
34:8 every wild *b* of the field
34:25 injurious wild *b* to cease
34:28 the wild *b* of the earth
Da 4:12 *b* of the field would seek
4:14 the *b* flee from under it
4:15 with the *b* let its portion be
4:16 heart of a *b* be given to it
5:21 was made like that of a *b*
7:5 *b*, a second one, it being like
7:6 *b*, one like a leopard, but it
7:6 And the *b* had four heads, and
7:7 fourth *b*, fearsome and
7:11 *b* was killed and its body was
7:19 fourth *b*, which proved to be
7:23 for the fourth *b*, there is a
Ho 2:12 wild *b* of the field will
2:18 with the wild *b* of the field
4:3 with the wild *b* of the field
13:8 a wild *b* of the field itself
Zep 1:3 finish off . . . man and *b*
Mt 21:5 offspring of a *b* of burden
Lu 10:34 mounted him upon his own *b*
Heb 12:20 And if a *b* touches the
Jas 3:7 wild *b* as well as bird and
2Pe 2:16 A voiceless *b* of burden
Re 11:7 the wild *b* that ascends out
13:1 I saw a wild *b* ascending out
13:2 wild *b* that I saw was like a
13:2 gave to the *b* its power
13:3 earth followed the wild *b*
13:4 the authority to the wild *b*
13:4 worshiped the wild *b* with
13:4 Who is like the wild *b*, and
13:11 wild *b* ascending out of the
13:12 of the first wild *b* in its
13:12 worship the first wild *b*
13:14 in the sight of the wild *b*
13:14 image to the wild *b* that
13:15 to the image of the wild *b*
13:15 image of the wild *b* should
13:15 the image of the wild *b*
13:17 name of the wild *b* or the
13:18 the number of the wild *b*
14:9 worships the wild *b* and its
14:11 worship the wild *b* and its
15:2 victorious from the wild *b*
16:2 had the mark of the wild *b*
16:10 the throne of the wild *b*
16:13 of the mouth of the wild *b*
17:3 upon a scarlet-colored wild *b*
17:7 wild *b* that is carrying her
17:8 wild *b* that you saw was, but
17:8 wild *b* was, but is not, and
17:11 wild *b* that was but is not
17:12 one hour with the wild *b*
17:13 and authority to the wild *b*
17:16 wild *b*, these will hate the
17:17 their kingdom to the wild *b*
19:19 I saw the wild *b* and the
19:20 the wild *b* was caught, and
19:20 mark of the wild *b* and
20:4 worshiped neither the wild *b*
20:10 wild *b* and the false prophet

Beasts

Ge 3:1 cautious of all the wild *b*
3:14 all the wild *b* of the field
7:21 animals and among the wild *b*
8:17 among the *b* and among all the
8:20 some of all the clean *b*
9:10 among fowls, among *b* and
36:6 Esau took . . . all his other *b*
45:17 Load your *b* of burden and go
Ex 13:2 among men and *b*. It is mine
22:5 send out his *b* of burden and
23:11 wild *b* of the field are to
23:29 wild *b* of the field really
Le 11:2 the *b* that are upon the earth
11:3 chews the cud among the *b*
22:8 torn by wild *b* so as to
26:22 send the wild *b* of the field
27:26 firstborn among *b*, which is
27:27 unclean *b* and he must redeem
27:28 from mankind or *b* or from
Nu 20:4 our *b* of burden to die there
20:8 and their *b* of burden drink
20:11 *b* of burden began to drink
35:3 and for all their wild *b*
De 7:22 *b* of the field may multiply
14:6 chewing the cud among the *b*
32:24 teeth of *b* I shall send upon
1Sa 17:44 and to the *b* of the field
17:46 to the wild *b* of the earth
2Sa 21:10 *b* of the field by night
1Ki 4:33 he would speak about the *b*
18:5 anymore of the *b* cut off
2Ch 32:28 all the different sorts of *b*
Job 18:3 should we be reckoned as *b*
28:8 *b* have not trodden it down
35:11 than the *b* of the earth
40:20 all the wild *b* of the field
41:34 over all majestic wild *b*
Ps 8:7 also the *b* of the open field
49:12 *b* that have been destroyed
49:20 *b* that have been destroyed
50:10 *b* upon a thousand mountains
73:22 mere *b* from your standpoint
78:48 *b* of burden even to the hail
79:2 loyal ones to the wild *b* of
104:11 wild *b* of the open field
104:14 grass sprout for the *b*
147:9 *b* he is giving their food
Pr 30:30 mightiest among the *b* and

Ec 3:18 that they themselves are *b*
Isa 30:6 against the *b* of the south
35:9 rapacious sort of wild *b*
46:1 come to be for the wild *b*
Jer 7:33 and for the *b* of the earth
12:4 *b* and the flying creatures
12:9 all you wild *b* of the field
15:3 the *b* of the earth to eat
16:4 for the *b* of the earth
19:7 and to the *b* of the earth
27:5 the *b* that are upon the
27:6 even the wild *b* of the field
28:14 the wild *b* of the field
34:20 for the *b* of the earth
Eze 5:17 famine and injurious wild *b*
8:10 and loathsome *b*, and all the
14:15 wild *b* pass through the
14:15 on account of the wild *b*
29:5 wild *b* of the earth and to
31:6 wild *b* of the field gave
31:13 all the wild *b* of the field
32:4 satisfy the wild *b* of the
38:20 the wild *b* of the field
39:4 and the wild *b* of the field
39:17 the wild *b* of the field
44:31 *b* should the priests eat
Da 2:38 the *b* of the field and the
4:21 *b* of the field would dwell
4:23 *b* of the field let its portion
4:25 *b* of the field your dwelling
4:32 with the *b* of the field your
7:3 four huge *b* were coming up
7:7 different from all the other *b*
7:12 for the rest of the *b*, their
7:17 huge *b*, because they are four
8:4 no wild *b* kept standing before
Joe 1:20 The *b* of the field also keep
2:22 Do not be fearful, you *b* of
Mic 5:8 lion among the *b* of a forest
Hab 2:17 rapacity upon the *b* that
Mr 1:13 and he was with the wild *b*
Ac 11:6 wild *b* and creeping things
23:24 *b* of burden that they may
1Co 15:32 I have fought with wild *b*
Tit 1:12 injurious wild *b*, unemployed
Re 6:8 and by the wild *b* of the earth

Beat
Ex 39:3 they *b* plates of gold to thin
Nu 16:39 *b* . . . into an overlaying
De 24:20 In case you *b* your olive tree
25:3 forty strokes he may *b* him
25:3 *b* him with many strokes in
Jg 4:21 and *b* it into the earth
Ru 2:17 *b* out what she had gleaned
2Sa 22:43 I shall *b* them flat
24:10 David's heart began to *b*
1Ki 6:32 *b* the gold down upon the
Job 37:18 can you *b* out the skies
Pr 23:13 case you *b* him with the rod
23:14 *b* him, that you may deliver
Ca 4:9 You have made my heart *b*, O
4:9 my heart *b* by one of your eyes
Isa 2:4 have to *b* their swords into
27:12 Jehovah will *b* off the
32:12 *B* yourselves upon the
Jer 4:8 *B* your breasts and howl
16:6 will people *b* themselves
Eze 24:16 should not *b* your breast
24:23 will not *b* yourselves nor
Joe 1:13 *b* your breasts, you priests
3:10 *B* your plowshares into
Mic 4:3 have to *b* their swords into
Mt 11:17 not *b* yourselves in grief
21:35 one they *b* up, another they
24:30 *b* themselves in lamentation
24:49 start to *b* his fellow slaves
Mr 12:3 *b* him up and sent him away
12:5 some of whom they *b* up and
Lu 12:45 start to *b* the menservants
20:11 That one also they *b* up and
Ac 16:22 command to *b* them with rods
Re 1:7 *b* themselves in grief because
7:16 neither will the sun *b* down
18:9 *b* themselves in grief over

Beaten
Ex 5:14 the officers . . . were *b*
5:16 and here your servants are *b*
27:20 pure, *b* olive oil for the
29:40 fourth of a hin of *b* oil, and
Le 24:2 *b* olive oil for the luminary
Nu 22:28 have *b* me these three times
22:32 Why have you *b* your she-ass
28:5 the fourth of a hin of *b* oil
De 25:2 wicked one deserves to be *b*
Isa 28:27 cummin is generally *b* out
49:9 all *b* paths their pasturing
Jer 3:2 eyes to the *b* paths and see
3:21 On the *b* paths there has
4:11 the *b* paths through the
10:9 Silver *b* into plates is what
12:12 the *b* paths through the
Mr 13:9 you will be *b* in synagogues
Lu 12:47 will be *b* with many strokes
12:48 will be *b* with few
2Co 11:25 times I was *b* with rods

Beaten-out
1Ki 5:11 twenty cor measures of *b* oil

Beating
Nu 22:25 and he went *b* her some more
22:27 *b* the ass with his staff
Jg 6:11 his son was *b* out wheat in
Ps 68:25 the maidens *b* tambourines
Isa 17:6 *b* off of the olive tree
24:13 the *b* off of the olive tree
Na 2:7 *b* repeatedly upon their hearts
Lu 8:52 all weeping and *b* themselves
18:13 kept *b* his breast, saying
20:10 away empty, after *b* him up
23:27 kept *b* themselves in grief
23:48 to return, *b* their breasts
Ac 18:17 went to *b* him in front of
21:32 they quit *b* Paul

Beatings
2Co 6:5 by *b*, by prisons, by disorders

Beauteous
1Ch 22:5 *b* distinction to all the
29:13 and praising your *b* name

Beautified
Isa 55:5 because he will have *b* you
60:9 for he will have *b* you
60:21 for me to be *b*
61:3 Jehovah, for him to be *b*

Beautifies
Ps 149:4 He *b* the meek ones with

Beautiful
Ge 12:11 are a woman *b* in appearance
12:14 woman, that she was very *b*
29:17 Rachel had become *b* in form
29:17 Rachel . . . *b* of countenance
39:6 Joseph grew to be *b* in form
39:6 in form and *b* in appearance
41:2 seven cows *b* in appearance
41:4 seven cows that were *b* in
41:18 seven cows fat-fleshed and *b*
De 21:11 a woman *b* in form, and you
1Sa 16:12 young man with *b* eyes and
17:42 and ruddy, of *b* appearance
25:3 the wife was . . . *b* in form
2Sa 13:1 *b* sister whose name was
14:25 no man so *b* in all Israel
14:27 woman most *b* in appearance
1Ki 1:3 went looking for a *b* girl
1:4 the girl was *b* in the extreme
Es 1:11 for she was *b* in appearance
2:2 virgins, *b* in appearance, for
2:3 virgins, *b* in appearance
2:7 and *b* in appearance, and at the
Ca 1:8 O you most *b* one among women
1:15 You are *b*, O girl companion
1:15 You are *b*. Your eyes are those
1:16 You are *b*, my dear one, also
2:10 my *b* one, and come away
2:13 my *b* one, and come away
4:1 You are *b*, O girl companion of
4:1 You are *b*. Your eyes are those
4:7 You are altogether *b*, O girl
4:10 How *b* your expressions of
5:9 O you most *b* one among women
6:1 O most *b* one among women
6:4 You are *b*, O girl companion of
6:10 *b* like the full moon, pure
7:1 How *b* your steps have become
7:6 *b* you are, and how pleasant
Isa 4:2 something *b* for those of
52:1 Put on your *b* garments
63:12 making His *b* arm go at the
63:14 *b* name for your own self
Jer 13:11 a praise and something *b*
13:20 gave to you, your *b* flock
Eze 16:12 and a *b* crown on your head
16:17 *b* articles from my gold and
16:39 and take your *b* articles and
23:26 take away your *b* articles
Eze 23:42 *b* crowns upon their heads
24:25 the *b* object of their
Mt 23:27 outwardly indeed appear *b*
Ac 3:2 temple door that was called *B*
3:10 at the *B* Gate of the temple
7:20 born, and he was divinely *b*
Heb 11:23 young child was *b* and they

Beautifully
2Ki 9:30 do her head up *b* and to

Beautify
Ezr 7:27 to *b* the house of Jehovah
Isa 60:7 *b* my own house of beauty
60:13 *b* the place of my sanctuary

Beautifying
Jg 4:9 the *b* thing will not become

Beauty
Ex 28:2 holy garments for . . . *b*
28:40 make headgears for . . . *b*
De 26:19 praise and reputation and *b*
2Sa 1:19 *b*, O Israel, is slain upon
1Ch 29:11 the *b* and the excellency and
2Ch 3:6 with precious stone for *b*
Es 1:4 the honor and the *b* of his
Ps 71:8 All day long with your *b*
78:61 *b* into the hand of the
89:17 are the *b* of their strength
96:6 and *b* are in his sanctuary
Pr 4:9 crown of *b* it will bestow
16:31 is a crown of *b* when it is
17:6 the *b* of sons is their fathers
19:11 is *b* on his part to pass over
20:29 The *b* of young men is their
28:12 exulting, there is abundant *b*
Isa 3:18 *b* of the bangles and the
13:19 *b* of the pride of the
20:5 and of Egypt their *b*
23:9 profane the pride of all *b*
28:1 decoration of *b* that is upon
28:4 decoration of *b* that is upon
28:5 garland of *b* to the ones
44:13 like the *b* of mankind, to
44:23 on Israel he shows his *b*
46:13 to Israel my *b*
49:3 in whom I shall show my *b*
60:7 beautify my own house of *b*
60:19 and your God your *b*
62:3 crown of *b* in the hand of
63:15 abode of holiness and *b*
64:11 Our house of holiness and *b*
Jer 13:18 your crown of *b* will
33:9 a *b* toward all the nations
48:17 been broken, the staff of *b*
La 2:1 heaven to earth the *b* of Israel
Eze 28:7 against the *b* of your wisdom
28:12 wisdom and perfect in *b*
28:17 haughty because of your *b*
Zec 12:7 the *b* of the house of David
12:7 *b* of the inhabitants of
Jas 1:11 *b* of its outward appearance

Bebai
Ezr 2:11 sons of *B*, six hundred and
8:11 of the sons of *B*, Zechariah
8:11 Zechariah the son of *B*
10:28 the sons of *B*, Jehohanan
Ne 7:16 sons of *B*, six hundred and
10:15 Bunni, Azgad, *B*

Became*
Ge 6:11 earth *b* filled with violence
19:26 and she *b* a pillar of salt
47:13 land of Canaan *b* exhausted
Ex 4:3 it *b* a serpent; and Moses
4:4 and it *b* a rod in his palm
7:10 his rod . . . *b* a big snake
7:12 his rod, and they *b* big snakes
7:13 Pharaoh's heart *b* obstinate
8:17 dust of the earth *b* gnats in
9:10 and it *b* boils with blisters
9:24 from the time it *b* a nation
15:25 and the water *b* sweet
2Sa 5:4 was David when he *b* king
1Ki 2:12 his kingship *b* very firmly
6:1 Solomon *b* king over Israel
15:1 Abijam *b* king over Judah
15:25 he *b* king over Israel in
15:29 as soon as he *b* king
15:33 Baasha . . . *b* king over all
16:8 Elah . . . *b* king over Israel
16:15 Zimri *b* king for seven days
16:23 Omri *b* king over Israel
16:29 he *b* king over Israel in
22:51 he *b* king over Israel in

2Ki 3:1 *b* king over Israel in Samaria
8:16 Jehoram . . . *b* king
8:17 when he *b* king, and for
8:25 Ahaziah . . . *b* king
12:1 Jehoash *b* king, and for
13:1 *b* king over Israel in
13:10 *b* king over Israel in
14:1 Amaziah . . . *b* king
14:23 *b* king in Samaria for
15:1 Azariah . . . *b* king
15:8 Zechariah . . . *b* king over
15:13 *b* king in the thirty-ninth
15:17 *b* king over Israel for ten
15:23 Pekahiah . . . *b* king over
15:27 Pekah . . . *b* king over Israel
15:32 Jotham . . . *b* king
16:1 Ahaz . . . *b* king
17:1 Hoshea . . . *b* king in Samaria
18:1 Hezekiah . . . *b* king
1Ch 17:22 Jehovah, *b* their God
2Ch 25:1 Amaziah *b* king, and for
29:1 Hezekiah himself *b* king at
Ps 114:2 Judah *b* his holy place
Mr 1:42 leprosy vanished . . . *b* clean
Joh 1:14 Word *b* flesh and resided
1Co 15:45 man Adam *b* a living soul
15:45 last Adam *b* a life-giving
Re 1:18 I *b* dead, but, look! I am
2:8 *b* dead and came to life again

Becher
Ge 46:21 sons of Benjamin were . . . *B*
Nu 26:35 of *B* the family of the
1Ch 7:6 of Benjamin were Bela and *B*
7:8 sons of *B* were Zemirah and
7:8 all these the sons of *B*

Becherites
Nu 26:35 Becher the family of the *B*

Beclouds
La 2:1 anger *b* the daughter of Zion

Become*
Ge 2:24 and they must *b* one flesh
3:22 man has *b* like one of us in
Ex 7:3 let Pharaoh's heart *b* obstinate
7:9 rod . . . will *b* a big snake
8:16 dust . . . must *b* gnats in all
9:9 *b* a powder upon all the land
9:9 must *b* boils breaking out with
9:12 Pharaoh's heart *b* obstinate
De 28:23 Your skies . . . *b* copper
28:25 *b* a frightful object to all
28:26 dead body must *b* food for
28:29 *b* one who gropes about at
28:29 *b* only one who is always
28:30 will *b* engaged to a woman
28:33 *b* one who is only defrauded
28:34 *b* maddened at the sight of
28:37 *b* an object of astonishment
28:44 He will *b* the head, while
28:44 you will *b* the tail
Jos 11:20 let their hearts *b* stubborn
2Sa 3:21 *b* king over all that your
15:10 Absalom has *b* king in
1Ki 1:11 the son of Haggith has *b* king
11:37 certainly *b* king over Israel
14:21 he had *b* king in Judah
22:41 Jehoshaphat . . . had *b* king
2Ki 9:13 and say: Jehu has *b* king!
9:29 Ahaziah had *b* king over Judah
1Ch 16:31 Jehovah himself has *b* king!
Ps 2:7 today, I have *b* your father
47:8 God has *b* king over the
93:1 Jehovah himself has *b* king!
96:10 Jehovah himself has *b* king
97:1 Jehovah himself has *b* king!
99:1 Jehovah himself has *b* king
Isa 24:23 Jehovah . . . has *b* king
52:7 to Zion: Your God has *b* king!
Eze 34:24 Jehovah, will *b* their God
Zec 14:9 Jehovah must *b* king over all
Mt 10:25 disciple to *b* as his teacher
11:29 *b* my disciples, for I am
20:26 wants to *b* great among you
Lu 3:5 curves must *b* straight ways
4:3 tell this stone to *b* a loaf
Ro 9:18 wishes he lets *b* obstinate
1Co 13:11 now that I have *b* a man
2Co 5:20 we beg: *B* reconciled to God
Eph 5:31 and the two will *b* one flesh
Heb 1:5 he himself will *b* my son
2:17 *b* like his brothers in all
5:5 today, I have *b* your father

Becomes
Ex 21:14 *b* heated against his fellow
Le 5:5 in case he *b* guilty as respects
6:4 he sins and indeed *b* guilty
15:32 so that he *b* unclean by it
22:4 *b* clean, neither he who
25:47 settler with you *b* wealthy
De 15:7 your brothers *b* poor among
1Sa 21:5 when one *b* holy in his
Job 18:12 His vigor *b* famished, And
24:14 night he *b* a regular thief
Ps 93:1 land also *b* firmly
96:10 land also *b* firmly
118:14 And to me he *b* salvation
Pr 2:10 knowledge itself *b* pleasant
14:33 it *b* known
19:3 *b* enraged against Jehovah
21:11 the inexperienced *b* wise
Ec 7:3 of the face the heart *b* better
12:4 of the grinding mill *b* low
Isa 2:9 man bows down, and man *b* low
18:5 bloom *b* a ripening grape
24:9 liquor *b* bitter to those
25:5 tyrannical ones *b* suppressed
29:11 *b* like the words of the
29:13 *b* men's commandment that
32:19 city *b* low in an abased
44:16 eats, and he *b* satisfied
Jer 15:16 your word *b* to me the
23:36 the burden itself *b* to each
La 4:1 how the gold that shines *b* dim
4:3 daughter of my people *b* cruel
4:6 *b* greater than the punishment
Mt 13:22 and he *b* unfruitful
13:32 *b* a tree, so that the birds
23:15 when he *b* one you make him
Mr 2:21 and the tear *b* worse
3:24 a kingdom *b* divided against
3:25 if a house *b* divided against
4:19 the word, and it *b* unfruitful
4:32 comes up and *b* greater than
8:38 For whoever *b* ashamed of me
Lu 9:26 whoever *b* ashamed of me and
22:16 *b* fulfilled in the kingdom
Ro 7:3 adulteress if she *b* another
10:20 Isaiah *b* very bold and says
1Co 16:10 see that he *b* free of fear
Heb 11:6 *b* the rewarder of those
1Pe 1:24 the grass *b* withered, and

Becoming
Ge 10:8 He made the start in *b* a
48:1 Look, your father is *b* weak
Ex 1:20 people kept . . . *b* very mighty
2:11 as Moses was *b* strong, that
23:1 by *b* a witness who schemes
Jg 19:9 has declined toward *b* evening
1Ki 14:2 reference to me as to *b* king
2Ki 25:27 in the year of his *b* king
1Ch 1:10 *b* a mighty one in the earth
Ne 6:6 you are *b* a king to them
Pr 14:16 the stupid is *b* furious and
15:6 there is a *b* ostracized
17:21 *b* father to a stupid child
23:24 one *b* father to a wise one
26:17 *b* furious at the quarrel that
Jer 2:5 vain idol and *b* vain
2:25 foot back from *b* barefoot
44:8 your *b* a malediction and a
52:31 in the year of his *b* king
Joe 2:26 eat, eating and *b* satisfied
Mt 6:16 fasting, stop *b* sad-faced
Lu 6:36 Continue *b* merciful, just as
Ac 10:4 *b* frightened, said: What is
13:9 *b* filled with holy spirit
19:28 *b* full of anger, the men
19:36 it is *b* for you to keep calm
1Co 7:23 stop *b* slaves of men
7:35 to that which is *b* and that
10:32 Keep from *b* causes for
Ga 3:13 *b* a curse instead of us
Eph 5:4 things which are not *b*, but
5:17 cease *b* unreasonable, but
Php 4:14 *b* sharers with me in my
Col 3:18 as it is *b* in the Lord
Heb 5:5 by *b* a high priest, but was
Jas 1:12 *b* approved he will receive
1Pe 5:3 *b* examples to the flock

Becorath
1Sa 9:1 son of *B*, the son of Aphiah

Bed
Ge 49:4 gone up to your father's *b*
Ex 21:18 but must keep to his *b*
Le 15:4 *b* upon which the one having
15:5 touch his *b* should wash his
15:21 touching her *b* should wash
15:23 upon the *b* or upon another
15:24 any *b* upon which he might
15:26 Any *b* upon which she may lie
15:26 *b* of her menstrual impurity
De 24:12 not go to *b* with his pledge
24:13 must go to *b* in his garment
2Sa 4:11 in his own house upon his *b*
11:2 rise from his *b* and walk
11:13 lie down on his *b* with the
13:5 on your *b* and play sick
1Ki 1:47 king bowed down upon the *b*
2Ch 16:14 *b* that had been filled with
Job 7:13 *b* will help carry my concern
33:15 During slumbers upon the *b*
33:19 with pain upon his *b*
Ps 4:4 Have your say . . . upon your *b*
36:4 he keeps scheming upon his *b*
41:3 All his *b* you will certainly
Pr 7:17 besprinkled my *b* with myrrh
22:27 take your *b* from under you
Ca 3:1 On my *b* during the nights I
5:13 are like a garden *b* of spice
Isa 57:7 you set your *b*. There also
57:8 you made your *b* spacious
57:8 You loved a *b* with them
Eze 23:17 the *b* of expressions of love
32:25 they have set a *b* for her
Da 2:28 of your head upon your *b*
2:29 on your *b* your own thoughts
4:5 mental images upon my *b* and
4:10 visions of my head upon my *b*
4:13 visions of my head upon my *b*
7:1 visions of his head upon his *b*
Mt 9:2 a paralyzed man lying on a *b*
9:6 pick up your *b*, and go to your
Mr 4:21 measuring basket or under a *b*
7:30 the young child laid on the *b*
Lu 5:18 carrying on a *b* a man who
5:19 down with the little *b*
5:24 and pick up your little *b* and
8:16 or puts it underneath a *b*
11:7 children are with me in *b*
17:34 two men will be in one *b*
Ac 9:34 Rise and make up your *b*
Heb 13:4 the marriage *b* be without

Bedad
Ge 36:35 Hadad son of *B*, who defeated
1Ch 1:46 and Hadad the son of *B*

Bedan
1Sa 12:11 *B* and Jephthah and Samuel
1Ch 7:17 And the sons of Ulam were *B*

Bedchamber
Ac 12:20 charge of the *b* of the king

Bedecked
Pr 7:16 coverlets I have *b* my divan

Bedeiah
Ezr 10:35 Benaiah, *B*, Cheluhi

Bedroom
Ex 8:3 frogs . . . your inner *b* and upon
2Sa 4:7 his couch in his inner *b*
2Ki 6:12 you speak in your inner *b*
Ec 10:20 in your *b* do not call down

Beds
2Sa 17:28 *b* and basins and potter's
22:16 stream *b* of the sea became
Ps 18:15 *b* of waters became visible
126:4 Like stream *b* in the Negeb
149:5 cry out joyfully on their *b*
Ca 6:2 to the garden *b* of spice plants
Isa 8:7 up over all his stream *b*
57:2 they take rest upon their *b*
Eze 6:3 stream *b* and to the valleys
17:7 the garden *b* where it was
17:10 the garden *b* of its sprout
31:12 the stream *b* of the earth
32:6 stream *b* themselves will be
34:13 by the stream *b* and by all
35:8 and all your stream *b*
36:4 to the stream *b* and to the
36:6 stream *b* and to the valleys
Ho 7:14 they kept howling on their *b*
Joe 3:18 the very stream *b* of Judah
Mic 2:1 what is bad, upon their *b*
Ac 5:15 there upon little *b* and cots

Beeliada
1Ch 14:7 Elishama and *B* and Eliphelet

Beelzebub
Mt 10:25 called the householder *B*
12:24 *B*, the ruler of the demons
12:27 if I expel . . . by means of *B*
Mr 3:22 were saying: He has *B*, and he
Lu 11:15 *B* the ruler of the demons
11:18 the demons by means of *B*
11:19 If it is by means of *B* I

Beer
Nu 21:16 Next from there on to *B*
Jg 9:21 and made his way to *B*, and he
Isa 1:22 Your wheat *b* is diluted with
Ho 4:18 Their wheat *b* being gone
Na 1:10 drunken as with their wheat *b*

Beera
1Ch 7:37 and Shilshah and Ithran and *B*

Beerah
1Ch 5:6 *B* his son, whom

Beer-elim
Isa 15:8 howling . . . is clear to *B*

Beeri
Ge 26:34 Judith the daughter of *B*
Ho 1:1 Hosea the son of *B* in the days

Beer-lahai-roi
Ge 16:14 why the well was called *B*
24:62 from the way that goes to *B*
25:11 was dwelling close by *B*

Beeroth
De 10:6 away from *B* Bene-jaakan for
Jos 9:17 and *B* and Kiriath-jearim
18:25 Gibeon and Ramah and *B*
2Sa 4:2 *B*, too, used to be counted as
Ezr 2:25 sons of Kiriath-jearim . . . *B*
Ne 7:29 the men of . . . *B*

Beerothite
2Sa 4:2 sons of Rimmon the *B*, of
4:5 sons of Rimmon the *B*, Rechab
4:9 sons of Rimmon the *B*, and
23:37 Naharai the *B*

Beerothites
2Sa 4:3 *B* went running away to

Beer-sheba
Ge 21:14 about in the wilderness of *B*
21:31 why he called that place *B*
21:32 concluded a covenant at *B*
21:33 a tamarisk tree at *B*
22:19 their way together to *B*
22:19 continued to dwell at *B*
26:23 he went up from there to *B*
26:33 the name of the city is *B*
28:10 from *B* and kept going to
46:1 pulled out and came to *B*
46:5 Jacob got up out of *B*, and
Jos 15:28 *B* and Biziothiah
19:2 have in their inheritance *B*
Jg 20:1 from Dan down to *B* along
1Sa 3:20 And all Israel from Dan to *B*
8:2 they were judging in *B*
2Sa 3:10 over Judah from Dan to *B*
17:11 from Dan to *B*, as the sand
24:2 from Dan to *B*, and you men
24:7 in the Negeb of Judah at *B*
24:15 the people from Dan to *B*
1Ki 4:25 from Dan to *B*, all the days
19:3 to *B*, which belongs to Judah
2Ki 12:1 name was Zibiah from *B*
23:8 from Geba as far as *B*
1Ch 4:28 to dwell in *B* and Moladah
21:2 count Israel from *B* to Dan
2Ch 19:4 from *B* to the mountainous
24:1 name was Zibiah from *B*
30:5 Israel, from *B* to Dan, to
Ne 11:27 in *B* and its dependent towns
11:30 from *B* clear to the valley
Am 5:5 to *B* you must not pass over
8:14 As the way of *B* is alive!

Bees
De 1:44 chasing you, just as *b* do
Jg 14:8 a swarm of *b* in the lion's
Ps 118:12 They surrounded me like *b*
Isa 7:18 *b* that are in the land of

Beeshterah
Jos 21:27 *B* and its pasture ground

Befall
Ge 42:4 a fatal accident may *b* him
42:38 If a fatal accident should *b*
44:29 fatal accident were to *b* him
Ex 1:10 in case war should *b* us
Le 10:19 as these began to *b* me
De 31:29 calamity will be bound to *b*
1Sa 28:10 error will not *b* you in this
Ps 91:10 No calamity will *b* you
Pr 12:21 hurtful will *b* the righteous
Ec 9:11 unforeseen occurrence *b* them
Jer 32:23 this calamity to *b* them
Da 4:24 must *b* my lord the king
10:14 *b* your people in the final
Mr 10:32 things destined to *b* him

Befallen
Ge 42:29 the things that had *b* them
Ex 18:8 hardship that had *b* them in
Es 4:7 things that had *b* him and the
6:13 everything that had *b* him
Jer 13:22 that these things have *b* me
44:23 *b* you this calamity as at

Befalling
Isa 51:19 Those two things were *b* you
1Co 10:11 went on *b* them as examples
1Pe 4:12 strange thing were *b* you

Befalls
Nu 11:23 whether what I say *b* you or

Befell
Da 4:28 *b* Nebuchadnezzar the king
Ac 20:19 and trials that *b* me by the

Befit
Lu 3:8 fruits that *b* repentance
Ac 26:20 works that *b* repentance

Befits
Mt 3:8 fruit that *b* repentance
Eph 5:3 just as it *b* holy people
1Ti 2:10 way that *b* women professing

Befitting
Ps 93:5 Holiness is *b* to your own

Before*
Ex 16:9 Come near *b* Jehovah, because
Le 24:8 set it in order *b* Jehovah
Mt 26:34 this night, *b* a cock crows
26:75 *B* a cock crows, you will
Mr 14:30 *b* a cock crows twice, even
14:72 *B* a cock crows twice, you
Lu 1:17 will go *b* him with Elijah's
12:8 union with me *b* men
12:8 union with him *b* the angels
12:9 disowns me *b* men will be
12:9 disowned *b* the angels of God
22:61 *B* a cock crows today you
Joh 1:15 because he existed *b* me
8:58 *B* Abraham came into
2Co 5:10 *b* the judgment seat of the
Heb 9:24 *b* the person of God for us
Re 7:9 standing *b* the throne and
7:9 *b* the Lamb, dressed in white
7:11 upon their faces *b* the throne
7:15 they are *b* the throne of God
8:3 altar that was *b* the throne
9:13 the golden altar that is *b* God
14:3 as if a new song *b* the throne
14:3 *b* the four living creatures
20:12 small, standing *b* the throne

Beforehand
Mr 13:11 do not be anxious *b* about
13:23 I have told you all things *b*
14:8 *b* to put perfumed oil on my
Lu 21:14 not to rehearse *b* how to
Ac 1:16 holy spirit spoke *b* by
2:31 he saw *b* and spoke concerning
3:18 he announced *b* through the
10:41 witnesses appointed *b* by
Ro 9:23 he prepared *b* for glory
1Co 11:21 his own evening meal *b*, so
Ga 3:8 the good news *b* to Abraham
4:2 day his father appointed *b*
1Th 3:4 we used to tell you *b* that
4:6 just as we told you *b* and
1Pe 1:11 bearing witness *b* about the

Befouled
2Sa 1:21 shield of mighty ones was *b*
Eze 34:19 water *b* by the stamping
Zec 3:3 clothed in *b* garments and
3:4 Remove the *b* garments from

Beg
Mt 9:38 *b* the Master of the harvest
Lu 8:28 I *b* you, do not torment me
9:38 I *b* you to take a look at my
10:2 *b* the Master of the harvest
14:18 in common started to *b* off
16:3 I am ashamed to *b*
Joh 9:8 man that used to sit and *b*
Ac 8:34 eunuch said to Philip: I *b* you
21:39 I *b* you, permit me to speak
25:11 I do not *b* off from dying
26:3 I *b* you to hear me patiently
2Co 5:20 substitutes for Christ we *b*
10:2 I *b* that, when present, I
Ga 4:12 I *b* you, Become as I am
Heb 12:25 See that you do not *b* off

Began*
Ge 36:33 Jobab . . . *b* to reign instead
36:34 Husham . . . *b* to reign
36:36 Samlah . . . *b* to reign
36:37 Shaul . . . *b* to reign instead
36:38 Baal-hanan . . . *b* to reign
36:39 Hadar *b* to reign instead of
1Ki 14:21 Rehoboam . . . *b* to reign
2Ki 18:2 when he *b* to reign, and for
Jer 52:1 old when he *b* to reign, and
Joh 8:44 was a manslayer when he *b*

Beggar
Mr 10:46 a blind *b*, was sitting
Lu 16:20 *b* named Lazarus used to be
16:22 course of time the *b* died
Joh 9:8 used to see he was a *b* began

Beggarly
Ga 4:9 weak and *b* elementary things

Begged
Lu 5:12 fell upon his face and *b* him
9:40 I *b* your disciples to expel it
Heb 12:25 did not escape who *b* off

Begging
Jg 19:7 father-in-law kept *b* him, so
Ps 109:10 And they must do *b*
Pr 20:4 he will be *b* in reaping time
Lu 8:38 kept *b* to continue with him
18:35 sitting beside the road *b*
Ro 1:10 *b* that if at all possible I
2Co 8:4 *b* us with much entreaty for

Beginning
Ge 1:1 In the *b* God created the
10:10 *b* of his kingdom came to be
49:3 the *b* of my generative power
De 11:12 from the *b* of the year to
21:17 *b* of his generative power
1Sa 3:12 from *b* to end
Job 8:7 *b* may . . . be a small thing
40:19 the *b* of the ways of God
42:12 afterward more than his *b*
Ps 78:51 *b* of their generative power
105:36 *b* of all their generative
111:10 Jehovah is the *b* of wisdom
Pr 1:7 fear of Jehovah is the *b* of
8:22 *b* of his way, the earliest
17:14 The *b* of contention is as one
Ec 7:8 of a matter than its *b*
Isa 46:10 from the *b* the finale
Jer 26:1 In the *b* of the royal rule
27:1 In the *b* of the kingdom of
28:1 *b* of the kingdom of Zedekiah
49:34 *b* of the kingship of
49:35 the *b* of their mightiness
Ho 9:10 on a fig tree in its *b*
Mic 1:13 The *b* of sin was what she
Mt 19:4 who created them from the *b*
19:8 not been the case from the *b*
24:8 are a *b* of pangs of distress
24:21 since the world's *b* until
Mr 1:1 *b* of the good news about Jesus
10:6 from the *b* of creation He
13:8 are a *b* of pangs of distress
13:19 from the *b* of the creation
Lu 1:2 those who from the *b* became
Joh 1:1 In the *b* the Word was, and
1:2 one was in the *b* with God
2:11 as the *b* of his signs, and
6:64 from the *b* Jesus knew who
Ac 11:15 it did also upon us in the *b*
26:4 from the *b* among my nation
Col 1:18 He is the *b*, the firstborn
2Th 2:13 God selected you from the *b*
Heb 1:10 at the *b*, O Lord, laid the
3:14 confidence we had at the *b*
5:12 from the *b* the elementary
7:3 having neither a *b* of days
2Pe 3:4 exactly as from creation's *b*
1Jo 1:1 That which was from the *b*
2:7 which you have had from the *b*
2:13 know him who is from the *b*
2:14 know him who is from the *b*
2:24 heard from the *b* remain in

1Jo 2:24 heard from the *b* remains in
3:8 Devil . . . sinning from the *b*
3:11 you have heard from the *b*
2Jo 5 one which we had from the *b*
6 heard from the *b*, that you
Re 3:14 the *b* of the creation by God
21:6 I am . . . the *b* and the end
22:13 last, the *b* and the end

Begins
Job 37:1 my heart *b* to tremble
Ps 104:22 The sun *b* to shine—they
Pr 7:13 and she *b* to say to him

Begotten
Mt 1:20 *b* in her is by holy spirit

Begun
De 20:6 vineyard and not *b* to use it
1Sa 3:2 his eyes had *b* to grow dim
3:7 not yet *b* to be revealed to
1Ki 11:33 *b* to bow down to Ashtoreth
1Ch 17:1 David had *b* dwelling in his
Jer 8:16 the whole land has *b* to rock
15:17 playing jokes and *b* exulting
23:9 All my bones have *b* shaking
49:21 the earth has *b* to rock
1Co 4:8 You have *b* ruling as kings
4:8 that you had *b* ruling as kings
Re 11:17 and *b* ruling as king
19:6 Jehovah . . . *b* to rule as king

Behalf
Ex 8:28 Make entreaty in my *b*
30:16 give it in *b* of the service
Le 9:7 make atonement in your own *b*
9:7 and in *b* of your house; and
9:7 make atonement in their *b*
16:6 atonement in *b* of himself
16:11 atonement in *b* of himself
16:17 atonement in *b* of himself
16:17 and in *b* of his house and
16:17 *b* of the entire congregation
16:24 atonement in his own *b* and in
16:24 and in *b* of the people
26:45 remember in their *b* the
Nu 21:7 interceding in *b* of the people
27:21 he must inquire in his *b* by
De 9:20 also in *b* of Aaron at that
23:5 God in your *b* changed the
Jos 22:26 Let us take action in our *b*
Jg 6:32 a legal defense in his own *b*
1Sa 7:5 may pray in your *b* to Jehovah
7:9 for aid in *b* of Israel, and
12:19 Pray in *b* of your servants
12:23 by ceasing to pray in your *b*
2Sa 10:12 courageous in *b* of our
10:12 *b* of the cities of our God
12:16 true God in *b* of the boy
1Ki 13:6 pray in my *b* that my hand
2Ki 11:7 in *b* of the king
19:4 prayer in *b* of the remnant
22:13 in my own *b* and in
22:13 and in *b* of the people and
22:13 and in *b* of all Judah
1Ch 19:13 in *b* of our people and in
19:13 in *b* of the cities of our
2Ch 16:9 strength in *b* of those whose
20:17 of Jehovah in your *b*
34:21 in my own *b* and in
34:21 in *b* of what is left in
Ne 5:19 have done in *b* of this people
11:23 of the king in *b* of them
Es 4:16 fast in my *b* and neither eat
8:8 write in *b* of the Jews
Job 2:4 said: Skin in *b* of skin, and
2:4 he will give in *b* of his soul
6:22 make a present in my *b*
42:8 sacrifice in your own *b*
42:10 in *b* of his companions
Ps 72:15 in his *b* let prayer be made
138:8 complete what is in my *b*
Pr 6:26 *b* of a woman prostitute one
9:12 become wise in your own *b*
Isa 8:19 in *b* of living persons
11:4 reproof in *b* of the meek
22:14 atoned for in your *b* until
30:6 *b* of the people they will
37:4 prayer in *b* of the remnant
Jer 7:16 pray in *b* of this people
7:16 in their *b* an entreating cry
11:14 do not pray in *b* of this
11:14 in their *b* an entreating cry
14:11 pray in *b* of this people
21:2 inquire in our *b* of Jehovah
29:7 and pray in its *b* to Jehovah
Jer 37:3 in our *b* to Jehovah our God
42:2 pray in our *b* to Jehovah
42:2 *b* of all this remnant, for
42:20 Pray in our *b* to Jehovah
Eze 13:5 in *b* of the house of Israel
22:30 before me in *b* of the land
45:17 *b* of the house of Israel
45:22, 22 own *b* and in *b* of all
Da 12:1 *b* of the sons of your people
Hag 1:9 one in *b* of his own house
Zec 11:7 in your *b*, O afflicted ones
Mt 26:28 be poured out in *b* of many
Mr 1:44 offer in *b* of your cleansing
14:24 be poured out in *b* of many
Lu 22:19 is to be given in your *b*
22:20 to be poured out in your *b*
Joh 6:51 my flesh in *b* of the life of
10:11 his soul in *b* of the sheep
10:15 my soul in *b* of the sheep
11:50 die in *b* of the people and
13:37 surrender my soul in your *b*
13:38 surrender your soul in my *b*
15:13 soul in *b* of his friends
17:19 myself in their *b*, that
18:14 to die in *b* of the people
Ac 5:41 dishonored in *b* of his name
26:1 to speak in *b* of yourself
Ro 9:3 in *b* of my brothers, my
15:8 circumcised in *b* of God's
1Co 11:24 my body which is in your *b*
2Co 1:11 given by many in our *b* for
12:8 In this *b* I three times
Eph 3:1 in *b* of you, the people of
3:13 tribulations . . . in your *b*
6:18 in *b* of all the holy ones
Php 1:29 was given in *b* of Christ
1:29 but also to suffer in his *b*
4:10 your thinking in my *b*
Col 1:7 of the Christ on our *b*
1:24 on *b* of his body, which is
2:1 in *b* of you and of those at
4:12 exerting himself in your *b*
4:13 to great effort in *b* of you
1Th 3:2 in *b* of your faith
Heb 5:1 is appointed in *b* of men over
6:20 has entered in our *b*, Jesus
3Jo 7 it was in *b* of his name that

Behave
Ex 23:21 Do not *b* rebelliously against
Le 6:2 *b* unfaithfully toward Jehovah
De 1:26 you began to *b* rebelliously
1:43 to *b* rebelliously against
17:12 *b* with presumptuousness in
1Sa 1:14 How long will you *b* drunk?
19:24 *b*, he also, like a prophet
21:15 this one to *b* crazy by me
Ps 105:25 *b* cunningly against his
106:43 *b* rebelliously in their
119:100 than older men I *b*
119:104 I *b* with understanding
Jer 9:17 *B* with understanding, you
Eze 5:6 to *b* rebelliously against my
1Co 13:5 does not *b* indecently, does
Php 1:27 *b* in a manner worthy of the
2Th 3:7 did not *b* disorderly among

Behaved
Le 26:40 *b* unfaithfully toward me
De 9:23 you *b* rebelliously against
1Sa 18:10 Saul . . . *b* like a prophet
2Ch 12:2 *b* unfaithfully toward
Ps 106:7 *b* rebelliously at the sea
107:11 *b* rebelliously against the
Isa 1:3 have not *b* understandingly
Jer 10:14 man has *b* so unreasoningly
10:21 have *b* unreasoningly, and
51:17 man has *b* so unreasoningly
La 3:42 and we have *b* rebelliously
Eze 39:23 they *b* unfaithfully toward
Ac 23:1 I have *b* before God with a

Behaves
Le 5:15 a soul *b* unfaithfully in that
Jos 1:18 Any man that *b* rebelliously

Behaving
Ex 9:17 *b* haughtily against my people
1Sa 19:20 they began *b* like prophets
19:21 they began *b* like prophets
19:21 they began *b* like prophets
19:23 *b* like a prophet until he
21:14 you see a man *b* crazy
1Ki 18:29 they continued *b* as prophets
Isa 3:8 *b* rebelliously in the eyes
Jer 29:26 and *b* like a prophet
Jer 29:27 *b* as a prophet to you people
1Co 7:36 he is *b* improperly toward

Behavior
De 9:7 proved rebellious in your *b*
9:24 rebellious in *b* with Jehovah
31:27 rebellious in *b* toward
Jg 2:19 and their stubborn *b*
Job 17:2 amid their rebellious *b* my
Mt 16:27 each one according to his *b*
Tit 2:3 aged women be reverent in *b*

Beheaded
Mt 14:10 and had John *b* in the prison
Mr 6:16 The John that I *b*, this one
6:27 and *b* him in the prison
Lu 9:9 Herod said: John I *b*

Beheld
Job 15:17 I have *b*, so let me relate
24:1 have not *b* his days
Ps 58:10 he has *b* the vengeance
63:2 *b* you in the holy place
Pr 22:29 *b* a man skillful in his work
29:20 *b* a man hasty with his
Isa 57:8 The male organ you *b*
Da 2:26 dream that I *b*, and its
2:41 *b* the feet and the toes to be
2:41 *b* the iron mixed with moist
2:43 *b* iron mixed with moist clay
2:45 *b* that out of the mountain
4:5 dream that I *b*, and it began
4:9 dream that I have *b* and its
4:18 dream . . . Nebuchadnezzar, *b*
4:20 tree that you *b*, that grew
4:23 king *b* a watcher, even a holy
7:1 Daniel himself *b* a dream and
Mr 5:15 *b* the demon-possessed man
5:38 he *b* the noisy confusion and
16:4 they *b* that the stone had
Lu 5:27 *b* a tax collector named Levi
23:48 *b* the things that occurred
24:12 he *b* the bandages alone
24:37 imagining they *b* a spirit
Joh 1:29 *b* Jesus coming toward him
6:19 *b* Jesus walking upon the sea
11:45 *b* what he did put faith in
20:1 *b* the stone already taken
20:5 *b* the bandages lying, yet
21:9 *b* lying there a charcoal fire
Ac 1:11 have *b* him going into the sky
4:13 *b* the outspokenness of Peter
10:11 *b* heaven opened and some
22:9 *b*, indeed, the light but did
28:6 *b* nothing hurtful happen
Heb 11:1 of realities though not *b*
11:3 what is *b* has come to be out
11:7 warning of things not yet *b*
1Jo 4:12 no time has anyone *b* God
4:14 *b* and are bearing witness
Re 11:12 and their enemies *b* them

Behemoth
Job 40:15 *B* that I have made as well

Behind*
Ge 7:16 Jehovah shut the door *b* him
19:6 but he shut the door *b* him
19:17 Do not look *b* you and do not
19:26 to look around from *b* him
Ne 9:26 casting your law *b* their back
Ps 139:5 *B* and before, you have
Isa 30:21 hear a word *b* you saying
37:22 *B* you the daughter of
Eze 23:35 to cast me *b* your back
Joe 2:3 and *b* it a flame consumes
2:3 *b* it is a desolate wilderness
Mt 16:23 to Peter: Get *b* me, Satan!
21:17 And leaving them *b* he went
Mr 8:33 Get *b* me, Satan, because you
13:16 return to the things *b* to
Lu 5:28 leaving everything *b* he rose
9:62 looks at the things *b* is well
15:4 leave the ninety-nine *b* in
17:31 not return to the things *b*
Joh 1:15 one coming *b* me has advanced
1:27 the one coming *b* me, but the
1:30 *B* me there comes a man who
6:66 went off to the things *b*
Php 3:13 Forgetting the things *b* and
Re 1:10 I heard *b* me a strong voice
4:6 full of eyes in front and *b*

Behold
Ge 27:39 *B*, away from the fertile
Nu 23:9 And from the hills I *b* them
23:24 *B*, a people will get up like

Nu 24:17 I shall *b* him, but not near
De 10:14 *B*, to Jehovah your God belong
Job 7:8 him that sees me will not *b*
19:26 I shall *b* God
19:27 even I shall *b* for myself
20:9 no more will his place *b*
23:9 but I cannot *b* him
24:15 Saying, No eye will *b* me
34:29 his face, who can *b* him
34:32 I *b* nothing, instruct me
35:5 *b* the clouds, that they are
35:13 Almighty himself does not *b*
35:14 you say you do not *b* him
36:26 *B!* God is more exalted than
Ps 11:4 His own eyes *b*, his own
11:7 the ones that will *b* his face
17:2 your own eyes *b* uprightness
17:15 I shall *b* your face
27:4 *b* the pleasantness of Jehovah
46:8 *b* the activities of Jehovah
58:8 will certainly not *b* the sun
Pr 24:32 I proceeded to *b*, I myself
Ca 6:13 come back, that we may *b* you
6:13 people *b* in the Shulammite
Isa 26:11 but they do not *b* it
26:11 *b* and be ashamed at the
33:17 is what your eyes will *b*
33:20 *B* Zion, the town of our
48:6 You have heard. *B* it all
Mt 11:7 out into the wilderness to *b*
13:16 your eyes because they *b*
18:10 *b* the face of my Father who
24:2 Do you not *b* all these things?
Mr 3:11 whenever they would *b* him
13:2 you *b* these great buildings
Lu 7:24 out into the wilderness to *b*
7:44 Do you *b* this woman?
8:16 stepping in may *b* the light
10:18 *b* Satan already fallen like
10:23 eyes that *b* the things you
11:33 stepping in may *b* the light
24:39 just as you *b* that I have
Joh 6:62 *b* the Son of man ascending
7:3 also may *b* the works you do
14:19 world will *b* me no more
14:19 but you will *b* me, because
16:10 you will *b* me no longer
16:16 you will *b* me no longer
16:17 you will not *b* me, and
16:19 you will not *b* me, and
17:24 *b* my glory that you have
Ac 3:16 whom you *b* and know, and
7:56 I *b* the heavens opened up
13:41 *B* it, you scorners, and
17:22 I *b* that in all things you
19:26 you *b* and hear how not only
20:38 going to *b* his face no more
21:20 You *b*, brother, how many
Ro 7:23 *b* in my members another law
1Co 1:26 For you *b* his calling of you
Heb 2:9 we *b* Jesus, who has been
7:4 *B*, then, how great this man
10:25 you *b* the day drawing near
Jas 2:22 You *b* that his faith worked

Beholding
Eze 21:29 *b* for you an unreality
Da 2:31 *b*, and, look! a certain
3:25 I am *b* four able-bodied men
3:27 *b* these able-bodied men, that
4:10 *b*, and, look! a tree in the
4:13 *b* in the visions of my head
5:5 king was *b* the back of the
5:23 *b* nothing or hearing nothing
7:2 *b* in my visions during the
7:4 *b* until its wings were plucked
7:6 *b*, and, see there! another
7:7 *b* in the visions of the night
7:9 *b* until there were thrones
7:11 *b* at that time because of the
7:11 *b* until the beast was killed
7:13 I kept on *b* in the visions of
7:21 *b* when that very horn made
Mt 13:17 to see the things you are *b*
Lu 10:23 behold the things you are *b*
10:24 to see the things you are *b*
21:6 these things that you are *b*
23:49 were standing *b* these things
Joh 6:2 *b* the signs he was performing
Ac 8:13 *b* great signs and powerful
9:7 voice, but not *b* any man
17:16 *b* that the city was full of
21:27 on *b* him in the temple began
25:24 *b* this man concerning whom

Col 2:5 rejoicing and *b* your good
Re 11:11 fear fell upon those *b* them

Beholds
Nu 12:8 appearance of Jehovah . . . he *b*
Job 8:17 A house of stones he *b*
17:15 my hope—who is it that *b*
Joh 5:19 what he *b* the Father doing
6:40 everyone that *b* the Son and
10:12 *b* the wolf coming and
12:45 and he that *b* me
12:45 *b* also him that sent me
14:17 it neither *b* it nor knows
1Jo 3:17 *b* his brother having need

Being*
Ac 17:29 the Divine *B* is like gold or
Heb 1:3 representation of his very *b*

Bel
Isa 46:1 *B* has bent down, Nebo is
Jer 50:2 *B* has been put to shame
51:44 attention upon *B* in Babylon

Bela
Ge 14:2 *B* (that is to say, Zoar)
14:8 on the march . . . king of *B*
36:32 *B* son of Beor proceeded to
36:33 When *B* died, Jobab son of
46:21 sons of Benjamin were *B* and
Nu 26:38 *B* the family of the Belaites
26:40 sons of *B* came to be Ard and
1Ch 1:43 *B* the son of Beor
1:44 Eventually *B* died, and Jobab
5:8 and *B* the son of Azaz
7:6 sons of Benjamin were *B* and
7:7 sons of *B* were Ezbon and Uzzi
8:1 Benjamin . . . father to *B* his
8:3 *B* came to have sons, Addar

Belaites
Nu 26:38 Of Bela the family of the *B*

Belial
2Co 6:15 harmony . . . Christ and *B*

Belief
Ac 24:24 on the *b* in Christ Jesus

Believe
Ge 45:26 because he did not *b* them
Ex 4:1 suppose they do not *b* me and
4:5 *b* that Jehovah . . . appeared to
4:8 if they will not *b* you and
4:8 *b* the voice of the later sign
4:9 if they will not *b* even these
Job 9:16 not *b* that he would give ear
15:22 He does not *b* that he will
29:24 they would not *b* it
39:24 it does not *b* that it is the
Pr 26:25 voice gracious, do not *b* in
Jer 40:14 Gedaliah . . . did not *b* them
Hab 1:5 which you people will not *b*
Mt 21:25 Why, then, did you not *b*
21:32 but you did not *b* him
21:32 regret afterwards so as to *b*
24:23 or, There! do not *b* it
24:26 do not *b* it
27:42 and we will *b* on him
Mr 9:42 these little ones that *b*
11:31 you did not *b* him
13:21 There he is, do not *b* it
15:32 that we may see and *b*
Lu 1:20 you did not *b* my words
8:12 may not *b* and be saved
8:13 they *b* for a season, but in a
20:5 Why is it you did not *b* him?
22:67 you would not *b* it at all
24:11 they would not *b* the women
24:25 and slow in heart to *b* on
Joh 1:7 people of all sorts might *b*
1:50 do you *b?* You will see
3:12 and yet you do not *b*, how
3:12 how will you *b* if I tell you
4:21 *B* me, woman, The hour is
4:42 not *b* any longer on account
4:48 you will by no means *b*
5:38 dispatched you do not *b*
5:44 How can you *b*, when you are
5:46 you would *b* me, for that one
5:47 if you do not *b* the writings
5:47 how will you *b* my sayings?
6:30 for us to see it and *b* you
6:36 seen me and yet do not *b*
6:64 some of you that do not *b*
8:24 if you do not *b* that I am he
8:45 the truth, you do not *b* me
8:46 why is it you do not *b* me?

Joh 9:18 Jews did not *b* concerning
10:25 and yet you do not *b*
10:26 you do not *b*, because you
10:37 do not *b* me
10:38 though you do not *b* me
10:38 *b* the works, in order that
11:15 in order for you to *b*
11:26 Do you *b* this?
11:40 *b* you would see the glory
11:42 *b* that you sent me forth
12:39 they were not able to *b*
13:19 you may *b* that I am he
14:10 *b* that I am in union with
14:11 *B* me that I am in union
14:11 *b* on account of the works
14:29 it does occur, you may *b*
16:30 *b* that you came out from
16:31 Do you *b* at present?
17:21 world may *b* that you sent
19:35 order that you also may *b*
20:25 I will certainly not *b*
20:29 who do not see and yet *b*
20:31 *b* that Jesus is the Christ
Ac 9:26 did not *b* he was a disciple
13:41 that you will by no means *b*
14:2 Jews that did not *b* stirred
15:7 word of the good news and *b*
16:31 *B* on the Lord Jesus and you
18:8 began to *b* and be baptized
19:4 *b* in the one coming after him
24:14 I *b* all the things set forth
26:27 King Agrippa, *b* the Prophets
26:27 Prophets? I know you *b*
27:25 I *b* God that it will be
28:24 began to *b* the things said
28:24 others would not *b*
Ro 4:24 we *b* on him who raised Jesus
6:8 we *b* that we shall also live
1Co 11:18 and in some measure I *b* it
2Th 2:12 they did not *b* the truth but
2Ti 3:14 and were persuaded to *b*
Heb 11:6 *b* that he is and that he
Jas 2:19 You *b* there is one God, do
2:19 yet the demons *b* and shudder
1Jo 4:1 do not *b* every inspired

Believed
Ex 4:31 At this the people *b*
1Sa 27:12 Achish *b* David, saying to
La 4:12 not *b* That the adversary and
Mt 21:32 and the harlots *b* him, and
Lu 1:45 Happy too is she that *b*
Joh 2:22 *b* the Scripture and the
4:41 *b* on account of what he said
4:50 man *b* the word that Jesus
4:53 and his whole household *b*
5:46 if you *b* Moses you would
6:69 *b* and come to know that you
8:31 to the Jews that had *b* him
11:27 *b* that you are the Christ
16:27 *b* that I came out as the
17:8 *b* that you sent me forth
20:8 went in, and he saw and *b*
20:29 you have seen me have you *b*
Ac 4:4 had listened to the speech *b*
4:32 those who had *b* had one heart
8:12 when they *b* Philip, who was
11:17 have *b* upon the Lord Jesus
15:5 Pharisees that had *b* rose up
16:34 now that he had *b* God
18:27 had *b* on account of God's
1Co 15:11 preaching and so you have *b*
Eph 1:13 after you *b*, you were sealed
1Ti 3:16 was *b* upon in the world
2Ti 1:12 I know the one whom I have *b*
Tit 3:8 who have *b* God may keep their
1Jo 4:16 have *b* the love that God has

Believer
Ac 8:13 also became a *b*, and, after
13:12 became a *b*, as he was
18:8 Crispus . . . became a *b* in the

Believers
Ac 2:44 those who became *b* were
5:14 *b* in the Lord kept on being
9:42 many became *b* on the Lord
11:21 great number that became *b*
13:48 rightly disposed . . . *b*
14:1 Jews and Greeks became *b*
14:23 in whom they had become *b*
17:4 some of them became *b* and
17:12 many of them became *b*, and
17:33 to him and became *b*
19:2 holy spirit when you became *b*
19:18 *b* would come and confess and

Ac 21:20 thousands of *b* . . . Jews
21:25 the *b* from among the nations
Ro 13:11 the time when we became *b*
1Co 3:5 through whom you became *b*
14:22 sign, not to the *b*, but to
14:22 prophesying is . . . for the *b*
15:2 you became *b* to no purpose
Eph 1:19 his power is toward us *b*
1Th 1:7 to all the *b* in Macedonia
2:10 we proved to be to you *b*
2:13 is also at work in you *b*
1Ti 6:2 are *b* and beloved
1Pe 1:21 through him are *b* in God
2:7 precious, because you are *b*

Believes
Joh 5:24 that hears my word and *b*
6:47 He that *b* has everlasting
Ac 13:39 who *b* is declared guiltless
1Co 13:7 *b* all things, hopes all

Believing
Lu 24:41 not *b* for sheer joy and
Joh 3:15 everyone *b* in him may have
6:64 who were the ones not *b*
20:27 but become *b*
20:31 *b*, you may have life by
Ac 16:1 the son of a *b* Jewish woman
19:9 not *b*, speaking injuriously
22:19 used to imprison . . . those *b*
Ro 15:13 joy and peace by your *b*, that
1Co 1:21 is preached to save those *b*
2Th 2:11 they may get to *b* the lie
1Ti 5:16 If any *b* woman has widows
6:2 let those having *b* owners not
Tit 1:6 having *b* children that were
1Pe 2:7 but to those not *b*, the
1Jo 5:1 *b* that Jesus is the Christ

Belittle
Job 37:23 righteousness he will not *b*
Heb 12:5 do not *b* the discipline from

Bell
Ex 28:34 *b* of gold and a pomegranate
28:34 *b* of gold and a pomegranate
39:26 a *b* and a pomegranate, a
39:26 a *b* and a pomegranate upon the

Bellies
Ge 41:21 So these came into their *b*
41:21 they had come into their *b*
Ro 16:18 slaves . . . of their own *b*

Belligerent
1Ti 3:3 not *b*, not a lover of money
Tit 3:2 not to be *b*, to be reasonable

Bellows
Jer 6:29 The *b* have been scorched

Bells
Ex 28:33 *b* of gold in between them
39:25 made *b* of pure gold and put
39:25 and put the *b* in between
Zec 14:20 upon the *b* of the horse

Belly
Ge 3:14 Upon your *b* you will go and
25:23 Two nations are in your *b*
25:24 look! twins were in her *b*
30:2 held back the fruit of the *b*
38:27 there were twins in her *b*
Le 11:42 creature that goes upon the *b*
Nu 5:21 fall away, and your *b* swell
5:22 cause your *b* to swell and the
5:27 and her *b* must swell, and her
De 7:13 and bless the fruit of your *b*
28:4 the fruit of your *b* and the
28:11 the fruit of your *b* and the
28:18 the fruit of your *b* and the
28:53 eat the fruit of your *b*
30:9 the fruit of your *b* and the
Jg 3:21 and plunged it into his *b*
3:22 draw the sword out of his *b*
13:5 will become on leaving the *b*
13:7 will become on leaving the *b*
16:17 from my mother's *b*
1Ki 7:20 the *b* that was adjoining the
Job 1:21 I came out of my mother's *b*
3:10 the doors of my mother's *b*
3:11 come forth from the *b* itself
10:19 From the *b* to the burial
15:2 fill his *b* with the east
15:35 *b* itself prepares deceit
19:17 the sons of my mother's *b*
20:15 out from his very *b*
20:20 know no ease in his *b*
Job 20:23 to fill his *b*, He will send
31:15 the One making me in the *b*
31:18 from the *b* of my mother I
32:18 pressure upon me in my *b*
32:19 My *b* is like wine that has
38:29 Out of whose *b* does the ice
40:16 in the tendons of its *b*
Ps 17:14 whose *b* you fill with your
22:9 drawing me forth from the *b*
22:10 From the *b* of my mother you
31:9 weak, my soul and my *b*
44:25 *b* has clung to the very earth
58:3 wandered about from the *b*
71:6 supported myself from the *b*
127:3 fruitage of the *b* is a
132:11 Of the fruitage of your *b*
139:13 in the *b* of my mother
Pr 13:25 *b* of the wicked ones will be
18:8 the innermost parts of the *b*
18:20 his *b* will be satisfied
20:27 the innermost parts of the *b*
20:30 the innermost parts of the *b*
22:18 should keep them in your *b*
26:22 the innermost parts of the *b*
31:2 and what, O son of my *b*, and
Ec 5:15 forth from his mother's *b*
11:5 the *b* of her that is pregnant
Ca 7:2 Your *b* is a heap of wheat
Isa 13:18 fruitage of the *b* they will
44:2 helping you even from the *b*
44:24 Former of you from the *b*
46:3 conveyed by me from the *b*
48:8 transgressor from the *b* you
49:1 called me even from the *b*
49:5 forming me from the *b* as a
49:15 pity the son of her *b*
Jer 1:5 I was forming you in the *b*
Eze 3:3 cause your own *b* to eat, that
Da 2:32 *b* and its thighs were of
Ho 9:11 no pregnant *b* and no
9:16 desirable things of their *b*
12:3 In the *b* he seized his brother
Jon 2:2 Out of the *b* of Sheol I cried
Mic 6:7 the fruitage of my *b* for the
Hab 3:16 my *b* began to be agitated
Mt 12:40 in the *b* of the huge fish
1Co 6:13 Foods for the *b*, and the
6:13 and the *b* for foods; but God
Php 3:19 and their god is their *b*
Re 10:9 it will make your *b* bitter
10:10 my *b* was made bitter

Belong
Ge 32:17 To whom do you *b*, and where
32:17 these ahead of you *b*
38:25 the man to whom these *b*
38:25 to whom these *b*, the seal
40:8 interpretations *b* to God
49:10 to him the obedience . . . *b*
Ex 13:12 The males *b* to Jehovah
Nu 30:6 *b* to a husband, and her vow
36:3 to which they may come to *b*
36:4 to which they may come to *b*
De 10:14 to . . . your God *b* the heavens
18:1 come to *b* to the priests, the
18:2 inheritance should come to *b*
29:29 things concealed *b* to
29:29 things revealed *b* to us and
33:8 *b* to the man loyal to you
Jos 2:13 and all who *b* to them
6:22 the woman and all who *b* to
14:14 come to *b* to Caleb the son
17:1 and Bashan came to *b* to him
17:11 came to *b* to Manasseh in
21:4 to *b* to the sons of Aaron
21:10 *b* to the sons of Aaron out
21:40 the cities that came to *b* to
24:32 it came to *b* to the sons
Jg 14:20 to *b* to a groomsman of his
Ru 1:12 to get to *b* to a husband
2:5 whom does this young woman *b*
1Sa 2:8 to Jehovah *b* earth's supports
9:20 that is desirable of Israel *b*
14:21 to *b* to the Philistines
25:7 shepherds that *b* to you
27:6 Ziklag has come to *b* to the
30:13 To whom do you *b*, and
2Sa 3:12 To whom does the land *b*?
4:2 *b* to the son of Saul, the
9:9 *b* to Saul and to all his house
1Ki 21:1 *b* to Naboth the Jezreelite
2Ki 6:11 who from those who *b* to us
10:6 If you *b* to me, and it is
12:16 came to *b* to the priests
2Ki 24:7 *b* to the king of Egypt from
1Ch 21:3 *b* to my lord as servants
Ne 5:5 and our vineyards *b* to others
Job 12:16 *b* the one making a mistake
Ps 24:1 To Jehovah *b* the earth and
47:9 the shields of the earth *b*
50:12 land and its fullness *b*
68:20 *b* the ways out from death
95:4 the peaks of the mountains *b*
115:16 to Jehovah the heavens *b*
Pr 16:1 *b* the arrangings of the heart
16:11 and scales *b* to Jehovah
Ca 8:12 thousand *b* to you, O Solomon
Isa 44:5 will say: I *b* to Jehovah
Jer 3:23 mountains *b* to falsehood
5:10 for they do not *b* to Jehovah
10:23 his way does not *b*
10:23 It does not *b* to man who
Eze 16:49 happened to *b* to her and her
18:4 All the souls—to me they *b*
18:4 to me they *b*. The soul that
44:30 priests it will come to *b*
45:6 Israel it will come to *b*
46:17 *b* to their own selves
48:21 will *b* to the chieftain
48:22 come to *b* to the chieftain
Da 2:20 mightiness—for they *b* to him
5:23 to whom all your ways *b* you
9:9 God *b* the mercies and the
Ho 3:3 not come to *b* to another man
Ob 20 to the sons of Israel will *b*
Zec 6:14 come to *b* to Helem and to
Mr 9:41 ground that you *b* to Christ
Joh 10:12 sheep do not *b* as his own
Ac 1:7 *b* to you to get knowledge of
27:23 of the God to whom I *b*
Ro 1:6 called to *b* to Jesus Christ
8:9 this one does not *b* to him
9:4 *b* the adoption as sons and the
9:5 to whom the forefathers *b* and
14:8 if we die, we *b* to Jehovah
1Co 1:12 one of you says: I *b* to Paul
3:4 when one says: I *b* to Paul
3:21 for all things *b* to you
3:22 all things *b* to you
3:23 in turn you *b* to Christ
6:19 you do not *b* to yourselves
10:26 to Jehovah *b* the earth and
15:23 those who *b* to the Christ
2Co 1:21 that you and we *b* to Christ
Ga 3:29 if you *b* to Christ, you are
5:24 those who *b* to Christ Jesus
Eph 5:11 works that *b* to the darkness
1Th 5:5 We *b* neither to night nor to
5:8 as for us who *b* to the day
1Ti 1:20 and Alexander *b* to these, and
2Ti 2:19 knows those who *b* to him
Re 19:1 and the power *b* to our God

Belonged
Ge 29:9 sheep that *b* to her father
31:1 taken everything that *b* to
31:1 from what *b* to our father he
31:19 stole the teraphim that *b*
40:5 baker who *b* to the king of
Ex 38:30 the copper grating that *b* to
39:39 grating of copper that *b* to
Nu 16:32 humankind that *b* to Korah
16:33 and all who *b* to them, alive
Jos 6:23 and all who *b* to her, yes
6:25 father and all who *b* to her
17:8 *b* to the sons of Ephraim
Jg 6:11 *b* to Joash the Abi-ezrite
18:28 plain that *b* to Beth-rehob
Ru 4:3 tract of field that *b* to our
4:9 buy all that *b* to Elimelech
4:9 and all that *b* to Chilion and
1Sa 20:40 attendant that *b* to him
21:7 shepherds that *b* to Saul
24:4 coat that *b* to Saul
24:5 coat that *b* to Saul
2Sa 2:8 army that had *b* to Saul
23:8 mighty men that *b* to David
1Ki 1:8 mighty men that *b* to David
15:27 Gibbethon, which *b* to the
16:15 which *b* to the Philistines
2Ki 11:10 that had *b* to King David
1Ch 11:10 mighty men that *b* to David
11:11 mighty men that *b* to David
12:20 that *b* to Manasseh
27:31 goods that *b* to King David
2Ch 1:6 copper altar that *b* to the
8:10 deputies that *b* to King
12:4 cities that *b* to Judah and

2Ch 23:9 that had *b* to King David
26:23 field that *b* to the kings
33:11 army that *b* to the king of
34:33 lands that *b* to the sons of
Es 1:9 house that *b* to King Ahasuerus
9:3 the business that *b* to the king
Jer 52:17 *b* to the house of Jehovah
Eze 41:6 the wall that *b* to the house
41:9 that *b* to the side chamber
41:9 chambers that *b* to the house
41:24 leaves *b* to the doors
42:3 that *b* to the inner courtyard
42:3 that *b* to the outer courtyard
Zec 7:3 who *b* to the house of Jehovah
Ac 9:2 he found who *b* to The Way

Belonging
Ex 12:7 doorway *b* to the houses in
14:28 *b* to all of Pharaoh's
Nu 31:42 half *b* to the sons of Israel
31:42 *b* to the men who waged war
31:47 half *b* to the sons of Israel
32:33 land *b* to its cities in the
De 33:2 right hand warriors *b* to them
Jos 13:3 as *b* to the Canaanites
16:2 from Bethel *b* to Luz and
22:11 side *b* to the sons of Israel
Ru 2:3 tract of the field *b* to Boaz
1Sa 6:18 *b* to the five axis lords
9:3 the she-asses *b* to Kish the
13:22 *b* to Saul and to Jonathan
14:16 the watchmen *b* to Saul in
17:8 and you servants *b* to Saul
17:46 exists a God *b* to Israel
2Sa 2:15 twelve *b* to Benjamin and
9:10 *b* to the grandson of your
15:36 Ahimaaz *b* to Zadok and
15:36 Jonathan *b* to Abiathar
1Ki 7:8 the house *b* to the Porch
7:21 pillars *b* to the porch of the
1Ch 5:13 brothers *b* to the house of
6:54 the sons of Aaron *b* to the
8:6 *b* to the inhabitants of Geba
8:13 *b* to the inhabitants of
25:9 first *b* to Asaph for Joseph
26:8 sixty-two *b* to Obed-edom
26:21 of the Gershonite *b* to Ladan
26:21 paternal houses *b* to Ladan
2Ch 2:13 *b* to Hiram-abi
4:9 the doors *b* to the enclosure
5:12 singers *b* to all of them
9:21 ships *b* to the king were
35:5 house *b* to the Levites
Ne 3:7 *b* to the throne of the
Job 12:6 *B* to one who has brought a
Ps 96:8 the glory *b* to his name
Pr 1:14 just one bag *b* to all of us
Ec 5:12 plenty *b* to the rich one is
Ca 3:7 couch, the one *b* to Solomon
Isa 2:12 day *b* to Jehovah of armies
17:14 lot *b* to those plundering
44:5 upon his hand: *B* to Jehovah
44:21 You are a servant *b* to me
49:5 as a servant *b* to him, has
Jer 6:25 the sword *b* to the enemy
12:12 the sword *b* to Jehovah is
26:16 no judgment of death *b* to
51:6 of vengeance *b* to Jehovah
La 1:10 the congregation *b* to you
1:15 winepress *b* to the virgin
Eze 10:8 was seen *b* to the cherubs
13:18 the ones *b* to my people
13:18 souls *b* to you the ones that
23:20 concubines *b* to those whose
30:3 a day *b* to Jehovah is near
45:19 ledge *b* to the altar and
46:19 those *b* to the priests
Da 6:15 law *b* to the Medes and the
11:14 robbers *b* to your people
Mic 4:8 the kingdom *b* to the daughter
Hab 1:6 of residences not *b* to it
Zec 14:1 a day coming, *b* to Jehovah
14:7 is known as *b* to Jehovah
14:21 something holy *b* to Jehovah
Lu 12:33 Sell the things *b* to you and
Ro 12:5 members *b* individually to one
13:12 off the works *b* to darkness
Ga 4:3 things *b* to the world
4:28 children *b* to the promise
Eph 4:25 members *b* to one another
Heb 11:16 that is, one *b* to heaven
1Pe 2:2 milk *b* to the word, that

Belongings
Mt 19:21 sell your *b* and give to the
Mt 24:47 appoint him over all his *b*
25:14 and committed to them his *b*
Lu 8:3 ministering . . . from their *b*
11:21 his *b* continue in peace
12:44 appoint him over all his *b*
14:33 say good-bye to all his *b*
19:8 half of my *b*, Lord, I am
1Co 13:3 if I give all my *b* to feed
Heb 10:34 the plundering of your *b*

Belongs
Ex 9:4 not a thing of all that *b* to
9:29 that the earth *b* to Jehovah
19:5 the whole earth *b* to me
20:17 that *b* to your fellowman
28:36 seal, Holiness *b* to Jehovah
39:30 a seal: Holiness *b* to Jehovah
Le 2:3 *b* to Aaron and his sons
2:10 *b* to Aaron and his sons, as
3:16 All the fat *b* to Jehovah
7:9 *b* to the priest who presents
14:13 guilt offering *b* to the
14:35 one to whom the house *b* must
27:24 possession of the land *b*
27:26 or sheep, it *b* to Jehovah
27:30 fruit . . . *b* to Jehovah
Nu 1:50 everything that *b* to it
5:8 *b* to the priest, except the
16:5 make known who *b* to him and
16:26 not touch anything that *b* to
16:30 everything that *b* to them
18:11 *b* to you: the contribution
De 1:17 for the judgment *b* to God
5:21 that *b* to your fellowman
21:17 firstborn's position *b* to
Jos 6:17 everything . . . *b* to Jehovah
7:15 he and all that *b* to him
13:4 which *b* to the Sidonians as
Jg 6:25 the bull that *b* to your father
19:14 Gibeah, which *b* to Benjamin
20:4 Gibeah, which *b* to Benjamin
1Sa 17:1 at Socoh, which *b* to Judah
17:47 to Jehovah *b* the battle, and
25:21 everything that *b* to this
25:21 all that *b* to him showed up
30:14 that which *b* to Judah and
2Sa 3:8 dog's head that *b* to Judah
16:4 that *b* to Mephibosheth
20:11 whoever *b* to David, let him
1Ki 1:33 the she-mule that *b* to me
17:9 Zarephath, which *b* to Sidon
19:3 Beer-sheba, which *b* to Judah
20:4 I am with all that *b* to me
22:3 Ramoth-gilead *b* to us
2Ki 8:6 Return all that *b* to her and
14:11 Beth-shemesh . . . *b* to Judah
1Ch 13:6 which *b* to Judah, to bring
29:16 and to you it all *b*
2Ch 25:21 Beth-shemesh . . . *b* to Judah
Ne 2:8 the park that *b* to the king
2:8 Castle that *b* to the house
3:25 *b* to the Courtyard of the
Ps 3:8 Salvation *b* to Jehovah
22:28 For the kingship *b* to Jehovah
25:14 *b* to those fearful of him
50:10 to me *b* every wild animal
60:7 Gilead *b* to me and Manasseh
60:7 and Manasseh *b* to me
62:11 That strength *b* to God
62:12 loving-kindness *b* to you
74:16 To you the day *b*; also, to
74:16 also, to you the night *b*
89:18 For our shield *b* to Jehovah
89:18 king *b* to the Holy One of
95:5 To whom the sea . . . *b*
108:8 Gilead *b* to me, Manasseh
108:8 Manasseh *b* to me
115:1 To us *b* nothing, O Jehovah
115:1 Jehovah, to us *b* nothing
119:165 Abundant peace *b* to those
146:3 man, to whom no salvation *b*
149:9 splendor *b* to all his loyal
Pr 21:31 but salvation *b* to Jehovah
Ca 6:9 there is who *b* to her mother
8:12 My vineyard, which *b* to me
Jer 26:11 the judgment of death *b*
32:7 right of repurchase *b* to you
46:10 day *b* to the Sovereign Lord
Eze 11:15 To us it *b*; the land has
29:3 My Nile River *b* to me
29:9 To me the Nile River *b*
40:40 *b* to the porch of the gate
48:22 what *b* to the chieftain it
Da 9:7 to you, O Jehovah there *b* the
Da 9:8 to us *b* the shame of face, to
Jon 2:9 Salvation *b* to Jehovah
Na 2:11 cave that *b* to the maned
Zec 14:20 Holiness *b* to Jehovah
Mt 5:3 kingdom of the heavens *b* to
5:10 kingdom of the heavens *b* to
19:14 kingdom of the heavens *b* to
20:23 *b* to those for whom it has
Mr 10:14 for the kingdom of God *b* to
10:40 it *b* to those for whom it
Lu 18:16 the kingdom of God *b* to
Joh 1:14 *b* to an only-begotten son
7:16 but *b* to him that sent me
14:24 *b* to the Father who sent me
Ac 21:11 man to whom this girdle *b*
1Co 3:23 Christ, in turn, *b* to God
2Co 10:7 that he *b* to Christ, let him
10:7 just as he *b* to Christ, so do
Eph 4:13 *b* to the fullness of the
4:18 the life that *b* to God
Php 1:25 the joy that *b* to your faith
Col 2:11 circumcision that *b* to the
2:17 the reality *b* to the Christ
Heb 5:14 solid food *b* to mature
Jas 1:25 law that *b* to freedom and
3:13 a mildness that *b* to wisdom

Beloved
De 33:12 Let the *b* one of Jehovah
Ps 45:*super* A song of the *b* women
60:5 your *b* ones may be rescued
108:6 your *b* ones may be rescued
127:2 sleep even to his *b* one
Ca 7:6 how pleasant you are, O *b* girl
Isa 5:1 to my *b* one a song of my
5:1 vineyard that my *b* one came
Jer 11:15 What business does my *b* one
12:7 I have given the *b* one my
Mt 3:17 This is my Son, the *b*, whom
12:18 servant whom I chose, my *b*
17:5 This is my Son, the *b*, whom
Mr 1:11 You are my Son, the *b*; I have
9:7 This is my Son, the *b*; listen
12:6 One more he had, a *b* son
Lu 3:22 You are my Son, the *b*; I have
20:13 I will send my son the *b*
Ro 1:7 are in Rome as God's *b* ones
9:25, 25 and her who was not *b* *b*
11:28 *b* for the sake of their
12:19 Do not avenge yourselves, *b*
16:5 Greet my *b* Epaenetus, who is
16:8 Ampliatus my *b* in the Lord
16:9 Greet . . . my *b* Stachys
16:12 Persis our *b* one, for she
1Co 4:14 you as my *b* children
4:17 is my *b* and faithful child
10:14 my *b* ones, flee from
15:58 my *b* brothers, become
2Co 7:1 *b* ones, let us cleanse
12:19 *b* ones, all things are for
Eph 5:1 of God, as *b* children
6:21 a *b* brother and faithful
Php 2:12 my *b* ones, in the way that
4:1 my brothers *b* and longed for
4:1 in the Lord, *b* ones
Col 1:7 Epaphras our *b* fellow slave
4:7 Tychicus, my *b* brother and
4:9 my faithful and *b* brother
4:14 Luke the *b* physician sends
1Th 2:8 because you became *b* to us
1Ti 6:2 are believers and *b*
2Ti 1:2 to Timothy, a *b* child
Phm 1 Philemon, our *b* one and fellow
16 as a brother *b*, especially so
Heb 6:9 *b* ones, we are convinced of
Jas 1:16 not be misled, my *b* brothers
1:19 Know this, my *b* brothers
2:5 Listen, my *b* brothers. God
1Pe 2:11 *B*, I exhort you as aliens
4:12 *B* ones, do not be puzzled
2Pe 1:17 This is my son, my *b*, whom
3:1 *B* ones, this is now the second
3:8 escaping your notice, *b* ones
3:14 *b* ones, since you are
3:15 just as our *b* brother Paul
3:17 *b* ones, having this advance
1Jo 2:7 *B* ones, I am writing you, not
3:2 *B* ones, now we are children
3:21 *B* ones, if our hearts do
4:1 *B* ones, do not believe every
4:7 *B* ones, let us continue loving
4:11 *B* ones, if this is how God
3Jo 1 Gaius, the *b*, whom I truly love
2 *B* one, I pray that in all things

3Jo 5 *B* one, you are doing a faithful
11 *B* one, be an imitator, not of
Jude 3 *B* ones, though I was making
17 *b* ones, call to mind the
20 *b* ones, by building up
Re 20:9 holy ones and the *b* city

Below
Ge 49:25 watery deep lying down *b*
Ex 28:27 from *b*, on its forefront
30:4 *b* its border upon two of its
37:27 *b* its border upon two of its
39:20 pieces of the ephod from *b*
De 33:13 the watery deep lying down *b*
Jg 7:8 down *b* him in the low plain
1Ki 4:12 beside Zarethan *b* Jezreel
7:24 down *b* its brim all around
7:32 were down *b* the sidewalls
Pr 15:24 turn away from Sheol down *b*
Jer 31:37 earth *b* could be searched
Eze 31:14 to the land down *b*, in the
31:16 *b* all the trees of Eden
31:18 to the land down *b*
32:18 to the land down *b*
32:24 to the land down *b*, those
42:9 *b* these dining rooms the
Am 2:9 fruitage above and his roots *b*
Mr 14:66 while Peter was *b* in the
Joh 8:23 You are from the realms *b*
Ac 2:19 and signs on earth *b*, blood
Jude 12 rocks hidden *b* water in your

Belshazzar
Da 5:1 As regards *B* the king, he made
5:2 *B*, under the influence of the
5:9 *B* was very much frightened
5:22 *B*, you have not humbled your
5:29 *B* commanded, and they clothed
5:30 *B* the Chaldean king was
7:1 first year of *B* the king of
8:1 kingship of *B* the king, there

Belt
1Sa 18:4 sword and his bow and his *b*
2Sa 18:11 ten pieces of silver and a *b*
1Ki 2:5 put the blood of war on his *b*
2Ki 1:8 a leather *b* girded about his
3:21 many as were girding on a *b*
Job 12:18 he binds a *b* upon their hips
Isa 3:24 instead of a *b*, a rope
5:27 *b* around their loins will
11:5 prove to be the *b* of his hips
11:5 faithfulness the *b* of his
Jer 13:1 get for yourself a linen *b*
13:2 got the *b* in accord with the
13:4 Take the *b* that you got, that
13:6 take from there the *b* that
13:7 took the *b* from the place
13:7 look! the *b* had been ruined
13:10 become just like this *b*
13:11 *b* clings to the hips of a man

Belteshazzar
Da 1:7 to Daniel the name of *B*
2:26 Daniel, whose name was *B*
4:8 Daniel, whose name is *B*
4:9 O *B* the chief of the
4:18 O *B*, say what the
4:19 name is *B*, was astonished
4:19 *B*, do not let the dream and
4:19 *B* was answering and saying
5:12 the king himself named *B*
10:1 whose name was called *B*

Belts
Pr 31:24 and *b* she has given to the
Eze 23:15 girded with *b* on their hips

Bemoaning
Jer 31:18 heard Ephraim *b* himself

Ben
1Ch 15:18 Zechariah, *B* and Jaaziel and

Benaiah
2Sa 8:18 *B* the son of Jehoiada was
20:23 *B* the son of Jehoiada was
23:20 *B* the son of Jehoiada the
23:22 *B* the son of Jehoiada did
23:30 *B* a Pirathonite, Hiddai of
1Ki 1:8 *B* the son of Jehoiada and
1:10 *B* and the mighty men and
1:26 *B* the son of Jehoiada and
1:32 *B* the son of Jehoiada. So they
1:36 *B* the son of Jehoiada
1:38 *B* the son of Jehoiada and the
1:44 *B* the son of Jehoiada and the
2:25 *B* the son of Jehoiada; and
1Ki 2:29 Solomon sent *B* the son of
2:30 *B* came to the tent of
2:30 *B* brought word back to the
2:34 *B* the son of Jehoiada went
2:35 *B* the son of Jehoiada in
2:46 the king commanded *B* the son
4:4 *B* the son of Jehoiada was
1Ch 4:36 and Adiel and Jesimiel and *B*
11:22 *B* the son of Jehoiada, the
11:24 *B* the son of Jehoiada did
11:31 *B* the Pirathonite
15:18 Eliab and *B* and Maaseiah
15:20 and *B* with stringed
15:24 *B* and Eliezer the priests
16:5 *B* and Obed-edom and Jeiel
16:6 *B* and Jahaziel the priests
18:17 *B* the son of Jehoiada was
27:5 *B* the son of Jehoiada the
27:6 *B* was a mighty man of the
27:14 *B* the Pirathonite of the
27:34 Jehoiada the son of *B* and
2Ch 20:14 *B* the son of Jeiel the
31:13 and *B* were commissioners
Ezr 10:25 of the sons of Parosh . . . *B*
10:30 sons of Pahath-moab . . . *B*
10:35 *B*, Bedeiah, Cheluhi
10:43 the sons of Nebo . . . *B*
Eze 11:1 and Pelatiah the son of *B*
11:13 Pelatiah the son of *B*

Ben-ammi
Ge 19:38 then called his name *B*

Benches
Mt 21:12 the *b* of those selling doves
Mr 11:15 the *b* of those selling doves

Bend
Ge 49:15 he will *b* down his shoulder
Nu 20:17 not *b* toward the right or
Jg 11:35 You have indeed made me *b*
2Sa 19:14 *b* the heart of all the men
22:10 *b* the heavens down and to
Ps 7:12 His bow he will certainly *b*
11:2 wicked ones . . . *b* the bow
18:9 he proceeded to *b* the heavens
22:29 to the dust will *b* down
58:7 *b* the bow for his arrows as
144:5 Jehovah, *b* down your heavens
Pr 17:23 to *b* the paths of judgment
Isa 45:23 to me every knee will *b*
46:2 they must each alike *b* down
60:14 *b* down at the very soles of
Jer 9:3 *b* their tongue as their bow
Ro 14:11 to me every knee will *b*
Eph 3:14 I *b* my knees to the Father
Php 2:10 every knee should *b* of those

Bended
Mr 1:40 entreating him even on *b* knee

Bending
1Ki 8:54 from *b* down upon his knees
1Ch 5:18 *b* the bow and trained in war
8:40 mighty men, *b* the bow, and
2Ch 14:8 *b* the bow were two hundred
29:30 *b* down and prostrating
Mr 15:19 *b* their knees, they would do
Ac 7:60 *b* his knees, he cried out
9:40 *b* his knees, he prayed, and

Bends
Jg 7:5 one that *b* down upon his knees
Job 40:17 It *b* down its tail like a

Beneath*
Ge 1:7 should be *b* the expanse and the
Isa 51:6 and look at the earth *b*
La 3:34 crushing *b* one's feet all the
Mt 22:44 put your enemies *b* your feet
Mr 6:11 dirt that is *b* your feet for
12:36 put your enemies *b* your feet
Re 12:1 moon was *b* her feet, and on

Bene-berak
Jos 19:45 and *B* and Gath-rimmon

Benediction
Ne 13:2 the malediction into a *b*

Benefactors
Lu 22:25 over them are called *B*

Beneficial
Job 30:13 *b* only for adversity to me
Jer 16:19 which there was nothing *b*
Mt 5:29 more *b* to you for one of your
5:30 it is more *b* for one of your
18:6 more *b* for him to have hung
1Co 12:7 to each one for a *b* purpose
2Co 12:1 I have to boast. It is not *b*
1Ti 4:8 bodily training is *b* for a
4:8 godly devotion is *b* for all
2Ti 3:16 and *b* for teaching, for
Tit 3:8 things are fine and *b* to men

Benefit
Ge 25:32 what *b* . . . is a birthright?
1Sa 12:21 unrealities that are of no *b*
2Ch 32:25 according to the *b* rendered
Job 15:3 utterances will be of no *b*
21:15 And how do we *b* ourselves
35:3 What *b* do I have more than
Pr 10:2 wicked one will be of no *b*
11:4 no *b* on the day of fury, but
Isa 1:11 Of what *b* to me is the
30:5 people that bring no *b* to one
30:5 and bring no *b*, but are a
30:6 they will prove of no *b*
44:9 themselves will be of no *b*
44:10 no *b* at all has it been
47:12 you might be able to *b*
48:17 teaching you to *b* yourself
57:12 that they will not *b* you
Jer 2:8 those who could bring no *b*
2:11 for what can bring no *b*
7:8 certainly be of no *b* at all
12:13 they will be of no *b*
23:32 by no means *b* this people
Hab 2:18 Of what *b* has a carved image
Mt 15:5 by which you might get *b*
16:26 what *b* will it be to a man
Mr 7:11 which you may get *b* from me
8:36 of what *b* is it for a man to
Lu 9:25 what does a man *b* himself if
Joh 4:38 into the *b* of their labor
11:50 your *b* for one man to die
16:7 for your *b* I am going away
18:14 their *b* for one man to die
Ro 2:25 of *b* only if you practice law
3:1 is the *b* of the circumcision
2Co 8:10 this matter is of *b* to you
Ga 5:2 Christ will be of no *b* to you
1Ti 6:2 receiving the *b* of their good
Heb 4:2 was heard did not *b* them
Jas 2:14 what *b* is it, my brothers
2:16 of what *b* is it?
Jude 16 the sake of their own *b*

Benefited
Mr 5:26 had not been *b* but, rather
Heb 13:9 with them have not been *b*

Benefits
Ps 116:12 For all his *b* to me

Bene-jaakan
Nu 33:31 and went camping in *B*
33:32 pulled away from *B* and went
De 10:6 pulled away from Beeroth *B*

Benevolently
Ac 28:7 entertained us *b* three days

Ben-hadad
1Ki 15:18 *B* the son of Tabrimmon the
15:20 *B* listened to King Asa and
20:1 As for *B* the king of Syria
20:2 This is what *B* has said
20:5 This is what *B* has said
20:9 said to messengers of *B*
20:10 *B* now sent to him and said
20:16 *B* was drinking himself
20:17 *B* at once sent out
20:20 *B* the king of Syria got to
20:26 *B* proceeded to muster the
20:30 *B*, he fled and finally came
20:32 *B* has said, Please, let my
20:33 to say: *B* is your brother
20:33 *B* went out to him
20:34 *B* now said to him: The
2Ki 6:24 *B* the king of Syria proceeded
8:7 *B* the king of Syria was sick
8:9 *B*, the king of Syria
13:3 *B* the son of Hazael all their
13:24 *B* his son began to reign in
13:25 *B* the son of Hazael
2Ch 16:2 sent to *B* the king of Syria
16:4 *B* listened to King Asa and
Jer 49:27 dwelling towers of *B*
Am 1:4 the dwelling towers of *B*

Ben-hail
2Ch 17:7 princes, namely, *B* and

Ben-hanan
1Ch 4:20 the sons of Shimon . . . *B*

Beninu
Ne 10:13 Hodiah, Bani and *B*

Benjamin
Ge 35:18 but his father called him *B*
35:24 sons by Rachel were . . . *B*
42:4 But Jacob did not send *B*
42:36 *B* you are going to take
43:14 your other brother and *B*
43:15 money in their hand and *B*
43:16 When Joseph saw *B* with them
43:29 raised his eyes and saw *B*
45:12 the eyes of my brother *B* are
45:14 he fell upon the neck of *B*
45:14 and *B* wept upon his neck
45:22 to *B* he gave three hundred
46:19 The sons of Rachel . . . *B*
46:21 sons of *B* were Bela and
49:27 *B* will keep on tearing like
Ex 1:3 Issachar, Zebulun and *B*
Nu 1:11 of *B*, Abidan the son of
1:36 sons of *B*, their births
1:37 registered . . . tribe of *B*
2:22 And the tribe of *B*
2:22 for the sons of *B* is Abidan
7:60 chieftain for the sons of *B*
10:24 the tribe of the sons of *B*
13:9 of the tribe of *B*, Palti the
26:38 sons of *B* by their families
26:41 sons of *B* by their families
34:21 of the tribe of *B*, Elidad the
De 27:12 Issachar and Joseph and *B*
33:12 As to *B* he said: Let the
Jos 18:11 tribe of the sons of *B*
18:20 inheritance of the sons of *B*
18:21 tribe of the sons of *B*
18:28 sons of *B* by their families
21:4 out of the tribe of *B*
21:17 out of the tribe of *B*
Jg 1:21 the sons of *B* did not drive
1:21 with the sons of *B* in
5:14 O *B*, among your peoples
10:9 against Judah and *B* and the
19:14 Gibeah, which belongs to *B*
20:3 sons of *B* got to hear that
20:4 to Gibeah, which belongs to *B*
20:10 by going against Gibeah of *B*
20:12 to all the tribesmen of *B*
20:13 sons of *B* did not want to
20:14 the sons of *B* went gathering
20:15 sons of *B* got to be mustered
20:17 were mustered apart from *B*
20:18 battle against the sons of *B*
20:20 went out to battle against *B*
20:21 sons of *B* came on out from
20:23 battle against the sons of *B*
20:24 drew near to the sons of *B*
20:25 *B* came on out from Gibeah to
20:28 battle against the sons of *B*
20:30 go up against the sons of *B*
20:31 the sons of *B* went on out to
20:32 the sons of *B* began to say
20:35 to defeat *B* before Israel
20:35 brought down to ruin in *B*
20:36 the sons of *B* imagined that
20:36 they kept giving ground to *B*
20:39 *B* started to strike down
20:40 when *B* turned his face back
20:41 the men of *B* were disturbed
20:43 They surrounded *B*
20:44 eighteen thousand men of *B*
20:46 those of *B* that fell on that
20:48 back against the sons of *B*
21:1 give his daughter to *B* as a
21:6 began to feel regret over *B*
21:13 and spoke to the sons of *B*
21:14 *B* came back at that time
21:15 the people felt regret over *B*
21:16 been annihilated out of *B*
21:17 those who have escaped of *B*
21:18 one that gives a wife to *B*
21:20 they commanded the sons of *B*
21:21 you must go to the land of *B*
21:23 sons of *B* did just that way
1Sa 4:12 a man of *B* went running
9:1 happened to be a man of *B*
9:16 a man from the land of *B*
9:21 families of the tribe of *B*
10:2 the territory of *B* at Zelzah
10:20 *B* came to be picked
10:21 *B* draw near by its families
13:2 with Jonathan at Gibeah of *B*
13:15 from Gilgal to Gibeah of *B*
13:16 were dwelling in Geba of *B*
1Sa 14:16 to Saul in Gibeah of *B*
2Sa 2:9 *B* and over Israel, all of it
2:15 twelve belonging to *B* and
2:25 sons of *B* went collecting
2:31 struck down those of *B* and
3:19 also spoke in the ears of *B*
3:19 of the whole house of *B*
4:2 of the sons of *B*
4:2 to be counted as part of *B*
19:17 a thousand men from *B*
21:14 in the land of *B* in Zela
23:29 of Gibeah of the sons of *B*
1Ki 4:18 Shimei the son of Ela, in *B*
12:21 Judah and the tribe of *B*
12:23 the house of Judah and *B*
15:22 Geba in *B*, and Mizpah
1Ch 2:2 *B*, Naphtali, Gad and Asher
6:60 from the tribe of *B* Geba
6:65 the tribe of the sons of *B*
7:6 the sons of *B* were Bela and
7:10 sons of Bilhan . . . *B* and Ehud
8:1 *B*, he became father to Bela
8:40 were from the sons of *B*
9:3 and some of the sons of *B*
9:7 of the sons of *B*, Sallu the
11:31 of Gibeah of the sons of *B*
12:2 the brothers of Saul, of *B*
12:16 the sons of *B* and Judah
12:29 sons of *B*, the brothers of
21:6 and *B* he did not register in
27:21 of *B*, Jaasiel the son of
2Ch 11:1 the house of Judah and *B*
11:3 all Israel in Judah and *B*
11:10 which were in Judah and *B*
11:12 Judah and *B* continued his
11:23 the lands of Judah and of *B*
14:8 out of *B* those bearing the
15:2 O Asa and all Judah and *B*
15:8 all the land of Judah and *B*
15:9 together all Judah and *B* and
17:17 of *B* there was the valiant
25:5 hundreds for all Judah and *B*
31:1 out of all Judah and *B* and
34:9 from all Judah and *B* and the
34:32 found in Jerusalem and *B*
Ezr 1:5 the fathers of Judah and of *B*
4:1 adversaries of Judah and *B*
10:9 the men of Judah and *B*
10:32 *B*, Malluch and Shemariah
Ne 3:23 *B* and Hasshub did repair work
11:4 and some of the sons of *B*
11:7 sons of *B:* Sallu the son of
11:31 sons of *B* were from Geba
11:36 divisions of Judah for *B*
12:34 Judah and *B* and Shemaiah
Ps 68:27 There is little *B* subduing
80:2 *B* and Manasseh do rouse up
Jer 1:1 Anathoth in the land of *B*
6:1 shelter, O you sons of *B*
17:26 from the land of *B* and from
20:2 in the upper gate of *B*
32:8 is in the land of *B*, for
32:44 in the land of *B* and in
33:13 in the land of *B* and in
37:12 to go to the land of *B*
37:13 he was in the gate of *B*
38:7 sitting in the gate of *B*
Eze 48:22 boundary of *B* it should
48:23 border, *B* one portion
48:24 by the boundary of *B*, from
48:32 the gate of *B*, one
Ho 5:8 at Beth-aven—after you, O *B*
Ob 19 and *B* must take possession of
Zec 14:10 from the gate of *B* all the
Ac 13:21 Saul . . . of the tribe of *B*
Ro 11:1 of Abraham, of the tribe of *B*
Php 3:5 of the tribe of *B*, a Hebrew
Re 7:8 out of . . . *B* twelve thousand

Benjaminite
1Sa 9:1 a *B*, a man mighty in wealth
9:21 Am I not a *B* of the smallest
2Sa 16:11 and how much more now a *B*
19:16 the son of Gera the *B*
20:1 Sheba, the son of Bichri a *B*
1Ki 2:8 Gera the *B* from Bahurim, and
Es 2:5 of Shimei the son of Kish a *B*
Ps 7:*super* the words of Cush the *B*

Benjaminites
1Sa 9:4 on through the land of the *B*
22:7 Listen, please, you *B*
1Ch 27:12 the Anathothite of the *B*

Benjamin's
Ge 43:34 *B* portion five times the
Ge 44:12 the cup was found in *B* bag

Benjamite
Jg 3:15 Ehud the son of Gera, a *B*

Benjamites
Jg 19:16 the men of the place were *B*
20:34 *B* did not know that calamity

Beno
1Ch 24:26 the sons of Jaaziah, *B*
24:27 Of Jaaziah, *B* and Shoham

Ben-oni
Ge 35:18 she called his name *B;* but

Bent
Nu 21:15 *b* itself toward the seat of
Jg 7:6 they *b* down upon their knees
16:30 *b* himself with power, and
Ru 3:8 So he *b* himself forward, and
1Ki 19:18 have not *b* down to Baal
22:34 a man that *b* the bow in his
2Ki 1:13 *b* down upon his knees in
4:34 *b* over him, and gradually
4:35 he went up and *b* over him
2Ch 18:33 *b* the bow in his innocence
Ps 37:14 and have *b* their bow
Ec 12:3 men of vital energy have *b*
Isa 5:28 and all their bows are *b*
21:15 and because of the *b* bow
46:1 Bel has *b* down, Nebo is
Hab 3:14 *b* on devouring an afflicted
Lu 13:11 she was *b* double and was
22:41 *b* his knees and began to pray
Ro 11:4 have not *b* the knee to Baal

Ben-zoheth
1Ch 4:20 the sons of Ishi were . . . *B*

Beon
Nu 32:3 and Sebam and Nebo and *B*

Beor
Ge 36:32 Bela son of *B* proceeded to
Nu 22:5 Balaam the son of *B* at Pethor
24:3 of Balaam the son of *B*, And
24:15 Balaam the son of *B*, And the
31:8 killed Balaam the son of *B*
De 23:4 Balaam the son of *B* from
Jos 13:22 And Balaam the son of *B*
24:9 Balaam the son of *B* to call
1Ch 1:43 Bela the son of *B*
Mic 6:5 Balaam the son of *B* answered
2Pe 2:15 path of Balaam, the son of *B*

Bera
Ge 14:2 these made war with *B* king

Beracah
1Ch 12:3 *B* and Jehu the Anathothite
2Ch 20:26 at the low plain of *B*
20:26 Low Plain of *B*—until today

Beraiah
1Ch 8:21 and *B* . . . the sons of Shimei

Bereave
Le 26:22 *b* you of children and cut off
De 32:25 Outdoors a sword will *b* them
Jer 15:7 certainly *b* them of children
Eze 5:17 they must *b* you of children
36:12 will not *b* them again of
36:14 no more *b* of children
Ho 9:12 will also *b* them of children

Bereaved
Ge 27:45 Why should I be *b* also of
42:36 It is I you have *b!* Joseph is
43:14, 14 *b*, I shall certainly be *b*
1Sa 15:33 your sword has *b* women of
15:33 your mother will be most *b*
Pr 17:12 a bear *b* of its cubs rather
Isa 49:20 the sons of your *b* state
49:21 a woman *b* of children and
Jer 18:21 become women *b* of children
Eze 14:15 *b* it of children and it
Joh 14:18 I shall not leave you *b*
1Th 2:17 when we were *b* of you for

Bereavement
Ps 35:12 bad for good, *B* to my soul
Jer 50:9 man causing *b* of children
La 1:20 sword caused *b* of children

Bereaving
Eze 36:13 *b* your nations of children

Berechiah
1Ch 3:20 Hashubah and Ohel and *B*
6:39 Asaph was the son of *B*, the
9:16 and *B* the son of Asa the son

1Ch 15:17 Asaph the son of *B*
15:23 and *B* and Elkanah the
2Ch 28:12 *B* the son of Meshillemoth
Ne 3:4 *B* the son of Meshezabel
3:30 Meshullam the son of *B*
6:18 Meshullam the son of *B*
Zec 1:1 to Zechariah the son of *B*
1:7 *B* the son of Iddo the prophet

Bered
Ge 16:14 it is between Kadesh and *B*
1Ch 7:20 Shuthelah and *B* his son and

Beri
1Ch 7:36 The sons of Zophah . . . *B* and

Beriah
Ge 46:17 the sons of Asher were . . . *B*
46:17 sons of *B* were Heber and
Nu 26:44 *B* the family of the Beriites
26:45 of the sons of *B*: Of Heber
1Ch 7:23 But he called his name *B*
7:30 The sons of Asher were . . . *B*
7:31 sons of *B* were Heber and
8:13 and *B* and Shema. These were
8:16 and Joha, the sons of *B*
23:10 of Shimei . . Jeush and *B*
23:11 and *B*, they did not have

Beriites
Nu 26:44 Beriah the family of the *B*

Bernice
Ac 25:13 *B* arrived in Caesarea for a
25:23 Agrippa and *B* came with
26:30 *B* and the men seated with

Berodach-baladan
2Ki 20:12 *B* the son of Baladan

Beroea
Ac 17:10 both Paul and Silas out to *B*
17:13 published also in *B* by Paul
20:4 the son of Pyrrhus of *B*

Berothah
Eze 47:16 *B*, Sibraim, which is

Berothai
2Sa 8:8 from Betah and *B*, cities of

Berothite
1Ch 11:39 Naharai the *B*, the

Berry
Ec 12:5 and the caper *b* bursts

Beryl
Re 21:20 the eighth *b*, the ninth

Besai
Ezr 2:49 the sons of *B*
Ne 7:52 the sons of *B*, the sons of

Beseech
Ge 50:17 I *b* you, pardon, please, the
2Ki 20:3 I *b* you, O Jehovah, remember
Isa 38:3 to say: I *b* you, O Jehovah
Jer 7:16 nor *b* me, for I shall not
27:18 *b* Jehovah of armies
Ac 24:4 I *b* you to hear us briefly

Beside
Ge 39:15 he then left his garment *b*
39:16 garment laid up *b* her until
39:18 left his garment *b* me and
Le 1:16 and throw it *b* the altar, to
6:10 must place them *b* the altar
De 11:30 *b* the big trees of Moreh
Jos 12:9 Ai, which was *b* Bethel, one
Jg 6:28 pole that was *b* it had been
Ru 2:14 she sat down *b* the harvesters
1Sa 4:18 backward *b* the gate, and his
5:2 and station it *b* Dagon
17:30 he turned about from *b* him
2Sa 14:30 Joab's tract of land *b* mine
1Ki 1:9 which is *b* En-rogel, and
2:29 and there he is *b* the altar
3:20 took my son from *b* me while
4:12 *b* Zarethan below Jezreel
7:20 up close *b* the belly that
10:19 standing *b* the armrests
13:24 the ass was standing *b* it
13:24 lion was standing *b* the
13:25 standing *b* the dead body
13:28 standing *b* the dead body
13:31 *B* his bones deposit my own
20:36 he went away from *b* him
21:1 *b* the palace of Ahab the king
2Ki 12:9 put it *b* the altar on the
2Ch 9:18 were standing *b* the armrests
2Ch 26:19 *b* the altar of incense
28:15 *b* their brothers
Ne 2:6 consort was sitting *b* him
Pr 8:30 *b* him as a master worker
Isa 19:19 a pillar to Jehovah *b* its
Jer 17:2 poles *b* a luxuriant tree
35:4 *b* the dining room of the
41:17 that was *b* Bethlehem, in
Eze 1:15 earth *b* the living creatures
1:19 the wheels would go *b* them
3:13 of the wheels close *b* them
9:2 and stand *b* the copper altar
10:6 enter and stand *b* the wheel
10:9 four wheels *b* the cherubs
10:9 one wheel *b* the one cherub
10:9 one wheel *b* the other cherub
32:13 from *b* many waters, and
33:30 *b* the walls and in the
39:15 also build *b* it a marker
40:7 the gate *b* the porch of the
43:6 come to be standing *b* me
43:8 their doorpost *b* my doorpost
45:7 *b* the holy contribution and
45:7 *b* the possession of the city
Da 8:17 came *b* where I was standing
10:13 there *b* the kings of Persia
Am 2:8 stretch . . . out *b* every altar
Mt 4:13 in Capernaum *b* the sea in
20:30 blind men sitting *b* the road
Mr 2:13 Again he went out *b* the sea
4:1 started teaching *b* the sea
4:1 crowd *b* the sea were on the
5:21 and he was *b* the sea
5:42 were *b* themselves with great
10:46 was sitting *b* the road
Lu 5:1 he was standing *b* the lake of
8:56 her parents were *b* themselves
9:47 young child, set it *b* him
18:35 blind man was sitting *b* the
Ac 16:13 outside the gate *b* a river
Ro 5:20 Law came in *b* in order that

Besiege
De 20:12 and you have to *b* it
28:52 *b* you within all your gates
28:52 they will certainly *b* you
1Sa 23:8 to Keilah, to *b* David and
2Ki 6:24 and to go up and *b* Samaria
1Ch 20:1 *b* Rabbah, while David was
2Ch 6:28 in case their enemies *b* them
Eze 4:3 you must *b* it. It is a sign

Besieged
De 20:19 the tree . . . a man to be *b*
Ps 60:9 will bring me to the *b* city
139:5 and before, you have *b* me

Besieges
1Ki 8:37 in case their enemy *b* them

Besieging
1Ki 15:27 all Israel were *b* Gibbethon
2Ki 6:25 *b* it until an ass's head got

Besmeared
Isa 44:18 eyes have been *b* so as not

Besodeiah
Ne 3:6 Meshullam the son of *B*

Besor
1Sa 30:9 torrent valley of *B*, and the
30:10 over the torrent valley of *B*
30:21 by the torrent valley of *B*

Besprinkled
Pr 7:17 I have *b* my bed with myrrh

Best
Ge 47:6 in the very *b* of the land
47:11 in the very *b* of the land
Ex 22:5 with the *b* of his own field
22:5 the *b* of his own vineyard
23:19 *b* of the first ripe fruits of
34:26 *b* of the first ripe fruits
Nu 18:12 All the *b* of the oil and all
18:12 *b* of the new wine and the
18:29 *b* of it, as some holy thing
18:30 contribute the *b* of them
18:32 you contribute the *b* from
1Sa 2:29 *b* of every offering of Israel
8:14 the *b* ones, he will take and
8:16 your *b* herds, and your asses
15:9 upon the *b* of the flock and
15:15 compassion upon the *b* of
1Ki 20:3 the *b* looking, are mine
2Ki 10:3 *b* and most upright of the
Es 2:9 *b* place of the house of the
Ps 33:3 Do your *b* at playing on the
63:5 As with the *b* part, even
Ec 5:18 The *b* thing that I myself
Ca 7:9 your palate like the *b* wine
Isa 23:16 Do your *b* at playing on
Eze 31:16 and the *b* of Lebanon
34:18 on the very *b* pasturage
Mic 7:4 Their *b* one is like a brier
Lu 15:22 bring out a robe, the *b* one

Bestirring
Pr 28:22 A man of envious eye is *b*

Bestow
1Ch 22:9 peace and quietness I shall *b*
Job 32:21 man I shall not *b* a title
32:22 know how I can *b* a title
Pr 4:9 crown of beauty it will *b*
Hag 2:19 this day I shall *b* blessing

Bestowed
Ge 27:37 grain and new wine I have *b*
2Co 8:1 *b* upon the congregations of

Bestower
Isa 23:8 Tyre, the *b* of crowns

Bestowing
1Pe 3:9 *b* a blessing, because you

Betah
2Sa 8:8 from *B* and Berothai, cities

Beten
Jos 19:25 Hali and *B* and Achshaph

Beth-anath
Jos 19:38 and *B* and Beth-shemesh
Jg 1:33 inhabitants of *B*, but they
1:33 *B* became theirs for forced

Beth-anoth
Jos 15:59 Maarath and *B* and Eltekon

Bethany
Mt 21:17 to *B* and passed the night
26:6 Jesus happened to be in *B* in
Mr 11:1 *B* at the Mount of Olives
11:11 he went out to *B* with the
11:12 they had come out from *B*
14:3 at *B* in the house of Simon
Lu 19:29 got near to Bethphage and *B*
24:50 he led them out as far as *B*
Joh 1:28 in *B* across the Jordan
11:1 Lazarus of *B*, of the village
11:18 *B* was near Jerusalem at
12:1 *B*, where Lazarus was whom

Beth-arabah
Jos 15:6 passed over at the north of *B*
15:61 the wilderness *B*, Middin
18:22 and *B* and Zemaraim and

Beth-aven
Jos 7:2 Ai, which is close by *B*, to
18:12 at the wilderness of *B*
1Sa 13:5 in Michmash to the east of *B*
14:23 itself passed over to *B*
Ho 4:15 neither go up to *B* nor swear
5:8 Shout a war cry at *B*—after
10:5 For the calf idol of *B* the
10:8 the high places of *B*, the

Beth-azmaveth
Ne 7:28 the men of *B*, forty-two

Beth-baal-meon
Jos 13:17 Dibon and Bamoth-baal and *B*

Beth-barah
Jg 7:24 as far as *B* and the Jordan
7:24 as far as *B* and the Jordan

Beth-biri
1Ch 4:31 and in Hazar-susim and in *B*

Beth-car
1Sa 7:11 as far as south of *B*

Beth-dagon
Jos 15:41 Gederoth, *B* and Naamah
19:27 to *B* and reached to Zebulun

Beth-diblathaim
Jer 48:22 against Nebo and against *B*

Beth-eden
Am 1:5 holder of the scepter from *B*

Bethel
Ge 12:8 region to the east of *B* and
12:8 his tent with *B* on the west
13:3 he made his way . . . to *B*, to
13:3 at first between *B* and Ai
28:19 called . . . that place *B*

Ge 31:13 I am the true God of *B*
35:1 go up to *B* and dwell there
35:3 let us rise and go up to *B*
35:6 Luz . . . that is to say, *B*
35:8 was buried at the foot of *B*
35:15 name of the place . . . *B*
35:16 Then he pulled away from *B*
Jos 7:2 Beth-aven, to the east of *B*
8:9 took up quarters between *B*
8:12 an ambush between *B* and Ai
8:17 not a man remaining in . . . *B*
12:9 of Ai, which was beside *B*
12:16 the king of *B*, one
16:1 the mountainous region of *B*
16:2 from *B* belonging to Luz and
18:13 Luz, that is to say, *B*
18:22 and Zemaraim and *B*
Jg 1:22 also went up against *B*, and
1:23 Joseph began to spy on *B*
4:5 tree between Ramah and *B* in
20:18 up to *B* and to inquire of God
20:26 came to *B* and wept and sat
20:31 one of which goes up to *B*
21:2 the people came to *B* and kept
21:19 which is to the north of *B*
21:19 goes up from *B* to Shechem
1Sa 7:16 circuit of *B* and Gilgal and
10:3 going up to the true God at *B*
13:2 the mountainous region of *B*
30:27 those who were in *B*, and
1Ki 12:29 placed the one in *B*, and
12:32 altar that he had made in *B*
12:32 at *B* the priests of the high
12:33 altar that he had made in *B*
13:1 out of Judah . . . to *B*
13:4 against the altar in *B*
13:10 by which he had come to *B*
13:11 prophet was dwelling in *B*
13:11 had done that day in *B*
13:32 the altar that is in *B*
2Ki 2:2 has sent me clear to *B*
2:2 So they went down to *B*
2:3 prophets that were at *B* came
2:23 to go up from there to *B*
10:29 one was in *B* and one in Dan
17:28 and began dwelling in *B*
23:4 the dust of them to *B*
23:15 the altar that was in *B*
23:17 done against the altar of *B*
23:19 doings that he had done at *B*
1Ch 7:28 dwelling places were *B* and
2Ch 13:19 *B* and its dependent towns
Ezr 2:28 men of *B* and Ai, two hundred
Ne 7:32 men of *B* and Ai, a hundred
11:31 *B* and its dependent towns
Jer 48:13 ashamed of *B* their
Ho 10:15 do to you people, O *B*
12:4 At *B* He got to find him
Am 3:14 against the altars of *B*
4:4 to *B* and commit transgression
5:5 do not search for *B*, and to
5:5 as regards *B*, it will become
5:6 *B* may not be with no one to
7:10 Amaziah the priest of *B*
7:13 at *B* you must no longer do
Zec 7:2 *B* proceeded to send Sharezer

Bethelite
1Ki 16:34 Hiel the *B* built Jericho

Beth-emek
Jos 19:27 to *B* and Neiel, and it

Beth-ezel
Mic 1:11 The wailing of *B* will take

Beth-gader
1Ch 2:51 Hareph the father of *B*

Beth-gamul
Jer 48:23 against *B* and against

Beth-gilgal
Ne 12:29 from *B* and from the fields

Beth-haccherem
Ne 3:14 prince of the district of *B*
Jer 6:1 over *B* raise a fire signal

Beth-haram
Jos 13:27 low plain *B* and Beth-nimrah

Beth-haran
Nu 32:36 Beth-nimrah and *B*, cities

Beth-hoglah
Jos 15:6 the boundary went up to *B*
18:19 northern slope of *B*
18:21 Jericho and *B* and

Beth-horon
Jos 10:10 by way of the ascent of *B*
10:11 were on the descent of *B*
16:3 boundary of Lower *B* and
16:5 as far as Upper *B*
18:13 south of Lower *B*
18:14 the mountain that faces *B*
21:22 *B* and its pasture ground
1Sa 13:18 would turn to the road of *B*
1Ki 9:17 build Gezer and Lower *B*
1Ch 6:68 *B* with its pasture grounds
7:24 Sheerah . . . got to build *B*
2Ch 8:5 went on to build Upper *B* and
8:5 Lower *B*, fortified cities
25:13 from Samaria clear to *B*

Beth-jeshimoth
Nu 33:49 from *B* to Abel-shittim on
Jos 12:3 east in the direction of *B*
13:20 the slopes of Pisgah and *B*
Eze 25:9 *B*, Baal-meon, even to

Beth-lebaoth
Jos 19:6 and *B* and Sharuhen

Bethlehem
Ge 35:19 Ephrath, that is to say, *B*
48:7 Ephrath, that is to say, *B*
Jos 19:15 Shimron and Idalah and *B*
Jg 12:8 Ibzan from *B* began to judge
12:10 Ibzan . . . was buried in *B*
17:7 a young man of *B* in Judah of
17:8 city of *B* in Judah to reside
17:9 a Levite from *B* in Judah and
19:1 a concubine from *B* in Judah
19:2 her father at *B* in Judah and
19:18 *B* in Judah to the remotest
19:18 I went to *B* in Judah; and it
Ru 1:1 go from *B* in Judah to reside
1:2 Ephrathites from *B* in Judah
1:19 until they came to *B*
1:19 as soon as they came to *B*
1:22 and they came to *B* at the
2:4 Boaz came from *B* and proceeded
4:11 and make a notable name in *B*
1Sa 16:4 When he came to *B* the older
17:12 Ephrathite from *B* of Judah
17:15 the sheep of his father at *B*
20:6 run to *B* his city, because
20:28 absence from me to go to *B*
2Sa 2:32 which is at *B*
23:14 outpost . . . was then in *B*
23:15 water from the cistern of *B*
23:16 water from the cistern of *B*
23:24 Elhanan the son of Dodo of *B*
1Ch 2:51 Salma the father of *B*
2:54 The sons of Salma were *B*
4:4 Ephrathah the father of *B*
11:16 Philistines was then in *B*
11:17 water from the cistern of *B*
11:18 water from the cistern of *B*
11:26 Elhanan the son of Dodo of *B*
2Ch 11:6 rebuilt *B* and Etam and Tekoa
Ezr 2:21 sons of *B*, a hundred and
Ne 7:26 men of *B* and Netophah
Jer 41:17 that was beside *B*, in order
Mic 5:2 *B* Ephrathah . . . too little
Mt 2:1 born in *B* of Judea in the
2:5 In *B* of Judea; for this is
2:6 O *B* of the land of Judah
2:8 sending them to *B*, he said
2:16 had all the boys in *B* and in
Lu 2:4 city, which is called *B*
2:15 go clear to *B* and see this
Joh 7:42 from *B* the village where

Bethlehemite
1Sa 16:1 shall send you to Jesse the *B*
16:18 a son of Jesse the *B* is
17:58 of your servant Jesse the *B*
2Sa 21:19 Jaare-oregim the *B* got to

Beth-maacah
2Sa 20:14 Sheba went . . . to Abel of *B*
20:15 against him in Abel of *B*

Beth-marcaboth
Jos 19:5 and Ziklag and *B* and
1Ch 4:31 in *B* and in Hazar-susim

Beth-meon
Jer 48:23 Beth-gamul and against *B*

Beth-merhak
2Sa 15:17 they came to a stop at *B*

Beth-nimrah
Nu 32:36 *B* and Beth-haran, cities
Jos 13:27 plain of Beth-haram and *B*

Beth-pazzez
Jos 19:21 and En-haddah and *B*

Beth-pelet
Jos 15:27 and Heshmon and *B*
Ne 11:26 in Moladah and in *B*

Beth-peor
De 3:29 in the valley in front of *B*
4:46 in the valley in front of *B*
34:6 land of Moab in front of *B*
Jos 13:20 *B* and the slopes of Pisgah

Bethphage
Mt 21:1 at *B* on the Mount of Olives
Mr 11:1 to *B* and Bethany at the Mount
Lu 19:29 he got near to *B* and Bethany

Beth-rapha
1Ch 4:12 in turn, became father to *B*

Beth-rehob
Jg 18:28 low plain that belonged to *B*
2Sa 10:6 and hire Syrians of *B* and

Bethsaida
Mt 11:21 Woe to you, *B!* because if
Mr 6:45 the opposite shore toward *B*
8:22 Now they put in at *B*
Lu 9:10 into a city called *B*
10:13 Woe to you, *B!* because if
Joh 1:44 Philip was from *B*, from the
12:21 from *B* of Galilee, and they

Beth-shan
1Sa 31:10 fastened on the wall of *B*
31:12 sons off the wall of *B* and
2Sa 21:12 from the public square of *B*

Beth-shean
Jos 17:11 *B* and its dependent towns
17:16 *B* and its dependent towns
Jg 1:27 take possession of *B* and its
1Ki 4:12 *B*, which is beside Zarethan
4:12 from *B* to Abel-meholah to
1Ch 7:29 *B* and its dependent towns

Beth-shemesh
Jos 15:10 went down to *B* and passed
19:22 Shahazumah and *B* and
19:38 and Beth-anath and *B*
21:16 *B* and its pasture ground
Jg 1:33 *B* and the inhabitants of
1:33 the inhabitants of *B* and of
1Sa 6:9 that it goes up, to *B*
6:12 ahead on the road to *B*
6:12 as far as the boundary of *B*
6:13 people of *B* were reaping the
6:15 men of *B*, for their part
6:19 striking down the men of *B*
6:20 Further, the men of *B* said
1Ki 4:9 and *B* and Elon-beth-hanan
2Ki 14:11 *B*, which belongs to Judah
14:13 captured at *B*, after
1Ch 6:59 *B* with its pasture grounds
2Ch 25:21 at *B*, which belongs to Judah
25:23 king of Israel seized at *B*
28:18 capture *B* and Aijalon and
Jer 43:13 *B*, which is in the land of

Beth-shemite
1Sa 6:14 the field of Joshua the *B*
6:18 in the field of Joshua the *B*

Beth-shittah
Jg 7:22 their flight as far as *B*, on

Beth-tappuah
Jos 15:53 Janim and *B* and Aphekah

Bethuel
Ge 22:22 Pildash and Jidlaph and *B*
22:23 *B* . . . the father of Rebekah
24:15 *B* the son of Milcah the wife
24:24 *B* the son of Milcah, whom
24:47 daughter of *B* the son of
24:50 Laban and *B* answered and said
25:20 Rebekah the daughter of *B*
28:2 the house of *B* the father of
28:5 Laban the son of *B* the Syrian
1Ch 4:30 in *B* and in Hormah and in

Bethul
Jos 19:4 and Eltolad and *B* and Hormah

Bethzatha
Joh 5:2 a pool designated in Hebrew *B*

Beth-zur
Jos 15:58 Halhul, *B* and Gedor
1Ch 2:45 Maon was the father of *B*

2Ch 11:7 *B* and Soco and Adullam
Ne 3:16 of half the district of *B*

Betitle
Isa 44:5 Israel one will *b* himself

Betonim
Jos 13:26 and *B* and from Mahanaim to

Betray
1Ch 12:17 to *b* me to my adversaries
Isa 16:3 do not *b* anyone fleeing
Mt 24:10 will *b* one another and will
26:15 What will you give me to *b*
26:16 a good opportunity to *b* him
26:21 One of you will *b* me
26:23 is the one that will *b* me
26:25 Judas, who was about to *b*
Mr 14:10 in order to *b* him to them
14:11 began seeking how to *b* him
14:18 eating with me, will *b* me
Lu 22:4 the effective way to *b* him
22:6 opportunity to *b* him to them
22:48 *b* the Son of man with a kiss
Joh 6:64 the one that would *b* him
6:71 this one was going to *b* him
12:4 was about to *b* him, said
13:2 Judas Iscariot . . . to *b* him
13:21 One of you will *b* me

Betrayed
Mt 10:4 Judas Iscariot, who later *b*
17:22 to be *b* into men's hands
26:24 whom the Son of man is b
26:45 Son of man to be *b* into the
27:3 Judas, who *b* him, seeing he
27:4 when I *b* righteous blood
Mr 3:19 Judas Iscariot, who later *b*
14:21 the Son of man is *b*
14:41 The Son of man is *b* into
Lu 22:22 man through whom he is *b*

Betrayer
Mt 26:46 Look! My *b* has drawn near
26:48 his *b* had given them a sign
Mr 14:42 Look! My *b* has drawn near
14:44 his *b* had given them an
Lu 22:21 the hand of my *b* is with me
Joh 18:2 Judas, his *b*, also knew the
18:5 Judas, his *b*, was also

Betrayers
Ac 7:52 whose *b* and murderers you
2Ti 3:4 *b*, headstrong, puffed up with

Betraying
Joh 13:11 knew, indeed, the man *b*
21:20 Lord, who is the one *b* you?

Better
Ge 29:19 It is *b* for me to give her
Ex 14:12 *b* . . . to serve the Egyptians
Nu 14:3 *b* for us to return to Egypt
Jg 8:2 gleanings of Ephraim *b* than
9:2 Which is *b* for you, for
11:25 are you any *b* than Balak the
15:2 Is not her younger sister *b*
18:19 Which is *b*, for you to
Ru 2:22 It is *b*, my daughter, that
3:10 your loving-kindness *b* in the
4:15 is *b* to you than seven sons
1Sa 1:8 I not *b* to you than ten sons
15:22 obey is *b* than a sacrifice
15:28 of yours who is *b* than you
27:1 nothing *b* for me than that I
2Sa 14:32 *b* for me that I should
17:14 *b* than the counsel of
18:3 *b* if you would be of service
1Ki 2:32 righteous and *b* than he was
19:4 am no *b* than my forefathers
21:2 a vineyard *b* than it
2Ki 5:12 *b* than all the waters of
2Ch 21:13 who were *b* than you
Es 1:19 a woman *b* than she is
Ps 37:16 *B* is the little of the
63:3 loving-kindness is *b* than life
84:10 *b* than a thousand elsewhere
118:8 *b* to take refuge in Jehovah
118:9 *b* to take refuge in Jehovah
Pr 3:14 *b* than having silver as gain
8:11 wisdom is *b* than corals, and
8:19 My fruitage is *b* than gold
12:9 *B* is the one lightly esteemed
15:16 *B* is a little in the fear of
15:17 *B* is a dish of vegetables
16:8 *B* is a little with
16:16 wisdom . . . much *b* than gold
16:19 *B* is it to be lowly in
Pr 16:32 is slow to anger is *b* than a
17:1 *B* is a dry piece of bread
19:1 *b* than the one crooked in his
19:22 is *b* than a lying man
21:9 *B* is it to dwell upon a
21:19 *B* is it to dwell in a
22:1 favor is *b* than even silver
25:7 *b* for him to say to you: Come
25:24 *B* is it to dwell upon a
27:5 *B* is a revealed reproof than a
27:10 *B* is a neighbor that is near
28:6 *B* is the one of little means
Ec 2:24 With a man there is nothing *b*
2:25 and who drinks *b* than I do
3:12 is nothing *b* for them than to
3:22 nothing *b* than that the man
4:3 *b* than both of them is the one
4:6 *B* is a handful of rest than a
4:9 Two are *b* than one, because
4:13 *B* is a needy but wise child
5:5 *B* is it that you vow not than
6:3 one prematurely born is *b* off
6:9 *B* is the seeing by the eyes
7:1 A name is *b* than good oil, and
7:2 *B* is it to go to the house of
7:3 *B* is vexation than laughter
7:3 the face the heart becomes *b*
7:5 *B* is it to hear the rebuke of
7:8 *B* is the end afterward of a
7:8 *B* is one who is patient than
7:10 former days proved to be *b*
7:18 *b* that you should take hold of
8:1 his face is changed for the *b*
8:15 nothing *b* under the sun than
9:4 a live dog is *b* off than a dead
9:16 Wisdom is *b* than mightiness
9:18 Wisdom is *b* than implements
Ca 1:2 of endearment are *b* than wine
4:10 How much *b* your expressions
Isa 52:7 good news of something *b*
56:5 *b* than sons and daughters
La 4:9 *B* have those slain with the
Da 1:15 countenances appeared *b* and
1:20 ten times *b* than all the
Ho 2:7 I had it *b* at that time than
Am 6:2 Are they *b* than these kingdoms
Jon 4:3 my dying is *b* than my being
4:8 is *b* than my being alive
Na 3:8 Are you *b* than No-amon, that
Joh 4:52 in which he got *b* in health
Ro 3:9 Are we in a *b* position?
1Co 7:9 for it is *b* to marry than to
7:38 not . . . marriage will do *b*
11:17 not for the *b*, but for the
Php 1:23 this, to be sure, is far *b*
Heb 1:4 has become *b* than the angels
6:9 we are convinced of *b* things
7:19 a *b* hope did, through which
7:22 in pledge of a *b* covenant
8:6 a correspondingly *b* covenant
8:6 established upon *b* promises
9:23 sacrifices that are *b* than
10:34 *b* and an abiding possession
11:16 reaching out for a *b* place
11:35 attain a *b* resurrection
11:40 God foresaw something *b* for
12:24 which speaks in a *b* way
1Pe 3:17 it is *b* to suffer because you
2Pe 2:21 been *b* for them not to have

Between*
Ge 1:4 God brought about a division *b*
1:6 come to be in *b* the waters and
1:6 dividing occur *b* the waters
1:7 make a division *b* the waters
1:14 make a division *b* the day and
1:18 make a division *b* the light
3:8 in *b* the trees of the garden
3:15 enmity *b* you and the woman
3:15 *b* your seed and her seed
9:13 covenant *b* me and the earth
9:15 covenant which is *b* me and
9:16 *b* God and every living soul
9:17 covenant . . . *b* me and all
17:2 give my covenant *b* me and you
17:7 my covenant *b* me and you and
17:10 *b* me and you men, even your
17:11 sign of the covenant *b* me
26:28 oath of obligation occur *b* us
26:28 *b* us and you, and let us
31:48 heap is a witness *b* me and
31:53 the god of Nahor judge *b* us
49:10 staff from *b* his feet, until
Ex 8:23 demarcation *b* my people and
Ex 9:4 distinction *b* the livestock of
11:7 distinction *b* the Egyptians
12:6 slaughter it *b* the two
13:9 as a memorial *b* your eyes
13:16 a frontlet band *b* your eyes
16:12 *B* the two evenings you will
29:39 young ram *b* the two evenings
29:41 young ram *b* the two evenings
31:13 sign *b* me and you during
31:17 *B* me and the sons of Israel
Le 10:10 distinction *b* the holy thing
10:10 *b* the unclean thing and the
11:47 *b* the unclean and the clean
20:25 *b* the clean beast and the
20:25 *b* the unclean fowl and the
23:5 *b* the two evenings is the
Nu 28:4 render up *b* the two evenings
28:8 male lamb *b* the two evenings
Ro 2:15 *b* their own thoughts, they

Bewail
Ge 23:2 Abraham came in to *b* Sarah
1Sa 25:1 *b* him and bury him at his
28:3 Israel had proceeded to *b*
1Ki 13:29 prophet to *b* and bury him
14:13 Israel will indeed *b* him
Jer 16:5 do not go to *b* and do not

Bewailed
Jer 16:4 They will not be *b*, neither
25:33 They will not be *b*, neither

Bewailing
Lu 23:27 in grief and *b* him

Beware
1Co 10:12 thinks he is standing *b* that
Heb 3:12 *B*, brothers, for fear there

Bewildered
Job 41:25 consternation they get *b*
Isa 19:3 Egypt must become *b* in the
Ac 2:6 came together and were *b*

Bewilderment
De 28:28 loss of sight and *b* of heart
Zec 12:4 strike every horse with *b*

Beyond
Ge 35:21 distance *b* the tower of Eder
Nu 14:41 you are passing *b* the order
22:18 pass *b* the order of Jehovah
24:13 pass *b* the order of Jehovah
32:19 the side of the Jordan and *b*
1Sa 20:36 to make it pass *b* him
2Sa 16:1 over a little *b* the summit
1Ki 14:15 scatter them *b* the River
1Ch 22:3 quantity as to be *b* weighing
Ezr 4:10 and the rest *b* the River
4:11 the men *b* the River
4:16 have no share *b* the River
4:17 and the rest *b* the River
4:20 governing all *b* the River
5:3 the governor *b* the River and
5:6 the governor *b* the River and
5:6 that were *b* the River
6:6 the governor *b* the River
6:6 governors that are *b* the River
6:8 of the tax *b* the River
6:13 the governor *b* the River
7:21 that are *b* the River
7:25 people that are *b* the River
8:36 the governors *b* the River
Ne 2:7 to the governors *b* the River
2:9 governors *b* the River and
3:7 the governor *b* the River
Job 14:5 decree . . . he may not go *b*
36:26 his years are *b* searching
Ps 104:9 *b* which they should not pass
147:5 understanding is *b* recounting
Pr 8:29 should not pass *b* his order
Isa 5:14 mouth wide *b* bounds
Jer 8:18 A grief that is *b* curing
22:19 *b* the gates of Jerusalem
Da 2:1 made to be something *b* him
Am 5:27 to go into exile *b* Damascus
Ac 7:43 I will deport you *b* Babylon
19:39 searching for anything *b* that
20:12 were comforted *b* measure
26:13 light *b* the brilliance of
Ro 4:18 Although *b* hope, yet based
1Co 4:6 Do not go *b* the things that
10:13 tempted *b* what you can bear
2Co 1:8 pressure *b* our strength, so
4:7 power *b* what is normal may
4:8 but not cramped *b* movement
8:3 *b* their actual ability this

2Co 10:16 news to the countries *b*
Ga 1:8 *b* what we declared to you as
1:9 something *b* what you accepted
Eph 3:20 *b* all the things we ask or

Bezai
Ezr 2:17 sons of *B*, three hundred and
Ne 7:23 the sons of *B*, three hundred
10:18 Hodiah, Hashum, *B*

Bezalel
Ex 31:2 do call by name *B* the son of
35:30 *B* the son of Uri the son of
36:1 *B* must work, also Oholiab
36:2 Moses . . . call *B* and Oholiab
37:1 *B* now made the Ark of acacia
38:22 and *B* the son of Uri the son
1Ch 2:20 in turn, became father to *B*
2Ch 1:5 altar that *B* the son of Uri
Ezr 10:30 sons of Pahath-moab . . . *B*

Bezek
Jg 1:4 they defeated them in *B*, ten
1:5 they found Adoni-bezek in *B*
1Sa 11:8 he took the sum of them in *B*

Bezer
De 4:43 *B* in the wilderness on the
Jos 20:8 toward the east they gave *B*
21:36 *B* and its pasture ground
1Ch 6:78 *B* in the wilderness with its
7:37 *B* and Hod and Shamma and

Biased
1Ti 5:21 according to a *b* leaning

Bichri
2Sa 20:1 Sheba, the son of *B* a
20:2 follow Sheba the son of *B*
20:6 Sheba the son of *B* will be
20:7 after Sheba the son of *B*
20:10 after Sheba the son of *B*
20:13 after Sheba the son of *B*
20:21 Sheba the son of *B*, has
20:22 Sheba the son of *B* and pitch

Bichrites
2Sa 20:14 the *B*, they then congregated

Bidden
Ac 20:1 and *b* them farewell, he went

Bidding
Jer 20:10 mortal man *b* me Peace!
Lu 5:5 at your *b* I will lower the

Bidkar
2Ki 9:25 now said to *B* his adjutant

Bier
De 3:11, 11 His *b* was a *b* of iron
Lu 7:14 approached and touched the *b*

Big
Ge 12:6 near the *b* trees of Moreh
13:18 dwelt among the *b* trees of
14:13 *b* trees of Mamre the Amorite
18:1 among the *b* trees of Mamre
21:8 then prepared a *b* feast on
35:4 hid them under the *b* tree
Ex 7:9 rod . . . will become a *b* snake
7:10 his rod . . . became a *b* snake
7:12 rod, and they became *b* snakes
18:18 is too *b* a load for you
18:22 every *b* case they will bring
29:20 the *b* toe of their right foot
Le 8:23 the *b* toe of his right foot
8:24 the *b* toe of their right foot
14:14 the *b* toe of his right foot
14:17 the *b* toe of his right foot
14:25 the *b* toe of his right foot
14:28 the *b* toe of his right foot
De 11:30 beside the *b* trees of Moreh
32:33 is the venom of *b* snakes
Jos 7:26 over him a *b* pile of stones
10:27 they placed *b* stones at the
19:33 the *b* tree in Zaanannim
Jg 4:11 tent pitched near the *b* tree
6:11 sat under the *b* tree that was
6:19 under the *b* tree and served it
6:20 set them on the *b* rock there
9:6 by the *b* tree, the pillar that
9:37 the *b* tree of Meonenim
11:2 sons of the wife got *b*, they
1Sa 10:3 as far as the *b* tree of Tabor
20:2 father will not do a *b* thing
2Sa 18:9 boughs of a massive *b* tree
18:9 got caught fast in the *b* tree
18:10 Absalom hung in a *b* tree
18:14 in the heart of the *b* tree
2Sa 18:17 into a *b* hollow and raised
18:17 a very *b* pile of stones
1Ki 13:14 sitting under the *b* tree
1Ch 10:12 under the *b* tree in Jabesh
Ne 2:13 the Fountain of the *B* Snake
Job 8:11 a reed grow *b* without water
39:4 they get *b* in the open field
Ps 35:18 in the *b* congregation
40:9 in the *b* congregation
40:10 in the *b* congregation
91:13 young lion and the *b* snake
92:12 Lebanon does, he will grow *b*
140:11 The *b* talker—let him not
Ec 2:21 is vanity and a *b* calamity
Isa 1:30 will become like a *b* tree
6:13 burning down, like a *b* tree
13:22 *b* snake will be in the
30:25 *b* slaughter when the towers
33:23 actually take a *b* plunder
44:14 keeps making it get *b*
57:5 passion among *b* trees, under
61:3 *b* trees of righteousness
Jer 51:34 like a *b* snake
Eze 6:13 under every branchy *b* tree
16:7 A very *b* multitude like the
16:7 so that you would grow *b* and
29:19 make a *b* spoil of it and
31:4 were what made it get *b*
38:12 to get a *b* spoil and to do
38:13 Is it to get a *b* spoil that
43:14 to the *b* surrounding ledge
Da 2:48 many *b* gifts he gave to him
5:1 made a *b* feast for a thousand
7:7 it had teeth of iron, *b* ones
Ho 4:13 and storax tree and *b* tree
Ob 12 ought not to maintain a *b* mouth
Jon 4:10 not toil upon or make get *b*
Mt 27:60 rolling a *b* stone to the
Mr 8:1 a *b* crowd and they had nothing
Lu 5:29 Levi spread a *b* reception
Joh 21:11 to land full of *b* fishes
Jas 3:4 boats, although they are so *b*

Bigger
Ge 25:27 And the boys got *b*, and Esau
Jg 13:24 and the boy kept getting *b*
1Sa 2:26 Samuel was growing *b* and
Da 7:20 *b* than that of its fellows
Am 6:2 is their territory *b* than your
Lu 12:18 storehouses and build *b* ones

Bigtha
Es 1:10 *B* and Abagtha, Zethar and

Bigthan
Es 2:21 *B* and Teresh, two court

Bigthana
Es 6:2 had reported concerning *B* and

Bigvai
Ezr 2:2 Mispar, *B*, Rehum, Baanah
2:14 sons of *B*, two thousand and
8:14 of the sons of *B*, Uthai and
Ne 7:7 Mispereth, *B*, Nehum, Baanah
7:19 the sons of *B*, two thousand
10:16 Adonijah, *B*, Adin

Bikath-aven
Am 1:5 cut off the inhabitant from *B*

Bildad
Job 2:11 *B* the Shuhite and Zophar the
8:1 *B* the Shuhite proceeded to
18:1 *B* the Shuhite proceeded to
25:1 *B* the Shuhite proceeded to
42:9 *B* the Shuhite and Zophar the

Bileam
1Ch 6:70 *B* with its pasture grounds

Bilgah
1Ch 24:14 for *B* the fifteenth, for
Ne 12:5 Mijamin, Maadiah, *B*
12:18 for *B*, Shammua; for

Bilgai
Ne 10:8 Maaziah, *B* and Shemaiah

Bilhah
Ge 29:29 Laban gave *B* his
30:3 Here is my slave girl *B*
30:4 With that she gave him *B*
30:5 *B* became pregnant and in time
30:7 *B*, Rachel's maidservant
35:22 went and lay down with *B*
35:25 the sons by *B*, Rachel's
37:2 he was with the sons of *B*
46:25 the sons of *B*, whom Laban
1Ch 4:29 in *B* and in Ezem and in
7:13 and Shallum, the sons of *B*

Bilhan
Ge 36:27 sons of Ezer: *B* and Zaavan
1Ch 1:42 The sons of Ezer were *B*
7:10 the sons of Jediael were *B*
7:10 sons of *B* were Jeush and

Bill
Ge 8:11 leaf freshly plucked in its *b*

Billhook
Isa 44:12 carver of iron with the *b*
Jer 10:3 the craftsman with the *b*

Billow
1Sa 2:28 make sacrificial smoke *b* up

Billowing
Isa 9:18 aloft as the *b* of smoke

Bilshan
Ezr 2:2 *B*, Mispar, Bigvai, Rehum
Ne 7:7 *B*, Mispereth, Bigvai, Nehum

Bimhal
1Ch 7:33 of Japhlet were Pasach and *B*

Bind
Ex 28:28 *b* the breastpiece by its
Nu 30:2 oath to *b* a vow of abstinence
30:3 does *b* herself with a vow of
De 11:18 *b* them as a sign upon your
2Ki 12:10 *b* it up and count the money
2Ch 36:6 *b* him with two fetters of
Job 31:36 *b* it around me like a grand
39:10 *b* a wild bull fast with its
40:13 *B* their very faces in the
Ps 105:22 *b* his princes agreeably to
118:27 *B* the festival procession
149:8 *b* their kings with shackles
Pr 6:21 *b* them upon your throat
Isa 22:21 sash I shall firmly *b* about
49:18 *b* them on yourself like a
61:1 to *b* up the brokenhearted
Eze 3:25 put cords upon you and *b* you
24:17 Your headdress *b* on yourself
Da 3:20 said to *b* Shadrach, Meshach
Ho 6:1 striking, but he will *b* us up
Mt 13:30 weeds and *b* them in bundles
16:19 whatever you may *b* on earth
18:18 things you may *b* on earth
22:13 *B* him hand and foot and
23:4 They *b* up heavy loads and put
Mr 5:3 nobody was able to *b* him fast
6:9 to *b* on sandals, and not to
Ac 12:8 *b* your sandals on. He did so
21:11 Jews will *b* in this manner

Binding
Ge 37:7 we were *b* sheaves in the
2Ki 10:12 *b* house of the shepherds
10:14 the cistern of the *b* house
Ps 58:5 someone wise is *b* with
147:3 is *b* up their painful spots
Eze 30:21 putting a bandage on for *b*
Mt 23:23 These things it was *b* to do
27:2 after *b* him, they led him
Ac 22:4 *b* and handing over to prisons

Binds
De 18:11 one who *b* others with a spell
Job 5:18 causes pain, but *b* up the
12:18 he *b* a belt upon their hips
Isa 30:26 Jehovah *b* up the breakdown
Mt 12:29 first he *b* the strong man
Mr 3:27 first he *b* the strong man

Binea
1Ch 8:37 Moza . . . became father to *B*
9:43 Moza, he became father to *B*

Binnui
Ezr 8:33 the son of *B* the Levites
10:30 sons of Pahath-moab . . . *B*
10:38 of the sons of *B*, Shimei
Ne 3:24 *B* the son of Henadad repaired
7:15 sons of *B*, six hundred and
10:9 *B* of the sons of Henadad
12:8 the Levites were Jeshua, *B*

Bird
Ge 7:14 every *b*, every winged
Le 14:5 one *b* must be killed in an
14:6 living *b*, he should take it
14:6 the living *b* in the blood of
14:6 *b* that was killed over the
14:7 living *b* over the open field
14:50 must kill the one *b* in an

Le 14:51 *b* and dip them in the blood
14:51 of the *b* that was killed
14:52 the blood of the *b* and the
14:52 the live *b* and the cedarwood
14:53 send the live *b* away outside
De 4:17 any winged *b* that flies in
14:11 Any clean *b* you may eat
Job 22:10 *b* traps are all around you
28:7 no *b* of prey has known it
41:5 play with it as with a *b*
Ps 11:1 Flee as a *b* to your mountain!
84:3 *b* itself has found a house
102:7 like a *b* isolated upon a roof
124:7 Our soul is like a *b* that
Pr 6:5 like a *b* from the hand of the
7:23 *b* hastens into the trap
26:2 as a *b* has cause for fleeing
27:8 *b* fleeing away from its nest
Ec 12:4 gets up at the sound of a *b*
Isa 18:6 *b* of prey of the mountains
18:6 upon it the *b* of prey will
46:11 the sunrising a *b* of prey
Jer 12:9 as a many-colored *b* of prey
La 3:52 hunted for me just as for a *b*
Ho 11:11 Like a *b* they will come
Am 3:5 Will a *b* fall into a trap on
Jas 3:7 *b* and creeping thing and sea
Re 18:2 of every unclean and hated *b*

Birdcatcher
Ps 91:3 from the trap of the *b*
Pr 6:5 bird from the hand of the *b*
Ho 9:8 there is the trap of a *b* on all

Birdcatchers
Jer 5:26 as when *b* crouch down

Birdhouse
Isa 60:8 like doves to their *b* holes

Bird's
De 22:6 In case a *b* nest happens to

Birds
Ge 15:10 young *b* he did not cut in
15:11 *b* of prey began to descend
Le 14:4 two live clean *b* and
14:49 take two *b* and cedarwood and
Ne 5:18 six select sheep and *b*
Ps 8:8 The *b* of heaven and the fish of
104:17 *b* themselves make nests
148:10 things and winged *b*
Ec 9:12 like *b* that are being taken in
Isa 31:5 Like *b* flying, Jehovah of
Jer 12:9 the *b* of prey are round about
Eze 17:23 all the *b* of every wing
39:4, 4 *b* of prey, *b* of every sort
39:17 *b* of every sort of wing
Da 4:12 *b* of the heavens would dwell
4:14 and the *b* from its boughs
4:21 *b* of the heavens would reside
Mt 6:26 Observe intently the *b* of
8:20 and *b* of heaven have roosts
13:4 the *b* came and ate them up
13:32 *b* of heaven come and find
Mr 4:4 and the *b* came and ate it up
4:32 *b* of the heaven are able to
Lu 8:5 the *b* of heaven ate it up
9:58 and *b* of heaven have roosts
12:24 more worth are you than *b*
13:19 *b* of heaven took up lodging
Ac 10:12 of the earth and *b* of heaven
11:6 things and *b* of heaven
Ro 1:23 *b* and four-footed creatures
1Co 15:39 and another flesh of *b*, and
Re 19:17 said to all the *b* that fly
19:21 *b* were filled from the

Birds'
Da 4:33 and his nails like *b* claws

Birsha
Ge 14:2 *B* king of Gomorrah, Shinab

Birth
Ge 3:16 in *b* pangs you will bring
4:1 In time she gave *b* to Cain
4:2 gave *b*, to his brother Abel
4:17 became pregnant and gave *b*
4:20 In time Adah gave *b* to Jabal
4:22 Zillah, she too gave *b* to
4:25 she gave *b* to a son and
11:28 land of his *b*, in Ur of the
16:11 you shall give *b* to a son
17:17 and will Sarah . . . give *b*?
18:13 give *b* although I have
19:38 she too gave *b* to a son
21:7 I have given *b* to a son in his
Ge 22:24 gave *b* to Tebah and Gaham
25:24 came to the full for giving *b*
25:26 at her giving them *b*
29:32 and brought a son to *b*
29:33 brought a son to *b*
29:34 brought a son to *b* and then
29:35 brought a son to *b*
29:35 she left off giving *b*
30:3 she may give *b* upon my knees
30:9 she had left off giving *b*
30:23 and brought a son to *b*
30:25 Rachel had given *b* to Joseph
31:13 return to the land of your *b*
35:16 Rachel proceeded to give *b*
38:27 in the time of her giving *b*
38:28 when she was giving *b* one
Ex 1:16 the Hebrew women to give *b*
1:19 they have already given *b*
2:2 woman . . . brought a son to *b*
15:14 *B* pangs must take hold on
Nu 11:12 I who have given them *b*, so
Jg 13:3 pregnant and give *b* to a son
13:5 certainly give *b* to a son
13:7 certainly give *b* to a son
13:24 gave *b* to a son and called
Ru 4:15 has given *b* to him
1Sa 1:20 and brought a son to *b* and
2:5 barren has given *b* to seven
2:21 gave *b* to three sons and two
4:19 pregnant near to giving *b*
4:19 began giving *b*, because her
1Ki 3:17 I gave *b* close by her in the
3:18 the third day after I gave *b*
3:18 also proceeded to give *b*
2Ki 4:17 and gave *b* to a son at this
19:3 there is no power to give *b*
1Ch 1:32 she gave *b* to Zimran and
2:17 Abigail, she gave *b* to Amasa
2:46 she gave *b* to Haran and Moza
2:48 gave *b* to Sheber and Tirhanah
4:9 I have given him *b* in pain
4:18 she gave *b* to Jered the
7:18 gave *b* to Ishhod and Abi-ezer
7:23 pregnant and gave *b* to a son
Job 15:35 giving *b* to what is hurtful
38:28 who gave *b* to the dewdrops
38:29 who indeed brings it to *b*
39:1 goats of the crag to give *b*
39:1 hinds bring forth with *b*
39:2 time that they give *b*
Ps 7:14 bound to give *b* to falsehood
29:9 the hinds writhe with *b* pains
48:6 *B* pangs like those of a woman
48:6 of a woman giving *b*
51:5 brought forth with *b* pains
Pr 17:25 to her that gave him *b*
23:22 father who caused your *b*
23:25 gave *b* to you will be joyful
27:1 what a day will give *b* to
Ec 3:2 time for *b* and a time to die
Ca 6:9 of the one giving *b* to her
8:5 your mother was in *b* pangs
8:5 she that was giving *b* to you
8:5 experienced *b* pangs
Isa 7:14 is giving *b* to a son, and she
8:3 and in time gave *b* to a son
13:8 *b* pains themselves grab hold
13:8 woman that is giving *b* they
21:3 of a woman that is giving *b*
23:4 I have not had *b* pains, and I
23:4 I have not given *b*, nor
26:17 draws near to giving *b*
26:17 cries out in her *b* pangs
26:18 we have given *b* to wind
26:18 proceed to fall in *b*
26:19 in death drop in *b*
33:11 give *b* to stubble
37:3 there is no power to give *b*
42:14 Like a woman giving *b* I am
45:10 are you in *b* pains with
51:18 sons that she brought to *b*
54:1 woman that did not give *b*
59:4 what is hurtful to *b*
65:23 bring to *b* for disturbance
66:7 labor pains she gave *b*
66:7 Before *b* pangs could come to
66:8 given *b* to her sons
66:9 and not cause the giving *b*
66:9 am I causing a giving *b* and
Jer 2:27 You yourself brought me to *b*
4:31 giving *b* to her first child
6:24 those of a woman giving *b*
13:21 *b* pangs themselves seize
13:21 those of a wife giving *b*
Jer 14:5 in the field has given *b*
15:9 The woman giving *b* to seven
15:10 you have given *b* to me
16:3 who are giving them *b*
16:3 causing their *b* in this land
20:14 that my mother gave me *b*
22:23 there come to you *b* pangs
22:23 of a woman giving *b*
22:26 your mother who gave you *b*
29:6 that they may give *b* to sons
30:6 whether a male is giving *b*
30:6 a female that is giving *b*
31:8 one giving *b*, all together
49:24 Distress and *b* pangs
49:24 a woman that is giving *b*
50:12 She that gave you *b* has
50:43 just like a woman giving *b*
Eze 16:3 Your origin and your *b* were
16:4 as regards your *b*, on the day
23:4 give *b* to sons and daughters
23:15 the land of their *b*
31:6 beasts of the field gave *b*
Da 11:6 he who caused her *b*, and the
Ho 1:6 and to give *b* to a daughter
1:8 pregnant and give *b* to a son
9:11 so that there is no giving *b*
9:16 in case they bring to *b*
13:13 pangs of a woman giving *b*
Mic 4:9 those of a woman giving *b*
4:10 like a woman giving *b*, for
5:3 that she who is giving *b*
5:3 actually gives *b*. And the
Zep 2:2 Before the statute gives *b* to
Zec 13:3 the ones who caused his *b*
13:3 the ones who caused his *b*
Mt 1:18 *b* of Jesus Christ was in this
1:21 give *b* to a son, and you must
1:23 will give *b* to a son, and
1:25 until she gave *b* to a son
Lu 1:14 many will rejoice over his *b*
1:31 and give *b* to a son, and you
1:57 due for Elizabeth to give *b*
2:6 to the full for her to give *b*
2:7 she gave *b* to her son, the
19:12 man of noble *b* traveled to
23:29 wombs that did not give *b*
Joh 9:1 he saw a man blind from *b*
16:21 when she is giving *b*, has
1Co 1:26 not many of noble *b*
Ga 4:27 woman who does not give *b*
Heb 11:23 by his parents after his *b*
Jas 1:15 fertile, gives *b* to sin; in
1Pe 1:3 he gave us a new *b* to a
1:23 been given a new *b*, not by
Re 12:2 and in her agony to give *b*
12:4 who was about to give *b*
12:4 when she did give *b*, it
12:5 she gave *b* to a son, a male
12:13 woman that gave *b* to the

Birthday
Ge 40:20 turned out to be Pharaoh's *b*
Mt 14:6 But when Herod's *b* was being
Mr 6:21 an evening meal on his *b* for

Birthright
Ge 25:32 of what benefit to me is a *b*?
25:34 So Esau despised the *b*
27:36 my *b* he has already taken

Births
Ex 28:10 in the order of their *b*
Nu 1:20 *b* according to their families
1:22 sons of Simeon, their *b*
1:24 *b* according to their families
1:26 *b* according to their families
1:28 *b* according to their families
1:30 *b* according to their families
1:32 *b* according to their families
1:34 *b* according to their families
1:36 their *b* according to their
1:38 Dan, their *b* according to
1:40 their *b* according to their
1:42 their *b* according to their

Birzaith
1Ch 7:31 who was the father of *B*

Bishlam
Ezr 4:7 *B*, Mithredath, Tabeel and the

Bit
Ex 5:11 of your services one *b*
5:19 one *b* of anyone's daily rate
Jg 19:5 your heart with a *b* of bread
1Sa 14:29 this little *b* of honey
1Ki 17:11 Please, get me a *b* of bread

1Ch 29:10 David *b* Jehovah before the
29:10 *B* may you be, O Jehovah the
2Ch 2:12 *B* be Jehovah the God of
6:4 *B* be Jehovah the God of Israel
9:8 Jehovah your God come to be *b*
20:26 for there they *b* Jehovah
30:27 stood up and *b* the people
31:10 Jehovah himself has *b* his
Ezr 7:27 *B* be Jehovah the God of our
Ne 8:6 Ezra *b* Jehovah the true God
11:2 the people *b* all the men who
Job 1:10 work of his hands you have *b*
1:21 the name of Jehovah . . . be *b*
42:12 Jehovah, he *b* the end of Job
Ps 10:3 one making undue profit has *b*
18:46 *b* be my Rock, And let the
21:6 constitute him highly *b*
28:6 *B* be Jehovah, for he has
31:21 *B* be Jehovah, For he has
37:22 those being *b* by him will
41:13 *B* be Jehovah the God of
45:2 has *b* you to time indefinite
66:20 *B* be God, who has not turned
68:19 *B* be Jehovah, who daily
68:35 to the people. *B* be God
72:15 All day long let him be *b*
72:18 *B* be Jehovah God, Israel's
72:19 *b* be his glorious name to
89:52 *B* be Jehovah to time
106:48 *B* be Jehovah the God of
112:2 upright ones, it will be *b*
113:2 May Jehovah's name become *b*
115:15 are the ones *b* by Jehovah
118:26 *B* be the One coming in the
118:26 *b* you people out of the
119:12 *B* you are, O Jehovah
124:6 *B* be Jehovah, who has not
128:4 able-bodied man will be *b*
129:8 *b* you in the name of Jehovah
135:21 *B* out of Zion be Jehovah
144:1 *B* be Jehovah my Rock
147:13 *b* your sons in the midst of
Pr 5:18 water source prove to be *b*
20:21 its own future will not be *b*
22:9 kindly in eye will be *b*
Isa 19:25, 25 *b* it, saying: *B* be my
61:9 offspring whom Jehovah has *b*
Jer 17:7 *B* is the able-bodied man who
20:14 birth not become *b*
Eze 3:12 *B* be the glory of Jehovah
Da 2:19 Daniel himself *b* the God of
2:20 name of God become *b* from
3:28 *B* be the God of Shadrach
4:34 and I *b* the Most High himself
Zec 11:5 May Jehovah be *b*, while I
Mt 21:9 *B* is he that comes in
23:39 until you say, *B* is he that
25:34 have been *b* by my Father
Mr 8:7 having *b* these, he told them
11:9 *B* is he that comes in
11:10 *B* is the coming kingdom of
14:61 Christ the Son of the *B* One
Lu 1:42 *B* are you among women, and
1:42 *b* is the fruit of your womb
1:68 *B* be Jehovah the God of Israel
2:28 received it . . . *b* God and said
2:34 Simeon *b* them, but said to
9:16 *b* them and broke them up and
13:35 *B* is he that comes in
19:38 *B* is the One coming as the
24:30 loaf, *b* it, broke it and
24:50 lifted up his hands and *b*
Joh 12:13 *B* is he that comes in
Ac 3:25 of the earth will be *b*
Ro 1:25 One who created, who is *b*
9:5 God, who is over all, be *b*
2Co 1:3 *B* be the God and Father of
Ga 3:8 all the nations will be *b*
3:9 *b* together with faithful
Eph 1:3 *B* be the God and Father of
1:3 *b* us with every spiritual
Heb 7:1 met Abraham . . . and *b* him
7:6 from Abraham and *b* him who
7:7 the less is *b* by the greater
11:20 Isaac *b* Jacob and Esau
11:21 *b* each of the sons of Joseph
1Pe 1:3 *B* be the God and Father of our

Blesses
1Sa 9:13 the one that *b* the sacrifice
Ps 107:38 *b* them so that they become
Pr 3:33 of the righteous ones he *b*

Blessing
Ge 12:2 and prove yourself a *b*
26:12 as Jehovah was *b* him
27:12 a malediction and not a *b*
27:29 each one of those *b* you
27:30 as Isaac had finished *b* Jacob
27:35 get the *b* meant for you
27:36 this time he has taken my *b*
27:36 you not reserved a *b* for me
27:38 just one *b* that you have
27:41 on account of the *b*
28:4 give to you the *b* of Abraham
30:27 Jehovah is *b* me due to you
33:11 the gift conveying my *b*
39:5 Jehovah kept *b* the house of
39:5 Jehovah's *b* came to be upon
48:20 repeatedly pronounce *b*
49:28 when he was *b* them
49:28 according to his own *b*
Ex 32:29 confer a *b* upon you today
Le 25:21 *b* for you in the sixth year
Nu 24:9 Those *b* you are the ones
De 11:26 *b* and malediction
11:27 the *b*, provided you will
11:29 the *b* upon Mount Gerizim
12:15 the *b* of Jehovah your God
16:17 the *b* of Jehovah your God
23:5 the malediction into a *b*
28:8 *b* on your stores of supply
30:1 the *b* and the malediction
30:19 the *b* and the malediction
33:1 is the *b* with which Moses
33:7 And this was Judah's *b*, as he
33:23 And full of the *b* of Jehovah
Jos 8:34 the *b* and the malediction
15:19 Do give me a *b*, for it is
Jg 1:15 Do grant me a *b*, for it is a
1Sa 25:27 regards this gift *b* that
30:26 gift *b* for you from the
2Sa 6:11 Jehovah kept *b* Obed-edom and
7:29 due to your *b* let the house
2Ki 5:15 a *b* gift from your servant
1Ch 13:14 Jehovah kept *b* the household
23:13 pronounce *b* in his name to
Ne 9:5 exalted above all *b* and praise
Job 29:13 *b* of the one about to perish
Ps 3:8 Your *b* is upon your people
24:5 carry away *b* from Jehovah
37:26 offspring are in line for a *b*
49:18 he kept *b* his own soul
109:17 not take delight in the *b*
109:28 your part, pronounce a *b*
129:8 *b* of Jehovah be upon you men
133:3 Jehovah commanded the *b* to
Pr 10:7 righteous one is due for a *b*
10:22 The *b* of Jehovah—that is
11:11 *b* of the upright ones a town
11:26 *b* for the head of the one
24:25 will come the *b* of good
27:14 *b* his fellowman with a loud
Isa 19:24 *b* in the midst of the earth
44:3 my *b* upon your descendants
65:8 there is a *b* in it
65:16 anyone *b* himself in the
66:3 a *b* with uncanny words
Eze 34:26 surroundings of my hill a *b*
34:26 Pouring rains of *b* there
44:30 *b* to rest upon your house
Joe 2:14 let remain after it a *b*
Hag 2:19 this day I shall bestow *b*
Zec 8:13 and you must become a *b*
Mal 2:2 I have even cursed the *b*
3:10 empty out upon you a *b* until
Mt 14:19 said a *b* and, after breaking
26:26 a loaf and, after saying a *b*
Mr 6:41 a *b*, and broke the loaves
10:16 *b* them, laying his hands
14:22 he took a loaf, said a *b*
Lu 1:64 and he began to speak, *b* God
24:51 As he was *b* them he was
24:53 in the temple *b* God
Ro 12:14 *b* those who persecute
12:14 be *b* and do not be cursing
15:29 measure of *b* from Christ
1Co 10:16 The cup of *b* which we bless
Ga 3:14 *b* of Abraham might come to
Eph 1:3 us with every spiritual *b*
Heb 6:7 in return a *b* from God
6:14 in *b* I will bless you, and
12:17 wanted to inherit the *b* he
Jas 3:10 come forth *b* and cursing
1Pe 3:9 bestowing a *b*, because you
3:9 so that you might inherit a *b*
Re 5:12 and honor and glory and *b*
5:13 to the Lamb be the *b* and the
7:12 The *b* and the glory and the

Blessings
Ge 49:25 the *b* of the heavens above
49:25 the *b* of the watery deep
49:25 *b* of the breasts and womb
49:26 *b* of your father will indeed
49:26 *b* of the eternal mountains
De 28:2 these *b* must come upon you
Ps 21:3 to meet him with *b* of good
84:6 with *b* the instructor enwraps
Pr 10:6 *B* are for the head of the
28:20 faithful acts . . . get many *b*
Mal 2:2 and I will curse your *b*

Blew
Ex 15:10 You *b* with your breath, the
Jos 6:8 passed on and *b* the horns, and
6:16 that the priests *b* the horns
Jg 7:20 *b* the horns and shattered the
2Sa 2:28 Joab now *b* the horn, and
18:16 Joab now *b* the horn, that
20:22 Upon that he *b* the horn
Hag 1:9 *b* upon it—for what reason
Mt 7:25 winds *b* and lashed against
7:27 floods came and the winds *b*
Joh 20:22 *b* upon them and said to
Ac 27:13 south wind *b* softly, they
Re 8:7 the first one *b* his trumpet
8:8 the second angel *b* his trumpet
8:10 the third angel *b* his trumpet
8:12 fourth angel *b* his trumpet
9:1 the fifth angel *b* his trumpet
9:13 the sixth angel *b* his trumpet
11:15 seventh angel *b* his trumpet

Blind
Ex 4:11 or who appoints . . . the *b*?
Le 19:14 before a *b* man you must not
21:18 man *b* or lame or with his
De 15:21 lame or *b*, any bad defect
27:18 causes the *b* to go astray
28:29 just as a *b* man gropes about
2Sa 5:6 *b* and the lame ones will
5:8 lame and the *b*, hateful to
5:8 *b* one and the lame one will
Job 29:15 Eyes I became to the *b* one
Ps 146:8 opening the eyes of the *b*
Isa 29:9 *b* yourselves, and be blinded
29:18 of the *b* ones will see
35:5 eyes of the *b* ones will be
42:7 to open the *b* eyes, to bring
42:16 make the *b* ones walk in a
42:18 forth to see, you *b* ones
42:19 Who is *b*, if not my servant
42:19 *b* as the one rewarded
42:19 *b* as the servant of Jehovah
43:8 *b* though eyes themselves
56:10 His watchmen are *b*. None of
59:10 just like *b* men, and like
Jer 31:8 *b* and the lame, the pregnant
La 4:14 They have wandered about as *b*
Zep 1:17 walk like *b* men
Mal 1:8 a *b* animal for sacrificing
Mt 9:27 two *b* men followed him
9:28 the *b* men came to him, and
11:5 The *b* are seeing again, and
12:22 a demon-possessed man, *b*
15:14 *B* guides is what they are
15:14, 14 a *b* man guides a *b* man
15:30 lame, maimed, *b*, dumb, and
15:31 and the *b* seeing, and they
20:30 two *b* men sitting beside
21:14 *b* and lame persons came up
23:16 Woe to you, *b* guides, who
23:17 Fools and *b* ones! Which, in
23:19 *B* ones! Which, in fact, is
23:24 *B* guides, who strain out the
23:26 *B* Pharisee, cleanse first
Mr 8:22 people brought him a *b* man
8:23 took the *b* man by the hand
10:46 a *b* beggar, was sitting
10:49 they called the *b* man
10:51 The *b* man said to him
Lu 4:18 a recovery of sight to the *b*
6:39 A *b* man cannot guide a
6:39 cannot guide a *b* man, can he
7:21 *b* persons the favor of seeing
7:22 the *b* are receiving sight
14:13 people, crippled, lame, *b*
14:21 poor and crippled and *b* and
18:35 *b* man was sitting beside the
Joh 5:3 a multitude of the sick, *b*
9:1 he saw a man *b* from birth
9:2 so that he was born *b*
9:17 they said to the *b* man again

Joh 9:18 been *b* and had gained sight
9:19 son who you say was born *b*
9:20 son and that he was born *b*
9:24 the man that had been *b* and
9:25 I was *b*, I see at present
9:32 the eyes of one born *b*
9:39 those seeing might become *b*
9:40 We are not *b* also, are we?
9:41 If you were *b*, you would
10:21 cannot open *b* people's eyes
11:37 the eyes of the *b* man
Ac 13:11 and you will be *b*, not
Ro 2:19 you are a guide of the *b*, a
1Pe 2:16 not as a *b* for badness, but
2Pe 1:9 he is *b*, shutting his eyes
Re 3:17 and poor and *b* and naked

Blinded
2Ki 25:7 and Zedekiah's eyes he *b*
Isa 29:9 blind yourselves, and be *b*
Jer 39:7 eyes of Zedekiah he *b*, after
52:11 And the eyes of Zedekiah he *b*
Joh 12:40 He has *b* their eyes and he
2Co 4:4 *b* the minds . . . unbelievers
1Jo 2:11 the darkness has *b* his eyes

Blindness
Ge 19:11 they struck with *b* the men
Le 22:22 No case of *b* or fracture or
2Ki 6:18 strike this nation with *b*
6:18 So he struck them with *b*

Blinds
Ex 23:8 the bribe *b* clear-sighted men
De 16:19 *b* the eyes of wise ones and

Blinking
Pr 16:30 *b* with his eyes to scheme up

Blisters
Ex 9:9 boils breaking out with *b*
9:10 and it became boils with *b*

Block
1Sa 25:31 stumbling *b* to the heart of
Ps 5:11 you will *b* approach to them
91:4 pinions he will *b* approach to
119:165 there is no stumbling *b*
Ca 8:9 *b* her up with a cedar plank
Isa 14:21 slaughtering *b* for his own
Eze 3:20 put a stumbling *b* before him
7:19 a stumbling *b* causing their
14:3 stumbling *b* causing their
14:4 places the very stumbling *b*
14:7 sets the very stumbling *b*
18:30 a stumbling *b* causing error
42:1 the dining-room *b* that was
44:12 stumbling *b* into error
Mt 16:23 You are a stumbling *b* to me
18:7 whom the stumbling *b* comes
Ro 11:9 stumbling *b* and a retribution
14:13 a stumbling *b* or a cause
1Co 8:9 a stumbling *b* to those who
Ga 5:11 stumbling *b* of the torture
Re 2:14 stumbling *b* before the sons

Blockaded
Isa 1:8 like a *b* city

Blocked
Job 19:8 My very path he has *b* with a
40:22 lotus trees keep it *b* off
La 3:7 *b* me up as with a stone wall
3:9 *b* up my ways with hewn stone
3:43 have *b* approach with anger
3:44 *b* approach to yourself with a

Blocks
Jer 6:21 for this people stumbling *b*
Zep 1:3 stumbling *b* with the wicked
Mt 18:7 world due to the stumbling *b*
18:7 stumbling *b* must . . . come

Blood
Ge 4:10 Your brother's *b* is crying
4:11 to receive your brother's *b*
9:4 flesh with its soul—its *b*
9:5 your *b* of your souls shall I
9:6 Anyone shedding man's *b*, by
9:6 by man will his own *b* be shed
37:22 Do not spill *b*. Pitch him
37:26 and did cover over his *b*
37:31 the long garment in the *b*
42:22 And now his *b*, here it is
49:11 garment in the *b* of grapes
Ex 4:9 become *b* on the dry land
4:25 are a bridegroom of *b* to me
4:26 A bridegroom of *b* because of
7:17 will certainly turn into *b*
Ex 7:19 that they may become *b*
7:19 be *b* in all the land of Egypt
7:20 Nile River was turned into *b*
7:21 *b* came to be in all the land
12:7 *b* and splash it upon the two
12:13 *b* must serve as your sign
12:13 see the *b* and pass over you
12:22 hyssop and dip it into the *b*
12:22 two doorposts some of the *b*
12:23 *b* upon the upper part of the
23:18 the *b* of my sacrifice
24:6 Moses took half the *b* and put
24:6 half the *b* he sprinkled upon
24:8 took the *b* and sprinkled it
24:8 *b* of the covenant that Jehovah
29:12 take some of the bull's *b*
29:12 rest of the *b* you will pour
29:16 take its *b* and sprinkle it
29:20 ram and take some of its *b*
29:20 sprinkle the *b* round about
29:21 the *b* that is upon the altar
30:10 the *b* of the sin offering of
34:25 the *b* of my sacrifice
Le 1:5 present the *b* and sprinkle the
1:5 and sprinkle the *b* round about
1:11 sprinkle its *b* round about
1:15 its *b* must be drained out
3:2 sprinkle the *b* round about upon
3:8 its *b* round about upon the
3:13 sprinkle its *b* round about
3:17 must not eat any fat or any *b*
4:5 the bull's *b* and bring it into
4:6 in the *b* and spatter some of
4:6 spatter some of the *b* seven
4:7 *b* upon the horns of the altar
4:7 the rest of the bull's *b* he
4:16 the bull's *b* into the tent of
4:17 *b* and spatter it seven times
4:18 some of the *b* upon the horns
4:18 rest of the *b* he will pour
4:25 of the *b* of the sin offering
4:25 pour the rest of its *b* at the
4:30 of its *b* with his finger and
4:30 its *b* at the base of the altar
4:34 of the *b* of the sin offering
4:34 its *b* at the base of the altar
5:9 the *b* of the sin offering upon
5:9 the remainder of the *b* will be
6:27 of its *b* upon the garment
6:27 wash what he spatters *b* upon
6:30 some of the *b* will be
7:2 its *b* one will sprinkle round
7:14 priest who sprinkles the *b* of
7:26 must not eat any *b* in any
7:27 Any soul who eats any *b*, that
7:33 *b* of the communion sacrifices
8:15 take the *b* and put it with
8:15 the rest of the *b* he poured
8:19 sprinkled the *b* round about
8:23 its *b* and put it upon the lobe
8:24 some of the *b* upon the lobe of
8:24 the *b* round about upon the
8:30 *b* that was upon the altar and
9:9 sons presented the *b* to him
9:9 he dipped his finger in the *b*
9:9 the rest of the *b* he poured at
9:12 Aaron's sons handed him the *b*
9:18 the *b* and he sprinkled it
10:18 Look! Its *b* has not been
12:4 stay in the *b* of purification
12:5 with the *b* of purification
12:7 from the source of her *b*
14:6 *b* of the bird that was killed
14:14 the *b* of the guilt offering
14:17 the *b* of the guilt offering
14:25 the *b* of the guilt offering
14:28 the *b* of the guilt offering
14:51 *b* of the bird that was killed
14:52 the *b* of the bird and the
15:19 discharge . . . proves to be *b*
15:25 her *b* should be flowing many
16:14 bull's *b* and spatter it with
16:14 spatter some of the *b* with
16:15 bring its *b* inside the
16:15 its *b* the same as he did
16:15 as he did with the bull's *b*
16:18 take some of the bull's *b*
16:18 some of the goat's *b* and put
16:19 spatter some of the *b* upon
16:27 *b* of both of which was
17:4 He has shed *b*, and that man
17:6 priest must sprinkle the *b*
17:10 eats any sort of *b*, I shall
17:10 soul that is eating the *b*, and
Le 17:11 soul of the flesh is in the *b*
17:11 *b* that makes atonement by
17:12 No soul of you must eat *b*
17:12 in your midst should eat *b*
17:13 pour its *b* out and cover it
17:14 every sort of flesh is its *b*
17:14 must not eat the *b* of any
17:14 every sort of flesh is its *b*
18:12 She is the *b* relation of your
18:13 *b* relation of your mother
18:17 are cases of *b* relationship
19:16 up against your fellow's *b*
19:26 eat nothing along with *b*
20:9 His own *b* is upon him
20:11 Their own *b* is upon them
20:12 Their own *b* is upon them
20:13 Their own *b* is upon them
20:16 Their own *b* is upon them
20:18 laid bare the source of her *b*
20:19 his *b* relation that one has
20:27 Their own *b* is upon them
21:2 *b* relation of his who is
25:49 *b* relative of his flesh, one
Nu 18:17 Their *b* you should sprinkle
19:4 *b* with his finger and spatter
19:4 and spatter some of its *b*
19:5 *b* together with its dung will
23:24 the *b* of the slain ones it will
27:11 inheritance to his *b* relation
35:12 a refuge from the *b* avenger
35:19 avenger of *b* is the one who
35:21 avenger of *b* will put the
35:24 striker and the avenger of *b*
35:25 the hand of the avenger of *b*
35:27 avenger of *b* does find him
35:27 avenger of *b* does slay the
35:33 is *b* that pollutes the land
35:33 *b* that has been spilled upon
35:33 the *b* of the one spilling it
De 12:16 Only the *b* you must not eat
12:23 resolved not to eat the *b*
12:23 the *b* is the soul and you
12:27 the flesh and the *b*, upon the
12:27 the *b* of your sacrifices
15:23 Only its *b* you must not eat
17:8 one in which *b* has been shed
19:6 Otherwise, the avenger of *b*
19:10 no innocent *b* may be spilled
19:12 the hand of the avenger of *b*
19:13 the guilt of innocent *b* out
21:7 Our hands did not shed this *b*
21:8 put the guilt of innocent *b*
21:9 the guilt of innocent *b* from
27:25 when it is innocent *b*
32:14 the *b* of the grape you kept
32:42 intoxicate my arrows with *b*
32:42 the *b* of the slain and the
32:43 avenge the *b* of his servants
Jos 2:19 his *b* will be upon his own
2:19 his *b* will be on our heads
20:3 refuge from the avenger of *b*
20:5 avenger of *b* chases after
20:9 the hand of the avenger of *b*
Jg 9:24 he might put their *b* upon
1Sa 14:32 to eating along with the *b*
14:33 by eating along with the *b*
14:34 by eating along with the *b*
19:5 sin against innocent *b* in
25:31 shedding of *b* without cause
26:20 my *b* fall to the earth
2Sa 1:22 *b* of the slain, from the fat
3:27 because of the *b* of Asahel
4:11 his *b* from your hands
14:11 avenger of *b* may not be
20:12 was wallowing in the *b* in
23:17 *b* of the men going at the
1Ki 2:5 the *b* of war in peacetime and
2:5 put the *b* of war on his belt
2:9 hairs down to Sheol with *b*
2:31 *b* undeservedly shed that Joab
2:32 his *b* upon his own head
2:33 their *b* must come back upon
16:11 avengers of *b* or his friends
18:28 they caused *b* to flow out
21:19 dogs licked up the *b* of
21:19 dogs will lick up your *b*
22:35 *b* of the wound kept pouring
22:38 dogs went licking up his *b*
2Ki 3:22 saw the water red like *b*
3:23 began to say: This is *b*!
9:7 avenge the *b* of my servants
9:7 the *b* of all the servants of
9:26 the *b* of Naboth and the
9:26 Naboth and the *b* of his sons

2Ki 9:33 her *b* went spattering upon
16:13 the *b* of the communion
16:15 all the *b* of burnt offering
16:15 all the *b* of a sacrifice
21:16 innocent *b* that Manasseh
24:4 innocent *b* that he had shed
24:4 Jerusalem with innocent *b*
1Ch 11:19 Is it the *b* of these men
22:8 *B* in great quantity you have
22:8 a great deal of *b* you have
28:3 and *b* you have spilled
2Ch 19:10 involving the shedding of *b*
24:25 *b* of the sons of Jehoiada
29:22 priests received the *b* and
29:22 the *b* upon the altar
29:22 the *b* upon the altar
29:24 sin offering with their *b*
30:16 priests sprinkling the *b*
35:11 sprinkle the *b* from their
Job 16:18 O earth, do not cover my *b*
39:30 young . . . keep sipping up *b*
Ps 16:4 their drink offerings of *b*
30:9 What profit is there in my *b*
50:13 *b* of he-goats shall I drink?
58:10 bathe in the *b* of the wicked
68:23 you may wash your foot in *b*
72:14 *b* will be precious in his
78:44 changing to *b* their Nile
79:3 poured out their *b* like water
79:10 avenging of the *b* of your
94:21 the *b* of the innocent one
105:29 changed their waters into *b*
106:38 kept spilling innocent *b*
106:38 *b* of their sons and their
Pr 1:11 let us lie in ambush for *b*
1:16 keep hastening to shed *b*
1:18 ambush for the very *b* of
6:17 that are shedding innocent *b*
12:6 are a lying in wait for *b*
30:33 nose is what brings forth *b*
Isa 1:11 *b* of young bulls and male
9:5 mantle rolled in *b* have even
15:9 Dimon have become full of *b*
34:3 must melt because of their *b*
34:6 it must be filled with *b*
34:6 *b* of young rams and he-goats
34:7 must be drenched with *b*
49:26 drunk with their own *b*
59:3 have become polluted with *b*
59:7 in a hurry to shed innocent *b*
63:3 spurting *b* kept spattering
63:6 to the earth their spurting *b*
66:3 a gift—the *b* of a pig
Jer 2:34 the *b* marks of the souls of
7:6 innocent *b* you will not shed
19:4 the *b* of the innocent ones
22:3 do not shed any innocent *b*
22:17 upon the *b* of the innocent
26:15 it is innocent *b* that you
46:10 take its fill of their *b*
48:10 holding . . . his sword from *b*
51:35 *b* be upon the inhabitants
La 4:13 pouring out the *b* of righteous
4:14 have become polluted with *b*
Eze 3:18 his *b* I shall ask back from
3:20 his *b* I shall ask back from
5:17 pestilence and *b* themselves
14:19 my rage upon it with *b*, in
16:6 kicking about in your *b*, and
16:6 to say to you in your *b*, Keep
16:6 say to you in your *b*, Keep
16:9 rinsed away your *b* from off
16:22 kicking about in your *b* you
16:36 with the *b* of your sons
16:38 and women shedding *b*, and I
16:38 the *b* of rage and jealousy
18:10 a shedder of *b*, who has
18:13 On him his own *b* will come
19:10 was like a vine in your *b*
21:32 own *b* will prove to be in
22:3 O city that is shedding *b* in
22:4 *b* that you have shed you
22:6 for the purpose of shedding *b*
22:9 for the purpose of shedding *b*
22:12 the purpose of shedding *b*
22:27 tearing prey in shedding *b*
23:37 there is *b* on their hands
23:45 for female shedders of *b*
23:45 there is *b* on their hands
24:7 its very *b* has come to be
24:8 I have put her *b* upon the
28:23 and *b* into her streets
32:6 matter, from your *b*, upon
33:4 his own *b* will come to be
Eze 33:5 His own *b* will come to be
33:6 its *b* I shall ask back from
33:8 his *b* I shall ask back at
33:25 With the *b* you keep eating
33:25 *b* you keep pouring out
35:6 for *b* that I was preparing
35:6 *b* itself will also pursue
35:6 it was *b* that you hated
35:6 and *b* itself will pursue you
36:18 *b* that they had poured out
38:22 with pestilence and with *b*
39:17 eat flesh and drink *b*
39:18 the *b* of the chieftains of
39:19 to drink *b* to drunkenness
43:18 and to sprinkle upon it *b*
43:20 *b* and put it upon its four
44:7 present my bread, fat and *b*
44:15 present to me fat and the *b*
45:19 *b* of the sin offering and
Ho 6:8 their footprints are *b*
Joe 2:30 *b* and fire and columns of
2:31 and the moon into *b*
3:19 they shed innocent *b*
3:21 consider innocent their *b*
Jon 1:14 do not put upon us innocent *b*
Hab 2:8 the shedding of *b* of mankind
2:17 the shedding of *b* of mankind
Zep 1:17 *b* will actually be poured
Zec 9:11 by the *b* of your covenant
Mt 9:20 years from a flow of *b*
16:17 flesh and *b* did not reveal
23:30 in the *b* of the prophets
23:35 righteous *b* spilled on earth
23:35 from the *b* of righteous Abel
23:35 to the *b* of Zechariah son of
26:28 means my *b* of the covenant
27:4 when I betrayed righteous *b*
27:6 they are the price of *b*
27:8 called Field of *B* to this
27:24 am innocent of the *b* of this
27:25 His *b* come upon us and upon
27:49 and *b* and water came out
Mr 5:25 woman subject to a flow of *b*
5:29 her fountain of *b* dried up
14:24 means my *b* of the covenant
Lu 8:43 a flow of *b* for twelve years
8:44 her flow of *b* stopped
11:50 the *b* of all the prophets
11:51 from the *b* of Abel down to
11:51 down to the *b* of Zechariah
13:1 Galileans whose *b* Pilate had
22:20 covenant by virtue of my *b*
22:44 sweat became as drops of *b*
Joh 1:13 born, not from *b* or from a
6:53 Son of man and drink his *b*
6:54 drinks my *b* has everlasting
6:55 and my *b* is true drink
6:56 my flesh and drinks my *b*
19:34 *b* and water came out
Ac 1:19 *A·kel′da·ma* . . . Field of *B*
2:19 *b* and fire and smoke mist
2:20 moon into *b* before the great
5:28 the *b* of this man upon us
15:20 to abstain . . . from *b*
15:29 keep abstaining . . . from *b*
18:6 your *b* be upon your own heads
20:26 clean from the *b* of all men
20:28 with the *b* of his own Son
21:25 keep themselves from . . . *b*
22:20 *b* of Stephen your witness
Ro 3:15 feet are speedy to shed *b*
3:25 through faith in his *b*
5:9 righteous now by his *b*
1Co 10:16 a sharing in the *b* of the
11:25 covenant by virtue of my *b*
11:27 body and the *b* of the Lord
15:50 flesh and *b* cannot inherit
Ga 1:16 conference with flesh and *b*
Eph 1:7 ransom through the *b* of that
2:13 near by the *b* of the Christ
6:12 not against *b* and flesh, but
Col 1:20 peace through the *b* he shed
Heb 2:14 are sharers of *b* and flesh
9:7 *b*, which he offers for
9:12 the *b* of goats and of young
9:12 but with his own *b*, once for
9:13 the *b* of goats and of bulls
9:14 the *b* of the Christ, who
9:18 inaugurated without *b*
9:19 *b* of the young bulls and of
9:20 *b* of the covenant that God
9:21 he sprinkled . . . with the *b*
9:22 cleansed with *b* according to
9:22 unless *b* is poured out no
Heb 9:25 with *b* not his own
10:4 *b* of bulls and of goats to
10:19 holy place by the *b* of Jesus
10:29 *b* of the covenant by which
11:28 and the splashing of the *b*
12:4 yet resisted as far as *b*
12:24 and the *b* of sprinkling
12:24 a better way than Abel's *b*
13:11 animals whose *b* is taken
13:12 the people with his own *b*
13:20 *b* of an everlasting covenant
1Pe 1:2 sprinkled with the *b* of Jesus
1:19 But it was with precious *b*
1Jo 1:7 *b* of Jesus his Son cleanses us
5:6 came by means of water and *b*
5:6 the water and with the *b*
5:8 spirit . . . water and the *b*
Re 1:5 by means of his own *b*
5:9 with your *b* you bought persons
6:10 judging and avenging our *b*
6:12 the entire moon became as *b*
7:14 white in the *b* of the Lamb
8:7 hail and fire mingled with *b*
8:8 third of the sea became *b*
11:6 waters to turn them into *b*
12:11 because of the *b* of the Lamb
14:20 *b* came out of the winepress
16:3 became *b* as of a dead man
16:4 the waters. And they became *b*
16:6 poured out the *b* of holy ones
16:6 *b* to drink. They deserve it
17:6 with the *b* of the holy ones
17:6 *b* of the witnesses of Jesus
18:24 *b* of prophets and of holy
19:2 avenged the *b* of his slaves
19:13 garment sprinkled with *b*

Bloodguilt
Ex 22:2 die, there is no *b* for him
22:3 there is *b* for him.) He is to
Le 17:4 *b* will be counted to that man
Nu 35:27 the avenger . . . has no *b*
De 19:10 no *b* has to be upon you
21:8 *b* must not be set to their
22:8 not place *b* upon your house
1Sa 25:26 from entering into *b* and
25:33 entering into *b* and
2Sa 1:16 *b* for you be upon your own
3:28 of *b* for Abner the son of
16:8 the *b* for the house of Saul
21:1 upon his house there is *b*
1Ki 2:37 *B* for you will itself come
Pr 28:17 with the *b* for a soul

Bloodguiltiness
Ps 51:14 Deliver me from *b*, O God

Bloodguilty
2Sa 16:7 get out, you *b* man and
16:8 because you are a *b* man
Ps 26:9 Nor my life along with *b* men
55:23 As for *b* and deceitful men
59:2 And from *b* men save me
139:19 *b* men will certainly depart
Eze 22:2 will you judge the *b* city

Bloodshed
Ps 5:6 A man of *b* and deception
9:12 when looking for *b*, he will
106:38 came to be polluted with *b*
Isa 1:15 With *b* your very hands have
4:4 even the *b* of Jerusalem from
26:21 expose her *b* and will no
33:15 ear from listening to *b*
Eze 9:9 the land is filled with *b* and
22:13 over your acts of *b* that
24:6 to the city of deeds of *b*
24:9 the city of deeds of *b*
Ho 1:4 accounting for the acts of *b*
4:2 acts of *b* have touched other
4:2 touched other acts of *b*
12:14 his deeds of *b* he leaves
Mic 3:10 acts of *b* and Jerusalem
7:2 for *b* they lie in wait
Na 3:1 Woe to the city of *b*. She is
Hab 2:12 that is building a city by *b*

Bloodstained
Eze 7:23 become full of *b* judgment
Zec 9:7 remove his *b* things from

Bloodthirsty
Pr 29:10 *B* men hate anyone blameless

Bloom
Isa 18:5 *b* becomes a ripening grape
1Co 7:36 that is past the *b* of youth

Bloomed
Ca 7:12 the pomegranate trees have *b*

Blossom
1Ki 7:26 the brim of a cup, a lily *b*
2Ch 4:5 the brim of a cup, a lily *b*
Job 14:2 Like a *b* he has come forth
Ps 72:16 *b* like the vegetation of
92:7 of what is hurtful *b* forth
92:12 righteous himself will *b*
92:13 our God, they will *b* forth
103:15 *b* of the field is the way
Ca 7:12 the *b* has burst open, the
Isa 5:24 *b* itself will go up just
18:5 *b* comes to perfection and
28:1 fading *b* of its decoration
35:1 joyful and *b* as the saffron
35:2 Without fail it will *b*
40:6 is like the *b* of the field
40:7 the *b* has withered, because
40:8 the *b* has withered; but as
Eze 17:24 have made the dry tree *b*
Ho 14:5 He will *b* like the lily, and
Na 1:4 very *b* of Lebanon has withered
Hab 3:17 fig tree itself may not *b*
1Pe 1:24 glory is like a *b* of grass

Blossomed
Ca 6:11 the pomegranate trees had *b*
Eze 7:10 rod has *b*. Presumptuousness

Blossoming
Nu 17:8 buds and *b* flowers and was

Blossoms
Ge 40:10 Its *b* pushed forth
Ex 25:31 its *b* are to proceed out
25:33 with knobs and *b* alternating
25:33 with knobs and *b* alternating
25:34 knobs and its *b* alternating
37:17 its knobs and its *b* proceeded
37:19 knobs and *b* alternating
37:19 with knobs and *b* alternating
37:20 knobs and its *b* alternating
Nu 8:4 up to its *b* it was hammered
1Ki 6:18 ornaments and garlands of *b*
6:29 engravings of *b*, inside and
6:32 the engravings of *b*, and he
6:35 engravings of *b*, and overlaid
7:49 the *b* and the lamps and the
2Ch 4:21 the *b* and the lamps and the
Job 15:33 cast off his *b* just like an
Ps 90:6 puts forth *b* and must change
103:15 is the way he *b* forth
Ec 12:5 the almond tree carries *b*
Ca 2:12 *B* themselves have appeared in
Isa 27:6 Israel will put forth *b* and

Blot
Re 3:5 *b* out his name from the book

Blotch
Le 13:2 an eruption or a scab or a *b*
13:4 if the *b* is white in the skin
13:19 a reddish-white *b*, he must
13:23 if in its place the *b* should
13:24 become a reddish-white *b* or
13:25 hair . . . white in the *b*
13:26 is no white hair in the *b*
13:28 if the *b* stands in its place
14:56 and the scab and the *b*

Blotches
Le 13:38 *b* develop in the skin of
13:38 skin of their flesh, white *b*
13:39 if the *b* in the skin of their

Blotted
Ac 3:19 as to get your sins *b* out
Col 2:14 and *b* out the handwritten

Blow
Ge 2:7 *b* into his nostrils the breath
4:23 young man for giving me a *b*
8:21 deal every living thing a *b*
Ex 10:13 east wind to *b* upon the land
21:25, 25 wound for wound, *b* for *b*
Nu 10:3 *b* on them both, and the whole
10:4 *b* on just one, the chieftains
10:5 *b* a fluctuating blast, and
10:6 *b* a fluctuating blast a second
10:6 *b* a fluctuating blast for each
10:7 you should *b*, but you must
10:8 *b* on the trumpets, and the
10:10 *b* on the trumpets over your
Jos 6:4 the priests should *b* the horns
6:20 they proceeded to *b* the horns
8:15 all Israel suffered a *b*
Jg 7:18 must *b* the horns, you too
7:19 *b* the horns, and there was a
7:20 on the horns to *b* them, and
7:22 to *b* the horns, and Jehovah
1Sa 26:10 Jehovah . . . deal him a *b*
2Sa 12:15 deal a *b* to the child that
20:1 he proceeded to *b* the horn
1Ki 1:34 you must *b* the horn and say
1:39 they began to *b* the horn
2Ki 9:13 began to *b* the horn and say
2Ch 13:20 Jehovah dealt him a *b*, so
21:14 great *b* to your people and
Ne 4:18 the one to *b* the horn was
Ps 78:26 south wind *b* by his own
81:3 On the new moon, *b* the horn
147:18 He causes his wind to *b*
Isa 19:22 certainly deal Egypt a *b*
19:22 a dealing of a *b* and a
40:24 *b* upon them and they dry up
Jer 4:5 *b* a horn throughout the land
6:1 and in Tekoa *b* the horn
51:27 *B* a horn among the nations
Eze 21:31 my fury I shall *b* upon you
22:20 *b* upon it with fire to
22:20 I will *b* and cause you
22:21 *b* upon you with the fire of
24:16 to your eyes by a *b*
33:6 does not *b* the horn and the
37:9 *b* upon these killed people
Ho 5:8 *B* a horn in Gibeah, a trumpet
Joe 2:1 *B* a horn in Zion, O men
2:15 *B* a horn in Zion, O men
Zec 9:14 Jehovah himself will *b*
Mt 6:2 do not *b* a trumpet ahead of
Re 7:1 that no wind might *b* upon the
8:6 trumpets prepared to *b* them
8:13 about to *b* their trumpets
10:7 he is about to *b* his trumpet

Blowing
Ex 19:13 At the *b* of the ram's horn
Nu 31:6 trumpets for *b* calls were in
Jos 6:9 of the priests *b* the horns
6:9 a continual *b* on the horns
6:13 continually *b* the horns, and
6:13 a continual *b* on the horns
Jg 3:27 he began *b* the horn in the
6:34 he went *b* the horn, and the
2Ki 11:14 and *b* the trumpets
2Ch 23:13 and *b* the trumpets, and
Ps 150:3 with the *b* of the horn
Isa 18:3 there is the *b* of a horn
27:13 *b* on a great horn, and
54:16 *b* upon the fire of charcoal
Lu 12:55 see that a south wind is *b*
Joh 6:18 a strong wind was *b*

Blown
Jg 7:18 I have *b* the horn, I and all
1Sa 13:3 the horn *b* throughout all the
Isa 40:7 spirit of Jehovah has *b* upon
Jer 1:13 cooking pot *b* upon is what
Eze 7:14 They have *b* the trumpet and
Am 3:6 If a horn is *b* in a city
Jas 1:6 driven by the wind and *b*

Blows
Ex 9:14 sending all my *b* against your
Le 26:21 inflict seven times more *b*
Job 39:25 as the horn *b* it says Aha!
Ps 89:23 him I kept dealing out *b*
Eze 33:3 *b* the horn and warns the
Lu 10:30 stripped him and inflicted *b*
Joh 3:8 The wind *b* where it wants to
Ac 16:23 inflicted many *b* upon them
1Co 9:26 directing my *b* is so as not
2Co 11:23 in *b* to an excess, in

Blue
Ex 25:4 *b* thread, and wool dyed
26:1 and *b* thread and wool dyed
26:4 make loops of *b* thread upon
26:31 make a curtain of *b* thread
26:36 of *b* thread and wool dyed
27:16 of *b* thread and wool dyed
28:5 take the gold and the *b* thread
28:6 ephod of gold, *b* thread and
28:8 of gold, *b* thread and wool
28:15 Of gold, *b* thread and wool
28:28 of the ephod with a *b* string
28:31 coat . . . of *b* thread
28:33 pomegranates of *b* thread and
28:37 fasten it with a *b* string
35:6 and *b* thread and wool dyed
35:23 found *b* thread and wool dyed
35:25 *b* thread and the wool dyed
Ex 35:35 of a weaver in *b* thread and
36:8 *b* thread and wool dyed reddish
36:11 made loops of *b* thread upon
36:35 a curtain of *b* thread and
36:37 out of *b* thread and wool
38:18 of *b* thread and wool dyed
38:23 the *b* thread and the wool
39:1 out of the *b* thread and wool
39:2 *b* thread and wool dyed
39:3 the *b* thread and the wool
39:5 of gold, *b* thread, and wool
39:8 *b* thread and wool dyed reddish
39:21 of the ephod with a *b* string
39:22 loom worker, all of *b* thread
39:24 of *b* thread and wool dyed
39:29 and *b* thread and wool dyed
39:31 put a string of *b* thread to
Nu 4:6 spread out an entire cloth of *b*
4:7 spread out a cloth of *b* over
4:9 take a cloth of *b* and cover the
4:11 spread out a cloth of *b*
4:12 put them in a cloth of *b* and
15:38 *b* string above the fringed
2Ch 2:7 and crimson and *b* thread, and
2:14 in *b* thread and in fine
3:14 curtain of *b* thread and wool
Es 1:6 *b* held fast in ropes of fine
8:15 royal apparel of *b* and linen
Jer 10:9 their clothing is *b* thread
Eze 23:6 clothed with *b* material
27:7 *B* thread and wool dyed
27:24 in wraps of *b* material and

Blunt
Ec 10:10 If an iron tool has become *b*

Blunted
Ro 11:7 had their sensibilities *b*

Boanerges
Mr 3:17 *B* . . . means Sons of Thunder

Boar
Ps 80:13 *b* out of the woods keeps

Board
Mt 14:22 to *b* the boat and go ahead
Mr 6:45 disciples to *b* the boat and
Joh 21:11 on *b* and drew the net to
Ac 27:6 and he made us *b* it

Boarded
Mr 8:10 *b* the boat with his disciples
Joh 6:24 *b* their little boats and

Boarding
Mt 9:1 So, *b* the boat, he proceeded
Mr 5:18 as he was *b* the boat, the
Joh 6:17 *b* a boat, they set out across

Boards
1Ki 6:15 inside it with *b* of cedar
6:15 with *b* of juniper
6:16 *b* of cedar, from the floor

Boast
1Ki 20:11 *b* about himself like one
1Ch 16:10 your *b* in his holy name
Ps 34:2 my soul will make its *b*
52:1 make your *b* over what is bad
63:11 one swearing by him will *b*
64:10 the upright in heart will *b*
97:7 their *b* in valueless gods
105:3 Make your *b* in his holy name
106:5 I may make my *b* with your
Pr 27:1 your *b* about the next day
Isa 41:16 of Israel you will *b*
45:25 will *b* about themselves
Jer 4:2 they will *b* about themselves
1Co 1:29 no flesh might *b* in the
1:31 let him *b* in Jehovah
4:7 why do you *b* as though you
9:16 it is no reason for me to *b*
13:3 I may *b*, but do not have
2Co 1:12 the thing we *b* of is this
1:14 we are a cause for you to *b*
5:12 who *b* over the outward
7:14 made any *b* to him about you
10:8 *b* a bit too much about the
10:13 we will *b*, not outside our
10:16 not to *b* in someone else's
10:17 let him *b* in Jehovah
11:12 the office of which they *b*
11:18 to the flesh, I too will *b*
11:30 I will *b* of the things
12:1 I have to *b*. It is not
12:5 Over such a man I will *b*
12:5 I will not *b* over myself
12:6 if I ever do want to *b*

2Co 12:9 *b* as respects my weaknesses
Ga 6:14 I should *b*, except in the

Boasted
2Co 8:24 what we *b* about you, before

Boaster
Job 11:2 a mere *b* be in the right

Boasters
Ps 5:5 No *b* may take their stand in
73:3 I became envious of the *b*

Boastful
Pr 29:8 Men of *b* talk inflame a town

Boasting
Ps 49:6 keep *b* about the abundance of
Pr 25:14 man *b* himself about a gift
Jer 23:32 and because of their *b*
Ro 3:27 Where, then, is the *b*? It is
4:2 ground for *b*; but not with
1Co 3:21 Hence let no one be *b* in men
5:6 Your cause for *b* is not fine
9:15 make my reason for *b* void
2Co 5:12 for *b* in respect to us, that
7:4 have great *b* in regard to you
7:14 our *b* before Titus has
9:2 *b* to the Macedonians about
9:3 that our *b* about you might
10:15 not *b* outside our assigned
11:10 *b* of mine in the regions
11:16 I too may do some little *b*
11:17 cocksureness peculiar to *b*
11:18 are *b* according to the flesh
11:30 If *b* there must be, I will
Ga 6:13 cause for *b* in your flesh
Eph 2:9 man should have ground for *b*
Php 3:3 have our *b* in Christ Jesus
Heb 3:6 and our *b* over the hope firm

Boasts
Pr 20:14 that he *b* about himself
1Co 1:31 He that *b*, let him boast in
2Co 10:17 he that *b*, let him boast in

Boat
Mt 4:21 in the *b* with Zebedee their
4:22 leaving the *b* and their
8:23 when he got aboard a *b*, his
8:24 *b* was being covered by the
9:1 boarding the *b*, he proceeded
13:2 went aboard a *b* and sat down
14:13 withdrew from there by *b*
14:22 to board the *b* and go ahead
14:24 the *b* was many hundreds of
14:29 getting down off the *b*
14:32 after they got up into the *b*
14:33 those in the *b* did obeisance
15:39 he got into the *b* and came
Mr 1:19 in their *b* mending their nets
1:20 Zebedee in the *b* with the
3:9 *b* continually at his service
4:1 he went aboard a *b* and sat out
4:36 they took him in the *b*, just
4:37 waves kept dashing into the *b*
4:37 *b* was close to being swamped
5:2 after he got out of the *b* a
5:18 as he was boarding the *b*, the
5:21 crossed back again in the *b*
6:32 went in the *b* for a lonely
6:45 disciples to board the *b* and
6:47 the *b* was in the midst of
6:51 got up into the *b* with them
6:54 as they got out of the *b*
8:10 he boarded the *b* with his
8:14 nothing with them in the *b*
Lu 5:3 from the *b* he began teaching
5:7 partners in the other *b* to
8:22 his disciples got into a *b*
8:37 aboard the *b* and turned away
Joh 6:17 boarding a *b*, they set out
6:19 and getting near the *b*
6:21 to take him into the *b*
6:21 the *b* was at the land to
6:22 no *b* there except a little
6:22 had not entered into the *b*
21:3 and got aboard the *b*, but
21:6 on the right side of the *b*
21:8 came in the little *b*, for
Ac 20:13 We now went ahead to the *b*
20:38 to conduct him to the *b*
21:2 found a *b* that was crossing
21:3 the *b* was to unload its cargo
21:6 and we went up into the *b* but
27:2 a *b* from Adramyttium that
27:6 *b* from Alexandria that was
27:10 cargo and the *b* but also of
Ac 27:15 *b* was violently seized and
27:17 helps to undergird the *b*
27:19 away the tackling of the *b*
27:22 be lost, only the *b* will
27:30 to escape from the *b*
27:31 remain in the *b*, you cannot
27:37 souls in the *b* were about
27:38 lighten the *b* by throwing
27:39 they could, to beach the *b*
27:44 certain things from the *b*
28:11 in a *b* from Alexandria that

Boats
Job 9:26 have moved on like reed *b*
Isa 2:16 and upon all desirable *b*
Jer 51:32 papyrus *b* they have burned
Mr 4:36 there were other *b* with him
Lu 5:2 he saw two *b* docked at the
5:3 Going aboard one of the *b*
5:7 they filled both *b*, so that
5:11 brought the *b* back to land
Joh 6:23 *b* from Tiberias arrived
6:24 boarded their little *b* and
Jas 3:4 *b*, although they are so big
Re 8:9 a third of the *b* were wrecked
18:19 all those having *b* at sea

Boaz
Ru 2:1 and his name was *B*
2:3 of the field belonging to *B*
2:4 *B* came from Bethlehem and
2:5 *B* said to the young man who
2:8 *B* said to Ruth: You have heard
2:11 *B* answered and said to her
2:14 *B* proceeded to say to her at
2:15 *B* now commanded his young
2:19 The name of the man . . . is *B*
2:23 close by the young women of *B*
3:2 is not *B* . . . our kinsman?
3:7 Meantime *B* ate and drank, and
4:1 As for *B*, he went up to the
4:1 whom *B* had mentioned
4:5 *B* said: On the day that you buy
4:8 when the repurchaser said to *B*
4:9 *B* said to the older men and
4:13 *B* took Ruth and she became
4:21 and Salmon became father to *B*
4:21 and *B* became father to Obed
1Ki 7:21 and called its name *B*
1Ch 2:11 in turn, became father to *B*
2:12 *B*, in turn, became father to
2Ch 3:17 name of the left-hand one *B*
Mt 1:5 Salmon became father to *B* by
1:5 *B* became father to Obed by
Lu 3:32 son of *B*, son of Salmon

Bocheru
1Ch 8:38 *B* . . . the sons of Azel
9:44 *B* . . . the sons of Azel

Bochim
Jg 2:1 from Gilgal to *B* and said
2:5 the name of that place *B*

Bodies
Ge 47:18 but our *b* and our land
Le 11:24 touching their dead *b*
11:25 their dead *b* will wash his
11:27 dead *b* will be unclean until
11:28 who carries their dead *b*
11:35 dead *b* may fall will be
11:36 dead *b* will be unclean
11:37 their dead *b* fall upon any
11:38 their dead *b* had fallen upon
Ne 9:37 our *b* they are ruling and
Ps 110:6 cause a fullness of dead *b*
Isa 5:25 dead *b* will become like
Jer 7:33 dead *b* of this people must
9:22 The dead *b* of mankind must
16:4 their dead *b* will actually
19:7 give their dead *b* as food
34:20 dead *b* must become food
Eze 1:11 two were covering their *b*
1:23 covering on that side their *b*
Da 3:27 had had no power over their *b*
3:28 gave over their *b*, because
Na 3:3 there is no end to the dead *b*
3:3 stumbling among their dead *b*
Mt 6:25 *b* as to what you will wear
27:52 many *b* of the holy ones that
Lu 12:22 or about your *b* as to what
Joh 19:31 *b* might not remain upon
19:31 and the *b* taken away
Ro 1:24 *b* might be dishonored among
6:12 rule as king in your mortal *b*
8:11 make your mortal *b* alive
Ro 8:23 release from our *b* by ransom
12:1 present your *b* a sacrifice
1Co 6:15 your *b* are members of Christ
15:40 there are heavenly *b*, and
15:40 and earthly *b*; but the glory
15:40 the glory of the heavenly *b*
15:40 earthly *b* is a different
Eph 5:28 their wives as their own *b*
Heb 10:22 *b* bathed with clean water
13:11 *b* of those animals whose

Bodily
Lu 3:22 spirit in *b* shape like a dove
Col 2:9 the divine quality dwells *b*
1Ti 4:8 *b* training is beneficial for

Body
Ge 26:14 and a large *b* of servants, so
Le 5:2 dead *b* of an unclean wild
5:2 dead *b* of an unclean domestic
5:2 dead *b* of an unclean swarming
7:24 fat of a *b* already dead and
11:8 must not touch their dead *b*
11:11 are to loathe their dead *b*
11:39 he who touches its dead *b*
11:40 eats any of its dead *b* will
11:40 who carries off its dead *b*
17:15 any soul that eats a *b*
22:8 eat any *b* already dead or
De 14:21 not eat any *b* already dead
21:23 *b* should not stay all night
28:26 dead *b* must become food for
Jos 8:29 took his dead *b* down from
1Ki 13:22 your dead *b* will not come
13:24 dead *b* came to be thrown
13:24 standing beside the dead *b*
13:25 dead *b* thrown onto the road
13:25 standing beside the dead *b*
13:28 found the dead *b* of him
13:28 standing beside the dead *b*
13:28 had not eaten the dead *b*
13:29 dead *b* of the man of the
13:30 dead *b* in his own burial
2Ki 9:37 the dead *b* of Jezebel will
Job 1:3 a very large *b* of servants
Ps 79:2 dead *b* of your servants as
Isa 20:4 *b* of captives of Egypt and
49:24 the *b* of captives of the
49:25 Even the *b* of captives of
Jer 26:23 dead *b* into the graveyard
29:14 gather your *b* of captives
29:22 entire *b* of exiles of Judah
36:30 his own dead *b* will become
Eze 4:14 neither a *b* already dead nor
44:31 No *b* already dead and no
Da 4:33 own *b* got to be wet, until
5:21 his own *b* got to be wet
7:11 and its *b* was destroyed and
10:6 his *b* was like chrysolite
Am 1:6 a complete *b* of exiles to
1:9 complete *b* of exiles to Edom
Mt 5:29 your whole *b* to be pitched
5:30 *b* to land in Gehenna
6:22 The lamp of the *b* is the eye
6:22 your whole *b* will be bright
6:23 your whole *b* will be dark
6:25 and the *b* than clothing
10:28 of those who kill the *b* but
10:28 can destroy both soul and *b*
26:12 this perfumed oil upon my *b*
26:26 Take, eat. This means my *b*
27:27 the whole *b* of troops
27:58 and asked for the *b* of Jesus
27:59 Joseph took the *b*, wrapped
Mr 5:29 she sensed in her *b* that she
6:27 dispatched a *b* guardsman
14:8 perfumed oil on my *b* in view
14:22 Take it, this means my *b*
14:51 garment over his naked *b*
15:16 called the whole *b* of troops
15:43 and asked for the *b* of Jesus
Lu 11:34 lamp of the *b* is your eye
11:34 your whole *b* is also bright
11:34 wicked, your *b* is also dark
11:36 if your whole *b* is bright
12:4 those who kill the *b* and
12:23 and the *b* than clothing
12:42 over his *b* of attendants to
14:32 sends out a *b* of ambassadors
17:37 *b* is, there also the eagles
19:14 sent out a *b* of ambassadors
22:19 This means my *b* which is to
23:52 and asked for the *b* of Jesus
23:55 and how his *b* was laid
24:3 not find the *b* of the Lord

Lu 24:23 did not find his *b* and they
Joh 2:21 the temple of his *b*
19:38 take away the *b* of Jesus
19:38 came and took his *b* away
19:40 took the *b* of Jesus and
20:12 *b* of Jesus had been lying
Ac 8:36 came to a certain *b* of water
8:36 A *b* of water; what prevents
9:40 turning to the *b*, he said
19:12 aprons were borne from his *b*
Ro 4:19 he considered his own *b*, now
6:6 our sinful *b* might be made
7:4 through the *b* of the Christ
7:24 *b* undergoing this death
8:10 *b* indeed is dead on account
8:13 practices of the *b* to death
12:4 have in one *b* many members
12:5 one *b* in union with Christ
15:27 things for the fleshly *b*
1Co 5:3 absent in *b* but present in
6:13 the *b* is not for fornication
6:13 and the Lord is for the *b*
6:16 joined to a harlot is one *b*
6:18 other sin . . . outside his *b*
6:18 is sinning against his own *b*
6:19 the *b* of you people is the
6:20 glorify God in the *b* of you
7:4 authority over her own *b*, but
7:4 authority over his own *b*, but
7:34 be holy both in her *b* and in
9:27 pummel my *b* and lead it as
10:16 sharing . . . *b* of the Christ
10:17 although many, are one *b*
11:24 This means my *b* which is in
11:27 be guilty respecting the *b*
11:29 if he does not discern the *b*
12:12 just as the *b* is one but has
12:12 all the members of that *b*
12:12 are one *b*, so also is the
12:13 all baptized into one *b*
12:14 the *b*, indeed, is not one
12:15 I am no part of the *b*, it
12:15 this reason no part of the *b*
12:16 I am no part of the *b*
12:16 this reason no part of the *b*
12:17 If the whole *b* were an eye
12:18 set the members in the *b*
12:19 where would the *b* be?
12:20 many members, yet one *b*
12:22 the members of the *b* which
12:23 the parts of the *b* which we
12:24 God compounded the *b*
12:25 be no division in the *b*, but
12:27 Now you are Christ's *b*, and
13:3 if I hand over my *b*, that I
15:35 what sort of *b* are they
15:37 not the *b* that will develop
15:38 God gives it a *b* just as it
15:38 each of the seeds its own *b*
15:44 It is sown a physical *b*
15:44 is raised up a spiritual *b*
15:44 If there is a physical *b*
2Co 4:10 in our *b* the death-dealing
4:10 be made manifest in our *b*
5:6 we have our home in the *b*
5:8 become absent from the *b* and
5:10 things done through the *b*
12:2 in the *b* I do not know, or
12:2 out of the *b* I do not know
12:3 in the *b* or apart from the
12:3 or apart from the *b*, I do
Ga 6:17 on my *b* the brand marks of a
Eph 1:23 which is his *b*, the fullness
2:16 both peoples in one *b* to
3:6 fellow members of the *b* and
4:4 One *b* there is, and one spirit
4:12 the building up of the *b* of
4:16 From him all the *b*, by being
4:16 for the growth of the *b* for
5:23 he being a savior of this *b*
5:30 we are members of his *b*
Php 1:20 magnified by means of my *b*
3:21 refashion our humiliated *b*
3:21 conformed to his glorious *b*
Col 1:18 and he is the head of the *b*
1:22 that one's fleshly *b* through
1:24 on behalf of his *b*, which
2:11 stripping off the *b* of the
2:19 one from whom all the *b*
2:23 a severe treatment of the *b*
3:5 Deaden . . . your *b* members
3:15 called to it in one *b*
1Th 5:23 the spirit and soul and *b* of
1Ti 4:14 *b* of older men laid their
Heb 10:5 but you prepared a *b* for me
10:10 offering of the *b* of Jesus
13:3 also are still in a *b*
Jas 2:16 the necessities for their *b*
2:26 *b* without spirit is dead, so
3:2 to bridle also his whole *b*
3:3 we manage also their whole *b*
3:6 it spots up all the *b* and sets
1Pe 2:24 bore our sins in his own *b*
Jude 9 was disputing about Moses' *b*

Bodyguard
Ge 37:36 Potiphar . . . chief of the *b*
39:1 chief of the *b*, an Egyptian
40:3 house of the chief of the *b*
40:4 chief of the *b* assigned Joseph
41:10 house of the chief of the *b*
41:12 servant of the chief of the *b*
1Sa 22:14 chief over your *b* and
2Sa 23:23 appointed him to his own *b*
2Ki 11:4 of the Carian *b* and of the
11:19 Carian *b* and the runners
25:8 the chief of the *b*
25:10 chief of the *b* pulled down
25:11 the chief of the *b* took
25:12 chief of the *b* let remain
25:15 chief of the *b* took the
25:18 chief of the *b* took Seraiah
25:20 the chief of the *b* then
1Ch 11:25 put him over his own *b*
Jer 39:9 chief of the *b* took into
39:10 chief of the *b* let remain in
39:11 chief of the *b*, saying
39:13 chief of the *b* and
40:1 chief of the *b* sent him
40:2 chief of the *b* took Jeremiah
40:5 chief of the *b* then gave
41:10 chief of the *b* had put in
43:6 chief of the *b* had let stay
52:12 the chief of the *b*, who
52:14 chief of the *b* pulled down
52:15 chief of the *b* took into
52:16 chief of the *b* let remain
52:19 the chief of the *b* took
52:24 chief of the *b* took Seraiah
52:26 chief of the *b* took and
52:30 chief of the *b* took Jews
Da 2:14 chief of the king's *b*, who

Bohan
Jos 15:6 *B* the son of Reuben
18:17 *B* the son of Reuben

Boil
Ex 16:23, 23 and what you can *b*, *b*
23:19 not *b* a kid in its mother's
29:31 you must *b* its flesh in a
34:26 You must not *b* a kid in its
Le 8:31 *B* the flesh at the entrance of
13:18 in case a *b* develops in its
13:19 the *b* a white eruption has
13:20 It has broken out in the *b*
13:23 the inflammation of the *b*
De 14:21 You must not *b* a kid in its
28:27 the *b* of Egypt and piles and
28:35 a malignant *b* upon both
2Ki 4:38 *b* stew for the sons of the
20:7 took and put it upon the *b*
Job 2:7 malignant *b* from the sole of
30:27 intestines were made to *b*
41:31 depths to *b* just like a pot
Isa 38:21 and rub it in upon the *b*
64:2 fire makes the very water *b*
Eze 24:5 *B* its pieces, also cook its
24:10 *B* the flesh thoroughly
46:20 *b* the guilt offering and
46:24 *b* the sacrifice of the

Boiled
Ex 12:9 Do not eat any of it . . . *b*
Le 6:28 may be *b* is to be shattered
6:28 it was *b* in a copper vessel
Nu 6:19 priest must take a *b* shoulder
11:8 *b* it in cooking pots or made
1Sa 2:15 not *b* meat, but raw
1Ki 19:21 the bulls he *b* their flesh
2Ki 6:29 we *b* my son and ate him
2Ch 35:13 they *b* in cooking pots and
La 4:10 have *b* their own children

Boiling
Ge 25:29 Jacob was *b* up some stew
De 16:7 do the *b* and the eating in the
1Sa 2:13 just when the meat was *b*
2Ch 35:13 *b* the passover offering over
Eze 46:23 *b* places made beneath the
Eze 46:24 houses of those doing the *b*
Zec 14:21 and must do *b* in them

Boils
Ex 9:9 *b* breaking out with blisters
9:10 and it became *b* with blisters
9:11 result of the *b*, because the
9:11 the *b* had developed on the

Boisterous
Ps 39:6 Surely they are *b* in vain
42:5 And why are you *b* within me?
42:11 why are you *b* within me?
43:5 And why are you *b* within me?
46:3 its waters be *b*, foam over
46:6 The nations became *b*, the
77:3 will remember God and be *b*
Pr 7:11 She is *b* and stubborn
9:13 A woman of stupidity is *b*
20:1 intoxicating liquor is *b*, and
Ca 5:4 my inward parts . . . became *b*
Isa 16:11 inwards are *b* just like a
17:12 peoples, who are *b* as with
22:2 you were full, a *b* city, an
51:15 sea that its waves may be *b*
Jer 4:19 My heart is *b* within me
5:22 they do become *b*, still
31:20 intestines have become *b*
31:35 its waves may become *b*
48:36 heart will be *b* for Moab
48:36 heart will be *b*, just like
50:42 like the sea that is *b*
51:55 waves will actually be *b*
Zec 9:15 drink—be *b*—as if there

Boisterousness
Isa 17:12 as with the *b* of the seas

Bold
2Ch 17:6 heart became *b* in the ways
Ps 138:3 *b* in my soul with strength
Pr 7:13 She has put on a *b* face, and
21:29 wicked . . . put on a *b* face
Lu 11:8 because of his *b* persistence
Ro 10:20 Isaiah becomes very *b* and
2Co 10:1 when absent I am *b* toward
10:2 taking *b* measures against
11:21 if anyone else acts *b* in
11:21 I too am acting *b* in it

Boldly
Ac 9:27 spoken *b* in the name of Jesus
9:28 speaking *b* in the name of the
18:26 man started to speak *b* in

Boldness
Ac 4:29 speaking your word with all *b*
4:31 the word of God with *b*
13:46 so, talking with *b*, Paul and
14:3 time speaking with *b* by the
19:8 spoke with *b* for three months
2Co 10:2 I may not use *b* with that
Eph 6:20 with *b* as I ought to speak
1Th 2:2 we mustered up *b* by means of
Heb 10:19 *b* for the way of entry into

Bolt
Ne 7:3 shut the doors and *b* them

Bolts
Ne 3:3 set up its doors, its *b* and its
3:6 its doors and its *b* and its
3:13 its doors, its *b* and its bars
3:14 its doors, its *b* and its bars
3:15 set up its doors, its *b* and

Bond
Eze 20:37 into the *b* of the covenant
Lu 13:16 loosed from this *b* on the
Ac 8:23 and a *b* of unrighteousness
Eph 4:3 in the uniting *b* of peace
Col 3:14 it is a perfect *b* of union

Bonds
2Ki 23:33 got to put him in *b* at
Job 12:18 *b* of kings he . . . loosens
38:31 tie fast the *b* of the Kimah
Mr 15:7 Barabbas in *b* with the
Lu 8:29 he would burst the *b* and be
Ac 9:14 put in *b* all those calling
16:26 the *b* of all were loosened
20:23 says that *b* and tribulations
23:29 thing deserving of death or *b*
26:29 the exception of these *b*
26:31 nothing deserving death or *b*
Php 1:7 both in my prison *b* and in
1:13 my *b* have become public
1:14 by reason of my prison *b*
1:17 for me in my prison *b*

Col 4:3 in fact, I am in prison *b*
4:18 bearing my prison *b* in mind
2Ti 2:9 to the point of prison *b* as
Phm 10 while in my prison *b*
13 prison *b* I bear for the sake
Heb 11:36 more than that, by *b* and
13:3 in mind those in prison *b*
Jude 6 eternal *b* under dense darkness

Bone

Ge 2:23 This is at last *b* of my bones
29:14 indeed my *b* and my flesh
Ex 12:46 you must not break a *b* in it
Nu 9:12 they should break no *b* in it
19:16 or a *b* of a man or a burial
19:18 one who touched the *b* or the
Jg 9:2 your *b* and your flesh I am
2Sa 5:1 are your *b* and your flesh
19:12 my *b* and my flesh you are
19:13 Are you not my *b* and my
1Ch 11:1 We are your *b* and your flesh
Job 2:5 touch as far as his *b* and his
31:22 broken from its upper *b*
Pr 25:15 tongue itself can break a *b*
Eze 37:7, 7 to approach, *b* to its *b*
39:15 actually see the *b* of a man
Joh 19:36 *b* of his will be crushed

Bones

Ge 2:23 This is at last bone of my *b*
50:25 take my *b* up out of here
Ex 13:19 Moses was taking Joseph's *b*
13:19 take my *b* up out of here
Nu 24:8 their *b* he will gnaw, and he
Jos 24:32 Joseph's *b*, which the sons
Jg 19:29 her *b* into twelve pieces
1Sa 31:13 their *b* and buried them
2Sa 21:12 took the *b* of Saul and the
21:12 the *b* of Jonathan his son
21:13 the *b* of Saul and the
21:13 the *b* of Jonathan his son
21:13 *b* of the men being exposed
21:14 they buried the *b* of Saul
1Ki 13:2 men's *b* he will burn upon
13:31 Beside his *b* deposit my own
13:31 deposit my own *b*
2Ki 13:21 touched the *b* of Elisha
23:14 their places with human *b*
23:16 *b* from the burial places
23:18 not let anyone disturb his *b*
23:18 they let his *b* alone along
23:18 the *b* of the prophet that
23:20 burned human *b* upon them
1Ch 10:12 buried their *b* under the big
2Ch 34:5 *b* of priests he burned upon
Job 4:14 my *b* it filled with dread
7:15 Death rather than my *b*
10:11 with *b* and sinews to weave
19:20 to my flesh my *b* actually
20:11 *b* have been full of his
21:24 marrow of his *b* . . . moist
30:17 my very *b* have been bored
30:30 *b* became hot from dryness
33:19 the quarreling of his *b* is
33:21 his *b* that were not seen
40:18 Its *b* are tubes of copper
40:18 *b* are like wrought-iron
Ps 6:2 for my *b* have been disturbed
22:14 all my *b* have been separated
22:17 I can count all my *b*
31:10 my very *b* have become weak
32:3 I kept silent my *b* wore out
34:20 guarding all the *b* of that
35:10 Let all my *b* themselves say
38:3 no peace in my *b* on account
42:10 With murder against my *b*
51:8 the *b* that you have crushed
53:5 scatter the *b* of anyone
102:3 *b* have been made red-hot
102:5 My *b* have stuck to my flesh
109:18 And like oil into his *b*
139:15 *b* were not hidden from you
141:7 *b* have been scattered at the
Pr 3:8 and a refreshment to your *b*
12:4 rottenness in his *b* is she
14:30 is rottenness to the *b*
15:30 that is good makes the *b* fat
16:24 and a healing to the *b*
17:22 is stricken makes the *b* dry
Ec 11:5 spirit in the *b* in the belly
Isa 38:13 he keeps breaking all my *b*
58:11 will invigorate your very *b*
66:14 your very *b* will sprout
Jer 8:1 the *b* of the kings of Judah
8:1 and the *b* of its princes
Jer 8:1 the *b* of the priests and the
8:1 and the *b* of the prophets
8:1 the *b* of the inhabitants of
20:9 fire shut up in my *b*
23:9 All my *b* have begun shaking
50:17 Babylon has gnawed on his *b*
La 1:13 he has sent fire into my *b*
3:4 He has broken my *b*
4:8 skin has shriveled upon their *b*
Eze 6:5 your *b* all around your altars
24:4 even with the choicest *b*
24:5 cook its *b* in the midst of
24:10 let the *b* themselves become
32:27 come to be upon their *b*
37:1 plain, and it was full of *b*
37:3 can these *b* come to life?
37:4 Prophesy over these *b*, and
37:4 you dry *b*, hear the word of
37:5 said to these *b*: Here I am
37:7 and *b* began to approach
37:11 as regards these *b*, they are
37:11 Our *b* have become dry, and
Da 6:24 and all their *b* they crushed
Am 2:1 burning the *b* of the king
6:10 bring out the *b* from the
Mic 3:2 organism from off their *b*
3:3 to pieces their very *b*, and
Hab 3:16 began to enter into my *b*
Zep 3:3 not gnaw *b* till the morning
Mt 23:27 full of dead men's *b* and of
Lu 24:39 not have flesh and *b* just
Ac 3:7 his ankle *b* were made firm
Heb 11:22 command concerning his *b*

Book

Ge 5:1 This is the *b* of Adam's
Ex 17:14 as a memorial in the *b* and
24:7 took the *b* of the covenant and
32:32 your *b* that you have written
32:33 shall wipe him out of my *b*
Nu 5:23 write . . . cursings in the *b*
21:14 the *b* of the Wars of Jehovah
De 17:18 write in a *b* for himself a
28:58 law . . . written in this *b*
28:61 written in the *b* of this law
29:20 oath written in this *b* will
29:21 written in this *b* of the law
29:27 malediction . . . in this *b*
30:10 written in this *b* of the law
31:24 the words of this law in a *b*
31:26 *b* of the law, you must place
Jos 1:8 This *b* of the law should not
8:31 in the *b* of the law of Moses
8:34 written in the *b* of the law
10:13 written in the *b* of Jashar
18:9 mapped it out . . . in a *b*
23:6 the *b* of the law of Moses
24:26 in the *b* of God's law and
1Sa 10:25 and wrote it in a *b* and
2Sa 1:18 written in the *b* of Jashar
1Ki 11:41 in the *b* of the affairs of
14:19 in the *b* of the affairs of
14:29 in the *b* of the affairs of
15:7 *b* of the affairs of the days
15:23 *b* of the affairs of the days
15:31 in the *b* of the affairs of
16:5 *b* of the affairs of the days
16:14 *b* of the affairs of the
16:20 *b* of the affairs of the
16:27 *b* of the affairs of the
22:39 *b* of the affairs of the days
22:45 *b* of the affairs of the days
2Ki 1:18 *b* of the affairs of the days
8:23 *b* of the affairs of the days
10:34 the *b* of the affairs of the
12:19 the *b* of the affairs of the
13:8 the *b* of the affairs of the
13:12 the *b* of the affairs of the
14:6 *b* of Moses' law that Jehovah
14:15 the *b* of the affairs of the
14:18 the *b* of the affairs of the
14:28 the *b* of the affairs of the
15:6 the *b* of the affairs of the
15:11 *b* of the affairs of the
15:15 *b* of the affairs of the days
15:21 the *b* of the affairs of the
15:26 the *b* of the affairs of the
15:31 the *b* of the affairs of the
15:36 the *b* of the affairs of the
16:19 the *b* of the affairs of the
20:20 *b* of the affairs of the days
21:17 *b* of the affairs of the days
21:25 *b* of the affairs of the days
22:8 The very *b* of the law I have
2Ki 22:8 Hilkiah gave the *b* to Shaphan
22:10 *b* that Hilkiah the priest
22:11 words of the *b* of the law
22:13 the words of this *b* that
22:13 words of this *b* by doing
22:16 the *b* that the king of Judah
23:2 the *b* of the covenant that
23:3 that were written in this *b*
23:21 this *b* of the covenant
23:24 *b* that Hilkiah the priest
23:28 *b* of the affairs of the days
24:5 *b* of the affairs of the days
1Ch 9:1 the *B* of the Kings of Israel
2Ch 16:11 *B* of the Kings of Judah and
17:9 was the *b* of Jehovah's law
20:34 *B* of the Kings of Israel
24:27 of the *B* of the Kings
25:4 the law, in the *b* of Moses
25:26 *B* of the Kings of Judah
27:7 *B* of the Kings of Israel
28:26 *B* of the Kings of Judah and
32:32 *B* of the Kings of Judah and
34:14 *b* of Jehovah's law by the
34:15 *b* of the law I have found
34:15 gave the *b* to Shaphan
34:16 brought the *b* to the king
34:18 a *b* that Hilkiah the priest
34:21 the words of the *b* that has
34:21 that is written in this *b*
34:24 *b* that they read before the
34:30 the *b* of the covenant
34:31 that were written in this *b*
35:12 written in the *b* of Moses
35:27 the *B* of the Kings of Israel
36:8 *B* of the Kings of Israel and
Ezr 4:15 the *b* of records of your
4:15 *b* of records and learn that
6:18 of the *b* of Moses
Ne 7:5 *b* of genealogical enrollment
8:1 the *b* of the law of Moses
8:3 to the *b* of the law
8:5 to open the *b* before the eyes
8:8 reading aloud from the *b*, from
8:18 *b* of the law of the true God
9:3 *b* of the law of Jehovah their
12:23 the *b* of the affairs of the
13:1 reading from the *b* of Moses
Es 2:23 *b* of the affairs of the days
6:1 *b* of the records of the affairs
9:32 it was written down in a *b*
10:2 *B* of the affairs of the times
Job 19:23 O that in a *b* . . . inscribed
Ps 40:7 In the roll of the *b* it being
56:8 Are they not in your *b*?
69:28 the *b* of the living ones
139:16 And in your *b* all its parts
Isa 29:11 *b* that has been sealed up
29:12 *b* must be given to someone
29:18 hear the words of the *b*
30:8 and inscribe it even in a *b*
34:4 just like a *b* scroll
34:16 *b* of Jehovah and read out
Jer 25:13 written in this *b* that
30:2 Write for yourself in a *b*
36:2 take . . . a roll of a *b*
36:4 to him, on the roll of the *b*
36:8 read aloud from the *b* the
36:10 from the *b* the words of
36:11 from out of the *b*
36:13 read aloud from the *b* in
36:18 writing in the *b* with ink
36:32 *b* that Jehoiakim the king
45:1 wrote in a *b* these words
51:60 in one *b* all the calamity
51:63 completed reading this *b*
Eze 2:9 there was the roll of a *b*
Da 12:1 found written down in the *b*
12:4 the words and seal up the *b*
Na 1:1 The *b* of the vision of Nahum
Mal 3:16 a *b* of remembrance began to
Mt 1:1 *b* of the history of Jesus
Mr 12:26 read in the *b* of Moses, in
Lu 3:4 the *b* of the words of Isaiah
20:42 David himself says in the *b*
Ac 1:20 written in the *b* of Psalms
7:42 in the *b* of the prophets
Php 4:3 names are in the *b* of life
Heb 9:19 sprinkled the *b* itself and
10:7 *b* it is written about me
Re 3:5 his name from the *b* of life
20:15 written in the *b* of life

Books

Ec 12:12 making of many *b* there is no
Da 7:10 there were *b* that were opened

Da 9:2 Daniel, discerned by the *b* the
Ac 19:19 *b* together and burned them

Booming
Job 36:33 His *b* tells about him

Boot
Isa 9:5 *b* of the one tramping with

Booth
Job 27:18 *b* that a watchman has made
36:29 The crashings from his *b*
Ps 18:11 All around him as his *b*
31:20 You will hide them in your *b*
Isa 1:8 like a *b* in a vineyard
4:6 *b* for a shade by day from
La 2:6 he treats his *b* violently like
Am 9:11 shall raise up the *b* of David
Jon 4:5 he made for himself there a *b*
Ac 15:16 and rebuild the *b* of David

Booths
Ge 33:17 and for his herd he made *b*
Le 23:34 festival of *b* for seven days
23:42 *b* you should dwell seven
23:42 Israel should dwell in the *b*
23:43 *b* that I made the sons of
De 16:13 the festival of *b* you should
16:16 weeks and the festival of *b*
31:10 release, in the festival of *b*
2Sa 11:11 and Judah are dwelling in *b*
22:12 darkness around him as *b*
1Ki 20:12 were drinking in the *b*
20:16 drunk in the *b*, he together
2Ch 8:13 at the festival of the *b*
Ezr 3:4 they held the festival of *b*
Ne 8:14 should dwell in *b* during the
8:15 of branchy trees to make *b*
8:16 make *b* for themselves, each
8:17 made *b* and took up dwelling
8:17 took up dwelling in the *b*
Zec 14:16 the festival of the *b*
14:18 the festival of the *b*
14:19 the festival of the *b*

Booty
Nu 31:11 *b* in the way of humans and
31:12 captives and the *b* and the
31:26 Take the sum of the *b*, the
31:27 divide the *b* in two between
31:32 And the *b* . . . the plunder
Jg 8:24 the nose ring of his *b*
Zep 3:8 day of my rising up to the *b*

Borashan
1Sa 30:30 and to those in *B*, and to

Border
Ex 25:11 make a *b* of gold round about
25:24 a *b* of gold round about
25:25 *b* of gold for its rim round
28:32 Its opening should have a *b*
30:3 make a *b* of gold round about
30:4 below its *b* upon two of its
37:2 a *b* of gold round about for it
37:11 *b* of gold round about for it
37:12 *b* of gold for its rim round
37:26 a *b* of gold round about for
37:27 its *b* upon two of its sides
39:23 opening had a *b* round about
Nu 20:23 by the *b* of the land of Edom
21:13 from the *b* of the Amorites
21:15 leaned against the *b* of Moab
21:24 the *b* of the sons of Ammon
33:44 Iye-abarim on the *b* of Moab
34:11 *b* must go down and strike
34:12 *b* must go down to the Jordan
De 2:4 along by the *b* of your brothers
3:17 the Jordan and the *b*, from
Jos 4:19 on the eastern *b* of Jericho
13:3 and up to the *b* of Ekron to
13:4 as the *b* of the Amorites
13:10 the *b* of the sons of Ammon
13:26 Mahanaim to the *b* of Debir
13:27 Jordan being the *b* as far as
18:19 (the *b*) proved to be at the
19:12 the *b* of Chisloth-tabor and
19:22 *b* proved to be at the Jordan
19:41 the *b* of their inheritance
19:46 the *b* in front of Joppa
Isa 56:11 unjust gain from his own *b*
Eze 11:10 On the *b* of Israel I shall
11:11 On the *b* of Israel I shall
43:13 *b* is upon its lip round
43:17 *b* surrounding it is half
43:20 upon the *b* round about and
48:1 prove to have an eastern *b*
Eze 48:2 from the eastern *b* to the
48:2 to the western *b*, Asher one
48:3 from the eastern *b* even to
48:3 to the western *b*, Naphtali
48:4 from the eastern *b* to the
48:4 to the western *b*, Manasseh
48:5 from the eastern *b* to the
48:5 to the western *b*, Ephraim
48:6 from the eastern *b* even to
48:6 to the western *b*, Reuben one
48:7 from the eastern *b* to the
48:7 to the western *b*, Judah one
48:8 from the eastern *b* to the
48:8 to the western *b*, the
48:8 portions from the eastern *b*
48:8 to the western *b*
48:16 northern *b* four thousand
48:16 southern *b* four thousand
48:16 eastern *b* four thousand
48:16 western *b* four thousand five
48:23 from the eastern *b* to the
48:23 to the western *b*, Benjamin
48:24 from the eastern *b* to the
48:24 to the western *b*, Simeon
48:25 from the eastern *b* to the
48:25 western *b*, Issachar one
48:26 eastern *b* to the western
48:26 to the western *b*, Zebulun
48:27 from the eastern *b* to the
48:27 to the western *b*, Gad one
48:28 Gad, to the southern *b*, it
48:30 On the northern *b*, four
48:32 eastern *b* there will be
48:33 southern *b* will be four
48:34 western *b* will be four
Zec 9:2 Hamath itself will also *b*

Borders
De 33:20 one widening the *b* of Gad
Ps 48:10 To the *b* of the earth
65:5 The Trust of all the *b* of the
Isa 26:15 afar all the *b* of the land

Bore
Ge 6:4 they *b* sons to them, they
16:15 Hagar *b* to Abram a son and
16:15 his son whom Hagar *b* Ishmael
21:2 *b* a son to Abraham in his old
22:23 eight Milcah *b* to Nahor the
24:24 whom she *b* to Nahor
24:36 *b* a son to my master after
24:47 whom Milcah *b* to him
25:2 she *b* him Zimran and Jokshan
25:12 the maidservant of Sarah *b*
30:5 and in time *b* Jacob a son
30:7 *b* a second son to Jacob
30:10 Leah's maidservant, *b* a son
30:12 Zilpah . . . *b* a second son
30:17 *b* to Jacob a fifth son
30:19 Leah . . . *b* a sixth son to
30:21 she *b* a daughter . . . Dinah
36:4 and Basemath *b* Reuel
36:5 Oholibamah *b* Jeush and Jalam
36:12 she *b* to Eliphaz Amalek
36:14 she *b* to Esau Jeush and
38:3 she *b* a son and he called his
38:4 *b* a son and called his name
38:5 Achzib at the time she *b* him
41:50 whom Asenath . . . *b* to him
43:3 unmistakably *b* witness to us
44:27 wife *b* but two sons to me
46:15 sons of Leah, whom she *b* to
46:18 In time she *b* these to Jacob
46:20 Asenath . . . *b* to him
46:25 In time she *b* these to Jacob
Ex 2:22 Later she *b* a son and he
6:20 she *b* him Aaron and Moses
6:23 she *b* him Nadab and Abihu
6:25 Later she *b* him Phinehas
Nu 16:14 eyes . . . you want to *b* out
26:59 his wife *b* to Levi in Egypt
26:59 she *b* to Amram Aaron and
Jg 8:31 she too *b* him a son. So he
Ru 4:12 Perez, whom Tamar *b* to Judah
4:13 conception and she *b* a son
2Sa 11:27 *b* to him a son, but the
12:24 *b* a son, and his name came
21:8 whom she *b* to Saul, Armoni
21:8 she *b* to Adriel the son of
1Ki 11:20 Tahpenes *b* him Genubath his
1Ch 2:4 *b* to him Perez and Zerah
2:19 who in time *b* Hur to him
2:21 but she *b* Segub to him
2:24 *b* him Ashhur the father of
2:29 *b* him Ahban and Molid
1Ch 2:35 who in time *b* him Attai
2:49 she *b* Shaaph the father of
4:6 Naarah *b* to him Ahuzzam and
7:14 whom his Syrian concubine *b*
7:14 She *b* Machir the father of
7:16 Maacah, Machir's wife, *b* a
2Ch 11:19 she *b* him sons, Jeush and
11:20 she *b* him Abijah and Attai
Ne 9:26 *b* witness against them to
9:34 you *b* witness against them
Job 40:24 can anyone *b* its nose?
41:2 with a thorn can you *b* its
Isa 53:4 as for our pains, he *b* them
Eze 3:14 And the spirit *b* me along
8:8 *b*, please, through the wall
12:5 *b* your way through the wall
12:12 wall they will *b* in order
31:8 *b* no resemblance as respects
Ho 1:3 and in time *b* to him a son
Mt 20:12 who *b* the burden of the day
Joh 1:15 John *b* witness about him
1:32 John also *b* witness, saying
4:44 *b* witness that in his own
13:21 and he *b* witness and said
Ac 2:40 *b* thorough witness and kept
13:22 whom he *b* witness and said
14:3 who *b* witness to the word of
15:8 *b* witness by giving them the
20:21 *b* witness both to Jews and
Heb 13:13 bearing the reproach he *b*
1Pe 2:24 He himself *b* our sins in
3Jo 3 and *b* witness to the truth you
Re 1:2 *b* witness to the word God
20:4 witness they *b* to Jesus and

Bored
Jg 16:21 Philistines . . . *b* his eyes
2Ki 12:9 took a chest and *b* a hole in
Job 30:17 bones have been *b* through
Eze 8:8 gradually *b* through the wall
12:7 I *b* my way through the wall

Boring
1Sa 11:2 of *b* out every right eye of

Born
Ge 4:18 Later there was *b* to Enoch
4:26 Seth also there was *b* a son
6:1 and daughters were *b* to them
10:1 sons began to be *b* to them
10:21 to Shem . . . also progeny *b*
10:25 Eber there were two sons *b*
14:14 slaves *b* in his household
17:12 anyone *b* in the house and
17:13 Every man *b* in your house
17:17 child *b*, and will Sarah, yes
17:23 all the men *b* in his house
17:27 anyone *b* in the house and
21:3 *b* to him, whom Sarah had
21:5 Isaac his son was *b* to him
24:15 Rebekah, who had been *b* to
35:26 Jacob's sons who were *b* to
36:5 sons of Esau who were *b* to
41:50 *b* to Joseph two sons
46:20 *b* to Joseph in the land of
46:22 sons of Rachel who were *b* to
46:27 Joseph's sons who were *b* to
48:5 *b* to you in the land of Egypt
50:23 were *b* upon Joseph's knees
Le 18:9 *b* in the same household or
18:9 same household or *b* outside it
22:11 slaves *b* in his house, they
22:27 or a goat be *b*, then it must
25:45 had *b* to them in your land
27:26 *b* as the firstborn for
Nu 13:22 those *b* of Anak, were there
13:28 those *b* of Anak we saw there
26:60 *b* to Aaron Nadab and Abihu
De 15:19 firstborn that will be *b* in
23:8 sons that may be *b* to them
Jos 5:5 people *b* in the wilderness on
15:14 and Talmai, those *b* of Anak
Jg 13:8 to the child that will be *b*
18:29 who had been *b* to Israel
Ru 4:17 A son has been *b* to Naomi
1Sa 14:49 the one *b* first was Merab
2Sa 3:2 sons were *b* to David in
3:5 ones *b* to David in Hebron
5:13 continued to be *b* to David
5:14 names of those *b* to him in
12:14 son himself, just *b* to you
14:27 *b* to Absalom three sons and
21:16 those *b* of the Rephaim, the
21:18 those *b* of the Rephaim
21:20 had been *b* to the Rephaim

2Sa 21:22 *b* to the Rephaim in Gath
1Ki 13:2 A son *b* to the house of David
1Ch 1:19 to Eber two sons were *b*
2:3 The three were *b* to him from
2:9 sons of Hezron that were *b* to
3:1 sons of David that were *b* to
3:4 were six *b* to him in Hebron
3:5 these *b* to him in Jerusalem
7:21 men of Gath that were *b* in
20:4 of those *b* of the Rephaim
20:6 had been *b* to the Rephaim
20:8 *b* to the Rephaim in Gath
22:9 There is a son being *b* to you
26:6 sons *b* that were rulers of
Ezr 10:3 wives and those *b* from them
Job 1:2 daughters came to be *b* to him
3:3 on which I came to be *b*, Also
5:7 man himself is *b* for trouble
11:12 an asinine zebra be *b* a man
14:1 Man, *b* of woman, Is
15:7 the very first man to be *b*
15:14 Or that anyone *b* of a woman
25:4 one *b* of a woman be clean
38:21 that time you were being *b*
Ps 22:31 the people that is to be *b*
78:6 sons that were to be *b*, might
87:4 This is one who was *b* there
87:5 and every one was *b* in her
87:6 This is one who was *b* there
90:2 mountains themselves were *b*
Pr 17:17 *b* for when there is distress
Ec 4:14 been *b* as one of little means
6:3 one prematurely *b* is better
7:1 than the day of one's being *b*
Isa 9:6 there has been a child *b* to us
66:8 a nation be *b* at one time
Jer 2:14 a slave *b* in the household
16:3 daughters that are *b* in this
20:14 the day on which I was *b*
20:15 *b* to you a son, a male
22:26 land in which . . . not *b*
La 2:20 the children *b* fully formed
Eze 16:4 on the day of your being *b*
16:5 in the day of your being *b*
Ho 2:3 as in the day of her being *b*
Mt 1:16 Mary, of whom Jesus was *b*
2:1 Jesus . . . *b* in Bethlehem of
2:2 is the one *b* king of the Jews
2:4 where the Christ was to be *b*
11:11 Among those *b* of women
19:12 are eunuchs that were *b* such
26:24 if that man had not been *b*
Mr 14:21 finer . . . he had not been *b*
Lu 1:35 what is *b* will be called holy
2:11 was *b* to you today a Savior
7:28 Among those *b* of women there
Joh 1:13 *b*, not from blood or from
3:3 Unless anyone is *b* again, he
3:4 How can a man be *b* when he
3:4 a second time and be *b*, can
3:5 Unless anyone is *b* from water
3:6 *b* from the flesh is flesh
3:6 *b* from the spirit is spirit
3:7 You people must be *b* again
3:8 has been *b* from the spirit
8:41 were not *b* from fornication
9:2 so that he was *b* blind
9:19 son who you say was *b* blind
9:20 son and that he was *b* blind
9:32 the eyes of one *b* blind
9:34 were altogether *b* in sins
16:21 has been *b* into the world
18:37 For this I have been *b*, and
Ac 2:8 language in which we were *b*
7:20 time Moses was *b*, and he was
22:3 Jew, *b* in Tarsus of Cilicia
22:28 But I was even *b* in them
Ro 9:11 when they had not yet been *b*
1Co 15:8 as if to one *b* prematurely
Ga 4:23 *b* in the manner of flesh
4:29 one *b* in the manner of flesh
4:29 one *b* in the manner of spirit
Php 3:5 a Hebrew *b* from Hebrews
Heb 11:12 there were *b* children just
2Pe 2:12 animals *b* naturally to be
1Jo 2:29 has been *b* from him
3:9 has been *b* from God does not
3:9 he has been *b* from God
4:7 has been *b* from God and gains
5:1 has been *b* from God, and
5:1 the one that caused to be *b*
5:1 who has been *b* from that one
5:4 *b* from God conquers the world
5:18 been *b* from God does not
1Jo 5:18 One *b* from God watches him

Borne
Ge 16:1 Abram's wife, had *b* him no
21:3 whom Sarah had *b* to him
21:9 she had *b* to Abraham, poking
22:20 Milcah herself has also *b*
29:34 I have *b* him three sons
30:1 she had *b* nothing to Jacob
30:20 I have *b* him six sons
31:43 children whom they have *b*
34:1 whom she had *b* to Jacob, used
De 21:15 have *b* sons to him, and the
Jg 13:2 was barren and had *b* no child
13:3 are barren and have *b* no child
1Sa 4:20 it is a son that you have *b*
2Sa 12:15 wife of Uriah had *b* to
1Ki 1:6 had *b* him after Absalom
3:21 to be my son that I had *b*
Job 34:31 I have *b*, although I do not
Ps 69:7 I have *b* reproach
88:15 *b* frightful things from you
Isa 9:18 *b* aloft as the billowing of
Jer 42:19 *b* witness against you
Eze 16:20 daughters whom you had *b* to
23:37 sons whom they had *b* to
36:6 humiliation . . . you have *b*
39:26 have *b* their humiliation
Hag 2:19 olive tree—it has not *b*, has
Mal 2:14 Jehovah . . . has *b* witness
Lu 11:46 with loads hard to be *b*
24:51 began to be *b* up to heaven
Joh 1:34 *b* witness that this one is
3:26 to whom you have *b* witness
5:33 has *b* witness to the truth
5:37 Father . . . *b* witness about
19:35 has *b* witness, and his
Ac 19:12 aprons were *b* from his body
27:15 gave way and were *b* along
Ro 3:21 is *b* witness to by the Law
1Co 15:15 *b* witness against God that
15:49 as we have *b* the image of
1Ti 5:10 having a witness *b* to her
2Ti 3:11 sort of persecutions I have *b*
Heb 11:2 had witness *b* to them
11:4 he had witness *b* to him
11:39 witness *b* to them through
2Pe 1:17 *b* to him by the magnificent
1:18 these words we heard *b* from
1:21 were *b* along by holy spirit
1Jo 5:9 *b* witness concerning his Son
3Jo 6 *b* witness to your love before
12 Demetrius has had witness *b*
Re 2:3 *b* up for my name's sake and

Borrow
De 15:6 you yourself will not *b*
28:12 you yourself will not *b*
Mt 5:42 *b* from you without interest

Borrowed
2Ki 6:5 my master, for it was *b*
Ne 5:4 *b* money for the king's tribute

Borrower
Pr 22:7 *b* is servant to the man doing
Isa 24:2 for the lender as for the *b*

Borrowing
Ps 37:21 *b* and does not pay back

Bosom
Ge 16:5 my maidservant over to your *b*
Nu 11:12 Carry them in your *b*, just
Ru 4:16 and to put it in her *b*, and
2Sa 12:3 in his *b* it would lie, and
12:8 of your lord into your *b*
1Ki 1:2 she must lie in your *b*, and
3:20 and laid him in her own *b*
3:20 dead son she laid in my *b*
17:19 he took him from her *b* and
Ne 5:13 my *b* I shook out and then
Ps 35:13 upon my *b* my own prayer
74:11 midst of your *b* to make an
79:12 seven times into their *b*
89:50 in my *b* the reproach of all
129:7 gathering sheaves his own *b*
Pr 5:20 embrace the *b* of a foreign
6:27 rake together fire into his *b*
17:23 take even a bribe from the *b*
21:14 bribe in the *b*, strong rage
Ec 7:9 in the *b* of the stupid ones
Isa 40:11 in his *b* he will carry them
49:22 bring your sons in the *b*
65:6 the reward into their own *b*
65:7 into their own *b*
Jer 32:18 *b* of their sons after them
La 2:12 into the *b* of their mothers
Mic 7:5 her who is lying in your *b*
Lu 16:22 to the *b* position of Abraham
16:23 and Lazarus in the *b* position
Joh 1:18 *b* position with the Father
13:23 in front of Jesus' *b* one

Bosoms
Eze 23:3 the *b* of their virginity
23:8 the *b* of her virginity
23:21 pressing of your *b* from

Bosses
Job 13:12 Your shield *b* are as shield
13:12 are as shield *b* of clay
15:26 the thick *b* of his shields

Bother
Mr 5:35 Why *b* the teacher any longer?
Lu 7:6 Sir, do not *b*, for I am not
8:49 not *b* the teacher any longer

Bottle
Ge 21:14 skin water *b* and gave it to
21:15 in the skin *b* and she
21:19 fill the skin *b* with water
Jg 4:19 she opened a skin *b* of milk
1Sa 16:20 a skin *b* of wine and a kid
Ps 56:8 put my tears in your skin *b*
119:83 like a skin *b* in the smoke

Bottle-gourd
Jon 4:6 God appointed a *b* plant, that
4:6 rejoice greatly over the *b*
4:7 should strike the *b* plant
4:9 with anger over the *b* plant
4:10 felt sorry for the *b* plant

Bottles
Job 32:19 Like new skin *b* it wants to

Bottom
Ex 26:24 should be duplicates at the *b*
36:29 duplicates at the *b* and
De 28:13 not come to be on the *b*
Eze 43:13 And its *b* is a cubit
43:14 *b* on the floor to the lower
43:17 its *b* is a cubit round about
Da 6:24 reached the *b* of the pit
Mt 27:51 rent in two, from top to *b*
Mr 15:38 rent in two from top to *b*

Bottoms
Ps 107:26 They go down to the *b*
Jon 2:6 To the *b* of the mountains I

Bough
Job 14:9 produce a *b* like a new plant
18:16 up above, his *b* will wither
29:19 stay overnight upon my *b*
Eze 31:3 cedar in Lebanon, pretty in *b*
Mal 4:1 not leave . . . root or *b*

Boughs
Le 23:40 *b* of branchy trees and
De 24:20 you must not go over its *b*
2Sa 18:9 *b* of a massive big tree
Ps 80:10 the cedars of God with its *b*
80:11 sent forth its *b* as far as
118:27 festival procession with *b*
Isa 10:33 lopping off *b* with a
17:6 five on the fruit-bearing *b*
27:10 actually consume her *b*
Eze 17:8 produce *b* and to bear fruit
17:23 bear *b* and produce fruit and
31:5 its *b* kept multiplying, and
31:6 its *b* all the flying
31:8 as respects its *b*
36:8 your very own *b* and bear
Da 4:12 on its *b* the birds of the
4:14 tree down, and cut off its *b*
4:14 and the birds from its *b*
4:21 *b* of which the birds of the

Bought
Ge 47:20 Joseph *b* all the land of the
47:23 I have today *b* you and your
Le 25:30 *b* back before the complete
25:33 property . . . is not *b* back
27:20 it may not be *b* back again
27:24 one from whom he *b* it, to
27:27 not be *b* back, it must then
27:28 devoted thing may be *b* back
27:33 It may not be *b* back
2Sa 12:3 small one, that he had *b*
24:24 David *b* the threshing floor
Ne 5:8 *b* back our own Jewish brothers
Pr 11:26 the one letting it be *b*
Isa 43:24 have *b* no sweet cane with
Jer 32:15 and vineyards will yet be *b*

Jer 32:43 fields will certainly be *b*
Mt 13:46 the things he had and *b* it
27:7 *b* with them the potter's
Mr 15:46 he *b* fine linen and took him
16:1 *b* spices in order to come and
Lu 14:18 I *b* a field and need to go
14:19 I *b* five yoke of cattle and
Ac 7:16 tomb that Abraham had *b* for
1Co 6:20 for you were *b* with a price
7:23 You were *b* with a price
2Pe 2:1 even the owner that *b* them
Re 5:9 with your blood you *b* persons
14:3 have been *b* from the earth
14:4 *b* from among mankind as

Bound*
Ge 22:9 *b* Isaac his son hand and foot
42:16 while you have been *b*
42:19 *b* in your house of custody
42:24 and *b* him before their eyes
44:30 *b* up with this one's soul
Ex 39:21 they *b* the breastpiece by its
Le 8:7 *b* it closely to him with it
Nu 30:4 that she has *b* upon her soul
30:4 that she has *b* upon her soul
30:5 vows that she has *b* upon her
30:6 that she has *b* upon her soul
30:7 vows that she has *b* upon her
30:8 that she *b* upon her soul
30:9 that she has *b* upon her
30:10 *b* an abstinence vow upon her
30:11 that she has *b* upon her soul
Jg 15:13 *b* him with two new ropes
16:21 *b* him with two fetters of
1Sa 18:1 *b* up with the soul of David
2Sa 3:34 hands had not been *b* ones
2Ki 5:23 *b* up two talents of silver
17:4 *b* in the house of detention
25:7 *b* him with copper fetters
2Ch 33:11 *b* him with two fetters of
Job 36:8 if they are *b* in fetters
36:13 help because he has *b* them
Ps 146:7 releasing those who are *b*
Ca 7:5 king is held *b* by the flowings
Isa 1:6 not been squeezed out or *b* up
Jer 39:7 *b* him with copper fetters
40:1 he was *b* with handcuffs in
52:11 king of Babylon *b* him with
Eze 30:21 will not be *b* up at all
Da 3:21 men were *b* in their mantles
3:23 *b* in the . . . fiery furnace
3:24 *b* into the midst of the fire
Na 3:10 have all been *b* with fetters
Mt 14:3 had arrested John and *b* him
16:19 the thing *b* in the heavens
18:18 will be things *b* in heaven
Mr 5:4 been *b* with fetters and chains
6:17 John and *b* him in prison on
15:1 they *b* Jesus and led him off
Lu 2:7 she *b* him with cloth bands and
2:12 an infant *b* in cloth bands
8:29 repeatedly *b* with chains and
10:34 *b* up his wounds, pouring oil
13:16 and whom Satan held *b*, look!
Joh 11:44 hands *b* with wrappings, and
11:44 countenance was *b* about
18:12 seized Jesus and *b* him
18:24 Annas sent him away *b* to
19:40 *b* it up with bandages with
Ac 9:2 bring *b* to Jerusalem any whom
9:21 lead them *b* to the . . . priests
12:6 sleeping *b* with two chains
20:22 look! *b* in the spirit, I am
21:11 *b* his own feet and hands and
21:13 I am ready not only to be *b*
21:33 him to be *b* with two chains
22:5 also those who were there *b*
22:29 Roman and that he had *b* him
23:12 *b* themselves with a curse
23:14 *b* ourselves with a curse not
23:21 they have *b* themselves with
24:27 Felix . . . left Paul *b*
Ro 7:2 married woman is *b* by law to
1Co 7:27 Are you *b* to a wife? Stop
7:39 A wife is *b* during all the
2Ti 2:9 the word of God is not *b*
Heb 13:3 as though you have been *b*
Re 9:14 the four angels that are *b*
20:2 *b* him for a thousand years

Boundaries
Ge 23:17 within all its *b* round about
Ex 10:4 locusts within your *b*
13:7 with you within all your *b*
Nu 34:2 Canaan according to its *b*
Nu 34:12 your land according to its *b*
De 19:14 set the *b* in your inheritance
Jos 18:20 by its *b* all around
Ps 74:17 all the *b* of the earth
Isa 10:13 remove the *b* of peoples
54:12 *b* of delightsome stones
60:18 breakdown within your *b*
Eze 45:1 holy portion in all its *b*
Ac 13:50 threw them outside their *b*
2Co 10:13 not outside our assigned *b*
10:15 outside our assigned *b* in

Boundary
Ge 10:19 *b* of the Canaanite came to
Ex 23:31 fix your *b* from the Red Sea
Nu 21:13 the Arnon is the *b* of Moab
34:3 your south *b* must prove to be
34:4 *b* must change direction from
34:5 *b* must change direction at
34:6 As for a west *b*, it must
34:6 This will become your west *b*
34:7 this will become your north *b*
34:7 mark out to Mount Hor as a *b*
34:8 will mark out the *b* to the
34:8 the termination of the *b* must
34:9 the *b* must go out to Ziphron
34:9 This will become your north *b*
34:10 as your *b* on the east from
34:11 *b* must go down from Shepham
35:26 the *b* of his city of refuge
35:27 outside the *b* of his city of
De 3:14 the *b* of the Geshurites and
3:16 the torrent valley being a *b*
3:16 the *b* of the sons of Ammon
11:24 to the western sea your *b*
19:14 not move back the *b* marks
27:17 who moves back the *b* mark
32:8 to fix the *b* of the peoples
Jos 12:2 the *b* of the sons of Ammon
12:5 as the *b* of the Geshurites
13:23 the *b* of the sons of Reuben
15:1 to the *b* of Edom, the
15:2 southern *b* came to be from
15:4 came to be their southern *b*
15:5 eastern *b* was the Salt Sea
15:5 the *b* at the northern corner
15:6 the *b* went up to Beth-hoglah
15:6 *b* went up to the stone of
15:7 *b* went up to Debir at the
15:7 *b* passed over to the waters
15:8 the *b* went up to the valley
15:8 *b* went up to the top of the
15:9 the *b* was marked out from
15:9 *b* was marked out to Baalah
15:10 *b* went around from Baalah
15:11 *b* went out to the slope of
15:11 the *b* was marked out to
15:12 *b* was at the Great Sea and
15:12 *b* all around, of the sons of
15:21 the *b* of Edom in the south
16:2 *b* of the Archites at Ataroth
16:3 the *b* of the Japhletites
16:3 the *b* of Lower Beth-horon
16:5 *b* of the sons of Ephraim by
16:5 the *b* of their inheritance
16:6 the *b* went out to the sea
16:6 *b* went around eastward to
16:8 the *b* moved on westward to
17:7 the *b* of Manasseh came to be
17:7 the *b* moved to the right to
17:8 *b* of Manasseh belonged to
17:9 *b* went down to the torrent
17:9 the *b* of Manasseh was on the
17:10 the sea came to be his *b*
18:12 their *b* came to be at the
18:12 *b* went up to the slope of
18:13 *b* passed over from there to
18:13 *b* . . . to Ataroth-addar
18:14 the *b* was marked out and
18:15 *b* went out westward and
18:16 the *b* went down to the
18:19 the *b* passed over to the
18:19 This was the southern *b*
18:20 the Jordan served as its *b*
19:10 *b* of their inheritance came
19:11 *b* went up westward also to
19:14 *b* went around it on the
19:18 *b* came to be to Jezreel and
19:22 the *b* reached to Tabor and
19:25 *b* came to be Helkath and
19:29 *b* went back to Ramah and
19:29 *b* went back to Hosah, and
19:33 *b* came to be from Heleph
19:34 *b* went back westward to
Jos 22:25 a *b* that Jehovah has put
Jg 11:18 the *b* of Moab, because Arnon
11:18 Arnon was the *b* of Moab
1Sa 6:12 far as the *b* of Beth-shemesh
13:18 the *b* that looks toward the
1Ki 4:21 and to the *b* of Egypt
2Ki 3:21 they began standing at the *b*
14:25 restored the *b* of Israel
2Ch 9:26 down to the *b* of Egypt
Job 24:2 those who move back *b* marks
38:20 you should take it to its *b*
Ps 104:9 *b* you set, beyond which they
Pr 15:25 will fix the *b* of the widow
22:28 move back a *b* of long ago
23:10 move back the *b* of long ago
Isa 19:19 to Jehovah beside its *b*
28:25 and spelt as his *b*
Jer 5:22 the sand as the *b* for the sea
Eze 29:10 and to the *b* of Ethiopia
45:7 from the western *b* to the
45:7 to the eastern *b*
47:15 *b* of the land to the
47:16 between the *b* of Damascus
47:16 and the *b* of Hamath
47:16 toward the *b* of Hauran
47:17 *b* from the sea must prove
47:17 *b* of Damascus and north
47:17 and the *b* of Hamath
47:18 Jordan, from the *b* to the
47:20 from the *b* straight ahead
48:1 *b* of Damascus northward, on
48:2 on the *b* of Dan, from the
48:3 on the *b* of Asher, from the
48:4 on the *b* of Naphtali, from
48:5 on the *b* of Manasseh, from
48:6 on the *b* of Ephraim, from
48:7 on the *b* of Reuben, from
48:8 on the *b* of Judah, from
48:12 on the *b* of the Levites
48:21 to the eastern *b*
48:21 cubits to the western *b*
48:22 Between the *b* of Judah and
48:22 *b* of Benjamin it should
48:24 by the *b* of Benjamin, from
48:25 *b* of Simeon, from the
48:26 *b* of Issachar, from the
48:27 *b* of Zebulun, from the
48:28 by the *b* of Gad, to the
48:28 *b* must prove to be from
Ho 5:10 like those moving back a *b*
Ob 7 As far as the *b* they have sent
2Co 10:13 *b* of the territory that God

Boundary's
Jos 15:4 the *b* termination proved to
15:11 the *b* termination proved to

Bounds
Ex 19:12 set *b* for the people round
19:23 Set *b* for the mountain
1Sa 9:17 keep my people within *b*
Isa 5:14 its mouth wide beyond *b*

Bountiful
2Co 9:5 *b* gift previously promised
9:5 be ready as a *b* gift and not

Bountifully
2Co 9:6, 6 sows *b* will also reap *b*

Bouts
Ro 13:13 in revelries and drunken *b*
Ga 5:21 envies, drunken *b*, revelries

Bow
Ge 18:2 proceeded to *b* down to the
24:26 *b* down and prostrate himself
24:48 *b* down and prostrate myself
27:3 your quiver and your *b*, and
27:29 national groups *b* low to you
27:29 sons of your mother *b* low
33:3 *b* down to the earth seven
37:7 and *b* down to my sheaf
37:10 *b* down to the earth to you
48:22 by my sword and by my *b*
49:24 yet his *b* was dwelling in a
Ex 20:5 must not *b* down to them nor
23:24 not *b* down to their gods or
24:1 must *b* down from a distance
34:8 Moses at once hurried to *b*
Le 26:1 in order to *b* down toward it
Nu 25:2 and to *b* down to their gods
De 4:19 *b* down to them and serve
5:9 You must not *b* down to them
8:19 and *b* down to them, I do bear
11:16 gods and *b* down to them
17:3 worship other gods and *b* down

De 26:10 *b* down before Jehovah your
29:26 other gods and to *b* down to
30:17 and *b* down to other gods and
Jos 23:7 serve them nor *b* down to
24:12 sword and not with your *b*
Jg 2:19 to serve them and *b* down to
1Sa 1:28 to *b* down there to Jehovah
2:4 men of the *b* are filled with
2:36 come and *b* down to him for
18:4 even his sword and his *b* and
24:8 David proceeded to *b* low
28:14 *b* low with his face to the
2Sa 1:18 Judah should be taught The *B*
1:22 *b* of Jonathan did not turn
15:5 drew near to *b* down to him
15:32 where people used to *b* down
16:4 I do *b* down. Let me find
22:35 pressed down a *b* of copper
1Ki 9:6 other gods and *b* down to them
9:9 other gods and *b* down to
11:33 to *b* down to Ashtoreth the
16:31 Baal and to *b* down to him
22:34 bent the *b* in his innocence
2Ki 4:37 *b* down to him to the earth
5:18 the house of Rimmon to *b*
5:18 have to *b* down at the house
5:18 I *b* down at the house of
6:22 your sword and with your *b*
9:24 filled his hand with a *b* and
13:15 Take a *b* and arrows
13:15 to himself a *b* and arrows
13:16 Put your hand to the *b*
17:16 began to *b* down to all the
17:35 must not *b* down to them
17:36 to him you should *b* down
18:22 this altar you should *b*
21:3 to *b* down to all the army of
1Ch 5:18 bending the *b* and trained in
8:40 mighty men, bending the *b*
10:3 those shooting with the *b*
12:2 armed with the *b*, using the
12:2 or with arrows in the *b*
16:29 *B* down to Jehovah in holy
29:20 and *b* low and prostrate
2Ch 7:19 other gods and *b* down to
7:22 other gods and *b* down to
14:8 bending the *b* were two
17:17 equipped with the *b* and
18:33 bent the *b* in his innocence
24:17 to *b* down to the king
25:14 before them he began to *b*
32:12 one altar you should *b*
33:3 *b* down to all the army of
Es 3:2 Mordecai, he would neither *b*
Job 1:20 fall to the earth and *b* down
9:13 helpers of a stormer must *b*
20:24 *b* of copper will cut him up
29:20 my *b* in my hand will shoot
39:3 They *b* down when they cast
Ps 5:7 I shall *b* down toward your
7:12 His *b* he will certainly bend
11:2 wicked ones . . . bend the *b*
17:13 Make him *b* down; do provide
18:34 pressed down a *b* of copper
22:27 nations will *b* down before
22:29 shall eat and will *b* down
29:2 *B* down to Jehovah in holy
37:14 and have bent their *b*
44:6 in my *b* that I kept trusting
45:11 your lord, So *b* down to him
46:9 The *b* he breaks apart and does
58:7 bend the *b* for his arrows
60:4 zigzag on account of the *b*
66:4 the earth will *b* down to you
72:9 inhabitants . . . will *b* down
76:3 the flaming shafts of the *b*
78:9 armed shooters of the *b*
78:57 turned around like a loose *b*
81:9 not *b* down to a foreign god
86:9 *b* down before you, O Jehovah
95:6 let us worship and *b* down
96:9 *B* down to Jehovah in holy
97:7 *B* down to him, all you gods
99:5 *b* down yourselves at his
99:9 *b* down yourselves at his holy
132:7 us *b* down at his footstool
138:2 *b* down toward your holy
Pr 12:25 will cause it to *b* down
14:19 *b* down before the good ones
Isa 2:8 work of one's hands they *b*
2:11 the loftiness of men must *b*
2:17 earthling man must *b* down
2:20 *b* before to the shrewmice
5:15 earthling man will *b* down

Isa 7:24 With arrows and the *b* he
10:4 *b* down under the prisoners
21:15 and because of the bent *b*
22:3 Without need of a *b* they
27:13 *b* down to Jehovah in the
36:7 this altar you should *b* down
41:2 like mere stubble with his *b*
44:15 a god to which he may *b*
45:14 and to you they will *b* down
46:6 yes, they *b* down
49:7 *b* down, by reason of Jehovah
49:23 to the earth they will *b*
51:23 *B* down that we may cross
65:12 *b* down to being slaughtered
66:19 those drawing the *b*, Tubal
66:23 *b* down before me, Jehovah
Jer 4:29 the horsemen and *b* shooters
6:23 The *b* and the javelin they
7:2 to *b* down to Jehovah
9:3 bend their tongue as their *b*
13:10 and to *b* down to them
22:9 *b* down to other gods and to
25:6 serve them and to *b* down
26:2 *b* down at the house of
46:9 handling and treading the *b*
49:35 I am breaking the *b* of Elam
50:14 you who are treading the *b*
50:29 all who are treading the *b*
50:42 *B* and javelin they handle
51:3 Let the one treading his *b*
La 2:4 trodden his *b* like an enemy
3:12 He has trodden his *b*, and he
3:20 remember and *b* low over me
Eze 1:28 the *b* that occurs in a cloud
39:3 your *b* out of your left hand
46:2 *b* down upon the threshold
46:3 people of the land must *b*
46:9 in order to *b* down should
Ho 1:5 break the *b* of Israel in the
1:7 not save them by a *b* or by a
2:18 *b* and the sword and war I
7:16 had become like a loose *b*
Am 2:15 no one handling the *b* will
Mic 5:13 no more *b* down to the work
6:6 I *b* myself to God on high
Hab 3:9 your *b* comes to be uncovered
Zep 2:11 people will *b* down to him
Zec 9:10 the battle *b* must be cut off
9:13 I will tread as my *b* Judah
9:13 *b* I will fill with Ephraim
10:4 out of him is the battle *b*
14:16 to *b* down to the King
14:17 to *b* down to the King, Jehovah
Ro 11:10 always *b* down their back
Re 6:2 the one seated upon it had a *b*

Bowed

Ge 19:1 *b* down with his face to the
23:7 *b* down to the natives, to the
23:12 Abraham *b* down before the
33:6 they and their children . . . *b*
33:7 they *b* down, and afterward
33:7 and Rachel, and they *b* down
42:6 Joseph's brothers came and *b*
43:28 they *b* down and prostrated
48:12 *b* down with his face to the
49:9 *b* down, he stretched himself
Ex 4:31 they *b* down and prostrated
12:27 people *b* low and prostrated
33:10 the people rose and *b* down
Nu 22:31 *b* low and prostrated himself
24:9 He *b* down, he lay down like
Jos 23:16 served other gods and *b*
Ru 2:10 and *b* down to the earth and
1Sa 4:19 *b* herself and began giving
20:41 and *b* three times; and they
25:23 and *b* to the earth
25:41 *b* with her face to the
2Sa 18:21 the Cushite *b* to Joab and
18:28 he *b* to the king with his
24:20 *b* down to the king with his
1Ki 1:16 Bath-sheba *b* low and
1:31 Bath-sheba *b* low with her
1:47 the king *b* down upon the bed
1:53 *b* down to King Solomon
2:19 meet her and *b* down to her
2Ki 2:15 *b* down to him to the earth
1Ch 21:21 *b* down to David with his
2Ch 7:3 *b* low with their faces to the
20:18 Jehoshaphat *b* low with his
29:29 *b* low and prostrated
Ne 8:6 then *b* low and prostrated
Ps 35:14 Saddened, I *b* down
38:6 I have *b* low to an extreme

Ps 44:25 *b* down to the dust itself
57:6 My soul has become *b* down
106:19 *b* down to a molten image
145:14 up all who are *b* down
146:8 raising up the ones *b* down
Jer 8:2 and that they have *b* down to
Hab 3:6 indefinitely lasting hills *b*

Bowels

Job 20:23 upon him, into his *b*
Zep 1:17 their *b* like the dung

Bowing

Ge 37:9 eleven stars were *b* down to
Ex 32:8 and keep *b* down to it and
Jg 2:12 they began *b* down to them
2:17 and went *b* down to them
1Ki 22:53 serving Baal and *b* down to
2Ki 19:37 *b* down at the house of
21:21 and *b* down to them
2Ch 29:28 *b* down while the song was
Ne 9:3 *b* down to Jehovah their God
9:6 the heavens are *b* down to you
Es 3:2 were *b* low and prostrating
3:5 Mordecai was not *b* low and
Isa 37:38 *b* down at the house of
58:5 *b* down his head just like a
60:14 you must go, *b* down
Jer 1:16 *b* down to the works of their
16:11 serving them and *b* down
Eze 8:16 *b* down to the east, to the
Zep 1:5 *b* down upon the roofs to the
1:5 *b* down, making sworn oaths
Joh 19:30 *b* his head, he delivered

Bowl

Nu 7:13 silver *b* of seventy shekels
7:19 silver *b* of seventy shekels
7:25 silver *b* of seventy shekels
7:31 silver *b* of seventy shekels
7:37 silver *b* of seventy shekels by
7:43 silver *b* of seventy shekels
7:49 silver *b* of seventy shekels
7:55 silver *b* of seventy shekels
7:61 silver *b* of seventy shekels
7:67 silver *b* of seventy shekels
7:73 silver *b* of seventy shekels
7:79 silver *b* of seventy shekels
7:85 and seventy to each *b*, all
Jg 5:25 large banquet *b* of majestic
6:38 a large banquet *b* with water
2Ki 2:20 a small new *b* and put salt
21:13 the handleless *b* clean
Pr 19:24 his hand in the banquet *b*
26:15 his hand in the banquet *b*
Ec 12:6 and the golden *b* gets crushed
Ca 7:2 Your navel roll is a round *b*
Isa 22:24 vessels of the *b* sort as
Zec 4:2 lampstand . . . with a *b* on top
4:3 one on the right side of the *b*
9:15 filled like the *b*, like the
12:2 a *b* causing reeling to all
Mt 26:23 his hand with me in the *b*
Mr 14:20 with me into the common *b*
Re 16:2 out his *b* into the earth
16:3 poured out his *b* into the sea
16:4 poured out his *b* into the
16:8 poured out his *b* upon the sun
16:10 poured . . . *b* upon the throne
16:12 his *b* upon the great river
16:17 poured . . . *b* upon the air

Bowls

Ex 24:6 half the blood and put it in *b*
25:29 its pitchers and its *b* with
27:3 its *b*, and its forks, and its
37:16 its *b* and its pitchers with
38:3 the *b*, the forks and the fire
Nu 4:7 *b* and the pitchers of the drink
4:14 and the *b*, all the utensils
7:84 twelve silver *b*, twelve
1Ki 7:40 and the shovels and the *b*
7:45 the *b* and all these utensils
7:50 the *b* and the cups and the
2Ki 12:13 extinguishers, *b*, trumpets
25:15 the fire holders and the *b*
1Ch 28:17 *b* and the pitchers of pure
28:17 small gold *b* by weight for
28:17 for the different small *b*
28:17 small silver *b* by weight
28:17 for the different small *b*
2Ch 4:8 and made a hundred *b* of gold
4:11 and the shovels and the *b*
4:22 the *b* and the cups and the
35:13 pots and in banquet *b*
Ezr 1:10 thirty small *b* of gold

Ezr 1:10 small secondary *b* of silver
8:27 twenty small gold *b* worth
Ne 7:70 fifty *b*, five hundred and
Jer 52:18 *b* and the cups and all the
52:19 *b* and the cans and the
52:19 *b* that were of genuine gold
Am 6:6 drinking out of *b* of wine
Zec 14:20 like the *b* before the altar
Re 5:8 *b* that were full of incense
15:7 *b* that were full of the anger
16:1 seven *b* of the anger of God
17:1 angels that had the seven *b*
21:9 angels who had the seven *b*

Bowl-shaped
1Ki 7:41 pillars and the *b* capitals
7:42 to cover the two *b* capitals

Bowmen
1Sa 31:3 *b*, finally found him, and
Isa 21:17 over of the number of *b*

Bows
2Ch 26:14 and *b* and slingstones
Ne 4:13 their lances and their *b*
4:16 the shields and the *b* and the
Ps 10:10 He is crushed, he *b* down
37:15 their own *b* will be broken
Isa 2:9 And earthling man *b* down, and
5:28 and all their *b* are bent
13:18 *b* will dash even young men
44:17 *b* down and prays to it and
Jer 51:56 *b* must be shattered, for
Eze 39:9 the *b* and with the arrows

Bowshot
Ge 21:16 about the distance of a *b*

Bowstring
Job 30:11 he loosened my own *b* and
Ps 11:2 ready their arrow upon the *b*

Bowstrings
Ps 21:12 *b* that you make ready

Box
1Sa 6:8 put into a *b* at the side of it
6:11 the *b* and the golden jerboas
6:15 and the *b* that was with it
Joh 12:6 thief and had the money *b*
13:29 was holding the money *b*

Boy
Ge 19:4 from *b* to old man, all the
21:12 about the *b* and about your
21:17 God heard the voice of the *b*
21:17 to the voice of the *b*
21:18 lift up the *b* and take hold
21:19 and to give the *b* a drink
21:20 *b*, and he kept growing and
22:5 I and the *b* want to go on
22:12 hand against the *b* and do not
37:2 being but a *b*, he was with
43:8 Send the *b* with me, that we
44:22 The *b* is not able to leave
44:30 without the *b* along with us
44:31 he sees that the *b* is not
44:32 became surety for the *b*
44:33 slave stay instead of the *b*
44:33 the *b* may go up with his
44:34 without the *b* along with me
Ex 2:6 and here the *b* was weeping
22:22 any widow or fatherless *b*
De 10:18 fatherless *b* and the widow
14:29 fatherless *b* and the widow
16:11 fatherless *b* and the widow
16:14 the fatherless *b* and the
24:17 or of the fatherless *b*
24:19 for the fatherless *b* and for
24:20 the fatherless *b* and for the
24:21 the fatherless *b* and for the
26:12 the fatherless *b* and the
26:13 the fatherless *b* and the
27:19 a fatherless *b* and a widow
Jg 13:24 and the *b* kept getting bigger
16:26 the *b* that was holding him
1Sa 1:22 As soon as the *b* is weaned
1:24 And the *b* was with her
1:25 and brought the *b* to Eli
1:27 was with reference to this *b*
2:11 as for the *b*, he became a
2:18 was ministering . . . as a *b*
2:21 *b* Samuel continued growing
3:1 the *b* Samuel was ministering
3:8 Jehovah . . . was calling the *b*
4:21 But she called the *b* Ichabod
17:33 you are but a *b*, and he is a
17:42 proved to be a *b* and ruddy
1Sa 17:55 Whose son is the *b*, Abner?
17:58 Whose son are you, *b*?
2Sa 12:16 true God in behalf of the *b*
1Ki 3:7 and I am but a little *b*
11:17 while Hadad was a young *b*
14:3 is going to happen to the *b*
14:17 the *b* himself died
2Ki 4:29 staff upon the face of the *b*
4:30 At this the mother of the *b*
4:31 The *b* did not wake up
4:32 and there the *b* was dead
4:35 the *b* began to sneeze as
4:35 the *b* opened his eyes
5:14 like the flesh of a little *b*
2Ch 34:3 while he was still a *b*, he
Job 24:9 snatch away a fatherless *b*
29:12 the fatherless *b* and anyone
31:17 the fatherless *b* did not eat
31:21 against the fatherless *b*
Ps 10:14 the fatherless *b*, commits
10:18 To judge the fatherless *b* and
82:3 and the fatherless *b*
146:9 fatherless *b* and the widow
Pr 20:11 by his practices a *b* makes
22:6 Train up a *b* according to the
22:15 with the heart of a *b*
23:13 discipline from the mere *b*
29:15 a *b* let on the loose will be
Ec 10:16 when your king is a *b* and
Ca 5:16 and this is my *b* companion
Isa 1:17 for the fatherless *b*
1:23 For a fatherless *b* they do
3:5 the *b* against the old man
7:16 *b* will know how to reject
8:4 *b* will know how to call out
10:19 mere *b* will be able to
11:6 little *b* will be leader over
65:20 one will die as a mere *b*
Jer 1:6 for I am but a *b*
1:7 Do not say, I am but a *b*
5:28 case of the fatherless *b*
7:6 no fatherless *b* and no widow
22:3 fatherless *b* or widow
51:22 dash old man and *b* to
La 2:21 *B* and old man have lain down
Eze 22:7 Fatherless *b* and widow they
Ho 11:1 When Israel was a *b*, then I
14:3 a fatherless *b* is shown mercy
Zec 7:10 defraud no . . . fatherless *b*
Mal 3:5 and with the fatherless *b*
Mt 17:18 *b* was cured from that hour
Lu 2:43 the *b* Jesus remained behind
9:42 healed the *b* and delivered
Joh 4:51 to say that his *b* was living
6:9 little *b* that has five barley
Ac 20:12 they took the *b* away alive

Boyhood
1Sa 17:33 is a man of war from his *b*
Ps 88:15 about to expire from *b* on

Boy's
2Ki 4:31 put the staff upon the *b* face

Boys
Ge 25:27 And the *b* got bigger, and Esau
48:16 bless the *b*. And let my name
Ex 22:24 and your sons fatherless *b*
1Sa 16:11 Are these all the *b*?
2Ki 2:23 small *b* that came out from
Job 16:11 God hands me over to young *b*
19:18 young *b* . . . rejected me
21:11 sending out their young *b*
22:9 the arms of fatherless *b* are
24:3 the male ass of fatherless *b*
24:5 to each one bread for the *b*
29:8 The *b* saw me and hid
Ps 68:5 A father of fatherless *b* and
94:6 the fatherless *b* they murder
109:9 his sons become fatherless *b*
109:12 favor to his fatherless *b*
148:12 old men together with *b*
Pr 23:10 field of fatherless *b* do not
Isa 3:4 make *b* their princes, and
9:17 upon their fatherless *b* and
10:2 plunder even the fatherless *b*
20:4 *b* and old men, naked and
40:30 *B* will both tire out and
Jer 49:11 Do leave your fatherless *b*
La 5:13 mere *b* have stumbled
Zec 8:5 with *b* and girls playing in
Mt 2:16 had all the *b* in Bethlehem
21:15 *b* that were crying out in

Bozez
1Sa 14:4 the name of the one was *B*

Bozkath
Jos 15:39 Lachish and *B* and Eglon
2Ki 22:1 daughter of Adaiah from *B*

Bozrah
Ge 36:33 Jobab son of Zerah from *B*
1Ch 1:44 the son of Zerah from *B*
Isa 34:6 Jehovah has a sacrifice in *B*
63:1 of glowing colors from *B*
Jer 48:24 Kerioth and against *B*
49:13 malediction will *B* become
49:22 spread out his wings over *B*
Am 1:12 the dwelling towers of *B*

Brace
2Ki 18:21 should *b* himself upon it
2Ch 32:8 people began to *b* themselves
Isa 36:6 man should *b* himself upon it
1Pe 1:13 *b* up your minds for activity

Braced
Jg 16:29 Samson *b* himself against the

Bracelet
2Sa 1:10 *b* that was upon his arm

Bracelets
Ge 24:22 and two *b* for her hands
24:30 *b* on the hands of his sister
24:47 and the *b* on her hands
Nu 31:50 *b*, signet rings, earrings
Isa 3:19 eardrops and the *b* and the
Eze 16:11 put *b* upon your hands and a
23:42 put *b* on the hands of the

Brag
Jg 7:2 Israel would *b* about itself
Jer 9:23 Let not the wise man *b* about
9:23 let not the mighty man *b*
9:23 Let not the rich man *b*
9:24 *b* about himself because of
49:4 *b* about the low plains, your
1Co 13:4 Love . . . does not *b*

Braggart
Pr 21:24 self-assuming *b* is the name

Braggarts
Isa 28:14 word of Jehovah, you *b*

Bragger
Isa 29:20 *b* must come to his finish

Bragging
Ps 94:4 keep *b* about themselves
Jer 9:24 let the one *b* about himself
Jas 3:14 do not be *b* and lying against

Brags
Jas 3:5 the tongue . . . makes great *b*
4:16 in your self-assuming *b*

Braided
Mt 27:29 they *b* a crown out of thorns
Mr 15:17 *b* a crown of thorns and put
Joh 19:2 soldiers *b* a crown of thorns

Braiding
1Ti 2:9 not with styles of hair *b* and
1Pe 3:3 the external *b* of the hair and

Braids
Jg 16:13 weave the seven *b* of my head
16:19 shave off the seven *b* of his
Ca 1:10 are comely among the hair *b*

Bramble
Jg 9:14 said to the *b*, You come, be
9:15 the *b* said to the trees, If it
9:15 let fire come out of the *b*
Ps 58:9 pots feel the kindled *b*

Branch
Jos 13:3 the *b* of the Nile that is in
Jg 9:48 cut down a *b* of the trees and
9:49 each one a *b* for himself and
Isa 17:6 olives in the top of the *b*
17:9 the *b* that they have left
Mt 24:32 as its young *b* grows tender
Mr 13:28 *b* grows tender and puts
Joh 15:2 *b* in me not bearing fruit
15:4 *b* cannot bear fruit of itself
15:6 he is cast out as a *b* and

Branches
Ge 49:22 propels its *b* up over a wall
Ex 25:31 its *b*, its cups, its knobs
25:32 six *b* are running out from
25:32 three *b* of the lampstand
25:32 three *b* of the lampstand
25:33 are on the one set of *b*
25:33 on the other set of *b*, with

Ex 25:33 six *b* running out from the
25:35 the knob under two *b* is out
25:35 knob under the two other *b*
25:35 the knob under two more *b* is
25:35 for the six *b* running out
25:36 *b* are to proceed out from it
37:17 Its sides and its *b*, its cups
37:18 six *b* were running out from
37:18 three *b* of the lampstand out
37:18 three *b* of the lampstand out
37:19 on the one set of *b*
37:19 on the other set of *b*
37:19 six *b* running out from the
37:21 the knob under two *b* was
37:21 two other *b* was out of it
37:21 knob under two more *b* was
37:21 six *b* running out from the
37:22 their *b* proceeded out from it
Isa 16:8 down its bright-red *b*
Jer 11:16 they have broken its *b*
Eze 17:6 shoots and sent forth *b*
19:10 and full of *b* she became
19:11 became tall up among *b*, and
31:5 *b* continued getting longer
31:6 under its *b* all the wild
31:8 not prove to be like it in *b*
31:12 its *b* will be broken among
31:13 upon its *b* there will
Mt 13:32 and find lodging among its *b*
21:8 began cutting down *b* from
Mr 4:32 produces great *b*, so that the
Lu 13:19 took up lodging in its *b*
Joh 12:13 took the *b* of palm trees
15:5 I am the vine, you are the *b*
15:6 men gather those *b* up and
Ro 11:16 root is holy, the *b* are also
11:17 *b* were broken off but you
11:18 not be exulting over the *b*
11:19 *B* were broken off that I
11:21 did not spare the natural *b*
Re 7:9 were palm *b* in their hands

Branchy
Le 23:40 boughs of *b* trees and poplars
Ne 8:15 leaves of *b* trees to make
Eze 6:13 and under every *b* big tree
20:28 hill and every *b* tree, then

Brand
Isa 3:24 a *b* mark instead of
Ga 6:17 *b* marks of a slave of Jesus

Branding
Ex 21:25, 25 *b* for *b*, wound for wound
1Ti 4:2 marked . . . as with a *b* iron

Brandish
Isa 10:26 *b* against him a whip as at
Eze 32:10 *b* my sword in their faces

Brandishing
2Sa 23:8 *b* his spear over eight
23:18 *b* his spear over three
1Ch 11:11 He was *b* his spear over
11:20 he was *b* his spear over
Isa 30:32 with battles of *b* he will

Brass
1Co 13:1 a sounding piece of *b* or a

Brawler
1Ti 3:3 not a drunken *b*, not a smiter
Tit 1:7 not a drunken *b*, not a smiter

Brazier
Jer 36:22 *b* burning before him
36:23 fire that was in the *b*
36:23 fire that was in the *b*

Breach
2Ki 14:13 *b* in the wall of Jerusalem
2Ch 25:23 *b* in the wall of Jerusalem
Job 16:14, 14 with *b* after *b*

Breached
2Ki 25:4 And the city got to be *b*

Breaches
Ps 60:2 Heal its *b*, for it has
Isa 22:9 *b* of the city of David
Eze 26:10 into a city opened by *b*
30:16 come to be for capture by *b*
Am 4:3 And by *b* you will go forth
9:11 certainly repair their *b*

Bread
Ge 3:19 you will eat *b* until you
14:18 king of Salem brought out *b*
18:5 let me get a piece of *b*, and
21:14 and took *b* and a skin water
25:34 Jacob gave Esau *b* and lentil
27:17 gave the tasty dish and the *b*
28:20 *b* to eat and garments to
31:54 invited his brothers to eat *b*
31:54 ate *b* and passed the night
37:25 they sat down to eat *b*
39:6 except the *b* he was eating
40:16 three baskets of white *b*
41:54 Egypt there was found *b*
41:55 began to cry to Pharaoh for *b*
43:25 they were going to eat *b*
45:23 carrying grain and *b* and
47:12 Joseph kept supplying . . . *b*
47:13 was no *b* in all the land
47:15 Give us *b*! And why should we
47:16 *b* in exchange for your
47:17 Joseph kept giving them *b*
47:17 *b* in exchange for all their
47:19 Buy us and our land for *b*
49:20 Out of Asher his *b* will be
Ex 2:20 Call him, that he may eat *b*
16:3 were eating *b* to satisfaction
16:4 I am raining down *b* for you
16:8 *b* to satisfaction, because
16:12 you will be satisfied with *b*
16:15 *b* that Jehovah has given you
16:22 picked up twice as much *b*
16:29 sixth day the *b* of two days
16:32 the *b* that I made you eat
18:12 *b* with Moses' father-in-law
23:25 bless your *b* and your water
29:2 unfermented *b* and unfermented
29:23 also a round loaf of *b* and a
29:23 a ring-shaped cake of oiled *b*
29:32 *b* that is in the basket at
29:34 the *b* should be left over
34:28 He ate no *b* and he drank no
40:23 arranged the row of *b* upon
Le 7:13 cakes of leavened *b* he will
8:26 cake of oiled *b* and one wafer
8:31 will eat it and the *b* that is
8:32 flesh and the *b* you will burn
21:6 offerings made by fire, the *b*
21:8 presenting the *b* of your God
21:17 to present the *b* of his God
21:21 to present the *b* of his God
21:22 eat the *b* of his God from
22:7 holy things . . . it is his *b*
22:11 may share in eating his *b*
22:13 eat some of her father's *b*
22:25 present as the *b* of your God
23:14 eat no *b* nor roasted grain
24:7 as the *b* for a remembrancer
26:5 eat your *b* to satisfaction and
26:26 bake your *b* in but one oven
26:26 give back your *b* by weight
Nu 4:7 constant *b* should continue on
14:9 for they are *b* to us
15:19 eat any of the *b* of the land
21:5 there is no *b* and no water
21:5 to abhor the contemptible *b*
28:2 my *b*, for my offerings made
28:24 daily for the seven days as *b*
De 8:3 not by *b* alone does man live
8:9 will not eat *b* with scarcity
9:9 neither ate *b* nor drank water
9:18 I neither ate *b* nor drank
10:18 give him *b* and a mantle
16:3 the *b* of affliction, because
23:4 to your aid with *b* and water
29:6 *B* you did not eat, and wine
Jos 9:5 all the *b* of their provisions
9:12 This *b* of ours, it was hot
Jg 7:13 cake of barley *b* turning over
8:5 loaves of *b* to the people that
8:6 *b* has to be given to your army
8:15 *b* has to be given to your
13:16 not feed myself on your *b*
19:5 with a bit of *b* and afterward
19:19 *b* and wine for me and your
Ru 1:6 to his people by giving them *b*
2:14 you must eat some of the *b*
1Sa 2:5 hire themselves out for *b*
2:36 money and a round loaf of *b*
2:36 to eat a piece of *b*
9:7 *b* itself has disappeared from
10:3 three round loaves of *b* and
14:24 man that eats *b* before the
14:24 none of the people tasted *b*
14:28 the man that eats *b* today
16:20 Jesse took an ass, *b* and a
17:17 and these ten loaves of *b*
20:34 not eat *b* on the second day
21:3 are five loaves of *b* at your
1Sa 21:4 There is no ordinary *b* under
21:4 there is holy *b*; provided
21:6 happened to be no *b* there
21:6 place fresh *b* there on the
22:13 giving him *b* and a sword
25:11 take my *b* and my water and
25:18 two hundred loaves of *b*
28:22 set before you a piece of *b*
30:11 gave him *b* that he might
30:12 not eaten *b* or drunk water
2Sa 3:29 or one in need of *b*
3:35 people came to give David *b*
3:35 shall taste *b* or anything at
6:19 ring-shaped cake of *b* and a
9:7 eat *b* at my table constantly
9:10 eat *b* at my table constantly
12:17 did not take *b* in company
12:20 set *b* before him and he
12:21 got up and began to eat *b*
13:5 give me *b* as a patient, and
13:5 make the *b* of consolation
13:6 take *b* as a patient from her
13:7 make the *b* of consolation
13:10 Bring the *b* of consolation
16:1 two hundred loaves of *b* and
16:2 the *b* and the load of summer
1Ki 11:18 *b* he assigned to him, and
13:8 eat *b* or drink water in this
13:9 not eat *b* or drink water
13:15 to the house and eat *b*
13:16 not eat *b* or drink water
13:17 not eat *b* or drink water
13:18 may eat *b* and drink water
13:19 eat *b* in his house and drink
13:22 eat *b* and drink water in
13:22 Do not eat *b* or drink water
13:23 after his eating *b* and after
14:3 loaves of *b* and sprinkled
17:6 *b* and meat in the morning
17:6 *b* and meat in the evening
17:11 Please, get me a bit of *b*
18:4 he supplied them *b* and water
18:13 supplying them *b* and water
21:4 and he did not eat *b*
21:5 and you are not eating *b*
21:7 eat *b* and let your heart be
22:27 reduced allowance of *b* and
2Ki 4:8 to constrain him to eat *b*
4:8 turn aside there to eat *b*
4:42 *b* of the first ripe fruits
4:42 and new grain in his *b* bag
6:22 Set *b* and water before them
18:32 a land of *b* and vineyards
25:3 no *b* for the people of the
25:29 ate *b* constantly before him
1Ch 9:32 in charge of the layer *b*
16:3 a round loaf of *b* and a date
23:29 even for the layer *b* and for
23:29 the wafers of unfermented *b*
28:16 the tables of the layer *b*
2Ch 2:4 with the constant layer *b* and
13:11 layers of *b* are upon the
18:26 reduced allowance of *b* and
29:18 table of the layer *b* and all
Ezr 10:6 ate no *b* and drank no water
Ne 5:14 not eat the *b* due the governor
5:15 *b* and wine daily forty silver
5:18 *b* due the governor I did not
9:15 *b* from heaven you gave them
10:33 the layer *b* and the constant
13:2 with *b* and with water
Job 15:23 search of *b*—where is it?
22:7 hungry one you hold back *b*
24:5 to each one *b* for the boys
33:20 certainly makes *b* loathsome
42:11 eat *b* with him in his house
Ps 14:4 as they have eaten *b*
37:25 his offspring looking for *b*
41:9 Who was eating my *b*, has
53:4 people as they have eaten *b*
78:20 able also to give *b* itself
78:25 the very *b* of powerful ones
80:5 made them eat the *b* of tears
102:9 eaten ashes . . . just like *b*
104:15 *b* that sustains the very
105:40 with *b* from heaven he kept
132:15 I shall satisfy with *b*
146:7 giving *b* to the hungry ones
Pr 4:17 with the *b* of wickedness
6:26 down to a round loaf of *b*
9:5 feed yourselves with my *b* and
9:17 and *b* eaten in secrecy—it is
12:9 himself but in want of *b*
12:11 be satisfied with *b*, but

Pr 17:1 Better is a dry piece of *b*
20:13 be satisfied with *b*
20:17 *B* gained by falsehood is
25:21 is hungry, give him *b* to eat
28:19 have his sufficiency of *b*
28:21 over a mere piece of *b*
31:27 *b* of laziness she does not
Ec 10:19 *B* is for the laughter of the
11:1 Send out your *b* upon the
Isa 3:1 whole support of *b* and the
3:7 my house there is neither *b*
4:1 eat our own *b* and wear our
21:14 fleeing away with *b* for
30:20 *b* in the form of distress
30:23 produce of the ground *b*
33:16 *b* will certainly be given
36:17 a land of *b* and vineyards
44:15 fire and actually bakes *b*
44:19 coals I have also baked *b*
51:14 his *b* may not be lacking
55:2 money for what is not *b*
55:10 and *b* to the eater
58:7 your *b* out to the hungry one
Jer 5:17 your harvest and your *b*
16:7 not deal out to them any *b*
37:21 round loaf of *b* to him
37:21 *b* was exhausted from the
38:9 no *b* anymore in the city
41:1 eat *b* together in Mizpah
42:14 *b* we shall not go hungry
44:17 used to be satisfied with *b*
52:6 *b* for the people of the land
52:33 and he ate *b* before him
La 1:11 they are looking for *b*
4:4 Children . . . have asked for *b*
4:10 as *b* of consolation to one
5:6 to get satisfaction with *b*
5:9 we bring in our *b*, because of
Eze 4:9 and make them into *b* for you
4:13 eat their *b* unclean among
4:15 you must make your *b* upon it
4:16 will have to eat *b* by weight
4:17 may be lacking *b* and water
12:18 with quaking your *b* . . . eat
12:19 their *b* they will eat, and
13:19 and for the morsels of *b*
16:19 *b* that I had given to you
16:49 Pride, sufficiency of *b* and
18:7 he would give his own *b*
18:16 he has given his own *b*, and
24:17 *b* of men you should not eat
24:22 *b* of men you will not eat
44:3 to eat *b* before Jehovah
44:7 present my *b*, fat and blood
48:18 *b* for the ones serving the
Da 10:3 Dainty *b* I did not eat, and
Ho 2:5 those giving my *b* and my
9:4 the *b* of times of mourning
9:4 their *b* is for their own soul
Am 4:6 want of *b* in all your places
7:12 eat *b*, and there you may
8:11 a famine, not for *b*, and a
Hag 2:12 touches with his skirt *b* or
Mal 1:7 upon my altar polluted *b*
Mt 4:3 stones to become loaves of *b*
4:4 Man must live, not on *b* alone
6:11 Give us today our *b* for this
7:9 son asks for *b*—he will not
15:26 take the *b* of the children
Mr 6:8 no *b*, no food pouch, no copper
7:27 take the *b* of the children
Lu 4:3 stone to become a loaf of *b*
4:4 Man must not live by *b* alone
7:33 come neither eating *b* nor
9:3 pouch, nor *b* nor silver money
11:3 Give us our *b* for the day
14:15 eats *b* in the kingdom of God
15:17 are abounding with *b*, while
Joh 6:23 ate the *b* after the Lord had
6:31 *b* from heaven to eat
6:32 Moses did not give you the *b*
6:32 the true *b* from heaven
6:33 the *b* of God is the one who
6:34 Lord, always give us this *b*
6:35 I am the *b* of life. He that
6:41 I am the *b* that came down
6:48 I am the *b* of life
6:50 *b* that comes down from
6:51 I am the living *b* that came
6:51 if anyone eats of this *b* he
6:51 *b* that I shall give is my
6:58 This is the *b* that came down
6:58 feeds on this *b* will live
13:18 used to feed on my *b* has
Joh 21:9 and fish lying upon it and *b*
21:13 Jesus came and took the *b*
2Co 9:10 and *b* for eating will supply

Breadstuff
Isa 28:28 *b* itself generally crushed

Breadth
Ge 13:17 its length and through its *b*
Job 37:10 the *b* of waters is under
Isa 8:8 fill the *b* of your land
Eze 40:5 the *b* of the thing built
40:25 *b* was twenty-five cubits
Da 3:1 the *b* of which was six cubits
Zec 2:2 to see what her *b* amounts to
5:2 *b* of which is ten cubits
Eph 3:18 what is the *b* and length and
Re 20:9 over the *b* of the earth
21:16 length is as great as its *b*
21:16 length and *b* and height are

Break
Ge 19:9 getting near to *b* in the door
27:40 *b* his yoke off your neck
Ex 12:46 you must not *b* a bone in it
13:13 then you must *b* its neck
14:15 that they should *b* camp
19:21 *b* through to Jehovah to take
19:22 that Jehovah may not *b* out
19:24 *b* through to come up to
19:24 he may not *b* out upon them
23:24 *b* down their sacred pillars
34:20 then you must *b* its neck
40:36 sons of Israel would *b* camp
40:37 not *b* camp until the day
Le 14:43 it does *b* out in the house
26:13 *b* the bars of your yoke and
26:19 *b* the pride of your strength
Nu 9:12 they should *b* no bone in it
24:8 he will *b* them to pieces
24:17 *b* apart the temples of
De 7:5 sacred pillars you should *b*
21:4 *b* the neck of the young cow
31:16 *b* my covenant that I have
31:20 disrespect and *b* my covenant
Jg 2:1 Never shall I *b* my covenant
2Sa 18:19 and *b* the news to the king
18:20 *b* the news on another day
18:20 you must not *b* the news
22:39 *b* them in pieces, that they
1Ki 15:19 do *b* your covenant with
2Ki 3:26 to *b* through to the king of
1Ch 16:33 of the forest *b* out joyfully
2Ch 16:3 *b* your covenant with Baasha
20:37 certainly *b* down your works
26:6 *b* through the wall of Gath
31:1 *b* up the sacred pillars
Ne 4:3 *b* down their wall of stones
Job 29:17 I would *b* the jawbones of
38:10 *b* up my regulation upon it
Ps 2:9 *b* them with an iron scepter
3:7 wicked ones you will have to *b*
10:15 *B* the arm of the wicked and
18:38 I shall *b* them in pieces so
58:6 *B* down the very jawbones of
68:21 *b* the head of his enemies
85:4 *b* off your vexation with us
89:33 loving-kindness I shall not *b*
96:12 the forest *b* out joyfully
105:33 *b* the trees of their
110:5 *b* kings to pieces on the day
110:6 *b* to pieces the head one over
Pr 18:1 against . . . wisdom he will *b*
18:24 companions disposed to *b* one
25:15 tongue itself can *b* a bone
Ec 3:3 time to *b* down and a time to
Isa 14:25 *b* the Assyrian in my land
14:27 counseled, and who can *b* it
27:11 *b* them off, lighting them
30:14 *b* it as in the breaking of
42:3 No crushed reed will he *b*
45:2 doors I shall *b* in pieces
54:3 you will *b* forth, and your
58:8 *b* forth just like the dawn
Jer 14:21 do not *b* your covenant with
15:12 Can one *b* iron in pieces
17:18 *b* them even with twice as
19:10 *b* the flask before the eyes
19:11 I shall *b* this people and
28:2 will *b* the yoke of the king
28:4 *b* the yoke of the king of
28:11 *b* the yoke of Nebuchadnezzar
30:8 I shall *b* one's yoke from
33:20 *b* my covenant of the day
43:13 *b* to pieces the pillars of
La 1:15 to *b* my young men to pieces
Eze 5:16 I will *b* your rods around
14:13 *b* for it the rods around
30:18 I *b* there the yoke bars of
30:21 I shall certainly *b*, and
30:22 and I will *b* his arms
30:24 *b* the arms of Pharaoh
34:27 *b* the bars of their yoke
Da 8:7 ram and to *b* its two horns
Ho 1:5 *b* the bow of Israel in the low
2:18 war I shall *b* out of the land
10:2 one who will *b* their altars
Joe 2:8 the others do not *b* off course
Am 1:5 will *b* the bar of Damascus
Mic 2:13 they will actually *b* through
Na 1:13 I shall *b* his carrying bar
Zep 3:14 *B* out in cheers, O Israel
Zec 11:10 in order to *b* my covenant
11:14 order to *b* the brotherhood
Mt 6:19 where thieves *b* in and steal
6:20 thieves do not *b* in and steal
Joh 2:19 *B* down this temple, and in
19:33 they did not *b* his legs
1Co 10:16 The loaf which we *b*, is it
Ga 4:27 *b* out and cry aloud, you
1Jo 3:8 *b* up the works of the Devil

Breakdown
Isa 30:13 *b* of which may come
30:26 Jehovah binds up the *b* of
51:19 Despoiling and *b*, and hunger
59:7 despoiling and *b* are in their
60:18 despoiling or *b* within your
65:14 howl because of sheer *b*
Jer 6:14 to heal the *b* of my people
8:11 heal the *b* of the daughter
8:21 the *b* of the daughter of my
10:19 to me on account of my *b*
17:18 even with twice as much *b*
30:12 There is no cure for your *b*
30:15 on account of your *b*
48:5 outcry over the *b* that people
50:22 in the land, and a great *b*
La 2:13 *b* is just as great as the sea
3:47 ours, desolateness and *b*
3:48 the *b* of the daughter of my
4:10 the *b* of the daughter of my
Da 11:26 will bring his *b*

Breakers
Ps 42:7 All your *b* and your waves
Jon 2:3 All your *b* and your waves

Breakfast
Joh 21:12 Come, take your *b*

Breakfasted
Joh 21:15 they had *b*, Jesus said to

Breaking
Ex 9:9 boils *b* out with blisters
9:10 blisters, *b* out on man and
22:2 found in the act of *b* in and
Le 2:6 a *b* of it up into pieces, and
13:42 leprosy *b* out in the baldness
13:57 article of skin, it is *b* out
Nu 10:2 and for *b* up the camps
1Sa 5:9 and piles began *b* out on them
25:10 servants that are *b* away
2Sa 22:5 deadly *b* waves encircled me
1Ki 19:11 wind was . . . *b* crags
1Ch 20:4 war began *b* out at Gezer
Ezr 9:14 *b* your commandments again
Job 16:14 He keeps *b* through me with
Ps 29:5 voice of Jehovah is *b* the
44:2 You went *b* national groups
88:7 *b* waves you have afflicted me
93:4 majestic *b* waves of the sea
Pr 15:4 means a *b* down in the spirit
Ec 10:8 is *b* through a stone wall
Isa 5:5 *b* down of its stone wall, and
5:7 *b* of law; for righteousness
30:14 *b* of a large jar of the
38:13 he keeps *b* all my bones
66:3 is as one *b* the neck of a dog
66:9 cause the *b* through and not
Jer 2:34 Not in the act of *b* in have
48:3 despoiling and great *b* down
49:35 Here I am *b* the bow of Elam
Eze 4:16 I am *b* the rods around which
16:59 the oath in *b* my covenant
17:18 in *b* a covenant, and, look!
44:7 *b* my covenant on account of
Ho 13:13 the *b* forth of sons from the
Mt 14:19 *b* the loaves, he distributed
Mr 14:3 *B* open the alabaster case she

Lu 24:35 to them by the *b* of the loaf
Joh 5:18 not only . . . *b* the Sabbath

Breaks
Le 13:12 *b* out in the skin
Job 5:18 He *b* to pieces, but his own
34:24 He *b* powerful ones without
Ps 29:5 Jehovah *b* the cedars of
46:9 The bow he *b* apart and does
Jer 19:11 *b* the vessel of the potter
Mt 5:19 *b* one of these least

Breakthrough
2Ch 32:1 of making them his by a *b*
Mic 2:13 The one making a *b* will

Breakthroughs
Isa 7:6 and by *b* take it for ourselves

Breast
Ex 29:26 *b* of the ram of installation
29:27 sanctify the *b* of the wave
Le 7:30 by fire the fat upon the *b*
7:30 bring it with the *b* to wave
7:31 the *b* must become Aaron's
7:34 the *b* of the wave offering
8:29 take the *b* and to wave it to
10:14 the *b* of the wave offering
10:15 the *b* of the wave offering
Nu 6:20 *b* of the wave offering and
18:18 the *b* of the wave offering
Job 24:9 boy even from the *b*
Isa 60:16 *b* of kings you will suck
66:11 get satisfaction from the *b*
Eze 24:16 should not beat your *b*
Lu 18:13 kept beating his *b*, saying
Joh 13:25 upon the *b* of Jesus and said
21:20 leaned back upon his *b* and

Breastbands
Isa 3:20 step chains and the *b* and
Jer 2:32 a bride her *b*

Breastpiece
Ex 25:7 setting stones for the . . . *b*
28:4 make: a *b*, and an ephod and
28:15 must make the *b* of judgment
28:22 upon the *b* wreathed chains
28:23 make upon the *b* two rings of
28:23 the two extremities of the *b*
28:24 at the extremities of the *b*
28:26 the two extremities of the *b*
28:28 bind the *b* by its rings to
28:28 *b* may not get displaced from
28:29 on the *b* of judgment over
28:30 and the Thummim into the *b*
29:5 and with the ephod and the *b*
35:9 for the ephod and for the *b*
35:27 for the ephod and the *b*
39:8 he made the *b* with the
39:9 made the *b*, when doubled
39:15 upon the *b* wreathed chains
39:16 the two extremities of the *b*
39:17 at the extremities of the *b*
39:19 the two extremities of the *b*
39:21 bound the *b* by its rings to
39:21 *b* might not get displaced
Le 8:8 placed the *b* upon him and put
8:8 put in the *b* the Urim and the

Breastplate
Eph 6:14 on the *b* of righteousness
1Th 5:8 the *b* of faith and love

Breastplates
Re 9:9, 9 they had *b* like iron *b*
9:17 sulphur-yellow *b*; and the

Breasts
Ge 49:25 the blessings of the *b* and
Le 9:20 the fatty pieces upon the *b*
9:21 the *b* and the right leg Aaron
Job 3:12 *b* that I should take suck
Ps 22:9 upon the *b* of my mother
Pr 5:19 her own *b* intoxicate you at
Ca 1:13 between my *b* he will spend
4:5 two *b* are like two young ones
7:3 two *b* are like two young ones
7:7 and your *b*, date clusters
7:8 *b* become like clusters of the
8:1 sucking the *b* of my mother
8:8 sister that does not have any *b*
8:10 and my *b* are like towers
Isa 28:9 moved away from the *b*
32:12 upon the *b* in lamentation
Jer 4:8 Beat your *b* and howl, because
Eze 16:7 *b* themselves were firmly
23:3 There their *b* were squeezed

Eze 23:21 sake of the *b* of your youth
23:34 your *b* you will tear out
Da 2:32 *b* and its arms were of silver
Ho 2:2 adultery from between her *b*
9:14 and *b* shriveling up
Joe 1:13 beat your *b*, you priests
2:16 and those sucking the *b*
Lu 11:27 and the *b* that you sucked
23:29 and the *b* that did not nurse
23:48 to return, beating their *b*
Re 1:13 girded at the *b* with a
15:6 girded about their *b* with

Breath
Ge 2:7 blow into his nostrils the *b*
7:22 Everything in which the *b* of
Ex 15:8 And by a *b* from your nostrils
15:10 You blew with your *b*, the
2Sa 22:16 of the *b* of his nostrils
1Ki 17:17 there was no *b* left in him
Job 4:9 Through the *b* of God they
9:18 my taking of a fresh *b*
19:17 My *b* . . . loathsome to my
26:4 whose *b* has come forth from
27:3 my *b* is yet whole within me
32:8 the *b* of the Almighty that
33:4 Almighty's own *b* proceeded
34:14 If that one's spirit and *b*
37:10 By the *b* of God the ice is
Ps 18:15 the *b* of your nostrils
Pr 20:27 *b* of earthling man is the
Isa 2:22 whose *b* is in his nostrils
30:33 *b* of Jehovah, like a torrent
42:5 One giving *b* to the people
Jer 4:31 who keeps gasping for *b*
15:9 her soul has struggled for *b*
La 4:20 The very *b* of our nostrils
Eze 37:5 I am bringing into you *b*
37:6 and put in you *b*, and you
37:8 as regards *b*, there was none
37:10 *b* proceeded to come into
Da 5:23 God in whose hand your *b* is
10:17 no *b* . . . was left remaining
Hab 2:19 no *b* at all in the midst of
Ac 17:25 to all persons life and *b* and
Re 13:15 give *b* to the image of the

Breathe
Ca 4:16 *B* upon my garden. Let its

Breathed
Jos 10:40 everything that *b* he devoted
11:14 let anyone that *b* remain

Breathes
Ca 2:17 Until the day *b* and the
4:6 Until the day *b* and the

Breathing
De 20:16 preserve any *b* thing alive
Jos 11:11 no *b* thing at all was left
1Ki 15:29 not let anyone *b* remain of
Ps 150:6 Every *b* thing—let it praise
Isa 57:16 *b* creatures that I myself
Ac 9:1 Saul, still *b* threat and

Bred
Jer 6:2 comely and daintily *b* woman

Breed
Ex 16:20 it would *b* worms and stink
De 32:14 male sheep, the *b* of Bashan

Breeze
Ac 2:2 that of a rushing stiff *b*

Breezy
Ge 3:8 about the *b* part of the day

Bribe
Ex 23:8 You are not to accept a *b*, for
23:8 *b* blinds clear-sighted men
De 10:17 nor accepts a *b*
16:19 not be partial or accept a *b*
16:19 for the *b* blinds the eyes
27:25 a *b* to strike a soul fatally
1Sa 8:3 would accept a *b* and pervert
2Ki 16:8 sent the king of Assyria a *b*
2Ch 19:7 partiality or taking of a *b*
Ps 15:5 a *b* against the innocent one
Pr 17:23 take even a *b* from the bosom
21:14 *b* in the bosom, strong rage
Isa 1:23 lover of a *b* and a chaser
5:23 in consideration of a *b*
33:15 from taking hold on a *b*
Eze 16:33 you offer a *b* to them to
22:12 A *b* they have taken in you
Mic 3:11 judge merely for a *b*, and

Bribery
Job 15:34 must eat up the tents of *b*
Ps 26:10 right hand is full of *b*
Isa 45:13 for a price nor for *b*

Bribes
Pr 29:4 a man out for *b* tears it down

Brick
Ge 11:3 *b* served as stone for them
Eze 4:1 take for yourself a *b*, and you
Na 3:14 grab hold of the *b* mold

Brickmaking
2Sa 12:31 he made them serve at *b*

Bricks
Ge 11:3 Come on! Let us make *b* and
Ex 1:14 slavery at clay mortar and *b*
5:7 people to make *b* as formerly
5:8 amount of *b* that they were
5:14 task in making *b* as formerly
5:16 they are saying to us, Make *b*!
5:18 give the fixed amount of *b*
5:19 must not deduct from your *b*
Isa 9:10 *B* are what have fallen, but
65:3 sacrificial smoke upon the *b*
Jer 43:9 mortar in the terrace of *b*

Bride
De 21:13 possession of her as your *b*
Ca 4:8 With me from Lebanon, O *b*
4:9 O my sister, my *b*, you have
4:10 O my sister, my *b*! How much
4:11 lips keep dripping, O my *b*
4:12 my *b*, a garden barred in, a
5:1 my *b*. I have plucked my myrrh
Isa 49:18 bind them on . . . like a *b*
61:10 the *b* who decks herself
62:5 of a bridegroom over a *b*
Jer 2:32 a *b* her breastbands
7:34 and the voice of the *b*
16:9 and the voice of the *b*
25:10 and the voice of the *b*
33:11 and the voice of the *b*
Joe 2:16 *b* from her nuptial chamber
Mal 2:11 of a foreign god as a *b*
Joh 3:29 has the *b* is the bridegroom
Re 18:23 *b* will ever be heard in you
21:2 as a *b* adorned for her husband
21:9 I will show you the *b*, the
22:17 and the *b* keep on saying

Bridegroom
Ex 4:25 you are a *b* of blood to me
4:26 A *b* of blood, because of the
Ps 19:5 it is like a *b* when coming
Isa 61:10 like the *b* who, in a
62:5 exultation of a *b* over a
Jer 7:34 the voice of the *b* and the
16:9 the voice of the *b* and the
25:10 the voice of the *b* and the
33:11 the voice of the *b* and
Joe 2:16 Let the *b* go forth from his
Mt 9:15 The friends of the *b* have no
9:15 as long as the *b* is with
9:15 the *b* will be taken away
25:1 and went out to meet the *b*
25:5 While the *b* was delaying
25:6 Here is the *b*! Be on your way
25:10 *b* arrived, and the virgins
Mr 2:19 While the *b* is with them the
2:19 friends of the *b* cannot fast
2:19 As long as they have the *b*
2:20 *b* will be taken away from
Lu 5:34 the friends of the *b* fast
5:34 while the *b* is with them
5:35 days will come when the *b*
Joh 2:9 director . . . called the *b*
3:29 that has the bride is the *b*
3:29 the friend of the *b*, when
3:29 account of the voice of the *b*
Re 18:23 no voice of a *b* and of a

Bridle
2Ki 19:28 my *b* between your lips
Job 30:11 the *b* they left loose on my
Ps 32:9 curbed even by *b* or halter
Pr 26:3 a *b* is for the ass, and the
Isa 30:28 *b* that causes one to wander
37:29 my *b* between your lips
Jas 1:26 yet does not *b* his tongue
3:2 able to *b* also his whole body

Bridles
Jas 3:3 put *b* in the mouths of horses
Re 14:20 blood . . . as high up as the *b*

Brief
Eph 3:3 as I wrote previously in *b*
Briefly
Ac 24:4 I beseech you to hear us *b*
Brier
Pr 15:19 lazy one is like a *b* hedge
Mic 7:4 Their best one is like a *b*
Briers
Jg 8:7 of the wilderness and the *b*
8:16 and *b*, and with them he put
Bright
Job 25:5 the moon, and it is not *b*
Ps 90:8 things before your *b* face
Pr 4:18 *b* light that is getting
Eze 1:13 the fire was *b*, and out of
Am 8:9 cause darkness . . . on a *b* day
Zec 1:8 horses red, *b* red, and white
Mt 6:22 your whole body will be *b*
17:5 a *b* cloud overshadowed them
Mr 14:54 warming . . . before a *b* fire
Lu 11:34 your whole body is also *b*
11:36 if your whole body is *b* with
11:36 it will all be as *b* as when
22:56 sitting by the *b* fire and
23:11 by clothing . . . a *b* garment
Ac 10:30 man in *b* raiment stood
Re 15:6 clothed with clean, *b* linen
19:8 in *b*, clean, fine linen
22:16 and the *b* morning star
Brighten
Job 9:27 alter my countenance and *b*
10:20 that I may *b* up a little
Ps 39:13 Look away . . . that I may *b* up
Brighter
Job 11:17 And *b* than midday will your
Brightly
Mt 13:43 shine as *b* as the sun in the
Brightness
2Sa 22:13 From the *b* in front of him
23:4 From *b*, from rain, there is
Ps 18:12 Out of the *b* in front of him
Pr 15:30 The *b* of the eyes makes the
Isa 4:5 *b* of a flaming fire by night
8:22 and gloominess with no *b*
50:10 whom there has been no *b*
59:9 for *b*, but in continuous
60:3 the *b* of your shining forth
60:19 for *b* the moon itself will
62:1 goes forth just like the *b*
Eze 1:4 and it had a *b* all around, and
1:27 and he had a *b* all around
1:28 the appearance was of the *b*
10:4 the *b* of the glory of Jehovah
Da 2:31 *b* of which was extraordinary
4:36 *b* themselves began to return
12:3 like the *b* of the expanse
Joe 2:10 stars have withdrawn their *b*
3:15 stars . . . withdraw their *b*
Am 5:20 not have gloom, and not *b*
Hab 3:4 his *b*, it got to be just like
3:11 your spear served for *b*
Bright-red
Isa 16:8 smitten down its *b* branches
Brilliance
Ac 26:13 light beyond the *b* of the sun
Brilliant
Job 16:4 I be *b* in words against you
37:21 It is *b* in the skies
Mt 17:2 his outer garments became *b*
Brim
1Ki 7:23, 23 its one *b* to its other *b*
7:24 down below its *b* all around
7:26 *b* was like the workmanship
7:26 *b* of a cup, a lily blossom
2Ch 4:2, 2 its one *b* to its other *b*
4:5 *b* was like the workmanship
4:5 *b* of a cup, a lily blossom
Joh 2:7 And they filled them to the *b*
Bring
Ge 2:22 woman and to *b* her to the
3:16 in birth pangs you will *b*
4:3 Cain proceeded to *b* some
5:29 This one will *b* us comfort
6:17 deluge . . . to *b* to ruin all
6:19 you will *b* into the ark to
8:17 *b* out with you, as they must
9:11 deluge to *b* the earth to ruin
9:14 I *b* a cloud over the earth
Ge 9:15 deluge to *b* all flesh to ruin
18:19 *b* upon Abraham what he has
18:28 *b* the whole city to ruin
18:28 I shall not *b* it to ruin if
18:31 not *b* it to ruin on account
18:32 I shall not *b* it to ruin on
19:5 *B* them out to us that we may
19:8 let me *b* them out to you
19:12 *b* out of the place!
19:13 Jehovah sent us to *b* the city
19:16 *b* him out and to station
24:53 *b* out articles of silver and
27:4 *b* it to me and, ah, let me
27:5 to hunt game and to *b* it in
27:7 *B* me some game and make me
27:10 must *b* it to your father
27:12 *b* upon myself a malediction
27:25 *B* it near to me that I may
31:39 I did not *b* to you. I myself
37:14 Go . . . and *b* me back word
38:24 Judah said: *B* her out and let
41:14 *b* him quickly from the
42:20 *b* your youngest brother to
42:34 *b* your youngest brother to
42:37 death if I do not *b* him back
42:38 *b* down my gray hairs with
43:7 *B* your brother down
43:9 If I fail to *b* him to you
44:21 *B* him down to me that I may
44:29 *b* down my gray hairs with
44:31 *b* down the gray hairs of
44:32 If I fail to *b* him back
45:13 must hurry and *b* my father
46:4 shall surely *b* you up also
48:9 *B* them, please, to me that I
50:24 *b* you up out of this land to
Ex 3:8 *b* them up out of that land to
3:10 *b* . . . Israel out of Egypt
3:11 *b* the sons of Israel out of
3:17 *b* you up out of affliction
6:6 I shall certainly *b* you out
6:8 *b* you into the land that I
6:13 to *b* the sons of Israel out
6:26 *B* the sons of Israel out from
6:27 *b* the sons of Israel out from
7:4 upon Egypt and *b* my armies
7:5 *b* the sons of Israel out from
8:18 in order to *b* forth gnats, but
9:19 *b* all your livestock and all
11:1 to *b* upon Pharaoh and Egypt
12:17 *b* your armies out from the
15:17 You will *b* them and plant
16:5 prepare what they will *b* in
18:19 *b* the cases to the true God
18:22 big case they will *b* to you
18:26 they would *b* to Moses, but
19:4 of eagles and *b* you to myself
21:6 master must *b* him near to
21:6 *b* him up against the door or
22:13 he is to *b* it as evidence
23:19 to *b* to the house of Jehovah
23:20 to *b* you into the place that
23:23 *b* you to the Amorites and
26:33 *b* the ark of the testimony
28:1 *b* near to yourself Aaron your
29:8 *b* his sons near and you must
32:2 daughters and *b* them to me
32:34 *b* punishment upon them for
34:26 *b* to the house of Jehovah
35:5 *b* it as Jehovah's contribution
35:29 hearts incited them to *b*
39:33 to *b* the tabernacle to Moses
40:4 must *b* the table in and set
40:4 must *b* in the lampstand and
40:12 *b* Aaron and his sons near to
40:14 *b* his sons near and you must
Le 2:2 must *b* it to the sons of Aaron
2:8 must *b* the grain offering that
2:8 he must *b* it near to the altar
4:3 sins so as to *b* guiltiness upon
4:4 *b* the bull to the entrance of
4:5 the bull's blood and *b* it into
4:14 must *b* it before the tent of
4:16 *b* some of the bull's blood
4:23 *b* as his offering a male kid
4:28 *b* as his offering a female
4:32 *b* a lamb as his offering for
4:32 lamb is what he should *b*
5:6 *b* his guilt offering to Jehovah
5:7 *b* as his guilt offering for
5:8 he must *b* them to the priest
5:11 must *b* as his offering for
5:12 he must *b* it to the priest
5:15 must *b* as his guilt offering
Le 5:18 he must *b* a sound ram from
6:6 will *b* to Jehovah a sound ram
6:21 You will *b* it well mixed
7:29 *b* his offering to Jehovah
7:30 *b* as Jehovah's offerings made
7:30 He will *b* it with the breast
10:15 *b* the leg of the sacred
12:6 *b* a young ram in its first
14:23 *b* them for establishing his
15:29 must *b* them to the priest at
16:12 *b* them inside the curtain
16:15 *b* its blood inside the
17:4 *b* it to the entrance of the
17:5 may *b* their sacrifices
17:5 *b* them to Jehovah to the
17:9 does not *b* it to the entrance
18:25 *b* punishment for its error
19:21 *b* his guilt offering to
23:10 *b* a sheaf of the firstfruits
23:17 *b* two loaves as a wave
24:14 *B* forth the one who called
26:10 *b* out the old ahead of the
26:16 *b* upon you disturbance with
26:25 *b* upon you a sword wreaking
26:36 *b* timidity into their hearts
26:41 *b* them into the land of
Nu 3:6 *B* the tribe of Levi near, and
5:15 man must *b* his wife to the
5:15 *b* her offering along with her
5:16 priest must *b* her forward and
5:25 he must *b* it near the altar
6:10 *b* two turtledoves or two male
6:12 *b* a young ram in its first
14:8 *b* us into this land and give
14:16 *b* this people into the land
14:24 *b* him into the land where he
14:31 also I shall certainly *b* in
16:10 that he should *b* you and all
18:2 *b* near, also, your brothers of
18:13 which they will *b* to Jehovah
20:5 to *b* us into this evil place
20:8 *b* out water for them from
20:10 we shall *b* out water for you
20:12 will not *b* this congregation
20:25 and *b* them up into Mount Hor
27:17 who will *b* them out and who
27:17 and who will *b* them in
De 1:22 *b* us back word concerning the
1:25 and to *b* it down to us, and
4:20 *b* you out of the iron furnace
4:31 *b* you to ruin or forget the
4:38 so as to *b* you in, to give you
5:15 God proceeded to *b* you out
6:10 God will *b* you into the land
6:21 *b* us out of Egypt with a
6:23 *b* us here to give us the land
7:26 must not *b* a detestable thing
9:26 do not *b* to ruin your people
9:28 *b* them into the land that he
10:10 not want to *b* you to ruin
12:6 *b* your burnt offerings and
12:11 *b* all about which I am
14:28 *b* out the entire tenth part
17:5 *b* that man or that woman who
19:16 *b* a charge of revolt against
21:12 *b* her into the midst of
21:19 *b* him out to the older men
22:2 *b* it home into the midst of
22:15 *b* forth the evidence of the
22:21 *b* the girl out to the
22:24 *b* them both out to the gate
23:18 not *b* the hire of a harlot
24:11 *b* the pledge outside to you
26:2 *b* in from the land of yours
28:41 daughters you will *b* forth
28:60 *b* back upon you all the
28:61 *b* them upon you until you
28:68 *b* you back to Egypt by ships
30:3 *b* back your captives and show
30:5 *b* you into the land of which
31:7 you will *b* this people into
31:20 *b* them to the ground that I
31:21 *b* them into the land about
31:23 *b* the sons of Israel into the
33:7 may you *b* him to his people
Jos 2:3 *B* out the men that came to
6:18 and *b* ostracism upon it
6:22 *b* out of there the woman and
7:7 why did you *b* this people all
7:25 will *b* ostracism upon you
8:23 to *b* him near to Joshua
10:22 *b* out these five kings from
18:6 must *b* them here to me, and
23:15 Jehovah will *b* . . . evil

Jg 2:1 to *b* you up out of Egypt and
2:1 to *b* you into the land about
6:30 *B* your son out that he may
16:18 *b* up the money in their hand
19:3 so as to *b* her back
19:22 *B* out the man that came into
19:24 Let me *b* them out, please
Ru 3:15 *B* the cloak that is on you
1Sa 1:22 boy is weaned, I must *b* him
2:14 that the fork might *b* up the
5:2 *b* it into the house of Dagon
9:7 what shall we *b* to the man?
9:7 *b* to the man of the true God
10:27 did not *b* any gift to him
13:9 *B* near to me the burnt
14:18 Do *b* the ark of the true God
14:34 *B* near to me, each one of
15:32 *B* Agag the king of Amalek
16:17 and you must *b* him to me
17:18 should *b* to the chief of the
17:57 and *b* him before Saul with
19:15 *B* him on his couch up to me
20:8 that you should *b* me
21:14 Why should you *b* him to me?
23:9 Do *b* the ephod near
26:9 Do not *b* him to ruin, for
26:15 *b* the king your lord to ruin
27:11 any alive to *b* them to Gath
28:8 *b* up for me the one whom I
28:11 Whom shall I *b* up for you?
28:11 *B* up Samuel for me
30:7 *b* the ephod near to me
2Sa 1:10 I might *b* them to my lord
1:14 *b* the anointed of Jehovah to
2:8 *b* him across to Mahanaim
3:13 first you *b* Michal, Saul's
6:2 *b* up from there the ark of
6:12 *b* the ark of the true God out
11:1 *b* the sons of Ammon to ruin
12:23 Am I able to *b* him back
13:10 *B* the bread of consolation
14:10 *b* him to me, and he will
14:13 king does not *b* back his
14:21 *b* the young man Absalom
15:8 *b* me back to Jerusalem
15:14 *b* down upon us what is bad
15:25 *b* me back and let me see it
17:3 *b* all the people back to you
17:14 *b* calamity upon Absalom
19:10 nothing to *b* the king back
19:11 *b* the king back to his house
19:12 last ones to *b* the king back
19:36 *b* the king along to the
19:40 might *b* the king across
19:41 *b* the king and his household
19:43 for us to *b* our king back
20:20 and that I should *b* to ruin
21:13 *b* up from there the bones
22:20 *b* me out into a roomy place
22:28 that you may *b* them low
24:16 Jerusalem to *b* it to ruin
1Ki 1:42 and you *b* good news
2:9 *b* his gray hairs down to
2:32 *b* back his blood upon his
3:1 Pharaoh's daughter and *b* her
5:9 *b* them down out of Lebanon to
7:51 Solomon began to *b* in the
8:1 *b* up the ark of the covenant
8:31 *b* him under liability to the
8:34 *b* them back to the ground
9:28 and *b* it in to King Solomon
12:21 so as to *b* the kingship back
13:29 and to *b* him back
15:15 began to *b* in the things
17:13 you must *b* it out to me
17:18 to *b* my error to mind and
17:20 *b* injury by putting her son
21:10 And *b* him out and stone him
21:29 not *b* the calamity in his
21:29 *b* the calamity upon his
22:9 *B* Micaiah the son of Imlah
2Ki 4:6 Do *b* still another vessel near
8:19 not want to *b* Judah to ruin
9:2 *b* him into the innermost
10:22 *B* out garments for all the
11:19 *b* the king down from the
12:4 to *b* to the house of Jehovah
13:23 not want to *b* them to ruin
17:4 did not *b* the tribute up to
18:25 this place to *b* it to ruin
18:25 and you must *b* it to ruin
19:25 formed it. Now I will *b* it
22:20 to *b* the king the reply
23:4 *b* out from the temple of
2Ki 24:16 *b* them as exiled people to
1Ch 9:28 by number that they would *b*
13:3 let us *b* the ark of our God
13:5 to *b* the ark of the true God
13:6 *b* up from there the ark of
13:12 How shall I *b* the ark of
15:3 to *b* the ark of Jehovah up to
15:12 must *b* the ark of Jehovah
15:14 to *b* up the ark of Jehovah
15:25 *b* up the ark of the covenant
19:16 *b* out the Syrians that were
21:2 *b* it to me that I may know
21:15 to Jerusalem to *b* ruin to
22:2 said to *b* together the alien
22:19 to *b* the ark of the covenant
2Ch 2:16 *b* them to you as rafts by
5:1 Solomon began to *b* in the
5:2 to *b* the ark of the covenant
6:22 *b* him under liability to the
6:25 *b* them back to the ground
8:18 and *b* it to King Solomon
11:1 *b* the kingdom back to
12:7 I shall not *b* them to ruin
15:18 *b* the things made holy by
18:8 *B* Micaiah the son of Imlah
19:4 *b* them back to Jehovah the
20:23 *b* his own fellow to ruin
21:7 Jehovah did not want to *b*
24:9 *b* to Jehovah the sacred tax
24:11 *b* the chest to the care of
24:19 *b* them back to Jehovah
25:16 *b* you to ruin, because you
28:13 not *b* in the captives here
28:27 *b* him into the burial
29:5 *b* the impure thing out from
29:31 Approach, and *b* sacrifices
29:31 congregation began to *b*
31:10 *b* the contribution into the
35:21 not let him *b* you to ruin
36:10 to *b* him to Babylon with
Ezr 1:8 to *b* them forth under the
3:7 *b* cedar timbers from Lebanon
7:15 to *b* the silver and the gold
8:17 *b* to us ministers for the
8:30 to *b* them to Jerusalem to
Ne 1:9 *b* them to the place that I
3:5 not *b* the back of their neck
4:2 Will they *b* the stones to life
8:1 to *b* the book of the law of
8:15 *b* in olive leaves and the
8:16 *b* them in and make booths for
9:26 to *b* them back to you; and
9:29 to *b* them back to your law
10:34 *b* to the house of our God
10:35 *b* the first ripe fruits of
10:36 *b* them to the house of our
10:37 *b* to the priests to the
10:39 *b* the contribution of the
11:1 *b* in one out of every ten to
12:27 to *b* them out of all their
Es 1:11 to *b* Vashti the queen in the
1:17 said to *b* in Vashti the queen
6:1 to *b* the book of the records of
6:8 let them *b* royal apparel with
6:14 to *b* Haman to the banquet
Job 8:10 will they not *b* forth words?
10:17 *b* forth new witnesses of
10:18 why from a womb did you *b*
14:3 me you *b* into judgment with
21:10 His cows *b* forth and suffer
33:4 proceeded to *b* me to life
38:32 *b* forth the Mazzaroth
39:1 hinds *b* forth with birth
39:12 it will *b* back your seed
40:11 haughty and *b* him low
40:19 Maker can *b* near his sword
Ps 18:19 *b* me out into a roomy place
25:17 stresses upon me O *b* me out
31:4 You will *b* me out of the net
35:17 *b* back my soul from their
37:6 *b* forth your righteousness
38:*super* to *b* to remembrance
40:2 *b* me up out of a roaring pit
43:3 *b* me to your holy mountain
55:23 *b* them down to the lowest
56:7 *b* down even the peoples
57:*super* Do not *b* to ruin. Of David
58:*super* Do not *b* to ruin. Of David
59:*super* Do not *b* to ruin. Of David
59:11 *b* them down, O our shield
59:13 *B* them to an end in rage
59:13 *B* them to an end, that they
60:9 *b* me to the besieged city
66:12 to *b* us forth to relief
Ps 68:22 From Bashan I shall *b* back
68:22 *b* them back from the depths
68:29 Kings will *b* gifts to you
70:*super* to *b* to remembrance
71:20 may you again *b* me up
75:*super* Do not *b* to ruin
76:11 Let them *b* a gift in fear
78:29 he proceeded to *b* to them
78:38 the error and not *b* ruin
78:45 these might *b* them to ruin
78:54 *b* them to his holy territory
80:3 O God, *b* us back; And light
80:7 O God of armies, *b* us back
80:19 God of armies, *b* us back
90:2 *b* forth as with labor pains
90:12 may *b* a heart of wisdom in
94:2 *B* back a retribution upon the
105:37 *b* them out with silver and
105:40 he proceeded to *b* quails
108:10 *b* me to the fortified city
142:7 *b* my soul out of the very
143:11 *b* forth my soul out of
Pr 19:24 cannot *b* it back even to his
21:22 *b* down the strength of its
23:12 Do *b* your heart to discipline
26:15 too weary to *b* it back to
29:17 and he will *b* you rest
Ec 3:5 a time to *b* stones together
3:22 who will *b* him in to look on
5:2 not be hasty to *b* forth a word
11:9 God will *b* you into judgment
12:14 will *b* every sort of work
Ca 8:2 I would *b* you into the house
8:11 would *b* in for its fruitage a
Isa 1:26 *b* back again judges for you
5:29 prey and *b* it safely away
7:17 Jehovah will *b* against you
10:13 *b* down the inhabitants just
10:18 orchard He will *b* to an end
13:11 *b* home its own badness upon
14:2 *b* them to their own place
16:3 *B* in counsel, you men
21:14 the thirsty one *b* water
23:7 *b* her far away to reside as
25:12 *b* it into contact with the
30:5 people that *b* no benefit to
30:5 and *b* no benefit, but are
31:2 *b* in what is calamitous
36:10 this land to *b* it to ruin
36:10 and you must *b* it to ruin
37:26 Now I will *b* it in
41:21 *B* your controversial case
42:1 Justice . . . what he will *b*
42:3 he will *b* forth justice
42:7 to *b* forth out of the dungeon
42:22 anyone to say: *B* back!
43:5 I shall *b* your seed, and
43:6 *B* my sons from far off, and
43:8 *B* forth a people blind though
45:20 *B* yourselves up close
46:11 I shall also *b* it in
49:5 to *b* back Jacob to him
49:6 *b* back even the safeguarded
49:8 to *b* about the repossessing
49:22 *b* your sons in the bosom
51:13 all set to *b* you to ruin
53:11 will *b* a righteous standing
56:7 *b* them to my holy mountain
58:7 *b* the afflicted, homeless
60:9 to *b* your sons from far away
60:11 *b* to you the resources of
60:17 I shall *b* in gold, and
60:17 I shall *b* in silver, and
63:6 to *b* down to the earth their
65:8 not to *b* everybody to ruin
65:9 *b* forth out of Jacob an
65:23 to *b* to birth for disturbance
66:4 I shall *b* upon them
66:20 *b* all your brothers out of
66:20 sons of Israel *b* the gift
Jer 2:8 those who could *b* no benefit
2:11 for what can *b* no benefit
3:14 and I will *b* you to Zion
6:5 *b* to ruin her dwelling towers
6:20 *b* in even frankincense from
8:1 *b* forth the bones of the kings
8:13 shall *b* them to their finish
11:12 *b* no salvation to them in
11:19 Let us *b* to ruin the tree
11:23 I shall *b* calamity upon the
12:9 *b* them to eat
12:15 will *b* them back, each one
13:1 must not *b* it into any water
13:9 *b* to ruin the pride of Judah

Jer 15:3 to eat and to *b* to ruin
15:6 and *b* you to ruin. I have
15:8 I will *b* for them, upon
15:19 then I shall *b* you back
15:19 *b* forth what is precious
16:15 *b* them back to their soil
17:18 *B* upon them the day of
17:21 *b* in through the gates of
17:22 *b* no load out of your
17:24 to *b* in no load through the
18:22 *b* upon them suddenly a
20:5 and *b* them to Babylon
23:3 *b* them back to their pasture
23:12 *b* upon them a calamity
24:1 he might *b* them to Babylon
25:9 *b* them against this land
25:13 *b* in upon that land all
26:23 to *b* Urijah out from Egypt
26:23 to *b* him to King Jehoiakim
27:11 *b* its neck under the yoke
27:12 *B* your necks under the yoke
27:22 *b* them up and restore them
28:3 he might *b* them to Babylon
29:14 I will *b* you back to the
30:3 *b* them back to the land that
30:17 *b* up a recuperation for you
31:9 for favor I shall *b* them
31:32 *b* them forth out of the
32:21 *b* forth your people Israel
32:37 *b* them back to this place
32:44 shall *b* back their captives
33:7 *b* back the captives of Judah
33:11 *b* back the captives of the
34:11 *b* back the menservants and
34:16 *b* back each one his
34:22 *b* them back to this city
35:2 *b* them into the house of
35:4 *b* them into the house of
36:29 *b* this land to ruin and
36:31 *b* upon them and upon the
39:7 in order to *b* him to Babylon
39:14 *b* him forth to his house
40:3 Jehovah might *b* it true and
41:5 *b* to the house of Jehovah
48:18 *b* your fortified places to
48:44 *b* upon her, upon Moab
49:8 disaster of Esau I will *b*
49:16 from there I shall *b* you
49:32 I shall *b* in their disaster
49:36 *b* in upon Elam the four
49:37 *b* upon them a calamity
50:19 I will *b* Israel back to
51:11 in order to *b* her to ruin
51:20 will *b* kingdoms to ruin
51:40 *b* them down like male
51:44 *b* forth out of his mouth
52:31 *b* him forth from the prison
La 1:21 You will certainly *b* the day
2:13 Who can *b* healing to you?
3:21 I shall *b* back to my heart
4:17 nation that can *b* no salvation
5:9 risk of our soul we *b* in our
5:21 *B* us back, O Jehovah, to
5:21 *B* new days for us as in the
Eze 5:13 I *b* my rage to its finish
5:16 send to *b* you people to ruin
5:17 sword I shall *b* in upon you
6:12 will *b* to its finish my rage
7:3 *b* upon you all your detestable
7:4 you I shall *b* your own ways
7:8 *b* my anger against you to its
7:8 *b* upon you all your detestable
7:24 *b* in the worst ones of the
9:10 *b* upon their own head
11:1 *b* me to the eastern gate of
11:8 a sword I shall *b* upon you
11:9 *b* you forth out of the midst
11:21 certainly *b* their own way
12:4 must *b* out your luggage like
12:13 and I will *b* him to Babylon
13:14 *b* it into contact with the
13:15 *b* my rage to its finish
14:17 sword that I should *b* upon
16:40 they must *b* up against you
16:42 *b* my rage to its rest in
17:12 and *b* them to himself at
17:19 even *b* it upon his head
17:20 I will *b* him to Babylon and
19:4 *b* him by means of hooks to
19:9 *b* him by means of hunting
20:6 *b* them forth from the land
20:8 to *b* my anger to its finish
20:15 not to *b* them into the land
20:21 to *b* my anger to its finish

Eze 20:28 *b* them into the land that I
20:34 will *b* you forth from the
20:35 *b* you into the wilderness
20:37 *b* you into the bond of the
20:38 I shall *b* them forth, but
20:41 *b* you forth from the
20:42 *b* you onto the soil of
21:3 I will *b* forth my sword out
21:17 *b* my rage to its rest
21:26 *b* low even the high one
22:4 And you *b* your days near
22:21 *b* you together and blow
22:30 for me not to *b* it to ruin
22:31 *b* upon their own head
23:22 *b* them in against you on
23:49 *b* your loose conduct upon
24:6 *b* it out; no lot must be
24:8 order to *b* up rage for the
25:14 *b* my vengeance on Edom by
25:17 when I *b* my vengeance on
26:3 *b* up against you many
26:4 *b* the walls of Tyre to ruin
26:19 *b* up over you the watery
26:20 *b* you down with those going
27:30 *b* up dust upon their heads
28:8 to the pit they will *b* you
28:18 I shall *b* forth a fire from
29:4 *b* you up out of the midst
29:14 *b* back the captive group
29:14 *b* them back to the land of
30:14 *b* Pathros to desolation
31:16 when I *b* it down to Sheol
32:3 *b* you in my dragnet
32:9 *b* the captives from you
32:18 crowd of Egypt and *b* it
33:2 in case I *b* upon it a sword
34:13 *b* them out from the peoples
34:13 *b* them in onto their soil
34:16 dispersed one I shall *b* back
36:24 and *b* you in upon your soil
37:12 *b* you up out of your burial
37:12 *b* you in upon the soil of
37:13 *b* you up out of your burial
37:21 *b* them onto their soil
38:4 hooks in your jaws and *b* you
38:16 *b* you against my land, for
38:22 *b* myself into judgment
39:2 *b* you in upon the mountains
39:25 *b* back the captive ones of
39:27 I *b* them back from the
39:28 *b* them together upon their
40:3 he proceeded to *b* me there
40:35 *b* me into the north gate
40:48 *b* me into the porch of the
41:1 to *b* me into the temple
42:1 *b* me to the dining-room
43:3 came to *b* the city to ruin
43:5 *b* me into the inner
43:22 *b* near a buck of the goats
43:23 *b* near a young bull, the
43:24 *b* them near before Jehovah
44:1 *b* me back by way of the
44:7 *b* in the foreigners
46:19 *b* me in by the entryway
46:21 *b* me out to the outer
Da 1:3 *b* some of the sons of Israel
1:18 king had said to *b* them in
1:18 *b* . . . before Nebuchadnezzar
3:13 fury, said to *b* in Shadrach
4:6 *b* in before me all the wise
5:2 to *b* in the vessels of gold
5:7 *b* in the conjurers, the
8:24 *b* mighty ones to ruin, also
8:25 he will *b* many to ruin
9:24 *b* in righteousness for times
9:26 will *b* to their ruin
11:17 to him to *b* her to ruin
11:26 will *b* his breakdown
Ho 4:9 I shall *b* back upon them
7:1 I would *b* healing to Israel
7:12 I shall *b* them down
9:12 although they *b* up their sons
9:16 in case they *b* to birth
10:6 *b* to Assyria itself as a gift
11:9 shall not *b* Ephraim to ruin
13:9 will certainly *b* you to ruin
Joe 2:23 *b* down upon you people a
3:1 I shall *b* back the captive
3:2 *b* them down to the low plain
3:11 *b* your powerful ones down
Am 3:11 *b* your strength down from
4:1 Do *b*, and let us drink!
4:4 *b* your sacrifices in the
6:3 do you *b* near the dwelling of

Am 6:10 *b* out the bones from the
8:10 *b* up upon all hips sackcloth
9:2 there I shall *b* them down
9:7 *b* Israel itself up out of the
Ob 3 Who will *b* me down to the earth?
4 down from there I would *b* you
Jon 1:13 *b* the ship back to the dry
2:6 proceeded to *b* up my life
Mic 1:15 dispossessor I shall yet *b*
5:6 *b* about deliverance from the
7:9 will *b* me forth to the light
Hab 3:2 O *b* it to life! In the midst
Zep 3:10 will *b* a gift to me
3:20 I shall *b* you people in
Hag 1:8 and you must *b* in lumber
1:11 the ground would *b* forth
Zec 4:7 *b* forth the headstone
8:8 *b* them in, and they must
10:10 *b* them back from the land
10:10 and Lebanon I shall *b* them
13:9 *b* the third part through the
Mal 1:8 *B* it near, please, to your
3:10 *B* all the tenth parts into
Mt 6:13 do not *b* us into temptation
14:18 He said: *B* them here to me
17:17 *B* him here to me
21:2 untie them and *b* them to me
21:41 will *b* an evil destruction
Mr 2:4 to *b* him right to Jesus on
6:27 commanded him to *b* his head
9:19 put up with you? *B* him to me
11:2 yet sat; loose it and *b* it
12:15 *B* me a denarius to look at
Lu 5:18 *b* him in and place him before
5:19 finding a way to *b* him in on
7:3 *b* his slave safely through
8:14 and *b* nothing to perfection
11:4 do not *b* us into temptation
12:11 when they *b* you in before
14:21 *b* in here the poor and
15:22 *b* out a robe, the best one
15:23 *b* the fattened young bull
18:15 to *b* him also their infants
19:27 *B* here and slaughter them
19:30 colt tied . . . Loose it and *b*
Joh 7:45 Why is it you did not *b* him
10:16 those also I must *b*, and
14:26 *b* back to your minds all
18:29 accusation do you *b* against
19:4 I *b* him outside to you in
21:10 *B* some of the fish you just
Ac 4:34 *b* the values of the things
5:26 *b* them, but without violence
5:28 *b* the blood of this man upon
7:26 *b* them together again in
9:2 *b* bound to Jerusalem any whom
16:37 come themselves and *b* us out
19:38 *b* charges against one another
21:16 to *b* us to the man at whose
22:5 I was on my way to *b* also
23:10 and *b* him into the soldiers'
23:15 why he should *b* him down to
23:20 *b* Paul down to the Sanhedrin
24:17 arrived to *b* gifts of mercy
27:43 *b* Paul safely through and
Ro 7:5 should *b* forth fruit to death
10:6 that is, to *b* Christ down
10:7 *b* Christ up from the dead
1Co 1:28 *b* to nothing the things that
4:5 both *b* the secret things of
6:13 God will *b* both it and them
1Th 4:14 God will *b* with him
2Th 2:8 and to *b* to nothing by the
2Ti 4:11 Take Mark and *b* him with
4:13 *b* the cloak I left at Troas
Heb 2:14 *b* to nothing the one having
8:9 *b* them forth out of the land
2Pe 2:1 quietly *b* in destructive sects
2:11 *b* against them an accusation
2Jo 10 and does not *b* this teaching
Jude 9 did not dare to *b* a judgment
Re 11:18 *b* to ruin those ruining the
21:24 will *b* their glory into it
21:26 *b* the glory and the honor

Bringer

1Sa 2:6 A *B* down to Sheol, and He
2Sa 4:10 became like a *b* of good news
1Ki 18:17 *b* of ostracism upon Israel
1Ch 2:7 *b* of ostracism upon Israel
Isa 41:27 shall give a *b* of good news

Bringing

Ge 1:10 *b* together of the waters he
2:19 he began *b* them to the man

Ge 6:13 I am *b* them to ruin together
6:17 I am *b* the deluge of waters
19:13 we are *b* this place to ruin
19:14 Jehovah is *b* the city to ruin
27:33 hunted for game and came *b*
29:23 Leah his daughter and *b* her
47:14 Joseph kept *b* the money into
47:17 *b* their livestock to Joseph
Ex 6:7 your God who is *b* you out
10:4 I am *b* locusts within your
12:42 *b* them out of the land of
16:32 was *b* you out of the land of
20:5 *b* punishment for the error of
32:3 gold earrings . . . *b* them to
32:34 the day of my *b* punishment I
34:7 *b* punishment for the error of
35:25 *b* as yarn the blue thread
36:5 people are *b* much more than
36:6 were restrained from *b* it in
Le 18:3 into which I am *b* you, you
20:22 *b* you to dwell in it may not
22:33 *b* you out of the land of
23:14 *b* the offering of your God
23:15 your *b* the sheaf of the wave
23:43 *b* them out of the land of
Nu 5:15 *b* error to remembrance
13:26 came *b* back word to them
13:32 *b* forth to the sons of Israel
14:3 why is Jehovah *b* us to this
14:18 *b* punishment for the error
14:36 *b* forth a bad report against
14:37 men *b* forth the bad report
15:18 the land where I am *b* you
17:8 and it was *b* forth buds and
22:41 and *b* him up to Bamoth-baal
23:22 God is *b* them out of Egypt
24:8 God is *b* him out of Egypt
25:6 was *b* near to his brothers a
31:12 *b* to Moses and Eleazar the
De 1:25 they came *b* us back word and
5:9 *b* punishment for the error of
8:7 God is *b* you into a good land
29:27 *b* upon it . . . malediction
32:18 *b* you forth with childbirth
Jos 14:7 I came *b* him back word just
24:6 *b* your fathers out of Egypt
Jg 11:3 idle men kept *b* themselves
11:9 If you are *b* me back to fight
20:42 *b* them down to ruin in their
1Sa 6:5 that are *b* the land to ruin
8:8 of my *b* them up out of Egypt
18:27 came *b* their foreskins and
30:7 Abiathar came *b* the ephod
2Sa 4:8 *b* the head of Ish-bosheth
5:2 Israel out and *b* it in
6:15 *b* up the ark of Jehovah with
7:6 *b* the sons of Israel up out
22:48 *b* the peoples down under me
22:49 *b* me out from my enemies
23:16 carrying and *b* it to David
24:16 the angel that was *b* ruin
1Ki 4:21 *b* gifts and serving Solomon
4:28 *b* to wherever the place
5:13 King Solomon kept *b* up those
8:4 they came *b* up the ark of
8:4 the Levites came *b* them up
8:21 *b* them out from the land of
8:53 *b* our forefathers out from
10:25 were *b* each his gift
14:10 I am *b* calamity upon the
17:6 *b* him bread and meat in
20:39 he came *b* a man to me and
21:21 I am *b* calamity upon you
2Ki 4:5 *b* the vessels near to her
4:42 *b* to the man of the true God
5:6 *b* the letter to the king of
10:6 men of the city that were *b*
10:24 I am *b* into your hands
21:12 *b* a calamity upon Jerusalem
22:16 *b* calamity upon this place
22:20 calamity that I am *b* upon
1Ch 11:2 Israel out and *b* it in
11:18 carrying and *b* it to David
12:40 *b* food upon asses and upon
15:28 *b* up the ark of the covenant
21:12 Jehovah's angel *b* ruin in
21:15 soon as he began *b* the ruin
21:15 angel that was *b* the ruin
2Ch 5:5 *b* up the Ark and the tent of
9:14 merchants who were *b* in and
9:14 *b* in gold and silver to
9:24 *b* each his gift, articles of
9:28 *b* out horses to Solomon from
12:12 *b* them to ruin completely
2Ch 17:11 *b* to Jehoshaphat presents
17:11 Arabs also were *b* to him
24:6 for *b* in from Judah and
24:10 *b* and casting it into the
29:21 *b* seven bulls and seven
31:12 *b* in the contribution and
32:23 many *b* gifts to Jehovah
34:14 *b* out the money that was
34:24 *b* calamity upon this place
34:28 calamity that I am *b* upon
Ezr 1:11 *b* up of the exiled people
Ne 10:31 *b* in wares and every kind of
13:15 *b* in grain heaps and loading
13:15 *b* them into Jerusalem on the
13:16 *b* in fish and every sort of
Es 3:9 *b* it into the king's treasury
Job 9:22 he is *b* to their end
Ps 19:7 perfect, *b* back the soul
57:2 God who is *b* them to an end
68:6 He is *b* forth prisoners into
69:4 Those *b* me to silence, being
78:16 *b* forth streams out of a
78:49 of angels *b* calamity
81:10 One *b* you up out of the land
106:23 rage from *b* them to ruin
107:14 *b* them out from darkness
135:7 *b* forth the wind from his
136:11 One *b* Israel out of the
Pr 6:32 is *b* his own soul to ruin
10:18 one *b* forth a bad report is
11:17 cruel person is *b* ostracism
11:29 *b* ostracism upon his own
15:27 unjust profit is *b* ostracism
Ec 2:26 *b* together merely to give to
Isa 1:13 Stop *b* in any more valueless
8:7 Jehovah is *b* up against them
29:21 *b* a man into sin by his
40:9 woman *b* good news for Zion
40:9 *b* good news for Jerusalem
40:26 One who is *b* forth the army
43:17 *b* forth the war chariot and
52:7 feet of the one *b* good news
52:7 one *b* good news of something
54:16 *b* forth a weapon as his
59:4 a *b* of what is hurtful to
Jer 2:6 One *b* us up out of the land
4:6 calamity that I am *b* in from
4:7 who is *b* the nations to ruin
5:15 *b* in upon you men a nation
6:19 *b* in calamity upon this
7:22 *b* them out from the land of
11:4 *b* them out of the land of
11:7 *b* them up out of the land
11:11 *b* upon them a calamity that
13:14 keep from *b* them to ruin
14:12 I am *b* them to their end
17:26 *b* whole burnt offering and
17:26 *b* thanksgiving sacrifice
19:3 *b* a calamity upon this place
19:15 I am *b* upon this city and
22:7 those *b* ruin, each one and
25:29 starting off in *b* calamity
28:3 I am *b* back to this place
28:4 I am *b* back to this place
28:6 by *b* back the utensils of
29:10 my good word in *b* you back
31:8 *b* them from the land of the
32:42 *b* in upon them all the
33:6 *b* up for her a recuperation
33:11 *b* a thanksgiving offering
34:13 *b* them out of the land of
35:17 *b* upon Judah and upon all
38:23 are *b* out to the Chaldeans
39:16 *b* true my words upon this
42:17 calamity that I am *b* in
45:5 *b* in a calamity upon all
48:35 *b* up an offering upon the
49:5 *b* in upon you a dreadful
50:9 *b* up against Babylon a
51:64 calamity that I am *b* in
La 2:8 *b* the wall . . . of Zion to ruin
Eze 6:3 I am *b* upon you a sword, and
7:9 shall I do the *b* upon you
9:1 weapon in his hand for *b* ruin
9:8 Are you *b* to ruin all the
9:11 *b* back word, saying: I have
11:7 will be a *b* forth of you
12:5 must do the *b* out through it
12:6 you will do the *b* out
12:7 the darkness I did the *b* out
12:12 do the *b* forth through it
17:4 *b* it to the land of Canaan
20:9 *b* them forth from the land
20:17 from *b* them to ruin
Eze 23:46 the *b* up of a congregation
26:7 *b* against Tyre Nebuchadrezzar
28:7 *b* upon you strangers, the
29:8 I am *b* upon you a sword
29:16 *b* error to remembrance by
37:5 I am *b* into you breath
38:17 as to *b* you in upon them
Da 9:12 *b* upon us great calamity
11:6 and those *b* her in, and he
12:3 *b* the many to righteousness
Ho 9:9 gone down deep in *b* ruin
9:13 *b* out of his sons even to a
Na 1:15 the feet of one *b* good news
Hag 1:6 but there is a *b* of little in
Zec 3:8 I am *b* in my servant Sprout
Mt 5:23 *b* your gift to the altar and
9:2 *b* him a paralyzed man lying
Mr 1:32 people began *b* him all those
2:3 *b* him a paralytic carried by
10:13 *b* him young children for
15:4 charges they are *b* against
Lu 23:14 charges you are *b* against
Joh 19:39 *b* a roll of myrrh and aloes
Ac 16:39 *b* them out, they requested
26:20 *b* the message that they
2Co 10:5 we are *b* every thought into
Eph 6:4 *b* them up in the discipline
Heb 2:10 *b* many sons to glory, to
7:19 *b* in besides of a better
2Pe 2:1 *b* speedy destruction upon

Brings

Ex 13:11 Jehovah *b* you into the land
Nu 5:18 bitter water that *b* a curse
5:19 bitter water that *b* a curse
5:22 water that *b* a curse must
5:24 bitter water that *b* a curse
5:24 water that *b* a curse must
5:27 water that *b* a curse must
De 7:1 at last *b* you into the land to
11:29 God *b* you into the land
1Sa 2:6 down to Sheol, and He *b* up
Job 12:22 *b* forth to the light deep
28:11 he *b* forth to the light
38:29 who indeed *b* it to birth
Ps 25:15 *b* my feet out of the net
73:10 *b* his people back hither
74:5 *b* up axes on high against a
107:28 upon them he *b* them forth
147:2 ones of Israel he *b* together
Pr 11:9 apostate *b* his fellowman to
16:30 *b* mischief to completion
21:27 one *b* it along with loose
25:23 wind from the north *b* forth
30:33 milk is what *b* forth butter
30:33 nose is what *b* forth blood
30:33 is what *b* forth quarreling
31:14 far away she *b* in her food
Isa 26:5 *b* it in touch with the dust
61:11 *b* forth its sprout, and
Jer 10:13 he *b* forth the wind from
50:25 *b* forth the weapons of his
51:16 *b* forth the wind from his
Eze 14:4 *b* up his dungy idols upon his
14:7 *b* up his dungy idols upon his
26:3 as the sea *b* up its waves
Mt 13:52 *b* out of his treasure store
Lu 6:45 A good man *b* forth good out
6:45 a wicked man *b* forth what is
Ro 3:5 *b* God's righteousness to the
Ga 4:24 *b* forth children for slavery
Php 4:17 fruitage that *b* more credit
2Th 1:8 as he *b* vengeance upon those
Tit 2:11 *b* salvation to all sorts of
Heb 1:6 he again *b* his Firstborn into
6:7 *b* forth vegetation suitable
Jas 1:15 sin . . . *b* forth death

Bristle

Job 4:15 hair of my flesh began to *b*
Jer 2:12 *b* up in very great horror

Bristly

Jer 51:27 horses . . . like *b* locusts

Broad

2Sa 17:28 *b* beans and lentils and
Ne 3:8 Jerusalem as far as the *B* Wall
9:35 the *b* and fat land that you
12:38 and on to the *B* Wall
Job 38:18 the *b* spaces of the earth
Ps 4:1 you must make *b* space for me
119:96 Your commandment is very *b*
Pr 11:12 man of *b* discernment is one
Jer 51:58 wall of Babylon, although *b*
Eze 4:9 barley and *b* beans and lentils

1Th 4:6 the rights of his *b* in this
2Th 3:6 every *b* walking disorderly
3:15 admonishing him as a *b*
Phm 1 and Timothy, our *b*, to
7 been refreshed through you, *b*
16 more than a slave, as a *b*
20 Yes, *b*, may I derive profit
Heb 8:11 each one his *b*, saying
13:23 our *b* Timothy has been
Jas 1:9 the lowly *b* exult over his
2:15 If a *b* or a sister is in a
4:11 He who speaks against a *b*
4:11 judges his *b* speaks against
1Pe 5:12 Silvanus, a faithful *b*, as I
2Pe 3:15 just as our beloved *b* Paul
1Jo 2:9 yet hates his *b* is in the
2:10 He that loves his *b* remains
2:11 that hates his *b* is in the
3:10 he who does not love his *b*
3:12 Cain . . . slaughtered his *b*
3:12 of his *b* were righteous
3:15 hates his *b* is a manslayer
3:17 beholds his *b* having need
4:20 and yet is hating his *b*, he
4:20 he who does not love his *b*
4:21 should be loving his *b* also
5:16 his *b* sinning a sin that does
Jude 1 *b* of James, to the called ones
Re 1:9 I John, your *b* and a sharer

Brotherhood
Zec 11:14 in order to break the *b*

Brother-in-law
Ge 38:8 perform *b* marriage with her
De 25:5 Her *b* should go to her, and
25:5 perform *b* marriage with her
25:7 perform *b* marriage with me

Brotherly
Ro 12:10 In *b* love have tender
1Th 4:9 with reference to *b* love
Heb 13:1 Let your *b* love continue
1Pe 1:22 unhypocritical *b* love as the
3:8 having *b* affection, tenderly
2Pe 1:7 godly devotion *b* affection
1:7 to your *b* affection love

Brother's
Ge 4:9 not know. Am I my *b* guardian?
4:10 Listen! Your *b* blood is
4:11 to receive your *b* blood at
32:11 from my *b* hand, from Esau's
38:8 relations with your *b* wife
38:9 relations with his *b* wife he
Le 18:16 nakedness of your *b* wife you
18:16 It is your *b* nakedness
20:21 man takes his *b* wife, it is
De 22:3 anything lost of your *b*
25:7 delight in taking his *b* widow
25:7 his *b* widow must then go up
25:7 preserve his *b* name in Israel
25:9 his *b* widow must approach
25:9 not build up his *b* household
1Ki 2:15 turned and came to be my *b*
Mt 7:3 the straw in your *b* eye, but
7:5 the straw from your *b* eye
Lu 6:41 straw that is in your *b* eye
6:42 straw that is in your *b* eye

Brothers
Ge 9:22 went telling it to his two *b*
9:25 the lowest slave to his *b*
13:8 for we men are *b*
16:12 before the face of all his *b*
19:7 my *b*, do not act badly
24:27 house of the *b* of my master
25:18 In front of all his *b* he
27:29 Become master over your *b*
27:37 his *b* I have given to him as
29:4 *b*, from what place are you?
31:23 took his *b* with him and
31:25 Laban had encamped his *b* in
31:32 Before our *b*, examine for
31:37, 37 front of my *b* and your *b*
31:46 Jacob said to his *b*: Pick up
31:54 invited his *b* to eat bread
34:11 to her *b*: Let me find favor
34:25 Simeon and Levi, *b* of Dinah
37:2 tending sheep with his *b*
37:4 *b* came to see that their
37:4 loved him more than all his *b*
37:5 dream and told it to his *b*
37:8 And his *b* began to say to him
37:9 he related it to his *b* and
37:10 his father as well as his *b*
37:10 your *b* for certain going to
Ge 37:11 his *b* grew jealous of him
37:12 His *b* now went to feed the
37:13 Your *b* are tending flocks
37:14 your *b* are safe and sound
37:16 It is my *b* I am looking for
37:17 Joseph kept on after his *b*
37:23 as Joseph came to his *b*
37:26 Judah said to his *b*: What
37:30 he returned to his other *b*
38:1 Judah went down from his *b*
38:11 He too may die like his *b*
42:3 ten *b* of Joseph went down to
42:4 with his other *b*, because he
42:6 Joseph's *b* came and bowed
42:7 When Joseph got to see his *b*
42:8 Joseph recognized his *b*, but
42:13 Your servants are twelve *b*
42:19 one of your *b* be kept bound
42:28 said to his *b*: My money has
42:32 We are twelve *b*, the sons of
44:14 Judah and his *b* went on into
44:33 boy may go up with his *b*
45:1 made himself known to his *b*
45:3 Joseph said to his *b*: I am
45:3 his *b* were unable to answer
45:4 Joseph said to his *b*: Come
45:15 kiss all his *b* and to weep
45:15 his *b* spoke with him
45:16 Joseph's *b* have come! And it
45:17 Say to your *b*, Do this: Load
45:24 Thus he sent his *b* off
46:31 Joseph said to his *b* and to
46:31 My *b* and my father's
47:1 My father and my *b* and their
47:2 the whole number of his *b*
47:3 Pharaoh said to his *b*
47:5 your *b* have come here to you
47:6 your father and your *b* dwell
47:11 had his father and his *b*
47:12 his father and his *b* and the
48:6 the name of their *b* they will
48:22 more than to your *b*, which I
49:5 Simeon and Levi are *b*
49:8 Judah, your *b* will laud you
49:26 one singled out from his *b*
50:8 Joseph's household and his *b*
50:14 he and his *b* and all those
50:15 When the *b* of Joseph saw
50:17 the revolt of your *b* and
50:18 *b* also came and fell down
50:24 Joseph said to his *b*: I am
Ex 1:6 his *b* and all that generation
2:11 Moses . . . went out to his *b*
2:11 a certain Hebrew of his *b*
4:18 want to . . . return to my *b*
Le 10:4 *b* from in front of the holy
10:6 your *b* of the whole house of
21:10 of his *b* upon whose head the
25:46 upon your *b* . . . not tread
25:48 One of his *b* may buy him
Nu 8:26 minister to his *b* in the tent
16:10 all your *b* the sons of Levi
18:2 your *b* of the tribe of Levi
18:6 have taken your *b*, the Levites
20:3 our *b* expired before Jehovah
25:6 was bringing near to his *b* a
27:4 the midst of our father's *b*
27:7 the midst of their father's *b*
27:9 give his inheritance to his *b*
27:10 has no *b*, you must then give
27:10 inheritance to his father's *b*
27:11 if his father has no *b*, you
32:6 Are your *b* to go to war while
36:11 the sons of their father's *b*
De 1:16 a hearing between your *b*
1:28 Our *b* have caused our heart to
2:4 along by the border of your *b*
2:8 we passed on away from our *b*
3:18 your *b*, the sons of Israel
3:20 Jehovah gives your *b* rest
10:9 inheritance with his *b*
15:7 one of your *b* becomes poor
17:15 From among your *b* you should
17:20 not exalt itself above his *b*
18:2 to him in the midst of his *b*
18:7 the same as all his *b*, the
18:15 from your *b*, like me, is
18:18 from the midst of their *b*
20:8 the hearts of his *b* to melt
24:7 kidnapping a soul of his *b*
24:14 your *b* or of your alien
25:5 In case *b* dwell together and
33:9 his *b* he did not acknowledge
33:16 one singled out from his *b*
De 33:24 become one approved by his *b*
Jos 1:14 formation before your *b*
1:15 gives rest to your *b* the
2:13 my *b* and my sisters and all
2:18 *b* and all the household of
6:23 her *b* and all who belonged
14:8 my *b* who went up with me
17:4 in the midst of our *b*
17:4 of the *b* of their father
22:3 You have not left your *b*
22:4 God has given your *b* rest
22:7 a gift with their *b* on the
22:8 enemies together with your *b*
Jg 8:19 They were my *b*, the sons of
9:1 the *b* of his mother and began
9:3 So the *b* of his mother began
9:5 and killed his *b*, the sons of
9:24 his hands to kill his *b*
9:26 his *b* came and crossed over
9:31 Ebed and his *b* are now come
9:41 drive Gaal and his *b* out from
9:56 by killing his seventy *b* come
11:3 ran away because of his *b* and
14:3 among the daughters of your *b*
16:31 his *b* and all the household
18:8 their *b* at Zorah and Eshtaol
18:8 their *b* began to say to them
18:14 said to their *b*: Did you
19:23 *b*, do not do anything wrong
20:13 their *b*, the sons of Israel
21:22 *b* come to conduct a legal
Ru 4:10 be cut off from among his *b*
1Sa 16:13 in the midst of his *b*
17:17 Take, please, to your *b* this
17:17 to the camp to your *b*
17:18 look after your own *b* as
17:22 about the welfare of his *b*
20:29 that I may see my *b*
22:1 *b* and the entire house of
30:23 not do that way, my *b*
2Sa 2:26 back from following their *b*
3:8 to his *b* and his personal
15:20 take your *b* back with you
19:12 My *b* you are; my bone and
19:41 Why did our *b* the men of
1Ki 1:9 invite all his *b* the king's
12:24 your *b* the sons of Israel
2Ki 9:2 from the midst of his *b* and
10:13 encountered the *b* of Ahaziah
10:13 We are the *b* of Ahaziah
23:9 cakes in among their *b*
1Ch 4:9 more honorable than his *b*
4:27 his *b* did not have many sons
5:2 to be superior among his *b*
5:7 *b* by their families in the
5:13 And their *b* belonging to the
6:44 their *b* on the left hand
6:48 their *b* the Levites were the
7:5 their *b* of all the families
7:22 *b* kept coming in to comfort
8:32 dwelt in front of their *b* in
8:32 along with *b* of theirs
9:6 and six hundred and ninety *b*
9:9 And the *b* of theirs by their
9:13 their *b*, heads of the house
9:19 his *b* of the house of his
9:25 their *b* in their settlements
9:32 the Kohathites, their *b*
9:38 their *b* in Jerusalem along
9:38 along with *b* of theirs
12:2 the *b* of Saul, of Benjamin
12:29 of Benjamin, the *b* of Saul
12:32 *b* were at their orders
12:39 *b* had made preparation for
13:2 let us send to our *b* that are
15:5 Uriel the chief and his *b*
15:6 Asaiah the chief and his *b*
15:7 Joel the chief and his *b*
15:8 Shemaiah the chief and his *b*
15:9 Eliel the chief and his *b*
15:10 the chief and his *b*, a
15:12 you and your *b*, and you
15:16 station their *b* the singers
15:17 of his *b*, Asaph the son of
15:17 the sons of Merari their *b*
15:18 *b* of the second division
16:7 by means of Asaph and his *b*
16:37 Asaph and his *b* to minister
16:38 and Obed-edom and his *b*
16:39 Zadok the priest and his *b*
23:22 their *b* took them as wives
23:32 sons of Aaron their *b* for
24:31 their *b* the sons of Aaron
25:7 *b* trained in song to Jehovah

1Ch 25:9 he and his *b* and his sons
25:10 Zaccur, his sons and his *b*
25:11 for Izri, his sons and his *b*
25:12 his sons and his *b*, twelve
25:13 Bukkiah, his sons and his *b*
25:14 his sons and his *b*, twelve
25:15 Jeshaiah, his sons and his *b*
25:16 his sons and his *b*, twelve
25:17 Shimei, his sons and his *b*
25:18 Azarel, his sons and his *b*
25:19 his sons and his *b*, twelve
25:20 Shubael, his sons and his *b*
25:21 his sons and his *b*, twelve
25:22 his sons and his *b*, twelve
25:23 Hananiah, his sons and his *b*
25:24 his sons and his *b*, twelve
25:25 Hanani, his sons and his *b*
25:26 his sons and his *b*, twelve
25:27 Eliathah, his sons and his *b*
25:28 Hothir, his sons and his *b*
25:29 Giddalti, his sons and his *b*
25:30 his sons and his *b*, twelve
25:31 his sons and his *b*, twelve
26:7 whose *b* were capable men
26:8 and their *b*, capable men
26:9 Meshelemiah had sons and *b*
26:11 sons and *b* of Hosah were
26:12 exactly as their *b* did, to
26:25 As regards his *b*, of Eliezer
26:26 Shelomoth and his *b* were
26:28 of Shelomith and his *b*
26:30 Hashabiah and his *b*, capable
26:32 his *b*, capable men, were
27:18 Elihu, one of David's *b*
28:2 Hear me, my *b* and my people
2Ch 5:12 to their sons and to their *b*
11:4 and fight against your *b*
11:22 leader among his *b*, for
19:10 *b* who are dwelling in their
19:10 you and against your *b*
21:2 *b*, Jehoshaphat's sons
21:4 killed all his *b* with the
21:13 even your own *b*, the
22:8 sons of the *b* of Ahaziah
28:8 hundred thousand of their *b*
28:11 captured from your *b*, for
28:15 beside their *b*
29:15 *b* together and sanctified
29:34 *b* the Levites helped them
30:7 *b* that acted unfaithfully
30:9 your *b* and your sons will be
31:15 *b* in the divisions, equally
35:5 *b*, the sons of the people
35:6 preparation for your *b* to
35:9 Shemaiah and Nethanel his *b*
35:15 their *b* the Levites
Ezr 3:2 and his *b* the priests and
3:2 and his *b* proceeded to rise up
3:8 and the rest of their *b*, the
3:9 Jeshua, his sons and his *b*
3:9 and their *b*, the Levites
6:20 for their *b* the priests and
7:18 good to you and to your *b*
8:17 to speak to Iddo and his *b*
8:18 his sons and his *b*, eighteen
8:19 *b*, and their sons, twenty
8:24 with them ten of their *b*
10:18 his *b*, Maaseiah and Eliezer
Ne 1:2 Hanani, one of my *b*, came in
3:1 the high priest and his *b*
3:18 *b* did repair work, Bavvai
4:2 his *b* and the military force
4:14 fight for your *b*, your sons
4:23 my *b* and my attendants and
5:1 against their Jewish *b*
5:5 same as the flesh of our *b*
5:8 Jewish *b* who were sold to the
5:8 sell your own *b*, and must they
5:10 my *b* and my attendants are
5:14 my *b* did not eat the bread
10:10 their *b* Shebaniah, Hodiah
10:29 were adhering to their *b*
11:12 *b* the doers of the work
11:13 *b*, heads of paternal houses
11:14 *b*, mighty men of valor
11:17 was second of his *b*, and
11:19 *b* who were keeping guard
12:7 the priests and their *b* in
12:8 thanks, he and his *b*
12:9 Bakbukiah and Unni their *b*
12:24 their *b* opposite them to
12:36 his *b* Shemaiah and Azarel
13:13 the distributing to their *b*
Es 10:3 by the multitude of his *b*

Job 6:15 *b* have dealt treacherously
19:13 My own *b* he has put far
22:6 seize a pledge from your *b*
42:11 his *b* and all his sisters
42:15 in among their *b*
Ps 22:22 declare your name to my *b*
69:8 become one estranged to my *b*
122:8 the sake of my *b* and my
133:1 *b* to dwell together in unity
Pr 6:19 forth contentions among *b*
17:2 in among the *b* he will have a
19:7 *b* of one of little means have
Isa 66:5 Your *b* that are hating you
66:20 bring all your *b* out of
Jer 7:15 as I threw out all your *b*
12:6 For even your own *b* and the
29:16 your *b* that have not gone
35:3 and his *b*, and all his sons
41:8 in the midst of their *b*
49:10 his *b* and his neighbors
Eze 11:15 as regards your *b*, your
11:15 your *b*, the men concerned
Ho 2:1 Say to your *b*, My people! and
Am 1:9 remember the covenant of *b*
Mic 5:3 the rest of his *b* will return
Mt 1:2 father to Judah and his *b*
1:11 and to his *b* at the time of
4:18 two *b*, Simon who is called
4:21 saw two others who were *b*
5:47 if you greet your *b* only
12:46 his mother and *b* took up a
12:47 Your mother and your *b* are
12:48 mother, and who are my *b*?
12:49 Look! My mother and my *b*!
13:55 his *b* James and Joseph and
19:29 left houses or *b* or sisters
20:24 indignant at the two *b*
22:25 there were seven *b* with us
23:8 whereas all you are *b*
25:40 of the least of these my *b*
28:10 Go, report to my *b*, that
Mr 3:31 his mother and his *b* came
3:32 mother and your *b* outside
3:33 Who are my mother and my *b*?
3:34 See, my mother and my *b*!
10:29 left house or *b* or sisters
10:30 *b* and sisters and mothers
12:20 There were seven *b*; and the
Lu 8:19 Now his mother and *b* came
8:20 Your mother and your *b* are
8:21 My mother and my *b* are these
14:12 or your *b* or your relatives
14:26 wife and children and *b* and
16:28 for I have five *b*, in order
18:29 left house or wife or *b* or
20:29 seven *b*; and the first took
21:16 delivered up even by . . . *b*
22:32 returned, strengthen your *b*
Joh 2:12 his mother and *b* and his
7:3 his *b* said to him: Pass on
7:5 His *b* were, in fact, not
7:10 *b* had gone up to the festival
20:17 to my *b* and say to them
21:23 saying went out among the *b*
Ac 1:14 of Jesus and with his *b*
1:15 in the midst of the *b* and
1:16 *b*, it was necessary for the
2:29 *b*, it is allowable to speak
2:37 Men, *b*, what shall we do?
3:17 *b*, I know that you acted in
3:22 from among your *b* a prophet
6:3 *b*, search out for yourselves
7:2 Men, *b* and fathers, hear
7:13 was made known to his *b*
7:23 inspection of his *b*, the sons
7:25 his *b* would grasp that God
7:26 Men, you are *b*. Why do you
7:37 your *b* a prophet like me
9:30 When the *b* detected this
10:23 *b* that were from Joppa went
11:1 *b* that were in Judea heard
11:12 six *b* also went with me
11:29 relief ministration to the *b*
12:17 things to James and the *b*
13:15 *b*, if there is any word of
13:26 *b*, you sons of the stock
13:38 *b*, that through this One a
14:2 influenced . . . against the *b*
15:1 teach the *b*: Unless you get
15:3 great joy to all the *b*
15:7 *b*, you well know that from
15:13 saying: Men, *b*, hear me
15:22 leading men among the *b*
15:23 and the older men, *b*, to

Ac 15:23 to those *b* in Antioch and
15:32 encouraged the *b* with many a
15:33 let go in peace by the *b* to
15:36 let us return and visit the *b*
15:40 entrusted by the *b* to the
16:2 the *b* in Lystra and Iconium
16:40 saw the *b* they encouraged
17:6 dragged Jason and certain *b* to
17:10 *b* sent both Paul and Silas
17:14 *b* immediately sent Paul off
18:18 Paul said good-bye to the *b*
18:27 the *b* wrote the disciples
21:7 we greeted the *b* and stayed
21:17 the *b* received us gladly
22:1 Men, *b* and fathers, hear my
22:5 letters to the *b* in Damascus
23:1 *b*, I have behaved before God
23:5 *B*, I did not know he was high
23:6 *b*, I am a Pharisee, a son of
28:14 Here we found *b* and were
28:15 *b*, when they heard the news
28:17 *b*, although I had done
28:21 *b* that has arrived reported
Ro 1:13 you to fail to know, *b*, that
7:1 be that you do not know, *b*
7:4 *b*, you also were made dead to
8:12 *b*, we are under obligation
8:29 the firstborn among many *b*
9:3 in behalf of my *b*, my
10:1 *B*, the goodwill of my heart
11:25 *b*, to be ignorant of this
12:1 *b*, to present your bodies
15:14 am persuaded about you, my *b*
15:30 I exhort you, *b*, through our
16:14 Hermas, and the *b* with them
16:17 *b*, to keep your eye on those
1Co 1:10 exhort you, *b*, through the
1:11 disclosure was made . . . *b*
1:26 calling of you, *b*, that not
2:1 to you, *b*, did not come with
3:1 *b*, I was not able to speak to
4:6 Now, *b*, these things I have
6:5 able to judge between his *b*
6:8 defraud, and your *b* at that
7:24 *b*, let him remain in it
7:29 *b*, the time left is reduced
8:12 sin against your *b* and wound
9:5 and the Lord's *b* and Cephas
10:1 not . . . be ignorant, *b*, that
11:33 *b*, when you come together
12:1 *b*, I do not want you to be
14:6 at this time, *b*, if I should
14:20 *B*, do not become young
14:26 What is to be done, then, *b*?
14:39 my *b*, keep zealously
15:1 I make known to you, *b*, the
15:6 five hundred *b* at one time
15:31 exultation over you, *b*
15:50 I say, *b*, that flesh and
15:58 beloved *b*, become steadfast
16:11 waiting for him with the *b*
16:12 to come to you with the *b*
16:15 I exhort you, *b*: you know
16:20 All the *b* greet you
2Co 1:8 *b*, about the tribulation that
8:1 we let you know, *b*, about the
8:23 our *b*, they are apostles of
9:3 I am sending the *b*, that our
9:5 encourage the *b* to come to
11:9 *b* that came from Macedonia
11:26 in dangers among false *b*
13:11 *b*, continue to rejoice, to
Ga 1:2 all the *b* with me, to the
1:11 I put you on notice, *b*
2:4 But because of the false *b*
3:15 *B*, I speak with a human
4:12 *B*, I beg you, Become as I
4:28 we, *b*, are children belonging
4:31 *b*, we are children, not of a
5:11 *b*, if I am still preaching
5:13 called for freedom, *b*; only
6:1 *B*, even though a man takes
6:18 with the spirit you show, *b*
Eph 6:23 the *b* have peace and love
Php 1:12 I desire you to know, *b*
1:14 most of the *b* in the Lord
3:1 my *b*, continue rejoicing in
3:13 *B*, I do not yet consider
3:17 imitators of me, *b*, and keep
4:1 my *b* beloved and longed for
4:8 *b*, whatever things are true
4:21 *b* who are with me send you
Col 1:2 and faithful *b* in union with
4:15 my greetings to the *b* at

1Th 1:4 For we know, *b* loved by God
2:1 know, *b*, how our visit to
2:9 bear in mind, *b*, our labor
2:14 you became imitators, *b*, of
2:17 *b*, when we were bereaved of
3:7 *b*, we have been comforted
4:1 *b*, we request you and exhort
4:10 the *b* in all of Macedonia
4:10 we exhort you, *b*, to go on
4:13 *b*, we do not want you to be
5:1 *b*, you need nothing to be
5:4 *b*, you are not in darkness
5:12 we request you, *b*, to have
5:14 *b*, admonish the disorderly
5:23 and soul and body of you *b*
5:25 *B*, continue in prayer for us
5:26 Greet all the *b* with a holy
5:27 to be read to all the *b*
2Th 1:3 God thanks always for you, *b*
2:1 *b*, respecting the presence of
2:13 for you, *b* loved by Jehovah
2:15 *b*, stand firm and maintain
3:1 *b*, carry on prayer for us
3:6 giving you orders, *b*, in the
3:13 *b*, do not give up in doing
1Ti 4:6 giving these advices to the *b*
5:1 younger men as *b*
6:2 because they are *b*
2Ti 4:21 and Claudia and all the *b*
Heb 2:11 not ashamed to call them *b*
2:12 declare your name to my *b*
2:17 like his *b* in all respects
3:1 holy *b*, partakers of the
3:12 Beware, *b*, for fear there
7:5 from their *b*, even if these
10:19 *b*, since we have boldness
13:22 I exhort you, *b*, to bear
Jas 1:2 Consider it all joy, my *b*
1:16 not be misled, my beloved *b*
1:19 Know this, my beloved *b*
2:1 My *b*, you are not holding
2:5 Listen, my beloved *b*. God
2:14 what benefit is it, my *b*
3:1 my *b*, knowing that we shall
3:10 my *b*, for these things to go
3:12 My *b*, a fig tree cannot
4:11 against one another, *b*
5:7 patience, therefore, *b*, until
5:9 sighs against one another, *b*
5:10 *B*, take as a pattern of the
5:12 my *b*, stop swearing, yes
5:19 My *b*, if anyone among you is
1Pe 2:17 the whole association of *b*
5:9 entire association of your *b*
2Pe 1:10 *b*, all the more do your
1Jo 3:13 Do not marvel, *b*, that the
3:14 because we love the *b*
3:16 surrender our souls for our *b*
3Jo 3 when *b* came and bore witness
5 in whatever you do for the *b*
10 receive the *b* with respect
Re 6:11 *b* who were about to be killed
12:10 accuser of our *b* has been
19:10 *b* who have the work of
22:9 slave of you and of your *b*

Brought

Ge 1:4 God *b* about a division between
1:9 Let the waters . . . be *b*
4:4 as for Abel, he too *b* some
8:9 took it and *b* it to himself
13:10 Jehovah *b* Sodom and Gomorrah
14:18 king of Salem *b* out bread
15:5 He now *b* him outside and said
15:7 I am Jehovah, who *b* you out
19:10 *b* Lot in to them, into the
19:17 they had *b* them forth to the
19:29 when God *b* the cities of the
20:9 *b* upon me and my kingdom a
24:67 Isaac *b* her into the tent of
26:10 would have *b* guilt upon us
27:14 and *b* them to his mother
27:25 he *b* it near to him and he
27:25 he *b* him wine and he began
27:31 *b* it to his father and said
29:13 and *b* him on into his house
29:32 and *b* a son to birth
29:33 *b* a son to birth and then
29:34 *b* a son to birth and then
29:35 *b* a son to birth and then
30:14 he *b* them to Leah his mother
30:23 and *b* a son to birth
32:23 *b* them over the torrent
32:23 and he *b* over what he had
Ge 33:11 blessing which was *b* to you
34:30 have *b* ostracism upon me
37:2 Joseph *b* a bad report about
37:28 these *b* Joseph into Egypt
37:32 had it *b* to their father and
38:25 As she was being *b* out she
39:1 he was *b* down to Egypt, and
39:1 Ishmaelites who had *b* him
39:14 He *b* to us a man, a Hebrew
39:17 Hebrew servant whom you *b*
43:2 cereals they had *b* from Egypt
43:18 we are being *b* here for them
43:22 more money we have *b* down
43:23 he *b* out Simeon to them
43:24 *b* the men into Joseph's
43:26 they *b* the gift that was in
44:8 *b* back to you from the land
46:7 he *b* his sons and his sons'
46:32 they have *b* here
47:7 Joseph *b* in Jacob his father
48:10 *b* them close to him, and he
48:12 Joseph *b* them out away from
48:13 and *b* them close to him
Ex 2:2 woman became pregnant and *b*
2:10 *b* him to Pharaoh's daughter
3:12 have *b* the people out of Egypt
10:8 Moses and Aaron were *b* back
11:6 will never be *b* about again
12:39 they had *b* out from Egypt
12:51 Jehovah *b* the sons of Israel
13:3 Jehovah *b* you out from here
13:5 when Jehovah will have *b* you
13:9 Jehovah *b* you out of Egypt
13:14 Jehovah *b* me out of Egypt
13:16 Jehovah *b* us out of Egypt
15:19 Jehovah *b* back the waters of
16:3 *b* us out into this wilderness
16:6 Jehovah who has *b* you out
17:3 have *b* us up out of Egypt to
18:1 had *b* Israel out of Egypt
19:17 Moses now *b* the people out
20:2 *b* you out of the land of Egypt
22:8 *b* near to the true God to
29:46 *b* them out of the land of
32:11 people whom you *b* out of the
32:12 With evil intent he *b* them
32:21 that you have *b* a great sin
35:21 *b* . . . Jehovah's contribution
35:22 *b* brooches and earrings and
35:23 red and sealskins, *b* them
35:24 *b* Jehovah's contribution, and
35:24 work of the service *b* it
35:27 chieftains *b* onyx stones and
35:29 *b* a voluntary offering to
36:3 *b* for the work of the holy
36:3 *b* to him a voluntary offering
40:21 *b* the Ark into the tabernacle
Le 6:30 blood will be *b* into the tent
8:6 Moses *b* Aaron and his sons
8:13 *b* Aaron's sons near and
8:18 now *b* the ram of the burnt
8:22 he *b* the second ram, the ram
8:24 Moses *b* Aaron's sons near and
10:1 *b* each one his fire holder
10:18 blood has not been *b* into
13:2 be *b* to Aaron the priest or
13:9 must then be *b* to the priest
14:2 he must be *b* to the priest
16:27 blood of both of which was *b*
19:36 *b* you out of the land of
24:11 So they *b* him to Moses
24:23 *b* forth the one who had
25:38 *b* you out of the land of
25:42 slaves whom I *b* out of the
25:55 *b* out of the land of Egypt
26:13 *b* you out of the land of
26:45 ancestors whom I *b* forth
Nu 6:13 *b* to the entrance of the tent
7:3 *b* their offering before Jehovah
15:25 *b* as their offering an
15:33 *b* him up to Moses and Aaron
15:36 *b* him forth outside the camp
15:41 *b* you out of the land of
16:13 have *b* us up out of a land
16:14 have not *b* us into any land
16:29 punishment will be *b* upon
17:9 Moses then *b* out all the rods
20:4 *b* Jehovah's congregation into
20:16 and *b* us out of Egypt; and
21:5 Why have you *b* us up out of
31:54 and *b* it into the tent of
32:17 have *b* them to their place
De 1:27 he *b* us out of the land of
4:32 great thing *b* about like this
De 4:37 and *b* you out of Egypt in his
5:6 *b* you out of the land of Egypt
6:12 *b* you out of the land of Egypt
6:23 *b* us out from there in order
7:8 Jehovah *b* you out with a
7:19 Jehovah your God *b* you out
8:14 *b* you out of the land of Egypt
8:15 *b* forth water for you out of
9:4 Jehovah has *b* me in to take
9:12 people whom you *b* out of
9:26 you *b* out of Egypt with a
9:28 land out of which you *b* them
9:28 *b* them out to put them to
9:29 *b* out with your great power
13:5 *b* you out of the land of
13:10 *b* you out of the land of
16:1 God *b* you out of Egypt by
19:18 *b* a false charge against
20:1 *b* you up out of the land of
22:14 *b* forth a bad name upon her
22:19 he *b* forth a bad name upon a
26:8 Jehovah *b* us out of Egypt
26:9 he *b* us to this place and
26:10 I have *b* the firstfruits of
29:25 he *b* them out of the land of
30:1 *b* them back to your heart
Jos 6:23 *b* out Rahab and her father
6:23 her family . . . they *b* out
7:23 and *b* them to Joshua and all
7:24 *b* them up to the low plain
7:25 have you *b* ostracism upon us
10:23 *b* out to him from the cave
10:24 *b* out these kings to Joshua
22:32 and *b* back word to them
24:5 and afterward I *b* you out
24:7 and *b* the sea upon them and
24:8 I *b* you to the land of the
24:17 our God who *b* us and our
24:32 Israel had *b* up out of
Jg 1:7 they *b* him to Jerusalem and
2:12 who had *b* them out of the
6:8 I who *b* you up from Egypt and
6:8 thus *b* you out of the house of
6:13 Egypt that Jehovah *b* us up
6:18 I have *b* out my gift and set
6:19 he *b* it out to him under the
7:25 they *b* the head of Oreb and
12:9 *b* in thirty daughters for his
15:13 and *b* him up out of the crag
16:8 *b* up to her seven still-moist
16:21 *b* him down to Gaza and bound
16:31 and *b* him up and buried him
18:3 Who *b* you here, and what are
19:21 he *b* him into his house and
19:25 *b* her forth to them outside
19:30 never been *b* about or been
20:3 this bad thing been *b* about
20:12 thing that has been *b* about
20:21 *b* twenty-two thousand men
20:25 *b* a further eighteen thousand
20:35 *b* down to ruin in Benjamin
21:12 *b* them to the camp at Shiloh
Ru 3:18 *b* the matter to an end today
1Sa 1:20 pregnant and *b* a son to birth
1:24 she *b* him up with her, along
1:25 and *b* the boy to Eli
2:19 *b* it up to him from year to
3:14 not be *b* to exemption from
5:1 *b* it from Ebenezer to Ashdod
5:8 *b* the ark of the God of Israel
5:9 after they had *b* it around to
5:10 They have *b* the ark of the
7:1 *b* the ark of Jehovah up and
9:22 *b* them to the dining hall
10:18 *b* Israel up out of Egypt
12:6 *b* your forefathers up out
14:29 My father has *b* ostracism
14:34 *b* near each one his bull
15:15 Amalekites they have *b* them
15:20 I *b* Agag the king of Amalek
17:54 and *b* it to Jerusalem, and
19:7 Jonathan *b* David to Saul
20:8 you have *b* your servant with
21:15 *b* this one to behave crazy
25:27 maidservant has *b* to my
25:35 what she had *b* him, and to
28:15 by having me *b* up
2Sa 2:3 David *b* up, each with his
3:22 spoil that they *b* with them
6:17 *b* the ark of Jehovah in and
7:18 that you have *b* me thus far
8:7 and *b* them to Jerusalem
10:16 Hadadezer sent and *b* out
12:30 he *b* out was very much

2Sa 12:31 *b* out that he might put
13:10 *b* them in to Amnon her
14:23 *b* Absalom to Jerusalem
16:8 Jehovah has *b* back upon you
17:28 *b* beds and basins and
17:29 they *b* forward for David
1Ki 1:3 then *b* her in to the king
1:27 this thing has been *b* about
1:38 and then *b* him to Gihon
1:53 *b* him down from off the
2:30 Benaiah *b* word back to the
2:40 Shimei went and *b* his slaves
3:24 *b* the sword before the king
8:6 the priests *b* in the ark of
8:16 *b* my people Israel out from
8:51 whom you *b* out from Egypt
9:9 *b* their forefathers out from
9:9 *b* upon them all this calamity
10:11 *b* from Ophir timbers of
12:24 this thing has been *b* about
12:28 that *b* you up out of the
13:20 prophet that had *b* him back
13:23 prophet whom he had *b* back
13:26 prophet that had *b* him back
17:23 *b* him down from the roof
18:18 not *b* ostracism upon Israel
18:40 Elijah then *b* them down to
20:9 and *b* word back to him
21:13 *b* him out to the outskirts
22:37 he was *b* to Samaria, then
2Ki 4:20 and *b* him to his mother
5:20 from his hand what he *b*
10:8 They have *b* the heads of the
10:22 *b* the attire out for them
10:26 *b* out the sacred pillars of
11:4 the runners and *b* them to
11:12 he *b* the son of the king out
12:4 is *b* to the house of Jehovah
12:9 *b* into the house of Jehovah
12:13 *b* to the house of Jehovah
12:16 *b* to the house of Jehovah
15:20 Menahem *b* forth the silver
16:14 *b* near from in front of the
17:7 *b* them up out of the land of
17:24 king of Assyria *b* people
17:36 Jehovah, who *b* you up out
19:12 forefathers *b* to ruin
20:20 *b* the water into the city
22:4 *b* into the house of Jehovah
23:4 *b* the dust of them to Bethel
23:6 he *b* out the sacred pole
23:8 he *b* all the priests from
23:30 *b* him to Jerusalem and
23:34 took and then *b* to Egypt
24:13 he *b* out from there all the
25:6 seized the king and *b* him
25:7 fetters and *b* him to Babylon
1Ch 4:10 God *b* to pass what he had
5:26 *b* them to Halah and Habor
10:12 *b* them to Jabesh and buried
11:8 Joab himself *b* to life the
11:19 the risk . . . that they *b* it
16:1 *b* the ark of the true God in
17:5 day that I *b* Israel up until
17:16 that you have *b* me thus far
18:7 and *b* them to Jerusalem
20:2 spoil of the city that he *b*
20:3 people that were in it he *b*
22:4 Tyrians *b* in cedar timbers
2Ch 1:4 *b* up from Kiriath-jearim to
1:17 *b* up and exported from Egypt
3:5 he *b* up upon it palm-tree
5:5 priests the Levites *b* them up
5:7 the priests *b* the ark of the
6:5 *b* my people out from the land
7:22 *b* them out of the land of
7:22 *b* upon them all this
8:11 Pharaoh's daughter Solomon *b*
9:10 servants of Solomon who *b*
9:10 *b* timbers of almug trees and
9:12 what she *b* to the king
11:4 this thing has been *b* about
15:11 from the spoil they had *b*
16:2 Asa now *b* out silver and
22:9 and they . . . *b* him to Jehu
23:11 *b* the king's son out and
23:14 priest *b* out the chiefs of
23:20 *b* the king down from the
24:14 *b* before the king and
24:23 *b* all the princes of the
25:12 *b* them to the top of the
25:14 *b* the gods of the sons of
25:23 *b* him to Jerusalem and
28:5 and *b* them to Damascus
2Ch 28:8 they *b* the spoil to Samaria
28:15 *b* them to Jericho, the
29:4 *b* the priests and the Levites
29:16 *b* out all the uncleanness
29:23 *b* the male goats of the sin
29:32 congregation *b* came to be
30:15 *b* burnt offerings to the
31:5 they *b* in abundantly
31:6 *b* in the tenth of cattle and
31:6 *b* in and so gave heaps upon
33:11 Jehovah *b* against them the
34:9 money that was being *b* to
34:11 kings of Judah had *b* to ruin
34:14 *b* to the house of Jehovah
34:16 Shaphan *b* the book to the
34:28 *b* the reply to the king
35:13 they *b* it quickly to all the
35:24 and *b* him to Jerusalem
36:4 Necho took and *b* to Egypt
36:7 *b* to Babylon and then put
36:17 *b* up against them the king
36:18 everything he *b* to Babylon
Ezr 1:7 *b* forth the utensils of the
1:7 had *b* out from Jerusalem and
1:11 Everything Sheshbazzar *b* up
4:2 Assyria, who *b* us up here
5:14 *b* to the temple of Babylon
6:5 and *b* to Babylon be returned
8:18 they *b* to us, according to
Ne 6:8 saying have not been *b* about
8:2 Ezra the priest *b* the law
9:7 Abram and *b* him out of Ur of
9:15 out of the crag you *b* forth
9:23 *b* them into the land that you
12:31 I *b* up the princes of Judah
13:12 *b* in the tenth of the grain
13:18 *b* upon us all this calamity
Es 5:10 and Zeresh his wife *b* in
5:12 Esther the queen *b* in with
Job 4:12 a word was stealthily *b*, And
10:19 I should have been *b*
12:6 who has *b* a god in his hand
15:7 before the hills were you *b*
21:32 the graveyard he will be *b*
24:24 And they have been *b* low
30:19 has *b* me down to the clay
32:18 Spirit has *b* pressure upon
Ps 30:3 *b* up my soul from Sheol
44:3 was not what *b* them salvation
45:14 she will be *b* to the king
45:14 are being *b* in to you
45:15 will be *b* with rejoicing
51:5 With error I was *b* forth
66:11 have *b* us into a hunting net
73:19 *b* to their finish through
78:33 *b* their days to an end as
78:71 *b* him in to be a shepherd
85:1 *b* back the ones taken captive
88:16 have *b* me to silence
103:10 *b* upon us what we deserve
105:43 So he *b* out his people with
106:43 be *b* low for their error
Pr 8:24 *b* forth as with labor pains
8:25 *b* forth as with labor pains
Ca 1:4 The king has *b* me into his
2:4 He *b* me into the house of wine
3:4 *b* him into my mother's house
Isa 1:2 Sons I have *b* up and raised
6:5 I am as good as *b* to silence
14:11 Sheol your pride has been *b*
14:15 down to Sheol you will be *b*
14:20 you *b* your own land to ruin
18:7 gift will be *b* to Jehovah
23:4 *b* up young men, raised up
37:12 my forefathers *b* to ruin
43:23 not *b* me the sheep of your
46:13 *b* near my righteousness
48:15 I have *b* him in, and there
49:21 who has *b* them up?
51:2 *b* you forth with childbirth
51:18 sons that she *b* to birth
51:18 all the sons that she *b* up
53:7 *b* just like a sheep to the
55:12 with peace you will be *b* in
63:11 *b* them up out of the sea
66:8 land be *b* forth with labor
Jer 2:7 *b* you to a land of the orchard
2:27 You yourself *b* me to birth
3:17 nations must be *b* together
5:30 has been *b* to be in the land
10:9 *b* in even from Tarshish
11:8 I *b* upon them all the words
11:19 that is *b* to slaughter
12:10 have *b* my vineyard to ruin
Jer 16:14 *b* the sons of Israel up out
16:15 who *b* the sons of Israel up
20:15 the man that *b* good news
23:7 *b* the sons of Israel up out
23:8 Jehovah is alive who *b* up
23:8 *b* in the offspring of the
27:16 *b* back from Babylon soon
27:22 is where they will be *b*
32:42 *b* in upon this people all
37:14 *b* him in to the princes
38:13 *b* him up out of the cistern
38:22 *b* out to the princes of
39:5 *b* him up to Nebuchadrezzar
41:16 people whom they *b* back
41:16 he *b* back from Gibeon
44:2 calamity that I have *b* in
48:19 Say, What has been *b* about?
49:26 *b* to silence in that day
50:30 will be *b* to silence in
51:10 Jehovah has *b* forth deeds
52:9 *b* him up to the king of
52:11 *b* him to Babylon and put
La 1:5 Jehovah himself has *b* grief to
2:2 *b* into contact with the earth
2:5 *b* his fortified places to ruin
2:6 He has *b* his festival to ruin
2:10 have *b* up dust upon their head
2:10 *b* their head down to the very
2:22 whom I *b* forth fully formed
3:13 He has *b* into my kidneys the
Eze 8:3 and *b* me to Jerusalem in the
8:7 *b* me to the entrance of the
8:14 *b* me to the entrance of the
8:16 *b* me to the inner courtyard
11:24 finally *b* me to Chaldea to
12:4 those being *b* forth for exile
12:7 My luggage I *b* out, just
14:3 *b* up their dungy idols upon
14:4 myself be *b* to answer him
14:7 *b* to answer him by myself
14:22 those being *b* forth
14:22 shall have *b* upon Jerusalem
14:22 that I shall have *b* upon her
17:13 and *b* him into an oath
19:3 she *b* up one of her cubs
19:9 *b* him to the king of Babylon
20:10 I *b* them forth from the
20:10 *b* them into the wilderness
20:14 I had *b* them forth
20:22 I had *b* them out
21:5 *b* forth my sword from its
21:7 come and be *b* to occur
23:42 drunkards being *b* in from
27:26 those rowing you have *b* you
27:32 *b* to silence in the midst
28:17 *b* your wisdom to ruin on
30:11 *b* in to reduce the land to
31:18 *b* down with the trees of
34:4 one you have not *b* back
37:1 *b* me forth in the spirit of
38:8 people *b* back from the sword
38:8 *b* forth from the peoples
39:8 come and it must be *b* to be
40:1 he *b* me to that place
40:2 *b* me to the land of Israel
40:4 you have been *b* here
40:17 *b* me into the outer
40:24 *b* me toward the south
40:28 *b* me into the inner
40:32 *b* me into the inner
42:1 *b* me forth to the outer
42:15 *b* me out by the way of the
44:4 *b* me by way of the north
47:1 *b* me back to the entrance
47:2 *b* me forth by the way of
47:8 *b* forth into the sea itself
Da 1:2 *b* them to the land of Shinar
1:2 *b* to the treasure-house of
2:44 that will never be *b* to ruin
3:13 men were *b* in before the king
5:3 *b* in the vessels of gold that
5:13 was *b* in before the king
5:13 king my father *b* out of Judah
5:15 *b* in before me the wise men
5:20 *b* down from the throne of
5:23 *b* before you even the vessels
6:16 *b* Daniel and threw him into
6:17 stone was *b* and placed on
6:18 musical instruments were *b*
6:22 they have not *b* me to ruin
6:24 *b* these able-bodied men who
6:26 that will not be *b* to ruin
7:13 *b* him up close even before
7:14 that will not be *b* to ruin

Da 8:14 be *b* into its right condition
9:14 and finally *b* it upon us, for
9:15 *b* your people out from the
Ho 7:6 *b* their heart near as to a
11:4 gently I *b* food to each one
12:1 and to Egypt oil itself is *b*
12:13 *b* up Israel out of Egypt
Joe 3:5 *b* my own desirable good
Am 2:10 I myself *b* you people up out
3:1 family that I *b* up out of the
5:25 offerings that you people *b*
Mic 6:4 I *b* you up out of the land of
Hab 1:15 *b* up with a mere fishhook
Hag 1:9 you have *b* it into the house
Zec 10:11 Assyria must be *b* down
Mal 1:13 have *b* something torn away
1:13 you have *b* it as a gift
Mt 4:24 *b* him all those faring badly
8:16 *b* him many demon-possessed
9:32 people *b* him a dumb man
12:22 *b* him a demon-possessed man
14:11 his head was *b* on a platter
14:11 and she *b* it to her mother
14:35 *b* him all those who were
17:1 and *b* them up into a lofty
17:16 I *b* him to your disciples
18:24 *b* in a man who owed him
19:13 young children were *b* to
21:7 they *b* the ass and its colt
22:19 They *b* him a denarius
25:20 *b* five additional talents
Mr 4:21 A lamp is not *b* to be put
4:21 *b* to be put upon a lampstand
6:28 and *b* his head on a platter
7:32 they *b* him a man deaf and
8:22 people *b* him a blind man
8:23 *b* him outside the village
9:2 *b* them up into a lofty
9:17 Teacher, I *b* my son to you
9:20 So they *b* him to him. But at
11:7 they *b* the colt to Jesus
12:16 They *b* one. And he said to
15:22 *b* him to the place Golgotha
Lu 1:52 has *b* down men of power from
2:22 they *b* him up to Jerusalem
2:27 *b* the young child Jesus in to
4:5 *b* him up and showed him all
4:40 *b* them to him. By laying his
5:11 they *b* the boats back to land
7:37 she *b* an alabaster case of
10:34 *b* him to an inn and took
22:54 *b* him into the house of the
23:14 You *b* this man to me as one
Joh 4:33 No one has *b* him anything to
16:21 *b* forth the young child, she
18:16 doorkeeper and *b* Peter in
19:13 *b* Jesus outside, and he
19:29 and *b* it to his mouth
20:18 *b* the news to the disciples
Ac 4:37 *b* the money and deposited it
5:2 he *b* just a part and deposited
5:15 *b* the sick out even into the
5:19 Jehovah's angel . . . *b* them
5:21 to the jail to have them *b*
5:27 *b* them and stood them in the
6:13 *b* forward false witnesses
7:21 and *b* him up as her own son
7:41 *b* up a sacrifice to the idol
7:45 *b* it in with Joshua into the
8:32 he was *b* to the slaughter
9:30 *b* him down to Caesarea and
11:26 he *b* him to Antioch
12:17 Jehovah *b* him out of the
13:17 *b* them out of it with an
13:23 *b* to Israel a savior, Jesus
14:13 *b* bulls and garlands to the
16:30 he *b* them outside and said
16:34 he *b* them into his house and
17:5 them *b* forth to the rabble
17:15 those conducting Paul *b* him
19:19 *b* their books together and
19:27 to be *b* down to nothing
19:33 *b* Alexander out of the crowd
19:37 you have *b* these men who are
21:28 *b* Greeks into the temple and
21:29 had *b* him into the temple
21:34 *b* to the soldiers' quarters
22:24 *b* into the soldiers' quarters
22:30 he *b* Paul down and stood him
23:28 I *b* him down into their
23:31 *b* him by night to Antipatris
25:6 and commanded Paul to be *b* in
25:15 *b* information about him
25:17 commanded the man to be *b*
Ac 25:23 Paul was *b* in
25:26 I *b* him forth before you
27:44 all were *b* safely to land
1Co 6:12 be *b* under authority by
15:24 *b* to nothing all government
15:26 death is to be *b* to nothing
2Co 3:11 was *b* in with glory, much
4:11 *b* face to face with death
7:7 he *b* us word again of your
Ga 2:4 the false brothers *b* in quietly
3:1 that *b* you under evil influence
1Ti 6:7 *b* nothing into the world
2Ti 1:16 he often *b* me refreshment
Tit 3:5 the bath that *b* us to life
Heb 13:20 *b* up from the dead the
Jas 1:18 he *b* us forth by the word
1Pe 1:13 kindness that is to be *b* to
2Pe 1:21 prophecy was at no time *b* by
2:5 he *b* a deluge upon a world
Re 10:7 is indeed *b* to a finish
15:1 anger of God is *b* to a finish

Brow
Lu 4:29 to the *b* of the mountain upon

Brown
Ge 30:33 dark *b* among the . . . rams
30:35 every one dark *b* among the

Bruise
Ge 3:15 He will *b* you in the head and
3:15 you will *b* him in the heel

Bruised
Mt 12:20 No *b* reed will he crush

Bruises
Job 9:17 Who with a storm *b* me And
Isa 1:6 Wounds and *b* and fresh

Bruising
Pr 20:30 *B* wounds are what scours
Lu 9:39 withdraws from him after *b*

Brushwood
Isa 64:2 as when a fire ignites the *b*

Bubble
Ps 19:2 causes speech to *b* forth
78:2 riddles of long ago to *b* forth
119:171 May my lips *b* forth praise
145:7 goodness they will *b* over
Pr 1:23 cause my spirit to *b* forth
Ec 10:1 to stink, to *b* forth
Jas 3:11 to *b* out of the same opening

Bubbles
Pr 15:2 *b* forth with foolishness
15:28 wicked ones *b* forth with bad

Bubbling
Ps 59:7 a *b* forth with their mouth
94:4 They keep *b* forth, they keep
Pr 18:4 wisdom is a torrent *b* forth
Joh 4:14 a fountain of water *b* up to

Buck
Eze 43:22 bring near a *b* of the goats
45:23 *b* of the goats daily

Bucket
Isa 40:15 are as a drop from a *b*
Joh 4:11 Sir, you have not even a *b*

Buckets
Nu 24:7 from his two leather *b*

Buckler
1Ki 10:17 to lay upon each *b*
2Ch 9:16 to lay upon each *b*
14:8 bearing the *b* and bending
Ps 35:2 Take hold of *b* and large
Jer 46:3 *b* and large shield, and
Eze 23:24 with large shield and *b*
38:4 with large shield and *b*
38:5 with *b* and helmet

Bucklers
1Ki 10:17 three hundred *b* of alloyed
2Ch 9:16 hundred *b* of alloyed gold
Eze 39:9 and *b* and large shields

Bud
Nu 17:5 his rod will *b*, and I shall
Job 8:12 yet in its *b*, not plucked off
Ho 14:7 and will *b* like the vine
Lu 21:30 they are already in the *b*

Budded
Nu 17:8 Aaron's rod . . . had *b*, and it
Heb 9:4 the rod of Aaron that *b* and

Budge
Mt 23:4 are not willing to *b* them

Buds
Ex 9:31 and the flax had flower *b*
Nu 17:8 *b* and blossoming flowers and
Ca 6:11 the *b* in the torrent valley

Build
Ge 2:22 God proceeded to *b* the rib
8:20 Noah began to *b* an altar to
11:4 Let us *b* ourselves a city and
13:18 he proceeded to *b* an altar
33:17 to *b* himself a house and
Ex 17:15 to *b* an altar and to call its
20:25 not *b* them as hewn stones
Nu 23:1 *B* for me on this spot seven
23:14 to *b* seven altars and to
23:29 *B* for me on this spot seven
32:16 *b* here stone flock pens for
32:24 *B* for yourselves cities for
32:34 *b* Dibon and Ataroth and Aroer
De 6:10 cities that you did not *b*
8:12 *b* good houses and indeed
20:20 cut it down and *b* siegeworks
22:8 In case you *b* a new house
25:9 *b* up his brother's household
27:5 *b* an altar there to Jehovah
27:6 *b* the altar of Jehovah your
28:30 You will *b* a house, but you
Jos 6:26 gets up and does *b* this city
8:30 to *b* an altar to Jehovah the
19:50 *b* up the city and dwell in
22:23 *b* for ourselves an altar
Jg 6:26 must *b* an altar to Jehovah
21:4 get up early and to *b* an altar
1Sa 2:35 *b* for him a lasting house
7:17 *b* an altar there to Jehovah
14:35 Saul proceeded to *b* an altar
2Sa 5:9 David began to *b* all around
5:11 began to *b* a house for David
7:5 *b* me a house for me to dwell
7:7 people not *b* me a house of
7:13 *b* a house for my name, and
7:27 A house I shall *b* for you
24:25 *b* there an altar to Jehovah
1Ki 2:36 *B* . . . a house in Jerusalem
5:3 *b* a house to the name of
5:5 will *b* the house to my name
5:18 and the stones to *b* the house
6:1 to *b* the house to Jehovah
6:15 *b* the walls of the house
6:36 *b* the inner courtyard with
7:2 to *b* the House of the Forest
7:8 to *b* for Pharaoh's daughter
8:16 to *b* a house for my name to
8:17 David my father to *b* a house
8:18 to *b* a house to my name
8:19 you . . . will not *b* the house
8:19 one that will *b* the house
8:20 *b* the house to the name of
9:15 to *b* the house of Jehovah
9:17 Solomon went on to *b* Gezer
9:19 desired to *b* in Jerusalem
11:7 to *b* a high place to Chemosh
11:38 will *b* you a lasting house
12:25 to *b* Shechem in the
15:17 and began to *b* Ramah, to
15:22 and King Asa began to *b*
16:24 *b* on the mountain and call
18:32 *b* the stones into an altar
2Ki 16:11 to *b* the altar
21:5 *b* altars to all the army of
1Ch 7:24 and she got to *b* Beth-horon
11:8 And he began to *b* the city
14:1 to *b* him a house
17:4 will not be you that will *b*
17:10 a house Jehovah will *b* for
17:12 one that will *b* me a house
17:25 purpose to *b* him a house
21:22 *b* in it an altar to Jehovah
22:6 command him to *b* a house to
22:7 to *b* a house to the name of
22:8 not *b* a house to my name
22:10 will *b* a house to my name
22:11 *b* the house of Jehovah your
22:19 *b* the sanctuary of Jehovah
28:2 *b* a resting house for the ark
28:2 I had made preparation to *b*
28:3 not *b* a house to my name
28:6 the one that will *b* my house
28:10 to *b* a house as a sanctuary
29:16 to *b* for you a house for
29:19 to *b* the castle for which
2Ch 2:1 *b* a house to Jehovah's name

2Ch 2:3 to *b* himself a house in which
2:6 retain power to *b* him a house
2:6 that I should *b* him a house
2:12 will *b* a house to Jehovah
3:1 Solomon started to *b* the
3:2 he started to *b* in the second
6:5 to *b* a house for my name to
6:7 to *b* a house to the name of
6:8 to *b* a house to my name
6:9 not *b* the house, but your son
6:9 the one that will *b* the house
6:10 that I might *b* the house to
8:5 *b* Upper Beth-horon and Lower
8:6 desired to *b* in Jerusalem and
11:5 *b* fortified cities in Judah
14:6 *b* fortified cities in Judah
14:7 *b* these cities and make
16:1 and began to *b* Ramah, so as
16:6 *b* with them Geba and Mizpah
20:8 *b* in it for you a sanctuary
33:5 *b* altars to all the army of
34:11 *b* with beams the houses
36:23 *b* him a house in Jerusalem
Ezr 1:2 to *b* him a house in Jerusalem
3:2 and *b* the altar of the God of
4:2 Let us *b* along with you; for
4:3 *b* to Jehovah the God of Israel
5:3 to *b* this house and to finish
5:9 to *b* this house and to finish
Ne 2:8 trees to *b* with timber the
2:18 Let us get up, and we must *b*
2:20 and we must *b*; but you
3:1 get up and *b* the Sheep Gate
3:15 to *b* it and to roof it over
4:10 not able to *b* on the wall
Job 20:19 that he did not proceed to *b*
Ps 28:5 down and not *b* them up
51:18 you *b* the walls of Jerusalem
69:35 will *b* the cities of Judah
78:69 *b* his sanctuary just like
89:4 *b* your throne to generation
102:16 will certainly *b* up Zion
Pr 24:27 also *b* up your household
Ec 3:3 to break down and a time to *b*
Ca 8:9 *b* upon her a battlement of
Isa 5:2 *b* a tower in the middle of it
9:10 with hewn stone we shall *b*
45:13 the one that will *b* my city
58:12 *b* up the places devastated
60:10 will actually *b* your walls
65:21 *b* houses and have occupancy
65:22 not *b* and someone else have
66:1 house that you people can *b*
Jer 1:10 to *b* and to plant
18:9 a kingdom to *b* it up and to
22:14 *b* for myself a roomy house
24:6 I will *b* them up, and I
29:5 *B* houses and inhabit them
29:28 *B* houses and inhabit them
31:28 alert toward them to *b* up
33:7 *b* them just as at the start
35:7 no house must you *b*, and
42:10 *b* you up and I shall not
49:16 *b* your nest high up just
52:4 *b* against her a siege wall
Eze 4:2 *b* a siege wall against it and
13:5 *b* up a stone wall in behalf
21:22 to *b* a siege wall
28:26 and *b* houses and plant
39:9 *b* fires with the armor and
39:15 also *b* beside it a marker
Am 9:11 *b* it up as in the days of
9:14 *b* the desolated cities and
Zep 1:13 *b* houses, but they will not
Hag 1:8 lumber. And *b* the house
Zec 5:11 *b* for her a house in the
6:12 *b* the temple of Jehovah
6:13 will *b* the temple of Jehovah
6:15 *b* in the temple of Jehovah
9:3 to *b* a rampart for herself
Mal 1:4 and *b* the devastated places
1:4 They, for their part, will *b*
Mt 16:18 on this rock-mass I will *b*
23:29 *b* the graves of the prophets
26:61 and *b* it up in three days
Mr 14:58 three days I will *b* another
Lu 11:47 you *b* the memorial tombs
12:18 storehouses and *b* bigger ones
14:28 wants to *b* a tower does not
14:30 *b* but was not able to finish
19:43 enemies will *b* around you a
Ac 7:49 of house will you *b* for me
20:32 which word can *b* you up and
1Co 10:23 but not all things *b* up
2Co 10:8 gave us to *b* you up and not
13:10 *b* up and not to tear down
Ga 2:18 once threw down I *b* up again

Builder
2Ki 24:14 craftsman and *b* of bulwarks
Mt 27:40 and *b* of it in three days
Mr 15:29 *b* of it in three days' time
Heb 11:10 *b* and maker of which city

Builders
1Ki 5:18 Solomon's *b* and Hiram's
5:18 Hiram's *b* and the Gebalites
2Ki 12:11 the *b* that were working at
22:6 and the *b* and the masons
24:16 *b* of bulwarks, a thousand
1Ch 14:1 cedar timbers and *b* of walls
2Ch 34:11 *b* to buy hewn stones and
Ezr 3:10 the *b* laid the foundation of
Ne 4:5 offense against the *b*
4:17 the *b* on the wall and those
4:18 the *b* were girded, each one
Ps 118:22 stone that the *b* rejected
127:1 *b* have worked hard on it
Jer 24:1 and the *b* of bulwarks, from
29:2 the *b* of bulwarks had gone
Eze 27:4 *b* have perfected your
Mt 21:42 stone that the *b* rejected
Mr 12:10 stone that the *b* rejected
Lu 20:17 stone which the *b* rejected
Ac 4:11 treated by you *b* as of no
1Pe 2:7 stone that the *b* rejected has

Building
Ge 4:17 he engaged in *b* a city and
10:11 and set himself to *b* Nineveh
11:8 gradually left off *b* the city
Ex 1:11 *b* cities as storage places for
32:5 went to *b* an altar before it
Jos 22:16 *b* for yourselves an altar
22:19 *b* for yourselves an altar
22:26 by *b* the altar, not for
22:29 by *b* an altar for burnt
1Sa 14:35 started altar *b* to Jehovah
2Sa 24:21 for *b* an altar to Jehovah
1Ki 3:1 he finished *b* his own house
5:5 *b* a house to the name of
6:9 *b* the house that he might
6:12 this house that you are *b*
6:14 Solomon continued *b* the
6:38 he was seven years at *b* it
9:1 Solomon had finished *b* the
14:23 *b* for themselves high
15:21 immediately quit *b* Ramah
15:22 which Baasha had been *b*
2Ki 17:9 *b* themselves high places in
25:1 *b* against it a siege wall
1Ch 15:1 *b* houses for himself in the
22:2 *b* the house of the true God
2Ch 2:4 I am *b* a house to the name of
2:5 the house that I am *b* will be
2:9 house that I am *b* will be
3:3 foundation for *b* the house of
14:7 went *b* and proving successful
16:5 quit *b* Ramah and stopped his
17:12 *b* fortified places and
27:3 he did a great deal of *b*
Ezr 4:1 *b* a temple to Jehovah the God
4:3 in *b* a house to our God
4:4 and disheartening them from *b*
4:12 *b* the rebellious and bad
5:4, 4 men that are *b* this *b*
6:14 men of the Jews were *b*
Ne 3:2 the men of Jericho did *b*
3:2 Zaccur the son of Imri did *b*
3:14 went *b* it and setting up its
4:3 Even what they are *b*, if a
4:6 So we kept *b* the wall, and
4:18 sword upon his hip, while *b*
6:6 That is why you are *b* the wall
Job 3:14 Those *b* desolate places for
12:14 that there may be no *b* up
Ps 104:3 *b* his upper chambers with
147:2 Jehovah is *b* Jerusalem
Jer 22:13 Woe to the one *b* his house
35:9 *b* houses for us to dwell
Eze 11:3 the *b* of houses close at hand
13:10 that is *b* a partition wall
16:24 *b* for yourself a mound and
17:17 by *b* a siege wall, in order
41:12 the *b* that was before the
41:12 the wall of the *b* was five
41:13 separated area and the *b*
41:15 the length of the *b* before
42:1 front of the *b* to the north
42:5 as regards the *b*
Eze 42:10 and before the *b*, there
Ho 8:14 Israel began . . . *b* temples
Am 9:6 *b* in the heavens his stairs
Mic 3:10 *b* Zion with acts of
7:11 day for *b* your stone walls
Hab 2:12 the one that is *b* a city
Lu 6:48 He is like a man *b* a house
11:48 but you are *b* their tombs
17:28 were planting, they were *b*
Ro 15:20 not be *b* on another man's
1Co 3:9 You people are . . . God's *b*
3:10 but someone else is *b* on it
3:10 keep watching how he is *b* on
2Co 5:1 we are to have a *b* from God
Eph 2:21 *b*, being harmoniously joined
4:12 for the *b* up of the body of
4:16 the *b* up of itself in love
4:29 *b* up as the need may be
1Th 5:11 and *b* one another up, just
Jude 20 *b* up yourselves on your most

Buildings
Mt 24:1 show him the *b* of the temple
Mr 13:1 stones and what sort of *b*
13:2 Do you behold these great *b*?

Builds
Job 39:27 that it *b* its nest high up
Ps 127:1 Jehovah himself *b* the house
Isa 44:15 *b* a fire and actually bakes
1Co 3:12 *b* on the foundation gold
8:1 puffs up, but love *b* up

Built
Ge 11:5 tower . . . sons of men had *b*
12:7 he *b* an altar there to Jehovah
12:8 he *b* an altar there to Jehovah
22:9 Abraham *b* an altar there and
26:25 *b* an altar there and called
35:7 he *b* an altar there and began
Ex 24:4 *b* at the foot of the mountain
Nu 13:22 Hebron had been *b* seven years
21:27 Let the city of Sihon be *b*
32:37 sons of Reuben *b* Heshbon and
32:38 of the cities that they *b*
De 20:5 man that has *b* a new house
Jos 22:10 *b* there an altar by the
22:11 *b* an altar on the frontier
24:13 cities that you had not *b*
Jg 1:26 and *b* a city and called its
6:24 So Gideon *b* an altar there to
6:28 on the altar that had been *b*
18:28 they *b* the city and took up
21:23 and *b* the cities and took up
Ru 4:11 *b* the house of Israel
1Ki 3:2 a house had not been *b* to the
6:2 the house that King Solomon *b*
6:5 he *b* against the wall of the
6:7 house, while it was being *b*
6:7 of quarry stone . . . it was *b*
6:7 while it was being *b*
6:10 *b* the side chambers against
6:16 he *b* twenty cubits at the
6:16 and *b* for it inside the
7:1 Solomon *b* in thirteen years
8:13 *b* a house of lofty abode for
8:27 this house that I have *b*
8:43 upon this house that I have *b*
8:44 house that I have *b* to your
8:48 house that I have *b* to your
9:3 this house that you have *b*
9:10 Solomon *b* the two houses
9:24 house that he had *b* for her
9:24 then that he *b* the Mound
9:25 altar that he had *b* for
10:4 and the house that he had *b*
11:27 had *b* the Mound
11:38 just as I have *b* for David
12:25 from there and *b* Penuel
15:23 the cities that he *b*, are
16:24 city that he *b* by the name
16:32 house of Baal that he *b* in
16:34 Hiel the Bethelite *b* Jericho
22:39 the house of ivory that he *b*
22:39 all the cities that he *b*
2Ki 14:22 *b* Elath and got to restore
15:35 *b* the upper gate of the
16:18 had *b* in the house and the
21:3 *b* again the high places that
21:4 he *b* altars in the house of
23:13 had *b* to Ashtoreth the
23:19 the kings of Israel had *b*
1Ch 6:10 the house that Solomon *b* in
6:32 until Solomon *b* the house of
8:12 Shemed, who *b* Ono and Lod
17:6 not *b* me a house of cedars

1Ch 21:26 David *b* there an altar to
22:5 the house to be *b* to Jehovah
22:19 *b* to the name of Jehovah
2Ch 6:2 *b* a house of lofty abode for
6:18 this house that I have *b*
6:33 this house that I have *b*
6:34 house that I have *b* to your
6:38 house that I have *b* to your
8:1 Solomon had *b* the house of
8:4 that he had *b* in Hamath
8:11 house that he had *b* for her
8:12 he had *b* before the porch
9:3 and the house that he had *b*
16:6 with which Baasha had *b*
26:6 *b* cities in Ashdod territory
26:9 Uzziah *b* towers in Jerusalem
26:10 *b* towers in the wilderness
27:3 *b* the upper gate of
27:4 And cities he *b* in the
27:4 *b* fortified places and
32:5 *b* up all the broken-down
33:3 *b* again the high places that
33:4 *b* altars in the house of
33:14 *b* an outer wall for the
33:15 altars that he had *b* in the
33:19 *b* high places and set up the
35:3 the king of Israel *b*
Ezr 5:8 *b* with stones rolled into
5:11 house that had been *b* many
5:11 king of Israel *b* and finished
6:14 *b* and finished it due to the
Ne 3:3 the sons of Hassenaah *b*
3:13 *b* it and then set up its
7:4 and there were no houses *b*
12:29 that the singers had *b* for
Job 22:23 you will be *b* up
27:18 *b* his house like a mere
Ps 89:2 Loving-kindness will stay *b*
122:3 Jerusalem is one that is *b*
Pr 9:1 True wisdom has *b* its house
14:1 woman has *b* up her house
24:3 wisdom a household will be *b*
Ec 2:4 I *b* houses for myself
9:14 *b* against it great strongholds
Ca 4:4 *b* in courses of stone, upon
Jer 7:31 they have *b* the high places
12:16 *b* up in the midst of my
19:5 they *b* the high places of
31:38 *b* to Jehovah from the tower
32:31 day that they *b* it, clear
32:35 *b* the high places of Baal
45:4 have *b* up I am tearing down
La 3:5 He has *b* against me, that he
Eze 16:25 you *b* your height and you
16:31 *b* your mound at the head
27:5 they *b* for you all the planks
36:36 have *b* the things torn down
40:5 the breadth of the thing *b*
Da 4:30 *b* for the royal house with
Am 5:11 houses . . . you have *b*
Hag 1:2 house of Jehovah . . . to be *b*
Zec 1:16 My own house will be *b* in
8:9 for the temple to be *b*
Mal 3:15 of wickedness have been *b* up
Mt 7:24 who *b* his house upon the
7:26 *b* his house upon the sand
Lu 4:29 which their city had been *b*
6:48 because of its being well *b*
6:49 *b* a house upon the ground
7:5 *b* the synagogue for us
Joh 2:20 temple was *b* in forty-six
18:18 they had *b* a charcoal fire
Ac 7:47 Solomon *b* a house for him
9:31 period of peace, being *b* up
1Co 3:14 anyone's work that he has *b*
8:10 be *b* up to the point of
14:17 other man is not being *b* up
Eph 2:20 *b* up upon the foundation
2:22 *b* up together into a place
Col 2:7 rooted and being *b* up in him
1Pe 2:5 being *b* up a spiritual house

Bukki
Nu 34:22 *B* the son of Jogli
1Ch 6:5 Abishua . . . father to *B*
6:5 *B* . . . became father to Uzzi
6:51 *B* his son, Uzzi his son
Ezr 7:4 son of Uzzi the son of *B*

Bukkiah
1Ch 25:4 the sons of Heman, *B*
25:13 the sixth for *B*, his sons

Bul
1Ki 6:38 *B*, that is the eighth month

Bulbul
Isa 38:14 the *b*, so I keep chirping
Jer 8:7 the swift and the *b*—they

Bulged
Ps 73:7 Their eye has *b* from fatness

Bull
Ge 18:7 get a tender and good young *b*
18:8 young *b* that he had got ready
Ex 20:17 must not desire . . . his *b*
21:28 in case a *b* should gore a
21:28 *b* is to be stoned without
21:28 owner of the *b* is free from
21:29 if a *b* was formerly in the
21:29 *b* is to be stoned and also
21:32 a slave girl that the *b* gored
21:32 and the *b* will be stoned
21:33 a *b* or an ass does fall into
21:35, 35 *b* should hurt another's *b*
21:35 sell the live *b* and divide
21:36 *b* was in the habit of goring
21:36, 36 with *b* for *b*, and the
22:1 steal a *b* or a sheep and he
22:1 five of the herd for the *b* and
22:4 stolen, from *b* to ass and to
22:9 transgression, concerning a *b*
22:10 an ass or *b* or sheep or any
22:30 with your *b* and your sheep
23:4 your enemy's *b* or his ass
23:12 your *b* and your ass may rest
29:1 Take a young *b*, and two rams
29:3 also the *b* and the two rams
29:10 present the *b* before the tent
29:11 must slaughter the *b* before
29:36 *b* of the sin offering daily
34:19 the male firstling of *b* and
Le 1:5 young *b* must be slaughtered
4:3 young *b* to Jehovah as a sin
4:4 bring the *b* to the entrance of
4:4 slaughter the *b* before Jehovah
4:8 of the *b* of the sin offering
4:10 *b* of the communion sacrifice
4:11 the skin of the *b* and all its
4:12 the entire *b* taken out to the
4:14 a young *b* for a sin offering
4:15 the *b* must be slaughtered
4:20 do to the *b* just as he did to
4:20 other *b* of the sin offering
4:21 *b* taken out to the outskirts
4:21 just as he burned the first *b*
7:23 not eat any fat of a *b* or a
8:2 the *b* of the sin offering and
8:14 the *b* of the sin offering
8:14 the *b* of the sin offering
8:17 had the *b* and its skin and its
9:4 a *b* and a ram for communion
9:18 slaughtered the *b* and the ram
9:19 the fatty pieces of the *b* and
16:3 a young *b* for a sin offering
16:6 the *b* of the sin offering
16:11 Aaron must present the *b* of
16:11 slaughter the *b* of the sin
16:27 *b* of the sin offering and the
17:3 slaughters a *b* or a young ram
22:23 *b* or a sheep having a member
22:27 *b* or a young ram or a goat
22:28 *b* and a sheep, you must not
23:18 and one young *b* and two rams
27:26 *b* or sheep, it belongs to
Nu 7:3 chieftains and a *b* for each one
7:15 one young *b*, one ram, one
7:21 one young *b*, one ram, one
7:27 one young *b*, one ram, one
7:33 young *b* . . . burnt offering
7:39 young *b* . . . burnt offering
7:45 young *b* . . . burnt offering
7:51 young *b* . . . burnt offering
7:57 young *b* . . . burnt offering
7:63 young *b* . . . burnt offering
7:69 young *b* . . . burnt offering
7:75 young *b* . . . a burnt offering
7:81 young *b* . . . burnt offering
8:8 young *b* and its grain offering
8:8 young *b* for a sin offering
15:11 for each *b* or for each ram
15:24 young *b* as a burnt offering
18:17 Only the firstborn *b* or
22:4 *b* licking up the green growth
23:2 a *b* and a ram on each altar
23:4 a *b* and a ram on each altar
23:14 to offer up a *b* and a ram on
23:22 course like that of a wild *b*
23:30 offering up a *b* and a ram on
Nu 24:8 The swift course of a wild *b*
28:12 with oil for each *b*
28:14 half a hin of wine for a *b*
28:20 three tenth measures for a *b*
28:28 grain offering . . . for each *b*
29:2 render up . . . one young *b*, one
29:3 tenth measures for the *b*
29:8 one young *b*, one ram, seven
29:9 grain offering . . . for the *b*
29:14 grain offering . . . for each *b*
29:36 to Jehovah, one *b*, one ram
29:37 drink offerings for the *b*
De 5:14 nor your *b* nor your ass nor
5:21 his *b* or his ass or anything
14:4 the *b*, the sheep and the goat
15:19 the firstborn of your *b*
17:1 a *b* or a sheep in which there
18:3 a victim, whether a *b* or a
22:1 the *b* of your brother or his
22:4 his *b* fall down on the road
22:10 not plow with a *b* and an ass
25:4 You must not muzzle a *b*
28:31 Your *b* slaughtered there
33:17 firstborn of a *b* his splendor
33:17 are the horns of a wild *b*
Jos 6:21 and to *b* and sheep and ass
7:24 his *b* and his ass and his
Jg 6:4 or *b* or ass remain in Israel
6:25, 25 Take the young *b*, the *b*
6:25 young *b* of seven years, and
6:26 young *b* and offer it up as a
6:28 young *b* had been offered up on
1Sa 1:24 with a three-year-old *b*
1:25 Then they slaughtered the *b*
12:3 Whose *b* have I taken or
14:34 each one of you, his *b* and
14:34 brought near each one his *b*
15:3 *b* as well as sheep, camel as
22:19 *b* and ass and sheep with
2Sa 6:13 sacrificed a *b* and a fatling
1Ki 18:23 one young *b* and cut it in
18:23 dress the other young *b*
18:25 one young *b* and dress it
18:26 young *b* that he gave them
18:33 cut the young *b* in pieces
2Ch 13:9 power by means of a young *b*
Ne 5:18 one *b*, six select sheep and
Job 6:5 Or a *b* low over its fodder
21:10 own *b* actually impregnates
24:3 the widow's *b* as a pledge
39:9 a wild *b* want to serve you
39:10 bind a wild *b* fast with its
40:15 grass it eats just as a *b*
Ps 50:9 take out of your house a *b*
66:15 render up a *b* with he-goats
69:31 more pleasing . . . than a *b*
69:31 a young *b* displaying horns
92:10 horn like that of a wild *b*
106:20 representation of a *b*, an
Pr 7:22 *b* that comes even to the
14:4 because of the power of a *b*
15:17 a manger-fed *b* and hatred
Isa 1:3 A *b* well knows its buyer, and
11:7 eat straw just like the *b*
32:20 feet of the *b* and of the ass
65:25 eat straw just like the *b*
66:3 The one slaughtering the *b* is
Eze 43:19 young *b*, the son of the herd
43:21 young *b*, the sin offering
43:22 from sin with the young *b*
43:23 young *b*, the son of the herd
43:25 *b*, the son of the herd
45:18 should take a young *b*
45:22 young *b* as a sin offering
45:24 ephah for the young *b* and
46:6 young *b*, the son of the herd
46:7 ephah for the young *b* and
46:11 ephah for the young *b* and
Lu 13:15 on the sabbath untie his *b*
14:5 son or *b* falls into a well
15:23 bring the fattened young *b*
15:27 the fattened young *b*, because
15:30 slaughtered . . . young *b* for
1Co 9:9 must not muzzle a *b* when it
1Ti 5:18 must not muzzle a *b* when it
Re 4:7 creature is like a young *b*

Bull's
Ex 29:10 their hands upon the *b* head
29:12 take some of the *b* blood and
29:14 *b* flesh and its skin and its
Le 4:4 lay his hand upon the *b* head
4:5 the *b* blood and bring it into
4:7 the rest of the *b* blood he

Le 4:15 their hands upon the *b* head
4:16 bring some of the *b* blood
16:14 *b* blood and spatter it with
16:15 as he did with the *b* blood
16:18 take some of the *b* blood
Eze 1:10 had a *b* face on the left

Bulls
Ge 32:5 come to have *b* and asses
32:15 ten *b*, twenty she-asses and
49:6 they hamstrung *b*
Ex 24:5 and sacrificed *b* as sacrifices
Nu 7:87 burnt offering being twelve *b*
7:88 sacrifice being twenty-four *b*
8:12 hands upon the heads of the *b*
23:1 on this spot seven *b* and seven
23:29 seven *b* and seven rams
28:11 two young *b* and one ram
28:19 two young *b* and one ram and
28:27 two young *b*, one ram, seven
29:13 thirteen young *b*, two rams
29:14 each bull of the thirteen *b*
29:17 second day twelve young *b*
29:18 drink offerings for the *b*
29:20 And on the third day eleven *b*
29:21 drink offerings for the *b*
29:23 the fourth day ten *b*, two
29:24 drink offerings for the *b*
29:26 And on the fifth day nine *b*
29:27 drink offerings for the *b*
29:29 And on the sixth day eight *b*
29:30 drink offerings for the *b*
29:32 on the seventh day seven *b*
29:33 drink offerings for the *b*
1Sa 11:7 a pair of *b* and cut them in
1Ki 1:19 he sacrificed *b* and fatlings
1:25 sacrifice *b* and fatlings and
7:25 standing upon twelve *b*
7:29 were lions, *b* and cherubs
7:29 beneath the lions and the *b*
7:44 twelve *b* beneath the sea
18:23 give us two young *b*, and
19:20 left the *b* and went running
19:21 the *b* and sacrificed them
19:21 the *b* he boiled their flesh
2Ki 16:17 off the copper *b* that were
1Ch 13:9 the *b* nearly caused an upset
15:26 to sacrifice seven young *b*
29:21 a thousand young *b*, a
2Ch 4:4 It was standing upon twelve *b*
4:15 sea and the twelve *b* under
29:21 bringing seven *b* and
30:24 a thousand *b* and seven
30:24 a thousand *b* and ten
Ezr 6:9 young *b* as well as rams and
6:17 hundred *b*, two hundred rams
7:17 *b*, rams, lambs and their
8:35 twelve *b* for all Israel
Job 42:8 take for yourselves seven *b*
Ps 22:12 young *b* have surrounded me
22:21 from the horns of wild *b*
29:6 like the sons of wild *b*
50:13 eat the flesh of powerful *b*
51:19 *b* will be offered up on your
68:30 reeds, the assembly of *b*
Isa 1:11 blood of young *b* and male
7:25 place for letting *b* loose
34:7 wild *b* must come down with
34:7 young *b* with the powerful
Jer 50:27 Massacre all her young *b*
52:20 twelve copper *b* that were
Eze 39:18 and he-goats, young *b*
45:23 to Jehovah seven young *b*
Da 4:25 to you to eat just like *b*
4:32 even to you to eat just like *b*
4:33 began to eat just like *b*
5:21 give him to eat just like *b*
Ho 12:11 they have sacrificed even *b*
14:2 the young *b* of our lips
Am 6:4 *b* from among fattened calves
Mt 22:4 my dinner, my *b* and fattened
Ac 14:13 brought *b* and garlands to
1Co 9:9 Is it *b* God is caring for?
Heb 9:12 of goats and of young *b*
9:13 the blood of goats and of *b*
9:19 blood of the young *b* and
10:4 blood of *b* and of goats to

Bulwark
Ps 91:4 will be a large shield and *b*
Hab 2:1 stationed upon the *b*; and I

Bulwarks
2Sa 22:46 quaking out from their *b*
2Ki 24:14 craftsman and builder of *b*
2Ki 24:16 builders of *b*, a thousand
Ps 18:45 quaking out from their *b*
Jer 24:1 and the builders of *b*, from
29:2 the builders of *b* had gone
Mic 7:17 in agitation out of their *b*

Bump
Joh 11:9 does not *b* against anything

Bumps
Joh 11:10 the night, he *b* against

Bunah
1Ch 2:25 sons of Jerahmeel . . . *B*

Bunch
Ex 12:22 take a *b* of hyssop and dip

Bunches
Zec 4:12 What are the two *b* of twigs

Bundle
Ge 42:35 each one's *b* of money in his
Ac 28:3 *b* of sticks and laid it upon

Bundles
Ge 42:35 got to see their *b* of money
Ru 2:16 some from the *b* of ears for
Mt 13:30 weeds and bind them in *b* to

Bunni
Ne 9:4 *B*, Sherebiah, Bani and Chenani
10:15 *B*, Azgad, Bebai
11:15 Hashabiah the son of *B*

Burden
Ge 45:17 Load your beasts of *b* and go
Ex 22:5 send out his beasts of *b* and
Nu 20:4 our beasts of *b* to die there
20:8 and their beasts of *b* drink
20:11 beasts of *b* began to drink
De 1:12 carry by myself the *b* of you
2Sa 13:25 we may not be a *b* upon you
19:35 a *b* anymore to my lord the
1Ki 5:15 seventy thousand *b* bearers
2Ch 2:2 men as *b* bearers and eighty
2:18 thousand of them *b* bearers
34:13 over the *b* bearers, and the
35:3 as a *b* upon the shoulder
Ne 4:10 power of the *b* bearer has
4:17 carrying the *b* of load bearers
13:15 and figs and every sort of *b*
13:19 no *b* might come in on the
Job 7:20 so that I should become a *b*
Ps 55:22 Throw your *b* upon Jehovah
78:48 beasts of *b* even to the hail
81:6 his shoulder even from the *b*
Isa 1:14 To me they have become a *b*
46:1 a *b* for the tired animals
46:2 to furnish escape for the *b*
Jer 23:33 What is the *b* of Jehovah?
23:33 You people are—O what a *b*!
23:34 who say, The *b* of Jehovah!
23:36 the *b* of Jehovah you people
23:36 the *b* itself becomes to
23:38 And if The *b* of Jehovah!
23:38 This word is the very *b* of
23:38 not say: The *b* of Jehovah!
Ho 8:10 the *b* of king and princes
Mt 20:12 who bore the *b* of the day
21:5 the offspring of a beast of *b*
Ac 15:28 favored adding no further *b*
23:24 beasts of *b* that they may
2Co 11:9 become a *b* to a single one
12:13 did not become a *b* to you
12:14 I will not become a *b*
12:16 I did not *b* you down
1Th 2:6 an expensive *b* as apostles of
2:9 not to put an expensive *b* upon
2Th 3:8 an expensive *b* upon any one
1Ti 5:16 not be under the *b*
2Pe 2:16 A voiceless beast of *b*
Re 2:24 putting upon you any other *b*

Burden-bearing
Ex 1:11 oppressing them in their *b*

Burdened
Pr 28:17 man *b* with the bloodguilt

Burdens
Ge 49:15 his shoulder to bear *b* and he
Ex 2:11 at the *b* they were bearing
5:4 Go bearing your *b*
5:5 desist from their bearing of *b*
6:6 under the *b* of the Egyptians
6:7 out from under the *b* of Egypt
Job 37:11 he *b* the cloud, His light
Ga 6:2 carrying the *b* of one another

Burdensome
Ex 10:14 locusts . . . were very *b*
Zec 12:3 Jerusalem a *b* stone to all
1Jo 5:3 his commandments are not *b*

Burial
Ge 23:4 *b* place among you that I may
23:6 choicest of our *b* places bury
23:6 hold back his *b* place from
23:9 the possession of a *b* place
23:20 *b* place at the hands of the
49:30 the possession of a *b* place
50:5 In my *b* place which I have
50:13 a *b* place from Ephron the
Ex 14:11 no *b* places at all in Egypt
Nu 19:16 or a *b* place will be unclean
19:18 or the corpse or the *b* place
Jg 8:32 buried in the *b* place of Joash
16:31 in the *b* place of Manoah his
2Sa 2:32 in the *b* place of his father
3:32 *b* of Abner in Hebron
3:32 weep at Abner's *b* place, and
4:12 *b* place of Abner in Hebron
17:23 *b* place of his forefathers
19:37 the *b* place of my father
21:14 *b* place of Kish his father
1Ki 13:22 *b* place of your forefathers
13:30 in his own *b* place
13:31 bury me in the *b* place in
14:13 will come into a *b* place
2Ki 13:21 man into Elisha's *b* place
23:6 its dust upon the *b* place of
23:16 he got to see the *b* places
23:16 the bones from the *b* places
23:17 *b* place of the man of the
2Ch 16:14 grand *b* place that he had
21:20 not in the *b* places of the
24:25 in the *b* places of the kings
26:23 *b* field that belonged to
28:27 *b* places of the kings of
32:33 *b* places of the sons of
34:4 surface of the *b* places
Ne 2:3 the *b* places of my forefathers
2:5 the *b* places of my forefathers
3:16 front of the *B* Places of David
Job 3:22 because they find a *b* place
5:26 come in vigor to the *b* place
10:19 the belly to the *b* place I
Ps 5:9 throat is an opened *b* place
88:5 ones lying in the *b* place
88:11 declared in the *b* place
Isa 14:19 without a *b* place for you
22:16 for yourself here a *b* place
22:16 is hewing out his *b* place
53:9 make his *b* place even with
65:4 among the *b* places, who also
Jer 5:16 is like an open *b* place
20:17 become to me my *b* place
22:19 With the *b* of a he-ass he
Eze 32:22 *b* places are round about
32:23 her *b* places have been put
32:25 Her *b* places are round about
32:26 Her *b* places are round about
37:12 I am opening your *b* places
37:12 up out of your *b* places
37:13 when I open your *b* places
37:13 up out of your *b* places
39:11 a *b* place in Israel, the
Na 1:14 shall make a *b* place for you
Mt 26:12 the preparation of me for *b*
Mr 14:8 my body in view of the *b*
Joh 12:7 view of the day of my *b*
19:40 custom of preparing for *b*
Ac 8:2 men carried Stephen to the *b*

Buried
Ge 15:15 you will be *b* at a good old
23:19 Abraham *b* Sarah his wife in
25:9 *b* him in the cave of
25:10 Abraham was *b*, and also
35:8 *b* at the foot of Bethel under
35:19 Rachel died and was *b* on the
35:29 Esau and Jacob . . . *b* him
48:7 I *b* her there on the way to
49:31 they *b* Abraham and Sarah his
49:31 they *b* Isaac and Rebekah
49:31 and there I *b* Leah
50:13 *b* him in the cave of the
50:14 after he had *b* his father
Nu 11:34 there they *b* the people who
20:1 died and there that she was *b*
De 10:6 died, and he got to be *b* there
Jos 24:30 So they *b* him in the
24:32 they *b* in Shechem in the
24:33 they *b* him in the Hill of

Jg 2:9 they *b* him in the territory
8:32 was *b* in the burial place of
10:2 he died and was *b* in Shamir
10:5 Jair died and was *b* in Kamon
12:7 died and was *b* in his city in
12:10 Ibzan . . . was *b* in Bethlehem
12:12 Elon . . . was *b* in Aijalon in
12:15 Abdon . . . was *b* in Pirathon
16:31 and *b* him between Zorah and
Ru 1:17 there is where I shall be *b*
1Sa 31:13 bones and *b* them under the
2Sa 2:4 were the ones that *b* Saul
2:5 Saul, in that you *b* him
4:12 *b* in the burial place of
17:23 he was *b* in the burial place
21:14 they *b* the bones of Saul
1Ki 2:10 was *b* in the city of David
2:34 *b* at his own house in the
11:43 was *b* in the city of David
13:31 man of the true God is *b*
14:18 they *b* him, and all Israel
14:31 was *b* with his forefathers
15:8 *b* him in the city of David
15:24 *b* with his forefathers in
16:6 and was *b* in Tirzah
16:28 and was *b* in Samaria
22:37 they *b* the king in Samaria
22:50 *b* with his forefathers in
2Ki 8:24 was *b* with his forefathers
9:28 *b* him in his grave with his
10:35 they *b* him in Samaria
12:21 *b* him with his forefathers
13:9 and they *b* him in Samaria
13:13 Jehoash was *b* in Samaria
13:20 Elisha died and they *b* him
14:16 *b* in Samaria with the kings
14:20 he was *b* in Jerusalem with
15:7 *b* him with his forefathers
15:38 *b* with his forefathers in
16:20 *b* with his forefathers in
21:18 *b* in the garden of his house
21:26 *b* him in his grave in the
23:30 and *b* him in his grave
1Ch 10:12 *b* their bones under the big
2Ch 9:31 *b* him in the city of David
12:16 *b* in the city of David
14:1 *b* him in the city of David
16:14 *b* him in his grand burial
21:1 *b* with his forefathers in
21:20 *b* him in the city of David
22:9 put him to death and *b* him
24:16 *b* him in the city of David
24:25 *b* him in the city of David
25:28 *b* him with his forefathers
26:23 *b* him with his forefathers
27:9 *b* him in the city of David
28:27 *b* him in the city, in
32:33 *b* him in the ascent to the
33:20 *b* him at his house
35:24 *b* in the graveyard of his
Job 27:15 *b* during a deadly plague
Ec 8:10 seen the wicked ones being *b*
Jer 8:2 gathered, nor will they be *b*
16:4 neither will they be *b*
16:6 They will not be *b*, neither
20:6 be *b* with all your lovers
22:19 he will be *b*, with a
25:33 be gathered up or be *b*
Eze 39:15 *b* it in the Valley of Gog's
Mt 14:12 *b* him and came and reported
Lu 16:22 the rich man died and was *b*
Ac 2:29 *b* and his tomb is among us
5:6 and carried him out and *b* him
5:9 of those who *b* your husband
5:10 *b* her alongside her husband
Ro 6:4 we were *b* with him through
1Co 15:4 he was *b*, yes, that he has
Col 2:12 *b* with him in his baptism

Burn

Ex 12:10 you should *b* with fire
29:14 *b* with fire outside the camp
29:34 must *b* what is left over
Le 4:12 *b* it upon wood in the fire
4:21 of the camp and must *b* it
6:12 *b* wood on it morning by
8:32 bread you will *b* with fire
10:6 which Jehovah has made *b*
13:52 he must *b* the garment or the
13:55 is unclean. You should *b* it
13:57 *b* in the fire whatever it is
16:27 *b* their skins and their
20:14 *b* him and them in the fire
Nu 24:22 to be one to *b* Kain down
De 7:5 images you should *b* with fire
7:25 their gods you should *b* in
9:21 *b* it in the fire and to crush
12:3 should *b* their sacred poles
12:31 *b* in the fire to their gods
13:16 *b* in the fire the city and
32:22 And it will *b* down to Sheol
Jos 11:6 their chariots you will *b* in
11:13 that Israel did not *b*
11:13 Joshua did *b* Hazor by itself
Jg 9:52 entrance of the tower to *b* it
12:1 we shall *b* over you with fire
14:15 we shall *b* you and the house
1Sa 30:1 Ziklag and *b* it with fire
1Ki 13:2 men's bones he will *b* upon
2Ki 25:9 *b* the house of Jehovah and
2Ch 2:4 *b* perfumed incense before him
26:16 *b* incense upon the altar of
26:18 *b* incense to Jehovah, but
26:18 sanctified, to *b* incense
28:3 *b* up his sons in the fire
29:7 incense they did not *b*, and
36:19 to *b* the house of the true
Ne 10:34 *b* upon the altar of Jehovah
Ps 79:5 your ardor *b* just like fire
Isa 47:14 will certainly *b* them up
Jer 4:4 *b* with no one to do the
7:20 it must *b*, and it will not
7:31 in order to *b* their sons
19:5 to *b* their sons in the fire
21:10 certainly *b* it with fire
21:12 like a fire and actually *b*
32:29 and must *b* it down and the
34:2 and he must *b* it with fire
34:22 and *b* it with fire; and the
36:25 king not to *b* the roll
37:8 capture it and *b* it with
37:10 *b* this city with fire
38:18 actually *b* it with fire
43:12 *b* them and lead them
43:13 Egypt he will *b* with fire
52:13 *b* the house of Jehovah and
Eze 5:2 A third you will *b* in the
16:41 *b* your houses with fire and
23:47 their houses they will *b*
39:9 *b* and build fires with the
43:21 *b* it in the appointed place
Na 2:13 I will *b* up her war chariot
Mt 3:12 chaff he will *b* up with fire
13:30 in bundles to *b* them up
Lu 3:17 the chaff he will *b* up with
Re 17:16 completely *b* her with fire

Burned

Ge 30:2 Jacob's anger *b* against Rachel
38:24 and let her be *b*
Ex 22:6 without fail for what was *b*
Le 4:12 are poured out it should be *b*
4:21 just as he *b* the first bull
6:30 It is to be *b* with fire
7:17 is to be *b* with fire
7:19 It is to be *b* with fire
8:17 dung *b* with fire outside the
9:11 he *b* the flesh and the skin
10:16 and, look! it had been *b* up
13:52 It should be *b* in the fire
16:28 one who *b* them should wash
19:6 should be *b* in the fire
21:9 She should be *b* in the fire
Nu 16:39 those who had been *b* up had
19:5 cow must be *b* under his eyes
19:5 with its dung will be *b*
19:8 one who *b* it will wash his
31:10 walled camps they *b* with
Jos 6:24 they *b* the city with fire
7:15 will be *b* with fire, he and
7:25 they *b* them with fire
8:28 Joshua *b* Ai and reduced it to
11:9 chariots he *b* in the fire
11:11 he *b* Hazor in the fire
Jg 15:6 and *b* her and her father with
18:27 the city they *b* with fire
1Sa 30:3 there it was *b* with fire
30:14 and Ziklag we *b* with fire
31:12 to Jabesh and *b* them there
2Sa 23:7 they will thoroughly be *b* up
1Ki 9:16 captured Gezer and *b* it with
15:13 her horrible idol and *b* it
16:18 *b* the king's house over
2Ki 10:26 house of Baal and *b* each one
23:4 *b* them outside Jerusalem on
23:6 *b* it in the torrent valley
23:11 chariots of the sun he *b* in
23:15 Then he *b* the high place
23:15 and *b* the sacred pole
23:16 *b* them upon the altar
2Ki 23:20 and *b* human bones upon them
23:26 his anger *b* against Judah
25:9 house of every great man he *b*
1Ch 14:12 so they were *b* in the fire
2Ch 15:16 *b* it in the torrent valley
34:5 he *b* upon their altars
36:19 dwelling towers they *b*
Ne 1:3 gates have been *b* with fire
2:17 gates have been *b* with fire
4:2 rubbish when they are *b*
Ps 74:8 of God must be *b* in the land
80:16 It is *b* with fire, cut off
Pr 6:27 his very garments not be *b*
Isa 1:7 your cities are *b* with fire
3:14 *b* down the vineyard
44:19 half of it I have *b* up in a
Jer 9:10 *b* so that there is no man
9:12 *b* like the wilderness
36:27 king had *b* up the roll
36:28 king of Judah *b* up
36:29 *b* up this roll, saying
36:32 king of Judah had *b* in the
38:17 city itself will not be *b*
38:23 city will be *b* with fire
39:8 Chaldeans *b* with fire, and
44:6 *b* in the cities of Judah and
51:32 papyrus boats they have *b*
52:13 great house he *b* with fire
Mic 1:7 will be *b* in the fire
Mt 13:40 weeds are collected and *b*
22:7 and *b* their city
Joh 15:6 into the fire and they are *b*
Ac 19:19 books together and *b* them up
1Co 3:15 if anyone's work is *b* up, he
Heb 6:8 and it ends up with being *b*
13:11 are *b* up outside the camp
Re 8:7 a third of the earth was *b* up
8:7 a third of the trees was *b* up
8:7 the green vegetation was *b* up
18:8 and she will be completely *b*

Burning

Ge 11:3 bake them with a *b* process
Ex 3:2 here the thornbush was *b* with
15:7 You send out your *b* anger, it
30:1 an altar . . . for *b* incense
32:12 Turn from your *b* anger and
Le 6:12 the altar will be kept *b* on
6:13 kept constantly *b* on the altar
10:6 do the weeping over the *b*
16:12 *b* coals of fire from off the
26:16 *b* fever, causing the eyes to
Nu 19:6 the midst of the *b* of the cow
19:17 of the *b* of the sin offering
25:4 that the *b* anger of Jehovah
32:14 *b* anger of Jehovah against
De 4:11 the mountain was *b* with fire
5:23 the mountain was *b* with fire
9:15 the mountain was *b* with fire
13:17 may turn from his *b* anger
28:22 *b* fever and inflammation
29:23 sulphur and salt and *b*, so
32:24 and eaten up by *b* fever And
1Sa 28:18 execute his *b* anger against
2Sa 22:13 *b* coals of fire blazed up
2Ki 17:31 *b* their sons in the fire to
23:26 the great *b* of his anger
2Ch 16:14 great funeral *b* for him
21:19 make a *b* for him like the
21:19 the *b* for his forefathers
26:19 was a censer for *b* incense
28:11 Jehovah's *b* anger is
28:13 is *b* anger against Israel
29:10 *b* anger may turn back from
30:8 his *b* anger may turn back
Ezr 10:14 the *b* anger of our God from
Ne 13:18 the *b* anger against Israel
Job 20:23 send his *b* anger upon him
Ps 18:12 Hail and *b* coals of fire
18:13 Hail and *b* coals of fire
38:7 loins have become full of *b*
39:3 the fire kept *b*
58:9 live green as well as the *b*
69:24 own *b* anger overtake them
78:49 sending . . . them his *b* anger
88:16 flashes of *b* anger have
89:46 keep on *b* just like a fire
106:18 fire went *b* among their
120:4 *b* coals of the broom trees
124:3 anger was *b* against us
140:10 *b* coals be dropped upon
Isa 4:4 and by the spirit of *b* down
5:5 be destined for *b* down
6:13 become something for *b* down
9:5 for *b* as food for fire

Isa 10:16, 16 a *b* will keep *b* away
10:16 away like the *b* of a fire
13:9 fury and with *b* anger, in
13:13 the day of his *b* anger
30:27 *b* with his anger and with
30:33 sulphur, is *b* against it
34:9 land must become as *b* pitch
40:16 for keeping a fire *b*, and
44:15 for man to keep a fire *b*
64:11 something for *b* in the fire
65:5 a fire *b* all day long
Jer 4:8 the *b* anger of Jehovah has not
4:26 because of his *b* anger
12:13 the *b* anger of Jehovah
20:9 a *b* fire shut up in my bones
25:37 the *b* anger of Jehovah
25:38 because of his *b* anger
30:24 *b* anger of Jehovah will
34:5 they will make a *b* for you
36:22 with a brazier *b* before him
49:37 calamity, my *b* anger
51:45 the *b* anger of Jehovah
La 1:12 in the day of his *b* anger
2:3 he keeps *b* like a flaming fire
4:11 He has poured out his *b* anger
Eze 1:13 was like *b* coals of fire
Da 3:6 into the *b* fiery furnace
3:11 into the *b* fiery furnace
3:15 into the *b* fiery furnace
3:17 Out of the *b* fiery furnace
3:20 into the *b* fiery furnace
3:21 into the *b* fiery furnace
3:23 midst of the *b* fiery furnace
3:26 door of the *b* fiery furnace
7:9 its wheels were a *b* fire
7:11 it was given to the *b* fire
Ho 7:4 like a furnace set *b* by a baker
7:6 it is *b* inside them
7:6 *b* as with a flaming fire
11:9 shall not express my *b* anger
Am 2:1 *b* the bones of the king of
4:11 a log snatched out of the *b*
6:10 be *b* them one by one
Jon 3:9 turn back from his *b* anger
Hab 3:5 *b* fever would go forth at his
Zep 2:2 the *b* anger of Jehovah
3:8 denunciation, all my *b* anger
Mal 4:1 that is *b* like the furnace
Mt 20:12 of the day and the *b* heat
Lu 12:35 and your lamps be *b*
24:32 hearts *b* as he was speaking
Joh 5:35 was a *b* and shining lamp
Eph 6:16 the wicked one's *b* missiles
Jas 1:11 sun rises with its *b* heat
1Pe 4:12 puzzled at the *b* among you
Re 4:5 seven lamps of fire *b* before
8:8 a great mountain *b* with fire
8:10 a great star *b* as a lamp fell
18:9 the smoke from the *b* of her
18:18 the smoke from the *b* of her

Burnings
Isa 33:12 become as the *b* of lime
Jer 34:5 *b* for your fathers, the

Burnished
Eze 1:7 as with the glow of *b* copper
Da 10:6 like the sight of *b* copper

Burns
Ps 46:9 The wagons he *b* in the fire
83:14 fire that *b* up the forest
Isa 44:16 Half of it he actually *b* up
62:1 salvation like a torch that *b*
Re 19:20 lake that *b* with sulphur
21:8 lake that *b* with fire and

Burnt
Ge 8:20 offer *b* offerings upon the
22:2 offer him up as a *b* offering
22:3 wood for the *b* offering
22:6 wood of the *b* offering and
22:7 the sheep for the *b* offering
22:8 sheep for the *b* offering, my
22:13 *b* offering in place of his
Ex 3:3 why the thornbush is not *b* up
10:25 sacrifices and *b* offerings
18:12 a *b* offering and sacrifices
20:24 your *b* offerings and your
24:5 offered up *b* offerings and
29:18 It is a *b* offering to Jehovah
29:25 upon the *b* offering as a
29:42 is a constant *b* offering
30:9 a *b* offering or a grain
30:28 the altar of *b* offering and
31:9 altar of *b* offering and all
Ex 32:6 offering up *b* offerings and
32:20 and he *b* it with fire and
35:16 altar of *b* offering and the
38:1 make the altar of *b* offering
40:6 altar of *b* offering before the
40:10 the altar of *b* offering
40:29 the altar of *b* offering at
40:29 offer up the *b* offering and
Le 1:3 a *b* offering from the herd, a
1:4 upon the head of the *b* offering
1:6 the *b* offering must be skinned
1:9 on the altar as a *b* offering
1:10 a *b* offering is from the flock
1:13 is a *b* offering, an offering
1:14 as a *b* offering to Jehovah
1:17 It is a *b* offering, an
3:5 upon the *b* offering that is
4:7 of the altar of *b* offering
4:10 upon the altar of *b* offering
4:18 of the altar of *b* offering
4:24 the *b* offering is regularly
4:25 of the altar of *b* offering
4:25 of the altar of *b* offering
4:29 same place as the *b* offering
4:30 of the altar of *b* offering
4:33 where the *b* offering is
4:34 of the altar of *b* offering
5:7 and one for a *b* offering
5:10 *b* offering according to the
6:9 is the law of the *b* offering
6:9 The *b* offering will be on the
6:10 fatty ashes of the *b* offering
6:12 set the *b* offering in order
6:25 place where the *b* offering is
7:2 slaughter the *b* offering they
7:8 presents the *b* offering of any
7:8 the skin of the *b* offering
7:37 law concerning the *b* offering
8:18 the ram of the *b* offering
8:21 a *b* offering for a restful
8:28 altar on top of the *b* offering
9:2 and a ram for a *b* offering
9:3 sound ones, for a *b* offering
9:7 your *b* offering, and make
9:12 slaughtered the *b* offering and
9:13 handed him the *b* offering
9:14 the *b* offering on the altar
9:16 he presented the *b* offering
9:17 the *b* offering of the morning
9:22 and the *b* offering and the
9:24 consuming the *b* offering
10:19 *b* offering before Jehovah
12:6 for a *b* offering and a male
12:8 one for a *b* offering and one
14:13 the *b* offering are regularly
14:19 slaughter the *b* offering
14:20 offer up the *b* offering and
14:22 and the other as a *b* offering
14:31 a *b* offering along with the
15:15 the other as a *b* offering
15:30 a *b* offering; and the priest
16:3 and a ram for a *b* offering
16:5 and one ram for a *b* offering
16:24 render up his *b* offering and
16:24 people's *b* offering and make
17:8 offers up a *b* offering or a
22:18 present to Jehovah for a *b*
23:12 for a *b* offering to Jehovah
23:18 *b* offering to Jehovah along
23:37 *b* offering and the grain
Nu 6:11 other as a *b* offering and
6:14 young ram . . . as a *b* offering
6:16 and his *b* offering
7:15 lamb . . . for a *b* offering
7:21 male lamb . . . for a *b* offering
7:27 for a *b* offering
7:33 young bull . . . *b* offering
7:39 for a *b* offering
7:45 for a *b* offering
7:51 young bull . . . *b* offering
7:57 male lamb . . . *b* offering
7:63 male lamb . . . *b* offering
7:69 one ram . . . for a *b* offering
7:75 young bull . . . *b* offering
7:81 one young bull . . . *b* offering
7:87 cattle for the *b* offering
8:12 *b* offering to Jehovah to make
10:10 over your *b* offerings
15:3 a *b* offering or a sacrifice to
15:5 with the *b* offering or for
15:8 *b* offering or a sacrifice to
15:24 young bull as a *b* offering
23:3 yourself by your *b* offering
23:6 stationed by his *b* offering
Nu 23:15 here by your *b* offering, and
23:17 stationed by his *b* offering
28:3 as a *b* offering constantly
28:6 the constant *b* offering
28:10 as a sabbath *b* offering on
28:10 with the constant *b* offering
28:11 as a *b* offering to Jehovah
28:13 a *b* offering, a restful odor
28:14 is the monthly *b* offering in
28:15 constant *b* offering together
28:19 a *b* offering to Jehovah, two
28:23 the morning *b* offering
28:23 for the constant *b* offering
28:24 with the constant *b* offering
28:27 *b* offering for a restful odor
28:31 constant *b* offering and its
29:2 *b* offering for a restful odor
29:6 the monthly *b* offering and
29:6 and the constant *b* offering
29:8 present as a *b* offering to
29:11 and the constant *b* offering
29:13 present as a *b* offering, an
29:16 the constant *b* offering, its
29:19 the constant *b* offering and
29:22 constant *b* offering and its
29:25 the constant *b* offering, its
29:28 the constant *b* offering and
29:31 the constant *b* offering, its
29:34 aside from the constant *b*
29:36 must present as a *b* offering
29:38 the constant *b* offering and
29:39 as your *b* offerings and your
De 12:6 bring your *b* offerings and
12:11 your *b* offerings and your
12:13 offer up your *b* offerings in
12:14 offer up your *b* offerings
12:27 render up your *b* offerings
27:6 offer *b* offerings to Jehovah
Jos 8:31 went offering up *b* offerings
22:23 to offer up *b* offerings and
22:26 altar, not for *b* offering
22:27 with our *b* offerings and
22:28 made, not for *b* offering
22:29 an altar for *b* offering
Jg 6:26 offer it up as a *b* offering on
11:31 that one up as a *b* offering
13:16 render up a *b* offering to
13:23 accepted a *b* offering and
20:26 offered up *b* offerings and
21:4 *b* offerings and communion
1Sa 6:14 as a *b* offering to Jehovah
6:15 offered up *b* offerings, and
7:9 offered it up as a *b* offering
7:10 offering up the *b* offering
10:8 to offer up *b* sacrifices, to
13:9 near to me the *b* sacrifice
13:9 offering up the *b* sacrifice
13:10 offering up the *b* sacrifice
13:12 offering up the *b* sacrifice
15:22 delight in *b* offerings and
2Sa 6:17 David offered up *b* sacrifices
6:18 offering up the *b* sacrifices
24:22 cattle for the *b* offering
24:24 *b* sacrifices without cost
24:25 offer up *b* sacrifices and
1Ki 3:4 thousand *b* sacrifices Solomon
3:15 offered up *b* sacrifices and
8:64 render up the *b* sacrifice and
8:64 to contain the *b* sacrifice
9:25 to offer up *b* sacrifices and
10:5 drinks and his *b* sacrifices
18:33 pour it upon the *b* offering
18:38 eating up the *b* offering
2Ki 3:27 offered . . . as a *b* sacrifice upon
5:17 a *b* offering or a sacrifice
10:24 sacrifices and *b* offerings
10:25 rendering up the *b* offering
16:13 make his *b* offering and
16:15 altar make the *b* offering
16:15 *b* offering of the king and
16:15 *b* offering of all the people
16:15 all the blood of *b* offering
1Ch 6:49 upon the altar of *b* offering
16:1 began to present *b* offerings
16:2 offering up the *b* offering
16:40 to offer up *b* offerings to
16:40 on the altar of *b* offering
21:23 the cattle for *b* offerings
21:24 *b* sacrifices without cost
21:26 offered up *b* sacrifices and
21:26 upon the altar of *b* offering
21:29 and the altar of *b* offering
22:1 an altar for *b* offering for
23:31 the *b* sacrifices to Jehovah

1Ch 29:21 *b* offerings to Jehovah on
2Ch 1:6 upon it a thousand *b* offerings
2:4 *b* offerings in the morning and
4:6 to do with the *b* offering
7:1 consume the *b* offering and
7:7 rendered up the *b* offerings
7:7 contain the *b* offering and the
8:12 offered up *b* sacrifices
9:4 *b* sacrifices that he regularly
13:11 *b* offerings smoke to
23:18 *b* sacrifices of Jehovah
24:14 offerers of *b* sacrifices
29:7 *b* sacrifice they did not
29:18 altar of *b* offering and all
29:24 king said the *b* offering
29:27 *b* sacrifice on the altar
29:27 time that the *b* offering
29:28 until the *b* offering was
29:31 to bring . . . *b* offerings
29:32 number of the *b* offerings
29:32 all these as a *b* offering
29:34 to skin all the *b* offerings
29:35 *b* offerings were in great
29:35 for the *b* offerings
30:15 brought *b* offerings to the
31:2 as regards the *b* offering and
31:3 goods for the *b* offerings
31:3 *b* offerings of the morning
31:3 *b* offerings for the sabbaths
35:12 prepared the *b* offerings so
35:14 offering up the *b* sacrifices
35:16 *b* offerings upon the altar
Ezr 3:2 offer up *b* sacrifices upon it
3:3 offering up *b* sacrifices to
3:3 *b* sacrifices of the morning
3:4 *b* sacrifices day by day in
3:5 the constant *b* offering and
3:6 *b* sacrifices to Jehovah
6:9 the *b* offerings to the God of
8:35 presented *b* sacrifices to
8:35 as a *b* offering to Jehovah
Ne 10:33 the constant *b* offering of
Job 1:5 and offered up *b* sacrifices
42:8 offer up a *b* sacrifice in
Ps 20:3 accept your *b* offering as
40:6 *B* offering and sin offering
50:8 your whole *b* offerings that
51:16 *b* offering you do not find
51:19 With *b* sacrifice and whole
66:13 with whole *b* offerings
66:15 *b* offerings of fatlings
Isa 1:11 enough of whole *b* offerings
40:16 sufficient for a *b* offering
43:23 of your whole *b* offerings
56:7 whole *b* offerings and their
Jer 6:20 *b* offerings of you people
7:21 Add those whole *b* offerings
7:22 *b* offering and sacrifice
14:12 the whole *b* offering and
17:26 bringing whole *b* offering
19:5 *b* offerings to the Baal
33:18 offer up whole *b* offering
Eze 40:38 rinse the whole *b* offering
40:39 the whole *b* offering and
40:42 for the whole *b* offering
40:42 the whole *b* offering and
43:18 upon it whole *b* offerings
43:24 whole *b* offering to Jehovah
43:27 whole *b* offerings of you
44:11 whole *b* offering and the
45:15 for the whole *b* offering
45:17 whole *b* offerings and the
45:17 whole *b* offering and the
45:23 whole *b* offering to Jehovah
45:25 as the whole *b* offering
46:2 his whole *b* offering and
46:4 whole *b* offering that the
46:12 a whole *b* offering, or
46:12 his whole *b* offering and
46:13 whole *b* offering daily to
46:15 constant whole *b* offering
Ho 6:6 than in whole *b* offerings
Am 5:22 to me whole *b* offerings
Mic 6:6 with whole *b* offerings, with
Mr 12:33 *b* offerings and sacrifices
Heb 10:6 approve of whole *b* offerings
10:8 whole *b* offerings and sin

Burnt-out
Jer 51:25 and make you a *b* mountain

Burst
Ge 27:38 Esau . . . *b* into tears
29:11 Jacob . . . *b* into tears
33:4 and they *b* into tears
50:1 *b* into tears over him and
50:17 Joseph *b* into tears when
Nu 11:31 wind *b* forth from Jehovah
Jos 9:4 worn out and *b* and tied up
9:13 wine skin-bottles . . . have *b*
2Ch 25:12 they, one and all, *b* apart
Job 32:19 belly . . . wants to *b* open
38:8 when it *b* out from the womb
40:23 the Jordan should *b* forth
Ps 78:26 east wind *b* forth in the
Pr 17:14 so before the quarrel has *b*
20:3 everyone foolish will *b* out
Ca 7:12 the blossom has *b* open, the
Isa 24:19 land has absolutely *b* apart
35:6 waters will have *b* out
Eze 13:13 windstorms to *b* forth in
Mic 4:10 *b* forth, O daughter of Zion
Mt 9:17 wineskins *b* and the wine
Lu 5:37 wine will *b* the wineskins
8:29 he would *b* the bonds and be
Joh 21:11 so many the net did not *b*
Ac 1:18 he noisily *b* in his midst
15:39 occurred a sharp *b* of anger

Burst-open
Jer 29:17 make them like the *b* figs

Bursts
Ec 12:5 and the caper berry *b*
Mr 2:22 the wine *b* the skins, and the

Bury
Ge 23:4 I may *b* my dead out of my
23:6 burial places *b* your dead
23:8 your souls agree to *b* my dead
23:11 give it to you. *B* your dead
23:13 that I may *b* my dead there
23:15 So *b* your dead
47:29 do not *b* me in Egypt
47:30 and *b* me in their grave
49:29 *B* me with my fathers in the
50:5 Canaan . . . you are to *b* me
50:5 let me go up and *b* my father
50:6 *b* your father just as he made
50:7 Joseph went up to *b* his
50:14 up with him to *b* his father
De 21:23 *b* him on that day, because
34:6 to *b* him in the valley in the
1Sa 25:1 *b* him at his house in Ramah
28:3 *b* him in Ramah his own city
2Sa 2:32 Asahel and *b* him in the
1Ki 2:31 must *b* him and remove from
11:15 came up to *b* those slain
13:29 to bewail and *b* him
13:31 *b* me in the burial place in
14:13 indeed bewail him and *b* him
2Ki 9:34 this accursed one and *b* her
9:35 went to *b* her, they did not
2Ch 24:25 *b* him in the burial places
Jer 7:32 will have to *b* in Topheth
19:11 in Topheth they will *b*
19:11 there is no more place to *b*
Eze 39:11 to *b* Gog and all his crowd
39:12 *b* them for the purpose of
Ho 9:6 Memphis, for its part, will *b*
Mt 8:21 to leave and *b* my father
8:22 let the dead *b* their dead
27:7 potter's field to *b* strangers
Lu 9:59 to leave and *b* my father
9:60 Let the dead *b* their dead

Burying
Ge 23:6 to prevent *b* your dead
Nu 33:4 Egyptians were *b* those whom
1Ki 13:31 after his *b* him that he
2Ki 9:10 there will be no one *b* her
13:21 as they were *b* a man
Ps 79:3 there is no one to do the *b*
Jer 14:16 with no one to do the *b*
Eze 39:13 will have to do the *b*
39:14 through the land, *b*, with
39:15 those who do the *b* will

Bush
Ge 2:5 no *b* of the field found in the

Bushes
Ge 21:15 the child under one of the *b*
2Sa 5:23 in front of the baca *b*
5:24 in the tops of the baca *b*
1Ch 14:14 in front of the baca *b*
14:15 in the tops of the baca *b*
Job 30:4 the salt herb by the *b*
30:7 Among the *b* they would cry
Ps 84:6 the low plain of the baca *b*
Isa 32:13 spiny *b* come up, for they
Ho 9:6 *b* will be in their tents

Business
Ge 34:10 and carry on *b* in it and get
34:21 and carry on *b* in it, as the
39:11 into the house to do his *b*
42:34 may carry on *b* in the land
Ex 18:14 What kind of *b* is this that
18:18 this *b* is too big a load for
1Ki 19:9 What is your *b* here, Elijah?
19:13 is your *b* here, Elijah
2Ki 23:5 put out of *b* the foreign-god
1Ch 26:29 the outside *b* as officers
29:6 chiefs of the *b* of the king
2Ch 26:18 not your *b*, O Uzziah, to
26:18 *b* of the priests the sons
Ezr 10:13 the *b* will not take one day
Ne 11:16 outside *b* of the house of the
Es 9:3 the *b* that belonged to the king
Ps 107:23 Doing *b* on vast waters
Isa 44:14 *b* is to cut down cedars
Jer 11:15 What *b* does my beloved one
Mic 3:1 not your *b* to know justice
Mt 22:5 another to his commercial *b*
25:16 did *b* with them and gained
Lu 19:13 Do *b* till I come
19:15 had gained by *b* activity
Ac 6:3 them over this necessary *b*
19:25 that from this *b* we have our
Ro 12:11 Do not loiter at your *b*
1Th 4:11 and to mind your own *b* and
Jas 4:13 engage in *b* and make profits

Businesses
2Ti 2:4 in the commercial *b* of life

Busy
Isa 44:12 been *b* at it with the coals
44:12 he keeps *b* at it with his

Busybody
1Pe 4:15 *b* in other people's matters

Butcher
Job 5:5 from *b* hooks one takes it
Am 4:2 lift you up with *b* hooks and

Butchered
1Sa 25:11 meat that I have *b* for my

Butt
2Sa 2:23 the *b* end of the spear

Butter
Ge 18:8 He then took *b* and milk and
De 32:14 *B* of the herd and milk of
2Sa 17:29 *b* and sheep and curds of
Job 20:17 streams of honey and *b*
29:6 When I washed my steps in *b*
Ps 55:21 Smoother than *b* are the
Pr 30:33 milk is what brings forth *b*
Isa 7:15 *B* and honey he will eat by
7:22 he will eat *b*; because
7:22 *b* and honey are what

Buttocks
2Sa 10:4 garments in half to their *b*
1Ch 19:4 garments in half to their *b*
Isa 20:4 and with *b* stripped, the

Buttress
2Ch 26:9 Valley Gate and by the *B*
Ne 3:19 to the Armory at the *B*
3:20 the *B* as far as the entrance
3:24 the *B* and as far as the corner
3:25 repair work in front of the *B*

Buy
Ge 39:1 an Egyptian, got to *b* him
41:57 came to Egypt to *b* from
42:2 Go down there and *b* for us
42:3 down to *b* grain from Egypt
42:5 others who were coming to *b*
42:7 From the land of Canaan to *b*
42:10 your servants have come to *b*
43:2 Return, *b* a little food for us
43:4 go down and *b* food for you
43:20 down at the start to *b* food
43:22 And more money . . . to *b* food
44:25 *b* a little food for us
47:19 *B* us and our land for bread
47:22 the priests he did not *b*
Ex 21:2 case you should *b* a Hebrew
Le 25:15 *b* from your associate
25:25 *b* back what his brother sold
25:44 *b* a slave man and a slave
25:45 from them you may *b*, and
25:48 his brothers may *b* him back
25:49 may *b* him back, or any blood
25:49 his family, may *b* him
25:49 he must also *b* himself back

Le 25:54 *b* himself back on these
27:13 *b* it back at all, he must
27:15 sanctifier wants to *b* his
27:19 *b* the field back, he must
27:20 not *b* the field back but if
27:31 *b* any of his tenth part back
De 2:6 food you may *b* from them for
Ru 4:4 saying, *B* it in front of the
4:5 On the day that you *b* the field
4:5 *b* it so as to cause the name
4:8 said to Boaz: *B* it for yourself
4:9 I do *b* all that belonged to
4:10 I do *b* for myself as a wife
2Sa 24:21 To *b* from you the threshing
24:24 *b* it from you for a price
1Ki 16:24 *b* the mountain of Samaria
2Ki 12:12 *b* timbers and hewn stones
22:6 to *b* timbers and hewn stones
2Ch 34:11 builders to *b* hewn stones
Ezr 7:17 *b* with this money bulls
Pr 23:23 *B* truth itself and do not
Isa 55:1 no money! Come, *b* and eat
55:1 Yes, come, *b* wine and milk
Jer 32:7 *B* for yourself the field of
32:8 *B*, please, the field of mine
32:8 *B* it for yourself. At that
32:9 *b* from Hanamel the son of
32:25 *B* for yourself the field
32:44 people will *b* fields
Am 8:6 *b* lowly people for mere silver
Mic 4:10 Jehovah will *b* you back out
Mt 14:15 *b* themselves things to eat
25:9 to those who sell it and *b*
25:10 they were going off to *b*
Mr 6:36 and *b* . . . something to eat
6:37 *b* two hundred denarii worth
Lu 9:13 *b* foodstuffs for all these
22:36 his outer garment and *b* one
Joh 4:8 into the city to *b* foodstuffs
6:5 *b* loaves for these to eat
13:29 *B* what things we need for
1Co 7:30 and those who *b* as those not
Re 3:18 *b* from me gold refined by
13:17 able to *b* or sell except a
18:11 no one to *b* their full stock

Buyer
De 28:68 but there will be no *b*
Pr 20:14 It is bad, bad! says the *b*
Isa 1:3 A bull well knows its *b*, and
24:2 for the *b* as for the seller
Eze 7:12 the *b*, let him not rejoice

Buyers
Zec 11:5 *b* of which proceed to kill

Buying
Ge 47:14 cereals which people were *b*
Le 25:14 *b* from your associate's hand
25:24 grant . . . the right of *b* back
Jer 32:7 belongs to you for *b* it
Mt 21:12 selling and *b* in the temple
Mr 11:15 selling and *b* in the temple
Lu 17:28 were *b*, they were selling
Eph 5:16 *b* out the opportune time for
Col 4:5 *b* out the opportune time for

Buys
Mt 13:44 and *b* that field

Buz
Ge 22:21 Uz his firstborn and *B* his
1Ch 5:14 son of Jahdo, the son of *B*
Jer 25:23 Dedan and Tema and *B* and

Buzi
Eze 1:3 to Ezekiel the son of *B* the

Buzite
Job 32:2 the son of Barachel the *B*
32:6 the son of Barachel the *B*

Bygone
2Ki 19:25 From *b* days I have even
Ne 12:46 in *b* time there were heads
Isa 37:26 From *b* days I have even

Bypassed
Isa 24:5 have *b* the laws, changed

Byword
Job 30:9 And I am to them for a *b*

Cab
2Ki 6:25 a *c* measure of dove's dung

Cabbon
Jos 15:40 *C* and Lahmam and Chitlish

Cabul
Jos 19:27 went out to *C* on the left
1Ki 9:13 called the Land of *C* down to

Caesar
Mt 22:17 lawful to pay head tax to *C*
22:21 Caesar's things to *C*, but
Mr 12:14 lawful to pay head tax to *C*
12:17 Pay . . . Caesar's things to *C*
Lu 2:1 a decree went forth from *C*
3:1 the reign of Tiberius *C*, when
20:22 for us to pay tax to *C* or not
20:25 pay back Caesar's things to *C*
23:2 the paying of taxes to *C* and
Joh 19:12 you are not a friend of *C*
19:12 a king speaks against *C*
19:15 We have no king but *C*
Ac 17:7 opposition to the decrees of *C*
25:8 against *C* have I committed
25:10 the judgment seat of *C*
25:11 I appeal to *C!*
25:12 To *C* you have appealed; to
25:12 to *C* you shall go
25:21 should send him on up to *C*
26:32 if he had not appealed to *C*
27:24 You must stand before *C*
28:19 compelled to appeal to *C*
Php 4:22 those of the household of *C*

Caesarea
Mt 16:13 into the parts of *C* Philippi
Mr 8:27 left for the villages of *C*
Ac 8:40 cities until he got to *C*
9:30 brought him down to *C* and
10:1 in *C* there was a certain man
10:24 after that he entered into *C*
11:11 dispatched from *C* to me
12:19 went down from Judea to *C*
18:22 came down to *C*. And he went
21:8 we set out and arrived in *C*
21:16 disciples from *C* also went
23:23 ready to march clear to *C*
23:33 horsemen entered into *C*
25:1 later to Jerusalem from *C*
25:4 Paul was to be kept in *C* and
25:6 he went down to *C*, and the
25:13 Bernice arrived in *C* for a

Caesar's
Mt 22:21 They said: *C*. Then he said
22:21 *C* things to Caesar, but
Mr 12:16 They said to him: *C*
12:17 Pay back *C* things to Caesar
Lu 20:24 Whose image . . . They said: *C*
20:25 pay back *C* things to Caesar

Cage
Jer 5:27 As a *c* is full of flying
Eze 19:9 in the *c* by means of hooks

Caiaphas
Mt 26:3 high priest who was called *C*
26:57 away to *C* the high priest
Lu 3:2 chief priest Annas and of *C*
Joh 11:49 *C*, who was high priest that
18:13 *C*, who was high priest that
18:14 *C* was, in fact, the one
18:24 bound to *C* the high priest
18:28 they led Jesus from *C* to
Ac 4:6 Annas the chief priest and *C*

Cain
Ge 4:1 In time she gave birth to *C*
4:2 *C* became a cultivator of the
4:3 *C* proceeded to bring some
4:5 any favor upon *C* and upon his
4:5 And *C* grew hot with great anger
4:6 Jehovah said to *C:* Why are you
4:8 *C* said to Abel his brother
4:8 *C* proceeded to assault Abel
4:9 Jehovah said to *C:* Where is
4:13 At this *C* said to Jehovah: My
4:15 that reason anyone killing *C*
4:15 Jehovah set up a sign for *C*
4:16 *C* went away from the face of
4:17 *C* had intercourse with his
4:24 If seven times *C* is to be
4:25 in place of Abel, because *C*
Heb 11:4 of greater worth than *C*
1Jo 3:12 *C*, who originated with the
Jude 11 have gone in the path of *C*

Cainan
Lu 3:36 son of *C*, son of Arpachshad
3:37 son of Mahalaleel, son of *C*

Cake
Ex 29:23 ring-shaped *c* of oiled bread
Le 8:26 one unfermented ring-shaped *c*
8:26 *c* of oiled bread and one
24:5 go to each ring-shaped *c*
Nu 6:19 unfermented ring-shaped *c* out
11:8 the taste of an oiled sweet *c*
Jg 7:13 *c* of barley bread turning over
1Sa 30:12 slice of a *c* of pressed figs
2Sa 6:19 ring-shaped *c* of bread and
6:19 and a date *c* and a raisin
6:19 and a raisin *c*, after which
1Ki 17:12 I have no round *c*, but a
17:13 make me a small round *c*
19:6 a round *c* upon heated stones
2Ki 20:7 a *c* of pressed dried figs
1Ch 16:3, 3 a date *c* and a raisin *c*
Ps 35:16 apostate mockers for a *c*
Isa 38:21 a *c* of pressed dried figs
Eze 4:12 as a round *c* of barley you
Ho 7:8 a round *c* not turned on the

Cakes
Ge 18:6 the dough and make round *c*
19:3 he baked unfermented *c*, and
Ex 12:8 unfermented *c* along with
12:15 to eat unfermented *c* only
12:17 festival of unfermented *c*
12:18 eat unfermented *c* down till
12:20 you are to eat unfermented *c*
12:39, 39 round *c*, unfermented *c*
13:6 you are to eat unfermented *c*
13:7 Unfermented *c* are to be eaten
16:31 that of flat *c* with honey
23:15 festival of unfermented *c*
23:15 eat unfermented *c* seven days
29:2 and unfermented ring-shaped *c*
29:23 basket of unfermented *c* that
34:18 festival of unfermented *c* you
34:18 eat unfermented *c*, just as I
Le 2:4 unfermented ring-shaped *c*
6:16 unfermented *c* in a holy place
7:12 unfermented ring-shaped *c*
7:12 ring-shaped *c* moistened with
7:13 ring-shaped *c* of leavened
8:2 the basket of unfermented *c*
8:26 the basket of unfermented *c*
23:6 festival of unfermented *c* to
23:6 you should eat unfermented *c*
24:5 twelve ring-shaped *c*. Two
Nu 6:15 of unfermented ring-shaped *c*
6:17 the basket of unfermented *c*
9:11 unfermented *c* and bitter
11:8 made it into round *c*, and its
15:20 coarse meal as ring-shaped *c*
28:17 Seven days unfermented *c*
De 16:3 along with it unfermented *c*
16:8 eat unfermented *c;* and on the
16:16 unfermented *c* and the
Jos 5:11 unfermented *c* and roasted
Jg 6:19 flour as unfermented *c*
6:20 unfermented *c* and set them
6:21 unfermented *c*, and fire began
6:21 and the unfermented *c*. As for
1Sa 25:18 hundred *c* of raisins and
25:18 hundred *c* of pressed figs
28:24 baked it into unfermented *c*
30:12 and two *c* of raisins
2Sa 13:6 bake two heart-shaped *c*
13:8 made the *c* under his eyes
13:8 cooked the heart-shaped *c*
13:10 heart-shaped *c* that she had
16:1 a hundred *c* of raisins and a
1Ki 14:3 sprinkled *c* and a flask of
2Ki 23:9 they ate unfermented *c* in
1Ch 12:40 *c* of pressed figs and
12:40 *c* of raisins and wine and
23:29 for the griddle *c* and for
2Ch 8:13 festival of unfermented *c*
30:13 of the unfermented *c* in the
30:21 of the unfermented *c*
35:17 unfermented *c* for seven
Ezr 6:22 festival of unfermented *c*
Job 20:7 Like his manure *c* he
Ca 2:5 refresh me with *c* of raisins
Isa 16:7 raisin *c* of Kir-hareseth
Jer 7:18 sacrificial *c* to the queen of
44:19 make for her sacrificial *c*
Eze 4:12 dung *c* of the excrement of
4:15 of the dung *c* of mankind
45:21 seven days unfermented *c*
Ho 3:1 and are loving raisin *c*
Mt 26:17 day of the unfermented *c* the
Mr 14:1 the festival of unfermented *c*
14:12 first day of unfermented *c*
Lu 22:1 festival of the unfermented *c*

Lu 22:7 day of the unfermented *c*
Ac 12:3 days of the unfermented *c*
20:6 the days of the unfermented *c*
1Co 5:8 unfermented *c* of sincerity

Calah
Ge 10:11 building Nineveh . . . and *C*
10:12 Resen between Nineveh and *C*

Calamities
De 31:17 many *c* and distresses must
31:17 these *c* have come upon us
31:21 many *c* and distresses will
32:23 I shall increase *c* upon them
Ps 34:19 the *c* of the righteous one
40:12 *c* encircled me until there
71:20 see many distresses and *c*
88:3 soul has had enough of *c*
141:5 my prayer during their *c*

Calamitous
De 6:22 miracles, great and *c*, upon
Ec 1:13 the *c* occupation that God has
2:17 was *c* from my standpoint
4:3 who has not seen the *c* work
4:8 and it is a *c* occupation
5:14 because of a *c* occupation
7:14 on a *c* day see that the true
8:5 will not know any *c* thing, and
9:3 is *c* in all that has been done
9:12 being ensnared at a *c* time
10:5 exists something *c* that I
10:13 of his mouth is *c* madness
12:1 before the *c* days proceed to
Isa 31:2 and will bring in what is *c*
Jer 10:5 for they can do nothing *c*
Eze 6:10 doing to them this *c* thing
Am 5:13 for it will be a *c* time
6:3 out of your mind the *c* day
Jon 4:6 deliver him from his *c* state
Hab 2:9 from the grasp of what is *c*
Zec 8:14 do what was *c* to you people

Calamity
Ge 19:19 fear *c* may keep close to me
44:29 gray hairs with *c* to Sheol
44:34 I may look upon the *c* that
48:16 been recovering me from all *c*
Nu 11:15 let me not look upon my *c*
De 29:21 separate him for *c* from all
31:29 *c* will be bound to befall
Jg 2:15 against them for *c*, just as
20:34 *c* was impending over them
20:41 saw that *c* had reached them
Ru 1:21 Almighty that has caused me *c*
1Sa 25:17 *c* has been determined
2Sa 12:11 *c* out of your own house
16:8 And here you are in your *c*
17:14 might bring *c* upon Absalom
24:16 to feel regret over the *c*
1Ki 9:9 brought upon them all this *c*
14:10 bringing *c* upon the house of
20:7 is *c* that this one is seeking
21:21 I am bringing *c* upon you
21:29 not bring the *c* in his own
21:29 bring the *c* upon his house
22:23 has spoken *c* concerning you
2Ki 6:33 this is the *c* from Jehovah
21:12 bringing a *c* upon Jerusalem
22:16 bringing *c* upon this place
22:20 the *c* that I am bringing
1Ch 4:10 really preserve me from *c*
7:23 it was with *c* that she
21:15 to feel regret over the *c*
2Ch 7:22 upon them all this *c*
18:22 Jehovah . . . has spoken *c*
20:9 come upon us *c*, sword
34:24 bringing *c* upon this place
34:28 *c* that I am bringing upon
Ne 13:18 brought upon us all this *c*
Es 8:6 the *c* that will find my people
Job 2:11 *c* that had come upon him
42:11 *c* that Jehovah had let come
Ps 10:6 shall be one who is in no *c*
27:5 hide me . . . in the day of *c*
34:21 *C* will put the wicked one
35:4 who are scheming *c* for me
35:26 Who are joyful at my *c*
37:19 ashamed in the time of *c*
38:12 those working for a *c* to me
40:14 who are delighting in my *c*
41:1 In the day of *c* Jehovah will
70:2 are taking delight in my *c*
71:13 who are seeking *c* for me
71:24 who are seeking *c* for me
78:49 of angels bringing *c*
Ps 90:15 years that we have seen *c*
91:10 No *c* will befall you
94:13 quietness from days of *c*
94:23 them with their own *c*
107:26 Because of the *c* their very
107:39 Owing to restraint, *c* and
121:7 guard you against all *c*
Pr 1:33 undisturbed from dread of *c*
12:21 certainly be filled with *c*
13:21 the ones whom *c* pursues
17:20 his tongue will fall into *c*
21:12 the wicked ones to their *c*
22:3 is the one that has seen the *c*
24:16 be made to stumble by *c*
27:12 has seen the *c* has concealed
28:14 will fall into *c*
Ec 2:21 This too is vanity and a big *c*
5:13 grave *c* that I have seen under
5:13 riches being kept . . . to his *c*
5:16 *c*: exactly as one has come
6:1 exists a *c* that I have seen
8:6 *c* of mankind is abundant upon
11:2 not know what *c* will occur
11:10 ward off *c* from your flesh
Isa 3:9 dealt out to themselves *c*
3:11 *C*; for the treatment
45:7 making peace and creating *c*
47:11 And upon you *c* must come
57:1 it is because of the *c* that
Jer 1:14 Out of the north the *c* will
2:3 *C* itself would come upon
2:27 in the time of their *c* they
2:28 in the time of your *c*
4:6 *c* that I am bringing in from
4:18 *c* upon you, for it is bitter
5:12 upon us no *c* will come
6:1 *c* itself has looked down out
6:19 *c* upon this people as the
7:6 you will not walk for *c*
11:11 a *c* that they will not be
11:12 in the time of their *c*
11:14 in regard to their *c*
11:15 upon you, when your *c* comes
11:17 spoken against you a *c*
11:23 *c* upon the men of Anathoth
14:16 pour out upon them their *c*
15:11 in the time of *c* and in
16:10 this great *c*, and what is
17:17 my refuge in the day of *c*
17:18 upon them the day of *c*
18:8 feel regret over the *c*
18:11 forming against you a *c*
19:3 bringing a *c* upon this place
19:15 all the *c* that I have spoken
21:10 for *c* and not for good
22:22 because of all your *c*
23:12 I shall bring upon them a *c*
23:17 No *c* will come upon you
24:9 *c*, in all the kingdoms of
25:6 I may not cause *c* to you
25:7 for *c* to yourselves
25:29 starting off in bringing *c*
25:32 A *c* is going forth from
26:3 feel regret for the *c* that I
26:13 feel regret for the *c* that
26:19 the *c* that he had spoken
26:19 great *c* against our souls
28:8 and of *c* and of pestilence
29:11 of peace, and not of *c*
32:23 all this *c* to befall them
32:42 all this great *c*
35:17 *c* that I have spoken against
36:3 *c* that I am thinking of
36:31 *c* that I have spoken against
38:4 of this people but for *c*
39:16 upon this city for *c* and
40:2 spoke this *c* against this
42:10 *c* that I have caused to you
42:17 *c* that I am bringing in
44:2 *c* that I have brought in
44:7 great *c* to your souls, in
44:11 for *c* and for cutting off
44:17 did not see any *c* at all
44:23 befallen you this *c* as at
44:27 alert toward them for *c* and
44:29 come true upon you for *c*
45:5 in a *c* upon all flesh
48:2 thought out against her a *c*
48:16 *c* is actually hurrying up
49:37 will bring upon them a *c*
51:2 all sides in the day of *c*
51:60 write in one book all the *c*
51:64 *c* that I am bringing in
La 1:21 themselves have heard of my *c*
Eze 7:5 Lord Jehovah has said, A *c*, a
7:5 unique *c*, look! it is coming
14:22 be comforted over the *c*
Da 9:12 bringing upon us great *c*
9:13 all this *c*—it has come upon
9:14 Jehovah kept alert to the *c*
Joe 2:13 regret on account of the *c*
Am 3:6 If a *c* occurs in the city
9:10 The *c* will not come near or
Ob 13 ought not to peer at his *c* in
Jon 1:7 whose account we have this *c*
1:8 that we are having this *c*
3:10 felt regret over the *c* that
4:2 feeling regret over the *c*
Mic 2:3 a *c* from which you people
2:3 because it is a time of *c*
3:11 will come upon us no *c*
Zep 3:15 You will fear *c* no more
Zec 1:15 they . . . helped toward *c*
8:17 *c* to one another do not you

Calamus
Ex 30:23 sweet *c* two hundred and

Calcol
1Ki 4:31 wiser than . . . Heman and *C*
1Ch 2:6 the sons of Zerah were . . . *C*

Calculate
Le 25:27 *c* the years from when he
27:18 priest must then *c* for him
27:23 *c* for him the amount of the
Lu 14:28 sit down and *c* the expense
Re 13:18 *c* the number of the wild

Calculated
Pr 23:7 that has *c* within his soul
Ac 19:19 they *c* together the prices of

Calculation
Le 25:52 then make a *c* for himself

Caldron
1Sa 2:14 or the *c* or the one-handled

Caleb
Nu 13:6 *C* the son of Jephunneh
13:30 *C* tried to still the people
14:6 and *C* the son of Jephunneh
14:24 As for my servant *C*, because
14:30 except *C* the son of Jephunneh
14:38 *C* . . . will certainly live on
26:65 except *C* the son of Jephunneh
32:12 except *C* the son of Jephunneh
34:19 tribe of Judah, *C* the son of
De 1:36 except *C* the son of Jephunneh
Jos 14:6 *C* the son of Jephunneh the
14:13 to *C* the son of Jephunneh
14:14 has come to belong to *C*
15:13 to *C* the son of Jephunneh
15:14 So *C* drove away from there
15:16 *C* proceeded to say: Whoever
15:18 At this *C* said to her
21:12 *C* the son of Jephunneh as
Jg 1:12 Then *C* said: Whoever strikes
1:14 *C* said to her: What do you
1:15 *C* gave her Upper Gulloth and
1:20 they gave *C* Hebron, just as
3:9 the younger brother of *C*
1Sa 30:14 upon the south of *C*; and
1Ch 2:18 As for *C* the son of Hezron
2:19 *C* took to himself Ephrath
2:42 *C* the brother of Jerahmeel
2:46 Ephah the concubine of *C*
2:50 These became the sons of *C*
4:15 *C* the son of Jephunneh
6:56 to *C* the son of Jephunneh

Caleb-ephrathah
1Ch 2:24 the death of Hezron in *C*

Calebite
1Sa 25:3 and he was a *C*

Caleb's
Jos 15:17 *C* brother, captured it
Jg 1:13 *C* younger brother, got to
1Ch 2:48 *C* concubine Maacah, she gave
2:49 And *C* daughter was Achsah

Calf
Ex 32:4 into a molten statue of a *c*
32:8 made a molten statue of a *c*
32:19 see the *c* and the dances
32:20 he took the *c* that they had
32:24 and this *c* came on out
32:35 because they had made the *c*
Le 9:2 a young *c* for a sin offering
9:3 a *c* and a young ram, each a

Le 9:8 the *c* of the sin offering
De 9:16 made yourselves a molten *c*
9:21 the *c*, I took, and I proceeded
1Sa 28:24 woman had a fattened *c* in
Ne 9:18 a molten statue of a *c* and
Ps 29:6 skip about like a *c*
106:19 they made a *c* in Horeb
Isa 11:6 *c* and the maned young lion
27:10 There the *c* will graze, and
Jer 31:18 like a *c* that has not been
34:18 *c* that they cut in two
34:19 between the pieces of the *c*
Eze 1:7 the sole of the foot of a *c*
Ho 8:5 Your *c* has been cast off
8:6 the *c* of Samaria will become
10:5 the *c* idol of Beth-aven the
Ac 7:41 they made a *c* in those days

Calkers
Eze 27:9 as *c* for your seams. All the
27:27 the *c* of your seams and

Call
Ge 1:8 God began to *c* the expanse
2:19 see what he would *c* each one
2:19 whatever the man would *c* it
4:26 he proceeded to *c* his name
5:29 proceeded to *c* his name Noah
8:21 Never again shall I *c* down
12:8 to *c* on the name of Jehovah
13:4 Abram proceeded to *c* there on
16:11 must *c* his name Ishmael
16:13 she began to *c* the name of
17:15 must not *c* her name Sarai
17:19 you must *c* his name Isaac
20:8 to *c* all his servants and to
22:14 Abraham began to *c* the name
22:15 *c* to Abraham the second time
24:57 *c* the young woman and
35:7 began to *c* the place El-bethel
35:10 began to *c* his name Israel
35:15 Jacob continued to *c* the
41:14 to send and to *c* Joseph
41:43 *c* out ahead of him, *A·vrékh!*
46:33 when Pharaoh will *c* you and
Ex 2:7 *c* for you a nursing woman
2:10 *c* his name Moses and to say
2:20 *C* him, that he may eat bread
16:31 began to *c* its name manna
17:15 to *c* its name Jehovah-nissi
19:3 Jehovah began to *c* to him out
22:28 not *c* down evil upon God nor
31:2 *c* by name Bezalel the son of
34:31 Moses proceeded to *c* them
36:2 to *c* Bezalel and Oholiab and
Le 1:1 to *c* Moses and speak to him
13:45 and *c* out, Unclean, unclean!
19:14 not *c* down evil upon a deaf
24:11 and to *c* down evil upon it
Nu 10:9 sound a war *c* on the trumpets
13:16 Moses continued to *c* Hoshea
16:12 Moses sent to *c* Dathan and
20:8 and *c* the assembly together
22:5 to *c* him, saying: Look!
22:20 If it is to *c* you that the
22:37 sent to you to *c* you
32:38 to *c* by their own names the
32:41 began to *c* them Havvoth-jair
32:42 *c* it Nobah by his own name
De 2:11 used to *c* them Emim
2:20 used to *c* them Zamzummim
3:9 used to *c* Hermon Sirion, and
3:9 Amorites used to *c* it Senir
3:14 *c* those villages of Bashan by
4:39 must *c* back to your heart
5:1 *c* all Israel and to say to
15:9 and he has to *c* out to Jehovah
23:4 Balaam . . . to *c* down evil
25:8 *c* him and speak to him, and
29:2 *c* all Israel and to say to
31:7 to *c* Joshua and say to him
31:14 *C* Joshua, and station
33:19 to the mountain they will *c*
Jos 10:24 to *c* all the men of Israel
19:47 began to *c* Leshem Dan
22:1 Joshua proceeded to *c* the
23:2 Joshua proceeded to *c* all
24:1 and to *c* the older men of
24:9 to *c* down evil upon you
Jg 3:9 Israel began to *c* to Jehovah
3:15 Israel began to *c* to Jehovah
4:6 proceeded to send and *c* Barak
4:10 Barak began to *c* Zebulun and
6:6 began to *c* to Jehovah for aid
6:32 *c* him Jerubbaal on that day
Jg 7:3 And now *c* out, please, in the
10:4 continue to *c* Havvoth-jair
10:10 began to *c* to Jehovah for aid
10:14 *c* for aid to the gods whom
12:1 not issue a *c* to go with you
12:2 to *c* to you for aid, and you
15:18 he began to *c* on Jehovah and
16:25 *C* Samson that he may offer
Ru 1:20 Do not *c* me Naomi
1:20 *C* me Mara, for the Almighty
1:21 Why should you *c* me Naomi
4:17 they began to *c* his name Obed
1Sa 1:20 to *c* his name Samuel
3:4 Jehovah proceeded to *c* Samuel
3:5 I did not *c*. Lie down again
3:6 And Jehovah went on to *c* yet
3:6 Here I am, for you did *c* me
3:6 I did not *c*, my son. Lie down
3:9 if he should *c* you, you must
6:2 *c* the priests and the diviners
7:12 began to *c* its name Ebenezer
9:26 Samuel proceeded to *c* to
10:17 Samuel proceeded to *c* the
12:10 to *c* to Jehovah for aid and
12:17 I shall *c* to Jehovah that he
15:2 *c* to account what Amalek did
16:3 *c* Jesse to the sacrifice
17:8 to *c* to the battle lines of
20:37 Jonathan began to *c* from
22:11 king sent to *c* Ahimelech
26:14 David began to *c* out to the
2Sa 2:26 Abner began to *c* to Joab and
3:8 *c* me to account for an error
15:2 Absalom would *c* him and say
16:9 *c* down evil upon my lord
16:10 Thus let him *c* down evil
16:10 *C* down evil upon David
16:11 that he may *c* down evil
16:13 that he might *c* down evil
17:5 *C*, please, Hushai the Archite
20:4 *C* the men of Judah together
20:5 Amasa went to *c* Judah
20:16 a wise woman began to *c*
22:4 Jehovah, I shall *c*, And from
1Ki 1:28 men, *c* Bath-sheba for me
1:32 *c* for me Zadok the priest
8:52 all for which they *c* to you
13:21 began to *c* out to the man
16:24 *c* the name of the city that
17:11 to *c* to her and say: Please
17:21 and *c* to Jehovah and say
18:24 *c* upon the name of your god
18:24 *c* upon the name of Jehovah
18:25 *c* upon the name of your god
18:27 *C* at the top of your voice
22:13 that had gone to *c* Micaiah
2Ki 4:12 *C* this Shunammite woman
4:15 he said: *C* her. So he called
4:36 *C* this Shunammite woman
5:11 *c* upon the name of Jehovah
10:19 *c* all the prophets of Baal
12:15 not *c* for an accounting
18:18 began to *c* out to the king
18:28 and *c* out in a loud voice
19:4 *c* him to account for the
20:11 began to *c* out to Jehovah
1Ch 4:10 *c* upon the God of Israel
6:65 they proceeded to *c* by names
16:4 to *c* to remembrance and to
16:8 *c* upon his name, Make his
21:26 to *c* upon Jehovah, who now
2Ch 14:11 Asa began to *c* to Jehovah
18:12 messenger that went to *c*
20:9 *c* to you for aid out of our
24:9 issued a *c* throughout Judah
30:5 *c* pass through all Israel
Ezr 10:7 *c* to pass throughout Judah
Ne 6:7 to *c* out concerning you
8:15 cause a *c* to pass throughout
9:28 return and *c* to you for aid
13:2 to *c* down evil upon them
13:25 and *c* down evil upon them
Es 6:9 and they must *c* out before him
6:11 *c* out before him: This is how
Job 3:1 to *c* down evil upon his day
5:1 *C*, please! Is there anyone
13:22 *c* that I myself may answer
14:15 You will *c*, and I myself
17:14 the pit I shall have to *c*
27:10 *c* to God at all times
Ps 3:4 I shall *c* to Jehovah himself
4:1 When I *c*, answer me, O my
4:3 will hear when I *c* to him
17:6 I myself do *c* upon you
Ps 18:3 praised, Jehovah, I shall *c*
20:9 in the day that we *c*
27:7 when I *c* with my voice
50:1 And he proceeds to *c* the earth
50:15 *c* me in the day of distress
55:16 to God I shall *c* out
56:9 back, on the day that I *c*
57:2 I *c* to God the Most High, to
62:4 they *c* down evil. *Se'lah*
80:18 we may *c* upon your own name
86:7 distress I will *c* upon you
91:15 He will *c* upon me, and I
102:2 day that I *c*, hurry, answer
105:1 to Jehovah, *c* upon his name
105:16 *c* for a famine upon the
116:2 throughout my days I shall *c*
116:4 of Jehovah I proceeded to *c*
116:13 name of Jehovah I shall *c*
116:17 name of Jehovah I shall *c*
141:1 to my voice when I *c* to you
142:1 I proceeded to *c* for aid
145:18 who *c* upon him in trueness
Pr 2:3 *c* out for understanding itself
7:4 you *c* understanding itself
9:3 *c* out on top of the heights
9:15 *c* out to those passing along
21:13 will *c* and not be answered
30:10 may not *c* down evil upon you
Ec 10:20 *c* down evil upon the king
10:20 *c* down evil upon anyone rich
Isa 7:14 *c* his name Immanuel
8:3 said to me: *C* his name
8:4 *c* out, My father! and My
8:21 *c* down evil upon his king
12:4 *C* upon his name. Make known
21:8 *c* out like a lion
22:12 *c* in that day for weeping
22:20 *c* my servant, namely
26:21 *c* to account the error of
34:12 will *c* to the kingship
34:14 demon will *c* to its
36:13 *c* out in a loud voice in
37:4 *c* him to account for the
40:2 and *c* out to her that her
40:6 Someone is saying: *C* out!
40:6 What shall I *c* out?
41:2 to *c* him to His feet, to
41:25 he will *c* upon my name
44:5 *c* himself by the name of
44:7 Let him *c* out, that he may
45:4 to *c* you by your name
47:1 people *c* you delicate and
47:5 *c* you Mistress of Kingdoms
55:5 you will *c*, and those of a
55:6 *C* to him while he proves to
58:1 *C* out full-throated; do not
58:5 *c* a fast and a day acceptable
58:9 *c*, and Jehovah himself would
58:13 *c* the sabbath an exquisite
60:14 *c* you the city of Jehovah
60:18 *c* your own walls Salvation
62:12 *c* them the holy people
65:15 he will *c* by another name
65:24 occur that before they *c* out
Jer 2:2 must *c* out in the ears of
3:17 *c* Jerusalem the throne of
3:19 you people will *c* out to me
4:5 *C* out loudly and say: Gather
6:30 people will certainly *c* them
7:27 you must *c* to them, but they
9:17 *c* the dirge-chanting women
11:11 certainly *c* to me for aid
11:12 *c* for aid to the gods to
20:8 despoiling are what I *c* out
25:12 *c* to account against the
29:12 *c* me and come and pray to
31:6 *c* out, Rise up, O men, and
33:3 *C* to me, and I shall answer
36:4 *c* Baruch the son of Neriah
36:31 *c* to account against him
La 2:22 to *c* out my places of alien
3:8 I *c* for aid and cry for help
Eze 8:18 *c* out in my ears with a loud
9:1 *c* out in my ears with a loud
36:29 *c* to the grain and make it
38:21 *c* forth against him
39:11 *c* it the Valley of Gog's
Da 2:2 *c* the magic-practicing priests
8:16 *c* out and say: Gabriel, make
Ho 1:4 *C* his name Jezreel, for yet a
1:6 *C* her name Lo-ruhamah, for I
1:9 *C* his name Lo-ammi, because
2:16 *c* me My husband, and you will
2:16 no longer *c* me My owner

Ho 7:14 they did not *c* to me for aid
11:7 upward they *c* it; no one at
Joe 1:14 *C* together a solemn assembly
1:19 To you, O Jehovah, I shall *c*
2:15 *C* together a solemn assembly
Am 5:16 to *c* a farmer to mourning
Jon 1:5 *c* for aid, each one to his god
1:6 Get up, *c* out to your god
1:14 *c* out to Jehovah and to say
3:8 *c* out to God with strength
Mic 3:4 will *c* to Jehovah for aid
3:5 that actually *c* out, Peace!
Hab 1:2 *c* to you for aid from
Zep 3:7 must *c* to account against her
3:9 to *c* upon the name of Jehovah
Zec 1:14 *C* out, saying, This is what
1:17 *C* out further, saying, This
3:10 *c*, each one to the other
7:13 *c* and I would not listen
13:9 will *c* upon my name, and I
Mal 1:4 *c* them the territory of
Mt 1:21 you must *c* his name Jesus
1:23 will *c* his name Immanuel
9:13 I came to *c*, not righteous
10:25 *c* those of his household so
20:8 *C* the workers and pay them
22:3 to *c* those invited to the
23:9 do not *c* anyone your father
Mr 2:17 I came to *c*, not righteous
3:31 they sent in to him to *c* him
10:18 Why do you *c* me good?
10:49 *C* him. And they called the
15:12 you *c* the king of the Jews
Lu 1:13 you are to *c* his name John
1:31 you are to *c* his name Jesus
1:54 to *c* to mind mercy
1:59 *c* it by the name of its
1:72 *c* to mind his holy covenant
5:32 have come to *c*, not righteous
6:46 Why, then, do you *c* me Lord!
8:8 to *c* out: Let him that has
14:12 do not *c* your friends or your
18:19 Why do you *c* me good? Nobody
Joh 4:16 *c* your husband and come to
15:15 I no longer *c* you slaves
Ac 2:39 Jehovah our God may *c* to him
9:21 who *c* upon this name, and
10:28 *c* no man defiled or unclean
10:32 to Joppa and *c* for Simon
12:13 came to attend to the *c*
20:26 I *c* you to witness this very
24:14 the way that they *c* a sect
Ro 9:25 I will *c* my people, and her
10:14 *c* on him in whom they have
1Co 14:8 sounds an indistinct *c*, who
2Co 1:23 I *c* upon God as a witness
Php 3:14 upward *c* of God by means of
1Th 4:16 with a commanding *c*, with
2Ti 2:22 *c* upon the Lord out of a
Heb 2:11 to *c* them brothers
8:12 *c* their sins to mind anymore
10:17 *c* their sins and their
Jas 5:14 Let him *c* the older men of
3Jo 10 I will *c* to remembrance his
Jude 17 *c* to mind the sayings that

Called

Ge 1:5 but the darkness he *c* Night
1:10 of the waters he *c* Seas
2:23 This one will be *c* Woman
3:20 Adam *c* his wife's name Eve
4:17 *c* the city's name by the name
4:25 a son and *c* his name Seth
5:2 and *c* their name Man in the
5:3 and *c* his name Seth
11:9 why its name was *c* Babel
12:18 Pharaoh *c* Abram and said
16:14 well was *c* Beer-lahai-roi
16:15 Abram *c* the name of his son
17:5 name will not be *c* Abram
19:22 *c* the name of the city Zoar
19:37 to a son and *c* his name Moab
19:38 *c* his name Ben-ammi. He is
20:9 Abimelech *c* Abraham and said
21:3 Abraham *c* the name of his son
21:12 what will be *c* your seed
21:17 God's angel *c* to Hagar out of
21:31 he *c* that place Beer-sheba
21:33 *c* there upon the name of
24:58 *c* Rebekah and said to her
25:25 so they *c* his name Esau
25:26 so he *c* his name Jacob
25:30 why his name was *c* Edom
26:9 Abimelech *c* Isaac and said
Ge 26:18 that his father had *c* them
26:20 he *c* the name of the well
26:21 Hence he *c* its name Sitnah
26:22 Hence he *c* its name Rehoboth
26:25 *c* on the name of Jehovah
26:33 Hence he *c* its name Shibah
27:1 he then *c* Esau his older son
27:36 why his name is *c* Jacob
27:42 she at once sent and *c* Jacob
28:1 Isaac *c* Jacob and blessed him
28:19 *c* . . . that place Bethel
29:32 then *c* his name Reuben
29:33 Hence she *c* his name Simeon
29:34 name was therefore *c* Levi
29:35 therefore *c* his name Judah
30:6 why she *c* his name Dan
30:8 So she *c* his name Naphtali
30:11 So she *c* his name Gad
30:13 So she *c* his name Asher
30:18 So she *c* his name Issachar
30:20 So she *c* his name Zebulun
30:21 then *c* her name Dinah
30:24 she *c* his name Joseph
31:4 Jacob sent and *c* Rachel
31:47 but Jacob *c* it Galeed
31:48 why he *c* its name Galeed
32:2 *c* . . . that place Mahanaim
32:28 no longer be *c* Jacob but
32:30 Jacob *c* . . . the place Peniel
33:17 *c* the name of the place
33:20 *c* it God the God of Israel
35:8 he *c* its name Allon-bacuth
35:10 No longer . . . *c* Jacob, but
35:18 she *c* his name Ben-oni; but
35:18 his father *c* him Benjamin
38:3 a son and he *c* his name Er
38:4 a son and *c* his name Onan
38:5 and then *c* his name Shelah
38:29 Hence his name was *c* Perez
38:30 his name came to be *c* Zerah
41:8 *c* all the magic-practicing
41:45 Pharaoh *c* Joseph's name
41:51 Joseph *c* the name of the
41:52 the second he *c* Ephraim
47:29 he *c* his son Joseph and said
48:6 will be *c* in their inheritance
48:16 let my name be *c* upon them
49:1 Jacob *c* his sons and said
50:11 its name was *c* Abel-mizraim
Ex 1:18 king of Egypt *c* the midwives
2:8 went and *c* the child's mother
2:22 and he *c* his name Gershom
3:4 God at once *c* to him out of
7:11 Pharaoh also *c* for the wise
8:8 Pharaoh *c* Moses and Aaron and
8:25 Pharaoh *c* Moses and Aaron and
9:27 Pharaoh sent and *c* Moses and
10:16 Pharaoh hurriedly *c* Moses
10:24 Pharaoh *c* Moses and said: Go
12:21 Moses *c* all the older men of
12:31 *c* Moses and Aaron by night
15:23 is why he *c* its name Marah
17:7 he *c* the name of the place
19:7 Moses came and *c* the older
19:20 Jehovah *c* Moses to the top
24:16 *c* to Moses from the midst
32:5 Aaron *c* out and said
33:7 he *c* it a tent of meeting
35:1 Moses *c* the entire assembly
35:30 has *c* by name Bezalel the
Le 9:1 Moses *c* Aaron and his sons and
10:4 Moses *c* Mishael and Elzaphan
20:9 upon whom he has *c* down evil
24:14 *c* down evil to the outside
24:23 one who had *c* down evil to
Nu 1:16 ones *c* of the assembly, the
11:3 *c* Taberah, because a fire of
11:34 to be *c* Kibroth-hattaavah
12:5 and *c* Aaron and Miriam
13:24 They *c* that place the torrent
20:10 *c* the congregation together
21:3 they *c* the name of the place
24:10 execrate my enemies that I *c*
De 3:13 *c* the land of the Rephaim
15:2 a release . . . must be *c*
25:10 his name must be *c* in Israel
28:10 name has been *c* upon you
Jos 4:4 Joshua *c* twelve men whom he
5:9 place came to be *c* Gilgal
6:6 *c* the priests and said to
7:26 been *c* Low Plain of Achor
8:16 *c* out to chase after them
9:22 Joshua now *c* them and spoke
21:9 cities that were *c* by name
Jg 1:17 the city was *c* Hormah
1:26 a city and *c* its name Luz
2:5 they *c* the name of that place
4:13 Sisera *c* together all his
6:7 Israel *c* to Jehovah for aid on
6:24 be *c* Jehovah-shalom down to
6:34 to be *c* together after him
6:35 to be *c* together after him
7:23 men of Israel were *c* together
7:24 Ephraim were *c* together, and
9:7 raised his voice and *c* out and
9:27 *c* down evil upon Abimelech
9:54 *c* the attendant bearing his
10:17 the sons of Ammon were *c*
12:1 Ephraim were *c* together and
13:24 a son and *c* his name Samson
15:17 and *c* that place Ramath-lehi
15:19 he *c* its name En-hakkore
16:18 *c* the Philistine axis lords
16:19 she *c* the man and had him
16:25 *c* Samson out of the prison
16:28 Samson now *c* to Jehovah and
18:12 have *c* that place Mahaneh-dan
18:22 *c* together and tried to catch
18:23 that you have been *c* together
18:29 *c* the name of the city Dan
1Sa 3:5 Here I am, for you *c* me
3:8 Jehovah *c* again for the third
3:8 for you must have *c* me
3:10 and *c* as at the other times
3:16 But Eli *c* Samuel and said
4:21 But she *c* the boy Ichabod
9:9 be *c* a seer in former times
12:18 Samuel *c* to Jehovah, and
13:4 *c* together to follow Saul to
14:20 all the people . . . were *c*
16:5 he *c* them to the sacrifice
16:8 Jesse *c* Abinadab and had him
17:43 *c* down evil upon David by
19:7 Afterward Jonathan *c* David
23:28 *c* that place the Crag of the
24:8 *c* out after Saul, saying
26:14 that have *c* out to the king
29:6 Achish *c* David and said to
2Sa 1:7 he *c* me, and I said, Here I
1:15 David *c* one of the young men
2:16 that place came to be *c*
5:9 be *c* the city of David
5:20 *c* the name of that place
6:2 where a name is *c* on, the
6:8 came to be *c* Perez-uzzah
9:2 *c* him to David, and the king
9:9 king now *c* Ziba, Saul's
11:13 David *c* him that he might
12:24 name came to be *c* Solomon
12:25 *c* his name Jedidiah, for
12:28 not have to be *c* upon it
13:17 *c* his attendant who waited
14:33 Then he *c* Absalom, who now
15:11 *c* and going unsuspectingly
16:7 Shimei said as he *c* down
18:18 he *c* the pillar by his own
18:18 to be *c* Absalom's Monument
18:25 the watchman *c* and told the
18:26 *c* to the gatekeeper and said
18:28 Ahimaaz *c* and said to the
19:21 he *c* evil down upon the
21:2 the king *c* the Gibeonites
1Ki 2:8 *c* down evil upon me with a
2:36 the king sent and *c* Shimei
2:42 the king sent and *c* Shimei
7:21 pillar and *c* its name Jachin
7:21 pillar and *c* its name Boaz
8:43 *c* upon this house that I
9:13 *c* the Land of Cabul down to
12:3 then they sent and *c* him
12:20 *c* him to the assembly and
13:2 he *c* out against the altar
13:4 *c* out against the altar in
13:32 he *c* out by the word of
17:10 he *c* to her and said: Please
18:3 Ahab *c* Obadiah, who was over
20:7 *c* all the older men of the
22:9 king of Israel *c* a certain
2Ki 2:24 *c* down evil upon them in the
3:10 has *c* these three kings to
3:13 has *c* these three kings to
3:21 *c* together men from as many
4:12 he *c* her that she might
4:15 So he *c* her, and she kept
4:22 now *c* her husband and said
4:36 He now *c* Gehazi and said
4:36 So he *c* her and she came in
6:11 he *c* his servants and said

2Ki 7:10 and *c* to the gatekeepers of
7:11 the gatekeepers *c* out and
8:1 Jehovah has *c* for a famine
9:1 *c* one of the sons of the
12:7 King Jehoash *c* Jehoiada the
14:7 *c* Joktheel down to this day
18:4 *c* the copper serpent-idol
1Ch 4:9 mother that *c* his name Jabez
5:20 to God that they *c* for aid in
7:16 a son and *c* his name Peresh
7:23 But he *c* his name Beriah
11:7 they *c* it the city of David
13:6 where his name is *c* on
13:11 came to be *c* Perez-uzzah
14:11 *c* the name of that place
15:11 David *c* Zadok and Abiathar
22:6 he *c* Solomon his son that he
23:14 *c* among the tribe of the
2Ch 3:17 *c* the name of the right-hand
6:33 name has been *c* upon this
7:14 whom my name has been *c*
10:3 *c* him, and Jeroboam and all
18:8 king of Israel *c* a court
20:26 *c* the name of that place
24:6 king *c* Jehoiada the head and
Ezr 2:61 came to be *c* by their name
Ne 5:12 *c* the priests and made them
7:63 came to be *c* by their name
12:44 portions *c* for by the law
Es 2:14 and she had been *c* by name
3:12 secretaries were then *c*
4:5 Esther *c* Hathach, one of the
4:11 inner courtyard who is not *c*
4:11 I have not been *c* to come in
8:9 secretaries of the king were *c*
9:26 why they *c* these days Purim
Job 9:16 If I *c* him, would he answer
19:16 To my servant I have *c*, but
35:15 his anger has not *c* for an
36:23 *c* his way to account
Ps 14:4 have not *c* even upon Jehovah
31:17 for I have *c* on you
34:6 afflicted one *c*, and Jehovah
37:22 those upon whom evil is *c*
49:11 *c* their landed estates by
53:4 have not *c* even upon Jehovah
66:17 To him I *c* with my mouth
79:6 not *c* upon your own name
81:7 In distress you *c*, and I
88:9 *c* on you, O Jehovah, all day
118:5 I *c* upon Jah
119:145 *c* with my whole heart
119:146 I have *c* upon you. O save
120:1 Jehovah I *c* in the distress
130:1 I have *c* upon you, O Jehovah
138:3 On the day that I *c*, you
141:1 Jehovah, I have *c* upon you
142:5 I *c* to you, O Jehovah, for
Pr 1:24 *c* out but you keep refusing
3:18 those . . . are to be *c* happy
9:18 those *c* in by her are in the
16:21 wise . . . *c* understanding
24:8 *c* a mere master at evil ideas
Ec 7:22 you, have *c* down evil upon
Ca 5:6 I *c* him, but he did not answer
Isa 1:26 be *c* City of Righteousness
4:1 *c* by your name to take away
6:3 *c* to that one and said
9:6 *c* Wonderful Counselor
13:3 *c* my mighty ones for
19:18 will one city be *c*
30:7 I have *c* this one: Rahab
31:2 not *c* back his own words
31:4 *c* out against it a full
32:5 no longer be *c* generous
35:8 Way of Holiness it will be *c*
41:9 I have *c* even from the
42:6 have *c* you in righteousness
43:1 I have *c* you by your name
43:7 that is *c* by my name and
43:22 you have not *c* even me
48:2 *c* themselves as being from
48:8 the belly you have been *c*
48:12 and you Israel my *c* one
48:15 Moreover, I have *c* him
49:1 has *c* me even from the belly
50:2 When I *c*, there was nobody
51:2 For he was one when I *c* him
54:5 whole earth he will be *c*
54:6 Jehovah *c* you as if you were
56:7 *c* even a house of prayer for
58:12 *c* the repairer of the gap
61:3 *c* big trees of righteousness
61:6 of Jehovah you will be *c*
Isa 62:2 be *c* by a new name, which
62:4 be *c* My Delight Is in Her
62:12 will be *c* Searched For
63:19 your name had not been *c*
65:12 *c*, but you did not answer
65:17 will not be *c* to mind
65:20 have evil *c* down upon him
66:4 *c*, but there was no one
Jer 3:4 from now on *c* out to me
4:20 crash is what has been *c*
7:10 which my name has been *c*
7:11 which my name has been *c*
7:14 which my name has been *c*
7:30 which my name has been *c*
10:25 not *c* even upon your name
11:16 Jehovah has *c* your name
12:6 *c* out loudly behind you
14:9 your own name has been *c*
15:16 name has been *c* upon me
19:6 will be *c* no more Topheth
20:3 Jehovah has *c* your name, not
23:6 with which he will be *c*
25:29 upon which my name is *c*
30:17 chased away is what they *c*
32:34 my own name has been *c*
33:16 *c*, Jehovah Is Our
34:15 which my name has been *c*
42:8 *c* for Johanan the son of
44:26 *c* out by the mouth of any
La 1:15 He has *c* against me a meeting
1:19 *c* to those intensely loving
3:55 *c* out your name, O Jehovah
4:15 Unclean! they have *c* out to
Eze 10:13 it was *c* out in my ears
20:29 should be *c* a High Place
21:24 being *c* to remembrance you
Da 5:12 Now let Daniel himself be *c*
9:18 that has been *c* by your name
9:19 has been *c* upon your city
10:1 name was *c* Belteshazzar
Ho 7:11 To Egypt they have *c*
11:1 out of Egypt I *c* my son
11:2 They *c* them. To that same
Am 9:12 my name has been *c*
Jon 2:2 I *c* out to Jehovah, and he
Zec 1:4 the former prophets *c*, saying
7:7 Jehovah *c* out by means of the
7:13 he *c* and they did not listen
8:3 be *c* the city of trueness
11:7 The one I *c* Pleasantness
11:7 and the other I *c* Union
Mt 1:16 Jesus . . . who is *c* Christ
1:25 and he *c* his name Jesus
2:15 Out of Egypt I *c* my son
2:23 He will be *c* a Nazarene
4:18 Simon who is *c* Peter and
4:21 mending their nets, and he *c*
5:9 they will be *c* sons of God
5:19 be *c* least in relation to the
5:19 *c* great in relation to the
10:2 Simon, the one *c* Peter, and
10:25 *c* the householder Beelzebub
13:55 Is not his mother *c* Mary
15:10 he *c* the crowd near and said
15:32 Jesus *c* his disciples to him
20:32 Jesus stopped, *c* them and
21:13 will be *c* a house of prayer
23:7 and to be *c* Rabbi by men
23:8 do not you be *c* Rabbi, for
23:10 Neither be *c* leaders, for
26:3 priest who was *c* Caiaphas
26:14 the one *c* Judas Iscariot
26:36 to the spot *c* Gethsemane
26:75 Peter *c* to mind the saying
27:8 *c* Field of Blood to this very
27:16 prisoner *c* Barabbas
27:33 came to a place *c* *Gol'go·tha*
27:46 the ninth hour Jesus *c* out
27:63 we have *c* to mind that that
Mr 1:20 and without delay he *c* them
8:34 *c* the crowd to him with his
9:35 *c* the twelve and said to
10:49 *c* the blind man, saying to
11:17 be *c* a house of prayer
12:43 he *c* his disciples to him
15:16 *c* the whole body of troops
15:34 *c* out with a loud voice
Lu 1:32 be *c* Son of the Most High
1:35 what is born will be *c* holy
1:42 she *c* out with a loud cry and
1:60 but he shall be *c* John
1:61 that is *c* by this name
1:62 what he wanted it to be *c*
1:76 *c* a prophet of the Most High
Lu 2:4 which is *c* Bethlehem, because
2:21 his name was also *c* Jesus
2:21 name *c* by the angel before
2:23 must be *c* holy to Jehovah
6:13 he *c* his disciples to him and
6:15 Simon who is *c* the zealous
7:11 he traveled to a city *c* Nain
8:54 took her by the hand and *c*
9:1 he *c* the twelve together and
9:10 into a city *c* Bethsaida
10:39 also had a sister *c* Mary
15:19 worthy of being *c* your son
15:21 worthy of being *c* your son
15:26 *c* one of the servants to him
16:2 *c* him and said to him, What
16:24 *c* and said, Father Abraham
18:16 Jesus *c* the infants to him
19:2 man *c* by the name Zacchaeus
19:15 commanded to be *c* to him
19:29 mountain *c* Mount of Olives
21:37 *c* the Mount of Olives
22:3 Judas, the one *c* Iscariot
22:25 over them are *c* Benefactors
22:47 the man *c* Judas, one of the
23:13 Pilate then *c* the chief
23:20 Again Pilate *c* out to them
23:33 they got to the place *c* Skull
23:46 Jesus *c* with a loud voice
24:8 they *c* his sayings to mind
Joh 1:42 you will be *c* Cephas
1:48 Before Philip *c* you, while
2:9 director . . . *c* the bridegroom
2:17 disciples *c* to mind that it
2:22 disciples *c* to mind that he
4:5 a city of Samaria *c* Sychar
4:25 Messiah . . . who is *c* Christ
9:11 man *c* Jesus made a clay and
9:18 *c* the parents of the man
9:24 *c* the man that had been
10:35 If he *c* gods those against
11:16 Thomas, who was *c* The Twin
11:28 *c* Mary her sister, saying
11:54 into a city *c* Ephraim, and
12:16 *c* to mind that these things
12:17 he *c* Lazarus out of the
15:15 I have *c* you friends
18:33 *c* Jesus and said to him
19:13 place *c* The Stone Pavement
19:17 is *c* *Gol'go·tha* in Hebrew
20:24 who was *c* The Twin, was
21:2 Thomas, who was *c* The Twin
Ac 1:12 *c* the Mount of Olives, which
1:19 that field was *c* in their
1:23 Joseph *c* Barsabbas, who was
3:2 door that was *c* Beautiful
3:11 was *c* Solomon's colonnade
4:18 they *c* them and charged them
5:21 *c* together the Sanhedrin and
6:2 the twelve *c* the multitude
7:14 Joseph sent out and *c* Jacob
7:58 feet of a young man *c* Saul
8:10 God, which can be *c* Great
9:11 go to the street *c* Straight
9:41 he *c* the holy ones and the
10:1 the Italian band, as it was *c*
10:7 *c* two of his house servants
10:18 they *c* out and inquired
10:24 *c* together his relatives and
11:16 I *c* to mind the saying of
11:26 in Antioch . . . *c* Christians
13:1 Symeon who was *c* Niger, and
13:2 work to which I have *c* them
15:17 people who are *c* by my name
15:22 Judas who was *c* Barsabbas
15:37 also John, who was *c* Mark
16:28 Paul *c* out with a loud voice
20:17 and *c* for the older men of
23:17 So Paul *c* one of the army
23:18 *c* me to him and requested
24:2 When he was *c*, Tertullus
26:6 I stand *c* to judgment
27:8 place *c* Fair Havens, near
27:14 wind *c* Euroaquilo rushed
27:16 small island *c* Cauda, and
28:1 that the island was *c* Malta
28:17 he *c* together those who
Ro 1:1 and *c* to be an apostle
1:6 *c* to belong to Jesus Christ
1:7 beloved ones, *c* to be holy
8:28 *c* according to his purpose
8:30 are the ones he also *c*; and
8:30 those whom he *c* are the ones
9:7 *c* your seed will be through
9:24 *c* not only from among Jews

Ro 9:26 be *c* sons of the living God
1Co 1:1 Paul, *c* to be an apostle of
1:2 *c* to be holy ones, together
1:9 *c* into a sharing with his Son
1:24 to those who are the *c*, both
1:26 in a fleshly way were *c*
5:11 anyone *c* a brother that is a
7:15 but God has *c* you to peace
7:17 one so walk as God has *c* him
7:18 Was any man *c* circumcised?
7:18 man been *c* in uncircumcision
7:20 In whatever state . . . was *c*
7:21 Were you *c* when a slave?
7:22 that was *c* when a slave is
7:22 that was *c* when a free man
7:24 each one was *c*, brothers
8:5 those who are *c* gods, whether
15:9 not fit to be *c* an apostle
Ga 1:6 *c* you with Christ's undeserved
1:15 *c* me through his undeserved
5:13 *c* for freedom, brothers
Eph 1:18 the hope to which he *c* you
2:11 uncircumcision you were *c* by
2:11 that which is *c* circumcision
4:1 calling with which you were *c*
4:4 you were *c* in the one hope
4:4 one hope to which you were *c*
Col 3:15 you were, in fact, *c* to it
4:11 and Jesus who is *c* Justus
1Th 4:7 God *c* us, not with allowance
2Th 2:4 who is *c* god or an object of
2:14 *c* you through the good news
1Ti 6:12 life for which you were *c*
6:20 of the falsely *c* knowledge
2Ti 1:9 and *c* us with a holy calling
Heb 3:13 as long as it may be *c* Today
5:4 when he is *c* by God, just as
5:10 *c* by God a high priest
9:2 and it is *c* the Holy Place
9:3 compartment *c* the Most Holy
9:15 ones who have been *c* might
11:8 Abraham, when he was *c*
11:16 to be *c* upon as their God
11:18 *c* your seed will be through
11:24 refused to be *c* the son of
Jas 2:7 name by which you were *c*
2:23 he came to be *c* Jehovah's
1Pe 1:15 the Holy One who *c* you, do
2:9 one that *c* you out of darkness
2:21 to this course you were *c*
3:9 you were *c* to this course, so
5:10 *c* you to his everlasting
2Pe 1:3 one who *c* us through glory
1Jo 3:1 should be *c* children of God
Jude 1 the *c* ones who are loved in
Re 1:9 in the isle that is *c* Patmos
8:11 of the star is *c* Wormwood
11:8 in a spiritual sense *c* Sodom
12:9 one *c* Devil and Satan, who
14:18 he *c* out with a loud voice
16:16 is *c* in Hebrew Har–Magedon
17:14 those *c* and chosen and
18:5 God has *c* her acts of
19:11 *c* Faithful and True, and
19:13 he is *c* is The Word of God

Calling
Ge 1:5 God began *c* the light Day, but
1:10 God began *c* the dry land Earth
2:20 man was *c* the names of all
3:9 God kept *c* to the man
4:26 of *c* on the name of Jehovah
19:5 they kept *c* out to Lot and
22:11 Jehovah's angel began *c* to
26:18 resumed *c* their names by the
31:47 began *c* it Jegar-sahadutha
Nu 10:7 *c* the congregation together
25:2 *c* the people to the sacrifices
De 4:7 God is in all our *c* upon him
Jg 7:20 began *c* out: Jehovah's sword
8:1 in not *c* us when you went to
1Sa 3:8 Jehovah that was *c* the boy
3:13 are *c* down evil upon God
7:8 *c* to Jehovah our God for aid
7:9 Samuel began *c* to Jehovah for
12:8 began *c* to Jehovah for aid
20:38 Jonathan went on *c* from
28:15 *c* you to let me know what
2Sa 16:5 *c* down evil as he came out
22:7 I kept *c* upon Jehovah, And
22:7 And to my God I kept *c*
1Ki 17:20 began *c* to Jehovah and
18:26 *c* upon the name of Baal
18:28 began *c* at the top of their
2Ch 32:18 *c* with a loud voice in the
Job 12:4 One *c* to God that he should
35:9 they keep *c* for aid
42:14 *c* the name of the first
Ps 18:6 I kept *c* upon Jehovah
22:2 O my God, I keep *c* by day
28:1 To you, O Jehovah, I keep *c*
30:8 To you, O Jehovah, I kept *c*
42:7 deep to watery deep is *c*
59:4 Do rouse yourself at my *c*
69:3 have become tired by my *c* out
86:3 to you I keep *c* all day long
86:5 to all those *c* upon you is
99:6 Samuel was among those *c*
99:6 *c* to Jehovah, and he himself
107:13 *c* to Jehovah for help in
107:19 *c* to Jehovah for help in
145:18 near to all those *c* upon
147:9 young ravens that keep *c*
Pr 1:28 time they will keep *c* me
8:1 Does not wisdom keep *c* out
8:4 men, I am *c*, and my voice is
20:20 *c* down evil upon his father
Ec 7:21 servant *c* down evil upon you
Isa 1:13 the *c* of a convention—I
6:4 at the voice of the one *c*
21:11 is one *c* out from Seir
40:3 is *c* out in the wilderness
41:4 *c* out the generations from
45:3 the One *c* you by your name
46:11 One *c* from the sunrising
48:1 *c* yourselves by the name of
48:13 I am *c* to them, that they
59:4 no one *c* out in righteousness
64:7 is no one *c* upon your name
65:1 that was not *c* upon my name
Jer 1:15 *c* for all the families of
7:13 kept *c* you, but you did not
11:14 *c* out to me in regard to
15:10 are *c* down evil upon me
25:29 a sword that I am *c* against
35:17 *c* to them but they did not
La 3:57 in the day that I kept *c* you
Eze 9:3 *c* out to the man that was
21:23 *c* error to remembrance
23:19 *c* to mind the days of her
23:21 *c* attention to the loose
Da 4:14 *c* out loudly, and this is
5:7 king was *c* out loudly to bring
Ho 7:7 none among them is *c* out to
Joe 2:32 survivors, whom Jehovah is *c*
Am 5:8 *c* for the waters of the sea
7:4 Jehovah was *c* for a contention
9:6 *c* for the waters of the sea
Hag 1:11 *c* for dryness upon the earth
Mt 18:2 *c* a young child to him, he
20:25 Jesus, *c* them to him, said
27:47 to say: This man is *c* Elijah
Mr 3:23 So, after *c* them to him, he
7:14 *c* the crowd to him again, he
10:42 Jesus, after *c* them to him
10:49 courage, get up, he is *c*
15:35 See! He is *c* Elijah
Lu 16:5 *c* to him each one of the
19:13 *C* ten slaves of his he gave
Joh 5:18 also *c* God his own Father
11:28 is present and is *c* you
Ac 9:14 all those *c* upon your name
10:15 You stop *c* defiled the
11:9 You stop *c* defiled the things
13:7 *C* Barnabas and Saul to him
14:12 they went *c* Barnabas Zeus
22:16 by your *c* upon his name
Ro 10:12 rich to all those *c* upon him
11:29 *c* of God are not things he
1Co 1:2 *c* upon the name of our Lord
1:26 For you behold his *c* of you
Ga 5:8 is not from the One *c* you
Eph 4:1 *c* with which you were called
1Th 2:12 God . . . *c* you to his kingdom
5:24 He who is *c* you is faithful
2Th 1:11 count you worthy of his *c*
2Ti 1:9 called us with a holy *c*, not
Heb 3:1 partakers of the heavenly *c*
1Pe 1:17 if you are *c* upon the Father
3:6 to obey Abraham, *c* him lord
2Pe 1:10 *c* and choosing of you sure

Calls
Ge 12:3 him that *c* down evil upon you
Ex 21:17 one who *c* down evil upon his
Le 20:9 *c* down evil upon his father
24:15 *c* down evil upon his God, he
Nu 31:6 trumpets for blowing *c* were
1Ki 8:43 which the foreigner *c* to you
2Ch 6:33 which the foreigner *c* to you
Job 11:10 And *c* a court, then who can
31:14 when he *c* for an accounting
Ps 50:4 He *c* to the heavens above and
89:26 *c* out to me, You are my
147:4 All of them he *c* by their
Pr 1:21 of the noisy streets it *c* out
12:23 is one that *c* out foolishness
18:6 very mouth *c* even for strokes
30:11 generation that *c* down evil
Isa 40:26 whom he *c* even by name
Joe 2:32 who *c* on the name of Jehovah
Mic 6:9 voice of Jehovah *c* out, and
Mt 22:43 by inspiration *c* him Lord
22:45 David *c* him Lord, how is he
Mr 12:37 David himself *c* him Lord
Lu 15:6 he *c* his friends and
15:9 she *c* the women who are her
20:37 he *c* Jehovah the God of
20:44 David, therefore, *c* him Lord
Joh 10:3 *c* his own sheep by name and
Ac 2:21 who *c* on the name of Jehovah
Ro 4:17 *c* the things that are not as
9:11 but upon the One who *c*
10:13 *c* on the name of Jehovah
13:7 him who *c* for the tax, the
13:7 to him who *c* for the tribute
13:7 to him who *c* for fear, such
13:7 him who *c* for honor, such
2Co 7:15 *c* to mind the obedience of
Jas 5:4 *c* for help on the part of the
Re 2:20 who *c* herself a prophetess

Calm
1Ki 19:12 there was a *c*, low voice
Job 4:16 There was a *c*, and I now
Ps 89:9 waves you yourself *c* them
107:29 windstorm to stand at a *c*
Pr 14:30 A *c* heart is the life of the
29:11 wise keeps it *c* to the last
Isa 57:20 when it is unable to *c* down
Mt 8:26 sea, and a great *c* set in
Mr 4:39 abated, and a great *c* set in
Lu 8:24 they subsided, and a *c* set in
Ac 19:36 becoming for you to keep *c*
1Ti 2:2 leading a *c* and quiet life

Calmed
Jg 8:3 their spirit *c* down toward

Calmness
Pr 15:4 *c* of the tongue is a tree of
Ec 10:4 for *c* itself allays great sins

Calms
Ge 27:44 rage of your brother *c* down

Calneh
Ge 10:10 Erech and Accad and *C*, in
Am 6:2 Make your way over to *C*, and

Calno
Isa 10:9 not *C* just like Carchemish

Calves
1Sa 14:32 and *c* and slaughtering them
1Ki 12:28 made two golden *c* and said
12:32 to sacrifice to the *c* that
2Ki 10:29 the golden *c* of which one
17:16 molten statues, two *c*
2Ch 11:15 for the *c* that he had made
13:8 golden *c* that Jeroboam made
Ps 68:30 With the *c* of the peoples
Jer 46:21 soldiers . . . like fattened *c*
Ho 13:2 sacrificers . . . kiss mere *c*
Am 6:4 bulls from among fattened *c*
Mic 6:6 offerings, with *c* a year old
Mal 4:2 paw . . . like fattened *c*

Came*
Ge 2:1 all their army *c* to their
2:2 God *c* to the completion of his
7:10 waters of the deluge *c* upon
8:11 dove *c* to him about the time
9:18 sons who *c* out of the ark
11:2 it *c* about that in their
12:5 they *c* to the land of Canaan
13:18 Later on he *c* and dwelt
14:5 Chedorlaomer *c*, and also the
14:7 *c* to En-mishpat, that is
14:13 man who had escaped *c* and
15:1 word of Jehovah *c* to Abram in
15:17 dense darkness *c* and, look! a
19:3 to him and *c* into his house
19:5 Where are the men who *c* in
19:9 lone man *c* here to reside as
20:3 God *c* to Abimelech in a dream

Ge 25:24 days *c* to the full for giving
25:25 the first *c* out red all over
25:26 his brother *c* out and his
25:29 Esau *c* along from the field
27:30 Esau his brother *c* back from
27:35 brother *c* with deception
28:11 In time he *c* across a place
29:9 Rachel *c* with the sheep that
31:24 God *c* to Laban the Syrian in
33:18 Jacob *c* safe and sound to the
34:7 sons of Jacob *c* in from the
35:6 Jacob *c* to Luz, which is in
35:27 Jacob *c* to Isaac his father
37:23 as Joseph *c* to his brothers
38:28 This one *c* out first
38:29 why, here his brother *c* out
39:16 his master *c* to his house
41:27 cows that *c* up after them
41:57 *c* to Egypt to buy from
42:5 Israel's sons *c* along with
42:6 Joseph's brothers *c* and bowed
42:29 they *c* to Jacob their father
43:21 we *c* to the lodging place
43:23 Your money *c* first to me
44:18 Judah now *c* near to him and
44:24 it *c* about that we went up
45:4 With that they *c* close to him
45:25 *c* into the land of Canaan
46:1 *c* to Beer-sheba, and he
46:6 Eventually they *c* into Egypt
46:8 sons who *c* into Egypt: Jacob
46:26 All the souls who *c* to Jacob
46:27 *c* into Egypt were seventy
46:28 *c* into the land of Goshen
47:1 Joseph *c* and reported to
48:1 it *c* about after these things
48:5 I *c* here to you into Egypt
50:9 camp *c* to be very numerous
50:10 they *c* to the threshing floor
50:18 *c* and fell down before him
Ex 1:1 Israel's sons who *c* into Egypt
1:1 each man and his household *c*
2:5 *c* down to bathe in the Nile
2:16 they *c* and drew water and
2:17 shepherds *c* and drove them
2:18 *c* home to Reuel their father
3:1 he *c* at length to the mountain
5:20 as they *c* out from Pharaoh
7:21 blood *c* to be in all the land
9:24 *c* hail, and fire quivering
10:13 morning *c* and the east wind
13:8 to me when I *c* out of Egypt
14:20 it *c* in between the camp of
15:23 they *c* to Marah, but they
15:27 After that they *c* to Elim
16:1 *c* to the wilderness of Sin
16:22 *c* about on the sixth day that
16:22 *c* and reported it to Moses
18:5 and his wife *c* to Moses into
18:12 *c* to eat bread with Moses'
19:1 *c* out of the land of Egypt
19:1 they *c* into the wilderness of
19:7 Moses *c* and called the older
19:16 it *c* about that thunders and
24:3 Moses *c* and related to the
34:31 So Aaron . . . *c* back to him
34:32 sons of Israel *c* near to him
Le 9:5 *c* near and stood before Jehovah
9:22 *c* down from rendering the sin
9:23 *c* out and blessed the people
9:24 fire *c* out from before
10:2 a fire *c* out from before
10:5 *c* near and carried them in
16:9 the lot *c* up for Jehovah
16:10 the lot *c* up for Azazel
Nu 8:22 Levites *c* in to carry on their
10:11 *c* about that in the second
11:25 Jehovah *c* down in a cloud
11:25 *c* about that as soon as the
12:5 Jehovah *c* down in the pillar
13:22 they then *c* to Hebron
13:23 When they *c* to the torrent
13:26 they walked and *c* to Moses
14:45 *c* on down and began striking
16:27 and Dathan and Abiram *c* out
16:35 a fire *c* out from Jehovah
20:6 Moses and Aaron *c* from before
21:7 the people *c* to Moses and
21:23 *c* to Jahaz and began fighting
21:33 Og the king of Bashan *c* out
22:9 Then God *c* to Balaam and said
22:14 got up and *c* to Balak and
22:16 they *c* to Balaam and said to
22:20 God *c* to Balaam by night and

Nu 22:39 and they *c* to Kiriath-huzoth
25:6 a man of the sons of Israel *c*
27:1 daughters of Zelophehad . . . *c*
31:12 they *c* bringing to Moses and
32:2 sons of Reuben *c* and said this
32:11 men who *c* up out of Egypt
32:13 generation . . . *c* to their end
De 1:19 eventually *c* to Kadesh-barnea
1:22 all of you *c* near to me and
1:44 *c* out to meet you and went
2:15 until they *c* to their end
11:10 Egypt out of which you *c*
16:3 you *c* out of the land of Egypt
32:44 Moses *c* and spoke all the
33:2 Jehovah—from Sinai he *c*, And
Jos 2:1 *c* to the house of a prostitute
2:10 when you *c* out of Egypt, and
2:22 *c* to the mountainous region
3:15 *c* as far as the Jordan and
4:19 people *c* up out of the Jordan
5:4 people that *c* out of Egypt
5:6 men of war who *c* out of Egypt
8:22 *c* out of the city to meet
8:24 until they *c* to their end
10:20 until these *c* to their end
14:7 I *c* bringing him back word
16:1 the lot *c* out for the sons of
17:6 *c* into an inheritance in the
18:9 they *c* to Joshua at the camp
21:45 it all *c* true
22:10 they *c* to the regions of the
22:15 In time they *c* to the sons
22:20 there *c* indignation? And he
24:6 you *c* to the sea, then the
24:11 and *c* to Jericho. And the
Jg 1:16 *c* up out of the city of palm
1:30 and *c* to be subject to forced
3:24 And his servants *c* and began
4:18 Jael *c* on out to meet Sisera
5:13 the survivors *c* down to the
5:13 people *c* down to me against
5:19 Kings *c*, they fought; It was
6:3 the Easterners *c* up, yes, they
6:3 yes, they *c* up against them
6:11 angel *c* and sat under the big
7:13 Gideon now *c*, and, look!
7:13 it *c* to a tent and struck it
7:19 Gideon *c* with the hundred men
8:4 *c* to the Jordan, crossing it
9:26 and his brothers *c* and crossed
11:13 they *c* up out of Egypt, from
11:16 they *c* up out of Egypt
11:29 spirit now *c* upon Jephthah
13:9 *c* again to the woman while
13:10 the man that *c* the other day
13:11 and *c* to the man and said to
15:9 Philistines *c* up and camped
15:14 *c* as far as Lehi, and the
16:1 woman there and *c* in to her
16:18 axis lords *c* up to her that
17:8 he *c* into the mountainous
18:2 they *c* into the mountainous
18:13 and *c* as far as the house of
19:10 *c* as far as in front of Jebus
19:22 man that *c* into your house
19:26 the woman *c* as it was
20:4 I *c*, I and my concubine, to
20:21 *c* on out from Gibeah and
20:25 Benjamin *c* on out from
20:26 *c* to Bethel and wept and sat
20:34 Israel *c* in front of Gibeah
20:48 men of Israel *c* back against
21:2 people *c* to Bethel and kept
21:14 Benjamin *c* back at that time
Ru 1:2 *c* to the fields of Moab and
1:19 until they *c* to Bethlehem
1:19 soon as they *c* to Bethlehem
1:22 they *c* to Bethlehem at the
2:4 Boaz *c* from Bethlehem and
1Sa 1:19 *c* into their house at Ramah
2:13 attendant of the priest *c*
2:15 attendant of the priest *c* and
3:10 Then Jehovah *c* and took his
5:10 the ark of the true God *c* to
6:14 the wagon itself *c* into the
7:1 men of Kiriath-jearim *c* and
8:4 and *c* to Samuel at Ramah
9:5 *c* into the land of Zuph
10:14 So we *c* to Samuel
11:4 messengers *c* to Gibeah of
11:7 that they *c* out as one man
11:9 the messengers *c* and told
14:20 they *c* as far as the battle
14:25 *c* into the woods, when

1Sa 14:26 the people *c* into the woods
15:12 Saul *c* to Carmel, and, look!
15:13 At length Samuel *c* to Saul
16:4 When he *c* to Bethlehem the
16:6 as they *c* in and he caught
16:21 David *c* to Saul and attended
17:20 he *c* to the camp enclosure
17:22 When he *c*, he began asking
17:34 there *c* a lion, and also a
18:13 regularly went out and *c* in
19:24 why they *c* to say: Is Saul
20:1 *c* and said in front of
20:33 Jonathan *c* to know that it
20:37 attendant *c* as far as the
20:38 and then *c* to his master
20:42 Jonathan himself *c* into the
21:1 David *c* into Nob to
21:10 *c* to Achish the king of Gath
22:2 *c* to be with him about four
22:5 David went away and *c* into
22:11 all of them *c* to the king
23:26 Saul *c* to this side of the
23:27 messenger that *c* to Saul
24:1 *c* reporting to him, saying
24:3 *c* to the stone sheepfolds
24:3 Saul *c* in to ease nature
25:8 upon a good day that we *c*
25:9 David's young men *c* and
25:12 *c* and reported to him in
25:36 Abigail *c* in to Nabal, and
26:1 men of Ziph *c* to Saul at
26:15 *c* in to bring the king your
27:9 he returned and *c* to Achish
28:4 *c* and pitched camp in Shunem
28:8 *c* to the woman by night
28:21 woman now *c* to Saul and
29:10 your lord that *c* with you
30:3 David *c* with his men to the
30:21 David *c* to the two hundred
30:21 *c* out to meet David and to
30:21 David *c* near to the people
30:23 marauder band that *c*
30:26 When David *c* to Ziklag he
31:6 *c* to die together on that
31:7 Philistines *c* on in and took
31:8 Philistines *c* to strip the
31:12 *c* to Jabesh and burned them
2Sa 1:2 *c* to David, he at once fell
2:4 men of Judah *c* and anointed
2:4 they *c* telling David, saying
2:23 *c* to the place where Asahel
2:24 *c* to the hill of Ammah
2:29 and finally *c* to Mahanaim
3:20 Abner *c* to David at Hebron
3:23 army that was with him *c* in
3:23 Abner the son of Ner *c* to
3:25 to fool you that he *c* and to
3:35 people *c* to give David bread
4:4 report . . . *c* from Jezreel
4:6 *c* into the middle of the
5:1 Israel *c* to David at Hebron
5:3 older men of Israel *c* to the
5:13 after he *c* from Hebron
5:20 David *c* to Baal-perazim
6:16 ark of Jehovah *c* into the
6:20 Michal, Saul's daughter, *c*
7:4 word of Jehovah *c* to Nathan
7:18 King David *c* in and sat down
8:5 Syria of Damascus *c* to help
8:13 *c* back from striking down
8:14 Edomites *c* to be servants of
10:14 and hence *c* into the city
10:14 Joab . . . *c* to Jerusalem
10:16 then they *c* to Helam, with
10:17 the Jordan and *c* to Helam
11:7 When Uriah *c* to him, David
11:17 men of the city *c* on out
11:22 *c* and told David all about
11:23 *c* out against us into the
12:1 *c* in to him and said to him
12:3 *c* to be as a daughter to him
12:4 visitor *c* to the rich man
12:16 *c* in and spent the night
12:20 *c* to the house of Jehovah
12:20 *c* into his own house and
12:24 *c* in to her and lay down
13:24 Absalom *c* in to the king
13:30 report itself *c* to David
14:31 *c* to Absalom at the house
14:33 Joab *c* in to the king and
14:33 Absalom, who now *c* in to
15:13 an informer *c* to David
15:20 Yesterday was when you *c*
15:32 when David himself *c* to the

2Sa 15:37 companion, *c* into the city
16:5 David *c* as far as Bahurim
16:5 calling down evil as he *c*
16:16 Hushai . . . *c* in to Absalom
17:6 So Hushai *c* in to Absalom
17:18 *c* to the house of a man in
17:20 *c* to the woman at her house
17:24 for David, he *c* to Mahanaim
17:27 as David *c* to Mahanaim
18:15 *c* around and struck Absalom
19:15 they *c* to Gilgal to go and
19:24 the day that he *c* in peace
19:25 he *c* to Jerusalem to meet
20:5 *c* later than the fixed time
22:11 he *c* riding upon a cherub
22:11 upon a cherub and *c* flying
23:16 *c* carrying and bringing it
24:6 they *c* on to Gilead and the
24:7 *c* to the fortress of Tyre
24:7 *c* to the terminating point
24:8 *c* to Jerusalem at the end of
24:11 Jehovah's word . . . *c* to Gad
24:13 Gad *c* in to David and told
24:18 Gad *c* in to David on that
1Ki 1:4 she *c* to be the king's nurse
1:22 the prophet himself *c* in
1:23 he *c* in before the king and
1:28 she *c* in before the king and
1:32 So they *c* in before the king
1:42 son of Abiathar the priest *c*
1:53 he *c* in and bowed down to
2:13 Adonijah . . . *c* to Bath-sheba
2:19 Bath-sheba *c* in to King
2:30 Benaiah *c* to the tent of
3:15 he *c* to Jerusalem and stood
6:1 *c* out from the land of Egypt
6:11 word of Jehovah *c* to Solomon
7:14 he *c* to King Solomon and
8:3 the older men of Israel *c*
10:1 she *c* to test him with
10:2 *c* on in to Solomon and began
10:10 never *c* anymore the like of
10:14 gold that *c* to Solomon in
11:18 and *c* into Paran and took
11:18 *c* into Egypt to Pharaoh the
12:1 Israel *c* to make him king
12:3 *c* and began to speak to
12:22 *c* to Shemaiah the man of
13:11 his sons now *c* in and
13:20 *c* to the prophet that had
13:25 they *c* in and spoke of it in
14:4 and *c* to the house of Ahijah
14:17 went her way and *c* to Tirzah
14:25 *c* up against Jerusalem
14:28 the king *c* to the house of
15:17 *c* up against Judah and
16:1 word of Jehovah now *c* to
16:18 *c* into the dwelling tower
17:2 word of Jehovah now *c* to him
17:22 soul of the child *c* back
17:22 the child . . . *c* to life
18:1 Jehovah's own word *c* to
18:38 fire of Jehovah *c* falling
19:3 and *c* to Beer-sheba, which
19:4 at length *c* and sat down
21:4 Ahab *c* into his house, sullen
21:5 Jezebel his wife *c* in to
21:13 *c* in and sat down in front
21:17 word *c* to Elijah the
21:28 *c* to Elijah the Tishbite
22:15 he *c* in to the king, and
22:21 a spirit *c* out and stood
22:33 *c* back from following him
2Ki 1:5 the messengers *c* back to him
1:6 a man that *c* up to meet us
2:4 So they *c* on to Jericho
2:15 *c* to meet him and bowed
2:23 that *c* out from the city
2:24 two she-bears *c* out from the
3:24 *c* into the camp of Israel
3:24 they *c* into Moab, striking
4:27 she *c* to the man of the true
4:27 *c* near to push her away
4:32 Elisha *c* into the house
4:42 that *c* from Baal-shalishah
5:4 *c* and reported to his lord
5:9 Naaman *c* with his horses and
5:15 *c* and stood before him and
5:24 *c* to Ophel, he immediately
5:25 *c* in and then stood by his
6:4 they finally *c* to the Jordan
7:10 We *c* into the camp of the
9:24 the arrow *c* out at his heart
9:30 At length Jehu *c* to Jezreel
2Ki 9:31 Jehu himself *c* in by the
9:34 *c* on in and ate and drank
10:7 as soon as the letter *c* to
10:8 messenger *c* in and told him
10:17 Finally he *c* to Samaria
10:21 worshipers of Baal *c* in
10:24 *c* in to render up sacrifices
11:9 *c* in to Jehoiada the priest
11:13 *c* to the people at the house
11:16 she *c* by the way of the
11:18 *c* to the house of Baal and
13:21 *c* to life and stood upon his
14:11 the king of Israel *c* up
14:13 *c* to Jerusalem and he made
15:14 *c* up from Tirzah
15:14 *c* to Samaria and struck
15:29 the king of Assyria *c* in and
16:11 King Ahaz *c* from Damascus
16:12 the king *c* from Damascus
17:3 the king of Assyria *c* up
17:28 *c* and began dwelling in
19:1 *c* into the house of Jehovah
19:5 servants . . . *c* in to Isaiah
20:4 Jehovah's word itself *c* to
21:15 *c* out from Egypt down to
23:29 *c* up to the king of Assyria
24:1 the king of Babylon *c* up
24:10 Babylon *c* up to Jerusalem
24:10 the city *c* under siege
25:1 the king of Babylon *c*
25:8 king of Babylon, *c* to
25:23 *c* to Gedaliah at Mizpah
25:26 rose up and *c* into Egypt
1Ch 2:53 and the Eshtaolites *c* out
2:55 Kenites that *c* from Hammath
4:9 Jabez *c* to be more honorable
4:38 *c* in by names were the
10:7 Philistines *c* on in and took
10:8 *c* to strip the slain, they
11:3 *c* to the king at Hebron and
11:21 he *c* to be a chief to them
12:1 that *c* to David at Ziklag
12:19 he *c* with the Philistines
12:20 When he *c* to Ziklag there
12:23 that *c* to David at Hebron
12:38 *c* to Hebron to make David
14:9 *c* in and kept making raids
15:25 chiefs of the thousands *c*
15:29 *c* as far as the city of
17:3 the word of God *c* to Nathan
17:16 King David *c* in and sat
18:5 Syria of Damascus *c* to help
19:7 they *c* in and camped before
19:7 and now *c* in for the war
19:15 Later Joab *c* into Jerusalem
19:17 *c* to them and drew up in
20:8 they *c* to fall by the hand of
21:4 Joab . . . *c* to Jerusalem
21:21 So David *c* as far as Ornan
22:8 Jehovah's word *c* against me
27:1 divisions of those that *c* in
2Ch 1:13 Solomon *c* from the high
1:15 king *c* to make the silver
5:4 all the older men of Israel *c*
5:11 priests *c* out from the holy
7:1 fire itself *c* down from the
7:3 spectators when the fire *c*
9:1 she *c* in to Solomon and spoke
9:13 gold that *c* to Solomon in
10:1 Israelites *c* to make him
10:2 Jeroboam immediately *c* back
10:3 Jeroboam and all Israel *c*
11:2 word of Jehovah *c* to Shemaiah
12:5 *c* to Rehoboam and the
12:7 word of Jehovah *c* to
12:9 *c* up against Jerusalem and
12:11 king *c* to the house of
12:11 runners *c* in and carried
14:9 and *c* as far as Mareshah
16:1 Baasha the king of Israel *c*
16:7 Hanani the seer *c* to Asa the
18:20 spirit *c* out and stood
18:32 *c* back from following him
20:2 *c* and told Jehoshaphat
20:4 they *c* to consult Jehovah
20:24 *c* to the watchtower of the
20:25 people *c* to plunder the
20:28 *c* to Jerusalem with
21:12 *c* a writing to him from
21:17 they *c* up into Judah and
21:19 intestines *c* out during his
22:1 band that *c* with the Arabs
22:7 *c*, he went out with Jehoram
23:2 So they *c* to Jerusalem
2Ch 23:12 *c* to the people at the house
23:15 *c* to the entry of the horse
23:17 *c* to the house of Baal and
23:20 *c* right through the upper
24:11 *c* and then emptied the
24:12 they *c* to be hirers of the
24:17 princes of Judah *c* in and
24:23 military force of Syria *c*
25:7 man of the true God *c* to
25:14 Amaziah *c* from striking
26:16 *c* into the temple of
26:17 valiant men, *c* in after him
28:17 Edomites themselves *c* in
28:20 king of Assyria *c* against
29:8 Jehovah's indignation *c* to
29:15 *c* according to the king's
29:16 priests now *c* inside the
29:17 *c* to the porch of Jehovah
29:18 *c* inside to Hezekiah the
29:21 *c* bringing seven bulls and
30:11 so that they *c* to Jerusalem
30:25 that *c* from Israel and
30:25 *c* from the land of Israel
30:27 their prayer *c* to his holy
31:8 *c* and saw the heaps, they
32:1 king of Assyria *c* and
32:25 *c* to be indignation against
35:22 *c* to fight in the valley
36:6 *c* up that he might bind
36:16 rage of Jehovah *c* up
Ezr 2:2 *c* with Zerubbabel, Jeshua
3:3 fright *c* upon them because
4:12 the Jews who *c* up here from
5:3 their colleagues *c* to them
5:16 *c* he laid the foundations
7:8 *c* to Jerusalem in the fifth
7:9 he *c* to Jerusalem, according
8:32 we *c* to Jerusalem and dwelt
9:4 they *c* gathering themselves
Ne 1:2 Hanani, one of my brothers, *c*
2:9 I *c* to the governors beyond
2:11 At length I *c* to Jerusalem
2:15 I *c* back and entered by the
4:21 dawn until the stars *c* out
9:13 upon Mount Sinai you *c* down
9:24 sons *c* in and took the land
12:39 *c* to a stand at the Gate of
12:40 *c* to a stand at the house of
13:3 So it *c* about that, as soon as
13:6 I *c* to the king, and sometime
13:7 I *c* to Jerusalem and got to
Es 2:13 young woman herself *c* in to
2:14 the evening she herself *c* in
2:17 king *c* to love Esther more
4:9 Hathach now *c* in and told
5:2 Esther now *c* near and touched
5:5 and Haman *c* to the banquet
5:10 Haman . . . *c* into his house
6:6 When Haman *c* in, the king
7:1 king and Haman *c* in to banquet
8:1 Mordecai himself *c* in before
9:1 king's word and his law *c* due
9:11 number . . . *c* before the king
9:25 Esther *c* in before the king he
Job 1:14 *c* a messenger to Job, and
1:15 Sabeans *c* making a raid and
1:17 another one *c* and proceeded
1:19 there *c* a great wind from
1:21 Naked I *c* out of my mother's
4:14 A dread *c* over me, and a
30:26 good I waited, yet bad *c*
30:26 the light, but gloom *c*
42:16 *c* to see his sons and his
Ps 18:6 now *c* into his ears
18:10 he *c* riding upon a cherub
18:10 upon a cherub and *c* flying
18:10 he *c* darting upon the wings
33:9 he himself said, and it *c* to
105:18 Into irons his soul *c*
105:19 the time that his word *c*
106:11 waters *c* covering their
106:40 *c* to detest his inheritance
109:18 *c* like waters into the
Ec 5:15 go away again, just as one *c*
8:10 how they *c* in and how they
9:14 and there *c* to it a great king
Isa 7:1 *c* up to Jerusalem for war
16:12 *c* to his sanctuary to pray
20:1 year that Tartan *c* to Ashdod
36:1 king of Assyria *c* up against
36:3 *c* out to him Eliakim the son
36:22 *c* to Hezekiah with their
37:1 *c* into the house of Jehovah
37:5 *c* in to Isaiah

Isa 37:34 the way by which he *c* he
38:1 *c* in to him and said to
39:3 *c* in to King Hezekiah and
39:3 they *c* to me, from Babylon
50:2 when I *c* in, there was no
Jer 2:7 you *c* in and defiled my land
8:15 for peace, but no good *c*
14:19 for peace, but no good *c*
16:19 *c* to possess sheer falsehood
20:3 it *c* about on the following
26:21 ran away and *c* into Egypt
32:8 son of my paternal uncle *c*
33:19 word of Jehovah *c* further
35:11 *c* up against the land that
36:14 and *c* in to them
36:20 *c* in to the king, to the
36:23 *c* about that as soon as
37:5 force of Pharaoh that *c*
37:16 Jeremiah *c* into the house
38:27 princes *c* in to Jeremiah
39:1 *c* to Jerusalem and began
39:4 *c* about that as soon as
40:6 Jeremiah *c* to Gedaliah the
40:8 *c* to Gedaliah at Mizpah
40:13 *c* to Gedaliah at Mizpah
41:1 *c* to Gedaliah the son of
41:5 *c* men from Shechem, from
41:7 *c* into the midst of the city
43:7 *c* into the land of Egypt
43:7 *c* gradually as far as
49:9 grape gatherers . . . *c* in
49:9 thieves *c* in by night, they
52:12 *c* into Jerusalem
Eze 16:1 word of Jehovah *c* further to
17:3 great eagle . . . *c* to Lebanon
20:1 *c* in to inquire of Jehovah
23:44 they *c* in to Oholah and to
33:21 *c* to me the escaped one
36:20 they *c* in to the nations
36:20 the nations where they *c* in
37:8 flesh itself *c* up and skin
40:6 he *c* to the gate, the front
43:3 *c* to bring the city to ruin
43:4 glory of Jehovah itself *c*
46:9 gate by which he *c* in, for
Da 1:1 *c* to Jerusalem and proceeded
2:29 thoughts *c* up as regards what
4:8 *c* in before me Daniel, whose
5:5 fingers of a man's hand *c*
7:8 horn, a small one, *c* up in
7:20 horn that *c* up and before
7:22 the Ancient of Days *c* and
8:2 *c* about, while I was seeing
8:3 the one that *c* up afterward
8:6 *c* running toward it in its
8:17 *c* beside where I was standing
8:17 but when he *c* I got terrified
10:13 princes, *c* to help me; and
Ob 5 if despoilers *c* in by night
5 grape gatherers that *c* in to
Jon 1:3 he finally *c* down to Joppa
2:7 Then my prayer *c* in to you
Mt 2:1 from eastern parts *c* to
2:9 *c* to a stop above where the
2:23 *c* and dwelt in a city named
3:1 John the Baptist *c* preaching
3:13 Jesus *c* from Galilee to the
3:16 *c* up from the water; and
4:3 the Tempter *c* and said to him
4:11 angels *c* and began to
4:13 *c* and took up residence in
5:1 his disciples *c* to him
5:17 Do not think I *c* to destroy
5:17 I *c*, not to destroy, but to
7:25 floods *c* and the winds blew
7:27 floods *c* and the winds blew
8:2 a leprous man *c* up and began
8:5 an army officer *c* to him
8:19 certain scribe *c* up and said
8:25 *c* and woke him up, saying
8:32 They *c* out and went off into
9:10 *c* and began reclining with
9:13 I *c* to call, not righteous
9:14 John's disciples *c* to him and
9:20 *c* up behind and touched the
9:23 he *c* into the ruler's house
9:28 the blind men *c* to him, and
10:34 not think I *c* to put peace
10:34 I *c* to put, not peace, but a
10:35 I *c* to cause division, with
11:18 John *c* neither eating nor
12:42 *c* from the ends of the earth
13:4 the birds *c* and ate them up
13:7 thorns *c* up and choked them
Mt 13:10 the disciples *c* up and said
13:25 enemy *c* and oversowed weeds
13:27 slaves of the householder *c*
13:36 disciples *c* to him and said
14:12 disciples *c* up and removed
14:12 and *c* and reported to Jesus
14:15 disciples *c* to him and said
14:25 he *c* to them, walking over
14:34 and *c* to land in Gennesaret
15:1 *c* to Jesus from Jerusalem
15:12 disciples *c* up and said to
15:22 *c* out and cried aloud
15:39 and *c* into the regions of
17:7 Jesus *c* near and, touching
17:14 they *c* toward the crowd
17:18 and the demon *c* out of him
17:19 the disciples *c* up to Jesus
18:1 disciples *c* near to Jesus and
19:1 *c* to the frontiers of Judea
19:3 Pharisees *c* up to him, intent
19:16 a certain one *c* up to him
20:9 When the eleventh-hour men *c*
20:10 So, when the first *c*, they
20:28 as the Son of man *c*, not to
21:14 lame persons *c* up to him
21:23 older men of the people *c* up
21:32 John *c* to you in a way of
21:34 the season of the fruits *c*
22:11 the king *c* in to inspect the
22:23 *c* up to him and asked him
22:34 they *c* together in one group
24:39 flood *c* and swept them all
25:11 rest of the virgins also *c*
25:19 master of those slaves *c* and
25:20 *c* forward and brought five
25:22 *c* forward and said, Master
25:24 *c* forward and said, Master
25:36 in prison and you *c* to me
26:17 the disciples *c* up to Jesus
26:36 Jesus *c* with them to the
26:40 *c* to the disciples and found
26:43 he *c* again and found them
26:45 *c* to the disciples and said
26:47 Judas, one of the twelve, *c*
26:50 *c* forward and laid hands on
26:60 false witnesses *c* forward
26:60 Later on two *c* forward
26:69 a servant girl *c* up to him
26:73 *c* up and said to Peter
27:33 they *c* to a place called
27:49 and blood and water *c* out
27:57 *c* a rich man of Arimathea
28:1 Mary *c* to view the grave
28:13 disciples *c* in the night and
Mr 1:9 Jesus *c* from Nazareth of
1:11 a voice *c* out of the heavens
1:26 unclean spirit . . . *c* on out
1:40 There also *c* to him a leper
2:3 *c* bringing him a paralytic
2:17 I *c* to call, not righteous
2:18 *c* and said to him: Why is it
2:27 sabbath *c* into existence for
3:8 great multitude . . . *c* to him
3:31 his mother and his brothers *c*
4:4 and the birds *c* and ate it up
4:7 the thorns *c* up and choked it
5:13 unclean spirits *c* out and
5:22 Jairus by name, *c* and, on
5:38 So they *c* to the house of the
6:1 and *c* into his home territory
6:29 *c* and took up his corpse and
6:53 they *c* into Gennesaret and
9:7 and a voice *c* out of the cloud
9:14 *c* toward the other disciples
9:33 And they *c* into Capernaum
10:1 *c* to the frontiers of Judea
10:1 crowds *c* together to him
10:45 even the Son of man *c*, not
10:46 they *c* into Jericho. But as
11:15 Now they *c* to Jerusalem
11:27 they *c* again to Jerusalem
11:27 and the older men *c* to him
12:18 Sadducees *c* to him, who say
14:17 he *c* with the twelve
14:41 he *c* the third time and said
14:45 And he *c* straight up and
14:66 girls of the high priest *c*
15:43 there *c* Joseph of Arimathea
16:2 they *c* to the memorial tomb
16:8 when they *c* out they fled
Lu 2:51 and *c* to Nazareth, and he
3:2 God's declaration *c* to John
3:3 he *c* into all the country
3:22 like a dove *c* down upon him
Lu 3:22 and a voice *c* out of heaven
4:16 And he *c* to Nazareth, where
4:35 the demon *c* out of him
4:42 *c* out as far as he was, and
6:17 he *c* down with them and took
6:17 who *c* to hear him and be
7:4 *c* up to Jesus began to entreat
7:20 they *c* up to him the men said
7:45 from the hour that I *c* in
8:19 mother and brothers *c* toward
8:35 they *c* to Jesus and found the
8:35 from whom the demons *c* out
8:41 a man named Jairus *c*, and
8:47 the woman *c* trembling and
8:49 officer of the synagogue *c*
9:12 The twelve now *c* up and said
9:35 a voice *c* out of the cloud
10:40 she *c* near and said: Lord
11:14 After the demon *c* out, the
11:31 *c* from the ends of the earth
12:49 I *c* to start a fire on the
12:51 imagine I *c* to give peace
13:6 he *c* looking for fruit on it
13:31 Pharisees *c* up, saying to
14:21 the slave *c* up and reported
15:17 When he *c* to his senses
15:24 son was dead and *c* to life
15:25 he *c* and got near the house
15:28 his father *c* out and began to
15:32 was dead and *c* to life
17:29 day that Lot *c* out of Sodom
19:10 Son of man *c* to seek and to
19:18 second *c*, saying, Your mina
22:14 At length when the hour *c*
Joh 1:3 *c* into existence through him
1:3 one thing *c* into existence
1:7 This man *c* for a witness
1:10 the world *c* into existence
1:11 He *c* to his own home, but
1:31 I *c* baptizing in water
3:26 So they *c* to John and said
4:5 he *c* to a city of Samaria
4:7 *c* to draw water. Jesus said
4:40 the Samaritans *c* to him
4:46 he *c* again to Cana of Galilee
4:54 *c* out of Judea into Galilee
6:24 *c* to Capernaum to look for
6:41 the bread that *c* down from
6:51 living bread that *c* down
6:58 bread that *c* down from
8:14 I know where I *c* from and
8:14 do not know where I *c* from
8:58 Before Abraham *c* into
9:39 I *c* into this world: that
10:35 whom the word of God *c*
10:41 many people *c* to him, and
11:33 Jews that *c* with her
11:38 *c* to the memorial tomb
12:9 *c*, not on account of Jesus
12:20 Greeks among those that *c*
12:22 Philip *c* and told Andrew
12:22 and Philip *c* and told Jesus
12:28 a voice *c* out of heaven
12:47 I *c*, not to judge the world
13:3 he *c* forth from God and was
13:6 And so he *c* to Simon Peter
16:27 *c* out as the Father's
16:28 I *c* out from the Father and
16:30 that you *c* out from God
17:8 *c* out as your representative
18:3 *c* there with torches and
18:29 Pilate *c* outside to them
19:5 Jesus *c* outside, wearing the
19:34 blood and water *c* out
19:38 *c* and took his body away
20:2 she ran and *c* to Simon
20:19 Jesus *c* and stood in their
20:24 not with them when Jesus *c*
20:26 Jesus *c*, although the doors
21:8 disciples *c* in the little
21:13 Jesus *c* and took the bread
Ac 2:6 multitude *c* together and were
4:1 the Sadducees *c* upon them
7:11 famine *c* upon the whole of
7:23 *c* into his heart to make an
7:31 Jehovah's voice *c*
7:38 he that *c* to be among the
8:36 *c* to a certain body of water
9:27 Barnabas *c* to his aid and led
9:32 *c* down also to the holy ones
10:13 voice *c* to him: Rise, Peter
10:29 Hence I *c*, really without
11:20 *c* to Antioch and began
13:14 and *c* to Antioch in Pisidia

Ac 14:24 Pisidia and *c* into Pamphylia
15:1 men *c* down from Judea and
16:11 and *c* with a straight run to
16:18 And it *c* out that very hour
24:1 Ananias *c* down with some
25:23 *c* with much pompous show
27:8 *c* to a certain place called
28:3 viper *c* out due to the heat
28:14 this way we *c* toward Rome
28:15 *c* to meet us as far as the
28:23 *c* in greater numbers to him
28:30 receive all those who *c* in
Ro 5:20 Law *c* in beside in order
14:9 Christ died and *c* to life
1Co 2:1 when I *c* to you, brothers
2:3 *c* to you in weakness and in
2:8 *c* to know, for if they had
14:36 word of God *c* forth, or was
2Co 3:7 *c* about in a glory, so that
11:9 brothers that *c* from
Ga 1:17 I *c* back again to Damascus
2:11 when Cephas *c* to Antioch, I
Eph 2:17 *c* and declared the good news
Php 2:7 *c* to be in the likeness of
1Ti 1:15 Jesus *c* into the world to
2:14 and *c* to be in transgression
2Ti 4:16 no one *c* to my side, but
Heb 7:28 oath that *c* after the Law
9:11 Christ *c* as a high priest of
Jas 2:23 he *c* to be called Jehovah's
2Pe 2:1 *c* to be false prophets among
1Jo 5:6 *c* by means of water and blood
3Jo 3 *c* and bore witness to the truth
Jude 14 *c* with his holy myriads
Re 2:8 became dead and *c* to life
4:2 *c* to be in the power of the
9:3 locusts *c* forth upon the earth
11:18 your own wrath *c*, and the
12:16 earth *c* to the woman's help
14:20 blood *c* out of the winepress
20:4 *c* to life and ruled as kings
20:9 fire *c* down out of heaven
21:9 *c* one of the seven angels

Camel
Ge 24:64 herself down from off the *c*
31:34 saddle basket of the *c*
Le 11:4 the *c*, because it is a chewer
De 14:7 you must not eat . . . the *c*
1Sa 15:3 *c* as well as ass
Zec 14:15 the *c*, and the male ass
Mt 19:24 *c* to get through a needle's
23:24 but gulp down the *c*
Mr 10:25 *c* to go through a needle's
Lu 18:25 *c* to get through the eye of

Camel's
Mt 3:4 clothing of *c* hair and a
Mr 1:6 John was clothed with *c* hair

Camels
Ge 12:16 and she-asses and *c*
24:10, 10 took ten *c* from the *c* of
24:11 he had the *c* kneel down
24:14 I shall also water your *c*
24:19 For your *c* too I shall draw
24:20 kept drawing for all his *c*
24:22 *c* had finished drinking, then
24:30 was, standing by the *c* at the
24:31 ready and room for the *c*
24:32 unharnessing the *c* and giving
24:32 fodder to the *c* and water to
24:35 maidservants and *c* and asses
24:44 also draw water for your *c*
24:46 and I shall also water your *c*
24:46 and she also watered the *c*
24:61 went riding on the *c* and
24:63 why, there *c* were coming
30:43 menservants and *c* and asses
31:17 lifted . . . wives onto the *c*
32:7 the cattle and the *c* into two
32:15 thirty *c* giving suck and
37:25 *c* were carrying labdanum and
Ex 9:3 their *c*, the herd and the flock
Jg 6:5 their *c* were without number
7:12 their *c* were without number
8:21 on the necks of their *c*
8:26 on the necks of the *c*
1Sa 27:9 herds and asses and *c* and
30:17 men that rode upon *c* and
1Ki 10:2 *c* carrying balsam oil and
2Ki 8:9 the load of forty *c*, and came
1Ch 5:21 their *c* fifty thousand, and
12:40 upon *c* and upon mules and
27:30 over the *c* there was Obil
2Ch 9:1 *c* carrying balsam oil, and
14:15 in great number and *c*
Ezr 2:67 their *c* four hundred and
Ne 7:69 The *c* were four hundred and
Job 1:3 and three thousand *c* and five
1:17 dashing against the *c* and
42:12 six thousand *c* and a
Isa 21:7 a war chariot of *c*
30:6 humps of *c* their supplies
60:6 The heaving mass of *c*
60:6 young male *c* of Midian and
Jer 49:29 *c* will be carried off from
49:32 *c* must become a plunder
Eze 25:5 Rabbah a pasture ground of *c*

Camp
Ge 12:9 Abram broke *c*, going then
13:11 Lot moved his *c* to the east
20:1 Abraham moved *c* from there to
32:2 The *c* of God this is! Hence
32:8 to the one *c* and assault it
32:8 a *c* remaining to make an
32:21 lodged that night in the *c*
33:8 all this *c* of travelers that
33:18 pitched *c* in front of the
50:9 *c* came to be very numerous
Ex 14:15 that they should break *c*
14:19 ahead of the *c* of Israel
14:20 the *c* of the Egyptians and
14:20 and the *c* of Israel
14:24 upon the *c* of the Egyptians
14:24 the *c* of the Egyptians into
16:13 to come up and cover the *c*
16:13 dew round about the *c*
19:16 the people who were in the *c*
19:17 out of the *c* to meet the
29:14 burn with fire outside the *c*
32:17 is a noise of battle in the *c*
32:19 as soon as he got near the *c*
32:26 stand in the gate of the *c*
32:27 in the *c* and kill each one
33:7 outside the *c*, far away from
33:7 far away from the *c*; and he
33:7 which was outside the *c*
33:11 When he returned to the *c*, his
36:6 to pass through the *c*, saying
40:36 sons of Israel would break *c*
40:37 not break *c* until the day
Le 4:12 the outskirts of the *c* to a
4:21 of the *c* and must burn it
6:11 a clean place outside the *c*
8:17 with fire outside the *c*
9:11 skin with fire outside the *c*
10:4 holy place to outside the *c*
10:5 their robes to outside the *c*
13:46 Outside the *c* is his dwelling
14:3 outside the *c*, and the priest
14:8 he may come into the *c*
16:26 he may come into the *c*
16:27 taken forth outside the *c*
16:28 he may come into the *c*
17:3 in the *c* or who slaughters
17:3 slaughters it outside the *c*
24:10 with each other in the *c*
24:14 outside of the *c*; and all
24:23 *c*, and they pelted him with
Nu 1:50 around the tabernacle . . . *c*
1:52 with reference to his *c*, and
2:3 *c* of Judah in their armies
2:9 of the *c* of Judah are one
2:10 *c* of Reuben will be toward
2:16 ones of the *c* of Reuben are
2:17 *c* of the Levites will be in
2:18 of the *c* of Ephraim
2:24 *c* of Ephraim are one hundred
2:25 *c* of Dan will be toward the
2:31 ones of the *c* of Dan are
4:5 when the *c* is departing, and
4:15 when the *c* is departing, and
5:2 send out of the *c* every leprous
5:3 send them outside the *c*, that
5:4 to send them outside the *c*
10:14 *c* of the sons of Judah pulled
10:18 *c* of Reuben pulled away in
10:22 *c* of the sons of Ephraim
10:25 *c* of the sons of Dan pulled
11:1 in the extremity of the *c*
11:9 dew descended upon the *c* by
11:26 the men remaining in the *c*
11:26 to act as prophets in the *c*
11:27 acting as prophets in the *c*
11:30 Moses withdrew to the *c*
11:31 fall above the *c* about a
11:31 all around the *c*, and about
Nu 11:32 all around the *c* for
12:14 seven days outside the *c*
12:15 quarantined outside the *c*
14:44 from the midst of the *c*
15:35 pelting him . . . outside the *c*
15:36 outside the *c* and pelted him
19:3 lead it forth outside the *c*
19:7 he may come into the *c*; but
19:9 outside the *c* in a clean place
31:12 booty and the spoil, to the *c*
31:13 to meet them outside the *c*
31:19 you yourselves, *c* outside the
31:19 outside the *c* seven days
31:24 you may come into the *c*
De 1:33 a place for you to *c*, by fire
2:14 from the midst of the *c*, just
2:15 out of the midst of the *c*
23:9 into *c* against your enemies
23:10 must also go outside the *c*
23:10 come into the midst of the *c*
23:11 come into the midst of the *c*
23:12 at your service outside the *c*
23:14 within your *c* to deliver you
23:14 your *c* must prove to be holy
29:11 who is in the midst of your *c*
Jos 1:11 through the midst of the *c*
3:2 through the midst of the *c*
5:8 in the *c* until they revived
5:10 continued to *c* in Gilgal, and
6:11 went to the *c* and stayed
6:11 and stayed overnight in the *c*
6:14 they returned to the *c*
6:18 the *c* of Israel a thing
6:23 outside the *c* of Israel
8:11 *c* to the north of Ai, with
8:13 the people set the main *c*
9:6 Joshua at the *c* at Gilgal and
10:5 *c* against Gibeon and to war
10:6 to Joshua at the *c* at Gilgal
10:15 returned to the *c* at Gilgal
10:21 return to the *c*, to Joshua
10:43 returned to the *c* at Gilgal
18:9 Joshua at the *c* in Shiloh
Jg 4:15 all the *c* into confusion by
4:16 the *c* as far as Harosheth of
4:16 the *c* of Sisera fell by the
6:4 they would *c* against them and
6:33 *c* in the low plain of Jezreel
7:1 the *c* of Midian happened to be
7:8 *c* of Midian, it happened to be
7:9 descend upon the *c*, for I have
7:10 Purah your attendant, to the *c*
7:11 certain to descend upon the *c*
7:11 formation who were in the *c*
7:13 the *c* of Midian. Then it came
7:14 and all the *c* into his hand
7:15 returned to the *c* of Israel
7:15 *c* of Midian into your hand
7:17 to the edge of the *c*, it must
7:18 round about all the *c*, and you
7:19 to the edge of the *c* at the
7:21 around the *c*, and the whole
7:21 whole *c* got on the run and
7:22, 22 in all the *c*; and the *c*
8:10 *c* of the Easterners; and those
8:11 began to strike the *c* while
8:11 the *c* happened to be off guard
8:12 and he drove all the *c* into
9:50 and to *c* against Thebez and
10:17 Ammon . . . pitched *c* in Gilead
10:17 and pitched *c* in Mizpah
21:8 into the *c* from Jabesh-gilead
21:12 to the *c* at Shiloh, which is
1Sa 4:3 When the people came to the *c*
4:5 the ark . . . came into the *c*
4:6 in the *c* of the Hebrews
4:6 ark . . . had come into the *c*
4:7 said: God has come into the *c*
11:1 *c* against Jabesh in Gilead
11:11 into the middle of the *c*
13:17 the *c* of the Philistines
14:15 trembling occurred in the *c*
14:19 in the *c* of the Philistines
14:21 up with them into the *c*
17:17 carry them quickly to the *c*
17:20 he came to the *c* enclosure
17:46 of the *c* of the Philistines
26:5 and Saul was lying in the *c*
26:6 with me to Saul into the *c*
26:7 asleep in the *c* enclosure
28:1 go out into the *c*, you and
28:4 and pitched *c* in Shunem
28:4 and they pitched *c* in Gilboa
28:5 *c* of the Philistines he

1Sa 28:19 *c* of Israel Jehovah will
29:6 coming in with me in the *c*
2Sa 1:2 coming from the *c*, from Saul
1:3 From the *c* of Israel I have
5:24 the *c* of the Philistines
23:16 the *c* of the Philistines
1Ki 16:16 on that day in the *c*
20:27 sons of Israel went into *c*
22:34 and take me out from the *c*
22:36 began to pass through the *c*
2Ki 3:9 no water for the *c* and for
3:24 came into the *c* of Israel
5:15 he with all his *c*, and came
6:24 to collect all his *c* together
7:4 invade the *c* of the Syrians
7:5 enter the *c* of the Syrians
7:5 the *c* of the Syrians
7:6 caused the *c* of the Syrians
7:7 the *c* just as it was
7:8 the outskirts of the *c*
7:10 into the *c* of the Syrians
7:12 went out from the *c* to hide
7:14 after the *c* of the Syrians
7:16 plunder the *c* of the Syrians
19:35 in the *c* of the Assyrians
1Ch 9:19 over the *c* of Jehovah, the
11:15 a *c* of the Philistines was
11:18 the *c* of the Philistines
12:22 until it was a great *c*
12:22 like the *c* of God
14:15 the *c* of the Philistines
14:16 the *c* of the Philistines
2Ch 14:13 Jehovah and before his *c*
18:33 take me out from the *c*
22:1 with the Arabs to the *c*
32:1 *c* against the fortified
32:21 *c* of the king of Assyria
Job 19:12 they *c* round about my tent
Ps 68:13 between the *c* ash heaps
69:25 walled *c* become desolate
78:28 fall in the middle of his *c*
106:16 to envy Moses in the *c*
Isa 37:36 the *c* of the Assyrians
Jer 52:4 *c* against her and to build
Joe 2:11 for his *c* is very numerous
Heb 13:11 burned up outside the *c*
13:13 forth to him outside the *c*
Re 20:9 the *c* of the holy ones and

Campaign
2Ch 28:12 from the military *c*

Camped
Nu 33:9 came to Elim . . . *c* there
Jg 15:9 *c* in Judah and went tramping
20:19 and *c* against Gibeah
1Ch 19:7 came in and *c* before Medeba

Camping
Ex 14:9 *c* by the sea, by Pihahiroth
15:27 went *c* there by the water
17:1 Israel . . . *c* at Rephidim
18:5 wilderness where he was *c*
19:2 Israel went *c* there in front
Nu 2:3 those *c* eastward toward the
2:5 *c* alongside him will be the
2:12 *c* alongside him will be the
2:27 ones *c* alongside him will be
3:38 those *c* before the tabernacle
10:5 *c* to the east must pull away
10:6 *c* to the south must pull away
12:16 *c* in the wilderness of Paran
21:12 *c* by the torrent valley of
21:13 *c* in the region of the Arnon
33:5 Israel . . . went *c* in Succoth
33:6 and went *c* in Etham, which
33:7 and they went *c* before Migdol
33:8 and took up *c* at Marah
33:10 and went *c* by the Red Sea
33:11 *c* in the wilderness of Sin
33:12 and went *c* at Dophkah
33:13 and went *c* at Alush
33:14 and went *c* in Rephidim
33:15 *c* in the wilderness of Sinai
33:16 went *c* at Kibroth-hattaavah
33:17 and went *c* in Hazeroth
33:18 and went *c* in Rithmah
33:19 took up *c* in Rimmon-perez
33:20 and went *c* in Libnah
33:21 and went *c* in Rissah
33:22 and went *c* in Kehelathah
33:23 and went *c* in Mount Shepher
33:24 and went *c* in Haradah
33:25 and went *c* in Makheloth
33:26 and went *c* in Tahath
Nu 33:27 and went *c* in Terah
33:28 and went *c* in Mithkah
33:29 and went *c* in Hashmonah
33:30 and went *c* in Moseroth
33:31 and went *c* in Bene-jaakan
33:32 and went *c* in Hor-haggidgad
33:33 and went *c* in Jotbathah
33:34 and went *c* in Abronah
33:35 and went *c* in Ezion-geber
33:36 *c* in the wilderness of Zin
33:37 went *c* in Mount Hor, on the
33:41 and went *c* in Zalmonah
33:42 and went *c* in Punon
33:43 and went *c* in Oboth
33:44 and went *c* in Iye-abarim on
33:45 and went *c* in Dibon-gad
33:46 went *c* in Almon-diblathaim
33:47 *c* in the mountains of Abarim
33:48 *c* on the desert plains of
33:49 continued *c* by the Jordan
Jos 4:19 *c* at Gilgal on the eastern
10:31 *c* against it and warring
10:34 *c* against it and warring
Jg 7:1 took up *c* at the well of Harod
11:18 *c* in the region of the Arnon
11:20 and *c* in Jahaz and fighting
18:12 went *c* at Kiriath-jearim in
1Sa 4:1 *c* alongside Ebenezer, and the
13:5 *c* in Michmash to the east of
17:1 *c* between Socoh and Azekah
17:2 *c* in the low plain of Elah
26:3 Saul took up *c* on the hill
26:5 the people *c* all around him
29:1 Israelites were *c* by the
2Sa 11:11 *c* on the face of the field
17:26 *c* in the land of Gilead
24:5 took up *c* at Aroer to the
2Ki 25:1 began *c* against it and
1Ch 11:15 Philistines was *c* in the
Ne 11:30 *c* from Beer-sheba clear to
Ps 34:7 *c* all around those fearing
53:5 bones of anyone *c* against you
Na 3:17 *c* in the stone pens in a cold

Camps
Ge 25:16 and by their walled *c*
32:7 and the camels into two *c*
32:10 and now I have become two *c*
Nu 2:17 be in the middle of the *c*
2:32 registered ones of the *c* in
5:3 not contaminate the *c* of those
10:2 and for breaking up the *c*
10:5 *c* of those . . . to the east
10:6 *c* of those camping to the
10:25 rear guard for all the *c* in
31:10 walled *c* they burned with
Jos 10:5 these and all their *c*, and
11:4 they and all their *c* with
Jg 8:10 and their *c* with them, about
1Sa 17:1 collecting their *c* together
17:4 the *c* of the Philistines
17:53 and went pillaging their *c*
28:1 collect their *c* for the army
29:1 collect all their *c* together
1Ch 6:54 walled *c* in their territory
9:18 of the *c* of the sons of Levi
2Ch 31:2 praise in the gates of the *c*
Ca 6:13 like the dance of two *c*
Eze 25:4 set up their walled *c* in you
Am 4:10 the stink of your *c* ascend
Zec 14:15 happens to be in those *c*

Cana
Joh 2:1 took place in *C* of Galilee
2:11 Jesus performed this in *C* of
4:46 came again to *C* of Galilee
21:2 Nathanael from *C* of Galilee

Canaan
Ge 9:18 Later Ham was the father of *C*
9:22 Ham the father of *C* saw his
9:25 Cursed be *C*. Let him become
9:26 let *C* become a slave to him
9:27 Let *C* become a slave to him
10:6 the sons of Ham . . . *C*
10:15 *C* became father to Sidon
11:31 to go to the land of *C*
12:5 go to the land of *C*
12:5 they came to the land of *C*
13:12 Abram dwelt in the land of *C*
16:3 dwelling in the land of *C*
17:8 the entire land of *C*, for a
23:2 land of *C*, and Abraham came
23:19 Hebron, in the land of *C*
28:1 wife from the daughters of *C*
Ge 28:6 wife from the daughters of *C*
28:8 saw that the daughters of *C*
31:18 to the land of *C*
33:18 which is in the land of *C*
35:6 which is in the land of *C*
36:2 wives from the daughters of *C*
36:5 born . . . in the land of *C*
36:6 accumulated in the land of *C*
37:1 in the land of *C*
42:5 famine . . . in the land of *C*
42:7 From the land of *C* to buy
42:13 sons of but one man in . . . *C*
42:29 to the land of *C* and told
42:32 our father in the land of *C*
44:8 to you from the land of *C*
45:17 go enter the land of *C*
45:25 came into the land of *C*
46:6 in the land of *C*
46:12 Onan died in the land of *C*
46:31 were in the land of *C*
47:1 have come from the land of *C*
47:4 famine . . . in the land of *C*
47:13 land of *C* became exhausted
47:14 Egypt and in the land of *C*
47:15 Egypt and the land of *C*
48:3 Luz in the land of *C*
48:7 in the land of *C* on the way
49:30 Mamre in the land of *C*, the
50:5 in the land of *C* is where you
50:13 into the land of *C* and buried
Ex 6:4 to give them the land of *C*
15:15 All the inhabitants of *C*
16:35 the frontier of the land of *C*
Le 14:34 you come into the land of *C*
18:3 the way the land of *C* does
25:38 *C*, to prove myself your God
Nu 13:2 may spy out the land of *C*
13:17 to spy out the land of *C*, he
26:19 Onan died in the land of *C*
32:30 your midst in the land of *C*
32:32 to the land of *C*, and the
33:40 the Negeb, in the land of *C*
33:51 into the land of *C*
34:2 are going into the land of *C*
34:2 *C* according to its boundaries
34:29 landholders in the land of *C*
35:10 crossing the Jordan to . . . *C*
35:14 will give in the land of *C*
De 32:49 see the land of *C*, which I
Jos 5:12 produce of the land of *C* in
14:1 possession in the land of *C*
21:2 in Shiloh in the land of *C*
22:9 Shiloh . . . in the land of *C*
22:10 regions . . . in the land of *C*
22:11 frontier of the land of *C*
22:32 of *C* to the other sons of
24:3 through all the land of *C*
Jg 3:1 any of the wars of *C*
4:2 Jabin the king of *C*, who
4:23 Jabin the king of *C* before the
4:24 against Jabin the king of *C*
4:24 cut off Jabin the king of *C*
5:19 kings of *C* fought In Taanach
21:12 which is in the land of *C*
1Ch 1:8 sons of Ham were . . . *C*
1:13 *C*, he became father to Sidon
16:18 I shall give the land of *C*
Ps 105:11 shall give the land of *C*
106:38 sacrificed to the idols of *C*
135:11 And all the kingdoms of *C*
Isa 19:18 speaking the language of *C*
Eze 16:29 abound toward the land of *C*
17:4 bringing it to the land of *C*
Zep 2:5 *C*, the land of the Philistines
Ac 7:11 *C*, even a great tribulation
13:19 nations in the land of *C*

Canaanite
Ge 10:18 families of the *C* were
10:19 boundary of the *C* came to
12:6 the *C* was in the land
13:7 *C* . . . dwelling in the land
38:2 a daughter of a certain *C*
46:10 Shaul the son of a *C* woman
Ex 6:15 Shaul the son of a *C* woman
Nu 21:1 Now the *C* the king of Arad
33:40 Now the *C*, the king of Arad
Eze 16:3 were from the land of the *C*
Zec 14:21 no more prove to be a *C* in

Canaanites
Ge 15:21 the *C* and the Girgashites and
24:3 daughters of the *C* in among
24:37 daughters of the *C* in whose
34:30 the *C* and the Perizzites

Ge 50:11 *C*, got to see the mourning
Ex 3:8 to the locality of the *C* and
3:17 to the land of the *C* and the
13:5 into the land of the *C* and the
13:11 you into the land of the *C*
23:23 indeed bring you to the . . . *C*
23:28 drive the Hivites, the *C* and
33:2 drive out the *C*, the Amorites
34:11 driving out . . . the *C*
Nu 13:29 *C* are dwelling by the sea
14:25 *C* are dwelling in the low
14:43 the *C* are there before you
14:45 *C* who were dwelling in that
21:3 and gave the *C* over; and they
De 1:7 the land of the *C*, and Lebanon
7:1 the *C* and the Perizzites and
11:30 *C* dwelling in the Arabah
20:17 the *C* and the Perizzites
Jos 3:10 the *C* and the Hittites and
5:1 kings of the *C*, who were by
7:9 the *C* and all the inhabitants
9:1 the *C*, the Perizzites, the
11:3 the *C* to the east and the
12:8 the *C*, the Perizzites, the
13:3 as belonging to the *C*
13:4 all the land of the *C*; and
16:10 *C* . . . dwelling in Gezer
16:10 *C* . . . in among Ephraim
17:12 *C* persisted in dwelling in
17:13 the *C* at forced labor
17:16 *C* dwelling in the land of
17:18 should drive away the *C*
24:11 the *C* and the Hittites and
Jg 1:1 to the *C* to fight against
1:3 let us fight against the *C*
1:4 Jehovah gave the *C* and the
1:5 and defeated the *C* and the
1:9 fight against the *C* inhabiting
1:10 the *C* who were dwelling in
1:17 to strike the *C* inhabiting
1:27 the *C* persisted in dwelling
1:28 the *C* to forced labor, and
1:29 the *C* who were dwelling in
1:29 the *C* continued to dwell in
1:30 the *C* continued to dwell in
1:32 the *C* inhabiting the land
1:33 to dwell in among the *C*
3:3 all the *C*, even the Sidonians
3:5 Israel dwelt in among the *C*
2Sa 24:7 the Hivites and of the *C*
1Ki 9:16 *C* dwelling in the city he
Ezr 9:1 the *C*, the Hittites, the
Ne 9:8 give him the land of the *C*
9:24 inhabitants of the land, the *C*
Ob 20 what the *C* possessed as far as

Canaanitess
1Ch 2:3 Shua's daughter, the *C*

Canal
Ne 3:15 the wall of the Pool of the *C*

Canals
Ex 7:19 rivers, over their Nile *c* and
8:5 over the rivers, the Nile *c*
2Ki 19:24 all the Nile *c* of Egypt
Ps 78:44 to blood their Nile *c*
Isa 7:18 of the Nile *c* of Egypt and
19:6 Nile *c* of Egypt must become
33:21 place of rivers, of wide *c*
37:25 all the Nile *c* of Egypt
Eze 29:3 in the midst of his Nile *c*
29:4 the fish of your Nile *c* to
29:4 the midst of your Nile *c*
29:4 the fish of your Nile *c* that
29:5 the fish of your Nile *c*
29:10 and against your Nile *c*
30:12 make the Nile *c* dry ground
Na 3:8 that was sitting by the Nile *c*

Cananaean
Mt 10:4 Simon the *C*, and Judas
Mr 3:18 and Thaddaeus and Simon the *C*

Canceled
Mt 18:27 let him off and *c* his debt
18:32 I *c* all that debt for you

Candace
Ac 8:27 *C* queen of the Ethiopians

Cane
Ca 4:14 *c* and cinnamon, along with
Isa 43:24 have bought no sweet *c* with
Jer 6:20 *c* from the land far away
Eze 27:19 cassia and *c*—for your

Canneh
Eze 27:23 Haran and *C* and Eden, the

Canopies
Eze 41:26 of the house and the *c*

Canopy
1Ki 7:6 and a *c* in front of them
10:19 throne had a round *c* behind
Eze 41:25 a *c* of wood over the front

Cans
Ex 27:3 make its *c* for clearing away
38:3 the *c* and the shovels and the
1Ki 7:45 *c* and the shovels and the
2Ki 25:14 the *c* and the shovels and
2Ch 4:11 Hiram made the *c* and the
4:16 *c* and the shovels and the
Jer 52:18 *c* and the shovels and the
52:19 *c* and the lampstands and

Capable
Ex 18:21 out of all the people *c* men
18:25 *c* men out of all Israel and
1Ch 26:6 for they were *c*, mighty men
26:7 whose brothers were *c* men
26:8 *c* men with the power for
26:9 brothers, *c* men, eighteen
26:30 *c* men, a thousand seven
26:32 his brothers, *c* men, were
Ne 11:6 and sixty-eight, *c* men
Pr 12:4 *c* wife is a crown to her
31:10 A *c* wife who can find?
Da 5:11 *c* man in your kingdom in
Mr 9:18 expel it, but they were not *c*
Ac 15:10 nor we were *c* of bearing

Capableness
Pr 31:29 daughters that have shown *c*

Capacity
1Jo 5:20 has given us intellectual *c*

Caper
Ec 12:5 and the *c* berry bursts

Capernaum
Mt 4:13 took up residence in *C* beside
8:5 When he entered into *C*, an
11:23 you, *C*, will you perhaps be
17:24 After they arrived in *C* the
Mr 1:21 they went their way into *C*
2:1 he again entered into *C* and he
9:33 And they came into *C*
Lu 4:23 heard as having happened in *C*
4:31 to *C*, a city of Galilee
7:1 he entered into *C*
10:15 *C*, will you . . . be exalted
Joh 2:12 disciples went down to *C*
4:46 whose son was sick in *C*
6:17 out across the sea for *C*
6:24 came to *C* to look for Jesus
6:59 in public assembly at *C*

Caphtor
De 2:23 came out from *C*, annihilated
Jer 47:4 ones from the island of *C*

Caphtorim
Ge 10:14 Pathrusim and Casluhim . . . *C*
De 2:23 the *C*, who came out from
1Ch 1:12 Casluhim . . . and *C*

Capital
1Ki 7:16 the height of the one *c*
7:16 the height of the other *c*
7:17 seven for the one *c*, and
7:17 and seven for the other *c*
7:18 what he did for the other *c*
7:20 rows all around upon each *c*
2Ki 25:17 the *c* upon it was of copper
25:17 the *c* was three cubits
25:17 all around upon the *c*
2Ch 3:15 *c* that was upon the top of
Jer 52:22 *c* upon it was of copper
52:22 height of the one *c* was
52:22 the pomegranates upon the *c*

Capitals
1Ki 7:16 two *c* he made to put upon
7:17 the *c* that were upon the top
7:18 to cover the *c* that were
7:19 the *c* that were upon the top
7:20 *c* were upon the two pillars
7:41 the bowl-shaped *c* that were
7:41 to cover the two round *c*
7:42 cover the two bowl-shaped *c*
2Ch 4:12 two pillars and the round *c*
4:12 to cover the two round *c*
4:13 *c* that were upon the pillars

Zep 2:14 right among her pillar *c*

Capitulation
2Ki 18:31 Make a *c* to me, and come
Isa 36:16 Make a *c* to me and come

Cappadocia
Ac 2:9 Judea and *C*, Pontus and the
1Pe 1:1 in Pontus, Galatia, *C*, Asia

Caps
Da 3:21 *c* and their other clothing

Captain
Jon 1:6 the ship *c* came near to him
Ac 4:1 the *c* of the temple and the
5:24 *c* of the temple and the chief
5:26 *c* went off with his officers
Re 18:17 every ship *c* and every man

Captains
Lu 22:4 chief priests and temple *c*
22:52 and *c* of the temple and

Captive
Ge 14:14 his brother had been taken *c*
34:29 wives they carried off *c*
Ex 12:29 the firstborn of the *c* who
Nu 24:22 will carry you away *c*
31:9 Midian and their little ones *c*
De 21:10 you have carried them away *c*
1Sa 30:2 *c* the women and all that
30:3 they had been carried off *c*
30:5 wives had been carried off *c*
1Ki 8:46 carry them off *c* to the land
8:47 they have been carried off *c*
8:48 who carried them off *c*
2Ki 5:2 *c* from the land of Israel a
6:22 taken *c* with your sword
1Ch 5:21 got to take *c* their livestock
2Ch 6:36 *c* to a land distant or
6:37 have been carried off *c*, and
6:38 those who carried them off *c*
14:15 took *c* flocks in great
21:17 took *c* all the goods that
28:8 thousand of their brothers *c*
30:9 before those holding them *c*
36:20 *c* to Babylon, and they came
Job 42:10 the *c* condition of Job
Ps 14:7 Jehovah gathers back the *c*
53:6 Jehovah gathers back the *c*
85:1 the ones taken *c* of Jacob
106:46 those holding them *c*
126:1 back the *c* ones of Zion
137:3 those holding us *c* asked
Isa 14:2 of those holding them *c*
52:2 O *c* daughter of Zion
61:1 liberty to those taken *c*
Jer 13:17 will have been carried *c*
30:3 I will gather the *c* ones
30:18 gathering the *c* ones of the
41:10 Ishmael took *c* all the
41:10 took them *c* and went off
41:14 Ishmael had led *c* from
43:12 burn them and lead them *c*
48:47 gather the *c* ones of Moab
49:6 gather the *c* ones of the
49:39 gather the *c* ones of Elam
50:33 those taking them *c* have
La 1:5 walked *c* before the adversary
Eze 6:9 they will have been taken *c*
16:53 I will gather their *c* ones
16:53 the *c* ones of Sodom and of
16:53 and the *c* ones of Samaria
16:53 gather your *c* ones in the
29:14 bring back the *c* group
39:25 the *c* ones of Jacob and
Ho 6:11 gather back the *c* ones of my
Joe 3:1 the *c* ones of Judah and
Am 4:10 the taking *c* of your horses
9:14 gather back the *c* ones of my
Zep 2:7 gather back the *c* ones of
3:20 gather back your *c* ones
Lu 21:24 led *c* into all the nations
Ro 7:23 leading me *c* to sin's law
Col 4:10 Aristarchus my fellow *c*
Phm 23 Epaphras my fellow *c* in union

Captives
Ge 31:26 like *c* taken by the sword
Nu 21:1 carry away some of them as *c*
31:12 the *c* and the booty and the
31:19 purify . . . you and your *c*
31:26 *c* both of humankind and of
De 21:11 seen among the *c* a woman
30:3 bring back your *c* and show
32:42 blood of the slain and the *c*
Jg 5:12 lead your *c* away, you son of

2Ch 6:37 in the land where they are *c*
6:38 the land where they are *c*
28:5 great number of *c* and
28:11 return the *c* that you have
28:13 not bring in the *c* here
28:14 armed men left the *c* and
28:15 took hold of the *c*, and
28:17 Judah and carrying off *c*
Ps 68:18 You have carried away *c*
126:4 Jehovah, our company of *c*
Isa 20:4 body of *c* of Egypt and
49:24 the body of *c* of the tyrant
49:25 *c* of the mighty man will
Jer 29:14 gather your body of *c*
31:23 I shall gather their *c*
32:44 shall bring back their *c*
33:7 bring back the *c* of Judah
33:7 and the *c* of Israel, and
33:11 back the *c* of the land just
33:26 gather their *c* and will
48:46 sons have been taken as *c*
48:46 and your daughters as *c*
Eze 32:9 bring the *c* from you among
Da 11:8 the *c* he will come to Egypt
Hab 1:9 gathers up *c* just like the
Lu 4:18 to preach a release to the *c*
Ro 16:7 fellow *c*, who are men of
Eph 4:8 he carried away *c*; he gave
2Ti 3:6 lead as their *c* weak women

Captivity
Nu 21:29 in the *c* to the king of the
De 21:13 remove the mantle of her *c*
28:41 they will go off into *c*
2Ch 29:9 our wives were in *c* for this
Ezr 2:1 out of the *c* of the exiled
3:8 out of the *c* to Jerusalem
8:35 out of the *c*, the former
9:7 the *c* and with the plunder
Ne 1:2 had been left over of the *c*
1:3 been left over from the *c*
4:4 plunder in the land of *c*
7:6 *c* of the exiled people whom
8:17 who had come back from the *c*
Ps 78:61 give his strength even to *c*
Isa 46:2 *c* their own soul must go
Jer 15:2 And whoever is for the *c*
15:2 to the *c*
20:6 you will go into *c*; and to
22:22 they will go into *c* itself
30:10 from the land of their *c*
30:16 into *c* they will all of
43:11 is due for *c* will be for
43:11 will be for *c*, and whoever
46:27 from the land of their *c*
La 1:18 young men have gone into *c*
2:14 in order to turn back your *c*
Eze 12:11 exile, into *c* they will go
30:17 into *c* the cities
30:18 into *c* her own dependent
Da 11:33 by *c* and by plundering, for
Am 9:4 go into *c* before their enemies
Ob 11 his military force into *c*
Na 3:10 for exile; she went into *c*
2Co 10:5 every thought into *c* to make
Re 13:10 If anyone is meant for *c*
13:10 he goes away into *c*

Captors
1Ki 8:46 *c* actually carry them off
8:47 in the land of their *c*
8:50 before their *c* and they must
2Ch 6:36 *c* actually carry them off
Isa 14:2 *c* of those holding them

Capture
Nu 32:39 march to Gilead and to *c* it
De 20:19 against it so as to *c* it
Jos 8:19 enter the city and *c* it
10:35 got to *c* it on that day and
10:37 they got to *c* it and went
10:39 got to *c* it and its king
15:16 Kiriath-sepher and does *c* it
19:47 *c* it and strike it with the
Jg 1:8 Jerusalem and got to *c* it
1:12 and does *c* it, why, I will
1:13 younger brother, got to *c* it
3:28 *c* the fords of the Jordan
7:24 *c* ahead of them the waters as
7:24 got to *c* the waters as far
7:25 got to *c* the two princes of
8:12 got to *c* Midian's two kings
9:45 and got to *c* the city; and he
9:50 camp against Thebez and *c* it
12:5 to *c* the fords of the Jordan
2Sa 5:7 David proceeded to *c* the
8:4 David got to *c* from him one
12:26 *c* the city of the kingdom
12:28 against the city, and *c* it
12:28 one to *c* the city, and my
2Ki 12:17 fight against Gath and *c* it
18:10 got to *c* it at the end of
1Ch 11:5 to *c* the stronghold of Zion
2Ch 12:4 *c* the fortified cities that
13:19 *c* cities from him, Bethel
28:18 *c* Beth-shemesh and Aijalon
32:18 that they might *c* the city
Pr 3:26 keep your foot against *c*
Isa 20:1 against Ashdod and to *c* it
Jer 18:22 excavated a pit to *c* me
32:3 he will certainly *c* it
32:24 come to the city to *c* it
32:28 and he must *c* it
34:22 fight against it and *c* it
37:8 *c* it and burn it with fire
38:3 and he will certainly *c* it
Eze 30:16 to be for *c* by breaches
Da 11:15 *c* a city with fortifications
11:18 and will actually *c* many

Captured
Nu 21:32 they *c* its dependent towns
De 2:35 the cities that we had *c*
Jos 6:20 and *c* the city
8:21 the ambush had *c* the city
10:1 Joshua had *c* Ai and then
10:28 Joshua *c* Makkedah on that
10:32 they *c* it on the second day
10:42 Joshua *c* all these kings
11:10 and *c* Hazor; and its king
11:12 all their kings Joshua *c*
11:17 he *c* all their kings and
15:17 Caleb's brother, *c* it
Jg 1:18 After that Judah *c* Gaza and
8:14 he *c* a young man of the men
1Sa 4:11 the ark of God itself was *c*
4:17 ark of the true God . . . *c*
4:19 ark of the true God was *c*
4:21 ark of the true God's being *c*
4:22 the ark . . . has been *c*
2Sa 12:27 also *c* the city of waters
12:29 fought against it and *c* it
1Ki 9:16 then *c* Gezer and burned it
16:18 that the city had been *c*
2Ki 14:13 *c* at Beth-shemesh, after
16:9 went up to Damascus and *c* it
17:6 king of Assyria *c* Samaria
18:10 Samaria was *c*
1Ch 18:4 David *c* from him a thousand
2Ch 15:8 cities that he had *c* from
17:2 that Asa his father had *c*
22:9 *c* him, as he was hiding in
25:12 the sons of Judah *c* alive
28:11 *c* from your brothers, for
33:11 *c* Manasseh in the hollows
Job 36:8 *c* with ropes of affliction
Ec 7:26 is sinning if one is *c* by her
Jer 38:28 day that Jerusalem was *c*
38:28 just when Jerusalem was *c*
48:1 put to shame, has been *c*
48:7 yourself will also be *c*
48:41 towns will actually be *c*
50:2 Babylon has been *c*
50:9 From there she will be *c*
51:31 city has been *c* at every
51:41 how Sheshach has been *c*
51:56 men will certainly be *c*
La 4:20 has been *c* in their large pit
Zec 14:2 the city will actually be *c*

Captures
Hab 1:10 it piles up dust and *c* it

Capturing
Nu 32:41 went *c* their tent villages
32:42 marched and went *c* Kenath
De 2:34 we went *c* all his cities at
3:4 we went *c* all his cities at
Ne 9:25 they went *c* fortified cities
Pr 16:32 than the one *c* a city

Caravan
Ge 37:25 a *c* of Ishmaelites that was

Caravans
Job 6:19 The *c* of Tema have looked
Isa 21:13 *c* of men of Dedan
Eze 27:25 *c* for your articles of

Carcass
Jg 14:8 to look at the *c* of the lion
Isa 14:19 like a *c* trodden down
Am 8:3 There will be many a *c*
Mt 24:28 the *c* is, there the eagles

Carcasses
Ge 15:11 birds of prey . . . upon the *c*
Le 26:30 lay your own *c* upon the
26:30 the *c* of your dungy idols
Nu 14:29 your *c* will fall, yes
14:32 the *c* of you yourselves will
14:33 your *c* come to their end
De 14:8 their *c* you must not touch
1Sa 17:46 give the *c* of the camp of
2Ki 19:35 all of them were dead *c*
2Ch 20:24 their *c* fallen to the earth
Isa 34:3 *c*, their stink will ascend
37:36 all of them were dead *c*
66:24 look upon the *c* of men that
Jer 31:40 the low plain of the *c* and
33:5 *c* of the men whom I have
41:9 Ishmael threw all the *c*
Eze 6:5 *c* of the sons of Israel before
43:7 *c* of their kings at their
43:9 *c* of their kings far from
Na 3:3 and the heavy mass of *c*
Heb 3:17 *c* fell in the wilderness

Carchemish
2Ch 35:20 came up to fight at *C* by
Isa 10:9 Is not Calno just like *C*?
Jer 46:2 by the river Euphrates at *C*

Carded
Isa 19:9 workers in *c* flax must

Care
Ge 2:15 cultivate it and to take *c* of
42:37 Give him over to my *c*, and I
Nu 3:8 take *c* of all the utensils of
3:10 take *c* of their priesthood
3:28 taking *c* of the obligation to
3:32 taking *c* of the obligation to
3:38 taking *c* of the obligation to
8:26 *c* of the obligation, but he
23:12 that I should take *c* to speak
28:2 take *c* to present to me my
De 4:9 take good *c* of your soul, that
4:15 take good *c* of your souls
5:32 take *c* to do just as Jehovah
6:3 take *c* to do them, that it may
6:25 *c* to do all this commandment
24:8 take good *c* and do according
28:15 by taking *c* to do all his
28:58 take *c* to carry out all the
31:12 take *c* to carry out all the
32:10 take *c* of him, To safeguard
32:46 take *c* to do all the words
Jos 1:7 take *c* to do according to all
1:8 take *c* to do according to all
22:24 rather out of anxious *c* for
1Sa 17:22 to the *c* of the keeper of
2Sa 15:16 to take *c* of the house
16:21 to take *c* of the house
20:3 to take *c* of the house
1Ki 2:4 If your sons will take *c* of
8:25 sons will take *c* of their
2Ki 9:34 take *c* of this accursed one
10:31 not take *c* to walk in the
17:37 should take *c* to do always
1Ch 22:13 if you take *c* to carry out
23:32 they took *c* of the guarding
25:8 the things to be taken *c* of
28:8 take *c* and search for all the
2Ch 6:16 sons will take *c* of their
24:11 *c* of the king by the hand
33:8 take *c* to do all that I have
35:2 the things under their *c* and
Ne 12:45 taking *c* of the obligation of
Es 2:20 happened to be under *c* by him
Job 10:12 own *c* has guarded my spirit
36:18 take *c* that rage does not
Ps 8:4 man that you take *c* of him
80:14 see and take *c* of this vine
106:4 *c* of me with your salvation
122:6 city, will be free from *c*
122:7 Freedom from *c* within your
Pr 12:25 Anxious *c* in the heart of a
Isa 40:11 suck he will conduct with *c*
60:4 be taken *c* of on the flank
Jer 22:21 during your freedom from *c*
49:23 sea there is anxious *c*
Eze 4:16 by weight and in anxious *c*
12:18 with anxious *c* your water
12:19 With anxious *c* . . . eat
34:11 my sheep and *c* for them
34:12 *c* of one feeding his drove
34:12 I shall *c* for my sheep

Eze 40:45 taking *c* of the obligation
40:46 taking *c* of the obligation
44:8 taken *c* of the obligation
44:15 took *c* of the obligation of
44:16 take *c* of the obligation
48:11 took *c* of the obligation
Da 8:25 during a freedom from *c* he
11:21 in during a freedom from *c*
11:24 during freedom from *c*, even
Mt 6:1 Take good *c* not to practice
22:16 and you do not *c* for anybody
Mr 4:38 Teacher, do you not *c* that we
12:14 you do not *c* for anybody
Lu 10:34 to an inn and took *c* of him
10:35 Take *c* of him, and whatever
Joh 10:13 and does not *c* for the sheep
Ac 21:24 and take *c* of their expenses
27:3 his friends and enjoy their *c*
1Co 12:25 the same *c* for one another
Php 2:20 who will genuinely *c* for the
1Ti 3:5 take *c* of God's congregation
Heb 2:6 man that you take *c* of him
Jas 2:20 do you *c* to know, O empty
1Pe 5:2 the flock of God in your *c*

Cared
1Ch 13:3 not *c* for it in the days of

Carefree
Job 3:26 I have not been *c*, nor have I
12:5 the *c* one has contempt for
21:23 When he is altogether *c* and
Pr 11:15 handshaking is keeping *c*

Carefreeness
Eze 16:49 the *c* of keeping undisturbed

Careful
De 2:4 and you must be very *c*
5:1 learn them and be *c* to do them
8:1 you should be *c* to keep, in
11:32 *c* to carry out all the
12:1 you should be *c* to carry out
12:32 what you should be *c* to do
15:5 *c* to do all this commandment
17:10 *c* to do according to all
24:8 you should be *c* to do
28:1 *c* to do all his commandments
Jos 22:5 be very *c* to carry out the
2Ki 21:8 *c* to do according to all
2Ch 19:7 Be *c* and act, for with
Ezr 4:22 be *c* that there be no
Ec 10:9 will have to be *c* with them
Mt 2:8 a *c* search for the young child
1Pe 1:10 *c* search were made by the
Re 19:10 Be *c*! Do not do that! All I
22:9 Be *c*! Do not do that! All I

Carefully
Ge 31:35 searched on *c*, but did not
44:12 And he went searching *c*
1Sa 23:23 search for him *c* among all
1Ki 20:6 must *c* search your house and
2Ki 10:23 Search *c* and see that there
Job 11:18 certainly look *c* around
21:29 *c* inspect their very signs
Ps 77:6 And my spirit will *c* search
119:4 your orders To be *c* kept
Pr 20:27 lamp of Jehovah, *c* searching
Isa 17:11 *c* fence about the plantation
Am 9:3 shall *c* search and be certain
Zep 1:12 *c* search Jerusalem with
Mt 2:7 and *c* ascertained from them
2:16 had *c* ascertained from the
Mr 4:22 has become *c* concealed but
Lu 2:51 *c* kept all these sayings in
8:17 anything *c* concealed that
10:21 have *c* hidden these things
12:2 there is nothing *c* concealed
15:8 search *c* until she finds it
Ac 15:29 *c* keep yourselves from these
17:11 *c* examining the Scriptures
17:23 *c* observing your objects of
Col 2:3 *C* concealed in him are all
Tit 3:13 *C* supply Zenas, who is
Heb 12:15 *c* watching that no one may

Careless
Isa 32:9 *c* daughters, give ear to my
32:10 you *c* ones will be agitated
32:11 Be agitated, you *c* ones!

Cares
1Pe 5:7 because he *c* for you

Caretaker
2Ki 22:14 the *c* of the garments
2Ch 34:22 the *c* of the garments

Es 2:7 came to be the *c* of Hadassah

Caretakers
2Ki 10:1 older men and the *c* of Ahab
10:5 older men and the *c* sent to
Isa 49:23 kings must become *c* for you
Eze 44:8 *c* of my obligation in my
44:14 *c* of the obligation of the

Cargo
Ac 21:3 the boat was to unload its *c*
27:10 loss not only of the *c* and

Carian
2Ki 11:4 of the *C* bodyguard and of
11:19 the *C* bodyguard and the

Caring
De 11:12 Jehovah your God is *c* for
Pr 12:10 *c* for the soul of his
Jon 1:6 God will show himself *c* about
1Co 9:9 Is it bulls God is *c* for?
Heb 8:9 I stopped *c* for them, says

Carkas
Es 1:10 *C*, the seven court officials

Carmel
Jos 12:22 king of Jokneam in *C*, one
15:55 Maon, *C* and Ziph and Juttah
19:26 reached westward to *C* and
1Sa 15:12 Saul came to *C*, and, look!
25:2 and his work was in *C*
25:2 shearing his sheep at *C*
25:5 Go up to *C*, and you must
25:7 they happened to be in *C*
25:40 Abigail at *C* and spoke to
1Ki 18:19 all Israel to me at Mount *C*
18:20 together at Mount *C*
18:42 went up to the top of *C*
2Ki 2:25 going from there to Mount *C*
4:25 of the true God at Mount *C*
2Ch 26:10 and vinedressers . . . in *C*
Ca 7:5 Your head upon you is like *C*
Isa 33:9 and *C* are shaking off their
35:2 splendor of *C* and of Sharon
Jer 46:18 and like *C* by the sea he
50:19 graze on *C* and on Bashan
Am 1:2 the summit of *C* must dry up
9:3 hide . . . on the top of *C*
Na 1:4 Bashan and *C* have withered

Carmelite
1Sa 30:5 Abigail . . . the *C*
2Sa 2:2 the wife of Nabal the *C*
3:3 the wife of Nabal the *C*
23:35 Hezro the *C*, Paarai the
1Ch 11:37 Hezro the *C*, Naarai the son

Carmelitess
1Sa 27:3 Abigail, Nabal's wife, the *C*
1Ch 3:1 Abigail the *C*

Carmi
Ge 46:9 sons of Reuben were . . . *C*
Ex 6:14 The sons of Reuben . . . *C*
Nu 26:6 of *C* the family of the
Jos 7:1 Achan the son of *C*, the son
7:18 *C*, the son of Zabdi, the son
1Ch 2:7 the sons of *C* were Achar
4:1 sons of Judah were . . . *C*
5:3 the sons of Reuben . . . *C*

Carmites
Nu 26:6 of Carmi the family of the *C*

Carob
Lu 15:16 *c* pods which the swine were

Carpenter
Mr 6:3 This is the *c* the son of Mary

Carpenter's
Mt 13:55 Is this not the *c* son?

Carpets
Jg 5:10 You who sit on rich *c*, And
Eze 27:24 in *c* of two-colored stuff

Carpus
2Ti 4:13 cloak I left at Troas with *C*

Carriage
1Ki 7:27 being the length of each *c*
7:30 wheels of copper to each *c*
7:32 wheels were by the *c*
7:34 the four corners of each *c*
7:34 were of one piece with the *c*
7:35 on top of the *c* there was a
7:35 upon the top of the *c* its
7:38 one basin upon each *c* for

Carriages
1Ki 7:27 make the ten *c* of copper
7:28 the workmanship of the *c*
7:37 he made the ten *c*
7:38 for the ten *c*
7:39 five *c* on the right side of
7:43 the ten *c* and the ten basins
7:43 the ten basins upon the *c*
2Ki 16:17 cut the sidewalls of the *c*
25:13 the *c* and the copper sea
25:16 *c* that Solomon had made
2Ch 4:14 the ten *c* and the ten basins
4:14 and the ten basins upon the *c*
Jer 27:19 concerning the *c* and
52:17 *c* and the copper sea that
52:20 *c* that King Solomon had

Carried
Ge 34:29 wives they *c* off captive
37:34 *c* on mourning over his son
43:34 portions *c* from before him
50:10 *c* on a very great and heavy
50:13 sons *c* him into the land of
Ex 10:13 the east wind *c* the locusts
10:19 it *c* the locusts away and
12:34 people *c* their flour dough
Le 10:5 and *c* them in their robes to
14:45 *c* forth outside the city to
18:30 customs that have been *c* on
Nu 24:20 he *c* further his proverbial
24:21 he *c* further his proverbial
24:23 he *c* further his proverbial
31:9 *c* off the women of Midian
De 1:31 Jehovah your God *c* you just as
21:10 you have *c* them away captive
Jg 1:8 the sons of Judah *c* on war
11:39 he *c* out his vow that he had
20:6 they had *c* on loose conduct
1Sa 4:4 *c* from there the ark of the
15:11 my words he has not *c* out
15:13 *c* out the word of Jehovah
17:34 each *c* off a sheep from the
30:3 they had been *c* off captive
30:5 wives had been *c* off captive
2Sa 6:4 *c* it from Abinadab's house
6:10 David had it *c* aside to the
19:42 has a gift been *c* to us?
1Ki 2:26 *c* the ark of the Sovereign
8:47 where they have been *c* off
8:48 who *c* them off captive
10:11 that *c* gold from Ophir
17:19 and *c* him up to the roof
2Ki 4:20 he *c* him and brought him to
7:8 *c* things from there and went
9:28 servants *c* him in a chariot
14:20 *c* him upon horses and he
20:17 actually be *c* to Babylon
1Ch 7:22 *c* on mourning for many days
10:12 *c* off the corpse of Saul and
13:13 *c* it aside to the house of
18:11 *c* off from all the nations
2Ch 6:37 have been *c* off captive, and
6:38 those who *c* them off captive
12:11 runners came in and *c* them
14:13 *c* off a very great deal of
25:28 *c* him upon horses and
28:5 *c* off from him a great
36:20 *c* off those remaining from
Ezr 4:19 and revolt have been *c* on
Job 5:13 counsel of astute ones is *c*
Ps 24:4 Who has not *c* My soul to
68:18 You have *c* away captives
Ec 8:14 exists a vanity that is *c* out
8:16 the occupation that is *c* on in
Isa 39:6 actually be *c* to Babylon
46:3 the ones *c* from the womb
53:4 sicknesses . . . he himself *c*
53:12 *c* the very sin of many
58:2 that *c* on righteousness
66:12 the flank you will be *c*
Jer 10:5 they are *c*, for they cannot
13:17 will have been *c* captive
23:20 until he will have *c* out
24:1 *c* into exile Jeconiah the
27:20 when he *c* Jeconiah the
29:1 *c* into exile from Jerusalem
29:23 *c* on senselessness in Israel
30:24 *c* out the ideas of his heart
31:19 *c* the reproach of my youth
35:16 *c* out the commandment of
49:29 camels will be *c* off from
Eze 8:3 a spirit *c* me between the
10:7 and *c* and put it into the
16:51 things that you *c* on

Eze 18:17 decisions he has *c* out
22:9 Loose conduct they have *c* on
22:29 *c* on a scheme of defrauding
23:8 prostitutions *c* from Egypt
23:27 *c* from the land of Egypt
33:16 Justice . . . he has *c* on
Da 2:35 wind *c* them away so that
11:12 crowd will certainly be *c*
11:14 *c* along to try making a
Ho 6:9 *c* on nothing but loose conduct
13:1 himself *c* weight in Israel
Na 2:7 she will certainly be *c* away
Hab 1:3 and why is strife *c*?
Mt 8:17 sicknesses and *c* our diseases
12:23 crowds were simply *c* away
Mr 2:3 a paralytic *c* by four
2:12 they were all simply *c* away
Lu 2:39 *c* out all the things according
7:12 a dead man being *c* out, the
8:14 *c* away by anxieties and
11:27 Happy is the womb that *c* you
16:22 *c* off by the angels to the
Joh 20:15 if you have *c* him off, tell
Ac 3:2 man that was lame . . . being *c*
5:6 and *c* him out and buried him
5:10 *c* her out and buried her
8:2 reverent men *c* Stephen to the
12:5 prayer . . . *c* on intensely
12:25 fully *c* out the relief
13:49 being *c* throughout the whole
21:35 being *c* along by the soldiers
2Co 10:6 obedience has been fully *c*
Eph 4:8 he *c* away captives; he gave
4:14 *c* hither and thither by every
Heb 13:9 *c* away with various and
1Pe 3:20 *c* safely through the water
Jude 12 waterless clouds *c* this way
Re 17:3 *c* me away in the power of
21:10 he *c* me away in the power

Carrier
Am 9:13 the *c* of the seed; and the

Carriers
Nu 10:17 as *c* of the tabernacle
10:21 Kohathites as *c* of the
De 31:9 the *c* of the ark of Jehovah's
31:25 Levites, the *c* of the ark of
Jos 3:15 the *c* of the Ark came as far
2Sa 6:13 *c* of the ark of Jehovah had

Carries
Le 11:28 he who *c* their dead bodies
11:40 he who *c* off its dead body
15:10 he who *c* them will wash his
Nu 11:12 male nurse *c* the suckling
De 1:31 just as a man *c* his son, in
32:11 *C* them on its pinions
2Sa 19:1 *c* on mourning over Absalom
Job 27:8 In case God *c* off his soul
Ps 10:9 He *c* off the afflicted one by
68:19 who daily *c* the load for us
Ec 12:5 the almond tree *c* blossoms
Isa 44:26 One that *c* out completely
Eze 33:14 and *c* on justice and
33:19 actually *c* on justice and
Hag 2:12 If a man *c* holy flesh in the
1Jo 3:7 he who *c* on righteousness is
3:8 *c* on sin originates with the
Re 19:11 *c* on war in righteousness
21:27 *c* on a disgusting thing and

Carry
Ge 4:13 punishment . . . too great to *c*
17:7 And I will *c* out my covenant
26:3 *c* out the sworn statement
34:10 Dwell and *c* on business in
34:21 and *c* on business in it, as
42:34 you may *c* on business in the
43:11 *c* them down to the man as a
44:1 extent they are able to *c* it
45:27 Joseph had sent to *c* him
47:30 *c* me out of Egypt and bury
Ex 18:22 must *c* the load with you
19:4 *c* you on wings of eagles and
25:14 in order to *c* the Ark with
25:27 for the poles to *c* the table
25:28 must *c* the table with them
28:12 and Aaron must *c* their names
28:29 Aaron must *c* the names of
28:30 Aaron must *c* the judgments
30:4 the poles with which to *c* it
31:16 so as to *c* out the sabbath
34:22 *c* on your festival of weeks
37:27 poles with which to *c* it
Le 10:4 *c* your brothers from in front
Le 16:22 goat must *c* upon itself all
18:4 decisions you should *c* out
18:30 *c* on any of the detestable
22:9 *c* sin because of it and have
25:18 *c* out my statutes and you
25:18 and you must *c* them out
26:3 commandments and you do *c*
26:9 *c* out my covenant with you
Nu 1:50 *c* the tabernacle and all its
4:15 come in to *c* them, but they
4:25 *c* the tent cloths of the
5:30 priest must *c* out toward her
8:19 *c* on the service of the sons
8:22 *c* on their service in the tent
11:12 *C* them in your bosom, just
11:14 *c* all this people, because
11:17 that you may not *c* it, just
16:9 *c* on the service of Jehovah's
18:6 *c* on the service of the tent
18:23 *c* on the service of the tent
21:1 and *c* away some of them as
23:19 and will he not *c* it out?
24:22 till Assyria will *c* you away
De 1:9 am not able by myself to *c* you
1:12 *c* by myself the burden of you
5:15 to *c* on the sabbath day
6:24 *c* out all these regulations
7:12 keep them and do *c* them out
8:18 in order to *c* out his covenant
9:5 to *c* out the word that Jehovah
10:8 the tribe of Levi to *c* the ark
11:32 *c* out all the regulations
12:1 you should be careful to *c* out
12:26 vow offerings you should *c*
14:24 you will not be able to *c* it
16:12 *c* out these regulations
26:16 *c* out these regulations
26:16 *c* them out with all your
27:10 *c* out his commandments and
28:20 that you try to *c* out
28:58 *c* out all the words of this
29:29 may *c* out all the words of
31:12 *c* out all the words of this
Jos 4:3 must *c* them over with you and
5:10 to *c* out the passover on the
6:4 should *c* seven rams' horns
6:6 should *c* seven rams' horns
22:5 be very careful to *c* out the
Jg 21:21 *c* off for yourselves by force
21:23 *c* off wives for their number
1Sa 1:23 may Jehovah *c* out his word
3:12 I shall *c* out toward Eli all
17:17 *c* them quickly to the camp
30:2 *c* off captive the women and
2Sa 2:32 *c* Asahel and bury him in the
4:4 nurse began to *c* him and flee
6:3 *c* it from the house of
7:25 *c* out to time indefinite and
8:2 David's servants to *c* tribute
8:6 David's servants to *c* tribute
17:13 Israel must also *c* ropes
1Ki 2:4 *c* out his word that he spoke
5:9 for your part, will *c* them
6:12 *c* out my word with you that
8:3 the priests began to *c* the Ark
8:20 *c* out his word that he had
8:46 captors actually *c* them off
8:65 Solomon proceeded to *c* on at
12:15 *c* out his word that Jehovah
14:28 the runners would *c* them
15:22 to *c* the stones of Ramah
18:12 will *c* you away to where
20:31 *c* sackcloth upon our loins
2Ki 4:19 *C* him to his mother
5:23 might *c* them before him
7:8 *c* from there silver and gold
15:29 *c* them into exile in
18:14 impose upon me I shall *c*
23:24 *c* out the words of the law
1Ch 15:2 No one is to *c* the ark of the
15:2 to *c* the ark of Jehovah and
15:15 Levites began to *c* the ark
16:29 *C* a gift and come in before
21:24 *c* what is yours to Jehovah
22:13 *c* out the regulations and
23:26 Levites will not have to *c*
2Ch 5:4 the Levites began to *c* the Ark
6:10 to *c* out his word that he
6:36 captors actually *c* them off
10:15 Jehovah might *c* out his word
16:6 *c* away the stones of Ramah
20:25 until they could *c* no more
36:6 to *c* him off to Babylon
Ne 5:13 that does not *c* out this word
Ne 8:12 to *c* on a great rejoicing
9:8 to *c* out your words, because
12:27 to *c* on an inauguration and
Job 7:13 bed will help *c* my concern
13:14 I *c* my flesh in my teeth
15:12 does your heart *c* you away
23:14 he will *c* out completely
24:10 have to *c* the reaped ears
27:21 *c* him off and he will go
31:36 upon my shoulder I would *c*
32:22 my Maker would *c* me away
36:3 *c* my knowledge from far off
Ps 10:9 *c* off some afflicted one by
16:4 not *c* their names upon my lips
21:11 they are unable to *c* out
24:5 *c* away blessing from Jehovah
28:9 and *c* them to time indefinite
58:9 *c* them off as a stormy wind
62:3 *c* on frantically against the
72:3 Let the mountains *c* peace to
83:3 *c* on their confidential talk
91:12 Upon their hands they will *c*
96:8 *C* a gift and come into his
103:18 orders so as to *c* them out
119:38 *C* out to your servant your
119:106 and I will *c* it out
141:4 *c* on notorious deeds in
Pr 20:18 direction *c* on your war
21:3 To *c* on righteousness and
24:6 you will *c* on your war, and
Ec 5:15 nothing at all can one *c* away
5:19 to *c* off his portion and to
Isa 8:4 *c* away the resources of
30:1 disposed to *c* out counsel
30:6 asses they *c* their resources
40:11 his bosom he will *c* them
40:24 itself will *c* them away
41:16 wind itself will *c* them
44:28 he will completely *c* out
46:4 that I myself may *c* and that
46:7 They *c* it upon the shoulder
49:22 will *c* your own daughters
57:13 a wind will *c* even all of
60:6 and frankincense they will *c*
63:9 *c* them all the days of long
64:6 *c* us away just like a wind
Jer 1:12 my word in order to *c* it out
4:27 *c* out a sheer extermination
5:18 not *c* out an extermination
7:5 will positively *c* out justice
10:19 sickness, and I shall *c* it
17:21 do not *c* on the sabbath day
18:12 going to *c* out each one the
22:17 in order to *c* them on
33:14 *c* out the good word that I
34:18 not *c* out the words of the
44:25 *c* out your vows, and
La 3:27 *c* the yoke during his youth
4:22 not *c* you off into exile again
Eze 4:4 you will *c* their error
4:5 *c* the error of the house of
4:6 *c* the error of the house of
11:20 and actually *c* them out
16:43 not *c* on any loose conduct
16:50 to *c* on a detestable thing
20:24 not *c* out my own judicial
29:19 he must *c* off its wealth
36:27 keep and actually *c* out
37:24 will certainly *c* them out
38:13 to *c* off silver and gold
39:10 not *c* sticks of wood from
43:11 may actually *c* them out
45:11 bath to *c* a tenth of a
46:20 *c* nothing out to the outer
Da 9:12 *c* out his words that he had
11:23 *c* on deception and actually
Ho 2:2 *C* on a legal case with your
2:2 *c* on a legal case, for she is
5:14 and I shall go and *c* off
Am 5:26 *c* Sakkuth your king and
6:10 *c* them forth one by one
Mic 6:14 will not *c* them safely away
6:14 you would *c* away safely
Zec 6:13 he . . . will *c* the dignity
7:9 and *c* on with one another
Mal 2:3 will actually *c* you away to
Mt 3:15 *c* out all that is righteous
4:6 will *c* you on their hands
Mr 6:8 to *c* nothing for the trip
6:55 started to *c* about on cots
11:16 *c* a utensil through the
Lu 4:11 will *c* you on their hands
9:3 *C* nothing for the trip, neither
10:4 Do not *c* a purse, nor a food

Lu 22:40 *C* on prayer, that you do not
22:46 Rise and *c* on prayer, that
Joh 5:10 not lawful for you to *c* the
12:6 *c* off the monies put in it
Ac 5:9 and they will *c* you out
1Co 16:3 send to *c* your kind gift to
16:13 *c* on as men, grow mighty
Ga 5:16 *c* out no fleshly desire at
6:5 each one will *c* his own load
Eph 6:18 you *c* on prayer on every
Php 1:6 will *c* it to completion until
Col 2:8 will *c* you off as his prey
2Th 3:1 brothers, *c* on prayer for us
1Ti 2:8 the men *c* on prayer, lifting
6:7 neither can we *c* anything out
Heb 13:18 *C* on prayer for us, for we
Jas 4:1 that *c* on a conflict in your
5:13 Let him *c* on prayer
1Pe 2:11 *c* on a conflict against the
1Jo 3:9 does not *c* on sin, because
3:10 does not *c* on righteousness
Re 17:17 hearts to *c* out his thought
17:17 *c* out their one thought by

Carrying
Ge 7:17 waters . . . began *c* the ark
37:25 camels were *c* labdanum and
45:23 ten asses *c* good things of
45:23 ten she-asses *c* grain and
Ex 27:7 sides of the altar when *c* it
37:5 sides of the Ark for *c* the Ark
37:14 for the poles for *c* the table
37:15 with gold for *c* the table
38:7 the altar for *c* it with them
Le 11:25 *c* any of their dead bodies
Nu 4:24 as to serving and as to *c*
4:47 service of *c* loads in the tent
7:5 *c* on the service of the tent of
7:9 did their *c* on the shoulder
8:11 *c* on the service of Jehovah
11:17 help you in *c* the load of
13:23 they went *c* it with a bar on
14:27 they are *c* on against me
18:21 service that they are *c* on
Jos 3:3 the priests, the Levites, *c* it
3:8 the priests *c* the ark of the
3:13 priests *c* the ark of Jehovah
3:14 *c* the ark of the covenant
3:15 priests *c* the Ark were dipped
3:17 the priests *c* the ark of
4:9 *c* the ark of the covenant, and
4:10 the priests *c* the Ark were
4:16 the priests *c* the ark of the
4:18 when the priests *c* the ark
6:8 priests *c* seven rams' horns
6:12 priests went *c* the ark of
6:13 priests *c* seven rams' horns
8:33 the Levites, *c* the ark of the
Jg 9:27 in *c* on a festal exultation
16:3 went *c* them up to the top of
1Sa 10:3 one *c* three kids and one
10:3 one *c* three round loaves of
10:3 one *c* a large jar of wine
14:1 the attendant *c* his weapons
14:3 Ahijah . . . was *c* the ephod
17:41 man *c* the large shield was
2Sa 15:24 the Levites *c* the ark of the
18:15 attendants *c* Joab's weapons
23:16 *c* and bringing it to David
1Ki 10:2 camels *c* balsam oil and very
10:22 *c* gold and silver, ivory
2Ki 23:3 by *c* out the words of this
24:16 the mighty men *c* on war
25:13 *c* the copper of them to
1Ch 5:18 men *c* shield and sword and
11:18 *c* and bringing it to David
12:24 sons of Judah *c* the . . . shield
15:22 chief of the Levites in *c*
15:22 he giving instruction in *c*
15:26 Levites while *c* the ark of
15:27 all the Levites *c* the Ark
15:27 Chenaniah the chief of the *c*
2Ch 9:1 camels *c* balsam oil, and gold
9:21 *c* gold and silver, ivory
28:17 Judah and *c* off captives
Ne 4:17 *c* the burden of load bearers
Ps 37:7 At the man *c* out his ideas
89:50 *c* in my bosom the reproach
103:20 angels . . . *c* out his word
126:6 *C* along a bagful of seed
126:6 *C* along his sheaves
Pr 10:23 *c* on of loose conduct is
Isa 15:7 *c* them away right over the
45:20 *c* the wood of their carved
52:11 *c* the utensils of Jehovah
Jer 11:5 *c* out the oath that I swore
17:27 and not *c* a load, but there
35:14 *c* out of the words of
48:10 *c* out the mission of
52:17 *c* all the copper of them
Eze 12:6 do the *c* on the shoulder
12:7 On my shoulder I did the *c*
12:12 do *c* in the darkness and go
Joe 2:11 For he who is *c* out his word
Na 1:13 I shall break his *c* bar from
Hab 1:5 activity that one is *c* on in
Mr 14:13 man *c* an earthenware vessel
Lu 5:18 men *c* on a bed a man who was
14:27 is not *c* his torture stake
22:10 a man *c* an earthenware
Ro 2:27 by *c* out the Law, judge you
Ga 6:2 *c* the burdens of one another
6:17 *c* on my body the brand marks
Tit 3:3 *c* on in badness and envy
Heb 12:4 In *c* on your contest against
Jas 2:8 *c* out the kingly law
Re 17:7 wild beast that is *c* her and
22:15 liking and *c* on a lie

Carshena
Es 1:14 those closest to him were *C*

Carve
Ex 34:1 *C* out for yourself two tablets
De 10:1 *C* for yourself two tablets of

Carved
Ex 20:4 a *c* image or a form like
34:4 Moses *c* out two tablets of
Le 26:1 not set up a *c* image or a
De 4:16 a *c* image, the form of any
4:23 do not make . . . a *c* image
4:25 a *c* image, a form of anything
5:8 a *c* image, any form like
10:3 and *c* two tablets of stone
27:15 the man who makes a *c* image
Jg 17:3 a *c* image and a molten statue
17:4 he went making a *c* image and
18:14 and a *c* image and a molten
18:17 take the *c* image and the
18:18 take the *c* image, the ephod
18:20 the teraphim and the *c* image
18:30 stood up the *c* image for
18:31 kept the *c* image of Micah
1Ki 6:29 *c* with engraved carvings of
6:32 *c* upon them carvings of
6:35 he *c* cherubs and palm-tree
2Ki 21:7 *c* image of the sacred pole
2Ch 33:7 *c* image that he had made in
Ps 97:7 serving any *c* image be
144:12 corners *c* in palace style
Isa 40:20 a *c* image that may not be
42:17 trust in the *c* image
44:9 formers of the *c* image are
44:15 has made it into a *c* image
44:17 into his *c* image
45:20 the wood of their *c* image
48:5 and my own *c* image and my
Jer 10:14 because of the *c* image
51:17 because of the *c* image
Eze 23:14 images of Chaldeans *c* in
41:18 *c* cherubs and palm-tree
41:19 *c* on the whole house all
41:20 *c* cherubs and palm-tree
Na 1:14 I shall cut off *c* image and
Hab 2:18 benefit has a *c* image been
2:18 the former of it has *c* it
Lu 23:53 in a tomb *c* in the rock

Carver
Isa 44:12 the *c* of iron with the
44:13 As for the wood *c*, he has

Carving
Eze 8:10 *c* being upon the wall all

Carvings
1Ki 6:18 *c* of gourd-shaped ornaments
6:29 *c* of cherubs and palm-tree
6:32 *c* of cherubs and palm-tree
7:31 upon its mouth there were *c*
Pr 25:11 As apples of gold in silver *c*
Eze 23:14 men in *c* upon the wall

Case
Ge 9:3 As in the *c* of green vegetation
32:17 In *c* that Esau my brother
37:26 in *c* we killed our brother
42:16 as the truth in your *c*
43:11 If, then, that is the *c*
43:14 in *c* I must be bereaved, I
44:26 in *c* our youngest brother is
Ex 1:10 in *c* war should befall us
7:9 In *c* that Pharaoh speaks to
12:48 And in *c* an alien resident
13:14 in *c* your son should inquire
15:25 a *c* for judgment and there
18:16 they have a *c* arise, it must
18:22 every big *c* they will bring
18:22 small *c* they themselves
18:26 A hard *c* they would bring to
18:26 small *c* they themselves
20:5 in the *c* of those who hate me
20:6 in the *c* of those who love me
21:2 In *c* you should buy a Hebrew
21:7 in *c* a man should sell his
21:14 And in *c* a man becomes
21:18 in *c* men should get into a
21:20 in *c* a man strikes his slave
21:22 And in *c* men should struggle
21:26 in *c* a man should strike the
21:28 in *c* a bull should gore a
21:33 in *c* a man should open a pit
21:33 in *c* a man should excavate a
21:35 in *c* a man's bull should
22:1 In *c* a man should steal a
22:6 In *c* a fire should spread out
22:7 In *c* a man should give his
22:9 regards any *c* of transgression
22:9 *c* of them both is to come to
22:10 In *c* a man should give his
22:14 in *c* anybody should ask for
22:16 in *c* a man seduces a virgin
23:33 In *c* you should serve their
24:14 Whoever has a *c* at law, let
31:14 In *c* there is anyone doing
Le 1:2 In *c* some man of you would
2:1 in *c* some soul would present
2:4 And in *c* you would present as
4:2 In *c* a soul sins by mistake in
5:1 in *c* a soul sins in that he has
5:3 in *c* he touches the uncleanness
5:4 Or in *c* a soul swears to the
5:5 that in *c* he becomes guilty as
5:15 In *c* a soul behaves
6:2 In *c* a soul sins in that he
6:4 that in *c* he sins and indeed
7:21 in *c* a soul touches anything
11:38 *c* water should be put upon
11:39 in *c* any beast that is yours
12:2 In *c* a woman conceives seed
13:2 In *c* a man develops in the
13:9 In *c* the plague of leprosy
13:16 in *c* the living flesh goes
13:18 in *c* a boil develops in its
13:24 in *c* there comes to be a
13:29 in *c* a plague develops in
13:31 in *c* the priest sees the
13:38 in *c* blotches develop in the
13:40 in *c* his head grows bald, it
13:42 in *c* a reddish-white plague
13:47 in *c* the plague of leprosy
15:2 In *c* any man has a running
15:8 the *c* of the one who has a
15:8 in that *c* wash his garments
15:13 in *c* the one having a running
15:16 in *c* a man has an emission
15:19 in *c* a woman is having a
15:25 in *c* the running discharge
15:25 in *c* she should have a flow
17:13 in that *c* pour its blood out
17:15 in that *c* wash his garments
18:29 In *c* anyone does any of all
19:5 in *c* you should sacrifice a
19:20 *c* a man lies down with a
19:23 *c* you people come into the
19:33 *c* an alien resident resides
20:9 *c* there should be any man who
21:9 *c* the daughter of a priest
21:18 *c* there is any man in whom
22:11 in *c* a priest should purchase
22:12 in *c* the daughter of a priest
22:13 in *c* the daughter of a priest
22:14 in *c* a man eats a holy thing
22:21 in *c* a man should present a
22:22 No *c* of blindness or fracture
22:29 in *c* you should sacrifice a
24:15 *c* any man calls down evil
24:17 *c* a man strikes any soul of
24:19 *c* a man should cause a
25:14 *c* you should sell
25:20 *c* you should say: What are
25:21 *c* I shall certainly command
25:25 *c* your brother grows poor
25:26 *c* anyone proves to have no
25:29 in *c* a man should sell a

Le 25:35 in *c* your brother grows poor
25:39 in *c* your brother grows poor
25:47 in *c* the hand of the alien
25:48 will continue in his *c*
27:2 In *c* a man makes a special
27:14 in *c* a man should sanctify
Nu 5:6 *c* they do any of all the sins of
5:12 *c* any man's wife turns aside
5:20 *c* you have turned aside while
5:20 *c* you have defiled yourself
5:30 *c* of a man where the spirit
6:2 *c* a man or a woman takes a
6:9 *c* anyone dying should die quite
9:14 *c* an alien resident should be
10:9 *c* you should enter into war
10:32 *c* you should come with us
15:8 in *c* you should render up a
15:14 in *c* there should be residing
15:22 Now in *c* you should make a
15:30 in that *c* that soul must be
19:14 in *c* a man should die in a
23:3 In that *c* whatever he will
27:5 Moses presented their *c*
27:8 In *c* any man should die
30:2 In *c* a man makes a vow to
30:3 in *c* a woman makes a vow to
30:9 the *c* of the vow of a widow
32:15 In *c* you should turn back
32:23 In that *c* know that your sin
De 1:17 the *c* that is too hard for you
4:3 in the *c* of the Baal of Peor
4:25 In *c* you become father to
5:9 in the *c* of those who hate me
5:10 in the *c* of those who love me
6:20 In *c* your son should ask you
7:9 in the *c* of those who love him
7:17 In *c* you say in your heart
12:21 In *c* the place that Jehovah
13:1 In *c* a prophet or a dreamer
13:6 In *c* your brother, the son of
13:12 In *c* you hear it said in one
14:24 in *c* the journey should be
15:7 In *c* some one of your
15:12 In *c* there should be sold to
15:13 in *c* you should send him out
15:16 in *c* he says to you, I shall
15:21 in *c* there should prove to be
17:2 In *c* there should be found in
17:8 In *c* a matter for judicial
18:6 in *c* the Levite goes out of
18:21 in *c* you should say in
19:4 the *c* of the manslayer who
19:11 in *c* there should happen to
19:15 in the *c* of any sin that he
19:16 In *c* a witness scheming
20:1 In *c* you go out to the battle
20:10 In *c* you draw near to a
20:19 In *c* you lay siege to a city
21:1 In *c* someone is found slain
21:10 In *c* you go out to the battle
21:15 In *c* a man comes to have
21:18 In *c* a man happens to have a
21:22 in *c* there comes to be in
22:6 In *c* a bird's nest happens to
22:8 In *c* you build a new house
22:13 In *c* a man takes a wife and
22:22 In *c* a man is found lying
22:23 In *c* there happened to be a
22:26 so it is with this *c*
22:28 In *c* a man finds a girl, a
23:9 In *c* you go out into camp
23:10 In *c* there happens to be in
23:21 In *c* you vow a vow to
23:22 in *c* you omit making a vow
23:24 In *c* you go into the vineyard
23:25 In *c* you go into the standing
24:1 In *c* a man takes a woman and
24:3 in *c* the latter man who took
24:5 In *c* a man takes a new wife
24:7 In *c* a man is found
24:10 In *c* you lend your fellowman
24:19 In *c* you reap your harvest
24:20 In *c* you beat your olive tree
24:21 In *c* you gather the grapes of
25:1 In *c* a dispute arises
25:5 In *c* brothers dwell together
25:11 In *c* men struggle together
Jos 4:6 In *c* your sons should ask in
8:5 in *c* they should come out to
20:5 in *c* the avenger of blood
22:28 in *c* they should say that
24:20 In *c* you should leave
Jg 14:12 in that *c* have to give you
15:3 in *c* I am dealing with them
Jg 21:22 conduct a legal *c* against us
1Sa 20:13 *c* it should seem good to my
23:3 in *c* we should go to Keilah
24:15 conduct the legal *c* for me
24:19 *c* where a man finds his
25:39 legal *c* of my reproach to
2Sa 15:2 legal *c* to come to the king
15:4 have a legal *c* or judgment
19:6 in that *c* it would be right
19:7 in *c* you are not going out
1Ki 8:37 In *c* a famine occurs in the
8:37 in *c* a pestilence occurs
8:37 in *c* scorching, mildew
8:37 in *c* their enemy besieges
8:44 In *c* your people go out to
8:46 In *c* they sin against you
2Ki 4:29 In *c* you encounter anyone
4:29 in *c* anyone should greet you
5:3 In that *c* he would recover
13:19 In that *c* you would
17:4 find conspiracy in Hoshea's *c*
18:22 in *c* you men should say to
1Ch 22:13 In that *c* you will prove
2Ch 6:28 *c* a famine occurs in the
6:28 in *c* a pestilence occurs, in
6:28 in *c* scorching and mildew
6:28 in *c* their enemies besiege
6:34 In *c* your people go out to
6:36 In *c* they sin against you
19:10 every legal *c* that will
28:15 *c* of anyone tottering, they
Es 4:11 only in *c* the king holds out
4:16 in *c* I must perish, I must
Job 9:2 in the right in a *c* with God
9:14 in *c* I myself answer him
10:16 yourself marvelous in my *c*
13:18 presented a *c* of justice
13:20 In that *c* I shall not
23:4 before him a *c* of justice
27:8 in *c* he cuts him off
27:8 In *c* God carries off his
27:9 In *c* distress comes upon him
29:16 the legal *c* of one whom I
31:13 in their *c* at law with me
31:35 individual in the *c* at law
33:29 *c* of an able-bodied man
35:14 The legal *c* is before him
38:5 measurements, in *c* you know
Ps 19:13 that *c* I shall be complete
27:10 In *c* my own father and my
35:1 Do conduct my *c*, O Jehovah
35:23 Jehovah, to my *c* at law
43:1 legal *c* against a nation not
51:19 In that *c* you will be
51:19 In that *c* bulls will be
62:10 In *c* the means of
74:22 conduct your own *c* at law
102:*super* in *c* he grows feeble and
119:6 In that *c* I should not be
119:154 do conduct my legal *c* and
Pr 2:5 in that *c* you will understand
2:9 In that *c* you will understand
3:23 In that *c* you will walk in
18:17 one first in his legal *c* is
20:16 *c* one has gone surety for a
21:6 the *c* of those seeking death
23:1 *c* you should sit down to feed
23:13 *c* you beat him with the rod
23:18 *c* there will exist a future
24:12 In *c* you should say: Look!
25:8 to conduct a legal *c* hastily
27:13 *c* one has gone surety for a
30:4 of his son, in *c* you know
Ca 8:10 In this *c* I have become in
Isa 1:23 legal *c* of a widow does not
7:9 *c* not be of long duration
8:19 *c* they should say to you
10:2 lowly ones from a legal *c*
28:15 flood, in *c* it should pass
30:21 *c* you people should go to
30:21 *c* you should go to the left
34:8 for the legal *c* over Zion
36:7 in *c* you should say to me
41:21 Bring your controversial *c*
42:20 a *c* of seeing many things
42:20 a *c* of opening the ears
43:2 In *c* you should pass through
43:2 In *c* you should walk through
58:7 in *c* you should see someone
58:8 In that *c* your light would
58:9 In that *c* you would call
58:14 will in that *c* find your
66:13 in the *c* of Jerusalem you
Jer 5:28 No legal *c* have they pleaded
Jer 5:28 legal *c* of the fatherless boy
11:20 I have revealed my *c* at law
20:12 I have revealed my *c* at law
22:15 In that *c* it went well
22:16 In that *c* it went well
22:16 not that a *c* of knowing me
25:28 in *c* they refuse to take the
30:11 in your *c* I shall make no
33:17 in David's *c* a man to sit
33:18 *c* of the priests, the
38:15 In *c* I should tell you
38:15 in *c* I advise you, you will
38:25 in *c* the princes hear that
50:34 conduct their legal *c*, in
51:36 am conducting your legal *c*
La 3:36 a man crooked in his legal *c*
Eze 2:7 for they are a *c* of rebellion
3:19 in *c* you have warned someone
3:21 in *c* you have warned someone
4:6 right side in the second *c*
14:9 prophet, in *c* he gets fooled
14:13 in *c* it commits sin against
16:32 *c* of the wife that commits
16:34 in your *c* the opposite thing
18:5 *c* he happens to be righteous
18:11 in *c* he has eaten also upon
18:21 wicked, in *c* he should turn
21:7 in *c* they say to you
24:13 come to its rest in your *c*
33:2 in *c* I bring upon it a sword
33:6 in *c* he sees the sword
33:9 in *c* you actually warn
44:24 And in a legal *c* they
46:12 in *c* the chieftain should
46:16 *c* the chieftain should give
46:17 in *c* he should give a gift
Da 6:17 be changed in the *c* of Daniel
Ho 2:2 Carry on a legal *c* with your
2:2 carry on a legal *c*, for she
3:1 *c* of Jehovah's love for the
4:1 Jehovah has a legal *c* with the
8:9 In Ephraim's *c*, they have
9:16 in *c* they bring to birth, I
12:2 has a legal *c* with Judah
13:15 In *c* he himself as the son
Mic 2:7 in the *c* of the one walking
6:1 a legal *c* with the mountains
6:2 the legal *c* of Jehovah, also
6:2 Jehovah has a legal *c* with
7:9 until he conducts my legal *c*
Zec 13:3 in *c* a man should prophesy
Mt 13:52 That being the *c*, every
16:9 in the *c* of the five thousand
16:10 the *c* of the four thousand
19:8 such has not been the *c* from
26:7 with an alabaster *c* of costly
26:54 In that *c*, how would the
Mr 14:3 alabaster *c* of perfumed oil
14:3 Breaking open the alabaster *c*
Lu 7:37 alabaster *c* of perfumed oil
Joh 9:3 be made manifest in his *c*
Ac 4:2 resurrection . . . the *c* of Jesus
19:38 do have a *c* against someone
21:22 In any *c* they are going to
Ro 3:3 What, then, is the *c*? If some
7:21 this law in my *c*: that when
9:10 not that *c* alone, but also
1Co 4:2 in this *c*, what is looked for
4:6 in our *c* you may learn the
6:1 has a *c* against the other dare
9:15 it should become so in my *c*
12:22 But much rather is it the *c*
2Co 1:19 Yes has become Yes in his *c*
11:10 in my *c* that no stop shall
Ga 3:16 seeds, as in the *c* of many
3:16 but as in the *c* of one: And
Eph 1:20 in the *c* of the Christ when
Php 1:21 in my *c* to live is Christ
1:30 as you saw in my *c* and as
1:30 you now hear about in my *c*
1Ti 1:16 me as the foremost *c*
3:15 but in *c* I am delayed, that
Heb 6:9 in your *c*, beloved ones, we
7:8 the one *c* it is men who are
7:8 in the other *c* it is someone
1Jo 2:8 a fact that is true in his *c*
2:10 cause for stumbling in his *c*
4:9 was made manifest in our *c*
4:16 love that God has in our *c*
5:10 witness given in his own *c*

Cases
Ex 18:19 bring the *c* to the true God
Le 18:17 are *c* of blood relationship

1Ki 3:11 to hear judicial *c*
2Ch 19:8 legal *c* of the inhabitants
28:10 *c* of guilt against Jehovah
Es 1:13 versed in law and legal *c*
Eze 26:10 in the *c* of entering into
Am 3:9 *c* of defrauding inside her
Mt 23:5 scripture-containing *c* that
2Co 6:4 by *c* of need, by difficulties
12:10 pleasure in . . . *c* of need
12:20 *c* of anger, contentions
12:20 *c* of being puffed up
1Ti 5:23 your frequent *c* of sickness

Casiphia
Ezr 8:17 the head one in the place *C*
8:17 the Nethinim in the place *C*

Casluhim
Ge 10:14 *C* (from among whom the
1Ch 1:12 Pathrusim and *C* (from among

Cassia
Ex 30:24 and *c* five hundred units by
Ps 45:8 myrrh and aloeswood and *c*
Eze 27:19 *c* and cane—for your

Cast
Ex 15:4 he has *c* into the sea
25:12 *c* four rings of gold for it
26:37 must *c* for them five socket
36:36 *c* four socket pedestals of
37:3 he *c* four rings of gold for it
37:13 he *c* four rings of gold for
38:5 he *c* four rings on the four
Jos 18:6 must *c* lots here for you
1Sa 14:42 *C* lots to decide between me
2Sa 20:12 he *c* a garment over him
20:15 *c* up a siege rampart
1Ki 7:15 *c* the two pillars of copper
7:16 the pillars, *c* in copper
7:24 ornaments *c* in its casting
7:30 *c* with wreaths across from
7:33 their hubs, they were all *c*
7:37 they all had one *c*, one
7:46 king *c* them in the clay mold
14:9 you have *c* behind your back
2Ki 13:23 not *c* them away from
17:20 he had *c* them away from
19:32 nor *c* up a siege rampart
23:6 *c* its dust upon the burial
23:12 he *c* their dust into the
24:20 *c* them out of his sight
1Ch 24:31 to *c* lots exactly as their
25:8 *c* lots as to the things to be
26:13 *c* lots for the small the
26:14 they *c* the lots, and his lot
28:9 he will *c* you off forever
2Ch 4:3 being *c* in its casting
4:17 *c* them in the thick ground
Ne 10:34 lots we *c* concerning the
11:1 they *c* lots to bring in one
Es 3:7 *c* Pur, that is, the Lot
9:24 had Pur, that is, the Lot, *c*
Job 6:27 *c* lots even over someone
15:33 And *c* off his blossoms just
18:7 his counsel will *c* him off
19:12 *c* up their way against me
29:24 face they would not *c* down
30:12 *c* up against me their
39:3 they *c* forth their young
41:24 Its heart is *c* like stone
41:24 *c* like a lower millstone
Ps 2:3 *c* their cords away from us
22:18 upon my clothing they *c* lots
43:2 Why have you *c* me off?
44:9 *c* off and keep humiliating us
56:7 *c* them forth. In anger bring
60:1 O God, you have *c* us off
60:10 O God, who have *c* us off
74:1 O God, have you *c* off forever
88:14 that you *c* off my soul
89:38 you have *c* off and you keep
108:11 O God, who have *c* us off
Pr 1:14 Your lot you ought to *c* in
15:19 upright ones is a way *c* up
16:33 Into the lap the lot is *c*
Isa 34:17 has *c* for them the lot
37:33 *c* up a siege rampart
40:19 *c* a mere molten image
44:10 or *c* a mere molten image
Jer 14:16 *c* out into the streets
26:23 *c* his dead body into the
52:3 *c* them out from before his
La 2:7 Jehovah has *c* off his altar
Eze 23:35 to *c* me behind your back
24:6 no lot must be *c* over it
Ho 8:3 Israel has *c* off good
8:5 Your calf has been *c* off
Am 5:7 ones who have *c* righteousness
Ob 11 over Jerusalem they *c* lots
Jon 1:7 let us *c* lots, that we may
Na 3:10 they *c* lots, and her great
Zec 1:21 to *c* down the horns of the
10:6 whom I had not *c* off
Mt 13:50 will *c* them into the fiery
17:27 *c* a fishhook, and take the
21:21 lifted up and *c* into the sea
Lu 6:22 *c* out your name as wicked
12:28 tomorrow is *c* into an oven
23:34 his garments, they *c* lots
Joh 12:31 of this world will be *c* out
15:6 *c* out as a branch and is
19:24 my apparel they *c* lots
21:6 *C* the net on the right side
21:6 Then they *c* it, but they
Ac 1:26 So they *c* lots over them
26:10 I *c* my vote against them
27:26 *c* ashore on a certain island
27:29 *c* somewhere upon the rocks
27:29 *c* out four anchors from the
27:43 *c* themselves into the sea
1Co 7:35 not that I may *c* a noose
Re 4:10 *c* their crowns before the
11:2 *c* it clear out and do not

Casting
Ex 38:27 the *c* of the socket pedestals
1Ki 7:24 ornaments cast in its *c*
2Ch 4:3 two rows, being cast in its *c*
24:10 *c* it into the chest until
Ne 9:26 *c* your law behind their back
Job 41:23 They are as a *c* upon it
Ps 44:23 Do not keep *c* off forever
77:7 that Jehovah keeps *c* off
Isa 19:8 *c* fishhooks into the Nile
28:2 *c* down to the earth with
La 3:17 You also do a *c* off so that
3:31 will Jehovah keep on *c* off
Joe 3:3 they kept *c* lots; and they
Jon 1:7 they kept *c* lots; and finally
Mic 2:5 to have no one *c* out the cord
Mt 27:35 his outer garments by *c* lots
Mr 1:16 *c* their nets about in the sea
15:24 by *c* the lot over them as
Lu 13:32 I am *c* out demons and
Ac 7:58 they began *c* stones at him
7:59 *c* stones at Stephen as he
19:13 the *c* out of demons also
Ro 11:15 the *c* of them away means

Castle
1Ch 29:1 the *c* is not for man, but
29:19 to build the *c* for which I
Ne 1:1 happened to be in Shushan the *c*
2:8 gates of the *C* that belongs to
7:2 Hananiah the prince of the *C*
Es 1:2 which was in Shushan the *c*
1:5 were found in Shushan the *c*
2:3 at Shushan the *c*, at the house
2:5 happened to be in Shushan the *c*
2:8 at Shushan the *c* in charge of
3:15 was given in Shushan the *c*
8:14 given out in Shushan the *c*
9:6 And in Shushan the *c* the Jews
9:11 those killed in Shushan the *c*
9:12 In Shushan the *c* the Jews
Da 8:2 Shushan the *c*, which is in

Castrated
De 23:1 No man *c* by crushing the

Casts
Mr 4:26 *c* the seed upon the ground
Re 6:13 *c* its unripe figs

Catastrophe
Isa 15:5 arouse the outcry about the *c*
Am 6:6 made sick at the *c* of Joseph
Na 3:19 There is no relief for your *c*

Catch
Ex 22:6 and it does *c* thorns, and
Nu 32:23 your sin will *c* up with you
Jg 15:4 to *c* three hundred foxes and
18:22 to *c* up with the sons of Dan
1Sa 15:8 to *c* Agag the king of Amalek
2Sa 15:14 actually *c* up with us and
2Ki 7:9 guilt must also *c* up with us
7:12 shall *c* them alive, and into
Ps 35:8 own net that he hid *c* him
71:11 Pursue and *c* him, for there
Pr 5:22 errors will *c* the wicked one
Isa 9:18 *c* fire in the thickets of the
Isa 59:9 does not *c* up with us
Jer 5:26 It is men that they *c*
42:16 *c* up with you in the land
Zec 1:6 not *c* up with your fathers
Mt 24:15 *c* sight of the disgusting
Mr 12:13 to *c* him in his speech
13:14 *c* sight of the disgusting
Lu 5:4 let down your nets for a *c*
5:9 *c* of fish which they took up
11:54 *c* something out of his mouth
20:20 might *c* him in speech, so as
20:26 not able to *c* him in this

Catches
Le 17:13 *c* a wild beast or a fowl
1Co 3:19 He *c* the wise in their own
1Jo 5:16 *c* sight of his brother

Catching
Job 5:13 One *c* the wise in their own
18:10 *c* device . . . on his pathway
Eze 14:5 of *c* the house of Israel by
Mr 5:6 But on *c* sight of Jesus from a
5:22 on *c* sight of him, he fell at
6:49 At *c* sight of him walking on
Lu 5:10 you will be *c* men alive
Ac 28:15 *c* sight of them, Paul
Re 17:6 *c* sight of her I wondered

Caterpillar
Joe 1:4 What was left by the *c*
2:25 and the *c* have eaten
Am 4:9 olive trees the *c* would devour

Cattle
Ge 12:16 he came to have sheep and *c*
13:5 Lot . . . owned sheep and *c*
20:14 Abimelech took sheep and *c*
21:27 Abraham took sheep and *c* and
24:35 giving him sheep and *c* and
26:14 herds of *c* and a large body
32:7 the *c* and the camels into two
33:13 *c* that are giving suck are in
47:6 appoint them *c* chiefs over
Ex 10:9 with our sheep and our *c* we
10:24 and your *c* will be detained
12:21 *c* according to your families
Nu 7:3 and twelve *c*, a wagon for two
7:6 accepted the wagons and the *c*
7:7 wagons and four *c* he gave to
7:8 and eight *c* he gave to the
7:17 communion sacrifice two *c*
7:23 communion sacrifice two *c*
7:29 communion sacrifice two *c*
7:35 communion sacrifice two *c*
7:41 communion sacrifice two *c*
7:47 communion sacrifice two *c*
7:53 communion sacrifice two *c*
7:59 communion sacrifice two *c*
7:65 communion sacrifice two *c*
7:71 communion sacrifice two *c*
7:77 communion sacrifice two *c*
7:83 communion sacrifice two *c*
7:87 *c* for the burnt offering being
7:88 *c* of the communion sacrifice
22:40 to sacrifice *c* and sheep and
De 14:26 crave in the way of *c* and
28:4 the young of your *c* and the
28:18 the young of your *c* and the
28:51 no young of your *c* or
Jg 3:31 Shamgar . . . with a *c* goad
1Sa 11:7 way it will be done to his *c*
14:32 and taking sheep and *c* and
15:21 and *c*, the choicest of them
2Sa 6:6 *c* nearly caused an upset
12:2 have very many sheep and *c*
12:4 and his own *c* to get such
17:29 curds of *c* they brought
24:22 *c* for the burnt offering
24:22 implements of the *c* for
24:24 threshing floor and the *c*
1Ki 1:9 a sacrifice of sheep and *c*
4:23 ten fat *c* and twenty
4:23 twenty pastured *c* and a
8:5 sacrificing sheep and *c* that
8:63 twenty-two thousand *c* and a
2Ki 5:26 vineyards or sheep or *c* or
1Ch 12:40 upon *c*, eatables of flour
12:40 and *c* and sheep in great
21:23 I do give the *c* for burnt
2Ch 5:6 sacrificing sheep and *c* that
7:5 twenty-two thousand *c* and a
15:11 seven hundred *c* and
18:2 sacrifice sheep and *c* in
29:22 slaughtered the *c* and the
29:32 came to be seventy *c*, a

2Ch 29:33 six hundred *c* and three
31:6 tenth of *c* and sheep and the
35:7 and *c*, three thousand
35:8 and three hundred *c*
35:9 and five hundred *c*
35:12 and thus also with the *c*
Job 1:3 five hundred spans of *c* and
1:14 *c* themselves happened to be
42:12 a thousand spans of *c* and
Ps 8:7 Small *c* and oxen, all of them
107:38 not let their *c* become few
144:14 Our *c* loaded down, without
Pr 14:4 no *c* the manger is clean
Ec 2:7 *c* and flocks in great quantity
Isa 22:13 the killing of *c* and the
30:24 *c* and the full-grown asses
65:10 Achor a resting-place for *c*
Jer 31:12 ones of the flock and the *c*
Eze 4:15 given you *c* manure instead
Joe 1:18 *c* have wandered in confusion
Am 6:12 will one plow there with *c*?
Lu 14:19 I bought five yoke of *c* and
Joh 2:14 temple those selling *c* and
2:15 and *c* out of the temple, and
4:12 sons and his *c* drank out of
1Co 15:39 there is another flesh of *c*
Re 18:13 *c* and sheep, and horses and

Cauda
Ac 27:16 small island called *C*, and

Caught
Ge 18:2 he *c* sight of them he began
19:1 Lot *c* sight of them, then he
21:19 she *c* sight of a well of
22:13 was a ram *c* by its horns in a
24:64 she *c* sight of Isaac and she
31:23 and *c* up with him in the
37:18 they *c* sight of him from a
38:15 When Judah *c* sight of her
Ex 2:5 she *c* sight of the ark in the
2:11 *c* sight of a certain Egyptian
Nu 5:13 she herself has not been *c*
11:22 all the fish of the sea be *c*
25:7 When Phinehas . . . *c* sight of
Jos 8:23 the king of Ai they *c* alive
Jg 9:36 Gaal *c* sight of the people, he
11:35 he *c* sight of her, he began
1Sa 16:6 and he *c* sight of Eliab, he
25:23 Abigail *c* sight of David
2Sa 1:6 mounted men had *c* up with
11:2 *c* sight of a woman bathing
18:9 head got *c* fast in the big
Job 20:9 eye that has *c* sight of him
28:7 a black kite *c* sight of it
Ps 9:15 their own foot has been *c*
10:2 They get *c* by the ideas that
59:12 may they be *c* in their pride
Pr 6:2 *c* by the sayings of your mouth
11:6 will themselves be *c*
Ca 1:6 the sun has *c* sight of me
Isa 8:15 and to be snared and *c*
13:15 *c* in the sweep will fall
24:18 will be *c* in the trap
28:13 broken and ensnared and *c*
Jer 6:11 for they will also be *c*
8:9 terrified and will be *c*
34:3 without fail be *c* and into
48:44 will be *c* in the trap
50:24 also been *c*, O Babylon
Eze 12:13 must be *c* in my hunting net
13:21 something *c* in the hunt
17:20 be *c* in my hunting net
19:4 In their pit he was *c*, and
19:8 In their pit he was *c*
21:23 in order for them to be *c*
Am 3:4 if it has *c* nothing at all
3:5 it has absolutely *c* nothing
Mt 3:7 he *c* sight of many of the
9:9 Jesus *c* sight of a man named
9:23 *c* sight of the flute players
14:26 *c* sight of him walking on
14:31 Jesus *c* hold of him and said
21:19 he *c* sight of a fig tree by
22:11 *c* sight there of a man not
28:9 and *c* him by his feet and did
Mr 2:14 he *c* sight of Levi the son of
9:15 the crowd *c* sight of him
11:13 he *c* sight of a fig tree
Lu 5:12 When he *c* sight of Jesus he
7:13 the Lord *c* sight of her, he
15:20 his father *c* sight of him
20:14 cultivators *c* sight of him
Joh 11:32 Jesus was and *c* sight of
21:3 that night they *c* nothing
Joh 21:10 the fish you just now *c*
21:21 he *c* sight of him, Peter
Ac 1:9 cloud *c* him up from their
3:3 he *c* sight of Peter and John
7:24 *c* sight of a certain one being
7:55 *c* sight of God's glory and of
9:40 as she *c* sight of Peter
20:14 he *c* up with us in Assos, we
21:32 they *c* sight of the military
28:4 *c* sight of the venomous
Ro 9:30 *c* up with righteousness, the
2Co 12:2 *c* away as such to the third
12:4 *c* away into paradise and
12:16 I *c* you by trickery
1Th 4:17 *c* away in clouds to meet the
2Ti 2:26 *c* alive by him for the will
2Pe 2:12 born naturally to be *c* and
Re 12:5 child was *c* away to God and
17:3 I *c* sight of a woman sitting
19:20 the wild beast was *c*, and

Cause
Ge 1:11 Let the earth *c* grass to shoot
24:12 *c* it to happen, please
Ex 5:4 you *c* the people to leave off
9:16 for this *c* I have kept you in
20:24 *c* my name to be remembered
22:5 and *c* a consuming in another
23:33 not *c* you to sin against me
33:18 *c* me to see, please, your
33:19 *c* all my goodness to pass
36:6 *c* an announcement to pass
Le 22:16 actually *c* them to bear the
24:19 *c* a defect in his associate
24:20 defect he may *c* in the man
25:9 *c* the horn of loud tone to
25:9 people should *c* the horn to
Nu 5:22 *c* your belly to swell and
8:11 Aaron must *c* the Levites to
8:13 *c* them to move to and fro as
8:15 *c* them to move to and fro as
27:7 *c* their father's inheritance
27:8 *c* his inheritance to pass to
35:23 *c* it to fall upon him, so
De 1:38 he will *c* Israel to inherit it
3:28 *c* them to inherit the land
20:8 *c* the hearts of his brothers
28:7 Jehovah will *c* your enemies
28:21 *c* the pestilence to cling to
28:25 *c* you to be defeated before
Jos 1:6 *c* this people to inherit the
Ru 4:5 *c* the name of the dead man to
4:10 to *c* the name of the dead man
1Sa 2:33 to *c* your eyes to fail and to
3:19 not *c* any of all his words
8:22 you must *c* a king to reign
12:1 *c* a king to reign over you
12:8 and *c* them to dwell in
25:31 *c* for staggering or a
25:31 shedding of blood without *c*
2Sa 7:21 *c* your servant to know them
13:13 where shall I *c* my reproach
22:33 *c* my way to be perfect
1Ki 12:30 came to be a *c* for sin
13:34 there came to be a *c* of sin
17:21 *c* the soul of this child to
2Ki 18:30 *c* you to trust in Jehovah
19:7 *c* him to fall by the sword
23:19 had built to *c* offense
1Ch 15:16 to *c* a sound of rejoicing to
17:14 *c* him to stand in my house
21:3 a *c* of guilt to Israel
21:8 *c* your servant's error to
2Ch 15:8 *c* the disgusting things to
21:11 *c* the inhabitants of
21:13 *c* Judah and the inhabitants
25:8 God could *c* you to stumble
25:8 to help and to *c* stumbling
28:23 *c* for making him and all
29:8 *c* for whistling, just as you
35:21 I should *c* disturbance
36:19 so as to *c* ruin
Ezr 2:68 to *c* it to stand on its own
4:13 *c* loss to the treasuries of
Ne 4:8 Jerusalem and *c* me disturbance
8:15 *c* a call to pass throughout
Job 2:3 to swallow him up without *c*
5:8 to God I would submit my *c*
9:23 should *c* death suddenly
10:2 *C* me to know why it is that
22:6 seize a pledge . . . without *c*
30:22 wind, you *c* me to ride it
31:16 widow I would *c* to fail
34:11 will *c* it to come upon him
Job 34:28 *c* the outcry of the lowly
36:31 he pleads the *c* of peoples
38:12 *c* the dawn to know its
38:27 *c* the growth of grass to
39:20 *c* it to leap like a locust
Ps 7:5 *c* my own glory to reside in
9:4 executed my judgment and my *c*
10:18 may no more *c* trembling
16:11 *c* me to know the path of
25:9 *c* the meek ones to walk in
25:14 covenant, to *c* them to know
26:7 To *c* thanksgiving to be heard
31:16 Do *c* your face to shine upon
35:7 without *c* they have hid for
35:7 Without *c* they have dug it
35:19 those hating me without *c*
36:8 pleasures you *c* them to drink
37:14 To *c* the afflicted and poor
39:4 *C* me, O Jehovah, to know my
41:10 favor and *c* me to get up
45:4 Ride in the *c* of truth and
50:23 will *c* him to see salvation
51:6 *c* me to know sheer wisdom
51:8 *c* me to hear exultation and
54:1 may you plead my *c*
59:10 *c* me to look upon my foes
64:8 And they *c* one to stumble
65:4 you choose and *c* to approach
65:8 you *c* to cry out joyfully
66:8 *c* the voice of praise to him
69:4 Those hating me without a *c*
69:23 *c* their very hips to wobble
72:2 plead the *c* of your people
78:2 *c* riddles of long ago to
78:15 *c* them to drink an abundance
91:16 *c* him to see salvation by
96:10 plead the *c* of the peoples
104:14 *c* food to go forth from the
104:20 You *c* darkness, that it may
109:3 against me without *c*
110:6 *c* a fullness of dead bodies
119:10 *c* me to go astray from
119:35 *C* me to tread in the
119:78 without *c* they have misled
119:86 Without *c* they have
119:161 persecuted me for no *c*
132:17 *c* the horn of David to grow
135:14 Jehovah will plead the *c*
137:6 my chief *c* for rejoicing
143:8 *c* me to hear your
Pr 1:11 innocent men without any *c*
1:23 *c* my spirit to bubble forth
3:30 quarrel with a man without *c*
4:11 *c* you to tread in the tracks
4:16 they *c* someone to stumble
8:21 *c* those loving me to take
10:3 *c* the soul of the righteous
12:25 what will *c* it to bow down
13:5 shamefully and *c* disgrace for
22:23 Jehovah . . . plead their *c*
23:11 will plead their *c* with you
25:9 Plead your own *c* with your
26:2 as a bird has *c* for fleeing
26:2 does not come without real *c*
31:5 pervert the *c* of any of the
31:8 *c* of all those passing away
31:9 plead the *c* of the afflicted
Ec 2:24 *c* his soul to see good because
5:6 mouth to *c* your flesh to sin
5:17 his part and *c* for indignation
6:10 not able to plead his *c* with
7:16 you *c* desolation to yourself
10:1 Dead flies are what *c* the oil
Isa 1:17 plead the *c* of the widow
11:9 *c* any ruin in all my holy
11:15 *c* people to walk in their
13:10 not *c* its light to shine
13:11 *c* the pride of the
13:13 *c* heaven itself to become
17:11 *c* the seed of yours to
19:17 to Egypt a *c* for reeling
30:3 Egypt a *c* for humiliation
30:5 and also a *c* for reproach
30:11 *C* the Holy One of Israel to
30:32 Jehovah will *c* to settle
31:5 must also *c* her to escape
32:6 *c* the soul of the hungry one
36:15 Hezekiah *c* you to trust in
37:7 *c* him to fall by the sword
41:22 *c* us to hear even the things
42:9 I *c* you people to hear them
42:16 I shall *c* them to tread
43:9 can they *c* us to hear even
43:14 *c* the bars of the prisons

Isa 43:20 to *c* my people, my chosen
45:8 heavens, *c* a dripping from
45:8 and let it *c* righteousness
48:20 *c* this to be heard. Make it
51:4 I shall *c* to repose even as
52:4 without *c* Assyria, for its
58:14 I will *c* you to eat from
61:11 *c* the sprouting of
64:7 *c* us to melt by the power
65:18 a *c* for joyfulness and her
65:18 people a *c* for exultation
65:25 do no harm nor *c* any ruin
66:9 shall I *c* the breaking
66:9 and not *c* the giving birth
66:9 do I actually *c* a shutting up?
Jer 2:37 For this *c* also you will go
5:10 her vine rows and *c* ruin
7:34 I will *c* to cease from the
10:18 I will *c* them distress in
15:8 I will *c* to fall upon them
15:14 I will *c* them to pass over
16:21 *c* them to know my hand
18:2 *c* you to hear my words
19:7 *c* them to fall by the sword
20:8 *c* for reproach and for
22:7 *c* them to fall into the fire
23:32 *c* my people to wander about
24:6 *c* them to return to this
25:6 I may not *c* calamity to you
30:13 no one pleading your *c*
30:21 *c* him to come near, and
31:18 *C* me to turn back, and I
32:31 *c* of anger in me and a
32:31 and a *c* of rage in me
36:29 *c* man and beast to cease
42:9 *c* your request for favor to
48:35 *c* to cease from Moab, is
49:2 *c* the alarm signal of war to
49:9 *c* only as much ruin as they
50:32 one to *c* it to rise up
50:34 and *c* agitation to the
50:45 *c* their abiding place to be
51:49 Babylon the *c* for the slain
La 2:18 *C* tears to descend just like a
3:52 just as for a bird, for no *c*
Eze 3:3 *c* your own belly to eat, that
6:4 *c* your slain ones to fall
7:24 *c* the pride of the strong
12:23 *c* this proverbial saying to
13:11 windstorms . . . *c* a splitting
13:13 *c* a blast of windstorms to
14:23 not without *c* that I shall
16:41 I will *c* you to cease from
16:43 you would *c* me agitation
18:30 *c* a turning back from all
18:32 So *c* a turning back and keep
20:4 *C* them to know the
21:28 polished to *c* it to devour
22:2 *c* her to know all her
22:20 with fire to *c* a liquefying
22:20 *c* you people to liquefy
23:27 *c* your loose conduct to
23:48 *c* loose conduct to cease
24:13 I *c* my rage to come to its
25:15 in order to *c* ruin, with
26:13 *c* the turmoil of your
26:20 I will *c* you to dwell in
29:4 and *c* the fish of your Nile
29:21 shall *c* a horn to sprout
30:10 *c* the crowd of Egypt to
30:12 *c* the land and its fullness
30:13 *c* the valueless gods to
30:22 *c* the sword to fall out of
31:15 certainly *c* a mourning
31:16 *c* nations to rock when I
32:4 *c* all the flying creatures
32:6 *c* the land to drink up your
32:10 *c* many peoples to be
32:12 *c* your crowd to fall by
34:25 *c* the injurious wild beast
34:26 *c* the pouring rain to
36:11 *c* you to be inhabited as
36:12 will *c* humankind to walk
36:15 *c* no further humiliating
36:15 will no more *c* to stumble
36:33 *c* the cities to be inhabited
37:6 *c* to come upon you flesh
37:17 *c* them to approach each
39:2 *c* you to come up from the
39:3 arrows I shall *c* to fall out
44:23 they should *c* them to know
44:30 *c* a blessing to rest
48:14 one *c* the choicest of the
48:29 *c* to fall by lot for
Da 8:24 way he will *c* ruin, and he
8:25 *c* deception to succeed in his
9:17 *c* your face to shine upon
9:27 *c* sacrifice and gift offering
10:14 *c* you to discern what will
11:12 *c* tens of thousands to fall
Ho 1:4 *c* the royal rule of the house
2:11 *c* all her exultation, her
2:14 *c* her to go into the
Am 5:27 I will *c* you to go into exile
8:4 *c* the meek ones of the earth
8:9 *c* darkness for the land on
Jon 3:10 and he did not *c* it
Mic 1:16 *C* baldness, and shear your
Na 3:5 I will *c* nations to see your
Hab 3:19 he will *c* me to tread
Zep 1:17 *c* distress to mankind, and
Zec 8:12 *c* the remaining ones of this
13:2 *c* to pass out of the land
Mt 10:35 I came to *c* division, with
11:6 no *c* for stumbling in me
13:41 all things that *c* stumbling
17:27 we do not *c* them to stumble
Mr 1:17 *c* you to become fishers of
Lu 8:47 *c* for which she touched him
18:7 shall not God *c* justice to be
18:8 He will *c* justice to be done
Joh 15:25 They hated me without *c*
Ac 10:21 *c* for which you are present
13:28 they found no *c* for death
19:40 no single *c* existing that
22:24 what *c* they were shouting
23:28 wishing to ascertain the *c*
28:18 was no *c* for death in me
Ro 9:17 very *c* I have let you remain
14:13 or a *c* for tripping
15:17 I have *c* for exulting in
16:17 those who *c* divisions and
1Co 1:23 a *c* for stumbling but to
5:6 *c* for boasting is not fine
2Co 1:14 we are a *c* for you to boast
6:3 giving any *c* for stumbling
Ga 4:18 sought for in a fine *c* at all
6:4 *c* for exultation in regard to
6:13 *c* for boasting in your flesh
Php 2:16 I may have *c* for exultation
Col 2:18 puffed up without proper *c*
3:13 anyone has a *c* for complaint
1Th 3:12 the Lord *c* you to increase
2Ti 1:6 For this very *c* I remind you
1:12 For this very *c* I am also
Tit 1:13 For this very *c* keep on
Heb 2:11 for this *c* he is not ashamed
2:14 having the means to *c* death
12:15 *c* trouble and that many
Jas 3:11 fountain does not *c* the
1Pe 1:7 found a *c* for praise and glory
3:6 not fearing any *c* for terror
1Jo 2:10 there is no *c* for stumbling
3Jo 4 No greater *c* for thankfulness
Re 11:3 *c* my two witnesses to
12:15 *c* her to be drowned by the
13:15 *c* to be killed all those who

Caused

Ge 8:1 God *c* a wind to pass over the
20:13 God *c* me to wander from the
27:20 God *c* it to meet up with me
41:28 he has *c* Pharaoh to see
41:39 God has *c* you to know all
Ex 4:25 *c* it to touch his feet and
5:22 Jehovah, why have you *c* evil
9:20 *c* his own servants and his
10:13 Jehovah *c* an east wind to
15:22 Moses *c* Israel to depart
Le 24:20 is what should be *c* in him
Nu 8:21 Aaron *c* them to move to and
11:11 Why have you *c* evil to your
De 1:28 *c* our heart to melt, saying
8:15 *c* you to walk through the
34:4 I have *c* you to see it with
Jos 13:32 Moses *c* them to inherit
14:1 Israel *c* them to inherit
14:8 *c* the heart of the people to
Ru 1:21 that has *c* me calamity
1Sa 7:10 Jehovah now *c* it to thunder
15:11 I have *c* Saul to reign as
2Sa 6:6 cattle nearly *c* an upset
1Ki 1:27 not *c* your servant to know
14:16 which he *c* Israel to sin
15:26 he *c* Israel to sin
15:30 he *c* Israel to sin and by
15:34 which he *c* Israel to sin
16:2 *c* my people Israel to sin
1Ki 16:13 they *c* Israel to sin by
16:26 *c* Israel to sin by offending
18:28 they *c* blood to flow out
21:22 and then *c* Israel to sin
22:52 who had *c* Israel to sin
2Ki 3:3 with which he *c* Israel to sin
7:6 *c* the camp of the Syrians to
10:29 which he *c* Israel to sin
10:31 he *c* Israel to sin
13:2 which he *c* Israel to sin
13:6 he *c* Israel to sin. In it he
14:24 which he *c* Israel to sin
15:9 he *c* Israel to sin
15:18 he *c* Israel to sin, all his
15:24 he *c* Israel to sin
15:28 he *c* Israel to sin
17:21 *c* them to sin with a great
21:16 he *c* Judah to sin by doing
23:11 *c* the horses that the kings
23:15 who *c* Israel to sin, had
1Ch 13:9 the bulls nearly *c* an upset
2Ch 8:2 *c* the sons of Israel to dwell
20:11 possession that you *c* us to
21:13 Ahab *c* the having of
28:20 *c* him distress, and did
33:12 *c* him distress, he softened
36:22 *c* a cry to pass through all
Ezr 1:1 *c* a cry to pass through all
6:12 God who has *c* his name to
6:22 Jehovah *c* them to rejoice
10:7 *c* a call to pass throughout
Ne 12:43 *c* them to rejoice with
13:26 the foreign wives *c* to sin
Job 15:13 And you have *c* words to go
29:3 he *c* his lamp to shine upon
31:39 its owners I have *c* to pant
37:15 he *c* the light of his cloud
Ps 21:7 He will not be *c* to totter
60:2 You have *c* the earth to rock
60:3 *c* your people to see hardship
76:8 heaven you *c* the legal contest
78:11 works that he *c* them to see
78:13 *c* the waters to stand like
78:52 *c* his people to depart just
78:55 *c* the tribes of Israel to
79:7 *c* his own abiding place to
89:42 *c* all his enemies to rejoice
89:43 *c* him not to gain ground
106:32 *c* provocation at the waters
107:17 *c* themselves affliction
136:14 *c* Israel to pass through
143:3 *c* me to dwell in dark places
Pr 7:26 she has *c* to fall down slain
8:28 *c* the fountains of the watery
10:30 he will not be *c* to stagger
12:3 it will not be *c* to stagger
23:5 *c* your eyes to glance at it
23:22 your father who *c* your birth
24:17 and when he is *c* to stumble
Isa 9:1 time one *c* it to be honored
16:10 Shouting I have *c* to cease
19:13 *c* Egypt to wander about
19:14 *c* Egypt to wander about in
21:2 due to her I have *c* to cease
23:11 *c* kingdoms to be agitated
43:12 have *c* it to be heard
44:8 *c* you individually to hear
45:21 *c* this to be heard from a
48:5 I *c* you to hear it, that
48:21 he *c* to flow forth for them
53:6 *c* the error of us all to
59:2 *c* the concealing of his
62:11 *c* it to be heard to the
Jer 1:9 *c* it to touch my mouth
7:12 I *c* my name to reside at
11:18 *c* me to see their dealings
12:14 I *c* my people, even Israel
13:11 *c* the whole house of Israel
23:22 *c* them to turn back from
28:15 *c* this people to trust in a
29:4 *c* to go into exile from
29:7 I have *c* you to go into exile
29:14 I *c* you to go into exile
31:9 will not be *c* to stumble
32:23 *c* all this calamity to
38:21 Jehovah has *c* me to see
38:22 *c* your foot to sink down
42:10 calamity that I have *c* to
48:4 have *c* a cry to be heard
48:33 I have *c* the wine itself to
49:16 shuddering you *c* has
50:6 shepherds have *c* them to
La 1:12 Jehovah has *c* grief in the day
1:20 the sword *c* bereavement of

La 2:6 Jehovah has *c* to be forgotten
3:4 He has *c* my flesh and my skin
3:32 although he has *c* grief, he
Eze 1:18 that they *c* fearfulness
11:6 You have *c* your slain ones
11:25 that he had *c* me to see
13:22 myself had not *c* him pain
27:10 ones that *c* your splendor
29:7 you *c* a split in their entire
29:7 *c* all their hips to wobble
31:4 watery deep *c* it to grow
32:23 *c* terror in the land of
32:24 *c* their terror in the land
32:25 terror was *c* in the land of
32:26 *c* their terror in the land
32:32 *c* his terror in the land of
Da 3:30 that time the king himself *c*
8:10 *c* some of the army and some
11:6 he who *c* her birth, and the
Ho 4:12 fornication has *c* them to
12:14 Ephraim *c* offense to
Am 4:11 I *c* an overthrow among you
7:1 Jehovah *c* me to see, and, look!
7:4 Jehovah *c* me to see, and
7:7 This is what he *c* me to see
8:1 Jehovah *c* me to see, and, look!
Hab 3:6 and then *c* nations to leap
Zec 3:4 *c* your error to pass away
5:4 I have *c* it to go forth
6:8 *c* the spirit of Jehovah to
13:3 the ones who *c* his birth
13:3 the ones who *c* his birth
Mal 1:13 you have *c* a sniffing at it
2:8 *c* many to stumble in the law
Ac 7:4 God *c* him to change his
15:24 *c* you trouble with speeches
2Co 2:5 Now if anyone has *c* sadness
Eph 1:8 he *c* to abound toward us in
1Jo 5:1 the one that *c* to be born

Causes
Ex 21:8 but *c* her to be redeemed, he
22:5 man *c* a field or a vineyard
Nu 24:23 will survive when God *c* it
De 27:18 *c* the blind to go astray in
Jg 11:24 your god *c* you to dispossess
Job 5:18 he himself *c* pain, but binds
20:12 If he *c* it to melt away
34:29 When he himself *c* quietness
41:31 It *c* the depths to boil just
Ps 19:2 *c* speech to bubble forth
107:25 *c* a tempestuous wind to
107:29 *c* the windstorm to stand
107:36 *c* the hungry ones to dwell
147:18 He *c* his wind to blow
Pr 12:26 *c* them to wander about
13:10 one only *c* a struggle, but
16:7 *c* even his enemies themselves
16:23 *c* his mouth to show insight
16:29 *c* him to go in a way that is
19:15 Laziness *c* a deep sleep to
26:28 and a flattering mouth *c* an
Ec 8:1 wisdom of a man itself *c* his
Isa 30:28 bridle that *c* one to
32:6 *c* even the thirsty one to go
Jer 10:13 he *c* vapors to ascend from
13:16 before he *c* darkness and
51:16 *c* vapors to ascend from the
La 2:8 he *c* rampart and wall to go
2:17 he *c* the enemy to rejoice
Eze 44:18 with what *c* sweat
Mt 24:15 thing that *c* desolation, as
Mr 13:14 thing that *c* desolation
Lu 17:1 *c* for stumbling should come
1Co 10:32 becoming *c* for stumbling to
Jude 13 their own *c* for shame

Causing
Ex 9:18 *c* it to rain down tomorrow
Le 26:16 *c* the eyes to fail and
1Sa 2:24 people . . . are *c* to circulate
5:6 he began *c* panic and striking
2Sa 14:11 *c* ruin and that they may
1Ki 16:19 by *c* Israel to sin
2Ki 2:19 the land is *c* miscarriages
2:21 or any *c* of miscarriages
1Ch 19:3 and *c* an overthrow and for
2Ch 5:13 *c* one sound to be heard in
26:16 to the point of *c* ruin
28:22 *c* him distress, he acted
Ezr 4:15 and *c* loss to kings and
Ne 9:27 who kept *c* them distress
Ps 19:8 *c* the heart to rejoice
68:6 God is *c* the solitary ones
68:9 downpour you began *c* to fall
Ps 78:16 *c* waters to descend just
91:3 the pestilence *c* adversities
94:20 throne *c* adversities be
106:29 *c* offense by their dealings
113:9 *c* the barren woman to dwell
135:7 *c* vapors to ascend from the
Pr 10:17 is *c* to wander
15:1 a word *c* pain makes anger to
17:4 to the tongue *c* adversities
18:9 is a brother to the one *c* ruin
26:21 man for *c* a quarrel to glow
28:10 is *c* the upright ones to go
28:24 partner of a man *c* ruination
29:15 will be *c* his mother shame
Ec 4:8 and *c* my soul to lack in good
6:11 things that are *c* much vanity
Isa 3:12 are *c* you to wander, and
8:13 the One *c* you to tremble
9:16 the ones *c* them to wander
41:26 is no one *c* one to hear
48:17 *c* you to tread in the way
51:17 goblet, the cup *c* reeling
51:22 cup *c* reeling. The goblet
59:2 *c* division between you and
66:9 am I *c* a giving birth and
Jer 2:30 like a lion that is *c* ruin
16:3 who are *c* their birth
16:9 *c* to cease out of this place
16:21 I am *c* them to know
30:10 will be no one *c* trembling
44:7 *c* a great calamity to your
44:8 *c* a cutting off of yourselves
46:27 without anyone *c* trembling
50:9 mighty man *c* bereavement of
Eze 7:19 a stumbling block *c* their
14:3 block *c* their error they have
14:4 stumbling block *c* his error
14:7 stumbling block *c* his error
18:30 a stumbling block *c* error
21:24 your *c* your error to be
Da 8:13 transgression *c* desolation, to
8:19 *c* you to know what will
9:27 will be the one *c* desolation
11:20 *c* an exactor to pass through
11:31 thing that is *c* desolation
12:11 thing that is *c* desolation
Am 5:9 *c* a despoiling to flash forth
Jon 3:10 he had spoken of *c* to them
Mic 3:5 *c* my people to wander, that
Na 1:9 *c* an outright extermination
Zec 11:6 *c* mankind to find themselves
12:2 a bowl *c* reeling to all the
Mr 5:39 Why are you *c* noisy confusion
Ac 15:3 were *c* great joy to all the
24:12 nor *c* a mob to rush together
Ro 8:15 spirit of slavery *c* fear
Ga 1:7 ones who are *c* you trouble
5:10 one who is *c* you trouble
Heb 3:8 the occasion of *c* bitter anger
3:15 occasion of *c* bitter anger

Cautious
Ge 3:1 proved to be the most *c* of all
Mt 10:16 prove . . . *c* as serpents

Cavalry
Re 9:16 the number of the armies of *c*

Cavalryman
2Ki 9:17 Take a *c* and send him to
Eze 26:10 the sound of *c* and wheel

Cavalrymen
Ex 14:9 Pharaoh and his *c* and his
14:17 Pharaoh . . . and his *c*
14:18 his war chariots and his *c*
14:23 *c* began going in after them
14:26 war chariots and their *c*
14:28 the war chariots and the *c*
15:19 and his *c* went into the sea
Jos 24:6 with war chariots and *c* to
Eze 23:6 *c* riding horses
23:12 *c* riding horses—desirable
26:7 and *c* and a congregation

Cave
Ge 19:30 he began dwelling in a *c*, he
23:9 give me the *c* of Machpelah
23:11 *c* that is in it to you I do
23:17 *c* that was in it and all the
23:19 in the *c* of the field of
23:20 the *c* that was in it became
25:9 in the *c* of Machpelah in the
49:29 *c* that is in the field of
49:30 *c* that is in the field of
49:32 The field purchased and the *c*
50:13 *c* of the field of Machpelah
Jos 10:16 hiding themselves in the *c*
10:17 hidden in the *c* at Makkedah
10:18 up to the mouth of the *c*
10:22 Open the mouth of the *c* and
10:22 five kings from the *c* to me
10:23 from the *c* these five kings
10:27 the *c* where they had hid
10:27 at the mouth of the *c*
1Sa 22:1 escape to the *c* of Adullam
24:3 the road, where a *c* was
24:3 parts of the *c* farthest back
24:7 Saul, he rose up from the *c*
24:8 and went out from the *c* and
24:10 into my hand in the *c*
2Sa 23:13 David at the *c* of Adullam
1Ki 18:4 hid by fifties in a *c*, and
18:13 men by fifties in a *c*, and
19:9 finally entered into a *c*
19:13 at the entrance of the *c*
1Ch 11:15 David at the *c* of Adullam
Ps 57:*super* ran away . . . into the *c*
142:*super* happened to be in the *c*
Jer 7:11 a mere *c* of robbers in your
Na 2:11 the *c* that belongs to the
Mt 7:25 house, but it did not *c* in
21:13 are making it a *c* of robbers
Mr 11:17 have made it a *c* of robbers
Lu 19:46 you made it a *c* of robbers
Joh 11:38 *c*, and a stone was lying

Caved
Mt 7:27 that house and it *c* in, and

Caves
Jg 6:2 the *c* and the places difficult
1Sa 13:6 hiding themselves in the *c*
Isa 2:19 enter into the *c* of the rocks
Eze 33:27 and in the *c* will die by
Heb 11:38 wandered about in . . . *c* of
Re 6:15 the *c* and in the rock-masses

Cease
Ge 8:22 day and night, will never *c*
Le 26:6 wild beast *c* out of the land
Nu 17:10 that their murmurings may *c*
De 15:11 poor will never *c* to be in
32:26 mention of them *c* from
Jg 20:28 my brother or shall I *c* to
1Sa 2:5 hungry actually *c* to hunger
2Ki 23:11 *c* from entering the house
Ne 6:3 Why should the work *c* while I
Job 7:16 *C* from me, for my days are
14:7 own twig will not *c* to be
16:6 And if I do *c* doing so, what
Ps 46:9 He is making wars to *c* to the
89:44 him *c* from his luster
119:119 ones of the earth to *c*
Pr 19:27 *C*, my son, to listen to
22:10 contest and dishonor may *c*
23:4 *C* from your own understanding
Isa 1:16 *c* to do bad
13:11 presumptuous ones to *c*, and
16:10 Shouting I have caused to *c*
17:3 city has been made to *c* out
21:2 to her I have caused to *c*
30:11 Holy One of Israel to *c*
Jer 7:34 *c* from the cities of Judah
16:9 to *c* out of this place
31:36 *c* from proving to be a
36:29 cause man and beast to *c*
44:27 famine, until they *c* to be
48:33 caused the wine itself to *c*
48:35 cause to *c* from Moab, is
Eze 6:6 dungy idols . . . made to *c*
7:24 pride of the strong ones to *c*
12:23 this proverbial saying to *c*
16:41 *c* from being a prostitute
23:27 loose conduct to *c* from you
23:48 cause loose conduct to *c*
26:13 of your singing to *c*
30:10 the crowd of Egypt to *c* by
30:13 gods to *c* out of Noph
30:18 actually be made to *c*
33:28 must be made to *c* and the
34:10 *c* from feeding my sheep
34:25 injurious wild beast to *c*
Da 9:27 and gift offering to *c*
11:18 reproach from him *c* for
Ho 1:4 royal rule . . . of Israel to *c*
2:11 her every festal season to *c*
Am 8:4 meek ones of the earth to *c*
1Co 13:8 are tongues, they will *c*
Eph 1:16 not *c* giving thanks for you
5:17 *c* becoming unreasonable, but

Ceased
Jos 5:12 the manna c on the following
Jg 5:7 The dwellers in open country c
5:7 in Israel they c, Until I
Job 3:17 have c from agitation, And
19:14 acquaintances have c to be
32:1 men c from answering Job
Ps 36:3 He has c to have insight for
49:8 it has c to time indefinite
Isa 24:8 of the tambourines has c
24:8 exultation of the harp has c
33:8 passing over the path has c
Jer 44:18 c to make sacrificial smoke
51:30 of Babylon have c to fight
La 5:14 have c even out of the gate
5:15 exultation of our heart has c
Lu 5:4 he c speaking, he said to
Col 1:9 have not c praying for you and

Ceases
Ho 7:4 c poking after kneading dough

Ceasing
1Sa 12:23 by c to pray in your behalf
Ro 1:9 how without c I always make

Cedar
2Sa 5:11 also c trees and workers in
1Ki 4:33 the c that is in Lebanon
5:8 matter of timbers of c trees
5:10 giver of timbers of c trees
6:10 by timbers of c trees
6:15 inside it with boards of c
6:16 boards of c, from the floor
9:11 with timbers of c trees and
2Ki 14:9 the c that was in Lebanon
1Ch 14:1 to David and c timbers and
22:4 c timbers without number
22:4 Tyrians brought in c timbers
2Ch 2:8 And send me timbers of c
25:18 c that was in Lebanon
Ezr 3:7 bring c timbers from Lebanon
Job 40:17 its tail like a c
Ps 92:12 c in Lebanon does, he will
Ca 8:9 block her up with a c plank
Isa 41:19 I shall set the c tree
Jer 22:14 paneling will be with c
22:15 competing by use of c
Eze 17:3 to take the treetop of the c
17:22 the lofty treetop of the c
17:23 and become a majestic c and
27:5 A c from Lebanon they took
31:3 An Assyrian, a c in Lebanon
Zec 11:2 for the c has fallen

Cedars
Nu 24:6 Like c by the waters
Jg 9:15 and consume the c of Lebanon
2Sa 7:2 I am dwelling in a house of c
7:7 not build me a house of c
1Ki 5:6 cut for me c from Lebanon
2Ki 19:23 shall cut down its lofty c
1Ch 17:1 am dwelling in a house of c
17:6 not built me a house of c
Ps 29:5 Jehovah is breaking the c
29:5 breaks the c of Lebanon in
80:10 c of God with its boughs
104:16 c of Lebanon that he planted
148:9 fruit trees and all you c
Ca 1:17 beams of our . . . house are c
5:15 Lebanon, choice like the c
Isa 2:13 c of Lebanon that are lofty
9:10 c we shall make replacement
14:8 the c of Lebanon, saying
37:24 cut down its lofty c, its
44:14 business is to cut down c
Jer 22:7 the choicest of your c
22:23 being nested in the c
Eze 31:8 Other c were no match for
Am 2:9 was like the height of c
Zec 11:1 fire may devour among your c

Cedarwood
Le 14:4 c and coccus scarlet material
14:6 the c and the coccus scarlet
14:49 and c and coccus scarlet
14:51 take the c and the hyssop and
14:52 the c and the hyssop and the
Nu 19:6 priest must take c and hyssop
1Ki 6:9 with beams and rows in c
6:18 the c on the house inside
6:18 All of it was c; there was
6:20 overlay the altar with c
6:36 and a row of beams of c
7:2 four rows of pillars of c
7:2 beams of c upon the pillars
1Ki 7:3 it was paneled in with c
7:7 they covered it in with c
7:11 stones . . . and also c
7:12 and a row of beams of c
10:27 c he made like the sycamore
2Ch 1:15 c he made like the sycamore
2:3 kept sending him c to build
9:27 c he made like the sycamore

Ceiling
1Ki 6:15 up to the rafters of the c

Celebrate
Ge 29:27 C to the full the week of
Ex 5:1 they may c a festival to me
12:14 c it as a festival to Jehovah
12:14 time indefinite you should c
12:47 assembly of Israel are to c
12:48 c the passover to Jehovah
12:48 he may come near to c it
23:14 are to c a festival to me
Le 23:39 c the festival of Jehovah
23:41 c it as a festival to Jehovah
23:41 c it in the seventh month
Nu 29:12 c a festival to Jehovah seven
De 16:1 you must c the passover to
16:10 c the festival of weeks to
16:13 c for yourself seven days
16:15 Seven days you will c the
2Sa 6:21 I will c before Jehovah
Na 1:15 O Judah, c your festivals
Zec 14:16 c the festival of the booths
14:18 c the festival of the booths
14:19 c the festival of the booths
Mt 26:18 I will c the passover with

Celebrated
Ge 11:4 let us make a c name for
29:28 Jacob did so and c fully the
Mt 14:6 Herod's birthday was being c
Heb 11:28 faith he had c the passover

Celebrating
1Sa 18:7 the women that were c kept
2Sa 6:5 Israel were c before Jehovah
1Ch 13:8 David and all Israel were c
15:29 David skipping about and c
Ps 42:4 Of a crowd c a festival

Celestial
Jas 1:17 the Father of the c lights

Cell
Ac 12:7 light shone in the prison c

Cenchreae
Ac 18:18 hair . . . clipped short in C
Ro 16:1 the congregation that is in C

Censer
2Ch 26:19 c for burning incense
Eze 8:11 with his c in his hand, and
Heb 9:4 golden c and the ark of the

Census
Ex 30:12 the sons of Israel as a c
30:12 when taking a c of them
30:12 when taking a c of them
2Ch 2:17 the c that David his father

Center
Ex 26:28 at the c of the panel frames
27:5 be toward the c of the altar
38:4 its rim, down toward its c
Jg 9:37 out of the c of the land, and
1Ki 7:25 hind parts were toward the c
Isa 66:17 gardens behind one in the c
Eze 27:24 made, in your trading c
38:12 in the c of the earth
Mr 3:3 Get up and come to the c
Lu 6:8 Get up and stand in the c

Cephas
Joh 1:42 you will be called C
1Co 1:12 But I to Apollos, But I to C
3:22 Apollos or C or the world or
9:5 the Lord's brothers and C, do
15:5 to C, then to the twelve
Ga 1:18 up to Jerusalem to visit C
2:9 James and C and John, the ones
2:11 when C came to Antioch, I
2:14 I said to C before them all

Cereal
Ne 10:31 wares and every kind of c on

Cereals
Ge 42:1 there were c in Egypt
42:2 that there are c in Egypt
42:19 take c for the famine in
42:26 their c upon their asses
Ge 43:2 had finished eating up the c
44:2 and the money for his c
47:14 c which people were buying
Am 8:5 moon passes and we may sell c

Ceremonial
Ac 21:26 for the c cleansing, until

Ceremonially
Joh 11:55 to cleanse themselves c
Ac 21:24 cleanse yourself c with them
21:26 and cleansed himself c with
24:18 found me c cleansed in the

Ceremonies
Mt 22:10 room for the wedding c was

Certain*
Ge 4:14 c that anyone finding me will
12:13 soul will be c to live due
37:8 to be king over us for c
37:8 dominate over us for c
37:10 c going to come and bow
44:31 c to occur that as soon as
Ex 34:15 will be c to invite you, and
34:16 daughters will be c to have
Nu 14:43 are c to fall by the sword
16:30 know for c that these men
32:9 Jehovah was c to give them
De 12:20 c to say, Let me eat meat
Isa 8:15 c to stumble and to fall and
19:3 c to resort to the valueless
20:6 c to say in that day, There
49:21 for c say in your heart
51:3 will for c comfort all her
55:11 have c success in that for
60:16 c to know that I, Jehovah

Certainly*
Ge 9:14 rainbow will c appear in the
9:15 I shall c remember my
9:16 I shall c see it to remember
12:3 c bless themselves by means
15:13 c afflict them for four
17:4 you will c become a father of
17:20 He will c produce twelve
21:7 Sarah will c suckle children
22:18 c bless themselves due to
26:4 nations of the earth will c
28:3 c become a congregation of
28:14 seed will c become like the
28:14 c spread abroad to the west
28:14 will c bless themselves
40:13 c return you to your office
40:13 c give Pharaoh's cup into
40:19 will c hang you upon a stake
40:19 c eat your flesh from off
41:30 seven years of famine will c
49:11 c wash his clothing in wine
50:24 c bring you up out of this
Ex 4:9 c become . . . blood on the dry
6:6 I shall c bring you out from
6:7 c take you to me as a people
6:7 c know that I am Jehovah your
6:8 c bring you into the land that
7:3 shall c multiply my signs and
7:5 Egyptians will c know that I
7:19 c be blood in all the land of
8:3 frogs . . . c come up and enter
8:11 frogs will c turn away from
8:22 c make the land of Goshen
8:29 gadflies will c turn away
9:4 And Jehovah will c make a
10:2 c know that I am Jehovah
10:5 c eat every sprouting tree of
11:6 will c occur a great outcry
11:8 servants of yours will c come
12:23 Jehovah will c pass over the
13:17 and will c return to Egypt
14:4 he will c chase after them
14:4 Egyptians will c know that I
14:18 c know that I am Jehovah
14:25 Jehovah c fights for them
16:6 c know that it is Jehovah who
16:12 c know that I am Jehovah
18:23 then c be able to stand it
19:5 c become my special property
20:24 you and shall c bless you
22:24 c kill you with the sword
22:27 I shall c hear, because I am
23:23 and I shall c efface them
23:25 c bless your bread and your
23:27 shall c throw into confusion
29:46 c know that I am Jehovah
32:34 I shall c bring punishment
Le 18:28 c vomit the nations out who
20:5 c fix my face against that

Le 20:6 *c* set my face against that
25:18 *c* dwell on the land in
25:19 *c* eat to satisfaction and
25:21 *c* command my blessing for
26:4 *c* give your showers of rain
26:5 threshing will *c* reach to
26:7 *c* chase your enemies, and
26:8 five . . . *c* chase a hundred
26:10 *c* eat the old of the
26:11 *c* put my tabernacle in the
26:16 *c* bring upon you disturbance
26:16 enemies will *c* eat it up
26:17 *c* be defeated before your
26:22 *c* bereave you of children and
26:25 *c* bring upon you a sword
26:36 *c* bring timidity into their
Nu 11:18 Jehovah will *c* give you meat
15:40 *c* do all my commandments
24:17 *c* step forth out of Jacob
De 4:27 Jehovah will *c* scatter you
7:2 God will *c* abandon them to you
7:4 they will *c* serve other gods
7:4 *c* annihilate you in a hurry
7:13 *c* love you and bless you
7:15 Jehovah will *c* remove from
7:22 God will *c* push these nations
9:23 land that I shall *c* give you
11:14 *c* give rain for your land
11:15 I shall *c* give vegetation in
11:23 *c* dispossess nations greater
12:1 will *c* allow you to take
12:10 he will *c* give you rest from
13:17 he may *c* show you mercy
15:6 *c* lend on pledge to many
18:18 he will *c* speak to them all
20:13 *c* give it into your hand
28:1 God also will *c* put you high
28:8 *c* bless you in the land that
28:12 will *c* lend to many nations
28:22 *c* pursue you until you have
28:39 will plant and *c* cultivate
28:45 maledictions will *c* come
28:64 *c* scatter you among all the
28:68 *c* bring you back to Egypt by
30:7 *c* put all these oaths upon
31:16 will *c* forsake me and break
31:17 *c* forsake them and conceal
32:37 *c* say, Where are their gods
Jos 1:3 to you people I shall *c* give
2:9 will *c* give you the land, and
2:12 you also will *c* exercise
2:14 *c* exercise loving-kindness
8:7 *c* give it into your hands
14:12 I shall *c* dispossess them
Jg 4:7 I shall *c* draw to you at the
4:14 Jehovah will *c* give Sisera
6:14 you will *c* save Israel out of
6:16 you will *c* strike down Midian
1Sa 2:35 *c* build for him a lasting
2:35 *c* walk before my anointed
24:20 Israel will *c* endure
25:29 *c* prove to be wrapped up
2Sa 7:9 *c* make for you a great name
7:10 *c* appoint a place for my
7:12 *c* raise up your seed after
7:13 *c* establish the throne of
7:16 kingdom will *c* be steadfast
1Ki 2:32 *c* bring back his blood upon
3:12 shall *c* give you a wise and
11:31 shall *c* give you ten tribes
11:35 *c* take the kingship out of
11:37 *c* become king over Israel
14:10 *c* cut off from Jeroboam
14:12 the child will *c* die
14:14 Jehovah will *c* raise up to
16:3 *c* constitute his house like
17:4 *c* command to supply you food
20:13 *c* know that I am Jehovah
20:28 *c* know that I am Jehovah
2Ki 3:18 *c* give Moab into your hand
1Ch 17:11 *c* raise up your seed after
22:10 *c* establish the throne of
Job 18:17 *c* perish from the earth
Ps 1:3 he will *c* become like a tree
67:6 will *c* give its produce
69:35 they will *c* dwell there and
Pr 8:35 finding me will *c* find life
1Co 9:2 I most *c* am to you, for you
2Co 4:16 *c* the man we are inside is

Certainty
Lu 1:4 know fully the *c* of the things
22:59 For a *c* this man also was
Joh 1:47 See, an Israelite for a *c*
Joh 4:42 a *c* the savior of the world
6:14 for a *c* the prophet that was
7:26 a *c* that this is the Christ
7:40 This is for a *c* The Prophet
Ac 2:36 *c* that God made him both Lord
10:34 *c* I perceive that God is not

Certificate
De 24:1 write out a *c* of divorce for
24:3 written out a *c* of divorce
Isa 50:1 the divorce *c* of the mother
Jer 3:8 give the *c* of her full divorce
Mt 5:31 give her a *c* of divorce
19:7 giving a *c* of dismissal and
Mr 10:4 writing of a *c* of dismissal

Certified
Ac 6:3 seven *c* men from among you

Cessation
Ezr 6:8 able-bodied men without *c*
Isa 38:11 inhabitants of the land of *c*

Chaff
Job 21:18 like *c* that a stormwind has
Ps 1:4 *c* that the wind drives away
35:5 like *c* before the wind
Isa 17:13 like the *c* of the mountains
29:5 tyrants just like the *c* that
41:15 will make just like the *c*
Da 2:35 *c* from the summer threshing
Ho 13:3 like *c* that is stormed away
Zep 2:2 day has passed by just like *c*
Mt 3:12 *c* he will burn up with fire
Lu 3:17 the *c* he will burn up with

Chain
Eze 7:23 Make the *c*, for the land
Mr 5:3 bind him fast even with a *c*
Ac 28:20 this *c* I have around me
Re 20:1 and a great *c* in his hand

Chainlets
Nu 31:50 gold, ankle *c*, and bracelets

Chains
Ex 28:14 and two *c* of pure gold
28:14 attach the ropelike *c* to the
28:22 wreathed *c*, in rope work, of
39:15 the breastpiece wreathed *c*
2Ch 3:5 palm-tree figures and *c*
3:16 made *c* in necklace style and
3:16 and put them on the *c*
Isa 3:20 step *c* and the breastbands
40:19 and silver *c* he is forging
51:14 The one stooping in *c* will
Mr 5:4 been bound with fetters and *c*
5:4 *c* were snapped apart by him
Lu 8:29 bound with *c* and fetters
Ac 12:6 sleeping bound with two *c*
12:7 and his *c* fell off his hands
21:33 him to be bound with two *c*
Eph 6:20 acting as an ambassador in *c*
2Ti 1:16 not become ashamed of my *c*

Chainwork
1Ki 6:21 *c* of gold pass across in
7:17 twisted ornaments in *c*, for

Chair
2Ki 4:10 a couch and a table and a *c*

Chalcedony
Re 21:19 foundation . . . third *c*

Chaldea
Jer 50:10 *C* must become a spoil
51:24 all the inhabitants of *C*
51:35 be upon the inhabitants of *C*
Eze 11:24 to *C* to the exiled people
23:16 messengers to them in *C*

Chaldean
Ezr 5:12 king of Babylon, the *C*, and
Da 2:10 priest or conjurer or *C*
5:30 Belshazzar the *C* king was

Chaldeans
Ge 11:28 in Ur of the *C*
11:31 with him out of Ur of the *C*
15:7 Ur of the *C* to give you this
2Ki 24:2 marauder bands of *C* and
25:4 *C* were all around against
25:5 a military force of *C* went
25:10 entire military force of *C*
25:13 the *C* broke in pieces and
25:24 being servants to the *C*
25:25 *C* that happened to be with
25:26 afraid because of the *C*
2Ch 36:17 the king of the *C*
Ne 9:7 brought him out of Ur of the *C*
Job 1:17 *C* made up three bands and
Isa 13:19 beauty of the pride of the *C*
23:13 Look! The land of the *C*
43:14 the *C* in the ships with
47:1 O daughter of the *C*
47:5 O daughter of the *C*; for you
48:14 own arm will be upon the *C*
48:20 Run away from the *C*. Tell
Jer 21:4 the *C* who are laying siege
21:9 the *C* who are laying siege
22:25 into the hand of the *C*
24:5 to the land of the *C*, in a
25:12 against the land of the *C*
32:4 from the hand of the *C*
32:5 warring against the *C*, you
32:24 into the hand of the *C*
32:25 into the hand of the *C*
32:28 city into the hand of the *C*
32:29 *C* who are fighting against
32:43 into the hand of the *C*
33:5 to fight against the *C* and
35:11 military force of the *C*
37:5 *C* that were laying siege
37:8 *C* will certainly come back
37:9 *C* will without fail go away
37:10 military force of the *C*
37:11 military force of the *C*
37:13 to the *C* that you are
37:14 not falling away to the *C*
38:2 one going out to the *C* is the
38:18 into the hand of the *C*
38:19 have fallen away to the *C*
38:23 are bringing out to the *C*
39:5 military force of the *C*
39:8 the *C* burned with fire, and
40:9 afraid of serving the *C*
40:10 *C* who will come to us
41:3 *C* who were found there
41:18 because of the *C*; for they
43:3 us into the hand of the *C*
50:1 concerning the land of the *C*
50:8 out of the land of the *C*
50:25 has in the land of the *C*
50:35 sword against the *C*, is the
50:45 against the land of the *C*
51:4 slain in the land of the *C*
51:54 from the land of the *C*
52:7 *C* were all around against
52:8 military force of the *C* went
52:14 military forces of the *C*
52:17 *C* broke to pieces and went
Eze 1:3 in the land of the *C* by the
12:13 to the land of the *C*, but
16:29 abound . . . toward the *C*
23:14 images of *C* carved in
23:15 *C* as respects the land of
23:23 Babylon and all the *C*
Da 1:4 and the tongue of the *C*
2:2 *C* to tell the king his dreams
2:4 *C* spoke to the king in the
2:5 saying to the *C*: The word is
2:10 *C* answered before the king
3:8 *C* approached and accused the
4:7 the *C* and the astrologers were
5:7 bring in the conjurers, the *C*
5:11 the *C* and the astrologers
9:1 over the kingdom of the *C*
Hab 1:6 here I am raising up the *C*
Ac 7:4 out from the land of the *C*

Chalk
Isa 44:13 traces it out with red *c*

Chalkstones
Isa 27:9 *c* that have been pulverized

Challenge
Jer 49:19 and who will *c* me
50:44 who will *c* me, and who

Chamber
Jg 3:20 sitting in his cool roof *c*
3:23 doors of the roof *c* behind
3:24 the doors of the roof *c* were
3:25 the doors of the roof *c*
2Sa 18:33 went up to the roof *c*
1Ki 6:6 side *c* was five cubits in
6:8 the lowest side *c* was on the
14:28 the guard *c* of the runners
17:19 to the roof *c*, where he was
17:23 from the roof *c* into the
20:30 into the innermost *c*
22:25 the innermost *c* to hide
2Ki 1:2 the grating in his roof *c*
4:10 make a little roof *c* on the

2Ki 4:11 turned aside to the roof *c*
9:2 him into the innermost *c*
23:12 the roof *c* of Ahaz that the
2Ch 12:11 to the guard *c* of the
18:24 innermost *c* to hide
Ne 3:31 the roof *c* of the corner
3:32 the roof *c* of the corner
Ps 19:5 coming out of his nuptial *c*
Eze 40:7 guard *c* was one reed in
40:12 guard *c* was six cubits
40:13 one guard *c* to the roof
41:5 the width of the side *c*
41:6, 6 side *c* upon side *c*, three
41:9 that belonged to the side *c*
41:11 entrance of the side *c* was
Da 6:10 windows in his roof *c* being
Joe 2:16 the bride from her nuptial *c*
Ac 1:13 upper *c*, where they were
9:37 and laid her in an upper *c*
9:39 led him up into the upper *c*
20:8 in the upper *c* where we were
25:23 entered into the audience *c*

Chambers
1Ki 6:5 made side *c* all around
6:10 the side *c* against the
1Ch 28:11 its roof *c* and its dark
2Ch 3:9 roof *c* he covered with gold
Ps 104:3 building his upper *c* with
104:13 mountains from his upper *c*
Jer 22:13 his upper *c*, but not with
22:14 and commodious upper *c*
Eze 40:7 between the guard *c* there
40:10 the guard *c* of the gate
40:12 in front of the guard *c*
40:16 for the guard *c* and for
40:21 its guard *c* were three on
40:29 its guard *c* and its side
40:33 its guard *c* and its side
40:36 guard *c*, its side pillars
41:6 And the side *c* were side
41:6 the side *c* all around
41:7 upward to the side *c*
41:8 foundations of the side *c*
41:9 construction of the side *c*
41:26 the side *c* of the house
Mt 24:26 Look! He is in the inner *c*

Chameleon
Le 11:30 the sand lizard and the *c*

Chamois
De 14:5 antelope and wild sheep and *c*

Champion
1Sa 17:4 *c* . . . his name being Goliath
17:23 *c*, his name being Goliath

Chance
Ge 31:28 a *c* to kiss my children and
Ru 2:3 by *c* she lighted on the tract
Mt 13:29 by no *c*, while collecting
Ac 25:16 a *c* to speak in his defense

Chanced
2Sa 1:6 *c* to be on Mount Gilboa, and

Chances
Nu 35:19 When he *c* upon him he
35:21 to death when he *c* upon him

Change
Ge 35:2 Jacob said . . . *c* your mantles
Le 13:16 back and it does *c* to white
Nu 34:4 boundary must *c* direction
34:5 boundary must *c* direction at
De 1:40 *c* your direction and pull
2:3 *C* your direction to the north
Job 1:11 for a *c*, thrust out your hand
2:5 For a *c*, thrust out your hand
12:15 and they *c* the earth
30:18 my garment takes on a *c*
30:21 *c* yourself to become cruel
Ps 41:3 his bed you will certainly *c*
46:2 though the earth undergo *c*
89:34 out of my lips I shall not *c*
90:6 forth blossoms and must *c*
105:25 heart *c* to hate his people
Pr 24:21 With those who are for a *c*
24:22 of those who are for a *c*
Jer 13:23 Can a Cushite *c* his skin?
31:13 *c* their mourning into
Eze 10:11 not *c* direction when they
10:11 not *c* direction when they
10:16 would not *c* direction, even
Da 7:25 intend to *c* times and law
Mic 4:13 horn I shall *c* into iron
4:13 hoofs I shall *c* into copper
Zep 3:9 the *c* to a pure language
Ac 6:14 *c* the customs that Moses
7:4 God caused him to *c* his
Heb 7:12 a *c* also of the law
12:17 sought a *c* of mind with

Changed
Ge 31:7 he has *c* my wages ten times
41:14 he shaved and *c* his mantles
Ex 14:5 heart of Pharaoh . . . was *c*
Le 13:17 plague has been *c* to white
13:25 hair . . . *c* white in the blotch
13:55 plague has not *c* its look and
Nu 32:38 their names being *c*
De 23:5 *c* the malediction into a
1Sa 10:6 and be *c* into another man
2Sa 12:20 *c* his mantles and came to
2Ki 23:34 and *c* his name to Jehoiakim
24:17 he *c* his name to Zedekiah
2Ch 36:4 *c* his name to Jehoiakim
Ne 13:2 God *c* the malediction into
Es 9:22 month that was *c* for them
Job 20:14 be *c* in his own intestines
41:28 slingstones have been *c* for
Ps 30:11 *c* my mourning into dancing
32:4 My life's moisture has been *c*
66:6 has *c* the sea into dry land
105:29 *c* their waters into blood
Ec 8:1 sternness of his face is *c* for
Isa 24:5 *c* the regulation, broken
34:9 torrents must be *c* into
63:10 *c* into an enemy of theirs
Jer 2:21 been *c* toward me into the
23:36 *c* the words of the living
48:11 very scent has not been *c*
La 5:15 dancing has been *c* into mere
Da 2:9 until the time itself is *c*
3:19 expression of his face was *c*
3:27 mantles had not been *c* and
3:28 *c* the very word of the king
4:16 its heart be *c* from that of
5:6 his very complexion was *c* in
5:10 nor let your complexion be *c*
6:8 in order for it not to be *c*
6:15 establishes is not to be *c*
6:17 be *c* in the case of Daniel
7:28 my very complexion *c* in me
10:8 my own dignity became *c* upon
Ho 11:8 My heart has *c* within me
Zec 14:10 The whole land will be *c*
Mal 3:6 I am Jehovah; I have not *c*
Ac 28:6 they *c* their mind and began
Ro 1:26 females *c* the natural use of
1Co 15:51 but we shall all be *c*
15:52 and we shall be *c*
Heb 1:12 they will be *c*, but you are
7:12 the priesthood is being *c*

Changers
Mt 21:12 the tables of the money *c*
Mr 11:15 the tables of the money *c*
Joh 2:15 the coins of the money *c*

Changes
Ge 45:22 gave individual *c* of mantles
45:22 and five *c* of mantles
2Ki 5:5 and ten *c* of garments
5:22 and two *c* of garments
5:23 with two *c* of garments
Ps 90:5 just like green grass that *c*

Changing
Ge 31:41 kept *c* my wages ten times
1Sa 10:9 God began *c* the heart of his
Ps 77:10 *c* of the right hand of the
78:44 *c* to blood their Nile canals
114:8 *c* the rock into a reedy pool
Jer 2:36 the *c* of your way
Da 2:21 *c* times and seasons, removing
5:9 complexion was *c* within him
1Co 7:31 the scene of this world is *c*

Changings
Ps 55:19 with whom there are no *c*

Channel
Job 6:15 *c* of winter torrents that
38:25 divided a *c* for the flood

Channeled
Job 28:10 *c* water-filled galleries

Channels
Ca 5:12 like doves by the *c* of water
Eze 31:4 its *c* it sent forth to all
Joe 1:20 the *c* of water have dried up

Chant
2Sa 1:17 David proceeded to *c* this
2Sa 3:33 king went on to *c* over Abner
2Ch 35:25 began to *c* over Josiah
Eze 27:32 a dirge and *c* over you
32:16 people will certainly *c* it
32:16 the nations will *c* it
32:16 its crowd they will *c* it

Characters
Ezr 4:7 was written in Aramaic *c*

Charcoal
Pr 26:21 *c* for the embers and wood
Isa 54:16 blowing upon the fire of *c*
Joh 18:18 they had built a *c* fire
21:9 *c* fire and fish lying upon

Charcoals
2Sa 14:7 glow of my *c* that has
Isa 47:14 will be no glow of *c* for

Charge
Ge 33:13 cattle . . . are in my *c*, and
39:5 in *c* of all that was his
Ex 21:2 out as one set free without *c*
Le 6:2 about something in his *c* or a
6:4 the thing in his *c* which was
6:4 which was put in his *c* or the
Nu 31:49 men of war who are in our *c*
De 17:18 in the *c* of the priests
19:16 a *c* of revolt against him
19:18 a false *c* against his brother
Jg 20:33 were making a *c* out of their
1Sa 17:20 the sheep to the keeper's *c*
17:28 in whose *c* did you leave
2Ki 7:17 to have *c* of the gateway
1Ch 9:26 in *c* of the dining rooms and
9:27 *c* of the key, even to open up
9:28 in *c* of the utensils of the
9:32 were in *c* of the layer bread
2Ch 30:17 Levites were in *c* of
31:12 was in *c* of them as leader
31:14 *c* of the voluntary offerings
Ne 13:4 priest in *c* of a dining hall
13:13 Levites in *c* of the stores
Es 2:3 women in *c* of Hegai the king's
2:8 in *c* of Hegai, then Esther was
2:8 in *c* of Hegai the guardian of
2:14 in *c* of Shaashgaz the king's
6:9 *c* of one of the king's noble
Jer 38:10 Take in your *c* from this
38:11 took the men in his *c* and
Mt 4:6 He will give his angels a *c*
20:8 said to his man in *c*, Call
27:37 *c* against him, in writing
Mr 7:36 the more he would *c* them
15:26 *c* against him was written
Lu 4:10 his angels a *c* concerning you
8:3 Chuza, Herod's man in *c*, and
12:48 people put in *c* of much
19:19 be in *c* of five cities
Joh 19:16 Then they took *c* of Jesus
Ac 7:60 Jehovah, do not *c* this sin
12:20 *c* of the bedchamber of the
15:5 *c* them to observe the law of
19:13 I solemnly *c* you by Jesus
25:18 no *c* of the wicked things
Ro 3:9 *c* that Jews as well as Greeks
Ga 4:2 he is under men in *c* and
1Ti 5:21 I solemnly *c* you before God
2Ti 4:1 I solemnly *c* you before God
Tit 1:6 not under a *c* of debauchery
Heb 9:20 God has laid as a *c* upon you

Charged
De 22:14 *c* her with notorious deeds
Pr 8:24 springs heavily *c* with water
Mt 9:30 Jesus sternly *c* them, saying
12:16 strictly *c* them not to make
16:20 *c* the disciples not to say
Mr 3:12 sternly *c* them not to make
7:36 he *c* them not to tell anyone
8:30 *c* them not to tell anyone
Ac 4:18 *c* them, nowhere to make any
19:40 *c* with sedition over today's
23:29 not *c* with a single thing
Ro 3:8 it is falsely *c* to us and just
5:13 sin is not *c* against anyone
Phm 18 keep this *c* to my account

Charges
2Sa 10:9 Joab saw that the battle *c*
11:15 of the heaviest battle *c*
1Ch 19:10 the battle *c* had come to be
Job 4:18 he *c* with faultiness
Mr 15:4 See how many *c* they are
Lu 23:14 *c* you are bringing against
Ac 19:38 bring *c* against one another

Ac 25:7 many and serious *c* for which
25:27 signify the *c* against him

Charging
De 22:17 *c* her with notorious deeds
2Ti 2:14 *c* them before God as witness

Chariot
Ge 41:43 ride in the second *c* of honor
46:29 Joseph had his *c* made ready
Ex 14:9 all the *c* horses of Pharaoh
Jg 4:15 off the *c* and took to flight
5:28 his war *c* delayed in coming
1Sa 8:12 and his *c* instruments
2Sa 8:4 hamstring all the *c* horses
8:4 hundred *c* horses of them
15:1 to have a *c* made for himself
1Ki 1:5 have a *c* made for himself
7:33 workmanship of a *c* wheel
9:19 the *c* cities and the cities
10:26 stationed in the *c* cities
10:29 a *c* customarily came up and
12:18 get up into the *c* to flee
20:25, 25 equal to . . . *c* for *c*
20:33 had him get up into the *c*
22:35 in the *c* facing the Syrians
22:35 the interior of the war *c*
22:38 wash off the war *c* by the
2Ki 2:11 a fiery war *c* and fiery
2:12 the war *c* of Israel and his
5:21 got down from his *c* to meet
5:26 down off his *c* to meet you
9:21 his war *c* was hitched up
9:21 each in his own war *c*
9:24 he collapsed in his war *c*
9:27 in the *c* on the way up to
9:28 servants carried him in a *c*
10:15 made him get up into the *c*
10:16 with him in his war *c*
13:14 war *c* of Israel and his
23:30 dead in a *c* from Megiddo
1Ch 18:4 hamstrung all the *c* horses
18:4 a hundred *c* horses of them
28:18 the representation of the *c*
2Ch 1:14 stationed in *c* cities and
1:17 a *c* for six hundred silver
8:6 all the *c* cities and the
9:25 stationed in the *c* cities
10:18 into his *c* to flee to
18:34 standing position in the *c*
35:24 took him down from the *c*
35:24 ride in the second war *c*
Ps 77:18 thunder was like *c* wheels
104:3 Making the clouds his *c*
Isa 21:7 war *c* with a span of steeds
21:7 a war *c* of asses
21:7 a war *c* of camels
21:9 war *c* of men, with a span
22:6 war *c* of earthling man
43:17 the war *c* and the horse
Jer 17:25 riding in the *c* and upon
51:21 dash the war *c* and its
Eze 26:10 and wheel and war *c*
Mic 1:13 the *c* to the team of horses
Na 2:3 the war *c* in the day of his
2:13 I will burn up her war *c*
3:2 horse and the leaping *c*
Hag 2:22 the *c* and its riders, and
Zec 6:2 first *c* there were red horses
6:2 the second *c*, black horses
6:3 And in the third *c* there were
6:3 fourth *c*, horses speckled
9:10 the war *c* from Ephraim and
Ac 8:28 sitting in his *c* and reading
8:29 and join yourself to this *c*
8:38 he commanded the *c* to halt

Charioteer
1Ki 22:34 said to his *c:* Turn your
2Ch 18:33 said to the *c:* Turn your
Ps 76:6 *c* and the horse have fallen

Charioteers
2Sa 1:6 *c* and the mounted men had
10:18 Syrians seven hundred *c* and
1Ki 9:22 chiefs of his *c* and of his
1Ch 19:18 seven thousand *c* and forty
2Ch 8:9 chiefs of his *c* and of his
Eze 39:20 horses and *c*, mighty

Chariots
Ge 50:9 with him both *c* and horsemen
Ex 14:6 to make his war *c* ready, and
14:7 to take six hundred chosen *c*
14:7 *c* of Egypt and warriors upon
14:17 Pharaoh and . . . his war *c*
14:18 Pharaoh, his war *c* and his
Ex 14:23 his war *c* and his cavalrymen
14:25 taking wheels off their *c*
14:26 Egyptians, their war *c* and
14:28 they covered the war *c* and
15:4 Pharaoh's *c* and his military
15:19 his war *c* and his cavalrymen
De 11:4 his war *c* against the faces
20:1 see horses and war *c*, a
Jos 11:4 very many horses and war *c*
11:6 *c* you will burn in the fire
11:9 *c* he burned in the fire
17:16 are war *c* with iron scythes
17:18 war *c* with iron scythes and
24:6 with war *c* and cavalrymen
Jg 1:19 they had war *c* with iron
4:3 he had nine hundred war *c*
4:7 Jabin's army and his war *c*
4:13 all his war *c*, the nine
4:13 war *c* with iron scythes, and
4:15 all his war *c* and all the
4:16 chased after the war *c* and
5:28 hoofbeats of his *c* be so late
1Sa 8:11 Your sons . . . as his in his *c*
8:11 have to run before his *c*
13:5 thirty thousand war *c* and
1Ki 4:26 stalls of horses for his *c*
10:26 gathering more *c* and steeds
10:26 a thousand four hundred *c*
16:9 the chief of half the *c*
20:1 and horses and *c*, and he
20:21 horses and the *c*, and he
22:31 two chiefs of the *c* that
22:32 soon as the chiefs of the *c*
22:33 the chiefs of the *c* saw
2Ki 5:9 his horses and his war *c*
6:14 he sent horses and war *c*
6:15 city with horses and war *c*
6:17 full of horses and war *c*
7:6 to hear the sound of war *c*
7:14 took two *c* with horses and
8:21 to Zair, also all the *c* with
8:21 and the chiefs of the *c*
10:2 the war *c* and the horses and
13:7 fifty horsemen and ten *c* and
18:24 for *c* and for horsemen
19:23 the multitude of my war *c*
23:11 *c* of the sun he burned in
1Ch 18:4 a thousand *c* and seven
19:6 hire for themselves *c* and
19:7 thirty-two thousand *c* and
2Ch 1:14 Solomon kept gathering *c* and
1:14 a thousand four hundred *c* and
9:25 *c* and twelve thousand steeds
12:3 twelve hundred *c* and with
14:9 three hundred *c*, and came
16:8 in *c* and in horsemen
18:30 chiefs of the *c* that were
18:31 the chiefs of the *c* saw
18:32 chiefs of the *c* saw that it
21:9 and also all the *c* with him
21:9 also the chiefs of the *c*
Ps 20:7 Some concerning *c* and others
68:17 The war *c* of God are in
Ca 1:9 of mine in the *c* of Pharaoh
6:12 at the *c* of my willing people
Isa 2:7 there is no limit to their *c*
22:7 become full of war *c*, and
22:18 *c* of your glory will be
31:1 put their trust in war *c*
36:9 trust in Egypt for *c* and for
37:24 multitude of my war *c* I
66:15 his *c* are like a stormwind
66:20 on horses and in *c* and in
Jer 4:13 his *c* are like a stormwind
22:4 riding in *c* and on horses
46:9 and drive madly, O you *c!*
47:3 rattling of his war *c*, the
50:37 against their war *c* and
Eze 23:24 rattling of war *c* and
26:7 with horses and war *c* and
Da 11:40 will storm with *c* and with
Joe 2:5 sound of *c* on . . . mountains
Mic 5:10 and destroy your *c*
Na 2:4 the war *c* keep driving madly
Hab 3:8 your *c* were salvation
Zec 6:1 four *c* coming forth from
Re 9:9 the sound of *c* of many horses

Charm
Ps 45:2 *C* has been poured out upon
Pr 3:22 and *c* to your throat
4:9 it will give a wreath of *c*
11:16 woman of *c* is the one that
22:11 for the *c* of his lips the
Pr 31:30 *C* may be false, and
Na 3:4 prostitute, attractive with *c*

Charmer
Isa 3:3 arts, and the skilled *c*

Charmers
Ps 58:5 not listen to the voice of *c*
Isa 19:3 valueless gods and to the *c*
47:15 as your *c* from your youth

Charming
Pr 5:19 hind and a *c* mountain goat
Ec 10:11 the serpent bites when no *c*
Isa 47:11 know no *c* against it
Jer 8:17 for which there is no *c*
Zec 4:7, 7 to it: How *c!* How *c!*

Chase
Ge 35:5 not *c* after the sons of Jacob
44:4 Get up! *C* after the men and
Ex 14:4 will certainly *c* after them
Le 26:7 *c* your enemies, and they will
26:8 five . . . certainly *c* a hundred
26:8 a hundred . . . *c* ten thousand
26:36 will indeed *c* them away, and
De 19:6 *c* after the manslayer and
Jos 2:5 *C* after them quickly, for you
8:16 *c* after them, and they went
10:19 *C* after your enemies, and
23:10 one man of you will *c* a
1Sa 30:8 Shall I *c* . . . this marauder
30:8 Go in *c*, for you will
30:10 David kept up the *c*, he and
2Sa 17:1 and *c* after David tonight
20:6 *c* after him, that he may not
20:7 to *c* after Sheba the son of
20:13 *c* after Sheba the son of
Job 18:11 indeed *c* him at his feet
18:18 they will *c* him away
41:28 An arrow does not *c* it away
Ho 2:7 *c* after her passionate lovers
Lu 17:23 Do not go out or *c* after

Chased
Jos 2:7 *c* after them in the direction
Jg 4:16 And Barak *c* after the war
2Sa 20:10 *c* after Sheba the son of
23:6 *c* away, like thornbushes
1Ch 8:13 *c* away the inhabitants of
12:15 *c* away all those of the low
Ne 13:28 So I *c* him away from me
Job 6:13 effectual working . . . *c* away
20:8 *c* away like a vision of the
30:15 My noble bearing is *c* like
Isa 13:14 like a gazelle *c* away and
16:2 *c* away from its nest, the
17:13 *c* like the chaff of the
Jer 30:17 a woman *c* away is what

Chaser
Isa 1:23 a bribe and a *c* after gifts

Chases
Jos 20:5 avenger of blood *c* after him
1Sa 26:20 *c* a partridge upon the
Pr 19:26 and that *c* a mother away is

Chasing
Ge 31:23 *c* after him for a distance
Ex 14:8 *c* after the sons of Israel
14:9 Egyptians went *c* after them
Le 26:36 and fall without anyone *c*
26:37 stumble . . . without anyone *c*
De 1:44 went *c* you, just as bees do
11:4 when they were *c* after them
Jos 2:7 after those *c* after them had
8:16 they went *c* after Joshua and
8:17 and went *c* after Israel
24:6 Egyptians went *c* after your
Jg 1:6 they went *c* after him and got
7:23 and they went *c* after Midian
8:5 and I am *c* after Zebah and
1Sa 23:25 *c* after David into the
23:28 back from *c* after David and
24:14 After whom are you *c?*
26:18 *c* after his servant, for
2Sa 2:19 Asahel went *c* after Abner
2:24 Joab and Abishai went *c*
2:28 not continue *c* after Israel
18:16 return from *c* after Israel
2Ki 5:21 Gehazi went *c* after Naaman
25:5 went *c* after the king
2Ch 13:19 And Abijah kept *c* after
Job 13:25 *c* after mere dry stubble
Pr 11:19 one *c* after what is bad is
Jer 39:5 Chaldeans went *c* after them
52:8 went *c* after the king, and

Ho 12:1 *c* after the east wind all day

Chasm
Lu 16:26 a great *c* has been fixed

Chaste
2Co 7:11 to be *c* in this matter
11:2 as a *c* virgin to the Christ
Php 4:8 whatever things are *c*
1Ti 5:22 preserve yourself *c*
Tit 2:5 *c*, workers at home, good
Jas 3:17 wisdom from above is . . . *c*
1Pe 3:2 *c* conduct together with deep

Chasteness
1Ti 4:12 in love, in faith, in *c*
5:2 women as sisters with all *c*

Chastise
Le 26:18 *c* you seven times as much for
26:28 *c* you seven times for your
1Ki 12:11 shall *c* you with scourges
12:14 shall *c* you with scourges
Pr 19:18 *C* your son while there
29:17 *C* your son and he will bring
Jer 46:28 *c* you to the proper degree
Lu 23:16 *c* him and release him
23:22 *c* and release him

Chastised
1Ki 12:11 *c* you with whips, but I
12:14 *c* you with whips, but I
2Ch 10:11 *c* you with whips, but I
10:14 his part, *c* you with whips

Chastisement
Isa 30:32 swing of his rod of *c* that
53:5 The *c* meant for our peace
Jer 30:14 with the *c* of someone cruel

Chastity
2Co 11:3 the *c* that are due the Christ

Chatterer
Ac 17:18 What is it this *c* would like

Chattering
3Jo 10 *c* about us with wicked words

Cheap
La 1:8 treated her as something *c*

Cheating
Pr 11:1 *c* pair of scales is something
20:23 *c* pair of scales is not good

Chebar
Eze 1:1 by the river *C*, that the
1:3 the Chaldeans by the river *C*
3:15 were dwelling by the river *C*
3:23 I had seen by the river *C*
10:15 I had seen at the river *C*
10:20 at the river *C*, so that I
10:22 I had seen by the river *C*
43:3 saw by the river *C*, and I

Check
Pr 10:19 one keeping his lips in *c*
Isa 48:9 I shall *c* my anger, and for
64:12 keeping yourself in *c*
Jer 14:10 they have not kept in *c*
Da 4:35 no one that can *c* his hand

Checkerwork
Ex 28:4 a robe of *c*, a turban and a
28:39 weave in *c* the robe of fine

Chedorlaomer
Ge 14:1 *C* king of Elam, and Tidal
14:4 Twelve years . . . served *C*
14:5 *C* came, and also the kings
14:9 against *C* king of Elam and
14:17 he returned from defeating *C*

Cheek
1Ki 22:24 struck Micaiah upon the *c*
2Ch 18:23 struck Micaiah on the *c* and
La 3:30 his *c* to the very one striking
Mic 5:1 strike upon the *c* the judge
Mt 5:39 slaps you on your right *c*
Lu 6:29 strikes you on the one *c*

Cheeks
Job 16:10 they have struck my *c*
Ca 1:10 *c* are comely among the hair
5:13 His *c* are like a garden bed of
Isa 50:6 my *c* to those plucking off
La 1:2 and her tears are upon her *c*

Cheer
Ac 2:28 fill me with good *c* with
14:17 full with food and good *c*
27:22 be of good *c*, for not a
27:25 be of good *c*, men; for I
2Co 2:2 who indeed is there to *c* me

Cheerful
Ps 98:4 Be *c* and cry out joyfully and
Isa 14:7 People have become *c* with
44:23 Become *c*, you mountains
49:13 Let the mountains become *c*
52:9 Become *c*, cry out joyfully
54:1 *c* with a joyful outcry and
55:12 will become *c* before you
Ac 2:26 my heart became *c* and my
27:36 they all became *c* and
2Co 9:7 for God loves a *c* giver
Php 2:19 that I may be a *c* soul when

Cheerfulness
Ro 12:8 let him do it with *c*

Cheering
Ec 2:3 by *c* my flesh even with wine

Cheers
Zep 3:14 Break out in *c*, O Israel

Cheese
Job 10:10 And like *c* to curdle me

Chelal
Ezr 10:30 sons of Pahath-moab . . . *C*

Chelub
1Ch 4:11 *C* the brother of Shuhah
27:26 there was Ezri the son of *C*

Chelubai
1Ch 2:9 the sons of Hezron . . . *C*

Cheluhi
Ezr 10:35 Benaiah, Bedeiah, *C*

Chemosh
Nu 21:29 perish, O people of *C*
Jg 11:24 *C* your god causes you to
1Ki 11:7 *C* the disgusting thing of
11:33 to *C* the god of Moab and
2Ki 23:13 *C* the disgusting thing of
Jer 48:7 *C* will certainly go forth
48:13 have to be ashamed of *C*
48:46 people of *C* have perished

Chenaanah
1Ki 22:11 Zedekiah the son of *C* made
22:24 Zedekiah the son of *C* now
1Ch 7:10 sons of Bilhan were . . . *C*
2Ch 18:10 Zedekiah the son of *C* made
18:23 Zedekiah the son of *C* now

Chenani
Ne 9:4 Bani and *C* proceeded to rise

Chenaniah
1Ch 15:22 *C* the chief of the Levites
15:27 *C* the chief of the carrying
26:29 Of the Izharites, *C* and his

Chephar-ammoni
Jos 18:24 and *C* and Ophni and Geba

Chephirah
Jos 9:17 cities were Gibeon and *C* and
18:26 Mizpeh and *C* and Mozah
Ezr 2:25 sons of Kiriath-jearim, *C*
Ne 7:29 *C* and Beeroth, seven hundred

Cheran
Ge 36:26 sons of Dishon . . . *C*
1Ch 1:41 sons of Dishon were . . . *C*

Cherethites
1Sa 30:14 raid on the south of the *C*
2Sa 8:18 was over the *C* and the
15:18 all the *C* and all the
20:7 the men of Joab and the *C*
20:23 Benaiah . . . was over the *C*
1Ki 1:38 the *C* and the Pelethites
1:44 the *C* and the Pelethites, and
1Ch 18:17 was over the *C* and the
Eze 25:16 cut off the *C* and destroy
Zep 2:5 Woe to . . . the nation of *C*

Cherished
De 13:6 your *c* wife or your companion
28:54 his brother and his *c* wife
28:56 toward her *c* husband and her

Cherishes
Eph 5:29 but he feeds and *c* it, as
1Th 2:7 mother *c* her own children

Cherishing
De 33:3 He was also *c* his people; All

Cherith
1Ki 17:3 *C* that is east of the Jordan
1Ki 17:5 *C* that is east of the Jordan

Cherub
Ex 25:19 make one *c* on this end and
25:19 and one *c* on that end
37:8 One *c* was on the end over
37:8 other *c* on the end over here
2Sa 22:11 he came riding upon a *c* and
1Ki 6:24 was the one wing of the *c*
6:24 was the other wing of the *c*
6:25 the second *c* was ten cubits
6:26 the one *c* was ten cubits
6:26 that was so of the other *c*
6:27 the wing of the other *c* was
2Ch 3:11 to the wing of the other *c*
3:12 wing of the one *c* of five
3:12 with the wing of the other *c*
Ezr 2:59 Tel-harsha, *C*, Addon and
Ne 7:61 *C*, Addon and Immer, and they
Ps 18:10 he came riding upon a *c* and
Eze 10:7 *c* thrust his hand out from
10:9 one wheel beside the one *c*
10:9 one wheel beside the other *c*
10:14 face was the face of the *c*
28:14 anointed *c* that is covering
28:16 O *c* that is covering
41:18, 18 between a *c* and a *c*
41:18 and the *c* had two faces

Cherubs
Ge 3:24 *c* and the flaming blade of a
Ex 25:18 you must make two *c* of gold
25:19 make the *c* at its two ends
25:20 the *c* must be spreading out
25:20 the faces of the *c* should be
25:22 from between the two *c* that
26:1 *c*, the work of an embroiderer
26:31 He will make it with *c*, the
36:8 with *c*, the work of an
36:35 he made it with *c*
37:7 further made two *c* of gold
37:8 *c* on the cover on both of its
37:9 *c* spreading out two wings
37:9 faces of the *c* proved to be
Nu 7:89 between the two *c*; and he
1Sa 4:4 Jehovah . . . upon the *c*
2Sa 6:2 sitting on the *c*
1Ki 6:23 two *c* of oil-tree wood
6:25 two *c* had the same measure
6:27 *c* inside the inner house
6:27 the wings of the *c*
6:28 he overlaid the *c* with gold
6:29 carvings of *c* and palm-tree
6:32 carvings of *c* and palm-tree
6:32 the gold down upon the *c*
6:35 he carved *c* and palm-tree
7:29 were lions, bulls and *c*
7:36 *c*, lions and palm-tree
8:6 underneath the wings of the *c*
8:7 the *c* were spreading out
8:7 *c* kept the Ark and its poles
2Ki 19:15 sitting upon the *c*
1Ch 13:6 Jehovah, sitting on the *c*
28:18 the *c* of gold for spreading
2Ch 3:7 he engraved *c* upon the walls
3:10 the Most Holy two *c* in the
3:11 As for the wings of the *c*
3:13 wings of these *c* were spread
3:14 and worked in *c* upon it
5:7 underneath the wings of the *c*
5:8 *c* were continually spreading
5:8 *c* covered over the Ark and its
Ps 80:1 who are sitting upon the *c*
99:1 He is sitting upon the *c*
Isa 37:16 sitting upon the *c*, you
Eze 9:3 was taken up from over the *c*
10:1 was over the head of the *c*
10:2 in under the *c*, and fill the
10:2 fire from between the *c* and
10:3 *c* were standing to the right
10:4 to rise up from the *c* to the
10:5 sound of the wings of the *c*
10:6 from between the *c*, that he
10:7 from between the *c* to the
10:7 fire that was between the *c*
10:8 was seen belonging to the *c*
10:9 four wheels beside the *c*
10:15 *c* would rise—it was the
10:16 *c* went, the wheels would
10:16 *c* lifted up their wings to
10:18 to stand still over the *c*
10:19 *c* now lifted up their wings
10:20 to know that they were *c*
11:22 *c* now lifted up their wings
41:18 carved *c* and palm-tree

La 2:11 the fainting away of c and
Eze 9:6 little c and women you should
20:26 every c opening the womb
Joe 3:3 the male c for a prostitute
3:3 female c they sold for wine
Mt 2:8 careful search for the young c
2:9 above where the young c was
2:11 young c with Mary its mother
2:13 the young c and its mother
2:13 for the young c to destroy it
2:14 took along the young c and
2:20 the young c and its mother
2:20 the soul of the young c are
2:21 the young c and its mother
9:2 Take courage, c; your sins are
10:21 a father his c, and children
18:2 calling a young c to him, he
18:4 like this young c is the one
18:5 receives one such young c on
21:28 C, go work today in the
Mr 2:5 C, your sins are forgiven
5:39 young c has not died, but is
5:40 in where the young c was
5:41 the hand of the young c, he
7:30 found the young c laid on the
9:20 threw the c into convulsions
9:24 the father of the young c was
9:36 he took a young c, stood it
10:15 like a young c will by no
12:19 but does not leave a c, his
13:12 a father a c, and children
Lu 1:7 But they had no c, because
1:59 to circumcise the young c
1:66 What . . . will this young c be?
1:76 young c, you will be called a
1:80 the young c went on growing
2:5 at present heavy with c
2:17 concerning this young c
2:27 brought the young c Jesus in
2:38 speaking about the c to all
2:40 the young c continued growing
2:48 C, why did you treat us this
9:47 took a young c, set it beside
9:48 Whoever receives this young c
15:31 C, you have always been with
16:25 Abraham said, C, remember
18:17 like a young c will by no
Joh 4:49 before my young c dies
16:21 brought forth the young c
Ac 7:5 while as yet he had no c
1Co 4:17 beloved and faithful c in the
Php 2:22 like a c with a father he
1Ti 1:2 a genuine c in the faith
1:18 I commit to you, c, Timothy
2Ti 1:2 to Timothy, a beloved c
2:1 my c, keep on acquiring power
Tit 1:4 Titus, a genuine c according
Phm 10 c, to whom I became a father
Heb 11:23 young c was beautiful and
Re 12:4 it might devour her c
12:5 c was caught away to God and
12:13 gave birth to the male c

Childbearing
1Ti 2:15 will be kept safe through c

Childbirth
Ex 1:16 on the stool for c, if it is a
De 2:25 have pains like those of c
32:18 bringing you forth with c
Isa 51:2 you forth with c pains
54:1 you that had no c pains
Jer 48:41 wife having c distress
49:22 wife having distress in c
Ga 4:19 I am again in c pains until
4:27 who does not have c pains

Childhood
Mr 9:21 He said: From c on

Childless
Ge 15:2 I am going c and the one who
Le 20:20 their sin. They should die c
20:21 They should become c
Jer 22:30 Write down this man as c
Lu 20:28 but this one remained c
20:29 first took a wife and died c

Children
Ge 3:16 you will bring forth c, and
16:1 Sarai . . . had borne him no c
16:2 shut me off from bearing c
16:2 Perhaps I may get c from her
20:17 and they began bearing c
21:7 Sarah will . . . suckle c
30:1 say to Jacob: Give me c or
30:3 I, may get c from her
30:26 Give over my wives and my c
31:17 Jacob got up and lifted his c
31:28 a chance to kiss my c and
31:43, 43 the c my c and the flock
31:43 against their c whom they
31:55 Laban . . . kissed his c
32:11 mother together with c
33:1 the c to Leah and to Rachel
33:2 maidservants and their c
33:2 Leah and her c after them
33:5 saw the women and the c and
33:5 The c with whom God has
33:6 they and their c, and bowed
33:7 came forward, and her c, and
33:13 that the c are delicate and
33:14 pace of the c until I shall
34:29 little c and their wives
36:25 the c of Anah: Dishon and
43:8 you and our little c
50:8 little c and their flocks and
50:21 your little c with food
Ex 1:17 preserve the male c alive
1:18 you preserved the male c
2:6 one of the c of the Hebrews
21:4 wife and her c will become
21:22 and her c do come out but no
Le 26:22 bereave you of c and cut off
De 2:34 men and women and little c
3:6 men, women and little c
20:14 the women and the little c
24:16 put to death on account of c
24:16 c should not be put to death
32:5 not his c, the defect is their
Ru 1:5 without her two c and her
1Sa 1:2 And Peninnah came to have c
1:2 but Hannah had no c
15:33 has bereaved women of c, in
15:33 be most bereaved of c among
2Ki 2:24 forty-two c of their number
4:1 take both my c for his slaves
8:12 c you will dash to pieces
1Ch 8:8 became father to c in the
14:4 names of the c that became
Ezr 10:1 men and women and c, for the
Ne 12:43 also the women and the c
Job 3:16 c that have seen no light
21:11 own male c go skipping
Ps 8:2 Out of the mouth of c and
17:14 lay up for their c what they
137:9 Your c against the crag
Isa 2:6 with the c of foreigners they
8:18 I and the c whom Jehovah has
13:16 c will be dashed to pieces
29:23 his c, the work of my hands
47:8 shall not know the loss of c
47:9 loss of c and widowhood
49:21 a woman bereaved of c and
57:4 the c of transgression, the
57:5 slaughtering the c in the
Jer 15:7 certainly bereave them of c
18:21 become women bereaved of c
40:7 little c and some of the
41:16 wives and the little c
43:6 wives and the little c and
50:9 causing bereavement of c
La 1:5 Her own c have walked captive
1:20 sword caused bereavement of c
2:19 account of the soul of your c
2:20 the c born fully formed
4:4 C themselves have asked for
4:10 have boiled their own c
Eze 5:17 they must bereave you of c
14:15 bereaved it of c and it
36:12 bereave . . . of any more c
36:13 bereaving your nations of c
36:14 no more bereave of c
Da 1:4 c in whom there was no defect
1:10 c who are of the same age as
1:13 c who are eating the
1:15 c who were eating the
1:17 c, the four of them, to them
Ho 1:2 and c of fornication, because
9:12 will also bereave them of c
13:16 c will be dashed to pieces
Joe 2:16 Gather c and those sucking
Mic 2:9 From off her c you take my
Na 3:10 c also came to be dashed to
Mt 2:18 Rachel weeping for her c
3:9 to raise up c to Abraham from
7:11 to give good gifts to your c
10:21 and c will rise up against
11:16 like young c sitting in the
14:21 besides women and young c
Mt 15:26 to take the bread of the c
15:38 besides women and young c
18:3 and become as young c, you
18:25 him and his wife and his c
19:13 young c were brought to him
19:14 Let the young c alone, and
19:29 or c or lands for the sake
21:28 A man had two c. Going up
22:24 man dies without having c
23:37 I wanted to gather your c
27:25 come upon us and upon our c
Mr 7:27 First let the c be satisfied
7:27 to take the bread of the c
7:28 the crumbs of the little c
9:37 one of such young c on the
10:13 young c for him to touch
10:14 Let the young c come to me
10:16 took the c into his arms
10:24 C, how difficult a thing it
10:29 mother or father or c or
10:30 and mothers and c and fields
13:12 c . . . against parents
Lu 1:17 the hearts of fathers to c
3:8 God has power to raise up c
7:32 c sitting in a marketplace
7:35 proved righteous by all its c
11:7 young c are with me in bed
11:13 to give good gifts to your c
13:34 I wanted to gather your c
14:26 wife and c and brothers and
18:16 Let the young c come to me
18:29 or parents or c for the sake
19:44 will dash you and your c
20:31 did not leave c behind, but
20:34 c of this system of things
20:36 and they are God's c by being
20:36 being c of the resurrection
23:28 weep . . . for your c
Joh 1:12 authority to become God's c
8:39 If you are Abraham's c, do
11:52 c of God who are scattered
13:33 Little c, I am with you a
21:5 Young c, you do not have
Ac 2:39 and to your c and to all
13:33 fulfilled it to us their c
21:5 with the women and c
21:21 to circumcise their c nor to
Ro 8:16 that we are God's c
8:17 If, then, we are c, we are
8:21 freedom of the c of God
9:7 Abraham's seed are they all c
9:8 the c in the flesh are not
9:8 are not really the c of God
9:8 c by the promise are counted
1Co 4:14 you as my beloved c
7:14 c would really be unclean
14:20 do not become young c in
2Co 6:13 I speak as to c—you, too
12:14 c ought not to lay up for
12:14 the parents for their c
Ga 4:19 my little c, with whom I
4:24 brings forth c for slavery
4:25 she is in slavery with her c
4:27 c of the desolate woman are
4:28 c belonging to the promise
4:31 c, not of a servant girl, but
Eph 2:3 c of wrath even as the rest
5:1 of God, as beloved c
5:8 Go on walking as c of light
6:1 C, be obedient to your parents
6:4 do not be irritating your c
Php 2:15 c of God without a blemish
Col 3:20 You c, be obedient to your
3:21 not be exasperating your c
1Th 2:7 mother cherishes her own c
2:11 as a father does his c, we
1Ti 3:4 having c in subjection with
3:12 presiding . . . over c and
5:4 if any widow has c or
5:10 if she reared c, if she
5:14 widows to marry, to bear c
Tit 1:6 having believing c that were
2:4 to love their c
Heb 2:13 c, whom Jehovah gave me
2:14 young c are sharers of blood
11:12 there were born c just as
12:8 are really illegitimate c
1Pe 1:14 As obedient c, quit being
3:6 And you have become her c
2Pe 2:14 They are accursed c
1Jo 2:1 My little c, I am writing
2:12 I am writing you, little c
2:13 I write you, young c
2:18 Young c, it is the last hour

1Jo 2:28 little *c*, remain in union
3:1 should be called *c* of God
3:2 now we are *c* of God, but as
3:7 Little *c*, let no one mislead
3:10 The *c* of God and the
3:10 *c* of the Devil are evident
3:18 Little *c*, let us love
4:4 originate with God, little *c*
5:2 we are loving the *c* of God
5:21 Little *c*, guard yourselves
2Jo 1 her *c*, whom I truly love
4 your *c* walking in the truth
13 The *c* of your sister, the
3Jo 4 my *c* go on walking in the truth
Re 2:23 her *c* I will kill with

Children's
Ge 31:16 are ours and our *c*. So now

Child's
Ex 2:8 went and called the *c* mother
Jg 13:12 *c* mode of life and his work
2Ki 4:34 the *c* flesh grew warm
Mr 5:40 the young *c* father and mother

Chileab
2Sa 3:3 second was *C* by Abigail the

Chilion
Ru 1:2 two sons were Mahlon and *C*
1:5 Mahlon and *C*, also died, so
4:9 and all that belonged to *C* and

Chilmad
Eze 27:23 and *C* were your traders

Chimham
2Sa 19:37 But here is your servant *C*
19:38 With me *C* will go across
19:40 *C* himself crossed with him
Jer 41:17 lodging place of *C* that

Chin
Le 13:29 on the head or on the *c*
13:30 leprosy . . . of the *c*
14:9 hair on his head and his *c*

Chinnereth
Nu 34:11 eastern slope of the sea of *C*
De 3:17 *C* to the sea of the Arabah
Jos 11:2 desert plains south of *C*
12:3 as far as the sea of *C*
13:27 the sea of *C* on the side of
19:35 Hammath, Rakkath and *C*
1Ki 15:20 *C*, as far as all the land

Chios
Ac 20:15 we arrived opposite *C*, but

Chirp
Isa 29:4 dust your own saying will *c*

Chirping
Isa 8:19 who are *c* and making
10:14 or opening his mouth or *c*
38:14 the bulbul, so I keep *c*

Chisel
Ex 20:25 you do wield your *c* upon it

Chislev
Ne 1:1 month *C*, in the twentieth year
Zec 7:1 ninth month, that is, in *C*

Chislon
Nu 34:21 Elidad the son of *C*

Chisloth-tabor
Jos 19:12 the border of *C* and went

Chitlish
Jos 15:40 Cabbon and Lahmam and *C*

Chloe
1Co 1:11 by those of the house of *C*

Choice
Ge 24:53 he gave *c* things to her
49:11 his own she-ass to a *c* vine
Ex 15:4 the *c* of his warriors have
De 12:11 *c* of your vow offerings
33:13 With the *c* things of heaven
33:14 And with the *c* things, the
33:14 the *c* things, the yield of
33:15 *c* things of the indefinitely
33:16 *c* things of the earth and its
2Sa 6:1 all the *c* men in Israel
10:9 all the *c* men in Israel and
1Ki 12:21 *c* men able-bodied for war
2Ki 3:19 and every *c* city, and every
8:12 their *c* men you will kill
19:23 its *c* juniper trees
1Ch 19:10 of all the *c* men in Israel
2Ch 11:1 *c* men able-bodied for war
21:3 in *c* things along with
25:5 hundred thousand *c* men going
32:23 *c* things to Hezekiah the
Ezr 1:6 animals and with *c* things
Pr 8:10 knowledge rather than *c* gold
8:19 and my produce than *c* silver
10:20 righteous one is *c* silver
Ca 5:15 Lebanon, *c* like the cedars
Isa 5:2 plant it with a *c* red vine
37:24 its *c* juniper trees
48:10 have made *c* of you in the
Jer 2:21 planted you as a *c* red vine
Ac 15:7 God made the *c* among you that

Choicest
Ge 23:6 *c* of our burial places bury
Ex 30:23 to yourself the *c* perfumes
De 33:15 the *c* from the mountains of
1Sa 15:21 sheep and cattle, the *c* of
Job 22:25 And silver, the *c*, to you
Ca 4:13 with the *c* fruits, henna
4:16 garden and eat its *c* fruits
7:13 are all sorts of the *c* fruits
Isa 22:7 *c* of your low plains must
Jer 22:7 the *c* of your cedars
48:15 *c* young men themselves have
Eze 23:7 the *c* sons of Assyria
24:4 even with the *c* bones
24:5 a taking of the *c* sheep
31:16 *c* and the best of Lebanon
48:14 *c* of the land to pass away
Am 6:6 the *c* oils do their anointing

Choir
Ne 12:38 thanksgiving *c* was walking

Choirs
Ne 12:31 *c* and processions
12:40 the two thanksgiving *c* came

Choke
Mt 13:22 riches *c* the word, and
18:28 he began to *c* him, saying
Mr 4:19 make inroads and *c* the word

Choked
Mt 13:7 thorns came up and *c* them
Mr 4:7 the thorns came up and *c* it
Lu 8:7 the thorns . . . *c* it off
8:14 they are completely *c* and

Choose
Ex 17:9 *C* men for us and go out
18:25 to *c* capable men out of all
Nu 16:5 whoever he may *c* will come
16:7 the man whom Jehovah will *c*
17:5 man whom I shall *c*, his rod
35:11 must *c* cities convenient for
De 12:5 *c* out of all your tribes
12:11 *c* to have his name reside
12:14 place that Jehovah will *c*
12:18 Jehovah your God will *c*
12:21 God will *c* to put his name
12:26 place that Jehovah will *c*
14:23 he will *c* to have his name
14:24 God will *c* to place his name
14:25 Jehovah your God will *c*
15:20 place that Jehovah will *c*
16:2 *c* to have his name reside
16:6 *c* to have his name reside
16:7 Jehovah your God will *c*
16:11 *c* to have his name reside
16:15 place that Jehovah will *c*
16:16 in the place that he will *c*
17:8 Jehovah your God will *c*
17:10 place which Jehovah will *c*
17:15 Jehovah your God will *c*
18:6 the place that Jehovah will *c*
23:16 in whatever place he may *c*
26:2 *c* to have his name reside
30:19 must *c* life in order that
31:11 in the place that he will *c*
Jos 8:3 to *c* thirty thousand men
9:27 the place that he should *c*
24:15 *c* for yourselves today
Jg 5:8 They proceeded to *c* new gods
1Sa 13:2 Saul proceeded to *c* for
17:8 *C* a man for yourselves, and
17:40 *c* . . . five smoothest stones
2Sa 15:15 my lord the king may *c*
17:1 *c*, please, twelve thousand
19:38 all that you may *c* to lay
24:12 *C* for yourself one of them
1Ki 8:16 *c* David to come to be over
18:23 *c* for themselves one young
18:25 *C* for yourselves one young
1Ch 21:10 *C* for yourself one of them
2Ch 6:6 *c* Jerusalem for my name to
6:6 I shall *c* David to come to be
7:16 *c* and sanctify this house
Job 9:14 I will *c* my words with him
15:5 you *c* the tongue of shrewd
29:25 I would *c* the way for them
34:4 Judgment let us *c* for
34:33 you yourself *c*, and not I
Ps 25:12 in the way that he will *c*
47:4 will *c* for us our inheritance
65:4 Happy is the one you *c* and
78:67 of Ephraim he did not *c*
Pr 1:29 of Jehovah they did not *c*
3:31 nor *c* any of his ways
Isa 7:15 reject the bad and *c* the good
7:16 reject the bad and *c* the good
14:1 yet certain to *c* Israel
58:5 Should the fast that I *c*
58:6 Is not this the fast that I *c*?
66:4 *c* ways of ill-treating them
Zec 1:17 yet actually *c* Jerusalem
2:12 and he must yet *c* Jerusalem
Joh 15:16 You did not *c* me, but I
Ac 26:16 to *c* you as an attendant

Chooses
Job 7:15 my soul *c* suffocation, Death
Isa 40:20 that is not rotten, he *c*
41:24 thing is anyone that *c* you
49:7 Holy One of Israel, who *c*

Choosing
1Sa 2:28 a *c* of him out of all the
20:30 *c* the son of Jesse to your
Eze 20:5 In the day of my *c* Israel, I
Zec 3:2 he who is *c* Jerusalem
Lu 14:7 *c* the most prominent places
Ac 15:25 favored *c* men to send to you
Ro 9:11 of God respecting the *c*
11:5 *c* due to undeserved kindness
11:28 reference to God's *c* they
1Th 1:4 loved by God, his *c* of you
Heb 11:25 *c* to be ill-treated with
2Pe 1:10 calling and *c* of you sure

Chop
1Sa 2:31 *c* off your arm and the arm
Da 4:14 *C* the tree down, and cut off
4:23 *C* the tree down, and ruin it

Chopped
Jg 21:6 one tribe has been *c* off from

Chopping
Isa 10:15 over the one *c* with it, or

Chorazin
Mt 11:21 Woe to you, *C*! Woe to you
Lu 10:13 Woe to you, *C*! Woe to you

Chose
Ge 6:2 namely, all whom they *c*
13:11 Lot *c* for himself the whole
De 4:37 he *c* their seed after them
7:7 so that he *c* you, for you were
10:15 he *c* their offspring after
2Sa 6:21 Jehovah, who *c* me rather
10:9 *c* some of all the choice men
1Ki 11:34 David my servant whom I *c*
1Ch 19:10 *c* some of all the choice
28:4 *c* me out of all the house of
28:4 Judah that he *c* as leader
28:5 *c* Solomon my son to sit upon
Ne 9:7 *c* Abram and brought him out of
Ps 78:68 *c* the tribe of Judah, Mount
78:70 so he *c* David his servant
Isa 65:12 I took no delight you *c*
66:4 I took no delight they *c*
Mt 12:18 Look! My servant whom I *c*
Lu 6:13 and *c* from among them twelve
10:42 Mary *c* the good portion, and
Joh 6:70 I *c* you twelve, did I not?
15:16 I *c* you, and I appointed
Ac 1:2 to the apostles whom he *c*
13:17 God . . . *c* our forefathers
1Co 1:27 God *c* the foolish things of
1:27 God *c* the weak things of the
1:28 God *c* the ignoble things of
Eph 1:4 he *c* us in union with him
Jas 2:5 God *c* the ones who are poor

Chosen
Ex 14:7 to take six hundred *c* chariots
De 7:6 God has *c* to become his people
14:2 Jehovah has *c* you to become
18:5 *c* out of all your tribes
21:5 God has *c* to minister to him

Jos 24:22 you . . . have *c* Jehovah
Jg 10:14 to the gods whom you have *c*
20:15 seven hundred *c* men were
20:16 were seven hundred *c* men
20:34 ten thousand *c* men out of
1Sa 8:18 king, whom you have *c* for
10:24 the one whom Jehovah has *c*
12:13 the king whom you have *c*
16:8 Neither has Jehovah *c* this
16:9 Neither has Jehovah *c* this
16:10 Jehovah has not *c* these
24:2 three thousand *c* men out of
26:2 the *c* ones of Israel, to
2Sa 16:18 the one whom Jehovah has *c*
21:6 Saul, the *c* one of Jehovah
1Ki 3:8 people whom you have *c*
8:16 I have not *c* a city out of
8:44 the city that you have *c*
8:48 the city that you have *c* and
11:13 Jerusalem which I have *c*
11:32 the city that I have *c* out
11:36 the city that I have *c* for
14:21 the city that Jehovah had *c*
2Ki 21:7 *c* out of all the tribes of
23:27 this city that I have *c*
1Ch 15:2 has *c* to carry the ark of
16:13 sons of Jacob, his *c* ones
28:6 for I have *c* him as my son
28:10 Jehovah himself has *c* you
29:1 the one whom God has *c*, is
2Ch 6:5 I have not *c* a city out of all
6:5 not *c* a man to become leader
6:34 city that you have *c* and the
6:38 city that you have *c* and the
7:12 *c* this place for myself as
12:13 city that Jehovah had *c* out
13:3 mighty men of war, *c* men
13:3 eight hundred thousand *c* men
13:17 five hundred thousand *c* men
29:11 Jehovah has *c* to stand
33:7 Jerusalem, which I have *c*
Ne 1:9 place that I have *c* to have my
Job 36:21 this you have *c* rather than
Ps 33:12 The people whom he has *c* as
84:10 *c* to stand at the threshold
89:3 covenant toward my *c* one
89:19 exalted a *c* one from among
105:6 sons of Jacob, his *c* ones
105:26 Aaron whom he had *c*
105:43 *c* ones even with a joyful
106:5 goodness to your *c* ones
106:23 been for Moses his *c* one
119:30 faithfulness I have *c*
119:173 your orders I have *c*
132:13 For Jehovah has *c* Zion
135:4 Jah has *c* even Jacob for
Pr 16:16 understanding is to be *c*
22:1 A name is to be *c* rather than
Isa 1:29 the gardens that you have *c*
41:8 O Jacob, whom I have *c*
41:9 my servant; I have *c* you
42:1 My *c* one, whom my soul has
43:10 my servant whom I have *c*
43:20 my people, my *c* one, to
44:1 you, O Israel, whom I have *c*
44:2 Jeshurun, whom I have *c*
45:4 and of Israel my *c* one
56:4 *c* what I have delighted in
65:9 *c* ones must take possession
65:15 for an oath by my *c* ones
65:22 *c* ones will use to the full
65:23 the *c* ones of Jehovah, and
66:3 that have *c* their own ways
Jer 8:3 death will certainly be *c*
33:24 families whom Jehovah has *c*
49:19 who is *c* I shall appoint
50:44 who is *c* I shall appoint
Hag 2:23 are the one whom I have *c*
Mt 22:14 are many invited, but few *c*
24:22 but on account of the *c* ones
24:24 mislead . . . even the *c* ones
24:31 gather his *c* ones together
Mr 13:20 on account of the *c* ones
13:20 ones whom he has *c* he has
13:22 lead astray . . . the *c* ones
13:27 gather his *c* ones together
Lu 9:35 Son, the one that has been *c*
18:7 for his *c* ones who cry out to
23:35 the Christ of God, the *C* One
Joh 13:18 I know the ones I have *c*
15:19 *c* you out of the world, on
Ac 1:24 of these two men you have *c*
9:15 *c* vessel to me to bear my
15:22 favored sending *c* men from
Ac 22:14 God . . . has *c* you to come to
Ro 8:33 accusation against God's *c*
11:7 but the ones *c* obtained it
16:13 Rufus the *c* one in the Lord
Col 3:12 God's *c* ones, holy and loved
1Ti 5:21 Christ Jesus and the *c* angels
2Ti 2:10 for the sake of the *c* ones
Tit 1:1 the faith of God's *c* ones and
1Pe 1:1 and Bithynia, to the ones *c*
2:4 but *c*, precious, with God
2:6 laying in Zion a stone, *c*, a
2:9 a *c* race, a royal priesthood
5:13 a *c* one like you, sends you
2Jo 1 The older man to the *c* lady
13 your sister, the *c* one, send
Re 17:14 *c* and faithful with him

Christ

Mt 1:1 Jesus *C*, son of David, son of
1:16 Jesus . . . who is called *C*
1:17 until the *C* fourteen
1:18 birth of Jesus *C* was in this
2:4 where the *C* was to be born
11:2 about the works of the *C*
16:16 You are the *C*, the Son of
16:20 not to say . . . he was the *C*
16:21 Jesus *C* commenced showing
22:42 the *C*? Whose son is he?
23:10 your Leader is one, the *C*
24:5 saying, I am the *C*, and will
24:23 Here is the *C*, or, There! do
26:63 whether you are the *C* the
26:68 Prophesy to us, you *C*
27:17 or Jesus the so-called *C*
27:22 with Jesus the so-called *C*
Mr 1:1 of the good news about Jesus *C*
1:34 demons . . . knew him to be *C*
8:29 said to him: You are the *C*
9:41 that you belong to *C*, I truly
12:35 that the *C* is David's son
13:21 See! Here is the *C*, See!
14:61 Are you the *C* the Son of the
15:32 the *C* the King of Israel now
Lu 2:11 a Savior, who is *C* the Lord
2:26 he had seen the *C* of Jehovah
3:15 May he perhaps be the *C*?
4:41 they knew him to be the *C*
9:20 said in reply: The *C* of God
20:41 that the *C* is David's son
22:67 If you are the *C*, tell us
23:2 saying he himself is *C* a king
23:35 if this one is the *C* of God
23:39 You are the *C*, are you not?
24:26 the *C* to suffer these things
24:46 the *C* would suffer and rise
Joh 1:17 came to be through Jesus *C*
1:20 confessed: I am not the *C*
1:25 not the *C* or Elijah or The
1:41 Messiah . . . translated, *C*
3:28 I am not the *C*, but, I have
4:25 coming, who is called *C*
4:29 This is not perhaps the *C*
7:26 certainty that this is the *C*
7:27 *C* comes, no one is to know
7:31 When the *C* arrives, he will
7:41 were saying: This is the *C*
7:41 *C* is not actually coming out
7:42 the *C* is coming from the
9:22 if anyone confessed him as *C*
10:24 If you are the *C*, tell us
11:27 you are the *C* the Son of God
12:34 that the *C* remains forever
17:3 whom you sent forth, Jesus *C*
20:31 Jesus is the *C* the Son of
Ac 2:31 resurrection of the *C*, that
2:36 both Lord and *C*, this Jesus
2:38 *C* for forgiveness of your
3:6 name of Jesus *C* the Nazarene
3:18 that his *C* would suffer
3:20 the *C* appointed for you, Jesus
4:10 name of Jesus *C* the Nazarene
5:42 good news about the *C*, Jesus
8:5 began to preach the *C* to them
8:12 and of the name of Jesus *C*
9:22 logically that this is the *C*
9:34 Aeneas, Jesus *C* heals you
10:36 of peace through Jesus *C*
10:48 in the name of Jesus *C*
11:17 upon the Lord Jesus *C*
15:26 the name of our Lord Jesus *C*
16:18 in the name of Jesus *C* to
17:3 necessary for the *C* to suffer
17:3 This is the *C*, this Jesus
18:5 to prove that Jesus is the *C*
Ac 18:28 that Jesus was the *C*
24:24 on the belief in *C* Jesus
26:23 *C* was to suffer and, as the
28:31 concerning the Lord Jesus *C*
Ro 1:1 Paul, a slave of Jesus *C* and
1:4 from the dead—yes, Jesus *C*
1:6 called to belong to Jesus *C*
1:7 Father and the Lord Jesus *C*
1:8 to my God through Jesus *C*
2:16 God through *C* Jesus judges
3:22 through the faith in Jesus *C*
3:24 the ransom paid by *C* Jesus
5:1 God through our Lord Jesus *C*
5:6 *C*, while we were yet weak
5:8 yet sinners, *C* died for us
5:11 God through our Lord Jesus *C*
5:15 by the one man Jesus *C*
5:17 the one person, Jesus *C*
5:21 life in view through Jesus *C*
6:3 who were baptized into *C* Jesus
6:4 *C* was raised up from the dead
6:8 if we have died with *C*, we
6:9 *C*, now that he has been raised
6:11 reference to God by *C* Jesus
6:23 everlasting life by *C* Jesus
7:4 through the body of the *C*
7:25 Thanks to God through Jesus *C*
8:1 those in union with *C* Jesus
8:2 life in union with *C* Jesus
8:10 if *C* is in union with you
8:11 raised up *C* Jesus from the
8:17 but joint heirs with *C*
8:34 *C* Jesus is the one who died
8:35 us from the love of the *C*
8:39 God's love that is in *C* Jesus
9:1 I am telling the truth in *C*
9:3 from the *C* in behalf of my
9:5 and from whom *C* sprang
10:4 *C* is the end of the Law, so
10:6 that is, to bring *C* down
10:7 to bring *C* up from the dead
10:17 is through the word about *C*
12:5 one body in union with *C*
13:14 put on the Lord Jesus *C*
14:9 to this end *C* died and came
14:15 that one for whom *C* died
14:18 slaves for *C* is acceptable
15:3 *C* did not please himself
15:5 same mental attitude that *C*
15:6 Father of our Lord Jesus *C*
15:7 the *C* also welcomed us, with
15:8 *C* actually became a minister
15:16 a public servant of *C* Jesus
15:17 exulting in *C* Jesus when it
15:18 those things which *C* worked
15:19 the good news about the *C*
15:20 where *C* had already been
15:29 measure of blessing from *C*
15:30 through our Lord Jesus *C* and
16:3 my fellow workers in *C* Jesus
16:5 is a firstfruits of Asia for *C*
16:7 in union with *C* longer than I
16:9 our fellow worker in *C*, and
16:10 the approved one in *C*
16:16 congregations of the *C* greet
16:18 are slaves, not of our Lord *C*
16:25 and the preaching of Jesus *C*
16:27 be the glory through Jesus *C*
1Co 1:1 to be an apostle of Jesus *C*
1:2 union with *C* Jesus, called
1:2 name of our Lord, Jesus *C*
1:3 Father and the Lord Jesus *C*
1:4 given to you in *C* Jesus
1:6 the witness about the *C* has
1:7 revelation of . . . Jesus *C*
1:8 the day of our Lord Jesus *C*
1:9 with his Son Jesus *C* our Lord
1:10 the name of our Lord Jesus *C*
1:12 I to Cephas, But I to *C*
1:13 The *C* exists divided. Paul
1:17 *C* dispatched me, not to go
1:17 the torture stake of the *C*
1:23 but we preach *C* impaled, to
1:24 *C* the power of God and the
1:30 are in union with *C* Jesus
2:2 Jesus *C*, and him impaled
2:16 but we do have the mind of *C*
3:1 fleshly men, as to babes in *C*
3:11 foundation . . . is Jesus *C*
3:23, 23 belong to *C*; *C* in turn
4:1 subordinates of *C* and
4:10 We are fools because of *C*
4:10 but you are discreet in *C*
4:15 ten thousand tutors in *C*, you

1Co 4:15 in *C* Jesus I have become
4:17 methods in connection with *C*
5:7 *C* our passover . . . sacrificed
6:11 name of our Lord Jesus *C* and
6:15 your bodies are members of *C*
6:15 take the members of the *C*
7:22 a free man is a slave of *C*
8:6 and there is one Lord, Jesus *C*
8:11 for whose sake *C* died
8:12 you are sinning against *C*
9:12 to the good news about the *C*
9:21 but under law toward *C*, that
10:4 that rock-mass meant the *C*
10:16 in the blood of the *C*
10:16 sharing in the body of the *C*
11:1 even as I am of *C*
11:3 head of every man is the *C*
11:3 the head of the *C* is God
12:12 one body, so also is the *C*
15:3 *C* died for our sins according
15:12 if *C* is being preached that
15:13 neither has *C* been raised
15:14 if *C* has not been raised
15:15 he raised up the *C*, but
15:16 neither has *C* been raised
15:17 if *C* has not been raised up
15:18 in death in union with *C*
15:19 we have hoped in *C*, we are
15:20 now *C* has been raised up
15:22 in the *C* all will be made
15:23 *C* the firstfruits
15:23 those who belong to the *C*
15:31 I have in *C* Jesus our Lord
15:57 through our Lord Jesus *C*
16:24 all of you in union with *C*
2Co 1:1 Paul, an apostle of *C* Jesus
1:2 and the Lord Jesus *C*
1:3 Father of our Lord Jesus *C*
1:5 sufferings for the *C* abound in
1:5 also abounds through the *C*
1:19 *C* Jesus, who was preached
1:21 that you and we belong to *C*
2:12 the good news about the *C*
2:14 in company with the *C* and
2:15 are a sweet odor of *C* among
2:17 in company with *C*, we are
3:3 a letter of *C* written by us
3:4 through the *C* we have this
3:14 done away with by . . . *C*
4:4 good news about the *C*, who
4:5 preaching . . . *C* Jesus as Lord
4:6 of God by the face of *C*
5:10 the judgment seat of the *C*
5:14 love the *C* has compels us
5:16 *C* according to the flesh
5:17 in union with *C*, he is a new
5:18 reconciled us . . . through *C*
5:19 by means of *C* reconciling
5:20 substituting for *C*, as
5:20 As substitutes for *C* we beg
6:15 harmony is there between *C*
8:9 kindness of our Lord Jesus *C*
8:23 our brothers . . . a glory of *C*
9:13 to the good news about the *C*
10:1 and kindness of the *C*, lowly
10:5 to make it obedient to the *C*
10:7 that he belongs to *C*, let
10:7 just as he belongs to *C*, so
10:14 the good news about the *C*
11:2 as a chaste virgin to the *C*
11:3 chastity that are due the *C*
11:10 It is a truth of *C* in my
11:13 into apostles of *C*
11:23 Are they ministers of *C?*
12:2 man in union with *C* who
12:9 power of the *C* may like a
12:10 and difficulties, for *C*
12:19 in connection with *C*
13:3 proof of *C* speaking in me
13:3 *C* who is not weak toward
13:5 Jesus *C* is in union with you
13:14 kindness of the Lord Jesus *C*
Ga 1:1 through Jesus *C* and God the
1:3 Father and the Lord Jesus *C*
1:7 the good news about the *C*
1:12 revelation by Jesus *C*
1:22 that were in union with *C*
2:4 we have in union with *C* Jesus
2:16 through faith toward *C* Jesus
2:16 have put our faith in *C* Jesus
2:16 due to faith toward *C*, and
2:17 righteous by means of *C*, have
2:17 is *C* . . . sin's minister?
2:20 I am impaled along with *C*
Ga 2:20 is *C* that is living in union
2:21 *C* actually died for nothing
3:1 before whose eyes Jesus *C* was
3:13 *C* by purchase released us
3:14 by means of Jesus *C* for the
3:16 And to your seed, who is *C*
3:22 from faith toward Jesus *C*
3:24 our tutor leading to *C*
3:26 through your faith in *C* Jesus
3:27 who were baptized into *C*
3:27 have put on *C*
3:28 one person in union with *C*
3:29 if you belong to *C*, you are
4:14 angel of God, like *C* Jesus
4:19 until *C* is formed in you
5:1 For such freedom *C* set us free
5:2 *C* will be of no benefit to you
5:4 You are parted from *C*
5:6 as regards *C* Jesus neither
5:24 those who belong to *C* Jesus
6:2 thus fulfill the law of the *C*
6:12 torture stake of the *C*, Jesus
6:14 *C*, through whom the world
6:18 kindness of our Lord Jesus *C*
Eph 1:1 Paul, an apostle of *C* Jesus
1:1 ones in union with *C* Jesus
1:2 Father and the Lord Jesus *C*
1:3 Father of our Lord Jesus *C*
1:3 places in union with *C*
1:5 adoption through Jesus *C* as
1:10 together again in the *C*, the
1:12 been first to hope in the *C*
1:17 God of our Lord Jesus *C*, the
1:20 operated in the case of the *C*
2:5 alive together with the *C*
2:6 in union with *C* Jesus
2:7 toward us in union with *C*
2:10 created in union with *C*
2:12 without *C*, alienated from
2:13 now in union with *C* Jesus
2:13 be near by the blood of the *C*
2:20 *C* Jesus himself is the
3:1 Paul, the prisoner of *C* Jesus
3:4 in the sacred secret of the *C*
3:6 in union with *C* Jesus through
3:8 unfathomable riches of the *C*
3:11 in connection with the *C*
3:17 to have the *C* dwell through
3:19 to know the love of the *C*
3:21 by means of *C* Jesus to all
4:7 *C* measured out the free gift
4:12 building . . . body of the *C*
4:13 to the fullness of the *C*
4:15 him who is the head, *C*
4:20 did not learn the *C* to be so
4:32 God also by *C* freely forgave
5:2 just as the *C* also loved you
5:5 kingdom of the *C* and of God
5:14 the *C* will shine upon you
5:20 name of our Lord Jesus *C*
5:21 to one another in fear of *C*
5:23 as the *C* also is head of the
5:24 is in subjection to the *C*
5:25 *C* also loved the congregation
5:29 *C* also does the congregation
5:32 speaking with respect to *C*
6:5 be obedient . . . as to the *C*
6:23 Father and the Lord Jesus *C*
6:24 those loving our Lord Jesus *C*
Php 1:1 slaves of *C* Jesus, to all
1:1 holy ones in union with *C*
1:2 Father and the Lord Jesus *C*
1:6 until the day of Jesus *C*
1:8 tender affection as *C* Jesus
1:10 up to the day of *C*
1:11 which is through Jesus *C*
1:13 in association with *C* among
1:15 preaching the *C* through envy
1:16 publicizing the *C* out of love
1:18 *C* is being publicized, and
1:19 of the spirit of Jesus *C*
1:20 *C* will . . . be magnified by
1:21 For in my case to live is *C*
1:23 and the being with *C*, for
1:26 overflow in *C* Jesus by
1:27 the good news about the *C*
1:29 was given in behalf of *C*
2:1 is any encouragement in *C*
2:5 that was also in *C* Jesus
2:11 Jesus *C* is Lord to the glory
2:21 interests, not those of *C*
3:3 have our boasting in *C* Jesus
3:7 loss on account of the *C*
3:8 knowledge of *C* Jesus my Lord
Php 3:8 that I may gain *C*
3:9 which is through faith in *C*
3:12 laid hold on by *C* Jesus
3:14 of God by means of *C* Jesus
3:18 of the torture stake of the *C*
3:20 a savior, the Lord Jesus *C*
4:7 by means of *C* Jesus
4:19 in glory by means of *C* Jesus
4:21 holy one in union with *C*
4:23 the Lord Jesus *C* be with the
Col 1:1 Paul, an apostle of *C* Jesus
1:2 in union with *C* at Colossae
1:3 the Father of our Lord Jesus *C*
1:4 faith in connection with *C*
1:7 faithful minister of the *C*
1:24 tribulations of the *C* in my
1:27 It is *C* in union with you
1:28 complete in union with *C*
2:2 secret of God, namely, *C*
2:5 of your faith toward *C*
2:6 as you have accepted *C* Jesus
2:8 and not according to *C*
2:11 that belongs to the *C*
2:17 the reality belongs to the *C*
2:20 If you died together with *C*
3:1 you were raised up with the *C*
3:1 where the *C* is seated at the
3:3 hidden with the *C* in union
3:4 When the *C*, our life, is made
3:11 *C* is all things and in all
3:15 let the peace of the *C*
3:16 the word of the *C* reside in
3:24 Slave for the Master, *C*
4:3 the sacred secret about the *C*
4:12 a slave of *C* Jesus, sends
1Th 1:1 and the Lord Jesus *C*
1:3 hope in our Lord Jesus *C*
2:6 burden as apostles of *C*
2:14 in union with *C* Jesus
3:2 the good news about the *C*
4:16 dead in union with *C* will
5:9 salvation through . . . Jesus *C*
5:18 in union with *C* Jesus
5:23 presence of our Lord Jesus *C*
5:28 our Lord Jesus *C* be with you
2Th 1:1 and the Lord Jesus *C*
1:2 and the Lord Jesus *C*
1:12 and of the Lord Jesus *C*
2:1 presence of our Lord Jesus *C*
2:14 glory of our Lord Jesus *C*
2:16 may our Lord Jesus *C* himself
3:5 into the endurance for the *C*
3:6 the name of the Lord Jesus *C*
3:12 in the Lord Jesus *C* that by
3:18 Jesus *C* be with all of you
1Ti 1:1 Paul, an apostle of *C* Jesus
1:1 and of *C* Jesus, our hope
1:2 and *C* Jesus our Lord
1:12 grateful to *C* Jesus our Lord
1:14 in connection with *C* Jesus
1:15 *C* Jesus came into the world
1:16 *C* Jesus might demonstrate
2:5 a man, *C* Jesus
3:13 faith in connection with *C*
4:6 a fine minister of *C* Jesus
5:11 come between them and the *C*
5:21 before God and *C* Jesus and
6:3 those of our Lord Jesus *C*
6:13 *C* Jesus, who as a witness
6:14 of our Lord Jesus *C*
2Ti 1:1 Paul, an apostle of *C* Jesus
1:1 that is in union with *C* Jesus
1:2 from God the Father and *C*
1:9 in connection with *C* Jesus
1:10 our Savior, *C* Jesus, who has
1:13 in connection with *C* Jesus
2:1 in connection with *C* Jesus
2:3 As a fine soldier of *C* Jesus
2:8 *C* was raised up from the dead
2:10 is in union with *C* Jesus
3:12 in association with *C* Jesus
3:15 faith in connection with *C*
4:1 before God and *C* Jesus, who
Tit 1:1 Paul . . . apostle of Jesus *C*
1:4 and *C* Jesus our Savior
2:13 the Savior of us, *C* Jesus
3:6 through Jesus *C* our Savior
Phm 1 prisoner for the sake of *C*
3 peace from . . . Lord Jesus *C*
6 as related to *C*
8 speech in connection with *C* to
9 a prisoner for the sake of *C*
20 in connection with *C*
23 captive in union with *C*

Phm 25 the Lord Jesus C be with the
Heb 3:6 C was faithful as a Son over
3:14 partakers of the C only if
5:5 C did not glorify himself by
5:7 C offered up supplications and
6:1 primary doctrine about the C
9:11 C came as a high priest of
9:14 the blood of the C, who
9:24 C entered, not into a holy
9:28 C was offered once for all
10:10 body of Jesus C once for
11:26 reproach of the C as riches
13:8 C is the same yesterday and
13:21 in us through Jesus C that
Jas 1:1 God and of the Lord Jesus C
2:1 faith of our Lord Jesus C
1Pe 1:1 Peter, an apostle of Jesus C
1:2 with the blood of Jesus C
1:3 Father of our Lord Jesus C
1:3 the resurrection of Jesus C
1:7 at the revelation of Jesus C
1:11 was indicating concerning C
1:11 about the sufferings for C
1:13 at the revelation of Jesus C
2:5 to God through Jesus C
2:21 even C suffered for you
3:15 sanctify the C as Lord in
3:16 conduct in connection with C
3:18 C died once for all time
3:21 the resurrection of Jesus C
4:1 since C suffered in the flesh
4:11 glorified through Jesus C
4:13 in the sufferings of the C
4:14 for the name of C, you are
5:1 of the sufferings of the C
5:10 glory in union with C
5:14 in union with C have peace
2Pe 1:1 apostle of Jesus C, to those
1:1 and the Savior Jesus C
1:8 knowledge of our Lord Jesus C
1:11 kingdom of . . . Jesus C
1:14 Jesus C signified to me
1:16 presence of our Lord Jesus C
2:20 the Lord and Savior Jesus C
3:18 our Lord and Savior Jesus C
1Jo 1:3 and with his Son Jesus C
2:1 Jesus C, a righteous one
2:22 denies that Jesus is the C
3:23 the name of his Son Jesus C
4:2 C as having come in the flesh
4:15 Jesus C is the Son of God
5:1 believing that Jesus is the C
5:6 water and blood, Jesus C
5:20 by means of his Son Jesus C
2Jo 3 Jesus C the Son of the Father
7 Jesus C as coming in the flesh
9 remain in the teaching of the C
Jude 1 Jude, a slave of Jesus C, but
1 and preserved for Jesus C
4 only Owner and Lord, Jesus C
17 apostles of our Lord Jesus C
21 mercy of our Lord Jesus C
25 through Jesus C our Lord
Re 1:1 revelation by Jesus C, which
1:2 to the witness Jesus C gave
1:5 Jesus C, the Faithful Witness
11:15 of our Lord and of his C
12:10 and the authority of his C
20:4 ruled as kings with the C
20:6 priests of God and of the C
22:21 C be with the holy ones

Christian
Ac 26:28 persuade me to become a C
1Pe 4:16 if he suffers as a C, let

Christians
Ac 11:26 by divine providence called C

Christ's
Ro 8:9 anyone does not have C spirit
1Co 12:27 Now you are C body, and
2Co 2:10 for your sakes in C sight
Ga 1:6 with C undeserved kindness
1:10 I would not be C slave
Eph 6:6 as C slaves, doing the will
Php 2:16 cause for exultation in C day
1Pe 1:19 spotless lamb, even C

Christs
Mt 24:24 false C and false prophets
Mr 13:22 false C and false prophets

Chronic
Le 13:11 it is c leprosy in the skin
Jer 15:18 my pain become c and my
30:12 Your stroke is c

Chrysolite
Ex 28:20 fourth row is c and onyx and
39:13 fourth row was c and onyx
Ca 5:14 of gold, filled with c
Eze 1:16 it was like the glow of c
10:9 like the glow of a c stone
28:13 c, onyx and jade; sapphire
Da 10:6 his body was like c, and his
Re 21:20 the seventh c, the eighth

Chrysoprase
Re 21:20 the tenth c, the eleventh

Chub
Eze 30:5 all the mixed company and C

Churning
Pr 30:33 the c of milk is what brings

Chuza
Lu 8:3 C, Herod's man in charge, and

Cilicia
Ac 6:9 C and Asia, to dispute with
15:23 in Antioch and Syria and C
15:41 he went through Syria and C
21:39 a Jew, of Tarsus in C, a
22:3 am a Jew, born in Tarsus of C
23:34 that he was from C
27:5 open sea along C and
Ga 1:21 the regions of Syria and of C

Cinnamon
Ex 30:23 sweet c in half that amount
Pr 7:17 bed with myrrh, aloes and c
Ca 4:14 cane and c, along with all
Re 18:13 also c and Indian spice and

Circle
Jg 21:21 out to dance in c dances
1Ki 7:23 thirty cubits to c all around
2Ch 4:2 line of thirty cubits to c all
Job 26:10 described a c upon the face
Ps 87:7 well as dancers of c dances
150:4 tambourine and the c dance
Pr 8:27 c upon the face of the watery
Isa 40:22 above the c of the earth
Eze 24:5 stack the logs in a c under
Mr 3:34 sitting around him in a c

Circlets
Ca 1:11 C of gold we shall make for

Circling
Ec 1:6 and it is c around to the north
1:6 and round it is continually c

Circlings
Ec 1:6 to its c the wind is returning

Circuit
1Sa 7:16 c of Bethel and Gilgal and
Job 1:5 days had gone round the c
Ps 19:6 its finished c is to their
Mt 10:23 c of the cities of Israel
Mr 6:6 about to the villages in a c
Ro 15:19 in a c as far as Illyricum

Circular
2Sa 8:7 David took the c shields of
1Ki 7:23 molten sea . . . c all around
7:35 a stand . . . c all around
2Ki 11:10 and the c shields that had
1Ch 18:7 took the c shields of gold
2Ch 4:2 molten sea . . . c all around
23:9 c shields that had belonged
Ca 4:4 c shields of the mighty men
Jer 51:11 Fill the c shields, O men
Eze 27:11 Their c shields they hung up
Zec 5:7 c lid of lead was lifted up

Circulate
Nu 36:7 no inheritance . . . should c
36:9 no inheritance should c from
1Sa 2:24 people . . . are causing to c

Circumcise
Ge 21:4 Abraham proceeded to c Isaac
Ex 12:44 any slave man . . . you must c
De 10:16 c the foreskin of your hearts
30:6 to c your heart and the heart
Jos 5:2 and c the sons of Israel again
Lu 1:59 came to c the young child
Joh 7:22 and you c a man on a sabbath
Ac 15:5 It is necessary to c them and
21:21 neither to c their children

Circumcised
Ge 17:10 male of yours must get c
17:11 you must get c in the flesh
17:12 eight days old must be c
17:13 must without fail get c
17:14 c, even that soul must be
17:24 the flesh of his foreskin c
17:25 the flesh of his foreskin c
17:26 day Abraham got c, and also
17:27 the men . . . got c with him
34:15 male of yours getting c
34:17 not listen to us to get c
34:22 every male of ours gets c
34:22 just the way they are c
34:24 and all the males got c, all
Le 12:3 his foreskin will be c
Jos 5:3 and c the sons of Israel at
5:5 proved to be c, but all the
5:5 they had not c
5:7 These Joshua c, because they
5:7 had not c them on the road
Jer 4:4 Get yourselves c to Jehovah
9:25 accounting with everyone c
Ac 7:8 Isaac and c him on the eighth
10:45 of those c were amazed
11:3 house of men that were not c
15:1 Unless you get c according to
16:3 and c him because of the Jews
Ro 3:30 declare c people righteous
4:9 come upon c people or also
4:12 father of c offspring, not
15:8 minister of those who are c
1Co 7:18 Was any man called c?
7:18 Let him not get c
Ga 2:3 not . . . compelled to be c
2:7 had it for those who are c
2:8 apostleship to those who are c
2:9 but they to those who are c
2:12 fear of those of the c class
5:2 if you become c, Christ will
5:3 to every man getting c that
6:12 try to compel you to get c
6:13 those who are getting c keep
6:13 they want you to be c that
Php 3:5 c the eighth day, out of the
Col 2:11 also c with a circumcision
4:11 these being of those c

Circumcising
Ge 17:23 he went to c the flesh of
Ex 12:48 there be a c of every male
Jos 5:4 reason why Joshua did the c
5:8 completed c all the nation
Lu 2:21 days came to the full for c

Circumcision
Ex 4:26 of blood, because of the c
Joh 7:22 Moses has given you the c
7:23 man receives c on a sabbath
Ac 7:8 also gave him a covenant of c
11:2 supporters of c began to
Ro 2:25 C is, in fact, of benefit
2:25 c has become uncircumcision
2:26 will be counted as c, will it
2:27 with its written code and c
2:28 c . . . which is on the outside
2:29 c is that of the heart by
3:1 what is the benefit of the c?
4:10 When he was in c or in
4:10 Not in c, but in
4:11 received a sign, namely, c
4:12 only to those who adhere to c
1Co 7:19 C does not mean a thing, and
Ga 5:6 neither c is of any value nor
5:11 if I am still preaching c
6:15 neither is c anything nor is
Eph 2:11 by that which is called c
Php 3:3 we are those with the real c
Col 2:11 c performed without hands
2:11 c that belongs to the Christ
3:11 c nor uncircumcision
Tit 1:10 men who adhere to the c

Circumstances
Ps 116:3 the distressing c of Sheol
118:5 Out of the distressing c I
La 1:3 among distressing c
Mt 12:45 final c of that man become
Mr 15:39 he had expired under these c
Lu 11:26 the final c of that man
Ac 5:38 under the present c, I say
Ro 4:10 what c, then, was it counted
1Co 7:15 not in servitude under such c
Php 4:11 in whatever c I am, to be
4:12 in all c I have learned the

Cistern
1Sa 19:22 great c that is in Secu
2Sa 3:26 from the c of Sirah
23:15 from the c of Bethlehem

2Sa 23:16 and drew water from the *c*
2Ki 10:14 the *c* of the binding house
18:31 the water of his own *c*
1Ch 11:17 from the *c* of Bethlehem
11:18 from the *c* of Bethlehem
Pr 5:15 water out of your own *c*, and
Ec 12:6 the water wheel for the *c* has
Isa 36:16 the water of his own *c*
Jer 6:7 As a *c* keeps its waters cool
37:16 into the house of the *c*
38:6 into the *c* of Malchijah
38:6 *c* there was no water, but
38:7 put Jeremiah into the *c*
38:9 have thrown into the *c*, so
38:10 out of the *c* before he dies
38:11 to Jeremiah into the *c* by
38:13 brought him up out of the *c*
41:7 into the midst of the *c*
41:9 *c* into which Ishmael threw
41:9 great *c*, the one that King

Cisterns
De 6:11 *c* hewn out that you did not
2Ch 26:10 and hewed out many *c*
Ne 9:25 *c* hewn out, vineyards and
Jer 2:13 to hew out for themselves *c*
2:13 *c*, that cannot contain the

Cities
Ge 13:12 among the *c* of the District
19:25 overthrowing these *c*, even
19:25 all the inhabitants of the *c*
19:29 God brought the *c* of the
19:29 *c* among which Lot had been
35:5 the *c* that were round about
41:35 as foodstuffs in the *c*, and
41:48 put the foodstuffs in the *c*
47:21 he removed them into *c* from
Ex 1:11 building *c* as storage places
Le 25:32 *c* of the Levites with the
25:32 houses of the *c* of their
25:33 the *c* of the Levites are
25:34 pasture ground of their *c*
26:25 gather yourselves into your *c*
26:31 give your *c* to the sword and
26:33 *c* will become a desolate
Nu 13:19 what the *c* are in which
13:28 fortified *c* are very great
21:2 devote their *c* to destruction
21:3 and their *c* to destruction
21:25 Israel took all these *c*, and
21:25 in all the *c* of the Amorites
31:10 *c* in which they had settled
32:16 and *c* for our little ones
32:17 in the *c* with fortifications
32:24 *c* for your little ones and
32:26 stay there in the *c* of Gilead
32:33 land belonging to its *c* in
32:33 the *c* of the land round about
32:36 *c* with fortifications, and
32:38 the names of the *c* that they
35:2 give the Levites *c* to inhabit
35:2 the pasture ground of the *c*
35:3 the *c* must serve for them to
35:4 the pasture grounds of the *c*
35:5 as pasture grounds of the *c*
35:6 These are the *c* that you will
35:6 six *c* of refuge, which you
35:6 will give forty-two other *c*
35:7 *c* that you will give to the
35:7 Levites will be forty-eight *c*
35:8 *c* that you will give will be
35:8 some of his *c* to the Levites
35:11 must choose *c* convenient for
35:11 *c* of refuge they will serve
35:12 *c* must serve you as a refuge
35:13 the *c* that you will give
35:13 six *c* of refuge, will be at
35:14 Three *c* you will give on
35:14 three *c* you will give
35:14 *c* of refuge they will serve
35:15 six *c* will serve as a refuge
De 1:22 the *c* to which we will come
1:28 *c* great and fortified to the
2:34 we went capturing all his *c*
2:35 the *c* that we had captured
2:37 *c* of the mountainous region
3:4 we went capturing all his *c*
3:4 sixty *c*, all the region
3:5 *c* fortified with a high wall
3:7 the spoil of the *c* we took as
3:10 the *c* of the tableland and all
3:10 the *c* of the kingdom of Og in
3:12 its *c* I have given to the
3:19 your *c* that I have given you
De 4:41 set apart three *c* on the side
4:42 must flee to one of these *c*
6:10 great and good-looking *c* that
9:1 *c* great and fortified to the
13:12 hear it said in one of your *c*
15:7 in one of your *c*, in your
16:5 in any one of your *c* that
17:2 *c* that Jehovah your God is
18:6 one of your *c* of all Israel
19:1 dwelt in their *c* and their
19:2 set apart three *c* for
19:5 flee to one of these *c* and
19:7 Three *c* you will set apart
19:9 then add three other *c* for
19:11 fled to one of these *c*
20:15 you will do to all the *c*
20:15 not of the *c* of these nations
20:16 the *c* of these peoples that
21:2 *c* that are all around the
23:16 choose in one of your *c*
Jos 9:17 and came to their *c* on the
9:17 and their *c* were Gibeon and
10:2 like one of the royal *c*, and
10:19 to enter into their *c*
10:20 into the fortified *c*
11:12 all the *c* of these kings
11:13 all the *c* standing on their
11:14 all the spoil of these *c*
11:21 their *c* Joshua devoted them
13:10 the *c* of Sihon the king of
13:21 the *c* of the tableland and
13:23 the *c* and their settlements
13:25 all the *c* of Gilead and
13:28 the *c* and their settlements
13:31 *c* of the royal realm of Og
14:4 except *c* to dwell in and
14:12 and great fortified *c*
15:9 the *c* of Mount Ephron
15:21 *c* at the extremity of the
15:32 all the *c* being twenty-nine
15:36 fourteen *c* and their
15:41 sixteen *c* and their
15:44 nine *c* and their
15:51 eleven *c* and . . . settlements
15:54 nine *c* and . . . settlements
15:57 ten *c* and their settlements
15:59 six *c* and their settlements
15:60 two *c* and their settlements
15:62 six *c* and their settlements
16:9 enclave *c* in the midst of
16:9 the *c* and their settlements
17:9 torrent valley of these *c*
17:9 midst of the *c* of Manasseh
17:12 take possession of these *c*
18:9 mapped it out by *c* in seven
18:21 the *c* of the tribe of the
18:24 *c* and their settlements
18:28 fourteen *c* and their
19:6 *c* and their settlements
19:7 four *c* and their settlements
19:8 all around these *c* as far as
19:15 twelve *c* and . . . settlements
19:16 the *c* and their settlements
19:22 *c* and their settlements
19:23 the *c* and their settlements
19:30 twenty-two *c* and their
19:31 the *c* and their settlements
19:35 fortified *c* were Ziddim
19:38 nineteen *c* and their
19:39 the *c* and their settlements
19:48 the *c* and their settlements
20:2 the *c* of refuge of which I
20:4 flee to one of these *c* and
20:9 became the *c* appointed for
21:2 commanded *c* to be given us
21:3 *c* and their pasture grounds
21:4 thirteen *c* came to belong to
21:5 ten *c* out of the families of
21:6 thirteen *c* out of the
21:7 twelve *c* out of the tribe of
21:8 gave the Levites these *c* and
21:9 *c* that were called by name
21:16 *c* out of these two tribes
21:18 its pasture ground; four *c*
21:19 *c* of the sons of Aaron
21:19 *c* and their pasture grounds
21:20 *c* out of the tribe of
21:22 pasture ground; four *c*
21:24 pasture ground; four *c*
21:25 its pasture ground; two *c*
21:26 All the *c* together with
21:27 its pasture ground; two *c*
21:29 its pasture ground; four *c*
21:31 its pasture ground; four *c*
Jos 21:32 its pasture ground; three *c*
21:33 the *c* of the Gershonites
21:33 thirteen *c* and their pasture
21:35 its pasture ground; four *c*
21:37 its pasture ground; four *c*
21:39 all the *c* being four
21:40 *c* that came to belong to
21:40 as their lot, twelve *c*
21:41 All the *c* of the Levites in
21:41 forty-eight *c* together with
21:42 *c* came to be each a city
21:42 thus as to all these *c*
24:13 *c* that you had not built
Jg 10:4 they had thirty *c*. These they
11:26 *c* that are by the banks of
11:33 twenty *c*—and as far as
20:14 out of the *c* to Gibeah
20:15 mustered . . . from the *c*
20:42 the men from out of the *c*
20:48 all the *c* that were found
21:23 and built the *c* and took up
1Sa 6:18 all the *c* of the Philistines
7:14 *c* that the Philistines had
18:6 out from all the *c* of Israel
27:5 place in one of the *c* of the
30:29 *c* of the Jerahmeelites
30:29 in the *c* of the Kenites
31:7 leave the *c* and flee, after
2Sa 2:1 one of the *c* of Judah
2:3 dwelling in the *c* of Hebron
8:8 *c* of Hadadezer, King David
10:12 behalf of the *c* of our God
12:31 the *c* of the sons of Ammon
20:6 find for himself fortified *c*
24:7 all the *c* of the Hivites
1Ki 4:13 sixty large *c* with wall and
9:11 twenty *c* in the land of
9:12 *c* that Solomon had given him
9:13 What sort of *c* are these
9:19 the storage *c* that became
9:19 and the chariot *c* and the
9:19 and the *c* for the horsemen
10:26 stationed in the chariot *c*
12:17 dwelling in the *c* of Judah
13:32 in the *c* of Samaria will
15:20 against the *c* of Israel and
15:23 the *c* that he built, are
20:34 The *c* that my father took
22:39 all the *c* that he built
2Ki 3:25 *c* they went throwing down
13:25 *c* that he had taken from
13:25 to recover the *c* of Israel
17:6 and in the *c* of the Medes
17:9 high places in all their *c*
17:24 dwell in the *c* of Samaria
17:24 and to dwell in its *c*
17:26 settled in the *c* of Samaria
17:29 *c* where they were dwelling
18:11 in the *c* of the Medes
18:13 the fortified *c* of Judah
19:13 king of the *c* of Sepharvaim
19:25 *c* desolate as piles of ruins
23:5 high places in the *c* of Judah
23:8 priests from the *c* of Judah
23:19 were in the *c* of Samaria
1Ch 2:22 *c* in the land of Gilead
2:23 dependent towns, sixty *c*
4:31 *c* down till David reigned
4:32 Tochen and Ashan, five *c*
4:33 *c* were as far as Baal
6:57 the *c* of refuge, Hebron, and
6:60 All their *c* were thirteen
6:60 were thirteen *c* among their
6:61 sons of Kohath . . . ten *c*
6:62 Gershom . . . thirteen *c*
6:63 sons of Merari . . . twelve *c*
6:64 Israel gave the Levites the *c*
6:65 by the lot they gave . . . *c*
6:66 Kohath came to have the *c* of
6:67 *c* of refuge, Shechem with
9:2 in their possession in their *c*
10:7 to leave their *c* and flee
13:2 their *c* with pasture grounds
18:8 *c* of Hadadezer, David took
19:7 from their *c* and now came
19:13 behalf of the *c* of our God
20:3 the *c* of the sons of Ammon
27:25 in the *c* and in the villages
2Ch 1:14 stationed in chariot *c* and
8:2 *c* that Hiram had given to
8:4 all the storage *c* that he had
8:5 fortified *c* with walls, doors
8:6 storage *c* that had become
8:6 all the chariot *c* and the

2Ch 8:6 *c* for the horsemen and every
9:25 stationed in the chariot *c*
10:17 dwelling in the *c* of Judah
11:5 build fortified *c* in Judah
11:10 fortified *c*, which were in
11:12 *c* large shields and lances
11:23 to all the fortified *c*, and
12:4 capture the fortified *c* that
13:19 capture *c* from him, Bethel
14:5 from all the *c* of Judah
14:6 build fortified *c* in Judah
14:7 build these *c* and make walls
14:14 struck all the *c* round about
14:14 plundering all the *c*
15:8 *c* that he had captured from
16:4 against the *c* of Israel, so
16:4 places of the *c* of Naphtali
17:2 the fortified *c* of Judah
17:2 *c* of Ephraim that Asa his
17:7 teach in the *c* of Judah
17:9 through all the *c* of Judah
17:12 and storage *c* in Judah
17:13 his in the *c* of Judah
17:19 fortified *c* throughout all
19:5 fortified *c* of Judah, city
19:10 who are dwelling in their *c*
20:4 all the *c* of Judah they came
21:3 with fortified *c* in Judah
23:2 Levites from all the *c* of
24:5 Go out to the *c* of Judah and
25:13 raids upon the *c* of Judah
26:6 built *c* in Ashdod territory
27:4 And *c* he built in the
28:18 upon the *c* of the Shephelah
28:25, 25 *c*, even the *c* of Judah
31:1 went out to the *c* of Judah
31:1 Israel returned to their *c*
31:6 dwelling in the *c* of Judah
31:15 in the *c* of the priests, in
31:19 pasture ground of their *c*
31:19 in all the different *c* there
32:1 against the fortified *c*, and
32:29 *c* he acquired for himself
33:14 the fortified *c* in Judah
34:6 *c* of Manasseh and Ephraim
Ezr 2:70 took up dwelling in their *c*
2:70 and all Israel in their *c*
3:1 Israel were in their *c*
4:10 settled in the *c* of Samaria
10:14 all in our *c* who have given
Ne 7:73 took up dwelling in their *c*
7:73 Israel were then in their *c*
8:15 pass throughout all their *c*
9:25 went capturing fortified *c*
10:37 in all our agricultural *c*
11:1 other parts in the other *c*
11:3 in the *c* of Judah there dwelt
11:3 in their *c*, Israel, the
11:20 in all the other *c* of Judah
12:44 out of the fields of the *c*
Es 8:11 were in all the different *c*
8:17 all the different *c* wherever
9:2 *c* in all the jurisdictional
9:19 *c* of the outlying districts
Job 15:28 in *c* that are to be effaced
Ps 9:6 the *c* that you have uprooted
69:35 will build the *c* of Judah
Isa 1:7 your *c* are burned with fire
6:11 *c* actually crash in ruins
14:17 overthrew its very *c*, that
14:21 the productive land with *c*
17:2 *c* of Aroer that have been
17:9 fortress *c* will become like
19:18 *c* in the land of Egypt
33:8 he has contemned the *c*
36:1 the fortified *c* of Judah
37:26 fortified *c* become desolate
40:9 Say to the *c* of Judah
42:11 and its *c* raise their voice
44:26 and of the *c* of Judah
54:3 inhabit even the desolated *c*
61:4 make anew the devastated *c*
64:10 *c* have become a wilderness
Jer 1:15 against all the *c* of Judah
2:15 own *c* have been set afire
2:28 the number of your *c* your
4:5 enter into the fortified *c*
4:7 Your own *c* will fall in ruins
4:16 against the very *c* of Judah
4:26 *c* of it had all been torn
5:6 is keeping awake at their *c*
5:17 *c* in which you are trusting
7:17 are doing in the *c* of Judah
7:34 cease from the *c* of Judah
Jer 8:14 enter into the fortified *c*
9:11 the *c* of Judah I shall make
10:22 the *c* of Judah a desolate
11:6 words in the *c* of Judah
11:12 And the *c* of Judah and the
11:13 become as many as your *c*
13:19 *c* of the south themselves
17:26 come from the *c* of Judah
19:15 and upon all its *c* all the
20:16 become like *c* that Jehovah
22:6 as for the *c*, not one will
25:18 the *c* of Judah and her
26:2 speak concerning all the *c*
31:21 back to these *c* of yours
31:23 land of Judah and in his *c*
31:24 Judah and all his *c* will
32:44 and in the *c* of Judah and
32:44 *c* of the mountainous region
32:44 *c* of the lowland and in
32:44 in the *c* of the south
33:10 *c* of Judah and in the
33:12 *c* there will yet come to be
33:13 *c* of the mountainous region
33:13 *c* of the lowland and in
33:13 in the *c* of the south and
33:13 in the *c* of Judah flocks
34:1 against all her *c*, saying
34:7 against all the *c* of Judah
34:7 for they, the fortified *c*
34:7 over among the *c* of Judah
34:22 *c* of Judah I shall make a
36:6 coming in from their *c* you
36:9 in from the *c* of Judah
40:5 over the *c* of Judah, and
40:10 your *c* that you have seized
44:2 upon all the *c* of Judah
44:6 burned in the *c* of Judah and
44:17 did in the *c* of Judah and
44:21 in the *c* of Judah and in the
48:9 *c* will become a mere object
48:15 gone up against her own *c*
48:24 the *c* of the land of Moab
48:28 Leave the *c* and reside on
49:1 dwelling in Israel's very *c*
49:13 *c* will become devastated
50:32 set a fire ablaze in its *c*
51:43 *c* have become an object of
La 5:11 the virgins in the *c* of Judah
Eze 6:6 *c* will become devastated and
12:20 inhabited *c* . . . be devastated
19:7 he devastated even their *c*
25:9 slope of Moab at the *c*
25:9 at his *c* to his frontier
26:19 the *c* that are actually not
29:12 *c* will become a desolate
29:12 devastated *c* for forty years
30:7 its own *c* will come to be
30:7 in the midst of devastated *c*
30:17 into captivity the *c*
35:4 Your *c* I shall set as a
35:9 own *c* will not be inhabited
36:4 abandoned *c* that have come
36:10 the *c* must become inhabited
36:33 cause the *c* to be inhabited
36:35 the *c* that were a waste
36:38 *c* that had been a waste
39:9 the *c* of Israel will
Ho 8:14 multiplied fortified *c*
8:14 send fire into his *c* and it
10:14 *c* will all be despoiled
11:6 whirl about in his *c* and
13:10 may save you in all your *c*
Am 4:6 in all your *c* and want of
4:8 two or three *c* staggered
9:14 build the desolated *c* and
Ob 20 possession of the *c* of the Negeb
Mic 5:11 cut off the *c* of your land
5:14 and annihilate your *c*
7:12 Assyria and the *c* of Egypt
Zep 1:16 against the fortified *c* and
3:6 Their *c* were laid waste
Zec 1:12 and to the *c* of Judah, whom
1:17 My *c* will yet overflow with
7:7 with her *c* all around her
8:20 inhabitants of many *c* will
Mt 9:35 on a tour of all the *c* and
10:23 circuit of the *c* of Israel
11:1 teach and preach in their *c*
11:20 he started to reproach the *c*
14:13 on foot from the *c*
Mr 6:33 from all the *c* they ran there
6:56 enter into villages or *c* or
Lu 4:43 to other *c* I must declare the
5:12 while he was in one of the *c*
Lu 19:17 hold authority over ten *c*
19:19 be in charge of five *c*
Ac 5:16 from the *c* around Jerusalem
8:40 good news to all the *c* until
14:6 fled to the *c* of Lycaonia
15:36 *c* in which we published the
16:4 they traveled on through the *c*
26:11 persecuting . . . in outside *c*
2Pe 2:6 the *c* Sodom and Gomorrah to
Jude 7 and Gomorrah and the *c* about
Re 16:19 *c* of the nations fell; and

Citizen
Ac 21:39 a *c* of no obscure city
22:28 purchased these rights as a *c*
Heb 8:11 teach each one his fellow *c*

Citizens
Lu 15:15 one of the *c* of that country
19:14 his *c* hated him and sent out
Eph 2:19 fellow *c* of the holy ones

Citizenship
Php 3:20 our *c* exists in the heavens

City
Ge 4:17 he engaged in building a *c*
10:12 this is the great *c*
11:4 build ourselves a *c* and also
11:5 go down to see the *c* and the
11:8 left off building the *c*
18:24 men in the midst of the *c*
18:26 midst of the *c* I will pardon
18:28 bring the whole *c* to ruin
19:4 of the *c*, the men of Sodom
19:12 all who are yours in the *c*
19:13 us to bring the *c* to ruin
19:14 is bringing the *c* to ruin
19:15 away in the error of the *c*
19:16 station him outside the *c*
19:20 *c* is nearby to flee there and
19:21 *c* of which you have spoken
19:22 called the name of the *c* Zoar
23:10 entering the gate of his *c*
23:18 entering the gate of his *c*
24:10 to the *c* of Nahor
24:11 outside the *c* at a well of
24:13 daughters . . . of the *c* are
26:33 name of the *c* is Beer-sheba
33:18 to the *c* of Shechem, which
33:18 camp in front of the *c*
34:20 went to the gate of their *c*
34:20 speak to the men of their *c*
34:24 out by the gate of his *c*
34:24 out by the gate of his *c*
34:25 to the *c* and to kill every
34:27 and went plundering the *c*
34:28 and what was in the *c* and
36:32 name of his *c* was Dinhabah
36:35 name of his *c* was Avith
36:39 the name of his *c* was Pau
41:48 that was round about a *c*
44:4 They went out of the *c*
44:13 and returned to the *c*
Ex 9:29 As soon as I go out of the *c*
9:33 Moses now went out of the *c*
Le 14:40 outside the *c* into an unclean
14:41 the *c* into an unclean place
14:45 outside the *c* to an unclean
14:53 outside the *c* into the open
25:29 house in a walled *c*, his
25:30 house that is in the *c* that
25:33 house sold in the *c* of his
Nu 20:16 Kadesh, a *c* at the extremity
21:26 Heshbon was the *c* of Sihon
21:27 Let the *c* of Sihon be built
22:36 meet him at the *c* of Moab
24:19 any survivor from the *c*
35:4 from the wall of the *c* and
35:5 measure outside the *c* on the
35:5 with the *c* in the middle
35:25 to his *c* of refuge to which
35:26 boundary of his *c* of refuge
35:27 boundary of his *c* of refuge
35:28 to dwell in his *c* of refuge
35:32 has fled to his *c* of refuge
De 2:34 every *c* to destruction, men
2:36 the *c* that is in the torrent
3:6 devoting every *c* to destruction
13:13 the inhabitants of their *c*
13:15 the inhabitants of that *c*
13:16 burn in the fire the *c* and
19:12 the older men of his *c* must
20:10 draw near to a *c* to fight
20:14 happens to be in the *c*, all
20:19 lay siege to a *c* many days

De 20:20 siegeworks against the *c*
21:3 the *c* nearest to the slain one
21:3 the older men of that *c* must
21:4 the older men of that *c*
21:6 the older men of that *c* who
21:19 to the older men of his *c*
21:20 to the older men of his *c*
21:21 the men of his *c* must pelt
22:15 to the older men of the *c*
22:17 the older men of the *c*
22:18 the older men of that *c* must
22:21 the men of her *c* must pelt
22:23 found her in the *c* and lay
22:24 to the gate of that *c* and
22:24 she did not scream in the *c*
25:8 the older men of his *c* must
28:3 Blessed will you be in the *c*
28:16 Cursed will you be in the *c*
34:3 the *c* of the palm trees, as
Jos 3:16 *c* at the side of Zarethan
6:3 must march round the *c*, going
6:3 going round the *c* once
6:4 march round the *c* seven times
6:5 wall of the *c* must fall down
6:7 Pass on and march round the *c*
6:11 go marching round the *c*
6:14 went marching round the *c* on
6:15 went marching round the *c* in
6:15 round the *c* seven times
6:16 Jehovah has given you the *c*
6:17 *c* must become a thing
6:20 people went up into the *c*
6:20 and captured the *c*
6:21 all that was in the *c*, from
6:24 they burned the *c* with fire
6:26 build this *c*, even Jericho
8:1 people and his *c* and his land
8:2 ambush of yours against the *c*
8:4 lying in ambush against the *c*
8:4 to the rear of the *c*
8:4 not . . . far away from the *c*
8:5 we shall go close to the *c*
8:6 drawn them away from the *c*
8:7 must take possession of the *c*
8:8 soon as you have seized the *c*
8:8 you should set the *c* on fire
8:11 and get in front of the *c*
8:12 and Ai, to the west of the *c*
8:13 to the north of the *c* and
8:13 was to the west of the *c*
8:14 men of the *c* got in a hurry
8:14 to the rear of the *c*
8:16 the people who were in the *c*
8:16 to be drawn away from the *c*
8:17 they left the *c* wide open
8:18 was in his hand toward the *c*
8:19 enter the *c* and capture it
8:19 hurried and set the *c* on fire
8:20 smoke of the *c* ascended to
8:21 ambush had captured the *c*
8:21 the smoke of the *c* ascended
8:22 came out of the *c* to meet
8:27 the spoil of that *c* Israel
8:29 entrance of the gate of the *c*
10:2 because Gibeon was a great *c*
11:19 proved to be no *c* that made
13:9 *c* that is in the middle of
13:16 *c* that is in the middle of
15:62 the *C* of Salt and En-gedi
18:14 a *c* of the sons of Judah
19:29 the fortified *c* of Tyre
19:50 *c* for which he asked
19:50 build up the *c* and dwell in
20:4 entrance of the gate of the *c*
20:4 the older men of that *c*
20:4 must receive him into the *c*
20:6 must dwell in that *c* until
20:6 he must enter into his *c*
20:6 the *c* from which he had fled
21:12 *c* and its settlements they
21:13 the *c* of refuge for the
21:21 the *c* of refuge for the
21:27 the *c* of refuge for the
21:32 the *c* of refuge for the
21:38 the *c* of refuge for the
21:42 cities came to be each a *c*
Jg 1:8 *c* they consigned to the fire
1:16 the *c* of palm trees with the
1:17 the *c* was called Hormah
1:23 name of the *c* before that
1:24 see a man going out of the *c*
1:24 the way to get into the *c*
1:25 the way to get into the *c*
1:25 went striking the *c* with the
Jg 1:26 and built a *c* and called its
3:13 possession of the *c* of palm
6:27 men of the *c* too much to do
6:28 men of the *c* got up early in
6:30 the men of the *c* said to Joash
8:16 took the older men of the *c*
8:17 to kill the men of the *c*
8:27 to exhibit it in his *c* Ophrah
9:30 prince of the *c* got to hear
9:31 are massing the *c* against you
9:33 dash against the *c*; and when
9:35 at the entrance of the *c* gate
9:43 were going out of the *c*
9:44 at the entrance of the *c* gate
9:45 fought against the *c* all that
9:45 and got to capture the *c*; and
9:45 pulled the *c* down and sowed
9:51 in the middle of the *c*, there
9:51 landowners of the *c* went
12:7 was buried in his *c* in Gilead
14:18 So the men of the *c* said to
16:2 all night long in the *c* gate
16:3 doors of the *c* gate and the
17:8 go from the *c* of Bethlehem in
18:27 the *c* they burned with fire
18:28 they built the *c* and took up
18:29 called the name of the *c* Dan
19:11 *c* of the Jebusites and stay
19:12 a *c* of foreigners who are no
19:15 in the public square of the *c*
19:17 in the public square of the *c*
19:22 look! the men of the *c*, mere
20:11 against the *c* as one man, as
20:31 were drawn away from the *c*
20:32 draw them away from the *c*
20:37 struck all the *c* with the
20:38 signal go up from the *c*
20:40 go up from the *c* as a pillar
20:40 whole *c* went up heavenward
20:48 those of the *c*, from men to
Ru 1:19 *c* became stirred up over them
2:18 and went into the *c*, and her
3:15 he went into the *c*
4:2 of the older men of the *c* and
1Sa 1:3 that man went up out of his *c*
4:13 went in to report in the *c*
4:13 the whole *c* began crying out
5:9 came to be upon the *c* with a
5:9 striking the men of the *c*
5:11 had occurred in the whole *c*
5:12 cry of the *c* for help kept
6:18 fortified *c* to the village of
8:22 Go each one to his *c*
9:6 is a man of God in this *c*
9:10 they went their way to the *c*
9:11 up on the ascent to the *c*
9:12 today he has come to the *c*
9:13 as you men come into the *c*
9:14 they went on up to the *c*
9:14 into the middle of the *c*
9:25 from the high place to the *c*
9:27 by the edge of the *c* Samuel
10:5 your coming there to the *c*
15:5 as far as the *c* of Amalek
16:4 older men of the *c* began to
20:6 run to Bethlehem his *c*
20:29 family sacrifice in the *c*
20:40 Go, take them to the *c*
20:42 himself came into the *c*
22:19 Nob the *c* of the priests he
23:7 into a *c* with doors and bar
23:10 Keilah to lay the *c* in ruin
27:5 in the royal *c* with you
28:3 bury him in Ramah his own *c*
30:3 with his men to the *c*, why
2Sa 5:7 that is, the *c* of David
5:9 be called the *c* of David
6:10 to him at the *c* of David
6:12 *c* of David with rejoicing
6:16 came into the *c* of David
10:3 of searching through the *c*
10:14 and hence came into the *c*
11:16 keeping guard over the *c*
11:17 men of the *c* came on out
11:20 so near to the *c* to fight
11:25 battle against the *c* and
12:1 happened to be in one *c*
12:26 capture the *c* of the
12:27 captured the *c* of waters
12:28 encamp against the *c*, and
12:28 one to capture the *c*, and
12:30 spoil of the *c* that he
15:2 From what *c* are you? and he
15:12 counselor, from his *c* Giloh
2Sa 15:14 strike the *c* with the edge
15:24 crossing over from the *c*
15:25 the ark . . . back to the *c*
15:27 Do return to the *c* in peace
15:34 if you return to the *c* and
15:37 companion, came into the *c*
17:13 if it is into some *c* that
17:13 also carry ropes to that *c*
17:17 to appear entering the *c*
17:23 to his house at his own *c*
18:3 to give help from the *c*
19:3 that day to come into the *c*
19:37 let me die in my *c* close
20:15 siege rampart against the *c*
20:16 began to call from the *c*
20:19 seeking to put to death a *c*
20:21 I will withdraw from the *c*
20:22 were scattered from the *c*
24:5 Aroer to the right of the *c*
1Ki 2:10 buried in the *c* of David
3:1 bring her to the *c* of David
8:1 *c* of David, that is to say
8:16 I have not chosen a *c* out of
8:44 the *c* that you have chosen
8:48 the *c* that you have chosen
9:16 in the *c* he had killed
9:24 out of the *c* of David to her
11:27 the *c* of David his father
11:32 the *c* that I have chosen
11:36 the *c* that I have chosen
11:43 buried in the *c* of David
13:25 and spoke of it in the *c* in
13:29 the *c* of the old prophet to
14:11 in the *c*, the dogs will eat
14:12 your feet come into the *c*
14:21 *c* that Jehovah had chosen
14:31 in the *c* of David
15:8 buried him in the *c* of David
15:24 *c* of David his forefather
16:4 is dying in the *c* the dogs
16:18 the *c* had been captured
16:24 the *c* that he built by the
17:10 into the entrance of the *c*
20:2 king of Israel at the *c*
20:12 to get set against the *c*
20:19 that came out from the *c*
20:30 fleeing to Aphek, to the *c*
20:30 came into the *c* into the
21:8 nobles that were in his *c*
21:11 men of his *c*, the older men
21:11 that were dwelling in his *c*
21:13 to the outskirts of the *c*
21:24 dying in the *c* the dogs
22:26 Amon the chief of the *c* and
22:36 Everyone to his *c*, and
22:50 *c* of David his forefather
2Ki 2:19 men of the *c* said to Elisha
2:19 situation of the *c* is good
2:23 that came out from the *c* and
3:19 every fortified *c* and every
3:19 and every choice *c*, and
6:14 and close in upon the *c*
6:15 surrounding the *c* with
6:19 and this is not the *c*
7:4 Let us enter the *c*, when the
7:4 when the famine is in the *c*
7:10 the gatekeepers of the *c* and
7:12 will come out from the *c*
7:12 into the *c* we shall enter
7:13 that have remained in the *c*
8:24 buried . . . in the *c* of David
9:15 in escape from the *c* to go
9:28 forefathers in the *c* of David
10:2 a fortified *c* and the armor
10:5 one who was over the *c*
10:6 distinguished men of the *c*
10:25 the *c* of the house of Baal
11:20 the *c*, for its part, had no
12:21 in the *c* of David
14:20 in the *c* of David
15:7 in the *c* of David
15:38 in the *c* of David his
16:20 in the *c* of David
17:9 clear to the fortified *c*
18:8 clear to the fortified *c*
18:30 this *c* will not be given
19:32 will not come into this *c*
19:33 into this *c* he will not
19:34 defend this *c* to save it
20:6 shall deliver you and this *c*
20:6 defend this *c* for my own
20:20 the water into the *c*
23:8 Joshua, the chief of the *c*
23:8 came into the gate of the *c*

2Ki 23:17 men of the *c* said to him
23:27 this *c* that I have chosen
24:10 the *c* came under siege
24:11 to come against the *c*
25:2 the *c* came to be under siege
25:3 famine was severe in the *c*
25:4 the *c* got to be breached
25:4 all around against the *c*
25:11 were left behind in the *c*
25:19 *c* he took one court official
25:19 that were found in the *c*
25:19 were to be found in the *c*
1Ch 1:43 whose *c* was Dinhabah
1:46 name of his *c* was Avith
1:50 the name of his *c* was Pau
6:56 the field of the *c* and its
11:5 Zion . . . the *c* of David
11:7 they called it the *c* of David
11:8 And he began to build the *c*
11:8 to life the rest of the *c*
13:13 at the *c* of David, but he
15:1 houses . . . in the *c* of David
15:29 as far as the *c* of David
19:9 at the entrance of the *c*, and
19:15 came into the *c*. Later Joab
20:2 the spoil of the *c* that he
2Ch 5:2 *c* of David, that is to say
6:5 I have not chosen a *c* out of
6:34 in the direction of this *c*
6:38 *c* that you have chosen and
8:11 *c* of David to the house that
9:31 buried him in the *c* of David
12:13 Jerusalem, the *c* that
12:16 buried in the *c* of David
14:1 buried him in the *c* of David
15:6, 6 *c* against *c*, because God
16:14 in the *c* of David
18:25 Amon the chief of the *c* and
19:5, 5 cities of Judah, *c* by *c*
21:1 forefathers in the *c* of David
21:20 buried . . . in the *c* of David
23:21 *c* itself had no disturbance
24:16 buried . . . in the *c* of David
24:25 buried . . . in the *c* of David
25:28 in the *c* of Judah
27:9 buried him in the *c* of David
28:15 Jericho, the *c* of palm
28:27 buried him in the *c*, in
29:20 princes of the *c* together
30:10, 10 along from *c* to *c*
32:3 that were outside the *c*
32:5 the Mound of the *c* of David
32:6 square of the gate of the *c*
32:18 they might capture the *c*
32:30 to the *c* of David, and
33:14 wall for the *c* of David
33:15 them thrown outside the *c*
34:8 Maaseiah the chief of the *c*
Ezr 2:1 each one to his own *c*
4:12 the rebellious and bad *c*
4:13 if this *c* should be rebuilt
4:15, 15 *c* is a *c* rebellious and
4:15 that *c* has been laid waste
4:16 if that *c* should be rebuilt
4:19 that *c* has from the days of
4:21 that *c* may not be rebuilt
10:14 individual *c* and its judges
Ne 2:3 the *c*, the house of the burial
2:5 to the *c* of the burial places
2:8 and for the wall of the *c* and
3:6 the Gate of the Old *C* was what
3:15 goes down from the *C* of David
7:4 the *c* was wide and great, and
7:6 to Judah, each to his own *c*
11:1 dwell in Jerusalem the holy *c*
11:9 Hassenuah over the *c* as second
11:18 the Levites in the holy *c*
12:37 Stairway of the *C* of David
12:39 the Gate of the Old *C* and
13:16 Tyrians . . . dwelt in the *c*
13:18 and also upon this *c*
Es 3:15 the *c* of Shushan, it was in
4:1 into the middle of the *c* and
4:6 the public square of the *c*
6:9 in the public square of the *c*
6:11 in the public square of the *c*
8:15 *c* of Shushan itself cried out
9:28 and each *c*, and these days of
Job 24:12 From out of the *c* the dying
Ps 31:21 to me in a *c* under stress
46:4 make the *c* of God rejoice
46:5 God is in the midst of the *c*
48:1 In the *c* of our God, in his
48:8 In the *c* of Jehovah of armies
Ps 48:8 in the *c* of our God
55:9 and disputing in the *c*
59:6 and go all around the *c*
59:14 and go all around the *c*
60:9 bring me to the besieged *c*
72:16 those who are from the *c*
87:3 you, O *c* of the true God
101:8 from the *c* of Jehovah
107:4 any way to a *c* of habitation
107:7 to come to a *c* of habitation
107:36 establish a *c* of habitation
108:10 bring me to the fortified *c*
122:3 is one that is built like a *c*
122:6 Those loving you, O *c*
127:1 Jehovah himself guards the *c*
Pr 1:21 of the gates into the *c* it
16:32 than the one capturing a *c*
21:22 even the *c* of mighty men
25:28 a *c* broken through, without
Ec 7:19 who happened to be in a *c*
8:10 forgotten in the *c* where they
9:14 There was a little *c*, and the
9:15 provided escape for the *c* by
10:15 to know how to go to the *c*
Ca 3:2 and go round about in the *c*
3:3 going around in the *c* found me
5:7 that were going about in the *c*
6:4 like Pleasant *C*, comely like
Isa 1:8 like a blockaded *c*
1:26 be called *C* of Righteousness
14:31 Howl, O gate! Cry out, O *c!*
17:1 removed from being a *c*, and
17:3 fortified *c* has been made to
19:2, 2 *c* against *c*, kingdom
19:18 *C* of Tearing Down will one
19:18 will one *c* be called
22:2 were full, a boisterous *c*
22:9 breaches of the *c* of David
23:7 your *c* that was exultant
23:16 a harp, go around the *c*
24:12 In the *c* an astonishing
25:2 made a *c* a pile of stones
25:2 of strangers to be no *c*
25:12 fortified *c*, with your high
26:1 Judah: We have a strong *c*
27:10 *c* will be solitary
32:14 hubbub of the *c* has been
32:19 *c* becomes low in an abased
36:15 *c* will not be given into
37:13 of the *c* of Sepharvaim
37:33 will not come into this *c*
37:34 this *c* he will not come
37:35 defend this *c* to save it for
38:6 shall deliver you and this *c*
38:6 and I will defend this *c*
45:13 one that will build my *c*
48:2 as being from the holy *c*
52:1 O Jerusalem, the holy *c*
60:14 call you the *c* of Jehovah
62:12 a *C* Not Left Entirely
66:6 sound of uproar out of the *c*
Jer 1:18 made you today a fortified *c*
3:14 one out of a *c* and two out
4:29 the entire *c* is running away
4:29 Every *c* is left, and there is
6:6 She is the *c* with which an
8:16 the *c* and its inhabitants
14:18 actually come into the *c*
17:24 through the gates of this *c*
17:25 by the gates of this *c*
17:25 this *c* will certainly be
19:8 *c* an object of astonishment
19:11 break this people and this *c*
19:12 to make this *c* like Topheth
19:15 I am bringing upon this *c*
20:5 stored-up things of this *c*
21:4 into the middle of this *c*
21:6 the inhabitants of this *c*
21:7 remaining over in this *c*
21:9 one sitting still in this *c*
21:10 set my face against this *c*
22:8 pass along by this *c* and say
22:8 do like this to this great *c*
23:39 I will desert you and the *c*
25:29 *c* upon which my name is
26:6 this *c* I shall make a
26:9 very *c* will be devastated
26:11 prophesied concerning this *c*
26:12 concerning this *c* and all
26:15 blood . . . upon this *c* and
26:20 prophesying against this *c*
27:17 *c* become a devastated place
27:19 remaining over in this *c*
29:7 seek the peace of the *c*
Jer 29:16 people dwelling in this *c*
30:18 *c* will actually be rebuilt
31:38 *c* will certainly be built
32:3 giving this *c* into the hand
32:24 to the *c* to capture it
32:24 *c* will certainly be given
32:25 *c* itself must be given into
32:28 *c* into the hand of the
32:29 fighting against this *c*
32:29 set this *c* aflame with fire
32:31 this *c*, from the day that
32:36 *c* which you persons are
33:4 the houses of this *c* and
33:5 my face from this *c*
34:2 giving this *c* into the hand
34:22 bring them back to this *c*
37:8 fight against this *c* and
37:10 burn this *c* with fire
37:21 was exhausted from the *c*
38:2 to dwell in this *c* is the
38:3 this *c* will be given into
38:4 left remaining in this *c*
38:9 no bread anymore in the *c*
38:17 *c* itself will not be burned
38:18 *c* must also be given into
38:23 *c* will be burned with fire
39:2 the *c* was broken through
39:4 by night from the *c* by the
39:9 left remaining in the *c*
39:16 true my words upon this *c*
41:7 into the midst of the *c*
46:8 I shall readily destroy the *c*
47:2 *c* and those inhabiting it
48:8 will come in on every *c*
48:8 *c* that can make its escape
49:25 *c* of praise has not been
51:31 *c* has been captured at
52:5 *c* came under siege until the
52:6 famine . . . severe in the *c*
52:7 *c* was broken through
52:7 from the *c* by night by the
52:7 all around against the *c*
52:15 remaining in the *c* and the
52:25 from the *c* he took one
52:25 who were found in the *c*
52:25 found in the midst of the *c*
La 1:1 the *c* that was abundant with
1:19 In the *c* my own priests and
2:12 in the public squares of the *c*
2:15 *c* of which they used to say
3:51 of all the daughters of my *c*
Eze 4:1 and engrave upon it a *c*, even
4:3 wall between you and the *c*
5:2 fire in the midst of the *c* as
5:8 Here I am against you, O *c*
7:15 whoever are in the *c*, famine
7:23 *c* . . . full of violence
9:1 their attention to the *c*
9:4 through the midst of the *c*
9:5 Pass through the *c* after him
9:7 forth and struck in the *c*
9:9 the *c* is full of crookedness
10:2 and toss them over the *c*
11:2 bad counsel against this *c*
11:6 slain ones in this *c* to be
11:23 over the midst of the *c* and
11:23 that is to the east of the *c*
17:4 in a *c* of traders he placed
21:19 head of the way to the *c* it
22:2 judge the bloodguilty *c* and
22:3 O *c* that is shedding blood
24:6 *c* of deeds of bloodshed
24:9 the *c* of deeds of bloodshed
26:10 into a *c* opened by breaches
26:17 O praised *c*, who became a
26:19 make you a devastated *c*
33:21 The *c* has been struck down!
39:16 *c* will also be Hamonah
40:1 the *c* had been struck down
40:2 structure of a *c* to the south
43:3 came to bring the *c* to ruin
45:6 as the possession of the *c*
45:7 of the possession of the *c*
45:7 the possession of the *c*
48:15 something profane for the *c*
48:15 *c* must come to be in the
48:17 *c* must come to have a
48:18 for the ones serving the *c*
48:19 serving the *c* out of all
48:20 the possession of the *c*
48:21 of the possession of the *c*
48:22 and the possession of the *c*
48:30 be the outlets of the *c*
48:31 gates of the *c* will be

Eze 48:35 name of the c from that day
Da 9:16 back from your c Jerusalem
9:18 c that has been called by your
9:19 has been called upon your c
9:24 upon your holy c, in order to
9:26 c and the holy place the
11:15 a c with fortifications
Joe 2:9 Into the c they rush
Am 3:6 If a horn is blown in a c
3:6 If a calamity occurs in the c
4:7 I made it rain on one c
4:7 on another c I would not make
4:8 to one c in order to drink
5:3 c that was going forth with a
6:8 I will deliver up the c and
7:17 in the c she will become a
Jon 1:2 go to Nineveh the great c, and
3:2 go to Nineveh the great c, and
3:3 proved to be a c great to God
3:4 started to enter into the c
4:5 Jonah went out of the c and
4:5 and sat down east of the c
4:5 what would become of the c
4:11 sorry for Nineveh the great c
Mic 6:9 To the c the very voice of
Na 2:10 voidness, and a c laid waste
3:1 Woe to the c of bloodshed
Hab 2:12 building a c by bloodshed
Zep 2:4 Gaza, an abandoned c is what
2:15 c that was sitting in
3:1 herself, the oppressive c
Zec 8:3 be called the c of trueness
8:5 the public squares of the c
8:21 inhabitants of one c will
14:2 c will actually be captured
14:2 half of the c must go forth
14:2 not be cut off from the c
Mt 2:6 the most insignificant c
2:23 dwelt in a c named Nazareth
4:5 took him along into the holy c
5:14 A c cannot be hid when
5:35 it is the c of the great King
8:33 and, going into the c, they
8:34 all the c turned out to meet
9:1 and went into his own c
10:5 not enter into a Samaritan c
10:11 Into whatever c or village
10:14 out of that house or that c
10:15 Judgment Day than for that c
10:23 persecute you in one c, flee
12:25 c . . . divided against itself
21:10 c was set in commotion
21:17 outside the c to Bethany
21:18 While returning to the c
22:7 and burned their c
22:9 roads leading out of the c
23:34, 34 persecute from c to c
26:18 Go into the c to So-and-so
27:53 entered into the holy c
28:11 went into the c and reported
Mr 1:33 whole c was gathered right
1:45 to enter openly into a c, but
5:14 reported it in the c and in
11:19 they would go out of the c
14:13 Go into the c, and a man
14:16 they entered the c and found
Lu 1:26 a c of Galilee named Nazareth
1:39 with haste, to a c of Judah
2:3 each one to his own c
2:4 out of the c of Nazareth, into
2:4 David's c, which is called
2:11 the Lord, in David's c
2:39 to their own c Nazareth
4:29 hurried him outside the c
4:29 upon which their c had been
4:31 Capernaum, a c of Galilee
7:11 he traveled to a c called Nain
7:12 got near the gate of the c
7:12 crowd from the c was also
7:37 known in the c to be a sinner
8:1, 1 journeying from c to c and
8:4, 4 went to him from c after c
8:27 a certain man from the c who
8:34 reported it to the c and to
8:39 throughout the whole c what
9:5 on going out of that c shake
9:10 into a c called Bethsaida
10:1 into every c and place to
10:8 wherever you enter into a c
10:10 wherever you enter into a c
10:11 dust . . . from your c
10:12 in that day than for that c
13:22, 22 from c to c and from
14:21 and the lanes of the c, and
Lu 18:2 c there was a certain judge
18:3 widow in that c and she kept
19:41 he viewed the c and wept
22:10 When you enter into the c a
23:19 sedition occurring in the c
23:51 from Arimathea, a c of the
24:49 abide in the c until you
Joh 1:44 the c of Andrew and Peter
4:5 to a c of Samaria called
4:8 into the c to buy foodstuffs
4:28 into the c and told the men
4:30 went out of the c and began
4:39 Samaritans out of that c put
11:54 into a c called Ephraim
19:20 impaled was near the c
Ac 4:27 gathered together in this c
7:58 throwing him outside the c
8:5 went down to the c of Samaria
8:8 great deal of joy in that c
8:9 in the c there was a certain
9:6 rise and enter into the c, and
9:38 that Peter was in this c
10:9 approaching the c, Peter went
11:5 I was in the c of Joppa
12:10 iron gate leading into the c
13:44 nearly all the c gathered
13:50 the principal men of the c
14:4 multitude of the c was split
14:13 temple was before the c
14:19 dragged him outside the c
14:20 and entered into the c
14:21 the good news to that c and
15:21, 21 in c after c those who
16:12 principal c of . . . Macedonia
16:12 We continued in this c
16:14 Lydia . . . the c of Thyatira
16:20 men are disturbing our c
16:39 them to depart from the c
17:5 to throw the c into an uproar
17:6 brothers to the c rulers
17:8 the crowd and the c rulers
17:16 that the c was full of idols
18:10 I have many people in this c
19:29 So the c became filled with
19:35 c recorder had quieted the
19:35 the c of the Ephesians is the
20:23, 23 c to c the holy spirit
21:5 as far as outside the c
21:29 Ephesian in the c with him
21:30 whole c was set in an uproar
21:39 a citizen of no obscure c
22:3 educated in this c at the feet
24:12 or throughout the c
25:23 men of eminence in the c
27:8 near which was the c Lasea
Ro 16:23 Erastus the c steward greets
2Co 11:26 in dangers in the c, in
11:32 the c of the Damascenes to
Tit 1:5, 5 of older men in c after c
Heb 11:10 awaiting the c having real
11:10 maker of which c is God
11:16 has made a c ready for them
12:22 and a c of the living God
13:14 have here a c that continues
Jas 4:13 we will journey to this c
Re 3:12 name of the c of my God
11:2 trample the holy c underfoot
11:8 the broad way of the great c
11:13 and a tenth of the c fell
14:20 was trodden outside the c
16:19 great c split into three
17:18 woman . . . means the great c
18:10 too bad, you great c, Babylon
18:10 Babylon you strong c
18:16 great c, clothed with fine
18:18 What c is like the great
18:18 is like the great c
18:19 great c, in which all those
18:21 Babylon the great c be
20:9 holy ones and the beloved c
21:2 the holy c, New Jerusalem
21:10 holy c Jerusalem coming
21:14 The wall of the c also had
21:15 measure the c and its gates
21:16 the c lies foursquare, and
21:16 measured the c with the reed
21:18 c was pure gold like clear
21:21 way of the c was pure gold
21:23 c has no need of the sun nor
22:3 throne . . . will be in the c
22:14 into the c by its gates
22:19 and out of the holy c

City's
Ge 4:17 called the c name by the name
28:19 Luz was the c name formerly
Jg 18:29 Laish was the c name at
Eze 48:16 are the c measurements
Re 21:19 c wall were adorned with

Civil
Ac 16:20 to the c magistrates, they
16:22 c magistrates, after tearing
16:35 c magistrates dispatched the
16:36 to Paul: The c magistrates
16:38 sayings to the c magistrates

Clad
1Sa 17:5 was c with a coat of mail

Claim
Ge 31:39 you would put in a c for it
De 17:8 a legal c has been raised
23:19 on which one may c interest
2Sa 19:28 just c even for crying out
Ne 2:20 nor just c, nor memorial in
Ps 140:12 legal c of the afflicted
Pr 29:7 the legal c of the lowly ones
Jer 22:16 legal c of the afflicted one
Joh 8:53 Who do you c to be?

Claiming
Hab 2:7 those c interest of you rise

Clamor
Ac 20:10 Stop raising a c, for his

Clamps
1Ch 22:3 and for c David prepared
2Ch 34:11 timbers for c and to build

Clan
Nu 18:2 of Levi, the c of your father

Clans
Ge 25:16 according to their c
Nu 25:15 the c of a paternal house in
Ps 117:1 Commend him, all you c

Clap
2Ki 11:12 began to c their hands and
Job 27:23 One will c his hands at him
Ps 47:1 All you peoples, c your hands
98:8 rivers . . . c their hands
Isa 55:12 will all c their hands
Eze 6:11 C your hands and stamp with
Na 3:19 certainly c their hands at you

Clapped
Nu 24:10 c his hands, and Balak went
Jos 15:18 she c her hands while upon
Jg 1:14 she c her hands while upon
La 2:15 have c their hands. They have
Eze 25:6 c the hands and you stamped

Claps
Job 34:37 Among us he c his hands and

Clarified
Ps 12:6 silver . . . c seven times

Clarify
Mal 3:3 must c them like gold and

Clashing
Ps 150:5 with the c cymbals
1Co 13:1 piece of brass or a c cymbal

Class
2Ki 24:14 the lowly c of the people
1Ch 23:11 house for one official c
Isa 53:9 with the rich c in his death
Jer 5:4 Surely they are of low c
2Co 10:12 do not dare to c ourselves
Ga 2:12 of those of the circumcised c
Jas 2:4 you have c distinctions

Classes
2Ch 35:5 the c of the house of the
35:12 c by the paternal house
Ezr 6:18 the priests in their c and

Claudia
2Ti 4:21 Pudens and Linus and C and

Claudius
Ac 11:28 place in the time of C
18:2 C had ordered all the Jews to
23:26 C Lysias to his excellency

Claws
Ps 10:10 has to fall into his strong c
Da 4:33 and his nails like birds' c
7:19 c of which were of copper

Clay
Ex 1:14 hard slavery at c mortar and

Le 14:41 pour the *c* mortar that they
14:42 have different *c* mortar
14:45 the *c* mortar of the house
1Ki 7:46 king cast them in the *c* mold
Job 4:19 dwelling in houses of *c*
10:9 out of *c* you have made me
13:12 are as shield bosses of *c*
27:16 prepare attire just as if *c*
30:19 brought me down to the *c*
33:6 From the *c* I was shaped, I
38:14 like *c* under a seal
Isa 10:6 like the *c* of the streets
29:16 accounted just like the *c*
41:25 as if they were *c* and just
45:9 the *c* say to its former
64:8 We are the *c*, and you are
Jer 18:4 the *c* was spoiled by the
18:6 *c* in the hand of the potter
Da 2:33 iron and partly of molded *c*
2:34 feet of iron and of molded *c*
2:35 molded *c*, the copper, the
2:41 toes to be partly of molded *c*
2:41 the iron mixed with moist *c*
2:42 and partly of molded *c*, the
2:43 iron mixed with moist *c*
2:43 is not mixing with molded *c*
2:45 molded *c*, the silver and the
Na 3:14 and trample down in the *c*
Joh 9:6 and made a *c* with the saliva
9:6 put his *c* upon the man's eyes
9:11 Jesus made a *c* and smeared
9:14 Jesus made the *c* and opened
9:15 He put a *c* upon my eyes, and
Ro 9:21 authority over the *c* to make
Re 2:27 to pieces like *c* vessels

Clean
Ge 7:2 Of every *c* beast you must take
7:2 every beast that is not *c* just
7:8 Of every *c* beast and of every
7:8 every beast that is not *c* and
8:20 some of all the *c* beasts
8:20 of all the *c* flying creatures
Le 4:12 of the camp to a *c* place
6:11 out to a *c* place outside the
7:19 everybody *c* may eat the flesh
10:10 the unclean thing and the *c*
10:14 sacred portion in a *c* place
11:32 the evening and then be *c*
11:36 waters will continue *c*, but
11:37 that is to be sown, it is *c*
11:47 the unclean and the *c* and
12:7 she must be *c* from the source
12:8 for her, and she must be *c*
13:6 must also pronounce him *c*
13:6 wash his garments and be *c*
13:13 then pronounce the plague *c*
13:13 it has turned white. He is *c*
13:17, 17 pronounce . . . *c*. He is *c*
13:23 priest must pronounce him *c*
13:28 priest must pronounce him *c*
13:34 must then pronounce him *c*
13:34 wash his garments and be *c*
13:37 He is *c*, and the priest must
13:37 priest must pronounce him *c*
13:39 He is *c*
13:40 it is baldness. He is *c*
13:41 forehead baldness. He is *c*
13:58 washed . . . and it must be *c*
13:59 pronounce it *c* or to declare
14:4 live *c* birds and cedarwood and
14:7 he must pronounce him *c*, and
14:8 bathe in water and must be *c*
14:9 bathe . . . and he must be *c*
14:11 pronounces him *c* must
14:20 for him; and he must be *c*
14:48 house *c*, because the plague
14:53 the house; and it must be *c*
14:57 and when something is *c*
15:8 spitting upon someone *c*, he
15:13 *c* from his running discharge
15:13 bathe his flesh . . . be *c*
15:28 *c* from her running discharge
15:28 and afterward she will be *c*
16:30 for you to pronounce you *c*
16:30 You will be *c* from all your
17:15 and he must be *c*
20:25 between the *c* beast and the
20:25 the unclean fowl and the *c*
22:4 *c*, neither he who touches
22:7 *c*, and afterward he may eat
Nu 5:28 not defiled . . . but she is *c*
9:13 man was *c* or did not happen
18:11 Everyone *c* in your house may
Nu 18:13 Everyone *c* . . . may eat it
19:9 a *c* man must gather up the
19:9 outside the camp in a *c* place
19:12 the seventh day he will be *c*
19:12 seventh day he will not be *c*
19:18 a *c* man must take hyssop and
19:19 the *c* person must spatter it
19:19 he must be *c* in the evening
31:23 and it must be *c*. Only it
31:24 on the seventh day and be *c*
De 12:15 and the *c* one may eat it
12:22 the unclean one and the *c* one
14:11 Any *c* bird you may eat
14:20 Any *c* flying creature you
15:22 unclean one and the *c* one
23:10 man who does not continue *c*
1Sa 20:26 happened so that he is not *c*
2Sa 22:27 the one keeping *c* you will
22:27 you will show yourself *c*
1Ki 14:10 a *c* sweep behind the house
16:3 I am making a *c* sweep after
21:21 a *c* sweep after you and cut
2Ki 5:10 come back to you; and be *c*
5:12 and certainly be *c*
5:13 said to you, Bathe and be *c*
5:14 little boy and he became *c*
21:13 wipe Jerusalem *c* just as
21:13 the handleless bowl *c*
21:13 wiping it *c* and turning it
2Ch 30:17 for all that were not *c*
Ezr 6:20 they were all of them *c*
Job 11:4 proved really *c* in your eyes
14:4 *c* out of someone unclean
15:14 man that he should be *c*
15:15 heavens . . . not *c* in his
17:9 the one with *c* hands keeps
25:4 can one born of a woman be *c*
25:5 have not proved *c* in his eyes
33:9 *C* I am, and I have no error
Ps 18:26 the one keeping *c* you will
18:26 you will show yourself *c*
19:8 commandment of Jehovah is *c*
24:4 in his hands and *c* in heart
51:7 hyssop, that I may be *c*
73:1 Israel, to those *c* in heart
Pr 14:4 are no cattle the manger is *c*
15:26 but pleasant sayings are *c*
Ec 9:2 the good one and the *c* one
Isa 1:16 make yourselves *c*; remove
52:11 keep yourselves *c*, you who
66:20 bring the gift in a *c* vessel
Jer 4:14 heart *c* of sheer badness
13:27 You cannot be *c*—after how
Eze 20:38 will *c* out from you the
22:26 the unclean thing and the *c*
24:13 but you did not become *c*
24:13 You will become *c* no more
36:25 sprinkle upon you *c* water
36:25 and you will become *c*
44:23 is unclean and what is *c*
Da 7:9 of his head was like *c* wool
Mic 6:11 *c* with wicked scales and
Zec 3:5 put a *c* turban upon his head
3:5 the *c* turban upon his head
Mal 1:11 to my name, even a *c* gift
Mt 3:12 *c* up his threshing floor
8:2 Lord . . . you can make me *c*
8:3 I want to. Be made *c*
10:8 make lepers *c*, expel demons
12:44 unoccupied but swept *c* and
23:26 outside . . . may become *c*
27:59 wrapped . . . in *c* fine linen
Mr 1:40 want to, you can make me *c*
1:41 I want to. Be made *c*
1:42 from him, and he became *c*
7:19 Thus he declared all foods *c*
Lu 3:17 to *c* up his threshing floor
5:12 want to, you can make me *c*
5:13 I want to. Be made *c*
11:25 arriving it finds it swept *c*
11:41 all other things are *c* about
Joh 13:10 washed, but is wholly *c*
13:10 you men are *c*, but not all
13:11 Not all of you are *c*
15:3 *c* because of the word that I
Ac 18:6 I am *c*. From now on I will
20:26 *c* from the blood of all men
Ro 14:20 all things are *c*, but it is
1Co 6:11 But you have been washed *c*
1Ti 1:5 love out of a *c* heart and
3:9 the faith with a *c* conscience
2Ti 1:3 with a *c* conscience, that I
2:22 the Lord out of a *c* heart
Tit 1:15, 15 things are *c* to *c* persons
Tit 1:15 and faithless nothing is *c*
Heb 10:22 bodies bathed with *c* water
Jas 1:27 form of worship that is *c*
Re 15:6 clothed with *c*, bright linen
19:8 in bright, *c*, fine linen
19:14 in white, *c*, fine linen

Cleaned
Isa 3:26 she will certainly be *c* out

Cleaner
Job 4:17 man be *c* than his own Maker
Mr 9:3 than any clothes *c* on earth

Cleanness
2Sa 22:21 the *c* of my hands he repays
22:25 my *c* in front of his eyes
Job 22:30 for the *c* of your hands
Ps 18:20 the *c* of my hands he repays
18:24 the *c* of my hands in front
Am 4:6 gave you people *c* of teeth
Heb 9:13 the extent of *c* of the flesh

Cleans
Joh 15:2 every one bearing fruit he *c*

Cleanse
Ge 35:2 *c* yourselves and change your
Le 16:19 *c* it and sanctify it from
Nu 8:6 Israel, and you must *c* them
8:7 should do to them to *c* them
8:7 they must . . . *c* themselves
8:15 *c* them and cause them to move
8:21 atonement for them to *c* them
2Ch 29:15 to *c* the house of Jehovah
34:3 he started to *c* Judah and
Ne 12:30 proceeded to *c* themselves
12:30 *c* the people and the gates
Job 37:21 and proceeded to *c* them
Ps 51:2 And *c* me even from my sin
119:9 a young man *c* his path
Eze 24:13 I had to *c* you, but you did
36:25 I shall *c* you
37:23 sinned, and I will *c* them
39:14 earth, in order to *c* it
39:16 will have to *c* the land
43:26 must *c* it and install it
Da 12:10 Many will *c* themselves and
Mal 3:3 and must *c* the sons of Levi
Mt 23:25 you *c* the outside of the cup
23:26 *c* first the inside of the
Mr 7:4 *c* themselves by sprinkling
Lu 11:39 you *c* the outside of the cup
Joh 11:55 *c* themselves ceremonially
Ac 21:24 *c* yourselves ceremonially with
2Co 7:1 let us *c* ourselves of every
Tit 2:14 *c* for himself a people
Heb 9:14 *c* our consciences from dead
Jas 4:8 *C* your hands, you sinners
1Jo 1:9 *c* us from all unrighteousness

Cleansed
Jos 22:17 we have not *c* ourselves
1Sa 20:26 for he has not been *c*
2Ch 29:18 *c* the whole house of
30:18 and Zebulun, that had not *c*
34:5 he *c* Judah and Jerusalem
34:8 *c* the land and the house, he
Ezr 6:20 *c* themselves as one group
Ne 13:9 they *c* the dining halls
Job 9:30 *c* my hands in potash
Ps 73:13 vain that I have *c* my heart
Pr 20:9 can say: I have *c* my heart
Eze 22:24 You are a land not being *c*
Joe 2:24 must be full of *c* grain
Mt 8:3 his leprosy was *c* away
11:5 the lepers are being *c* and
Lu 4:27 not one of them was *c*, but
7:22 the lepers are being *c* and the
17:17 ten were *c*, were they not?
Ac 10:15 the things God has *c*
11:9 defiled the things God has *c*
21:26 *c* himself ceremonially with
24:18 ceremonially *c* in the temple
Heb 9:22 *c* with blood according to
9:23 be *c* by these means, but
10:2 been *c* once for all time

Cleanser
Mal 3:3 as a refiner and *c* of silver

Cleanses
1Jo 1:7 blood of Jesus his Son *c* us

Cleansing
Le 14:4 for *c* himself two live clean
14:7 *c* himself from the leprosy
14:8 one *c* himself must wash his

Le 14:11 c himself, and the things
14:14 of the one c himself and
14:17 the one c himself and upon
14:18 head of the one c himself
14:19 c himself from his impurity
14:25 ear of the one c himself and
14:28 of the one c himself and
14:29 head of the one c himself
14:31 one c himself before Jehovah
Nu 19:9 be kept for the water for c
19:13 the water for c has not been
19:20 The water for c was not
19:21 spattering the water for c
19:21 one touching the water for c
31:23 purified by the water for c
2Ch 29:16 house of Jehovah to do the c
Isa 66:17 c themselves for the
Jer 4:11 for winnowing, nor for c
Eze 16:4 had not been washed for c
36:33 c you from all your errors
39:12 c the land, for seven
Da 11:35 do a c and to do a whitening
Mr 1:44 offer in behalf of your c the
Lu 5:14 in connection with your c
17:14 going off their c occurred
Ac 21:26 for the ceremonial c, until
Eph 5:26 c it with the bath of water
2Pe 1:9 c from his sins of long ago

Clear
Le 14:36 c out the house before the
Nu 4:13 c away the fatty ashes of
De 4:32 one end of the heavens c to
7:1 c away populous nations from
13:5 you must c out what is evil
17:7 c out what is bad from your
17:12 you must c out what is bad
19:13 you must c away the guilt of
19:19 c away what is bad from
21:9 c away the guilt of innocent
21:21 c away what is bad from
22:21 c away what is bad from
22:22 c away what is bad out of
22:24 c away what is evil from
24:7 you must c away what is bad
27:8 making them quite c
Jg 20:13 let us c out what is bad
1Sa 17:52 c to the valley and as far
2Sa 4:11 I not c you out of the earth
13:18 lead her c outside, and he
1Ki 2:28 report itself came c to Joab
5:9 by sea c to the place that
7:36 according to the c space of
2Ki 2:2 has sent me c to Bethel
11:11 c to the left side of the
14:13 c to the corner gate
14:25 c to the sea of the Arabah
17:9 c to the fortified city
18:8 c to Gaza and also its
18:8 c to the fortified city
1Ch 4:39 c to the east of the valley
7:28 c to Gaza and its dependent
12:16 to come c to the place
2Ch 4:3 ornaments under it c around
23:10 c to the left side of the
25:13 Samaria c to Beth-horon
25:23 c to the Corner Gate, four
28:9 reached c to the heavens
34:6 Simeon and c to Naphtali, in
Ne 4:6 together c to half its height
11:30 c to the valley of Hinnom
12:37 c to the Water Gate to the
12:39 c to the Fish Gate and the
Job 6:20 have come c to the place and
13:17 Hear my word c through, And
23:3 come c to his fixed place
31:12 would eat c to destruction
Ps 51:4 be in the c when you judge
69:1 have come c to the soul
Isa 10:18 the soul c to the flesh, and
15:8 howling . . . is c to Eglaim
15:8 howling . . . is c to Beer-elim
30:28 that reaches c to the neck
32:4 quick in speaking c things
33:15 c from taking hold on a
40:3 C up the way of Jehovah
57:14 C the way. Remove any
62:10 C the way of the people
Jer 4:10 has reached c to the soul
4:18 has reached c to your heart
25:31 come c to the farthest part
25:33 c to the other end of the
31:40 c to . . . the Horse Gate
32:31 c down to this day, has
Jer 36:2 Josiah, c down to this day
48:34 in Heshbon c to Elealeh
48:34 c to Jahaz they have given
48:34 from Zoar c to Horonaim
51:9 c to the heavens her
La 3:40 do let us return c to Jehovah
Eze 32:14 make their waters c up
34:18 c waters you drink but the
Jon 2:5 Waters encircled me c to the
Hab 3:13 c up to the neck. *Se'lah*
Mal 3:1 he must c up a way before me
Mt 12:18 justice is he will make c
18:31 made c to their master all
Lu 2:15 go c to Bethlehem and see
Ac 11:5 and it came c to me
23:1 with a perfectly c conscience
23:15 c to the military commander
23:22 made these things c to me
23:23 ready to march c to Caesarea
1Co 5:7 C away the old leaven, that
2Ti 2:21 keeps c of the latter ones
Heb 7:15 still more abundantly c that
2Pe 3:1 I am arousing your c thinking
Re 11:2 cast it c out and do not
18:5 sins . . . c up to heaven
21:18 was pure gold like c glass
22:1 c as crystal, flowing out

Cleared
Ge 20:16 and you are c of reproach
24:41 you will be c of obligation
De 26:13 I have c away what is holy
1Ki 22:46 he c out from the land
2Ki 16:6 he c out the Jews from Elath
23:24 Josiah c out, in order that
2Ch 19:3 c out the sacred poles from
Isa 7:25 mountains that used to be c

Clearing
Ex 27:3 for c away its fatty ashes
Ps 80:9 made a c before it, that it
2Co 7:11 yes, c of yourselves, yes

Clearly
Mt 7:5 see c how to extract the
Mr 8:25 the man saw c, and he was
Lu 6:42 you will see c how to extract
Ro 1:20 qualities are c seen from the
2Ti 1:10 made c evident through the

Clears
1Ki 14:10 as one c away the dung

Clear-sighted
Ex 4:11 who appoints . . . the c or the
23:8 the bribe blinds c men and

Cleave
Le 1:17 And he must c it at its wings
Nu 36:7 c each one to the inheritance
36:9 c each to its own inheritance
Jos 23:8 God that you should c, just
23:12 you do c to what is left
Job 19:20 my bones actually c, And I

Cleaved
Job 29:10 tongue c to their palate
Ps 119:31 I have c to your reminders
La 4:4 tongue of the suckling has c to

Cleaves
Pr 7:23 arrow c open his liver, just

Cleaving
De 4:4 you who are c to Jehovah your
Jos 22:5 by c to him and by serving
2Sa 23:10 hand kept c to the sword
Ps 119:25 soul has been c to the very
141:7 one is doing c and splitting

Cleft
Le 11:3 splits the hoof and forms a c
11:7 a former of a c in the hoof
11:26 but is not a former of a c
De 14:6 forms a c into two hoofs
Jg 15:8 in a c of the crag Etam
15:11 the c of the crag Etam and
Jer 13:4 hide it there in a c of the

Clefts
Isa 2:21 into the c of the crags
7:19 upon the c of the crags and
57:5 under the c of the crags
Jer 16:16 out of the c of the crags

Clement
Php 4:3 with C as well as the rest

Cleopas
Lu 24:18 the one named C said to

Climb
2Sa 22:30 By my God I can c a wall
Ps 18:29 by my God I can c a wall
Isa 35:6 lame one will c up just as

Climbed
Jg 9:51 c onto the roof of the tower
Lu 5:19 they c up to the roof, and
9:28 c up into the mountain to
19:4 c a fig-mulberry tree in

Climbing
Nu 20:27 they went c Mount Hor
Ca 2:8 coming, c upon the mountains
Zep 1:9 c upon the platform in that

Climbs
Joh 10:1 c up some other place, that

Cling
De 10:20 and to him you should c
11:22 love Jehovah . . . c to him
13:4 and to him you should c
28:21 cause the pestilence to c to
Job 41:23 folds of its flesh do c
Ps 101:3 It does not c to me
Jer 13:11 of Judah to c even to me
Eze 29:4 to c to your scales
29:4 that c to your very scales
Ro 12:9 c to what is good

Clinging
Ge 34:3 his soul began c to Dinah the
Joh 20:17 said to her: Stop c to me

Clings
Jer 13:11 belt c to the hips of a man

Clip
Eze 44:20 c the hair of their heads

Clipped
Isa 15:2 baldness; every beard is c
Jer 9:26 with hair c at the temples
25:23 with hair c at the temples
48:37 and every beard is c
49:32 their hair c at the temples
Ac 18:18 he had the hair of his head c

Cloak
Ru 3:15 Bring the c that is on you
Es 8:15 a fine-fabric c, even of wool
Mt 27:28 draped him with a scarlet c
27:31 they took the c off and put
2Ti 4:13 bring the c I left at Troas
Heb 1:12 wrap them up just as a c

Cloaks
Isa 3:22 and the c and the purses

Clods
Job 21:33 the c of earth of a torrent
38:38 c of earth themselves get
Ps 65:10 a leveling off of its c

Clopas
Joh 19:25 Mary the wife of C, and

Close
Ge 19:19 calamity may keep c to me
25:11 and Isaac was dwelling c by
35:4 tree that was c by Shechem
37:12 flock of their father c by
37:13 tending flocks c by Shechem
37:18 before he could get c by
45:4 Come c to me, please
45:4 With that they came c to him
47:18 that year came to its c
48:10 he brought them c to him
48:13 and brought them c to him
Ex 12:4 he and his neighbor c by must
14:10 When Pharaoh got c by, the
25:27 rings should be c by the rim
28:8 is upon it for tying it c
39:5 the girdle . . . for tying it c
Le 18:6 any c fleshly relative of his
21:2 c to him, for his mother and
21:3 virgin who is c to him, who
De 2:19 c in front of the sons of
4:30 at the c of the days, then
11:12 to the c of the year
15:9 release, has come c, and your
31:29 at the c of the days, because
Jos 7:2 Ai, which is c by Beth-aven
8:5 we shall go c to the city
Jg 9:6 c by the big tree, the pillar
9:52 on up c to the entrance of the
18:3 c by the house of Micah, they
18:22 c by the house of Micah were
18:25 your voice be heard c to us
19:11 they were c by Jebus, as the

Ru 2:8 keep *c* by my young women
2:21 *C* by the young people that are
2:23 *c* by the young women of Boaz
1Sa 10:2 men *c* by the tomb of Rachel
17:26 men that were standing *c* by
23:19 David concealing himself *c*
31:2 *c* range of Saul and his sons
2Sa 6:7 *c* by the ark of the true God
11:21 have to go so *c* to the wall
13:23 which is *c* by Ephraim
19:37 *c* by the burial place of
20:8 *c* by the great stone that is
24:16 *c* by the threshing floor of
1Ki 1:9 *c* by the stone of Zoheleth
3:17 I gave birth *c* by her in the
7:20 up *c* beside the belly that
8:17 *c* to the heart of David my
8:18 *c* to your heart to build a
8:18 proved to be *c* to your heart
10:2 to be *c* to her heart
10:26 *c* by the king in Jerusalem
21:2 it is *c* by my house
2Ki 4:4 go and *c* the door behind
6:14 and *c* in upon the city
6:32 *c* the door, and you must
1Ch 10:2 kept in *c* range of Saul and
21:15 *c* by the threshing floor of
22:7 *c* to my heart to build a
26:16 *c* by the gate Shallecheth
28:2 was *c* to my heart to build a
2Ch 1:11 proved to be *c* to your heart
1:14 *c* by the king at Jerusalem
6:7 *c* to the heart of David my
6:8 *c* to your heart to build a
6:8 proved to be *c* to your heart
9:1 happened to be *c* to her heart
9:25 *c* by the king in Jerusalem
24:4 *c* to the heart of Jehoash
29:10 *c* to my heart to conclude
Ne 3:23 work *c* by his own house
4:12 Jews dwelling *c* by them
6:10 *c* the doors of the temple
Job 3:10 *c* the doors of my mother's
Ps 38:11 *c* acquaintances themselves
69:15 well *c* its mouth over me
Isa 14:16 *c* examination even to you
34:1 Come up *c*, you nations
41:1 come up *c* together for the
45:20 *c* together, you escapees
57:3 you men, come up *c* here
65:5 saying, Keep *c* to yourself
Jer 50:21 destruction *c* upon them
La 5:5 *C* onto our neck we have been
Eze 1:20 lifted up *c* alongside them
1:21 wheels would be lifted up *c*
3:13 sound of the wheels *c* beside
10:19 the wheels also were *c*
11:3 building of houses *c* at hand
11:22 the wheels were *c* by them
42:7 was *c* by the dining rooms
Da 7:13 him up *c* even before that One
7:16 *c* to one of those who were
8:7 into *c* touch with the ram
Mt 21:1 when they got *c* to Jerusalem
Mr 4:37 boat was *c* to being swamped
Lu 5:1 when the crowd was pressing *c*
23:36 coming *c* and offering him
24:28 they got *c* to the village
Ac 9:23 days were coming to a *c*
22:6 drawing *c* to Damascus, about
27:33 *c* to the approach of day
Jas 4:8 Draw *c* to God, and he will
4:8 and he will draw *c* to you
5:8 presence of the Lord . . . *c*
1Pe 4:7 end of all . . . drawn *c*
2Pe 3:12 *c* in mind the presence of

Closed
Ge 2:21 *c* up the flesh over its place
Ex 14:3 The wilderness has *c* in upon
Jg 3:22 so that the fat *c* in over the
3:23 he *c* the doors of the roof
1Sa 1:5 Jehovah, he had *c* up her womb
1:6 Jehovah had *c* up her womb
4:2 in *c* battle line in the field
1Ki 11:27 *c* up the gap of the city
2Ki 4:5 she *c* the door behind herself
4:21 *c* the door upon him and went
4:33 *c* the door behind them both
2Ch 28:24 *c* the doors of the house
29:7 *c* the doors of the porch and
Ne 13:19 and the doors began to be *c*
Job 17:4 their heart you have *c* to
19:6 hunting net he has *c* in upon
Job 41:15 *C* as with a tight seal
Ps 88:17 *c* in upon me all at one time
Ec 12:4 onto the street have been *c*
Isa 60:11 not be *c* even by day or by
Ac 21:30 the doors were *c*
Re 21:25 gates will not be *c* at all

Closefisted
De 15:7 not . . . be *c* toward your poor

Close-fitting
Isa 30:22 *c* covering of your molten

Closely
Ex 29:5 tie it *c* to him with the
Le 8:7 ephod and bound it *c* to him
25:25 repurchaser *c* related to him
Jg 20:42 battle followed them up *c*
20:45 kept following *c* after them
1Sa 14:22 went pursuing *c* after them
2Sa 19:42 the king is *c* related to us
20:3 they continued shut up *c*
1Ki 3:21 So I examined him *c* in the
Job 41:16 One to the other they fit *c*
Ps 18:32 God is the One girding me *c*
63:8 My soul has *c* followed you
Isa 45:5 I shall *c* gird you, although
Jer 42:16 *c* follow after you to Egypt
Eze 3:13 were *c* touching each other
Mr 3:2 watching him *c* to see whether
Lu 6:7 watching him *c* to see whether
7:11 *C* following this he traveled
8:45 crowds are . . . *c* pressing you
14:1 they were *c* watching him
20:20 after observing him *c*, they
Ac 9:24 *c* watching also the gates
1Co 14:24 he is *c* examined by all
1Ti 4:6 which you have followed *c*
2Ti 3:10 have *c* followed my teaching
Heb 12:3 consider *c* the one who has
1Pe 2:21 you to follow his steps *c*
Re 6:8 And Hades was *c* following him

Closer
Ge 27:41 for my father are getting *c*
Ru 3:12 repurchaser *c* related than I
Pr 18:24 sticking *c* than a brother

Closes
Isa 29:10 *c* your eyes, the prophets

Closest
Nu 27:11 blood relation who is *c* to
Es 1:14 those *c* to him were Carshena

Closing
Jos 2:5 at the *c* of the gate by dark
1Sa 23:26 Saul and his men were *c* in
Ps 17:9 enemies . . . *c* in upon me
Pr 17:28 anyone *c* up his own lips, as
Isa 33:15 *c* his eyes so as not to

Cloth
Ex 26:2 each tent *c* is twenty-eight
26:2 of each tent *c* is four cubits
26:4 the edge of the one tent *c* at
26:4 edge of the outermost tent *c*
26:5 fifty loops on the one tent *c*
26:5 the extremity of the tent *c*
26:8 each tent *c* is thirty cubits
26:8 of each tent *c* is four cubits
26:9 fold double the sixth tent *c*
26:10 the edge of the one tent *c*
26:10 upon the edge of the tent *c*
26:12 tent *c* that remains over is
36:9 each tent *c* was twenty-eight
36:9 each tent *c* four cubits
36:11 the edge of the one tent *c* at
36:11 outermost tent *c* at the
36:12 fifty loops on the one tent *c*
36:12 extremity of the tent *c* that
36:15 tent *c* was thirty cubits
36:15 each tent *c* four cubits
36:17 edge of the outermost tent *c*
36:17 tent *c* that joined with
Nu 4:6 spread out an entire *c* of blue
4:7 spread out a *c* of blue over the
4:8 *c* of coccus scarlet over them
4:9 take a *c* of blue and cover the
4:11 spread out a *c* of blue
4:12 put them in a *c* of blue and
4:13 spread out a *c* of wool dyed
Ps 104:2 the heavens like a tent *c*
Isa 1:18 should be red like crimson *c*
Jer 38:11 worn-out pieces of *c* and
38:12 the pieces of *c* under your
Eze 27:7 your *c* expanse happened to be
Mt 9:16 sews a patch of unshrunk *c*
Mr 2:21 sews a patch of unshrunk *c*
Lu 2:7 she bound him with *c* bands and
2:12 an infant bound in *c* bands
19:20 mina . . . laid away in a *c*
Joh 11:44 was bound about with a *c*
20:7 *c* that had been upon his head

Clothe
Ge 3:21 garments . . . to *c* them
Ex 28:41 with them you must *c* Aaron
29:5 *c* Aaron with the robe and the
29:8 must *c* them with the robes
40:13 must *c* Aaron with the holy
40:14 you must *c* them with robes
Le 6:10 priest must *c* himself with
Nu 20:26 *c* with them Eleazar his son
Es 4:4 sent garments to *c* Mordecai
6:8 which the king does *c* himself
6:9 *c* the man in whose honor the
6:11 *c* Mordecai and make him ride
Job 10:11 flesh you proceeded to *c* me
27:17 be the one to *c* himself
39:19 *c* its neck with a rustling
40:10 splendor may you *c* yourself
Ps 132:16 shall *c* with salvation
132:18 I shall *c* with shame
Pr 23:21 will *c* one with mere rags
Isa 22:21 will *c* him with your robe
49:18 you will *c* yourself just
50:3 I *c* the heavens with
51:9 *c* yourself with strength
Jer 4:30 to *c* yourself with scarlet
46:4 *C* yourselves with coats of
Eze 7:27 *c* himself with desolation
16:10 I went on to *c* you with an
34:3 wool you *c* your own selves
42:14 *c* themselves with other
Zec 3:5 and to *c* him with garments
Mt 6:30 he not much rather *c* you
25:38 or naked, and *c* you
25:43 naked, but you did not *c* me
Lu 12:28 much rather will he *c* you
15:22 and *c* him with it, and put
Col 3:10 *c* yourselves with the new
3:12 *c* yourselves with the tender
3:14 *c* yourselves with love, for

Clothed
Ge 38:19 *c* herself with the garments
41:42 *c* him with garments of fine
Le 8:7 *c* him with the sleeveless coat
8:13 *c* them with robes and girded
Nu 20:28 *c* Eleazar his son with them
1Sa 17:38 *c* him with a coat of mail
28:8 *c* himself with other
2Sa 1:24 *c* you in scarlet with finery
20:8 girded, *c* with a garment
1Ki 22:10 *c* in garments, in the
2Ch 5:12 *c* in fine fabric with
6:41 be *c* with salvation, and let
18:9 his throne, *c* in garments
28:15 naked ones they *c* from the
28:15 *c* them and furnished them
Job 7:5 My flesh . . . *c* with maggots
8:22 will be *c* with shame
29:14 righteousness I *c* myself
Ps 35:26 Let those be *c* with shame
65:13 pastures have become *c* with
93:1 With eminence he is *c*
93:1 Jehovah is *c*—with strength
104:1 splendor you have *c* yourself
109:18 *c* with malediction as his
109:29 be *c* with humiliation
132:9 be *c* with righteousness
Pr 31:21 are *c* with double garments
Isa 14:19 *c* with killed men stabbed
61:10 *c* me with the garments of
Eze 9:2 in among them *c* with linen
9:3 man . . . *c* with the linen
9:11 the man *c* with the linen, at
10:2 to the man *c* with the linen
10:6 man *c* with the linen, saying
10:7 of the one *c* with the linen
23:6 governors *c* with blue
23:12 *c* with perfect taste
38:4 *c* in perfect taste
Da 5:7 with purple he will be *c*
5:16 with purple you will be *c*
5:29 they *c* Daniel with purple
10:5 man *c* in linen, with his hips
12:6 to the man *c* with the linen
12:7 hear the man *c* with the linen
Zec 3:3 *c* in befouled garments and
Mt 22:11 *c* with a marriage garment
25:36 naked, and you *c* me. I fell

Mr 1:6 John was *c* with camel's hair
5:15 *c* and in his sound mind, this
16:5 *c* in a white robe, and they
Lu 8:35 *c* and in his sound mind
24:49 *c* with power from on high
Ac 12:21 Herod *c* himself with royal
1Co 4:11 continue . . . to be scantily *c*
Re 1:13 son of man, *c* with a garment
15:6 *c* with clean, bright linen
18:16 city, *c* with fine linen and
19:14 *c* in white, clean, fine

Clothes
2Sa 13:31 ripped his *c* apart and lay
Isa 51:8 the *c* moth will eat them up
Hag 1:6 There is a putting on of *c*
Mt 6:30 *c* the vegetation of the field
Mr 9:3 far whiter than any *c* cleaner
Lu 12:28 God thus *c* the vegetation in

Clothing
Ge 49:11 certainly wash his *c* in wine
Ex 21:10 her *c* and her marriage due
De 22:12 four extremities of your *c*
Jg 14:12 and thirty outfits of *c*
14:13 and thirty outfits of *c*
1Sa 17:38 Saul now went *c* David with
2Sa 1:24 gold upon your *c*
2Ch 20:25 abundance both goods and *c*
Ezr 3:10 the priests in official *c*
Es 4:2 king's gate in *c* of sackcloth
Job 29:14 and it was *c* me
38:14 take their station as in *c*
41:13 uncovered the face of its *c*
Ps 22:18 And upon my *c* they cast lots
35:13 my *c* was sackcloth
45:13 *c* is with settings of gold
69:11 When I made sackcloth my *c*
102:26 like *c* you will replace
Pr 27:26 young rams are for your *c*
31:22 Her *c* is of linen and wool
31:25 and splendor are her *c*, and
Isa 63:1 who is honorable in his *c*
63:2 Why is it that your *c* is red
63:3 all my *c* I have polluted
Jer 10:9 their *c* is blue thread and
Da 3:21 their other *c* and were thrown
7:9 *c* was white just like snow
Zec 3:4 *c* of you with robes of state
Mt 3:4 *c* of camel's hair and a
6:25 and the body than *c*
6:28 Also, on the matter of *c*
28:3 and his *c* as white as snow
Lu 8:27 he had not worn *c*, and he was
12:23 and the body than *c*
23:11 *c* him with a bright garment
24:4 two men in flashing *c* stood
Jas 2:2 and in splendid *c* enters in
2:2 poor man in filthy *c* also
2:3 one wearing the splendid *c*

Cloths
Ex 26:1 are to make of ten tent *c*, of
26:2 measure for all the tent *c*
26:3 Five tent *c* are to form a
26:3 tent *c* a series with the one
26:6 join the tent *c* one to the
26:7 make *c* of goat's hair for the
26:7 You will make eleven tent *c*
26:8 measure for the eleven tent *c*
26:9 you must join five tent *c* by
26:9 six tent *c* by themselves, and
26:12 of the *c* of the tent is an
26:13 length of the *c* of the tent
36:8 tent *c* of fine twisted linen
36:9 measure for all the tent *c*
36:10 five tent *c* one to another
36:10 five other tent *c* he joined
36:13 joined the tent *c* to one
36:14 make tent *c* of goat's hair
36:14 Eleven tent *c* were what he
36:15 for the eleven tent *c*
36:16 joined five tent *c* together
36:16 six other tent *c* by
Nu 4:25 tent *c* of the tabernacle and
2Sa 7:2 in the middle of tent *c*
1Ch 17:1 the ark . . . is under tent *c*
Ca 1:5 yet like the tent *c* of Solomon
Isa 54:2 stretch out the tent *c* of
Jer 4:20 in a moment my tent *c*
10:20 or raising up my tent *c*
49:29 tent *c* and all their
Hab 3:7 tent *c* of the land of Midian
Ac 5:6 wrapped him in *c*, and carried
19:12 *c* and aprons were borne from

Cloud
Ge 9:13 My rainbow I do give in the *c*
9:14 I bring a *c* over the earth
9:14 certainly appear in the *c*
9:16 rainbow must occur in the *c*
Ex 13:21 a pillar of *c* to lead them
13:22 pillar of *c* would not move
14:19 pillar of *c* departed from
14:20 a *c* together with darkness
14:24 the pillar of fire and *c*
16:10 glory appeared in the *c*
19:9 am coming to you in a dark *c*
19:16 a heavy *c* upon the mountain
20:21 went near to the dark *c* mass
24:15 *c* was covering the mountain
24:16 *c* continued to cover it for
24:16 from the midst of the *c*
24:18 into the midst of the *c* and
33:9 the pillar of *c* would come
33:10 people saw the pillar of *c*
34:5 to come down in the *c* and
40:34 the *c* began to cover the tent
40:35 the *c* resided over it and
40:36 the *c* lifted itself up from
40:37 if the *c* did not lift itself
40:38 *c* was over the tabernacle
Le 16:2 in a *c* I shall appear over
16:13 and the *c* of the incense must
Nu 9:15 the *c* covered the tabernacle
9:16 *c* would cover it by day, and
9:17 *c* would go up from over the
9:17 *c* would reside, there is
9:18 *c* would reside over the
9:19 *c* prolonged its stay over
9:20 *c* would continue a few days
9:21 *c* would continue from evening
9:21 *c* lifted itself in the
9:21 by night that the *c* lifted
9:22 *c* prolonged its stay over the
10:11 *c* lifted itself from over
10:12 *c* proceeded to reside in the
10:34 Jehovah's *c* was over them by
11:25 Jehovah came down in a *c*
12:5 down in the pillar of *c* and
12:10 *c* turned away from over the
14:14 your *c* is standing over them
14:14 pillar of *c* by day and in the
16:42 *c* covered it, and Jehovah's
De 1:33 and by a *c* in daytime
4:11 darkness, *c* and thick gloom
5:22 the *c* and the thick gloom
31:15 the tent in the pillar of *c*
31:15 pillar of *c* began to stand by
1Ki 8:10 *c* itself filled the house of
8:11 ministering because of the *c*
18:44 small *c* like a man's palm
2Ch 5:13 house . . . filled with a *c*
5:14 not able . . . because of the *c*
Ne 9:12 by a pillar of *c* you led them
9:19 The pillar of *c* itself did not
Job 3:5 Let a rain *c* reside over it
7:9 *c* certainly comes to its end
26:8 *c* mass is not split under
26:9 Spreading out over it his *c*
28:26 for the thunderous storm *c*
30:15 like a *c* my salvation has
36:29 can understand the *c* layers
37:11 he burdens the *c*, His light
37:11 light scatters the *c* mass
37:15 the light of his *c* to beam
37:16 about the poisings of the *c*
38:9 I put the *c* as its garment
38:25 for the thunderous storm *c*
38:34 your voice even to the *c*
38:36 put wisdom in the *c* layers
Ps 78:14 lead them with a *c* by day
99:7 In the pillar of *c* he
105:39 spread out a *c* for a screen
Pr 8:28 made firm the *c* masses above
16:15 goodwill is like the *c* of
Isa 4:5 place a *c* by day and a smoke
18:4 *c* of dew in the heat of
19:1 riding on a swift *c* and
25:5 heat with the shadow of a *c*
44:22 just as with a *c*, and
44:22 sins just as with a *c* mass
60:8 come flying just like a *c*
La 3:44 *c* mass, that prayer may not
Eze 1:4 a great *c* mass and quivering
1:28 bow that occurs in a *c* mass
8:11 of the *c* of the incense was
10:3 the *c* was filling the inner
10:4 became filled with the *c*
Na 1:3 the *c* mass is the powder of

Mt 17:5 a bright *c* overshadowed them
17:5 a voice out of the *c*, saying
Mr 9:7 a *c* formed, overshadowing
9:7 and a voice came out of the *c*
Lu 9:34 a *c* formed and began to
9:34 As they entered into the *c*
9:35 a voice came out of the *c*
12:54 see a *c* rising in western
21:27 Son of man coming in a *c*
Ac 1:9 *c* caught him up from their
1Co 10:1 were all under the *c* and all
10:2 by means of the *c* and of the
Heb 12:1 so great a *c* of witnesses
12:18 with fire, and a dark *c* and
Re 10:1 arrayed with a *c*, and a
11:12 went up into heaven in the *c*
14:14 a white *c*, and upon the
14:14 upon the *c* someone seated
14:15 to the one seated on the *c*
14:16 one seated on the *c* thrust

Cloudburst
Isa 30:30 fire and *c* and rainstorm

Clouds
Jg 5:4 *C* also dripped with water
2Sa 22:12 Dark waters, thick *c*
23:4 A morning without *c*
1Ki 18:45 darkened up with *c* and wind
Job 20:6 very head reaches to the *c*
22:14 *C* are a concealment place
26:8 the waters in his *c*, So that
35:5 behold the *c*, that they are
36:28 So that the *c* trickle
38:37 number the *c* in wisdom
Ps 18:11 Dark waters, thick *c*
18:12 there were his *c* that passed
36:5 faithfulness is up to the *c*
68:34 and his strength is in the *c*
77:17 *c* have thunderously poured
97:2 *C* and thick gloom are all
104:3 Making the *c* his chariot
147:8 covering the heavens with *c*
Pr 25:14 As vaporous *c* and a wind
Ec 11:3 the *c* are filled with water
11:4 looking at the *c* will not
12:2 *c* have returned, afterward
Isa 5:6 the *c* I shall lay a command
14:14 the high places of the *c*
30:27 anger and with heavy *c*
Jer 4:13 Like rain *c* he will come up
Eze 30:3 A day of *c*, an appointed
30:18 *c* themselves will cover her
31:3 among the *c* its treetop
31:10 treetop even among the *c*
31:14 treetops even among the *c*
32:7 sun, with *c* I shall cover it
34:12 day of *c* and thick gloom
38:9 Like *c* to cover the land
38:16 like *c* to cover the land
Da 7:13 with the *c* of the heavens
Ho 6:4 is like the morning *c* and like
13:3 like the *c* of morning
Joe 2:2 a day of *c* and thick gloom
Zep 1:15 day of *c* and of thick gloom
Zec 10:1 who is making the storm *c*
Mt 24:30 Son of man coming on the *c*
26:64 coming on the *c* of heaven
Mr 13:26 the Son of man coming in *c*
14:62 coming with the *c* of heaven
1Th 4:17 in *c* to meet the Lord in the
Jude 12 waterless *c* carried this way
Re 1:7 He is coming with the *c*, and

Cloudy
De 33:26 upon *c* skies in his eminence
Ps 77:17 sound the *c* skies have given
78:23 command the *c* skies above
Pr 3:20 *c* skies keep dripping down
Isa 45:8 let the *c* skies themselves
Jer 51:9 lifted up to the *c* skies

Cloven
De 14:7 that split the hoof, *c*

Club
Job 41:29 A *c* has been regarded by
Pr 25:18 As a war *c* and a sword and a
Jer 51:20 You are a *c* for me, as

Clubs
Mt 26:47 crowd with swords and *c*
26:55 and *c* as against a robber to
Mr 14:43 a crowd with swords and *c*
14:48 come out with swords and *c*
Lu 22:52 and *c* as against a robber

Collect
Ge 41:35 *c* all the foodstuffs of
De 13:16 its spoil you should *c* into
30:3 show you mercy and *c* you
30:4 your God will *c* you and from
1Sa 7:5 *C* all Israel together at
22:2 began to *c* together to him
25:1 *c* together and bewail him
28:1 Philistines began to *c* their
29:1 Philistines proceeded to *c*
2Sa 2:30 to *c* all the people together
3:21 *c* all Israel together to my
1Ki 18:19 *c* together all Israel to me
18:20 and *c* the prophets together
2Ki 6:24 to *c* all his camp together
1Ch 13:2 *c* themselves together to us
16:35 *c* us together and deliver
2Ch 15:9 *c* together all Judah and
24:5 *c* money from all Israel to
25:5 *c* Judah together and to have
32:6 *c* them to him at the public
Ezr 7:28 *c* out of Israel the head ones
8:15 *c* them at the river that
10:7 the former exiles to *c*
Ne 1:9 I shall *c* them and certainly
4:20 will *c* yourselves together to
7:5 *c* together the nobles and the
Es 2:3 *c* together all the young women
Ps 106:47 *c* us together from the
Isa 11:12 *c* together from the four
13:14 flock without anyone to *c*
22:9 *c* the waters of the lower
34:15 gledes must *c* themselves
40:11 will *c* together the lambs
43:5 I shall *c* you together
44:11 *c* themselves together
45:20 *C* yourselves and come
54:7 I shall *c* you together
56:8 I shall *c* together to him
66:18 *c* all the nations and
Jer 23:3 *c* together the remnant of
29:14 *c* you together out of all
31:8 *c* them together from the
31:10 himself *c* him together
49:14 *C* yourselves together, and
Eze 11:17 I will also *c* you from the
16:37 *c* them together against you
20:34 *c* you together out of the
20:41 *c* you together from the
22:20 *c* them together in my anger
28:25 *c* together the house of
29:13 *c* the Egyptians together
34:13 *c* them together from the
36:24 *c* you together out of all
37:21 I will *c* them together
39:17 *C* yourselves together and
39:27 *c* them together out of the
Ho 8:10 I shall now *c* them together
9:6 Egypt itself will *c* them
Joe 2:6 *c* a glow of excitement
2:16 *C* the old men together
3:2 *c* together all the nations
3:11 and *c* yourselves together
Mic 2:12 *c* the remaining ones of
4:6 I will *c* together, even her
4:12 *c* them together like a row
Zep 3:8 to *c* together kingdoms
3:19 dispersed I shall *c* together
Zec 10:8 whistle . . . *c* them together
10:10 I shall *c* them together
Mt 13:28 then, to go out and *c* them
13:30 *c* the weeds and bind them
13:41 *c* out from his kingdom all
Heb 7:5 to *c* tithes from the people

Collected
Jos 10:6 have *c* together against us
Jg 9:47 of Shechem had *c* together
12:4 *c* all the men of Gilead
1Sa 7:6 were *c* together at Mizpah
7:7 Israel had *c* themselves
8:4 *c* themselves together and
13:5 *c* themselves together to
13:11 Philistines were being *c*
17:1 were *c* together at Socoh
17:2 Israel, they *c* themselves
28:4 Philistines *c* together and
28:4 Saul *c* all Israel together
1Ki 20:1 he *c* all his military forces
22:6 *c* the prophets together
2Ki 10:18 *c* all the people together
1Ch 11:1 the Israelites *c* themselves
2Ch 15:10 *c* together at Jerusalem in
18:5 king of Israel *c* the prophets
2Ch 20:4 Judah were *c* together to
23:2 *c* together the Levites from
24:5 *c* the priests and the Levites
32:4 people were *c* together, and
Ezr 10:1 *c* themselves together to him
10:9 *c* themselves together at
Ne 5:16 *c* together there for the work
13:11 *c* them together and
Es 2:8 young women were *c* together
2:19 virgins were *c* together a
Ps 102:22 peoples are *c* all together
107:3 *c* together even from the
Isa 34:16 that has *c* them together
43:9 nations all be *c* together
48:14 Be *c* together, all you
49:18 all of them been *c* together
56:8 those already *c* together
60:4 have . . . been *c* together
60:7 will be *c* together to you
Jer 40:15 Judah who are being *c*
Eze 29:5 nor be *c* together
38:8 *c* together out of many
Ho 1:11 Israel will certainly be *c*
Mic 1:7 she *c* them, and to the thing
Na 2:10 have *c* a glow of excitement
Mt 13:40 weeds are *c* and burned with
13:48 *c* the fine ones into vessels
Lu 8:4 a great crowd had *c* together
19:23 have *c* it with interest
Ac 28:3 Paul *c* a certain bundle of

Collecting
Ge 41:48 he kept *c* all the foodstuffs
Nu 11:32 one *c* least gathered ten
15:32 *c* . . . wood on the sabbath
15:33 found him *c* pieces of wood
1Sa 17:1 the Philistines went *c* their
2Sa 2:25 Benjamin went *c* together
1Ki 11:24 kept *c* men to his side and
2Ch 13:7 *c* themselves together by him
Pr 13:11 *c* by the hand is the one
Isa 22:11 *c* basin that you must make
56:8 *c* together the dispersed ones
62:9 ones *c* it will drink it in
Jer 32:37 I am *c* them together out
49:5 *c* together those running
Eze 16:37 I am *c* together all those
22:19 *c* you together into the
22:20 As in *c* silver and copper
Na 3:18 no one *c* them together
Hab 2:5 *c* together to himself all the
Zep 3:20 time of my *c* you together
Mt 13:29 chance, while *c* the weeds
17:24 *c* the two drachmas tax

Collection
Isa 57:13 your *c* of things will not
1Co 16:1 *c* that is for the holy ones

Collections
Ec 12:11 indulging in *c* of sentences
1Co 16:2 *c* will not take place then

Collector
Mt 10:3 Thomas and Matthew the tax *c*
18:17 of the nations and as a tax *c*
Lu 5:27 beheld a tax *c* named Levi
18:10 and the other a tax *c*
18:11 or even as this tax *c*
18:13 tax *c* standing at a distance
19:2 and he was a chief tax *c*

Collectors
Mt 5:46 tax *c* doing the same thing
9:10 tax *c* and sinners came and
9:11 your teacher eats with tax *c*
11:19 friend of tax *c* and sinners
21:31 tax *c* and the harlots are
21:32 the tax *c* . . . believed him
Mr 2:15 many tax *c* and sinners were
2:16 he was eating with . . . tax *c*
2:16 Does he eat with the tax *c*
Lu 3:12 tax *c* came to be baptized
5:29 great crowd of tax *c* and
5:30 eat and drink with tax *c*
7:29 all the people and the tax *c*
7:34 a friend of tax *c* and sinners
15:1 tax *c* and the sinners kept

Collects
Pr 28:8 usury *c* them merely for the

Colonnade
Joh 10:23 temple in the *c* of Solomon
Ac 3:11 what was called Solomon's *c*
5:12 one accord in Solomon's *c*

Colonnades
Joh 5:2 Bethzatha, with five *c*

Colony
Ac 16:12 from there to Philippi, a *c*

Color
Ge 30:32 sheep speckled and with *c*
Pr 23:31 when it exhibits a red *c*
Ca 2:13 a mature *c* for its early figs
Eze 17:3 plumage, which had *c* variety

Color-patched
Ge 30:32 any *c* and speckled one among
30:33 not speckled and *c* among
30:35 he-goats striped and *c*
30:35 the she-goats speckled and *c*
30:39 speckled and *c* ones

Colors
Isa 63:1 garments of glowing *c* from
Eze 16:16 high places of varied *c* and
27:7 Linen in various *c* from
27:16 material of various *c* and
27:24 material of various *c* and

Colossae
Col 1:2 in union with Christ at *C*

Colt
Mt 21:2 an ass tied, and a *c* with her
21:5 upon an ass, yes, upon a *c*
21:7 brought the ass and its *c*
Mr 11:2 you will find a *c* tied, on
11:4 found the *c* tied at the door
11:5 are you doing loosing the *c*
11:7 they brought the *c* to Jesus
Lu 19:30 you will find a *c* tied, on
19:33 loosing the *c* the owners
19:33 Why are you loosing the *c*?
19:35 outer garments upon the *c*
Joh 12:15 seated upon an ass's *c*

Columns
Ca 3:6 *c* of smoke, being perfumed
Joe 2:30 and fire and *c* of smoke

Comb
Pr 24:13 let sweet *c* honey be upon
27:7 will tread down *c* honey, but
Ca 4:11 With *c* honey your lips keep

Combat
Nu 31:14 men of the *c* forces, the
2Sa 2:14 put on a *c* before us
1Ch 20:1 lead the *c* force of the army

Combating
Col 2:23 *c* the satisfying of the flesh

Combine
1Co 2:13 we *c* spiritual matters with

Combined
Ps 136:9 and the stars for *c* dominion

Combs
Ps 19:10 the flowing honey of the *c*

Come*
Ge 11:3 *C* on! Let us make bricks and
11:4 said: *C* on! Let us build
11:7 *C* now! Let us go down and
17:6 and kings will *c* out of you
Ex 1:10 *C* on! Let us deal shrewdly
3:5 Do not *c* near here. Draw your
3:18 must *c*, you and the older
3:18 Jehovah . . . has *c* in touch
5:3 God of the Hebrews has *c* in
19:22 regularly *c* near to Jehovah
20:20 the true God has *c*, and in
20:24 I shall *c* to you and shall
32:34 now, *c*, lead the people to
33:9 pillar of cloud would *c* down
34:5 to *c* down in the cloud and
Nu 6:5 the days . . . *c* to the full
6:13 Naziriteship *c* to the full, he
10:29 *c* with us, and we shall
11:20 that we have *c* out of Egypt
15:2 eventually *c* into the land of
18:4 no stranger may *c* near to you
19:7 he may *c* into the camp
22:5 A people has *c* out of Egypt
De 12:26 *c* to the place that Jehovah
15:9 year of the release, has *c*
17:14 *c* into the land that Jehovah
23:1 may *c* into the congregation
23:2 *c* into the congregation of
Jos 4:21 their fathers in time to *c*
10:24 *C* forward. Place your feet
14:11 to go out and to *c* in

Jos 23:14 They have all *c* true for
Jg 6:5 *c* into the land to ruin it
Ru 3:17 Do not *c* empty-handed to your
Sa 4:7 said: God has *c* into the camp!
9:16 for their outcry has *c* to me
13:11 *c* within the appointed days
25:26 hand *c* to your salvation
26:10 his day will *c* and he will
Sa 5:6 David will not *c* in here
7:12 days *c* to the full, and you
7:12 *c* out of your inward parts
14:29 did not consent to *c* to him
Ki 15:19 *C*, do break your covenant
18:31 Jehovah's word had *c*
22:27 until I *c* in peace
Ki 14:8 Do *c*. Let us look each other
Ch 24:19 *c* into the house of Jehovah
Ch 6:32 *c* and pray toward this house
6:37 *c* to their senses in the land
7:11 *c* into Solomon's heart to do
8:11 the ark of Jehovah has *c*
30:1 *c* to the house of Jehovah
zr 3:8 had *c* out of the captivity to
Ne 8:17 had *c* back from the captivity
13:1 not *c* into the congregation
ob 1:7 Satan: Where do you *c* from?
7:9 down to Sheol will not *c* up
20:22 misfortune itself will *c*
38:11 This far you may *c*, and no
s 24:7 the glorious King may *c* in
24:9 the glorious King may *c* in
32:9 they will *c* near to you
34:11 *C*, you sons, listen to me
36:11 haughtiness *c* against me
42:2 *c* and appear before God
43:4 I will *c* to the altar of God
46:8 *C*, you people, behold the
66:5 *C*, you people, and see the
66:16 *C*, listen, all you who fear
68:31 things will *c* out of Egypt
78:4 even to the generation to *c*
83:4 *C* and let us efface them from
88:2 Before you my prayer will *c*
95:6 *c* in, let us worship and bow
95:10 have not *c* to know my ways
96:8 gift and *c* into his courtyards
96:13 Jehovah. For he has *c*
96:13 he has *c* to judge the earth
98:9 Jehovah, for he has *c* to judge
100:2 *C* in before him with a
100:4 *C* into his gates with
101:2 When will you *c* to me?
102:1 may my own cry for help *c*
102:13 the appointed time has *c*
105:23 proceeded to *c* into Egypt
119:77 Let your mercies *c* to me
121:1 From where will my help *c*?
126:6 *c* in with a joyful cry
132:7 *c* into his grand tabernacle
r 2:19 None . . . will *c* back
3:28 *c* back and tomorrow I shall
7:18 *c*, let us drink our fill of
11:2 Has presumptuousness *c*?
11:2 Then dishonor will *c*
a 2:13 Rise up, *c*, O girl companion
6:13, 13 *C* back, *c* back, O
6:13 O Shulammite! *C* back
a 1:18 *C*, now, you people, and let
2:3 *C*, you people, and let us go
2:5 *c* and let us walk in the
19:23 will actually *c* into Egypt
21:12 inquire. *C* again!
27:13 *c* and bow down to Jehovah
34:1 *C* up close, you nations
35:4 God will *c* with vengeance
35:4 will *c* and save you people
35:10 *c* to Zion with a joyful cry
49:9 say to the prisoners, *C* out!
51:11 return and must *c* to Zion
55:1 *C* to the water. And the ones
55:1 no money! *C*, buy and eat
55:1 Yes, *c*, buy wine and milk
55:3 Incline your ear and *c* to me
60:6 from Sheba—they will *c*
r 3:16 will it *c* up into the heart
4:13 Like rain clouds he will *c*
5:12 upon us no calamity will *c*
7:31 had not *c* up into my heart
18:18 *C*, men, and let us think
19:5 had not *c* up into my heart
20:6 to Babylon you will *c* and
25:31 A noise will certainly *c*
25:33 *c* to be in that day from
27:18 may not *c* into Babylon

Jer 28:4 who have *c* to Babylon
29:12 *c* and pray to me, and I
31:9 With weeping they will *c*
31:21 *C* back, O virgin of Israel
34:3 and to Babylon you will *c*
36:29 The king of Babylon will *c*
37:8 Chaldeans will certainly *c*
51:61 soon as you *c* to Babylon
La 1:10 not *c* into the congregation
3:22 mercies . . . not *c* to an end
5:21 and we shall readily *c* back
Eze 7:6 An end itself must *c*. The end
14:12 word of Jehovah . . . *c* to me
21:7 Look! It will certainly *c*
23:39 *c* into my sanctuary on that
32:11 Babylon will *c* upon you
46:9 *c* in before Jehovah in the
Da 9:13 calamity—it has *c* upon us
Ho 3:5 the sons of Israel will *c* back
14:1 Do *c* back, O Israel, to
14:2 words and *c* back to Jehovah
Joe 1:15 the Almighty One it will *c*
2:12 *c* back to me with all your
2:13 *c* back to Jehovah your God
Am 8:2 The end has *c* to my people
Mic 4:2 *C*, you people, and let us go
7:12 they will *c* from Assyria
Hab 3:3 God . . . to *c* from Teman
Hag 2:7 desirable things . . . *c* in
Zec 8:22 *c* to seek Jehovah of armies
Mal 3:1 *c* to His temple the true Lord
3:1 He will certainly *c*, Jehovah
3:5 I will *c* near to you people
Mt 6:10 Let your kingdom *c*. Let your
8:9 I say . . . *C*! and he comes
11:14 Elijah who is destined to *c*
11:23 Down to Hades you will *c*
11:28 *C* to me, all you who are
12:32 system of things . . . to *c*
15:18 *c* out of the heart, and
17:10 say that Elijah must *c* first
17:12 Elijah has already *c* and
18:7 stumbling blocks must . . . *c*
19:21 and *c* be my follower
22:4 *C* to the marriage feast
23:36 will *c* upon this generation
24:5 *c* on the basis of my name
24:14 and then the end will *c*
24:17 not *c* down to take the goods
24:50 master of that slave will *c*
25:34 *C*, you who have been blessed
27:25 His blood *c* upon us and upon
27:40 *c* down off the torture stake
Mr 1:17 *C* after me, and I shall cause
8:34 If anyone wants to *c* after me
9:1 kingdom of God already *c* in
9:11 say that first Elijah must *c*
10:21 and *c* be my follower
13:6 *c* on the basis of my name
14:38 you do not *c* into temptation
14:41 It is enough! The hour has *c*
Lu 1:35 Holy spirit will *c* upon you
5:35 Yet days will *c* when the
7:8 to another, *C*! and he comes
10:9 The kingdom of God has *c* near
10:15 Down to Hades you will *c*
11:2 Let your kingdom *c*
18:22 and *c* be my follower
19:13 Do business till I *c*
19:43 days will *c* upon you when
20:16 He will *c* and destroy these
21:8 *c* on the basis of my name
Joh 1:46 Can anything good *c* out of
1:46 said to him: *C* and see
3:2 as a teacher have *c* from God
3:19 light has *c* into the world
3:20 does not *c* to the light
5:29 *c* out . . . to a resurrection
5:43 *c* in the name of my Father
6:14 the prophet that was to *c*
6:38 *c* down from heaven to do
6:42 I have *c* down from heaven
6:44 No man can *c* to me unless
6:65 No one can *c* to me unless
6:69 believed and *c* to know that
7:8 due time has not yet fully *c*
7:28 not *c* of my own initiative
7:30 his hour had not yet *c*
7:34 and where I am you cannot *c*
7:36 and where I am you cannot *c*
7:37 let him *c* to me and drink
7:50 who had *c* to him previously
8:20 his hour had not yet *c*
8:21 I am going you cannot *c*

Joh 8:22 I am going you cannot *c*
8:42 I *c* of my own initiative at
9:22 *c* to an agreement that, if
10:10 I have *c* that they might
11:25 he dies, will *c* to life
11:43 Lazarus, *c* on out!
12:27 why I have *c* to this hour
12:46 *c* as a light into the world
13:33 Where I go you cannot *c*
16:7 helper will by no means *c* to
17:1 Father, the hour has *c*
18:37 I have *c* into the world
Ac 1:11 *c* thus in the same manner as
3:19 seasons of refreshing may *c*
14:11 gods . . . have *c* down to us
16:15 And she just made us *c*
19:32 why they had *c* together
22:14 you to *c* to know his will
24:25 and the judgment to *c*
Ro 8:38 nor things to *c* nor powers
11:26 deliverer will *c* out of Zion
1Co 3:22 or things to *c*, all things
4:19 will *c* to you shortly, if
4:21 Shall I *c* to you with a rod
11:18 when you *c* together in a
14:23 or unbelievers *c* in, will
16:22 O our Lord, *c*!
2Co 1:22 us the token of what is to *c*
5:5 token of what is to *c*, that
12:14 I am ready to *c* to you
Eph 1:21 but also in that to *c*
2:13 *c* to be near by the blood of
Col 2:17 a shadow of the things to *c*
1Ti 3:14 hoping to *c* to you shortly
4:8 now and that which is to *c*
2Ti 4:9 utmost to *c* to me shortly
Heb 2:5 the inhabited earth to *c*
10:1 of the good things to *c*
10:7 I am *c* (in the roll of the
10:9 I am *c* to do your will
13:14 seeking the one to *c*
2Pe 2:6 a pattern . . . of things to *c*
3:10 day will *c* as a thief
1Jo 5:20 that the Son of God has *c*
2Jo 12 I am hoping to *c* to you and
Re 3:3 I shall *c* as a thief, and you
3:10 hour of test, which is to *c*
4:1 *C* on up here, and I shall
6:1 with a voice as of thunder: *C*!
6:3 second living creature say: *C*!
6:5 third living creature say: *C*!
6:7 fourth living creature say: *C*!
6:17 day of their wrath has *c*, and
7:14 *c* out of the great tribulation
11:12 say to them: *C* on up here
12:12 Devil has *c* down to you
15:4 nations will *c* and worship
16:17 saying: It has *c* to pass!
18:8 in one day her plagues will *c*
22:17 bride keep on saying: *C*!
22:17 let anyone hearing say: *C*!
22:17 And let anyone thirsting *c*
22:20 Amen! *C*, Lord Jesus

Comeliness

1Co 12:23 have the more abundant *c*

Comely

Ca 1:5 A black girl I am, but *c*, O
1:10 cheeks are *c* among the hair
2:14 and your form is *c*
6:4 *c* like Jerusalem, awesome as
Isa 52:7 How *c* upon the mountains are
Jer 6:2 a *c* and daintily bred woman
Ro 10:15 How *c* are the feet of those
1Co 12:24 our *c* parts do not need

Comes*

Ge 49:10 until Shiloh *c*; and to him
Ex 28:29 when he *c* into the Holy as a
28:30 when he *c* in before Jehovah
Le 14:46 whoever *c* into the house any
22:3 who *c* near to the holy things
De 31:11 *c* to see the face of Jehovah
1Ki 8:42 *c* and prays toward this
Job 3:25 dreaded, and it *c* upon me
3:25 what I have been scared of *c*
14:14 wait, Until my relief *c*
27:9 In case distress *c* upon him
37:8 beast *c* into the ambush
37:9 Out of the interior room *c*
37:22 the north golden splendor *c*
Ps 49:19 His soul finally *c* only as
Pr 1:26 mock when what you dread *c*
1:27 dread *c* just like a storm
6:26 *c* down to a round loaf of

COMMANDED

Nu 1:54 all that Jehovah had *c* Moses
2:33 just as Jehovah had *c* Moses
2:34 all that Jehovah had *c* Moses
3:16 just as he had been *c*
3:42 as Jehovah had *c* him, to
3:51 just as Jehovah had *c* Moses
4:49 just as Jehovah had *c* Moses
8:3 just as Jehovah had *c* Moses
8:20 that Jehovah had *c* Moses as
8:22 as Jehovah had *c* Moses
9:5 all that Jehovah had *c* Moses
15:23 has *c* you by means of Moses
15:23 from the day that Jehovah *c*
15:36 just as Jehovah had *c* Moses
17:11 just as Jehovah had *c* him
19:2 the law that Jehovah has *c*
20:9 just as he had *c* him
20:27 did just as Jehovah had *c*
26:4 just as Jehovah had *c* Moses
27:11 just as Jehovah has *c* Moses
27:22 just as Jehovah had *c* him
29:40 that Jehovah had *c* Moses
30:1 the word that Jehovah has *c*
30:16 regulations that Jehovah *c*
31:7 just as Jehovah had *c* Moses
31:21 the law that Jehovah *c* Moses
31:31 just as Jehovah had *c* Moses
31:41 just as Jehovah had *c* Moses
31:47 just as Jehovah had *c* Moses
34:13 Moses *c* the sons of Israel
34:13 Jehovah has *c* to give to the
34:29 ones whom Jehovah *c* to make
36:2 Jehovah *c* my lord to give the
36:2 was *c* by Jehovah to give the
36:5 Moses *c* the sons of Israel at
36:6 word that Jehovah has *c* for
36:10 Just as Jehovah had *c* Moses
36:13 Jehovah *c* by means of Moses
De 1:3 all that Jehovah had *c* him for
1:19 as Jehovah our God had *c* us
1:41 Jehovah our God has *c* us! So
3:18 So I *c* you men at that
3:21 I *c* Joshua at that particular
4:5 as Jehovah my God has *c* me
4:13 covenant, which he *c* you to
4:14 Jehovah *c* at that particular
4:23 Jehovah your God has *c* you
5:12 just as Jehovah your God *c* you
5:15 *c* you to carry on the sabbath
5:16 Jehovah your God has *c* you
5:32 Jehovah your God has *c* you
5:33 all the way . . . God has *c* you
6:1 God has *c* to teach you, so as
6:17 regulations that he has *c* you
6:20 Jehovah our God has *c* you
6:24 Jehovah *c* us to carry out all
6:25 just as he has *c* us
9:12 the way about which I *c* them
9:16 which Jehovah had *c* you
10:5 just as Jehovah had *c* me
12:21 just as I have *c* you, and you
13:5 God has *c* you to walk
17:3 a thing that I have not *c*
18:20 a word that I have not *c* him
20:17 Jehovah your God has *c* you
24:8 Just as I have *c* them, you
26:13 commandment that you have *c*
26:14 all that you have *c* me
28:45 his statutes that he *c* you
29:1 Jehovah *c* Moses to conclude
31:5 commandment that I have *c*
31:29 way about which I have *c*
34:9 just as Jehovah had *c* Moses
Jos 1:7 that Moses my servant *c* you
1:9 Have I not *c* you?
1:13 servant of Jehovah *c* you
1:16 you have *c* us we shall do
4:8 just as Joshua had *c*, and
4:10 that Jehovah had *c* Joshua to
4:10 all that Moses had *c* Joshua
4:17 Joshua *c* the priests, saying
6:10 Joshua had *c* the people
8:8 See, I have *c* you
8:31 had *c* the sons of Israel
8:33 the servant of Jehovah had *c*
8:35 that Moses had *c* that Joshua
9:24 had *c* Moses his servant to
10:27 Joshua *c*, and they went
10:40 the God of Israel had *c*
11:12 the servant of Jehovah had *c*
11:15 as Jehovah had *c* Moses his
11:15 so Moses *c* Joshua, and so
11:15 that Jehovah had *c* Moses
11:20 as Jehovah had *c* Moses
Jos 13:6 just as I have *c* you
14:2 Jehovah had *c* by means of
14:5 Just as Jehovah had *c* Moses
17:4 Jehovah it was who *c* Moses
21:2 *c* cities to be given us in
21:8 as Jehovah had *c* by means of
22:2 all that Moses . . . *c* you
22:2 in all that I have *c* you
22:5 servant of Jehovah *c* you by
23:16 that he *c* you, and because
Jg 2:20 my covenant that I *c* their
3:4 that he had *c* their fathers
13:14 I have *c* her let her keep
21:20 they *c* the sons of Benjamin
Ru 2:9 *c* the young men not to touch
2:15 Boaz now *c* his young men
3:6 her mother-in-law had *c* her
1Sa 2:29 my offering that I have *c* in
13:13 commandment . . . that he *c*
13:14 not keep what Jehovah *c* you
17:20 just as Jesse had *c* him
18:22 Further, Saul *c* his servants
20:29 my own brother that *c* me
21:2 king himself *c* me as to a
21:2 which I have *c* you. And I
2Sa 4:12 David *c* the young men and
5:25 as Jehovah had *c* him, and he
7:7 *c* to shepherd my people
13:28 Absalom *c* his attendants
13:28 Have not I myself *c* you?
13:29 just as Absalom had *c*
14:19 Joab that *c* me, and he it
18:5 the king *c* all the chiefs
18:12 the king *c* you and Abishai
21:14 that the king had *c*
24:19 what Jehovah had *c*
1Ki 2:46 the king *c* Benaiah the son of
5:17 *c* that they should quarry
9:4 according to all that I have *c*
11:10 *c* him not to go after other
11:10 that which Jehovah had *c*
13:9 way he *c* me by the word of
13:21 Jehovah your God *c* you
15:5 He had *c* him all the days of
22:31 *c* the thirty-two chiefs of
2Ki 11:9 Jehoiada the priest had *c*
11:15 Jehoiada the priest *c* the
16:16 all that King Ahaz had *c*
17:13 that I *c* your forefathers
17:15 *c* them not to do like them
17:27 king of Assyria *c*, saying
17:34 *c* the sons of Jacob
17:35 covenant with them and *c*
18:6 that Jehovah had *c* Moses
18:12 the servant of Jehovah had *c*
21:8 all that I have *c* them
21:8 my servant Moses *c* them
22:12 king *c* Hilkiah the priest
23:21 king now *c* all the people
1Ch 6:49 servant of the true God had *c*
14:16 just as the true God had *c*
15:15 as Moses had *c* by Jehovah's
16:15 The word that he *c*, to a
17:6 I *c* to shepherd my people
22:13 Jehovah *c* Moses respecting
24:19 the God of Israel had *c* him
2Ch 7:17 to all that I have *c* you, and
18:30 *c* the chiefs of the chariots
23:8 Jehoiada the priest had *c*
25:4 Jehovah *c*, saying: Fathers
33:8 *c* them concerning all the
34:20 king *c* Hilkiah and Ahikam
Ezr 4:3 Cyrus the king of Persia has *c*
9:11 *c* by means of your servants
Ne 1:8 word that you *c* Moses your
8:1 which Jehovah had *c* Israel
8:14 Jehovah had *c* by means of
9:14 *c* them by means of Moses
Es 3:2 the king had *c* respecting him
3:12 Haman *c* the king's satraps
4:10 and *c* him concerning Mordecai
8:9 all that Mordecai *c* to the
Job 38:12 that you *c* the morning
Ps 33:9 *c*, and it proceeded to stand
78:5 that he *c* our forefathers
105:8 The word that he *c*, to a
111:9 he has *c* his covenant
119:138 have *c* your reminders in
133:3 Jehovah *c* the blessing to be
148:5 *c*, and they were created
Isa 45:12 the army of them I have *c*
48:5 molten image have *c* them
Jer 7:31 a thing that I had not *c*
11:4 which I *c* your forefathers
Jer 11:8 this covenant that I *c* them
13:5 just as Jehovah had *c* me
13:6 the belt that I *c* you to hide
14:14 *c* them or spoken to them
17:22 as I *c* your forefathers
19:5 I had not *c* or spoken of
26:8 *c* him to speak to all the
32:13 *c* Baruch before their eyes
32:23 things that you *c* them to
35:8 in everything that he *c* us
35:10 Jonadab our forefather *c* us
35:14 that he *c* his sons, to drink
35:16 forefather that he *c* them
35:18 according to all that he *c*
36:5 Jeremiah *c* Baruch, saying
36:8 Jeremiah the prophet had *c*
36:26 king *c* Jerahmeel the son
37:21 King Zedekiah *c*, and they
38:10 king *c* Ebed-melech the
38:27 words that the king had *c*
50:21 to all that I have *c* you
51:59 Jeremiah the prophet *c*
La 1:10 you *c* that they should not
2:17 *c* from the days of long ago
3:37 Jehovah himself has not *c*
Eze 9:11 done just as you have *c* me
10:6 *c* the man clothed with the
12:7 the way that I had been *c*
24:18 just as I had been *c*
37:7 just as I had been *c*
37:10 prophesied just as he had *c*
Da 5:29 Belshazzar *c*, and they clothed
6:16 the king himself *c*, and they
6:23 Daniel himself he *c* to be
6:24 king *c*, and they brought these
Jon 2:10 Jehovah *c* the fish, so that
Na 1:14 concerning you Jehovah has *c*
Zec 1:6 *c* my servants, the prophets
Mal 4:4 which I *c* him in Horeb
Mt 14:9 the king . . . *c* it to be given
14:19 *c* the crowds to recline on
17:9 Jesus *c* them, saying: Tell
27:10 to what Jehovah had *c* me
27:58 Pilate *c* it to be given over
28:20 all the things I have *c* you
Mr 6:27 and *c* him to bring his head
13:34 *c* the doorkeeper to keep on
Lu 18:40 *c* the man to be led to him
19:15 he *c* to be called to him
Ac 4:15 *c* them to go outside the
8:38 he *c* the chariot to halt, and
10:33 been *c* by Jehovah to say
10:48 *c* them to be baptized in the
12:19 *c* them to be led off to
21:34 *c* him to be brought to the
22:30 *c* the chief priests and all
23:10 *c* the force of soldiers to go
23:35 he *c* that he be kept under
25:6 and *c* Paul to be brought in
25:17 *c* the man to be brought in
25:21 I *c* him to be kept until I
27:43 he *c* those able to swim to

Commander

Jg 11:6 and serve as our *c*, and let us
11:11 over them as head and *c*
Pr 6:7 it has no *c*, officer or ruler
25:15 By patience a *c* is induced
Isa 55:4 as a leader and *c* to the
Da 11:18 *c* will have to make the
Joh 18:12 *c* and the officers of the
Ac 21:31 came up to the *c* of the band
21:32 sight of the military *c* and
21:33 the military *c* came near and
21:37 Paul said to the military *c*
22:24 military *c* ordered him to
22:26 he went to the military *c*
22:27 military *c* approached and
22:28 *c* responded: I purchased
22:29 military *c* became afraid on
23:10 the military *c* became afraid
23:15 clear to the military *c* why
23:17 man off to the military *c*
23:18 led him to the military *c*
23:19 The military *c* took him by
23:22 the military *c* let the young
24:22 Lysias the military *c* comes

Commander's

Ge 49:10 neither the *c* staff from
Nu 21:18 With a *c* staff, with their
Ps 60:7 Judah is my *c* staff
108:8 Judah is my *c* staff

Commanders

Jos 10:24 the *c* of the men of war

Jg 5:9 heart is for the *c* of Israel
5:14 Out of Machir the *c* went
Mic 3:1 you *c* of the house of Israel
3:9 you *c* of the house of Israel
Mr 6:21 and the military *c* and the
Ac 25:23 with military *c* as well as
Re 6:15 military *c* and the rich and
19:18 fleshy parts of military *c*

Commanding

Ge 27:8 listen . . . in what I am *c* you
Ex 34:11 keep what I am *c* you today
34:32 *c* them all that Jehovah had
Le 7:38 *c* the sons of Israel to
Nu 32:25 will do just as my lord is *c*
De 4:2 the word that I am *c* you
4:2 commandments . . . that I am *c*
4:40 commandments that I am *c* you
6:2 commandments that I am *c* you
6:6 these words that I am *c* you
7:11 decisions that I am *c* you
8:1 commandment that I am *c* you
8:11 statutes that I am *c* you
10:13 his statutes that I am *c* you
11:8 commandment that I am *c* you
11:13 commandments that I am *c*
11:22 commandment that I am *c* you
11:27 that I am *c* you today
11:28 the way about which I am *c*
12:11 all about which I am *c* you
12:14 do all that I am *c* you
12:28 these words that I am *c* you
12:32 Every word that I am *c* you
13:18 I am *c* you today, so as to
15:5 commandment that I am *c* you
15:11 I am *c* you, saying, You
15:15 I am *c* you this thing today
19:7 That is why I am *c* you
19:9 commandment that I am *c* you
24:18 I am *c* you to do this thing
24:22 I am *c* you to do this thing
26:16 God is *c* you to carry out
27:1 commandment that I am *c* you
27:4 just as I am *c* you today
27:10 which I am *c* you today
28:1 commandments that I am *c* you
28:13 I am *c* you today to observe
28:14 words that I am *c* you today
28:15 statutes that I am *c* you
30:2 all that I am *c* you today
30:8 that I am *c* you today
30:11 I am *c* you today is not too
30:16 I am *c* you today, so as to
Jer 34:22 Here I am *c*, is the
Am 6:11 For here is Jehovah *c*, and he
9:9 look! I am *c*, and I will
Joh 15:14 if you do what I am *c* you
Ac 23:30 *c* the accusers to speak
2Co 8:8 not in the way of *c* you, but
1Th 4:16 from heaven with a *c* call
1Ti 4:3 *c* to abstain from foods which

Commandingly

Ps 119:4 have *c* given your orders

Commandment

Ex 24:12 law and the *c* that I must
Le 4:23 the *c* has been made known to
Nu 15:31 and his *c* that he has broken
De 5:31 let me speak to you all the *c*
6:1 the *c*, the regulations and the
6:25 take care to do all this *c*
7:11 you must keep the *c* and the
8:1 Every *c* that I am commanding
11:8 you must keep the whole *c*
11:22 strictly keep all this *c*
15:5 be careful to do all this *c*
17:20 not turn aside from the *c*
19:9 keep all this *c* that I am
26:13 in accord with all your *c*
27:1 an observing of every *c* that
30:11 this *c* that I am commanding
31:5 the *c* that I have commanded
Jos 22:3 the *c* of Jehovah your God
22:5 carry out the *c* and the law
1Sa 13:13 not kept the *c* of Jehovah
1Ki 2:43 the *c* that I solemnly laid
13:21 the *c* with which Jehovah
2Ki 17:34 law and the *c* that Jehovah
17:37 the law and the *c* that he
18:36 *c* of the king was, saying
1Ch 22:12 give you *c* concerning Israel
2Ch 8:13 *c* of Moses for the sabbaths
8:14 *c* of David the man of the
8:15 king's *c* to the priests
14:4 and to do the law and the *c*
2Ch 17:4 in his *c* he walked, and
19:10 involving law and *c* and
24:21 pelted . . . at the king's *c*
29:15 according to the king's *c*
29:25 by the *c* of David and of Gad
29:25 *c* was by means of his
30:6 *c* of the king, saying
30:12 perform the *c* of the king
31:21 *c* to search for his God
35:10 according to the king's *c*
35:15 to the *c* of David and of
35:16 the *c* of King Josiah
Ezr 10:3 those trembling at the *c* of
Ne 11:23 *c* of the king in behalf of
12:24 *c* of David the man of the
12:45 the *c* of David and Solomon
Es 3:3 sidestepping the king's *c*
Job 23:12 From the *c* of his lips I do
Ps 19:8 The *c* of Jehovah is clean
119:96 Your *c* is very broad
119:98 your *c* makes me
Pr 6:20 son, the *c* of your father
6:23 *c* is a lamp, and a light the
13:13 one fearing the *c* is the
19:16 He that is keeping the *c* is
Ec 8:5 keeping the *c* will not know
Isa 29:13 men's *c* that is being
36:21 for the *c* of the king was
Jer 32:11 sealed according to the *c*
35:14 the *c* of their forefather
35:16 the *c* of their forefather
35:18 obeyed the *c* of Jehonadab
Mal 2:1 this *c* is to you, O priests
2:4 I have sent to you this *c*
Mt 15:3 also overstep the *c* of God
22:36 which is the greatest *c* in
22:38 is the greatest and first *c*
Mr 7:8 Letting go the *c* of God, you
7:9 you set aside the *c* of God
10:5 he wrote you this *c*
12:28 Which *c* is first of all?
12:31 There is no other *c* greater
Lu 15:29 never . . . transgress your *c*
23:56 sabbath according to the *c*
Joh 10:18 *c* on this I received from
12:49 *c* as to what to tell and
12:50 *c* means everlasting life
13:34 I am giving you a new *c*
14:31 Father has given me *c*
15:12 my *c*, that you love one
Ac 1:2 given *c* through holy spirit
13:47 Jehovah has laid *c* upon us
Ro 7:8 an inducement through the *c*
7:9 when the *c* arrived, sin came
7:10 *c* which was to life, this I
7:11 inducement through the *c*
7:12 *c* is holy and righteous and
7:13 more sinful through the *c*
13:9 whatever other *c* there is
1Co 14:37 they are the Lord's *c*
1Ti 6:14 observe the *c* in a spotless
Heb 7:5 *c* to collect tithes from the
7:16 law of a *c* depending upon
7:18 aside of the preceding *c* on
9:19 every *c* according to the Law
2Pe 2:21 turn away from the holy *c*
3:2 the *c* of the Lord and Savior
1Jo 2:7, 7 not a new *c*, but an old *c*
2:7 This old *c* is the word which
2:8 I am writing you a new *c*
3:23 *c*, that we have faith in the
3:23 just as he gave us *c*
4:21 this *c* we have from him
2Jo 4 we received *c* from the Father
5 not a new *c*, but one which we
6 This is the *c*, just as you

Commandments

Ex 15:26 give ear to his *c* and keep
16:28 people refuse to keep my *c*
20:6 who love me and keep my *c*
Le 22:31 keep my *c* and do them. I am
26:3 keeping my *c* and you do carry
26:14 nor do all these *c*
26:15 not to do all my *c*, to the
27:34 *c* that Jehovah gave Moses as
Nu 15:22 and not do all these *c*
15:39 the *c* of Jehovah and do them
15:40 certainly do all my *c* and
36:13 These are the *c* and the
De 4:2 keep the *c* of Jehovah your God
4:40 his regulations and his *c*
5:10 love me and keep my *c*
5:29 to keep all my *c* always
De 6:2 keep all his statutes and his *c*
6:17 keep the *c* of Jehovah your God
7:9 and those who keep his *c*
8:2 you would keep his *c* or not
8:6 keep the *c* of Jehovah your
8:11 so as not to keep his *c* and
10:13 keep the *c* of Jehovah and
11:1 judicial decisions and his *c*
11:13 will without fail obey my *c*
11:27 obey the *c* of Jehovah your
11:28 the *c* of Jehovah your God
13:4 and his *c* you should keep, and
13:18 by keeping all his *c* that
26:13 have not overstepped your *c*
26:17 observe his . . . *c*
26:18 you will observe all his *c*
27:10 carry out his *c* and his
28:1 being careful to do all his *c*
28:9 keep the *c* of Jehovah your
28:13 keep obeying the *c* of Jehovah
28:15 do all his *c* and his statutes
28:45 keeping his *c* and his
30:8 do all his *c* that I am
30:10 keep his *c* and his statutes
30:16 listen to the *c* of Jehovah
30:16 his *c* and his statutes and
Jos 22:5 and by keeping his *c* and by
Jg 2:17 by obeying the *c* of Jehovah
3:4 obey Jehovah's *c* that he had
1Ki 2:3 his *c* and his judicial
3:14 my regulations and my *c*
6:12 keep all my *c* by walking in
8:58 his *c* and his regulations
8:61 keeping his *c* as at this day
9:6 not keep my *c* and my statutes
11:34 kept my *c* and my statutes
11:38 my statutes and my *c*
14:8 kept my *c* and who walked
18:18 left the *c* of Jehovah, and
2Ki 17:13 and keep my *c*, my statutes
17:16 leaving all the *c* of Jehovah
17:19 not keep the *c* of Jehovah
18:6 *c* that Jehovah had commanded
23:3 his *c* and his testimonies
1Ch 28:7 strongly resolved to do my *c*
28:8 all the *c* of Jehovah your God
29:19 heart to keep your *c*, your
2Ch 7:19 leave my statutes and my *c*
24:20 overstepping the *c* of
34:31 to keep his *c* and his
Ezr 7:11 words of the *c* of Jehovah
9:10 For we have left your *c*
9:14 go breaking your *c* again
Ne 1:5 loving him and keeping his *c*
1:7 have not kept the *c* and the
1:9 kept my *c* and done them
9:13 good regulations and *c*
9:14 *c* and regulations and a law
9:16 they did not listen to your *c*
9:29 and did not listen to your *c*
9:34 nor paid attention to your *c*
10:29 *c* of Jehovah our Lord and
10:32 imposed upon ourselves *c* to
Ps 78:7 but observe his own *c*
89:31 they do not keep my own *c*
112:1 *c* he has taken very much
119:6 When I look to all your *c*
119:10 me to go astray from your *c*
119:19 not conceal from me your *c*
119:21 are straying from your *c*
119:32 run the very way of your *c*
119:35 in the pathway of your *c*
119:47 show a fondness for your *c*
119:48 your *c* that I have loved
119:60 not delay To keep your *c*
119:66 *c* I have exercised faith
119:73 that I may learn your *c*
119:86 your *c* are faithfulness
119:115 observe the *c* of my God
119:127 why I have loved your *c*
119:131 for your *c* I have longed
119:143 Your *c* I was fond of
119:151 And all your *c* are truth
119:166 I have done your own *c*
119:172 your *c* are righteousness
119:176 not forgotten your own *c*
Pr 2:1 treasure up my own *c* with
3:1 my *c* may your heart observe
4:4 Keep my *c* and continue living
7:1 treasure up my own *c* with you
7:2 Keep my *c* and continue living
10:8 wise in heart will accept *c*
Ec 12:13 the true God and keep his *c*
Isa 48:18 pay attention to my *c*

Jer 35:18 continue keeping all his *c*
Da 9:4 and to those keeping his *c*
9:5 turning aside from your *c* and
Mt 5:19 breaks one of these least *c*
19:17 observe the *c* continually
22:40 On these two *c* the whole
Mr 10:19 You know the *c*, Do not
Lu 1:6 in accord with all the *c*
18:20 You know the *c*, Do not
Joh 14:15 you will observe my *c*
14:21 He that has my *c* and
15:10 If you observe my *c*, you
15:10 observed the *c* of the Father
1Co 7:19 observance of God's *c* does
Eph 2:15 Law of *c* consisting in
Tit 1:14 Jewish fables and *c* of men
1Jo 2:3 we continue observing his *c*
2:4 and yet is not observing his *c*
3:22 we are observing his *c* and
3:24 who observes his *c* remains
5:2 are loving God and doing his *c*
5:3 that we observe his *c*
5:3 yet his *c* are not burdensome
2Jo 6 on walking according to his *c*
Re 12:17 who observe the *c* of God
14:12 observe the *c* of God and

Commands
Ge 12:20 Pharaoh issued *c* to men
26:5 my *c*, my statutes, and my
49:33 Jacob finished giving *c* to
Le 4:2 that Jehovah *c* should not be
4:13 Jehovah *c* should not be done
4:22 God *c* should not be done
4:27 that Jehovah *c* should not be
5:17 all the things that Jehovah *c*
27:34 Moses as *c* to the sons of
2Sa 9:11 king *c* for his servant is
17:23 he gave *c* to his household
2Ki 20:1 Give *c* to your household
Job 37:12 he *c* them upon the face of
Isa 38:1 Give *c* to your household
Mt 15:9 teach *c* of men as doctrines
Mr 7:7 teach as doctrines *c* of men
Col 2:22 the *c* and teachings of men
4:10 received *c* to welcome him
1Ti 4:11 Keep on giving these *c* and
5:7 So keep on giving these *c*

Commemoration
Es 9:28 *c* itself of them not come to

Commenced
Mt 4:17 Jesus *c* preaching and saying
16:21 Jesus Christ *c* showing his
16:22 Peter . . . *c* rebuking him
26:22 they *c* each and every one to
Mr 14:71 he *c* to curse and swear
Lu 3:23 when he *c* his work, was
Joh 7:31 *c* saying: When the Christ
Ac 11:4 this Peter *c* and went on to

Commencement
Ru 1:22 at the *c* of barley harvest

Commencements
Nu 10:10 at the *c* of your months, you
28:11 And at the *c* of your months

Commencing
Lu 24:27 *c* at Moses and all the

Commend
Job 40:14 And I, even I, shall *c* you
Ps 63:3 My own lips will *c* you
117:1 *C* him, all you clans
145:4 generation will *c* your works
147:12 *C* Jehovah, O Jerusalem
1Co 8:8 But food will not *c* us to God
11:2 I *c* you because in all things
11:17 I do not *c* you because it is
11:22 Shall I *c* you? In this I do
11:22 In this I do not *c* you

Commendation
Jg 11:40 to give *c* to the daughter of
Da 2:23 I am giving praise and *c*

Commended
Ec 8:15 I myself *c* rejoicing, because
Lu 16:8 master *c* the steward, though

Commending
1Pe 4:19 *c* their souls to a faithful

Comment
Isa 33:18 heart will *c* in low tones
Ac 28:25 while Paul made this one *c*

Commercial
Mt 22:5 another to his *c* business
2Ti 2:4 in the *c* businesses of life

Commission
Nu 27:19 must *c* him before their eyes
De 3:28 *c* Joshua and encourage him
31:14 Joshua . . . that I may *c* him
31:23 to *c* Joshua the son of Nun
1Sa 13:14 Jehovah will *c* him as a
25:30 *c* you as leader over Israel
1Ki 1:35 *c* to become leader over
4:28 each one according to his *c*
1Ch 6:32 service according to their *c*
Jer 15:3 *c* over them four families
51:27 *C* against her a recruiting
Hag 1:13 messenger's *c* from Jehovah
Ac 26:12 *c* from the chief priests

Commissioned
Nu 27:23 his hands upon him and *c* him
1Ch 23:24 by their *c* ones, in the
2Ch 36:23 *c* me to build him a house
Ezr 1:2 *c* me to build him a house in
Ne 5:14 *c* me to become their governor
Isa 62:6 I have *c* watchmen. All day
Jer 1:10 I have *c* you this day to be
40:5 king of Babylon has *c* over
40:7 *c* Gedaliah the son of
40:7 *c* him over the men and women
40:11 *c* over them Gedaliah the
41:2 Babylon had *c* over the land
41:18 Babylon had *c* over the land

Commissioner
Jg 9:28 and is not Zebul a *c* of his?
2Ch 24:11 *c* of the chief priest came
Jer 20:1 *c* in the house of Jehovah
52:25 *c* over the men of war, and

Commissioners
2Ch 31:13 *c* at the side of Conaniah
Es 2:3 let the king appoint *c* in all
Ac 19:31 the *c* of festivals and games

Commit
Ge 39:9 could I *c* this great badness
Ex 20:14 You must not *c* adultery
Le 4:22 he does *c* unintentionally one
19:29 land may not *c* prostitution
19:35 not *c* injustice in judging
Nu 5:12 *c* an act of unfaithfulness
31:16 Israel to *c* unfaithfulness
De 4:25 *c* evil in the eyes of Jehovah
5:18 Neither must you *c* adultery
19:15 any sin that he may *c*
Jg 19:2 to *c* fornication against him
19:23 not *c* this disgraceful folly
Ezr 6:12 to *c* a violation and destroy
Ne 9:18 *c* great acts of disrespect
13:27 *c* all this great badness in
Job 42:8 *c* disgraceful folly with you
Pr 14:17 will *c* foolishness, but the
Isa 23:17 and *c* prostitution with
Jer 3:6 she may *c* prostitution there
3:8 began to go and *c* prostitution
Ho 3:3 You must not *c* fornication
4:13 your daughters *c* fornication
4:13 daughters-in-law *c* adultery
4:14 because they *c* fornication
4:14 because they *c* adultery
6:9 they *c* murder at Shechem
13:2 they *c* additional sin and
Am 4:4 to Bethel and *c* transgression
Mt 5:27 You must not *c* adultery
19:18 You must not *c* adultery, You
Mr 3:28 they blasphemously *c*
10:19 Do not *c* adultery, Do not
Lu 18:20 Do not *c* adultery, Do not
Ac 20:32 *c* you to God and to the word
26:9 *c* many acts of opposition
Ro 2:22 saying Do not *c* adultery, do
2:22 do you *c* adultery?
6:15 Shall we *c* a sin because we
13:9 You must not *c* adultery
1Co 6:18 sin that a man may *c* is
7:28 marry, you would *c* no sin
7:28 such one would *c* no sin
2Co 11:7 I *c* a sin by humbling myself
1Ti 1:18 This mandate I *c* to you
2Ti 2:2 things *c* to faithful men
Jas 2:11 You must not *c* adultery
2:11 not *c* adultery but you do
1Jo 2:1 that you may not *c* a sin
2:1 yet, if anyone does *c* a sin
Re 2:14 and to *c* fornication
Re 2:20 my slaves to *c* fornication

Commits
Le 20:10 a man who *c* adultery with
20:10 *c* adultery with the wife of
Ps 10:14 fatherless boy, *c* himself
Pr 6:30 *c* thievery to fill his soul
Isa 57:3 woman that *c* prostitution
Eze 14:13 *c* sin against me in acting
16:32 of the wife that *c* adultery
Mt 5:21 whoever *c* a murder will be
5:32 divorced woman *c* adultery
18:15 if your brother *c* a sin, go
19:9 marries another *c* adultery
Mr 10:11 marries another *c* adultery
10:12 marries . . . she *c* adultery
Lu 16:18 marries another *c* adultery
16:18 from a husband *c* adultery
17:3 If your brother *c* a sin give

Committed
Ge 20:9 and what sin have I *c* against
34:7 he had *c* a disgraceful folly
40:3 he *c* them to the jail of the
41:10 he *c* me to the jail of the
44:5 It is a bad deed you have *c*
Ex 28:38 the error *c* against the holy
Le 4:3 sin that he has *c* a sound young
4:14 *c* against it has become known
4:23 sin that he has *c* against the
4:28 his sin that he has *c* has
4:28 for his sin that he has *c*
4:35 for his sin that he has *c*
5:6 for his sin that he has *c*
5:7 for the sin that he has *c*
5:10 for his sin that he has *c*
5:11 offering for the sin he has *c*
5:13 for his sin that he has *c*
5:16 sin he has *c* against the holy
5:18 his mistake that he *c*
19:22 for his sin that he *c*; and
19:22 sin that he *c* must be
20:12 *c* a violation of what is
24:12 *c* him into custody till
Nu 5:27 *c* an act of unfaithfulness
12:11 the sin . . . which we have *c*
15:34 So they *c* him into custody
25:18 they *c* against you cunningly
De 9:18 sin that you had *c* in doing
17:8 a violent deed has been *c*
22:21 she has *c* a disgraceful folly
Jos 7:15 has *c* a disgraceful folly in
1Sa 20:1 sin have I *c* before your
1Ki 14:27 he *c* them to the control of
16:7 the badness that he *c* in the
18:9 What sin have I *c* that you
1Ch 2:7 *c* an act of unfaithfulness
2Ch 12:10 *c* them to the control of
36:14 *c* unfaithfulness on a large
Ne 4:5 *c* offense against the builders
13:7 badness that Eliashib had *c*
Job 6:24 And what mistake I have *c*
34:32 unrighteousness I have *c*
36:23 You have *c* unrighteousness
Ps 22:8 He *c* himself to Jehovah
Pr 30:20 has said: I have *c* no wrong
Jer 3:1 *c* prostitution with many
3:8 Israel had *c* adultery
11:17 *c* on their own part
42:20 you have *c* error against
51:24 badness that they have *c* in
La 1:8 Jerusalem has *c* outright sin
Eze 16:34 no prostitution has been *c*
18:18 he *c* outright defrauding
18:21 his sins that he has *c* and
18:22 transgressions that he has *c*
18:24 unfaithfulness that he has *c*
18:27 wickedness that he has *c*
23:3 youth they *c* prostitution
23:37 they have *c* adultery and
23:37 idols they have *c* adultery
Ho 2:5 their mother has *c* fornication
Mic 3:4 *c* badness in their dealings
Mal 2:11 detestable thing has been *c*
Mt 5:28 *c* adultery with her in his
25:14 and *c* to them his belongings
25:20 Master, you *c* five talents
25:22 you *c* to me two talents
Mr 15:7 their sedition had *c* murder
Lu 23:15 has been *c* by him
Joh 5:22 *c* all the judging to the Son
Ac 14:23 they *c* them to Jehovah in
25:8 have I *c* any sin
25:11 *c* anything deserving of death
25:25 *c* nothing deserving of death

1Co 5:2 man that *c* this deed should
10:8 some of them *c* fornication
2Co 5:19 and he *c* the word of the
Jas 5:15 if he has *c* sins, it will be
1Pe 2:22 *c* no sin, nor was deception
Jude 7 *c* fornication excessively and
Re 17:2 of the earth *c* fornication
18:3 of the earth *c* fornication
18:9 *c* fornication with her and

Committing
Le 21:9 profane by *c* prostitution, it
Nu 5:6 *c* an act of unfaithfulness
De 22:21 *c* prostitution in the house
Jos 7:1 *c* an act of unfaithfulness
Ne 9:26 *c* acts of great disrespect
Pr 6:32 *c* adultery with a woman
Jer 3:3 a wife *c* prostitution
3:9 *c* adultery with stones and
5:7 they continued *c* adultery
7:9 murdering and *c* adultery and
12:1 those who are *c* treachery
23:14 *c* adultery and walking in
29:23 *c* adultery with the wives
Eze 23:43 keep on *c* her prostitution
Ho 3:1 *c* adultery, as in the case of
4:2 stealing and *c* of adultery
4:15 you are *c* fornication, O
Am 4:4 frequent in *c* transgression
Ac 24:16 *c* no offense against God and
Tit 2:10 not *c* theft, but exhibiting
1Pe 2:23 kept on *c* himself to the one
Re 2:22 those *c* adultery with her

Commodious
Jer 22:14 house and *c* upper chambers

Common
Pr 21:9 although in a house in *c*
25:24 although in a house in *c*
Eze 22:26 the holy thing and the *c*
Mr 14:20 dipping . . . into the *c* bowl
Lu 14:18 all in *c* started to beg off
Ac 2:44 in having all things in *c*
4:32 they had all things in *c*
1Co 10:13 except what is *c* to men
Tit 1:4 a faith shared in *c*
Jude 3 the salvation we hold in *c*

Commonplace
Pr 22:29 station himself before *c* men

Commotion
2Sa 18:29 *c* at the time Joab sent the
Isa 16:14 disgraced with much *c* of
17:12 *c* of many peoples, who are
31:4 in spite of their *c* he will
63:15 the *c* of your inward parts
Mt 21:10 the whole city was set in *c*
Heb 12:26 I will set in *c* not only

Communicated
Job 37:20 man said that it will be *c*

Communication
2Sa 3:17 *c* by Abner with the older

Communion
Ex 20:24 *c* sacrifices, your flock and
24:5 as *c* sacrifices to Jehovah
29:28 From their *c* sacrifices
32:6 and presenting *c* sacrifices
Le 3:1 his offering is a *c* sacrifice
3:3 the *c* sacrifice as an offering
3:6 for a *c* sacrifice to Jehovah
3:9 from the *c* sacrifice he must
4:10 of a bull of the *c* sacrifice
4:26 the fat of the *c* sacrifice
4:31 from off the *c* sacrifice
4:35 young ram of the *c* sacrifice
6:12 pieces of the *c* sacrifices
7:11 law of the *c* sacrifice that
7:13 sacrifice of his *c* sacrifices
7:14 blood of the *c* sacrifices, it
7:15 of his *c* sacrifices is to be
7:18 flesh of his *c* sacrifice
7:20 the flesh of the *c* sacrifice
7:21 the flesh of the *c* sacrifice
7:29 presents his *c* sacrifice to
7:29 from his *c* sacrifice
7:32 priest from your *c* sacrifices
7:33 blood of the *c* sacrifices
7:34 from their *c* sacrifices
7:37 and the *c* sacrifice
9:4 and a ram for *c* sacrifices to
9:18 ram of the *c* sacrifice that
9:22 offering and the *c* sacrifices
10:14 *c* sacrifices of the sons of
Le 17:5 as *c* sacrifices to Jehovah
19:5 sacrifice a *c* sacrifice to
22:21 *c* sacrifice to Jehovah in
23:19 lambs . . . as a *c* sacrifice
Nu 6:14 sound ram as a *c* sacrifice
6:17 the ram as a *c* sacrifice
6:18 that is under the *c* sacrifice
7:17 *c* sacrifice two cattle, five
7:23 *c* sacrifice two cattle, five
7:29 *c* sacrifice two cattle, five
7:35 *c* sacrifice two cattle, five
7:41 *c* sacrifice two cattle, five
7:47 *c* sacrifice two cattle, five
7:53 *c* sacrifice two cattle, five
7:59 *c* sacrifice two cattle, five
7:65 *c* sacrifice two cattle, five
7:71 *c* sacrifice two cattle, five
7:77 *c* sacrifice two cattle, five
7:83 *c* sacrifice two cattle, five
7:88 cattle of the *c* sacrifice
10:10 and your *c* sacrifices; and
15:8 or *c* sacrifices to Jehovah
29:39 and your *c* sacrifices
De 27:7 sacrifice *c* sacrifices and eat
Jos 8:31 and sacrificing *c* sacrifices
22:23 render up *c* sacrifices on
22:27 our *c* sacrifices, that your
Jg 20:26 *c* offerings before Jehovah
21:4 offer up burnt offerings and *c*
1Sa 10:8 to render up *c* sacrifices
11:15 rendered up *c* sacrifices
13:9 Bring . . . the *c* sacrifices
2Sa 6:17 *c* sacrifices before Jehovah
6:18 *c* sacrifices, he then blessed
24:25 *c* sacrifices, and Jehovah
1Ki 3:15 rendered up *c* offerings and
8:63 offer the *c* sacrifices
8:64 pieces of the *c* sacrifices
8:64 pieces of the *c* sacrifices
9:25 *c* sacrifices upon the altar
2Ki 16:13 blood of the *c* sacrifices
1Ch 16:1 *c* sacrifices before the true
16:2 and the *c* sacrifices, he
21:26 and *c* sacrifices, and he
2Ch 7:7 pieces of the *c* sacrifices
29:35 pieces of the *c* sacrifices
30:22 sacrificing *c* sacrifices and
31:2 as regards . . . *c* sacrifices
33:16 upon it *c* sacrifices and
Pr 7:14 *C* sacrifices were incumbent
Eze 43:27 and your *c* sacrifices
45:15 *c* sacrifices, in order to
45:17 *c* sacrifices, in order to
46:2 and his *c* sacrifices, and he
46:12 or *c* sacrifices as a
46:12 his *c* sacrifices just as he
Am 5:22 your *c* sacrifices of fatlings

Community
Job 30:5 From the *c* they would be
Ps 68:10 tent *c*—they have dwelt

Compact
Job 38:30 watery deep makes itself *c*

Compactly
2Pe 3:5 earth standing *c* out of water

Companies
Ca 6:4 awesome as *c* gathered around
6:10 as *c* gathered around banners
Mr 6:39 the people to recline by *c*

Companion
Ge 38:12 he and Hirah his *c* the
38:20 hand of his *c* the Adullamite
Ex 2:13 should you strike your *c*
11:2 should ask every man of his *c*
11:2 ask . . . every woman of her *c*
De 13:6 your *c* who is like your own
Jg 7:13 man relating a dream to his *c*
7:14 his *c* answered and said: This
2Sa 13:3 Amnon had a *c* whose name
15:37 Hushai, David's *c*, came
16:16 the Archite, David's *c*
16:17 toward your *c*, is it
16:17 did you not go with your *c*
1Ch 27:33 Hushai . . . was the king's *c*
Es 1:19 the king give to a *c* of hers
Job 6:27 And barter over your *c*
30:29 a *c* to the daughters of the
31:9 very entranceway of my *c*
Ps 15:3 To his *c* he has done nothing
35:14 As for a *c*, as for a brother
88:18 away from me friend and *c*
101:5 slandering his *c* in secrecy
Pr 17:17 a true *c* is loving all the
17:18 full surety before his *c*
19:4 separated even from his *c*
19:6 a *c* to the man making gifts
22:11 lips the king will be his *c*
27:9 sweetness of one's *c* due to
27:10 Do not leave your own *c* or
27:10 or the *c* of your father, and
29:5 man that is flattering his *c*
Ca 1:9 likened you, O girl *c* of mine
1:15 beautiful, O girl *c* of mine
2:2 my girl *c* among the daughters
2:10 Rise up, you girl *c* of mine
2:13 come, O girl *c* of mine, my
4:1 beautiful, O girl *c* of mine
4:7 beautiful, O girl *c* of mine
5:2 my sister, my girl *c*, my dove
5:16 and this is my boy *c*, O
6:4 beautiful, O girl *c* of mine
Isa 19:2 and each one against his *c*
34:14 demon will call to its *c*
41:6 went helping each one his *c*
Jer 3:20 gone from her *c*, so you
5:8 each one to the wife of his *c*
6:21 the neighbor and his *c*—they
7:5 between a man and his *c*
9:4 each one against his own *c*
9:4 every *c* himself would walk
9:5 trifling each one with his *c*
9:8 keeps speaking with his own *c*
9:20 teach . . . her *c* a dirge
23:30 words, each one from his *c*
31:34 teach each one his *c*
34:15 liberty each one to his *c*
34:17 and each one to his *c*
Eze 22:11 wife of his *c* a man has
33:26 each one the wife of his *c*
Ho 3:1 love a woman loved by a *c*
Mic 7:5 Do not put your faith in a *c*
Zec 11:6 one in the hand of his *c*
11:9 each one the flesh of her *c*
14:13 of the hand of his *c*, and
14:13 against the hand of his *c*
Mal 3:16 each one with his *c*, and
2Co 8:19 to be our traveling *c* in

Companion's
Eze 18:6 *c* wife he did not defile and
18:11 his *c* wife he has defiled
18:15 *c* wife he has not defiled

Companions
Jg 11:37 I and my girl *c*
11:38 she with her girl *c*, and
Job 2:11 three *c* of Job got to hear
16:20 *c* are spokesmen against me
17:5 tell *c* to take their shares
19:21 O you my *c*, For God's own
32:3 against his three *c* his anger
35:4 And to your *c* with you
42:7 against you and your two *c*
42:10 prayed in behalf of his *c*
Ps 28:3 speaking peace with their *c*
38:11 As for my lovers and my *c*
45:14 virgins in her train as her *c*
122:8 sake of my brothers and my *c*
Pr 18:24 exist *c* disposed to break one
19:4 Wealth is what adds many *c*
Ca 5:1 Eat, O *c*! Drink and become
Jer 3:1 prostitution with many *c*
29:23 with the wives of their *c*
La 1:2 own *c* have dealt treacherously
Eze 22:12 gain of your *c* with
Da 2:13 looked for Daniel and his *c*
2:17 *c* he made known the matter
2:18 not destroy Daniel and his *c*
Hab 2:15 his *c* something to drink
Zec 3:8 *c* who are sitting before you
Ac 19:29 traveling *c* of Paul

Companionship
Job 34:8 *c* with practicers of what is
Pr 22:24 *c* with anyone given to anger
28:7 *c* with gluttons humiliates
29:3 *c* with prostitutes destroys

Company
Ge 11:28 Haran died while in *c* with
44:28 one went out from my *c* and
Ex 12:38 a vast mixed *c* also went up
Nu 8:24 *c* in the service of the tent
8:25 retire from the service *c* and
De 15:16 shall not go out from your *c*
15:18 send him out from your *c* as
1Sa 18:13 removed him from his *c* and
2Sa 2:25 they came to be one *c* and

2Sa 12:17 take bread in *c* with them
1Ki 10:28 *c* of the king's merchants
2Ch 1:16 *c* of the king's merchants
Ne 13:3 separate all the mixed *c* from
Job 6:19 traveling *c* of Sabeans have
Ps 110:3 *c* of young men just like
126:4 Jehovah, our *c* of captives
Jer 25:20 all the mixed *c*, and all
25:24 the kings of the mixed *c*
50:37 against all the mixed *c*
Eze 14:22 an escaped *c*, those being
23:18 disgusted from *c* with her
23:18 from *c* with her sister
30:5 all the mixed *c* and Chub and
Lu 2:44 Assuming that he was in the *c*
Joh 21:2 in *c* Simon Peter and Thomas
Ac 17:5 took into their *c* certain
18:26 they took him into their *c*
Ro 15:24 been satisfied with your *c*
1Co 5:9 mixing in *c* with fornicators
5:11 quit mixing in *c* with anyone
2Co 2:14 in *c* with the Christ and
2:17 in *c* with Christ, we are
Re 1:9 endurance in *c* with Jesus

Comparable
Ps 49:12 *c* with the beasts that have
49:20 *c* with the beasts that have
143:7 *c* with those going down into
Pr 27:15 and a contentious wife are *c*
Isa 14:10 that you have been made *c*

Compare
Isa 46:5 make me equal or *c* me that
Mt 11:16 shall I *c* this generation
Lu 7:31 *c* the men of this generation
13:18 with what shall I *c* it?
13:20 shall I *c* the kingdom of God
2Co 10:12 or *c* ourselves with some

Compared
2Sa 14:25 *c* with Absalom there proved
Job 28:17 and glass cannot be *c* to it
28:19 topaz of Cush cannot be *c*
Ps 40:5 There is none to be *c* to you
89:6 can be *c* to Jehovah
Eze 32:19 *C* with whom are you more

Comparing
2Co 10:12 and *c* themselves with

Comparison
Jg 8:2 What now have I done in *c*
8:3 do in *c* with you? It was then
Da 1:10 in *c* with the children who
Hag 2:3 in *c* with that, as nothing
Joh 10:6 Jesus spoke this *c* to them
16:29 and are uttering no *c*
Ro 8:18 in *c* with the glory that is
Ga 6:4 not in *c* with the other person

Comparisons
Joh 16:25 these things to you in *c*
16:25 speak to you no more in *c*

Compartment
Heb 9:2 constructed a first tent *c*
9:3 tent *c* called the Most Holy
9:6 priests enter the first tent *c*
9:7 second *c* the high priest alone

Compartments
Ge 6:14 You will make *c* in the ark

Compass
Isa 44:13 with a *c* he keeps tracing

Compassion
Ge 19:16 then in the *c* of Jehovah
42:21 he implored *c* on our part
Ex 2:6 At that she felt *c* for him
De 13:8 nor must you feel *c*, nor
1Sa 15:3 you must not have *c* upon him
15:9 people had *c* upon Agag and
15:15 people had *c* upon the best
23:21 for you have had *c* on me
2Sa 12:6 because he did not have *c*
21:7 felt *c* upon Mephibosheth
2Ch 36:15 felt *c* for his people and
36:17 feel *c* for young man or
Job 6:10 Though he would have no *c*
16:13 and feels no *c*; He pours out
19:16 I keep imploring him for *c*
20:13 If he has *c* upon it and does
27:22 at him and have no *c*
Pr 6:34 *c* in the day of vengeance
Isa 9:19 show *c* even on his brother
63:9 In his love and in his *c* he
Jer 13:14 I shall show no *c*, nor feel
Jer 15:5 who will show *c* upon you
21:7 show *c* or have any mercy
51:3 any *c* for her young men
La 2:2 shown no *c* upon any abiding
2:17 has torn down and shown no *c*
2:21 slaughtered; you have had no *c*
3:43 killed; you have shown no *c*
Eze 5:11 myself also will not show *c*
7:4 neither will I feel *c*, for
7:9 feel sorry nor shall I feel *c*
8:18 neither shall I feel *c*
9:5 and do not feel any *c*
9:10 neither shall I show *c*
16:5 these things in *c* upon you
24:21 the object of your soul's *c*
36:21 have *c* on my holy name
Ho 13:14 *C* itself will be concealed
Joe 2:18 show *c* upon his people
Hab 1:17 while he shows no *c*
Zec 11:5 shepherds do not show any *c*
11:6 I shall show *c* no more upon
Mal 3:17 I will show *c* upon them
3:17 man shows *c* upon his son
Lu 1:78 the tender *c* of our God
1:78 With this *c* a daybreak will
Ro 9:15 I will show *c* to whomever
9:15 to whomever I do show *c*
Col 3:12 the tender affections of *c*
Heb 10:28 dies without *c*, upon the

Compassionate
La 4:10 *c* women have boiled their
Eph 4:32 tenderly *c*, freely forgiving
1Pe 3:8 tenderly *c*, humble in mind

Compassions
Ho 11:8 my *c* have grown hot
Ro 12:1 I entreat you by the *c* of God
Php 2:1 any tender affections and *c*
1Jo 3:17 the door of his tender *c*

Compel
Lu 14:23 and *c* them to come in, that
Ga 6:12 to *c* you to get circumcised

Compelled
1Sa 13:12 *c* myself and went offering
Isa 43:23 not *c* you to serve me with
43:24 you have *c* me to serve
Mt 14:22 *c* his disciples to board the
Mr 6:45 he *c* his disciples to board
Ac 28:19 I was *c* to appeal to Caesar
2Co 12:11 You *c* me to, for I ought
Ga 2:3 not . . . *c* to be circumcised

Compelling
Es 1:8 there was no one *c*, for that
Ro 13:5 *c* reason for you people to be
Ga 2:14 are *c* people of the nations to

Compels
2Co 5:14 love the Christ has *c* us

Compensate
Ex 22:1 to *c* with five of the herd for

Compensation
Ex 21:19 *c* only for the time lost
21:26 set free in *c* for his eye
21:27 set free in *c* for his tooth
21:34 The owner . . . is to make *c*
21:36 make *c* with bull for bull
22:3 He is to make *c* without fail
22:4 alive, he is to make double *c*
22:5 make *c* with the best of his
22:6 make *c* without fail for what
22:7 found, he is to make double *c*
22:9 make double *c* to his fellow
22:11 the other is not to make *c*
22:12 is to make *c* to their owner
22:13 he is not to make *c*
22:14 he is to make *c* without fail
22:15 he is not to make *c*
Le 5:16 will make *c* for the sin he
6:5 *c* for it in its full amount
24:18 *c* for it, soul for soul
24:21 beast should make *c* for it
2Sa 12:6 should make *c* with four, as
Isa 57:18 make *c* with comfort to him
Eze 29:20 his *c* for service that he
Joe 2:25 make *c* to you for the years
1Ti 5:4 due *c* to their parents and

Competent
Da 2:26 *c* enough to make known to me
4:18 you are *c*, because the spirit
5:8 *c* enough to read the writing
5:15 *c* enough to show the very
2Ti 3:17 may be fully *c*, completely

Competing
Jer 22:15 *c* by use of cedar

Competition
Ga 5:26 stirring up *c* with one

Compile
Lu 1:1 to *c* a statement of the facts

Complain
Nu 11:1 something evil to *c* about in

Complainant
Mt 5:25 that somehow the *c* may not

Complainers
Jude 16 *c* about their lot in life

Complaining
Pr 21:13 the *c* cry of the lowly one
Mt 5:25 with the one *c* against you

Complaint
Ge 18:20 cry of *c* about Sodom and
Ex 2:23 slavery and to cry out in *c*
Jer 12:1 when I make my *c* to you
Ac 25:16 defense concerning the *c*
Col 3:13 a cause for *c* against another

Complaints
La 3:39 can a living man indulge in *c*

Complement
Ge 2:18 helper for him, as a *c* of him
2:20 found no helper as a *c* of him

Complete
Ge 6:16 you will *c* it to the extent
Ex 31:15 day is a sabbath of *c* rest
35:2 sabbath of *c* rest to Jehovah
Le 16:31 sabbath of *c* rest for you
23:3 is a sabbath of *c* rest, a holy
23:15 They should prove to be *c*
23:24 *c* rest, a memorial by the
23:32 sabbath of *c* rest for you
23:39 first day is a *c* rest and
23:39 the eighth day is a *c* rest
25:4 sabbath of *c* rest for the
25:5 sabbath of *c* rest for the land
25:30 *c* year has come to the full
1Ki 8:61 heart must prove to be *c*
11:4 not prove to be *c* with
15:3 heart did not prove to be *c*
15:14 heart . . . *c* with Jehovah
2Ki 20:3 and with a *c* heart, and
22:4 *c* the money that is being
1Ch 12:38 with a *c* heart they came to
28:9 serve him with a *c* heart and
29:9 with a *c* heart that they
29:19 my son give a *c* heart to
2Ch 8:16 So the house of Jehovah was *c*
15:17 heart itself proved to be *c*
16:9 those whose heart is *c*
19:9 and with a *c* heart
25:2 only not with a *c* heart
Ps 19:13 In that case I shall be *c*
138:8 will *c* what is in my behalf
139:22 With a *c* hatred I do hate
Pr 11:1 *c* stone-weight is a pleasure
Isa 38:3 and with a *c* heart, and
47:9 In their *c* measure they must
Eze 4:6 *c* them. And you must lie upon
43:27 And they will *c* the days
Da 7:1 *c* account of the matters he
Am 1:6 into exile a *c* body of exiles
1:9 a *c* body of exiles to Edom
Na 1:12 they were in *c* form and there
Mt 10:23 by no means *c* the circuit of
Lu 1:45 there will be a *c* performance
14:28 if he has enough to *c* it
Ac 3:16 *c* soundness in the sight of
1Co 13:10 that which is *c* arrives
2Co 8:6 *c* this same kind giving on
Eph 4:2 with *c* lowliness of mind and
6:11 Put on the *c* suit of armor
6:13 take up the *c* suit of armor
Col 1:28 *c* in union with Christ
4:12 *c* and with firm conviction
Jas 1:4 endurance have its work *c*
1:4 *c* and sound in all respects
Re 6:2 and to *c* his conquest

Completed
De 34:8 period for Moses were *c*
Jos 3:17 had *c* passing over the Jordan
4:1 had *c* passing over the Jordan
4:10 the whole matter had been *c*
4:11 the people had *c* passing over

Jos 5:8 when they had *c* circumcising
2Sa 15:24 people *c* crossing over from
1Ki 6:7 of quarry stone already *c*
6:22 until all the house was *c*
7:22 the pillars was gradually *c*
9:25 and he *c* the house
Ezr 5:16 rebuilt but it has not been *c*
6:15 *c* this house by the third day
Ps 102:27 own years will not be *c*
Jer 26:8 when Jeremiah had *c* speaking
51:63 *c* reading this book, you
Eze 4:8 have *c* the days of your siege
Lu 2:43 and *c* the days. But when they
7:1 he had *c* all his sayings in the
18:31 things written . . . be *c*
Ac 19:21 when these things had been *c*
21:5 when we had *c* the days, we
21:7 then *c* the voyage from Tyre
Ga 3:3 are you now being *c* in flesh?

Completely
Ex 17:14 *c* wipe out the remembrance
21:19 until he gets him *c* healed
28:31 coat . . . *c* of blue thread
Le 19:9 reap the edge of your field *c*
23:22 not do *c* the edge of your
Jg 1:28 did not drive them out *c*
2Ch 12:12 bringing them to ruin *c*
Job 23:14 he will carry out *c* what
Isa 2:18 gods . . . will pass away *c*
44:26 carries out *c* the counsel
44:28 he will *c* carry out
Jer 13:19 taken into exile *c*
Eze 17:10 Will it not dry up *c*, even
Am 9:8 *c* annihilate the house of
Mt 3:12 *c* clean up his threshing
14:36 touched it were made *c* well
Lu 3:17 clean up his threshing floor *c*
8:14 *c* choked and bring nothing
Joh 7:23 made a man *c* sound in health
Ac 3:23 *c* destroyed from among the
Ro 8:37 *c* victorious through him that
11:11 stumble so that they fell *c*
2Co 12:15 be *c* spent for your souls
Ga 2:4 that they might *c* enslave us
1Th 5:23 God of peace sanctify you *c*
2Th 1:11 perform *c* all he pleases
2Ti 3:8 men *c* corrupted in mind
3:17 *c* equipped for every good
Heb 7:25 to save *c* those who are
10:11 able to take sins away *c*
1Pe 1:13 keep your senses *c*
Re 17:16 will *c* burn her with fire
18:8 and she will be *c* burned with

Completing
Da 10:3 *c* of the three full weeks

Completion
Ge 2:1 all their army came to their *c*
2:2 God came to the *c* of his work
15:16 has not yet come to *c*
Ex 39:32 work . . . all came to its *c*
De 31:24 law in a book until their *c*
31:30 of this song until their *c*
1Ki 7:51 work . . . was at its *c*
2Ch 5:1 house of Jehovah was at its *c*
Ne 6:15 wall came to *c* on the
Pr 16:30 brings mischief to *c*
Isa 60:20 will have come to *c*
Jer 1:3 until the *c* of the eleventh
Da 8:23 transgressors act to a *c*
Php 1:6 will carry it to *c* until the
Heb 8:5 about to make the tent in *c*

Complexion
Da 5:6 king, his very *c* was changed
5:9 his *c* was changing within him
5:10 nor let your *c* be changed
7:28 my very *c* changed in me; but

Compliance
Phm 21 Trusting in your *c*, I am

Complimentary
Ro 16:18 by smooth talk and *c* speech

Compose
Eze 17:2 *c* a proverbial saying toward
24:3 *c* a proverbial saying

Composed
Ge 4:23 Lamech *c* these words for his
Ac 1:1 I *c* about all the things Jesus
Heb 13:22 *c* a letter to you in few

Composing
Eze 20:49 *c* proverbial sayings

Composition
Ex 30:32 with its *c* you must not make
30:37 this *c*, you must not make

Compounded
1Co 12:24 God *c* the body, giving honor

Comprehension
Eph 3:4 *c* I have in the sacred secret
Col 1:9 all wisdom and spiritual *c*

Compulsion
2Co 9:7 not grudgingly or under *c*
Phm 14 not as under *c*, but of your
1Pe 5:2 not under *c*, but willingly
Re 13:16 puts under *c* all persons

Compulsory
1Ki 11:28 *c* service of the house of
2Ki 25:12 vinedressers and *c* laborers
Job 7:1 a *c* labor for mortal man on
14:14 the days of my *c* service
Jer 39:10 and *c* services on that day
52:16 and as *c* laborers

Compute
Ex 12:4 *c* each one proportionate to

Conaniah
2Ch 31:12 *C* the Levite was in charge
31:13 side of *C* and Shimei his
35:9 *C* and Shemaiah and Nethanel

Conceal
Ex 2:3 was no longer able to *c* him
De 31:17 forsake them and *c* my face
31:18 *c* my face in that day
32:20 Let me *c* my face from them
1Sa 20:2 father *c* this matter from
20:5 I must *c* myself in the field
20:24 to *c* himself in the field
1Ki 17:3 *c* yourself at the torrent
Job 3:10 so *c* trouble from my eyes
13:20 not *c* myself just on your
13:24 Why do you *c* your very face
14:13 in Sheol you would *c* me
34:22 to *c* themselves there
Ps 13:1 How long will you *c* your face
17:8 your wings may you *c* me
27:5 *c* me in the secret place of
27:9 Do not *c* your face from me
31:20 *c* them in the secret place
51:9 *C* your face from my sins
55:12 I could *c* myself from him
56:6 attack, they *c* themselves
64:2 *c* me from the confidential
69:17 do not *c* your face from your
102:2 Do not *c* your face from me
104:29 If you *c* your face, they get
119:19 Do not *c* from me your
143:7 Do not *c* your face from me
Pr 22:3 calamity and proceeds to *c*
Isa 16:3 *C* the dispersed ones; do not
29:14 discreet men will *c* itself
50:6 My face I did not *c* from
Jer 36:19 *c* yourself, you and
Eze 39:29 no longer *c* my face from
Am 9:3 if they *c* themselves from in
Mic 3:4 he will *c* his face from them

Concealed
Ge 4:14 from your face I shall be *c*
Ex 2:2 she kept him *c* for three lunar
3:6 Then Moses *c* his face, because
De 29:29 things *c* belong to Jehovah
Jos 2:4 took the two men and *c* them
1Sa 20:19 place where you *c* yourself
2Ki 11:2 *c* from the face of Athaliah
2Ch 22:11 *c* because of Athaliah, and
Job 3:23 whose way has been *c*, And
10:13 you have *c* in your heart
28:11 the *c* thing he brings forth
28:21 of the heavens it has been *c*
40:21 In the *c* place of reeds
Ps 10:8 From *c* places he will kill
10:9 lying in wait in the *c* place
10:11 He has *c* his face
17:12 lion sitting in *c* places
17:14 fill with your *c* treasure
19:6 nothing *c* from its heat
19:12 From *c* sins pronounce me
22:24 has not *c* his face from him
30:7 You *c* your face; I became
38:9 sighing itself has not been *c*
44:24 do you keep your very face *c*
64:4 To shoot from *c* places at
81:7 in the *c* place of thunder
83:3 conspire against your *c* ones
Ps 88:14 keep your face *c* from me
89:46 keep yourself *c*? For all
Pr 27:5 revealed reproof than a *c* love
27:12 has seen the calamity has *c*
Ca 2:14 the *c* place of the steep way
Isa 28:15 in falsehood have *c*
40:27 has been *c* from Jehovah
45:15 a God keeping yourself *c*
49:2 He *c* me in his own quiver
54:8 I *c* my face from you for but
64:7 have *c* your face from us
65:16 actually be *c* from my eyes
Jer 16:17 They have not been *c* from
23:24 any man be *c* in places of
33:5 all whose badness I have *c*
36:26 But Jehovah kept them *c*
Eze 7:22 actually profane my *c* place
39:23 I *c* my face from them and
Da 2:22 and the *c* things, knowing
Ho 13:14 will be *c* from my eyes
Ob 6 his *c* treasures have been sought
Zep 2:3 *c* in the day of Jehovah's
Mr 4:22 has become carefully *c* but
Lu 8:17 *c* that will never become
9:45 it was *c* from them that they
12:2 *c* that will not be revealed
Col 2:3 Carefully *c* in him are all

Concealing
De 7:20 were *c* themselves before you
1Sa 23:19 David *c* himself close by us
26:1 David *c* himself on the hill
Ps 54:*super* David *c* himself with us
Isa 8:17 *c* his face from the house
29:15 in *c* counsel from Jehovah
53:3 the *c* of one's face from us
57:17 *c* my face, while I was
59:2 the *c* of his face from you
Eze 39:24 I kept *c* my face from them

Concealment
De 32:38 become a *c* place for you
Job 22:14 Clouds are a *c* place for
Ps 18:11 made darkness his *c* place
32:7 You are a place of *c* for me
61:4 refuge in the *c* of your wings
119:114 place of *c* and my shield
Pr 1:11 lie in *c* for the innocent
1:18 lie in *c* for their souls
Isa 16:4 place of *c* to them because
28:17 out the very place of *c*
32:2 of *c* from the rainstorm
45:3 treasures in the *c* places
45:19 In a place of *c* I spoke not
48:16 spoken in no place of *c*
Jer 13:17 in places of *c* my soul will
23:24 concealed in places of *c*
37:17 his house in a place of *c*
38:16 Jeremiah in the place of *c*
40:15 in a place of *c* in Mizpah
49:10 uncover his places of *c*
La 3:10 as a lion in places of *c*
Hab 3:14 afflicted one in a place of *c*

Conceals
Job 34:29 when he *c* his face, who can
Pr 28:28 the wicked rise up, a man *c*

Conceivable
Le 7:24 be used for anything else *c*

Conceive
1Ch 4:17 she got to *c* Miriam and
Isa 33:11 You people *c* dried grass
Lu 1:31 you will *c* in your womb and
Eph 3:20 all the things we ask or *c*
Heb 11:11 received power to *c* seed

Conceived
Nu 11:12 I myself *c* all this people
Job 3:3 An able-bodied man has been *c*
Ps 7:14 he has *c* trouble and is bound
51:5 And in sin my mother *c* me
Lu 1:36 *c* a son, in her old age
2:21 before he was *c* in the womb
Ro 9:10 also when Rebekah *c* twins
1Co 2:9 *c* in the heart of man the

Conceives
Le 12:2 *c* seed and does bear a male

Conceiving
Job 15:35 There is a *c* of trouble and
Isa 59:4 has been a *c* of trouble
59:13 *c* and a muttering of words

Conception
Ru 4:13 Jehovah granted her *c* and she
Ho 9:11 no pregnant belly and no *c*

Concern
Nu 18:7 regards every c of the altar
1Sa 1:16 out of the abundance of my c
1Ch 16:9 C yourselves with all his
Job 7:13 My bed will help carry my c
9:27 said, Let me forget my c
10:1 I will give vent to my c
12:8 Or show your c to the earth
15:4 having of any c before God
21:4 is my c expressed to man?
23:2 state of c is rebelliousness
Ps 55:2 I am driven . . . about by my c
55:17 cannot but show c and I moan
64:1 O God, my voice in my c
77:3 I will show c, that my spirit
77:6 With my heart I will show c
77:12 dealings I will c myself
102:*super* pours out his c before
105:2 C yourselves with all his
119:15 orders I will c myself
119:27 I may c myself with your
119:48 I will c myself with your
119:78 I c myself with your orders
119:97 All day long it is my c
119:99 reminders are a c to me
119:148 c myself with your saying
142:2 I kept pouring out my c
145:5 works I will make my c
Pr 6:22 itself will make you its c
23:29 Who has c? Who has wounds
Isa 53:8 and who will c himself even
Jer 2:18 now what c should you have
2:18 And what c should you have
Am 4:13 man what his mental c is
Joh 21:22 of what c is that to you?
21:23 of what c is that to you?
Ac 18:17 Gallio would not c himself
Php 1:27 the things which c you, that
4:8 things are of serious c
2Th 3:11 with what does not c them
2Pe 1:3 things that c life and godly

Concerned
1Ki 18:27 he must be c with a matter
Job 7:11 c with the bitterness of my
Ps 143:5 c with the work of your own
Eze 11:15 men c with your right to
Joh 12:6 he was c about the poor
Ga 3:20 where only one person is c

Concerns
Ps 119:23 he c himself with your
Lu 22:37 that which c me is having

Concert
Lu 15:25 heard a music c and dancing

Concession
Mt 19:8 c to you of divorcing your
1Co 7:6 I say this by way of c, not

Conclude
Ge 21:27 proceeded to c a covenant
26:28 let us c a covenant with you
31:44 come, let us c a covenant, I
Ex 23:32 not to c a covenant with
34:12 do not c a covenant with the
34:15 that you may c a covenant
34:27 do c a covenant with you and
De 7:2 c no covenant with them nor
29:1 to c with the sons of Israel
Jos 9:6 And now, c a covenant with us
9:7 how could we c a covenant
9:11 now c a covenant with us
24:25 Joshua proceeded to c a
Jg 2:2 you must not c a covenant
1Sa 11:1 C a covenant with us that we
11:2 On this condition I shall c
18:3 proceeded to c a covenant
2Sa 3:12 c your covenant with me, and
3:13 shall c a covenant with you
3:21 c a covenant with you, and
1Ki 5:12 proceeded to c a covenant
2Ch 29:10 c a covenant with Jehovah
34:31 to c the covenant before
Ezr 10:3 c a covenant with our God
Job 41:4 c a covenant with you
Ps 83:5 to c even a covenant
Isa 55:3 I shall readily c with you
61:8 I shall c toward them
Jer 31:31 c with the house of Israel
31:33 c with the house of Israel
32:40 c with them an indefinitely
34:15 c a covenant before me in
Eze 34:25 c with them a covenant of
37:26 will c with them a covenant
Ho 2:18 c a covenant in that day in
12:1 covenant with Assyria they c
Heb 8:8 c with the house of Israel

Concluded
Ge 15:18 Jehovah c with Abram a
21:32 So they c a covenant at
Ex 24:8 covenant that Jehovah has c
De 4:23 that he c with you and that
5:2 God c a covenant with us in
5:3 Jehovah c this covenant, but
9:9 covenant that Jehovah had c
29:1 he had c with them in Horeb
29:25 c with them when he brought
31:16 covenant that I have c with
Jos 9:16 had c a covenant with them
1Sa 23:18 two of them c a covenant
2Sa 5:3 David c a covenant with them
1Ki 8:21 he c with our forefathers
20:34 he c a covenant with him
2Ki 11:4 and c a covenant with them
11:17 Jehoiada c the covenant
17:15 covenant that he had c with
17:35 Jehovah c a covenant with
17:38 covenant that I have c with
23:3 c the covenant before Jehovah
1Ch 11:3 David c a covenant with them
16:16 covenant he c with Abraham
2Ch 6:11 he c with the sons of Israel
21:7 he had c with David, and
23:3 congregation c a covenant
23:16 Jehoiada c a covenant
Job 31:1 covenant I have c with my
Ps 89:3 c a covenant toward my chosen
105:9 covenant he c with Abraham
Isa 28:15 c a covenant with Death
Jer 11:10 my covenant that I c with
31:32 c with their forefathers
34:8 Zedekiah c a covenant with
34:13 c a covenant with your
34:18 c before me with the calf
Eze 17:13 royal seed and c a covenant
Hag 2:5 Remember the thing that I c
Zec 11:10 covenant that I had c with
Mt 20:10 c they would receive more
Lu 4:2 days . . . were c, he felt hungry
4:13 having c all the temptation
Ac 21:27 days were about to be c, the

Concludes
1Sa 22:8 own son c a covenant with

Concluding
Ex 34:10 Here I am c a covenant
De 29:12 your God is c with you today
29:14 c this covenant and this oath
Jos 9:15 and c a covenant with them
Ps 50:5 Those c my covenant over
Isa 57:8 went c a covenant with them
Ho 10:4 false oaths, c a covenant
Ro 9:28 c it and cutting it short

Conclusion
Ec 12:13 c of the matter, everything
Mt 13:39 harvest is a c of a system
13:40 c of the system of things
13:49 c of the system of things
24:3 the c of the system of things
28:20 c of the system of things
Mr 13:4 are destined to come to a c
Ac 16:10 c that God had summoned us
Heb 9:26 c of the systems of things

Conclusions
Lu 2:19 drawing c in her heart
20:5 they drew c, saying: If we

Concubine
Ge 22:24 his c too, whose name was
35:22 with Bilhah his father's c
36:12 Timna . . . the c of Eliphaz
Ex 21:8 does not designate her as a c
Jg 8:31 c of his that was in Shechem
19:1 he took as his wife a c from
19:2 And his c began to commit
19:9 he and his c and his attendant
19:10 and his c and his attendant
19:24 my virgin daughter and his c
19:25 the man took hold of his c
19:27 his c, fallen at the entrance
19:29 laid hold of his c and cut
20:4 I and my c, to stay overnight
20:5 it was my c that they raped
20:6 I grasped my c and cut her up
2Sa 3:7 Saul had had a c whose name
3:7 with the c of my father
21:11 daughter of Aiah, Saul's c
1Ch 1:32 Keturah, Abraham's c, she
2:46 Ephah the c of Caleb
2:48 As for Caleb's c Maacah
7:14 whom his Syrian c bore

Concubines
Ge 25:6 sons of the c that Abraham
2Sa 5:13 taking more c and wives out
15:16 c, to take care of the house
16:21 with the c of your father
16:22 with the c of his father
19:5 and the soul of your c
20:3 c whom he had left behind
1Ki 11:3 and three hundred c
1Ch 3:9 the sons of the c, and Tamar
2Ch 11:21 his other wives and his c
11:21 also sixty c, so that he
Es 2:14 eunuch, the guardian of the c
Ca 6:8 eighty c and maidens without
6:9 queens and c, and they
Eze 23:20 c belonging to those whose
Da 5:2 his c and his secondary wives
5:3 c and his secondary wives
5:23 c and your secondary wives

Condemn
Job 34:29 who, then, can c?
Isa 54:17 in the judgment you will c
Mt 12:41 Men of Nineveh . . . will c
12:42 queen of the south . . . c it
20:18 they will c him to death
Mr 10:33 will c him to death and
Lu 11:31 and will c them; because she
11:32 generation and will c it
Ro 2:1 you c yourself, inasmuch as
8:34 Who is he that will c?
2Co 7:3 I do not say this to c you
1Jo 3:20 our hearts may c us in
3:21 if our hearts do not c us

Condemnation
1Sa 14:47 he administered c
Ac 25:15 asking a judgment of c
Ro 5:16 from one trespass in c, but
5:18 to men of all sorts was c
8:1 with Christ Jesus have no c
2Co 3:9 the code administering c was

Condemned
Mt 12:7 not have c the guiltless ones
12:37 by your words you will be c
27:3 seeing he had been c, felt
Mr 14:64 c him to be liable to death
Lu 6:37 you will by no means be c
Ro 8:3 c sin in the flesh
14:23 he is already c if he eats
1Co 11:32 become c with the world
Ga 2:11 to face, because he stood c
Tit 2:8 speech which cannot be c
Heb 11:7 this faith he c the world
Jas 5:6 You have c, you have murdered
2Pe 2:6 he c them, setting a pattern

Condemning
Lu 6:37 stop c, and you will by no

Condemns
2Co 3:6 the written code c to death

Condescending
Ps 113:6 c to look on heaven and

Condition
Ge 34:15 on this c can we give
34:19 not delay to perform the c
34:22 on this c will the men give
42:9 the exposed c of the land
42:12 the exposed c of the land
Ex 14:27 to come back to its normal c
1Sa 11:2 On this c I shall conclude it
11:2 c of boring out every right
Job 42:10 the captive c of Job when
Ps 136:23 Who during our low c
Ec 10:6 dwelling merely in a low c
Isa 1:5 The whole head is in a sick c
6:12 deserted c does become very
24:12 astonishing c has been left
65:14 the good c of the heart
Jer 3:22 shall heal your renegade c
Eze 36:11 as in your former c and
Da 8:14 brought into its right c
Mr 5:23 daughter is in an extreme c
Ro 5:4 in turn, an approved c; the
5:4 the approved c, in turn, hope
1Co 7:24 In whatever c each one was

Conditions
2Ki 14:10 under unfavorable c and have

Eph 5:32 respect to Christ and the *c*
Php 3:6 zeal, persecuting the *c*
4:15 not a *c* took a share with
Col 1:18 the head of the body, the *c*
1:24 his body, which is the *c*
1:25 became a minister of this *c*
4:15 and to the *c* at her house
4:16 in the *c* of the Laodiceans
1Th 1:1 to the *c* of the Thessalonians
2Th 1:1 to the *c* of the Thessalonians
1Ti 3:5 will he take care of God's *c*
3:15 the *c* of the living God, a
5:16 *c* not be under the burden
Phm 2 to the *c* that is in your house
Heb 2:12 in the middle of the *c* I
12:23 the *c* of the firstborn who
Jas 5:14 call the older men of the *c*
3Jo 6 borne witness . . . before the *c*
9 I wrote something to the *c*, but
10 and to throw out of the *c*
Re 2:1 angel of the *c* in Ephesus
2:8 angel of the *c* in Smyrna
2:12 angel of the *c* in Pergamum
2:18 angel of the *c* in Thyatira
3:1 angel of the *c* in Sardis
3:7 angel of the *c* in Philadelphia
3:14 angel of the *c* in Laodicea

Congregations
Ac 15:41 Cilicia, strengthening the *c*
16:5 *c* continued to be made firm
Ro 16:4 the *c* of the nations render
16:16 the *c* of the Christ greet you
1Co 7:17 thus I ordain in all the *c*
11:16 neither do the *c* of God
14:33 all the *c* of the holy ones
14:34 women keep silent in the *c*
16:1 orders to the *c* of Galatia
16:19 *c* of Asia send . . . greetings
2Co 8:1 upon the *c* of Macedonia
8:18 has spread through all the *c*
8:19 appointed by the *c* to be our
8:23 are apostles of *c* and a glory
8:24 before the face of the *c*
11:8 Other *c* I robbed by accepting
11:28 the anxiety for all the *c*
12:13 less than the rest of the *c*
Ga 1:2 to the *c* of Galatia
1:22 to the *c* of Judea that were
1Th 2:14 *c* of God that are in Judea
2Th 1:4 take pride in you among the *c*
Re 1:4 John to the seven *c* that are
1:11 send it to the seven *c*, in
1:20 the angels of the seven *c*
1:20 lampstands mean seven *c*
2:7 what the spirit says to the *c*
2:11 what the spirit says to the *c*
2:17 what the spirit says to the *c*
2:23 *c* will know that I am he
2:29 what the spirit says to the *c*
3:6 what the spirit says to the *c*
3:13 what the spirit says to the *c*
3:22 the spirit says to the *c*
22:16 these things for the *c*

Congregator
Ec 1:1 of the *c*, the son of David the
1:2 *c* has said, the greatest vanity
1:12 I, the *c*, happened to be king
7:27 This I have found, said the *c*
12:8 greatest vanity! said the *c*
12:9 that the *c* had become wise
12:10 The *c* sought to find the

Coniah
Jer 22:24 *C* the son of Jehoiakim
22:28 *C* a mere form despised
37:1 *C* the son of Jehoiakim

Conjurer
Da 2:10 priest or *c* or Chaldean

Conjurers
Da 1:20 *c* that were in all his royal
2:2 *c* and the sorcerers and the
2:27 *c*, the magic-practicing
4:7 the *c*, the Chaldeans and the
5:7 bring in the *c*, the Chaldeans
5:11 the *c*, the Chaldeans and the
5:15 *c*, that they may read this

Connection
Ge 20:9 you have done in *c* with me
Le 18:23 a beast to have *c* with it
20:16 any beast to have a *c*
1Sa 24:18 you have done in *c* with me
2Sa 21:4 in *c* with Saul and his
1Ki 10:1 *c* with the name of Jehovah
2Ki 4:16 in *c* with your maidservant
1Ch 17:20 in *c* with all that we have
Ne 13:14 performed in *c* with the
Ho 2:18 *c* with the wild beast of the
Mt 26:31 be stumbled in *c* with me on
26:33 are stumbled in *c* with you
Lu 1:72 the mercy in *c* with our
5:14 in *c* with your cleansing
16:11 in *c* with the unrighteous
16:12 faithful in *c* with what is
Joh 13:31 God is glorified in *c* with
14:13 glorified in *c* with the Son
Ro 1:9 in *c* with the good news about
9:17 in *c* with you I may show my
11:2 says in *c* with Elijah, as he
1Co 4:17 my methods in *c* with Christ
11:11 in *c* with the Lord neither
15:58 vain in *c* with the Lord
2Co 8:18 praise in *c* with the good
8:19 in *c* with this kind gift to
8:20 find fault with us in *c* with
12:19 speaking in *c* with Christ
Ga 1:16 to reveal his Son in *c* with
Eph 3:11 formed in *c* with the Christ
5:8 now light in *c* with the Lord
6:20 may speak in *c* with it with
Php 4:9 saw in *c* with me, practice
Col 1:4 faith in *c* with Christ Jesus
1Th 4:7 but in *c* with sanctification
5:18 In *c* with everything give
2Th 1:10 in *c* with his holy ones
1:10 in *c* with all those who
1Ti 1:4 by God in *c* with faith
1:14 is in *c* with Christ Jesus
3:13 the faith in *c* with Christ
2Ti 1:9 was given us in *c* with Christ
1:13 that are in *c* with Christ
2:1 is in *c* with Christ Jesus
2:9 *c* with which I am suffering
3:15 the faith in *c* with Christ
Phm 8 speech in *c* with Christ to
20 in *c* with the Lord: refresh
20 affections in *c* with Christ
1Pe 3:16 conduct in *c* with Christ

Conquer
Re 11:7 make war with them and *c*
13:7 war with the holy ones and *c*
17:14 the Lamb will *c* them

Conquered
Joh 16:33 I have *c* the world
Ro 12:21 yourself be *c* by the evil
Col 2:15 in open public as *c*, leading
1Jo 2:13 you have *c* the wicked one
2:14 you have *c* the wicked one
4:4 you have *c* those persons
5:4 conquest that has *c* the world
Re 3:21 I *c* and sat down with my
5:5 *c* so as to open the scroll and
12:11 *c* him because of the blood

Conquering
Ro 12:21 *c* the evil with the good
Re 6:2 *c* and to complete his conquest
21:7 Anyone *c* will inherit these

Conqueror
Jg 18:7 was no oppressive *c* that was

Conquers
Lu 11:22 comes against him and *c* him
1Jo 5:4 born from God *c* the world
5:5 one that *c* the world but he
Re 2:7 him that *c* I will grant to
2:11 He that *c* will by no means
2:17 him that *c* I will give some
2:26 him that *c* and observes my
3:5 He that *c* will thus be arrayed
3:12 one that *c*—I will make him
3:21 one that *c* I will grant to

Conquest
1Jo 5:4 the *c* that has conquered the
Re 6:2 and to complete his *c*

Conscience
Ac 23:1 with a perfectly clear *c* down
Ro 2:15 *c* is bearing witness with
9:1 my *c* bears witness with me in
13:5 also on account of your *c*
1Co 8:7 *c*, being weak, is defiled
8:10 *c* of that one who is weak
8:12 their *c* that is weak, you
10:25 inquiry on account of your *c*
10:27 inquiry on account of your *c*
1Co 10:28 and on account of *c*
10:29 *C*, I say, not your own, but
10:29 by another person's *c*
2Co 1:12 to which our *c* bears witness
4:2 human *c* in the sight of God
1Ti 1:5 and out of a good *c* and
1:19 holding faith and a good *c*
3:9 of the faith with a clean *c*
4:2 marked in their *c* as with a
2Ti 1:3 and with a clean *c*, that I
Heb 9:9 perfect as respects his *c*
10:22 sprinkled from a wicked *c*
13:18 we have an honest *c*, as
1Pe 2:19 because of *c* toward God
3:16 Hold a good *c*, so that in the
3:21 request . . . for a good *c*

Consciences
2Co 5:11 manifest also to your *c*
Tit 1:15 and their *c* are defiled
Heb 9:14 cleanse our *c* from dead

Conscious
Ec 9:5 living are *c* that they will
9:5 the dead, they are *c* of nothing
Mt 5:3 Happy are those *c* of their
1Co 4:4 am not *c* of anything against

Consciousness
Ac 24:16 *c* of committing no offense
Heb 10:2 have no *c* of sins anymore

Conscripted
2Sa 20:24 Adoram was over those *c*
1Ki 4:6 over those *c* for forced labor
5:13 those *c* for forced labor out
5:13 those *c* for forced labor
5:14 Adoniram was over those *c*
9:15 *c* for forced labor that King
12:18 those *c* for forced labor
2Ch 10:18 those *c* for forced labor

Consent
Ge 34:15 on this condition . . . give *c*
34:22 *c* to dwell with us so as to
34:23 let us give them our *c* that
Ex 10:27 did not *c* to send them away
Jg 11:17 and he did not *c*. And Israel
19:10 the man did not *c* to stay
2Sa 12:17 he did not *c* and did not
13:14 not *c* to listen to her voice
13:16 did not *c* to listen to her
13:25 not *c* to go but blessed
14:29 he did not *c* to come to him
14:29 and he did not *c* to come
23:16 he did not *c* to drink it
23:17 he did not *c* to drink it
1Ki 20:8 and you should not *c*
22:49 Jehoshaphat did not *c*
2Ki 24:4 not *c* to grant forgiveness
1Ch 11:18 David did not *c* to drink it
11:19 And he did not *c* to drink it
Pr 1:10 try to seduce you, do not *c*
1:30 They did not *c* to my counsel
Eze 20:8 did not *c* to listen to me
Lu 11:48 yet you give *c* to them
Ac 18:20 longer time, he would not *c*
Ro 1:32 *c* with those practicing them
1Co 7:5 except by mutual *c* for an
Phm 14 without your *c* I do not want

Consented
De 25:7 He has not *c* to perform
2Ki 12:8 the priests *c* not to take
Lu 22:6 *c*, and he began to seek a good

Consequence
2Sa 12:6 *c* of the fact that he has
12:10 *c* of the fact that you
Ps 40:15 in *c* of their shame
Am 4:12 As a *c* of the fact that I
Joh 21:23 In *c*, this saying went out

Consequences
Job 13:26 *c* of the errors of my youth

Consider
Ex 33:13 *c* that this nation is your
Le 19:23 *c* its fruitage impure as its
De 32:7 *C* the years back from
32:29 would *c* their end afterward
Jg 5:10 you who walk on the road, *C*
Job 14:21 but he does not *c* them
23:5 would *c* what he says to me
Pr 23:1 *c* what is before you
29:7 wicked does not *c* such
Isa 32:4 overhasty will *c* knowledge
Joe 3:21 will *c* innocent their blood

Mt 7:3 *c* the rafter in your own eye
Lu 7:7 I did not *c* myself worthy to
2Co 11:5 I *c* that I have not in a
Php 2:25 I *c* it necessary to send to
3:8 *c* all things to be loss on
3:8 I *c* them as a lot of refuse
3:13 not yet *c* myself as having
Phm 17 If . . . you *c* me a sharer
Heb 3:1 *c* the apostle and high priest
10:24 *c* one another to incite to
12:3 *c* closely the one who has
Jas 1:2 *C* it all joy, my brothers
2Pe 1:13 I *c* it right, as long as I
2:13 *c* luxurious living in the
3:9 as some people *c* slowness
3:15 *c* the patience of our Lord

Considerable
Ps 25:11 my error, for it is *c*
Mr 10:46 his disciples and a *c* crowd
Lu 7:12 A *c* crowd from the city was
8:27 for a *c* time he had not worn
8:32 a herd of a *c* number of swine
20:9 he traveled abroad for *c* time
23:8 over a *c* time he was wanting
Ac 11:24 *c* crowd was added to the
14:3 spent *c* time speaking with
19:26 Paul has persuaded a *c* crowd
27:9 As *c* time had passed and by

Considerably
Jg 19:11 the daylight had gone down *c*

Consideration
Ge 19:21 show you *c* to this extent
Le 19:32 *c* for the person of an old
Jos 11:20 come to have no favorable *c*
1Sa 25:35 may have *c* for your person
2Ki 3:14 for which I am having *c*
16:15 for me to take under *c*
Ne 5:7 my heart took *c* within me
Job 34:19 more *c* to the noble one
Ps 41:1 with *c* toward the lowly one
Pr 6:35 *c* for any sort of ransom
21:12 *c* to the house of the wicked
Isa 5:23 righteous in *c* of a bribe
43:18 things do not turn your *c*
52:15 they must turn their *c*
Jer 2:10 and give your special *c*
23:20 will give your *c* to it
30:24 will give your *c* to it
La 4:16 no *c* even for the priests
Da 9:23 So give *c* to the matter, and
11:30 give *c* to those leaving the
11:37 he will give no *c*; and to
11:37 other god he will give no *c*
Php 2:6 gave no *c* to a seizure
1Th 5:13 more than extraordinary *c* in

Considered
Ge 31:15 really *c* as foreigners to
41:16 I need not be *c*! God will
De 2:11 also were *c* like the Anakim
2:20 Rephaim it also used to be *c*
1Ki 10:21 *c* in the days of Solomon as
2Ch 9:20 silver; it was *c* as nothing
Ne 13:13 for they were *c* faithful
Job 34:27 his ways have they *c*
38:18 *c* the broad spaces of the
Ps 119:30 I have *c* appropriate
119:59 I have *c* my ways
119:128 *c* all orders regarding all
139:2 *c* my thought from far off
Pr 31:16 She has *c* a field and
Isa 43:4 you have been *c* honorable
Jer 4:28 I have spoken, I have *c*
Da 4:35 being *c* as merely nothing
Joe 3:21 that I had not *c* innocent
Hab 2:16 and be *c* uncircumcised
Mt 12:12 All *c*, of how much more
Lu 18:9 who *c* the rest as nothing
Ac 12:12 after he *c* it, he went to
Ro 4:19 he *c* his own body, now
Php 3:7 have *c* loss on account of the
1Ti 1:12 *c* me faithful by assigning

Considering
Ps 33:15 He is *c* all their works
73:16 kept *c* so as to know this
Da 7:8 I kept on *c* the horns, and
8:5 my part, kept on *c*, and, look!
Php 2:3 *c* that the others are superior
4:8 continue *c* these things
2Th 3:15 not be *c* him as an enemy
1Ti 6:1 keep on *c* their owners

Considers
Job 13:1 My ear has heard and *c* it
24:12 And God himself *c* it not as
Pr 14:15 the shrewd one *c* his steps
Ro 14:14 a man *c* something to be

Consign
2Ki 8:12 you will *c* to the fire

Consigned
Jg 1:8 the city they *c* to the fire
20:48 cities . . . they *c* to the fire
2Ki 19:18 *c* their gods to the fire

Consigning
Isa 37:19 *c* of their gods to the fire

Consisted
Col 2:14 which *c* of decrees and which

Consisting
Eph 2:15 commandments *c* in decrees

Consists
Eph 5:9 *c* of every sort of goodness
Php 3:19 their glory *c* in their shame

Consolation
2Sa 3:35 give David bread for *c* while
13:5 make the bread of *c* under my
13:7 make the bread of *c* for him
13:10 Bring the bread of *c* to
Job 16:5 *c* of my own lips would hold
21:2 And let this become your *c*
36:16 the *c* of your table will
Isa 66:11 the breast of full *c* by her
Jer 16:7 the cup of *c* to drink
La 4:10 as bread of *c* to one during
Lu 2:25 waiting for Israel's *c*, and
6:24 having your *c* in full
Php 2:1 if any *c* of love, if any

Consolations
Job 15:11 *c* of God not enough for you
Ps 94:19 *c* began to fondle my soul

Console
Joh 11:19 in order to *c* them

Consoles
1Co 14:3 and *c* men by his speech

Consoling
Joh 11:31 and that were *c* her, on
1Th 2:11 *c* and bearing witness to you

Consolingly
Jg 19:3 speak *c* to her so as to bring
1Th 5:14 speak *c* to the depressed

Consort
Ne 2:6 queenly *c* was sitting beside
Ps 45:9 The queenly *c* has taken her

Conspicuous
Ca 5:10 the most *c* of ten thousand
Da 8:5 was a *c* horn between its eyes

Conspicuously
Da 8:8 come up *c* four instead of it

Conspicuousness
Jos 22:10 an altar great in *c*

Conspiracy
2Sa 15:12 the *c* kept getting stronger
1Ki 16:20 Zimri and his *c* with which
2Ki 11:14, 14 began crying: *C! C!*
12:20 leagued together in a *c* and
14:19 leagued against him in a *c*
15:15 Shallum and his *c* with
15:30 a *c* against Pekah the son
17:4 to find *c* in Hoshea's case
2Ch 23:13, 13 Athaliah . . . said: *C! C!*
25:27 *c* against him in Jerusalem
Isa 8:12 A *c*! respecting all that of
8:12 people keep saying, A *c*!
Jer 11:9 *C* has been found among the
Eze 22:25 a *c* of her prophets in the
Ac 23:12 day, the Jews formed a *c* and
23:13 that formed this oathbound *c*

Conspirators
2Ki 21:24 the *c* against King Amon
2Ch 24:26 *c* against him: Zabad the
33:25 *c* against King Amon, and

Conspire
1Ki 15:27 began to *c* against him
16:9 began to *c* against him
2Ki 9:14 to *c* against Jehoram
Ne 4:8 began to *c* together to come
Ps 83:3 *c* against your concealed ones

Conspired
1Sa 22:8 *c*, all of you, against me
22:13 Why have you men *c* against
1Ki 16:16 Zimri has *c* and also struck
16:20 conspiracy with which he *c*
2Ki 10:9 I myself *c* against my lord
15:10 *c* against him and struck
15:15 conspiracy with which he *c*
15:25 adjutant *c* against him
21:23 servants of Amon *c* against
2Ch 24:21 *c* against him and pelted
24:25 own servants *c* against him
33:24 servants *c* against him and
Am 7:10 Amos has *c* against you right

Conspiring
2Sa 15:31 among those *c* with Absalom

Constables
Ac 16:35 dispatched the *c* to say
16:38 *c* reported these sayings to

Constancy
Da 6:16 you are serving with *c*, he
6:20 whom you are serving with *c*
Eph 6:18 keep awake with all *c* and

Constant
Ex 29:42 It is a *c* burnt offering
Nu 4:7 *c* bread should continue on it
4:16 *c* grain offering and the
28:6 the *c* burnt offering, which
28:10 with the *c* burnt offering
28:15 *c* burnt offering together
28:23 is for the *c* burnt offering
28:24 with the *c* burnt offering it
28:31 the *c* burnt offering and its
29:6 *c* burnt offering and its grain
29:11 and the *c* burnt offering and
29:16 aside from the *c* burnt
29:19 the *c* burnt offering and its
29:22 the *c* burnt offering and its
29:25 the *c* burnt offering, its
29:28 aside from the *c* burnt
29:31 aside from the *c* burnt
29:34 aside from the *c* burnt
29:38 aside from the *c* burnt
Jos 23:11 be on *c* guard for your
2Ch 2:4 with the *c* layer bread and
Ezr 3:5 the *c* burnt offering and that
Ne 10:33 the *c* grain offering and
10:33 the *c* burnt offering of the
Jer 52:34 *c* allowance given him from
Eze 46:15 *c* whole burnt offering
Da 8:11 *c* feature was taken away, and
8:12 together with the *c* feature
8:13 vision be of the *c* feature
11:31 and remove the *c* feature
12:11 *c* feature has been removed
Lu 2:47 were in *c* amazement at his
Ac 2:46 *c* attendance at the temple
8:13 in *c* attendance upon Philip
10:7 were in *c* attendance upon him
1Co 7:35 *c* attendance upon the Lord
1Ti 4:16 Pay *c* attention to yourself
2Ti 2:7 Give *c* thought to what I am

Constantly
Ex 25:30 upon the table before me *c*
27:20 to light up the lamps *c*
28:29 memorial before Jehovah *c*
28:30 his heart before Jehovah *c*
28:38 stay upon his forehead *c*, to
29:38 offer upon the altar . . . *c*
30:8 incense *c* before Jehovah
Le 6:13 kept *c* burning on the altar
6:20 as a grain offering *c*, half
24:2 to light up the lamp *c*
24:3 before Jehovah *c*
24:4 in order before Jehovah *c*
24:8 in order before Jehovah *c*
Nu 9:16 it went on *c*: The cloud would
28:3 lambs . . . a burnt offering *c*
De 11:12 eyes of Jehovah . . . *c* upon it
2Sa 9:7 will eat bread at my table *c*
9:10 will eat bread at my table *c*
9:13 *c* at the table of the king
1Ki 10:8 are standing before you *c*
2Ki 4:9 that is passing by us *c*
25:29 ate bread *c* before him all
25:30 allowance was *c* given him
1Ch 16:6 trumpets *c* before the ark of
16:11 Seek his face *c*
16:37 minister before the Ark *c*
16:40 *c* morning and evening and
23:31 *c* before Jehovah

2Ch 9:7 standing before you *c* and
24:14 *c* all the days of Jehoiada
Ne 2:13 I was *c* examining the walls
Ps 16:8 Jehovah in front of me *c*
25:15 My eyes are *c* toward Jehovah
34:1 *C* his praise will be in my
35:27 And let them say *c*
38:17 pain was in front of me *c*
40:11 trueness . . . *c* safeguard me
40:16 say *c*: May Jehovah be
50:8 that are in front of me *c*
51:3 my sin is in front of me *c*
69:23 their very hips to wobble *c*
70:4 say *c*: God be magnified!
71:3 into which to enter *c*
71:6 In you my praise is *c*
71:14 as for me, I shall wait *c*
72:15 behalf let prayer be made *c*
73:23 But I am *c* with you
74:23 against you is ascending *c*
105:4 Seek his face *c*
109:15 be in front of Jehovah *c*
109:19 girded about himself *c*
119:44 I will keep your law *c*
119:109 My soul is in my palm *c*
119:117 upon your regulations *c*
Pr 5:19 may you be in an ecstasy *c*
6:21 Tie them upon your heart *c*
15:15 good at heart has a feast *c*
28:14 man that is feeling dread *c*
Isa 10:1 those who, *c* writing, have
21:8 I am standing *c* by day, and
49:16 walls are in front of me *c*
51:13 you were in dread *c* the
52:5 and *c*, all day long, my name
58:11 bound to lead you *c* and to
60:11 kept open *c*; they will not
62:6 *c*, let them not keep still
65:3 *c*, sacrificing in the gardens
Jer 6:7 plague are before my face *c*
52:33 ate bread before him *c*
Eze 38:8 a *c* devastated place
46:14 lasting statute, *c*
Da 6:4 *c* seeking to find some pretext
Ho 12:6 a hoping in your God *c*
Am 5:24 like a *c* flowing torrent
Ob 16 the nations will keep drinking *c*
Na 3:19 badness did not pass over *c*
Hab 1:17 have to kill nations *c*
Ac 2:25 had Jehovah *c* before my eyes
Ro 13:6 *c* serving this very purpose
1Co 9:13 those *c* attending at the
2Th 3:16 peace *c* in every way
Tit 3:8 to make firm assertions *c*

Constellation
Job 9:9 Making the Ash *c*, the Kesil
9:9 the Kesil *c*, And the Kimah
9:9 the Kimah *c* and the interior
38:31 the bonds of the Kimah *c*
38:31 very cords of the Kesil *c*
38:32 bring forth the Mazzaroth *c*
38:32 Ash *c* alongside its sons
Am 5:8 The Maker of the Kimah *c* and
5:8 the Kesil *c*, and the One

Constellations
2Ki 23:5 to the *c* of the zodiac and
Isa 13:10 and their *c* of Kesil will

Consternation
Job 41:25 Due to *c* they get

Constitute
Ge 13:16 I will *c* your seed like the
21:13 *c* him a nation, because he
21:18 I shall *c* him a great nation
32:12 *c* your seed like the grains
46:3 *c* you there into a great
48:20 May God *c* you like Ephraim
De 21:16 *c* the son of the loved one
Jos 6:18 do *c* the camp of Israel a
24:25 to *c* for them a regulation
1Ki 14:7 *c* you a leader over my
16:2 *c* you leader over my people
16:3 *c* his house like the house of
21:22 *c* your house like the house
2Ki 9:9 I must *c* the house of Ahab
1Ch 17:22 to *c* your people Israel as
Ps 21:6 *c* him highly blessed forever
21:9 *c* them as a fiery furnace at

Constituted
De 10:22 *c* you like the stars of the
Jos 9:27 Joshua *c* them on that day
1Ki 9:22 that Solomon *c* slaves
2Ch 2:11 he has *c* you king over them
2Ch 8:9 Solomon *c* slaves for his work
25:16 of the king that we *c* you
29:8 *c* them an object at which to
30:7 he *c* them an object of
Ne 9:7 and *c* his name Abraham
13:26 God *c* him king over all
Ro 5:19 many were *c* sinners
5:19 many will be *c* righteous
Jas 3:6 The tongue is *c* a world of

Constituting
Jas 4:4 *c* himself an enemy of God

Constrain
2Ki 4:8 began to *c* him to eat bread

Constraint
Job 36:16 Broader space, not *c*, will
37:10 waters is under *c*

Constructed
Heb 3:4 every house is *c* by someone
3:4 he that *c* all things is God
9:2 *c* a first tent compartment in
9:6 things had been *c* this way
11:7 *c* an ark for the saving of
1Pe 3:20 while the ark was being *c*

Construction
Eze 41:9 the *c* of the side chambers

Constructs
Heb 3:3 he who *c* it has more honor

Consult
Le 19:31 *c* professional foretellers
1Sa 28:7 will go to her and *c* her
2Sa 21:1 to *c* the face of Jehovah
1Ch 13:1 David proceeded to *c* with
21:30 to go before it to *c* God
2Ch 20:4 they came to *c* Jehovah
Ezr 7:10 to *c* the law of Jehovah and
Ne 6:7 come, and let us *c* together
Isa 40:14 *c* together that one might
45:21 *c* together in unity

Consultation
Mt 27:1 held a *c* against Jesus so as
Mr 15:1 conducted a *c*, and they bound

Consulting
Pr 13:10 *c* together there is wisdom
Mt 27:7 After *c* together, they bought
Ac 4:15 began *c* with one another

Consults
De 18:11 anyone who *c* a spirit medium

Consume
Ge 41:30 famine will simply *c* the
Nu 11:1 *c* some in the extremity of
16:35 *c* the two hundred and fifty
24:8 He will *c* the nations, his
De 5:25 this great fire may *c* us
7:16 you must *c* all the peoples
32:22 *c* the earth and its produce
Jg 6:21 and to *c* the meat and the
9:15 and *c* the cedars of Lebanon
9:20 *c* the landowners of Shechem
9:20 of Millo and *c* Abimelech
2Ch 7:1 *c* the burnt offering and the
Ps 39:11 you *c* his desirable things
Isa 27:10 actually *c* her boughs
Mt 6:19 where moth and rust *c*, and
Heb 10:27 *c* those in opposition

Consumed
Ge 31:40 by day the heat *c* me and
Ex 3:2 yet the thornbush was not *c*
22:6 or a field gets *c*, the one
Le 10:2 from before Jehovah and *c*
Nu 21:28 It has *c* Ar of Moab, the
26:10 fire *c* two hundred and fifty
De 31:17 become something to be *c*
Eze 24:11 Let its rust get *c*
47:12 will their fruitage be *c*
Joe 1:19 flame has *c* all the trees

Consumes
Le 6:10 fire regularly *c* upon the
Ps 97:3 *c* his adversaries all around
Joe 2:3 and behind it a flame *c*
Mt 6:20 neither moth nor rust *c*
Lu 12:33 does not get near nor moth *c*

Consuming
Ex 22:5 and cause a *c* in another field
Le 9:24 began *c* the burnt offering
De 4:24 Jehovah your God is a *c* fire
9:3 A *c* fire he is
Isa 42:25 it kept *c* him all around
Heb 12:29 our God is also a *c* fire

Contact
Ex 14:25 flee from any *c* with Israel
Jos 2:16 may not come in *c* with you
1Sa 14:9 until we make *c* with you
2Sa 5:8 make *c* with both the lame
2Ch 3:12 in *c* with the wing of the
Isa 25:12 *c* with the earth, to the
La 2:2 brought into *c* with the earth
Eze 13:14 into *c* with the earth, and

Contain
1Ki 7:26 were what it would *c*
7:38 what each basin would *c*
8:27 heavens . . . cannot *c* you
8:64 to *c* the burnt sacrifice
2Ch 2:6 heaven of the heavens cannot *c*
4:5 were what it could *c*
6:18 heavens themselves, cannot *c*
7:7 *c* the burnt offering and the
Jer 2:13 that cannot *c* the water
Joh 21:25 not *c* the scrolls written

Contained
1Pe 2:6 it is *c* in Scripture: Look! I

Containing
Eze 23:32 the cup *c* much

Contaminate
Nu 5:3 not *c* the camps of those in

Contemned
Ps 78:59 so he *c* Israel very much
Isa 33:8 he has *c* the cities

Contemning
Ps 89:38 cast off and you keep *c*
106:24 got to *c* the desirable land

Contemplate
Pr 5:6 path of life she does not *c*
Heb 13:7 *c* how their conduct turns

Contemplating
Pr 5:21 and he is *c* all his tracks

Contemporaries
Ge 6:9 Noah . . . faultless among his *c*

Contempt
Ge 38:23 we may not fall into *c*
De 27:16 father or his mother with *c*
2Sa 19:43 have you treated us with *c*
Ne 4:4 have become an object of *c*
Es 1:18 plenty of *c* and indignation
Job 12:5 has *c* for extinction itself
12:21 is pouring out *c* upon nobles
31:34 *c* itself of families would
Ps 31:18 in haughtiness and *c*
107:40 pouring out *c* upon nobles
119:22 Roll off me reproach and *c*
123:3 we have been glutted with *c*
123:4 *c* on the part of the
Pr 12:8 will come to be for *c*
18:3 wicked one comes in, *c* also
Isa 9:1 one treated with *c* the land
23:9 to treat with *c* all the
Eze 22:7 they have treated with *c* in
Mt 5:22 an unspeakable word of *c*
Ga 4:14 you did not treat with *c*
1Th 5:20 treat prophesyings with *c*
Heb 10:29 undeserved kindness with *c*

Contemptible
Nu 21:5 has come to abhor the *c* bread
Ps 15:4 In his eyes anyone *c* is
119:141 I am insignificant and *c*
2Co 10:10 is weak and his speech *c*

Contend
De 33:8 to *c* with him by the waters
Jg 11:25 Did he ever *c* with Israel
Job 13:8 will you *c* at law
13:19 one that will *c* with me
23:6 an abundance of power *c* with
Isa 3:13 stationing himself to *c* and
27:8 *c* with her when sending her
49:25 I myself shall *c*, and your
50:8 Who can *c* with me? Let us
57:16 indefinite that I shall *c*
Jer 2:9 *c* further with you people
2:9 sons of your sons I shall *c*
Ho 4:4 let no man *c*, neither let a
Ac 11:2 began to *c* with him

Contended
Ge 26:20 they had *c* with him
32:28 *c* with God and with men so
De 33:7 His arms have *c* for what is

Job 33:13 against him that you *c*
Isa 45:9 has *c* with his Former, as an
Ho 12:3 dynamic energy he *c* with God
2Ti 2:5 *c* according to the rules

Contender
Jg 12:2 I became a special *c*, I and

Contending
1Sa 2:10 those *c* against him will be
Job 9:3 If he should find delight in *c*
10:2 that you are *c* with me
40:2 be any *c* of a faultfinder
Isa 49:25 anyone *c* against you I
Jer 2:29 people keep *c* against me
Ho 4:4 who are *c* against a priest
12:4 he kept *c* with an angel
Joh 6:52 the Jews began *c* with one
Ac 23:9 *c* fiercely, saying: We find

Contends
Isa 51:22 God, who *c* for his people
2Ti 2:5 *c* even in the games, he is

Content
1Ti 6:8 shall be *c* with these things
Heb 13:5 *c* with the present things
3Jo 10 not being *c* with these things

Contention
Pr 15:18 An enraged man stirs up *c*
16:28 keeps sending forth *c*, and a
17:14 The beginning of *c* is as one
22:10 that *c* may go out and that
26:20 no slanderer *c* grows still
28:25 arrogant in soul stirs up *c*
29:22 given to anger stirs up *c*
Am 7:4 for a *c* by means of fire

Contentions
Pr 6:14 keeps sending out merely *c*
6:19 forth *c* among brothers
10:12 Hatred is what stirs up *c*
18:18 The lot puts even *c* to rest
18:19 *c* that are like the bar of a
19:13 *c* of a wife are as a leaking
23:29 Who has *c*? Who has concern?
2Co 12:20 *c*, backbitings, whisperings
Ga 5:20 anger, *c*, divisions, sects

Contentious
Pr 21:9 a roof than with a *c* wife
21:19 a *c* wife along with vexation
25:24 of a roof than with a *c* wife
26:21 *c* man for causing a quarrel
27:15 and a *c* wife are comparable
Ro 2:8 for those who are *c* and who

Contentiousness
Php 1:17 the former do it out of *c*
2:3 doing nothing out of *c* or out
Jas 3:14 jealousy and *c* in your hearts
3:16 For where jealousy and *c* are

Contest
Ps 76:8 caused the legal *c* to be heard
Pr 22:10 legal *c* and dishonor may
1Co 9:25 every man taking part in a *c*
Heb 10:32 you endured a great *c* under
12:4 In carrying on your *c* against

Contests
La 3:58 the *c* of my soul. You have

Continual
Jos 6:9 with a *c* blowing on the horns
6:13 a *c* blowing on the horns
Job 33:19 quarreling of his bones is *c*
Isa 33:15 walking in *c* righteousness
50:10 has walked in *c* darkness
Eze 39:14 men for *c* employment whom

Continually
Ge 3:24 sword that was turning itself *c*
31:15 he keeps eating *c* even from
39:4 waited upon him *c*, so that he
Ex 19:19 the horn became *c* louder and
40:15 their anointing must serve *c*
De 33:13 May his land be *c* blessed
Jos 6:13 *c* blowing the horns, and the
1Sa 18:9 And Saul was *c* looking
18:14 And David was *c* acting
2Sa 3:6 *c* strengthening his position
7:6 *c* walking about in a tent and
8:15 David was *c* rendering
14:11 may not be *c* causing ruin
15:12 the people were *c* growing
2Ki 4:1 servant had *c* feared Jehovah
18:4 *c* been making sacrificial
21:15 *c* offending me from the
1Ch 18:14 he was *c* rendering judicial
2Ch 5:8 cherubs were *c* spreading out
10:6 *c* attending upon Solomon his
26:5 *c* tended to search for God
30:10 *c* speaking in mockery of
36:16 *c* making jest at the
Ezr 4:4 *c* weakening the hands of the
6:9 be given them *c* day by day
6:10 *c* be presenting soothing
7:25 may *c* judge all the people
Ne 1:4 *c* fasting and praying before
6:14 *c* trying to make me afraid
6:19 they were *c* saying before me
6:19 were *c* taking out to him
Es 1:22 husband to be *c* acting as
2:15 Esther was *c* gaining favor in
Ps 104:11 *c* give drink to all the
Ec 1:6 Round and round it is *c*
12:9 taught the people knowledge *c*
Jer 35:13 *c* receive exhortation to
Da 6:2 satraps might *c* be giving to
7:25 will harass *c* the holy ones
Jon 1:11 *c* growing more tempestuous
1:13 *c* growing more tempestuous
Mt 10:6 go *c* to the lost sheep of the
16:24 stake and *c* follow me
19:17 observe the commandments *c*
26:41 Keep on the watch and pray *c*
Mr 3:9 little boat *c* at his service
5:5 And *c*, night and day, he was
8:34 stake and follow me *c*
11:18 *c* being astounded at his
Lu 9:23 and follow me *c*
12:31 seek *c* his kingdom, and
18:5 widow's *c* making me trouble
24:53 *c* in the temple blessing
Ac 10:2 made supplication to God *c*
24:16 I am exercising myself *c* to
Heb 1:11 you yourself are to remain *c*
10:1 which they offer *c* make

Continue
Ge 2:18 is not good for the man to *c*
9:2 terror of you will *c* upon
13:8 do not let any quarreling *c*
26:3 I shall *c* with you and bless
28:20 If God will *c* with me and
30:31 I shall *c* guarding it
31:3 and I shall *c* with you
33:9 Let *c* yours what is yours
33:14 *c* the journey at my leisure
39:10 alongside her, to *c* with her
45:10 and you must *c* near me
48:21 God will certainly *c* with
49:26 *c* upon the head of Joseph
Ex 9:2 if you *c* refusing to send them
9:29 hail will not *c* any longer
10:4 *c* refusing to send my people
12:6 it must *c* under safeguard by
18:14 Why do you alone *c* sitting
18:14 people *c* taking their stand
20:20 fear of him may *c* before
22:30 it will *c* with its mother
28:28 *c* above the girdle of the
30:31 to *c* as a holy anointing oil
30:32 *c* as something holy for you
30:37 is to *c* as something holy to
39:21 it might *c* above the girdle
Le 11:36 waters will *c* clean
15:19 should *c* seven days in her
19:23 will *c* uncircumcised for you
20:14 loose conduct may not *c* in
22:27 *c* under its mother seven
25:28 what he sold must also *c* in
25:29 repurchase must also *c*
25:29 right of repurchase should *c*
25:31 Right of repurchase should *c*
25:32 *c* to time indefinite for the
25:48 repurchase will *c* in his
25:50 he should *c* with him
25:53 *c* with him like a hired
26:3 *c* walking in my statutes and
26:44 they *c* in the land of their
Nu 4:7 constant bread should *c* on it
9:20 cloud would *c* a few days over
9:21 cloud would *c* from evening to
12:12 let her *c* like someone dead
14:43 Jehovah will not *c* with you
36:12 inheritance might *c* together
De 3:19 *c* dwelling in your cities
4:37 *c* to live, because he loved
7:12 *c* listening to these judicial
8:1 *c* living and indeed multiply
10:5 that they might *c* there
De 17:19 it must *c* with him, and he
18:3 *c* as the due right of the
22:2 *c* with you until your brother
22:19 she will *c* to be his wife
23:10 a man who does not *c* clean
24:5 *c* exempt at his house for one
25:3 *c* to beat him with many
25:15 you should *c* to have
25:15 you should *c* to have
28:9 *c* to keep the commandments
28:41 but they will not *c* yours
28:46 *c* on you and your offspring
31:8 He himself will *c* with you
31:23 I myself shall *c* with you
Jos 4:9 they *c* there until this day
15:63 Jebusites *c* dwelling with
16:10 Canaanites *c* dwelling in
23:13 will not *c* to dispossess
Jg 5:17 why did he *c* to dwell for the
10:4 they *c* to call Havvoth-jair
17:12 *c* in the house of Micah
18:19 to *c* a priest to the house
1Sa 21:5 of the young men *c* holy
2Sa 2:28 not *c* chasing after Israel
7:29 it to *c* to time indefinite
1Ki 5:14 they would *c* in Lebanon, for
8:8 there they *c* down to this day
8:16 house for my name to *c* there
11:32 will *c* his for the sake of
11:36 may *c* having a lamp always
2Ki 11:8 *c* with the king when he goes
20:19 will *c* in my own days
23:27 My name will *c* there
1Ch 5:26 to *c* until this day
17:27 it to *c* to time indefinite
2Ch 5:9 they *c* there down to this day
23:7 *c* with the king when he
23:16 *c* as the people of Jehovah
29:11 *c* as his ministers and
Ne 2:17 no longer *c* to be a reproach
Job 1:21 Let the name of Jehovah *c* to
21:12 They *c* raising their voice
32:16 for they do not *c* speaking
33:31 I myself shall *c* speaking
Ps 36:10 *C* your loving-kindness to
37:18 inheritance will *c* even to
92:14 and fresh they will *c* to be
102:28 servants will *c* residing
119:8 regulations I *c* to keep
122:7 peace *c* within your rampart
Pr 4:4 commandments and *c* living
7:2 my commandments and *c* living
Isa 39:8 truth will *c* in my own days
64:12 *c* keeping yourself in check
Jer 22:15 Will you *c* reigning because
25:5 *c* dwelling upon the ground
27:22 there they will *c* to be
32:5 *c* until I turn my attention
33:24 no more *c* being a nation
35:18 and *c* keeping all his
38:20 your soul will *c* to live
40:9 *C* dwelling in the land and
Eze 13:9 they will not *c* on, and in
18:3 will no more *c* to be yours
21:13 This will not *c* existing
36:3 you *c* being talked about
37:22 longer *c* to be two nations
44:2 gate, shut is how it will *c*
44:2 and it must *c* shut
46:1 *c* shut for the six workdays
46:17 *c* to belong to their own
Da 11:17 she will not *c* to be his
Ho 9:3 not *c* dwelling in the land
9:4 *c* pouring out wine to Jehovah
9:15 I will not *c* on loving them
Mic 5:12 will you *c* to have
Mal 2:4 my covenant with Levi may *c*
Mt 5:44 *C* to love your enemies and
12:5 as not sacred and *c* guiltless
17:17 how long must I *c* with you?
Mr 3:14 that they might *c* with him
4:17 they *c* for a time; then as
5:18 that he might *c* with him
9:19 how long must I *c* with you?
Lu 6:27 *C* to love your enemies, to do
6:35 *c* to love your enemies and
6:36 *C* becoming merciful, just as
8:38 kept begging to *c* with him
9:41 how long must I *c* with you
11:21 his belongings *c* in peace
Joh 7:33 I *c* a little while longer
10:38 *c* knowing that the Father
21:19 to him: *C* following me
21:22 You *c* following me

Ac 2:24 to *c* to be held fast by it
5:4 it not *c* in your control
11:23 *c* in the Lord with hearty
13:43 *c* in the undeserved kindness
26:22 I *c* to this day bearing
Ro 6:1 Shall we *c* in sin, that
6:12 do not let sin *c* to rule as
9:11 *c* dependent, not upon works
1Co 4:11 we *c* to hunger and also to
7:26 for a man to *c* as he is
2Co 1:13 *c* to recognize to the end
13:11 brothers, *c* to rejoice, to
Ga 2:5 the good news might *c* with you
3:10 *c* in all the things written
Eph 1:16 I *c* mentioning you in my
5:25 *c* loving your wives, just
Php 1:9 I *c* praying, that your love
3:1 *c* rejoicing in the Lord
4:8 *c* considering these things
Col 1:23 that you *c* in the faith
3:13 *C* putting up with one another
4:18 *C* bearing my prison bonds in
1Th 3:6 *c* having good remembrance of
5:25 Brothers, *c* in prayer for us
2Th 3:5 May the Lord *c* directing your
3:15 but *c* admonishing him as a
1Ti 2:15 provided they *c* in faith and
4:13 *c* applying yourself to public
2Ti 3:14 *c* in the things that you
Tit 3:1 *C* reminding them to be in
Heb 6:10 holy ones and *c* ministering
8:9 did not *c* in my covenant
12:28 let us *c* to have undeserved
13:1 Let your brotherly love *c*
Jas 1:12 to those who *c* loving him
2:9 if you *c* showing favoritism
1Pe 3:7 husbands, *c* dwelling in like
4:4 not *c* running with them in
1Jo 2:3 *c* observing his commandments
4:7 let us *c* loving one another
4:12 If we *c* loving one another
Jude 22 *c* showing mercy to some that
23 *c* showing mercy to others
Re 3:3 *c* mindful of how you have

Continued

Ge 2:25 both of them *c* to be naked
5:7 Seth *c* to live eight hundred
5:10 Enosh *c* to live eight hundred
5:13 Kenan *c* to live eight hundred
5:16 Mahalalel *c* to live eight
5:19 Jared *c* to live eight hundred
5:26 Methuselah *c* to live seven
5:30 Lamech *c* to live five hundred
6:4 sons of the true God *c* to
7:24 waters *c* overwhelming the
8:7 raven, and it *c* flying outdoors
9:28 Noah *c* to live three hundred
11:1 earth *c* to be of one language
11:11 Shem *c* to live five hundred
11:13 Arpachshad *c* to live four
11:15 Shelah *c* to live four hundred
11:17 Eber *c* to live four hundred
11:19 Peleg *c* to live two hundred
11:21 Reu *c* to live two hundred and
11:23 Serug *c* to live two hundred
11:25 Nahor *c* to live a hundred and
11:30 Sarai *c* to be barren
13:18 So Abram *c* to live in tents
14:12 Lot . . . and his goods and *c*
17:3 and God *c* to speak with him
18:10 he *c*: I am surely going to
18:30 he *c*: May Jehovah, please
18:31 he *c* on: Please, here I have
21:20 God *c* to be with the boy
22:7 he *c*: Here are the fire and
22:19 Abraham *c* to dwell at
25:11 God *c* to bless Isaac his son
25:32 Esau *c*: Here I am simply
26:5 *c* to keep his obligations to
26:10 Abimelech *c*: What is this
27:37 in answer to Esau Isaac *c*
28:10 Jacob *c* on his way out from
31:12 he *c*, Raise your eyes, please
33:11 he *c* to urge him, so that he
35:15 Jacob *c* to call the name of
37:1 Jacob *c* to dwell in the land
37:17 the man *c*: They have pulled
37:35 his father *c* weeping for him
38:11 Tamar went and *c* to dwell
38:18 he *c*: What is the security
39:20 he *c* there in the prison
39:21 Jehovah *c* with Joseph and
40:4 they *c* in jail for some days
Ge 40:21 he *c* to give the cup into
41:49 Joseph *c* piling up grain in
43:34 *c* banqueting and drinking
46:5 *c* transporting Jacob their
46:34 *c* to be stock raisers from
47:27 Israel *c* to dwell in the
48:20 *c* to bless them on that day
50:3 the Egyptians *c* to shed tears
50:22 Joseph *c* to dwell in Egypt
Ex 2:23 the sons of Israel *c* to sigh
5:5 Pharaoh *c*: Look! The people of
6:13 Jehovah *c* to speak to Moses
7:22 Pharaoh's heart *c* to be
8:19 But Pharaoh's heart *c* to be
9:7 Pharaoh's heart *c* to be
9:35 Pharaoh's heart *c* obstinate
16:8 And Moses *c*: It will be when
24:16 Jehovah's glory *c* to reside
24:16 cloud *c* to cover it for six
24:18 And Moses *c* in the mountain
30:22 Jehovah *c* to speak to Moses
31:1 Jehovah *c* to speak to Moses
34:28 *c* there with Jehovah forty
40:38 and a fire *c* upon it by night
Le 5:14 Jehovah *c* to speak to Moses
6:8 Jehovah *c* to speak to Moses
7:22 Jehovah *c* to speak to Moses
14:1 Jehovah *c* to speak to Moses
15:1 Jehovah *c* to speak to Moses
18:1 Jehovah *c* to speak to Moses
21:16 Jehovah *c* to speak to Moses
22:17 Jehovah *c* to speak to Moses
23:9 Jehovah *c* to speak to Moses
23:33 Jehovah *c* to speak to Moses
27:1 Jehovah *c* to speak to Moses
Nu 3:4 Eleazar and Ithamar *c* to act
3:11 Jehovah *c* to speak to Moses
3:44 Jehovah *c* to speak to Moses
5:5 Jehovah *c* speaking to Moses
9:15 *c* over the tabernacle until
11:35 and they *c* in Hazeroth
13:16 Moses *c* to call Hoshea the
14:1 people *c* giving vent to their
20:15 we *c* to dwell in Egypt many
20:29 Israel *c* weeping for Aaron
21:4 *c* trekking from Mount Hor by
22:35 And Balaam *c* going with the
33:49 they *c* camping by the Jordan
35:9 Jehovah *c* to speak to Moses
De 3:26 Jehovah *c* to be furious
33:9 covenant they *c* to observe
Jos 5:10 sons of Israel *c* to camp in
7:5 *c* striking them down on the
7:7 *c* dwelling on the other side
10:26 *c* hanging upon the stakes
24:31 Israel *c* to serve Jehovah
Jg 1:19 Jehovah *c* with Judah, so
1:29 the Canaanites *c* to dwell in
1:30 the Canaanites *c* to dwell in
1:32 the Asherites *c* to dwell in
1:33 they *c* to dwell in among the
2:7 And the people *c* to serve
3:8 the sons of Israel *c* to serve
3:14 Israel *c* to serve Eglon the
7:22 the three hundred *c* to blow
8:8 he *c* on his way up from there
8:11 Gideon *c* on up by the way of
8:29 and *c* to dwell in his house
9:41 Abimelech *c* to dwell in
10:2 And he *c* to judge Israel for
10:3 and he *c* to judge Israel for
12:7 Jephthah *c* to judge Israel for
12:9 he *c* to judge Israel for seven
12:11 *c* to judge Israel ten years
12:14 he *c* to judge Israel eight
13:24 and Jehovah *c* to bless him
14:7 And he *c* on his way down and
14:10 his father *c* on his way down
14:17 that the banquet *c* for them
14:19 And his anger *c* hot, and he
15:20 he *c* to judge Israel in the
18:31 the house . . . *c* in Shiloh
19:2 and *c* there fully four months
19:4 he *c* to dwell with him three
20:47 *c* to dwell on the crag of
21:2 and *c* to raise their voice and
Ru 1:2 the fields of Moab and *c* there
1:7 from the place where she had *c*
1:19 they both *c* on their way
2:17 she *c* to glean in the field
2:23 she *c* to keep close by the
3:2 whose young women you have *c*
1Sa 2:21 Samuel *c* growing up with
3:15 Samuel *c* lying down until
1Sa 3:19 Samuel *c* growing up, and
4:1 word of Samuel *c* to come to
6:15 *c* rendering up sacrifices on
7:13 the hand of Jehovah *c* to be
9:25 he *c* speaking with Saul on
10:27 *c* like one grown speechless
11:15 Israel *c* rejoicing to a
13:8 he *c* waiting for seven days
14:19 turmoil . . . *c* to go on
14:52 warfare *c* heavy against the
17:51 David *c* running and got to
19:7 he *c* before him the same as
19:23 *c* behaving like a prophet
20:27 David's place *c* vacant
21:10 David rose up and *c* running
22:4 *c* dwelling with him all the
23:13 *c* walking about wherever
23:15 David *c* in fear because
23:25 and *c* dwelling in the
27:3 David *c* to dwell with Achish
2Sa 1:1 David *c* to dwell at Ziklag
5:13 *c* to be born to David
8:6 Jehovah *c* to save David
12:18 child *c* alive we did speak
12:26 Joab *c* to fight against
13:37 David *c* to mourn over his
14:28 Absalom *c* dwelling in
15:17 the king *c* on his way out
15:29 and they *c* to dwell there
18:6 the people *c* on their way
19:4 the king *c* crying out with a
20:3 they *c* shut up closely until
24:6 *c* on to Dan-jaan and went
1Ki 2:15 he *c*: You yourself well know
3:3 Solomon *c* to love Jehovah
3:6 you *c* keeping toward him this
4:1 Solomon *c* king over all
4:25 and Israel *c* to dwell in
4:29 *c* giving Solomon wisdom and
6:9 he *c* building the house that
6:14 Solomon *c* building the house
9:25 Solomon *c* three times in
11:19 Hadad *c* to find favor in
11:20 *c* at the house of Pharaoh
11:25 he *c* reigning over Syria
11:40 *c* in Egypt until Solomon's
12:6 men who had *c* attending
12:6 while he *c* alive, saying
12:17 Rehoboam *c* to reign over
15:21 and *c* dwelling in Tirzah
15:25 *c* to reign over Israel two
16:29 *c* to reign over Israel in
17:15 and she *c* to eat, she
18:7 As Obadiah *c* on the way
18:29 they *c* behaving as prophets
20:29 *c* encamped for seven days
22:1 they *c* dwelling without war
22:51 Ahaziah . . . *c* to reign over
22:53 *c* serving Baal and bowing
2Ki 3:1 *c* to reign for twelve years
9:21 they *c* on out to meet Jehu
9:27 he *c* his flight to Megiddo
11:3 he *c* with her at the house
11:20 people . . . *c* to rejoice
12:2 *c* doing what was right in
13:2 *c* to do what was bad in
13:5 Israel *c* to dwell in their
13:11 *c* to do what was bad in
14:3 *c* to do what was upright in
14:17 *c* to live after the death of
14:24 *c* to do what was bad in
15:3 *c* to do what was upright in
15:5 he *c* to be a leper until the
15:13 *c* to reign for a full lunar
15:18 he *c* to do what was bad in
15:24 *c* to do what was bad in
15:28 *c* to do what was bad in
15:34 *c* to do what was right in
16:13 he *c* to make his burnt
17:2 *c* to do what was bad in
17:11 *c* to make sacrificial smoke
17:12 they *c* to serve dungy idols
17:15 *c* rejecting his regulations
17:17 *c* to make their sons and
18:3 he *c* to do what was right in
18:6 *c* keeping his commandments
18:28 Rabshakeh *c* to stand and
21:20 *c* to do what was bad in
21:21 *c* serving the dungy idols
23:37 he *c* to do what was bad in
24:9 *c* to do what was bad in
24:19 *c* to do what was bad in
1Ch 3:4 *c* to reign there seven years
4:28 *c* to dwell in Beer-sheba and

1Ch 4:43 *c* to dwell there down to
5:16 they *c* to dwell in Gilead
5:22 *c* to dwell in their place
12:39 *c* there with David three
15:1 And he *c* building houses for
17:5 I *c* from tent to tent and
18:14 David *c* to reign over all
21:28 he *c* to sacrifice there
23:14 *c* to be called among the
24:2 Ithamar *c* to act as priests
29:21 *c* to sacrifice sacrifices to
29:22 *c* eating and drinking before
29:25 Jehovah *c* to make Solomon
2Ch 1:1 David *c* to get strength in
1:13 and *c* to reign over Israel
9:30 Solomon *c* to reign in
10:6 his father while he *c* alive
10:17 Rehoboam *c* to reign over
11:5 Rehoboam *c* to dwell in
11:12 Judah and Benjamin *c* his
12:13 Rehoboam *c* to make his
13:21 And Abijah *c* to strengthen
14:5 *c* without disturbance before
14:13 Ethiopians *c* falling down
15:15 Jehovah *c* to give them rest
17:3 Jehovah *c* with Jehoshaphat
17:5 all Judah *c* to give presents
17:12 Jehoshaphat *c* advancing
19:4 Jehoshaphat *c* dwelling in
20:30 God *c* to give him rest all
21:6 he *c* to do what was bad in
22:12 *c* with them in the house of
23:21 of the land *c* to rejoice
25:2 *c* to do what was right in
25:25 *c* to live after the death
26:7 true God *c* to help him
26:14 Uzziah *c* to prepare for
26:21 Uzziah the king *c* to be a
30:10 runners *c* on, passing
30:25 in Judah *c* rejoicing
31:20 *c* to do what was good and
32:30 and Hezekiah *c* to prove
33:22 and he *c* serving them
36:5 *c* to do what was bad in the
36:9 *c* to do what was bad in
36:12 *c* to do what was bad in the
Ezr 4:24 *c* stopped until the second
Ne 2:11 and I *c* there for three days
4:6 *c* to have a heart for working
8:3 *c* to read aloud from it before
8:8 *c* reading aloud from the book
8:8 *c* giving understanding in the
Job 34:1 Elihu *c* to answer and say
35:1 Elihu *c* answering and saying
42:16 Job *c* living after this a
Ps 78:14 he *c* to lead them with a
99:7 cloud he *c* speaking to them
142:2 I *c* to tell about my own
Isa 36:13 Rabshakeh *c* to stand and
36:21 *c* to keep silent and did not
42:14 long time. I *c* silent
43:10 after me there *c* to be none
57:9 *c* sending your envoys far off
Jer 1:11 word of Jehovah *c* to occur
3:13 *c* scattering your ways to
5:7 they *c* committing adultery
16:1 word of Jehovah *c* to occur
18:5 the word of Jehovah *c* to
33:23 word of Jehovah *c* to occur
37:16 Jeremiah *c* dwelling there
37:21 Jeremiah *c* dwelling in the
38:13 Jeremiah *c* to dwell in the
38:28 Jeremiah *c* to dwell in
44:24 Jeremiah *c* on to say
52:2 *c* to do what was bad in
Eze 3:4 he *c* saying to me: Son of man
4:16 *c* saying to me: Son of man
6:1 word of Jehovah *c* to occur to
7:1 word of Jehovah *c* to occur to
8:13 *c* on to say to me: You will
10:1 I *c* to see, and, look! upon
10:9 I *c* to see, and, look! there
11:14 word of Jehovah *c* to occur
12:1 word of Jehovah *c* to occur
12:8 word of Jehovah *c* to occur
12:17 word of Jehovah *c* to occur
12:26 word of Jehovah *c* to occur
13:1 word of Jehovah *c* to occur
14:12 word of Jehovah *c* to come
15:1 word of Jehovah *c* to occur
16:19 and it *c* to occur, is the
16:26 *c* making your prostitution
16:50 they *c* to be haughty and to
17:1 word of Jehovah *c* to occur
Eze 17:11 word of Jehovah *c* to occur
18:1 word of Jehovah *c* to occur
20:45 word of Jehovah *c* to occur
21:1 *c* to occur to me, saying
21:8 word of Jehovah *c* to occur
21:18 *c* to occur to me, saying
22:1 word of Jehovah *c* to occur
22:17 word of Jehovah *c* to come
22:23 word of Jehovah *c* to come
23:7 she *c* giving forth her
23:17 *c* getting defiled by them
23:21 *c* calling attention to the
24:1 *c* to occur to me in the
24:15 *c* to occur to me, saying
25:1 *c* to occur to me, saying
27:1 word of Jehovah *c* to occur
28:1 word of Jehovah *c* to occur
28:11 the word of Jehovah *c* to
28:20 word of Jehovah *c* to occur
30:1 word of Jehovah *c* to occur
31:5 its branches *c* getting longer
34:1 word of Jehovah *c* to occur
34:5 and they *c* to be scattered
34:8 sheep *c* to be food for every
35:1 word of Jehovah *c* to occur
36:16 word of Jehovah *c* to occur
37:15 word of Jehovah *c* to occur
38:1 word of Jehovah *c* to occur
47:4 *c* measuring a thousand and
47:4 *c* measuring a thousand and
47:5 he *c* measuring a thousand
Da 1:19 *c* to stand before the king
1:21 Daniel *c* on until the first
4:13 I *c* beholding in the visions
Hag 1:3 *c* to come by means of Haggai
Zec 1:5 indefinite that they *c* to live
4:8 *c* to occur to me, saying
6:9 word of Jehovah *c* to occur to
7:4 *c* to occur to me, saying
7:8 word of Jehovah *c* to occur to
8:1 word . . . *c* to occur, saying
8:18 *c* to occur to me, saying
Mal 2:5 And he *c* fearing me
Mt 26:26 *c* eating, Jesus took a loaf
27:61 and the other Mary *c* there
Mr 1:13 he *c* in the wilderness forty
1:45 he *c* outside in lonely places
6:20 yet he *c* to hear him gladly
6:52 their hearts *c* dull of
14:22 as they *c* eating, he took a
15:47 *c* looking at where he had
Lu 1:21 *c* waiting for Zechariah, and
1:80 he *c* in the deserts until the
2:33 *c* wondering at the things
2:40 *c* growing and getting strong
2:40 and God's favor *c* upon him
2:51 and he *c* subject to them
3:18 *c* declaring good news to the
4:30 and *c* on his way
5:16 he *c* in retirement in the
6:12 *c* the whole night in prayer
9:45 they *c* without understanding
22:44 *c* praying more earnestly
23:12 had *c* at enmity between
Joh 7:1 Jesus *c* walking about in
Ac 2:42 *c* devoting themselves to the
2:47 Jehovah *c* to join to them
4:33 apostles *c* giving forth the
5:12 portents *c* to occur among the
5:42 *c* without letup teaching and
9:28 *c* with them, walking in and
13:52 the disciples *c* to be filled
15:3 these men *c* on their way
15:35 *c* spending time in Antioch
16:5 *c* to be made firm in the
16:12 We *c* in this city, spending
2Co 7:5 we *c* to be afflicted in every
Ga 4:3 *c* enslaved by the elementary
Heb 11:27 he *c* steadfast as seeing

Continues

Ge 8:22 For all the days the earth *c*
Nu 19:13 he *c* unclean. His uncleanness
Jos 2:19 who *c* with you in the house
Jg 6:24 altar . . . *c* to be called
2Sa 18:18 it *c* to be called Absalom's
1Ki 12:27 people *c* going up to render
2Ki 2:22 the water *c* healed down to
6:31 *c* standing upon him today
Mt 5:22 everyone who *c* wrathful with
13:21 but *c* for a time, and after
1Co 14:38 is ignorant, he *c* ignorant
2Co 9:9 his righteousness *c* forever
Heb 13:14 have here a city that *c*

Continuing

Nu 15:32 *c* in the wilderness, they
Jos 10:1 and were *c* in their midst
1Sa 15:26 from *c* as king over Israel
Ec 7:15 one *c* long in his badness
8:12 *c* a long time as he pleases
Jer 38:2 one *c* to dwell in this city
Lu 13:22 and *c* on his journey to
Ac 27:33 you are *c* without food
Heb 7:23 prevented by death from *c* as
7:24 because of *c* alive forever
2Pe 3:4 all things are *c* exactly as

Continuous

Isa 26:3 will safeguard in *c* peace
54:4 reproach of your *c* widowhood
57:19 *C* peace there will be to
58:12 foundations of *c* generations
59:9 in *c* gloom we kept walking

Continuously

Ec 7:28 which my soul has *c* sought

Contracting

Ne 9:8 a *c* of the covenant with him
9:38 *c* a trustworthy arrangement

Contradict

Tit 1:9 and to reprove those who *c*

Contradicting

Ac 13:45 blasphemously *c* the things

Contradictions

1Ti 6:20 the *c* of the falsely called

Contrary

Ex 10:10 on the *c*, something evil is
Es 9:1 to the *c*, in that the Jews
Lu 6:35 To the *c*, continue to love
23:28 On the *c*, weep for
Joh 7:27 On the *c*, we know where
Ac 2:16 On the *c*, this is what was
15:11 On the *c*, we trust to get
18:13 *C* to the law this person
27:4 because the winds were *c*
28:17 *c* to the people or the
Ro 1:26 into one *c* to nature
3:31 On the *c*, we establish law
8:37 To the *c*, in all these things
11:24 grafted *c* to nature into
16:17 *c* to the teaching that you
1Co 6:8 To the *c*, you wrong and
2Co 2:7 on the *c* now, you should
Ga 2:7 on the *c*, when they saw that I
1Th 2:7 To the *c*, we became gentle
2Th 3:8 To the *c*, by labor and toil
1Ti 4:12 On the *c*, become an example
5:1 To the *c*, entreat him as a
6:2 On the *c*, let them the more
2Ti 1:17 On the *c*, when he happened
Heb 10:3 To the *c*, by these sacrifices
12:3 has endured such *c* talk by
1Pe 3:9 the *c*, bestowing a blessing
4:13 On the *c*, go on rejoicing

Contribute

Le 22:15 which they may *c* to Jehovah
Nu 15:20 is the way you should *c* it
18:19 Israel will *c* to Jehovah
18:24 tenth part . . . *c* to Jehovah
18:26 *c* from it as a contribution
18:28 *c* a contribution to Jehovah
18:29 *c* every sort of contribution
18:30 When you *c* the best of them
18:32 incur sin for it when you *c*
Eze 48:8 that you people should *c*
48:9 you should *c* to Jehovah
48:20 *c* as the holy contribution

Contributed

Ex 29:27 that was *c* from the ram of
Nu 31:52 they *c* to Jehovah amounted
2Ch 30:24 *c* for the congregation a
30:24 princes themselves *c* for
35:7 *c* to the sons of the people
35:9 *c* to the Levites for passover
Ezr 8:25 who were to be found had *c*

Contributing

Ex 35:24 all those *c* the contribution
2Pe 1:5 *c* in response all earnest

Contribution

Ex 25:2 they may take up a *c* for me
25:2 are to take up the *c* of mine
25:3 this is the *c* that you are to
30:13 half shekel is the *c* to
30:14 will give Jehovah's *c*
30:15 give Jehovah's *c* so as to

Ex 35:5 take up a *c* for Jehovah
35:5 as Jehovah's *c*, namely, gold
35:21 Jehovah's *c* for the work of
35:24 the *c* of silver and copper
35:24 brought Jehovah's *c*
36:3 the *c* that the sons of Israel
36:6 any more stuff for the holy *c*
Le 22:12 eat of the *c* of the holy
Nu 5:9 every *c* of all the holy things
6:20 and the leg of the *c*
15:19 should make a *c* to Jehovah
15:20 make a *c* of the firstfruits
15:20 the *c* of a threshing floor
15:21 *c* to Jehovah throughout your
18:11 the *c* of their gift together
18:24 as a *c* . . . to the Levites
18:26 as a *c* to Jehovah a tenth
18:27 be reckoned to you as your *c*
18:28 *c* to Jehovah from all your
18:28 give the *c* . . . to Aaron the
18:29 every sort of *c* to Jehovah
31:29 give it . . . as Jehovah's *c*
31:41 gave the tax as Jehovah's *c*
31:52 all the gold of the *c* that
De 12:6 the *c* of your hand and your
12:11 your tenth parts and the *c*
12:17 or the *c* of your hand
1Ch 16:7 David made a *c* for the first
2Ch 31:10 bring the *c* into the house
31:12 bringing in the *c* and the
31:14 give Jehovah's *c* and the
35:8 a *c* as a voluntary offering
Ezr 8:25 the *c* to the house of our God
Ne 10:39 bring the *c* of the grain
13:5 and the *c* for the priests
Isa 40:20 A certain tree as a *c*
Eze 44:30 every *c* of everything out
45:1 offer a *c* to Jehovah, a holy
45:6 exactly as the holy *c*
45:7 that side of the holy *c*
45:7 beside the holy *c* and
45:13 *c* that you should offer
45:16 *c* to the chieftain in Israel
48:8 *c* that you people should
48:9 *c* that you should contribute
48:10 holy *c* for the priests, to
48:12 they must come to have a *c*
48:12 *c* of the land as something
48:18 exactly as the holy *c*, ten
48:18 exactly as the holy *c*, and
48:20 whole *c* is twenty-five
48:20 as the holy *c* with the
48:21 side of the holy *c* and of
48:21 *c* to the eastern boundary
48:21 holy *c* and the sanctuary
Ro 15:26 a *c* to the poor of the holy
2Co 8:20 with this liberal *c* to be
9:13 generous in your *c* to them
Php 1:5 *c* you have made to the good

Contributions
Nu 18:8 custody of the *c* made to me
18:19 holy *c* . . . given to you
2Sa 1:21 there be fields of holy *c*
Ne 10:37 our *c* and the fruitage of
12:44 for the stores, for the *c*
Eze 20:40 I shall require your *c* and
44:30 *c*—to the priests it will
Mal 3:8 the tenth parts and in the *c*

Contrite
Isa 66:2 afflicted and *c* in spirit

Contrivance
Ac 17:29 by the art and *c* of man

Contrived
2Pe 1:16 artfully *c* false stories

Contriving
Eph 4:14 means of cunning in *c* error

Control
Ge 43:31 kept *c* of himself and said
45:1 no longer able to *c* himself
2Sa 8:3 *c* back again at the river
1Ki 14:27 the *c* of the chiefs of the
1Ch 18:3 his *c* at the river Euphrates
25:2 under the *c* of Asaph the one
25:2 under the *c* of the king
25:3 *c* of their father Jeduthun
25:6 the *c* of their father in song
25:6 Under the *c* of the king were
26:28 under the *c* of Shelomith
29:8 *c* of Jehiel the Gershonite
2Ch 12:10 *c* of the chiefs of the
17:15 And under his *c* there was
17:16 under his *c* there was
17:18 under his *c* there was
26:11 *c* of Hananiah of the king's
26:13 under their *c* the army
31:15 under his *c* there were
Ezr 1:8 under the *c* of Mithredath the
Ne 13:13 under their *c* there was
Es 5:10 Haman kept *c* of himself and
Job 34:17 anyone hating justice *c*
Ec 2:19 take *c* over all my hard work
8:4 of the king is the power of *c*
8:8 power of *c* in the day of death
Ac 5:4 it not continue in your *c*
Col 3:15 peace of the Christ *c* in your

Controlled
Ps 85:3 You have *c* all your fury
1Co 14:32 are to be *c* by the prophets

Controlling
Pr 16:32 he that is *c* his spirit than

Controversial
Isa 41:21 Bring your *c* case forward

Controversially
Ac 17:18 to conversing with him *c*

Controversies
Ac 18:15 *c* over speech and names and
26:3 well as the *c* among Jews

Controversy
Ex 23:2 not testify over a *c* so as to
23:3 not show preference in a *c* of
23:6 of your poor man in his *c*
2Ch 22:8 *c* with the house of Ahab
Isa 66:16 for a fact take up the *c*
Jer 2:35 entering into *c* with you
25:31 there is a *c* that Jehovah

Convenient
Nu 35:11 cities *c* for yourselves
Mr 6:21 *c* day came along when Herod
Lu 4:13 until another *c* time

Conveniently
Mr 14:11 seeking how to betray him *c*

Convening
Nu 10:2 service for *c* the assembly

Convention
Ex 12:16 take place for you a holy *c*
12:16 on the seventh day a holy *c*
Le 23:3 of complete rest, a holy *c*
23:7 you will have a holy *c* occur
23:8 there will be a holy *c*
23:21 Jehovah's holy *c* for
23:24 trumpet blast, a holy *c*
23:27 holy *c* should take place for
23:35 first day is a holy *c*
23:36 occur a holy *c* for you, and
Nu 28:18 there will be a holy *c*
28:25 you should hold a holy *c*
28:26 you should hold a holy *c*
29:1 you should hold a holy *c*
29:7 you should hold a holy *c*, and
29:12 you should hold a holy *c*
Isa 1:13 the calling of a *c*—I cannot
4:5 over her *c* place a cloud by

Conventions
Le 23:2 festivals . . . are holy *c*
23:4 holy *c*, which you should
23:37 proclaim as holy *c*, for

Converse
Lu 4:36 *c* with one another, saying
Ac 24:26 and would *c* with him

Conversed
Ac 10:27 as he *c* with him he went in

Conversing
Nu 7:89 *c* with him from above the
Mt 17:3 Moses and Elijah, *c* with him
Mr 9:4 and they were *c* with Jesus
Lu 9:30 two men were *c* with him, who
24:14 *c* with each other over all
24:15 they were *c* and discussing
Ac 17:18 *c* with him controversially
20:11 after *c* for quite a while

Conversion
Ac 15:3 *c* of people of the nations

Converted
1Ti 3:6 not a newly *c* man, for fear

Converting
Ex 14:21 and *c* the sea basin into dry

Converts
Ps 107:33 *c* rivers into a wilderness
107:35 *c* a wilderness into a reedy
107:41 *c* him into families just

Convey
Ec 10:20 *c* the sound and something
Isa 65:5 shall certainly *c* holiness
Ac 23:24 *c* him safely to Felix the

Conveyed
2Ki 23:30 his servants *c* him dead in
Es 1:12 was *c* by means of the court
Isa 46:3 ones *c* by me from the belly

Conveying
Ge 33:11 the gift *c* my blessing which

Convict
Jude 15 *c* all the ungodly concerning

Conviction
Col 4:12 *c* in all the will of God
1Th 1:5 with holy spirit and strong *c*

Convicts
Joh 8:46 Who of you *c* me of sin?

Convinced
Ro 4:21 *c* that what he had promised
8:38 I am *c* that neither death nor
14:5 be fully *c* in his own mind
Heb 6:9 we are *c* of better things and

Convincing
Joh 16:8 *c* evidence concerning sin

Convulsed
Lu 9:42 and violently *c* him

Convulsion
Mr 1:26 throwing him into a *c* and

Convulsions
Isa 13:8 *C* and birth pains themselves
21:3 *C* themselves have grabbed
21:3 *c* of a woman that is giving
Da 10:16 my *c* were turned within me
Mr 9:20 threw the child into *c*
9:26 going through many *c* it got
Lu 9:39 throws him into *c* with foam

Cooing
Isa 38:14 I keep *c* like the dove
59:11 doves we mournfully keep *c*

Cook
1Sa 9:23 Later Samuel said to the *c*
9:24 *c* lifted off the leg and
Eze 24:5 *c* its bones in the midst of

Cooked
Ex 12:9 not eat any . . . *c* in water
2Sa 13:8 and *c* the heart-shaped cakes

Cooking
Nu 11:8 boiled it in *c* pots or made
Jg 6:19 the broth he put in the *c* pot
1Sa 2:14 or the two-handled *c* pot or
2:14 or the one-handled *c* pot
2Ki 4:38 Put the large *c* pot on and
2Ch 35:13 they boiled in *c* pots and
Jer 1:13 A widemouthed *c* pot blown
Eze 11:3 She is the widemouthed *c* pot
11:7 she is the widemouthed *c* pot
11:11 for you a widemouthed *c* pot
24:3 the widemouthed *c* pot on
24:6 widemouthed *c* pot, the rust
Mic 3:3 flesh in the midst of a *c* pot
Zec 14:20 widemouthed *c* pots in the
14:21 every widemouthed *c* pot

Cooks
1Sa 8:13 for ointment mixers and *c*

Cool
Jg 3:20 he was sitting in his *c* roof
3:24 just easing nature in the *c*
Pr 17:27 discernment is *c* of spirit
Jer 6:7 a cistern keeps its waters *c*
6:7 she has kept her badness *c*
18:14 waters, *c*, trickling
Mt 24:12 greater number will *c* off
Lu 16:24 in water and *c* my tongue

Coolness
Pr 25:13 the *c* of snow in the day of

Cooperate
Ex 23:1 Do not *c* with a wicked one
Ro 8:28 God makes all his works *c*
Eph 4:16 to *c* through every joint

Cooperating
1Co 16:16 everyone *c* and laboring
Cope
Lu 14:31 ten thousand troops to *c*
Coping
1Ki 7:9 the foundation up to the *c*
Copious
De 32:2 as *c* showers upon vegetation
Ps 65:10 With *c* showers you soften it
68:9 *c* downpour you began causing
72:6 Like *c* showers that wet the
Jer 3:3 So *c* showers are withheld
14:22 heavens . . . give *c* showers
Mic 5:7 *c* showers upon vegetation
Copper
Ge 4:22 every sort of tool of *c* and
Ex 25:3 gold and silver and *c*
26:11 make fifty hooks of *c* and
26:37 five socket pedestals of *c*
27:2 you must overlay it with *c*
27:3 make all its utensils of *c*
27:4 a network of *c*; and you must
27:4 upon the net four rings of *c*
27:6 you must overlay them with *c*
27:10 socket pedestals are of *c*
27:11 socket pedestals being of *c*
27:17 but socket pedestals of *c*
27:18 socket pedestals being of *c*
27:19 and all the pins . . . are of *c*
30:18 make a basin of *c* and its
30:18 its stand of *c* for washing
31:4 in gold and silver and *c*
35:5 gold and silver and *c*
35:16 the *c* grating that is for it
35:24 contribution of silver and *c*
35:32 in gold and silver and *c*
36:18 fifty hooks of *c* for joining
36:38 socket pedestals were of *c*
38:2 Next he overlaid it with *c*
38:3 All its utensils he made of *c*
38:4 a network of *c*, under its rim
38:5 near the grating of *c*, as
38:6 wood and overlaid them with *c*
38:8 he made the basin of *c* and
38:8 and its stand of *c*, by
38:10 socket pedestals were of *c*
38:11 socket pedestals were of *c*
38:17 for the pillars were of *c*
38:19 socket pedestals were of *c*
38:20 tent pins . . . of *c*
38:29 the *c* of the wave offering
38:30 and the *c* altar and the
38:30 the *c* grating that belonged
39:39 altar of *c* and the grating
39:39 grating of *c* that belonged to
Le 6:28 it was boiled in a *c* vessel
26:19 and your earth like *c*
Nu 16:39 took the *c* fire holders
21:9 a serpent of *c* and placed it
21:9 and he gazed at the *c* serpent
31:22 the *c*, the iron, the tin and
De 8:9 of which you will mine *c*
28:23 Your skies . . . become *c*
33:25 and *c* are your gate locks
Jos 6:19 the articles of *c* and iron
6:24 articles of *c* and iron they
22:8 silver and gold and *c* and
Jg 16:21 two fetters of *c*, and he
1Sa 17:5 a helmet of *c* on his head
17:5 five thousand shekels of *c*
17:6 greaves of *c* above his feet
17:6 a javelin of *c* between his
17:38 he put a *c* helmet upon his
2Sa 3:34 been put into fetters of *c*
8:8 David took *c* in very great
8:10 and articles of *c*
21:16 three hundred shekels of *c*
22:35 pressed down a bow of *c*
1Ki 4:13 cities with wall and *c* bar
7:14 a Tyrian man, a worker in *c*
7:14 every sort of work in *c*
7:15 he cast the two pillars of *c*
7:16 the pillars, cast in *c*
7:27 make the ten carriages of *c*
7:30 four wheels of *c* to each
7:30 carriage, with axles of *c*
7:38 to make ten basins of *c*
7:45 Hiram made of polished *c* for
7:47 The weight of the *c* was not
8:64 the *c* altar that is before
14:27 in place of them *c* shields
2Ki 16:14 the *c* altar that was before
2Ki 16:15 the *c* altar, it will become
16:17 took down off the *c* bulls
18:4 crushed . . . the *c* serpent
18:4 called the *c* serpent-idol
25:7 bound him with *c* fetters
25:13 pillars of *c* that were in
25:13 the carriages and the *c* sea
25:13 the *c* of them to Babylon
25:14 all the utensils of *c* with
25:16 the *c* of all these utensils
25:17 capital upon it was of *c*
25:17 the whole of it, was *c*
1Ch 15:19 the *c* cymbals to play aloud
18:8 David took very much *c*
18:8 Solomon made the *c* sea and
18:8 pillars and the *c* utensils
18:10 of gold and silver and *c*
22:3 *c* in such quantity as to be
22:14 *c* and the iron there is no
22:16 the silver and the *c* and the
29:2 and the *c* for the copperwork
29:7 *c* worth eighteen thousand
2Ch 1:5 *c* altar that Bezalel the son
1:6 the *c* altar that belonged to
2:7 in gold and in silver and in *c*
2:14 in *c*, in iron, in stones and
4:1 *c* altar, twenty cubits being
4:9 doors he overlaid with *c*
4:16 made . . . of polished *c*
4:18 the weight of the *c* was not
6:13 had made a platform of *c* and
7:7 *c* altar that Solomon had made
12:10 in their place *c* shields
24:12 workers in iron and *c* for
33:11 two fetters of *c* and took
36:6 two fetters of *c* to carry
Ezr 8:27 and two utensils of good *c*
Job 6:12 Or is my flesh of *c*?
20:24 A bow of *c* will cut him up
28:2 from stone *c* is being poured
40:18 Its bones are tubes of *c*
41:27 *C* as mere rotten wood
Ps 18:34 pressed down a bow of *c*
107:16 has broken the doors of *c*
Isa 45:2 *c* doors I shall break in
48:4 and your forehead is *c*
60:17 Instead of the *c* I shall
60:17 instead of the wood, *c*
Jer 1:18 an iron pillar and *c* walls
6:28 slanderers—*c* and iron
15:12 out of the north, and *c*
15:20 a fortified *c* wall
39:7 bound him with *c* fetters
52:11 bound him with *c* fetters
52:17 *c* pillars that belonged to
52:17 *c* sea that was in the house
52:17 carrying all the *c* of them
52:18 *c* utensils with which they
52:20 twelve *c* bulls that were
52:20 no weight taken of the *c* of
52:22 capital upon it was of *c*
52:22 the whole was of *c*
La 3:7 He has made my *c* fetters heavy
Eze 1:7 with the glow of burnished *c*
9:2 and stand beside the *c* altar
22:18 are *c* and tin and iron and
22:20 *c* and iron and lead and
24:11 its *c* must become heated up
27:13 articles of *c* your articles
40:3 was like the appearance of *c*
Da 2:32 and its thighs were of *c*
2:35 *c*, the silver and the gold
2:39 kingdom, a third one, of *c*
2:45 crushed the iron, the *c*, the
4:15 a banding of iron and of *c*
4:23 a banding of iron and of *c*
5:4 praised the gods of . . . *c*
5:23 praised mere gods of . . . *c*
7:19 claws of which were of *c*
10:6 like the sight of burnished *c*
Mic 4:13 hoofs I shall change into *c*
Zec 6:1 mountains were *c* mountains
Mt 10:9 or *c* for your girdle purses
Mr 6:8 *c* money in their girdle purses
7:4 and pitchers and *c* vessels
Re 1:15 feet were like fine *c* when
2:18 and his feet are like fine *c*
9:20 silver and *c* and stone and
18:12 *c* and of iron and of marble
Coppersmith
2Ti 4:14 Alexander the *c* did me many
Copperwork
1Ch 29:2 and the copper for the *c*, the
Copulation
Jer 2:24 at her time for *c*, who can
Copy
De 17:18 a *c* of this law from that
Jos 8:32 a *c* of the law of Moses that
Ezr 4:11 this is a *c* of the letter
4:23 *c* of the official document
5:6 *c* of the letter that Tattenai
7:11 this is a *c* of the letter
Es 3:14 *c* of the writing to be given
4:8 a *c* of the writing of the law
8:13 A *c* of the writing was to be
Heb 9:24 which is a *c* of the reality
Copyist
Ezr 7:6 skilled *c* in the law of Moses
7:11 gave Ezra the priest the *c*
7:11 a *c* of the words of the
7:12 the *c* of the law of the God
7:21 the *c* of the law of the God
Ne 8:1 to Ezra the *c* to bring the book
8:4 Ezra the *c* kept standing upon
8:9 and Ezra the priest, the *c*
8:13 together to Ezra the *c*
12:26 Ezra the priest, the *c*
12:36 Ezra the *c* before them
13:13 the priest and Zadok the *c*
Ps 45:1 the stylus of a skilled *c*
Jer 36:10 son of Shaphan the *c*, in
Cor
1Ki 4:22 thirty *c* measures of fine
4:22 sixty *c* measures of flour
5:11 thousand *c* measures of wheat
5:11 and twenty *c* measures of
2Ch 27:5 *c* measures of wheat
Ezr 7:22 hundred *c* measures of wheat
Eze 45:14 bath is a tenth of the *c*
Lu 16:7 hundred *c* measures of wheat
Coral
Job 28:18 *C* and rock crystal
Corals
Pr 3:15 more precious than *c*, and
8:11 wisdom is better than *c*, and
20:15 gold, also an abundance of *c*
31:10 is far more than that of *c*
La 4:7 were in fact more ruddy than *c*
Eze 27:16 fine fabric and *c* and rubies
Corban
Mr 7:11 *c*, (that is, a gift dedicated
Cord
Ge 38:18 Your seal ring and your *c*
38:25 seal ring and the *c* and the
Jos 2:18 This *c* of scarlet thread you
2:21 she tied the scarlet *c* in the
Job 4:21 not their tent *c* within them
18:10 *c* for him is hidden on the
Ec 4:12 threefold *c* cannot quickly be
12:6 the silver *c* is removed, and
Eze 40:3 was a flax *c* in his hand
Mic 2:5 have no one casting out the *c*
Cords
Ex 28:14 As *c* you will make them
35:18 the courtyard and their *c*
39:40 its tent *c* and its tent pins
Nu 3:26 and its tent *c*, for all its
3:37 pins and their tent *c*
4:26 tent *c* and all their service
4:32 tent *c* together with all their
Job 38:31 loosen the very *c* of the
Ps 2:3 cast their *c* away from us
Isa 5:18 as with wagon *c* sin
54:2 Lengthen out your tent *c*
Jer 10:20 tent *c* have all been torn
Eze 3:25 put *c* upon you and bind you
4:8 I will put *c* upon you that
Ho 11:4 with the *c* of love, so that I
Coriander
Ex 16:31 manna . . . was white like *c*
Nu 11:7 manna was like *c* seed, and
Corinth
Ac 18:1 from Athens and came to *C*
19:1 while Apollos was in *C*, Paul
1Co 1:2 that is in *C*, to you who have
2Co 1:1 congregation . . . that is in *C*
1:23 I have not yet come to *C*
2Ti 4:20 Erastus stayed in *C*, but I
Corinthians
Ac 18:8 And many of the *C* that heard
2Co 6:11 *C*, our heart has widened

Cormorant
Le 11:17 the little owl and the *c*
De 14:17 the vulture and the *c*

Cornelius
Ac 10:1 *C*, an army officer of the
10:3 to him and say to him: *C!*
10:17 men dispatched by *C* had
10:22 *C*, an army officer, a man
10:24 *C*, of course, was expecting
10:25 *C* met him, fell down at his
10:30 *C* said: Four days ago
10:31 *C*, your prayer has been

Corner
Ex 26:23 two panel frames as *c* posts
26:24 will serve as two *c* posts
36:28 two panel frames as *c* posts
36:29 to the two *c* posts
Jos 15:5 boundary at the northern *c*
18:12 northern *c* from the Jordan
2Ki 14:13 clear to the *c* gate
2Ch 25:23 clear to the *C* Gate, four
26:9 Jerusalem by the *C* Gate and
28:24 at every *c* in Jerusalem
Ne 3:24 Buttress and as far as the *c*
3:31 the roof chamber of the *c*
3:32 the roof chamber of the *c* and
Ps 118:22 become the head of the *c*
Pr 7:8 on the street near her *c*, and
7:12 near every *c* she lies in wait
21:9 to dwell upon a *c* of a roof
25:24 to dwell upon a *c* of a roof
Isa 28:16 *c* of a sure foundation
Jer 31:38 of Hananel to the *C* Gate
31:40 *c* of the Horse Gate toward
51:26 from you a stone for a *c*
Eze 41:22 and it had its *c* posts
46:21 to the four *c* posts of the
46:21 *c* post of the courtyard
46:21 *c* post of the courtyard
46:22 *c* posts of the courtyard
46:22 *c* structures had the same
Zep 1:16 against the high *c* towers
3:6 their *c* towers were desolated
Zec 14:10 all the way to the *C* Gate
Lu 4:37 *c* of the surrounding country
Ac 4:11 has become the head of the *c*
26:26 has not been done in a *c*
1Pe 2:7 become the head of the *c*

Cornerpieces
1Ki 7:30 its four *c* were supports for

Corners
Ex 25:26 the rings on the four *c* that
27:2 its horns upon its four *c*
37:13 put the rings upon the four *c*
38:2 its horns upon its four *c*
1Ki 7:34 four *c* of each carriage
2Ch 26:15 upon the *c*, to shoot arrows
Job 1:19 the four *c* of the house, so
Ps 144:12 *c* carved in palace style
Eze 43:20 four *c* of the surrounding
45:19 upon the four *c* of the
Zec 9:15 like the *c* of the altar
Mt 6:5 on the *c* of the broad ways to
Re 7:1 upon the four *c* of the earth
20:8 in the four *c* of the earth

Cornerstone
Job 38:6 Or who laid its *c*
Mt 21:42 that has become the chief *c*
Mr 12:10 has become the chief *c*
Lu 20:17 this has become the chief *c*
Eph 2:20 Jesus . . . the foundation *c*
1Pe 2:6 a foundation *c*, precious

Corpse
Nu 19:11 touching the *c* of any human
19:13 Everyone touching a *c*, the
19:16 a *c* or a bone of a man or a
19:18 or the *c* or the burial place
Jg 14:8 bees in the lion's *c*, and
14:9 out of the *c* of the lion that
1Sa 31:10 his *c* they fastened on the
31:12 took the *c* of Saul and the
1Ch 10:12 carried off the *c* of Saul
Isa 26:19 A *c* of mine—they will rise
Mt 14:12 and removed the *c* and buried
Mr 6:29 *c* and laid it in a memorial
15:45 he granted the *c* to Joseph

Corpses
1Sa 31:12 *c* of his sons off the wall
1Ch 10:12 Saul and the *c* of his sons
Jer 16:18 the *c* of their disgusting

Re 11:8 *c* will be on the broad way
11:9 nations will look at their *c*
11:9 their *c* be laid in a tomb

Correct
De 4:36 hear his voice so as to *c* you
Ps 6:1 do not in your rage *c* me
38:1 Nor in your rage *c* me
94:12 man whom you *c*, O Jah
Ec 12:10 writing of *c* words of truth
Jer 2:19 Your badness should *c* you
10:24 *C* me, O Jehovah, however
30:11 *c* you to the proper degree
Tit 1:5 might *c* the things that were

Corrected
Le 26:23 let yourselves be *c* by me
De 21:18 *c* him but he will not listen
Job 4:3 Look! You have *c* many, And
Ps 2:10 Let yourselves be *c*, O judges
16:7 my kidneys have *c* me
39:11 against error you have *c* man
118:18 Jah *c* me severely
Pr 29:19 be *c* by mere words, for he
Jer 6:8 Be *c*, O Jerusalem, that my
31:18 You have *c* me, that I may
31:18 that I may be *c*, like a
Eze 23:48 to let themselves be *c*
Heb 12:5 give out when you are *c* by

Correcting
De 8:5 Jehovah your God was *c* you
Ps 94:10 One *c* the nations, can he not
Pr 9:7 *c* the ridiculer is taking to

Correction
Ps 73:14 And my *c* is every morning
Pr 31:1 his mother gave to him in *c*

Correctly
Jg 12:6 was unable to say the word *c*
Lu 7:43 He said to him: You judged *c*
10:28 You answered *c*; keep on doing
20:21 know you speak and teach *c*
Ac 18:26 way of God more *c* to him

Correctness
Ac 18:25 speaking and teaching with *c*

Corrector
Ro 2:20 *c* of the unreasonable ones

Corrects
De 8:5 just as a man *c* his son
Isa 28:26 *c* him according to what is

Correspond
Le 25:50 sale must *c* with the number
De 25:2 to *c* with his wicked deed
Jos 4:8 to *c* with the number of the

Corresponding
Ex 24:4 *c* with the twelve tribes of
1Ch 26:16 guard group *c* with guard
Ne 12:24 *c* with guard group
Eze 42:12 before the *c* stone wall
1Ti 2:6 gave himself a *c* ransom for

Correspondingly
Ps 90:15 rejoice *c* to the days that
Isa 59:18 he will reward *c*, rage to
Jer 23:29 my word *c* like a fire
Mt 11:18 *C*, John came neither eating
Lu 7:33 *C*, John the Baptist has come
16:25 but Lazarus *c* the injurious
Heb 8:6 of a *c* better covenant

Corresponds
Pr 27:19 As in water face *c* with face
Ga 4:25 she *c* with the Jerusalem
1Pe 3:21 That which *c* to this is also

Corrupt
Job 15:16 one is detestable and *c*
Ps 14:3 they are all alike *c*
53:3 they are all alike *c*
Da 6:4 no pretext or *c* thing at all
6:4 *c* thing at all was found in

Corrupted
Eze 20:44 your *c* dealings, O house
2Co 7:2 we have *c* no one, we have
11:3 your minds might be *c* away
Eph 4:22 being *c* according to his
1Ti 6:5 men *c* in mind and despoiled
2Ti 3:8 men completely *c* in mind
Re 19:2 harlot who *c* the earth with

Corruptible
Ro 1:23 the image of *c* man and of
1Co 9:25 that they may get a *c* crown
15:53 this which is *c* must put on

1Co 15:54 this which is *c* puts on
1Pe 1:18 it was not with *c* things
1:23 a new birth, not by *c*, but

Corrupting
Jude 10 they go on *c* themselves

Corruption
Le 22:25 because their *c* is in them
Ac 2:27 your loyal one to see *c*
2:31 nor did his flesh see *c*
13:34 no more to return to *c*
13:35 your loyal one to see *c*
13:36 forefathers and did see *c*
13:37 raised up did not see *c*
Ro 8:21 free from enslavement to *c*
1Co 15:42 It is sown in *c*, it is
15:50 does *c* inherit incorruption
Ga 6:8 will reap *c* from his flesh
2Pe 1:4 the *c* that is in the world
2:19 existing as slaves of *c*

Corruptly
Ne 1:7 acted *c* against you and have
Job 34:31 although I do not act *c*

Cors
2Ch 2:10 wheat . . . twenty thousand *c*
2:10 and barley twenty thousand *c*

Cos
Ac 21:1 straight course and came to *C*

Cosam
Lu 3:28 son of *C*, son of Elmadam

Cost
Le 27:14 so much it should *c*
27:17 it should *c* according to the
2Sa 24:24 burnt sacrifices without *c*
1Ch 21:24 burnt sacrifices without *c*
1Co 9:18 the good news without *c*, to
2Co 11:7 without *c* I gladly declared

Costliness
Re 18:19 rich by reason of her *c*

Costly
Eze 16:10 cover you with *c* material
16:13 fine linen and *c* material
Mt 26:7 case of *c* perfumed oil
Joh 12:3 oil, genuine nard, very *c*

Cot
Mr 2:4 they lowered the *c* on which
2:9 and pick up your *c* and walk
2:11 Get up, pick up your *c*, and
2:12 immediately picked up his *c*
Joh 5:8 pick up your *c* and walk
5:9 picked up his *c* and began to
5:10 for you to carry the *c*
5:11 Pick up your *c* and walk
Ac 9:33 lying flat on his *c* for eight

Cots
Mr 6:55 to carry about on *c* those who
Ac 5:15 there upon little beds and *c*

Cotton
Es 1:6 There were linen, fine *c* and

Couch
Ge 47:31 over the head of the *c*
48:2 Israel . . . sat up on his *c*
49:33 his feet up onto the *c* and
Ex 8:3 frogs . . . upon your *c* and into
1Sa 19:13 placed it on the *c*, and a
19:15 Bring him on his *c* up to me
19:16 teraphim image on the *c* and
28:23 and sat on the *c*
2Sa 3:31 was walking behind the *c*
4:7 he was lying upon his *c* in
1Ki 17:19 laid him upon his own *c*
21:4 lay down upon his *c* and kept
2Ki 1:4 As regards the *c* upon which
1:6 as regards the *c* upon which
1:16 *c* upon which you have gone
4:10 put there for him a *c* and
4:21 *c* of the man of the true God
4:32 dead, being laid upon his *c*
2Ch 24:25 kill him upon his own *c*
Es 4:3 spread out as a *c* for many
7:8 Haman was fallen upon the *c* on
Ps 6:6 I make my *c* swim
139:8 spread out my *c* in Sheol
Pr 26:14 and the lazy one upon his *c*
Ca 3:7 It is his *c*, the one belonging
Isa 14:11 are spread out as a *c*
28:20 *c* has proved too short for
58:5 sackcloth and ashes as his *c*

Eze 23:41 sat down upon a glorious *c*
Am 3:12 on a splendid *c* and on a

Couches
2Ki 11:2 the inner room for the *c*
2Ch 22:11 the inner room for the *c*
Es 1:6 *c* of gold and silver upon a
Am 6:4 lying down on *c* of ivory and

Council
Mr 3:6 *c* with the party followers of
Lu 23:50 who was a member of the *C*

Counsel
De 32:28 a nation on whom *c* perishes
Jg 19:30 upon it, take *c* and speak
20:7 give your word and *c* here
2Sa 15:31 the *c* of Ahithophel into
15:34 the *c* of Ahithophel
16:20 men, give *c* on your part
16:23 And the *c* of Ahithophel
16:23 all the *c* of Ahithophel was
17:7 The *c* with which Ahithophel
17:11 say in *c*: Let all Israel
17:14 The *c* of Hushai the Archite
17:14 the *c* of Ahithophel
17:14 the *c* of Ahithophel although
17:23 *c* had not been acted upon
1Ki 1:12 let me, please, solemnly *c*
12:6 take *c* with the older men
12:8 left the *c* of the older men
12:8 take *c* with the young men
12:9 offering in *c* that we may
12:13 the *c* of the older men
12:14 to the *c* of the young men
12:28 the king took *c* and made
2Ki 6:8 took *c* with his servants
18:20 *c* and mightiness for the
1Ch 12:19 on *c* the axis lords of the
2Ch 10:6 Rehoboam began to take *c*
10:8 left the *c* of the older men
10:8 take *c* with the young men
10:9 you are offering in *c* that
10:13 Rehoboam left the *c* of the
10:14 *c* of the young men, saying
20:21 took *c* with the people and
22:5 in their *c* that he walked
25:16 have not listened to my *c*
25:17 took *c* and sent to Jehoash
Ezr 4:5 to frustrate their *c* all the
10:3 according to the *c* of Jehovah
10:8 the *c* of the princes and the
Ne 4:15 God had frustrated their *c*
Job 5:13 *c* of astute ones is carried
10:3 upon the *c* of wicked ones
12:13 He has *c* and understanding
18:7 Even his *c* will cast him off
21:16 *c* of wicked ones has kept
22:18 *c* of wicked ones has kept
29:21 would keep silent for my *c*
38:2 obscuring *c* By words without
42:3 that is obscuring *c* without
Ps 1:1 in the *c* of the wicked ones
14:6 The *c* of the afflicted one
20:4 And all your *c* may he fulfill
33:10 the *c* of the nations
33:11 *c* of Jehovah will stand
71:10 have jointly exchanged *c*
73:24 your *c* you will lead me
83:5 have unitedly exchanged *c*
106:13 They did not wait for his *c*
107:11 *c* of the Most High they had
119:24 As men of my *c*
Pr 1:25 keep neglecting all my *c*
1:30 They did not consent to my *c*
8:14 I have *c* and practical wisdom
12:15 one listening to *c* is wise
19:20 Listen to *c* and accept
19:21 *c* of Jehovah . . . will stand
20:5 *C* in the heart of a man is as
20:18 By *c* plans themselves are
21:30 nor any *c* in opposition to
27:9 due to the *c* of the soul
Isa 5:19 *c* of the Holy One of Israel
11:2 the spirit of *c* and of
14:26 This is the *c* that is
16:3 Bring in *c*, you men, execute
19:3 I shall confuse its own *c*
19:11 their *c* is something
19:17 *c* of Jehovah of armies that
23:8 given this *c* against Tyre
23:9 given this *c*, to profane
28:29 has been wonderful in *c*
29:15 concealing *c* from Jehovah
30:1 disposed to carry out *c*, but
Isa 32:7 *c* for acts of loose conduct
32:8 that he has given *c*
36:5 *c* and mightiness for the war
40:13 who as his man of *c* can
41:28 no one that was giving *c*
44:26 the *c* of his own messengers
46:10 My own *c* will stand, and
46:11 the man to execute my *c*
Jer 18:18 *c* from the wise one or the
18:23 *c* against me for my death
19:7 make void the *c* of Judah
32:19 great in *c* and abundant in
49:7 *c* perished from those having
49:20 *c* of Jehovah that he has
49:30 formulated a *c* even against
50:45 *c* of Jehovah that he has
Eze 7:26 and *c* from elderly men
11:2 bad *c* against this city
Da 2:14 addressed himself with *c* and
4:27 may my *c* seem good to you
6:7 *c* together to establish a royal
Ho 10:6 will be ashamed of its *c*
Mic 4:12 not come to understand his *c*
Zec 6:13 *c* of peace will prove to be
Mt 12:14 took *c* against him that they
22:15 took *c* together in order to
26:4 *c* together to seize Jesus
28:12 and taken *c*, they gave a
Lu 7:30 disregarded the *c* of God to
14:31 first sit down and take *c*
Joh 11:53 they took *c* to kill him
12:10 took *c* to kill Lazarus also
Ac 2:23 *c* and foreknowledge of God
4:28 *c* had foreordained to occur
9:23 Jews took *c* together to do
20:27 telling you all the *c* of God
Heb 6:17 the unchangeableness of his *c*

Counseled
2Sa 16:23 which he *c* in those days
17:7 with which Ahithophel has *c*
17:15 Ahithophel *c* Absalom and
17:15 the way that I myself *c*
17:21 Ahithophel *c* against you
1Ki 12:13 older men who had *c* him
Isa 14:24 just as I have *c*, that is
14:26 *c* against all the earth, and
14:27 *c*, and who can break it up?
19:12 Jehovah of armies has *c*
Mic 6:5 Balak the king of Moab *c*
Hab 2:10 have *c* something shameful
Joh 18:14 *c* the Jews that it was to

Counseling
Pr 12:20 those *c* peace have rejoicing
Isa 19:17 that he is *c* against him
Na 1:11 *c* what is not worth while

Counselings
Pr 22:20 written . . . with *c* and

Counselor
2Sa 15:12 David's *c*, from his city
1Ch 26:14 a *c* with discretion, they
27:32 a *c*, a man of understanding
27:33 Ahithophel was a *c* of the
2Ch 22:3 mother herself became his *c*
25:16 *c* of the king that we
Isa 3:3 *c* and expert in magical arts
9:6 Wonderful *C*, Mighty God
Mic 4:9 or has your own *c* perished
Ro 11:34 or who has become his *c*

Counselors
2Ch 22:4 *c* to him after the death
Ezr 4:5 and hiring *c* against them to
7:14 the king and his seven *c* an
7:15 that the king and his *c* have
7:28 before the king and his *c*
8:25 the king and his *c* and his
Job 3:14 kings and *c* of the earth
12:17 He is making *c* go barefoot
Pr 11:14 in the multitude of *c*
15:22 in the multitude of *c* there
24:6 of *c* there is salvation
Isa 1:26 and *c* for you as at the start
19:11 wise ones of Pharaoh's *c*
47:13 the multitude of your *c*
Da 3:2 *c*, the treasurers, the judges
3:3 the *c*, the treasurers, the
Ac 25:12 the assembly of *c*, replied

Counsels
Ps 5:10 will fall due to their own *c*
81:12 walking in their own *c*
Pr 1:31 glutted with their own *c*
Isa 25:1 *c* from early times, in
Jer 7:24 they went walking in the *c*
Ho 11:6 devour because of their *c*
Mic 6:16 you people walk in their *c*
1Co 4:5 and make the *c* of the hearts
Eph 1:11 to the way his will *c*

Count
Ge 13:16 *c* the dust particles of the
15:5 and *c* the stars, if you are
15:5 if you are possibly able to *c*
15:6 *c* it to him as righteousness
Le 15:13 *c* for himself seven days for
15:28 also *c* for herself seven days
23:15 *c* for yourselves from the
23:16 *c*, fifty days, and you must
25:8 *c* for yourself seven sabbaths
De 16:9 Seven weeks you should *c* for
16:9 start to *c* seven weeks
1Sa 13:15 to take the *c* of the people
14:17 Take the *c*, please, and see
14:17 When they took the *c*, why
15:4 took the *c* of them in Telaim
2Sa 24:1 take a *c* of Israel and Judah
1Ki 20:15 the *c* of the young men of
20:15 took the *c* of all the people
2Ki 12:10 *c* the money that was being
1Ch 21:2 David said . . . Go, *c* Israel
27:24 started to take the *c*, but
2Ch 2:17 Solomon took a *c* of all the
Job 31:4 And *c* even all my steps
39:2 *c* the lunar months that they
Ps 22:17 I can *c* all my bones
48:12 go about it, *C* its towers
90:12 *c* our days in such a way
139:18 I to try to *c* them, they
Isa 22:10 you will actually *c*
Jer 33:13 of the one taking the *c*
Ac 26:2 I *c* myself happy that it is
2Th 1:11 *c* you worthy of his calling

Counted
Le 17:4 bloodguilt will be *c* to that
Nu 23:10 *c* the fourth part of Israel
Jg 21:9 When the people were *c*, well
2Sa 4:2 Beeroth, too, used to be *c* as
1Ki 3:8 numbered or *c* for multitude
8:5 cattle that could not be *c*
2Ki 12:11 money that had been *c* off
2Ch 2:2 *c* off seventy thousand men
5:6 could not be *c* or numbered
Job 7:3 nights of trouble they have *c*
Ps 106:31 *c* to him as righteousness
Ec 1:15 wanting cannot possibly be *c*
Isa 53:12 that he was *c* in; and he
Jer 33:22 of the heavens cannot be *c*
Lu 20:35 *c* worthy of gaining that
Ac 5:41 *c* worthy to be dishonored in
Ro 2:26 *c* as circumcision, will it
4:3 was *c* to him as righteousness
4:4 man that works the pay is *c*
4:5 his faith is *c* as righteousness
4:9 faith was *c* to Abraham as
4:10 circumstances, then, was it *c*
4:11 righteousness to be *c* to them
4:22 was *c* to him as righteousness
4:23 That it was *c* to him was
4:24 whom it is destined to be *c*
9:8 children by the promise are *c*
Ga 3:6 was *c* to him as righteousness
2Th 1:5 *c* worthy of the kingdom of
Heb 3:3 *c* worthy of more glory than
10:29 man be *c* worthy who has
Jas 2:23 *c* to him as righteousness

Countenance
Ge 4:5 anger, and his *c* began to fall
4:6 and why has your *c* fallen?
29:17 Rachel . . . beautiful of *c*
De 28:50 a nation fierce in *c*, who
Job 9:27 Let me alter my *c* and
Pr 15:13 has a good effect on the *c*
La 3:36 Jehovah himself has had no *c*
Da 1:13 *c* of the children who are
8:23 stand up a king fierce in *c*
Joh 11:44 *c* was bound about with a
Re 1:16 his *c* was as the sun when it

Countenances
Da 1:13 and let our *c* and the
1:15 *c* appeared better and fatter

Counterarguments
Job 13:6 Hear, please, my *c*, And to
23:4 mouth I would fill with *c*
Ps 38:14 in my mouth there were no *c*

Counterfeit
2Pe 2:3 exploit you with *c* words

Counting
Ge 41:49 finally they gave up *c* it
Job 14:16 you keep *c* my very steps
Ps 147:4 *c* the number of the stars
Isa 33:18 the one *c* the towers
Ac 10:30 days ago *c* from this hour
2Co 10:2 confidence with which I am *c*

Countries
2Co 10:16 to the *c* beyond you, so as

Country
Ge 12:1 Go your way out of your *c* and
12:1 the *c* that I shall show you
24:4 will go to my *c* and to my
30:25 go to my place and to my *c*
42:30 lord of the *c* spoke harshly
42:30 for men spying on the *c*
42:33 the lord of the *c* said to us
Ex 1:10 and go up out of the *c*
Le 25:31 part of the field of the *c*
Nu 10:30 I shall go to my own *c* and
22:13 Go to your *c*, because Jehovah
De 23:7 an alien resident in his *c*
Jg 5:7 The dwellers in open *c* ceased
5:11 dwellers in open *c* in Israel
1Sa 6:18 to the village of the open *c*
1Ch 5:10 all the *c* east of Gilead
2Ch 3:6 gold was gold from the gold *c*
Es 9:19 *c* Jews, inhabiting the cities
Job 39:6 dwelling places the salt *c*
Ps 107:34 Fruitful land into salt *c*
Isa 25:5 the heat in a waterless *c*
32:2 of water in a waterless *c*
Jer 17:6 in a salt *c* that is not
48:21 land of level *c*, to Holon
Eze 27:28 the open *c* will rock
38:11 the land of open rural *c*
Jon 1:8 What is your *c*, and from
Zec 2:4 As open rural *c* Jerusalem
Mt 2:12 to their *c* by another way
3:5 all the *c* around the Jordan
8:28 into the *c* of the Gadarenes
13:53 he went across *c* from there
14:35 into all that surrounding *c*
15:29 Crossing *c* from there, Jesus
Mr 1:28 the *c* round about in Galilee
5:1 into the *c* of the Gerasenes
5:10 send the spirits out of the *c*
15:21 Simon . . . coming from the *c*
Lu 1:39 went into the mountainous *c*
1:65 whole mountainous *c* of Judea
2:8 in that same *c* shepherds
3:1 ruler of the *c* of Ituraea and
3:3 all the *c* around the Jordan
4:14 through all the surrounding *c*
4:37 corner of the surrounding *c*
6:17 the maritime *c* of Tyre and
7:17 and all the surrounding *c*
8:26 in the *c* of the Gerasenes
8:37 surrounding *c* of the Gerasenes
15:13 abroad into a distant *c*
15:14 famine . . . throughout that *c*
15:15 one of the citizens of that *c*
21:21 let those in the *c* places not
23:26 Simon . . . coming from the *c*
Joh 3:22 went into Judean *c*, and
11:54 the *c* near the wilderness
11:55 out of the *c* to Jerusalem
Ac 10:39 in the *c* of the Jews and in
12:20 *c* was supplied with food
13:49 throughout the whole *c*
14:6 Derbe and the *c* round about
16:6 Phrygia and the *c* of Galatia
18:23 through the *c* of Galatia and
26:20 over all the *c* of Judea, and

Countrymen
1Th 2:14 at the hands of your own *c*

Countryside
1Sa 27:5 in one of the cities of the *c*
27:7 David dwelt in the *c* of the
27:11 in the *c* of the Philistines
Mr 5:14 in the city and in the *c*
6:36 off into the *c* and villages
6:56 into villages or cities or *c*
Lu 8:34 to the city and to the *c*
9:12 villages and *c* round about

Counts
Ro 4:6 God *c* righteousness apart

Couple
Jg 19:3 and a *c* of he-asses
Jg 19:10 the *c* of he-asses saddled up
2Sa 16:1 meet him with a *c* of asses

Courage
Nu 24:18 Israel is displaying his *c*
2Ch 15:8 he took *c* and proceeded to
25:11 took *c* and proceeded to
32:5 took *c* and built up all the
Isa 46:8 you people may muster up *c*
Jer 49:24 Damascus has lost *c*
Mt 8:28 nobody had the *c* to pass by
9:2 Take *c*, child; your sins are
9:22 Take *c*, daughter; your faith
14:27 Take *c*, it is I; have no
Mr 6:50 Take *c*, it is I; have no fear
10:49 Take *c*, get up, he is
12:34 *c* anymore to question him
15:43 *c* to go in before Pilate and
Lu 20:40 the *c* to ask him a single
Joh 16:33 take *c*! I have conquered
21:12 disciples had the *c* to
Ac 5:13 *c* to join himself to them
23:11 Be of good *c*! For as you have
28:15 Paul thanked God and took *c*
2Co 5:6 always of good *c* and know
5:8 we are of good *c* and are
7:16 have good *c* by reason of you
Php 1:14 *c* to speak the word of God
Heb 13:6 we may be of good *c* and say

Courageous
Ge 47:6 there are among them *c* men
Nu 13:20 show yourselves *c* and take
De 31:6 Be *c* and strong. Do not be
31:7 Be *c* and strong, because you
31:23 Be *c* and strong, because you
Jos 1:6 Be *c* and strong, for you are
1:7 be *c* and very strong to take
1:9 Be *c* and strong. Do not suffer
1:18 Only be *c* and strong.
10:25 Be *c* and strong, for it is
23:6 be very *c* to keep and to do
Jg 20:22 Israel, showed themselves *c*
1Sa 4:9 Show yourselves *c* and prove
2Sa 10:12 *c* in behalf of our people
1Ch 19:13 *c* in behalf of our people
22:13 Be *c* and strong. Do not be
28:10 Be *c* and act
28:20 Be *c* and strong and act
2Ch 15:7 be *c* and do not let your
23:1 Jehoiada showed himself *c*
25:8 act, be *c* for the war
32:7 Be *c* and strong. Do not be
Ps 27:14 be *c* and let your heart be
31:24 Be *c*, and may your heart be

Couriers
Es 3:13 the letters by means of *c* to
3:15 *c* themselves went out, being
8:10 by the hand of the *c* on horses
8:14 The *c* themselves, riding post

Course
Nu 23:22 *c* like that of a wild bull
24:8 swift *c* of a wild bull is his
Jos 11:20 proved to be Jehovah's *c* to
2Sa 2:22 Turn your *c* aside from
1Ki 10:25 as a yearly matter of *c*
2Ch 6:23 putting his *c* upon his own
8:13 a daily matter of *c* to make
8:14 as a daily matter of *c*, and
9:24 as a yearly matter of *c*
31:16 as a daily matter of *c*
32:1 this faithful *c* Sennacherib
Ps 106:43 in their disobedient *c*
Pr 2:9 the entire *c* of what is good
2:15 devious in their general *c*
4:26 Smooth out the *c* of your foot
Ec 11:1 *c* of many days you will find
Isa 26:7 very *c* of a righteous one
Jer 5:23 and keep walking in their *c*
8:6 back into the popular *c*
23:10 *c* of action proves to be bad
Joe 2:8 an able-bodied man in his *c*
2:8 the others do not break off *c*
Mt 9:26 Of *c*, the talk about this
18:7 Of *c*, the stumbling blocks
26:41 The spirit, of *c*, is eager
Mr 1:9 In the *c* of those days Jesus
4:5 of *c*, did not have much soil
14:38 The spirit, of *c*, is eager
Lu 2:4 Of *c*, Joseph also went up from
5:17 In the *c* of one of the days
6:6 In the *c* of another sabbath he
8:22 In the *c* of one of the days
16:22 *c* of time the beggar died
Lu 23:56 of *c*, they rested on the
Joh 4:27 Of *c*, no one said: What are
7:13 No one, of *c*, would speak
21:4 not, of *c*, discern that it
Ac 10:24 Cornelius, of *c*, was
13:25 John was fulfilling his *c*
19:1 In the *c* of events, while
20:24 if only I may finish my *c*
21:1 we ran with a straight *c* and
Ro 12:13 Follow the *c* of hospitality
1Co 9:25 of *c*, do it that they may
Ga 1:13 You, of *c*, heard about my
5:13 of *c*, called for freedom
Eph 4:22 your former *c* of conduct and
Col 1:23 provided, of *c*, that you
2Ti 3:10 my *c* of life, my purpose
4:7 have run the *c* to the finish
Heb 3:4 Of *c*, every house is
1Pe 2:21 to this *c* you were called
3:9 you were called to this *c*, so
4:4 *c* to the same low sink of
2Pe 2:12 their own *c* of destruction
2:16 hindered the prophet's mad *c*
Jude 11 the erroneous *c* of Balaam
13 stars with no set *c*, for

Courses
Ca 4:4 built in *c* of stone, upon

Court
Ge 37:36 Potiphar a *c* official of
39:1 Potiphar, a *c* official of
1Sa 8:15 give them to his *c* officials
1Ki 22:9 a certain *c* official and said
2Ki 8:6 king gave her a *c* official
9:32 two or three *c* officials
20:4 middle *c* when Jehovah's
20:18 *c* officials in the palace of
23:11 the *c* official
24:12 princes and his *c* officials
24:15 his *c* officials and the
25:19 he took one *c* official that
1Ch 28:1 with the *c* officials and the
2Ch 18:8 called a *c* official and said
Es 1:10 seven *c* officials that were
1:12 by means of the *c* officials
1:15 by means of the *c* officials
2:21 two *c* officials of the king
6:2 two *c* officials of the king
6:14 king's *c* officials themselves
7:9 Harbona, one of the *c* officials
Job 11:10 And calls a *c*, then who can
Isa 39:7 *c* officials in the palace of
59:4 gone to *c* in faithfulness
Jer 29:2 the lady and the *c* officials
34:19 *c* officials and the priests
41:16 *c* officials, whom he
52:25 took one *c* official that
Da 1:3 Ashpenaz his chief *c* official
1:7 principal *c* official went
1:8 principal *c* official that he
1:9 before the principal *c* official
1:10 principal *c* official said to
1:11 principal *c* official had
1:18 the principal *c* official also
2:49 Daniel was in the *c* of the
7:10 The *C* took its seat, and there
7:26 *C* itself proceeded to sit
Mt 5:21 accountable to the *c* of
5:22 accountable to the *c* of
5:22 accountable to the Supreme *C*
5:25 judge to the *c* attendant
5:40 if a person wants to go to *c*
Mr 14:65 the *c* attendants took him
Lu 12:58 deliver you to the *c* officer
12:58 *c* officer throw you into
Ac 17:34 of the *c* of the Areopagus
19:38 *c* days are held and there are
1Co 6:1 dare to go to *c* before
6:6 but brother goes to *c* with

Courtesy
2Sa 11:8 king's *c* gift went out
Ac 25:13 a visit of *c* to Festus

Courts
Mt 10:17 deliver you up to local *c*
Mr 13:9 deliver you up to local *c*
Jas 2:6 they drag you before law *c*

Courtyard
Ex 27:9 make the *c* of the tabernacle
27:9 the *c* has hangings of fine
27:12 As for the width of the *c*
27:13 width of the *c* on the east
27:16 And for the gate of the *c*

Ex 27:17 All the pillars of the *c*
27:18 The length of the *c* is a
27:19 and all the pins of the *c* are
35:17 the *c*, its pillars and its
35:17 screen of the gate of the *c*
35:18 the tent pins of the *c* and
38:9 he proceeded to make the *c*
38:9 the hangings of the *c* were of
38:15 of the gate of the *c*, the
38:16 of the *c* round about were of
38:17 for all the pillars of the *c*
38:18 screen of the gate of the *c*
38:18 with the hangings of the *c*
38:20 *c* round about were of copper
38:31 the socket pedestals of the *c*
38:31 of the gate of the *c*, and all
38:31 tent pins of the *c* round
39:40 the hangings of the *c*, its
39:40 screen for the gate of the *c*
40:8 place the *c* round about and
40:8 screen of the gate of the *c*
40:33 *c* round about the tabernacle
40:33 screen of the gate of the *c*
Le 6:16 eat it in the *c* of the tent of
6:26 the *c* of the tent of meeting
Nu 3:26 hangings of the *c* and the
3:26 *c* that is round about the
3:37 pillars of the *c* round about
4:26 hangings of the *c* and the
4:26 *c* that is round about the
4:32 pillars of the *c* round about
2Sa 17:18 who had a well in his *c*
1Ki 6:36 inner *c* with three rows of
7:8 at the other *c*, it was away
7:9 outside as far as the great *c*
7:12 the great *c*, round about
7:12 for the inner *c* of the house
8:64 sanctify the middle of the *c*
2Ch 4:9 he made the *c* of the priests
7:7 *c* that was before the house
20:5 Jehovah before the new *c*
24:21 in the *c* of Jehovah's house
29:16 *c* of the house of Jehovah
Ne 3:25 belongs to the *C* of the Guard
13:7 *c* of the house of the true God
Es 1:5 the *c* of the garden of the
2:11 *c* of the house of the women
4:11 to the king at the inner *c*
5:1 took her stand in the inner *c*
5:2 the queen standing in the *c*
6:4 Who is in the *c*? Now Haman
6:4 the outer *c* of the king's house
6:5 is Haman standing in the *c*
Isa 34:13 the *c* for the ostriches
Jer 19:14 *c* of the house of Jehovah
26:2 *c* of the house of Jehovah
32:2 *C* of the Guard that is in
32:8 into the *C* of the Guard
32:12 in the *C* of the Guard
33:1 shut up in the *C* of the Guard
36:10 in the upper *c*, at the
36:20 to the king, to the *c*
37:21 in the *C* of the Guard
37:21 in the *C* of the Guard
38:6 was in the *C* of the Guard
38:13 dwell in the *C* of the Guard
38:28 *C* of the Guard until the
39:14 out of the *C* of the Guard
39:15 up in the *C* of the Guard
Eze 8:7 to the entrance of the *c*, and
8:16 brought me to the inner *c* of
10:3 was filling the inner *c*
10:4 the *c* itself was full of the
10:5 heard to the outer *c*, like
40:14 the side pillars of the *c*
40:17 brought me into the outer *c*
40:17 pavement made for the *c*
40:19 the front of the inner *c*
40:20 the outer *c* had a gate the
40:23 the gate of the inner *c*
40:27 And the inner *c* had a gate
40:28 into the inner *c* by the gate
40:31 porch was to the outer *c*
40:32 inner *c* by way of the east
40:34 was toward the outer *c*
40:37 to the outer *c* were its
40:44 singers, in the inner *c*
40:47 measuring the inner *c*
41:15 and the porches of the *c*
42:1 outer *c* by the way toward
42:3 that belonged to the inner *c*
42:3 that belonged to the outer *c*
42:7 toward the outer *c* before
42:8 outer *c* was fifty cubits
Eze 42:9 in to them from the outer *c*
42:10 the stone wall of the *c*
42:14 go . . . to the outer *c*
43:5 bring me into the inner *c*
44:17 the gates of the inner *c*
44:17 gates of the inner *c* and
44:19 go forth to the outer *c*
44:19 outer *c* to the people, they
44:21 they come into the inner *c*
44:27 inner *c*, to minister in
45:19 the gate of the inner *c*
46:1 gate of the inner *c* that is
46:20 out to the outer *c* so as
46:21 outer *c* and make me pass
46:21 four corner posts of the *c*
46:21 *c* by this corner post of
46:21 this corner post of the *c*
46:21 a *c* by that corner post of
46:21 corner post of the *c*
46:22 corner posts of the *c* there
Mt 26:3 in the *c* of the high priest
26:58 as the *c* of the high priest
26:69 was sitting outside in the *c*
Mr 14:54 in the *c* of the high priest
14:66 Peter was below in the *c*
15:16 led him off into the *c*, that
Lu 22:55 fire in the midst of the *c*
Joh 18:15 the *c* of the high priest
Re 11:2 *c* that is outside the temple

Courtyards
Ge 25:16 names by their *c* and by their
Ex 8:13 houses, the *c* and the fields
2Ki 21:5 *c* of the house of Jehovah
23:12 in two *c* of the house of
1Ch 23:28 over the *c* and over the
28:6 build my house and my *c*
28:12 for the *c* of Jehovah's house
2Ch 23:5 people will be in the *c* of
33:5 *c* of the house of Jehovah
Ne 8:16 own roof and in their *c* and
8:16 *c* of the house of the true
Ps 65:4 That he may reside in your *c*
84:2 for the *c* of Jehovah
84:10 day in your *c* is better than
92:13 *c* of our God, they will
96:8 a gift and come into his *c*
100:4 Into his *c* with praise
116:19 *c* of the house of Jehovah
135:2 *c* of the house of our God
Isa 1:12 to trample my *c*
62:9 will drink it in my holy *c*
Eze 9:7 and fill the *c* with the slain
42:6 like the pillars of the *c*
46:22 small *c*, forty cubits in
Zec 3:7 also keep my *c*; and I shall

Cousin
Col 4:10 Mark the *c* of Barnabas

Covenant
Ge 6:18 I do establish my *c* with you
9:9 I am establishing my *c* with
9:11 Yes, I do establish my *c*
9:12 the sign of the *c* that I am
9:13 must serve as a sign of the *c*
9:15 certainly remember my *c*
9:16 see it to remember the *c* to
9:17 the sign of the *c* that I do
15:18 concluded with Abram a *c*
17:2 I will give my *c* between me
17:4 my *c* is with you, and you
17:7 And I will carry out my *c*
17:7 *c* to time indefinite, to prove
17:9 you are to keep my *c*, you and
17:10 This is my *c* that you men
17:11 sign of the *c* between me and
17:13 my *c* in the flesh of you
17:13 must serve as a *c* to time
17:14 He has broken my *c*
17:19 I will establish my *c* with
17:19 *c* to time indefinite to his
17:21 my *c* I shall establish with
21:27 proceeded to conclude a *c*
21:32 So they concluded a *c* at
26:28 let us conclude a *c* with you
31:44 come, let us conclude a *c*
Ex 2:24 and God remembered his *c* with
6:4 established my *c* with them
6:5 and I remember my *c*
19:5 will indeed keep my *c*, then
23:32 not to conclude a *c* with
24:7 took the book of the *c* and
24:8 blood of the *c* that Jehovah
31:16 It is a *c* to time indefinite
Ex 34:10 Here I am concluding a *c*
34:12 do not conclude a *c* with the
34:15 conclude a *c* with the
34:27 a *c* with you and Israel
34:28 words of the *c*, the Ten
Le 2:13 the salt of the *c* of your God
24:8 *c* to time indefinite with the
26:9 will carry out my *c* with you
26:15 of your violating my *c*
26:25 wreaking vengeance for the *c*
26:42 remember my *c* with Jacob
26:42 and even my *c* with Isaac
26:42 my *c* with Abraham I shall
26:44 violate my *c* with them; for
26:45 *c* of the ancestors whom I
Nu 10:33 ark of Jehovah's *c*
14:44 ark of Jehovah's *c* and Moses
18:19 is a *c* of salt before Jehovah
25:12 am giving him my *c* of peace
25:13 as the *c* of a priesthood to
De 4:13 state to you his *c*, which he
4:23 not forget the *c* of Jehovah
4:31 the *c* of your forefathers that
5:2 God concluded a *c* with us in
5:3 Jehovah concluded this *c*, but
7:2 conclude no *c* with them nor
7:9 keeping *c* and loving-kindness
7:12 keep toward you the *c* and the
8:18 his *c* that he swore to your
9:9 the tablets of the *c* that
9:11 the tablets of the *c*
9:15 the two tablets of the *c* were
10:8 carry the ark of Jehovah's *c*
17:2 so as to overstep his *c*
29:1 *c* that Jehovah commanded Moses
29:1 *c* that he had concluded with
29:9 words of this *c* and do them
29:12 enter into the *c* of Jehovah
29:14 concluding this *c* and this
29:21 *c* that is written in this
29:25 abandoned the *c* of Jehovah
31:9 of the ark of Jehovah's *c*
31:16 my *c* that I have concluded
31:20 disrespect and break my *c*
31:25 of the ark of Jehovah's *c*
31:26 ark of the *c* of Jehovah your
33:9 *c* they continued to observe
Jos 3:3 the ark of the *c* of Jehovah
3:6 the ark of the *c* and pass
3:6 they took up the ark of the *c*
3:8 carrying the ark of the *c*
3:11 the ark of the *c* of the Lord
3:14 carrying the ark of the *c*
3:17 the ark of Jehovah's *c* kept
4:7 before the ark of Jehovah's *c*
4:9 carrying the ark of the *c*
4:18 the ark of the *c* of Jehovah
6:6 Take up the ark of the *c*, and
6:8 the ark of the *c* of Jehovah
7:11 *c* that I laid as a command
7:15 overstepped the *c* of Jehovah
8:33 the ark of the *c* of Jehovah
9:6 And now, conclude a *c* with us
9:7 could we conclude a *c* with
9:11 now conclude a *c* with us
9:15 and concluding a *c* with them
9:16 had concluded a *c* with them
23:16 your overstepping the *c* of
24:25 to conclude a *c* with the
Jg 2:1 Never shall I break my *c* with
2:2 you must not conclude a *c*
2:20 have overstepped my *c* that
20:27 ark of the *c* of the true God
1Sa 4:3 the ark of Jehovah's *c*, that
4:4 the ark of the *c* of Jehovah
4:4 ark of the *c* of the true God
4:5 ark of the *c* of Jehovah came
11:1 Conclude a *c* with us that we
18:3 proceeded to conclude a *c*
20:8 into a *c* of Jehovah that you
22:8 own son concludes a *c* with
23:18 two of them concluded a *c*
2Sa 3:12 conclude your *c* with me, and
3:13 shall conclude a *c* with you
3:21 conclude a *c* with you, and
5:3 David concluded a *c* with them
15:24 carrying the ark of the *c*
23:5 an indefinitely lasting *c*
1Ki 3:15 the ark of the *c* of Jehovah
5:12 proceeded to conclude a *c*
6:19 put there the ark of the *c*
8:1 bring up the ark of the *c* of
8:6 brought in the ark of the *c* of
8:21 for the Ark where the *c*

1Ki 8:23 *c* and the loving-kindness
11:11 have not kept my *c* and my
15:19 is a *c* between me and you
15:19 do break your *c* with Baasha
19:10 Israel have left your *c*
19:14 Israel have left your *c*
20:34 in a *c* I shall send you
20:34 he concluded a *c* with him
2Ki 11:4 and concluded a *c* with them
11:17 Jehoiada concluded the *c*
13:23 his *c* with Abraham, Isaac
17:15 *c* that he had concluded
17:35 Jehovah concluded a *c* with
17:38 the *c* that I have concluded
18:12 kept overstepping his *c*
23:2 words of the book of the *c*
23:3 the *c* before Jehovah
23:3 the words of this *c*
23:3 took their stand in the *c*
23:21 in this book of the *c*
1Ch 11:3 David concluded a *c* with
15:25 the ark of the *c* of Jehovah
15:26 carrying the ark of the *c*
15:28 bringing up the ark of the *c*
15:29 the ark of the *c* of Jehovah
16:6 ark of the *c* of the true God
16:15 Remember his *c* even to
16:16 *c* he concluded with Abraham
16:17 an indefinitely lasting *c*
16:37 the ark of the *c* of Jehovah
17:1 the ark of the *c* of Jehovah
22:19 to bring the ark of the *c* of
28:2 the ark of the *c* of Jehovah
28:18 the ark of the *c* of Jehovah
2Ch 5:2 the ark of the *c* of Jehovah
5:7 the ark of the *c* of Jehovah
6:11 ark where the *c* of Jehovah
6:14 keeping the *c* and the
13:5 his sons, by a *c* of salt
15:12 *c* to search for Jehovah the
16:3 *c* between me and you and
16:3 break your *c* with Baasha the
21:7 *c* that he had concluded with
23:1 with him into the *c*
23:3 congregation concluded a *c*
23:16 Jehoiada concluded a *c*
29:10 conclude a *c* with Jehovah
34:30 words of the book of the *c*
34:31 the *c* before Jehovah
34:31 perform the words of the *c*
34:32 the *c* of God, the God of
Ezr 10:3 conclude a *c* with our God
Ne 1:5 keeping the *c* and
9:8 contracting of the *c* with him
9:32 the *c* and loving-kindness
13:29 and the *c* of the priesthood
Job 5:23 with the stones . . . your *c*
31:1 A *c* I have concluded with
41:4 conclude a *c* with you
Ps 25:10 those observing his *c* and
25:14 his *c*, to cause them to know
44:17 not acted falsely in your *c*
50:5 Those concluding my *c* over
50:16 may bear my *c* in your mouth
55:20 He has profaned his *c*
74:20 Take a look at the *c*
78:10 did not keep the *c* of God
78:37 not prove faithful in his *c*
83:5 to conclude even a *c*
89:3 concluded a *c* toward my
89:28 *c* will be faithful to him
89:34 I shall not profane my *c*
89:39 have spurned the *c* of your
103:18 Toward those keeping his *c*
105:8 remembered his *c* even to
105:9 *c* he concluded with Abraham
105:10 indefinitely lasting *c* even
106:45 concerning them his *c*
111:5 he will remember his *c*
111:9 he has commanded his *c*
132:12 your sons will keep my *c*
Pr 2:17 forgotten the very *c* of her
Isa 24:5 the indefinitely lasting *c*
28:15 concluded a *c* with Death
28:18 your *c* with Death will
33:8 He has broken the *c*
42:6 as a *c* of the people, as a
49:8 give you as a *c* for the
54:10 nor will my *c* of peace
55:3 an indefinitely lasting *c*
56:4 are laying hold of my *c*
56:6 and laying hold of my *c*
57:8 concluding a *c* with them
59:21 *c* with them, Jehovah has
Isa 61:8 an indefinitely lasting *c*
Jer 3:16 The ark of the *c* of Jehovah!
11:2 Hear the words of this *c*
11:3 listen to the words of this *c*
11:6 the words of this *c*, and you
11:8 all the words of this *c*
11:10 my *c* that I concluded with
14:21 do not break your *c* with us
22:9 they left the *c* of Jehovah
31:31 house of Judah a new *c*
31:32 *c* that I concluded with
31:32 *c* of mine they themselves
31:33 *c* that I shall conclude
32:40 an indefinitely lasting *c*
33:20 break my *c* of the day and
33:20 and my *c* of the night, even
33:21 *c* be broken with David
33:25 *c* of the day and night
34:8 Zedekiah concluded a *c* with
34:10 *c* to let each one his
34:13 *c* with your forefathers in
34:15 conclude a *c* before me in
34:18 men sidestepping my *c*, in
34:18 the words of the *c*
50:5 indefinitely lasting *c* that
Eze 16:8 and enter into a *c* with you
16:59 the oath in breaking my *c*
16:60 remember my *c* with you in
16:60 an indefinitely lasting *c*
16:61 but not owing to your *c*
16:62 establish my *c* with you
17:13 royal seed and concluded a *c*
17:14 by keeping his *c* it might
17:15 and who has broken a *c*
17:16 and that broke his *c*, with
17:18 in breaking a *c*, and, look!
17:19 and my *c* that he has broken
20:37 into the bond of the *c*
30:5 sons of the land of the *c*
34:25 with them a *c* of peace
37:26 conclude . . . a *c* of peace
37:26 an indefinitely lasting *c*
44:7 breaking my *c* on account of
Da 9:4 keeping the *c* and the
9:27 *c* in force for the many for
11:22 also the Leader of the *c*
11:28 will be against the holy *c*
11:30 against the holy *c* and act
11:30 those leaving the holy *c*
11:32 wickedly against the *c*, he
Ho 2:18 conclude a *c* in that day in
6:7 man, have overstepped the *c*
8:1 they have overstepped my *c*
10:4 false oaths, concluding a *c*
12:1 a *c* with Assyria they conclude
Am 1:9 remember the *c* of brothers
Ob 7 The very men in *c* with you
Zec 9:11 by the blood of your *c*
11:10 in order to break my *c* that
Mal 2:4 my *c* with Levi may continue
2:5 my *c*, it proved to be with
2:8 You have ruined the *c* of Levi
2:10 the *c* of our forefathers
2:14 and the wife of your *c*
3:1 the messenger of the *c* in
Mt 26:28 means my blood of the *c*
Mr 14:24 means my blood of the *c*
Lu 1:72 call to mind his holy *c*
22:20 new *c* by virtue of my blood
22:29 I make a *c* with you, just
22:29 a *c* with me, for a kingdom
Ac 3:25 *c* which God covenanted with
7:8 gave him a *c* of circumcision
Ro 11:27 *c* on my part with them
1Co 11:25 This cup means the new *c* by
2Co 3:6 to be ministers of a new *c*
3:14 at the reading of the old *c*
Ga 3:15 A validated *c*, though it is
3:17 *c* previously validated by
Heb 7:22 given in pledge of a better *c*
8:6 of a correspondingly better *c*
8:7 if that first *c* had been
8:8 the house of Judah a new *c*
8:9 the *c* that I made with their
8:9 did not continue in my *c*
8:10 this is the *c* that I shall
8:10 *c* with the house of Israel
8:13 In his saying a new *c* he has
9:1 the former *c* used to have
9:4 the ark of the *c* overlaid
9:4 and the tablets of the *c*
9:15 he is a mediator of a new *c*
9:15 under the former *c*, the
9:16 there is a *c*, the death
Heb 9:17 For a *c* is valid over dead
9:18 the former *c* inaugurated
9:20 blood of the *c* that God has
10:16, 16 the *c* that I shall *c*
10:29 blood of the *c* by which he
12:24 the mediator of a new *c*
13:20 blood of an everlasting *c*
Re 11:19 ark of his *c* was seen in his

Covenanted
1Ki 8:9 *c* with the sons of Israel
2Ch 5:10 Jehovah *c* with the sons of
7:18 as I *c* with David your
Ac 3:25 God *c* with your forefathers

Covenanter
Heb 9:16 death of the human *c* needs
9:17 while the human *c* is living

Covenants
Ro 9:4 *c* and the giving of the Law
Ga 4:24 these women mean two *c*
Eph 2:12 strangers to the *c* of the

Cover
Ge 6:14 you must *c* it inside and
24:65 headcloth and to *c* herself
37:26 and did *c* over his blood
Ex 8:6 frogs began . . . to *c* the land
10:5 *c* the visible surface of the
15:5 waters proceeded to *c* them
16:13 to come up and *c* the camp
21:33 a pit and should not *c* it
24:16 to *c* it for six days
25:17 must make a *c* of pure gold
25:18 on both ends of the *c*
25:19 On the *c* you are to make the
25:20 screening over the *c* with
25:20 Toward the *c* the faces of
25:21 place the *c* above upon the
25:22 with you from above the *c*
26:13 to *c* it on this side and on
26:34 put the *c* upon the ark of the
28:42 them to *c* the naked flesh
30:6 *c* that is over the Testimony
31:7 the *c* that is upon it, and all
35:12 the *c* and the curtain of the
37:6 to make the *c* of pure gold
37:7 them on both ends of the *c*
37:8 cherubs on the *c* on both of
37:9 over the *c* with their wings
37:9 cherubs . . . toward the *c*
39:35 and its poles and the *c*
40:20 put the *c* above upon the Ark
40:34 cloud began to *c* the tent of
Le 13:12 leprosy does *c* all the skin
13:45 *c* over the mustache and call
16:2 the *c* which is upon the Ark
16:2 I shall appear over the *c*
16:13 overspread the Ark *c*, which
16:14 front of the *c* on the east
16:14 seven times before the *c*
16:15 spatter it toward the *c*
16:15 and before the *c*
17:13 pour its blood out and *c* it
Nu 4:5 *c* the ark of the testimony
4:8 *c* it with a covering of
4:9 *c* the lampstand of the
4:11 *c* it with a covering of
4:12 *c* them with a covering of
7:89 above the *c* that was upon the
9:16 cloud would *c* it by day, and
De 13:8 nor *c* him protectively
22:12 with which you *c* yourself
23:13 turn and *c* your excrement
1Ki 1:1 would *c* him with garments
7:18 to *c* the capitals that were
7:41 to *c* the two round capitals
7:42 to *c* the two bowl-shaped
1Ch 28:11 house of the propitiatory *c*
2Ch 3:7 he went on to *c* the house
4:12 to *c* the two round capitals
4:13 to *c* the two round capitals
Ne 4:5 do not *c* over their error and
Job 16:18 O earth, do not *c* my blood
21:26 maggots . . . a *c* over them
33:17 that he may *c* pride itself
38:34 water itself may *c* you
Ps 32:5 and my error I did not *c*
44:19 *c* us over with deep shadow
65:3 you yourself will *c* them
71:13 *c* themselves with reproach
78:38 *c* the error and not bring
79:9 *c* over our sins on account of
104:9 not again *c* the earth
140:9 of their own lips *c* them

Ps 143:9 I have taken *c* even with you
Isa 26:21 *c* over her killed ones
51:16 hand I shall certainly *c* you
58:7 naked, you must *c* him
59:6 nor will they *c* themselves
60:2 *c* the earth, and thick gloom
60:6 camels itself will *c* you
Jer 13:22 have been taken off as a *c*
18:23 Do not *c* over their error
46:8 I shall *c* the earth
Eze 12:6 *c* your very face that you
12:12 His face he will *c* in order
16:8 to *c* your nudeness and to
16:10 *c* you with costly material
16:18 embroidered garments and *c*
18:7 naked one he would *c* with a
24:7 order to *c* it over with dust
24:17 not *c* over the mustache
24:22 Mustaches you will not *c*
26:10 their dust will *c* you
30:18 clouds themselves will *c*
31:15 will *c* the watery deep
32:7 *c* the heavens and darken
32:7 sun, with clouds I shall *c*
38:9 Like clouds to *c* the land
38:16 like clouds to *c* the land
Ho 10:8 say to the mountains, *C* us!
Ob 10 shame will *c* you, and you
Jon 3:8 *c* themselves with sackcloth
Mic 3:7 have to *c* over the mustache
7:10 shame will *c* her, who was
Hab 2:14 waters . . . *c* over the sea
2:17 the violence . . . will *c* you
Mr 14:65 *c* his whole face and hit
Lu 23:30 and to the hills, *C* us over!
1Co 11:6 a woman does not *c* herself
Heb 9:5 the propitiatory *c*
Jas 5:20 will *c* a multitude of sins

Covered

Ge 7:19 mountains . . . came to be *c*
7:20 and the mountains became *c*
9:23 Thus they *c* their father's
18:17 Am I keeping *c* from Abraham
38:14 *c* herself with a shawl and
38:15 because she had *c* her face
Ex 14:28 *c* the war chariots and the
15:10 the sea *c* them; They sank
Le 13:13 leprosy has *c* all his flesh
Nu 7:3 six *c* wagons and twelve cattle
9:15 the cloud *c* the tabernacle of
16:42 the cloud *c* it, and Jehovah's
22:5 They have *c* the earth as far
Jos 24:7 sea upon them and *c* them
Jg 4:18 she *c* him with a blanket
4:19 drink, after which she *c* him
1Sa 19:13 she *c* it with a garment
28:14 *c* with a sleeveless coat
2Sa 15:30 David . . . with his head *c*
15:30 *c* each one his head, and
19:4 king himself *c* up his face
1Ki 6:9 *c* in the house with beams
7:7 they *c* it in with cedarwood
2Ki 16:18 *c* structure for the sabbath
19:1 *c* himself with sackcloth and
19:2 priests *c* with sackcloth
1Ch 21:16 older men, *c* with sackcloth
2Ch 3:5 house he *c* with juniper wood
3:5 he *c* it with good gold, and
3:8 he *c* it with good gold to the
3:9 roof chambers he *c* with gold
5:8 cherubs *c* over the Ark and its
Es 6:12 mourning and with his head *c*
7:8 and Haman's face they *c*
Job 23:17 gloom has *c* my own face
31:33 I *c* over my transgressions
36:30 roots of the sea he has *c*
36:32 he has *c* over the lightning
Ps 32:1 pardoned, whose sin is *c*
40:10 righteousness I have not *c*
44:15 shame of my own face has *c*
68:13 a dove *c* with silver
69:7 Humiliation has *c* my face
78:53 the sea *c* their enemies
80:10 were *c* with its shadow
85:2 You have *c* all their sin
104:6 just like a garment you *c* it
106:17 *c* over the assembly of
Pr 24:31 Nettles *c* its very surface
26:26 Hatred is *c* over by deceit
Ec 6:4 his own name will be *c*
Ca 5:14 ivory plate *c* with sapphires
Isa 6:2 With two he kept his face *c*
6:2 with two he kept his feet *c*
Isa 29:10 he has *c* even your heads
37:1 *c* himself with sackcloth
37:2 priests *c* with sackcloth
66:20 in chariots and in *c* wagons
Jer 14:3 they have *c* their head
14:4 they have *c* their head
51:42 its waves she has been *c*
51:51 Humiliation has *c* our faces
Eze 7:18 and shuddering has *c* them
18:16 naked one he has *c* with a
24:8 that it may not be *c* over
26:19 vast waters will have *c* you
41:16 the windows were *c* ones
Jon 3:6 *c* himself with sackcloth and
Hab 3:3 His dignity *c* the heavens
Mal 2:16 has *c* over his garment
Mt 8:24 boat . . . being *c* by the waves
10:26 nothing *c* over that will not
Lu 2:44 they *c* a day's distance and
Ro 4:7 and whose sins have been *c*
1Co 11:6 or shaved, let her be *c*
11:7 ought not to have his head *c*

Covering

Ge 8:13 remove the *c* of the ark and
20:16 for you a *c* of the eyes to
Ex 10:15 went *c* the visible surface
22:27 his only *c*. It is his mantle
24:15 the cloud was *c* the mountain
26:14 *c* for the tent of ram skins
26:14 a *c* of sealskins up on top
35:11 with its tent and its *c*
36:19 a *c* for the tent out of ram
36:19 *c* out of sealskins up on top
39:34 its *c* of ram skins dyed red
39:34 its *c* of sealskins and the
40:19 the *c* of the tent above upon
Le 9:19 fat *c* and the kidneys and
Nu 3:25 the tent, its *c* and the screen
4:6 put a *c* of sealskins over it
4:8 *c* of sealskins and put in its
4:10 into a *c* of sealskins and put
4:11 *c* of sealskins and put in its
4:12 *c* of sealskins and put them
4:14 over it a *c* of sealskins and
4:15 finish *c* the holy place and
4:25 tent of meeting, its *c* and
4:25 sealskin *c* that is on top
16:33 the earth went *c* them over
22:11 they go *c* the earth as far as
1Ki 11:29 Ahijah was *c* himself with
Job 24:7 without any *c* in the cold
24:15 over his face he puts a *c*
26:6 place of destruction has no *c*
31:19 the poor one had no *c*
Ps 106:11 came *c* their adversaries
147:8 One who is *c* the heavens
Pr 10:18 *c* over hatred there are lips
11:13 in spirit is *c* over a matter
12:16 is *c* over a dishonor
12:23 shrewd man is *c* knowledge
17:9 one *c* over transgression is
28:13 is *c* over his transgressions
Isa 11:9 waters are *c* the very sea
14:11 and worms are your *c*
23:18 and for elegant *c*
30:22 *c* of your molten statue of
50:3 sackcloth itself their *c*
Jer 3:25 our humiliation keeps *c* us
Eze 1:11 and two were *c* their bodies
1:23 had two wings *c* on this side
1:23 *c* on that side their bodies
27:7 your deck *c* proved to be
28:13 precious stone was your *c*
28:14 anointed cherub that is *c*
28:16 O cherub that is *c*, from
Ho 2:9 linen for *c* her nakedness
Na 3:5 will put the *c* of your skirts
Mal 2:13 *c* with tears the altar of
Mt 7:15 come to you in sheep's *c*
Lu 22:64 after *c* him over they would
1Ti 6:8 So, having sustenance and *c*

Coverings

Ge 3:7 and made loin *c* for themselves

Coverlet

2Ki 8:15 a *c* and dip it in water and

Coverlets

Pr 7:16 *c* I have bedecked my divan
31:22 *C* she has made for herself

Covers

Ex 29:13 the fat that *c* the intestines
29:22 the fat that *c* the intestines
Le 3:3 the fat that *c* the intestines
Le 3:9 the fat that *c* the intestines
3:14 the fat that *c* the intestines
4:8 fat that *c* over the intestines
7:3 the fat that *c* the intestines
Job 9:24 The face of its judges he *c*
15:27 *c* his face with his
22:11 mass of water itself *c* you
Ps 55:5 and shuddering *c* me
Pr 10:6 it *c* up violence
10:11 it *c* up violence
10:12 love *c* over even all
Lu 8:16 *c* it with a vessel or puts it
1Pe 4:8 love *c* a multitude of sins

Covert

Job 38:40 in the *c* for an ambush
Ps 10:9 like a lion in his *c*
27:5 he will hide me in his *c*
76:2 *c* proves to be in Salem
Jer 25:38 left his *c* just like a

Covet

Ro 7:7 had not said: You must not *c*
13:9 You must not *c*, and whatever

Coveted

Ac 20:33 I have *c* no man's silver or

Coveting

Jas 4:2 go on murdering and *c*, and

Covetings

Mr 7:22 *c*, acts of wickedness, deceit

Covetous

1Th 4:5 not in *c* sexual appetite such

Covetousness

Lu 12:15 guard against every sort of *c*
Ro 1:29 *c*, badness, being full of
7:7 would not have known *c* if the
7:8 worked out in me *c* of every
Col 3:5 hurtful desire, and *c*, which
1Th 2:5 or with a false front for *c*
2Pe 2:3 with *c* they will exploit you
2:14 have a heart trained in *c*

Cow

Nu 19:2 take for you a sound red *c* in
19:5 *c* must be burned under his
19:6 midst of the burning of the *c*
19:9 gather up the ashes of the *c*
19:10 gathering the ashes of the *c*
De 21:3 take a young *c* of the herd
21:4 lead the young *c* down to a
21:4 break the neck of the young *c*
21:6 young *c*, the neck of which
Jg 14:18 not plowed with my young *c*
1Sa 16:2 A young *c* of the herd you
Isa 7:21 young *c* of the herd and two
11:7 *c* and the bear themselves
Ho 4:16 like a stubborn *c*, Israel has

Cowardice

2Ti 1:7 God gave us not a spirit of *c*

Cowards

Re 21:8 *c* and those without faith and

Cower

La 3:16 has made me *c* in the ashes

Cows

Ge 32:15 forty *c* and ten bulls
41:2 seven *c* beautiful in
41:3 seven other *c* ascending after
41:3 *c* by the bank of the river
41:4 the *c* that were ugly in
41:4 seven *c* that were beautiful
41:18 seven *c* fat-fleshed and
41:19 seven other *c* ascending after
41:20 bad *c* began to eat up the
41:20 eat up the first seven fat *c*
41:26 seven good *c* are seven years
41:27 the seven skinny and bad *c*
De 7:13 the young of your *c* and the
1Sa 6:7 two *c* that are giving suck
6:7 must hitch the *c* to the wagon
6:10 two *c* that were giving suck
6:12 *c* began to go straight ahead
6:14 *c* they offered up as a burnt
Job 21:10 His *c* bring forth and suffer
Am 4:1 you *c* of Bashan, who are on

Cozbi

Nu 25:15 woman fatally struck was *C*
25:18 Peor and in the affair of *C*

Cozeba

1Ch 4:22 Jokim and the men of *C*

Crack
2Ki 12:5 wherever any *c* is found

Cracked
2Sa 17:19 heaped up *c* grain upon it
Pr 27:22 a mortar, in among *c* grain

Cracks
2Ki 12:5 repair the *c* of the house
12:6 repaired the *c* of the house
12:7 repairing the *c* of the house
12:7 the *c* of the house you should
12:8 repair the *c* of the house
12:12 *c* of the house of Jehovah
22:5 to repair the *c* of the house

Craftiness
Ex 21:14 point of killing him with *c*

Craftsman
Ex 28:11 the work of a *c* in stones
35:35 work of a *c* and an
38:23 a *c* and embroiderer and
2Ki 24:14 *c* and builder of bulwarks
Isa 40:19 *c* has cast a mere molten
40:20 A skillful *c* he searches out
41:7 the *c* went strengthening the
54:16 have created the *c*, the one
Jer 10:3 the *c* with the billhook
10:9 the workmanship of a *c* and
Ho 8:6 A mere *c* made it, and it is
Re 18:22 no *c* of any trade will ever

Craftsmanship
Ex 31:3 and in every kind of *c*
35:31 and in every sort of *c*

Craftsmen
2Ki 22:6 to the *c* and the builders and
24:16 *c* and the builders of
1Ch 4:14 *c* are what they became
29:5 work by the hand of the *c*
2Ch 24:12 *c* for renovating Jehovah's
34:11 gave it to the *c* and
Ezr 3:7 the cutters and to the *c*
Ne 11:35 and Ono, the valley of the *c*
Isa 44:11 *c* are from earthling men
Jer 24:1 the *c* and the builders of
29:2 the *c* and the builders of
Eze 21:31 the *c* of ruination
Ho 13:2 the work of *c*, all of it
Zec 1:20 Jehovah showed me four *c*
Ac 19:24 furnished the *c* no little
19:38 if Demetrius and the *c* with

Crafty
Mt 26:4 to seize Jesus by *c* device
Mr 14:1 to seize him by *c* device
2Co 12:16 you say, I was *c* and I

Crag
Nu 20:8 speak to the *c* before their
20:8 water for them from the *c*
20:10 together before the *c*
20:10 Is it from this *c* that we
20:11 struck the *c* with his rod
24:21 set on the *c* is your abode
De 32:13 suck honey out of a *c*
Jg 15:8 in a cleft of the *c* Etam
15:11 the cleft of the *c* Etam and
15:13 brought him up out of the *c*
20:45 to the *c* of Rimmon
20:47 to the *c* of Rimmon, and they
20:47 to dwell on the *c* of Rimmon
21:13 were on the *c* of Rimmon
1Sa 14:4 toothlike *c* here on this side
14:4 a toothlike *c* there on that
23:25 at once went down to the *c*
23:28 the *C* of the Divisions
2Sa 22:2 Jehovah is my *c* and my
2Ch 25:12 them to the top of the *c*
25:12 them from the top of the *c*
Ne 9:15 waters out of the *c* you
Job 39:1 goats of the *c* to give birth
39:28 on a *c* it resides and stays
39:28 Upon the tooth of a *c* and
Ps 18:2 Jehovah is my *c* and my
31:3 my *c* and my stronghold
40:2 raised up my feet upon a *c*
42:9 I will say to God my *c*
71:3 are my *c* and my stronghold
78:16 forth streams out of a *c*
137:9 children against the *c*
141:6 down by the sides of the *c*
Pr 30:26 *c* is where they put their
Ca 2:14 dove in the retreats of the *c*
Isa 22:16 in a *c* he is cutting out a
31:9 *c* will pass away out of
Isa 32:2 shadow of a heavy *c* in an
42:11 inhabitants of the *c* cry out
Jer 5:3 their faces harder than a *c*
13:4 there in a cleft of the *c*
23:29 hammer that smashes the *c*
48:28 and reside on the *c*, you
49:16 in the retreats of the *c*
Eze 24:7 bare surface of a *c* she
24:8 shining, bare surface of a *c*
26:4 bare surface of a *c*
26:14 shining, bare surface of a *c*
Am 6:12 On a *c* will horses run, or
Ob 3 residing in the retreats of the *c*

Craggy
Isa 33:16 *c* places difficult to

Crags
1Sa 13:6 hiding themselves in . . . *c*
1Ki 19:11 wind was . . . breaking *c*
Ps 104:18 *c* are a refuge for the rock
Isa 2:21 into the clefts of the *c*
7:19 upon the clefts of the *c* and
57:5 under the clefts of the *c*
Jer 16:16 out of the clefts of the *c*
51:25 roll you away from the *c*

Cramp
2Sa 1:9 *c* has seized me, because all

Cramped
Jos 19:47 territory . . . too *c* for
2Ki 6:1 dwelling before you is too *c*
Job 18:7 steps of vigor will become *c*
Pr 4:12 your pace will not be *c*
Isa 49:19 are too *c* to be dwelling
49:20 place has become too *c* for
Mt 7:14 and *c* the road leading off
2Co 4:8 but not *c* beyond movement
6:12 not *c* for room within us
6:12 *c* for room in your own

Cranium
Nu 24:17 *c* of all the sons of tumult

Crash
Job 30:22 you dissolve me with a *c*
Pr 16:18 Pride is before a *c*, and a
17:19 entryway high is seeking a *c*
18:12 Before a *c* the heart of a
Isa 1:28 the *c* of revolters and that
6:11 cities actually *c* in ruins
10:33 boughs with a terrible *c*
Jer 4:6 the north, even a great *c*
4:20, 20 *C* upon *c* is what has
6:1 the north, even a great *c*
14:17 with a great *c* the virgin
51:54 great *c* from the land of
La 2:11 the *c* of the daughter of my

Crashing
Zep 1:10 a great *c* from the hills

Crashings
Job 36:29 The *c* from his booth

Crave
De 5:21 *c* your fellowman's house
14:26 may *c* in the way of cattle
1Sa 2:16 whatever your soul may *c*

Craved
Pr 21:10 wicked one has *c* what is bad

Craves
De 12:15 whenever your soul *c* it you
12:20 your soul *c* to eat meat
12:20 whenever your soul *c* it
12:21 whenever your soul *c* it
2Sa 3:21 over all that your soul *c*
1Ki 11:37 over all that your soul *c*

Craving
Ge 3:16 your *c* will be for your
4:7 for you is its *c*; and will you
Nu 11:34 people who showed selfish *c*
De 18:6 because of any *c* of his soul
1Sa 23:20 *c* of your soul, O king
2Sa 23:15 David expressed his *c* and
1Ch 11:17 David showed his *c* and said
Pr 10:3 *c* of the wicked ones he will
11:6 by their *c* those dealing
21:25 *c* of the lazy will put him
21:26 has shown himself eagerly *c*
23:3 yourself *c* his tasty dishes
23:6 yourself *c* his tasty dishes
24:1 *c* to get in with them
Ca 7:10 and toward me is his *c*
Jer 2:24 *c* of her soul, snuffing up
17:16 I did not show any *c*
Ho 10:10 When it is my *c* I shall also
Am 5:18 who are *c* the day of Jehovah
Mic 7:3 the *c* of his soul, his very

Cravings
Ps 140:8 the *c* of the wicked one
Jas 4:1 your *c* for sensual pleasure
4:3 your *c* for sensual pleasure

Crazed
Jer 25:16 act like *c* men because of
51:7 the nations keep acting *c*

Crazily
Isa 44:25 diviners themselves act *c*

Crazy
1Sa 21:14 you see a man behaving *c*
21:15 in need of people driven *c*
21:15 this one to behave *c* by me
2Ki 9:11 Why did this *c* man come in
Job 12:17 judges themselves go *c*
Ec 7:7 may make a wise one act *c*
Jer 50:38 visions they keep acting *c*

Create
Ge 1:21 God proceeded to *c* the great
1:27 God proceeded to *c* the man
Nu 16:30 created that Jehovah will *c*
Ps 51:10 *C* in me even a pure heart
Isa 4:5 *c* over every established place
45:18 not *c* it simply for nothing
Eph 2:15 *c* the two peoples in union

Created
Ge 1:1 God *c* the heavens and the earth
1:27 in God's image he *c* him
1:27 male and female he *c* them
2:3 his work that God has *c* for
2:4 time of their being *c*, in the
5:2 Male and female he *c* them
5:2 in the day of their being *c*
6:7 wipe men whom I have *c* off
Ex 34:10 never been *c* in all the earth
Nu 16:30 if it is something *c* that
De 4:32 the day that God *c* man on the
Ps 89:12 south—you yourself *c* them
89:47 in vain that you have *c* all
102:18 people that is to be *c* will
104:30 your spirit, they are *c*
148:5 commanded, and they were *c*
Isa 40:26 Who has *c* these things?
41:20 Holy One of Israel . . . *c* it
43:7 have *c* for my own glory
45:8 myself, Jehovah, have *c* it
45:12 have *c* even man upon it
48:7 they must be *c*, and not
54:16 have *c* the craftsman
54:16 have *c* the ruinous man for
Jer 31:22 Jehovah has *c* a new thing
Eze 21:30 the place that you were *c*
28:13 In the day of your being *c*
28:15 the day of your being *c*
Mal 2:10 one God that has *c* us
Mt 19:4 that he who *c* them from the
Mr 13:19 the creation which God *c*
Ro 1:25 One who *c*, who is blessed
1Co 11:9 man was not *c* for the sake
Eph 2:10 *c* in union with Christ Jesus
3:9 in God, who *c* all things
4:24 *c* according to God's will
Col 1:16 all other things were *c* in
1:16 *c* through him and for him
3:10 image of the One who *c* it
1Ti 4:3 God *c* to be partaken of with
Re 4:11 because you *c* all things, and
4:11 they existed and were *c*
10:6 who *c* the heaven and the

Creating
Ge 5:1 In the day of God's *c* Adam he
Isa 45:7 Forming light and *c* darkness
45:7 making peace and *c* calamity
57:19 *c* the fruit of the lips
65:17 *c* new heavens and a new
65:18 forever in what I am *c*
65:18 I am *c* Jerusalem a cause

Creation
Mr 10:6 from the beginning of *c* He
13:19 from the beginning of the *c*
Ro 1:20 from the world's *c* onward
1:25 sacred service to the *c*
8:19 eager expectation of the *c*
8:20 *c* was subjected to futility
8:21 *c* itself also will be set
8:22 *c* keeps on groaning together
8:39 *c* will be able to separate

2Co 5:17 with Christ, he is a new *c*
Ga 6:15 but a new *c* is something
Col 1:15 the firstborn of all *c*
1:23 all *c* that is under heaven
1Ti 4:4 that every *c* of God is fine
Heb 4:13 not a *c* that is not manifest
9:11 that is, not of this *c*
1Pe 2:13 to every human *c*: whether to
Re 3:14 the beginning of the *c* by God

Creation's
2Pe 3:4 exactly as from *c* beginning

Creator
Ec 12:1 Remember, now, your Grand *C*
Isa 40:28 Jehovah, the *C* of the
42:5 the *C* of the heavens and the
43:1 your *C*, O Jacob, and your
43:15 the *C* of Israel, your King
45:18 the *C* of the heavens, He the
Am 4:13 and the *C* of the wind
1Pe 4:19 their souls to a faithful *C*

Creature
Ge 1:21 and every winged flying *c*
1:28 every living *c* that is moving
1:30 flying *c* of the heavens
2:19 flying *c* of the heavens
6:7 to flying *c* of the heavens
6:19 every living *c* of every sort
7:14 every flying *c* of the heavens
7:14 every bird, every winged *c*
7:23 wiped out . . . flying *c* of
8:17 Every living *c* that is with
8:19 Every living *c* . . . went out
8:19 every flying *c* . . . went out
9:2 every living *c* of the earth
9:2 every flying *c* of the heavens
9:5 hand of every living *c* shall I
9:10 every living *c* of the earth
Le 5:2 body of an unclean swarming *c*
11:2 living *c* that you may
11:3 Every *c* that splits the hoof
11:10 swarming *c* of the waters
11:20 swarming *c* that goes on all
11:23 other winged swarming *c* that
11:27 every *c* going upon its paws
11:41 swarming *c* that swarms upon
11:42 *c* that goes upon the belly
11:42 any *c* that goes on all fours
11:43 any swarming *c* that swarms
11:44 swarming *c* that moves upon
11:46 flying *c* and every living
11:47 living *c* that is eatable and
11:47 the living *c* that may not be
De 14:19 every winged swarming *c* is
14:20 clean flying *c* you may eat
28:26 food for every flying *c*
Ps 50:11 I well know every winged *c*
Ec 10:20 a flying *c* of the heavens
Isa 16:2 like a fleeing winged *c*
Jer 9:10 the flying *c* of the heavens
Eze 1:20 spirit of the living *c* was
1:21 spirit of the living *c* was
10:15 same living *c* that I had
10:17 spirit of the living *c* was
10:20 the living *c* that I had seen
44:31 no *c* torn to pieces of the
Da 7:6 four wings of a flying *c* on
Ho 2:18 flying *c* of the heavens and
4:3 the flying *c* of the heavens
9:11 like a flying *c* their glory
Zep 1:3 the flying *c* of the heavens
Ac 28:4 venomous *c* hanging from his
28:5 he shook the venomous *c* off
Jas 3:7 and sea *c* is to be tamed and
Re 4:7 first living *c* is like a lion
4:7 living *c* is like a young bull
4:7 *c* has a face like a man's
4:7 fourth living *c* is like a
5:13 every *c* that is in heaven and
6:3 heard the second living *c* say
6:5 heard the third living *c* say
6:7 voice of the fourth living *c*

Creatures
Ge 1:20 let flying *c* fly over the
1:22 let the flying *c* become many
1:26 the flying *c* of the heavens
1:28 the flying *c* of the heavens
2:20 the flying *c* of the heavens
6:20 flying *c* according to their
7:3 flying *c* of the heavens by
7:8 of the flying *c* and everything
7:21 expired, among the flying *c*
8:17 among the flying *c* and among
Ge 8:20 clean flying *c* and to offer
9:10 all living *c* of the earth
Le 11:13 loathe among the flying *c*
11:21 the winged swarming *c* that
11:27 *c* that go on all fours, they
11:29 to you among the swarming *c*
11:31 among all the swarming *c*
11:42 the swarming *c* that swarm
1Ki 4:33 about the flying *c* and about
Job 12:7 winged *c* . . . will tell you
28:21 from the flying *c* of the
35:11 the flying *c* of the heavens
Ps 78:27 winged flying *c* just like
104:12 roost the flying *c* of the
104:25 Living *c*, small as well as
Isa 57:16 *c* that I myself have made
Jer 4:25 the flying *c* of the heavens
5:27 cage is full of flying *c*
7:33 food for the flying *c*
12:4 the beasts and the flying *c*
15:3 the flying *c* of the heavens
16:4 as food for the flying *c*
19:7 as food to the flying *c*
34:20 flying *c* of the heavens
50:6 perishing *c* my people has
Eze 1:5 the likeness of four living *c*
1:13 the likeness of the living *c*
1:13 between the living *c*, and
1:14 on the part of the living *c*
1:15 As I kept seeing the living *c*
1:15 the earth beside the living *c*
1:19 *c* went, the wheels would go
1:19 living *c* were lifted up from
1:22 the heads of the living *c*
3:13 wings of the living *c* that
29:5 the flying *c* of the heavens
31:6 flying *c* of the heavens
31:13 flying *c* of the heavens
32:4 flying *c* of the heavens to
38:20 the flying *c* of the heavens
44:31 of the flying *c*
Da 2:38 winged *c* of the heavens
Ho 7:12 flying *c* of the heavens
Ac 10:12 four-footed *c* and creeping
11:6 four-footed *c* of the earth
Ro 1:23 birds and four-footed *c* and
Jas 1:18 certain firstfruits of his *c*
Re 4:6 four living *c* that are full of
4:8 as for the four living *c*, each
4:9 living *c* offer glory and honor
5:6 throne and of the four living *c*
5:8 the four living *c* and the
5:11 living *c* and the elders, and
5:14 four living *c* went saying
6:1 one of the four living *c* say
6:6 midst of the four living *c*
7:11 and the four living *c*, and
8:9 the *c* that are in the sea
14:3 before the four living *c*
15:7 one of the four living *c*
19:4 four living *c* fell down

Credence
Lu 1:1 that are given full *c* among us

Credit
Lu 6:32 of what *c* is it to you?
6:33 really of what *c* is it to you?
6:34 of what *c* is it to you?
1Co 8:8 we have no *c* to ourselves
2Co 12:6 my *c* more than what he sees
Php 4:17 more *c* to your account

Creditor
De 15:2 a releasing by every *c* of
1Sa 22:2 all men who had a *c* and all
2Ki 4:1 *c* himself has come to take

Creditors
Isa 50:1 which one of my *c* is it to

Creeping
Ps 148:10 *c* things and winged birds
Eze 8:10 representation of *c* things
38:20, 20 *c* things that are *c* on
Ho 2:18 *c* thing of the ground, and
Joe 1:4 *c*, unwinged locust has eaten
1:4 what the *c*, unwinged locust
2:25 the *c*, unwinged locust, and
Hab 1:14 *c* things over whom no one
Ac 10:12 *c* things of the earth and
11:6 *c* things and birds of heaven
Ro 1:23 creatures and *c* things
Jas 3:7 *c* thing and sea creature is to

Creepy
Ps 119:120 flesh has had a *c* feeling

Crescens
2Ti 4:10 *C* to Galatia, Titus to

Cretans
Ac 2:11 *C* and Arabians, we hear them
Tit 1:12 said: *C* are always liars

Crete
Am 9:7 and the Philistines out of *C*
Ac 27:7 under the shelter of *C* at
27:12 a harbor of *C* that opens
27:13 coasting inshore along *C*
27:21 put out to sea from *C* and
Tit 1:5 this reason I left you in *C*

Cricket
Le 11:22 the *c* according to its kind

Cried
Ge 45:1 So he *c* out: Have everybody go
Ex 8:12 and Moses *c* out to Jehovah
15:25 Then he *c* out to Jehovah
17:4 Moses *c* out to Jehovah
Nu 20:16 we *c* out to Jehovah and he
1Ki 20:39 he *c* out to the king and
2Ki 4:1 *c* out to Elisha, saying
4:40 *c* out and began saying
6:26 certain woman *c* out to him
Es 8:15 Shushan itself *c* out shrilly
Job 38:7 morning stars joyfully *c* out
Ps 22:5 To you they *c* out, and they
22:24 when he *c* to him for help he
30:2 I *c* to you for help, and you
31:22 when I *c* to you for help
34:17 They *c* out, and Jehovah
88:1 By day I have *c* out
88:13 I myself have *c* for help
Pr 20:25 rashly *c* out, Holy! and after
Isa 33:7 heroes have *c* out in the
La 2:18 heart has *c* out to Jehovah
Da 6:20 *c* out with a sad voice even
Jon 2:2 Out of the belly of Sheol I *c*
Mt 14:26 And they *c* out in their fear
14:30 he *c* out: Lord, save me!
15:22 *c* aloud, saying: Have mercy
20:30 *c* out, saying: Lord, have
20:31 yet they *c* all the louder
27:50 Again Jesus *c* out with a
Mr 5:7 he had *c* out with a loud voice
6:49 apparition! and they *c* aloud
15:13 they *c* out: Impale him!
15:14 *c* out all the more: Impale
Lu 8:28 he *c* aloud and fell down
9:38 a man *c* out from the crowd
18:38 he *c* out, saying: Jesus, Son
23:18 whole multitude they *c* out
Joh 1:15 actually *c* out—this was the
7:28 *c* out as he was teaching in
7:37 Jesus . . . *c* out, saying
11:43 he *c* out with a loud voice
12:44 Jesus *c* out and said
Ac 7:57 *c* out at the top of the voice
7:60 he *c* out with a strong voice
24:21 one utterance which I *c* out
Re 6:10 *c* with a loud voice, saying
7:2 he *c* with a loud voice to the
10:3 he *c* out with a loud voice
10:3 when he *c* out, the seven
18:2 *c* out with a strong voice
18:18 *c* out as they looked at the
18:19 dust upon their heads and *c*
19:17 he *c* out with a loud voice

Cries
Ex 22:23 if he *c* out to me at all
Job 3:24 And like waters my roaring *c*
24:12 wounded ones *c* for help
Ps 32:7 joyful *c* at providing escape
63:5 with lips of joyful *c* my
Pr 29:6 righteous *c* out joyfully and
Isa 10:30 your voice out in shrill *c*
14:7 cheerful with joyful *c*
15:5 own heart *c* out over Moab
26:17 *c* out in her birth pangs
43:14 whining *c* on their part
46:7 One even *c* out to it, but
Zep 3:17 joyful over you with happy *c*
Lu 9:39 he *c* out, and it throws him
Ro 9:27 Isaiah *c* out concerning Israel
Ga 4:6 and it *c* out: *Abba*, Father!
Re 12:2 she *c* out in her pains and in

Crime
Lu 23:4 I find no *c* in this man

Crimson
2Ch 2:7 and *c* and blue thread, and

2Ch 2:14 in fine fabric and in *c* and
3:14 dyed reddish purple and *c*
Isa 1:18 should be red like *c* cloth
Na 2:3 are dressed in *c* stuff

Cringe
De 33:29 enemies will *c* before you

Cringing
2Sa 22:45 Foreigners . . . will come *c*
Ps 18:44 Foreigners . . . will come *c*
66:3 enemies will come *c* to you
81:15 they will come *c* to him

Crippled
Lu 14:13 poor people, *c*, lame, blind
14:21 the poor and *c* and blind and

Crispus
Ac 18:8 *C* the presiding officer of
1Co 1:14 baptized none . . . except *C* and

Critical
2Ti 3:1 last days *c* times hard to

Criticize
1Ti 5:1 not severely *c* an older man

Criticized
Ge 21:25 When Abraham *c* Abimelech

Crook
Le 27:32 that passes under the *c*, the

Crooked
De 32:5 A generation *c* and twisted!
2Sa 22:27 with the *c* one you will act
Job 9:20 then he would declare me *c*
Ps 18:26 the *c* one you will show
101:4 *c* heart departs from me
125:5 aside to their *c* ways
146:9 the wicked ones he makes *c*
Pr 2:15 whose paths are *c* and who
8:8 there is nothing twisted or *c*
10:9 making his ways *c* will make
11:20 *c* at heart are something
14:2 *c* in his ways is despising
17:20 is *c* at heart will not find
19:1 than the one *c* in his lips
21:8 a stranger, is *c* in his way
22:5 are in the way of the *c* one
28:6 than anyone *c* in his ways
28:18 *c* in his ways will fall at
Ec 1:15 *c* cannot be made straight
7:13 straight what he has made *c*
Isa 27:1 Leviathan, the *c* serpent
59:8 roadways they have made *c*
La 3:36 a man *c* in his legal case
Mic 3:9 everything that is straight *c*
Hab 1:4 reason justice goes forth *c*
Ac 2:40 saved from this *c* generation
Php 2:15 a *c* and twisted generation

Crookedness
Pr 4:24 yourself the *c* of speech
6:12 is walking with *c* of speech
Eze 9:9 and the city is full of *c*

Crop
Le 1:16 must remove its *c* with its
25:21 yield its *c* for three years
25:22 eat from the old *c* until the
25:22 coming of its *c* you will eat
Pr 14:4 *c* is abundant because of the

Crops
Le 25:15 years of the *c* he should sell
25:16 number of the *c* is what he
25:20 not sow seed or gather our *c*
Ps 107:37 they may yield fruitful *c*
Lu 12:17 have nowhere to gather my *c*
Re 22:2 producing twelve *c* of fruit

Cross
Ge 31:21 to get up and *c* the River
32:16 *C* over ahead of me, and you
Nu 32:5 Do not make us *c* the Jordan
34:4 and *c* over to Zin, and its
De 2:24 *c* the torrent valley of Arnon
4:21 I should not *c* the Jordan or
12:10 *c* the Jordan and dwell in
27:2 *c* the Jordan into the land
31:2 You will not *c* this Jordan
34:4 as you will not *c* over there
Jos 1:2 now get up, *c* this Jordan
2:23 to *c* over and come to Joshua
3:1 there before they would *c*
Jg 6:33 to *c* over and camp in the low
10:9 would *c* the Jordan to fight
Ru 2:8 not *c* over from this place
1Sa 14:1 *c* over to the outpost of the
1Sa 14:4 to *c* over against the outpost
14:6 *c* over to the outpost of
21:13 making *c* marks on the doors
2Sa 15:22 to Ittai: Go and *c* over
17:16 *c* over without fail, for
19:18 was about to *c* the Jordan
19:33 *c* over with me, and I shall
19:37 *c* over with my lord the
19:39 now began to *c* the Jordan
Isa 23:6 *C* over to Tarshish
23:10 *C* over your land like the
23:12 *c* over to Kittim itself
47:2 *C* over the rivers
51:23 that we may *c* over, so that
Jer 41:10 *c* over to the sons of Ammon
Mr 4:35 Let us *c* to the other shore
Lu 8:22 Let us *c* to the other side of
16:26 neither may people *c* over

Crossbars
1Ki 7:28 were between the *c*
7:29 between the *c* there were
7:29 over the *c* it was like that

Crossed
Ge 32:10 with but my staff I *c* this
32:22 *c* over the ford of Jabbok
De 2:14 *c* the torrent valley of Zered
27:3 when you have *c*, in order
27:4 when you have *c* the Jordan
27:12 when you have *c* the Jordan
Jg 9:26 *c* over into Shechem, and the
12:1 *c* over northward and said to
12:1 you *c* over to fight against
1Sa 13:7 Hebrews even *c* the Jordan to
2Sa 10:17 Israel and *c* the Jordan and
15:22 Ittai the Gittite *c* over
16:1 David himself had *c* over a
17:24 *c* the Jordan, he and all the
19:18 he *c* the ford to conduct
19:39 and the king himself *c*
19:40 Chimham himself *c* with
24:5 they *c* the Jordan and took
1Ki 19:19 So Elijah *c* over to him and
1Ch 12:15 the ones that *c* the Jordan
19:17 *c* the Jordan and came to
Ne 9:11 *c* over through the midst of
Jer 48:32 shoots have *c* over the sea
Mt 16:5 disciples *c* to the other side
Mr 5:21 Jesus had *c* back again in the

Crossing
Ge 32:21 the gift went *c* over ahead
Nu 32:7 from *c* into the land that
33:51 You are *c* the Jordan into the
35:10 You are *c* the Jordan to the
De 2:13 *c* the torrent valley of Zered
4:22 I am not *c* the Jordan, but
4:22 but you are *c*, and you must
4:26 *c* the Jordan to take
9:1 *c* the Jordan to go in and
9:3 your God is *c* before you
11:8 land to which you are *c* to
11:11 *c* to take possession of it
11:31 you are *c* the Jordan to go
30:18 ground to which you are *c*
31:3 God is the one *c* before you
31:3 Joshua is the one *c* before you
31:13 soil to which you are *c* the
32:47 are *c* the Jordan to take
Jos 1:11 are *c* this Jordan to go in
24:11 you went *c* the Jordan and
Jg 8:4 to the Jordan, *c* it, he and the
11:20 *c* through his territory, and
1Sa 14:8 we are *c* over to the men
2Sa 2:29 *c* the Jordan and marching
15:18 servants were *c* at his side
15:18 *c* before the king's face
15:23 the people were *c* over
15:23 the people were *c* over upon
15:24 *c* over from the city
17:22 kept *c* the Jordan until the
Ps 66:6 the river they went *c* over on
Pr 8:2 *c* of the roadways it has
Isa 23:2 the ones *c* over the sea
51:23 the street for those *c* over
Mt 15:29 *C* country from there, Jesus
Ac 21:2 boat that was *c* to Phoenicia

Crossness
Ec 7:3 by the *c* of the face the heart

Crossways
Eze 21:21 stood still at the *c*, at

Crouch
Job 38:40 they *c* in the hiding places
Ps 107:39 they become few and *c* down
Jer 5:26 as when birdcatchers *c* down

Crouching
Ge 4:7 there is sin *c* at the entrance
1Ki 18:42 *c* to the earth and keeping

Crow
Lu 22:34 cock will not *c* today until
Joh 13:38 A cock will by no means *c*

Crowd
Ge 17:4 a father of a *c* of nations
17:5 a father of a *c* of nations
Ex 23:2 follow after the *c* for evil
23:2 to turn aside with the *c* in
Nu 11:4 mixed *c* that was in the midst
Jg 4:7 his war chariots and his *c*
2Sa 6:19 to the whole *c* of Israel
1Ki 20:13 you seen all this great *c*
20:28 this great *c* into your hand
2Ki 7:13 same as all the *c* of Israel
7:13 same as all the *c* of Israel
25:11 and the rest of the *c*
2Ch 13:8 when you are a large *c* and
14:11 we have come against this *c*
20:2 large *c* from the region of
20:12 large *c* that is coming
20:15 because of this large *c*
20:24 their faces toward the *c*
32:7 all the *c* that is with him
Job 31:34 suffer a shock at a large *c*
Ps 42:4 Of a *c* celebrating a festival
68:27 Judah with their shouting *c*
Isa 5:13 *c* will be parched with
5:14 *c* and her uproar and the
13:4 Listen! A *c* in the mountains
29:5 *c* of those strange to you
29:5 *c* of the tyrants just like
29:7 *c* of all the nations that
29:8 *c* of all the nations that
Eze 7:12 hot feeling against all its *c*
7:13 the vision is for all its *c*
7:14 feeling is against all its *c*
23:42 the sound of a *c* at ease
30:10 the *c* of Egypt to cease
30:15 cut off the *c* of No
31:2 king of Egypt and to his *c*
31:18 Pharaoh and all his *c*, is
32:12 *c* to fall by the very
32:12 her *c* must be annihilated
32:16 over all its *c* they will
32:18 lament over the *c* of Egypt
32:24 are Elam and all her *c*
32:25 for her among all her *c*
32:26 and Tubal and all her *c* are
32:31 be comforted over all his *c*
32:32 even Pharaoh and all his *c*
39:11 to bury Gog and all his *c*
39:11 the Valley of Gog's *C*
39:15 in the Valley of Gog's *C*
Da 10:6 was like the sound of a *c*
11:10 *c* of large military forces
11:11 have a large *c* stand up
11:11 *c* will actually be given
11:12 *c* will certainly be carried
11:13 set up a *c* larger than the
Mt 8:18 Jesus saw a *c* around him
9:23 and the *c* in noisy confusion
9:25 the *c* had been sent outside
13:2 *c* was standing on the beach
14:5 he feared the *c*, because they
14:14 a great *c*; and he felt pity
15:10 he called the *c* near and
15:31 *c* felt amazement as they
15:32 said: I feel pity for the *c*
15:33 loaves to satisfy a *c* of
15:35 instructing the *c* to recline
17:14 when they came toward the *c*
20:29 a great *c* followed him
20:31 *c* sternly told them to keep
21:8 Most of the *c* spread their
21:26 we have the *c* to fear, for
26:47 *c* with swords and clubs
27:15 release a prisoner to the *c*
27:24 before the *c*, saying: I am
Mr 2:4 to Jesus on account of the *c*
2:13 all the *c* kept coming to him
3:9 *c* might not press upon him
3:20 Once more the *c* gathered, so
3:32 a *c* was sitting around him
4:1 great *c* gathered near him, so
4:1 *c* beside the sea were on the
4:36 they had dismissed the *c*
5:21 a great *c* gathered together

Mr 5:24 a great *c* was following him
5:27 she came behind in the *c* and
5:30 he turned about in the *c* and
5:31 You see the *c* pressing in
6:34 he saw a great *c*, but he was
6:45 he himself dismissed the *c*
7:14 calling the *c* to him again
7:17 a house away from the *c*
7:33 he took him away from the *c*
8:1 a big *c* and they had nothing
8:2 I feel pity for the *c*, because
8:6 he instructed the *c* to recline
8:6 and they served them to the *c*
8:34 called the *c* to him with his
9:14 they noticed a great *c* about
9:15 the *c* caught sight of him
9:17 one of the *c* answered him
9:25 Jesus, now noticing that a *c*
10:46 *c* were going out of Jericho
11:18 all the *c* was continually
11:32 They were in fear of the *c*
12:12 they feared the *c*, for they
12:37 the great *c* was listening to
12:41 the *c* was dropping money
14:43 a *c* with swords and clubs
15:8 the *c* came on up and started
15:11 stirred up the *c* to have him
15:15 wishing to satisfy the *c*
Lu 5:1 when the *c* was pressing close
5:19 on account of the *c*, they
5:29 great *c* of tax collectors and
6:17 a great *c* of his disciples
6:19 the *c* were seeking to touch
7:9 turned to the *c* following him
7:11 a great *c* were traveling with
7:12 considerable *c* from the city
8:4 great *c* had collected together
8:19 to him because of the *c*
8:40 the *c* received him kindly
9:12 Dismiss the *c*, that they may
9:16 to set before the *c*
9:37 a great *c* met him
9:38 a man cried out from the *c*
11:27 woman out of the *c* raised
12:1 the *c* had gathered together
12:13 one of the *c* said to him
13:14 began to say to the *c*
13:17 the *c* began to rejoice at all
18:36 he heard a *c* moving through
19:3 but he could not for the *c*
19:39 Pharisees from the *c* said to
22:6 without a *c* around
22:47 a *c*, and the man called
Joh 5:13 there being a *c* in the place
6:2 a great *c* kept following him
6:5 a great *c* was coming to him
6:22 *c* that was standing on the
6:24 *c* saw that neither Jesus was
7:12 but he misleads the *c*
7:20 *c* answered: You have a demon
7:31 the *c* put faith in him
7:32 The Pharisees heard the *c*
7:40 *c* that heard these words
7:43 division . . . among the *c*
7:49 *c* that does not know the Law
11:42 account of the *c* standing
12:9 great *c* of the Jews got to
12:12 great *c* that had come to
12:17 *c* that was with him when
12:18 *c*, because they heard he
12:29 *c* that stood about and heard
12:34 *c* answered him: We heard
Ac 1:15 *c* of persons was all together
6:7 great *c* of priests began to
11:24 *c* was added to the Lord
11:26 and taught quite a *c*, and
14:14 and leaped out into the *c*
16:22 *c* rose up together against
17:8 agitated the *c* and the city
19:26 persuaded a considerable *c*
19:33 Alexander out of the *c*, the
19:35 recorder had quieted the *c*
21:27 all the *c* into confusion
21:34 some in the *c* began shouting
21:35 of the violence of the *c*
24:18 not with a *c* or with a
Re 7:9 a great *c*, which no man was
19:1 voice of a great *c* in heaven
19:6 as a voice of a great *c* and

Crowded
Da 6:11 *c* in and found Daniel

Crowds
Eze 32:20 and all her *c*, you men
Joe 3:14, 14 *C*, *c* are in the low
Mt 4:25 great *c* followed him from
5:1 When he saw the *c* he went up
7:28 *c* were astounded at his way
8:1 great *c* followed him
9:8 the *c* were struck with fear
9:33 *c* felt amazement and said
9:36 On seeing the *c* he felt pity
11:7 Jesus started to say to the *c*
12:23 *c* were simply carried away
12:46 he was yet speaking to the *c*
13:2 and great *c* gathered to him
13:34 Jesus spoke to the *c* by
13:36 after dismissing the *c* he
14:13 the *c*, getting to hear of it
14:15 send the *c* away, that they
14:19 commanded the *c* to recline
14:19 disciples in turn to the *c*
14:22 while he sent the *c* away
14:23 having sent the *c* away, he
15:30 Then great *c* approached him
15:36 disciples in turn to the *c*
15:39 after sending the *c* away, he
19:2 great *c* followed him, and he
21:9 As for the *c*, those going
21:11 *c* kept telling: This is the
21:46 they feared the *c*, because
22:33 the *c* were astounded at his
23:1 Jesus spoke to the *c* and to
26:55 Jesus said to the *c*: Have
27:20 older men persuaded the *c* to
Mr 10:1 again *c* came together to him
Lu 3:7 *c* coming out to be baptized by
3:10 And the *c* would ask him
4:42 the *c* began hunting about for
5:3 he began teaching the *c*
5:15 great *c* would come together
7:24 say to the *c* concerning John
8:42 the *c* thronged him
8:45 the *c* are hemming you in and
9:11 But the *c*, getting to know it
9:18 Who are the *c* saying that I
11:14 spoke. And the *c* marveled
11:29 the *c* were massing together
12:54 went on to say also to the *c*
14:25 great *c* were traveling with
23:4 to the chief priests and the *c*
23:48 the *c* that were gathered
Joh 7:12 talk about him among the *c*
Ac 8:6 *c* were paying attention to
13:45 the Jews got sight of the *c*
14:11 the *c*, seeing what Paul had
14:13 offer sacrifices with the *c*
14:18 scarcely restrained the *c*
14:19 persuaded the *c*, and they
Re 17:15 mean peoples and *c* and

Crowed
Mt 26:74 And immediately a cock *c*
Mr 14:72 a cock *c* a second time
Lu 22:60 was yet speaking, a cock *c*
Joh 18:27 and immediately a cock *c*

Crown
Ge 49:26 the *c* of the head of the one
Le 13:42 in the baldness of the *c*
13:42 baldness of his *c* or of his
13:43 in the baldness of his *c* or
De 28:35 to the *c* of your head
33:16 the *c* of the head of the one
33:20 yes, the *c* of the head
2Sa 12:30 *c* of Malcam off its head
14:25 to the *c* of his head there
1Ch 20:2 David took the *c* of Malcam
Es 8:15 with a great *c* of gold, and a
Job 2:7 his foot to the *c* of his head
19:9 takes away the *c* of my head
31:36 around me like a grand *c*
Ps 7:16 upon the *c* of his head his
21:3 a *c* of refined gold
68:21 The hairy *c* of the head of
Pr 4:9 *c* of beauty it will bestow
12:4 capable wife is a *c* to her
14:24 The *c* of the wise is their
16:31 Gray-headedness is a *c* of
17:6 *c* of old men is the grandsons
Isa 3:17 *c* of the head of the
28:1 Woe to the eminent *c* of the
28:5 become as a *c* of decoration
62:3 *c* of beauty in the hand of
Jer 2:16 feeding on you at the *c* of
13:18 your *c* of beauty will
48:45 *c* of the head of the sons
La 5:16 The *c* of our head has fallen
Eze 16:12 a beautiful *c* on your head
Eze 21:26 and lift off the *c*
Zec 6:11 make a grand *c* and put it
6:14 grand *c* itself will come to
Mt 27:29 braided a *c* out of thorns
Mr 15:17 braided a *c* of thorns and
Joh 19:2 braided a *c* of thorns and
19:5 wearing the thorny *c* and
1Co 9:25 they may get a corruptible *c*
Php 4:1 my joy and *c*, stand firm in
1Th 2:19 or joy or *c* of exultation
2Ti 4:8 for me the *c* of righteousness
Jas 1:12 will receive the *c* of life
1Pe 5:4 the unfadable *c* of glory
Re 2:10 will give you the *c* of life
3:11 that no one may take your *c*
6:2 and a *c* was given him, and he
12:1 head was a *c* of twelve stars
14:14 golden *c* on his head and a

Crowned
Ps 8:5 and splendor you then *c* him
65:11 You have *c* the year with
2Ti 2:5 not *c* unless he has contended
Heb 2:7 glory and honor you *c* him
2:9 *c* with glory and honor for

Crowning
Ps 103:4 *c* you with loving-kindness

Crowns
Isa 23:8 Tyre, the bestower of *c*
28:3 eminent *c* of the drunkards
Eze 23:42 beautiful *c* upon their heads
Re 4:4 upon their heads golden *c*
4:10 cast their *c* before the throne
9:7 what seemed to be *c* like gold

Crows
Mt 26:34 this night, before a cock *c*
26:75 Before a cock *c*, you will
Mr 14:30 before a cock *c* twice, even
14:72 before a cock *c* twice, you
Lu 22:61 Before a cock *c* today you

Cruel
Ge 49:7 their anger, because it is *c*
De 32:33 And the *c* poison of cobras
Job 30:21 to become *c* to me
Pr 5:9 nor your years to what is *c*
11:17 *c* person is bringing
12:10 the wicked ones are *c*
17:11 *c* is the messenger that is
Isa 13:9 *c* both with fury and with
Jer 6:23 It is a *c* one, and they will
30:14 chastisement of someone *c*
50:42 *c* and will show no mercy
La 4:3 becomes *c*, like ostriches in

Cruelty
Pr 27:4 There is the *c* of rage, also

Crumbling
Isa 23:13 has set her as a *c* ruin
25:2 fortified town a *c* ruin

Crumbs
Mt 15:27 little dogs do eat of the *c*
Mr 7:28 the *c* of the little children

Crumby
Jos 9:5 proved to be dry and *c*
9:12 it is dry and has become *c*

Crush
De 9:21 *c* it, grinding it thoroughly
1Ki 13:26 *c* him and put him to death
2Ch 16:10 Asa began to *c* some others
Job 6:9 God would go ahead and *c* me
39:15 that some foot may *c* them
Ps 72:4 And let him *c* the defrauder
Pr 22:22 not *c* the afflicted one in
Isa 3:15 in that you *c* my people
28:28 but he will not *c* it
41:15 the mountains and *c* them
Da 2:40 *c* and shatter even all these
2:44 *c* and put an end to all these
7:23 trample it down and *c* it
Zec 11:6 *c* to pieces the land, and I
Mt 12:20 No bruised reed will he *c*
Ro 16:20 will *c* Satan under your feet

Crushed
Ex 32:20 and *c* it till it was fine
Le 22:24 testicles squeezed or *c* or
De 28:33 defrauded and *c* always
1Sa 12:3 or whom have I *c* or from
12:4 nor have you *c* us, nor have
1Ki 13:28 nor had it *c* the ass
2Ki 18:4 *c* to pieces the copper
18:21 this *c* reed, Egypt

2Ki 23:12 *c* them there, and he cast
2Ch 15:6 they were *c* to pieces, nation
34:7 graven images he *c* and
Job 4:20 they are *c* to pieces
5:4 are *c* in the gate without a
20:19 For he has *c* to pieces, he
22:9 of fatherless boys are *c*
34:25 at night, and they get *c*
Ps 9:9 a secure height for anyone *c*
10:10 He is *c*, he bows down
10:18 fatherless boy and the *c* one
34:18 who are *c* in spirit he saves
38:8 *c* to an extreme degree
44:19 *c* us in the place of jackals
51:8 the bones that you have *c*
51:17 A heart broken and *c*, O God
74:14 *c* to pieces the heads of
74:21 *c* one not return humiliated
89:10 have *c* Rahab, even as someone
89:23 I *c* his adversaries to pieces
90:3 man go back to *c* matter
119:20 My soul is *c* with longing
143:3 *c* my life to the very earth
Pr 26:28 false hates the one *c* by it
Ec 12:6 and the golden bowl gets *c*
12:6 for the cistern has been *c*
Isa 19:10 her weavers must become *c*
24:12 gate has been *c* to a mere
28:28 itself generally *c*
30:14 *c* to pieces without one's
30:14 among its *c* pieces a
36:6 support of this *c* reed, in
42:3 No *c* reed will he break
42:4 will not grow dim nor be *c*
53:5 was being *c* for our errors
57:15 one *c* and lowly in spirit
57:15 heart of the ones being *c*
58:6 send away the *c* ones free
Jer 44:10 they did not feel *c*, and
46:5 are *c* to pieces; and they
Eze 29:7 you got to be *c*, and you
Da 2:34 struck . . . and *c* them
2:35 *c* and became like the chaff
2:45 *c* the iron, the copper, the
6:24 and all their bones they *c*
Ho 5:11 Ephraim is . . . *c* in justice
Mic 1:7 images will all be *c* to
3:3 *c* them to pieces like what
Lu 4:18 *c* ones away with a release
Joh 19:36 not a bone of his will be *c*

Crushes
Job 4:19 One *c* them more quickly than

Crushing
De 23:1 No man castrated by *c* the
Job 19:2 And keep *c* me with words
Ps 94:5 Jehovah, they keep *c*
Isa 53:10 took delight in *c* him
La 3:34 *c* beneath one's feet all the
Da 2:40 as iron is *c* and grinding
7:7 It was devouring and *c*, and
7:19 which was devouring and *c*
Am 4:1 who are *c* the poor ones

Crusts
Job 7:5 My skin itself has formed *c*

Cry
Ge 18:20 *c* of complaint about Sodom
27:34 Esau began to *c* out in an
39:14 *c* out to the men of her
39:14 *c* out at the top of my voice
39:18 began to *c* out, he then left
41:55 people began to *c* to Pharaoh
Ex 2:23 and to *c* out in complaint
2:23 *c* for help kept going up
5:15 and began to *c* out to Pharaoh
14:10 and began to *c* out to Jehovah
22:27 he will *c* out to me, and I
Nu 11:2 began to *c* out to Moses
12:13 And Moses began to *c* out to
De 24:15 *c* out to Jehovah against you
26:7 we began to *c* out to Jehovah
Jos 6:5 should shout a great war *c*
6:20 began to shout a great war *c*
24:7 And they began to *c* out to
Jg 4:3 Israel began to *c* out to
1Sa 5:10 the Ekronites began to *c* out
5:12 *c* of the city for help kept
8:18 *c* out in that day by reason
2Sa 22:7 my *c* for help in his ears
22:42 They *c* for help, but there
1Ki 8:28 listen to the entreating *c*
22:32 began to *c* for aid
22:36 the ringing *c* began to pass
2Ki 6:5 And he began to *c* out and say
8:3 *c* out to the king for her
2Ch 6:19 entreating *c* and to the
13:14 *c* out to Jehovah, while the
13:15 broke out shouting a war *c*
13:15 of Judah shouted a war *c*
18:31 Jehoshaphat began to *c* for
20:22 the joyful *c* and praise
36:22 a *c* to pass through all his
Ezr 1:1 a *c* to pass through all his
Ne 9:4 *c* out with a loud voice to
9:27 they would *c* out to you
Es 4:1 *c* out with a loud and bitter
9:31 the fasts and their *c* for aid
Job 3:7 Let no joyful *c* come in it
6:5 Will a zebra *c* out over grass
20:5 joyful *c* of wicked people is
30:7 they would *c* out
30:20 I *c* to you for help, but
30:24 a *c* for help respecting
31:38 own ground would *c* for aid
36:13 should not *c* for help
36:19 your *c* for help take effect
38:41 young ones *c* to God for help
39:25 of chiefs and the war *c*
Ps 5:2 to the sound of my *c* for help
5:11 they will *c* out joyfully
17:1 attention to my entreating *c*
18:6 my own *c* before him for help
18:41 They *c* for help, but there
20:5 We will *c* out joyfully
28:2 when I *c* to you for help
30:5 morning there is a joyful *c*
32:11 And *c* out joyfully, all you
33:1 *C* out joyfully, O you
34:15 are toward their *c* for help
35:27 *c* out joyfully and rejoice
39:12 to my *c* for help do give ear
40:1 and heard my *c* for help
42:4 With the voice of a joyful *c*
47:1 with the sound of a joyful *c*
61:1 hear, O God, my entreating *c*
61:2 I shall *c*, even to you, when
63:7 I *c* out joyfully
65:8 cause to *c* out joyfully
67:4 rejoice and *c* out joyfully
71:23 My lips will *c* out joyfully
77:1 I will even *c* out to God
81:1 O *c* out joyfully, you people
84:2 *c* out joyfully to the living
88:2 your ear to my entreating *c*
89:12 name they *c* out joyfully
90:14 *c* out joyfully and may
92:4 of your hands I *c* out joyfully
95:1 us *c* out joyfully to Jehovah
98:4 *c* out joyfully and make
98:8 very mountains *c* out joyfully
100:2 before him with a joyful *c*
102:1 may my own *c* for help
105:43 ones even with a joyful *c*
106:44 he heard their entreating *c*
107:22 his works with a joyful *c*
118:15 voice of a joyful *c* and
119:147 that I may *c* for help
119:169 entreating *c* come near
126:2 our tongue with a joyful *c*
126:5 reap even with a joyful *c*
126:6 come in with a joyful *c*
132:9 loyal ones *c* out joyfully
132:16 without fail *c* out joyfully
142:1 I began to *c* for favor
142:6 to my entreating *c*
145:7 they will *c* out joyfully
145:19 *c* for help he will hear
149:5 *c* out joyfully on their beds
Pr 11:10 perish there is a joyful *c*
21:13 complaining *c* of the lowly
30:15 daughters that *c*: Give! Give!
Ec 9:17 *c* of one ruling among stupid
Isa 12:6 *C* out shrilly and shout for
14:31 Howl, O gate! *C* out, O city!
15:4 Heshbon and Elealeh *c* out
19:20 *c* out to Jehovah because
22:5 and the *c* to the mountain
24:14 they will *c* out joyfully
24:14 *c* out shrilly from the sea
26:19 Awake and *c* out joyfully
27:8 With a scare *c* you will
35:6 will *c* out in gladness
35:10 to Zion with a joyful *c*
42:2 not *c* out or raise his voice
42:11 of the crag *c* out in joy
42:11 let people *c* aloud
42:13 he will let out a war *c*
Isa 44:23 Joyfully *c* out, you heavens
48:20 the sound of a joyful *c*
49:13 Give a glad *c*, you heavens
52:9 *c* out joyfully in unison
54:1 *C* out joyfully, you barren
54:1 and *c* shrilly, you that had
57:13 When you *c* for aid your
58:9 you would *c* for help, and he
61:7 *c* out joyfully over their
65:14 will *c* out joyfully
65:19 the sound of a plaintive *c*
Jer 7:16 an entreating *c* or a prayer
8:19 the sound of the *c* for help
11:14 an entreating *c* or a prayer
14:12 to their entreating *c*
18:22 Let a *c* be heard out of
20:8 as often as I speak, I *c* out
22:20 Go up onto Lebanon and *c* out
22:20 And *c* out from Abarim
25:34 Howl, you shepherds, and *c*
30:15 Why do you *c* out on account
31:7 *C* out loudly to Jacob with
31:7 *c* shrilly at the head of
31:12 *c* out joyfully on the height
47:2 men will certainly *c* out
48:4 have caused a *c* to be heard
48:20 Howl and *c* out. Tell in
48:31 in his entirety I shall *c*
48:34 *c* in Heshbon clear to
49:3 *C* out, O dependent towns of
49:29 *c* out to them, Fright is
50:15 Shout a war *c* against her
51:48 *c* out joyfully, for out
La 3:8 I call for aid and *c* for help
3:56 my relief, to my *c* for help
Eze 9:8 fall upon my face and *c* out
11:13 *c* with a loud voice and say
21:12 *C* out and howl, O son of
27:30 and will *c* out bitterly
Ho 5:8 Shout a war *c* at Beth-aven
Joe 1:14 and *c* to Jehovah for aid
2:1 a war *c* in my holy mountain
Jon 3:7 he had the *c* made, and he had
Hab 1:2 O Jehovah, must I *c* for help
2:11 a stone itself will *c* out
Zep 1:14 man is letting out a *c*
3:14 Joyfully *c* out, O daughter
Zec 2:10 *C* out loudly and rejoice
6:8 *c* out to me and speak to me
Mt 11:16 *c* out to their playmates
12:19 not wrangle, nor *c* aloud
25:6 a *c*, Here is the bridegroom!
Mr 3:11 *c* out, saying: You are the
15:37 Jesus let out a loud *c* and
Lu 1:42 called out with a loud *c* and
18:7 chosen ones who *c* out to him
19:40 the stones would *c* out
Ac 8:7 *c* out with a loud voice and
19:34 one *c* arose from them all as
23:6 to *c* out in the Sanhedrin
Ro 8:15 spirit we *c* out: *Abba*, Father!
Ga 4:27 *c* aloud, you woman who does

Crying
Ge 4:10 Your brother's blood is *c*
39:15 raised my voice and began *c*
Ex 5:8 *c* out, saying, We want to go
14:15 Why do you keep *c* out to me?
Jg 10:12 and you went *c* out to me
18:23 kept *c* out to the sons of Dan
1Sa 4:13 the whole city began *c* out
15:11 he kept *c* out to Jehovah all
28:12 *c* out at the top of her
2Sa 13:19 *c* out as she walked
19:4 *c* out with a loud voice
19:28 *c* out further to the king
2Ki 2:12 *c* out: My father, my father
8:5 *c* out to the king for her
11:14 *c*: Conspiracy! Conspiracy!
2Ch 32:20 *c* to the heavens for aid
Job 19:7 I keep *c* out, Violence! but I
19:7 I keep *c* for help, but there
29:12 the afflicted one *c* for help
30:28 I kept *c* for help
35:9 They keep *c* for help
35:12 they keep *c* out, but he
Ps 18:6 to my God I kept *c* for help
72:12 the poor one *c* for help
107:6 *c* out to Jehovah in their
107:28 *c* out to Jehovah in their
Pr 1:20 wisdom itself keeps *c* aloud
8:3 entrances it keeps *c* loudly
Isa 16:10 there is no joyful *c* out
35:2 joyousness and with glad *c*

Isa 52:8 they keep *c* out joyfully
Da 3:4 the herald was *c* out loudly
Ho 8:2 To me they keep *c*, O my God
Mt 3:3 is *c* out in the wilderness
9:27 *c* out and saying: Have mercy
15:23 she keeps *c* out after us
21:9 kept *c* out: Save, we pray
21:15 boys . . . *c* out in the temple
27:23 *c* out all the more: Let him
Mr 1:3 is *c* out in the wilderness
5:5 he was *c* out in the tombs and
9:24 *c* out, the father of the
9:26 after *c* out and going through
11:9 those coming behind kept *c*
Lu 3:4 is *c* out in the wilderness
4:41 *c* out and saying: You are the
7:32 *c* out to one another, and who
Joh 1:23 *c* out in the wilderness
Ac 14:14 out into the crowd, *c* out
16:17 and *c* out with the words
17:6 *c* out: These men that have
19:28 began *c* out, saying: Great is
19:32 some were *c* out one thing
21:28 *c* out: Men of Israel, help!
21:36 *c* out: Take him away!
22:23 they were *c* out and throwing
Jas 5:4 keep *c* out, and the calls
Re 7:10 *c* with a loud voice, saying
14:15 *c* with a loud voice to the

Crystal
Job 28:18 Coral and rock *c* themselves
Re 4:6 a glassy sea like *c*
22:1 clear as *c*, flowing out from

Crystal-clear
Re 21:11 as a jasper stone shining *c*

Cub
Ge 49:9 A lion *c* Judah is. From the
De 33:22 he said: Dan is a lion *c*
Na 2:11 where the lion's *c* was, and

Cubit
Ge 6:16 to the extent of a *c* upward
Ex 25:10 and a *c* and a half its width
25:10 and a *c* and a half its height
25:17 and a *c* and a half its width
25:23 and a *c* its width and a
25:23 and a *c* and a half its height
26:13 And the *c* on this side and
26:13 and the *c* on that side in
26:16 a *c* and a half is the width
30:2 A *c* in length and a
30:2 a *c* in width, it should be
36:21 one *c* and a half the width
37:1 and a *c* and a half its width
37:1 and a *c* and a half its height
37:6 and a *c* and a half its width
37:10 and a *c* its width, and a
37:10 and a *c* and a half its height
37:25 A *c* was its length and a
37:25 length and a *c* its width
De 3:11 its width, by the *c* of a man
Jg 3:16 its length being a *c*
1Ki 7:24 ten in a *c*, enclosing the sea
7:35 a stand a half a *c* in height
2Ch 4:3 ten in a *c*, enclosing the sea
Eze 40:5 by a *c* and a handbreadth
40:12 guard chambers was one *c*
40:12 area of one *c* on either side
40:42 length was one *c* and a half
40:42 width one *c* and a half
40:42 and the height one *c*
42:4 the inside, a way of one *c*
43:13, 13 *c* being a *c* and a
43:13 And its bottom is a *c*
43:13 And a *c* is the width
43:14 and the width is one *c*
43:14 and its width is a *c*
43:17 surrounding it is half a *c*
43:17 bottom is a *c* round about
Mt 6:27 add one *c* to his life-span
Lu 12:25 can add a *c* to his life-span

Cubits
Ge 6:15 make it: three hundred *c* the
6:15 ark, fifty *c* its width, and
6:15 ark . . . thirty *c* its height
7:20 Up to fifteen *c* the waters
Ex 25:10 two and a half *c* its length
25:17 two and a half *c* its length
25:23 two *c* its length and a cubit
26:2 tent cloth is twenty-eight *c*
26:2 of each tent cloth is four *c*
26:8 each tent cloth is thirty *c*
26:8 of each tent cloth is four *c*
Ex 26:16 Ten *c* is the length of a
27:1 five *c* its length and five
27:1 five *c* its width. The altar
27:1 and its height three *c*
27:9 a hundred *c* being the length
27:11 for a hundred *c* of length
27:12 the hangings are of fifty *c*
27:13 the width . . . is fifty *c*
27:14 fifteen *c* of hangings to one
27:15 are fifteen *c* of hangings
27:16 is a screen twenty *c* long
27:18 courtyard is a hundred *c*, and
27:18 the width fifty *c*, and the
27:18 and the height five *c*, of
30:2 and its height two *c*
36:9 tent cloth was twenty-eight *c*
36:9 each tent cloth four *c*
36:15 each tent cloth was thirty *c*
36:15 each tent cloth four *c*
36:21 Ten *c* . . . a panel frame
37:1 Two *c* and a half was its
37:6 Two *c* and a half was its
37:10 Two *c* was its length, and a
37:25 and two *c* was its height
38:1 Five *c* was its length, and
38:1 five *c* its width, it
38:1 and three *c* was its height
38:9 linen, for a hundred *c*
38:11 side there were a hundred *c*
38:12 hangings were for fifty *c*
38:13 sunrising there were fifty *c*
38:14 fifteen *c* to the one wing
38:15 hangings were for fifteen *c*
38:18 and twenty *c* was the length
38:18 its extent was five *c*
Nu 11:31 two *c* above the surface of
35:4 for a thousand *c* all around
35:5 the east side two thousand *c*
35:5 the south side two thousand *c*
35:5 the west side two thousand *c*
35:5 the north side two thousand *c*
De 3:11 Nine *c* is its length, and four
3:11 four *c* its width, by the
Jos 3:4 two thousand *c* by measure
1Sa 17:4 height being six *c* and a span
1Ki 6:2 was sixty *c* in its length
6:2 and thirty *c* in its height
6:3 was twenty *c* in its length
6:3 Ten *c* it was in its depth
6:6 was five *c* in its width
6:6 was six *c* in its width, and
6:6 was seven *c* in its width
6:10 five *c* in their height
6:16 twenty *c* at the rear sides
6:17 forty *c* that the house proved
6:20 was twenty *c* in length, and
6:20 and twenty *c* in width
6:20 and twenty *c* in its height
6:23 ten *c* being the height of
6:24 five *c* was the one wing of
6:24 five *c* was the other wing
6:24 Ten *c* it was from the tip of
6:25 the second cherub was ten *c*
6:26 the one cherub was ten *c*
7:2 a hundred *c* in its length
7:2 fifty *c* in its width, and
7:2 and thirty *c* in its height
7:6 made fifty *c* in its length
7:6 and thirty *c* in its width
7:10 stones of ten *c*, and
7:10 and stones of eight *c*
7:15 eighteen *c* being the height
7:15 twelve *c* would measure
7:16 Five *c* was the height of
7:16 five *c* was the height of
7:19 of lily work, of four *c*
7:23 make the molten sea ten *c*
7:23 and its height was five *c*
7:23 thirty *c* to circle all around
7:27 four *c* being the length of
7:27 and four *c* its width
7:27 and three *c* its height
7:31 and upward was [?] *c*
7:31 a stand of one and a half *c*
7:32 wheel was one and a half *c*
7:38 Each basin was four *c*
2Ki 14:13 corner gate, four hundred *c*
25:17 Eighteen *c* was the height
25:17 the capital was three *c*
1Ch 11:23 a man of . . . five *c*
2Ch 3:3 the length in *c* by the former
3:3 measurement being sixty *c*
3:3 and the width twenty *c*
3:4 was twenty *c* in front of the
2Ch 3:8 being twenty *c*, and its own
3:8 its own width being twenty *c*
3:11 their length was twenty *c*
3:11 one wing of five *c* reaching
3:11 and the other wing of five *c*
3:12 of the one cherub of five *c*
3:12 other wing of five *c* was in
3:13 were spread out twenty *c*
3:15 two pillars, thirty-five *c*
3:15 the capital . . . was five *c*
4:1 twenty *c* being its length
4:1 and twenty *c* its width, and
4:1 and ten *c* its height
4:2 molten sea ten *c* from its one
4:2 and its height was five *c*
4:2 line of thirty *c* to circle all
6:13 Its length was five *c*, and
6:13 its width five *c*, and its
6:13 and its height three *c*
25:23 Gate, four hundred *c*
Ezr 6:3 its height being sixty *c*, its
6:3 its width sixty *c*
Ne 3:13 a thousand *c* in the wall as
Es 5:14 make a stake fifty *c* high
7:9 the stake . . . fifty *c* high
Jer 52:21 eighteen *c* in height was
52:21 thread of twelve *c* itself
52:22 one capital was five *c*
Eze 40:5 the measuring reed of six *c*
40:7 there were five *c*; and the
40:9 the gate, eight *c*
40:9 its side pillars, two *c*
40:11 entrance of the gate, ten *c*
40:11 of the gate, thirteen *c*
40:12 guard chamber was six *c*
40:12 and six *c* on that side
40:13 a width of twenty-five *c*
40:14 side pillars of sixty *c*
40:15 inner gate was fifty *c*
40:19 Outside it was a hundred *c*
40:21 Fifty *c* was its length
40:21 width was twenty-five in *c*
40:23 gate to gate a hundred *c*
40:25 Fifty *c* was the length
40:25 breadth was twenty-five *c*
40:27 the south a hundred *c*
40:29 Fifty *c* was the length
40:29 width was twenty-five *c*
40:30 length was twenty-five *c*
40:30 and the width five *c*
40:33 The length was fifty *c*
40:33 the width twenty-five *c*
40:36 The length was fifty *c*
40:36 the width twenty-five *c*
40:47 The length was a hundred *c*
40:47 the width a hundred *c*
40:48 five *c* on this side and five
40:48 and five *c* on that side
40:48 gate was three *c* on this
40:48 and three *c* on that side
40:49 the porch was twenty *c*
40:49 and the width eleven *c*
41:1 six *c* being the width over
41:1 and six *c* the width over
41:2 the entrance was ten *c*
41:2 the entrance were five *c*
41:2 and five *c* over there
41:2 its length, forty *c*
41:2 and the width, twenty *c*
41:3 of the entrance, two *c*
41:3 and the entrance, six *c*
41:3 the entrance was seven *c*
41:4 its length, twenty *c*
41:4 and its width, twenty *c*
41:5 wall of the house, six *c*
41:5 the side chamber was four *c*
41:8 reed of six *c* to the joining
41:9 the outside, was five *c*
41:10 width was twenty *c* round
41:11 space left open was five *c*
41:12 was seventy *c* wide
41:12 was five *c* in width
41:12 and its length was ninety *c*
41:13 house, a hundred *c* in length
41:13 a hundred *c* in length
41:14 area . . . was a hundred *c*
41:15 on that side, a hundred *c*
41:22 wooden altar was three *c*
41:22 and its length was two *c*
42:2 the length of a hundred *c*
42:2 and the width was fifty *c*
42:3 In front of the twenty *c*
42:4 a walkway ten *c* in width
42:7 Its length was fifty *c*

Lu 6:7 he would *c* on the sabbath
8:43 not been able to get a *c*
9:1 authority . . . to *c* sicknesses
9:11 he healed those needing a *c*
10:9 *c* the sick ones in it, and go
13:14 Jesus did the *c* on the
14:3 lawful on the sabbath to *c* or

Cured
Le 14:3 leprosy has been *c* in the
Mt 4:24 paralyzed persons, and he *c*
8:16 *c* all who were faring badly
12:15 and he *c* them all
12:22 *c* him, so that the dumb man
14:14 and he *c* their sick ones
15:30 at his feet, and he *c* them
17:18 boy was *c* from that hour
19:2 followed him, and he *c* them
21:14 in the temple, and he *c*
Mr 1:34 he *c* many that were ill with
3:10 he *c* many, with the result
Lu 5:15 to be *c* of their sicknesses
6:18 with unclean spirits were *c*
7:21 In that hour he *c* many of
8:2 been *c* of wicked spirits and
13:14 *c*, and not on the sabbath day
Joh 5:10 began to say to the *c* man
Ac 4:14 man that had been *c* standing
5:16 they would one and all be *c*
8:7 paralyzed and lame were *c*
28:9 to come to him and be *c*

Curer
Pr 17:22 is joyful does good as a *c*

Cures
Lu 9:6 and performing *c* everywhere

Curing
Jer 8:18 A grief that is beyond *c*
Mt 4:23 and *c* every sort of disease
9:35 *c* every sort of disease and
Re 22:2 were for the *c* of the nations

Current
Ge 23:16 shekels *c* with the merchants

Curse
Ge 12:3 down evil upon you I shall *c*
Ex 22:28 nor *c* a chieftain among your
Nu 5:18 bitter water that brings a *c*
5:19 bitter water that brings a *c*
5:22 water that brings a *c* must
5:24 bitter water that brings a *c*
5:24 water that brings a *c* must
5:27 water that brings a *c* must
22:6 do *c* this people for me, for
22:6 the one whom you *c* is cursed
22:12 You must not *c* the people
23:7 Do come, do *c* Jacob for me
De 28:20 will send upon you the *c*
Jg 5:23 *C* Meroz, said the angel of
5:23 *C* its inhabitants incessantly
17:2 pronounced a *c* and also said
1Ki 8:31 under liability to the *c*
8:31 actually comes within the *c*
2Ch 6:22 him under liability to the *c*
6:22 comes within the *c* before
Ne 10:29 coming into liability to a *c*
Job 1:11 not *c* you to your very face
2:5 see whether he will not *c* you
2:9 your integrity? *C* God and die!
Pr 3:33 *c* of Jehovah is on the house
29:24 An oath involving a *c* he may
Isa 24:6 the *c* itself has eaten up the
Jer 23:10 because of the *c* the land
29:18 a *c* and for an object of
42:18 will certainly become a *c*
44:12 they must become a *c*, an
La 3:65 insolence of heart, your *c* to
Da 9:11 poured out upon us the *c* and
Zec 5:3 *c* that is going forth over
Mal 2:2 send upon you the *c*, and I
2:2 and I will *c* your blessings
3:9 With the *c* you are cursing
Mt 26:74 he started to *c* and swear
Mr 14:71 he commenced to *c* and swear
Ac 23:12 bound themselves with a *c*
23:14 bound ourselves with a *c* not
23:21 with a *c* neither to eat nor
Ga 3:10 under a *c*; for it is written
3:13 us from the *c* of the Law by
3:13 becoming a *c* instead of us
Jas 3:9 with it we *c* men who have
Re 22:3 no more will there be any *c*

Cursed
Ge 3:14 you are the *c* one out of all
3:17 *c* is the ground on your
4:11 you are *c* in banishment
5:29 ground which Jehovah has *c*
9:25 *C* be Canaan. Let him become
27:29 *C* be each one of those
49:7 *C* be their anger, because it
Nu 22:6 the one whom you curse is *c*
24:9 cursing you are the ones *c*
De 27:15 *C* is the man who makes a
27:16 *C* is the one who treats his
27:17 *C* is the one who moves back
27:18 *C* is the one who causes the
27:19 *C* is the one who perverts the
27:20 *C* is the one who lies down
27:21 *C* is the one who lies down
27:22 *C* is the one who lies down
27:23 *C* is the one who lies down
27:24 *C* is the one who fatally
27:25 *C* is the one who accepts a
27:26 *C* is the one who will not
28:16 *C* will you be in the city
28:16 *c* will you be in the field
28:17 *C* will be your basket and
28:18 *C* will be the fruit of your
28:19 *C* will you be when you come
28:19 *c* will you be when you go
Jos 6:26 *C* may the man be before
9:23 And now you are a *c* people
Jg 21:18 *C* is the one that gives a
1Sa 14:24 *C* is the man that eats
14:28 *C* is the man that eats
26:19 *c* before Jehovah, because
1Ki 21:10 You have *c* God and the king!
21:13 has *c* God and the king
Job 1:5 and have *c* God in their heart
24:18 land will be *c* in the earth
Ps 119:21 rebuked the *c* presumptuous
Jer 11:3 *C* is the man that does not
17:5 *C* is the able-bodied man who
20:14 *C* be the day on which I was
20:15 *C* be the man that brought
48:10 *C* be the one that is
48:10 *c* be the one that is holding
Mal 1:14 *c* is the one acting
2:2 I have even *c* the blessing
Mt 25:41 you who have been *c*, into
Mr 11:21 the fig tree that you *c*
Ro 9:3 separated as the *c* one from
Ga 3:10 *C* is every one that does not
Heb 6:8 and is near to being *c*

Curses
2Ch 34:24 all the *c* that are written
Job 3:8 Let *c* of the day execrate it
Pr 28:27 hiding his eyes . . . many *c*
Ho 4:2 pronouncing of *c* and practicing

Cursing
Ge 27:29 each one of those *c* you
Le 5:1 has heard public *c* and he is
Nu 5:21 with an oath involving *c*
5:21 Jehovah set you for a *c* and
5:27 woman must become a *c* in
24:9 And those *c* you are the ones
1Ki 8:31 lays a *c* upon him to bring
2Ch 6:22 lays a *c* upon him to bring
Ps 59:12 *c* and the deception that they
Mal 3:9 With the curse you are *c* me
Lu 6:28 to bless those *c* you, to
Ro 3:14 mouth is full of *c* and
12:14 blessing and do not be *c*
Jas 3:10 come forth blessing and *c*

Cursings
Nu 5:23 priest must write these *c* in

Curtain
Ex 26:31 must make a *c* of blue thread
26:33 put the *c* under the hooks and
26:33 the ark . . . within the *c*
26:33 *c* must make a division for
26:35 set the table outside the *c*
27:21 *c* that is by the Testimony
30:6 put it before the *c* that is
35:12 the *c* of the screen
36:35 make a *c* of blue thread and
38:27 socket pedestals of the *c*
39:34 and the *c* of the screen
40:3 to the Ark with the *c*
40:21 the *c* of the screen in place
40:22 to the north outside the *c*
40:26 tent of meeting before the *c*
Le 4:6 front of the *c* of the holy
4:17 Jehovah in front of the *c*
16:2 the holy place inside the *c*
16:12 bring them inside the *c*
16:15 blood inside the *c* and do
21:23 not come in near the *c*, and
24:3 *c* of the Testimony in the
Nu 4:5 take down the screening *c* and
18:7 regards what is inside the *c*
2Ch 3:14 *c* of blue thread and wool
Mt 27:51 *c* of the sanctuary was rent
Mr 15:38 *c* of the sanctuary was rent
Lu 23:45 *c* of the sanctuary was rent
Heb 6:19 it enters in within the *c*
9:3 behind the second *c* was the
10:20 the *c*, that is, his flesh

Curves
Lu 3:5 *c* must become straight ways

Curvings
Ca 7:1 The *c* of your thighs are like

Cush
Ge 2:13 the entire land of *C*
10:6 And the sons of Ham were *C*
10:7 sons of *C* were Seba and
10:8 *C* became father to Nimrod
1Ch 1:8 sons of Ham were *C* and
1:9 sons of *C* were Seba and
1:10 *C* himself became father to
Job 28:19 The topaz of *C* cannot be
Ps 7:*super* words of *C* the Benjaminite
68:31 *C* itself will quickly
87:4 and Tyre, together with *C*
Isa 11:11 remnant . . . from *C* and
Jer 46:9 mighty men go forth, *C* and

Cushan
Hab 3:7 I saw the tents of *C*

Cushan-rishathaim
Jg 3:8 into the hand of *C* the king of
3:8 to serve *C* eight years
3:10 *C* the king of Syria into his
3:10 that his hand overpowered *C*

Cushi
Jer 36:14 Shelemiah the son of *C*
Zep 1:1 *C* the son of Gedaliah the

Cushite
Nu 12:1 account of the *C* wife whom he
12:1 it was a *C* wife he had taken
2Sa 18:21 Joab said to the *C*: Go, tell
18:21 the *C* bowed to Joab and
18:22 please, run behind the *C*
18:23 eventually passed by the *C*
18:31 here was the *C* coming in
18:31 and the *C* began to say
18:32 the king said to the *C*
18:32 the *C* said: May the enemies
Jer 13:23 Can a *C* change his skin?

Cushites
Am 9:7 like the sons of the *C* to me

Custody
Ge 42:17 together in *c* for three days
42:19 bound in your house of *c*
Le 24:12 into *c* till there should be a
Nu 15:34 they committed him into *c*
18:8 *c* of the contributions made
Jer 37:21 put Jeremiah in *c* in the
41:10 put in the *c* of Gedaliah
52:11 put him in the house of *c*
Mt 26:48 this is he; take him into *c*
26:50 on Jesus and took him into *c*
26:55 you did not take me into *c*
26:57 Those who took Jesus into *c*
Mr 14:44 take him into *c* and lead
14:46 and took him into *c*
14:49 you did not take me into *c*
Lu 22:63 the men that had him in *c*
Ac 4:3 put them in *c* till the next
5:18 in the public place of *c*
24:23 have some relaxation of *c*
Ga 3:22 together to the *c* of sin
3:23 delivered up together into *c*

Custom
Ge 40:13 according to the former *c*
Jg 18:7 the *c* of the Sidonians, quiet
Ru 4:7 *c* of former times in Israel
1Ki 18:28 according to their *c* with
2Ki 11:14 pillar according to the *c*
1Ch 15:13 according to the *c*
2Ch 35:13 according to the *c*
Jer 49:12 not their *c* to drink the cup
Mt 27:15 *c* of the governor to release
Lu 2:42 the *c* of the festival
4:16 his *c* on the sabbath day, he
Joh 18:39 *c* that I should release a

Joh 19:40 *c* of preparing for burial
Ac 15:1 according to the *c* of Moses
17:2 according to Paul's *c* he went
1Co 11:16 dispute for some other *c*
Heb 10:25 as some have the *c*

Customarily
Ge 22:14 it is *c* said today: In the
50:3 *c* take for the embalming
De 21:4 *c* no tilling or sowing of
1Ki 10:29 a chariot *c* came up and was
2Ch 1:17 *c* brought up and exported
Eze 42:14 in which they *c* minister
Mr 14:12 they *c* sacrificed the
Lu 22:39 he went as *c* to the Mount

Customary
Ge 29:26 not *c* to do this way in our
31:35 the *c* thing with women is
Da 3:19 than it was *c* to heat it up
Lu 2:27 the *c* practice of the law
Php 2:29 the *c* welcome in the Lord

Customs
Le 18:30 detestable *c* that have been
Jer 10:3 the *c* of the peoples are
Ac 6:14 change the *c* that Moses
16:21 publishing *c* that it is not
21:21 nor to walk in the solemn *c*
26:3 expert on all the *c* as well
28:17 or the *c* of our forefathers

Cut
Ge 9:11 No more will all flesh be *c*
15:10 *c* them in two and put each
15:10 birds he did not *c* in pieces
17:14 soul must be *c* off from his
41:36 not be *c* off by the famine
Ex 4:25 Zipporah took a flint and *c*
8:9 *c* the frogs off from you and
12:15 must be *c* off from Israel
12:19 that soul must be *c* off
29:17 *c* up the ram into its pieces
30:33 be *c* off from his people
30:38 be *c* off from his people
31:14 be *c* off from the midst of
34:13 sacred poles you are to *c*
39:3 he *c* out threads to work in
Le 1:6 be skinned and *c* up into its
1:12 must *c* it up into its parts
7:20 that soul must be *c* off from
7:21 must be *c* off from his people
7:25 must be *c* off from his people
7:27 must be *c* off from his people
8:20 *c* up the ram into its pieces
14:41 clay mortar that they *c* off
14:43 having *c* off the house and
17:4 man must be *c* off from among
17:9 must be *c* off from his people
17:10 *c* him off from among his
17:14 Anyone eating it will be *c*
18:29 *c* off from among their people
19:8 soul must be *c* off from his
19:27 not *c* your sidelocks short
20:3 *c* him off from among his
20:5 *c* him and all those who have
20:6 *c* him off from among his
20:17 *c* off before the eyes of the
20:18 be *c* off from among their
22:3 soul must be *c* off from
22:22 having a *c* or wart or
22:24 the testicles . . . *c* off
23:29 be *c* off from his people
26:22 *c* off your domestic animals
26:30 *c* off your incense stands and
Nu 4:18 Kohathites be *c* off from
9:13 soul must then be *c* off from
11:23 hand of Jehovah is *c* short
13:23 *c* down from there a shoot
13:24 sons of Israel *c* down from
15:30 *c* off from among his people
15:31 soul . . . *c* off without fail
19:13 must be *c* off from Israel
19:20 that soul must be *c* off from
De 7:5 sacred poles you should *c* down
12:3 *c* down the graven images of
12:29 God will *c* off from before
19:5 strike with the ax to *c* the
20:19 you must not *c* them down
20:20 you must *c* it down and build
23:1 having his male member *c* off
Jos 3:13 of the Jordan will be *c* off
3:16 *c* off, and the people passed
4:7 waters of the Jordan were *c*
4:7 waters . . . were *c* off
7:9 *c* our name off from the earth
Jos 9:23 will never be *c* off from you
11:21 went and *c* off the Anakim
17:15 must *c* it down for yourself
17:18 forest, you must *c* it down
23:4 all the nations that I *c* off
Jg 1:6 and *c* off the thumbs of his
1:7 great toes of their feet *c* off
4:24 they had *c* off Jabin the king
5:26 she . . . *c* up his temples
6:25 sacred pole . . . you should *c*
6:26 sacred pole that you will *c*
6:28 it had been *c* down, and the
6:30 he has *c* down the sacred pole
9:48 *c* down a branch of the trees
9:49 the people *c* down also each
19:29 *c* her up according to her
20:6 my concubine and *c* her up and
Ru 4:10 name . . . not be *c* off from
1Sa 2:33 not *c* off from being at my
5:4 palms of both his hands *c* off
11:7 bulls and *c* them in pieces
17:51 he *c* his head off with it
20:15 you will not *c* off your own
20:16 name of Jonathan be *c* off
24:4 *c* off the skirt of the
24:5 *c* off the skirt of the
24:11 I *c* off the skirt of your
24:21 not *c* off my seed after me
28:9 *c* off the spirit mediums
31:9 *c* off his head and strip off
2Sa 3:29 *c* off from Joab's house a
4:12 *c* off their hands and their
7:9 *c* off all your enemies from
10:4 *c* their garments in half to
20:22 *c* off the head of Sheba the
1Ki 2:4 there will not be *c* off a man
5:6 *c* for me cedars from Lebanon
5:6 to *c* trees like the Sidonians
8:25 will not be *c* off a man
9:5 *c* off from sitting upon the
9:7 *c* Israel off from upon the
11:16 *c* off every male in Edom
14:10 *c* off from Jeroboam anyone
14:14 *c* off the house of Jeroboam
15:13 *c* down her horrible idol
18:4 *c* off Jehovah's prophets
18:5 anymore of the beasts *c* off
18:23 bull and *c* it in pieces
18:33 *c* the young bull in pieces
21:21 *c* off from Ahab anyone
2Ki 6:4 and began to *c* down the trees
6:6 he *c* off a piece of wood and
9:8 must *c* off from Ahab anyone
10:32 *c* off Israel piece by piece
16:17 King Ahaz *c* the sidewalls
18:4 and *c* down the sacred pole
18:16 Hezekiah *c* off the doors of
19:23 *c* down its lofty cedars
23:14 *c* down the sacred poles and
24:13 *c* to pieces all the gold
1Ch 17:8 shall *c* off all your enemies
19:4 *c* their garments in half to
2Ch 2:7 knowing how to *c* engravings
2:16 *c* down trees from Lebanon
6:16 not be *c* off a man of yours
7:18 man of yours be *c* off from
14:3 and *c* down the sacred poles
15:16 Asa *c* down her horrible
22:7 *c* off the house of Ahab
28:24 *c* to pieces the utensils
31:1 *c* down the sacred poles and
34:4 he *c* down from off them
34:7 incense stands he *c* down in
Job 1:20 *c* the hair off his head and
6:9 release his hand and *c* me off
8:14 Whose confidence is *c* off
14:2 has come forth and is *c* off
14:7 If it gets *c* down, it will
20:24 A bow of copper will *c* him
21:21 his months . . . *c* in two
24:24 they are *c* off
Ps 12:3 will *c* off all smooth lips
34:16 *c* off the mention of them
37:9 evildoers . . . will be *c* off
37:22 called by him will be *c* off
37:28 they will indeed be *c* off
37:34 the wicked ones are *c* off
37:38 people will indeed be *c* off
46:9 and does *c* the spear in pieces
75:10 of the wicked ones I shall *c*
80:16 is burned with fire, *c* off
101:8 To *c* off from the city of
102:23 He *c* short my days
107:16 *c* down even the bars of
Ps 109:15 *c* off the remembrance of
129:4 *c* in pieces the ropes of the
Pr 2:22 wicked, they will be *c* off
10:27 wicked ones will be *c* short
10:31 perverseness will be *c* off
23:18 own hope will not be *c* off
24:14 own hope will not be *c* off
Isa 9:10 trees are what have been *c*
9:14 Jehovah will *c* off from
9:20 *c* down on the right and will
10:7 to *c* off nations not a few
10:33 in growth are being *c* down
11:13 to Judah will be *c* off
11:15 *c* off the tongue of the
14:12 been *c* down to the earth
14:22 *c* off from Babylon name
18:5 *c* off the sprigs with
22:25 upon it must be *c* off
29:20 to do harm must be *c* off
33:12 As thorns *c* away, they will
37:24 *c* down its lofty cedars
38:12 to *c* me off from the very
44:14 is to *c* down cedars; and
45:2 the iron bars I shall *c* down
48:19 *c* off or be annihilated
55:13 that will not be *c* off
56:5 one that will not be *c* off
Jer 6:6 *C* down wood and throw up
7:28 been *c* off from their mouth
9:21 in order to *c* off the child
9:22 like a row of newly *c* grain
10:3 tree . . . that one has *c* down
11:19 *c* him off from the land of
22:7 *c* down the choicest of your
33:17 *c* off in David's case a man
33:18 *c* off a man from before me
34:18 calf that they *c* in two
35:19 *c* off from Jonadab the
44:7 *c* off from yourselves man
46:23 certainly *c* down her forest
47:4 to *c* off from Tyre and from
48:2 *c* her off from being a
48:25 Moab has been *c* down
50:16 *C* off the sower from
50:23 been *c* down and gets broken
51:62 place, in order to *c* it off
La 2:3 *c* down every horn of Israel
3:54 I shall certainly be *c* off
Eze 6:6 your incense stands *c* down
14:8 *c* him off from the midst of
14:13 *c* off from it earthling man
14:17 *c* off from it earthling man
14:19 *c* off from it earthling man
14:21 *c* off from it earthling man
16:4 navel string had not been *c*
17:17 order to *c* off many souls
21:3 *c* off from you righteous one
21:4 *c* off from you righteous one
21:19 index hand should be *c* out
21:19 it should be *c* out
25:7 *c* you off from the peoples
25:13 and *c* off from it man and
25:16 *c* off the Cherethites and
29:8 *c* off from you earthling man
30:15 *c* off the crowd of No
31:12 the nations, will *c* it down
35:7 *c* off from it the one
Da 2:34 stone was *c* out not by hands
2:45 stone was *c* not by hands, and
4:14 down, and *c* off its boughs
9:26 Messiah will be *c* off, with
Ho 8:4 that they may be *c* off
Joe 1:5 *c* off from your mouths
1:9 drink offering have been *c* off
1:16 food itself been *c* off before
Am 1:5 *c* off the inhabitant from
1:8 I will *c* off the inhabitant
2:3 I will *c* off the judge from
2:13 with a row of newly *c* grain
3:14 horns of the altar . . . *c* off
9:1 And *c* them off at the head
Ob 9 *c* off from the mountainous
10 to be *c* off to time indefinite
14 in order to *c* off his escapees
Mic 4:12 like a row of newly *c* grain
5:9 enemies . . . will be *c* off
5:10 I will *c* off your horses
5:11 *c* off the cities of your
5:12 *c* off sorceries out of your
5:13 *c* off your graven images and
Na 1:12 they must be *c* down; and one
1:14 I shall *c* off carved image
1:15 he will certainly be *c* off
2:13 *c* off from the earth your

Na 3:15 A sword will *c* you off
Zep 1:3 *c* off mankind from the
1:4 *c* off from this place the
1:11 silver have been *c* off
3:6 I *c* off nations; their corner
3:7 dwelling might not be *c* off
Zec 9:6 *c* off the pride of the
9:10 *c* off the war chariot from
9:10 battle bow must be *c* off
11:10 and *c* it to pieces, in order
11:14 *c* in pieces my second staff
12:6 in a row of newly *c* grain
13:2 *c* off the names of the idols
13:8 will be *c* off and expire
14:2 not be *c* off from the city
Mal 2:12 Jehovah will *c* off each one
Mt 3:10 *c* down and thrown into the
5:30 making you stumble, *c* it off
7:19 *c* down and thrown into the
18:8 *c* it off and throw it away
24:22 those days were *c* short, no
24:22 those days will be *c* short
Mr 9:43 makes you stumble, *c* it off
9:45 foot makes you stumble, *c* it
11:8 *c* down foliage from the
13:20 had *c* short the days, no
13:20 he has *c* short the days
Lu 3:9 *c* down and thrown into the
6:44 they *c* grapes off a thornbush
13:7 have found none. *C* it down!
13:9 if not, you shall *c* it down
Joh 18:10 and *c* his right ear off
18:26 man whose ear Peter *c* off
Ac 5:33 they felt deeply *c* and were
7:54 they felt *c* to their hearts
27:20 hope . . . began to be *c* off
27:32 *c* away the ropes of the
Ro 11:24 you were *c* out of the olive
2Co 11:12 *c* off the pretext from
1Th 2:18 but Satan *c* across our path
2Pe 2:9 day of judgment to be *c* off

Cutbacks
1Ki 6:6 *c* that he gave to the house

Cuth
2Ki 17:30 men of *C*, for their part

Cuthah
2Ki 17:24 people from Babylon and *C*

Cut-off
Ru 2:7 among the *c* ears of grain
2:15 among the *c* ears of grain

Cuts
Le 19:28 make *c* in your flesh for a
De 19:1 God *c* off the nations whose
1Sa 20:15 Jehovah *c* off the enemies
Job 27:8 in case he *c* him off
Jer 16:6 anyone make *c* upon himself
41:5 *c* made upon themselves
47:5 keep making *c* upon yourself
48:37 Upon all hands there are *c*
Lu 5:36 No one *c* a patch from a new

Cutters
1Ki 5:15 thousand *c* in the mountain
2Ch 2:2 men as *c* in the mountain, and
2:10 the *c* of the trees, I do give
2:18 *c* in the mountain and three
Ezr 3:7 to give money to the *c* and

Cutting
1Ki 5:18 the Gebalites did the *c*
18:28 *c* themselves according to
2Ch 2:8 *c* down the trees of Lebanon
2:14 at *c* every sort of engraving
Ps 109:13 his posterity be for *c* off
Isa 6:13 *c* down of them, there is a
22:16 crag he is *c* out a residence
48:9 there may be no *c* you off
Jer 44:8 causing a *c* off of yourselves
44:11 and for *c* off all Judah
Eze 23:47 will be a *c* of them down
Hab 2:10 the *c* off of many peoples
Mt 21:8 began *c* down branches from
Ac 27:40 *c* away the anchors, they
Ro 9:28 concluding it and *c* it short

Cutting-off
Mt 25:46 depart into everlasting *c*

Cuttings
De 14:1 You must not make *c* upon
Mic 5:1 you make *c* upon yourself

Cylinders
Ca 5:14 His hands are *c* of gold

Cymbal
1Co 13:1 of brass or a clashing *c*

Cymbals
2Sa 6:5 with sistrums and with *c*
1Ch 13:8 with *c* and with trumpets
15:16 harps and *c*, playing aloud
15:19 the copper *c* to play aloud
15:28 with trumpets and with *c*
16:5 with the *c* playing aloud
16:42 the trumpets and *c* and
25:1 prophesying . . . with the *c*
25:6 with *c*, stringed instruments
2Ch 5:12 with *c* and with stringed
5:13 the trumpets and with the *c*
29:25 house of Jehovah, with *c*
Ezr 3:10 sons of Asaph, with the *c*
Ne 12:27 *c* and stringed instruments
Ps 150:5 the *c* of melodious sound
150:5 with the clashing *c*

Cypress
Isa 41:19 the *c* at the same time
60:13 the ash tree and the *c* at
Eze 27:6 made with ivory in *c* wood

Cyprus
Ac 4:36 a Levite, a native of *C*
11:19 as far as Phoenicia and *C*
11:20 men of *C* and Cyrene that
13:4 they sailed away to *C*
15:39 along and sailed away to *C*
21:3 in sight of the island of *C*
21:16 Mnason of *C*, an early
27:4 sailed under the shelter of *C*

Cyrene
Mt 27:32 a native of *C* named Simon
Mr 15:21 Simon of *C*, coming from the
Lu 23:26 Simon, a certain native of *C*
Ac 2:10 Libya, which is toward *C*
11:20 men of Cyprus and *C* that
13:1 and Lucius of *C*, and Manaen

Cyrenians
Ac 6:9 *C* and Alexandrians and of those

Cyrus
2Ch 36:22 *C* the king of Persia
36:22 *C* the king of Persia
36:23 *C* the king of Persia has
Ezr 1:1 *C* the king of Persia
1:1 spirit of *C* the king of Persia
1:2 what *C* the king of Persia has
1:7 King *C* himself brought forth
1:8 *C* the king of Persia
3:7 by *C* the king of Persia
4:3 as King *C* the king of Persia
4:5 days of *C* the king of Persia
5:13 *C* the king of Babylon
5:13 *C* the king put an order
5:14 *C* the king took out of the
5:17 from *C* the king an order was
6:3 the first year of *C* the king
6:3 *C* the king put an order
6:14 order of *C* and Darius and
Isa 44:28 *C*, He is my shepherd
45:1 to his anointed one, to *C*
Da 1:21 first year of *C* the king
6:28 the kingdom of *C* the Persian
10:1 third year of *C* the king of

Dabbesheth
Jos 19:11 to Mareal and reached to *D*

Daberath
Jos 19:12 and went out to *D* and went
21:28 *D* and its pasture ground
1Ch 6:72 *D* with its pasture grounds

Dagger
Ac 21:38 led the four thousand *d* men

Daggers
1Ki 18:28 with *d* and with lances

Dagon
Jg 16:23 sacrifice to *D* their god and
1Sa 5:2 bring it into the house of *D*
5:2 and station it beside *D*
5:3 *D* was fallen upon his face to
5:3 took *D* and returned him to
5:4 *D* was fallen upon his face to
5:4 head of *D* and the palms of
5:5 the priests of *D* and all those
5:5 going into the house of *D*
5:5 the threshold of *D* in Ashdod
5:7 and against *D* our god
1Ch 10:10 fastened to the house of *D*

Daily
Ex 5:19 one bit of anyone's *d* rate
29:36 bull of the sin offering *d*
Le 23:37 according to the *d* schedule
Nu 28:24 render up *d* for the seven
2Ki 25:30 *d* as due, all the days of
2Ch 8:13 *d* matter of course to make
8:14 as a *d* matter of course
31:16 as a *d* matter of course
Ne 5:15 *d* forty silver shekels
5:18 happened to be made ready *d*
12:47 according to the *d* need and
Ps 68:19 *d* carries the load for us
Jer 7:25 *d* getting up early and
37:21 loaf of bread to him *d*
52:34 *d* as due, until the day
Eze 45:23 *d* for the seven days, and
45:23 a buck of the goats *d*
46:13 burnt offering *d* to Jehovah
Da 1:5 king appointed a *d* allowance
Lu 19:47 teaching *d* in the temple
Ac 2:47 to them *d* those being saved
3:2 *d* put him near the temple door
6:1 in the *d* distribution
17:11 examining the Scriptures *d*
19:9 *d* giving talks in the school
1Co 15:31 *D* I face death. This I
Heb 7:27 He does not need *d*, as those

Dainties
Ge 49:20 he will give the *d* of a king
Ps 141:4 not feed myself on their *d*

Daintily
Jer 6:2 a comely and *d* bred woman

Dainty
De 28:54 delicate and *d* man among you
28:56 the delicate and *d* woman
28:56 being of *d* habit and for
Isa 47:1 call you delicate and *d*
Da 10:3 *D* bread I did not eat, and
Re 18:14 all the *d* things and the

Dalmanutha
Mr 8:10 came into the parts of *D*

Dalmatia
2Ti 4:10 to Galatia, Titus to *D*

Dalphon
Es 9:7 Parshandatha and *D* and Aspatha

Dam
Ex 15:8 stood still like a *d* of floods
Jos 3:13 will stand still as one *d*
3:16 They rose up as one *d* very
Ps 33:7 as by a *d* the waters
78:13 waters to stand like a *d*

Damage
Es 7:4 when with *d* to the king
Jer 31:28 to destroy and to do *d*, so I
Lu 9:25 his own self or suffers *d*
Ac 27:10 with *d* and great loss not
27:21 sustained this *d* and loss
2Co 7:9 no *d* in anything due to us

Damaged
Ps 31:12 have become like a *d* vessel

Damages
Ex 21:22 he is to have *d* imposed upon

Damaging
Heb 13:17 for this would be *d* to you

Damaris
Ac 17:34 and a woman named *D*, and

Damascene
Am 3:12 and on a *D* divan

Damascenes
2Co 11:32 guarding the city of the *D*

Damascus
Ge 14:15 Hobah, which is north of *D*
15:2 is a man of *D*, Eliezer
2Sa 8:5 When Syria of *D* came to help
8:6 put garrisons in Syria of *D*
1Ki 11:24 to *D* and took up dwelling
11:24 and began reigning in *D*
15:18 who was dwelling in *D*
19:15 to the wilderness of *D*
20:34 assign to yourself in *D* the
2Ki 5:12 the rivers of *D*, better than
8:7 Elisha proceeded to come to *D*
8:9 every sort of good thing of *D*
14:28 restored *D* and Hamath to
16:9 went up to *D* and captured it
16:10 the king of Assyria at *D*

2Ki 16:10 the altar that was in *D*
16:11 King Ahaz had sent from *D*
16:11 King Ahaz came from *D*
16:12 the king came from *D*
1Ch 18:5 When Syria of *D* came to help
18:6 put garrisons in Syria of *D*
2Ch 16:2 who was dwelling at *D*
24:23 they sent to the king of *D*
28:5 and brought them to *D*
28:23 sacrifice to the gods of *D*
Ca 7:4 which is looking out toward *D*
Isa 7:8 head of Syria is *D*, and
7:8 the head of *D* is Rezin
8:4 carry away the resources of *D*
10:9 Is not Samaria just like *D?*
17:1 The pronouncement against *D*
17:1 *D* removed from being a city
17:3 and the kingdom out of *D*
Jer 49:23 For *D:* Hamath and Arpad
49:24 *D* has lost courage
49:27 ablaze on the wall of *D*
Eze 27:18 *D* was your merchant in the
47:16 between the boundary of *D*
47:17 boundary of *D* and north
47:18 between Hauran and *D* and
48:1 boundary of *D* northward, on
Am 1:3 account of three revolts of *D*
1:5 I will break the bar of *D*
5:27 to go into exile beyond *D*
Zec 9:1 and *D* is where it rests
Ac 9:2 letters to the synagogues in *D*
9:3 he approached *D*, when suddenly
9:8 and conducted him into *D*
9:10 in *D* a certain disciple named
9:19 with the disciples in *D*
9:22 Jews that dwelt in *D* as he
9:27 in *D* he had spoken boldly in
22:5 letters to the brothers in *D*
22:6 and drawing close to *D*, about
22:10 Rise, go your way into *D*
22:11 I arrived in *D*, being led by
26:12 as I was journeying to *D*
26:20 those in *D* first and to
2Co 11:32 In *D* the governor under
Ga 1:17 and I came back again to *D*

Dammed
Job 28:11 he has *d* up, And the

Dan
Ge 14:14 and went in pursuit up to *D*
30:6 why she called his name *D*
35:25 sons by Bilhah . . . were *D*
46:23 the sons of *D* were Hushim
49:16 *D* will judge his people as
49:17 Let *D* prove to be a serpent
Ex 1:4 *D* and Naphtali, Gad and Asher
31:6 Ahisamach of the tribe of *D*
35:34 Ahisamach of the tribe of *D*
38:23 Ahisamach of the tribe of *D*
Le 24:11 of Dibri of the tribe of *D*
Nu 1:12 of *D*, Ahiezer the son of
1:38 the sons of *D*, their births
1:39 registered . . . the tribe of *D*
2:25 *D* will be toward the north
2:25 for the sons of *D* is Ahiezer
2:31 ones of the camp of *D* are
7:66 chieftain for the sons of *D*
10:25 sons of *D* pulled away as
13:12 of the tribe of *D*, Ammiel
26:42 sons of *D* by their families
26:42 the families of *D* by their
34:22 of the tribe of the sons of *D*
De 27:13 Zebulun, *D* and Naphtali
33:22, 22 *D* he said: *D* is a lion
34:1 the land, Gilead as far as *D*
Jos 19:40 the tribe of the sons of *D*
19:47 territory of the sons of *D*
19:47 sons of *D* proceeded to go
19:47 they began to call Leshem *D*
19:47 name of *D* their forefather
19:48 the tribe of the sons of *D*
21:5 and out of the tribe of *D* and
21:23 from the tribe of *D*, Elteke
Jg 1:34 pressing the sons of *D* into
5:17 And *D*, why did he continue to
18:2 the sons of *D* sent five men
18:16 sons of *D*, were standing at
18:22 catch up with the sons of *D*
18:23 crying out to the sons of *D*
18:25 the sons of *D* said to him
18:26 sons of *D* kept going on their
18:29 the name of the city *D* by the
18:29 the name of their father, *D*
18:30 the sons of *D* stood up the
Jg 20:1 from *D* down to Beer-sheba
1Sa 3:20 Israel from *D* to Beer-sheba
2Sa 3:10 Judah from *D* to Beer-sheba
17:11 from *D* to Beer-sheba, as
24:2 Israel, from *D* to Beer-sheba
24:15 people from *D* to Beer-sheba
1Ki 4:25 from *D* to Beer-sheba, all
12:29 and the other he put in *D*
12:30 before the one as far as *D*
15:20 striking down Ijon and *D*
2Ki 10:29 was in Bethel and one in *D*
1Ch 2:2 *D*, Joseph and Benjamin
21:2 Israel from Beer-sheba to *D*
27:22 of *D*, Azarel the son of
2Ch 2:14 of a woman of the sons of *D*
16:4 struck Ijon and *D* and
30:5 from Beer-sheba to *D*, to
Jer 4:15 a voice is telling from *D*
8:16 From *D* has been heard the
Eze 48:1 *D* one portion
48:2 on the boundary of *D*, from
48:32 the gate of *D*, one
Am 8:14 As your god is alive, O *D!*

Dance
Jg 21:21 out to *d* in circle dances
Ps 150:4 tambourine and the circle *d*
Ca 6:13 like the *d* of two camps
Jer 31:4 *d* of those who are laughing
31:13 will rejoice in the *d*
Mt 11:17 for you, but you did not *d*
Lu 7:32 but you did not *d;* we wailed

Danced
Mt 14:6 daughter of Herodias *d* at it
Mr 6:22 *d* and pleased Herod and those

Dancers
Ps 87:7 well as *d* of circle dances

Dances
Ex 15:20 with tambourines and in *d*
32:19 could see the calf and the *d*
Jg 21:21 out to dance in circle *d*
1Sa 18:6 with song and *d* to meet Saul
21:11 responding with *d*, saying
29:5 responding in the *d*, saying
Ps 87:7 well as dancers of circle *d*

Dancing
Jg 11:34 tambourine playing and *d*
21:23 from the women *d* around
2Sa 6:14 David was *d* around before
6:16 King David leaping and *d*
Ps 30:11 changed my mourning into *d*
149:3 them praise his name with *d*
La 5:15 Our *d* has been changed into
Lu 15:25 heard a music concert and *d*

Danger
Lu 8:23 with water and to be in *d*
Ac 19:27 *d* exists not only that this
19:40 in *d* of being charged with
Ro 8:35 or nakedness or *d* or sword
Php 2:30 exposing his soul to *d*, that

Dangers
2Co 11:26 in *d* from rivers, in
11:26 in *d* from highwaymen, in
11:26 in *d* from my own race, in
11:26 in *d* from the nations
11:26 in *d* in the city, in
11:26 in *d* in the wilderness, in
11:26 in *d* at sea, in
11:26 in *d* among false brothers

Dangled
Job 28:4 swung down, they have *d*

Daniel
1Ch 3:1 the second, *D*, of Abigail
Ezr 8:2 of the sons of Ithamar, *D*
Ne 10:6 *D*, Ginnethon, Baruch
Eze 14:14 midst of it, Noah, *D* and Job
14:20 even were Noah, *D* and Job
28:3 look! you are wiser than *D*
Da 1:6 sons of Judah, *D*, Hananiah
1:7 to *D* the name of Belteshazzar
1:8 *D* determined in his heart that
1:9 gave *D* over to loving-kindness
1:10 court official said to *D*
1:11 *D* said to the guardian whom
1:11 official had appointed over *D*
1:17 *D* himself had understanding
1:19 no one was found like *D*
1:21 *D* continued on until the
2:13 they looked for *D* and his
2:14 *D*, for his part, addressed
2:15 made known the matter . . . to *D*
Da 2:16 *D* himself went in and asked
2:17 *D* went to his own house
2:18 destroy *D* and his companions
2:19 to *D* in a night vision the
2:19 *D* himself blessed the God of
2:20 *D* was answering and saying
2:24 *D* himself went in to Arioch
2:25 Arioch, in a hurry, took *D*
2:26 saying to *D*, whose name was
2:27 *D* was answering before the
2:46 to *D* he paid homage, and he
2:47 king was answering *D* and
2:48 king made *D* someone great
2:49 *D*, for his part, made a
2:49 *D* was in the court of the
4:8 *D*, whose name is Belteshazzar
4:19 *D* himself, whose name is
5:12 had been found in him, in *D*
5:12 Now let *D* himself be called
5:13 *D* himself was brought in
5:13 and saying to *D:* Are you the
5:13 Are you the *D* that is of the
5:17 *D* was answering and saying
5:29 they clothed *D* with purple
6:2 officials, of whom *D* was one
6:3 *D* was steadily distinguishing
6:4 to find some pretext against *D*
6:5 find in this *D* no pretext at
6:10 *D*, as soon as he knew that
6:11 *D* petitioning and imploring
6:13 *D*, who is of the exiles of
6:14 toward *D* he set his mind in
6:16 *D* and threw him into the pit
6:16 saying to *D:* Your God whom
6:17 be changed in the case of *D*
6:20 with a sad voice even to *D*
6:20 speaking up and saying to *D*
6:20 *D*, servant of the living God
6:21 *D* himself spoke even with the
6:23 *D* himself he commanded to be
6:23 *D* was lifted up out of the
6:24 men who had accused *D*, and
6:26 fearing before the God of *D*
6:27 rescued *D* from the paw of the
6:28 this *D*, he prospered in the
7:1 *D* himself beheld a dream and
7:2 *D* was speaking up and saying
7:15 *D*, my spirit was distressed
7:28 *D*, my own thoughts kept
8:1 appeared to me, even me, *D*
8:15 *D*, was seeing the vision and
8:27 *D*, I felt exhausted and was
9:2 *D*, discerned by the books the
9:22 *D*, now I have come forth to
10:1 was a matter revealed to *D*
10:2 *D*, happened to be mourning
10:7 I *D* by myself, the appearance
10:11 *D*, you very desirable man
10:12 Do not be afraid, O *D*, for
12:4 *D*, make secret the words and
12:5 I saw, I *D*, and, look!
12:9 Go, *D*, because the words are
Mt 24:15 through *D* the prophet

Danites
Jg 13:2 family of the *D*, and his name
18:1 tribe of the *D* was looking
18:11 family of the *D*, departed
18:30 priests to . . . the *D* until
1Ch 12:35 of the *D* those drawing up

Dan-jaan
2Sa 24:6 continued on to *D* and went

Dannah
Jos 15:49 *D* and Kiriath-sannah

Dara
1Ch 2:6 the sons of Zerah were . . . *D*

Darda
1Ki 4:31 wiser than . . . Calcol and *D*

Dare
Jg 16:15 How *d* you say, I do love you
Ps 11:1 How *d* you men say to my soul
Jer 48:14 How *d* you people say: We
Mt 22:46 nor did anyone *d* from that
Mr 11:32 But *d* we say, From men?
Ac 7:32 Moses did not *d* to
1Co 6:1 *d* to go to court before
2Co 10:12 do not *d* to class ourselves
Jude 9 not *d* to bring a judgment

Dares
Ge 49:9 like a lion, who *d* rouse him?
Nu 24:9 like a lion, who *d* rouse him?
Ro 5:7 someone even *d* to die

Darics
1Ch 29:7 talents and ten thousand *d*
Ezr 8:27 bowls worth a thousand *d*

Daring
2Pe 2:10 *D*, self-willed, they do not

Darius
Ezr 4:5 reign of *D* the king of Persia
4:24 reign of *D* the king of Persia
5:5 report could go to *D* and
5:6 sent to *D* the king
5:7 To *D* the king: All peace!
6:1 *D* the king put an order
6:12 I, *D*, do put through an order
6:13 *D* the king had sent word
6:14 order of Cyrus and *D* and
6:15 the reign of *D* the king
Ne 12:22 kingship of *D* the Persian
Da 5:31 *D* the Mede himself received
6:1 It seemed good to *D*, and he
6:6 *D* the king, live on even for
6:9 King *D* himself signed the
6:25 *D* the king himself wrote to
6:28 prospered in the kingdom of *D*
9:1 *D* the son of Ahasuerus of the
11:1 first year of *D* the Mede I
Hag 1:1 the second year of *D* the king
1:15 second year of *D* the king
2:10 in the second year of *D*
Zec 1:1 in the second year of *D* the
1:7 in the second year of *D*, the
7:1 fourth year of *D* the king

Dark
Ge 30:33 *d* brown among the . . . rams
30:35 every one *d* brown among the
49:12 *D* red are his eyes from wine
Ex 10:15 land grew *d;* and they went
19:9 am coming to you in a *d* cloud
20:21 near to the *d* cloud mass
Jos 2:5 by *d* that the men went out
2Sa 22:12 *D* waters, thick clouds
1Ch 28:11 its *d* inner rooms and the
Job 3:9 stars of its twilight grow *d*
6:16 They are *d* from ice, Upon
18:6 certainly grow *d* in his tent
Ps 18:11 *D* waters, thick clouds
74:20 *d* places of the earth have
88:6 In *d* places, in a large abyss
88:18 acquaintances are a *d* place
105:28 sent darkness . . . made it *d*
139:12 not prove too *d* for you
143:3 to dwell in *d* places
Ec 12:2 the moon and the stars grow *d*
12:3 the windows have found it *d*
Isa 5:30 light has grown *d* because of
13:10 sun will actually grow *d*
29:15 have occurred in a *d* place
42:16 turn a *d* place before them
45:19 in a *d* place of the earth
Jer 4:28 the heavens . . . become *d*
La 3:6 In *d* places he has made me sit
Eze 30:18 day will actually grow *d*
Joe 2:10 Sun and moon . . . become *d*
3:15 Sun and moon . . . become *d*
Am 5:8 made day itself *d* as night
Mic 3:6 the day must get *d* upon them
Mt 6:23 your whole body will be *d*
Mr 1:35 while it was still *d*, he
Lu 11:34 wicked, your body is also *d*
11:36 bright with no part at all *d*
Joh 6:17 grown *d* and Jesus had not
Heb 12:18 with fire, and a *d* cloud
2Pe 1:19 a lamp shining in a *d* place

Dark-brown
Ge 30:32 *d* sheep among the young rams
30:40 the *d* ones among the flocks

Darken
Job 3:5 things that *d* a day terrorize
Eze 31:15 I shall *d* Lebanon, and
32:7 the heavens and *d* their stars
32:8 *d* them on your account

Darkened
1Ki 18:45 the heavens themselves *d*
Ps 69:23 eyes become *d* so as not to
Mt 24:29 the sun will be *d*, and the
Mr 13:24 the sun will be *d*, and the
Ro 1:21 unintelligent heart became *d*
11:10 eyes become *d* so as not to
Re 8:12 third of them might be *d*
9:2 the sun was *d*, also the air
16:10 its kingdom became *d*, and

Darker
La 4:8 has become *d* than blackness

Darkness
Ge 1:2 there was *d* upon the surface
1:4 between the light and the *d*
1:5 but the *d* he called Night. And
1:18 between the light and the *d*
15:12 great *d* was falling upon him
15:17 dense *d* came and, look! a
Ex 10:21 that *d* may occur over the
10:21 Egypt and the *d* may be felt
10:22 gloomy *d* began to occur in
14:20 a cloud together with *d*
De 4:11 was *d*, cloud and thick gloom
5:23 out of the middle of the *d*
Jos 24:7 he placed a *d* between you
1Sa 2:9 wicked ones . . . silenced in *d*
30:17 from the morning *d* until
2Sa 22:12 *d* around him as booths
22:29 that makes my *d* shine
2Ki 7:5 rose up in the evening *d* to
7:7 fleeing in the evening *d*
Job 3:4 for that day, let it become *d*
3:5 Let *d* and deep shadow reclaim
5:14 They encounter *d* even by day
10:21 To the land of *d* and deep
11:17 *D* . . . like the morning
12:22 deep things from the *d*
12:25 They grope in *d*, where
15:22 he will come back out of *d*
15:23 day of *d* is ready at his
15:30 will not turn away from *d*
17:12 is near on account of *d*
17:13 In the *d* I shall have to
18:18 out of the light into the *d*
19:8 upon my roadways he puts *d*
20:26 *d* will be reserved for his
22:11 *d*, so that you cannot see
23:17 put to silence because of *d*
24:15 has watched for evening *d*
24:16 *d* he has dug into houses
26:10 To where light ends in *d*
28:3 An end to the *d* he has set
29:3 walk through *d* by his light
34:22 no *d* nor any deep shadow
37:19 produce words because of *d*
38:19 *d*, where, now, is its place
Ps 18:11 made *d* his concealment place
18:28 God . . . will make my *d* shine
35:6 Let their way become *d* and
82:5 In *d* they keep walking about
88:12 be known in the *d* itself
104:20 You cause *d*, that it may
105:28 sent *d* and so made it dark
107:10 dwelling in *d* and deep
107:14 bringing them out from *d*
112:4 in the *d* as a light to the
139:11 *d* itself will hastily seize
139:12 *d* itself would not prove
139:12 *d* might just as well be the
Pr 2:13 to walk in the ways of *d*
20:20 at the approach of *d*
Ec 2:13 advantage for light than for *d*
2:14 stupid one . . . in sheer *d*
5:17 all his days he eats in *d*
6:4 one come and in *d* he goes away
6:4 with *d* his own name will be
11:8 him remember the days of *d*
Isa 5:11 till late in the evening *d*
5:20 putting *d* for light and
5:20 and light for *d*, those who
5:30 there is distressing *d*
8:22 *d*, obscurity, hard times and
9:2 walking in the *d* have seen
29:18 of the *d* even the eyes of
42:7 detention those sitting in *d*
45:3 the treasures in the *d* and
45:7 Forming light and creating *d*
47:5 come into the *d*, O daughter
49:9 in the *d*, Reveal yourselves!
50:10 has walked in continual *d*
58:10 flash up even in the *d*, and
59:9 for light, but, look! *d*
59:10 just as in evening *d*
60:2 *d* itself will cover the
Jer 2:31 or a land of intense *d*
13:16 before he causes *d* and
La 3:2 makes to walk in *d* and not in
Eze 8:12 Israel are doing in the *d*
12:6 During the *d* you will do the
12:7 During the *d* I did the
12:12 do carrying in the *d* and go
32:8 will put *d* upon your land

Da 2:22 knowing what is in the *d*
Joe 2:2 a day of *d* and gloominess
2:31 The sun . . . turned into *d*
Am 5:18 It will be *d*, and no light
5:20 day of Jehovah be *d*, and
8:9 cause *d* for the land on a
Mic 3:6 *d* you will have, so as not
7:8 although I dwell in the *d*
Na 1:8 *d* will pursue his very enemies
Zep 1:15 a day of *d* and of gloominess
Mt 4:16 people sitting in *d* saw a
6:23 the light that is in you is *d*
6:23 how great that *d* is!
8:12 be thrown into the *d* outside
10:27 What I tell you in the *d*
22:13 throw him out into the *d*
25:30 slave out into the *d* outside
27:45 a *d* fell over all the land
Mr 15:33 a *d* fell over the whole land
Lu 1:79 in *d* and death's shadow, to
11:35 light that is in you is *d*
12:3 things you say in the *d* will
22:53 hour and the authority of *d*
23:44 a *d* fell over all the earth
Joh 1:5 the light is shining in the *d*
1:5 the *d* has not overpowered it
3:19 men have loved the *d* rather
8:12 will by no means walk in *d*
12:35 *d* does not overpower you
12:35 walks in the *d* does not
12:46 may not remain in the *d*
20:1 while there was still *d*
Ac 2:20 sun will be turned into *d*
13:11 and *d* fell upon him, and he
26:18 turn them from *d* to light
Ro 2:19 a light for those in *d*
13:12 off the works belonging to *d*
1Co 4:5 secret things of *d* to light
2Co 4:6 light shine out of *d*, and
6:14 does light have with *d*
Eph 4:18 they are in *d* mentally, and
5:8 for you were once *d*, but you
5:11 works that belong to the *d*
6:12 the world rulers of this *d*
Col 1:13 from the authority of the *d*
1Th 5:4 brothers, you are not in *d*
5:5 neither to night nor to *d*
Heb 12:18 and thick *d* and a tempest
1Pe 2:9 one that called you out of *d*
2Pe 2:4 to pits of dense *d* to be
2:17 *d* has been reserved
1Jo 1:5 God is light and there is no *d*
1:6 we go on walking in the *d*
2:8 the *d* is passing away and
2:9 is in the *d* up to right now
2:11 hates his brother is in the *d*
2:11 and is walking in the *d*
2:11 the *d* has blinded his eyes
Jude 6 eternal bonds under dense *d*
13 *d* stands reserved forever

Darkon
Ezr 2:56 the sons of *D*
Ne 7:58 the sons of *D*, the sons of

Darlings
Isa 44:9 their *d* themselves will be

Dart
Job 41:26 Nor spear, *d* or arrowhead

Darting
1Sa 14:32 *d* greedily at the spoil and
15:19 *d* greedily at the spoil and
Ps 18:10 *d* upon the wings of a spirit

Darts
Job 9:26 an eagle that *d* to and fro

Dash
Jg 9:33 make a *d* against the city
9:44 made a *d* that they might
9:44 made a *d* against all who
2Ki 8:12 you will *d* to pieces
Ps 2:9 you will *d* them to pieces
137:9 ahold and does *d* to pieces
Isa 13:18 bows will *d* even young men
Jer 13:14 I will *d* them one against
48:12 jars they will *d* to pieces
51:20 *d* nations to pieces, and
51:21 *d* the horse and his rider
51:21 will *d* the war chariot and
51:22 *d* man and woman to pieces
51:22 *d* old man and boy to pieces
51:22 *d* young man and virgin to
51:23 *d* shepherd and his drove to
51:23 *d* farmer and his span of

Jer 51:23 *d* governors and deputy
Ho 7:1 makes a *d* on the outside
Lu 19:44 will *d* you and your children

Dashed
Isa 13:16 children will be *d* to
Jer 22:28 despised, *d* to pieces
Ho 10:14 a mother herself was *d* to
13:16 children will be *d* to pieces
Na 3:10 children also came to be *d* to
Lu 6:48 the river *d* against that house
6:49 Against it the river *d*, and
9:42 the demon *d* him to the ground

Dashes
Mr 9:18 it *d* him to the ground, and

Dashing
Jg 7:19 a *d* to pieces of the large
20:37 and went *d* toward Gibeah
Job 1:17 *d* against the camels and
Jer 8:6 a horse . . . *d* into the battle
Da 12:7 *d* of the power of the holy
Na 3:2 the *d* horse and the leaping
Mr 4:37 waves kept *d* into the boat

Dashings
Jg 5:22, 22 *d* upon *d* of his stallions

Date
2Sa 6:19 and a *d* cake and a raisin
1Ch 16:3 a *d* cake and a raisin cake
Ca 5:11 of his hair are *d* clusters
7:7 and your breasts, *d* clusters

Dates
Ca 7:8 hold of its fruit stalks of *d*

Dathan
Nu 16:1 *D* and Abiram the sons of
16:12 Moses sent to call *D* and
16:24 tabernacles of Korah, *D* and
16:25 went to *D* and Abiram, and
16:27 tabernacle of Korah, *D* and
16:27 and *D* and Abiram came out
26:9 sons of Eliab: Nemuel and *D*
26:9 *D* and Abiram were summoned
De 11:6 what he did to *D* and Abiram
Ps 106:17 and swallowed down *D*

Daughter
Ge 11:29 Milcah, the *d* of Haran, the
20:12 *d* of my father, only not the
20:12 only not the *d* of my mother
24:23 Whose *d* are you? Tell me
24:24 I am the *d* of Bethuel the
24:47 Whose *d* are you? to which
24:47 *d* of Bethuel the son of Nahor
24:48 take the *d* of the brother of
25:20 at his taking Rebekah the *d*
26:34 Judith the *d* of Beeri the
26:34 Basemath the *d* of Elon the
28:9 Mahalath the *d* of Ishmael
29:6 Rachel his *d* coming with the
29:10 saw Rachel the *d* of Laban
29:18 Rachel your younger *d*
29:23 resorted to taking Leah his *d*
29:24 even to Leah his *d*
29:28 Rachel his *d* as his wife
29:29 Rachel his *d* as her
30:21 *d* . . . called her name Dinah
34:1 Dinah the *d* of Leah, whom she
34:3 Dinah the *d* of Jacob, and he
34:5 had defiled Dinah his *d*
34:7 in lying down with Jacob's *d*
34:8 his soul is attached to your *d*
34:17 we will take our *d* and go
34:19 did find delight in Jacob's *d*
36:2 Adah the *d* of Elon the Hittite
36:2 Oholibamah the *d* of Anah
36:3 Basemath, Ishmael's *d*, the
36:14 Oholibamah the *d* of Anah
36:18 Oholibamah the *d* of Anah
36:25 Oholibamah the *d* of Anah
36:39 Mehetabel the *d* of Matred
36:39 Matred the *d* of Mezahab
38:2 Judah got to see a *d* of a
38:12 *d* of Shua, Judah's wife
41:45 Asenath the *d* of Potiphera
41:50 Asenath the *d* of Potiphera
46:15 together with his *d* Dinah
46:18 Laban gave to his *d* Leah
46:20 Asenath the *d* of Potiphera
46:25 Laban gave to his *d* Rachel
Ex 1:16 it is a *d*, it must also live
1:22 every *d* you are to preserve
2:1 man . . . took a *d* of Levi
2:5 Pharaoh's *d* came down to bathe
Ex 2:7 his sister said to Pharaoh's *d*
2:8 So Pharaoh's *d* said to her
2:9 Pharaoh's *d* then said to her
2:10 brought him to Pharaoh's *d*
2:21 gave Zipporah his *d* to Moses
6:23 Elisheba, Amminadab's *d*, the
20:10 you nor your son nor your *d*
21:7 sell his *d* as a slave girl
21:31 it gored a son or gored a *d*
Le 12:6 or for a *d* she will bring a
18:9 *d* of your father or the
18:9 or the *d* of your mother
18:10 nakedness of the *d* of your
18:10, 10 the *d* of your *d*, you
18:11 nakedness of the *d* of your
18:17 of a woman and her *d* you
18:17 The *d* of her son and the
18:17, 17 *d* of her *d* . . . not take
19:29 profane your *d* by making her
20:17 takes . . . *d* of his father
20:17 or the *d* of his mother, and
21:2 for his *d* and for his brother
21:9 *d* of a priest should make
22:12 *d* of a priest should become
22:13 *d* of a priest should become
24:11 Shelomith, the *d* of Dibri of
Nu 25:15 was Cozbi the *d* of Zur
25:18 *d* of a chieftain of Midian
26:46 name of Asher's *d* was Serah
26:59 Jochebed, Levi's *d*, whom his
27:8 inheritance to pass to his *d*
27:9 has no *d*, you must then give
30:16 between a father and his *d*
36:8 every *d* getting possession of
De 5:14 your son nor your *d* nor your
7:3 Your *d* you must not give to
7:3 his *d* you must not take for
12:18 your son and your *d* and your
13:6 your *d* or your cherished wife
16:11 you and your son and your *d*
16:14 you and your son and your *d*
18:10 his *d* pass through the fire
22:16 my *d* to this man as a wife
22:17 *d* does not have evidence of
27:22 the *d* of his father or the
27:22 or the *d* of his mother
28:56 husband and her son and her *d*
Jos 15:16 give him Achsah my *d* as a
15:17 gave him Achsah his *d* as a
Jg 1:12 Achsah my *d* as a wife
1:13 he gave him Achsah his *d* as
11:34 his *d* coming out to meet
11:34 he had neither son nor *d*
11:35 my *d*! You have indeed made
11:40 commendation to the *d* of
19:24 virgin *d* and his concubine
21:1 give his *d* to Benjamin as a
Ru 2:2 So she said to her: Go, my *d*
2:8 have heard, have you not, my *d*
2:22 It is better, my *d*, that you
3:1 My *d*, ought I not to look for
3:10 Blessed may you be . . . my *d*
3:11 now, my *d*, do not be afraid
3:16 now said: Who are you, my *d*?
3:18 Sit still, my *d*, until you
1Sa 14:50 Ahinoam the *d* of Ahimaaz
17:25 his own *d* he will give him
18:17 Here is my oldest *d* Merab
18:19 Merab, Saul's *d*, to David
18:20 Michal, Saul's *d*, was in
18:27 Saul gave him Michal his *d*
18:28 Michal, Saul's *d*, she loved
25:44 Michal his *d*, David's wife
2Sa 3:3 Maacah the *d* of Talmai the
3:7 was Rizpah the *d* of Aiah
3:13 bring Michal, Saul's *d*, when
6:16 Michal, Saul's *d*, herself
6:20 Michal, Saul's *d*, came on
6:23 Michal, Saul's *d*, she came
11:3 Bath-sheba the *d* of Eliam
12:3 it came to be as a *d* to him
14:27 one *d* whose name was Tamar
17:25 Abigail the *d* of Nahash
21:8 sons of Rizpah the *d* of Aiah
21:8 Michal the *d* of Saul whom
21:10 Rizpah the *d* of Aiah took
21:11 Rizpah the *d* of Aiah, Saul's
1Ki 3:1 take Pharaoh's *d* and bring her
4:11 Taphath, Solomon's *d*
4:15 took Basemath, Solomon's *d*
7:8 to build for Pharaoh's *d*
9:16 his *d*, the wife of Solomon
9:24 Pharaoh's *d* herself came up
11:1 with the *d* of Pharaoh
1Ki 16:31 Jezebel the *d* of Ethbaal
22:42 Azubah the *d* of Shilhi
2Ki 8:18 Ahab's *d* that became his
9:34 for she is the *d* of a king
11:2 the *d* of King Jehoram
14:9 your *d* to my son as a wife
15:33 Jerusha the *d* of Zadok
18:2 Abi the *d* of Zechariah
19:21 The virgin *d* of Zion has
19:21 *d* of Jerusalem has wagged
21:19 Meshullemeth the *d* of Haruz
22:1 Jedidah the *d* of Adaiah
23:10 *d* pass through the fire to
23:31 Hamutal the *d* of Jeremiah
23:36 Zebidah the *d* of Pedaiah
24:8 Nehushta the *d* of Elnathan
24:18 Hamutal the *d* of Jeremiah
1Ch 1:50 Mehetabel, the *d* of Matred
1:50 Matred, the *d* of Mezahab
2:3 Shua's *d*, the Canaanitess
2:21 the *d* of Machir the father
2:35 Sheshan gave his *d* to Jarha
2:49 And Caleb's *d* was Achsah
3:2 Maacah the *d* of Talmai the
3:5 Bath-sheba the *d* of Ammiel
4:18 Bithiah the *d* of Pharaoh
7:24 And his *d* was Sheerah, and
15:29 Michal, Saul's *d*, herself
2Ch 8:11 Pharaoh's *d* Solomon brought
11:18 Mahalath the *d* of Jerimoth
11:18 Abihail the *d* of Eliab the
13:2 Micaiah the *d* of Uriel of
20:31 Azubah the *d* of Shilhi
21:6 *d* had become his wife, and
22:11 Jehoshabeath the *d* of the
22:11 Jehoshabeath the *d* of King
25:18 give your *d* to my son as a
27:1 Jerushah the *d* of Zadok
29:1 Abijah the *d* of Zechariah
Ne 6:18 taken the *d* of Meshullam the
Es 2:7 the *d* of his father's brother
2:7 Mordecai took her as his *d*
2:15 Esther the *d* of Abihail the
2:15 whom he had taken as his *d*
9:29 the queen, the *d* of Abihail
Ps 9:14 In the gates of the *d* of Zion
45:10 Listen, O *d*, and see, and
45:12 *d* of Tyre also with a gift
45:13 The king's *d* is all glorious
137:8 O *d* of Babylon, who are to
Ca 7:1 in your sandals, O willing *d*
Isa 1:8 the *d* of Zion has been left
10:30 shrill cries, O *d* of Gallim
10:32 mountain of the *d* of Zion
16:1 mountain of the *d* of Zion
22:4 of the *d* of my people
23:10 O *d* of Tarshish
23:12 the virgin *d* of Sidon
37:22 *d* of Zion has despised you
37:22 *d* of Jerusalem has wagged
47:1 O virgin *d* of Babylon
47:1 O *d* of the Chaldeans
47:5 O *d* of the Chaldeans
52:2 O captive *d* of Zion
62:11 to the *d* of Zion, Look!
Jer 4:11 to the *d* of my people
4:31 the voice of the *d* of Zion
6:2 The *d* of Zion has resembled
6:23 against you, O *d* of Zion
6:26 O *d* of my people, gird on
8:11 the breakdown of the *d* of my
8:19 the *d* of my people from a
8:21 the breakdown of the *d* of my
8:22 recuperation of the *d* of my
9:1 of the *d* of my people
9:7 account of the *d* of my people
14:17 the virgin *d* of my people
31:22 and that, O unfaithful *d*
46:11 O virgin *d* of Egypt
46:19 inhabitress, the *d* of Egypt
46:24 *d* of Egypt will certainly
48:18 of the *d* of Dibon
49:4 O *d* unfaithful, you the one
50:42 against you, O *d* of Babylon
51:33 *d* of Babylon is like a
52:1 Hamutal the *d* of Jeremiah
La 1:6 from the *d* of Zion there goes
1:15 to the virgin *d* of Judah
2:1 anger beclouds the *d* of Zion
2:2 places of the *d* of Judah
2:4 Into the tent of the *d* of Zion
2:5 And in the *d* of Judah he makes
2:8 wall of the *d* of Zion to ruin
2:10 older men of the *d* of Zion

La 2:11 crash of the *d* of my people
2:13 to you, O *d* of Jerusalem
2:13 O virgin *d* of Zion
2:15 at the *d* of Jerusalem, saying
2:18 O wall of the *d* of Zion
3:48 of the *d* of my people
4:3 *d* of my people becomes cruel
4:6 error of the *d* of my people
4:10 of the *d* of my people
4:21 and rejoice, O *d* of Edom
4:22 Your error, O *d* of Zion, has
4:22 to your error, O *d* of Edom
Eze 14:20 nor *d* would they deliver
16:44 Like mother is her *d*
16:45 are the *d* of your mother
22:11 the *d* of his own father, a
44:25 for *d* or for brother or
Da 11:6 *d* of the king of the south
11:17 regards the *d* of womankind
Ho 1:3 Gomer the *d* of Diblaim, so
1:6 and to give birth to a *d*
Mic 1:13 she was to the *d* of Zion
4:8 the mound of the *d* of Zion
4:8 to the *d* of Jerusalem
4:10 burst forth, O *d* of Zion
4:13 up and thresh, O *d* of Zion
5:1 O *d* of an invasion; a siege
7:6 a *d* is rising up against her
Zep 3:10 the *d* of my scattered ones
3:14 Joyfully cry out, O *d* of Zion!
3:14 Rejoice . . . O *d* of Jerusalem!
Zec 2:7 with the *d* of Babylon
2:10 and rejoice, O *d* of Zion
9:9 Be very joyful, O *d* of Zion
9:9 in triumph, O *d* of Jerusalem
Mal 2:11 *d* of a foreign god as a
Mt 9:18 By now my *d* must be dead
9:22 Take courage, *d;* your faith
10:35 and a *d* against her mother
10:37 affection for son or *d* than
14:6 *d* of Herodias danced at it
15:22 My *d* is badly demonized
15:28 her *d* was healed from that
21:5 Tell the *d* of Zion, Look!
Mr 5:23 My little *d* is in an extreme
5:34 *D,* your faith has made you
5:35 Your *d* died! Why bother the
6:22 *d* of this very Herodias came
7:25 *d* had an unclean spirit
7:26 expel the demon from her *d*
7:29 demon has gone out of your *d*
Lu 2:36 Anna a prophetess, Phanuel's *d*
8:42 *d* about twelve years old and
8:48 *D,* your faith has made you
8:49 Your *d* has died; do not bother
12:53 mother against *d* and
12:53 and *d* against her mother
13:16 woman who is a *d* of Abraham
Joh 12:15 Have no fear, *d* of Zion
Ac 7:21 *d* of Pharaoh picked him up
Heb 11:24 the son of the *d* of Pharaoh

Daughter-in-law
Ge 11:31 and Sarai his *d,* the wife of
38:11 Judah said to Tamar his *d*
38:16 not know that she was his *d*
38:24 Tamar your *d* has played the
Le 18:15 nakedness of your *d* you must
20:12 a man lies down with his *d*
Ru 1:22 the Moabite woman, her *d*
2:20 At that Naomi said to her *d*
2:22 So Naomi said to Ruth her *d*
4:15 your *d* who does love you
1Sa 4:19 his *d,* the wife of Phinehas
1Ch 2:4 Tamar his *d* it was that bore
Eze 22:11 his own *d* a man has defiled
Mic 7:6 *d* against her mother-in-law
Lu 12:53 mother-in-law against her *d*
12:53 *d* against her mother-in-law

Daughter's
De 22:17 evidence of my *d* virginity

Daughters
Ge 5:4 Adam . . . father to sons and *d*
5:7 Seth . . . father to sons and *d*
5:10 Enosh . . . father to sons and *d*
5:13 Kenan . . . father to sons and *d*
5:16 Mahalalel . . . to sons and *d*
5:19 Jared . . . father to sons and *d*
5:22 Enoch . . . father to sons and *d*
5:26 Methuselah . . . sons and *d*
5:30 Lamech . . . sons and *d*
6:1 and *d* were born to them
6:2 began to notice the *d* of men
Ge 6:4 relations with the *d* of men
11:11 Shem . . . to sons and *d*
11:13 Arpachshad . . . sons and *d*
11:15 Shelah . . . sons and *d*
11:17 Eber . . . father to sons and *d*
11:19 Peleg . . . sons and *d*
11:21 Reu . . . father to sons and *d*
11:23 Serug . . . sons and *d*
11:25 Nahor . . . to sons and *d*
19:8 I have two *d* who have never
19:12 *d* and all who are yours in
19:14 who were to take his *d,* and
19:15 two *d* who are found here
19:16 hands of his two *d* and they
19:30 his two *d* along with him
19:30 Lot . . . and his two *d*
19:36 *d* of Lot became pregnant
24:3 *d* of the Canaanites in among
24:13 *d* of the men of the city are
24:37 *d* of the Canaanites in whose
27:46 because of the *d* of Heth
27:46 a wife from the *d* of Heth
27:46 like . . . the *d* of the land
28:1 wife from the *d* of Canaan
28:2 wife from the *d* of Laban
28:6 a wife from the *d* of Canaan
28:8 Esau saw that the *d* of Canaan
29:16 Laban had two *d*
30:13 *d* will certainly pronounce me
31:26 driving my *d* off like
31:28 kiss my children and my *d*
31:31 tear your *d* away from me
31:41 years for your two *d* and six
31:43, 43 The *d* are my *d* and the
31:50 If you go to afflicting my *d*
31:50 wives in addition to my *d*
31:55 kissed . . . his *d* and blessed
34:1 out to see the *d* of the land
34:9 your *d* you are to give to us
34:9 our *d* you are to take for
34:16 certainly give our *d* to you
34:16 your *d* we shall take for
34:21 Their *d* we can take as wives
34:21 our own *d* we can give to
36:2 wives from the *d* of Canaan
36:6 Esau took . . . his *d* and all
37:35 *d* kept rising up to comfort
46:7, 7 his *d* and his sons' *d*
46:15 of his sons and of his *d*
Ex 2:16 priest of Midian had seven *d*
2:20 Then he said to his *d*
3:22 upon your sons and your *d*
6:25 one of the *d* of Putiel as his
10:9 With our sons and our *d,* with
21:4 she does bear him sons or *d*
21:9 to the due right of *d*
32:2 of your sons and of your *d*
34:16 their *d* for your sons, and
34:16 their *d* will be certain to
Le 10:14 your sons and your *d* with
26:29 will eat the flesh of your *d*
Nu 18:11 you and your sons and your *d*
18:19 sons and your *d* with you
21:29 his *d* in the captivity to the
25:1 relations with the *d* of Moab
26:33 proved to have no sons, but *d*
26:33 the *d* of Zelophehad were
27:1 *d* of Zelophehad the son of
27:1 these were the names of his *d*
27:7 *d* of Zelophehad are speaking
36:2 the inheritance . . . to his *d*
36:6 for the *d* of Zelophehad
36:10 way the *d* of Zelophehad did
36:11 the *d* of Zelophehad, became
De 12:12 your sons and your *d* and
12:31 their sons and their *d* they
23:17 None of the *d* of Israel may
28:32 Your sons and your *d* given
28:41 Sons and *d* you will bring
28:53 flesh of your sons and your *d*
32:19 his sons and his *d* gave
Jos 17:3 his sons and his *d* and his
17:3 to have, not sons, but *d*
17:3 were the names of his *d*
17:6 the *d* of Manasseh came into
Jg 3:6 to take their *d* as wives for
3:6 and their own *d* they gave to
11:40 the *d* of Israel would go to
12:9 have thirty sons and thirty *d*
12:9 brought in thirty *d* for his
14:1 the *d* of the Philistines
14:2 the *d* of the Philistines, and
14:3 among the *d* of your brothers
21:7 give them any of our *d* as
Jg 21:18 give them wives from our *d*
21:21 *d* of Shiloh come on out to
21:21 wife from the *d* of Shiloh
Ru 1:11 But Naomi said: Return, my *d*
1:12 Return, my *d,* go, for I have
1:13 my *d,* for it is very bitter
1Sa 1:4 to all her sons and her *d*
2:21 to three sons and two *d*
8:13 And your *d* he will take for
14:49 for the names of his two *d*
30:3 their *d,* they had been
30:6 of his sons and his *d*
30:19 to sons and *d* and from the
2Sa 1:20 *d* of the Philistines may
1:20 *d* of the uncircumcised men
1:24 *d* of Israel, weep over Saul
5:13 more sons and *d* continued
13:18 way the *d* of the king, the
19:5 escape for . . . your *d*
2Ki 17:17 *d* pass through the fire and
1Ch 2:34 came to have no sons, but *d*
4:27 had sixteen sons and six *d*
7:15 Zelophehad came to have *d*
14:3 father to more sons and *d*
23:22 to have, not sons, but *d*
25:5 fourteen sons and three *d*
2Ch 11:21 sons and sixty *d*
13:21 sons and sixteen *d*
24:3 father to sons and *d*
28:8 captive, women, sons and *d*
29:9 *d* and our wives were in
31:18 sons and their *d,* for all
Ezr 2:61 *d* of Barzillai the Gileadite
9:2 *d* for themselves and for
9:12 your *d* do not you people give
9:12 *d* do you accept for your sons
Ne 3:12 repair work, he and his *d*
4:14 your sons and your *d,* your
5:2 sons and our *d* we are giving
5:5 our sons and our *d* to slaves
5:5 some of our *d* already reduced
7:63 wife from the *d* of Barzillai
10:28 their sons and their *d*
10:30 not give our *d* to the peoples
10:30 their *d* we should not take
13:25 not give your *d* to their sons
13:25 any of their *d* for your sons
Job 1:2 seven sons and three *d* came
1:13 sons and his *d* were eating
1:18 sons and your *d* were eating
30:29 to the *d* of the ostrich
42:13 seven sons and three *d*
42:15 as pretty as Job's *d* in all
Ps 45:9 The *d* of kings are among your
106:37 And their *d* to demons
106:38 of their sons and their *d*
144:12 *d* like corners carved in
Pr 30:15 leeches have two *d* that cry
31:29 are many *d* that have shown
Ec 12:4 all the *d* of song sound low
Ca 1:5 comely, O you *d* of Jerusalem
2:2 my girl companion among the *d*
2:7 under oath, O *d* of Jerusalem
3:5 under oath, O *d* of Jerusalem
3:10 by the *d* of Jerusalem
3:11 and look, O you *d* of Zion
5:8 under oath, O *d* of Jerusalem
5:16 companion, O *d* of Jerusalem
6:9 The *d* have seen her, and they
8:4 under oath, O *d* of Jerusalem
Isa 3:16 *d* of Zion have become
3:17 head of the *d* of Zion scabby
4:4 excrement of the *d* of Zion
16:2 the *d* of Moab will become
32:9 careless *d,* give ear to my
43:6 my *d* from the extremity of
49:22 they will carry your own *d*
56:5 better than sons and *d*
60:4 your *d* who will be taken
Jer 3:24 their sons and their *d*
5:17 eat up your sons and your *d*
7:31 burn their sons and their *d*
9:20 teach your *d* a lamentation
11:22 Their sons and their *d*
14:16 and their sons and their *d*
16:2 come to have sons and *d* in
16:3 concerning the *d* that are
19:9 and the flesh of their *d*
29:6 father to sons and to *d*
29:6 give your own *d* to husbands
29:6 give birth to sons and to *d*
32:35 *d* pass through the fire
35:8 wives, our sons and our *d*
41:10 *d* of the king and all the

Jer 43:6 *d* of the king and every soul
48:46 and your *d* as captives
La 3:51 of all the *d* of my city
Eze 13:17 against the *d* of your people
14:16 nor *d* would they deliver
14:18 deliver neither sons nor *d*
14:22 Sons and *d*, here they are
16:20 *d* . . . you would sacrifice
16:27 the *d* of the Philistines
16:57 reproach of the *d* of Syria
16:57 *d* of the Philistines, those
16:61 give them to you as *d*, but
23:2 the *d* of one mother
23:4 to give birth to sons and *d*
23:10 sons and her *d* they took
23:25 Your sons and your *d* they
23:47 and their *d* they will kill
24:21 your sons and your *d* whom
24:25 their sons and their *d*
32:16 Even the *d* of the nations
32:18 the *d* of majestic nations
Ho 4:13 your *d* commit fornication
4:14 an accounting against your *d*
Joe 2:28 *d* will certainly prophesy
3:8 sell your sons and your *d*
Am 7:17 your *d*, by the sword they
Lu 1:5 a wife from the *d* of Aaron
23:28 *D* of Jerusalem, stop weeping
Ac 2:17 and your *d* will prophesy and
21:9 *d*, virgins, that prophesied
2Co 6:18 you will be sons and *d* to me

Daughters'

Ge 31:43 everything . . . mine and my *d*

Daughters-in-law

Ru 1:6 with her *d* and to return from
1:7 both of her *d* were with her
1:8 Naomi said to both of her *d*
Ho 4:13 your own *d* commit adultery
4:14 against your *d* because they

David

Ru 4:22 and Jesse became father to *D*
1Sa 16:13 operative upon *D* from that
16:19 Do send to me *D* your son
16:20 by the hand of *D* his son to
16:21 *D* came to Saul and attended
16:22 saying: Let *D*, please, keep
16:23 *D* took the harp and played
17:12 *D* was the son of . . . Jesse
17:14 *D* was the youngest, and the
17:15 *D* was going and returning
17:17 Then Jesse said to *D* his son
17:20 *D* got up early in the
17:22 *D* left the baggage from off
17:23 and *D* got to listen in
17:26 *D* began to say to the men
17:28 anger grew hot against *D*
17:29 *D* said: What have I done
17:31 words that *D* spoke came to
17:32 *D* proceeded to say to Saul
17:33 Saul said to *D*: You are not
17:34 *D* went on to say to Saul
17:37 Then *D* added: Jehovah, who
17:37 Saul said to *D*: Go, and may
17:38 Saul now went clothing *D*
17:39 *D* girded his sword on over
17:39 *D* said to Saul: I am unable
17:39 So *D* removed them off him
17:41 nearer and nearer to *D*, and
17:42 Philistine looked and saw *D*
17:43 Philistine said to *D*: Am I
17:43 called down evil upon *D* by
17:44 went on to say to *D*: Just come
17:45 *D* said to the Philistine
17:48 drawing nearer to meet *D*
17:48 *D* began hurrying and running
17:49 *D* thrust his hand into his
17:50 *D*, with a sling and a stone
17:51 *D* continued running and got
17:54 Then *D* took the head of the
17:55 Saul saw *D* going out to
17:57 as soon as *D* returned from
17:58 *D* said: The son of your
18:1 bound up with the soul of *D*
18:3 Jonathan and *D* proceeded to
18:4 gave it to *D*, and also his
18:5 And *D* began going out
18:6 *D* returned from striking the
18:7 And *D* his tens of thousands
18:8 given *D* tens of thousands
18:9 looking suspiciously at *D*
18:10 *D* was playing music with
18:11 will pin *D* even to the wall
18:11 *D* turned aside from before
1Sa 18:12 And Saul grew afraid of *D*
18:14 *D* was continually acting
18:16 and Judah were lovers of *D*
18:17 Finally Saul said to *D*
18:18 *D* said to Saul: Who am I
18:19 Saul's daughter, to *D*
18:20 Michal . . . in love with *D*
18:21 Saul said to *D*: By one of
18:22 Speak to *D* secretly, saying
18:23 words in the ears of *D*
18:23 *D* said: Is it an easy thing
18:24 like these that *D* spoke
18:25 what you men will say to *D*
18:25 schemed to have *D* fall by
18:26 reported these words to *D*
18:27 *D* rose and he and his men
18:27 and *D* came bringing their
18:28 that Jehovah was with *D*
18:29 more fear because of *D*
18:29 to be an enemy of *D* always
18:30 *D* acted most prudently of
19:1 of putting *D* to death
19:2 he took great delight in *D*
19:2 So Jonathan told *D*, saying
19:4 Jonathan spoke well of *D* to
19:4 sin against his servant *D*
19:5 having *D* put to death for
19:7 Afterward Jonathan called *D*
19:7 Jonathan brought *D* to Saul
19:8 *D* went sallying forth and
19:9 *D* was playing music with his
19:10 pin *D* to the wall with the
19:10 *D* himself fled that he
19:11 Michal his wife told *D*
19:12 Michal had *D* descend
19:14 messengers to take *D*, but
19:15 the messengers to see *D*
19:18 *D*, he ran away and made his
19:19 *D* is in Naioth in Ramah
19:20 sent messengers to take *D*
19:22 Where are Samuel and *D*?
20:1 *D* went running away from
20:3 *D* swore in addition and said
20:4 Jonathan went on to say to *D*
20:5 At this *D* said to Jonathan
20:6 *D* earnestly asked leave of
20:10 *D* said to Jonathan: Who
20:11 Jonathan said to *D*: Just
20:12 say to *D*: Jehovah the God
20:12 is well-disposed toward *D*
20:15 cuts off the enemies of *D*
20:16 off from the house of *D*
20:17 Jonathan swore again to *D*
20:24 *D* proceeded to conceal
20:28 *D* earnestly asked leave of
20:33 father to put *D* to death
20:34 had been hurt respecting *D*
20:39 Jonathan and *D* themselves
20:41 *D*, he rose up from nearby
20:41 *D* had done it the most
20:42 say to *D*: Go in peace, since
20:42 *D* rose up and went his way
21:1 *D* came into Nob to Ahimelech
21:1 tremble at meeting *D* and
21:2 *D* said to Ahimelech the
21:4 priest answered *D* and said
21:5 *D* answered the priest and
21:8 *D* went on to say to
21:9 *D* went on to say: There is
21:10 *D* rose up and continued
21:11 Is not this *D* the king of
21:11 And *D* his tens of thousands
21:12 *D* began to take these words
22:1 *D* proceeded to go from there
22:3 *D* went from there to Mizpeh
22:4 *D* happened to be in the
22:5 Gad the prophet said to *D*
22:5 *D* went away and came into
22:6 *D* and the men that were with
22:14 And who . . . is like *D*
22:17 their hand also is with *D*
22:20 running away to follow *D*
22:21 Abiathar told *D*: Saul has
22:22 *D* said to Abiathar: I well
23:1 came reporting to *D*, saying
23:2 *D* proceeded to inquire of
23:2 Jehovah said to *D*: Go, and
23:3 the men of *D* said to him
23:4 *D* inquired yet again of
23:5 *D* went with his men to
23:5 *D* came to be the savior of
23:6 ran away to *D* at Keilah
23:7 *D* has come to Keilah
23:8 to besiege *D* and his men
1Sa 23:9 *D* got to know that Saul was
23:10 *D* went on to say: O Jehovah
23:12 *D* went on to say: Will the
23:13 *D* rose up with his men
23:13 *D* had escaped from Keilah
23:14 *D* took up dwelling in the
23:15 *D* continued in fear because
23:15 *D* was in the wilderness of
23:16 went to *D* at Horesh, that
23:18 *D* kept dwelling in Horesh
23:19 *D* concealing himself close
23:24 *D* and his men were in the
23:25 told *D*, he at once went
23:25 chasing after *D* into the
23:26 *D* and his men were on that
23:26 *D* became hurried to go away
23:26 men were closing in on *D*
23:28 from chasing after *D* and
23:29 *D* made his way up from
24:1 *D* is in the wilderness of
24:2 looking for *D* and his men
24:3 *D* and his men were in the
24:4 *D* rose up and quietly cut
24:7 *D* dispersed his men with
24:8 *D* rose up afterward and went
24:8 *D* proceeded to bow low with
24:9 *D* went on to say to Saul
24:9 *D* is seeking your hurt
24:16 *D* finished speaking these
24:16 this your voice, my son *D*
24:17 say to *D*: You are more
24:22 *D* swore to Saul, after
24:22 *D* and his men, they went
25:1 *D* rose up and went down to
25:4 *D* got to hear in the
25:5 *D* sent ten young men and
25:5 *D* said to the young men
25:8 and to your son *D*
25:9 words in the name of *D* and
25:10 Who is *D*, and who is the
25:13 *D* said to his men: Gird on
25:13 *D* also girded on his own
25:13 go up after *D*, about four
25:14 *D* sent messengers from the
25:20 *D* and his men coming down
25:21 *D*, he had said: It was
25:22 God do to the enemies of *D*
25:23 Abigail caught sight of *D*
25:23 fell upon her face before *D*
25:32 *D* said to Abigail: Blessed
25:35 *D* accepted from her hand
25:39 *D* got to hear that Nabal
25:39 *D* proceeded to send and
25:40 *D* himself has sent us to
25:42 messengers of *D* and then
25:43 *D* had also taken Ahinoam
26:1 *D* concealing himself on the
26:2 look for *D* in the wilderness
26:3 while *D* was dwelling in the
26:4 *D* sent spies that he might
26:5 *D* rose up and went to the
26:5 *D* got to see the place where
26:6 *D* answered and said to
26:7 *D* made his way with Abishai
26:8 Abishai now said to *D*: God
26:9 *D* said to Abishai: Do not
26:10 *D* went on to say: As
26:12 *D* took the spear and the
26:13 *D* passed on to the other
26:14 *D* began to call out to the
26:15 *D* went on to say to Abner
26:17 recognize the voice of *D*
26:17 this your voice, my son *D*
26:17 To this *D* said: It is my
26:21 my son *D*, for I shall no
26:22 *D* answered and said: Here
26:25 Saul said to *D*: Blessed may
26:25 Blessed . . . be, my son *D*
26:25 *D* proceeded to go his way
27:1 *D* said in his heart: Now I
27:2 *D* rose up and he and six
27:3 *D* continued to dwell with
27:3 *D* and his two wives
27:4 *D* had run away to Gath, and
27:5 *D* said to Achish: If, now
27:7 *D* dwelt in the countryside
27:8 *D* proceeded to go up with
27:9 *D* struck the land, but he
27:10 *D* said: Upon the south of
27:11 *D* was not preserving any
27:11 This is the way *D* did
27:12 Achish believed *D*, saying
28:1 Achish said to *D*
28:2 *D* said to Achish: That is

1Sa 28:2 Achish said to *D*: That is
28:17 give it to your fellowman *D*
29:2 *D* and his men were passing
29:3 *D* the servant of Saul king
29:5 *D* to whom they kept
29:5 *D* his tens of thousands
29:6 Achish called *D* and said to
29:8 *D* said to Achish: Why, what
29:9 said to *D*: I well know that
29:11 *D* rose up early, he and
30:1 *D* and his men were coming to
30:3 *D* came with his men to the
30:4 *D* and the people that were
30:6 distressing to *D*, because
30:6 *D* took to strengthening
30:7 *D* said to Abiathar the priest
30:7 the ephod near to *D*
30:8 *D* began to inquire of
30:9 *D* got on his way, he and the
30:10 *D* kept up the chase, he
30:11 took him to *D* and gave him
30:13 *D* now said to him: To whom
30:15 *D* said to him: Will you
30:17 *D* went striking them down
30:18 *D* got to deliver all that
30:18 his two wives *D* delivered
30:19 Everything *D* recovered
30:20 *D* took all the flocks and
30:21 *D* came to the two hundred
30:21 tired to go along with *D*
30:21 came out to meet *D* and to
30:21 *D* came near to the people
30:22 men that had gone with *D*
30:23 *D* said: You must not do
30:26 When *D* came to Ziklag he
30:31 places where *D* had walked
2Sa 1:1 *D* himself had returned from
1:1 *D* continued to dwell at
1:2 came to *D*, he at once fell
1:3 *D* proceeded to say to him
1:4 *D* went on to say to him
1:5 *D* said to the young man that
1:11 *D* took hold of his garments
1:13 *D* now said to the young man
1:14 *D* said to him: How was it
1:15 *D* called one of the young
1:16 *D* then said to him: The
1:17 *D* proceeded to chant this
2:1 *D* proceeded to inquire of
2:1 *D* went on to say: Where shall
2:2 *D* went up there and also his
2:3 *D* brought up, each with his
2:4 anointed *D* there as king over
2:4 they came telling *D*, saying
2:5 *D* sent messengers to the men
2:10 themselves followers of *D*
2:11 days that *D* proved to be king
2:13 and the servants of *D*, they
2:15 from the servants of *D*
2:17 before the servants of *D*
2:30 from the servants of *D*
2:31 servants of *D*, for their part
3:1 and the house of *D* came to be
3:1 *D* kept getting stronger, and
3:2 sons were born to *D* in Hebron
3:5 ones born to *D* in Hebron
3:6 of Saul and the house of *D*
3:8 in the hand of *D*
3:9 just as Jehovah swore to *D*
3:10 the throne of *D* over Israel
3:12 sent messengers to *D* on the
3:14 *D* sent messengers to
3:17 seeking *D* as king over you
3:18 Jehovah himself said to *D*
3:18 By the hand of *D* my servant
3:19 speak in the ears of *D* at
3:20 Abner came to *D* at Hebron
3:20 *D* proceeded to make a feast
3:21 Abner said to *D*: Let me rise
3:21 *D* sent Abner off, and he got
3:22 Abner, he was not with *D* in
3:26 Joab went out from *D* and
3:26 *D* himself did not know of it
3:28 *D* heard of it afterward, he
3:31 *D* said to Joab and all the
3:31 Even King *D* was walking
3:35 people came to give *D* bread
3:35 *D* swore, saying: So may God
4:8 head of Ish-bosheth to *D* at
4:9 *D* answered Rechab and Baanah
4:12 *D* commanded the young men
5:1 Israel came to *D* at Hebron
5:3 King *D* concluded a covenant
5:3 anointed *D* as king over Israel

2Sa 5:4 Thirty years old was *D* when
5:6 say to *D*: You will not come
5:6 *D* will not come in here
5:7 *D* proceeded to capture the
5:7 that is, the city of *D*
5:8 *D* said on that day: Anyone
5:8 hateful to the soul of *D*
5:9 *D* took up dwelling in the
5:9 be called the city of *D*
5:9 *D* began to build all around
5:10 *D* went on getting greater
5:11 send messengers to *D*, and
5:11 began to build a house for *D*
5:12 *D* came to know that Jehovah
5:13 *D* went on taking more
5:13 continued to be born to *D*
5:17 anointed *D* as king over
5:17 came up to look for *D*
5:17 *D* heard of it, then he went
5:19 *D* began to inquire of Jehovah
5:19 Jehovah said to *D*: Go up
5:20 *D* came to Baal-perazim, and
5:20 *D* got to strike them down
5:21 *D* and his men took them
5:23 *D* inquired of Jehovah, but
5:25 *D* did that way, just as
6:1 *D* proceeded again to gather
6:2 *D* and all the people that
6:5 *D* and all the house of Israel
6:8 *D* became angry over the fact
6:9 *D* became afraid of Jehovah
6:10 *D* was not willing to remove
6:10 to him at the city of *D*
6:10 *D* had it carried aside to
6:12 report was made to King *D*
6:12 *D* proceeded to go and bring
6:12 the city of *D* with rejoicing
6:14 *D* was dancing around before
6:14 *D* being girded with an ephod
6:15 *D* and all the house of Israel
6:16 came into the city of *D*
6:16 King *D* leaping and dancing
6:17 tent that *D* had pitched for
6:17 *D* offered up burnt sacrifices
6:18 *D* was finished with offering
6:20 *D* now returned to bless his
6:20 out to meet *D* and then said
6:21 *D* said to Michal: It was
7:5 say to my servant *D*, This is
7:8 say to my servant *D*, This is
7:17 way that Nathan spoke to *D*
7:18 King *D* came in and sat down
7:20 *D* add and speak to you, when
7:26 house of your servant *D*
8:1 *D* proceeded to strike the
8:1 *D* got to take Metheg-ammah
8:3 *D* went on to strike down
8:4 *D* got to capture from him one
8:4 *D* proceeded to hamstring all
8:5 *D* then struck down among the
8:6 *D* put garrisons in Syria of
8:6 Jehovah continued to save *D*
8:7 *D* took the circular shields
8:8 *D* took copper in very great
8:9 *D* had struck down all the
8:10 son to King *D* to ask him
8:11 King *D* sanctified to Jehovah
8:13 *D* proceeded to make a name
8:14 came to be servants of *D*
8:14 Jehovah kept saving *D*
8:15 *D* kept reigning over all
8:15 *D* was continually rendering
8:18 sons of *D* . . . became priests
9:1 *D* proceeded to say: Is there
9:2 called him to *D*, and the king
9:5 *D* sent and took him from the
9:6 came in to *D*, he at once fell
9:6 *D* said: Mephibosheth!
9:7 *D* went on to say to him
10:2 *D* said: I shall exercise
10:2 *D* sent by means of his
10:2 servants of *D* proceeded to
10:3 *D* honoring your father in
10:3 *D* has sent his servants to
10:4 Hanun took the servants of *D*
10:5 people reported it to *D*, and
10:6 become foul-smelling to *D*
10:7 *D* heard of it, then he sent
10:17 report was made to *D*, he
10:17 in formation to meet *D*
10:18 *D* got to kill of the Syrians
11:1 *D* proceeded to send Joab and
11:1 *D* was dwelling in Jerusalem
11:2 *D* proceeded to rise from his

2Sa 11:3 *D* sent and inquired about
11:4 *D* sent messengers that he
11:5 told *D* and said: I am
11:6 *D* sent to Joab, saying: Send
11:6 So Joab sent Uriah to *D*
11:7 *D* began to ask how Joab was
11:8 *D* said to Uriah: Go down to
11:10 told *D*, saying: Uriah did
11:10 *D* said to Uriah: It is from
11:11 Uriah said to *D*: The Ark
11:12 *D* said to Uriah: Dwell here
11:13 *D* called him that he might
11:14 *D* proceeded to write a
11:17 servants of *D*, fell and
11:18 report to *D* all the matters
11:22 told *D* all about which Joab
11:23 say to *D*: The men proved
11:25 *D* said to the messenger
11:27 *D* immediately sent and took
11:27 *D* had done appeared bad in
12:1 to send Nathan to *D*. So he
12:7 Nathan said to *D*: You
12:13 *D* now said to Nathan: I
12:13 At this Nathan said to *D*
12:15 had borne to *D* so that
12:16 *D* began to seek the true
12:16 *D* went on a strict fast and
12:18 servants of *D* were afraid
12:19 *D* got to see that his
12:19 *D* began to discern that the
12:19 *D* said to his servants: Has
12:20 *D* got up from the earth and
12:24 *D* . . . comfort Bath-sheba
12:27 Joab sent messengers to *D*
12:29 *D* gathered all the people
12:31 *D* and all the people
13:1 Absalom the son of *D* had a
13:1 Amnon the son of *D* fell in
13:7 *D* sent to Tamar at the house
13:21 King *D* himself heard about
13:30 report itself came to *D*
13:37 *D* continued to mourn over
13:39 soul of *D* the king longed
15:13 an informer came to *D*
15:14 *D* said to all his servants
15:22 At that *D* said to Ittai
15:30 *D* was going up by the
15:31 to *D* the report was made
15:31 *D* said: Turn, please, the
15:32 when *D* himself came to the
15:33 *D* said to him: If you
16:1 *D* himself had crossed over
16:5 *D* came as far as Bahurim
16:6 began throwing stones at *D*
16:6 all the servants of King *D*
16:10 Call down evil upon *D*
16:11 *D* went on to say to Abishai
16:13 *D* and his men kept going
16:23 both to *D* and to Absalom
17:1 and chase after *D* tonight
17:16 tell *D*, saying, Do not lodge
17:17 as they had to tell King *D*
17:21 went on and told King *D*
17:21 said to *D*: You people, rise
17:22 *D* rose up and also all the
17:24 *D*, he came to Mahanaim, and
17:27 as *D* came to Mahanaim
17:29 they brought forward for *D*
18:1 *D* proceeded to number the
18:2 *D* sent one third of the
18:7 before the servants of *D*
18:9 before the servants of *D*
18:24 *D* was sitting between the
19:11 As for King *D*, he sent to
19:16 hurried . . . to meet King *D*
19:22 *D* said: What do I have to
19:41 all the men of *D* with him
19:43 even in *D* we are more than
20:1 We have no share in *D*, and
20:2 to go up from following *D*
20:3 *D* came to his house at
20:6 *D* said to Abishai: Now Sheba
20:11 whoever belongs to *D*, let
20:21 his hand against King *D*
20:26 also became a priest of *D*
21:1 a famine in the days of *D*
21:1 *D* proceeded to consult the
21:3 *D* went on to say to the
21:7 between *D* and Jonathan the
21:11 reported to *D* what Rizpah
21:12 *D* went and took the bones
21:15 *D* and his servants with him
21:15 and *D* grew tired
21:16 to think of striking *D* down

2Sa 21:17 the men of *D* swore to him
21:22 fall by the hand of *D* and
22:1 *D* proceeded to speak to
22:51 To *D* and to his seed for
23:1 the last words of *D*
23:1 *D* the son of Jesse, And the
23:8 men that belonged to *D*
23:9 the three mighty men with *D*
23:13 to *D* at the cave of Adullam
23:14 *D* was then in the place
23:15 *D* expressed his craving and
23:16 bringing it to *D*
23:23 *D* appointed him to his own
24:1 incited *D* against them
24:10 *D* said to Jehovah: I have
24:11 *D* proceeded to rise up in
24:12 Go, and you must say to *D*
24:13 Gad came in to *D* and told
24:14 So *D* said to Gad: It is
24:17 *D* proceeded to say to
24:18 Gad came in to *D* on that
24:19 *D* began to go up in accord
24:21 *D* said: To buy from you the
24:22 Araunah said to *D*: Let my
24:24 *D* bought the threshing floor
24:25 *D* proceeded to build there
1Ki 1:1 King *D* was old, advanced in
1:8 mighty men that belonged to *D*
1:11 *D* does not know of it at all
1:13 Go and enter in to King *D*
1:28 *D* now answered and said
1:31 *D* live to time indefinite
1:32 *D* said: You men, call for me
1:37 the throne of my lord King *D*
1:38 upon the she-mule of King *D*
1:43 *D* himself has made Solomon
1:47 wish our lord King *D* well
2:1 the days of *D* gradually drew
2:10 Then *D* lay down with his
2:10 was buried in the city of *D*
2:11 the days that *D* had reigned
2:12 the throne of *D* his father
2:24 seated upon the throne of *D*
2:26 carried the ark . . . before *D*
2:32 *D* himself had not known of
2:33 for *D* and for his offspring
2:44 that you did to *D* my father
2:45 the throne of *D* itself will
3:1 bring her to the city of *D*
3:3 walking in the statutes of *D*
3:6 your servant *D* my father
3:7 in the place of *D* my father
3:14 just as *D* your father walked
5:1 a lover of *D* Hiram had always
5:3 *D* my father was not able to
5:5 just as Jehovah promised to *D*
5:7 he has given *D* a wise son
6:12 I spoke to *D* your father
7:51 things made holy by *D* his
8:1 city of *D*, that is to say
8:15 with *D* my father, and by his
8:16 *D* to come to be over my
8:17 *D* my father to build a house
8:18 Jehovah said to *D* my father
8:20 rise up in the place of *D*
8:24 kept toward your servant *D*
8:25 keep toward your servant *D*
8:26 promised to your servant *D*
8:66 performed for *D* his servant
9:4 just as *D* your father walked
9:5 just as I promised *D* your
9:24 came up out of the city of *D*
11:4 like the heart of *D* his
11:6 like *D* his father
11:12 the sake of *D* your father
11:13 the sake of *D* my servant
11:15 when *D* struck down Edom
11:21 that *D* had lain down with
11:24 when *D* killed them
11:27 the city of *D* his father
11:32 the sake of my servant *D*
11:33 like *D* his father
11:34 the sake of *D* my servant
11:36 that *D* my servant may
11:38 just as *D* my servant did
11:38 just as I have built for *D*
11:39 the offspring of *D* on
11:43 buried in the city of *D* his
12:16 What share do we have in *D*?
12:16 to your own house, O *D*
12:19 against the house of *D*
12:20 follower of the house of *D*
12:26 return to the house of *D*
13:2 A son born to the house of *D*

1Ki 14:8 away from the house of *D*
14:8 not become like my servant *D*
14:31 forefathers in the city of *D*
15:3 heart of *D* his forefather
15:4 on account of *D*, Jehovah his
15:5 *D* did what was right in the
15:8 buried him in the city of *D*
15:11 like *D* his forefather
15:24 city of *D* his forefather
22:50 city of *D* his forefather
2Ki 8:19 for the sake of *D* his servant
8:24 buried . . . in the city of *D*
9:28 forefathers in the city of *D*
11:10 had belonged to King *D*
12:21 forefathers in the city of *D*
14:3 not like *D* his forefather
14:20 in the city of *D*
15:7 in the city of *D*
15:38 city of *D* his forefather
16:2 like *D* his forefather
16:20 forefathers in the city of *D*
17:21 from the house of *D*
18:3 *D* his forefather had done
19:34 the sake of *D* my servant
20:5 God of *D* your forefather has
20:6 for the sake of *D* my servant
21:7 had said to *D* and to Solomon
22:2 walk in all the way of *D* his
1Ch 2:15 the sixth, *D* the seventh
3:1 sons of *D* that were born to
3:9 all the sons of *D* besides
4:31 cities down till *D* reigned
6:31 *D* gave positions for the
7:2 Their number in the days of *D*
9:22 These *D* and Samuel the seer
10:14 over to *D* the son of Jesse
11:1 to *D* at Hebron, saying: Look!
11:3 *D* concluded a covenant with
11:3 they anointed *D* as king over
11:4 *D* and all Israel went to
11:5 of Jebus began to say to *D*
11:5 *D* proceeded to capture the
11:5 Zion . . . the city of *D*
11:6 *D* said: Anyone striking the
11:7 *D* took up dwelling in the
11:7 they called it the city of *D*
11:9 *D* went on getting greater
11:10 men that belonged to *D*
11:11 men that belonged to *D*
11:13 to be with *D* at Pas-dammim
11:15 to *D* at the cave of Adullam
11:16 *D* was then in the place
11:17 *D* showed his craving and
11:18 and bringing it to *D*
11:18 *D* did not consent to drink
11:25 *D* put him over his own
12:1 that came to *D* at Ziklag
12:16 difficult to approach, to *D*
12:17 *D* went out before them and
12:18 Yours we are, O *D*, and with
12:18 *D* received them and put
12:19 deserted to *D* when he came
12:21 were of help to *D* against
12:22 people kept coming to *D* to
12:23 that came to *D* at Hebron
12:31 to come to make *D* king
12:33 for flocking together to *D*
12:38 to Hebron to make *D* king
12:38 one heart for making *D* king
12:39 with *D* three days, eating
13:1 *D* proceeded to consult with
13:2 *D* went on to say to all the
13:5 *D* congregated all Israel
13:6 *D* and all Israel proceeded to
13:8 And *D* and all Israel were
13:11 And *D* became angry because
13:12 *D* became afraid of the true
13:13 *D* did not remove the Ark to
13:13 to himself at the city of *D*
14:1 messengers to *D* and cedar
14:2 *D* came to know that Jehovah
14:3 And *D* went on to take more
14:3 *D* came to be father to more
14:8 *D* had been anointed as king
14:8 came up to look for *D*
14:8 When *D* heard of it, then he
14:10 *D* began to inquire of God
14:11 *D* went up to Baal-perazim
14:11 *D* said: The true God has
14:12 Then *D* said the word, and
14:14 *D* inquired again of God, and
14:16 *D* did just as the true God
15:1 houses . . . in the city of *D*
15:2 *D* said: No one is to carry

1Ch 15:3 *D* congregated all Israel at
15:4 *D* proceeded to gather the
15:11 *D* called Zadok and Abiathar
15:16 *D* now said to the chiefs of
15:25 And *D* and the older men of
15:27 And *D* was dressed in a
15:27 upon *D* there was an ephod
15:29 as far as the city of *D*
15:29 to see King *D* skipping about
16:1 tent that *D* had pitched for
16:2 *D* finished offering up the
16:7 *D* made a contribution for
16:43 *D* went around to bless his
17:1 *D* had begun dwelling in his
17:1 *D* proceeded to say to Nathan
17:2 Upon that Nathan said to *D*
17:4 you must say to *D* my servant
17:7 you will say to my servant *D*
17:15 way that Nathan spoke to *D*
17:16 King *D* came in and sat down
17:18 What more could *D* say to
17:24 the house of *D* your servant
18:1 *D* proceeded to strike down
18:3 And *D* went on to strike down
18:4 *D* captured from him a
18:4 *D* hamstrung all the chariot
18:5 *D* went striking down among
18:6 *D* put garrisons in Syria of
18:6 kept giving salvation to *D*
18:7 *D* took the circular shields
18:8 *D* took very much copper
18:9 *D* had struck down all the
18:10 Hadoram his son to King *D*
18:11 King *D* sanctified to Jehovah
18:13 And Jehovah kept saving *D*
18:14 *D* continued to reign over
18:17 sons of *D* were the first in
19:2 *D* said: I shall exercise
19:2 *D* sent messengers to comfort
19:2 servants of *D* proceeded to
19:3 Is *D* honoring your father in
19:4 Hanun took the servants of *D*
19:5 and told *D* about the men
19:6 become foul-smelling to *D*
19:8 When *D* heard of it, he
19:17 the report was made to *D*
19:17 When *D* drew up in battle
19:18 and *D* went killing of the
19:19 promptly made peace with *D*
20:1 *D* was dwelling in Jerusalem
20:2 *D* took the crown of Malcam
20:3 the way *D* proceeded to do
20:3 *D* and all the people returned
20:7 of Shimea the brother of *D*
20:8 to fall by the hand of *D* and
21:1 to incite *D* to number Israel
21:2 *D* said to Joab and the chiefs
21:5 gave the number . . . to *D*
21:8 *D* said to the true God
21:10 and you must speak to *D*
21:11 Gad went in to *D* and said
21:13 *D* said to Gad: It is very
21:16 When *D* raised his eyes, he
21:16 and *D* and the older men
21:17 *D* proceeded to say to the
21:18 said to Gad to say to *D*
21:18 *D* should go up to erect an
21:19 *D* went up at the word of
21:21 So *D* came as far as Ornan
21:21 When Ornan looked and saw *D*
21:21 bowed down to *D* with his
21:22 *D* said to Ornan: Do give me
21:23 Ornan said to *D*: Take it as
21:24 King *D* said to Ornan
21:25 *D* gave Ornan for the place
21:26 *D* built there an altar to
21:28 when *D* saw that Jehovah had
21:30 *D* had not been able to go
22:1 *D* said: This is the house of
22:2 *D* now said to bring together
22:3 and for clamps *D* prepared
22:4 in great quantity to *D*
22:5 *D* said: Solomon my son is
22:5 *D* made preparation in great
22:7 *D* went on to say to Solomon
22:17 *D* went on to command all
23:1 *D* himself had grown old and
23:5 that *D* said I have made for
23:6 Then *D* distributed them in
23:25 *D* had said: Jehovah the God
23:27 For by the last words of *D*
24:3 *D*, and Zadok from the sons
24:31 before *D* the king and Zadok
25:1 *D* and the chiefs of the

1Ch 26:26 *D* the king and the heads of
26:32 *D* the king assigned them
27:23 *D* did not take the number
27:24 of the days of King *D*
27:31 that belonged to King *D*
28:1 *D* proceeded to congregate all
28:2 *D* the king rose to his feet
28:11 *D* proceeded to give Solomon
28:20 *D* went on to say to Solomon
29:1 *D* the king now said to all
29:9 *D* the king himself rejoiced
29:10 *D* blessed Jehovah before the
29:10 *D* said: Blessed may you be
29:20 *D* went on to say to all the
29:22 Solomon the son of *D* king
29:23 as king in place of *D* his
29:24 also all the sons of King *D*
29:26 As for *D* the son of Jesse
29:29 the affairs of *D* the king
2Ch 1:1 And Solomon the son of *D*
1:4 the ark of the true God *D* had
1:4 the place that *D* had prepared
1:8 loving-kindness toward *D* my
1:9 your promise with *D* my father
2:3 as you dealt with *D* my father
2:7 *D* my father has prepared
2:12 to *D* the king a wise son
2:14 men of my lord *D* your father
2:17 census that *D* his father had
3:1 had appeared to *D* his father
3:1 place that *D* had prepared on
5:1 made holy by *D* his father
5:2 up from the city of *D*, that
6:4 with *D* my father and by his
6:6 I shall choose *D* to come to
6:7 close to the heart of *D* my
6:8 Jehovah said to *D* my father
6:10 in the place of *D* my father
6:15 *D* my father what you
6:16 keep toward your servant *D*
6:17 promised to your servant *D*
6:42 loving-kindnesses to *D* your
7:6 *D* the king had made to thank
7:6 *D* would render praise by
7:10 had performed toward *D*
7:17 as *D* your father walked
7:18 covenanted with *D* your
8:11 city of *D* to the house that
8:11 not dwell in the house of *D*
8:14 rule of *D* his father, and
8:14 commandment of *D* the man of
9:31 in the city of *D* his father
10:16 What share do we have in *D*?
10:16 to your own house, O *D*
10:19 against the house of *D*
11:17 way of *D* and Solomon for
11:18 Jerimoth the son of *D* and
12:16 buried in the city of *D*
13:5 kingdom to *D* over Israel to
13:6 of Solomon the son of *D*
13:8 hand of the sons of *D*, when
14:1 buried him in the city of *D*
16:14 in the city of *D*
17:3 in the former ways of *D* his
21:1 forefathers in the city of *D*
21:7 bring the house of *D* to ruin
21:7 he had concluded with *D*, and
21:12 God of *D* your forefather has
21:20 buried him in the city of *D*
23:3 concerning the sons of *D*
23:9 that had belonged to King *D*
23:18 *D* had put in divisions over
23:18 song by the hands of *D*
24:16 buried him in the city of *D*
24:25 buried him in the city of *D*
27:9 buried him in the city of *D*
28:1 like *D* his forefather
29:2 *D* his forefather had done
29:25 commandment of *D* and of
29:26 with the instruments of *D*
29:27 of *D* the king of Israel
29:30 words of *D* and of Asaph the
30:26 Solomon the son of *D* the
32:5 the Mound of the city of *D*
32:30 to the city of *D*, and
32:33 places of the sons of *D*
33:7 God had said to *D* and to
33:14 wall for the city of *D*
34:2 ways of *D* his forefather
34:3 the God of *D* his forefather
35:3 Solomon the son of *D*
35:4 *D* the king of Israel
35:15 the commandment of *D* and of
Ezr 3:10 *D* the king of Israel
Ezr 8:2 of the sons of *D*, Hattush
8:20 whom *D* and the princes gave
Ne 3:15 goes down from the City of *D*
3:16 the Burial Places of *D* and
12:24 *D* the man of the true God
12:36 instruments of song of *D*
12:37 Stairway of the City of *D* by
12:37 wall above the House of *D*
12:45 *D* and Solomon his son
12:46 in the days of *D* and Asaph
Ps 3:*super* A melody of *D* when he was
4:*super* A melody of *D*
5:*super* A melody of *D*
6:*super* A melody of *D*
7:*super* A dirge of *D* that he sang
8:*super* A melody of *D*
9:*super* A melody of *D*
11:*super* To the Director. Of *D*
12:*super* A melody of *D*
13:*super* Director. A melody of *D*
14:*super* To the director. Of *D*
15:*super* A melody of *D*
16:*super* A miktam of *D*
17:*super* A prayer of *D*
18:*super* Of Jehovah's servant, of *D*
18:50 To *D* and to his seed to time
19:*super* director. A melody of *D*
20:*super* director. A melody of *D*
21:*super* director. A melody of *D*
22:*super* A melody of *D*
23:*super* A melody of *D*
24:*super* Of *D*. A melody
25:*super* Of *D*
26:*super* Of *D*
27:*super* Of *D*
28:*super* Of *D*
29:*super* A melody of *D*
30:*super* A melody . . . Of *D*
31:*super* director. A melody of *D*
32:*super* Of *D*. Maskil
34:*super* Of *D*, at the time of his
35:*super* Of *D*
36:*super* Of Jehovah's servant, *D*
37:*super* Of *D*
38:*super* A melody of *D*, to bring
39:*super* A melody of *D*
40:*super* Of *D*, a melody
41:*super* A melody of *D*
51:*super* melody of *D*. When Nathan
52:*super* Of *D*, when Doeg the
52:*super* *D* had come to the house
53:*super* Maskil. Of *D*
54:*super* Of *D*. When the Ziphites
54:*super* *D* concealing himself with
55:*super* Maskil. Of *D*
56:*super* Of *D*. Miktam. When the
57:*super* Do not bring to ruin. Of *D*
58:*super* Do not bring to ruin. Of *D*
59:*super* Of *D*. Miktam. When Saul
60:*super* Of *D*. For teaching
61:*super* Of *D*
62:*super* A melody of *D*
63:*super* A melody of *D*, when he
64:*super* director. A melody of *D*
65:*super* A melody of *D*. A song
68:*super* Of *D*. A melody, a song
69:*super* on The Lilies. Of *D*
70:*super* Of *D*, to bring to
72:20 prayers of *D*, the son of
78:70 so he chose *D* his servant
86:*super* A prayer of *D*
89:3 I have sworn to *D* my servant
89:20 I have found *D* my servant
89:35 To *D* I will not tell lies
89:49 About which you swore to *D*
101:*super* Of *D*. A melody
103:*super* Of *D*
108:*super* A song. A melody of *D*
109:*super* To the director. Of *D*
110:*super* Of *D*. A melody
122:*super* Song of the Ascents. Of *D*
122:5 Thrones for the house of *D*
124:*super* Song of the Ascents. Of *D*
131:*super* Song of the Ascents. Of *D*
132:1 O Jehovah, concerning *D*
132:10 account of *D* your servant
132:11 Jehovah has sworn to *D*
132:17 cause the horn of *D* to grow
133:*super* Song of the Ascents. Of *D*
138:*super* Of *D*
139:*super* For the director. Of *D*
140:*super* A melody of *D*
141:*super* A melody of *D*
142:*super* Of *D*, when he happened
Ps 143:*super* A melody of *D*
144:*super* Of *D*
144:10 setting *D* his servant free
145:*super* A praise, of *D*
Pr 1:1 son of *D*, the king of Israel
Ec 1:1 congregator, the son of *D* the
Ca 4:4 neck is like the tower of *D*
Isa 7:2 made to the house of *D*
7:13 Listen, please, O house of *D*
9:7 throne of *D* and upon his
16:5 trueness in the tent of *D*
22:9 breaches of the city of *D*
22:22 key of the house of *D* upon
29:1 the town where *D* encamped
37:35 the sake of *D* my servant
38:5 Jehovah the God of *D* your
55:3 to *D* that are faithful
Jer 13:13 kings that are sitting for *D*
17:25 sitting on the throne of *D*
21:12 O house of *D*, this is what
22:2 sitting on the throne of *D*
22:4 sitting for *D* upon his throne
22:30 sitting upon the throne of *D*
23:5 I will raise up to *D* a
29:16 sitting on the throne of *D*
30:9 and *D* their king, whom I
33:15 for *D* a righteous sprout
33:21 covenant be broken with *D*
33:22 seed of *D* my servant and
33:26 and of *D* my servant, so
36:30 upon the throne of *D*, and
Eze 34:23 even my servant *D*
34:24 my servant *D* a chieftain
37:24 my servant *D* will be king
37:25 *D* my servant will be their
Ho 3:5 and for *D* their king
Am 6:5 like *D*, have devised for
9:11 raise up the booth of *D* that
Zec 12:7 the beauty of the house of *D*
12:8 become in that day like *D*
12:8 and the house of *D* like God
12:10 pour out upon the house of *D*
12:12 family of the house of *D* by
13:1 to the house of *D* and to the
Mt 1:1 Jesus Christ, son of *D*, son of
1:6 Jesse became father to *D* the
1:6 *D* became father to Solomon by
1:17 from Abraham until *D* were
1:17 from *D* until the deportation
1:20 Joseph, son of *D*, do not be
9:27 Have mercy on us, Son of *D*
12:3 Have you not read what *D* did
12:23 not perhaps be the Son of *D*
15:22 mercy on me, Lord, Son of *D*
20:30 have mercy on us, Son of *D*!
20:31 have mercy on us, Son of *D*!
21:9 Save, we pray, the Son of *D*!
21:15 Save, we pray, the Son of *D*!
22:43 *D* by inspiration calls him
22:45 *D* calls him Lord, how is he
Mr 2:25 *D* did when he fell in need
10:47 Son of *D*, Jesus, have mercy
10:48 Son of *D*, have mercy on me!
11:10 kingdom of our father *D*
12:36 *D* himself said, Jehovah said
12:37 *D* himself calls him Lord
Lu 1:32 the throne of *D* his father
1:69 the house of *D* his servant
2:4 the house and family of *D*
3:31 son of Nathan, son of *D*
6:3 the very thing *D* did when he
18:38 Jesus, Son of *D*, have mercy
18:39 Son of *D*, have mercy on me
20:42 *D* himself says in the book
20:44 *D*, therefore, calls him Lord
Joh 7:42 from the offspring of *D*, and
7:42 village where *D* used to be
Ac 2:25 *D* says respecting him, I had
2:29 family head *D*, that he both
2:34 *D* did not ascend to the
4:25 holy spirit said by . . . *D*
7:45 remained until the days of *D*
13:22 raised up for them *D* as king
13:22 *D* the son of Jesse, a man
13:34 to *D* that are faithful
13:36 *D*, on the one hand, served
15:16 and rebuild the booth of *D*
Ro 1:3 who sprang from the seed of *D*
4:6 *D* also speaks of the happiness
11:9 *D* says: Let their table
Heb 11:32 go on to relate about . . . *D*
Re 3:7 has the key of *D*, who opens
5:5 tribe of Judah, the root of *D*
22:16 root and the offspring of *D*

David's

Ru 4:17 the father of Jesse, *D* father
1Sa 17:50 was no sword in *D* hand
18:26 the matter was to *D* liking
19:11 messengers to *D* house to
20:16 at the hand of *D* enemies
20:25 but *D* place was vacant
20:27 *D* place continued vacant
20:35 field of *D* appointed place
24:4 *D* men began to say to him
24:5 *D* heart kept striking him for
25:9 *D* young men came and spoke
25:10 Nabal answered *D* servants
25:12 *D* young men turned around
25:40 *D* servants came to Abigail
25:44 *D* wife, to Palti the son of
30:5 *D* two wives had been carried
30:20 This is *D* spoil
2Sa 3:5 Ithream by Eglah, *D* wife
3:22 *D* servants and Joab were
8:2 *D* servants to carry tribute
8:6 Syrians came to be *D* servants
12:5 *D* anger grew very hot
12:30 it came to be upon *D* head
13:3 of Shimeah, *D* brother
13:32 of Shimeah, *D* brother
15:12 *D* counselor, from his city
15:37 Hushai, *D* companion, came
16:16 Hushai . . . *D* companion
21:21 *D* brother, struck him down
24:10 *D* heart began to beat him
24:11 Gad the prophet, *D* visionary
1Ch 12:8 separated themselves to *D*
14:17 *D* fame began to go out into
18:2 *D* servants bearing tribute
18:6 *D* servants bearing tribute
18:13 the Edomites came to be *D*
20:2 and it came to be on *D* head
21:9 to speak to Gad, *D* visionary
26:31 fortieth year of *D* kingship
27:18 Elihu, one of *D* brothers
27:32 Jonathan, *D* nephew, was a
Jer 33:17 cut off in *D* case a man
Mt 22:42 They said to him: *D*
Mr 12:35 that the Christ is *D* son
Lu 1:27 man named Joseph of *D* house
2:4 into Judea, to *D* city, which
2:11 Christ the Lord, in *D* city
20:41 that the Christ is *D* son
Ac 1:16 by *D* mouth about Judas, who
2Ti 2:8 and was of *D* seed, according
Heb 4:7 so long a time in *D* psalm

Dawn

Ge 19:15 *d* ascended, then the angels
32:24 grapple with him until the *d*
32:26 for the *d* has ascended
Jos 6:15 as soon as the *d* ascended
Jg 19:25 off at the ascending of the *d*
1Sa 9:26 as soon as the *d* ascended
Ne 4:21 ascending of the *d* until the
Job 3:9 let it not see the beams of *d*
38:12 the *d* to know its place
41:18 are like the beams of *d*
Ps 22:*super* upon the Hind of the *D*
57:8 I will awaken the *d*
108:2 I will awaken the *d*
110:3 from the womb of the *d*
139:9 to take the wings of the *d*
Ca 6:10 is looking down like the *d*
Isa 8:20 will have no light of *d*
14:12 shining one, son of the *d*
58:8 break forth just like the *d*
Da 6:19 at *d*, proceeded to get up
Ho 6:3 Like *d*, his going forth is
10:15 In the *d* the king of Israel
Joe 2:2 like light of *d* spread out
Am 4:13 One making *d* into obscurity
Jon 4:7 at the ascending of the *d* on
Mr 15:1 at *d* the chief priests with

Dawns

2Pe 1:19 day *d* and a daystar rises

Day

Ge 1:5 God began calling the light *D*
1:5 came to be morning, a first *d*
1:8 came to be morning, a second *d*
1:13 came to be morning, a third *d*
1:14 make a division between the *d*
1:16 luminary for dominating the *d*
1:18 to dominate by *d* and by night
1:19 to be morning, a fourth *d*
1:23 to be morning, a fifth *d*
1:31 came to be morning, a sixth *d*
Ge 2:2 And by the seventh *d* God came
2:2 to rest on the seventh *d* from
2:3 God . . . bless the seventh *d*
2:4 *d* that Jehovah God made earth
2:17 for in the *d* you eat from it
3:5 God knows that in the very *d*
3:8 about the breezy part of the *d*
4:14 driving me this *d* from off
5:1 In the *d* of God's creating
5:2 their name Man in the *d* of
7:11 seventeenth *d* of the month
7:11 *d* all the springs of the vast
7:13 On this very *d* Noah went in
8:4 the seventeenth *d* of the month
8:13 on the first *d* of the month
8:14 on the twenty-seventh *d* of
8:22 *d* and night, will never cease
15:18 On that *d* Jehovah concluded
17:23 in this very *d*, just as God
17:26 In this very *d* Abraham got
18:1 about the heat of the *d*
19:34 next *d* that the firstborn
19:37 father of Moab, to this *d*
19:38 sons of Ammon, to this *d*
21:8 *d* of Isaac's being weaned
22:4 third *d* that Abraham raised
24:12 before me this *d* and perform
26:32 Now on that *d* it occurred
26:33 Beer-sheba, down to this *d*
27:2 do not know the *d* of my death
27:45 bereaved . . . of you in one *d*
29:7 Why, it is yet full *d*
30:33 future *d* you may come to
30:35 he set aside on that *d* the
31:22 Later, on the third *d*, it
31:39 Whether one was stolen by *d*
31:40 by *d* the heat consumed me
32:32 down to this *d*, because he
33:13 too quickly for one *d*, then
33:16 on that *d* Esau turned back on
34:25 on the third *d*, when they
35:3 in the *d* of my distress
35:20 pillar . . . down to this *d*
39:10, 10 spoke to Joseph *d* after *d*
39:11 on this *d* as other days he
40:20 on the third *d* it turned out
42:18 said to them on the third *d*
47:26 a decree down to this *d*
48:15 my existence until this *d*
48:20 bless them on that *d*, saying
50:20 this *d* to preserve many
Ex 2:13 went out on the following *d*
5:6 on that *d* Pharaoh commanded
5:13, 13 one his work, *d* for *d*
6:28 *d* that Jehovah spoke to Moses
8:22 on that *d* I shall certainly
9:6 did this thing on the next *d*
9:18 from the *d* it was founded
10:6 from the *d* of their existing
10:6 upon the ground until this *d*
10:13 all that *d* and all night
10:28 the *d* of your seeing my face
12:3 On the tenth *d* of this month
12:6 fourteenth *d* of this month
12:14 *d* must serve as a memorial
12:15 On the first *d* you are to
12:15 first *d* down to the seventh
12:16 the first *d* there is to take
12:16 seventh *d* a holy convention
12:17 on this very *d* I must bring
12:17 keep this *d* throughout your
12:18 fourteenth *d* of the month
12:18 twenty-first *d* of the month
12:41 came about on this very *d*
12:51 it came about on this very *d*
13:3 *d* on which you went out of
13:6 the seventh *d* is a festival to
13:8 tell your son on that *d*
14:30 that *d* Jehovah saved Israel
16:1 the fifteenth *d* of the second
16:4, 4 his amount *d* for *d*, in
16:5 it must occur on the sixth *d*
16:5, 5 they keep picking up *d* by *d*
16:22 it came about on the sixth *d*
16:26 on the seventh *d* is a sabbath
16:27 came about on the seventh *d*
16:29 on the sixth *d* the bread of
16:29 his locality on the seventh *d*
16:30 the sabbath on the seventh *d*
18:13 next *d* that Moses sat down
19:1 on the same *d*, they came into
19:11 prove ready for the third *d*
19:11 on the third *d* Jehovah will
19:16 And on the third *d* when it
Ex 20:8 sabbath *d* to hold it sacred
20:10 the seventh *d* is a sabbath to
20:11 to rest on the seventh *d*
20:11 Jehovah blessed the sabbath *d*
21:21 if he lingers for a *d* or two
22:30 eighth *d* you are to give it
23:12 seventh *d* you are to desist
24:16 seventh *d* he called to Moses
29:38 young rams . . . two a *d*
31:15 seventh *d* is a sabbath of
31:15 work on the sabbath *d* will
31:17 on the seventh *d* he rested
32:6 the next *d* they were early in
32:28 fell of the people on that *d*
32:30 next *d* that Moses proceeded
32:34 *d* of my bringing punishment
34:21 *d* you will keep sabbath
35:2 seventh *d* . . . something holy
35:3 places on the sabbath *d*
40:2 On the *d* of the first month
40:17 on the first *d* of the month
40:37 not break camp until the *d*
40:38 was over the tabernacle by *d*
Le 6:5 on the *d* his guilt is proved
6:20 present to Jehovah on the *d* of
7:15 eaten on the *d* of his offering
7:16 on the *d* of his presenting
7:16 the next *d* what is left of it
7:17 sacrifice on the third *d* is to
7:18 all be eaten on the third *d*
7:35 on the *d* that he presented
7:36 the *d* of his anointing them
7:38 in the *d* of his commanding
8:33 until the *d* of fulfilling the
8:34 as it has been done this *d*
8:35 *d* and night for seven days
9:1 the eighth *d* that Moses called
12:3 on the eighth *d* the flesh of
13:5 look at him on the seventh *d*
13:6 look at him on the seventh *d*
13:14 on the *d* the living flesh
13:27 look at him on the seventh *d*
13:32 the plague on the seventh *d*
13:34 must look . . . the seventh *d*
13:51 seventh *d*, that the plague
14:2 the *d* for establishing his
14:9 seventh *d* that he should shave
14:10 on the eighth *d* he will take
14:23 the eighth *d* he must bring
14:39 the seventh *d* and must take a
15:14 on the eighth *d* he should
15:29 the eighth *d* she should take
16:30 on this *d* atonement will be
19:6 On the *d* of your sacrifice and
19:6 next *d* it should be eaten, but
19:6 left over till the third *d*
19:7 eaten on the third *d*, it is a
22:27 eighth *d* and forward it will
22:28 its young one on the one *d*
22:30 On that *d* it should be eaten
23:3 seventh *d* is a sabbath of
23:5 fourteenth *d* of the month
23:6 fifteenth *d* of this month is
23:7 first *d* you will have a
23:8 seventh *d* there will be a
23:11 the *d* after the sabbath the
23:12 *d* of your having the sheaf
23:14 until this very *d*
23:15 *d* after the sabbath, from
23:15 *d* of your bringing the sheaf
23:16 *d* after the seventh sabbath
23:21 proclaim on this very *d*
23:27 is the *d* of atonement
23:28 sort of work on this very *d*
23:28 it is a *d* of atonement to
23:29 afflicted on this very *d*
23:30 work on this very *d*, I must
23:34 fifteenth *d* of this seventh
23:35 first *d* is a holy convention
23:36 eighth *d* there should occur
23:39 fifteenth *d* of the seventh
23:39 first *d* is a complete rest
23:39 eighth *d* is a complete rest
23:40 first *d* the fruit of splendid
24:8 one sabbath *d* after another he
25:9 *d* of atonement you people
27:23 estimated value on that *d*
Nu 1:1 first *d* of the second month
1:18 assembly on the first *d* of
3:1 *d* that Jehovah spoke with
3:13 *d* that I struck every
6:9 shave his head in the *d* of
6:9 seventh *d* he should shave it
6:10 eighth *d* he should bring two

Ps 22:2 O my God, I keep calling by *d*
25:5 In you I have hoped all *d* long
27:5 in the *d* of calamity
32:3 my groaning all *d* long
32:4 *d* and night your hand was
35:28 All *d* long your praise
37:13 sees that his *d* will come
37:26 All *d* long he is showing
38:6 All *d* long I have walked
38:12 keep muttering all *d* long
41:1 In the *d* of calamity Jehovah
42:3 have become food *d* and night
42:3 they say to me all *d* long
42:8 By *d* Jehovah will command
42:10 they say to me all *d* long
44:8 will offer praise all *d* long
44:15 All *d* long my humiliation
44:22 have been killed all *d* long
50:15 call me in the *d* of distress
52:1 loving-kindness . . . all *d* long
55:10 *D* and night they go round
56:1 Warring all *d* long, he keeps
56:2 have kept snapping all *d* long
56:3 Whatever *d* I get afraid, I
56:5 All *d* long they keep hurting
56:9 turn back, on the *d* that I
59:16 flee in the *d* of my distress
61:8, 8 may pay my vows *d* after *d*
71:8 All *d* long with your beauty
71:15 All *d* long your salvation
71:24 my own tongue, all *d* long
72:15 All *d* long let him be
73:14 to be plagued all *d* long
74:16 To you the *d* belongs; also
74:22 the senseless one all *d* long
77:2 the *d* of my distress I have
78:9 Retreated in the *d* of fight
78:14 lead them with a cloud by *d*
78:42 *d* that he redeemed them
81:3 for the *d* of our festival
84:10 *d* in your courtyards is
86:3 I keep calling all *d* long
86:7 In the *d* of my distress I
88:1 By *d* I have cried out
88:9 on you, O Jehovah, all *d* long
88:17 like waters all *d* long
89:16 they are joyful all *d* long
91:5 of the arrow that flies by *d*
92:*super* a song, for the sabbath *d*
95:8 *d* of Massah in the wilderness
96:2, 2 From *d* to *d* tell the good
102:2 *d* that I am in sore straits
102:2 *d* that I call, hurry, answer
102:8 All *d* long my enemies have
110:3 *d* of your military force
110:5 pieces on the *d* of his anger
118:24 the *d* that Jehovah has made
119:97 All *d* long it is my concern
119:164 Seven times in the *d* I
121:6 By *d* the sun itself will not
136:8 the sun for dominion by *d*
137:7 the *d* of Jerusalem, Who
138:3 On the *d* that I called, you
139:12 shine just as the *d* does
140:2 all *d* long keep attacking
140:7 in the *d* of the armed force
145:2 All *d* long I will bless you
146:4 that *d* his thoughts do perish
Pr 4:18 the *d* is firmly established
6:34 in the *d* of vengeance
7:9 in the evening of the *d*, at
7:20 *d* of the full moon he will
8:30, 30 specially fond of *d* by *d*
8:34, 34 awake at my doors *d* by *d*
11:4 no benefit on the *d* of fury
12:16 his vexation in the same *d*
16:4 the wicked one for the evil *d*
21:26 All the *d* he has shown
21:31 prepared for the *d* of battle
23:17 fear of Jehovah all *d* long
24:10 in the *d* of distress
25:13 of snow in the *d* of harvest
25:19 in the *d* of distress
25:20 a garment on a cold *d* is as
27:1 your boast about the next *d*
27:1 what a *d* will give birth to
27:10 on the *d* of your disaster
27:15 in the *d* of a steady rain and
31:25 and she laughs at a future *d*
Ec 7:1 and the *d* of death than the
7:1 than the *d* of one's being born
7:14 On a good *d* prove yourself to
7:14 a calamitous *d* see that the
8:8 of control in the *d* of death
Ec 8:16 either by *d* or by night
11:8 *d* that has come in is vanity
12:3 *d* when the keepers of the
Ca 2:17 Until the *d* breathes and the
3:11 on the *d* of his marriage and
3:11 the *d* of the rejoicing of his
4:6 Until the *d* breathes and the
8:8 *d* that she will be spoken for
Isa 2:11 be put on high in that *d*
2:12 is the *d* belonging to Jehovah
2:17 be put on high in that *d*
2:20 In that *d* the earthling man
3:7 raise his voice in that *d*
3:18 In that *d* Jehovah will take
4:1 hold of one man in that *d*
4:2 *d* what Jehovah makes sprout
4:5 place a cloud by *d* and a
4:6 booth for a shade by *d* from
5:30 growl over it in that *d* as
7:17 since the *d* of Ephraim's
7:18 *d* that Jehovah will whistle
7:20 In that *d*, by means of a
7:21 *d* that an individual will
7:23 *d* that every place where
9:4 pieces as in the *d* of Midian
9:14 shoot and rush, in one *d*
10:3 *d* of being given attention
10:17 his thornbushes in one *d*
10:20 *d* that those remaining over
10:27 And it must occur in that *d*
10:32 *d* in Nob to make a halt
11:10 *d* that there will be the
11:11 *d* that Jehovah will again
11:16 *d* of his coming up out of
12:1 *d* you will be sure to say
12:4 *d* you will certainly say
13:6 *d* of Jehovah is near
13:9 *d* of Jehovah itself is
13:13 *d* of his burning anger
14:3 *d* when Jehovah gives you
17:4 *d* that the glory of Jacob
17:7 *d* earthling man will look
17:9 *d* his fortress cities will
17:11 *d* you may carefully fence
17:11 *d* of the disease and
19:16 *d* Egypt will become like
19:18 *d* there will prove to be
19:19 *d* there will prove to be
19:21 must know Jehovah in that *d*
19:23 *d* there will come to be a
19:24 *d* Israel will come to be
20:6 certain to say in that *d*
21:8 standing constantly by *d*, and
22:5 *d* of confusion and of
22:8 look in that *d* toward the
22:12 call in that *d* for weeping
22:20 *d* that I will call my
22:25 In that *d*, is the utterance
23:15 *d* that Tyre must be
24:21 *d* that Jehovah will turn
25:9 in that *d* one will certainly
26:1 *d* this song will be sung in
27:1 *d* Jehovah, with his hard
27:2 In that *d* sing to her
27:3 even night and *d*
27:8 in the *d* of the east wind
27:12 *d* that Jehovah will beat
27:13 *d* that there will be a
28:5 *d* Jehovah of armies will
28:19 during the *d* and during the
28:24 Is it all *d* long that the
29:18 that *d* the deaf ones will
30:8 it may serve for a future *d*
30:23 graze in that *d* in a
30:25 *d* of the big slaughter when
30:26 *d* that Jehovah binds up the
31:7 *d* they will reject each one
34:8 Jehovah has a *d* of vengeance
34:10 By night or by *d* it will
37:3, 3 This *d* is a *d* of distress
38:19 Just as I can this *d*
39:6 stored up down to this *d*
47:9 will come suddenly, in one *d*
49:8 in a *d* of salvation I have
51:13 the whole *d* long on account
52:5 all *d* long, my name was
52:6 for that reason in that *d*
58:2, 2 *d* after *d* it was I whom
58:3 in the very *d* of your fasting
58:4 as in the *d* for making your
58:5 as a *d* for earthling man to
58:5 and a *d* acceptable to Jehovah
58:13 own delights on my holy *d*
58:13 a holy *d* of Jehovah, one
Isa 60:11 even by *d* or by night
60:19 prove to be a light by *d*
61:2 *d* of vengeance on the part
62:6 All *d* long and all night long
63:4 the *d* of vengeance is in my
65:2 my hands all *d* long to a
65:5 a fire burning all *d* long
66:8 with labor pains in one *d*
Jer 1:10 commissioned you this *d* to
3:25 to this *d*, and we have not
4:9 And it must occur in that *d*
6:4 the *d* has declined, for the
7:22 in the *d* of my bringing them
7:25 the *d* that your forefathers
7:25 land of Egypt until this *d*
9:1 weep *d* and night for the
11:4 in the *d* of my bringing
11:5 and honey, as in this *d*
11:7 in the *d* of my bringing them
11:7 down to this *d*, rising up
12:3 apart for the *d* of killing
14:17 with tears night and *d*
15:9 has set while it is yet *d*
16:13 serve other gods *d* and night
16:19 flight in the *d* of distress
17:16 for the desperate *d* I did
17:17 refuge in the *d* of calamity
17:18 upon them the *d* of calamity
17:21 carry on the sabbath *d*
17:22 your homes on the sabbath *d*
17:22 must sanctify the sabbath *d*
17:24 no load . . . on the sabbath *d*
17:24 to sanctify the sabbath *d*
17:27 by sanctifying the sabbath *d*
17:27 Jerusalem on the sabbath *d*
18:17 in the *d* of their disaster
20:3 the following *d* that Pashhur
20:7 object of laughter all *d* long
20:8 and for jeering all *d* long
20:14 the *d* on which I was born
20:14 the *d* that my mother gave
25:3 down to this *d*, these
25:18 just as at this *d*
25:33 in that *d* from one end of
27:22 the *d* of my turning my
30:7 For that *d* is a great one
30:8 And it must occur in that *d*
31:6 *d* when the lookouts in the
31:32 *d* of my taking hold of
31:35 the sun for light by *d*
32:20 Egypt down to this *d* and
32:20 own self, just as at this *d*
32:31 *d* that they built it, clear
32:31 clear down to this *d*, has
33:20 break my covenant of the *d*
33:20 *d* and night not to occur
33:25 covenant of the *d* and night
34:13 *d* of my bringing them out
35:14 drunk none down to this *d*
36:2 since the *d* that I spoke
36:2 Josiah, clear down to this *d*
36:6 in the *d* of fast; and also
36:30 thrown out to the heat by *d*
38:28 the *d* that Jerusalem was
39:2 on the ninth *d* of the month
39:10 services on that *d*
39:16 happen before you in that *d*
39:17 will deliver you in that *d*
41:4 second *d* of the putting of
44:2 a devastated place this *d*
44:6 desolate waste, as at this *d*
44:10 down to this *d* they did not
44:22 inhabitant, as at this *d*
44:23 calamity as at this *d*
46:10 *d* belongs to the Sovereign
46:10 *d* of vengeance for avenging
46:21 *d* of their disaster has
47:4 *d* that is coming to despoil
48:41 in that *d* like the heart of
49:22 that *d* like the heart of the
49:26 brought to silence in that *d*
50:27 for their *d* has come
50:30 brought to silence in that *d*
50:31 for your *d* must come, the
51:2 in the *d* of calamity
52:4 on the tenth *d* of the month
52:6 on the ninth *d* of the month
52:11 until the *d* of his death
52:12 on the tenth *d* of the month
52:31 twenty-fifth *d* of the month
52:34 until the *d* of his death
La 1:12 in the *d* of his burning anger
1:13 desolate. All the *d* I am ill
1:21 will certainly bring the *d*

La 2:1 footstool in the *d* of his anger
2:7 as in the *d* of a festival
2:16 the *d* that we have hoped for
2:18 like a torrent *d* and night
2:21 killed in the *d* of your anger
2:22 As in the *d* of a festival you
2:22 the *d* of the wrath of Jehovah
3:3 repeatedly turns his hand all *d*
3:14 the theme of their song all *d*
3:57 the *d* that I kept calling you
3:62 whispering against me all *d*
Eze 1:1 fourth month, on the fifth *d*
1:2 On the fifth *d* of the month
1:28 on the *d* of a pouring rain
2:3 down to this selfsame *d*
4:6, 6 *d* for a year, a *d* for a
4:10 weight—twenty shekels a *d*
7:7 must come, the *d* is near
7:10 The *d!* Look! It is coming
7:12 the *d* must arrive
7:19 in the *d* of Jehovah's fury
8:1 sixth month, on the fifth *d*
13:5 battle in the *d* of Jehovah
16:4 on the *d* of your being born
16:5 in the *d* of your being born
16:56 in the *d* of your pride
20:1 on the tenth *d* of the month
20:5 the *d* of my choosing Israel
20:6 that *d* I lifted up my hand
20:29 a High Place down to this *d*
21:25 *d* has come in the time of
21:29 whose *d* has come in the
22:24 in the *d* of denunciation
23:38 my sanctuary in that *d*
23:39 into my sanctuary on that *d*
24:1 tenth month, on the tenth *d*
24:2 the name of the *d*, this
24:2 this selfsame *d*. The king of
24:2 Jerusalem on this selfsame *d*
24:25 in the *d* of my taking away
24:26 in that *d* there will come
24:27 In that *d* your mouth will
26:1 on the first *d* of the month
26:18 in the *d* of your downfall
27:27 in the *d* of your downfall
28:13 the *d* of your being created
28:15 *d* of your being created
29:1 the twelfth *d* of the month
29:17 first month, on the first *d*
29:21 In that *d* I shall cause a
30:2 Howl . . . Alas for the *d!*
30:3 for a *d* is near, yes, a
30:3 a *d* belonging to Jehovah is
30:3 A *d* of clouds, an appointed
30:9 In that *d* messengers will
30:9 in the *d* of Egypt, for, look!
30:18 *d* will actually grow dark
30:20 the seventh *d* of the month
31:1 on the first *d* of the month
31:15 *d* of its going down to
32:1 on the first *d* of the month
32:10 on the *d* of your downfall
32:17 fifteenth *d* of the month
33:12 in the *d* of his revolt
33:12 the *d* of his turning back
33:12 in the *d* of his sinning
33:21 fifth *d* of the month of
34:12 in the *d* of his coming to
34:12 *d* of clouds and thick gloom
36:33 In the *d* of my cleansing
38:10 must occur in that *d* that
38:14 *d* when my people Israel
38:18 it must occur in that *d*
38:18 in the *d* when Gog comes in
38:19 in that *d* a great quaking
39:8 the *d* of which I have spoken
39:11 must occur in that *d* that
39:13 *d* that I glorify myself
39:22 God from that *d* and forward
40:1 on the tenth *d* of the month
40:1 same *d* the hand of Jehovah
43:18 altar on the *d* of its being
43:22 second *d* you will bring
43:25 as a sin offering for the *d*
43:27 eighth *d* and from then on
44:27 *d* of his coming into the
45:18 first *d* of the month, you
45:20 seventh *d* in the month
45:21 fourteenth *d* of the month
45:22 that *d*, in his own behalf
45:25 fifteenth *d* of the month
46:1 sabbath *d* it should be opened
46:1 *d* of the new moon it should
46:4 to Jehovah on the sabbath *d*
Eze 46:6 *d* of the new moon there
46:12 as he does on the sabbath *d*
48:35 from that *d* on will be
Da 6:10 even three times in a *d* he
6:13 three times in a *d* he is
9:7 shame of face as at this *d*
9:15 for yourself as at this *d*
10:4 twenty-fourth *d* of the first
10:12 *d* that you gave your heart
Ho 1:5 *d* that I must break the bow of
1:11 will be the *d* of Jezreel
2:3 as in the *d* of her being born
2:15 *d* of her coming up out of the
2:16 must occur in that *d*, is the
2:18 conclude a covenant in that *d*
2:21 in that *d* that I shall answer
5:9 become in the *d* of rebuke
6:2 third *d* he will make us get up
7:5 On the *d* of our king, princes
9:5 people do in the *d* of meeting
9:5 *d* of the festival of Jehovah
10:14 in the *d* of battle when a
12:1 after the east wind all *d*
Joe 1:15 Alas for the *d;* because the
1:15 the *d* of Jehovah is near
2:1 the *d* of Jehovah is coming
2:2 *d* of darkness and gloominess
2:2 a *d* of clouds and thick gloom
2:11 the *d* of Jehovah is great
2:31 fear-inspiring *d* of Jehovah
3:14 for the *d* of Jehovah is near
3:18 it must occur in that *d* that
Am 1:14 signal in the *d* of battle
1:14 in the *d* of stormwind
2:16 how he will flee in that *d*
3:14 in the *d* of my holding an
4:4 the third *d*, your tenth parts
5:8 made *d* itself dark as night
5:18 are craving the *d* of Jehovah
5:18 the *d* of Jehovah mean to you
5:20 the *d* of Jehovah be darkness
6:3 the calamitous *d*, and do you
8:3 be a howling in that *d*
8:9 it must occur in that *d*, is
8:9 for the land on a bright *d*
8:10 result of it as a bitter *d*
8:13 In that *d* the pretty virgins
9:11 In that *d* I shall raise up
Ob 8 Will it not be in that *d?*
11 *d* when you stood off on the
11 in the *d* when strangers took
12 sight in the *d* of your brother
12 in the *d* of his misfortune
12 in the *d* of their perishing
12 in the *d* of their distress
13 in the *d* of their disaster
13 in the *d* of his disaster
13 in the *d* of his disaster
14 survivors in the *d* of distress
15 the *d* of Jehovah against all
Jon 3:4 the walking distance of one *d*
4:7 of the dawn on the next *d*
Mic 2:4 In that *d* one will raise up
3:6 *d* must get dark upon them
4:6 In that *d*, is the utterance
5:10 And it must occur in that *d*
7:4 The *d* of your watchmen, of
7:11 The *d* for building your
7:11 at that *d* the decree will
7:12 At that *d* even all the way
Na 1:7 stronghold in the *d* of distress
2:3 in the *d* of his getting ready
3:17 in the stone pens in a cold *d*
Hab 3:16 wait for the *d* of distress
Zep 1:7 the *d* of Jehovah is near
1:8 the *d* of Jehovah's sacrifice
1:9 upon the platform in that *d*
1:10 must occur on that *d*, is the
1:14 great *d* of Jehovah is near
1:14 the *d* of Jehovah is bitter
1:15, 15 That *d* is a *d* of fury
1:15 *d* of distress and of anguish
1:15 *d* of storm and of desolation
1:15 *d* of darkness and of
1:15 *d* of clouds and of thick
1:16 a *d* of horn and of alarm
1:18 in the *d* of Jehovah's fury
2:2 *d* has passed by just like
2:2 the *d* of Jehovah's anger
2:3 in the *d* of Jehovah's anger
3:8 the *d* of my rising up to the
3:11 In that *d* you will not be
3:16 In that *d* it will be said to
Hag 1:1 on the first *d* of the month
Hag 1:15 twenty-fourth *d* of the sixth
2:1 twenty-first *d* of the month
2:10 twenty-fourth *d* of the ninth
2:15 from this *d* and forward
2:18 from this *d* and forward
2:18 twenty-fourth *d* of the ninth
2:18 *d* that the foundation of the
2:19 From this *d* I shall bestow
2:20 twenty-fourth *d* of the month
2:23 In that *d*, is the utterance
Zec 1:7 On the twenty-fourth *d* of the
2:11 joined to Jehovah in that *d*
3:9 error of that land in one *d*
3:10 In that *d*, is the utterance
4:10 despised the *d* of small
6:10 must come in that *d*, and you
7:1 fourth *d* of the ninth month
8:9 *d* on which the foundation of
9:16 save them in that *d* like the
11:11 came to be broken in that *d*
12:3 must occur in that *d* that I
12:4 In that *d*, is the utterance
12:6 In that *d* I shall make the
12:8 In that *d* Jehovah will be a
12:8 become in that *d* like David
12:9 must occur in that *d* that I
12:11 In that *d* the wailing in
13:1 In that *d* there will come
13:2 And it must occur in that *d*
13:4 And it must occur in that *d*
14:1 is a *d* coming, belonging
14:3 as in the *d* of his warring
14:3 warring, in the *d* of fight
14:4 stand in that *d* upon the
14:6 must occur in that *d* that
14:7 one *d* that is known as
14:7 It will not be *d*, neither
14:8 must occur in that *d* that
14:9 In that *d* Jehovah will prove
14:13 must occur in that *d* that
14:20 that *d* there will prove to
14:21 Jehovah of armies in that *d*
Mal 3:2 the *d* of his coming, and
3:17 the *d* when I am producing a
4:1 *d* is coming that is burning
4:1 the *d* that is coming will
4:3 the *d* on which I am acting
4:5 fear-inspiring *d* of Jehovah
Mt 6:11 Give . . . bread for this *d*
6:34 anxious about the next *d*, for
6:34 the next *d* will have its own
6:34 Sufficient for each *d* is its
7:22 say to me in that *d*, Lord
10:15 and Gomorrah on Judgment *D*
11:22 Tyre and Sidon on Judgment *D*
11:23 remained until this very *d*
11:24 land of Sodom on Judgment *D*
12:36 concerning it on Judgment *D*
13:1 On that *d* Jesus, having left
16:21 on the third *d* be raised up
17:23 third *d* he will be raised up
20:2 workers for a denarius a *d*
20:6 here all *d* unemployed
20:12 who bore the burden of the *d*
20:19 third *d* he will be raised up
22:23 On that *d* Sadducees, who say
22:46 anyone dare from that *d* on
24:20 nor on the sabbath *d*
24:36 that *d* and hour nobody knows
24:38 *d* that Noah entered into the
24:42 what *d* your Lord is coming
24:50 a *d* that he does not expect
25:13 you know neither the *d* nor
26:17 first *d* of the unfermented
26:29 *d* when I drink it new with
26:49 Good *d*, Rabbi! and kissed
26:55, 55 *D* after *d* I used to sit
27:8 Field of Blood to this very *d*
27:29 Good *d*, you King of the Jews!
27:62 next *d*, which was after the
27:64 secure until the third *d*
28:1 on the first *d* of the week
28:9 met them and said: Good *d!*
28:15 the Jews up to this very *d*
Mr 2:20 then they will fast in that *d*
4:27 rises up by *d*, and the seed
4:35 on that *d*, when evening had
5:5 night and *d*, he was crying out
6:21 *d* came along when Herod
11:12 The next *d*, when they had
11:19 it became late in the *d*
13:32 *d* or the hour nobody knows
13:35 late in the *d* or at midnight
14:12 first *d* of unfermented cakes

Mr 14:25 until that *d* when I drink
14:49, 49 *D* after *d* I was with you
15:18 Good *d*, you King of the Jews!
15:42 the *d* before the sabbath
16:2 on the first *d* of the week
Lu 1:20 the *d* that these things take
1:28 Good *d*, highly favored one
1:59 on the eighth *d* they came to
1:80 *d* of showing himself openly
2:37 sacred service night and *d*
4:16 his custom on the sabbath *d*
4:42 when it became *d*, he went
6:13 when it became *d* he called
6:23 Rejoice in that *d* and leap
9:12 Then the *d* started to decline
9:22 on the third *d* be raised up
9:23, 23 *d* after *d* and follow me
9:37 the succeeding *d*, when they
10:12 for Sodom in that *d* than
10:35 And the next *d* he took out
11:3 Give us our bread for the *d*
12:46 *d* that he is not expecting
13:14 and not on the sabbath *d*
13:16 this bond on the sabbath *d*
13:32 third *d* I shall be finished
13:33 and the following *d*
14:5 pull him out on the sabbath *d*
16:19, 19 enjoying . . . from *d* to *d*
17:4 if he sins seven times a *d*
17:27 that *d* when Noah entered
17:29 on the *d* that Lot came out
17:30 that *d* when the Son of man
17:31 On that *d* let the person
18:7 cry out to him *d* and night
18:33 on the third *d* he will rise
19:9 This *d* salvation has come to
19:42 had discerned in this *d* the
21:34 suddenly that *d* be instantly
21:37 by *d* he would be teaching
21:38 come early in the *d* to him
22:7 *d* of the unfermented cakes
22:53, 53 in the temple *d* after *d*
22:66 At length when it became *d*
23:12 each other on that very *d*
23:54 it was the *d* of Preparation
24:1 On the first *d* of the week
24:7 and yet on the third *d* rise
24:13 on that very *d* two of them
24:21 third *d* since these things
24:29 the *d* has already declined
24:46 and rise . . . on the third *d*
Joh 1:29 The next *d* he beheld Jesus
1:35 next *d* John was standing
1:39 they stayed with him that *d*
1:43 The next *d* he desired to
2:1 on the third *d* a marriage
5:9 on that *d* it was a sabbath
6:22 The next *d* the crowd that
6:39 resurrect it at the last *d*
6:40 resurrect him at the last *d*
6:44 resurrect him in the last *d*
6:54 resurrect him at the last *d*
7:37 Now on the last *d*, the great
7:37 the great *d* of the festival
8:56 prospect of seeing my *d*, and
9:4 that sent me while it is *d*
9:14 Sabbath on the *d* that Jesus
11:24 resurrection on the last *d*
11:53 *d* on they took counsel to
12:7 view of the *d* of my burial
12:12 next *d* the great crowd
12:48 judge him in the last *d*
14:20 In that *d* you will know
16:23 *d* you will ask me no
16:26 *d* you will ask in my name
18:28 It was now early in the *d*
19:3 Good *d*, you king of the Jews!
19:31 *d* of that Sabbath was a
20:1 the first *d* of the week Mary
20:19 when it was late on that *d*
Ac 1:2 the *d* that he was taken up
1:22 *d* he was received up from
2:1 *d* of the festival of Pentecost
2:15 it is the third hour of the *d*
2:20 illustrious *d* of Jehovah
2:29 tomb is among us to this *d*
2:41 *d* about three thousand souls
2:46, 46 *d* after *d* they were in
4:3 in custody till the next *d*
4:5 next *d* there took place in
4:9 are this *d* being examined, on
5:42 every *d* in the temple and
7:8 circumcised . . . on the eighth *d*
7:26 next *d* he appeared to them

Ac 8:1 *d* great persecution arose
9:24 gates both *d* and night in
10:3 ninth hour of the *d* he saw
10:9 next *d* as they were pursuing
10:23 next *d* he rose and went off
10:24 *d* after that he entered into
10:40 this One up on the third *d*
12:18 when it became *d*, there was
12:21 on a set *d* Herod clothed
13:14 synagogue on the sabbath *d*
13:33 become your Father this *d*
14:20 next *d* he left with Barnabas
16:5, 5 increase . . . from *d* to *d*
16:11 the following *d* to Neapolis
16:13 And on the sabbath *d* we went
16:35 When it became *d*, the civil
17:17 every *d* in the marketplace
17:31 a *d* in which he purposes to
20:7 On the first *d* of the week
20:7 going to depart the next *d*
20:15 from there the succeeding *d*
20:15 next *d* we touched at Samos
20:15 following *d* we arrived at
20:16 on the *d* of the festival of
20:18 *d* that I stepped into the
20:26 witness this very *d* that I
20:31 for three years, night and *d*
21:1 on the next *d* to Rhodes, and
21:7 and stayed one *d* with them
21:8 next *d* we set out and arrived
21:18 the following *d* Paul went in
21:26 next *d* and cleansed himself
22:3 just as all of you are this *d*
22:30 the next *d*, as he desired to
23:1 clear conscience . . . to this *d*
23:12 when it became *d*, the Jews
23:32 The next *d* they permitted
25:6 the next *d* he sat down on the
25:17 the next *d* I sat down on the
25:23 on the next *d*, Agrippa and
26:2 am to make my defense this *d*
26:7 sacred service night and *d*
26:22 to this *d* bearing witness
27:3 next *d* we landed at Sidon
27:9 fast of atonement *d* had
27:18 *d* they began to lighten the
27:19 third *d*, with their own
27:29 wishing for it to become *d*
27:33 approach of *d* Paul began
27:33 fourteenth *d* you have been
27:39 when it became *d*, they
28:13 *d* later a south wind sprang
28:13 Puteoli on the second *d*
28:23 arranged for a *d* with him
Ro 2:5 on the *d* of wrath and of the
2:16 *d* when God through Christ
8:36 being put to death all *d* long
10:21 All *d* long I have spread
11:8 hear, down to this very *d*
13:12 the *d* has drawn near
14:5 judges one *d* as above another
14:5 judges one *d* as all others
14:6 He who observes the *d*
1Co 1:8 in the *d* of our Lord Jesus
3:13 for the *d* will show it up
5:5 be saved in the *d* of the Lord
10:8 thousand of them in one *d*
15:4 been raised up the third *d*
16:2 Every first *d* of the week
2Co 1:14 in the *d* of our Lord Jesus
3:14 to this present *d* the same
4:16, 16 renewed from *d* to *d*
6:2 *d* of salvation I helped you
6:2 Now is the *d* of salvation
11:25 a *d* I have spent in the deep
11:28, 28 *d* to *d*, the anxiety for
Ga 4:2 the *d* his father appointed
Eph 4:30 sealed for a *d* of releasing
6:13 to resist in the wicked *d*
Php 1:5 the first *d* until this moment
1:6 until the *d* of Jesus Christ
1:10 up to the *d* of Christ
2:16 for exultation in Christ's *d*
3:5 circumcised the eighth *d*, out
Col 1:6 from the *d* you heard and
1:9 from the *d* we heard of it
1Th 2:9 was with working night and *d*
3:10 while night and *d* we make
5:2 Jehovah's *d* is coming exactly
5:4 so that that *d* should overtake
5:5 sons of light and sons of *d*
5:8 as for us who belong to the *d*
2Th 1:10 regarded in that *d* with
2:2 that the *d* of Jehovah is here

2Th 3:8 by labor and toil night and *d*
1Ti 5:5 and prayers night and *d*
2Ti 1:3 my supplications, night and *d*
1:12 trust with him until that *d*
1:18 mercy from Jehovah in that *d*
4:8 a reward in that *d*, yet not
Heb 3:8 the *d* of making the test in
3:13 exhorting one another each *d*
4:4 he has said of the seventh *d*
4:4 God rested on the seventh *d*
4:7 marks off a certain *d* by
4:8 have spoken of another *d*
8:9 *d* of my taking hold of their
10:11, 11 station from *d* to *d* to
10:25 behold the *d* drawing near
Jas 2:15 the food sufficient for the *d*
5:5 hearts on the *d* of slaughter
1Pe 2:12 in the *d* for his inspection
2Pe 1:19 *d* dawns and a daystar rises
2:8, 8 dwelling . . . from *d* to *d*
2:9 *d* of judgment to be cut off
3:4 *d* our forefathers fell asleep
3:7 reserved to the *d* of judgment
3:8 one *d* is with Jehovah as a
3:8 a thousand years as one *d*
3:10 *d* will come as a thief
3:12 presence of the *d* of Jehovah
3:18 now and to the *d* of eternity
1Jo 4:17 in the *d* of judgment
Jude 6 the judgment of the great *d*
Re 1:10 I came to be in the Lord's *d*
4:8 they have no rest *d* and night
6:17 great *d* of their wrath has
7:15 sacred service *d* and night in
8:12 the *d* might not have
9:15 prepared for the hour and *d*
12:10 accuses them *d* and night
14:11 *d* and night they have no
16:14 war of the great *d* of God
18:8 in one *d* her plagues will
20:10 be tormented *d* and night
21:25 not be closed at all by *d*

Daybreak
Ne 8:3 from *d* till midday, in front
Lu 1:78 *d* will visit us from on high
Ac 5:21 into the temple at *d* and
20:11 after conversing . . . until *d*

Daylight
Jg 19:11 as the *d* had gone down
19:26 fell down . . . until *d*
2Sa 2:32 *d* for them at Hebron
Job 3:4 Nor let *d* beam upon it
24:14 At *d* the murderer gets up
24:16 They have not known *d*
Isa 38:12 From *d* till night you keep
38:13 From *d* till night you keep
Da 6:19 to get up in the *d*, and in
Zep 3:5 At *d* it did not prove lacking
Joh 11:9 There are twelve hours of *d*
11:9 anyone walks in *d* he does

Day's
Nu 11:31 about a *d* journey this way
11:31 about a *d* journey that way
1Ki 19:4 the wilderness a *d* journey
Lu 2:44 they covered a *d* distance and
11:3 to the *d* requirement
Ac 1:12 a sabbath *d* journey away

Days
Ge 1:14 seasons and for *d* and years
3:14 what you will eat all the *d*
3:17 eat its produce all the *d* of
5:4 *d* of Adam after his fathering
5:5 all the *d* of Adam that he
5:8 So all the *d* of Seth amounted
5:11 all the *d* of Enosh amounted
5:14 all the *d* of Kenan amounted
5:17 *d* of Mahalalel amounted to
5:20 all the *d* of Jared amounted
5:23 all the *d* of Enoch amounted
5:27 all the *d* of Methuselah
5:31 all the *d* of Lamech amounted
6:3 his *d* shall amount to a
6:4 The Nephilim . . . in those *d*
7:4 in just seven *d* more I am
7:4 rain . . . forty *d* and forty
7:10 seven *d* later it turned out
7:12 downpour . . . for forty *d* and
7:17 deluge went on for forty *d*
7:24 earth a hundred and fifty *d*
8:3 end of a hundred and fifty *d*
8:6 end of forty *d* Noah proceeded
8:10 waiting still another seven *d*

Ge 8:12 waiting still another seven *d*
8:22 all the *d* the earth continues
9:29 *d* of Noah amounted to nine
10:25 in his *d* the earth was
11:32 *d* of Terah came to be two
14:1 in the *d* of Amraphel king of
17:12 every male of yours eight *d*
21:4 Isaac his son when eight *d*
21:34 of the Philistines many *d*
24:55 stay with us at least ten *d*
25:7 *d* of the years of Abraham's
25:24 her *d* came to the full for
26:1 famine that occurred in the *d*
26:8 it came about that as his *d*
26:15 dug in the *d* of Abraham his
26:18 dug in the *d* of Abraham his
27:41 *d* of the period of mourning
27:44 dwell with him for some *d*
29:20 like some few *d* because of
29:21 my wife, because my *d* are up
30:14 the *d* of the wheat harvest
35:28 *d* of Isaac came to be a
35:29 old and satisfied with *d*
37:34 over his son for many *d*
38:12 the *d* became many and the
39:11 on this day as other *d* he
40:4 continued in jail for some *d*
40:12 The three twigs are three *d*
40:13 three *d* from now Pharaoh
40:18 The three baskets are three *d*
40:19 three *d* from now Pharaoh
42:17 in custody for three *d*
47:8 *d* of the years of your life
47:9 The *d* of the years of my
47:9 the *d* of the years of my life
47:9 the *d* of the years of the
47:9 *d* of their alien residences
47:28 Jacob's *d*, the years of his
47:29 the *d* approached for Israel
49:1 in the final part of the *d*
50:3 took fully forty *d* for him
50:3 this many *d* they customarily
50:3 shed tears for him seventy *d*
50:4 *d* of weeping for him passed
50:10 rites for his father seven *d*
Ex 2:11 Now it came about in those *d*
2:23 about during those many *d*
3:18 a journey of three *d* into the
5:3 of three *d* into the wilderness
7:25 seven *d* came to be fulfilled
8:27 journey of three *d* into the
10:22 darkness . . . for three *d*
10:23 from his own place three *d*
12:15 Seven *d* you are to eat
12:19 Seven *d* no sour dough is to
13:6 Seven *d* you are to eat
13:7 to be eaten for the seven *d*
15:22 three *d* in the wilderness
16:26 Six *d* you will pick it up
16:29 sixth day the bread of two *d*
19:15 Get ready during the three *d*
20:9 must do all your work six *d*
20:11 in six *d* Jehovah made the
20:12 your *d* may prove long upon
21:21 lingers for a day or two *d*
22:30 Seven *d* it will continue
23:12 Six *d* you are to do your
23:15 unfermented cakes seven *d*
23:26 the number of your *d* full
24:16 to cover it for six *d*
24:18 in the mountain forty *d* and
29:30 Seven *d* the priest who
29:35 take seven *d* to fill their
29:37 seven *d* to make atonement
31:15 Six *d* may work be done, but
31:17 in six *d* Jehovah made the
34:18 seven *d* at the appointed time
34:21 Six *d* you are to labor, but
34:28 forty *d* and forty nights
35:2 Six *d* may work be done, but
Le 8:33 tent of meeting for seven *d*
8:33 the *d* of your installation
8:33 take seven *d* to fill your hand
8:35 day and night for seven *d*
12:2 she must be unclean seven *d*
12:2 as in the *d* of the impurity
12:4 thirty-three *d* more she will
12:4 of the *d* of her purification
12:5 then be unclean fourteen *d*
12:5 sixty-six *d* more she will
12:6 of the *d* of her purification
13:4 quarantine the plague seven *d*
13:5 quarantine him another seven *d*
13:21 then quarantine him seven *d*
Le 13:26 then quarantine him seven *d*
13:31 falling off of hair seven *d*
13:33 falling off of hair seven *d*
13:46 All the *d* that the plague is
13:50 quarantine the plague seven *d*
13:54 quarantine . . . seven *d*
14:8 outside his tent seven *d*
14:38 quarantine the house seven *d*
14:46 of the *d* of quarantining it
15:13 seven *d* for his purification
15:19 seven *d* in her menstrual
15:24 must then be unclean seven *d*
15:25 flowing many *d* when it is
15:25 all the *d* of her unclean
15:25 *d* of her menstrual impurity
15:26 *d* of her running discharge
15:28 count for herself seven *d*
22:27 under its mother seven *d*
23:3 Six *d* may work be done, but
23:6 Seven *d* you should eat
23:8 by fire to Jehovah seven *d*
23:16 count, fifty *d*, and you must
23:34 festival of booths for seven *d*
23:36 Seven *d* you should present an
23:39 festival of Jehovah seven *d*
23:40 Jehovah your God seven *d*
23:41 festival to Jehovah seven *d*
23:42 you should dwell seven *d*
25:8 *d* of the seven sabbaths of
26:34 the *d* of its lying desolated
26:35 *d* of its lying desolated it
Nu 6:4 *d* of his Naziriteship he should
6:5 *d* of the vow of his
6:5 *d* that he should be separated
6:6 *d* of his keeping separate to
6:8 *d* of his Naziriteship he is
6:12 for the *d* of his Naziriteship
6:12 former *d* will go uncounted
6:13 *d* of his Naziriteship come to
9:18 *d* that the cloud would reside
9:19 over the tabernacle many *d*
9:20 cloud would continue a few *d*
9:22 Whether it was two *d* or a
9:22 or a month or more *d* during
10:33 for a journey of three *d*, and
10:33 journey of three *d* to search
11:19, 19 nor two *d* nor five *d*
11:19, 19 nor ten *d* nor twenty *d*
11:20 to a month of *d*, until it
11:21 eat for a month of *d*
12:14 not be humiliated seven *d*
12:14 quarantined seven *d* outside
12:15 outside the camp seven *d*
13:20 Now the *d* were the
13:20 *d* of the first ripe fruits
13:25 end of forty *d* they returned
14:34 *d* that you spied out the land
14:34 forty *d*, a day for a year, a
19:11 must also be unclean seven *d*
19:14 will be unclean seven *d*
19:16 will be unclean seven *d*
20:15 to dwell in Egypt many *d*
20:29 weeping for Aaron thirty *d*
24:14 in the end of the *d*
28:17 Seven *d* unfermented cakes
28:24 daily for the seven *d* as
29:12 festival to Jehovah seven *d*
31:19 outside the camp seven *d*
De 1:2 it being eleven *d* from Horeb
1:46, 46 many *d*, as many *d* as you
2:1 *d* in going around Mount Seir
2:14 the *d* that we walked from
4:9 your heart all the *d* of your
4:10 fear me all the *d* that they
4:26 not lengthen your *d* on it
4:30 at the close of the *d*, then
4:32 the former *d* that occurred
4:40 lengthen your *d* on the soil
5:13 must do all your work six *d*
5:16 your *d* may prove long and it
5:33 lengthen your *d* in the land
6:2 all the *d* of your life, and in
6:2 that your *d* may prove long
9:9 in the mountain forty *d* and
9:11 at the end of the forty *d* and
9:18 as at first, forty *d* and
9:25 before Jehovah forty *d* and
10:10 the same as the first *d*
10:10 forty *d* and forty nights
11:9 lengthen your *d* on the soil
11:21 in order that your *d* and the
11:21 the *d* of your sons may be
11:21 as the *d* of the heavens over
12:1 all the *d* that you are alive
De 12:19 all your *d* on your soil
16:3 for seven *d*. You should eat
16:3 all the *d* of your life
16:4 in all your territory seven *d*
16:8 Six *d* you should eat
16:13 seven *d* when you make an
16:15 Seven *d* you will celebrate
17:9 will be acting in those *d*
17:19 in it all the *d* of his life
17:20 that he may lengthen his *d*
19:17 judges . . . acting in those *d*
20:19 lay siege to a city many *d*
22:7 may indeed lengthen your *d*
22:19 not . . . divorce her all his *d*
22:29 not . . . divorce her all his *d*
23:6 all your *d* to time indefinite
25:15 that your *d* may become long
26:3 who will be acting in those *d*
30:18 not lengthen your *d* on the
30:20 life and the length of your *d*
31:13 all the *d* that you are living
31:14 *d* have drawn near for you to
31:29 at the close of the *d*
32:7 Remember the *d* of old
32:47 may lengthen your *d* upon the
33:25 in proportion to your *d* is
34:8 plains of Moab thirty *d*
34:8 the *d* of weeping of the
Jos 1:5 all the *d* of your life
1:11 three *d* from now you are
2:16 must keep hid there three *d*
2:22 kept dwelling there three *d*
3:2 at the end of the three *d*
3:15 all the *d* of harvest
4:14 Moses all the *d* of his life
6:3 way you should do for six *d*
6:14 the way they did for six *d*
9:16 at the end of three *d*, after
11:18 Many *d* it was that Joshua
20:6 who happens to be in those *d*
22:3 many *d* down to this day
23:1 many *d* after Jehovah had
23:1 Joshua was . . . advanced in *d*
23:2 old, I have advanced in *d*
24:7 in the wilderness many *d*
24:31 serve Jehovah all the *d* of
24:31 all the *d* of the older men
24:31 who extended their *d* after
Jg 2:7 serve Jehovah all the *d* of
2:7 all the *d* of the older men
2:7 who extended their *d* after
2:18 all the *d* of the judge; for
5:6 In the *d* of Shamgar the son of
5:6 In the *d* of Jael, pathways had
5:21 The torrent of ancient *d*, the
8:28 forty years in the *d* of Gideon
11:40 four *d* in the year
14:12 the seven *d* of the banquet
14:14 tell the riddle for three *d*
14:17 weeping over him the seven *d*
15:1 in the *d* of wheat harvest
15:20 in the *d* of the Philistines
17:6 In those *d* there was no king
18:1 In those *d* there was no king
18:1 in those *d* the tribe of the
18:31 the *d* that the house of the
19:1 *d* that there was no king in
19:4 to dwell with him three *d*
20:27 the ark . . . was in those *d*
20:28 standing before it in those *d*
21:25 In those *d* there was no king
Ru 1:1 *d* when the judges administered
1Sa 1:11 all the *d* of his life, and no
1:28 All the *d* that he does happen
2:31 *D* are coming when I shall
3:1 had become rare in those *d*
7:2 *d* kept multiplying, so that
7:13 all the *d* of Samuel
7:15 all the *d* of his life
9:20 were lost to you three *d* ago
10:8 Seven *d* you should keep
13:8 waiting for seven *d* to the
13:11 come within the appointed *d*
14:52 all the *d* of Saul
17:12 And in the *d* of Saul
17:16 his position for forty *d*
18:10 music . . . as in former *d*
18:26 the *d* had not yet expired
20:31 *d* that the son of Jesse is
22:4 *d* that David happened to be
25:7 *d* they happened to be in
25:15 *d* of our walking about with
25:16 all the *d* that we happened
25:28 in you throughout your *d*

Lu 17:22 *D* will come when you will
17:22 the *d* of the Son of man but
17:26 it occurred in the *d* of Noah
17:26 in the *d* of the Son of man
17:28 it occurred in the *d* of Lot
19:43 the *d* will come upon you
20:1 On one of the *d* while he was
21:6 the *d* will come in which not
21:22 *d* for meting out justice
21:23 suckling a baby in those *d*
23:7 in Jerusalem in these *d*
23:29 *d* are coming in which people
24:18 occurred in her in these *d*
Joh 2:12 did not stay there many *d*
2:19 in three *d* I will raise it
2:20 you raise it up in three *d*
4:40 and he stayed there two *d*
4:43 After the two *d* he left
11:6 remained two *d* in the place
11:17 four *d* in the memorial
11:39 smell, for it is four *d*
12:1 six *d* before the passover
20:26 eight *d* later his disciples
Ac 1:3 by them throughout forty *d*
1:5 spirit not many *d* after this
1:15 during these *d* Peter rose up
2:17 in the last *d*, God says, I
2:18 some of my spirit in those *d*
3:24 plainly declared these *d*
5:36 before these *d* Theudas rose
5:37 the *d* of the registration
6:1 *d*, when the disciples were
7:41 they made a calf in those *d*
7:45 remained until the *d* of David
9:9 for three *d* he did not see
9:19 some *d* with the disciples in
9:23 many *d* were coming to a
9:37 in those *d* she happened to
9:43 few *d* he remained in Joppa
10:30 Cornelius said: Four *d* ago
10:48 him to remain for some *d*
11:27 in these *d* prophets came
12:3 *d* of the unfermented cakes
13:31 many *d* he became visible to
13:41 am working a work in your *d*
15:7 from early *d* God made the
15:36 after some *d* Paul said to
16:12 this city, spending some *d*
16:18 she kept doing for many *d*
18:18 staying quite some *d* longer
19:38 court *d* are held and there
20:6 *d* of the unfermented cakes
20:6 in Troas within five *d*; and
20:6 in Troas . . . we spent seven *d*
21:4 and remained here seven *d*
21:5 when we had completed the *d*
21:10 quite a number of *d*, a
21:15 after these *d* we prepared
21:26 the *d* to be fulfilled for the
21:27 the seven *d* were about to be
21:38 before these *d* stirred up a
24:1 Five *d* later the high priest
24:11 twelve *d* since I went up to
24:24 Some *d* later Felix arrived
25:1 three *d* later to Jerusalem
25:6 or ten *d* among them, he went
25:13 Now when some *d* had passed
25:14 spending a number of *d* there
27:7 slowly quite a number of *d*
27:20 stars appeared for many *d*
28:7 entertained us . . . three *d*
28:12 we remained three *d*
28:14 remain with them seven *d*
28:17 three *d* later he called
Ga 1:18 stayed with him for fifteen *d*
4:10 scrupulously observing *d* and
Eph 5:16 because the *d* are wicked
2Ti 3:1 last *d* critical times hard to
Heb 1:2 has at the end of these *d*
5:7 In the *d* of his flesh Christ
7:3 neither a beginning of *d* nor
8:8 *d* coming, says Jehovah, and I
8:10 after those *d*, says Jehovah
10:16 covenant . . . after those *d*
10:32 remembering the former *d*
11:30 been encircled for seven *d*
12:10 they for a few *d* used to
Jas 5:3 stored up in the last *d*
1Pe 3:10 love life and see good *d*, let
3:20 waiting in Noah's *d*, while
2Pe 3:3 in the last *d* there will come
Re 2:10 may have tribulation ten *d*
2:13 *d* of Antipas, my witness
9:6 in those *d* the men will seek
Re 10:7 in the *d* of the sounding of
11:3 two hundred and sixty *d*
11:6 the *d* of their prophesying
11:9 for three and a half *d*, and
11:11 after the three and a half *d*
12:6 two hundred and sixty *d*

Days'

Ge 30:36 a distance of three *d* journey
31:23 a distance of seven *d* journey
1Sa 11:3 Give us seven *d* time, and we
Ezr 10:8 not come in three *d* time
Mr 15:29 builder of it in three *d*

Daystar

2Pe 1:19 a *d* rises, in your hearts

Daytime

Ex 13:21 in the *d* in a pillar of cloud
13:21 to go in the *d* and nighttime
13:22 before the people in the *d*
De 1:33 and by a cloud in *d*
Eze 12:3 go into exile in the *d* before
12:4 in the *d* before their eyes
12:7 luggage for exile, in the *d*
30:16 be adversaries during the *d*
Ho 4:5 certainly stumble in the *d*
Ro 13:13 As in the *d* let us walk
2Pe 2:13 living in the *d* a pleasure

Dazzling

Ca 5:10 My dear one is *d* and ruddy
Isa 18:4 *d* heat along with the light

Dead

Ge 20:3 you are as good as *d* because
23:3 got up from before his *d*
23:4 bury my *d* out of my sight
23:6 burial places bury your *d*
23:6 to prevent burying your *d*
23:8 your souls agree to bury my *d*
23:11 give it to you. Bury your *d*
23:13 that I may bury my *d* there
23:15 So bury your *d*
30:1 I shall be a *d* woman
42:38 his brother is *d* and he has
44:20 his brother is *d* so that he
50:15 saw that their father was *d*
Ex 4:19 hunting for your soul are *d*
12:30 where there was not one *d*
12:33 we are all as good as *d*
14:30 Egyptians *d* on the seashore
21:34 *d* animal will become his
21:35 the *d* one they should divide
21:36 *d* one will become his own
Le 5:2 *d* body of an unclean wild
5:2 *d* body of an unclean domestic
5:2 *d* body of an unclean swarming
7:24 fat of a body already *d* and
11:8 must not touch their *d* body
11:11 are to loathe their *d* body
11:24 touching their *d* bodies will
11:25 their *d* bodies will wash his
11:27 *d* bodies will be unclean
11:28 carries their *d* bodies will
11:35 their *d* bodies may fall
11:36 *d* bodies will be unclean
11:37 their *d* bodies fall upon any
11:38 their *d* bodies had fallen
11:39 he who touches its *d* body
11:40 eats any of its *d* body will
11:40 who carries off its *d* body
17:15 body already *d* or
21:11 should not come to any *d* soul
22:8 body already *d* or anything
Nu 6:6 not come toward any *d* soul
6:11 sinned because of the *d* soul
12:12 like someone *d*, whose flesh
16:48 between the *d* and the living
16:49 *d* from the scourge amounted
16:49 those *d* on account of Korah
De 14:1 baldness . . . for a *d* person
14:21 not eat any body already *d*
18:11 anyone who inquires of the *d*
21:23 his *d* body should not stay
25:5 the wife of the *d* one should
25:6 to the name of his *d* brother
26:14 given any of it for anyone *d*
28:26 *d* body must become food for
Jos 1:2 Moses my servant is *d*; and
8:29 took his *d* body down from
Jg 3:25 was fallen to the earth *d*
4:1 now that Ehud was *d*
4:22 there was Sisera fallen *d*
16:30 the *d* that he put to death in
Ru 1:8 toward the men now *d* and
Ru 2:20 toward the living and the *d*
4:5 the wife of the *d* man, that
4:5 name of the *d* man to rise upon
4:10 the name of the *d* man to rise
4:10 name of the *d* man may not be
1Sa 24:14 you chasing? After a *d* dog?
25:37 heart came to be *d* inside
2Sa 2:7 your lord Saul is *d*, and it
4:10 Here Saul is *d*, and he
9:8 turned your face to the *d* dog
13:39 Amnon, because he was *d*
14:2 many days over someone *d*
14:5 now that my husband is *d*
16:9 this *d* dog call down evil
19:6 others were today *d*
1Ki 3:20 *d* son she laid in my bosom
3:21 he was *d*. So I examined him
3:22 and your son is the *d* one!
3:22 but your son is the *d* one
3:23 and your son is the *d* one!
3:23 but your son is the *d* one
13:22 your *d* body will not come
13:24 *d* body came to be thrown
13:24 standing beside the *d* body
13:25 the *d* body thrown onto the
13:25 standing beside the *d* body
13:28 and found the *d* body of him
13:28 standing beside the *d* body
13:28 had not eaten the *d* body
13:29 *d* body of the man of the
13:30 *d* body in his own burial
21:14 Naboth has been stoned . . . *d*
21:15 no longer alive, but *d*
21:16 heard that Naboth was *d*
2Ki 4:1 servant, my husband, is *d*
4:32 and there the boy was *d*
8:5 how he had revived the *d* one
9:37 the *d* body of Jezebel will
19:35 all . . . were *d* carcasses
23:30 *d* in a chariot from Megiddo
Ps 31:12 Like someone *d* and not in
79:2 *d* body of your servants as
88:5 Set free among the *d*
88:10 those who are *d* will you do
106:28 sacrifices of the *d* ones
110:6 cause a fullness of *d* bodies
115:17 *d* themselves do not praise
143:3 those *d* for time indefinite
Ec 4:2 the *d* who had already died
9:3 and after it—to the *d* ones
9:4 dog is better off than a *d* lion
9:5 the *d*, they are conscious of
10:1 *D* flies are what cause the
Isa 5:25 *d* bodies will become like
8:19 application to *d* persons in
22:2 nor those *d* in battle
26:14 They are *d*; they will not
26:19 Your *d* ones will live
37:36 all . . . were *d* carcasses
57:1 are being gathered to the *d*
59:10 we are just like *d* people
Jer 7:33 the *d* bodies of this people
9:22 The *d* bodies of mankind must
16:4 their *d* bodies will actually
16:7 comfort someone over the *d*
19:7 give their *d* bodies as food
22:10 Do not weep for the *d* one
26:23 cast his *d* body into the
34:20 *d* bodies must become food
36:30 his own *d* body will become
La 3:6 sit like men *d* for a long time
Eze 4:14 neither a body already *d* nor
24:17 For the *d* ones no mourning
44:25 *d* person of mankind he
44:31 No body already *d* and no
Na 3:3 there is no end to the *d* bodies
3:3 stumbling among their *d* bodies
Mt 2:20 of the young child are *d*
8:22, 22 let the *d* bury their *d*
9:18 By now my daughter must be *d*
10:8 raise up *d* persons, make
11:5 and the *d* are being raised up
14:2 He was raised up from the *d*
17:9 is raised up from the *d*
22:31 the resurrection of the *d*
22:32 God, not of the *d*, but of
23:27 full of *d* men's bones and
27:64 He was raised up from the *d*!
28:4 trembled and became as *d* men
28:7 he was raised up from the *d*
Mr 6:14 has been raised up from the *d*
9:9 had risen from the *d*
9:10 this rising from the *d* meant
9:26 he became as *d*, so that the

Mr 9:26 were saying: He is *d!*
12:25 when they rise from the *d*
12:26 concerning the *d,* that they
12:27 He is a God, not of the *d*
15:44 whether he was already *d*
Lu 7:12 a *d* man being carried out
7:15 the *d* man sat up and started
7:22 the *d* are being raised up
9:7 had been raised up from the *d*
9:60, 60 Let the *d* bury their *d*
15:24 son was *d* and came to life
15:32 brother was *d* and came to
16:30 if someone from the *d* goes
16:31 if someone rises from the *d*
20:35 resurrection from the *d*
20:37 the *d* are raised up even
20:38 He is a God, not of the *d*
24:5 the living One among the *d*
24:46 rise from among the *d* on
Joh 2:22 he was raised up from the *d*
5:21 the Father raises the *d* up
5:25 *d* will hear the voice of the
11:44 man that had been *d* came
12:1 had raised up from the *d*
12:9 he raised up from the *d*
12:17 raised him up from the *d*
19:33 saw that he was already *d*
20:9 that he must rise from the *d*
21:14 being raised up from the *d*
Ac 3:15 God raised him up from the *d*
4:2 resurrection from the *d* in the
4:10 God raised up from the *d,* by
5:10 they found her *d,* and they
10:41 after his rising from the *d*
10:42 judge of the living and the *d*
13:30 raised him up from the *d*
13:34 resurrected him from the *d*
14:19 imagining he was *d*
17:3 suffer and to rise from the *d*
17:31 resurrected him from the *d*
17:32 of a resurrection of the *d*
20:9 fell . . . and was picked up *d*
23:6 hope of resurrection of the *d*
24:21 the resurrection of the *d*
25:19 Jesus who was *d* but who
26:8 that God raises up the *d*
26:23 to be resurrected from the *d*
28:6 or suddenly drop *d*
Ro 1:4 of resurrection from the *d*
4:17 God, who makes the *d* alive
4:24 Jesus our Lord up from the *d*
6:4 was raised up from the *d*
6:9 has been raised up from the *d*
6:11 *d* indeed with reference to
6:13 God as those alive from the *d*
7:4 made *d* to the Law through the
7:4 who was raised up from the *d*
7:8 for apart from law sin was *d*
8:10 is *d* on account of sin, but
8:11 raised up Jesus from the *d*
8:11 up Christ Jesus from the *d*
8:34 who was raised up from the *d*
10:7 bring Christ up from the *d*
10:9 God raised him up from the *d*
11:15 mean but life from the *d*
14:9 Lord over both the *d* and the
1Co 15:12 been raised up from the *d*
15:12 no resurrection of the *d*
15:13 no resurrection of the *d*
15:15 if the *d* are really not to
15:16 the *d* are not to be raised
15:20 been raised up from the *d*
15:21 resurrection of the *d* is
15:29 the purpose of being *d* ones
15:29 *d* are not to be raised up
15:32 the *d* are not to be raised
15:35 How are the *d* to be raised
15:42 the resurrection of the *d*
15:52 the *d* will be raised up
2Co 1:9 the God who raises up the *d*
Ga 1:1 raised him up from the *d*
Eph 1:20 raised him up from the *d* and
2:1 were *d* in your trespasses and
2:5 when we were *d* in trespasses
5:14 and arise from the *d,* and
Php 3:11 resurrection from the *d*
Col 1:18 the firstborn from the *d*
2:12 raised him up from the *d*
2:13 *d* in your trespasses and in
1Th 1:10 whom he raised up from the *d*
4:16 *d* in union with Christ will
1Ti 5:6 is *d* though she is living
2Ti 2:8 was raised up from the *d* and
4:1 to judge the living and the *d*
Heb 6:1 repentance from *d* works, and
6:2 the resurrection of the *d* and
9:14 our consciences from *d* works
9:17 is valid over *d* victims
11:12 man, and him as good as *d*
11:19 him up even from the *d*
11:35 Women received their *d* by
13:20 brought up from the *d* the
Jas 2:17 faith . . . is *d* in itself
2:26 body without spirit is *d,* so
2:26 faith without works is *d*
1Pe 1:3 Jesus Christ from the *d*
1:21 raised him up from the *d* and
4:5 those living and those *d*
4:6 was declared also to the *d*
Re 1:5 The firstborn from the *d,* and
1:17 I fell as *d* at his feet
1:18 I became *d,* but, look! I am
2:8 became *d* and came to life
3:1 you are alive, but you are *d*
11:18 time for the *d* to be judged
14:13 Happy are the *d* who die in
16:3 became blood as of a *d* man
20:5 rest of the *d* did not come
20:12 I saw the *d,* the great and
20:12 *d* were judged out of those
20:13 sea gave up those *d* in it
20:13 Hades gave up those *d* in

Deaden
Col 3:5 *D,* therefore, your body

Deadened
Ro 4:19 his own body, now already *d*

Deadly
Ex 10:17 this *d* plague from upon me
2Sa 22:5 *d* breaking waves encircled
Job 24:12 the soul of *d* wounded ones
27:15 buried during a *d* plague
Jer 15:2 Whoever is for *d* plague
15:2 to *d* plague! And whoever is
18:21 those killed with *d* plague
43:11 due for *d* plague will
43:11 will be for *d* plague, and
Eze 21:25 *d* wounded, wicked chieftain
30:24 as a *d* wounded one he will
Re 2:23 I will kill with *d* plague, so
6:8 food shortage and . . . *d* plague

Deadness
Ro 4:19 the *d* of the womb of Sarah

Deaf
Ex 4:11 who appoints . . . the *d* or the
Le 19:14 call down evil upon a *d* man
Ps 28:1 O my Rock, do not be *d* to me
38:13 like someone *d,* I would not
58:4 *D* like the cobra that stops
Isa 29:18 *d* ones will certainly hear
35:5 ears of the *d* ones will be
42:18 Hear, you *d* ones; and look
42:19 who is *d* as my messenger
43:8 ones *d* though they have ears
Mic 7:16 very ears will become *d*
Mt 11:5 *d* are hearing, and the dead
Mr 7:32 a man *d* and with a speech
7:37 He even makes the *d* hear and
9:25 *d* spirit, I order you, get
Lu 7:22 the *d* are hearing, the dead

Deal
Ge 8:21 never again shall I *d* every
21:23 *d* with me and with the land
32:9 and I will *d* well with you
32:12 I shall *d* well with you and
Ex 1:10 Let us *d* shrewdly with them
5:15 Why do you *d* this way with
Le 19:11 and you must not *d* falsely
Nu 14:39 began to mourn a great *d*
De 3:19 a great *d* of livestock
21:14 You must not *d* tyrannically
Jg 9:23 proceeded to *d* treacherously
21:2 in a great *d* of weeping
1Sa 26:10 Jehovah himself will *d* him
31:4 and *d* abusively with me
2Sa 12:15 *d* a blow to the child that
18:5 *D* gently for my sake with
22:26 you will *d* faultlessly
1Ki 10:10 very great *d* of balsam oil
2Ki 10:18 will worship him a great *d*
12:10 great *d* of money in the
1Ch 10:4 *d* abusively with me
22:8 a great *d* of blood you have
2Ch 14:13 a very great *d* of spoil
26:10 great *d* of livestock that
27:3 he did a great *d* of building
2Ch 28:8 great *d* of spoil they took
32:4 find a great *d* of water
Ne 4:10 there is a great *d* of rubbish
Job 19:3 that you *d* so hard with me
Ps 18:25 you will *d* faultlessly
37:3 and *d* with faithfulness
51:18 do *d* well with Zion
109:21 *D* with me for the sake of
142:7 you *d* appropriately with me
Pr 13:23 yields a great *d* of food
Ec 1:16 saw a great *d* of wisdom and
5:17 with a great *d* of vexation
Isa 19:22 certainly *d* Egypt a blow
33:1 they will *d* treacherously
53:12 *d* him a portion among the
Jer 16:7 not *d* out to them any bread
38:19 *d* abusively with me
La 1:22 *d* severely with them, Just as
Eze 29:19 do a great *d* of plundering
30:24 do a great *d* of groaning
Da 7:28 kept frightening me a great *d*
11:13 and with a great *d* of goods
Zec 8:15 to *d* well with Jerusalem
Mal 2:10 we *d* treacherously with one
2:15 may no one *d* treacherously
2:16 must not *d* treacherously
Mt 18:35 heavenly Father will also *d*
26:9 have been sold for a great *d*
Mr 1:45 to proclaim it a great *d* and
Joh 3:29 a great *d* of joy on account
Ac 8:3 to *d* outrageously with the
8:8 great *d* of joy in that city
Ro 3:2 A great *d* in every way
1Th 2:2 with a great *d* of struggling
2Ti 3:1 critical times hard to *d* with
Heb 5:2 He is able to *d* moderately
Re 5:4 a great *d* of weeping because

Dealer
Isa 21:2 treacherous *d* is dealing

Dealers
Isa 24:16 treacherous *d* have dealt
24:16 treacherous *d* have dealt
Jer 9:2 assembly of treacherous *d*

Dealing
Ex 21:8 his treacherously *d* with her
Jg 11:27 you are *d* wrong with me by
15:3 *d* with them to their injury
2Ch 21:14 Jehovah is *d* a great blow
Ps 14:1 acted detestably in their *d*
25:3 *d* treacherously without
66:5 His *d* with the sons of men is
89:23 him I kept *d* out blows
119:158 who are treacherous in *d*
Pr 11:3 those *d* treacherously will
11:6 those *d* treacherously will
11:17 *d* rewardingly with his own
13:2 those *d* treacherously is
13:15 *d* treacherously is rugged
21:18 one *d* treacherously takes the
Isa 3:12 task assigners are *d* severely
19:22 a *d* of a blow and a healing
21:2 treacherous dealer is *d*
33:1 *d* treacherously, without
33:1 done with *d* treacherously
48:8 you kept *d* treacherously
Jer 3:8 treacherously *d* Judah her
3:11 than treacherously *d* Judah
La 4:4 is no one *d* it out to them
Hab 1:13 look on those *d* treacherously
2:5 the wine is *d* treacherously
Col 4:1 keep *d* out what is righteous
Heb 12:7 God is *d* with you as with

Dealings
1Ki 1:7 came to have *d* with Joab the
Job 24:21 *d* with a barren woman who
Ps 77:12 with your *d* I will concern
78:11 also began to forget his *d*
103:7 *d* even to the sons of Israel
105:1 among the peoples his *d*
106:29 causing offense by their *d*
106:39 intercourse by their *d*
Pr 13:20 *d* with the stupid ones will
14:14 with the results of his *d*
Isa 1:16 remove the badness of your *d*
3:8 *d* are against Jehovah
3:10 very fruitage of their *d*
12:4 among the peoples his *d*
59:18 In accordance with the *d* he
Jer 4:4 the badness of your *d*
4:18 Your way and your *d*—there
7:3 your ways and your *d* good
7:5 your ways and your *d* good

Jer 11:18 caused me to see their *d*
17:10 to the fruitage of his *d*
18:11 your ways and your *d* good
21:12 the badness of your *d*
21:14 the fruitage of your *d*
23:2 for the badness of your *d*
23:22 the badness of their *d*
25:5 from the badness of your *d*
26:3 the badness of their *d*
26:13 your ways and your *d* good
32:19 to the fruitage of his *d*
35:15 and make your *d* good
44:22 badness of your *d*, because
Eze 14:22 see their way and their *d*
14:23 see their way and their *d*
20:43 *d* by which you defiled
20:44 corrupted *d*, O house of
21:24 according to all your *d*
24:14 and according to your *d*
36:17 their way and with their *d*
36:19 to their *d* I judged them
36:31 your *d* that were not good
Ho 4:9 their *d* I shall bring back
5:4 Their *d* do not permit of a
7:2 their *d* have surrounded them
9:15 account of the evil of their *d*
12:2 to his *d* he will repay him
Mic 2:7 or are these his *d*?
3:4 committed badness in their *d*
7:13 of the fruit of their *d*
Zep 3:7 making all their *d* ruinous
3:11 your *d* with which you
Zec 1:4 bad ways and from your bad *d*
1:6 ways and according to our *d*
Joh 4:9 have no *d* with Samaritans

Dealt

Ge 21:23 love with which I have *d*
Ex 1:20 So God *d* well with the
10:2 severely I have *d* with Egypt
Nu 22:29 have *d* ruthlessly with me
De 24:7 has *d* tyrannically with him
1Sa 6:6 He *d* severely with them that
14:33 You have *d* treacherously
2Sa 18:13 *d* treacherously against his
2Ch 2:3 as you *d* with David my father
13:20 Jehovah *d* him a blow, so
Job 6:15 brothers have *d* treacherously
Ps 13:6 he has *d* rewardingly with me
119:65 *d* well indeed with your
Isa 3:9 *d* out to themselves calamity
24:16 treacherous dealers have *d*
24:16 treacherous dealers have *d*
33:1 having *d* treacherously with
Jer 3:20 have *d* treacherously with
5:11 *d* treacherously with me
12:6 *d* treacherously with you
La 1:2 have *d* treacherously with her
1:12 pain that has been severely *d*
1:22 you have *d* severely with me
2:20 to whom you have *d* severely
3:51 My own eye has *d* severely
Ho 5:7 they have *d* treacherously
6:7 they have *d* treacherously
Mal 2:11 Judah has *d* treacherously
2:14 have *d* treacherously
Lu 1:25 way Jehovah has *d* with me

Dear

Ca 1:13 As a bag of myrrh my *d* one is
1:14 henna my *d* one is to me
1:16 my *d* one, also pleasant
2:3 so is my *d* one among the sons
2:8 The sound of my *d* one! Look!
2:9 *d* one is resembling a gazelle
2:10 My *d* one has answered and
2:16 *d* one is mine and I am his
2:17 my *d* one; be like the gazelle
4:16 my *d* one come into his garden
5:2 the sound of my *d* one knocking
5:4 My *d* one himself pulled back
5:5 even I, to open to my *d* one
5:6 I opened, even I, to my *d* one
5:6 my *d* one himself had turned
5:8 if you find my *d* one, you
5:9 How is your *d* one more than
5:9 more than any other *d* one
5:9 How is your *d* one more than
5:9 more than any other *d* one
5:10 *d* one is dazzling and ruddy
5:16 This is my *d* one, and this is
6:1 Where has your *d* one gone, O
6:1 Where has your *d* one turned
6:2 My own *d* one has gone down to
6:3 I am my *d* one's, and my
Ca 6:3 and my *d* one is mine. He is
7:9 with a slickness for my *d* one
7:10 I am my *d* one's, and toward
7:11 Do come, O my *d* one, let us
7:13 my *d* one, I have treasured up
8:5 leaning upon her *d* one
8:14 Run away, my *d* one, and make
Lu 7:2 slave, who was *d* to him, was
Ac 20:24 my soul of any account as *d*
Php 2:29 holding men of that sort *d*

Death

Ge 18:25 put to *d* the righteous man
25:11 after Abraham's *d* God
26:11 wife will surely be put to *d*
26:18 after Abraham's *d*
27:2 I do not know the day of my *d*
27:7 before Jehovah before my *d*
27:10 may bless you before his *d*
37:18 against him to put him to *d*
38:7 hence Jehovah put him to *d*
38:10 hence he put him also to *d*
42:37 two sons you may put to *d* if
50:16 the command before his *d*
Ex 1:16 you must also put it to *d*
4:24 for a way to put him to *d*
16:3 congregation to *d* by famine
17:3 our livestock to *d* by thirst
19:12 will positively be put to *d*
21:12 to be put to *d* without fail
21:15 to be put to *d* without fail
21:16 to be put to *d* without fail
21:17 to be put to *d* without fail
21:29 put a man or a woman to *d*
21:29 its owner is to be put to *d*
22:19 is positively to be put to *d*
31:14 will positively be put to *d*
31:15 will positively be put to *d*
35:2 work on it will be put to *d*
Le 11:31 *d* state will be unclean
11:32 fall in its *d* state will be
16:1 the *d* of Aaron's two sons
19:20 They should not be put to *d*
20:2 be put to *d* without fail
20:2 pelt him to *d* with stones
20:4 by not putting him to *d*
20:9 be put to *d* without fail
20:10 *d* without fail, the
20:11 be put to *d* without fail
20:12 be put to *d* without fail
20:13 be put to *d* without fail
20:15 be put to *d* without fail
20:16 be put to *d* without fail
20:27 be put to *d* without fail
20:27 pelt them to *d* with stones
24:16 be put to *d* without fail
24:16 *d* for his abusing the Name
24:17 be put to *d* without fail
24:21 of a man should be put to *d*
27:29 be put to *d* without fail
Nu 1:51 near should be put to *d*
3:10 near should be put to *d*
3:38 coming near would be put to *d*
14:15 put this people to *d* as one
15:35 the man should be put to *d*
16:13 to *d* in the wilderness
16:29 the *d* of all mankind
16:41 put Jehovah's people to *d*
18:7 the stranger . . . put to *d*
23:10 die the *d* of the upright ones
26:10 at the *d* of the assembly
33:39 at his *d* on Mount Hor
35:16 murderer should be put to *d*
35:17 murderer should be put to *d*
35:18 murderer should be put to *d*
35:19 will put the murderer to *d*
35:19 himself will put him to *d*
35:21 striker should be put to *d*
35:21 will put the murderer to *d*
35:25 the *d* of the high priest who
35:28 until the high priest's *d*
35:28 and after the high priest's *d*
35:31 he should be put to *d*
35:32 the *d* of the high priest
De 9:28 to *d* in the wilderness
13:5 should be put to *d*
13:9 to put him to *d*, and the hand
17:6 one dying should be put to *d*
17:6 He will not be put to *d* at
17:7 to put him to *d*, and the hand
19:6 no sentence of *d* for him
21:22 deserving the sentence of *d*
21:22 and he has been put to *d*
22:26 has no sin deserving of *d*
De 24:16 not be put to *d* on account of
24:16 to *d* on account of fathers
24:16 be put to *d* for his own sin
30:15 life and good, and *d* and bad
30:19 put life and *d* before you
31:27 how much more so after my *d*
31:29 after my *d* you will without
32:39 I put to *d*, and I make alive
33:1 blessed . . . before his *d*
34:7 and twenty years old at his *d*
Jos 1:1 after the *d* of Moses the
1:18 command us will be put to *d*
2:13 deliver our souls from *d*
10:26 put them to *d* and hang them
11:17 and putting them to *d*
20:6 the *d* of the high priest
Jg 1:1 after the *d* of Joshua it came
5:18 their souls to the point of *d*
6:31 be put to *d* even this morning
9:54 put me to *d*, for fear they
13:7 until the day of his *d*
13:23 only to put us to *d*, he
15:13 by no means put you to *d*
16:30, 30 put to *d* in his own *d*
16:30 put to *d* during his lifetime
20:13 that we may put them to *d*
21:5 be put to *d* without fail
Ru 1:17 if anything but *d* should make
2:11 after the *d* of your husband
1Sa 2:25 now pleased to put them to *d*
4:20 And about the time of her *d*
5:10 put me and my people to *d*
5:11 put me and my people to *d*
11:12 that we may put them to *d*
11:13 be put to *d* on this day
14:13 putting them to *d* behind
15:3 and you must put them to *d*
15:32 experience of *d* has departed
15:35 until the day of his *d*
17:35 and put it to *d*
17:50 David . . . put him to *d*
17:51 definitely put him to *d*
19:1 of putting David to *d*
19:2 seeking to have you put to *d*
19:5 David put to *d* for nothing
19:6 he will not be put to *d*
19:11 put to *d* in the morning
19:11 you will be a man put to *d*
19:15 to me to have him put to *d*
19:17 Why should I put you to *d*?
20:3 a step between me and *d*
20:8 put me to *d* yourself, since
20:31 for he is destined for *d*
20:32 Why should he be put to *d*?
20:33 father to put David to *d*
22:17 put to *d* the priests of
22:18 put to *d* on that day
28:9 to have me put to *d*
30:2 not put anyone to *d*, but
30:15 not put me to *d*, and that
2Sa 1:1 after Saul's *d*, and when
1:9 definitely put me to *d*, for
1:10 definitely put him to *d*, for
1:16 the anointed of Jehovah to *d*
1:23 in their *d* they were not
3:30 Asahel their brother to *d* at
3:33 *d* of a senseless person
3:37 Abner the son of Ner put to *d*
4:7 so that they put him to *d*
6:23 down to the day of her *d*
8:2 two lines to put them to *d*
13:28 you must then put him to *d*
13:32 that they have put to *d*
14:6 other down and put him to *d*
14:7 that we may put him to *d*
14:32 he must then put me to *d*
15:21 whether for *d* or for life
18:15 they might put him to *d*
19:21 Shimei be put to *d*, in that
19:22 today be put to *d* in Israel
19:28 nothing but doomed to *d*
20:19 seeking to put to *d* a city
21:1 he put the Gibeonites to *d*
21:4 to put a man to *d* in Israel
21:9 put to *d* in the first days
21:17 and put him to *d*
22:6 snares of *d* confronted me
1Ki 1:51 servant to *d* by the sword
2:8 put you to *d* by the sword
2:24 Adonijah will be put to *d*
2:26 you are deserving of *d*
2:26 I shall not put you to *d*
2:34 Benaiah . . . put him to *d*
3:26 Do not . . . put him to *d*

1Ki 3:27 by no means put him to *d*
11:40 to put Jeroboam to *d*
11:40 in Egypt until Solomon's *d*
13:24 put him to *d*, and his dead
13:26 crush him and put him to *d*
15:28 So Baasha put him to *d* in
16:10 and put him to *d* in the
16:22 Tibni met *d*, and Omri began
17:18 and to put my son to *d*
17:20 by putting her son to *d*
18:9 hand of Ahab to put me to *d*
19:17 Jehu will put to *d*
19:17 Elisha will put to *d*
2Ki 1:1 Israel after the *d* of Ahab
2:21 No more will *d* or any
4:40 There is *d* in the pot, O man
5:7 put to *d* and to preserve alive
7:4 but if they put us to *d*
11:2 that were to be put to *d*
11:2 and he was not put to *d*
11:8 will be put to *d*
11:15 there be an execution of *d*
11:15 Do not let her be put to *d*
11:16 she got put to *d* there
11:20 put to *d* with the sword at
14:6 he did not put to *d*
14:6 not be put to *d* for sons
14:6 not be put to *d* for fathers
14:6 each one be put to *d*
14:17 *d* of Jehoash the son of
14:19 and put him to *d* there
15:5 leper until the day of his *d*
15:10 put him to *d* and began to
15:14 in Samaria and put him to *d*
15:25 he put him to *d* and began
15:30 struck him and put him to *d*
16:9 and Rezin he put to *d*
17:26 they are putting them to *d*
21:23 king to *d* in his own house
23:29 he put him to *d* at Megiddo
25:21 put them to *d* at Riblah
1Ch 2:3 so that he put him to *d*
2:24 And after the *d* of Hezron
10:14 put him to *d* and turned the
19:18 and Shophach . . . he put to *d*
22:5 preparation . . . before his *d*
2Ch 15:13 put to *d*, whether small or
22:4 after the *d* of his father
22:9 put him to *d* and buried him
22:11 were to be put to *d*, and
22:11 and she did not put him to *d*
23:7 he should be put to *d*
23:14 put to *d* with the sword!
23:14 put her to *d* at the house
23:15 at once put her to *d* there
23:21 Athaliah they had put to *d*
24:15 thirty years old at his *d*
24:17 after Jehoiada's *d* the
25:4 sons he did not put to *d*
25:25 live after the *d* of Jehoash
25:27 and put him to *d*
26:21 until the day of his *d*
32:33 rendered to him at his *d*
33:24 to *d* in his own house
Ezr 7:26 for *d* or for banishment, or
Es 2:7 *d* of her father and her mother
4:11 law is to have him put to *d*
Job 3:21 waiting for *d*, and it is not
5:2 envying will put to *d*
5:20 certainly redeem you from *d*
7:15 my soul chooses . . . *D* rather
9:23 flood itself should cause *d*
18:13 firstborn of *d* will eat his
26:5 impotent in *d* keep trembling
28:22 Destruction and *d*
30:23 to *d* you will make me turn
33:22 to those inflicting *d*
38:17 gates of *d* been uncovered to
Ps 6:5 in *d* there is no mention of
7:13 prepare the instruments of *d*
9:13 up from the gates of *d*
13:3 I may not fall asleep in *d*
18:4 The ropes of *d* encircled me
18:5 The snares of *d* confronted me
22:15 in the dust of *d* you are
33:19 deliver their soul from *d*
34:21 the wicked one himself to *d*
37:32 is seeking to put him to *d*
49:14 *D* itself will shepherd them
49:17 at his *d* he cannot take along
55:4 the frights of *d* itself have
56:13 delivered my soul from *d*
59:*super* to put him to *d*
68:20 belong the ways out from *d*
Ps 78:50 hold back their soul from *d*
79:11 preserve those appointed to *d*
88:10 impotent in *d* themselves
89:48 alive who will not see *d*
102:20 loosen those appointed to *d*
105:29 to put their fish to *d*
107:18 arriving at the gates of *d*
109:16 to put him to *d*
116:3 The ropes of *d* encircled me
116:8 have rescued my soul from *d*
116:15 Is the *d* of his loyal ones
118:18 not give me over to *d*
Pr 2:18 down to *d* her house does sink
2:18 down to those impotent in *d*
5:5 Her feet are descending to *d*
7:27 to the interior rooms of *d*
8:36 the ones that do love *d*
9:18 those impotent in *d* are
10:2 is what will deliver from *d*
11:4 will deliver from *d*
11:19 is in line for his own *d*
12:28 in its pathway means no *d*
13:14 away from the snares of *d*
14:12 ways of *d* are the end of it
14:27 away from the snares of *d*
16:14 means messengers of *d*, but
16:25 ways of *d* are the end of it
18:21 *D* and life are in the power
19:16 will be put to *d*
19:18 to the putting of him to *d*
21:6 in the case of those seeking *d*
21:16 of those impotent in *d*
21:25 the lazy will put him to *d*
24:11 are being taken away to *d*
26:18 fiery missiles, arrows and *d*
Ec 7:1 day of *d* than the day of one's
7:26 More bitter than *d* I found
8:8 of control in the day of *d*
Ca 8:6 love is as strong as *d* is
Isa 11:4 put the wicked one to *d*
14:9 awakened those impotent in *d*
14:30 I will put your root to *d*
25:8 swallow up *d* forever, and the
26:14 Impotent in *d*, they will
26:19 those impotent in *d* drop
28:15 concluded a covenant with *D*
28:18 your covenant with *D* will
38:18 *d* itself cannot praise you
51:14 may not go in *d* to the pit
53:9 with the rich class in his *d*
53:12 his soul to the very *d*
65:15 put you individually to *d*
Jer 8:3 *d* will certainly be chosen
9:21 *d* has come up through our
18:23 counsel against me for my *d*
20:17 put me to *d* from the womb
21:8 way of life and the way of *d*
26:11 the judgment of *d* belongs
26:15 if you are putting me to *d*
26:16 There is no judgment of *d*
26:19 by any means put him to *d*
26:21 seeking to put him to *d*
26:24 to have him put to *d*
38:4 man, please, be put to *d*
38:15 without fail put me to *d*
38:16 I will not put you to *d*
38:25 shall not put you to *d*
41:2 put to *d* the one whom the
41:4 putting of Gedaliah to *d*
41:8 Do not put us to *d*, for
41:8 not put them to *d* in the
43:3 put us to *d* or to take us
52:11 until the day of his *d*
52:27 put them to *d* in Riblah
52:34 until the day of his *d*
La 1:20 the house it is the same as *d*
Eze 13:19 to put to *d* the souls that
18:13 will positively be put to *d*
18:23 in the *d* of someone wicked
18:32 delight in the *d* of someone
28:8 die the *d* of someone slain
31:14 all of them be given to *d*
33:11 in the *d* of the wicked one
43:7 of their kings at their *d*
Ho 2:3 and put her to *d* with thirst
4:3 will be gathered in *d*
9:16 put to *d* the desirable things
13:14 from *d* I shall recover them
13:14 Where are your stings, O *D*?
Jon 4:9 anger, to the point of *d*
Hab 2:5 like *d* and cannot be satisfied
Mt 10:21 will deliver up brother to *d*
10:21 and will have them put to *d*
15:4 that reviles . . . end up in *d*
Mt 16:28 not taste *d* at all until
20:18 they will condemn him to *d*
26:38 is deeply grieved, even to *d*
26:59 in order to put him to *d*
26:66 answer: He is liable to *d*
27:1 Jesus so as to put him to *d*
Mr 7:10 reviles . . . end up in *d*
9:1 not taste *d* at all until first
10:33 they will condemn him to *d*
13:12 deliver brother over to *d*
13:12 and have them put to *d*
14:34 deeply grieved, even to *d*
14:55 Jesus to put him to *d*
14:64 condemned . . . liable to *d*
Lu 2:26 would not see *d* before he
9:27 not taste *d* at all until first
21:16 will put some of you to *d*
22:33 both into prison and into *d*
23:15 nothing deserving of *d* has
23:22 nothing deserving of *d* in
24:20 sentence of *d* and impaled
Joh 5:24 passed over from *d* to life
8:51 he will never see *d* at all
8:52 he will never taste *d* at all
11:4 not with *d* as its object
11:13 however, about his *d*
12:33 sort of *d* he was about to
18:32 *d* he was destined to die
21:19 what sort of *d* he would
Ac 2:24 by loosing the pangs of *d*
7:60 this he fell asleep in *d*
13:28 they found no cause for *d*
13:36 fell asleep in *d* and was
22:4 persecuted this Way to the *d*
23:29 a single thing deserving of *d*
25:11 anything deserving of *d*
25:25 nothing deserving of *d*
26:31 nothing deserving *d* or bonds
28:18 was no cause for *d* in me
Ro 1:32 are deserving of *d*, they not
5:10 God through the *d* of his Son
5:12 and *d* through sin, and thus
5:12 *d* spread to all men because
5:14 *d* ruled as king from Adam
5:17 *d* ruled as king through that
5:21 as sin ruled as king with *d*
6:3 were baptized into his *d*
6:4 our baptism into his *d*, in
6:5 in the likeness of his *d*, we
6:9 *d* is master over him no more
6:10 *d* that he died, he died with
6:16 of sin with *d* in view or of
6:21 the end of those things is *d*
6:23 the wages sin pays is *d*, but
7:5 should bring forth fruit to *d*
7:10 this I found to be to *d*
7:13 what is good become *d* to me
7:13 sin working out *d* for me
7:24 the body undergoing this *d*
8:2 from the law of sin and of *d*
8:6 minding of the flesh means *d*
8:13 practices of the body to *d*
8:36 being put to *d* all day long
8:38 neither *d* nor life nor angels
1Co 3:22 or *d* or things now here or
4:9 men appointed to *d*, because
6:14 raise us up out of *d* through
7:39 should fall asleep in *d*, she
11:26 the *d* of the Lord, until he
11:30 a few are sleeping in *d*
15:6 some have fallen asleep in *d*
15:18 fell asleep in *d* in union
15:20 have fallen asleep in *d*
15:21 since *d* is through a man
15:26 *d* is to be brought to
15:31 Daily I face *d*. This I
15:51 not all fall asleep in *d*
15:54 *D* is swallowed up forever
15:55 *D*, where is your victory?
15:55 *D*, where is your sting?
15:56 The sting producing *d* is sin
2Co 1:9 had received the sentence of *d*
1:10 From such a great thing as *d*
2:16, 16 odor issuing from *d* to *d*
3:6 written code condemns to *d*
3:7 code which administers *d* and
4:11 face to face with *d* for
4:12 *d* is at work in us, but life
6:9 and yet not delivered to *d*
7:10 of the world produces *d*
Php 1:20 through life or through *d*
2:8 became obedient as far as *d*
2:8 yes, *d* on a torture stake
2:27 sick nearly to the point of *d*

Php 2:30 he came quite near to *d*
3:10 submitting . . . to a *d* like
Col 1:22 through his *d*, in order to
1Th 4:13 those who are sleeping in *d*
4:14 who have fallen asleep in *d*
4:15 who have fallen asleep in *d*
2Ti 1:10 Jesus, who has abolished *d*
Heb 2:9 honor for having suffered *d*
2:9 might taste *d* for every man
2:14 through his *d* he might bring
2:14 having the means to cause *d*
2:15 for fear of *d* were subject
5:7 able to save him out of *d*
7:23 prevented by *d* from
9:15 *d* has occurred for their
9:16 *d* of the human covenanter
11:5 so as not to see *d*, and he
Jas 1:15 sin . . . brings forth *d*
5:20 save his soul from *d* and
1Pe 3:18 being put to *d* in the flesh
2Pe 3:4 forefathers fell asleep in *d*
1Jo 3:14 passed over from *d* to life
3:14 does not love remains in *d*
5:16 sin that does not incur *d*
5:16 not sinning so as to incur *d*
5:16 is a sin that does incur *d*
5:17 a sin that does not incur *d*
Re 1:18 I have the keys of *d* and of
2:10 faithful even to *d*, and I
2:11 be harmed by the second *d*
6:8 seated upon it had the name *D*
9:6 the men will seek *d* but will
9:6 but *d* keeps fleeing from them
12:11 souls even in the face of *d*
13:3 as though slaughtered to *d*
18:8 plagues . . . *d* and mourning
20:6 second *d* has no authority
20:13 *d* and Hades gave up those
20:14 *d* and Hades were hurled into
20:14 This means the second *d*
21:4 *d* will be no more, neither
21:8 This means the second *d*

Death-dealing
1Sa 5:11 a *d* confusion had occurred in
2Co 4:10 *d* treatment given to Jesus
Jas 3:8 it is full of *d* poison

Deathly
Ps 73:4 For they have no *d* pangs
Mt 4:16 in a region of *d* shadow

Death's
Lu 1:79 in darkness and *d* shadow, to

Deaths
Jer 16:4 *d* from maladies they will
Eze 28:10 The *d* of uncircumcised ones

Death-stroke
Re 13:3 its *d* got healed, and all the
13:12 beast, whose *d* got healed

Debater
1Co 1:20 Where the *d* of this system

Debates
1Ti 2:8 apart from wrath and *d*
6:4 and *d* about words

Debating
Lu 24:17 these matters that you are *d*

Debauched
Lu 15:13 by living a *d* life

Debauchery
Eph 5:18 wine, in which there is *d*
Tit 1:6 not under a charge of *d* nor
1Pe 4:4 to the same low sink of *d*

Debir
Jos 10:3 to *D* the king of Eglon
10:38 came back to *D* and began
10:39 so he did to *D* and its king
11:21 from *D*, from Anab and from
12:13 the king of *D*, one
13:26 Mahanaim to the border of *D*
15:7 boundary went up to *D* at
15:15 to the inhabitants of *D*
15:15 name of *D* before that was
15:49 that is to say, *D*
21:15 and *D* and its pasture ground
Jg 1:11 the inhabitants of *D*
1:11 the name of *D* before that
1Ch 6:58 *D* with its pasture grounds

Deborah
Ge 35:8 *D* the nursing woman of
Jg 4:4 *D*, a prophetess, the wife of
Jg 4:9 *D* got up and went with Barak
4:10 and *D* went on up with him
4:14 *D* now said to Barak: Get up
5:1 *D* along with Barak the son of
5:7 Until I, *D*, rose up, Until I
5:12 *D*; Awake, awake, utter a song
5:15 Issachar were with *D*, And as

Deborah's
Jg 4:5 she was dwelling under *D* palm

Debris
Am 6:11 and the small house into *d*

Debt
De 15:2 every creditor of the *d*
Ne 10:31 and the *d* of every hand
Hab 2:6 *d* heavy against himself
Mt 18:27 and canceled his *d*
18:32 canceled all that *d* for you
Lu 7:41 the one was in *d* for five
11:4 everyone that is in *d* to us
Ro 4:4 undeserved kindness, but as a *d*

Debtor
Ro 1:14 to senseless ones I am a *d*

Debtor's
Pr 13:13 a *d* pledge will be seized

Debtors
Mt 6:12 we also have forgiven our *d*
Lu 7:41 were *d* to a certain lender
13:4 they were proved greater *d*
16:5 one of the *d* of his master
Ro 15:27 and yet they were *d* to them

Debts
2Ki 4:7 and pay off your *d*, and you
Mt 6:12 and forgive us our *d*, as we

Decapolis
Mt 4:25 from Galilee and *D* and
Mr 5:20 started to proclaim in the *D*
7:31 the midst of the regions of *D*

Decay
Job 21:20 His eyes will see his *d*
30:24 Nor during one's *d* is there

Decaying
Isa 17:1 become a heap, a *d* ruin

Decease
Mt 2:15 there until the *d* of Herod

Deceased
Le 19:28 cuts in your flesh for a *d*
21:1 For a *d* soul no one may defile
22:4 unclean by a *d* soul or a man
Nu 5:2 everyone unclean by a *d* soul
Hag 2:13 someone unclean by a *d* soul
Mt 2:19 When Herod had *d*, look!
22:25 the first married and *d*, and
Joh 11:39 Martha, the sister of the *d*
Ac 2:29 *d* and was buried and his tomb
7:15 Jacob . . . *d*; and so did our

Deceit
Ge 34:13 answer . . . with *d* and to
Job 13:7 for him will you speak *d*?
15:35 belly itself prepares *d*
27:4 tongue will mutter no *d*
Ps 32:2 whose spirit there is no *d*
Pr 26:26 Hatred is covered over by *d*
Mr 7:22 *d*, loose conduct, an envious
Joh 1:47 in whom there is no *d*
Ro 1:29 *d*, malicious disposition
3:13 used *d* with their tongues
1Th 2:3 from uncleanness or with *d*

Deceitful
Ps 52:4 words, O you *d* tongue
55:23 *d* men, they will not live
Pr 14:25 a *d* one launches forth mere
Jer 15:18 like something *d*, like
Mic 1:14 *d* to the kings of Israel
2Co 11:13 false apostles, *d* workers

Deceitfully
Ps 24:4 Nor taken an oath *d*
52:2 Working *d*

Deceitfulness
1Pe 2:1 all *d* and hypocrisy and envies

Deceive
Le 6:2 does *d* his associate about
19:11 you must not *d*, and you must
2Ki 18:29 Do not let Hezekiah *d* you
19:10 *d* you, saying: Jerusalem
2Ch 32:15 Hezekiah *d* you or allure
Isa 36:14 not let Hezekiah *d* you
37:10 you are trusting *d* you
Jer 29:8 Let not your prophets . . . *d*
37:9 Do not *d* your souls, saying
Eph 5:6 Let no man *d* you with empty

Deceived
Ge 3:13 The serpent—it *d* me and so I
1Ki 13:18 a prophet . . . (He *d* him.)
Isa 19:13 princes of Noph have been *d*
Jer 4:10 *d* this people and Jerusalem
49:16 shuddering you caused has *d*
Ob 3 your heart is what has *d* you
7 have all *d* you. The men at
1Ti 2:14 Adam was not *d*, but the
2:14 the woman was thoroughly *d*

Deceiver
2Jo 7 is the *d* and the antichrist

Deceivers
2Co 6:8 as *d* and yet truthful
Tit 1:10 *d* of the mind, especially
2Jo 7 many *d* have gone forth into the

Deceiving
Zec 13:4 for the purpose of *d*
Ga 6:3 he is *d* his own mind
Jas 1:22 *d* yourselves with false
1:26 goes on *d* his own heart

Decently
Ro 13:13 let us walk *d*, not in
1Co 14:40 *d* and by arrangement
1Th 4:12 walking *d* as regards people

Deception
Ge 27:35 Your brother came with *d*
Job 31:5 And my foot hastens to *d*
Ps 5:6 A man of bloodshed and *d*
17:1 my prayer without lips of *d*
33:17 horse is a *d* for salvation
34:13 your lips against speaking *d*
35:20 *d* they keep scheming
36:3 words of his mouth are . . . *d*
43:1 man of *d* and unrighteousness
50:19 tongue you keep attached to *d*
55:11 and *d* have not moved away
59:12 the *d* that they rehearse
109:2 mouth of *d* have opened
Pr 12:5 by the wicked ones is *d*
12:17 but a false witness, *d*
12:20 *D* is in the heart of those
14:8 of stupid ones is *d*
26:24 but inside of him he puts *d*
Isa 53:9 there was no *d* in his mouth
Jer 5:27 their houses are full of *d*
9:6 sitting is in the midst of *d*
9:6 Through *d* they have refused
9:8 *D* is what it has spoken
Da 8:25 *d* to succeed in his hand
11:23 carry on *d* and actually come
Ho 4:2 practicing of *d* and murdering
10:13 eaten the fruitage of *d*
11:12 with *d* the house of Israel
12:7 his hand are the scales of *d*
Am 8:5 to falsify the scales of *d*
Na 3:1 is all full of *d* and of robbery
Zep 1:9 with violence and *d*
Col 2:8 the philosophy and empty *d*
2Th 2:10 with every unrighteous *d* for
1Pe 2:22 nor was *d* found in his mouth
3:10 and his lips from speaking *d*

Deceptions
Ps 10:7 full of oaths and of *d* and
38:12 *d* they keep muttering all
Ho 7:3 and, by their *d*, princes

Deceptive
Le 6:3 *d* about it and does swear
1Ki 22:22 a *d* spirit in the mouth of
22:23 put a *d* spirit into the
2Ch 18:21 *d* spirit in the mouth of
18:22 *d* spirit in the mouth of
Isa 30:10 envision *d* things
Mic 6:11 a bag of *d* stone weights
Mt 13:22 *d* power of riches choke the
Mr 4:19 the *d* power of riches and the
Eph 4:22 according to his *d* desires
Heb 3:13 by the *d* power of sin
2Pe 2:13 delight in their *d* teachings

Decide
Ge 31:37 let them *d* between us two
De 32:31 enemies being the ones to *d*
1Sa 14:42 *d* between me and Jonathan
Job 9:33 no person to *d* between us
22:28 And you will *d* on something

Ac 24:22 I shall *d* upon these matters

Decided

1Ki 20:40 You yourself have *d*
2Ch 30:5 *d* to have a call pass through
30:23 congregation *d* to hold it
32:3 *d* with his princes and his
Es 2:1 what had been *d* against her
Job 14:5 If his days are *d*, The
Isa 10:22 extermination *d* upon will
28:22 even something *d* upon, that
Da 9:26 is *d* upon is desolations
9:27 thing *d* upon will go pouring
11:36 thing *d* upon must be done
Ac 3:13 he had *d* to release him
16:4 decrees that had been *d* upon
19:39 be *d* in a regular assembly
20:16 For Paul had *d* to sail past
25:25 I *d* to send him
27:1 *d* for us to sail away to
1Co 2:2 *d* not to know anything among
2Co 2:1 I have *d* for myself, not to
Tit 3:12 is where I have *d* to winter

Decision

Ex 21:31 according to this judicial *d*
23:6 judicial *d* of your poor man
Le 24:22 *d* should hold good for you
Nu 15:16 one judicial *d* for you and
27:11 as a statute by judicial *d*
De 17:8 a matter for judicial *d*
17:9 the word of the judicial *d*
17:11 according to the judicial *d*
Jos 24:25 and judicial *d* in Shechem
1Sa 30:25 judicial *d* for Israel down
2Sa 5:24 act with *d*, because at that
8:15 rendering judicial *d* and
1Ki 3:28 *d* that the king had handed
3:28 to execute judicial *d*
10:9 as king to render judicial *d*
20:33 as a *d* of his own accord
2Ki 25:6 pronounce a judicial *d* upon
1Ch 18:14 rendering judicial *d* and
2Ch 9:8 king to execute judicial *d*
Ezr 5:17 the *d* of the king concerning
Job 16:21 the *d* is to be made between
Ps 25:9 to walk in his judicial *d*
36:6 *d* is a vast watery deep
72:2 ones with judicial *d*
81:4 judicial *d* of the God of Jacob
94:15 judicial *d* will return even
119:43 for your own judicial *d*
119:132 your judicial *d* toward
119:149 judicial *d* preserve me
119:160 righteous judicial *d* of
149:9 the judicial *d* written
Pr 16:10 Inspired *d* should be upon the
16:33 *d* by it is from Jehovah
Isa 10:23 strict *d* the Sovereign Lord
16:3 you men, execute the *d*
28:7 they have reeled as to *d*
51:4 and my judicial *d* I shall
Joe 3:14 in the low plain of the *d*
3:14 in the low plain of the *d*
Zep 2:3 practiced His own judicial *d*
3:5 giving his own judicial *d*
3:8 judicial *d* is to gather
Ac 15:19 my *d* is not to trouble those
21:25 rendering our *d* that they
25:21 the *d* by the August One
Ro 14:13 make this your *d*, not to
1Co 7:37 made this *d* in his own heart

Decisions

Ex 18:16 the *d* of the true God and
21:1 these are the judicial *d* that
24:3 and all the judicial *d*, and
Le 18:4 My judicial *d* you should carry
18:5 my statutes and my judicial *d*
18:26 judicial *d*, and you must not
19:37 judicial *d*, and you must do
20:22 my judicial *d* and do them
25:18 keep my judicial *d* and you
26:15 abhor my judicial *d* so as
26:43 rejected my judicial *d*, and
26:46 judicial *d* and the laws that
Nu 36:13 the judicial *d* that Jehovah
De 4:1 judicial *d* that I am teaching
4:5 regulations and judicial *d*
4:8 judicial *d* like all this law
4:14 regulations and judicial *d*
4:45 judicial *d* that Moses spoke
5:1 *d* that I am speaking in your
5:31 the judicial *d* that you should
6:1 the judicial *d* that Jehovah
6:20 judicial *d* mean that Jehovah
De 7:11 regulations and the judicial *d*
7:12 listening to these judicial *d*
8:11 judicial *d* and his statutes
11:1 his judicial *d* and his
11:32 *d* that I am putting before
12:1 the judicial *d* that you should
26:16 regulations and judicial *d*
26:17 his judicial *d* and listen to
30:16 statutes and his judicial *d*
33:10 Jacob in your judicial *d*
33:21 his judicial *d* with Israel
2Sa 22:23 For all his judicial *d* are
1Ki 2:3 his judicial *d* and his
6:12 perform my judicial *d* and
8:58 and his judicial *d*, which
9:4 regulations and my judicial *d*
11:33 my judicial *d* like David
2Ki 17:34 statutes and his judicial *d*
17:37 the judicial *d* and the law
1Ch 16:12 the judicial *d* of his mouth
16:14 are his judicial *d*
22:13 the judicial *d* that Jehovah
28:7 and my judicial *d*, as at
2Ch 7:17 and my judicial *d*
19:10 judicial *d*, you must warn
33:8 judicial *d* by the hand of
Ne 1:7 regulations and the judicial *d*
9:13 upright judicial *d* and laws
9:29 against your own judicial *d*
10:29 his judicial *d* and his
Ps 10:5 Your judicial *d* are high up
18:22 judicial *d* are in front of
19:9 judicial *d* of Jehovah are true
48:11 account of your judicial *d*
72:1 judicial *d* to the king
89:30 my judicial *d* they do not
97:8 your judicial *d*, O Jehovah
103:6 judicial *d* for all those
105:5 the judicial *d* of his mouth
105:7 judicial *d* are in all the
119:7 your righteous judicial *d*
119:13 judicial *d* of your mouth
119:20 For your judicial *d* all the
119:30 your judicial *d* I have
119:39 your judicial *d* are good
119:52 remembered your judicial *d*
119:62 your righteous judicial *d*
119:75 that your judicial *d* are
119:91 to your judicial *d* they
119:102 From your judicial *d* I
119:106 your righteous judicial *d*
119:108 your own judicial *d*
119:120 judicial *d* I have been
119:137 judicial *d* are upright
119:156 to your judicial *d*
119:164 your righteous judicial *d*
119:175 your own judicial *d* help
147:19 his judicial *d* to Israel
147:20 judicial *d*, they have not
Jer 39:5 upon him judicial *d*
52:9 pronounce . . . judicial *d*
Eze 5:6 against my judicial *d* in
5:6 my judicial *d* they rejected
5:7 and my judicial *d* you did not
5:7 judicial *d* of the nations that
5:8 I will execute . . . judicial *d*
11:20 keep my own judicial *d* and
18:9 and my judicial *d* he kept in
18:17 judicial *d* he has carried
20:11 my judicial *d* I made known
20:13 my judicial *d* they rejected
20:16 rejected my own judicial *d*
20:19 keep my own judicial *d* and
20:21 my judicial *d* they did not
20:24 carry out my own judicial *d*
20:25 judicial *d* by which they
36:27 judicial *d* you will keep
37:24 judicial *d* they will walk
44:24 with my judicial *d* they
Da 9:5 and from your judicial *d*
Mal 4:4 regulations and judicial *d*
Ro 14:1 *d* on inward questionings
Jas 2:4 judges rendering wicked *d*
Re 16:5 you have rendered these *d*
16:7 righteous are your judicial *d*

Deck

Job 40:10 *D* yourself, please, with
Jer 4:30 *d* yourself with ornaments
31:4 *d* yourself with your
Eze 16:11 to *d* you with ornaments
27:7 your *d* covering proved to be
Lu 16:19 to *d* himself with purple

Decked

Eze 23:40 *d* yourself with ornaments
Jon 1:5 parts of the *d* vessel
Mr 15:17 they *d* him with purple and

Decking

Eze 16:13 kept *d* yourself with gold
Ho 2:13 *d* herself with her ring and

Decks

Isa 61:10 bride who *d* herself with

Declaration

Le 24:12 distinct *d* to them according
Job 13:17 let my *d* be in your ears
Lu 1:37 no *d* will be an impossibility
1:38 according to your *d*. At that
2:29 in peace according to your *d*
3:2 God's *d* came to John the son
Ro 5:16 in a *d* of righteousness
10:10 public *d* for salvation
1Ti 6:12 *d* in front of many witnesses
6:13 *d* before Pontius Pilate
Heb 10:23 the public *d* of our hope
13:15 make public *d* to his name

Declare

Ex 10:2 *d* in the ears of your son and
23:7 *d* the wicked one righteous
33:19 will *d* the name of Jehovah
34:5 and *d* the name of Jehovah
Le 13:3 and he must *d* him unclean
13:8 must then *d* him unclean
13:11 priest must *d* him unclean
13:15 and he must *d* him unclean
13:20 must then *d* him unclean
13:22 must then *d* him unclean
13:25 priest must *d* him unclean
13:27 must then *d* him unclean
13:30 must then *d* such one unclean
13:44 the priest should *d* him
13:59 it clean or to *d* it unclean
14:36 not *d* unclean everything that
De 32:3 I shall *d* the name of Jehovah
Jos 11:20 as to *d* war against Israel
Es 5:11 Haman proceeded to *d* to them
Job 9:20 then he would *d* me crooked
12:8 fishes of the sea will *d* it
15:17 I shall *d* it to you
27:5 should *d* you men righteous
32:6 *d* my knowledge to you men
32:10 I shall *d* my knowledge
32:17 I shall *d* my knowledge
36:2 and I shall *d* to you That
Ps 9:1 *d* all your wonderful works
9:14 *d* all your praiseworthy deeds
22:22 *d* your name to my brothers
26:7 to *d* all your wonderful works
73:28 refuge, To *d* all your works
75:1 Men have to *d* your wondrous
79:13 we shall *d* your praise
87:6 Jehovah himself will *d*, when
96:3 *D* among the nations his glory
107:22 *d* his works with a joyful
118:17 I may *d* the works of Jah
145:6 your greatness, I will *d* it
Da 4:2 it has seemed good to me to *d*
Lu 1:19 *d* the good news of these
4:18 *d* good news to the poor
4:43 I must *d* the good news of the
9:60 *d* abroad the kingdom of God
16:15 who *d* yourselves righteous
Joh 4:25 *d* all things to us openly
16:13 *d* to you the things coming
16:14 and will *d* it to you
Ac 10:36 *d* to them the good news of
16:10 to *d* the good news to them
23:8 Pharisees publicly *d* them all
Ro 1:15 *d* the good news also to you
2:16 to the good news I *d*
3:30 will *d* circumcised people
10:9 publicly *d* that word in your
10:15 *d* good news of good things
15:20 *d* the good news where Christ
16:25 with the good news I *d* and
1Co 9:16 if I did not *d* the good news
2Co 2:12 in Troas to *d* the good news
4:3 news we *d* is in fact veiled
9:13 as you publicly *d* you are
10:16 to *d* the good news to the
Ga 1:8 were to *d* to you as good news
1:16 *d* the good news about him to
3:8 would *d* people of the nations
Eph 3:8 *d* to the nations the good
2Th 2:14 through the good news we *d*
Tit 1:16 publicly *d* they know God

Heb 2:12 *d* your name to my brothers
1Pe 2:9 *d* abroad the excellencies
Re 14:6 *d* as glad tidings to those

Declared
Ex 9:16 my name *d* in all the earth
Ps 22:30 will be *d* concerning Jehovah
40:10 your salvation I have *d*
88:11 loving-kindness be *d* in the
102:21 name of Jehovah to be *d* in
119:13 *d* All the judicial decisions
119:26 I have *d* my own ways, that
Isa 43:9 that they may be *d* righteous
Mt 11:5 the good news *d* to them
12:37 you will be *d* righteous
Mr 7:19 Thus he *d* all foods clean
Lu 7:29 *d* God to be righteous, they
16:16 kingdom . . . *d* as good news
Ac 3:24 also plainly *d* these days
7:17 God had openly *d* to Abraham
8:35 *d* to him the good news about
13:39 not to be *d* guiltless by means
13:39 who believes is *d* guiltless
Ro 1:4 *d* God's Son according to the
2:13 doers of law . . . *d* righteous
3:20 no flesh will be *d* righteous
3:24 *d* righteous by his undeserved
3:28 *d* righteous by faith apart
4:2 Abraham were *d* righteous as a
5:1 *d* righteous as a result of
5:9 *d* righteous now by his blood
8:30 he also *d* to be righteous
8:30 those whom he *d* righteous
9:17 name may be *d* in all the
1Co 6:11 but you have been *d* righteous
15:1 good news which I *d* to you
15:2 I *d* the good news to you, if
2Co 11:7 I gladly *d* the good news of
Ga 1:8 we *d* to you as good news
1:11 good news which was *d* by me
2:16 *d* righteous, not due to works
2:16 be *d* righteous due to faith
2:16 no flesh will be *d* righteous
2:17 in seeking to be *d* righteous
3:8 *d* the good news beforehand
3:11 one is *d* righteous with God
3:24 be *d* righteous due to faith
4:13 I *d* the good news to you the
5:4 *d* righteous by means of law
Eph 2:17 *d* the good news of peace
1Ti 3:16 was *d* righteous in spirit
Tit 3:7 *d* righteous by virtue of the
Heb 4:2 the good news *d* to us also
4:6 the good news was first *d* did
11:13 *d* that they were strangers
Jas 2:21 Abraham . . . *d* righteous by
2:24 be *d* righteous by works, and
2:25 harlot *d* righteous by works
1Pe 1:12 *d* the good news to you with
1:25 been *d* to you as good news
4:6 good news was *d* also to the
Re 10:7 the good news which he *d* to

Declares
Joh 16:15 and *d* it to you
Ro 4:5 *d* the ungodly one righteous
8:33 One who *d* them righteous

Declaring
Ex 34:6 *d*: Jehovah, Jehovah, a God
Le 20:25 for you in *d* them unclean
Es 8:17 *d* themselves Jews, for the
Job 32:2 *d* his own soul righteous
Ps 19:1 The heavens are *d* the glory of
Isa 50:8 One *d* me righteous is near
Jer 36:18 *d* to me all these words
Lu 2:10 I am *d* to you good news of a
3:18 *d* good news to the people
8:1 preaching and *d* the good news
9:6 *d* the good news and performing
20:1 and *d* the good news, the
Ac 4:2 *d* the resurrection from the
5:42 *d* the good news about the
8:4 *d* the good news of the word
8:12 Philip, who was *d* the good
8:25 *d* the good news to many
8:40 *d* the good news to all the
11:20 *d* the good news of the Lord
13:32 *d* to you the good news about
14:7 they went on *d* the good news
14:15 are *d* the good news to you
14:21 And after *d* the good news to
15:35 and *d*, with many others also
17:18 was *d* the good news of Jesus
Ro 3:26 *d* righteous the man that has
4:25 the sake of *d* us righteous
5:18 *d* of them righteous for life
1Co 1:17 but to go *d* the good news
2:1 *d* the sacred secret of God to
9:16 If . . . I am *d* the good news
9:18 That while *d* the good news I
14:25 and worship God, *d*: God is
2Co 10:14 in *d* the good news about the
Ga 1:9 *d* to you as good news
1:23 *d* the good news about the
Php 4:15 start of *d* the good news

Decline
Ps 90:9 days have come to their *d* in
Lu 9:12 Then the day started to *d*

Declined
Jg 19:9 The day has *d* toward becoming
Ps 102:11 like a shadow that has *d*
Jer 6:4 the day has *d*, for the
Lu 24:29 and the day has already *d*

Declines
Ps 109:23 Like a shadow when it *d*

Declining
2Sa 3:1 house of Saul kept *d* more and

Decorate
Mt 23:29 *d* the memorial tombs of the

Decoration
Isa 4:2 to be for *d* and for glory
13:19 Babylon, the *d* of kingdoms
24:16 *D* to the Righteous One!
28:1 blossom of its *d* of beauty
28:4 *d* of beauty that is upon
28:5 become as a crown of *d*
Eze 7:20 *d* of one's ornament—one has
20:6 was the *d* of all the lands
20:15 is the *d* of all the lands
25:9 the *d* of the land
26:20 *d* in the land of those alive
Da 8:9 sunrising and toward the *D*
11:16 stand in the land of the *D*
11:41 enter into the land of the *D*
11:45 and the holy mountain of *D*

Decrease
Ro 11:12 their *d* means riches to

Decreased
Isa 24:6 have *d* in number, and very

Decreasing
Joh 3:30 but I must go on *d*

Decree
Ge 47:26 a *d* down to this day over
De 28:8 *d* for you the blessing
Ezr 6:11 anybody that violates this *d*
Es 1:20 *d* of the king that he will
Job 14:5 A *d* for him you have made
Ps 2:7 refer to the *d* of Jehovah
94:20 it is framing trouble by *d*
Pr 8:29 *d* that the waters themselves
Da 4:17 By the *d* of watchers the
4:24 *d* of the Most High is that
Jon 3:7 by the *d* of the king and his
Mic 7:11 the *d* will be far away
Lu 2:1 a *d* went forth from Caesar
Ro 1:32 righteous *d* of God, that those

Decreed
Pr 8:27 *d* a circle upon the face of
8:29 *d* the foundations of the earth
31:5 drink and forget what is *d* and
Ac 10:42 One *d* by God to be judge of
17:26 he *d* the appointed times and

Decreeing
Pr 8:15 keep *d* righteousness

Decrees
Ac 16:4 *d* that had been decided upon
17:7 opposition to the *d* of Caesar
Eph 2:15 the Law . . . consisting in *d*
Col 2:14 which consisted of *d* and
2:20 subject yourselves to the *d*
Re 15:4 righteous *d* have been made

Decrepit
2Ch 36:17 man or virgin, old or *d*

Dedan
Ge 10:7 sons of Raamah . . . *D*
25:3 Jokshan became father . . . *D*
25:3 sons of *D* became Asshurim and
1Ch 1:9 sons of Raamah were . . . *D*
1:32 sons of Jokshan . . . *D*
Isa 21:13 caravans of men of *D*
Jer 25:23 *D* and Tema and Buz and all
49:8 O inhabitants of *D*! For the
Eze 25:13 from Teman, even to *D*
27:15 sons of *D* were your traders
27:20 *D* was your trader in
38:13 Sheba and *D* and the

Dedicate
Ho 9:10 *d* themselves to the shameful

Dedicated
Mt 15:5 is a gift *d* to God
Mr 7:11 that is, a gift *d* to God
Lu 21:5 fine stones and *d* things

Dedication
Ex 29:6 sign of *d* upon the turban
39:30 holy sign of *d*, out of pure
Le 8:9 the holy sign of *d*, just as
21:12 sign of *d*, the anointing oil
Joh 10:22 festival of *d* took place in

Deduct
Ex 5:19 must not *d* from your bricks

Deduction
Le 27:18 *d* should be made from the

Deed
Ge 44:5 a bad *d* you have committed
44:15 What sort of *d* is this that
De 2:7 God has blessed you in every *d*
14:29 in every *d* of your hand that
15:10 bless you in every *d* of yours
16:15 in every *d* of your hand
17:8 violent *d* has been committed
21:5 dispute over every violent *d*
24:19 God may bless you in every *d*
25:2 correspond with his wicked *d*
28:12 bless every *d* of your hand
Job 33:17 turn aside a man from his *d*
Isa 28:21 that he may do his *d*
28:21 his *d* is strange—and that
Jer 32:10 wrote in a *d* and affixed
32:11 I took the *d* of purchase
32:12 *d* of purchase to Baruch
32:12 in the *d* of purchase, before
32:14 this *d* of purchase, even
32:14 and the other *d* left open
32:16 given the *d* of purchase to
32:44 recording in the *d* and a
Mt 26:10 she did a fine *d* toward me
Mr 3:4 on the sabbath to do a good *d*
3:4 do a bad *d*, to save or to kill
14:6 She did a fine *d* toward me
Joh 7:21 One *d* I performed, and you
Ac 4:9 basis of a good *d* to an ailing
5:4 purposed such a *d* as this in
Ro 13:3 of fear, not to the good *d*
15:18 obedient, by my word and *d*
1Co 5:2 man that committed this *d*
2Th 2:17 firm in every good *d* and
1Jo 3:18 but in *d* and truth

Deeds
Ge 20:9 *D* that should not have been
Nu 16:28 sent me to do all these *d*
25:18 with their *d* of cunning
De 3:24 *d* like yours and mighty
11:3 *d* that he did in the midst of
11:7 all the great *d* of Jehovah
22:14 charged her with notorious *d*
22:17 charging . . . notorious *d*
1Sa 2:3 *d* are rightly estimated
2Sa 22:49 From the man of violent *d*
23:20 who did many *d* in Kabzeel
1Ch 11:22 who did many *d* in Kabzeel
16:8 Make his *d* known among the
Ezr 9:13 upon us for our bad *d* and
Ne 6:14 according to these *d* of each
Ps 9:11 Tell among the peoples his *d*
9:14 all your praiseworthy *d*
99:8 against their notorious *d*
140:1 the man of *d* of violence
140:4 the man of *d* of violence
141:4 notorious *d* in wickedness
Isa 29:15 *d* have occurred in a dark
Jer 32:14 Taking these *d*, this
44:9 forgotten the bad *d* of your
44:9 bad *d* of the kings of Judah
44:9 bad *d* of their wives and
44:9 your own bad *d* and the
44:9 the bad *d* of your wives
51:10 *d* of righteousness for us
Eze 24:6 the city of *d* of bloodshed
24:9 the city of *d* of bloodshed
Ho 12:14 his *d* of bloodshed he leaves

Mt 23:3 not do according to their *d*
Lu 1:49 has done great *d* for me, and
3:19 the wicked *d* that Herod did
3:20 added also this to all those *d*
11:48 you are witnesses of the *d*
Ac 3:26 one away from your wicked *d*
7:22 powerful in his words and *d*
9:36 She abounded in good *d* and
Ro 4:7 lawless *d* have been pardoned
2Ti 4:14 repay . . . according to his *d*
Heb 8:12 to their unrighteous *d*
10:17 lawless *d* to mind anymore
1Pe 4:3 in *d* of loose conduct, lusts
2Pe 2:8 by reason of their lawless *d*
3:11 and *d* of godly devotion
Jude 15 ungodly *d* that they did in
Re 2:2 I know your *d*, and your labor
2:5 repent and do the former *d*
2:6 the *d* of the sect of Nicolaus
2:19 I know your *d*, and your love
2:19 *d* of late are more than
2:22 unless they repent of her *d*
2:23 give . . . according to your *d*
2:26 observes my *d* down to the end
3:1 I know your *d*, that you have
3:2 *d* fully performed before my
3:8 I know your *d*—look! I have
3:15 I know your *d*, that you are
20:12 scrolls according to their *d*
20:13 according to their *d*

Deep
Ge 1:2 the surface of the watery *d*
2:21 Jehovah God had a *d* sleep
7:11 springs of the vast watery *d*
8:2 springs of the watery *d* and
15:12 a *d* sleep fell upon Abram
22:13 *d* in the foreground, there
49:25 blessings of the watery *d*
De 33:13 watery *d* lying down below
1Sa 26:12 *d* sleep from Jehovah that
2Sa 13:9 took the *d* pan and poured
Job 3:5 darkness and *d* shadow reclaim
4:13 When *d* sleep falls upon men
10:21 of darkness and *d* shadow
10:22 To the land . . . of *d* shadow
11:7 find out the *d* things of God
12:22 He is uncovering *d* things
12:22 forth to the light *d* shadow
16:16 eyelids there is *d* shadow
19:27 have failed *d* within me
24:17 morning . . . as *d* shadow for
24:17 sudden terrors of *d* shadow
28:3 in the gloom and *d* shadow
28:14 watery *d* itself has said
33:15 When *d* sleep falls upon men
34:22 darkness nor any *d* shadow
38:16 in search of the watery *d*
38:17 the gates of *d* shadow can
38:30 surface of the watery *d*
41:32 watery *d* as gray-headedness
Ps 22:14 melted *d* in my inward parts
23:4 in the valley of *d* shadow
36:6 decision is a vast watery *d*
38:2 arrows have sunk themselves *d*
42:7, 7 Watery *d* to watery *d* is
44:19 cover us over with *d* shadow
64:6 even his heart, is *d*
69:2 I have sunk down in *d* mire
69:14 and from the *d* waters
92:5 Very *d* your thoughts are
104:6 watery *d* just like a garment
106:9 them through the watery *d* as
107:10 in darkness and *d* shadow
107:14 from darkness and *d* shadow
Pr 8:27 upon the face of the watery *d*
8:28 fountains of the watery *d* to
18:4 a man's mouth are *d* waters
19:15 Laziness causes a *d* sleep to
20:5 Counsel . . . is as *d* waters
22:14 of strange women is a *d* pit
23:27 For a prostitute is a *d* pit
Ec 7:24 is far off and exceedingly *d*
Isa 7:11 making it as *d* as Sheol or
9:2 in the land of *d* shadow
29:10 poured a spirit of *d* sleep
29:15 *d* in concealing counsel
30:33 He has made its pile *d*
31:6 have gone *d* in their revolt
33:19 too *d* in language to listen
44:27 One saying to the watery *d*
51:10 the waters of the vast *d*
Jer 2:6 of no water and of *d* shadow
13:16 actually make it *d* shadow
Jer 49:8 Go down *d* in order to dwell
49:30 go down *d* in order to dwell
Eze 23:32 the *d* and wide one
26:19 up over you the watery *d*
31:4 watery *d* caused it to grow
31:15 I will cover the watery *d*
Da 2:22 He is revealing the *d* things
Ho 5:2 have gone *d* down, and I was
9:9 gone down *d* in bringing ruin
Am 5:8 *d* shadow into the morning
7:4 eating up the vast watery *d*
Jon 2:5 the watery *d* itself kept
Hab 3:10 watery *d* gave forth its
Zec 1:8 that were in the *d* place
Lu 5:4 Pull out to where it is *d*, and
6:48 down *d* and laid a foundation
Joh 4:11 and the well is *d*
Ac 20:9 Eutychus fell into a *d* sleep
Ro 11:8 them a spirit of *d* sleep
1Co 2:10 even the *d* things of God
2Co 8:2 *d* poverty made the riches of
11:25 a day I have spent in the *d*
Eph 5:33 wife should have *d* respect
1Pe 3:2 together with *d* respect
3:15 a mild temper and *d* respect
Re 2:24 know the *d* things of Satan

Deeper
Le 13:3 the plague is *d* than the skin
13:4 appearance is not *d* than the
13:21 not *d* than the skin and it
13:25 appearance is *d* than the skin
13:30 appearance is *d* than the skin
13:31 is not *d* than the skin and
13:32 hair is not *d* than the skin
13:34 is not *d* than the skin
Job 11:8 It is *d* than Sheol. What can
Pr 17:10 rebuke works *d* in one having

Deep-fat
Le 2:7 offering out of the *d* kettle
7:9 one made in the *d* kettle and

Deeply
Mt 26:38 My soul is *d* grieved, even
Mr 6:26 *d* grieved, yet the king did
7:34 he sighed *d* and said to him
8:12 he groaned *d* with his spirit
14:34 My soul is *d* grieved, even
Lu 1:29 was *d* disturbed at the saying
18:23 *d* grieved, for he was very
Ac 5:33 they felt *d* cut and were

Deeps
De 8:7 watery *d* issuing forth in the
Ps 71:20 the watery *d* of the earth
77:16 watery *d* began to be
78:15 just like watery *d*
135:6 seas and all the watery *d*
148:7 and all you watery *d*
Pr 3:20 watery *d* themselves were
8:24 there were no watery *d* I

Defamed
1Co 4:13 when being *d*, we entreat

Defeat
Ex 32:18 sound of the singing of *d*
De 7:2 and you must *d* them
Jg 20:32 are suffering *d* before us
20:35 to *d* Benjamin before Israel
20:36 imagined . . . Israel faced *d*
20:39 suffering nothing but *d*
1Sa 4:3 Why did Jehovah *d* us today
4:17 a great *d* among the people
2Sa 17:9 A *d* has taken place among
Isa 10:26 *d* of Midian by the rock
1Co 6:7 means altogether a *d* for you

Defeated
Ge 14:7 *d* the whole field of the
14:15 *d* them and kept in pursuit
36:35 Hadad . . . *d* the Midianites
Le 26:17 *d* before your enemies
Nu 14:42 not be *d* before your enemies
32:4 the land that Jehovah *d* before
De 1:42 not be *d* before your enemies
2:33 we *d* him and his sons and
4:46 *d* on their coming out of
28:7 enemies . . . *d* before you
28:25 be *d* before your enemies
29:7 battle, but we *d* them
Jos 12:1 whom the sons of Israel *d*
12:6 sons of Israel who *d* them
12:7 Israel *d* on the side of the
Jg 1:4 they *d* them in Bezek, ten
1:5 and *d* the Canaanites and the
1Sa 4:2 so that Israel was *d* before
4:10 Israel was *d*, and they went
7:10 and they got *d* before Israel
2Sa 2:17 Israel were finally *d* before
10:15 had been *d* before Israel
10:19 had been *d* before Israel
18:7 the people of Israel were *d*
1Ki 8:33 your people Israel are *d*
2Ki 14:12 Judah came to be *d* before
1Ch 1:46 *d* Midian in the field of
19:16 had been *d* before Israel
19:19 had been *d* before Israel
2Ch 6:24 Israel are *d* before an enemy
13:15 true God himself *d* Jeroboam
14:12 Jehovah *d* the Ethiopians
25:22 Judah came to be *d* before
Jer 46:2 king of Babylon *d* in the
Heb 11:33 through faith *d* kingdoms in

Defeating
Ge 14:17 returned from *d* Chedorlaomer
De 1:4 after his *d* Sihon the king of

Defeats
Ge 14:5 inflicted *d* on the Rephaim

Defect
Le 21:17 No man . . . *d* may come near
21:18 man in whom there is a *d*
21:21 in whom there is a *d*
21:21 is a *d* in him. He may not
21:23 *d* in him; and he should not
22:20 is a *d* you must not present
22:21 no *d* at all should prove to
22:25 There is a *d* in them
24:19 cause a *d* in his associate
24:20 *d* he may cause in the man
Nu 19:2 cow in which there is no *d*
De 15:21 should prove to be in it a *d*
15:21 lame or blind, any bad *d*
17:1 which there proves to be a *d*
32:5 children, the *d* is their own
2Sa 14:25 proved to be no *d* in him
Job 11:15 raise your face without *d*
31:7 *d* has stuck in my own palms
Pr 9:7 giving a reproof . . . *d* in him
Ca 4:7 and there is no *d* in you
Da 1:4 in whom there was no *d*

Defective
Tit 1:5 correct the things . . . *d*

Defend
2Ki 19:34 shall certainly *d* this city
20:6 *d* this city for my own sake
Isa 31:5 in the same way *d* Jerusalem
37:35 *d* this city to save it for
38:6 and I will *d* this city
Zec 9:15 will *d* them, and they will

Defended
Ac 7:24 *d* him and executed vengeance

Defender
Ro 16:2 *d* of many, yes, of me myself

Defending
Isa 31:5 *D* her, he will also
Php 1:7 *d* and legally establishing of

Defense
Jg 6:31 to make a legal *d* for Baal to
6:31 a legal *d* for him ought to be
6:31 make a legal *d* for himself
6:32 Baal make a legal *d* in his
Zec 12:8 Jehovah will be a *d* around
Lu 12:11 or what you will speak in *d*
21:14 how to make your *d*
Ac 19:33 to make his *d* to the people
22:1 fathers, hear my *d* to you now
24:10 readily speak in my *d* the
25:8 But Paul said in *d*
25:16 a chance to speak in his *d*
26:1 proceeded to say in his *d*
26:2 I am to make my *d* this day
26:24 saying these things in his *d*
1Co 9:3 My *d* to those who examine me
2Co 12:19 been making our *d* to you
Php 1:16 for the *d* of the good news
2Ti 4:16 In my first *d* no one came
1Pe 3:15 make a *d* before everyone

Defiant
Ps 40:4 turned his face to *d* people

Deficiency
2Co 8:14 now might offset their *d*
8:14 also come to offset your *d*
11:9 abundantly supplied my *d*

Deficient
Da 5:27 balances and have been found *d*

Defile
Le 21:1 a deceased soul no one may *d*
21:3 for her he may *d* himself
21:4 not *d* himself for a woman
21:11 mother he may not *d* himself
Nu 5:29 and she does *d* herself
6:7 or his sister may he *d* himself
35:34 must not *d* the land in which
De 21:23 you must not *d* your soil
Isa 30:22 must *d* the overlaying of
Jer 7:30 in order to *d* it
32:34 in order to *d* it
Eze 9:7 *D* the house and fill the
18:6 companion's wife . . . not *d*
20:7 of Egypt do not *d* yourselves
20:18 do not you *d* yourselves
37:23 no longer *d* themselves with
43:7 Israel, *d* my holy name, they
Ho 9:4 those eating it will *d*
Mt 15:18 and those things *d* a man
15:20 unwashed hands does not *d* a
Mr 7:15 into him that can *d* him
7:15 are the things that *d* a man
7:18 into a man can *d* him
7:23 from within and *d* a man
2Pe 2:10 with the desire to *d* it
Re 3:4 in Sardis that did not *d* their
14:4 not *d* themselves with women

Defiled
Ge 34:5 heard that he had *d* Dinah
34:13 he had *d* Dinah their sister
34:27 they had *d* their sister
Nu 5:13 *d* herself but there is no
5:14 she in fact has *d* herself, or
5:14 she in fact has not *d* herself
5:20 *d* yourself and some man has
5:27 occur that if she has *d*
5:28 woman has not *d* herself but
6:9 *d* the head of his Naziriteship
6:12 because he *d* his Naziriteship
19:13 has *d* Jehovah's tabernacle
19:20 sanctuary that he has *d*
De 24:4 his wife after she has been *d*
2Ch 36:14 *d* the house of Jehovah
Ps 79:1 they have *d* your holy temple
Jer 2:7 you came in and *d* my land
2:23 say, I have not *d* myself
Eze 4:14 Look! My soul is not a *d* one
5:11 my sanctuary that you *d* with
18:11 companion's wife he has *d*
18:15 companion's wife . . . not *d*
20:26 become *d* by their gifts
20:43 by which you *d* yourselves
22:11 daughter-in-law a man has *d*
23:7 dungy idols—she *d* herself
23:13 because she had *d* herself
23:17 continued getting *d* by them
23:30 you *d* yourself with their
23:38 *d* my sanctuary in that day
33:26 *d* each one the wife of his
43:8 *d* my holy name by their
Ho 5:3 Israel has *d* itself
6:10 Israel has *d* itself
Mr 7:2 *d* hands, that is, unwashed
7:5 take their meal with *d* hands
Joh 18:28 that they might not get *d*
Ac 10:14 never have I eaten anything *d*
10:15 You stop calling *d* the
10:28 call no man *d* or unclean
11:8 *d* or unclean thing has never
11:9 You stop calling *d* the things
21:28 and has *d* this holy place
Ro 14:14 that nothing is *d* in itself
14:14 considers something to be *d*
14:14 to him it is *d*
1Co 8:7 conscience, being weak, is *d*
Tit 1:15 to persons *d* and faithless
1:15 and their consciences are *d*
Heb 9:13 on those who have been *d*
12:15 many may not be *d* by it

Defilement
Ne 13:29 the *d* of the priesthood and
2Co 7:1 every *d* of flesh and spirit
Heb 13:4 marriage bed be without *d*

Defilements
2Pe 2:20 from the *d* of the world

Defiles
Mt 15:11 Not what enters . . . mouth *d*
15:11 what proceeds out . . . *d*
Mr 7:20 out of a man is what *d* a man

Defiling
Le 15:31 for their *d* of my tabernacle
18:28 *d* it the same way as it will
20:3 purpose of *d* my holy place
Eze 14:11 no more go *d* themselves
20:30 are you people *d* yourselves
20:31 *d* yourselves for all your
23:17 *d* her with their immoral
Mt 15:20 These are the things *d* a man
Jude 8 *d* the flesh and disregarding

Definite
Da 7:22 *d* time arrived that the holy

Definitely
Ex 8:27 *d* sacrifice to Jehovah our God
1Sa 17:51 *d* put him to death when he
23:10 has *d* heard that Saul
2Sa 1:9 *d* put me to death, for the
1:10 *d* put him to death, for I
1:16 *d* put the anointed of Jehovah
1Ki 9:6 sons should *d* turn back from
Jer 20:17 *d* put me to death from the
1Ti 4:1 the inspired utterance says *d*

Deflected
Ro 3:12 All men have *d*, all of them

Defraud
Le 6:2 a robbery or he does *d* his
19:13 You must not *d* your fellow
De 24:14 not *d* a hired laborer who is
1Ch 16:21 not allow anyone to *d* them
Ps 105:14 allow any human to *d* them
119:122 presumptuous ones not *d* me
Ho 12:7 to *d* is what he has loved
Zec 7:10 *d* no widow or fatherless boy
Mr 10:19 Do not *d*, Honor your father
1Co 6:8 you wrong and *d*, and your

Defrauded
De 28:29 one who is always *d* and
28:33 one who is only *d* and
1Sa 12:3 or whom have I *d* or whom
12:4 they said: You have not *d* us
Ps 103:6 for all those being *d*
146:7 judgment for the *d* ones
Eze 22:29 alien resident they have *d*
Mic 2:2 *d* an able-bodied man and his
1Co 6:7 rather let yourselves be *d*

Defrauder
Ps 72:4 And let him crush the *d*
119:134 Redeem me from any *d* of
Jer 21:12 out of the hand of the *d*
22:3 out of the hand of the *d*

Defrauding
Ps 62:10 Do not put your trust in *d*
73:8 About *d* they speak in an
119:121 abandon me to those *d* me
Pr 14:31 He that is *d* the lowly one
22:16 is *d* the lowly one to supply
28:3 *d* the lowly ones is as a rain
Isa 30:12 men trust in *d* and in what
Jer 22:17 upon *d* and upon extortion
Eze 18:18 he committed outright *d*
22:7 acted with *d* in the midst of
22:12 your companions with *d*
22:29 carried on a scheme of *d*
Am 3:9 and cases of *d* inside her
4:1 who are *d* the lowly ones

Degenerate
Jer 2:21 *d* shoots of a foreign vine

Degenerating
Ho 10:1 Israel is a *d* vine. Fruit he

Degree
1Sa 11:15 rejoicing to a great *d*
2Ch 11:12 them to a very great *d*
17:12 great to a superior *d*
26:8 to an extraordinary *d*
Ps 38:6 bowed low to an extreme *d*
38:8 crushed to an extreme *d*
Jer 30:11 correct you to the proper *d*
46:28 chastise you to the proper *d*
2Ti 4:15 our words to an excessive *d*

Deities
Ac 17:18 be a publisher of foreign *d*
17:22 given to the fear of the *d*

Deity
Ac 25:19 their own worship of the *d*

Dejected
Ge 40:6 here they were looking *d*
1Ki 20:43 sullen and *d*, and came to
21:4 Ahab . . . sullen and *d* over
Ps 10:10 army of *d* ones has to fall
109:16 one *d* at heart, to put him
Jer 14:2 have become *d* to the earth
Eze 21:7 every spirit must become *d*
Da 11:30 he will have to become *d*

Dejected-looking
Da 1:10 see your faces *d* in

Dejectedly
Mal 3:14 have walked *d* on account of

Dejecting
Eze 13:22 *d* the heart of a righteous

Dejection
Ex 23:28 send the feeling of *d* ahead
De 7:20 send the feeling of *d* upon
Jos 24:12 the feeling of *d* ahead of
Jas 4:9 and your joy into *d*

Deker
1Ki 4:9 the son of *D*, in Makaz and in

Delaiah
1Ch 3:24 sons of Elioenai were . . . *D*
24:18 for *D* the twenty-third
Ezr 2:60 the sons of *D*
Ne 6:10 *D* the son of Mehetabel
7:62 the sons of *D*, the sons of
Jer 36:12 *D* the son of Shemaiah and
36:25 *D* and Gemariah themselves

Delay
Ge 34:19 did not *d* to perform the
45:9 Come down to me. Do not *d*
Ps 119:60 hurried up, and I did not *d*
Da 9:19 Do not *d*, for your own sake
Hab 2:3 Even if it should *d*, keep in
Mt 14:22 without *d*, he compelled his
Mr 1:20 and without *d* he called them
6:45 without *d*, he compelled his
Ac 16:33 his were baptized without *d*
25:17 I made no *d*, but the next
Heb 10:37 will arrive and will not *d*
Re 10:6 There will be no *d* any longer

Delayed
Jg 5:28 his war chariot *d* in coming
Ac 19:22 he himself *d* for some time
1Ti 3:15 but in case I am *d*, that you

Delaying
Mt 24:48 My master is *d*
25:5 While the bridegroom was *d*
Lu 1:21 at his *d* in the sanctuary
Ac 22:16 now why are you *d*? Rise, get

Delays
Lu 12:45 My master *d* coming, and

Deliberately
Le 20:4 *d* hide their eyes from that
Nu 15:30 soul that does something *d*
De 22:1 sheep straying about and *d*
22:4 and *d* withdraw from them

Delicacies
Da 1:5 from the *d* of the king and
1:8 pollute himself with the *d*
1:13 eating the *d* of the king
1:15 eating the *d* of the king
1:16 taking away their *d* and their
11:26 ones eating his *d* will bring

Delicate
Ge 33:13 that the children are *d* and
De 28:54 *d* and dainty man among you
28:56 the *d* and dainty woman
1Ch 22:5 Solomon . . . is young and *d*
29:1 Solomon . . . is young and *d*
Isa 47:1 people call you *d* and dainty

Delicateness
De 28:56 dainty habit and for *d*

Delight
Ge 34:19 find *d* in Jacob's daughter
Nu 14:8 If Jehovah has found *d* in us
De 21:14 you have found no *d* in her
25:7 no *d* in taking his brother's
25:8 have found no *d* in taking her
Ru 3:13 not take *d* in repurchasing you
1Sa 15:22 Does Jehovah have as much *d*
18:22 The king has found *d* in you
18:25 king has *d*, not in marriage
19:2 he took great *d* in David
2Sa 15:26 I have found no *d* in you
20:11 Whoever has found *d* in Joab
22:20 he had found *d* in me
23:5 my salvation and all my *d*
24:3 has he found *d* in this thing

1Ki 5:8 your *d* in the matter of timbers
5:9 my *d* by giving the food for
5:10 according to all his *d*
9:1 that he took *d* in making
10:9 taken *d* in you by putting
10:13 all her *d* for which she
2Ch 9:8 taken *d* in you by putting you
9:12 queen of Sheba all her *d* for
Ne 1:11 take *d* in fearing your name
Es 2:14 the king had taken *d* in her
6:6 the king himself has taken a *d*
6:6 take *d* in rendering an honor
6:7 the king himself has taken a *d*
6:9 the king himself has taken a *d*
6:9 the king himself has taken a *d*
6:11 king himself has taken a *d*
Job 9:3 find *d* in contending with him
13:3 arguing with God . . . find *d*
21:14 we have found no *d*
21:21 For what will his *d* be in
22:3 Does the Almighty have any *d*
22:26 will find your exquisite *d*
27:10 will he find exquisite *d*
31:16 lowly ones from their *d*
33:32 *d* in your righteousness
Ps 1:2 his *d* is in the law of Jehovah
5:4 you are not a God taking *d* in
16:3 the ones in whom is all my *d*
18:19 because he had found *d* in me
22:8 since he has taken *d* in him
35:27 takes *d* in the peace of his
37:4 take exquisite *d* in Jehovah
37:11 *d* in the abundance of peace
37:23 in his way He takes *d*
40:6 offering you did not *d* in
41:11 that you have found *d* in me
51:6 have taken *d* in truthfulness
51:16 do not take *d* in sacrifice
68:30 peoples that take *d* in fights
70:2 are taking *d* in my calamity
73:25 no other *d* on the earth
107:30 to the haven of their *d*
109:17 not take *d* in the blessing
112:1 he has taken very much *d*
119:35 For in it I have taken *d*
147:10 the horse does he take *d*
Pr 18:2 finds no *d* in discernment
31:13 is the *d* of her hands
Ec 5:4 is no *d* in the stupid ones
12:1 say: I have no *d* in them
Isa 1:11 he-goats I have taken no *d*
13:17 gold, take no *d* in it
13:22 the palaces of exquisite *d*
42:21 has taken a *d* in that he
44:28 all that I *d* in he will
46:10 that is my *d* I shall do
48:14 what is his *d* upon Babylon
53:10 took *d* in crushing him
53:10 what is the *d* of Jehovah
55:2 exquisite *d* in fatness itself
58:2 that they would express *d*
58:2 to God in whom they had *d*
58:3 *d* in the very day of your
58:13 an exquisite *d*, a holy day
58:14 your exquisite *d* in Jehovah
62:4 be called My *D* Is in Her
62:4 will have taken *d* in you
65:12 I took no *d* you chose
66:3 very soul has taken a *d*
66:4 thing in which I took no *d*
66:11 experience exquisite *d* from
Jer 6:10 word they can take no *d*
9:24 in these things I do take *d*
22:28 in which there is no *d*
42:22 *d* to enter to reside as
48:38 in which there is no *d*
Eze 18:23 any *d* at all in the death of
18:32 *d* in the death of someone
33:11 *d*, not in the death of the
Ho 6:6 taken *d*, and not in sacrifice
8:8 vessel in which there is no *d*
Mic 1:16 your sons of exquisite *d*
2:9 a woman has exquisite *d*
Mal 1:10 No *d* do I have in you
2:17 he himself has taken *d*
3:12 will become a land of *d*
Ro 7:22 I really *d* in the law of God
Col 2:18 takes *d* in a mock humility
2Pe 2:13 *d* in their deceptive

Delighted
Jg 13:23 If Jehovah had been *d* only to
1Ki 9:11 with gold as much as he *d* in
Ps 40:8 your will, O my God, I have *d*
51:19 will be *d* with sacrifices
115:3 Everything that he *d* to do
135:6 Jehovah *d* to do he has done
Isa 55:11 do that in which I have *d*
56:4 chosen what I have *d* in and
Jon 1:14 according to what you have *d*

Delightful
1Ch 28:9 complete heart . . . a *d* soul
Ec 12:10 sought to find the *d* words

Delighting
1Ki 13:33 anyone *d* in it, he would
Ps 34:12 the man that is *d* in life
35:27 are *d* in my righteousness
40:14 who are *d* in my calamity
111:2 part of all those *d* in them
Mic 7:18 he is *d* in loving-kindness
Mal 3:1 in whom you are *d*. Look! He

Delights
Pr 3:15 all other *d* of yours cannot
8:11 all other *d* themselves cannot
21:1 that he *d* to, he turns it
Ec 2:8 *d* of the sons of mankind, a
8:3 all that he *d* to do he will do
Ca 7:6 girl, among exquisite *d*
Isa 58:13 doing your own *d* on my holy
58:13 rather than finding what *d*

Delightsome
Isa 54:12 your boundaries of *d* stones

Delilah
Jg 16:4 and her name was *D*
16:6 *D* said to Samson: Do tell me
16:10 *D* said to Samson: Look! You
16:12 So *D* took new ropes and tied
16:13 *D* said to Samson: Up till
16:18 *D* got to see that he had

Delinquent
Jos 18:3 to be *d* about going in to

Deliver
Ge 32:11 *D* me, I pray you, from my
37:21 *d* him out of their hand
37:22 *d* him out of their hand in
Ex 3:8 to go down to *d* them out of
6:6 and *d* you from their slavery
Nu 35:25 *d* the manslayer out of the
De 19:12 *d* him into the hand of the
23:14 within your camp to *d* you
25:11 *d* her husband out of the hand
Jos 2:13 must *d* our souls from death
9:26 to *d* them from the hand of
Jg 9:17 *d* you out of Midian's hand
10:15 Only *d* us, please, this day
1Sa 7:3 he will *d* you from the hand
12:10 *d* us out of the hand of our
12:11 and *d* you out of the hand of
12:21 no benefit and that do not *d*
14:48 *d* Israel out of the hand of
17:37 will *d* me from the hand of
26:24 *d* me out of all distress
30:18 David got to *d* all that the
2Sa 14:16 *d* his slave girl out of the
22:49 you will *d* me
2Ki 17:39 *d* you out of the hand of all
18:29 not able to *d* you out of my
18:30 Jehovah will *d* us, and this
18:32 Jehovah himself will *d* us
18:35 *d* Jerusalem out of my hand
20:6 shall *d* you and this city
1Ch 16:35 and *d* us from the nations
2Ch 25:15 *d* their own people out of
32:11 God himself will *d* us out
32:13 *d* their land out of my hand
32:14 *d* his people out of my hand
32:14 to *d* you out of my hand
32:15 *d* his people out of my hand
32:15 God *d* you out of my hand
32:17 *d* their people out of my
32:17 *d* his people out of my
Ezr 7:19 *d* in full before God at
Ne 9:28 *d* them in accord with your
Job 5:19 In six distresses he will *d*
Ps 7:1 Save me . . . and *d* me
18:48 you will *d* me
22:8 Let him *d* him, since he has
22:20 Do *d* from the sword my soul
25:20 Do guard my soul and *d* me
31:2 *D* me speedily. Become for me
31:15 *D* me from the hand of my
33:19 To *d* their soul from death
39:8 From . . . transgressions *d* me
40:13 pleased, O Jehovah, to *d* me
Ps 51:14 *D* me from bloodguiltiness
59:1 *D* me from my enemies, O my
59:2 *D* me from the practicers of
69:14 *D* me from the mire, that I
70:1 O God, to *d* me, O Jehovah, to
71:2 *d* me and provide me with
72:12 *d* the poor one crying for
79:9 *d* us and cover over our sins
82:4 of the wicked ones *d* them
91:3 *d* you from the trap of the
106:43 Many times he would *d* them
107:6 he proceeded to *d* them
109:21 Sovereign Lord . . . *d* me
119:170 your saying, O *d* me
120:2 Jehovah, do *d* my soul from
142:6 *D* me from my persecutors
143:9 *D* me from my enemies, O
144:7 *d* me from the many waters
144:11 *d* me from the hand of the
Pr 2:12 *d* you from the bad way
2:16 *d* you from the strange woman
6:3 *d* yourself, for you have come
6:5 *D* yourself like a gazelle
10:2 righteousness is what will *d*
11:4 righteousness itself will *d*
11:6 is what will *d* them, but by
12:6 is what will *d* them
19:19 for if you would *d* him, you
23:14 *d* his very soul from Sheol
24:11 *D* those who are being taken
Isa 19:4 *d* up Egypt into the hand of
19:20 who will actually *d* them
31:5 he will also certainly *d* her
36:14 he is not able to *d* you
36:15 Jehovah will *d* us
36:18 Jehovah himself will *d* us
36:20 *d* Jerusalem out of my hand
38:6 I shall *d* you and this city
44:17 *D* me, for you are my god
44:20 he does not *d* his soul
47:14 not *d* their soul from the
50:2 is there in me no power to *d*?
57:13 things will not *d* you
Jer 1:8 I am with you to *d* you
1:19 Jehovah, to *d* you
15:20 to save you and to *d* you
15:21 *d* you out of the hand of the
18:21 *d* them over to the power of
21:12 *d* the one being robbed out
22:3 *d* the one that is being
39:17 I will *d* you in that day
42:11 *d* you out of his hand
Eze 7:19 will be able to *d* them in
13:21 and *d* my people out of your
13:23 I will *d* my people out of
14:14 would *d* their soul, is the
14:16 nor daughters would they *d*
14:18 *d* neither sons nor daughters
14:20 nor daughter would they *d*
14:20 righteousness would *d* their
33:9 certainly *d* your own soul
33:12 *d* him in the day of his
34:10 *d* my sheep out of their
34:12 *d* them out of all the
Da 3:29 god . . . able to *d* like this
6:14 he kept on striving to *d* him
Ho 11:8 How can I *d* you up, O Israel?
Am 6:8 *d* up the city and what fills
Jon 4:6 *d* him from his calamitous
Zep 1:18 to *d* them in the day of
Mt 6:13 but *d* us from the wicked one
10:17 *d* you up to local courts
10:19 when they *d* you up, do not
10:21 brother will *d* up brother to
20:19 will *d* him up to men of the
24:9 will *d* you up to tribulation
Mr 10:33 *d* him to men of the nations
13:9 will *d* you up to local courts
13:11 leading you along to *d* you
13:12 will *d* brother over to death
Lu 12:58 *d* you to the court officer
24:21 the one destined to *d* Israel
Ac 7:34 I have come down to *d* them
16:4 they would *d* to those there
21:11 *d* into the hands of people of
26:17 I *d* you from this people
Ga 1:4 *d* us from the present wicked
2Ti 4:18 *d* me from every wicked work
Tit 2:14 *d* us from every sort of
2Pe 2:9 Jehovah knows how to *d* people

Deliverance
1Sa 30:8 will without fail make a *d*
Es 4:14 and *d* themselves will stand

Isa 43:13 is no one effecting *d*
66:7 gave *d* to a male child
Mic 5:6 *d* from the Assyrian, when
Lu 1:68 performed *d* toward his people
2:38 waiting for Jerusalem's *d*
21:28 your *d* is getting near
Heb 9:12 an everlasting *d* for us

Delivered
Ge 14:20 Most High God, who has *d* your
32:30 and yet my soul was *d*
Ex 2:19 A certain Egyptian *d* us
5:23 by no means *d* your people
12:27 but he *d* our houses
18:4 he *d* me from Pharaoh's sword
18:9 *d* them from the hand of Egypt
18:10 *d* you from the hand of Egypt
18:10 *d* the people from under the
Jos 22:31 Now you have *d* the sons of
24:10 I *d* you out of his hand
Jg 6:9 So I *d* you out of the hand of
8:34 had *d* them out of the hand
1Sa 7:14 Israel *d* from the hand of
17:37 Jehovah, who *d* me from the
30:18 and his two wives David *d*
30:22 none of the spoil that we *d*
2Sa 12:7 *d* you out of the hand of
19:9 It was the king that *d* us
22:1 Jehovah had *d* him out of the
23:12 *d* it and kept striking down
2Ki 18:33 *d* each one his own land out
18:34 *d* Samaria out of my hand
18:35 *d* their land out of my hand
19:11 and will you yourself be *d*
19:12 *d* them, even Gozan and
1Ch 11:14 middle of the tract and *d*
Ezr 8:31 he *d* us out of the palm of
Job 21:30 At the day of fury he is *d*
Ps 18:*super* day that Jehovah had *d*
33:16 not *d* by the abundance of
34:4 out of all my frights he *d* me
34:17 their distresses he *d* them
54:7 out of every distress he *d* me
56:13 have *d* my soul from death
56:13 *d* my feet from stumbling
63:10 *d* over to the power of the
69:14 *d* from those hating me and
86:13 *d* my soul out of Sheol
Isa 20:6 *d* because of the king of
36:18 gods of the nations *d* each
36:19 *d* Samaria out of my hand
36:20 *d* their land out of my hand
37:11 will you yourself be *d?*
37:12 *d* them, even Gozan and
Jer 7:10 We shall certainly be *d*
20:13 *d* the soul of the poor one
Eze 3:19 will have *d* your own soul
3:21 will have *d* your own soul
14:16 they themselves, would be *d*
14:18 they themselves, would be *d*
34:27 *d* them out of the hand of
Mic 4:10 There you will be *d*
Hab 2:9 to be *d* from the grasp of
Mt 11:27 been *d* to me by my Father
18:34 *d* him to the jailers, until
20:18 Son of man will be *d* up to
26:2 is to be *d* up to be impaled
Mr 9:31 The Son of man is to be *d*
10:33 *d* to the chief priests and
Lu 1:2 the message *d* these to us
4:6 because it has been *d* to me
9:42 and *d* him to his father
9:44 to be *d* into the hands of men
10:22 All things have been *d* to
18:32 *d* up to men of the nations
21:16 be *d* up even by parents and
24:7 *d* into the hands of sinful
Joh 18:30 not have *d* him up to you
18:35 chief priests *d* you up to
18:36 not be *d* up to the Jews
19:30 he *d* up his spirit
Ac 2:23 one *d* up by the determined
3:13 *d* up and disowned before
7:10 he *d* him out of all his
12:11 *d* me out of Herod's hand
15:26 *d* up their souls for the
23:33 *d* the letter to the governor
28:17 I was *d* over as a prisoner
Ro 4:25 He was *d* up for the sake of
8:32 Son but *d* him up for us all
15:31 be *d* from the unbelievers in
2Co 6:9 and yet not *d* to death
Ga 3:22 Scripture *d* up all things
3:23 *d* up together into custody
Eph 5:2 Christ . . . *d* himself up for
5:25 and *d* up himself for it
Col 1:13 *d* us from the authority of
2Th 3:2 be *d* from harmful and wicked
2Ti 3:11 out of . . . all the Lord *d* me
4:17 was *d* from the lion's mouth
1Pe 1:18 *d* from your fruitless form
2Pe 2:4 *d* them to pits of dense
2:7 he *d* righteous Lot, who was
2:21 holy commandment *d* to them
Jude 3 all time *d* to the holy ones

Deliverer
Jg 18:28 And there was no *d*, for it
1Sa 14:39 who is the *D* of Israel
2Sa 14:6 was no *d* to part them
Job 5:4 in the gate without a *d*
Ps 7:2 when there is no *d*
50:22 without there being any *d*
71:11 catch him, for there is no *d*
Isa 5:29 and there will be no *d*
42:22 for plunder without a *d*
Da 8:7 ram proved to have no *d* out of
Ho 5:14 and there will be no *d*
Mic 5:8 and there is no *d*
Ac 7:35 sent off as both ruler and *d*
Ro 11:26 *d* will come out of Zion and

Delivering
Ex 18:8 and yet Jehovah was *d* them
1Sa 10:18 *d* you from the hand of
2Sa 22:18 *d* me from my strong enemy
Job 10:7 no one *d* out of your . . . hand
Ps 18:17 *d* me from my strong enemy
35:10 *D* the afflicted one from one
Pr 14:25 A true witness is *d* souls
Eze 35:5 kept *d* the sons of Israel
Da 6:27 *d* and performing signs and
8:4 doing any *d* out of its hand
Zec 11:6 do no *d* out of their hand
Lu 21:12 *d* you up to the synagogues

Delivers
Ps 34:19 out of them all Jehovah *d*
97:10 of the wicked ones he *d* them
1Th 1:10 *d* us from the wrath which

Delivery
Ge 35:16 with her in making the *d*
35:17 difficulty in making the *d*

Delude
Col 2:4 may *d* you with persuasive

Deluge
Ge 6:17 bringing the *d* of waters
7:6 *d* of waters occurred on the
7:7 ahead of the waters of the *d*
7:10 waters of the *d* came upon
7:17 *d* went on for forty days upon
9:11 cut off by waters of a *d*
9:11 no more will there occur a *d*
9:15 a *d* to bring all flesh to ruin
9:28 Noah continued . . . after the *d*
10:1 born to them after the *d*
10:32 in the earth after the *d*
11:10 two years after the *d*
Ps 29:10 Upon the *d* Jehovah has seated
2Pe 2:5 brought a *d* upon a world of

Deluged
2Pe 3:6 when it was *d* with water

Demand
Ne 5:18 due the governor I did not *d*
Lu 3:13 Do not *d* anything more than
12:48 *d* more than usual of him
23:24 for their *d* to be met

Demanded
Lu 12:48 much will be *d* of him; and
22:31 Satan has *d* to have you men
Ac 13:21 then on they *d* a king, and
13:28 they *d* of Pilate that he be

Demanding
Lu 12:20 they are *d* your soul from
23:23 *d* that he be impaled; and
23:25 and whom they were *d*, but

Demands
1Pe 3:15 *d* of you a reason for the

Demarcation
Ex 8:23 *d* between my people and your

Demas
Col 4:14 greetings, and so does *D*
2Ti 4:10 *D* has forsaken me because
Phm 24 *D*, Luke, my fellow workers

Demetrius
Ac 19:24 *D*, a silversmith, by making
19:38 *D* and the craftsmen with
3Jo 12 *D* has had witness borne to

Demolished
Ezr 5:12 *d* this house and took the
Jer 51:58 will without fail be *d*

Demolisher
Isa 22:5 There is the *d* of the wall

Demon
Isa 34:14 goat-shaped *d* will call to
Mt 9:32 a dumb man possessed of a *d*
9:33 after the *d* had been expelled
11:18 yet people say, He has a *d*
17:18 and the *d* came out of him
Mr 7:26 asking him to expel the *d*
7:29 the *d* has gone out of your
7:30 on the bed and the *d* gone out
Lu 4:33 with a spirit, an unclean *d*
4:35 the *d* came out of him
7:33 but you say, He has a *d*
8:29 driven by the *d* into the
9:42 *d* dashed him to the ground
11:14 he was expelling a dumb *d*
11:14 After the *d* came out, the
Joh 7:20 crowd answered: You have a
8:48 are a Samaritan and have a *d*
8:49 I do not have a *d*, but I
8:52 we do know you have a *d*
10:20 He has a *d* and is mad
10:21 *d* cannot open blind
Ac 16:16 a spirit, a *d* of divination

Demonic
Jas 3:15 is the earthly, animal, *d*

Demonized
Mt 15:22 My daughter is badly *d*
Joh 10:21 not the sayings of a *d* man

Demon-possessed
Mt 4:24 *d* and epileptic and paralyzed
8:16 brought him many *d* persons
8:28 two *d* men coming out from
8:33 the affair of the *d* men
12:22 brought him a *d* man, blind
Mr 1:32 who were ill and those *d*
5:15 they beheld the *d* man sitting
5:16 had happened to the *d* man and
5:18 the man that had been *d* began
Lu 8:36 the *d* man had been made well

Demons
Le 17:7 goat-shaped *d* with which they
De 32:17 went sacrificing to *d*, not
2Ch 11:15 for the goat-shaped *d* and
Ps 106:37 And their daughters to *d*
Isa 13:21 goat-shaped *d* themselves
Mt 7:22 and expel *d* in your name, and
8:31 *d* began to entreat him
9:34 It is by the ruler of the *d*
9:34 that he expels the *d*
10:8 make lepers clean, expel *d*
12:24 not expel the *d* except by
12:24 Beelzebub . . . ruler of the *d*
12:27 if I expel the *d* by means of
12:28 spirit that I expel the *d*
Mr 1:34 and he expelled many *d*, but
1:34 he would not let the *d* speak
1:39 Galilee and expelling the *d*
3:15 have authority to expel the *d*
3:22 expels the *d* by means of the
3:22 means of the ruler of the *d*
6:13 they would expel many *d* and
9:38 expelling *d* by the use of
Lu 4:41 *D* also would come out of
8:2 from whom seven *d* had come
8:27 man . . . who had *d* met him
8:30 Legion, because many *d* had
8:33 Then the *d* went out of the
8:35 the man from whom the *d* came
8:38 the man from whom the *d* had
9:1 authority over all the *d* and
9:49 a certain man expelling *d*
10:17 the *d* are made subject to us
11:15 He expels the *d* by means of
11:15 Beelzebub the ruler of the *d*
11:18 the *d* by means of Beelzebub
11:19 I expel the *d*, by whom do
11:20 I expel the *d*, the kingdom
13:32 I am casting out *d* and
Ac 19:13 the casting out of *d* also
1Co 10:20 they sacrifice to *d*, and not
10:20 become sharers with the *d*

1Co 10:21 of Jehovah and the cup of *d*
10:21 and the table of *d*
1Ti 4:1 utterances and teachings of *d*
Jas 2:19 yet the *d* believe and shudder
Re 9:20 should not worship the *d* and
16:14 expressions inspired by *d*
18:2 dwelling place of *d* and a

Demonstrate
Ro 2:15 *d* the matter of the law to be
9:22 the will to *d* his wrath and
2Co 8:24 *d* to them the proof of your
Ga 2:18 *d* myself to be a transgressor
1Ti 1:16 *d* all his long-suffering for
Heb 6:17 *d* more abundantly to the

Demonstrated
Ac 18:28 he *d* by the Scriptures that
2Co 7:11 *d* yourselves to be chaste
Eph 2:7 *d* the surpassing riches of his

Demonstrating
Ps 118:15 Jehovah is *d* vital energy
118:16 Jehovah is *d* vital energy

Demonstration
1Co 2:4 with a *d* of spirit and power
Heb 11:1 the evident *d* of realities

Denarii
Mt 18:24 talents [=60,000,000 *d*]
18:28 was owing him a hundred *d*
Mr 6:37 buy two hundred *d* worth of
14:5 upward of three hundred *d*
Lu 7:41 in debt for five hundred *d*
10:35 next day he took out two *d*
Joh 6:7 Two hundred *d* worth of loaves
12:5 sold for three hundred *d* and

Denarius
Mt 20:2 the workers for a *d* a day
20:9 they each received a *d*
20:10 pay at the rate of a *d*
20:13 You agreed with me for a *d*
22:19 They brought him a *d*
Mr 12:15 Bring me a *d* to look at
Lu 20:24 Show me a *d*. Whose image
Re 6:6 A quart of wheat for a *d*, and
6:6 three quarts of barley for a *d*

Denied
Job 31:28 should have *d* the true God
Jer 5:12 They have *d* Jehovah, and they
Mt 26:70 But he *d* it before them all
26:72 again he *d* it, with an oath
Mr 14:68 he *d* it, saying: Neither do
Lu 22:34 three times *d* knowing me
22:57 he *d* it, saying: I do not
Joh 18:25 He *d* it and said: I am not
18:27 Peter *d* it again; and

Denies
1Jo 2:22 *d* that Jesus is the Christ
2:22 *d* the Father and the Son
2:23 Everyone that *d* the Son does

Denounce
Nu 23:7 Yes, do come, do *d* Israel
23:8 could I *d* those whom Jehovah
Pr 24:24 national groups will *d* him
Isa 66:14 will actually *d* his enemies

Denounced
Nu 23:8 those whom Jehovah has not *d*
Pr 22:14 one *d* by Jehovah will fall
25:23 away a secret, a *d* face
Mic 6:10 ephah measure that is *d*
Zec 1:12 have *d* these seventy years
Mal 1:4 people whom Jehovah has *d*

Dens
Mt 8:20 Foxes have *d* and birds of
Lu 9:58 Foxes have *d* and birds of
Heb 11:38 wandered about in . . . *d*

Dense
Ge 15:17 *d* darkness came and, look! a
2Pe 2:4 to pits of *d* darkness to be
Jude 6 eternal bonds under *d* darkness

Denuding
Ezr 4:14 to see the *d* of the king

Denunciation
Ps 38:3 because of your *d*
69:24 Pour out upon them your *d*
78:49 Fury and *d* and distress
102:10 Because of your *d* and your
Isa 10:5 in their hand for my *d*
10:25 *d* will have come to an end
13:5 weapons of his *d*, to wreck
Isa 26:20 moment until the *d* passes
30:27 they have become full of *d*
Jer 10:10 will hold up under his *d*
15:17 with *d* that you have filled
50:25 forth the weapons of his *d*
La 2:6 And in his angry *d* he shows no
Eze 21:31 pour out upon you my *d*
22:24 in the day of *d*
22:31 pour out my *d* upon them
Da 8:19 in the final part of the *d*
11:36 *d* will have come to a finish
Ho 7:16 the *d* of their tongue
Na 1:6 In the face of his *d* who can
Hab 3:12 With *d* you went marching
Zep 3:8 pour out upon them my *d*

Denunciations
Ps 7:11 God is hurling *d* every day
Da 11:30 hurl *d* against the holy

Deny
Ge 18:15 Sarah began to *d* it, saying
Jos 24:27 you may not *d* your God
Job 8:18 *d* him, saying, I have not
Pr 30:9 satisfied and I actually *d* you
Joh 1:20 he confessed and did not *d*
Ac 4:16 and we cannot *d* it
2Ti 2:12, 12 we *d*, he also will *d* us
2:13 for he cannot *d* himself
Re 2:13 *d* your faith in me even in

Denying
Isa 59:13 and a *d* of Jehovah
Mr 14:70 Again he was *d* it. And once
Lu 8:45 When they were all *d* it

Depart
Ex 12:37 Israel proceeded to *d* from
13:20 proceeded to *d* from Succoth
15:22 Moses caused Israel to *d*
17:1 *d* from the wilderness of Sin
De 4:9 not *d* from your heart all the
Jos 1:8 law should not *d* from your
Jg 16:17 power also would certainly *d*
1Sa 15:6 Go, *d*, go down from the
2Sa 7:15 my loving-kindness . . . not *d*
12:10 sword will not *d* from your
2Ki 3:3 He did not *d* from them
13:6 not *d* from the sin of the
13:11 did not *d* from all the sins
14:24 did not *d* from all the sins
15:9 did not *d* from the sins of
15:18 did not *d* from all the sins
15:24 did not *d* from the sins of
15:28 did not *d* from the sins of
17:22 They did not *d* from them
Ne 9:19 cloud itself did not *d* from
Job 34:20 powerful ones *d* by no hand
Ps 78:52 people to *d* just like a flock
80:8 make a vine *d* from Egypt
139:19 men will certainly *d* from
Pr 27:22 his foolishness will not *d*
Isa 10:27 load will *d* from upon your
11:13 jealousy of Ephraim must *d*
14:25 yoke may actually *d* from
14:25 load may *d* from upon their
Am 6:7 sprawling ones must *d*
Na 3:1 of robbery. Prey does not *d!*
Zec 10:2 certainly *d* like a flock
10:11 scepter of Egypt will *d*
Mt 2:22 became afraid to *d* for there
25:46 will *d* into everlasting
Lu 5:8 *D* . . . I am a sinful man
9:57 to wherever you may *d*
Joh 1:43 he desired to *d* for Galilee
Ac 16:39 requested them to *d* from the
18:2 all the Jews to *d* from Rome
20:7 was going to *d* the next day
25:4 about to *d* shortly for there
28:25 they began to *d*, while Paul
Ro 15:28 *d* by way of you for Spain
1Co 7:10 wife should not *d* from her
7:11 if she should actually *d*, let
7:15 unbelieving one proceeds to *d*
7:15 let him *d*; a brother or a
2Co 12:8 that it might *d* from me

Departed
Ex 14:19 *d* and went to their rear
14:19 the pillar of cloud *d* from
16:1 Later they *d* from Elim, and
Jg 16:20 Jehovah that had *d* from him
18:11 *d* . . . from Zorah and Eshtaol
1Sa 15:6 Kenites *d* from the midst of
15:32 experience of death has *d*
16:14 spirit . . . *d* from Saul, and
16:23 bad spirit *d* from upon him
1Sa 18:12 but from Saul he had *d*
28:15 God himself has *d* from me
28:16 Jehovah himself has *d* from
2Sa 22:22 not wickedly *d* from my God
Ps 18:21 not wickedly *d* from my God
Pr 27:25 The green grass has *d*, and
Isa 6:7 your error has *d* and your sin
24:11 exultation of the land has *d*
Mt 19:1 he *d* from Galilee and came
Mr 6:1 he *d* from there and came into
9:30 they *d* and went their way
Lu 1:38 At that the angel *d* from her
2:15 when the angels had *d* from
19:32 *d* and found it just as he
22:13 *d* and found it just as he
Joh 4:3 and *d* again for Galilee
6:1 Jesus *d* across the sea of
11:54 *d* from there to the country
Ac 12:10 immediately the angel *d*
15:38 *d* from them from Pamphylia
16:40 they encouraged them and *d*
17:15 they *d*
18:1 he *d* from Athens and came to
18:23 he *d* and went from place to
20:11 he at length *d*
2Co 2:13 good-bye to them and *d* for
Php 4:15 when I *d* from Macedonia
Re 6:14 heaven *d* as a scroll that is
18:14 has *d* from you, and all the

Departing
Nu 4:5 when the camp is *d*, and they
4:15 when the camp is *d*, and after
Jg 16:19 his power kept *d* from upon
Mt 12:9 After *d* from that place he
24:1 *D* now, Jesus was on his way

Departs
Ps 101:4 A crooked heart *d* from me

Departure
Nu 33:2 the *d* places by their stages
33:2 from one *d* place to another
Lu 9:31 *d* that he was destined to
2Pe 1:15 after my *d*, you may be able

Departures
Nu 10:12 manner of their *d* from the
10:28 *d* of the sons of Israel in

Depend
Ne 4:2 Will they *d* upon themselves?
Ga 3:10 *d* upon works of law are under

Depended
Eze 33:26 You have *d* upon your sword

Dependent
Nu 21:25 Heshbon and all its *d* towns
21:32 So they captured its *d* towns
32:42 Kenath and its *d* towns; and
Jos 15:45 Ekron and its *d* towns and
15:47 Ashdod, its *d* towns and its
15:47 Gaza, its *d* towns and its
17:11 Beth-shean and its *d* towns
17:11 Ibleam and its *d* towns
17:11 Dor and its *d* towns and
17:11 En-dor and its *d* towns
17:11 Taanach and its *d* towns
17:11 Megiddo and its *d* towns
17:16 Beth-shean and its *d* towns
Jg 1:27 Beth-shean and its *d* towns
1:27 Taanach and its *d* towns and
1:27 Dor and its *d* towns and the
1:27 Ibleam and its *d* towns and
1:27 Megiddo and its *d* towns, but
11:26 Heshbon and its *d* towns and
11:26 Aroer and its *d* towns and in
1Ch 2:23 Kenath and its *d* towns
5:16 in Bashan and in its *d* towns
7:28 Bethel and its *d* towns and
7:28 west, Gezer and its *d* towns
7:28 and Shechem and its *d* towns
7:28 to Gaza and its *d* towns
7:29 Beth-shean and its *d* towns
7:29 Taanach and its *d* towns
7:29 Megiddo and its *d* towns
7:29 Dor and its *d* towns
8:12 Ono and Lod and its *d* towns
18:1 take Gath and its *d* towns
2Ch 13:19 Bethel and its *d* towns, and
13:19 Jeshanah and its *d* towns
13:19 Ephrain and its *d* towns
28:18 and Soco and its *d* towns
28:18 Timnah and its *d* towns and
28:18 Gimzo and its *d* towns and
Ne 11:25 Kiriath-arba and its *d* towns
11:25 in Dibon and its *d* towns

Ne 11:27 Beer-sheba and its *d* towns
11:28 in Meconah and its *d* towns
11:30 Azekah and its *d* towns
11:31 Bethel and its *d* towns
Ps 48:11 *d* towns of Judah be joyful
97:8 *d* towns of Judah began to
Jer 49:2 *d* towns themselves will be
49:3 Cry out, O *d* towns of Rabbah
Eze 16:46 with her *d* towns, who is
16:46 is Sodom with her *d* towns
16:48 she with her *d* towns, has
16:48 you and your *d* towns
16:49 to her and her *d* towns, and
16:53 of Sodom and of her *d* towns
16:53 Samaria and of her *d* towns
16:55 Sodom and her *d* towns
16:55 and Samaria and her *d* towns
16:55 own *d* towns will return
26:6 her *d* towns that are in the
26:8 Your *d* towns in the field
30:18 her own *d* towns will go
Ro 9:11 continue *d*, not upon works
1Pe 4:11 *d* on the strength that God

Depending
Heb 7:16 *d* upon the flesh, but

Depends
Ro 9:16 it *d*, not upon the one
12:18 as far as it *d* upon you, be

Deport
Ac 7:43 I will *d* you beyond Babylon

Deportation
Mt 1:11 time of the *d* to Babylon
1:12 After the *d* to Babylon
1:17 until the *d* to Babylon
1:17 from the *d* to Babylon until

Deported
Es 2:6 *d* people who were taken into

Deposit
Ex 16:33 and *d* it before Jehovah as
16:34 *d* it before the Testimony as
Le 6:2 or a *d* in hand or a robbery
Nu 17:4 *d* them in the tent of meeting
19:9 *d* them outside the camp in a
De 14:28 *d* it inside your gates
26:4 *d* it before the altar of
26:10 *d* it before Jehovah your God
Jos 4:3 *d* them in the lodging place
1Ki 13:29 to *d* him upon the ass and
13:31 Beside his bones *d* my own
Ezr 5:15 *d* them in the temple that is
Isa 46:7 and *d* it in its place that
Eze 40:42 also *d* the implements with
40:43 *d* the flesh of the gift
42:13 *d* the most holy things and
42:14 they will *d* their garments
44:19 *d* them in the holy dining
Lu 19:21 take up what you did not *d*
19:22 taking up what I did not *d*
Ac 4:35 *d* them at the feet of the

Deposited
Nu 17:7 Moses *d* the rods before
1Sa 10:25 and *d* it before Jehovah
1Ki 8:9 Moses had *d* there in Horeb
13:30 he *d* his dead body in his
2Ki 5:24 *d* them in the house and sent
17:29 *d* in the house of the high
Ezr 6:1 records of the treasures *d*
6:5 and be *d* in the house of God
Zec 5:11 be *d* there upon her proper
Mt 25:27 to have *d* my silver monies
Ac 4:37 *d* it at the feet of the
5:2 a part and *d* it at the feet

Depositing
Jos 4:8 lodging place and *d* them

Depositories
Ge 41:56 to open up all the grain *d*

Deposits
Isa 10:28 Michmash he *d* his articles

Depressed
Php 2:26 *d* because you heard he had
1Th 5:14 consolingly to the *d* souls

Depressions
Le 14:37 yellowish-green or reddish *d*

Deprive
Col 2:18 no man *d* you of the prize

Deprived
Isa 38:10 *d* of the remainder of my
Heb 12:15 *d* of the undeserved kindness

Depriving
1Co 7:5 Do not be *d* each other of it

Depth
1Ki 6:3 Ten cubits it was in its *d*
Ps 69:15 Nor the *d* swallow me up
Pr 25:3 the earth for *d*, and the heart
Mt 13:5 not having *d* of soil
Mr 4:5 of not having *d* of soil
Ac 27:28 sounded the *d* and found it
Ro 8:39 nor *d* nor any other creation
11:33 *d* of God's riches and wisdom
Eph 3:18 length and height and *d*

Depths
Ex 15:5 went into the *d* like a stone
Ne 9:11 hurled into the *d* like a stone
Job 41:31 *d* to boil just like a pot
Ps 68:22 back from the *d* of the sea
88:6 in a pit of the lowest *d*
95:4 are the inmost *d* of the earth
107:24 wonderful works in the *d*
130:1 Out of the *d* I have called
Isa 51:10 made the *d* of the sea a way
Eze 27:34 in the *d* of the waters
Jon 2:3 When you threw me to the *d*
Mic 7:19 throw into the *d* of the sea
Zec 10:11 all the *d* of the Nile

Deputations
Ps 78:49 *D* of angels bringing

Deputies
1Ki 4:5 Azariah . . . was over the *d*
4:7 Solomon had twelve *d* over all
4:19 *d* that were in the land
4:27 *d* supplied food to King
5:16 Solomon's princely *d* who
9:23 the chiefs of the *d* who
2Ch 8:10 chiefs of the *d* that belonged

Deputy
1Ki 4:19 one *d* over all the other
22:47 in Edom; a *d* was king
Ezr 9:2 the *d* rulers has proved to
Ne 2:16 the *d* rulers themselves did
2:16 the nobles and the *d* rulers
4:14 the nobles and the *d* rulers
4:19 to the nobles and the *d* rulers
5:7 the nobles and the *d* rulers
5:17 the Jews and the *d* rulers
7:5 the nobles and the *d* rulers
12:40 half of the *d* rulers with
13:11 find fault with the *d* rulers
Isa 41:25 will come upon *d* rulers as
Jer 51:23 and *d* rulers to pieces
51:28 its *d* rulers and all the
51:57 her *d* rulers and her mighty
Eze 23:6 *d* rulers—desirable young
23:12 governors and *d* rulers who
23:23 governors and *d* rulers all

Derbe
Ac 14:6 Lycaonia, Lystra and *D* and
14:20 he left with Barnabas for *D*
16:1 So he arrived at *D* and also at
20:4 and Gaius of *D*, and Timothy

Deride
Ne 2:19 began to *d* us and look on us
Job 21:3 you may each *d*
Pr 3:34 ridiculers, he himself will *d*

Derided
Ps 119:51 have *d* me to the extreme

Deriders
Ho 7:5 drawn his hand along with *d*

Derides
Pr 19:28 good-for-nothing witness *d*

Deriding
2Ch 30:10 mockery of them and *d* them
Ne 4:1 and he kept *d* the Jews
Job 11:3 keep *d* without . . . rebuke
Ps 80:6 enemies keep *d* as they please

Derision
2Ki 19:21 she has held you in *d*
Job 22:19 will hold them in *d*
34:7 drinks up *d* like water
Ps 2:4 will hold them in *d*
22:7 seeing me, they hold me in *d*
44:13 A *d* and jeering to those all
59:8 hold all the nations in *d*
79:4 *d* and a jeering to those
123:4 *d* of those who are at ease
Pr 14:9 those who make a *d* of guilt
Pr 17:5 the one of little means in *d*
30:17 eye that holds a father in *d*
Isa 37:22 she has held you in *d*
Jer 20:7 everyone is holding me in *d*
Eze 23:32 object of laughter and *d*
Ho 7:16 their *d* in the land of Egypt

Derive
Phm 20 may I *d* profit from you in

Descend
Ge 15:11 birds of prey began to *d*
Ex 19:24 Go, *d*, and you must come up
32:7 said to Moses: Go, *d*, because
Nu 11:9 by night, the manna would *d*
Jos 2:15 had them *d* by a rope through
2:18 by which you have had us *d*
2:23 *d* again from the mountainous
Jg 7:9 *d* upon the camp, for I have
7:10, 10 afraid to *d*, *d*, you with
7:11 be certain to *d* upon the camp
11:37 I will *d* upon the mountains
1Sa 19:12 Michal had David *d* through
2Sa 22:10 the heavens down and to *d*
Job 17:16 must *d* to the very dust
21:13 down to Sheol they *d*
Ps 7:16 his own violence will *d*
18:9 bend the heavens down and *d*
72:6 *d* like the rain upon the mown
78:16 waters to *d* just like rivers
104:8 Valley plains proceeded to *d*
144:5 your heavens that you may *d*
Pr 30:4 to heaven that he may *d*
Ca 4:8 *d* from the top of Anti-Lebanon
Isa 34:5 Upon Edom it will *d*, and
57:9 to *d* toward Melech with oil
Jer 21:13 Who will *d* against us?
La 2:18 tears to *d* just like a torrent
Eze 34:26 rain to *d* in its time
Joe 3:13 *d*, for the winepress has
Ro 10:7 Who will *d* into the abyss?
1Th 4:16 Lord himself will *d* from

Descendant
Ge 49:11 the *d* of his own she-ass

Descendants
1Ch 5:7 enrollment by their *d* were
7:2 mighty men, by their *d*
7:4 And with them by their *d*
7:9 enrollment by their *d* as
8:28 by their *d*, headmen
9:9 brothers of theirs by their *d*
9:34 Levites by their *d*, headmen
Job 5:25 *d* like the vegetation of the
21:8 And their *d* before their eyes
27:14 his *d* themselves will not
31:8 my own *d* be rooted out
Isa 22:24 the *d* and the offshoots
44:3 my blessing upon your *d*
48:19 *d* from your inward parts
61:9 their *d* in among the peoples
65:23 and their *d* with them

Descended
Ex 19:25 Moses *d* to the people and
Nu 11:9 dew *d* upon the camp by night
1Sa 15:12 went across and *d* to Gilgal
2Sa 23:20 *d* and struck down a lion
1Ch 11:22 *d* and struck down a lion
Mt 28:2 Jehovah's angel had *d* from
Lu 8:23 a violent windstorm *d* upon
Joh 3:13 but he that *d* from heaven
Eph 4:9 also *d* into the lower regions
4:10 The very one that *d* is also
Re 16:21 *d* out of heaven upon the men

Descending
Ge 28:12 God's angels ascending and *d*
De 9:21 torrent that was *d* from the
28:43 keep *d* lower and lower
Jos 3:13 the waters *d* from above, and
3:16 waters *d* from above began
3:16 those *d* toward the sea of
Jg 4:14 And Barak went *d* from Mount
1Sa 9:27 *d* by the edge of the city
2Ki 1:10 fire came *d* from the heavens
1:12 fire of God came *d* from the
Ps 133:3 *d* upon the mountains of Zion
Pr 5:5 Her feet are *d* to death
7:27 *d* to the interior rooms of
Ec 3:21 whether it is *d* downward to
Isa 30:30 *d* of his arm to be seen
Mt 3:16 *d* like a dove God's spirit
17:9 *d* from the mountain, Jesus
Joh 1:51 ascending and *d* to the Son
Ac 10:11 vessel *d* like a great linen

Ac 11:5 *d* like a great linen sheet
Re 10:1 strong angel *d* from heaven
18:1 angel *d* from heaven, with

Descends
Isa 55:10 just as the pouring rain *d*
Re 3:12 new Jerusalem which *d* out

Descent
Nu 1:18 *d* acknowledged as regards
Jos 7:5 striking them down on the *d*
10:11 were on the *d* of Beth-horon
Jg 7:11 made their *d* to the edge of

Descents
Ge 10:32 according to their family *d*
Ex 6:16 according to their family *d*
6:19 according to their family *d*

Described
Job 26:10 *d* a circle upon the face of

Desert
Le 16:22 errors into a *d* land, and
Nu 22:1 on the *d* plains of Moab
26:3 in the *d* plains of Moab by
26:63 in the *d* plains of Moab by
31:12 to the *d* plains of Moab
33:48 on the *d* plains of Moab by
33:49 on the *d* plains of Moab
33:50 on the *d* plains of Moab by
35:1 on the *d* plains of Moab by
36:13 the *d* plains of Moab by the
De 1:1 the *d* plains in front of Suph
4:31 He will not *d* you or bring
31:6 neither *d* you nor leave you
31:8 neither *d* you nor leave you
32:10 And in an empty, howling *d*
34:1 from the *d* plains of Moab
34:8 the *d* plains of Moab
Jos 1:5 neither *d* you nor leave you
4:13 onto the *d* plains of Jericho
5:10 on the *d* plains of Jericho
8:14 before the *d* plain
11:2 *d* plains south of Chinnereth
13:32 on the *d* plains of Moab on
1Sa 12:22 For Jehovah will not *d* his
2Sa 17:16 Do not lodge in the *d* plains
2Ki 25:5 in the *d* plains of Jericho
1Ch 12:19 he will *d* to his lord Saul
28:20 He will not *d* you or leave
Job 24:5 The *d* plain gives to each one
39:6 I have appointed the *d* plain
Ps 68:4 riding through the *d* plains
68:7 you marched through the *d*
78:40 make him feel hurt in the *d*
106:14 God to the proof in the *d*
107:4 in the wilderness, in the *d*
138:8 not *d* the works of your own
Isa 21:13 against the *d* plain
21:13 forest in the *d* plain you
23:13 her for the *d* haunters
33:9 Sharon has become like the *d*
35:1 *d* plain will be joyful and
35:6 and torrents in the *d* plain
40:3 through the *d* plain straight
41:19 In the *d* plain I shall
43:19 a way, through the *d* rivers
43:20 rivers in the *d*, to cause
51:3 her *d* plain like the garden
Jer 2:6 through a land of *d* plain
5:6 a wolf itself of the *d* plains
7:29 will *d* the generation with
17:6 solitary tree in the *d* plain
23:39 I will *d* you and the city
39:5 in the *d* plains of Jericho
50:12 wilderness and a *d* plain
51:43 land and a *d* plain
52:8 in the *d* plains of Jericho
Ac 8:26 This is a *d* road

Deserted
Jg 6:13 Jehovah has *d* us, and he gives
1Ch 12:19 of Manasseh that *d* to David
12:20 *d* to him from Manasseh
2Ch 15:9 *d* to him from Israel in
Isa 6:12 *d* condition does become very
24:10 *d* town has been broken down
Jer 12:7 I have *d* my inheritance
15:6 You yourself have *d* me

Deserters
2Ki 25:11 *d* that had gone over to the
Jer 39:9 *d* that had fallen away to
52:15 *d* that had fallen away to

Deserting
1Sa 29:3 day of his *d* to me until

Deserts
Lu 1:80 he continued in the *d* until
5:16 in retirement in the *d*
Heb 11:38 wandered about in *d* and

Deserve
1Sa 26:16 you men *d* to die, because
Ps 103:10 brought upon us what we *d*
Lu 23:41 we *d* for things we did
Re 16:6 blood to drink. They *d* it

Deserved
Jg 9:16 as the doing of his hands *d*
Isa 66:6 what is *d* to his enemies

Deservedly
Ca 1:4 *D* they have loved you

Deserves
De 25:2 the wicked one *d* to be beaten
2Sa 12:5 the man doing this *d* to die
Mt 10:10 for the worker *d* his food

Deserving
Nu 35:31 a murderer who is *d* to die
De 21:22 a sin *d* the sentence of death
22:26 has no sin *d* of death
1Ki 2:26 For you are *d* of death
Mt 10:11 search out who in it is *d*
10:13 if the house is *d*, let the
10:13 but if it is not *d*, let the
Lu 12:48 did things *d* of strokes
23:15 nothing *d* of death has been
23:22 nothing *d* of death in him
Ac 23:29 thing *d* of death or bonds
25:11 anything *d* of death
25:25 committed nothing *d* of death
26:31 practices nothing *d* death
Ro 1:32 are *d* of death, they not only
1Ti 1:15 *d* of full acceptance is the
4:9 *d* of full acceptance is that

Design
2Ki 16:10 the *d* of the altar and its
Lu 23:51 voted in support of their *d*

Designate
Ge 22:2 mountains that I shall *d* to
Ex 21:8 does not *d* her as a concubine
1Sa 16:3 the one whom I *d* to you
28:8 one whom I shall *d* to you
Isa 62:2 mouth of Jehovah will *d*
Ac 1:24 *d* which one of these two

Designated
Ge 22:3 that the true God *d* to him
22:9 God had *d* to him, and Abraham
26:2 in the land that I *d* to you
Ex 32:13 land that I have *d* I shall
Le 19:20 maidservant *d* for another
Nu 1:17 men who had been *d* by names
1Ch 12:31 *d* by name to come to make
16:41 *d* by names to thank Jehovah
2Ch 28:15 *d* by their names rose up
31:19 been *d* by their names, to
Ezr 8:20 had been *d* by their names
Jer 47:7 where he has *d* it to be
Mic 6:9 who it was that *d* it, O you
Lu 10:1 the Lord *d* seventy others and
Joh 5:2 pool *d* in Hebrew Bethzatha

Designates
Ex 21:9 to his son that he *d* her, he

Designing
Ex 31:4 for *d* devices, for working in
35:32 for *d* devices, for working
35:35 men . . . *d* devices
2Ch 2:14 at *d* every sort of device

Designs
2Co 2:11 we are not ignorant of his *d*

Desirable
Ge 2:9 every tree *d* to one's sight
3:6 the tree was *d* to look upon
27:15 garments . . . most *d* ones
1Sa 9:20 that is *d* of Israel belong
1Ki 9:1 every *d* thing of Solomon that
9:19 the *d* things of Solomon that
20:6 *d* to your eyes they will put
2Ch 8:6 every *d* thing of Solomon that
20:25 clothing and *d* articles; and
32:27 for all the *d* articles
36:10 *d* articles of the house of
36:19 and also all its *d* articles
Ezr 8:27 gleaming red, as *d* as gold
Job 20:20 By means of his *d* things he
33:20 And his own soul *d* food
Ps 39:11 you consume his *d* things

Ps 106:24 to contemning the *d* land
Pr 19:22 *d* thing in earthling man is
21:20 *D* treasure and oil are in the
Ca 5:16 about him is altogether *d*
Isa 2:16 and upon all *d* boats
32:12 over the *d* fields, over the
64:11 every one of our *d* things
Jer 3:19 and to give you the *d* land
12:10 turned my *d* share into a
25:34 must fall like a *d* vessel
La 1:7 *d* things that happened to be
1:10 hand against all her *d* things
1:11 *d* things for something to eat
2:4 killing all those *d* to the eyes
Eze 23:6 *d* young men all of them
23:12 *d* young men all of them
23:23 *d* young men, governors and
24:16 the thing *d* to your eyes
24:21 the thing *d* to your eyes
24:25 the thing *d* to their eyes
26:12 *d* houses they will pull
Da 9:23 you are someone very *d*
10:11 Daniel, you very *d* man
10:19 not be afraid, O very *d* man
11:8 *d* articles of silver and of
11:38 and by means of *d* things
11:43 all the *d* things of Egypt
Ho 9:6 their *d* things of silver
9:16 put to death the *d* things
13:15 pillage . . . all *d* articles
Joe 3:5 my own *d* good things into
Am 5:11 *d* vineyards you have planted
Na 2:9 of all sorts of *d* articles
Hag 2:7 *d* things of all the nations
Zec 7:14 the *d* land an object of
Mt 18:14 *d* thing with my Father who

Desire
Ex 20:17 not *d* your fellowman's house
20:17 not *d* your fellowman's wife
34:24 and nobody will *d* your land
De 5:21 *d* your fellowman's wife
7:25 You must not *d* the silver
Jos 6:18 may get a *d* and you do take
Job 23:13 his own soul has a *d*, and
Ps 10:17 The *d* of the meek ones you
21:2 *d* of his heart you have given
38:9 in front of you is all my *d*
78:30 turned aside from their *d*
106:14 showed their selfish *d* in
112:10 *d* of the wicked ones will
145:16 satisfying the *d* of every
145:19 *d* of those fearing him he
Pr 1:22 ridiculers *d* for yourselves
6:25 *d* her prettiness in your heart
10:24 *d* of the righteous ones will
11:23 *d* of the righteous ones is
13:19 *D* when realized is
19:18 do not lift up your soulful *d*
23:2 are the owner of soulful *d*
Isa 26:8 the *d* of the soul has been
53:2 so that we should *d* him
56:11 dogs strong in soulful *d*
58:10 your own soulful *d*, and
Jer 44:14 lifting up their soulful *d*
Eze 16:27 the soulful *d* of the women
23:11 her sensual *d* more
Da 11:37 *d* of women and to every
Mic 7:1 fig, that my soul would *d*
Lu 15:16 he used to *d* to be filled
17:22 you will *d* to see one of
20:46 *d* to walk around in robes
Ac 13:22 will do all the things I *d*
16:3 Paul expressed the *d* for this
17:20 we *d* to get to know what
Ga 5:16 carry out no fleshly *d* at all
5:17 against the spirit in its *d*
Php 1:12 I *d* you to know, brothers
1:23 what I do *d* is the releasing
Col 3:5 hurtful *d*, and covetousness
1Th 2:17 see your faces with great *d*
1Ti 2:8 I *d* that in every place the
2:9 I *d* the women to adorn
5:14 I *d* the younger widows to
Tit 3:8 these things I *d* you to make
Heb 6:11 *d* each one of you to show
Jas 1:14 and enticed by his own *d*
1:15 *d* . . . has become fertile
4:2 You *d*, and yet you do not have
2Pe 2:10 flesh with the *d* to defile
3:9 does not *d* any to be destroyed
1Jo 2:16 the *d* of the flesh and the
2:16 and the *d* of the eyes and
2:17 passing away and so is its *d*

2Jo 12 not *d* to do so with paper and
Jude 5 I *d* to remind you, despite
Re 9:6 they will *d* to die but death

Desired
1Ki 9:19 *d* to build in Jerusalem and
2Ch 8:6 *d* to build in Jerusalem and
21:20 went away without being *d*
Ps 19:10 are more to be *d* than gold
68:16 The mountain that God has *d*
78:29 what they *d* he proceeded to
Pr 12:12 *d* the netted prey of bad men
13:12 thing *d* is a tree of life
Ca 2:3 His shade I have passionately *d*
Isa 1:29 trees that you people *d*, and
26:9 I have *d* you in the night
Da 7:19 *d* to make certain concerning
Mic 2:2 *d* fields and have seized them
Mt 13:17 righteous men *d* to see the
Lu 10:24 *d* to see the things you are
22:15 *d* to eat this passover with
Joh 1:43 he *d* to depart for Galilee
Ac 22:30 he *d* to know for sure just
24:27 Felix *d* to gain favor with
27:43 officer *d* to bring Paul
1Co 10:6 even as they *d* them
Re 18:14 fruit that your soul *d* has

Desires
Eze 33:31 expressing lustful *d* and
Mr 4:19 *d* for the rest of the things
Joh 7:17 If anyone *d* to do His will
8:44 to do the *d* of your father
Ro 1:24 God, in keeping with the *d*
6:12 that you should obey their *d*
13:14 ahead for the *d* of the flesh
Ga 5:24 with its passions and *d*
Eph 2:3 with the *d* of our flesh
4:22 according to his deceptive *d*
1Ti 6:9 many senseless and hurtful *d*
2Ti 2:22 the *d* incidental to youth
3:6 led by various *d*
4:3 in accord with their own *d*
Tit 2:12 ungodliness and worldly *d*
3:3 being slaves to various *d* and
1Pe 1:14 the *d* you formerly had in
2:11 abstaining from fleshly *d*
4:2 no more for the *d* of men, but
2Pe 2:18 by the *d* of the flesh and by
3:3 according to their own *d*
3:9 *d* all to attain to repentance
Jude 16 according to their own *d*
18 according to their own *d*

Desiring
Lu 16:21 *d* to be filled with the
Ac 14:13 *d* to offer sacrifices with
18:27 *d* to go across into Achaia
25:9 Festus, *d* to gain favor with
1Co 10:6 persons *d* injurious things
2Co 5:2 *d* to put on the one for us
2Ti 3:12 *d* to live with godly
1Pe 1:12 angels are *d* to peer

Desirous
Pr 13:4 lazy one is showing himself *d*
Ac 28:18 *d* of releasing me, as there
1Co 14:12 *d* of gifts of the spirit
1Ti 3:1 he is *d* of a fine work

Desist
Ex 5:5 *d* from their . . . burdens
23:12 seventh day you are to *d*, in
Jos 22:25 our sons *d* from fearing
Ps 8:2 one taking his vengeance *d*
Pr 20:3 for a man to *d* from disputing
2Pe 2:14 unable to *d* from sin, and

Desisted
1Pe 4:1 in the flesh has *d* from sins

Desolate
Ge 47:19 and our land not be laid *d*
Ex 23:29 may not become a *d* waste
Le 26:31 lay your sanctuaries *d*, and
26:32 lay the land *d*, and your
26:33 cities will become a *d* ruin
2Ki 19:25 cities *d* as piles of ruins
Job 3:14 Those building *d* places for
16:7 those assembling with me *d*
38:27 storm-stricken and *d* places
Ps 69:25 their walled camp become *d*
109:10 food from their *d* places
Isa 5:17 *d* places of well-fed animals
17:9 must become a *d* waste
33:8 highways have been made *d*
37:26 cities become *d* as piles of
Isa 61:4 places *d* for generation after
62:4 no more be said to be *d*
64:10 Jerusalem a *d* waste
Jer 4:27 A *d* waste is what the whole
6:8 not set you as a *d* waste
9:11 Judah I shall make a *d* waste
10:22 Judah a *d* waste, the lair
12:10 wilderness of a *d* waste
12:11 One has made it a *d* waste
12:11 whole land has been made *d*
25:12 I will make it *d* wastes
32:43 *d* waste without man and
34:22 make a *d* waste without an
44:6 a *d* waste, as at this day
49:2 become a mound of *d* waste
49:20 dwelling place become *d*
49:33 lair of jackals, a *d* waste
50:13 *d* waste in her entirety
51:26 *d* wastes to time indefinite
51:62 *d* wastes to time indefinite
La 1:4 All her gates are laid *d*
1:13 has made me a woman laid *d*
1:16 sons have become those laid *d*
3:11 He has made me one laid *d*
Eze 6:4 your altars must be made *d*
6:14 and make the land a *d* waste
12:19 land may be laid *d* of its
12:20 will become a mere *d* waste
14:15 a *d* waste without anybody
14:16 would become a *d* waste
15:8 make the land a *d* waste
19:7 the land was laid *d* and he
20:26 that I might make them *d*
25:3 because it has been laid *d*
29:9 must become a *d* waste and
29:12 the land of Egypt a *d* waste
29:12 will become a *d* waste
30:7 made *d* in the midst of
32:15 land of Egypt a *d* waste
33:28 make the land a *d* waste
33:28 Israel must be laid *d*
33:29 make the land a *d* waste
35:3 and make you a *d* waste
35:4 become a sheer *d* waste
35:7 region of Seir a *d* waste
35:9 *d* wastes are what I shall
35:12 They have been laid *d*
35:14 *d* waste is what I shall
35:15 because it was laid *d*
35:15 *d* waste is what you will
36:3 lying *d* and a snapping at you
36:4 places that were laid *d*
36:34 it had become a *d* waste
36:35 was laid *d* has become like
36:35 waste and that were laid *d*
36:36 what has been laid *d*
Da 9:27 also upon the one lying *d*
Ho 2:12 lay *d* her vine and her fig
Joe 1:17 Storehouses have been laid *d*
2:3 behind it is a *d* wilderness
3:19 a *d* waste it will become
3:19 of *d* waste it will become
Am 7:9 will certainly be laid *d*
Mic 1:7 idols I shall make a *d* waste
7:13 land must become a *d* waste
Zep 1:13 their houses for a *d* waste
2:4 Ashkelon is to be a *d* waste
2:9 and a salt pit, and a *d* waste
2:13 make Nineveh a *d* waste, a
Zec 7:14 land itself has been left *d*
Ac 1:20 his lodging place become *d*
Ga 4:27 children of the *d* woman are

Desolated
Le 26:22 roads will actually be *d*
26:34 days of its lying *d*, while
26:35 lying *d* it will keep sabbath
26:43 lying *d* without them and
2Ch 36:21 All the days of lying *d*
Ezr 9:9 to restore its *d* places and
Ps 79:7 own abiding place to be *d*
102:6 a little owl of *d* places
Isa 44:26 *d* places I shall raise up
49:8 the *d* hereditary possessions
49:19 *d* places and the land of
54:1 for the sons of the *d* one
54:3 inhabit even the *d* cities
61:4 the *d* places of former times
Jer 10:25 place they have *d*
12:11 withered away; it is *d* to
33:10 *d* without man and without
50:45 their abiding place to be *d*
La 5:18 Zion's mountain that is *d*
Eze 6:6 high places . . . will become *d*
Eze 6:6 your altars may lie *d* and be
29:10 *d* waste, from Migdol to
29:12 in the midst of *d* lands
30:7 in the midst of *d* lands
30:12 *d* by the hand of strangers
32:15 land is *d* of its fullness
36:34 the *d* land itself will be
Da 9:17 your sanctuary that is *d*, for
9:18 and see our *d* conditions and
Joe 2:20 waterless land and *d* waste
Am 9:14 build the *d* cities and
Zep 3:6 their corner towers were *d*
Mal 1:3 his mountains a *d* waste and

Desolateness
La 3:47 become ours, *d* and breakdown

Desolating
Mic 6:13 a *d* of you, on account of
Lu 21:20 *d* of her has drawn near

Desolation
Le 26:33 land must become a *d*, and
Jos 8:28 as a *d* down to this day
Job 30:3 there were storm and *d*
Ec 7:16 should you cause *d* to yourself
Isa 1:7 Your land is a *d*, your cities
1:7 the *d* is like an overthrow by
6:11 itself is ruined into a *d*
Eze 6:14 *d* worse than the wilderness
7:27 will clothe himself with *d*
23:33 of astonishment and of *d*
30:14 will bring Pathros to *d*
33:28 even a *d*, and the pride of
33:29 even a *d*, on account of all
35:3 desolate waste, even a *d*
35:7 desolate waste, even a *d*
Da 8:13 transgression causing *d*, to
9:27 will be the one causing *d*
11:31 thing that is causing *d*
12:11 thing that is causing *d*
Zep 1:15 a day of storm and of *d*
Mt 12:25 against itself comes to *d*
24:15 thing that causes *d*, as
Mr 13:14 thing that causes *d* standing
Lu 11:17 against itself comes to *d*

Desolations
Ps 9:6 your *d* have come to their
55:15 *D* be upon them! Let them go
74:3 steps to the long-lasting *d*
Isa 15:6 of Nimrim become sheer *d*
Jer 48:34 will become mere *d*
Da 9:26 what is decided upon is *d*

Despair
De 28:65 of the eyes and *d* of soul
1Sa 27:1 Saul must *d* of me in looking
Job 6:26 sayings of one in *d* are for
9:23 At the very *d* of the innocent
41:22 And before it *d* leaps
Ps 42:5 Why are you in *d*, O my soul
42:6 my very soul is in *d*
42:11 Why are you in *d*, O my soul
43:5 Why are you in *d*, O my soul
Ec 2:20 *d* over all the hard work at

Desperate
Jer 17:9 The heart . . . is *d*
17:16 for the *d* day I did not

Despicable
1Sa 15:9 all the goods that were *d*
Es 3:6 *d* in his eyes to lay hand upon
Ps 22:6 A reproach to men and *d* to
Na 3:6 I will make you *d*; and I will
Mt 5:22 whoever says, You *d* fool!

Despise
2Sa 6:16 began to *d* him in her heart
12:9 *d* the word of Jehovah by
1Ch 15:29 began to *d* him in her heart
Es 1:17 *d* their owners in their own
Ps 51:17 O God, you will not *d*
69:33 not *d* his very own prisoners
73:20 you will *d* their very image
102:17 And not *d* their prayer
Pr 6:30 People do not *d* a thief just
23:9 he will *d* your discreet words
23:22 do not *d* your mother just
Ca 8:1 People would not even *d* me
8:7 persons would positively *d*
Jer 14:21 do not *d* your glorious
Mt 6:24 stick to the one and *d* the
18:10 not *d* one of these little
Lu 16:13 stick to the one and *d* the
Ro 2:4 *d* the riches of his kindness
1Co 11:22 do you *d* the congregation of

Tit 2:15 Let no man ever *d* you

Despised

Ge 16:4 began to be *d* in her eyes
16:5 I began to be *d* in her eyes
25:34 So Esau *d* the birthright
Nu 15:31 Jehovah's word that he has *d*
De 32:15 *d* the Rock of his salvation
1Sa 10:27 they *d* him, and they did
2Sa 12:10 *d* me so that you took the
2Ki 19:21 Zion has *d* you, she has
Ps 22:24 For he has neither *d* Nor
Pr 1:7 are what mere fools have *d*
11:12 has *d* his own fellowman
13:13 He that has *d* the word, from
Ec 9:16 wisdom of the needy one is *d*
Isa 37:22 Zion has *d* you, she has held
49:7 to him that is *d* in soul
53:3 *d* and was avoided by men
53:3 He was *d*, and we held him
Jer 22:28 Coniah a mere form *d*
49:15 nations, *d* among mankind
Eze 16:59 *d* the oath in breaking my
17:16 king the one that *d* his oath
17:18 has *d* an oath in breaking a
17:19 my oath that he has *d* and
22:8 My holy places you have *d*
Da 11:21 one who is to be *d*, and
Ob 2 You are *d* very much
Zec 4:10 *d* the day of small things
Mal 1:6 In what way have we *d* your
1:7 table of Jehovah . . . *d*
1:12 fruit is something to be *d*
2:9 *d* and low to all the people

Despises

Pr 30:17 that *d* obedience to a mother

Despising

1Sa 2:30 those *d* me will be of little
17:42 saw David, he began *d* him
2Ch 36:16 *d* his words and mocking
Pr 14:2 crooked in his ways is *d* Him
14:21 one *d* his own fellowman is
15:20 stupid man is *d* his mother
19:16 he that is *d* his ways will
Mic 7:6 For a son is *d* a father
Mal 1:6 O priests who are *d* my name
Heb 12:2 *d* shame, and has sat down at

Despisingly

Ne 2:19 and look on us *d* and say

Despite

Le 26:18 *d* these things, you will not
De 1:32 But *d* this word you were not
Ps 78:32 *D* all this they sinned some
Isa 53:9 *d* the fact that he had done
Mr 9:31 *d* being killed, he will rise
Joh 4:9 *d* being a Jew, ask me for a
1Pe 1:7 gold that perishes *d* its being
Jude 5 *d* your knowing all things

Despoil

Job 24:6 vineyard . . . they hastily *d*
Pr 11:3 treacherously will *d* them
24:15 do not *d* his resting-place
Jer 47:4 to *d* all the Philistines
49:28 *d* the sons of the East
Eze 32:12 *d* the pride of Egypt
Ho 10:2 he will *d* their pillars
Hab 2:8 will *d* you, because of the

Despoiled

Ps 7:4 *d* anyone showing hostility to
17:9 the wicked who have *d* me
76:5 powerful in heart have been *d*
137:8 Babylon, who are to be *d*
Isa 15:1 in the night it has been *d*
15:1 in the night it has been *d*
23:1 been *d* from being a port
23:14 your stronghold has been *d*
33:1 you yourself being *d*, and to
33:1 you will be *d*
59:15 from badness is being *d*
Jer 4:13 because we have been *d*
4:20 the whole land has been *d*
4:20 my tents have been *d*
4:30 Now that you are *d*, what
9:19 How we have been *d!*
10:20 My own tent has been *d*
48:1 Nebo, for she has been *d*
48:15 Moab has been *d*, and one
48:20 that Moab has been *d*
49:3 Heshbon, for Ai has been *d*
49:10 will certainly be *d*
Ho 10:14 cities will all be *d*
Joe 1:10 The field has been *d*, the
1:10 for the grain has been *d*
Mic 2:4 We have positively been *d!*
Na 3:7 Nineveh has been *d!* Who will
Hab 2:8 you yourself *d* many nations
Zec 11:2 have been *d!* Howl, you
11:3 their majesty has been *d*
11:3 along the Jordan have been *d*
Lu 11:22 divides out the things he *d*
1Ti 6:5 and *d* of the truth, thinking

Despoiler

Job 15:21 During peace a *d* . . . comes
Isa 16:4 to them because of the *d*
21:2 and the *d* is despoiling
33:1 you have finished as a *d*
Jer 6:26 the *d* will come upon us
15:8 bring for them . . . the *d*
48:8 *d* will come in on every city
48:18 *d* of Moab has come up
48:32 *d* himself has fallen
51:56 upon Babylon, the *d*, and

Despoilers

Job 12:6 tents of the *d* are unworried
Jer 12:12 the *d* have come. For the
51:48 will come to her the *d*
51:53 the *d* will come to her, is
Ob 5 if *d* came in by night, to what

Despoiling

Job 5:21 not be afraid of *d* when it
5:22 At *d* and hunger . . . laugh
Ps 12:5 the *d* of the afflicted ones
Pr 21:7 *d* by the wicked ones will
24:2 *d* is what their heart keeps
Isa 13:6 *d* from the Almighty it will
16:4 the *d* has terminated
21:2 and the despoiler is *d*
22:4 *d* of the daughter of my
33:1 Woe to you who are *d*
51:19 *D* and breakdown, and hunger
59:7 *d* and breakdown are in their
60:18 *d* or breakdown within your
Jer 5:6 a wolf . . . keeps *d* them
6:7 Violence and *d* are heard in
20:8 Violence and *d* are what I
25:36 Jehovah is *d* their pasturage
47:4 Jehovah is *d* the Philistines
48:3 *d* and great breaking down
51:55 for Jehovah is *d* Babylon
Eze 45:9 the violence and the *d*
Ho 7:13 *D* to them, for they have
9:6 will have to go because of *d*
10:14 the *d* by Shalman of the
12:1 Lying and *d* are what he
Joe 1:15 like a *d* from the Almighty
Am 3:10 *d* in their dwelling towers
5:9 causing a *d* to flash forth
5:9 *d* itself may come upon even
Hab 1:3 why are *d* and violence in
Zec 2:8 nations . . . *d* you people

Despoils

Ps 91:6 destruction that *d* at midday

Despondently

1Ki 21:27 in sackcloth and walking *d*

Despot

Eze 31:11 hand of the *d* of the nations

Despots

Ex 15:15 *d* of Moab, trembling will

Destine

Isa 65:12 *d* you men to the sword

Destined

1Sa 20:31 for he is *d* for death
Job 15:28 prove *d* for heaps of stones
Pr 22:16 is surely *d* for want
Isa 5:5 be *d* for burning down
5:5 *d* for a place of trampling
Ho 9:13 Ephraim is *d* to a bringing
Mt 11:14 is Elijah who is *d* to come
16:27 Son of man is *d* to come in
17:12 Son of man is *d* to suffer at
17:22 *d* to be betrayed into men's
Mr 10:32 these things *d* to befall him
13:4 are *d* to come to a conclusion
Lu 9:31 departure that he was *d* to
9:44 the Son of man is *d* to be
21:7 these things are *d* to occur
21:36 things that are *d* to occur
24:21 the one *d* to deliver Israel
Joh 11:51 Jesus was *d* to die for the
18:32 of death he was *d* to die
Ac 13:34 *d* no more to return to
Ro 4:24 to whom it is *d* to be counted
2Co 8:4 ministry *d* for the holy ones
Ga 3:23 that was *d* to be revealed
Col 2:22 things that are all *d* to
1Th 3:4 were *d* to suffer tribulation
2Ti 4:1 *d* to judge the living and the
Heb 11:8 place he was *d* to receive

Destiny

Isa 65:11 mixed wine for the god of *D*
Mt 16:22 will not have this *d* at all
2Th 2:14 To this very *d* he called you

Destitute

1Ti 5:5 actually a widow and left *d*

Destroy

Le 19:27 not *d* the extremity of your
23:30 *d* that soul from among his
Nu 24:19 *d* any survivor from the city
33:52 *d* all their stone figures
33:52 and all their images . . . *d*
De 7:24 you must *d* their names from
9:3 dispossess them and *d* them
11:4 Jehovah proceeded to *d* them
12:2 *d* all the places where the
12:3 *d* their names from that place
28:63 *d* you and to annihilate you
Jos 7:7 the Amorites for them to *d* us
2Ki 24:2 against Judah to *d* it
Ezr 6:12 to commit a violation and *d*
Es 3:13 to kill and to *d* all the Jews
4:7 against the Jews, to *d* them
8:5 he wrote to *d* the Jews that
8:11 *d* all the force of the people
9:24 against the Jews to *d* them
9:24 to disquiet them and *d* them
Job 12:23 great, that he may *d* them
Ps 5:6 will *d* those speaking a lie
21:10 Their fruitage you will *d*
119:95 wicked have waited, to *d*
143:12 must *d* all those showing
Pr 1:32 stupid is what will *d* them
Ec 7:7 and a gift can *d* the heart
9:18 one sinner can *d* much good
Isa 26:14 and *d* all mention of them
Jer 1:10 to *d* and to tear down
15:7 I will *d* my people, since
18:7 to pull it down and to *d* it
25:10 I will *d* out of them the
31:28 to *d* and to do damage, so I
46:8 I shall readily *d* the city
49:38 *d* out of there the king and
51:55 *d* out of her the great voice
Eze 6:3 certainly *d* your high places
22:15 *d* your uncleanness out of
25:7 and *d* you from the lands
25:16 *d* the rest of the seacoast
28:16 *d* you, O cherub that is
30:13 *d* the dungy idols and cause
32:13 *d* all her domestic animals
Da 2:12 *d* all the wise men of Babylon
2:18 *d* Daniel and his companions
2:24 *d* the wise men of Babylon
2:24 *d* any wise men of Babylon
7:26 and to *d* him totally
Ob 8 *d* the wise ones out of Edom
Mic 5:10 and *d* your chariots
Zep 2:5 I will also *d* you, so that
2:13 and he will *d* Assyria
Mt 2:13 for the young child to *d* it
5:17 Do not think I came to *d* the
5:17 not to *d*, but to fulfill
10:28 can *d* both soul and body in
12:14 that they might *d* him
Mr 1:24 Did you come to *d* us? I know
3:6 against him, in order to *d*
9:22 into the water to *d* him
11:18 began to seek how to *d* him
12:9 come and *d* the cultivators
Lu 4:34 Did you come to *d* us? I know
6:9 to save or to *d* a soul
19:47 were seeking to *d* him
20:16 come and *d* these cultivators
Joh 10:10 to steal and slay and *d*
1Co 3:17 God will *d* him; for the
Jas 4:12 who is able to save and to *d*

Destroyed

De 28:51 until they have *d* you
2Ki 11:1 *d* all the offspring of the
13:7 the king of Syria had *d* them
19:18 so that they *d* them
21:3 Hezekiah his father had *d*
2Ch 22:10 *d* all the royal offspring
Es 3:9 be a writing that they be *d*

Es 7:4 to be annihilated, killed and *d*
Job 14:19 *d* the very hope of mortal
Ps 9:5 you have *d* the wicked one
49:12 the beasts that have been *d*
49:20 the beasts that have been *d*
Isa 5:6 shall set it as a thing *d*
37:19 so that they *d* them
La 2:9 *d* and broken her bars in pieces
Da 7:11 and its body was *d* and it was
Mt 22:7 *d* those murderers and burned
27:20 but to have Jesus *d*
Lu 13:3 you will all likewise be *d*
13:5 all be *d* in the same way
13:33 to be *d* outside of Jerusalem
17:27 flood arrived and *d* them all
17:29 from heaven and *d* them all
Joh 3:16 not be *d* but have everlasting
10:28 will by no means ever be *d*
11:50 the whole nation to be *d*
17:12 not one of them is *d* except
Ac 3:23 *d* from among the people
2Co 4:9 are thrown down, but not *d*
Eph 2:14 *d* the wall in between that
2Pe 2:12 naturally to be caught and *d*
3:9 does not desire any to be *d*
Jude 5 *d* those not showing faith

Destroyer
1Co 10:10 only to perish by the *d*
Heb 11:28 *d* might not touch their

Destroying
De 7:10 repaying . . . him by *d* him
8:20 the nations that Jehovah is *d*
2Ki 10:19 *d* the worshipers of Baal
Es 9:6 was a *d* of five hundred men
9:12 a *d* of five hundred men and
Jer 12:17 uprooting and *d* it, is the
23:1 *d* and scattering the sheep
Eze 22:27 in *d* souls for the purpose
Ac 13:19 *d* seven nations in the land

Destroys
Pr 29:3 with prostitutes *d* valuable
Joh 12:25 is fond of his soul *d* it
1Co 3:17 anyone *d* the temple of God

Destruction
Ex 22:20 is to be devoted to *d*
Le 27:28 devote to Jehovah for *d* out
27:29 devoted to *d* from among
Nu 21:2 devote their cities to *d*
21:3 them and their cities to *d*
De 2:34 devoting every city to *d*
3:6 we devoted them to *d*, just as
3:6 in devoting every city to *d*
7:2 without fail devote them to *d*
7:26 become a thing devoted to *d*
7:26 it is something devoted to *d*
13:15 *d* at the edge of the sword
20:17 devote them to *d*, the
32:24 burning fever And bitter *d*
Jos 2:10 Og, whom you devoted to *d*
6:17 a thing devoted to *d*
6:18 the thing devoted to *d*, for
6:18 the thing devoted to *d* and
6:18 a thing devoted to *d* and
6:21 *d* by the edge of the sword
7:1 the thing devoted to *d* in that
7:1 of the thing devoted to *d*
7:11 the thing devoted to *d* and
7:12 become a thing devoted to *d*
7:12 thing devoted to *d* out of
7:13 A thing devoted to *d* is in
7:13 the thing devoted to *d* from
7:15 the thing devoted to *d* will
8:26 the inhabitants of Ai to *d*
10:1 and then devoted it to *d*
10:28 soul that was in it to *d*
10:35 soul that was in it to *d*
10:37 soul that was in it to *d*
10:39 soul that was in it to *d*
10:40 he devoted to *d*, just as
11:11 devoting them to *d*
11:12 He devoted them to *d*, just
11:20 he might devote them to *d*
11:21 Joshua devoted them to *d*
22:20 the thing devoted to *d*
Jg 1:17 to devote it to *d*. Hence the
21:11 you should devote to *d*
1Sa 15:3 devote him to *d* with all
15:8 *d* with the edge of the sword
15:9 not wish to devote them to *d*
15:9 these they devoted to *d*
15:15 we have devoted to *d*
15:18 the Amalekites, to *d*, and
1Sa 15:20 Amalek I have devoted to *d*
15:21 as something devoted to *d*
30:17 devote them to *d*; and not
1Ki 9:21 been unable to devote to *d*
20:42 the man devoted to me for *d*
2Ki 19:11 by devoting them to *d*
1Ch 2:7 the thing devoted to *d*
4:41 they devoted them to *d*
2Ch 20:23 devote them to *d* and
32:14 forefathers devoted to *d*
Es 8:6 upon the *d* of my relatives
9:5 with a killing and *d*, and they
Job 21:17 does he apportion *d*
26:6 place of *d* has no covering
28:22 *D* and death themselves have
31:12 that would eat clear to *d*
Ps 88:11 in the place of *d*
91:6 *d* that despoils at midday
Pr 15:11 Sheol and the place of *d* are
27:20 Sheol and the place of *d*
Isa 34:2 he must devote them to *d*
34:5 people devoted by me to *d*
37:11 lands by devoting them to *d*
43:28 as a man devoted to *d* and
Jer 25:9 and I will devote them to *d*
50:21 devoting to *d* close upon
50:26 and devote her to *d*
51:3 Devote to *d* all her army
Da 11:44 and to devote many to *d*
Zec 14:11 no more any banning to *d*
Mal 4:6 with a devoting of it to *d*
Mt 7:13 the road leading off into *d*
21:41 bring an evil *d* upon them
Joh 17:12 except the son of *d*, in
Ro 9:22 of wrath made fit for *d*
1Co 5:5 the *d* of the flesh, in order
Php 1:28 is a proof of *d* for them
3:19 and their finish is *d*, and
Col 2:22 destined to *d* by being used
1Th 5:3 saying: Peace . . . sudden *d*
2Th 1:9 punishment of everlasting *d*
2:3 gets revealed, the son of *d*
1Ti 6:9 which plunge men into *d* and
Heb 10:39 sort that shrink back to *d*
2Pe 2:1 bringing speedy *d* upon
2:3 *d* of them is not slumbering
2:12 suffer *d* in their own course
2:12 in their own course of *d*
3:6 *d* when it was deluged with
3:7 and of *d* of the ungodly men
3:16 Scriptures, to their own *d*
Re 17:8 and it is to go off into *d*
17:11 and it goes off into *d*

Destructive
Isa 28:2 a *d* storm, like a thunderous
Na 1:3 In *d* wind and in storm is his
2Pe 2:1 will quietly bring in *d* sects

Destructiveness
Ho 13:14 Where is your *d*, O Sheol?

Detail
Joh 21:25 were written in full *d*
Ac 9:27 he told them in *d* how on the
12:17 told them in *d* how Jehovah
13:41 relates it to you in *d*
15:3 relating in *d* the conversion
21:19 giving in *d* an account of the
Heb 9:5 not the time to speak in *d*

Details
1Ki 6:38 all its *d* and all its plan
Isa 53:8 with the *d* of his generation
Ac 8:33 tell the *d* of his generation

Detain
Ge 24:56 Do not *d* me, seeing that
Jg 13:15 *d* you and fix up a kid of the
13:16 If you *d* me, I shall not
1Ki 18:44 the downpour may not *d* you
Lu 4:42 to *d* him from going

Detained
Ex 10:24 and your cattle will be *d*
Nu 22:16 Do not be *d*, please, from
1Sa 21:7 *d* before Jehovah, and his

Detected
Lu 20:23 *d* their cunning and said to
Ac 9:30 When the brothers *d* this

Detecting
Mr 12:15 *D* their hypocrisy, he said

Detection
2Sa 4:6 brother themselves escaped *d*

Detention
1Ki 22:27 in the house of *d* and feed
2Ki 17:4 bound in the house of *d*
25:27 out of the house of *d*
2Ch 18:26 fellow in the house of *d*
Isa 42:7 out of the house of *d* those
42:22 and in the houses of *d*
Jer 37:4 put him in the house of *d*
37:15 had made the house of *d*
37:18 me into the house of *d*

Determination
Nu 26:56 By the *d* of the lot one's
Ac 27:42 *d* of the soldiers to kill

Determine
Joh 19:24 *d* by lots over it whose it
Ac 23:15 to *d* more accurately the

Determined
Ge 18:21 I am quite *d* to go down
Jg 12:3 I *d* to put my soul in my own
1Sa 20:7 bad has been *d* upon by him
20:9 evil has been *d* upon by my
20:33 *d* upon by his father to put
25:17 calamity has been *d* against
2Sa 6:22 I am *d* to glorify myself
1Ki 18:1 I am *d* to give rain upon the
Es 7:7 bad had been *d* against him
Da 1:8 Daniel *d* in his heart that he
9:24 weeks that have been *d* upon
Ac 2:23 *d* counsel and foreknowledge
5:28 *d* to bring the blood of this
11:29 disciples *d*, each of them
15:37 Barnabas was *d* to take along
27:39 *d*, if they could, to beach
1Ti 6:9 those who are *d* to be rich

Detest
De 7:26 loathe it and absolutely *d* it
23:7 You must not *d* an Edomite
23:7 You must not *d* an Egyptian
Job 9:31 garments would certainly *d*
19:19 my intimate group *d* me
Ps 106:40 came to *d* his inheritance
107:18 soul got to *d* even every
Am 5:10 a speaker . . . they *d*

Detestable
Ge 43:32 a *d* thing to the Egyptians
46:34 herder of sheep is a *d* thing
Ex 8:26 a thing *d* to the Egyptians
8:26 a thing *d* to the Egyptians
Le 18:22 lie down with a male . . . *d*
18:26 not do any of all these *d*
18:27 *d* things the men of the land
18:29 any of all these *d* things
18:30 *d* customs that have been
20:13 both . . . have done a *d* thing
De 7:25 it is a thing *d* to Jehovah
7:26 must not bring a *d* thing into
12:31 everything *d* to Jehovah that
13:14 this *d* thing has been done
14:3 You must eat no *d* thing of
17:1 a thing *d* to Jehovah your God
17:4 this *d* thing has been done in
18:9 the *d* things of those nations
18:12 something *d* to Jehovah, and
18:12 on account of these *d* things
20:18 all their *d* things, which
22:5 *d* to Jehovah your God
23:18 something *d* to Jehovah your
24:4 something *d* before Jehovah
25:16 doer of injustice, is . . . *d*
27:15 a molten statue, a thing *d*
32:16 With *d* things they kept
1Ki 14:24 the *d* things of the nations
2Ki 16:3 the *d* things of the nations
21:2 the *d* things of the nations
21:11 has done these *d* things
23:13 Milcom the *d* thing of the
1Ch 21:6 king's word had been *d* to
2Ch 28:3 *d* things of the nations
33:2 *d* things of the nations that
34:33 removed all the *d* things
36:8 Jehoiakim and his *d* things
36:14 *d* things of the nations
Ezr 9:1 their *d* things, namely, the
9:11 their *d* things with which
9:14 peoples of these *d* things
Job 15:16 much less so when one is *d*
Ps 88:8 as something very *d* to them
Pr 3:32 devious person is a *d* thing
6:16 are things *d* to his soul
8:7 wickedness is something *d* to
11:1 something *d* to Jehovah, but
11:20 are something *d* to Jehovah

Pr 12:22 False lips are something *d*
13:19 *d* to the stupid ones to turn
15:8 sacrifice of the wicked . . . *d*
15:9 way of the wicked . . . *d* to
15:26 schemes of the bad . . . *d* to
16:5 proud in heart is something *d*
16:12 is something *d* to kings, for
17:15 are something *d* to Jehovah
20:10 something *d* to Jehovah
20:23 are something *d* to Jehovah
21:27 wicked ones is something *d*
24:9 ridiculer . . . *d* to mankind
26:25 seven *d* things in his heart
28:9 his prayer is something *d*
29:27 injustice is something *d* to
29:27 something *d* to a wicked one
Isa 1:13 Incense . . . is something *d*
41:24 A *d* thing is anyone that
44:19 make into a mere *d* thing
Jer 2:7 you made something *d*
6:15 something *d* that they had
7:10 doing all these *d* things
8:12 had done even what was *d*
16:18 and their *d* things they had
32:35 heart to do this *d* thing
44:4 *d* sort of thing that I have
44:22 *d* things that you had done
Eze 5:9 by reason of all your *d* things
5:11 and with all your *d* things
6:9 done in all their *d* things
6:11 bad *d* things of the house of
7:3 upon you all your *d* things
7:4 your own *d* things will come
7:8 upon you all your *d* things
7:9 your own *d* things will come
7:20 *d* images, their disgusting
8:6 *d* things they are doing, the
8:6 will see again great *d* things
8:9 see the bad *d* things that they
8:13 *d* things that they are doing
8:15 *d* things worse than these
8:17 *d* things that they have done
9:4 over all the *d* things that
11:18 all its *d* things out of it
11:21 and their *d* things, upon
12:16 recount all their *d* things
14:6 even from all your *d* things
16:2 known to Jerusalem her *d*
16:22 in all your *d* things and
16:25 your prettiness something *d*
16:36 all your *d* dungy idols, even
16:43 alongside all your *d* things
16:47 their *d* things that you did
16:50 to carry on a *d* thing before
16:51 your *d* things abound more
16:51 *d* things that you carried on
16:58 *d* things, you yourself must
18:12 a *d* thing is what he has
18:13 these *d* things he has done
18:24 *d* things that the wicked
20:4 *d* things of their forefathers
22:2 to know all her *d* things
22:11 a man has done a *d* thing
23:36 tell them their *d* things
33:26 You have done a *d* thing
33:29 *d* things that they have
36:31 on account of your *d* things
43:8 their *d* things that they did
44:6 *d* things, O house of Israel
44:7 account of all your *d* things
44:13 their *d* things that they
Mal 2:11 *d* thing has been committed
Tit 1:16 they are *d* and disobedient

Detestably
1Ki 21:26 went acting very *d* by going
Ps 14:1 have acted *d* in their dealing
53:1 acted *d* in unrighteousness
Eze 16:52 you acted more *d* than they

Detested
Job 30:10 They have *d* me, they have
Isa 14:19 like a *d* sprout, clothed
49:7 him that is *d* by the nation

Detesting
Ps 119:163 and I do keep *d* it
Am 6:8 I am *d* the pride of Jacob
Mic 3:9 the ones *d* justice and the

Detests
Ps 5:6 and deception Jehovah *d*

Deuel
Nu 1:14 of Gad, Eliasaph the son of *D*
7:42 Eliasaph the son of *D*
7:47 of Eliasaph the son of *D*
Nu 10:20 Eliasaph the son of *D*

Devastate
Isa 42:15 *d* mountains and hills, and

Devastated
2Ki 19:17 *d* the nations and their land
2Ch 34:6 their *d* places all around
Ne 2:3 places of my forefathers, is *d*
2:17 Jerusalem is *d* and its gates
Isa 37:18 Assyria have *d* all the lands
48:21 walk even through *d* places
49:19 your *d* places and your
51:3 comfort all her *d* places
52:9 you *d* places of Jerusalem
58:12 the places *d* a long time
61:4 the long-standing *d* places
61:4 make anew the *d* cities, the
Jer 7:34 become nothing but a *d* place
22:5 will become a mere *d* place
25:9 places *d* to time indefinite
25:11 land must become a *d* place
25:18 to make them a *d* place
26:9 this very city will be *d*
27:17 this city become a *d* place
44:2 they are a *d* place this day
44:6 they came to be a *d* place
44:22 land came to be a *d* place
49:13 cities will become *d* places
Eze 5:14 I shall make you a *d* place
6:6 cities will become *d* and the
6:6 in order that they may lie *d*
12:20 inhabited cities . . . be *d*
13:4 Like foxes in the *d* places
19:7 and he *d* even their cities
25:13 make it a *d* place from
26:2 be filled—she has been *d*
26:19 When I make you a *d* city
26:20 places *d* for a long time
29:9 desolate waste and a *d* place
29:10 the land of Egypt *d* places
29:12 midst of *d* cities for forty
30:7 in the midst of *d* cities
33:24 of these *d* places are
33:27 who are in the *d* places
35:4 shall set as a *d* place
36:4 *d* places that were laid
36:10 the *d* places themselves
36:33 *d* places must be rebuilt
38:8 to be a constantly *d* place
38:12 *d* places reinhabited and
Am 7:9 Israel will be *d*; and I will
Zep 3:6 I *d* their streets, so that
Mal 1:4 return and build the *d* places
Ga 1:23 the faith which he formerly *d*
Re 17:16 harlot and will make her *d*
18:17 such great riches have been *d*
18:19 in one hour she has been *d*

Devastating
Isa 49:17 tearing you down and *d* you
Ga 1:13 congregation of God and *d* it

Devastation
Isa 60:12 without fail come to *d*
64:11 things has become a *d*
Jer 49:13 *d* and a malediction will
50:38 is a *d* upon her waters
Zep 2:14 be *d* at the threshold

Devastations
Da 9:2 fulfilling the *d* of Jerusalem

Devastator
Jg 16:24 the *d* of our land and the one

Develop
Ge 41:36 *d* in the land of Egypt
Ex 16:24 nor did maggots *d* in it
Le 13:2 does *d* in the skin of his
13:38 blotches *d* in the skin of
13:49 plague does *d* in the garment
13:52 in which the plague may *d*
De 5:29 *d* this heart of theirs to fear
Jg 9:23 let *d* a bad spirit between
2Sa 2:26 bitterness is what will *d*
1Co 15:37 not the body that will *d*
Heb 3:12 *d* in any one of you a wicked

Developed
Ge 25:11 it *d* that after Abraham's
38:27 it *d* that in the time of her
38:29 it *d* that as soon as he drew
41:8 *d* in the morning that his
41:54 famine *d* in all the lands
Ex 9:11 boils had *d* on . . . Egyptians
16:13 *d* a layer of dew round about
Le 13:19 a white eruption has *d* or a
Le 13:32 no yellow hair has *d* in it
1Sa 14:15 *d* into a trembling from God
2Ch 16:12 *d* an ailment in his feet
Eze 16:7 breasts . . . were firmly *d*
Joh 7:43 a division over him *d* among

Developing
De 31:21 inclination that they are *d*

Develops
Le 13:2 *d* in the skin of his flesh an
13:9 plague of leprosy *d* in a man
13:18 in case a boil *d* in its skin
13:29 in case a plague *d* in such
13:42 plague *d* in the baldness of
13:47 plague of leprosy *d* in it

Deviate
Job 23:11 I have kept, and I do not *d*
Ps 44:18 footsteps *d* from your path
Isa 30:11 the way; *d* from the path

Deviated
Ps 119:51 From your law I have not *d*
119:157 reminders I have not *d*
Ac 1:25 Judas *d* to go to his own
1Ti 6:21 some have *d* from the faith
2Ti 2:18 men have *d* from the truth

Deviates
Job 31:7 my stepping *d* from the way

Deviating
1Ti 1:6 By *d* from these things

Device
2Ch 2:14 at designing every sort of *d*
Job 18:10 catching *d* for him on his
Ps 64:6 They have hidden a shrewd *d*
Jer 11:15 do this thing, the evil *d*
Mt 26:4 to seize Jesus by crafty *d*
Mr 14:1 to seize him by crafty *d*
Ac 8:22 the *d* of your heart may be

Devices
Ex 31:4 designing *d*, for working in
35:32 designing *d*, for working in
35:35 men . . . designing *d*

Devil
Mt 4:1 to be tempted by the *D*
4:5 *D* took him along into the holy
4:8 the *D* took him along to an
4:11 the *D* left him, and, look!
13:39 that sowed them is the *D*
25:41 fire prepared for the *D* and
Lu 4:2 while being tempted by the *D*
4:3 the *D* said to him: If you are
4:6 the *D* said to him: I will give
4:13 So the *D*, having concluded all
8:12 *D* comes and takes the word
Joh 8:44 are from your father the *D*
13:2 *D* having already put it into
Ac 10:38 all those oppressed by the *D*
13:10 you son of the *D*, you enemy
Eph 4:27 neither allow place for the *D*
6:11 the machinations of the *D*
1Ti 3:6 judgment passed upon the *D*
3:7 reproach and a snare of the *D*
2Ti 2:26 out from the snare of the *D*
Heb 2:14 cause death, that is, the *D*
Jas 4:7 oppose the *D* . . . he will flee
1Pe 5:8 Your adversary, the *D*, walks
1Jo 3:8 sin originates with the *D*
3:8 *D* has been sinning from the
3:8 break up the works of the *D*
3:10 the children of the *D* are
Jude 9 had a difference with the *D*
Re 2:10 *D* will keep on throwing some
12:9 one called *D* and Satan, who
12:12 *D* has come down to you
20:2 serpent, who is the *D* and
20:10 *D* who was misleading them

Devious
Pr 2:15 are *d* in their general course
3:32 *d* person is a detestable
Isa 30:12 what is *d* and you support

Deviousness
Pr 4:24 *d* of lips put far away from

Devised
Am 6:5 *d* for themselves instruments

Devising
Job 4:8 those *d* what is hurtful And
Pr 14:22 *d* mischief go wandering
14:22 as regards those *d* good
Ec 9:10 no work nor *d* nor knowledge

Devolve
1Ki 4:7 *d* upon each one to provide the
Eze 45:17 upon the chieftain will *d*

Devolved
Ne 13:13 it *d* to do the distributing

Devolves
Ezr 7:20 that it *d* upon you to give
10:4 for the matter *d* upon you
10:12 your word it *d* upon us to

Devote
Ex 13:12 *d* everyone that opens the
Le 27:28 *d* to Jehovah for destruction
Nu 21:2 *d* their cities to destruction
De 7:2 *d* them to destruction
13:15 *D* it and everything that is
20:17 *d* them to destruction, the
Jos 11:20 might *d* them to destruction
Jg 1:17 Zephath and to *d* it to
21:11 you should *d* to destruction
1Sa 15:3 and *d* him to destruction
15:9 to *d* them to destruction
15:18 and you must *d* the sinners
30:17 *d* them to destruction; and
1Ki 9:21 unable to *d* to destruction
2Ch 20:23 *d* them to destruction and
Isa 34:2 *d* them to destruction
Jer 25:9 I will *d* them to destruction
50:26 and *d* her to destruction
51:3 *D* to destruction all her
Da 11:44 to *d* many to destruction
Mic 4:13 *d* to Jehovah their unjust
Ac 6:4 *d* ourselves to prayer and to
1Co 7:5 may *d* time to prayer and may

Devoted
Ex 22:20 is to be *d* to destruction
Le 27:21 as a field that is *d*
27:28 *d* thing that a man might
27:28 *d* thing may be bought back
27:29 *d* person who might be
27:29 person who might be *d* to
Nu 18:14 Every *d* thing in Israel
21:3 *d* them and their cities to
De 3:6 we *d* them to destruction, just
7:26 a thing *d* to destruction
7:26 something *d* to destruction
Jos 2:10 whom you *d* to destruction
6:17 a thing *d* to destruction
6:18 the thing *d* to destruction
6:18 the thing *d* to destruction
6:18 a thing *d* to destruction and
7:1 the thing *d* to destruction in
7:1 of the thing *d* to destruction
7:11 the thing *d* to destruction
7:12 a thing *d* to destruction
7:12 the thing *d* to destruction
7:13 A thing *d* to destruction is
7:13 the thing *d* to destruction
7:15 the thing *d* to destruction
8:26 *d* all the inhabitants of Ai
10:1 and then *d* it to destruction
10:28 he *d* him and every soul
10:35 *d* every soul that was in it
10:37 he *d* it and every soul that
10:40 he *d* to destruction, just
11:12 He *d* them to destruction
11:21 *d* them to destruction
22:20 the thing *d* to destruction
1Sa 15:8 people he *d* to destruction
15:9 these they *d* to destruction
15:15 we have *d* to destruction
15:20 I have *d* to destruction
15:21 something *d* to destruction
1Ki 20:42 man *d* to me for destruction
1Ch 2:7 the thing *d* to destruction
4:41 they *d* them to destruction
2Ch 32:14 forefathers *d* to destruction
Isa 34:5 *d* by me to destruction
43:28 as a man *d* to destruction
Eze 44:29 every *d* thing in Israel

Devoting
Le 18:21 *d* of any of your offspring
De 2:34 *d* every city to destruction
3:6 in *d* every city to destruction
Jos 6:21 *d* all that was in the city
10:39 *d* every soul that was in it
11:11 *d* them to destruction
2Ki 19:11 by *d* them to destruction
Isa 37:11 by *d* them to destruction
Jer 50:21 *d* to destruction close upon
Mal 4:6 with a *d* of it to destruction
Ac 2:42 *d* themselves to the teaching

Devotion
Ex 20:5 am a God exacting exclusive *d*
Nu 25:11 my insistence on exclusive *d*
De 4:24 a God exacting exclusive *d*
5:9 a God exacting exclusive *d*
6:15 a God exacting exclusive *d*
Jos 24:19 God exacting exclusive *d*
Ec 12:12 much *d* to them is wearisome
Ca 8:6 insistence on exclusive *d* is as
Eze 5:13 my insistence on exclusive *d*
39:25 exclusive *d* for my holy
Na 1:2 a God exacting exclusive *d*
Ac 3:12 godly *d* we have made him
17:23 unknowingly giving godly *d*
1Ti 2:2 full godly *d* and seriousness
3:16 sacred secret of this godly *d*
4:7 with godly *d* as your aim
4:8 godly *d* is beneficial for all
5:4 learn first to practice godly *d*
6:3 that accords with godly *d*
6:5 thinking that godly *d* is a
6:6 this godly *d* along with
6:11 pursue righteousness, godly *d*
2Ti 3:5 having a form of godly *d* but
3:12 to live with godly *d*
Tit 1:1 which accords with godly *d*
2:12 godly *d* amid this present
2Pe 1:3 concern life and godly *d*
1:6 to your endurance godly *d*
1:7 to your godly *d* brotherly
2:9 deliver people of godly *d*
3:11 and deeds of godly *d*

Devour
De 28:38 because the locust will *d* it
Job 20:21 nothing left over . . . to *d*
Ps 21:9 and the fire will *d* them
Pr 30:8 *d* the food prescribed for me
Isa 31:8 of earthling man, will *d*
Jer 5:14 and it will certainly *d* them
17:27 *d* the dwelling towers of
21:14 *d* all the things round about
46:10 sword will certainly *d* and
46:14 sword will certainly *d* all
48:45 *d* the temples of Moab and
49:27 *d* the dwelling towers of
50:32 must *d* all its surroundings
Eze 7:15 famine and pestilence . . . *d*
15:7 the fire itself will *d* them
20:47 and it must *d* in you every
21:28 to *d*, in order to glitter
22:25 A soul they actually *d*
28:18 It is what must *d* you
34:28 it will not *d* them, and
36:14 you will no more *d*, and
Da 7:23 it will *d* all the earth and
Ho 2:12 wild beast . . . *d* them
5:7 *d* them with their portions
7:7 they actually *d* their judges
8:14 must *d* the dwelling towers
11:6 *d* because of their counsels
13:8 *d* them there like a lion
Am 1:4 and it must *d* the dwelling
1:7 must *d* her dwelling towers
1:10 must *d* her dwelling towers
1:12 must *d* the dwelling towers
1:14 must *d* her dwelling towers
2:2 it must *d* the dwelling towers
2:5 it must *d* the dwelling towers
4:9 trees the caterpillar would *d*
5:6 and it may not actually *d*
Ob 18 set them ablaze and *d* them
Na 2:13 *d* your own maned young lions
3:13 Fire will certainly *d* your
3:15 Even there fire will *d* you
3:15 *d* you like the locust species
Zec 9:15 *d* and subdue the slingstones
11:1 fire may *d* among your cedars
11:9 let them *d*, each one the
12:6 must *d* on the right hand and
Mal 4:1 certainly *d* them, Jehovah
Lu 20:47 *d* the houses of the widows
1Pe 5:8 lion, seeking to *d* someone
Re 12:4 birth, it might *d* her child

Devoured
Ge 37:20 a vicious wild beast *d* him
37:33 wild beast must have *d* him
Jer 2:30 Your sword has *d* your
30:16 be *d*; and as for all your
50:17 king of Assyria has *d* him
La 2:3 fire that has *d* all around
Eze 15:5 when fire itself has *d* it
16:20 to be *d*—is that not enough
Eze 19:3 He *d* even earthling man
19:6 He *d* even earthling man
19:12 Fire itself *d* it
19:14 It *d* her very shoots, her
23:25 you will be *d* by the fire
Joe 1:19 fire itself has *d* the pasture
1:20 fire itself has *d* the pasture
2:3 Ahead of it a fire has *d*
Na 1:10 *d* like stubble fully dry
Zep 1:18 the whole earth will be *d*
3:8 all the earth will be *d*
Zec 9:4 in the fire she . . . will be *d*
Re 20:9 fire . . . out of heaven and *d*

Devourer
Eze 36:13 A *d* of humankind is what

Devourers
Ps 57:4 I cannot but lie down among *d*

Devouring
Ex 24:17 a *d* fire on the mountaintop
2Sa 22:9 fire itself . . . kept *d*
Ps 18:8 fire . . . from his mouth kept *d*
52:4 You have loved all *d* words
104:4 His ministers a *d* fire
106:18 went *d* the wicked ones
Isa 29:6 and the flame of a *d* fire
30:27 his tongue is like a *d* fire
30:30 flame of a *d* fire and
33:14 any time with a *d* fire
Jer 2:3 Any persons *d* him would make
12:12 *d* from one end of the land
30:16 those *d* you will themselves
Da 7:7 It was *d* and crushing, and
7:19 which was *d* and crushing
Ho 4:8 sin . . . is what they keep *d*
Joe 2:5 fire that is *d* stubble
Hab 3:14 bent on *d* an afflicted one
Mal 3:11 rebuke for you the *d* one
Mr 12:40 *d* the houses of the widows
Ga 5:15 you keep on biting and *d* one

Devours
Ps 50:3 Before him there *d* a fire
Eze 15:4 the fire certainly *d*, and the
2Co 11:20 whoever *d* what you have
Re 11:5 fire . . . *d* their enemies

Devout
Ac 10:2 *d* man and one fearing God
10:7 *d* soldier from among those

Dew
Ge 27:39 away from the *d* of the
Ex 16:13 a layer of *d* round about the
16:14 the layer of *d* evaporated and
Nu 11:9 *d* descended upon the camp by
De 32:2 saying will trickle as the *d*
33:13 things of heaven, with *d*
33:28 will let the *d* drip down
Jg 6:37 *d* comes to be on the fleece
6:38 drain off enough *d* from the
6:39 earth let there come to be *d*
6:40 upon all the earth *d* occurred
2Sa 1:21 let no *d*, let no rain be
17:12 the *d* falls upon the ground
1Ki 17:1 neither *d* nor rain, except
Job 29:19 And *d* itself will stay
Ps 133:3 It is like the *d* of Hermon
Pr 19:12 his goodwill is like the *d*
Ca 5:2 For my head is filled with *d*
Isa 18:4 cloud of *d* in the heat of
26:19, 19 *d* . . . the *d* of mallows
Da 4:15 with the *d* of the heavens let
4:23 with the *d* of the heavens let
4:25 with the *d* of the heavens you
4:33 with the *d* of the heavens his
5:21 with the *d* of the heavens his
Ho 6:4 the *d* that early goes away
13:3 the *d* that early goes away
14:5 become like the *d* to Israel
Mic 5:7 peoples like *d* from Jehovah
Hag 1:10 heavens kept back their *d*
Zec 8:12 heavens . . . give their *d*

Dewdrops
Job 38:28 Or who gave birth to the *d*?
Ps 110:3 of young men just like *d*

Dews
Ge 27:28 God give you the *d* of the

Diadem
2Sa 1:10 *d* that was upon his head and
2Ki 11:12 the *d* and the Testimony
2Ch 23:11 put upon him the *d* and the
Ps 89:39 profaned his *d* to the very

Ps 132:18 his *d* will flourish
Pr 27:24 nor a *d* for all generations
Zec 9:16 the stones of a *d* glittering

Diadems
Re 12:3 and upon its heads seven *d*
13:1 and upon its horns ten *d*
19:12 upon his head are many *d*

Dialect
Mt 26:73 your *d* gives you away

Diamond
Jer 17:1 With a *d* point it is
Eze 3:9 Like a *d*, harder than flint, I

Diblah
Eze 6:14 than the wilderness toward *D*

Diblaim
Ho 1:3 Gomer the daughter of *D*, so

Dibon
Nu 21:30 certainly perish up to *D*
32:3 Ataroth and *D* and Jazer and
32:34 build *D* and Ataroth and Aroer
Jos 13:9 Medeba as far as *D*
13:17 *D* and Bamoth-baal and
Ne 11:25 in *D* and its dependent towns
Isa 15:2 up to The House and to *D*
Jer 48:18 of the daughter of *D*
48:22 against *D* and against Nebo

Dibon-gad
Nu 33:45 and went camping in *D*
33:46 pulled away from *D* and went

Dibri
Le 24:11 Shelomith, the daughter of *D*

Dictator
Isa 3:6 *d* you ought to become to us
3:7 set me as *d* over the people

Dictators
Isa 1:10 you *d* of Sodom. Give ear to
22:3 *d* themselves have fled at

Die
Ge 2:17 you will positively *d*
3:3 not touch it that you do not *d*
3:4 You positively will not *d*
19:19 to me and I certainly *d*
20:7 *d*, you and all who are
25:32 Here I am simply going to *d*
26:9 I said it for fear I should *d*
27:4 soul may bless you before I *d*
33:13 whole flock will certainly *d*
38:11 too may *d* like his brothers
42:2 may keep alive and not *d* off
42:20 and you will not *d*
43:8 keep alive and not *d* off
44:9 with whom it may be found *d*
44:22 he would certainly *d*
44:31 he will simply *d*, and your
45:28 go and see him before I *d*
46:30 This time I am willing to *d*
47:15 why should we *d* in front of
47:19 should we *d* before your eyes
47:19 that we may live and not *d*
47:29 the days . . . for Israel to *d*
Ex 7:18 fish . . . Nile River will *d*
8:13 frogs began to *d* off from the
9:4 to the sons of Israel will *d*
9:6 livestock of Egypt began to *d*
9:19 and they will have to *d*
10:28 seeing my face you will *d*
11:5 every firstborn . . . must *d*
14:11 here to *d* in the wilderness
14:12 us to *d* in the wilderness
20:19 with us for fear we may *d*
21:14 from being at my altar to *d*
21:18 he does not *d* but must keep
21:35 and it does *d*, then they
22:2 and he does get struck and *d*
22:10 and it does *d* or get maimed
22:14 or *d* while its owner is not
28:35 comes out, that he may not *d*
28:43 incur error and certainly *d*
30:20 that they may not *d*
30:21 wash . . . that they may not *d*
Le 8:35 that you may not *d*; for so I
10:6 that you may not *d* and that
10:7 not go out for fear you may *d*
10:9 meeting, that you may not *d*
11:39 should *d*, he who touches
15:31 that they may not *d* in their
16:2 the Ark, that he may not *d*
16:13 that he may not *d*
Le 20:20 sin. They should *d* childless
22:9 *d* for it because they were
Nu 4:15 so that they have to *d*
4:19 not *d* for their approaching
4:20 and so they have to *d*
6:7 defile himself when they *d*
6:9 *d* quite suddenly alongside him
14:35 and there they will *d*
14:37 will *d* by the scourge before
16:29 these people will *d* and with
17:10 that they may not *d*
17:13 will *d!* Must we end up in
18:3 come near that they may not *d*
18:22 to incur sin so as to *d*
18:32 that you may not *d*
19:13 soul of whatever man may *d*
19:14 a man should *d* in a tent
20:4 beasts of burden to *d* there
20:26 Aaron . . . must *d* there
21:5 us up out of Egypt to *d* in the
23:10 *d* the death of the upright
26:11 the sons of Korah did not *d*
26:65 They will *d* without fail in
27:8 *d* without his having a son
33:38 *d* there in the fortieth year
35:12 that the manslayer may not *d*
35:17 stone by which he could *d*
35:18 wood by which he could *d*
35:20 that he might *d*
35:21 he might *d*, without fail
35:23 stone by which he could *d*
35:30 against a soul for him to *d*
35:31 who is deserving to *d*, for
De 5:25 why should we *d*, for this
5:25 we are also certain to *d*
13:10 and he must *d*, because he
17:5 and such one must *d*
17:12 that man must *d*; and you
18:16 that I may not *d*
18:20 that prophet must *d*
19:12 and he must *d*
20:5 he may *d* in the battle and
20:6 he may *d* in the battle and
20:7 he may *d* in the battle and
21:21 with stones, and he must *d*
22:21 she must *d*, because she has
22:22 both of them must then *d*
22:24 they must *d*, the girl for
22:25 must also *d* by himself
24:3 in case the latter . . . should *d*
24:7 that kidnapper must also *d*
31:14 have drawn near for you to *d*
32:50 Then *d* on the mountain
33:6 Let Reuben live and not *d* off
Jos 2:14 Our souls are to *d* instead
20:9 not *d* by the hand of the
Jg 6:23 Do not fear. You will not *d*
6:30 your son out that he may *d*
13:22 We shall positively *d*
15:18 shall I *d* of thirst and must
16:30 Let my soul *d* with the
Ru 1:17, 17 Where you *d* I shall *d*
1Sa 2:33 all *d* by the sword of men
2:34 one day both of them will *d*
5:12 men that did not *d* had been
12:19 as we do not want to *d*
14:39 yet he will positively *d*
14:43 Here I am! Let me *d*
14:44 if you do not positively *d*
14:45 Is Jonathan to *d*, who has
14:45 Jonathan, and he did not *d*
20:2 You will not *d*. Look! My
20:14 toward me, that I may not *d*
22:16 positively *d*, Ahimelech
26:10 and he will have to *d*
26:16 you men deserve to *d*
31:6 *d* together on that day
2Sa 3:33 should Abner *d*
10:1 came to *d*, and Hanun his son
11:15 must be struck down and *d*
12:5 man doing this deserves to *d*
12:13 sin pass by. You will not *d*
12:14 son . . . will positively *d*
14:14 *d* without fail and be like
18:3 and if half of us would *d*
19:23 to Shimei: You will not *d*
19:37 let me *d* in my city close
1Ki 1:52 he will also have to *d*
2:1 drew near for him to *d*
2:30 For here is where I shall *d*
2:37 that you will positively *d*
2:42 that you will positively *d*
13:31 I *d* you must bury me in the
14:12 the child will certainly *d*
1Ki 17:12 shall have to eat it and *d*
19:4 ask that his soul might *d*
21:10 and stone him that he may *d*
2Ki 1:4 because you will positively *d*
1:6 because you will positively *d*
1:16 you will positively *d*
7:4 we would also have to *d* there
7:4 we shall also have to *d*
7:4 then we shall have to *d*
8:10 that he will positively *d*
9:27 Megiddo and got to *d* there
13:14 with which he was to *d*
18:32 living that you may not *d*
20:1 indeed *d* and will not live
1Ch 19:1 king . . . of Ammon came to *d*
2Ch 25:4 Fathers should not *d* for sons
25:4 sons themselves *d* for
25:4 own sin that they should *d*
32:11 *d* by famine and by thirst
Job 2:9 Curse God and *d*
3:11 did I not proceed to *d*
4:21 They *d* for lack of wisdom
12:2 with you wisdom will *d* out
21:23 one will *d* during his full
21:25 will *d* with a bitter soul
34:20 In a moment they *d*, even
36:14 Their soul will *d* in youth
Ps 41:5 When will he *d* and his name
48:14 will guide us until we *d*
49:10 that even the wise ones *d*
82:7 you will *d* just as men do
118:17 I shall not *d*, but I shall
Pr 5:23 one to *d* because there is no
15:10 anyone hating reproof will *d*
23:13 with the rod, he will not *d*
30:7 them from me before I *d*
Ec 2:16 and how will the wise one *d?*
3:2 time for birth and a time to *d*
7:17 *d* when it is not your time
9:5 are conscious that they will *d*
Isa 22:13 for tomorrow we shall *d*
22:14 behalf until you people *d*
22:18 There you will *d*, and
38:1 indeed *d* and will not live
50:2 and they *d* because of thirst
51:6 will *d* like a mere gnat
51:12 a mortal man that will *d*
59:5 would *d*, and the egg that
65:20 one will *d* as a mere boy
66:24 worms upon them will not *d*
Jer 11:21 you may not *d* at our hand
11:22 will *d* by the sword
11:22 will *d* by the famine
16:4 from maladies they will *d*
16:6 they will certainly *d*, the
20:6 and there you will *d* and
21:6 great pestilence they will *d*
21:9 will *d* by the sword and by
22:12 he will *d*, and this land he
22:26 there is where you will *d*
26:8 You will positively *d*
27:13 your people *d* by the sword
28:16 you yourself must *d*, for
31:30 own error that one will *d*
34:4 You will not *d* by the sword
34:5 In peace you will *d*; and as
37:20 that I may not *d* there
38:2 one that will *d* by the sword
38:9 he will *d* where he is
38:24 so that you do not *d*
38:26 house of Jehonathan to *d*
42:16 there is where you will *d*
42:17 ones to *d* by the sword, by
42:22 you will *d* in the place
44:12 by the famine they will *d*
Eze 3:18 You will positively *d*, and
3:18 in his error he will *d*, but
3:19 for his error will *d*
3:20 *d* because you did not warn
3:20 For his sin he will *d*, and
5:12 the pestilence they will *d*
6:12 by the pestilence he will *d*
6:12 by the famine he will *d*, and
7:15 by the sword he will *d*, and
12:13 Babylon . . . there he will *d*
13:19 souls that ought not to *d*
17:16 midst of Babylon he will *d*
18:4 soul that is sinning . . . *d*
18:17 not *d* because of the error
18:18 he must *d* for his error
18:20 soul that is sinning . . . *d*
18:21 keep living. He will not *d*
18:24 sinned, for them he will *d*
18:26 for his injustice . . . *d*

Eze 18:28 keep living. He will not *d*
18:31 why should you *d,* O house
28:8 *d* the death of someone slain
28:10 *d* by the hand of strangers
33:8 you will positively *d!*
33:8 will *d* in his own error
33:9 will *d* in his own error
33:11 that you should *d,* O house
33:13 for this he will *d*
33:14 You will positively *d,* and
33:15 keep living. He will not *d*
33:18 he must also *d* for them
33:27 will *d* by the pestilence
Ho 13:1 guilty in regard to Baal and *d*
Am 2:2 and with noise Moab must *d*
6:9 in one house, they must also *d*
7:11 By the sword Jeroboam will *d*
7:17 on unclean ground you will *d*
9:10 By the sword they will *d*
Jon 4:8 asking that his soul might *d*
Hab 1:12 my Holy One, you do not *d*
Zec 11:9 one that is dying, let her *d*
Mt 9:24 the little girl did not *d*
26:35 I should have to *d* with you
Mr 9:48 their maggot does not *d*
14:31 If I have to *d* with you, I
Lu 8:52 she did not *d* but is sleeping
20:36 neither can they *d* anymore
Joh 6:50 may eat of it and not *d*
8:21 yet you will *d* in your sin
8:24 You will *d* in your sins
8:24 you will *d* in your sins
11:16 go, that we may *d* with him
11:26 faith in me will never *d*
11:50 one man to *d* in behalf of
11:51 Jesus was destined to *d* for
12:33 of death he was about to *d*
18:14 *d* in behalf of the people
18:32 death he was destined to *d*
19:7 he ought to *d,* because he
21:23 that disciple would not *d*
21:23 to him that he would not *d*
Ac 9:37 happened to fall sick and *d*
21:13 also to *d* at Jerusalem for
Ro 5:7 anyone *d* for a righteous man
5:7 someone even dares to *d*
8:13 the flesh you are sure to *d*
14:8, 8 if we *d,* we *d* to Jehovah
14:8 both if we live and if we *d*
1Co 9:15 be finer for me to *d* than
15:32 for tomorrow we are to *d*
2Co 7:3 to *d* and to live with us
Php 1:21 to live is Christ, and to *d*
Heb 9:27 men to *d* once for all time
11:21 Jacob, when about to *d*
Re 3:2 that were ready to *d,* for I
9:6 they will desire to *d* but
14:13 dead who *d* in union with the

Died

Ge 5:5 Adam . . . years and he *d*
5:8 Seth . . . years and he *d*
5:11 Enosh . . . years and he *d*
5:14 Kenan . . . years and he *d*
5:17 Mahalalel . . . years and he *d*
5:20 Jared . . . years and he *d*
5:27 of Methuselah . . . and he *d*
5:31 seventy-seven years and he *d*
7:22 all . . . on the dry ground, *d*
9:29 days of Noah . . . and he *d*
11:28 Later Haran *d* while in
11:32 Then Terah *d* in Haran
23:2 Sarah *d* in Kiriath-arba, that
25:8 Abraham expired and *d* in a
25:17 Then he expired and *d* and
35:8 nursing woman of Rebekah *d*
35:18 soul was going out . . . she *d*
35:19 Rachel *d* and was buried on
35:29 Isaac expired and *d* and was
36:33 When Bela *d,* Jobab son of
36:34 When Jobab *d,* Husham from
36:35 When Husham *d,* Hadad son of
36:36 When Hadad *d,* Samlah from
36:37 When Samlah *d,* Shaul from
36:38 When Shaul *d,* Baal-hanan
36:39 Baal-hanan son of Achbor *d*
38:12 Judah's wife, *d;* and Judah
46:12 Onan *d* in the land of Canaan
48:7 Rachel *d* alongside me in the
50:26 Joseph *d* at the age of
Ex 1:6 Joseph *d,* and also all his
2:23 the king of Egypt finally *d*
7:21 fish . . . in the Nile River *d*
9:6 not one of the livestock . . . *d*
9:7 not so much as one . . . had *d*
Ex 16:3 If only we had *d* by Jehovah's
Le 10:2 that they *d* before Jehovah
16:1 before Jehovah so that they *d*
Nu 3:4 Nadab and Abihu *d* before
14:2 If only we had *d* in the land
14:2 we had *d* in this wilderness
15:36 pelted him . . . so that he *d*
20:1 It was there that Miriam *d*
20:28 Aaron *d* there on the top of
21:6 that many people of Israel *d*
25:9 those who *d* from the scourge
26:10 As for Korah, he *d* at the
26:19 Onan *d* in the land of Canaan
26:61 Nadab and Abihu *d* for their
27:3 has *d* in the wilderness, and
27:3 but for his own sin he has *d*
35:23 fall upon him, so that he *d*
De 10:6 There Aaron *d,* and he got to
19:5 hit his fellowman and . . . *d*
19:11 struck his soul . . . he has *d*
25:5 *d* without his having a son
32:50 your brother *d* on Mount Hor
34:5 *d* there in the land of Moab
Jos 5:4 had *d* in the wilderness on
10:11 so that they *d*
10:11 who *d* from the hailstones
24:29 Joshua . . . *d* at the age of
24:33 Eleazar the son of Aaron *d*
Jg 1:7 to Jerusalem and he *d* there
2:8 servant of Jehovah, *d* at the
2:19 when the judge *d* they would
2:21 Joshua left behind when he *d*
3:11 Othniel the son of Kenaz *d*
4:21 asleep and weary. So he *d*
8:32 son of Joash *d* at a good old
8:33 Gideon had *d* the sons of
9:49 *d* too, about a thousand men
9:54 ran him through, so that he *d*
9:55 Abimelech had *d,* they now
10:2 he *d* and was buried in Shamir
10:5 Jair *d* and was buried in
12:7 Jephthah . . . *d* and was buried
12:10 Ibzan *d* and was buried in
12:12 Elon . . . *d* and was buried in
12:15 Abdon . . . *d* and was buried
20:5 raped, and she gradually *d*
Ru 1:3 the husband of Naomi *d*
1:5 Mahlon and Chilion, also *d,* so
1Sa 4:11 Hophni and Phinehas, *d*
4:17 your own two sons have *d*
4:18 neck got broken so that he *d*
4:19 and her husband had *d*
17:51 that their mighty one had *d*
25:1 Samuel *d;* and all Israel
25:38 struck Nabal, so that he *d*
25:39 hear that Nabal had *d,* and
28:3 Samuel himself had *d,* and
31:5 saw that Saul had *d,* then
31:5 upon his own sword and *d*
31:7 Saul and his sons had *d,* then
2Sa 1:4 fallen so that they *d,* and
1:4 and Jonathan his son have *d*
1:5 Saul has *d* and also Jonathan
1:15 struck him down so that he *d*
2:23 fell there and *d* where he
2:23 Asahel fell and then *d*
2:31 hundred and sixty men that *d*
3:27 in the abdomen, so that he *d*
4:1 that Abner had *d* in Hebron
6:7 *d* there close by the ark of
10:18 struck down so that he *d*
11:17 Uriah the Hittite also *d*
11:21 so that he *d* at Thebez
11:21 servant Uriah the Hittite *d*
11:24 servants of the king *d*
11:24 Uriah the Hittite also *d*
11:26 Uriah her husband had *d*
12:18 that the child gradually *d*
12:18 that the child had *d*
12:18 say to him, The child has *d*
12:19 discern that the child had *d*
12:19 Has the child *d?*
12:19 this they said: He has *d*
12:21 child had *d* you got up and
12:23 he has *d,* why is it I am
13:32 is Amnon alone that has *d*
13:33 sons themselves have *d*
13:33 is Amnon alone that has *d*
17:23 strangled himself and . . . *d*
18:20 the king's own son has *d*
18:33 O that I might have *d*
19:10 he has *d* in the battle
20:10 So he *d.* And Joab and
24:15 seventy thousand persons *d*
1Ki 2:25 fall upon him, so that he *d*
2:46 fell upon him, so that he *d*
3:19 the son of this woman *d* at
11:21 the chief of the army had *d*
12:18 pelted him . . . so that he *d*
14:17 the boy himself *d*
16:18 with fire, so that he *d*
21:13 with stones, so that he *d*
21:15 been stoned so that he *d*
22:35 he *d* in the evening
22:37 Thus the king *d*
2Ki 1:17 he gradually *d,* according
3:5 as soon as Ahab *d,* the king
4:20 and gradually he *d*
7:3 sitting here until we have *d*
7:17 so that he *d,* just as the
7:20 in the gateway, so that he *d*
8:15 over his face, so that he *d*
11:1 she saw that her son had *d*
12:21 struck him . . . so that he *d*
13:20 Elisha *d* and they buried
13:24 Hazael the king of Syria *d*
23:34 where he eventually *d*
25:25 Gedaliah, so that he *d*
1Ch 1:44 Bela *d,* and Jobab the son of
1:45 Jobab *d,* and Husham from the
1:46 Husham *d,* and Hadad the son
1:47 Hadad *d,* and Samlah from
1:48 Samlah *d,* and Shaul from
1:49 Shaul *d,* and Baal-hanan the
1:50 Baal-hanan *d,* and Hadad began
1:51 Eventually Hadad *d*
2:19 Azubah *d.* So Caleb took to
2:30 But Seled *d* without sons
2:32 But Jether *d* without sons
10:5 saw that Saul had *d,* then he
10:5 fell upon the sword and *d*
10:6 Saul and three sons of his *d*
10:6 those of his house *d* together
10:7 that Saul and his sons had *d*
10:13 Thus Saul *d* for his
13:10 and he *d* there before God
23:22 Eleazar *d;* and he had come
24:2 Abihu *d* before their father
29:28 he *d* in a good old age
2Ch 10:18 with stones, so that he *d*
13:20 a blow, so that he *d*
16:13 *d* in the forty-first year
18:34 *d* at the time of the
21:19 *d* in his bad maladies
22:10 she saw that her son had *d*
24:15 *d,* being a hundred and
24:25 own couch, so that he *d*
35:24 he *d* and was buried in the
Job 1:19 the young people and they *d*
42:17 Job *d,* old and satisfied
Ec 4:2 the dead who had already *d*
Isa 6:1 year that King Uzziah *d* I
14:28 year that King Ahaz *d* this
Jer 28:17 Hananiah the prophet *d* in
Eze 11:13 son of Benaiah himself *d*
24:18 wife gradually *d* in the
Mt 8:32 the sea and *d* in the waters
22:27 Last of all the woman *d*
Mr 5:35 Your daughter *d!* Why bother
5:39 young child has not *d,* but is
12:20 he *d* he left no offspring
12:21 the second took her, but *d*
12:22 the woman also *d*
15:44 whether he had already *d*
Lu 8:49 Your daughter has *d;* do not
8:53 they knew she had *d*
16:22 course of time the beggar *d*
16:22 rich man *d* and was buried
20:29 took a wife and *d* childless
20:31 children behind, but *d* off
20:32 Lastly, the woman also *d*
Joh 6:49 ate the manna . . . yet *d*
6:58 forefathers ate and yet *d*
8:52 Abraham *d,* also the prophets
8:53 our father Abraham, who *d*
8:53 Also, the prophets *d.* Who do
11:14 outspokenly: Lazarus has *d*
11:21 my brother would not have *d*
11:32 my brother would not have *d*
Ac 7:4 his father *d,* God caused him
Ro 5:6 Christ . . . *d* for ungodly men
5:8 yet sinners, Christ *d* for us
5:15 by one man's trespass many *d*
6:2 we *d* with reference to sin
6:7 who has *d* has been acquitted
6:8 if we have *d* with Christ, we
6:10 For the death that he *d,* he
6:10 he *d* with reference to sin

Ro 7:6 *d* to that by which we were
7:9 came to life again, but I *d*
8:34 Jesus is the one who *d*, yes
14:9 Christ *d* and came to life
14:15 that one for whom Christ *d*
1Co 8:11 for whose sake Christ *d*
15:3 that Christ *d* for our sins
2Co 5:14 one man *d* for all; so
5:14 so, then, all had *d*
5:15 he *d* for all that those who
5:15 *d* for them and was raised
Ga 2:19 through law I *d* toward law
2:21 Christ actually *d* for nothing
Col 2:20 you *d* together with Christ
3:3 For you *d*, and your life has
1Th 4:14 if our faith is that Jesus *d*
5:10 He *d* for us, that, whether
2Ti 2:11 *d* together, we shall also
Heb 11:4 although he *d*, yet speaks
11:13 In faith all these *d*
11:37 they *d* by slaughter with
1Pe 3:18 Christ *d* once for all time
Jude 12 fruitless, having *d* twice
Re 8:9 which have souls *d*, and a
8:11 of the men *d* from the waters
16:3 every living soul *d*, yes, the

Dies
Ge 21:16 not see it when the child *d*
Ex 21:12 so that he actually *d* is to
21:20 actually *d* under his hand
21:28 actually *d*, the bull is to be
Nu 35:16 has struck him so that he *d*
35:17 has struck him so that he *d*
35:18 has struck him so that he *d*
Job 14:8 And in the dust its stump *d*
14:10 man *d* and lies vanquished
14:14 man *d* can he live again
Pr 11:7 wicked man *d*, his hope
Ec 3:19, 19 the one *d*, so the other *d*
Jer 38:10 of the cistern before he *d*
Eze 18:26 does injustice and *d* on
Mt 22:24 *d* without having children
Mr 12:19 if someone's brother *d* and
Lu 20:28 If a man's brother *d* having
Joh 4:49 before my young child *d*
11:25 he *d*, will come to life
12:24 falls into the ground and *d*
12:24 if it *d*, it then bears much
Ro 6:9 Christ . . . *d* no more; death is
7:2 but if her husband *d*, she is
7:3 if her husband *d*, she is free
14:7 no one *d* with regard to
1Co 15:36 alive unless first it *d*
Heb 10:28 *d* without compassion, upon

Differ
1Co 4:7 makes you to *d* from another
Ga 4:1 not *d* at all from a slave

Difference
2Ch 12:8 *d* between my service and the
Eze 44:23 *d* between a holy thing and
44:23 *d* between what is unclean
Jon 4:11 the *d* between their right
Ga 2:6 makes no *d* to me—God does not
Jude 9 archangel had a *d* with the

Different
Le 14:42 have *d* clay mortar taken
Nu 14:24 a *d* spirit has proved to be
1Ki 18:21 limping upon two *d* opinions
2Ki 17:29 each *d* nation came to be a
17:29 *d* nation, in their cities
1Ch 26:13 lots . . . for the *d* gates
28:14 utensils for the *d* services
28:14 utensils for the *d* services
28:15 weight of the *d* lampstands
28:15 service of the *d* lampstands
28:16 for the *d* tables, and silver
28:17 for the *d* small bowls
28:17 for the *d* small bowls
2Ch 8:14 divisions for the *d* gates
11:12 *d* cities large shields and
16:14 *d* sorts of ointment mixed
31:19 *d* cities there were men
32:28 all the *d* sorts of beasts
34:13 work for the *d* services
35:15 were at the *d* gates
Ne 13:24 the tongue of the *d* peoples
Es 1:7 the vessels were *d* from one
3:8 their laws are *d* from all
3:12 the *d* jurisdictional districts
3:12 the princes of the *d* peoples
3:14 the *d* jurisdictional districts
4:3 the *d* jurisdictional districts
Es 8:11 that were in all the *d* cities
8:13 the *d* jurisdictional districts
8:17 the *d* jurisdictional districts
8:17 in all the *d* cities wherever
Isa 28:11 *d* tongue he will speak to
41:16 will drive them *d* ways
Eze 15:2 the vine tree happen to be *d*
Da 7:3 one being *d* from the others
7:7 *d* from all the other beasts
7:19 proved to be *d* from all the
7:23 *d* from all the other kingdoms
7:24 *d* from the first ones, and
Mt 11:3 or are we to expect a *d* one?
12:45 seven *d* spirits more wicked
Lu 7:19 or are we to expect a *d* one?
9:29 his face became *d* and his
9:56 So they went to a *d* village
11:26 along seven *d* spirits more
19:20 a *d* one came, saying, Lord
20:11 and sent them a *d* slave
Joh 19:37 again, a *d* scripture says
Ac 2:4 to speak with *d* tongues, just
2:13 *d* ones mocked at them and
7:18 *d* king over Egypt, who did
1Co 12:10 to another *d* tongues, and to
12:28 to direct, *d* tongues
15:40 earthly bodies is a *d* sort
Ga 4:20 and to speak in a *d* way
1Ti 1:3 ones not to teach *d* doctrine

Differing
Ro 12:6 gifts *d* according to the

Differs
1Co 15:41 star *d* from star in glory

Difficult
De 30:11 is not too *d* for you, nor is
Jg 6:2 and the places *d* to approach
1Sa 23:14 places *d* to approach, and
23:19 places *d* to approach at
23:29 places *d* to approach at
24:22 to the place *d* to approach
2Sa 13:2 *d* in the eyes of Amnon to do
1Ki 3:9 able to judge this *d* people
2Ki 2:10 You have asked a *d* thing
1Ch 11:7 in the place *d* to approach
12:8 at the place *d* to approach in
12:16 to the place *d* to approach
Isa 33:16 craggy places *d* to approach
Da 2:11 king himself is asking is *d*
Zec 8:6 seem too *d* in the eyes of the
8:6 seem too *d* also in my eyes
Mt 19:23 a *d* thing for a rich man to
Mr 10:23 How *d* a thing it will be
10:24 how *d* a thing it is to enter
Lu 18:24 How *d* a thing it will be

Difficulties
2Co 6:4 by cases of need, by *d*
12:10 I take pleasure in . . . *d*

Difficulty
Ge 35:17 had *d* in making the delivery
Ex 14:25 were driving them with *d*
Ps 119:143 and *d* themselves found me
Ac 27:7 and coming to Cnidus with *d*
27:8 coasting along it with *d* we
1Pe 4:18 righteous . . . saved with *d*

Dig
Ge 26:18 Isaac proceeded to *d* again
De 23:13 *d* a hole with it and turn
2Ki 19:24 shall certainly *d* and drink
Ps 7:15 and he proceeded to *d* it
Isa 5:2 *d* it up and to rid it of
37:25 *d* and drink waters
Am 9:2 If they *d* down into Sheol
Lu 13:8 *d* around it and put on manure
16:3 I am not strong enough to *d*

Digging
Ge 26:19 *d* in the torrent valley and
26:21 they went *d* another well
Ex 7:24 Egyptians went *d* round about
Job 3:21 keep *d* for it more than for
Pr 16:27 man is *d* up what is bad, and
Ec 10:8 is *d* a pit will himself fall

Dignity
Ge 49:3 the excellence of *d* and the
Nu 27:20 put some of your *d* upon him
1Ch 16:27 *D* and splendor are before
29:11 the excellency and the *d*
29:25 put upon him such royal *d*
Es 1:19 her royal *d* let the king give
4:14 you have attained to royal *d*
Job 13:11 Will not his very *d* make
Job 31:23 against his *d* I could not
37:22 Upon God *d* is fear-inspiring
39:20 The *d* of its snorting is
40:10 with *d* and splendor may you
Ps 8:1 whose *d* is recounted above the
21:5 *D* and splendor you put upon
45:3 With your *d* and your splendor
62:4 allure from one's own *d*
96:6 *D* and splendor are before
104:1 With *d* and splendor you have
111:3 activity is *d* and splendor
145:5 glorious splendor of your *d*
148:13 *d* is above earth and heaven
Pr 5:9 not give to others your *d*, nor
Isa 30:30 *d* of his voice to be heard
Jer 22:18 O master! And alas, his *d!*
Da 2:6 much *d* you will receive on my
2:37 the strength and the *d*
4:30 and for the *d* of my majesty
4:36 for the *d* of my kingdom my
5:18 and the *d* and the majesty
5:20 *d* was taken away from him
7:14 rulership and *d* and kingdom
10:8 my own *d* became changed upon
11:21 the *d* of the kingdom
Ho 14:6 his *d* will become like that
Hab 1:7 justice and its own *d* go
3:3 His *d* covered the heavens
Zec 6:13 he . . . will carry the *d*
10:3 like his horse of *d* in the

Diklah
Ge 10:27 Hadoram and Uzal and *D*
1Ch 1:21 Hadoram and Uzal and *D*

Dilean
Jos 15:38 *D* and Mizpeh and Joktheel

Diligent
Pr 10:4 hand of the *d* one is what
12:24 hand of the *d* ones is the
12:27 *d* one is a man's precious
13:4 soul of the *d* ones will be
21:5 The plans of the *d* one surely
Lu 2:45 making a *d* search for him
Ac 12:19 Herod made *d* search for him
1Pe 1:10 a *d* inquiry and a careful

Diligently
Pr 23:1 *d* consider what is before you
1Ti 5:10 if she *d* followed every good
2Ti 1:17 he *d* looked for me and found

Dill
Mt 23:23 and the *d* and the cummin

Diluted
Isa 1:22 wheat beer is *d* with water

Dim
Ge 27:1 his eyes were too *d* to see
De 34:7 His eye had not grown *d*, and
1Sa 3:2 his eyes had begun to grow *d*
Isa 42:3 and as for a *d* flaxen wick
42:4 not grow *d* nor be crushed
La 4:1 the gold that shines becomes *d*
5:17 our eyes have grown *d*
Zec 11:17 will without fail grow *d*

Diminish
Job 15:4 *d* the having of any concern
Eze 5:11 am the One that will *d* you
16:27 I shall *d* your allowance

Diminished
Ex 21:10 marriage due are not to be *d*

Dimmer
Job 17:7 vexation my eye grows *d*

Dimnah
Jos 21:35 *D* and its pasture ground

Dimon
Isa 15:9 waters of *D* have become full
15:9 *D* I shall place additional

Dimonah
Jos 15:22 Kinah and *D* and Adadah

Din
Isa 14:11 the *d* of your stringed
17:12 *d* just like the noise of
17:13 *d* just like the noise of

Dinah
Ge 30:21 then called her name *D*
34:1 Now *D* the daughter of Leah
34:3 his soul began clinging to *D*
34:5 heard that he had defiled *D*
34:13 he had defiled *D* their sister

Mt 26:35 other *d* also said the same
26:36 he said to the *d:* Sit down
26:40 he came to the *d* and found
26:45 he came to the *d* and said to
26:56 the *d* abandoned him and fled
27:64 *d* may never come and steal
28:7 tell his *d* that he was raised
28:8 they ran to report to his *d*
28:13 Say, His *d* came in the night
28:16 eleven *d* went into Galilee
28:19 make *d* of people of all the
Mr 2:15 with Jesus and his *d,* for
2:16 saying to his *d:* Does he eat
2:18 John's *d* and the Pharisees
2:18 Why is it the *d* of John and
2:18 *d* of the Pharisees practice
2:18 *d* do not practice fasting
2:23 *d* started to make their way
3:7 Jesus with his *d* withdrew to
3:9 he told his *d* to have a little
4:34 to his *d* he would explain all
5:31 But his *d* began to say to him
6:1 and his *d* followed him
6:29 When his *d* heard of it they
6:35 his *d* came up to him and
6:41 began giving them to the *d*
6:45 *d* to board the boat and go
7:2 *d* eat their meal with defiled
7:5 your *d* do not conduct
7:17 his *d* began to question him
8:1 he summoned the *d* and said
8:4 *d* answered him: From where
8:6 give them to his *d* to serve
8:10 boarded the boat with his *d*
8:27 Jesus and his *d* now left for
8:27 questioning his *d,* saying to
8:33 looked at his *d* and rebuked
8:34 crowd to him with his *d* and
9:14 came toward the other *d*
9:18 I told your *d* to expel it
9:28 his *d* proceeded to ask him
9:31 he was teaching his *d* and
10:10 the *d* began to question him
10:13 but the *d* reprimanded them
10:23 Jesus said to his *d*
10:24 the *d* gave way to surprise
10:46 *d* and a considerable crowd
11:1 he dispatched two of his *d*
11:14 And his *d* were listening
12:43 he called his *d* to him and
13:1 one of his *d* said to him
14:12 his *d* said to him: Where do
14:13 he sent forth two of his *d*
14:14 eat the passover with my *d*
14:16 So the *d* went out, and they
14:32 said to his *d:* Sit down here
16:7 go, tell his *d* and Peter, He
Lu 5:30 murmuring to his *d,* saying
5:33 The *d* of John fast frequently
6:1 his *d* were plucking and eating
6:13 called his *d* to him and chose
6:17 a great crowd of his *d,* and
6:20 eyes upon his *d* and began to
7:11 his *d* and a great crowd were
7:18 John's *d* reported to him
7:19 a certain two of his *d* and
8:9 his *d* began to ask him what
8:22 he and his *d* got into a boat
9:14 But he said to his *d*
9:16 began to give them to the *d*
9:18 the *d* came together to him
9:40 I begged your *d* to expel it
9:43 he said to his *d*
9:54 When the *d* James and John
10:23 he turned to the *d* by
11:1 one of his *d* said to him
11:1 as John also taught his *d*
12:1 by saying first to his *d*
12:22 he said to his *d:* On this
16:1 went on to say also to the *d*
17:1 Then he said to his *d:* It is
17:22 he said to the *d:* Days will
18:15 *d* began to reprimand them
19:29 he sent forth two of the *d*
19:37 *d* started to rejoice and
19:39 Teacher, rebuke your *d*
20:45 listening he said to the *d*
22:11 eat the passover with my *d*
22:39 and the *d* also followed him
22:45 went to the *d* and found them
Joh 1:35 standing with two of his *d*
1:37 the two *d* heard him speak
2:2 Jesus and his *d* were also
2:11 his *d* put their faith in him
Joh 2:12 *d* went down to Capernaum
2:17 *d* called to mind that it is
2:22 *d* called to mind that he
3:22 Jesus and his *d* went into
3:25 on the part of the *d* of John
4:1 baptizing more *d* than John
4:2 no baptizing but his *d* did
4:8 his *d* had gone off into the
4:27 his *d* arrived, and they
4:31 *d* were urging him, saying
4:33 *d* began saying to one another
6:3 he was sitting with his *d*
6:8 One of his *d,* Andrew the
6:12 he said to his *d:* Gather
6:16 his *d* went down to the sea
6:22 into the boat with his *d*
6:22 that only his *d* had left
6:24 Jesus was there nor his *d*
6:60 many of his *d,* when they
6:61 his *d* were murmuring about
6:66 many of his *d* went off to
7:3 in order that your *d* also may
8:31 you are really my *d*
9:2 his *d* asked him: Rabbi, who
9:27 not want to become his *d*
9:28 but we are *d* of Moses
11:7 this he said to the *d:* Let
11:8 *d* said to him: Rabbi, just
11:12 *d* said to him: Lord, if he
11:16 said to his fellow *d*
11:54 he remained with the *d*
12:4 one of his *d,* who was about
12:16 *d* took no note of at first
13:5 wash the feet of the *d* and
13:22 *d* began to look at one
13:23 Jesus' bosom one of his *d*
13:35 know that you are my *d,* if
15:8 and prove yourselves my *d*
16:17 his *d* said to one another
16:29 *d* said: See! Now you are
18:1 Jesus went out with his *d*
18:1 and his *d* entered into it
18:2 times met there with his *d*
18:17 also one of this man's *d*
18:19 questioned Jesus about his *d*
18:25 not also one of his *d,* are
20:10 *d* went back to their homes
20:18 brought the news to the *d*
20:19 where the *d* were for fear
20:20 *d* rejoiced at seeing the
20:25 *d* would say to him: We
20:26 his *d* were again indoors
20:30 signs also before the *d*
21:1 *d* at the sea of Tiberias
21:2 and two others of his *d*
21:4 *d* did not, of course, discern
21:8 *d* came in the little boat
21:12 *d* had the courage to inquire
21:14 Jesus appeared to the *d*
Ac 6:1 when the *d* were increasing
6:2 called the multitude of the *d*
6:7 of the *d* kept multiplying
9:1 against the *d* of the Lord
9:19 days with the *d* in Damascus
9:25 *d* took him and let him down
9:26 to join himself to the *d*
9:38 *d* heard that Peter was in
11:26 *d* were by divine providence
11:29 *d* determined, each of them
13:52 the *d* continued to be filled
14:20 when the *d* surrounded him
14:21 and making quite a few *d*
14:22 souls of the *d,* encouraging
14:28 a little time with the *d*
15:10 upon the neck of the *d* a
18:23 strengthening all the *d*
18:27 the brothers wrote the *d*
19:1 to Ephesus, and found some *d*
19:9 and separated the *d* from them
19:30 the *d* would not permit him
20:1 Paul sent for the *d,* and when
20:30 to draw away the *d* after
21:4 By a search we found the *d*
21:16 *d* from Caesarea also went

Discipline
De 11:2 have not seen the *d* of Jehovah
22:18 take the man and *d* him
Job 5:17 *d* of the Almighty do not you
Ps 50:17 Why, you—you have hated *d*
Pr 1:2 one to know wisdom and *d*
1:3 the *d* that gives insight
1:7 *d* are what mere fools have
1:8 to the *d* of your father, and
Pr 3:11 *d* of Jehovah, O my son, do
4:1 sons, to the *d* of a father and
4:13 Take hold on *d;* do not let
5:12 I have hated *d* and my heart
5:23 to die because there is no *d*
6:23 of *d* are the way of life
7:22 for the *d* of a foolish man
8:10 Take my *d* and not silver
8:33 Listen to *d* and become wise
10:17 holding to *d* is a path to
12:1 A lover of *d* is a lover of
13:1 where there is a father's *d*
13:18 one neglecting *d* comes to
13:24 does look for him with *d*
15:5 the *d* of his father, but
15:10 *D* is bad to the one leaving
15:32 shunning *d* is rejecting his
15:33 The fear of Jehovah is a *d*
16:22 the *d* of the foolish ones is
19:20 to counsel and accept *d,* in
19:27 to listen to *d* and it will
22:15 *d* is what will remove it
23:12 Do bring your heart to *d* and
23:13 Do not hold back *d* from the
23:23 and *d* and understanding
24:32 I saw, I took the *d*
Jer 2:30 No *d* did they take
5:3 They refused to take *d*
7:28 and have not taken *d*
17:23 in order to receive no *d*
32:33 listening to receive *d*
Ho 7:12 *d* them in agreement with the
10:10 I shall also *d* them
Zep 3:2 she did not accept *d*
3:7 fear me; you will accept *d*
Eph 6:4 the *d* and mental-regulating
1Ti 1:20 taught by *d* not to blaspheme
Heb 12:5 belittle the *d* from Jehovah
12:7 It is for *d* you are enduring
12:7 that a father does not *d*
12:8 *d* of which all have become
12:9 fathers . . . of our flesh to *d* us
12:10 to *d* us according to what
12:11 no *d* seems for the present
Re 3:19 affection I reprove and *d*

Disciplined
1Co 11:32 we are *d* by Jehovah, that
2Co 6:9 as *d* and yet not delivered

Disciplines
Heb 12:6 for whom Jehovah loves he *d*

Disciplining
Isa 26:16 when they had your *d*
Ho 7:15 And I, for my part, did *d*
2Ti 3:16 for *d* in righteousness

Disclose
Ru 4:4 I thought that I should *d* it to
1Sa 20:2 little thing and not *d* it to
20:12 certainly *d* it to your ear
20:13 *d* it to your ear and send
22:17 did not *d* it to my ear
Joh 11:57 he should *d* it, in order

Disclosed
Jg 16:17 he *d* to her all his heart and
16:18 he had *d* to her all his heart
16:18 he has *d* to me all his heart
Lu 8:47 *d* before all the people the
20:37 Moses *d,* in the account
Ac 23:30 a plot . . . has been *d* to me
1Co 10:28 of the one that *d* it and on
Col 1:8 also *d* to us your love in a

Disclosing
1Sa 22:8 no one *d* it to my ear when
22:8 *d* to my ear that my own son

Disclosure
Ps 119:130 *d* of your words gives
1Co 1:11 *d* was made to me about you

Disconcerted
1Sa 1:6 the sake of making her feel *d*
Ps 38:6 I have become *d,* I have bowed
Isa 21:3 *d* so that I do not hear

Disconcertedness
Isa 19:14 of her the spirit of *d*

Discontented
Mic 2:7 spirit of Jehovah become *d*

Discontinued
Isa 24:8 the highly elated ones has *d*

Discouraged
Pr 24:10 *d* in the day of distress

Discouragement
Ex 6:9 did not listen . . . out of *d*
Discourse
Ac 15:32 many a *d* and strengthened
Discoursing
Ac 20:7 Paul began *d* to them, as he
Discover
Ps 17:3 *d* that I have not schemed
Ec 7:14 mankind may not *d* anything at
Discovered
Ge 11:2 they eventually *d* a valley
1Sa 22:6 men . . . with him had been *d*
2Pe 3:10 the works in it will be *d*
Discredited
Lu 23:11 *d* him, and he made fun of
Discreet
Ge 41:33 a man *d* and wise and set
41:39 no one as *d* and wise as you
De 1:13 *d* and experienced men of your
Pr 19:14 but a *d* wife is from Jehovah
23:9 he will despise your *d* words
Isa 5:21 *d* even in front of their own
29:14 of their *d* men will conceal
Ho 14:9 *D*, that he may know them
Mt 7:24 will be likened to a *d* man
24:45 is the faithful and *d* slave
25:2 and five were *d*
25:4 whereas the *d* took oil in
25:8 foolish said to the *d*, Give
25:9 *d* answered with the words
Lu 12:42 the *d* one, whom his master
Ro 11:25 to be *d* in your own eyes
12:16 become *d* in your own eyes
1Co 4:10 but you are *d* in Christ; we
Discreetly
Pr 10:19 lips in check is acting *d*
Discretion
1Sa 25:3 the wife was good in *d* and
1Ch 22:12 may Jehovah give you *d* and
26:14 a counselor with *d*, they
2Ch 2:12 a wise son, experienced in *d*
30:22 acting with fine *d* toward
Ezr 8:18 a man of *d* from the sons of
Job 17:4 heart you have closed to *d*
Ps 47:7 Make melody, acting with *d*
101:2 I will act with *d* in a
Pr 12:8 mouth of *d* a man will be
Jer 23:5 reign and act with *d* and
Discuss
Lu 22:23 to *d* among themselves the
Discussed
Mr 9:10 *d* among themselves what this
Heb 8:1 as to the things being *d*
Discussing
Lu 24:15 they were conversing and *d*
Discussion
Mr 1:27 began a *d* among themselves
Disdaining
Eze 16:31 a prostitute in *d* hire
Disease
Job 6:7 They are like *d* in my food
Ps 106:15 wasting *d* into their soul
Isa 10:16 his fat ones a wasting *d*
17:11 of the *d* and incurable pain
Mt 4:23 and curing every sort of *d*
9:35 curing every sort of *d* and
10:1 to cure every sort of *d* and
Diseased
Le 21:20 *d* in his eyes or scabby or
1Ki 15:23 he got *d* in his feet
1Ti 6:4 mentally *d* over questionings
Diseases
De 7:15 all the evil *d* of Egypt that
28:60 all the *d* of Egypt before
2Ch 24:25 left him with many *d*
Mt 4:24 distressed with various *d*
8:17 sicknesses and carried our *d*
Mr 3:10 all those who had grievous *d*
Lu 4:40 people sick with various *d*
7:21 of sicknesses and grievous *d*
Ac 19:12 and the *d* left them, and the
Disembarked
Joh 21:9 when they *d* onto land
Disfigure
Mt 6:16 they *d* their faces that they

Disfigurement
Isa 52:14 *d* as respects his appearance
Disfiguring
Job 14:20 *d* his face so that you send
Disgorged
Re 12:15 serpent *d* water like a
12:16 river that the dragon *d*
Disgrace
Ex 32:25 for a *d* among their opposers
Pr 13:5 and cause *d* for themselves
Hab 2:16 be *d* upon your glory
Disgraced
De 25:3 your brother is actually *d*
2Sa 19:3 steal away when they felt *d*
Isa 16:14 Moab must also be *d* with
Disgraceful
Ge 34:7 he had committed a *d* folly
De 22:21 she has committed a *d* folly
Jos 7:15 a *d* folly in Israel
Jg 19:23 Do not commit this *d* folly
19:24 not do this *d*, foolish thing
20:6 loose conduct and *d* folly in
20:10 in view of all the *d* folly
2Sa 13:12 Do not do this *d* folly
Job 42:8 commit *d* folly with you
Pr 14:34 sin . . . *d* to national groups
Ro 1:26 *d* sexual appetites, for both
1Co 11:6 if it is *d* for a woman to be
14:35 for it is *d* for a woman to
Disgracefully
Pr 19:26 son acting shamefully and *d*
Disguise
1Ki 14:2 *d* yourself that they may not
Disguised
1Sa 21:13 *d* his sanity under their
28:8 Saul *d* himself and clothed
1Ki 20:38 *d* with a bandage over his
22:30 king of Israel *d* himself
2Ch 18:29 king of Israel *d* himself
35:22 he *d* himself and did not
Disguises
Pr 28:12 rise up, a man *d* himself
Disguising
1Ki 22:30 a *d* and entering into the
2Ch 18:29 *d* and entering into the
Ps 34:*super* time of his *d* his sanity
Disgust
Eze 23:22 has turned away in *d*
Ga 4:14 contempt or spit at in *d*
Disgusted
Jer 6:8 my soul may not turn away *d*
Eze 23:17 to turn away *d* from them
23:18 *d* from company with her
23:18 *d* from company with her
23:28 soul has turned away *d*
Heb 3:10 *d* with this generation and
3:17 God become *d* for forty years
Disgusting
De 29:17 see their *d* things and their
1Ki 11:5 Milcom the *d* thing of the
11:7 Chemosh the *d* thing of Moab
11:7 Molech the *d* thing of the
2Ki 23:13 Ashtoreth the *d* thing of
23:13 Chemosh the *d* thing of Moab
23:24 *d* things that had appeared
2Ch 15:8 *d* things to vanish from all
Isa 66:3 in their *d* things their very
Jer 4:1 take away your *d* things on
7:30 set their *d* things in the
13:27 I have seen your *d* things
16:18 corpses of their *d* things
32:34 *d* things in the house upon
Eze 5:11 with all your *d* things and
7:20 *d* things, they have made
11:18 remove all its *d* things and
11:21 heart is walking in their *d*
20:7 the *d* things of his eyes, and
20:8 The *d* things of their eyes
20:30 after their *d* things are you
37:23 with their *d* things and
Da 9:27 upon the wing of *d* things
11:31 *d* thing that is causing
12:11 the *d* thing that is causing
Ho 9:10 *d* like the thing of their love
Na 3:6 I will throw *d* things upon you
Zec 9:7 *d* things from between his
Mt 24:15 catch sight of the *d* thing

Mr 13:14 the *d* thing that causes
Lu 16:15 is a *d* thing in God's sight
Re 17:4 was full of *d* things and the
17:5 of the *d* things of the earth
21:8 who are *d* in their filth
21:27 carries on a *d* thing and a
Dish
Ge 27:4 make me a tasty *d* such as I
27:7 make me a tasty *d* and, ah
27:9 a tasty *d* for your father
27:14 his mother made a tasty *d*
27:17 she gave the tasty *d* and the
27:31 went about making a tasty *d*
Nu 7:13 offering was one silver *d*, its
7:19 one silver *d*, its weight
7:25 one silver *d*, its weight
7:31 offering was one silver *d*
7:37 offering was one silver *d*
7:43 offering was one silver *d*, its
7:49 offering was one silver *d*
7:55 offering was one silver *d*
7:61 offering was one silver *d*
7:67 offering was one silver *d*
7:73 His offering was one silver *d*
7:79 offering was one silver *d*
7:85 shekels to each silver *d*
Pr 15:17 Better is a *d* of vegetables
Mt 23:25 of the cup and of the *d*, but
23:26 of the cup and of the *d*
Lu 11:39 the outside of the cup and *d*
Dishan
Ge 36:21 Ezer and *D* . . . sons of Seir
36:28 the sons of *D*: Uz and Aran
36:30 *D* . . . sheiks of the Horite
1Ch 1:38 sons of Seir were . . . *D*
1:42 sons of *D* were Uz and Aran
Dishearten
Nu 32:7 you *d* the sons of Israel from
Disheartened
Ex 15:15 Canaan will indeed be *d*
Nu 32:9 then they *d* the sons of Israel
Jos 2:9 have become *d* because of you
2:24 also grown *d* because of us
Isa 14:31 become *d*, O Philistia
Disheartening
Ezr 4:4 and *d* them from building
Dishes
Ex 25:29 make its *d* and its cups and
37:16 its *d* and its cups and its
Nu 4:7 put upon it the *d* and the cups
7:84 twelve silver *d*, twelve
Pr 23:3 yourself craving his tasty *d*
23:6 yourself craving his tasty *d*
Isa 25:6 a banquet of well-oiled *d*
25:6 well-oiled *d* filled with
Dishon
Ge 36:21 *D* and Ezer . . . sons of Seir
36:25 children of Anah: *D* and
36:26 sons of *D*: Hemdan and Eshban
36:30 *D* . . . sheiks of the Horite
1Ch 1:38 sons of Seir were . . . *D*
1:41 sons of Anah were *D*
1:41 sons of *D* were Hemdan
Dishonest
1Ti 3:8 not greedy of *d* gain
Tit 1:7 not greedy of *d* gain
1:11 for the sake of *d* gain
1Pe 5:2 neither for love of *d* gain
Dishonor
Job 10:15 Glutted with *d* and
Ps 83:16 Fill their faces with *d*
Pr 3:35 stupid ones are exalting *d*
6:33 A plague and *d* he will find
9:7 is taking to himself *d*, and
11:2 Then *d* will come; but wisdom
12:16 is covering over a *d*
13:18 comes to poverty and *d*, but
18:3 with *d* there is reproach
22:10 contest and *d* may cease
Isa 22:18 *d* of the house of your
Jer 13:26 your *d* will certainly be
46:12 nations have heard your *d*
Ho 4:7 they have exchanged for mere *d*
4:18 have positively loved *d*
Na 3:5 and kingdoms your *d*
Hab 2:16 with *d* instead of glory
Joh 8:49 honor my Father, and you *d*
Ro 2:23 of the Law *d* God
1Co 4:10 good repute, but we are in *d*

1Co 11:14 long hair, it is a *d* to him
15:43 It is sown in *d*, it is
2Co 6:8 through glory and *d*, through
11:21 I say this to our *d*, as

Dishonorable
Ro 9:21 another for a *d* use

Dishonored
Mr 12:4 struck on the head and *d*
Lu 20:11 beat up and *d* and sent away
Ac 5:41 be *d* in behalf of his name
Ro 1:24 bodies might be *d* among them
Jas 2:6 though, have *d* the poor man

Disintegrated
Jer 49:23 Hamath and Arpad . . . have *d*

Disintegration
Isa 38:17 kept it from the pit of *d*

Disloyal
2Ti 3:2 unthankful, *d*

Dismembered
Da 2:5 *d* is what you will be, and
3:29 should be *d*, and its house

Dismiss
De 24:1 and *d* her from his house
Lu 9:12 *D* the crowd, that they may go

Dismissal
Mt 19:7 giving a certificate of *d* and
Mr 10:4 writing of a certificate of *d*

Dismissed
Ge 21:14 So Abraham . . . then *d* her
De 24:3 and *d* her from his house
24:4 first owner of her who *d* her
Mr 4:36 after they had *d* the crowd
6:45 while he himself *d* the crowd
Lu 8:38 he *d* the man, saying
Ac 19:41 he *d* the assembly

Dismissing
Mt 13:36 after *d* the crowds he went

Disobedience
Ro 5:19 through the *d* of the one man
11:30 mercy because of their *d*
11:32 them all up together in *d*
2Co 10:6 punishment for every *d*, as
Eph 2:2 operates in the sons of *d*
5:6 wrath . . . upon the sons of *d*
Heb 4:6 did not enter in because of *d*
4:11 in the same pattern of *d*

Disobedient
Ne 9:26 became *d* and rebelled against
Ps 106:43 in their *d* course
Lu 1:17 the *d* ones to the practical
Ac 26:19 *d* to the heavenly sight
Ro 1:30 *d* to parents
10:21 people that is *d* and talks
11:30 once *d* to God but have now
11:31 these now have been *d* with
2Ti 3:2 blasphemers, *d* to parents
Tit 1:16 they are detestable and *d*
3:3 we were once senseless, *d*
Heb 2:2 transgression and *d* act
1Pe 2:8 stumbling because they are *d*
3:20 been *d* when the patience of

Disobediently
Heb 3:18 except to those who acted *d*
11:31 with those who acted *d*

Disobey
Jer 42:13 *d* the voice of Jehovah your
Ro 2:8 and who *d* the truth but obey

Disobeys
Joh 3:36 *d* the Son will not see life

Disorder
2Ch 15:6 *d* with every sort of
Job 10:22 of deep shadow And *d*
1Co 14:33 God, not of *d*, but of peace
Jas 3:16 there *d* and every vile thing

Disorderly
1Sa 30:16 they were spread *d* over the
Ac 19:40 a reason for this *d* mob
1Th 5:14 brothers, admonish the *d*
2Th 3:6 every brother walking *d* and
3:7 did not behave *d* among you
3:11 are walking *d* among you

Disorders
2Ch 15:5 were many *d* among all the
Am 3:9 many *d* in the midst of her
Lu 21:9 hear of wars and *d*, do not be

2Co 6:5 by beatings, by prisons, by *d*
12:20 cases of being puffed up, *d*

Disown
Mt 10:33 also *d* him before my Father
16:24 let him *d* himself and pick
26:34 you will *d* me three times
26:35 I will by no means *d* you
26:75 you will *d* me three times
Mr 8:34 let him *d* himself and pick
14:30 you will *d* me three times
14:31 I will by no means *d* you
14:72 you will *d* me three times
Lu 9:23 let him *d* himself and pick
22:61 you will *d* me three times
Tit 1:16 they *d* him by their works
2Pe 2:1 *d* even the owner that bought

Disowned
Lu 12:9 *d* before the angels of God
Joh 13:38 you have *d* me three times
Ac 3:13 *d* before Pilate's face, when
3:14 you *d* that holy and righteous
7:35 Moses, whom they *d*, saying
1Ti 5:8 *d* the faith and is worse than

Disowns
Mt 10:33 but whoever *d* me before men
Lu 12:9 he that *d* me before men will

Dispatch
Ac 11:13 *D* men to Joppa and send for

Dispatched
2Ch 13:13 *d* an ambush around to come
Mt 21:34 he *d* his slaves to the
21:36 Again he *d* other slaves
21:37 Lastly he *d* his son to them
22:16 *d* to him their disciples
Mr 6:27 *d* a body guardsman and
11:1 he *d* two of his disciples
Lu 7:20 John the Baptist *d* us to you
22:8 he *d* Peter and John, saying
Joh 4:38 I *d* you to reap what you
5:33 You have *d* men to John, and
5:36 that the Father *d* me
5:38 one whom he *d* you do not
7:32 *d* officers to get hold of
10:36 and *d* into the world
11:3 his sisters *d* word to him
Ac 8:14 *d* Peter and John to them
9:38 *d* two men to him to entreat
10:8 and *d* them to Joppa
10:17 men *d* by Cornelius had made
10:20 because I have *d* them
11:11 having been *d* from Caesarea
16:35 *d* the constables to say
16:36 civil magistrates have *d* men
19:22 So he *d* to Macedonia two of
1Co 1:17 *d* me, not to go baptizing
2Co 12:17 those I have *d* to you, I
12:18 I *d* the brother with him

Dispatching
Ac 11:30 *d* it to the older men by
15:27 *d* Judas and Silas, that they

Dispensing
1Ti 1:4 a *d* of anything by God in

Disperse
De 32:26 I shall *d* them, I will make
Jg 21:24 Israel began to *d* from there
Jer 24:9 to which I shall *d* them
27:10 I shall have to *d* you
27:15 I shall *d* you, and you will
29:18 I shall certainly *d* them
Eze 4:13 nations to which I shall *d*
12:15 I *d* them among the nations
20:23 to *d* them among the lands
22:15 *d* you among the lands
29:12 *d* them among the lands
30:23 and *d* them among the lands
30:26 *d* them among the lands
Joe 2:20 *d* him to a waterless land
Zec 1:21 Judah, in order to *d* her

Dispersed
De 30:1 Jehovah your God has *d* you
30:4 If your *d* people should be at
1Sa 13:11 people had been *d* from me
24:7 David *d* his men with these
Ne 1:9 though your *d* people should
Ps 147:2 *d* ones of Israel he brings
Isa 11:12 gather the *d* ones of Israel
16:3 Conceal the *d* ones; do not
16:4 *d* ones reside as aliens even
27:13 *d* in the land of Egypt

Isa 33:3 nations have been *d*
51:6 must be *d* in fragments
56:8 the *d* ones of Israel
Jer 8:3 where I will have *d* them
16:15 lands to which he had *d*
23:3 lands to which I had *d* them
23:8 lands to which I have *d* them
29:14 to which I have *d* you
32:37 have *d* them in my anger
40:12 to which they had been *d*
43:5 to which they had been *d*, in
46:28 nations to which I have *d*
49:5 people will certainly be *d*
49:36 *d* ones of Elam will not
Eze 34:4 *d* one you have not brought
34:16 *d* one I shall bring back
36:19 were *d* among the lands
Da 9:7 the lands to which you *d* them
Mic 4:6 her that was *d* I will
Zep 3:19 is *d* I shall collect together
Zec 1:19 horns that *d* Judah, Israel
1:21 the horns that *d* Judah to
Joh 7:35 Jews *d* among the Greeks and
Ac 5:36 were *d* and came to nothing

Dispersing
Ps 5:10 let there be a *d* of them
Jer 23:2 you kept *d* them, and you
50:17 Lions . . . have done the *d*

Displaced
Ex 28:28 breastpiece may not get *d*
39:21 not get *d* from on top the

Display
Mt 16:1 *d* to them a sign from heaven
Lu 19:11 going to *d* itself instantly
Heb 9:2 and the *d* of the loaves
12:21 the *d* was so fearsome that
1Jo 2:16 *d* of one's means of life

Displayed
Ge 10:9 He *d* himself a mighty hunter
2Ch 26:8 for he *d* strength to an
Joh 10:32 I *d* to you many fine works

Displaying
Nu 24:18 Israel is *d* his courage
Ps 69:31 Than a young bull *d* horns

Displeasing
Ge 21:11 very *d* to Abraham as regards
21:12 *d* to you about the boy and
28:8 daughters of Canaan were *d*
48:17 it was *d* to him, and he
Ex 21:8 *d* in the eyes of her master
Da 6:14 it was very *d* to him, and
Jon 4:1 To Jonah . . . it was highly *d*

Displeasure
Ps 2:5 in his hot *d* he will disturb
Mr 14:5 were feeling great *d* at her

Disposal
Ge 16:6 Your maidservant is at your *d*
33:15 at your *d* some of the people
47:6 The land of Egypt is at your *d*
1Sa 21:3 bread at your *d*, just give
21:8 your *d*, a spear or a sword
2Ki 10:24 at his *d* and went on to say
Ca 8:12 My vineyard . . . is at my *d*

Disposed
De 21:5 violent deed should be *d* of
1Ki 14:10 the dung until it is *d* of
Job 9:35 For I am not so *d* in myself
Ps 55:21 But his heart is *d* to fight
Pr 18:24 companions *d* to break one
20:25 he is *d* to make examination
29:22 anyone *d* to rage has many a
Isa 30:1 those *d* to carry out counsel
Jer 44:19 *d* to pour out drink
Na 1:2 vengeance and is *d* to rage
Ac 13:48 rightly *d* for everlasting
2Ti 2:25 those not favorably *d*; as
2Pe 1:12 *d* always to remind you of

Disposition
Ge 49:6 do not become united, O my *d*
1Ch 23:28 *d* of the sons of Aaron for
Joh 8:44 according to his own *d*
Ro 1:29 deceit, malicious *d*, being
Php 2:20 no one else of a *d* like his
1Pe 4:1 with the same mental *d*

Dispossess
De 2:12 sons of Esau proceeded to *d*
2:21 *d* them and dwell in their
2:22 *d* them and dwell in their

De 9:1 *d* nations greater and mightier
9:3 you must *d* them and destroy
11:23 *d* nations greater and more
12:29 you are going to *d* them
12:29 you must also *d* them and
Jos 13:6 shall *d* them from before the
13:13 did not *d* the Geshurites
14:12 I shall certainly *d* them
17:13 did not *d* them entirely
23:13 to *d* these nations on your
Jg 1:19 but he could not *d* the
11:23 and you . . . would *d* them
11:24 god causes you to *d* that you
11:24 that you will *d*
11:24 the one we shall *d*
Zec 9:4 Jehovah himself will *d* her

Dispossessed
Nu 21:32 *d* the Amorites who were
De 19:1 you have *d* them and have
Jos 23:5 he *d* them on your account
Jg 11:23 *d* the Amorites from before
11:24 God has *d* from before us is

Dispossesses
Pr 30:23 when she *d* her mistress

Dispossessing
De 12:2 the nations whom you are *d*
18:14 these nations whom you are *d*
Jos 13:12 striking them and *d* them

Dispossessor
Mic 1:15 The *d* I shall yet bring to

Dispute
De 17:8 matters of *d*, inside your
19:17 the two men who have the *d*
21:5 *d* over every violent deed
25:1 a *d* arises between men, and
2Sa 19:9 *d* in all the tribes of Israel
Lu 12:58 to rid yourself of the *d*
21:15 not be able to resist or *d*
22:24 arose a heated *d* among them
Joh 3:25 a *d* arose on the part of the
Ac 6:9 and Asia, to *d* with Stephen
15:2 in Jerusalem regarding this *d*
25:20 being perplexed as to the *d*
1Co 11:16 man seems to *d* for some
Heb 6:16 oath is the end of every *d*
7:7 without any *d*, the less is

Disputes
Ac 25:19 *d* with him concerning their
1Ti 6:5 violent *d* about trifles on

Disputing
Ps 55:9 I have seen violence and *d*
Pr 20:3 for a man to desist from *d*
Mr 8:11 *d* with him, seeking . . . sign
9:14 and scribes *d* with them
9:16 What are you *d* with them?
12:28 come up and heard them *d*
Ac 9:29 *d* with the Greek-speaking
15:2 *d* by Paul and Barnabas with
15:7 much *d* had taken place, Peter
Jude 9 and was *d* about Moses' body

Disquiet
De 2:15 to *d* them out of the midst
Es 9:24 to *d* them and destroy them

Disquieting
Job 4:13 *d* thoughts from visions of
20:2 own *d* thoughts themselves
Ps 94:19 *d* thoughts became many
139:23 and know my *d* thoughts

Disquietude
Ps 55:2 And I cannot but show *d*

Disregard
Mt 23:23 not to *d* the other things
Mr 6:26 king did not want to *d* her
1Th 4:8 the man that shows *d* is

Disregarded
Mt 23:23 *d* the weightier matters of
Lu 7:30 *d* the counsel of God to them
1Ti 5:12 *d* their first expression of
Heb 10:28 *d* the law of Moses dies

Disregarding
1Th 4:8 is *d*, not man, but God
Jude 8 *d* lordship and speaking

Disregards
Lu 10:16, 16 he that *d* you *d* me too
10:16, 16 he that *d* me *d* also him
Joh 12:48 He that *d* me and does not

Disrepute
Ac 19:27 occupation . . . come into *d*

Disrespect
De 31:20 treat me with *d* and break
32:19 then he came to *d* them
1Sa 2:17 offering of Jehovah with *d*
2Sa 12:14 treated Jehovah with *d*
Ne 9:18 to commit great acts of *d*
9:26 committing acts of great *d*
Ps 74:10 treating your name with *d*
74:18 treated your name with *d*
Isa 1:4 the Holy One of Israel with *d*
52:5 was being treated with *d*
Jer 14:21 Do not *d* us for the sake
33:24 they keep treating with *d*

Disrespected
Ps 10:3 He has *d* Jehovah
10:13 the wicked one has *d* God
107:11 of the Most High they had *d*
Pr 1:30 they *d* all my reproof
5:12 heart has *d* even reproof
Isa 5:24 One of Israel they have *d*

Disrespectful
Jer 23:17 those who are *d* of me
Eze 35:12 heard all your *d* things

Disrespectfully
Nu 16:30 men have treated Jehovah *d*
Isa 60:14 those treating you *d* must

Disrespects
Pr 15:5 foolish *d* the discipline of

Disrobing
Mt 27:28 *d* him, they draped him with

Dissension
Ac 15:2 had occurred no little *d* and
23:7 *d* arose between the Pharisees
23:10 Now when the *d* grew great

Dissensions
1Co 1:11 that *d* exist among you

Dissolve
Job 30:22 you *d* me with a crash
Ps 58:7 *d* as into waters that go

Dissolved
Ps 75:3 all its inhabitants being *d*
Isa 28:18 will certainly be *d*
Na 2:6 palace itself will . . . be *d*
Ac 13:43 synagogue assembly was *d*
2Co 5:1 this tent, should be *d*, we
2Pe 3:10 intensely hot will be *d*
3:11 these things are thus to be *d*
3:12 will be *d* and the elements

Dissolves
Job 7:5 skin . . . formed crusts and *d*

Dissolving
Job 8:19 That is the *d* of his way

Dissuaded
Ac 21:14 When he would not be *d*, we

Distaff
Pr 31:19 she has thrust out to the *d*

Distance
Ge 18:2 men were standing some *d*
21:16 about the *d* of a bowshot
21:16 she sat down at a *d* and began
22:4 to see the place from a *d*
30:36 set a *d* of three days'
31:23 a *d* of seven days' journey
35:21 a *d* beyond the tower of Eder
37:18 caught sight of him from a *d*
Ex 2:4 stationed herself at a *d*
20:18 quivered and stood at a *d*
20:21 people kept standing at a *d*
24:1 you must bow down from a *d*
De 32:52 a *d* you will see the land
Jos 3:4 a *d* between you and it of
Jg 18:22 a *d* away from the house of
1Sa 26:13 top of the mountain at a *d*
2Ki 2:7 standing in view at a *d*
2Ch 26:15 fame went out to a great *d*
Ezr 3:13 heard even to a great *d*
6:6 keep your *d* from there
Job 39:29 Far into the *d* its eyes
Ps 38:11 have stood off at a *d*
138:6 he knows only from a *d*
Pr 7:19 traveling on a way of some *d*
Jon 3:3 a walking *d* of three days
3:4 the walking *d* of one day
Mt 26:58 following him at a good *d*
27:55 were there viewing from a *d*
Mr 5:6 sight of Jesus from a *d* he ran
11:13 from a *d* he caught sight of
14:54 from a good *d*, followed him
15:40 women viewing from a *d*
Lu 2:44 they covered a day's *d* and
18:13 collector standing at a *d*
22:54 Peter was following at a *d*
23:49 were standing at a *d*
Joh 11:18 at a *d* of about two miles
Ac 27:28 proceeded a short *d* and
Re 14:20 *d* of a thousand six hundred
18:10 at a *d* because of their fear
18:15 at a *d* because of their fear
18:17 stood at a *d*

Distant
Nu 9:10 off on a *d* journey, he too
De 29:22 who will come from a *d* land
Jos 9:6 from a *d* land that we have
9:9 from a very *d* land that your
2Sa 7:19 down to a *d* future time
1Ki 8:41 comes from a *d* land by
8:46 land of the enemy *d* or
2Ki 20:14 From a *d* land they came
1Ch 17:17 down to a *d* future time
2Ch 6:32 comes from a *d* land by
6:36 captive to a land *d* or nearby
Es 9:20 the nearby and the *d* ones
Pr 25:25 a good report from a *d* land
Isa 8:9 you in *d* parts of the earth
39:3 From a *d* land they came to
46:11 from a *d* land the man to
Zec 10:9 in the *d* places they will
Lu 15:13 abroad into a *d* country
19:12 traveled to a *d* land to
24:13 village about seven miles *d*
Ac 1:8 the most *d* part of the earth

Distinct
Ge 47:26 priests as a *d* group did not
Ex 8:22 make the land of Goshen . . . *d*
33:16 your people . . . made *d*
Le 24:12 be a *d* declaration to them

Distinction
Ex 9:4 *d* between the livestock of
11:7 *d* between the Egyptians and
Le 10:10 make a *d* between the holy
11:47 a *d* between the unclean and
20:25 *d* between the clean beast
1Ch 22:5 beauteous *d* to all the lands
Eze 22:26 they have made no *d*
Mal 3:18 the *d* between a righteous
Ac 15:9 no *d* at all between us and
Ro 3:22 For there is no *d*
10:12 no *d* between Jew and Greek

Distinctions
Jas 2:4 you have class *d* among
3:17 not making partial *d*, not

Distinctly
Nu 15:34 *d* stated what should be done
Ezr 4:18 has been *d* read before me
Mr 8:25 he was seeing everything *d*

Distinguish
2Sa 14:17 *d* what is good and what is
Ps 4:3 will certainly *d* his loyal one
Heb 5:14 to *d* both right and wrong

Distinguished
Ex 24:11 *d* men of the sons of Israel
2Sa 23:19 *d* even more than the rest
23:23 *d* even more than the thirty
2Ki 10:6 the *d* men of the city that
10:11 and all his *d* men and his
1Ch 11:21 more *d* than the two others
11:25 was more *d* than the thirty
Am 6:1 the *d* ones of the chief part
Lu 14:8 someone more *d* than you may

Distinguishing
Ezr 3:13 people were not *d* the sound
Da 6:3 Daniel was steadily *d* himself

Distort
Ex 23:8 *d* the words of righteous men

Distorting
Ac 13:10 *d* the right ways of Jehovah

Distortion
Pr 11:3 *d* by those dealing
15:4 *d* in it means a breaking down

Distorts
De 16:19 *d* the words of righteous
Pr 19:3 earthling man that *d* his way

Distracted
Lu 10:40 Martha . . . *d* with attending
Distraction
1Co 7:35 upon the Lord without *d*
Distress
Ge 35:3 in the day of my *d*
42:21 we saw the *d* of his soul
42:21 why this *d* has come upon us
Jg 10:14 in the time of your *d*
11:7 just when you are in *d*
1Sa 22:2 And all men in *d* and all
26:24 deliver me out of all *d*
2Sa 4:9 redeemed my soul out of all *d*
22:7 In my *d* I kept calling upon
1Ki 1:29 my soul out of all *d*
2Ki 19:3 This day is a day of *d* and
2Ch 15:4 in their *d* they returned to
15:6 with every sort of *d*
20:9 to you for aid out of our *d*
28:20 caused him *d*, and did not
28:22 causing him *d*, he acted
33:12 caused him *d*, he softened
Ne 9:27 who kept causing them *d*
9:27 in the time of their *d* they
9:37 and we are in great *d*
Es 7:4 But the *d* is not appropriate
Job 7:11 speak in the *d* of my spirit
15:24 *D* . . . keep terrifying him
27:9 In case *d* comes upon him
36:16 from the mouth of *d*
36:19 No, nor in *d* Even all your
38:23 kept back for the time of *d*
Ps 4:1 In the *d* you must make broad
9:9 secure height in times of *d*
10:1 yourself hid in times of *d*
18:6 In my *d* I kept calling upon
20:1 answer you in the day of *d*
22:11 because *d* is nearby
32:7 safeguard me from *d* itself
37:39 fortress in the time of *d*
50:15 And call me in the day of *d*
54:7 out of every *d* he delivered
59:16 flee in the day of my *d*
60:11 Do give us assistance from *d*
77:2 In the day of my *d* I have
78:49 Fury and denunciation and *d*
81:7 In *d* you called, and I
86:7 In the day of my *d* I will
91:15 I shall be with him in *d*
106:44 would see the *d* of theirs
107:6 out to Jehovah in their *d*
107:13 Jehovah for help in their *d*
107:19 Jehovah for help in their *d*
107:28 out to Jehovah in their *d*
108:12 give us assistance from *d*
116:3 *D* and grief I kept finding
119:143 *D* and difficulty
120:1 Jehovah I called in the *d*
138:7 walk in the midst of *d*
142:2 to tell about my own *d*
143:11 forth my soul out of *d*
Pr 1:27 *d* and hard times come upon
11:8 one rescued even from *d*
12:13 righteous one gets out of *d*
17:17 is born for when there is *d*
24:10 discouraged in the day of *d*
25:19 treacherous in the day of *d*
Isa 8:22 lo! *d* and darkness, obscurity
25:4 poor one in the *d* that he has
26:16 during *d* they have turned
30:6 land of *d* and hard conditions
30:20 bread in the form of *d*
33:2 salvation in the time of *d*
37:3 day of *d* and of rebuke and
46:7 out of one's *d* it does not
63:9 During all their *d* it was
Jer 4:31 the *d* like that of a woman
6:24 *D* itself has seized hold of
10:18 I will cause them *d* in
14:8 in the time of *d*, why do you
15:11 and in the time of *d*
16:19 for flight in the day of *d*
30:7 the time of *d* for Jacob
48:41 wife having childbirth *d*
49:22 wife having *d* in childbirth
49:24 *D* and birth pangs
50:43 There is *d*! Severe pains
Da 12:1 time of *d* such as has not
Ob 12 in the day of their *d*
14 his survivors in the day of *d*
Jon 2:2 Out of my *d* I called out to
Na 1:7 a stronghold in the day of *d*
1:9 *D* will not rise up a second
Hab 3:16 wait for the day of *d*
Zep 1:15 a day of *d* and of anguish
1:17 will cause *d* to mankind, and
Zec 10:11 pass through the sea with *d*
Mt 24:8 are a beginning of pangs of *d*
Mr 13:8 a beginning of pangs of *d*
Lu 2:48 in mental *d* have been looking
19:43 will encircle you and *d* you
Ro 2:9 *d*, upon the soul of every man
8:35 *d* or persecution or hunger or
1Th 5:3 just as the pang of *d* upon a
Distressed
Jg 10:9 and Israel was greatly *d*
2Sa 1:26 *d* over you, my brother
Da 7:15 Daniel, my spirit was *d*
Mt 4:24 *d* with various diseases and
Lu 4:38 *d* with a high fever, and they
12:50 being *d* until it is finished
Ac 28:8 *d* with fever and dysentery
2Pe 2:7 Lot, who was greatly *d* by the
Distresses
De 31:17 calamities and *d* must come
31:21 many calamities and *d* will
1Sa 10:19 all your evils and your *d*
Job 5:19 In six *d* he will deliver you
Ps 25:17 *D* of my heart have
25:22 Israel out of all his *d*
31:7 known about the *d* of my soul
34:6 out of all his *d* He saved him
34:17 out of all their *d* he
46:1 readily to be found during *d*
71:20 have made me see many *d* and
Pr 21:23 is keeping his soul from *d*
Isa 65:16 former *d* will actually be
Distressing
Ge 47:9 Few and *d* the days of the
1Sa 15:11 it was *d* to Samuel, and he
30:6 very *d* to David, because the
2Sa 13:2 so *d* to Amnon that he felt
24:14 It is very *d* to me
1Ch 21:13 very *d* to me. Please, let
Ps 116:3 *d* circumstances of Sheol
118:5 Out of the *d* circumstances
Isa 5:30 there is *d* darkness
59:19 will come in like a *d* river
63:9 all their distress it was *d*
Jer 48:5 *d* outcry over the breakdown
La 1:3 among *d* circumstances
Distribute
Jg 5:30 ought they not to *d* spoil, A
Lu 18:22 and *d* to poor people, and
23:34 *d* his garments, they cast
Ac 6:2 to *d* food to tables
Eph 4:28 to *d* to someone in need
Distributed
Jos 19:51 *d* as a possession by lot in
1Ch 23:6 David *d* them in divisions to
24:4 they *d* them to the sons of
24:5 they *d* them by lots, these
2Ch 11:23 *d* some out of all his sons
Ps 112:9 He has *d* widely; he has
Mt 14:19 loaves, he *d* them to the
27:35 they *d* his outer garments by
Mr 15:24 *d* his outer garments by
Joh 6:11 giving thanks, he *d* them to
Ac 2:3 And tongues . . . were *d* about
13:19 *d* the land of them by lot
Ro 12:3 as God has *d* to him a measure
2Co 9:9 He has *d* widely, he has given
Distributes
Job 38:24 by which the light *d* itself
Ro 12:8 he that *d*, let him do it with
Distributing
Ne 13:13 it devolved to do the *d*
Mt 15:36 and began *d* to the disciples
Ac 2:45 properties and *d* the proceeds
Distribution
Ac 4:35 *d* would be made to each one
6:1 overlooked in the daily *d*
1Co 12:11 making a *d* to each one
Distributions
Heb 2:4 and with *d* of holy spirit
Distributors
Jg 5:11 voices of the water *d* among
District
Ge 13:10 saw the whole *D* of the Jordan
13:11 whole *D* of the Jordan
13:12 among the cities of the *D*
19:17 not stand still in all the *D*
19:25 even the entire *D* and all the
19:28 land of the *D* and saw a
19:29 cities of the *D* to ruin God
De 34:3 and the Negeb and the *D*, the
2Sa 18:23 run by the way of the *D*
1Ki 7:46 In the *D* of the Jordan it
2Ch 4:17 In the *D* of the Jordan the
Ezr 2:1 sons of the jurisdictional *d*
5:8 the jurisdictional *d* of Judah
6:2 the jurisdictional *d* of Media
7:16 jurisdictional *d* of Babylon
Ne 1:3 there in the jurisdictional *d*
3:9 half the *d* of Jerusalem
3:12 half the *d* of Jerusalem
3:14 the *d* of Beth-haccherem
3:15 a prince of the *d* of Mizpah
3:16 of half the *d* of Beth-zur
3:17 half the *d* of Keilah, did
3:17 did repair work for his *d*
3:18 half the *d* of Keilah
3:22 men of the Jordan *D*, did
7:6 sons of the jurisdictional *d*
11:3 heads of the jurisdictional *d*
12:28 the *D*, from all around
Es 1:22 to each jurisdictional *d* in
3:12 each jurisdictional *d*, in its
8:9 to each jurisdictional *d* in its
8:11 jurisdictional *d* that were
9:28 each jurisdictional *d* and each
Ec 5:8 in a jurisdictional *d*, do not
Da 2:48 jurisdictional *d* of Babylon
2:49 jurisdictional *d* of Babylon
3:1 the jurisdictional *d* of Babylon
3:12 jurisdictional *d* of Babylon
3:30 jurisdictional *d* of Babylon
8:2 in Elam the jurisdictional *d*
11:24 jurisdictional *d* he will
Mt 14:1 Herod, the *d* ruler, heard the
Lu 3:1 Herod was *d* ruler of Galilee
3:1 Philip his brother was *d* ruler
3:1 was *d* ruler of Abilene
3:19 Herod the *d* ruler, for being
9:7 Herod the *d* ruler heard of
Ac 2:9 Pontus and the *d* of Asia
13:1 with Herod the *d* ruler, and
16:6 the word in the *d* of Asia
16:12 city of the *d* of Macedonia
19:10 inhabiting the *d* of Asia
19:22 some time in the *d* of Asia
19:26 in nearly all the *d* of Asia
19:27 the whole *d* of Asia and the
20:4 from the *d* of Asia Tychicus
20:16 any time in the *d* of Asia
20:18 I stepped into the *d* of Asia
24:18 Jews from the *d* of Asia
27:2 the coast of the *d* of Asia
2Co 1:8 to us in the *d* of Asia
2Ti 1:15 all the men in the *d* of Asia
Re 1:4 that are in the *d* of Asia
Districts
1Ki 20:14 of the jurisdictional *d*
20:15 of the jurisdictional *d*
20:17 of the jurisdictional *d*
20:19 of the jurisdictional *d*
Ezr 4:15 to kings and jurisdictional *d*
Es 1:1 twenty-seven jurisdictional *d*
1:3 princes of the jurisdictional *d*
1:16 the jurisdictional *d* of King
1:22 the king's jurisdictional *d*
2:3 jurisdictional *d* of his realm
2:18 for the jurisdictional *d* he
3:8 jurisdictional *d* of your realm
3:12 the different jurisdictional *d*
3:13 the king's jurisdictional *d*
3:14 the different jurisdictional *d*
4:3 the different jurisdictional *d*
4:11 of the king's jurisdictional *d*
8:5 the king's jurisdictional *d*
8:9 princes of the jurisdictional *d*
8:9 jurisdictional *d*, to each
8:12 in all the jurisdictional *d*
8:13 the different jurisdictional *d*
8:17 the different jurisdictional *d*
9:2 all the jurisdictional *d* of
9:3 princes of the jurisdictional *d*
9:4 all the jurisdictional *d*
9:12 rest of the jurisdictional *d*
9:16 jurisdictional *d* of the king
9:19 the cities of the outlying *d*
9:20 *d* of King Ahasuerus, the
9:30 *d*, the realm of Ahasuerus
Ec 2:8 and the jurisdictional *d*
La 1:1 among the jurisdictional *d* has

Eze 19:8 from the jurisdictional *d*
Da 3:2 the jurisdictional *d* to come
3:3 of the jurisdictional *d* were
Mt 2:16 Bethlehem and in all its *d*
4:13 the *d* of Zebulun and Naphtali
8:34 to move out from their *d*
Mr 5:17 him to go away from their *d*

Disturb
2Ki 23:18 not let anyone *d* his bones
2Ch 32:18 to *d* them, in order that
Ps 2:5 hot displeasure he will *d* them
83:15 *d* them with your own
Da 11:44 reports that will *d* him, out

Disturbance
Le 26:16 bring upon you *d* with
Jos 11:23 the land had no *d* from war
14:15 land had no *d* from war
Jg 3:11 land had no *d* for forty years
3:30 the land had no further *d*
5:31 the land had no further *d* for
8:28 the land had no further *d* for
2Ki 11:20 city, for its part, had no *d*
1Ch 4:40 and having no *d* but at ease
2Ch 14:1 land had no *d* for ten years
14:5 without *d* before him
14:6 for the land had no *d*
20:30 Jehoshaphat had no *d*, and
23:21 the city itself had no *d*
35:21 that I should cause *d*
Ne 4:8 Jerusalem and cause me *d*
Ps 78:33 And their years by the *d*
Isa 14:7 has become free of *d*
65:23 they bring to birth for *d*
Jer 30:10 free of *d* and be at ease
46:27 have no *d* and be at ease
Eze 38:11 upon those having no *d*
Zec 1:11 sitting still and having no *d*
Ac 19:23 *d* concerning The Way

Disturbances
Jer 15:8 suddenly excitement and *d*

Disturbed
Ge 45:3 they were *d* by reason of him
Ex 15:15 Edom will indeed be *d*; As
Jg 20:41 the men of Benjamin were *d*
1Sa 28:15 *d* me by having me brought
28:21 that he had been greatly *d*
2Sa 4:1 Israelites themselves were *d*
7:10 and no more will they be *d*
18:33 the king became *d* and went
1Ch 17:9 and no more will they be *d*
Job 4:5 even you, and you get *d*
21:6 I have also become *d*
23:15 why I feel *d* because of him
23:16 Almighty himself has *d* me
Ps 6:2 for my bones have been *d*
6:3 own soul has been very much *d*
6:10 be very much ashamed and *d*
30:7 I became one that is *d*
48:5 They got *d*, they were sent
83:17 and be *d* for all times
90:7 by your rage we have been *d*
104:29 your face, they get *d*
Isa 13:8 And people have become *d*
21:3 *d* so that I do not see
Jer 51:32 themselves have become *d*
Eze 7:27 hands of the people . . . get *d*
26:18 *d* owing to your going out
Lu 1:29 was deeply *d* at the saying
10:41 you are anxious and *d* about
Joh 5:7 pool when the water is *d*

Disturbing
Ac 16:20 These men are *d* our city

Disturbs
Job 22:10 And sudden dread *d* you

Ditches
2Ki 3:16 torrent valley full of *d*
Isa 30:25 to be streams, water *d*, in
44:4 like poplars by the water *d*
Jer 14:3 They have come to the *d*

Divan
Job 7:13 said, My *d* will comfort me
Ps 6:6 With my tears I make my own *d*
41:3 upon a *d* of illness
132:3 on the *d* of my grand lounge
Pr 7:16 I have bedecked my *d*, with
Ca 1:16 Our *d* also is one of foliage
Am 3:12 and on a Damascene *d*

Divans
Am 6:4 sprawling on their *d*, and are

Diversified
Eph 3:10 greatly *d* wisdom of God

Divide
Ge 49:27 at evening he will *d* spoil
Ex 15:9 I shall *d* spoil! My soul will
21:35 and *d* the price paid for it
21:35 the dead one they should *d*
Le 1:17 He must not *d* it
20:26 *d* you off from the peoples
Nu 31:27 *d* the booty in two between
34:17 *d* the land to you people for
34:18 to *d* the land for a
De 19:3 you must *d* up the territory
1Ki 16:21 people of Israel began to *d*
Job 41:6 *d* it up among tradesmen
Ps 55:9 O Jehovah, *d* their tongue
Pr 16:19 than to *d* spoil with the
Isa 9:3 when they *d* up the spoil
56:3 *d* me off from his people
Eze 5:1 and *d* the hair in portions
39:14 whom they will *d* off
Lu 12:13 to *d* the inheritance with me

Divided
Ge 10:25 in his days the earth was *d*
32:7 *d* the people who were with
33:1 he *d* off the children to Leah
Le 20:24 *d* you off from the peoples
20:25 *d* off for you in declaring
Nu 31:42 Moses *d* from that belonging
Jg 7:16 he *d* the three hundred men up
9:43 *d* them up into three bands
1Ki 18:6 *d* between themselves the
2Ki 2:8 were *d* this way and that way
2:14 *d* this way and that way
1Ch 1:19 in his days the earth was *d*
Job 38:25 *d* a channel for the flood
Pr 30:27 all of them *d* into groups
Isa 33:23 will have to be *d* up
La 4:16 face of Jehovah has *d* them up
Eze 37:22 be *d* any longer into two
Da 2:41 kingdom . . . prove to be *d*
5:28 your kingdom has been *d* and
11:4 *d* toward the four winds of
Mt 12:25 kingdom *d* against itself
12:25 house *d* against itself will
12:26 Satan . . . *d* against himself
Mr 3:24 kingdom . . . *d* against itself
3:25 a house . . . *d* against itself
3:26 against himself and become *d*
6:41 *d* up the two fishes for all
Lu 11:17 kingdom *d* against itself
11:17 house *d* against itself falls
11:18 if Satan is also *d* against
12:52 *d*, three against two and
12:53 *d*, father against son and
15:12 *d* his means of living to
1Co 1:13 The Christ exists *d*. Paul
7:34 and he is *d*. Further, the

Divides
Lu 11:22 *d* out the things he despoiled

Dividing
Ge 1:6 *d* occur between the waters and
14:15 he resorted to *d* his forces
Jos 19:49 finished *d* the land for a
Isa 58:7 *d* of your bread out to the
Heb 4:12 to the *d* of soul and spirit

Divination
Nu 22:7 payments for *d* in their hands
23:23 Nor any *d* against Israel
De 18:10 anyone who employs *d*, a
1Sa 15:23 is the same as the sin of *d*
28:8 Employ *d*, please, for me by
2Ki 17:17 practice *d* and to look for
2Ch 33:6 and used *d* and practiced
Isa 3:2 practicer of *d* and elderly
Jer 14:14 A false vision and *d* and a
27:9 your practicers of *d* and to
29:8 practicers of *d* deceive you
Eze 12:24 nor double-faced *d* in the
13:6 what is untrue and a lying *d*
13:7 a lying *d* that you have said
13:23 *d* you will divine no longer
21:21 in order to resort to *d*
21:22 the *d* proved to be for
21:23 an untrue *d* in their eyes
Mic 3:6 so as not to practice *d*
3:11 practice *d* simply for money
Zec 10:2 practicers of *d*, for their
Ac 16:16 with a spirit, a demon of *d*

Divine
De 18:14 and to those who *d*; but as
Jos 22:22, 22 *D* One, God, Jehovah, *D*
Ps 50:1 The *D* One, God, Jehovah, has
82:1 the assembly of the *D* One
83:1 do not stay quiet, O *D* One
118:27 Jehovah is the *D* One, And
118:28 You are my *D* One, and
Isa 46:9 I am the *D* One and there is
Eze 13:23 you will *d* no longer
Mt 2:12 given *d* warning in a dream
2:22 given *d* warning in a dream
Ac 10:22 *d* instructions by a holy
11:26 were by *d* providence called
17:29 that the *D* Being is like gold
Ro 11:4 *d* pronouncement say to him
Col 2:9 the fullness of the *d* quality
Heb 8:5 was given the *d* command
11:7 given *d* warning of things
12:25 giving *d* warning upon earth
2Pe 1:3 *d* power has given us freely
1:4 become sharers in *d* nature

Divinely
Lu 2:26 it had been *d* revealed to him
Ac 7:20 born, and he was *d* beautiful

Diviner
Jos 13:22 the son of Beor, the *d*

Diviners
1Sa 6:2 to call the priests and the *d*
Isa 44:25 *d* themselves act crazily
Mic 3:7 the *d* will certainly be

Divining
Eze 13:9 untruth and that are *d* a lie
21:29 their *d* for you a lie
22:28 *d* for them a lie, saying

Division
Ge 1:4 God brought about a *d* between
1:7 make a *d* between the waters
1:14 make a *d* between the day and
1:18 to make a *d* between the light
Ex 26:33 curtain must make a *d* for
Nu 1:52 three-tribe *d* by their armies
2:2 by his three-tribe *d*, by the
2:3 three-tribe *d* of the camp of
2:10 three-tribe *d* of the camp of
2:18 three-tribe *d* of the camp of
2:25 three-tribe *d* of the camp of
10:14 three-tribe *d* of the camp of
10:18 three-tribe *d* of the camp of
10:22 three-tribe *d* of the camp of
10:25 three-tribe *d* of the camp
1Ch 15:18 brothers of the second *d*
27:1 *d* was twenty-four thousand
27:2 first *d* of the first month
27:2 his *d* there were twenty-four
27:4 the *d* of the second month
27:4 Dodai the Ahohite with his *d*
27:4 his *d* there were twenty-four
27:5 and in his *d* there were
27:6 and over his *d* there was
27:7 and in his *d* there were
27:8 and in his *d* there were
27:9 and in his *d* there were
27:10 and in his *d* there were
27:11 and in his *d* there were
27:12 and in his *d* there were
27:13 and in his *d* there were
27:14 and in his *d* there were
27:15 and in his *d* there were
Isa 59:2 causing *d* between you and
Eze 42:20 *d* between what is holy and
Mt 10:35 I came to cause *d*, with a
Lu 1:5 Zechariah of the *d* of Abijah
1:8 assignment of his *d* before God
12:51 I tell you, but rather *d*
Joh 7:43 a *d* over him developed among
9:16 So there was a *d* among them
10:19 *d* resulted among the Jews
1Co 12:25 should be no *d* in the body

Divisions
Nu 2:17 to their three-tribe *d*
2:31 to their three-tribe *d*
2:34 in their three-tribe *d*
Jg 5:15 Among the *d* of Reuben great
5:16 For the *d* of Reuben there were
1Sa 23:28 place the Crag of the *D*
2Ki 11:7 two *d* among you that are all
1Ch 23:6 David distributed them in *d*
24:1 the sons of Aaron had their *d*
24:3 *d* of them for their office
26:1 For the *d* of gatekeepers
26:12 these *d* of the gatekeepers
26:19 *d* of the gatekeepers of the

1Ch 27:1 *d* of those that came in and
28:1 *d* of those ministering to
28:13 for the *d* of the priests and
28:21 *d* of the priests and of the
2Ch 5:11 was no need to observe the *d*
8:14 set the *d* of the priests
8:14 gatekeepers in their *d* for the
23:8 set the *d* free from duty
23:18 David had put in *d* over the
31:2 *d* of the priests and of the
31:2 Levites in their *d*, each one
31:15 to their brothers in the *d*
31:16 according to their *d*
31:17 obligations in their *d*
35:4 according to your *d*, by the
35:10 and the Levites by their *d*
Ezr 6:18 and the Levites in their *d*
Ne 11:36 *d* of Judah for Benjamin
Ro 16:17 who cause *d* and occasions
1Co 1:10 should not be *d* among you
11:18 I hear *d* exist among you
Ga 5:20 anger, contentions, *d*, sects

Divorce
De 22:19 will not be allowed to *d* her
22:29 He will not be allowed to *d*
24:1 write out a certificate of *d*
24:3 a certificate of *d* for her
Isa 50:1 the *d* certificate of the
Jer 3:8 certificate of her full *d* to
Mt 1:19 intended to *d* her secretly
5:31 give her a certificate of *d*
19:3 Is it lawful for a man to *d*
Mr 10:2 lawful for a man to *d* a wife

Divorced
Le 21:7 woman *d* from her husband they
21:14 or a *d* woman and one violated
22:13 a *d* when she has no offspring
Nu 30:9 vow of a widow or a *d* woman
Eze 44:22 *d* woman should they take
Mt 5:32 marries a *d* woman commits
Lu 16:18 he that marries a woman *d*

Divorces
Mt 5:31 whoever *d* his wife, let him
19:9 whoever *d* his wife, except
Mr 10:11 *d* his wife and marries
Lu 16:18 *d* his wife and marries

Divorcing
Mal 2:16 For he has hated a *d*
Mt 5:32 everyone *d* his wife, except
19:7 Moses prescribe . . . *d* her
19:8 concession to you of *d* your
Mr 10:4 of dismissal and *d* her
10:12 after *d* her husband, marries

Dizahab
De 1:1 and Laban and Hazeroth and *D*

Docked
Lu 5:2 two boats *d* at the lakeside

Doctrine
1Ti 1:3 not to teach different *d*
6:3 If any man teaches other *d*
Heb 6:1 primary *d* about the Christ

Doctrines
Mt 15:9 teach commands of men as *d*
Mr 7:7 teach as *d* commands of men

Document
Ezr 4:18 the official *d* that you have
4:23 the copy of the official *d*
5:5 an official *d* concerning this
Es 9:25 he said with the written *d*
Job 31:35 had written a *d* itself
Col 2:14 the handwritten *d* against

Documents
Es 1:22 he sent written *d* to all the
8:5 to undo the written *d*, the
8:10 written *d* by the hand of the
9:20 written *d* to all the Jews
9:30 written *d* to all the Jews in

Dodai
1Ch 27:4 was *D* the Ahohite with his

Dodanim
Ge 10:4 the sons of Javan . . . *D*

Dodavahu
2Ch 20:37 Eliezer the son of *D* of

Dodged
1Sa 19:10 he *d* from before Saul, so

Dodo
Jg 10:1 Puah, the son of *D*, a man of
2Sa 23:9 Eleazar the son of *D* the
23:24 Elhanan the son of *D* of
1Ch 11:12 the son of *D* the Ahohite
11:26 Elhanan the son of *D* of

Doeg
1Sa 21:7 name was *D* the Edomite, the
22:9 *D* the Edomite, being
22:18 king said to *D*: You turn and
22:18 *D* the Edomite turned and
22:22 *D* the Edomite was there
Ps 52:*super* when *D* the Edomite came

Doer
De 25:16 every *d* of injustice, is
2Sa 3:39 repay the *d* of what is bad
Ezr 7:26 not become a *d* of the law
Ps 106:21 *D* of great things in Egypt
136:4 *D* of wonderful, great things
Ec 3:9 advantage is there for the *d*
Joh 8:34 Every *d* of sin is a slave of
Jas 1:23 of the word, and not a *d*
1:25 *d* of the work, will be happy
4:11 not a *d* of law, but a judge

Doers
2Ki 12:11 the hands of *d* of the work
12:14 to the *d* of the work that
12:15 give to the *d* of the work
22:9 hand of the *d* of the work
1Ch 22:15 in great number *d* of work
23:24 *d* of the work for the
27:26 the *d* of work in the field
2Ch 24:12 *d* of the work of the
24:13 *d* of the work began
34:10 hand of the *d* of the work
34:10 *d* of the work who were
34:13 *d* of the work for the
34:17 hand of the *d* of the work
Ezr 3:9 *d* of the work in the house of
Ne 2:16 the rest of the *d* of the work
11:12 *d* of the work of the house
Es 9:3 *d* of the business that belonged
Jer 32:30 *d* of what was bad in my
Mal 3:15 the *d* of wickedness have
Ro 2:13 *d* of law will be declared
Jas 1:22 become *d* of the word, and
1Pe 2:14 but to praise *d* of good

Dog
Ex 11:7 no *d* move eagerly its tongue
De 23:18 a harlot or the price of a *d*
Jg 7:5 just as a *d* laps, you will set
1Sa 17:43 said to David: Am I a *d*, so
24:14 you chasing? After a dead *d*?
2Sa 9:8 turned your face to the dead *d*
16:9 this dead *d* call down evil
2Ki 8:13 servant, who is a mere *d*
Ps 22:20 from the very paw of the *d*
59:6 They keep barking like a *d*
59:14 Let them bark like a *d* and
Pr 26:11 a *d* returning to its vomit
26:17 hold of the ears of a *d* is
Ec 9:4 a live *d* is better off than a
Isa 66:3 one breaking the neck of a *d*
2Pe 2:22 *d* has returned to its own

Dog's
2Sa 3:8 Am I a *d* head that belongs to

Dogs
Ex 22:31 You should throw it to the *d*
1Ki 14:11 in the city, the *d* will eat
16:4 in the city the *d* will eat
21:19 *d* licked up the blood of
21:19 *d* will lick up your blood
21:23 *d* will eat up Jezebel in
21:24 in the city the *d* will eat
22:38 *d* went licking up his blood
2Ki 9:10 Jezebel the *d* will eat up
9:36 *d* will eat the flesh of
Job 30:1 place with the *d* of my flock
Ps 22:16 For *d* have surrounded me
68:23 the tongue of your *d* may
Isa 56:10 are speechless *d*; they are
56:11 *d* strong in soulful desire
Jer 15:3 the *d* to drag away, and the
Mt 7:6 Do not give what is holy to *d*
15:26 and throw it to little *d*
15:27 *d* do eat of the crumbs
Mr 7:27 throw it to the little *d*
7:28 *d* underneath the table eat
Lu 16:21 *d* would come and lick his
Php 3:2 Look out for the *d*, look out
Re 22:15 Outside are the *d* and those

Doing*
Ge 4:7 If you turn to *d* good, will
41:25 What the true God is *d* he
41:28 What the true God is *d* he
Ex 15:11 the One *d* marvels
Nu 31:31 went *d* just as Jehovah had
32:13 generation that was *d* evil
1Ki 14:22 *d* what was bad in the eyes
15:26 kept *d* what was bad in the
Ne 13:17 bad thing that you are *d*
Job 5:9 *d* great things unsearchable
9:10 *D* great things unsearchable
9:12 say to him, What are you *d*?
Ps 14:1 There is no one *d* good
14:3 There is no one *d* good
28:4 Pay back to them their own *d*
37:1 those *d* unrighteousness
119:68 You are good and are *d* good
Pr 8:36 is *d* violence to his soul
12:14 very *d* of a man's hands will
Ec 8:4 may say . . . What are you *d*?
8:12 sinner may be *d* bad a hundred
Isa 44:24 I, Jehovah, am *d* everything
45:7 Jehovah, am *d* all these
64:5 exulting and *d* righteousness
65:12 *d* what was bad in my eyes
66:4 *d* what was bad in my eyes
Jer 5:1 there exists anyone *d* justice
35:18 *d* according to all that he
Eze 7:9 I am Jehovah *d* the smiting
8:6 detestable things they are *d*
8:6 that the house of Israel are *d*
12:9 say to you, What are you *d*?
18:19 statutes . . . he keeps *d*
20:11 man who keeps *d* them might
33:15 by not *d* injustice, he will
33:32 there are none *d* them
Da 4:35 *d* according to his own will
4:35 to him, What have you been *d*?
Am 9:12 Jehovah, who is *d* this
Mt 5:47 extraordinary thing are you *d*
6:3 know what your right is *d*
7:21 one *d* the will of my Father
7:26 sayings of mine and not *d*
12:2 *d* what it is not lawful to
13:41 who are *d* lawlessness
15:25 she began *d* obeisance to him
16:8 Why are you *d* this reasoning
Mr 2:24 *d* on the sabbath what is not
11:3 Why are you *d* this?
11:5 What are you *d* loosing the
Lu 10:28 keep on *d* this and you will
Joh 6:30 What work are you *d*?
7:51 come to know what he is *d*
10:25 works that I am *d* in the
10:37 *d* the works of my Father
10:38 But if I am *d* them, even
Ac 10:38 through the land *d* good
14:15 Why are you *d* these things?
15:17 says Jehovah, who is *d* these
Ro 13:3 Keep *d* good, and you will
13:4 *d* what is bad, be in fear
1Co 10:31 or *d* anything else, do all
11:24 Keep *d* this in remembrance
11:25 Keep *d* this, as often as you
2Co 8:10 not only the *d* but also the
13:7 you may be *d* what is fine
Eph 4:28 *d* with his hands what is
1Th 4:10 are *d* it to all the brothers
Heb 13:16 not forget the *d* of good
Jas 1:25 will be happy in his *d* it
2:19 You are *d* quite well
1Pe 2:15 by *d* good you may muzzle the
4:19 while they are *d* good
Re 22:11 He that is *d* unrighteousness

Doings
1Sa 8:8 In accord with all their *d*
2Ki 23:19 *d* that he had done at Bethel
2Ch 34:25 all the *d* of their hands
Ps 103:2 And do not forget all his *d*

Domestic
Ge 1:24 *d* animal and moving animal
1:25 *d* animal according to its
1:26 *d* animals and all the earth
2:20 names of all the *d* animals
3:14 cursed . . . of all the *d* animals
6:7 from man to *d* animal, to
6:20 *d* animals according to their
7:14 every *d* animal according to
7:21 among the *d* animals and
8:1 every *d* animal that was with
47:18 stock of *d* animals have been

x 20:10 nor your *d* animal nor your
22:10 any *d* animal to keep, and it
e 1:2 offering . . . from the *d* animals
5:2 body of an unclean *d* animal
19:19 interbreed your *d* animals
24:18 of the soul of a *d* animal
25:7 *d* animal and for the wild
26:22 cut off your *d* animals and
u 3:41 *d* animals of the Levites in
3:41 firstborn among the *d* animals
3:45 *d* animals of the Levites in
3:45 in place of their *d* animals
31:9 all their *d* animals and all
31:11 way of humans and *d* animals
31:26 captives . . . of *d* animals
31:30 of every sort of *d* animal
31:47 humankind and of *d* animals
32:26 *d* animals will stay there
35:3 serve for their *d* animals
e 2:35 Only the *d* animals did we
3:7 the *d* animals and the spoil
5:14 nor your ass nor any *d* animal
7:14 nor among your *d* animals
11:15 field for your *d* animals
13:15 *d* animals, to destruction
20:14 the *d* animals and everything
28:4 the fruit of your *d* beast
28:11 the fruit of your *d* animals
28:51 fruit of your *d* animals
30:9 fruit of your *d* animals and
s 8:2 its spoil and its *d* animals
8:27 the *d* animals and the spoil
11:14 and the *d* animals the sons
21:2 grounds for our *d* animals
; 20:48 from men to *d* animal up to
i 3:9 camp and for the *d* animals
3:17 livestock and your *d* animals
r 1:4 goods and with *d* animals
1:6 with *d* animals and with
e 2:12 no *d* animal with me except
2:12 except the *d* animal on which
2:14 no place for the *d* animal
9:37 and over our *d* animals
10:36 sons and of our *d* animals
b 12:7 *d* animals . . . will instruct
s 148:10 and all you *d* animals
r 12:10 for the soul of his *d* animal
a 46:1 and for the *d* animals
r 7:20 upon *d* animal, and upon the
31:27 with the seed of *d* animal
32:43 without man and *d* animal
33:10 man and without *d* animal
33:10 without *d* animal, there
33:12 man and even *d* animal and
50:3 *d* animal have taken flight
51:62 or even *d* animal, but
ze 14:13 earthling man and *d* animal
14:17 earthling man and *d* animal
14:19 earthling man and *d* animal
14:21 earthling man and *d* animal
25:13 man and *d* animal, and
29:8 earthling man and *d* animal
29:11 the foot of *d* animal pass
32:13 destroy all her *d* animals
32:13 a *d* animal muddy them
e 1:18 the *d* animal has sighed
n 3:7 No man and no *d* animal, no
3:8 sackcloth, man and *d* animal
4:11 besides many *d* animals
ag 1:11 and upon *d* animal, and upon
c 2:4 *d* animals in the midst of
8:10 for the wages of *d* animals
14:15 every sort of *d* animal that

omestics
t 24:45 master appointed over his *d*

ominate
e 1:18 to *d* by day and by night and
3:16 husband, and he will *d* you
37:8 Are you going to *d* over us
e 15:6 you must *d* over many nations
15:6 over you they will not *d*
s 8:6 *d* over the works of your hands
19:13 Do not let them *d* me

ominated
c 8:9 man has *d* man to his injury

ominating
e 1:16 luminary for *d* the day
1:16 lesser luminary for *d* the
45:8 one *d* over all the land of
45:26 *d* over all the land of Egypt
h 29:12 and you are *d* everything
h 20:6 *d* over all the kingdoms of
Ps 22:28 And he is *d* the nations

Domination
Ps 103:19 own kingship has held *d*
103:22 In all places of his *d*

Domineer
Es 9:1 had waited to *d* over them
Ps 119:133 of hurtful thing *d* over me

Domineered
Ne 5:15 themselves *d* over the people
Es 9:1 Jews themselves *d* over those

Domineering
Eze 16:30 of a woman, a *d* prostitute

Dominion
1Ki 9:19 in all the land of his *d*
2Ki 20:13 own house and in all his *d*
2Ch 8:6 and in all the land of his *d*
Ps 114:2 Israel his grand *d*
136:8 Even the sun for *d* by day
136:9 and the stars for combined *d*
145:13 your *d* is throughout all
Isa 22:21 *d* I shall give into his
39:2 own house and in all his *d*
Jer 34:1 the *d* under his hand, and
51:28 all the land of each one's *d*
Da 6:26 every *d* of my kingdom, people
6:26 and his *d* is forever
11:3 rule with extensive *d* and do
11:4 *d* with which he had ruled
11:5 rule with extensive *d* greater
Mic 4:8 first *d* will certainly come

Doomed
2Sa 19:28 nothing but *d* to death

Door
Ge 7:16 Jehovah shut the *d* behind him
19:6 but he shut the *d* behind him
19:9 getting near to break in the *d*
19:10 and they shut the *d*
Ex 21:6 against the *d* or the doorpost
De 15:17 through his ear and to the *d*
Jg 19:22 one another against the *d*
2Sa 13:17 and lock the *d* behind her
13:18 he locked the *d* behind her
1Ki 6:34 two leaves of the one *d*
6:34 two leaves of the other *d*
2Ki 4:4 close the *d* behind yourself
4:5 closed the *d* behind herself
4:21 closed the *d* upon him and
4:33 closed the *d* behind them
6:32 close the *d*, and you must
6:32 press him back with the *d*
9:3 open the *d* and flee and not
9:10 opened the *d* and went
Ps 141:3 watch over the *d* of my lips
Pr 26:14 A *d* keeps turning upon its
Ca 5:4 hand from the hole of the *d*
8:9 if she should be a *d*, we shall
Isa 57:8 behind the *d* and the doorpost
Eze 41:24 two *d* leaves belonged to
41:24, 24 One *d* had two *d* leaves
41:24 the other had two *d* leaves
Da 3:26 *d* of the burning fiery furnace
Mt 6:6 after shutting your *d*, pray to
25:10 and the *d* was shut
27:60 the *d* of the memorial tomb
Mr 1:33 was gathered right at the *d*
2:2 room, not even about the *d*
11:4 found the colt tied at the *d*
15:46 the *d* of the memorial tomb
16:3 the *d* of the memorial tomb
Lu 11:7 The *d* is already locked, and
13:24 get in through the narrow *d*
13:25 has got up and locked the *d*
13:25 to knock at the *d*, saying
Joh 10:1 sheepfold through the *d*
10:2 enters through the *d* is
10:7 I am the *d* of the sheep
10:9 I am the *d*; whoever enters
18:16 standing outside at the *d*
Ac 3:2 *d* that was called Beautiful
5:9 are at the *d*, and they will
12:6 and guards before the *d* were
12:13 he knocked at the *d* of the
14:27 the nations the *d* to faith
1Co 16:9 *d* that leads to activity
2Co 2:12 a *d* was opened to me in the
Col 4:3 God may open a *d* of utterance
1Jo 3:17 *d* of his tender compassions
Re 3:8 have set before you an opened *d*
3:20 I am standing at the *d* and
3:20 my voice and opens the *d*, I
4:1 an opened *d* in heaven, and

Doorkeeper
Jer 35:4 son of Shallum the *d*
Mr 13:34 the *d* to keep on the watch
Joh 10:3 The *d* opens to this one
18:16 spoke to the *d* and brought
18:17 servant girl, the *d*, then

Doorkeepers
2Ki 12:9 there the priests, the *d*
22:4 *d* have gathered from the
23:4 the *d* to bring out from the
25:18 second priest and three *d*
1Ch 9:19 the *d* of the tent, and their
2Ch 23:4 Levites, will be for *d*
34:9 *d* had gathered from the hand
Ezr 7:24 the *d*, the Nethinim, and the
Es 2:21 court officials of the king, *d*
6:2 *d*, who had sought to lay hand
Jer 52:24 and the three *d*

Doorpost
Ex 21:6 against the door or the *d*; and
1Sa 1:9 seat by the *d* of the temple
Isa 57:8 behind the door and the *d*
Eze 41:21 temple, the *d* was squared
43:8, 8 their *d* beside my *d*
45:19 upon the *d* of the House
45:19 *d* of the gate of the inner
46:2 stand by the *d* of the gate

Doorposts
Ex 12:7 splash it upon the two *d* and
12:22 the two *d* some of the blood
12:23 blood upon . . . the two *d*
De 6:9 write them upon the *d* of your
11:20 write them upon the *d* of
1Ki 6:31 side pillars, *d* and a fifth
6:33 the *d* of oil-tree wood
7:5 the *d* were squared with the
2Ki 18:16 the *d* that Hezekiah the king

Doors
Ex 21:19 does walk about out of *d*
De 3:5 with a high wall, *d* and bar
Jos 2:19 out of the *d* of your house
6:26 let him put up its *d*
Jg 3:23 he closed the *d* of the roof
3:24 the *d* of the roof chamber
3:25 one opening the *d* of the roof
11:31 *d* of my house to meet me
16:3 the *d* of the city gate and the
19:27 opened the *d* of the house
1Sa 3:15 the *d* of Jehovah's house
9:26 Samuel, went forth out of *d*
21:13 making cross marks on the *d*
23:7 into a city with *d* and bar
1Ki 6:31 with *d* of oil-tree wood
6:32 two *d* were of oil-tree wood
6:34 two *d* were of juniper wood
7:50 the sockets for the *d* of the
7:50 the *d* of the house of the
16:34 he put up its *d*, according
2Ki 18:16 cut off the *d* of the temple
1Ch 22:3 nails for the *d* of the gates
2Ch 3:7 its walls and its *d* with gold
4:9 *d* belonging to the enclosure
4:9 *d* he overlaid with copper
4:22 inner *d* for the Most Holy
4:22 *d* of the house of the temple
8:5 cities with walls, *d* and bar
14:7 towers, double *d* and bars
28:24 *d* of the house of Jehovah
29:3 opened the *d* of the house
29:7 closed the *d* of the porch
Ne 3:1 and went setting up its *d*
3:3 set up its *d*, its bolts and
3:6 set up its *d* and its bolts and
3:13 built it and then set up its *d*
3:14 setting up its *d*, its bolts
3:15 set up its *d*, its bolts and
6:1 *d* themselves I had not set up
6:10 close the *d* of the temple
7:1 I at once set up the *d*
7:3 shut the *d* and bolt them
13:19 the *d* began to be closed
Job 3:10 the *d* of my mother's belly
31:32 *d* I kept open to the path
38:8 barricaded the sea with *d*
38:10 And to set a bar and *d*
41:14 The *d* of its face who has
Ps 31:11 When seeing me out of *d*
78:23 opened the very *d* of heaven
107:16 has broken the *d* of copper
Pr 5:16 springs be scattered out of *d*
8:34 keeping awake at my *d* day by
24:27 Prepare your work out of *d*

Ec 12:4 *d* onto the street have been
Isa 26:20 shut your *d* behind you
45:1 before him the two-leaved *d*
45:2 copper *d* I shall break in
Jer 49:31 No *d* and no bar does it have
Eze 26:2 broken, the *d* of the peoples
38:11 not have even bar and *d*
41:23 the holy place had two *d*
41:24 leaves belonged to the *d*
41:25 upon the *d* of the temple
Zec 11:1 Open up your *d*, O Lebanon
Mal 1:10 Who . . . will shut the *d*?
Mt 24:33 that he is near at the *d*
Mr 13:29 that he is near, at the *d*
Lu 2:8 shepherds living out of *d* and
Joh 20:19 *d* were locked where the
20:26 the *d* were locked, and he
Ac 5:19 Jehovah's angel opened the *d*
5:23 guards standing at the *d*, but
16:26 the *d* were instantly opened
16:27 the prison *d* were open, drew
21:30 the *d* were closed
Jas 5:9 Judge is standing before the *d*

Doorway
Ex 12:7 and the upper part of the *d*
12:22 upon the upper part of the *d*
12:23 see the blood upon . . . the *d*

Dophkah
Nu 33:12 and went camping at *D*
33:13 they pulled away from *D* and

Dor
Jos 11:2 mountain ridges of *D* to the
12:23 king of *D* on the mountain
12:23 the mountain ridge of *D*
17:11 *D* and its dependent towns
Jg 1:27 *D* and its dependent towns
1Ki 4:11 all the mountain ridge of *D*
1Ch 7:29 *D* and its dependent towns

Dorcas
Ac 9:36 when translated, means *D*
9:39 garments that *D* used to make

Dothan
Ge 37:17 Let us go to *D*. So Joseph
37:17 and found them at *D*
2Ki 6:13 saying: There he is in *D*

Double
Ge 43:12 *d* the money in your hand
43:15 took *d* the money in their
Ex 16:5 *d* what they keep picking up
22:4 he is to make *d* compensation
22:7 he is to make *d* compensation
22:9 *d* compensation to his fellow
26:9 fold *d* the sixth tent cloth at
De 15:18 *d* the value of a hired
2Ki 25:4 the gate between the *d* wall
1Ch 12:33 they were not of a *d* heart
2Ch 14:7 towers, *d* doors and bars
Job 41:13 Into its *d* jaw who will
42:10 had been Job's, in *d* amount
Ps 12:2 speaking even with a *d* heart
35:3 draw spear and *d* ax to meet
Pr 31:21 are clothed with *d* garments
Ec 4:6 than a *d* handful of hard work
Isa 61:7 there will be a *d* portion
61:7 of even a *d* portion
Jer 39:4 gate between the *d* wall
52:7 gate between the *d* wall that
Zec 9:12 O woman, a *d* portion
Lu 13:11 she was bent *d* and was
1Ti 5:17 reckoned worthy of *d* honor

Doubled
Ex 28:16 should be foursquare when *d*
39:9 to be foursquare when *d*
39:9 the breastpiece, when *d*, a

Double-edged
Isa 41:15 instrument having *d* teeth

Double-faced
Eze 12:24 nor *d* divination in the

Double-size
Eze 47:9 to which the *d* torrent comes

Double-tongued
1Ti 3:8 be serious, not *d*, not giving

Doubt
Isa 56:3 Without *d* Jehovah will
Mt 14:31 why did you give way to *d*?
21:21 you have faith and do not *d*
Mr 11:23 does not *d* in his heart
Lu 4:23 No *d* you will apply this

Doubted
Mt 28:17 did obeisance, but some *d*

Doubting
Ac 10:20 not *d* at all, because I have
11:12 go with them, not *d* at all
Jas 1:6 asking in faith, not *d* at all

Doubtless
Ge 20:11 *D* there is no fear of God in

Doubts
Lu 24:38 why is it *d* come up in your
Ro 14:23 if he has *d*, he is already
Jas 1:6 he who *d* is like a wave of
Jude 22 mercy to some that have *d*

Dough
Ge 18:6 knead the *d* and make round
Ex 12:15 take away sour *d* from your
12:19 no sour *d* is to be found in
12:34 people carried their flour *d*
12:39 began to bake the flour *d*
13:7 no sour *d* is to be seen with
Le 2:11 make no sour *d* and no honey
De 16:4 no sour *d* should be seen
1Sa 28:24 kneaded *d* and baked it into
2Sa 13:8 flour *d* and kneaded it and
1Ch 23:29 for the mixed *d* and for all
Jer 7:18 kneading flour *d* in order to
Ho 7:4 ceases poking after kneading *d*

Dove
Ge 8:8 he sent out from him a *d* to
8:9 And the *d* did not find any
8:10 sent out the *d* from the ark
8:11 *d* came to him about the time
8:12 he sent out the *d*, but it did
Ps 55:6 that I had wings as a *d* has
56:*super* director on the Silent *D*
68:13 wings of a *d* covered with
Ca 2:14 my *d* in the retreats of the
5:2 my girl companion, my *d*, my
6:9 One there is who is my *d*, my
Isa 38:14 I keep cooing like the *d*
Jer 48:28 *d* that makes its nest in
Ho 7:11 a simple-minded *d* without
11:11 like a *d* out of the land of
Mt 3:16 like a *d* God's spirit coming
Mr 1:10 like a *d*, the spirit coming
Lu 3:22 in bodily shape like a *d*
Joh 1:32 spirit . . . as a *d* out of

Dove's
2Ki 6:25 *d* dung was worth five silver

Doves
Ca 1:15 Your eyes are those of *d*
4:1 Your eyes are those of *d*
5:12 His eyes are like *d* by the
Isa 59:11 like *d* we mournfully keep
60:8 *d* to their birdhouse holes
Eze 7:16 like the *d* of the valleys
Na 2:7 like the sound of *d*, beating
Mt 10:16 and yet innocent as *d*
21:12 benches of those selling *d*
Mr 11:15 benches of those selling *d*
Joh 2:14 selling . . . sheep and *d* and
2:16 said to those selling the *d*

Down*
Ge 11:5 Jehovah proceeded to go *d* to
18:2 proceeded to bow *d* to the
De 5:9 You must not bow *d* to them
11:16 gods and bow *d* to them
32:22 And it will burn *d* to Sheol
Jg 15:16 I have struck *d* a thousand
2Sa 22:48 bringing the peoples *d* under
2Ki 17:36 to him you should bow *d*
Ps 80:14 Look *d* from heaven and see
102:19 looked *d* from his holy
145:14 up all who are bowed *d*
146:8 raising up the ones bowed *d*
Pr 12:25 what will cause it to bow *d*
14:32 the wicked will be pushed *d*
Isa 19:18 City of Tearing *D* will one
63:3 trampling them *d* in my rage
1Co 16:11 no one . . . look *d* upon him
2Co 5:4 groan, being weighed *d*
13:10 build up and not to tear *d*
1Ti 4:12 ever look *d* on your youth
5:11 turn *d* younger widows, for
6:2 not look *d* on them, because
2Ti 2:23 turn *d* foolish and ignorant
Heb 11:30 the walls of Jericho fell *d*
Jas 3:15 wisdom that comes *d* from

Downcast
2Sa 13:4 son of the king, so *d* as
Job 22:29 with *d* eyes he will save

Downfall
2Ch 22:7 *d* of Ahaziah occurred by
Pr 29:16 will look on their very *d*
Eze 26:15 At the sound of your *d*
26:18 in the day of your *d*
27:27 in the day of your *d*
31:16 At the sound of its *d* I
32:10 on the day of your *d*

Downhearted
Isa 61:3 instead of the *d* spirit
Col 3:21 so that they do not become *d*

Downpour
Ge 7:12 *d* upon the earth went on for
8:2 so the *d* from the heavens was
1Ki 17:7 occurred no *d* upon the earth
17:14 *d* upon the surface of the
18:41 sound of the turmoil of a *d*
18:44 the *d* may not detain you
18:45 a great *d* began to occur
2Ki 3:17 and you will not see a *d*
Job 37:6 to the *d* of rain, even to
37:6 the *d* of his strong rains
Ps 68:9 *d* you began causing to fall
Pr 25:14 and a wind without any *d*
25:23 as with labor pains a *d*
Ec 11:3 empty out a sheer *d* upon the
12:2 returned, afterward the *d*
Ca 2:11 the *d* itself is over, it has
Jer 5:24 giving the *d* and the autumn
14:4 there has occurred no *d* upon
Eze 13:11 A flooding *d* will certainly
13:13 will occur a flooding *d*
38:22 flooding *d* and hailstones
Joe 2:23 down upon you people a *d*
Am 4:7 I also withheld . . . the *d*
Zec 10:1 gives a *d* of rain to them

Downpours
Ps 105:32 He made their *d* hail

Downstairs
Ac 10:20 go *d* and be on your way
10:21 Peter went *d* to the men
20:10 Paul went *d*, threw himself

Downtreading
Isa 22:5 confusion and of *d* and of

Downward
2Ki 19:30 take root *d* and produce
Ec 3:21 whether it is descending *d* to
Isa 37:31 take root *d* and produce
Eze 1:27 appearance of his hips and *d*
8:2 hips even *d* there was fire

Drachma
Lu 15:8 woman with ten *d* coins, if
15:8 if she loses one *d* coin, does
15:9 found the *d* coin that I lost

Drachmas
Ezr 2:69 sixty-one thousand *d*, and
Ne 7:70 treasure a thousand gold *d*
7:71 twenty thousand gold *d*
7:72 twenty thousand gold *d* and
Mt 17:24 collecting the two *d* tax
17:24 teacher not pay the two *d*

Drag
2Sa 17:13 *d* it down to the torrent
Job 21:33 after him . . . *d* all mankind
Pr 21:7 will *d* them away, for they
Jer 15:3 the dogs to *d* away, and the
Eze 32:20 *D* her away and all her
Jas 2:6 they *d* you before law courts

Dragged
Jer 49:20 the flock will be *d* about
50:45 the flock will be *d* about
Ac 14:19 they stoned Paul and *d* him
16:19 *d* them into the marketplace
17:6 *d* Jason and certain brothers
21:30 and *d* him outside the temple

Dragging
Jer 22:19 a *d* about and a throwing
Joh 21:8 *d* the net of fishes
Ac 8:3 *d* out both men and women, he

Dragnet
Eze 32:3 certainly bring you in my *d*
Mic 7:2 hunt . . . brother, with a *d*
Hab 1:15 he drags them away in his *d*
1:16 he offers sacrifice to his *d*
1:17 why he will empty out his *d*
Mt 13:47 the kingdom . . . is like a *d*

Dragnets
Ec 7:26 and whose heart is *d* and
Eze 26:5 A drying yard for *d* is
26:14 A drying yard for *d* is what
47:10 be a drying yard for *d*

Dragon
Re 12:3 great fiery-colored *d*, with
12:4 *d* kept standing before the
12:7 angels battled with the *d*
12:7 the *d* and its angels battled
12:9 down the great *d* was hurled
12:13 *d* saw that it was hurled
12:16 river that the *d* disgorged
12:17 *d* grew wrathful at the
13:2 *d* gave to the beast its
13:4 worshiped the *d* because it
13:11 it began speaking as a *d*
16:13 out of the mouth of the *d*
20:2 he seized the *d*, the original

Drags
Ec 12:5 the grasshopper *d* itself along
Hab 1:15 *d* them away in his dragnet
Re 12:4 tail *d* a third of the stars

Drain
Jg 6:38 he got to *d* off enough dew
Ps 75:8 will *d* them out, drink them
Eze 23:34 have to drink it and *d* it
Ho 13:15 his well and *d* his spring

Drained
Ge 8:13 waters had *d* from off the
8:13 surface of the ground had *d*
Le 1:15 its blood must be *d* out upon
5:9 the blood will be *d* out at the
Ps 73:10 waters of what is full are *d*
Isa 51:17 have drunk, you have *d* out

Drains
Job 14:11 a river itself *d* off and

Drama
Ga 4:24 stand as a symbolic *d*; for

Drank
Ge 24:54 ate and *d*, he and the men
26:30 and they ate and *d*
Ex 24:11 the true God and ate and *d*
34:28 and he *d* no water
De 9:9 neither ate bread nor *d* water
9:18 neither ate bread nor *d* water
Jg 9:27 and *d* and called down evil
Ru 3:7 Meantime Boaz ate and *d*, and
2Sa 19:35 what I ate and what I *d*
1Ki 19:8 he rose up and ate and *d*
2Ki 9:34 came on in and ate and *d*
Ezr 10:6 ate no bread and *d* no water
Da 5:3 and his secondary wives *d*
5:4 They *d* wine, and they praised
Mr 14:23 and they all *d* out of it
Lu 13:26 We ate and *d* in front of you
Joh 4:12 and his cattle *d* out of it
Ac 9:9 and he neither ate nor *d*
10:41 *d* with him after his rising
1Co 10:4 *d* the same spiritual drink

Draped
Mt 27:28 *d* him with a scarlet cloak

Draw
Ge 24:11 the women who *d* water were
24:13 are coming out to *d* water
24:19 *d* water until they are done
24:20 to the well to *d* water, and
24:43 coming out to *d* water to
24:44 and I shall also *d* water for
24:45 *d* water. Then I said to her
Ex 3:5 *D* your sandals from off your
12:21 *D* out . . . small cattle
15:9 I shall *d* my sword! My hand
Le 16:8 *d* lots over the two goats
De 20:10 *d* near to a city to fight
25:9 *d* his sandal off his foot and
Jos 5:15 *D* your sandals from off your
8:26 did not *d* back his hand with
18:8 I shall *d* lots for you
Jg 3:22 he did not *d* the sword out
4:7 I shall certainly *d* to you at
8:10 men who used to *d* the sword
8:20 did not *d* his sword, because
9:54 *D* your sword and put me to
20:20 to *d* up in battle formation
20:30 to *d* up in formation against
20:32 *d* them away from the city
Ru 2:9 what the young men will *d*
4:7 *d* his sandal off and give it to
Ru 4:8 proceeded to *d* his sandal off
1Sa 4:2 to *d* up in formation to meet
9:11 girls going out to *d* water
10:20 the tribes of Israel *d* near
10:21 tribe of Benjamin *d* near by
17:8 to *d* up in battle formation
31:4 *D* your sword and run me
2Sa 10:8 *d* up in battle formation at
10:10 *d* them up in formation to
1Ki 13:4 was not able to *d* it back to
1Ch 10:4 *D* your sword and run me
19:9 and *d* up in battle formation
19:11 *d* up in formation to meet
Job 24:22 *d* away strong people by his
41:1 Can you *d* out Leviathan
Ps 28:3 Do not *d* me along with wicked
35:3 *d* spear and double ax to meet
85:5 *d* out your anger to generation
91:10 plague will *d* near to your
132:11 he will not *d* back from it
Pr 20:5 is one that will *d* it up
Ca 1:4 *D* me with you; let us run
Isa 5:19 *d* near and come, that we
12:3 *d* water out of the springs
20:2 sandals you should *d* from
Eze 5:2 I shall *d* out a sword itself
5:12 sword is what I shall *d* out
12:14 a sword I shall *d* out after
18:8 he would *d* back his hand
28:7 *d* their swords against the
30:11 *d* their swords against
Joe 3:9 Let them *d* near! Let them
Na 3:14 Water for a siege *d* out for
Zep 3:2 To her God she did not *d* near
Hag 2:16 *d* off fifty measures of the
Joh 2:8 *D* some out now and take it
4:7 came to *d* water. Jesus said
4:15 to this place to *d* water
12:32 *d* men of all sorts to me
21:6 no longer able to *d* it in
Ac 20:30 *d* away the disciples after
Jas 4:8 *D* close to God, and he will
4:8 and he will *d* close to you

Drawer
De 29:11 to the *d* of your water

Drawers
Ex 28:42 make *d* of linen for them to
39:28 linen *d* of fine twisted linen
Le 6:10 the linen *d* on over his flesh
16:4 linen *d* should come upon his
Jos 9:21 and *d* of water for all the
9:23 *d* of water for the house of
9:27 *d* of water for the assembly
Eze 44:18 linen *d* are what should

Drawing
Ge 24:20 and kept *d* for all his camels
Nu 18:7 stranger *d* near should be put
De 20:3 *d* near today to the battle
Jos 18:10 *d* lots for them in Shiloh
Jg 5:11 among the places of *d* water
20:15 men *d* sword, apart from the
20:17 hundred thousand men *d* sword
20:22 *d* up in battle formation in
20:25 all of these *d* sword
20:33 went *d* up in formation at
20:35 all of these *d* sword
20:46 men *d* sword, all . . . valiant
1Sa 7:6 went *d* water and pouring it
17:2 *d* up in battle formation to
17:21 began *d* up battle line to
17:48 and *d* nearer to meet David
2Sa 22:17 *d* me out of great waters
24:9 valiant men *d* sword, and the
2Ki 3:26 men *d* sword to break through
1Ch 12:33 *d* up in battle formation
12:35 *d* up in battle formation
12:36 *d* up in battle formation
21:5 hundred thousand men *d* sword
21:5 seventy thousand men *d* sword
Ps 18:16 *d* me out of great waters
22:9 One *d* me forth from the belly
73:28 *d* near to God is good for me
Pr 20:2 *d* his fury against himself is
Ec 5:1 let there be a *d* near to hear
Isa 5:18 Woe to those *d* error with
58:2 *d* near to God in whom they
66:19 those *d* the bow, Tubal and
Ho 11:4 I kept *d* them, with the cords
Zep 1:6 *d* back from following Jehovah
Lu 2:19 *d* conclusions in her heart
15:1 kept *d* near to him to hear
Joh 4:11 a bucket for *d* water, and
Ac 16:10 *d* the conclusion that God had
22:6 *d* close to Damascus, about
27:27 were *d* near to some land
Heb 3:12 *d* away from the living God
7:19 we are *d* near to God
10:25 you behold the day *d* near

Drawn
Ex 2:10 have *d* him out of the water
Nu 22:23 with his *d* sword in his hand
22:31 with his *d* sword in his hand
De 20:2 you have *d* near to the battle
25:10 one who had his sandal *d* off
31:14 have *d* near for you to die
Jos 4:18 feet of the priests were *d*
5:13 with his *d* sword in his hand
8:6 *d* them away from the city
8:16 to be *d* away from the city
Jg 20:22 had *d* up in formation on the
20:31 were *d* away from the city
2Sa 3:1 came to be long *d* out
1Ch 21:16 his *d* sword in his hand
Ps 30:1 for you have *d* me up
37:14 wicked ones have *d* a sword
55:21 But they are *d* swords
Pr 26:7 of the lame one *d* up water
Isa 18:2 to a nation *d* out and scoured
18:7 a people *d* out and scoured
21:15 because of the *d* sword
Jer 6:23 *d* up in battle order like a
29:28 saying: It is long *d* out
31:3 *d* you with loving-kindness
La 3:57 You have *d* near in the day
4:18 Our end has *d* near. Our days
Eze 12:23 The days have *d* near, and
18:17 he has *d* back his hand
21:28 a sword *d* for a slaughter
36:8 *d* near to the point of
Ho 5:6 He had *d* away from them
7:5 *d* his hand along with deriders
Joe 2:5 mighty people, *d* up in battle
Mt 3:2 of the heavens has *d* near
4:17 the kingdom . . . has *d* near
10:7 kingdom of the heavens has *d*
26:45 hour has *d* near for the Son
26:46 Look! My betrayer has *d* near
Mr 1:15 the kingdom of God has *d* near
14:42 My betrayer has *d* near
Lu 21:20 desolating of her has *d* near
Joh 2:9 had *d* out the water knew
Ro 13:12 the day has *d* near
Jas 1:14 one is tried by being *d* out
5:8 presence of the Lord has *d*
1Pe 4:7 end of all things has *d* close

Draws
Job 33:22 his soul *d* near to the pit
36:27 he *d* up the drops of water
Ps 10:9 when he *d* his net shut
Isa 26:17 *d* near to giving birth
Joh 6:44 Father, who sent me, *d* him

Dread
Ge 31:42 *D* of Isaac, had not proved
31:53 Jacob swore by the *D* of his
Ex 1:12 a sickening *d* as a result of
15:16 Fright and *d* will fall upon
Nu 22:3 a sickening *d* of the sons of
De 2:25 the *d* of you and the fear of
11:25 The *d* of you and the fear of
28:66 and be in *d* night and day
28:67 of the *d* of your heart
28:67 with which you will be in *d*
1Sa 11:7 the *d* of Jehovah began to fall
1Ch 14:17 the *d* of him upon all the
2Ch 14:14 *d* of Jehovah had come to be
17:10 *d* of Jehovah came to be
19:7 *d* of Jehovah come to be upon
20:29 *d* of God came to be upon
Es 8:17 *d* of the Jews had fallen upon
9:2 *d* of them had fallen upon all
9:3 *d* of Mordecai had fallen upon
Job 4:14 A *d* came over me, and a
4:14 my bones it filled with *d*
13:11 very *d* of him fall upon you
21:9 peace itself, free from *d*
22:10 And sudden *d* disturbs you
23:15 and am in *d* of him
31:23 disaster from God was a *d*
39:16 because she has no *d*
39:22 It laughs at *d*, and is not
Ps 14:5 were filled with a great *d*
27:1 Of whom shall I be in *d*?
31:11 And a *d* to my acquaintances
36:1 no *d* of God in front of his

Ps 53:5 were filled with a great *d*
53:5 there had proved to be no *d*
78:53 security, and they felt no *d*
105:38 *d* of them had fallen upon
119:120 *d* of you my flesh has had
119:161 in *d* of your own words
Pr 1:26 mock when what you *d* comes
1:27 what you *d* comes just like a
1:33 from *d* of calamity
3:24 lie down you will feel no *d*
28:14 that is feeling *d* constantly
Ca 3:8 because of *d* during the nights
Isa 7:16 are feeling a sickening *d*
12:2 I shall trust and be in no *d*
19:16 be in *d* because of the
19:17 *d* because of the counsel of
24:17 *D* and the hollow and the
33:14 have come to be in *d*
44:8 Do not be in *d*, you people
44:11 They will be in *d*
51:13 you were in *d* constantly
Jer 2:19 no *d* of me has resulted to
30:5 *d*, and there is no peace
33:9 be in *d* and be agitated on
36:16 looked at one another in *d*
36:24 they felt no *d*; neither
48:43 *D* and the hollow and the
48:44 fleeing because of the *d*
La 3:47 *D* and the hollow themselves

Dreaded
Job 3:25 a dreadful thing I have *d*
Isa 24:18 sound of the *d* thing will

Dreadful
Job 3:25 a *d* thing I have dreaded, and
15:21 sound of *d* things is in his
Ps 91:5 afraid of anything *d* by night
Pr 3:25 afraid of any sudden *d* thing
Jer 49:5 in upon you a *d* thing
Da 2:31 and its appearance was *d*

Dreadfulness
Job 25:2 Rulership and *d* are with him
Ps 64:1 From the *d* of the enemy may
Isa 2:10 because of the *d* of Jehovah
2:19 because of the *d* of Jehovah
2:21 because of the *d* of Jehovah

Dream
Ge 20:3 God came to Abimelech in a *d*
20:6 true God said to him in the *d*
28:12 he began to *d*, and, look!
31:10 saw a sight in a *d* and here
31:11 angel . . . said to me in the *d*
31:24 in a *d* by night and said to
37:5 Joseph had a *d* and told it to
37:6 Listen, please, to this *d* that
37:9 he had still another *d*, and
37:9 I have had a *d* once more, and
37:10 What does this *d* that you
40:5, 5 to *d* a *d*, each one his own
40:5 each one his own *d* in the one
40:5 *d* with its own interpretation
40:8 We have dreamed a *d*, and
40:9 to relate his *d* to Joseph
40:9 In my *d*, why, here there was
40:16 I too was in my *d*, and here
41:7 and here it was a *d*
41:11 we both dreamed a *d* in the
41:11 We dreamed each one his *d*
41:12 to each according to his *d*
41:15 I have dreamed a *d*, but
41:15 can hear a *d* and interpret it
41:17 In my *d* here I was standing
41:22 saw in my *d* and here there
41:25 The *d* of Pharaoh is but one
41:26 The *d* is but one
41:32 *d* was repeated to Pharaoh
Nu 12:6 In a *d* I would speak to him
De 13:1 dreamer of a *d* arises in your
13:3 or to the dreamer of that *d*
13:5 that dreamer of the *d* should
Jg 7:13 was a man relating a *d* to his
7:13 say: Here is a *d* that I have
7:15 the relating of the *d* and its
1Ki 3:5 appeared to Solomon in a *d*
3:15 here it had been a *d*
Job 20:8 Like a *d* he will fly off
33:15 a *d*, a vision of the night
Ps 73:20 Like a *d* after awaking
Ec 5:3 a *d* certainly comes in because
Isa 29:7 occur just as in a *d*, in
Jer 23:25, 25 a *d!* I have had a *d!*
23:28 with whom there is a *d*
23:28 let him relate the *d*
Da 2:3 *d* that I have dreamed, and my
2:3 is agitated to know the *d*
2:4 Say what the *d* is to your
2:5 make the *d* known to me, and
2:6 *d* and its interpretation you
2:6 show me the very *d* and its
2:7 king say what the *d* is to his
2:9 make known to me the very *d*
2:9 tell me the very *d*, and I
2:26 make known to me the *d* and
2:28 Your *d* and the visions of
2:36 This is the *d*, and its
2:45 the *d* is reliable, and the
4:5 *d* that I beheld, and it began
4:6 very interpretation of the *d*
4:7 saying . . . what the *d* was
4:8 him I said what the *d* was
4:9 tell me the visions of my *d*
4:18 the *d* that I myself, King
4:19 *d* and the interpretation
4:19 *d* apply to those hating you
7:1 Daniel himself beheld a *d* and
7:1 time he wrote down the *d*
Joe 2:28 old men, dreams they will *d*
Mt 1:20 angel appeared to him in a *d*
2:12 given divine warning in a *d*
2:13 appeared in a *d* to Joseph
2:19 appeared in a *d* to Joseph
2:22 given divine warning in a *d*
27:19 suffered a lot today in a *d*
Ac 2:17 your old men will *d* dreams

Dreamed
Ge 37:6 this dream that I have *d*
37:10 dream that you have *d* mean
40:8 We have *d* a dream, and there
41:5 to sleep and *d* a second time
41:11 we both *d* a dream in the one
41:11 We *d* each one his dream with
41:15 I have *d* a dream, but there
42:9 dreams that he had *d*
Jg 7:13 a dream that I have *d*
Da 2:1 Nebuchadnezzar *d* dreams
2:3 is a dream that I have *d*, and

Dreamer
Ge 37:19 Look! Here comes that *d*
De 13:1 In case a prophet or a *d* of
13:3 or to the *d* of that dream
13:5 that *d* of the dream should be

Dreamers
Jer 27:9 divination and to your *d*

Dreaming
Ge 41:1 Pharaoh was *d* and here he was
Ps 126:1 like those who were *d*
Jer 29:8 dreams that they are *d*

Dreams
Ge 37:8 reason to hate him over his *d*
37:20 what will become of his *d*
41:8 to relate his *d* to them
41:12 to interpret our *d* to us
42:9 Joseph remembered the *d* that
1Sa 28:6 by *d* or by the Urim or by
28:15 by . . . the prophets or by *d*
Job 7:14 have terrified me with *d*
Ec 5:7 of occupation there are *d*, and
Isa 29:8 someone hungry *d* and here
29:8 someone thirsty *d* and here
Jer 23:27 by means of their *d* that
23:32 the prophets of false *d*
29:8 do not you listen to their *d*
Da 1:17 in all sorts of visions and *d*
2:1 Nebuchadnezzar dreamed *d*
2:2 to tell the king his *d*
5:12 insight to interpret *d* and
Joe 2:28 old men, *d* they will dream
Zec 10:2 valueless *d* are what they
Ac 2:17 your old men will dream *d*
Jude 8 indulging in *d*, are defiling

Dregs
Ps 75:8 *d* will be poured out from it
Isa 25:6 of wine kept on the *d*
25:6 of wine kept on the *d*
Jer 48:11 undisturbed on their *d*
Zep 1:12 are congealing upon their *d*

Drench
Isa 16:9 With my tears I shall *d* you

Drenched
Job 24:8 From the rainstorm . . . get *d*
Isa 34:5 sword will certainly be *d*
34:7 land must be *d* with blood

Drenching
Ps 65:10 There is a *d* of its furrows

Dress
Le 6:10 his official *d* of linen, and
2Sa 13:18 virgins, used to *d* with
14:2 *d* yourself, please, with
1Ki 18:23 shall *d* the other young bull
18:25 young bull and *d* it first
Lu 7:25 in splendid *d* and existing in
1Ti 2:9 in well-arranged *d*, with

Dressed
1Sa 25:18 five sheep *d* and
1Ki 18:26 they *d* it, and they kept
1Ch 15:27 David was *d* in a sleeveless
Na 2:3 are *d* in crimson stuff
Mt 11:8 A man *d* in soft garments?
Lu 7:25 man *d* in soft outer garments
Re 3:18 that you may become *d* and
4:4 *d* in white outer garments, and
7:9 great crowd . . . *d* in white
7:13 who are *d* in the white robes
11:3 days *d* in sackcloth

Dresser
Isa 3:7 shall not become a wound *d*

Dresses
Ex 30:7 when he *d* the lamps, he will

Dressing
Es 5:1 that Esther went *d* up royally

Drew
Ge 14:8 they *d* up in battle order
37:28 they *d* and lifted up Joseph
38:29 as soon as he *d* back his hand
Ex 2:16 they came and *d* water and
2:19 he actually *d* water for us
4:6 *d* it out . . . hand was stricken
4:7 *d* it out of the upper fold
Jg 20:2 men on foot who *d* the sword
20:24 sons of Israel *d* near to the
1Sa 7:10 *d* near for battle against
14:27 and *d* his hand back to his
2Sa 10:9 *d* them up in formation to
10:17 Syrians now *d* up in
15:5 *d* near to bow down to him
23:16 *d* water from the cistern
1Ki 2:1 days of David gradually *d* near
2:7 the way they *d* near to me
1Ch 11:18 *d* water from the cistern of
19:10 *d* them up in formation to
19:17 *d* up in formation against
19:17 When David *d* up in battle
2Ch 13:3 *d* up in battle formation
14:10 *d* up in battle formation in
Job 32:6 why I *d* back and was afraid
Isa 41:5 *d* near and kept coming
Jer 38:13 *d* out Jeremiah by means of
Eze 20:22 I *d* back my hand and went
Mt 26:51 *d* his sword and struck the
Mr 14:47 *d* his sword and struck the
Lu 20:5 they *d* conclusions, saying
22:41 *d* away from them about a
Joh 18:6 they *d* back and fell to the
18:10 *d* it and struck the slave
21:11 *d* the net to land full of
Ac 5:37 he *d* off people after him
16:27 *d* his sword and was about to

Dried
Ge 8:7 the waters *d* off the earth
8:14 the earth had *d* off
Nu 6:3 eat grapes either fresh or *d*
11:6 But now our soul is *d* away
Jos 2:10 *d* up the waters of the Red
4:23 God *d* up the waters of the
4:23 Red Sea when he *d* it up from
5:1 *d* up the waters of the Jordan
Jg 16:7 sinews that have not been *d*
16:8 sinews that had not been *d*
1Ki 13:4 his hand . . . became *d* up
2Ki 20:7 a cake of pressed *d* figs
Job 6:17 it grows hot they are *d* up
Ps 22:15 *d* up just like a fragment of
74:15 *d* up ever-flowing rivers
102:4 like vegetation and is *d* up
102:11 *d* up like mere vegetation
106:9 and it was gradually *d* up
129:6 has been torn out has *d* up
Isa 5:24 mere *d* grass sinks down
15:6 green grass has *d* up, the
19:5 water will certainly be *d* up
27:11 When her sprigs have *d* up
29:8 tired and his soul is *d* out

Isa 33:11 You people conceive *d* grass
38:21 a cake of pressed *d* figs and
40:7 The green grass has *d* up
40:8 The green grass has *d* up
51:10 the one that *d* up the sea
Jer 18:14 trickling, be *d* up
23:10 of the wilderness have *d* up
50:38 waters, and they must be *d*
Eze 17:24 *d* up the still-moist tree
19:12 wind that *d* up her fruit
Joe 1:10 the new wine has been *d* up
1:12 all the trees . . . have *d* up
1:17 *D* figs have shriveled under
1:17 for the grain has *d* up
1:20 the channels of water have *d*
Am 4:7 a tract of land . . . *d* up
Jon 4:7 plant; and it gradually *d* up
Mr 5:29 her fountain of blood *d* up
Lu 8:6 it *d* up because of not having
Joh 15:6 as a branch and is *d* up
Re 16:12 and its water was *d* up, that

Dried-out
Ps 107:9 he has satisfied the *d* soul
Isa 44:19 the *d* wood of a tree shall

Dried-up
Mr 3:1 a man was there with a *d* hand

Dries
Job 14:11 river . . . drains off and *d*
Ps 90:6 withers and certainly *d* up
Na 1:4 the sea, and he *d* it up

Drift
Heb 2:1 that we may never *d* away

Drink
Ge 19:32 give our father wine to *d*
19:33 their father wine to *d*
19:34 give him wine to *d* tonight
19:35 gave their father wine to *d*
21:19 and to give the boy a *d*
24:14 that I may take a *d*, and who
24:14 Take a *d*, and I shall also
24:18 *D*, my lord. With that she
24:18 she . . . gave him a *d*
24:19 giving him a *d*, then she said
24:43 let me *d* a little water from
24:44 take a *d*, and I shall also
24:45 to her, Give me a *d*, please
24:46 Take a *d*, and I shall also
24:46 I took a *d*, and she also
27:25 wine and he began to *d*
30:38 the flocks would come to *d*
30:38 when they came to *d*
35:14 poured a *d* offering upon it
Ex 7:21 Egyptians were unable to *d*
7:24 the Nile River for water to *d*
7:24 unable to *d* . . . of the Nile
15:23 to *d* the water from Marah
15:24 saying: What are we to *d*?
17:1 no water for the people to *d*
17:2 Give us water that we may *d*
17:6 and the people must *d* it
29:40 *d* offering of the fourth of a
29:41 and with a *d* offering
30:9 not pour a *d* offering upon it
32:6 people sat down to eat and *d*
32:20 made the sons of Israel *d* it
Le 10:9 Do not *d* wine or intoxicating
11:34 any *d* that may be drunk in
23:13 *d* offering a fourth of a hin
23:18 *d* offerings as an offering
23:37 *d* offerings according to the
Nu 4:7 pitchers of the *d* offering; and
5:24 woman *d* the bitter water that
5:26 make the woman *d* the water
5:27 made her *d* the water, it
6:3 not *d* the vinegar of wine or
6:3 *d* any liquid made from grapes
6:15 and their *d* offerings
6:17 render . . . its *d* offering
6:20 the Nazirite may *d* wine
15:5 wine as a *d* offering, the
15:7 present wine as a *d* offering
15:10 present wine as a *d* offering
15:24 its *d* offering according to
20:5 and there is no water to *d*
20:8 and their beasts of burden *d*
20:11 beasts of burden began to *d*
20:17 not *d* the water of a well
20:19 should *d* your water, I shall
21:22 We shall *d* water of no well
23:24 blood of slain ones . . . *d*
28:7 along with its *d* offering
Nu 28:7 *d* offering of intoxicating
28:8 with its same *d* offering you
28:9 together with its *d* offering
28:10 and its *d* offering
28:14 as their *d* offerings there
28:15 together with its *d* offering
28:24 rendered, and its *d* offering
28:31 with their *d* offerings
29:6 with their *d* offerings
29:11 with their *d* offerings
29:16 offering and its *d* offering
29:18 *d* offerings for the bulls
29:19 with their *d* offerings
29:21 *d* offerings for the bulls
29:22 and its *d* offering
29:24 *d* offerings for the bulls
29:25 and its *d* offering
29:27 *d* offerings for the bulls
29:28 and its *d* offering
29:30 *d* offerings for the bulls
29:31 and its *d* offerings
29:33 *d* offerings for the bulls
29:34 and its *d* offering
29:37 *d* offerings for the bull, the
29:38 and its *d* offering
29:39 and your *d* offerings and your
33:14 there for the people to *d*
De 2:6 water you may purchase . . . *d*
2:28 I must *d*. Only let me pass
28:39 but you will *d* no wine and
29:6 liquor you did not *d*, in order
32:38 To *d* the wine of their
32:38 wine of their *d* offerings
Jg 4:19 a little water to *d*, for I
4:19 of milk and gave him a *d*
7:5 bends down upon his knees to *d*
7:6 upon their knees to *d* water
13:4 do not *d* wine or intoxicating
13:7 and now do not *d* wine or
13:14 no wine . . . let her *d*, and
15:19 and he proceeded to *d*
19:4 they would eat and *d*, and he
19:6 began to eat and to *d* together
19:21 and began to eat and *d*
Ru 2:9 *d* from what the young men
1Sa 30:11 and gave him water to *d*
2Sa 11:11 *d* and to lie down with my
11:13 eat before him and *d*
12:3 and from his cup it would *d*
16:2 the one tired out . . . to *d*
23:15 O that I might have a *d* of
23:16 he did not consent to *d* it
23:17 *d* the blood of the men
23:17 he did not consent to *d* it
1Ki 13:8 eat bread or *d* water in this
13:9 not eat bread or *d* water
13:16 not eat bread or *d* water
13:17 not eat bread or *d* water
13:18 may eat bread and *d* water
13:19 in his house and *d* water
13:22 eat bread and *d* water in
13:22 Do not eat bread or *d* water
17:4 torrent valley you should *d*
17:10 in a vessel that I may *d*
18:41 Go up, eat and *d*
18:42 to go up to eat and *d*
19:6 And he began to eat and *d*
2Ki 3:17 men will certainly *d* from
6:22 eat and *d* and go to their
6:23 they began to eat and *d*
7:8 to eat and *d* and carry from
16:13 to pour out his *d* offering
16:15 and their *d* offerings
18:27 and *d* their own urine with
18:31 *d* each one the water of his
19:24 dig and *d* strange waters
1Ch 11:17 a *d* of the water from the
11:18 David did not consent to *d*
11:19 *d* at the risk of their souls
11:19 he did not consent to *d* it
29:21 lambs and their *d* offerings
2Ch 28:15 gave them *d* and greased
29:35 with the *d* offerings for
Ezr 3:7 and *d* and oil to the Sidonians
7:17 and their *d* offerings and
Ne 8:10 and *d* the sweet things, and
8:12 to eat and *d* and to send out
Es 1:7 wine to *d* in gold vessels
3:15 and Haman, they sat down to *d*
4:16 neither eat nor *d* for three
Job 1:4 sisters to eat and *d* with
21:20 rage of the Almighty . . . *d*
22:7 not give the tired one a *d* of
Ps 16:4 their *d* offerings of blood
Ps 36:8 *d* their fill of the fatness
36:8 pleasures you cause them to *d*
50:13 blood of he-goats shall I *d*?
60:3 *d* wine sending us reeling
69:21 tried to make me *d* vinegar
75:8 will drain them out, *d* them
78:15 cause them to *d* an abundance
78:44 *d* from their own streams
80:5 making them *d* tears upon
102:9 things I *d* I have mingled
104:11 *d* to all the wild beasts of
110:7 valley in the way he will *d*
Pr 4:17 acts of violence . . . they *d*
5:15 *D* water out of your own
7:18 *d* our fill of love until the
23:7 Eat and *d*, he says to you, but
25:21 thirsty, give him water to *d*
31:4 it is not for kings to *d* wine
31:5 may not *d* and forget what is
31:7 one *d* and forget one's poverty
Ec 2:24 *d* and cause his soul to see
3:13 *d* and see good for all his
5:18 eat and *d* and see good for all
8:15 than to eat and *d* and rejoice
9:7 *d* your wine with a good heart
Ca 5:1 *D* and become drunk with
8:2 give you a *d* of spiced wine
Isa 24:9 no song that they *d* wine
32:6 thirsty one to go without *d*
36:12 *d* their own urine with you
36:16 *d* each one the water of his
37:25 certainly dig and *d* waters
43:20 people, my chosen one, to *d*
56:12 let us *d* intoxicating liquor
57:6 you poured out a *d* offering
62:8 foreigners *d* your new wine
62:9 *d* it in my holy courtyards
65:13 own servants will *d*, but
Jer 2:18 to *d* the waters of Shihor
2:18 to *d* the waters of the River
7:18 pouring out of *d* offerings
8:14 gives us poisoned water to *d*
9:15 make them *d* poisoned water
16:7 the cup of consolation to *d*
16:8 with them to eat and to *d*
19:13 *d* offerings to other gods
22:15 father, did he not eat and *d*
23:15 poisoned water to *d*
25:15 all the nations . . . *d* it
25:16 *d* and shake back and forth
25:17 make all the nations *d* to
25:26 Sheshach himself will *d*
25:27 *D* and get drunk and puke
25:28 cup out of your hand to *d*
25:28 You will *d* without fail
32:29 *d* offerings to other gods
35:2 must give them wine to *d*
35:5 and said to them: *D* wine
35:6 We shall *d* no wine, because
35:6 You must *d* no wine, neither
35:14 sons, to *d* no wine, and
44:17 pour out to her *d* offerings
44:18 *d* offerings to her we have
44:19 pour out *d* offerings to her
44:19 pour out *d* offerings to her
44:25 to pour out *d* offerings to
49:12 their custom to *d* the cup
49:12 they will *d* without fail
49:12 you will *d* without fail
La 5:4 For money we have had to *d* our
Eze 4:11 will *d* merely by measure
4:11 time to time you will *d*
4:16 in horror that they will *d*
12:18 your water you should *d*
12:19 with horror . . . they will *d*
20:28 their *d* offerings
23:32 cup . . . you will *d*
23:34 have to *d* it and drain it
25:4 will *d* your milk
32:6 *d* up your discharged matter
34:18 clear waters you *d* but the
34:19 water befouled . . . they *d*
39:17 eat flesh and *d* blood
39:18 you will *d*, rams, young
39:19 *d* blood to drunkenness
44:21 wine should any priests *d*
45:17 and the *d* offering during
Da 1:10 your food and your *d*
1:12 and water that we may *d*
5:2 his secondary wives might *d*
Ho 2:5 my linen, my oil and my *d*
Joe 1:9 *d* offering have been cut off
1:13 and *d* offering have been
2:14 a *d* offering for Jehovah your

Joe 3:3 for wine, that they might *d*
Am 2:8 *d* at the house of their gods
2:12 the Nazirites wine to *d*
4:1 Do bring, and let us *d!*
4:8 one city in order to *d* water
9:14 vineyards and *d* the wine
Ob 16 *d* and gulp down and become as
Jon 3:7 Even water they should not *d*
Mic 6:15 but you will not *d* wine
Hab 2:15 companions something to *d*
2:16 *D* also, you yourself, and be
Zep 1:13 will not *d* the wine of them
Zec 7:6 and when you would *d*, were
9:15 *d*—be boisterous—as if
Mt 6:25 will eat or what you will *d*
6:31 What are we to *d?* or, What
10:42 a cup of cold water to *d*
20:22 Can you *d* the cup that I am
20:22 the cup that I am about to *d*
20:23 You will indeed *d* my cup
24:49 and *d* with the confirmed
25:35 you gave me something to *d*
25:37 and give you something to *d*
25:42 but you gave me nothing to *d*
26:27 *D* out of it, all of you
26:29 by no means *d* henceforth any
26:29 when I *d* it new with you in
26:42 to pass away except I *d* it
27:34 wine mixed with gall to *d*
27:34 tasting it, he refused to *d*
27:48 and went giving him a *d*
Mr 9:41 you a cup of water to *d*
10:38 Are you able to *d* the cup
10:39 you will *d*, and with the
14:25 *d* any more of the product of
14:25 when I *d* . . . in the kingdom
15:36 began giving him a *d*, saying
Lu 1:15 he must *d* no wine and strong
1:15 no wine and strong *d* at all
5:30 eat and *d* with tax collectors
5:33 but yours eat and *d*
12:19 ease, eat, *d*, enjoy yourself
12:29 eat and what you might *d*
12:45 to eat and *d* and get drunk
13:15 lead it away to give it *d*
17:8 afterward you can eat and *d*
22:18 not *d* again from the product
22:30 eat and *d* at my table in my
Joh 4:7 said to her: Give me a *d*
4:9 ask me for a *d*, when I am
4:10 says to you, Give me a *d*
6:53 Son of man and *d* his blood
6:55 and my blood is true *d*
7:37 let him come to me and *d*
18:11 I not by all means *d* it
Ac 23:12 nor *d* until they had killed
23:21 neither to eat nor to *d*
Ro 12:20 give him something to *d*
14:21 not to eat flesh or to *d*
1Co 9:4 have authority to eat and *d*
10:4 drank the same spiritual *d*
10:4 For they used to *d* from the
10:7 sat down to eat and *d*, and
11:25 as often as you *d* it, in
11:26 eat this loaf and *d* this cup
11:28 of the loaf and *d* of the cup
12:13 all made to *d* one spirit
15:32 let us eat and *d*, for
Php 2:17 poured out like a *d* offering
1Ti 5:23 Do not *d* water any longer
2Ti 4:6 poured out like a *d* offering
Re 14:8 *d* of the wine of the anger
14:10 *d* of the wine of the anger
16:6 blood to *d*. They deserve it

Drinkers

Ps 69:12 subject of the songs of *d*
Pr 23:20 to be among heavy *d* of wine
Joe 1:5 and howl, all you wine *d*

Drinking

Ge 9:21 he began *d* of the wine and
24:19 water until they are done *d*
24:20 jar into the *d* trough and ran
24:22 camels had finished *d*, then
25:34 and he went to eating and *d*
30:38 in the water *d* troughs
43:34 continued banqueting and *d*
Ex 7:18 no stomach for *d* water from
De 32:14 the grape you kept *d* as wine
Ru 3:3 he has finished eating and *d*
1Sa 1:9 and after the *d*, while Eli
30:16 *d* and having a feast on
1Ki 1:25 eating and *d* before him and
4:20 eating and *d* and rejoicing
1Ki 10:21 *d* vessels of King Solomon
13:23 after his *d* that he at once
16:9 *d* himself drunk at the house
17:6 torrent valley he kept *d*
20:12 kings were *d* in the booths
20:16 *d* himself drunk in the
1Ch 12:39 eating and *d*, for their
29:22 eating and *d* before Jehovah
2Ch 9:4 *d* service and their attire
9:20 *d* vessels of King Solomon
Es 1:8 time of *d* according to the law
Job 1:13 eating and *d* wine in the
1:18 eating and *d* wine in the
6:4 venom . . . my spirit is *d*
15:16 *d* in unrighteousness just
Pr 9:5 share in *d* the wine that I
26:6 one that is *d* mere violence
Ec 10:17 mightiness, not for mere *d*
Isa 5:22 mighty in *d* wine, and to
21:5 an eating, a *d!* Get up, you
22:13 and the *d* of wine
22:13 Let there be eating and *d*
24:9 bitter to those *d* it
29:8 dreams and here he is *d*, and
51:22 will not repeat the *d* of it
Jer 35:8 *d* no wine all our days
Eze 31:14 none *d* water may stand up
31:16 all those *d* water, will be
Da 1:5 and from his *d* wine, even to
1:8 and with his *d* wine
1:16 and their *d* wine and giving
5:1 Belshazzar . . . he was *d* wine
5:23 have been *d* wine from them
Am 5:11 you will not keep *d* the wine
6:6 are *d* out of bowls of wine
Ob 16 nations will keep *d* constantly
Hag 1:6 *d*, but not to the point of
Zec 7:6 not you the ones doing the *d*
Mt 11:18 came neither eating nor *d*
11:19 did come eating and *d*, still
11:19 given to *d* wine, a friend
24:38 eating and *d*, men marrying
Mr 10:38 the cup which I am *d*, or
10:39 The cup I am *d* you will
Lu 7:33 eating bread nor *d* wine
7:34 has come eating and *d*, but
7:34 A man . . . given to *d* wine
10:7 eating and *d* the things they
17:8 through eating and *d*, and
17:27 were eating, they were *d*
17:28 were eating, they were *d*
21:34 with overeating and heavy *d*
Joh 4:13 Everyone *d* from this water
Ro 14:17 does not mean eating and *d*
1Co 10:21 You cannot be *d* the cup of
10:31 are eating or *d* or doing
11:22 have houses for eating and *d*
Col 2:16 judge you in eating and *d* or
1Pe 4:3 revelries, *d* matches, and

Drinks

Ge 44:5 thing that my master *d* from
De 11:11 rain of the heavens it *d*
1Ki 10:5 *d* and his burnt sacrifices
Job 34:7 *d* up derision like water
Ec 2:25 and who *d* better than I do?
Joh 4:14 *d* from the water that I
6:54 *d* my blood has everlasting
6:56 my flesh and *d* my blood
1Co 11:27 or *d* the cup of the Lord
11:29 For he that eats and *d*
11:29 eats and *d* judgment against
Heb 6:7 ground that *d* in the rain
9:10 with foods and *d* and various

Drip

De 32:2 instruction will *d* as the
33:28 will let the dew *d* down
Job 29:22 upon them my word would *d*
36:28 *d* upon mankind abundantly
Ps 65:11 very tracks *d* with fatness
Eze 20:46 and *d* words to the south
21:2 *d* words toward the holy
21:7 knees themselves will *d*
Joe 3:18 will *d* with sweet wine
Am 9:13 must *d* with sweet wine, and

Dripped

Jg 5:4 heavens also *d*, Clouds also
5:4 Clouds also *d* with water
Ps 68:8 Heaven itself also *d* because
Ca 5:5 my own hands *d* with myrrh and

Dripping

1Sa 14:26 there was a *d* of honey, but
Ps 65:12 the wilderness keep *d*
Pr 3:20 skies keep *d* down light rain
5:3 lips of a strange woman keep *d*
Ca 4:11 comb honey your lips keep *d*
5:13 lilies, *d* with liquid myrrh
Isa 45:8 heavens, cause a *d* from
Eze 7:17 they keep *d* with water

Drive

Ge 21:10 *D* out this slave girl and her
33:13 and should they *d* them too
Ex 3:7 of those who *d* them to work
6:1 he will *d* them out of his land
11:1 literally *d* you out from here
15:9 My hand will *d* them away
23:28 will simply *d* the Hivites
23:29 I shall not *d* them out from
23:30 *d* them out from before you
23:31 will certainly *d* them out
33:2 and *d* out the Canaanites, the
34:24 *d* the nations away from
Nu 14:12 pestilence and *d* them away
22:6 I may *d* them out of the land
22:11 I shall actually *d* them out
32:39 *d* away the Amorites who
33:52 *d* away all the inhabitants
33:55 *d* the inhabitants of the land
De 4:27 Jehovah will *d* you away
4:38 *d* away nations greater and
7:17 be able to *d* them away
11:23 *d* away all these nations on
31:3 and you must *d* them away
33:27 *d* away from before you the
Jos 3:10 *d* away from before you the
15:63 not able to *d* them away
16:10 not *d* away the Canaanites
17:18 *d* away the Canaanites
23:9 Jehovah will *d* away great
24:18 Jehovah proceeded to *d* out
Jg 1:21 Benjamin did not *d* out the
1:28 and they did not *d* them out
1:29 Neither did Ephraim *d* out
1:30 Zebulun did not *d* out the
1:31 Asher did not *d* out the
1:32 they did not *d* them out
1:33 Naphtali did not *d* out the
2:3 I shall not *d* them away from
2:21 shall not *d* out again from
9:41 to *d* Gaal and his brothers out
11:2 to *d* Jephthah out and to say
2Sa 7:23 *d* out because of your people
17:2 *d* him into trembling
18:14 *d* them through the heart of
2Ki 4:24 *D* and go ahead. Do not hold
2Ch 20:7 *d* away the inhabitants of
20:11 to *d* us out from your
21:11 that he might *d* Judah away
Job 20:15 God will *d* it out from his
24:3 *d* off even the male ass of
Ps 68:2 may you *d* them away
Pr 22:10 *D* away the ridiculer, that
Isa 22:23 *d* him in as a peg in a
41:16 will *d* them different ways
Jer 46:9 *d* madly, O you chariots!
Eze 30:9 *d* self-confident Ethiopia
31:11 wickedness I will *d* it out
Ho 9:15 *d* them away from my own
Mic 2:9 you *d* out from the house in
Zep 2:4 high noon they will *d* her out
Joh 6:37 I will by no means *d* away
Ga 4:30 *D* out the servant girl and

Driven

Ex 10:11 *d* out from before Pharaoh
12:39 they had been *d* out of Egypt
Le 26:36 the sound of a leaf *d* about
1Sa 21:15 in need of people *d* crazy
26:19 *d* me out today from feeling
1Ki 14:24 Jehovah had *d* out from
2Ki 17:8 whom Jehovah had *d* out from
21:2 nations that Jehovah had *d*
2Ch 13:9 *d* out Jehovah's priests, the
28:3 nations that Jehovah had *d*
33:2 nations that Jehovah had *d*
Job 13:25 a mere leaf *d* about quiver
30:5 they would be *d* away
Ps 55:2 I am *d* restlessly about by my
68:2 As smoke is *d* away, may you
Pr 21:6 is an exhalation *d* away
Ec 12:11 like nails *d* in are those
Isa 19:7 be *d* away, and it will be no
22:25 *d* in a lasting place will
41:2 *d* about like mere stubble
59:19 spirit of Jehovah has *d*
Jer 4:9 priests . . . *d* to astonishment
Da 4:33 from mankind he was being *d*

Da 5:21 sons of mankind he was *d* away
Jon 2:4 I have been *d* away from in
Lu 8:29 *d* by the demon into the
Ac 27:17 and thus were *d* along
Jas 1:6 wave of the sea *d* by the
3:4 big and are *d* by hard winds
2Pe 2:17 mists *d* by a violent storm

Drives
Nu 32:21 until he *d* away his enemies
2Ki 9:20 is with madness that he *d*
Job 32:13 It is God that *d* him away
Ps 1:4 chaff that the wind *d* away
Pr 19:13 leaking roof that *d* one away
27:15 leaking roof that *d* one away

Driving
Ge 4:14 Here you are actually *d* me
15:11 but Abram kept *d* them away
31:18 he began *d* all his herd and
31:26 *d* my daughters off like
Ex 3:1 While he was *d* the flock to
14:25 were *d* them with difficulty
34:11 am *d* out from before you the
Nu 11:31 *d* quails from the sea and
De 9:4 Jehovah is *d* them away from
9:5 God is *d* them away from
18:12 God is *d* them away from
Jg 2:23 nations stay by not *d* them
2Ki 9:20, 20 *d* is like the *d* of Jehu
1Ch 17:21 *d* out nations from before
Job 3:18 voice of one *d* them to work
Ps 80:8 kept *d* out the nations, that
Isa 9:4 of the one *d* them to work
14:2 who were *d* them to work
14:4 one *d* others to work come
58:3 that you kept *d* to work
Da 4:25 will be *d* away from men, and
4:32 they are *d* even you away
Na 2:4 the war chariots keep *d* madly
Ac 26:24 Great learning is *d* you into

Drop
De 28:40 your olives will *d* off
2Sa 24:16 enough! Now let your hand *d*
2Ki 9:33 he said: Let her *d!*
9:33 Then they let her *d*, and
1Ch 21:15 enough! Now let your hand *d*
2Ch 15:7 not let your hands *d* down
Ne 6:9 hands will *d* . . . from the work
Isa 13:7 hands themselves will *d* down
26:19 in death *d* in birth
40:15 are as a *d* from a bucket
Jer 3:12 not have my face *d* angrily
Eze 21:7 and all hands must *d* down
Am 7:16 let no word *d* against the
Mic 2:6 Do not you people let words *d*
2:6 They let words *d*. They will
2:6 They will not let words *d*
2:11 I shall let words *d* to you
2:11 words *d* for this people
Zep 3:16 May your hands not *d* down
Mt 27:6 is not lawful to *d* them into
Lu 21:2 widow *d* two small coins of
Ac 28:6 or suddenly *d* dead

Dropped
Job 30:17 and *d* from off me
30:30 skin became black and *d* off
Ps 140:10 burning coals be *d* upon
Jer 6:24 Our hands have *d*
50:43 his hands have *d* down
Mr 12:42 and *d* in two small coins
12:43 this poor widow *d* in more
12:44 *d* in out of their surplus
12:44 *d* in all of what she had
Lu 21:3 *d* in more than they all did
21:4 these *d* in gifts out of their
21:4 *d* in all the means of living

Dropping
Ps 55:3 *d* upon me what is hurtful
Jer 47:3 of the *d* down of their hands
Eze 7:17 the hands, they keep *d* down
Mr 12:41 *d* money into the treasury
12:41 were *d* in many coins
12:43 *d* money into the treasury
Lu 16:21 *d* from the table of the rich
21:1 rich *d* their gifts into the

Drops
Ex 30:23 myrrh in congealed *d* five
30:34 stacte *d* and onycha and
Job 36:27 he draws up the *d* of water
Ca 5:2 hair with the *d* of the night
Isa 5:30 the *d* falling on it
Lu 22:44 sweat became as *d* of blood

Jas 1:11 flower *d* off and the beauty

Dropsy
Lu 14:2 a certain man who had *d*

Dross
Ps 119:119 scummy *d* you have made
Pr 25:4 a removing of scummy *d* from
Isa 1:22 silver . . . become scummy *d*
1:25 smelt away your scummy *d* as
Eze 22:18 have become as scummy *d*
22:18 scummy *d*, that of silver
22:19 become as much scummy *d*

Drought
Job 24:19 *d* . . . snatch away the snow
Jer 17:8 the year of *d* he will not

Droughts
Jer 14:1 the matters of the *d*

Drove
Ge 3:24 he *d* the man out and posted
32:16 to his servants one *d* after
32:16, 16 interval between *d* and *d*
Ex 2:17 shepherds came and *d* them
5:6 those who *d* the people to work
5:10 who *d* the people to work
5:13 those who *d* them to work
10:19 the locusts away and *d* them
Jos 15:14 Caleb *d* away from there the
24:12 it gradually *d* them out
Jg 1:20 then he *d* out from there the
4:21 *d* the pin into his temples
6:9 and *d* them out from before you
8:12 *d* all the camp into trembling
11:7 you *d* me out of my father's
1Sa 17:34 a sheep from the *d*
23:5 *d* off with their livestock
30:2 *d* them along and went on
30:20 they *d* before that other
1Ki 2:27 Solomon *d* out Abiathar from
10:28 the horse *d* for a price
21:26 *d* out from before the sons
2Ki 16:3 whom Jehovah *d* out because
2Ch 1:16 take the horse *d* for a price
Job 24:2 A *d* they have snatched away
Ps 34:*super* he *d* him out, and he went
44:2 your hand *d* away even nations
78:52 conducted them like a *d* in
78:55 gradually *d* out the nations
Ca 4:1 Your hair is like a *d* of goats
4:2 like a *d* of freshly-shorn ewes
6:5 Your hair is like a *d* of goats
6:6 teeth are like a *d* of ewes
Isa 40:11 he will shepherd his own *d*
Jer 13:17 the *d* of Jehovah will have
13:20 the *d* that one gave to you
31:10 as a shepherd does his *d*
31:24 have set out with the *d*
51:23 shepherd and his *d* to pieces
Eze 34:12 feeding his *d* in the day of
Mic 2:12 like a *d* in the midst of its
4:8 O tower of the *d*, the mound
Zec 10:3 turned his attention to his *d*
Mal 1:14 in his *d* a male animal
Joh 2:15 *d* all those with the sheep
Ac 18:16 With that he *d* them away

Droves
Ge 29:2 three *d* of sheep were lying
29:2 accustomed to water the *d*
29:3 all the *d* had been gathered
29:8 until all the *d* are gathered
30:40 set his own *d* by themselves
32:19 all those following the *d*
2Ch 32:28 and stalls for the *d*
Pr 27:23 Set your heart to your *d*
Ca 1:7 among the *d* of your partners
Isa 17:2 become mere places for *d*
32:14 zebras, the pasture of *d*
Jer 6:3 and their *d* proceeded to come
Joe 1:18 *d* of cattle have wandered
1:18 the *d* of the sheep have been
Mic 5:8 young lion among *d* of sheep
Zep 2:14 *d* will certainly lie

Drowned
Mr 5:13 they *d* one after another in
Lu 8:33 herd . . . into the lake and *d*
Re 12:15 her to be *d* by the river

Drowsed
Ps 76:5 have *d* away to their sleep

Drowsiness
Pr 23:21 *d* will clothe one with mere

Drowsy
Ps 121:3 you cannot possibly be *d*
121:4 He will not be *d* nor go to
Isa 5:27 No one is *d* and no
Na 3:18 Your shepherds have become *d*

Drugged
Mr 15:23 give him wine *d* with myrrh

Drunk
Le 11:34 any drink that may be *d* in
1Sa 1:13 But Eli took her for *d*
1:14 How long will you behave *d?*
1:15 liquor I have not *d*, but I
25:36 he was as *d* as could be
30:12 or *d* water for three days
2Sa 11:13 So he got him *d*
1Ki 16:9 drinking himself *d* at the
20:16 drinking himself *d* in the
Ca 5:1 *d* my wine along with my milk
5:1 become *d* with expressions of
Isa 19:14 someone *d* is made to
44:12 He has not *d* water; so he
49:26 *d* with their own blood
51:17 *d* at the hand of Jehovah his
51:17 you have *d*, you have drained
51:21 O woman afflicted and *d*
63:6 make them *d* with my rage
Jer 23:9 become like a man that is *d*
25:27 Drink and get *d* and puke
35:14 *d* none down to this day
48:26 Make him *d*, O men, for he
51:7 she making all the earth *d*
51:7 her wine the nations have *d*
51:39 and I will make them *d*
51:57 and her mighty men *d*, and
La 4:21 You will become *d* and show
Ob 16 the way that you people have *d*
Na 3:11 become *d;* you will become
Hab 2:15 in order to make them *d*
Lu 5:39 No one that has *d* old wine
12:45 to eat and drink and get *d*
Ac 2:15 not *d*, as you suppose, for
Eph 5:18 not be getting *d* with wine
1Th 5:7, 7 *d* are usually *d* at night
Re 17:2 made *d* with the wine of her
17:6 woman was *d* with the blood

Drunkard
De 21:20 being a glutton and a *d*
Pr 23:21 *d* and a glutton will come to
26:9 come up into the hand of a *d*
1Co 5:11 in company with . . . a *d*

Drunkards
Isa 28:1 crown of the *d* of Ephraim
28:3 crowns of the *d* of Ephraim
Eze 23:42 *d* being brought in from the
Joe 1:5 Wake up, you *d*, and weep
Mt 24:49 drink with the confirmed *d*
1Co 6:10 nor *d*, nor revilers, nor

Drunken
Job 12:25 wander about like a *d* man
Ps 107:27 unsteadily like a *d* man
Isa 24:20 unsteadily like a *d* man
Na 1:10 *d* as with their wheat beer
Ro 13:13 not in revelries and *d* bouts
Ga 5:21 envies, *d* bouts, revelries
1Ti 3:3 not a *d* brawler, not a smiter
Tit 1:7 not a *d* brawler, not a smiter

Drunkenness
Jer 13:13 Jerusalem with *d*
Eze 23:33 With *d* and grief you will
39:19 and to drink blood to *d*

Drusilla
Ac 24:24 Felix arrived with *D* his

Dry
Ge 1:9 and let the *d* land appear
1:10 God began calling the *d* land
7:22 all that were on the *d* ground
8:13 the ground had drained *d*
26:15 would fill them with *d* earth
Ex 4:9 and pour it out on the *d* land
4:9 become blood on the *d* land
14:16 midst of the sea on *d* land
14:21 the sea basin into *d* ground
14:22 midst of the sea on *d* land
14:29 walked on *d* land in the
15:19 Israel walked on *d* land
Le 7:10 is moistened with oil or *d*
Jos 3:17 immovable on *d* ground in the
3:17 passing over on *d* ground
4:18 drawn out onto the *d* ground

Jos 4:22 On the *d* land it was that
9:5 provisions proved to be *d* and
9:12 is *d* and has become crumby
1Ki 17:7 the torrent valley became *d*
2Ki 2:8 went across on the *d* ground
19:24 shall *d* up with the soles
Ne 9:11 of the sea on the *d* land
Job 8:12 in its bud . . . it will *d* up
12:15 upon the waters and they *d*
13:25 chasing . . . mere *d* stubble
15:30 His twig a flame will *d* up
18:16 will his very roots *d* up
Ps 32:4 as in the *d* heat of summer
63:1 In a land *d* and exhausted
66:6 changed the sea into *d* land
95:5 own hands formed the *d* land
Pr 17:1 Better is a *d* piece of bread
17:22 stricken makes the bones *d*
Isa 4:6 shade by day from the *d* heat
19:5 parched and actually run *d*
19:7 of the Nile River will *d* up
37:25 *d* up with the soles of my
40:24 they *d* up; and like stubble
41:17 very tongue has become *d*
42:15 vegetation I shall *d* up
42:15 and reedy pools I shall *d* up
44:3 streams upon the *d* place
44:27 all your rivers I shall *d* up
50:2 I *d* up the sea; I make
56:3 say, Look! I am a *d* tree
Jer 12:4 of all the field *d* up
51:30 Their mightiness has run *d*
51:36 And I will *d* up her sea
51:36 I will make her wells *d*
La 4:8 has become just as *d* as a tree
Eze 17:9 plucked sprouts become *d*
17:9 It will become *d*. Neither by
17:10 Will it not *d* up completely
17:10 of its sprout it will *d* up
17:24 made the *d* tree blossom
19:12 was torn off and became *d*
20:47 and every *d* tree
30:12 the Nile canals *d* ground
37:2 look! they were very *d*
37:4 you *d* bones, hear the word
37:11 Our bones have become *d*
Da 2:10 not exist a man on the *d* land
Ho 9:16 Their very root must *d* up
13:15 it will *d* up his well and
Am 1:2 summit of Carmel must *d* up
Jon 1:9 made the sea and the *d* land
1:13 the ship back to the *d* land
2:10 Jonah onto the *d* land
Na 1:4 rivers he actually makes run *d*
1:10 devoured like stubble fully *d*
Hag 2:6 and the sea and the *d* ground
Zec 10:11 depths of the Nile must *d*
11:17 arm will without fail *d* up
Mt 23:15 you traverse sea and *d* land
Joh 11:2 his feet *d* with her hair
12:3 wiped his feet *d* with her
13:5 *d* them off with the towel
Heb 11:29 Red Sea as on *d* land, but on

Drying
Eze 26:5 A *d* yard for dragnets is
26:14 A *d* yard for dragnets is
47:10 to be a *d* yard for dragnets

Dryness
Jg 6:37 on all the earth there is *d*
6:39 *d* occur to the fleece alone
6:40 *d* came to be on the fleece
Job 30:30 bones became hot from *d*
Eze 29:10 *d*, a desolated waste, from
Joe 1:12 The vine itself has shown *d*
Hag 1:11 calling for *d* upon the earth

Due
Ge 12:13 be certain to live *d* to you
22:18 *d* to the fact that you have
26:5 *d* to the fact that Abraham
30:27 Jehovah is blessing me *d* to
39:5 *d* to Joseph, and Jehovah's
Ex 19:18 *d* to the fact that Jehovah
21:9 to the *d* right of daughters
21:10 and her marriage *d* are not
Nu 1:53 service *d* to the tabernacle
25:13 *d* to the fact that he
De 18:3 the *d* right of the priests
22:29 his wife *d* to the fact that
28:47 *d* to the fact that you did
Jg 6:2 *D* to Midian the sons of Israel
6:6 impoverished *d* to Midian; and
1Sa 2:13 the *d* right of the priests
1Sa 8:9 rightful *d* of the king who
8:11 rightful *d* of the king that
10:25 rightful *d* of the kingship
24:19 *d* to the fact that this day
2Sa 4:10 *d* for me to give him the
7:29 *d* to your blessing let the
2Ki 22:17 *d* to the fact that they have
25:30 daily as *d*, all the days of
1Ch 24:19 according to their *d* right
2Ch 21:12 *D* to the fact that you have
34:25 *d* to the fact that they
Ezr 3:4 rule of what was *d* each day
6:14 *d* to the order of the God of
6:14 *d* to the order of Cyrus and
Ne 5:14 eat the bread *d* the governor
5:18 bread *d* the governor I did not
Es 9:1 law came *d* to be performed
Job 6:17 In *d* season they become
41:25 *D* to its rising up the
41:25 *D* to consternation they get
Ps 5:10 fall *d* to their own counsels
38:8 *d* to the groaning of my heart
39:10 *D* to the hostility of your
44:16 *D* to the voice of the one
49:14 forms are *d* to wear away
55:3 *D* to the voice of the enemy
107:17 *d* to the way of their
107:17 *d* to their errors, finally
Pr 10:7 righteous one is *d* for a
27:9 *d* to the counsel of the soul
Ec 7:10 not *d* to wisdom that you have
Isa 7:22 *d* to the abundance of the
21:2 sighing *d* to her I have
40:26 *D* to the abundance of
48:4 *D* to my knowing that you are
50:2 *d* to there being no water
53:12 *d* to the fact that he
59:18 *d* treatment to his enemies
59:18 recompense *d* treatment
Jer 5:19 *D* to what fact has Jehovah
8:16 *D* to the sound of the
29:19 *d* to the fact that they have
43:11 *d* for deadly plague will
43:11 is *d* for captivity will be
43:11 is *d* for the sword will be
50:7 *d* to the fact that they have
52:34 daily as *d*, until the day
Ho 9:7 the *d* payment must come
Hab 1:11 its power is *d* to its god
Mt 18:7 *d* to the stumbling blocks
18:19 *d* to my Father in heaven
21:41 fruits when they become *d*
Mr 12:2 in *d* season he sent forth a
Lu 1:57 *d* for Elizabeth to give birth
13:16 Was it not *d*, then, for this
20:10 in *d* season he sent out a
21:8 The *d* time has approached
Joh 7:6 My *d* time is not yet present
7:6 your *d* time is always at hand
7:8 my *d* time has not yet fully
Ac 28:3 viper came out *d* to the heat
Ro 1:27 which was *d* for their error
11:5 *d* to undeserved kindness
11:6 it is no longer *d* to works
1Co 1:30 it is *d* to him that you are
4:5 judge . . . before the *d* time
7:3 render to his wife her *d*; but
2Co 1:11 *d* to many prayerful faces
7:9 damage in anything *d* to us
7:13 *d* to the joy of Titus
8:22 *d* to his great confidence in
11:3 the chastity that are *d* the
Ga 2:16 not *d* to works of law, but
2:16 declared righteous *d* to faith
2:16 and not *d* to works of law
2:16 *d* to works of law no flesh
3:2 the spirit *d* to works of law
3:2 or *d* to a hearing by faith
3:8 nations righteous *d* to faith
3:18 the inheritance is *d* to law
3:18 is no longer *d* to promise
3:24 declared righteous *d* to faith
6:9 *d* season we shall reap if we
Eph 4:16 in *d* measure, makes for the
Col 3:24 will receive the *d* reward
1Th 1:3 *d* to your hope in our Lord
2Th 2:6 revealed in his own *d* time
1Ti 5:4 keep paying a *d* compensation
2Ti 4:6 *d* time for my releasing is
Tit 1:3 in his own *d* times he made
Jas 5:4 The wages *d* the workers who
1Pe 2:18 with all *d* fear, not only to
5:6 he may exalt you in *d* time
Re 16:21 blasphemed God *d* to . . . hail
Re 18:3 rich *d* to the power of her

Dues
Ro 13:7 Render to all their *d*, to

Dug
Ge 21:30 witness for me that I have *d*
26:15 servants of his father had *d*
26:18 water that they had *d* in the
26:22 and *d* another well, but they
26:32 the well that they had *d*
Nu 21:18 A well, princes *d* it
Job 24:16 he has *d* into houses
Ps 35:7 they have *d* it for my soul
Isa 51:1 from which you were *d* out
Jer 13:7 went to the Euphrates and *d*
Mt 21:33 and *d* a winepress in it and
25:18 *d* in the ground and hid the
Mr 2:4 and having *d* an opening they
12:1 *d* a vat for the winepress and
Lu 6:48 *d* and went down deep and laid
Ro 11:3 they have *d* up your altars

Dukes
Jos 13:21 the *d* of Sihon, who were
Ps 83:11 like Zalmunna all their *d*
Eze 32:30 where the *d* of the north
Mic 5:5 yes, eight *d* of mankind

Dull
Ge 48:10 eyes of Israel were *d* from
Le 13:6 if the plague has grown *d* and
13:21 than the skin and it is *d*
13:26 than the skin and it is *d*
13:28 in the skin and it is *d*, it
13:39 of their flesh are *d* white
13:56 plague is *d* after it has been
Mr 6:52 hearts . . . *d* of understanding
8:17 hearts *d* of understanding
Heb 5:11 become *d* in your hearing

Dulled
2Co 3:14 their mental powers were *d*

Dulling
Ro 11:25 a *d* of sensibilities has

Dullness
Pr 23:29 Who has *d* of eyes?

Dumah
Ge 25:14 and Mishma and *D* and Massa
Jos 15:52 Arab and *D* and Eshan
1Ch 1:30 *D*, Massa, Hadad and Tema
Isa 21:11 pronouncement against *D*

Dumb
Hab 2:19 to a *d* stone: O wake up!
Mt 9:32 people brought him a *d* man
9:33 expelled the *d* man spoke
12:22 blind and *d*; and he cured
12:22 the *d* man spoke and saw
15:30 lame, maimed, blind, *d*, and
15:31 saw the *d* speaking and the
Lu 1:22 signs to them, but remained *d*
11:14 he was expelling a *d* demon
11:14 demon came out, the *d* man

Dung
Ex 29:14 and its *d* you will burn with
Le 4:11 and its intestines and its *d*
8:17 and its *d* burned with fire
16:27 and their *d* in the fire
Nu 19:5 with its *d* will be burned
1Ki 14:10 as one clears away the *d*
2Ki 6:25 dove's *d* was worth five
Eze 4:12 *d* cakes of the excrement of
4:15 the *d* cakes of mankind
Zep 1:17 their bowels like the *d*
Mal 2:3 scatter *d* upon your faces
2:3 the *d* of your festivals

Dungeon
Ps 142:7 my soul out of the very *d*
Isa 24:22 and be shut up in the *d*
42:7 out of the *d* the prisoner

Dungy
Le 26:30 carcasses of your *d* idols
De 29:17 to see . . . their *d* idols
1Ki 15:12 removed all the *d* idols
21:26 by going after the *d* idols
2Ki 17:12 continued to serve *d* idols
21:11 Judah sin with his *d* idols
21:21 serving the *d* idols that
23:24 teraphim and the *d* idols
Jer 50:2 *d* idols have become
Eze 6:4 to fall before your *d* idols
6:5 before their *d* idols, and I
6:6 your *d* idols may be actually

Eze 6:9 going . . . after their *d* idols
6:13 the midst of their *d* idols
6:13 odor to all their *d* idols
8:10 the *d* idols of the house of
14:3 *d* idols upon their heart
14:4 his *d* idols upon his heart
14:4 the multitude of his *d* idols
14:5 through their *d* idols—all of
14:6 back from your *d* idols and
14:7 his *d* idols upon his heart
16:36 all your detestable *d* idols
18:6 the *d* idols of the house of
18:12 to the *d* idols he lifted up
18:15 the *d* idols of the house of
20:7 with the *d* idols of Egypt do
20:8 *d* idols of Egypt they did not
20:16 *d* idols that their heart
20:18 with their *d* idols do not
20:24 *d* idols of their forefathers
20:31 *d* idols down till today
20:39 each . . . his own *d* idols
20:39 gifts and by your *d* idols
22:3 has made *d* idols within
22:4 *d* idols that you have made
23:7 *d* idols—she defiled herself
23:30 with their *d* idols
23:37 with their *d* idols they
23:39 their sons to their *d* idols
23:49 the sins of your *d* idols
30:13 destroy the *d* idols and
33:25 to your *d* idols, and blood
36:18 unclean with their *d* idols
36:25 from all your *d* idols I
37:23 with their *d* idols and
44:10 after their *d* idols, they
44:12 before their *d* idols and

Duplicates
Ex 26:24 should be *d* at the bottom
26:24 should be *d* up to the top of
36:29 *d* at the bottom and

Dura
Da 3:1 set it up in the plain of *D* in

Durable
Nu 24:21 *D* is your dwelling, and set
Jer 49:19 to the *d* abiding place
50:44 to the *d* abiding place
Mic 6:2 *d* objects, you foundations

Duration
2Ch 20:20 prove yourselves of long *d*
Job 11:17 will your life's *d* arise
Ps 39:5 my life's *d* is as nothing in
78:66 reproach of indefinite *d* he
89:47 Remember of what *d* of life
Isa 7:9 that case not be of long *d*

Dust
Ge 2:7 form the man out of *d* from
3:14 *d* is what you will eat all
3:19, 19 For *d* you are and to *d*
13:16 seed like the *d* particles
13:16 able to count the *d* particles
18:27 whereas I am *d* and ashes
28:14 seed . . . like the *d* particles
Ex 8:16 strike the *d* of the earth
8:17 and struck the *d* of the earth
8:17 *d* of the earth became gnats
Le 17:13 blood . . . cover it with *d*
Nu 5:17 will take some of the *d*
19:17 *d* of the burning of the sin
23:10 the *d* particles of Jacob
De 9:21 it had become fine like *d*
9:21 threw its *d* into the torrent
28:24 powder and *d* as the rain
32:24 venom of reptiles of the *d*
Jos 7:6 putting *d* upon their heads
1Sa 2:8 of a lowly one from the *d*
2Sa 16:13 and he threw a lot of *d*
22:43 pound them fine like the *d*
1Ki 16:2 raised you up out of the *d*
18:38 the stones and the *d*, and
20:10 if the *d* of Samaria will be
2Ki 13:7 like the *d* at threshing
23:4 the *d* of them to Bethel
23:6 and ground it to *d* and cast
23:6 cast its *d* upon the burial
23:12 their *d* into the torrent
23:15 he ground it to *d* and burned
2Ch 1:9 numerous as the *d* particles
Job 2:12 toss *d* toward the heavens
4:19 Whose foundation is in the *d*
5:6 not from mere *d* does what is
7:5 with maggots and lumps of *d*
7:21 now in *d* I shall lie down
Job 8:19 from the *d* others spring up
10:9 to *d* you . . . make me return
14:8 And in the *d* its stump dies
14:19 washes off earth's *d*
16:15 thrust my horn in the . . . *d*
17:16 must descend to the very *d*
19:25 he will rise up over the *d*
20:11 it will lie down in mere *d*
21:26 in the *d* they will lie down
22:24 precious ore in the *d* And
27:16 pile up silver like *d*
28:2 taken from the very *d* And
28:6 And it has gold *d*
30:6 holes of the *d* and in rocks
30:19 I show myself like *d* and
34:15 will return to the very *d*
38:38 *d* pours out as into a
39:14 in the *d* she keeps them
40:13 Hide them together in the *d*
41:33 Upon the *d* there is not the
42:6 I do repent in *d* and ashes
Ps 7:5 glory to reside in the *d* itself
18:42 shall pound them fine like *d*
22:15 in the *d* of death you are
22:29 those going down to the *d*
30:9 Will the *d* laud you? Will it
44:25 bowed down to the *d* itself
72:9 enemies will lick the *d*
78:27 rain upon them just like *d*
102:14 to her *d* they direct their
103:14 Remembering that we are *d*
104:29 And back to their *d* they go
113:7 lowly one from the very *d*
119:25 been cleaving to the very *d*
Pr 8:26 *d* masses of the productive
Ec 3:20 all come to be from the *d*
3:20 are all returning to the *d*
12:7 *d* returns to the earth just as
Isa 2:10 and hide yourself in the *d*
2:19 and into the holes of the *d*
25:12 with the earth, to the *d*
26:5 it in touch with the *d*
26:19 you residents in the *d*
29:4 from the *d* your saying will
29:4 from the *d* your own saying
34:7 *d* will be made greasy with
34:9 and her *d* into sulphur
40:12 measure the *d* of the earth
40:15 the film of *d* on the scales
40:15 as mere fine *d*
41:2 kept giving them like *d* to
47:1 down and sit down in the *d*
49:23 *d* of your feet they will
52:2 free from the *d*, rise up
65:25 serpent, his food will be *d*
La 2:10 brought up *d* upon their head
3:29 put his mouth in the very *d*
Eze 24:7 to cover it over with *d*
26:4 scrape her *d* away from her
26:10 their *d* will cover you
26:12 *d* they will place in the
27:30 bring up *d* upon their heads
Da 12:2 asleep in the ground of *d*
Am 2:7 panting for the *d* of the earth
Mic 1:10 wallow in the very *d*
7:17 lick up *d* like the serpents
Hab 1:10 it piles up *d* and captures it
Zep 1:17 be poured out like *d*, and
Zec 9:3 silver like *d* and gold like
Mt 10:14 shake the *d* off your feet
Lu 9:5 shake the *d* off your feet for
10:11 Even the *d* that got stuck
Ac 13:51 shook the *d* off their feet
22:23 and tossing *d* into the air
1Co 15:47 of the earth and made of *d*
15:48 As the one made of *d* is
15:48 so those made of *d* are also
15:49 image of the one made of *d*
Re 18:19 threw *d* upon their heads

Dusty
Ne 4:2 out of the heaps of *d* rubbish

Duties
2Ki 15:5 in his house exempt from *d*
1Ch 26:12 the headmen had *d* exactly
2Ch 26:21 exempt from *d*, as a leper
Ne 12:9 opposite them for guard *d*
13:30 assign *d* to the priests and
Mt 17:25 receive *d* or head tax
Lu 10:40 with attending to many *d*
1Co 9:13 men performing sacred *d* eat

Duty
1Ch 9:33 those set free from *d*
2Ch 7:6 standing at their posts of *d*
8:14 Levites at their posts of *d*
23:8 the divisions free from *d*

Dwell
Ge 4:20 those who *d* in tents and
13:6 did not allow for them to *d*
13:6 not able to *d* all together
20:15 *D* where it is good in your
22:19 Abraham continued to *d* at
27:44 And you must *d* with him for
34:10 And with us you may *d*, and
34:10 *D* and carry on business in it
34:16 *d* with you and become one
34:21 let them *d* in the land and
34:22 consent to *d* with us so as
34:23 that they may *d* with us
35:1 go up to Bethel and *d* there
36:7 too great for them to *d*
37:1 Jacob continued to *d* in the
38:11 *D* as a widow in the house of
38:11 *d* at her own father's house
45:10 must *d* in the land of Goshen
46:34 *d* in the land of Goshen
47:4 *d*, please, in the land of
47:6 *d* in the very best of the land
47:6 *d* in the land of Goshen, and
47:11 his father and his brothers *d*
47:27 to *d* in the land of Egypt
50:22 Joseph continued to *d* in
Ex 2:15 *d* in the land of Midian
2:21 showed willingness to *d*
23:33 should not *d* in your land
Le 7:26 in any places where you *d*
13:46 *d* isolated. Outside the camp
14:8 *d* outside his tent seven days
20:22 *d* in it may not vomit you
23:3 in all places where you *d*
23:14 in all places where you *d*
23:31 in all places where you *d*
23:42 booths you should *d* seven
23:42 Israel should *d* in the booths
23:43 sons of Israel to *d* when I was
25:18 *d* on the land in security
25:19 and *d* in security on it
26:5 and *d* in security in your land
Nu 13:28 people who *d* in the land are
20:15 to *d* in Egypt many days; and
21:31 Israel began to *d* in the land
21:34 who used to *d* in Heshbon
32:17 while our little ones must *d*
33:53 and *d* in it, because to you I
35:25 *d* in it until the death of
35:28 *d* in his city of refuge until
De 1:46 as many days as you did *d*
2:12 and to *d* in their place, just
2:21 dispossess them and *d* in
2:22 *d* in their place until this
2:23 they might *d* in their place
8:12 houses and indeed *d* in them
11:31 take possession of it and *d*
12:10 *d* in the land that Jehovah
12:10 will indeed *d* in security
12:29 and *d* in their land
13:12 God is giving you to *d* there
21:13 *d* in your house and weep for
25:5 In case brothers *d* together
28:30 but you will not *d* in it
30:20 may *d* upon the ground that
Jos 1:14 *d* in the land that Moses
14:4 except cities to *d* in and
19:50 the city and *d* in it
20:4 and he must *d* with them
20:6 must *d* in that city until
21:2 be given us in which to *d*
21:43 of it and to *d* in it
Jg 1:29 to *d* in among them in Gezer
1:30 Canaanites continued to *d* in
1:32 Asherites continued to *d* in
1:33 they continued to *d* in among
5:17 to *d* for the time in ships
8:29 continued to *d* in his house
9:41 continued to *d* in Arumah, and
15:8 began to *d* in a cleft of the
17:10 Do *d* with me and serve as a
17:11 to *d* with the man, and the
18:1 inheritance for itself to *d*
19:4 to *d* with him three days
20:47 to *d* on the crag of Rimmon
1Sa 1:22 before Jehovah and *d* there
5:7 not let the ark . . . *d* with us
12:8 cause them to *d* in this
12:11 you might *d* in security
19:2 must *d* in secrecy and keep

Pr 8:26 had not made the *e* and the
8:29 the foundations of the *e*
8:31 productive land of his *e*, and
10:30 not keep residing on the *e*
11:31 in the *e* he will be rewarded
17:24 at the extremity of the *e*
25:3 the *e* for depth, and the heart
30:4 all the ends of the *e* to rise
30:14 the afflicted ones off the *e*
30:21 the *e* has been agitated, and
30:24 are the smallest of the *e*
Ec 1:4 the *e* is standing even to time
3:21 descending downward to the *e*
5:2 you are on the *e*. That is why
5:9 profit of the *e* is among them
7:20 is no man righteous in the *e*
8:14 that is carried out on the *e*
8:16 that is carried on in the *e*
10:7 princes walking on the *e* just
11:2 calamity will occur on the *e*
11:3 a sheer downpour upon the *e*
12:7 dust returns to the *e* just as
Isa 1:2 and give ear, O *e*, for Jehovah
2:19 the *e* to suffer shocks
2:21 for the *e* to suffer shocks
3:26 will sit down on the very *e*
5:26 at the extremity of the *e*
6:3 all the *e* is his glory
8:9 you in distant parts of the *e*
8:22 to the *e* he will look, and
10:14 gather up even all the *e*
11:4 of the meek ones of the *e*
11:4 strike the *e* with the rod of
11:9 *e* will certainly be filled
11:12 four extremities of the *e*
12:5 is made known in all the *e*
13:5 to wreck all the *e*
13:13 *e* will rock out of its
14:7 whole *e* has come to rest
14:9 goatlike leaders of the *e*
14:12 have been cut down to the *e*
14:16 that was agitating the *e*
14:21 take possession of the *e* and
14:26 counseled against all the *e*
16:4 have been finished off the *e*
18:3 and you residents of the *e*
18:6 for the beast of the *e*
18:6 beast of the *e* will pass the
19:24 in the midst of the *e*
21:9 gods he has broken to the *e*
23:8 the honorable ones of the *e*
23:9 the honorable ones of the *e*
23:17 all the kingdoms of the *e*
25:8 take away from all the *e*
25:12 contact with the *e*, to the
26:5 he abases it to the *e*
26:9 judgments from you for the *e*
26:19 *e* itself will let even
28:2 casting down to the *e* with
29:4 speak from the very *e*, and
29:4 become even from the *e*
34:1 *e* and that which fills it
37:16 all the kingdoms of the *e*
37:16 made the heavens and the *e*
37:20 *e* may know that you
40:12 measure the dust of the *e*
40:21 the foundations of the *e*
40:22 above the circle of the *e*
40:23 judges of the *e* as a mere
40:24 stump taken root in the *e*
40:28 of the extremities of the *e*
41:5 extremities of the *e* began
41:9 the extremities of the *e*
42:4 he sets justice in the *e*
42:5 the *e* and its produce
42:10 from the extremity of the *e*
43:6 from the extremity of the *e*
44:23 you lowest parts of the *e*
44:24 by myself, laying out the *e*
45:8 Let the *e* open up, and let
45:12 made the *e* and have created
45:18 the Former of the *e* and the
45:19 in a dark place of the *e*
45:22 all you at the ends of the *e*
47:1 *e* where there is no throne
48:13 laid the foundation of the *e*
48:20 to the extremity of the *e*
49:6 to the extremity of the *e*
49:13 and be joyful, you *e*
49:23 With faces to the *e* they
51:6 and look at the *e* beneath
51:6 the *e* itself will wear out
51:13 the foundation of the *e*
51:16 lay the foundation of the *e*
Isa 51:23 your back just like the *e*
52:10 *e* must see the salvation
54:5 The God of the whole *e* he
54:9 no more pass over the *e*
55:9 heavens are higher than the *e*
55:10 saturates the *e* and makes
58:14 the high places of the *e*
60:2 cover the *e*, and thick gloom
61:11 *e* itself brings forth its
62:7 as a praise in the *e*
62:11 the farthest part of the *e*
63:6 to the *e* their spurting blood
65:16 blessing himself in the *e*
65:16 a sworn statement in the *e*
65:17 new heavens and a new *e*
66:1 and the *e* is my footstool
66:22 the new *e* that I am making
Jer 6:19 Listen, O *e*! Here I am
6:22 the remotest parts of the *e*
7:33 for the beasts of the *e*
9:24 and righteousness in the *e*
10:10 the *e* will rock, and no
10:11 very heavens and the *e*
10:11 who will perish from the *e*
10:12 Maker of the *e* by his power
10:13 the extremity of the *e*
10:17 Gather up from the *e* your
10:18 the inhabitants of the *e*
14:2 become dejected to the *e*
15:3 and the beasts of the *e*
15:4 to all the kingdoms of the *e*
15:10 strife with all the *e*
16:4 for the beasts of the *e*
16:19 come from the ends of the *e*
17:13 written down even in the *e*
19:7 and to the beasts of the *e*
22:29, 29, 29 O *e*, *e*, *e*, hear the
23:24 the *e* that I . . . fill
24:9 in all the kingdoms of the *e*
25:26 the other kingdoms of the *e*
25:29 all the inhabitants of the *e*
25:30 all the inhabitants of the *e*
25:31 the farthest part of the *e*
25:32 the remotest parts of the *e*
25:33 from one end of the *e* clear
25:33 to the other end of the *e*
26:6 to all the nations of the *e*
27:5 I myself have made the *e*
27:5 upon the surface of the *e*
29:18 all the kingdoms of the *e*
31:8 the remotest parts of the *e*
31:22 created a new thing in the *e*
31:37 foundations of the *e* below
32:17 made the heavens and the *e*
33:2 Jehovah the Maker of *e* has
33:9 nations of the *e* who will
33:25 statutes of heaven and *e*
34:1 all the kingdoms of the *e*
34:17 all the kingdoms of the *e*
34:20 for the beasts of the *e*
44:8 all the nations of the *e*
46:8 I shall cover the *e*
49:21 the *e* has begun to rock
50:23 forge hammer of all the *e*
50:41 remotest parts of the *e*
50:46 *e* will certainly be set
51:7 she making all the *e* drunk
51:15 Maker of the *e* by his power
51:16 the extremity of the *e*
51:25 you ruiner of the whole *e*
51:29 *e* rock and be in severe
51:41 Praise of the whole *e* gets
51:46 violence in the *e* and ruler
51:48 *e* and all that is in them
51:49 slain ones of all the *e*
La 2:1 thrown down from heaven to *e*
2:2 into contact with the *e*
2:9 have sunk down into the very *e*
2:10 sit down on the *e*, where they
2:10 their head down to the very *e*
2:11 been poured out to the very *e*
2:15 an exultation for all the *e*
2:21 down on the *e* of the streets
3:34 all the prisoners of the *e*
4:12 The kings of the *e* and all the
Eze 1:15 one wheel on the *e* beside
1:19 were lifted up from the *e*
1:21 were lifted up from the *e*
7:21 to the wicked ones of the *e*
8:3 between the *e* and the heavens
10:16 to be high above the *e*
10:19 rose from the *e* before my
12:6 that you may not see the *e*
12:12 see with his own eye the *e*
Eze 13:14 into contact with the *e*
19:12 To the *e* she was thrown
24:7 not pour it out upon the *e*
26:11 to the *e* your own pillars
26:16 Upon the *e* they will sit
26:17 all the inhabitants of the *e*
28:17 Onto the *e* I will throw you
28:18 make you ashes upon the *e*
29:5 wild beasts of the *e* and to
31:12 the stream beds of the *e*
31:12 all the peoples of the *e*
32:4 wild beasts of the whole *e*
34:6 on all the surface of the *e*
34:28 the wild beast of the *e*
35:14 that all the *e* rejoices
38:12 in the center of the *e*
38:20 to the *e* even every wall
39:14 on the surface of the *e*
39:18 of the chieftains of the *e*
43:2 *e* itself shone because of
Da 2:35 and filled the whole *e*
2:39 will rule over the whole *e*
4:1 are dwelling in all the *e*
4:10 a tree in the midst of the *e*
4:11 the extremity of the whole *e*
4:15 its rootstock itself in the *e*
4:15 among the vegetation of the *e*
4:20 was visible to all the *e*
4:22 to the extremity of the *e*
4:23 its rootstock itself in the *e*
4:35 inhabitants of the *e* are being
4:35 and the inhabitants of the *e*
6:25 are dwelling in all the *e*
6:27 in the heavens and on the *e*
7:4 was lifted up from the *e* and
7:17 that will stand up from the *e*
7:23 will come to be on the *e*
7:23 it will devour all the *e* and
8:5 the surface of the whole *e*
8:5 and it was not touching the *e*
8:7 threw it to the *e* and trampled
8:10 stars to fall to the *e*, and
8:12 throwing truth to the *e*, and
8:18 asleep on my face on the *e*
10:9 with my face to the *e*
10:15 I had set my face to the *e*
Ho 2:21 part, will answer the *e*
2:22 *e*, for its part, will answer
2:23 like seed for me in the *e*
6:3 rain that saturates the *e*
Joe 2:30 in the heavens and on the *e*
3:16 and *e* certainly will rock
Am 2:7 panting for the dust of the *e*
3:5 bird fall into a trap on the *e*
3:14 and must fall to the *e*
5:7 righteousness itself to the *e*
5:8 out upon the surface of the *e*
8:4 cause the meek ones of the *e*
9:6 over the *e* that he founded
9:6 out upon the surface of the *e*
9:9 not a pebble falls to the *e*
Ob 3 Who will bring me down to the *e*?
Jon 2:6 As for the *e*, its bars were
Mic 1:2 pay attention, O *e* and what
4:13 the true Lord of the whole *e*
5:4 as far as the ends of the *e*
6:2 Hear . . . foundations of the *e*
7:2 has perished from the *e*
7:17 like reptiles of the *e* they
Na 1:5 the *e* will be upheaved because
2:13 cut off from the *e* your prey
Hab 1:6 to the wide-open places of *e*
2:8 the violence to the *e*, the
2:14 the *e* will be filled with
2:17 the violence done to the *e*
2:20 Keep silence . . . all the *e*
3:3 praise the *e* became filled
3:6 that he might shake up the *e*
3:9 you proceeded to split the *e*
3:12 went marching through the *e*
Zep 1:18 the whole *e* will be devoured
1:18 all the inhabitants of the *e*
2:3 all you meek ones of the *e*
2:11 emaciate . . . gods of the *e*
3:8 all the *e* will be devoured
3:20 all the peoples of the *e*
Hag 1:10 *e* itself kept back its yield
1:11 for dryness upon the *e*, and
2:6 rocking the heavens and the *e*
2:21 rocking the heavens and the *e*
Zec 1:10 to walk about in the *e*
1:11 walked about in the *e*, and
1:11 the whole *e* is sitting still
4:10 are roving about in all the *e*

Zec 4:14 the Lord of the whole *e*
5:3 over the surface of all the *e*
5:6 is their aspect in all the *e*
5:9 between the *e* and the heavens
6:5 the Lord of the whole *e*
6:7 order to walk about in the *e*
6:7 said: Go, walk about in the *e*
6:7 began walking about in the *e*
8:12 *e* itself will give its yield
9:10 River to the ends of the *e*
12:1 the foundation of the *e* and
12:3 the nations of the *e* will
14:9 become king over all the *e*
14:17 of the families of the *e* to
Mal 4:6 strike the *e* with a devoting
Mt 5:5 since they will inherit the *e*
5:13 You are the salt of the *e*
5:18 would heaven and *e* pass away
5:35 nor by *e*, because it is the
6:10 as in heaven, also upon *e*
6:19 treasures upon the *e*, where
9:6 authority on *e* to forgive sins
10:34 came to put peace upon the *e*
11:25 Father, Lord of heaven and *e*
12:40 in the heart of the *e* three
12:42 from the ends of the *e* to
16:19 whatever you may bind on *e*
16:19 whatever you may loose on *e*
17:25 the kings of the *e* receive
18:18 things you may bind on *e*
18:18 things you may loose on *e*
18:19 If two of you on *e* agree
23:9 call anyone your father on *e*
23:35 righteous blood spilled on *e*
24:14 in all the inhabited *e* for a
24:30 tribes of the *e* will beat
24:35 Heaven and *e* will pass away
27:51 and the *e* quaked, and the
28:18 in heaven and on the *e*
Mr 2:10 to forgive sins upon the *e*
4:31 the seeds that are on the *e*
9:3 clothes cleaner on *e* could
13:31 Heaven and *e* will pass away
Lu 2:1 inhabited *e* to be registered
2:14 upon *e* peace among men of
4:5 kingdoms of the inhabited *e*
5:24 on the *e* to forgive sins
10:21 Father, Lord of heaven and *e*
11:31 came from the ends of the *e*
12:49 to start a fire on the *e*
12:51 to give peace on the *e*? No
12:56 outward appearance of *e* and
16:17 heaven and *e* to pass away
18:8 really find the faith on the *e*
21:25 on the *e* anguish of nations
21:26 coming upon the inhabited *e*
21:33 Heaven and *e* will pass away
21:35 upon the face of all the *e*
23:44 darkness fell over all the *e*
Joh 3:31 He that is from the *e* is
3:31 from the *e* and speaks of
3:31 and speaks of things of the *e*
12:32 I am lifted up from the *e*
17:4 have glorified you on the *e*
Ac 1:8 most distant part of the *e*
2:19 and signs on *e* below, blood
3:25 families of the *e* will be
4:24 who made the heaven and the *e*
4:26 kings of the *e* took their
7:49 and the *e* is my footstool
8:33 life is taken away from the *e*
10:11 four extremities upon the *e*
10:12 creeping things of the *e* and
11:6 four-footed creatures of the *e*
11:28 upon the entire inhabited *e*
13:47 to the extremity of the *e*
14:15 made the heaven and the *e*
17:6 overturned the inhabited *e*
17:24 One is, Lord of heaven and *e*
17:26 the entire surface of the *e*
17:31 to judge the inhabited *e* in
19:27 of Asia and the inhabited *e*
22:22 such a man away from the *e*
24:5 throughout the inhabited *e*
Ro 9:17 may be declared in all the *e*
9:28 make an accounting on the *e*
10:18 into all the *e* their sound
10:18 inhabited *e* their utterances
1Co 8:5 whether in heaven or on *e*
10:26 to Jehovah belong the *e* and
15:47 first man is out of the *e*
Eph 1:10 and the things on the *e*
3:15 in heaven and on *e* owes its
4:9 lower regions, that is, the *e*
Eph 6:3 endure a long time on the *e*
Php 2:10 in heaven and those on *e* and
3:19 minds upon things on the *e*
Col 1:16 in the heavens and upon the *e*
1:20 the things upon the *e* or the
3:2 not on the things upon the *e*
3:5 body members . . . upon the *e*
Heb 1:6 Firstborn into the inhabited *e*
1:10 laid the foundations of the *e*
2:5 the inhabited *e* to come
8:4 If, now, he were upon *e*, he
11:38 and dens and caves of the *e*
12:25 divine warning upon *e*
12:26 his voice shook the *e*, but
12:26 not only the *e* but also the
Jas 5:5 lived in luxury upon the *e* and
5:7 the precious fruit of the *e*
5:12 by heaven or by *e* or by any
2Pe 3:5 *e* standing compactly out of
3:7 the heavens and the *e* that
3:10 *e* and the works in it will
3:13 new heavens and a new *e*
Re 1:5 Ruler of the kings of the *e*
1:7 all the tribes of the *e* will
3:10 upon the whole inhabited *e*
3:10 those dwelling on the *e*
5:3 neither in heaven nor upon *e*
5:3 nor underneath the *e* was there
5:6 sent forth into the whole *e*
5:10 to rule as kings over the *e*
5:13, 13 on *e* and underneath the *e*
6:4 to take peace away from the *e*
6:8 over the fourth part of the *e*
6:8 by the wild beasts of the *e*
6:10 upon those who dwell on the *e*
6:13 stars of heaven fell to the *e*
6:15 And the kings of the *e* and
7:1 upon the four corners of the *e*
7:1 the four winds of the *e*, that
7:1 blow upon the *e* or upon the
7:2 to harm the *e* and the sea
7:3 Do not harm the *e* or the sea
8:5 altar and hurled it to the *e*
8:7 and it was hurled to the *e*
8:7 a third of the *e* was burned up
8:13 to those dwelling on the *e*
9:1 fallen from heaven to the *e*
9:3 locusts came forth upon the *e*
9:3 the scorpions of the *e* have
9:4 harm no vegetation of the *e*
10:2 but his left one upon the *e*
10:5 on the *e* raised his right hand
10:6 the *e* and the things in it
10:8 on the sea and on the *e*
11:4 before the Lord of the *e*
11:6 to strike the *e* with every
11:10 those dwelling on the *e*
11:10 those dwelling on the *e*
11:18 to ruin those ruining the *e*
12:4 it hurled them down to the *e*
12:9 the entire inhabited *e*; he
12:9 he was hurled down to the *e*
12:12 Woe for the *e* and for the
12:13 it was hurled down to the *e*
12:16 *e* came to the woman's help
12:16 *e* opened its mouth and
13:3 *e* followed the wild beast
13:8 all those who dwell on the *e*
13:11 beast ascending out of the *e*
13:12 *e* and those who dwell in it
13:13 out of heaven to the *e* in
13:14 those who dwell on the *e*
13:14 those who dwell on the *e* to
14:3 have been bought from the *e*
14:6 to those who dwell on the *e*
14:7 made the heaven and the *e*
14:15 harvest of the *e* . . . ripe
14:16 thrust in his sickle on the *e*
14:16 and the *e* was reaped
14:18 clusters of the vine of the *e*
14:19 his sickle into the *e* and
14:19 gathered the vine of the *e*
16:1 the anger of God into the *e*
16:2 out his bowl into the *e*
16:14 of the entire inhabited *e*
16:18 men came to be on the *e*, so
17:2 kings of the *e* committed
17:2 those who inhabit the *e* were
17:5 the disgusting things of the *e*
17:8 those who dwell on the *e*
17:18 over the kings of the *e*
18:1 *e* was lighted up from his
18:3 kings of the *e* committed
18:3 traveling merchants of the *e*
Re 18:9 kings of the *e* who committed
18:11 merchants of the *e* are
18:23 top-ranking men of the *e*
18:24 been slaughtered on the *e*
19:2 harlot who corrupted the *e*
19:19 kings of the *e* and their
20:8 in the four corners of the *e*
20:9 over the breadth of the *e*
20:11 *e* and the heaven fled away
21:1 a new heaven and a new *e*
21:1 former *e* had passed away, and
21:24 kings of the *e* will bring

Earthen

2Co 4:7 this treasure in *e* vessels

Earthenware

Le 6:28 the *e* vessel in which it may
11:33 As for any *e* vessel into
14:5 killed in an *e* vessel over
14:50 *e* vessel over running water
15:12 an *e* vessel that the one
Nu 5:17 holy water in an *e* vessel
Job 2:8 fragment of *e* with which to
41:30 As pointed *e* fragments are
Ps 22:15 just like a fragment of *e*
Pr 26:23 upon a fragment of *e* are
Isa 30:14 *e* with which to rake the
45:9 as an *e* fragment with the
45:9 *e* fragments of the ground
Jer 19:1 get an *e* flask of a potter
32:14 put them into an *e* vessel
La 4:2 reckoned as large jars of *e*
Eze 23:34 its *e* fragments you will
Mr 14:13 a man carrying an *e* vessel
Lu 22:10 a man carrying an *e* vessel
2Ti 2:20 but also of wood and *e*

Earthling

1Sa 15:29 *e* man so as to feel regrets
Job 14:10 *e* man expires, and where is
31:33 If like an *e* man I covered
32:21 on an *e* man I shall not
34:11 the way *e* man acts he will
34:15 *e* man himself will return
35:8 to a son of *e* man
37:7 On the hand of every *e* man
38:26 in which there is no *e* man
Ps 8:4 *e* man that you take care of
39:5 *e* man, though standing firm
39:11 every *e* man is an exhalation
49:12 yet *e* man, though in honor
49:20 *E* man, although in honor
56:11 What can *e* man do to me?
60:11 salvation by *e* man is
62:9 the sons of *e* man are an
64:9 all *e* men will become afraid
78:60 he resided among *e* men
108:12 salvation by *e* man is
115:4 of the hands of *e* man
118:6 What can *e* man do to me?
118:8 Than to trust in *e* man
135:15 work of the hands of *e* man
146:3 *e* man, to whom no salvation
Pr 3:4 eyes of God and of *e* man
16:1 *e* man belong the arrangings
16:9 *e* man may think out his way
19:3 *e* man that distorts his way
19:22 desirable thing in *e* man is
20:24 *e* man, how can he discern
20:25 *e* man has rashly cried out
20:27 breath of *e* man is the lamp
24:12 pay back to *e* man according
29:23 very haughtiness of *e* man
Ec 2:12 what can the *e* man do who
Isa 2:9 And *e* man bows down, and man
2:11 haughty eyes of *e* man must
2:17 the haughtiness of the *e* man
2:20 the *e* man will throw his
2:22 *e* man, whose breath is in
5:15 *e* man will bow down, and
6:11 houses be without *e* man
6:12 removes *e* men far away
13:12 *e* man rarer than the gold
17:7 *e* man will look up to his
22:6 the war chariot of *e* man
31:3 are *e* men, and not God
31:8 sword, not that of *e* man
44:11 craftsmen are from *e* men
58:5 *e* man to afflict his soul
Jer 2:6 in which no *e* man dwelt
4:25 there was not an *e* man, and
10:23 to *e* man his way does not
16:20 Can *e* man make for himself
17:5 who puts his trust in *e* man

Eastward
Ge 11:2 in their journeying *e* they
13:14 look . . . *e* and westward
25:6 *e*, to the land of the East
Nu 2:3 *e* toward the sunrising will be
34:15 *e* toward the sunrising
Jos 16:1 to the waters of Jericho *e*
16:6 around *e* to Taanath-shiloh
16:6 and passed over *e* to Janoah
19:12 it went back from Sarid *e*
19:13 *e* toward the sunrise to
1Ki 7:39 right side of the house *e*
17:3 you must turn your way *e*
Eze 11:1 gate . . . that is facing *e*
45:7 something on the east side *e*
47:1 threshold of the House *e*
47:3 man went forth *e* with a

Easy
De 1:41 *e* to go up into the mountain
1Sa 18:23 Is it an *e* thing in your
2Ki 20:10 *e* thing for the shadow to
Pr 14:6 knowledge is an *e* thing
2Co 8:13 for it to be *e* for others

Easygoingness
Pr 1:32 *e* of the stupid is what will

Eat
Ge 2:16 tree of the garden you may *e*
2:17 you must not *e* from it, for
2:17 day you *e* from it you will
3:1 God said you must not *e* from
3:2 trees of the garden we may *e*
3:3 God has said, You must not *e*
3:11 I commanded you not to *e*
3:14 dust is what you will *e* all
3:17 You must not *e* from it
3:17 In pain you will *e* its produce
3:18 must *e* the vegetation of the
3:19 you will *e* bread until you
3:22 from the tree of life and *e*
9:4 its blood—you must not *e*
24:33 something to *e* was set
24:33 I shall not *e* until I have
27:4 let me *e*, in order that my
27:7 let me *e*, that I may bless
27:10 he must *e* it, in order that
27:19 Sit down and *e* some of my
27:25 I may *e* some of the game
27:25 he began to *e*, and he brought
27:31 Let my father get up and *e*
28:20 bread to *e* and garments to
31:54 invited his brothers to *e*
32:32 to *e* the sinew of the thigh
37:25 they sat down to *e* bread
40:19 *e* your flesh from off you
41:4 began to *e* up the seven cows
41:20 to *e* up the first seven fat
43:16 the men are to *e* with me at
43:25 they were going to *e* bread
43:32 not able to *e* a meal with
45:18 *e* the fat part of the land
47:24 for your little ones to *e*
49:27 he will *e* the animal seized
Ex 2:20 Call him, that he may *e*
10:5 *e* up the rest of what has
10:5 *e* every sprouting tree of
10:12 *e* up all the vegetation of
12:7 houses in which they will *e*
12:8 *e* the flesh on this night
12:8 *e* it roasted with fire and
12:9 Do not *e* any of it raw or
12:11 in this way you should *e* it
12:11 and you must *e* it in haste
12:15 *e* unfermented cakes only
12:16 what every soul needs to *e*
12:18 to *e* unfermented cakes down
12:20 Nothing leavened are you to *e*
12:20 are to *e* unfermented cakes
12:43 No foreigner may *e* of it
12:45 a hired laborer may not *e* of
12:48 no uncircumcised man may *e*
13:6 are to *e* unfermented cakes
16:8 in the evening meat to *e* and
16:12 you will *e* meat and in the
16:25 *E* it today, because today is
16:32 made you *e* in the wilderness
18:12 came to *e* bread with Moses'
22:31 not *e* flesh in the field that
23:11 poor ones . . . must *e* of it
23:11 beasts of the field are to *e*
23:15 *e* unfermented cakes seven
29:32 must *e* the flesh of the ram
29:33 must *e* the things with
29:33 stranger may not *e* them
Ex 32:6 sat down to *e* and drink
34:15 *e* some of his sacrifice
34:18 *e* unfermented cakes, just
Le 3:17 not *e* any fat or any blood at
6:16 Aaron and his sons will *e*
6:16 will *e* it in the courtyard of
6:18 the sons of Aaron will *e* it
6:26 offers it for sin will *e* it
6:29 among the priests will *e* it
7:6 male among the priests will *e*
7:19 clean may *e* the flesh
7:23 not *e* any fat of a bull or a
7:24 but you must not *e* it at all
7:26 must not *e* any blood in any
8:31 there is where you will *e* it
8:31 Aaron and his sons will *e* it
10:12 and *e* it unfermented near
10:13 must *e* it in a holy place
10:14 *e* the breast of the wave
10:17 you not *e* the sin offering
11:2 may *e* of all the beasts that
11:3 that is what you may *e*
11:4 must not *e* among the chewers
11:8 must not *e* any of their flesh
11:9 *e* of everything that is in
11:9 those you may *e*
11:11 not *e* any of their flesh
11:21 what you may *e* of all the
11:22 the ones of them you may *e*
11:42 you must not *e* them, because
17:12 No soul of you must *e* blood
17:12 in your midst should *e* blood
17:14 You must not *e* the blood of
19:25 fifth year you may *e* its
19:26 You must *e* nothing along
21:22 *e* the bread of his God from
22:4 *e* of the holy things until
22:6 may not *e* any of the holy
22:7 *e* some of the holy things
22:8 *e* any body already dead or
22:10 no stranger at all may *e*
22:10 laborer may *e* anything holy
22:12 *e* of the contribution of the
22:13 *e* some of her father's bread
23:6 should *e* unfermented cakes
23:14 *e* no bread nor roasted grain
24:9 *e* it in a holy place, because
25:12 you may *e* what the land
25:19 *e* to satisfaction and dwell
25:20 *e* in the seventh year seeing
25:22 *e* from the old crop until
25:22 crop you will *e* the old
26:5 *e* your bread to satisfaction
26:10 *e* the old of the preceding
26:16 enemies will certainly *e* it
26:26 *e* but . . . not be satisfied
26:29 *e* the flesh of your sons, and
26:29 *e* the flesh of your daughters
26:38 land of your enemies must *e*
Nu 6:3 *e* grapes either fresh or
6:4 *e* anything at all that is made
9:11 bitter greens they should *e*
11:4 Who will give us meat to *e*?
11:5 fish that we used to *e* in
11:13 give us meat, and let us *e*
11:18 certainly *e* meat, because
11:18 Who will give us meat to *e*
11:18 and you will indeed *e*
11:19 *e*, not one day nor two days
11:21 *e* for a month of days
15:19 when you *e* any of the bread
18:10 holy place you should *e* it
18:10 Every male should *e* it
18:11 Everyone clean . . . may *e* it
18:13 Everyone clean . . . may *e* it
18:31 you must *e* it in every place
23:24 not lie down until it may *e*
25:2 to *e* and to bow down to their
De 2:6 What food you may buy . . . *e*
2:28 I must *e*; and what water you
4:28 cannot see or hear or *e* or
8:9 will not *e* bread with scarcity
8:12 *e* and indeed satisfy yourself
11:15 indeed *e* and be satisfied
12:7 *e* before Jehovah your God and
12:15 *e* meat according to the
12:15 and the clean one may *e* it
12:16 the blood you must not *e*
12:17 not be allowed to *e* inside
12:18 you will *e* it, in the place
12:20 Let me *e* meat, because your
12:20 your soul craves to *e* meat
12:20 craves it you may *e* meat
12:21 you must *e* inside your gates
De 12:22 so you may *e* it: the unclean
12:22 together may *e* it
12:23 resolved not to *e* the blood
12:23 must not *e* the soul with the
12:24 You must not *e* it
12:25 You must not *e* it, in order
12:27 but the flesh you may *e*
14:3 must *e* no detestable thing
14:4 sort of beast that you may *e*
14:6 It you may *e*
14:7 Only this sort you must not *e*
14:8 of their flesh must you *e*
14:9 you may *e*: Everything that has
14:9 has fins and scales you may *e*
14:10 must not *e*. It is unclean
14:11 Any clean bird you may *e*
14:12 ones of which you must not *e*
14:20 flying creature you may *e*
14:21 not *e* any body already dead
14:21 he must *e* it; or there may
14:23 *e* the tenth part of your
14:26 *e* there before Jehovah your
14:29 *e* and satisfy themselves; in
15:20 you should *e* it year by year
15:22 you should *e* it, the unclean
15:23 its blood you must not *e*
16:3 *e* nothing leavened along with
16:3 *e* along with it unfermented
16:8 *e* unfermented cakes; and on
18:1 inheritance, they should *e*
18:8 An equal share he should *e*
20:14 *e* the spoil of your enemies
20:19 for you should *e* from them
23:24 *e* only enough grapes for you
26:12 must *e* it within your gates
27:7 sacrifices and *e* them there
28:31 but you will not *e* any of it
28:33 production a people will *e*
28:39 the worm will *e* it up
28:51 *e* the fruit of your domestic
28:53 *e* the fruit of your belly
28:55 his sons that he will *e*
28:57 she will *e* them in secrecy
29:6 Bread you did not *e*, and wine
31:20 *e* and be satisfied and grow
32:38 Who used to *e* the fat of
32:42 While my sword will *e* flesh
Jos 5:11 began to *e* some of the yield
5:12 to *e* some of the produce of
Jg 13:4 and do not *e* anything unclean
13:7 and do not *e* any unclean thing
13:14 wine vine should she *e*, and
13:14 of any sort let her *e*
14:9 they began to *e*. And he did
14:14 something to *e* came forth
19:4 they would *e* and drink, and
19:6 to *e* and to drink together
19:21 and began to *e* and drink
Ru 2:14 you must *e* some of the bread
2:14 she would *e*, so that she was
1Sa 1:7 that she would weep and not *e*
1:8 and why do you not *e*, and why
1:18 to go on her way and to *e*
2:36 to *e* a piece of bread
9:13 up to the high place to *e*
9:13 may not *e* until his coming
9:13 those who are invited may *e*
9:19 you men must *e* with me
9:24 *E*, because to the appointed
9:24 you may *e* with those invited
20:5 sitting with the king to *e*
20:24 his seat at the meal to *e*
20:34 did not *e* bread on the second
28:22 and you *e*, that power may
28:23 said: I am not going to *e*
30:11 bread that he might *e*
2Sa 2:26 sword going to *e* endlessly
9:7 will *e* bread at my table
9:10 and they must *e*
9:10 *e* bread at my table
11:11 *e* and drink and to lie down
11:13 *e* before him and drink
12:3 From his morsel it would *e*
12:20 and he began to *e*
12:21 and began to *e* bread
13:5 have to *e* from her hand
13:9 Amnon refused to *e* and said
13:11 near to him for him to *e*
16:2 are for the young men to *e*
17:29 for David . . . to *e*
1Ki 13:8 *e* bread or drink water in
13:9 must not *e* bread or drink
13:15 to the house and *e* bread
13:16 may not *e* bread or drink

1Ki 13:17 not *e* bread or drink water
13:18 may *e* bread and drink water
13:19 *e* bread in his house and
13:22 *e* bread and drink water in
13:22 Do not *e* bread or drink
14:11 the city, the dogs will *e*
14:11 fowls of the heavens will *e*
16:4 in the city the dogs will *e*
16:4 fowls of the heavens will *e*
17:12 shall have to *e* it and die
17:15 she continued to *e*
18:41 Go up, *e* and drink
18:42 to go up to *e* and drink
19:5 he said to him: Rise up, *e*
19:6 began to *e* and drink, after
19:7 Rise up, *e*, for the journey
19:21 and they proceeded to *e*
21:4 and he did not *e* bread
21:7 *e* bread and let your heart
21:23 dogs will *e* up Jezebel in
21:24 in the city the dogs will *e*
21:24 fowls of the heavens will *e*
2Ki 1:10 *e* up you and your fifty
1:12 and *e* up you and your fifty
4:8 to constrain him to *e* bread
4:8 turn aside there to *e* bread
4:40 for the men to *e*. And it
4:40 And they were not able to *e*
4:41 the people that they may *e*
4:42 the people that they may *e*
4:43 the people that they may *e*
4:44 and they began to *e*, and they
6:22 *e* and drink and go to their
6:23 they began to *e* and drink
6:28 Give your son that we may *e*
6:28 own son we shall *e* tomorrow
6:29 your son that we may *e* him
7:2 but from it you will not *e*
7:8 to *e* and drink and carry from
7:19 but from it you will not *e*
9:10 Jezebel the dogs will *e* up
9:36 will *e* the flesh of Jezebel
18:27 *e* their own excrement and
18:31 *e* each one from his own
19:29 and *e* their fruitage
2Ch 7:13 grasshoppers to *e* up the land
30:18 *e* the passover according to
30:22 *e* the appointed feast for
Ezr 2:63 not *e* from the most holy
4:14 do *e* the salt of the palace
9:12 *e* the good of the land and
Ne 5:2 get grain and *e* and keep alive
5:14 did not *e* the bread due the
7:65 not *e* from the most holy
8:10 Go, *e* the fatty things and
8:12 to *e* and drink and to send
9:25 to *e* and to be satisfied and
9:36 to *e* its fruitage and its good
Es 4:16 neither *e* nor drink for three
Job 1:4 sisters to *e* and drink with
9:26 and fro for something to *e*
15:34 fire itself must *e* up the
18:13 *e* the pieces of his skin
18:13 firstborn of death will *e*
20:26 A fire . . . will *e* him up
22:20 a fire will certainly *e* up
31:8 sow seed and someone else *e*
31:12 fire that would *e* clear to
31:17 I used to *e* my morsel by
31:17 the fatherless boy did not *e*
38:41 there is nothing to *e*
42:11 began to *e* bread with him
Ps 22:26 will *e* and be satisfied
22:29 shall *e* and will bow down
27:2 against me to *e* up my flesh
44:11 sheep, as something to *e*
50:13 Shall I *e* the flesh of
59:15 wander . . . for something to *e*
78:18 to *e* for their soul
78:24 raining upon them manna to *e*
78:45 gadflies, that these might *e*
80:5 them *e* the bread of tears
102:4 have forgotten to *e* my food
106:28 *e* the sacrifices of the dead
128:2 *e* the toil of your own hands
Pr 1:31 *e* from the fruitage of their
13:2 a man will *e* good
18:21 will *e* its fruitage
23:7 *E* and drink, he says to you
24:13 son, *e* honey, for it is good
25:16 *E* what is sufficient for you
25:21 hungry, give him bread to *e*
27:18 will himself *e* its fruit
30:14 *e* up the afflicted ones off

Pr 30:17 sons of the eagle will *e* it
31:27 of laziness she does not *e*
Ec 2:24 should *e* and indeed drink and
3:13 every man should *e* and indeed
5:18 *e* and drink and see good for
5:19 empowered him to *e* from it
6:2 God does not enable him to *e*
6:2 a mere foreigner may *e* it
8:15 to *e* and drink and rejoice
9:7 *e* your food with rejoicing and
10:17 princes *e* at the proper time
Ca 4:16 and *e* its choicest fruits
5:1 *E*, O companions! Drink and
Isa 1:19 good of the land you will *e*
3:10 *e* the very fruitage of their
4:1 *e* our own bread and wear our
5:17 alien residents will *e*
7:15 Butter and honey he will *e*
7:22 he will *e* butter; because
7:22 the midst of the land will *e*
9:12 *e* up Israel with open mouth
9:18 and weeds it will *e* up
9:20 one will *e* on the left, and
9:20 *e* the flesh of his own arm
10:17 blaze up and *e* up his weeds
11:7 even the lion will *e* straw
26:11 fire . . . will *e* them up
30:24 *e* fodder seasoned with
33:11 as a fire, will *e* you up
36:12 *e* their own excrement and
36:16 *e* each one from his own
37:30 vineyards and *e* their
44:19 I roast flesh and *e*. But the
49:26 *e* their own flesh
50:9 A mere moth will *e* them up
51:8 the moth will *e* them up
51:8 clothes moth will *e* them up
55:1 no money! Come, buy and *e*
55:2 and *e* what is good, and let
56:9 come to *e*, all you wild
58:14 *e* from the hereditary
61:6 you people will *e*, and in
62:9 ones gathering it will *e* it
65:13 servants will *e*, but you
65:21 plant vineyards and *e* their
65:25 lion will *e* straw just like
Jer 2:7 to *e* its fruitage and its
5:17 *e* up your harvest and your
5:17 The men will *e* up your sons
5:17 They will *e* up your flocks
5:17 *e* up your vine and your fig
7:21 your sacrifices and *e* flesh
8:16 come in and *e* up the land
9:15 this people, *e* wormwood
12:9 bring them to *e*
15:3 to *e* and to bring to ruin
15:16 and I proceeded to *e* them
16:8 with them to *e* and to drink
19:9 *e* the flesh of their sons
19:9 *e* each one the flesh of his
22:15 your father, did he not *e*
23:15 making them *e* wormwood
29:5 gardens and *e* their fruitage
29:28 gardens and *e* their fruitage
41:1 *e* bread together in Mizpah
La 1:11 things for something to *e*, in
1:19 to look for something to *e*
Eze 2:8 and *e* what I am giving you
3:1 Son of man, what you find, *e*
3:1 *E* this roll, and go, speak to
3:2 gradually made me *e* this roll
3:3 cause your own belly to *e*
3:3 I began to *e* it, and it came
4:9 and ninety days you will *e* it
4:10 food that you will *e* will be
4:10 time to time you will *e* it
4:12 cake of barley you will *e* it
4:13 *e* their bread unclean among
4:16 have to *e* bread by weight
5:10 will *e* sons in the midst of
5:10 will *e* their fathers, and I
12:18 with quaking . . . you should *e*
12:19 With anxious care . . . *e*
16:19 honey that I had had you *e*
18:2 Fathers . . . *e* unripe grapes
18:6 on the mountains . . . not *e*
24:17 bread . . . you should not *e*
24:22 bread of men you will not *e*
25:4 will *e* your fruitage, and
34:3 The fat is what you *e*, and
39:17 *e* flesh and drink blood
39:18 mighty ones you will *e*
39:19 to *e* fat to satisfaction
42:13 *e* the most holy things

Eze 44:3 *e* bread before Jehovah
44:29 the ones who will *e* them
44:31 beasts should the priests *e*
Da 1:12 vegetables that we may *e* and
4:25 to you to *e* just like bulls
4:32 to you to *e* just like bulls
4:33 vegetation he began to *e* just
5:21 give him to *e* just like bulls
7:5 to it, Get up, *e* much flesh
10:3 Dainty bread I did not *e*, and
Ho 4:10 *e*, but will not get satisfied
9:3 they will *e* what is unclean
Joe 2:26 you will certainly *e*, eating
Am 7:12 *e* bread, and there you may
9:14 and *e* the fruit of them
Mic 6:14 will *e* and not get satisfied
7:1 no grape cluster to *e*
Hab 1:8 like the eagle speeding to *e*
Zec 7:6 when you would *e* and when
11:16 of the fat one he will *e*
Mt 6:25 *e* or what you will drink
6:31 What are we to *e?* or, What
12:1 pluck heads of grain and to *e*
12:4 was not lawful for him to *e*
14:15 buy themselves things to *e*
14:16 give them something to *e*
15:2 hands when about to *e* a meal
15:27 dogs do *e* of the crumbs
15:32 and they have nothing to *e*
24:49 should *e* and drink with the
25:35 you gave me something to *e*
25:42 but you gave me nothing to *e*
26:17 for you to *e* the passover
26:26 Take, *e*. This means my body
Mr 2:16 he *e* with the tax collectors
2:26 not lawful for anybody to *e*
3:20 not able even to *e* a meal
5:43 should be given her to *e*
6:31 time even to *e* a meal
6:36 and buy . . . something to *e*
6:37 You give them something to *e*
6:37 give them to the people to *e*
7:2 *e* their meal with defiled
7:3 do not *e* unless they wash
7:4 they do not *e* unless they
7:28 *e* of the crumbs of the little
8:1 and they had nothing to *e*
8:2 and they have nothing to *e*
11:14 Let no one *e* fruit from you
14:12 for you to *e* the passover
14:14 where I may *e* the passover
Lu 3:11 let him that has things to *e*
5:30 you *e* and drink with tax
5:33 but yours *e* and drink
6:4 no one to *e* but for the priests
8:55 to be given her to *e*
9:13 You give them something to *e*
10:8 *e* the things set before you
12:19 *e*, drink, enjoy yourself
12:22 what you will *e* or about
12:29 seeking what you might *e*
12:45 to *e* and drink and get drunk
14:1 on the sabbath to *e* a meal
15:23 let us *e* and enjoy ourselves
17:8 afterward you can *e* and drink
22:8 passover ready for us to *e*
22:11 *e* the passover with my
22:15 to *e* this passover with you
22:16 I will not *e* it again until
22:30 *e* and drink at my table in
24:41 have something there to *e*
Joh 2:17 zeal . . . will *e* me up
4:31 urging him, saying: Rabbi, *e*
4:32 I have food to *e* of which
4:33 brought him anything to *e*
6:5 buy loaves for these to *e*
6:31 bread from heaven to *e*
6:50 may *e* of it and not die
6:52 man give us his flesh to *e*
6:53 *e* the flesh of the Son of
18:28 but might *e* the passover
21:5 do not have anything to *e*
Ac 10:10 hungry and wanted to *e*
10:13 Rise, Peter, slaughter and *e*
11:7 Rise, Peter, slaughter and *e*
23:12 saying they would neither *e*
23:21 neither to *e* nor to drink
Ro 14:2 has faith to *e* everything
14:6 and he who does not *e* does
14:6 does not *e* to Jehovah
14:21 It is well not to *e* flesh
14:23 he does not *e* out of faith
1Co 3:2 not something to *e*, for you
8:7 *e* food as something

1Co 8:8 if we do not *e*, we do not
8:8 if we *e*, we have no credit to
8:13 will never again *e* flesh at
9:4 have authority to *e* and drink
9:7 and does not *e* of its fruit
9:7 does not *e* some of the milk
9:13 *e* the things of the temple
10:7 sat down to *e* and drink, and
10:18 those who *e* the sacrifices
10:27 proceed to *e* everything that
10:28 Do not *e* on account of the
11:20 *e* the Lord's evening meal
11:21 when you *e* it, each one
11:26 as often as you *e* this loaf
11:28 let him *e* of the loaf and
11:33 come together to *e* it, wait
11:34 let him *e* at home, that you
15:32 let us *e* and drink, for
Ga 2:12 used to *e* with people of the
2Th 3:8 nor did we *e* food . . . free
3:10 to work, neither let him *e*
3:12 *e* food they themselves earn
Heb 13:10 have no authority to *e*
Jas 5:3 and will *e* your fleshy parts
Re 2:7 grant to *e* of the tree of life
2:14 *e* things sacrificed to idols
2:20 *e* things sacrificed to idols
10:9 Take it and *e* it up, and it
17:16 will *e* up her fleshy parts
19:18 *e* the fleshy parts of kings

Eatable
Le 11:47 living creature that is *e* and

Eatables
Ge 40:17 all sorts of *e* for Pharaoh
1Ch 12:40 *e* of flour, cakes of pressed
Ezr 3:7 and *e* and drink and oil to
Heb 13:9 not by *e*, by which those

Eaten
Ge 3:11 From the tree . . . have you *e*?
6:21 every sort of food that is *e*
14:24 the young men have already *e*
Ex 12:46 In one house it is to be *e*
13:3 So nothing leavened may be *e*
13:7 cakes are to be *e* for the
21:28 but its flesh is not to be *e*
29:34 It must not be *e*, because
Le 6:16 be *e* as unfermented cakes in
6:23 It must not be *e*
6:26 In a holy place it will be *e*
6:30 no sin offering . . . must be *e*
7:6 In a holy place it will be *e*
7:15 *e* on the day of his offering
7:16 to be *e* on the day of his
7:16 is left of it also may be *e*
7:18 sacrifice should at all be *e*
7:19 unclean is not to be *e*
10:18 You should have *e* it without
10:19 had I *e* the sin offering
11:13 They should not be *e*
11:34 food that may be *e* upon
11:41 It must not be *e*
11:47 creature that may not be *e*
17:13 fowl that may be *e*, he must
19:6 next day it should be *e*, but
19:7 *e* on the third day, it is a
19:23 It should not be *e*
22:30 On that day it should be *e*
Nu 12:12 whose flesh . . . is half *e*
28:17 unfermented cakes will be *e*
De 6:11 have *e* and become satisfied
8:10 When you have *e* and satisfied
12:22 and the stag may be *e*
14:19 They should not be *e*
26:14 *e* of it during my mourning
32:24 *e* up by burning fever And
Jos 5:12 had *e* some of the yield of
1Sa 1:9 after they had *e* in Shiloh
14:30 if the people had but *e*
28:20 not *e* food the whole day
30:12 not *e* bread or drunk water
2Sa 19:42 Have we *e* at all at the
1Ki 13:28 lion had not *e* the dead body
Ne 2:3 gates have been *e* up with fire
2:13 it had been *e* up by fire
Job 6:6 things be *e* without salt
21:25 he has not *e* of good things
31:39 its fruitage I have *e*
Ps 14:4 as they have *e* bread
53:4 people as they have *e* bread
69:9 zeal for your house has *e* me
79:7 For they have *e* up Jacob
102:9 I have *e* ashes themselves
Pr 9:17 and bread *e* in secrecy—it is
Pr 23:8 Your morsel that you have *e*
30:20 she has *e* and has wiped her
Ca 5:1 I have *e* my honeycomb along
Isa 1:20 with a sword you will be *e*
24:6 itself has *e* up the land
Jer 3:24 has *e* up the toil of our
10:25 For they have *e* up Jacob
10:25 Yes, they have *e* him up
24:2 could not be *e* for badness
24:3 they cannot be *e* for badness
24:8 figs that cannot be *e* for
29:17 figs that cannot be *e* for
50:7 have *e* them up, and their
51:34 Babylon has *e* me up
Eze 4:14 nor a torn animal have I *e*
18:11 *e* also upon the mountains
18:15 On the mountains . . . not *e*
22:9 mountains they have *e* in you
45:21 cakes are what should be *e*
Ho 7:9 Strangers have *e* up his power
10:13 *e* the fruitage of deception
Joe 1:4 the locust has *e*
1:4 unwinged locust has *e*
1:4 the cockroach has *e*
2:25 and the caterpillar have *e*
Mic 3:3 *e* the organism of my people
Joh 6:13 left over by those who had *e*
Ac 10:14 I *e* anything defiled and
11:3 not circumcised and had *e*
12:23 *e* up with worms and expired
Re 10:10 when I had *e* it up, my belly

Eater
Jg 14:14 Out of the *e* something to
Ps 106:20 bull, an *e* of vegetation
Isa 55:10 and bread to the *e*
Na 3:12 fall into the mouth of an *e*

Eaters
Pr 23:20 are gluttonous *e* of flesh

Eating
Ge 3:3 But as for *e* of the fruit of
3:5 that in the very day of your *e*
3:6 taking of its fruit and *e* it
3:6 with her and he began *e* it
3:17 took to *e* from the tree
18:8 under the tree as they were *e*
19:3 cakes, and they went to *e*
25:34 he went to *e* and drinking
31:15 he keeps *e* continually even
39:6 except the bread he was *e*
40:17 there were fowls *e* them
43:2 had finished *e* up the cereals
43:32 the Egyptians who were *e*
Ex 10:15 *e* up all the vegetation of
12:4 proportionate to his *e* as
12:15 anyone *e* what is leavened
12:44 Then first he may share in *e*
16:3 were *e* bread to satisfaction
16:16 in proportion to his *e*
16:18 in proportion to his *e*
16:21 in proportion to his *e*
Le 7:25 anyone *e* fat from the beast
17:10 soul that is *e* the blood, and
17:14 Anyone *e* it will be cut off
19:8 one *e* it will answer for his
22:11 he as such may share in *e* it
22:11 may share in *e* his bread
22:16 of their *e* their holy things
25:7 its produce should serve for *e*
De 16:7 do the boiling and the *e* in
Jos 24:13 are what you are *e*
Jg 14:9 and walked on, *e* as he walked
19:8 And both of them kept *e*
Ru 3:3 until he has finished *e*
1Sa 14:32 to *e* along with the blood
14:33 by *e* along with the blood
14:34 in this place and the *e*, and
14:34 by *e* along with the blood
30:16 *e* and drinking and having
2Sa 9:11 Mephibosheth is *e* at my
9:13 that he was *e*
18:8 the forest did more in *e* up
18:8 than the sword did in *e* them
19:28 among those *e* at your table
1Ki 1:25 *e* and drinking before him
1:41 had finished *e*. When Joab
2:7 among those *e* at your table
4:20 *e* and drinking and rejoicing
13:23 after his *e* bread and after
18:19 *e* at the table of Jezebel
18:38 *e* up the burnt offering
21:5 sad and you are not *e* bread
2Ki 1:10 went *e* up him and his fifty
2Ki 1:12 went *e* up him and his fifty
1:14 *e* up the two former chiefs
4:43 *e* and a having of leftovers
19:29 *e* this year of the growth
1Ch 12:39 with David three days, *e*
29:22 continued *e* and drinking
2Ch 31:10 *e* and getting satisfied and
Job 1:13 *e* and drinking wine in the
1:16 and *e* them up; and I got to
1:18 *e* and drinking wine in the
34:3 as the palate tastes when *e*
Ps 14:4 *E* up my people as they have
41:9 *e* my bread, has magnified
53:4 *E* up my people as they have
78:29 *e* and satisfying themselves
80:13 keeps *e* it away
105:35 *e* all the vegetation in
105:35 *e* the fruitage of their
127:2 you are *e* food with pains
Pr 13:25 righteous is *e* to the
25:27 *e* of too much honey is not
Ec 4:5 stupid . . . is *e* his own flesh
5:11 *e* them certainly become many
10:16 own princes keep *e* even in
Isa 1:7 front of you strangers are *e*
21:5 an *e*, a drinking! Get up
22:13 the *e* of flesh and the
22:13 Let there be *e* and drinking
23:18 *e* to satisfaction and for
29:8 dreams and here he is *e*
37:30 *e* this year of the growth
59:5 *e* some of their eggs would
65:4 *e* the flesh of the pig
65:22 and someone else do the *e*
66:17 *e* the flesh of the pig and
Jer 31:30 Any man *e* the unripe grape
La 2:20 the women keep *e* their own
4:5 that were *e* pleasant things
Eze 33:25 With the blood you keep *e*
Da 1:13 *e* the delicacies of the king
1:15 children who were *e* the
11:26 ones *e* his delicacies will
Ho 8:13 *e* what Jehovah himself took
9:4 those *e* it will defile
Joe 2:26 *e* and becoming satisfied
Am 6:4 are *e* the rams out of a flock
7:2 finished *e* up the vegetation
7:4 *e* up the vast watery deep and
Ob 7 Those *e* food with you will place
Hag 1:6 There is an *e*, but it is not
Zec 7:6 you the ones doing the *e*
Mt 11:18 John came neither *e* nor
11:19 Son of man did come *e* and
14:21 *e* were about five thousand
15:38 those *e* were four thousand
24:38 days before the flood, *e* and
26:21 While they were *e*, he said
26:26 As they continued *e*, Jesus
Mr 1:6 was *e* insect locusts and wild
2:16 he was *e* with the sinners
14:18 reclining at the table and *e*
14:18 *e* with me, will betray me
14:22 as they continued *e*, he took
Lu 6:1 *e* the heads of grain, rubbing
7:33 come neither *e* bread nor
7:34 has come *e* and drinking, but
10:7 in that house, *e* and drinking
15:16 pods which the swine were *e*
17:8 through *e* and drinking, and
17:27 were *e*, they were drinking
17:28 were *e*, they were drinking
Ac 27:35 and broke it and started *e*
Ro 14:3 one *e* not look down on the
14:3 look down on the one not *e*
14:3 one not *e* not judge the one
14:3 not judge the one *e*, for God
14:17 kingdom . . . does not mean *e*
1Co 5:11 not even *e* with such a man
8:4 *e* of foods offered to idols
8:10 *e* foods offered to idols
10:25 keep *e*, making no inquiry
10:31 whether you are *e* or
11:22 houses for *e* and drinking
2Co 9:10 and bread for *e* will supply
Col 2:16 let no man judge you in *e*

Eats
Ex 15:7 your burning anger . . . *e* them
Le 7:18 the soul that *e* some of it
7:20 the soul who *e* the flesh of
7:21 actually *e* some of the flesh
7:25 soul that *e* must be cut off
7:27 Any soul who *e* any blood
11:40 he who *e* any of its dead

Le 14:47 *e* in the house should wash
17:10 *e* any sort of blood, I shall
17:15 any soul that *e* a body
22:14 man *e* a holy thing by
Nu 13:32 that *e* up its inhabitants
1Sa 14:24 Cursed is the man that *e*
14:28 Cursed is the man that *e*
2Sa 11:25 sword *e* up one as well as
Job 5:5 he harvests the hungry one *e*
13:28 garment that a moth . . . *e*
40:15 grass it *e* just as a bull
Ec 2:25 who *e* and who drinks better
5:12 is little or much that he *e*
5:17 all his days he *e* in darkness
Isa 5:24 fire *e* up the stubble and
44:16 the flesh that he *e*, and he
La 4:11 which *e* up her foundations
Mt 9:11 *e* with tax collectors and
Lu 14:15 Happy is he who *e* bread in
15:2 sinners and *e* with them
Joh 6:51 if anyone *e* of this bread
Ro 14:2 man who is weak *e* vegetables
14:6, 6 he who *e*, *e* to Jehovah
14:20 occasion for stumbling *e*
14:23 condemned if he *e*, because
1Co 11:27 whoever *e* the loaf or
11:29 For he that *e* and drinks
11:29 *e* and drinks judgment

Ebal
Ge 36:23 sons of Shobal . . . *E*, Shepho
De 11:29 the malediction upon Mount *E*
27:4 commanding . . . in Mount *E*
27:13 the malediction on Mount *E*
Jos 8:30 an altar . . . in Mount *E*
8:33 in front of Mount *E*, (just as
1Ch 1:40 sons of Shobal were . . . *E*

Ebed
Jg 9:26 the son of *E* and his brothers
9:28 the son of *E* went on to say
9:30 Gaal the son of *E*. Then his
9:31 the son of *E* and his brothers
9:35 son of *E* went out and stood
Ezr 8:6 *E* the son of Jonathan, and

Ebed-melech
Jer 38:7 *E* the Ethiopian, a man
38:8 *E* went out of the house of
38:10 *E* the Ethiopian, saying
38:11 *E* took the men in his
38:12 *E* the Ethiopian said to
39:16 say to *E* the Ethiopian

Ebenezer
1Sa 4:1 took up camping alongside *E*
5:1 brought it from *E* to Ashdod
7:12 and began to call its name *E*

Eber
Ge 10:21 forefather of . . . sons of *E*
10:24 Shelah became father to *E*
10:25 to *E* there were two sons
11:14 Shelah . . . father to *E*
11:15 after his fathering *E* Shelah
11:16 *E* lived on for thirty-four
11:17 after his fathering Peleg *E*
Nu 24:24 they will indeed afflict *E*
1Ch 1:18 Shelah . . . father to *E*
1:19 to *E* two sons were born
1:25 *E*, Peleg, Reu
5:13 Jacan and Zia and *E*, seven
8:12 sons of Elpaal were *E* and
8:22 and Ishpan and *E* and Eliel
Ne 12:20 Kallai; for Amok, *E*
Lu 3:35 son of Peleg, son of *E*, son of

Ebez
Jos 19:20 Rabbith and Kishion and *E*

Ebiasaph
1Ch 6:23 Elkanah his son and *E* his son
6:37 son of *E*, the son of Korah
9:19 son of *E* the son of Korah and

Ebony
Eze 27:15 horns of ivory and *e* they

Ebron
Jos 19:28 and to *E* and Rehob and

Ecbatana
Ezr 6:2 at *E*, in the fortified place

Ecstasy
Pr 5:19 may you be in an *e* constantly
5:20 *e* with a strange woman or
Mr 5:42 themselves with great *e*
Lu 5:26 Then an *e* seized one and all
Ac 3:10 *e* at what had happened to him

Eczema
De 28:27 piles and *e* and skin eruption

Eden
Ge 2:8 God planted a garden in *E*
2:10 river issuing out of *E* to
2:15 garden of *E* to cultivate it
3:23 put him out of . . . *E*
3:24 garden of *E* the cherubs and
4:16 Fugitiveness to the east of *E*
2Ki 19:12 the sons of *E* that were in
2Ch 29:12 *E* the son of Joah
31:15 *E* . . . in office of trust
Isa 37:12 sons of *E* that were in
51:3 make her wilderness like *E*
Eze 27:23 and *E*, the traders of Sheba
28:13 In *E*, the garden of God, you
31:9 all the other trees of *E* that
31:16 below all the trees of *E*
31:18 among the trees of *E*
31:18 down with the trees of *E*
36:35 become like the garden of *E*
Joe 2:3 Like the garden of *E* the land

Eder
Ge 35:21 beyond the tower of *E*
Jos 15:21 Kabzeel and *E* and Jagur
1Ch 8:15 and Zebadiah and Arad and *E*
23:23 of Mushi were Mahli and *E*
24:30 of Mushi were Mahli and *E*

Edge
Ge 34:26 with the *e* of the sword
Ex 7:15 meet him by the *e* of the Nile
13:20 at the *e* of the wilderness
17:13 with the *e* of the sword
19:12 and do not touch the *e* of it
26:4 the *e* of the one tent cloth at
26:4 *e* of the outermost tent cloth
26:10 the *e* of the one tent cloth
26:10 fifty loops upon the *e* of the
28:26 upon its *e* that is on the
36:11 the *e* of the one tent cloth
36:11 the *e* of the outermost tent
36:17 *e* of the outermost tent cloth
36:17 made fifty loops upon the *e*
39:19 its *e* that is on the side
Le 19:9 must not reap the *e* of your
23:22 *e* of your field when you are
Nu 15:38 string above the fringed *e* of
15:39 serve as a fringed *e* for you
21:24 with the *e* of the sword and
33:6 is on the *e* of the wilderness
De 13:15 with the *e* of the sword
13:15 destruction at the *e* of the
20:13 with the *e* of the sword
Jos 3:8 as far as the *e* of the waters
3:15 in the *e* of the waters
6:21 by the *e* of the sword
8:24 by the *e* of the sword until
8:24 with the *e* of the sword
10:28 with the *e* of the sword
10:30 with the *e* of the sword
10:32 with the *e* of the sword
10:35 with the *e* of the sword
10:37 with the *e* of the sword
10:39 with the *e* of the sword
11:11 with the *e* of the sword
11:12 with the *e* of the sword
11:14 struck with the *e* of the
19:47 with the *e* of the sword
Jg 1:8 striking it with the *e* of the
1:25 city with the *e* of the sword
4:15 by the *e* of the sword before
4:16 fell by the *e* of the sword
7:11 to the *e* of those in battle
7:17 come to the *e* of the camp, it
7:19 to the *e* of the camp at the
18:27 with the *e* of the sword, and
20:37 city with the *e* of the sword
20:48 with the *e* of the sword
21:10 with the *e* of the sword
1Sa 9:27 by the *e* of the city Samuel
15:8 with the *e* of the sword
22:19 with the *e* of the sword
22:19 with the *e* of the sword
2Sa 15:14 with the *e* of the sword
2Ki 10:25 with the *e* of the sword and
Job 1:15 with the *e* of the sword
1:17 with the *e* of the sword
Ec 10:10 has not whetted its *e*, then
Jer 21:7 with the *e* of the sword
31:29 the sons that got set on *e*
31:30 teeth that will be set on *e*
Eze 18:2 the sons that get set on *e*
Lu 21:24 fall by the *e* of the sword
Heb 11:34 escaped the *e* of the sword

Edges
Nu 15:38 fringed *e* upon the skirts of
Jg 3:16 and it had two *e*, its length

Edible
Le 11:22 the *e* locust after its kind

Edom
Ge 25:30 is why his name was called *E*
32:3 land of Seir, the field of *E*
36:1 Esau, that is to say, *E*
36:8 region of Seir. Esau is *E*
36:9 Esau the father of *E* in the
36:16 sheiks . . . in the land of *E*
36:17 sheiks . . . in the land of *E*
36:19 He is *E*
36:21 sheiks . . . in the land of *E*
36:31 reigned in the land of *E*
36:32 proceeded to reign in *E*
36:43 sheiks of *E* according to
36:43 This is Esau the father of *E*
Ex 15:15 the sheiks of *E* will indeed
Nu 20:14 from Kadesh to the king of *E*
20:18 *E* said to him: You must not
20:20 *E* came on out to encounter
20:21 *E* refused to grant Israel to
20:23 the border of the land of *E*
21:4 to go around the land of *E*
24:18 *E* must become a possession
33:37 the frontier of the land of *E*
34:3 alongside *E*, and your south
Jos 15:1 to the boundary of *E*
15:21 boundary of *E* in the south
Jg 5:4 marching out of the field of *E*
11:17 messengers to the king of *E*
11:17 the king of *E* did not listen
11:18 the land of *E* and the land of
1Sa 14:47 against *E* and against the
2Sa 8:14 kept garrisons placed in *E*
8:14 In all *E* he placed garrisons
1Ki 9:26 Red Sea in the land of *E*
11:14 He was in *E*
11:15 when David struck down *E*
11:15 strike down every male in *E*
11:16 cut off every male in *E*
22:47 king, there was none in *E*
2Ki 3:8 way of the wilderness of *E*
3:9 the king of *E* proceeded to go
3:12 king of *E* went down to him
3:20 from the direction of *E*
3:26 through to the king of *E*
8:20 In his days *E* revolted from
8:22 *E* kept up its revolt from
14:10 unmistakably struck down *E*
16:6 restored Elath to *E*
1Ch 1:43 reigned in the land of *E*
1:51 the sheiks of *E* came to be
1:54 These were the sheiks of *E*
18:11 from *E* and from Moab and
18:13 So he put garrisons in *E*
2Ch 8:17 of the sea in the land of *E*
20:2 region of the sea, from *E*
21:8 *E* revolted from under the
21:10 *E* kept up its revolt from
25:19 Here you have struck down *E*
25:20 searched for the gods of *E*
Ps 60:*super* and strike down *E* in the
60:8 Over *E* I shall throw my
60:9 certainly lead me as far as *E*
83:6 tents of *E* and the
108:9 *E* I shall throw my sandal
108:10 lead me as far as *E*
137:7 regarding the sons of *E* the
Isa 11:14 *E* and Moab will be those
34:5 Upon *E* it will descend, and
34:6 slaughtering in the land of *E*
63:1 is this one coming from *E*
Jer 9:26 upon Judah and upon *E* and
25:21 *E* and Moab and the sons of
27:3 send them to the king of *E*
40:11 sons of Ammon and in *E*
49:7 For *E* this is what Jehovah
49:17 *E* must become an object of
49:20 has formulated against *E*
49:22 the mighty men of *E* will
La 4:21 and rejoice, O daughter of *E*
4:22 your error, O daughter of *E*
Eze 25:12 the reason that *E* has acted
25:13 against *E* and cut off from
25:14 bring my vengeance on *E* by
25:14 do in *E* according to my
27:16 *E* was your merchant because

Eze 32:29 *E*, her kings and all her
35:15 Seir, even all *E*, all of it
36:5 and against *E*, all of it
Da 11:41 *E* and Moab and the main part
Joe 3:19 *E*, a wilderness of desolate
Am 1:6 exiles to hand over to *E*
1:9 complete body of exiles to *E*
1:11 account of three revolts of *E*
2:1 the bones of the king of *E*
9:12 what is left remaining of *E*
Ob 1 Lord Jehovah has said regarding *E*
8 destroy the wise ones out of *E*
Mal 1:4 *E* keeps saying, We have been

Edomite
De 23:7 You must not detest an *E*
1Sa 21:7 Doeg the *E*, the principal one
22:9 Doeg the *E*, being stationed
22:18 Doeg the *E* turned and
22:22 Doeg the *E* was there, that
1Ki 11:1 foreign wives . . . *E*
11:14 Hadad the *E* of the offspring
11:17 *E* men of the servants of
Ps 52:*super* when Doeg the *E* came and

Edomites
2Sa 8:13 striking down the *E* in the
8:14 *E* came to be servants of
2Ki 8:21 got to strike down the *E*
14:7 the *E* in the Valley of Salt
16:6 the *E*, for their part
1Ch 18:12 he struck down the *E* in the
18:13 the *E* came to be David's
2Ch 21:9 striking down the *E* that
25:14 from striking down the *E*
28:17 *E* themselves came in and

Edrei
Nu 21:33 to the battle of *E*
De 1:4 dwelling in Ashtaroth, in *E*
3:1 to meet us in battle at *E*
3:10 Bashan as far as Salecah and *E*
Jos 12:4 who dwelt in Ashtaroth and *E*
13:12 in Ashtaroth and in *E*
13:31 and *E*, the cities of the
19:37 Kedesh and *E* and En-hazor

Educated
Ac 13:1 Manaen who was *e* with Herod
22:3 *e* in this city at the feet of

Efface
Ex 23:23 and I shall certainly *e* them
2Ch 32:21 *e* every valiant, mighty man
Ps 83:4 *e* them from being a nation

Effaced
Ex 9:15 you might be *e* from the earth
Job 4:7 have the upright ever been *e*
15:28 in cities that are to be *e*
22:20 our antagonists have been *e*
Zec 11:8 *e* three shepherds in one
11:9 And the one that is being *e*
11:9 let her be *e*
11:16 To the sheep being *e* he

Effacing
1Ki 13:34 *e* them and annihilating

Effect
Ge 30:27 taken the omens to the *e*
Ex 6:9 Moses spoke to this *e* to the
Nu 5:19 be free of the *e* of this
1Sa 23:17 has knowledge to that *e*
Ezr 6:2 memorandum to this *e* was
Job 5:12 hands do not work with *e*
36:19 your cry for help take *e*
Pr 3:26 be, in *e*, your confidence
15:13 joyful heart has a good *e* on
Jer 2:30 To no *e* I have struck your
Mt 5:19 and teaches mankind to that *e*
7:28 the *e* was that the crowds
Ac 7:6 God spoke to this *e*, that his
20:13 giving instructions to this *e*
Ro 3:3 faithfulness of God without *e*
2Th 2:2 to the *e* that the day of

Effected
Ps 99:4 are what you yourself have *e*
Isa 28:15 Sheol we have *e* a vision
Heb 11:33 *e* righteousness, obtained

Effecting
Isa 43:13 is no one *e* deliverance

Effective
Eze 17:17 not make him *e* in the war
Lu 19:48 did not find the *e* thing for
22:2 seeking the *e* way for them
22:4 the *e* way to betray him to

Effectively
Da 8:24 prove successful and do *e*
11:17 and he will act *e*
11:28 act *e* and certainly go back
11:30 the holy covenant and act *e*
11:32 they will prevail and act *e*
11:39 act *e* against the most

Effects
Job 37:13 he makes it produce *e*

Effectual
Job 6:13 *e* working . . . chased away
Isa 28:29 done greatly in *e* working

Effort
Col 4:13 to great *e* in behalf of you
2Pe 1:5 in response all earnest *e*
Jude 3 every *e* to write you about

Efforts
Job 36:19 Even all your powerful *e*
Ac 9:26 he made *e* to join himself
16:7 made *e* to go into Bithynia
26:12 Amid these *e* as I was

Egg
Isa 59:5 *e* that was smashed would
Lu 11:12 Or if he also asks for an *e*

Egged
1Ki 21:25 whom Jezebel his wife *e* on

Eggs
De 22:6 with young ones or *e*, and the
22:6 the young ones or the *e*
Job 39:14 leaves her *e* to the earth
Isa 10:14 gathers *e* that have been
34:15 made its nest and lays *e*
59:5 The *e* of a poisonous snake
59:5 eating some of their *e* would

Eglah
2Sa 3:5 Ithream by *E*, David's wife
1Ch 3:3 Ithream, of *E* his wife

Eglaim
Isa 15:8 howling . . . is clear to *E*

Eglath-shelishiyah
Isa 15:5 far along as Zoar and *E*
Jer 48:34 clear to Horonaim, to *E*

Eglon
Jos 10:3 Debir the king of *E*, saying
10:5 the king of *E*, these and all
10:23 the king of *E*
10:34 passed on from Lachish to *E*
10:36 went up from *E* to Hebron
10:37 all that he had done to *E*
12:12 the king of *E*, one
15:39 Lachish and Bozkath and *E*
Jg 3:12 let *E* the king of Moab grow
3:14 to serve *E* the king of Moab
3:15 to *E* the king of Moab
3:17 the tribute to *E* the king of
3:17 Now *E* was a very fat man

Egotism
Php 2:3 out of *e*, but with lowliness

Egotistical
Ga 5:26 us not become *e*, stirring up

Egypt
Ge 12:10 toward *E* to reside there as
12:11 as he got near to entering *E*
12:14 as soon as Abram entered *E*
13:1 Abram went up out of *E*
13:10 the land of *E* as far as Zoar
15:18 river of *E* to the great river
21:21 for him from the land of *E*
25:18 which is in front of *E*
26:2 and said: Do not go down to *E*
37:25 to take it down to *E*
37:28 these brought Joseph into *E*
37:36 sold him into *E* to Potiphar
39:1 he was brought down to *E*, and
40:1 cupbearer of the king of *E*
40:1 their lord the king of *E*
40:5 who belonged to the king of *E*
41:8 magic-practicing priests of *E*
41:19 in all the land of *E*
41:29 plenty in all the land of *E*
41:30 the plenty in the land of *E*
41:33 set him over the land of *E*
41:34 one fifth of the land of *E*
41:36 develop in the land of *E*
41:41 you over all the land of *E*
41:43 over all the land of *E*
41:44 in all the land of *E*
Ge 41:45 go out over the land of *E*
41:46 before Pharaoh the king of *E*
41:46 in all the land of *E*
41:48 came upon the land of *E* and
41:53 obtained in the land of *E*
41:54 but in all the land of *E*
41:55 land of *E* became famished
41:56 strong grip on the land of *E*
41:57 came to *E* to buy from Joseph
42:1 there were cereals in *E*
42:2 that there are cereals in *E*
42:3 down to buy grain from *E*
43:2 cereals . . . brought from *E*
43:15 went their way down to *E*
45:4 whom you sold into *E*
45:8 over all the land of *E*
45:9 appointed me lord for all *E*
45:13 about all my glory in *E*
45:18 the good of the land of *E*
45:19 wagons from the land of *E*
45:20 the good of all the land of *E*
45:23 carrying good things of *E*
45:25 they began going up out of *E*
45:26 over all the land of *E*
46:3 not be afraid to go down to *E*
46:4 shall go down with you to *E*
46:6 Eventually they came into *E*
46:7 offspring, with him into *E*
46:8 sons who came into *E*: Jacob
46:20 to Joseph in the land of *E*
46:26 came to Jacob into *E*
46:27 born to him in *E* were two
46:27 came into *E* were seventy
46:34 a detestable thing to *E*
47:6 land of *E* is at your disposal
47:11 possession in the land of *E*
47:13 the land of *E* and the land of
47:14 to be found in the land of *E*
47:15 the money from the land of *E*
47:21 one end of the territory of *E*
47:26 over the landed estate of *E*
47:27 dwell in the land of *E*, in
47:28 lived on in the land of *E*
47:29 do not bury me in *E*
47:30 carry me out of *E* and bury
48:5 born to you in the land of *E*
48:5 I came here to you into *E*
50:7 older men of the land of *E*
50:14 Joseph returned to *E*, he and
50:22 continued to dwell in *E*, he
50:26 he was put in a coffin in *E*
Ex 1:1 Israel's sons who came into *E*
1:5 but Joseph was already in *E*
1:8 there arose over *E* a new king
1:15 king of *E* said to the Hebrew
1:17 did not do as the king of *E*
1:18 the king of *E* called the
2:23 the king of *E* finally died
3:7 of my people who are in *E*
3:10 the sons of Israel out of *E*
3:11 bring . . . Israel out of *E*
3:12 brought the people out of *E*
3:16 is being done to you in *E*
3:18 come . . . to the king of *E*
3:19 king of *E* will not give you
3:20 I shall have to . . . strike *E*
4:18 to my brothers who are in *E*
4:19 Go, return to *E*, because all
4:20 to return to the land of *E*
4:21 After you . . . returned to *E*
5:4 the king of *E* said to them
5:12 over all the land of *E*
6:7 from under the burdens of *E*
6:13 Israel out from the land of *E*
6:26 Israel out from the land of *E*
6:27 sons of Israel out from *E*
6:28 to Moses in the land of *E*
6:29 Speak to Pharaoh king of *E*
7:3 my miracles in the land of *E*
7:4 have to lay my hand upon *E* and
7:4 Israel, out from the land of *E*
7:5 stretch out my hand against *E*
7:11 magic-practicing priests of *E*
7:19 hand out over the waters of *E*
7:19 be blood in all the land of *E*
7:21 blood . . . in all the land of *E*
7:22 magic-practicing priests of *E*
8:5 frogs . . . over the land of *E*
8:6 waters of *E*, and the frogs
8:6 frogs . . . cover the land of *E*
8:7 frogs . . . over the land of *E*
8:16 gnats in all the land of *E*
8:17 gnats in all the land of *E*
8:21 gadfly; and the houses of *E*

Ex 8:24 gadflies began to invade . . . E
9:4 Israel and the livestock of E
9:6 livestock of E began to die
9:9 powder upon all the land of E
9:9 in all the land of E
9:18 never occurred in E from the
9:22 hail . . . on all the land of E
9:22 hail . . . in the land of E
9:23 hail upon the land of E
9:24 hail . . . in all the land of E
9:25 striking at all the land of E
10:2 severely I have dealt with E
10:6 the houses of all E will be
10:7 yet know that E has perished
10:12 hand out over the land of E
10:12 come up over the land of E
10:13 rod out over the land of E
10:14 up over all the land of E
10:14 upon all the territory of E
10:15 in all the land of E
10:19 in all the territory of E
10:21 darkness . . . the land of E
10:22 occur in all the land of E
11:1 to bring upon Pharaoh and E
11:3 very great in the land of E
11:4 going out into the midst of E
11:5 firstborn in the land of E
11:6 outcry in all the land of E
11:9 miracles . . . in the land of E
12:1 and Aaron in the land of E
12:12 pass through the land of E
12:12 firstborn in the land of E
12:12 and on all the gods of E
12:13 I strike at the land of E
12:17 armies out from the land of E
12:27 sons of Israel in E when he
12:29 firstborn in the land of E
12:39 they had brought out from E
12:39 they had been driven out of E
12:40 Israel, who had dwelt in E
12:41 went out of the land of E
12:42 out of the land of E. With
12:51 armies out of the land of E
13:3 on which you went out of E
13:8 to me when I came out of E
13:9 Jehovah brought you out of E
13:14 Jehovah brought me out of E
13:15 firstborn in the land of E
13:16 Jehovah brought us out of E
13:17 will certainly return to E
13:18 went up out of the land of E
14:5 was reported to the king of E
14:7 chariots of E and warriors
14:8 king of E become obstinate
14:11 no burial places at all in E
14:11 to us in leading us out of E
14:12 word we spoke to you in E
16:1 coming out of the land of E
16:3 in the land of E while we
16:6 you out from the land of E
16:32 you out of the land of E
17:3 have brought us up out of E
18:1 had brought Israel out of E
18:8 had done to Pharaoh and E on
18:9 them from the hand of E
18:10 from the hand of E and from
18:10 from under the hand of E
19:1 came out of the land of E, on
20:2 out of the land of E, out of
22:21 residents in the land of E
23:9 residents in the land of E
23:15 in it you came out of E
29:46 out of the land of E that
32:1 up out of the land of E
32:4 up out of the land of E
32:7 out of the land of E have
32:8 you up out of the land of E
32:11 out of the land of E with
32:23 out of the land of E, we
33:1 led up out of the land of E
34:18 Abib that you came out of E
Le 11:45 up out of the land of E to
18:3 The way the land of E does
19:34 residents in the land of E
19:36 you out of the land of E
22:33 E to prove myself God to you
23:43 out of the land of E. I am
25:38 out of the land of E to give
25:42 brought out of the land of E
25:55 brought out of the land of E
26:13 out of the land of E
26:45 out of the land of E
Nu 1:1 coming out of the land of E
3:13 firstborn in the land of E I

Nu 8:17 firstborn in the land of E
9:1 coming out of the land of E
11:5 eat in E for nothing, the
11:18 it was well with us in E
11:20 that we have come out of E
13:22 seven years before Zoan of E
14:2 died in the land of E, or if
14:3 better for us to return to E
14:4 and let us return to E
14:19 from E onward until now
14:22 performed in E and in the
15:41 out of the land of E in order
20:5 conducted us up out of E to
20:15 proceeded to go down to E
20:15 to dwell in E many days; and
20:16 and brought us out of E; and
21:5 brought us up out of E to die
22:5 A people has come out of E
22:11 who are coming out of E, and
23:22 is bringing them out of E
24:8 God is bringing him out of E
26:4 who went out of the land of E
26:59 his wife bore to Levi in E
32:11 men who came up out of E
33:1 went out of the land of E in
33:38 Israel from the land of E
34:5 to the torrent valley of E
De 1:27 out of the land of E to give
1:30 all that he did with you in E
4:20 the iron furnace, out of E
4:34 God has done for you in E
4:37 and brought you out of E in
4:45 on their coming out of E
4:46 on their coming out of E
5:6 out of the land of E, out of
5:15 a slave in the land of E and
6:12 out of the land of E, out of
6:21 became slaves to Pharaoh in E
6:21 to bring us out of E with a
6:22 signs and miracles . . . upon E
7:8 hand of Pharaoh the king of E
7:15 all the evil diseases of E
7:18 God did to Pharaoh and all E
8:14 you out of the land of E
9:7 you went out of the land of E
9:12 whom you brought out of E
9:26 out of E with a strong hand
10:19 residents in the land of E
10:22 went down into E, and now
11:3 in the midst of E to Pharaoh
11:3 to Pharaoh the king of E and
11:4 to the military forces of E
11:10 not like the land of E
13:5 out of the land of E and has
13:10 out of the land of E, out
15:15 a slave in the land of E
16:1 God brought you out of E
16:3 you came out of the land of E
16:3 coming out of the land of E
16:6 time of your coming out of E
16:12 you became a slave in E, and
17:16 make the people go back to E
20:1 up out of the land of E
23:4 when you were going out of E
24:9 you were coming out of E
24:18 you became a slave in E, and
24:22 a slave in the land of E
25:17 you were coming out of E
26:5 to E and to reside there as
26:8 Jehovah brought us out of E
28:27 the boil of E and piles and
28:60 all the diseases of E before
28:68 bring you back to E by ships
29:2 in the land of E to Pharaoh
29:16 dwelt in the land of E and
29:25 brought them out of . . . E
34:11 in the land of E to Pharaoh
Jos 2:10 when you came out of E, and
5:4 the people that came out of E
5:4 they were coming out of E
5:5 they were coming out of E
5:6 men of war who came out of E
5:9 rolled away the reproach of E
9:9 and of all that he did in E
13:3 Nile that is in front of E
15:4 to the torrent valley of E
15:47 to the torrent valley of E
24:4 and his sons went down to E
24:5 and I went plaguing E with
24:6 your fathers out of E and
24:7 to see what I did in E; and
24:14 and in E, and serve Jehovah
24:17 out of the land of E, out
24:32 had brought up out of E

Jg 2:1 out of E and to bring you into
2:12 out of the land of E and
6:8 who brought you up from E and
6:9 the hand of E and out of the
6:13 out of E that Jehovah brought
10:11 Was it not from E and from
11:13 came up out of E, from the
11:16 they came up out of E
19:30 up out of the land of E
1Sa 2:27 in E as slaves to the house
4:8 God that was the smiter of E
6:6 the way E and Pharaoh made
8:8 my bringing them up out of E
10:18 brought Israel up out of E
10:18 from the hand of E and from
12:6 up out of the land of E
12:8 as Jacob had come into E and
12:8 your forefathers out from E
15:2 he was coming up out of E
15:6 of their coming up out of E
15:7 Shur, which is in front of E
27:8 and down to the land of E
2Sa 7:6 Israel up out of E to this
7:23 redeemed to yourself from E
1Ki 3:1 with Pharaoh the king of E
4:21 and to the boundary of E
4:30 than all the wisdom of E
6:1 came out from the land of E
8:9 coming out from the land of E
8:16 my people Israel out from E
8:21 out from the land of E
8:51 whom you brought out from E
8:53 our forefathers out from E
8:65 to the torrent valley of E
9:9 out from the land of E
9:16 Pharaoh the king of E
10:28 that Solomon had from E
10:29 and was exported from E for
11:17 to come into E, while Hadad
11:18 came into E to Pharaoh the
11:18 to Pharaoh the king of E
11:21 heard in E that David had
11:40 running off to E to Shishak
11:40 to Shishak the king of E
11:40 in E until Solomon's death
12:2 while he was yet in E
12:2 Jeroboam might dwell in E
12:28 up out of the land of E
14:25 Shishak the king of E came
2Ki 7:6 kings of E to come against us
17:4 to So the king of E and
17:7 out of the land of E from
17:7 Pharaoh the king of E
17:36 out of the land of E with
18:21 this crushed reed, E
18:21 way Pharaoh the king of E
18:24 put your trust in E for
19:24 all the Nile canals of E
21:15 came out from E down to
23:29 Pharaoh Nechoh the king of E
23:34 E, where he eventually died
24:7 king of E come out from his
24:7 to belong to the king of E
24:7 the torrent valley of E up to
25:26 rose up and came into E
1Ch 13:5 from the river of E as far
17:21 you have redeemed from E
2Ch 1:16 that Solomon had from E
1:17 exported from E a chariot
5:10 they were coming out from E
6:5 people out from the land of E
7:8 to the torrent valley of E
7:22 out of the land of E, and
9:26 down to the boundary of E
9:28 horses to Solomon from E and
10:2 while he was yet in E
10:2 came back from E
12:2 Shishak the king of E came
12:3 came with him out of E
12:9 Shishak the king of E came
20:10 out of the land of E, but
26:8 fame went even as far as E
35:20 Necho the king of E came
36:3 the king of E removed him
36:4 the king of E made Eliakim
36:4 Necho took and brought to E
Ne 9:9 of our forefathers in E
9:17 return to their servitude in E
9:18 God who led you up out of E
Ps 68:31 things will come out of E
78:12 In the land of E, the field
78:43 How he put his signs in E
78:51 struck . . . the firstborn in E
80:8 make a vine depart from E

's 81:5 going forth over the land of *E*
81:10 up out of the land of *E*
105:23 proceeded to come into *E*
105:38 *E* rejoiced when they went
106:7 for our forefathers in *E*
106:21 Doer of great things in *E*
114:1 Israel went forth from *E*
135:8 down the firstborn ones of *E*
135:9 into the midst of you, O *E*
136:10 the One striking down *E* in
'r 7:16 divan, with . . . linen of *E*
sa 7:18 of the Nile canals of *E*
10:24 you in the way that *E* did
10:26 the way that he did with *E*
11:11 remnant . . . from *E* and
11:16 up out of the land of *E*
19:1 The pronouncement against *E*
19:1 and coming into *E*
19:1 valueless gods of *E* will
19:1 heart of *E* will melt in the
19:3 spirit of *E* must become
19:4 *E* into the hand of a hard
19:6 Nile canals of *E* must become
19:12 has counseled concerning *E*
19:13 caused *E* to wander about
19:14 *E* to wander about in all
19:15 *E* will not come to have
19:16 *E* will become like women
19:17 to *E* a cause for reeling
19:18 cities in the land of *E*
19:19 midst of the land of *E*
19:20 in the land of *E*; for they
19:22 certainly deal *E* a blow
19:23 highway out of *E* to Assyria
19:23 will actually come into *E*
19:23 and *E* into Assyria; and they
19:23 service, *E* with Assyria
19:24 be the third with *E* and
19:25 Blessed be my people, *E*
20:3 sign and a portent against *E*
20:4 body of captives of *E* and
20:4 the nakedness of *E*
20:5 and of *E* their beauty
23:5 at the report pertaining to *E*
27:12 to the torrent valley of *E*
27:13 dispersed in the land of *E*
30:2 setting out to go down to *E*
30:2 refuge in the shadow of *E*
30:3 *E* a cause for humiliation
31:1 down to *E* for assistance
36:6 this crushed reed, in *E*
36:6 king of *E* is to all those
36:9 trust in *E* for chariots and
37:25 all the Nile canals of *E*
43:3 given *E* as a ransom for you
45:14 The unpaid laborers of *E* and
52:4 to *E* that my people went
Jer 2:6 up out of the land of *E*
2:18 for the way of *E* in order
2:36 Of *E*, too, you will become
7:22 out from the land of *E*
7:25 out of the land of *E* until
9:26 upon *E* and upon Judah and
11:4 out of the land of *E*, out of
11:7 up out of the land of *E* and
16:14 up out of the land of *E*
23:7 up out of the land of *E*
24:8 dwelling in the land of *E*
25:19 Pharaoh the king of *E* and
26:21 ran away and came into *E*
26:22 Jehoiakim sent men to *E*
26:22 other men with him to *E*
26:23 to bring Urijah out from *E*
31:32 forth out of the land of *E*
32:20 miracles in the land of *E*
32:21 Israel out of the land of *E*
34:13 them out of the land of *E*
37:5 Pharaoh that came out of *E*
37:7 go back to their land, *E*
41:17 to go on and enter into *E*
42:14 land of *E* we shall enter
42:15 to enter into *E* and
42:16 with you in the land of *E*
42:16 follow after you to *E*; and
42:17 enter into *E* to reside there
42:18 of your entering into *E*, and
42:19 Do not enter into *E*
43:2 into *E* to reside there as
43:7 came into the land of *E*
43:11 and strike the land of *E*
43:12 houses of the gods of *E*
43:12 up in the land of *E*, just
43:13 which is in the land of *E*
43:13 houses of the gods of *E*

Jer 44:1 dwelling in the land of *E*
44:8 other gods in the land of *E*
44:12 into the land of *E* to reside
44:12 finish in the land of *E*
44:13 dwelling in the land of *E*
44:14 aliens, in the land of *E*
44:15 in the land of *E*, in Pathros
44:24 who are in the land of *E*
44:26 dwelling in the land of *E*
44:26 in all the land of *E*
44:27 that are in the land of *E*
44:28 return from the land of *E*
44:28 the land of *E* to reside
44:30 Hophra, the king of *E*
46:2 For *E*, concerning the
46:2 Pharaoh Necho the king of *E*
46:8 *E* itself comes up just like
46:11 O virgin daughter of *E*
46:13 strike down the land of *E*
46:14 Tell it in *E*, O men
46:17 Pharaoh the king of *E* is a
46:19 the daughter of *E*
46:20 *E* is as a very pretty heifer
46:24 *E* will certainly feel shame
46:25 upon *E* and upon her gods and
La 5:6 To *E* we have given the hand
Eze 16:26 yourself to the sons of *E*
17:15 sending his messengers to *E*
19:4 by . . . hooks to the land of *E*
20:5 to them in the land of *E*
20:6 from the land of *E* to a land
20:7 with the dungy idols of *E* do
20:8 idols of *E* they did not leave
20:8 the midst of the land of *E*
20:9 forth from the land of *E*
20:10 forth from the land of *E*
20:36 wilderness of the land of *E*
23:3 prostitute themselves in *E*
23:8 prostitutions carried from *E*
23:19 in the land of *E*
23:21 your bosoms from *E* onward
23:27 carried from the land of *E*
23:27 and *E* you will remember no
27:7 in various colors from *E*
29:2 Pharaoh the king of *E* and
29:2 against *E* in its entirety
29:3 Pharaoh, king of *E*, the
29:6 *E* will have to know that I
29:9 land of *E* must become a
29:10 land of *E* devastated places
29:12 land of *E* a desolate waste
29:19 the land of *E*, and he
29:20 given him the land of *E*
30:4 will certainly come into *E*
30:4 when one falls slain in *E*
30:6 supporters of *E* must also
30:8 set a fire in *E* and all its
30:9 in the day of *E*, for, look!
30:10 the crowd of *E* to cease
30:11 draw their swords against *E*
30:13 out of the land of *E*
30:13 put fear in the land of *E*
30:15 Sin, the fortress of *E*
30:16 I will set a fire in *E*
30:18 the yoke bars of *E*
30:19 acts of judgment in *E*
30:21 Pharaoh the king of *E*
30:22 Pharaoh the king of *E*
30:25 against the land of *E*
31:2 say to Pharaoh the king of *E*
32:2 Pharaoh the king of *E*, and
32:12 despoil the pride of *E*
32:15 land of *E* a desolate waste
32:16 over *E* and over all its
32:18 lament over the crowd of *E*
Da 9:15 people out from the land of *E*
11:8 captives he will come to *E*
11:42 and as regards the land of *E*
11:43 the desirable things of *E*
Ho 2:15 up out of the land of *E*
7:11 To *E* they have called
7:16 derision in the land of *E*
8:13 To *E* they themselves
9:3 Ephraim must return to *E*, and
9:6 *E* itself will collect them
11:1 out of *E* I called my son
11:5 not return to the land of *E*
11:11 come trembling out of *E*
12:1 to *E* oil itself is brought
12:9 your God from the land of *E*
12:13 brought up Israel out of *E*
13:4 your God from the land of *E*
Joe 3:19 *E*, a desolate waste it will
Am 2:10 up out of the land of *E*

Am 3:1 up out of the land of *E*
3:9 towers in the land of *E*
4:10 in the nature of that of *E*
8:8 sink down like the Nile of *E*
9:5 sink down like the Nile of *E*
9:7 up out of the land of *E*
Mic 6:4 you up out of the land of *E*
7:12 Assyria and the cities of *E*
7:12 from *E* even all the way to
7:15 from the land of *E* I shall
Na 3:9 her full might, also *E*
Hag 2:5 when you came forth from *E*
Zec 10:10 back from the land of *E*
10:11 scepter of *E* will depart
14:18 if the family of *E* itself
14:19 punishment for the sin of *E*
Mt 2:13 flee into *E*, and stay there
2:14 by night and withdrew into *E*
2:15 Out of *E* I called my son
2:19 in a dream to Joseph in *E*
Ac 2:10 *E* and the parts of Libya
7:9 of Joseph and sold him into *E*
7:10 sight of Pharaoh king of *E*
7:10 appointed him to govern *E*
7:11 came upon the whole of *E* and
7:12 there were foodstuffs in *E*
7:15 Jacob went down into *E*
7:17 grew and multiplied in *E*
7:18 different king over *E*, who
7:34 of my people who are in *E*
7:34 I will send you off to *E*
7:36 signs in *E* and in the Red Sea
7:39 they turned back to *E*
7:40 led us out of the land of *E*
13:17 residence in the land of *E*
Heb 3:16 went out of *E* under Moses
8:9 forth out of the land of *E*
11:26 than the treasures of *E*
11:27 By faith he left *E*, but not
Jude 5 people out of the land of *E*
Re 11:8 called Sodom and *E*, where

Egyptian

Ge 16:1 she had an *E* maidservant and
16:3 took Hagar, her *E* maidservant
21:9 son of Hagar the *E*, whom she
39:1 an *E*, got to buy him from the
39:2 house of his master, the *E*
39:5 blessing the house of the *E*
Ex 1:19 are not like the *E* women
2:11 caught sight of a certain *E*
2:12 he struck the *E* down and
2:14 me just as you killed the *E*
2:19 A certain *E* delivered us
Le 24:10 son of an *E* man, went out
De 23:7 You must not detest an *E*
1Sa 30:11 find a man, an *E*, in the
30:13 I am an *E* attendant, a
2Sa 23:21 that struck down the *E* man
23:21 spear in the hand of the *E*
1Ch 2:34 Sheshan had an *E* servant
11:23 that struck down the *E* man
11:23 in the hand of the *E* there
Isa 11:15 tongue of the *E* sea, and
Ac 7:24 by striking the *E* down
7:28 did away with the *E* yesterday
21:38 Are you not really the *E* who

Egyptian's

2Sa 23:21 spear away from the *E* hand
1Ch 11:23 spear away from the *E* hand

Egyptians

Ge 12:12 *E* will see you and will say
12:14 *E* got to see the woman, that
41:55 Pharaoh said to all the *E*
41:56 and to sell to the *E*, as the
43:32 for the *E* who were eating
43:32 the *E* were not able to eat a
43:32 a detestable thing to the *E*
45:2 the *E* got to hear it and
47:15 the *E* began coming to Joseph
47:20 bought all the land of the *E*
47:20 the *E* sold each one his field
50:3 *E* continued to shed tears for
50:11 a heavy mourning for the *E*
Ex 1:13 the *E* made the sons of Israel
3:8 out of the hand of the *E* and to
3:9 oppression with which the *E*
3:17 up out of affliction by the *E*
3:21 favor in the eyes of the *E*
3:22 and you must strip the *E*
6:5 whom the *E* are enslaving
6:6 under the burdens of the *E*
7:5 *E* . . . know that I am Jehovah

Ex 7:18 *E* will . . . have no stomach
7:21 *E* were unable to drink water
7:24 *E* went digging round about
8:26 a thing detestable to the *E*
8:26 a thing detestable to the *E*
9:11 boils . . . on all the *E*
11:3 favor in the eyes of the *E*
11:7 distinction between the *E* and
12:23 plague the *E* and does see
12:27 when he plagued the *E*, but
12:30 his servants and all other *E*
12:30 a great outcry among the *E*
12:33 *E* began to urge the people
12:35 they went asking from the *E*
12:36 favor in the eyes of the *E*
12:36 and they stripped the *E*
14:4 *E* will certainly know that I
14:9 the *E* went chasing after them
14:10 *E* were marching after them
14:12 that we may serve the *E*
14:12 better for us to serve the *E*
14:13 *E* whom you do see today you
14:17 the hearts of the *E* become
14:18 *E* will certainly know that I
14:20 in between the camp of the *E*
14:23 *E* took up the pursuit, and
14:24 upon the camp of the *E* from
14:24 camp of the *E* into confusion
14:25 *E* began to say: Let us flee
14:25 for them against the *E*
14:26 come back over the *E*, their
14:27 the *E* were fleeing from
14:27 shook the *E* off into the
14:30 from the hand of the *E*, and
14:30 Israel got to see the *E* dead
14:31 in action against the *E*; and
15:26 that I put upon the *E*
19:4 have seen what I did to the *E*
32:12 should the *E* say, With evil
Nu 14:13 *E* will be bound to hear that
20:15 *E* began doing harm to us and
33:3 before the eyes of all the *E*
33:4 *E* were burying those whom
De 26:6 the *E* went treating us badly
Jos 24:6 the *E* went chasing after
24:7 between you and the *E* and
Ezr 9:1 the *E* and the Amorites
Isa 19:2, 2 I will goad *E* against *E*
19:21 become known to the *E*
19:21 *E* must know Jehovah in
30:7 *E* are mere vanity, and they
31:3 *E*, though, are earthling men
Eze 29:12 I will scatter the *E* among
29:13 collect the *E* together
29:14 the captive group of the *E*
30:23 scatter the *E* among the
30:26 scatter the *E* among the
Ac 7:22 in all the wisdom of the *E*
Heb 11:29 the *E* were swallowed up

Egypt's
Ex 6:11 speak to Pharaoh, *E* king, that
6:13 Pharaoh, *E* king, in order to
6:27 speaking to Pharaoh, *E* king

Ehi
Ge 46:21 sons of Benjamin were . . . *E*

Ehud
Jg 3:15 a savior, *E* the son of Gera
3:16 *E* made a sword for himself
3:20 And *E* came to him as he was
3:20 *E* went on to say: A word of
3:21 *E* thrust in his left hand and
3:23 *E* proceeded to go out through
3:26 As for *E*, he escaped while
4:1 now that *E* was dead
1Ch 7:10 sons of Bilhan were . . . *E*
8:6 And these were the sons of *E*

Eight
Ge 5:4 Adam . . . *e* hundred years
5:7 Seth . . . *e* hundred and seven
5:10 Enosh continued to live *e*
5:13 Kenan . . . *e* hundred and forty
5:16 live *e* hundred and thirty
5:17 *e* hundred and ninety-five
5:19 Jared . . . *e* hundred years
17:12 male of yours *e* days old
21:4 Isaac his son when *e* days old
22:23 *e* Milcah bore to Nahor the
Ex 26:25 there must be *e* panel frames
36:30 amounted to *e* panel frames
Nu 2:24 one hundred and *e* thousand one
3:28 *e* thousand six hundred, taking
4:48 *e* thousand five hundred and
Nu 7:8 and *e* cattle he gave to the
29:29 And on the sixth day *e* bulls
Jg 3:8 serve Cushan-rishathaim *e*
12:14 to judge Israel *e* years
1Sa 17:12 Jesse. And he had *e* sons
2Sa 23:8 *e* hundred slain at one time
24:9 *e* hundred thousand valiant
1Ki 7:10 and stones of *e* cubits
2Ki 8:17 and for *e* years he reigned in
22:1 *E* years old was Josiah when
1Ch 12:24 were six thousand *e* hundred
12:30 twenty thousand *e* hundred
24:4 for their paternal houses, *e*
2Ch 13:3 *e* hundred thousand chosen
21:5 *e* years he reigned in
21:20 for *e* years he reigned in
29:17 house of Jehovah in *e* days
34:1 *E* years old was Josiah when
Ezr 2:6 two thousand *e* hundred and
Ne 7:11 two thousand *e* hundred and
7:13 *e* hundred and forty-five
11:12 *e* hundred and twenty-two
Ec 11:2 portion to seven, or even to *e*
Jer 41:15 he escaped with *e* men from
52:29 *e* hundred and thirty-two
Eze 40:9 the gate, *e* cubits
40:31 and its ascent was *e* steps
40:34 And its ascent was *e* steps
40:37 And its ascent was *e* steps
40:41 side of the gate—*e* tables
Mic 5:5 yes, *e* dukes of mankind
Lu 2:21 when *e* days came to the full
9:28 *e* days after these words
Joh 20:26 *e* days later his disciples
Ac 9:33 flat on his cot for *e* years
25:6 not more than *e* or ten days
1Pe 3:20 *e* souls, were carried safely

Eighteen
Ge 14:14 three hundred and *e* slaves
Jg 3:14 the king of Moab *e* years
10:8 for *e* years all the sons of
20:25 *e* thousand men among the
20:44 *e* thousand men of Benjamin
2Sa 8:13 striking . . . *e* thousand
1Ki 7:15 *e* cubits being the height of
2Ki 24:8 *E* years old was Jehoiachin
25:17 *E* cubits was the height of
1Ch 12:31 *e* thousand that had been
18:12 struck down . . . *e* thousand
26:9 and brothers, capable men, *e*
29:7 worth *e* thousand talents
2Ch 11:21 *e* wives that he had taken
36:9 *E* years old was Jehoiachin
Ezr 8:9 two hundred and *e* males
8:18 his sons and his brothers, *e*
Ne 7:11 thousand eight hundred and *e*
Jer 52:21 pillars, *e* cubits in height
Eze 48:35 *e* thousand cubits
Lu 13:4 those *e* upon whom the tower
13:11 of weakness for *e* years
13:16 held bound, look! *e* years

Eighteenth
1Ki 15:1 *e* year of King Jeroboam
2Ki 3:1 the *e* year of Jehoshaphat
22:3 the *e* year of King Josiah
23:23 *e* year of King Josiah this
1Ch 24:15 for Happizzez the *e*
25:25 for the *e*, for Hanani, his
2Ch 13:1 *e* year of King Jeroboam it
34:8 *e* year of his reigning
35:19 *e* year of Josiah's reign
Jer 32:1 the *e* year of Nebuchadrezzar
52:29 *e* year of Nebuchadrezzar

Eighth
Ex 22:30 *e* day you are to give it to
Le 9:1 on the *e* day that Moses called
12:3 on the *e* day the flesh of his
14:10 *e* day he will take two sound
14:23 on the *e* day he must bring
15:14 on the *e* day he should take
15:29 on the *e* day she should take
22:27 *e* day and forward it will be
23:36 *e* day there should occur a
23:39 the *e* day is a complete rest
25:22 sow seed the *e* year and you
Nu 6:10 *e* day he should bring two
7:54 On the *e* day there was the
29:35 the *e* day you should hold a
1Ki 6:38 Bul, that is, the *e* month
8:66 On the *e* day he sent the
12:32 *e* month on the fifteenth
12:33 day in the *e* month
2Ki 24:12 *e* year of his being king
1Ch 12:12 Johanan the *e*, Elzabad the
24:10 for Abijah the *e*
25:15 the *e* for Jeshaiah, his sons
26:5 the seventh, Peullethai the *e*
27:11, 11 The *e* for the *e* month
2Ch 7:9 *e* day they held a solemn
29:17 *e* day of the month they
34:3 *e* year of his reigning
Ne 8:18 *e* day there was a solemn
Eze 43:27 *e* day and from then on that
Zec 1:1 *e* month in the second year
Lu 1:59 on the *e* day they came to
Ac 7:8 circumcised him on the *e* day
Php 3:5 circumcised the *e* day, out of
Re 17:11 it is also itself an *e* king
21:20 the *e* beryl, the ninth

Eightieth
1Ki 6:1 the four hundred and *e* year

Eighty
Ge 35:28 to be a hundred and *e* years
Ex 7:7 And Moses was *e* years old and
Nu 4:48 thousand five hundred and *e*
Jg 3:30 disturbance for *e* years
2Sa 19:32 Barzillai . . . *e* years of age
19:35 I am *e* years old today
1Ki 5:15 *e* thousand cutters in the
12:21 a hundred and *e* thousand
2Ki 6:25 worth *e* silver pieces
10:24 stationed *e* men outside at
1Ch 15:9 of the sons of Hebron . . . *e*
2Ch 2:2 *e* thousand men as cutters in
2:18 and *e* thousand cutters in the
11:1 hundred and *e* thousand choice
14:8 two hundred and *e* thousand
17:15 two hundred and *e* thousand
17:18 hundred and *e* thousand men
26:17 *e* valiant men, came in
Ezr 8:8 and with him *e* males
Es 1:4 a hundred and *e* days
Ps 90:10 mightiness they are *e* years
Ca 6:8 and *e* concubines and maidens
Jer 41:5 *e* men with their beards
Lu 16:7 agreement back and write *e*

Eighty-eight
1Ch 25:7 came to be two hundred and *e*
Ne 7:26 and Netophah, a hundred and *e*

Eighty-five
Jos 14:10 here I am today *e* years old
1Sa 22:18 *e* men bearing an ephod of
2Ki 19:35 a hundred and *e* thousand
Isa 37:36 a hundred and *e* thousand

Eighty-four
Ne 11:18 were two hundred and *e*
Lu 2:37 a widow now *e* years old

Eighty-seven
Ge 5:25 for a hundred and *e* years
1Ch 7:5 mighty men, *e* thousand by

Eighty-six
Ge 16:16 Abram was *e* years old at
Nu 2:9 one hundred *e* thousand four

Eighty-three
Ex 7:7 and Aaron was *e* years old at

Eighty-two
Ge 5:26 seven hundred and *e* years
5:28 for a hundred and *e* years

Eker
1Ch 2:27 sons of Ram . . . Jamin and *E*

Ekron
Jos 13:3 and up to the border of *E* to
15:11 went out to the slope of *E*
15:45 *E* and its dependent towns
15:46 From *E* westward all that
19:43 and Elon and Timnah and *E*
Jg 1:18 and *E* and its territory
1Sa 5:10 the ark of the true God to *E*
5:10 the ark . . . came to *E*
6:16 and went their way back to *E*
6:17 golden piles . . . for *E* one
7:14 back to Israel from *E* to
17:52 and as far as the gates of *E*
17:52 far as Gath and as far as *E*
2Ki 1:2 Baal-zebub the god of *E*
1:3 Baal-zebub the god of *E*
1:6 Baal-zebub the god of *E*
1:16 Baal-zebub the god of *E*
Jer 25:20 kings of the land of . . . *E*
Am 1:8 turn my hand back upon *E*
Zep 2:4 *E*, she will be uprooted

Zec 9:5 *E* also, because her looked-for
9:7 and *E* like the Jebusite

Ekronites
Jos 13:3 the *E*; and the Avvim
1Sa 5:10 the *E* began to cry out

Ela
1Ki 4:18 Shimei the son of *E*, in

Elah
Ge 36:41 sheik Oholibamah, sheik *E*
1Sa 17:2 in the low plain of *E*
17:19 were in the low plain of *E*
21:9 down in the low plain of *E*
1Ki 16:6 *E* his son began to reign in
16:8 *E* . . . became king over
16:13 the sins of *E* his son
16:14 rest of the affairs of *E*
2Ki 15:30 Hoshea the son of *E*
17:1 Hoshea the son of *E* became
18:1 *E* the king of Israel
18:9 *E* the king of Israel
1Ch 1:52 sheik Oholibamah, sheik *E*
4:15 the sons of Caleb . . . *E*
4:15 and the sons of *E*, Kenaz
9:8 *E* the son of Uzzi the son of

Elam
Ge 10:22 sons of Shem were *E* and
14:1 Chedorlaomer king of *E*
14:9 Chedorlaomer king of *E* and
1Ch 1:17 sons of Shem were *E* and
8:24 and Hananiah and *E* and
26:3 *E* the fifth, Jehohanan the
Ezr 2:7 sons of *E*, a thousand two
2:31 the sons of the other *E*
8:7 of the sons of *E*, Jeshaiah
10:2 sons of *E* answered and said
10:26 of the sons of *E*, Mattaniah
Ne 7:12 sons of *E*, a thousand two
7:34 sons of the other *E*
10:14 heads of the people . . . *E*
12:42 Malchijah and *E* and Ezer
Isa 11:11 remnant . . . from *E* and
21:2 Go up, O *E*! Lay siege
22:6 *E* itself has taken up the
Jer 25:25 all the kings of *E* and all
49:34 concerning *E* in the
49:35 I am breaking the bow of *E*
49:36 bring in upon *E* the four
49:36 dispersed ones of *E* will
49:38 I will set my throne in *E*
49:39 the captive ones of *E*
Eze 32:24 *E* and all her crowd round
Da 8:2 *E* the jurisdictional district

Elamites
Ezr 4:9 of Susa, that is, the *E*
Jer 49:37 shatter the *E* before their
Ac 2:9 Parthians and Medes and *E*, and

Elapsed
1Sa 25:38 ten days *e* and then Jehovah
Ac 24:27 when two years had *e*, Felix

Elasah
Jer 29:3 *E* the son of Shaphan and

Elated
Ps 68:3 Let them be *e* before God
Pr 11:10 righteous ones a town is *e*
Isa 24:8 noise of the highly *e* ones
32:13 yes, the highly *e* town

Elatedly
Isa 61:6 speak *e* about yourselves

Elath
De 2:8 from *E* and from Ezion-geber
2Ki 14:22 built *E* and got to restore
16:6 restored *E* to Edom
16:6 cleared out the Jews from *E*
16:6 entered *E* and kept dwelling

El-berith
Jg 9:46 the vault of the house of *E*

El-bethel
Ge 35:7 began to call the place *E*

Elbow
Mr 7:3 wash their hands up to the *e*

Elbows
Eze 13:18 bands together upon all *e*

Eldaah
Ge 25:4 sons of Midian were . . . *E*
1Ch 1:33 sons of Midian . . . *E*

Eldad
Nu 11:26 name of the one was *E*, and
11:27 *E* and Medad are acting as

Elderly
1Sa 19:20 *e* ones of the prophets
Ps 105:22 wisdom to even his *e* men
107:32 seat of the *e* men let them
Isa 3:2 of divination and *e* man
3:14 judgment with the *e* ones of
24:23 front of his *e* men with
Eze 7:26 and counsel from *e* men
8:11 seventy men of the *e* ones
8:12 *e* ones of the house of Israel
14:1 from the *e* ones of Israel
20:1 the *e* ones of Israel came in
20:3 with the *e* men of Israel

Elders
Re 4:4 I saw seated twenty-four *e*
4:10 twenty-four *e* fall down
5:5 But one of the *e* says to me
5:6 in the midst of the *e* a lamb
5:8 twenty-four *e* fell down before
5:11 living creatures and the *e*
5:14 the *e* fell down and worshiped
7:11 around the throne and the *e*
7:13 one of the *e* said to me
11:16 twenty-four *e* who were
14:3 new song before the . . . *e*
19:4 twenty-four *e* and the four

Elead
1Ch 7:21 his son and Ezer and *E*

Eleadah
1Ch 7:20 *E* his son and Tahath his son

Elealeh
Nu 32:3 *E* and Sebam and Nebo and
32:37 sons of Reuben built . . . *E*
Isa 15:4 And Heshbon and *E* cry out
16:9 drench you, O Heshbon and *E*
Jer 48:34 cry in Heshbon clear to *E*

Eleasah
1Ch 2:39 in turn, became father to *E*
2:40 *E*, in turn, became father to
8:37 *E* his son, Azel his son
9:43 *E* his son, Azel his son
Ezr 10:22 the sons of Pashhur . . . *E*

Eleazar
Ex 6:23 Later she bore him . . . *E*
6:25 *E*, Aaron's son, took for
28:1 *E* and Ithamar, the sons of
Le 10:6 Moses said to Aaron and to *E*
10:12 *E* and Ithamar, his sons that
10:16 *E* and Ithamar, Aaron's sons
Nu 3:2 Aaron's sons . . . Abihu, *E* and
3:4 *E* and Ithamar continued to act
3:32 was *E* the son of Aaron the
4:16 oversight of *E* the son of
16:37 Say to *E* the son of Aaron the
16:39 *E* the priest took the copper
19:3 must give it to *E* the priest
19:4 *E* the priest must take some
20:25 Take Aaron and *E* his son and
20:26 clothe with them *E* his son
20:28 clothed *E* his son with them
20:28 Moses and *E* came on down
25:7 Phinehas the son of *E* the son
25:11 Phinehas the son of *E* the son
26:1 to say this to Moses and *E*
26:3 And Moses and *E* the priest
26:60 born to Aaron . . . *E* and
26:63 registered by Moses and *E*
27:2 before *E* the priest and before
27:19 before *E* the priest and
27:21 it is before *E* the priest
27:22 and stood him before *E* the
31:6 and Phinehas the son of *E* the
31:12 bringing to Moses and *E* the
31:13 Moses and *E* the priest and
31:21 *E* the priest then said to the
31:26 you and *E* the priest and the
31:29 give it to *E* the priest as
31:31 Moses and *E* the priest went
31:41 Jehovah's contribution to *E*
31:51 *E* the priest accepted the
31:54 *E* the priest accepted the
32:2 to Moses and *E* the priest and
32:28 to *E* the priest and to Joshua
34:17 *E* the priest and Joshua the
De 10:6 *E* his son began to act as
Jos 14:1 *E* the priest and Joshua
17:4 *E* the priest and Joshua the
Jos 19:51 *E* the priest and Joshua the
21:1 approached *E* the priest and
22:13 Phinehas the son of *E* the
22:31 the son of *E* the priest said
22:32 Phinehas the son of *E* the
24:33 *E* the son of Aaron died
Jg 20:28 Now Phinehas the son of *E*
1Sa 7:1 *E* his son was the one whom
2Sa 23:9 *E* the son of Dodo the son of
1Ch 6:3 sons of Aaron were . . . *E* and
6:4 As for *E*, he became father
6:50 sons of Aaron: *E* his son
9:20 it was Phinehas the son of *E*
11:12 was *E* the son of Dodo the
23:21 of Mahli were *E* and Kish
23:22 *E* died; and he had come to
24:1 The sons of Aaron . . . *E* and
24:2 *E* and Ithamar continued to
24:3 and Zadok from the sons of *E*
24:4 sons of *E* were found to be
24:4 to the sons of *E*, as heads
24:5 from the sons of *E* and from
24:6 one paternal house . . . for *E*
24:28 Of Mahli, *E*, who did not
Ezr 7:5 *E* the son of Aaron the chief
8:33 *E* the son of Phinehas and
10:25 of the sons of Parosh . . . *E*
Ne 12:42 and *E* and Uzzi and
Mt 1:15 Eliud became father to *E*
1:15 *E* became father to Matthan

Electrum
Eze 1:4 something like the look of *e*
1:27 something like the glow of *e*
8:2 shining, like the glow of *e*

Elegance
Ge 49:21 He is giving words of *e*

Elegant
Isa 23:18 and for *e* covering

Elementary
Ga 4:3 enslaved by the *e* things
4:9 weak and beggarly *e* things
Col 2:8 the *e* things of the world and
2:20 the *e* things of the world
Heb 5:12 the *e* things of the sacred

Elements
2Pe 3:10 the *e* being intensely hot
3:12 the *e* being intensely hot

Elevate
Da 6:3 king was intending to *e* him

Elevated
Ps 73:8 they speak in an *e* style
Isa 26:5 the height, the *e* town
30:25 upon every *e* hill there
52:13 be *e* and exalted very much

Elevation
Isa 49:11 themselves will be on an *e*

Eleven
Ge 32:22 took . . . his *e* young sons
37:9 *e* stars were bowing down to
Ex 26:7 You will make *e* tent cloths
26:8 measure for the *e* tent cloths
36:14 *E* tent cloths were what he
36:15 for the *e* tent cloths
Nu 29:20 And on the third day *e* bulls
De 1:2 it being *e* days from Horeb by
Jos 15:51 *e* cities and their
2Ki 23:36 *e* years he reigned in
24:18 Zedekiah . . . *e* years he
2Ch 36:5 Jehoiakim . . . *e* years he
36:11 Zedekiah . . . *e* years he
Jer 52:1 *e* years he reigned in
Eze 40:49 and the width *e* cubits
Mt 28:16 the *e* disciples went into
Lu 24:9 to the *e* and to all the rest
24:33 found the *e* and those with
Ac 1:26 along with the *e* apostles
2:14 Peter stood up with the *e* and

Eleventh
Nu 7:72 On the *e* day . . . Asher
De 1:3 fortieth year, in the *e* month
1Ki 6:38 *e* year, in the lunar month
2Ki 9:29 *e* year of Jehoram the son of
25:2 *e* year of King Zedekiah
1Ch 12:13 the tenth, Machbannai the *e*
24:12 for Eliashib the *e*, for
25:18 the *e* for Azarel, his sons
27:14, 14 The *e* for the *e* month
Jer 1:3 the *e* year of Zedekiah the
39:2 *e* year of Zedekiah, in the

Jer 52:5 *e* year of King Zedekiah
Eze 26:1 the *e* year, on the first day
30:20 *e* year, in the first month
31:1 *e* year, in the third month
Zec 1:7 of the *e* month, that is, the
Mt 20:6 *e* hour he went out and found
Re 21:20 the *e* hyacinth, the twelfth

Eleventh-hour
Mt 20:9 When the *e* men came, they

Elhanan
2Sa 21:19 *E* the son of Jaare-oregim
23:24 *E* the son of Dodo of
1Ch 11:26 *E* the son of Dodo of
20:5 and *E* the son of Jair got to

Eli
1Sa 1:3 the two sons of *E*, Hophni and
1:9 *E* the priest was sitting
1:12 *E* was watching her mouth
1:13 But *E* took her for drunk
1:14 *E* said to her: How long will
1:17 *E* answered and said: Go in
1:25 and brought the boy to *E*
2:11 minister of Jehovah before *E*
2:12 Now the sons of *E* were
2:20 *E* blessed Elkanah and his
2:22 *E* was very old, and he had
2:27 to come to *E* and say to him
3:1 boy Samuel was . . . before *E*
3:2 that *E* was lying in his place
3:5 And he went running to *E* and
3:6 Samuel got up and went to *E*
3:8 he got up and went to *E* and
3:8 *E* began to discern that it
3:9 *E* said to Samuel: Go, lie
3:12 I shall carry out toward *E*
3:14 have sworn to the house of *E*
3:14 the error of the house of *E*
3:15 Samuel was afraid to tell *E*
3:16 But *E* called Samuel and said
4:4 two sons of *E* were there
4:11 the two sons of *E* . . . died
4:13 there was *E* sitting on the
4:14 *E* got to hear the sound of
4:14 might go in and report to *E*
4:15 *E* was ninety-eight years old
4:16 man proceeded to say to *E*
14:3 *E*, the priest of Jehovah in
1Ki 2:27 against the house of *E* in
Mt 27:46, 46 saying: *E*, *E*, *la'ma*
Mr 15:34, 34 loud voice: *E*, *E*, *la'ma*

Eliab
Nu 1:9 *E* the son of Helon
2:7 *E* the son of Helon
7:24 chieftain for . . . Zebulun, *E*
7:29 offering of *E* the son of Helon
10:16 *E* the son of Helon
16:1 and Abiram the sons of *E*
16:12 and Abiram the sons of *E*
26:8 And the son of Pallu was *E*
26:9 sons of *E*: Nemuel and Dathan
De 11:6 sons of *E* the son of Reuben
1Sa 16:6 and he caught sight of *E*, he
17:13 *E* the firstborn, and his
17:28 *E* his oldest brother got to
1Ch 2:13 father to his firstborn *E*
6:27 *E* his son, Jeroham his son
12:9 the second, *E* the third
15:18 *E* and Benaiah and Maaseiah
15:20 and Jehiel and Unni and *E*
16:5 *E* and Benaiah and Obed-edom
2Ch 11:18 Abihail the daughter of *E*

Eliab's
1Sa 17:28 *E* anger grew hot against

Eliada
2Sa 5:16 Elishama and *E* and Eliphelet
1Ki 11:23 Rezon the son of *E*, who had
1Ch 3:8 Elishama and *E* and Eliphelet
2Ch 17:17 valiant, mighty man *E*

Eliahba
2Sa 23:32 *E* the Shaalbonite, the sons
1Ch 11:33 *E* the Shaalbonite

Eliakim
2Ki 18:18 *E* the son of Hilkiah
18:26 *E* the son of Hilkiah and
18:37 *E* the son of Hilkiah
19:2 sent *E*, who was over the
23:34 Pharaoh Nechoh made *E* the
2Ch 36:4 made *E* his brother king over
Ne 12:41 the priests *E*, Maaseiah
Isa 22:20 *E* the son of Hilkiah
Isa 36:3 *E* the son of Hilkiah, who
36:11 *E* and Shebna and Joah said
36:22 *E* the son of Hilkiah, who
37:2 sent *E*, who was over the
Mt 1:13 Abiud became father to *E*
1:13 *E* became father to Azor
Lu 3:30 son of Jonam, son of *E*

Eliam
2Sa 11:3 Bath-sheba the daughter of *E*
23:34 *E* the son of Ahithophel the

Eliasaph
Nu 1:14 of Gad, *E* the son of Deuel
2:14 is *E* the son of Reuel
3:24 was *E* the son of Lael
7:42 *E* the son of Deuel
7:47 offering of *E* the son of Deuel
10:20 there was *E* the son of Deuel

Eliashib
1Ch 3:24 sons of Elioenai were . . . *E*
24:12 for *E* the eleventh, for
Ezr 10:6 Jehohanan the son of *E*
10:24 and of the singers, *E*
10:27 of the sons of Zattu . . . *E*
10:36 Vaniah, Meremoth, *E*
Ne 3:1 And *E* the high priest and his
3:20 house of *E* the high priest
3:21 entrance of the house of *E*
12:10 Joiakim . . . father to *E*
12:10 and *E* to Joiada
12:22 The Levites in the days of *E*
12:23 Johanan the son of *E*
13:4 *E* the priest in charge of a
13:7 badness that *E* had committed
13:28 *E* the high priest was a

Eliashib's
Ne 3:21 as far as the end of *E* house

Eliathah
1Ch 25:4 the sons of Heman . . . *E*
25:27 for the twentieth, for *E*

Elidad
Nu 34:21 of Benjamin, *E* the son of

Elieho-enai
1Ch 26:3 the sixth, *E* the seventh
Ezr 8:4 *E* the son of Zerahiah, and

Eliel
1Ch 5:24 Epher and Ishi and *E* and
6:34 son of *E*, the son of Toah
8:20 Elienai and Zillethai and *E*
8:22 and Ishpan and Eber and *E*
11:46 *E* the Mahavite, and Jeribai
11:47 *E* and Obed and Jaasiel the
12:11 the sixth, *E* the seventh
15:9 sons of Hebron, *E* the chief
15:11 Levites . . . Shemaiah and *E*
2Ch 31:13 and *E* . . . commissioners at

Elienai
1Ch 8:20 and *E* and Zillethai and Eliel

Eliezer
Ge 15:2 is a man of Damascus, *E*
Ex 18:4 the name of the other was *E*
1Ch 7:8 the sons of Becher were . . . *E*
15:24 and *E* the priests loudly
23:15 The sons of Moses . . . *E*
23:17 the sons of *E* came to be
23:17 and *E* did not come to have
26:25 of *E* there was Rehabiah his
27:16 *E* the son of Zichri was
2Ch 20:37 *E* the son of Dodavahu of
Ezr 8:16 sent for *E*, Ariel, Shemaiah
10:18 *E* and Jarib and Gedaliah
10:23 of the Levites . . . and *E*
10:31 the sons of Harim, *E*
Lu 3:29 son of Jesus, son of *E*, son of

Elihoreph
1Ki 4:3 *E* and Ahijah, the sons of

Elihu
1Sa 1:1 *E*, the son of Tohu, the son
1Ch 12:20 from Manasseh . . . *E* and
26:7 were capable men, *E* and
27:18 *E*, one of David's brothers
Job 32:2 anger of *E* the son of
32:4 *E* himself had waited for Job
32:5 *E* gradually saw that there
32:6 *E* the son of Barachel the
34:1 *E* continued to answer and
35:1 *E* continued answering and
36:1 *E* proceeded to say further

Elijah
1Ki 17:1 *E* the Tishbite from the
17:13 *E* said to her: Do not be
17:16 had spoken by means of *E*
17:18 she said to *E*: What do I
17:23 *E* now took the child and
17:23 *E* then said: See, your son
17:24 the woman said to *E*
18:1 came to *E* in the third year
18:2 *E* went to show himself to
18:7 there was *E* to meet him
18:7 Is this you, my lord *E*?
18:8 say to your lord, Here is *E*
18:11 say to your lord: Here is *E*
18:14 to your lord: Here is *E*
18:15 *E* said: As Jehovah of
18:16 so Ahab went to meet *E*
18:17 as soon as Ahab saw *E*
18:21 *E* approached all the people
18:22 *E* went on to say to the
18:25 *E* now said to the prophets
18:27 *E* began to mock them and
18:30 *E* said to all the people
18:31 So *E* took twelve stones
18:36 *E* the prophet began to
18:40 *E* said to them: Seize the
18:40 *E* then brought them down to
18:41 *E* now said to Ahab: Go up
18:42 As for *E*, he went up to
18:46 proved to be upon *E*, so
19:1 all that *E* had done and all
19:2 sent a messenger to *E*
19:9 is your business here, *E*
19:13 that as soon as *E* heard it
19:13 is your business here, *E*
19:19 So *E* crossed over to him
19:20 went running after *E* and
19:21 following *E* and began to
21:17 came to *E* the Tishbite
21:20 say to *E*: Have you found me
21:28 came to *E* the Tishbite
2Ki 1:3 he spoke to *E* the Tishbite
1:4 With that *E* went off
1:8 said: It was *E* the Tishbite
1:10 *E* answered and spoke to the
1:12 *E* answered and spoke to them
1:13 upon his knees in front of *E*
1:15 angel of Jehovah spoke to *E*
1:17 word of Jehovah that *E* had
2:1 to take *E* in a windstorm up
2:1 *E* and Elisha proceeded to go
2:2 *E* began to say to Elisha
2:4 *E* now said to him: Elisha
2:6 *E* now said to him: Sit here
2:8 *E* took his official garment
2:9 *E* himself said to Elisha
2:11 and *E* went ascending in the
2:13 the official garment of *E*
2:14 the official garment of *E*
2:14 Jehovah the God of *E*
2:15 The spirit of *E* has settled
3:11 water upon the hands of *E*
9:36 his servant *E* the Tishbite
10:10 by means of his servant *E*
10:17 that he had spoken to *E*
1Ch 8:27 and *E* . . . sons of Jeroham
2Ch 21:12 writing to him from *E* the
Ezr 10:21 sons of Harim . . . *E*
10:26 of the sons of Elam . . . *E*
Mal 4:5 to you people *E* the prophet
Mt 11:14 *E* who is destined to come
16:14 others *E*, still others
17:3 appeared to them Moses and *E*
17:4 three tents . . . one for *E*
17:10 say that *E* must come first
17:11 *E*, indeed, is coming and
17:12 *E* has already come and they
27:47 say: This man is calling *E*
27:49 whether *E* comes to save him
Mr 6:15 others were saying: It is *E*
8:28 *E*, still others, One of the
9:4 Also, *E* with Moses appeared
9:5 one for Moses and one for *E*
9:11 say that first *E* must come
9:12 *E* does come first and restore
9:13 *E*, in fact, has come, and
15:35 See! He is calling *E*
15:36 Let us see whether *E* comes
Lu 4:25 in the days of *E*, when the
4:26 *E* was sent to none of those
9:8 but by others that *E* had
9:19 others, *E*, and still others
9:30 who were Moses and *E*
9:33 one for Moses and one for *E*

Joh 1:21 Are you *E?* And he said
1:25 Christ or *E* or The Prophet
Ro 11:2 *E*, as he pleads with God
Jas 5:17 *E* was a man with feelings

Elijah's
1Ki 17:15 did according to *E* word
17:22 Jehovah listened to *E* voice
Lu 1:17 with *E* spirit and power, to

Elika
2Sa 23:25 *E* the Harodite

Elim
Ex 15:27 After that they came to *E*
16:1 Later they departed from *E*
16:1 which is between *E* and Sinai
Nu 33:9 from Marah and came to *E*
33:9 *E* there were twelve springs
33:10 pulled away from *E* and went

Elimelech
Ru 1:2 And the man's name was *E*, and
1:3 *E* the husband of Naomi died
2:1 of the family of *E*, and his
2:3 who was of the family of *E*
4:3 that belonged to our brother *E*
4:9 I do buy all that belonged to *E*

Elioenai
1Ch 3:23 sons of Neariah were *E*
3:24 the sons of *E* were Hodaviah
4:36 and *E* and Jaakobah and
7:8 the sons of Becher were . . . *E*
Ezr 10:22 the sons of Pashhur, *E*
10:27 of the sons of Zattu, *E*
Ne 12:41 *E*, Zechariah, Hananiah

Eliphal
1Ch 11:35 *E* the son of Ur

Eliphaz
Ge 36:4 Adah proceeded to bear *E* to
36:10 sons of Esau: *E*
36:11 the sons of *E* came to be
36:12 Timna . . . the concubine of *E*
36:12 she bore to *E* Amalek
36:15 sons of *E*, Esau's firstborn
36:16 sheiks of *E* . . . of Edom
1Ch 1:35 sons of Esau were *E*, Reuel
1:36 sons of *E* were Teman and
Job 2:11 *E* the Temanite and Bildad
4:1 *E* the Temanite proceeded to
15:1 *E* the Temanite proceeded to
22:1 *E* the Temanite proceeded to
42:7 to say to *E* the Temanite
42:9 *E* the Temanite and Bildad

Eliphelehu
1Ch 15:18 and *E* and Mikneiah, and
15:21 and Mattithiah and *E* and

Eliphelet
2Sa 5:16 Elishama and Eliada and *E*
23:34 *E* the son of Ahasbai the son
1Ch 3:6 Ibhar and Elishama and *E*
3:8 and Eliada and *E*, nine
8:39 sons of Eshek . . . *E* the third
14:7 Elishama and Beeliada and *E*
Ezr 8:13 sons of Adonikam . . . *E*
10:33 the sons of Hashum . . . *E*

Elisha
1Ki 19:16 *E* the son of Shaphat from
19:17 *E* will put to death
19:19 found *E* the son of Shaphat
2Ki 2:1 Elijah and *E* proceeded to go
2:2 Elijah began to say to *E*
2:2 *E* said: As Jehovah is living
2:3 came out to *E* and said to him
2:4 *E*, sit here, please, because
2:5 approached *E* and said to him
2:9 Elijah himself said to *E*
2:9 *E* said: Please, that two
2:12 *E* was seeing it, and he was
2:14 so that *E* went across
2:15 has settled down upon *E*
2:19 men of the city said to *E*
3:11 is here *E* the son of Shaphat
3:13 *E* proceeded to say to the
3:14 To this *E* said: As Jehovah
4:1 cried out to *E*, saying: Your
4:2 *E* said to her: What shall I
4:8 *E* went passing along to
4:17 just as *E* had spoken to her
4:32 *E* came into the house
4:38 *E* himself returned to Gilgal
5:8 *E* the man of the true God
5:9 the entrance of the house of *E*
2Ki 5:10 *E* sent a messenger to him
5:20 *E* the man of the true God
5:25 *E* now said to him: Where
6:1 to say to *E*: Look, now! The
6:12 *E* the prophet who is in
6:17 *E* began to pray and say
6:17 chariots of fire all around *E*
6:18 *E* went on to pray to Jehovah
6:18 according to the word of *E*
6:19 *E* now said to them
6:20 *E* then said: O Jehovah, open
6:21 king of Israel now said to *E*
6:31 if the head of *E* the son of
6:32 *E* was sitting in his own
7:1 *E* now said: Listen, you men
8:1 *E* himself had spoken to the
8:4 great things that *E* has done
8:5 is her son whom *E* revived
8:7 *E* proceeded to come to
8:10 *E* said to him: Go, say to
8:13 *E* said: Jehovah has shown me
8:14 went from *E* and came to his
8:14 What did *E* say to you?
9:1 *E* the prophet, for his part
13:14 *E*, he had taken sick with
13:15 *E* proceeded to say to him
13:16 *E* laid his hands upon the
13:17 *E* said: Shoot! So he shot
13:20 *E* died and they buried him
13:21 man touched the bones of *E*
Lu 4:27 in the time of *E* the prophet

Elishah
Ge 10:4 sons of Javan were *E* and
1Ch 1:7 sons of Javan were *E* and
Eze 27:7 from the islands of *E* are

Elishama
Nu 1:10 *E* the son of Ammihud
2:18 is *E* the son of Ammihud
7:48 *E* the son of Ammihud
7:53 of *E* the son of Ammihud
10:22 *E* the son of Ammihud was
2Sa 5:16 *E* and Eliada and Eliphelet
2Ki 25:25 Nethaniah the son of *E*
1Ch 2:41 in turn, became father to *E*
3:6 Ibhar and *E* and Eliphelet
3:8 *E* and Eliada and Eliphelet
7:26 Ammihud his son, *E* his son
14:7 *E* and Beeliada and Eliphelet
2Ch 17:8 *E* and Jehoram the priests
Jer 36:12 *E* the secretary and Delaiah
36:20 room of *E* the secretary
36:21 room of *E* the secretary
41:1 Nethaniah the son of *E* of

Elishaphat
2Ch 23:1 *E* the son of Zichri, with

Elisha's
2Ki 2:22 to *E* word that he spoke
13:21 the man into *E* burial place

Elisheba
Ex 6:23 Aaron took *E* . . . as his wife

Elishua
2Sa 5:15 *E* and Nepheg and Japhia
1Ch 14:5 and Ibhar and *E* and Elpelet

Eliud
Mt 1:14 Achim became father to *E*
1:15 *E* became father to Eleazar

Elizabeth
Lu 1:5 and her name was *E*
1:7 *E* was barren, and they both
1:13 *E* will become mother to a
1:24 *E* his wife became pregnant
1:36 *E* your relative has also
1:40 Zechariah and greeted *E*
1:41 *E* heard the greeting of Mary
1:41 *E* was filled with holy spirit
1:57 due for *E* to give birth

Elizaphan
Nu 3:30 was *E* the son of Uzziel
34:25 of Zebulun a chieftain, *E* the
1Ch 15:8 of the sons of *E*, Shemaiah
2Ch 29:13 sons of *E*, Shimri and Jeuel

Elizur
Nu 1:5 Of Reuben, *E* the son of Shedeur
2:10 is *E* the son of Shedeur
7:30 *E* the son of Shedeur
7:35 of *E* the son of Shedeur
10:18 *E* the son of Shedeur was

Elkanah
Ex 6:24 the sons of Korah were . . . *E*
1Sa 1:1 *E*, the son of Jeroham, the
1:4 *E* proceeded to sacrifice, and
1:8 *E* her husband proceeded to say
1:19 *E* now had intercourse with
1:21 man *E* went up with all his
1:23 *E* her husband said to her
2:11 *E* went to Ramah to his house
2:20 Eli blessed *E* and his wife
1Ch 6:23 *E* his son and Ebiasaph his
6:25 sons of *E* were Amasai and
6:26 As for *E*, the sons of
6:26 sons of *E* were Zophai his
6:27 Jeroham his son, *E* his son
6:34 son of *E*, the son of Jeroham
6:35 son of *E*, the son of Mahath
6:36 the son of *E*, the son of Joel
9:16 the son of Asa the son of *E*
12:6 *E* and Isshiah and Azarel and
15:23 and *E* the gatekeepers for
2Ch 28:7 *E* the one next to the king

Elkoshite
Na 1:1 the vision of Nahum the *E*

Ellasar
Ge 14:1 days of . . . Arioch king of *E*
14:9 and Arioch king of *E*; four

Elmadam
Lu 3:28 son of Cosam, son of *E*, son

Elnaam
1Ch 11:46 and Joshaviah the sons of *E*

Elnathan
2Ki 24:8 Nehushta the daughter of *E*
Ezr 8:16, 16 *E* and Jarib and *E* and
8:16 Joiarib and *E*, instructors
Jer 26:22 *E* the son of Achbor and
36:12 *E* the son of Achbor and
36:25 even *E* and Delaiah and

Elon
Ge 26:34 daughter of *E* the Hittite
36:2 Adah the daughter of *E*
46:14 sons of Zebulun were . . . *E*
Nu 26:26 *E* the family of the Elonites
Jos 19:43 and *E* and Timnah and Ekron
Jg 12:11 *E* the Zebulunite began to
12:12 *E* the Zebulunite died and

Elon-beth-hanan
1Ki 4:9 and Beth-shemesh and *E*

Elonites
Nu 26:26 of Elon the family of the *E*

Eloquent
Ac 18:24 named Apollos . . . an *e* man

Eloth
1Ki 9:26 Ezion-geber, which is by *E*
2Ch 8:17 *E* upon the shore of the sea
26:2 rebuilt *E* and then restored

Elpaal
1Ch 8:11 father to Abitub and *E*
8:12 the sons of *E* were Eber and
8:18 and Jobab, the sons of *E*

El-paran
Ge 14:6 *E*, which is at the wilderness

Elpelet
1Ch 14:5 and Ibhar and Elishua and *E*

Else
Ge 19:12 Do you have anyone *e* here?
28:17 nothing *e* but the house of
45:1 And no one *e* stood with him
Ex 8:10 is no one *e* like Jehovah our
34:3 let nobody *e* be seen in all
Le 7:24 for anything *e* conceivable
De 24:5 anything *e* be imposed onto
Jos 22:24 care for something *e* that
Jg 7:14 is nothing *e* but the sword of
Ru 4:4 there is no one *e* but you to do
1Sa 17:30 toward someone *e* and went
1Ki 20:39 or *e* a talent of silver you
Job 17:3 Who *e* is there that will
24:24 like everyone *e* they are
31:8 sow seed and someone *e* eat
Ps 16:4 when there is someone *e*, do
109:8 oversight let someone *e* take
143:7 Or *e* I must become
Pr 4:23 all *e* that is to be guarded
30:2 unreasoning than anyone *e*
Isa 1:5 Where *e* will you be struck
42:8 to no one *e* shall I give my
45:5 and there is no one *e*
45:6 and there is no one *e*

Isa 45:14 no one *e*; there is no other
45:18 and there is no one *e*
45:22 God, and there is no one *e*
47:8 I am, and there is nobody *e*
47:10 I am, and there is nobody *e*
48:11 to no one *e* shall I give
65:22 someone *e* have occupancy
65:22 someone *e* do the eating
Jer 17:9 anything *e* and is desperate
Da 2:11 nobody *e* exists who can show
2:40 and grinding everything *e*, so
Zep 2:15 I am, and there is nobody *e*
Mr 1:38 Let us go somewhere *e*, into
Joh 5:43 if someone *e* arrived in his
15:24 works that no one *e* did
Ac 1:20 oversight let someone *e* take
4:12 is no salvation in anyone *e*
Ro 2:21 the one teaching someone *e*
1Co 1:16 whether I baptized anybody *e*
3:10 someone *e* is building on it
10:31 or doing anything *e*, do all
2Co 10:15 in the labors of someone *e*
11:21 if anyone *e* acts bold in
Ga 1:19 saw no one *e* of the apostles
Php 2:20 no one *e* of a disposition
1Th 5:15 injury for injury to anyone *e*
Re 3:15 I wish you were cold or *e* hot

Else's
2Co 10:16 someone *e* territory where

Elsewhere
Ps 84:10 is better than a thousand *e*

Elteke
Jos 21:23 *E* and its pasture ground

Eltekeh
Jos 19:44 *E* and Gibbethon and Baalath

Eltekon
Jos 15:59 and Beth-anoth and *E*

Eltolad
Jos 15:30 *E* and Chesil and Hormah
19:4 and *E* and Bethul and Hormah

Eludes
Isa 40:27 and justice to me *e* my God

Elul
Ne 6:15 on the twenty-fifth day of *E*

Eluzai
1Ch 12:5 *E* and Jerimoth and Bealiah

Elymas
Ac 13:8 *E* the sorcerer (that, in fact

Elzabad
1Ch 12:12 the eighth, *E* the ninth
26:7 The sons of Shemaiah . . . *E*

Elzaphan
Ex 6:22 sons of Uzziel were . . . *E* and
Le 10:4 and *E*, the sons of Uzziel

Emaciate
Zep 2:11 *e* all the gods of the earth

Emaciated
Ps 102:7 I have grown *e*, And I am

Emancipate
Heb 2:15 *e* all those who for fear

Emasculated
Ga 5:12 would even get themselves *e*

Embalm
Ge 50:2 physicians, to *e* his father

Embalmed
Ge 50:2 So the physicians *e* Israel
50:26 and they had him *e*, and he

Embalming
Ge 50:3 customarily take for the *e*

Embarrassed
2Ki 2:17 urging him until he was *e*
Ezr 9:6 *e* to raise my face to you

Embarrassment
2Ki 8:11 set to the point of *e*

Embers
Pr 26:21 charcoal for the *e* and wood

Embitter
Da 11:11 king of the south will *e*

Embittered
Ps 106:33 For they *e* his spirit

Emboldened
Es 7:5 has *e* himself to do that way

Ac 5:3 Ananias, why has Satan *e* you

Embrace
Ge 33:4 *e* him and fall upon his neck
Pr 4:8 glorify you because you *e* it
5:20 *e* the bosom of a foreign
Ec 3:5 a time to *e* and a time to keep
Ca 8:3 his right hand—it would *e* me
La 4:5 have had to *e* ash heaps
Lu 10:4 and do not *e* anybody in

Embraced
Ge 29:13 he *e* him and kissed him and
48:10 then kissed them and *e* them
Ac 2:41 *e* his word heartily were
20:10 *e* him and said: Stop raising

Embraces
Ca 2:6 and his right hand—it *e* me

Embracing
2Ki 4:16 year you will be *e* a son
Ec 3:5 a time to keep away from *e*

Embroidered
Jg 5:30 An *e* garment, dyed stuff, two
5:30 two *e* garments For the necks
Eze 16:10 with an *e* garment and to
16:13 material and an *e* garment
16:18 would take your *e* garments
26:16 their own *e* garments

Embroiderer
Ex 26:1 cherubs, the work of an *e*
26:31 cherubs, the work of an *e*
28:6 linen, the work of an *e*
28:15 the workmanship of an *e*
35:35 an *e* and of a weaver in blue
36:8 the work of an *e*
36:35 With the work of an *e* he
38:23 a craftsman and *e* and weaver
39:3 as the work of an *e*
39:8 with the workmanship of an *e*

Embryo
Ps 139:16 eyes saw even the *e* of me

Emek-keziz
Jos 18:21 and Beth-hoglah and *E*

Emerald
Ex 28:17 row of ruby, topaz and *e* is
39:10 A row of ruby, topaz and *e*
Eze 28:13 sapphire, turquoise and *e*
Re 4:3 there is a rainbow like an *e*
21:19 foundation . . . the fourth *e*

Emerged
Re 14:15 angel *e* from the temple
14:17 angel *e* from the temple
14:18 angel *e* from the altar and
15:6 *e* from the sanctuary, clothed

Emery
Zec 7:12 heart they set as an *e* stone

Emim
Ge 14:5 inflicted defeats on . . . *E*
De 2:10 *E* dwelt in it in former
2:11 Moabites used to call them *E*

Eminence
De 33:26 upon cloudy skies in his *e*
Ps 68:34 Over Israel his *e* is and his
93:1 With *e* he is clothed
Isa 26:10 not see the *e* of Jehovah
Ac 25:23 men of *e* in the city, and

Eminency
Eze 7:11 nor is there any *e* in them

Eminent
De 33:29 the One who is your *e* sword
Isa 28:1 Woe to the *e* crown of the
28:3 *e* crowns of the drunkards

Eminently
Isa 13:3 my *e* exultant ones

Emission
Le 15:16 man has an *e* of semen go
15:17 upon which the *e* of semen
15:18 lie down with an *e* of semen
15:32 from whom an *e* of semen may
18:20 not give your *e* as semen to
18:23 not give your *e* to any beast
19:20 and has an *e* of semen, when
20:15 seminal *e* to a beast, he
22:4 there goes out a seminal *e*
Nu 5:13 and has an *e* of semen
5:20 has put in you his seminal *e*

Emitted
Ex 34:29 the skin of his face *e* rays

Ex 34:30 skin of his face *e* rays and
34:35 skin of Moses' face *e* rays

Emmaus
Lu 24:13 from Jerusalem and named *E*

Emotion
Mr 16:8 strong *e* were gripping them

Emotions
Ge 43:30 his inward *e* were excited
1Ki 3:26 her inward *e* were excited

Employ
1Sa 28:8 *E* divination, please, for
Eze 27:15 were merchants in your *e*
27:21 merchants in your *e*

Employed
1Ch 20:3 *e* at sawing stones and at

Employing
Jer 23:31 ones who are *e* their tongue

Employment
2Ch 29:19 removed from *e* during his
Eze 39:14 be men for continual *e*

Employs
De 18:10 anyone who *e* divination, a

Empowered
Ec 5:19 *e* him to eat from it and to

Emptied
Ge 24:20 she quickly *e* her jar into
2Ch 24:11 *e* the chest and lifted it
Isa 24:3 the land will be *e*, and
Jer 48:11 *e* from one vessel into
Na 2:2 those emptying out have *e* them
Php 2:7 *e* himself and took a slave's

Emptiness
Isa 34:11 measuring line of *e* and the
Mic 6:14 *e* will be in the midst of
Na 2:10 *E* and voidness, and a city

Empty
Ge 37:24 At the time the pit was *e*
41:27 the seven *e* ears of grain
De 32:10 And in an *e*, howling desert
Jg 7:16 and large *e* jars, and torches
2Ki 4:3 all your neighbors, *e* vessels
Ne 5:13 become shaken out and *e*
Job 6:18 into the *e* place and perish
11:3 Will your *e* talk itself put
12:24 wander about in an *e* place
26:7 the north over the *e* place
Ps 2:1 kept muttering an *e* thing
4:2 you keep loving *e* things
Pr 13:25 the wicked ones will be *e*
Ec 11:3 *e* out a sheer downpour upon
Isa 16:6 his *e* talk will not be so
29:8 awakes and his soul is *e*
29:21 one with *e* arguments
32:6 hungry one to go *e*, and he
44:25 the signs of the *e* talkers
Jer 4:23 the land . . . was *e* and waste
14:3 with their vessels *e*
48:12 vessels they will *e* out
48:30 his *e* talk—they will not
50:36 sword against the *e* talkers
51:2 who will make her land *e*
51:34 has set me as an *e* vessel
Eze 24:10 And *e* out the broth, and
24:11 Stand it *e* upon its coals
Hab 1:17 he will *e* out his dragnet
Mal 3:10 *e* out upon you a blessing
Mr 12:3 and sent him away *e*
Lu 1:53 sent away *e* those who had
20:10 sent him away *e*, after
20:11 dishonored and sent away *e*
Ac 4:25 meditate upon *e* things
2Co 9:3 not prove *e* in this respect
Eph 5:6 man deceive you with *e* words
Col 2:8 the philosophy and *e* deception
1Ti 6:20 *e* speeches that violate what
2Ti 2:16 *e* speeches that violate
Jas 2:20 to know, O *e* man, that faith

Empty-handed
Ge 31:42 now have sent me away *e*
Ex 3:21 you go, you will not go *e*
23:15 must not appear before me *e*
34:20 not appear before me *e*
De 15:13 you must not send him out *e*
16:16 appear before Jehovah *e*
Ru 1:21 it is *e* that Jehovah has made
3:17 come *e* to your mother-in-law
Job 22:9 Widows you have sent away *e*

:mpty-headed
Sa 6:20 as one of the *e* men uncovers
:o 1:21 became *e* in their reasonings

:mptying
:e 42:35 when they were *e* their sacks
sa 24:1 Jehovah is *e* the land and
:a 2:2 those *e* out have emptied them

:nable
:c 6:2 God does not *e* him to eat

:nacting
sa 10:1 are *e* harmful regulations

:naim
:e 38:14 at the entrance of *E*, which
38:21 temple prostitute in *E* along

:nam
os 15:34 En-gannim, Tappuah and *E*

:nan
:u 1:15 Ahira the son of *E*
2:29 Ahira the son of *E*
7:78 Ahira the son of *E*
7:83 offering of Ahira the son of *E*
10:27 Ahira the son of *E*

:ncamp
:x 13:20 to *e* at Etham at the edge of
14:2 *e* before Pihahiroth between
14:2 you are to *e* by the sea
19:2 and to *e* in the wilderness
:u 1:52 Israel must *e* each with
1:53 Levites should *e* around the
2:2 *e*, each man by his three-tribe
2:2 in front of the tent . . . *e*
2:17 *e*, so they should set out
9:17 the sons of Israel would *e*
9:18 order of Jehovah they would *e*
9:23 order of Jehovah they would *e*
10:31 we may *e* in the wilderness
Sa 12:28 *e* against the city, and
Ki 6:8 you will *e* with me
sa 29:3 *e* on all sides against you
er 50:29 *E* against her all around
ec 9:8 *e* as an outpost for my house

:ncamped
:e 26:17 Isaac moved from there and *e*
31:25 Laban had *e* his brothers in
:u 2:34 *e* in their three-tribe
3:23 They were *e* to the west
3:29 Kohath were *e* on the side of
3:35 were *e* on the side of the
9:18 they would remain *e*
9:20 they would remain *e*, and at
9:22 Israel remained *e* and would
21:10 pulled away and *e* in Oboth
21:11 and *e* in Iye-abarim, in the
22:1 and *e* on the desert plains of
os 11:5 *e* together at the waters of
Sa 4:1 Philistines themselves *e* in
13:16 they had *e* in Michmash
26:5 place where Saul had *e*, and
Sa 23:13 *e* in the low plain of the
Ki 16:16 people that were *e* heard
20:29 continued *e* for seven days
:zr 8:15 kept *e* there three days
sa 29:1 the town where David *e*
:u 21:20 surrounded by *e* armies

:ncamping
Ki 16:15 were *e* against Gibbethon

:ncampment
:e 12:9, 9 *e* to *e* toward the Negeb
13:3, 3 *e* to *e* out of the Negeb
:u 10:34 marching out from the *e*
's 27:3 an *e* should pitch tent
:ze 1:24 like the sound of an *e*

:ncampments
:u 13:19 in *e* or in fortifications
:ze 4:2 and set *e* against it and put

:ncamps
:u 1:51 tabernacle *e*, the Levites

:ncircle
:e 37:7 sheaves proceeded to *e* and
:e 32:10 began to *e* him, to take care
Ki 11:8 must *e* the king all around
Ch 23:7 Levites must *e* the king all
ob 16:13 His archers *e* me; He splits
:a 3:5 *e* me with poisonous plant and
:u 19:43 will *e* you and distress you

:ncircled
Sa 22:5 deadly breaking waves *e* me
Ps 18:4 The ropes of death *e* me
40:12 calamities *e* me until there
116:3 The ropes of death *e* me
Jon 2:3 Then a very river *e* me
2:5 Waters *e* me clear to the soul
Joh 10:24 Jews *e* him and began to say
Heb 11:30 had been *e* for seven days
Re 20:9 *e* the camp of the holy ones

Encirclement
Eze 21:14 is making an *e* of them

Encircling
Ge 2:11 *e* the entire land of Havilah
2:13 *e* the entire land of Cush
1Ki 7:24 *e* it, ten in a cubit

Enclave
Jos 16:9 sons of Ephraim had *e* cities

Enclosed
Ps 17:10 *e* themselves with their own
22:16 evildoers . . . have *e* me
Lu 5:6 *e* a great multitude of fish

Enclosing
1Ki 7:24 ten in a cubit, *e* the sea
2Ch 4:3 ten in a cubit, *e* the sea all
Job 26:9 *E* the face of the throne
Jon 2:5 watery deep itself kept *e* me

Enclosure
1Sa 17:20 When he came to the camp *e*
26:5 lying in the camp *e* with
26:7 asleep in the camp *e* with
2Ch 4:9 the great *e* and the doors
4:9 the doors belonging to the *e*
6:13 in the middle of the *e*
Ho 13:8 rip apart the *e* of their heart

Enclosures
Hab 3:17 may be no herd in the *e*

Encounter
Nu 20:20 Edom came on out to *e* him
1Sa 10:3 *e* you three men going up to
2Ki 4:29 In case you *e* anyone, you
10:15 *e* Jehonadab the son of
2Ch 35:20 Josiah went out to an *e*
Job 5:14 They *e* darkness even by day
Ho 13:8 I shall *e* them like a bear
Mr 14:13 a man . . . will *e* you

Encountered
Ex 5:20 that they *e* Moses and Aaron
1Sa 25:20 So she *e* them
2Ki 10:13 *e* the brothers of Ahaziah
Jer 41:6 soon as he *e* them he

Encountering
Ge 32:19 speak to Esau on your *e* him
Ex 14:27 were fleeing from *e* it, but
Pr 17:12 be an *e* by a man of a bear

Encounters
Pr 27:16 oil is what his right hand *e*

Encourage
De 3:28 *e* him and strengthen him
2Sa 11:25 throw it down. And *e* him
Ac 11:23 *e* them all to continue in
27:33 Paul began to *e* one and all
27:34 I *e* you to take some food
2Co 8:6 led us to *e* Titus that, just
9:5 to *e* the brothers to come to

Encouraged
2Ch 35:2 *e* them in the service of the
Ac 15:32 *e* the brothers with many a
16:40 saw the brothers they *e* them
20:1 he had *e* them and bidden them
1Co 14:31 all may learn and all be *e*
1Ti 1:3 *e* you to stay in Ephesus when

Encouragement
Ac 13:15 word of *e* for the people
15:31 they rejoiced over the *e*
Ro 1:12 interchange of *e* among you
2Co 8:17 has indeed responded to the *e*
Php 2:1 there is any *e* in Christ
Heb 6:18 *e* to lay hold on the hope set
13:22 bear with this word of *e*
1Pe 5:12 to give *e* and an earnest

Encourages
1Co 14:3 *e* and consoles men by his

Encouraging
Ac 14:22 *e* them to remain in the
20:2 *e* the ones there with many a
Heb 10:25 *e* one another, and all the

Encroach
1Th 4:6 and *e* upon the rights of his

End
Ge 6:13 The *e* of all flesh has come
8:3 *e* of a hundred and fifty days
8:6 at the *e* of forty days Noah
16:3 *e* of ten years of Abram's
27:25 to the *e* that my soul may
41:1 at the *e* of two full years
47:21, 21 one *e* . . . to its other *e*
Ex 9:14 to the *e* that you may know
12:41 *e* of the four hundred and
25:19 make one cherub on this *e*
25:19 and one cherub on that *e*
26:4 cloth at the *e* of the series
26:15 acacia wood, standing on *e*
26:28, 28 through from *e* to *e*
36:11 tent cloth at the junction *e*
36:20 acacia wood, standing on *e*
36:33 frames from one *e* to the
37:8 One cherub was on the *e* over
37:8 cherub on the *e* over here
Nu 13:25 at the *e* of forty days they
14:33 to their *e* in the wilderness
14:35 they will come to their *e*
16:40 to the *e* that no strange man
17:13 *e* up in expiring that way
23:10 let my *e* turn out afterward
24:14 in the *e* of the days
24:20 his *e* afterward will be even
32:13 came to their *e*
De 2:14 had come to their *e* from the
2:15 until they came to their *e*
4:32 one *e* of the heavens clear to
4:32 to the other *e* of the heavens
9:11 at the *e* of the forty days
13:7 from one *e* of the land to the
13:7 to the other *e* of the land
14:28 At the *e* of three years you
15:1 At the *e* of every seven years
28:49 from the *e* of the earth
28:64 one *e* of the earth to the
28:64 to the other *e* of the earth
30:4 people should be at the *e* of
31:10 At the *e* of every seven years
32:20 see what their *e* will be
32:29 consider their *e* afterward
Jos 3:2 at the *e* of the three days
8:24 until they came to their *e*
9:16 at the *e* of three days, after
10:20 until these came to their *e*
15:1 the Negeb at its southern *e*
15:5 up to the *e* of the Jordan
15:5 at the *e* of the Jordan
18:19 the southern *e* of the Jordan
Jg 11:39 at the *e* of two months that
Ru 2:23 the harvest . . . came to an *e*
3:18 brought the matter to an *e*
1Sa 3:12 from beginning to *e*
2Sa 2:23 with the butt *e* of the spear
14:26 *e* of every year that he
15:7 at the *e* of forty years
20:18 will certainly *e* the matter
24:8 *e* of nine months and twenty
1Ki 2:39 at the *e* of three years
8:40 to the *e* that they may fear
8:60 to the *e* that all the peoples
9:10 at the *e* of twenty years
17:7 at the *e* of some days that
2Ki 8:3 at the *e* of seven years
10:21, 21 to be full from *e* to *e*
18:10 at the *e* of three years
21:16, 16 Jerusalem from *e* to *e*
2Ch 6:31 *e* that they may fear you by
8:1 *e* of twenty years, in which
20:16 *e* of the torrent valley in
Ezr 9:11, 11 filled it from *e* to *e*
Ne 1:9 to be at the *e* of the heavens
3:21 as the *e* of Eliashib's house
Es 9:28 not come to an *e* among their
Job 4:9 they come to an *e*
6:11 what is my *e*, that I should
7:6 My days . . . *e* in hopelessness
7:9 certainly comes to its *e*
8:7 your own *e* afterward would
9:22 he is bringing to their *e*
16:3 Is there an *e* to windy words?
18:2 at putting an *e* to words
22:5 there be no *e* to your errors
28:3 *e* to the darkness he has set
31:40 words of Job . . . to an *e*
42:12 he blessed the *e* of Job
Ps 7:9 wicked ones come to an *e*

Ps 12:1 loyal one has come to an *e*
31:10 my life has come to an *e*
37:20 They must come to their *e*
37:20 they must come to their *e*
39:4 O Jehovah, to know my *e*
39:10 I myself have come to an *e*
57:2 bringing them to an *e* on my
59:13 Bring them to an *e* in rage
59:13 Bring them to an *e*, that
71:13 may those come to their *e*
72:20 prayers . . . come to their *e*
73:19 they have reached their *e*
74:11 to make an *e* of us
78:33 an *e* as if a mere exhalation
90:7 come to an *e* in your anger
102:3 days have come to an *e* just
105:45 *e* that they might keep his
119:96 perfection I have seen an *e*
119:139 ardor has made an *e* of me
143:7 My spirit has come to an *e*
Pr 1:21 upper *e* of the noisy streets
5:11 your organism come to an *e*
14:12 ways of death are the *e* of
16:25 ways of death are the *e* of
22:8 his fury will come to its *e*
23:32 At its *e* it bites just like a
Ec 4:8 is no *e* to all his hard work
4:16 is no *e* to all the people
7:2 that is the *e* of all mankind
7:8 Better is the *e* afterward of a
10:13 *e* afterward of his mouth is
12:12 of many books there is no *e*
Isa 7:3 *e* of the conduit of the upper
9:7 to peace there will be no *e*
10:18 He will bring to an *e*
10:25 will have come to an *e*
15:6 the grass has come to an *e*
16:4 oppressor has reached his *e*
21:16 must even come to its *e*
23:15 *e* of seventy years it will
23:17 at the *e* of seventy years
24:13 gathering has come to an *e*
29:20 tyrant must reach his *e*
31:3 all of them come to an *e*
32:10 will have come to an *e*
66:17 all together reach their *e*
Jer 8:20 the summer has come to an *e*
12:12 from one *e* of the land even
12:12 to the other *e* of the land
13:6 at the *e* of many days that
14:12 bringing them to their *e*
16:4 they will come to an *e*
20:18 days should come to their *e*
25:33 from one *e* of the earth
25:33 to the other *e* of the earth
27:15 to the *e* that I shall
34:14 *e* of seven years you men
36:3 *e* that they may return
42:7 *e* of ten days that the word
51:13 your *e* has come, the
51:31 been captured at every *e*
La 2:11 to their *e* in sheer tears
3:22 mercies . . . not come to an *e*
4:18 Our *e* has drawn near
4:18 for our *e* has come
Eze 3:16 at the *e* of seven days that
5:12 come to their *e* in the midst
7:2, 2 An *e*, the *e*, has come upon
7:3 Now the *e* is upon you, and I
7:6 An *e* itself must come
7:6 *e* must come; it must awaken
13:14 you must come to an *e* in
21:25 time of the error of the *e*
21:29 time of the error of the *e*
29:13 At the *e* of forty years I
31:14 to the *e* that none of the
39:14 To the *e* of seven months
43:23 *e* of the purifying from sin
46:18 *e* that my people may not
Da 1:5 *e* of these they might stand
1:15 at the *e* of ten days their
1:18 *e* of the days that the king
2:44 an *e* to all these kingdoms
4:29 *e* of twelve lunar months he
4:34 And at the *e* of the days I
7:28 point is the *e* of the matter
8:17 is for the time of the *e*
8:19 the appointed time of the *e*
9:26 *e* of it will be by the flood
9:26 until the *e* there will be war
11:6 *e* of some years they will
11:13 and at the *e* of the times
11:27 *e* is yet for the time
11:35 until the time of the *e*
Da 11:40 time of the *e* the king of
11:45 come all the way to his *e*
12:4 book, until the time of the *e*
12:6 the *e* of the wonderful things
12:9 up until the time of the *e*
12:13 go toward the *e;* and you
12:13 lot at the *e* of the days
Ho 8:4 idols, to the *e* that they may
11:6 make an *e* of his bars and
Am 5:14 to the *e* that you people may
8:2 The *e* has come to my people
8:10 *e* result of it as a bitter day
9:12 to the *e* that they may take
Mic 6:16 to the *e* that I may make
Na 3:3 is no *e* to the dead bodies
Hab 2:3 it keeps panting on to the *e*
Zec 12:7 to the *e* that the beauty of
Mt 10:22 he that has endured to the *e*
15:4 *e* up in death
24:6 but the *e* is not yet
24:13 he that has endured to the *e*
24:14 and then the *e* will come
Mr 3:26 Satan . . . is coming to an *e*
7:10 reviles . . . *e* up in death
13:7 but the *e* is not yet
13:13 he that has endured to the *e*
Lu 1:33 will be no *e* of his kingdom
21:9 *e* does not occur immediately
Joh 13:1 loved them to the *e*
Ac 26:16 to this *e* I have made
Ro 5:21 To what *e?* That, just as sin
6:21 *e* of those things is death
6:22 and the *e* everlasting life
10:4 Christ is the *e* of the Law
14:9 For to this *e* Christ died
1Co 1:8 also make you firm to the *e*
9:18 to the *e* that I may not
15:24 the *e*, when he hands over
2Co 1:13 to recognize to the *e*
2:9 to this *e* also I write to
3:13 not gaze intently at the *e* of
11:15 their *e* shall be according
Eph 3:10 This was to the *e* that now
3:16 to the *e* that he may grant
6:18 to that *e* keep awake with
Col 1:10 to the *e* of fully pleasing
1:29 To this *e* I am indeed
1Th 2:12 to the *e* that you should go
3:13 to the *e* that he may make
2Th 1:11 To that very *e* indeed we
1Ti 1:4 which *e* up in nothing, but
4:10 For to this *e* we are working
Heb 1:2 has at the *e* of these days
3:6 the hope firm to the *e*
3:14 firm to the *e*
6:11 the hope down to the *e*
6:16 oath is the *e* of every
7:3 nor an *e* of life, but having
11:22 Joseph, nearing his *e*
1Pe 1:9 receive the *e* of your faith
1:20 at the *e* of the times for
2:8 To this very *e* they were also
4:2 to the *e* that he may live the
4:7 *e* of all things has drawn
4:17 *e* be of those who are not
Re 2:26 my deeds down to the *e* I
21:6 I am . . . beginning and the *e*
22:13 the beginning and the *e*

Endearment
Ca 1:2 expressions of *e* are better
1:4 mention your expressions of *e*
4:10 your expressions of *e* are, O
4:10 better your expressions of *e*
5:1 drunk with expressions of *e*
7:12 my expressions of *e* to you

Endeavored
Ga 2:10 have also earnestly *e* to do
1Th 2:17 *e* far more than is usual

Endeavoring
Eph 4:3 earnestly *e* to observe the

Ended
Ge 41:53 seven years . . . gradually *e*
Jer 36:23 roll *e* up in the fire that
Re 20:3 the thousand years were *e*
20:5 the thousand years were *e*
20:7 thousand years have been *e*

Endlessly
2Sa 2:26 the sword going to eat *e*

En-dor
Jos 17:11 *E* and its dependent towns
1Sa 28:7 spirit mediumship in *E*
Ps 83:10 They were annihilated at *E*

Endowed
Ge 30:20 God has *e* me, yes, me, with

Endowment
Ge 30:20 endowed . . . with a good *e*

Ends
Ex 23:2 after the crowd for evil *e*
25:18 them on both *e* of the cover
25:19 the cherubs at its two *e*
28:25 the two *e* of the two ropes
37:7 them on both *e* of the cover
37:8 cherubs . . . on both of its *e*
39:18 two *e* of the two ropes
De 33:17 to the *e* of the earth
1Sa 2:10 judge the *e* of the earth
Job 26:10 where light *e* in darkness
28:24 to the very *e* of the earth
Ps 2:8 the *e* of the earth as your own
22:27 All the *e* of the earth will
59:13 to the *e* of the earth. *Se'lah*
67:7 *e* of the earth will fear him
72:8 River to the *e* of the earth
98:3 *e* of the earth have seen the
Pr 14:13 grief is what rejoicing *e* up
30:4 all the *e* of the earth to rise
Isa 45:22 you at the *e* of the earth
52:10 all the *e* of the earth must
Jer 16:19 from the *e* of the earth
Eze 15:4 Both *e* of it the fire
Mic 5:4 as far as the *e* of the earth
Zec 9:10 River to the *e* of the earth
Mt 12:42 from the *e* of the earth to
Lu 11:31 came from the *e* of the earth
1Co 10:11 *e* of the systems of things
Heb 6:8 it *e* up with being burned

Endurable
Mt 10:15 will be more *e* for the land
11:22 be more *e* for Tyre and Sidon
11:24 *e* for the land of Sodom
Lu 10:12 more *e* for Sodom in that day
10:14 more *e* for Tyre and Sidon

Endurance
Lu 8:15 and bear fruit with *e*
21:19 By *e* on your part you will
Ro 2:7 by *e* in work that is good
5:3 that tribulation produces *e*
5:4 *e*, in turn, an approved
8:25 on waiting for it with *e*
15:4 through our *e* and through
15:5 supplies *e* and comfort grant
2Co 6:4 *e* of much, by tribulations
12:12 among you by all *e*
1Th 1:3 *e* due to your hope in our
2Th 1:4 because of your *e* and faith
3:5 into the *e* for the Christ
1Ti 6:11 love, *e*, mildness of temper
2Ti 3:10 closely followed . . . my *e*
Tit 2:2 in faith, in love, in *e*
Heb 10:36 you have need of *e*, in
12:1 run with *e* the race that is
Jas 1:3 of your faith works out *e*
1:4 *e* have its work complete
5:11 have heard of the *e* of Job
2Pe 1:6 to your self-control *e*, to
1:6 to your *e* godly devotion
Re 1:9 *e* in company with Jesus, came
2:2 your labor and *e*, and that
2:3 You are also showing *e*, and
2:19 faith and ministry and *e*
3:10 you kept the word about my *e*
13:10 *e* and faith of the holy ones
14:12 it means *e* for the holy ones

Endure
1Sa 24:20 Israel will certainly *e*
Job 20:21 his well-being will not *e*
Ps 101:5 arrogant heart . . . I cannot *e*
Pr 30:21 four it is not able to *e*
Jer 20:9 and I was unable to *e* it
Ro 12:12 *E* under tribulation
1Co 10:13 for you to be able to *e* it
2Co 1:6 *e* the same sufferings that we
4:10 *e* everywhere in our body
Eph 6:3 *e* a long time on the earth
Col 1:11 *e* fully and be long-suffering
1Pe 2:20 and being slapped, you *e* it
2:20 and you suffer, you *e* it

Endured
Mt 10:22 he that has *e* to the end is
24:13 he that has *e* to the end is
Mr 13:13 he that has *e* to the end is
Heb 10:32 you *e* a great contest under

Ieb 12:2 he *e* a torture stake
12:3 has *e* such contrary talk by
'as 5:11 happy those who have *e*

:ndures
Co 13:7 *e* all things
Pe 1:25 saying of Jehovah *e* forever

:nduring
er 5:15 It is an *e* nation. It is a
8:5 with an *e* unfaithfulness
:ze 22:14 Will your heart keep *e*
)a 6:26 One *e* to times indefinite
Ti 2:10 *e* all things for the sake of
2:12 if we go on *e*, we shall
Ieb 12:7 is for discipline you are *e*
as 1:12 man that keeps on *e* trial
Pe 1:23 the living and *e* God

:n-eglaim
:ze 47:10 from En-gedi even up to *E*

:nemies
ie 22:17 take . . . the gate of his *e*
49:8 the back of the neck of your *e*
:x 23:22 hostile to your *e* and harass
23:27 the neck of all your *e* to you
.e 26:7 chase your *e*, and they will
26:8 *e* will indeed fall before you
26:16 *e* will certainly eat it up
26:17 defeated before your *e*
26:32 *e* who are dwelling in it
26:34 are in the land of your *e*
26:36 in the lands of their *e*
26:37 in resistance before your *e*
26:38 land of your *e* must eat you
26:39 error in the lands of your *e*
26:41 into the land of their *e*
26:44 in the land of their *e*, I
Iu 10:9 and be saved from your *e*
10:35 let your *e* be scattered; and
14:42 not be defeated before your *e*
23:11 to execrate my *e* that I took
24:10 It was to execrate my *e* that
24:18 the possession of his *e*
32:21 until he drives away his *e*
)e 1:42 not be defeated before your *e*
6:19 by pushing away all your *e*
12:10 rest from all your *e*
20:1 battle against your *e* and you
20:3 the battle against your *e*
20:4 fight for you against your *e*
20:14 must eat the spoil of your *e*
21:10 to the battle against your *e*
23:9 into camp against your *e*
23:14 and to abandon your *e* to you
25:19 *e* round about in the land
28:7 Jehovah will cause your *e*
28:25 defeated before your *e*
28:31 Your sheep given to your *e*
28:48 serve your *e* whom Jehovah
28:68 to your *e* as slave men and
30:7 these oaths upon your *e* and
32:31 our *e* being the ones to
33:29 your *e* will cringe before
os 7:8 turned his back before his *e*
7:12 to rise up against their *e*
7:12 will turn before their *e*
7:13 to rise up against your *e*
10:13 take vengeance on its *e*
10:19 Chase after your *e*, and you
10:25 your *e* against whom you are
21:44 not one of all their *e* stood
21:44 All their *e* Jehovah gave
22:8 share of the spoil of your *e*
23:1 rest from all their *e* all
'g 2:14 into the hand of their *e*
2:14 able to stand before their *e*
2:18 out of the hand of their *e*
3:28 your *e*, the Moabites, into
5:31 Thus let all your *e* perish, O
8:34 of all their *e* round about
11:36 vengeance . . . upon your *e*
Sa 2:1 is widened against my *e*
4:3 from the palm of our *e*
12:10 out of the hand of our *e*
12:11 out of the hand of your *e*
14:24 taken vengeance upon my *e*
14:30 from the spoil of their *e*
14:47 about against all his *e*
18:25 on the *e* of the king
20:15 Jehovah cuts off the *e* of
20:16 at the hand of David's *e*
25:22 God do to the *e* of David
25:26 *e* and those seeking injury
25:29 soul of your *e*, he will

1Sa 29:8 fight against the *e* of my
30:26 the spoil of Jehovah's *e*
2Sa 3:18 the hand of all their *e*
5:20 broken through my *e* ahead
7:1 rest from all his *e* round
7:9 cut off all your *e* from
7:11 you rest from all your *e*
18:19 from the hand of his *e*
18:32 May the *e* of my lord the
19:9 out of the palm of our *e*
22:1 out of the palm of all his *e*
22:4 from my *e* I shall be saved
22:38 I will pursue my *e*, that I
22:41 And as for my *e*, you will
22:49 bringing me out from my *e*
1Ki 3:11 requested the soul of your *e*
8:48 in the land of their *e*
2Ki 17:39 the hand of all your *e*
21:14 into the hand of their *e*
21:14 and pillage to all their *e*
1Ch 14:11 God has broken through my *e*
17:8 I shall cut off all your *e*
17:10 I . . . humble all your *e*
21:12 of your *e* to overtake you
22:9 give him rest from all his *e*
2Ch 6:28 in case their *e* besiege them
6:34 war against their *e* in the
20:27 them rejoice over their *e*
20:29 against the *e* of Israel
Ne 4:15 *e* heard that it had become
5:9 reproach of the nations, our *e*
6:1 the rest of our *e* that I had
6:16 as soon as all our *e* heard
9:28 to the hand of their *e*
Es 8:13 themselves upon their *e*
9:1 *e* of the Jews had waited to
9:5 went striking down all their *e*
9:16 upon their *e* and a killing
9:22 Jews had rested from their *e*
Ps 3:7 strike all my *e* on the jaw
6:10 *e* will be very much ashamed
9:3 When my *e* turn back, They
17:9 *e* against my soul themselves
18:*super* of the palm of all his *e*
18:3 from my *e* I shall be saved
18:37 pursue my *e* and overtake
18:40 And as for my *e*, you will
18:48 escape . . . from my angry *e*
21:8 hand will find all your *e*
25:2 May my *e* not exult over me
25:19 how many my *e* have become
27:2 my adversaries and my *e*
27:6 above my *e* all around me
30:1 not let my *e* rejoice over me
31:15 Deliver me from . . . my *e*
35:19 who for no reason are my *e*
37:20 *e* of Jehovah will be like
38:19 my *e* who are alive became
41:2 over to the soul of his *e*
41:5 As for my *e*, they say what is
45:5 heart of the *e* of the king
54:7 upon my *e* my eye has looked
56:9 my *e* will turn back, on the
59:1 Deliver me from my *e*, O my
66:3 *e* will come cringing to you
68:1 arise, let his *e* be scattered
68:21 break the head of his *e*
68:23 have its portion from the *e*
69:4 being my *e* for no reason
69:18 account of my *e* redeem me
71:10 my *e* have said in regard to
72:9 *e* will lick the dust itself
78:53 the sea covered their *e*
80:6 *e* keep deriding as they please
81:14 *e* I would easily subdue
83:2 your very *e* are in an uproar
89:10 you have scattered your *e*
89:42 caused all his *e* to rejoice
89:51 How your *e* have reproached
92:9 look! your *e*, O Jehovah
92:9 your own *e* will perish
102:8 my *e* have reproached me
106:42 their *e* might oppress them
110:1 *e* as a stool for your feet
110:2 in the midst of your *e*
119:98 Wiser than my *e* your
127:5 speak with *e* in the gate
132:18 *e* I shall clothe with shame
138:7 of the anger of my *e* you
139:22 have become to me real *e*
143:9 Deliver me from my *e*
143:12 may you silence my *e*
Pr 16:7 *e* themselves to be at peace
Isa 1:24 will avenge myself on my *e*

Isa 9:11 *e* of that one he will goad
42:13 over his *e* he will show
59:18 due treatment to his *e*
62:8 grain as food to your *e*
66:6 what is deserved to his *e*
66:14 actually denounce his *e*
Jer 12:7 soul into the palm of her *e*
15:9 before their *e*, is the
15:14 to pass over with your *e*
17:4 will make you serve your *e*
19:7 before their *e* and by the
19:9 stress with which their *e*
20:4 by the sword of their *e*
20:5 into the hand of their *e*
21:7 into the hand of their *e*
34:20 into the hand of their *e*
34:21 into the hand of their *e*
44:30 into the hand of his *e*
49:37 Elamites before their *e*
La 1:2 They have become *e* to her
1:5 who are her *e* are unconcerned
1:21 All my *e* themselves have
2:16 *e* have opened their mouth
3:46 our *e* have opened their mouth
3:52 My *e* have positively hunted
Eze 39:27 out of the lands of their *e*
Am 9:4 into captivity before their *e*
Mic 4:10 out of the palm of your *e*
5:9 *e* of yours will be cut off
7:6 a man's *e* are the men of his
Na 1:2 he is resentful toward his *e*
1:8 will pursue his very *e*
3:13 To your *e* the gates of your
Mt 5:44 to love your *e* and to pray
10:36 a man's *e* will be persons of
22:44 put your *e* beneath your feet
Mr 12:36 put your *e* beneath your feet
Lu 1:71 a salvation from our *e* and
1:74 rescued from the hands of *e*
6:27 Continue to love your *e*, to
6:35 continue to love your *e* and
19:27 *e* of mine that did not want
19:43 *e* will build around you a
20:43 *e* as a stool for your feet
Ac 2:35 *e* as a stool for your feet
Ro 5:10 *e*, we became reconciled to
11:28 they are *e* for your sakes
1Co 15:25 put all *e* under his feet
Php 3:18 as the *e* of the torture stake
Col 1:21 were once alienated and *e*
Heb 1:13 *e* as a stool for your feet
10:13 *e* should be placed as a
Re 11:5 fire . . . devours their *e*
11:12 and their *e* beheld them

Enemy
Ex 15:6 Jehovah, can shatter an *e*
15:9 The *e* said, I shall pursue
Le 26:25 given into the hand of an *e*
De 28:53 your *e* will hem you in
28:55 your *e* will hem you in
28:57 your *e* will hem you in
32:27 vexation from the *e*
32:42 heads of the leaders of the *e*
33:27 away from before you the *e*
Jg 16:23 into our hand Samson our *e*
16:24 our *e* and the devastator of
1Sa 18:29 to be an *e* of David always
19:17 sent my *e* away that he
24:4 giving your *e* into your hand
24:19 man finds his *e*, will he
26:8 surrendered your *e* into your
2Sa 4:8 Saul your *e* who looked for
22:18 from my strong *e*, From
1Ki 8:33 are defeated before the *e*
8:37 in case their *e* besieges
8:44 to the war against their *e*
8:46 and abandon them to the *e*
8:46 captive to the land of the *e*
21:20 found me, O *e* of mine
2Ch 6:24 are defeated before an *e*
6:36 abandon them to an *e*, and
25:8 you to stumble before an *e*
26:13 help the king against the *e*
Ezr 8:22 to help us against the *e* in
8:31 out of the palm of the *e* and
Es 7:6 and *e*, is this bad Haman
Job 13:24 regard me as an *e* of yours
27:7 *e* become in every way a
33:10 He takes me for an *e* of his
Ps 7:5 Let an *e* pursue my soul
8:2 the *e* and the one taking his
9:6 O you *e*, your desolations have
13:2 How long will my *e* be exalted

Ps 13:4 my *e* may not say: I have won
18:17 from my strong *e*, And from
31:8 into the hand of the *e*
41:11 *e* does not shout in triumph
42:9 the oppression of the *e*
43:2 the oppression by the *e*
44:16 *e* and the one taking his
55:3 Due to the voice of the *e*
55:12 *e* that proceeded to reproach
61:3 tower in the face of the *e*
64:1 the dreadfulness of the *e*
74:3 *e* has treated badly in the
74:10 *e* keep treating your name
74:18 *e* himself has reproached
89:22 *e* will make exactions upon
106:10 them from the hand of the *e*
143:3 For the *e* has pursued my soul
Pr 24:17 your *e* falls, do not rejoice
Isa 63:10 changed into an *e* of theirs
Jer 6:25 the sword belonging to the *e*
15:11 distress, against the *e*
18:17 scatter them before the *e*
30:14 with the stroke of an *e*
31:16 from the land of the *e*
44:30 king of Babylon, his *e* and
La 1:9 for the *e* has put on great airs
1:16 the *e* has put on great airs
2:3 back from before the *e*
2:4 has trodden his bow like an *e*
2:5 Jehovah has become like an *e*
2:7 Into the hand of the *e* he has
2:17 he causes the *e* to rejoice
2:22 *e* himself exterminated them
4:12 *e* would come into the gates
Eze 36:2 reason that the *e* has said
Ho 8:3 Let one who is an *e* pursue him
Mic 2:8 to rise up as an outright *e*
7:8 O you woman *e* of mine
7:10 my *e* will see, and shame
Na 3:11 seek a stronghold from the *e*
Zep 3:15 He has turned away your *e*
Mt 5:43 You heard . . . hate your *e*
13:25 *e* came and oversowed weeds
13:28 An *e*, a man, did this
13:39 *e* that sowed them is the
Lu 10:19 over all the power of the *e*
Ac 13:10 *e* of everything righteous
Ro 12:20 if your *e* is hungry, feed
1Co 15:26 the last *e*, death is to be
Ga 4:16 *e* because I tell you the truth
2Th 3:15 considering him as an *e*, but
Jas 4:4 himself an *e* of God

Enemy's
Ex 23:4 *e* bull or his ass going astray

Energetic
Es 10:2 his *e* work and his mightiness

Energies
Ec 10:10 will exert his own vital *e*

Energy
De 33:11 Bless . . . his vital *e*
1Sa 2:4 do gird on vital *e*
2Sa 22:40 with vital *e* for the battle
Job 40:16 *e* in the tendons of its
Ps 18:32 girding me . . . with vital *e*
18:39 with vital *e* for warfare
33:17 its vital *e* it does not
59:11 By your vital *e* make them
60:12 we shall gain vital *e*
84:7, 7 on from vital *e* to vital *e*
108:13 we shall gain vital *e*
118:15 is demonstrating vital *e*
118:16 is demonstrating vital *e*
Pr 31:3 give your vital *e* to women
Ec 12:3 the men of vital *e* have bent
Isa 5:22 men with vital *e* for
40:26 the abundance of dynamic *e*
40:29 one without dynamic *e* he
Jer 46:22 with vital *e* men will go
48:14 men of vital *e* for the war
Da 3:20 men of vital *e* who were in
Ho 12:3 with his dynamic *e* he
Joe 2:22 must give their vital *e*
Na 2:3 his men of vital *e* are
Hab 3:19 Sovereign Lord is my vital *e*

Enfeebled
Heb 12:12 hang down and the *e* knees

Enforce
Da 6:7 and to *e* an interdict, that

Engage
De 2:5 Do not *e* in strife with them
2:9 molest Moab or *e* in war with
De 2:19 molest them or *e* in strife
2:24 and *e* in war with him
2Ki 14:10 should you *e* in strife under
2Ch 25:19 *e* in strife in a bad
Da 11:40 *e* with him in a pushing, and
Ho 2:19 I will *e* you to me for time
2:19 *e* you to me in righteousness
2:20 *e* you to me in faithfulness
Jas 4:13 *e* in business and make

Engaged
Ge 4:17 he *e* in building a city and
Ex 19:14 *e* in washing their mantles
22:16 a virgin who is not *e*, and
Nu 26:9 *e* in a struggle against Moses
26:9 they *e* in a struggle against
De 20:7 *e* to a woman and has not
22:23 a virgin girl *e* to a man
22:25 found the girl who was *e*
22:27 The girl who was *e* screamed
22:28 a virgin who has not been *e*
28:30 will become *e* to a woman
Jg 9:27 *e* in gathering the grapes of
13:1 Israel *e* again in doing what
1Sa 25:2 *e* in shearing his sheep at
2Sa 3:14 Michal, whom I *e* to myself
2Ch 13:3 Abijah *e* in the war with
35:14 were *e* in offering up the
Ps 60:*super* he *e* in a struggle with
Ec 2:4 I *e* in greater works. I built
Jer 2:2 during your being *e* to marry
Zec 10:5 get *e* in battle, for Jehovah

Engagement
1Ki 20:14 Who will open the battle *e*?
20:29 that the *e* in battle began

Engaging
2Ch 26:11 have a force *e* in war
26:13 men *e* in war with the
Ro 15:16 *e* in the holy work of the

En-gannim
Jos 15:34 Zanoah and *E*, Tappuah and
19:21 Remeth and *E* and En-haddah
21:29 *E* and its pasture ground

En-gedi
Jos 15:62 the City of Salt and *E*
1Sa 23:29 difficult to approach at *E*
24:1 is in the wilderness of *E*
2Ch 20:2 that is to say, *E*
Ca 1:14 among the vineyards of *E*
Eze 47:10 from *E* even up to En-eglaim

Engine
Eze 26:9 the strike of his attack *e*

Engineers
2Ch 26:15 the invention of *e*, that

Engines
2Ch 26:15 *e* of war, the invention of

Engirdles
Job 30:18 my long garment it *e* me

Engrave
Ex 28:9 *e* upon them the names of the
28:11 *e* the two stones with the
28:36 *e* upon it with the engravings
Eze 4:1 and *e* upon it a city, even

Engraved
Ex 32:16 writing of God *e* upon the
39:6 *e* with the engravings of a
1Ki 6:29 *e* carvings of cherubs and
7:36 he *e* upon the plates of its
2Ch 3:7 he *e* cherubs upon the walls
Isa 49:16 Upon my palms I have *e* you
Jer 17:1 *e* on the tablet of their
2Co 3:7 was *e* in letters in stones

Engraving
2Ch 2:14 at cutting every sort of *e*
Zec 3:9, 9 Here I am *e* its *e*, is the

Engravings
Ex 28:11 with the *e* of a seal, you
28:21 With the *e* of a seal they
28:36 upon it with the *e* of a seal
39:6 with the *e* of a seal according
39:14 with the *e* of a seal, each
39:30 with the *e* of a seal
1Ki 6:29 *e* of blossoms, inside and
6:32 the *e* of blossoms, and he
6:35 *e* of blossoms, and overlaid
2Ch 2:7 and knowing how to cut *e*
Ps 74:6 *e* of it, one and all, they

En-haddah
Jos 19:21 and *E* and Beth-pazzez

En-hakkore
Jg 15:19 he called its name *E*

Enhance
Isa 10:15 ax *e* itself over the one

En-hazor
Jos 19:37 Kedesh and Edrei and *E*

Enjoy
Ex 30:38 to *e* its smell must be cut
2Ki 14:10 *E* your honor and dwell in
Job 20:18 but which he will not *e*
Ps 55:14 we used to *e* sweet intimacy
Pr 7:18 *e* each other with love
Am 5:21 I shall not *e* the smell of
Lu 12:19 ease, eat, drink, *e* yourself
15:23 let us eat and *e* ourselves
15:24 they started to *e* themselves
15:29 *e* myself with my friends
15:32 just had to *e* ourselves and
Ac 7:41 *e* themselves in the works of
24:2 Seeing that we *e* great peace
27:3 his friends and *e* their care
Ro 5:1 *e* peace with God through our
Re 11:10 *e* themselves, and they will

Enjoyed
1Ch 29:17 *e* seeing make offerings

Enjoying
De 33:29 people *e* salvation in Jehovah
Lu 16:19 *e* himself from day to day

Enjoyment
Isa 11:3 *e* by him in the fear of
1Ti 6:17 all things richly for our *e*
Heb 11:25 the temporary *e* of sin

Enlarge
1Ch 4:10 actually *e* my territory
Ps 71:21 May you *e* my greatness
Jer 4:30 *e* your eyes with black paint
Mt 23:5 and *e* the fringes of their

Enlightened
Job 33:30 he may be *e* with the light
Eph 1:18 your heart having been *e*
Heb 6:4 have once for all been *e*
10:32 you were *e*, you endured

Enliven
Ps 85:6 yourself not *e* us again

En-mishpat
Ge 14:7 came to *E*, that is, Kadesh

Enmities
Ga 5:20 *e*, strife, jealousy, fits of

Enmity
Ge 3:15 I shall put *e* between you
Nu 35:21 in *e* he has struck him with
35:22 without *e* that he has pushed
35:23 he was not at *e* with him
Eze 25:15 an indefinitely lasting *e*
35:5 an indefinitely lasting *e*
Lu 23:12 had continued at *e* between
Ro 8:7 of the flesh means *e* with God
Eph 2:15 he abolished the *e*, the Law
2:16 killed off the *e* by means of
Jas 4:4 with the world is *e* with God

Enoch
Ge 4:17 and gave birth to *E*
4:17 by the name of his son *E*
4:18 Later there was born to *E*
5:18 Jared . . . became father to *E*
5:19 after his fathering *E* Jared
5:21 *E* lived on for sixty-five
5:22 *E* went on walking with the
5:23 all the days of *E* amounted
5:24 *E* kept walking with the
1Ch 1:3 *E*, Methuselah, Lamech
Lu 3:37 son of *E*, son of Jared, son of
Heb 11:5 By faith *E* was transferred
Jude 14 *E*, prophesied also regarding

Enosh
Ge 4:26 proceeded to call his name *E*
5:6 Seth . . . became father to *E*
5:7 And after his fathering *E* Seth
5:9 And *E* lived on for ninety years
5:10 after his fathering Kenan *E*
5:11 days of *E* amounted to nine
1Ch 1:1 Adam, Seth, *E*
Lu 3:38 son of *E*, son of Seth, son of

Enough
Ge 45:28 It is *e*! Joseph my son is
Ex 9:28 *e* . . . of God's thunders and
36:7 *e* for all the work to be done

Ex 36:7 proved to be . . . more than *e*
Le 5:7 he cannot afford *e* for a sheep
12:8 cannot afford *e* for a sheep
14:21 and does not have *e* means
25:26 find *e* for its repurchase
25:28 not find *e* to give back to
Nu 16:3 That is *e* of you, because the
16:7 *e* of you, you sons of Levi
De 1:6 You have dwelt long *e* in this
2:3 around this mountain long *e*
3:26 That is *e* of you! Never speak
23:24 *e* grapes for you to satisfy
30:9 more than *e* in every work of
Jos 17:16 mountainous region is not *e*
Jg 6:38 he got to drain off *e* dew
21:14 they did not find *e* for them
2Sa 12:8 if it were not *e*, I was
22:37 room large *e* for my steps
24:16 It is *e*! Now let your hand
1Ki 19:4 It is *e*! Now, O Jehovah
1Ch 21:15 It is *e*! Now let your hand
2Ch 30:3 because not *e* priests, on
Ne 8:2 all intelligent *e* to listen
Job 15:11 consolations of God not *e*
27:14 will not have *e* food
Ps 18:36 room large *e* for my steps
34:12 loving *e* days to see what is
88:3 soul has had *e* of calamities
129:1 Long *e* they have shown
129:2 Long *e* they have shown
Pr 30:15 four that have not said: *E*!
30:16 and fire that has not said: *E*!
Ec 4:13 come to know *e* to be warned
8:17 say they are wise *e* to know
Isa 1:11 *e* of whole burnt offerings
Jer 7:32 there being *e* place
Eze 16:20 is that not *e* of your acts
44:6 *e* of you because of all your
45:9 *e* of you, O chieftains of
Da 2:26 competent *e* to make known to
5:8 competent *e* to read the
5:15 not competent *e* to show the
Na 2:12 to pieces *e* for his whelps
Mt 10:25 It is *e* for the disciple to
25:9 may not be quite *e* for us and
Mr 14:41 It is *e*! The hour has come!
Lu 6:48 was not strong *e* to shake it
14:28 if he has *e* to complete it
16:3 I am not strong *e* to dig
22:38 He said to them: It is *e*
Joh 6:7 of loaves is not *e* for them
14:8 show us the Father . . . is *e*
1Co 3:2 for you were not yet strong *e*
3:2 neither are you strong *e* now
2Ti 1:18 you know well *e*

Enraged
2Ki 6:11 king of Syria became *e* over
2Ch 26:19 Uzziah became *e* while in
Pr 15:18 An *e* man stirs up contention
19:3 becomes *e* against Jehovah

Enraging
Job 12:6 ones *e* God have the safety

Enrich
1Sa 17:25 king will *e* him with great
Ps 65:9 You *e* it very much

Enriched
1Co 1:5 *e* in him, in full ability to
2Co 9:11 you are being *e* for every

Enricher
1Sa 2:7 Jehovah is . . . an *E*

En-rimmon
Ne 11:29 in *E* and in Zorah and in

En-rogel
Jos 15:7 termination proved to be *E*
18:16 and went down to *E*
2Sa 17:17 were standing at *E*
1Ki 1:9 Zoheleth, which is beside *E*

Enrolled
1Ch 5:1 not to be *e* genealogically for
5:17 all of them *e* genealogically
9:1 they were *e* genealogically
Ne 7:5 themselves *e* genealogically
2Ti 2:4 one who *e* him as a soldier
Heb 12:23 firstborn who have been *e*

Enrollment
1Ch 5:7 the genealogical *e* by their
7:5 genealogical *e* of them all
7:7 and their genealogical *e* was
7:9 their genealogical *e* by their
7:40 their genealogical *e* was in
1Ch 9:22 by their genealogical *e*
2Ch 12:15 by genealogical *e*
31:16 genealogical *e* of the males
31:17 genealogical *e* of the
31:18 *e* among all their little
31:19 *e* among the Levites
Ezr 8:1 genealogical *e* of those going
8:3 *e* of a hundred and fifty
Ne 7:5 the book of genealogical *e* of

Enrollments
1Ch 4:33 genealogical *e* for them

En route
Jg 8:14 *E* he captured a young man of

En-shemesh
Jos 15:7 the waters of *E*, and its
18:17 to *E* and went out to

Enslave
Ac 7:6 people would *e* them and
Ga 2:4 they might completely *e* us

Enslaved
Ga 4:3 *e* by the elementary things
Tit 2:3 neither *e* to a lot of wine
2Pe 2:19 by another is *e* by this one

Enslavement
Ro 8:21 free from *e* to corruption

Enslaves
2Co 11:20 put up with whoever *e* you

Enslaving
Ex 6:5 whom the Egyptians are *e*, and

Ensnared
De 7:25 for fear you may be *e* by it
Ps 9:16 the wicked one has been *e*
Pr 6:2 *e* by the sayings of your mouth
12:13 the lips the bad person is *e*
Ec 9:12 being *e* at a calamitous time
Isa 28:13 broken and *e* and caught

Ensnaring
Na 3:4 she who is *e* nations by her

Entangles
Heb 12:1 and the sin that easily *e* us

En-Tappuah
Jos 17:7 to the inhabitants of *E*

Enter
Ge 45:17 go *e* the land of Canaan
Ex 8:3 frogs . . . *e* into your house and
12:23 *e* into your houses to plague
Nu 4:23 *e* into the service group to
4:30 *e* into the service group to
5:22 *e* into your intestines to
5:24 *e* into her as something
5:27 *e* into her as something
8:24 *e* into the company in the
10:9 *e* into war in your land
14:30 you will not *e* into the land
20:24 he will not *e* into the land
De 6:18 *e* and take possession of the
11:8 *e* in and take possession of
24:10 must not *e* into his house
26:1 *e* into the land that Jehovah
27:3 *e* into the land that Jehovah
29:12 to *e* into the covenant of
Jos 8:19 *e* the city and capture it
10:19 to *e* into their cities
20:6 and he must *e* into his city
Jg 18:17 *e* in there to take the carved
1Sa 1:24 *e* the house of Jehovah in
1Ki 1:13 Go and *e* in to King David
22:25 *e* the innermost chamber to
2Ki 7:4 Let us *e* the city, when the
7:5 to *e* the camp of the Syrians
7:9 let us *e* and make report at
7:12 and into the city we shall *e*
18:21 *e* into his palm and pierce
19:23 I will *e* its final lodging
2Ch 7:2 priests were unable to *e* into
18:24 *e* the innermost chamber to
23:6 *e* the house of Jehovah but
23:6 ones that will *e*, because
23:19 no one unclean . . . might *e*
Ne 2:8 the house into which I am to *e*
6:11 *e* into the temple and live
6:11 I shall not *e*!
9:15 *e* and possess the land that
9:23 should *e* to take possession
Job 1:6 Satan proceeded to *e* right
2:1 and Satan also proceeded to *e*
3:6 the lunar months let it not *e*
41:13 its double jaw who will *e*?
Ps 37:15 sword will *e* into their
45:15 will *e* into the palace of
71:3 fortress into which to *e*
95:11 not *e* into my resting-place
119:170 request for favor *e* in
143:2 *e* into judgment with your
Pr 4:14 of the wicked ones do not *e*
18:6 stupid *e* into quarreling, and
22:24 fits of rage you must not *e*
23:10 of fatherless boys do not *e*
27:10 not *e* the house of your own
Isa 2:10 *E* into the rock and hide
2:19 people will *e* into the caves
2:21 *e* into the holes in the
3:14 Jehovah himself will *e* into
22:15 *e* in to this steward, to
23:1 from being a place to *e* in
26:2 faithful conduct may *e*
26:20 *e* into your interior rooms
30:29 *e* into the mountain of
36:6 *e* into his palm and pierce
37:24 *e* its final height, the
44:7 the things that will *e* in
59:14 is unable to *e*
Jer 4:5 *e* into the fortified cities
8:14 *e* into the fortified cities
16:5 Do not *e* into the house of
16:8 *e* no house of banqueting
17:19 the kings of Judah *e* in and
17:25 *e* in by the gates of this
35:11 let us *e* into Jerusalem
36:5 unable to *e* into the house
36:6 *e* in and read aloud from
41:17 to go on and *e* into Egypt
42:14 land of Egypt we shall *e*
42:15 to *e* into Egypt and
42:15 *e* in to reside there as
42:17 *e* into Egypt to reside
42:19 Do not *e* into Egypt
42:22 *e* to reside as aliens
43:2 Do not *e* into Egypt to reside
44:12 to *e* into the land of Egypt to
Eze 3:4 go, *e* in among the house of
3:11 *e* in among the exiled people
10:2 *E* in between the wheelwork
10:6 *e* and stand beside the wheel
16:8 *e* into a covenant with you
21:19 the king of Babylon to *e*
21:20 sword to *e* against Rabbah
Da 11:24 he will *e* in and actually do
11:40 *e* into the lands and flood
11:41 *e* into the land of the
Jon 3:4 started to *e* into the city
Hab 3:16 began to *e* into my bones
Hag 1:14 to *e* in and to do the work
Zec 5:4 *e* into the house of the thief
14:18 and does not actually *e*
Mt 5:20 no means *e* into the kingdom
7:21 will *e* into the kingdom of
8:8 for you to *e* under my roof
10:5 not *e* into a Samaritan city
10:11 or village you *e*, search
18:3 no means *e* into the kingdom
18:8 *e* into life maimed or lame
18:9 to *e* one-eyed into life than
19:17 want to *e* into life, observe
25:21 *E* into the joy of your
25:23 *E* into the joy of your
26:41 may not *e* into temptation
Mr 1:45 no longer able to *e* openly
5:12 swine, that we may *e* into
6:10 you *e* into a home, stay there
6:56 *e* into villages or cities
8:26 But do not *e* into the village
9:25 get out of him and *e* into
9:43 finer for you to *e* into life
9:45 *e* into life lame than with
9:47 finer for you to *e* one-eyed
10:15 will by no means *e* into it
10:23 to *e* into the kingdom of God
10:24 to *e* into the kingdom of God
10:25 to *e* into the kingdom of God
Lu 8:32 permit them to *e* into those
8:41 to *e* into his house
9:4 wherever you *e* into a home
10:5 Wherever you *e* into a house
10:8 wherever you *e* into a city
10:10 wherever you *e* into a city
21:21 in the country places not *e*
22:10 When you *e* into the city a
22:40 do not *e* into temptation
22:46 do not *e* into temptation
24:26 and to *e* into his glory
Joh 3:4 He cannot *e* into the womb of

Joh 3:5 cannot *e* into the kingdom of
10:1 not *e* into the sheepfold
18:28 *e* into the governor's palace
Ac 9:6 rise and *e* into the city, and
14:22 *e* into the kingdom of God
16:15 *e* into my house and stay
20:29 oppressive wolves will *e* in
Heb 3:11 shall not *e* into my rest
3:18 should not *e* into his rest
3:19 not *e* in because of lack of
4:3 do *e* into the rest, just as
4:3 They shall not *e* into my rest
4:5 They shall not *e* into my rest
4:6 for some to *e* into it, and
4:6 did not *e* in because of
4:11 utmost to *e* into that rest
9:6 the priests *e* the first tent
Re 15:8 able to *e* into the sanctuary
21:27 lie will in no way *e* into

Entered
Ge 12:14 as soon as Abram *e* Egypt
Ex 24:18 Moses *e* into the midst of
Nu 4:35 *e* into the service group for
4:39 *e* into the service group for
13:27 We *e* into the land to which
De 18:9 *e* into the land that Jehovah
Jg 19:29 he *e* his house and took the
Ru 2:3 *e* and began to glean in the
2:7 she *e* and kept on her feet
2Sa 16:15 Absalom . . . *e* Jerusalem
1Ki 19:9 finally *e* into a cave that
22:30 and *e* into the battle
2Ki 7:8 *e* into one tent and began to
7:8 *e* into another tent and
10:23 Jehu *e* with Jehonadab the
16:6 *e* Elath and kept dwelling
2Ch 15:12 *e* into a covenant to search
18:29 they *e* into the battle
22:8 Jehu had *e* into controversy
32:21 *e* the house of his god and
Ne 2:15 *e* by the Valley Gate, and
6:10 *e* the house of Shemaiah the
Job 1:6 sons of the true God *e* to take
2:1 sons of the true God *e* to take
38:22 *e* into the storehouses of
Pr 29:9 man having *e* into judgment
Jer 4:29 They have *e* into the thickets
34:10 *e* into the covenant to let
Eze 3:15 *e* in among the exiled people
3:24 spirit *e* into me and made
10:2 So he *e* in before my eyes
10:3 the man *e*, and the cloud
Da 5:10 *e* right into the banqueting
6:6 *e* as a throng to the king, and
6:10 *e* into his house, and, the
6:15 *e* as a throng to the king, and
10:3 or wine *e* into my mouth
Ob 11 outright foreigners *e* his gate
Na 2:11 where the lion walked and *e*
Mt 2:21 *e* into the land of Israel
8:5 When he *e* into Capernaum
12:4 he *e* into the house of God
17:25 when he *e* the house Jesus
21:10 when he *e* into Jerusalem
21:12 Jesus *e* into the temple and
24:38 until the day that Noah *e*
27:53 *e* into the holy city,) and
Mr 1:21 he *e* into the synagogue and
2:1 he again *e* into Capernaum and
2:26 he *e* into the house of God
3:1 *e* into a synagogue, and a man
5:13 out and *e* into the swine
7:17 he had *e* a house away from
7:24 he *e* into a house and did not
9:28 after he *e* into a house his
11:11 he *e* into Jerusalem, into
11:15 he *e* into the temple and
14:16 they *e* the city and found it
16:5 *e* into the memorial tomb
Lu 1:9 *e* into the sanctuary of
1:40 *e* into the home of Zechariah
4:16 he *e* into the synagogue, and
4:38 he *e* into Simon's home
6:4 he *e* into the house of God and
6:6 he *e* into the synagogue and
7:1 he *e* into Capernaum
7:36 he *e* into the house of the
7:44 I *e* into your house; you gave
8:30 many demons had *e* into him
8:33 *e* into the swine, and the
9:34 As they *e* into the cloud, they
9:46 a reasoning *e* among them as
9:52 and *e* into a village of

Lu 10:38 he *e* into a certain village
17:27 when Noah *e* into the ark
19:1 he *e* Jericho and was going
19:45 he *e* into the temple and
22:3 Satan *e* into Judas, the one
24:3 *e* they did not find the body
Joh 4:38 *e* into the benefit of their
6:22 Jesus had not *e* into the boat
13:27 Satan *e* into the latter
18:1 and his disciples *e* into it
18:33 Pilate *e* into the governor's
19:9 *e* into the governor's palace
20:6 he *e* into the memorial tomb
Ac 1:13 So, when they had *e*, they
3:8 *e* with them into the temple
5:21 *e* into the temple at daybreak
9:17 *e* into the house, and he laid
9:31 *e* into a period of peace
10:24 after that he *e* into Caesarea
10:25 As Peter *e*, Cornelius met
11:8 has never *e* into my mouth
11:12 *e* into the house of the man
14:1 *e* together into the synagogue
14:20 rose up and *e* into the city
18:19 *e* into the synagogue and
21:8 *e* into the house of Philip the
23:16 *e* into the soldiers' quarters
23:33 horsemen *e* into Caesarea
25:23 *e* into the audience chamber
28:16 we *e* into Rome, Paul was
Ro 5:12 one man sin *e* into the world
1Th 1:9 the way we first *e* in among
Heb 4:10 has *e* into God's rest has
6:20 has *e* in our behalf, Jesus
9:12 he *e*, no, not with the blood
9:24 Christ *e*, not into a holy
Jas 5:4 *e* into the ears of Jehovah
Re 11:11 spirit of life from God *e*

Entering
Ge 12:11 as he got near to *e* Egypt
23:10 those *e* the gate of his city
23:18 those *e* the gate of his city
Nu 4:43 *e* into the service group for
13:21 Rehob to the *e* in of Hamath
34:8 to the *e* in of Hamath, and
Jos 6:1 no one going out and no one *e*
10:20 *e* into the fortified cities
13:5 far as to the *e* in of Hamath
Jg 3:3 far as to the *e* in of Hamath
1Sa 25:26 from *e* into bloodguilt and
25:33 *e* into bloodguilt and
2Sa 17:17 able to appear *e* the city
1Ki 8:65 from the *e* in of Hamath
22:30 *e* into the battle for me
2Ki 11:8 anyone *e* within the rows
14:25 from the *e* in of Hamath
23:11 *e* the house of Jehovah by
1Ch 13:5 as far as the *e* of Hamath
2Ch 7:8 *e* in of Hamath down to the
18:29 *e* into the battle for me
Isa 24:10 has been shut up from *e*
Jer 2:35 *e* into controversy with you
7:2 *e* into these gates to bow
17:20 are *e* in by these gates
42:18 of your *e* into Egypt, and
44:8 *e* to reside as aliens
44:14 *e* in to reside there as
Eze 26:10 *e* into a city opened by
41:6 were *e* into the wall that
47:20 to the *e* in to Hamath
48:1 to the *e* in to Hamath
Da 4:7 and the astrologers were *e*
Am 6:14 the *e* in of Hamath down to
Mt 10:12 you are *e* into the house
15:17 everything *e* into the mouth
Lu 17:12 *e* into a certain village
Ac 3:2 from those *e* into the temple
19:8 *E* into the synagogue, he spoke
25:1 after *e* upon the government
Heb 4:1 of *e* into his rest, let us

Enters
1Ch 5:9 one *e* the wilderness at the
Ps 55:5 trembling itself *e* into me
Pr 2:10 wisdom *e* into your heart and
Isa 57:2 He *e* into peace; they take
Mt 15:11 Not what *e* into his mouth
Lu 22:10 the house into which he *e*
Joh 10:2 *e* through the door is
10:9 *e* through me will be saved
Heb 6:19 *e* in within the curtain
9:7 priest alone *e* once a year
9:25 high priest *e* into the holy
Jas 2:2 *e* into a gathering of you

Jas 2:2 man in filthy clothing also *e*

Entertain
Ac 24:15 these men themselves also *e*
2Co 10:15 but we *e* hope that, as your

Entertained
Ac 10:6 *e* by a certain Simon, a
10:18 Peter was being *e* there
10:23 invited them in and *e* them
10:32 *e* in the house of Simon
21:16 whose home we were to be *e*
28:7 *e* us benevolently three days
1Ti 5:10 if she *e* strangers, if she
Heb 13:2 some . . . *e* angels

Enthroned
Ps 55:19 sitting *e* as in the past

Entice
2Pe 2:14 and they *e* unsteady souls
2:18 they *e* those who are just

Enticed
De 11:16 for fear your heart may be *e*
Job 5:2 one easily *e* envying will put
31:9 has been *e* toward a woman
31:27 began to be *e* in secrecy
Pr 20:19 one that is *e* with his lips
Jas 1:14 and *e* by his own desire

Entire
Ge 2:6 it watered the *e* surface of
2:11 the *e* land of Havilah, where
2:13 encircling the *e* land of Cush
7:3 on the surface of the *e* earth
17:8 even the *e* land of Canaan, for
19:25 even the *e* District and all
47:12 the *e* household of his father
Ex 10:15 visible surface of the *e* land
12:3 to the *e* assembly of Israel
16:1 the *e* assembly of the sons of
16:2 the *e* assembly of the sons of
16:9 the *e* assembly of the sons of
16:10 *e* assembly of the sons of
17:1 the *e* assembly of the sons of
29:18 *e* ram smoke upon the altar
35:1 Moses called the *e* assembly
35:4 the *e* assembly of the sons of
Le 3:9 The *e* fatty tail is what he
4:12 have the *e* bull taken out to
4:13 if the *e* assembly of Israel
8:21 made the *e* ram smoke upon the
16:17 behalf of the *e* congregation
19:2 the *e* assembly of the sons of
24:14 *e* assembly must pelt him
24:16 *e* assembly should without
Nu 4:6 spread out an *e* cloth of blue
16:5 Korah and to his *e* assembly
16:6 Korah and his *e* assembly
16:22 against the *e* assembly
18:3 their obligation to the *e* tent
20:1 the *e* assembly, proceeded to
20:22 Israel, the *e* assembly
De 14:28 bring out the *e* tenth part
18:1 the *e* tribe of Levi
26:12 the *e* tenth of your produce
33:5 The *e* number of the tribes of
Jos 22:18 against the *e* assembly of
Jg 8:10 the *e* camp of the Easterners
Ru 2:21 finished the *e* harvest that I
1Sa 22:1 *e* house of his father got to
22:15 *e* house of my father, for
2Sa 2:29 marching through the *e* gully
3:29 the *e* house of his father
1Ki 11:34 not take the *e* kingdom out
2Ki 25:10 the *e* military force of
1Ch 28:19 insight for the *e* thing in
2Ch 26:12 *e* number of the heads of
26:14 for the *e* army, shields and
31:19 *e* genealogical enrollment
Ezr 2:64 The *e* congregation as one
Ne 4:6 the *e* wall came to be joined
7:66 *e* congregation as one group
Pr 2:9 the *e* course of what is good
Jer 4:29 the *e* city is running away
29:22 *e* body of exiles of Judah
31:37 reject the *e* seed of Israel
40:4 The *e* land is before you
Eze 29:7 a split in their *e* shoulder
43:12 *e* territory all around is
Da 11:17 of his *e* kingdom, and there
Mt 8:32 the *e* herd rushed over the
26:59 the *e* Sanhedrin were looking
Ac 11:28 upon the *e* inhabited earth
15:12 *e* multitude became silent
17:26 the *e* surface of the earth

Ps 61:1 Do hear, O God, my *e* cry
88:2 Incline your ear to my *e* cry
106:44 when he heard their *e* cry
119:169 *e* cry come near before
142:6 pay attention to my *e* cry
Jer 7:16 in their behalf an *e* cry
11:14 in their behalf an *e* cry
14:12 listening to their *e* cry
Zep 3:10 the ones *e* me, namely, the
Mt 8:5 officer came to him, *e* him
14:36 *e* him that they might just
Mr 1:40 leper, *e* him even on bended
5:18 *e* him that he might continue
Lu 8:31 they kept *e* him not to order
Ac 13:42 the people began *e* for these
16:9 *e* him and saying: Step over
21:12 began *e* him not to go up to

Entreaty
Ex 8:9 when I shall make *e* for you
8:28 Make *e* in my behalf
8:29 indeed make *e* to Jehovah, and
8:30 Moses . . . made *e* to Jehovah
10:18 and made *e* to Jehovah
2Ch 33:19 *e* was granted him and all
Job 22:27 You will make *e* to him
33:26 make *e* to God that he may
Ps 30:8 I kept making *e* for favor
143:1 Do give ear to my *e*
Ac 16:15 she said with *e*: If you men
2Co 5:20 God were making *e* through
8:4 *e* for the privilege of kindly

Entrenched
2Co 10:4 overturning strongly *e* things

Entrust
Ps 31:5 Into your hand I *e* my spirit
Lu 16:11 *e* you with what is true
23:46 your hands I *e* my spirit

Entrusted
Nu 12:7 is being *e* with all my house
Jer 36:20 the roll they *e* to the
Ac 14:26 *e* to the undeserved kindness
15:40 been *e* by the brothers to the
Ro 3:2 they were *e* with the sacred
1Co 9:17 have a stewardship *e* to me
Ga 2:7 had *e* to me the good news for
1Th 2:4 to be *e* with the good news
1Ti 1:11 good news . . . I was *e*
Tit 1:3 preaching with which I was *e*

Entrusting
Joh 2:24 was not *e* himself to them

Entry
2Ki 11:16 horse *e* of the king's house
2Ch 23:13 by his pillar at the *e*
23:15 *e* of the horse gate of the
Ac 13:24 advance of the *e* of that One
Heb 10:19 *e* into the holy place by

Entryway
2Ki 16:18 outer *e* he shifted from the
1Ch 4:39 to go to the *e* of Gedor
9:19 the keepers of the *e*
Pr 17:19 his *e* high is seeking a crash
Jer 38:14 to him to the third *e*
Eze 40:15 front of the gate of the *e*
42:9 the *e* was to the east
44:5 *e* of the House with all the
46:19 *e* that was by the side of

Entryways
Eze 43:11 its *e*, and all its ground

Enumerate
Ps 50:16 you have to *e* my regulations

Enveloped
Jg 6:34 Jehovah's spirit *e* Gideon so
1Ch 12:18 spirit itself *e* Amasai, the
2Ch 24:20 spirit itself *e* Zechariah
Ps 65:13 low plains . . . *e* with grain
76:4 You are *e* with light, more

Enveloping
Isa 25:7 is *e* over all the peoples

Envelopment
Isa 25:7 face of the *e* that is

Envelops
Ps 73:6 Violence *e* them as a garment

Envies
Ga 5:21 *e*, drunken bouts, revelries
1Pe 2:1 *e* and all sorts of backbiting

Envious
Ps 37:1 Do not be *e* of those doing
Ps 73:3 I became *e* of the boasters
Pr 3:31 *e* of the man of violence
23:17 heart not be *e* of sinners
24:1 Do not be *e* of bad men, and
24:19 become *e* of wicked people
28:22 *e* eye is bestirring himself
Mr 7:22 loose conduct, an *e* eye

Enviously
Ps 68:16 keep watching *e*

Envision
Isa 30:10 You must not *e* for us any
30:10 *e* deceptive things

Envoy
Pr 13:17 a faithful *e* is a healing
25:13 faithful *e* to those sending
Jer 49:14 *e* that is sent among the
Ob 1 an *e* that has been sent among
Php 2:25 your *e* and private servant

Envoys
Isa 18:2 sending forth *e* by means of
30:4 his own *e* reach even Hanes
57:9 sending your *e* far off, so

Envy
Ge 26:14 Philistines began to *e* him
Ps 106:16 to *e* Moses in the camp
Mt 27:18 out of *e* they had handed him
Mr 15:10 because of *e* the chief
Ro 1:29 full of *e*, murder, strife
Php 1:15 preaching . . . through *e* and
1Ti 6:4 From these things spring *e*
Tit 3:3 carrying on in badness and *e*
Jas 4:5 tendency to *e* that the spirit

Envying
Job 5:2 *e* will put to death
Eze 31:9 other trees . . . kept *e* it
Ga 5:26 *e* one another

Enwrap
Ps 109:29 *e* themselves with their

Enwrapped
Ps 89:45 You have *e* him with shame
Isa 59:17 *e* himself with zeal as if
61:10 *e* me, like the bridegroom

Enwrapping
Ps 104:2 *E* yourself with light as

Enwraps
Ps 84:6 blessings the instructor *e*
109:19 garment with which he *e*

Epaenetus
Ro 16:5 Greet my beloved *E*, who is a

Epaphras
Col 1:7 *E* our beloved fellow slave
4:12 *E*, who is from among you
Phm 23 *E* my fellow captive in union

Epaphroditus
Php 2:25 to send to you *E*, my brother
4:18 received from *E* the things

Ephah
Ge 25:4 sons of Midian were *E* and
Ex 16:36 an omer is a tenth of an *e*
29:40 a tenth part of an *e* measure
Le 5:11 tenth of an *e* of fine flour
6:20 tenth of an *e* of fine flour
14:10 an *e* of fine flour as a
14:21 one tenth of an *e* of fine
19:36 accurate *e* and an accurate
23:13 offering two tenths of an *e*
23:17 *e* of fine flour they should
24:5 Two tenths of an *e* should go
Nu 5:15 tenth of an *e* of barley flour
15:4 fine flour, a tenth of an *e*
28:5 tenth of an *e* of fine flour as
De 25:15 An *e* accurate and just
Jg 6:19 an *e* of flour as unfermented
Ru 2:17 to be about an *e* of barley
1Sa 1:24 one *e* of flour and a large
17:17 this *e* of roasted grain and
1Ch 1:33 sons of Midian were *E* and
2:46 *E* the concubine of Caleb
2:47 sons of Jahdai were . . . *E*
Pr 20:10 and two sorts of *e* measures
Isa 5:10 produce but an *e* measure
60:6 camels of Midian and of *E*
Eze 45:10 scales and an accurate *e*
45:11 regards the *e* and the bath
45:11 tenth of a homer an *e*
45:13 sixth part of the *e* from
45:13 *e* from the homer of barley
Eze 45:24 *e* for the young bull and
45:24 *e* for the ram he should
45:24 oil, a hin to the *e*
46:5 offering an *e* for the ram
46:5 regards oil, a hin to the *e*
46:7 *e* for the young bull and
46:7 *e* for the ram he should
46:7 regards oil, a hin to the *e*
46:11 *e* for the young bull and
46:11 and an *e* for the ram, and
46:11 regards oil, a hin to the *e*
46:14 sixth of an *e* and, as
Am 8:5 in order to make the *e* small
Mic 6:10 the scrimped *e* measure that
Zec 5:6 *e* measure that is going forth
5:7 sitting in the midst of the *e*
5:8 back into the midst of the *e*
5:9 raised the *e* up between the
5:10 Where are they taking the *e*?

Ephahs
De 25:14 two sorts of *e*, a great one

Ephai
Jer 40:8 sons of *E* the Netophathite

Epher
Ge 25:4 sons of Midian were . . . *E* and
1Ch 1:33 sons of Midian . . . *E*
4:17 the sons of Ezrah . . . *E*
5:24 *E* and Ishi and Eliel and

Ephesdammim
1Sa 17:1 took up camping . . . in *E*

Ephesian
Ac 21:29 seen Trophimus the *E* in the

Ephesians
Ac 19:28 Great is Artemis of the *E*!
19:34 Great is Artemis of the *E*!
19:35 city of the *E* is the temple

Ephesus
Ac 18:19 So they arrived at *E*, and he
18:21 And he put out to sea from *E*
18:24 Apollos . . . arrived in *E*
19:1 and came down to *E*, and found
19:17 the Greeks that dwelt in *E*
19:26 not only in *E* but in nearly
19:35 Men of *E*, who really is
20:16 had decided to sail past *E*
20:17 from Miletus he sent to *E*
1Co 15:32 with wild beasts at *E*
16:8 I am remaining in *E* until
Eph 1:1 the holy ones who are in *E*
1Ti 1:3 I encouraged you to stay in *E*
2Ti 1:18 the services he rendered in *E*
4:12 have sent Tychicus off to *E*
Re 1:11 the seven congregations, in *E*
2:1 *E* write: These are the things

Ephlal
1Ch 2:37 in turn, became father to *E*
2:37 *E*, in turn, became father to

Ephod
Ex 25:7 setting stones for the *e* and
28:4 an *e* and a sleeveless coat and
28:6 *e* of gold, blue thread and
28:12 the shoulder pieces of the *e*
28:15 the workmanship of the *e*
28:25 the shoulder pieces of the *e*
28:26 the side toward the *e* inward
28:27 two shoulder pieces of the *e*
28:27 above the girdle of the *e*
28:28 to the rings of the *e* with a
28:28 above the girdle of the *e* and
28:28 displaced from on top the *e*
28:31 the sleeveless coat of the *e*
29:5 the sleeveless coat of the *e*
29:5 the *e* and the breastpiece, and
29:5 with the girdle of the *e*
35:9 setting stones for the *e* and
35:27 for the *e* and the breastpiece
39:2 *e* of gold, blue thread and
39:7 the shoulder pieces of the *e*
39:8 of the *e*, out of gold, blue
39:18 the shoulder pieces of the *e*
39:19 the side toward the *e* inward
39:20 two shoulder pieces of the *e*
39:20 above the girdle of the *e*
39:21 to the rings of the *e* with a
39:21 above the girdle of the *e*
39:21 displaced from on top the *e*
39:22 the sleeveless coat of the *e*
Le 8:7 put the *e* upon him and girded
8:7 girdle of the *e* and bound it

Nu 34:23 Hanniel the son of *E*
Jg 8:27 to make it into an *e* and to
17:5 to make an *e* and teraphim and
18:14 an *e* and teraphim and a
18:17 carved image and the *e* and
18:18 the *e* and the teraphim and
18:20 took the *e* and the teraphim
1Sa 2:18 having a linen *e* girded on
2:28 to bear an *e* before me, that
14:3 Ahijah . . . carrying the *e*
21:9 in a mantle, behind the *e*
22:18 men bearing an *e* of linen
23:6 *e* that went down in his hand
23:9 Do bring the *e* near
30:7 bring the *e* near to me
30:7 Abiathar came bringing the *e*
2Sa 6:14 David being girded with an *e*
1Ch 15:27 there was an *e* of linen
Ho 3:4 without an *e* and teraphim

Ephphatha
Mr 7:34 to him: *E*, that is, Be opened

Ephraim
Ge 41:52 the second he called *E*
46:20 Manasseh and *E*, whom Asenath
48:1 his two sons Manasseh and *E*
48:5 *E* and Manasseh will become
48:13 *E* by his right hand to
48:20 God constitute you like *E*
48:20 putting *E* before Manasseh
Nu 1:10 of *E*, Elishama the son of
1:32 *E*, their births according to
1:33 registered . . . tribe of *E*
2:18 division of the camp of *E*
2:18 for the sons of *E* is Elishama
2:24 camp of *E* are one hundred and
7:48 chieftain for the sons of *E*
10:22 *E* pulled away in their
13:8 of the tribe of *E*, Hoshea the
26:28 sons of Joseph . . . *E*
26:35 sons of *E* by their families
26:37 families of the sons of *E*
34:24 of *E* a chieftain, Kemuel the
De 33:17 the tens of thousands of *E*
34:2 the land of *E* and Manasseh
Jos 14:4 two tribes, Manasseh and *E*
16:4 Joseph, Manasseh and *E*
16:5 boundary of the sons of *E* by
16:8 tribe of the sons of *E* by
16:9 sons of *E* had enclave cities
16:10 Canaanites . . . in among *E*
17:8 belonged to the sons of *E*
17:9 these cities of *E* in the
17:15 mountainous region of *E*
17:17 Joshua said . . . to *E* and
19:50 the mountainous region of *E*
20:7 the mountainous region of *E*
21:5 families of the tribe of *E*
21:20 cities out of the tribe of *E*
21:21 mountainous region of *E*
24:30 mountainous region of *E*
24:33 mountainous region of *E*
Jg 1:29 Neither did *E* drive out the
2:9 mountainous region of *E*, on
3:27 the mountainous region of *E*
4:5 the mountainous region of *E*
5:14 Out of *E* was their origin in
7:24 the mountainous region of *E*
7:24 *E* were called together, and
8:1 men of *E* said to him: What
8:2 gleanings of *E* better than the
10:1 the mountainous region of *E*
10:9 house of *E*; and Israel was
12:1 *E* were called together and
12:4 and fought *E*; and the men of
12:4 striking *E* down, for they had
12:4 Men escaped from *E* is what
12:4 *E*, inside of Manasseh
12:5 fords of the Jordan ahead of *E*
12:5 escaping men of *E* would say
12:6 forty-two thousand out of *E*
12:15 Pirathon in the land of *E* in
17:1 the mountainous region of *E*
17:8 the mountainous region of *E*
18:2 the mountainous region of *E*
18:13 the mountainous region of *E*
19:1 the mountainous region of *E*
19:16 the mountainous region of *E*
19:18 the mountainous region of *E*
1Sa 1:1 the mountainous region of *E*
9:4 the mountainous region of *E*
14:22 the mountainous region of *E*
2Sa 2:9 king over . . . *E* and Benjamin
13:23 which is close by *E*
2Sa 18:6 battle . . . in the forest of *E*
20:21 mountainous region of *E*
1Ki 4:8 the mountainous region of *E*
12:25 the mountainous region of *E*
2Ki 5:22 the mountainous region of *E*
14:13 the gate of *E* clear to the
1Ch 6:66 from the tribe of *E*
6:67 the mountainous region of *E*
7:20 sons of *E* were Shuthelah and
7:22 *E* their father carried on
9:3 and some of the sons of *E* and
12:30 of the sons of *E* there were
27:10 Pelonite of the sons of *E*
27:14 Pirathonite of the sons of *E*
27:20 of the sons of *E*, Hoshea the
2Ch 13:4 mountainous region of *E*, and
15:8 mountainous region of *E* and
15:9 from *E* and Manasseh and
17:2 in the cities of *E* that Asa
19:4 mountainous region of *E*
25:7 all the sons of *E*
25:10 come to him from *E*, to
25:23 from the Gate of *E* clear to
28:7 Zichri, a mighty man of *E*
28:12 heads of the sons of *E*
30:1 letters he wrote to *E* and
30:10 land of *E* and Manasseh
30:18 people, many from *E* and
31:1 in *E* and Manasseh until they
34:6 cities of Manasseh and *E* and
34:9 the hand of Manasseh and *E*
Ne 8:16 public square of the Gate of *E*
12:39 over the Gate of *E* and on
Ps 60:7 *E* is the fortress of my head
78:9 sons of *E*, though armed
78:67 of *E* he did not choose
80:2 Before *E* and Benjamin and
108:8 *E* is the fortress of my head
Isa 7:2 Syria has leaned upon *E*
7:5 *E* and the son of Remaliah
7:8 *E* will be shattered to pieces
7:9 head of *E* is Samaria, and
9:9 *E* and the inhabitant of
9:21, 21 Manasseh *E*, and *E*
11:13 jealousy of *E* must depart
11:13 *E* itself will not be
11:13 show hostility toward *E*
17:3 made to cease out of *E*
28:1 crown of the drunkards of *E*
28:3 crowns of the drunkards of *E*
Jer 4:15 the mountainous region of *E*
7:15 the whole offspring of *E*
31:6 the mountainous region of *E*
31:9 as for *E*, he is my firstborn
31:18 heard *E* bemoaning himself
31:20 Is *E* a precious son to me
50:19 mountainous region of *E*
Eze 37:16 For Joseph, the stick of *E*
37:19 which is in the hand of *E*
48:5 to the western border, *E* one
48:6 on the boundary of *E*, from
Ho 4:17 *E* is joined with idols
5:3 I personally have known *E*
5:3 *E*, you have treated women like
5:5 Israel and *E* themselves are
5:9 O *E*, a mere object of
5:11 *E* is oppressed, crushed in
5:12 I was like the moth to *E*
5:13 *E* got to see his sickness
5:13 *E* proceeded to go to Assyria
5:14 be like a young lion to *E*
6:4 What shall I do to you, O *E*?
6:10 fornication on the part of *E*
7:1 the error of *E* is also actually
7:8 As for *E*, it is among the
7:8 *E* . . . has become a round cake
7:11 *E* proves to be like a
8:11 For *E* has multiplied altars
9:3 *E* must return to Egypt, and
9:8 The watchman of *E* was with
9:11 As regards *E*, like a flying
9:13 *E*, whom I have seen like Tyre
9:13 even *E* is destined to a
9:16 *E* must be struck down
10:6 Shame is what *E* himself will
10:11 *E* was a trained heifer
10:11 I make someone ride *E*
11:3 I taught *E* to walk, taking
11:8 How can I give you up, O *E*?
11:9 I shall not bring *E* to ruin
11:12 *E* has surrounded me
12:1 *E* is feeding on wind and
12:8 *E* keeps saying, Indeed, I
12:14 *E* caused offense to
Ho 13:1 *E* spoke, there was trembling
13:12 The error of *E* is wrapped
14:8 *E* will say, What do I have
Ob 19 possession of the field of *E*
Zec 9:10 the war chariot from *E* and
9:13 The bow I will fill with *E*
10:7 those of *E* must become just
Joh 11:54 into a city called *E*, and

Ephraimite
Jg 12:5 say to each one: Are you an *E*?
1Sa 1:1 name was Elkanah . . . an *E*
1Ki 11:26 Nebat an *E* from Zeredah

Ephraim's
Ge 48:14 and placed it on *E* head
48:17 right hand placed on *E* head
48:17 from *E* head to Manasseh's
50:23 Joseph got to see *E* sons
Jos 17:10 To the south it was *E*
Isa 7:17 day of *E* turning away from
Ho 8:9 In *E* case, they have hired

Ephrain
2Ch 13:19 *E* and its dependent towns

Ephrath
Ge 35:16 before coming to *E*, Rachel
35:19 *E*, that is to say, Bethlehem
48:7 land before coming to *E*
48:7 *E*, that is to say, Bethlehem
1Ch 2:19 Caleb took to himself *E*

Ephrathah
Ru 4:11 and you prove your worth in *E*
1Ch 2:50 Hur the firstborn of *E*
4:4 *E* the father of Bethlehem
Ps 132:6 We have heard it in *E*
Mic 5:2 Bethlehem *E* . . . too little

Ephrathite
1Sa 17:12 *E* from Bethlehem of Judah

Ephrathites
Ru 1:2 *E* from Bethlehem in Judah

Ephron
Ge 23:8 urge *E* the son of Zohar for
23:10 *E* was sitting among the sons
23:10 So *E* the Hittite answered
23:13 spoke to *E* in the hearing of
23:14 *E* answered Abraham, saying
23:16 Abraham listened to *E*, and
23:16 Abraham weighed out to *E* the
23:17 the field of *E* that was in
25:9 field of *E* the son of Zohar
49:29 the field of *E* the Hittite
49:30 Abraham purchased from *E* the
50:13 a burial place from *E* the
Jos 15:9 to the cities of Mount *E*

Epicurean
Ac 17:18 *E* and the Stoic philosophers

Epileptic
Mt 4:24 and *e* and paralyzed persons
17:15 he is an *e* and is ill, for

Equal
Ex 30:13 Twenty gerahs *e* a shekel
De 18:8 An *e* share he should eat
1Ki 20:25 *e* to the military force
1Ch 12:14 The least one was *e* to a
Job 41:26 does not prove *e*
Ps 55:13 mortal man who was as my *e*
Pr 3:15 cannot be made *e* to it
8:11 cannot be made *e* to it
26:4 also may not become *e* to him
Isa 40:25 I should be made his *e*
46:5 make me *e* or compare me
La 2:13 What shall I make *e* to you
Mt 20:12 made them *e* to us who bore
Joh 5:18 making himself *e* to God
2Co 11:12 *e* to us in the office of
Php 2:6 that he should be *e* to God
2Pe 1:1 in *e* privilege with ours
Re 21:16 breadth and height are *e*

Equaled
Ex 38:27 A hundred socket pedestals *e*

Equalizing
2Co 8:14 an *e* your surplus just now
8:14 that an *e* might take place

Equally
Ex 38:18 its extent was five cubits *e*
2Ch 31:15 *e* to great and small

Equip
Nu 31:3 *E* men from among you for the
32:20 *e* yourselves before Jehovah

De 15:14 *e* him with something from
Heb 13:21 *e* you with every good thing

Equipment

Ge 45:20 feel sorry over your *e*
Nu 4:32 their *e* and all their service
4:32 assign the *e* for which they
Jg 5:14 handling the *e* of a scribe
Eph 6:15 *e* of the good news of peace

Equipped

Nu 31:5 twelve thousand *e* for the
32:17 go *e* in battle formation
32:21 every *e* one of yours will
32:27 everyone *e* for the army
32:29 everyone *e* for the war
32:30 if they do not pass over *e*
32:32 pass over *e* before Jehovah
De 3:18 You will pass over, *e*, before
Jos 4:13 forty thousand *e* for the
1Ch 12:23 those *e* for the army that
12:24 hundred, *e* for the army
2Ch 17:17 *e* with the bow and shield
2Ti 3:17 *e* for every good work

Equitable

Da 11:6 to make an *e* arrangement
11:17 will be *e* terms with him

Equivalent

Ge 48:19 become the full *e* of nations
2Sa 17:3 *E* to the returning of all is

Er

Ge 38:3 and he called his name *E*
38:6 Judah took a wife for *E*
38:7 But *E*, Judah's firstborn
46:12 the sons of Judah were *E*
46:12 *E* and Onan died in the land
Nu 26:19 sons of Judah were *E* and
26:19 *E* and Onan died in the land
1Ch 2:3 sons of Judah were *E* and Onan
2:3 *E* the firstborn of Judah came
4:21 *E* the father of Lecah and
Lu 3:28 son of Elmadam, son of *E*

Eran

Nu 26:36 *E* the family of the Eranites

Eranites

Nu 26:36 Of Eran the family of the *E*

Erastus

Ac 19:22 dispatched . . . Timothy and *E*
Ro 16:23 *E* the city steward greets
2Ti 4:20 *E* stayed in Corinth, but I

Erech

Ge 10:10 Babel and *E* and Accad and
Ezr 4:9 people of *E*, the Babylonians

Erect

Ge 37:7 sheaf got up and also stood *e*
Le 26:13 and make you walk *e*
1Ch 21:18 to *e* an altar to Jehovah on
Isa 33:23 will not hold firmly *e*
Mt 17:4 I will *e* three tents here
Mr 9:5 let us *e* three tents, one for
Lu 9:33 let us *e* three tents, one for
21:28 raise yourselves *e* and lift
Ac 14:10 Stand up *e* on your feet
15:16 rebuild its ruins and *e* it

Erected

Ge 31:51 the pillar that I have *e*
Isa 23:13 have *e* their siege towers
Mt 21:33 *e* a tower, and let it out to
Mr 12:1 *e* a tower, and let it out

Erecting

1Sa 15:12 *e* a monument for himself

Eri

Ge 46:16 the sons of Gad were . . . *E*
Nu 26:16 *E* the family of the Erites

Erites

Nu 26:16 of Eri the family of the *E*

Erred

1Ki 8:47 We have sinned and *e*, we
2Ch 6:37 we have *e* and we have acted

Erring

Isa 29:24 who are *e* in their spirit
Heb 5:2 with the ignorant and *e* ones

Erroneous

Jer 4:14 your *e* thoughts lodge within
Jude 11 the *e* course of Balaam for

Erroneousness

Isa 57:17 At the *e* of his unjust gain

Error

Ge 4:13 My punishment for *e* is too
15:16 *e* of the Amorites has not
19:15 away in the *e* of the city
44:16 God has found out the *e* of
Ex 20:5 for the *e* of fathers upon sons
28:38 Aaron must answer for the *e*
28:43 not incur *e* and certainly die
34:7 pardoning *e* and transgression
34:7 bringing punishment for the *e*
34:9 forgive our *e* and our sin, and
Le 5:1 then he must answer for his *e*
5:17 and must answer for his *e*
7:18 will answer for his *e*
10:17 the *e* of the assembly so as
17:16 must then answer for his *e*
18:25 punishment for its *e* upon it
19:8 will answer for his *e*
20:17 He should answer for his *e*
20:19 should answer for their *e*
26:39 rot away because of their *e*
26:40 confess their own *e*
26:40 and the *e* of their fathers in
26:41 they will pay off their *e*
26:43 paying for their *e*, because
Nu 5:15 bringing *e* to remembrance
5:31 man must be innocent of *e*
5:31 wife will answer for her *e*
14:18 pardoning *e* and transgression
14:18 punishment for the *e* of the
14:19 Forgive, please, the *e* of
15:31 His own *e* is upon him
18:1 *e* against the sanctuary
18:1 for *e* against your priesthood
18:23 should answer for their *e*
30:15 he also actually bears her *e*
De 5:9 *e* of fathers upon sons and upon
19:15 respecting any *e* or any sin
Jos 22:17 Was the *e* of Peor too
22:20 man to expire in his *e*
1Sa 3:13 for the *e* that he has known
3:14 the *e* of the house of Eli
20:1 What is my *e*, and what sin
20:8 But if there is *e* in me
25:24 Upon me . . . be the *e*
28:10 guilt for *e* will not befall
2Sa 3:8 *e* concerning a woman today
14:9 Upon me . . . be the *e*, and
14:32 if there is any *e* in me
19:19 let my lord attribute *e*
22:24 I will keep myself from *e*
24:10 let your servant's *e* pass
1Ki 17:18 to bring my *e* to mind and
1Ch 21:8 cause your servant's *e* to
Ezr 9:13 have underestimated our *e*
Ne 4:5 their *e* and their sin from
Job 7:21 And overlook my *e*? For now
10:6 you should try to find my *e*
10:14 of my *e* you do not hold me
11:6 your *e* to be forgotten for
14:17 you apply glue over my *e*
15:5 For your *e* trains your mouth
20:27 Heaven will uncover his *e*
31:11 an *e* for attention by the
31:28 an *e* for attention by the
31:33 By hiding my *e* in my shirt
33:9 Clean I am, and I have no *e*
Ps 18:23 I shall keep myself from *e*
25:11 You must even forgive my *e*
31:10 Because of my *e* my power
32:2 Jehovah does not put *e*
32:5 and my *e* I did not cover
32:5 pardoned the *e* of my sins
36:2 find out his *e* so as to hate
38:18 to tell about my own *e*
39:11 against *e* you have corrected
49:5 *e* of my supplanters surrounds
51:2 Thoroughly wash me from my *e*
51:5 With *e* I was brought forth
59:4 Though there is no *e*, they
65:3 Things of *e* have proved
69:27, 27 Do give *e* upon their *e*
78:38 cover the *e* and not bring
85:2 pardoned the *e* of your people
89:32 their *e* even with strokes
103:3 who is forgiving all your *e*
106:43 brought low for their *e*
109:14 *e* of his forefathers be
Pr 16:6 and trueness *e* is atoned for
Isa 1:4 the people heavy with *e*, an
5:18 *e* with ropes of untruth
6:7 *e* has departed and your sin
13:11 own *e* upon the wicked
14:21 the *e* of their forefathers
Isa 22:14 *e* will not be atoned for in
26:21 call to account the *e* of
27:9 *e* of Jacob will be atoned
30:13 this *e* will become like a
33:24 those pardoned for their *e*
40:2 her *e* has been paid off
53:6 caused the *e* of us all to
59:3 and your fingers with *e*
64:7 melt by the power of our *e*
64:9 not forever remember our *e*
Jer 2:22 your *e* would certainly be a
3:13 Only take note of your *e*
13:22 the abundance of your *e*
14:10 he will remember their *e*
14:20 the *e* of our forefathers
16:10 what is our *e* and what is
16:17 their *e* been hid from in
16:18 full amount of their *e*
18:23 Do not cover over their *e*
25:12 their *e*, even against the
30:14 the abundance of your *e*
30:15 the abundance of your *e*
31:30 each one for his own *e* that
31:34 I shall forgive their *e*
32:18 *e* of the fathers into the
33:8 purify them from all their *e*
36:3 forgive their *e* and their
36:31 his servants their *e*, and
42:20 you have committed *e*
50:20 *e* of Israel will be
51:6 inanimate through her *e*
La 2:14 not uncovered your *e* in order
4:6 The punishment for the *e* of
4:22 Your *e*, O daughter of Zion
4:22 turned his attention to your *e*
Eze 3:18 in his *e* he will die, but
3:19 for his *e* will die
4:4 lay the *e* of the house of
4:4 you will carry their *e*
4:5 to you the years of their *e*
4:5 the *e* of the house of Israel
4:6 *e* of the house of Judah forty
4:17 and rot away in their *e*
7:13 his own life by his own *e*
7:16 each one in his own *e*
7:19 block causing their *e*
9:9 *e* of the house of Israel and
14:3 block causing their *e* they
14:4 block causing his *e* in front
14:7 block causing his *e* in front
14:10 will have to bear their *e*
14:10 The *e* of the inquirer will
14:10 as the *e* of the prophet
16:49 the *e* of Sodom your sister
18:17 of the *e* of his father
18:18 then he must die for his *e*
18:19 the *e* of the father
18:20 the *e* of the father, and a
18:20 because of the *e* of the son
18:30 a stumbling block causing *e*
21:23 is calling *e* to remembrance
21:24 *e* to be remembered by your
21:25 come in the time of the *e*
21:29 time of the *e* of the end
29:16 bringing *e* to remembrance
33:6 for its own *e* it itself
33:8 one will die in his own *e*
33:9 will die in his own *e*
35:5 the time of their final *e*
39:23 it was because of their *e*
44:10 must also bear their *e*
44:12 stumbling block into *e*
44:12 and they must bear their *e*
Da 9:13 turning back from our *e* and
9:24 and to make atonement for *e*
Ho 4:8 *e* they keep lifting up their
5:5 made to stumble in their *e*
7:1 the *e* of Ephraim is also
8:13 he will remember their *e*
9:7 the abundance of your *e*
9:9 He will remember their *e*
12:8 on my part, no *e* that is sin
13:12 The *e* of Ephraim is wrapped
14:1 you have stumbled in your *e*
14:2 May you pardon *e*; and accept
Mic 7:18 one pardoning *e* and passing
Zec 3:4 caused your *e* to pass away
3:9 take away the *e* of that land
Mal 2:6 whom he turned back from *e*
Ro 1:27 recompense . . . for their *e*
Eph 4:14 of cunning in contriving *e*
1Th 2:3 does not arise from *e* or from
2Th 2:11 God lets an operation of *e*
Jas 5:20 back from the *e* of his way

2Pe 2:18 who conduct themselves in *e*
3:17 by the *e* of the law-defying
1Jo 4:6 the inspired expression of *e*

Errors
Le 16:21 the *e* of the sons of Israel
16:22 upon itself all their *e* into
26:39 *e* of their fathers with them
Nu 14:34 answer for your *e* forty
Ezr 9:6 *e* themselves have multiplied
9:7 because of our *e* we have been
Ne 9:2 and the *e* of their fathers
Job 13:23 In what way do I have *e* and
13:26 of the *e* of my youth
19:29 means a raging against *e*
22:5 there be no end to your *e*
Ps 38:4 my own *e* have passed over my
40:12 More *e* of mine overtook me
51:9 And wipe out even all my *e*
79:8 against us the *e* of ancestors
90:8 set our *e* right in front of
103:10 according to our *e* has he
107:17 due to their *e*, finally
130:3 If *e* were what you watch
130:8 Israel out of all his *e*
Pr 5:22 own *e* will catch the wicked
Isa 43:24 made me weary with your *e*
50:1 Because of your own *e* you
53:5 was being crushed for our *e*
53:11 *e* he himself will bear
59:2 the very *e* of your people
59:12 our *e*, we well know them
64:6 our *e* themselves will carry
65:7 for their own *e* and for the
65:7 the *e* of their forefathers
Jer 5:25 *e* have turned these things
11:10 the *e* of their forefathers
14:7 if our own *e* do testify
33:8 I will forgive all their *e*
La 4:13 the *e* of her priests, There
5:7 it is their *e* that we . . . bear
Eze 24:23 have to rot away in your *e*
28:18 to the abundance of your *e*
32:27 *e* will come to be upon
36:31 on account of your *e* and
36:33 cleansing . . . all your *e*
43:10 because of their *e*, and
Da 9:16 of the *e* of our forefathers
Ho 10:10 to their two *e*
Am 3:2 against you for all your *e*
Mic 7:19 he will subject our *e*

Eruption
Le 13:2 his flesh an *e* or a scab or
13:10 is a white *e* in the skin and
13:10 the living flesh is in the *e*
13:19 a white *e* has developed or
13:28 it is an *e* of the scar
13:39 it is a harmless *e*. It has
13:43 is an *e* of the reddish-white
14:56 *e* and the scab and the blotch
De 28:27 piles and eczema and skin *e*

Esar-haddon
2Ki 19:37 *E* his son began to reign in
Ezr 4:2 days of *E* the king of Assyria
Isa 37:38 *E* his son began to reign in

Esau
Ge 25:25 so they called his name *E*
25:26 holding onto the heel of *E*
25:27 *E* became a man knowing how
25:28 And Isaac had love for *E*
25:29 *E* came along from the field
25:30 *E* said to Jacob: Quick
25:32 And *E* continued: Here I am
25:34 Jacob gave *E* bread and lentil
25:34 So *E* despised the birthright
26:34 *E* grew to be forty years old
27:1 he then called *E* his older
27:5 while Isaac spoke to *E* his
27:5 *E* went on out into the field
27:6 your father speaking to *E*
27:11 *E* my brother is a hairy man
27:15 Rebekah took garments of *E*
27:19 I am *E* your firstborn
27:21 really my son *E* or not
27:22 the hands are the hands of *E*
27:23 hairy like the hands of *E*
27:24 You are really my son *E*?
27:30 *E* his brother came back from
27:32 your son, your firstborn, *E*
27:34 *E* began to cry out in an
27:37 But in answer to *E* Isaac
27:38 *E* said to his father: Is
27:38 *E* raised his voice and burst
Ge 27:41 *E* harbored animosity for
27:41 *E* kept saying in his heart
27:42 words of *E* her older son
27:42 *E* your brother is comforting
28:5 mother of Jacob and *E*
28:6 *E* saw that Isaac had blessed
28:8 *E* saw that the daughters of
28:9 *E* went to Ishmael and took as
32:3 messengers ahead of him to *E*
32:4 you will say to my lord, to *E*
32:6 We got to your brother *E*, and
32:8 If *E* should come to the one
32:13 a gift for *E* his brother
32:17 In case that *E* my brother
32:18 sent to my lord, to *E*, and
32:19 word you are to speak to *E*
33:1 *E* was coming and with him
33:4 *E* went running to meet him
33:9 *E* said: I have a great many
33:15 *E* said: Let me, please, put
33:16 *E* turned back on his way to
35:1 you were running away from *E*
35:29 *E* and Jacob his sons buried
36:1 And this is the history of *E*
36:2 *E* took his wives from the
36:4 proceeded to bear Eliphaz to *E*
36:5 These are the sons of *E* who
36:6 *E* took his wives and his sons
36:8 So *E* took up dwelling in the
36:8 region of Seir. *E* is Edom
36:9 And this is the history of *E*
36:10 the names of the sons of *E*
36:14 she bore to *E* Jeush and
36:15 the sheiks of the sons of *E*
36:19 These are the sons of *E*
36:40 the names of the sheiks of *E*
36:43 This is *E* the father of Edom
De 2:4 sons of *E*, who are dwelling
2:5 I have given Mount Seir to *E*
2:8 sons of *E*, who are dwelling in
2:12 and the sons of *E* proceeded to
2:22 he did for the sons of *E*, who
2:29 sons of *E* dwelling in Seir
Jos 24:4 to Isaac I gave Jacob and *E*
24:4 *E* I gave Mount Seir to take
1Ch 1:34 sons of Isaac were *E* and
1:35 sons of *E* were Eliphaz
Jer 49:8 disaster of *E* I will bring
49:10 I will strip *E* bare
Ob 6 extent to which those of *E*
8 the mountainous region of *E*
9 the mountainous region of *E*
18 and the house of *E* as stubble
18 no survivor to the house of *E*
19 of the mountainous region of *E*
21 the mountainous region of *E*
Mal 1:2 *E* the brother of Jacob
1:3 and *E* I have hated; and I
Ro 9:13 I loved Jacob, but *E* I hated
Heb 11:20 Isaac blessed Jacob and *E*
12:16 like *E*, who in exchange for

Esau's
Ge 32:11 Deliver me . . . from *E* hand
36:10 the son of Adah, *E* wife
36:10 the son of Basemath, *E* wife
36:12 concubine of Eliphaz, *E* son
36:12 the sons of Adah, *E* wife
36:13 sons of Basemath, *E* wife
36:14 *E* wife, in that she bore to
36:15 sons of Eliphaz, *E* firstborn
36:17 the sons of Reuel, *E* son
36:17 sons by Basemath, *E* wife
36:18 sons of Oholibamah, *E* wife
36:18 daughter of Anah, *E* wife

Escape
Ge 19:17 *E* for your soul! Do not look
19:17 *E* to the mountainous region
19:19 I am not able to *e* to the
19:20 *e* there—is it not a small
19:22 *E* there, because I am not
32:8 camp remaining to make an *e*
45:7 keep you alive by a great *e*
Jg 3:26 and made his *e* to Seirah
1Sa 19:10 might *e* during that night
19:11 soul *e* tonight, tomorrow
19:12 go and run away and *e*
19:17 enemy away that he might *e*
19:18 *e* and got to come to Samuel
22:1 *e* to the cave of Adullam
22:20 Abiathar, made his *e* and
27:1 *e* without fail to the land
27:1 certainly *e* from his hand
2Sa 19:5 providing *e* for your soul
2Sa 19:9 he it was that provided *e*
20:6 cities and *e* before our eyes
22:2 and the Provider of *e* for me
22:44 *e* from the faultfinding of
1Ki 1:12 provide *e* for your own soul
18:40 a single one of them *e*
20:20 king of Syria got to *e* upon
2Ki 9:15 in *e* from the city to go
19:30 who *e* of the house of Judah
19:31 those who *e* from Mount Zion
2Ch 12:7 give them an *e*, and my rage
Ezr 9:8 leaving over . . . those who *e*
Es 4:13 the king's household will *e*
Job 1:15 I got to *e*, only I by myself
1:16 I got to *e*, only I by myself
1:17 I got to *e*, only I by myself
1:19 I got to *e*, only I by myself
19:20 *e* with the skin of my teeth
20:20 he will not *e*
41:19 sparks of fire make their *e*
Ps 17:13 do provide *e* for my soul
18:2 and the Provider of *e* for me
18:43 *e* from the faultfinding of
18:48 providing *e* for me from my
22:4 kept providing them with *e*
22:8 Let Him provide him with *e*!
31:1 provide *e* for me
32:7 joyful cries at providing *e*
33:17 it does not afford *e*
37:40 and provide them with *e*
37:40 He will provide them with *e*
40:17 and the Provider of *e* for me
41:1 Jehovah will provide *e* for
43:1 may you provide me with *e*
55:8 hasten to a place of *e* for me
70:5 and the Provider of *e* for me
71:2 and provide me with *e*
71:4 O my God, provide me with *e*
82:4 Provide *e* for the lowly one
89:48 *e* for his soul from the hand
91:14 also provide him with *e*
107:20 provide them *e* out of their
116:4 do provide my soul with *e*
144:2 my Provider of *e* for me
Pr 11:21 righteous . . . certainly *e*
19:5 forth lies will not *e*
28:26 is the one that will *e*
Ec 8:8 wickedness will provide no *e*
9:15 *e* for the city by his wisdom
Isa 15:9 of Moab who *e* and for the
20:6 how shall we ourselves *e*?
31:5 must also cause her to *e*
37:31 who *e* of the house of Judah
37:32 who *e* out of Mount Zion
46:2 unable to furnish *e* for the
46:4 may bear up and furnish *e*
49:24 of the tyrant make their *e*
49:25 will make their *e*
Jer 25:35 *e* from the majestic ones
32:4 king of Judah, will not *e*
34:3 will not *e* out of his hand
38:18 not *e* out of their hand
38:23 not *e* out of their hand
39:18 furnish you an *e*, and by
46:6 not the mighty man try to *e*
48:6 provide *e* for your souls
48:8 no city that can make its *e*
48:19 her that is making her *e*
51:6 *e* each one for his own soul
51:45 each one his soul with *e*
Eze 7:16 make their *e* and become
17:15 Will he *e*, he who is doing
17:15 And will he actually *e*?
17:18 He will not make his *e*
Da 11:41 *e* out of his hand, Edom and
12:1 your people will *e*, every one
Am 2:14 will provide his soul with *e*
2:15 no one swift . . . will *e*
2:15 will provide his soul with *e*
Zec 2:7 Zion! Make your *e*, you who
Mr 7:24 Yet he could not *e* notice
Ac 27:30 sailors began seeking to *e*
27:42 one might swim away and *e*
Ro 2:3 you will *e* the judgment of God
1Th 5:3 and they will by no means *e*
Heb 2:3 how shall we *e* if we have
12:25 For if they did not *e* who

Escaped
Ge 14:13 a man who had *e* came and
Ex 10:5 eat up the rest of what has *e*
Nu 21:29 give his sons as *e* ones and
Jos 10:20 *e* and went entering into
Jg 3:26 Ehud, he *e* while they were

Jg 3:29 and not a single one *e*
12:4 Men *e* from Ephraim is what
21:17 those who have *e* of Benjamin
1Sa 23:13 David had *e* from Keilah
30:17 not a man of them *e* except
2Sa 1:3 camp of Israel I have *e*
4:6 themselves *e* detection
2Ki 19:37 *e* to the land of Ararat
1Ch 4:43 remnant that had *e* of Amalek
2Ch 16:7 Syria has *e* out of your hand
30:6 *e* ones that are left of you
Ezr 9:13 those who have *e* such as
9:15 an *e* people as at this day
Ne 1:2 the Jews, those who had *e*
Ps 124:7 like a bird that is *e* From
124:7 And we ourselves have *e*
Isa 4:2 those of Israel who have *e*
10:20 *e* of the house of Jacob
37:38 *e* to the land of Ararat
66:19 who are *e* to the nations
Jer 41:15 he *e* with eight men from
44:14 return, except some *e* ones
Eze 6:9 your *e* ones will certainly
14:22 an *e* company, those being
24:26 come to you the *e* one for
24:27 will be opened to the *e* one
33:5 his own soul would have *e*
33:21 the *e* one from Jerusalem
33:22 the coming of the *e* one
Joe 2:32 prove to be the *e* ones
Lu 8:47 that she had not *e* notice
Ac 16:27 that the prisoners had *e*
2Co 11:33 basket and *e* his hands
Heb 11:34 *e* the edge of the sword
2Pe 1:4 *e* from the corruption that is
2:20 *e* from the defilements of

Escapee
Jos 8:22 either a survivor or an *e*
Jer 42:17 to have a survivor or an *e*
44:14 will come to be no *e* or
La 2:22 proved to be no *e* or survivor
Da 11:42 will not prove to be an *e*

Escapees
Isa 15:9 lion for the *e* of Moab who
45:20 you *e* from the nations
Jer 50:29 there prove to be no *e*
51:50 *e* from the sword, keep
Eze 7:16 their *e* will certainly make
Ob 14 in order to cut off his *e*

Escapes
De 23:15 he *e* from his master to you
2Ki 10:24 man that *e* from the men
Ec 7:26 if one *e* from her, but one is
Ac 26:26 things *e* his notice, for
2Pe 3:5 this fact *e* their notice

Escaping
Jg 12:5 the *e* men of Ephraim would
2Sa 15:14 there will prove to be no *e*
1Ki 19:17 one *e* from Hazael's sword
19:17 one *e* from Jehu's sword
2Ch 20:24 without anyone *e*
Ezr 9:14 none remaining and none *e*
Jer 44:28 ones *e* from the sword, they
50:28 *e* from the land of Babylon
Eze 6:8 the ones *e* from the sword
Joe 2:3 to be nothing thereof *e*
Am 9:1 no one *e* of them will make
Ob 17 where those *e* will prove to be
Lu 21:36 may succeed in *e* all these
2Pe 2:18 *e* from people who conduct
3:8 one fact not be *e* your notice

Escort
Ge 18:16 walking with them to *e* them
2Sa 19:31 to *e* him to the Jordan

Escorted
Ro 15:24 be *e* part way there by you

Escorting
Ge 12:20 they went *e* him and his wife

Esek
Ge 26:20 the name of the well *E*

Eshan
Jos 15:52 Arab and Dumah and *E*

Eshbaal
1Ch 8:33 father to Jonathan . . . and *E*
9:39 father to Jonathan and . . . *E*

Eshban
Ge 36:26 sons of Dishon: Hemdan and *E*
1Ch 1:41 sons of Dishon were . . . *E*

Eshcol
Ge 14:13 Mamre . . . the brother of *E*
14:24 who went with me, Aner, *E*
Nu 13:23 to the torrent valley of *E*
13:24 the torrent valley of *E*, on
32:9 up to the torrent valley of *E*
De 1:24 far as the torrent valley of *E*

Eshek
1Ch 8:39 sons of *E* his brother were

Eshtaol
Jos 15:33 *E* and Zorah and Ashnah
19:41 Zorah and *E* and Ir-shemesh
Jg 13:25 between Zorah and *E*
16:31 between Zorah and *E* in the
18:2 men . . . from Zorah and *E*
18:8 their brothers at Zorah and *E*
18:11 departed from . . . *E*

Eshtaolites
1Ch 2:53 the Zorathites and the *E*

Eshtemoa
Jos 21:14 *E* and its pasture ground
1Sa 30:28 and to those in *E*
1Ch 4:17 Ishbah the father of *E*
4:19 and *E* the Maacathite
6:57 *E* with its pasture grounds

Eshtemoh
Jos 15:50 Anab and *E* and Anim

Eshton
1Ch 4:11 who was the father of *E*
4:12 *E*, in turn, became father to

Esli
Lu 3:25 son of *E*, son of Naggai

Especially
Ge 25:21 entreating Jehovah *e* for his
Ex 31:13 *E* my sabbaths you are to
De 28:59 the plagues . . . *e* severe
Ac 20:38 were *e* pained at the word he
25:26 *e* before you, King Agrippa
26:3 *e* as you are expert on all
2Co 1:12 but more *e* toward you
2:4 that I have more *e* for you
6:2 Now is the *e* acceptable time
8:12 *e* acceptable according to
Ga 6:10 *e* toward those related to
Php 4:22 *e* those of the household of
1Ti 4:10 Savior . . . *e* of faithful ones
5:8 *e* for those who are members
5:17 *e* those who work hard in
2Ti 4:13 scrolls, *e* the parchments
Tit 1:10 *e* those men who adhere to
Phm 16 brother beloved, *e* so to me
Heb 13:19 I exhort you more *e* to do
2Pe 2:10 *e*, however, those who go on

Establish
Ge 6:18 I do *e* my covenant with you
9:11 Yes, I do *e* my covenant with
9:17 covenant that I do *e* between
17:19 I will *e* my covenant with
17:21 covenant I shall *e* with
Nu 30:13 her husband should *e* it or
De 28:9 *e* you as a holy people to
Ru 4:7 to *e* every sort of thing
2Sa 3:10 *e* the throne of David over
7:12 firmly *e* his kingdom
7:13 *e* the throne of his kingdom
7:24 *e* your people Israel firmly
1Ki 9:5 *e* the throne of your kingdom
1Ch 17:11 firmly *e* his kingship
17:12 *e* his throne firmly to time
22:10 *e* the throne of his kingship
28:7 *e* his kingship firmly to
2Ch 7:18 *e* the throne of your kingship
Ezr 2:62 to *e* their genealogy publicly
Ne 7:64 to *e* their genealogy publicly
Ps 7:9 may you *e* the righteous one
48:8 God himself will firmly *e* it
87:5 himself will firmly *e* her
89:4 I shall firmly *e* your seed
90:17 hands do you firmly *e* upon
90:17 hands, do you firmly *e* it
107:36 *e* a city of habitation
Pr 21:29 that will firmly *e* his ways
Isa 9:7 *e* it firmly and to sustain it
Jer 28:6 May Jehovah *e* your words
29:10 *e* toward you my good word
33:2 to *e* it firmly, Jehovah
Eze 16:60 *e* for you an indefinitely
16:62 *e* my covenant with you
Da 6:7 *e* a royal statute and to
Da 6:8 king, may you *e* the statute
Ro 3:31 On the contrary, we *e* law
10:3 but seeking to *e* their own
Heb 10:9 he may *e* what is second

Established
Ge 41:32 the thing is firmly *e* on
Ex 6:4 also *e* my covenant with them
10:2 my signs that I have *e* among
15:17 An *e* place that you have
15:17 that your hands have *e*
15:25 He *e* for them a regulation
Nu 30:14 he has also *e* all her vows
30:14 He has *e* them because he
De 13:14 the thing is *e* as the truth
17:4 the thing is *e* as the truth
Jg 16:26 the house is firmly *e* and
16:29 the house was firmly *e*
1Sa 20:31 will not be firmly *e*
2Sa 5:12 Jehovah had firmly *e* him as
7:16 firmly *e* to time indefinite
7:26 David become firmly *e* before
1Ki 2:12 kingship . . . very firmly *e*
2:24 firmly *e* me and keeps me
2:45 *e* before Jehovah forever
2:46 the kingdom was firmly *e*
8:13 an *e* place for you to dwell
8:39 your *e* place of dwelling
8:43 your *e* place of dwelling
8:49 your *e* place of dwelling
1Ch 14:2 Jehovah had firmly *e* him as
16:30 productive land is firmly *e*
2Ch 6:2 *e* place for you to dwell in
6:33 your *e* place of dwelling
6:39 your *e* place of dwelling
12:1 Rehoboam was firmly *e*
12:14 *e* his heart to search for
17:5 kingdom firmly *e* in his hand
Ezr 3:3 *e* the altar firmly upon its
Job 11:15 you will certainly become *e*
21:8 their offspring are firmly *e*
Ps 24:2 he keeps it firmly *e*
33:14 the *e* place where he dwells
40:2 He firmly *e* my steps
89:2 faithfulness firmly *e* in them
89:14 the *e* place of your throne
89:37 moon it will be firmly *e*
93:1 land also becomes firmly *e* so
93:2 throne is firmly *e* from long
96:10 firmly *e* so that it cannot
97:2 *e* place of his throne
99:4 have firmly *e* uprightness
101:7 he will not be firmly *e*
102:28 offspring will be firmly *e*
103:19 firmly *e* his throne in the
104:5 the earth upon its *e* places
119:5 that my ways were firmly *e*
140:11 firmly *e* in the earth
Pr 4:18 until the day is firmly *e*
4:26 your own ways be firmly *e*
12:3 firmly *e* by wickedness
12:19 truth that will be firmly *e*
16:3 your plans will be firmly *e*
16:12 is the throne firmly *e*
19:29 Judgments have been firmly *e*
20:18 plans . . . are firmly *e*
22:18 *e* together upon your lips
24:3 it will prove firmly *e*
25:5 be firmly *e* by righteousness
29:14 his throne will be firmly *e*
Isa 2:2 firmly *e* above the top of the
4:5 *e* place of Mount Zion and
16:5 will certainly be firmly *e*
18:4 and look upon my *e* place
45:18 the One who firmly *e* it
54:14 firmly *e* in righteousness
Jer 30:20 assembly will be firmly *e*
Da 6:12 matter is well *e* according
8:11 *e* place of his sanctuary was
Ho 6:3 his going forth is firmly *e*
Mic 4:1 firmly *e* above the top of the
Na 2:5 the barricade . . . firmly *e*
Hab 2:12 *e* a town by unrighteousness
Zec 5:11 and it must be firmly *e*
Mt 18:16 every matter may be *e*
2Co 13:1 every matter must be *e*
Eph 3:17 and *e* on the foundation
Col 1:23 *e* on the foundation and
Heb 8:6 *e* upon better promises

Establishes
Da 6:15 king himself *e* is not to be

Establishing
Ge 9:9 I am *e* my covenant with you
Le 14:2 the day for *e* his purification

Le 14:23 for *e* his purification to the
14:32 when *e* his purification
Nu 6:9 the day of *e* his purification
De 29:13 purpose of *e* you today as his
Ps 9:7 *e* his throne for judgment
65:6 He is firmly *e* the mountains
Jer 10:12 *e* the productive land
51:15 One firmly *e* the productive
Php 1:7 legally *e* of the good news

Establishment
Le 13:7 for the *e* of his purification
13:35 the *e* of his purification

Estate
Ge 47:26 over the landed *e* of Egypt

Estates
Ps 49:11 called their landed *e* by

Esteem
2Ki 5:1 held in *e*, because it was by
Pr 4:8 Highly *e* it, and it will exalt

Esteemed
1Sa 18:23 little means and lightly *e*
2Sa 6:22 even more lightly *e* than
Pr 12:9 one lightly *e* but having a
Isa 3:5 lightly *e* one against the
Ac 5:34 teacher *e* by all the people
19:27 Artemis will be *e* as nothing
Heb 10:29 *e* as of ordinary value the
11:11 she *e* him faithful who had
11:26 *e* the reproach of the

Esther
Es 2:7 Hadassah, that is, *E*, the
2:8 then *E* was taken to the king's
2:10 *E* had not told about her
2:15 *E* the daughter of Abihail the
2:15 *E* was continually gaining
2:16 *E* was taken to King Ahasuerus
2:17 king came to love *E* more than
2:18 the banquet of *E*
2:20 *E* was not telling about her
2:20 the saying of Mordecai *E* was
2:22 immediately told *E* the queen
2:22 In turn *E* talked to the king
4:5 *E* called Hathach, one of the
4:8 show *E* and to tell her and to
4:9 and told *E* Mordecai's words
4:10 Then *E* said to Hathach and
4:12 tell Mordecai the words of *E*
4:13 Mordecai said to reply to *E*
4:15 *E* said to reply to Mordecai
4:17 *E* had laid in command upon
5:1 *E* went dressing up royally
5:2 as soon as the king saw *E* the
5:2 king held out to *E* the golden
5:2 *E* now came near and touched
5:3 What do you have, O *E* the
5:4 *E* said: If to the king it does
5:5 act quickly on the word of *E*
5:5 to the banquet that *E* had made
5:6 In time the king said to *E*
5:7 To this *E* answered and said
5:12 *E* the queen brought in with
6:14 the banquet that *E* had made
7:1 in to banquet with *E* the queen
7:2 king now said to *E* also on the
7:2 What is your petition, O *E* the
7:3 *E* the queen answered and said
7:5 went on to say to *E* the queen
7:6 *E* said: The man, the adversary
7:7 request for his soul from *E*
7:8 upon the couch on which *E* was
8:1 gave to *E* the queen the house
8:1 *E* had told what he was to her
8:2 *E* went on to place Mordecai
8:3 *E* spoke again before the king
8:4 the golden scepter out to *E*
8:4 *E* rose and stood before the
8:7 Ahasuerus said to *E* the queen
8:7 house of Haman . . . given to *E*
9:12 king proceeded to say to *E* the
9:13 *E* said: If to the king it does
9:25 *E* came in before the king he
9:29 *E* the queen, the daughter of
9:31 and *E* the queen had imposed
9:32 saying of *E* confirmed these

Esther's
Es 2:11 to know of *E* welfare and
4:4 *E* young women and her eunuchs

Estimate
Pr 16:2 is making an *e* of spirits
21:2 is making an *e* of hearts
Pr 24:12 is making an *e* of hearts

Estimated
Le 5:15 the *e* value in silver shekels
5:18 flock according to the *e* value
6:6 *e* value, for a guilt offering
27:2 according to the *e* value
27:3 *e* value has to be of a male
27:3 *e* value must then become
27:4 female, the *e* value must then
27:5 *e* value of the male must then
27:6 *e* value of the male must then
27:6 female the *e* value must be
27:7 male, the *e* value must then
27:8 too poor for the *e* value, he
27:12 value *e* by the priest, so it
27:13 in addition to the *e* value
27:15 money of the *e* value in
27:16 *e* in proportion to its seed
27:17 cost according to the *e* value
27:18 be made from the *e* value
27:19 money of the *e* value in
27:23 give the *e* value on that day
27:25 value should be *e* in the
27:27 according to the *e* value
27:27 sold according to the *e* value
Nu 18:16 redeem it, by the *e* value
1Sa 2:3 by him deeds are rightly *e*

Estranged
Nu 14:34 know what my being *e* means
Ps 69:8 become one *e* to my brothers

Etam
Jg 15:8 in a cleft of the crag *E*
15:11 the cleft of the crag *E* and
1Ch 4:3 sons of the father of *E*
4:32 their settlements were *E* and
2Ch 11:6 rebuilt Bethlehem and *E* and

Eternal
Ge 49:26 blessings of the *e* mountains
Isa 9:6 *E* Father, Prince of Peace
Hab 3:6 the *e* mountains got to be
Ro 1:20 his *e* power and Godship
Eph 3:11 *e* purpose that he formed in
Jude 6 *e* bonds under dense darkness

Eternity
Isa 45:17 the indefinite times of *e*
1Ti 1:17 the King of *e*, incorruptible
2Pe 3:18 now and to the day of *e*
Jude 25 authority for all past *e* and
25 and now and into all *e*
Re 15:3 are your ways, King of *e*

Etham
Ex 13:20 encamp at *E* at the edge of
Nu 33:6 and went camping in *E*, which
33:7 pulled away from *E* and turned
33:8 in the wilderness of *E* and

Ethan
1Ki 4:31 wiser than . . . *E* the Ezrahite
1Ch 2:6 the sons of Zerah were . . . *E*
2:8 the sons of *E* were Azariah
6:42 son of *E*, the son of Zimmah
6:44 *E* the son of Kishi, the son
15:17 *E* the son of Kushaiah
15:19 singers Heman, Asaph and *E*
Ps 89:*super* Maskil. Of *E* the Ezrahite

Ethanim
1Ki 8:2 month of *E* in the festival

Ethbaal
1Ki 16:31 *E* the king of the Sidonians

Ether
Jos 15:42 Libnah and *E* and Ashan
19:7 Ain, Rimmon and *E* and Ashan

Ethiopia
2Ki 19:9 Tirhakah the king of *E*
Es 1:1 as king from India to *E*
8:9 that were from India to *E*
Isa 18:1 region of the rivers of *E*
20:3 Egypt and against *E*
20:4 and the exiles of *E*, boys and
20:5 *E* their looked-for hope and
37:9 Tirhakah the king of *E*
43:3 *E* and Seba in place of you
45:14 and the merchants of *E* and
Eze 29:10 and to the boundary of *E*
30:4 severe pains must occur in *E*
30:5 *E* and Put and Lud and all
30:9 drive self-confident *E* into
38:5 Persia, *E* and Put with them
Na 3:9 *E* was her full might, also
Zep 3:10 the region of the rivers of *E*

Ethiopian
2Ch 14:9 Zerah the *E* went out against
Jer 38:7 Ebed-melech the *E*, a man
38:10 Ebed-melech the *E*, saying
38:12 Ebed-melech the *E* said to
39:16 say to Ebed-melech the *E*
Ac 8:27 an *E* eunuch, a man in power

Ethiopians
2Ch 12:3 of Egypt . . . Sukkiim and *E*
14:12 Jehovah defeated the *E*
14:12 and the *E* took to flight
14:13 *E* continued falling down
16:8 *E* and the Libyans themselves
21:16 were by the side of the *E*
Da 11:43 the *E* will be at his steps
Zep 2:12 *E* . . . will be people slain by
Ac 8:27 under Candace queen of the *E*

Eth-kazin
Jos 19:13 to Gath-hepher, to *E*, and

Ethnan
1Ch 4:7 sons of Helah were . . . *E*

Ethni
1Ch 6:41 son of *E*, the son of Zerah

Eubulus
2Ti 4:21 *E* sends you his greetings

Eunice
2Ti 1:5 and your mother *E*, but which

Eunuch
Es 2:3 in charge of Hegai the king's *e*
2:14 Shaashgaz the king's *e*, the
2:15 king's *e*, the guardian of the
Isa 56:3 Neither let the *e* say, Look!
Jer 38:7 man who was a *e* and who was
Ac 8:27 Ethiopian *e*, a man in power
8:34 *e* said to Philip: I beg you
8:36 *e* said: Look! A body of water
8:38 both Philip and the *e*; and he
8:39 *e* did not see him anymore

Eunuchs
Es 4:4 Esther's young women and her *e*
4:5 Hathach, one of the king's *e*
Isa 56:4 Jehovah has said to the *e*
Mt 19:12 are *e* that were born such
19:12 there are *e* that were made
19:12 that were made *e* by men
19:12 *e* that have made themselves
19:12 that have made themselves *e*

Euodia
Php 4:2 *E* I exhort and Syntyche I

Euphrates
Ge 2:14 And the fourth river is the *E*
15:18 the great river, the river *E*
De 1:7 the great river, the river *E*
11:24 the river *E*, to the western
Jos 1:4 the great river, the river *E*
2Sa 8:3 back again at the river *E*
2Ki 23:29 by the river *E*, and King
24:7 Egypt up to the river *E*
1Ch 5:9 the wilderness at the river *E*
18:3 his control at the river *E*
2Ch 35:20 at Carchemish by the *E*
Jer 13:4 go to the *E*, and hide it
13:5 hid it by the *E*, just as
13:6 go to the *E* and take from
13:7 I went to the *E* and dug and
46:2 by the river *E* at Carchemish
46:6 bank of the river *E* they
46:10 the north by the river *E*
51:63 it into the midst of the *E*
Re 9:14 bound at the great river *E*
16:12 bowl upon the great river *E*

Euroaquilo
Ac 27:14 wind called *E* rushed down

Eutychus
Ac 20:9 *E* fell into a deep sleep

Evangelizer
Ac 21:8 Philip the *e*, who was one of
2Ti 4:5 do the work of an *e*, fully

Evangelizers
Eph 4:11 some as *e*, some as shepherds

Evaporated
Ex 16:14 In time the layer of dew *e*
Isa 44:27 to the watery deep, Be *e*

Eve
Ge 3:20 called his wife's name *E*
4:1 Adam had intercourse with *E*

2Co 11:3 the serpent seduced *E* by its
1Ti 2:13 was formed first, then *E*

Even

Ge 4:4 flock, *e* their fatty pieces
17:8 *e* the entire land of Canaan
17:10 you men, *e* your seed after
17:14 *e* that soul must be cut off
19:25 *e* the entire District and all
27:34 Bless me, *e* me too, my
27:38 Bless me, *e* me too, my
29:24 *e* to Leah his daughter
30:3 I, *e* I, may get children from
31:15 *e* from the money given for
37:23 *e* the long striped garment
46:7 *e* all his offspring, with him
49:26 *e* upon the crown of the head
Ex 3:19 *e* I, well know that the king
4:9 not believe *e* these two signs
6:5 I, *e* I, have heard the groaning
9:30 *e* then show fear because of
12:41 it *e* came about on this very
15:18 time indefinite, *e* forever
21:14 take him *e* from being at my
25:22 *e* all that I shall command
Le 3:3 *e* all the fat that is over the
3:9 *e* all the fat that is upon the
3:14 *e* all the fat that is upon
4:8 *e* all the fat that is over the
26:24 I, *e* I, shall have to strike
26:39 *e* because of the errors of
26:40 yes, *e* when they walked in
26:42 and *e* my covenant with Isaac
26:42 *e* my covenant with Abraham
26:43 *e* because, they had rejected
Nu 3:8 *e* the obligation of the sons
5:4 *e* to send them outside the
6:7 Not *e* for his father or his
14:4 They *e* went to saying to one
16:38 *e* the fire holders of these
22:33 *e* you I should have killed
24:20 will be *e* his perishing
De 1:37 *E* against me Jehovah got
9:8 *E* in Horeb you provoked
9:26 *e* your private property
10:14 *e* the heavens of the heavens
10:15 offspring after them, *e* you
12:31 *e* their sons and their
18:1 *e* his inheritance, they should
20:11 it must *e* occur that all the
22:26 indeed murders him, *e* a soul
23:2 *E* to the tenth generation
23:3 *E* to the tenth generation
23:18 your God, *e* both of them
28:57 *e* toward her afterbirth
28:58 fear . . . *e* Jehovah, your God
29:22 *e* when they have seen the
32:31 *E* our enemies being the
33:9 *E* his brothers he did not
Jos 6:26 build this city, *e* Jericho
9:4 they, *e* of their own accord
24:18 *e* the Amorites, dwelling
Jg 2:17 *e* to their judges they did
3:3 Canaanites, *e* the Sidonians
6:31 put to death *e* this morning
10:9 to fight *e* against Judah and
20:26 Israel, *e* all the people
21:10 *e* the women and the little
1Sa 2:5 *E* the barren has given birth
13:7 Hebrews *e* crossed the Jordan
14:15 pillagers trembled, *e* they
14:21 *e* they too were for proving
14:39 *e* if it is in Jonathan my
18:4 and *e* his sword and his bow
18:11 pin David *e* to the wall
22:19 *E* Nob the city of the
25:11 I do not *e* know from where
25:43 *e* both of them, his wives
28:19 *E* the camp of Israel
30:19 *e* to anything that they had
30:24 *e* so will the share of the
31:6 *e* all his men, came to die
2Sa 1:4 *e* Saul and Jonathan his son
2:7 *e* I whom the house of Judah
3:31 *E* King David was walking
6:22 *e* more lightly esteemed than
7:11 *e* from the day that I put
7:19 *e* be something little in
13:36 *e* the king and all his
14:7 let us *e* annihilate the heir
15:34 servant of your father, *e* I
15:34 now *e* I am your servant
17:5 what is in his mouth, *e* his
17:10 *e* the valiant man whose
17:12 not be left *e* a single one
2Sa 17:13 be found there *e* a pebble
19:28 just claim *e* for crying out
19:30 Let him *e* take the whole
19:43 *e* in David we are more than
23:19 distinguished *e* more than
23:23 *e* more than the thirty
24:3 God *e* add to the people a
1Ki 2:22 the kingship . . . *e* for him and
4:24 *e* all the kings this side of
4:34 *e* from all the kings of the
8:36 *e* of your people Israel
11:35 give it to you, *e* ten tribes
14:24 And *e* the male temple
15:13 *e* Maacah his grandmother
21:19 lick up your blood, *e* yours
2Ki 2:14 the God of Elijah, *e* He
7:19 *E* if Jehovah were making
8:9 *e* every sort of good thing of
10:33 *e* Gilead and Bashan
11:2 *e* him and his nursing woman
13:6 *e* the sacred pole itself
13:17 *e* the arrow of salvation
16:3 *e* his own son he made pass
16:15 *e* Urijah the priest, saying
17:15 *e* in imitation of the
17:19 *E* Judah itself did not keep
18:5 *e* those who had happened to
18:12 *e* all that Moses the
19:12 *e* Gozan and Haran and
19:25 I have *e* formed it
21:8 *e* concerning all the law
21:11 make *e* Judah sin with his
22:16 *e* all the words of the book
22:19 I, *e* I, have heard, is the
23:15 *e* that altar and the
23:27 I have chosen, *e* Jerusalem
1Ch 5:9 *E* to the east he dwelt as far
5:26 stirred . . . *e* the spirit of
9:23 *e* the house of the tent, for
9:27 charge of the key, *e* to open
11:2 *e* while Saul happened to be
11:8 *e* to the parts round about
16:15 *e* to time indefinite
16:17 as a regulation *e* to Jacob
16:17 lasting covenant *e* to Israel
17:10 *e* since the days that I put
21:12 *e* pestilence, in the land
22:12 *e* to keep the law of
23:29 *e* for the layer bread and
26:24 *e* Shebuel the son of
28:1 *e* every valiant, mighty man
28:12 *e* the architectural plan of
28:19 *e* for all the works of the
29:9 *e* David the king himself
29:10 time indefinite *e* to time
29:21 *e* sacrifices in great
2Ch 1:11 neither is it *e* many days
2:9 *e* for preparing timbers for
6:27 *e* of your people Israel
7:17 *e* by doing according to all
8:13 *e* as a daily matter of
13:22 *e* his ways and his words
14:15 *e* the tents with livestock
15:16 *e* Maacah his grandmother
16:12 *e* in his sickness he
17:6 *e* removed the high places
20:4 *E* from all the cities of
20:13 *e* their little ones, their
21:13 *e* your own brothers, the
21:19 *e* when the term of two
23:10 *e* each one with his missile
24:6 *e* that of the congregation
24:7 *e* all the holy things of the
26:8 fame went *e* as far as Egypt
26:16 *e* to the point of causing
28:2 *e* molten statues he made
28:25 *e* the cities of Judah, he
29:27 *e* under the direction of the
29:30 praise *e* with rejoicing
30:1 *e* letters he wrote to
30:6 *e* according to the
30:10 passing . . . *e* to Zebulun
30:21 instruments, *e* to Jehovah
31:6 *e* they themselves brought in
32:17 *E* letters he wrote to
34:7 *e* went pulling down the
34:27 I, *e* I, have heard, is the
36:13 *e* against King
36:14 *E* all the chiefs of the
Ezr 1:5 *e* everyone whose spirit the
3:13 heard *e* to a great distance
7:22 *e* to a hundred talents of
7:25 *e* all those knowing the laws
9:6 grown great *e* to the heavens
Ezr 10:16 *e* all of them by their
Ne 4:3 *E* what they are building, if a
6:7 are *e* prophets that you have
6:10 *e* by night they are coming in
8:7 *e* the Levites, were explaining
8:13 *e* to gain insight into the
9:6 *e* the heaven of the heavens
9:16 *e* our forefathers, acted
9:19 *e* you, in your abundant mercy
9:22 *e* the land of the king of
9:24 *e* their kings and the peoples
9:29 *e* acted presumptuously and
12:23 *e* down till the days of
12:27 *e* with thanksgivings and
12:28 *e* from the District, from
13:17 *e* profaning the sabbath day
13:26 *E* him the foreign wives
13:31 *e* for the supply of the wood
Es 5:3 let it *e* be given to you!
5:6 Let it *e* be granted you!
5:6 let it *e* be done!
7:2 Let it *e* be given to you
7:2 the kingship—let it *e* be done!
8:15 *e* of wool dyed reddish
9:1 *e* a turning to the contrary
9:12 Let it *e* be given to you
9:12 request? Let it *e* be done
Job 1:6 and *e* Satan proceeded to enter
2:3 *E* yet he is holding fast his
4:5 It touches *e* you, and you get
4:6 *e* the integrity of your ways
5:5 And *e* from butcher hooks one
5:14 encounter darkness *e* by day
6:3 heavier *e* than the sands of
6:8 God would grant *e* my hope
6:10 *E* it would still be my
6:14 *e* the fear of the Almighty
6:27 *e* over someone fatherless
7:14 You *e* have terrified me with
8:12 *E* ahead of all other grass it
9:5 people do not *e* know of them
9:15 I would not answer, *e* though
10:18 not *e* an eye could see me
11:12 *E* a hollow-minded man
13:15 *E* if he would slay me
14:7 exists hope for *e* a tree
14:7 it will *e* sprout again
14:18 And *e* a rock will be moved
14:19 rubs away *e* stones
15:17 *E* this I have beheld, so let
15:20 *E* the very number of years
17:8 And *e* the innocent one gets
18:7 *E* his counsel will cast him
18:20 *e* the people in the East
19:13 have *e* turned aside from me
19:23 they were *e* inscribed
19:27 *e* I shall behold for myself
20:2 *E* on account of my inward
20:25 *e* go out through his back
20:29 *E* his stated inheritance
21:22 he teach knowledge *e* to God
22:6 *e* the garments of naked
23:2 *E* today my state of concern
23:16 *E* God himself has made my
24:3 *e* the male ass of fatherless
24:9 boy *e* from the breast
25:5 *e* the moon . . . is not bright
28:19 *e* with gold in its purity
28:21 hidden *e* from the eyes of
29:8 *e* the aged ones rose up
30:2 *E* the power of their hands
30:9 *e* the theme of their song
31:4 And count *e* all my steps
32:10 declare my knowledge, *e* I
32:17 give in answer my part, *e* I
32:17 declare my knowledge, *e* I
34:13 productive land, *e* all of it
34:20 *e* in the middle of the
34:33 *E* what you well know
34:34 *E* a wise able-bodied man
35:11 wiser than *e* the flying
36:7 *E* kings on the throne
36:12 pass away *e* by a missile
36:19 *E* all your powerful efforts
37:6 *e* to the downpour of his
38:22 see *e* the storehouses of the
38:34 your voice *e* to the cloud
39:15 *e* a wild beast of the field
40:14 I, *e* I, shall commend you
41:16 not *e* air can come in
41:19 *E* sparks of fire make
41:20 set aflame *e* with rushes
41:21 *e* a flame goes forth out of
Ps 2:6 I, *e* I, have installed my king

Ps 9:5 to time indefinite, e forever
9:17 E all the nations forgetting
10:16 time indefinite, e forever
12:2 e with a double heart
14:3 no one doing good, Not e one
14:4 have not called e upon Jehovah
16:3 e the majestic ones, are the
21:4 time indefinite, e forever
21:7 E in the loving-kindness of
23:4 E though I walk in the valley
25:11 You must e forgive my error
27:3 E then I shall be trusting
27:10 E Jehovah himself would take
32:9 curbed e by bridle or halter
33:22 E as we have kept waiting
35:16 their teeth e against me
35:17 E my only one from the
35:21 their mouth e against me
35:23 O my God, e Jehovah, to my
37:18 will continue e to time
40:5 God, e your wonderful works
41:13 e to time indefinite
44:2 hand drove away e nations
45:6 your throne . . . e forever
45:17 laud you . . . e forever
48:14 time indefinite, e forever
49:7 redeem e a brother
49:10 that e the wise ones die
50:18 thief, you were e pleased
51:2 cleanse me e from my sin
51:7 become whiter e than snow
51:9 And wipe out e all my errors
51:10 Create in me e a pure heart
51:12 e with a willing spirit
52:8 to time indefinite, e forever
53:3 no one doing good, Not e one
53:4 have not called e upon Jehovah
55:19 E He that is sitting
56:3 shall trust e in you
56:7 bring down e the peoples
57:4 devourers, e the sons of men
59:12 E for the cursing and the
60:super e twelve thousand
61:2 I shall cry, e to you, when
62:11 twice I have heard e this
63:5 the best part, e fatness
64:6 e his heart, is deep
65:2 e to you people of all flesh
67:2 e among all the nations
68:9 e when it was weary—you
68:12 E the kings of armies flee
68:16 E Jehovah himself will
68:18 Yes, e the stubborn ones
68:35 e might to the people
69:4 e more than the hairs of my
71:6 e from the inward parts of
71:18 And e until old age and
71:23 E my soul that you have
73:5 e in the trouble of mortal
73:24 you will take me e to glory
74:6 they strike e with hatchet
74:8 e their offspring, have said
74:11 e your right hand, withdrawn
74:16 luminary, e the sun
77:1 I will e cry out to God
78:4 Relating them e to the
78:27 E winged flying creatures
78:41 pained e the Holy One of
78:47 their vine e by the hail
78:48 of burden e to the hail
78:50 life he handed over e to the
78:61 his strength e to captivity
79:11 come in e before you
81:6 turned aside his shoulder e
81:6 to be free e from the basket
83:5 to conclude e a covenant
84:3 E the bird itself has found
84:6 E with blessings the
88:3 come in touch e with Sheol
89:1 sing about e to time
89:2 built e to time indefinite
89:4 E to time indefinite I shall
89:10 Rahab, e as someone slain
89:32 transgression e with a rod
89:32 their error e with strokes
89:36 to be e to time indefinite
90:2 E from time indefinite to
91:10 e a plague will draw near to
94:10 E the One teaching men
94:15 return e to righteousness
94:21 pronounce wicked e the blood
97:11 rejoicing e for the ones
98:1 right hand, e his holy arm
102:8 have sworn e by me

Ps 102:9 have mingled e with weeping
102:19 has looked e at the earth
103:1 E everything within me, his
103:7 e to the sons of Israel
103:10 e according to our sins
103:17 e to time indefinite
105:8 e to time indefinite
105:10 as a regulation e to Jacob
105:10 lasting covenant e to Israel
105:22 wisdom to e his elderly
105:34 of locust, e without number
105:43 ones e with a joyful cry
106:16 E Aaron the holy one of
106:48 e to time indefinite
107:3 together e from the lands
107:14 tearing e their bands apart
107:16 cut down e the bars of iron
107:18 detest e every sort of food
107:27 e all their wisdom proves
108:1 make melody, E my glory
112:7 not be afraid e of bad news
116:6 he proceeded to save e me
119:23 E princes have sat
119:29 Remove . . . e the false way
119:44 time indefinite, e forever
119:45 searched e for your orders
119:56 E this has become mine
119:127 More than gold, e refined
124:3 swallowed us up e alive
125:1 dwells e to time indefinite
125:4 E to the ones upright in
126:5 reap e with a joyful cry
126:6 goes forth, e weeping
127:2 sleep e to his beloved one
133:3 E life to time indefinite
135:4 Jah has chosen e Jacob for
135:7 made e sluices for the rain
135:11 E Sihon the king of the
135:14 regret e over his servants
136:8 E the sun for dominion by
136:19 E Sihon the king of the
138:2 saying e above all your name
139:3 familiar e with all my ways
139:12 E the darkness itself would
139:16 Your eyes saw e the embryo
139:18 than e the grains of sand
139:19 e the bloodguilty men will
140:1 safeguard me e from the man
140:4 e from the man of deeds of
141:5 e my prayer during their
143:9 have taken cover e with you
145:1 time indefinite, e forever
145:2 time indefinite, e forever
145:21 time indefinite, e forever
Pr 1:12 e whole, like those going
3:12 e as a father does a son in
3:23 e your foot will not strike
4:11 instruct you e in the way of
5:12 has disrespected e reproof
6:1 handshake e to the stranger
6:8 food e in the summer
6:8 food supplies e in the harvest
6:26 hunts e for a precious soul
7:22 that comes e to the slaughter
8:12 I find e the knowledge of
8:19 better than gold, e than
10:12 love covers over e all
11:7 e expectation based on
11:8 one rescued e from distress
14:13 E in laughter the heart may
14:20 E to his fellowman one who
16:4 e the wicked one for the evil
16:7 he causes e his enemies
17:15 e both of them are something
17:23 e a bribe from the bosom to
17:28 E anyone foolish, when
18:6 mouth calls e for strokes
18:16 him e before great people
18:18 puts e contentions to rest
18:18 it separates e the mighty
18:20 satisfied e with the produce
19:4 lowly gets separated e from
19:24 it back e to his own mouth
20:11 E by his practices a boy
20:12 Jehovah himself has made e
21:8 man, e a stranger, is crooked
21:22 scaled e the city of mighty
21:28 will speak e forever
22:1 favor is better than e silver
22:6 e when he grows old he will
22:19 you knowledge today, e you
23:15 heart will rejoice, e mine
23:34 e like one lying down at the
24:16 one may fall e seven times

Pr 27:22 E if you should pound the
28:9 e his prayer is something
28:17 himself flee e to the pit
29:21 e become a thankless one
30:11 evil e upon its father and
30:11 does not bless e its mother
31:24 She has made e undergarments
31:31 praise her e in the gates
Ec 1:4 earth is standing e to time
1:11 be no remembrance e of them
1:16 I, e I, spoke with my heart
2:1 I said, e I, in my heart
2:3 cheering my flesh e with wine
2:3 e to lay hold on folly until I
2:8 of mankind, a lady, e ladies
2:11 I, e I, turned toward all the
2:12 e I, turned to see wisdom and
2:13 I saw, e I, that there exists
2:18 e I, hated all my hard work
2:24 This too I have seen, e I
3:1 e a time for every affair
3:11 E time indefinite he has put
3:18 I, e I, have said in my heart
5:19 e empowered him to eat from
6:3 e the grave has not become his
6:5 E the sun itself he has not
6:6 E supposing that he has lived
6:7 e their own soul does not get
7:14 made e this exactly as that
7:22 own heart well knows e many
7:22 e you, have called down evil
7:25 turned around, e my heart did
8:1 e the sternness of his face is
8:6 judgment e for every affair
8:17 e if they should say they are
9:1 e to search out all this, that
9:11 do e those having knowledge
10:16 keep eating e in the morning
10:20 E in your bedroom do not
11:2 to seven, or e to eight
11:8 man should live e many years
Ca 3:6 e with every sort of scent
4:8 the top of Senir, e Hermon
5:5 I got up, e I, to open to my
5:6 I opened, e I, to my dear one
8:1 People would not e despise me
Isa 1:6 sole of the foot e to the head
1:15 E though you make many
1:18 will become e like wool
1:23 e the legal case of a widow
3:5 e each one over his fellowman
4:4 rinse away e the bloodshed
5:10 e ten acres of vineyard will
5:10 e a homer measure of seed
5:15 e the eyes of the high ones
5:21 e in front of their own
5:23 e the righteousness of the
5:30 e the light has grown dark
7:20 e by means of the king of
7:20 away e the beard itself
8:7 e therefore, look! Jehovah is
9:5 e come to be for burning as
9:9 e all of them, Ephraim and
9:17 rejoice e over their young
9:19 compassion e on his brother
10:2 plunder e the fatherless boys
10:11 e so I shall do to
10:14 gather up e all the earth
10:18 e from the soul clear to the
11:7 e the lion will eat straw
11:10 e the nations will turn
11:13 e those showing hostility
13:18 bows will dash e young men
14:8 E the juniper trees have also
14:9 E Sheol underneath has
14:16 will gaze e at you
14:16 close examination e to you
14:17 homeward e for his
16:4 aliens e in you, O Moab
16:7 Moab; e all of it will howl
16:9 shouting e over your summer
16:11 harp e over Moab, and
17:4 e the fatness of his flesh
17:5 e become like one gleaning
17:9 e the branch that they have
18:6 and upon it e every beast of
18:7 e from a people
19:8 e those spreading fishing
19:20 savior, e a grand one, who
21:16 Kedar must e come to its
23:12 E there it will not be
24:16 E with treachery the
25:2 not be rebuilt e to time
26:12 e all our works you have

Isa 26:19 *e* those impotent in death
27:1 *e* to Leviathan, the crooked
27:3 safeguard her *e* night and day
28:22 *e* something decided upon
29:4 become *e* from the earth
29:7 Ariel, *e* all those waging
29:10 has covered *e* your heads
29:18 *e* the eyes of the blind ones
29:19 *e* the poor ones of mankind
29:21 *e* for the one reproving in
29:24 *e* those who are grumbling
30:3 *e* for you men a reason for
30:4 own envoys reach *e* Hanes
30:8 and inscribe it *e* in a book
30:26 heals *e* the severe wound
30:31 strike it *e* with a staff
31:4 *e* the maned young lion, over
32:4 and *e* the tongue of the
32:6 *e* the thirsty one to go
32:7 *e* when someone poor speaks
33:12 be set ablaze *e* with fire
33:23 *e* spoil in abundance will
34:14 *e* the goat-shaped demon
35:4 God *e* with a repayment
35:8 highway there, *e* a way; and
37:12 delivered them, *e* Gozan and
37:26 I have *e* formed it
38:11 I shall not see Jah, *e* Jah
40:9 *e* onto a high mountain
40:9 your voice *e* with power
40:10 will come *e* as a strong one
40:16 *E* Lebanon is not sufficient
40:26 army of them *e* by number
40:26 whom he calls *e* by name
41:2 make him go subduing *e* kings
41:9 *e* from the remote parts of
41:14 *e* your Repurchaser, the
41:22 hear *e* the things that are
42:12 tell forth *e* his praise
43:9 to hear *e* the first things
43:10 *e* my servant whom I have
43:16 a roadway *e* through strong
43:20 water *e* in the wilderness
43:22 you have not called *e* me
44:2 helping you *e* from the belly
44:14 *e* a massive tree, and he
44:25 turns *e* their knowledge into
44:28 *e* in my saying of Jerusalem
45:1 ungird *e* the hips of kings
45:1 *e* the gates will not be shut
45:4 I *e* proceeded to call you by
45:11 Ask me *e* about the things
45:12 have created *e* man upon it
45:14 come over *e* to you, and
45:16 ashamed and *e* be humiliated
45:18 formed it *e* to be inhabited
46:4 *E* to one's old age I am the
46:7 One *e* cries out to it
46:11 I have *e* spoken it; I shall
48:1 make mention *e* of the God of
48:3 I have told *e* from that time
48:6 *e* things kept in reserve
48:7 *e* things that before today
48:16 has sent me, *e* his spirit
48:20 *e* with the sound of a
48:21 *e* through devastated places
49:1 called me *e* from the belly
49:6 bring back *e* the safeguarded
49:12 will come *e* from far away
49:15 *E* these women can forget
49:17 will go forth *e* from you
49:22 raise up my hand *e* to the
49:25 *E* the body of captives of
51:4 *e* as a light to the peoples
51:5 will judge *e* the peoples
51:6 to be *e* to time indefinite
51:8 to be *e* to time indefinite
51:22 Jehovah, *e* your God, who
52:6 *e* for that reason in that day
52:12 will be going *e* before you
53:8 *e* with the details of his
53:9 *e* with the wicked ones
54:3 take possession *e* of nations
54:3 inhabit *e* the desolated
54:4 forget *e* the shame of your
54:15 fall *e* on account of you
55:1 *e* without money and without
55:5 will run *e* to you, for the
56:5 *e* give to them in my house
56:7 *e* a house of prayer for all
56:11 are *e* dogs strong in
57:11 you were in no fear *e* of me
57:13 carry *e* all of them away
57:16 *e* the breathing creatures

Isa 58:10 flash up *e* in the darkness
58:11 *e* in a scorched land, and
58:12 raise up *e* the foundations
59:14 *e* in the public square
59:21 now on *e* to time indefinite
60:11 not be closed *e* by day or by
60:15 I will *e* set you as a thing
61:1 the eyes *e* to the prisoners
61:4 *e* the desolated places of
61:7 take possession of *e* a double
61:9 be known *e* among the nations
62:5 God will exult *e* over you
63:7 *e* the abundant goodness to
65:4 *e* in the watch huts, eating
65:4 *e* the broth of foul things
65:6 I will *e* render the reward
66:7 *e* gave deliverance to a male
66:17 *e* the jumping rodent, they
Jer 2:8 *e* the prophets prophesied by
2:10 send *e* to Kedar and give
2:11 *e* for those that are no gods
2:13 They have left *e* me, the
2:16 *E* the sons of Noph and
3:3 not *e* a spring rain has
3:7 she should return *e* to me
3:10 and *e* for all this her
4:1 you may return *e* to me
4:5 publish it *e* in Jerusalem
4:6 the north, *e* a great crash
4:12 comes *e* from these to me
4:17 has rebelled *e* against me
5:2 *E* if they should say
5:4 *E* I myself had said: Surely
5:18 And *e* in those days, is the
5:22 Do you not fear *e* me, is the
5:22 severe pains *e* because of me
5:24 guards *e* the prescribed
5:28 *e* the legal case of the
5:30 *e* a horrible thing, has
6:1 the north, *e* a great crash
6:13 *e* to the greatest one of
6:13 the prophet *e* to the priest
6:15 *e* how to feel humiliated
6:20 *e* frankincense from Sheba
6:25 do not walk *e* in the way
7:7 *e* to time indefinite
8:7 *E* the stork in the heavens
8:10 least one *e* to the greatest
8:10 the prophet *e* to the priest
8:12 done *e* what was detestable
8:12 *e* how to feel humiliated
9:3 and they ignored *e* me, is the
9:4 For *e* every brother would
9:12 *e* the one to whom the mouth
9:17 send *e* to the skilled women
10:2 *e* at the signs of the heavens
10:9 brought in *e* from Tarshish
10:13 made *e* sluices for the rain
10:21 not looked *e* for Jehovah
10:23 *e* to direct his step
10:25 not called *e* upon your name
11:23 not *e* a remnant will there
12:1 *e* about matters of judgment
12:6 *e* your own brothers and the
12:6 *e* they themselves have dealt
12:6 *E* they themselves have
12:8 her voice *e* against me
12:12 *e* to the other end of the
12:14 caused my people, *e* Israel
13:11 Judah to cling *e* to me
14:2 *e* the outcry of Jerusalem
14:5 For *e* the hind in the field
14:7 *E* if our own errors do
14:19 your soul abhorred *e* Zion
14:22 *e* the heavens themselves
15:13 *e* in all your territories
16:5 *e* loving-kindness and
17:4 loose, *e* of your own accord
17:10 *e* to give to each one
17:13 written down *e* in the earth
17:18 *e* with twice as much
18:20 speak good *e* concerning
19:12 *e* to make this city like
21:7 *e* into the hand of their
22:24 *e* if Coniah the son of
23:13 my people, *e* Israel, wander
23:19 *e* a whirling tempest
25:9 *e* sending to Nebuchadrezzar
25:12 error, *e* against the land
25:13 *e* all that is written in
25:14 For *e* they themselves, many
26:5 *e* rising up early and sending
27:6 *e* the wild beasts of the
27:7 the nations must serve *e* him

Jer 27:7 time *e* of his own land
27:8 *e* Nebuchadnezzar the king of
27:12 *E* to Zedekiah the king of
28:14 *e* the wild beasts of the
30:7 he will be saved *e* out of it
31:34 *e* to the greatest one of
32:4 see *e* the eyes of that one
32:14 *e* the sealed one, and
32:30 *e* offending me by the work
33:12 and *e* domestic animal and
33:20 *e* in order for day and
33:26 reject *e* the seed of Jacob
34:3 see *e* the eyes of the king
34:3 speak *e* with your mouth
36:25 *e* Elnathan and Delaiah
39:14 *e* proceeded to send and
40:8 *e* Ishmael the son of
42:1 *e* to the greatest one
42:8 *e* to the greatest one
42:15 *e* now therefore hear the
43:1 *e* all these words
43:6 *e* the able-bodied men and
44:12 *e* to the greatest one
44:14 *e* to return to the land of
45:4 uprooting, *e* all the land
46:25 her kings, *e* upon Pharaoh
48:17 *e* all those knowing their
48:26 of ridicule, *e* he himself
48:34 *e* the waters of Nimrim
49:2 *e* against Rabbah of the sons
49:3 will go *e* into exile, his
49:11 widows will trust *e* in me
49:21 been heard *e* at the Red Sea
49:30 counsel *e* against you and
50:8 *e* out of the land of the
50:30 *e* all her men of war will
51:16 made *e* sluices for the rain
51:19 *e* the staff of his
51:42 come up *e* over Babylon
51:53 *E* if Babylon should ascend
51:53 *e* if she should make the
51:60 *e* all these words written
51:62 *e* domestic animal, but
La 3:26 wait, *e* silently, for the
4:3 *E* jackals themselves have
4:16 no consideration *e* for the
4:16 no favor *e* to the old men
5:12 faces of *e* old men have not
5:13 *E* young men have lifted up a
5:14 have ceased *e* out of the gate
Eze 4:1 upon it a city, *e* Jerusalem
4:14 my youth up, *e* until now
5:8 I am against you, O city, *e* I
5:12 scatter *e* to every wind
5:16 *e* famine I shall increase
6:14 *e* a desolation worse than
7:27 *e* a chieftain will clothe
8:2 the appearance of his hips *e*
8:2 his hips *e* upward there was
10:2 *e* to say: Enter in between
10:16 not change direction, *e* they
12:28 speak, it will *e* be done
14:6 *e* from all your detestable
14:18 *e* were these three men in
14:20 *e* were Noah, Daniel and Job
14:22 *e* all that I shall have
16:29 *e* in this you did not get
16:34 *e* in your giving hire when
16:36 *e* with the blood of your
16:43 *e* here I also, for my part
16:47 you *e* began to act more
16:51 not sinned *e* up to half of
17:10 *e* as when the east wind
17:18 has done *e* all these things
17:19 *e* bring it upon his head
17:21 abroad *e* to every wind
19:3 He devoured *e* earthling man
19:6 He devoured *e* earthling man
19:7 he devastated *e* their cities
21:6 *E* with bitterness you should
21:24 be seized *e* by the hand
21:26 Put on high *e* what is low
21:26 bring low *e* the high one
23:10 they killed *e* with sword
23:25 will fall *e* by the sword
23:39 *e* proceeded to come into
23:43 her prostitution, *e* she
24:4 *e* with the choicest bones
25:9 Baal-meon, *e* to Kiriathaim
25:13 from Teman, *e* to Dedan
26:7 *e* a multitudinous people
26:8 will kill *e* with the sword
26:11 kill *e* with the sword
27:9 *E* old men of Gebal and her

Eze 27:11 *e* your military force
30:6 fall in it *e* by the sword
31:10 treetop *e* among the clouds
31:14 treetops *e* among the clouds
32:13 *e* the hoofs of a domestic
32:16 *E* the daughters of the
32:21 *e* to him, with his helpers
32:29 *e* with the uncircumcised
32:32 *e* Pharaoh and all his crowd
33:12 *e* anyone having
33:24 *e* concerning the soil of
33:28 *e* a desolation, and the
33:29 waste, *e* a desolation, on
34:4 subjection, *e* with tyranny
34:23 *e* my servant David
35:3 waste, *e* a desolation
35:7 waste, *e* a desolation
35:15 Seir, *e* all Edom, all of it
36:2 *E* the high places of old
36:3 *e* for the reason that there
36:12 *e* my people Israel, and
38:8 *e* a land that has been
38:11 not have *e* bar and doors
38:15 *e* a numerous military force
38:20 *e* every wall will fall
40:14 *e* to the side pillars of
41:18 *e* carved cherubs and
44:7 profane it, *e* my house
44:19 *e* to the outer courtyard
47:10 En-gedi *e* up to En-eglaim
48:3 *e* to the western border
48:6 *e* to the western border
48:32 *e* the gate of Joseph, one
Da 1:5 *e* to nourish them for three
1:20 *e* got to find them ten times
2:4 live on *e* for times indefinite
2:18 *e* for them to ask for mercies
2:20 *e* to time indefinite, for
2:40 crush and shatter *e* all these
2:46 offer *e* a present and incense
3:9 live on *e* for times indefinite
3:27 *e* their mantles had not been
4:13 watcher, *e* a holy one, coming
4:15 *e* with a banding of iron and
4:17 *e* the lowliest one of mankind
4:23 a watcher, *e* a holy one
4:25 *e* to you to eat just like
4:32 they are driving *e* you away
4:32 *e* to you to eat just like
4:36 *e* my high royal officers and
5:10 living *e* to times indefinite
5:11 *e* your father, O king
5:15 *e* to make known to me its
5:23 *e* the vessels of his house
6:6 live on *e* for times indefinite
6:10 *e* three times in a day he was
6:20 with a sad voice *e* to Daniel
6:21 himself spoke *e* with the king
6:21 live on *e* to times indefinite
7:13 up close *e* before that One
7:14 should all serve *e* him
7:18 *e* for time indefinite upon
7:19 treading down *e* what was left
7:20 *e* that horn that had eyes and
7:25 *e* words against the Most High
7:27 will serve and obey *e* them
8:1 appeared to me, *e* me, Daniel
11:4 uprooted, *e* for others than
11:5 strong, *e* one of his princes
11:24 *e* into the fatness of the
12:3 time indefinite, *e* forever
Ho 4:3 *e* the fishes of the sea
4:5 *e* a prophet must stumble with
4:6 I shall forget your sons, *e* I
7:13 have spoken lies *e* against me
8:6 For from Israel was *e* this
9:7 *e* animosity being abundant
9:13 *e* Ephraim is destined to a
9:13 his sons *e* to a killer
9:16 I will *e* put to death the
10:6 *E* it someone will bring to
12:2 *e* to hold an accounting
12:11 they have sacrificed *e* bulls
Joe 1:2 *e* in the days of your
1:12 *e* the fig tree has faded
2:8 fall *e* among the missiles
2:29 And *e* on the menservants and
Am 1:3 threshing Gilead *e* with iron
3:11 an adversary *e* round about
4:10 ascend *e* into your nostrils
5:9 come upon *e* a fortified place
5:12 poor people *e* in the gate
5:22 *e* in your gift offerings I
8:4 *e* in order to cause the meek
Am 8:12 from north *e* to the sunrise
Ob 13 *e* you, ought not to peer at his
19 *e* of the mountainous region of
19 Shephelah, *e* of the Philistines
Jon 3:5 *e* to the least one of them
3:7 *E* water they should not drink
Mic 1:5 *e* because of the sins of the
2:4 *e* a lamentation. One will
3:9 ones who make *e* everything
4:5 to time indefinite, *e* forever
4:6 *e* her whom I have treated
7:12 *e* all the way to you they
7:12 *e* all the way to the River
Na 1:10 interwoven *e* as thorns and
1:12 *e* in that state they must be
3:15 *E* there fire will devour you
Hab 1:10 laughs *e* at every fortified
2:3 *E* if it should delay, keep in
3:3 *e* a Holy One from Mount
Zep 2:9 waste, *e* to time indefinite
3:20 *e* in the time of my
Hag 2:17 *e* all the work of your hands
Zec 4:2 lamps are upon it, *e* seven
6:10 *e* from Heldai and from
7:3 and to the prophets, *e* saying
7:5 really fast to me, *e* me
9:9 *e* upon a full-grown animal
10:1 *e* of Jehovah who is making
12:2 siege, *e* against Jerusalem
13:7 *e* against the able-bodied
14:17 *e* upon them no pouring rain
Mal 1:11 sun's rising *e* to its setting
1:11 to my name, *e* a clean gift
2:2 I have *e* cursed the blessing
4:4 *e* regulations and judicial
Mt 6:29 not *e* Solomon in all his
8:27 *e* the winds and the sea obey
13:12 *e* what he has will be taken
18:17 listen *e* to the congregation
24:24 if possible, *e* the chosen
25:29 *e* what he has will be taken
26:35 *E* if I should have to die
26:38 deeply grieved, *e* to death
27:44 the same way *e* the robbers
Mr 1:27 orders *e* the unclean spirits
1:40 entreating him *e* on bended
2:2 room, not *e* about the door
2:28 is Lord *e* of the sabbath
3:8 *E* from Jerusalem and from
3:11 *E* the unclean spirits
3:20 not able *e* to eat a meal
4:25 *e* what he has will be taken
4:41 *e* the wind and the sea obey
5:3 bind him fast *e* with a chain
6:31 leisure time *e* to eat a meal
7:37 He *e* makes the deaf hear and
10:45 *e* the Son of man came, not
14:29 *E* if all the others are
14:30 *e* you will disown me three
14:34 deeply grieved, *e* to death
15:1 *e* the whole Sanhedrin
15:32 *E* those impaled together
Lu 3:12 *e* tax collectors came to be
6:18 *E* those troubled with unclean
6:29 withhold *e* the undergarment
6:32 *e* the sinners love those
6:33 *E* the sinners do the same
6:34 *E* sinners lend without
7:9 Not *e* in Israel have I found
7:49 this man who *e* forgives sins
8:18 *e* what he imagines he has
8:25 for he orders *e* the winds
9:42 *e* as he was approaching, the
10:11 *E* the dust that got stuck
10:17 *e* the demons are made
12:7 *e* the hairs of your heads are
12:15 *e* when a person has an
12:27 Not *e* Solomon in all his
12:38 watch, *e* if in the third
14:26 yes, and *e* his own soul
14:34 if *e* the salt loses its
15:15 He *e* went and attached
17:4 *E* if he sins seven times a
17:24 *e* as the lightning, by its
18:7 *e* though he is long-suffering
18:11 or *e* as this tax collector
18:13 not willing *e* to raise his
19:26 *e* what he has will be taken
19:42 If you, *e* you, had discerned
20:31 *e* the seven: they did not
20:37 *e* Moses disclosed, in the
21:16 delivered up *e* by parents and
22:50 one of them *e* did strike the
22:67 *E* if I told you, you would
Lu 23:5 *e* starting out from Galilee
23:36 *E* the soldiers made fun of
Joh 1:3 not *e* one thing came into
1:16 *e* undeserved kindness upon
1:31 *E* I did not know him, but
1:33 *E* I did not know him
4:11 Sir, you have not *e* a bucket
6:27 this one the Father, *e* God
6:36 *e* seen me and yet do not
6:57 *e* that one will live because
8:14 *E* if I do bear witness about
8:25 Why am I *e* speaking to you
10:33 blasphemy, *e* because you
10:38 *e* though you do not believe
11:25 *e* though he dies, will come
12:13 *e* the king of Israel
12:42 *e* of the rulers actually
12:43 than *e* the glory of God
14:31 *e* as the Father has given
Ac 2:18 *e* upon my men slaves and
2:26 *e* my flesh will reside in
4:27 *E* so, both Herod and Pontius
4:32 not *e* one would say that any
5:15 sick out *e* into the broad
7:11 *e* a great tribulation; and
10:47 holy spirit *e* as we have
13:33 *e* as it is written in the
13:41 *e* if anyone relates it to
17:28 *e* as certain ones of the
17:32 about this *e* another time
19:12 *e* cloths and aprons were
19:27 *e* her magnificence which the
19:31 *E* some of the commissioners
21:28 he *e* brought Greeks into the
22:28 Paul said: But I was *e* born
24:26 he sent for him *e* more
26:11 to persecuting them *e* in
27:9 *e* the fast of atonement day
Ro 1:13 *e* as among the rest of the
1:20 *e* his eternal power and
1:25 *e* those who exchanged the
1:27 *e* the males left the natural
2:15 being accused or *e* excused
3:4 *e* as it is written: That you
3:10 righteous man, not *e* one
3:26 *e* when declaring righteous
4:17 *e* of God, who makes the dead
5:7 someone *e* dares to die
5:14 *e* over those who had not
6:19 for *e* as you presented your
8:32 not *e* spare his own Son but
15:3 *e* Christ did not please
1Co 1:6 *e* as the witness about the
2:10 *e* the deep things of God
3:5 *e* as the Lord granted each
4:3 *E* I do not examine myself
5:1 fornication as is not *e* among
5:11 not *e* eating with such a man
7:8 that they remain *e* as I am
7:28 But *e* if you did marry, you
8:5 For *e* though there are those
9:5 *e* as the rest of the apostles
10:6 *e* as they desired them
10:33 *e* as I am pleasing all
11:1 *e* as I am of Christ
13:12 *e* as I am accurately known
14:21 not *e* then will they give
14:34 *e* as the Law says
15:45 *e* so written: The first man
16:6 *e* pass the winter with you
16:10 work of Jehovah, *e* as I am
2Co 1:8 very uncertain *e* of our lives
3:10 *e* that which has once been
4:16 *e* if the man we are outside
5:16 *E* if we have known Christ
7:8 *e* if I saddened you by my
7:8 *E* if I did at first regret it
10:8 *e* if I should boast a bit too
10:13 it reach *e* as far as you
10:14 to come *e* as far as you in
11:6 *e* if I am unskilled in
11:16 *e* if as unreasonable, that
11:31 *e* the One who is to be
12:11 *e* if I am nothing
Ga 1:8 *e* if we or an angel out of
2:3 not *e* Titus, who was with me
2:13 *e* Barnabas was led along with
2:16 *e* we have put our faith in
5:12 *e* get themselves emasculated
6:1 *e* though a man takes some
6:13 *e* do those who are getting
6:16 *e* upon the Israel of God
Eph 2:3 children of wrath *e* as the
2:5 *e* when we were dead in

Eph 4:4 *e* as you were called in the
5:3 greediness not *e* be mentioned
5:11 rather, *e* be reproving them
5:12 it is shameful *e* to relate
Php 2:17 *e* if I am being poured out
3:21 *e* to subject all things to
4:16 *e* in Thessalonica, you sent
Col 1:6 *e* as it is bearing fruit and
3:13 *E* as Jehovah freely forgave
1Th 2:15 who killed *e* the Lord Jesus
3:12 *e* as we also do to you
2Ti 2:5 contends *e* in the games, he
3:9 *e* as the madness of those
Tit 3:3 *e* we were once senseless
Phm 19 you owe me *e* yourself
21 knowing you will *e* do more
Heb 4:2 *e* as they also had; but the
4:12 *e* to the dividing of soul
7:5 their brothers, *e* if these
7:9 *e* Levi who receives tithes
11:11 *e* when she was past the
11:19 him up *e* from the dead
Jas 3:4 *E* boats, although they are so
3:9 bless Jehovah, *e* the Father
1Pe 1:19 spotless lamb, *e* Christ's
2:21 *e* Christ suffered for you
3:14 *e* if you should suffer for
3:18 *e* Christ died once for all
4:14 *e* the spirit of God, is
5:1 *e* of the glory that is to be
2Pe 2:1 *e* the owner that bought them
2:12 *e* suffer destruction in their
1Jo 2:18 *e* now there have come to be
Jude 23 hate *e* the inner garment
Re 1:2 *e* to all the things he saw
2:10 faithful *e* to death, and I
2:13 *e* in the days of Antipas, my
3:21 *e* as I conquered and sat
4:11 Jehovah, *e* our God, to receive
12:11 souls *e* in the face of death
13:6 *e* those residing in heaven
13:13 *e* make fire come down out
17:17 *e* to carry out their one
18:6 *e* as she herself rendered
19:16 *e* upon his thigh, he has a

Evening
Ge 1:5 came to be *e* and there came
1:8 And there came to be *e* and
1:13 And there came to be *e* and
1:19 came to be *e* and there came
1:23 came to be *e* and there came
1:31 And there came to be *e* and
8:11 to him about the time of *e*
19:1 angels arrived at Sodom by *e*
24:11 about *e* time, about the time
24:63 at about the falling of *e*
29:23 during the *e* he resorted to
30:16 from the field in the *e*
49:27 at *e* he will divide spoil
Ex 12:18 in the *e* you are to eat
12:18 day of the month in the *e*
16:6 At *e* you will certainly know
16:8 in the *e* meat to eat and in
16:13 in the *e* the quails began to
18:13 from the morning till the *e*
18:14 you from morning till *e*
27:21 from *e* till morning before
Le 6:20 and half of it in the *e*
11:24 will be unclean until the *e*
11:25 must be unclean until the *e*
11:27 will be unclean until the *e*
11:28 must be unclean until the *e*
11:31 will be unclean until the *e*
11:32 must be unclean until the *e*
11:39 will be unclean until the *e*
11:40 must be unclean until the *e*
11:40 must be unclean until the *e*
14:46 will be unclean until the *e*
15:5 and be unclean until the *e*
15:6 and be unclean until the *e*
15:7 and be unclean until the *e*
15:8 and be unclean until the *e*
15:10 will be unclean until the *e*
15:10 and be unclean until the *e*
15:11 and be unclean until the *e*
15:16 and be unclean until the *e*
15:17 and be unclean until the *e*
15:18 and be unclean until the *e*
15:19 will be unclean until the *e*
15:21 and be unclean until the *e*
15:22 and be unclean until the *e*
15:23 will be unclean until the *e*
15:27 and be unclean until the *e*
17:15 unclean until the *e*; and he
Le 22:6 must be unclean until the *e*
23:32 ninth of the month in the *e*
23:32, 32 *e* to *e* you should observe
24:3 *e* to morning before Jehovah
Nu 9:15 *e* what appeared to be fire
9:21 cloud would continue from *e*
19:7 must be unclean until the *e*
19:8 must be unclean until the *e*
19:10 and be unclean until the *e*
19:19 he must be clean in the *e*
19:21 will be unclean until the *e*
19:22 will be unclean until the *e*
De 16:4 sacrifice in the *e* on the
16:6 the passover in the *e* as soon
23:11 at the falling of *e* he should
28:67 say, If it only were *e*! and
28:67 in the *e* you will say, If it
Jos 5:10 in the *e*, on the desert
7:6 before the ark . . . until the *e*
8:29 upon a stake until the *e*
10:26 upon the stakes until the *e*
Jg 19:9 declined toward becoming *e*
19:16 his work in the field at *e*
20:23 before Jehovah until the *e*
20:26 and fasted . . . until the *e*
21:2 until the *e* and continued to
Ru 2:17 glean in the field until the *e*
1Sa 14:24 that eats bread before the *e*
17:16 at early morning and at *e*
20:5 in the field until *e* on the
30:17 morning . . . until the *e*
2Sa 1:12 fast until the *e* over Saul
11:2 time of *e* that David
11:13 out in the *e* to lie down on
1Ki 17:6 and bread and meat in the *e*
22:35 gradually he died in the *e*
2Ki 7:5 rose up in the *e* darkness to
7:7 fleeing in the *e* darkness
16:15 the grain offering of the *e*
1Ch 16:40 constantly morning and *e*
23:30 and likewise at *e*
2Ch 2:4 burnt offerings . . . in the *e*
13:11, 11 offerings . . . *e* by *e*
13:11, 11 to light up *e* by *e*
18:34 the Syrians until the *e*
31:3 burnt offerings of the . . . *e*
Ezr 3:3 of the morning and of the *e*
9:4 the grain offering of the *e*
9:5 the grain offering of the *e*
Es 2:14 In the *e* she herself came in
Job 4:20 From morning to *e* they are
7:4 *e* actually goes its measure
24:15 has watched for *e* darkness
Ps 30:5 In the *e* weeping may take up
55:17 *E* and morning and noontime
65:8 the morning and *e* you
90:6 At *e* it withers and certainly
104:23 And to his service until *e*
141:2 as the *e* grain offering
Pr 7:9 twilight, in the *e* of the day
Ec 11:6 until the *e* do not let your
Isa 5:11 till late in the *e* darkness
17:14 At *e* time, why, look! there
59:10 just as in *e* darkness
Jer 6:4 shadows of *e* keep extending
Eze 12:4 go out in the *e* before their
12:7 and in the *e* I bored my way
24:18 gradually died in the *e*
33:22 in the *e* before the coming
46:2 not be shut until the *e*
Da 8:26 seen concerning the *e* and the
9:21 time of the *e* gift offering
Hab 1:8 proved fiercer than *e* wolves
Zep 2:7 in the *e*, they will lie
3:3 Her judges were *e* wolves
Zec 14:7 *e* time it will become light
Mt 8:16 But after it became *e*, people
14:15 *e* fell his disciples came
16:2 *e* falls you are accustomed
20:8 When it became *e*, the master
23:6 prominent place at *e* meals
26:20 When, now, it had become *e*
Mr 1:32 After *e* had fallen, when the
4:35 when *e* had fallen, he said to
6:21 Herod spread an *e* meal on
6:47 *E* having now fallen, the boat
12:39 prominent places at *e* meals
14:17 After *e* had fallen he came
Lu 14:12 a dinner or *e* meal, do not
14:16 was spreading a grand *e* meal
14:17 at the hour of the *e* meal
14:24 have a taste of my *e* meal
17:8 for me to have my *e* meal
20:46 prominent places at *e* meals
Lu 22:20 after they had the *e* meal
23:54 *e* light of the sabbath was
24:29 toward *e* and the day has
Joh 6:16 When *e* fell, his disciples
12:2 they spread an *e* meal for
13:2 the *e* meal was going on
13:4 got up from the *e* meal and
21:20 who at the *e* meal had also
Ac 4:3 for it was already *e*
28:23 from morning till *e*
1Co 11:20 to eat the Lord's *e* meal
11:21 one takes his own *e* meal
11:25 after he had the *e* meal
Re 3:20 take the *e* meal with him
19:9 the *e* meal of the Lamb's
19:17 to the great *e* meal of God

Evenings
Ex 12:6 between the two *e*
16:12 Between the two *e* you will
29:39 young ram between the two *e*
29:41 young ram between the two *e*
30:8 lamps between the two *e*
Le 23:5 between the two *e* is the
Nu 9:3 between the two *e* you should
9:5 between the two *e*, in the
9:11 between the two *e*, they should
28:4 render up between the two *e*
28:8 male lamb between the two *e*
Da 8:14 two thousand three hundred *e*

Eveningtime
Ps 59:6 They keep returning at *e*
59:14 And let them return at *e*

Event
Ex 18:16 In the *e* that they have a
20:25 In the *e* that you do wield
Lu 16:27 In that *e* I ask you, father

Events
Le 19:31 professional foretellers of *e*
20:6 foretellers of *e* so as to have
De 18:11 professional foreteller of *e*
32:35 *e* in readiness for them
1Sa 28:3 professional foretellers of *e*
28:9 professional foretellers of *e*
2Ki 21:6 professional foretellers of *e*
23:24 foretellers of *e* and
2Ch 33:6 professional foretellers of *e*
Ps 46:8 astonishing *e* on the earth
Isa 19:3 professional foretellers of *e*
Lu 24:35 related the *e* on the road
Ac 19:1 In the course of *e*, while

Eventuality
Ec 2:14 one *e* that eventuates to them
2:15 An *e* like that upon the stupid
3:19 is an *e* as respects the sons
3:19 an *e* as respects the beast
3:19 and they have the same *e*
9:2 One *e* there is to the righteous
9:3 because there is one *e* to all

Eventually*
Ge 11:2 they *e* discovered a valley
46:6 *E* they came into Egypt, Jacob
Le 23:10 *e* come into the land that I
25:2 *e* come into the land that I
Nu 15:2 When you *e* come into the land
24:24 But he too will *e* perish
De 1:19 we *e* came to Kadesh-barnea
17:14 *e* come into the land that
29:7 *E* you came to this place, and

Eventuate
Ec 2:15 will *e* to me, yes, me

Eventuates
Ec 2:14 is one eventuality that *e* to

Ever-flowing
Ps 74:15 yourself dried up *e* rivers

Everlasting
Mt 18:8 two feet into the *e* fire
19:16 I do in order to get *e* life
19:29 and will inherit *e* life
25:41 the *e* fire prepared for the
25:46 depart into *e* cutting-off
25:46 righteous ones into *e* life
Mr 3:29 but is guilty of *e* sin
10:17 what . . . to inherit *e* life
10:30 coming system . . . *e* life
Lu 10:25 shall I inherit *e* life
16:9 into the *e* dwelling places
18:18 shall I inherit *e* life
18:30 system of things *e* life
Joh 3:15 believing . . . have *e* life

Joh 3:16 be destroyed but have *e* life
3:36 has *e* life; he that disobeys
4:14 bubbling up to impart *e* life
4:36 gathering fruit for *e* life
5:24 has *e* life, and he does not
5:39 you will have *e* life
6:27 food . . . for life *e*
6:40 should have *e* life, and I
6:47 He that believes has *e* life
6:54 drinks my blood has *e* life
6:68 You have sayings of *e* life
10:28 And I give them *e* life
12:25 safeguard it for *e* life
12:50 commandment means *e* life
17:2 he may give them *e* life
17:3 This means *e* life, their
Ac 13:46 yourselves worthy of *e* life
13:48 rightly disposed for *e* life
Ro 2:7 *e* life to those who are
5:21 *e* life in view through Jesus
6:22 and the end *e* life
6:23 gift God gives is *e* life
16:26 the command of the *e* God to
2Co 4:17 for us a glory that . . . is *e*
4:18 but the things unseen are *e*
5:1 house . . . *e* in the heavens
Ga 6:8 reap *e* life from the spirit
2Th 1:9 punishment of *e* destruction
2:16 gave *e* comfort and good hope
1Ti 1:16 faith on him for *e* life
6:12 firm hold on the *e* life
6:16 To him be honor and might *e*
2Ti 2:10 along with *e* glory
Tit 1:2 a hope of the *e* life which
3:7 to a hope of *e* life
Heb 5:9 responsible for *e* salvation
6:2 of the dead and *e* judgment
9:12 an *e* deliverance for us
9:14 *e* spirit offered himself
9:15 of the *e* inheritance
13:20 blood of an *e* covenant, our
1Pe 5:10 called you to his *e* glory in
2Pe 1:11 the *e* kingdom of our Lord
1Jo 1:2 *e* life which was with the
2:25 promised us, the life *e*
3:15 no manslayer has *e* life
5:11 that God gave us *e* life
5:13 know that you have life *e*
5:20 the true God and life *e*
Jude 7 judicial punishment of *e* fire
21 Christ with *e* life in view
Re 14:6 *e* good news to declare as

Every*
Ex 18:22 *e* big case they will bring
35:31 in *e* sort of craftsmanship
De 2:7 God has blessed you in *e* deed
Job 7:18 attention to him *e* morning
Ps 150:6 *E* breathing thing—let it
Joh 1:9 gives light to *e* sort of man
2Co 4:8 We are pressed in *e* way, but
6:4 but in *e* way we recommend
7:1 *e* defilement of flesh and
7:11 *e* respect you demonstrated
9:8 have plenty for *e* good work
10:5 *e* lofty thing raised up
10:5 are bringing *e* thought into
10:6 for *e* disobedience, as soon
11:6 in *e* way we manifested it to
11:9 in *e* way I kept myself
Eph 1:21 *e* government and authority
1:21 *e* name named, not only in
4:19 uncleanness of *e* sort with
5:3 uncleanness of *e* sort or
Php 1:18 *e* way, whether in pretense
2:10 in the name of Jesus *e* knee
2:11 *e* tongue should openly
Col 1:10 bearing fruit in *e* good work
1:28 admonishing *e* man and
1:28 teaching *e* man in all wisdom
1:28 present *e* man complete in
1Th 5:22 from *e* form of wickedness
2Th 2:10 with *e* unrighteous deception
1Ti 5:10 followed *e* good work
2Ti 2:21 prepared for *e* good work
3:17 equipped for *e* good work
4:18 deliver me from *e* wicked work
Tit 2:14 from *e* sort of lawlessness
3:1 to be ready for *e* good work
Phm 6 *e* good thing among us as
Heb 10:11 *e* priest takes his station
12:1 put off *e* weight and the sin
Jas 1:17 *e* perfect present is from
3:16 disorder and *e* vile thing are
1Pe 2:13 subject yourselves to *e* human

1Jo 4:2 *E* inspired expression that
5:18 *e* person that has been born
Re 1:7 and *e* eye will see him, and
5:9 out of *e* tribe and tongue and
5:13 *e* creature that is in heaven
6:14, 14 *e* mountain and *e* island
6:15, 15 *e* slave and *e* free person
16:3 *e* living soul died, yes, the
18:2 of *e* unclean and hated bird
21:4 wipe out *e* tear from their

Everyone*
Ge 3:20 the mother of *e* living
Job 30:23 meeting for *e* living
Pr 13:16 *E* shrewd will act with
Mt 5:22 *e* who continues wrathful
5:32 *e* divorcing his wife, except
Lu 11:4 forgive *e* that is in debt to
11:10 For *e* asking receives, and
11:10 and *e* seeking finds, and to
11:10 to *e* knocking it will be
14:11 *e* that exalts himself will
16:18 *E* that divorces his wife and
18:14 *e* that exalts himself will
19:26 To *e* that has, more will be
Joh 3:8 So is *e* that has been born
3:15 *e* believing in him may have
3:16 *e* exercising faith in him
4:13 *E* drinking from this water
12:46 *e* putting faith in me may
18:37 *E* that is on the side of
Ac 2:21 *e* who calls on . . . Jehovah
1Co 15:28 God may be all things to *e*
1Pe 3:15 make a defense before *e* that
1Jo 2:29 that *e* who practices
3:10 *E* who does not carry on
3:15 *E* who hates his brother is
5:1 *E* believing that Jesus is

Everything*
Ge 1:31 God saw *e* he had made and
6:17 *E* that is in the earth will
7:22 *E* in which the breath of the
9:2 *e* that goes moving on the
14:20 Abram gave him a tenth of *e*
21:22 God is with you in *e* you are
De 21:17 two parts in *e* he is found
28:47 for the abundance of *e*
28:48 and the want of *e*; and he
Jos 1:17 As we listened to Moses in *e*
1Ch 17:2 *E* that is in your heart do
28:12 architectural plan of *e* that
29:12 and you are dominating *e*
29:14 For *e* is from you, and out
Job 1:10 *e* that he has all around
1:11 and touch *e* he has and see
1:12 *E* that he has is in your hand
2:4 *e* that a man has he will give
Isa 46:10 *e* that is my delight I
Jer 10:16 he is the Former of *e*, and
Ro 14:2 One man has faith to eat *e*
2Co 8:7 you are abounding in *e*, in
9:8 full self-sufficiency in *e*
Eph 5:13 *e* . . . manifest is light
5:24 be to their husbands in *e*
Php 4:12 *e* and in all circumstances
Col 3:17 do *e* in the name of the Lord
3:20 obedient to your parents in *e*
3:22 slaves, be obedient in *e* to
1Th 5:18 In connection with *e* give
1Jo 2:16 *e* in the world—the desire
5:4 *e* that has been born from God

Everywhere
Jos 1:7 you may act wisely *e* you go
Jg 2:15 *E* that they went out, the
1Ki 2:3 you do and *e* that you turn
Pr 17:8 *E* that he turns he has success
21:1 *E* that he delights to, he
Isa 18:2 to a people fear-inspiring *e*
18:7 a people fear-inspiring *e*
Lu 9:6 and performing cures *e*
Ac 17:30 that they should all *e* repent
21:28 teaches everybody *e* against
28:22 *e* it is spoken against
1Co 1:2 all who *e* are calling upon
4:17 as I am teaching *e* in every
2Co 4:10 we endure *e* in our body the

Evi
Nu 31:8 kings of Midian . . . *E* and
Jos 13:21 chieftains of Midian, *E* and

Evidence
Ex 22:13 he is to bring it as *e*
De 22:14 did not find *e* of virginity
22:15 *e* of the girl's virginity to

De 22:17 does not have *e* of virginity
22:17 *e* of my daughter's virginity
22:20 *e* of virginity was not found
1Sa 23:23 return to me with the *e*
Lu 11:44 tombs which are not in *e*
Joh 16:8 convincing *e* concerning sin
Ac 25:7 they were unable to show *e*
1Ti 5:19 *e* of two or three witnesses
Heb 11:14 *e* that they are earnestly

Evident
Mr 14:64 What is *e* to you? They all
1Co 15:27 it is *e* that it is with the
Ga 3:11 righteous with God is *e*
2Ti 1:10 *e* through the manifestation
Heb 11:1 *e* demonstration of realities
1Jo 3:10 children of the Devil are *e*

Evil
Ge 8:21 I call down *e* upon the ground
12:3 him that calls down *e* upon
50:15 repay us for all the *e* that
50:17 they have rendered *e* to you
50:20 you had *e* in mind against me
Ex 5:19 saw themselves in an *e* plight
5:22 you caused *e* to this people
5:23 he has done *e* to this people
10:10 something *e* is your aim
21:17 calls down *e* upon his father
22:28 not call down *e* upon God nor
23:2 follow after the crowd for *e*
32:12 With *e* intent he brought
32:12 the *e* against your people
32:14 feel regret over the *e* that
33:4 got to hear this *e* word, they
Le 5:4 with his lips to do *e* or to do
19:14 call down *e* upon a deaf man
20:9 *e* upon his father and his
20:9 whom he has called down *e*
24:11 and to call down *e* upon it
24:14 called down *e* to the outside
24:15 calls down *e* upon his God, he
24:23 one who had called down *e* to
Nu 11:1 something *e* to complain
11:11 Why have you caused *e* to
14:27 this *e* assembly have this
14:35 do to all this *e* assembly
20:5 to bring us into this *e* place
32:13 generation that was doing *e*
De 1:35 men of this *e* generation will
4:25 *e* in the eyes of Jehovah
7:15 all the *e* diseases of Egypt
9:18 doing *e* in the eyes of Jehovah
13:5 you must clear out what is *e*
22:24 clear away what is *e* from
23:4 Balaam . . . to call down *e*
Jos 23:15 bring upon you all the *e*
24:9 to call down *e* upon you
Jg 9:27 called down *e* upon Abimelech
9:56 *e* of Abimelech that he had
9:57 the *e* of the men of Shechem
1Sa 3:13 are calling down *e* upon God
6:9 has done to us this great *e*
12:17 your *e* is abundant that you
12:19 added to all our sins an *e*
12:20 you have done all this *e*
17:43 called down *e* upon David by
20:9 to know that *e* has been
20:13 good to my father to do *e*
24:17 I who have rendered you *e*
25:21 repays me *e* in return for
2Sa 16:5 calling down *e* as he came
16:7 said as he called down *e*
16:9 call down *e* upon my lord
16:10 Thus let him call down *e*
16:10 Call down *e* upon David!
16:11 that he may call down *e*
16:13 that he might call down *e*
18:32 rose up against you for *e*
19:21 *e* down upon the anointed of
1Ki 2:8 called down *e* upon me with
2Ki 2:24 *e* . . . in the name of Jehovah
Ne 13:2 to call down *e* upon them
13:25 and call down *e* upon them
Job 3:1 to call down *e* upon his day
21:30 disaster an *e* one is spared
31:29 because *e* had found him
Ps 37:8 heated up only to do *e*
37:22 those upon whom *e* is called
49:5 be afraid in the days of *e*
62:4 they call down *e*. *Se'lah*
109:20 speaking *e* against my soul
140:11 *e* itself hunt him with
Pr 16:4 the wicked one for the *e* day
20:20 *e* upon his father and his

Pr 20:22 not say: I will pay back *e*
24:8 a mere master at *e* ideas
30:10 may not call down *e* upon you
30:11 generation that calls down *e*
Ec 7:21 servant calling down *e* upon
7:22 you, have called down *e* upon
9:12 are being taken in an *e* net
10:20 call down *e* upon the king
10:20 call down *e* upon anyone rich
Isa 8:21 call down *e* upon his king
65:20 have *e* called down upon him
Jer 11:15 do this thing, the *e* device
15:10 are calling down *e* upon me
Ho 9:15 the *e* of their dealings
Hab 2:9 making *e* gain for his house
Mt 21:41 Because they are *e*, he will
21:41 will bring an *e* destruction
24:48 if that *e* slave should say
Ro 12:17, 17 Return *e* for *e* to no one
12:21 be conquered by the *e*, but
12:21 conquering the *e* with the
13:10 Love does not work *e* to
16:19 but innocent as to what is *e*
Ga 3:1 brought you under *e* influence
2Ti 1:8 suffering *e* for the good news
2:3 take your part in suffering *e*
2:9 suffering *e* to the point of
2:24 himself restrained under *e*
4:5 suffer *e*, do the work of an
Jas 1:13 with *e* things God cannot be
5:10 pattern of the suffering of *e*
5:13 Is there anyone suffering *e*
1Pe 3:17 than because you are doing *e*

Evildoer
Pr 17:4 The *e* is paying attention to
2Ti 2:9 prison bonds as an *e*
1Pe 4:15 *e* or as a busybody in other

Evildoers
Job 8:20 he take hold of the hand of *e*
Ps 22:16 *e* . . . have enclosed me
26:5 hated the congregation of *e*
27:2 *e* approached against me to
37:1 heated up because of the *e*
37:9 *e* themselves will be cut off
64:2 the confidential talk of *e*
92:11 rise up against me, the *e*
94:16 up for me against the *e*
119:115 Get away from me, you *e*
Pr 24:19 show yourself heated up at *e*
Isa 9:17 and *e* and every mouth is
14:20 offspring of *e* will not be
31:2 against the house of *e*
Jer 20:13 out of the hand of *e*
23:14 strengthened the hands of *e*
Lu 23:32 *e*, were also being led to
23:33 *e*, one on his right and one
23:39 one of the hung *e* began to
1Pe 2:12 speaking against you as *e*
2:14 to inflict punishment on *e*

Evildoing
Isa 1:4 an *e* seed, ruinous sons

Evil-inclined
Ex 32:22 the people, that they are *e*
De 28:54 will be *e* toward his brother
28:56 *e* toward her . . . husband

Evil-merodach
2Ki 25:27 *E* the king of Babylon
Jer 52:31 *E* the king of Babylon, in

Evils
1Sa 10:19 your *e* and your distresses

Ewe
Isa 53:7 like a *e* that before her

Ewes
Ca 4:2 like a drove of freshly-shorn *e*
6:6 teeth are like a drove of *e*

Exact
Ge 43:9 you may *e* the penalty for him
Es 4:7 *e* statement of the money that
10:2 the *e* statement of Mordecai's
Heb 1:3 the *e* representation of his

Exacted
2Ki 23:35 individual tax rate he *e*
Re 18:20 has judicially *e* punishment

Exacting
Ex 20:5 a God *e* exclusive devotion
De 4:24 a God *e* exclusive devotion
5:9 a God *e* exclusive devotion
6:15 a God *e* exclusive devotion
Jos 24:19 he is a God *e* exclusive
Ne 5:7 Usury is what you are *e*, each
5:11 are *e* as interest from them
Na 1:2 a God *e* exclusive devotion and
Mt 25:24 I knew you to be an *e* man

Exactions
Ps 89:22 enemy will make *e* upon him

Exactly
Ge 44:10 *e* according to your words
50:12 *e* as he had commanded them
Ex 7:10 *e* as Jehovah had commanded
1Ch 24:31 to cast lots *e* as their
24:31 *e* as his younger brother
26:12 the headmen had duties *e* as
Ezr 10:12 *E* according to your word
Job 38:37 Who can *e* number the clouds
Ec 5:16 *e* as one has come, so one
7:14 has made even this *e* as that
Jer 42:5 that we shall *e* do
Eze 3:8 made your face *e* as hard as
3:8 your forehead *e* as hard as
40:18 *e* as the length of the gates
45:6 *e* as the holy contribution
45:7 *e* as one of the shares
48:18 *e* as the holy contribution
48:18 *e* as the holy contribution
48:21 *E* like the portions, it
Mr 1:24 I know *e* who you are, the
Lu 4:34 I know *e* who you are, the
Ac 27:25 be *e* as it has been told me
2Co 3:18 *e* as done by Jehovah the
1Th 5:2 day is coming *e* as a thief
2Pe 3:4 *e* as from creation's

Exactor
Da 11:20 *e* to pass through the

Exacts
1Th 4:6 is one who *e* punishment for

Exalt
De 17:20 his heart may not *e* itself
1Sa 2:10 *e* the horn of his anointed
Es 3:1 to *e* him and to put his throne
Job 17:4 is why you do not *e* them
Ps 30:1 I shall *e* you, O Jehovah, for
34:3 let us *e* his name together
37:34 *e* you to take possession of
75:4 Do not *e* the horn
75:5 Do not *e* your horn on high
92:10 *e* my horn like that of a
99:5 *E* Jehovah our God and bow
99:9 *E* Jehovah our God And bow
118:28 My God—I shall *e* you
145:1 I will *e* you, O my God the
148:14 *e* the horn of his people
Pr 4:8 esteem it, and it will *e* you
Isa 25:1 I *e* you, I laud your name
33:10 now I will *e* myself
Da 11:36 *e* himself and magnify
Jas 4:10 Jehovah, and he will *e* you
1Pe 5:6 he may *e* you in due time

Exaltation
Ge 4:7 will there not be an *e*?
Jas 1:9 brother exult over his *e*

Exalted
Ex 15:1 for he has become highly *e*
15:21 for he has become highly *e*
1Sa 2:1 horn is indeed *e* in Jehovah
2Sa 5:12 *e* his kingdom for the sake
22:47 rock of my salvation be *e*
1Ch 14:2 his kingship was highly *e* on
2Ch 32:23 *e* in the eyes of all the
Ne 9:5 *e* above all blessing and praise
Es 5:11 he had *e* him over the princes
Job 36:7 and they will be *e*
36:26 God is more *e* than we can
37:23 He is *e* in power, And
Ps 12:8 vileness is *e* among the sons
13:2 How long will my enemy be *e*
18:46 the God of my salvation be *e*
21:13 *e* in your strength, O Jehovah
46:10 will be *e* among the nations
46:10 I will be *e* in the earth
57:5 be *e* above the heavens, O God
57:11 Do be *e* above the heavens
66:7 not be *e* in themselves
75:10 the righteous one will be *e*
89:13 Your right hand is *e*
89:16 your righteousness they are *e*
89:17 your goodwill our horn is *e*
89:19 *e* a chosen one from among
89:24 And in my name his horn is *e*
Ps 89:42 *e* the right hand of his
108:5 *e* above the heavens, O God
112:9 His own horn will be *e* with
140:8 that they may not be *e*
Pr 11:11 upright ones a town is *e*
Isa 52:13 be elevated and *e* very much
Eze 20:28 they got to see every *e* hill
31:10 its heart became *e* because
Da 5:23 against the Lord . . . you *e*
11:12 His heart will become *e*, and
Ho 13:6 their heart began to be *e*
Mt 11:23 you perhaps be *e* to heaven
23:12 humbles himself will be *e*
Lu 1:52 from thrones and *e* lowly ones
10:15 you perhaps be *e* to heaven
14:11 humbles himself will be *e*
18:14 humbles himself will be *e*
Ac 2:33 *e* to the right hand of God and
5:31 God *e* this one as Chief Agent
13:17 he *e* the people during their
2Co 11:7 myself that you might be *e*
12:7 might not feel overly *e*
12:7 I might not be overly *e*
Php 2:9 *e* him to a superior position

Exaltedly
Job 36:22 God himself acts *e* with his

Exalter
1Sa 2:7 Jehovah is . . . an *E*

Exalting
Ps 75:6 from the south is there an *e*
118:16 right hand of Jehovah is *e*
Pr 3:35 stupid ones are *e* dishonor
14:29 impatient is *e* foolishness
Da 4:37 *e* and glorifying the King of
5:19 happened to want to, he was *e*

Exalts
Ps 75:7 abases, and that one he *e*
113:7 *e* the poor one from the
Pr 14:34 Righteousness . . . *e* a nation
Mt 23:12 Whoever *e* himself will be
Lu 14:11 everyone that *e* himself will
18:14 everyone that *e* himself will
2Co 11:20 whoever *e* himself over you

Examination
Le 13:36 not make *e* for yellow hair
Pr 20:25 he is disposed to make *e*
Isa 14:16 give close *e* even to you
Ac 24:8 by *e* find out about all these
25:26 judicial *e* has taken place
28:18 these, after making an *e*

Examine
Ge 31:32 *e* for yourself what is with
37:32 *E*, please, whether it is your
38:25 *E*, please, to whom these
Le 27:33 not *e* whether it is good or
Job 29:16 did not know—I would *e* it
Ps 11:4 eyes *e* the sons of men
26:2 *E* me, O Jehovah, and put me
139:23 *E* me, and know my
Jer 6:27 and you must *e* their way
9:7 and I have to *e* them, because
Zec 13:9 *e* them as in the examining
Lu 12:56 know how to *e* the outward
12:56 to *e* this particular time
14:19 and am going to *e* them
Ac 22:29 about to *e* him with torture
1Co 4:3 Even I do not *e* myself
9:3 my defense to those who *e* me

Examined
Ge 38:26 Judah *e* them and said: She
1Ki 3:21 *e* him closely in the morning
Ps 17:3 You have *e* my heart, you have
66:10 For you have *e* us, O God
95:9 They *e* me, they also saw my
Jer 12:3 you have *e* my heart in union
Lu 23:14 I *e* him in front of you but
Ac 4:9 *e*, on the basis of a good deed
12:19 *e* the guards and commanded
22:24 should be *e* under scourging
1Co 2:14 they are *e* spiritually
2:15 himself is not *e* by any man
4:3 be *e* by you or by a human
14:24 he is closely *e* by all

Examiner
1Ch 29:17 you are an *e* of the heart
Pr 17:3 but Jehovah is the *e* of hearts

Examines
Ps 11:5 *e* the righteous one as well
1Co 2:15 spiritual man *e* indeed all
4:4 but he that *e* me is Jehovah

Examining
Ge 37:33 he went *e* it and exclaimed
Ne 2:13 *e* the walls of Jerusalem
2:15 I kept on *e* the wall
Ps 81:7 *e* you at the waters of
Jer 11:20 *e* the kidneys and the heart
17:10 *e* the kidneys, even to give
20:12 are *e* the righteous one
Zec 13:9 as in the *e* of gold
Ac 17:11 *e* the Scriptures daily as to

Example
Eze 5:15 a warning *e* and a horror to
Mt 12:32 For *e*, whoever speaks a
15:2 For *e*, they do not wash their
15:4 For *e*, God said, Honor your
15:19 For *e*, out of the heart come
Mr 7:10 For *e*, Moses said, Honor your
Lu 6:44 For *e*, people do not gather
12:58 For *e*, when you are going
14:28 For *e*, who of you that wants
Ro 7:7 for *e*, I would not have known
1Co 12:8 For *e*, to one there is given
2Co 11:17 not after the Lord's *e*
Ga 4:22 For *e*, it is written that
Php 3:17 with the *e* you have in us
1Th 1:7 an *e* to all the believers in
2Th 3:9 as an *e* to you to imitate us
1Ti 4:12 an *e* to the faithful ones
Tit 2:7 an *e* of fine works; showing
Heb 1:5 For *e*, to which one of the
6:7 For *e*, the ground that drinks
Jude 7 before us as a warning *e* by

Examples
1Co 10:6 these things became our *e*
10:11 went on befalling them as *e*
1Pe 5:3 but becoming *e* to the flock

Exasperated
Ge 45:24 Do not get *e* at one another

Exasperating
Col 3:21 do not be *e* your children

Excavate
Ex 21:33 *e* a pit and should not cover

Excavated
Ge 50:5 burial place which I have *e*
Nu 21:18 The nobles of the people *e* it
2Ch 16:14 burial place that he had *e*
Ps 7:15 A pit he has *e*, and he
57:6 They *e* before me a pitfall
94:13 the wicked one a pit is *e*
119:85 have *e* pitfalls to get me
Jer 18:20 have *e* a pit for my soul
18:22 *e* a pit to capture me

Excavating
Ge 26:25 went *e* a well there
Pr 26:27 He that is *e* a pit will fall

Exceeded
Ps 73:7 *e* the imaginations of the

Exceeding
Ps 119:138 And in *e* faithfulness

Exceedingly
1Ch 23:17 themselves become *e* many
Ps 31:23 rewarding *e* anyone showing
50:3 has become *e* stormy weather
119:167 And I love them *e*
Ec 7:24 *e* deep. Who can find it out?
Isa 47:9 might of your spells—*e*
Da 11:25 *e* great and mighty military
2Th 1:3 your faith is growing *e* and
1Ti 1:14 abounded *e* along with faith

Excel
Ge 49:4 do not you *e*, because you have

Excellence
Ge 49:3 the *e* of dignity and the
49:3 and the *e* of strength

Excellencies
1Pe 2:9 should declare abroad the *e*

Excellency
1Sa 15:29 the *E* of Israel will not
1Ch 29:11 and the *e* and the dignity
Job 20:6 *e* ascends to heaven itself
La 3:18 My *e* has perished, and my
Ac 23:26 Claudius Lysias to his *e*
24:3 receive it, Your *E* Felix
26:25 Your *E* Festus, but I am

Excellent
Ru 3:11 that you are an *e* woman
Lu 1:3 to you, most *e* Theophilus
Ro 2:18 approve of things that are *e*
Heb 1:4 a name more *e* than theirs
8:6 a more *e* public service

Excelling
Php 3:8 *e* value of the knowledge of

Excels
2Co 3:10 because of the glory that *e*
Php 4:7 the peace of God that *e* all

Except
Ge 21:26 also not heard of it *e* today
39:6 *e* the bread he was eating
39:9 anything at all *e* you, because
42:15 *e* when your youngest brother
Ex 3:19 to go *e* by a strong hand
Nu 5:8 *e* the ram of atonement with
11:6 nothing at all *e* the manna
14:30 *e* Caleb the son of Jephunneh
26:65 *e* Caleb the son of Jephunneh
32:12 *e* Caleb the son of Jephunneh
35:33 *e* by the blood of the one
De 1:36 *e* Caleb the son of Jephunneh
Jos 11:13 *e* that Joshua did burn Hazor
14:4 *e* cities to dwell in and
1Sa 21:9 there is no other here *e* it
30:17 *e* four hundred
30:22 *e* to each one his wife and
2Sa 3:13 You may not see my face *e*
7:22 no God *e* you among all of
1Ki 12:20 David *e* the tribe of Judah
17:1 *e* at the order of my word
2Ki 24:14 *e* the lowly class of the
1Ch 17:20 there is no God *e* you in
2Ch 2:6 *e* for making sacrificial
Ne 2:12 *e* the domestic animal on
Es 2:15 *e* what Hegai the king's
Ps 18:31 who is a rock *e* our God?
Pr 18:2 *e* that his heart should
Ec 5:11 *e* looking at them with his
Isa 10:4 *e* it be that one must bow
64:4 eye itself seen a God, *e* you
Jer 44:14 return, *e* some escaped ones
Da 2:11 *e* the gods, whose own
2:30 *e* to the intent that the
3:28 any god at all *e* their own
6:5 *e* we have to find it against
6:7 for thirty days *e* to you
6:12 *e* from you, O king, he should
Ho 13:4 no God *e* me that you used to
Mt 5:32 *e* on account of fornication
12:24 *e* by means of Beelzebub
12:39 given it *e* the sign of Jonah
13:57 *e* in his home territory and
16:4 given it *e* the sign of Jonah
19:9 divorces his wife, *e* on the
21:19 nothing on it *e* leaves only
26:42 to pass away *e* I drink it
Mr 2:7 Who can forgive sins *e* one
2:26 to eat *e* the priests, and he
4:22 is nothing hidden *e* for the
5:37 *e* Peter and James and John
6:4 *e* in his home territory and
6:5 *e* to lay his hands upon a few
6:8 nothing for the trip *e* a staff
8:14 *e* for one loaf they had
9:8 no one . . . *e* Jesus alone
9:29 out by anything *e* by prayer
10:18 Nobody is good, *e* one, God
Lu 5:21 Who can forgive sins *e* God
8:51 *e* Peter and John and James
11:29 *e* the sign of Jonah
18:19 Nobody is good, *e* one, God
Joh 6:22 no boat there *e* a little one
6:46 *e* he who is from God
14:6 to the Father *e* through me
17:12 *e* the son of destruction
Ac 8:1 *e* the apostles were scattered
11:19 word to no one *e* to Jews
15:28 *e* these necessary things
20:23 *e* that from city to city the
24:21 *e* with respect to this one
26:22 *e* things the Prophets as
Ro 13:1 is no authority *e* by God
13:8 *e* to love one another; for
1Co 1:14 baptized none . . . *e* Crispus
2:2 *e* Jesus Christ, and him
2:11 *e* the spirit of man that is
2:11 *e* the spirit of God
7:5 *e* by mutual consent for an
10:13 *e* what is common to men
12:3 *e* by holy spirit
2Co 1:13 *e* those which you well know
2Co 2:2 *e* the one that is made sad by
12:5 *e* as respects my weaknesses
12:13 *e* that I myself did not
Ga 1:12 *e* through revelation by Jesus
6:14 *e* in the torture stake of our
Php 1:18 *e* that in every way, whether
4:15 and receiving, *e* you alone
1Ti 5:19 *e* only on the evidence of
Heb 3:18 not enter into his rest *e* to
Re 2:17 knows *e* the one receiving it
13:17 *e* a person having the mark

Excepting
Isa 45:21 there being none *e* me

Exception
2Sa 20:18 Without *e* they used to
1Ki 21:25 Without *e* no one has proved
Isa 45:5 the *e* of me there is no God
Ac 26:29 with the *e* of these bonds
1Co 15:27 with the *e* of the one who

Excess
Nu 3:46 who are in *e* of the Levites
3:48 those who are in *e* of them
3:49 those who were in *e* of the
Jer 18:13 Israel has done to an *e*
Da 3:22 the furnace was heated to *e*
Mt 5:37 in *e* of these is from the
1Co 15:10 I labored in *e* of them all
2Co 11:23 in blows to an *e*, in
12:7 of the *e* of the revelations
Ga 1:13 *e* I kept on persecuting the

Excesses
1Pe 4:3 lusts, *e* with wine, revelries

Excessive
Zec 14:14 garments in *e* abundance
2Ti 4:15 our words to an *e* degree

Excessively
Ec 7:16 nor show yourself *e* wise
Jude 7 committed fornication *e* and

Exchange
Ge 30:15 *e* for your son's mandrakes
47:16 bread in *e* for your livestock
47:17 bread in *e* for their horses
47:17 bread in *e* for all their
Le 27:10 may not *e* it with good for
27:10 *e* it at all with beast for
27:33 neither should he *e* it
27:33 if he would *e* it at all, it
Ru 4:7 repurchase and concerning the *e*
Job 15:31 to be what he gets in *e*
28:15 gold cannot be given in *e*
28:17 refined gold an *e* for it
Eze 27:9 to *e* articles of merchandise
27:13 articles of *e* were given
27:16 your stores were given in *e*
27:17 articles of *e* were given
27:19 articles of *e* they proved
27:25 for your articles of *e*
27:27 your articles of *e*, your
27:33 your articles of *e* you made
27:34 As for your articles of *e*
48:14 nor should one make an *e*
Mt 16:26 man give in *e* for his soul
20:28 soul a ransom in *e* for many
Mr 8:37 man give in *e* for his soul
10:45 a ransom in *e* for many
Heb 12:16 Esau, who in *e* for one meal

Exchanged
Le 27:10 what is *e* for it should
27:33 *e* for it should become
Ps 71:10 have jointly *e* counsel
83:5 they have unitedly *e* counsel
106:20 they *e* my glory For a
Jer 2:11 Has a nation *e* gods, even
2:11 people have *e* my glory for
Ho 4:7 My own glory they have *e* for
Ro 1:25 *e* the truth of God for the

Exchanging
Eze 27:27 those *e* your articles of

Excite
Pr 28:4 *e* themselves against them
Da 11:10 for his sons, they will *e*
11:10 *e* himself all the way to his
11:25 *e* himself for the war with

Excited
Ge 43:30 emotions were *e* toward his
1Ki 3:26 her inward emotions were *e*
Job 17:8 one gets *e* over the apostate
31:29 *e* because evil had found

Pr 29:9 become *e* and has also laughed
Jer 50:24 that you *e* yourself
Ro 7:5 sinful passions that were *e*
2Th 2:2 nor to be *e* either through

Excitedly
2Ch 26:20 *e* began to remove him from

Excitement
Job 20:2 on account of my inward *e*
39:24 With pounding and *e* it
Jer 15:8 fall upon them suddenly *e*
Ho 11:9 I shall not come in *e*
Joe 2:6 certainly collect a glow of *e*
Na 2:10 have collected a glow of *e*

Exciting
2Ki 19:27 your *e* yourself against me
19:28 your *e* yourself against me
Isa 37:28 your *e* yourself against me
37:29 *e* yourself against me and

Exclaimed
Ge 37:30 he *e*: The child is gone! And
37:33 he went examining it and *e*
38:29 she *e*: What do you mean by
42:36 Jacob their father *e* to them
43:6 Israel *e*: Why did you have to
44:16 Judah *e*: What can we say to
44:28 I *e*: Ah, he must surely be
45:28 Israel *e*: It is enough!
50:11 they *e*: This is a heavy
Ex 2:18 Reuel their father he *e*

Exclude
Lu 6:22 they *e* you and reproach you

Excluding
Isa 66:5 *e* you by reason of my name

Exclusive
Ex 20:5 am a God exacting *e* devotion
Nu 25:11 my insistence on *e* devotion
De 4:24 a God exacting *e* devotion
5:9 am a God exacting *e* devotion
6:15 a God exacting *e* devotion
Jos 24:19 he is a God exacting *e*
Ca 8:6 insistence on *e* devotion is as
Eze 5:13 my insistence on *e* devotion
39:25 *e* devotion for my holy name
Na 1:2 a God exacting *e* devotion and

Excrement
De 23:13 and turn and cover your *e*
1Ki 18:27 *e* and has to go to the privy
2Ki 18:27 eat their own *e* and drink
Pr 30:12 been washed from its own *e*
Isa 4:4 washed away the *e* of the
36:12 may eat their own *e* and
Eze 4:12 cakes of the *e* of mankind

Excuse
Ge 43:20 *E* us, my lord! We surely did
Ex 4:10 *E* me, Jehovah, but I am not a
4:13 *E* me, Jehovah, but send
Nu 12:11 Aaron said to Moses: *E* me
Jos 7:8 *E* me, O Jehovah, but what can
Jg 6:13 *E* me, my lord, but if Jehovah
6:15 *E* me, Jehovah. With what
13:8 and say: *E* me, Jehovah
1Sa 1:26 *E* me, my lord! By the life
1Ki 3:17 *E* me, my lord, I and this
3:26 *E* me, my lord! You men
Joh 15:22 they have no *e* for their sin
Jude 4 into an *e* for loose conduct

Excused
Lu 14:18 I ask you, Have me *e*
14:19 I ask you, Have me *e*
Ro 2:15 are being accused or even *e*

Excusing
Am 7:8 no more do any further *e* of it
8:2 shall no more do any further *e*

Execrate
Nu 22:11 do come, do *e* them for me
22:17 Do *e* this people for me
23:8 How could I *e* those whom God
23:11 to *e* my enemies that I took
23:13 *e* them for me from there
23:25 you cannot *e* him at all
23:27 *e* him for me from there
24:10 It was to *e* my enemies that
Job 3:8 Let curses of the day *e* it
5:3 I began to *e* his abiding place
Pr 11:26 the populace will *e* him
24:24 the peoples will *e* him

Execrated
Nu 23:8 those whom God has not *e*

Execute
Ex 12:12 I shall *e* judgments. I am
Nu 31:3 to *e* Jehovah's vengeance upon
De 33:21 righteousness . . . *e*
1Sa 28:18 *e* his burning anger against
1Ki 3:28 to *e* judicial decision
8:45 must *e* judgment for them
8:49 must *e* judgment for them
8:59 *e* judgment for his servant
2Ch 6:35 and you must *e* judgment for
6:39 *e* judgment for them and
9:8 king to *e* judicial decision
20:12 God, will you not *e*
Ps 50:4 to *e* judgment on his people
110:6 *e* judgment among the nations
119:84 *e* judgment against those
140:12 Jehovah will *e* The legal
149:7 *e* vengeance upon the nations
149:9 *e* upon them the judicial
Isa 16:3 you men, *e* the decision
46:11 the man to *e* my counsel
Jer 18:8 I had thought to *e* upon it
22:15 *e* justice and righteousness
23:5 *e* justice and righteousness
26:3 that I am thinking to *e* upon
33:15 *e* justice and righteousness
51:36 *e* vengeance for you
Eze 5:8 I will *e* in the midst of you
5:10 *e* in you acts of judgment
11:9 *e* upon you acts of judgment
16:41 *e* in you acts of judgment
18:8 true justice he would *e*
18:9 he kept in order to *e* truth
18:21 *e* justice and righteousness
18:27 *e* justice and righteousness
25:11 shall *e* acts of judgment
25:17 *e* in them great acts of
28:22 *e* acts of judgment in her
28:26 *e* acts of judgment upon
30:14 *e* acts of judgment in No
30:19 *e* acts of judgment in Egypt
Mic 5:15 I will *e* vengeance upon the
Jude 15 *e* judgment against all, and

Executed
Nu 33:4 Jehovah had *e* judgments
Jg 11:36 has *e* acts of vengeance for
2Ch 24:24 upon Jehoash they *e* acts of
Ezr 7:26 let judgment be promptly *e*
Ps 9:4 *e* my judgment and my cause
9:16 the judgment that he has *e*
119:121 I have *e* judgment and
Ec 8:11 has not been *e* speedily, that
Jer 30:24 until he will have *e* and
Eze 18:5 *e* justice and righteousness
18:19 and righteousness he has *e*
23:10 were what they *e* upon her
39:21 judgment that I have *e* and
Lu 23:32 being led to be *e* with him
Ac 7:24 *e* vengeance for the one being
13:28 of Pilate that he be *e*
26:10 when they were to be *e*, I
Re 19:2 he has *e* judgment upon the
20:4 souls of those *e* with the ax

Executes
Mic 7:9 actually *e* justice for me

Executing
De 10:18 *e* judgment for the
Ps 99:8 *e* vengeance against their
103:6 Jehovah is *e* acts of
146:7 One *e* judgment for the
Isa 10:23 will be *e* in the midst of
Eze 11:13 extermination . . . you are *e*
24:8 rage for the *e* of vengeance

Execution
2Ki 11:15 there be an *e* of death

Exempt
De 24:5 *e* at his house for one year
1Ki 15:22 all Judah—there was none *e*
2Ki 15:5 in his house *e* from duties
2Ch 26:21 *e* from duties, as a leper

Exemption
Ex 34:7 no means will he give *e* from
Nu 14:18 he give *e* from punishment
1Sa 3:14 brought to *e* from punishment

Exercise
Ge 20:13 loving-kindness . . . *e* toward
47:29 you must *e* loving-kindness
De 9:23 did not *e* faith toward him
Jos 2:12 *e* loving-kindness toward the
2:14 certainly *e* loving-kindness
Jg 1:24 shall certainly *e* kindness
8:35 they did not *e* loving-kindness
Ru 1:8 May Jehovah *e* loving-kindness
1Sa 20:14 *e* the loving-kindness of
2Sa 2:6 now may Jehovah *e* toward you
2:6 I too shall *e* to you this
9:1 *e* loving-kindness toward him
9:3 I may *e* . . . loving-kindness
9:7 *e* loving-kindness toward you
10:2 *e* loving-kindness toward
15:20 may Jehovah *e* toward you
1Ki 2:7 you should *e* loving-kindness
21:7 *e* the kingship over Israel
1Ch 19:2 I shall *e* loving-kindness
Ps 2:10 And now, O kings, *e* insight
109:16 to *e* loving-kindness
Mic 6:8 to *e* justice and to love
Mr 5:36 Have no fear, only *e* faith
Joh 3:18 He that does not *e* faith has
6:29 *e* faith in him whom that
12:36 *e* faith in the light, in
14:1 *E* faith in God
14:1 *e* faith also in me
Ro 10:9 *e* faith in your heart that
1Co 7:4 *e* authority over her own body
7:4 *e* authority over his own body
2Co 4:13 we too *e* faith and therefore
1Ti 2:12 or to *e* authority over a man
Jas 5:7 *E* patience, therefore
5:8 *e* patience; make your hearts
1Pe 1:8 you *e* faith in him and are

Exercised
Ge 19:19 which you have *e* with me to
32:10 faithfulness that you have *e*
De 34:12 awesomeness that Moses *e*
Jos 2:12 I have *e* loving-kindness
Jg 8:35 goodness that he had *e* toward
9:16 it is goodness that you have *e*
Ru 1:8 you have *e* it toward the men
1Sa 15:6 you *e* loving-kindness with
2Sa 2:5 *e* this loving-kindness toward
10:2 his father *e* loving-kindness
1Ki 3:6 have *e* great loving-kindness
2Ki 17:14 not *e* faith in Jehovah
1Ch 19:2 his father *e* loving-kindness
2Ch 1:8 that *e* great loving-kindness
24:22 Jehoiada his father had *e*
Ps 119:66 commandments I . . . *e* faith
Eze 23:11 *e* her sensual desire more
Joh 3:18 not *e* faith in the name of
Ro 4:3 Abraham *e* faith in Jehovah
2Co 4:13 I *e* faith, therefore I spoke
2Th 1:10 with all those who *e* faith
Heb 4:3 *e* faith do enter into the

Exercises
Joh 3:18 He that *e* faith in him is
3:36 He that *e* faith in the Son
6:35 *e* faith in me will never get
6:40 the Son and *e* faith in him
11:25 He that *e* faith in me
11:26 *e* faith in me will never
14:12 He that *e* faith in me, that
Ro 10:10 *e* faith for righteousness
1Co 9:25 *e* self-control in all things
1Jo 4:18 because fear *e* a restraint
Re 13:12 it *e* all the authority of

Exercising
Ge 24:49 *e* loving-kindness and
Ex 20:6 *e* loving-kindness toward the
De 5:10 *e* loving-kindness toward the
2Sa 3:8 *e* loving-kindness toward the
22:51 *e* loving-kindness to his
Ps 18:50 *e* loving-kindness to his
Isa 28:16 *e* faith will get panicky
42:14 I kept *e* self-control
Jer 9:24 the One *e* loving-kindness
32:18 One *e* loving-kindness
Joh 1:12 were *e* faith in his name
3:16 everyone *e* faith in him
7:5 in fact, not *e* faith in him
16:9 they are not *e* faith in me
Ac 24:16 I am *e* myself continually to
Ro 3:25 while God was *e* forbearance
10:4 everyone *e* faith may have
Ga 3:22 be given to those *e* faith
Jas 5:7 *e* patience over it until he
5:10 *e* of patience the prophets
1Pe 2:6 no one *e* faith in it will by

Exert
Ec 10:10 *e* his own vital energies
Lu 13:24 *E* yourselves vigorously to
Ro 15:30 you *e* yourselves with me in

Exerted
Ge 48:2 Israel *e* his strength and
Da 10:19 I *e* my strength and finally

Exerting
Col 1:29 *e* myself in accordance with
4:12 *e* himself in your behalf
1Ti 4:10 working hard and *e* ourselves

Exerts
Heb 4:12 word of God . . . *e* power and

Exhalation
Job 7:16 for my days are an *e*
Ps 39:5 man . . . is nothing but an *e*
39:11 every earthling man is an *e*
62:9 earthling man are an *e*
62:9 together lighter than an *e*
78:33 to an end as if a mere *e*
94:11 that they are as an *e*
144:4 resemblance to a mere *e*
Pr 21:6 by a false tongue is an *e*
Isa 57:13 An *e* will take them away
Jer 10:3 customs . . . are just an *e*
Re 18:2 place of every unclean *e* and

Exhausted
Ge 21:15 water became *e* in the skin
47:13 the land of Canaan became *e*
De 25:18 while you were *e* and weary
32:24 *E* from hunger they will be
Jos 3:16 Arabah, the Salt Sea, were *e*
1Ki 17:14 flour itself will not get *e*
17:16 flour itself did not get *e*
Ps 63:1 land dry and *e*, where there
143:6 My soul is like an *e* land to
Isa 32:2 heavy crag in an *e* land
Jer 37:21 bread was *e* from the city
Da 8:27 Daniel, I felt *e* and was made

Exhibit
Jg 8:27 and to *e* it in his city Ophrah
Ro 3:25 to *e* his own righteousness
3:26 *e* his own righteousness in

Exhibited
Ac 20:35 I have *e* to you in all things
Col 2:15 he *e* them in open public as

Exhibiting
Ac 9:39 *e* many inner garments and
Tit 2:10 *e* good fidelity to the full
3:2 reasonable, *e* all mildness

Exhibition
1Co 4:9 *e* as men appointed to death

Exhibits
Pr 23:31 wine when it *e* a red color

Exhort
Ro 15:30 *e* you, brothers, through our
16:17 I *e* you, brothers, to keep
1Co 1:10 *e* you, brothers, through
16:15 I *e* you, brothers: you know
2Co 2:8 I *e* you to confirm your love
Php 4:2, 2 Euodia I *e* and Syntyche I *e*
1Th 4:1 and *e* you by the Lord Jesus
4:10 we *e* you, brothers, to go
5:14 we *e* you, brothers, admonish
1Ti 2:1 I therefore *e*, first of all
2Ti 4:2 *e*, with all long-suffering
Tit 1:9 able both to *e* by the teaching
Heb 13:19 I *e* you more especially to
13:22 I *e* you, brothers, to bear
1Pe 2:11 I *e* you as aliens and
Jude 3 *e* you to put up a hard fight

Exhortation
Job 20:3 An insulting *e* to me I hear
33:16 on *e* to them he puts his
36:10 will uncover their ear to *e*
Jer 10:8 tree is a mere *e* of vanities
35:13 receive *e* to obey my words
Ho 5:2 I was an *e* to all of them
Ro 12:8 let him be at his *e*; he that
1Th 2:3 For the *e* we give does not
2Th 3:12 order and *e* in the Lord
1Ti 4:13 applying yourself to . . . *e*
Heb 12:5 the *e* which addresses you as
1Pe 5:1 I give this *e*, for I too am

Exhortations
Lu 3:18 many other *e* and continued
1Ti 6:2 and giving these *e*

Exhorting
Ac 2:40 witness and kept *e* them
18:27 *e* them to receive him kindly
1Th 2:11 we kept *e* each one of you
Tit 2:6 keep on *e* the younger men to
2:15 and *e* and reproving with
Phm 9 *e* you rather on the basis of
10 *e* you concerning my child
Heb 3:13 but keep on *e* one another

Exhorts
Ro 12:8 he that *e*, let him be at his

Exile
Jg 18:30 the land's being taken into *e*
1Sa 4:21 gone away from Israel into *e*
4:22 Glory has gone . . . into *e*
2Sa 15:19 you are an *e* from your
2Ki 15:29 into *e* in Assyria
16:9 its people into *e* at Kir
17:6 led Israel into *e* in Assyria
17:11 Jehovah had taken into *e*
17:23 into *e* in Assyria down to
17:26 into *e* and then settled in
17:27 you led into *e* from there
17:28 led into *e* from Samaria
17:33 they had led them into *e*
18:11 Israel into *e* in Assyria and
24:14 took into *e* all Jerusalem
24:14 he was taking into *e*
24:15 Jehoiachin into *e* to Babylon
25:11 the bodyguard took into *e*
25:21 Judah went into *e* from off
25:27 *e* of Jehoiachin the king
1Ch 5:6 king of Assyria took into *e*
5:22 down to the time of the *e*
5:26 he took into *e* those of the
6:15 Judah and Jerusalem into *e*
8:6 take them into *e* at Manahath
8:7 the one that took them into *e*
9:1 Judah itself was taken into *e*
Ezr 2:1 had taken into *e* at Babylon
4:1 sons of the *E* were building a
4:10 took into *e* and settled in
5:12 the people into *e* at Babylon
6:21 had returned from the *E* ate
Ne 7:6 taken into *e* and who later
Es 2:6 taken into *e* from Jerusalem
2:6 *e* with Jeconiah the king of
2:6 the king of Babylon took into *e*
Isa 5:13 will have to go into *e*
45:13 in *e* he will let go, not
49:21 into *e* and taken prisoner
Jer 1:3 Jerusalem went into *e* in the
13:19 has been taken into *e*
13:19 taken into *e* completely
20:4 take them into *e* in Babylon
22:12 they have taken him into *e*
24:1 carried into *e* Jeconiah the
27:20 king of Judah, into *e* from
29:1 into *e* from Jerusalem to
29:4 go into *e* from Jerusalem to
29:7 caused you to go into *e*
29:14 I caused you to go into *e*
29:16 gone forth with you into *e*
39:9 took into *e* to Babylon
40:1 taken into *e* in Babylon
40:7 taken into *e* in Babylon
43:3 take us into *e* in Babylon
46:19 mere baggage for *e*
48:7 go forth into *e*, his priests
48:11 into *e* they have not gone
49:3 will go even into *e*, his
52:15 the bodyguard took into *e*
52:27 Judah went into *e* from off
52:28 Nebuchadrezzar took into *e*
52:30 took Jews into *e*, seven
52:31 *e* of Jehoiachin the king
La 1:3 Judah has gone into *e* because
4:22 not carry you off into *e* again
Eze 1:2 of the *e* of King Jehoiachin
12:3 for yourself luggage for *e*
12:3 and go into *e* in the daytime
12:3 go into *e* from your place to
12:4 like luggage for *e* in the
12:4 being brought forth for *e*
12:7 just like the luggage for *e*
12:11 Into *e*, into captivity they
25:3 they have gone into *e*
33:21 day of the month of our *e*
39:23 Israel, went into *e*, on
39:28 when I send them in *e* to
40:1 twenty-fifth year of our *e*
Ho 10:5 it will have gone into *e*
Am 1:6 *e* a complete body of exiles
1:15 their king must go into *e*
5:5 will without fail go into *e*
5:27 go into *e* beyond Damascus
6:7 go into *e* at the head of those
Am 6:7 the head of those going into *e*
7:11 without fail go into *e*
7:17 without fail go into *e* from
Mic 1:16 gone away from you into *e*
Na 3:10 She, too, was meant for *e*
Zec 14:2 must go forth into the *e*

Exiled
2Ki 24:15 he led away as *e* people
24:16 as *e* people to Babylon
Ezr 1:11 the *e* people out of Babylon
2:1 captivity of the *e* people
9:4 unfaithfulness of the *e* people
10:6 of the *e* people
10:8 congregation of the *e* people
Ne 7:6 the captivity of the *e* people
Jer 28:6 the *e* people from Babylon
29:1 older men of the *e* people
29:4 has said to all the *e* people
29:20 all you *e* people, whom I
29:31 Send to all the *e* people
Eze 1:1 in the midst of the *e* people
3:11 enter in among the *e* people
3:15 the *e* people at Tel-abib
11:24 to Chaldea to the *e* people
11:25 to speak to the *e* people all
Zec 6:10 something from the *e* people

Exiles
Ezr 6:16 the former *e* held the
6:19 the former *e* proceeded to
6:20 for all the former *e* and for
8:35 captivity, the former *e*
10:7 the former *e* to collect
10:16 former *e* proceeded to do
Isa 20:4 and the *e* of Ethiopia, boys
Jer 24:5 I shall regard the *e* of Judah
28:4 and all the *e* of Judah
29:22 entire body of *e* of Judah
40:1 *e* of Jerusalem and of Judah
Da 2:25 man of the *e* of Judah who
5:13 Daniel that is of the *e* of
6:13 who is of the *e* of Judah
Am 1:5 will have to go as *e* to Kir
1:6 *e* to hand over to Edom
1:9 a complete body of *e* to Edom
Ob 20 as for the *e* of this rampart
20 the *e* of Jerusalem, who were in

Exist
Ex 8:22 that no gadfly may *e* there
12:49 One law is to *e* for the
23:26 nor a barren woman will *e* in
Nu 9:14 *e* one statute for you people
2Ch 16:9 will *e* wars against you
Job 38:28 *e* a father for the rain
Ps 73:11 *e* knowledge in the Most High
Pr 18:24 *e* companions disposed to
23:18 there will *e* a future, and
Ec 1:10 Does anything *e* of which one
6:11 there *e* many things that are
8:14 *e* righteous ones to whom
8:14 *e* wicked ones to whom it is
Isa 43:8 blind though eyes . . . *e*
44:8 Does there *e* a God besides
Jer 14:22 *e* among the vain idols of
23:26 *e* in the heart of the
27:18 the word of Jehovah does *e*
37:17 *e* a word from Jehovah
37:17 Jeremiah said: There does *e!*
41:8 *e* in our possession hidden
La 1:12 Does there *e* any pain like my
Da 2:10 not *e* a man on the dry land
2:11 does not *e* with flesh at all
3:12 *e* certain Jews whom you
3:29 there does not *e* another god
Joe 2:2 to *e* from the indefinite past
Jon 4:11 there *e* more than one
Mic 6:10 *e* in the house of a wicked
Zec 8:10 wages for mankind made to *e*
Ac 17:28 we have life and move and *e*
1Co 1:11 that dissensions *e* among you
11:18 hear divisions *e* among you
Col 1:17 other things were made to *e*
2Pe 1:8 things *e* in you and overflow
Re 21:25 for night will not *e* there

Existed
Ge 42:5 famine *e* in the land of
Job 16:4 your souls *e* where my soul
Joh 1:15 because he *e* before me
1:30 because he *e* before me
Re 4:11 because of your will they *e*

Existence
Ge 48:15 all my *e* until this day
Ex 9:16 kept you in *e*, for the sake of

1Ki 15:4 and keeping Jerusalem in *e*
Ec 1:10 had *e* for time indefinite
1:10 *e* is from time prior to us
Mr 2:27 sabbath came into *e* for the
Joh 1:3 came into *e* through him, and
1:3 even one thing came into *e*
1:3 What has come into *e*
1:10 world came into *e* through
8:58 Before Abraham came into *e*
2Co 5:17 new things have come into *e*
Jas 3:9 into *e* in the likeness of God

Existing
Ge 7:4 I will wipe every *e* thing that
7:23 he wiped out every *e* thing
Ex 10:6 from the day of their *e* upon
De 11:6 every *e* thing that stepped
Job 14:2 and does not keep *e*
Eze 21:13 This will not continue *e*
Lu 7:25 and *e* in luxury are in royal
16:23 he *e* in torments, and he saw
Ac 5:17 then *e* sect of the Sadducees
19:40 no single cause *e* that will
Ro 13:1 *e* authorities stand placed
Php 2:6 he was *e* in God's form, gave
2Pe 2:19 *e* as slaves of corruption

Exists
1Sa 17:46 *e* a God belonging to Israel
2Ki 3:12 word of Jehovah *e* with him
5:8 there *e* a prophet in Israel
2Ch 15:7 *e* a reward for your activity
25:8 *e* power with God to help
25:9 *e* with Jehovah the means to
Ezr 10:2 there *e* a hope for Israel
Job 9:33 There *e* no person to decide
11:18 trust because there *e* hope
14:7 there *e* hope for even a tree
28:1 for silver there *e* a place
33:23 there *e* for him a messenger
Ps 7:3 If there *e* any injustice in
14:2 there *e* anyone having insight
53:2 there *e* anyone having insight
58:11 there *e* a God that is judging
135:17 *e* no spirit in their mouth
Pr 11:24 *e* the one that is scattering
12:18 *e* the one speaking
13:7 *e* the one that is pretending
13:23 *e* the one that is swept away
14:12 *e* a way that is upright
16:25 *e* a way that is upright
18:24 *e* a friend sticking closer
19:18 your son while there *e* hope
20:15 *e* gold, also an abundance
24:14 then there *e* a future, and
Ec 2:13 *e* more advantage for wisdom
2:21 *e* the man whose hard work
4:8 *e* one, but not a second one
5:13 *e* a grave calamity that I
6:1 *e* a calamity that I have seen
7:15 *e* the righteous one perishing
7:15 *e* the wicked one continuing
8:6 *e* a time and judgment even for
8:14 *e* a vanity that is carried out
9:4 the living there *e* confidence
10:5 *e* something calamitous that I
Jer 5:1 there *e* anyone doing justice
31:6 *e* a day when the lookouts
31:16 *e* a reward for your
31:17 *e* a hope for your future
La 3:29 Perhaps there *e* a hope
Da 2:11 nobody else *e* who can show it
2:28 *e* a God in the heavens who
2:30 wisdom that *e* in me more
4:35 *e* no one that can check his
5:11 *e* a capable man in your
Mal 1:14 there *e* in his drove a male
Lu 12:28 that today *e* and tomorrow
Ac 19:27 danger *e* not only that this
25:11 none of those things *e* of
1Co 1:13 The Christ *e* divided. Paul
Php 3:20 citizenship *e* in the heavens

Exits
Eze 42:11 and all their *e* were alike
43:11 and its *e* and its entryways
44:5 all the *e* of the sanctuary

Exodus
Heb 11:22 *e* of the sons of Israel

Expand
Isa 60:5 will actually quiver and *e*

Expanding
Ge 30:30 it went *e* to a multitude

Expanse
Ge 1:6 Let an *e* come to be in between
1:7 God proceeded to make the *e*
1:7 beneath the *e* and the waters
1:7 that should be above the *e*
1:8 God began to call the *e* Heaven
1:14 luminaries . . . in the *e*
1:15 as luminaries in the *e* of the
1:17 God put them in the *e* of the
1:20 face of the *e* of the heavens
Ps 19:1 the work of his hands the *e*
150:1 in the *e* of his strength
Eze 1:22 the likeness of an *e* like the
1:23 under the *e* their wings were
1:25 a voice above the *e* that was
1:26 *e* that was over their head
10:1 *e* that was over the head of
27:7 your cloth *e* happened to be
Da 12:3 like the brightness of the *e*

Expect
Mt 11:3 are we to *e* a different one?
24:50 on a day that he does not *e*
Lu 7:19 are we to *e* a different one?
7:20 or are we to *e* another?

Expectation
Job 41:9 One's *e* about it will
Ps 33:20 soul has been in *e* of Jehovah
39:7 Jehovah? My *e* is toward you
Pr 10:28 *e* of the righteous ones is
11:7 *e* based on powerfulness has
13:12 *E* postponed is making the
Isa 8:17 will keep in *e* of Jehovah
30:18 in *e* of showing you favor
30:18 those keeping in *e* of him
64:4 one that keeps in *e* of him
La 3:18 and my *e* from Jehovah
Da 12:12 one who is keeping in *e* and
Hab 2:3 should delay, keep in *e* of it
Zep 3:8 in *e* of me, is the utterance
Lu 3:15 as the people were in *e* and
21:26 *e* of the things coming upon
Ro 8:19 eager *e* of the creation is
Php 1:20 in harmony with my eager *e*
Heb 10:27 fearful *e* of judgment and
11:1 Faith is the assured *e* of

Expecting
Lu 8:40 for they were all *e* him
12:46 a day that he is not *e* him
Ac 3:5 *e* to get something from them
10:24 Cornelius, of course, was *e*
12:11 people of the Jews were *e*
28:6 *e* he was going to swell up

Expedition
Nu 31:14 in from the military *e*
31:27 who went out on the *e* and
31:28 who went out on the *e*
31:32 people of the *e* had taken
31:36 those who went out on the *e*

Expel
Isa 27:8 *e* her with his blast, a hard
Mt 7:22 *e* demons in your name, and
8:31 If you *e* us, send us forth
10:1 to *e* these and to cure every
10:8 make lepers clean, *e* demons
12:24 not *e* the demons except by
12:27 if I *e* the demons by means
12:27 do your sons *e* them
12:28 spirit that I *e* the demons
17:19 Why is it we could not *e* it?
Mr 3:15 authority to *e* the demons
3:23 How can Satan *e* Satan?
6:13 they would *e* many demons and
7:26 asking him to *e* the demon
9:18 told your disciples to *e* it
9:28 Why could we not *e* it?
Lu 9:40 begged your disciples to *e* it
11:18 you say I *e* the demons by
11:19 I *e* the demons, by whom do
11:19 by whom do your sons *e* them?
11:20 I *e* the demons, the kingdom
Joh 16:2 *e* you from the synagogue

Expelled
Mt 8:16 *e* the spirits with a word
9:33 after the demon had been *e*
Mr 1:34 and he *e* many demons, but he
Joh 9:22 get *e* from the synagogue
12:42 to be *e* from the synagogue

Expelling
Mr 1:39 of Galilee and *e* the demons
9:38 *e* demons by the use of your

Lu 9:49 saw a certain man *e* demons
11:14 he was *e* a dumb demon

Expels
Mt 9:34 that he *e* the demons
12:26 if Satan *e* Satan, he has
Mr 3:22 *e* the demons by means of the
Lu 11:15 He *e* the demons by means of

Expend
Jas 4:3 *e* it upon your cravings for

Expended
Le 26:20 power will simply be *e* for
2Ki 12:12 *e* upon the house to repair

Expense
De 21:16 at the *e* of the hated one's
2Sa 19:42 eaten at all at the king's *e*
2Ki 15:20 silver at the *e* of Israel
15:20 the *e* of all the valiant
Ezr 6:4 let the *e* be given from the
6:8 *e* will promptly be given to
Lu 14:28 calculate the *e*, to see if
1Co 9:7 as a soldier at his own *e*

Expenses
Ac 21:24 take care of their *e*, that

Expensive
1Ki 5:17 *e* stones, to lay the
7:9 of *e* stones according to
7:10 *e* stones laid as a foundation
7:11 up above there were *e* stones
Mr 14:3 oil, genuine nard, very *e*
1Th 2:6 an *e* burden as apostles of
2:9 not to put an *e* burden upon
2Th 3:8 not to impose an *e* burden
1Ti 2:9 gold or pearls or very *e* garb

Experience
Ge 31:40 my *e* that by day the heat
Jg 3:2 Israel to have the *e*, so
8:16 men of Succoth through an *e*
1Sa 15:32 the bitter *e* of death has
Isa 47:1 you will not *e* again that
47:5 not *e* again that people call
66:11 *e* exquisite delight from
Zec 9:5 hope will have to *e* shame
10:5 horses will have to *e* shame
Heb 10:33 who were having such an *e*

Experienced
De 1:13 and *e* men of your tribes
1:15 men wise and *e*, and put them
Jg 3:1 who had not *e* any of the wars
3:2 that had not *e* such things
21:11 that has *e* lying with a male
2Ch 2:8 *e* at cutting down the trees
2:12 a wise son, *e* in discretion
2:13 *e* in understanding, belonging
2:14 *e*, to work in gold and in
Ca 8:5 birth to you *e* birth pangs
Am 5:16 those *e* in lamentation
2Co 11:25 three times I *e* shipwreck
1Ti 1:19 have *e* shipwreck concerning

Expert
1Ch 15:22 Chenaniah . . . he was *e*
25:8 the *e* along with the learner
2Ch 34:12 *e* with the instruments of
Isa 3:3 and *e* in magical arts, and
Ac 26:3 *e* on all the customs as well

Expertly
Ge 44:5 he *e* reads omens? It is a bad
44:15 a man as I am can *e* read

Experts
1Ch 25:7 in song to Jehovah, all *e*

Expiration
Ge 4:3 at the *e* of some time

Expire
Ge 6:17 that is in the earth will *e*
Nu 17:12 Now we are bound to *e*, we
Jos 22:20 not the only man to *e* in
Job 3:11 Why did I not . . . then *e*?
13:19 silent I should simply *e*
27:5 Until I *e* I shall not take
29:18 Within my nest I shall *e*
34:15 All flesh will *e* together
36:12 will *e* without knowledge
Ps 88:15 about to *e* from boyhood on
104:29 away their spirit, they *e*
Zec 13:8 will be cut off and *e*

Expired
Ge 7:21 flesh . . . upon the earth *e*
25:8 Then Abraham *e* and died in

Ge 25:17 Then he *e* and died and was
35:29 Isaac *e* and died and was
49:33 *e* and was gathered to his
Nu 20:3 If only we had *e* when our
20:3 our brothers *e* before Jehovah
20:29 got to see that Aaron had *e*
1Sa 18:26 and the days had not yet *e*
2Ch 21:19 two full years had *e*, his
Job 10:18 Could I have *e*, that not
La 1:19 and my own old men have *e*
Mr 15:37 let out a loud cry and *e*
15:39 *e* under these circumstances
Lu 23:46 When he had said this, he *e*
Ac 5:5 Ananias fell down and *e*
5:10 fell down at his feet and *e*
12:23 eaten up with worms and *e*

Expires
Job 14:10 man *e*, and where is he?

Expiring
Nu 17:13 we end up in *e* that way
Job 11:20 will be an *e* of the soul

Explain
De 1:5 Moses undertook to *e* this law
Mt 13:36 *E* to us the illustration of
Mr 4:34 to his disciples he would *e*
Ac 11:4 to *e* the particulars to them

Explained
Joh 1:18 the one that has *e* him
Ac 28:23 he *e* the matter to them by
Heb 5:11 much to say and hard to be *e*

Explaining
Ne 8:7 *e* the law to the people
Ac 17:3 *e* and proving by references

Explanation
Jg 7:15 the dream and its *e*, he began
Da 5:12 and the *e* of riddles and the

Exploit
Jer 27:7 must *e* him as a servant
30:8 strangers *e* him as a servant
2Pe 2:3 *e* you with counterfeit words

Exploited
Jer 25:14 have *e* them as servants

Explore
Jg 18:2 spy out the land and to *e* it
18:2 said to them: Go, *e* the land
Ec 1:13 heart to seek and *e* wisdom in
7:25 to *e* and to search for wisdom
La 3:40 search out our ways and *e*

Explored
Ec 2:3 I *e* with my heart by cheering

Explores
Job 39:8 It *e* mountains for its

Export
1Ki 10:28 the *e* of the horses that
2Ch 1:16 *e* of the horses that Solomon

Exported
1Ki 10:29 and was *e* from Egypt for
2Ch 1:17 *e* from Egypt a chariot for

Exporting
1Ki 10:29 that they did the *e*
2Ch 1:17 of them that they did the *e*

Expose
Nu 25:4 *e* them to Jehovah toward the
1Sa 14:8 let us *e* ourselves to them
2Sa 21:6 *e* them to Jehovah in Gibeah
21:9 *e* them on the mountain
Isa 26:21 *e* her bloodshed and will
Ac 7:19 fathers to *e* their infants
Heb 6:6 and *e* him to public shame

Exposed
Ge 42:9 the *e* condition of the land
42:12 the *e* condition of the land
Ex 20:26 private parts may not be *e*
Le 20:18 he has *e* her source, and she
20:19 blood relation that one has *e*
Jg 6:37 wool *e* on the threshing floor
1Sa 14:11 two of them *e* themselves
2Sa 21:13 bones of the men being *e*
Eze 13:14 its foundation must be *e*
16:57 own badness got to be *e*
Mr 4:22 for the purpose of being *e*
Ac 7:21 when he was *e*, the daughter
Heb 4:13 openly *e* to the eyes of him
10:33 *e* as in a theater both to

Exposing
Php 2:30 *e* his soul to danger, that

Exposition
2Ch 13:22 *e* of the prophet Iddo
24:27 *e* of the Book of the Kings

Expounded
Ne 8:8 it being *e*, and there being a
Ac 18:26 and *e* the way of God more

Express
Isa 3:26 mourn and *e* sorrow, and
19:8 must *e* sorrow, and even
58:2 that they would *e* delight
Jer 7:23 *e* in command upon them
Eze 18:3 to *e* this proverbial saying
23:25 *e* my ardor against you
Ho 11:9 shall not *e* my burning anger
Ac 13:36 served the *e* will of God in
Ro 3:3 If some did not *e* faith, will
9:19 has withstood his *e* will
13:4 avenger to *e* wrath upon the
1Co 10:5 God did not *e* his approval

Expressed
Ge 29:30 *e* more love for Rachel than
50:16 they *e* a command to Joseph
Nu 11:4 *e* selfish longing, and the
Ru 3:10 *e* your loving-kindness better
2Sa 23:15 David *e* his craving and said
Job 21:4 is my concern *e* to man?
Eze 35:11 jealousy that you have *e*
Mt 19:25 they *e* very great surprise
Ac 16:3 Paul *e* the desire for this
Heb 10:34 you both *e* sympathy for
1Pe 4:10 kindness *e* in various ways

Expressing
Isa 13:3 mighty ones for *e* my anger
Eze 18:2 are *e* this proverbial saying
33:31 are *e* lustful desires and
Mr 14:4 were some *e* indignation
Ro 2:22 one *e* abhorrence of the idols

Expression
Le 7:12 it in *e* of thanksgiving
Nu 30:12 *e* of her lips as her vows or
De 8:3 every *e* of Jehovah's mouth
Ps 89:34 *e* out of my lips I shall not
Isa 3:9 *e* of their faces actually
Jer 17:16 known the *e* of my lips
Da 3:19 *e* of his face was changed
Ho 9:7 the man of inspired *e* will be
Mr 9:23 That *e*, If you can! Why, all
Ro 3:14 full of cursing and bitter *e*
2Co 9:11 an *e* of thanks to God
Eph 4:9 the *e* he ascended, what does
2Th 2:2 through an inspired *e* or
1Ti 5:12 their first *e* of faith
Heb 7:9 *e*, through Abraham even Levi
12:27 Now the *e* Yet once more
1Jo 4:1 not believe every inspired *e*
4:2 knowledge of the inspired *e*
4:2 inspired *e* that confesses
4:3 inspired *e* that does not
4:3 the antichrist's inspired *e*
4:6 the inspired *e* of truth and
4:6 and the inspired *e* of error

Expressions
Ps 56:12 render *e* of thanksgiving to
89:1 Jehovah's *e* of loving-kindness
Pr 7:18 enjoy each other with love *e*
Ca 1:2 *e* of endearment are better
1:4 mention your *e* of endearment
4:10 your *e* of endearment are, O
4:10 better your *e* of endearment
5:1 drunk with *e* of endearment
7:12 my *e* of endearment to you
Eze 16:8 was the time for love's *e*
23:17 to the bed of *e* of love
2Co 9:12 many *e* of thanks to God
2Pe 2:18 swelling *e* of no profit
1Jo 4:1 test the inspired *e* to see
Re 16:13 three unclean inspired *e*
16:14 *e* inspired by demons and
22:6 God of the inspired *e* of the

Expressly
Da 2:16 time *e* to show the very
Mr 8:15 began to order them *e* and say
9:9 *e* ordered them not to relate

Expropriations
Eze 45:9 Lift your *e* off my people

Exquisite
Job 22:26 will find your *e* delight
27:10 will he find *e* delight
Ps 37:4 take *e* delight in Jehovah
Ps 37:11 find their *e* delight in the
Ec 2:8 the *e* delights of the sons of
Ca 7:6 beloved girl, among *e* delights
Isa 13:22 in the palaces of *e* delight
55:2 *e* delight in fatness itself
58:13 an *e* delight, a holy day
58:14 your *e* delight in Jehovah
66:11 experience *e* delight from
Mic 1:16 your sons of *e* delight
2:9 which a woman has *e* delight

Extend
Ge 10:30 dwelling came to *e* from
Ex 28:42 to the thighs they are to *e*
30:2 Its horns *e* out of it
2Ki 20:10 the shadow to *e* itself ten
Jer 43:10 *e* his state tent over them

Extended
Ge 21:34 Abraham *e* his residence as
26:8 his days there *e* themselves
38:28 one *e* his hand, and the
Nu 24:6 they have *e* a long way, Like
Jos 24:31 older men who *e* their days
Jg 2:7 older men who *e* their days
1Sa 27:8 land that *e* from Telam as
1Ch 21:16 his hand *e* toward Jerusalem
Ezr 7:28 has *e* loving-kindness before
Isa 26:15 *e* afar all the borders of
48:13 hand *e* out the heavens

Extendedly
1Sa 1:12 she prayed *e* before Jehovah

Extending
Ge 39:21 kept *e* loving-kindness to
Ps 109:12 no one *e* loving-kindness
Isa 66:12 *e* to her peace just like
Jer 6:4 shadows . . . keep *e* themselves
Mt 12:49 And *e* his hand toward his

Extends
Nu 21:13 wilderness that *e* from the
Ezr 9:9 *e* toward us loving-kindness
Eze 30:25 *e* it out against the land

Extensive
Ne 4:19 The work is large and *e*, and
Isa 6:12 *e* in the midst of the land
Da 11:3 rule with *e* dominion and do
11:5 rule with *e* dominion greater
Re 16:18 so *e* an earthquake, so great

Extensively
Nu 11:32 *e* all around the camp for
Eze 25:12 kept doing wrong *e* and

Extent
Ge 6:16 complete it to the *e* of a
19:21 consideration to this *e* also
44:1 *e* they are able to carry it
Ex 10:6 filled to an *e* that your
38:18 its *e* was five cubits
Le 5:4 swears to the *e* of speaking
26:15 to the *e* of your violating my
Jos 13:1 to a very great *e* the land
Ezr 10:13 rebelled to a great *e* in
Ps 119:107 afflicted to a great *e*
Isa 52:14 To the *e* that many have
Jer 31:20 *e* of my speaking against
Ho 11:2 To that same *e* they went
Ob 5 to what *e* would you have been
6 the *e* to which those of Esau
Hab 2:18 to the *e* of making valueless
Zec 1:15 indignant to only a little *e*
1:21 to such an *e* that no one at
Mt 25:40 To the *e* that you did it to
25:45 To the *e* that you did not do
2Co 1:14 recognized, to an *e*, that we
2:5 but all of you to an *e*—not to
Php 3:16 *e* we have made progress
4:19 to the *e* of his riches in
Col 1:11 to the *e* of his glorious
Heb 1:4 to the *e* that he has inherited
7:20 to the *e* that it was not
7:22 to that *e* also Jesus has
9:13 *e* of cleanness of the flesh
Re 18:7 *e* that she glorified herself
18:7 to that *e* give her torment

Exterminate
Ex 32:10 and I may *e* them, and let
32:12 to *e* them from the surface
33:3 may not *e* you on the way
33:5 of you and certainly *e* you
Le 26:44 abhor them so as to *e* them
Nu 16:21 I may *e* them in an instant
16:45 I may *e* them in an instant
Jos 24:20 do you injury and *e* you

2Sa 22:39 I shall *e* them and break
1Ki 22:11 Syrians until you *e* them
2Ch 18:10 Syrians until you *e* them
Eze 20:13 in order to *e* them
22:31 fire of my fury I will *e*
Zec 5:4 *e* it and its timbers and its

Exterminated
Nu 25:11 not *e* the sons of Israel in
De 7:24 until you have *e* them
28:21 *e* you from off the ground
1Sa 15:18 until you will have *e* them
2Sa 21:5 The man that *e* us and that
22:38 not return until they are *e*
2Ch 8:8 the sons of Israel had not *e*
Ps 18:37 not return until they are *e*
31:22 *e* from in front of your eyes
119:87 have *e* me in the earth
Jer 5:3 You *e* them. They refused to
9:16 until I shall have *e* them
49:37 until I shall have *e* them
La 2:22 my enemy himself *e* them

Exterminating
Isa 10:23 *e* and a strict decision the
Jer 10:25 and they keep at *e* him
Eze 43:8 I went *e* them in my anger

Extermination
Ne 9:31 did not make an *e* of them or
Isa 10:22 *e* decided upon will be
28:22 *e*, even something decided
Jer 4:27 not carry out a sheer *e*
5:10 you men make an actual *e*
5:18 not carry out an *e* of you
30:11 *e* among all the nations
30:11 your case I shall make no *e*
46:28 *e* among all the nations to
46:28 with you I shall make no *e*
Eze 11:13 Is it an *e* that you are
13:13 will be hailstones for an *e*
20:17 not make an *e* of them in
21:13 For an *e* has been made, and
Da 9:27 until an *e*, the very thing
11:16 will be *e* in his hand
Na 1:8 an outright *e* of her place
1:9 He is causing an outright *e*
Zep 1:18 he will make an *e*, indeed

External
2Co 11:28 those things of an *e* kind
1Pe 3:3 the *e* braiding of the hair and

Extinction
Job 12:5 has contempt for *e* itself
31:29 *e* of one intensely hating
Pr 24:22 who is aware of the *e* of

Extinguish
2Sa 14:7 *e* the glow of my charcoals
21:17 not *e* the lamp of Israel
Ca 8:7 are not able to *e* love, nor can
Isa 42:3 wick, he will not *e* it
Jer 21:12 there be no one to *e* it
Am 5:6 not be with no one to *e* it
Mt 12:20 no . . . wick will he *e*

Extinguished
1Sa 3:3 the lamp of God was not yet *e*
2Ki 22:17 my rage . . . will not be *e*
2Ch 29:7 kept the lamps *e*, and
34:25 this place and not be *e*
Job 17:1 my own days have been *e*
18:5 light also of wicked . . . *e*
18:6 his own lamp will be *e*
21:17 lamp of the wicked ones *e*
Ps 118:12 *e* like a fire of thornbushes
Pr 13:9 wicked ones—it will be *e*
20:20 his lamp will be *e* at the
24:20 lamp of wicked people . . . *e*
Isa 34:10 or by day it will not be *e*
43:17 They will certainly be *e*
66:24 fire itself will not be *e*
Jer 7:20 and it will not be *e*
17:27 and will not be *e*
Eze 20:47 flame will not be *e*
20:48 so that it will not be *e*
32:7 when you get *e* I will cover

Extinguishers
1Ki 7:50 the basins and the *e* and the
2Ki 12:13 *e*, bowls, trumpets, any
25:14 the *e* and the cups and all
2Ch 4:22 *e* and the bowls and the cups
Jer 52:18 *e* and the bowls and the

Extinguishing
Isa 1:31 with no one to do the *e*
Jer 4:4 burn with no one to do the *e*

Extol
Ps 107:32 *e* him in the congregation

Extolling
Ps 66:17 was an *e* with my tongue
149:6 songs *e* God be in their
Ac 5:13 the people were *e* them

Extorted
Le 6:4 the *e* thing which he has taken
Lu 19:8 whatever I *e* from anyone by
2Co 9:5 gift and not as something *e*

Extortion
Jer 22:17 upon defrauding and upon *e*

Extortioner
1Co 5:11 in company with . . . an *e*

Extortioners
Lu 18:11 rest of men, *e*, unrighteous
1Co 5:10 the greedy persons and *e* or
6:10 nor *e* will inherit God's

Extract
Mt 7:4 to *e* the straw from your eye
7:5 First *e* the rafter from your
7:5 to *e* the straw from your
Lu 6:42 allow me to *e* the straw that
6:42 *e* the rafter from your own
6:42 *e* the straw that is in your

Extracting
Am 5:11 *e* farm rent from someone

Extraordinarily
1Ki 7:47 of so *e* great a quantity
2Ch 16:14 *e* great funeral burning for
20:19 with an *e* loud voice
Da 7:19 *e* fearsome, the teeth of

Extraordinary
Ge 18:14 anything too *e* for Jehovah
Ex 1:7 mightier at a very *e* rate
Nu 13:32 are men of *e* size
De 17:8 a matter . . . too *e* for you
2Sa 21:20 a man of *e* size, with six
23:21 man that was of *e* size
1Ch 11:23 a man of *e* size, of five
20:6 man of *e* size whose fingers
2Ch 26:8 strength to an *e* degree
Da 2:31 the brightness of which was *e*
4:36 greatness *e* was added to me
5:12 *e* spirit and knowledge and
5:14 wisdom *e* have been found in
6:3 an *e* spirit was in him; and
Mt 5:47 what *e* thing are you doing?
Mr 7:37 astounded in a most *e* way
Ac 19:11 performing *e* works of power
28:2 showed us *e* human kindness
1Th 3:10 more than *e* supplications
5:13 more than *e* consideration in

Extravagance
1Co 2:1 not come with an *e* of speech

Extreme
Ge 27:33 great trembling in *e* measure
49:19 Gad . . . will raid the *e* rear
Jos 8:13 the city and the *e* rear of it
1Ki 1:4 girl was beautiful in the *e*
Job 35:15 taken note of the *e* rashness
Ps 38:6 have bowed low to an *e* degree
38:8 crushed to an *e* degree
119:51 have derided me to the *e*
Isa 64:9 not be indignant . . . to the *e*
64:12 let us be afflicted to the *e*
Da 8:8 put on great airs to an *e*
Ho 10:15 because of your *e* badness
Mr 5:23 daughter is in an *e* condition
2Co 1:8 under *e* pressure beyond our

Extremely
Ge 27:34 to cry out in an *e* loud and
2Sa 2:17 fighting came to be *e* hard
Jer 14:17 with an *e* sickish stroke
Ac 26:11 I was *e* mad against them

Extremities
Ex 27:4 rings of copper at its four *e*
28:7 to be joined at its two *e*
28:23 the two *e* of the breastpiece
28:24 at the *e* of the breastpiece
28:26 the two *e* of the breastpiece
38:5 on the four *e* near the grating
39:4 It was joined at its two *e*
39:16 the two *e* of the breastpiece
39:17 at the *e* of the breastpiece
39:19 the two *e* of the breastpiece
De 22:12 the four *e* of your clothing
Job 37:3 his lightning is to the *e* of
38:13 hold on the *e* of the earth
Ps 19:6 circuit is to their other *e*
Isa 11:12 the four *e* of the earth
40:28 the Creator of the *e* of
41:5 The very *e* of the earth began
41:9 from the *e* of the earth
Jer 49:36 the four *e* of the heavens
Eze 7:2 upon the four *e* of the land
Ac 10:11 let down by its four *e*
11:5 being let down by its four *e*
Ro 10:18 *e* of the inhabited earth

Extremity
Ge 23:9 is at the *e* of his field
Ex 26:5 on the *e* of the tent cloth
36:12 on the *e* of the tent cloth
Le 19:27 not destroy the *e* of your
21:5 *e* of their beard they should
Nu 11:1 some in the *e* of the camp
20:16 at the *e* of your territory
22:36 is on the *e* of the territory
23:13 the *e* of them you will see
34:3 *e* of the Salt Sea on the east
Jos 13:27 far as the *e* of the sea of
15:2 from the *e* of the Salt Sea
15:8 the *e* of the low plain of
15:21 cities at the *e* of the tribe
18:15 the *e* of Kiriath-jearim
18:16 the *e* of the mountain that
Ru 3:7 at the *e* of the grain heap
Ps 19:4 the *e* of the productive land
19:6 From one *e* of the heavens is
46:9 wars to cease to the *e* of the
61:2 From the *e* of the earth I
135:7 from the *e* of the earth
Pr 17:24 eyes . . . at the *e* of the earth
Isa 5:26 to it at the *e* of the earth
7:18 *e* of the Nile canals of Egypt
13:5 from the *e* of the heavens
24:16 From the *e* of the land
42:10 from the *e* of the earth
43:6 from the *e* of the earth
48:20 to the *e* of the earth
49:6 to the *e* of the earth
Jer 10:13 from the *e* of the earth
51:16 from the *e* of the earth
Eze 48:1 northern *e*, on the side by
Da 4:11 to the *e* of the whole earth
4:22 to the *e* of the earth
Mt 24:31 from one *e* of the heavens to
24:31 the heavens to their other *e*
Mr 13:27, 27 earth's *e* to heaven's *e*
Ac 13:47 to the *e* of the earth

Exult
De 28:63 *e* over you to destroy you
30:9 Jehovah will again *e* over you
1Sa 2:1 My heart does *e* in Jehovah
2Sa 1:20 daughters . . . may *e*
1Ch 16:32 Let the field *e* and all that
Job 3:22 *e* because they find a burial
Ps 5:11 loving your name will *e* in
9:2 I will rejoice and *e* in you
25:2 May my enemies not *e* over me
35:9 Let it *e* in his salvation
40:16 those *e* and rejoice in you
60:6 I will *e*, I will give out
68:3 let them *e* with rejoicing
70:4 May those *e* and rejoice in you
94:3 wicked themselves going to *e*
96:12 open field *e* and all that
108:7 I will *e*, I will give out
149:5 Let the loyal ones *e* in glory
Pr 23:16 my kidneys will *e* when your
Isa 23:12 never again *e*, O oppressed
35:1 waterless region will *e*
61:10 I shall *e* in Jehovah
62:5 God will *e* even over you
65:18 *e*, you people, and be joyful
65:19 and *e* in my people
66:10 *E* greatly with her, all you
66:14 heart will be bound to *e*
Jer 11:15 At that time will you *e*?
32:41 I will *e* over them to do
51:39 in order that they may *e*
La 4:21 *E* and rejoice, O daughter of
Eze 21:10 Or shall we *e*? Is it
Hab 3:18 I will *e* in Jehovah himself
Zep 3:14 and *e* with all the heart
3:17 *e* over you with rejoicing
Ro 5:2 *e*, based on hope of the glory
5:3 us *e* while in tribulations
Jas 1:9 let the lowly brother *e* over

Exultant
Ps 43:4 To God, my *e* rejoicing
Isa 5:14 her uproar and the *e* one
13:3 my eminently *e* ones
22:2 boisterous city, an *e* town
23:7 city that was *e* from days
Zep 2:15 *e* city that was sitting in
3:11 your haughtily *e* ones

Exultantly
Jg 15:14 shouted *e* at meeting him

Exultation
Le 19:24 thing of festal *e* to Jehovah
Jg 9:27 carrying on a festal *e*, after
Es 8:16 and rejoicing and *e* and honor
8:17 rejoicing and *e* for the Jews
Ps 45:7 with the oil of *e* more than
48:2 the *e* of the whole earth
51:8 to hear *e* and rejoicing
51:12 the *e* of salvation by you
105:43 out his people with *e*
119:111 are the *e* of my heart
Isa 8:6 *e* over Rezin and the son of
12:3 *e* you people will be certain
22:13 look! *e* and rejoicing
24:8 *e* of the tambourines has
24:8 *e* of the harp has ceased
24:11 *e* of the land has departed
32:13 upon all the houses of *e*
32:14 *e* of zebras, the pasture
35:10 *e* and rejoicing they will
51:3 *E* and rejoicing themselves
51:11 To *e* and rejoicing they
60:15 an *e* for generation after
61:3 oil of *e* instead of mourning
62:5 *e* of a bridegroom over a
65:18 her people a cause for *e*
Jer 7:34 the voice of *e* and the voice
15:16 word becomes to me the *e*
16:9 the voice of *e* and the voice
25:10 the sound of *e* and the
31:13 their mourning into *e*
33:9 become to me a name of *e*
33:11 sound of *e* and the sound of
49:25 abandoned, the town of *e*
La 2:15 an *e* for all the earth
5:15 The *e* of our heart has ceased
Eze 24:25 object of their *e*, the
Ho 2:11 certainly cause all her *e*
Joe 1:12 *e* has gone ashamed away
Zec 8:19 for the house of Judah an *e*
1Co 15:31 This I affirm by the *e* over
Ga 6:4 cause for *e* in regard to
Php 1:26 *e* may overflow in Christ
2:16 cause for *e* in Christ's day
1Th 2:19 hope or joy or crown of *e*
Heb 1:9 anointed . . . the oil of *e*

Exulted
De 28:63 *e* over you to do you good
30:9 as he *e* over your forefathers
Ps 119:14 your reminders I have *e*
La 1:21 They have *e*, because you

Exulting
Ps 119:162 I am *e* over your saying
Pr 28:12 the righteous ones are *e*
Isa 64:5 one *e* and doing righteousness
Jer 15:17 playing jokes and begun *e*
50:11 men kept *e* when pillaging
Ro 5:11 *e* in God through our Lord
11:18 not be *e* over the branches
11:18 If, though, you are *e* over
15:17 cause for *e* in Christ Jesus

Exultingly
1Ch 16:35 to speak *e* in your praise
Ps 106:47 To speak *e* in your praise

Exults
Job 39:21 low plain and *e* in power
Ps 19:5 *e* as a mighty man does to run
28:7 helped, so that my heart *e*
Jas 2:13 Mercy *e* triumphantly over

Eye
Ge 44:21 I may set my *e* upon him
45:20 do not let your *e* feel sorry
Ex 21:24, 24 *e* for *e*, tooth for tooth
21:26 strike the *e* of his slave
21:26 the *e* of his slave girl and
21:26 in compensation for his *e*
Le 24:20, 20 fracture, *e* for *e*, tooth
Nu 22:11 as far as the *e* can see
24:3 man with the *e* unsealed
24:15 the man with the *e* unsealed
De 7:16 Your *e* must not feel sorry
13:8 nor should your *e* feel sorry
15:9 your *e* should indeed become
19:13 Your *e* should not feel sorry
19:21 your *e* should not feel sorry
19:21, 21 *e* for *e*, tooth for tooth
25:12 Your *e* must feel no sorrow
28:54 his *e* will be evil-inclined
28:56 her *e* will be evil-inclined
32:10 as the pupil of his *e*
34:7 His *e* had not grown dim, and
1Sa 11:2 boring out every right *e* of
2Sa 16:12 Jehovah will see with his *e*
Ezr 5:5 the *e* of their God proved to
Job 7:7 my *e* will not see good again
7:8 *e* of him that sees me will
10:18 not even an *e* could see me
13:1 Look! All this my *e* has seen
14:3 you have opened your *e*, And
16:20 To God my *e* has looked
17:2 my *e* lodges
17:7 vexation my *e* grows dimmer
20:9 *e* that has caught sight of
24:15 for the *e* of the adulterer
24:15 Saying, No *e* will behold me
28:7 the *e* of a black kite caught
28:10 precious things his *e* has
29:11 the *e* itself saw and
42:5 now my own *e* does see you
Ps 6:7 my *e* has become weak
31:9 my *e* has become weak, my
32:8 I will give advice with my *e*
33:18 The *e* of Jehovah is toward
35:19 let them not wink the *e*
35:21 Aha! Aha! our *e* has seen it
54:7 upon my enemies my *e* has
73:7 *e* has bulged from fatness
88:9 own *e* has languished because
92:11 my *e* will look on my foes
94:9 One forming the *e*, can he not
116:8 My *e* from tears, my foot
Pr 6:13 winking with his *e*, making
10:10 winking his *e* will give pain
20:12 hearing ear and the seeing *e*
22:9 kindly in *e* will be blessed
23:6 food of anyone of ungenerous *e*
28:22 of envious *e* is bestirring
30:17 The *e* that holds a father in
Ec 1:8 *e* is not satisfied at seeing
Isa 13:18 their *e* will not feel sorry
52:8, 8 be *e* into *e* that they
64:4 nor has an *e* itself seen a
Jer 13:17 *e* will run down with tears
24:6 I will set my *e* upon them in
40:4 I shall keep my *e* upon you
La 1:16, 16 My *e*, my *e* is running
2:18 pupil of your *e* not keep quiet
3:48 water my *e* keeps running
3:49 My very *e* has been poured
3:51 My own *e* has dealt severely
Eze 5:11 my *e* will not feel sorry and
7:4 my *e* will not feel sorry for
7:9 Neither will my *e* feel sorry
8:18 My *e* will not feel sorry
9:5 Let not your *e* feel sorry, and
9:10 my *e* will not feel sorry
12:12 may not see with his own *e*
16:5 No *e* felt sorry for you to do
20:17 my *e* began to feel sorry
Zec 9:1 Jehovah has an *e* on earthling
11:17 arm and upon his right *e*
11:17 right *e* will . . . grow dim
Mt 5:29 right *e* of yours is making
5:38, 38 *E* for *e* and tooth for
6:22 The lamp of the body is the *e*
6:22 *e* is simple, your whole body
6:23 if your *e* is wicked, your
7:3 straw in your brother's *e*, but
7:3 the rafter in your own *e*
7:4 extract the straw from your *e*
7:4 a rafter is in your own *e*
7:5 the rafter from your own *e*
7:5 straw from your brother's *e*
18:9 your *e* is making you stumble
19:24 to get through a needle's *e*
20:15 *e* wicked because I am good
Mr 7:22 loose conduct, an envious *e*
9:47 if your *e* makes you stumble
10:25 to go through a needle's *e*
Lu 6:41 that is in your brother's *e*
6:41 rafter that is in your own *e*
6:42 the straw that is in your *e*
6:42 the rafter in that *e* of yours
6:42 the rafter from your own *e*
Lu 6:42 that is in your brother's *e*
11:34 lamp of the body is your *e*
11:34 *e* is simple, your whole body
18:25 the *e* of a sewing needle
Ro 16:17 keep your *e* on those who
1Co 2:9 *E* has not seen and ear has
12:16 Because I am not an *e*, I am
12:17 If the whole body were an *e*
12:21 The *e* cannot say to the hand
15:52 in the twinkling of an *e*
Ga 6:1 keep an *e* on yourself, for
Php 2:4 keeping an *e*, not in personal
3:17 keep your *e* on those who are
Re 1:7 and every *e* will see him, and

Eyeball
Ps 17:8 Keep me as the pupil of the *e*
Zec 2:8 touching you is touching my *e*

Eyebrows
Le 14:9 head and his chin and his *e*

Eyelids
Job 16:16 upon my *e* . . . deep shadow
Ps 77:4 You have seized hold of my *e*

Eyes
Ge 3:5 your *e* are bound to be opened
3:6 to be longed for to the *e*, yes
3:7 the *e* of both of them became
6:8 Noah found favor in the *e* of
13:10 Lot raised his *e* and saw the
13:14 Raise your *e*, please, and
16:4 began to be despised in her *e*
16:5 began to be despised in her *e*
16:6 to her what is good in your *e*
18:2 he raised his *e*, then he
18:3 I have found favor in your *e*
19:8 to them as is good in your *e*
19:14 in the *e* of his sons-in-law
19:19 favor in your *e* so that you
20:15 where it is good in your *e*
20:16 for you a covering of the *e*
21:19 God opened her *e* so that she
22:4 Abraham raised his *e* and
22:13 Abraham raised his *e* and
23:11 Before the *e* of the sons of
23:18 *e* of the sons of Heth among
24:63 *e* and looked, why, there
24:64 Rebekah raised her *e*, she
27:1 when Isaac was old and his *e*
27:12 become in his *e* like one
28:8 displeasing in the *e* of Isaac
29:17 the *e* of Leah had no luster
29:20 but in his *e* they proved
30:27 I have found favor in your *e*
30:41 before the *e* of the flocks
31:10 raised my *e* and saw a sight
31:12 Raise your *e*, please, and see
31:35 anger gleam in the *e* of my
31:40 sleep would flee from my *e*
32:5 I may find favor in your *e*
33:1 Jacob raised his *e* and looked
33:5 he raised his *e* and saw the
33:8 favor in the *e* of my lord
33:10 I have found favor in your *e*
33:15 favor in the *e* of my lord
34:11 Let me find favor in your *e*
34:18 good in the *e* of Hamor
34:18 in the *e* of Shechem, Hamor's
37:25 they raised their *e* and took
38:7 bad in the *e* of Jehovah; hence
38:10 was bad in the *e* of Jehovah
39:4 kept finding favor in his *e*
39:7 began to raise her *e* toward
39:21 find favor in the *e* of the
41:37 good in the *e* of Pharaoh and
42:24 and bound him before their *e*
43:29 he raised his *e* and saw
45:12 And here your *e* and the
45:12 *e* of my brother Benjamin
45:16 good in the *e* of Pharaoh
46:4 lay his hand upon your *e*
47:19 should we die before your *e*
47:25 favor in the *e* of my lord
47:29 I have found favor in your *e*
48:10 *e* of Israel were dull from
49:12 Dark red are his *e* from wine
50:4 I have found favor in your *e*
Ex 3:21 this people favor in the *e* of the
4:30 under the *e* of the people
7:20 under the *e* of Pharaoh and his
8:26 the Egyptians before their *e*
11:3 in the *e* of the Egyptians
11:3 in the *e* of Pharaoh's servants
11:3 and in the *e* of the people

Ex 12:36 in the *e* of the Egyptians, so
13:9 as a memorial between your *e*
13:16 frontlet band between your *e*
14:10 Israel began to raise their *e*
15:26 do what is right in his *e*
17:6 *e* of the older men of Israel
19:11 the *e* of all the people
21:8 displeasing in the *e* of her
24:17 to the *e* of the sons of
33:12 have found favor in my *e*
33:13 found favor in your *e*, make
33:13 I may find favor in your *e*
33:16 I have found favor in your *e*
33:17 have found favor in my *e*
34:9 favor in your *e*, O Jehovah, let
Le 4:13 been hidden from the *e* of the
10:19 satisfactory in Jehovah's *e*
10:20 proved satisfactory in his *e*
13:12 full sight of the priest's *e*
20:4 hide their *e* from that man
20:17 cut off before the *e* of the
21:20 diseased in his *e* or scabby
25:53 with tyranny before your *e*
26:16 *e* to fail and making the
26:45 under the *e* of the nations
Nu 5:13 hidden from the *e* of her
10:31 you must serve as *e* for us
11:6 *e* are on nothing at all except
11:10 the *e* of Moses it was bad
11:11 not found favor in your *e*
11:15 have found favor in your *e*
13:33 we became in our own *e* like
13:33 way we became in their *e*
15:24 done far from the *e* of the
15:39 following . . . your *e*, which
16:14 Is it the *e* of those men
19:5 must be burned under his *e*
20:8 to the crag before their *e*
20:12 before the *e* of the sons of
20:27 the *e* of all the assembly
22:31 to uncover Balaam's *e*, so
22:34 if it is bad in your *e*, let
23:27 in the *e* of the true God so
24:1 was good in the *e* of Jehovah
24:2 Balaam raised his *e* and saw
24:4 down with the *e* uncovered
24:16 with the *e* uncovered
25:6 before Moses' *e* and before
25:6 the *e* of all the assembly
27:14 by the waters before their *e*
27:19 stand him . . . before their *e*
32:5 we have found favor in your *e*
32:13 evil in the *e* of Jehovah
33:3 the *e* of all the Egyptians
33:55 as pricks in your *e* and as
36:6 To whom it is good in their *e*
De 1:23 proved to be good in my *e*, so
1:30 in Egypt under your own *e*
3:21 Your *e* are seeing all that
3:27 raise your *e* to the west and
3:27 see with your *e*, for you will
4:3 Your own *e* are the ones that
4:6 before the *e* of the peoples
4:9 things that your *e* have seen
4:19 raise your *e* to the heavens
4:25 evil in the *e* of Jehovah your
4:34 in Egypt before your *e*
6:8 a frontlet band between your *e*
6:18 right and good in Jehovah's *e*
6:22 miracles . . . before our *e*
7:19 great provings that your *e*
9:17 shattered them before your *e*
9:18 doing evil in the *e* of Jehovah
10:21 things that your *e* have seen
11:7 your *e* were the ones seeing
11:12 The *e* of Jehovah your God
11:18 frontlet band between your *e*
12:8 right in his own *e*
12:25 what is right in Jehovah's *e*
12:28 right in the *e* of Jehovah
13:18 right in the *e* of Jehovah
15:18 hard in your *e* when you send
16:19 blinds the *e* of wise ones
17:2 bad in the *e* of Jehovah your
21:7 neither did our *e* see it shed
21:9 what is right in Jehovah's *e*
24:1 no favor in his *e* because he
25:3 actually disgraced in your *e*
25:9 before the *e* of the older men
28:31 slaughtered . . . before your *e*
28:32 *e* looking on and yearning
28:34 at the sight of your *e* that
28:65 failing of the *e* and despair
28:67 the sight of your *e* that you
De 29:2 before your *e* in the land of
29:3 *e* saw, those great signs and
29:4 and *e* to see and ears to hear
31:7 before the *e* of all Israel
31:29 bad in the *e* of Jehovah
34:4 to see it with your own *e*
34:12 before the *e* of all Israel
Jos 3:7 great in the *e* of all Israel
4:14 great in the *e* of all Israel
5:13 to raise his *e* and look, and
9:25 good and right in your *e*
10:12 before the *e* of Israel
22:30 came to be good in their *e*
22:33 good in the *e* of the sons
23:13 as thorns in your *e* until
24:7 your *e* got to see what I
24:15 bad in your *e* to serve
24:17 great signs before our *e*
Jg 2:11 bad in the *e* of Jehovah and
3:7 what was bad in Jehovah's *e*
3:12 what was bad in Jehovah's *e*
3:12 what was bad in Jehovah's *e*
4:1 what was bad in Jehovah's *e*
6:1 bad in the *e* of Jehovah
6:17 I have found favor in your *e*
10:6 bad in the *e* of Jehovah, and
10:15 anything . . . good in your *e*
13:1 what was bad in Jehovah's *e*
14:3 the one just right in my *e*
14:7 was still right in Samson's *e*
16:21 Philistines . . . bored his *e*
16:28 for one of my two *e*
17:6 what was right in his own *e*
19:17 raised his *e* he got to see
19:24 what is good in your *e*
21:25 What was right in his own *e*
Ru 2:2 is in whose *e* I may find favor
2:9 Let your *e* be on the field that
2:10 I have found favor in your *e*
2:13 Let me find favor in your *e*
1Sa 1:18 find favor in your *e*
1:23 Do what is good in your *e*
2:33 to cause your *e* to fail and
3:2 his *e* had begun to grow dim
3:18 What is good in his *e* let
4:15 his *e* had set so that he was
6:13 raised their *e* and saw the
8:6 was bad in the *e* of Samuel
11:10 all that is good in your *e*
12:3 should hide my *e* with it
12:16 is doing before your *e*
12:17 evil . . . in the *e* of Jehovah
14:27 and his *e* began to beam
14:29 my *e* have beamed because I
14:36 that is good in your *e* do
14:40 What is good in your *e* do
15:17 were little in your own *e*
15:19 was bad in the *e* of Jehovah
16:7 sees what appears to the *e*
16:12 young man with beautiful *e*
16:22 he has found favor in my *e*
18:5 seemed good in the *e* of all
18:5 the *e* of the servants of Saul
18:23 an easy thing in your *e* to
20:3 I have found favor in your *e*
20:29 have found favor in your *e*
21:13 under their *e* and began
24:4 it may seem good in your *e*
24:10 *e* have seen how Jehovah
25:8 men may find favor in your *e*
26:21 precious in your *e* this day
26:24 was great this day in my *e*
26:24 great in the *e* of Jehovah
27:5 found favor in your *e*, let
29:6 has been good in my *e*
29:6 *e* of the axis lords you are
29:7 *e* of the axis lords of the
29:9 been good in my own *e*, like
2Sa 3:19 good in the *e* of Israel and
3:19 *e* of the whole house of
3:36 and it was good in their *e*
3:36 *e* of all the people good
4:10 in his own *e* became like
6:20 to the *e* of the slave girls
6:22 I will become low in my *e*
7:19 something little in your *e*
10:3 honoring . . . in your *e*
10:12 what is good in his own *e*
11:25 matter appear bad in your *e*
11:27 bad in the *e* of Jehovah
12:9 doing what is bad in his *e*
12:11 wives under your own *e* and
12:11 under the *e* of this sun
13:2 difficult in the *e* of Amnon
2Sa 13:5 of consolation under my *e*
13:6 cakes under my *e*, that I may
13:8 made the cakes under his *e*
13:34 watchman, raised his *e* and
14:22 I have found favor in your *e*
15:25 favor in the *e* of Jehovah
15:26 just as it is good in his *e*
16:4 Let me find favor in your *e*
16:22 under the *e* of all Israel
17:4 right in the *e* of Absalom
17:4 the *e* of all the older men
18:4 good in your *e* I shall do
18:24 he raised his *e* and saw and
19:6 it would be right in your *e*
19:18 do what was good in his *e*
19:27 do what is good in your *e*
19:37 what is good in your *e*
19:38 what is good in your *e*
20:6 and escape before our *e*
22:25 cleanness in front of his *e*
22:28 *e* are against the haughty
24:3 *e* of my lord the king are
24:22 what is good in his *e*
1Ki 1:20 *e* of all Israel are upon you
1:48 with my own *e* seeing it
3:10 pleasing in the *e* of Jehovah
8:29 *e* may prove to be opened
8:52 *e* may prove to be opened
9:3 *e* and my heart will certainly
9:12 were not just right in his *e*
10:7 that my own *e* might see
11:6 was bad in the *e* of Jehovah
11:19 favor in the *e* of Pharaoh
11:33 what is right in my *e* and
11:38 do what is right in my *e* by
14:4 *e* had set because of his age
14:8 only what was right in my *e*
14:22 bad in the *e* of Jehovah
15:5 right in the *e* of Jehovah
15:11 right in the *e* of Jehovah
15:26 bad in the *e* of Jehovah
15:34 was bad in the *e* of Jehovah
16:7 in the *e* of Jehovah by
16:19 was bad in the *e* of Jehovah
16:25 was bad in the *e* of Jehovah
16:30 worse in the *e* of Jehovah
20:6 desirable to your *e* they
20:38 with a bandage over his *e*
20:41 the bandage from over his *e*
21:2 if it is good in your *e*, I
21:20 is bad in the *e* of Jehovah
21:25 bad in the *e* of Jehovah
22:43 right in the *e* of Jehovah
22:52 what was bad in Jehovah's *e*
2Ki 1:13 be precious in your *e*
1:14 soul be precious in your *e*
3:2 what was bad in Jehovah's *e*
3:18 trivial thing in the *e* of
4:34, 34 and his own *e* upon his *e*
4:35 the boy opened his *e*
6:17 open his *e*, please, that he
6:17 opened the attendant's *e*
6:20 open the *e* of these that
6:20 Jehovah opened their *e*, and
7:2 seeing it with your own *e*
7:19 seeing it with your own *e*
8:18 what was bad in Jehovah's *e*
8:27 what was bad in Jehovah's *e*
9:30 paint her *e* with black paint
10:5 is good in your own *e* do
10:30 what is right in my *e*
12:2 was right in Jehovah's *e*
13:2 what was bad in Jehovah's *e*
13:11 what was bad in Jehovah's *e*
14:3 was upright in Jehovah's *e*
14:24 what was bad in Jehovah's *e*
15:3 was upright in Jehovah's *e*
15:9 was bad in Jehovah's *e*
15:18 was bad in Jehovah's *e*
15:24 was bad in Jehovah's *e*
15:28 was bad in Jehovah's *e*
15:34 was right in Jehovah's *e*
16:2 in the *e* of Jehovah his God
17:2 what was bad in Jehovah's *e*
17:17 was bad in the *e* of Jehovah
18:3 was right in Jehovah's *e*
19:16 Open your *e*, O Jehovah, and
19:22 do you raise your *e* on high
20:3 good in your *e* I have done
21:2 what was bad in Jehovah's *e*
21:6 what was bad in Jehovah's *e*
21:15 did what was bad in my *e*
21:16 was bad in the *e* of Jehovah
21:20 bad in Jehovah's *e*

2Ki 22:2 was right in Jehovah's *e* and
22:20 your *e* will not look upon
23:32 was bad in Jehovah's *e*
23:37 was bad in Jehovah's *e*
24:9 what was bad in Jehovah's *e*
24:19 was bad in Jehovah's *e*
25:7 slaughtered before his *e*
25:7 Zedekiah's *e* he blinded
1Ch 2:3 to be bad in the *e* of Jehovah
13:4 seemed right in the *e* of all
17:17 little in your *e*, O God, yet
19:3 honoring . . . father in your *e*
19:13 what is good in his own *e*
21:7 bad in the *e* of the true God
21:16 When David raised his *e*, he
21:23 what is good in his own *e*
28:8 before the *e* of all Israel
29:10 *e* of all the congregation
29:25 before the *e* of all Israel
2Ch 6:20 *e* may prove to be opened
6:40 *e* prove to be opened and
7:15 *e* will prove to be opened
7:16 and my *e* and my heart will
9:6 come that my own *e* might see
14:2 right in the *e* of Jehovah his
16:9 *e* are roving about through
20:12 but our *e* are toward you
20:32 was right in Jehovah's *e*
21:6 what was bad in Jehovah's *e*
22:4 was bad in Jehovah's *e*
24:2 was right in Jehovah's *e*
25:2 was right in Jehovah's *e*
26:4 was right in Jehovah's *e*
27:2 was right in Jehovah's *e*
28:1 was right in Jehovah's *e*
29:2 was right in Jehovah's *e*
29:6 bad in the *e* of Jehovah our
29:8 are seeing with your own *e*
30:4 right in the *e* of the king
30:4 *e* of all the congregation
32:23 *e* of all the nations after
33:2 what was bad in Jehovah's *e*
33:6 was bad in the *e* of Jehovah
33:22 was bad in Jehovah's *e*
34:2 right in Jehovah's *e* and
34:28 your *e* will not look upon
36:5 bad in the *e* of Jehovah his
36:9 what was bad in Jehovah's *e*
36:12 was bad in the *e* of Jehovah
Ezr 3:12 this house before their *e*
9:8 to make our *e* shine, O our
Ne 1:6 and your *e* opened, to listen
6:16 very much in their own *e*
8:5 before the *e* of all the people
Es 1:17 their owners in their own *e*
1:21 pleasing in the *e* of the king
2:4 seems pleasing in the king's *e*
2:4 was pleasing in the king's *e*
2:9 woman was pleasing in his *e*
2:15 the *e* of everyone seeing her
3:6 despicable in his *e* to lay hand
3:11 what is good in your own *e*
5:2 she gained favor in his *e*, so
5:8 found favor in the king's *e*
7:3 If I have found favor in your *e*
8:5 and I am good in his *e*, let it
8:8 what is good in your own *e* in
Job 2:12 raised their *e* from far off
3:10 so conceal trouble from my *e*
4:16 A form was in front of my *e*
7:8 Your *e* will be upon me, but I
10:4 Do you have *e* of flesh, Or is
11:4 proved really clean in your *e*
11:20 *e* of the wicked will fail
15:12 And why do your *e* flash?
15:15 actually not clean in his *e*
16:9 sharpens his *e* against me
17:5 very *e* of his sons will fail
18:3 regarded as unclean in your *e*
19:15 I have become in their *e*
19:27 my very *e* will certainly
21:8 descendants before their *e*
21:20 His *e* will see his decay
22:29 downcast *e* he will save
24:23 *e* will be upon their ways
25:5 not proved clean in his *e*
27:19 His *e* he has opened, but
28:21 hidden even from the *e* of
29:15 *E* I became to the blind one
31:1 I have concluded with my *e*
31:7 walked merely after my *e*
31:16 the *e* of the widow I would
32:1 was righteous in his own *e*
34:21 *e* are upon the ways of man
Job 36:7 his *e* from anyone righteous
39:29 distance its *e* keep looking
40:24 Before its *e* can anyone take
41:18 its *e* are like the beams
Ps 5:5 their stand in front of your *e*
10:8 His *e* are on the lookout for
11:4 His own *e* behold, his own
11:4 his own beaming *e* examine
13:3 make my *e* shine, that I may
15:4 In his *e* anyone contemptible
17:2 your own *e* behold uprightness
17:11 They fix their *e* to incline
18:24 my hands in front of his *e*
18:27 haughty *e* you will abase
19:8 clean, making the *e* shine
25:15 My *e* are constantly toward
26:3 is in front of my *e*
31:22 from in front of your *e*
34:15 The *e* of Jehovah are toward
36:1 dread of God in front of his *e*
36:2 to himself in his own *e*
38:10 the light of my own *e* also
50:21 things in order before your *e*
51:4 bad in your *e* I have done
66:7 Upon the nations his own *e*
69:3 *e* have failed while waiting
69:23 Let their *e* become darkened
72:14 will be precious in his *e*
73:16 It was a trouble in my *e*
79:10 there be known before our *e*
90:4 thousand years are in your *e*
91:8 with your *e* will you look on
98:2 *e* of the nations he has
101:3 set in front of my *e* any
101:5 Anyone of haughty *e* and of
101:6 My *e* are upon the faithful
101:7 established In front of my *e*
115:5 *E* . . . but they cannot see
116:15 Precious in the *e* of Jehovah
118:23 It is wonderful in our *e*
119:18 Uncover my *e*, that I may
119:37 *e* pass on from seeing what
119:82 *e* have pined away for your
119:123 *e* have pined away for your
119:136 water have run down my *e*
119:148 *e* have been ahead of the
121:1 raise my *e* to the mountains
123:1 To you I have raised my *e*
123:2 *e* of servants are toward the
123:2 *e* of a maidservant are
123:2 *e* are toward Jehovah our God
131:1 Nor have my *e* been lofty
132:4 will not give sleep to my *e*
132:4 slumber to my own beaming *e*
135:16 *E* they have, but they can
139:16 Your *e* saw even the embryo
141:8 my *e* are to you, O Jehovah
145:15 the *e* of all look hopefully
146:8 Jehovah is opening the *e* of
Pr 1:17 *e* of anything owning wings
3:4 good insight in the *e* of God
3:7 become wise in your own *e*
3:21 not get away from your *e*
4:21 they not get away from your *e*
4:25 your *e*, straight ahead they
4:25 beaming *e* should gaze
5:21 in front of the *e* of Jehovah
6:4 not give any sleep to your *e*
6:4 slumber to your beaming *e*
6:17 lofty *e*, a false tongue, and
6:25 take you with her lustrous *e*
7:2 law like the pupil of your *e*
10:26 and as smoke to the *e*, so
12:15 one is right in his own *e*
15:3 The *e* of Jehovah are in every
15:30 brightness of the *e* makes
16:2 a man are pure in his own *e*
16:30 He is blinking with his *e* to
17:8 in the *e* of its grand owner
17:24 *e* of the stupid one are at
20:8 all badness with his own *e*
20:13 Open your *e*; be satisfied
21:2 a man is upright in his own *e*
21:4 Haughty *e* and an arrogant
21:10 be shown no favor in his *e*
22:12 *e* of Jehovah himself have
23:5 caused your *e* to glance at it
23:26 *e* of yours take pleasure in
23:29 Who has dullness of *e*?
23:33 *e* will see strange things
24:18 and it be bad in his *e* and
25:7 a noble whom your *e* have seen
26:5 someone wise in his own *e*
26:12 a man wise in his own *e*
Pr 26:16 is wiser in his own *e* than
27:20 the *e* of a man get satisfied
28:11 man is wise in his own *e*
28:27 is hiding his *e* will get
29:13 Jehovah is lighting up the *e*
30:12 that is pure in its own *e*
30:13 *e* have become O how lofty
30:13 beaming *e* are lifted up
Ec 2:10 anything that my *e* asked for
2:14 wise, his *e* are in his head
4:8 *e* themselves are not satisfied
5:11 looking at them with his *e*
6:9 Better is the seeing by the *e*
8:16 seeing no sleep with his *e*
11:7 good for the *e* to see the sun
11:9 in the things seen by your *e*
Ca 1:15 Your *e* are those of doves
4:1 Your *e* are those of doves
4:9 my heart beat by one of your *e*
5:12 His *e* are like doves by the
6:5 Turn your *e* away from in front
7:4 *e* are like the pools in Heshbon
8:10 I have become in his *e* like
Isa 1:15 I hide my *e* from you
1:16 from in front of my *e*; cease
2:11 haughty *e* of earthling man
3:8 in the *e* of his glory
3:16 and ogling with their *e*
5:15 *e* of the high ones will
5:21 those wise in their own *e*
6:5 *e* have seen the King, Jehovah
6:10 paste their very *e* together
6:10 may not see with their *e*
10:12 of his loftiness of *e*
11:3 any mere appearance to his *e*
13:16 to pieces before their *e*
17:7 *e* will gaze at the Holy One
29:10 he closes your *e*, the
29:18 *e* of the blind ones will
30:20, 20 *e* must become *e* seeing
32:3 *e* of those seeing will not
33:15 closing his *e* so as not to
33:17 what your *e* will behold
33:20 *e* will see Jerusalem an
35:5 *e* of the blind ones will be
37:17 Open your *e*, O Jehovah
37:23 you raise your *e* on high
38:3 good in your *e* I have done
38:14 *e* have looked languishingly
40:26 Raise your *e* high up and
42:7 to open the blind *e*, to bring
43:4 have been precious in my *e*
43:8 blind though *e* . . . exist
44:18 *e* have been besmeared so
49:5 glorified in the *e* of Jehovah
49:18 Raise your *e* all around and
51:6 Raise your *e* to the heavens
52:10 before the *e* of all the
59:10 like those without *e* we
59:15 and it was bad in his *e*
60:4 Raise your *e* all around and
61:1 the wide opening of the *e*
65:12 what was bad in my *e*
65:16 be concealed from my *e*
66:4 doing what was bad in my *e*
Jer 3:2 Raise your *e* to the beaten
4:30 your *e* with black paint
5:3 those *e* of yours toward
5:21 They have *e*, but they cannot
7:11 cave of robbers in your *e*
7:30 done what is bad in my *e*
9:1 my *e* were a source of tears
9:18 our *e* run down with tears
9:18 *e* trickle with waters
13:20 Raise your *e* and see those
14:6 their *e* have failed because
14:17 my *e* run down with tears
16:9 before the *e* of you people
16:17 *e* are upon all their ways
16:17 hid from in front of my *e*
18:4 in the *e* of the potter
18:10 bad in my *e* by not obeying
19:10 break the flask before the *e*
20:4 your *e* will be looking on
22:17 your *e* and your heart are
26:14 what is right in your *e*
27:5 it has proved right in my *e*
28:1 before the *e* of the priests
28:5 before the *e* of the priests
28:5 before the *e* of all the
28:11 before the *e* of all the
29:21 down before your *e*
31:16 and your *e* from tears, for
32:4 his own *e* will see even the

Jer 32:4 see even the *e* of that one
32:12 *e* of Hanamel the son of my
32:12 the *e* of the witnesses
32:12 *e* of all the Jews who were
32:13 Baruch before their *e*
32:19 whose *e* are opened upon
32:30 of what was bad in my *e*
34:3 own *e* will see even the
34:3 the *e* of the king of Babylon
34:15 do what is upright in my *e*
39:6 in Riblah before his *e*, and
39:7 *e* of Zedekiah he blinded
39:12 your own *e* set upon him
40:4 good in your *e* to come with
40:4 bad in your *e* to come with
40:4 and right in your *e* to go, go
40:5 right in your *e* to go, go
42:2 as your *e* are seeing us
43:9 the *e* of the Jewish men
51:24 before the *e* of you people
52:2 bad in the *e* of Jehovah
52:10 slaughter . . . before his *e*
52:11 *e* of Zedekiah he blinded
La 2:4 all those desirable to the *e*
2:11 *e* have come to their end in
4:17 *e* keep pining away in vain
5:17 our *e* have grown dim
Eze 1:18 their rims were full of *e*
4:12 will bake it before their *e*
5:8 in the *e* of the nations
5:14 the *e* of every passerby
6:9 at their *e* that are going in
8:5 raise your *e* in the direction
8:5 *e* in the direction of the
10:2 So he entered in before my *e*
10:12 were full of *e* all around
10:19 from the earth before my *e*
12:2 *e* to see but they actually
12:3 into exile . . . before their *e*
12:3 another place before their *e*
12:4 the daytime before their *e*
12:4 in the evening before their *e*
12:5 Before their *e*, bore your
12:6 Before their *e* you will do
12:7 the carrying, before their *e*
16:41 before the *e* of many women
18:6 his *e* he did not raise to the
18:12 idols he lifted up his *e*
18:15 *e* he has not lifted up to
20:7 disgusting things of his *e*
20:8 disgusting things of their *e*
20:9 before the *e* of the nations
20:9 known to them before their *e*
20:14 before the *e* of the nations
20:14 before whose *e* I had
20:22 before the *e* of the nations
20:22 nations, before whose *e* I
20:24 that their *e* proved to be
20:41 before the *e* of the nations
21:6 should sigh before their *e*
21:23 untrue divination in their *e*
22:16 before the *e* of the nations
22:26 they have hidden their *e*
23:16 at the sight of her *e* and
23:27 not raise your *e* to them
23:40 painted your *e* and decked
24:16 thing desirable to your *e*
24:21 thing desirable to your *e*
24:25 thing desirable to their *e*
28:18 the *e* of all those seeing
28:25 in the *e* of the nations
33:25 your *e* you keep lifting to
36:23 among you before their *e*
36:34 the *e* of every passerby
37:20 in your hand before their *e*
38:16 before their *e*, O Gog
38:23 before the *e* of many
39:27 the *e* of many nations
40:4 Son of man, see with your *e*
43:11 write before their *e*, in
44:5 see with your *e*, and with
Da 4:34 lifted up to the heavens my *e*
7:8, 8 *e* like the *e* of a man in
7:20 horn that had *e* and a mouth
8:3 When I raised my *e*, then I
8:5 conspicuous horn between its *e*
8:21 horn that was between its *e*
9:18 Do open your *e* and see our
10:5 raise my *e* and see, and here
10:6 and his *e* like fiery torches
Ho 2:10 *e* of her passionate lovers
13:14 will be concealed from my *e*
Joe 1:16 cut off before our very *e*
Am 9:3 in front of my *e* on the floor
Am 9:4 I will set my *e* upon them
9:8 The *e* of the Sovereign Lord
Jon 2:4 away from in front of your *e*
Mic 4:11 may our *e* look upon Zion
7:10 My own *e* will look upon her
Hab 1:13 too pure in *e* to see . . . bad
Zep 3:20 captive ones before your *e*
Hag 2:3 as nothing in your *e*
Zec 1:18 to raise my *e* and see
2:1 to raise my *e* and see
3:9 one stone there are seven *e*
4:10 seven are the *e* of Jehovah
5:1 I raised my *e* again and saw
5:5 Raise your *e*, please, and see
5:9 I raised my *e* and saw, and
6:1 I raised my *e* again and saw
8:6 too difficult in the *e* of the
8:6 too difficult also in my *e*
9:8 now I have seen it with my *e*
11:12 If it is good in your *e*
12:4 I shall open my *e*, and every
14:12 *e* will rot away in their
Mal 1:5 And your own *e* will see it
2:17 is good in the *e* of Jehovah
Mt 9:29 he touched their *e*, saying
9:30 And their *e* received sight
13:15 and they have shut their *e*
13:15 never see with their *e* and
13:16 happy are your *e* because
16:6 Keep your *e* open and watch
17:8 When they raised their *e*
18:9 with two *e* into the fiery
20:33 Lord, let our *e* be opened
20:34 Jesus touched their *e*, and
21:42 and it is marvelous in our *e*
26:43 for their *e* were heavy
Mr 8:15 Keep your *e* open, look out
8:18 having *e*, do you not see
8:23 having spit upon his *e*, he
8:25 hands again upon the man's *e*
9:47 than with two *e* to be pitched
12:11 it is marvelous in our *e*
14:40 their *e* were weighed down
Lu 2:30 my *e* have seen your means of
4:20 the *e* of all in the synagogue
6:20 he lifted up his *e* upon his
10:23 Happy are the *e* that behold
12:15 Keep your *e* open and guard
16:23 in Hades he lifted up his *e*
18:13 to raise his *e* heavenward
19:42 have been hid from your *e*
24:16 *e* were kept from recognizing
24:31 their *e* were fully opened
24:43 and ate it before their *e*
Joh 4:35 Lift up your *e* and view the
6:5 Jesus raised his *e* and
9:6 put his clay upon the man's *e*
9:10 then, were your *e* opened
9:11 and smeared it on my *e* and
9:14 the clay and opened his *e*
9:15 He put a clay upon my *e*, and
9:17 seeing that he opened your *e*
9:21 who opened his *e* we do not
9:26 How did he open your *e*?
9:30 and yet he opened my *e*
9:32 opened the *e* of one born
10:21 cannot open blind people's *e*
11:37 opened the *e* of the blind
11:41 Jesus raised his *e*
12:40 He has blinded their *e* and
12:40 not see with their *e* and
17:1 raising his *e* to heaven, he
Ac 2:25 Jehovah . . . before my *e*
9:8 *e* were opened he was seeing
9:18 fell from his *e* what looked
9:40 She opened her *e* and, as she
26:18 open their *e*, to turn them
28:27 and they have shut their *e*
28:27 never see with their *e* and
Ro 3:18 fear of God before their *e*
11:8 *e* so as not to see and ears
11:10 *e* become darkened so as not
11:25 be discreet in your own *e*
12:16 discreet in your own *e*
2Co 4:18 our *e*, not on the things seen
Ga 3:1 before whose *e* Jesus Christ
4:15 have gouged out your *e* and
Eph 1:18 *e* of your heart having been
Heb 4:13 openly exposed to the *e* of
Jas 4:10 Humble yourselves in the *e*
1Pe 3:4 of great value in the *e* of God
3:12 For the *e* of Jehovah are upon
2Pe 1:9 shutting his *e* to the light
2:14 They have *e* full of adultery
1Jo 1:1 we have seen with our *e*
2:11 darkness has blinded his *e*
2:16 and the desire of the *e* and
3:22 that are pleasing in his *e*
Re 1:14 and his *e* as a fiery flame
2:18 has his *e* like a fiery flame
3:18 eyesalve to rub in your *e*
4:6 full of *e* in front and behind
4:8 underneath they are full of *e*
5:6 having seven horns and seven *e*
5:6 which *e* mean the seven spirits
7:17 out every tear from their *e*
19:12 His *e* are a fiery flame
21:4 out every tear from their *e*

Eyesalve
Re 3:18 *e* to rub in your eyes that

Eyeservice
Eph 6:6 by way of *e* as men pleasers
Col 3:22 not with acts of *e*, as men

Eyewitnesses
Lu 1:2 from the beginning became *e*
1Pe 2:12 works of which they are *e*
3:2 been *e* of your chaste conduct
2Pe 1:16 become *e* of his magnificence

Ezbai
1Ch 11:37 Naarai the son of *E*

Ezbon
Ge 46:16 the sons of Gad were . . . *E*
1Ch 7:7 sons of Bela were *E* and Uzzi

Ezekiel
Eze 1:3 *E* the son of Buzi the priest
24:24 *E* has become for you a

Ezem
Jos 15:29 Baalah and Iim and *E*
19:3 Hazar-shual and Balah and *E*
1Ch 4:29 in Bilhah and in *E* and in

Ezer
Ge 36:21 *E* and Dishan . . . sons of Seir
36:27 sons of *E*: Bilhan and Zaavan
36:30 *E* . . . sheiks of the Horite
1Ch 1:38 sons of Seir were . . . *E*
1:42 The sons of *E* were Bilhan
4:4 *E* the father of Hushah
7:21 his son and *E* and Elead
12:9 *E* was the head, Obadiah the
Ne 3:19 And *E* the son of Jeshua
12:42 Malchijah and Elam and *E*

Ezion-geber
Nu 33:35 and went camping in *E*
33:36 pulled away from *E* and went
De 2:8 Arabah, from Elath and from *E*
1Ki 9:26 *E*, which is by Eloth
22:48 the ships were wrecked at *E*
2Ch 8:17 Solomon went to *E* and to
20:36 they made ships in *E*

Ezra
Ezr 7:1 *E* the son of Seraiah the son
7:6 *E* himself went up from
7:10 *E* himself had prepared his
7:11 *E* the priest the copyist
7:12 to *E* the priest, the copyist
7:21 *E* the priest, the copyist of
7:25 *E*, according to the wisdom
10:1 as soon as *E* had prayed and
10:2 said to *E*: We—we have acted
10:5 *E* rose and had the chiefs of
10:6 *E* now rose from before the
10:10 *E* the priest rose and said
10:16 *E* the priest and the men
Ne 8:1 to *E* the copyist to bring the
8:2 *E* the priest brought the law
8:4 *E* the copyist kept standing
8:5 *E* proceeded to open the book
8:6 *E* blessed Jehovah the true God
8:9 and *E* the priest, the copyist
8:13 together to *E* the copyist
12:1 Seraiah, Jeremiah, *E*
12:13 for *E*, Meshullam; for
12:26 *E* the priest, the copyist
12:33 Azariah, *E* and Meshullam
12:36 *E* the copyist before them

Ezrah
1Ch 4:17 the sons of *E* were Jether

Ezrahite
1Ki 4:31 wiser than . . . Ethan the *E*
Ps 88:*super* Maskil of Heman the *E*
89:*super* Maskil. Of Ethan the *E*

Ezri
1Ch 27:26 was *E* the son of Chelub
Fables
Tit 1:14 no attention to Jewish *f*
Fabric
1Ch 4:21 fine *f* of the house of Ashbea
15:27 a sleeveless coat of fine *f*
2Ch 2:14 in fine *f* and in crimson and
3:14 *f*, and worked in cherubs
5:12 clothed in fine *f* with
Es 1:6 held fast in ropes of fine *f*
Eze 27:16 and fine *f* and corals and
Fabricate
Pr 3:29 *f* against your fellowman
Fabricating
1Sa 23:9 Saul was *f* mischief against
Pr 6:14 *f* something bad all the time
6:18 heart *f* hurtful schemes, feet
12:20 heart of those *f* mischief
Fabrics
Isa 19:9 loom workers on white *f*
Face
Ge 1:20 *f* of the expanse of the
3:8 hiding from the *f* of Jehovah
3:19 In the sweat of your *f* you
4:14 from your *f* I shall be
4:16 Cain went away from the *f* of
16:12 before the *f* of all his
17:3 Abram fell upon his *f*, and
17:17 Abraham fell upon his *f* and
19:1 bowed down with his *f* to the
27:30 from before the *f* of Isaac
31:2 would look at the *f* of Laban
31:5 seeing the *f* of your father
31:21 he directed his *f* to the
32:20 afterward I shall see his *f*
32:30, 30 I have seen God *f* to *f*
33:10 I have seen your *f* as though
33:10 as though seeing God's *f*
38:15 because she had covered her *f*
43:3 You must not see my *f* again
43:5 You must not see my *f* again
43:31 he washed his *f* and went out
44:23 may not see my *f* anymore
44:26 not able to see the man's *f*
46:30 now that I have seen your *f*
48:11 no idea of seeing your *f*, but
48:12 with his *f* to the earth
50:1 Joseph fell upon the *f* of his
Ex 3:6 Then Moses concealed his *f*
10:28 Do not try to see my *f* again
10:28 seeing my *f* you will die
10:29 shall not try to see your *f*
20:3 any other gods against my *f*
23:17 the *f* of the true Lord
32:11 soften the *f* of Jehovah his
33:11, 11 spoke to Moses *f* to *f*
33:19 to pass before your *f*, and
33:20 are not able to see my *f*
33:23 But my *f* may not be seen
34:6 passing by before his *f* and
34:24 to see the *f* of Jehovah your
34:29 skin of his *f* emitted rays
34:30 skin of his *f* emitted rays
34:33 would put a veil over his *f*
34:35 sons of Israel saw Moses' *f*
34:35 Moses' *f* emitted rays; and
34:35 veil back over his *f* until he
Le 10:3 before the *f* of all the people
17:10 set my *f* against the soul
20:3 set my *f* against that man
20:5 *f* against that man and his
20:6 *f* against that soul and cut
26:17 set my *f* against you, and
Nu 6:25 Jehovah make his *f* shine
6:26 Jehovah lift up his *f* toward
12:14 to spit directly in her *f*
14:14, 14 who has appeared *f* to *f*
16:4 Moses . . . fell upon his *f*
16:46 from the *f* of Jehovah
21:20 toward the *f* of Jeshimon
22:31 prostrated himself on his *f*
24:1 his *f* to the wilderness
32:17 the *f* of the inhabitants of
De 5:4, 4 *F* to *f* Jehovah spoke with
5:7 any other gods against my *f*
7:10 repaying to his *f* the one who
7:10 he will repay him to his *f*
9:27 Do not turn your *f* to the
11:25 before the *f* of all the land
25:9 spit in his *f* and answer and
De 28:31 robbery from before your *f*
31:11 to see the *f* of Jehovah
31:17 and conceal my *f* from them
31:18 conceal my *f* in that day
32:20 Let me conceal my *f* from
34:10, 10 whom Jehovah knew *f* to *f*
Jos 5:14 fell on his *f* to the earth
7:6 fell upon his *f* to the earth
7:10 you are falling upon your *f*
Jg 5:5 from the *f* of Jehovah. This
5:5 the *f* of Jehovah, Israel's God
6:22, 22 Jehovah's angel *f* to *f*
20:40 Benjamin turned his *f* back
Ru 2:10 she fell upon her *f* and bowed
1Sa 1:18 *f* became self-concerned no
5:3 Dagon was fallen upon his *f*
5:4 Dagon was fallen upon his *f*
13:12 the *f* of Jehovah I have not
17:49 he went falling upon his *f*
20:41 fell on his *f* to the earth
24:8 *f* to the earth and prostrate
25:23 fell upon her *f* before David
25:41 bowed with her *f* to the
26:20 before the *f* of Jehovah
28:14 bow low with his *f* to the
2Sa 2:22 raise my *f* to Joab your
3:13 You may not see my *f* except
3:13 when you come to see my *f*
9:6 fell upon his *f* and prostrated
9:8 turned your *f* to the dead dog
11:11 on the *f* of the field, and
14:4 fall upon her *f* to the earth
14:20 altering the *f* of the
14:22 Joab fell upon his *f* to the
14:24 but my *f* he may not see
14:24 *f* of the king he did not see
14:28 *f* of the king he did not see
14:32 see the *f* of the king and
14:33 falling upon his *f* to the
15:18 crossing before the king's *f*
17:19 over the *f* of the well and
18:28 with his *f* to the earth
19:4 king . . . covered up his *f*
19:5 the *f* of all your servants
21:1 to consult the *f* of Jehovah
24:20 with his *f* to the earth
1Ki 1:23 with his *f* to the earth
1:31 with her *f* to the earth and
2:15 all Israel had set their *f*
2:16 Do not turn my *f* away
2:17 he will not turn your *f* away
2:20 Do not turn my *f* away
2:20 I shall not turn your *f* away
8:14 the king turned his *f* and
10:24 seeking the *f* of Solomon
13:6 the *f* of Jehovah your God and
13:6 softened the *f* of Jehovah
18:7 and fell upon his *f* and said
18:42 his *f* put between his knees
19:13 wrapped his *f* in . . . garment
21:4 and kept his *f* turned, and
2Ki 3:14 *f* of Jehoshaphat the king of
4:29 staff upon the *f* of the boy
4:31 the staff upon the boy's *f*
8:15 and spread it out over his *f*
9:32 his *f* toward the window and
9:37 upon the *f* of the field
11:2 from the *f* of Athaliah
12:17 Hazael set his *f* to go up
13:4 softened the *f* of Jehovah
13:14 to weep over his *f* and say
13:23 from before his *f* until now
14:8 look each other in the *f*
14:11 to look each other in the *f*
18:24 the *f* of one governor of the
20:2 turned his *f* to the wall and
1Ch 16:11 Seek his *f* constantly
21:21 with his *f* to the earth
2Ch 6:3 king turned his *f* and began to
6:42 back the *f* of your anointed
7:14 seek my *f* and turn back from
7:20 throw away from before my *f*
9:23 seeking the *f* of Solomon to
20:3 set his *f* to search for
20:18 low with his *f* to the earth
25:17 us look each other in the *f*
25:21 look each other in the *f*
29:6 turned around their *f* away
30:9 turn away the *f* from you if
32:2 his *f* set for war against
32:21 back with shame of *f* to his
33:12 softened the *f* of Jehovah
35:22 Josiah did not turn his *f*
Ezr 9:6 embarrassed to raise my *f* to
Ezr 9:7 and with shame of *f*, just as
Ne 2:2 Why is your *f* gloomy when you
2:3 my *f* become gloomy when the
Es 7:8 and Haman's *f* they covered
Job 1:11 not curse you to your very *f*
2:5 not curse you to your very *f*
4:15 went passing over my *f*
9:24 The *f* of its judges he covers
11:15 raise your *f* without defect
13:15 argue to his *f* for my own
13:24 do you conceal your very *f*
14:20 You are disfiguring his *f* so
15:27 covers his *f* with his
16:8 In my *f* it testifies
16:16 *f* . . . reddened from weeping
17:6 someone into whose *f* to spit
21:31 tell him . . . to his very *f*
22:26 will raise your *f* to God
23:17 gloom has covered my own *f*
24:15 over his *f* . . . a covering
26:9 Enclosing the *f* of the throne
26:10 upon the *f* of the waters
29:24 *f* they would not cast down
30:10 from my *f* they did not hold
33:26 will see his *f* with joyful
34:29 And when he conceals his *f*
37:12 the *f* of the productive land
41:13 the *f* of its clothing
41:14 The doors of its *f* who has
42:8 His *f* only I shall accept so
42:9 Jehovah accepted Job's *f*
Ps 4:6 Lift up the light of your *f*
9:19 be judged before your *f*
10:11 He has concealed his *f*
11:7 ones that will behold his *f*
13:1 will you conceal your *f* from
16:11 Rejoicing . . . is with your *f*
17:13 do confront him to the *f*
17:15 I shall behold your *f*
21:6 with the rejoicing at your *f*
21:12 make ready against their *f*
22:24 not concealed his *f* from him
24:6 Of those searching for your *f*
25:16 Turn your *f* to me, and show
27:8 Seek to find my *f*, you people
27:8 Your *f*, O Jehovah, I shall
27:9 Do not conceal your *f* from me
30:7 You concealed your *f*
31:16 *f* to shine upon your servant
34:16 The *f* of Jehovah is against
40:4 turned his *f* to defiant people
41:12 before your *f* to time
44:3 and the light of your *f*
44:15 the shame of my own *f* has
44:24 keep your very *f* concealed
45:12 will soften your own *f*
51:9 Conceal your *f* from my sins
51:11 away from before your *f*
61:3 tower in the *f* of the enemy
67:1 He will make his *f* shine upon
69:7 Humiliation has covered my *f*
69:17 not conceal your *f* from your
80:3 light up your *f*, that we may
80:7 And light up your *f*, that we
80:16 rebuke of your *f* they perish
80:19 Light up your *f*, that we
84:9 the *f* of your anointed one
88:14 your *f* concealed from me
89:14 come in before your *f*
89:15 light of your *f* they keep
90:8 things before your bright *f*
102:2 Do not conceal your *f* from
104:15 make the *f* shine with oil
104:29 If you conceal your *f*, they
104:30 the *f* of the ground new
105:4 Seek his *f* constantly
119:58 softened your *f* with all my
119:135 Make your own *f* shine upon
132:10 the *f* of your anointed one
139:7 can I run away from your *f*
140:13 will dwell before your *f*
143:7 not conceal your *f* from me
Pr 7:13 She has put on a bold *f*, and
7:15 meet you, to look for your *f*
8:27 upon the *f* of the watery deep
16:15 In the light of the king's *f*
17:24 *f* of the understanding one
19:6 who soften the *f* of a noble
21:29 wicked . . . put on a bold *f*
25:23 away a secret, a denounced *f*
27:17 sharpens the *f* of another
27:19, 19 *f* corresponds with *f*
29:26 seeking the *f* of a ruler, but
Ec 7:3 by the crossness of the *f* the

Ec 8:1 itself causes his *f* to shine
8:1 sternness of his *f* is changed
Isa 1:12 keep coming in to see my *f*
6:2 two he kept his *f* covered
8:17 concealing his *f* from the
14:21 *f* of the productive land
24:1 he has twisted the *f* of it
25:7 *f* of the envelopment that
29:22 his own *f* now grow pale
36:9 back the *f* of one governor
38:2 Hezekiah turned his *f* to the
50:6 My *f* I did not conceal from
50:7 I have set my *f* like a flint
53:3 concealing of one's *f* from
54:8 I concealed my *f* from you
57:17 concealing my *f*, while I
59:2 concealing of his *f* from you
64:7 concealed your *f* from us
64:12 In the *f* of these things
65:3 offending me right to my *f*
Jer 2:27 the neck and not the *f*
3:12 not have my *f* drop angrily
6:7 and plague are before my *f*
7:10 in the *f* of doing all these
7:15 out from before my *f*, just
8:2 As manure upon the *f* of the
9:22 upon the *f* of the field
13:26 your skirts over your *f*
15:1 from before my *f*, that they
17:16 in front of your *f* it has
18:17 The back, and not the *f*, I
21:10 set my *f* against this city
26:19 soften the *f* of Jehovah
32:31 remove it from before my *f*
32:33 the back and not the *f*
33:5 concealed my *f* from this
44:11 setting my *f* against you
52:3 out from before his *f*
La 2:19 heart before the *f* of Jehovah
3:35 before the *f* of the Most High
4:16 *f* of Jehovah has divided them
Eze 1:10 four of them had a man's *f*
1:10 with a lion's *f* to the right
1:10 had a bull's *f* on the left
1:10 the four . . . had an eagle's *f*
1:28 then I fell upon my *f*, and I
2:4 sons insolent of *f* and hard of
3:8 made your *f* exactly as hard
3:23 and I went falling upon my *f*
4:3 must fix your *f* against it
4:7 Jerusalem you will fix your *f*
6:2 your *f* toward the mountains
7:22 to turn away my *f* from them
9:8 to fall upon my *f* and cry out
10:11 to which the head would *f*
10:14 four faces. The first *f* was
10:14 was the *f* of the cherub
10:14 and the second *f* was the
10:14 was the *f* of earthling man
10:14 third was the *f* of a lion
10:14 was the *f* of an eagle
11:13 fall upon my *f* and cry with
12:6 cover your very *f* that you
12:12 His *f* he will cover in
13:17 set your *f* against the
14:4 in front of his *f* and that
14:7 in front of his *f* and that
14:8 set my *f* against that man
15:7 have set my *f* against them
15:7 I direct my *f* against them
20:35, 35 with you there *f* to *f*
20:46 set your *f* in the direction
21:2 set your *f* toward Jerusalem
21:16 wherever your *f* is directed
25:2 set your *f* toward the sons
28:21 set your *f* toward Sidon
29:2 set your *f* against Pharaoh
35:2 set your *f* against the
38:2 set your *f* against Gog of
39:23 I concealed my *f* from them
39:24 kept concealing my *f* from
39:29 no longer conceal my *f* from
41:19 the *f* of a man was toward
41:19 *f* of a maned young lion
43:3 I went falling upon my *f*
44:4 I went falling on my *f*
Da 2:46 fell down upon his *f*, and to
3:19 expression of his *f* was
8:17 so that I fell upon my *f*
8:18 asleep on my *f* on the earth
9:3 set my *f* to Jehovah the true
9:7 shame of *f* as at this day, to
9:8 to us belongs the shame of *f*
9:13 softened the *f* of Jehovah our
Da 9:17 *f* to shine upon your sanctuary
10:6 his *f* like the appearance of
10:9 fast asleep upon my *f*, with
10:9 with my *f* to the earth
10:15 I had set my *f* to the earth
11:17 set his *f* to come with the
11:18 turn his *f* back to the
11:19 his *f* back to the fortresses
Ho 5:5 Israel has testified to his *f*
5:15 they will certainly seek my *f*
7:2 In front of my *f* they have
7:10 Israel has testified to his *f*
Joe 2:20 his *f* to the eastern sea
Mic 3:4 will conceal his *f* from them
Na 1:5 be upheaved because of his *f*
1:6 In the *f* of his denunciation
2:1 has come up before your *f*
3:5 your skirts over your *f*
Zec 7:2 to soften the *f* of Jehovah
8:21 go to soften the *f* of Jehovah
8:22 to soften the *f* of Jehovah
Mal 1:9 please, soften the *f* of God
Mt 6:17 your head and wash your *f*
11:10 my messenger before your *f*
17:2 his *f* shone as the sun, and
18:10 behold the *f* of my Father
19:26 Looking them in the *f*, Jesus
26:39 he fell upon his *f*, praying
26:67 they spit into his *f* and hit
26:67 Others slapped him in the *f*
Mr 1:2 my messenger before your *f*
14:65 to cover his whole *f* and hit
14:65 slapping him in the *f*, the
Lu 5:12 he fell upon his *f* and begged
7:27 my messenger before your *f*
9:29 his *f* became different and
9:51 set his *f* to go to Jerusalem
9:53 his *f* was set for going to
17:16 fell upon his *f* at Jesus'
21:35 upon the *f* of all the earth
Joh 18:22 gave Jesus a slap in the *f*
19:3 give him slaps in the *f*
Ac 2:28 with good cheer with your *f*
3:13 disowned before Pilate's *f*
6:15, 15 his *f* was as an angel's *f*
20:25 will see my *f* no more
20:38 to behold his *f* no more
25:16, 16 his accusers *f* to *f*
1Co 13:12, 12 it will be *f* to *f*
14:25 fall upon his *f* and worship
15:31 Daily I *f* death. This I
2Co 3:7 not gaze . . . the *f* of Moses
3:7 because of the glory of his *f*
3:13 put a veil upon his *f*, that
4:6 of God by the *f* of Christ
4:11, 11 *f* to *f* with death for
8:24 the *f* of the congregations
10:7 according to their *f* value
11:20 strikes you in the *f*
Ga 1:22 But I was unknown by *f* to the
2:11, 11 I resisted him *f* to *f*
Eph 3:4 In the *f* of this you, when
Col 2:1 those who have not seen my *f*
Jas 1:23 at his natural *f* in a mirror
1Pe 3:12 *f* of Jehovah is against those
2Jo 12, 12 to speak with you *f* to *f*
3Jo 14, 14 we shall speak *f* to *f*
Re 4:7 creature has a *f* like a man's
6:16 the *f* of the One seated on the
10:1 and his *f* was as the sun
12:11 souls even in the *f* of death
12:14 from the *f* of the serpent
22:4 they will see his *f*, and his

Faced
Ex 16:10 and *f* toward the wilderness
Jg 6:14 Jehovah *f* him and said: Go in
20:36 Israel *f* defeat when they

Faces
Ge 9:23 their *f* were turned away
30:40 turned the *f* of the flocks
40:7 what reason are your *f* gloomy
42:6 with their *f* to the earth
44:14 fall upon their *f* to the
Ex 20:20 may continue before your *f*
25:20 their *f* one toward the other
25:20 *f* of the cherubs should be
37:9 their *f* were one to the other
37:9 *f* of the cherubs proved to be
Le 9:24 and went falling upon their *f*
Nu 14:5 fell upon their *f* before all
16:22 fell upon their *f* and said
16:45 they fell upon their *f*
20:6 and fell upon their *f*, and
De 11:4 *f* of which he made the
Jos 15:2 the bay that *f* southward
15:8 that *f* the valley of Hinnom
18:14 mountain that *f* Beth-horon
18:16 *f* the valley of the son of
Jg 13:20 they fell upon their *f* to the
18:23 they turned their *f* and said
1Sa 26:3 Hachilah, which *f* Jeshimon
1Ki 18:39 fell upon their *f* and said
1Ch 12:8, 8 *f* were the *f* of lions
21:16 fell down upon their *f*
2Ch 3:13 cherubs . . . their *f* inward
7:3 with their *f* to the earth
20:24 turned their *f* toward the
Ne 8:6 with their *f* to the earth
Job 6:28 I shall lie to your very *f*
21:5 Turn your *f* to me and stare
40:13 Bind their very *f* in the
Ps 34:5 *f* could not possibly be
83:16 Fill their *f* with dishonor
Isa 3:9 expression of their *f* actually
3:15 *f* of the afflicted ones
5:21 in front of their own *f*
13:8, 8 Their *f* are inflamed *f*
25:8 wipe the tears from all *f*
49:23 With *f* to the earth they
Jer 1:8 afraid because of their *f*
5:3 their *f* harder than a crag
7:19 purpose of shame to their *f*
30:6 and all *f* have turned pale
42:15 set your *f* to enter into
42:17 set their *f* to enter into
44:12 set their *f* to enter into
50:5 their *f* in that direction
51:51 has covered our *f*, for
La 5:12 *f* of even old men have not
Eze 1:6 each one had four *f*, and each
1:8 had their *f* and their wings
1:10 for the likeness of their *f*
1:11 That is the way their *f* were
1:15 by the four *f* of each
2:6 and at their *f* do not you be
3:8 exactly as hard as their *f* and
3:9 struck with terror at their *f*
6:9 feel a loathing in their *f* at
7:18 on all *f* there is shame and
8:16 and their *f* to the east, and
9:2 upper gate that *f* to the north
10:14 And each one had four *f*
10:21 each one had four *f* and each
10:22 for the likeness of their *f*
10:22 *f* the appearance of which I
14:3 have put in front of their *f*
14:6 turn your *f* back even from
20:43 a loathing at your own *f*
20:47 all *f* must be scorched from
27:35 *F* must become perturbed
32:10 my sword in their *f*, and
41:18 and the cherub had two *f*
Da 1:10 see your *f* dejected-looking
Joe 2:6 As for all *f*, they will
Na 2:10 as for the *f* of all of them
Hab 1:9 The assembling of their *f* is
Mal 2:3 will scatter dung upon your *f*
Mt 6:16 they disfigure their *f* that
17:6 disciples fell upon their *f*
Lu 24:5 their *f* turned to the ground
24:17 they stood still with sad *f*
2Co 1:11 us due to many prayerful *f*
3:18 with unveiled *f* reflect like
1Th 2:17 to see your *f* with great
3:10 to see your *f* and to make
Re 7:11 they fell upon their *f* before
9:7, 7 their *f* were as men's *f*
11:16 fell upon their *f* and

Facing
1Sa 14:5 on the north *f* Michmash
14:5 was on the south *f* Geba
20:25 Jonathan was *f* him, and
26:1 Hachilah, *f* Jeshimon
1Ki 7:25 twelve bulls, three *f* north
7:25 bulls . . . three *f* west
7:25 bulls . . . three *f* south
7:25 bulls . . . three *f* east
22:35 in the chariot *f* the Syrians
2Ch 4:4 bulls, three *f* the north and
4:4 bulls . . . three *f* the west
4:4 bulls . . . three *f* the south
4:4 bulls . . . three *f* the east
18:34 *f* the Syrians until the
Eze 8:3 gate that is *f* northward
11:1 gate . . . that is *f* eastward
43:1 gate that is *f* toward the
43:17 And its steps are *f* east

ze 44:1 the outer one *f* east, and
46:1 courtyard that is *f* east
46:12 gate that is *f* east, and
46:19 that were *f* to the north
47:2 gate that is *f* toward the

act

e 22:16 *f* that you have done this
22:18 due to the *f* that you have
26:5 due to the *f* that Abraham
28:19 *f* is, Luz was the city's
40:15 I was in *f* kidnapped from
41:32 the *f* that the dream was
x 9:16 in *f*, for this cause I have
16:29 Mark the *f* that Jehovah has
19:18 due to the *f* that Jehovah
22:12 should for a *f* be stolen
22:13 should for a *f* be torn by a
u 5:14 she in *f* has defiled herself
5:14 she in *f* has not defiled
22:37 for a *f* sent to you to call
25:13 the *f* that he tolerated no
32:1 livestock, very many, in *f*
e 1:36 the *f* that he has followed
9:5 in *f*, it is for the wickedness
22:29 the *f* that he humiliated her
28:47 the *f* that you did not serve
os 7:20 For a *f* I—I have sinned
u 3:12 a *f* that I am a repurchaser
Sa 2:27 for a *f* reveal myself to the
14:43 I did for a *f* taste a little
20:3 in *f*, as Jehovah is living
24:19 due to the *f* that this day
26:4 that Saul had for a *f* come
26:21 *f* that my soul has been
Sa 3:30 *f* that he had put Asahel
6:8 angry over the *f* that Jehovah
8:10 *f* that he had fought against
12:6 *f* that he has done this thing
12:10 *f* that you despised me so
13:22 *f* that he had humiliated
14:5 For a *f* I am a widowed
Ki 4:14 a *f*, a son she does not have
18:12 the *f* that they had not
19:17 It is a *f*, O Jehovah, the
22:13 *f* that our forefathers did
22:17 due to the *f* that they have
Ch 18:10 *f* that he had fought against
Ch 21:12 *f* that you have not walked
29:36 *f* that the true God had
34:21 the *f* that our forefathers
34:25 due to the *f* that they have
ob 9:2 For a *f* I do know that it is
12:2 For a *f* you men are the
19:5 If for a *f* against me you
32:3 the *f* that they had not found
34:12 for a *f*, God himself does
36:4 are for a *f* no falsehood
s 119:136 *f* that they have not kept
c 12:9 the *f* that the congregator had
a 37:18 It is a *f*, O Jehovah, that
43:4 the *f* that you have been
44:15 In *f* he builds a fire and
50:2 hand become in *f* so short
53:9 despite the *f* that he had
53:12 due to the *f* that he poured
66:16 a *f* take up the controversy
er 5:19 Due to what *f* has Jehovah
16:11 the *f* that your fathers
22:9 On account of the *f* that they
24:8 this in *f* is what Jehovah
29:19 the *f* that they have not
33:25 *f* that I had appointed my
44:23 *f* that you made sacrificial
50:7 *f* that they have sinned
a 4:7 in *f* more ruddy than corals
ze 23:30 the *f* that you defiled
39:23 the *f* that they behaved
a 2:8 For a *f*, I am aware that time
o 10:8 in *f* say to the mountains
m 4:12 the *f* that I shall do this
ic 2:10 the *f* that she has become
t 3:3 in *f*, is the one spoken of
5:26 I say to you for a *f*, You
7:12 this, in *f*, is what the Law
13:32 in *f*, the tiniest of all the
23:17 Which, in *f*, is greater, the
23:19 Which, in *f*, is greater, the
24:22 In *f*, unless those days were
26:73 in *f*, your dialect gives you
r 1:19 in *f*, while they were in
3:27 In *f*, no one that has got
8:16 the *f* that they had no loaves
9:6 In *f*, he did not know what
9:13 Elijah, in *f*, has come, and
Mr 10:26 Who, in *f*, can be saved?
13:20 In *f*, unless Jehovah had
14:70 in *f*, you are a Galilean
Lu 5:6 In *f*, their nets began ripping
9:14 They were, in *f*, about five
9:28 In actual *f*, about eight days
9:45 In *f*, it was concealed from
14:32 If, in *f*, he cannot do so
18:25 easier, in *f*, for a camel to
20:36 In *f*, neither can they die
22:59 in *f*, he is a Galilean!
23:15 In *f*, neither did Herod, for
24:34 For a *f* the Lord was raised
Joh 4:6 In *f*, Jacob's fountain was
5:46 In *f*, if you believed Moses
6:51 for a *f*, the bread that I
6:71 in *f*, speaking of Judas the
7:5 His brothers were, in *f*, not
8:26 As a matter of *f*, he that
11:2 in *f*, the Mary that greased
11:30 not yet, in *f*, come into
11:38 in *f*, a cave, and a stone
13:29 Some, in *f*, were imagining
16:2 *f*, the hour is coming when
18:14 in *f*, the one that counseled
19:36 In *f*, these things took
21:25 in *f*, many other things
Ac 2:15 in *f*, not drunk, as you
2:32 which *f* we are all witnesses
3:15 of which *f* we are witnesses
3:22 In *f*, Moses said, Jehovah
3:24 prophets, in *f*, from Samuel
4:16 for a *f*, a noteworthy sign
4:34 In *f*, there was not one in
7:22 In *f*, he was powerful in
12:9 In *f*, he supposed he was
13:8 in *f*, is the way his name is
13:34 *f* that he resurrected him
13:47 In *f*, Jehovah has laid
17:21 In *f*, all Athenians and the
17:27 in *f*, he is not far off from
18:2 *f* that Claudius had ordered
19:32 The *f* is, some were crying
21:39 Paul said: I am, in *f*, a Jew
26:10 in *f*, I did in Jerusalem
Ro 1:16 in *f*, God's power for
2:25 in *f*, of benefit only if you
7:9 In *f*, I was once alive apart
8:7 of God, nor, in *f*, can it be
10:18 in *f*, into all the earth
14:7 None of us, in *f*, lives with
1Co 3:2 In *f*, neither are you strong
4:18 as though I were in *f* not
14:5 in *f*, he translates, that the
14:9 *f*, be speaking into the air
15:2 in *f*, you became believers
15:18 In *f*, also, those who fell
15:41 in *f*, star differs from star
2Co 1:9 In *f*, we felt within
2:10 In *f*, as for me, whatever I
3:10 In *f*, even that which has
3:15 In *f*, down till today
4:3 we declare is in *f* veiled
5:4 In *f*, we who are in this
7:5 In *f*, when we arrived in
10:7 take this *f* into account for
11:1 in *f*, you are putting up
11:20 In *f*, you put up with
Ga 1:10 in *f*, men I am now trying
2:6 to me, in *f*, those outstanding
3:26 in *f*, sons of God through
Eph 5:24 In *f*, as the congregation
Php 1:18 In *f*, I will also keep on
2:27 in *f*, not only on him, but
4:15 In *f*, you Philippians, also
Col 3:15 you were, in *f*, called to it
4:3 in *f*, I am in prison bonds
1Th 1:8 The *f* is, not only has the
2:5 In *f*, at no time have we
2:19 why, is it not in *f* you?
3:4 In *f*, too, when we were with
4:1 just as you are in *f* walking
4:10 in *f*, you are doing it to
5:11 just as you are in *f* doing
2Th 3:1 just as it is in *f* with you
3:10 In *f*, also, when we were
1Ti 1:9 in the knowledge of this *f*
5:15 in *f*, some have been turned
2Ti 3:12 In *f*, all those desiring
Heb 3:16 Did not, in *f*, all do so
12:6 in *f*, he scourges every one
Jas 1:7 In *f*, let not that man
1Pe 1:6 In this *f* you are greatly
2:21 In *f*, to this course you
1Pe 4:6 In *f*, for this purpose the
2Pe 1:11 In *f*, thus there will be
3:5 this *f* escapes their notice
3:8 let this one *f* not be escaping
1Jo 2:8 a *f* that is true in his case
2:18 from which *f* we gain the
3:10 Devil are evident by this *f*
5:9 *f* that he has borne witness
3Jo 12 In *f*, we, also, are bearing
Re 14:4 in *f*, they are virgins
16:14 in *f*, expressions inspired

Facts

Ge 43:7 tell him according to these *f*
Nu 13:28 *f* are that the people who
Lu 1:1 compile a statement of the *f*

Faculties

2Pe 3:1 your clear thinking *f* by way

Fade

2Sa 22:46 Foreigners . . . will *f* away
Job 14:18 mountain itself . . . will *f*
Ps 18:45 Foreigners . . . will *f* away
37:2 like . . . grass they will *f*
Isa 19:8 will actually *f* away
64:6 shall *f* away like leafage
Ho 4:3 *f* away with the wild beast of
Jas 1:11 rich man will *f* away in his

Faded

1Sa 2:5 abundant in sons has *f* away
Isa 24:4 gone to mourning, has *f* away
24:4 has withered, has *f* away
Jer 14:2 its very gates have *f* away
15:9 has *f* away; her soul has
La 2:8 Together they have *f* away
Joe 1:10 the oil has *f* away
1:12 the fig tree has *f* away

Fading

Jg 19:8 until the *f* away of the day
Ps 6:2 O Jehovah, for I am *f* away
Isa 28:1 *f* blossom of its decoration
28:4 *f* flower of its decoration

Fail

Ge 17:13 without *f* get circumcised
28:22 without *f* give the tenth of
43:9 If I *f* to bring him to you
44:32 If I *f* to bring him back
50:24 God will without *f* turn his
50:25 without *f* turn his attention
Ex 3:16 without *f* give attention to
13:19 without *f* turn his attention
21:12 to be put to death without *f*
21:15 to be put to death without *f*
21:16 to be put to death without *f*
21:17 to be put to death without *f*
21:20 is to be avenged without *f*
21:22 without *f* according to what
21:28 is to be stoned without *f*
21:36 without *f* make compensation
22:3 make compensation without *f*
22:6 make compensation without *f*
22:14 make compensation without *f*
22:16 obtain her without *f* as his
23:4 to return it without *f* to him
23:5 are without *f* to get it loose
23:24 without *f* throw them down
23:24 without *f* break down their
Le 10:18 eaten it without *f* in the
20:2 be put to death without *f*
20:9 be put to death without *f*
20:10 put to death without *f*, the
20:11 be put to death without *f*
20:12 be put to death without *f*
20:13 be put to death without *f*
20:15 be put to death without *f*
20:16 be put to death without *f*
20:27 be put to death without *f*
24:16 be put to death without *f*
24:16 without *f* pelt him with
24:17 be put to death without *f*
26:16 eyes to *f* and making the
27:29 be put to death without *f*
Nu 15:31 should be cut off without *f*
15:35 Without *f* the man should be
18:15 should without *f* redeem the
21:2 without *f* give this people
22:17 without *f* honor you greatly
24:11 without *f* going to honor you
26:65 They will die without *f* in
35:16 Without *f* the murderer
35:17 Without *f* the murderer
35:18 Without *f* the murderer
35:21 without *f* the striker should

Nu 35:26 manslayer without *f* goes out
35:31 without *f* he should be put
De 7:2 without *f* devote them to
11:13 if you will without *f* obey
13:9 you should kill him without *f*
13:15 should without *f* strike the
14:22 Without *f* you should give a
15:4 Jehovah will without *f* bless
15:5 if you will without *f* listen
17:15 without *f* set over yourself
20:17 without *f* devote them to
23:21 God will without *f* require
28:1 without *f* listen to the voice
31:29 without *f* act ruinously, and
Jos 3:10 without *f* drive away from
Jg 4:9 Without *f* I shall go with you
11:30 without *f* give the sons of
14:12 without *f* tell it to me
17:3 without *f* sanctify the silver
21:5 be put to death without *f*
Ru 4:14 not let a repurchaser *f* for
1Sa 1:11 will without *f* look upon the
2:33 to cause your eyes to *f* and
9:6 he says comes true without *f*
20:5 without *f*, to be sitting
22:22 would without *f* tell Saul
24:20 without *f*, rule as king
25:28 Jehovah will without *f* make
26:25 without *f* work but you
26:25 without *f* come off the
27:1 escape without *f* to the land
30:8 without *f* overtake them, and
30:8 without *f* make a deliverance
2Sa 5:19 I shall without *f* give the
9:7 without *f* I shall exercise
14:14 die without *f* and be like
15:8 without *f* bring me back to
17:11 without *f* be gathered to
17:16 cross over without *f*, for
18:2 without *f* go out with you
24:24 without *f* I shall buy it
1Ki 11:11 without *f* rip the kingdom
11:22 to send me away without *f*
13:32 without *f* the word that he
17:14 will not *f* until the day of
17:16 jar of oil itself did not *f*
2Ki 18:30 Without *f* Jehovah will
1Ch 4:10 If you will without *f* bless
21:24 without *f* I shall make the
Ezr 6:9 day by day without *f*
Es 6:13 without *f* fall before him
Job 11:20 eyes of the wicked will *f*
17:5 very eyes of his sons will *f*
27:22 without *f* try to run away
31:16 widow I would cause to *f*
Ps 109:10 without *f* let his sons go
126:6 without *f* goes forth, even
126:6 without *f* come in with a
132:15 I shall bless without *f*
132:16 without *f* cry out joyfully
Pr 10:19 not *f* to be transgression
23:5 without *f* it makes wings for
23:24 will without *f* be joyful
Isa 22:7 steeds must without *f* set
22:18 Without *f* he will wrap you
24:3 Without *f* the land will be
24:3 without *f* it will be
30:19 without *f* show you favor
34:16 not *f* to have each one her
35:2 Without *f* it will blossom
36:15 Without *f* Jehovah will
40:30 will without *f* stumble
48:8 without *f* you kept dealing
60:12 *f* come to devastation
61:10 Without *f* I shall exult in
Jer 6:9 without *f* glean the remnant
10:5 Without *f* they are carried
12:16 without *f* learn the ways of
25:28 You will drink without *f*
25:30 Without *f* he will roar upon
31:20 without *f* remember him
32:4 without *f* be given into the
34:3 without *f* be caught and into
36:16 without *f* tell the king all
36:29 come without *f* and will
37:9 without *f* go away from
38:3 Without *f* this city will be
38:15 without *f* put me to death
38:17 without *f* go out to the
39:18 without *f* furnish you an
42:10 without *f* keep dwelling in
44:25 without *f* perform our vows
44:25 without *f* carry out your
44:25 without *f* perform your
Jer 44:29 without *f* come true upon
49:12 they will drink without *f*
49:12 you will drink without *f*
50:34 Without *f* he will conduct
51:56 Without *f* he will repay
51:58 without *f* be demolished
La 3:20 Without *f* your soul will
Eze 3:21 without *f* keep on living
28:9 without *f* say, I am god
30:16 without *f* be in severe
31:11 Without *f* he will act
Am 5:5 will without *f* go into exile
7:11 will without *f* go into exile
7:17 without *f* go into exile from
Mic 2:12 I shall without *f* collect
Na 3:13 gates . . . without *f* be opened
Hab 2:3 it will without *f* come true
Zep 1:2 without *f* finish everything
Zec 6:15 without *f* listen to the
11:17 arm will without *f* dry up
11:17 will without *f* grow dim
12:3 will without *f* get severe
Lu 16:9 when such *f*, they may receive
Ro 1:13 not want you to *f* to know
10:18 did not *f* to hear, did they?
10:19 Israel did not *f* to know
Heb 11:32 time will *f* me if I go on
2Pe 1:10 you will by no means ever *f*

Failed
Jos 21:45 Not a promise *f* out of all
23:14 not one word . . . has *f*
23:14 Not one word of them has *f*
1Ki 8:56 There has not *f* one word of
Job 19:27 My kidneys have *f* deep
Ps 69:3 My eyes have *f* while waiting
73:26 organism and my heart have *f*
Jer 14:6 eyes have *f* because there is
Lu 23:45 because the sunlight *f*; then
Ro 9:6 though the word of God had *f*

Failing
De 28:65 a *f* of the eyes and despair
Ps 71:9 when my power is *f*, do not

Fails
1Co 13:8 Love never *f*. But whether

Failure
Hab 3:17 may actually turn out a *f*

Faint
Ps 63:1 my flesh has grown *f* with
77:3 that my spirit may *f* away
107:5 soul within them began to *f*
Lu 21:26 men become *f* out of fear

Fainted
Ps 142:3 my spirit *f* away within me
Jon 2:7 my soul *f* away within me

Fainthearted
De 20:8 the man that is fearful and *f*
2Ch 13:7 young and *f*, and he did not
Mt 8:26 Why are you *f*, you with
Mr 4:40 Why are you *f*? Do you not yet

Fainting
La 2:11 *f* away of child and suckling
2:12 *f* away like someone slain in
2:19 are *f* away because of famine

Faints
Ps 143:4 my spirit *f* away within me

Fair
Da 4:12 foliage was *f*, and its fruit
4:21 the foliage of which was *f*
Mt 16:2 It will be *f* weather, for
Ac 27:8 place called *F* Havens, near
Col 4:1 is righteous and what is *f*

Faith
Ge 15:6 he put *f* in Jehovah; and he
Ex 14:31 *f* in Jehovah and in Moses
19:9 may put *f* to time indefinite
Nu 14:11 *f* in me for all the signs
20:12 show *f* in me to sanctify me
De 1:32 not putting *f* in Jehovah
9:23 did not exercise *f* toward him
1Ki 10:7 did not put *f* in the words
2Ki 17:14 not exercised *f* in Jehovah
2Ch 9:6 I did not put *f* in their
20:20 Put *f* in Jehovah your God
20:20 Put *f* in his prophets and
32:15 do not put *f* in him
Job 4:18 In his servants he has no *f*
15:15 In his holy ones he has no *f*
15:31 put no *f* in worthlessness
Ps 27:13 *f* in seeing the goodness of
78:22 they did not put *f* in God
78:32 not put *f* in his wonderful
106:12 they had *f* in his word
106:24 They had no *f* in his word
116:10 I had *f*, for I proceeded to
119:66 I have exercised *f*
Pr 14:15 inexperienced puts *f* in every
Isa 7:9 people have *f*, you will in
28:16 one exercising *f* will get
43:10 may know and have *f* in me
53:1 *f* in the thing heard by us
65:16 bless . . . by the God of *f*
65:16 will swear by the God of *f*
Jer 12:6 Do not put any *f* in them
Jon 3:5 Nineveh began to put *f* in God
Mic 7:5 not put your *f* in a companion
Mt 6:30 clothe you, you with little *f*
8:10 have I found so great a *f*
8:13 Just as it has been your *f*
8:26 you with little *f*
9:2 On seeing their *f* Jesus said
9:22 your *f* has made you well
9:28 Do you have *f* that I can do
9:29 According to your *f* let it
13:58 account of their lack of *f*
14:31 You with little *f*, why did
15:28 O woman, great is your *f*
16:8 no loaves, you with little *f*
17:20 Because of your little *f*
17:20 have *f* the size of a mustard
18:6 little ones who put *f* in me
21:21 If only you have *f* and do
21:22 having *f*, you will receive
Mr 1:15 and have *f* in the good news
2:5 Jesus saw their *f* he said to
4:40 Do you not yet have any *f*?
5:34 your *f* has made you well
5:36 Have no fear, only exercise *f*
6:6 he wondered at their lack of *f*
9:23 all things . . . if one has *f*
9:24 I have *f*! Help me out where
9:24 Help me out where I need *f*
10:52 your *f* has made you well
11:22 said to them: Have *f* in God
11:23 has *f* that what he says
11:24 have *f* that you have
Lu 5:20 when he saw their *f* he said
7:9 have I found so great a *f*
7:50 Your *f* has saved you; go your
8:25 to them: Where is your *f*?
8:48 your *f* has made you well; go
8:50 no fear, only put forth *f*
12:28 you, you with little *f*
17:5 to the Lord: Give us more *f*
17:6 *f* the size of a mustard grain
17:19 your *f* has made you well
18:8 really find the *f* on the earth
18:42 your *f* has made you well
22:32 that your *f* may not give out
Joh 1:12 exercising *f* in his name
2:11 disciples put their *f* in him
2:23 put their *f* in his name
3:16 everyone exercising *f* in him
3:18 He that exercises *f* in him
3:18 He that does not exercise *f*
3:18 not exercised *f* in the name
3:36 exercises *f* in the Son has
4:39 put *f* in him on account of
6:29 exercise *f* in him whom that
6:35 exercises *f* in me will never
6:40 the Son and exercises *f* in
7:5 not exercising *f* in him
7:31 of the crowd put *f* in him
7:38 that puts *f* in me, just as
7:39 those who put *f* in him were
7:48 has put *f* in him, has he?
8:30 many put *f* in him
9:35 putting *f* in the Son of man
9:36 that I may put *f* in him
9:38 I do put *f* in him, Lord
10:42 many put *f* in him there
11:25 He that exercises *f* in me
11:26 exercises *f* in me will
11:45 beheld what he did put *f* in
11:48 they will all put *f* in him
12:11 and putting *f* in Jesus
12:36 exercise *f* in the light, in
12:37 were not putting *f* in him
12:38 Jehovah, who has put *f* in
12:42 rulers actually put *f* in
12:44 He that puts *f* in me
12:44 puts *f*, not in me only
12:46 everyone putting *f* in me

Joh 14:1 Exercise *f* in God
14:1 exercise *f* also in me
14:12 He that exercises *f* in me
16:9 are not exercising *f* in me
17:20 putting *f* in me through
Ac 3:16 by our *f* in his name, has
3:16 *f* that is through him has
6:5 Stephen, a man full of *f* and
6:7 began to be obedient to the *f*
10:43 everyone putting *f* in him
11:24 full of holy spirit and of *f*
13:8 proconsul away from the *f*
14:9 he had *f* to be made well
14:22 remain in the *f* and saying
14:27 to the nations the door to *f*
15:9 purified their hearts by *f*
16:5 to be made firm in the *f* and
20:21 and *f* in our Lord Jesus
26:18 sanctified by their *f* in me
Ro 1:5 of *f* among all the nations
1:8 *f* is talked about throughout
1:12 one through the other's *f*
1:16 everyone having *f*, to the
1:17 revealed by reason of *f* and
1:17 and toward *f*, just as it is
1:17 by means of *f* he will live
3:3 If some did not express *f*
3:3 their lack of *f* perhaps make
3:22 through the *f* in Jesus Christ
3:22 for all those having *f*
3:25 through *f* in his blood
3:26 the man that has *f* in Jesus
3:27 but through the law of *f*
3:28 righteous by *f* apart from
3:30 righteous as a result of *f*
3:30 righteous by means of their *f*
3:31 abolish law by means of our *f*
4:3 Abraham exercised *f* in Jehovah
4:5 *f* in him who declares the
4:5 *f* is counted as righteousness
4:9 *f* was counted to Abraham as
4:11 righteousness by the *f* he had
4:11 father of all those having *f*
4:12 in the footsteps of that *f*
4:13 through the righteousness by *f*
4:14 *f* has been made useless and
4:16 it was as a result of *f*
4:16 adheres to the *f* of Abraham
4:17 One in whom he had *f*, even
4:18 yet based on hope he had *f*
4:19 he did not grow weak in *f*
4:20 not waver in a lack of *f*
4:20 became powerful by his *f*
5:1 righteous as a result of *f*
5:2 gained our approach by *f* into
9:30 that results from *f*
9:32 he pursued it, not by *f*, but
9:33 rests his *f* on it will not
10:4 everyone exercising *f* may
10:6 resulting from *f* speaks in
10:8 the word of *f*, which we are
10:9 exercise *f* in your heart that
10:10 *f* for righteousness, but
10:11 None that rests his *f* on
10:14 in whom they have not put *f*
10:14 put *f* in him of whom they
10:16 put *f* in the thing heard
10:17 *f* follows the thing heard
11:20 For their lack of *f* they
11:20 but you are standing by *f*
11:23 remain in their lack of *f*
12:3 to him a measure of *f*
12:6 to the *f* proportioned to us
14:1 having weaknesses in his *f*
14:2 man has *f* to eat everything
14:22 *f* that you have, have it in
14:23 he does not eat out of *f*
14:23 is not out of *f* is sin
16:26 to promote obedience by *f*
1Co 2:5 *f* might be, not in men's
12:9 *f* by the same spirit
13:2 if I have all the *f* so as to
13:13 there remain *f*, hope, love
15:14 and our *f* is in vain
15:17 your *f* is useless; you are
16:13 stand firm in the *f*, carry
2Co 1:24 masters over your *f*, but we
1:24 it is by your *f* that you are
4:13 same spirit of *f* as that of
4:13 I exercised *f*, therefore I
4:13 we too exercise *f* and
5:7 walking by *f*, not by sight
8:7 in *f* and word and knowledge
10:15 as your *f* is being increased
2Co 13:5 whether you are in the *f*
Ga 1:23 news about the *f* which he
2:16 only through *f* toward Christ
2:16 have put our *f* in Christ Jesus
2:16 declared righteous due to *f*
2:20 live by the *f* that is toward
3:2 or due to a hearing by *f*
3:5 or owing to a hearing by *f*
3:6 Abraham put *f* in Jehovah, and
3:7 those who adhere to *f* are the
3:8 nations righteous due to *f*
3:9 those who adhere to *f* are
3:11 one will live by reason of *f*
3:12 Law does not adhere to *f*, but
3:14 spirit through our *f*
3:22 promise resulting from *f*
3:22 given to those exercising *f*
3:23 before the *f* arrived, we
3:23 *f* that was destined to be
3:24 declared righteous due to *f*
3:25 now that the *f* has arrived
3:26 through your *f* in Christ
5:5 righteousness as a result of *f*
5:6 *f* operating through love is
5:22 fruitage of the spirit . . . *f*
6:10 those related to us in the *f*
Eph 1:15 *f* you have in the Lord Jesus
2:8 you have been saved through *f*
3:12 through our *f* in him
3:17 through your *f* in your hearts
4:5 one Lord, one *f*, one baptism
4:13 to the oneness in the *f*
6:16 the large shield of *f*
6:23 love with *f* from God the
Php 1:25 joy that belongs to your *f*
1:27 for the *f* of the good news
1:29 not only to put your *f* in
2:17 to which *f* has led you
3:9 which is through *f* in Christ
3:9 from God on the basis of *f*
Col 1:4 *f* in connection with Christ
1:23 that you continue in the *f*
2:5 the firmness of your *f* toward
2:7 and being stabilized in the *f*
2:7 overflowing with *f* in
2:12 *f* in the operation of God
1Th 1:8 *f* toward God has spread
3:2 in behalf of your *f*
3:10 that are lacking about your *f*
4:14 our *f* is that Jesus died and
5:8 breastplate of *f* and love
2Th 1:3 your *f* is growing exceedingly
1:4 your endurance and *f* in all
1:10 all those who exercised *f*
1:10 witness we gave met with *f*
1:11 the work of *f* with power
2:13 and by your *f* in the truth
3:2 *f* is not a possession of all
1Ti 1:2 a genuine child in the *f*
1:4 by God in connection with *f*
1:5 out of *f* without hypocrisy
1:13 acted with a lack of *f*
1:14 along with *f* and love that
1:16 *f* on him for everlasting
1:19 *f* and a good conscience
1:19 shipwreck concerning their *f*
2:7 in the matter of *f* and truth
2:15 provided they continue in *f*
3:9 the sacred secret of the *f*
3:13 freeness of speech in the *f*
4:1 will fall away from the *f*
4:3 have *f* and accurately know
4:6 with the words of the *f* and
4:12 in love, in *f*, in chasteness
5:8 disowned the *f* and is worse
5:8 worse than a person without *f*
5:12 their first expression of *f*
6:10 been led astray from the *f*
6:11 *f*, love, endurance, mildness
6:12 the fine fight of the *f*
6:21 have deviated from the *f*
2Ti 1:5 I recollect the *f* which is in
1:13 the *f* and love that are in
2:18 are subverting the *f* of some
2:22 pursue righteousness, *f*, love
3:8 disapproved as regards the *f*
3:10 closely followed . . . my *f*
3:15 *f* in connection with Christ
4:7 I have observed the *f*
Tit 1:1 the *f* of God's chosen ones
1:4 a *f* shared in common
1:13 they may be healthy in the *f*
2:2 sound in mind, healthy in *f*
3:15 affection for us in the *f*
Phm 5 hearing of your love and *f*
6 the sharing of your *f* may go
Heb 3:12 a wicked heart lacking *f* by
3:19 because of lack of *f*
4:2 they were not united by *f*
4:3 exercised *f* do enter into the
6:1 and *f* toward God
6:12 through *f* and patience
10:22 in the full assurance of *f*
10:38 will live by reason of *f*
10:39 *f* to the preserving alive
11:1 *F* is the assured expectation
11:3 By *f* we perceive that the
11:4 By *f* Abel offered God a
11:4 through which *f* he had
11:5 By *f* Enoch was transferred
11:6 without *f* it is impossible
11:7 By *f* Noah, after being given
11:7 through this *f* he condemned
11:7 that is according to *f*
11:8 By *f* Abraham, when he was
11:9 By *f* he resided as an alien
11:11 By *f* also Sarah herself
11:13 In *f* all these died
11:17 By *f* Abraham, when he was
11:20 By *f* also Isaac blessed
11:21 By *f* Jacob, when about to
11:22 By *f* Joseph, nearing his
11:23 By *f* Moses was hid for
11:24 By *f* Moses, when grown up
11:27 By *f* he left Egypt, but not
11:28 By *f* he had celebrated the
11:29 By *f* they passed through
11:30 By *f* the walls of Jericho
11:31 By *f* Rahab the harlot did
11:33 through *f* defeated kingdoms
11:39 to them through their *f*
12:2 and Perfecter of our *f*, Jesus
13:7 turns out imitate their *f*
Jas 1:3 tested quality of your *f*
1:6 asking in *f*, not doubting at
2:1 *f* of our Lord Jesus Christ
2:5 rich in *f* and heirs of the
2:14 *f* but he does not have works
2:14 *f* cannot save him, can it?
2:17 *f*, if it does not have works
2:18 You have *f*, and I have works
2:18 Show me your *f* apart from
2:18 show you my *f* by my works
2:20 that *f* apart from works is
2:22 his *f* worked along with his
2:22 works his *f* was perfected
2:23 Abraham put *f* in Jehovah
2:24 by works, and not by *f* alone
2:26 also *f* without works is dead
5:15 the prayer of *f* will make
1Pe 1:5 God's power through *f* for a
1:7 the tested quality of your *f*
1:8 you exercise *f* in him and are
1:9 receive the end of your *f*
1:21 your *f* and hope might be in
2:6 no one exercising *f* in it
5:9 solid in the *f*, knowing that
2Pe 1:1 those who have obtained a *f*
1:5 supply to your *f* virtue, to
1Jo 3:23 *f* in the name of his Son
5:4 conquered the world, our *f*
5:5 *f* that Jesus is the Son of God
5:10 putting his *f* in the Son of
5:10 person not having *f* in God
5:10 not put his *f* in the witness
5:13 you who put your *f* in the
Jude 3 put up a hard fight for the *f*
5 destroyed those not showing *f*
20 on your most holy *f*, and
Re 2:13 not deny your *f* in me even
2:19 your love and *f* and ministry
13:10 endurance and *f* of the holy
14:12 of God and the *f* of Jesus
21:8 cowards and those without *f*

Faithful

De 7:9 the *f* God, keeping covenant and
1Sa 2:35 for myself a *f* priest
22:14 like David, *f*, and the
2Sa 20:19 the peaceable and *f* ones of
1Ch 17:23 prove *f* to time indefinite
17:24 let your name prove *f* and
2Ch 1:9 let your promise . . . prove *f*
31:20 *f* before Jehovah his God
32:1 this *f* course Sennacherib
Ne 9:8 And you found his heart *f*
13:13 for they were considered *f*
Job 12:20 removing speech from the *f*

Ps 12:1 *f* people have vanished from
31:23 The *f* ones Jehovah is
78:37 not prove *f* in his covenant
89:28 covenant will be *f* to him
89:37 as a *f* witness in the skies
101:6 My eyes are upon the *f* ones
Pr 11:13 one *f* in spirit is covering
13:17 but a *f* envoy is a healing
14:5 *f* witness is one that will
20:6 but a *f* man who can find?
25:13 *f* envoy to those sending him
27:6 inflicted by a lover are *f*
28:20 man of *f* acts will get many
Isa 1:21 how the *f* town has become a
1:26 Righteousness, *F* Town
8:2 *f* witnesses, Uriah the priest
26:2 keeping *f* conduct may enter
49:7 Jehovah, who is *f*, the Holy
55:3 to David that are *f*
Jer 42:5 true and *f* witness against
Mt 24:45 is the *f* and discreet slave
25:21 Well done, good and *f* slave!
25:21 were *f* over a few things
25:23 Well done, good and *f* slave!
25:23 were *f* over a few things
Lu 12:42 Who really is the *f* steward
16:10 person *f* in what is least
16:10 least is *f* also in much
16:11 *f* in connection with the
16:12 *f* in connection with what
19:17 you have proved yourself *f*
Ac 10:45 *f* ones that had come with
13:34 to David that are *f*
16:15 judged me to be *f* to Jehovah
1Co 1:9 God is *f*, by whom you were
4:2 is for a man to be found *f*
4:17 beloved and *f* child in the
7:25 him by the Lord to be *f*
10:13 God is *f*, and he will not
2Co 6:15 *f* person have with an
Ga 3:9 together with *f* Abraham
Eph 1:1 *f* ones in union with Christ
6:21 and *f* minister in the Lord
Col 1:2 and *f* brothers in union with
1:7 is a *f* minister of the Christ
4:7 *f* minister and fellow slave
4:9 Onesimus, my *f* and beloved
1Th 1:3 your *f* work and your loving
5:24 He who is calling you is *f*
2Th 3:3 the Lord is *f*, and he will
1Ti 1:12 considered me *f* by assigning
1:15 *F* and deserving of full
3:1 That statement is *f*. If any
3:11 *f* in all things
4:9 *F* and deserving of full
4:10 especially of *f* ones
4:12 an example to the *f* ones in
2Ti 2:2 these things commit to *f* men
2:11 *F* is the saying: Certainly
2:13 he remains *f*, for he cannot
Tit 1:9 holding firmly to the *f* word
3:8 *F* is the saying, and
Heb 2:17 a merciful and *f* high priest
3:2 *f* to the One that made him
3:5 Moses as an attendant was *f*
3:6 Christ was *f* as a Son over
10:23 for he is *f* that promised
11:11 she esteemed him *f* who had
1Pe 4:19 souls to a *f* Creator while
5:12 Silvanus, a *f* brother, as I
1Jo 1:9 is *f* and righteous so as to
3Jo 5 doing a *f* work in whatever you
Re 1:5 Jesus Christ, the *F* Witness
2:10 Prove yourself *f* even to
2:13 Antipas, my witness, the *f*
3:14 the *f* and true witness, the
17:14 chosen and *f* with him will
19:11 *F* and True, and he judges
21:5 these words are *f* and true
22:6 These words are *f* and true

Faithfully

Ne 9:33 *f* is how you have acted

Faithfulness

Ge 32:10 *f* that you have exercised
Nu 5:14 suspicious of his wife's *f*
5:14 suspicious of his wife's *f*
De 32:4 God of *f*, with whom there is
32:20 Sons in whom there is no *f*
1Sa 26:23 own *f*, in that Jehovah
2Ki 12:15 *f* that they were working
22:7 in *f* that they are working
2Ch 19:9 fear of Jehovah with *f* and
31:12 and the holy things in *f*
34:12 men were acting in *f* in the
Ps 33:4 And all his work is in *f*
36:5 your *f* is up to the clouds
37:3 and deal with *f*
40:10 Your *f* and your salvation I
88:11 Your *f* in the place of
89:1 make your *f* known with my
89:2 *f* firmly established in them
89:5 *f* in the congregation of the
89:8 your *f* is all around you
89:24 *f* and my loving-kindness are
89:33 false with regard to my *f*
89:49 swore to David in your *f*
92:2 about your *f* during the nights
96:13 And the peoples with his *f*
98:3 his *f* to the house of Israel
100:5 his *f* to generation after
119:30 The way of *f* I have chosen
119:75 *f* you have afflicted me
119:86 your commandments are *f*
119:90 *f* is for generation after
119:138 And in exceeding *f*
143:1 In your *f* answer me in your
Pr 12:17 He that launches forth *f*
12:22 acting in *f* are a pleasure
Isa 11:5 and *f* the belt of his loins
25:1 from early times, in *f*
59:4 has gone to court in *f*
Jer 5:1 anyone seeking *f*, and I shall
5:3 those eyes of yours toward *f*
7:28 *F* has perished, and it has
9:3 but not for *f* have they proved
La 3:23 Your *f* is abundant
Ho 2:20 I will engage you to me in *f*
Hab 2:4 by his *f* he will keep living
Mt 23:23 justice and mercy and *f*
Ro 3:3 the *f* of God without effect
1Th 3:5 I sent to know of your *f*
3:6 good news about your *f* and
3:7 through the *f* you show

Faithless

Pr 14:14 The one *f* at heart will be
Mt 17:17 O *f* and twisted generation
Mr 9:19 O *f* generation, how long
Lu 9:41 Jesus said: O *f* and twisted
Tit 1:15 to persons defiled and *f*

Faithlessly

1Ch 10:13 had acted *f* against Jehovah
Ps 44:18 heart has not turned *f* back

Falcon

Le 11:16 the *f* according to its kind
De 14:15 the *f* according to its kind
Job 39:26 that the *f* soars up

Fall

Ge 2:21 God had a deep sleep *f*
4:5 his countenance began to *f*
33:4 *f* upon his neck and kiss him
38:23 we may not *f* into contempt
43:18 *f* upon us and attack us and
44:14 *f* upon their faces to the
Ex 15:16 and dread will *f* upon them
19:21 and many of them have to *f*
21:33 bull or an ass does *f* into it
Le 11:32 *f* in its death state will be
11:33 which any of them should *f*
11:35 dead bodies may *f* will be
11:37 dead bodies *f* upon any seed
26:7 *f* before you by the sword
26:8 enemies will indeed *f* before
26:36 and *f* without anyone chasing
Nu 5:21 letting your thigh *f* away
5:22 and the thigh to *f* away
5:27 and her thigh must *f* away
11:31 *f* above the camp about a
14:3 to *f* by the sword? Our wives
14:29 your carcasses will *f*, yes
14:32 will *f* in this wilderness
14:43 certain to *f* by the sword
34:2 the land that will *f* to you
35:23 cause it to *f* upon him, so
De 22:4 his bull *f* down on the road
22:8 falling might *f* from it
28:52 fortified walls . . . *f*
Jos 6:5 wall of the city must *f* down
6:20 wall began to *f* down flat
11:7 surprise and to *f* upon them
13:6 *f* to Israel as an inheritance
Jg 15:18 must I *f* into the hand of
1Sa 3:19 his words to *f* to the earth
4:18 to *f* from the seat backward
11:7 dread of Jehovah began to *f*
14:13 began to *f* before Jonathan
1Sa 14:45 will *f* to the earth
18:25 schemed to have David *f* by
26:20 my blood *f* to the earth
2Sa 4:4 he then had a *f* and was lamed
14:4 *f* upon her face to the earth
14:11 of your son will *f* to the
21:22 *f* by the hand of David and
22:39 they will *f* under my feet
24:14 *f*, please, into the hand of
24:14 of man do not let me *f*
1Ki 1:52 will not *f* a single hair
2:25 *f* upon him, so that he died
2:29 saying: Go, *f* upon him
2:31 *f* upon him; and you must
22:20 and *f* at Ramoth-gilead
2Ki 4:37 come in and *f* at his feet
6:6 Where did it *f*? So he showed
10:10 will *f* unfulfilled to the
14:10 have to *f*, you and Judah
19:7 *f* by the sword in his own
1Ch 5:10 came to *f* by their hand
20:8 to *f* by the hand of David and
21:13 *f* into the hand of Jehovah
21:13 hand of man do not let me *f*
2Ch 18:19 and *f* at Ramoth-gilead
25:19 bad position and have to *f*
Es 6:13 you have started to *f*, you
6:13 without fail *f* before him
Job 1:20 *f* to the earth and bow down
13:11 dread of him *f* upon you
31:22 my own shoulder blade *f*
37:6 to the snow he says, *F*
Ps 5:10 *f* due to their own counsels
7:15 he will *f* into the hole that
10:10 to *f* into his strong claws
13:3 I may not *f* asleep in death
18:38 They will *f* under my feet
35:8 With ruin let him *f* into it
37:14 afflicted and poor one to *f*
37:24 Although he may *f*, he will
68:9 you began causing to *f*
73:18 have made them *f* to ruins
78:28 them *f* in the middle of his
82:7 of the princes you will *f*
91:7 thousand will *f* at your very
101:3 doing of those who *f* away
106:26 them *f* in the wilderness
106:27 *f* among the nations
118:13 pushed . . . that I should *f*
140:10 made to *f* into the fire
141:10 wicked will *f* into their
Pr 7:26 has caused to *f* down slain
11:5 the wicked one will *f*
11:14 direction, the people *f*
11:28 riches—he himself will *f*
13:17 is wicked will *f* into bad
17:20 tongue will *f* into calamity
19:15 causes a deep sleep to *f*, and
22:14 denounced by Jehovah will *f*
24:16 the righteous one may *f* even
26:27 excavating a pit will *f* into
28:10 himself *f* into his own pit
28:14 will *f* into calamity
28:18 crooked in his ways will *f*
Ec 4:10 For if one of them should *f*
10:8 will himself *f* right into it
Isa 3:25 sword your own men will *f*
8:15 and to *f* and be broken
10:34 Lebanon itself will *f*
13:15 will *f* by the sword
22:25 must be hewn down and *f*
24:18 will *f* into the hollow
24:20 *f*, so that it will not rise
26:18 proceed to *f* in birth
30:13 broken section about to *f*
30:25 when the towers *f*
31:3 being helped will have to *f*
31:8 Assyrian must *f* by the sword
37:7 *f* by the sword in his own
47:11 upon you adversity will *f*
54:15 *f* even on account of you
Jer 4:7 own cities will *f* in ruins
6:15 *f* among those who are
8:4 Will they *f* and not get up
8:12 *f* among those who are
9:22 must also *f* like manure upon
15:8 I will cause to *f* upon them
19:7 cause them to *f* by the sword
20:4 *f* by the sword of their
22:7 to *f* into the fire
23:12 be pushed and certainly *f*
25:27 *f* so that you cannot get up
25:34 *f* like a desirable vessel
36:7 *f* before Jehovah and they

Jer 37:20 *f* before you, and do not
38:26 for favor *f* before the king
39:18 by the sword you will not *f*
42:2 for favor, please, *f* before
42:9 request for favor to *f* before
44:12 They will *f* by the sword
46:16 They also actually *f*
48:44 *f* into the hollow
49:26 *f* in her public squares, and
50:30 *f* in her public squares
50:32 certainly stumble and *f*
51:4 *f* slain in the land of the
51:44 wall . . . of Babylon must *f*
51:47 slain ones will *f* in the
51:49 slain ones of Israel to *f*
Eze 5:12 by the sword they will *f* all
6:4 to *f* before your dungy idols
6:7 *f* in the midst of you, and
6:11 the pestilence they will *f*
6:12 by the sword he will *f*
9:8 to *f* upon my face and cry out
11:10 By the sword you will *f*
11:13 *f* upon my face and cry with
13:11 plastering . . . it will *f*
13:11 you, O hailstones, will *f*
13:12 And, look! the wall must *f*
13:14 she will certainly *f*, and
17:21 by the sword they will *f*
23:25 will *f* even by the sword
24:21 by the sword they will *f*
25:13 By the sword they will *f*
27:27 *f* in the heart of the open
28:23 must *f* in the midst of her
29:5 Upon . . . field you will *f*
30:5 will *f* by the very sword
30:6 supporters of Egypt . . . *f*
30:6 *f* in it even by the sword
30:17 by the sword they will *f*
30:22 sword to *f* out of his hand
30:25 arms of Pharaoh will *f*
31:12 foliage will certainly *f*
32:12 to *f* by the very swords of
32:20 by the sword they will *f*
33:27 will *f* by the sword itself
35:8 slain by the sword will *f*
38:20 steep ways will have to *f*
38:20 even every wall will *f*
39:3 to *f* out of your own right
39:4 *f*, you and all your bands
39:5 you will *f*, for I myself
47:14 land must *f* to you by lot
47:22 they will *f* by lot into an
48:29 *f* by lot for inheritance
Da 3:5 *f* down and worship the image
3:6 does not *f* down and worship
3:10 *f* down and worship the image
3:11 would not *f* down and worship
3:15 *f* down and worship the image
8:10 stars to *f* to the earth, and
9:18 our entreaties *f* before you
9:20 request for favor *f* before
11:12 cause tens of thousands to *f*
11:19 will certainly stumble and *f*
11:26 will certainly *f* down slain
Ho 7:16 their princes will *f* because
10:8 and to the hills, *F* over us!
13:16 By the sword they will *f*
Joe 2:8 *f* even among the missiles
Am 3:5 Will a bird *f* into a trap
3:14 and must *f* to the earth
7:17 by the sword they will *f*
8:14 *f*, and they will rise up no
Na 3:12 *f* into the mouth of an eater
Mt 4:9 if you *f* down and do an act of
10:29 not one of them will *f* to
15:14 both will *f* into a pit
24:29 stars will *f* from heaven
Mr 14:35 *f* on the ground . . . praying
Lu 2:34 the *f* and the rising again of
8:13 in a season of testing they *f*
21:24 will *f* by the edge of the
23:30 to the mountains, *F* over us!
Ac 2:43 fear began to *f* upon every
5:15 shadow might *f* upon some one
9:37 happened to *f* sick and die
27:32 skiff and let it *f* off
27:40 anchors, they let them *f*
Ro 3:23 *f* short of the glory of God
1Co 1:7 do not *f* short in any gift at
7:39 husband should *f* asleep in
8:8 we do not *f* short, and, if we
10:8 only to *f*, twenty-three
10:12 beware that he does not *f*
14:25 *f* upon his face and worship
1Co 15:51 not all *f* asleep in death
1Ti 3:6 *f* into the judgment passed
3:7 *f* into reproach and a snare
4:1 will *f* away from the faith
6:9 *f* into temptation and a snare
Heb 4:11 *f* in the same pattern of
10:31 *f* into the hands of the
Jas 5:12 you do not *f* under judgment
2Pe 3:17 and *f* from your own
Re 4:10 *f* down before the One seated
6:16 *F* over us and hide us from
11:6 that no rain should *f* during

Fallacious

Jer 7:4 put your trust in *f* words
7:8 putting your trust in *f* words

Fallen

Ge 4:6 why has your countenance *f*?
Le 11:38 dead bodies had *f* upon it
De 21:1 *f* on the field, and it has not
Jos 2:9 fright of you has *f* upon us
Jg 3:25 their lord was *f* to the
4:22 there was Sisera *f* dead, with
8:10 and those already *f* were a
18:1 inheritance had not *f* to them
19:27 *f* at the entrance of the
1Sa 5:3 Dagon was *f* upon his face to
5:4 Dagon was *f* upon his face to
18:22 have *f* in love with you
19:24 lay *f* naked all that day
26:12 sleep . . . had *f* upon them
31:8 sons *f* upon Mount Gilboa
2Sa 1:4 people have *f* so that they
1:10 not live after he had *f*
1:12 they had *f* by the sword
1:19 How have the mighty men *f*
1:25 mighty ones *f* in the midst
1:27 have the mighty ones *f*
3:34 you have *f*
3:38 great man that has *f* this
2Ki 2:13 garment of Elijah that had *f*
2:14 garment of Elijah that had *f*
1Ch 5:22 were many that had *f* slain
10:8 to find Saul and his sons *f*
2Ch 20:24 carcasses *f* to the earth
Es 7:8 Haman was *f* upon the couch on
8:17 dread of the Jews had *f* upon
9:2 dread of them had *f* upon all
9:3 dread of Mordecai had *f* upon
Ps 16:6 *f* for me in pleasant places
20:8 have broken down and *f*
36:12 have *f*; They have been pushed
55:4 death itself have *f* upon me
57:6 have *f* into the midst of it
69:9 reproaches . . . have *f* upon me
76:6 the horse have *f* fast asleep
105:38 dread of them had *f* upon
Isa 3:8 and Judah itself has *f*
9:10 Bricks are what have *f*, but
14:12 you have *f* from heaven, you
16:9 over your harvest has *f* down
21:9, 9 She has *f*! Babylon has *f*
Jer 2:25 *f* in love with strangers
38:19 Jews that have *f* away to
39:9 deserters that had *f* away to
46:6 they have stumbled and *f*
46:12 Together they have *f* down
48:32 despoiler himself has *f*
50:15 Her pillars have *f*
51:8 Babylon has *f*, so that she is
51:49 ones of all the earth have *f*
52:15 deserters that had *f* away
La 2:21 *f* by the sword. You have
5:16 The crown of our head has *f*
Eze 27:34 midst of you they have *f*
31:13 Upon its *f* trunk all the
Ho 7:7 Their own kings have all *f*
Am 5:2 The virgin, Israel, has *f*
9:11 the booth of David that is *f*
Mic 7:8 Although I have *f*, I shall
Zec 11:2 for the cedar has *f*
Mt 27:52 holy ones that had *f* asleep
Mr 1:32 After evening had *f*, when the
4:35 when evening had *f*, he said
6:47 Evening having now *f*, the
14:17 After evening had *f* he came
Lu 10:18 Satan already *f* like
Ac 8:16 not yet *f* upon any one of
15:16 the booth of David that is *f*
26:14 we had all *f* to the ground
Ro 15:3 reproaches . . . have *f* upon me
1Co 15:6 some have *f* asleep in death
15:20 who have *f* asleep in death
Ga 5:4 *f* away from his undeserved
Php 2:26 you heard he had *f* sick
1Th 4:14 who have *f* asleep in death
4:15 who have *f* asleep in death
Heb 4:1 seem to have *f* short of it
6:6 who have *f* away, to revive
Re 2:5 from what you have *f*, and
9:1 I saw a star that had *f* from
14:8 She has *f*! Babylon the great
14:8 Babylon the great has *f*, she
17:10 seven kings: five have *f*
18:2 She has *f*! Babylon the Great
18:2 Babylon the Great has *f*, and
18:3 all the nations have *f* victim

Falling

Ge 14:10 flight and went *f* into them
15:12 great darkness was *f* upon
24:63 at about the *f* of evening
Le 9:24 and went *f* upon their faces
13:30 is an abnormal *f* off of hair
13:31 abnormal *f* off of hair
13:31 of abnormal *f* off of hair
13:32 *f* off of hair has not spread
13:32 *f* off of hair is not deeper
13:33 *f* off of hair shaved; and
13:33 *f* off of hair seven days
13:34 abnormal *f* off of hair on
13:34 abnormal *f* off of hair has
13:35 the abnormal *f* off of hair
13:36 abnormal *f* off of hair has
13:37 *f* off of hair has stood and
13:37 *f* off of hair has been healed
14:54 the abnormal *f* off of hair
Nu 24:4 While *f* down with the eyes
24:16 *f* down . . . the eyes uncovered
De 22:8 someone *f* might fall from it
23:11 at the *f* of evening he should
Jos 7:10 that you are *f* upon your face
8:24 they kept *f*, all of them
17:5 ten allotments *f* to Manasseh
Jg 9:40 the slain kept *f* in numbers
16:30 *f* upon the axis lords and
1Sa 17:49 he went *f* upon his face to
17:52 Philistines kept *f* on the
31:1 *f* down slain in Mount Gilboa
2Sa 3:29 one *f* by the sword or one
3:34 one *f* before the sons of
14:33 *f* upon his face to the earth
1Ki 18:38 fire of Jehovah came *f* and
20:30 the wall came *f* down upon
1Ch 10:1 kept *f* slain in Mount Gilboa
2Ch 13:17 slain of Israel kept *f*
14:13 Ethiopians continued *f* down
Job 14:18 mountain itself, *f*, will
Ps 40:4 Nor to those *f* away to lies
45:5 under you peoples keep *f*
145:14 support to all who are *f*
Isa 5:30 because of the drops *f* on it
10:4 people keep *f* under those
Jer 6:15 fall among those who are *f*
8:12 fall among those who are *f*
37:13 that you are *f* away
37:14 *f* away to the Chaldeans
48:9 *f* in ruins she will go forth
49:21 At the sound of their *f*
Eze 3:23 and I went *f* upon my face
32:22 those *f* by the sword
32:23 slain, *f* by the sword
32:24 those *f* by the sword, who
32:27 mighty ones, *f* from among
39:23 they kept *f*, all of them
43:3 I went *f* upon my face
44:4 I went *f* on my face
Da 3:7 *f* down and worshiping the
Ho 5:2 in slaughter work those *f* away
Mt 2:11 *f* down, they did obeisance
15:27 crumbs *f* from the table of
21:44 the person *f* upon this stone
Mr 3:10 were *f* upon him to touch him
9:20 after *f* on the ground he
13:25 stars . . . *f* out of heaven
Lu 20:18 Everyone *f* upon that stone
22:44 of blood *f* to the ground
Ac 28:2 of the rain that was *f*

Fallow

Ex 23:11 and you must let it lie *f*
La 3:11 and he makes me to lie *f*

Falls

Ge 49:17 so that its rider *f* backward
De 20:20 siegeworks . . . until it *f*
2Sa 17:9 he *f* upon them at the start
17:12 the dew *f* upon the ground
Job 4:13 When deep sleep *f* upon men

Job 33:15 When deep sleep *f* upon men
Pr 24:17 your enemy *f*, do not rejoice
Ec 4:10 with just the one who *f*
9:12 when it *f* upon them suddenly
11:3 if a tree *f* to the south or if
11:3 where the tree *f* there it
Jer 21:9 *f* away to the Chaldeans who
Eze 30:4 when one *f* slain in Egypt
Am 9:9 not a pebble *f* to the earth
Mt 12:11 *f* into a pit on the sabbath
16:2 evening *f* you are accustomed
17:15 he *f* often into the fire and
21:44 anyone upon whom it *f*, it
Lu 11:17 divided against itself *f*
14:5 son or bull *f* into a well
15:12 property that *f* to my share
20:18 it *f*, it will pulverize
Joh 12:24 of wheat *f* into the ground
Ro 14:4 own master he stands or *f*
1Pe 1:24 and the flower *f* off

False
Ge 21:23 you will not prove *f* to me
Ex 5:9 not pay attention to *f* words
23:7 are to keep far from a *f* word
De 19:18 the witness is a *f* witness
19:18 *f* charge against his brother
1Sa 15:29 will not prove *f*, and He
2Ki 4:28 not lead me to a *f* hope
9:12 It is *f*! Tell us, please
Ps 27:12 *f* witnesses have risen up
31:18 May *f* lips become speechless
89:33 *f* with regard to my
119:29 Remove . . . even the *f* way
119:104 I have hated every *f* path
119:128 Every *f* path I have hated
120:2 deliver my soul from *f* lips
Pr 6:17 a *f* tongue, and hands that
6:19 *f* witness that launches forth
11:18 one is making *f* wages
12:17 but a *f* witness, deception
12:22 *F* lips are something
13:5 *f* word is what the righteous
14:5 *f* witness launches forth mere
19:5 A *f* witness will not be free
19:9 *f* witness will not be free
21:6 treasures by a *f* tongue is an
25:18 fellowman as a *f* witness
26:28 A tongue that is *f* hates the
29:12 paying attention to *f* speech
31:30 Charm may be *f*, and
Isa 9:15 prophet giving *f* instruction
32:7 with *f* sayings
63:8 sons that will not prove *f*
Jer 8:8 *f* stylus of the secretaries
14:14 A *f* vision and divination
23:32 the prophets of *f* dreams
37:14 Jeremiah said: It is *f*!
Ho 10:4 making *f* oaths, concluding a
Zec 8:17 and do not love any *f* oath
Mt 7:15 *f* prophets that come to you
15:19 *f* testimonies, blasphemies
19:18 You must not bear *f* witness
24:11 many *f* prophets will arise
24:24, 24 *f* Christs and *f* prophets
26:59 for *f* witness against Jesus
26:60 although many *f* witnesses
Mr 10:19 Do not bear *f* witness
13:22 *f* Christs . . . will arise and
13:22 and *f* prophets will arise
14:56 *f* witness against him, but
14:57 *f* witness against him
Lu 6:26 did to the *f* prophets
18:20 Do not bear *f* witness, Honor
19:8 extorted . . . by *f* accusation
Ac 5:3 play *f* to the holy spirit and
5:4 You have played *f*, not to men
6:13 *f* witnesses, who said: This
13:6 a *f* prophet, a Jew whose
Ro 1:31 *f* to agreements, having no
11:11 by their *f* step there is
11:12 their *f* step means riches
1Co 15:15 found *f* witnesses of God
2Co 11:13 such men are *f* apostles
11:26 in dangers among *f* brothers
Ga 2:4 But because of the *f* brothers
6:1 *f* step before he is aware of
1Th 2:5 or with a *f* front for
1Ti 1:4 pay attention to *f* stories
1:10 liars, *f* swearers and
4:7 *f* stories which violate what
2Ti 3:5 but proving *f* to its power
4:4 be turned aside to *f* stories
Jas 1:22 yourselves with *f* reasoning
Jas 2:10 makes a *f* step in one point
2Pe 1:16 artfully contrived *f* stories
2:1 came to be *f* prophets among
2:1 also be *f* teachers among you
1Jo 4:1 *f* prophets have gone forth
Jude 4 proving *f* to our only Owner
Re 3:8 did not prove *f* to my name
16:13 the mouth of the *f* prophet
19:20 *f* prophet that performed in
20:10 and the *f* prophet already

Falsehood
De 5:20 a *f* against your fellowman
Job 13:4 you men are smearers of *f*
36:4 words are for a fact no *f*
Ps 7:14 is bound to give birth to *f*
52:3 *F* more than speaking
63:11 mouth of those speaking *f*
109:2 with the tongue of *f*
119:69 have smeared me with *f*
119:118 For their trickiness is *f*
119:163 *F* I have hated, and I do
144:8 is a right hand of *f*
144:11 is a right hand of *f*
Pr 10:18 hatred there are lips of *f*
12:19 tongue of *f* will be only as
17:7 for a noble the lip of *f*
20:17 Bread gained by *f* is
25:14 about a gift in *f*
Isa 28:15 in *f* we have concealed
44:20 a *f* in my right hand
57:4 transgression, the seed of *f*
59:3 Your own lips have spoken *f*
59:13 a muttering of words of *f*
Jer 3:23 on the mountains belong to *f*
5:2 be swearing to sheer *f*
5:31 actually prophesy in *f*
8:8 has worked in sheer *f*
9:3 tongue as their bow in *f*
9:5 their tongue to speak *f*
10:14 his molten image is a *f*
13:25 putting your trust in *f*
14:14 *F* is what the prophets are
16:19 came to possess sheer *f*
20:6 prophesied to them in *f*
23:14 adultery and walking in *f*
23:25 *f* in my own name
23:26 who are prophesying the *f*
27:10 *f* is what they are
27:14 because *f* is what they are
27:16 For *f* is what they are
28:15 this people to trust in a *f*
29:9 For it is in *f* that they are
29:21 are prophesying to you *f*
29:31 to make you trust in *f*
40:16 *f* that you are speaking
43:2 is a *f* that you are speaking
51:17 his molten image is a *f*
Eze 13:22 a righteous one with *f*
Ho 7:1 for they have practiced *f*
Mic 2:11 man, walking by wind and *f*
6:12 inhabitants have spoken *f*
Hab 2:18 and an instructor in *f*
Zec 10:2 their part, have visioned *f*
13:3 *f* is what you have spoken
Eph 4:25 put away *f*, speak truth
Re 14:5 no *f* . . . in their mouths

Falsehoods
Ps 101:7 for anyone speaking *f*, he
Jer 23:32 because of their *f*

Falsely
Ex 20:16 You must not testify *f* as a
Le 6:3 does swear *f* over any of all
6:5 over which he might swear *f*
19:11 you must not deal *f* anyone
Ps 44:17 not acted *f* in your covenant
Jer 3:10 with all her heart, only *f*
6:13 each one is acting *f*
7:9 adultery and swearing *f*
8:10 each one is acting *f*
27:15 prophesying in my name *f*
29:23 speaking *f* in my own name
Zec 5:4 a sworn oath in my name *f*
Mal 3:5 and against those swearing *f*
Lu 3:14 or accuse anybody *f*, but be
Ro 3:8 it is *f* charged to us and just
1Ti 6:20 the *f* called knowledge

Falsifier
Pr 17:4 *f* is giving ear to the tongue

Falsify
Am 8:5 *f* the scales of deception

Fame
Ge 6:4 mighty ones . . . the men of *f*
Nu 14:15 who have heard of your *f*
16:2 sons of Israel . . . men of *f*
Jos 6:27 his *f* came to be in all the
9:9 we have heard of his *f* and
1Ki 4:31 his *f* came to be in all the
1Ch 5:24 men of *f*, heads of the house
12:30 men of *f*, by the house of
14:17 David's *f* began to go out
2Ch 26:8 *f* went even as far as Egypt
26:15 his *f* went out to a great
Es 9:4 his *f* was traveling throughout
Eze 39:13 a matter of *f* in the day

Familiar
Ps 55:13 *f* to me and my acquaintance
139:3 *f* even with all my ways
Pr 16:28 separating those *f* with one
17:9 separating those *f* with one
22:25 may not get *f* with his paths

Families
Ge 8:19 according to their *f* they
10:5 according to their *f*, by their
10:18 *f* of the Canaanite were
10:20 Ham according to their *f*
10:31 Shem according to their *f*
10:32 *f* of the sons of Noah
12:3 all the *f* of the ground will
28:14 the *f* of the ground will
36:40 according to their *f*
Ex 1:21 later presented them with *f*
6:14 These are the *f* of Reuben
6:15 These are the *f* of Simeon
6:17 according to their *f*
6:19 were the *f* of the Levites
6:24 were the *f* of the Korahites
6:25 Levites, according to their *f*
12:21 cattle according to your *f*
Le 25:45 *f* that are with you whom
Nu 1:2 Israel according to their *f*
1:18 their *f* in the house of their
1:20 births according to their *f*
1:22 births according to their *f*
1:24 births according to their *f*
1:26 births according to their *f*
1:28 births according to their *f*
1:30 births according to their *f*
1:32 births according to their *f*
1:34 births according to their *f*
1:36 births according to their *f*
1:38 births according to their *f*
1:40 births according to their *f*
1:42 births according to their *f*
2:34 each one in his *f* with regard
3:15 their fathers by their *f*
3:18 sons of Gershon by their *f*
3:19 sons of Kohath by their *f*
3:20 sons of Merari by their *f*
3:20 *f* of the Levites according to
3:21 the *f* of the Gershonites
3:23 *f* of the Gershonites were
3:27 were the *f* of the Kohathites
3:29 *f* of the sons of Kohath were
3:30 for the *f* of the Kohathites
3:33 These were the *f* of Merari
3:35 for the *f* of Merari was
3:39 by their *f*, all the males
4:2 according to their *f* in the
4:18 *f* of the Kohathites be cut off
4:22 according to their *f*
4:24 *f* of the Gershonites as to
4:28 service of the *f* of the sons
4:29 register them by their *f* in
4:33 *f* of the sons of Merari
4:34 Kohathites by their *f* and by
4:36 registered . . . by their *f*
4:37 *f* of the Kohathites, all those
4:38 Gershon by their *f* and by the
4:40 registered of them by their *f*
4:41 *f* of the sons of Gershon, all
4:42 *f* of the sons of Merari by
4:42 Merari by their *f* by the
4:44 registered of them by their *f*
4:45 the *f* of the sons of Merari
4:46 Levites by their *f* and by the
11:10 people weeping in their *f*
26:7 were the *f* of the Reubenites
26:12 sons of Simeon by their *f*
26:14 were the *f* of the Simeonites
26:15 The sons of Gad by their *f*
26:18 the *f* of the sons of Gad
26:20 sons of Judah . . . by their *f*
26:22 These were the *f* of Judah

Nu 26:23 sons of Issachar by their *f*
26:25 These were the *f* of Issachar
26:26 sons of Zebulun by their *f*
26:27 the *f* of the Zebulunites, of
26:28 sons of Joseph by their *f*
26:34 These were the *f* of Manasseh
26:35 sons of Ephraim by their *f*
26:37 the *f* of the sons of Ephraim
26:37 the sons of Joseph by their *f*
26:38 sons of Benjamin by their *f*
26:41 sons of Benjamin by their *f*
26:42 the sons of Dan by their *f*
26:42, 42 the *f* of Dan by their *f*
26:43 All the *f* of the Shuhamites
26:44 The sons of Asher by their *f*
26:47 the *f* of the sons of Asher
26:48 sons of Naphtali by their *f*
26:50, 50 *f* of Naphtali by their *f*
26:57 of the Levites by their *f*
26:58 were the *f* of the Levites
27:1 the *f* of Manasseh the son of
33:54 by lot according to your *f*
36:1 of the *f* of the sons of Joseph
36:12 *f* of the sons of Manasseh
Jos 7:17 had the *f* of Judah come near
13:15 sons of Reuben by their *f*
13:23 sons of Reuben by their *f*
13:24 sons of Gad by their *f*
13:28 the sons of Gad by their *f*
13:29 sons of Manasseh by their *f*
13:31 sons of Machir by their *f*
15:1 the sons of Judah by their *f*
15:12 sons of Judah by their *f*
15:20 the sons of Judah by their *f*
16:5 sons of Ephraim by their *f*
16:8 sons of Ephraim by their *f*
17:2 over according to their *f*
17:2 males according to their *f*
18:11 sons of Benjamin by their *f*
18:20 sons of Benjamin by their *f*
18:21 sons of Benjamin by their *f*
18:28 sons of Benjamin by their *f*
19:1 sons of Simeon by their *f*
19:8 sons of Simeon by their *f*
19:10 sons of Zebulun by their *f*
19:16 sons of Zebulun by their *f*
19:17 sons of Issachar by their *f*
19:23 sons of Issachar by their *f*
19:24 sons of Asher by their *f*
19:31 sons of Asher by their *f*
19:32 sons of Naphtali by their *f*
19:39 sons of Naphtali by their *f*
19:40 the sons of Dan by their *f*
19:48 the sons of Dan by their *f*
21:4 the *f* of the Kohathites and
21:5 *f* of the tribe of Ephraim
21:6 *f* of the tribe of Issachar
21:7 sons of Merari by their *f*
21:10 of the *f* of the Kohathites
21:20 the *f* of the sons of Kohath
21:26 *f* of the sons of Kohath who
21:27 of the *f* of the Levites
21:33 Gershonites by their *f* were
21:34 *f* of the sons of Merari
21:40 sons of Merari by their *f*
21:40 from the *f* of the Levites
1Sa 9:21 *f* of the tribe of Benjamin
10:21 Benjamin draw near by its *f*
1Ch 2:53 *f* of Kiriath-jearim were
2:55 *f* of the scribes dwelling
4:2 were the *f* of the Zorathites
4:8 *f* of Aharhel the son of Harum
4:21 *f* of the house of the
4:27 none of their *f* had as many
4:38 the chieftains among their *f*
5:7 his brothers by their *f* in
6:19 the *f* of the Levites by their
6:60 cities among their *f*
6:62 Gershom by their *f* they gave
6:63 sons of Merari by their *f*
6:66 *f* of the sons of Kohath came
7:5 of all the *f* of Issachar were
16:28 to Jehovah, O *f* of peoples
Ne 4:13 the people posted by *f* with
Job 31:34 contempt itself of *f* would
Ps 22:27 *f* of the nations will bow
96:7 O you *f* of the peoples
107:41 converts him into *f* just
Jer 1:15 all the *f* of the kingdoms of
2:4 you *f* of the house of Israel
10:25 the *f* who have not called
15:3 commission over them four *f*
25:9 take all the *f* of the north
31:1 God to all the *f* of Israel
Jer 33:24 *f* whom Jehovah has chosen
Eze 20:32 like the *f* of the lands
Am 3:2 out of all the *f* of the ground
Na 3:4 and *f* by her sorceries
Zec 12:14 *f* that are left remaining
14:17 *f* of the earth to Jerusalem
Ac 3:25 the *f* of the earth will be

Family

Ge 10:32 according to their *f* descents
24:38 to my *f* and you must take a
24:40 from my *f* and from the house
24:41 when you get to my *f*, and if
25:13 *f* origins: Ishmael's firstborn
Ex 6:16 according to their *f* descents
6:19 according to their *f* descents
Le 20:5 against that man and his *f*
25:10 return each one to his *f*
25:41 return to his *f*, and he
25:47 the *f* of the alien resident
25:49 one of his *f*, may buy him
Nu 3:21 Of Gershon there were the *f*
3:21 the *f* of the Shimeites
3:27 *f* of the Amramites and the
3:27 and the *f* of the Izharites
3:27 and the *f* of the Hebronites
3:27 and the *f* of the Uzzielites
3:33 *f* of the Mahlites and the
3:33 and the *f* of the Mushites
26:5 the *f* of the Hanochites; of
26:5 Pallu the *f* of the Palluites
26:6 Hezron the *f* of the Hezronites
26:6 Carmi the *f* of the Carmites
26:12 the *f* of the Nemuelites
26:12 Jamin the *f* of the Jaminites
26:12 the *f* of the Jachinites
26:13 the *f* of the Zerahites; of
26:13 Shaul the *f* of the Shaulites
26:15 the *f* of the Zephonites
26:15 Haggi the *f* of the Haggites
26:15 Shuni the *f* of the Shunites
26:16 of Ozni the *f* of the Oznites
26:16 of Eri the *f* of the Erites
26:17 of Arod the *f* of the Arodites
26:17 Areli the *f* of the Arelites
26:20 the *f* of the Shelanites
26:20 Perez the *f* of the Perezites
26:20 Zerah the *f* of the Zerahites
26:21 the *f* of the Hezronites
26:21 Hamul the *f* of the Hamulites
26:23 Of Tola the *f* of the Tolaites
26:23 of Puvah the *f* of the Punites
26:24 the *f* of the Jashubites
26:24 the *f* of the Shimronites
26:26 Sered the *f* of the Seredites
26:26 of Elon the *f* of the Elonites
26:26 the *f* of the Jahleelites
26:29 the *f* of the Machirites
26:29 the *f* of the Gileadites
26:30 Iezer the *f* of the Iezerites
26:30 Helek the *f* of the Helekites
26:31 the *f* of the Asrielites
26:31 the *f* of the Shechemites
26:32 the *f* of the Shemidaites
26:32 the *f* of the Hepherites
26:35 the *f* of the Shuthelahites
26:35 the *f* of the Becherites
26:35 Tahan the *f* of the Tahanites
26:36 Of Eran the *f* of the Eranites
26:38 Of Bela the *f* of the Belaites
26:38 the *f* of the Ashbelites
26:38 the *f* of the Ahiramites
26:39 the *f* of the Shuphamites
26:39 the *f* of the Huphamites
26:40 Of Ard the *f* of the Ardites
26:40 Naaman the *f* of the Naamites
26:42 the *f* of the Shuhamites
26:44 Imnah the *f* of the Imnites
26:44 Ishvi the *f* of the Ishvites
26:44 Beriah the *f* of the Beriites
26:45 Heber the *f* of the Heberites
26:45 the *f* of the Malchielites
26:48 the *f* of the Jahzeelites
26:48 of Guni the *f* of the Gunites
26:49 Jezer the *f* of the Jezerites
26:49 the *f* of the Shillemites
26:57 the *f* of the Gershonites
26:57 the *f* of the Kohathites
26:57 the *f* of the Merarites
26:58 the *f* of the Libnites, the
26:58 the *f* of the Hebronites, the
26:58 the *f* of the Mahlites, the
26:58 the *f* of the Mushites, the
26:58 the *f* of the Korahites
Nu 27:4 away from the midst of his *f*
27:11 is closest to him of his *f*
36:1 the *f* of the sons of Gilead
36:6 to the *f* of the tribe of their
36:8 *f* of the tribe of her father
36:12 of the *f* of their father
De 29:18 a *f* or a tribe whose heart
Jos 6:23 all her *f* relationship they
7:14, 14 will come near, *f* by *f*
7:14 *f* that Jehovah will pick
7:17 picked the *f* of the Zerahites
7:17 *f* of the Zerahites come near
Jg 1:25 and all his *f* they let go
9:1 all the *f* of the house of his
13:2 the *f* of the Danites, and his
17:7 man . . . of the *f* of Judah
18:2 Dan sent five men of their *f*
18:11 *f* of the Danites, departed
18:19 priest to a tribe and *f* in
21:24 his own tribe and his own *f*
Ru 2:1 of the *f* of Elimelech, and his
2:3 who was of the *f* of Elimelech
1Sa 9:21 my *f* the most insignificant
10:21 *f* of the Matrites came to
18:18 my kinsfolk, my father's *f*
20:6 sacrifice there for all the *f*
20:29 we have a *f* sacrifice in
2Sa 14:7 all the *f* have risen up
16:5 man of the *f* of Saul's house
1Ch 1:29 These are their *f* origins
6:54 to the *f* of the Kohathites
6:61 gave from the *f* of the tribe
6:70 *f* of the sons of Kohath that
6:71 from the *f* of the half tribe
Es 9:28 every generation, each *f*, each
Job 32:2 the Buzite of the *f* of Ram
Jer 3:14 and two out of a *f*, and I
8:3 remaining out of this bad *f*
Am 3:1 the whole *f* that I brought up
Mic 2:3 against this *f* a calamity
Zec 12:12 wail, each *f* by itself
12:12 the *f* of the house of David
12:12 the *f* of the house of Nathan
12:13 the *f* of the house of Levi
12:13 the *f* of the Shimeites by
12:14 remaining, each *f* by itself
14:18 *f* of Egypt itself does not
Lu 2:4 of the house and *f* of David
Ac 2:29 *f* head David, that he both
7:8 Jacob of the twelve *f* heads
7:9 *f* heads became jealous of
7:13 *f* stock of Joseph became
Eph 3:15 to whom every *f* in heaven
Php 3:5 out of the *f* stock of Israel
Heb 7:4 Abraham, the *f* head, gave a

Famine

Ge 12:10 *f* arose in the land and
12:10 the *f* was severe in the land
26:1 there arose a *f* in the land
26:1 besides the first *f* that
41:27 to be seven years of *f*
41:30 But seven years of *f* will
41:30 *f* will simply consume the
41:31 as a result of that *f*
41:36 the seven *f* years, which
41:36 may not be cut off by the *f*
41:50 before the year of the *f*
41:54 the *f* started to come, just
41:54 the *f* developed in all the
41:56 the *f* obtained over all the
41:56 the *f* got a strong grip on
41:57 the *f* had a strong grip on
42:5 *f* existed in the land of
42:19 take cereals for the *f* in
42:33 take something for the *f*
43:1 the *f* was severe in the land
45:6 the second year of the *f*
45:11 there are yet five years of *f*
47:4 the *f* is severe in the land
47:13 the *f* was very severe; and
47:13 as a result of the *f*
47:20 the *f* had got a strong grip
Ex 16:3 congregation to death by *f*
Ru 1:1 a *f* arose in the land, and a
2Sa 21:1 a *f* in the days of David for
24:13 seven years of *f* in your
1Ki 8:37 a *f* occurs in the land
18:2 the *f* was severe in Samaria
2Ki 4:38 and there was *f* in the land
6:25 a great *f* arose in Samaria
7:4 when the *f* is in the city
8:1 Jehovah has called for a *f*
25:3 *f* was severe in the city

1Ch 21:12 three years there is . . . a *f*
2Ch 6:28 *f* occurs in the land, in
20:9 or *f*, let us stand before
32:11 to die by *f* and by thirst
Job 5:20 During *f* he will certainly
Ps 33:19 to preserve them alive in *f*
37:19 in the days of *f* they will
105:16 call for a *f* upon the land
Isa 14:30 with *f* I will put your
Jer 5:12 no sword or *f* shall we see
11:22 will die by the *f*
14:12 by *f* and by pestilence I am
14:13 no *f* to happen to you
14:15 no sword or *f* will occur
14:15 By sword and by *f* those
14:16 because of the *f* and the
14:18 the maladies from the *f*
15:2 And whoever is for the *f*
15:2 to the *f*! And whoever is for
16:4 by the sword and by *f* they
18:21 their sons over to the *f*
21:7 the sword and from the *f*
21:9 the *f* and by the pestilence
24:10 the *f* and the pestilence
27:8 the sword and with the *f*
27:13 the *f* and by the pestilence
29:17 the *f* and the pestilence
29:18 *f* and with the pestilence
32:24 *f* and the pestilence
32:36 *f* and by the pestilence
34:17 and to the *f*, and I shall
38:2 the *f* and by the pestilence
38:9 where he is because of the *f*
42:16 *f* at which you are in a
42:17 the *f* and by the pestilence
42:22 by the sword, by the *f* and
44:12 by the *f* they will come
44:12 by the *f* they will die
44:13 with the *f* and with the
44:18 by the *f* we have come to
44:27 *f*, until they cease to be
52:6 *f* also got to be severe in
La 2:19 because of *f* at the head of all
4:9 than those slain by *f*
Eze 5:12 by *f* they will come to their
5:16 injurious arrows of the *f*
5:16 *f* I shall increase upon you
5:17 send upon you people *f* and
6:11 by the sword, by the *f* and
6:12 safeguarded, by the *f* he
7:15 and the *f* are inside
7:15 in the city, *f* and pestilence
12:16 from the sword, from the *f*
14:13 send upon it *f* and cut off
14:21 sword and *f* and injurious
34:29 by *f* in the land, and
36:29 I shall put upon you no *f*
36:30 receive . . . reproach of *f*
Am 8:11 will send a *f* into the land
8:11 a *f*, not for bread, and a
Lu 4:25 great *f* fell upon all the land
15:14 severe *f* occurred throughout
15:17 I am perishing here from *f*
Ac 7:11 *f* came upon the whole of
11:28 great *f* was about to come
Re 18:8 her plagues . . . mourning and *f*

Famished
Ge 41:55 the land of Egypt became *f*
Job 18:12 His vigor becomes *f*, And
Isa 5:13 their glory will be *f* men

Famous
Isa 55:13 for Jehovah something *f*, a

Fanfoot
Le 11:30 the gecko *f* and the large

Fanned
Job 20:26 A fire that no one *f* will

Far
Ge 10:19 from Sidon as *f* as Gerar
10:19 as *f* as Sodom and Gomorrah
10:30 from Mesha as *f* as Sephar
12:6 Abram . . . as *f* as the site
13:10 land of Egypt as *f* as Zoar
25:18 of Egypt, as *f* as Assyria
26:16 you have grown *f* stronger
44:4 had not gone *f* when Joseph
Ex 1:16 he went so *f* as to say: When
8:28 do not make it quite so *f*
23:7 to keep *f* from a false word
33:7 *f* away from the camp; and he
Nu 12:3 Moses was by *f* the meekest
14:45 scattering them as *f* as
15:24 done *f* from the eyes of the
Nu 21:26 as *f* as the Arnon
22:5 as *f* as one can see, and they
22:11 as *f* as the eye can see
De 1:24 as *f* as the torrent valley of
1:44 in Seir as *f* as Hormah
2:23 in settlements as *f* as Gaza
2:36 as *f* as Gilead, there proved
3:8 Arnon as *f* as Mount Hermon
3:10 all Bashan as *f* as Salecah and
3:14 region of Argob as *f* as the
3:16 and as *f* as Jabbok, the
4:49 as *f* as the sea of the Arabah
12:21 should be *f* away from you
13:7 or those *f* away from you
14:24 will be too *f* away for you
20:15 the cities very *f* away from
28:49 a nation *f* away, from the
30:11 nor is it *f* away
34:1 the land, Gilead as *f* as Dan
34:2 Judah as *f* as the western sea
34:3 the palm trees, as *f* as Zoar
Jos 3:1 to come as *f* as the Jordan
3:8 come as *f* as the edge of the
3:15 came as *f* as the Jordan and
3:16 one dam very *f* away at Adam
7:5 the gate as *f* as Shebarim
8:4 not go very *f* away from the
9:22 We are very *f* away from you
10:10 slaying them as *f* as Azekah
10:11 as *f* as Azekah, so that
11:8 as *f* as populous Sidon and
11:17 as *f* as Baal-gad in the
12:2 half of Gilead as *f* as Jabbok
12:3 the Arabah as *f* as the sea of
12:3 as *f* as the sea of the Arabah
12:5 as *f* as the boundary of the
12:7 and as *f* as Mount Halak
13:4 Sidonians, as *f* as Aphek
13:4 as *f* as the border of the
13:5 as *f* as to the entering in of
13:9 Medeba as *f* as Dibon
13:11 Bashan as *f* as Salecah
13:25 of Ammon as *f* as Aroer
13:27 the border as *f* as the
16:3 as *f* as the boundary of
16:5 as *f* as Upper Beth-horon
19:8 as *f* as Baalath-beer, Ramah
19:10 came to be as *f* as Sarid
19:28 Kanah as *f* as populous Sidon
19:29 as *f* as the fortified city
19:33 and Jabneel as *f* as Lakkum
Jg 3:3 as *f* as to the entering in of
4:16 the camp as *f* as Harosheth
7:22 flight as *f* as Beth-shittah
7:22 Zererah, as *f* as the outskirts
7:24 the waters as *f* as Beth-barah
7:24 waters as *f* as Beth-barah and
9:40 as *f* as the entrance of the
11:13 Arnon as *f* as the Jabbok and
11:13 as *f* as the Jordan. And now
11:16 as *f* as the Red Sea and got
11:22 as *f* as the Jabbok and from
11:22 as *f* as the Jordan
11:33 as *f* as Abel-keramim with a
14:5 he got as *f* as the vineyards
15:14 came as *f* as Lehi, and the
17:8 as *f* as the house of Micah
18:2 as *f* as the house of Micah
18:7 *f* off from the Sidonians and
18:13 as *f* as the house of Micah
18:28 for it was *f* away from Sidon
19:10 as *f* as in front of Jebus
19:12 to pass on as *f* as Gibeah
20:45 after them as *f* as Gidom and
1Sa 6:12 as *f* as the boundary of
7:11 as *f* as south of Beth-car
10:3 as *f* as the big tree of Tabor
14:20 came as *f* as the battle
15:5 as *f* as the city of Amalek
15:7 from Havilah as *f* as Shur
17:52 as *f* as the gates of Ekron
17:52 both as *f* as Gath and as
17:52 as Gath and as *f* as Ekron
19:22 as *f* as the great cistern
20:37 attendant came as *f* as the
27:8 from Telam as *f* as Shur and
30:9 *f* as the torrent valley of
2Sa 3:16 after her as *f* as Bahurim
5:25 from Geba to as *f* as Gezer
6:6 as *f* as the threshing floor
7:18 you have brought me thus *f*
16:5 David came as *f* as Bahurim
19:15 come as *f* as the Jordan
20:16 Come near as *f* as here, and
1Ki 7:9 as *f* as the great courtyard
12:30 before the one as *f* as Dan
15:20 as *f* as all the land of
19:8 as *f* as the mountain of the
2Ki 4:22 as *f* as the man of the true
6:2 as *f* as the Jordan and take
7:5 come as *f* as the outskirts
7:8 as *f* as the outskirts of the
7:15 following them as *f* as the
8:7 has come as *f* as here
9:18 messenger came as *f* as to
9:20 He came as *f* as to them
10:25 kept going as *f* as the city
19:3 as *f* as the womb's mouth
23:8 from Geba as *f* as Beer-sheba
1Ch 4:33 cities were as *f* as Baal
5:8 as *f* as Nebo and Baal-meon
5:9 as *f* as where one enters the
5:11 Bashan as *f* as Salecah
5:16 as *f* as their terminations
12:40 as *f* as Issachar and Zebulun
13:5 *f* as the entering of Hamath
13:9 as *f* as the threshing floor
15:29 as *f* as the city of David
17:16 you have brought me thus *f*
21:21 So David came as *f* as Ornan
2Ch 12:4 came as *f* as Jerusalem
14:9 and came as *f* as Mareshah
14:13 pursuing them as *f* as Gerar
26:8 fame went even as *f* as Egypt
33:14 *f* as the Fish Gate, and he
Ne 3:1 as *f* as the Tower of Meah they
3:1 as *f* as the Tower of Hananel
3:8 Jerusalem as *f* as the Broad
3:13 as *f* as the Gate of the
3:15 as *f* as the Stairway that
3:16 repair work as *f* as in front
3:16 as *f* as the pool that had
3:16 as *f* as the House of the
3:20 Buttress as *f* as the entrance
3:21 as *f* as the end of Eliashib's
3:24 as *f* as the Buttress and as
3:24 and as *f* as the corner
3:26 as *f* as in front of the Water
3:27 as *f* as the wall of Ophel
3:31 as *f* as the house of the
3:31 as *f* as the roof chamber of
4:19 *f* apart from one another
5:8 as *f* as it was in our power
12:43 could be heard *f* away
Es 4:2 as *f* as in front of the king's
Job 2:5 touch as *f* as his bone and his
2:12 raised their eyes from *f* off
5:4 sons remain *f* from salvation
11:14 in your hand, put it *f* away
13:21 Put your own hand *f* away
19:13 brothers he has put *f* away
21:16 has kept *f* from me
22:18 counsel . . . kept *f* from me
22:23 keep unrighteousness *f* from
28:4 sunk a shaft *f* from where
28:4 Places forgotten *f* from the
30:10 kept themselves *f* from me
34:10 *F* be it from the true God
36:3 carry my knowledge from *f*
36:25 keeps looking from *f* off
38:11 This *f* you may come, and
39:25 *f* off it smells the battle
39:29 *F* into the distance its eyes
Ps 22:1 Why are you *f* from saving me
22:11 Do not keep *f* off from me
22:19 Jehovah, O do not keep *f* off
35:22 do not keep yourself *f* from
38:21 do not keep *f* away from me
49:19 comes only as *f* as the
55:7 I would go *f* away in flight
56:*super* among those *f* away
60:9 lead me as *f* as Edom
65:5 and those *f* away on the sea
71:12 do not keep *f* away from me
80:11 boughs as *f* as the sea
88:8 my acquaintances *f* away from
88:18 *f* away from me friend and
103:12 *f* off as the sunrise is
103:12 *f* off from us he has put
108:10 lead me as *f* as Edom
109:17 it became *f* away from him
118:27 *f* as the horns of the altar
119:150 *f* away from your own law
119:155 Salvation is *f* away from
139:2 my thought from *f* off
Pr 4:24 lips put *f* away from yourself
5:8 way *f* off from alongside her
15:29 Jehovah is *f* away from the

Pr 22:5 guarding his soul keeps *f*
22:15 will remove it *f* from him
27:10 than a brother that is *f*
30:8 lying word put *f* away from
31:10 Her value is *f* more than
31:14 From *f* away she brings in
Ec 7:23 But it was *f* from me
7:24 What has come to be is *f* off
Isa 5:26 to a great nation *f* away
6:12 earthling men *f* away
10:3 when it comes from *f* away
13:5 coming from the land *f* away
15:4 *f* as Jahaz their voice has
15:5 *f* along as Zoar and
16:8 *f* as Jazer they had reached
17:13 it must flee *f* away and be
22:3 *F* off they had run away
23:7 *f* away to reside as an alien
29:13 heart itself *f* away from
30:27 Jehovah is coming from *f*
33:13 you men who are *f* away
33:17 will see a land *f* away
37:3 as *f* as the womb's mouth
43:6 Bring my sons from *f* off
46:12 *f* away from righteousness
46:13 It is not *f* away, and my
49:1 you national groups *f* away
49:12 come even from *f* away
49:19 you down have been *f* away
54:14 be *f* away from oppression
57:9 sending your envoys *f* off, so
57:19 to the one that is *f* away
59:9 has come to be *f* away from
59:11 has stayed *f* away from us
59:14 kept standing simply *f* off
60:4 From *f* away your own sons
60:9 bring your sons from *f* away
Jer 2:5 have become *f* off from me
4:16 coming from a land *f* away
5:15 a nation from *f* away
6:20 cane from the land *f* away
8:19 people from a land *f* away
12:2 *f* away from their kidneys
23:23 and not a God *f* away
25:26 who are near and *f* away
27:10 taken *f* away from off your
30:10 I am saving you from *f* off
31:3 *f* away Jehovah himself
31:10 among the islands *f* away
31:40 *f* as the torrent valley of
43:7 gradually as *f* as Tahpanhes
46:27 am saving you from *f* away
48:24 those *f* away and those near
49:30 Flee, take flight *f* away
51:50 From *f* away remember
La 1:16 comforter has become *f* away
Eze 6:12 *f* away, by the pestilence he
8:6 *f* off from my sanctuary
11:15 Get *f* away from Jehovah
11:16 I have put them *f* away
12:27 respecting times *f* off he
22:5 lands nearby and those *f*
23:40 men coming from *f* away
41:17 and as *f* as the inner house
43:9 of their kings *f* from me
44:10 Levites who got *f* away
48:28 as *f* as the Great Sea
Da 9:7 *f* away in all the lands to
Joe 2:20 put *f* away from upon you
3:6 *f* from their own territory
3:8 to a nation *f* away
Am 9:10 come near or reach as *f* as us
Ob 7 As *f* as the boundary they
20 possessed as *f* as Zarephath
Mic 1:9 for it has come as *f* as Judah
1:9 the plague as *f* as the gate
1:9 my people, as *f* as Jerusalem
1:15 As *f* as Adullam the glory of
4:3 mighty nations *f* away
4:7 *f* off a mighty nation
4:8 as *f* as to you it will come
4:10 to come as *f* as to Babylon
5:4 as *f* as the ends of the earth
7:11 the decree will be *f* away
Hab 1:8 from *f* away its own steeds
Zec 6:15 those who are *f* away will
Mt 11:9 and *f* more than a prophet
14:15 hour is already *f* advanced
15:8 heart is *f* removed from me
26:58 as *f* as the courtyard of the
Mr 4:33 *f* as they were able to listen
7:6 hearts are *f* removed from me
8:3 some of them are from *f* away
9:3 *f* whiter than any clothes
12:33 worth *f* more than all the
12:34 are not *f* from the kingdom
14:54 as *f* as in the courtyard of
Lu 4:42 came out as *f* as he was, and
7:6 he was not *f* from the house
7:26 and *f* more than a prophet
14:32 while that one is yet *f* away
22:51 Let it go as *f* as this
24:50 led them out as *f* as Bethany
Ac 9:38 to come on as *f* as us
11:19 as *f* as Phoenicia and Cyprus
11:22 out Barnabas as *f* as Antioch
13:6 whole island as *f* as Paphos
17:14 off to go as *f* as the sea
17:15 brought him as *f* as Athens
17:27 he is not *f* off from each
21:5 as *f* as outside the city
22:21 send you out to nations *f* off
26:11 so *f* as to persecuting them
28:15 as *f* as the Marketplace of
Ro 7:13 might become *f* more sinful
12:18 as *f* as it depends upon you
15:19 a circuit as *f* as Illyricum
1Co 14:36 as *f* as you that it reached
2Co 10:13 it reach even as *f* as you
10:14 to come even as *f* as you in
Ga 1:14 was *f* more zealous for the
Eph 1:21 *f* above every government and
2:13 you who were once *f* off have
2:17 peace to you, the ones *f* off
4:10 *f* above all the heavens
Php 1:23 this, to be sure, is *f* better
2:8 became obedient as *f* as death
1Th 2:17 *f* more than is usual to see
Heb 12:4 yet resisted as *f* as blood

Faraway
Isa 66:19 the *f* islands, who have

Fare
Pr 11:15 positively *f* badly because
13:20 stupid ones will *f* badly
Jon 1:3 he paid its *f* and went down

Fared
Ge 30:29 your herd has *f* with me

Farewell
Ac 20:1 and bidden them *f*, he went

Faring
Mt 4:24 all those *f* badly, distressed
8:16 cured all who were *f* badly

Farm
Am 5:11 *f* rent from someone lowly

Farmer
Ge 9:20 Noah started off as a *f* and
Jer 51:23 dash *f* and his span of
Am 5:16 call a *f* to mourning, and to
2Ti 2:6 hardworking *f* must be the
Jas 5:7 the *f* keeps waiting for the

Farmers
2Ch 26:10 *f* and vinedressers in the
Isa 61:5 foreigners will be your *f*
Jer 14:4 the *f* have become ashamed
31:24 *f* and those who have set
Joe 1:11 *F* have felt shame

Farther
1Sa 10:3 pass on from there still *f*
20:22 arrows are *f* away from you
20:37 the arrow *f* away from you
2Ki 3:7 He went *f* and now sent to
Job 38:11 you may come, and no *f*
Pr 19:7 *f* have his personal friends
Mr 1:19 a little *f* he saw James the
Lu 24:28 as if he was journeying on *f*

Farthest
1Sa 24:3 parts of the cave *f* back
Isa 62:11 to the *f* part of the earth
Jer 25:31 to the *f* part of the earth
50:26 to her from the *f* part

Fashion
Php 2:8 found himself in *f* as a man

Fashioned
Ro 12:2 *f* after this system of things
1Pe 1:14 quit being *f* according to the

Fashioner
Job 36:3 to my *F* I shall ascribe

Fast
Le 27:19 and it must stand *f* as his
Jg 4:21 he was *f* asleep and weary
1Sa 7:6 and kept a *f* on that day
13:21 and for fixing *f* the oxgoad
2Sa 1:12 *f* until the evening over Saul
12:16 David went on a strict *f*
12:22 I did *f* and I kept weeping
18:9 got caught *f* in the big tree
1Ki 2:28 *f* to the horns of the altar
21:9 Proclaim a *f*, and have
21:12 a *f* and had Naboth sit at
21:27 went on a *f* and kept lying
2Ch 20:3 proclaimed a *f* for all Judah
Ezr 8:21 proclaimed a *f* there at the
Es 1:6 held *f* in ropes of fine fabric
4:16 *f* in my behalf and neither
4:16 I shall *f* likewise, and upon
Job 2:3 he is holding *f* his integrity
2:9 yet holding *f* your integrity
17:9 keeps holding *f* to his way
38:31 tie *f* the bonds of the
39:10 bind a wild bull *f* with its
Ps 16:5 You are holding *f* my lot
63:8 your right hand keeps *f* hold
76:6 horse have fallen *f* asleep
Pr 3:18 those keeping *f* hold of it
4:4 heart keep *f* hold of my words
10:5 acting shamefully is *f* asleep
Isa 41:10 keep *f* hold of you with my
42:1 on whom I keep *f* hold
58:3 For what reason did we *f* and
58:4 and struggle you would *f*
58:5 the *f* that I choose become
58:5 call a *f* and a day acceptable
58:6 this the *f* that I choose
Jer 14:12 When they *f*, I am not
36:6 in the day of *f*; and also
36:9 a *f* before Jehovah
Da 8:18 *f* asleep on my face on the
10:9 *f* asleep upon my face, with
Jon 1:5 to lie down and go *f* asleep
3:5 a *f* and to put on sackcloth
Zec 7:5 did you really *f* to me, even
8:19 The *f* of the fourth month
8:19 the *f* of the fifth month
8:19 the *f* of the seventh month
8:19 the *f* of the tenth month
Mt 9:14 but your disciples do not *f*
9:15 and then they will *f*
Mr 2:19 of the bridegroom cannot *f*
2:19 with them they cannot *f*
2:20 then they will *f* in that day
5:3 nobody was able to bind him *f*
7:3 holding *f* the tradition of
7:4 traditions . . . to hold *f*
7:8 hold *f* the tradition of men
Lu 5:33 disciples of John *f* frequently
5:34 friends of the bridegroom *f*
5:35 they will *f* in those days
8:29 a long time it had held him *f*
18:12 I *f* twice a week, I give
Joh 8:44 did not stand *f* in the truth
Ac 2:24 continue to be held *f* by it
16:24 their feet *f* in the stocks
27:9 *f* of atonement day had
Ro 7:6 by which we were being held *f*
1Co 11:2 holding *f* the traditions just
15:2 if you are holding it *f*
Ga 5:1 stand *f*, and do not let
Col 2:19 is not holding *f* to the head
1Th 5:21 hold *f* to what is fine
Heb 3:6 if we make *f* our hold on our
3:14 if we make *f* our hold on the
10:23 Let us hold *f* the public
Re 2:13 keep on holding *f* my name
2:14 holding *f* the teaching of
2:15 holding *f* the teaching of the
2:25 hold *f* what you have until I
3:11 holding *f* what you have, that

Fasted
Jg 20:26 and *f* on that day until the
2Sa 12:21 you *f* and kept weeping
Ezr 8:23 we *f* and made request of our
Zec 7:5 you *f* and there was a wailing
Mt 4:2 *f* forty days and forty nights
Ac 13:3 they *f* and prayed and laid

Fasten
Ex 28:37 must *f* it with a blue string
Jer 10:4 they *f* them down, that none
1Jo 5:18 does not *f* his hold on him

Fastened
1Sa 31:10 corpse they *f* on the wall
1Ch 10:10 skull they *f* to the house of
Isa 41:7 one *f* it with nails that it
Ac 2:23 you *f* to a stake by the hand
28:3 and *f* itself on his hand

Fastenings
Ex 27:17 round about have *f* of silver

Fasting
1Sa 31:13 they went *f* for seven days
2Sa 12:23 why is it I am *f*? Am I
1Ch 10:12 they went *f* for seven days
Ne 1:4 continually *f* and praying
9:1 with *f* and with sackcloth and
Es 4:3 and *f* and weeping and wailing
Ps 35:13 With *f* I afflicted my soul
69:10 weep with the *f* of my soul
109:24 have swayed from *f*
Isa 58:3 in the very day of your *f*
58:4 keep *f* as in the day for
Da 6:18 and spent the night *f*, and
9:3 with *f* and sackcloth and ashes
Joe 1:14 Sanctify a time of *f*
2:12 with *f* and with weeping and
2:15 Sanctify a time of *f*
Mt 6:16 *f*, stop becoming sad-faced
6:16 may appear to men to be *f*
6:17 when *f*, grease your head
6:18 appear to be *f*, not to men
9:14 Pharisees practice *f* but your
15:32 to send them away *f*
Mr 2:18 and the Pharisees practiced *f*
2:18 the Pharisees practice *f*, but
2:18 disciples do not practice *f*
8:3 off to their homes *f*, they
Ac 13:2 ministering to Jehovah and *f*

Fastings
Lu 2:37 with *f* and supplications
Ac 14:23 offering prayer with *f*, they

Fasts
Es 9:31 matters of the *f* and their

Fat
Ge 41:4 beautiful in appearance and *f*
41:5 on one stalk, *f* and good
41:7 to swallow up the seven *f* and
41:20 the first seven *f* cows
45:18 eat the *f* part of the land
49:20 Asher his bread will be *f*
Ex 23:18 *f* of my festival should not
29:13 *f* that covers the intestines
29:13 two kidneys and the *f* that is
29:22, 22 the *f* and the *f* tail and
29:22 *f* that covers the intestines
29:22 kidneys and the *f* that is
Le 3:3 *f* that covers the intestines
3:3 *f* that is over the intestines
3:4 two kidneys and the *f* that is
3:9 present its *f* as an offering
3:9 *f* that covers the intestines
3:9 *f* that is upon the intestines
3:10 the *f* that is upon them
3:14 *f* that covers the intestines
3:14 *f* that is upon the intestines
3:15 the two kidneys and the *f* that
3:16 All the *f* belongs to Jehovah
3:17 not eat any *f* or any blood
4:8 the *f* of the bull of the sin
4:8 the *f* that covers over the
4:8 *f* that is over the intestines
4:9 two kidneys and the *f* that is
4:19 lift up all its *f* from it
4:26 its *f* smoke on the altar like
4:26 like the *f* of the communion
4:31 And he will remove all its *f*
4:31 just as the *f* was removed
4:35 remove all its *f* the same as
4:35 as the *f* of the young ram of
7:3 As for all its *f*, he will
7:3 *f* that covers the intestines
7:4 two kidneys and the *f* that is
7:23 not eat any *f* of a bull or a
7:24 *f* of a body already dead
7:24 *f* of an animal torn to pieces
7:25 anyone eating *f* from the
7:30 the *f* upon the breast
7:31 the *f* smoke upon the altar
7:33 sacrifices and the *f*, the
8:16 all the *f* that was upon the
8:16 the two kidneys and their *f*
8:25, 25 the *f* and the *f* tail and
8:25 all the *f* that was upon the
8:25 the two kidneys and their *f*
9:10 the *f* and the kidneys and the
9:19 and the *f* tail of the ram
9:19 the *f* covering and the kidneys
16:25 *f* of the sin offering smoke
17:6 *f* smoke as a restful odor to
Nu 13:20 whether it is *f* or lean
18:17 *f* you should make smoke
De 31:20 and be satisfied and grow *f*
32:14 Together with the *f* of rams
32:14 with the kidney *f* of wheat
32:15 Jeshurun began to grow *f*
32:15 grown *f*, you have become
32:38 the *f* of their sacrifices
Jg 3:17 Now Eglon was a very *f* man
3:22 so that the *f* closed in over
1Sa 2:15 they could make the *f* smoke
2:16 to make the *f* smoke first
15:9 and the herd and the *f* ones
15:22 than the *f* of rams
2Sa 1:22 from the *f* of mighty ones
1Ki 4:23 ten *f* cattle and twenty
8:64 *f* pieces of the communion
8:64 *f* pieces of the communion
1Ch 4:40 found *f* and good pasturage
2Ch 7:7 *f* pieces of the communion
7:7 offering and the *f* pieces
29:35 *f* pieces of the communion
35:14 the *f* pieces until night
Ne 9:25 and a *f* soil and taking in
9:25 to grow *f* and to luxuriate in
9:35 the broad and *f* land that you
Job 15:27 he puts on *f* upon his loins
21:24 thighs . . . become full of *f*
Ps 17:10 with their own *f*
20:3 burnt offering as being *f*
22:29 the *f* ones of the earth shall
73:4 And their paunch is *f*
81:16 off the *f* of the wheat
92:14 *F* and fresh they will
119:70 unfeeling just like *f*
147:14 *f* of the wheat he keeps
Pr 11:25 soul will itself be made *f*
13:4 diligent ones will be made *f*
15:30 good makes the bones *f*
28:25 upon Jehovah will be made *f*
Isa 1:11 the *f* of well-fed animals
10:16 upon his *f* ones a wasting
30:23 must become *f* and oily
34:6 made greasy with the *f*
34:6 *f* of the kidneys of rams
34:7 be made greasy with the *f*
43:24 the *f* of your sacrifices
Jer 5:28 They have grown *f*
Eze 34:3 The *f* is what you eat, and
34:14 on a *f* pasturage they will
34:16 *f* one and the strong one I
39:19 to eat *f* to satisfaction
44:7 my bread, *f* and blood
44:15 present to me *f* and the
Zec 11:16 the *f* one he will eat, and

Fatal
Ge 42:4 a *f* accident may befall him
42:38 If a *f* accident should befall
44:29 a *f* accident were to befall
Ex 21:22 but no *f* accident occurs, he
21:23 if a *f* accident should occur
Le 24:18 *f* striker of the soul of a
24:21 *f* striker of a beast should
24:21 *f* striker of a man should be
Nu 35:30 Every *f* striker of a soul

Fatally
Ge 34:27 attacked the *f* wounded men
37:21 Let us not strike his soul *f*
Le 24:17 strikes any soul . . . *f*
Nu 25:14 *f* struck Israelite man who
25:14 who was *f* struck with the
25:15 Midianite woman *f* struck
25:18 *f* struck in the day of the
35:11 flee there who *f* strikes a
35:15 flee there that *f* strikes a
De 19:6 may indeed strike his soul *f*
19:11 and struck his soul *f* and he
21:1 known who struck him *f*
27:24 *f* strikes his fellowman
27:25 a bribe to strike a soul *f*
Jos 20:3 manslayer who *f* strikes a
20:5 he struck his fellowman *f*
20:9 who *f* strikes a soul
1Sa 17:52 and the *f* wounded of the
Eze 26:15 *f* wounded one groans

Fat-fleshed
Ge 41:2 seven cows beautiful . . . *f*
41:18 seven cows *f* and beautiful

Father
Ge 2:24 a man will leave his *f* and
4:18 Irad became *f* to Mehujael
4:18 Mehujael became *f* to
4:18 Methushael became *f* to
Ge 5:3 he became *f* to a son in his
5:4 Adam . . . became *f* to sons
5:6 Seth . . . became *f* to Enosh
5:7 Seth . . . became *f* to sons and
5:9 Enosh . . . became *f* to Kenan
5:10 Enosh . . . became *f* to sons
5:12 Kenan . . . *f* to Mahalalel
5:13 Kenan . . . became *f* to sons
5:15 Then he became *f* to Jared
5:16 *f* to sons and daughters
5:18 Jared . . . became *f* to Enoch
5:19 Jared . . . became *f* to sons
5:21 he became *f* to Methuselah
5:22 Enoch . . . became *f* to sons
5:25 Then he became *f* to Lamech
5:26 Methuselah . . . he became *f*
5:28 Lamech . . . became *f* to a son
5:30 Lamech . . . became *f* to sons
5:32 Noah became *f* to Shem, Ham
6:10 In time Noah became *f* to
9:18 Later Ham was the *f* of Canaan
9:22 Ham the *f* of Canaan saw his
10:8 And Cush became *f* to Nimrod
10:13 Mizraim became *f* to Ludim
10:15 Canaan became *f* to Sidon
10:24 Arpachshad . . . *f* to Shelah
10:24 Shelah became *f* to Eber
10:26 Joktan became *f* to Almodad
11:10 Shem . . . *f* to Arpachshad
11:11 Shem . . . became *f* to sons
11:12 Arpachshad . . . *f* to Shelah
11:13 Arpachshad . . . *f* to sons
11:14 Shelah . . . became *f* to Eber
11:15 Shelah . . . became *f* to sons
11:16 Eber . . . became *f* to Peleg
11:17 Eber . . . became *f* to sons
11:18 Peleg . . . became *f* to Reu
11:19 Peleg . . . became *f* to sons
11:20 Reu . . . became *f* to Serug
11:21 Reu . . . became *f* to sons and
11:22 Serug . . . became *f* to Nahor
11:23 Serug . . . *f* to sons and
11:24 Nahor . . . became *f* to Terah
11:25 Nahor . . . *f* to sons and
11:26 Terah . . . became *f* to Abram
11:27 Terah became *f* to Abram
11:27 and Haran became *f* to Lot
11:28 Terah his *f* in the land of
11:29 Haran, the *f* of Milcah and
11:29 Haran . . . *f* of Iscah
12:1 from the house of your *f* to
17:4 a *f* of a crowd of nations
17:5 a *f* of a crowd of nations
19:31 Our *f* is old and there is not
19:32 give our *f* wine to drink and
19:32 offspring from our *f*
19:33 giving their *f* wine to drink
19:33 lay down with her *f*, but he
19:34 I lay down with my *f* last
19:34 offspring from our *f*
19:35 gave their *f* wine to drink
19:36 became pregnant from their *f*
19:37 He is the *f* of Moab, to this
19:38 the *f* of the sons of Ammon
20:12 daughter of my *f*, only not
20:13 from the house of my *f*
22:7, 7 to Abraham his *f*: My *f*!
22:21 and Kemuel the *f* of Aram
22:23 And Bethuel became the *f* of
24:23 room at the house of your *f*
24:38 go to the house of my *f* and
24:40 and from the house of my *f*
25:3 Jokshan became *f* to Sheba
25:19 Abraham became *f* to Isaac
26:3 I swore to Abraham your *f*
26:15 the servants of his *f* had dug
26:15 in the days of Abraham his *f*
26:18 in the days of Abraham his *f*
26:18 names that his *f* had called
26:24 the God of Abraham your *f*
27:6 your *f* speaking to Esau your
27:9 a tasty dish for your *f*
27:10 must bring it to your *f*
27:12 What if my *f* feels me?
27:14 dish such as his *f* was fond
27:18 he went on in to his *f* and
27:18 and said: My *f*! to which he
27:19 went on to say to his *f*
27:22 came near to Isaac his *f*
27:26 Isaac his *f* said to him
27:30 the face of Isaac his *f*
27:31 brought it to his *f* and said
27:31 and said to his *f*
27:31 Let my *f* get up and eat some

Ge 27:32 Isaac his *f* said to him
27:34 say to his *f*: Bless me, even
27:34 Bless me, even me too, my *f*
27:38 Then Esau said to his *f*
27:38 just one blessing . . . my *f*
27:38 Bless me, even me too, my *f*
27:39 in answer Isaac his *f* said
27:41 his *f* had blessed him
27:41 period of mourning for my *f*
28:2 the house of Bethuel the *f*
28:7 Jacob was obeying his *f* and
28:8 in the eyes of Isaac his *f*
28:13 the God of Abraham your *f*
28:21 to the house of my *f*
29:9 sheep that belonged to her *f*
29:12 he was the brother of her *f*
29:12 running and telling her *f*
31:1 belonged to our *f*; and from
31:1 from what belonged to our *f*
31:5 seeing the face of your *f*
31:5 God of my *f* has proved to be
31:6 I have served your *f*
31:7 your *f* has trifled with me
31:9 herd of your *f* away and
31:14 in the house of our *f*
31:16 away from our *f* are ours
31:18 to go to Isaac his *f* to the
31:19 that belonged to her *f*
31:29 God of your *f* talked to me
31:30 house of your *f*, why, though
31:35 said to her *f*: Do not let
31:42 the God of my *f*, the God of
31:53 the god of their *f*. But Jacob
31:53 swore by the Dread of his *f*
32:9 O God of my *f* Abraham and God
32:9 God of my *f* Isaac, O Jehovah
33:19 Hamor the *f* of Shechem, for
34:4 Shechem said to Hamor his *f*
34:6 Hamor, Shechem's *f*, went out
34:11 Then Shechem said to her *f*
34:13 Shechem and Hamor his *f*
34:19 of the whole house of his *f*
35:18 his *f* called him Benjamin
35:27 Jacob came to Isaac his *f*
36:9 history of Esau the *f* of Edom
36:24 the asses for Zibeon his *f*
36:43 This is Esau the *f* of Edom
37:1 the alien residences of his *f*
37:2 the wives of his *f*. So Joseph
37:2 report about them to their *f*
37:4 their *f* loved him more than
37:10 he related it to his *f* as
37:10 his *f* began to rebuke him
37:11 his *f* observed the saying
37:12 feed the flock of their *f*
37:22 to return him to his *f*
37:32 had it brought to their *f*
37:35 *f* continued weeping for him
38:11 in the house of your *f* until
41:51 and all the house of my *f*
42:13 the youngest is with our *f*
42:29 they came to Jacob their *f*
42:32 twelve . . . sons of our *f*
42:32 our *f* in the land of Canaan
42:35 they as well as their *f* got
42:36 Jacob their *f* exclaimed to
42:37 Reuben said to his *f*: My own
43:2 their *f* proceeded to say to
43:7 Is your *f* yet alive? Do you
43:8 Judah said to Israel his *f*
43:11 Israel their *f* said to them
43:23 the God of your *f* gave you
43:27 Is your *f*, the aged man of
43:28 our *f* is getting along well
44:17 go up in peace to your *f*
44:19 Do you have a *f* or a brother?
44:20 We do have an aged *f* and a
44:20 and his *f* does love him
44:22 not able to leave his *f*
44:22 If he did leave his *f*, he
44:24 went up to your slave my *f*
44:25 our *f* said, Return, buy a
44:27 your slave my *f* said to us
44:30 come to your slave my *f*
44:31 hairs of your slave our *f*
44:32 when away from his *f*
44:32 sinned against my *f* forever
44:34 how can I go up to my *f*
44:34 that will find out my *f*
45:3 Is my *f* still alive?
45:8 appoint me a *f* to Pharaoh
45:9 Go up quickly to my *f*, and
45:13 tell my *f* about all my glory
45:13 must hurry and bring my *f*

Ge 45:18 your *f* and your households
45:19 you must lift your *f* on one
45:23 to his *f* he sent as follows
45:23 sustenance for his *f* for the
45:25 came . . . to Jacob their *f*
45:27 the spirit of Jacob their *f*
46:1 to the God of his *f* Isaac
46:3 God, the God of your *f*
46:5 transporting Jacob their *f*
46:29 meet Israel his *f* at Goshen
47:1 My *f* and my brothers and
47:5 Your *f* and your brothers have
47:6 Have your *f* and your brothers
47:7 Joseph brought in Jacob his *f*
47:11 Joseph had his *f* and his
47:12 Joseph kept supplying his *f*
47:12 the entire household of his *f*
48:1 Look, your *f* is becoming weak
48:6 you shall become *f* after them
48:9 Joseph said to his *f*: They are
48:17 Joseph saw that his *f* kept
48:18 Joseph said to his *f*: Not so
48:18 Not so, my *f*, because this
48:19 his *f* kept refusing and said
49:2 yes, listen to Israel your *f*
49:8 sons of your *f* will prostrate
49:25 He is from the God of your *f*
49:26 The blessings of your *f* will
49:28 this is what their *f* spoke
50:1 fell upon the face of his *f*
50:2 physicians, to embalm his *f*
50:5 My *f* made me swear, saying
50:5 let me go up and bury my *f*
50:6 Go up and bury your *f* just as
50:7 Joseph went up to bury his *f*
50:8 and the household of his *f*
50:10 mourning rites for his *f*
50:14 with him to bury his *f*
50:14 after he had buried his *f*
50:15 saw that their *f* was dead
50:16 Your *f* gave the command
50:22 he and the house of his *f*
Ex 2:18 came home to Reuel their *f*
3:6 I am the God of your *f*, the
18:4 the God of my *f* is my helper
20:12 Honor your *f* and your mother
21:15 one who strikes his *f* and
21:17 calls down evil upon his *f*
22:17 *f* flatly refuses to give her
40:15 just as you anointed their *f*
Le 16:32 priest as successor of his *f*
18:7 nakedness of your *f* and the
18:9 daughter of your *f* or the
18:11 offspring of your *f*, she
18:12 the blood relation of your *f*
19:3 each one his mother and his *f*
20:9 evil upon his *f* and his
20:9 *f* and his mother upon whom
20:11 bare the nakedness of his *f*
20:17 the daughter of his *f* or
21:2 *f* and for his son and for his
21:9 her *f* that she is profaning
21:11 *f* and his mother he may not
Nu 3:4 along with Aaron their *f*
6:7 even for his *f* or his mother
12:14 Were her *f* to spit directly
18:1 the house of your *f* with you
18:2 of Levi, the clan of your *f*
26:29 Machir became *f* to Gilead
26:58 Kohath became *f* to Amram
27:3 *f* has died in the wilderness
27:4 name of our *f* be taken away
27:11 if his *f* has no brothers, you
30:3 house of her *f* in her youth
30:4 her *f* actually hears her vow
30:4 her *f* does keep silent toward
30:5 if her *f* has forbidden her on
30:5 because her *f* forbade her
30:16 between a *f* and his daughter
30:16 youth in the house of her *f*
36:8 family of the tribe of her *f*
36:12 of the family of their *f*
De 4:25 *f* to sons and grandsons and
5:16 Honor your *f* and your mother
21:13 weep for her *f* and her
21:18 the voice of his *f* or the
21:19 his *f* and his mother must
22:15 the *f* of the girl and her
22:16 the girl's *f* must say to the
22:19 give them to the girl's *f*
22:21 in the house of her *f*. So you
22:29 give the girl's *f* fifty
22:30 uncover the skirt of his *f*
26:5 My *f* was a perishing Syrian

De 27:16 treats his *f* or his mother
27:20 uncovered the skirt of his *f*
27:22 the daughter of his *f* or the
32:6 your *F* who has produced you
32:7 *f*, and he can tell you; Your
33:9 said to his *f* and his mother
Jos 2:12 toward the household of my *f*
2:13 alive my *f* and my mother and
2:18 your *f* and your mother and
2:18 all the household of your *f*
6:23 Rahab and her *f* and her
6:25 household of her *f* and all
15:13 Arba being the *f* of Anak
15:18 ask a field from her *f*
17:1 Machir . . . the *f* of Gilead
17:4 of the brothers of their *f*
21:11 Arba being the *f* of Anak
24:2 Terah the *f* of Abraham and
24:2 Terah . . . the *f* of Nahor
24:32 Hamor, Shechem's *f*, for a
Jg 1:14 to ask a field from her *f*
6:25 bull that belongs to your *f*
6:27 feared the household of his *f*
8:32 burial place of Joash his *f* in
9:1 the house of his mother's *f*
9:5 house of his *f* at Ophrah and
9:17 my *f* fought for you and went
9:18 household of my *f* today that
9:28 men of Hamor, Shechem's *f*
9:56 that he had done to his *f*
11:1 came to be the *f* of Jephthah
11:2 in the household of our *f*, for
11:36 My *f*, if you have opened
11:37 to her *f*: Let this thing be
11:39 she made her return to her *f*
14:2 told his *f* and his mother and
14:3 his *f* and his mother said to
14:3 Samson said to his *f*: Get
14:4 *f* and his mother, they did
14:5 with his *f* and his mother to
14:6 not tell his *f* or his mother
14:9 rejoined his *f* and his mother
14:10 his *f* continued on his way
14:15 house of your *f* with fire
14:16 to my own *f* and my own
15:1 her *f* did not allow him to go
15:2 her *f* said: I really said to
15:6 and burned her and her *f* with
16:31 household of his *f* came
16:31 burial place of Manoah his *f*
17:10 serve as a *f* and priest for
18:19 become a *f* and a priest for
18:29 Dan by the name of their *f*
19:2 house of her *f* at Bethlehem
19:3 the *f* of the young woman got
19:4 young woman's *f*, took hold of
19:5 *f* of the young woman said to
19:6 *f* of the young woman said to
19:8 the *f* of the young woman then
19:9 young woman's *f*, said to him
Ru 2:11 leave your *f* and your mother
4:17 He is the *f* of Jesse, David's
4:17 of Jesse, David's *f*
4:18 Perez became *f* to Hezron
4:19 and Hezron became *f* to Ram
4:19 Ram became *f* to Amminadab
4:20 Amminadab became *f* to
4:20 Nahshon became *f* to Salmon
4:21 and Salmon became *f* to Boaz
4:21 and Boaz became *f* to Obed
4:22 and Obed became *f* to Jesse
4:22 and Jesse became *f* to David
1Sa 2:25 to the voice of their *f*
9:3 to Kish the *f* of Saul
9:5 my *f* may not quit attending
9:20 to the whole house of your *f*
10:2 now your *f* has given up the
10:12 said: But who is their *f*?
10:14 brother of Saul's *f* said to
14:1 to his *f* he did not tell it
14:27 his *f* put the people under
14:28 Your *f* solemnly put the
14:29 My *f* has brought ostracism
14:51 And Kish was the *f* of Saul
14:51 Ner the *f* of Abner was the
17:15 to tend the sheep of his *f*
17:25 house of his *f* he will set
17:34 became a shepherd of his *f*
19:2 Saul my *f* is seeking to have
19:3 stand at the side of my *f* in
19:3 speak for you to my *f*, and
19:4 Saul his *f* and said to him
20:1 I committed before your *f*
20:2 *f* will not do a big thing or

1Sa 20:2 f conceal this matter from
20:3 f must surely know that I
20:6 f should miss me at all
20:8 why should it be to your f
20:9 by my f to come upon you
20:10 what your f may answer you
20:12 sound out my f about this
20:13 good to my f to do evil
20:13 he proved to be with my f
20:32 answered Saul his f and
20:33 by his f to put David to
20:34 own f had humiliated him
22:1 house of his f got to hear of
22:3 f and my mother, please
22:11 house of his f, the priests
22:15 entire house of my f, for
22:16 all the house of your f
22:22 soul of the house of your f
23:17 Saul my f will not find you
23:17 Saul my f also has
24:11 my f, see, yes, see the
24:21 out of the house of my f
2Sa 2:32 the burial place of his f
3:7 with the concubine of my f
3:8 the house of Saul your f
3:29 the entire house of his f
6:21 chose me rather than your f
7:14 myself shall become his f
9:7 the sake of Jonathan your f
10:2 f exercised loving-kindness
10:2 comfort him over his f, and
10:3 Is David honoring your f in
13:5 your f will certainly come
14:9 upon the house of my f
15:34 the servant of your f, even
16:3 the royal rule of my f
16:19 as I served before your f
16:21 the concubines of your f
16:21 foul-smelling to your f
16:22 the concubines of his f
17:8 well know your f and the men
17:8 and your f is a warrior
17:10 your f is a mighty man and
19:28 the household of my f would
19:37 the burial place of my f
21:14 burial place of Kish his f
24:17 and upon the house of my f
1Ki 1:6 f did not hurt his feelings
2:12 the throne of David his f
2:24 the throne of David my f
2:26 before David my f, and
2:26 my f suffered affliction
2:31 from off the house of my f
2:32 my f David himself had not
2:44 that you did to David my f
3:3 in the statutes of David his f
3:6 your servant David my f
3:7 in the place of David my f
3:14 just as David your f walked
5:1 as king in place of his f
5:3 David my f was not able to
5:5 promised to David my f
6:12 I spoke to David your f
7:14 and his f was a Tyrian man
7:51 made holy by David his f
8:15 with David my f, and by his
8:17 David my f to build a house
8:18 Jehovah said to David my f
8:20 in the place of David my f
8:24 your servant David my f
8:25 your servant David my f
8:26 your servant David my f
9:4 just as David your f walked
9:5 I promised David your f
11:4 the heart of David his f
11:6 like David his f
11:12 the sake of David your f
11:17 the servants of his f with
11:27 the city of David his f
11:33 like David his f
11:43 the city of David his f
12:4 Your f, for his part, made
12:4 the hard service of your f
12:6 attending upon Solomon his f
12:9 yoke that your f put upon us
12:10 Your f, for his part, made
12:11 my f, for his part, loaded
12:11 f, for his part, chastised
12:14 My f, for his part, made
12:14 f, for his part, chastised
13:11 relating them to their f
13:12 Then their f spoke to them
15:3 in all the sins of his f
15:15 things made holy by his f
1Ki 15:19, 19 between my f and your f
15:26 walking in the way of his f
18:18 and the house of your f have
19:20 kiss my f and my mother
20:34 The cities that my f took
20:34 from your f I shall return
20:34 as my f assigned in Samaria
22:43 Asa his f. He did not turn
22:46 in the days of Asa his f
22:52 in the way of his f
22:53 all that his f had done
2Ki 2:12, 12 crying out: My f, my f
3:2 not like his f or like his
3:2 Baal that his f had made
3:13 the prophets of your f and
4:18 went out as usual to his f
4:19 And he kept saying to his f
5:13 My f, had it been a great
6:21 strike them down, my f
9:25 teams behind Ahab his f
10:3 upon the throne of his f
13:14, 14 My f, my f, the war
13:25 Jehoahaz his f in war
14:3 that Jehoash his f had done
14:5 struck down the king his f
14:21 in place of his f Amaziah
15:3 that Amaziah his f had done
15:34 that Uzziah his f had done
20:18 to whom you will become f
21:3 Hezekiah his f had destroyed
21:20 Manasseh his f had done
21:21 way that his f had walked
21:21 his f had served and bowing
23:30 king in place of his f
23:34 in place of Josiah his f
24:9 to all that his f had done
1Ch 1:10 Cush . . . f to Nimrod
1:11 Mizraim, he became f to
1:13 Canaan, he became f to Sidon
1:18 Arpachshad . . . f to Shelah
1:18 Shelah . . . became f to Eber
1:20 Joktan . . . f to Almodad and
1:34 Abraham came to be f to
2:10 Ram . . . f to Amminadab
2:10 f to Nahshon the chieftain
2:11 in turn, became f to Salma
2:11 in turn, became f to Boaz
2:12 in turn, became f to Obed
2:12 in turn, became f to Jesse
2:13 f to his firstborn Eliab
2:17 the f of Amasa was Jether
2:18 f to sons by Azubah his wife
2:20 Hur . . . became f to Uri
2:20 in turn, became f to Bezalel
2:21 Machir the f of Gilead
2:22 in turn, became f to Jair
2:23 Machir the f of Gilead
2:24 Ashhur the f of Tekoa
2:36 in turn, became f to Nathan
2:36 in turn, became f to Zabad
2:37 in turn, became f to Ephlal
2:37 in turn, became f to Obed
2:38 in turn, became f to Jehu
2:38 in turn, became f to Azariah
2:39 in turn, became f to Helez
2:39 in turn, became f to Eleasah
2:40 in turn, became f to Sismai
2:40 in turn, became f to Shallum
2:41 became f to Jekamiah
2:41 became f to Elishama
2:42 Mesha . . . f of Ziph
2:42 Mareshah the f of Hebron
2:44 in turn, became f to Raham
2:44 Raham the f of Jorkeam
2:44 became f to Shammai
2:45 Maon was the f of Beth-zur
2:46 Haran, he became f to Gazez
2:49 Shaaph the f of Madmannah
2:49 Sheva the f of Machbenah
2:49 and the f of Gibea
2:50 the f of Kiriath-jearim
2:51 Salma the f of Bethlehem
2:51 Hareph the f of Beth-gader
2:52 the f of Kiriath-jearim
2:55 the f of the house of Rechab
4:2 Reaiah . . . became f to Jahath
4:2 in turn, became f to Ahumai
4:3 the sons of the f of Etam
4:4 Penuel the f of Gedor and
4:4 Ezer the f of Hushah
4:4 Ephrathah the f of Bethlehem
4:5 Ashhur the f of Tekoa
4:8 Koz, he became f to Anub and
4:11 he became f to Mehir
1Ch 4:11 who was the f of Eshton
4:12 became f to Beth-rapha and
4:12 Tehinnah the f of Ir-nahash
4:14 he became f to Ophrah
4:14 Seraiah, he became f to Joab
4:14 Joab the f of Ge-harashim
4:17 Ishbah the f of Eshtemoa
4:18 Jered the f of Gedor and
4:18 Heber the f of Soco and
4:18 Jekuthiel the f of Zanoah
4:19 f of Keilah the Garmite and
4:21 Er the f of Lecah and Laadah
4:21 Laadah the f of Mareshah
5:1 profaning the lounge of his f
6:4 Eleazar . . . f to Phinehas
6:4 Phinehas . . . f to Abishua
6:5 Abishua . . . became f to Bukki
6:5 Bukki . . . became f to Uzzi
6:6 Uzzi . . . became f to Zerahiah
6:6 in turn, became f to Meraioth
6:7 Meraioth . . . f to Amariah
6:7 Amariah . . . f to Ahitub
6:8 Ahitub . . . became f to Zadok
6:8 Zadok . . . became f to Ahimaaz
6:9 Ahimaaz, in turn, became f to
6:9 Azariah . . . f to Johanan
6:10 Johanan . . . f to Azariah
6:11 Azariah . . . f to Amariah
6:11 Amariah . . . f to Ahitub
6:12 Ahitub . . . became f to Zadok
6:12 Zadok . . . f to Shallum
6:13 Shallum . . . f to Hilkiah
6:13 Hilkiah . . . f to Azariah
6:14 Azariah . . . f to Seraiah
6:14 Seraiah . . . f to Jehozadak
7:14 bore Machir the f of Gilead
7:22 Ephraim their f carried on
7:31 who was the f of Birzaith
7:32 As for Heber, he became f to
8:1 Benjamin, he became f to Bela
8:7 became f to Uzza and Ahihud
8:8 Shaharaim, he became f to
8:9 f to Jobab and Zibia and
8:11 f to Abitub and Elpaal
8:29 f of Gibeon, Jeiel, dwelt
8:32 As for Mikloth, he became f
8:33 Ner, he became f to Kish
8:33 Kish . . . became f to Saul
8:33 Saul . . . f to Jonathan
8:34 Merib-baal . . . f to Micah
8:36 As for Ahaz, he became f to
8:36 Jehoaddah, in turn, became f
8:36 Zimri, in turn, became f to
8:37 Moza, in turn, became f to
9:19 house of his f the Korahites
9:35 f of Gibeon, Jeiel, dwelt
9:38 Mikloth, he became f to
9:39 Ner, he became f to Kish
9:39 Kish, in turn, became f to
9:39 Saul, in turn, became f to
9:40 Merib-baal, he became f to
9:42 Ahaz, he became f to Jarah
9:42 Jarah, in turn, became f to
9:42 Zimri, in turn, became f to
9:43 Moza, he became f to Binea
14:3 David came to be f to more
17:13 I myself shall become his f
19:2 f exercised loving-kindness
19:2 to comfort him over his f
19:3 Is David honoring your f in
22:10 son to me, and I a f to him
24:2 and Abihu died before their f
25:3 control of their f Jeduthun
25:6 control of their f in song
26:6 of the house of their f
26:10 his f appointed him as head
28:4 out of all the house of my f
28:6 I myself shall become his f
28:9 know the God of your f and
29:10 the God of Israel our f
29:23 king in place of David his f
2Ch 1:8 toward David my f and that
1:9 your promise with David my f
2:3 as you dealt with David my f
2:7 whom David my f has prepared
2:14 whose f was a man of Tyre
2:14 men of my lord David your f
2:17 census that David his f had
3:1 had appeared to David his f
5:1 made holy by David his f
6:4 with David my f and by his
6:7 heart of David my f to build
6:8 Jehovah said to David my f
6:10 in the place of David my f

2Ch 6:15 David my *f* what you
6:16 David my *f* what you
7:17 as David your *f* walked, even
7:18 covenanted with David your *f*
8:14 rule of David his *f*, and the
9:31 in the city of David his *f*
10:4 Your *f*, for his part, made
10:4 hard service of your *f* and
10:6 attending upon Solomon his *f*
10:9 yoke that your *f* put upon
10:10 Your *f*, for his part, made
10:11 my *f*, for his part, loaded
10:11 My *f*, for his part
10:14 My *f*, for his part
11:21 *f* to twenty-eight sons
13:21 *f* to twenty-two sons and
15:18 things made holy by his *f*
16:3, 3 between my *f* and your *f*
17:2 that Asa his *f* had captured
17:4 God of his *f* that he searched
20:32 way of his *f* Asa, and he
21:3 *f* gave them many gifts in
21:4 over the kingdom of his *f*
21:12 Jehoshaphat your *f* or in
21:13 the household of your *f*
22:4 after the death of his *f*
24:3 *f* to sons and daughters
24:22 that Jehoiada his *f* had
25:3 struck down the king his *f*
26:1 in place of his *f* Amaziah
26:4 Amaziah his *f* had done
27:2 to all that Uzziah his *f*
33:3 Hezekiah his *f* had pulled
33:22 Manasseh his *f* had done
33:22 images that Manasseh his *f*
33:23 same as Manasseh his *f*
36:1 king in the place of his *f*
Ne 1:6 I and the house of my *f*
12:10 became *f* to Joiakim, and
12:10 Joiakim . . . *f* to Eliashib
12:11 Joiada . . . *f* to Jonathan
12:11 Jonathan . . . *f* to Jaddua
Es 2:7 she had neither *f* nor mother
2:7 death of her *f* and her mother
Job 15:10 greater than your *f* in days
17:14 To the pit . . . You are my *f*
29:16 a real *f* to the poor ones
31:18 with me as with a *f*, And
34:36 My *f*, let Job be tested out
38:28 there exist a *f* for the rain
42:15 their *f* proceeded to give
Ps 2:7 today, I have become your *f*
27:10 In case my own *f* and my own
68:5 A *f* of fatherless boys and
89:26 calls out . . . You are my *F*
103:13 *f* shows mercy to his sons
Pr 1:8 to the discipline of your *f*
3:12 even as a *f* does a son in
4:1 sons, to the discipline of a *f*
4:3 real son to my *f*, tender and
6:20 the commandment of your *f*
10:1 one that makes a *f* rejoice
15:5 the discipline of his *f*, but
15:20 one that makes a *f* rejoice
17:21 becoming *f* to a stupid child
17:21 *f* of a senseless child does
17:25 son is a vexation to his *f*
19:13 means adversities to his *f*
19:26 He that is maltreating a *f*
20:20 calling down evil upon his *f*
23:22 Listen to your *f* who caused
23:24 *f* of a righteous one will
23:24 one becoming *f* to a wise one
23:25 Your *f* and your mother will
27:10 or the companion of your *f*
28:7 gluttons humiliates his *f*
28:24 robbing his *f* and his mother
29:3 wisdom makes his *f* rejoice
30:11 evil even upon its *f* and that
30:17 that holds a *f* in derision
Ec 5:14 he has become *f* to a son when
6:3 become a *f* a hundred times
Isa 3:6 brother in the house of his *f*
7:17 against the house of your *f*
8:4 call out, My *f*! and My
9:6 Eternal *F*, Prince of Peace
22:21 *f* to the inhabitant of
22:23 glory to the house of his *f*
22:24 glory of the house of his *f*
38:19 The *f* himself can give
39:7 to whom you will become *f*
43:27 Your own *f*, the first one
45:10 to the one saying to a *f*
45:10 What do you become *f* to?
Isa 49:21 Who has become *f* to these
51:2 Look to Abraham your *f* and
63:16 For you are our *F*
63:16 you, O Jehovah, are our *F*
64:8 O Jehovah, you are our *F*
Jer 2:27 to a tree, You are my *f*
3:4 called out to me, My *F*
3:19 My *F*! you people will call
6:21 *f* and sons together
12:6 the household of your own *f*
16:7 on account of one's *f* and
20:15 brought good news to my *f*
22:11 instead of Josiah his *f*
22:15 your *f*, did he not eat and
29:6 become *f* to sons and to
31:9 I have become to Israel a *F*
La 5:3 mere orphans without a *f*
Eze 16:3 Your *f* was the Amorite, and
16:45 and your *f* was an Amorite
18:4 As the soul of the *f* so
18:10 *f* to a son who is a robber
18:14 become *f* to a son, who
18:14 seeing all the sins of his *f*
18:17 of the error of his *f*
18:18 his *f*, because he committed
18:19 the error of the *f*
18:20 the error of the *f*, and a
18:20 *f* himself will bear nothing
22:7 *F* and mother they have
22:10 nakedness of a *f* they have
22:11 the daughter of his own *f*
44:25 unclean, but for *f* or for
47:22 *f* to sons in the midst of
Da 5:2 Nebuchadnezzar his *f* had taken
5:11 and in the days of your *f*
5:11 King Nebuchadnezzar your *f*
5:11 even your *f*, O king
5:13 my *f* brought out of Judah
5:18 gave to Nebuchadnezzar your *f*
Ho 5:7 that they have become *f*
Am 2:7 a man and his own *f* have gone
Mic 7:6 For a son is despising a *f*
Zec 13:3 his *f* and his mother, the
13:3 *f* and his mother, the ones
Mal 1:6 son, for his part, honors a *f*
1:6 I am a *f*, where is the honor
2:10 one *f* that all of us have
Mt 1:2 Abraham became *f* to Isaac
1:2 Isaac became *f* to Jacob
1:2 Jacob became *f* to Judah and
1:3 Judah became *f* to Perez and
1:3 Perez became *f* to Hezron
1:3 Hezron became *f* to Ram
1:4 Ram became *f* to Amminadab
1:4 Amminadab became *f* to Nahshon
1:4 Nahshon became *f* to Salmon
1:5 Salmon became *f* to Boaz by
1:5 Boaz became *f* to Obed by Ruth
1:5 Obed became *f* to Jesse
1:6 Jesse became *f* to David the
1:6 David became *f* to Solomon by
1:7 Solomon became *f* to Rehoboam
1:7 Rehoboam became *f* to Abijah
1:7 Abijah became *f* to Asa
1:8 Asa became *f* to Jehoshaphat
1:8 Jehoshaphat became *f* to
1:8 Jehoram became *f* to Uzziah
1:9 Uzziah became *f* to Jotham
1:9 Jotham became *f* to Ahaz
1:9 Ahaz became *f* to Hezekiah
1:10 Hezekiah . . . *f* to Manasseh
1:10 Manasseh became *f* to Amon
1:10 Amon became *f* to Josiah
1:11 Josiah became *f* to Jeconiah
1:12 Jeconiah . . . *f* to Shealtiel
1:12 Shealtiel . . . *f* to Zerubbabel
1:13 Zerubbabel became *f* to Abiud
1:13 Abiud became *f* to Eliakim
1:13 Eliakim became *f* to Azor
1:14 Azor became *f* to Zadok
1:14 Zadok became *f* to Achim
1:14 Achim became *f* to Eliud
1:15 Eliud became *f* to Eleazar
1:15 Eleazar became *f* to Matthan
1:15 Matthan became *f* to Jacob
1:16 Jacob became *f* to Joseph
2:22 instead of his *f* Herod, he
3:9 As a *f* we have Abraham. For I
4:21 boat with Zebedee their *f*
4:22 leaving the boat and their *f*
5:16 and give glory to your *F* who
5:45 your *F* who is in the heavens
5:48 as your heavenly *F* is perfect
6:1 your *F* who is in the heavens
Mt 6:4 *F* who is looking on in secret
6:6 pray to your *F* who is in
6:6 your *F* who looks on in secret
6:8 God your *F* knows what things
6:9 Our *F* in the heavens, let your
6:14 heavenly *F* will also forgive
6:15 *F* forgive your trespasses
6:18 to your *F* who is in secrecy
6:18 your *F* who is looking on in
6:26 your heavenly *F* feeds them
6:32 heavenly *F* knows you need
7:11 your *F* who is in the heavens
7:21 one doing the will of my *F*
8:21 to leave and bury my *f*
10:20 spirit of your *F* that speaks
10:21 a *f* his child, and children
10:32 my *F* who is in the heavens
10:33 also disown him before my *F*
10:35 with a man against his *f*
10:37 greater affection for *f* or
11:25 I publicly praise you, *F*
11:26 Yes, O *F*, because to do thus
11:27 delivered to me by my *F*
11:27 knows the Son but the *F*
11:27 fully know the *F* but the Son
12:50 does the will of my *F* who
13:43 in the kingdom of their *F*
15:4 Honor your *f* and your mother
15:4 him that reviles *f* or mother
15:5 Whoever says to his *f* or
15:6 must not honor his *f* at all
15:13 my heavenly *F* did not plant
16:17 my *F* who is in the heavens
16:27 come in the glory of his *F*
18:10 behold the face of my *F* who
18:14 a desirable thing with my *F*
18:19 due to my *F* in heaven
18:35 heavenly *F* will also deal
19:5 a man will leave his *f* and
19:19 Honor your *f* and your mother
19:29 everyone that has left . . . *f*
20:23 it has been prepared by my *F*
21:31 two did the will of his *f*
23:9 do not call anyone your *f* on
23:9 one is your *F*, the heavenly
24:36 nor the Son, but only the *F*
25:34 have been blessed by my *F*
26:29 in the kingdom of my *F*
26:39 My *F*, if it is possible, let
26:42 My *F*, if it is not possible
26:53 appeal to my *F* to supply me
28:19 in the name of the *F* and of
Mr 1:20 they left their *f* Zebedee in
5:40 young child's *f* and mother
7:10 Honor your *f* and your mother
7:10 Let him that reviles *f* or
7:11 If a man says to his *f* or
7:12 do a single thing for his *f*
8:38 arrives in the glory of his *F*
9:21 he asked his *f*: How long has
9:24 the *f* of the young child was
10:7 a man will leave his *f* and
10:19 Honor your *f* and mother
10:29 mother or *f* or children or
11:10 kingdom of our *f* David
11:25 your *F* who is in the heavens
13:12 a *f* a child, and children
13:32 nor the Son, but the *F*
14:36 *F*, all things are possible
15:21 the *f* of Alexander and Rufus
Lu 1:32 the throne of David his *f*
1:59 call it by the name of its *f*
1:62 asking its *f* by signs what he
1:67 Zechariah its *f* was filled
2:33 its *f* and mother continued
2:48 your *f* and I in mental
2:49 be in the house of my *F*
3:8 As a *f* we have Abraham. For I
6:36 just as your *F* is merciful
8:51 and the girl's *f* and mother
9:26 in his glory and that of the *F*
9:42 and delivered him to his *f*
9:59 to leave and bury my *f*
10:21 I publicly praise you, *F*
10:21 Yes, O *F*, because to do thus
10:22 been delivered to me by my *F*
10:22 no one knows but the *F*; and
10:22 who the *F* is, no one knows
11:2 *F*, let your name be
11:11 which *f* is there among you
11:13 the *F* in heaven give holy
12:30 your *F* knows you need these
12:32 your *F* has approved of giving
12:53 divided, *f* against son and

Lu 12:53 divided . . . son against f
14:26 not hate his f and mother
15:12 younger . . . said to his f
15:12 F, give me the part of the
15:17 How many hired men of my f
15:18 journey to my f and say to
15:18 F, I have sinned against
15:20 he rose and went to his f
15:20 his f caught sight of him
15:21 F, I have sinned against
15:22 the f said to his slaves
15:27 f slaughtered the fattened
15:28 his f came out and began to
15:29 In reply he said to his f
16:24 F Abraham, have mercy on me
16:27 I ask you, f, to send him
16:27 him to the house of my f
16:30 f Abraham, but if someone
18:20 Honor your f and mother
22:29 my F has made a covenant
22:42 F, if you wish, remove this
23:34 F, forgive them, for they do
23:46 F, into your hands I entrust
24:49 which is promised by my F
Joh 1:14 only-begotten son from a f
1:18 bosom position with the F
2:16 making the house of my F a
3:35 The F loves the Son and has
4:21 you people worship the F
4:23 worship the F with spirit
4:23 F is looking for suchlike
4:53 f knew it was in the very
5:17 My F has kept working until
5:18 also calling God his own F
5:19 what he beholds the F doing
5:20 F has affection for the Son
5:21 the F raises the dead up
5:22 F judges no one at all, but
5:23 just as they honor the F
5:23 not honor the F who sent him
5:26 the F has life in himself
5:36 works that my F assigned me
5:36 that the F dispatched me
5:37 the F who sent me has
5:43 come in the name of my F
5:45 will accuse you to the F
6:27 this one the F, even God
6:32 my F does give you the true
6:37 Everything the F gives me
6:40 this is the will of my F
6:42 whose f and mother we know
6:44 unless the F, who sent me
6:45 has heard from the F and
6:46 seen the F, except he who
6:46 this one has seen the F
6:57 the living F sent me forth
6:57 I live because of the F
6:65 it is granted him by the F
8:16 F who sent me is with me
8:18 F who sent me bears witness
8:19 say to him: Where is your F?
8:19 know neither me nor my F
8:19 you would know my F also
8:27 talking to them about the F
8:28 as the F taught me I speak
8:38 have seen with my F I speak
8:38 you have heard from your f
8:39 Our f is Abraham. Jesus said
8:41 You do the works of your f
8:41 we have one F, God
8:42 If God were your F, you
8:44 are from your f the Devil
8:44 to do the desires of your f
8:44 liar and the f of the lie
8:49 but I honor my F, and you
8:53 greater than our f Abraham
8:54 It is my F that glorifies me
8:56 Abraham your f rejoiced
10:15 the F knows me and I know
10:15 and I know the F
10:17 why the F loves me, because
10:18 this I received from my F
10:25 doing in the name of my F
10:29 F has given me is something
10:29 out of the hand of the F
10:30 I and the F are one
10:32 many fine works from the F
10:36 me whom the F sanctified
10:37 doing the works of my F
10:38 F is in union with me and
10:38 I am in union with the F
11:41 F, I thank you that you have
12:26 the F will honor him
12:27 F, save me out of this hour
Joh 12:28 F, glorify your name
12:49 F himself who sent me has
12:50 just as the F has told me
13:1 out of this world to the F
13:3 F had given all things into
14:2 house of my F there are
14:6 to the F except through me
14:7 would have known my F also
14:8 Lord, show us the F, and it
14:9 seen me has seen the F also
14:9 you say, Show us the F
14:10 I am in union with the F
14:10 F is in union with me
14:10 F who remains in union
14:11 I am in union with the F
14:11 F is in union with me
14:12 I am going my way to the F
14:13 F may be glorified in
14:16 I will request the F and
14:20 I am in union with my F
14:21 will be loved by my F
14:23 and my F will love him
14:24 belongs to the F who sent
14:26 F will send in my name
14:28 I am going my way to the F
14:28 the F is greater than I am
14:31 to know that I love the F
14:31 F has given me commandment
15:1 and my F is the cultivator
15:8 My F is glorified in this
15:9 F has loved me and I have
15:10 the commandments of the F
15:15 I have heard from my F
15:16 you ask the F in my name
15:23 hates me hates also my F
15:24 hated me as well as my F
15:26 I will send you from the F
15:26 which proceeds from the F
16:3 know either the F or me
16:10 I am going to the F and you
16:15 that the F has are mine
16:17 I am going to the F
16:23 F for anything he will give
16:25 plainness concerning the F
16:26 make request of the F
16:27 F himself has affection
16:28 I came out from the F and
16:28 am going my way to the F
16:32 because the F is with me
17:1 F, the hour has come
17:5 F, glorify me alongside
17:11 Holy F, watch over them on
17:21 F, are in union with me and
17:24 F, as to what you have
17:25 Righteous F, the world has
18:11 cup that the F has given me
20:17 not yet ascended to the F
20:17 I am ascending to my F
20:17 and your F and to my God
20:21 as the F has sent me forth
Ac 1:4 for what the F has promised
1:7 the F has placed in his own
2:33 holy spirit from the F, he
7:4 after his f died, God caused
7:8 he became the f of Isaac and
7:14 called Jacob his f and all
7:29 he became the f of two sons
13:33 I have become your F this
16:1 Timothy . . . of a Greek f
16:3 knew that his f was a Greek
28:8 f of Publius was lying down
Ro 1:7 peace from God our F and the
4:11 f of all those having faith
4:12 f of circumcised offspring
4:12 state which our f Abraham had
4:16 Abraham. (He is the f of us
4:17 I have appointed you a f of
4:18 become the f of many nations
6:4 through the glory of the F
8:15 spirit we cry out: *Abba, F!*
15:6 glorify the God and F of our
1Co 1:3 peace from God our F and the
4:15 have become your f through
5:1 a certain man has of his f
8:6 to us one God the F, out of
15:24 kingdom to his God and F
2Co 1:2 peace from God our F and
1:3 Blessed be the God and F of
1:3 F of tender mercies and the
6:18 I shall be a f to you, and
11:31 and F of the Lord Jesus
Ga 1:1 God the F, who raised him up
1:3 peace from God our F and the
1:4 to the will of our God and F
Ga 4:2 day his f appointed beforehand
4:6 and it cries out: *Abba, F!*
Eph 1:2 peace from God our F and the
1:3 F of our Lord Jesus Christ
1:17 F of glory, may give you a
2:18 have the approach to the F
3:14 I bend my knees to the F
4:6 one God and F of all persons
5:20 thanks . . . to our God and F
5:31 leave his f and his mother
6:2 Honor your f and your mother
6:23 faith from God the F and
Php 1:2 and peace from God our F and
2:11 to the glory of God the F
2:22 like a child with a f he
4:20 to our God and F be the glory
Col 1:2 and peace from God our F
1:3 God the F of our Lord Jesus
1:12 thanking the F who rendered
3:17 thanking God the F through
1Th 1:1 in union with God the F and
1:3 before our God and F
2:11 as a f does his children, we
3:11 may our God and F himself
3:13 before our God and F at the
2Th 1:1 in union with God our F and
1:2 and peace from God the F and
2:16 God our F, who loved us and
1Ti 1:2 mercy, peace from God the F
5:1 entreat him as a f, younger
2Ti 1:2 peace from God the F and
Tit 1:4 peace from God the F and
Phm 3 peace from God our F and the
10 child, to whom I became a f
Heb 1:5 today, I have become your f
1:5 I myself shall become his f
5:5 today, I have become your f
12:7 what son is he that a f does
12:9 to the F of our spiritual
Jas 1:17 F of the celestial lights
1:27 standpoint of our God and F
2:21 not Abraham our f declared
3:9 bless Jehovah, even the F, and
1Pe 1:2 foreknowledge of God the F
1:3 Blessed be the God and F
1:17 if you are calling upon the F
2Pe 1:17 received from God the F
1Jo 1:2 life which was with the F
1:3 sharing of ours is with the F
2:1 we have a helper with the F
2:13 you have come to know the F
2:15 love of the F is not in him
2:16 not originate with the F
2:22 denies the F and the Son
2:23 does not have the F either
2:23 confesses the Son has the F
2:24 and in union with the F
3:1 love the F has given us
4:14 the F has sent forth his Son
2Jo 3 mercy and peace from God the F
3 Jesus Christ the Son of the F
4 commandment from the F
9 that has both the F and the Son
Jude 1 relationship with God the F
Re 1:6 priests to his God and F
2:27 as I have received from my F
3:5 of his name before my F and
3:21 with my F on his throne
14:1 name of his F written on

Fathered

De 32:18 The Rock who f you, you

Fathering

Ge 5:4 of Adam after his f Seth came
5:7 And after his f Enosh Seth
5:10 after his f Kenan Enosh
5:13 after his f Mahalalel Kenan
5:16 after his f Jared Mahalalel
5:19 And after his f Enoch Jared
5:22 after his f Methuselah Enoch
5:26 And after his f Lamech
5:30 And after his f Noah Lamech
11:11 after his f Arpachshad Shem
11:13 after his f Shelah Arpachshad
11:15 And after his f Eber Shelah
11:17 And after his f Peleg Eber
11:19 And after his f Reu Peleg
11:21 And after his f Serug Reu
11:23 And after his f Nahor Serug
11:25 And after his f Terah Nahor

Father-in-law

Ge 38:13 your f is going up to Timnah
38:25 sent to her f, saying: By

Ex 4:18 returned to Jethro his *f* and
18:1 Moses' *f*, got to hear about
18:2 Jethro, Moses' *f*, took
18:5 So Jethro, Moses' *f*, and his
18:6 I, your *f*, Jethro, am come to
18:7 went on out to meet his *f*
18:8 relating to his *f* all that
18:12 Then Jethro, Moses' *f*, took
18:12 to eat bread with Moses' *f*
18:14 Moses' *f* got to see all that
18:15 Moses said to his *f*: Because
18:17 Moses' *f* said to him: It is
18:24 to the voice of his *f* and did
18:27 Moses saw his *f* off, and he
Nu 10:29 Hobab . . . the *f* of Moses
Jg 19:4 *f*, the young woman's father
19:7 his *f* kept begging him, so
19:9 *f*, the young woman's father
1Sa 4:19 *f* and her husband had died
4:21 to her *f* and her husband
Joh 18:13 Annas; for he was *f* to

Fatherless
Ex 22:22 afflict any widow or *f* boy
22:24 widows and your sons *f* boys
De 10:18 judgment for the *f* boy and
14:29 the *f* boy and the widow
16:11 the *f* boy and the widow
16:14 the *f* boy and the widow
24:17 judgment . . . of the *f* boy
24:19 the *f* boy and for the widow
24:20 the *f* boy and for the widow
24:21 the *f* boy and for the widow
26:12 the *f* boy and the widow
26:13 the *f* boy and the widow
27:19 an alien resident, a *f* boy
Job 6:27 lots even over someone *f*
22:9 arms of *f* boys are crushed
24:3 even the male ass of *f* boys
24:9 snatch away a *f* boy even
29:12 the *f* boy and anyone that
31:17 While the *f* boy did not eat
31:21 to and fro against the *f* boy
Ps 10:14 the *f* boy, commits himself
10:18 To judge the *f* boy and the
68:5 A father of *f* boys and a judge
82:3 the lowly one and the *f* boy
94:6 the *f* boys they murder
109:9 Let his sons become *f* boys
109:12 showing favor to his *f* boys
146:9 *f* boy and the widow he
Pr 23:10 field of *f* boys do not enter
Isa 1:17 judgment for the *f* boy
1:23 For a *f* boy they do not
9:17 *f* boys and upon their widows
10:2 may plunder even the *f* boys
Jer 5:28 the legal case of the *f* boy
7:6 no *f* boy and no widow you
22:3 resident, *f* boy or widow
49:11 Do leave your *f* boys
Eze 22:7 *F* boy and widow they have
Ho 14:3 a *f* boy is shown mercy
Zec 7:10 defraud no widow or *f* boy
Mal 3:5 and with the *f* boy, and
Heb 7:3 being *f*, motherless, without

Father's
Ge 9:22 saw his *f* nakedness and went
9:23 they covered their *f* nakedness
9:23 did not see their *f* nakedness
24:7 took me from my *f* house and
27:34 On hearing his *f* words Esau
35:22 with Bilhah his *f* concubine
38:11 dwell at her own *f* house
46:31 to his *f* household: Let me
46:31 my *f* household who were in
48:17 take hold of his *f* hand to
49:4 you have gone up to your *f* bed
50:17 the servants of your *f* God
Ex 2:16 to water their *f* flock
6:20 took Jochebed his *f* sister as
15:2 I shall laud him; my *f* God
Le 18:8 nakedness of your *f* wife you
18:8 It is your *f* nakedness
18:11 daughter of your *f* wife, the
18:12 nakedness of your *f* sister
18:14 nakedness of your *f* brother
20:11 lies down with his *f* wife has
20:19 *f* sister you must not lay
22:13 *f* house as in her youth, she
22:13 may eat some of her *f* bread
Nu 27:4 the midst of our *f* brothers
27:7 the midst of their *f* brothers
27:7 *f* inheritance to pass to them
27:10 inheritance to his *f* brothers
Nu 36:11 the sons of their *f* brothers
De 22:21 the entrance of her *f* house
22:30 should take his *f* wife, that
27:20 lies down with his *f* wife
Jg 6:15 am the smallest in my *f* house
6:25 altar of Baal that is your *f*
11:7 drove me out of my *f* house
14:19 his way up to his *f* house
19:3 had him come into her *f* house
1Sa 18:2 to return to his *f* house
18:18 my kinsfolk, my *f* family
1Ki 12:10 be thicker than my *f* hips
1Ch 21:17 be upon me and my *f* house
28:4 of Judah my *f* house, and
28:4 among my *f* sons, I was the
2Ch 10:10 be thicker than my *f* hips
36:10 Zedekiah his *f* brother king
Es 2:7 the daughter of his *f* brother
4:14 as for you and your *f* house
Ps 45:10 your people and your *f* house
Pr 13:1 where there is a *f* discipline
Am 6:10 his *f* brother will have to
Mt 10:29 without your *F* knowledge
Joh 16:27 out as the *F* representative
Ac 7:20 three months in his *f* home

Fathers
Ge 31:3 Return to the land of your *f*
47:9 my *f* in the days of their
47:30 And I must lie with my *f*
48:15 my *f* Abraham and Isaac
48:16 my *f*, Abraham and Isaac
49:29 Bury me with my *f* in the
Ex 6:14 heads of the house of their *f*
6:25 heads of the *f* of the Levites
10:6, 6 your *f* and your fathers' *f*
20:5 punishment for the error of *f*
34:7 for the error of *f* upon sons
Le 26:39 errors of their *f* with them
26:40 error of their *f* in their
Nu 1:2 house of their *f*, by the
1:4 a head to the house of his *f*
1:16 of the tribes of their *f*
1:18 in the house of their *f*
1:20 in the house of their *f*
1:22 in the house of their *f*
1:24 in the house of their *f*
1:26 in the house of their *f*
1:28 in the house of their *f*
1:30 in the house of their *f*
1:32 in the house of their *f*
1:34 in the house of their *f*
1:36 in the house of their *f* by
1:38 in the house of their *f* by
1:40 in the house of their *f* by
1:42 in the house of their *f* by
1:44 one each the house of his *f*
1:45 house of their *f* from twenty
1:47 tribe of their *f* did not get
2:2 signs for the house of their *f*
2:32 to the house of their *f*
2:34 regard to the house of his *f*
3:15 the house of their *f*
3:20 the house of their *f*
4:2 in the house of their *f*
4:22 house of their *f* according to
4:29 in the house of their *f*
4:34 and by the house of their *f*
4:38 and by the house of their *f*
4:40 by the house of their *f*
4:42 by the house of their *f*
4:46 by the house of their *f*
7:2 heads of the house of their *f*
13:2 man for each tribe of his *f*
14:18 the error of the *f* upon sons
14:23 which I swore to their *f*
17:2 by the house of their *f*
17:3 head of the house of their *f*
17:6 by the house of their *f*
20:15 our *f* proceeded to go down
20:15 doing harm to us and our *f*
26:2 to the house of their *f*, all
26:55 of the tribes of their *f* they
31:26 of the *f* of the assembly
32:8 way your *f* did when I sent
32:14 in the place of your *f* as the
32:28 heads of the *f* of the tribes
33:54 By the tribes of your *f* you
34:14 by the house of their *f* and
34:14 by the house of their *f* have
36:1 *f* of the family of the sons
36:1 the *f* of the sons of Israel
36:3 from the inheritance of our *f*
36:4 of the tribe of our *f*
Nu 36:6 tribe of their *f* that they
De 1:8 which Jehovah swore to your *f*
1:35 I swore to give to your *f*
5:9 error of *f* upon sons and upon
8:3 nor your *f* had known; in
8:16 which your *f* had not known
24:16 *F* should not be put to death
24:16 put to death on account of *f*
30:5 your *f* took possession
30:5 multiply you more than your *f*
Jos 4:21 ask their *f* in time to come
14:1 heads of the *f* of the tribes
19:51 the *f* of the tribes of the
21:1 heads of the *f* of the Levites
21:1 heads of the *f* of the tribes
22:14 the house of their *f* of
22:28 altar that our *f* made, not
24:6 I was bringing your *f* out
24:6 chasing after your *f* with
24:17 our *f* up out of the land
Jg 2:10 were gathered to their *f*
2:12 the God of their *f* who had
2:19 more ruinously than their *f*
2:22 just as their *f* kept it, or
3:4 that he had commanded their *f*
6:13 acts that our *f* related to us
21:22 their *f* or their brothers
1Sa 12:15 to be against you and your *f*
1Ki 8:1 the chieftains of the *f*, of
2Ki 14:6 *F* should not be put to death
14:6 not be put to death for *f*
1Ch 9:9 heads of the *f* by the house of
9:19 *f* over the camp of Jehovah
9:33 heads of the *f* of the Levites
9:34 heads of the *f* of the Levites
15:12 of the *f* of the Levites
23:9 the heads of the *f* for Ladan
23:24 Levi by the house of their *f*
23:24 the heads of the *f*, by their
24:6 heads of the *f* of the priests
2Ch 25:4 *F* should not die for sons
25:4 sons themselves die for *f*
29:6 *f* have acted unfaithfully
31:17 by the house of their *f*
Ezr 1:5 *f* of Judah and of Benjamin
2:59 tell the house of their *f*
5:12 our *f* irritated the God of
8:29 princes of the *f* of Israel
10:16 *f* for their paternal house
Ne 7:61 tell the house of their *f*
8:13 the *f* of all the people
9:2 and the errors of their *f*
Job 8:8 things searched out by their *f*
15:18 it being from their *f*
30:1 Whose *f* I would have refused
Ps 22:4 In you our *f* trusted; They
78:3 own *f* have related to us
Pr 17:6 the beauty of sons is their *f*
19:14 The inheritance from *f* is a
Jer 2:5 What have your *f* found in me
3:25 our *f* from our youth on and
7:18 the *f* are lighting the fire
9:14 which their *f* had taught
9:16 they nor their *f* have known
13:14 both the *f* and the sons, at
16:3 *f* who are causing their
16:11 fact that your *f* left me
16:12 acted worse . . . than your *f*
16:13 not known, neither your *f*
23:27 their *f* forgot my name by
31:29 *f* were the ones that ate
32:18 error of the *f* into the
34:5 with the burnings for your *f*
47:3 *f* will actually not turn
Eze 5:10 *f* themselves will eat sons
5:10 will eat their *f*, and I will
18:2 *F* . . . eat unripe grapes, but
Da 11:24 actually do what his *f* and
11:24, 24 *f* of his *f* have not done
11:37 god of his *f* he will give
11:38 god that his *f* did not know
Zec 1:2 grew indignant at your *f*
1:4 Do not become like your *f* to
1:5 As for your *f*, where are they?
1:6 not catch up with your *f*
Mal 4:6 turn the heart of *f* back
4:6 heart of sons back toward *f*
Lu 1:17 turn back the hearts of *f* to
Ac 7:2 Men, brothers and *f*, hear
7:19 *f* to expose their infants
22:1 Men, brothers and *f*, hear my
1Co 4:15 do not have many *f*; for in
Ga 1:14 for the traditions of my *f*
Eph 6:4 *f*, do not be irritating your

Col 3:21 you *f*, do not be exasperating
1Ti 1:9 profane, murderers of *f* and
Heb 12:9 we used to have *f* who were
1Jo 2:13 I am writing you, *f*, because
2:14 I write you, *f*, because you

Fathers'

Ex 10:6 your *f* fathers have not seen

Fathoms

Ac 27:28 depth and found it twenty *f*
27:28 and found it fifteen *f*

Fatling

2Sa 6:13 sacrificed a bull and a *f*

Fatlings

1Ki 1:9 of sheep and cattle and *f*
1:19 he sacrificed bulls and *f*
1:25 sacrifice bulls and *f* and
Ps 66:15 offerings of *f* I shall offer
Eze 39:18 the *f* of Bashan all of them
Am 5:22 communion sacrifices of *f*

Fatness

Jg 9:9 give up my *f* with which they
Job 36:16 table will be full of *f*
Ps 36:8 fill of the *f* of your house
63:5 with the best part, even *f*
65:11 your very tracks drip with *f*
73:7 Their eye has bulged from *f*
Isa 17:4 *f* of his flesh will be made
55:2 exquisite delight in *f* itself
Jer 31:14 soul of the priests with *f*
Da 11:24 *f* of the jurisdictional
Ro 11:17 of the olive's root of *f*

Fattened

1Sa 28:24 woman had a *f* calf in the
1Ki 4:23 and roebucks and *f* cuckoos
Jer 46:21 soldiers . . . like *f* calves
Am 6:4 bulls from among *f* calves
Mal 4:2 paw the ground like *f* calves
Mt 22:4 and *f* animals are slaughtered
Lu 15:23 And bring the *f* young bull
15:27 slaughtered the *f* young bull
15:30 slaughtered the *f* young bull
Jas 5:5 You have *f* your hearts on the

Fattening

1Sa 2:29 *f* yourselves from the best

Fatter

Da 1:15 *f* in flesh than all the

Fattiness

Job 15:27 covers his face with his *f*

Fatty

Ge 4:4 his flock, even their *f* pieces
Ex 27:3 for clearing away its *f* ashes
Le 1:16 to the place for the *f* ashes
3:9 entire *f* tail is what he will
4:12 the *f* ashes are poured out
4:12 the *f* ashes are poured out
6:10 lift up the *f* ashes of the
6:11 take the *f* ashes out to a
6:12 make the *f* pieces of the
7:3 will present of it the *f* tail
8:26 the *f* pieces and the right
9:19 for the *f* pieces of the bull
9:20 placed the *f* pieces upon the
9:20 *f* pieces smoke upon the altar
9:24 the *f* pieces upon the altar
10:15 by fire, of the *f* pieces
Nu 4:13 clear away the *f* ashes of the
1Ki 13:3 the *f* ashes that are upon it
13:5 the *f* ashes were spilled out
Ne 8:10 eat the *f* things and drink the
Jer 31:40 carcasses and of the *f* ashes

Fault

Ex 5:16 your own people are at *f*
Ne 5:7 finding *f* with the nobles and
13:11 began to find *f* with the
13:17 find *f* with the nobles of
13:25 began to find *f* with them
Ps 50:20 you give away a *f*
103:9 for all time keep finding *f*
Mt 18:15 go lay bare his *f* between
Joh 18:38 I find no *f* in him
19:4 know I find no *f* in him
19:6 I do not find any *f* in him
Ro 9:19 Why does he yet find *f*?
2Co 6:3 ministry . . . be found *f* with
8:20 having any man find *f* with
Heb 8:8 does find *f* with the people

Faultfinder

Job 40:2 a *f* with the Almighty

Faultfinding

2Sa 22:44 from the *f* of my people
Ps 18:43 from the *f* of the people

Faultiness

Job 4:18 messengers he charges with *f*

Faultless

Ge 6:9 Noah . . . proved himself *f*
17:1 and prove yourself *f*
De 18:13 *f* with Jehovah your God
2Sa 22:24 prove myself *f* toward him
22:26 With the *f*, mighty one you
Ps 18:23 prove myself *f* with him
18:25 With the *f*, able-bodied man
37:18 the days of the *f* ones
101:2 with discretion in a *f* way
101:6 one walking in a *f* way
119:1 Happy are the ones *f* in their
119:80 my heart prove *f* in your
Pr 28:10 *f* ones themselves will come
28:18 is walking *f* will be saved
Eze 28:15 *f* in your ways from the day
Heb 8:7 first covenant had been *f*

Faultlessly

2Sa 22:26 mighty one you will deal *f*
Ps 15:2 walking *f* and practicing
18:25 you will deal *f*

Faultlessness

Jos 24:14 and serve him in *f* and in
Jg 9:16 in truth and in *f* that you
9:19 and in *f* that you have acted
Ps 84:11 good from those walking in *f*

Favor

Ge 4:4 Jehovah was looking with *f*
4:5 he did not look with any *f*
6:8 Noah found *f* in the eyes of
18:3 I have found *f* in your eyes
19:19 found *f* in your eyes so that
30:27 found *f* in your eyes,—I
32:5 I may find *f* in your eyes
33:8 In order to find *f* in the eyes
33:10 If, now, I have found *f* in
33:15 *f* in the eyes of my lord
34:11 Let me find *f* in your eyes
39:4 Joseph kept finding *f* in his
39:21 granting him to find *f* in
43:29 God show you his *f*, my son
47:25 *f* in the eyes of my lord
47:29 I have found *f* in your eyes
50:4 I have found *f* in your eyes
Ex 3:21 *f* in the eyes of the Egyptians
11:3 *f* in the eyes of the Egyptians
12:36 Jehovah gave the people *f* in
33:12 you have found *f* in my eyes
33:13 found *f* in your eyes, make
33:13 I may find *f* in your eyes
33:16 I have found *f* in your eyes
33:17 you have found *f* in my eyes
33:19, 19 *f* the one whom I may *f*
34:9 If, now, I have found *f* in
Nu 6:25 and may he *f* you
11:11 not found *f* in your eyes
11:15 have found *f* in your eyes
32:5 we have found *f* in your eyes
De 3:23 to implore *f* from Jehovah at
7:2 nor show them any *f*
24:1 should find no *f* in his eyes
28:50 show *f* to a young man
Jg 6:17 I have found *f* in your eyes
21:22 Do us a *f* for their sakes
Ru 2:2 in whose eyes I may find *f*
2:10 I have found *f* in your eyes
2:13 Let me find *f* in your eyes
1Sa 1:18 find *f* in your eyes
16:22 he has found *f* in my eyes
20:3 I have found *f* in your eyes
20:29 if I have found *f* in your
25:8 may find *f* in your eyes
27:5 found *f* in your eyes, let
29:4 himself in *f* with his lord
2Sa 12:22 Jehovah may show me *f*, and
14:22 I have found *f* in your eyes
15:25 *f* in the eyes of Jehovah
16:4 Let me find *f* in your eyes
1Ki 8:28 his request for *f*, O Jehovah
8:30 listen to the request for *f*
8:33 *f* toward you in this house
8:38 whatever request for *f* there
8:45 and their request for *f*
8:47 *f* in the land of their
8:49 their request for *f*, and you
8:52 opened to the request for *f*
8:52 request for *f* of your people
1Ki 8:54 this prayer and request for *f*
8:59 request for *f* before Jehovah
9:3 prayer and your request for *f*
9:3 you requested *f* before me
11:19 *f* in the eyes of Pharaoh
2Ki 1:13 began to implore *f* of him
13:23 Jehovah showed them *f* and
1Ch 5:20 entreated in their *f* because
2Ch 6:19 and to his request for *f*
6:24 make request for *f* before
6:29 whatever request for *f* there
6:35 their request for *f*, and you
6:37 make request to you for *f* in
6:39 and their requests for *f*
33:13 heard his request for *f* and
Ezr 9:8 *f* from Jehovah our God has
Es 2:15 *f* in the eyes of everyone
2:17 so that she gained more *f* and
4:8 in to the king and implore *f*
5:2 Esther . . . gained *f* in his eyes
5:8 have found *f* in the king's eyes
7:3 If I have found *f* in your eyes
8:3 wept and implored *f* of him to
8:5 if I have found *f* before him
Job 8:5 of the Almighty . . . implore *f*
9:15 I would implore *f*
19:21 Show me some *f*, show me
19:21 show me some *f*, O you my
20:10 seek the *f* of lowly people
Ps 4:1 Show me *f* and hear my prayer
6:2 Show me *f*, O Jehovah, for I
6:9 indeed hear my request for *f*
9:13 Show me *f*, O Jehovah; see my
25:16 face to me, and show me *f*
26:11 redeem me and show me *f*
27:7 And show me *f* and answer me
30:8 I kept making entreaty for *f*
30:10 O Jehovah, and show me *f*
31:9 Show me *f*, O Jehovah, for I
37:21 righteous one is showing *f*
37:26 he is showing *f* and lending
41:4 O Jehovah, show me *f*
41:10 show me *f* and cause me to
51:1 Show me *f*, O God, according
55:1 from my request for *f*
56:1 Show me *f*, O God, because
57:1, 1 *f*, O God, show me *f*
59:5 *f* to any hurtful traitors
67:1 will show us *f* and bless us
84:11 *F* and glory are what he
86:3 Show me *f*, O Jehovah
86:16 Turn to me and show me *f*
102:14 her dust they direct their *f*
109:12 *f* to his fatherless boys
119:29 *f* me with your own law
119:58 *f* according to your saying
119:132 Turn to me and show me *f*
119:170 request for *f* enter in
123:2 Until he shows us *f*
123:3 Show us *f*, O Jehovah
123:3 Jehovah, show us *f*
142:1 I began to cry for *f*
Pr 3:4 find *f* and good insight in
3:34 meek ones he will show *f*
13:15 Good insight itself gives *f*
14:21 showing *f* to the afflicted
14:31 one showing *f* to the poor
17:8 The gift is a stone winning *f*
19:17 showing *f* to the lowly one
21:10 fellow will be shown no *f*
22:1 *f* is better than even silver
28:8 one showing *f* to the lowly
28:23 will afterward find more *f*
Ec 9:11 having knowledge have the *f*
10:12 of the wise one mean *f*, but
Isa 26:10 *f*, he simply will not learn
27:11 Former will show it no *f*
30:18 of showing you *f*
30:19 show you *f* at the sound of
32:8 in *f* of generous things he
33:2 Jehovah, show us *f*
Jer 16:13 I shall not give you any *f*
31:2 found *f* in the wilderness
31:9 their entreaties for *f* I
36:7 request for *f* will fall
37:20 my request for *f*, please
38:26 request for *f* fall before
42:2 May our request for *f*
42:9 request for *f* to fall before
La 4:16 show no *f* even to the old men
Eze 16:52 argue in *f* of your sisters
36:9 For here I am in *f* of you
Da 6:11 imploring *f* before his God
7:22 given in *f* of the holy ones

Da 9:20 my request for *f* fall before
Ho 12:4 might implore *f* for himself
Am 5:15 show *f* to the remaining ones
Zec 12:10 spirit of *f* and entreaties
Mal 1:9 God, that he may show us *f*
Lu 1:30 you have found *f* with God
2:40 God's *f* continued upon him
2:52 in *f* with God and men
7:21 blind persons the *f* of seeing
Ac 2:47 finding *f* with all the people
7:46 found *f* in the sight of God
24:27 Felix desired to gain *f* with
25:3 as a *f* against the man that
25:9 Festus, desiring to gain *f*
25:11 hand me over to them as a *f*
25:16 to hand any man over as a *f*
2Co 4:6 in *f* of the one against the
Jas 2:3 *f* upon the one wearing the
1Pe 3:7 of the undeserved *f* of life

Favorable
Jos 11:20 to have no *f* consideration
Ps 77:9 Has God forgotten to be *f*
102:13 the season to be *f* to her
Lu 4:22 *f* witness about him and to
Ga 6:10 long as we have time *f* for it
Eph 4:29 impart what is *f* to the
2Ti 4:2 be at it urgently in *f* season

Favorably
Mr 4:20 to the word and *f* receive it
Lu 1:13 supplication has been *f* heard
Ac 10:31 prayer has been *f* heard and
2Ti 2:25 those not *f* disposed; as
Heb 5:7 *f* heard for his godly fear

Favored
Ge 33:5 God has *f* your servant
33:11 God has *f* me and because I
Lu 1:28 Good day, highly *f* one
Ac 15:22 *f* sending chosen men from
15:25 *f* choosing men to send to
15:28 *f* adding no further burden

Favoritism
Jas 2:1 with acts of *f*, are you
2:9 if you continue showing *f*

Favors
Job 33:24 Then he *f* him and says

Fear
Ge 9:2 a *f* of you and a terror of you
11:4 for *f* we may be scattered
15:1 not *f*, Abram. I am a shield
19:15 *f* you may be swept away in
19:17 for *f* you may be swept away
19:19 for *f* calamity may keep
20:11 no *f* of God in this place
26:7 afraid to say My wife for *f*
26:9 I said it for *f* I should die
42:18 I *f* the true God
44:34 for *f* that then I may look
45:11 for *f* you and your house
Ex 1:10 for *f* they may multiply, and
9:30 show *f* because of Jehovah God
14:31 the people began to *f* Jehovah
20:19 with us for *f* we may die
20:20 the *f* of him may continue
34:12 for *f* it may prove itself a
34:15 for *f* that you may conclude
Le 10:7 not go out for *f* you may die
19:3 *f* each one his mother and his
19:14 you must be in *f* of your God
19:32 must be in *f* of your God
25:17 be in *f* of your God, because
25:36 you must be in *f* of your God
25:43 you must be in *f* of your God
Nu 12:8 *f* to speak against my servant
14:9 do not you *f* the people of
14:9 Jehovah is with us. Do not *f*
20:18 for *f* I may come out with
De 2:25 dread of you and the *f* of you
4:10 learn to *f* me all the days
5:29 this heart of theirs to *f* me
6:2 *f* Jehovah your God so as to
6:13 Jehovah your God you should *f*
6:15 for *f* the anger of Jehovah
6:24 to *f* Jehovah our God for our
7:22 for *f* the wild beasts of the
7:25 *f* you may be ensnared by it
8:12 for *f* that you may eat and
9:28 for *f* the land out of which
10:12 *f* Jehovah your God, so as to
10:20 Jehovah your God you should *f*
11:16 for *f* your heart may be
11:25 dread of you and the *f* of you

De 12:13 for *f* you may offer up your
12:30 for *f* you may be entrapped
12:30 and for *f* you may inquire
13:4 and him you should *f*, and his
14:23 *f* Jehovah your God always
15:9 for *f* a base word should come
17:19 learn to *f* Jehovah his God
20:5 for *f* he may die in the
20:6 for *f* he may die in the
20:7 for *f* he may die in the
22:9 for *f* that the full produce
25:3 for *f* he should continue to
25:18 and he did not *f* God
28:58 so as to *f* this glorious and
31:12 *f* Jehovah your God and take
31:13 they must learn to *f* Jehovah
Jos 4:14 began to *f* him just as they
4:24 *f* Jehovah your God always
6:18 for *f* you may get a desire
24:14 *f* Jehovah and serve him in
Jg 6:10 You must not *f* the gods of
6:23 Do not *f*. You will not die
9:54 for *f* they should say about
18:25 for *f* that men bitter of
Ru 4:6 for *f* I may ruin my own
1Sa 12:14 If you will *f* Jehovah and
12:18 *f* of Jehovah and of Samuel
12:24 Only *f* Jehovah, and you
18:29 more *f* because of David
20:3 Jonathan know this for *f* he
23:15 David continued in *f*
2Sa 1:14 did not *f* to thrust your hand
1:20 *f* that the daughters of the
1:20 *f* that the daughters of the
15:14 for *f* he may hurry up and
17:16 for *f* that the king and all
23:3 Ruling in the *f* of God
1Ki 8:40 they may *f* you all the days
8:43 so as to *f* you the same as
2Ki 17:7 they began to *f* other gods
17:25 they did not *f* Jehovah
17:28 how they ought to *f* Jehovah
17:35 You must not *f* other gods
17:36 the One whom you should *f*
17:37 you must not *f* other gods
17:38 you must not *f* other gods
17:39 God that you should *f*
2Ch 6:31 *f* you by walking in your
6:33 may *f* you the same as your
19:9 in the *f* of Jehovah with
26:5 of the true God
Ne 4:14 I saw their *f* I immediately
5:9 Is it not in the *f* of our God
5:15 on account of the *f* of God
Job 6:14 leave . . . *f* of the Almighty
11:15 and you will not *f*
15:4 *f* before God to have no force
28:28 The *f* of Jehovah—that is
37:24 Therefore let men *f* him
Ps 2:11 Serve Jehovah with *f* And be
5:7 bow down . . . in *f* of you
9:20 Do put *f* into them, O Jehovah
19:9 The *f* of Jehovah is pure
23:4 I *f* nothing bad, For you are
27:1 Of whom shall I be in *f*?
27:3 My heart will not *f*
33:8 those of the earth be in *f* of
34:9 *F* Jehovah, you holy ones
34:11 The *f* of Jehovah is what I
40:3 Many will see it and will *f*
46:2 we shall not *f*, though the
55:5 *F*, yes, trembling itself
64:4 shoot at him and do not *f*
66:16 listen, all you who *f* God
67:7 ends of the earth will *f* him
72:5 *f* you as long as there is a
76:11 Let them bring a gift in *f*
86:11 my heart to *f* your name
90:11 according to the *f* of you
102:15 will *f* the name of Jehovah
111:10 *f* of Jehovah is the
112:1 is the man in *f* of Jehovah
115:11 You that *f* Jehovah, trust
118:6 on my side; I shall not *f*
119:38 That tends to the *f* of you
119:63 of all those who do *f* you
Pr 1:7 *f* of Jehovah is the beginning
1:29 *f* of Jehovah they did not
2:5 understand the *f* of Jehovah
3:7 *F* Jehovah and turn away from
8:13 *f* of Jehovah means the hating
9:10 *f* of Jehovah is the start of
10:27 *f* of Jehovah will add days
14:26 In the *f* of Jehovah there is

Pr 14:27 *f* of Jehovah is a well of
15:16 a little in the *f* of Jehovah
15:33 *f* of Jehovah is a discipline
16:6 in the *f* of Jehovah one turns
19:23 *f* of Jehovah tends toward
22:4 the *f* of Jehovah is riches and
23:17 be in the *f* of Jehovah all
24:21 son, *f* Jehovah and the king
31:21 does not *f* for her household
Ec 5:7 But *f* the true God himself
8:12 because they were in *f* of him
8:13 because he is not in *f* of God
12:13 *F* the true God and keep his
Isa 7:25 for *f* of thornbushes and
8:12 object of their *f* you men
8:12 you men must not *f*, nor
8:13 be the object of your *f*
11:2 and of the *f* of Jehovah
11:3 in the *f* of Jehovah
25:3 nations, they will *f* you
29:13 *f* toward me becomes men's
33:6 *f* of Jehovah, which is his
41:5 islands saw and began to *f*
50:10 people is in *f* of Jehovah
54:14 for you will *f* none—and
57:11 begin to *f*, so that you took
57:11 you were in no *f* even of me
59:19 to *f* the name of Jehovah
63:17 hard against the *f* of you
Jer 5:22 Do you not *f* even me, is the
5:24 *f* Jehovah our God, the One
10:7 *f* you, O King of the nations
26:19 Did he not *f* Jehovah and
32:39 in order to *f* me always
32:40 *f* of me I shall put in
38:19 *f* that they might give me
42:11 of whom you are in *f*
Eze 30:13 put *f* in the land of Egypt
Da 1:10 *f* of my lord the king, who
5:19 and showing *f* before him
Jon 1:5 the mariners began to *f* and
1:10 the men began to *f* greatly
1:16 the men began to *f* Jehovah
Mic 6:9 wisdom will *f* your name
Zep 3:7 Surely you will *f* me
3:15 You will *f* calamity no more
Hag 1:12 began to *f* because of Jehovah
Mal 1:6 where is the *f* of me?
2:5 giving them to him, with *f*
3:16 those in *f* of Jehovah spoke
3:16 for those in *f* of Jehovah
4:2 you who are in *f* of my name
Mt 9:8 the crowds were struck with *f*
10:26 do not *f* them; for there is
10:28 in *f* of him that can destroy
10:31 have no *f*: you are worth
14:26 they cried out in their *f*
14:27 courage, it is I; have no *f*
17:7 said: Get up and have no *f*
21:26 we have the crowd to *f*, for
28:4 for *f* of him the watchmen
28:8 with *f* and great joy, they
28:10 Have no *f*! Go, report to my
Mr 4:41 they felt an unusual *f*, and
5:36 Have no *f*, only exercise
6:20 For Herod stood in *f* of John
6:50 courage, it is I; have no *f*
10:32 who followed began to *f*
11:18 for they were in *f* of him
11:32 They were in *f* of the crowd
16:8 for they were in *f*
Lu 1:12 and *f* fell upon him
1:13 Have no *f*, Zechariah, because
1:30 Have no *f*, Mary, for you have
1:50 mercy is upon those who *f* him
1:65 *f* fell upon all those living
2:10 Have no *f*, for, look! I am
5:26 and they became filled with *f*
7:16 *f* seized them all, and they
8:25 struck with *f*, they marveled
8:37 were in the grip of great *f*
8:50 Have no *f*, only put forth
12:4 Do not *f* those who kill the
12:5 indicate to you whom to *f*
12:5 *F* him who after killing has
12:5 Yes, I tell you, *f* this One
12:7 Have no *f*; you are worth
12:32 Have no *f*, little flock
18:2 judge that had no *f* of God
18:4 not *f* God or respect a man
19:21 You see, I was in *f* of you
21:26 men become faint out of *f*
22:2 they were in *f* of the people
23:40 Do you not *f* God at all

Joh 6:20 It is I; have no *f*!
7:13 because of the *f* of the Jews
9:22 they were in *f* of the Jews
12:15 Have no *f*, daughter of Zion
14:27 nor let them shrink for *f*
19:38 out of his *f* of the Jews
20:19 were for *f* of the Jews
Ac 2:43 *f* began to fall upon every
5:5 great *f* came over all those
5:11 great *f* came over the whole
9:31 it walked in the *f* of Jehovah
13:16 you others that *f* God, hear
13:26 others among you who *f* God
17:22 given to the *f* of the deities
18:9 Have no *f*, but keep on
19:17 a *f* fell upon them all, and
27:17 *f* of running aground on the
27:24 Have no *f*, Paul. You must
Ro 3:18 no *f* of God before their eyes
8:15 spirit of slavery causing *f*
11:20 lofty ideas, but be in *f*
13:3 of *f*, not to the good deed
13:3 to have no *f* of the authority
13:4 doing what is bad, be in *f*
13:7, 7 who calls for *f*, such *f*
1Co 2:3 and in *f* and with much
16:10 that he becomes free of *f*
2Co 5:11 the *f* of the Lord, we keep
7:1 perfecting holiness in God's *f*
7:11 yes, indignation, yes, *f*
7:15 you received him with *f* and
Ga 2:2 *f* that somehow I was running
2:12 separating himself, in *f* of
4:11 I *f* for you, that somehow I
6:1 for *f* you also may be tempted
Eph 5:21 to one another in *f* of Christ
6:5 with *f* and trembling in the
Php 2:12 your own salvation with *f*
Col 3:22 with *f* of Jehovah
1Ti 3:6 *f* that he might get puffed
5:20 the rest also may have *f*
Heb 2:15 for *f* of death were subject
3:12 *f* there should ever develop
3:13 for *f* any one of you should
4:1 let us *f* that sometime
4:11 for *f* anyone should fall in
5:7 heard for his godly *f*
11:7 showed godly *f* and
11:23 not *f* the order of the king
12:28 service with godly *f* and
1Pe 1:17 conduct yourselves with *f*
2:17 be in *f* of God, have honor
2:18 with all due *f*, not only to
3:14 the object of their *f* do not
3:14 do not you *f*, neither become
1Jo 4:18 no *f* in love, but perfect
4:18 love throws *f* outside
4:18 *f* exercises a restraint
4:18 he that is under *f* has not
Jude 12 feed themselves without *f*
23 doing so with *f*, while you
Re 11:11 and great *f* fell upon those
14:7 *F* God and give him glory
15:4 not really *f* you, Jehovah
18:10 their *f* of her torment and
18:15 of their *f* of her torment
19:5 his slaves, who *f* him, the

Feared
Ex 1:17 the midwives *f* the true God
1:21 midwives had *f* the true God
9:20 Anyone who *f* Jehovah's word
15:11 The One to be *f* with songs
Jos 4:14 just as they had *f* Moses all
Jg 6:27 as he *f* the household of his
1Sa 15:24 I *f* the people and so obeyed
1Ki 18:12 *f* Jehovah from his youth
2Ki 4:1 continually *f* Jehovah, and
1Ch 16:25 *f* more than all other gods
Ne 7:2 *f* the true God more than many
Job 1:9 for nothing that Job has *f* God
Ps 55:19 And who have not *f* God
76:8 earth itself *f* and kept quiet
130:4 In order that you may be *f*
Eze 11:8 A sword you have *f*, and a
Ho 10:3 for we have not *f* Jehovah
Mal 3:5 while they have not *f* me
Mt 14:5 he *f* the crowd, because they
21:46 they *f* the crowds, because
Mr 12:12 they *f* the crowd, for they
Lu 20:19 but they *f* the people; for

Fearers
2Ki 17:32 came to be *f* of Jehovah
17:33 Jehovah that they became *f*
2Ki 17:41 came to be *f* of Jehovah
Ps 22:23 You *f* of Jehovah, praise him!
135:20 *f* of Jehovah, bless Jehovah

Fearful
Ge 28:17 And he grew *f* and added
De 20:8 Who is the man that is *f*
1Ki 3:28 became *f* because of the king
Ps 25:12 the man *f* of Jehovah
25:14 belongs to those *f* of him
Joe 2:21 Do not be *f*, O ground
2:22 Do not be *f*, you beasts of
Mt 10:28 *f* of those who kill the body
28:5 Do not you be *f*, for I know
Mr 5:15 and they grew *f*
9:6 for they became quite *f*
Lu 2:9 and they became very *f*
8:35 and they became *f*
9:34 the cloud, they became *f*
21:11 will be *f* sights and from
Joh 6:19 and they became *f*
19:8 he became more *f*
Ac 16:38 grew *f* when they heard that
Heb 10:27 *f* expectation of judgment
10:31 It is a *f* thing to fall
12:21 Moses said: I am *f* and
Re 1:17 Do not be *f*. I am the First

Fearfulness
Eze 1:18 height that they caused *f*

Fearing
Ex 18:21 *f* God, trustworthy men
De 8:6 in his ways and by *f* him
Jos 22:25 sons desist from *f* Jehovah
1Ki 18:3 to be one greatly *f* Jehovah
2Ki 17:34 none *f* Jehovah and none
Ne 1:11 take delight in *f* your name
Job 1:1 *f* God and turning aside from
1:8 *f* God and turning aside from
2:3 and upright, *f* God and turning
Ps 15:4 those *f* Jehovah he honors
22:25 pay in front of those *f* him
31:19 treasured up for those *f* you
33:18 Jehovah is toward those *f*
34:7 camping all around those *f*
34:9 there is no lack to those *f*
60:4 given to those *f* you a signal
61:5 of those *f* your name
85:9 salvation is near to those *f*
103:11 is superior toward those *f*
103:13 shown mercy to those *f* him
103:17 Toward those *f* him, And his
111:5 he has given to those *f* him
115:13 bless those *f* Jehovah
118:4 Let those *f* Jehovah now say
119:74 Those *f* you are the ones
119:79 those *f* you turn back to me
128:1 Happy is everyone *f* Jehovah
145:19 desire of those *f* him he
147:11 pleasure in those *f* him
Pr 13:13 one *f* the commandment is
14:2 uprightness is *f* Jehovah
Ec 8:12 well with those *f* the true
Da 6:26 *f* before the God of Daniel
Jon 1:9 the God of the heavens I am *f*
Mal 2:5 And he continued *f* me
Ac 10:2 one *f* God together with all
10:22 *f* God and well reported by
27:29 *f* we might be cast
Heb 11:27 not *f* the anger of the king
1Pe 3:6 and not *f* any cause for terror
Re 11:18 reward . . . those *f* your name

Fear-inspiring
Ge 28:17 How *f* this place is!
Ex 34:10 a *f* thing that I am doing
De 1:19 that great and *f* wilderness
7:21 a great and *f* God
8:15 the great and *f* wilderness
10:17 the God great, mighty and *f*
10:21 these great and *f* things
28:58 this glorious and *f* name
Jg 13:6 angel of the true God, very *f*
2Sa 7:23 for them great and *f* things
1Ch 17:21 achievements and *f* things
Ne 1:5 the God great and *f*, keeping
4:14 Jehovah the great and the *f*
9:32 the God great, mighty and *f*
Job 37:22 Upon God dignity is *f*
Ps 45:4 instruct you in *f* things
47:2 Jehovah, the Most High, is *f*
65:5 *f* things in righteousness
66:3 How *f* your works are!
66:5 dealing with . . . men is *f*
68:35 God is *f* out of your grand
Ps 76:7 You—*f* you are, And who can
76:12 *F* he is to the kings of the
89:7 He is grand and *f* over all
96:4 He is *f* above all other gods
99:3 Great and *f*, holy it is
106:22 *F* things at the Red Sea
111:9 His name is holy and *f*
139:14 *f* way I am wonderfully
145:6 of your own *f* things
Isa 18:2 to a people *f* everywhere
18:7 from a people *f* everywhere
21:1 coming, from a *f* land
64:3 you did *f* things for which
Da 9:4 the great One and the *f* One
Joe 2:11 day of Jehovah is . . . very *f*
2:31 great and *f* day of Jehovah
Hab 1:7 Frightful and *f* it is
Zep 2:11 Jehovah will be *f* against
Mal 1:14 my name will be *f* among
4:5 great and *f* day of Jehovah

Fearlessly
Lu 1:74 the privilege of *f* rendering
Php 1:14 to speak the word of God *f*

Fears
Ps 128:4 be blessed Who *f* Jehovah
Pr 14:16 wise one *f* and is turning
31:30 woman that *f* Jehovah is the
Ec 7:18 he that *f* God will go forth
Ac 10:35 man that *f* him and works
2Co 7:5 fights without, *f* within

Fearsome
Da 7:7 fourth beast, *f* and terrible
7:19 extraordinarily *f*, the teeth
Heb 12:21 the display was so *f* that

Fearsomeness
De 4:34 with great *f* like all that
26:8 with great *f* and with signs
Jer 32:21 and with great *f*

Feast
Ge 19:3 he made a *f* for them, and he
21:8 prepared a big *f* on the day
26:30 *f* for them and they ate and
29:22 and made a *f*
40:20 a *f* for all his servants
Nu 28:26 in your *f* of weeks you
1Sa 25:36 he was having a *f* in his
25:36 like the *f* of the king; and
30:16 *f* on account of all the
2Sa 3:20 David proceeded to make a *f*
1Ki 3:15 a *f* for all his servants
2Ki 6:23 he spread a great *f* for them
2Ch 30:22 eat the appointed *f* for
Pr 15:15 that is good at heart has a *f*
Jer 16:5 the house of a mourners' *f*
Da 5:1 made a big *f* for a thousand of
Mt 22:2 king, that made a marriage *f*
22:3 invited to the marriage *f*
22:4 Come to the marriage *f*
22:8 marriage *f* indeed is ready
22:9 invite to the marriage *f*
25:10 with him to the marriage *f*
Lu 5:29 Levi spread a big reception *f*
14:8 to a marriage *f*, do not lie
14:13 spread a *f*, invite poor
Joh 2:1 marriage *f* took place in Cana
2:2 invited to the marriage *f*
2:8 it to the director of the *f*
2:9 director of the *f* tasted the
2:9 director of the *f* called the
Jude 12 while they *f* with you

Feasting
2Pe 2:13 while *f* together with you

Feasts
Ne 10:33 the appointed *f* and for the
Isa 5:12 and wine at their *f*
Jude 12 in your love *f* while they

Feathers
Le 1:16 remove its crop with its *f*
Da 4:33 long just like eagles' *f* and

Feature
Da 8:11 constant *f* was taken away
8:12 together with the constant *f*
8:13 vision be of the constant *f*
11:31 and remove the constant *f*
12:11 constant *f* has been removed
Heb 7:11 as a *f* the people were given

Featureless
Ps 107:40 wander about in a *f* place

'ecal
g 3:22 *f* matter began to come out

'ed
)e 8:3 *f* you with the manna, which
8:16 who *f* you with manna in the
Ch 28:15 *f* them and gave them drink
'r 4:17 *f* themselves with the bread
Co 3:2 *f* you milk, not something to
as 2:16 keep warm and well *f*, but
e 12:14 *f* for a time and times and

'ee
Sa 4:10 give him the messenger's *f*

'eeble
e 30:42 *f* ones always came to be
Sa 4:1 his hands became *f* and all
17:2 weary and *f* in both hands
e 4:2 What are the *f* Jews doing?
's 61:2 when my heart grows *f*
102:*super* in case he grows *f* and
sa 1:5 and the whole heart is *f*
57:16 spirit itself would grow *f*

'eeble-handed
Ki 19:26 inhabitants will be *f*
sa 37:27 inhabitants will be *f*

'eebleness
e 30:42 flocks showed *f* he would not

'eed
e 29:7 Water the sheep . . . *f* them
37:12 brothers now went to *f* the
41:18 to *f* among the Nile grass
e 22:13 no stranger at all may *f* on
g 13:16 not *f* myself on your bread
Ki 22:27 and *f* him with a reduced
Ch 18:26 *f* him with a reduced
s 141:4 *f* myself on their dainties
r 9:5 *f* yourselves with my bread
23:1 to *f* yourself with a king
23:6 not *f* yourself with the food
sa 11:7 the bear themselves will *f*
14:30 lowly ones will certainly *f*
65:25 will *f* as one, and the lion
er 3:15 *f* you with knowledge and
ze 34:2 the shepherds ought to *f*
34:3 flock itself you do not *f*
34:8 my own sheep they did not *f*
34:10 shepherds will no longer *f*
34:13 *f* them on the mountains
34:14 pasturage I shall *f* them
34:14 fat pasturage they will *f*
34:15 I myself shall *f* my sheep
34:16 *f* that one with judgment
34:18 very best pasturage you *f*
34:19 should they *f* and the water
34:23 shepherd, and he must *f*
34:23 David . . . will *f* them
a 4:12 all flesh would *f* itself
o 9:2 and winepress do not *f* them
ic 7:14 *f* on Bashan and Gilead as
ep 2:7 Upon them they will *f*
3:13 *f* and actually lie stretched
t 25:37 we see you hungry and *f* you
oh 13:18 used to *f* on my bread has
21:15 He said to him: *F* my lambs
21:17 to him: *F* my little sheep
o 12:20 enemy is hungry, *f* him
Co 13:3 my belongings to *f* others
ude 12 shepherds that *f* themselves
e 12:6 *f* her there a thousand two

'eeders
ze 34:2 have become *f* of themselves

'eeding
e 41:2 they went *f* among the Nile
's 80:13 keep *f* upon it
81:16 *f* him off the fat of the
a 4:5 that are *f* among the lilies
sa 44:20 He is *f* on ashes
er 2:16 *f* on you at the crown of the
ze 34:8 shepherds kept *f* themselves
34:10 cease from *f* my sheep, and
34:12 *f* his drove in the day of
o 12:1 Ephraim is *f* on wind and
r 5:11 was there at the mountain *f*
u 8:32 was *f* there on the mountain

'eeds
t 6:26 your heavenly Father *f* them
u 12:24 and yet God *f* them
oh 6:54 He that *f* on my flesh and
6:56 He that *f* on my flesh and
6:57 he also that *f* on me, even
Joh 6:58 *f* on this bread will live
Eph 5:29 but he *f* and cherishes it

Feel
Ge 27:21 may *f* you, my son, to know
45:5 do not *f* hurt and do not be
45:20 do not let your eye *f* sorry
Ex 13:17 people will *f* regret when
32:12 and *f* regret over the evil
32:14 Jehovah began to *f* regret
Nu 22:3 Moab began to *f* a sickening
23:19 that he should *f* regret
De 7:16 Your eye must not *f* sorry for
13:8 nor should your eye *f* sorry
13:8 nor must you *f* compassion
19:13 Your eye should not *f* sorry
19:21 your eye should not *f* sorry
25:12 Your eye must *f* no sorrow
32:36 *f* regret over his servants
Jg 2:18 Jehovah would *f* regret over
11:20 Sihon did not *f* sure about
16:26 permit me to *f* the pillars
19:6 and let your heart *f* good
19:9 and let your heart *f* good
19:22 making their hearts *f* good
21:6 Israel began to *f* regret over
1Sa 1:6 making her *f* disconcerted
1:8 why does your heart *f* bad?
15:29 and He will not *f* regrets
15:29 man so as to *f* regrets
20:3 for fear he may *f* hurt
2Sa 24:16 Jehovah began to *f* regret
1Ki 1:1 but he would not *f* warm
1:2 king will certainly *f* warm
1Ch 21:15 began to *f* regret over the
2Ch 36:17 *f* compassion for young man
Ezr 9:6 O my God, I do *f* ashamed and
Ne 8:10 and do not *f* hurt, for the
8:11 day is holy; and do not *f* hurt
13:22 do *f* sorry for me according
Job 3:6 not *f* glad among the days of
23:15 *f* disturbed because of him
Ps 21:6 *f* glad with the rejoicing at
58:9 your pots *f* the kindled
72:13 *f* sorry for the lowly one
78:40 him *f* hurt in the desert
90:13 *f* regret over your servants
106:45 *f* regret according to the
110:4 and he will *f* no regret
115:7 Hands . . . but they cannot *f*
119:158 I do *f* a loathing, because
135:14 *f* regret even over his
139:21 *f* a loathing for those
Pr 3:24 lie down you will *f* no dread
Isa 8:21 has made himself *f* indignant
10:7 he will *f* inclined
13:18 their eye will not *f* sorry
50:7 not have to *f* humiliated
54:4 and do not *f* humiliated
63:10 made his holy spirit *f* hurt
Jer 3:3 have refused to *f* humiliated
6:15 Did they *f* shame because it
6:15 do not *f* any shame
6:15 even how to *f* humiliated
8:12 Did they *f* shame because
8:12 could not *f* ashamed
8:12 even how to *f* humiliated
10:14 *f* shame because of the
13:14 nor *f* any sorrow, and I
18:8 *f* regret over the calamity
18:10 also *f* regret over the good
21:7 He will not *f* sorry for them
22:22 *f* humiliated because of all
26:3 I shall have to *f* regret
26:13 *f* regret for the calamity
42:10 *f* regret over the calamity
44:10 they did not *f* crushed
46:24 will certainly *f* shame
51:17 *f* ashamed because of the
Eze 5:11 my eye will not *f* sorry and
6:9 *f* a loathing in their faces at
7:4 my eye will not *f* sorry for
7:4 neither will I *f* compassion
7:9 Neither will my eye *f* sorry
7:9 nor shall I *f* compassion
8:18 My eye will not *f* sorry
8:18 neither shall I *f* compassion
9:5 Let not your eye *f* sorry, and
9:5 and do not *f* any compassion
9:10 my eye will not *f* sorry
16:42 I shall no more *f* offended
16:54 and you must *f* humiliated
16:61 and *f* humiliated when you
20:17 my eye began to *f* sorry for
Eze 20:43 actually *f* a loathing at
24:14, 14 I *f* sorry nor *f* regret
36:31 bound to *f* a loathing at
36:32 ashamed and *f* humiliation
43:10 *f* humiliated because of
43:11 *f* humiliated because of all
Da 2:1 spirit began to *f* agitated
Joe 2:13 *f* regret on account of the
2:14 *f* regret and let remain
2:17 Do *f* sorry, O Jehovah, for
Jon 3:9 *f* regret and turn back from
4:11 *f* sorry for Nineveh the great
Zec 1:17 *f* regrets over Zion and yet
9:5 will also *f* very severe pains
Mt 15:32 said: I *f* pity for the crowd
21:32 did not *f* regret afterwards
Mr 8:2 I *f* pity for the crowd
Lu 13:17 opposers began to *f* shame
17:9 not *f* gratitude to the slave
24:39 *f* me and see, because a
2Co 12:7 not *f* overly exalted, there
Heb 7:21 and he will *f* no regret
1Pe 4:16 let him not *f* shame, but

Feeling
Ge 27:22 and he went *f* him, after
31:34 Laban went *f* through the
Ex 23:28 *f* of dejection ahead of you
Nu 11:29 Are you *f* jealous for me?
De 7:20 send the *f* of dejection upon
Jos 24:12 the *f* of dejection ahead
Ru 3:7 and his heart was *f* good
1Sa 25:36 Nabal's heart was *f* good
26:19 *f* myself attached to the
2Sa 10:5 men . . . *f* very humiliated
21:2 in his *f* jealous for the sons
1Ki 8:66 *f* merry of heart over all
2Ch 7:10 *f* good at heart over the
Job 20:22 he will be *f* anxious
Ps 95:10 *f* a loathing toward that
119:120 flesh has had a creepy *f*
Pr 28:14 that is *f* dread constantly
Isa 7:16 are *f* a sickening dread will
Jer 15:6 I have got tired of *f* regret
26:19 Jehovah got to *f* regret
Eze 7:12 hot *f* against all its crowd
7:14 my hot *f* is against all its
Jon 4:2 *f* regret over the calamity
Zec 1:15 I am *f* indignant against the
Mr 14:5 *f* great displeasure at her
Php 1:14 *f* confidence by reason of my
1Pe 3:8 showing fellow *f*, having

Feelings
Ge 34:7 hurt in their *f* and they grew
1Ki 1:6 his father did not hurt his *f*
Eze 35:11 owing to your *f* of hatred
Jas 5:17 Elijah was a man with *f*

Feels
Ge 27:12 What if my father *f* me?
Job 10:1 *f* a loathing toward my life
16:13 and *f* no compassion
Ca 2:7 love in me until it *f* inclined
3:5 love in me until it *f* inclined
8:4 love in me until it *f* inclined

Feet
Ge 18:4 you must have your *f* washed
19:2 and have your *f* washed
24:32 and water to wash his *f* and
24:32 *f* of the men who were with
29:1 Jacob set his *f* in motion
43:24 might have their *f* washed
49:10 staff from between his *f*
49:33 gathered his *f* up onto the
Ex 3:5 your sandals from off your *f*
4:25 caused it to touch his *f* and
12:11 sandals on your *f* and your
24:10 under his *f* there was what
25:12 put them above its four *f*
25:26 that are for the four *f*
30:19 wash their hands and their *f*
30:21 wash their hands and *f* that
37:3 for above its four *f*, with
37:13 that were for the four *f*
40:31 hands and their *f* at it
Le 11:21 leaper legs above their *f*
11:42 great number of *f* of all the
13:12 from his head to his *f*
Nu 20:19 than to pass through on my *f*
De 2:28 let me pass through on my *f*
33:3 they—they reclined at your *f*
Jos 3:13 soles of the *f* of the priests
3:15 the *f* of the priests carrying
4:3 priests' *f* stood motionless

Jos 4:9 f of the priests carrying the
4:18 soles of the f of the priests
5:15 your sandals from off your f
9:5 and patched sandals on their f
10:24 Place your f on the back of
10:24 f on the back of their necks
Jg 1:6 and the great toes of his f
1:7 great toes of their f cut off
5:27 Between her f he collapsed
5:27 Between her f he collapsed
19:21 washed their f and began
Ru 2:7 kept on her f from that time
3:4 come and uncover him at his f
3:7 uncovered him at his f and lay
3:8 look! a woman lying at his f
3:14 she kept lying at his f until
1Sa 2:9 f of his loyal ones he guards
14:13 up on his hands and his f
17:6 greaves of copper above his f
25:24 She then fell at his f and
25:41 maidservant to wash the f
2Sa 2:18 Asahel was swift on his f
3:34 f had not been put into
4:4 had a son lame in the f
4:12 off their hands and their f
9:3 of Jonathan, lame in the f
9:13 he was lame in both of his f
11:8 your house and bathe your f
15:16 all his household at his f
15:17 all the people at his f
19:24 he had not attended to his f
21:20 six toes on each of his f
22:10 gloom was beneath his f
22:34 f like those of the hinds
22:39 they will fall under my f
1Ki 2:5 sandals that were on his f
5:3 under the soles of his f
14:6 heard the sound of her f as
14:12 your f come into the city
15:23 he got diseased in his f
2Ki 4:27 took hold of him by his f
4:37 to come in and fall at his f
6:32 sound of the f of his lord
9:35 skull and the f and the
13:21 to life and stood upon his f
19:24 with the soles of my f all
1Ch 28:2 David the king rose to his f
2Ch 3:13 cherubs . . . upon their f
16:12 ailment in his f until he
Ne 9:21 f themselves did not become
Es 8:3 and fell down before his f and
Job 12:5 for those of wobbling f
13:27 keep my f put in the stocks
13:27 For the soles of my f you
18:8 let go into a net by his f
18:11 indeed chase him at his f
29:15 f to the lame one I was
30:12 My f they have let go
33:11 He puts my f in the stocks
Ps 8:6 you have put under his f
18:9 thick gloom was beneath his f
18:33 my f like those of the hinds
18:38 They will fall under my f
22:16 are at my hands and my f
25:15 brings my f out of the net
31:8 my f stand in a roomy place
40:2 raised up my f upon a crag
47:3 national groups under our f
56:13 my f from stumbling
73:2 my f had almost turned aside
105:18 fetters they afflicted his f
110:1 as a stool for your f
115:7 F . . . but they cannot walk
119:59 back my f to your reminders
119:101 I have restrained my f
122:2 Our f proved to be standing
Pr 1:16 f are those that run to sheer
5:5 Her f are descending to death
6:18 f that are in a hurry to run
6:28 f themselves not be scorched
7:11 house her f do not keep
19:2 that is hastening with his f
26:6 one that is mutilating his f
Ec 5:1 Guard your f whenever you go
Ca 5:3 I have washed my f. How can I
Isa 3:16 f they make a tinkling sound
6:2 two he kept his f covered
7:20 and the hair of the f, and
20:2 draw from off your f
23:7 f used to bring her far
26:6 f of the afflicted one, the
28:3 With the f the eminent
32:20 f of the bull and of the ass
37:25 with the soles of my f all
Isa 41:2 call him to His f, to give
41:3 on his f over the path by
49:23 the dust of your f they
52:7 f of the one bringing good
59:7 f keep running to sheer
60:13 the very place of my f
60:14 at the very soles of your f
Jer 13:16 your f strike up against
14:10 their f they have not kept
18:22 they have hid for my f
La 1:13 has spread out a net for my f
3:34 crushing beneath one's f all
Eze 1:7, 7 their f were straight f
1:7 the sole of their f was like
2:1 stand up upon your f that I
2:2 made me stand up upon my f
3:24 made me stand up on my f
16:25 sprawl out your f to every
24:17 you should put upon your f
24:23 your sandals be upon your f
25:6 and you stamped with the f
32:2 the waters with your f and
34:18 trample down with your f
34:18 stamping with your very f
34:19 ground trampled by your f
34:19 the stamping of your f
37:10 live and stand upon their f
43:7 place of the soles of my f
Da 2:33 its f were partly of iron and
2:34 struck the image on its f of
2:41 f and the toes to be partly of
2:42 toes of the f being partly of
7:4 stand up on two f just like
7:7 was treading down with its f
7:19 what was left with its f
10:6 place of his f were like the
Am 2:15 no one swift on his f will
Na 1:3 is the powder of his f
1:15 f of one bringing good news
Hab 3:5 fever would go forth at his f
3:19 f like those of the hinds
Zec 14:4 his f will actually stand
14:12 one is standing upon one's f
Mal 4:3 under the soles of your f in
Mt 5:35 it is the footstool of his f
7:6 trample them under their f
10:14 shake the dust off your f
15:30 threw them at his f, and he
18:8 with two hands or two f into
22:44 your enemies beneath your f
28:9 caught him by his f and did
Mr 5:22 Jairus . . . fell at his f
6:11 dirt that is beneath your f
7:25 prostrated herself at his f
9:45 lame than with two f to be
10:50 he leaped to his f and went
12:36 your enemies beneath your f
Lu 1:79 direct our f prosperously in
7:38 a position behind at his f
7:38 wet his f with her tears and
7:38 she tenderly kissed his f and
7:44 gave me no water for my f
7:44 wet my f with her tears and
7:45 tenderly kissing my f
7:46 greased my f with perfumed
8:35 sitting at the f of Jesus
8:41 he fell at the f of Jesus and
9:5 shake the dust off your f for
10:11 dust that got stuck to our f
10:39 down at the f of the Lord
15:22 and sandals on his f
17:16 upon his face at Jesus' f
20:43 as a stool for your f
24:39 See my hands and my f, that
24:40 showed . . . hands and his f
Joh 11:2 his f dry with her hair
11:32 fell at his f, saying to
11:44 his f and hands bound with
12:3 greased the f of Jesus and
12:3 wiped his f dry with her
13:5 wash the f of the disciples
13:6 Lord, are you washing my f?
13:8 certainly never wash my f
13:9 Lord, not my f only, but
13:10 have more than his f washed
13:12 he had washed their f and
13:14 Teacher, washed your f, you
13:14 wash the f of one another
20:12 one at the f where the
21:8 about three hundred f away
Ac 2:35 enemies as a stool for your f
3:7 soles of his f and his ankle
4:35 them at the f of the apostles
4:37 it at the f of the apostles
Ac 5:2 at the f of the apostles
5:9 f of those who buried your
5:10 she fell down at his f and
7:33 Take the sandals off your f
7:58 f of a young man called Saul
10:25 fell down at his f and did
13:25 sandal of whose f I am not
13:51 shook the dust off their f
14:8 man disabled in his f, lame
14:10 Stand up erect on your f
16:24 their f fast in the stocks
21:11 bound his own f and hands
22:3 at the f of Gamaliel
26:16 rise and stand on your f
Ro 3:15 f are speedy to shed blood
10:15 comely are the f of those
16:20 crush Satan under your f
1Co 12:21 the head cannot say to the f
15:25 put all enemies under his f
15:27 all things under his f
Eph 1:22 all things under his f, and
6:15 f shod with the equipment
1Ti 5:10 washed the f of holy ones
Heb 1:13 as a stool for your f
2:8 you subjected under his f
10:13 placed as a stool for his f
12:13 straight paths for your f
Re 1:13 that reached down to the f
1:15 f were like fine copper when
1:17 I fell as dead at his f
2:18 his f are like fine copper
3:9 do obeisance before your f and
10:1 his f were as fiery pillars
11:11 and they stood upon their f
12:1 moon was beneath her f, and
13:2 f were as those of a bear
19:10 I fell down before his f to
22:8 before the f of the angel

Felix
Ac 23:24 safely to F the governor
23:26 his excellency, Governor F
24:3 Your Excellency F, with the
24:22 F, knowing quite accurately
24:24 F arrived with Drusilla his
24:25 F became frightened and
24:27 F was succeeded by Porcius
24:27 F desired to gain favor
25:14 man left prisoner by F

Fell
Ge 15:12 a deep sleep f upon Abram
17:3 Abram f upon his face, and
17:17 Abraham f upon his face and
24:67 he f in love with her, and
26:20 the shepherds of Gerar f to
26:21 f to quarreling over it also
34:3 he f in love with the young
45:14 f upon the neck of Benjamin
46:29 at once f upon his neck and
50:1 Joseph f upon the face of his
50:18 f down before him and said
Ex 17:2 people f to quarreling with
32:28 there f of the people on that
Nu 14:5 Moses and Aaron f upon their
16:4 Moses . . . f upon his face
16:22 f upon their faces and said
16:45 they f upon their faces
20:6 and f upon their faces, and
Jos 5:14 Joshua f on his face to the
7:6 f upon his face to the earth
8:25 all those who f on that day
Jg 2:11 the sons of Israel f to doing
4:16 camp of Sisera f by the edge
5:27 he f, he lay down; Between
5:27 he f; Where he collapsed
5:27 there he f overcome
7:13 it f, and it went turning it
7:13 and the tent f flat
12:6 So there f at that time
13:20 they f upon their faces to
16:4 he f in love with a woman in
19:26 f down at the entrance of
20:44 there f eighteen thousand
20:46 those of Benjamin that f on
Ru 2:10 she f upon her face and bowed
1Sa 4:10 there f thirty thousand men
14:32 f to eating along with the
20:41 f on his face to the earth
25:23 f upon her face before David
25:24 She then f at his feet and
28:20 Saul quickly f down his
31:4 took the sword and f upon it
31:5 f upon his own sword and
2Sa 1:2 f down to the earth and

2Sa 2:16 so that they *f* down together
2:23 he *f* there and died where he
2:23 Asahel *f* and then died
9:6 *f* upon his face and prostrated
11:17 servants of David, *f* and
13:1 son of David *f* in love with
14:22 Joab *f* upon his face to the
19:18 he *f* down before the king
20:8 came forth, and so it *f* out
21:9 the seven of them *f* together
1Ki 2:32 he *f* upon two men more
2:34 *f* upon him and put him to
2:46 *f* upon him, so that he died
14:1 the son of Jeroboam *f* sick
17:17 *f* sick, and his sickness
18:7 and *f* upon his face and said
18:39 *f* upon their faces and said
19:5 *f* asleep under the broom
20:25 military force that *f* from
2Ki 1:2 *f* down through the grating
3:19 every good tree you should *f*
3:25 every good tree they would *f*
6:5 axhead itself *f* into the
1Ch 10:4 Saul took the sword and *f*
10:5 *f* upon the sword and died
21:14 seventy thousand persons *f*
21:16 *f* down upon their faces
26:14 the lot to the east *f* to
2Ch 20:18 *f* down before Jehovah to do
29:9 forefathers *f* by the sword
32:24 Hezekiah *f* sick to the point
Ne 6:16 once *f* very much in their
Es 8:3 and *f* down before his feet and
Job 1:16 very fire of God *f* from the
1:19 it *f* upon the young people
Ps 27:2 They . . . stumbled and *f*
78:64 they *f* by the very sword
Isa 9:8 and it *f* upon Israel
La 1:7 her people *f* into the hand of
Eze 1:28 then I *f* upon my face, and I
8:1 hand of . . . Jehovah *f* upon me
11:5 spirit of Jehovah *f* upon me
Da 2:46 Nebuchadnezzar himself *f* down
3:23 *f* down bound in the midst of
4:31 voice that *f* from the heavens
7:20 before which three *f*, even
8:17 so that I *f* upon my face
10:7 trembling that *f* upon them
Jon 1:7 finally the lot *f* upon Jonah
Mt 2:16 *f* into a great rage, and he
13:4 seeds *f* alongside the road
13:5 *f* upon the rocky places
13:7 *f* among the thorns, and the
13:8 others *f* upon the fine soil
14:15 evening *f* his disciples came
17:6 disciples *f* upon their faces
18:26 slave *f* down and began to do
18:29 his fellow slave *f* down and
25:36 I *f* sick and you looked
26:39 he *f* upon his face, praying
27:45 darkness *f* over all the land
Mr 2:25 David did when he *f* in need
4:4 some seed *f* alongside the road
4:5 seed *f* upon the rocky place
4:7 other seed *f* among the thorns
4:8 others *f* upon the fine soil
5:22 Jairus . . . *f* at his feet
5:33 *f* down before him and told
10:17 *f* upon his knees before him
15:33 darkness *f* over the whole
Lu 1:12 and fear *f* upon him
1:44 your greeting *f* upon my ears
1:65 fear *f* upon all those living
4:25 famine *f* upon all the land
4:36 astonishment *f* upon all, and
5:8 Peter *f* down at the knees of
5:12 he *f* upon his face and begged
8:5 *f* alongside the road and was
8:7 Some other *f* among the thorns
8:8 other *f* upon the good soil
8:14 that which *f* among the thorns
8:23 they were sailing he *f* asleep
8:28 he cried aloud and *f* down
8:41 he *f* at the feet of Jesus and
8:47 woman came trembling and *f*
10:30 *f* among robbers, who both
10:36 man that *f* among the robbers
13:4 tower in Siloam *f*, thereby
15:20 ran and *f* upon his neck and
17:16 he *f* upon his face at Jesus'
19:7 all *f* to muttering, saying
23:44 darkness *f* over all the earth
Joh 6:16 evening *f*, his disciples
7:15 the Jews *f* to wondering
Joh 11:32 *f* at his feet, saying to
18:6 back and *f* to the ground
Ac 1:26 and the lot *f* upon Matthias
5:5 Ananias *f* down and expired
5:10 she *f* down at his feet and
5:24 *f* into a quandary over these
7:60 this he *f* asleep in death
9:4 he *f* to the ground and heard
9:18 *f* from his eyes what looked
10:10 he *f* into a trance
10:25 Cornelius met him, *f* down
10:44 holy spirit *f* upon all those
11:15 holy spirit *f* upon them
12:7 his chains *f* off his hands
13:11 and darkness *f* upon him, and
13:36 *f* asleep in death and was
16:29 *f* down before Paul and Silas
19:17 a fear *f* upon them all, and
19:35 the image that *f* from heaven
20:9 Eutychus *f* into a deep sleep
20:9 *f* down from the third story
20:37 they *f* upon Paul's neck and
21:40 When a great silence *f*, he
22:7 I *f* to the ground and
22:17 praying . . . I *f* into a trance
27:27 fourteenth night *f* and we
Ro 11:11 so that they *f* completely
11:22 who *f* there is severity
1Co 15:18 who *f* asleep in death in
2Co 11:9 with you and I *f* in need
Php 2:27 he *f* sick nearly to the point
Heb 3:17 *f* in the wilderness
11:30 the walls of Jericho *f* down
2Pe 3:4 forefathers *f* asleep in death
Re 1:17 I *f* as dead at his feet
5:8 twenty-four elders *f* down
5:14 elders *f* down and worshiped
6:13 stars of heaven *f* to the earth
7:11 they *f* upon their faces before
8:10 star burning as a lamp *f* from
8:10 *f* upon a third of the rivers
11:11 and great fear *f* upon those
11:13 and a tenth of the city *f*
11:16 *f* upon their faces and
16:19 cities of the nations *f*; and
19:4 *f* down and worshiped God
19:10 I *f* down before his feet to
22:8 I *f* down to worship before

Felled
2Ch 32:21 *f* him with the sword

Felling
2Ki 6:5 a certain one was *f* his beam

Felloes
1Ki 7:33 their *f* and their spokes

Fellow
Ex 21:14 becomes heated against his *f*
21:18 strike his *f* with a stone or
22:7 give his *f* money or articles
22:8 hand upon the goods of his *f*
22:9 double compensation to his *f*
22:10 give his *f* an ass or bull
22:11 hand on the goods of his *f*
22:14 ask for something of his *f*
22:26 seize the garment of your *f*
32:27 kill . . . each one his *f* and
33:11 man would speak to his *f*
Le 19:13 You must not defraud your *f*
19:18 must love your *f* as yourself
De 4:42 slays his *f* without knowing
15:2 debt that he may let his *f*
15:2 press his *f* . . . for payment
Ru 4:7 sandal off and give it to his *f*
1Sa 25:17 a good-for-nothing *f* to
25:21 that belongs to this *f*
1Ki 22:27 *f* in the house of detention
2Ch 18:26 Put this *f* in the house of
20:23 to bring his own *f* to ruin
Job 6:14 from his own *f*, He will
16:21 a son of man and his *f*
Pr 16:29 violence will seduce his *f*
18:17 his *f* comes in and certainly
21:10 his *f* will be shown no favor
Jer 23:35 saying each one to his *f*
Mt 9:3 This *f* is blaspheming
12:24 *f* does not expel the demons
18:28 *f* slaves that was owing him
18:29 his *f* slave fell down and
18:31 his *f* slaves saw the things
18:33 had mercy on your *f* slave
20:13 said, *F*, I do you no wrong
22:12 *F*, how did you get in here
24:49 start to beat his *f* slaves
Mt 26:50 *F*, for what purpose are you
Lu 14:10 in front of all your *f* guests
14:15 one of the *f* guests said to
Joh 11:16 said to his *f* disciples
Ac 24:5 found this man a pestilent *f*
Ro 16:3 my *f* workers in Christ Jesus
16:7 *f* captives, who are men of
16:9 Urbanus our *f* worker in
16:21 Timothy my *f* worker greets
1Co 3:9 we are God's *f* workers
2Co 1:24 are *f* workers for your joy
8:23 *f* worker for your interests
Eph 2:19 *f* citizens of the holy ones
3:6 joint heirs and *f* members
Php 2:25, 25 *f* worker and *f* soldier
4:3 as the rest of my *f* workers
Col 1:7 Epaphras our beloved *f* slave
4:7 and *f* slave in the Lord
4:10 Aristarchus my *f* captive
4:11 *f* workers for the kingdom of
Phm 1 our beloved one and *f* worker
2 to Archippus, our *f* soldier
23 Epaphras my *f* captive in
24 Demas, Luke, my *f* workers
Heb 8:11 teach each one his *f* citizen
1Pe 3:8 showing *f* feeling, having
3Jo 8 become *f* workers in the truth
Re 6:11 *f* slaves and their brothers
19:10 *f* slave of you and of your
22:9 *f* slave of you and of your

Fellowman
Ex 20:16 as a witness against your *f*
20:17 that belongs to your *f*
Le 20:10 with the wife of his *f*
De 5:20 a falsehood against your *f*
5:21 that belongs to your *f*
19:4 he strikes his *f* without
19:5 with his *f* into the woods
19:5 hit his *f* and he has died
19:11 a man hating his *f*, and he
19:14 the boundary marks of your *f*
22:24 humiliated the wife of his *f*
22:26 a man rises up against his *f*
23:24 into the vineyard of your *f*
23:25 the standing grain of your *f*
23:25 the standing grain of your *f*
24:10 In case you lend your *f* a
27:17 the boundary mark of his *f*
27:24 who fatally strikes his *f*
Jos 20:5 he struck his *f* fatally
1Sa 14:20 come to be against his *f*
15:28 *f* of yours who is better
28:17 give it to your *f* David
2Sa 12:11 and give them to your *f*
1Ki 8:31 a man sins against his *f*
2Ch 6:22 If a man sins against his *f*
Job 12:4 a laughingstock to his *f* I
Pr 3:28 to your *f*: Go, and come back
3:29 fabricate against your *f*
6:1 have gone surety for your *f*
6:3 come into the palm of your *f*
6:3 and storm your *f* with
6:29 with the wife of his *f*
11:9 apostate brings his *f* to ruin
11:12 has despised his own *f*, but
14:20 Even to his *f* one who is of
14:21 The one despising his own *f*
24:28 a witness against your *f*
25:8 your *f* now humiliates you
25:9 your own cause with your *f*
25:17 rare at the house of your *f*
25:18 testifying against his *f* as
26:19 man that has tricked his *f*
27:14 blessing his *f* with a loud
Isa 3:5 even each one over his *f*
Jer 19:9 each one the flesh of his *f*
22:13 by use of his *f* who serves
Ro 13:8 for he that loves his *f* has

Fellowman's
Ex 20:17 must not desire your *f* house
20:17 must not desire your *f* wife
De 5:21 desire your *f* wife. Neither
5:21 crave your *f* house, his field

Fellow's
Le 19:16 stand up against your *f* blood

Fellows
Jg 14:10 way the young *f* used to do
18:2 men who were valiant *f*, out
Ru 3:10 in not going after the young *f*
1Ki 21:10 good-for-nothing *f*, sit in
21:13 *f*, came in and sat down in
1Ch 5:18 valiant *f*, men carrying

1Ch 5:24 mighty *f*, men of fame
2Ch 13:7 good-for-nothing *f*, kept
Da 7:20 bigger than that of its *f*

Fellowship
Pr 20:19 you must have no *f*
2Co 6:14 what *f* do righteousness and

Felt
Ge 6:6 Jehovah *f* regrets that he had
6:6 and he *f* hurt at his heart
31:37 you have *f* through all my
Ex 1:12 they *f* a sickening dread as a
2:6 she *f* compassion for him
10:21 and the darkness may be *f*
18:9 Jethro *f* glad over all the
Jg 21:15 *f* regret over Benjamin
1Sa 18:29 Saul *f* still more fear
24:10 I *f* sorry for you and said
2Sa 13:2 *f* sick on account of Tamar
19:2 king has *f* hurt over his son
19:3 when they *f* disgraced
21:7 the king *f* compassion upon
2Ch 36:15 he *f* compassion for his
Ezr 8:22 *f* ashamed to ask a military
Job 31:29 I *f* excited because evil had
Ps 78:53 security, and they *f* no dread
Jer 2:26 house of Israel have *f* shame
4:28 I have not *f* regret, nor
9:19 How much we have *f* shame
15:9 become ashamed and *f* abashed
20:16 while He has *f* no regret
31:19 turning back I *f* regret
31:19 I also *f* humiliated, for
36:24 And they *f* no dread
Eze 16:5 No eye *f* sorry for you to do
Da 8:27 Daniel, I *f* exhausted and was
Joe 1:11 Farmers have *f* shame
Am 7:3 Jehovah *f* regret over this
7:6 Jehovah *f* regret over this
Jon 3:10 *f* regret over the calamity
4:10 *f* sorry for the bottle-gourd
Zec 1:15 *f* indignant to only a little
8:14 has said, and I *f* no regret
11:8 their own soul *f* a loathing
Mt 4:2 forty nights, then he *f* hungry
9:33 crowds *f* amazement and said
9:36 seeing the crowds he *f* pity
14:14 he *f* pity for them, and he
15:31 crowd *f* amazement as they
21:30 he *f* regret and went out
27:3 *f* remorse and turned the
Mr 4:41 they *f* an unusual fear, and
10:21 *f* love for him and said to
10:32 they *f* amazement; but those
Lu 4:2 were concluded, he *f* hungry
Ac 5:33 they *f* deeply cut and were
7:54 they *f* cut to their hearts
2Co 1:9 *f* within ourselves that we
Heb 12:18 that which can be *f* and
1Jo 1:1 and our hands *f*, concerning

Female
Ge 1:27 male and *f* he created them
5:2 Male and *f* he created them
6:19 Male and *f* they will be
7:3 male and *f*, to preserve
7:9 inside the ark, male and *f*
7:16 male and *f* of every sort of
21:28 Abraham set seven *f* lambs of
21:29 of these seven *f* lambs
21:30 accept the seven *f* lambs at
31:38 *f* sheep and your she-goats
32:14 two hundred *f* sheep and
Ex 2:5 her *f* attendants were walking
35:22 rings and *f* ornaments, all
Le 3:1 herd, whether a male or a *f*
3:6 a male or a *f*, a sound one is
4:28 offering a *f* kid of the goats
4:32 a sound *f* lamb is what he
5:6, 6 *f* from the flock, a *f* lamb
5:6 *f* kid of the goats, for a sin
12:5 Now if she should bear a *f*
12:7 bears either a male or a *f*
14:10 and one sound *f* lamb, in its
15:33 whether a male or a *f*, and
27:4 *f*, the estimated value must
27:5 and for the *f* ten shekels
27:6 *f* the estimated value must be
27:7 and for the *f* ten shekels
Nu 5:3 male or a *f* you should send
6:14 one sound *f* lamb in its first
15:27 present a *f* goat in its first
31:15 you preserved alive every *f*
31:50 and *f* ornaments, in order to
De 4:16 representation of male or *f*
De 7:14 male or a *f* without offspring
2Sa 12:3 nothing but one *f* lamb
12:4 *f* lamb of the man of little
12:6 for the *f* lamb he should
17:8 like a *f* bear that has lost
19:26 saddle the *f* ass for me
19:35 voice of male and *f* singers
2Ch 35:25 male singers and *f* singers
Ezr 2:65 male singers and *f* singers
Ne 7:67 male singers and *f* singers
Job 39:13 the wing of the *f* ostrich
Ec 2:8 male singers and *f* singers
Ca 2:7 by the *f* gazelles or by the
3:5 by the *f* gazelles or by the
4:5 the twins of a *f* gazelle, that
7:3 the twins of a *f* gazelle
Jer 30:6 a *f* that is giving birth
31:22 mere *f* will press around an
Eze 23:45 for *f* shedders of blood
Ho 4:14 the *f* temple prostitutes that
Joe 3:3 *f* child they sold for wine
Mic 1:8 a mourning like *f* ostriches
Mt 19:4 made them male and *f*
Mr 10:6 He made them male and *f*
Ro 1:27 left the natural use of the *f*
Ga 3:28 is neither male nor *f*; for

Females
Ps 78:71 following the *f* giving suck
Ro 1:26 *f* changed the natural use of

Feminine
1Pe 3:7 a weaker vessel, the *f* one

Fence
Isa 17:11 *f* about the plantation of
Mt 21:33 put a *f* around it and dug a
Mr 12:1 vineyard, and put a *f* around

Fenced
Ca 7:2 wheat, *f* about with lilies
Eze 40:12 *f* area in front of the
40:12 *f* area of one cubit on
Eph 2:14 wall in between that *f* them

Fenced-in
Lu 14:23 the roads and the *f* places

Ferment
La 1:20 My very intestines are in a *f*
2:11 My intestines are in a *f*
1Co 5:7 as you are free from *f*

Fermented
Mt 13:33 until the whole mass was *f*
Lu 13:21 until the whole mass was *f*

Ferments
1Co 5:6 a little leaven *f* the whole
Ga 5:9 leaven *f* the whole lump

Fertile
Ge 27:28 the *f* soils of the earth and
27:39 away from the *f* soils of the
Isa 28:1 head of the *f* valley of
28:4 *f* valley must become like
Jas 1:15 *f*, gives birth to sin; in

Fervent
Pr 26:23 *f* lips along with a bad

Fervor
Ne 3:20 worked with *f* and repaired

Festal
Le 19:24 holy thing of *f* exultation to
Nu 10:10 your *f* seasons and at the
Jg 9:27 in carrying on a *f* exultation
Isa 1:14 *f* seasons my soul has hated
33:20 town of our *f* occasions
Jer 46:17 has let the *f* time pass by
Eze 36:38 Jerusalem in her *f* seasons
44:24 regard to all my *f* seasons
45:17 *f* seasons of the house of
46:9 Jehovah in the *f* seasons
46:11 in the *f* seasons the grain
Ho 2:11 her every *f* season to cease
Zep 3:18 absence from your *f* season
Zec 8:19 rejoicing and good *f* seasons

Festered
Ps 38:5 My wounds . . . they have *f*

Festival
Ex 5:1 they may celebrate a *f* to me
10:9 for we have a *f* to Jehovah
12:14 *f* to Jehovah throughout your
12:17 the *f* of unfermented cakes
13:6 seventh day is a *f* to Jehovah
23:14 are to celebrate a *f* to me
23:15 the *f* of unfermented cakes
Ex 23:16 the *f* of harvest of the first
23:16 the *f* of ingathering at the
23:18 fat of my *f* should not stay
32:5 is a *f* to Jehovah tomorrow
34:18 *f* of unfermented cakes you
34:22 carry on your *f* of weeks
34:22 the *f* of ingathering at the
34:25 the *f* of the passover should
Le 23:6 *f* of unfermented cakes to
23:34 *f* of booths for seven days
23:39 celebrate the *f* of Jehovah
23:41 *f* to Jehovah seven days in
Nu 28:17 the fifteenth day . . . a *f*
29:12 celebrate a *f* to Jehovah
De 16:10 the *f* of weeks to Jehovah
16:13 the *f* of booths you should
16:14 rejoice during your *f*, you
16:15 celebrate the *f* to Jehovah
16:16 *f* of the unfermented cakes
16:16 the *f* of weeks and the
16:16 the *f* of booths, and none
31:10 release, in the *f* of booths
Jg 21:19 There is a *f* of Jehovah from
1Ki 8:2 month of Ethanim in the *f*
8:65 carry on at that time the *f*
12:32 a *f* in the eighth month on
12:32 the *f* that was in Judah
12:33 a *f* for the sons of Israel
1Ch 23:31 and at the *f* seasons, by
2Ch 2:4 *f* seasons of Jehovah our God
5:3 *f*, that of the seventh month
7:8 *f* at that time for seven
7:9 and the *f* for seven days
8:13 *f* of unfermented cakes and
8:13 *f* of the weeks and at the
8:13 and at the *f* of the booths
30:13 *f* of the unfermented cakes
30:21 *f* of the unfermented cakes
31:3 and for the *f* seasons
35:17 *f* of the unfermented cakes
Ezr 3:4 they held the *f* of booths
3:5 *f* seasons of Jehovah
6:22 the *f* of unfermented cakes
Ne 8:14 dwell in booths during the *f*
8:18 holding the *f* seven days
Ps 42:4 Of a crowd celebrating a *f*
81:3 for the day of our *f*
118:27 Bind the *f* procession with
Isa 30:29 sanctifies oneself for a *f*
La 1:4 there are none coming to the *f*
2:6 He has brought his *f* to ruin
2:6 forgotten in Zion *f* and sabbath
2:7 voice, as in the day of a *f*
2:22 As in the day of a *f* you
Eze 45:21 As a *f* for seven days
45:23 seven days of the *f* he
45:25 during the *f*, he should
Ho 2:11 her *f*, her new moon and her
9:5 the day of the *f* of Jehovah
Zec 14:16 the *f* of the booths
14:18 the *f* of the booths
14:19 the *f* of the booths
Mt 26:5 Not at the *f*, in order that
27:15, 15 from *f* to *f* it was the
Mr 14:1 the *f* of unfermented cakes
14:2 Not at the *f*; perhaps there
15:6, 6 from *f* to *f* he used to
Lu 2:41 for the *f* of the passover
2:42 the custom of the *f*
22:1 *f* of the unfermented cakes
Joh 2:23 at the passover, at its *f*
4:45 in Jerusalem at the *f*
4:45 also had gone to the *f*
5:1 there was a *f* of the Jews
6:4 passover, the *f* of the Jews
7:2 However, the *f* of the Jews
7:2 *f* of tabernacles, was near
7:8 You go up to the *f*: I am not
7:8 not yet going up to this *f*
7:10 brothers had gone up to the *f*
7:11 looking for him at the *f* and
7:14 by now the *f* was half over
7:37 the great day of the *f*
10:22 *f* of dedication took place
11:56 not come to the *f* at all
12:12 that had come to the *f*
12:20 came up to worship at the *f*
13:1 before the *f* of the passover
13:29 things we need for the *f*
Ac 2:1 *f* of Pentecost was in progress
20:16 the day of the *f* of Pentecost
1Co 5:8 us keep the *f*, not with old
16:8 until the *f* of Pentecost
Col 2:16 or in respect of a *f* or of

Festivals
Le 23:2 *f* of Jehovah that you should
23:2 These are my seasonal *f*
23:4 seasonal *f* of Jehovah, holy
23:37 seasonal *f* of Jehovah that
23:44 spoke of the seasonal *f* of
Nu 15:3 during your seasonal *f*, in
29:39 at your seasonal *f*, besides
Ch 8:13 appointed *f* three times in
sa 29:1 let the *f* run the round
Eze 45:17 during the *f* and during the
46:11 And in the *f* and in the
Am 5:21 hated, I have rejected your *f*
8:10 turn your *f* into mourning
Na 1:15 O Judah, celebrate your *f*
Mal 2:3 the dung of your *f*
Ac 19:31 the commissioners of *f* and

Festus
Ac 24:27 was succeeded by Porcius *F*
25:1 *F*, after entering upon the
25:4 *F* answered that Paul was to
25:9 *F*, desiring to gain favor
25:12 Then *F*, after speaking with
25:13 a visit of courtesy to *F*
25:14 *F* laid before the king the
25:22 Agrippa said to *F*: I myself
25:23 when *F* gave the command
25:24 *F* said: King Agrippa and all
26:24 *F* said in a loud voice
26:25 Your Excellency *F*, but I am
26:32 Agrippa said to *F*: This

Fetch
Sa 16:11 Do send and *f* him, because
20:31 send and *f* him to me, for
26:22 men come on over and *f* it
Ki 7:13 send and *f* Hiram out of Tyre
20:33 he said: Come, *f* him
Ki 2:20 *F* me a small new bowl and
3:15 *f* me a string-instrument
4:41 So he said: *F*, then, flour

Fetched
Sa 17:31 before Saul. Hence he *f* him
Ki 2:20 So they *f* it for him

Fetching
Sa 4:6 of the house as men *f* wheat

Fettered
Pr 7:22 *f* for the discipline of a

Fetters
Jg 15:14 his *f* melted off his hands
16:21 two *f* of copper, and he came
Sa 3:34 been put into *f* of copper
Ki 25:7 bound him with copper *f*
Ch 33:11 two *f* of copper and took
36:6 two *f* of copper to carry
Job 36:8 if they are bound in *f*
Ps 105:18 *f* they afflicted his feet
149:8 ones with *f* of iron
Ec 7:26 and whose hands are *f*
Isa 45:14 in *f* they will come over
58:6 loosen the *f* of wickedness
Jer 37:15 into the house of *f*, in
39:7 bound him with copper *f*
52:11 bound him with copper *f* and
La 3:7 He has made my copper *f* heavy
Na 3:10 have all been bound with *f*
Mr 5:4 been bound with *f* and chains
5:4 the *f* were actually smashed
Lu 8:29 with chains and *f* under guard

Fever
Le 26:16 burning *f*, causing the eyes
De 28:22 burning *f* and inflammation
32:24 and eaten up by burning *f*
Ps 78:48 livestock to the flaming *f*
Hab 3:5 burning *f* would go forth at
Mt 8:14 lying down and sick with *f*
8:15 and the *f* left her, and she
Mr 1:30 was lying down sick with a *f*
1:31 the *f* left her, and she began
Lu 4:38 distressed with a high *f*, and
4:39 rebuked the *f*, and it left her
Joh 4:52 seventh hour the *f* left him
Ac 28:8 *f* and dysentery, and Paul

Feverish
De 28:22 inflammation and *f* heat

Fevers
Ho 13:5 wilderness, in the land of *f*

Few
Ge 29:20 like some *f* days because of
34:30 I am *f* in number, and they
Ge 47:9 *F* and distressing the days of
Le 25:52 *f* remain of the years until
Nu 9:20 cloud would continue a *f* days
13:18 whether they are *f* or many
26:56 between the many and the *f*
35:8, 8 from the *f* you will take *f*
De 4:27 *f* in number among the nations
26:5 alien with very *f* in number
28:62 left with very *f* in number
33:6 And let his men not become *f*
Jos 7:3 going there, for they are *f*
1Sa 14:6 to save by many or by *f*
17:28 did you leave those *f* sheep
1Ki 17:12 a *f* pieces of wood, and I
2Ki 4:3 Do not hold yourself to a *f*
1Ch 16:19 happened to be *f* in number
16:19 very *f*, and alien residents
2Ch 29:34 happened to be too *f*, and
Ne 2:12 I and a *f* men with me, and
7:4 *f* people inside it, and there
Job 10:20 Are not my days *f*? Let him
16:22 just a *f* years are to come
Ps 39:5 have made my days just a *f*
105:12 happened to be *f* in number
105:12 very *f*, and alien residents
107:38 let their cattle become *f*
107:39 become *f* and crouch down
109:8 Let his days prove to be *f*
Ec 5:2 words should prove to be *f*
9:14 and the men in it were *f*
12:3 because they have become *f*
Isa 1:9 to us just a *f* survivors, we
10:7 to cut off nations not a *f*
16:14 be a trifling *f*, not mighty
21:17 Kedar, will become *f*, for
24:6 *f* mortal men have remained
65:20 a suckling a *f* days old
Jer 29:6 and do not become *f*
30:19 they will not become *f*
42:2 remaining, a *f* out of many
44:28 land of Judah, *f* in number
Eze 5:3 take therefrom a *f* in number
12:16 remaining from them a *f*
29:15 I will make them so *f* as
Da 11:20 a *f* days he will be broken
Mt 7:14 *f* are the ones finding it
9:37 great, but the workers are *f*
15:34 Seven, and a *f* little fishes
22:14 many invited, but *f* chosen
25:21 faithful over a *f* things
25:23 faithful over a *f* things
Mr 6:5 lay his hands upon a *f* sickly
8:7 also had a *f* little fishes
Lu 10:2 great, but the workers are *f*
10:42 A *f* things, though, are
12:48 will be beaten with *f*
13:23 those who are being saved *f*
Ac 9:43 *f* days he remained in Joppa
12:12 quite a *f* were gathered
14:21 making quite a *f* disciples
17:4 and not a *f* of the principal
17:12 did not a *f* of the reputable
20:8 quite a *f* lamps in the upper
1Co 11:30 quite a *f* are sleeping in
Heb 12:10 they for a *f* days used to
13:22 letter to you in *f* words
1Pe 3:20 a *f* people, that is, eight
5:12 written you in *f* words, to
Re 2:14 I have a *f* things against you
3:4 *f* names in Sardis that did

Fewer
Pr 13:11 from vanity become *f*, but

Fewness
Le 25:16 *f* of years he should reduce
Nu 26:54 according to the *f* you should

Fidelity
Tit 2:10 exhibiting good *f* to the full

Field
Ge 2:5 no bush of the *f* found in the
2:5 no vegetation of the *f* was as
2:19 every wild beast of the *f*
2:20 every wild beast of the *f*
3:1 wild beasts of the *f* that
3:14 all the wild beasts of the *f*
3:18 eat the vegetation of the *f*
4:8 Let us go over into the *f*
4:8 while they were in the *f* Cain
14:7 defeated the whole *f* of the
23:9 at the extremity of his *f*
23:11 The *f* I do give to you, and
23:13 amount of silver for the *f*
23:17 the *f* of Ephron that was in
Ge 23:17 *f* and the cave that was in
23:17 the trees that were in the *f*
23:19 *f* of Machpelah in front of
23:20 *f* and the cave that was in it
24:63 meditate in the *f* at about
24:65 man there walking in the *f*
25:9 *f* of Ephron the son of Zohar
25:10 *f* that Abraham had purchased
25:27 a man of the *f*, but Jacob a
25:29 Esau came along from the *f*
27:3 go out to the *f* and hunt some
27:5 Esau went on out into the *f*
27:27 like the scent of the *f*
29:2 there was a well in the *f*
30:14 find mandrakes in the *f*
30:16 Jacob was coming from the *f*
31:4 out to the *f* to his flock
32:3 land of Seir, the *f* of Edom
33:19 he acquired a tract of the *f*
34:5 to be with his herd in the *f*
34:7 came in from the *f* as soon as
34:28 what was in the *f* they took
36:35 Midianites in the *f* of Moab
37:7 in the middle of the *f*
37:15 he was wandering in a *f*
39:5 had in the house and in the *f*
41:48 The foodstuffs of the *f* that
47:20 Egyptians sold each one his *f*
47:24 yours as seed for the *f* and
49:29 the *f* of Ephron the Hittite
49:30 in the *f* of Machpelah that
49:30 the *f* that Abraham purchased
49:32 The *f* purchased and the cave
50:13 cave of the *f* of Machpelah
50:13 *f* that Abraham had purchased
Ex 1:14 slavery in the *f*, yes, every
9:3 your livestock that is in the *f*
9:19 all that is yours in the *f*
9:19 be found in the *f* and not
9:21 and his livestock in the *f*
9:22 vegetation of the *f* in the
9:25 everything that was in the *f*
9:25 sorts of vegetation of the *f*
9:25 all sorts of trees of the *f*
10:5 sprouting tree . . . of the *f*
10:15 vegetation of the *f* in all
16:25 will not find it in the *f*
22:5 *f* or a vineyard to be grazed
22:5 a consuming in another *f*, he
22:5 with the best of his own *f* or
22:6 or a *f* gets consumed, the one
22:31 not eat flesh in the *f* that
23:11 wild beasts of the *f* are to
23:16 of what you sow in the *f*
23:16 in your labors from the *f*
23:29 wild beasts of the *f* really
Le 14:7 living bird over the open *f*
14:53 into the open *f* and
17:5 sacrificing in the open *f*
19:9 edge of your *f* completely
19:19 sow your *f* with seeds of two
23:22 edge of your *f* when you are
25:3 sow your *f* with seed, and six
25:4 *f* you must not sow with seed
25:12 *f* you may eat what the land
25:31 part of the *f* of the country
25:34 *f* of pasture ground of their
26:4 tree of the *f* will give its
26:22 beasts of the *f* among you
27:16 *f* of his possession that a
27:17 sanctify his *f* from the year
27:18 sanctifies his *f*, the priest
27:19 buy the *f* back, he must then
27:20 not buy the *f* back but if
27:20 *f* is sold to another man, it
27:21 *f* when it goes out in the
27:21 as a *f* that is devoted
27:22 sanctifies to Jehovah a *f*
27:22 of the *f* of his possession
27:24 *f* will return to the one
27:28 *f* of his possession, may be
Nu 16:14 give us an inheritance of *f*
19:16 who on the open *f* may touch
20:17 not pass through a *f* or a
21:20 that is in the *f* of Moab, at
21:22 shall not turn off into a *f*
22:4 the green growth of the *f*
22:23 that she might go into the *f*
23:14 took him to the *f* of Zophim
De 5:21 his *f* or his slave man or
7:22 beasts of the *f* may multiply
11:15 give vegetation in your *f*
14:22 which comes forth of the *f*
20:19 is the tree of the *f* a man

De 21:1 fallen on the *f*, and it has
22:25 in the *f* that the man found
22:27 in the *f* that he found her
24:19 reap your harvest in your *f*
24:19 forgotten a sheaf in the *f*
28:3 blessed will you be in the *f*
28:16 cursed will you be in the *f*
28:26 and to the beast of the *f*
28:38 you will take out to the *f*
32:13 he ate the produce of the *f*
Jos 8:24 inhabitants of Ai in the *f*
15:18 ask a *f* from her father
21:12 the *f* of the city and its
24:32 tract of the *f* that Jacob
Jg 1:14 to ask a *f* from her father
5:4 marching out of the *f* of Edom
5:18 on the heights of the *f*
9:27 into the *f* and engaged in
9:32 and lie in wait in the *f*
9:42 began to go out into the *f*
9:43 began to lie in wait in the *f*
9:44 all who were in the *f*, and
13:9 she was sitting in the *f*
19:16 his work in the *f* at evening
20:6 *f* of Israel's inheritance
20:31 in the *f*, about thirty men
Ru 1:6 she had heard in the *f* of Moab
2:2 Let me go, please, to the *f*
2:3 began to glean in the *f* behind
2:3 of the *f* belonging to Boaz
2:6 with Naomi from the *f* of Moab
2:8 go away to glean in another *f*
2:9 the *f* that they will harvest
2:17 continued to glean in the *f*
2:22 not annoy you in another *f*
4:3 tract of the *f* that belonged
4:3 returned from the *f* of Moab
4:5 On the day that you buy the *f*
1Sa 4:2 closed battle line in the *f*
6:1 in the *f* of the Philistines
6:14 came into the *f* of Joshua
6:18 *f* of Joshua the Beth-shemite
11:5 after the herd from the *f*
14:14 in an acre of *f*
14:15 in the camp in the *f* and
14:25 all the surface of the *f*
17:44 and to the beasts of the *f*
19:3 in the *f* where you will be
20:5 conceal myself in the *f*
20:11 let us go out into the *f*
20:11 them went out into the *f*
20:24 conceal himself in the *f*
20:35 the *f* of David's appointed
25:15 we happened to be in the *f*
30:11 an Egyptian, in the *f*
2Sa 2:18 that are in the open *f*
9:7 to you all the *f* of Saul your
10:8 themselves in the open *f*
11:11 on the face of the *f*, and
11:23 against us into the *f*
14:6 with each other in the *f*
17:8 has lost her cubs in the *f*
18:6 out to the *f* to meet Israel
19:29 Ziba should share in the *f*
20:12 from the highway to the *f*
21:10 wild beasts of the *f* by
23:11 the *f* full of lentils
1Ki 11:29 were by themselves in the *f*
14:11 the one dying in the *f*, the
16:4 in the *f* the fowls of the
21:24 dying in the *f* the fowls of
2Ki 4:39 to the *f* to pick mallows
7:12 hide themselves in the *f*
8:3 for her house and for her *f*
8:5 for her house and for her *f*
8:6 and all the products of the *f*
9:25 the tract of the *f* of Naboth
9:37 *f* in the tract of land
14:9 wild beast of the *f* that was
18:17 of the laundryman's *f*
19:26 as vegetation of the *f* and
1Ch 1:46 Midian in the *f* of Moab
6:56 And the *f* of the city and its
8:8 to children in the *f* of Moab
11:13 a tract of the *f* full of
16:32 Let the *f* exult and all that
19:9 by themselves in the open *f*
27:25 over the treasures in the *f*
27:26 the doers of work in the *f*
2Ch 25:18 wild beast of the *f* that
26:23 burial *f* that belonged to
31:5 all the produce of the *f*
Ne 5:16 not a *f* did we acquire
13:10 each one to his own *f*

Job 5:23 For with the stones of the *f*
5:23 And the wild beast of the *f*
24:6 In the *f* its fodder they
39:4 they get big in the open *f*
39:15 beast of the *f* may tread on
40:20 the wild beasts of the *f*
Ps 8:7 also the beasts of the open *f*
50:11 animal throngs of the open *f*
78:12 of Egypt, the *f* of Zoan
78:43 miracles in the *f* of Zoan
80:13 throngs of the open *f* keep
96:12 open *f* exult and all that
103:15 blossom of the *f* is the way
104:11 wild beasts of the open *f*
Pr 23:10 *f* of fatherless boys do not
24:27 ready for yourself in the *f*
24:30 the *f* of the lazy individual
27:26 are the price of the *f*
31:16 She has considered a *f* and
Ec 5:9 for a *f* the king himself has
Ca 2:7 or by the hinds of the *f*, that
3:5 by the hinds of the *f*, that you
7:11 let us go forth to the *f*
Isa 1:8 hut in a *f* of cucumbers
5:8, 8 those who annex *f* to *f*
7:3 highway of the laundryman's *f*
36:2 of the laundryman's *f*
37:27 as vegetation of the *f* and
40:6 like the blossom of the *f*
43:20 wild beast of the *f* will
55:12 trees of the *f* will all
56:9 wild animals of the open *f*
Jer 4:17 Like guards of the open *f*
6:25 Do not go out into the *f*
7:20 upon the tree of the *f* and
9:22 upon the face of the *f*
10:5 a scarecrow of a cucumber *f*
12:4 vegetation of all the *f*
12:9 all you wild beasts of the *f*
13:27 in the *f*, I have seen your
14:5 the hind in the *f* has given
14:18 actually go out into the *f*
17:3 on the mountains in the *f*
18:14 from the rock of the open *f*
26:18 plowed up as a mere *f*
27:6 the wild beasts of the *f*
28:14 the wild beasts of the *f*
32:7 *f* of mine that is in
32:8 *f* of mine that is in
32:9 *f* that was in Anathoth
32:25 Buy for yourself the *f* with
35:9 *f* or seed should become ours
40:7 forces who were in the *f*
40:13 forces who were in the *f*
41:8 hidden treasures in the *f*
La 4:9 of the produce of the open *f*
Eze 7:15 is in the *f*, by the sword he
16:5 upon the surface of the *f*
16:7 like the sprouting of the *f*
17:5 and put it in a *f* for seed
17:8 a good *f*, by vast waters
17:24 trees of the *f* will have to
20:46 forest of the *f* of the south
26:6 towns that are in the *f*
26:8 dependent towns in the *f*
29:5 surface of the *f* you will
31:4 to all the trees of the *f*
31:5 the other trees of the *f*
31:6 beasts of the *f* gave birth
31:13 the wild beasts of the *f*
31:15 trees of the *f* will all
32:4 Upon the surface of the *f* I
33:27 upon the surface of the *f*
34:5 every wild beast of the *f*
34:8 every wild beast of the *f*
34:27 tree of the *f* must give its
36:30 and the produce of the *f*
38:20 the wild beasts of the *f*
39:4 the wild beasts of the *f*
39:5 Upon the surface of the *f*
39:10 sticks of wood from the *f*
39:17 the wild beasts of the *f*
47:13 two pieces of *f* to Joseph
Da 2:38 the beasts of the *f* and the
4:12 beast of the *f* would seek
4:15 among the grass of the *f*
4:21 beasts of the *f* would dwell
4:23 among the grass of the *f*, and
4:23 beasts of the *f* let its
4:25 beasts of the *f* your dwelling
4:32 with the beasts of the *f* your
Ho 2:12 the wild beast of the *f*
2:18 with the wild beast of the *f*
4:3 with the wild beast of the *f*

Ho 10:4 in the furrows of the open *f*
12:11 in the furrows of the open *f*
12:12 run away to the *f* of Syria
13:8 a wild beast of the *f* itself
Joe 1:10 The *f* has been despoiled
1:11 the harvest of the *f* has
1:12 all the trees of the *f*
1:19 all the trees of the *f*
1:20 The beasts of the *f* also keep
2:22 you beasts of the open *f*
Ob 19 possession of the *f* of Ephraim
19 Ephraim and of the *f* of Samaria
Mic 1:6 a heap of ruins of the *f*
3:12 be plowed up as a mere *f*
4:10 have to reside in the *f*
Zec 10:1 each one vegetation in the *f*
Mal 3:11 the *f* prove fruitless for
Mt 6:28 from the lilies of the *f*
6:30 the vegetation of the *f*
13:24 sowed fine seed in his *f*
13:27 not sow fine seed in your *f*
13:31 took and planted in his *f*
13:36 Explain . . . weeds in the *f*
13:38 *f* is the world; as for the
13:44 a treasure hidden in the *f*
13:44 and buys that *f*
22:5 went off, one to his own *f*
24:18 man in the *f* not return to
24:40 two men will be in the *f*
27:7 potter's *f* to bury strangers
27:8 that *f* has been called
27:8 called *F* of Blood to this
27:10 gave them for the potter's *f*
Mr 13:16 let the man in the *f* not
Lu 12:28 the vegetation in the *f*
14:18 I bought a *f* and need to go
15:25 his older son was in the *f*
17:7 when he gets in from the *f*
17:31 the person out in the *f*
Joh 4:5 *f* that Jacob gave to Joseph
Ac 1:18 purchased a *f* with the wages
1:19 that *f* was called in their
1:19 that is, *F* of Blood
5:3 some of the price of the *f*
5:8 did you two sell the *f* for so
1Co 3:9 You people are God's *f* under

Fields

Ex 8:13 the courtyards and the *f*
Jg 15:5 the *f* of standing grain of the
Ru 1:1 as an alien in the *f* of Moab
1:2 they came to the *f* of Moab and
1:6 to return from the *f* of Moab
1:22 returning from the *f* of Moab
1Sa 8:14 And your *f* . . . he will take
8:15 of your *f* of seed and of your
22:7 give to all of you *f* and
2Sa 1:21 be *f* of holy contributions
1Ki 2:26 Go to Anathoth to your *f*
2Ch 31:19 *f* of pasture ground of their
Ne 5:3 Our *f* and our vineyards and
5:4 on our *f* and our vineyards
5:5 *f* and our vineyards belong to
5:11 their *f*, their vineyards
11:25 the settlements in their *f*
11:30 Lachish and its *f*
12:29 from the *f* of Geba and
12:44 out of the *f* of the cities
Job 5:10 waters upon the open *f*
Ps 107:37 sow *f* and plant vineyards
132:6 in the *f* of the forest
Isa 32:12 over the desirable *f*, over
32:14 have become bare *f*, for
Jer 6:12 the *f* and the wives at the
8:10 *f* to those taking possession
32:15 *f* and vineyards will yet be
32:43 *f* will certainly be bought
32:44 money people will buy *f*
Mic 2:2 desired *f* and have seized
2:4 he apportions out our own *f*
Mr 10:29 *f* for my sake and for the
10:30 mothers and children and *f*
11:8 cut down foliage from the *f*
Lu 15:15 into his *f* to herd swine
Joh 4:35 your eyes and view the *f*
Ac 4:34 possessors of *f* or houses
Jas 5:4 workers who harvested your *f*

Fierce

De 28:50 a nation *f* in countenance
Da 8:23 king *f* in countenance and
Mt 8:28 unusually *f*, so that nobody
2Ti 3:3 *f*, without love of goodness

'iercely
.c 23:9 and began contending *f*, saying
'iercer
Iab 1:8 proved *f* than evening wolves
'iery
.e 15:17 and a *f* torch that passed in
Iu 21:8 Make for yourself a *f* snake
Ki 2:11 look! a *f* war chariot and
2:11 war chariot and *f* horses
's 21:9 as a *f* furnace at the
r 26:18 that is shooting *f* missiles
sa 14:29 will be a flying *f* snake
30:6 viper and the flying *f* snake
54:12 gates of *f* glowing stones
ze 28:14 midst of *f* stones you
28:16 the midst of the *f* stones
a 3:6 into the burning *f* furnace
3:11 into the burning *f* furnace
3:15 into the burning *f* furnace
3:17 Out of the burning *f* furnace
3:20 into the burning *f* furnace
3:21 into the burning *f* furnace
3:22 ones that the *f* flame killed
3:23 of the burning *f* furnace
3:26 door of the burning *f* furnace
10:6 his eyes like *f* torches, and
ec 12:6 like a *f* torch in a row of
t 5:22 be liable to the *f* Gehenna
13:42 pitch . . . into the *f* furnace
13:50 cast them into the *f* furnace
18:9 two eyes into the *f* Gehenna
.c 7:30 angel in the *f* flame of a
.o 12:20 heap *f* coals upon his head
Ieb 10:27 *f* jealousy that is going
e 1:14 and his eyes as a *f* flame
2:18 has his eyes like a *f* flame
10:1 his feet were as *f* pillars
19:12 His eyes are a *f* flame, and
19:20 *f* lake that burns with
'iery-colored
.e 6:4 another came forth, a *f* horse
12:3 great *f* dragon, with seven
'ifteen
.e 5:10 Enosh . . . eight hundred and *f*
7:20 Up to *f* cubits the waters
x 27:14 *f* cubits of hangings to one
27:15 are *f* cubits of hangings
38:14 for *f* cubits to the one wing
38:15 hangings were for *f* cubits
.e 27:7 *f* shekels and for the female
g 8:10 *f* thousand being all who were
Sa 9:10 Ziba had *f* sons and twenty
19:17 *f* sons and twenty servants
Ki 7:3 There were *f* to a row
Ki 14:17 king of Israel for *f* years
20:6 add *f* years to your days
Ch 25:25 continued . . . *f* years
sa 38:5 adding onto your days *f* years
ze 45:12 *f* shekels should prove to
lo 3:2 for *f* silver pieces and a
c 27:28 and found it *f* fathoms
a 1:18 I stayed with him for *f* days
'ifteenth
x 16:1 *f* day of the second month
.e 23:6 *f* day of this month is the
23:34 *f* day of this seventh month
23:39 *f* day of the seventh month
Iu 28:17 on the *f* day of this month
29:12 *f* day of the seventh month
33:3 the *f* day of the first month
Ki 12:32 on the *f* day of the month
12:33 *f* day in the eighth month
Ki 14:23 In the *f* year of Amaziah
Ch 24:14 for Bilgah the *f*, for
25:22 for the *f*, for Jeremoth
Ch 15:10 of the *f* year of Asa's reign
s 9:18 there was a rest on the *f* day
9:21 *f* day of it in each and every
ze 32:17 the *f* day of the month
45:25 on the *f* day of the month
.u 3:1 In the *f* year of the reign of
'ifth
e 1:23 came to be morning, a *f* day
30:17 bore to Jacob a *f* son
41:34 take up one *f* of the land
47:24 give a *f* to Pharaoh, but four
47:26 have to the amount of a *f*
.e 5:16 he will add to it a *f* of it
6:5 he will add to it a *f* of it
19:25 *f* year you may eat its fruit
22:14 add the *f* of it to it and

Le 27:13 give a *f* of it in addition
27:15 give a *f* of the money of the
27:19 give a *f* of the money of the
27:27 give a *f* of it in addition
27:31 give a *f* of it in addition
Nu 5:7 also adding a *f* of it to it
7:36 *f* day there was the chieftain
29:26 on the *f* day nine bulls, two
33:38 in the *f* month, on the first
Jos 19:24 the *f* lot came out for the
Jg 19:8 he got up . . . on the *f* day to
2Sa 3:4 *f* was Shephatiah the son of
1Ki 6:31 pillars, doorposts and a *f*
14:25 the *f* year of King Rehoboam
2Ki 8:16 in the *f* year of Jehoram
25:8 the *f* month on the seventh
1Ch 2:14 the fourth, Raddai the *f*
3:3 the *f*, Shephatiah, of Abital
8:2 the fourth and Rapha the *f*
12:10 the fourth, Jeremiah the *f*
24:9 for Malchijah the *f*, for
25:12 the *f* for Nethaniah, his
26:3 Elam the *f*, Jehohanan the
26:4 the fourth and Nethanel the *f*
27:8, 8 *f* chief for the *f* month
2Ch 12:2 *f* year of King Rehoboam that
Ezr 7:8 to Jerusalem in the *f* month
7:9 the first day of the *f* month
Ne 6:5 with the same word a *f* time
Jer 1:3 into exile in the *f* month
28:1 in the *f* month, that
36:9 *f* year of Jehoiakim the son
52:12 in the *f* month, on the
Eze 1:1 fourth month, on the *f* day of
1:2 On the *f* day of the month
1:2 *f* year of the exile of King
8:1 sixth month, on the *f* day of
20:1 *f* month, on the tenth day of
33:21 *f* day of the month of our
Zec 7:3 Shall I weep in the *f* month
7:5 a wailing in the *f* month and
8:19 the fast of the *f* month, and
Re 6:9 when he opened the *f* seal, I
9:1 the *f* angel blew his trumpet
16:10 *f* one poured out his bowl
21:20 the *f* sardonyx, the sixth
Fifties
Ex 18:21 chiefs over *f* and chiefs over
18:25 chiefs of *f* and chiefs of
De 1:15 and chiefs of *f* and chiefs of
1Sa 8:12 chiefs over *f*, and some to
1Ki 18:4 keep them hid by *f* in a cave
18:13 hundred men by *f* in a cave
2Ki 1:14 chiefs of fifty and their *f*
Fiftieth
Le 25:10 sanctify the *f* year and
25:11 Jubilee is what that *f* year
2Ki 15:23 In the *f* year of Azariah
Fifty
Ge 6:15 ark, *f* cubits its width, and
7:24 a hundred and *f* days
8:3 the end of a hundred and *f* days
9:28 three hundred and *f* years
9:29 nine hundred and *f* years and
18:24 *f* righteous men in the midst
18:24 sake of the *f* righteous who
18:26 find in Sodom *f* righteous
18:28 *f* righteous should be lacking
Ex 26:5 *f* loops on the one tent cloth
26:5 *f* loops you will make on the
26:6 make *f* hooks of gold and join
26:10 *f* loops upon the edge of the
26:10 *f* loops upon the edge of the
26:11 make *f* hooks of copper and
27:12 the hangings are of *f* cubits
27:13 the width . . . is *f* cubits
27:18 the width *f* cubits, and the
30:23 two hundred and *f* units, and
30:23 two hundred and *f* units
36:12 *f* loops on the one tent cloth
36:12 *f* loops on the . . . tent cloth
36:13 made *f* hooks of gold and
36:17 made *f* loops upon the edge
36:17 made *f* loops upon the edge
36:18 *f* hooks of copper for joining
38:12 hangings were for *f* cubits
38:13 east side . . . *f* cubits
38:26 thousand five hundred and *f*
Le 23:16 count, *f* days, and you must
27:3 *f* shekels of silver by the
27:16 seed, then at *f* shekels of
Nu 1:25 thousand six hundred and *f*

Nu 1:46 thousand five hundred and *f*
2:15 thousand six hundred and *f*
2:16 thousand four hundred and *f*
2:32 thousand five hundred and *f*
4:3 upward to *f* years old, all
4:23 years old upward to *f* years
4:30 thirty years old upward to *f*
4:35 years old upward to *f* years
4:36 thousand seven hundred and *f*
4:39 years old upward to *f* years
4:43 thirty years old upward to *f*
4:47 upward to *f* years old
8:25 after the age of *f* years he
16:2 two hundred and *f* men of the
16:17 two hundred and *f* fire
16:35 the two hundred and *f* men
26:10 consumed two hundred and *f*
31:30 you should take one out of *f*
31:47 the one to be taken out of *f*
31:52 seven hundred and *f* shekels
De 22:29 give . . . *f* silver shekels
Jos 7:21 *f* shekels being its weight
1Sa 6:19 seventy men—*f* thousand men
2Sa 15:1 *f* men running before him
24:24 for *f* silver shekels
1Ki 1:5 *f* men running before him
7:2 *f* cubits in its width, and
7:6 made *f* cubits in its length
9:23 five hundred and *f*, the
10:29 a horse for a hundred and *f*
18:19 four hundred and *f* prophets
18:22 are four hundred and *f* men
2Ki 1:9, 9 a chief of *f* with his *f*
1:10 spoke to the chief of the *f*
1:10 eat up you and your *f*
1:10 went eating up him and his *f*
1:11, 11 chief of *f* with his *f*
1:12 and eat up you and your *f*
1:12 went eating up him and his *f*
1:13, 13 chief of *f* and his *f*
1:13 the third chief of *f* went up
1:13 the soul of these *f* servants
1:14 two former chiefs of *f* and
2:7 were *f* men of the sons of the
2:16 *f* men, valiant persons
2:17 *f* men; and they kept looking
13:7 *f* horsemen and ten chariots
15:20 *f* silver shekels for each
15:25 *f* men of the sons of Gilead
1Ch 5:21 their camels *f* thousand, and
5:21 two hundred and *f* thousand
8:40 grandsons, a hundred and *f*
12:33 there were *f* thousand, and
2Ch 1:17 a horse for a hundred and *f*
3:9 the nails was *f* gold shekels
8:10 two hundred and *f*, the
8:18 four hundred and *f* talents
Ezr 8:3 a hundred and *f* males
8:6 and with him *f* males
8:26 six hundred and *f* talents of
Ne 5:17 rulers, a hundred and *f* men
7:70 *f* bowls, five hundred and
Es 5:14 make a stake *f* cubits high
7:9 the stake . . . *f* cubits high
Isa 3:3 chief of *f* and highly
Eze 40:15 inner gate was *f* cubits
40:21 *F* cubits was its length
40:25 *F* cubits was the length
40:29 *F* cubits was the length
40:33 The length was *f* cubits
40:36 The length was *f* cubits
42:2 and the width was *f* cubits
42:7 Its length was *f* cubits
42:8 outer courtyard was *f* cubits
45:2 *f* cubits it will have as a
48:17 two hundred and *f* cubits
48:17 south two hundred and *f*
48:17 east two hundred and *f*
48:17 west two hundred and *f*
Hag 2:16 *f* measures of the wine
Mr 6:40 groups of a hundred and of *f*
Lu 7:41 but the other for *f*
9:14 in groups of about *f* each
16:6 sit down and quickly write *f*
Joh 8:57 You are not yet *f* years old
Ac 13:20 four hundred and *f* years
19:19 *f* thousand pieces of silver
Fifty-five
2Ki 21:1 Manasseh . . . *f* years he
2Ch 33:1 Manasseh . . . for *f* years he
Ne 7:20 six hundred and *f*
Fifty-four
Nu 1:29 *f* thousand four hundred

Nu 2:6 *f* thousand four hundred
Ezr 2:7 thousand two hundred and *f*
2:15 four hundred and *f*
2:31 a thousand two hundred and *f*
Ne 7:12 a thousand two hundred and *f*
7:34 a thousand two hundred and *f*

Fifty-nine
Nu 1:23 *f* thousand three hundred
2:13 *f* thousand three hundred

Fifty-one
Nu 2:16 one hundred and *f* thousand

Fifty-second
2Ki 15:27 In the *f* year of Azariah

Fifty-seven
Nu 1:31 *f* thousand four hundred
2:8 *f* thousand four hundred
2:31 one hundred *f* thousand six

Fifty-six
1Ch 9:9 were nine hundred and *f*
Ezr 2:14 two thousand and *f*
2:22 the men of Netophah, *f*
2:30 a hundred and *f*

Fifty-three
Nu 1:43 *f* thousand four hundred
2:30 *f* thousand four hundred
26:47 *f* thousand four hundred
2Ch 2:17 a hundred and *f* thousand six
Joh 21:11 fishes, one hundred and *f*

Fifty-two
Nu 26:34 *f* thousand seven hundred
2Ki 15:2 *f* years he reigned in
2Ch 26:3 Uzziah . . . *f* years he reigned
Ezr 2:29 the sons of Nebo, *f*
2:37 a thousand and *f*
2:60 six hundred and *f*
Ne 6:15 day of Elul, in *f* days
7:10 six hundred and *f*
7:33 the men of the other Nebo, *f*
7:40 of Immer, a thousand and *f*

Fig
Ge 3:7 they sewed *f* leaves together
Jg 9:10 said to the *f* tree, You come
9:11 the *f* tree said to them, Must
1Ki 4:25 and under his own *f* tree
2Ki 18:31 one from his own *f* tree
Ps 105:33 vines and their *f* trees
Pr 27:18 is safeguarding the *f* tree
Ca 2:13 the *f* tree, it has gained a
Isa 28:4 the early *f* before summer
34:4, 4 shriveled *f* off the *f* tree
36:16 one from his own *f* tree and
Jer 5:17 eat up your vine and your *f*
8:13 no figs on the *f* tree, and
Ho 2:12 her *f* tree, of which she has
9:10, 10 the early *f* on a *f* tree
Joe 1:7 and my *f* tree as a stump
1:12 the *f* tree has faded away
2:22 The *f* tree and the vine must
Am 4:9 your *f* trees and your olive
Mic 4:4 his vine and under his *f* tree
7:1 no early *f*, that my soul
Na 3:12 as *f* trees with the first
Hab 3:17 the *f* tree itself may not
Hag 2:19 the vine and the *f* tree and
Zec 3:10 and while under the *f* tree
Mt 21:19 he caught sight of a *f* tree
21:19 *f* tree withered instantly
21:20 *f* tree withered instantly
21:21 do what I did to the *f* tree
24:32 learn from the *f* tree as an
Mr 11:13 caught sight of a *f* tree
11:20 they saw the *f* tree already
11:21 the *f* tree that you cursed
13:28 from the *f* tree learn the
Lu 13:6 man had a *f* tree planted in
13:7 for fruit on this *f* tree, but
21:29 Note the *f* tree and all the
Joh 1:48 under the *f* tree, I saw you
1:50 you underneath the *f* tree
Jas 3:12 *f* tree cannot produce olives
Re 6:13 *f* tree shaken by a high wind

Fight
Ex 1:10 hate us and will *f* against us
14:14 Jehovah will himself *f* for
17:8 *f* against Israel in Rephidim
17:9 *f* against the Amalekites
17:10 to *f* against the Amalekites
Nu 21:1 he began to *f* with Israel
22:11 be able to *f* against them
De 1:30 Jehovah . . . will *f* for you
De 1:41 *f* in accord with all that
1:42 You must not go up and *f*
20:4 to *f* for you against your
20:10 draw near to a city to *f*
Jos 11:5 of Merom to *f* against Israel
Jg 1:1 first to the Canaanites to *f*
1:3 *f* against the Canaanites
1:9 to *f* against the Canaanites
5:20 From heaven did the stars *f*
8:1 to *f* against Midian? And they
9:38 Go . . . and *f* against them
9:39 the *f* against Abimelech
10:9 to *f* even against Judah and
11:4 began to *f* against Israel
11:5 *f* against Israel, the older
11:6 let us *f* against the sons of
11:8 *f* against the sons of Ammon
11:9 *f* against the sons of Ammon
11:12 against me to *f* in my land
11:25 did he ever *f* against them?
11:32 Ammon to *f* against them
12:1 *f* against the sons of Ammon
12:3 this day to *f* against me
1Sa 4:9 prove yourselves men and *f*
8:20 before us and *f* our battles
13:5 to *f* against Israel, thirty
15:18 and you must *f* against them
17:9 If he is able to *f* with me
17:10 and let us *f* together
17:32 *f* with this Philistine
17:33 against this Philistine to *f*
18:17 and *f* the wars of Jehovah
29:8 *f* against the enemies of my
2Sa 10:17 David and began to *f* against
11:20 so near to the city to *f*
12:26 Joab continued to *f* against
17:11 own person going into the *f*
1Ki 12:21 to *f* against the house of
12:24 not go up and *f* against your
20:1 Samaria and *f* against it
20:23 let us *f* against them on
20:25 *f* against them on the level
22:4 you go with me to the *f*
22:31 You must *f*, neither with
22:32 aside against him to *f*
2Ki 3:21 come up to *f* against them
10:3 *f* for the house of your lord
12:17 go up and *f* against Gath
16:5 they were not able to *f*
19:9 come out to *f* against you
1Ch 14:15 then you go out into the *f*
19:17 they began to *f* against him
2Ch 11:1 to *f* against Israel so as
11:4 *f* against your brothers
13:12 *f* against Jehovah the God
17:10 not *f* against Jehoshaphat
18:30 *f*, neither with the small
18:31 around against him to *f*
20:17 will not need to *f* in this
26:6 *f* against the Philistines and
32:8 help us and to *f* our battles
35:20 came up to *f* at Carchemish
35:21 that my *f* is and that God
35:22 but to *f* against him he
35:22 *f* in the valley plain of
Ne 4:8 come and *f* against Jerusalem
4:14 *f* for your brothers, your sons
4:20 Our God himself will *f* for us
Job 38:23 For the day of *f* and war
Ps 55:18 my soul in peace from the *f*
55:21 his heart is disposed to *f*
78:9 Retreated in the day of *f*
Isa 30:32 actually *f* against them
37:9 come out to *f* against you
Jer 1:19 be certain to *f* against you
15:20 certainly *f* against you
21:5 will *f* against you with a
33:5 *f* against the Chaldeans
34:22 *f* against it and capture
37:8 *f* against this city and
41:12 *f* against Ishmael the son
51:30 of Babylon have ceased to *f*
Da 10:20 *f* with the prince of Persia
11:11 go forth and *f* with him
Zec 14:3 warring, in the day of *f*
1Ti 6:12, 12 *F* the fine *f* of the faith
2Ti 2:14 not to *f* about words, a
2:24 does not need to *f*, but
4:7 I have fought the fine *f*
Jude 3 put up a hard *f* for the faith

Fighters
Ac 5:39 *f* actually against God

Fighting
Nu 21:23 and began *f* with Israel
De 3:22 God is the One *f* for you
20:19 by *f* against it so as to
Jos 10:14 Jehovah himself was *f* for
10:42 who was *f* for Israel
23:3 the one who was *f* for you
23:10 the one who is *f* for you
24:8 they went *f* against you
24:9 and went *f* against Israel
24:11 began *f* against you; but I
Jg 9:52 and began *f* against it, and he
10:18 the lead in *f* against the
11:20 and *f* against Israel
11:27 dealing wrong with me by *f*
20:34 and the *f* was heavy
1Sa 12:9 and they kept *f* against them
17:19 *f* against the Philistines
19:8 *f* against the Philistines
25:28 are what my lord is *f*; and
28:15 Philistines are *f* against
31:1 Philistines were *f* against
31:3 *f* became heavy against Saul
2Sa 2:17 *f* came to be extremely hard
2:28 not renew the *f* anymore
11:17 *f* against Joab, then some
2Ki 19:8 Assyria *f* against Libnah
1Ch 5:22 the true God that the *f* was
10:3 *f* became heavy against Saul
Ps 109:3 *f* against me without cause
144:1 teaching my hands for *f*
Ec 9:18 better than implements for *f*
Isa 37:8 king of Assyria *f* against
Jer 21:4 you are *f* the king of Babylon
32:24 Chaldeans who are *f* against
32:29 Chaldeans who are *f* against
34:1 *f* against Jerusalem and
34:7 *f* against Jerusalem and
37:10 Chaldeans who are *f* you
Ac 7:26 they were *f*, and he tried
12:20 *f* mood against the people
Jas 4:2 You go on *f* and waging war

Fights
Ex 14:25 Jehovah certainly *f* for them
Ps 68:30 that take delight in *f*
2Co 7:5 were *f* without, fears within
2Ti 2:23 knowing they produce *f*
Tit 3:9 and strife and *f* over the Law
Jas 4:1 from what source are there *f*

Fig-mulberry
Lu 19:4 climbed a *f* tree in order to

Figs
Nu 13:23 carrying . . . some of the *f*
20:5 It is no place of seed and *f*
De 8:8 barley and vines and *f* and
1Sa 25:18 hundred cakes of pressed *f*
30:12 of a cake of pressed *f*
2Ki 20:7 a cake of pressed dried *f*
1Ch 12:40 cakes of pressed *f* and cakes
Ne 13:15 *f* and every sort of burden
Ca 2:13 mature color for its early *f*
Isa 38:21 a cake of pressed dried *f*
Jer 8:13 no *f* on the fig tree, and
24:1 two baskets of *f* set before
24:2 the *f* were very good, like
24:2 very good, like early *f*
24:2 the *f* were very bad, so that
24:3, 3 *F*, the good *f* being very
24:5 Like these good *f*, so I shall
24:8 like the bad *f* that cannot
29:17 *f* that cannot be eaten for
Joe 1:17 Dried *f* have shriveled under
Am 7:14 nipper of *f* of sycamore trees
Mt 7:16 or *f* from thistles, do they
Mr 11:13 it was not the season of *f*
Lu 6:44 people do not gather *f* from
Jas 3:12 or a vine *f*, can it? Neither
Re 6:13 casts its unripe *f*

Figure
Eze 41:18 palm-tree *f* between a
41:19 palm-tree *f* on this side
41:19 palm-tree *f* on that side
Joh 5:37 nor seen his *f*

Figured
Nu 33:56 as I had *f* doing to them I
Jg 20:5 was I that they *f* on killing
Isa 14:24 just as I have *f*, so it

Figurehead
Ac 28:11 and with the *f* Sons of Zeus

Figures
Nu 33:52 destroy all their stone *f*
1Ki 6:29 cherubs and palm-tree *f* and
6:32 cherubs and palm-tree *f* and
6:32 cherubs and the palm-tree *f*
6:35 cherubs and palm-tree *f*
7:36 lions and palm-tree *f*
2Ch 3:5 upon it palm-tree *f* and
Eze 40:16 there were palm-tree *f*
40:22 and its palm-tree *f* were
40:26 it had palm-tree *f*, one on
40:31 palm-tree *f* were on its
40:34 palm-tree *f* were on its
40:37 and palm-tree *f* were on its
41:18 cherubs and palm-tree *f*
41:20 palm-tree *f*, on the wall of
41:25 cherubs and palm-tree *f*
41:26 palm-tree *f* over here and
Ac 7:43 *f* which you made to worship

File
Ro 8:33 *f* accusation against God's

Fill
Ge 1:22 become many and *f* the waters
1:28 become many and *f* the earth
9:1 become many and *f* the earth
21:19 *f* the skin bottle with water
24:16 *f* her water jar and then
26:15 would *f* them with dry earth
44:1 *F* the bags of the men with
Ex 16:32 *F* an omer measure of it as
28:17 *f* it with a filling of
28:41 and *f* their hand with power
29:9 you must *f* the hand of Aaron
29:29 *f* their hand with power
29:33 *f* their hand with power, in
29:35 *f* their hand with power
31:3 *f* him with the spirit of God
32:29 *F* your hand today with power
35:31 to *f* him with the spirit of
Le 8:33 seven days to *f* your hand
De 6:11 and that you did not *f*
Jg 6:38 *f* a large banquet bowl with
17:5 *f* the hand of one of his sons
1Sa 16:1 *F* your horn with oil and go
1Ki 13:33 *f* his hand with power
18:33 *F* four large jars with
2Ki 3:25 his stone and actually *f* it
23:14 *f* their places with human
1Ch 29:5 *f* his hand today with a gift
Job 3:15 *f* their houses with silver
15:2 *f* his belly with the east
20:23 to *f* his belly, He will
23:4 *f* with counterarguments
41:7 *f* its skin with harpoons
Ps 17:14 whose belly you *f* with your
36:8 drink their *f* of the fatness
72:19 his glory *f* the whole earth
80:9 take root and *f* the land
81:10 mouth wide, and I shall *f* it
83:16 *F* their faces with dishonor
Pr 1:13 *f* our houses with spoil
6:30 thievery to *f* his soul when
7:18 drink our *f* of love until the
Isa 8:8 *f* the breadth of your land
14:21 *f* the face of the productive
27:6 simply *f* the surface of the
33:5 *f* Zion with justice and
Jer 23:24 the earth that I . . . *f*
31:25 languishing soul I will *f*
33:5 *f* places with the carcasses
46:10 take its *f* of their blood
51:11 *F* the circular shields
51:14 I will *f* you with men
Eze 3:3 *f* your very intestines with
7:19 intestines they will not *f*
8:17 to *f* the land with violence
9:7 and *f* the courtyards with the
10:2 *f* the hollows of both your
24:4 *f* it even with the choicest
30:11 *f* the land with the slain
32:5 *f* the valleys with the
35:8 *f* its mountains with its
Hag 2:7 will *f* this house with glory
Zec 9:13 bow I will *f* with Ephraim
Mt 23:32 *f* up the measure of your
Lu 8:23 they began to *f* up with water
Joh 2:7 *F* the water jars with water
6:12 when they had their *f* he
Ac 2:28 *f* me with good cheer with
Ro 15:13 God who gives hope *f* you
1Co 4:8 already have your *f*, do you?
1Th 2:16 *f* up the measure of their

Filled
Ge 6:11 earth became *f* with violence
Ex 1:7 the land got to be *f* with them
2:16 drew water and *f* the gutters
10:6 Egypt will be *f* to an extent
15:9 My soul will be *f* with them
28:3 *f* with the spirit of wisdom
35:35 *f* them with wisdom of heart
39:10 *f* it with four rows of stones
40:34 glory *f* the tabernacle
40:35 glory *f* the tabernacle
Le 9:17 *f* his hand with some of it
16:32 hand will be *f* with power
19:29 be *f* with loose morals
21:10 hand was *f* with power to
Nu 3:3 hands had been *f* with power to
14:21 the earth will be *f* with the
Jos 9:13 wine skin-bottles that we *f*
Jg 17:12 Micah *f* the hand of the
1Sa 2:4 mighty men . . . *f* with terror
1Ki 8:10 cloud itself *f* the house of
8:11 glory of Jehovah *f* the house
18:35 trench also he *f* with water
20:27 Syrians . . . *f* the earth
2Ki 3:17 valley will be *f* with water
3:20 came to be *f* with the water
9:24 Jehu himself *f* his hand with
21:16 *f* Jerusalem from end to end
24:4 he *f* Jerusalem with innocent
2Ch 5:13 house . . . was *f* with a cloud
5:14 glory of Jehovah *f* the house
7:1 glory itself *f* the house
7:2 glory had *f* the house of
13:9 *f* his hand with power by
16:14 *f* with balsam oil and
29:31 *f* your hand with power for
Ezr 9:11 *f* it from end to end by
Es 3:5 and Haman became *f* with rage
5:9 *f* with rage against Mordecai
Job 4:14 my bones it *f* with dread
22:18 *f* their houses with good
36:17 you will certainly be *f*
Ps 14:5 were *f* with a great dread
23:5 My cup is well *f*
33:5 the earth is *f*
53:5 were *f* with a great dread
71:8 mouth is *f* with your praise
107:9 soul he has *f* with good
119:64 O Jehovah, has *f* the earth
126:2 came to be *f* with laughter
127:5 man that has *f* his quiver
129:7 reaper has not *f* his own
Pr 3:10 supply will be *f* with plenty
8:21 their storehouses I keep *f*
12:21 certainly be *f* with calamity
20:17 mouth will be *f* with gravel
24:4 interior rooms be *f* with all
Ec 1:8 is the ear *f* from hearing
6:7 their own soul does not get *f*
11:3 the clouds are *f* with water
Ca 5:2 For my head is *f* with dew
5:14 of gold, *f* with chrysolite
Isa 1:15 very hands have become *f*
2:7 land is *f* with silver and
2:7 their land is *f* with horses
2:8 land is *f* with valueless gods
6:4 gradually *f* with smoke
11:9 earth will certainly be *f*
13:21 houses must be *f* with eagle
23:2 they have *f* you
25:6 dishes *f* with marrow, of
34:6 sword; it must be *f* with
Jer 13:12 that gets *f* with wine
13:12 jar . . . gets *f* with wine
15:17 that you have *f* me
16:18 they had *f* my inheritance
19:4 *f* this place with the blood
41:9 *f* with those slain
46:12 own outcry has *f* the land
51:34 *f* his abdomen with my
Eze 9:9 the land is *f* with bloodshed
10:4 became *f* with the cloud, and
11:6 *f* her streets with the slain
16:30 I am *f* up with rage against
19:7 *f* it with the sound of his
23:33 and grief you will be *f*
26:2 be *f*—she has been devastated
27:25 get *f* and become very
28:16 they *f* the midst of you
32:6 will be *f* up from you
44:4 had *f* the house of Jehovah
Da 2:35 and *f* the whole earth
3:19 got *f* with fury, and
Na 2:12 he kept his holes *f* with prey
Hab 2:14 earth . . . *f* with the knowing
3:3 praise the earth became *f*
Zec 8:5 *f* with boys and girls playing
9:15 *f* like the bowl, like the
Mt 5:6 since they will be *f*
22:10 *f* with those reclining at
Lu 1:15 he will be *f* with holy spirit
1:41 Elizabeth was *f* with holy
1:67 *f* with holy spirit, and he
2:40 *f* with wisdom, and God's
3:5 Every gully must be *f* up, and
4:28 became *f* with anger
5:7 they *f* both boats, so that
5:26 and they became *f* with fear
6:11 they became *f* with madness
6:21 because you will be *f*
6:25 Woe to you who are *f* up now
14:23 that my house may be *f*
15:16 to be *f* with the carob pods
16:21 desiring to be *f* with the
Joh 2:7 And they *f* them to the brim
6:13 *f* twelve baskets with
12:3 became *f* with the scent of
16:6 grief has *f* your hearts
Ac 2:2 *f* the whole house in which
2:4 all became *f* with holy spirit
3:10 became *f* with astonishment
4:8 Peter, *f* with holy spirit
4:31 all *f* with the holy spirit
5:17 and became *f* with jealousy
5:28 have *f* Jerusalem with your
9:17 and be *f* with holy spirit
13:9 becoming *f* with holy spirit
13:45 they were *f* with jealousy
13:52 *f* with joy and holy spirit
19:29 city became *f* with confusion
Ro 1:29 *f* as they were with all
15:14 been *f* with all knowledge
2Co 7:4 I am *f* with comfort, I am
Eph 3:19 be *f* with all the fullness
5:18 keep getting *f* with spirit
Php 1:11 be *f* with righteous fruit
4:18 I am *f*, now that I have
Col 1:9 *f* with the accurate knowledge
2Ti 1:4 that I may get *f* with joy
Re 6:11 until the number was *f* also
8:5 *f* it with some of the fire of
15:8 sanctuary became *f* with smoke
19:21 the birds were *f* from the

Filling
Ge 42:25 *f* up their receptacles with
Ex 28:17 fill it with a *f* of stones
Isa 6:1 his skirts were *f* the temple
65:11 *f* up mixed wine for the god
Jer 13:13 *f* all the inhabitants of
Eze 10:3 the cloud was *f* the inner
Zep 1:9 *f* the house of their masters
Ac 14:17 *f* your hearts to the full
Col 1:24 am *f* up what is lacking of

Fillings
Ex 28:20 of gold should be in their *f*
39:13 settings of gold in their *f*

Fills
1Ch 16:32 and also that which *f* it
Job 8:21 *f* your mouth with laughter
Ps 24:1 the earth and that which *f* it
89:11 land and what *f* it—you
96:11 sea thunder and that which *f*
98:7 sea thunder and that which *f*
Isa 34:1 earth and that which *f* it
42:10 sea and to that which *f* it
Jer 8:16 the land and what *f* it
47:2 the land and what *f* it
Am 6:8 the city and what *f* it
Mic 1:2 O earth and what *f* you, and
1Co 10:26 earth and that which *f* it
Eph 1:23 who *f* up all things in all

Film
Isa 40:15 *f* of dust on the scales

Filter
Job 36:27 They *f* as rain for his mist

Filtered
Isa 25:6 wine kept on the dregs, *f*

Filth
1Pe 3:21 the *f* of the flesh, but the
Re 21:8 who are disgusting in their *f*

Filthiness
Jas 1:21 put away all *f* and that

Filthy
Isa 28:8 become full of *f* vomit
Jas 2:2 poor man in *f* clothing also
Re 22:11, 11 *f* one be made *f* still

Final
Ge 49:1 in the *f* part of the days
2Ki 19:23 enter its *f* lodging place
Isa 2:2 in the *f* part of the days that
37:24 enter its *f* height, the
Jer 23:20 In the *f* part of the days
30:24 *f* part of the days you
48:47 in the *f* part of the days
49:39 *f* part of the days that I
Eze 35:5 the time of their *f* error
38:8 In the *f* part of the years
38:16 In the *f* part of the days
Da 2:28 in the *f* part of the days
8:19 the *f* part of the denunciation
8:23 *f* part of their kingdom, as
10:14 in the *f* part of the days
12:8 be the *f* part of these things
Ho 3:5 in the *f* part of the days
Mic 4:1 in the *f* part of the days
Mt 12:45 *f* circumstances of that man
Lu 11:26 the *f* circumstances of that
2Pe 2:20 the *f* conditions have become

Finale
Isa 46:10 from the beginning the *f*
47:7 did not remember the *f* of
Jer 5:31 will you men do in the *f*
17:11 in his *f* he will prove to

Finality
Jer 23:39 people to neglect, with *f*

Finally*
Ge 3:10 *F* he said: Your voice I heard
12:5 *F* they came to the land of
30:22 *F* God remembered Rachel
41:55 *F* all the land of Egypt
50:4 *F* the days of weeping for him
Ex 14:26 *F* Jehovah said to Moses
17:4 *F* Moses cried out to Jehovah
Nu 20:16 *F* we cried out to Jehovah
Ps 32:5 My sin I *f* confessed to you
78:51 *F* he struck down all the
78:60 *f* forsook the tabernacle of
2Co 13:11 *F* . . . continue to rejoice
1Pe 3:8 *F*, all of you be like-minded
2Pe 3:14 be found *f* by him spotless

Financially
Le 25:35 he is *f* weak alongside you

Find
Ge 8:9 And the dove did not *f* any
18:26 If I shall *f* in Sodom fifty
18:28 ruin if I *f* there forty-five
18:30 not do it if I *f* thirty there
19:11 trying to *f* the entrance
30:14 to *f* mandrakes in the field
31:32 you may *f* your gods, let
31:33 but did not *f* them
31:34 but did not *f* them
31:35 but did not *f* the teraphim
32:5 I may *f* favor in your eyes
33:8 In order to *f* favor in the
33:15 Let me *f* favor in the eyes
34:11 Let me *f* favor in your eyes
34:19 *f* delight in Jacob's daughter
39:21 granting him to *f* favor in
44:34 the calamity that will *f*
47:25 *f* favor in the eyes of my
Ex 2:4 *f* out what would be done
5:11 straw . . . wherever you may *f*
15:22 but they did not *f* water
16:25 will not *f* it in the field
33:13 I may *f* favor in your eyes
Le 6:3 he does *f* something lost and
25:26 *f* enough for its repurchase
25:28 *f* enough to give back to him
Nu 35:27 avenger of blood does *f* him
De 4:29 you will also certainly *f* him
22:14 not *f* evidence of virginity
24:1 *f* no favor in his eyes because
32:10 *f* him in a wilderness land
Jos 2:22 and they did not *f* them
Jg 5:30 Ought they not to *f*, ought
17:8 wherever he might *f* a place
17:9 wherever I may *f* a place
21:14 did not *f* enough for them
Ru 1:9 *f* a resting-place each one in
2:2 in whose eyes I may *f* favor
2:13 Let me *f* favor in your eyes
1Sa 1:18 *f* favor in your eyes
1Sa 9:4 and they did not *f* them
9:4 and they did not *f* them
9:13 *f* him before he goes up to
9:13 just now you will *f* him
10:2 *f* two men close by the tomb
13:14 Jehovah will certainly *f*
20:21 saying, Go, *f* the arrows
20:36 *f* the arrows that I am
23:17 Saul . . . will not *f* you
25:8 my young men may *f* favor in
25:8 whatever your hand may *f*
30:11 *f* a man, an Egyptian, in
31:8 *f* Saul and his three sons
2Sa 3:8 *f* yourself in the hand of
15:25 *f* favor in the eyes of
16:4 Let me *f* favor in your eyes
17:20 they did not *f* them and so
20:6 he may not actually *f*
1Ki 11:19 to *f* favor in the eyes of
11:29 got to *f* him on the road
13:14 got to *f* him sitting under
18:5 we may *f* green grass, that
18:10 that they could not *f* you
18:12 Ahab, and he will not *f* you
20:36 the lion got to *f* him and
20:37 he went on to *f* another man
2Ki 2:17 but they did not *f* him
4:39 he got to *f* a wild vine and
9:21 got to *f* him in the tract of
9:35 did not *f* anything of her
17:4 to *f* conspiracy in Hoshea's
1Ch 10:8 to *f* Saul and his sons fallen
2Ch 20:16 *f* them at the end of the
20:25 *f* among them in abundance
22:8 *f* the princes of Judah and
32:4 *f* a great deal of water
Ezr 2:62 they did not *f* themselves
4:15 *f* in the book of records and
7:16 silver . . . gold that you *f* in
8:15 sons of Levi did I *f* there
Ne 5:8 and they did not *f* a word
13:10 *f* out that the very portions
13:11 began to *f* fault with the
13:17 *f* fault with the nobles of
13:25 began to *f* fault with them
Es 8:6 calamity that will *f* my
Job 3:22 because they *f* a burial place
9:3 *f* delight in contending with
10:6 you should try to *f* my error
11:7 *f* out the deep things of God
11:7 *f* out to the very limit of
13:3 I would *f* delight
17:10 not *f* anyone wise among you
20:8 and they will not *f* him
22:26 *f* your exquisite delight
23:3 knew where I might *f* him
27:10 will he *f* exquisite delight
28:1 there exists a place to *f* it
Ps 4:2 you keep seeking to *f* a lie
10:15 until you *f* no more
21:8 hand will *f* all your enemies
21:8 will *f* those hating you
27:8 Seek to *f* my face, you people
27:8 O Jehovah, I shall seek to *f*
34:14 Seek to *f* peace, and pursue
36:2 *f* out his error so as to hate
37:11 *f* their exquisite delight in
51:16 you do not *f* pleasure
107:4 *f* any way to a city of
119:52 And I *f* comfort for myself
132:5 Until I *f* a place for Jehovah
147:10 the man does he *f* pleasure
Pr 1:13 us *f* all sorts of precious
1:28 but they will not *f* me
2:5 *f* the very knowledge of God
3:4 *f* favor and good insight in
6:33 plague and dishonor he will *f*
7:15 that I may *f* you
8:12 I *f* even the knowledge of
8:17 are the ones that *f* me
8:35 will certainly *f* life, and
14:6 ridiculer has sought to *f*
16:20 showing insight . . . *f* good
17:20 crooked . . . will not *f* good
18:15 ear of wise ones seeks to *f*
19:8 is going to *f* good
20:6 but a faithful man who can *f*?
21:21 will *f* life, righteousness
28:23 will afterward *f* more favor
31:10 A capable wife who can *f*?
Ec 3:11 may never *f* out the work that
7:24 Who can *f* it out?
7:27 another, to *f* out the sumup
8:17 mankind are not able to *f* out
Ec 8:17 to seek, yet they do not *f* out
8:17 they would be unable to *f* out
11:1 many days you will *f* it again
12:10 to *f* the delightful words
Ca 3:1 sought him, but I did not *f*
3:2 I sought him, but I did not *f*
5:6 I sought him, but I did not *f*
5:8 if you *f* my dear one, you
8:1 Should I *f* you outside, I
Isa 34:14 *f* for itself a resting-place
41:12 but you will not *f* them
51:1 who are seeking to *f* Jehovah
55:2 soul *f* its exquisite delight
58:14 *f* your exquisite delight in
Jer 2:24 In her month they will *f* her
5:1 whether you can *f* a man
6:16 *f* ease for your souls
10:18 order that they may *f* out
29:13 actually seek me and *f* me
Eze 3:1 Son of man, what you *f*, eat
34:4 one you have not sought to *f*
34:6 with no one seeking to *f*
43:27 *f* pleasure in you
Da 1:20 *f* them ten times better than
6:4 *f* some pretext against Daniel
6:4 all that they were able to *f*
6:5 *f* in this Daniel no pretext at
6:5 *f* it against him in the law
Ho 2:6 own roadways she will not *f*
2:7 but she will not *f* them
5:6 but they could not *f* him
12:4 At Bethel He got to *f* him
12:8 they will *f*, on my part, no
Am 5:22 I shall *f* no pleasure
8:12 but they will not *f* it
9:13 all *f* themselves melting
Zec 11:6 causing mankind to *f*
Mal 1:8 Will he *f* pleasure in you
Mt 7:7 on seeking, and you will *f*
10:39 loses his soul . . . *f* it
11:29 *f* refreshment for your souls
13:32 *f* lodging among its branches
16:25 soul for my sake will *f* it
17:27 you will *f* a stater coin
18:13 And if he happens to *f* it, I
21:2 will at once *f* an ass tied
22:9 anyone you *f* invite to the
Mr 4:32 to *f* lodging under its shadow
11:2 you will *f* a colt tied, on
11:13 perhaps *f* something on it
13:36 he does not *f* you sleeping
Lu 2:12 *f* an infant bound in cloth
6:7 to *f* some way to accuse him
9:12 lodging and *f* provisions
11:9 on seeking, and you will *f*
18:8 will he really *f* the faith
19:30 you will *f* a colt tied, on
19:48 did not *f* the effective thing
23:4 I *f* no crime in this man
24:3 not *f* the body of the Lord
24:23 did not *f* his body and they
Joh 7:34 look . . . you will not *f* me
7:35 so that we shall not *f* him
7:36 but you will not *f* me, and
10:9 in and out and *f* pasturage
18:38 I *f* no fault in him
19:4 know I *f* no fault in him
19:6 I do not *f* any fault in him
21:6 and you will *f* some
Ac 4:21 *f* any ground on which to
5:22 did not *f* them in the prison
17:6 When they did not *f* them they
17:27 *f* him, although, in fact, he
23:9 *f* nothing wrong in this man
24:8 *f* out about all these things
24:11 are in a position to *f* out
Ro 7:21 I *f*, then, this law in my
9:19 Why does he yet *f* fault?
2Co 8:20 having any man *f* fault with
9:4 come with me and *f* you not
12:20 I may *f* you not as I could
2Ti 1:18 Lord grant him to *f* mercy
Heb 4:16 and *f* undeserved kindness for
8:8 does *f* fault with the people
Re 9:6 but will by no means *f* it
18:14 never again . . . people *f* them

Finding
Ge 4:14 anyone *f* me will kill me
4:15 no one *f* him should strike
27:20 so quick in *f* it, my son
39:4 Joseph kept *f* favor in his
Ne 5:7 began *f* fault with the nobles
Ps 103:9 for all time keep *f* fault

’s 116:3 Distress and grief I kept f
119:162 one does when f much spoil
147:11 Jehovah is f pleasure in
’r 4:22 life to those f them and
8:9 to the ones f knowledge
8:35 one f me will certainly find
14:32 be f refuge in his integrity
:c 7:26 f out: More bitter than death
:a 8:10 like her that is f peace
sa 58:3 f delight in the very day of
58:13 rather than f what delights
’er 50:7 those f them have eaten them
ſt 7:14 and few are the ones f it
13:46 f one pearl of high value
ſr 14:55 but they were not f any
.u 2:45 But, not f him, they returned
5:19 not f a way to bring him in
11:24 and, after f none, it says
’oh 9:35 on f him, he said: Are you
.c 2:47 f favor with all the people
7:11 were not f any provisions
12:19 not f him, he examined the
25:10 also are f out quite well
Co 2:13 not f Titus my brother, but

’inds

)e 22:28 In case a man f a girl, a
25:7 if the man f no delight in
g 9:33 as your hand f it possible
Sa 10:7 what your hand f possible
24:19 man f his enemy, will he
’ob 14:6 Until he f pleasure as a
33:10 opposition to me he f
’s 107:26 very soul f itself melting
’r 3:12 son in whom he f pleasure
18:2 Anyone stupid f no delight in
:c 9:10 All that your hand f to do, do
ſt 7:8 everyone seeking f, and to
10:39 that f his soul will lose it
11:6 f no cause for stumbling in
12:43 a resting-place, and f none
12:44 it f it unoccupied but swept
24:46 on arriving f him doing so
.u 11:10 and everyone seeking f, and
11:25 arriving it f it swept clean
12:37 on arriving f watching
12:38 and f them thus, happy are
12:43 if his master on arriving f
15:4 for the lost one until he f it
15:8 search carefully until she f

’ine

:e 18:6 seah measures of f flour
30:34 Laban said: Why, that is f!
41:42 with garments of f linen and
:x 16:14, 14 a f flaky thing, f like
25:4 and f linen, and goat’s hair
26:1 cloths, of f twisted linen
26:31 material and f twisted linen
26:36 material and f twisted linen
27:9 hangings of f twisted linen
27:16 f twisted linen, the work of
27:18 f twisted linen, and their
28:5 material and the f linen
28:6 material and f twisted linen
28:8 material and f twisted linen
28:15 and f twisted linen you will
28:39 the robe of f linen and make
28:39 and make a turban of f linen
29:2 Out of f wheat flour you will
29:40 ephah measure of f flour
30:36 into f powder and put some
32:20 and crushed it till it was f
35:6 f linen and goat’s hair
35:23 f linen and goat’s hair and
35:25 material and the f linen
35:35 scarlet material and f linen
36:8 cloths of f twisted linen
36:35 material and f twisted linen
36:37 material and f twisted linen
38:9 courtyard were of f twisted
38:16 were of f twisted linen
38:18 material and f twisted linen
38:23 scarlet material and f linen
39:2 material and f twisted linen
39:3 material and the f linen
39:5 material and f twisted linen
39:8 material and f twisted linen
39:27 made the robes of f linen
39:28 the turban of f linen and
39:28 headgears of f linen and the
39:28 drawers of f twisted linen
39:29 the sash of f twisted linen
.e 2:1 should prove to be f flour
2:2 his handful of its f flour and

Le 2:4 it should be of f flour
2:5 of f flour moistened with oil
2:7 be made of f flour with oil
5:11 tenth of an ephah of f flour
6:15 f flour of the grain offering
6:20 tenth of an ephah of f flour
7:12 f flour as ring-shaped cakes
14:10 f flour as a grain offering
14:21 ephah of f flour moistened
16:12 full of f perfumed incense
23:13 ephah of f flour moistened
23:17 ephah of f flour they should
24:5 f flour and bake it up into
Nu 6:15 cakes of f flour, moistened
7:13 full of f flour moistened
7:19 full of f flour moistened
7:25 full of f flour moistened
7:31 f flour moistened with oil
7:37 full of f flour moistened
7:43 f flour moistened with oil
7:49 f flour moistened with oil
7:55 full of f flour moistened
7:61 full of f flour moistened
7:67 full of f flour moistened
7:73 f flour moistened with oil
7:79 f flour moistened with oil
8:8 grain offering of f flour
15:4 a grain offering of f flour
15:6 of f flour, moistened with a
15:9 of three tenths of f flour
28:5 tenth of an ephah of f flour
28:9 two tenth measures of f flour
28:12 f flour as a grain offering
28:12 f flour as a grain offering
28:13 a tenth measure of f flour
28:20 grain offerings of f flour
28:28 f flour moistened with oil
29:3 grain offering of f flour
29:9 f flour moistened with oil
29:14 f flour moistened with oil
De 9:21 it had become f like dust
22:19 f him a hundred silver
Ru 3:13 if he will repurchase you, f
2Sa 22:43 pound them f like the dust
1Ki 4:22 cor measures of f flour
2Ki 7:1 a seah measure of f flour
7:16 a seah measure of f flour
7:18 a seah measure of f flour
23:33 imposed a f upon the land
1Ch 4:21 workers of f fabric of the
9:29 over the f flour and the
15:27 sleeveless coat of f fabric
23:29 for the f flour for the
2Ch 2:14 in f fabric and in crimson
3:14 and f fabric, and worked in
5:12 clothed in f fabric with
30:22 acting with f discretion
Ezr 7:26 money f or for imprisonment
Es 1:6 There were linen, f cotton and
1:6 held fast in ropes of f fabric
Ps 18:42 shall pound them f like dust
Pr 1:9 and a f necklace to your throat
17:26 f upon the righteous one is
19:19 rage will be bearing the f
21:11 of a f on the ridiculer the
27:22 pound the foolish one f with
Isa 29:5 become just like f powder
40:15 as mere f dust
40:22 heavens just as a f gauze
Eze 16:10 to wrap you in f linen and
16:13 your attire was f linen and
16:13 F flour and honey and oil
16:19 f flour and oil and honey
27:16 f fabric and corals and
46:14 for sprinkling the f flour
Mt 3:10 not produce f fruit is to be
5:16 may see your f works and
7:17 good tree produces f fruit
7:18 rotten tree produce f fruit
7:19 tree not producing f fruit
12:12 do a f thing on the sabbath
12:33, 33 tree f and its fruit f
13:8 others fell upon the f soil
13:23 the one sown upon the f soil
13:24 a man that sowed f seed in
13:27 did you not sow f seed in
13:37 sower of the f seed is the
13:38 f seed, these are the sons
13:45 merchant seeking f pearls
13:48 collected the f ones into
17:4 it is f for us to be here
26:10 she did a f deed toward me
27:59 wrapped . . . in clean f linen
Mr 4:8 others fell upon the f soil

Mr 4:20 that were sown on the f soil
9:5 f for us to be here, so let us
9:50 Salt is f; but if ever the
12:28 answered them in a f way
14:6 She did a f deed toward me
14:51 wearing a f linen garment
15:46 he bought f linen and took
15:46 wrapped him in the f linen
Lu 3:9 not producing f fruit is to be
6:38 into your laps a f measure
6:43 f tree producing rotten fruit
6:43 rotten tree producing f fruit
8:15 As for that on the f soil
8:15 with a f and good heart
9:33 it is f for us to be here, so
14:34 Salt, to be sure, is f
21:5 adorned with f stones and
23:53 wrapped it up in f linen
Joh 2:10 puts out the f wine first
2:10 reserved the f wine until
10:11 I am the f shepherd
10:11 f shepherd surrenders his
10:14 I am the f shepherd, and I
10:32 many f works from the
10:33 not for a f work, but for
Ro 7:16 I agree that the Law is f
7:18 ability to work out what is f
12:17 Provide f things in the sight
1Co 5:6 cause for boasting is not f
14:17 give thanks in a f way, but
2Co 13:7 you may be doing what is f
Ga 4:17 seek you, not in a f way
4:18 f for you to be zealously
4:18 sought for in a f cause at
6:9 give up in doing what is f
1Th 5:21 hold fast to what is f
1Ti 1:8 we know that the Law is f
1:18 go on waging the f warfare
2:3 This is f and acceptable in
3:1 he is desirous of a f work
3:4 own household in a f manner
3:7 also have a f testimony
3:12 presiding in a f manner over
3:13 who minister in a f manner
3:13 a f standing and great
4:4 every creation of God is f
4:6 a f minister of Christ Jesus
4:6 and of the f teaching which
5:10 to her for f works, if she
5:17 who preside in a f way be
5:25 the f works are publicly
6:12 the f fight of the faith
6:12 the f public declaration in
6:13 the f public declaration
6:18 to be rich in f works
6:19 a f foundation for the future
2Ti 1:14 This f trust guard through
2:3 As a f soldier of Christ Jesus
4:7 I have fought the f fight
Tit 2:7 an example of f works
2:14 zealous for f works
3:8 minds on maintaining f works
3:8 things are f and beneficial
3:14 learn to maintain f works
Heb 6:5 tasted the f word of God and
10:24 incite to love and f works
13:9 f for the heart to be given
Jas 2:3 this seat here in a f place
2:7 blaspheme the f name by
3:13 show out of his f conduct
1Pe 2:12 Maintain your conduct f
2:12 as a result of your f works
4:10 as f stewards of God’s
Re 1:15 feet were like f copper when
2:18 his feet are like f copper
18:12 f linen and purple and silk
18:13 f flour and wheat and cattle
18:14 the f fruit that your soul
18:16 city, clothed with f linen
19:8 in bright, clean, f linen
19:8 f linen stands for the
19:14 in white, clean, f linen

Fined

2Ch 36:3 f the land a hundred silver
Am 2:8 those who have been f

Fine-fabric

Es 8:15 a f cloak, even of wool dyed

Finer

Mt 18:8 f for you to enter into life
18:9 f for you to enter one-eyed
26:24 would have been f for him
Mr 9:42 it would be f for him if a

Mr 9:43 *f* for you to enter into life
9:45 *f* for you to enter into life
9:47 it is *f* for you to enter
14:21 *f* for that man if he had not
1Co 9:15 would be *f* for me to die

Finery
2Sa 1:24 clothed you in scarlet with *f*

Finest
Ge 43:11 Take the *f* products of the
Ca 4:14 along with all the *f* perfumes
Eze 16:7 come in with the *f* ornament
27:22 *f* of all sorts of perfumes

Finger
Ex 8:19 Pharaoh: It is the *f* of God!
29:12 blood and put it with your *f*
31:18 stone written on by God's *f*
Le 4:6 must dip his *f* in the blood
4:17 dip his *f* into some of the
4:25 the sin offering with his *f*
4:30 blood with his *f* and put it
4:34 with his *f* and put it upon
8:15 with his *f* upon the horns of
9:9 he dipped his *f* in the blood
14:16 dip his right *f* into the oil
14:16 the oil with his *f* seven
14:27 spatter with his right *f*
16:14 spatter it with his *f* in
16:14 some of the blood with his *f*
16:19 with his *f* seven times and
Nu 19:4 some of its blood with his *f*
De 9:10 written upon with God's *f*
1Ki 12:10 My little *f* itself will
2Ch 10:10 My own little *f* will
Isa 3:21 *f* rings and the nose rings
58:9 the poking out of the *f* and
Mt 23:4 to budge them with their *f*
Lu 11:20 by means of God's *f* I expel
16:24 the tip of his *f* in water
Joh 20:25 *f* into the print of the
20:27 Thomas: Put your *f* here

Fingerbreadths
Jer 52:21 thickness was four *f*, it

Fingers
2Sa 21:20 six *f* on each of his hands
1Ch 20:6 *f* and toes were in sixes
Ps 8:3 heavens, the works of your *f*
144:1 My *f* for warfare
Pr 6:13 indications with his *f*
7:3 Tie them upon your *f*, and
Ca 5:5 and my *f* with liquid myrrh
Isa 2:8 that which one's *f* have made
17:8 what his *f* have made he
59:3 and your *f* with error
Da 5:5 *f* of a man's hand came forth
Mr 7:33 put his *f* into the man's ears
Lu 11:46 loads with one of your *f*
Jas 2:2 with gold rings on his *f* and

Finish
Ex 5:13 *F* your works, each one his
5:14 not *f* your prescribed task in
34:33 Moses would *f* speaking with
Nu 4:15 *f* covering the holy place and
De 7:22 allowed to *f* them off quickly
26:12 When you *f* with tithing
Jos 5:6 had come to its *f*, to whom
2Sa 11:19 As soon as you *f* speaking
1Ki 6:9 the house that he might *f* it
6:14 the house that he might *f* it
1Ch 27:24 the count, but he did not *f*
Ezr 4:12 to *f* the walls and to repair
5:3 and to *f* this beam structure
5:9 to *f* this beam structure
Ne 4:2 Will they *f* up in a day?
Job 36:11 They will *f* their days in
Ps 9:6 have come to their perpetual *f*
73:19 *f* through sudden terrors
102:26 they will *f* their turn
Ec 3:11 made from the start to the *f*
Isa 1:28 will come to their *f*
29:20 bragger must come to his *f*
Jer 8:13 shall bring them to their *f*
14:15 will come to their *f*
24:10 until they come to their *f*
44:12 their *f* in the land of Egypt
44:12 they will come to their *f*
44:18 we have come to our *f*
44:27 their *f* by the sword
La 3:22 we have not come to our *f*
4:22 error . . . has come to its *f*
Eze 5:13 will certainly come to its *f*
5:13 I bring my rage to its *f*
Eze 6:12 will bring to its *f* my rage
7:8 my anger against you to its *f*
13:15 bring my rage to its *f* upon
20:8 my anger to its *f* upon them
20:21 to bring my anger to its *f*
Da 9:24 and to *f* off sin, and to
11:36 will have come to a *f*
12:7 things will come to their *f*
Am 3:15 will have to come to their *f*
Zep 1:2 without fail *f* everything off
1:3 *f* off earthling man and beast
1:3 *f* off the flying creature of
Zec 4:9 and his own hands will *f* it
Mal 3:6 you have not come to your *f*
Lu 14:29 but not be able to *f* it
14:30 build but was not able to *f*
18:5 and pummeling me to a *f*
Joh 4:34 sent me and to *f* his work
Ac 20:24 if only I may *f* my course
2Co 8:11 *f* up also the doing of it
Php 3:19 and their *f* is destruction
2Ti 4:7 I have run the course to the *f*
1Pe 5:10 will himself *f* your training
Re 10:7 is indeed brought to a *f*
15:1 anger of God is brought to a *f*

Finished
Ge 17:22 God *f* speaking with him and
18:33 he had *f* speaking to Abraham
24:15 before he had *f* speaking
24:19 *f* giving him a drink, then
24:22 camels had *f* drinking, then
24:45 Before I was *f* speaking in
27:30 as Isaac had *f* blessing Jacob
43:2 had *f* eating up the cereals
44:12 and *f* with the youngest
49:33 Jacob *f* giving commands to
Ex 31:18 had *f* speaking with him on
40:33 So Moses *f* the work
Le 16:20 *f* making atonement for the
Nu 7:1 Moses *f* setting up the
16:31 as soon as he had *f* speaking
De 2:16 *f* dying off from the midst
20:9 *f* speaking to the people
31:24 *f* writing the words of this
32:45 Moses *f* speaking all these
Jos 10:20 had *f* slaying them with a
19:49 *f* dividing the land for a
Jg 3:18 when he had *f* presenting the
15:17 when he *f* speaking, he
Ru 2:21 *f* the entire harvest that I
3:3 he has *f* eating and drinking
1Sa 10:13 he *f* speaking as a prophet
13:10 as soon as he had *f* offering
18:1 as he had *f* speaking to Saul
24:16 David *f* speaking these
2Sa 6:18 David was *f* with offering up
13:36 soon as he *f* speaking, here
1Ki 1:41 they themselves had *f* eating
3:1 he *f* building his own house
6:38 the house was *f* as regards
7:1 he *f* all his own house
7:40 Hiram *f* doing all the work
8:54 Solomon *f* praying to Jehovah
9:1 Solomon had *f* building the
2Ki 10:25 he *f* rendering up the burnt
1Ch 16:2 David *f* offering up the burnt
28:20 of Jehovah's house is *f*
2Ch 4:11 Hiram *f* doing the work that
7:1 Solomon *f* praying, the fire
7:11 Solomon *f* the house of
8:16 of Jehovah until it was *f*
20:23 *f* with the inhabitants of
24:14 they had *f* they brought
29:17 of the first month they *f*
29:28 the burnt offering was *f*
29:29 *f* offering it up, the king
29:34 until the work was *f* and
31:1 they *f* all this, all the
31:1 Manasseh until they had *f*
31:7 in the seventh month they *f*
Ezr 4:13 rebuilt and its walls be *f*
4:16 rebuilt and its walls be *f*
5:11 king of Israel built and *f*
6:14 built and *f* it due to the
9:1 these things were *f*, the
10:17 *f* with all the men that
Ps 19:6 its *f* circuit is to their
90:9 *f* our years just like a
104:35 sinners will be *f* off from
Isa 16:4 have been *f* off the earth
33:1 you have *f* as a despoiler
Jer 27:8 *f* them off by his hand
43:1 Jeremiah *f* speaking to all
Eze 42:15 *f* the measurements of the
Da 5:26 of your kingdom and has *f* it
Am 7:2 *f* eating up the vegetation
Mt 7:28 when Jesus *f* these sayings
11:1 *f* giving instructions to his
13:53 Now when Jesus had *f* these
19:1 when Jesus had *f* these words
26:1 Jesus had *f* all these sayings
Lu 12:50 distressed until it is *f*
13:32 the third day I shall be *f*
Joh 17:4 *f* the work you have given me
Ro 15:28 after I have *f* with this and
Heb 4:3 *f* from the founding of the
Re 11:7 they have *f* their witnessing
15:8 of the seven angels were *f*

Finishes
Le 25:29 time of his sale *f* out; his

Finishing
Jos 8:24 Israel was *f* the killing of
2Ki 13:17 at Aphek to the *f* point
13:19 Syria to the *f* point
Da 12:7 *f* of the dashing of the power
2Co 8:11 *f* up of it out of what you

Fins
Le 11:9 that has *f* and scales in the
11:10 that has no *f* and scales
11:12 has no *f* and scales is a
De 14:9 Everything that has *f* and
14:10 everything that has no *f* and

Fire
Ge 19:24 it rain sulphur and *f* from
22:6 took in his hands the *f* and
22:7 Here are the *f* and the wood
Ex 3:2 *f* in the midst of a thornbush
3:2 burning with the *f* and yet the
9:23 *f* would run down to the earth
9:24 *f* quivering in among the hail
12:8 should eat it roasted with *f*
12:9 but roast with *f*, its head
12:10 should burn with *f*
13:21 nighttime in a pillar of *f*
13:22 pillar of *f* in the nighttime
14:24 the pillar of *f* and cloud
19:18 came down upon it in *f*; and
22:6 In case a *f* should spread out
22:6 one who started the *f* is to
24:17 *f* on the mountaintop
25:38 *f* holders are of pure gold
27:3 its forks, and its *f* holders
29:14 burn with *f* outside the camp
29:18 is an offering made by *f* to
29:25 It is an offering made by *f*
29:34 burn what is left over with *f*
29:41 offering made by *f* to
30:20 offering made by *f* smoke
32:20 and he burnt it with *f* and
32:24 into the *f* and this calf
35:3 not light a *f* in any of your
37:23 *f* holders out of pure gold
38:3 the forks and the *f* holders
40:38 *f* continued upon it by night
Le 1:7 must put *f* on the altar and
1:7 and set wood in order on the *f*
1:8 on the *f* that is on the altar
1:9 offering made by *f* of a restful
1:12 the wood that is on the *f*
1:13 made by *f* of a restful odor
1:17 the wood that is on the *f*
1:17 an offering made by *f* of a
2:2 an offering made by *f* of a
2:3 Jehovah's offerings made by *f*
2:9 an offering made by *f* of a
2:10 of Jehovah's offerings by *f*
2:11 as an offering made by *f*
2:14 green ears roasted with *f*
2:16 offering made by *f* to Jehovah
3:3 offering made by *f* to Jehovah
3:5 over the wood that is on the *f*
3:5 an offering made by *f* of a
3:9 offering made by *f* to Jehovah
3:11 offering made by *f* to Jehovah
3:14 offering made by *f* to Jehovah
3:16 an offering made by *f* for a
4:12 burn it upon wood in the *f*
4:35 Jehovah's offerings made by *f*
5:12 Jehovah's offerings made by *f*
6:9 the *f* of the altar will be
6:10 the *f* regularly consumes upon
6:12 the *f* on the altar will be
6:13 *F* will be kept constantly
6:17 of my offerings made by *f*
6:18 Jehovah's offerings made by *f*

Le 6:30 It is to be burned with *f*
7:5 offering made by *f* to Jehovah
7:17 is to be burned with *f*
7:19 It is to be burned with *f*
7:25 offering made by *f* to Jehovah
7:30 Jehovah's offerings made by *f*
7:35 Jehovah's offerings made by *f*
8:17 burned with *f* outside the
8:21 offering made by *f* to Jehovah
8:28 offering made by *f* to Jehovah
8:32 bread you will burn with *f*
9:11 with *f* outside the camp
9:24 and *f* came out from before
10:1 brought each one his *f* holder
10:1 put *f* in them and placed
10:1 offering . . . illegitimate *f*
10:2 a *f* came out from before
10:12 offerings made by *f* and eat
10:13 offerings made by *f*
10:15 with the offerings made by *f*
13:24 skin of the flesh from the *f*
13:52 It should be burned in the *f*
13:55 You should burn it in the *f*
13:57 You should burn in the *f*
16:12 take the *f* holder full of
16:12 burning coals of *f* from off
16:13 upon the *f* before Jehovah
16:27 and their dung in the *f*
19:6 should be burned in the *f*
20:14 burn him and them in the *f*
21:6 offerings made by *f*, the
21:9 She should be burned in the *f*
21:21 offerings made by *f*. There is
22:22 no offering made by *f* from
22:27 offering made by *f* to
23:8 offering made by *f* to Jehovah
23:13 as an offering made by *f* to
23:18 offering made by *f*, of a
23:25 made by *f* to Jehovah
23:27 offering made by *f* to
23:36 offering made by *f* to
23:36 offering made by *f* to
23:37 offering made by *f* to
24:7 offering made by *f* to Jehovah
24:9 Jehovah's offerings made by *f*
Nu 3:4 offered illegitimate *f* before
4:9 and its *f* holders and all its
4:14 the *f* holders, the forks and
6:18 put it upon the *f* that is
9:15 appeared to be *f* continued
9:16 appearance of *f* by night
11:1 *f* of Jehovah began to blaze
11:2 and the *f* sank down
11:3 *f* of Jehovah had blazed
14:14 in the pillar of *f* by night
15:3 offering made by *f* to Jehovah
15:10 as an offering made by *f*, of
15:13 an offering made by *f*, of a
15:14 an offering made by *f*, of a
15:25 an offering made by *f* to
16:6 Take *f* holders for yourselves
16:7 put *f* in them and place
16:17 take each one his *f* holder
16:17 his *f* holder before Jehovah
16:17 *f* holders, and you and Aaron
16:17 and Aaron each his *f* holder
16:18 took each one his *f* holder
16:18 holder and put *f* upon them
16:35 *f* came out from Jehovah and
16:37 should take up the *f* holders
16:37 scatter the *f* over there; for
16:38 even the *f* holders of these
16:39 took the copper *f* holders
16:46 Take the *f* holder and put
16:46 put *f* from upon the altar in
18:9 out of the offering made by *f*
18:17 as an offering made by *f* for
21:28 a *f* has come out of Heshbon
26:10 *f* consumed two hundred and
26:61 illegitimate *f* before
28:2 my offerings made by *f* as a
28:3 the offering made by *f* that
28:6 offering made by *f* to Jehovah
28:8 an offering made by *f*, of a
28:13 an offering made by *f* to
28:19 as an offering made by *f*, a
28:24 bread, an offering made by *f*
29:6 an offering made by *f* to
29:13 an offering made by *f*, of a
29:36 an offering made by *f*, of a
31:10 camps they burned with *f*
31:23 that is processed with *f*, you
31:23 you should pass through the *f*
31:23 that is not processed with *f*

De 1:33 by *f* at night for you to see
4:11 mountain was burning with *f*
4:12 out of the middle of the *f*
4:15 out of the middle of the *f*
4:24 your God is a consuming *f*, a
4:33 out of the middle of the *f*
4:36 he made you see his great *f*
4:36 from the middle of the *f*
5:4 out of the middle of the *f*
5:5 afraid because of the *f* and
5:22 out of the middle of the *f*
5:23 mountain was burning with *f*
5:24 out of the middle of the *f*
5:25 this great *f* may consume us
5:26 out of the middle of the *f*
7:5 images you should burn with *f*
7:25 gods you should burn in the *f*
9:3 A consuming *f* he is
9:10 out of the middle of the *f*
9:15 mountain was burning with *f*
9:21 burn it in the *f* and to crush
10:4 out of the middle of the *f*
12:3 their sacred poles in the *f*
12:31 burn in the *f* to their gods
13:16 burn in the *f* the city and
18:1 The offerings made by *f* of
18:10 daughter pass through the *f*
18:16 *f* do not let me see anymore
32:22 a *f* has been ignited in my
Jos 6:24 they burned the city with *f*
7:15 be burned with *f*, he and
7:25 they burned them with *f*
8:8 you should set the city on *f*
8:19 hurried and set the city on *f*
11:6 chariots . . . burn in the *f*
11:9 chariots he burned in the *f*
11:11 he burned Hazor in the *f*
13:14 The offerings made by *f* of
Jg 1:8 city they consigned to the *f*
6:21 *f* began to ascend out of the
9:15 let *f* come out of the bramble
9:20 let *f* come out of Abimelech
9:20 *f* come out of the landowners
9:49 set the vault on *f*, so that
9:52 the tower to burn it with *f*
12:1 we shall burn over you with *f*
14:15 house of your father with *f*
15:5 he set *f* to the torches and
15:5 he set on *f* everything from
15:6 her and her father with *f*
15:14 threads . . . scorched with *f*
16:9 torn in two when it smells *f*
18:27 the city they burned with *f*
20:48 cities . . . consigned to the *f*
1Sa 2:28 offerings made by *f* of the
30:1 Ziklag and burn it with *f*
30:3 there it was burned with *f*
30:14 and Ziklag we burned with *f*
2Sa 14:30 Go and set it ablaze with *f*
14:30 tract of land ablaze with *f*
14:31 land . . . ablaze with *f*
22:9 *f* itself from his mouth kept
22:13 burning coals of *f* blazed up
23:7 with *f* they will thoroughly
1Ki 7:50 the cups and the *f* holders
9:16 Gezer and burned it with *f*
16:18 with *f*, so that he died
18:23 they should not put *f* to it
18:23 but I shall not put *f* to it
18:24 true God that answers by *f*
18:25 you must not put *f* to it
18:38 *f* of Jehovah came falling
19:12 after the quaking . . . a *f*
19:12 Jehovah was not in the *f*
19:12 after the *f* there was a
2Ki 1:10 let *f* come down from the
1:10 *f* came descending from the
1:12 let *f* come down from the
1:12 *f* of God came descending
1:14 *f* came down from the heavens
6:17 war chariots of *f* all around
8:12 you will consign to the *f*
16:3 he made pass through the *f*
17:17 daughters pass through the *f*
17:31 burning their sons in the *f*
19:18 their gods to the *f*, because
21:6 own son pass through the *f*
23:10 through the *f* to Molech
23:11 chariots . . . burned in the *f*
25:9 great man he burned with *f*
25:15 took the *f* holders and the
1Ch 14:12 they were burned in the *f*
21:26 *f* from the heavens upon the
2Ch 4:22 the *f* holders, of pure gold

2Ch 7:1 *f* itself came down from the
7:3 spectators when the *f* came
28:3 burn up his sons in the *f*
33:6 own sons pass through the *f*
35:13 passover offering over the *f*
36:19 towers they burned with *f*
Ne 1:3 gates have been burned with *f*
2:3 have been eaten up with *f*
2:13 it had been eaten up by *f*
2:17 gates have been burned with *f*
9:12 by a pillar of *f* by night
9:19 pillar of *f* by night to light
Job 1:16 very *f* of God fell from the
15:34 *f* itself must eat up the
18:5 spark of his *f* . . . not shine
20:26 A *f* . . . will eat him up
22:20 a *f* will certainly eat up
28:5 been upturned as if by *f*
31:12 a *f* that would eat clear to
41:19 Even sparks of *f* make their
Ps 11:6 upon the wicked ones traps, *f*
18:8 *f* itself from his mouth kept
18:12 Hail and burning coals of *f*
18:13 Hail and burning coals of *f*
21:9 and the *f* will devour them
29:7 hewing with the flames of *f*
39:3 the *f* kept burning
46:9 The wagons he burns in the *f*
50:3 Before him there devours a *f*
66:12 through *f* and through water
68:2 wax melts because of the *f*
74:7 sanctuary into the *f* itself
78:14 night with a light of *f*
78:21 *f* itself was kindled against
78:63 His young men a *f* ate up
79:5 your ardor burn just like *f*
80:16 is burned with *f*, cut off
83:14 *f* that burns up the forest
89:46 on burning just like a *f*
97:3 Before him a very *f* goes
104:4 His ministers a devouring *f*
105:32 A flaming *f* on their land
105:39 *f* to give light by night
106:18 *f* went burning among their
118:12 like a *f* of thornbushes
140:10 made to fall into the *f*
148:8 You *f* and hail, snow and
Pr 6:27 rake together *f* into his bosom
16:27 upon his lips . . . scorching *f*
26:20 is no wood the *f* goes out
26:21 and wood for the *f*, so is a
30:16 *f* that has not said: Enough!
Ca 8:6 blazings of a *f*, the flame of
Isa 1:7 your cities are burned with *f*
4:5 of a flaming *f* by night
5:24 *f* eats up the stubble and
9:5 for burning as food for *f*
9:18 become aflame just like a *f*
9:18 catch *f* in the thickets of
9:19 become as food for the *f*
10:16 like the burning of a *f*
10:17 Light must become a *f*, and
26:11 *f* for your own adversaries
27:4 such on *f* at the same time
29:6 the flame of a devouring *f*
30:14 to rake the *f* from the
30:27 tongue is like a devouring *f*
30:30 flame of a devouring *f* and
30:33 *F* and wood are in abundance
33:11 own spirit, as a *f*, will
33:12 be set ablaze even with *f*
33:14 with a devouring *f*
37:19 of their gods to the *f*
40:16 for keeping a *f* burning, and
43:2 should walk through the *f*
44:15 for man to keep a *f* burning
44:15 *f* and actually bakes bread
44:16 actually burns up in a *f*
44:19 it I have burned up in a *f*
47:14 A *f* itself will certainly
50:11 you who are igniting a *f*
50:11 walk in the light of your *f*
54:16 the one blowing upon the *f*
64:2 a *f* ignites the brushwood
64:2 *f* makes the very water boil
64:11 for burning in the *f*
65:5 a *f* burning all day long
66:15 comes as a very *f*, and his
66:15 his rebuke with flames of *f*
66:16 For as a *f* Jehovah himself
66:24 *f* itself will not be
Jer 4:4 not go forth just like a *f*
5:14 my words in your mouth a *f*
6:1 raise a *f* signal; because

Jer 6:29 from their *f* there is lead
7:18 fathers are lighting the *f*
7:31 their daughters in the *f*
11:16 set a *f* blazing against her
15:14 a *f* itself has been ignited
17:4 as a *f* you people have been
17:27 set a *f* ablaze in her gates
19:5 to burn their sons in the *f*
20:9 *f* shut up in my bones
21:10 certainly burn it with *f*
21:12 like a *f* and actually burn
21:14 set a *f* ablaze in her forest
22:7 to fall into the *f*
23:29 Is not my word . . . like a *f*
29:22 Ahab . . . roasted in the *f*
32:29 city aflame with *f* and
32:35 through the *f* to Molech
34:2 and he must burn it with *f*
34:22 and burn it with *f*; and the
36:23 *f* that was in the brazier
36:23 roll ended up in the *f*
36:32 had burned in the *f*
37:8 capture . . . burn it with *f*
37:10 burn this city with *f*
38:17 will not be burned with *f*
38:18 actually burn it with *f*
38:23 city will be burned with *f*
39:8 Chaldeans burned with *f*
43:12 set a *f* ablaze in the houses
43:13 Egypt he will burn with *f*
48:45 *f* will certainly go forth
49:2 be set aflame in the very *f*
49:27 set a *f* ablaze on the wall
50:32 set a *f* ablaze in its cities
51:30 residences . . . set on *f*
51:32 they have burned with *f*
51:58 will be set aflame with *f*
51:58 groups simply for the *f*
52:13 house he burned with *f*
52:19 *f* holders and the bowls
La 1:13 he has sent *f* into my bones
2:3 keeps burning like a flaming *f*
2:4 out his rage, just like *f*
4:11 he sets a *f* ablaze in Zion
Eze 1:4 cloud mass and quivering *f*
1:4 out of the midst of the *f*
1:13 was like burning coals of *f*
1:13 the *f* was bright, and out of
1:13 and out of the *f* there was
1:27 appearance of *f* all around
1:27 like the appearance of *f*, and
5:2 *f* in the midst of the city
5:4 into the midst of the *f* and
5:4 and incinerate them in the *f*
5:4 From one a *f* will go forth to
8:2 the appearance of *f*
8:2 even downward there was *f*
10:2 coals of *f* from between
10:6 Take *f* from between the
10:7 to the *f* that was between
15:4 Into the *f* is where it must
15:4 the *f* certainly devours, and
15:5 *f* itself has devoured it
15:6 have given to the *f* as fuel
15:7 Out of the *f* they have gone
15:7 but the *f* itself will devour
16:21 them pass through the *f*
16:41 burn your houses with *f* and
19:12 *F* itself devoured it
19:14 *f* proceeded to come forth
20:26 child . . . pass through the *f*
20:31 your sons pass through the *f*
20:47 setting a *f* ablaze against
21:31 the *f* of my fury I shall
21:32 For the *f* you will become
22:20 *f* to cause a liquefying
22:21 with the *f* of my fury
22:31 With the *f* of my fury I
23:25 will be devoured by the *f*
23:37 through the *f* to them as
23:47 with *f* their houses they
24:10 Kindle the *f*. Boil the flesh
24:12 Into the *f* with its rust!
28:18 a *f* from the midst of you
30:8 I set a *f* in Egypt and all
30:14 set a *f* in Zoan and
30:16 I will set a *f* in Egypt
36:5 in the *f* of my zeal I will
38:19 in the *f* of my fury, I
38:22 *f* and sulphur I shall rain
39:6 I will send *f* upon Magog and
Da 3:24 bound into the midst of the *f*
3:25 free in the midst of the *f*
3:26 out from the midst of the *f*
Da 3:27 *f* had had no power over their
3:27 smell of *f* itself had not
7:9 His throne was flames of *f*
7:9 its wheels were a burning *f*
7:10 stream of *f* flowing and going
7:11 it was given to the burning *f*
Ho 7:6 burning as with a flaming *f*
8:14 send *f* into his cities and
Joe 1:19 *f* itself has devoured the
1:20 *f* itself has devoured the
2:3 Ahead of it a *f* has devoured
2:5 *f* that is devouring stubble
2:30 blood and *f* and columns of
Am 1:4 a *f* onto the house of Hazael
1:7 a *f* onto the wall of Gaza
1:10 a *f* onto the wall of Tyre
1:12 I will send a *f* into Teman
1:14 set *f* to the wall of Rabbah
2:2 I will send a *f* into Moab
2:5 I will send a *f* into Judah
5:6 become operative just like *f*
7:4 a contention by means of *f*
Ob 18 house of Jacob must become a *f*
Mic 1:4 like wax because of the *f*
1:7 will be burned in the *f*
Na 1:6 rage . . . poured out like *f*
2:3 With the *f* of iron fittings
3:13 *F* will certainly devour your
3:15 Even there *f* will devour you
Hab 2:13 will toil on only for the *f*
Zep 1:18 by the *f* of his zeal the
3:8 by the *f* of my zeal all the
Zec 2:5 a wall of *f* all around, and
3:2 a log snatched out of the *f*
9:4 in the *f* she herself will be
11:1 a *f* may devour among your
12:6 like a *f* pot among trees and
13:9 the third part through the *f*
Mal 3:2 like the *f* of a refiner and
Mt 3:10 down and thrown into the *f*
3:11 with holy spirit and with *f*
3:12 chaff he will burn up with *f*
7:19 down and thrown into the *f*
13:40 collected and burned with *f*
17:15 he falls often into the *f*
18:8 feet into the everlasting *f*
25:41 everlasting *f* prepared for
Mr 9:22 throw him both into the *f* and
9:43 the *f* that cannot be put out
9:48 and the *f* is not put out
9:49 must be salted with *f*
14:54 before a bright *f*
Lu 3:9 cut down and thrown into the *f*
3:16 with holy spirit and *f*
3:17 with *f* that cannot be put out
9:54 do you want us to tell *f* to
12:49 I came to start a *f* on the
16:24 in anguish in this blazing *f*
17:29 it rained *f* and sulphur from
22:55 lit a *f* in the midst of the
22:56 sitting by the bright *f* and
Joh 15:6 and pitch them into the *f*
18:18 they had built a charcoal *f*
21:9 charcoal *f* and fish lying
Ac 2:3 tongues as if of *f* became
2:19 on earth below, blood and *f*
28:2 kindled a *f* and received all
28:3 sticks and laid it upon the *f*
28:5 creature off into the *f*
1Co 3:13 be revealed by means of *f*
3:13 *f* itself will prove what
3:15 it will be as through *f*
1Th 5:19 put out the *f* of the spirit
2Th 1:8 in a flaming *f*, as he brings
2Ti 1:6 stir up like a *f* the gift of
Heb 1:7 public servants a flame of *f*
11:34 stayed the force of *f*
12:18 has been set aflame with *f*
12:29 God is also a consuming *f*
Jas 3:5 How little a *f* it takes to
3:5 set so great a woodland on *f*
3:6 Well, the tongue is a *f*
5:3 *f* is what you have stored up
1Pe 1:7 despite its being proved by *f*
2Pe 3:7 stored up for *f* and are being
3:12 the heavens being on *f* will
Jude 7 punishment of everlasting *f*
23 snatching them out of the *f*
Re 3:18 from me gold refined by *f*
4:5 seven lamps of *f* burning
8:5 some of the *f* of the altar and
8:7 hail and *f* mingled with blood
8:8 great mountain burning with *f*
9:17 *f* and smoke and sulphur
Re 9:18 *f* and the smoke and the
11:5 *f* issues forth from their
13:13 *f* come down out of heaven
14:10 tormented with *f* and sulphur
14:18 he had authority over the *f*
15:2 glassy sea mingled with *f*
16:8 to scorch the men with *f*
17:16 completely burn her with *f*
18:8 be completely burned with *f*
20:9 *f* came down out of heaven
20:10 hurled into the lake of *f*
20:14 hurled into the lake of *f*
20:14 second death, the lake of *f*
20:15 hurled into the lake of *f*
21:8 lake that burns with *f* and

Firelight

Isa 44:16 I have seen the *f*
47:14 no *f* in front of which to

Fireplace

Ps 102:3 made red-hot just like a *f*
Isa 30:14 rake the fire from the *f*

Fire-red

Mt 16:2 weather, for the sky is *f*
16:3 sky is *f*, but gloomy-looking
Re 9:17 they had *f* and hyacinth-blue

Fires

Eze 39:9 build *f* with the armor and
39:9 have to light *f* seven years
39:10 the armor they will light *f*

Firewood

Eze 39:10 gather *f* out of the forests

Firm

Ex 14:13 Stand *f* and see the salvation
De 7:24 take a *f* stand against you
9:2 a *f* stand before the sons of
11:25 a *f* stand against you
Jos 1:5 will take a *f* stand before
1Sa 13:13 your kingdom *f* over Israel
2Ki 14:5 kingdom had become *f* in his
Job 4:4 knees . . . you would make *f*
Ps 39:5 man, though standing *f*, is
89:21 whom my own hand will be *f*
Pr 8:28 made *f* the cloud masses
Isa 35:3 knees that are wobbling *f*
Ac 3:7 his ankle bones were made *f*
16:5 to be made *f* in the faith and
Ro 1:11 in order for you to be made *f*
16:25 to him who can make you *f*
1Co 1:6 been rendered *f* among you
1:8 make you *f* to the end, that
16:13 stand *f* in the faith, carry
Eph 6:11 able to stand *f* against the
6:13 thoroughly, to stand *f*
6:14 Stand *f*, therefore, with
Php 1:27 are standing *f* in one spirit
4:1 stand *f* in this way in the
Col 4:12 with *f* conviction in all the
1Th 3:2 in order to make you *f* and
3:8 if you stand *f* in the Lord
3:13 he may make your hearts *f*
2Th 2:15 stand *f* and maintain your
2:17 *f* in every good deed and
3:3 he will make you *f* and keep
1Ti 6:12 get a *f* hold on the
6:19 a *f* hold on the real life
Tit 3:8 make *f* assertions constantly
Heb 2:2 proved to be *f*, and every
3:6 the hope *f* to the end
3:14 confidence . . . *f* to the end
6:19 hope . . . both sure and *f*
Jas 5:8 make your hearts *f*, because
1Pe 5:10 God . . . he will make you *f*
5:12 in which stand *f*

Firmly

Ge 41:32 thing is *f* established on
Nu 21:27 built and be proved *f* set up
De 12:23 be *f* resolved not to eat the
Jg 16:26 the house is *f* established
16:29 the house was *f* established
1Sa 20:31 will not be *f* established
2Sa 5:12 Jehovah had *f* established
7:12 *f* establish his kingdom
7:13 throne of his kingdom *f* to
7:16 one *f* established to time
7:24 people Israel *f* for yourself
7:26 David become *f* established
1Ki 2:12 became very *f* established
2:24 *f* established me and keeps
2:45 *f* established before Jehovah
2:46 kingdom was *f* established
1Ch 14:2 Jehovah had *f* established

Ch 16:30 land is *f* established: Never
17:11 *f* establish his kingship
17:12 establish his throne *f* to
22:10 his kingship *f* over Israel
28:7 establish his kingship *f* to
Ch 12:1 Rehoboam was *f* established
12:14 *f* established his heart to
17:5 kingdom *f* established in his
zr 3:3 altar *f* upon its own site
ob 21:8 offspring are *f* established
s 9:7 *F* establishing his throne for
24:2 he keeps it *f* established
40:2 He *f* established my steps
48:8 God himself will *f* establish
65:6 *f* establishing the mountains
87:5 himself will *f* establish her
89:2 faithfulness *f* established in
89:4 I shall *f* establish your seed
89:37 it will be *f* established
90:17 hands do you *f* establish
90:17 hands, do you *f* establish
93:1 *f* established so that it
93:2 throne is *f* established from
96:10 *f* established so that it
99:4 have *f* established uprightness
101:7 he will not be *f* established
102:28 will be *f* established
103:19 has *f* established his throne
107:36 they *f* establish a city of
119:5 my ways were *f* established
140:11 *f* established in the earth
: 4:18 until the day is *f* established
4:26 own ways be *f* established
11:19 *f* standing for righteousness
12:3 *f* established by wickedness
12:19 that will be *f* established
16:3 plans will be *f* established
16:12 is the throne *f* established
19:29 *f* established for ridiculers
20:18 plans . . . are *f* established
21:29 will *f* establish his ways
22:18 *f* established together upon
24:3 it will prove *f* established
25:5 *f* established by righteousness
29:14 throne will be *f* established
a 2:2 *f* established above the top of
9:7 establish it *f* and to sustain
16:5 certainly be *f* established
22:21 sash I shall *f* bind about
33:23 they will not hold *f* erect
45:18 One who *f* established it
54:14 prove to be *f* established
r 10:12 the One *f* establishing the
30:20 will be *f* established
33:2 to establish it *f*, Jehovah
51:15 One *f* establishing the
e 16:7 breasts . . . were *f* developed
40:43 *f* fixed on the interior
o 6:3 going forth is *f* established
ic 4:1 *f* established above the top
a 2:5 will have to be *f* established
c 5:11 and it must be *f* established
1 9:51 he *f* set his face to go to
t 1:9 *f* to the faithful word as
e 1:12 *f* set in the truth that is

irmness

ol 2:5 the *f* of your faith toward
eb 13:9 heart to be given *f* by

irst

1:5 came to be morning, a *f* day
2:11 The *f* one's name is Pishon
4:19 The name of the *f* was Adah
8:5 In the tenth month, on the *f*
8:13 in the six hundred and *f* year
8:13 in the *f* month, on the
8:13 on the *f* day of the month
13:3 where his tent had been at *f*
22:4 It was *f* on the third day that
25:25 the *f* came out red all over
25:31 Sell me, *f* of all, your
25:33 Swear to me *f* of all
26:1 besides the *f* famine that
32:17 commanded the *f* one, saying
32:26 let you go until you *f* bless
38:28 This one came out *f*
41:20 eat up the *f* seven fat cows
43:23 Your money came *f* to me
x 4:8 to the voice of the *f* sign
12:2 *f* of the months of the year
12:15 On the *f* day you are to take
12:15 *f* day down to the seventh
12:16 on the *f* day there is to take
12:18 *f* month, on the fourteenth

Ex 12:44 *f* he may share in eating it
12:48 *F* then he may . . . celebrate
23:16 harvest of the *f* ripe fruits
23:19 *f* ripe fruits of your ground
26:24 top of each one at the *f* ring
28:17 and emerald is the *f* row
29:40 will go for the *f* young ram
34:1 tablets of stone like the *f*
34:1 that appeared on the *f* tablets
34:4 tablets of stone like the *f*
34:19 *f* opens the womb is mine
34:22 *f* ripe fruits of the wheat
34:26 best of the *f* ripe fruits of
34:32 *F* after that all the sons of
36:29 top of each one at the *f* ring
39:10 and emerald was the *f* row
40:2 On the day of the *f* month, on
40:2 on the *f* of the month, you
40:17 about that in the *f* month
40:17 on the *f* day of the month
Le 2:14 offering of the *f* ripe fruits
2:14 offering of your *f* ripe fruits
4:21 just as he burned the *f* bull
5:8 present *f* the one for the sin
9:15 sin with it as with the *f*
12:6 a young ram in its *f* year
14:10 female lamb, in its *f* year
23:5 *f* month, on the fourteenth
23:7 *f* day you will have a holy
23:12 ram, in its *f* year, for a
23:17 as *f* ripe fruits to Jehovah
23:20 loaves of the *f* ripe fruits
23:24 *f* of the month, there should
23:35 *f* day is a holy convention
23:39 *f* day is a complete rest and
23:40 *f* day the fruit of splendid
Nu 1:1 *f* day of the second month in
1:18 assembly on the *f* day of the
2:9 camp of Judah . . . set out *f*
6:12 ram in its *f* year as a guilt
6:14 ram in its *f* year as a burnt
6:14 lamb in its *f* year as a sin
7:12 offering on the *f* day proved
7:15 one male lamb in its *f* year
7:21 one male lamb in its *f* year
7:27 male lamb in its *f* year, for
7:33 one male lamb in its *f* year
7:39 one male lamb in its *f* year
7:45 one male lamb in its *f* year
7:51 one male lamb in its *f* year
7:57 one male lamb in its *f* year
7:63 one male lamb in its *f* year
7:69 one male lamb in its *f* year
7:75 one male lamb in its *f* year
7:81 one male lamb in its *f* year
8:22 *F* after that the Levites came
9:1 land of Egypt, in the *f* month
9:5 *f* month, on the fourteenth day
10:13 pulling away for the *f* time
10:14 Judah pulled away *f* of all
13:20 *f* ripe fruits of the grapes
15:27 a female goat in its *f* year
18:13 *f* ripe fruits of all that is
20:1 the *f* month, and the people
24:20 Amalek was the *f* one of the
28:16 *f* month, on the fourteenth
28:18 On the *f* day there will be a
28:26 the day of the *f* ripe fruits
29:1 on the *f* of the month, you
33:3 the *f* month, on the fifteenth
33:3 fifteenth day of the *f* month
33:38 in the fifth month, on the *f*
De 1:3 eleventh month, on the *f* of
9:18 as at *f*, forty days and forty
10:1 tablets of stone like the *f*
10:2 appeared on the *f* tablets
10:3 tablets . . . like the *f* ones
10:4 the same writing as the *f*
10:10 the same as the *f* days
13:9 Your hand *f* of all should
16:4 in the evening on the *f* day
16:9 when the sickle is *f* put to
17:7 hand of the witnesses *f* of
18:4 The *f* of your grain, your new
18:4 the *f* of the shorn wool of
24:4 *f* owner of her who dismissed
33:21 the *f* part for himself
Jos 1:15 *F* when Jehovah gives rest
4:19 on the tenth of the *f* month
8:5 to meet us just as at the *f*
8:6 fleeing . . . just as at the *f*
8:33 bless the people of Israel *f*
21:10 the *f* lot became theirs
Jg 1:1 go up *f* to the Canaanites to

Jg 18:29 was the city's name at *f*
20:22 in formation on the *f* day
20:32 the same as at the *f*
20:39 just as in the *f* battle
Ru 3:10 than in the *f* instance, in not
1Sa 2:16 make the fat smoke *f* of all
9:13 *F* after that those who are
14:14 the *f* slaughter with which
14:33 *F* of all, roll a great stone
14:49 the one born *f* was Merab
2Sa 3:13 *f* you bring Michal, Saul's
7:10 again as they did at the *f*
18:27 the running style of the *f*
19:20 *f* of all the house of Joseph
19:43 matter become *f* for us to
21:9 in the *f* days of harvest
23:19 to the rank of the *f* three
1Ki 1:51 Solomon *f* of all swear to
13:6 and it came to be as at *f*
17:13 a small round cake *f*, and
18:25 young bull and dress it *f*
20:9 sent to your servant at *f*
20:17 came out *f*, Ben-hadad at
22:5 Inquire, please, *f* of all
2Ki 4:42 bread of the *f* ripe fruits
1Ch 9:2 *f* inhabitants that were in
11:6 striking the Jebusites *f*, he
11:6 got to go up *f*, and he came
11:21 not come up to the *f* three
11:25 to the rank of the *f* three
12:15 the Jordan in the *f* month
15:13 at the *f* time you did not
16:7 contribution for the *f* time
17:9 just as they did at the *f*
18:17 sons of David were the *f* in
24:7 the *f* for Jehoiarib; for
25:9 *f* belonging to Asaph for
27:2, 2 *f* division of the *f* month
27:3 were for the *f* month
29:29 the *f* ones and the last
2Ch 9:29 affairs of Solomon, the *f*
12:15 affairs, the *f* and the last
16:11 of Asa, the *f* and the last
18:4 inquire *f* of all for the
20:34 Jehoshaphat, the *f* and the
25:26 of Amaziah, the *f* and the
26:22 of Uzziah, the *f* and the
28:26 ways, the *f* and the last
29:3 *f* year of his reigning, in
29:3 *f* month, opened the doors
29:17 started on the *f* day of the
29:17 the *f* month at sanctifying
29:17 *f* month they finished
35:1 fourteenth day . . . *f* month
35:27 affairs, the *f* and the last
36:22 *f* year of Cyrus the king
Ezr 1:1 *f* year of Cyrus the king of
3:6 *f* day of the seventh month on
5:13 the *f* year of Cyrus the king
6:3 *f* year of Cyrus the king
6:19 fourteenth day . . . *f* month
7:9, 9 the *f* day of the *f* month
7:9 the *f* day of the fifth month
8:31 twelfth day of the *f* month
10:16 *f* day of the tenth month
10:17, 17 *f* day of the *f* month
Ne 7:5 those who came up at the *f*
8:2 *f* day of the seventh month
8:18 the *f* day until the last day
10:35 *f* ripe fruits of our ground
10:35 and the *f* ripe fruits of all
13:31 and for the *f* ripe fruits
Es 1:14 were sitting *f* in the kingdom
3:7 *f* month . . . the month Nisan
3:12 *f* month on the thirteenth day
Job 15:7 you the very *f* man to be born
41:11 has given me something *f*
42:14 name of the *f* Jemimah and
Pr 8:26 *f* part of the dust masses of
18:17 one *f* in his legal case is
20:21 is being got by greed at *f*
Isa 1:26 judges for you as at the *f*
41:4 I, Jehovah, the *F* One; and
41:22 The *f* things—what they
41:27 is one *f*, saying to Zion
42:9 The *f* things—here they have
43:9 to hear even the *f* things
43:18 not remember the *f* things
43:27 Your own father, the *f* one
44:6 I am the *f* and I am the last
46:9 *f* things of a long time ago
48:3 The *f* things I have told even
48:12 the same One. I am the *f*
52:4 in the *f* instance to reside

Isa 60:9 Tarshish also as at the *f*
65:7 wages *f* of all into their
Jer 2:3 Jehovah, the *f* yield to Him
4:31 giving birth to her *f* child
7:12 my name to reside at *f*
11:10 the *f* ones, who refused to
16:18 *f* of all, I will repay the
25:1 the *f* year of Nebuchadrezzar
36:28 write on it all the *f* words
36:28 proved to be on the *f* roll
50:17 In the *f* instance the king
Eze 10:14 *f* face was the face of the
26:1 on the *f* day of the month
29:17, 17 *f* month, on the *f* day
30:20 the *f* month, on the seventh
31:1 on the *f* day of the month
32:1 on the *f* day of the month
40:21 measurement of the *f* gate
44:30, 30 *f* of all the *f* ripe fruits
45:18, 18 *f* month, on the *f* day
45:21 *f* month, on the fourteenth
46:13 male lamb, in its *f* year
Da 1:21 *f* year of Cyrus the king
7:1 *f* year of Belshazzar the king
7:4 *f* one was like a lion, and it
7:8 three of the *f* horns that
7:24 different from the *f* ones
8:21 it stands for the *f* king
9:1 *f* year of Darius the son of
9:2 *f* year of his reigning I
10:4 twenty-fourth day . . . *f* month
10:12 *f* day that you gave your
11:1 *f* year of Darius the Mede I
11:13 crowd larger than the *f*; and
11:29 last the same as at the *f*
Ho 2:7 to my husband, the *f* one, for
Joe 2:23 and spring rain, as at the *f*
Mic 4:8 *f* dominion will certainly
Na 3:12 as fig trees with the *f* ripe
Hag 1:1 on the *f* day of the month
Zec 6:2 *f* chariot there were red
12:7 save the tents of Judah *f*
14:10 to the place of the *F* Gate
Mt 5:24 *f* make your peace with your
6:33 seeking *f* the kingdom and
7:5 *F* extract the rafter from your
8:21 permit me *f* to leave and
10:2 apostles are these: *F*, Simon
12:29 *f* he binds the strong man
12:45 become worse than the *f*
13:30 *F* collect the weeds and bind
16:28 *f* they see the Son of man
17:10 say that Elijah must come *f*
17:27 take the *f* fish coming up
19:30 *f* will be last and the last
19:30 will be last and the last *f*
20:8 from the last to the *f*
20:10 So, when the *f* came, they
20:16 last ones will be *f*, and the
20:16 and the *f* ones last
20:27 whoever wants to be *f* among
21:28 Going up to the *f*, he said
21:36 slaves, more than the *f*, but
22:25 the *f* married and deceased
22:38 greatest and *f* commandment
23:26 cleanse *f* the inside of the
26:17 the *f* day of the unfermented
27:64 will be worse than the *f*
28:1 on the *f* day of the week
Mr 3:27 *f* he binds the strong man
4:28 *f* the grass-blade, then the
7:27 *F* let the children be
9:1 until *f* they see the kingdom
9:11 say that *f* Elijah must come
9:12 Elijah does come *f* and
9:35 If anyone wants to be *f*, he
10:31 many . . . *f* will be last
10:31 will be last, and the last *f*
10:44 whoever wants to be *f* among
12:20 the *f* took a wife, but when
12:28 Which commandment is *f* of
12:29 The *f* is, Hear, O Israel
13:10 the good news . . . preached *f*
14:12 *f* day of unfermented cakes
16:2 on the *f* day of the week they
Lu 2:2 this *f* registration took place
6:42 *F* extract the rafter from
9:27 until *f* they see the kingdom
9:59 Permit me *f* to leave and bury
9:61 *f* permit me to say good-bye
10:5 say *f*, May this house have
11:26 become worse than the *f*
11:38 did not *f* wash before the
12:1 by saying *f* to his disciples
Lu 13:30 those last who will be *f*
13:30 those *f* who will be last
14:18 The *f* said to him, I bought
14:28 *f* sit down and calculate the
14:31 *f* sit down and take counsel
16:5 to say to the *f*, How much
17:25 *F*, however, he must undergo
19:16 the *f* one presented himself
20:29 the *f* took a wife and died
21:9 these things must occur *f*
24:1 On the *f* day of the week
Joh 1:41 *F* this one found his own
2:10 puts out the fine wine *f*
7:51 unless *f* it has heard from
10:40 John was baptizing at *f*
12:16 took no note of at *f*, but
16:4 I did not tell you at *f*
16:9 the *f* place, concerning sin
18:13 they led him *f* to Annas
19:32 the legs of the *f* man and
19:39 in the night the *f* time
20:1 the *f* day of the week Mary
20:4 reached the memorial tomb *f*
20:8 reached the memorial tomb *f*
20:19 the *f* of the week, and
Ac 1:1 The *f* account, O Theophilus
3:26 To you *f* God, after raising
7:12 forefathers out the *f* time
11:26 was *f* in Antioch that the
12:10 through the *f* sentinel guard
13:46 of God to be spoken *f* to you
15:14 God for the *f* time turned
17:9 and *f* after taking sufficient
20:7 On the *f* day of the week
20:18 *f* day that I stepped into the
26:5 with me from the *f* know, if
26:20 those in Damascus *f* and to
26:23 *f* to be resurrected from the
27:43 sea and make it to land *f*
Ro 1:8 *F* of all, I give thanks to my
1:16 having faith, to the Jew *f*
2:9 Jew *f* and also of the Greek
2:10 Jew *f* and also for the Greek
3:2 *F* of all, because they were
8:29 he gave his *f* recognition he
10:19 *F* Moses says: I will incite
11:2 people, whom he *f* recognized
11:35 Who has *f* given to him, so
15:24 have *f* in some measure been
1Co 11:18 For *f* of all, when you come
11:28 *F* let a man approve himself
12:28 *f*, apostles; second, prophets
14:30 let the *f* one keep silent
15:3 among the *f* things, that
15:36 unless *f* it dies
15:45 The *f* man Adam became a
15:46 the *f* is, not that which is
15:47 *f* man is out of the earth
16:2 Every *f* day of the week let
2Co 7:8 Even if I did at *f* regret it
8:5 *f* they gave themselves to
8:12 readiness is there *f*, it is
10:14 we were the *f* to come even
Ga 4:13 good news to you the *f* time
Eph 1:12 been *f* to hope in the Christ
6:2 the *f* command with a promise
Php 1:5 the *f* day until this moment
Col 1:18 one who is *f* in all things
1Th 1:9 the way we *f* entered in
2:2 after we had *f* suffered and
4:16 dead . . . will rise *f*
2Th 2:3 unless the apostasy comes *f*
1Ti 2:1 I therefore exhort, *f* of all
2:13 Adam was formed *f*, then Eve
3:10 be tested as to fitness *f*
5:4 learn *f* to practice godly
5:12 their *f* expression of faith
2Ti 1:5 *f* in your grandmother Lois
2:6 the *f* to partake of the fruits
4:16 In my *f* defense no one came
Tit 3:10 a *f* and a second admonition
Heb 4:6 good news was *f* declared did
7:2 is *f* of all, by translation
7:27 *f* for his own sins and then
8:7 if that *f* covenant had been
9:2 constructed a *f* tent
9:6 enter the *f* tent compartment
9:8 made manifest while the *f*
10:8 After *f* saying: You did not
10:9 He does away with what is *f*
Jas 3:17 is *f* of all chaste, then
1Pe 4:17 if it starts *f* with us, what
2Pe 1:20 For you know this *f*, that no
2:20 worse for them than the *f*
2Pe 3:1 as in my *f* one, I am arousing
3:3 know this *f*, that in the last
1Jo 4:19 we love, because he *f* loved
3Jo 9 likes to have the *f* place
Re 1:17 I am the *F* and the Last
2:4 left the love you had at *f*
2:8 the *F* and the Last, who
4:1 *f* voice that I heard was as
4:7 *f* living creature is like a
8:7 And the *f* one blew his trumpet
13:12 of the *f* wild beast in
13:12 worship the *f* wild beast
16:2 *f* one went off and poured
20:5 This is the *f* resurrection
20:6 part in the *f* resurrection
21:19 *f* foundation was jasper, the
22:13 Omega, the *f* and the last

Firstborn
Ge 10:15 Sidon his *f* and Heth
19:31 *f* proceeded to say to the
19:33 *f* went in and lay down with
19:34 *f* then said to the younger
19:37 *f* became mother to a son and
22:21 Uz his *f* and Buz his brother
25:13 Ishmael's *f* Nebaioth and
25:31 Sell me . . . your right as *f*
25:33 sell his right as *f* to Jacob
27:19 I am Esau your *f*
27:32 I am your son, your *f*, Esau
29:26 younger woman before the *f*
35:23 Jacob's *f* Reuben and Simeon
36:15 Eliphaz, Esau's *f*: Sheik
38:6 took a wife for Er his *f*
38:7 Judah's *f*, proved to be bad
41:51 name of the *f* Manasseh
43:33 the *f* according to his right
43:33 right as *f* and the youngest
46:8 Jacob's *f* was Reuben
48:14 since Manasseh was the *f*
48:18 this is the *f*. Put your right
49:3 Reuben, you are my *f*, my
Ex 4:22 said: Israel is my son, my *f*
4:23 I am killing your son, your *f*
6:14 sons of Reuben, Israel's *f*
11:5 *f* in the land of Egypt must
11:5 from the *f* of Pharaoh who is
11:5 *f* of the maidservant who is
11:5 and every *f* of beast
12:12 strike every *f* in the land of
12:29 Jehovah struck every *f* in the
12:29 from the *f* of Pharaoh
12:29 to the *f* of the captive who
12:29 Jehovah struck . . . *f* of beast
13:2 male *f* that opens each womb
13:13 redeem . . . every *f* of man
13:15 every *f* in the land of Egypt
13:15 from the *f* of man to the
13:15 to the *f* of beast. That is
13:15 every *f* of my sons I redeem
22:29 The *f* of your sons you are to
34:20 Every *f* of your sons you are
Le 27:26 *f* among beasts, which is
27:26 born as the *f* for Jehovah
Nu 1:20 sons of Reuben, Israel's *f*
3:2 Aaron's sons: the *f* Nadab and
3:12 place of all the *f* opening
3:13 For every *f* is mine. In the
3:13 day that I struck every *f* in
3:13 *f* in Israel from man to beast
3:40 Register all the *f* males of
3:41 in place of all the *f* among
3:41 *f* among the domestic animals
3:42 register all the *f* among the
3:43 *f* males by the number of the
3:45 place of all the *f* among the
3:46 the *f* of the sons of Israel
3:50 *f* of the sons of Israel he
8:16 *f* of the sons of Israel, you
8:17 every *f* among the sons of
8:17 striking every *f* in the land
8:18 *f* among the sons of Israel
18:15 redeem the *f* of mankind; and
18:15 the *f* of the unclean beast
18:17, 17 *f* bull or *f* male lamb or
18:17 *f* goat you should not redeem
26:5 Reuben, Israel's *f*; Reuben's
33:4 Egyptians were burying . . . *f*
De 12:6 the *f* ones of your herd
12:17 the *f* ones of your herd and
14:23 the *f* ones of your herd and
15:19 male *f* that will be born in
15:19 do no service with the *f* of
15:19 nor shear the *f* of your flock

De 21:15 the *f* son has come to be of
21:16 son of the loved one his *f*
21:16 the hated one's son, the *f*
21:17 recognize as the *f* the hated
25:6 the *f* whom she will bear
33:17 As the *f* of a bull his
Jos 6:26 At the forfeit of his *f* let
17:1 Manasseh . . . was Joseph's *f*
17:1 Machir the *f* of Manasseh
Jg 8:20 he said to Jether his *f*: Get
1Sa 8:2 his *f* son happened to be Joel
17:13 Eliab the *f*, and his second
2Sa 3:2 *f* came to be Amnon by
1Ki 16:34 the forfeit of Abiram his *f*
2Ki 3:27 took his *f* son who was going
1Ch 1:13 Sidon his *f* and Heth
1:29 Ishmael's *f* Nebaioth and
2:3 Er the *f* of Judah came to be
2:13 became father to his *f* Eliab
2:25 Jerahmeel the *f* of Hezron
2:25 Ram the *f* and
2:27 Ram the *f* of Jerahmeel
2:42 Mesha his *f*, who was the
2:50 Hur the *f* of Ephrathah
3:1 the *f* Amnon, of Ahinoam the
3:15 sons of Josiah were the *f*
4:4 Hur the *f* of Ephrathah
5:1 Reuben the *f* of Israel
5:1 Israel—for he was the *f*
5:1 his right as *f* was given to
5:1 for the right of the *f*
5:2 the right as *f* was Joseph's
5:3 Reuben the *f* of Israel
6:28 of Samuel were the *f* Joel
8:1 became father to Bela his *f*
8:30 his son, the *f*, was Abdon
8:39 sons of Eshek . . . Ulam his *f*
9:5 Shilonites, Asaiah the *f* and
9:31 *f* of Shallum the Korahite
9:36 his son, the *f*, was Abdon
26:2 Zechariah the *f*, Jediael the
26:4 Shemaiah the *f*, Jehozabad
26:10 did not happen to be the *f*
2Ch 21:3 Jehoram, for he was the *f*
Ne 10:36 the *f* of our sons and of our
10:36 the *f* of our herds and of
Job 1:13 house of their brother the *f*
1:18 house of their brother the *f*
18:13 The *f* of death will eat his
Ps 78:51 struck down all the *f* in
89:27 shall place him as *f*
105:36 down every *f* in their land
135:8 struck down the *f* ones of
136:10 down Egypt in their *f* ones
Isa 14:30 *f* ones of the lowly ones
Jer 31:9 as for Ephraim, he is my *f*
Mic 6:7 give my *f* son for my revolt
Zec 12:10 lamentation over the *f* son
Lu 2:7 gave birth to her son, the *f*
Ro 8:29 be the *f* among many brothers
Col 1:15 the *f* of all creation
1:18 the *f* from the dead, that he
Heb 1:6 his *F* into the inhabited earth
11:28 not touch their *f* ones
12:16 gave away his rights as *f*
12:23 congregation of the *f* who
Re 1:5 The *f* from the dead, and The

Firstborn's
De 21:17 the right of the *f* position

Firstfruits
Le 2:12 As an offering of the *f*, you
23:10 the *f* of your harvest to the
Nu 15:20 a contribution of the *f*
15:21 the *f* of your coarse meal
18:12 *f*, which they will give
De 26:2 take some of the *f* of all the
26:10 I have brought the *f* of the
2Ch 31:5 *f* of the grain, new wine
Ne 10:37 *f* of our coarse meal and our
12:44 for the *f* and for the tenths
Pr 3:9 the *f* of all your produce
Eze 20:40 the *f* of your presentations
44:30 *f* of your coarse meals you
Ro 8:23 the *f*, namely, the spirit
11:16 part taken as *f* is holy, the
16:5 Epaenetus, who is a *f* of Asia
1Co 15:20 the *f* of those who have
15:23 Christ the *f*, afterward
16:15 the *f* of Achaia and that
Jas 1:18 be certain *f* of his creatures
Re 14:4 as *f* to God and to the Lamb

Firstling
Ex 13:12 devote . . . every *f*, the young
Ex 13:13 every *f* ass you are to
34:19 the male *f* of bull and of
34:20 the *f* of an ass you are to

Firstlings
Ge 4:4 brought some *f* of his flock

Fish
Ge 1:26 subjection the *f* of the sea
1:28 subjection the *f* of the sea
Ex 7:18 *f* that are in the Nile River
7:21 *f* . . . in the Nile River died
Nu 11:5 remember the *f* that we used
11:22 *f* of the sea be caught for
De 4:18 any *f* that is in the waters
1Sa 5:4 Only the *f* part had been left
2Ch 33:14 far as the *F* Gate, and he
Ne 3:3 the *F* Gate was what the sons
12:39 clear to the *F* Gate and the
13:16 bringing in *f* and every sort
Job 41:7 Or its head with *f* spears
Ps 8:8 and the *f* of the sea
105:29 to put their *f* to death
Isa 50:2 *f* stink due to there being no
Jer 16:16 will certainly *f* for them
Eze 29:4 cause the *f* of your Nile
29:4 the *f* of your Nile canals
29:5 the *f* of your Nile canals
38:20 the *f* of the sea and the
47:9 there will be very many *f*
47:10 their *f* will prove to be
47:10 *f* of the Great Sea, very
Jon 1:17 a great *f* to swallow Jonah
1:17 in the inward parts of the *f*
2:1 the inward parts of the *f*
2:10 Jehovah commanded the *f*, so
Zep 1:10 outcry from the *F* Gate, and
Mt 7:10 perhaps, he will ask for a *f*
12:40 in the belly of the huge *f*
13:47 gathering up *f* of every kind
17:27 take the first *f* coming up
Lu 5:6 a great multitude of *f*
5:9 catch of *f* which they took up
11:11 his son asks for a *f*, will
11:11 a serpent instead of a *f*
24:42 handed . . . piece of broiled *f*
Joh 21:9 fire and *f* lying upon it
21:10 the *f* you just now caught
21:13 gave it to them, and the *f*
1Co 15:39 of birds, and another of *f*

Fishermen
Lu 5:2 the *f* had got out of them

Fishers
Isa 19:8 the *f* will have to mourn
Jer 16:16 I am sending for many *f*
Eze 47:10 *f* will actually stand
Mt 4:18 into the sea, for they were *f*
4:19 I will make you *f* of men
Mr 1:16 Simon and Andrew . . . were *f*
1:17 cause you to become *f* of men

Fishes
Ge 9:2 and upon all the *f* of the sea
1Ki 4:33 speak about . . . the *f*
Job 12:8 *f* of the sea will declare it
Ec 9:12 *f* that are being taken in an
Ho 4:3 and even the *f* of the sea
Hab 1:14 man like the *f* of the sea
Zep 1:3 and the *f* of the sea
Mt 14:17 but five loaves and two *f*
14:19 the five loaves and two *f*
15:34 Seven, and a few little *f*
15:36 the seven loaves and the *f*
Mr 6:38 Five, besides two *f*
6:41 the five loaves and the two *f*
6:41 divided up the two *f* for all
6:43 aside from the *f*
8:7 They also had a few little *f*
Lu 9:13 five loaves and two *f*
9:16 five loaves and the two *f*
Joh 6:9 loaves and two small *f*
6:11 as much of the small *f* as
21:6 of the multitude of the *f*
21:8 dragging the net of *f*
21:11 net to land full of big *f*

Fishhook
Job 41:1 draw out Leviathan with a *f*
Hab 1:15 has brought up with a mere *f*
Mt 17:27 cast a *f*, and take the first

Fishhooks
Isa 19:8 casting *f* into the Nile
Am 4:2 the last part of you with *f*

Fishing
Isa 19:8 those spreading *f* nets upon
Hab 1:15 he gathers them in his *f* net
1:16 sacrificial smoke to his *f*
Mt 4:18 letting down a *f* net into the
Joh 21:3 to them: I am going *f*

Fist
Isa 58:4 with the *f* of wickedness

Fists
Mt 26:67 and hit him with their *f*
Mr 14:65 hit him with their *f* and say

Fit
Job 41:16 One to the other they *f*
Jer 13:7 it was not *f* for anything
13:10 belt that is *f* for nothing
Eze 15:4 Is it *f* for any work?
16:13 became *f* for royal position
16:50 just as I saw *f*
Mt 3:11 sandals I am not *f* to take
8:8 I am not a *f* man for you to
Mr 1:7 I am not *f* to stoop and untie
Lu 3:16 sandals I am not *f* to untie
7:6 I am not *f* to have you come
Ac 22:22 for he was not *f* to live
Ro 9:22 wrath made *f* for destruction
1Co 15:9 not *f* to be called an apostle
1Th 2:4 *f* to be entrusted with the

Fitly
1Co 1:10 be *f* united in the same mind

Fitness
1Ti 3:10 be tested as to *f* first

Fits
Pr 22:24 with a man having *f* of rage
Ga 5:20 *f* of anger, contentions

Fitted
Ex 36:22 two tenons *f* one to the
Ca 3:10 interior being *f* out lovingly
Lu 9:62 well *f* for the kingdom of God

Fitting
Ps 33:1 upright ones praise is *f*
147:1 it is pleasant—praise is *f*
Pr 17:7 lip of uprightness is not *f*
19:10 Luxury is not *f* for anyone
26:1 so glory is not *f* for a stupid
Jer 10:7 for to you it is *f*
Ro 1:28 to do the things not *f*
1Co 11:13 Is it *f* for a woman to pray
16:4 if it is *f* for me to go
2Th 1:3 as it is *f*, because your
Tit 2:1 speaking what things are *f*
Heb 2:10 For it was *f* for the one for

Fittings
Na 2:3 With the fire of iron *f* is the

Five
Ge 5:6 Seth lived . . . a hundred and *f*
5:11 Enosh . . . nine hundred and *f*
5:30 *f* hundred and ninety-five
5:32 Noah got to be *f* hundred years
11:11 Shem . . . *f* hundred years
11:32 Terah . . . two hundred and *f*
14:9 four kings against the *f*
18:28 righteous should be lacking *f*
18:28 for the *f* bring the whole
43:34 Benjamin's portion *f* times
45:6 there are yet *f* years in
45:11 yet *f* years of famine
45:22 and *f* changes of mantles
47:2 took *f* men, that he might
Ex 22:1 compensate with *f* of the herd
26:3 *F* tent cloths are to form a
26:3 *f* tent cloths a series with
26:9 must join *f* tent cloths by
26:26 *f* for the panel frames of
26:27 *f* bars for the panel frames
26:27 *f* bars for the panel frames
26:37 *f* pillars of acacia and
26:37 *f* socket pedestals of copper
27:1 altar . . . *f* cubits its length
27:1 and *f* cubits its width
27:18 and the height *f* cubits, of
30:23 drops *f* hundred units
30:24 cassia *f* hundred units by
36:10 joined *f* tent cloths one to
36:10 *f* other tent cloths he
36:16 joined *f* tent cloths together
36:31 *f* for the panel frames of
36:32 *f* bars for the panel frames
36:32 *f* bars for the panel frames
36:38 its *f* pillars and their pegs

Ex 36:38 *f* socket pedestals were of
38:1 *F* cubits was its length, and
38:1 *f* cubits its width, it
38:18 its extent was *f* cubits
38:26 thousand *f* hundred and fifty
Le 26:8 *f* of you will certainly chase
27:5 age is from *f* years old up to
27:6 up to *f* years old, the
27:6 become *f* shekels of silver
Nu 1:21 forty-six thousand *f* hundred
1:33 forty thousand *f* hundred
1:41 forty-one thousand *f* hundred
1:46 thousand *f* hundred and fifty
2:11 forty-six thousand *f* hundred
2:19 forty thousand *f* hundred
2:28 forty-one thousand *f* hundred
2:32 three thousand *f* hundred and
3:22 were seven thousand *f* hundred
3:47 must take *f* shekels for each
4:48 eight thousand *f* hundred and
7:17, 17 *f* rams, *f* he-goats
7:17 *f* male lambs each a year old
7:23, 23 *f* rams, *f* he-goats
7:23 *f* male lambs each a year old
7:29 sacrifice . . . *f* rams
7:29 sacrifice . . . *f* he-goats
7:29 sacrifice . . . *f* male lambs
7:35 sacrifice . . . *f* rams
7:35 sacrifice . . . *f* he-goats
7:35 sacrifice . . . *f* male lambs
7:41 sacrifice . . . *f* rams
7:41 sacrifice . . . *f* he-goats
7:41 sacrifice . . . *f* male lambs
7:47 sacrifice . . . *f* rams
7:47 sacrifice . . . *f* he-goats
7:47 sacrifice . . . *f* male lambs
7:53 sacrifice . . . *f* rams
7:53 sacrifice . . . *f* he-goats
7:53 sacrifice . . . *f* male lambs
7:59 sacrifice . . . *f* rams
7:59 sacrifice . . . *f* he-goats
7:59 sacrifice . . . *f* male lambs
7:65 sacrifice . . . *f* rams
7:65 sacrifice . . . *f* he-goats
7:65 sacrifice . . . *f* male lambs
7:71 sacrifice . . . *f* rams
7:71 sacrifice . . . *f* he-goats
7:71 sacrifice . . . *f* male lambs
7:77 sacrifice . . . *f* rams
7:77 sacrifice . . . *f* he-goats
7:77 sacrifice . . . *f* male lambs
7:83 sacrifice . . . *f* rams
7:83 sacrifice . . . *f* he-goats
7:83 sacrifice . . . *f* male lambs
11:19 nor two days nor *f* days
18:16 *f* silver shekels by the
26:18 forty thousand *f* hundred
26:22 thousand *f* hundred
26:27 sixty thousand *f* hundred
26:37 thousand *f* hundred
31:8 the *f* kings of Midian; and
31:28 one soul out of *f* hundred, of
31:36 thousand *f* hundred of the
31:39 thirty thousand *f* hundred
31:43 thousand *f* hundred
31:45 thirty thousand *f* hundred
Jos 8:12 took about *f* thousand men
10:5 *f* kings of the Amorites
10:16 these *f* kings fled and went
10:17 The *f* kings have been found
10:22 bring out these *f* kings
10:23 from the cave these *f* kings
10:26 and hang them upon *f* stakes
13:3 *f* axis lords of the
Jg 3:3 The *f* axis lords of the
18:2 sent *f* men of their family
18:7 *f* men went on and came to
18:14 *f* men that had gone to spy
18:17 *f* men that had gone to spy
20:45 a gleaning of *f* thousand men
1Sa 6:4 *f* golden piles and
6:4 *f* golden jerboas, for every
6:16 And the *f* axis lords of the
6:18 belonging to the *f* axis lords
17:5 *f* thousand shekels of copper
17:40 the *f* smoothest stones from
21:3 *f* loaves of bread at your
25:18 *f* sheep dressed and
25:18 *f* seah measures of roasted
25:42 *f* maids of hers walking
2Sa 4:4 *F* years old he happened to be
21:8 the *f* sons of Michal the
24:9 were *f* hundred thousand men
1Ki 4:32 songs . . . a thousand and *f*
1Ki 6:6 was *f* cubits in its width
6:10 *f* cubits in their height
6:24 *f* cubits was the one wing of
6:24 and *f* cubits was the other
7:16 *F* cubits was the height of
7:16 *f* cubits was the height of
7:23 and its height was *f* cubits
7:39 *f* carriages on the right side
7:39 *f* on the left side of the
7:49 lampstands, *f* to the right
7:49 the right and *f* to the left
9:23 *f* hundred and fifty, the
2Ki 6:25 was worth *f* silver pieces
7:13 *f* of the remaining horses
13:19 to strike *f* or six times
25:19 *f* men from those having
1Ch 2:4 All the sons of Judah were *f*
2:6 There were *f* of them in all
3:20 and Hasadiah, Jushab-hesed, *f*
4:32 Tochen and Ashan, *f* cities
4:42 to Mount Seir, *f* hundred men
7:3 sons of Izrahiah were . . . *f*
7:7 the sons of Bela were . . . *f*
11:23 a man of . . . *f* cubits
29:7 worth *f* thousand talents
2Ch 3:11 the one wing of *f* cubits
3:11 the other wing of *f* cubits
3:12 of the one cherub of *f* cubits
3:12 other wing of *f* cubits was
3:15 the capital . . . was *f* cubits
4:2 and its height was *f* cubits
4:6 basins, and put *f* to the right
4:6 ten basins . . . *f* to the left
4:7 lampstands . . . *f* to the right
4:7 lampstands . . . *f* to the left
4:8 ten tables . . . *f* to the right
4:8 ten tables . . . *f* to the left
6:13 Its length was *f* cubits, and
6:13 its width *f* cubits, and its
13:17 *f* hundred thousand chosen
26:13 thousand *f* hundred men
35:9 passover victims *f* thousand
35:9 and *f* hundred cattle
Ezr 1:11 *f* thousand four hundred
2:69 *f* thousand minas, and a
Ne 7:70 *f* hundred and thirty priests'
Es 9:6 a destroying of *f* hundred men
9:12 a destroying of *f* hundred men
Job 1:3 *f* hundred spans of cattle and
1:3 and *f* hundred she-asses, along
Isa 17:6 *f* on the fruit-bearing boughs
19:18 *f* cities in the land of
30:17 account of the rebuke of *f*
Jer 52:22 one capital was *f* cubits
Eze 40:7 there were *f* cubits; and the
40:30 and the width *f* cubits
40:48 *f* cubits on this side and
40:48 and *f* cubits on that side
41:2 the entrance were *f* cubits
41:2 and *f* cubits over there
41:9 the outside, was *f* cubits
41:11 left open was *f* cubits
41:12 was *f* cubits in width
42:16 It was *f* hundred reeds, by
42:17 *f* hundred reeds, by the
42:18 *f* hundred reeds, by the
42:19 measured *f* hundred reeds
42:20 length of *f* hundred reeds
42:20 width of *f* hundred reeds
45:2, 2 *f* hundred by *f* hundred
45:6 give *f* thousand in width
48:15 *f* thousand cubits that is
48:16 four thousand *f* hundred
48:16 four thousand *f* hundred
48:16 four thousand *f* hundred
48:16 four thousand *f* hundred
48:30 four thousand *f* hundred
48:32 four thousand *f* hundred
48:33 four thousand *f* hundred
48:34 four thousand *f* hundred
Mt 14:17 but *f* loaves and two fishes
14:19 took the *f* loaves and two
14:21 were about *f* thousand men
16:9 *f* loaves in the case of the
16:9 in the case of the *f* thousand
25:2 *F* of them were foolish, and
25:2 and *f* were discreet
25:15 And to one he gave *f* talents
25:16 that received the *f* talents
25:16 with them and gained *f* more
25:20 that had received *f* talents
25:20 brought *f* additional talents
25:20 you committed *f* talents to
25:20 see, I gained *f* talents more
Mr 6:38 *F*, besides two fishes
6:41 the *f* loaves and the two
6:44 those who ate . . . *f* thousand
8:19 I broke the *f* loaves for the
8:19 loaves for the *f* thousand men
Lu 1:24 secluded for *f* months, saying
7:41 in debt for *f* hundred denarii
9:13 *f* loaves and two fishes
9:14 in fact, about *f* thousand men
9:16 *f* loaves and the two fishes
12:6 *F* sparrows sell for two
12:52 be *f* in one house divided
14:19 I bought *f* yoke of cattle
16:28 for I have *f* brothers, in
19:18 mina, Lord, made *f* minas
19:19 be in charge of *f* cities
Joh 4:18 For you have had *f* husbands
5:2 Bethzatha, with *f* colonnades
6:9 has *f* barley loaves and
6:10 about *f* thousand in number
6:13 from the *f* barley loaves
Ac 4:4 men became about *f* thousand
20:6 in Troas within *f* days; and
24:1 *F* days later the high priest
1Co 14:19 speak *f* words with my mind
15:6 upward of *f* hundred brothers
2Co 11:24 I *f* times received forty
Re 9:5 should be tormented *f* months
9:10 to hurt the men *f* months
17:10 seven kings: *f* have fallen

Fix
Ex 21:13 *f* for you a place where he
23:31 I will *f* your boundary from
Le 20:5 *f* my face against that man
De 32:8 *f* the boundary of the peoples
Jg 13:15 and *f* up a kid of the goats
Ps 17:11 They *f* their eyes to incline
119:73 proceeded to *f* me solidly
119:133 *F* my own steps solidly in
Pr 15:25 *f* the boundary of the widow
Jer 31:21 *F* your heart upon the
Eze 4:3 must *f* your face against it
4:7 you will *f* your face, with

Fixed
Ex 5:18 give the *f* amount of bricks
Jg 16:14 she *f* them with the pin
2Sa 20:5 came later than the *f* time
2Ki 8:11 he kept a *f* look and kept it
Ezr 6:3 its foundations are to be *f*
Ne 11:23 a *f* provision for the singers
Job 23:3 come clear to his *f* place
Ps 24:2 he himself has solidly *f* it
119:90 solidly *f* the earth, that
Pr 3:19 He solidly *f* the heavens in
30:32 have *f* your thought upon it
Eze 40:43 firmly *f* on the interior
45:11 to be but one *f* amount
Ho 6:11 a harvest has been *f* for you
Na 2:7 it has been *f*; she has been
Lu 4:20 eyes . . . intently *f* upon him
16:26 a great chasm has been *f*
Ac 3:5 he *f* his attention upon them
Col 3:2 minds *f* on the things above

Fixes
Isa 62:7 until he *f* solidly, yes

Fixing
1Sa 13:21 and for *f* fast the oxgoad

Flagrantly
1Sa 12:25 But if you *f* do what is bad

Flagstone
Ne 3:8 *f* Jerusalem as far as the

Flagstones
Ex 24:10 like a work of sapphire *f*

Flaky
Ex 16:14 *f* thing, fine like hoarfrost

Flame
Ex 3:2 angel appeared to him in a *f*
Nu 21:28 a *f* from the town of Sihon
Jg 13:20 as the *f* ascended from off
13:20 in the *f* of the altar while
Job 15:30 His twig a *f* will dry up
41:21 *f* goes forth out of its
Ps 83:14 *f* that scorches the
106:18 *f* itself went devouring the
Ca 8:6 of a fire, the *f* of Jah
Isa 10:17 and his Holy One a *f*
29:6 and the *f* of a devouring fire
30:30 *f* of a devouring fire and
43:2 will the *f* itself singe you

sa 47:14 from the power of the f
er 48:45 f from the midst of Sihon
ze 20:47 f will not be extinguished
a 3:22 ones that the fiery f killed
11:33 stumble by sword and by f
oe 1:19 f has consumed all the trees
2:3 and behind it a f consumes
b 18 and the house of Joseph a f
a 3:3 the f of the sword, and the
c 7:30 angel in the fiery f of a
eb 1:7 public servants a f of fire
e 1:14 and his eyes as a fiery f
2:18 has his eyes like a fiery f
19:12 His eyes are a fiery f, and

lames
s 29:7 hewing with the f of fire
sa 1:31 go up in f at the same time
5:24 into the f mere dried grass
66:15 his rebuke with f of fire
a 7:9 His throne was f of fire; its

laming
e 3:24 and the f blade of a sword
s 7:13 arrows he will make f ones
76:3 broke the f shafts of the bow
78:48 livestock to the f fever
105:32 A f fire on their land
sa 4:5 of a f fire by night
a 2:3 he keeps burning like a f fire
o 7:6 burning as with a f fire
e 2:5 the sound of a f fire that
Th 1:8 in a f fire, as he brings

lank
a 60:4 be taken care of on the f
66:12 Upon the f you will be
ze 34:21 with f and with shoulder

lanks
s 23:13 scourge on your f and as

lapped
b 39:13 female ostrich f joyously

laps
b 39:18 she f her wings on high

lared
s 1:12 his very rage f up within him

lares
s 2:12 For his anger f up easily

lash
e 32:31 the sun began to f upon him
sa 22:5 f floods of good-for-nothing
b 9:23 If a f flood itself should
15:12 And why do your eyes f?
31:26 light when it would f forth
41:18 sneezings f forth light
s 18:4 F floods of good-for-nothing
c 1:5 where it is going to f forth
a 13:10 not f forth their light
28:15 overflowing f flood, in
28:18 overflowing f flood, when
58:10 f up even in the darkness
m 5:9 a despoiling to f forth
c 26:13 f from heaven about me and

lashed
e 33:2 And he f forth from Seir upon
i 3:22 sun itself f upon the water
h 26:19 leprosy itself f up in his
s 97:11 Light itself has f up for
112:4 f up in the darkness as a
c 1:5 And the sun also has f forth
c 9:3 light from heaven f around
22:6 out of heaven a great light f

lashes
x 20:18 lightning f and the sound
b 41:19 there go lightning f
s 88:16 f of burning anger have

lashing
u 17:24 lightning, by its f, shines
24:4 two men in f clothing stood

lask
sa 10:1 then took the f of oil and
i 14:3 cakes and a f of honey
i 9:1 this f of oil in your hand and
9:3 f of oil and pour it out upon
r 19:1 an earthenware f of a potter
19:10 break the f before the eyes

lat
x 16:31 that of f cakes with honey
s 6:5 of the city must fall down f
6:20 wall began to fall down f

Jg 7:13 and the tent fell f
2Sa 22:43 I shall beat them f
Ac 9:33 lying f on his cot for eight

Flatly
Ex 22:17 father f refuses to give her

Flattering
Pr 26:28 f mouth causes an overthrow
28:23 that is f with his tongue
29:5 man that is f his companion
1Th 2:5 either with f speech, (just

Flawless
Php 1:10 be f and not be stumbling

Flax
Ex 9:31 f and the barley . . . struck
9:31 and the f had flower buds
Jos 2:6 stalks of f laid in rows for
Isa 19:9 workers in carded f must
Eze 40:3 was a f cord in his hand

Flaxen
Isa 42:3 and as for a dim f wick
43:17 Like a f wick they must be
Mt 12:20 no smoldering f wick will

Flea
1Sa 24:14 After a single f?
26:20 to look for a single f

Fled
Ge 14:10 those who remained f to the
Nu 16:34 f at the screaming of them
35:25 refuge to which he had f
35:32 has f to his city of refuge
De 19:11 has f to one of these cities
34:7 his vital strength had not f
Jos 10:16 these five kings f and went
20:6 the city from which he f
Jg 4:17 he f on foot to the tent of
1Sa 4:16 battle line that I have f
4:17 has f before the Philistines
19:10 David himself f that he
31:7 men of Israel had f, and that
2Sa 1:4 people have f from the battle
10:14 saw that the Syrians had f
18:17 they f each man to his home
19:3 because they f in the battle
19:8 had f each one to his home
23:11 f because of the Philistines
1Ki 2:29 Joab has f to the tent of
20:30 Ben-hadad, he f and finally
2Ki 25:4 the men of war f by night
1Ch 10:7 saw that they had f and that
11:13 f because of the Philistines
19:15 saw that the Syrians had f
2Ch 25:27 At length he f to Lachish
Es 6:1 that night the king's sleep f
Ps 31:11 they have f from me
Ca 2:17 and the shadows have f, turn
4:6 and the shadows have f, I
Isa 10:29 Gibeah of Saul itself has f
20:6 to which we f for assistance
21:15 f away, because of the
22:3 dictators themselves have f
33:3 of turmoil peoples have f
Jer 4:25 flying creatures . . . all f
9:10 and the beast will have f
46:5 they have positively f, and
46:21 they have f together
Da 6:18 his very sleep f from him
Ho 7:13 for they have f from me
Zec 14:5 f because of the earthquake
Mt 8:33 the herders f and, going into
26:56 Then all the disciples . . . f
Mr 5:14 But the herders of them f and
14:50 they all abandoned him and f
16:8 f from the memorial tomb
Lu 8:34 they f and reported it to the
Ac 14:6 f to the cities of Lycaonia
19:16 they f naked and wounded out
Heb 6:18 we who have f to the refuge
Re 12:6 woman f into the wilderness
16:20 Also, every island f, and
20:11 earth and the heaven f away

Fledglings
De 32:11 eagle . . . Hovers over its f

Flee
Ge 19:20 city is nearby to f there and
31:40 sleep would f from my eyes
39:13 that he might f outside
Ex 4:3 serpent; and Moses began to f
9:20 livestock to f into the houses
14:25 Let us f from any contact
21:13 a place where he can f
Le 26:17 f when no one is pursuing
26:36 f as in flight from a sword
Nu 10:35 hate you f from before you
35:6 give for the manslayer to f
35:11 the manslayer must f there
35:15 for anyone to f there that
35:26 of refuge to which he may f
De 4:42 manslayer to f there who
4:42 must f to one of these cities
19:3 for any manslayer to f there
19:4 the manslayer who may f there
19:5 f to one of these cities and
28:7 by seven ways they will f
28:25 by seven ways you will f
Jos 8:5 we must then f before them
8:6 And we must f before them
8:20 no ability in them to f this
20:3 f there; and they must serve
20:4 f to one of these cities and
20:9 f there who fatally strikes
Jg 20:32 Let us f, and we shall
1Sa 31:7 leave the cities and f
2Sa 4:4 began to carry him and f
4:4 running in panic to f, he
17:2 people . . . will have to f
18:3 for if we should at all f
1Ki 12:18 chariot to f to Jerusalem
2Ki 9:3 open the door and f and not
9:23 that he might f, and said to
1Ch 10:7 to leave their cities and f
2Ch 10:18 chariot to f to Jerusalem
Ps 11:1 F as a bird to your mountain!
59:16 f in the day of my distress
60:4 To f zigzag on account of the
68:1 hate him f because of him
68:12, 12 armies f, they f
104:7 your rebuke they began to f
Pr 28:1 wicked do f when there is no
28:17 himself f even to the pit
Isa 10:3 will you f for assistance
13:14 f, each one to his own land
17:11 harvest will certainly f in
17:13 it must f far away and be
30:16 but on horses we shall f
30:16 That is why you will f
30:17 rebuke of five you will f
31:8 f because of the sword
35:10 and sighing must f away
51:11 will certainly f away
Jer 25:35 a place to f to has perished
46:6 not the swift one try to f
49:8 F! Let yourselves give way!
49:24 She has turned to f, and
49:30 F, take flight far away
50:16 f each one to his own land
51:6 F out of the midst of
Da 4:14 the beast f from under it
Am 2:14 And a place to which to f
2:16 naked is how he will f in
Na 3:7 everyone seeing you will f
3:17 and away they certainly f
Zec 2:6 F, then, you people, from
14:5 f to the valley of my
14:5 have to f, just as you fled
Mt 2:13 f into Egypt, and stay there
3:7 to f from the coming wrath
10:23 persecute you in one city, f
23:33 how are you to f from the
Lu 3:7 to f from the coming wrath
Joh 10:5 will f from him, because
1Co 6:18 F from fornication
10:14 my beloved ones, f from
1Ti 6:11 f from these things
2Ti 2:22 So, f from the desires
Jas 4:7 oppose the Devil . . . he will f

Fleece
Jg 6:37 keeping a f of wool exposed
6:37 If dew comes to be on the f
6:38 wrung the f, he got to drain
6:38 enough dew from the f to fill
6:39 once more with the f
6:39 dryness occur to the f alone
6:40 on the f alone, and upon all

Fleeing
Ge 39:18 and went f outside
Ex 14:27 the Egyptians were f from
Jos 8:6 They are f before us just as
8:20 people that were f to the
10:11 were f from before Israel
Jg 7:21 into shouting and went f
9:40 he went f before him; and the
9:51 city went f, after which they
20:45 and went f to the wilderness

Jg 20:47 went *f* to the wilderness to
1Sa 4:10 went *f* each one to his tent
17:24 went *f* on account of him
2Sa 10:13 Syrians, and they went *f*
24:13 *f* before your adversaries
1Ki 2:28 Joab went *f* to the tent of
20:30 *f* to Aphek, to the city
2Ki 7:7 *f* in the evening darkness
7:7 they kept *f* for their soul
8:21 people went *f* to their tents
9:10 opened the door and went *f*
14:19 and he went *f* to Lachish
1Ch 10:1 men of Israel went *f* from
Pr 26:2 Just as a bird has cause for *f*
27:8 a bird *f* away from its nest
27:8 a man *f* away from his place
Isa 16:2 like a *f* winged creature
16:3 do not betray anyone *f*
21:14 confront the one *f* away
24:18 *f* from the sound of the
Jer 48:19 Ask him that is *f* and her
48:44 *f* because of the dread
48:45 those *f* have stood still
50:28 sound of those *f* and
Am 9:1 No one *f* of them will make
Na 2:8 but they are *f*. Stand still
Mt 24:16 let those in Judea begin *f*
Mr 13:14 let those in Judea begin *f*
Lu 21:21 let those in Judea begin *f*
Re 9:6 but death keeps *f* from them

Flees

Am 5:19 a man *f* because of the lion
Joh 10:12 and abandons the sheep and *f*

Fleet

1Ki 9:26 *f* of ships that King Solomon
9:27 sending in the *f* of ships
10:11 Hiram's *f* of ships that
10:22 a *f* of ships of Tarshish
10:22 with Hiram's *f* of ships
10:22 the *f* of ships of Tarshish
Isa 33:21 On it no galley *f* will go

Flesh

Ge 2:21 closed up the *f* over its place
2:23, 23 of my bones And *f* of my *f*
2:24 and they must become one *f*
6:3 man . . . is also *f*. Accordingly
6:12 all *f* had ruined its way
6:13 The end of all *f* has come
6:17 ruin all *f* in which the force
6:19 creature of every sort of *f*
7:15 two, of every sort of *f*
7:16 female of every sort of *f*
7:21 all *f* that was moving upon
8:17 every sort of *f* . . . bring out
9:4 Only *f* with its soul—its
9:11 No more will all *f* be cut off
9:15 every living soul among all *f*
9:15 deluge to bring all *f* to ruin
9:16 every living soul among all *f*
9:17 between me and all *f* that is
17:11 circumcised in the *f* of your
17:13 covenant in the *f* of you men
17:14 not get the *f* of his foreskin
17:23 circumcising the *f* of their
17:24 he had the *f* of his foreskin
17:25 the *f* of his foreskin
29:14 are indeed my bone and my *f*
37:27 he is our brother, our *f*
40:19 eat your *f* from off you
Ex 4:7 restored like the rest of his *f*
12:8 must eat the *f* on this night
12:46 not take any of the *f* out
21:28 but its *f* is not to be eaten
22:31 not eat *f* in the field that
28:42 them to cover the naked *f*
29:14 bull's *f* and its skin and its
29:31 boil its *f* in a holy place
29:32 must eat the *f* of the ram
29:34 the *f* of the installation
30:32 not to be rubbed in the *f* of
Le 4:11 the bull and all its *f* along
6:10 linen drawers on over his *f*
6:27 touch its *f* will become holy
7:15 the *f* of the thanksgiving
7:17 the *f* of the sacrifice on
7:18 of the *f* of his communion
7:19 the *f* that may touch anything
7:19 As for the *f*, everybody clean
7:19 everybody clean may eat the *f*
7:20 the soul who eats the *f* of
7:21 actually eats some of the *f*
8:17 its skin and its *f* and its
Le 8:31 Boil the *f* at the entrance of
8:32 *f* and the bread you will burn
9:11 he burned the *f* and the skin
11:8 must not eat any of their *f*
11:11 must not eat any of their *f*
12:3 the *f* of his foreskin will be
13:2 the skin of his *f* an eruption
13:2 develop in the skin of his *f*
13:3 plague in the skin of the *f*
13:3 deeper than the skin of his *f*
13:4 is white in the skin of his *f*
13:10 living *f* is in the eruption
13:11 leprosy in the skin of his *f*
13:13 leprosy has covered all his *f*
13:14 day the living *f* appears in
13:15 priest must see the living *f*
13:15 The living *f* is unclean
13:16 living *f* goes back and it
13:18 As for the *f*, in case a boil
13:24 a scar in the skin of the *f*
13:24 the raw *f* of the scar does
13:38 of their *f*, white blotches
13:39 of their *f* are dull white
13:43 leprosy in the skin of the *f*
14:9 bathe his *f* in water; and he
15:7 touches the *f* of the one
15:13 bathe his *f* in running water
15:16 bathe all his *f* in water and
15:19 discharge in her *f* proves to
16:4 upon his *f*, and he should gird
16:4 bathe his *f* in water and put
16:24 he must bathe his *f* in water
16:26 he must bathe his *f* in water
16:27 burn their skins and their *f*
16:28 he must bathe his *f* in water
17:11 soul of the *f* is in the blood
17:14 soul of every sort of *f* is
17:14 any sort of *f*, because the
17:14 soul of every sort of *f* is
17:16 not bathe his *f*, he must
19:28 make cuts in your *f* for a
21:5 their *f* they should not make an
22:6 he must bathe his *f* in water
25:49 relative of his *f*, one of his
26:29 eat the *f* of your sons, and
26:29 eat the *f* of your daughters
Nu 8:7 razor pass over all their *f*
12:12 like someone dead, whose *f*
16:22 spirits of every sort of *f*
18:15 of every sort of *f*, which
18:18 their *f* should become yours
19:5 skin and its *f* and its blood
19:7 and bathe his *f* in water, and
19:8 must bathe his *f* in water
27:16 the spirits of all sorts of *f*
De 5:26 all *f* that has heard the voice
12:23 not eat the soul with the *f*
12:27 the *f* and the blood, upon the
12:27 but the *f* you may eat
14:8 None of their *f* must you eat
16:4 neither should any of the *f*
28:53 the *f* of your sons and your
28:55 the *f* of his sons that he
32:42 While my sword will eat *f*
Jg 8:7 give your *f* a threshing with
9:2 your bone and your *f* I am
1Sa 17:44 give your *f* to the fowls
2Sa 5:1 are your bone and your *f*
19:12 my bone and my *f* you are
19:13 not my bone and my *f*
1Ki 19:21 the bulls he boiled their *f*
21:27 put sackcloth upon his *f*
2Ki 4:34 the child's *f* grew warm
5:10 your *f* may come back to you
5:14 his *f* came back like the
5:14 like the *f* of a little boy
6:30 was underneath upon his *f*
9:36 will eat the *f* of Jezebel
1Ch 11:1 We are your bone and your *f*
2Ch 32:8 there is an arm of *f*
Ne 5:5 our *f* is the same as the
5:5 same as the *f* of our brothers
Job 2:5 as far as his bone and his *f*
4:15 The hair of my *f* began to
6:12 Or is my *f* of copper?
7:5 *f* . . . clothed with maggots
10:4 Do you have eyes of *f*, Or is
10:11 With skin and *f* you
12:10 the spirit of all *f* of man
13:14 do I carry my *f* in my teeth
14:22 his own *f* while upon him
19:20 to my *f* my bones actually
19:22 satisfied with my very *f*
19:26 Yet reduced in my *f* I shall
Job 21:6 has taken hold of my *f*
33:21 *f* wastes away from sight
33:25 *f* become fresher than in
34:15 All *f* will expire together
41:23 folds of its *f* do cling
Ps 16:9 own *f* will reside in security
27:2 against me to eat up my *f*
38:3 no sound spot in my *f*
38:7 no sound spot in my *f*
50:13 eat the *f* of powerful bulls
56:4 What can *f* do to me?
63:1 my *f* has grown faint with
65:2 people of all *f* will come
78:39 that they were *f*
79:2 *f* of your loyal ones to the
84:2 very *f* cry out joyfully to
102:5 My bones have stuck to my *f*
109:24 *f* has grown lean, without
119:120 *f* has had a creepy feeling
136:25 One giving food to all *f*
145:21 all *f* bless his holy name
Pr 4:22 and health to all their *f*
5:11 *f* and your organism come to
23:20 are gluttonous eaters of *f*
Ec 2:3 cheering my *f* even with wine
4:5 stupid . . . is eating his own *f*
5:6 mouth to cause your *f* to sin
11:10 off calamity from your *f*
12:12 is wearisome to the *f*
Isa 9:20 one eat the *f* of his own arm
10:18 the soul clear to the *f*
17:4 fatness of his *f* will be
22:13 the eating of *f* and the
31:3 horses are *f*, and not spirit
40:5 all *f* must see it together
40:6 All *f* is green grass, and
44:16 he roasts well the *f* that
44:19 I roast *f* and eat. But the
49:26 eat their own *f*
49:26 all *f* will have to know
58:7 hide . . . from your own *f*
65:4 eating the *f* of the pig
66:16 his sword, against all *f*
66:17 eating the *f* of the pig and
66:23 all *f* will come in to bow
66:24 repulsive to all *f*
Jer 7:21 your sacrifices and eat *f*
11:15 with holy *f* will they make
12:12 There is no peace for any *f*
17:5 actually makes *f* his arm
19:9 eat the *f* of their sons and
19:9 and the *f* of their daughters
19:9 eat each one the *f* of his
25:31 in judgment with all *f*
32:27 Jehovah, the God of all *f*
45:5 in a calamity upon all *f*
La 3:4 my *f* and my skin to wear away
Eze 4:14 there has come no foul *f*
10:12 their *f* . . . full of eyes
11:3 cooking pot, and we are the *f*
11:7 they are the *f*, and she is
11:11 to be *f* in the midst of her
11:19 heart of stone from their *f*
11:19 and give them a heart of *f*
16:26 your neighbors great of *f*
20:48 all those of *f* must see
21:4 all *f* from south to north
21:5 *f* will have to know that I
24:10 Boil the *f* thoroughly
32:5 your *f* upon the mountains
36:26 heart of stone from your *f*
36:26 and give you a heart of *f*
37:6 cause to come upon you *f*
37:8 *f* itself came up and skin
39:17 eat *f* and drink blood
39:18 *f* of mighty ones you will
40:43 the *f* of the gift offering
44:7 and uncircumcised in *f*, in
44:9 uncircumcised in *f*, may
Da 1:15 fatter in *f* than all the
2:11 does not exist with *f* at all
4:12 it all *f* would feed itself
7:5 to it, Get up, eat much *f*
10:3 no *f* or wine entered into my
Ho 8:13 they kept sacrificing *f*, and
Joe 2:28 spirit on every sort of *f*
Mic 3:3 *f* in the midst of a cooking
Hag 2:12 If a man carries holy *f* in
Zec 2:13 Keep silence, all *f*, before
11:9 each one the *f* of her
11:16 *f* of the fat one he will
14:12 a rotting away of one's *f*
Mt 16:17 *f* and blood did not reveal
19:5 and the two will be one *f*

Mt 19:6 are no longer two, but one *f*
24:22 no *f* would be saved; but on
26:41 is eager, but the *f* is weak
Mr 10:8 the two will be one *f*; so
10:8 are no longer two, but one *f*
13:20 no *f* would be saved
14:38 eager, but the *f* is weak
Lu 3:6 all *f* will see the saving
24:39 a spirit does not have *f* and
Joh 1:14 Word became *f* and resided
3:6, 6 been born from the *f* is *f*
6:51 my *f* in behalf of the life
6:52 man give us his *f* to eat
6:53 eat the *f* of the Son of man
6:54 He that feeds on my *f* and
6:55 for my *f* is true food, and
6:56 He that feeds on my *f* and
6:63 the *f* is of no use at all
8:15 You judge according to the *f*
17:2 him authority over all *f*
Ac 2:17 spirit upon every sort of *f*
2:26 my *f* will reside in hope
2:31 nor did his *f* see corruption
Ro 1:3 seed of David according to the *f*
2:28 is on the outside upon the *f*
3:20 no *f* . . . declared righteous
4:1 forefather according to the *f*
6:19 of the weakness of your *f*
7:5 we were in accord with the *f*
7:18 in my *f*, there dwells
7:25 but with my *f* to sin's law
8:3 it was weak through the *f*
8:3 Son in the likeness of sinful *f*
8:3 condemned sin in the *f*
8:4 walk, not in accord with the *f*
8:5 who are in accord with the *f*
8:5 minds on the things of the *f*
8:6 minding of the *f* means death
8:7 minding of the *f* means enmity
8:8 who are in harmony with the *f*
8:9 harmony, not with the *f*, but
8:12 not to the *f* to live in accord
8:12 to live in accord with the *f*
8:13 live in accord with the *f*
9:3 relatives according to the *f*
9:5 sprang according to the *f*
9:8 children in the *f* are not
11:14 those who are my own *f* to
13:14 for the desires of the *f*
14:21 It is well not to eat *f* or
1Co 1:29 no *f* might boast in the
5:5 the destruction of the *f*, in
6:16 The two . . . will be one *f*
7:28 have tribulation in their *f*
8:13 will never again eat *f* at
9:11 reap things for the *f* from
15:39 Not all *f* is the same
15:39 is the same *f*, but there is
15:39 there is another *f* of cattle
15:39 and another *f* of birds, and
15:50 *f* and blood cannot inherit
2Co 1:17 according to the *f*, that
4:11 manifest in our mortal *f*
5:16 no man according to the *f*
5:16 Christ according to the *f*
7:1 defilement of *f* and spirit
7:5 our *f* got no relief, but we
10:2 to what we are in the *f*
10:3 though we walk in the *f*, we
10:3 to what we are in the *f*
11:18 boasting according to the *f*
12:7 thorn in the *f*, an angel of
Ga 1:16 into conference with *f* and
2:16 no *f* . . . declared righteous
2:20 life that I now live in *f* I
3:3 you now being completed in *f*
4:13 through a sickness of my *f*
4:14 trial to you in my *f*, you
4:23 born in the manner of *f*
4:29 one born in the manner of *f*
5:13 as an inducement for the *f*
5:17 *f* is against the spirit in
5:17 and the spirit against the *f*
5:19 works of the *f* are manifest
5:24 impaled the *f* together with
6:8 sowing with a view to his *f*
6:8 reap corruption from his *f*
6:12 pleasing appearance in the *f*
6:13 cause for boasting in your *f*
Eph 2:3 with the desires of our *f*
2:3 the things willed by the *f*
2:11 people of the nations as to *f*
2:11 made in the *f* with hands
2:15 means of his *f* he abolished
Eph 5:29 no man ever hated his own *f*
5:31 the two will become one *f*
6:12 not against blood and *f*, but
Php 1:22 if it be to live on in the *f*
1:24 for me to remain in the *f* is
3:2 for those who mutilate the *f*
3:3 not . . . confidence in the *f*
3:4 for confidence also in the *f*
3:4 for confidence in the *f*
Col 1:24 of the Christ in my *f* on
2:1 not seen my face in the *f*
2:5 though I am absent in the *f*
2:11 the body of the *f*, by the
2:13 state of your *f*
2:23 the satisfying of the *f*
1Ti 3:16 He was made manifest in *f*
Heb 2:14 are sharers of blood and *f*
5:7 In the days of his *f* Christ
7:16 depending upon the *f*, but
9:10 pertaining to the *f* and were
9:13 extent of cleanness of the *f*
10:20 the curtain, that is, his *f*
12:9 fathers who were of our *f* to
1Pe 1:24 all *f* is like grass, and all
3:18 being put to death in the *f*
3:21 the filth of the *f*, but the
4:1 since Christ suffered in the *f*
4:1 suffered in the *f* has desisted
4:2 time in the *f*, no more for
4:6 judged as to the *f* from the
2Pe 2:10 those who go on after *f* with
2:18 by the desires of the *f* and
1Jo 2:16 the desire of the *f* and the
4:2 Christ . . . come in the *f*
2Jo 7 Jesus Christ as coming in the *f*
Jude 7 out after *f* for unnatural use
8 are defiling the *f* and
23 that has been stained by the *f*

Fleshly
Le 18:6 any close *f* relative of his
Pr 14:30 the life of the *f* organism
Eze 23:20 those whose *f* member is as
23:20 *f* member of male asses
Joh 1:13 from blood or from a *f* will
Ro 7:14 but I am *f*, sold under sin
15:27 with things for the *f* body
1Co 1:26 not many wise in a *f* way
3:1 as to *f* men, as to babes in
3:3 you are yet *f*. For whereas
3:3 are you not *f* and are you not
10:18 which is Israel in a *f* way
2Co 1:12 not with *f* wisdom but with
3:3 but on *f* tablets, on hearts
10:4 the weapons . . . are not *f*
Ga 5:16 carry out no *f* desire at all
Eph 6:5 are your masters in a *f* sense
Col 1:22 means of that one's *f* body
2:18 by his *f* frame of mind
3:22 your masters in a *f* sense
Phm 16 in *f* relationship and in the
1Pe 2:11 abstaining from *f* desires

Fleshy
Jas 5:3 and will eat your *f* parts
Re 17:16 and will eat up her *f* parts
19:18 eat the *f* parts of kings and
19:18 the *f* parts of military
19:18 *f* parts of strong men
19:18 *f* parts of horses and of
19:18 and the *f* parts of all, of
19:21 filled from the *f* parts of

Flew
Isa 6:6 one of the seraphs *f* to me

Flies
De 4:17 bird that *f* in the heavens
Job 39:27 that an eagle *f* upward
Ps 91:5 of the arrow that *f* by day
Pr 23:5 and *f* away toward the heavens
Ec 10:1 Dead *f* are what cause the oil
Isa 7:18 *f* that are at the extremity
Ho 9:11 their glory *f* away, so that
Na 3:16 the locust . . . it *f* away

Flight
Ge 14:10 took to *f* and went falling
39:12 to *f* and went on outside
39:15 took to *f* and went on
Le 26:36 flee as in *f* from a sword
De 32:30 two put ten thousand to *f*
Jos 7:4 *f* before the men of Ai
8:15 they took to *f* by the way of
Jg 1:6 When Adoni-bezek took to *f*
4:15 Sisera . . . took to *f* on foot
Jg 7:22 camp kept up their *f* as far as
8:12 and Zalmunna took to *f*, he at
9:21 Jotham took to *f* and went
1Sa 14:22 Philistines had taken to *f*
17:51 Philistines . . . took to *f*
19:8 took to *f* from before him
30:17 upon camels and took to *f*
31:1 Israel took to *f* from before
2Sa 10:14 *f* from before Abishai and
10:18 Syrians took to *f* from
13:29 mount . . . and take to *f*
22:3 my place for *f*, my Savior
1Ki 20:20 the Syrians took to *f*
2Ki 3:24 took to *f* from before them
9:27 took to *f* by the way of the
9:27 continued his *f* to Megiddo
14:12 to *f*, each one to his tent
1Ch 19:14 took to *f* from before him
19:15 to *f* from before Abishai
19:18 Syrians took to *f* because of
2Ch 13:16 Israel took to *f* from
14:12 the Ethiopians took to *f*
25:22 to *f* each one to his tent
Job 11:20 place for *f* will certainly
Ps 21:12 turn their backs in *f*
55:7 I would go far away in *f*
114:3 sea . . . saw and took to *f*
114:5 O sea, that you took to *f*
142:4 place for *f* has perished
Isa 52:12 and you will go in no *f*
Jer 16:19 for *f* in the day of distress
48:6 Take to *f*; provide escape for
49:30 Flee, take *f* far away
50:3 domestic animal have taken *f*
50:8 Take your *f* out of the midst
Am 9:1 will make good his *f*, and no
Mt 24:20 Keep praying that your *f* may
Ac 7:29 Moses took to *f* and became

Flint
Ex 4:25 Zipporah took a *f* and cut off
Jos 5:2 *f* knives and circumcise the
5:3 Joshua made *f* knives for
Job 28:9 Upon the *f* he has thrust out
Isa 5:28 to be accounted as *f* itself
50:7 I have set my face like a *f*
Eze 3:9 harder than *f*, I have made

Flinty
De 8:15 water . . . out of the *f* rock
32:13 And oil out of a *f* rock
Ps 114:8 *f* rock into a spring of

Float
2Ki 6:6 and made the axhead *f*

Floating
Ge 7:17 ark and it was *f* high above

Flock
Ge 4:4 some firstlings of his *f*
21:28 seven female lambs of the *f*
30:31 resume shepherding your *f*
30:32 pass among your whole *f*
30:38 he placed in front of the *f*
31:4 out to the field to his *f*
31:8 whole *f* produced speckled
31:8 whole *f* produced striped ones
31:10 time when the *f* got in heat
31:10 he-goats springing upon the *f*
31:12 he-goats springing upon the *f*
31:38 rams of your *f* I never ate
31:41 and six years for your *f*
31:43, 43 *f* my *f*, and everything
33:13 whole *f* will certainly die
37:2 with his brothers among the *f*
37:12 feed the *f* of their father
37:14 whether the *f* is safe and
47:4 no pasturage for the *f* that
47:17 the livestock of the *f* and
Ex 2:16 to water their father's *f*
2:17 Moses . . . watered their *f*
2:19 that he might water the *f*
3:1 shepherd of the *f* of Jethro
3:1 While he was driving the *f* to
9:3 *f* . . . a very heavy pestilence
20:24 sacrifices, your *f* and your
22:1 four of the *f* for the sheep
34:3 no *f* or herd should be
Le 1:2 from the herd and from the *f*
1:10 burnt offering is from the *f*
3:6 if his offering is from the *f*
5:6 from the *f*, a female lamb or
5:15 a sound ram from the *f*
5:18 bring a sound ram from the *f*
6:6 a sound ram from the *f*
22:21 a sound one among . . . the *f*

Le 27:32 tenth part of the herd and *f*
Nu 15:3 from the herd or from the *f*
31:28 of the asses and of the *f*
31:30 of the asses and of the *f*, of
31:32 thousand of the *f*
31:36 five hundred of the *f*
31:37 tax for Jehovah from the *f*
31:43 from the *f* amounted to three
32:16 build here stone *f* pens for
32:36 and stone *f* pens
De 7:13 and the progeny of your *f*
8:13 herd and your *f* may increase
12:6 of your herd and of your *f*
12:17 your herd and of your *f* or
12:21 your *f* that Jehovah has given
14:23 of your herd and of your *f*
15:14 with something from your *f*
15:19 in your herd and in your *f*
15:19 shear the firstborn of your *f*
16:2 the *f* and of the herd, in the
18:4 the shorn wool of your *f* you
28:4 and the progeny of your *f*
28:18 and the progeny of your *f*
28:51 cattle or progeny of your *f*
32:14 the herd and milk of the *f*
Jos 7:24 and his *f* and his tent and
1Sa 15:9 upon the best of the *f* and
15:14 sound of the *f* in my ears
15:15 the best of the *f* and of the
16:19 David . . . who is with the *f*
17:34 a shepherd . . . among the *f*
25:16 shepherding the *f*
2Sa 7:8 following the *f* to become a
1Ch 17:7 from following the *f* to
2Ch 29:33 three thousand of the *f*
32:29 livestock of the *f* and of
Ezr 10:19 be a ram of the *f* for their
Job 21:11 young boys just like a *f*
30:1 place with the dogs of my *f*
Ps 74:1 the *f* of your pasturage
77:20 your people just like a *f*
78:52 to depart just like a *f*
78:70 from the pens of the *f*
79:13 and the *f* of your pasturage
80:1 Joseph just like a *f*
107:41 into families just like a *f*
Pr 27:23 the appearance of your *f*
Ca 1:7 make the *f* lie down at midday
1:8 in the footprints of the *f* and
Isa 13:14 *f* without anyone to collect
63:11 with the shepherds of his *f*
Jer 13:20 to you, your beautiful *f*
25:34 you majestic ones of the *f*
25:35 the majestic ones of the *f*
25:36 the majestic ones of the *f*
31:12 young ones of the *f* and the
33:12 are making the *f* lie down
49:20 little ones of the *f* will
50:6 *f* of perishing creatures my
50:8 leading animals before the *f*
50:45 little ones of the *f* will
Eze 25:5 Ammon a resting-place of a *f*
34:2 *f* that the shepherds ought
34:3 *f* itself you do not feed
36:37 like a *f* with men
36:38 Like a *f* of holy persons
36:38 like the *f* of Jerusalem in
36:38 become full of a *f* of men
43:23 ram from the *f*, a sound one
43:25 ram out of the *f*, perfect
45:15 one sheep out of the *f*, out
Ho 5:6 their *f* and with their herd
Am 6:4 eating the rams out of a *f*
7:15 take me from following the *f*
Jon 3:7 no *f*, should taste anything
Mic 2:12 like a *f* in the pen
7:14 the *f* of your inheritance
Hab 3:17 *f* may actually be severed
Zec 9:16 like the *f* of his people
10:2 certainly depart like a *f*
11:4 Shepherd the *f* meant for the
11:7 shepherd the *f* meant for the
11:7 O afflicted ones of the *f*
11:7 and I went shepherding the *f*
11:11 afflicted ones of the *f* who
11:17 shepherd . . . leaving the *f*
13:7 those of the *f* be scattered
Mt 26:31 the sheep of the *f* will be
Lu 12:32 Have no fear, little *f*
17:7 plowing or minding the *f*
Joh 10:16 become one *f*, one shepherd
Ac 20:28 Pay attention to . . . the *f*
20:29 treat the *f* with tenderness
1Co 9:7 shepherds a *f* and does not
1Co 9:7 eat some of the milk of the *f*
1Pe 5:2 Shepherd the *f* of God in your
5:3 becoming examples to the *f*

Flocking
1Ch 12:33 for *f* together to David they
12:38 *f* together in battle line

Flocks
Ge 26:14 he came to have *f* of sheep
29:3 and they watered the *f*
30:36 shepherding the *f* of Laban
30:38 the *f* would come to drink
30:39 the *f* would get in heat
30:39 the *f* would produce striped
30:40 turned the faces of the *f*
30:40 among the *f* of Laban
30:40 set them by the *f* of Laban
30:41 robust *f* would get in heat
30:41 before the eyes of the *f*
30:42 when the *f* showed feebleness
30:43 great *f* and maidservants and
32:7 the *f* and the cattle and the
34:28 Their *f* and their herds and
37:13 tending *f* close by Shechem
37:16 Where are they tending *f*?
45:10 your *f* and your herds and
46:32 their *f* and their herds and
47:1 my brothers and their *f* and
50:8 their *f* and their herds they
Ex 12:32 Take both your *f* and your
12:38 them, as well as *f* and herds
Nu 11:22 *f* and herds be slaughtered
32:24 and stone pens for your *f*
Jg 5:16 the pipings for the *f*? For the
1Sa 8:17 *f* he will take the tenth
27:9 took *f* and herds and asses
30:20 David took all the *f* and
1Ki 20:27 like two tiny *f* of goats
1Ch 4:39 for pasturage for their *f*
4:41 pasturage for their *f* there
27:31 over the *f* there was Jaziz
2Ch 14:15 captive *f* in great number
17:11 bringing to him *f*, seven
35:7 to the sons of the people *f*
Ne 10:36 of our herds and of our *f*
Ps 65:13 have become clothed with *f*
144:13 Our *f* multiplying by
Ec 2:7 cattle and *f* in great quantity
Isa 13:20 let their *f* lie down there
60:7 All the *f* of Kedar—they
61:5 shepherd the *f* of you people
Jer 3:24 their *f* and their herds
5:17 eat up your *f* and your herds
33:13 *f* will yet pass by under
49:29 their own *f* will be taken
Lu 2:8 in the night over their *f*

Flog
Ac 22:19 I used to imprison and *f* in

Flogged
Ac 5:40 apostles, *f* them, and ordered
16:37 *f* us publicly uncondemned

Flood
Job 9:23 *f* itself should cause death
38:25 divided a channel for the *f*
Ps 32:6 As for the *f* of many waters
78:20 torrents themselves might *f*
Pr 27:4 also the *f* of anger, but who
Isa 8:8 actually *f* and pass over
28:15 overflowing flash *f*, in
28:17 *f* out the very place of
28:18 overflowing flash *f*, when
43:2 they will not *f* over you
54:8 With a *f* of indignation I
Jer 47:2 *f* the land and what fills it
Da 9:26 end of it will be by the *f*
11:10 and *f* over and pass through
11:22 arms of the *f*, they will be
11:40 and *f* over and pass through
Na 1:8 by the *f* that is passing along
Mt 24:38 before the *f*, eating and
24:39 took no note until the *f*
Lu 6:48 when a *f* arose, the river
17:27 *f* arrived and destroyed them

Flooded
Da 11:22 *f* over on account of him
11:26 military force, it will be *f*

Floodgates
Ge 7:11 *f* of the heavens were opened
8:2 *f* of the heavens became
2Ki 7:2 were making *f* in the heavens
7:19 were making *f* in the heavens
Isa 24:18 *f* on high will actually be
Mal 3:10 the *f* of the heavens and

Flooding
Isa 10:22 *f* through in righteousness
28:2 storm of powerful, *f* waters
30:28 spirit is like a *f* torrent
66:12 just like a *f* torrent
Jer 47:2 have become a *f* torrent
Eze 13:11 A *f* downpour will certainly
13:13 will occur a *f* downpour
38:22 *f* downpour and hailstones

Floods
Ex 15:8 stood still like a dam of *f*
2Sa 22:5 *f* of good-for-nothing men
2Ch 32:4 *f* through the middle of the
Ps 18:4 *f* of good-for-nothing men
Mt 7:25 *f* came and the winds blew
7:27 *f* came and the winds blew

Floor
Ge 50:10 the threshing *f* of Atad
50:11 the threshing *f* of Atad, and
Nu 5:17 be on the *f* of the tabernacle
15:20 contribution of a threshing *f*
18:27 the grain of the threshing *f*
18:30 produce of the threshing *f*
De 15:14 your threshing *f* and your oil
16:13 your threshing *f* and your oil
Jg 6:37 exposed on the threshing *f*
Ru 3:2 at the threshing *f* tonight
3:3 and go down to the threshing *f*
3:6 to go down to the threshing *f*
3:14 came to the threshing *f*
2Sa 6:6 as the threshing *f* of Nacon
24:16 the threshing *f* of Araunah
24:18 threshing *f* of Araunah
24:21 the threshing *f* for building
24:24 David bought the threshing *f*
1Ki 6:15 From the *f* of the house up
6:15 overlay the *f* of the house
6:16 from the *f* up to the rafters
6:30 *f* of the house he overlaid
7:7 from the *f* to the rafters
22:10 threshing *f* at the entrance
2Ki 6:27 either from the threshing *f*
1Ch 13:9 the threshing *f* of Chidon
21:15 by the threshing *f* of Ornan
21:18 on the threshing *f* of Ornan
21:21 out of the threshing *f* and
21:22 the place of the threshing *f*
21:28 at the threshing *f* of Ornan
2Ch 3:1 on the threshing *f* of Ornan
18:9 threshing *f* at the entrance
Job 39:12 gather to your threshing *f*
Isa 21:10 the son of my threshing *f*
Jer 51:33 is like a threshing *f*
Eze 41:16 the *f* up to the windows
41:20 *f* to above the entrance
42:6 the middle ones from the *f*
43:14 on the *f* to the lower
Da 2:35 from the summer threshing *f*
Ho 9:2 Threshing *f* and winepress do
13:3 away from the threshing *f*
Am 9:3 on the *f* of the sea, down
Mic 4:12 cut grain to the threshing *f*
Mt 3:12 clean up his threshing *f*, and
Lu 3:17 to clean up his threshing *f*

Floors
1Sa 23:1 pillaging the threshing *f*
Ho 9:1 all the threshing *f* of grain
Joe 2:24 the threshing *f* must be full

Flour
Ge 18:6 fine *f*, knead the dough and
Ex 12:34 people carried their *f* dough
12:39 began to bake the *f* dough
29:2 Out of fine wheat *f* you will
29:40 ephah measure of fine *f*
Le 2:1 should prove to be fine *f*
2:2 his handful of its fine *f* and
2:4 be of fine *f*, unfermented
2:5 of fine *f* moistened with oil
2:7 be made of fine *f* with oil
5:11 of fine *f* for a sin offering
6:15 fine *f* of the grain offering
6:20 tenth of an ephah of fine *f*
7:12 fine *f* as ring-shaped cakes
14:10 fine *f* as a grain offering
14:21 fine *f* moistened with oil as
23:13 ephah of fine *f* moistened
23:17 ephah of fine *f* they should
24:5 fine *f* and bake it up into
Nu 5:15 tenth of an ephah of barley *f*

Nu 6:15 cakes of fine *f*, moistened
7:13 full of fine *f* moistened with
7:19 full of fine *f* moistened with
7:25 full of fine *f* moistened with
7:31 fine *f* moistened with oil for
7:37 fine *f* moistened with oil for
7:43 fine *f* moistened with oil for
7:49 fine *f* moistened with oil for
7:55 fine *f* moistened with oil for
7:61 full of fine *f* moistened with
7:67 full of fine *f* moistened with
7:73 fine *f* moistened with oil for
7:79 fine *f* moistened with oil for
8:8 offering of fine *f* moistened
15:4 a grain offering of fine *f*, a
15:6 of fine *f*, moistened with a
15:9 of three tenths of fine *f*
28:5 tenth of an ephah of fine *f* as
28:9 two tenth measures of fine *f*
28:12 fine *f* as a grain offering
28:12 fine *f* as a grain offering
28:13 a tenth measure of fine *f*
28:20 grain offerings of fine *f*
28:28 fine *f* moistened with oil
29:3 their grain offering of fine *f*
29:9 fine *f* moistened with oil
29:14 of fine *f* moistened with oil
Jg 6:19 an ephah of *f* as unfermented
1Sa 1:24 one ephah of *f* and a large
28:24 took *f* and kneaded dough
2Sa 13:8 *f* dough and kneaded it and
17:28 *f* and roasted grain and
1Ki 4:22 thirty cor measures of fine *f*
4:22 and sixty cor measures of *f*
17:12 *f* in the large jar and a
17:14 jar of *f* itself will not
17:16 jar of *f* itself did not get
2Ki 4:41 So he said: Fetch, then, *f*
7:1 a seah measure of fine *f* will
7:16 a seah measure of fine *f*
7:18 a seah measure of fine *f*
1Ch 9:29 over the fine *f* and the wine
12:40 eatables of *f*, cakes of
23:29 for the fine *f* for the grain
Isa 47:2 a hand mill and grind out *f*
Jer 7:18 kneading *f* dough in order to
Eze 16:13 Fine *f* and honey and oil
16:19 fine *f* and oil and honey
46:14 for sprinkling the fine *f*
Ho 8:7 No sprout produces *f*
Mt 13:33 in three large measures of *f*
Lu 13:21 in three large measures of *f*
Re 18:13 fine *f* and wheat and cattle

Flourish
Ps 132:18 upon him his diadem will *f*
Pr 11:28 the righteous ones will *f*
14:11 of the upright ones will *f*

Flourishing
Jer 48:32 own *f* shoots have crossed
Da 4:4 my house and *f* in my palace

Flow
Le 15:25 *f* longer than her menstrual
15:33 *f* of his running discharge
1Ki 18:28 caused blood to *f* out upon
Job 40:11 Let *f* the furious outburst
Ps 78:20 waters might *f* and torrents
105:41 and waters began to *f* out
Isa 48:21 he caused to *f* forth for
Joe 3:18 hills will *f* with milk
3:18 Judah will all *f* with water
Mt 9:20 years from a *f* of blood
Mr 5:25 to a *f* of blood twelve years
Lu 8:43 a *f* of blood for twelve years
8:44 her *f* of blood stopped
Joh 7:38 streams of . . . water will *f*

Flowed
Le 15:3 *f* with a running discharge or
Jg 5:5 Mountains *f* away from the face
La 3:54 Waters have *f* over my head

Flower
Ex 9:31 and the flax had *f* buds
Isa 28:4 fading *f* of its decoration
Jas 1:10 like a *f* of the vegetation
1:11 its *f* drops off and the
1Pe 1:24 and the *f* falls off

Flowers
Ex 25:33 Three cups shaped like *f* of
25:33 cups shaped like *f* of almond
25:34 cups shaped like *f* of almond
37:19 cups shaped like *f* of almond
37:19 cups shaped like *f* of almond
Ex 37:20 cups shaped like *f* of almond
Nu 17:8 blossoming *f* and was bearing

Flowing
Ex 3:8 a land *f* with milk and honey
3:17 land *f* with milk and honey
13:5 a land *f* with milk and honey
33:3 a land *f* with milk and honey
Le 15:25 her blood should be *f* many
20:24 land *f* with milk and honey
Nu 13:27 indeed *f* with milk and honey
14:8 that is *f* with milk and honey
16:13 out of a land *f* with milk
16:14 land *f* with milk and honey
De 6:3 the land *f* with milk and honey
11:9 a land *f* with milk and honey
26:9 a land *f* with milk and honey
26:15 land *f* with milk and honey
27:3 land *f* with milk and honey
Jos 5:6 a land *f* with milk and honey
Ps 19:10 and the *f* honey of the combs
69:2 a *f* stream itself has washed
69:15 *f* stream of waters wash me
Ca 7:9 softly *f* over the lips
Isa 27:12 *f* stream of the River to
47:2 Strip off the *f* skirt
Jer 11:5 land *f* with milk and honey
32:22 land *f* with milk and honey
49:4 your *f* low plain
Eze 20:6 one *f* with milk and honey
20:15 one *f* with milk and honey
Da 7:10 stream of fire *f* and going
Am 5:24 like a constantly *f* torrent
Re 22:1 *f* out from the throne of God

Flowings
Ca 7:5 The king is held bound by the *f*

Flows
De 31:20 which *f* with milk and honey

Fluctuating
Nu 10:5 blow a *f* blast, and the camps
10:6 blow a *f* blast a second time
10:6 blow a *f* blast for each time
10:7 you must not sound a *f* blast

Fluent
Ex 4:10 I am not a *f* speaker, neither

Fluently
Hab 2:2 reading . . . may do so *f*

Flung
De 9:17 two tablets and *f* them down

Flute
1Sa 10:5 tambourine and *f* and harp
Isa 5:12 tambourine and *f*, and wine
30:29 walking with a *f* to enter
Mt 9:23 caught sight of the *f* players
11:17 We played the *f* for you, but
Lu 7:32 We played the *f* for you, but
1Co 14:7 whether a *f* or a harp
14:7 played on the *f* or on the

Flutes
1Ki 1:40 the people were playing on *f*
Jer 48:36 just like *f*; and for the
48:36 boisterous, just like *f*

Flutists
Re 18:22 of *f* and of trumpeters will

Fluttering
Isa 10:14 no one *f* his wings or

Fly
Ge 1:20 flying creatures *f* over the
Job 5:7 As the very sparks *f* upward
20:8 Like a dream he will *f* off
Ps 55:6 I would *f* away and reside
90:10 pass by, and away we *f*
Isa 6:2 with two he would *f* about
11:14 *f* at the shoulder of the
Hab 1:8 *f* like the eagle speeding to
Re 12:14 *f* into the wilderness to her
19:17 birds that *f* in midheaven

Flying
Ge 1:20 let *f* creatures fly over the
1:21 and every winged *f* creature
1:22 let the *f* creatures become
1:26 *f* creatures of the heavens
1:28 the *f* creatures of the heavens
1:30 *f* creature of the heavens
2:19 *f* creature of the heavens
2:20 *f* creatures of the heavens
6:7 to *f* creature of the heavens
6:20 *f* creatures according to
Ge 7:3 *f* creatures of the heavens by
7:8 of the *f* creatures and
7:14 *f* creature of the heavens
7:21 expired, among the *f*
7:23 wiped out . . . *f* creature of
8:7 raven, and it continued *f*
8:17 among the *f* creatures and
8:19 every *f* creature . . . went out
8:20 of all the clean *f* creatures
9:2 upon every *f* creature of the
Le 11:13 loathe among the *f* creatures
11:46 the *f* creature and every
De 14:20 clean *f* creature you may eat
28:26 food for every *f* creature
2Sa 22:11 upon a cherub and came *f*
1Ki 4:33 about the *f* creatures and
Job 28:21 from the *f* creatures of the
35:11 *f* creatures of the heavens
Ps 18:10 upon a cherub and came *f*
78:27 winged *f* creatures just like
104:12 roost the *f* creatures of
Pr 26:2 and just as a swallow for *f*
Ec 10:20 a *f* creature of the heavens
Isa 14:29 will be a *f* fiery snake
30:6 viper and the *f* fiery snake
31:5 Like birds *f*, Jehovah of
60:8 come *f* just like a cloud
Jer 4:25 *f* creatures of the heavens
5:27 cage is full of *f* creatures
7:33 food for the *f* creatures
9:10 the *f* creature of the heavens
12:4 beasts and the *f* creatures
15:3 *f* creatures of the heavens
16:4 as food for the *f* creatures
19:7 as food to the *f* creatures
34:20 *f* creatures of the heavens
Eze 13:20 souls as though they were *f*
13:20 as though they were *f*
29:5 *f* creatures of the heavens
31:6 *f* creatures of the heavens
31:13 *f* creatures of the heavens
32:4 *f* creatures of the heavens to
38:20 *f* creatures of the heavens
44:31 of the *f* creatures
Da 7:6 four wings of a *f* creature on
Ho 2:18 *f* creature of the heavens and
4:3 the *f* creature of the heavens
7:12 *f* creatures of the heavens
9:11 like a *f* creature their glory
Zep 1:3 the *f* creature of the heavens
Zec 5:1 and, look! a *f* scroll
5:2 I am seeing a *f* scroll, the
Re 4:7 creature is like a *f* eagle
8:13 eagle *f* in midheaven say
14:6 angel *f* in midheaven, and he

Foam
Ps 46:3 waters be boisterous, *f* over
Lu 9:39 into convulsions with *f*, and
Jude 13 waves of the sea that *f* up

Foaming
Ps 75:8 wine is *f*, it is full of
Isa 27:2 A vineyard of *f* wine!
Mr 9:20 he kept rolling about, *f*

Foams
Mr 9:18 he *f* and grinds his teeth

Fodder
Ge 24:25 straw and much *f* with us
24:32 giving straw and *f* to the
42:27 opened his sack to give *f* to
43:24 he gave *f* for their asses
Jg 19:19 straw and *f* for our he-asses
Job 6:5 Or a bull low over its *f*
24:6 the field its *f* they harvest
Isa 30:24 eat *f* seasoned with sorrel

Foe
Ps 89:43 treat his sword as a *f*

Foes
Ps 5:8 by reason of my *f*
27:11 on account of my *f*
54:5 will repay the bad to my *f*
56:2 My *f* have kept snapping all
59:10 cause me to look upon my *f*
92:11 my eye will look on my *f*

Foil
1Ki 6:35 and overlaid gold *f* upon the

Fold
Ex 4:6 the upper *f* of your garment
4:6 the upper *f* of his garment
4:7 the upper *f* of your garment
4:7 the upper *f* of his garment

Ex 4:7 the upper *f* of his garment
26:9 *f* double the sixth tent cloth
Joh 10:16 which are not of this *f*

Folding
Pr 6:10 *f* of the hands in lying down
24:33 *f* of the hands to lie down
Ec 4:5 stupid one is *f* his hands and

Folds
Job 41:23 The *f* of its flesh do cling

Foliage
Ps 1:3 the *f* of which does not wither
104:12 among the thick *f* they
Pr 11:28 like *f* the righteous ones
Ca 1:16 Our divan also is one of *f*
Isa 1:30 the *f* of which is withering
Jer 8:13 the *f* itself will certainly
17:8 his *f* will actually prove
Eze 17:6 to turn its *f* inward
17:7 its *f* it thrust out to him
17:23 in the shadow of its *f* they
19:11 of the abundance of its *f*
31:7 in the length of its *f*
31:9 in the abundance of its *f*
31:12 its *f* will certainly fall
Da 4:12 Its *f* was fair, and its fruit
4:14 Shake off its *f*, and scatter
4:21 the *f* of which was fair, and
Mr 11:8 cut down *f* from the fields

Follow
Ex 11:8 the people who *f* your steps
23:2 must not *f* after the crowd
Jos 3:3 your place, and you must *f* it
Jg 3:28 *F* me, because Jehovah has
1Sa 8:3 inclined to *f* unjust profit
12:21 *f* the unrealities that are
13:4 together to *f* Saul to Gilgal
22:20 running away to *f* David
2Sa 20:2 *f* Sheba the son of Bichri
20:11 let him *f* Joab
1Ki 2:28 had inclined to *f* Adonijah
2:28 he had not inclined to *f*
11:2 your heart to *f* their gods
11:4 his heart to *f* other gods
11:6 did not *f* Jehovah fully like
20:10 all the people that *f* me
2Ki 6:19 *F* me, and let me conduct
Ps 94:15 upright in heart will *f* it
Jer 42:16 *f* after you to Egypt
Mt 8:19 Teacher, I will *f* you
9:9 he did rise up and *f* him
9:19 Jesus . . . began to *f* him
10:38 torture stake and *f* after me
16:24 stake and continually *f* me
Mr 5:37 he did not let anyone *f* along
8:34 stake and *f* me continually
10:52 began to *f* him on the road
14:13 will encounter you. *F* him
14:51 began to *f* him nearby; and
Lu 9:23 and *f* me continually
9:57 I will *f* you to wherever you
9:61 I will *f* you, Lord; but first
18:43 began to *f* him, glorifying
22:10 *F* him into the house into
Joh 10:4 sheep *f* him, because they
10:5 by no means *f* but will flee
10:27 know them, and they *f* me
12:26 let him *f* me, and where
13:36 you cannot *f* me now, but
13:36 but you will *f* afterwards
13:37 I cannot *f* you at present
Ro 12:13 *F* the course of hospitality
1Ti 5:15 turned aside to *f* Satan
1Pe 1:11 about the glories to *f* these
2:21 a model for you to *f* his
2Pe 2:2 *f* their acts of loose conduct

Followed
Ge 29:25 it *f* in the morning that
30:25 it *f* that when Rachel had
39:5 it *f* that from the time he
39:15 it *f* that as soon as he heard
39:18 it *f* that as soon as I raised
Nu 32:11 they have not *f* me wholly
32:12 they have *f* Jehovah wholly
De 1:36 he has *f* Jehovah fully
Jos 14:8 I *f* Jehovah my God fully
14:9 you have *f* Jehovah my God
14:14 he *f* Jehovah the God of
Jg 20:42 the battle *f* them up closely
2Sa 15:18 that had *f* him from Gath
Ps 63:8 My soul has closely *f* you
Mt 4:20 abandoning the nets, they *f*
4:22 leaving the boat . . . *f* him
4:25 great crowds *f* him from
8:1 great crowds *f* him
8:23 his disciples *f* him
9:27 two blind men *f* him, crying
12:15 Many also *f* him, and he
14:13 *f* him on foot from the
19:2 crowds *f* him, and he cured
19:27 left all things and *f* you
19:28 you who have *f* me will also
20:29 a great crowd *f* him
20:34 received sight, and they *f*
Mr 1:18 abandoned their nets and *f*
2:14 And rising up he *f* him
3:7 Galilee and from Judea *f* him
6:1 and his disciples *f* him
10:32 those who *f* began to fear
14:54 from a good distance, *f* him
Lu 5:11 abandoned everything and *f*
9:11 getting to know it, *f* him
18:28 left our own things and *f*
22:39 the disciples also *f* him
23:49 had *f* him from Galilee
23:55 *f* along and took a look at
Joh 1:37 two disciples . . . *f* Jesus
1:40 what John said and *f* Jesus
11:31 *f* her, supposing that she
Ac 13:43 *f* Paul and Barnabas, who in
1Co 10:4 rock-mass that *f* them, and
1Ti 4:6 which you have *f* closely
5:10 diligently *f* every good work
2Ti 3:10 have closely *f* my teaching
2Pe 2:15 *f* the path of Balaam, the
Re 13:3 earth *f* the wild beast with
14:8 second angel, *f*, saying: She
14:9 angel, a third, *f* them

Follower
1Sa 11:7 as a *f* of Saul and of Samuel
1Ki 12:20 a *f* of the house of David
Mt 9:9 and he said to him: Be my *f*
19:21 and come be my *f*
Mr 2:14 and he said to him: Be my *f*
10:21 and come be my *f*
Lu 5:27 and he said to him: Be my *f*
9:59 Be my *f*. The man said
18:22 and come be my *f*
Joh 1:43 and said to him: Be my *f*

Followers
1Sa 12:14 prove to be *f* of Jehovah
2Sa 2:10 proved themselves *f* of David
1Ki 1:7 offering help as *f* of Adonijah
16:21 *f* of Tibni the son of Ginath
16:21 the other part *f* of Omri
Mt 22:16 party *f* of Herod, saying
Mr 3:6 with the party *f* of Herod
12:13 of the party *f* of Herod

Following
Ge 13:1 *F* that Abram went up out of
18:5 *F* that, you can pass on
20:14 *F* that Abimelech took sheep
24:61 *f* the man; and the servant
32:19 also all those *f* the droves
45:21 *F* that the sons of Israel did
50:18 *F* that his brothers also
Ex 2:13 went out on the *f* day and
15:1 to say the *f*: Let me sing to
38:21 *f* are the things inventoried
Le 16:3 With the *f* Aaron should come
26:16 I . . . shall do the *f*
Nu 14:24 he kept *f* wholly after me
14:43 turned back from *f* Jehovah
15:39 *f* your hearts and your eyes
15:39 are *f* in immoral intercourse
32:15 turn back from *f* him, he
De 7:4 will turn your son from *f* me
24:20 go over its boughs *f* up
24:21 leftovers *f* up yourself
27:12 The *f* are the ones who will
27:13 the *f* are the ones who will
Jos 5:12 manna ceased on the *f* day
6:8 ark . . . was *f* them
6:9 the rear guard was *f* the Ark
6:13 the rear guard was *f* the ark
22:16 turning back . . . from *f*
22:18 today from *f* Jehovah; and
22:23 turn back from *f* Jehovah
22:29 from *f* Jehovah by building
Jg 2:12 *f* other gods from among the
3:28 they went *f* him and got to
4:10 men went on up *f* his steps
8:5 the people that are *f* my steps
9:49 and went *f* Abimelech
20:45 kept *f* closely after them as
Ru 2:2 *f* after whoever it is in whose
1Sa 6:7 go back home from *f* them
12:20 turn aside from *f* Jehovah
13:7 people trembled while *f* him
14:46 Saul withdrew from *f* the
15:11 has turned back from *f* me
24:1 Saul returned from *f* the
2Sa 2:19 or to the left from *f* Abner
2:21 to turn aside from *f* him
2:22 your course aside from *f* me
2:26 back from *f* their brothers
2:27 each one from *f* his brother
2:30 turned back from *f* Abner and
7:8 from *f* the flock to become a
11:8 courtesy gift went out *f* him
11:12 and the day *f*
15:1 *f* such things that Absalom
17:9 people that are *f* Absalom
20:2 began to go up from *f* David
20:13 *f* Joab to chase after Sheba
1Ki 1:35 And you must come up *f* him
1:40 the people came on up *f* him
9:6 turn back from *f* me and not
13:14 *f* the man of the true God
16:22 people that were *f* Omri
16:22 people that were *f* Tibni
18:18 you went *f* the Baals
18:21 the true God, go *f* him
18:21 but if Baal is, go *f* him
19:20 Then I will go *f* you
19:21 he returned from *f* him and
19:21 went *f* Elijah and began to
22:33 came back from *f* him
2Ki 3:9 that were *f* their steps
7:15 *f* them as far as the Jordan
10:29 not turn aside from *f* that
17:15 went *f* vain idols and
17:21 part Israel from *f* Jehovah
18:6 not turn aside from *f* him
1Ch 17:7 from *f* the flock to become a
29:21 on the day *f* that day, a
2Ch 11:16 *f* them from all the tribes
18:32 came back from *f* him
25:27 turned aside from *f* Jehovah
34:31 to go *f* Jehovah and to keep
34:33 *f* Jehovah the God of their
Job 34:27 turned aside from *f* him
Ps 78:71 *f* the females giving suck
109:13 *f* generation let their name
Jer 3:19 from *f* me you people will
17:16 being a shepherd *f* you
20:3 on the *f* day that Pashhur
Eze 14:7 withdraws himself from *f*
14:11 go wandering off from *f* me
41:21 like the *f* appearance
Ho 1:2 turns from *f* Jehovah
Joe 1:3 their sons to the *f* generation
Am 7:15 take me from *f* the flock
Zep 1:6 drawing back from *f* Jehovah
Zec 2:8 *F* after the glory he has sent
Mt 8:10 said to those *f* him: I tell
8:22 Keep *f* me, and let the dead
21:9 and those *f* kept crying out
26:58 Peter kept *f* him at a good
Mr 2:15 and sinners . . . began *f* him
5:24 a great crowd was *f* him and
10:28 left all things . . . *f* you
Lu 5:28 he rose up and went *f* him
7:9 turned to the crowd *f* him and
7:11 Closely *f* this he traveled
9:49 because he is not *f* with us
13:33 and tomorrow and the *f* day
22:54 Peter was *f* at a distance
23:27 *f* him a great multitude of
Joh 1:38 getting a view of them *f*
6:2 a great crowd kept *f* him
18:15 disciple was *f* Jesus
20:6 Simon Peter also came *f* him
21:19 to him: Continue *f* me
21:20 whom Jesus used to love *f*
21:22 You continue *f* me
Ac 12:8 garment on and keep *f* me
12:9 kept *f* him, but he did not
13:42 to them on the *f* sabbath
16:11 but on the *f* day to Neapolis
16:17 girl kept *f* Paul and us and
20:15 *f* day we arrived at Miletus
21:18 *f* day Paul went in with us
21:36 the people kept *f*, crying out
23:11 the *f* night the Lord stood by
27:18 *f* day they began to lighten
2Pe 1:16 *f* artfully contrived false
Re 6:8 And Hades was closely *f* him
14:4 *f* the Lamb no matter where
19:14 *f* him on white horses, and

Follows
Ge 45:23 to his father he sent as *f*
Ezr 4:8 to Artaxerxes the king, as *f*
Joh 8:12 *f* me will by no means walk
Ro 6:15 What *f*? Shall we commit a
9:9 promise was as *f*: At this
10:17 So faith *f* the thing heard
1Co 9:3 My defense to . . . as *f*
Heb 4:4 as *f*: And God rested on the

Folly
Ge 34:7 a disgraceful *f* against Israel
De 22:21 a disgraceful *f* in Israel
Jos 7:15 a disgraceful *f* in Israel
Jg 19:23 commit this disgraceful *f*
20:6 and disgraceful *f* in Israel
20:10 all the disgraceful *f* that
2Sa 13:12 not do this disgraceful *f*
Job 42:8 commit disgraceful *f* with
Ec 1:17 I have come to know *f*, that
2:3 lay hold on *f* until I could see
2:12 see wisdom and madness and *f*
2:13 for wisdom than for *f*, just

Fond
Ge 27:4 tasty dish such as I am *f* of
27:9 tasty dish . . . such as he is *f*
27:14 such as his father was *f* of
Ps 119:24 reminders are what I am *f*
119:70 been *f* of your own law
119:77 your law is what I am *f* of
119:92 not been what I am *f* of
119:143 commandments I was *f* of
119:174 And your law I am *f* of
Pr 8:30 one he was specially *f* of
8:31 things I was *f* of were with
Isa 5:7 plantation of which he was *f*
Joh 12:25 He that is *f* of his soul
15:19 *f* of what is its own

Fondle
Ps 94:19 consolations began to *f* my

Fondled
Isa 66:12 the knees you will be *f*

Fondly
Jer 31:20 or a *f* treated child

Fondness
Ps 119:16 statutes I shall show a *f*
119:47 a *f* for your commandments

Food
Ge 1:29 To you let it serve as *f*
1:30 all green vegetation for *f*
2:9 good for *f* and also the tree
3:6 that the tree was good for *f*
6:21 for yourself every sort of *f*
6:21 it must serve as *f* for you
9:3 may serve as *f* for you
14:11 and all their *f* and went on
43:2 Return, buy a little *f* for us
43:4 go down and buy *f* for you
43:20 down at the start to buy *f*
43:22 And more money . . . to buy *f*
44:1 *f* to the extent they are able
44:25 buy a little *f* for us
45:11 I will supply you with *f*
47:24 seed for the field and as *f*
50:21 your little children with *f*
Ex 16:15 Jehovah has given you for *f*
Le 3:11 it smoke on the altar as *f*
3:16 smoke upon the altar as *f*, an
11:34 Any sort of *f* that may be
11:39 beast that is yours for *f*
19:23 plant any tree for *f*, you
25:6 serve you people for *f*, for
25:37 not give your *f* out on usury
De 2:6 *f* you may buy from them for
2:28 *f* you will sell me for money
20:20 you know is not a tree for *f*
23:19 pay . . . interest on *f*
28:26 *f* for every flying creature
Jg 1:7 picking up *f* under my table
Ru 2:18 took out what *f* she had left
1Sa 28:20 not eaten *f* the whole day
2Sa 9:10 *f* for those belonging to the
19:32 supplied the king with *f*
19:33 certainly supply you with *f*
20:3 kept on supplying *f* to them
1Ki 4:7 and his household with *f*
4:7 the *f* one month in the year
4:22 Solomon's *f* for each day
4:27 supplied *f* to King Solomon
5:9 giving the *f* for my household
5:11 *f* supplies for his household
1Ki 10:5 and the *f* of his table and
17:4 command to supply you *f*
17:9 a widow, to supply you *f*
1Ch 12:40 bringing *f* upon asses and
2Ch 2:10 wheat as *f* for your servants
9:4 *f* of his table and the sitting
11:11 supplies of *f* and oil and
11:23 gave them *f* in abundance
Ne 5:3 get grain during the *f* shortage
9:21 with *f* in the wilderness
9:25 olive groves and trees for *f*
Es 2:9 massages and her appropriate *f*
Job 3:24 For before my *f* my sighing
6:7 They are like disease in my *f*
12:11 As the palate tastes *f*
20:14 His *f* itself will certainly
24:5 their activity, looking for *f*
27:14 will not have enough *f*
28:5 the earth, out of it *f* goes
30:4 broom trees was their *f*
31:31 satisfied from *f* of his
33:20 his own soul desirable *f*
36:31 He gives *f* in abundance
38:41 prepares for the raven its *f*
39:29 there it has to search for *f*
Ps 42:3 tears have become *f* day and
69:21 *f* they gave me a poisonous
74:14 give it as *f* to the people
78:30 *f* was yet in their mouth
79:2 *f* to the fowls of the heavens
102:4 have forgotten to eat my *f*
104:14 *f* to go forth from the
104:21 seeking their *f* from God
104:27 them their *f* in its season
107:18 detest even every sort of *f*
109:10 look for *f* from their
111:5 *F* he has given to those
127:2 you are eating *f* with pains
136:25 One giving *f* to all flesh
145:15 their *f* in its season
147:9 beasts he is giving their *f*
Pr 6:8 prepares its *f* even in the
6:8 *f* supplies even in the harvest
13:23 yields a great deal of *f*
22:9 given of his *f* to the lowly
23:3 as it is the *f* of lies
23:6 *f* of anyone of ungenerous eye
27:27 of goats' milk for your *f*
27:27 for the *f* of your household
28:3 away so that there is no *f*
30:8 the *f* prescribed for me
30:22 he has his sufficiency of *f*
30:25 summer they prepare their *f*
31:14 far away she brings in her *f*
31:15 gives *f* to her household and
Ec 9:7 eat your *f* with rejoicing and
9:11 nor do the wise . . . have the *f*
Isa 9:5 for burning as *f* for fire
9:19 become as *f* for the fire
62:8 no more give your grain as *f*
65:25 serpent, his *f* will be dust
Jer 7:33 *f* for the flying creatures
11:19 to ruin the tree with its *f*
16:4 as *f* for the flying creatures
19:7 give their dead bodies as *f*
34:20 *f* for the flying creatures
40:5 gave him a *f* allowance and
Eze 4:10 that you will eat will be
23:37 the fire to them as *f*
29:5 I will give you for *f*
33:27 certainly give him for *f*
34:5 became *f* for every wild
34:8 *f* for every wild beast of
34:10 will not become *f* for them
35:12 they have been given for *f*
39:4 I will give you for *f*
47:12 all sorts of trees for *f*
47:12 must prove to be for *f*
Da 1:10 appointed your *f* and your
4:12 and there was *f* for all on it
4:21 on which there was *f* for all
Ho 11:4 gently I brought *f* to each one
Joe 1:16 Has not *f* itself been cut off
Ob 7 Those eating *f* with you will
Jon 3:7 None should take *f*
Hab 1:16 and his *f* is healthful
3:17 the terraces . . . produce no *f*
Hag 2:12 wine or oil or any sort of *f*
Zec 11:16 he will not supply with *f*
Mal 1:12 to be despised, its *f*
3:10 come to be *f* in my house
Mt 3:4 his *f* too was insect locusts
6:25 the soul mean more than *f*
10:10 or a *f* pouch for the trip
Mt 10:10 the worker deserves his *f*
24:7 there will be *f* shortages and
24:45 their *f* at the proper time
Mr 6:8 no *f* pouch, no copper money in
13:8 there will be *f* shortages
Lu 9:3 neither staff nor *f* pouch
10:4 a purse, nor a *f* pouch, nor
12:23 soul is worth more than *f*
12:42 their measure of *f* supplies
21:11 pestilences and *f* shortages
22:35 without purse and *f* pouch
22:36 likewise also a *f* pouch
Joh 4:32 I have *f* to eat of which
4:34 My *f* is for me to do the
6:27 not for the *f* that perishes
6:27 the *f* that remains for life
6:55 for my flesh is true *f*, and
Ac 2:46 and partook of *f* with great
6:2 to distribute *f* to tables
9:19 he took *f* and gained strength
12:20 with *f* from that of the king
14:17 to the full with *f* and good
20:11 began the meal and took *f*
23:14 not to take a bite of *f* until
27:21 long abstinence from *f*
27:33 one and all to take some *f*
27:33 are continuing without *f*
27:34 you to take some *f*, for
27:36 began taking some *f*
27:38 had been satisfied with *f*
Ro 14:15 if because of *f* your brother
14:15 by your *f* ruin that one for
14:20 just for the sake of *f*
1Co 8:7 eat *f* as something sacrificed
8:8 *f* will not commend us to God
8:13 *f* makes my brother stumble
10:3 ate the same spiritual *f*
2Co 6:5 by times without *f*
11:27 abstinence from *f* many
2Th 3:8 nor did we eat *f* . . . free
3:12 eat *f* they themselves earn
Heb 5:12 as need milk, not solid *f*
5:14 solid *f* belongs to mature
Jas 2:15 the *f* sufficient for the day
Re 6:8 *f* shortage and with deadly

Foods
Mr 7:19 Thus he declared all *f* clean
1Co 6:13 *F* for the belly, and the
6:13 and the belly for *f*; but God
8:1 concerning *f* offered to idols
8:4 eating of *f* offered to idols
8:10 eating *f* offered to idols
1Ti 4:3 commanding to abstain from *f*
Heb 9:10 *f* and drinks and various

Foodstuff
Eze 27:17 special *f* and honey and oil

Foodstuffs
Ge 41:35 *f* of these coming good years
41:35 as *f* in the cities, and they
41:36 the *f* must serve as a supply
41:48 he kept collecting all the *f*
41:48 he would put the *f* in the
41:48 The *f* of the field that was
42:7 the land of Canaan to buy *f*
42:10 servants have come to buy *f*
Lu 9:13 buy *f* for all these people
Joh 4:8 off into the city to buy *f*
Ac 7:12 Jacob heard there were *f* in

Fool
Jg 14:15 *F* your husband that he may
16:5 *F* him and see in what his
2Sa 3:25 to *f* you that he came and to
1Ki 22:20 *f* Ahab, that he may go up
22:21 I myself shall *f* him
22:22 he said, You will *f* him
2Ch 18:19 Who will *f* Ahab the king
18:20 I myself shall *f* him
18:21 You will *f* him, and, what
Ps 78:36 to *f* him with their mouth
102:8 Those making a *f* of me have
Mt 5:22 says, You despicable *f*! will
1Co 3:18 let him become a *f*, that he

Fooled
Jer 20:7 You have *f* me, O Jehovah
20:7 O Jehovah, so that I was *f*
20:10 Perhaps he will be *f*, so
Eze 14:9 prophet, in case he gets *f*
14:9 Jehovah, have *f* that prophet

Foolish
Jg 19:24 do this disgraceful, *f* thing
Job 5:2 the *f* one vexation will kill

Job 5:3 seen the *f* one taking root
Ps 75:4 I said to the *f* ones: Do not
75:4 Do not be *f*
107:17 *f*, due to the way of their
Pr 7:22 the discipline of a *f* man
10:8 one *f* with his lips will be
10:10 one *f* with his lips will
10:14 mouth of the *f* one is near
10:21 *f* themselves keep dying
11:29 *f* person will be a servant
12:15 *f* one is right in his own
12:16 *f* person that makes known
14:1 *f* one tears it down with her
14:3 in the mouth of the *f* one
14:9 *F* are those who make a
15:5 *f* disrespects the discipline
16:22 the discipline of the *f* ones
17:28 *f*, when keeping silent, will
20:3 everyone *f* will burst out in
24:7 *f* one true wisdom is too high
24:28 have to be *f* with your lips
27:3 the vexation by someone *f* is
27:22 pound the *f* one fine with a
29:9 into judgment with a *f* man
Ec 2:19 he will prove to be wise or *f*
7:17 overmuch, nor become *f*
10:3 way the *f* one is walking, his
10:3 says to everybody that he is *f*
10:14 the *f* one speaks many words
Isa 19:11 princes of Zoan are indeed *f*
35:8 *f* ones will wander about on
Jer 4:22 For my people is *f*
Ho 9:7 The prophet will be *f*, the man
Mt 7:26 will be likened to a *f* man
25:2 Five of them were *f*, and
25:3 the *f* took their lamps but
25:8 *f* said to the discreet, Give
Ro 1:22 were wise, they became *f*
1Co 1:20 the wisdom of the world *f*
1:25 a *f* thing of God is wiser
1:27 God chose the *f* things of the
Eph 5:4 nor *f* talking nor obscene
2Ti 2:23 *f* and ignorant questionings
Tit 3:9 But shun *f* questionings and

Foolishly
Ge 31:28 Now you have acted *f*
Nu 12:11 sin in which we have acted *f*
1Sa 13:13 You have acted *f*
26:21 I have acted *f* and am very
2Sa 24:10 for I have acted very *f*
1Ch 21:8 for I have acted very *f*
2Ch 16:9 acted *f* respecting this, for
Isa 19:13 of Zoan have acted *f*, the
Jer 5:4 They acted *f*, for they have
50:36 they will certainly act *f*

Foolishness
2Sa 15:31 counsel of Ahithophel into *f*
Ps 38:5 festered, Because of my *f*
69:5 have come to know my *f*
Pr 5:23 of his *f* he goes astray
12:23 is one that calls out *f*
13:16 stupid will spread abroad *f*
14:8 *f* of stupid ones is deception
14:17 quick to anger . . . commit *f*
14:18 take possession of *f*, but the
14:24, 24 *f* of the stupid ones is *f*
14:29 is impatient is exalting *f*
15:2 bubbles forth with *f*
15:14 stupid . . . aspires to *f*
15:21 *F* is a rejoicing to one who
16:22 of the foolish ones is *f*
17:12 than anyone stupid in his *f*
18:13 that is *f* on his part and a
19:3 the *f* of an earthling man
22:15 *F* is tied up with the heart
24:9 The loose conduct of *f* is sin
26:4 stupid according to his *f*
26:5 stupid according to his *f*
26:11 stupid one is repeating his *f*
27:22 *f* will not depart from him
Ec 7:25 and the *f* of madness
10:1 a little *f* does to one who is
10:6 *F* has been put in many high
10:13 the words of his mouth is *f*
Isa 44:25 their knowledge into *f*
1Co 1:18 is *f* to those who are
1:21 *f* of what is preached to
1:23 but to the nations *f*
2:14 for they are *f* to him; and
3:19 wisdom of this world is *f*

Fools
Pr 1:7 are what mere *f* have despised
Mt 23:17 *F* and blind ones! Which, in
1Co 4:10 We are *f* because of Christ

Foot
Ge 8:9 for the sole of its *f*, and so
22:9 bound Isaac his son hand and *f*
35:8 buried at the *f* of Bethel
41:44 lift up his hand or his *f*
Ex 12:37 able-bodied men on *f*
21:24, 24 hand for hand, *f* for *f*
24:4 at the *f* of the mountain an
29:20 the big toe of their right *f*
32:19 at the *f* of the mountain
Le 8:23 the big toe of his right *f*
8:24 the big toe of their right *f*
14:14 the big toe of his right *f*
14:17 the big toe of his right *f*
14:25 the big toe of his right *f*
14:28 the big toe of his right *f*
21:19 to be a fracture of the *f* or
Nu 11:21 hundred thousand men on *f*
22:25 squeeze Balaam's *f* against
De 2:5 the width of the sole of the *f*
8:4 nor did your *f* become swollen
11:10 to do irrigating with your *f*
11:24 sole of your *f* will tread
19:21, 21 hand for hand, *f* for *f*
25:9 draw his sandal off his *f* and
28:35 from the sole of your *f* to
28:56 set the sole of her *f* upon
28:65 for the sole of your *f*
29:5 did not wear out upon your *f*
32:35 their *f* will move unsteadily
33:24 one dipping his *f* in oil
Jos 1:3 the sole of your *f* will tread
14:9 upon which your *f* has trod
Jg 4:15 and took to flight on *f*
4:17 he fled on *f* to the tent of
5:15 he was sent on *f*. Among the
20:2 men on *f* who drew the sword
1Sa 4:10 thirty thousand men on *f*
15:4 hundred thousand men on *f*
23:22 place where his *f* comes to
2Sa 8:4 twenty thousand men on *f*
10:6 twenty thousand men on *f*
14:25 sole of his *f* to the crown
1Ki 20:29 hundred thousand men on *f*
2Ki 13:7 and ten thousand men on *f*
21:8 the *f* of Israel wander from
1Ch 18:4 and twenty thousand men on *f*
19:18 and forty thousand men on *f*
2Ch 33:8 not remove the *f* of Israel
Job 2:7 boil from the sole of his *f*
23:11 steps my *f* has laid hold
28:4 forgotten far from the *f*
31:5 my *f* hastens to deception
39:15 that some *f* may crush them
Ps 9:15 their own *f* has been caught
26:12 *f* will certainly stand on a
36:11 may not the *f* of haughtiness
38:16 When my *f* moved unsteadily
66:6 they went crossing over on *f*
66:9 not allowed our *f* to totter
68:23 you may wash your *f* in blood
91:12 strike your *f* against any
94:18 My *f* will certainly move
116:8 my *f* from stumbling
119:105 word is a lamp to my *f*
121:3 allow your *f* to totter
Pr 1:15 Hold back your *f* from their
3:23 your *f* will not strike
3:26 keep your *f* against capture
4:26 out the course of your *f*, and
4:27 your *f* from what is bad
6:13 making signs with his *f*
25:17 your *f* rare at the house of
25:19 and a wobbling *f* is the
Isa 1:6 sole of the *f* even to the head
26:6 *f* will trample it down
58:13 turn back your *f* as regards
Jer 2:25 Hold your *f* back from
38:22 *f* to sink down into the
Eze 1:7 the sole of the *f* of a calf
6:11 stamp with your *f*, and say
29:11 the *f* of earthling man, nor
29:11 the *f* of domestic animal
32:13 and the *f* of earthling man
Mt 4:6 no time strike your *f* against
14:13 followed him on *f* from the
18:8 your *f* is making you stumble
22:13 Bind him hand and *f* and
Mr 6:33 they ran there together on *f*
9:45 if your *f* makes you stumble
Lu 4:11 strike your *f* against a stone
Ac 20:13 was intending to go on *f*
Ac 21:4 told Paul not to set *f* in
1Co 12:15 If the *f* should say: Because
Re 10:2 he set his right *f* upon the

Footbreadth
Ac 7:5 possession in it, no, not a *f*

Footmen
Jer 12:5 Because with *f* you have run

Footprints
Ps 77:19 *f* have not come to be known
89:51 *f* of your anointed one
Ca 1:8 yourself in the *f* of the flock
Ho 6:8 harmful; their *f* are blood

Footsteps
Ps 17:5 *f* will certainly not be made
44:18 our *f* deviate from your path
Ro 4:12 in the *f* of that faith while
2Co 12:18 In the same *f*, did we not?

Footstool
1Ch 28:2 and as the *f* of our God, and
2Ch 9:18 *f* in gold to the throne
Ps 99:5 bow down yourselves at his *f*
132:7 Let us bow down at his *f*
Isa 66:1 and the earth is my *f*
La 2:1 not remembered his *f* in the
Mt 5:35 it is the *f* of his feet
Ac 7:49 and the earth is my *f*
Jas 2:3 that seat there under my *f*

Forasmuch
Da 2:8 *f* as you have perceived that
2:10 *f* as no grand king or governor
2:40 *F* as iron is crushing and
2:41 *f* as you beheld the iron
2:45 *f* as you beheld that out of
3:29 *f* as there does not exist
4:18 *f* as all the other wise men
5:12 *f* as an extraordinary spirit
6:3 *f* as an extraordinary spirit
6:4 *f* as he was trustworthy and no
6:22 *f* as before him innocence
Ro 11:13 *F* as I am, in reality, an
1Pe 4:13 *f* as you are sharers in the
2Pe 1:3 *f* as his divine power has

Forbade
Nu 30:5 because her father *f* her

Forbearance
Ro 2:4 riches of his kindness and *f*
3:25 while God was exercising *f*

Forbid
Ac 10:47 anyone *f* water so that these
24:23 he *f* no one of his people
1Co 14:39 do not *f* the speaking in

Forbidden
Nu 30:5 if her father has *f* her on the
30:11 her husband . . . has not *f* her
Ac 16:6 *f* by the holy spirit to speak

Forbidding
Lu 23:2 and *f* the paying of taxes to
1Ti 4:3 *f* to marry, commanding to

Forbids
Nu 30:8 if her husband . . . *f* her

Force
Ge 1:2 God's active *f* was moving to
6:17 flesh in which the *f* of life
7:15 flesh in which the *f* of life
7:22 breath of the *f* of life
De 6:5 your soul and all your vital *f*
27:26 the words of this law in *f*
Jos 6:7 war-equipped *f* should pass on
6:9 the war-equipped *f* was going
6:13 war-equipped *f* was walking
Jg 21:21 carry off for yourselves by *f*
1Sa 2:16 I shall have to take it by *f*
13:17 And the *f* of pillagers
14:15 *f* of pillagers trembled
2Sa 8:9 the military *f* of Hadadezer
1Ki 20:25 number a military *f* for
20:25 equal to the military *f*
2Ki 6:14 a heavy military *f* there
6:15 military *f* was surrounding
7:6 sound of a great military *f*
9:5 the chiefs of the military *f*
11:15 ones of the military *f*
18:17 military *f* to Jerusalem
23:25 and with all his vital *f*
25:1 all his military *f*, against
25:5 a military *f* of Chaldeans
25:5 military *f* was scattered
25:10 military *f* of Chaldeans

1Ch 18:9 the military *f* of Hadadezer
20:1 the combat *f* of the army
2Ch 13:3 military *f* of four hundred
14:8 military *f* bearing the large
14:9 military *f* of a million men
16:7 military *f* of the king of
16:8 military *f* in multitude, in
23:14 ones of the military *f*, and
24:23 military *f* of Syria came up
24:24 military *f* of the Syrians
24:24 military *f* of very great
26:11 a *f* engaging in war, those
26:13 power of a military *f* to
33:14 chiefs of the military *f* in
Ezr 4:23 stopped them by *f* of arms
8:22 a military *f* and horsemen
Ne 2:9 chiefs of the military *f* and
4:2 the military *f* of Samaria
Es 1:3 military *f* of Persia and Media
8:11 all the *f* of the people and
Job 15:4 fear before God to have no *f*
Ps 10:9 carry off . . . one by *f*
10:9 the afflicted one by *f* when
110:3 the day of your military *f*
136:15 military *f* into the Red Sea
140:7 in the day of the armed *f*
Isa 28:2 down to the earth with *f*
36:2 with a heavy military *f*
43:17 military *f* and the strong
Jer 34:1 and all his military *f* and
35:11 military *f* of the Chaldeans
35:11 military *f* of the Syrians
37:5 military *f* of Pharaoh that
37:7 military *f* of Pharaoh that
37:10 military *f* of the Chaldeans
37:11 military *f* of the Chaldeans
37:11 the military *f* of Pharaoh
38:3 military *f* of the king of
39:1 all his military *f* came to
39:5 military *f* of the Chaldeans
46:2 military *f* of Pharaoh Necho
52:4 he and all his military *f*
52:8 military *f* of the Chaldeans
52:8 military *f* was scattered
Eze 17:17 by a great military *f* and
27:10 to be in your military *f*
27:11 even your military *f*, were
29:18 military *f* perform a great
29:18 his military *f* from Tyre
29:19 wages for his military *f*
32:31 and all his military *f* will
37:10 very, very great military *f*
38:4 your military *f*, horses and
38:15 even a numerous military *f*
46:18 *f* them out of their
Da 3:20 who were in his military *f* he
9:27 covenant in *f* for the many
11:7 come to the military *f* and
11:13 with a great military *f* and
11:25 with a great military *f*; and
11:25 great and mighty military *f*
11:26 military *f*, it will be
Joe 2:11 voice before his military *f*
2:25 military *f* that I have sent
Ob 11 his military *f* into captivity
Zec 4:6 Not by a military *f*, nor by
9:4 strike down her military *f*
Ac 6:12 they took him by *f* and led
23:10 commanded the *f* of soldiers
23:27 with a *f* of soldiers and
26:11 *f* them to make a recantation
1Co 14:11 the *f* of the speech sound
Eph 4:23 in the *f* actuating your mind
Heb 9:17 in *f* at any time while the
11:34 stayed the *f* of fire
Jas 5:16 it is at work, has much *f*

Forced
Ge 49:15 subject to slavish *f* labor
Ex 1:11 over them chiefs of *f* labor
De 20:11 become yours for *f* labor
Jos 16:10 subject to slavish *f* labor
17:13 the Canaanites at *f* labor
Jg 1:28 Canaanites to *f* labor, and
1:30 to be subject to *f* labor
1:33 became theirs for *f* labor
1:35 they were *f* into task work
2Sa 20:24 conscripted for *f* labor
23:16 *f* their way into the camp
1Ki 4:6 those conscripted for *f* labor
5:13 those conscripted for *f* labor
5:13 those conscripted for *f* labor
5:14 those conscripted for *f* labor
9:15 conscripted for *f* labor that
1Ki 9:21 for slavish *f* labor until
12:18 conscripted for *f* labor
1Ch 11:18 three *f* their way into the
2Ch 8:8 men for *f* labor until this
10:18 conscripted for *f* labor
21:17 into Judah and *f* it open
Es 10:1 lay *f* labor upon the land and
Pr 12:24 come to be for *f* labor
Isa 31:8 come to be for *f* labor
59:14 justice was *f* to move back
La 1:1 has come to be for *f* labor
Ac 7:19 *f* the fathers to expose their

Forceful
2Co 10:10 letters are weighty and *f*

Forcefulness
Es 9:29 write with all *f* to confirm
Da 11:17 the *f* of his entire kingdom

Forces
Ge 14:15 he resorted to dividing his *f*
Ex 14:4 military *f*; and the Egyptians
14:9 military *f* were overtaking
14:17 military *f*, his war chariots
14:28 all of Pharaoh's military *f*
15:4 military *f* he has cast into
Nu 31:14 men of the combat *f*, the
De 11:4 to the military *f* of Egypt
1Sa 17:20 military *f* were going out
2Sa 24:2 the chief of the military *f*
24:4 the chiefs of the military *f*
24:4 the chiefs of the military *f*
1Ki 15:20 chiefs of the military *f*
20:1 his military *f* together
20:19 military *f* that were behind
2Ki 25:23 chiefs of the military *f*
25:26 chiefs of the military *f*
1Ch 11:26 men of the military *f*
2Ch 16:4 chiefs of the military *f*
17:2 put military *f* in all the
26:13 army *f* were three hundred
Ps 33:16 the abundance of military *f*
Jer 32:2 military *f* of the king of
34:7 military *f* of the king of
34:21 military *f* of the king of
40:7 chiefs of the military *f*
40:13 *f* who were in the field
41:11 military *f* who were with
41:13 chiefs of the military *f*
41:16 chiefs of the military *f*
42:1 chiefs of the military *f* and
42:8 chiefs of the military *f*
43:4 chiefs of the military *f* and
43:5 chiefs of the military *f*
52:14 military *f* of the Chaldeans
Da 11:10 crowd of large military *f*
Eph 6:12 against the wicked spirit *f*

Forcibly
Isa 22:17 and grasping you *f*
Ac 19:29 taking *f* along with them

Ford
Ge 32:22 crossed over the *f* of Jabbok
2Sa 19:18 he crossed the *f* to conduct
Isa 10:29 have passed over the *f*

Fords
Jos 2:7 of the Jordan at the *f*, and
Jg 3:28 capture the *f* of the Jordan
12:5 to capture the *f* of the Jordan
12:6 at the *f* of the Jordan
2Sa 15:28 by the *f* of the wilderness
Isa 16:2 become at the *f* of Arnon
Jer 51:32 *f* themselves have been

Fore
Ro 3:5 God's righteousness to the *f*

Forefather
Ge 10:21 Shem, the *f* of all the sons
Jos 19:47 to the name of Dan their *f*
24:3 I took your *f* Abraham from
1Sa 2:27 to the house of your *f* while
2:28 give to the house of your *f*
2:30 and the house of your *f*, they
2:31 arm of the house of your *f*
1Ki 15:3 the heart of David his *f*
15:11 like David his *f*
15:24 the city of David his *f*
22:50 in the city of David his *f*
2Ki 14:3 only not like David his *f*
15:38 in the city of David his *f*
16:2 like David his *f*
18:3 that David his *f* had done
20:5 the God of David your *f*
22:2 all the way of David his *f*
1Ch 24:19 by the hand of Aaron their *f*
2Ch 17:3 former ways of David his *f*
21:12 God of David your *f* has said
28:1 like David his *f*
29:2 that David his *f* had done
34:2 in the ways of David his *f*
34:3 for the God of David his *f*
Isa 38:5 the God of David your *f* has
58:14 possession of Jacob your *f*
Jer 35:6 our *f*, was the one that laid
35:8 *f* in everything that he
35:10 Jonadab our *f* commanded us
35:14 commandment of their *f*
35:16 the commandment of their *f*
35:18 of Jehonadab your *f* and
Lu 1:73 he swore to Abraham our *f*
Joh 4:12 not greater than our *f* Jacob
Ac 4:25 our *f* David, your servant
7:2 appeared to our *f* Abraham
Ro 4:1 Abraham our *f* according to
9:10 the one man, Isaac our *f*
Heb 7:10 still in the loins of his *f*

Forefathers
Ge 15:15 go to your *f* in peace; you
46:34 both we and our *f*, in order
47:3 herders . . . both we and our *f*
48:21 you to the land of your *f*
Ex 3:13 God of your *f* has sent me to
3:15 Jehovah the God of your *f*, the
3:16 God of your *f* has appeared to
4:5 Jehovah the God of their *f*
13:5 swore to your *f* to give you
13:11 sworn to you and to your *f*
Le 25:41 to the possession of his *f*
Nu 11:12 you swore to their *f*
36:7 the inheritance . . . of his *f*
36:8 of the inheritance of his *f*
De 1:11 May Jehovah the God of your *f*
1:21 Jehovah the God of your *f* has
4:1 the God of your *f* is giving you
4:31 forget the covenant of your *f*
4:37 he loved your *f* so that he
5:3 It was not with our *f* that
6:3 Jehovah the God of your *f* has
6:10 he swore to your *f* Abraham
6:18 Jehovah has sworn to your *f*
6:23 which he had sworn to our *f*
7:8 he had sworn to your *f*, that
7:12 which he swore to your *f*
7:13 he swore to your *f* to give
8:1 which Jehovah swore to your *f*
8:18 that he swore to your *f*
9:5 Jehovah swore to your *f*
10:11 sworn to their *f* to give to
10:15 Only to your *f* did Jehovah
10:22 your *f* went down into Egypt
11:9 swore to your *f* to give to
11:21 Jehovah swore to your *f* to
12:1 Jehovah the God of your *f*
13:6 neither you nor your *f*
13:17 as he has sworn to your *f*
19:8 he swore to your *f*, and he
19:8 he promised to give to your *f*
26:3 swore to our *f* to give to us
26:7 to Jehovah the God of our *f*
26:15 just as you swore to our *f*
27:3 the God of your *f* has spoken
28:11 swore to your *f* to give you
28:36 neither you nor your *f*
28:64 neither you nor your *f*
29:13 sworn to your *f* Abraham
29:25 Jehovah the God of their *f*
30:9 as he exulted over your *f*
30:20 *f* Abraham, Isaac and Jacob
31:7 swore to their *f* to give to
31:16 are lying down with your *f*
31:20 have sworn about to their *f*
32:17 With whom your *f* were not
Jos 1:6 swore to their *f* to give to
5:6 Jehovah had sworn to their *f*
18:3 the God of your *f* has given
21:43 sworn to give to their *f*
21:44 he had sworn to their *f*
24:2 your *f* dwelt a long time
24:14 gods that your *f* served on
24:15 gods that your *f* who were
Jg 2:1 about which I swore to your *f*
2:17 the way in which their *f* had
2:20 that I commanded their *f* and
1Sa 12:6 *f* up out of the land of Egypt
12:7 with you and with your *f*
12:8 *f* began calling to Jehovah
12:8 lead your *f* out from Egypt

2Sa 7:12 lie down with your *f*, then
17:23 the burial place of his *f*
1Ki 1:21 king lies down with his *f*
2:10 David lay down with his *f*
8:21 concluded with our *f* when he
8:34 that you gave to their *f*
8:40 ground that you gave to our *f*
8:48 land that you gave to their *f*
8:53 our *f* out from Egypt
8:57 he proved to be with our *f*
8:58 he gave in command to our *f*
9:9 *f* out from the land of Egypt
11:21 had lain down with his *f*
11:43 lay down with his *f*
13:22 the burial place of your *f*
14:15 that he gave to their *f*
14:20 he lay down with his *f*
14:22 more than all that their *f*
14:31 lay down with his *f*
14:31 and was buried with his *f*
15:8 Abijam lay down with his *f*
15:12 idols that his *f* had made
15:24 Asa lay down with his *f*
15:24 buried with his *f* in the
16:6 Baasha lay down with his *f*
16:28 Omri lay down with his *f*
19:4 I am no better than my *f*
21:3 possession of my *f* to you
21:4 possession of my *f*
22:40 Ahab lay down with his *f*
22:50 lay down with his *f* and was
22:50 buried with his *f* in the
2Ki 8:24 Jehoram lay down with his *f*
8:24 buried with his *f* in the
9:28 his grave with his *f* in the
10:35 Jehu lay down with his *f*
12:18 Jehoram and Ahaziah his *f*
12:21 buried him with his *f* in
13:9 Jehoahaz lay down with his *f*
13:13 Jehoash lay down with his *f*
14:16 Jehoash lay down with his *f*
14:20 in Jerusalem with his *f*
14:22 king lay down with his *f*
14:29 lay down with his *f*
15:7 Azariah lay down with his *f*
15:7 buried him with his *f* in
15:9 just as his *f* had done
15:22 lay down with his *f*
15:38 Jotham lay down with his *f*
15:38 was buried with his *f* in
16:20 Ahaz lay down with his *f*
16:20 buried with his *f* in the
17:13 I commanded your *f* and
17:14 like the necks of their *f*
17:15 had concluded with their *f*
17:41 just as their *f* had done
19:12 that my *f* brought to ruin
20:17 that your *f* have stored up
20:21 lay down with his *f*
21:8 that I gave to their *f*
21:15 their *f* came out from Egypt
21:18 lay down with his *f* and
21:22 Jehovah the God of his *f*
22:13 *f* did not listen to the
22:20 am gathering you to your *f*
23:32 all that *f* of his had done
23:37 all that *f* of his had done
24:6 lay down with his *f*
1Ch 4:38 household itself of their *f*
5:13 to the house of their *f* were
5:15 head of the house of their *f*
5:24 heads of the house of their *f*
5:24 heads of the house of their *f*
5:25 toward the God of their *f*
6:19 the Levites by their *f*
7:2 heads of the house of their *f*
7:4 to the house of their *f*
7:7 heads of the house of their *f*
7:9 heads of the house of their *f*
7:11 heads of their *f*, valiant
7:40 heads of the house of the *f*
8:6 the heads of the houses of *f*
8:10 heads of the houses of *f*
8:13 heads of the houses of *f*
8:28 heads of the houses of *f*
9:9 by the house of their *f*
9:13 heads of the house of their *f*
12:17 let the God of our *f* see to
12:28 house of his *f*, twenty-two
12:30 by the house of their *f*
17:11 you to go to be with your *f*
26:31 by its generations by *f*
29:15 the same as all our *f*
29:18 God of . . . Israel our *f*
1Ch 29:20 Jehovah the God of their *f*
2Ch 6:25 gave to them and their *f*
6:31 ground that you gave to our *f*
6:38 land that you gave to their *f*
7:22 God of their *f* who had
9:31 Solomon lay down with his *f*
11:16 Jehovah the God of their *f*
12:16 lay down with his *f* and
13:12 Jehovah the God of your *f*
13:18 Jehovah the God of their *f*
14:1 Abijah lay down with his *f*
14:4 Jehovah the God of their *f*
15:12 Jehovah the God of their *f*
16:13 Asa lay down with his *f*
17:14 by the house of their *f*
19:4 Jehovah the God of their *f*
20:6 God of our *f*, are you not God
20:33 heart for the God of their *f*
21:1 lay down with his *f* and was
21:1 buried with his *f* in the
21:10 Jehovah the God of his *f*
21:19 like the burning for his *f*
24:18 Jehovah the God of their *f*
24:24 Jehovah the God of their *f*
25:5 house of the *f*, by the chiefs
25:28 buried him with his *f* in
26:2 had lain down with his *f*
26:23 Uzziah lay down with his *f*
26:23 they buried him with his *f*
27:9 Jotham lay down with his *f*
28:6 Jehovah the God of their *f*
28:9 Jehovah the God of your *f*
28:25 Jehovah the God of his *f*
28:27 Ahaz lay down with his *f*
29:5 Jehovah the God of your *f*
29:9 *f* fell by the sword, and our
30:7 not become like your *f* and
30:7 Jehovah the God of their *f*
30:8 stiffen your neck as your *f*
30:19 Jehovah, the God of his *f*
30:22 Jehovah the God of their *f*
32:13 *f* did to all the peoples of
32:14 *f* devoted to destruction
32:15 out of the hand of my *f*
32:33 lay down with his *f*
33:8 that I assigned to their *f*
33:12 because of the God of his *f*
33:20 lay down with his *f*
34:21 *f* did not keep the word of
34:28 gathering you to your *f*
34:32 the God of their *f*
34:33 Jehovah the God of their *f*
35:4 by the house of your *f*
35:5 the house of the *f* for your
35:24 in the graveyard of his *f*
36:15 Jehovah the God of their *f*
Ezr 7:27 Jehovah the God of our *f*
8:28 Jehovah the God of your *f*
9:7 From the days of our *f* we
10:11 Jehovah the God of your *f*
Ne 2:3 the burial places of my *f*
2:5 the burial places of my *f*
9:9 affliction of our *f* in Egypt
9:16 our *f*, acted presumptuously
9:23 you had promised to their *f*
9:32 and our prophets and our *f*
9:34 princes, our priests and our *f*
9:36 land that you gave to our *f*
10:34 by the house of our *f*, at
13:18 this way that your *f* did
Ps 39:12 settler the same as all my *f*
44:1 *f* themselves have recounted
45:16 In place of your *f* there
49:19 as the generation of his *f*
78:5 that he commanded our *f*
78:8 not become like their *f*
78:12 In front of their *f* he had
78:57 treacherously like their *f*
95:9 your *f* put me to the proof
106:6 just the same as our *f*
106:7 As for our *f* in Egypt
109:14 error of his *f* be
Pr 22:28 which your *f* have made
Isa 14:21 the error of their *f*
37:12 *f* brought to ruin delivered
39:6 that your *f* have stored up
64:11 in which our *f* praised you
65:7 for the errors of their *f*
Jer 3:18 possession to your *f*
3:24 of our *f* from our youth
7:7 land that I gave to your *f*
7:14 gave to you and to your *f*
7:22 I did not speak with your *f*
7:25 *f* came forth out of the land
Jer 7:26 acted worse than their *f*
11:4 which I commanded your *f*
11:5 oath that I swore to your *f*
11:7 solemnly admonished your *f*
11:10 to the errors of their *f*
11:10 I concluded with their *f*
14:20 the error of our *f*, for we
16:15 which I gave to their *f*
16:19 our *f* came to possess sheer
17:22 as I commanded your *f*
19:4 they and their *f* and the
23:39 to your *f*—from before me
24:10 gave to them and to their *f*
25:5 gave to you and to your *f*
30:3 land that I gave to their *f*
31:32 concluded with their *f* in
32:22 swore to their *f* to give to
34:13 covenant with your *f* in the
34:14 your *f* did not listen to me
35:15 given to you and to your *f*
44:3 neither you nor your *f*
44:9 the bad deeds of your *f*
44:10 you and before your *f*
44:17 and our *f*, our kings and our
44:21 you and your *f*, your kings
50:7 hope of their *f*, Jehovah
La 5:7 *f* are the ones that have sinned
Eze 2:3 *f* have transgressed against
20:4 detestable things of their *f*
20:18 In the regulations of your *f*
20:24 the dungy idols of their *f*
20:27 *f* spoke abusively of me
20:30 In the way of your *f* are
20:36 your *f* in the wilderness of
20:42 an oath to give to your *f*
36:28 land that I gave to your *f*
37:25 in which your *f* dwelt, and
47:14 oath to give to your *f*
Da 2:23 God of my *f*, I am giving
9:6 our *f* and to all the people
9:8 to our princes and to our *f*
9:16 because of the errors of our *f*
Ho 9:10 I saw the *f* of you people
Joe 1:2 even in the days of your *f*
Am 2:4 after which their *f* had walked
Mic 7:20 you swore to our *f* from the
Mal 2:10 the covenant of our *f*
3:7 From the days of your *f*
Mt 23:30 were in the days of our *f*
23:32 the measure of your *f*
Lu 1:55 just as he told to our *f*
1:72 in connection with our *f*
6:23 *f* used to do to the prophets
6:26 *f* did to the false prophets
11:47 prophets, but your *f* killed
11:48 of the deeds of your *f* and
Joh 4:20 *f* worshiped in this mountain
6:31 Our *f* ate the manna in the
6:49 *f* ate the manna in the
6:58 your *f* ate and yet died
7:22 but that it is from the *f*
Ac 3:13 the God of our *f*, has
3:25 God covenanted with your *f*
5:30 God of our *f* raised up Jesus
7:11 our *f* were not finding any
7:12 sent our *f* out the first time
7:15 deceased; and so did our *f*
7:32 I am the God of your *f*, the
7:38 and with our *f*, and he
7:39 *f* refused to become obedient
7:44 *f* had the tent of the witness
7:45 *f* who succeeded to it also
7:45 thrust out from before our *f*
7:51 as your *f* did, so you do
7:52 did your *f* not persecute
13:17 God . . . chose our *f*, and he
13:32 the promise made to the *f*
13:36 was laid with his *f* and did
15:10 yoke . . . our *f* nor we were
22:14 The God of our *f* has chosen
24:14 service to the God of my *f*
26:6 made by God to our *f* I stand
28:17 or the customs of our *f*
28:25 Isaiah the prophet to your *f*
Ro 9:5 to whom the *f* belong and
11:28 for the sake of their *f*
15:8 promises He made to their *f*
1Co 10:1 our *f* were all under the
2Ti 1:3 sacred service as my *f* did
Heb 1:1 to our *f* by means of the
3:9 *f* made a test of me with a
8:9 that I made with their *f*
1Pe 1:18 by tradition from your *f*
2Pe 3:4 our *f* fell asleep in death

Forefathers'
Zec 8:14 your *f* making me indignant

Forefront
Ex 26:9 cloth at the *f* of the tent
28:25 of the ephod, at the *f* of it
28:27 from below, on its *f*, near
28:37 On the *f* of the turban it
39:18 pieces of the ephod, at the *f*
39:20 on its *f*, near its place of
Le 8:9 upon the turban at the *f* of it
1Ki 7:5 *f* of the illumination opening

Forego
Ne 10:31 *f* the seventh year and the

Foregoing
Jude 7 same manner as the *f* ones had

Foreground
Ge 22:13 deep in the *f*, there was a

Forehead
Ex 28:38 come to be upon Aaron's *f*
28:38 stay upon his *f* constantly
Le 13:41 in front, it is *f* baldness
13:42 of the crown or of the *f*
13:42 of his crown or of his *f*
13:43 his crown or of his *f* like
1Sa 17:49 the Philistine in his *f* and
17:49 the stone sank into his *f*
2Ch 26:19 flashed up in his *f* before
26:20 with leprosy in his *f*
Isa 3:17 will lay their very *f* bare
48:4 and your *f* is copper
Jer 3:3 the *f* of a wife committing
Eze 3:8 your *f* exactly as hard as
3:9 I have made your *f*. You must
Re 13:16 right hand or upon their *f*
14:9 receives a mark on his *f* or
17:5 her *f* was written a name
20:4 the mark upon their *f* and

Foreheads
De 14:1 impose baldness on your *f* for
Eze 3:8 exactly as hard as their *f*
9:4 mark on the *f* of the men that
Re 7:3 have sealed . . . in their *f*
9:4 have the seal of God on their *f*
14:1 written on their *f*
22:4 his name will be on their *f*

Foreign
Ge 35:2 Put away the *f* gods that are
35:4 they gave Jacob all the *f* gods
Ex 2:22 have come to be in a *f* land
18:3 I have come to be in a *f* land
21:8 to sell her to a *f* people in
De 31:16 intercourse with *f* gods of
32:12 was no *f* god along with him
Jos 24:20 and you do serve *f* gods
24:23 remove the *f* gods that are
Jg 10:16 began to remove the *f* gods
1Sa 7:3 put away the *f* gods from your
1Ki 11:1 loved many *f* wives along
11:8 he did for all his *f* wives
2Ch 14:3 removed the *f* altars and the
33:15 remove the *f* gods and the
Ezr 10:2 gave a dwelling to *f* wives
10:10 gave a dwelling to *f* wives
10:11 and from the *f* wives
10:14 given a dwelling to *f* wives
10:17 given a dwelling to *f* wives
10:18 given a dwelling to *f* wives
10:44 had accepted *f* wives, and
Ne 13:26 the *f* wives caused to sin
13:27 giving a dwelling to *f* wives
13:30 them from everything *f*
Ps 81:9 will not bow down to a *f* god
137:4 song of Jehovah Upon *f* ground
Pr 2:16 *f* woman who has made her
5:20 the bosom of a *f* woman
6:24 the tongue of the *f* woman
20:16 in the instance of a *f* woman
23:27 a *f* woman is a narrow well
27:13 in the instance of a *f* woman
Jer 2:21 shoots of a *f* vine
5:19 serving a *f* god in your land
8:19 with their vain *f* gods
Da 11:39 along with a *f* god
Zep 1:8 to all those wearing *f* attire
Mal 2:11 daughter of a *f* god as a
Ac 7:6 residents in a *f* land and the
17:18 be a publisher of *f* deities
Heb 11:9 as in a *f* land, and dwelt in

Foreigner
Ge 17:12 any *f* who is not from your
Ge 17:27 purchased . . . from a *f*, got
Ex 12:43 passover: No *f* may eat of it
Le 22:25 of a *f* you must not present
De 14:21 a selling of it to a *f*
15:3 *f* you may press for payment
17:15 put over yourself a *f* who
23:20 may make a *f* pay interest
29:22 the *f* who will come from a
Ru 2:10 when I am a *f*
2Sa 15:19 for you are a *f* and, besides
1Ki 8:41 the *f*, who is no part of
8:43 for which the *f* calls to you
2Ch 6:32 *f* who is no part of your
6:33 for which the *f* calls to you
Job 19:15 A real *f* I have become in
Ps 69:8 a *f* to the sons of my mother
Pr 5:10 be in the house of a *f*
7:5 *f* who has made her own
27:2 *f*, and not your own lips, do
Ec 6:2 although a mere *f* may eat it
Isa 56:3 the *f* that has joined
Eze 44:9 No *f*, uncircumcised in heart
44:9 *f* who is in the midst of the
1Co 14:11 a *f* to the one speaking
14:11 speaking will be a *f* to me
Col 3:11 *f*, Scythian, slave, freeman

Foreigners
Ge 31:15 considered as *f* to him since
Jg 19:12 city of *f* who are no part of
2Sa 22:45 *F* themselves will come
22:46 *F* themselves will fade
Ne 9:2 from all the *f*, and to stand
Ps 18:44 *F* themselves will come
18:45 *F* themselves will fade away
144:7 From the hand of the *f*
144:11 from the hand of the *f*
Isa 2:6 with the children of *f* they
56:6 the *f* that have joined
60:10 *f* will actually build your
61:5 *f* will be your farmers and
62:8 nor will *f* drink your new
La 5:2 to strangers, our houses to *f*
Eze 44:7 *f* uncircumcised in heart and
Ob 11 outright *f* entered his gate
Ac 17:21 the *f* sojourning there would
1Co 14:21 With the tongues of *f* and
Heb 11:34 routed the armies of *f*

Foreign-god
2Ki 23:5 out of business the *f* priests
Ho 10:5 as well as its *f* priests
Zep 1:4 the name of the *f* priests

Foreign-speaking
Ac 28:2 the *f* people showed us
28:4 *f* people caught sight of the

Foreknowledge
Ac 2:23 counsel and *f* of God
1Pe 1:2 according to the *f* of God

Foreknown
1Pe 1:20 *f* before the founding of the

Foremen
1Ki 5:16 *f* over the people who were
9:23 the *f* over the people who
2Ch 8:10 the *f* over the people

Foremost
Ge 33:2 children *f* and Leah and her
2Ki 24:15 the *f* men of the land he
Ezr 9:2 to be *f* in this unfaithfulness
Pr 8:6 about the *f* things that I speak
Eze 17:13 *f* men of the land he took
32:21 *f* men of the mighty ones
Da 10:13 one of the *f* princes
Mr 6:21 and the *f* ones of Galilee
Ac 1:18 pitching head *f* he noisily
1Ti 1:15 Of these I am *f*
1:16 by means of me as the *f* case

Foreordained
Ac 4:28 and counsel had *f* to occur
Ro 8:29 *f* to be patterned after the
8:30 those whom he *f* are the ones
1Co 2:7 God *f* before the systems of
Eph 1:5 he *f* us to the adoption
1:11 *f* according to the purpose

Forerunner
Heb 6:20 a *f* has entered in our behalf

Foresail
Ac 27:40 hoisting the *f* to the wind

Foresaw
Heb 11:40 God *f* something better for

Foreskin
Ge 17:14 not get the flesh of his *f*
17:24 flesh of his *f* circumcised
17:25 flesh of his *f* circumcised
34:14 sister to a man who has a *f*
Ex 4:25 cut off her son's *f* and caused
Le 12:3 his *f* will be circumcised
19:23 fruitage impure as its *f*
De 10:16 the *f* of your hearts and

Foreskins
Ge 17:11 in the flesh of your *f*, and
17:23 flesh of their *f* in this very
1Sa 18:25 hundred *f* of the Philistines
18:27 David came bringing their *f*
2Sa 3:14 hundred *f* of the Philistines
Jer 4:4 away the *f* of your hearts

Forest
Jos 17:15 go your way up to the *f*
17:18 it is a *f*, you must cut it
1Sa 22:5 came into the *f* of Hereth
2Sa 18:6 in the *f* of Ephraim
18:8 the *f* did more in eating up
18:17 pitched him in the *f* into a
1Ki 7:2 the House of the *F* of Lebanon
10:17 House of the *F* of Lebanon
10:21 House of the *F* of Lebanon
2Ki 19:23 the *f* of its orchard
1Ch 16:33 trees of the *f* break out
2Ch 9:16 House of the *F* of Lebanon
9:20 House of the *F* of Lebanon
Ps 50:10 every wild animal of the *f*
83:14 fire that burns up the *f*
96:12 trees of the *f* break out
104:20 animals of the *f* move forth
132:6 in the fields of the *f*
Ec 2:6 to irrigate with them the *f*
Ca 2:3 tree among the trees of the *f*
Isa 7:2 of the trees of the *f* because
9:18 fire in the thickets of the *f*
10:18 glory of his *f* and of his
10:19 rest of the trees of his *f*
10:34 thickets of the *f* with an
21:13 *f* in the desert plain you
22:8 armory of the house of the *f*
29:17 be accounted just as a *f*
32:15 is accounted as a real *f*
32:19 hail when the *f* goes down
37:24 the *f* of its orchard
44:14 among the trees of the *f*
44:23 you *f* and all you trees in
56:9 you wild animals in the *f*
Jer 5:6 a lion out of the *f* has struck
10:3 a mere tree out of the *f*
12:8 like a lion in the *f*
21:14 set a fire ablaze in her *f*
26:18 for high places of a *f*
46:23 certainly cut down her *f*
Eze 15:2 be among the trees of the *f*
15:6 among the trees of the *f*
20:46 and prophesy to the *f* of
20:47 say to the *f* of the south
Ho 2:12 I will set them as a *f*, and
Am 3:4 Will a lion roar in the *f*
Mic 3:12 as the high places of a *f*
5:8 lion among the beasts of a *f*
7:14 residing alone in a *f*—in
Zec 11:2 impenetrable *f* has come

Forests
Ps 29:9 And strips bare the *f*
Eze 34:25 and sleep in the *f*
39:10 firewood out of the *f*

Foreteller
De 18:11 a professional *f* of events or

Foretellers
Le 19:31 consult professional *f* of
20:6 *f* of events so as to have
1Sa 28:3 professional *f* of events
28:9 professional *f* of events
2Ki 21:6 and professional *f* of events
23:24 the professional *f* of events
2Ch 33:6 professional *f* of events
Isa 19:3 professional *f* of events

Forethought
Ac 24:2 reforms . . . through your *f*

Forever
Ge 44:32 sinned against my father *f*
Ex 15:18 to time indefinite, even *f*
1Ki 2:45 established before Jehovah *f*
1Ch 28:9 he will cast you off *f*
Job 4:20 they perish *f*

Ezr 3:12 that had seen the *f* house
6:16 the *f* exiles held the
6:19 the *f* exiles proceeded to
6:20 for all the *f* exiles and for
8:35 captivity, the *f* exiles
10:7 all the *f* exiles to collect
10:16 *f* exiles proceeded to do
Ne 5:15 *f* governors that were prior
Job 8:8 ask . . . of the *f* generation
Ps 89:49 *f* acts of loving-kindness
Ec 1:11 of people of *f* times, nor
6:5 one has rest rather than the *f*
7:10 the *f* days proved to be better
Isa 9:1 *f* time when one treated with
27:11 *F* will show it no favor
29:16 say respecting its *f*: He
43:1 and your *F*, O Israel: Do not
43:18 to the *f* things do not turn
44:2 your Maker and your *F*
44:24 *F* of you from the belly
45:9 has contended with his *F*
45:9 Should the clay say to its *f*
45:11 of Israel and the *F* of him
45:18 the *F* of the earth and the
61:4 desolated places of *f* times
65:16 *f* distresses will actually
65:17 *f* things will not be called
Jer 10:16 he is the *F* of everything
30:20 become as in *f* times
33:2 Jehovah the *F* of it to
34:5 *f* kings who happened to be
51:19 he is the *F* of everything
Eze 16:55 return to their *f* state
16:55 return to their *f* state
16:55 will return to your *f* state
36:11 as in your *f* condition and
38:17 I spoke in the *f* days by
Am 4:13 the *F* of the mountains and
Hab 2:18 the *f* of it has carved it
2:18 *f* of its form has trusted
Hag 2:3 saw this house in its *f* glory
2:9 greater . . . than that of the *f*
Zec 1:4 the *f* prophets called, saying
7:7 by means of the *f* prophets
7:12 by means of the *f* prophets
8:11 not be as in the *f* days to
Mt 15:2 of the men of *f* times
Mr 7:3 of the men of *f* times
7:5 of the men of *f* times
2Co 2:16 the *f* ones an odor issuing
Eph 4:22 your *f* course of conduct and
Php 1:17 but the *f* do it out of
Heb 8:13 made the *f* one obsolete
9:1 the *f* covenant used to have
9:15 under the *f* covenant, the
9:18 *f* covenant inaugurated
10:32 *f* days in which, after you
Re 2:5 and repent and do the *f* deeds
21:1, 1 *f* heaven and the *f* earth
21:4 The *f* things have passed away

Formerly
Ge 28:19 Luz was the city's name *f*
31:2 it was not with him as *f*
31:5 not the same toward me as *f*
Ex 5:7 the people to make bricks as *f*
5:8 bricks that they were making *f*
5:14 task in making bricks as *f*
21:29 bull was *f* in the habit of
21:36 was in the habit of goring *f*
Nu 21:26 with the king of Moab *f*
De 4:42 he was not hating him *f*; and
19:4 he was no hater of him *f*
19:6 he was no hater of him *f*
Jos 4:18 all its banks as *f*
20:5 he was not hating him *f*
Ru 2:11 whom you had not known *f*
1Sa 10:11 knowing him *f* saw him
14:21 to the Philistines as *f*
17:30 the same reply as *f*
19:7 before him the same as *f*
21:5 same as *f* when I went out
2Ki 13:5 to dwell in their homes as *f*
Job 42:11 all those *f* knowing him
Isa 16:13 spoke concerning Moab *f*
Joh 9:8 who *f* used to see he was a
2Co 12:21 those who *f* sinned but
Ga 1:13 my conduct *f* in Judaism
1:23 man that *f* persecuted us is
1:23 faith which he *f* devastated
2:6 sort of men they *f* were makes
Eph 2:11 *f* you were people of the
1Ti 1:13 *f* I was a blasphemer and a
Phm 11 *f* useless to you but now
1Pe 1:14 the desires you *f* had in your
3:5 *f* the holy women who were
Re 2:19 are more than those *f*

Formers
Isa 44:9 *f* of the carved image are

Forming
Ge 2:19 God was *f* from the ground
Nu 10:25 *f* the rear guard for all the
Ezr 9:14 *f* marriage alliances with
Ps 33:15 *f* their hearts all together
94:9 One *f* the eye, can he not
Isa 22:11 one *f* it long ago you will
45:7 *F* light and creating darkness
49:5 Jehovah, the One *f* me from
Jer 1:5 I was *f* you in the belly I
18:11 *f* against you a calamity
Am 7:1 he was *f* a locust swarm at
Zec 12:1 *f* the spirit of man inside

Formless
Ge 1:2 Now the earth proved to be *f*

Forms
Le 11:3 splits the hoof and *f* a cleft
De 14:6 *f* a cleft into two hoofs
Ps 49:14 their *f* are due to wear away
Isa 45:16 manufacturers of idol *f*

Formulated
Jer 49:20 he has *f* against Edom
49:30 *f* a counsel even against you
50:45 he has *f* against Babylon and

Fornicating
Eze 6:9 *f* heart that has turned aside

Fornication
Nu 14:33 to answer for your acts of *f*
Jg 19:2 to commit *f* against him
Eze 6:9 eyes that are going in *f* after
23:11 more than the *f* of her
23:29 nudeness of your acts of *f*
43:7 kings, by their *f* and by
43:9 them remove their *f* and the
Ho 1:2 take to yourself a wife of *f*
1:2 and children of *f*, because by
1:2 by *f* the land positively turns
2:2 put away her *f* from before
2:4 for they are the sons of *f*
2:5 their mother has committed *f*
3:3 You must not commit *f*, and
4:11 *F* and wine and sweet wine
4:12 *f* has caused them to wander
4:12 by *f* they go out from under
4:13 your daughters commit *f*
4:14 because they commit *f*
4:15 you are committing *f*, O
5:4 *f* in the midst of them
6:10 *f* on the part of Ephraim
9:1 by *f* you have gone from
Mt 5:32 except on account of *f*, makes
19:9 except on the ground of *f*
Joh 8:41 We were not born from *f*
Ac 15:20 to abstain . . . from *f* and
15:29 keep abstaining . . . from *f*
21:25 keep themselves from . . . *f*
1Co 5:1 Actually *f* is reported among
5:1 such *f* as is not even among
6:13 body is not for *f*, but for
6:18 Flee from *f*. Every other sin
6:18 that practices *f* is sinning
7:2 because of prevalence of *f*
10:8 Neither let us practice *f*, as
10:8 as some of them committed *f*
2Co 12:21 *f* and loose conduct that
Ga 5:19 works of the flesh . . . *f*
Eph 5:3 Let *f* and uncleanness of every
Col 3:5 as respects *f*, uncleanness
1Th 4:3 that you abstain from *f*
Jude 7 committed *f* excessively and
Re 2:14 to idols and to commit *f*
2:20 my slaves to commit *f* and
2:21 willing to repent of her *f*
9:21 their *f* nor of their thefts
14:8 wine of the anger of her *f*
17:2 of the earth committed *f*
17:2 drunk with the wine of her *f*
17:4 unclean things of her *f*
18:3 wine of the anger of her *f*
18:3 of the earth committed *f*
18:9 committed *f* with her and
19:2 the earth with her *f*, and

Fornications
2Ki 9:22 the *f* of Jezebel your mother
Mt 15:19 out of the heart come . . . *f*
Mr 7:21 *f*, thieveries, murders

Fornicator
1Co 5:11 a brother that is a *f* or a
Eph 5:5 no *f* or unclean person or
Heb 12:16 may be no *f* nor anyone not

Fornicators
1Co 5:9 quit mixing . . . with *f*
5:10 the *f* of this world or the
6:9 Neither *f*, nor idolaters, nor
1Ti 1:10 *f*, men who lie with males
Heb 13:4 for God will judge *f* and
Re 21:8 murderers and *f* and those
22:15 *f* and the murderers and the

Forsake
De 31:16 *f* me and break my covenant
31:17 *f* them and conceal my face
1Ki 8:57 neither leave us nor *f* us
2Ki 21:14 indeed *f* the remnant of my
Ps 27:9 Do not *f* me and do not leave
94:14 Jehovah will not *f* his
Pr 1:8 not *f* the law of your mother
6:20 not *f* the law of your mother
2Ti 4:16 they all proceeded to *f* me
Heb 13:5 nor by any means *f* you

Forsaken
De 28:20 in that you have *f* me
Isa 2:6 you have *f* your people, the
32:14 tower itself has been *f*
Am 5:2 *f* upon her own ground
Mt 27:46 my God, why have you *f* me?
Mr 15:34 my God, why have you *f* me?
Ac 2:31 neither was he *f* in Hades
2Ti 4:10 Demas has *f* me because he

Forsaking
Heb 10:25 not *f* the gathering of

Forsook
De 32:15 So he *f* God, who made him
Ps 78:60 *f* the tabernacle of Shiloh
Jude 6 *f* their own proper dwelling

Fortieth
Nu 33:38 *f* year of the going out of
De 1:3 *f* year, in the eleventh month
1Ch 26:31 *f* year of David's kingship
Ac 7:23 time of his *f* year was being

Fortification
Lu 19:43 a *f* with pointed stakes and

Fortifications
Nu 13:19 in encampments or in *f*
32:17 dwell in the cities with *f*
32:36 cities with *f*, and stone
Ps 89:40 You have laid his *f* in ruin
Da 11:15 capture a city with *f*

Fortified
Nu 13:28 the *f* cities are very great
De 1:28 great and *f* to the heavens
3:5 cities *f* with a high wall
9:1 cities great and *f* to the
28:52 your high and *f* walls in
Jos 10:20 entering into the *f* cities
14:12 and great *f* cities
19:29 as far as the *f* city of Tyre
19:35 *f* cities were Ziddim, Zer
1Sa 6:18 *f* city to the village of the
2Sa 20:6 find for himself *f* cities
2Ki 3:19 strike down every *f* city and
8:12 *f* places you will consign to
10:2 a *f* city and the armor
17:9 clear to the *f* city
18:8 clear to the *f* city
18:13 all the *f* cities of Judah
19:25 make *f* cities desolate
2Ch 8:5 *f* cities with walls, doors
11:5 build *f* cities in Judah
11:10 *f* cities, which were in
11:11 reinforced the *f* places and
11:23 to all the *f* cities, and
12:4 to capture the *f* cities that
14:6 build *f* cities in Judah, for
17:2 all the *f* cities of Judah
17:12 building *f* places and
17:19 in the *f* cities throughout
19:5 *f* cities of Judah, city by
21:3 along with *f* cities in Judah
27:4 built *f* places and towers
32:1 camp against the *f* cities
33:14 all the *f* cities in Judah
Ezr 6:2 in the *f* place that was in
Ne 9:25 they went capturing *f* cities
Ps 108:10 will bring me to the *f* city

Isa 2:15 tower and upon every *f* wall
17:3 *f* city has been made to
25:2 *f* town a crumbling ruin
25:12 *f* city, with your high
27:10 *f* city will be solitary
34:13 weeds in her *f* places
36:1 all the *f* cities of Judah
37:26 *f* cities become desolate
Jer 1:18 made you today a *f* city and
4:5 let us enter into the *f* cities
5:17 *f* cities in which you are
8:14 enter into the *f* cities
15:20 this people a *f* copper wall
34:7 for they, the *f* cities, were
48:18 bring your *f* places to ruin
La 2:2 torn down the *f* places of the
2:5 brought his *f* places to ruin
Eze 21:20 against Jerusalem *f*
36:35 that were torn down are *f*
Da 11:24 against *f* places he will
11:39 the most *f* strongholds
Ho 8:14 Judah . . . multiplied *f* cities
10:14 your own *f* cities will all
Am 5:9 may come upon even a *f* place
Mic 5:11 tear down all your *f* places
Na 2:1 a safeguarding of the *f* place
3:12 your *f* places are as fig trees
3:14 Strengthen your *f* places
Hab 1:10 laughs even at every *f* place
Zep 1:16 against the *f* cities and

Fortify
Isa 41:10 I am your God. I will *f* you

Fortress
2Sa 22:33 God is my strong *f*, And he
24:7 they came to the *f* of Tyre
Ps 31:4 For you are my *f*
37:39 *f* in the time of distress
43:2 For you are the God of my *f*
52:7 does not put God as his *f*
60:7 Ephraim is the *f* of my head
71:3 rock *f* into which to enter
108:8 Ephraim is the *f* of my head
Isa 17:9 *f* cities will become like a
17:10 Rock of your *f* you have not
Eze 24:25 *f*, the beautiful object of
30:15 Sin, the *f* of Egypt, and
Da 11:1 and as a *f* to him
11:7 against the *f* of the king of
11:10 all the way to his *f*
11:31 profane the sanctuary, the *f*
Joe 3:16 a *f* for the sons of Israel

Fortresses
Da 11:19 turn his face back to the *f*
11:38 to the god of *f*, in his

Fortunatus
1Co 16:17 Stephanas and *F* and Achaicus

Fortune
Ge 30:11 Then Leah said: With good *f*

Forty
Ge 5:13 Kenan . . . eight hundred and *f*
7:4, 4 rain . . . *f* days and *f* nights
7:12, 12 downpour . . . *f* days and *f*
7:17 deluge went on for *f* days
8:6 end of *f* days Noah proceeded
18:29 Suppose *f* are found there
18:29 not do it on account of the *f*
25:20 Isaac happened to be *f* years
26:34 Esau grew to be *f* years old
32:15 *f* cows and ten bulls, twenty
50:3 took fully *f* days for him
Ex 16:35 Israel ate the manna *f* years
24:18, 18 *f* days and *f* nights
26:19 *f* socket pedestals of silver
26:21 *f* socket pedestals of silver
34:28, 28 with Jehovah *f* days and *f*
36:24 *f* socket pedestals of silver
36:26 *f* socket pedestals of silver
Nu 1:33 *f* thousand five hundred
2:19 *f* thousand five hundred
13:25 end of *f* days they returned
14:33 in the wilderness *f* years
14:34 *f* days, a day for a year, a
14:34 for your errors *f* years, as
26:18 *f* thousand five hundred
32:13 in the wilderness *f* years
De 2:7 These *f* years Jehovah your God
8:2 *f* years in the wilderness
8:4 become swollen these *f* years
9:9, 9 *f* days and *f* nights
9:11, 11 the *f* days and *f* nights
9:18, 18 *f* days and *f* nights
De 9:25, 25 *f* days and *f* nights
10:10, 10 *f* days and *f* nights
25:3 *f* strokes he may beat him
29:5 *f* years in the wilderness
Jos 4:13 *f* thousand equipped for the
5:6 *f* years in the wilderness
14:7 *F* years old I was when Moses
Jg 3:11 no disturbance for *f* years
5:8 Among *f* thousand in Israel
5:31 no . . . disturbance for *f* years
8:28 for *f* years in the days of
12:14 *f* sons and thirty grandsons
13:1 the Philistines for *f* years
1Sa 4:18 had judged Israel *f* years
17:16 his position for *f* days
2Sa 2:10 *F* years old Ish-bosheth
5:4 For *f* years he ruled as king
10:18 *f* thousand horsemen, and
15:7 at the end of *f* years that
1Ki 2:11 David had reigned . . . *f* years
4:26 *f* thousand stalls of horses
6:17 *f* cubits that the house
7:38 *F* bath measures were what
11:42 Solomon . . . *f* years
19:8, 8 for *f* days and *f* nights
2Ki 8:9 the load of *f* camels, and
12:1 for *f* years he reigned in
1Ch 12:36 to the army . . . *f* thousand
19:18 and *f* thousand men on foot
29:27 over Israel were *f* years
2Ch 9:30 over all Israel for *f* years
24:1 *f* years he reigned in
Ne 5:15 daily *f* silver shekels
9:21 for *f* years you provided them
Job 42:16 a hundred and *f* years and
Ps 95:10 *f* years I kept feeling a
Eze 4:6 of the house of Judah *f* days
29:11 for *f* years it will not be
29:12 devastated . . . for *f* years
29:13 At the end of *f* years I
41:2 its length, *f* cubits
46:22 *f* cubits in length and
Am 2:10 the wilderness *f* years
5:25 in the wilderness for *f* years
Jon 3:4 *f* days more, and Nineveh will
Mt 4:2, 2 fasted *f* days and *f* nights
Mr 1:13 in the wilderness *f* days
Lu 4:2 *f* days, while being tempted
Ac 1:3 by them throughout *f* days and
4:22 was more than *f* years old
7:30 when *f* years were fulfilled
7:36 in the wilderness for *f* years
7:42 *f* years in the wilderness
13:18 period of about *f* years he
13:21 gave them Saul . . . *f* years
23:13 more than *f* men that formed
23:21 more than *f* men of theirs
2Co 11:24 received *f* strokes less one
Heb 3:9 had seen my works for *f* years
3:17 become disgusted for *f* years

Forty-eight
Nu 35:7 the Levites will be *f* cities
Jos 21:41 *f* cities together with their
Ne 7:15 six hundred and *f*
7:44 of Asaph, a hundred and *f*

Forty-first
2Ch 16:13 *f* year of his reigning

Forty-five
Ge 18:28 to ruin if I find there *f*
Nu 1:25 *f* thousand six hundred and
2:15 *f* thousand six hundred and
26:41 were *f* thousand six hundred
26:50 were *f* thousand four hundred
Jos 14:10 these *f* years since Jehovah
1Ki 7:3 that were upon the *f* pillars
Ezr 2:8 nine hundred and *f*
2:34 three hundred and *f*
2:66 mules two hundred and *f*
Ne 7:13 eight hundred and *f*
7:36 three hundred and *f*
7:67 two hundred and *f* male
7:68 mules two hundred and *f*
Jer 52:30 seven hundred and *f* souls

Forty-four
1Ch 5:18 *f* thousand seven hundred and
Re 7:4 hundred and *f* thousand, sealed
14:1 a hundred and *f* thousand
14:3 the hundred and *f* thousand
21:17 one hundred and *f* cubits

Forty-nine
Le 25:8 amount to *f* years for you

Forty-one
Nu 1:41 *f* thousand five hundred
2:28 *f* thousand five hundred
1Ki 14:21 *F* years old Rehoboam was
15:10 *f* years he reigned in
2Ki 14:23 king in Samaria for *f* years
2Ch 12:13 Rehoboam was *f* years old

Forty-seven
Ge 47:28 Jacob . . . a hundred and *f*
Ezr 2:38 a thousand two hundred and *f*
Ne 7:41 thousand two hundred and *f*

Forty-six
Nu 1:21 *f* thousand five hundred
2:11 *f* thousand five hundred
Joh 2:20 temple was built in *f* years

Forty-three
Nu 26:7 *f* thousand seven hundred and
Ezr 2:25 seven hundred and *f*
Ne 7:29 seven hundred and *f*

Forty-two
Nu 35:6 you will give *f* other cities
Jg 12:6 *f* thousand out of Ephraim
2Ki 2:24 tearing to pieces *f* children
10:14 *f* men, and he did not let
Ezr 2:10 six hundred and *f*
2:24 the sons of Azmaveth, *f*
2:64 *f* thousand three hundred and
Ne 7:28 men of Beth-azmaveth, *f*
7:62 six hundred and *f*
7:66 *f* thousand three hundred and
11:13 two hundred and *f*, and
Re 11:2 city underfoot for *f* months
13:5 authority to act *f* months

Forward
Ge 33:6 the maidservants came *f*, they
33:7 Leah too came *f*, and her
33:7 Joseph came *f*, and Rachel
Le 22:27 eighth day and *f* it will be
Nu 5:16 priest must bring her *f* and
Jos 10:24 Come *f*. Place your feet on
10:24 came *f* and placed their
Ru 3:8 he bent himself *f*, and, look!
1Sa 16:13 upon David from that day *f*
17:16 Philistine kept coming *f*
18:9 at David from that day *f*
30:25 from that day *f* that he
2Sa 17:29 they brought *f* for David
2Ki 20:9 go *f* ten steps of the stairs
Ne 4:7 had gone *f*, for the gaps had
4:16 that day *f* half of my young
Es 8:14 urged *f* and being moved with
Isa 41:21 your controversial case *f*
Jer 7:24 backward . . . and not *f*
Eze 1:9 would go each one straight *f*
1:12 would go each one straight *f*
10:22 go each one straight *f*
39:22 God from that day and *f*
Hag 2:15 from this day and *f*
2:18 from this day and *f*, from
Mt 11:12 those pressing *f* are seizing
16:21 From that time *f* Jesus
25:20 came *f* and brought five
25:22 came *f* and said, Master
25:24 came *f* and said, Master, I
26:39 And going a little way *f*, he
26:50 they came *f* and laid hands
26:60 false witnesses came *f*
26:60 Later on two came *f*
Mr 14:35 And going a little way *f* he
Lu 16:16 person is pressing *f* toward
24:12 stooping *f*, he beheld the
Joh 20:5 stooping *f*, he beheld the
20:11 she stooped *f* to look into
Ac 6:13 brought *f* false witnesses
Php 3:13 *f* to the things ahead

Fought
Nu 21:26 who *f* with the king of Moab
Jg 1:5 then they *f* against him and
5:19 Kings came, they *f*; It was
5:19 kings of Canaan *f* In Taanach
5:20 they *f* against Sisera
9:17 my father *f* for you and went
9:45 Abimelech *f* against the city
12:4 and *f* Ephraim; and the men of
1Sa 4:10 Philistines *f* and Israel was
23:5 *f* against the Philistines
2Sa 8:10 *f* against Hadadezer so that
12:27 I have *f* against Rabbah
12:29 Rabbah and *f* against it and
21:15 down and *f* the Philistines
2Ki 8:29 *f* Hazael the king of Syria

2Ki 9:15 *f* Hazael the king of Syria
13:12 *f* against Amaziah the king
14:15 *f* against Amaziah the king
14:28 he *f* and how he restored
1Ch 18:10 he had *f* against Hadadezer
2Ch 20:29 Jehovah had *f* against the
22:6 *f* Hazael the king of Syria
Joh 18:36 my attendants would have *f*
1Co 15:32 I have *f* with wild beasts
2Ti 4:7 I have *f* the fine fight, I

Foul
Le 7:18 It will become a *f* thing
19:7 on the third day, it is a *f*
Isa 65:4 broth of *f* things being in
Eze 4:14 there has come no *f* flesh
34:18 *f* by stamping with your

Fouled
Pr 25:26 A *f* spring and a ruined well

Fouling
Eze 32:2 and *f* their rivers

Foul-smelling
1Sa 13:4 and now Israel has become *f*
2Sa 10:6 become *f* to David, and the
16:21 *f* to your father, and the
1Ch 19:6 they had become *f* to David
Job 19:17 I have become *f* to the sons

Found
Ge 2:5 no bush of the field *f* in the
2:20 for man there was *f* no helper
6:8 Noah *f* favor in the eyes of
16:7 Later Jehovah's angel *f* her
18:3 I have *f* favor in your eyes
18:29 Suppose forty are *f* there
18:30 Suppose thirty are *f* there
18:31 Suppose twenty are *f* there
18:32 Suppose ten are *f* there
19:15 daughters who are *f* here
19:19 servant has *f* favor in your
24:67 Isaac *f* comfort after the
26:19 *f* . . . a well of fresh water
26:32 We have *f* water
27:39 your dwelling will be *f*
30:27 *f* favor in your eyes,—I
31:37 goods of your house . . . *f*
33:10 If, now, I have *f* favor in
36:24 Anah who *f* the hot springs
37:5 *f* further reason to hate him
37:8 they *f* fresh reason to hate
37:15 a man *f* him and here he was
37:17 and *f* them at Dothan
37:32 and said: This is what we *f*
38:20 but he never *f* her
38:22 I never *f* her and, besides
38:23 but you—you never *f* her
41:38 Can another man be *f* like
41:54 Egypt there was *f* bread
42:20 words may be *f* trustworthy
44:8 the money that we *f* in the
44:9 slaves with whom it may be *f*
44:10 one with whom it may be *f*
44:12 cup was *f* in Benjamin's bag
44:16 God has *f* out the error of
44:16 in whose hand the cup was *f*
44:17 in whose hand the cup was *f*
47:14 money that was to be *f* in
47:29 I have *f* favor in your eyes
50:4 I have *f* favor in your eyes
Ex 9:19 that will be *f* in the field
12:19 no sour dough is to be *f* in
16:27 but they *f* none
21:16 in whose hand he has been *f*
22:2 *f* in the act of breaking in
22:4 *f* in his hand what was stolen
22:7 if the thief should be *f*, he
22:8 If the thief should not be *f*
33:12 you have *f* favor in my eyes
33:13 *f* favor in your eyes, make
33:16 have *f* favor in your eyes
33:17 you have *f* favor in my eyes
34:9 If, now, I have *f* favor in
35:23 *f* blue thread and wool dyed
35:24 there was *f* acacia wood for
Le 6:4 or the thing lost that he has *f*
Nu 11:11 why have I not *f* favor in
11:15 have *f* favor in your eyes
14:8 If Jehovah has *f* delight in us
15:32 *f* a man collecting pieces of
15:33 those who *f* him collecting
31:50 what he has *f* as Jehovah's
32:5 we have *f* favor in your eyes
De 4:30 these words have *f* you out at
De 17:2 *f* in your midst in one of
18:10 should not be *f* in you anyone
20:11 all the people *f* in it should
21:1 In case someone is *f* slain
21:14 have *f* no delight in her
21:17 everything he is *f* to have
22:3 and which you have *f*
22:17 I have *f* your daughter does
22:20 virginity was not *f* in the
22:22 In case a man is *f* lying
22:23 *f* her in the city and lay
22:25 *f* the girl who was engaged
22:27 in the field that he *f* her
22:28 and they have been *f* out
24:1 *f* something indecent on her
24:7 a man is *f* kidnapping a soul
25:8 *f* no delight in taking her
Jos 10:17 *f* hidden in the cave at
Jg 1:5 they *f* Adoni-bezek in Bezek
6:17 I have *f* favor in your eyes
15:15 *f* a moist jawbone of a male
20:48 striking . . . all that were *f*
20:48 all the cities that were *f*
21:12 they *f* out of the inhabitants
Ru 2:10 I have *f* favor in your eyes
1Sa 9:8 shekel of silver *f* in my hand
9:11 *f* girls going out to draw
9:20 the she-asses . . . have been *f*
10:2 The she-asses . . . have been *f*
10:16 the she-asses had been *f*
10:21 and he was not to be *f*
12:5 *f* nothing at all in my hand
13:15 those yet *f* with him, about
13:16 the people yet *f* with them
13:19 was not a smith to be *f* in
13:22 a sword or a spear was *f* in
13:22 *f* one belonging to Saul and
14:30 from the spoil . . . they *f*
16:22 he has *f* favor in my eyes
18:22 king has *f* delight in you
20:3 I have *f* favor in your eyes
20:29 if I have *f* favor in your
21:3 or whatever may be *f*
25:28 badness, it will not be *f*
27:5 *f* favor in your eyes, let
29:3 not *f* in him a single thing
29:6 not *f* badness in you from
29:8 *f* in your servant from the
31:3 bowmen, finally *f* him, and
2Sa 14:22 I have *f* favor in your eyes
15:26 I have *f* no delight in you
17:12 where he is certain to be *f*
17:13 not be *f* there even a pebble
18:9 Absalom *f* himself before the
18:22 no news being *f* for you
20:11 has *f* delight in Joab
22:20 he had *f* delight in me
24:3 he *f* delight in this thing
1Ki 1:3 *f* Abishag the Shunammite and
1:52 if what is bad should be *f*
13:24 a lion *f* him on the road
13:28 and *f* the dead body of him
14:13 been *f* in him in the house
19:19 *f* Elisha the son of Shaphat
21:20 Have you *f* me, O enemy of
21:20 he said: I have *f* you
2Ki 12:5 wherever any crack is *f*
12:10 *f* at the house of Jehovah
12:18 *f* in the treasures of the
14:14 *f* at the house of Jehovah
16:8 *f* at the house of Jehovah
18:15 *f* at the house of Jehovah
19:4 the remnant that are to be *f*
19:8 and *f* the king of Assyria
20:13 to be *f* in his treasures
22:8 book of the law I have *f* in
22:9 money . . . *f* in the house
22:13 this book that has been *f*
23:2 *f* in the house of Jehovah
23:24 *f* at the house of Jehovah
25:19 that were *f* in the city
25:19 were to be *f* in the city
1Ch 4:40 they *f* fat and good pasturage
4:41 Meunim that were to be *f*
10:3 the bow finally *f* him, and
17:25 *f* occasion to pray before
20:2 *f* it to be a talent of gold
24:4 *f* to be more numerous in
26:31 mighty men came to be *f*
28:9 will let himself be *f* by you
29:8 what stones were *f* with any
2Ch 2:17 *f* a hundred and fifty-three
5:11 priests that were to be *f*
15:2 let himself be *f* by you
2Ch 15:4 he let himself be *f* by them
15:15 himself be *f* by them
19:3 good things that have been *f*
21:17 goods that were to be *f* in
25:5 *f* them to be three hundred
25:24 *f* in the house of the true
29:16 uncleanness that they *f* in
29:29 those *f* with him bowed low
30:21 Israel that were *f* in
31:1 Israelites that were *f* there
34:14 Hilkiah the priest *f* the
34:15 book of the law I have *f*
34:17 is *f* in the house of Jehovah
34:21 the book that has been *f*
34:30 *f* at the house of Jehovah
34:32 who were *f* in Jerusalem
34:33 *f* in Israel take up service
35:7 all who were to be *f*
35:17 that were to be *f*
35:18 that were to be *f* and the
36:8 was to be *f* against him
Ezr 4:19 *f* that that city has from
6:2 Media, there was *f* a scroll
8:25 Israelites who were to be *f*
10:18 came to be *f* that had given
Ne 7:5 I *f* the book of genealogical
7:5 the first, and *f* written in it
7:64 it was not *f*, so that they
8:14 they *f* written in the law
9:8 you *f* his heart faithful before
9:32 the hardship that has *f* us
13:1 *f* written in it that the
Es 1:5 people that were *f* in Shushan
2:23 *f* out, and both of them got
4:16 the Jews that are to be *f* in
5:8 have *f* favor in the king's eyes
6:2 *f* written what Mordecai had
7:3 If I have *f* favor in your eyes
8:5 if I have *f* favor before him
Job 19:28 root of the matter is *f* in
21:14 we have *f* no delight
28:12 wisdom—where can it be *f*
28:13 it is not *f* in the land of
31:25 had *f* a lot of things
31:29 because evil had *f* him
32:3 they had not *f* an answer but
32:13 not say, We have *f* wisdom
33:24 I have *f* a ransom
37:23 Almighty, we have not *f* him
42:15 no women were *f* as pretty
Ps 18:19 he had *f* delight in me
32:6 a time only as you may be *f*
37:36 and he was not *f*
41:11 you have *f* delight in me
46:1 A help that is readily to be *f*
69:20 for comforters, but I *f* none
76:5 men have *f* their hands
84:3 bird itself has *f* a house
89:20 I have *f* David my servant
102:14 *f* pleasure in her stones
116:3 of Sheol themselves *f* me
119:143 difficulty themselves *f* me
132:6 *f* it in the fields of the
Pr 3:13 is the man that has *f* wisdom
6:31 when *f*, he will make it good
10:13 person wisdom is *f*, but the
16:31 when it is *f* in the way of
18:22 Has one *f* a good wife?
18:22 One has *f* a good thing, and
24:14 If you have *f* it, then there
25:16 Is it honey that you have *f*?
Ec 7:26 More bitter than death I *f*
7:27 I have *f*, said the congregator
7:28 sought, but I have not *f*
7:28 out of a thousand I have *f*
7:28 a woman . . . I have not *f*
7:29 This only I have *f*, that the
9:7 true God has *f* pleasure in your
9:15 *f* in it a man, needy but wise
12:3 at the windows have *f* it dark
Ca 3:3 going around in the city *f* me
3:4 I *f* the one whom my soul has
5:7 The watchmen . . . *f* me
Isa 13:15 *f* will be pierced through
22:3 *f* have been taken prisoner
30:14 *f* among its crushed pieces
35:9 None will be *f* there
37:4 remnant that are to be *f*
37:8 Rabshakeh returned and *f*
39:2 was to be *f* in his treasures
51:3 will be *f* in her
55:6 while he may be *f*. Call to
57:10 *f* a revival of your own
65:1 *f* by those who had not

Isa 65:8 new wine is *f* in the cluster
Jer 2:5 What have your fathers *f* in
2:26 a thief when he is *f* out
2:34 been *f* the blood marks of
2:34 breaking in have I *f* them
5:26 there have been *f* wicked men
11:9 Conspiracy has been *f* among
14:3 They have *f* no water
15:16 Your words were *f*, and I
23:11 I have *f* their badness
29:14 let myself be *f* by you
31:2 *f* favor in the wilderness
41:3 Chaldeans who were *f* there
41:8 ten men that were *f* among
41:12 *f* him by the abundant
45:3 and no resting-place have I *f*
48:27 *f* among outright thieves
50:20 and they will not be *f*
50:24 You were *f* and also taken
52:25 who were *f* in the city
52:25 *f* in the midst of the city
La 1:3 No resting-place has she *f*
1:6 stags that have *f* no pasturage
2:9 have *f* no vision from Jehovah
2:16 we have hoped for. We have *f*
Eze 22:30 and I *f* no one
26:21 no more be *f* to time
28:15 unrighteousness was *f* in
Da 1:19 no one was *f* like Daniel
2:25 *f* an able-bodied man of the
2:35 no trace at all was *f* of
5:11 wisdom of gods were *f* in him
5:12 been *f* in him, in Daniel
5:14 have been *f* in you
5:27 and have been *f* deficient
6:4 corrupt thing at all was *f* in
6:11 and *f* Daniel petitioning and
6:22 innocence itself was *f* in me
6:23 was no hurt at all *f* on him
11:19 and he will not be *f*
12:1 *f* written down in the book
Ho 9:10 in the wilderness I *f* Israel
10:2 now they will be *f* guilty
12:8 I have *f* valuable things for
14:8 must fruit for you be *f*
Jon 1:3 and *f* a ship going to Tarshish
Mic 1:13 revolts of Israel have been *f*
Na 1:5 hills *f* themselves melting
Zep 3:13 *f* in their mouths a tricky
Zec 10:10 no room will be *f* for them
Mal 2:6 no unrighteousness to be *f* on
Mt 1:18 she was *f* to be pregnant by
2:8 *f* it report back to me, that
8:10 have I *f* so great a faith
13:44 treasure . . . a man *f* and hid
18:28 *f* one of his fellow slaves
20:6 and *f* others standing, and he
21:19 he *f* nothing on it except
22:10 gathered together all they *f*
26:40 *f* them sleeping, and he said
26:43 again and *f* them sleeping
26:60 they *f* none, although many
27:32 *f* a native of Cyrene named
Mr 1:37 *f* him, and they said to him
7:30 *f* the young child laid on the
11:4 *f* the colt tied at the door
11:13 he *f* nothing but leaves, for
14:16 *f* it just as he said to them
14:37 he came and *f* them sleeping
14:40 he came and *f* them sleeping
Lu 1:30 you have *f* favor with God
2:16 *f* Mary as well as Joseph, and
2:46 they *f* him in the temple
4:17 he opened the scroll and *f* the
7:9 have I *f* so great a faith
7:10 *f* the slave in good health
8:35 *f* the man from whom the
9:36 Jesus was *f* alone
13:6 for fruit on it, but *f* none
13:7 have *f* none. Cut it down!
15:5 when he has *f* it he puts it
15:6 *f* my sheep that was lost
15:9 when she has *f* it she calls
15:9 *f* the drachma coin that I
15:24 he was lost and was *f*
15:32 and he was lost and was *f*
17:18 Were none *f* that turned back
19:32 *f* it just as he said to them
22:13 departed and *f* it just as he
22:45 *f* them slumbering from
23:2 This man we *f* subverting our
23:14 *f* in this man no ground for
23:22 *f* nothing deserving of death
24:2 *f* the stone rolled away from
Lu 24:24 and they *f* it so, just as
24:33 *f* the eleven and those with
Joh 1:41 this one *f* his own brother
1:41 We have *f* the Messiah
1:43 Jesus *f* Philip and said to
1:45 Philip *f* Nathanael and said
1:45 *f* the one of whom Moses
2:14 he *f* in the temple those
5:14 Jesus *f* him in the temple
6:25 they *f* him across the sea
11:17 *f* he had already been four
12:14 Jesus had *f* a young ass, he
Ac 5:10 they *f* her dead, and they
5:23 jail we *f* locked with all
5:23 opening up we *f* no one inside
5:39 be *f* fighters actually against
7:46 *f* favor in the sight of God
8:40 Philip was *f* to be in Ashdod
9:2 he *f* who belonged to The Way
9:33 *f* a certain man named Aeneas
10:27 and *f* many people assembled
11:26 after he *f* him, he brought
13:22 I have *f* David the son of
13:28 they *f* no cause for death
17:23 I also *f* an altar on which
18:2 *f* a certain Jew named Aquila
19:1 Ephesus, and *f* some disciples
19:19 *f* them worth fifty thousand
21:2 *f* a boat that was crossing to
21:4 a search we *f* the disciples
23:29 I *f* him to be accused about
24:5 *f* this man a pestilent fellow
24:12 *f* me neither in the temple
24:18 *f* me ceremonially cleansed
24:20 what wrong they *f* as I stood
27:6 army officer *f* a boat from
27:28 the depth and *f* it twenty
27:28 and *f* it fifteen fathoms
28:14 Here we *f* brothers and were
Ro 3:4 let God be *f* true, though
3:4 every man be *f* a liar, even
7:10 this I *f* to be to death
10:20 I was *f* by those who were
1Co 4:2 for a man to be *f* faithful
15:15 *f* false witnesses of God
2Co 5:3 we shall not be *f* naked
6:3 ministry might not be *f* fault
11:12 *f* equal to us in the office
Ga 2:17 also ourselves been *f* sinners
Php 2:8 *f* himself in fashion as a man
3:9 and be *f* in union with him
2Ti 1:17 looked for me and *f* me
Heb 11:5 he was nowhere to be *f*
12:17 he *f* no place for it
1Pe 1:7 *f* a cause for praise and glory
2:22 was deception *f* in his mouth
2Pe 3:14 *f* finally by him spotless
2Jo 4 *f* certain ones of your children
Jude 3 I *f* it necessary to write
Re 2:2 and you *f* them liars
3:2 *f* your deeds fully performed
5:4 no one was *f* worthy to open
12:8 place *f* for them any longer
14:5 no falsehood was *f* in their
16:20 and mountains were not *f*
18:21 she will never be *f* again
18:22 of any trade will ever be *f*
18:24 *f* the blood of prophets and
20:11 no place was *f* for them
20:15 not *f* written in the book of

Foundation

Jos 6:26 let him lay the *f* of it, and
1Ki 5:17 to lay the *f* of the house
6:37 house of Jehovah had its *f*
7:9 from the *f* up to the coping
7:10 expensive stones laid as a *f*
16:34 he laid the *f* of it, and at
2Ki 11:6 be at the gate of the *F*
2Ch 3:3 a *f* for building the house of
23:5 be at the gate of the *F*
Ezr 3:6 the *f* of Jehovah's temple
3:10 *f* of the temple of Jehovah
3:11 *f* of the house of Jehovah
3:12 laying of the *f* of this house
Job 4:19 Whose *f* is in the dust
22:16 Whose *f* is poured away just
Ps 87:1 *f* is in the holy mountains
137:7 Lay it bare to the *f* within
Pr 10:25 righteous one is a *f* to time
Isa 14:32 laid the *f* of Zion, and
28:16 as a *f* in Zion a stone
28:16 precious corner of a sure *f*
44:28 You will have your *f* laid
Isa 48:13 laid the *f* of the earth
51:13 laying the *f* of the earth
51:16 and lay the *f* of the earth
54:11 lay your *f* with sapphires
Eze 13:14 and its *f* must be exposed
Hab 3:13 a laying of the *f* bare
Hag 2:18 *f* of the temple of Jehovah
Zec 4:9 have laid the *f* of this house
8:9 *f* of the house of Jehovah of
12:1 laying the *f* of the earth
Lu 6:48 laid a *f* upon the rock-mass
6:49 a house . . . without a *f*
14:29 he might lay its *f* but not
Ro 15:20 building on another man's *f*
1Co 3:10 I laid a *f*, but someone else
3:11 no man can lay any other *f*
3:12 if anyone builds on the *f*
Eph 2:20 upon the *f* of the apostles
2:20 Jesus . . . the *f* cornerstone
3:17 and established on the *f*
Col 1:23 established on the *f* and
1Ti 6:19 a fine *f* for the future
2Ti 2:19 *f* of God stays standing
Heb 6:1 not laying a *f* again, namely
1Pe 2:6 a *f* cornerstone, precious
Re 21:14 also had twelve *f* stones
21:19 first *f* was jasper, the

Foundation-laying

2Ch 8:16 day of the *f* of the house of

Foundations

De 32:22 ablaze the *f* of mountains
2Sa 22:8 *f* of the heavens themselves
22:16 *f* of the productive land
Ezr 4:12 walls and to repair the *f*
5:16 laid the *f* of the house of
6:3 and its *f* are to be fixed
Ps 11:3 the *f* themselves are torn
18:7 And the *f* of the mountains
18:15 the *f* of the productive land
82:5 *f* of the earth are made to
102:25 laid the *f* of the earth
Pr 8:29 decreed the *f* of the earth
Isa 24:18 *f* of the land will rock
40:21 from the *f* of the earth
58:12 *f* of continuous generations
Jer 31:37 *f* of the earth below could
51:26 corner or a stone for *f*
La 4:11 in Zion, which eats up her *f*
Eze 30:4 take its wealth and its *f*
41:8 *f* of the side chambers
Mic 1:6 and her *f* I shall lay bare
6:2 Hear . . . you *f* of the earth
Ac 16:26 *f* of the jail were shaken
Heb 1:10 laid the *f* of the earth
11:10 city having real *f*, the
Re 21:19 *f* of the city's wall were

Founded

Ex 9:18 from the day it was *f* until
Job 38:4 when I *f* the earth
Ps 8:2 you have *f* strength
78:69 earth that he has *f* to time
89:11 you yourself have *f* them
104:5 *f* the earth upon its
104:8 place that you have *f* for
119:152 indefinite you have *f* them
Pr 3:19 in wisdom *f* the earth
Isa 23:13 *f* her for the desert
Am 9:6 over the earth that he *f*
Hab 1:12 for a reproving you have *f* it
Mt 7:25 had been *f* upon the rock-mass

Founder

Ge 4:20 *f* of those . . . in tents
4:21 He proved to be the *f* of all

Founding

2Ch 24:27 *f* of the house of the true
Mt 13:35 things hidden since the *f*
25:34 from the *f* of the world
Lu 11:50 from the *f* of the world
Joh 17:24 before the *f* of the world
Eph 1:4 before the *f* of the world
Heb 4:3 from the *f* of the world
9:26 from the *f* of the world
1Pe 1:20 before the *f* of the world
Re 13:8 from the *f* of the world
17:8 from the *f* of the world

Fountain

Ge 16:7 angel found her at a *f* of
16:7 at the *f* on the way to Shur
24:13 stationed at a *f* of water
24:16 down to the *f* and began to
24:29 man who was outside at the *f*

Ge 24:30 by the camels at the *f*
24:42 I got to the *f* today, then
24:43 am stationed at a *f* of water
24:45 to the *f* and began to draw
49:22 fruit-bearing tree by the *f*
De 33:28 The *f* of Jacob by itself
Ne 2:13 the *F* of the Big Snake and to
2:14 *F* Gate and to the King's Pool
3:15 the *F* Gate was what Shallun
12:37 the *F* Gate and straight ahead
Mr 5:29 her *f* of blood dried up, and
Joh 4:6 In fact, Jacob's *f* was there
4:6 was sitting at the *f* just as
4:14 a *f* of water bubbling up
Jas 3:11 A *f* does not cause the sweet
Re 21:6 *f* of the water of life free

Fountains
2Ch 32:4 stopping up all the *f* and
Pr 8:28 the *f* of the watery deep
2Pe 2:17 are *f* without water
Re 7:17 guide them to *f* of waters of
8:10 and upon the *f* of waters
14:7 One who made . . . *f* of waters
16:4 rivers and the *f* of the waters

Four
Ge 2:10 became, as it were, *f* heads
11:13 live *f* hundred and three
11:15 *f* hundred and three years
11:17 *f* hundred and thirty years
14:9 *f* kings against the five
15:13 afflict them for *f* hundred
23:15 plot worth *f* hundred silver
23:16 *f* hundred silver shekels
32:6 and *f* hundred men with him
33:1 and with him *f* hundred men
47:24 but *f* parts will become
Ex 12:40 *f* hundred and thirty years
12:41 *f* hundred and thirty years
22:1 *f* of the flock for the sheep
25:12 cast *f* rings of gold for it
25:12 put them above its *f* feet
25:26 make for it *f* rings of gold
25:26 the rings on the *f* corners
25:26 that are for the *f* feet
25:34 on the lampstand are *f* cups
26:2 of each tent cloth is *f* cubits
26:8 of each tent cloth is *f* cubits
26:32 it upon *f* pillars of acacia
26:32 *f* socket pedestals of silver
27:2 its horns upon its *f* corners
27:4 upon the net *f* rings of copper
27:4 copper at its *f* extremities
27:16 their pillars being *f* and
27:16 and their socket pedestals *f*
28:17 there being *f* rows of stones
36:9 each tent cloth *f* cubits
36:15 each tent cloth *f* cubits
36:36 made for it *f* acacia pillars
36:36 *f* socket pedestals of silver
37:3 he cast *f* rings of gold for it
37:3 for above its *f* feet, with
37:13 cast *f* rings of gold for it
37:13 the rings upon the *f* corners
37:13 that were for the *f* feet
37:20 *f* cups shaped like flowers
38:2 its horns upon its *f* corners
38:5 Then he cast *f* rings on the
38:5 on the *f* extremities near the
38:19 And their *f* pillars and
38:19 their *f* socket pedestals were
38:29 two thousand *f* hundred
39:10 it with *f* rows of stones
Le 11:23 *f* legs is a loathsome thing
Nu 1:29 fifty-four thousand *f* hundred
1:31 fifty-seven thousand *f* hundred
1:37 thirty-five thousand *f* hundred
1:43 fifty-three thousand *f* hundred
2:6 fifty-four thousand *f* hundred
2:8 fifty-seven thousand *f* hundred
2:9 eighty-six thousand *f* hundred
2:16 fifty-one thousand *f* hundred
2:23 thirty-five thousand *f* hundred
2:30 fifty-three thousand *f* hundred
7:7 wagons and *f* cattle he gave
7:8 *f* wagons and eight cattle he
7:85 two thousand *f* hundred
26:43 sixty-four thousand *f* hundred
26:47 thousand *f* hundred
26:50 forty-five thousand *f* hundred
De 3:11 *f* cubits its width, by the
22:12 on the *f* extremities of your
Jos 19:7 *f* cities and their
21:18 its pasture ground; *f* cities
Jos 21:22 pasture ground; *f* cities
21:24 pasture ground; *f* cities
21:29 pasture ground; *f* cities
21:31 pasture ground; *f* cities
21:35 pasture ground; *f* cities
21:37 pasture ground; *f* cities
21:39 all the cities being *f*
Jg 9:34 against Shechem in *f* bands
11:40 *f* days in the year
19:2 continued there . . . *f* months
20:2 *f* hundred thousand men on
20:17 *f* hundred thousand men
20:47 the crag of Rimmon *f* months
21:12 *f* hundred girls, virgins
1Sa 4:2 about *f* thousand men in
22:2 with him about *f* hundred men
25:13 about *f* hundred men, while
27:7 to be a year and *f* months
30:10 he and *f* hundred men, but
30:17 *f* hundred young men that
2Sa 12:6 make compensation with *f*
21:22 These *f* had been born to
1Ki 6:1 *f* hundred and eightieth year
7:2 upon *f* rows of pillars of
7:19 of lily work, of *f* cubits
7:27 *f* cubits being the length of
7:27 *f* cubits its width, and
7:30 *f* wheels of copper to each
7:30 and its *f* cornerpieces were
7:32 *f* wheels were down below
7:34 there were *f* supports upon
7:34 *f* corners of each carriage
7:38 Each basin was *f* cubits
7:42 *f* hundred pomegranates for
9:28 *f* hundred and twenty talents
10:26 thousand *f* hundred chariots
18:19 *f* hundred and fifty prophets
18:19 *f* hundred prophets of the
18:22 are *f* hundred and fifty men
18:33 Fill *f* large jars with
22:6 about *f* hundred men, and
2Ki 7:3 And there were *f* men, lepers
14:13 gate, *f* hundred cubits
1Ch 3:5 *f* of Bath-sheba the daughter
7:1 sons of Issachar were . . . *f*
9:24 to the *f* directions that the
9:26 there were *f* mighty men of
12:26 *f* thousand six hundred
21:5 Judah *f* hundred and seventy
21:20 his *f* sons with him were
23:5 *f* thousand gatekeepers and
23:5 *f* thousand givers of praise
23:10 *f* were the sons of Shimei
23:12 sons of Kohath were . . . *f*
26:17 to the north for a day, *f*
26:17 to the south for a day, *f*
26:18 *f* at the highway, two at
2Ch 1:14 a thousand *f* hundred chariots
4:13 *f* hundred pomegranates for
8:18 *f* hundred and fifty talents
9:25 *f* thousand stalls of horses
13:3 *f* hundred thousand mighty
18:5 *f* hundred men, and said to
25:23 Gate, *f* hundred cubits
Ezr 1:10 *f* hundred and ten small
1:11 were five thousand *f* hundred
2:15 *f* hundred and fifty-four
2:67 *f* hundred and thirty-five
6:17 *f* hundred lambs, and as a
Ne 6:4 sent me the same word *f* times
7:69 *f* hundred and thirty-five
11:6 *f* hundred and sixty-eight
Job 1:19 the *f* corners of the house
42:16 his grandsons—*f* generations
Pr 30:15 *f* that have not said: Enough!
30:18 *f* that I have not come to
30:21 *f* it is not able to endure
30:24 There are *f* things that are
30:29 *f* that do well in their
Isa 11:12 *f* extremities of the earth
17:6 branch; *f* or five on the
Jer 15:3 over them *f* families
36:23 three or *f* page-columns, he
49:36 upon Elam the *f* winds from
49:36 *f* extremities of the
52:21 *f* fingerbreadths, it being
52:30 *f* thousand and six hundred
Eze 1:5 likeness of *f* living creatures
1:6 each one had *f* faces, and each
1:6 and each one of them *f* wings
1:8 their wings on their *f* sides
1:8 *f* of them had their faces and
1:10 *f* of them had a man's face
1:10 *f* of them had a bull's face
Eze 1:10 the *f* . . . had an eagle's face
1:15 by the *f* faces of each
1:16 *f* of them had one likeness
1:17 on their *f* respective sides
1:18 full of eyes all around the *f*
7:2 the *f* extremities of the land
10:9 *f* wheels beside the cherubs
10:10 *f* of them had one likeness
10:11 would go, to their *f* sides
10:12 *f* of them had their wheels
10:14 And each one had *f* faces
10:21 As for the *f*, each one had
10:21 each one had *f* faces and
10:21 and each one had *f* wings
14:21 my *f* . . . acts of judgment
37:9 From the *f* winds come in
40:41 There were *f* tables over
40:41 and *f* tables over there at
40:42 *f* tables for the whole
41:5 side chamber was *f* cubits
42:20 *f* sides he measured it
43:14 ledge there are *f* cubits
43:15 the altar hearth is *f* cubits
43:15 there are the *f* horns
43:16 squared on its *f* sides
43:17 width, on its *f* sides
43:20 put it upon its *f* horns
43:20 *f* corners of the surrounding
45:19 upon the *f* corners of the
46:21 *f* corner posts of the
46:22 *f* corner posts of the
46:22 *f* of them with corner
46:23 round about the *f* of them
48:16 *f* thousand five hundred
48:16 *f* thousand five hundred, and
48:16 *f* thousand five hundred
48:16 *f* thousand five hundred
48:30 *f* thousand five hundred
48:32 *f* thousand five hundred
48:33 *f* thousand five hundred
48:34 *f* thousand five hundred
Da 1:17 children, the *f* of them, to
3:25 beholding *f* able-bodied men
7:2 *f* winds of the heavens were
7:3 *f* huge beasts were coming up
7:6 *f* wings of a flying creature
7:6 And the beast had *f* heads, and
7:17 beasts, because they are *f*
7:17 *f* kings that will stand up
8:8 come up conspicuously *f*
8:8 the *f* winds of the heavens
8:22 *f* that finally stood up
8:22 *f* kingdoms from his nation
11:4 divided toward the *f* winds
Am 1:3 on account of *f*, I shall not
1:6 on account of *f*, I shall not
1:9 on account of *f*, I shall not
1:11 and on account of *f*, I shall
1:13 on account of *f*, I shall not
2:1 on account of *f*, I shall not
2:4 on account of *f*, I shall not
2:6 on account of *f*, I shall not
Zec 1:18 look! there were *f* horns
1:20 showed me *f* craftsmen
2:6 the *f* winds of the heavens
6:1 *f* chariots coming forth from
6:5 *f* spirits of the heavens that
Mt 15:38 those eating were *f* thousand
16:10 the case of the *f* thousand
24:31 together from the *f* winds
Mr 2:3 a paralytic carried by *f*
8:9 were about *f* thousand men
8:20 for the *f* thousand men
13:27 together from the *f* winds
Joh 4:35 *f* months before the harvest
6:19 rowed about three or *f* miles
11:17 *f* days in the memorial
11:39 smell, for it is *f* days
19:23 garments and made *f* parts
Ac 5:36 men, about *f* hundred, joined
7:6 afflict them for *f* hundred
10:11 down by its *f* extremities
10:30 Cornelius said: *F* days ago
11:5 down by its *f* extremities
12:4, 4 *f* shifts of *f* soldiers each
13:20 *f* hundred and fifty years
21:9 had *f* daughters, virgins, that
21:23 have *f* men with a vow upon
21:38 the *f* thousand dagger men
27:29 cast out *f* anchors from the
Ga 3:17 *f* hundred and thirty years
Re 4:6 *f* living creatures that are
4:8 as for the *f* living creatures
5:6 *f* living creatures and in the

Ex 26:29 overlay the panel *f* with
35:11 its hooks and its panel *f*
36:20 panel *f* for the tabernacle
36:22 panel *f* of the tabernacle
36:23 panel *f* for the tabernacle
36:23 twenty panel *f* for the side
36:24 beneath the twenty panel *f*
36:25 he made twenty panel *f*
36:27 he made six panel *f*
36:28 two panel *f* as corner posts
36:30 amounted to eight panel *f*
36:31 panel *f* of the one side of
36:32 five bars for the panel *f* of
36:32 five bars for the panel *f* of
36:33 middle of the panel *f* from
36:34 the panel *f* with gold, and
39:33 its panel *f*, its bars and its
40:18 and placing its panel *f* and
Nu 3:36 panel *f* of the tabernacle and
4:31 panel *f* of the tabernacle and
1Ki 6:4 make windows of narrowing *f*
Eze 40:16 windows of narrowing *f* for
41:16 windows with narrowing *f*
41:26 windows of narrowing *f* and

Framework
Ro 2:20 *f* of the knowledge and of the

Framing
Ps 94:20 it is *f* trouble by decree

Frankincense
Ex 30:34 galbanum and pure *f*
Le 2:1 oil over it and put *f* upon it
2:2 its oil along with all its *f*
2:15 and place *f* upon it
2:16 along with all its *f*, as an
5:11 he must not place *f* upon it
6:15 its oil and all the *f* that is
24:7 put pure *f* upon each layer set
Nu 5:15 nor put *f* upon it, because
1Ch 9:29 and the *f* and the balsam oil
Ne 13:5 the *f* and the utensils and
13:9 the grain offering and the *f*
Ca 3:6 perfumed with myrrh and *f*
4:6 of myrrh and to the hill of *f*
4:14 with all sorts of trees of *f*
Isa 43:23 I made you weary with *f*
60:6 Gold and *f* they will carry
66:3 presenting a memorial of *f*
Jer 6:20 bring in even *f* from Sheba
17:26 and grain offering and *f*
41:5 *f* in their hand to bring to
Mt 2:11 gifts, gold and *f* and myrrh
Re 18:13 *f* and wine and olive oil and

Frantically
Ps 62:3 carry on *f* against the man

Fraud
Le 6:4 thing which he has taken by *f*
Ac 13:10 full of every sort of *f* and

Frauds
Isa 33:15 the unjust gain from *f*

Fraudulent
Pr 28:16 also abundant in *f* practices

Fraudulently
Mal 3:5 against those acting *f* with

Free
Ge 24:8 become *f* from this oath you
24:41 *f* of obligation to me by
Ex 21:2 as one set *f* without charge
21:5 want to go out as one set *f*
21:19 must be *f* from punishment
21:26 one set *f* in compensation
21:27 send him away as one set *f*
21:28 owner . . . *f* from punishment
Le 1:3 present it of his own *f* will
19:20 because she was not set *f*
Nu 5:19 be *f* of the effect of this
5:28 be *f* from such punishment
32:22 *f* from guilt against Jehovah
De 15:12 out from you as one set *f*
15:13 out from you as one set *f*
15:18 as one set *f*; because for
Jos 2:17 are *f* from guilt respecting
2:19 and we shall be *f* from guilt
2:20 *f* from guilt respecting this
Jg 15:3 I must be *f* of guilt against
16:20 I shall . . . shake myself *f*
1Sa 17:25 he will set *f* in Israel
24:15 to *f* me from your hand
25:39 *f* me from Nabal's hand and
2Sa 18:19 judged him to *f* him from
18:31 judged you today to *f* you
1Ch 9:33 those set *f* from duty
2Ch 23:8 the divisions *f* from duty
Job 3:19 the slave is set *f* from his
21:9 peace itself, *f* from dread
39:5 Who sent forth the zebra *f*
Ps 81:6 to be *f* even from the basket
88:5 Set *f* among the dead
122:6 city, will be *f* from care
144:7 Set me *f* and deliver me
144:10 David his servant *f* from
144:11 Set me *f* and deliver me
Pr 16:5 not be *f* from punishment
17:5 not be *f* from punishment
19:5 A false witness will not be *f*
19:9 false witness will not be *f*
Isa 14:7 has become *f* of disturbance
52:2 Shake . . . *f* from the dust
58:6 send away the crushed ones *f*
Jer 25:29 go *f* of punishment
25:29 will not go *f* of punishment
30:10 be *f* of disturbance and be
34:9 and Hebrew woman, go *f*, in
34:10 his maidservant go *f*
34:11 whom they had let go *f*
34:14 go *f* from being with you
34:16 go *f* agreeably to their soul
Da 3:25 walking about *f* in the midst
Ho 14:4 love them of my own *f* will
Zec 3:7 give you *f* access among these
5:3 has gone *f* of punishment
5:3 has gone *f* of punishment
Mt 10:8, 8 You received *f*, give *f*
28:14 will set you *f* from worry
Lu 2:29 letting your slave go *f* in
Joh 4:10 had known the *f* gift of God
8:32 the truth will set you *f*
8:33 you say, You will become *f*
8:36 if the Son sets you *f*, you
8:36 you will be actually *f*
Ac 2:38 *f* gift of the holy spirit
8:20 of the *f* gift of God
10:45 *f* gift of the holy spirit
11:17 God gave the same *f* gift to
Ro 3:24 as a *f* gift that they are
5:15 God and his *f* gift with the
5:16 it is not with the *f* gift
5:17 *f* gift of righteousness rule
6:18 you were set *f* from sin, you
6:20 were *f* as to righteousness
6:22 you were set *f* from sin but
7:3 if her husband dies, she is *f*
8:2 *f* from the law of sin and of
8:21 set *f* from enslavement to
1Co 5:7 as you are *f* from ferment
7:21 but if you can also become *f*
7:22 was called when a *f* man is
7:32 I want you to be *f* from
7:39 *f* to be married to whom she
9:1 Am I not *f*? Am I not an
9:19 though I am *f* from all
12:13 whether slaves or *f*, and we
16:10 he becomes *f* of fear among
2Co 6:6 by love *f* from hypocrisy
9:15 for his indescribable *f* gift
Ga 4:22 and one by the *f* woman
4:23 *f* woman through a promise
4:26 Jerusalem above is *f*, and she
4:30 with the son of the *f* woman
4:31 but of the *f* woman
5:1 such freedom Christ set us *f*
Eph 3:7 the *f* gift of the undeserved
4:7 measured out the *f* gift
Php 2:14 things *f* from murmurings
2:28 be the more *f* from grief
2Th 3:8 we eat food from anyone *f*
1Ti 3:10 they are *f* from accusation
Tit 1:6 is any man *f* from accusation
1:7 must be *f* from accusation as
Phm 14 but of your own *f* will
Heb 6:4 tasted the heavenly *f* gift
13:5 life be *f* of the love of
Jas 2:12 by the law of a *f* people
1Pe 2:16 Be as *f* people, and yet
Re 6:15 slave and every *f* person hid
13:16 *f* and the slaves, that they
21:6 of the water of life *f*
22:17 wishes take life's water *f*

Freedman
1Co 7:22 when a slave is the Lord's *f*

Freedmen
Ac 6:9 so-called Synagogue of the *F*

Freedom
Le 19:20 *f* been given her, punishment
Ps 122:7 *F* from care within your
Jer 22:21 I spoke to you during your *f*
Da 8:25 during a *f* from care he will
11:21 during a *f* from care and
11:24 during *f* from care, even
Ro 8:21 *f* of the children of God
1Co 10:29 my *f* is judged by another
2Co 3:17 of Jehovah is, there is *f*
Ga 2:4 sneaked in to spy upon our *f*
5:1 For such *f* Christ set us free
5:13 called for *f*, brothers; only
5:13 *f* as an inducement for the
Jas 1:25 law that belongs to *f* and
1Pe 2:16 and yet holding your *f*, not
2Pe 2:19 they are promising them *f*

Freely
Pr 11:25 one *f* watering others will
11:25 himself also be *f* watered
Lu 7:42 he *f* forgave them both
7:43 whom he *f* forgave the more
Ac 3:14 murderer, to be *f* granted to
27:24 God has *f* given you all
Eph 4:32 *f* forgiving one another just
4:32 God also by Christ *f* forgave
Col 3:13 *f* forgiving one another *f* if
3:13 Even as Jehovah *f* forgave you
2Pe 1:3 divine power has given us *f*
1:4 *f* given us the precious and

Freeman
Ga 3:28 there is neither slave nor *f*
Eph 6:8 whether he be slave or *f*
Col 3:11 slave, *f*, but Christ is all

Freemen
Re 19:18 of *f* as well as of slaves

Freeness
Ac 2:29 with *f* of speech to you
26:26 speaking with *f* of speech
28:31 the greatest *f* of speech
2Co 3:12 are using great *f* of speech
7:4 I have great *f* of speech
Eph 3:12 we have this *f* of speech
6:19 with all *f* of speech to
Php 1:20 in all *f* of speech Christ
1Ti 3:13 and great *f* of speech in the
Phm 8 great *f* of speech in connection
Heb 3:6 on our *f* of speech and our
4:16 approach with *f* of speech to
10:35 throw away your *f* of speech
1Jo 2:28 have *f* of speech and not be
3:21 have *f* of speech toward God
4:17 that we may have *f* of speech

Frequent
Ec 6:1 and it is *f* among mankind
Am 4:4 *f* in committing transgression
1Ti 5:23 and your *f* cases of sickness

Frequently
Lu 5:33 The disciples of John fast *f*
Ac 24:26 he sent for him even more *f*

Fresh
Ge 26:19 found . . . a well of *f* water
37:8 found *f* reason to hate him
Nu 6:3 nor eat grapes either *f* or
Jg 7:20 and took *f* hold on the torches
1Sa 21:6 place *f* bread there on the
Job 9:18 my taking of a *f* breath
29:20 My glory is *f* with me
Ps 92:10 moisten myself with *f* oil
92:14 Fat and *f* they will continue
Ca 4:15 gardens, a well of *f* water
8:2 the *f* juice of pomegranates
Isa 1:6 and bruises and *f* stripes

Fresher
Job 33:25 flesh become *f* than in

Freshly
Ge 8:11 olive leaf *f* plucked in its
Eze 17:9 *f* plucked sprouts become dry

Freshly-shorn
Ca 4:2 are like a drove of *f* ewes

Friend
Ge 26:26 Ahuzzath his confidential *f*
1Ki 4:5 a priest, the *f* of the king
20:35 prophets said to his *f* by
Ps 88:18 put far away from me *f* and
Pr 2:17 confidential *f* of her youth
18:24 a *f* sticking closer than a
Isa 41:8 the seed of Abraham my *f*
Jer 3:4 confidential *f* of my youth
Mic 7:5 trust in a confidential *f*
Mt 11:19 a *f* of tax collectors and

Lu 7:34 a *f* of tax collectors and
10:6 if a *f* of peace is there
11:5 will have a *f* and will go to
11:5 *F*, loan me three loaves
11:6 a *f* of mine has just come to
11:8 because of being his *f*
14:10 *F*, go on up higher. Then you
Joh 3:29 the *f* of the bridegroom
11:11 Lazarus our *f* has gone to
19:12 you are not a *f* of Caesar
Jas 2:23 to be called Jehovah's *f*
4:4 wants to be a *f* of the world

Friendly
Ac 19:31 who were *f* to him, sent to

Friends
1Sa 30:26 older men of Judah, his *f*
2Sa 3:8 brothers and his personal *f*
1Ki 16:11 avengers of blood or his *f*
Es 5:10 had his *f* and Zeresh his wife
5:14 his wife and all his *f* said
6:13 his wife and to all his *f*
Pr 14:20 many are the *f* of the rich
19:7 *f* kept away from him! He is
Jer 13:21 *f* right alongside you at
Mt 9:15 The *f* of the bridegroom have
Mr 2:19 *f* of the bridegroom cannot
Lu 5:34 *f* of the bridegroom fast
7:6 already sent *f* to say to him
12:4 my *f*, Do not fear those who
14:12 do not call your *f* or your
15:6 calls his *f* and his neighbors
15:9 her *f* and neighbors together
15:29 to enjoy myself with my *f*
16:9 Make *f* for yourselves by
21:16 delivered up even by . . . *f*
23:12 and Pilate now became *f*
Joh 15:13 soul in behalf of his *f*
15:14 You are my *f* if you do what
15:15 I have called you *f*, because
Ac 10:24 his relatives and intimate *f*
27:3 his *f* and enjoy their care
3Jo 14 *f* send you their greetings
14 my greetings to the *f* by name

Friendship
Jas 4:4 *f* with the world is enmity

Fright
Ex 15:16 *F* and dread will fall upon
23:27 send the *f* of me ahead of
De 32:25 bereave them, And indoors *f*
Jos 2:9 the *f* of you has fallen upon
Ezr 3:3 *f* came upon them because of
Job 7:14 you make me start up in *f*
13:11 make you start up with *f*
13:21 the *f* of you—may it not
18:11 make him start up in *f*
Ps 31:13 *F* being on all sides
Isa 31:9 pass away out of sheer *f*
Jer 6:25 there is *f* all around
20:3 not Pashhur, but *F* all around
20:4 I am making you a *f* to
20:10 There was *f* all around
38:19 I am in *f* of the Jews that
42:16 at which you are in a *f*
46:5 There is *f* all around
49:29 cry out . . . *F* is all around!

Frighten
Da 4:5 visions . . . that began to *f* me
4:19 very thoughts began to *f* him
4:19 interpretation themselves *f*
5:6 his own thoughts began to *f*
5:10 not let your thoughts *f* you
7:15 visions of my head began to *f*

Frightened
Nu 22:3 And Moab became very *f* at the
De 1:17 not become *f* because of a man
18:22 You must not get *f* at him
Job 19:29 Be *f* for yourselves because
41:25 the strong get *f*
Ps 22:23 *f* at him, all you the seed
33:8 all the inhabitants . . . be *f*
Isa 57:11 become *f* at and begin to
Da 3:24 king himself became *f* and he
5:9 Belshazzar was very much *f*
Ho 10:5 Samaria will get *f*
Mr 5:33 the woman, *f* and trembling
Lu 24:5 women became *f* and kept their
24:37 terrified, and had become *f*
Ac 10:4 becoming *f*, said: What is it
24:25 Felix became *f* and answered
Php 1:28 being *f* by your opponents
Re 11:13 the rest became *f* and gave

Frightening
Da 7:28 my own thoughts kept *f* me

Frightful
De 28:25 a *f* object to all the earth's
Job 20:25 *F* objects will go against
39:20 dignity of its snorting is *f*
41:14 Its teeth round about are *f*
Ps 88:15 borne *f* things from you very
Pr 10:24 thing *f* to the wicked one
Isa 33:18 in low tones on a *f* thing
66:4 things *f* to them I shall
Jer 50:38 because of their *f* visions
Eze 23:46 a making of them a *f* object
Hab 1:7 *F* and fear-inspiring it is

Frightfully
Ge 15:12 *f* great darkness was falling

Frightfulness
Job 9:34 his *f*, let it not terrify me
33:7 No *f* in me will terrify you
Pr 20:2 The *f* of a king is a growling

Frights
Ps 34:4 out of all my *f* he delivered
55:4 the *f* of death itself have

Fringe
Mt 9:20 touched the *f* of his outer
14:36 the *f* of his outer garment
Mr 6:56 the *f* of his outer garment
Lu 8:44 the *f* of his outer garment

Fringed
Nu 15:38 *f* edges upon the skirts of
15:38 blue string above the *f* edge
15:39 serve as a *f* edge for you

Fringes
Job 26:14 These are the *f* of his ways
Mt 23:5 the *f* of their garments

Frivolous
Jer 3:9 because of her *f* view

Fro
Ge 1:2 force was moving to and *f* over
Ex 29:24 to and *f* as a wave offering
29:26 to and *f* as a wave offering
Le 7:30 to and *f* as a wave offering
8:27 to and *f* as a wave offering
8:29 to and *f* as a wave offering
9:21 to and *f* as a wave offering
10:15 wave offering to and *f*
14:12 to and *f* as a wave offering
14:24 to and *f* as a wave offering
23:11 wave the sheaf to and *f*
23:11 should wave it to and *f*
23:12 sheaf waved to and *f* you
23:20 wave them to and *f* along
Nu 5:25 grain offering to and *f* before
6:20 *f* as a wave offering before
8:11 Levites to move to and *f*
8:13 to and *f* as a wave offering
8:15 to and *f* as a wave offering
8:21 move to and *f* as a wave
De 23:25 not swing to and *f* upon the
2Ki 5:11 move his hand to and *f* over
Job 9:26 an eagle that darts to and *f*
31:21 I waved my hand to and *f*
Isa 24:20 swayed to and *f* like a
30:28 nations to and *f* with a
Jer 2:23 running to and *f* in her ways
Ac 27:27 tossed to and *f* on the sea

Frogs
Ex 8:2 here I am plaguing . . . with *f*
8:3 River will fairly teem with *f*
8:4 on your people . . . *f* will come
8:5 make the *f* come up over the
8:6 Egypt, and the *f* began to come
8:7 priests . . . made the *f* come
8:8 remove the *f* from me and my
8:9 cut the *f* off from you and
8:11 *f* will certainly turn away
8:12 *f* that He had put upon Pharaoh
8:13 *f* began to die off from the
Ps 78:45 *f*, that these might bring
105:30 land swarmed with *f*
Re 16:13 that looked like *f* come out

Fronds
Le 23:40 the *f* of palm trees and the

Front
Ge 23:17 Machpelah, which is in *f* of
23:19 of Machpelah in *f* of Mamre
25:9 that is in *f* of Mamre
25:18 which is in *f* of Egypt
Ge 25:18 In *f* of all his brothers he
30:38 he placed in *f* of the flock
31:37 in *f* of my brothers and your
33:18 camp in *f* of the city
47:15 why should we die in *f* of
49:30 in *f* of Mamre in the land of
50:13 the field . . . in *f* of Mamre
Ex 8:20 a position in *f* of Pharaoh
9:13 a position in *f* of Pharaoh
14:2 In *f* of it you are to encamp
17:5 Pass in *f* of the people and
19:2 there in *f* of the mountain
25:37 shine upon the area in *f* of
34:3 in *f* of that mountain
40:24 of meeting in *f* of the table
Le 4:6 in *f* of the curtain of the holy
4:17 Jehovah in *f* of the curtain
5:8 nip off its head at the *f* of
6:14 Jehovah in *f* of the altar
10:4 in *f* of the holy place to
13:41 his head grows bald up in *f*
16:2 in *f* of the cover which is
16:14 *f* of the cover on the east
Nu 2:2 *f* of the tent of meeting they
8:2 the area in *f* of the lampstand
8:3 the area in *f* of the lampstand
19:4 the *f* of the tent of meeting
21:11 is toward the *f* of Moab
22:5 are dwelling right in *f* of me
De 1:1 the desert plains in *f* of Suph
2:19 get close in *f* of the sons of
3:29 the valley in *f* of Beth-peor
4:46 the valley in *f* of Beth-peor
11:30 the Arabah, in *f* of Gilgal
31:11 law in *f* of all Israel in
34:6 of Moab in *f* of Beth-peor
Jos 3:16 passed over in *f* of Jericho
5:13 a man standing in *f* of him
8:11 and get in *f* of the city
8:33 in *f* of the priests, the
8:33 in *f* of Mount Gerizim and
8:33 half of them in *f* of Mount
8:35 in *f* of all the congregation
9:1 Great Sea and in *f* of Lebanon
13:3 the Nile that is *f* of Egypt
13:25 which is in *f* of Rabbah
15:7 *f* of the ascent of Adummim
17:7 which is in *f* of Shechem
18:17 *f* of the ascent of Adummim
18:18 slope in *f* of the Arabah
19:11 that is in *f* of Jokneam
19:46 the border in *f* of Joppa
Jg 16:3 that is in *f* of Hebron
19:10 came as far as in *f* of Jebus
20:34 Israel came in *f* of Gibeah
20:43 directly in *f* of Gibeah
Ru 4:4 Buy it in *f* of the inhabitants
1Sa 12:3 against me in *f* of Jehovah
12:3 and in *f* of his anointed one
15:7 Shur, which is in *f* of Egypt
15:30 in *f* of the older men of my
15:30 in *f* of Israel and return
20:1 said in *f* of Jonathan: What
2Sa 2:24 *f* of Giah on the way to the
5:23 in *f* of the baca bushes
10:9 from the *f* and from the rear
11:15 *f* of the heaviest battle
12:12 thing in *f* of all Israel
12:12 and in *f* of the sun
22:13 the brightness in *f* of him
22:23 decisions are in *f* of me
22:25 cleanness in *f* of his eyes
1Ki 6:3 the porch in *f* of the temple
6:3 *f* of the width of the house
6:3 its depth, in *f* of the house
6:17 the temple in *f* of it
6:21 in *f* of the innermost room
7:6 porch was in *f* of them with
7:6 and a canopy in *f* of them
8:8 in *f* of the innermost room
8:22 in *f* of all the congregation
11:7 mountain . . . *f* of Jerusalem
20:27 in *f* of them like two tiny
20:29 these in *f* of those
21:10 sit in *f* of him, and let
21:13 and sat down in *f* of him
21:13 in *f* of the people, saying
2Ki 1:13 upon his knees in *f* of Elijah
16:14 from in *f* of the house
23:13 were in *f* of Jerusalem
1Ch 5:11 sons of Gad in *f* of them
8:32 dwelt in *f* of their brothers
9:38 dwelt in *f* of their brothers
14:14 in *f* of the baca bushes

1Ch 19:10 against him from the *f* and
2Ch 3:4 porch that was in *f* of the
3:4 *f* of the width of the house
3:17 pillars in *f* of the temple
5:9 in *f* of the innermost room
6:12 *f* of all the congregation of
6:13 *f* of all the congregation of
7:6 sounding the trumpets in *f*
8:14 minister in *f* of the priests
13:13 *f* of Judah and the ambush
13:14 the battle in *f* and behind
20:16 *f* of the wilderness of
Ne 2:13 in *f* of the Fountain of the
3:10 in *f* of his own house
3:16 in *f* of the Burial Places of
3:19 in *f* of the going up to the
3:23 in *f* of their own house
3:25 work in *f* of the Buttress
3:26 in *f* of the Water Gate on the
3:27 in *f* of the great protruding
3:28 in *f* of his own house
3:29 work in *f* of his own house
3:30 work in *f* of his own hall
3:31 in *f* of the Inspection Gate
7:3 each one in *f* of his own house
8:3 in *f* of the men and the women
12:38 choir was walking in *f*
13:21 the night in *f* of the wall
Es 4:2 far as in *f* of the king's gate
Job 4:16 A form was in *f* of my eyes
10:17 witnesses . . . in *f* of me
26:6 Sheol is naked in *f* of him
Ps 5:5 their stand in *f* of your eyes
16:8 Jehovah in *f* of me constantly
18:12 the brightness in *f* of him
18:22 decisions are in *f* of me
18:24 my hands in *f* of his eyes
22:25 in *f* of those fearing him
23:5 table in *f* of those showing
26:3 your loving-kindness is in *f*
31:19 In *f* of the sons of men
31:22 from in *f* of your eyes
36:1 dread of God in *f* of his eyes
38:9 in *f* of you is all my desire
38:17 my pain was in *f* of me
39:1 anyone wicked is in *f* of me
39:5 duration is as nothing in *f*
44:15 humiliation is in *f* of me
50:8 offerings that are in *f* of me
51:3 And my sin is in *f* of me
52:9 in *f* of your loyal ones
54:3 have not set God in *f* of them
68:25 The singers went in *f*
69:19 hostility to me are in *f* of
78:12 In *f* of their forefathers he
86:14 set you in *f* of themselves
88:1 In the night also in *f* of you
89:36 throne as the sun in *f* of me
90:8 our errors right in *f* of you
101:3 set in *f* of my eyes any
101:7 established In *f* of my eyes
109:15 in *f* of Jehovah constantly
116:14 in *f* of all his people
116:18 in *f* of all his people
119:46 reminders in *f* of kings
119:168 my ways are in *f* of you
138:1 *f* of other gods I shall
Pr 4:25 gaze straight in *f* of you
5:21 *f* of the eyes of Jehovah
14:7 in *f* of the stupid man, for
15:11 Sheol . . . in *f* of Jehovah
Ec 6:8 walk in *f* of the living ones
Ca 6:5 eyes away from in *f* of me
Isa 1:7 in *f* of you strangers are
1:16 from in *f* of my eyes; cease
5:21 in *f* of their own faces
24:23 *f* of his elderly men with
40:17 nonexistent in *f* of him
47:14 no firelight in *f* of which
49:16 Your walls are in *f* of me
59:12 become many in *f* of you
61:11 in *f* of all the nations
Jer 16:17 hid from in *f* of my eyes
17:16 in *f* of your face it has
Eze 2:10 written upon in *f* and on the
14:3 have put in *f* of their faces
14:4 in *f* of his face and that
14:7 in *f* of his face and that
40:6 the *f* of which is toward the
40:12 in *f* of the guard chambers
40:15 *f* of the gate of the
40:15 *f* of the porch of the inner
40:19 in *f* of the lower gate to
40:19 *f* of the inner courtyard
Eze 40:20 gate the *f* of which was
40:22 the gate the *f* of which is
40:22 its porch was to their *f*
40:26 its porch was to their *f*
40:44 *f* side was toward the south
40:44 The *f* was toward the north
40:45 *f* of which is toward the
40:46 *f* of which is toward the
41:14 width of the *f* of the house
41:16 In *f* of the threshold there
41:21 in *f* of the holy place
41:25 the *f* of the porch outside
42:1 in *f* of the separated area
42:1 in *f* of the building to the
42:3 In *f* of the twenty cubits
42:3 in *f* of the pavement that
42:15 gate the *f* of which was
43:4 gate the *f* of which was
47:1 *f* of the House was east
Da 2:31 was standing in *f* of you, and
3:3 standing in *f* of the image
5:1 in *f* of the thousand he was
5:5 writing in *f* of the lampstand
8:15 standing in *f* of me someone
10:16 who was standing in *f* of me
Ho 7:2 In *f* of my face they have come
Am 9:3 in *f* of my eyes on the floor
Jon 2:4 away from in *f* of your eyes
Mic 2:8 From the *f* of a garment you
Hab 1:3 and violence in *f* of me
Zec 14:4 which is in *f* of Jerusalem
Mt 5:24 gift there in *f* of the altar
6:1 in *f* of men in order to be
23:6 the *f* seats in the synagogues
Mr 2:12 walked out in *f* of them all
10:32 Jesus was going in *f* of
11:9 those going in *f* and those
12:39 *f* seats in the synagogues
Lu 5:19 among those in *f* of Jesus
11:43 the *f* seats in the synagogues
13:26 We ate and drank in *f* of you
14:10 have honor in *f* of all your
20:46 *f* seats in the synagogues
23:14 I examined him in *f* of you
Joh 1:15 has advanced in *f* of me
1:30 man who has advanced in *f* of
13:23 in *f* of Jesus' bosom one of
Ac 4:10 stand here sound in *f* of you
18:17 in *f* of the judgment seat
19:33 the Jews thrusting him up *f*
1Th 2:5 a false *f* for covetousness
1Ti 6:12 in *f* of many witnesses
Re 4:6 full of eyes in *f* and behind
19:20 in *f* of it the signs with

Frontier
Ex 16:35 the *f* of the land of Canaan
Nu 33:37 on the *f* of the land of Edom
Jos 22:11 built an altar on the *f* of
Eze 25:9 at his cities to his *f*

Frontiers
Mt 19:1 *f* of Judea across the Jordan
Mr 10:1 came to the *f* of Judea and

Frontlet
Ex 13:16 a *f* band between your eyes
De 6:8 a *f* band between your eyes
11:18 *f* band between your eyes

Fronts
De 32:49 which *f* toward Jericho, and
34:1 Pisgah, which *f* toward

Frost
Jer 36:30 and to the *f* by night

Fruit
Ge 1:11, 11 *f* trees yielding *f*
1:12 trees yielding *f*, the seed of
1:29 the *f* of a tree bearing seed
3:2 *f* of the trees of the garden
3:3 as for eating of the *f* of the
3:6 she began taking of its *f* and
3:12 she gave me *f* from the tree
3:22 actually take *f* also from the
30:2 held back the *f* of the belly
Ex 10:15 all the *f* of the trees that
Le 19:24 *f* will become a holy thing
19:25 eat its *f* in order to add its
23:40 *f* of splendid trees, the
26:4 tree . . . will give its *f*
26:20 earth will not give its *f*
27:30 *f* of the tree, belongs to
De 7:13 and bless the *f* of your belly
7:13 and the *f* of your soil, your
28:4 the *f* of your belly and the
De 28:4 the *f* of your ground and the
28:4 the *f* of your domestic beast
28:11 the *f* of your belly and the
28:11 *f* of your domestic animals
28:18 the *f* of your belly and the
28:51 *f* of your domestic animals
28:53 eat the *f* of your belly
29:18 the *f* of a poisonous plant
30:9 in the *f* of your belly and
30:9 *f* of your domestic animals
2Sa 16:1 a hundred loads of summer *f*
16:2 *f* are for the young men to
Ps 1:3 gives its own *f* in its season
72:16 His *f* will be as in Lebanon
148:9 *f* trees and all you cedars
Pr 10:31 it bears the *f* of wisdom
27:18 will himself eat its *f*, and
Ec 2:5 I planted in them *f* trees of
Ca 2:3 *f* has been sweet to my palate
7:8 hold of its *f* stalks of dates
Isa 14:29 *f* will be a flying fiery
27:9 *f* when he takes away his
27:12 Jehovah will beat off the *f*
32:10 no *f* gathering will come in
57:19 creating the *f* of the lips
Jer 3:16 bear *f* in the land in those
11:16 pretty with *f* and in form
12:2 they have also produced *f*
17:8 leave off from producing *f*
Eze 17:8 produce boughs and to bear *f*
17:9 and make its very *f* scaly
17:23 bear boughs and produce *f*
19:10 A bearer of *f* and full of
19:12 wind that dried up her *f*
19:14 her very shoots, her very *f*
47:12 they will bear new *f*
Da 4:12 and its *f* was abundant, and
4:21 the *f* of which was abundant
Ho 9:16 no *f* that they produce
10:1 *F* he keeps putting forth for
10:1 to the abundance of his *f*
14:8 must *f* for you be found
Am 8:1 was a basket of summer *f*
8:2 I said: A basket of summer *f*
9:14 gardens and eat the *f* of them
Mic 7:1 the gatherings of summer *f*
7:13 of the *f* of their dealings
Mal 1:12 its *f* is something to be
3:11 for you the *f* of the ground
Mt 3:8 then produce *f* that befits
3:10 not produce fine *f* is to be
7:17 good tree produces fine *f*
7:17 tree produces worthless *f*
7:18 tree cannot bear worthless *f*
7:18 a rotten tree produce fine *f*
7:19 tree not producing fine *f*
12:33 the tree fine and its *f* fine
12:33 tree rotten and its *f* rotten
12:33 by its *f* the tree is known
13:8 and they began to yield *f*
13:23 who really does bear *f* and
13:26 sprouted and produced *f*
21:19 no *f* come from you anymore
Mr 4:7 choked it, and it yielded no *f*
4:8 they began to yield *f*, and
4:20 bear *f* thirtyfold and sixty
4:28 the ground bears *f* gradually
4:29 as soon as the *f* permits it
11:14 Let no one eat *f* from you
Lu 1:42 blessed is the *f* of your womb
3:9 not producing fine *f* is to be
6:43 fine tree producing rotten *f*
6:43 rotten tree producing fine *f*
6:44 tree is known by its own *f*
8:8 it produced *f* a hundredfold
8:15 and bear *f* with endurance
13:6 came looking for *f* on it, but
13:7 looking for *f* on this fig tree
13:9 it produces *f* in the future
20:10 of the *f* of the vineyard
Joh 4:36 gathering *f* for everlasting
12:24 it then bears much *f*
15:2 branch in me not bearing *f*
15:2 one bearing *f* he cleans
15:2 that it may bear more *f*
15:4 branch cannot bear *f* of
15:5 this one bears much *f*
15:8 you keep bearing much *f*
15:16 and keep bearing *f* and that
15:16 that your *f* should remain
Ro 6:21 *f* that you used to have at
6:22 your *f* in the way of holiness
7:4 that we should bear *f* to God
7:5 should bring forth *f* to death

Ro 15:28 got this *f* securely to them
1Co 9:7 and does not eat of its *f*
Php 1:11 be filled with righteous *f*
Col 1:6 bearing *f* and increasing in
1:10 bearing *f* in every good work
Heb 12:11 yields peaceable *f*, namely
13:15 *f* of lips which make public
Jas 3:18 *f* of righteousness has its
5:7 the precious *f* of the earth
5:18 and the land put forth its *f*
Re 18:14 *f* that your soul desired has
22:2 producing twelve crops of *f*

Fruitage
Le 19:23 its *f* impure as its foreskin
25:19 land will indeed give its *f*
Nu 13:20 take some of the *f* of the
13:26 showing them the *f* of the
13:27 and honey, and this is its *f*
De 1:25 some of the *f* of the land in
26:2 of all the *f* of the soil
26:10 *f* of the ground that Jehovah
28:11 and the *f* of your ground
28:18 and the *f* of your ground
28:33 The *f* of your ground and
28:42 the *f* of your ground
28:51 and the *f* of your ground
30:9 and the *f* of your soil
2Ki 19:29 vineyards and eat their *f*
19:30 and produce *f* upward
Ne 9:36 to eat its *f* and its good
10:35 *f* of every sort of tree
10:37 *f* of every sort of tree
Job 31:39 its *f* I have eaten without
Ps 21:10 Their *f* you will destroy
58:11 there is *f* for the righteous
104:13 *f* of your works the earth
105:35 the *f* of their ground
127:3 *f* of the belly is a reward
132:11 Of the *f* of your belly
Pr 1:31 eat from the *f* of their way
8:19 My *f* is better than gold
11:30 *f* of the righteous one is
12:14 *f* of a man's mouth he is
13:2 *f* of his mouth a man will
18:20 From the *f* of a man's mouth
18:21 is loving it will eat its *f*
31:16 from the *f* of her hands she
31:31 of the *f* of her hands, and
Ca 8:11 for its *f* a thousand silver
8:12 to those keeping its *f*
Isa 3:10 very *f* of their dealings
4:2 *f* of the land will be
10:12 *f* of the insolence of the
13:18 *f* of the belly they will
37:30 vineyards and eat their *f*
37:31 and produce *f* upward
65:21 vineyards and eat their *f*
Jer 2:7 to eat its *f* and its good
6:19 as the *f* of their thoughts
7:20 and upon the *f* of the ground
17:10 to the *f* of his dealings
21:14 the *f* of your dealings
29:5 plant gardens and eat their *f*
29:28 gardens and eat their *f*
32:19 to the *f* of his dealings
48:32 Upon your summer *f* and upon
La 2:20 keep eating their own *f*
Eze 25:4 will eat your *f*, and they
34:27 the field must give its *f*
36:8 and bear your own *f* for my
36:30 the *f* of the tree abound
47:12 will their *f* be consumed
47:12 *f* must prove to be for
Da 4:14 foliage, and scatter its *f*
Ho 10:13 eaten the *f* of deception
Joe 2:22 tree will . . . give its *f*
Am 2:9 I went annihilating his *f*
6:12 the *f* of righteousness into
Mic 6:7 the *f* of my belly for the sin
Zec 8:12 vine itself will give its *f*
Ac 2:30 one from the *f* of his loins
Ro 1:13 some *f* also among you even
Ga 5:22 the *f* of the spirit is love
Eph 5:9 the *f* of the light consists
Php 1:22 this is a *f* of my work
4:17 *f* that brings more credit to

Fruit-bearing
Ge 49:22 Offshoot of a *f* tree, Joseph
49:22 the offshoot of a *f* tree
Ps 128:3 wife will be like a *f* vine
Isa 17:6 five on the *f* boughs thereof
32:12 fields, over the *f* vine

Fruitful
Ge 1:22 Be *f* and become many and fill
1:28 God said to them: Be *f* and
8:17 be *f* and become many upon
9:1 say to them: Be *f* and become
9:7 you men, be *f* and become many
17:6 make you very, very *f* and
17:20 bless . . . make him *f*
26:22 has made us *f* in the earth
28:3 make you *f* and multiply you
35:11 Be *f* and become many
41:52 God has made me *f* in the
47:27 *f* and grew to be very many
48:4 I am making you *f*, and I will
Ex 1:7 the sons of Israel became *f*
23:30 until you become *f* and
Le 26:9 *f* and multiply you, and I
Ps 105:24 making his people very *f*
107:34 *F* land into salt country
107:37 they may yield *f* crops
Isa 5:1 have on a *f* hillside
11:1 his roots a sprout will be *f*
45:8 let it be *f* with salvation
Jer 23:3 be *f* and become many
Eze 36:11 multiply and become *f*
Ac 14:17 and *f* seasons, filling your

Fruitfulness
Ho 13:15 reed plants should show *f*

Fruitless
Mal 3:11 the field prove *f* for you
1Pe 1:18 *f* form of conduct received
Jude 12 trees in late autumn, but *f*

Fruits
Ge 4:3 proceeded to bring some *f*
Ex 23:16 harvest of the first ripe *f*
23:19 first ripe *f* of your ground
34:22 first ripe *f* of the wheat
34:26 first ripe *f* of your soil you
Le 2:14 the first ripe *f* to Jehovah
2:14 offering of your first ripe *f*
23:17 as first ripe *f* to Jehovah
23:20 loaves of the first ripe *f*
Nu 13:20 first ripe *f* of the grapes
18:13 first ripe *f* of all that is
28:26 the day of the first ripe *f*
2Ki 4:42 bread of the first ripe *f*
Ne 10:35 first ripe *f* of our ground
10:35 and the first ripe *f* of all
13:31 and for the first ripe *f*
Ca 4:13 with the choicest *f*, henna
4:16 garden and eat its choicest *f*
7:13 all sorts of the choicest *f*
Jer 40:10 gather wine and summer *f*
40:12 summer *f* in very great
Eze 44:30 first ripe *f* of everything
Na 3:12 trees with the first ripe *f*
Mt 7:16 By their *f* you will recognize
7:20 by their *f* you will recognize
21:34 season of the *f* came around
21:34 his slaves . . . to get his *f*
21:41 who will render him the *f*
21:43 to a nation producing its *f*
Mr 12:2 the *f* of the vineyard from
Lu 3:8 produce *f* that befit repentance
2Ti 2:6 the first to partake of the *f*
Jas 3:17 full of mercy and good *f*
Re 22:2 yielding their *f* each month

Frustrate
2Sa 15:34 *f* the counsel of Ahithophel
17:14 *f* the counsel of Ahithophel
Ezr 4:5 to *f* their counsel all the

Frustrated
Ne 4:15 true God had *f* their counsel

Frustrating
Job 5:12 *f* the schemes of the shrewd
Pr 15:22 There is a *f* of plans where
Isa 44:25 *f* the signs of the empty

Fuel
Eze 15:4 where it must be put for *f*
15:6 have given to the fire as *f*
21:32 fire you will become *f*

Fugitive
Ge 4:12 A wanderer and a *f* you will
4:14 must become a wanderer and *f*
Ps 56:8 My being a *f* you yourself
Jer 4:1 then you will not go as a *f*

Fugitiveness
Ge 4:16 residence in the land of *F*

Fugitives
Eze 17:21 *f* of his in all his bands
Ho 9:17 become *f* among the nations

Fulfill
1Ki 2:27 to *f* Jehovah's word that he
2Ch 36:21 to *f* Jehovah's word by the
36:21 to *f* seventy years
Job 39:2 lunar months that they *f*
Ps 20:4 And all your counsel may he *f*
20:5 Jehovah *f* all your requests
Isa 65:20 that does not *f* his days
Mt 5:17 not to destroy, but to *f*
Lu 9:31 destined to *f* at Jerusalem
Ga 6:2 thus *f* the law of the Christ
Col 4:17 in the Lord, that you *f* it

Fulfilled
Ex 7:25 seven days came to be *f* after
Es 2:12 procedure were gradually *f*
Job 15:32 Before his day will it be *f*
Isa 40:2 military service has been *f*
Jer 25:12 seventy years have been *f*
25:34 your scatterings have been *f*
Da 4:33 was *f* upon Nebuchadnezzar
Mt 1:22 to be *f* which was spoken by
2:15 for that to be *f* which was
2:17 *f* which was spoken through
2:23 be *f* what was spoken through
4:14 be *f* what was spoken through
8:17 be *f* what was spoken through
12:17 *f* what was spoken through
13:35 that there might be *f* what
21:4 might be *f* what was spoken
26:54 Scriptures be *f* that it must
26:56 of the prophets to be *f*
27:9 was *f*, saying: And they took
Mr 1:15 The appointed time has been *f*
14:49 that the Scriptures may be *f*
Lu 1:20 be *f* in their appointed time
1:23 his public service were *f*
4:21 scripture . . . just heard is *f*
21:22 the things written may be *f*
21:24 times of the nations are *f*
22:16 *f* in the kingdom of God
24:44 Psalms about me must be *f*
Joh 12:38 Isaiah the prophet was *f*
13:18 the Scripture might be *f*
15:25 Law may be *f*, They hated
17:12 the scripture might be *f*
18:9 word might be *f* which he
18:32 word of Jesus might be *f*
19:24 *f*: They apportioned my
19:36 for the scripture to be *f*
Ac 1:16 for the scripture to be *f*
3:18 God has *f* the things he
7:23 fortieth year was being *f*
7:30 And when forty years were *f*
13:27 *f* the things voiced by the
13:33 God has entirely *f* it to us
21:26 notice of the days to be *f*
Ro 8:4 Law might be *f* in us who walk
13:8 he that loves . . . *f* the law
Ga 5:14 Law stands *f* in one saying
Jas 2:23 scripture was *f* which says

Fulfilling
Le 8:33 day of *f* the days of your
12:4 until the *f* of the days of her
12:6 at the *f* of the days of her
Jer 29:10 the *f* of seventy years at
Da 9:2 for *f* the devastations of
Ac 13:25 as John was *f* his course

Fulfillment
1Ki 8:15 by his own hand has given *f*
8:24 made the *f*, as at this day
2Ch 6:4 by his own hands has given *f*
6:15 have made *f* as at this day
Jer 44:25 you people have made a *f*
Mt 13:14 of Isaiah is having *f*, which
Ac 7:17 *f* of the promise that God
26:7 to the *f* of this promise
Ro 13:10 love is the law's *f*
Heb 10:36 the *f* of the promise
11:13 get the *f* of the promises
11:39 get the *f* of the promise

Full
Ge 6:13 earth is *f* of violence as a
23:9 For the *f* amount of silver
25:24 her days came to the *f* for
29:7 Why, it is yet *f* day
29:14 he dwelt with him a *f* month
29:27 Celebrate to the *f* the week
41:1 at the end of two *f* years

Ge 41:7 seven fat and *f* ears of grain
41:22 up on one stalk, *f* and good
43:21 our money in *f* weight
43:34 drinking with him to the *f*
48:19 the *f* equivalent of nations
Ex 8:21 simply be *f* of the gadfly
9:8 hands *f* of soot from a kiln
22:29 *f* produce and the overflow
23:26 the number of your days *f*
Le 6:5 compensation for it in its *f*
13:12 the *f* sight of the priest's
16:12 the fire holder *f* of burning
16:12 *f* of fine perfumed incense
25:30 year has come to the *f* for
Nu 6:5 the days . . . come to the *f*
6:13 Naziriteship come to the *f*, he
7:13 *f* of fine flour moistened
7:14 of ten shekels, *f* of incense
7:19 *f* of fine flour moistened
7:20 gold cup . . . *f* of incense
7:25 *f* of fine flour moistened
7:26 of ten shekels, *f* of incense
7:31 *f* of fine flour moistened
7:32 of ten shekels, *f* of incense
7:37 *f* of fine flour moistened
7:38 gold cup . . . *f* of incense
7:43 *f* of fine flour moistened
7:44 of ten shekels, *f* of incense
7:49 *f* of fine flour moistened
7:50 of ten shekels, *f* of incense
7:55 *f* of fine flour moistened
7:56 of ten shekels, *f* of incense
7:61 *f* of fine flour moistened
7:62 of ten shekels, *f* of incense
7:67 *f* of fine flour moistened
7:68 gold cup . . . *f* of incense
7:73 *f* of fine flour moistened
7:74 of ten shekels, *f* of incense
7:79 *f* of fine flour moistened
7:80 of ten shekels, *f* of incense
7:86 twelve gold cups *f* of incense
18:27 *f* produce of the wine or oil
22:18 house *f* of silver and gold
24:13 house *f* of silver and gold
De 6:11 houses *f* of all good things
8:17 the *f* might of my own hand
22:9 the *f* produce of the seed that
33:23 *f* of the blessing of Jehovah
34:9 was *f* of the spirit of wisdom
Jg 16:27 the house was *f* of men and
Ru 1:21 I was *f* when I went, and it
1Sa 18:27 giving them in *f* number to
28:20 his *f* length to the earth
2Sa 7:12 days come to the *f*, and you
8:2 *f* line to preserve them alive
13:23 two *f* years that Absalom
14:28 Jerusalem for two *f* years
23:11 the field *f* of lentils
1Ki 7:14 he was *f* of the wisdom and
2Ki 3:16 torrent valley *f* of ditches
4:4 *f* ones you should set aside
4:6 as soon as the vessels were *f*
4:39 wild gourds . . . garment *f*
6:17 *f* of horses and war chariots
7:15 the way was *f* of garments
10:21 house of Baal came to be *f*
15:13 reign for a *f* lunar month
1Ch 11:13 of the field *f* of barley
13:8 with *f* power and with songs
17:11 days have come to the *f* for
21:22 For the money in *f* give it
21:24 purchase for the money in *f*
2Ch 15:15 *f* pleasure on their part
21:19 two *f* years had expired
Ezr 7:19 deliver in *f* before God at
Ne 9:25 houses *f* of all good things
Es 1:5 these days had come to the *f*
Job 8:16 He is *f* of sap before the sun
20:11 been *f* of his youthful vigor
21:23 his *f* self-sufficiency
21:24 thighs have become *f* of fat
28:18 more than one *f* of pearls
30:21 the *f* might of your hand
32:18 I have become *f* of words
36:16 table will be *f* of fatness
Ps 10:7 His mouth is *f* of oaths and
26:10 right hand is *f* of bribery
38:7 loins have become *f* of
48:10 hand is *f* of righteousness
65:9 stream from God is *f* of water
68:6 prisoners into *f* prosperity
73:10 waters of what is *f* are
74:20 *f* of the abodes of violence
75:8 foaming, it is *f* of mixture
Ps 81:3 On the *f* moon, for the day of
104:24 earth is *f* of your
144:13 Our garners *f*, furnishing
Pr 7:20 *f* moon he will come to his
17:1 house *f* of the sacrifices of
17:18 going *f* surety before his
Ec 1:7 yet the sea itself is not *f*
9:3 sons of men is also *f* of bad
Ca 6:10 beautiful like the *f* moon
Isa 1:21 She was *f* of justice
2:6 *f* of what is from the East
15:9 Dimon have become *f* of blood
21:3 become *f* of severe pains
22:2 With turmoil you were *f*, a
22:7 become *f* of war chariots
24:23 *f* moon has become abashed
28:8 become *f* of filthy vomit
30:26 light of the *f* moon must
30:27 become *f* of denunciation
31:4 a *f* number of shepherds, and
32:18 residences of *f* confidence
40:2 *f* amount for all her sins
40:29 he makes *f* might abound
45:24 *f* righteousness and strength
47:9 the *f* might of your spells
51:20 *f* of the rage of Jehovah
63:15 your zeal and your *f* might
65:22 ones will use to the *f*
66:11 the breast of *f* consolation
Jer 3:8 certificate of her *f* divorce
4:12 The *f* wind itself comes even
5:27 cage is *f* of flying creatures
5:27 houses are *f* of deception
6:11 I have become *f*. I have
6:11 with one that is *f* of days
16:18 I will repay the *f* amount
23:10 that the land has become *f*
28:3 Within two *f* years more I
28:11 within two *f* years more
35:5 cups *f* of wine and goblets
51:5 been *f* of guilt from the
La 4:18 Our days have come to their *f*
Eze 1:18 their rims were *f* of eyes
5:2 the siege have come to the *f*
7:23 *f* of bloodstained judgment
7:23 has become *f* of violence
9:9 the city is *f* of crookedness
10:4 *f* of the brightness of the
10:12 were *f* of eyes all around
17:3 long pinions, *f* of plumage
19:10 *f* of branches she became
28:12 *f* of wisdom and perfect in
36:38 become *f* of a flock of men
37:1 plain, and it was *f* of bones
41:8 *f* reed of six cubits to the
43:5 *f* of the glory of Jehovah
Da 10:2 mourning for three *f* weeks
10:3 of the three *f* weeks
Joe 2:24 must be *f* of cleansed grain
3:13 the winepress has become *f*
Am 2:13 *f* up with a row of newly cut
Mic 3:8 *f* of power, with the spirit
6:12 have become *f* of violence
Na 3:1 *f* of deception and of robbery
3:9 Ethiopia was her *f* might, also
Mt 6:2 are having their reward in *f*
6:5 are having their reward in *f*
6:16 are having their reward in *f*
9:16 its *f* strength would pull
13:48 When it got *f* they hauled it
14:20 fragments, twelve baskets *f*
15:37 seven provision baskets *f*
23:25 inside they are *f* of plunder
23:27 *f* of dead men's bones and
23:28 you are *f* of hypocrisy and
Mr 2:21 its *f* strength pulls from it
4:28 the *f* grain in the head
6:43 fragments, twelve baskets *f*
8:8 seven provision baskets *f*
8:19 baskets *f* of fragments you
8:20 baskets *f* of fragments did
Lu 1:1 are given *f* credence among us
2:6 the days came to the *f* for her
2:21 when eight days came to the *f*
2:22 came to the *f*, they brought
4:1 Jesus, *f* of holy spirit
5:12 look! a man *f* of leprosy
6:24 having your consolation in *f*
9:51 were now coming to the *f*
11:22 takes away his *f* armament
11:39 inside of you is *f* of plunder
16:20 put at his gate, *f* of ulcers
16:25 received in *f* your good
23:41 in *f* what we deserve for
Joh 1:14 *f* of undeserved kindness
3:29 joy of mine has been made *f*
15:11 and your joy may be made *f*
16:24 your joy may be made *f*
17:13 joy in themselves to the *f*
19:29 vessel . . . *f* of sour wine
19:29 sponge *f* of the sour wine
21:11 net to land *f* of big fishes
21:25 were written in *f* detail
Ac 2:13 They are *f* of sweet wine
6:3 *f* of spirit and wisdom, that
6:5 Stephen, a man *f* of faith and
6:8 Stephen, *f* of graciousness and
7:55 he, being *f* of holy spirit
11:24 *f* of holy spirit and of faith
13:10 *f* of every sort of fraud and
14:17 filling your hearts to the *f*
17:16 that the city was *f* of idols
19:28 becoming *f* of anger, the men
Ro 1:27 *f* recompense, which was due
1:29 *f* of envy, murder, strife
1:32 know *f* well the righteous
3:14 mouth is *f* of cursing and
11:12 more will the *f* number of
11:25 *f* number of people of the
15:14 are also *f* of goodness, as
15:29 a *f* measure of blessing from
1Co 1:5 in *f* ability to speak and in
1:5 to speak and in *f* knowledge
7:31 those not using it to the *f*
2Co 9:8 have *f* self-sufficiency in
Ga 4:4 *f* limit of the time arrived
Eph 1:10 *f* limit of the appointed
Php 1:9 knowledge and *f* discernment
2:2 make my joy *f* in that you are
4:12 how to be *f* and how to
4:18 I have all things in *f* and
Col 2:2 the *f* assurance of their
1Ti 1:15 deserving of *f* acceptance is
2:2 with *f* godly devotion and
2:11 with *f* submissiveness
4:9 deserving of *f* acceptance is
6:1 worthy of *f* honor, that the
Tit 2:10 good fidelity to the *f*, so
2:15 reproving with *f* authority
Heb 6:11 the *f* assurance of the hope
10:22 in the *f* assurance of faith
Jas 3:8 is *f* of death-dealing poison
3:17 *f* of mercy and good fruits
2Pe 2:14 They have eyes *f* of adultery
1Jo 1:4 our joy may be in *f* measure
2Jo 8 that you may obtain a *f* reward
12 your joy may be in *f* measure
Re 4:6 *f* of eyes in front and behind
4:8 underneath they are *f* of eyes
5:8 bowls that were *f* of incense
15:7 were *f* of the anger of God
17:3 *f* of blasphemous names and
17:4 *f* of disgusting things and the
18:11 no one to buy their *f* stock
18:12 *f* stock of gold and silver
21:9 *f* of the seven last plagues

Fuller
1Th 4:10 go on doing it in *f* measure

Full-grown
Ge 32:15 she-asses and ten *f* asses
49:11 Tying his *f* ass to a vine
Jg 10:4 who rode on thirty *f* asses
12:14 who rode on seventy *f* asses
Isa 30:6 shoulders of *f* asses they
30:24 *f* asses cultivating the
Zec 9:9 upon a *f* animal the son of a
1Co 14:20 yet become *f* in powers of
Eph 4:13 to a *f* man, to the measure

Fullness
De 33:16 things of the earth and its *f*
Ps 50:12 the productive land and its *f*
110:6 cause a *f* of dead bodies
Isa 6:3 *f* of all the earth is his
Eze 12:19 be laid desolate of its *f*
30:12 the land and its *f* to be
32:15 land is desolated of its *f*
Joh 1:16 received from out of his *f*
Eph 1:23 the *f* of him who fills up
3:19 all the *f* that God gives
4:10 might give *f* to all things
4:13 to the *f* of the Christ
Col 1:19 for all *f* to dwell in him
2:9 the *f* of the divine quality
2:10 possessed of a *f* by means of

Full-throated
Isa 58:1 Call out *f*; do not hold back

Fully
Ge 29:28 Jacob did so and celebrated *f*
50:3 took *f* forty days for him
De 1:36 he has followed Jehovah *f*
Jos 14:8 I followed Jehovah my God *f*
14:9 followed Jehovah my God *f*
14:14 followed . . . the God of Israel *f*
Jg 19:2 continued there *f* four months
Ru 2:11 The report was *f* made to me
2Sa 23:7 *f* armed with iron and the
1Ki 11:6 did not follow Jehovah *f*
Ec 8:11 *f* set in them to do bad
La 2:20 the children born *f* formed
2:22 I brought forth *f* formed
Na 1:10 devoured like stubble *f* dry
Mt 11:27 no one *f* knows the Son but
11:27 *f* know the Father but the
Lu 1:4 know *f* the certainty of the
1:53 he has *f* satisfied hungry ones
9:32 but when they got *f* awake
24:31 their eyes were *f* opened
24:32 *f* opening up the Scriptures
24:45 opened up their minds *f* to
Joh 7:8 due time has not yet *f* come
Ac 12:25 *f* carried out the relief
14:26 work they had *f* performed
22:24 know *f* for what cause they
Ro 4:21 *f* convinced that what he had
14:5 *f* convinced in his own mind
2Co 10:6 obedience has been *f* carried
Eph 2:16 *f* reconcile both peoples in
Php 2:30 he might *f* make up for your
4:19 God will *f* supply all your
Col 1:10 to the end of *f* pleasing him
1:11 so as to endure *f* and be
1:25 to preach the word of God *f*
1Th 4:1 keep on doing it more *f*
2Ti 3:17 be *f* competent, completely
4:5 *f* accomplish your ministry
4:17 might be *f* accomplished and
Re 2:10 may be *f* put to the test
3:2 deeds *f* performed before my

Fume
Ps 80:4 how long must you *f* against

Fun
Ge 21:9 borne to Abraham, poking *f*
Pr 26:19 said: Was I not having *f*?
Mt 20:19 to make *f* of and to scourge
27:29 they made *f* of him, saying
27:31 when they had made *f* of him
27:41 making *f* of him and saying
Mr 10:34 they will make *f* of him and
15:20 when they had made *f* of him
15:31 chief priests were making *f*
Lu 18:32 will be made *f* of and be
22:63 make *f* of him, hitting him
23:11 made *f* of him by clothing
23:36 the soldiers made *f* of him

Function
1Ch 23:28 *f* was at the disposition of
Ro 12:4 do not all have the same *f*

Functionaries
2Ki 17:32 *f* for them in the house of

Functioning
Eph 4:16 *f* of each respective member

Funeral
2Ch 16:14 great *f* burning for him

Furious
De 3:26 Jehovah continued to be *f*
Job 40:11 the *f* outburst of your anger
Ps 78:21 heard and began to be *f*
78:59 God heard and got to be *f*
78:62 his inheritance he became *f*
89:38 *f* toward your anointed one
Pr 14:16 the stupid is becoming *f*
26:17 *f* at the quarrel that is not
Jer 7:29 generation with which . . . *f*
Da 2:12 angry and got very *f*, and

Furlongs
Re 14:20 of a thousand six hundred *f*
21:16 twelve thousand *f*; its

Furnace
Ge 15:17 smoking *f* and a fiery torch
De 4:20 bring you out of the iron *f*
1Ki 8:51 from inside the iron *f*
Job 41:20 a *f* set aflame even with
Ps 12:6 refined in a smelting *f*
21:9 constitute them as a fiery *f*
Pr 17:3 the *f* for gold, but Jehovah
Pr 27:21 and the *f* is for gold
Isa 31:9 and whose *f* is in Jerusalem
48:10 smelting *f* of affliction
Jer 11:4 out of the *f* of iron, saying
La 5:10 skin . . . hot just like a *f*
Eze 22:18 lead in the midst of a *f*
22:20 into the midst of a *f*
22:22 in the midst of a *f*, so
Da 3:6 into the burning fiery *f*
3:11 into the burning fiery *f*
3:15 into the burning fiery *f*
3:17 Out of the burning fiery *f*
3:19 heat up the *f* seven times
3:20 into the burning fiery *f*
3:21 into the burning fiery *f*
3:22 the *f* was heated to excess
3:23 midst of the burning fiery *f*
3:26 door of the burning fiery *f*
Ho 7:4 a *f* set burning by a baker
7:6 their heart near as to a *f*
7:6 by morning the *f* is burning as
7:7 hot, all of them, like the *f*
Mal 4:1 that is burning like the *f*
Mt 13:42 pitch them into the fiery *f*
13:50 cast them into the fiery *f*
Re 1:15 copper when glowing in a *f*
9:2 as the smoke of a great *f*

Furnish
Jos 18:4 *F* for yourselves three men
Isa 43:9 Let them *f* their witnesses
46:2 unable to *f* escape for the
46:4 may bear up and *f* escape
Jer 39:18 *f* you an escape, and by
Eze 22:14 hands *f* strength in the
Da 5:16 are able to *f* interpretations
Ac 16:16 to *f* her masters with much
1Co 9:18 may *f* the good news without
1Ti 1:4 *f* questions for research

Furnished
2Ch 28:15 *f* them with sandals and
Isa 63:5 So my arm *f* me salvation
Mt 21:16 mouth of babes . . . *f* praise
Mr 14:15 upper room, *f* in preparation
Lu 22:12 a large upper room *f*. Get it
Ac 17:31 *f* a guarantee to all men in
19:24 *f* the craftsmen no little
Heb 9:16 covenanter needs to be *f*

Furnishes
1Ti 6:17 *f* us all things richly for

Furnishing
Ps 144:13 *f* products of one sort

Furnishings
Ex 25:9 and pattern of all its *f*
Nu 7:1 sanctify it and all its *f* and

Furniture
Ne 13:8 *f* of Tobiah's house outside

Furrow
Job 39:10 with its ropes in the *f*

Furrows
Job 31:38 *f* themselves would weep
41:15 *F* of scales are its
Ps 65:10 There is a drenching of its *f*
129:3 have lengthened their *f*
Ho 10:4 in the *f* of the open field
12:11 like piles of stones in the *f*

Furtherance
Php 2:22 in *f* of the good news

Fury
Ge 49:7 *f*, because it acts harshly
Job 21:30 the day of *f* he is delivered
Ps 7:6 *f* of those showing hostility
78:49 *F* and denunciation and
85:3 have controlled all your *f*
90:9 to their decline in your *f*
90:11 *f* according to the fear of
Pr 11:4 no benefit on the day of *f*
11:23 hope of the wicked ones is *f*
14:35 his *f* comes to be toward one
20:2 drawing his *f* against himself
21:24 in a *f* of presumptuousness
22:8 rod of his *f* will come to its
Isa 9:19 *f* of Jehovah of armies the
10:6 against the people of my *f*
13:9 cruel both with *f* and with
13:13 at the *f* of Jehovah of
14:6 one striking peoples in *f*
16:6 his pride and his *f*—his
Jer 48:30 I myself have known his *f*
La 2:2 In his *f* he has torn down the
La 3:1 because of the staff of his *f*
Eze 7:19 in the day of Jehovah's *f*
19:12 was finally uprooted in *f*
20:13 I promised to pour out my *f*
21:31 the fire of my *f* I shall
22:21 with the fire of my *f*
22:31 With the fire of my *f* I
38:19 in the fire of my *f*, I
Da 3:13 in a rage and *f*, said to bring
3:19 got filled with *f*
Ho 5:10 pour out my *f* just like water
13:11 shall take him away in my *f*
Am 1:11 *f*—he has kept it perpetually
Hab 3:8 is your *f* against the sea
Zep 1:15 That day is a day of *f*
1:18 in the day of Jehovah's *f*

Futile
1Co 3:20 reasonings of the wise . . . *f*
Tit 3:9 they are unprofitable and *f*
Jas 1:26 man's form of worship is *f*

Futility
Ro 8:20 creation was subjected to *f*

Future
Ge 30:33 whatever *f* day you may come
De 6:20 son should ask you in a *f* day
29:22 the *f* generation, your sons
Jos 22:24 In a *f* day your sons will
22:27 say in a *f* day to our sons
22:28 in a *f* day, we must also
2Sa 7:19 down to a distant *f* time
1Ch 17:17 down to a distant *f* time
Ps 37:37 the *f* of that man will be
37:38 The *f* of wicked people will
48:13 to the *f* generation
73:17 I wanted to discern their *f*
102:18 for the *f* generation
Pr 5:11 *f* when your flesh and your
19:20 may become wise in your *f*
20:21 own *f* will not be blessed
23:18 there will exist a *f*, and
24:14 then there exists a *f*, and
24:20 to be no *f* for anyone bad
31:25 and she laughs at a *f* day
Isa 30:8 it may serve for a *f* day
41:22 and know the *f* of them
Jer 12:4 He does not see our *f*
29:11 give you a *f* and a hope
31:17 exists a hope for your *f*
La 1:9 did not remember the *f* for her
Lu 13:9 it produces fruit in the *f*
1Ti 6:19 a fine foundation for the *f*

Gaal
Jg 9:26 Then *G* the son of Ebed and his
9:28 *G* the son of Ebed went on to
9:30 words of *G* the son of Ebed
9:31 *G* the son of Ebed and his
9:35 *G* the son of Ebed went out
9:36 *G* caught sight of the people
9:37 *G* spoke once more and said
9:39 *G* went on out at the head of
9:41 drive *G* and his brothers out

Gaash
Jos 24:30 Ephraim, north of Mount *G*
Jg 2:9 on the north of Mount *G*
2Sa 23:30 the torrent valleys of *G*
1Ch 11:32 the torrent valleys of *G*

Gabbai
Ne 11:8 *G* and Sallai, nine hundred and

Gabbatha
Joh 19:13 but, in Hebrew, *G*

Gabriel
Da 8:16 *G*, make that one there
9:21 man *G*, whom I had seen in
Lu 1:19 I am *G*, who stands near
1:26 the angel *G* was sent forth

Gad
Ge 30:11 So she called his name *G*
35:26 sons by Zilpah . . . were *G*
46:16 sons of *G* were Ziphion and
49:19 As for *G*, a marauder band
Ex 1:4 Dan and Naphtali, *G* and Asher
Nu 1:14 of *G*, Eliasaph the son of
1:24 sons of *G*, their births
1:25 registered . . . tribe of *G*
2:14 And the tribe of *G*
2:14 chieftain for the sons of *G*
7:42 chieftain for the sons of *G*
10:20 tribe of the sons of *G* there
13:15 of the tribe of *G*, Geuel the

Nu 26:15 sons of *G* by their families
26:18 families of the sons of *G*
32:1 sons of *G* had come to have
32:2 the sons of *G* and the sons of
32:6 Moses said to the sons of *G*
32:25 sons of *G* and the sons of
32:29 If the sons of *G* and the sons
32:31 sons of *G* and the sons of
32:33 to the sons of *G* and to the
32:34 sons of *G* proceeded to build
De 27:13 *G* and Asher and Zebulun, Dan
33:20 And as to *G* he said: Blessed
33:20 widening the borders of *G*
Jos 4:12 sons of *G* and the half tribe
13:24 a gift to the tribe of *G*
13:24 sons of *G* by their families
13:28 inheritance of the sons of *G*
18:7 and *G* and Reuben and the half
20:8 Gilead out of the tribe of *G*
21:7 and out of the tribe of *G* and
21:38 And out of the tribe of *G*
22:9 sons of *G* and the half tribe
22:10 sons of *G* and the half tribe
22:11 sons of *G* and the half tribe
22:13 sons of *G* and the half
22:15 the sons of *G* and the half
22:21 the sons of *G* and the half
22:25 Reuben and the sons of *G*
22:30 sons of *G* and the sons of
22:31 said to . . . the sons of *G*
22:32 of *G* in the land of Gilead
22:33 sons of *G* were dwelling
22:34 sons of *G* began to name
1Sa 13:7 to the land of *G* and Gilead
22:5 *G* the prophet said to David
2Sa 24:11 *G* the prophet, David's
24:13 *G* came in to David and told
24:14 David said to *G*: It is very
24:18 *G* came in to David on that
24:19 accord with the word of *G*
1Ch 2:2 Naphtali, *G* and Asher
5:11 sons of *G* in front of them
6:63 from the tribe of *G* and from
6:80 from the tribe of *G*, Ramoth
12:14 of *G*, heads of the army
21:9 speak to *G*, David's visionary
21:11 *G* went in to David and said
21:13 David said to *G*: It is very
21:18 said to *G* to say to David
21:19 went up at the word of *G*
29:29 words of *G* the visionary
2Ch 29:25 *G* the king's visionary and
Jer 49:1 has taken possession of *G*
Eze 48:27 the western border, *G* one
48:28 by the boundary of *G*, to the
48:34 the gate of *G*, one
Re 7:5 out of . . . *G* twelve thousand

Gadarenes
Mt 8:28 into the country of the *G*

Gaddi
Nu 13:11 *G* the son of Susi

Gaddiel
Nu 13:10 of Zebulun, *G* the son of Sodi

Gadding
1Ti 5:13 *g* about to the houses

Gadflies
Ex 8:24 heavy swarms of *g* began to
8:24 ruin as a result of the *g*
8:29 *g* will certainly turn away
8:31 *g* turned away from Pharaoh
Ps 78:45 send upon them *g*, that
105:31 said that the *g* should come

Gadfly
Ex 8:21 and into your houses the *g*
8:21 will simply be full of the *g*
8:22 that no *g* may exist there

Gadi
2Ki 15:14 Menahem the son of *G* came
15:17 Menahem the son of *G*

Gadite
2Sa 23:36 Nathan of Zobah, Bani the *G*

Gadites
Nu 34:14 *G* . . . have already taken
De 3:12 to the Reubenites and the *G*
3:16 to the Reubenites and the *G*
4:43 Ramoth in Gilead for the *G*
29:8 the *G* and half the tribe of
Jos 1:12 to the Reubenites and the *G*
12:6 to the Reubenites and the *G*
13:8 the *G* took their inheritance
Jos 22:1 proceeded to call . . . the *G*
2Sa 24:5 toward the *G*, and to Jazer
2Ki 10:33 the *G* and the Reubenites
1Ch 5:18 sons of Reuben and the *G* and
5:26 took into exile . . . the *G*
12:8 *G* that separated themselves
12:37 of the Reubenites and the *G*
26:32 Reubenites and the *G* and the

Gaham
Ge 22:24 Tebah and *G* and Tahash

Gahar
Ezr 2:47 the sons of *G*
Ne 7:49 sons of Giddel, the sons of *G*

Gain
Ex 28:38 *g* approval for them before
Le 19:5 sacrifice it to *g* approval for
22:19 *g* approval for you it must
22:20 not serve to *g* approval for
22:21 in order to *g* approval
22:29 sacrifice it to *g* approval
23:11 before Jehovah to *g* approval
25:26 hand does make *g* and he does
Jg 5:19 No *g* of silver did they take
Ne 8:13 *g* insight into the words of
Job 22:3 any *g* in that you make your
Ps 60:12 we shall *g* vital energy
89:43 not to *g* ground in the battle
108:13 we shall *g* vital energy
Pr 3:14 it as *g* is better than having
3:14 better than having silver as *g*
21:17 and oil will not *g* riches
23:4 Do not toil to *g* riches
28:20 hastening to *g* riches will
31:11 and there is no *g* lacking
Isa 33:15 rejecting the unjust *g* from
56:11 each one for his unjust *g*
57:17 unjust *g* I grew indignant
Jer 5:27 great and they *g* riches
5:28 that they may *g* success
6:13 making for himself unjust *g*
8:10 each one is making unjust *g*
22:17 upon your unjust *g*, and
Eze 22:12 making *g* of your companions
22:13 unjust *g* that you have made
22:27 purpose of making unjust *g*
33:31 after their unjust *g* is
Da 2:8 what you men are trying to *g*
Hab 2:9 making evil *g* for his house
Zec 11:5 while I shall *g* riches
Mr 8:36 a man to *g* the whole world
Ac 16:16 much *g* by practicing the art
16:19 that their hope of *g* had left
19:24 the craftsmen no little *g*
24:27 Felix desired to *g* favor
25:9 Festus, desiring to *g* favor
1Co 7:32 he may *g* the Lord's approval
7:33 how he may *g* the approval of
7:34 *g* the approval of her husband
9:19 I may *g* the most persons
9:20 Jew, that I might *g* Jews
9:20 I might *g* those under law
9:21 that I might *g* those without
9:22 that I might *g* the weak
Php 1:21 is Christ, and to die, *g*
3:8 that I may *g* Christ
1Ti 3:8 not greedy of dishonest *g*
6:5 devotion is a means of *g*
6:6 it is a means of great *g*
2Ti 2:4 *g* the approval of the one who
Tit 1:7 not greedy of dishonest *g*
1:11 for the sake of dishonest *g*
1Pe 5:2 for love of dishonest *g*
1Jo 2:18 we *g* the knowledge that it
2:29 you *g* the knowledge that
3:24 by this we *g* the knowledge
4:2 You *g* the knowledge of the
4:9 we might *g* life through him
4:13 *g* the knowledge that we are
5:2 we *g* the knowledge that we
5:20 *g* the knowledge of the true
Re 22:14 *g* entrance into the city by

Gained
Es 2:9 she *g* loving-kindness before
2:17 so that she *g* more favor and
5:2 Esther . . . *g* favor in his eyes
Ps 98:1 arm, has *g* salvation for him
Pr 20:17 Bread *g* by falsehood is
Ca 2:13 has *g* a mature color for its
Da 7:13 Ancient of Days he *g* access
Mt 18:15 you have *g* your brother
25:16 with them and *g* five more
25:17 received the two *g* two more
Mt 25:20 see, I *g* five talents more
25:22 see, I *g* two talents more
Lu 19:15 had *g* by business activity
19:16 Lord, your mina *g* ten minas
Joh 9:11 went and washed and *g* sight
9:15 asking him how he *g* sight
9:18 been blind and had *g* sight
9:18 of the man that *g* sight
Ac 9:19 he took food and *g* strength
Ro 5:2 *g* our approach by faith into

Gaining
Es 2:15 *g* favor in the eyes of
Lu 20:35 worthy of *g* that system of

Gains
Ps 49:16 because some man *g* riches
Mt 16:26 if he *g* the whole world but
Lu 9:25 if he *g* the whole world but
Php 3:7 Yet what things were *g* to me
1Jo 4:6 that *g* the knowledge of God
4:7 and *g* the knowledge of God

Gaius
Ac 19:29 forcibly along with them *G*
20:4 and *G* of Derbe, and Timothy
Ro 16:23 *G*, my host and that of all
1Co 1:14 of you except Crispus and *G*
3Jo 1 *G*, the beloved, whom I truly

Galal
1Ch 9:15 and Bakbakkar, Heresh and *G*
9:16 son of *G* the son of Jeduthun
Ne 11:17 *G* the son of Jeduthun

Galatia
Ac 16:6 Phrygia and the country of *G*
18:23 through the country of *G* and
1Co 16:1 to the congregations of *G*
Ga 1:2 to the congregations of *G*
2Ti 4:10 Crescens to *G*, Titus to
1Pe 1:1 in Pontus, *G*, Cappadocia, Asia

Galatians
Ga 3:1 O senseless *G*, who is it that

Galbanum
Ex 30:34 and perfumed *g* and pure

Galeed
Ge 31:47 but Jacob called it *G*
31:48 why he called its name *G*

Galilean
Mt 26:69 too, were with Jesus the *G*
Mr 14:70 for, in fact, you are a *G*
Lu 22:59 for, in fact, he is a *G*!
23:6 whether the man was a *G*
Ac 5:37 Judas the *G* rose in the days

Galileans
Lu 13:1 *G* whose blood Pilate had
13:2 Do you imagine that these *G*
13:2 worse . . . than all other *G*
Joh 4:45 the *G* received him, because
Ac 2:7 these who are speaking are *G*

Galilee
Jos 20:7 to Kedesh in *G* in the
21:32 Kedesh in *G*, and its pasture
1Ki 9:11 cities in the land of *G*
2Ki 15:29 Hazor and Gilead and *G*
1Ch 6:76 Kedesh in *G* with its pasture
Isa 9:1 Jordan, *G* of the nations
Mt 2:22 into the territory of *G*
3:13 Jesus came from *G* to the
4:12 arrested, he withdrew into *G*
4:15 *G* of the nations
4:18 alongside the sea of *G* he
4:23 throughout the whole of *G*
4:25 followed him from *G* and
15:29 next came near the sea of *G*
17:22 were gathered together in *G*
19:1 he departed from *G* and came
21:11 Jesus, from Nazareth of *G*
26:32 will go ahead of you into *G*
27:55 accompanied Jesus from *G* to
28:7 is going ahead of you into *G*
28:10 that they may go off into *G*
28:16 eleven disciples went into *G*
Mr 1:9 Jesus came from Nazareth of *G*
1:14 Jesus went into *G*, preaching
1:16 alongside the sea of *G* he saw
1:28 the country round about in *G*
1:39 throughout the whole of *G* and
3:7 a great multitude from *G* and
6:21 and the foremost ones of *G*
7:31 Sidon to the sea of *G* in the
9:30 went their way through *G*
14:28 will go ahead of you into *G*

Mr 15:41 when he was in *G*, and many
16:7 going ahead of you into *G*
Lu 1:26 to a city of *G* named Nazareth
2:4 Joseph also went up from *G*
2:39 they went back into *G* to
3:1 Herod was district ruler of *G*
4:14 Jesus returned . . . into *G*
4:31 Capernaum, a city of *G*
5:17 every village of *G* and Judea
8:26 is on the side opposite *G*
17:11 the midst of Samaria and *G*
23:5 starting out from *G* to here
23:49 had followed him from *G*
23:55 had come with him out of *G*
24:6 spoke to you . . . in *G*
Joh 1:43 he desired to depart for *G*
2:1 marriage . . . in Cana of *G*
2:11 performed this in Cana of *G*
4:3 and departed again for *G*
4:43 two days he left there for *G*
4:45 arrived in *G*, the Galileans
4:46 he came again to Cana of *G*
4:47 come out of Judea into *G*
4:54 came out of Judea into *G*
6:1 the sea of *G*, or Tiberias
7:1 continued walking about in *G*
7:9 he remained in *G*
7:41 Christ is not . . . out of *G*
7:52 not also out of *G*, are you?
7:52 no prophet . . . out of *G*
12:21 from Bethsaida of *G*, and
21:2 Nathanael from Cana of *G*
Ac 1:11 Men of *G*, why do you stand
9:31 *G* and Samaria entered into a
10:37 from *G* after the baptism
13:31 him from *G* to Jerusalem

Gall
Job 16:13 He pours out my *g* bladder
20:14 the *g* of cobras within him
20:25 weapon out through his *g*
Mt 27:34 gave him wine mixed with *g*
Ac 8:23 I see you are a poisonous *g*

Galleries
Job 28:10 channeled water-filled *g*
Eze 41:15 its *g* on this side and on
41:16 *g* were round about the
42:5 *g* took away from them

Gallery
Eze 42:3, 3 *g* opposite *g* in three

Galley
Isa 33:21 On it no *g* fleet will go

Gallim
1Sa 25:44 who was from *G*
Isa 10:30 cries, O daughter of *G*

Gallio
Ac 18:12 *G* was proconsul of Achaia
18:14 *G* said to the Jews: If it
18:17 *G* would not concern himself

Galls
Job 16:3 what *g* you, that you answer?

Gamaliel
Nu 1:10 *G* the son of Pedahzur
2:20 is *G* the son of Pedahzur
7:54 *G* the son of Pedahzur
7:59 of *G* the son of Pedahzur
10:23 *G* the son of Pedahzur
Ac 5:34 Pharisee named *G*, a Law
22:3 at the feet of *G*, instructed

Game
Ge 25:28 it meant *g* in his mouth
27:5 to hunt *g* and to bring it in
27:7 Bring me some *g* and make me
27:19 eat some of my *g*, in order
27:25 that I may eat some of the *g*
27:31 eat some of his son's *g*
27:33 hunted for *g* and came
Pr 12:27 start up one's *g* animals

Games
Ac 19:31 commissioners of . . . *g*, who
2Ti 2:5 contends even in the *g*, he is

Gamul
1Ch 24:17 for *G* the twenty-second

Gangrene
2Ti 2:17 word will spread like *g*

Gap
2Sa 5:20 like a *g* made by waters
1Ki 11:27 the *g* of the city of David
1Ch 14:11 like a *g* made by waters
Ne 6:1 had not been left in it a *g*
Job 30:14 As through a wide *g* they
Ps 106:23 stood in the *g* before him
Isa 58:12 called the repairer of the *g*
Eze 22:30 standing in the *g* before me

Gaps
Ne 4:7 *g* had started to be stopped up
Eze 13:5 not go up into the *g*, neither

Garb
De 22:5 No *g* of an able-bodied man
1Ti 2:9 or pearls or very expensive *g*

Garden
Ge 2:8 Jehovah God planted a *g* in Eden
2:9 of life in the middle of the *g*
2:10 out of Eden to water the *g*
2:15 *g* of Eden to cultivate it and
2:16 From every tree of the *g* you
3:1 eat from every tree of the *g*
3:2 fruit of the trees of the *g*
3:3 is in the middle of the *g*
3:8 God walking in the *g* about
3:8 in between the trees of the *g*
3:10 Your voice I heard in the *g*
3:23 God put him out of the *g* of
3:24 at the east of the *g* of Eden
13:10 like the *g* of Jehovah, like
De 11:10 like a *g* of vegetables
1Ki 21:2 serve as a *g* of vegetables
2Ki 9:27 by the way of the *g* house
21:18 buried in the *g* of his house
21:18 in the *g* of Uzza; and Amon
21:26 his grave in the *g* of Uzza
25:4 wall that is by the king's *g*
Ne 3:15 to the King's *G* and as far as
Es 1:5 the *g* of the king's palace
7:7 to go to the *g* of the palace
7:8 returned from the *g* of the
Job 8:16 in his *g* his own twig goes
Ca 4:12 A *g* barred in is my sister
4:12 my bride, a *g* barred in, a
4:16 Breathe upon my *g*. Let its
4:16 my dear one come into his *g*
5:1 I have come into my *g*, O my
5:13 are like a *g* bed of spice
6:2 one has gone down to his *g*
6:2 to the *g* beds of spice plants
6:11 To the *g* of nut trees I had
Isa 1:30 like a *g* that has no water
51:3 plain like the *g* of Jehovah
58:11 like a well-watered *g*
61:11 *g* itself makes the things
Jer 31:12 like a well-watered *g*, and
39:4 the way of the *g* of the king
52:7 wall that is by the king's *g*
La 2:6 violently like that in a *g*
Eze 17:7 *g* beds where it was planted
17:10 In the *g* beds of its sprout
28:13 In Eden, the *g* of God, you
31:8 match for it in the *g* of God
31:8 No other tree in the *g* of God
31:9 in the *g* of the true God
36:35 become like the *g* of Eden
Joe 2:3 Like the *g* of Eden the land
Lu 13:19 a man took and put in his *g*
Joh 18:1 to where there was a *g*, and
18:26 I saw you in the *g* with
19:41 impaled there was a *g*, and
19:41 in the *g* a new memorial
Ro 11:24 into the *g* olive tree, how

Gardener
Joh 20:15 imagining it was the *g*

Gardens
Nu 24:6 Like *g* by the river. Like aloe
Ec 2:5 I made *g* and parks for myself
Ca 4:15 a spring of *g*, a well of
6:2 to shepherd among the *g*, and
8:13 you who are dwelling in the *g*
Isa 1:29 abashed because of the *g* that
65:3 sacrificing in the *g* and
66:17 the *g* behind one in the
Jer 29:5 plant *g* and eat their
29:28 plant *g* and eat their
Am 4:9 a multiplying of your *g*
9:14 make *g* and eat the fruit of

Gareb
2Sa 23:38 *G* the Ithrite
1Ch 11:40 *G* the Ithrite
Jer 31:39 ahead to the hill of *G*

Garland
Isa 28:5 and as a *g* of beauty to
Eze 7:7 The *g* must come to you, O
Eze 7:10 The *g* has gone forth. The rod

Garlands
1Ki 6:18 ornaments and *g* of blossoms
Ac 14:13 brought bulls and *g* to the

Garlic
Nu 11:5 eat in Egypt . . . and the *g*

Garment
Ge 25:25 like an official *g* of hair
37:3 a long, striped shirtlike *g*
37:23 Joseph of his long *g*
37:23 the long striped *g* that was
37:31 they took Joseph's long *g*
37:31 dipped the long *g* in the
37:32 sent the long striped *g*
37:32 it is your son's long *g*
37:33 It is my son's long *g!*
39:12 grabbed hold of him by his *g*
39:12 he left his *g* in her hand
39:13 he had left his *g* in her hand
39:15 he then left his *g* beside me
39:16 she kept his *g* laid up beside
39:18 left his *g* beside me and
49:11 his *g* in the blood of grapes
Ex 4:6 into the upper fold of your *g*
4:6 into the upper fold of his *g*
4:7 into the upper fold of your *g*
4:7 into the upper fold of his *g*
4:7 of the upper fold of his *g*
22:9 a sheep, a *g*, anything lost of
22:26 *g* of your fellow as a pledge
Le 6:27 some of its blood upon the *g*
11:32 or a *g* or a skin or sackcloth
13:47 a *g*, in case the plague of
13:47 leprosy . . . in a woolen *g*
13:47 leprosy . . . in a linen *g*
13:49 plague does develop in the *g*
13:51 plague has spread in the *g*
13:52 must burn the *g* or the warp
13:53 spread in the *g* or in the
13:56 tear it out of the *g* or the
13:57 still appears in the *g* or in
13:58 As for the *g* or the warp or
13:59 leprosy in a *g* of wool or of
14:55 leprosy of the *g* and in the
15:17 And any *g* and any skin upon
19:19 *g* of two sorts of thread
Nu 31:20 every *g* . . . you should purify
De 24:13 he must go to bed in his *g*
24:17 the *g* of a widow as a pledge
Jos 7:21 an official *g* from Shinar
7:24 the silver and the official *g*
Jg 3:16 he girded it underneath his *g*
5:30 An embroidered *g*, dyed stuff
1Sa 19:13 she covered it with a *g*
2Sa 20:8 girded, clothed with a *g*
20:12 he cast a *g* over him, as he
1Ki 11:29 Ahijah . . . with a new *g*
11:30 Ahijah now took . . . new *g*
19:13 wrapped his face in . . . *g*
19:19 his official *g* upon him
2Ki 1:8 A man possessing a hair *g*
2:8 Elijah took his official *g* and
2:13 the official *g* of Elijah that
2:14 official *g* of Elijah that had
4:39 gourds from it, his *g* full
9:13 took each one his *g* and put
Ezr 9:3 ripped apart my *g* and my
9:5 *g* and my sleeveless coat torn
Job 13:28 Like a *g* that a moth
24:7 pass the night without a *g*
24:10 to go about without a *g*
30:18 my *g* takes on a change
30:18 the collar of my long *g*
31:19 perishing from having no *g*
38:9 I put the cloud as its *g*
Ps 73:6 Violence envelops them as a *g*
102:26 just like a *g* they will
104:2 with light as with a *g*
104:6 watery deep just like a *g*
109:18 with malediction as his *g*
109:19 *g* with which he enwraps
Pr 7:10 *g* of a prostitute and cunning
20:16 Take one's *g*, in case one has
25:20 removing a *g* on a cold day
27:13 Take one's *g*, in case one has
Isa 3:24 instead of a rich *g*, a
50:9 like a *g*, will wear out
51:6 like a *g* the earth itself
51:8 eat them up just as if a *g*
59:6 cobweb will not serve as a *g*
64:6 are like a *g* for periods of
Jer 43:12 wraps himself up in his *g*
Eze 16:10 with an embroidered *g* and

Eze 16:13 and an embroidered *g*
18:7 naked . . . cover with a *g*
18:16 naked . . . covered with a *g*
Jon 3:6 put off his official *g* from
Mic 2:8 From the front of a *g* you
Hag 2:12 flesh in the skirt of his *g*
Zec 13:4 wear an official *g* of hair
Mal 2:16 has covered over his *g*
Mt 5:40 possession of your inner *g*
5:40 your outer *g* also go to him
9:16 cloth upon an old outer *g*
9:16 pull from the outer *g* and
9:20 the fringe of his outer *g*
9:21 only touch his outer *g* I
14:36 the fringe of his outer *g*
22:11 clothed with a marriage *g*
22:12 not having on a marriage *g*
24:18 to pick up his outer *g*
Mr 2:21 cloth upon an old outer *g*
5:27 and touched his outer *g*
6:56 the fringe of his outer *g*
10:50 Throwing off his outer *g*, he
13:16 to pick up his outer *g*
14:51 wearing a fine linen *g*
14:52 he left his linen *g* behind
Lu 5:36 a patch from a new outer *g*
5:36 sews it onto an old outer *g*
5:36 the patch from the new *g*
6:29 takes away your outer *g*, do
8:44 the fringe of his outer *g*, and
22:36 sell his outer *g* and buy one
23:11 clothing him with a bright *g*
Joh 19:2 him with a purple outer *g*
19:5 and the purple outer *g*
19:23 part, and the inner *g*
19:23 inner *g* was without a seam
21:7 about himself his top *g*
Ac 12:8 Put your outer *g* on and keep
Heb 1:11 just like an outer *g* they
1:12 as a cloak, as an outer *g*
Jude 23 inner *g* that has been stained
Re 1:13 son of man, clothed with a *g*
19:13 outer *g* sprinkled with blood
19:16 upon his outer *g*, even

Garments
Ge 3:21 to make long *g* of skin for
24:53 and *g* and to give them to
27:15 Rebekah took *g* of Esau
27:27 smell the scent of his *g*
28:20 bread to eat and *g* to wear
37:29 he ripped his *g* apart
38:14 *g* of her widowhood from her
38:19 the *g* of her widowhood
41:42 clothed him with *g* of fine
Ex 28:2 make holy *g* for Aaron your
28:3 Aaron's *g* for sanctifying him
28:4 these are the *g* that they
28:4 make the holy *g* for Aaron
29:5 take the *g* and clothe Aaron
29:21 upon Aaron and his *g* and upon
29:21 upon his sons and the *g* of
29:21 he and his *g* and his sons and
29:21 the *g* of his sons with him
29:29 holy *g* that are Aaron's
31:10 *g* of knitted work and the
31:10 holy *g* for Aaron the priest
31:10 the priest and the *g* of his
35:19 the *g* of knitted work for
35:19 holy *g* for Aaron the priest
35:19 *g* of his sons for acting as
35:21 contribution for the . . . *g*
39:1 made *g* of knitted work for
39:1 holy *g* that were for Aaron
39:41 the *g* of knitted work for
39:41 holy *g* for Aaron the priest
39:41 *g* of his sons for acting as
40:13 clothe Aaron with the holy *g*
Le 6:11 he must strip off his *g* and
6:11 and put on other *g*, and he
8:2 the *g* and the anointing oil
8:30 Aaron and his *g* and upon his
8:30 the *g* of his sons with him
8:30 he sanctified Aaron and his *g*
8:30 the *g* of his sons with him
10:6 you must not tear your *g*
11:25 dead bodies will wash his *g*
11:28 bodies will wash his *g*
11:40 dead body will wash his *g*
11:40 wash his *g*, and he must be
13:6 must wash his *g* and be clean
13:34 must wash his *g* and be clean
13:45 his *g* should be torn, and
14:8 wash his *g* and shave off all
Le 14:9 wash his *g* and bathe his
14:47 should wash his *g*
14:47 should wash his *g*
15:5 wash his *g*, and he must bathe
15:6 wash his *g*, and he must bathe
15:7 wash his *g*, and he must bathe
15:8 wash his *g* and bathe in water
15:10 wash his *g*, and he must
15:11 then wash his *g* and bathe in
15:13 wash his *g* and bathe his
15:21 should wash his *g*, and he
15:22 wash his *g*, and he must
15:27 wash his *g* and bathe in
16:4 linen turban. They are holy *g*
16:23 strip off the linen *g* that
16:24 put on his *g* and come out
16:26 he should wash his *g*, and he
16:28 wash his *g*, and he must
16:32 and must put on the linen *g*
16:32 They are holy *g*
17:15 wash his *g* and bathe in
21:10 with power to wear the *g*, he
21:10 he should not tear his *g*
Nu 8:7 must wash their *g* and cleanse
8:21 washed their *g*, after which
14:6 ripped their *g* apart
15:38 upon the skirts of their *g*
19:7 priest must wash his *g* and
19:8 wash his *g* in water and must
19:10 wash his *g* and be unclean
19:19 must wash his *g* and bathe in
19:21 should wash his *g*, also the
20:26 strip Aaron of his *g*, and you
20:28 stripped Aaron of his *g* and
31:24 wash your *g* on the seventh
De 29:5 your *g* did not wear out upon
Jos 9:5 worn-out *g* upon themselves
9:13 these *g* and sandals of ours
22:8 and *g* in very great quantity
Jg 5:30 two embroidered *g* For the
8:26 *g* of wool dyed reddish purple
11:35 he began to rip his *g* and to
17:10 usual outfit of *g* and your
1Sa 4:12 his *g* ripped apart and dirt
17:38 clothing David with his *g*
17:39 his sword on over his *g* and
18:4 to David, and also his *g*
19:24 strip off his *g* and behave
27:9 and asses and camels and *g*
28:8 clothed himself with other *g*
2Sa 1:2 *g* ripped apart and dirt upon
1:11 David took hold of his *g* and
3:31 Rip your *g* apart and tie on
10:4 cut their *g* in half to their
13:31 with their *g* ripped apart
14:2 with *g* of mourning, and do
19:24 nor had he washed his *g*
1Ki 1:1 they would cover him with *g*
10:25 *g* and armor and balsam oil
21:27 to rip his *g* apart and to
22:10 clothed in *g*, in the
22:30 put on your *g*
2Ki 2:12 own *g* and ripped them into
5:5 and ten changes of *g*
5:7 ripped his *g* apart and said
5:8 had ripped his *g* apart, he at
5:8 Why did you rip your *g* apart?
5:22 and two changes of *g*
5:23 with two changes of *g*, and
5:26 to accept *g* or olive groves
6:30 immediately ripped his *g*
7:8 silver and gold and *g* and
7:15 full of *g* and utensils that
10:22 *g* for all the worshipers of
11:14 Athaliah ripped her *g* apart
18:37 their *g* ripped apart and
19:1 ripped his *g* apart and
22:11 ripped his *g* apart
22:14 the caretaker of the *g*
22:19 you ripped your *g* apart
25:29 he took off his prison *g*
1Ch 19:4 cut their *g* in half to their
2Ch 9:24 *g*, armor and balsam oil
18:9 his throne, clothed in *g*
18:29 for your part, put on your *g*
23:13 Athaliah ripped her *g* apart
34:19 ripped his *g* apart
34:22 the caretaker of the *g*
34:27 ripped your *g* apart and
Ne 4:23 were not taking off our *g*
9:21 *g* did not wear out, and
Es 4:1 to rip his *g* apart and put on
4:4 she sent *g* to clothe Mordecai
Job 9:31 *g* would certainly detest me
Job 22:6 even the *g* of naked people
37:17 How your *g* are hot
Ps 22:18 They apportion my *g* among
45:8 *g* are myrrh and aloeswood
133:2 down to the collar of his *g*
Pr 6:27 yet his very *g* not be burned
31:21 are clothed with double *g*
Ec 9:8 let your *g* prove to be white
Ca 4:11 fragrance of your *g* is like
Isa 36:22 with their *g* ripped apart
37:1 ripped his *g* apart and
52:1 Put on your beautiful *g*
59:17 *g* of vengeance as raiment
61:10 with the *g* of salvation
63:1 *g* of glowing colors from
63:2 and your *g* are like those of
63:3 kept spattering upon my *g*
Jer 36:24 rip their *g* apart
41:5 their *g* ripped apart and
52:33 took off his prison *g* and
La 4:14 none are able to touch their *g*
Eze 16:16 to take some of your *g* and
16:18 take your embroidered *g* and
16:39 must strip you of your *g*
23:26 strip off you your *g* and
26:16 their own embroidered *g*
27:20 Dedan was your trader in *g*
27:24 your traders in gorgeous *g*
42:14 deposit their *g* in which
42:14 themselves with other *g*
44:17 linen *g* they should wear
44:19 *g* in which they were
44:19 and put on other *g*, that
44:19 the people with their *g*
Da 3:21 their *g* and their caps and
Joe 2:13 your hearts, and not your *g*
Am 2:8 on *g* seized as a pledge they
Zec 3:3 clothed in befouled *g* and
3:4 Remove the befouled *g* from
3:5 and to clothe him with *g*
14:14 *g* in excessive abundance
Mt 11:8 A man dressed in soft *g*?
11:8 those wearing soft *g* are in
17:2 his outer *g* became brilliant
21:7 put upon these their outer *g*
21:8 their outer *g* on the road
23:5 the fringes of their *g*
26:65 priest ripped his outer *g*
27:31 put his outer *g* upon him and
27:35 distributed his outer *g* by
Mr 5:28 If I touch just his outer *g*
5:30 say: Who touched my outer *g*?
9:3 his outer *g* became glistening
11:7 *g* upon it, and he sat on it
11:8 their outer *g* on the road
14:63 priest ripped his inner *g*
15:20 put his outer *g* upon him
15:24 distributed his outer *g* by
Lu 7:25 man dressed in soft outer *g*
19:35 outer *g* upon the colt and
19:36 their outer *g* on the road
23:34 his *g*, they cast lots
Joh 13:4 and laid aside his outer *g*
13:12 had put his outer *g* on and
19:23 outer *g* and made four parts
19:24 apportioned my outer *g*
Ac 1:10 two men in white *g* stood
7:58 outer *g* at the feet of a
9:39 exhibiting many inner *g* and
9:39 outer *g* that Dorcas used to
14:14 they ripped their outer *g*
16:22 tearing the outer *g* off them
18:6 he shook out his *g* and said
22:20 guarding the outer *g* of those
22:23 throwing their outer *g* about
Jas 5:2 *g* have become moth-eaten
1Pe 3:3 or the wearing of outer *g*
Re 3:4 defile their outer *g*, and
3:5 arrayed in white outer *g*
3:18 white outer *g* that you may
4:4 dressed in white outer *g*, and
16:15 and keeps his outer *g*, that

Garmite
1Ch 4:19 father of Keilah the *G* and

Garners
Ps 144:13 Our *g* full, furnishing

Garrison
1Sa 10:5 is a *g* of the Philistines
13:3 the *g* of the Philistines that
13:4 a *g* of the Philistines
1Ch 11:16 a *g* of the Philistines was

arrisons
Sa 8:6 David put *g* in Syria of
8:14 he kept *g* placed in Edom
8:14 In all Edom he placed *g*
Ch 18:6 David put *g* in Syria of
18:13 So he put *g* in Edom, and
Ch 17:2 *g* in the land of Judah and

asp
sa 42:14 going to groan, pant, and *g*

asping
er 4:31 who keeps *g* for breath

atam
e 36:11 sons of Eliphaz . . . *G*
36:16 sheik *G* . . . of Edom
Ch 1:36 sons of Eliphaz were . . . *G*

ate
e 19:1 Lot was sitting in the *g* of
22:17 of the *g* of his enemies
23:10 entering the *g* of his city
23:18 entering the *g* of his city
24:60 take possession of the *g*
28:17 this is the *g* of the heavens
34:20 went to the *g* of their city
34:24 those going out by the *g* of
34:24 those going out by the *g* of
x 27:16 for the *g* of the courtyard
32:26 his stand in the *g* of the
32:27, 27 from *g* to *g* in the camp
35:17 the *g* of the courtyard
38:15 of the *g* of the courtyard
38:18 the screen of the *g* of the
38:31 of the *g* of the courtyard
39:40 for the *g* of the courtyard
40:8 of the *g* of the courtyard
40:33 put up the screen of the *g* of
u 4:26 *g* of the courtyard that is
e 21:19 and to the *g* of his place
22:15 men of the city at the *g* of
22:24 bring them both out to the *g*
25:7 up to the *g* to the older men
33:25 and copper are your *g* locks
os 2:5 the closing of the *g* by dark
2:7 they shut the *g* immediately
7:5 from before the *g* as far as
8:29 of the *g* of the city and
20:4 entrance of the *g* of the city
g 9:35 at the entrance of the city *g*
9:40 the entrance of the *g*
9:44 at the entrance of the city *g*
16:2 all night long in the city *g*
16:3 doors of the city *g* and the
18:16 at the entrance of the *g*
18:17 at the entrance of the *g*
u 3:11 in the *g* of my people is
4:1 he went up to the *g* and began
4:10 and from the *g* of his place
4:11 the people that were in the *g*
Sa 4:18 backward beside the *g*, and
9:18 in the middle of the *g* and
21:13 marks on the doors of the *g*
Sa 3:27 led him aside inside the *g*
10:8 at the entrance of the *g*
11:23 to the entrance of the *g*
15:2 the side of the road to the *g*
18:4 standing at the side of the *g*
18:24 roof of the *g* by the wall
19:8 seated himself in the *g*, and
19:8 the king sitting in the *g*
23:15 cistern . . . that is at the *g*
23:16 that is at the *g* and came
Ki 22:10 of the *g* of Samaria
Ki 7:3 be at the entrance of the *g*
9:31 himself came in by the *g*
10:8 at the entrance of the *g*
11:6 at the *g* of the Foundation
11:6 at the *g* behind the runners
11:19 the *g* of the runners to
14:13 at the *g* of Ephraim clear
14:13 clear to the corner *g*
15:35 the upper *g* of the house of
23:8 entrance of the *g* of Joshua
23:8 came into the *g* of the city
25:4 by the way of the *g* between
Ch 9:18 in the king's *g* to the east
11:17 which is at the *g*
11:18 which is at the *g*, and came
16:42 sons of Jeduthun at the *g*
26:16 close by the *g* Shallecheth
Ch 18:9 entrance of the *g* of Samaria
23:5 be at the *g* of the Foundation
23:15 horse *g* of the king's house
23:20 upper *g* to the king's house

2Ch 24:8 *g* of the house of Jehovah
25:23 from the *G* of Ephraim clear
25:23 clear to the Corner *G*, four
26:9 Jerusalem by the Corner *G*
26:9 by the Valley *G* and by the
27:3 upper *g* of Jehovah's house
32:6 square of the *g* of the city
33:14 far as the Fish *G*, and he
Ne 2:13 to go out by the Valley *G* by
2:13 *G* of the Ash-heaps, and I
2:14 to the Fountain *G* and to the
2:15 entered by the Valley *G*, and
3:1 get up and build the Sheep *G*
3:3 the Fish *G* was what the sons
3:6 the *G* of the Old City was what
3:13 The Valley *G* was what Hanun
3:13 far as the *G* of the Ash-heaps
3:14 the *G* of the Ash-heaps was
3:15 Fountain *G* was what Shallun
3:26 the Water *G* on the east and
3:28 the Horse *G* the priests did
3:29 the keeper of the East *G*
3:31 in front of the Inspection *G*
3:32 the Sheep *G* the goldsmiths
8:1 that was before the Water *G*
8:3 that is before the Water *G*
8:16 public square of the Water *G*
8:16 square of the *G* of Ephraim
12:31 to the *G* of the Ash-heaps
12:37 the Fountain *G* and straight
12:37 to the Water *G* to the east
12:39 over the *G* of Ephraim and
12:39 the *G* of the Old City and
12:39 clear to the Fish *G* and the
12:39 and on to the Sheep *G*
12:39 a stand at the *G* of the Guard
Es 2:19 was sitting in the king's *g*
2:21 was sitting in the king's *g*
3:2 in the king's *g* were bowing
3:3 in the king's *g* began to say to
4:2 far as in front of the king's *g*
4:2 come into the king's *g* in
4:6 that was before the king's *g*
5:9 saw Mordecai in the king's *g*
5:13 Jew sitting in the king's *g*
6:10 is sitting in the king's *g*
6:12 returned to the king's *g*
Job 5:4 are crushed in the *g* without
29:7 to the *g* by the town
31:21 of my assistance in the *g*
Ps 69:12 Those sitting in the *g* began
118:20 This is the *g* of Jehovah
127:5 speak with enemies in the *g*
Pr 22:22 the afflicted one in the *g*
24:7 *g* he will not open his mouth
Ca 7:4 by the *g* of Bath-rabbim
Isa 14:31 Howl, O *g!* Cry out, O city!
22:7 in position at the *g*
24:12 *g* has been crushed to a
28:6 away the battle from the *g*
29:21 the one reproving in the *g*
Jer 7:2 the *g* of the house of Jehovah
17:19 stand in the *g* of the sons
19:2 the *G* of the Potsherds
20:2 in the upper *g* of Benjamin
26:10 entrance of the new *g* of
31:38 Hananel to the Corner *G*
31:40 corner of the Horse *G*
36:10 new *g* of the house of
37:13 he was in the *g* of Benjamin
38:7 sitting in the *g* of Benjamin
39:3 sit down in the Middle *G*
39:4 *g* between the double wall
52:7 *g* between the double wall
La 5:14 have ceased even out of the *g*
Eze 8:3 entrance of the inner *g* that
8:5 north of the *g* of the altar
8:14 the *g* of the house of Jehovah
9:2 the upper *g* that faces to the
10:19 *g* of the house of Jehovah
11:1 the eastern *g* of the house of
11:1 in the entrance of the *g*
40:3 he was standing in the *g*
40:6 he came to the *g*, the front
40:6 the threshold of the *g*
40:7 the *g* beside the porch of
40:7 porch of the *g* toward the
40:8 measure the porch of the *g*
40:9 measured the porch of the *g*
40:9 *g* was toward the interior
40:10 the guard chambers of the *g*
40:11 entrance of the *g*, ten
40:11 length of the *g*, thirteen
40:13 measure the *g* from the roof

Eze 40:15 the *g* of the entryway to
40:15 inner *g* was fifty cubits
40:16 inside of the *g* all around
40:19 in front of the lower *g* to
40:20 the outer courtyard had a *g*
40:21 measurement of the first *g*
40:22 the *g* the front of which is
40:23 the *g* of the inner courtyard
40:23 opposite the *g* to the north
40:23, 23 *g* to *g* a hundred cubits
40:24 was a *g* toward the south
40:27 the inner courtyard had a *g*
40:27, 27 *g* to *g* toward the south
40:28 the inner courtyard by the *g*
40:28 measure the *g* of the south
40:32 measure the *g* as of the
40:35 bring me into the north *g*
40:39 in the porch of the *g* there
40:40 the entrance of the north *g*
40:40 to the porch of the *g*
40:41 side of the *g*—eight tables
40:44 the outside of the inner *g*
40:44 on the side of the north *g*
40:44 on the side of the east *g*
40:48 the *g* was three cubits on
42:15 *g* the front of which was
43:1 he made me go to the *g*
43:1 *g* that is facing toward the
43:4 *g* the front of which was
44:1 the *g* of the sanctuary
44:2 As regards this *g*, shut is
44:3 way of the porch of the *g*
44:4 north *g* to before the House
45:19 *g* of the inner courtyard
46:1 *g* of the inner courtyard
46:2 porch of the *g*, from outside
46:2 by the doorpost of the *g*
46:2 upon the threshold of the *g*
46:2 *g* itself should not be shut
46:3 at the entrance of that *g*
46:8 way of the porch of the *g*
46:9 by the way of the north *g*
46:9 by the way of the south *g*
46:9 by the way of the south *g*
46:9 way of the *g* to the north
46:9 *g* by which he came in
46:12 *g* that is facing east, and
46:12 shut the *g* after his going
46:19 side of the *g* to the holy
47:2 by the way of the north *g*
47:2 outer *g* that is facing
48:31 the *g* of Reuben, one
48:31 the *g* of Judah, one
48:31 the *g* of Levi, one
48:32 even the *g* of Joseph, one
48:32 *g* of Benjamin, one
48:32 the *g* of Dan, one
48:33 the *g* of Simeon, one
48:33 the *g* of Issachar, one
48:33 the *g* of Zebulun, one
48:34 the *g* of Gad, one
48:34 the *g* of Asher, one
48:34 the *g* of Naphtali, one
Am 5:10 In the *g* they have hated a
5:12 poor people even in the *g*
5:15 give justice a place in the *g*
Ob 11 foreigners entered his *g*
13 come into the *g* of my people
Mic 1:9 the plague as far as the *g*
1:12 to the *g* of Jerusalem
2:13 they will pass through a *g*
Zep 1:10 outcry from the Fish *G*, and
Zec 14:10 from the *g* of Benjamin all
14:10 to the place of the First *G*
14:10 all the way to the Corner *G*
Mt 7:13 Go in through the narrow *g*
7:14 narrow is the *g* and cramped
Lu 7:12 got near the *g* of the city
16:20 put at his *g*, full of ulcers
Ac 3:10 Beautiful *G* of the temple
10:17 and stood there at the *g*
12:10 iron *g* leading into the city
12:14 she did not open the *g*, but
16:13 outside the *g* beside a river
Heb 13:12 suffered outside the *g*

Gatehouse
Mt 26:71 he had gone out to the *g*

Gatekeeper
2Sa 18:26 called to the *g* and said
1Ch 9:21 *g* of the entrance of the tent
2Ch 31:14 *g* to the east, in charge

Gatekeepers
2Ki 7:10 *g* of the city and reported

2Ki 7:11 the *g* called out and they
1Ch 9:17 *g* were Shallum and Akkub and
9:18 were the *g* of the camps of
9:22 as *g* at the thresholds were
9:23 *g* of the house of Jehovah
9:24 four directions that the *g*
9:26 four mighty men of the *g*
15:18 Obed-edom and Jeiel the *g*
15:23 Elkanah the *g* for the Ark
15:24 and Jehiah the *g* for the Ark
16:38 and Hosah as *g*
23:5 four thousand *g* and four
26:1 For the divisions of *g*
26:12 Of these divisions of the *g*
26:19 divisions of the *g* of the
2Ch 8:14 *g* in their divisions for the
23:19 *g* by the gates of the house
34:13 and officers and *g*
35:15 the *g* were at the different
Ezr 2:42 sons of the *g*, the sons of
2:70 the singers and the *g* and the
7:7 the *g* and the Nethinim went
10:24 the *g*, Shallum and Telem
Ne 7:1 the *g* and the singers and the
7:45 The *g*, the sons of Shallum
7:73 the *g* and the singers and
10:28 Levites, the *g*, the singers
10:39 the *g* and the singers are
11:19 the *g* were Akkub, Talmon and
12:25 were keeping guard as *g*
12:45 the singers and the *g*
12:47 the singers and of the *g*
13:5 the singers and the *g* are

Gates
Ex 20:10 who is inside your *g*
De 5:14 resident who is inside your *g*
6:9 write them . . . on your *g*
11:20 your house and on your *g*
12:12 Levite who is inside your *g*
12:15 inside all your *g*
12:17 allowed to eat inside your *g*
12:18 Levite who is inside your *g*
12:21 you must eat inside your *g*
14:21 alien . . . inside your *g*
14:27 Levite who is inside your *g*
14:28 deposit it inside your *g*
14:29 who are inside your *g*, must
15:22 Inside your *g* you should eat
16:11 Levite who is inside your *g*
16:14 who are inside your *g*
16:18 inside all your *g* that
17:5 out to your *g*, yes, the man
17:8 dispute, inside your *g*
24:14 in your land, within your *g*
26:12 must eat it within your *g*
28:52 within all your *g* until your
28:52 within all your *g* in all
28:55 hem you in within all your *g*
28:57 hem you in within your *g*
31:12 alien . . . within your *g*
Jg 5:8 then there was war in the *g*
5:11 made their way down to the *g*
1Sa 17:52 and as far as the *g* of Ekron
2Sa 18:24 sitting between the two *g*
1Ki 8:37 in the land of their *g*
2Ki 23:8 the high places of the *g*
1Ch 22:3 nails for the doors of the *g*
26:13 for the different *g*
2Ch 6:28 in the land of their *g*
8:14 divisions for the different *g*
23:19 *g* of the house of Jehovah
31:2 praise in the *g* of the camps
35:15 were at the different *g*
Ne 1:3 *g* have been burned with fire
2:3 *g* have been eaten up with fire
2:8 *g* of the Castle that belongs to
2:13 *g* of it had been eaten up by
2:17 *g* have been burned with fire
6:1 I had not set up in the *g*
7:3 The *g* of Jerusalem should not
11:19 keeping guard in the *g*
12:25 group by the stores of the *g*
12:30 cleanse the people and the *g*
13:19 the *g* of Jerusalem had grown
13:19 I stationed at the *g* that
13:22 keeping guard of the *g* to
Job 38:17 *g* of death been uncovered
38:17 *g* of deep shadow can you
Ps 9:13 up from the *g* of death
9:14 the *g* of the daughter of Zion
24:7 Raise your heads, O you *g*
24:9 Raise your heads, O you *g*
87:2 in love with the *g* of Zion
Ps 100:4 into his *g* with thanksgiving
107:18 arriving at the *g* of death
118:19 the *g* of righteousness
122:2 Within your *g*, O Jerusalem
147:13 the bars of your *g* strong
Pr 1:21 entrances of the *g* into the
8:3 At the side of the *g*, at the
14:19 at the *g* of the righteous one
31:23 is someone known in the *g*
31:31 praise her even in the *g*
Isa 26:2 Open the *g*, you men
38:10 will go into the *g* of Sheol
45:1 even the *g* will not be shut
54:12 *g* of fiery glowing stones
60:11 your *g* will actually be
60:18 Salvation and your *g* Praise
62:10 pass out through the *g*
Jer 1:15 the *g* of Jerusalem, and
7:2 entering into these *g* to bow
14:2 its very *g* have faded away
15:7 in the *g* of the land
17:19 in all the *g* of Jerusalem
17:20 are entering in by these *g*
17:21 through the *g* of Jerusalem
17:24 through the *g* of this city
17:25 by the *g* of this city
17:27 through the *g* of Jerusalem
17:27 set a fire ablaze in her *g*
22:2 coming in through these *g*
22:4 through the *g* of this house
22:19 beyond the *g* of Jerusalem
51:58 her *g*, although high, will
La 1:4 All her *g* are laid desolate
2:9 Her *g* have sunk down into the
4:12 come into the *g* of Jerusalem
Eze 21:15 overthrown at all their *g*
21:22 battering-rams against *g*
26:10 he comes in through your *g*
40:14 in the *g* all around
40:18 at the side of the *g* was
40:18 as the length of the *g*
40:38 the side pillars of the *g*
44:11 over the *g* of the House
44:17 *g* of the inner courtyard
44:17 *g* of the inner courtyard
48:31 *g* of the city will be
48:31 three *g* being on the north
48:32 three *g*, even the gate
48:33 three *g*, the gate of Simeon
48:34 three *g*, the gate of Gad
Na 2:6 The very *g* of the rivers will
3:13 *g* of your land . . . opened
Zec 8:16 do your judging in your *g*
Mt 16:18 and the *g* of Hades will not
Ac 9:24 closely watching also the *g*
14:13 bulls and garlands to the *g*
Re 21:12 wall and had twelve *g*, and
21:12 and at the *g* twelve angels
21:13 On the east were three *g*
21:13 and on the north three *g*
21:13 and on the south three *g*
21:13 and on the west three *g*
21:15 measure the city and its *g*
21:21 twelve *g* were twelve pearls
21:21 *g* was made of one pearl
21:25 *g* will not be closed at all
22:14 into the city by its *g*

Gateway
2Sa 18:33 roof chamber over the *g*
2Ki 7:1 in the *g* of Samaria
7:17 to have charge of the *g*
7:17 kept trampling him in the *g*
7:18 in the *g* of Samaria
7:20 kept trampling him in the *g*
Ac 12:13 knocked at the door of the *g*
12:14 was standing before the *g*

Gath
Jos 11:22 in *G* and in Ashdod that they
1Sa 5:8 Toward *G* let the ark of the
6:17 golden piles . . . for *G* one
7:14 to Israel from Ekron to *G*
17:4 name being Goliath, from *G*
17:23 Goliath . . . from *G*, was
17:52 as far as *G* and as far as
21:10 to Achish the king of *G*
21:12 of Achish the king of *G*
27:2 Achish . . . the king of *G*
27:3 to dwell with Achish in *G*
27:4 David had run away to *G*, and
27:11 alive to bring them to *G*
2Sa 1:20 not, you people, tell it in *G*
15:18 had followed him from *G*
21:20 war arose yet again at *G*
2Sa 21:22 born to the Rephaim in *G*
1Ki 2:39 Maacah the king of *G*
2:39 Look! Your slaves are at *G*
2:40 went to *G* to Achish to look
2:40 brought his slaves from *G*
2:41 gone out of Jerusalem to *G*
2Ki 12:17 fight against *G* and capture
1Ch 7:21 men of *G* that were born in
8:13 the inhabitants of *G*
18:1 and take *G* and its dependent
20:6 came to be war again at *G*
20:8 born to the Rephaim in *G*
2Ch 11:8 and *G* and Mareshah and Ziph
26:6 break through the wall of *G*
Ps 56:*super* laid hold of him in *G*
Am 6:2 down to *G* of the Philistines
Mic 1:10 In *G* do not you men tell it

Gather
Ge 6:21 and you must *g* it to yourself
34:30 *g* together against me and
49:1 *G* yourselves together that I
Ex 3:16 *g* the older men of Israel
5:7 not *g* straw to give to the
5:7 go and *g* straw for themselves
5:12 to *g* stubble for straw
23:10 and you must *g* its produce
23:16 *g* in your labors from the
Le 19:10 not *g* the leftovers of your
25:3 you must *g* the land's produce
25:5 unpruned vine you must not *g*
25:11 *g* the grapes of its unpruned
25:20 not sow seed or *g* our crops
26:25 *g* yourselves into your cities
Nu 11:16 *G* for me seventy men of the
19:9 *g* up the ashes of the cow and
21:16 *G* the people, and let me
De 11:14 *g* your grain and your sweet
19:5 into the woods to *g* wood
24:21 *g* the grapes of your vineyard
24:21 you must not *g* the leftovers
28:38 but little will you *g*
28:39 no wine and *g* nothing in
33:21 will *g* themselves together
Jos 2:18 *g* to yourself into the house
Ru 2:7 *g* among the cut-off ears of
1Sa 14:52 he would *g* him to himself
2Sa 6:1 David proceeded again to *g*
10:15 to *g* themselves together
12:28 *g* the rest of the people
23:11 to *g* themselves to Lehi
1Ch 15:4 *g* the sons of Aaron and the
23:2 *g* all the princes of Israel
2Ch 29:20 *g* the princes of the city
30:13 *g* themselves together at
34:29 *g* all the older men of
Ezr 3:1 *g* themselves as one man to
Ne 8:1 to *g* themselves as one man at
12:28 *g* themselves even from the
12:44 *g* into them out of the
Es 4:16 *g* all the Jews that are to be
Job 39:12 *g* to your threshing floor
Ps 41:6 *g* up for himself something
50:5 *G* to me my loyal ones, Those
85:4 *G* us back, O God of our
126:4 Do *g* back, O Jehovah, our
142:7 let the righteous ones *g*
Isa 10:14 *g* up even all the earth, and
11:12 *g* the dispersed ones of
34:15 *g* them together under its
Jer 4:5 *G* yourselves together, and let
8:14 *G* yourselves together, and
10:17 *G* up from the earth your
12:9 *g* together, all you wild
21:4 *g* them into the middle of
29:14 *g* your body of captives
30:3 I will *g* the captive ones
31:23 I shall *g* their captives
33:26 *g* their captives and will
40:10 *g* wine and summer fruits
48:47 *g* the captive ones of Moab
49:6 *g* the captive ones of the
49:39 *g* the captive ones of Elam
Eze 11:17 *g* you from the lands among
16:53 I will *g* their captive ones
16:53 *g* your captive ones in the
24:4 *G* pieces in it, every good
39:10 *g* firewood out of the
39:17 *G* yourselves together all
Da 11:10 *g* together a crowd of large
Ho 6:11 *g* back the captive ones of
Joe 1:14 *G* together the older men
2:16 *G* the people together
2:16 *G* children and those sucking

Am 9:14 will *g* back the captive ones
Mic 2:12 I shall positively *g* Jacob
4:6 *g* her that was limping
Na 2:2 certainly *g* the pride of Jacob
Zep 2:1 *G* yourselves together, yes
2:7 *g* back the captive ones of
3:8 decision is to *g* nations
3:18 I shall certainly *g* together
3:20 *g* back your captive ones
Zec 14:2 *g* all the nations against
Mt 3:12 will *g* his wheat into the
6:26 or reap or *g* into storehouses
7:16 people *g* grapes from thorns
12:30 does not *g* with me scatters
23:37 I wanted to *g* your children
24:31 *g* his chosen ones together
Mr 13:27 *g* his chosen ones together
Lu 3:17 to *g* the wheat into his
6:44 people do not *g* figs from
11:23 does not *g* with me scatters
12:17 I have nowhere to *g* my crops
12:18 I will *g* all my grain and
13:34 I wanted to *g* your children
Joh 6:12 *G* together the fragments
11:52 also *g* together in one
15:6 men *g* those branches up and
Eph 1:10 *g* all things together again
Re 14:18 *g* the clusters of the vine
16:14 *g* them together to the war
20:8 *g* them together for the war

Gathered
Ge 25:8 and was *g* to his people
25:17 died and was *g* to his people
29:3 all the droves had been *g*
29:8 until all the droves are *g*
29:22 Laban *g* all the men of the
35:29 died and was *g* to his people
49:29 I am being *g* to my people
49:33 *g* his feet up onto the couch
49:33 and was *g* to his people
Ex 4:29 Moses and Aaron went and *g*
9:19 and not *g* into the house, the
16:18 had *g* much had no surplus
16:18 had *g* little had no shortage
Le 23:39 *g* the produce of the land
Nu 11:32 collecting least *g* ten
14:35 have *g* together against me
20:24 will be *g* to his people
20:26 Aaron will be *g* and must die
21:23 Sihon *g* all his people and
27:13 you must be *g* to your people
27:13 as Aaron your brother was *g*
31:2 you will be *g* to your people
De 32:50 be *g* to your people, just as
32:50 and got to be *g* to his people
33:5 the heads of the people *g*
Jos 10:5 they *g* together and went on
Jg 2:10 were *g* to their fathers, and
3:13 he *g* against them the sons
6:33 Easterners *g* together as one
9:6 house of Millo *g* together and
10:17 Israel *g* themselves together
16:23 they *g* together to sacrifice
20:11 men of Israel were *g* against
1Sa 5:8 *g* all the axis lords of the
5:11 *g* all the axis lords of the
2Sa 10:17 *g* all Israel and crossed the
12:29 David *g* all the people and
14:14 which cannot be *g*
17:11 Israel without fail be *g* to
21:13 they *g* the bones of the men
23:9 *g* themselves there for the
2Ki 22:4 have *g* from the people
22:20 *g* to your own graveyard in
23:1 *g* together to him all the
1Ch 11:13 where the Philistines had *g*
19:7 *g* together from their cities
19:17 *g* all Israel together and
2Ch 12:5 *g* themselves at Jerusalem
24:11 they *g* money in abundance
28:24 Ahaz *g* together the
29:4 *g* them to the open place to
29:15 *g* their brothers together
30:3 *g* themselves to Jerusalem
34:9 *g* from the hand of Manasseh
34:28 *g* to your graveyard in peace
Ne 8:13 *g* themselves together to Ezra
9:1 sons of Israel *g* themselves
Job 27:19 but nothing will be *g*
Ps 35:15 they rejoiced and *g* together
35:15 They *g* together against me
47:9 peoples themselves have *g*
126:1 Jehovah *g* back the captive
Pr 6:8 *g* its food supplies even in the
27:25 the vegetation . . . has been *g*
30:4 *g* the wind in the hollow of
Ca 6:4 as companies *g* around banners
6:10 as companies *g* around banners
Isa 13:4 of nations *g* together
24:22 they will certainly be *g*
33:4 *g* like the cockroaches when
43:9 national groups be *g* together
49:5 Israel itself may be *g*
57:1 are being *g* to the dead
57:1 one has been *g* away
Jer 8:2 They will not be *g*, nor will
17:11 As the partridge that has *g*
25:33 neither will they be *g* up
Eze 29:5 not be *g* up nor be collected
38:12 people *g* together out of
Ho 4:3 will be *g* in death
10:10 peoples will certainly be *g*
Am 3:9 Be *g* together against the
Mic 4:11 *g* against you many nations
Zec 12:3 all the nations . . . be *g*
14:14 nations . . . certainly be *g*
Mt 13:2 and great crowds *g* to him
17:22 were *g* together in Galilee
18:20 three *g* together in my name
22:10 *g* together all they found
22:41 Pharisees were *g* together
24:28 eagles will be *g* together
25:26 *g* where I did not winnow
25:32 the nations will be *g* before
26:3 the older men of the people *g*
26:57 and the older men were *g*
27:17 they were *g* together Pilate
27:27 *g* the whole body of troops
27:62 *g* together before Pilate
28:12 *g* together with the older
Mr 1:33 city was *g* right at the door
2:2 many *g*, so much so that there
3:20 Once more the crowd *g*, so
4:1 a very great crowd *g* near him
5:21 crowd *g* together to him
6:30 the apostles *g* together
7:1 Pharisees . . . *g* about him
Lu 12:1 the crowd had *g* together in
15:13 *g* all things together and
17:37 the eagles will be *g* together
22:66 and scribes, *g* together, and
23:48 crowds that were *g* together
Joh 6:13 they *g* them together, and
11:47 Pharisees *g* the Sanhedrin
Ac 4:27 *g* together in this city
4:31 place in which they were *g*
11:26 whole year they *g* together
12:12 were *g* together and praying
13:44 *g* together to hear the word
14:27 *g* the congregation together
15:6 older men *g* together to see
15:30 *g* the multitude together and
19:25 and he *g* them and those who
20:7 *g* together to have a meal
20:8 where we were *g* together
1Co 5:4 when you are *g* together, also
2Th 2:1 our being *g* together to him
Re 14:19 and *g* the vine of the earth
16:16 *g* them together to the place
19:17 *g* together to the great
19:19 armies *g* together to wage

Gatherer
De 29:11 the *g* of your wood to the

Gatherers
Jos 9:21 let them become *g* of wood
9:23 *g* of wood and drawers of
9:27 *g* of wood and drawers of
2Ch 2:10 the *g* of wood, the cutters
Jer 49:9 grape *g* . . . actually came in
Ob 5 grape *g* that came in to you

Gathering
Ge 29:7 not the time for *g* the herds
Ex 16:17, 17 *g* much and some *g* little
32:26 all the sons of Levi began *g*
Le 26:5 reach to your grape *g*
26:5 grape *g* will reach to the
Nu 11:24 *g* seventy men from the older
11:32 and kept *g* the quail
16:11 are *g* together are against
19:10 one *g* the ashes of the cow
Jg 8:2 the grape *g* of Abi-ezer
9:27 and engaged in *g* the grapes of
11:20 Sihon went *g* all his people
20:14 the sons of Benjamin went *g*
2Sa 9:10 do the *g* in, and it must
1Ki 10:26 *g* more chariots and steeds
17:10 *g* up pieces of wood
17:12 *g* up a few pieces of wood
2Ki 22:20 *g* you to your forefathers
2Ch 1:14 Solomon kept *g* chariots and
34:28 *g* you to your forefathers
Ezr 9:4 to me they came *g* themselves
Ps 33:7 is *g* as by a dam the waters
39:6 not know who will be *g* them
129:7 *g* sheaves his own bosom
Pr 10:5 *g* during the summertime
Ec 2:26 of *g* and bringing together
Isa 17:5 harvester is *g* the standing
24:13 grape *g* has come to an end
24:22 *g* as of prisoners into the
32:10 no fruit *g* will come in
33:4 cockroaches when *g* in, like
62:9 ones *g* it will eat it
Jer 6:9 *g* grapes upon the vine
8:13 When doing the *g*, I shall
9:22 with no one to do the *g* up
30:18 *g* the captive ones of the
40:12 *g* wine and summer fruits
46:22 who are *g* pieces of wood
48:32 grape *g* the despoiler
Mic 7:1 the gleaning of a grape *g*
Hab 2:5 *g* to himself all the nations
Zep 2:1 do the *g*, O nation not paling
Mt 2:4 *g* together all the chief
13:30 then go to *g* the wheat into
13:47 and *g* up fish of every kind
25:24 *g* where you did not winnow
Joh 4:36 *g* fruit for everlasting life
Ac 4:5 *g* together of their rulers and
Heb 10:25 *g* of ourselves together, as
Jas 2:2 enters into a *g* of you, but

Gatherings
Mic 7:1 like the *g* of summer fruit

Gathers
Job 34:14 and breath he *g* to himself
Ps 14:7 Jehovah *g* back the captive
53:6 Jehovah *g* back the captive
Isa 10:14 *g* eggs that have been left
52:8 see when Jehovah *g* back Zion
Hab 1:9 *g* up captives just like the
1:15 he *g* them in his fishing net
Mt 23:37 the way a hen *g* her chicks
Lu 13:34 that a hen *g* her brood of

Gath-hepher
Jos 19:13 toward the sunrise to *G*
2Ki 14:25 the prophet that was from *G*

Gath-rimmon
Jos 19:45 and Bene-berak and *G*
21:24 *G* and its pasture ground
21:25 *G* and its pasture ground
1Ch 6:69 *G* with its pasture grounds

Gauze
Isa 40:22 heavens just as a fine *g*

Gave
Ge 3:6 *g* some also to her husband
3:12 The woman whom you *g* to be
3:12 she *g* me fruit from the tree
3:17 I *g* you this command, You
4:1 In time she *g* birth to Cain
4:2 Later she again *g* birth, to his
4:17 became pregnant and *g* birth
4:20 In time Adah *g* birth to Jabal
4:22 Zillah, she too *g* birth to
4:25 she *g* birth to a son and
14:20 At that Abram *g* him a tenth
16:3 *g* her to Abram her husband as
16:5 *g* my maidservant over to your
19:35 *g* their father wine to drink
19:38 she too *g* birth to a son
20:14 *g* them to Abraham and
21:14 *g* it to Hagar, setting it
21:27 *g* them to Abimelech, and
22:24 she herself also *g* birth to
24:8 free from this oath you *g* me
24:18 she . . . *g* him a drink
24:53 he *g* choice things to her
25:5 Abraham *g* everything he had
25:6 Abraham had Abraham *g* gifts
25:34 Jacob *g* Esau bread and lentil
27:17 she *g* the tasty dish and the
29:24 Laban *g* to her Zilpah his
29:28 after which he *g* him Rachel
29:29 Laban *g* Bilhah his
29:33 so he *g* me also this one
30:4 she *g* him Bilhah her
30:6 so that he *g* me a son

Ge 30:35 *g* them over into the hands
35:4 *g* Jacob all the foreign gods
38:18 he *g* them to her and had
39:4 all that was his he *g* into
39:20 *g* him over to the prison
39:22 *g* over into Joseph's hand
40:11 I *g* the cup into Pharaoh's
41:45 *g* him Asenath the daughter
41:49 finally they *g* up counting it
42:25 Joseph *g* the command, and
43:23 the God of your father *g*
43:24 *g* water that they might have
43:24 he *g* fodder for their asses
43:30 and *g* way to tears there
45:14 *g* way to weeping, and
45:21 and Joseph *g* them wagons
45:21 *g* them provisions for the
45:22 he *g* individual changes of
45:22 *g* three hundred silver pieces
46:18 Laban *g* to his daughter Leah
46:25 Bilhah, whom Laban *g* to his
46:29 *g* way to tears upon his neck
47:11 he *g* them a possession in
47:22 rations that Pharaoh *g* them
50:16 Your father *g* the command
Ex 2:21 he *g* Zipporah his daughter to
9:23 Jehovah *g* thunders and hail
11:3 Jehovah *g* the people favor in
12:36 Jehovah *g* the people favor
Le 27:34 Jehovah *g* Moses as commands
Nu 3:51 Moses *g* the money of the
7:6 and *g* them to the Levites
7:7 *g* to the sons of Gershon in
7:8 he *g* to the sons of Merari in
7:9 the sons of Kohath he *g* none
21:3 *g* the Canaanites over
31:41 Moses *g* the tax as Jehovah's
31:47 and *g* them to the Levites
32:28 Moses *g* a command
32:33 At this Moses *g* to them
32:40 Moses *g* Gilead to Machir the
De 3:3 God *g* into our hand also Og
5:22 tablets of stone and *g* me
9:10 Jehovah *g* me the two tablets
9:11 Jehovah *g* me the two tablets
10:4 tablets . . . which Jehovah *g*
22:16 I *g* my daughter to this man
26:9 *g* us this land, a land
29:8 *g* it as an inheritance to the
31:9 law and *g* it to the priests
32:8 *g* the nations an inheritance
32:19 his sons and his daughters *g*
Jos 6:24 copper and iron they *g* to the
8:29 Joshua *g* the command, and
10:30 Jehovah *g* it also and its
10:32 *g* Lachish into Israel's hand
11:8 *g* them into Israel's hand
11:23 *g* it as an inheritance to
12:6 *g* it as a holding to the
12:7 *g* it to the tribes of Israel
13:8 inheritance that Moses *g*
14:13 and *g* Hebron to Caleb the
15:13 he *g* a share in the midst
15:17 *g* him Achsah his daughter
15:19 he *g* her Upper Gulloth and
17:4 he *g* them, at the order of
19:49 *g* an inheritance to Joshua
19:50 they *g* him the city for
20:7 *g* a sacred status to Kedesh
20:8 toward the east they *g* Bezer
21:3 sons of Israel *g* the Levites
21:8 sons of Israel *g* the Levites
21:9 they *g* these cities that
21:11 they *g* them Kiriath-arba
21:12 settlements they *g* to Caleb
21:13 they *g* the city of refuge
21:21 they *g* them the city of
21:43 Jehovah *g* Israel all the
21:44 Jehovah *g* them rest all
21:44 their enemies Jehovah *g* into
22:4 the servant of Jehovah *g* you
24:3 seed many. So I *g* him Isaac
24:4 to Isaac I *g* Jacob and Esau
24:4 Esau I *g* Mount Seir to take
24:8 I *g* them into your hand
24:11 I *g* them into your hand
24:13 I *g* you a land for which
Jg 1:4 Jehovah *g* the Canaanites and
1:13 For that he *g* him Achsah his
1:15 Caleb *g* her Upper Gulloth
1:20 they *g* Caleb Hebron, just as
2:14 he *g* them into the hands of
3:6 daughters they *g* to their sons
3:10 Jehovah *g* Cushan-rishathaim

Jg 4:19 and *g* him a drink, after
5:25 Water he asked, milk she *g*
6:1 Jehovah *g* them into the hand
6:9 before you and *g* you their land
8:3 God *g* Midian's princes Oreb
9:4 they *g* him seventy pieces of
11:21 *g* Sihon and all his people
12:3 Jehovah *g* them into my hand
13:1 *g* them into the hand of the
13:24 woman *g* birth to a son and
14:9 *g* them some, and they began
14:19 *g* the outfits to the tellers
15:2 I *g* her to your groomsman
15:6 then *g* her to his groomsman
15:18 *g* this great salvation into
16:24 *g* way to praising their god
17:3 Accordingly he *g* back the
17:4 and *g* them to the silversmith
21:14 they *g* them the women that
Ru 2:18 and *g* it to her
3:17 measures of barley he *g* me
4:17 neighbor ladies *g* it a name
1Sa 1:4 *g* to Peninnah his wife and to
1:5 to Hannah he *g* one portion
2:21 *g* birth to three sons and
6:13 *g* way to rejoicing at seeing
8:21 Samuel *g* a hearing to all
9:22 *g* them a place at the head
11:9 and they *g* way to rejoicing
17:30 people *g* him the same reply
18:4 *g* it to David, and also his
18:27 In turn Saul *g* him Michal
19:5 and you *g* way to rejoicing
20:40 Jonathan *g* his weapons to
21:6 priest *g* him what was holy
22:10 provisions he *g* him, and
22:10 sword of Goliath . . . *g* him
23:13 and so he *g* up going out
24:10 Jehovah *g* you today into
26:23 Jehovah today *g* you into my
27:6 Achish *g* him Ziklag on that
30:11 *g* him bread that he might
30:11 *g* him water to drink
30:12 *g* him a slice of a cake of
30:23 *g* the marauder band that
2Sa 3:32 the people *g* way to weeping
10:10 people he *g* into the hand
17:23 *g* commands to his household
18:33 and *g* way to weeping
21:9 he *g* them into the hand of
24:9 Joab now *g* the number of the
24:15 Jehovah *g* a pestilence in
1Ki 3:6 *g* him a son to sit upon his
3:17 I *g* birth close by her in
3:18 the third day after I *g* birth
5:11 *g* Hiram twenty thousand cor
5:12 *g* Solomon wisdom, just as he
6:6 he *g* to the house all around
8:34 you *g* to their forefathers
8:40 ground that you *g* to our
8:48 land that you *g* to their
8:58 which he *g* in command to
9:16 *g* it as a parting gift to his
10:10 she *g* the king a hundred and
10:10 the queen of Sheba *g* to King
10:13 *g* the queen of Sheba all her
10:13 apart from what he *g* her
11:18 who then *g* him a house
11:18 and land he *g* him
11:19 that he *g* him a wife, the
13:3 he *g* a portent on that day
13:8 If you *g* me half of your
13:26 Jehovah *g* him to the lion
14:15 he *g* to their forefathers
15:4 God *g* him a lamp in
17:23 and *g* him to his mother
18:26 young bull that he *g* them
19:21 then *g* it to the people
2Ki 4:17 *g* birth to a son at this
5:23 and *g* them to two of his
8:6 king *g* her a court official
8:11 *g* way to weeping
10:15 So he *g* him his hand
11:10 priest now *g* the chiefs of
12:11 *g* the money that had been
13:3 *g* them into the hand of
13:5 Jehovah *g* Israel a savior
14:6 Jehovah *g* in command, saying
15:19 Menahem *g* Pul a thousand
18:15 Hezekiah *g* all the silver
18:16 *g* them to the king of
21:8 the ground that I *g* to their
22:8 Hilkiah *g* the book to Shaphan
23:35 gold Jehoiakim *g* to Pharaoh

1Ch 1:32 she *g* birth to Zimran and
2:17 Abigail, she *g* birth to
2:35 Sheshan *g* his daughter to
2:46 she *g* birth to Haran and
2:48 she *g* birth to Sheber and
4:18 she *g* birth to Jered the
6:31 David *g* positions for the
6:55 *g* them Hebron in the land of
6:56 they *g* to Caleb the son of
6:57 they *g* the cities of refuge
6:61 *g* from the family of the
6:62 *g* from the tribe of Issachar
6:63 *g* from the tribe of Reuben
6:64 sons of Israel *g* the Levites
6:65 by the lot they *g* from the
6:67 *g* them the cities of refuge
6:71 the sons of Gershom they *g*
6:77 *g* from the tribe of Zebulun
7:18 She *g* birth to Ishhod and
7:23 pregnant and *g* birth to a son
19:11 *g* into the hand of Abishai
21:5 Joab now *g* the number of the
21:14 Jehovah *g* a pestilence in
21:25 David *g* Ornan for the place
28:19 He *g* insight for the entire
29:7 *g* to the service of the house
29:8 they *g* to the treasure of the
29:9 people *g* way to rejoicing
2Ch 2:1 Solomon now *g* the word to
6:25 ground that you *g* to them
6:31 that you *g* to our forefathers
6:38 you *g* to their forefathers
9:9 *g* the king a hundred and
9:9 queen of Sheba *g* to King
9:12 Solomon himself *g* the queen
11:23 *g* them food in abundance
13:5 God of Israel himself *g* a
13:16 God *g* them into their hand
14:6 for Jehovah *g* him rest
15:15 Judah *g* way to rejoicing
21:3 father *g* them many gifts in
21:3 kingdom he *g* to Jehoram, for
23:9 Jehoiada the priest *g* the
24:24 *g* into their hand a
27:5 sons of Ammon *g* him in
28:5 God *g* him into the hand of
28:9 *g* them into your hand, so
28:15 *g* them drink and greased
28:15 *g* them transportation on
31:6 and so *g* heaps upon heaps
32:22 and *g* them rest all around
32:24 and a portent He *g* him
32:29 God *g* him very many goods
34:11 *g* it to the craftsmen and
34:15 Hilkiah *g* the book to
34:18 Hilkiah the priest *g* me
35:8 *g* to the priests for the
36:17 He *g* into his hand
Ezr 2:69 *g* gold for the working
5:11 word that they *g* back to us
5:12 he *g* them into the hand of
7:11 *g* Ezra the priest the copyist
8:17 *g* them a command concerning
8:20 *g* to the service of the
8:36 *g* the laws of the king to
10:2 *g* a dwelling to foreign
10:10 *g* a dwelling to foreign
Ne 1:7 *g* in command to Moses your
2:1 the wine and *g* it to the king
2:6 I *g* him the appointed time
2:8 So the king *g* them to me
2:9 *g* them the letters of the king
7:70 houses that *g* to the work
7:70 *g* to the treasure a thousand
7:71 *g* to the treasure for the
7:72 the rest of the people *g* was
9:10 *g* signs and miracles against
9:15 bread from heaven you *g* them
9:20 your good spirit you *g* to
9:20 water you *g* them for their
9:27 *g* them into the hand of their
9:30 you *g* them into the hand of
9:35 good things that you *g* to
9:36 the land that you *g* to our
Es 3:10 and *g* it to Haman the son of
4:8 he *g* him to show Esther and to
8:1 *g* to Esther the queen the house
8:2 *g* it to Mordecai; and Esther
Job 38:28 who *g* birth to the dewdrops?
38:36 *g* understanding to the sky
Ps 21:4 Life he asked of you. You *g* it
69:21 they *g* me a poisonous plant
78:24 grain of heaven he *g* to them
78:66 of indefinite duration he *g*

Ps 99:7 regulation that he *g* to them
105:44 *g* them the lands of the
106:41 *g* them into the hand of the
135:12 who *g* their land as an
136:21 who *g* their land as an
Pr 17:25 to her that *g* him birth
23:25 she that *g* birth to you will
31:1 mother *g* to him in correction
Ec 12:7 returns to the true God who *g*
Ca 8:11 He *g* the vineyard over to the
Isa 8:3 and in time *g* birth to a son
50:6 My back I *g* to the strikers
66:7 labor pains she *g* birth
66:7 *g* deliverance to a male
Jer 3:18 *g* as a hereditary possession
7:7 in the land that I *g* to your
7:14 place that I *g* to you and to
9:13 my law that I *g* to be before
13:20 the drove that one *g* to you
16:15 I *g* to their forefathers
20:14 that my mother *g* me birth
22:26 your mother who *g* you birth
23:39 the city that I *g* to you
24:10 ground that I *g* to them
25:5 ground that Jehovah *g* to you
30:3 the land that I *g* to their
32:12 *g* the deed of purchase to
32:22 you *g* them this land that
36:32 *g* it to Baruch the son of
39:11 *g* command concerning
40:5 *g* him a food allowance and
50:12 She that *g* you birth has
Eze 16:36 sons whom you *g* to them
20:12 sabbaths I also *g* to them
23:9 I *g* her into the hand of
26:17 *g* their terror to all the
27:19 they *g*. Iron in wrought
28:25 I *g* to my servant, to Jacob
31:6 beasts of the field *g* birth
36:28 dwell in the land that I *g*
37:25 *g* to my servant, to Jacob
39:23 *g* them into the hand of
Da 1:2 Jehovah *g* into his hand
1:9 true God *g* Daniel over to
1:17 true God *g* knowledge and
2:48 many big gifts he *g* to him
3:28 *g* over their bodies, because
5:18 *g* to Nebuchadnezzar your
5:19 greatness that He *g* him, all
10:12 *g* your heart to understanding
Am 4:6 *g* you people cleanness of
Hab 3:10 watery deep *g* forth its
Mt 1:25 until she *g* birth to a son
8:18 *g* the command to shove off
9:8 God, who *g* such authority to
10:1 *g* them authority over unclean
21:23 who *g* you this authority?
25:15 And to one he *g* five talents
25:35 you *g* me something to eat
25:35 you *g* me something to drink
25:42 but you *g* me nothing to eat
25:42 you *g* me nothing to drink
26:27 *g* it to them, saying: Drink
27:10 they *g* them for the potter's
27:34 *g* him wine mixed with gall
28:12 they *g* a sufficient number
Mr 1:43 he *g* him strict orders and at
2:26 *g* some also to the men who
3:16 he also *g* the surname Peter
3:17 *g* these the surname Boanerges
6:8 *g* them orders to carry nothing
6:28 and he *g* it to the maiden
6:28 maiden *g* it to her mother
8:6 seven loaves, *g* thanks, broke
10:24 disciples *g* way to surprise
11:28 who *g* you this authority to
13:34 *g* the authority to his
14:22 broke it and *g* it to them
14:23 offered thanks and *g* it to
14:72 and *g* way to weeping
Lu 2:7 she *g* birth to her son, the
3:16 John *g* the answer, saying to
3:18 *g* many other exhortations and
5:14 he *g* the man orders to tell
6:4 *g* some to the men with him
7:15 and he *g* him to his mother
7:44 *g* me no water for my feet
7:45 You *g* me no kiss; but this
8:32 And he *g* them permission
9:1 *g* them power and authority
10:35 *g* them to the innkeeper, and
15:29 never once *g* a kid for me to
18:43 at seeing it, *g* praise to God
19:13 he *g* them ten minas and told
Lu 20:2 who . . . *g* you this authority
22:17 he *g* thanks and said: Take
22:19 took a loaf, *g* thanks, broke
22:19 broke it, and *g* it to them
23:24 Pilate *g* sentence for their
Joh 1:12 *g* authority to become God's
3:16 he *g* his only-begotten Son
4:5 field that Jacob *g* to Joseph
4:12 Jacob, who *g* us the well and
6:31 He *g* them bread from heaven
7:19 Moses *g* you the Law, did he
11:35 Jesus *g* way to tears
13:26 *g* it to Judas, the son of
17:6 men you *g* me out of the
17:6 you *g* them to me, and they
17:7 things you *g* me are from you
17:8 sayings that you *g* me I have
18:22 *g* Jesus a slap in the face
19:9 But Jesus *g* him no answer
19:38 Pilate *g* him permission
21:13 bread and *g* it to them
Ac 1:4 he *g* them the orders: Do not
5:34 *g* the command to put the men
5:40 they *g* heed to him, and they
7:8 also *g* him a covenant of
7:10 *g* him graciousness and
7:44 *g* orders when speaking to
9:21 *g* way to astonishment and
11:17 God *g* the same free gift to
13:20 *g* them judges until Samuel
13:21 God *g* them Saul son of Kish
16:22 *g* the command to beat them
21:33 and *g* command for him to be
21:40 After he *g* permission, Paul
24:1 they *g* information to the
25:2 *g* him information against
25:23 when Festus *g* the command
27:15 *g* way and were borne along
27:35 *g* thanks to God before
Ro 1:24 *g* them up to uncleanness
1:26 God *g* them up to disgraceful
1:28 God *g* them up to a
8:29 he *g* his first recognition
1Co 16:1 *g* orders to the congregations
2Co 5:5 God, who *g* us the token of
5:18 *g* us the ministry of the
8:5 *g* themselves to the Lord and
10:8 authority that the Lord *g* us
13:10 authority that the Lord *g*
Ga 1:4 He *g* himself for our sins
2:8 who *g* Peter powers necessary
2:8 *g* powers also to me for those
2:9 *g* me and Barnabas the right
Eph 4:8 he *g* gifts in men
4:11 he *g* some as apostles, some
4:19 *g* themselves over to loose
Php 2:6 *g* no consideration to a
2:9 kindly *g* him the name that is
2:22 the proof he *g* of himself
1Th 4:2 orders we *g* you through the
4:6 also *g* you a thorough witness
2Th 1:10 witness we *g* met with faith
2:16 *g* everlasting comfort and
1Ti 2:6 *g* himself a corresponding
2Ti 1:7 God *g* us not a spirit of
Tit 1:5 as I *g* you orders
2:14 *g* himself for us that he
Heb 2:13 children, whom Jehovah *g* me
7:4 *g* a tenth out of the chief
11:22 *g* a command concerning his
12:16 *g* away his rights as
Jas 5:11 seen the outcome Jehovah *g*
5:18 heaven *g* rain and the land
1Pe 1:3 he *g* us a new birth to a
1:21 *g* him glory; so that your
1Jo 3:23 just as he *g* us commandment
3:24 to the spirit which he *g* us
5:11 God *g* us everlasting life
Re 1:1 A revelation . . . God *g* him, to
1:2 witness to the word God *g*
1:2 to the witness Jesus Christ *g*
2:21 I *g* her time to repent, but
5:4 I *g* way to a great deal of
11:13 *g* glory to the God of heaven
12:5 she *g* birth to a son, a male
12:13 woman that *g* birth to the
13:2 dragon *g* to the beast its
13:4 *g* the authority to the wild
15:7 *g* the seven angels seven
20:13 sea *g* up those dead in it
20:13 Hades *g* up those dead in

Gaza
Ge 10:19 near *G*, as far as Sodom and
De 2:23 in settlements as far as *G*
Jos 10:41 to *G* and all the land of
11:22 was only in *G*, in Gath and
15:47 *G*, its dependent towns and
Jg 1:18 Judah captured *G* and its
6:4 all the way to *G*, and they
16:1 Samson went to *G* and saw a
16:21 brought him down to *G* and
1Sa 6:17 golden piles . . . for *G* one
1Ki 4:24 from Tiphsah to *G*, even all
2Ki 18:8 to *G* and also its territories
1Ch 7:28 to *G* and its dependent towns
Jer 25:20 kings of the land of . . . *G*
47:1 proceeded to strike down *G*
47:5 Baldness must come to *G*
Am 1:6 account of three revolts of *G*
1:7 a fire onto the wall of *G*
Zep 2:4 *G*, an abandoned city is what
Zec 9:5 *G*, she will also feel very
9:5 will certainly perish from *G*
Ac 8:26 down from Jerusalem to *G*

Gaze
Job 7:19 you not turn your *g* from me
10:20 Let him turn his *g* from me
14:6 Turn your *g* from upon him
Ps 22:17 look, they *g* upon me
119:117 *g* upon your regulations
Pr 4:25 eyes should *g* straight in
Isa 5:30 actually *g* at the land, and
14:16 will *g* even at you
17:7 *g* at the Holy One of Israel
17:8 have made he will not *g*
22:4 Turn your *g* away from me
41:10 Do not *g* about, for I am
41:23 *g* about and see it at the
Jon 2:4 *g* again upon your holy temple
2Co 3:7 not *g* intently at the face of
3:13 might not *g* intently at the

Gazed
Ex 33:8 they *g* after Moses until he
Nu 21:9 and he *g* at the copper serpent
Job 36:25 mankind themselves have *g*
Ps 33:14 *g* at all those dwelling on
Ac 3:4 Peter, together with John, *g*
6:15 in the Sanhedrin *g* at him
7:55 *g* into heaven and caught
10:4 man *g* at him and, becoming

Gazelle
De 12:15 like the *g* and like the stag
12:22 *g* and the stag may be eaten
14:5 the stag and *g* and roebuck
15:22 like the *g* and like the stag
Pr 6:5 Deliver yourself like a *g* from
Ca 2:9 My dear one is resembling a *g*
2:17 my dear one; be like the *g* or
4:5 the twins of a female *g*, that
7:3 the twins of a female *g*
8:14 and make yourself like a *g* or
Isa 13:14 like a *g* chased away and

Gazelles
2Sa 2:18 *g* that are in the open field
1Ki 4:23 stags and *g* and roebucks and
1Ch 12:8 they were like the *g* upon
Ca 2:7 by the female *g* or by the
3:5 by the female *g* or by the

Gazez
1Ch 2:46 Haran and Moza and *G*
2:46 Haran, he became father to *G*

Gazing
Ge 24:21 man was *g* at her in wonder
Ca 2:9 *g* through the windows
Ac 1:10 they were *g* into the sky
3:12 *g* at us as though by personal
11:6 *G* into it, I made

Gazites
Jos 13:3 the *G* and the Ashdodites
Jg 16:2 And report was made to the *G*

Gazzam
Ezr 2:48 the sons of *G*
Ne 7:51 the sons of *G*, the sons of

Gear
Ac 27:17 lowered the *g* and thus

Geba
Jos 18:24 and Ophni and *G*
21:17 *G* and its pasture ground
1Sa 13:3 Philistines that was in *G*
13:16 dwelling in *G* of Benjamin
14:5 was on the south facing *G*
2Sa 5:25 from *G* to as far as Gezer

1Ki 15:22 *G* in Benjamin, and Mizpah
2Ki 23:8 from *G* as far as Beer-sheba
1Ch 6:60 *G* with its pasture grounds
8:6 to the inhabitants of *G*, and
2Ch 16:6 build with them *G* and
Ezr 2:26 the sons of Ramah and *G*
Ne 7:30 the men of Ramah and *G*, six
11:31 of Benjamin were from *G*
12:29 the fields of *G* and Azmaveth
Isa 10:29 *G* is a place for them to
Zec 14:10 from *G* to Rimmon to the

Gebal
Ps 83:7 *G* and Ammon and Amalek
Eze 27:9 Even old men of *G* and her

Gebalites
Jos 13:5 the land of the *G* and all of
1Ki 5:18 the *G* did the cutting, and

Geber
1Ki 4:13 son of *G*, in Ramoth-gilead
4:19 *G* the son of Uri, in the land

Gebim
Isa 10:31 inhabitants of *G* themselves

Gecko
Le 11:30 the *g* fanfoot and the large
Pr 30:28 *g* lizard takes hold with its

Gedaliah
2Ki 25:22 *G* the son of Ahikam the
25:23 king . . . had appointed *G*
25:23 came to *G* at Mizpah, that
25:24 *G* swore to them and their
25:25 they got to strike down *G*
1Ch 25:3 sons of Jeduthun, *G* and Zeri
25:9 for *G* the second (he and his
Ezr 10:18 Eliezer and Jarib and *G*
Jer 38:1 *G* the son of Pashhur and
39:14 *G* the son of Ahikam the
40:5 *G* the son of Ahikam the
40:6 *G* the son of Ahikam at
40:7 *G* the son of Ahikam over the
40:8 came to *G* at Mizpah, even
40:9 *G* the son of Ahikam the
40:11 *G* the son of Ahikam the
40:12 of Judah to *G* at Mizpah
40:13 they came to *G* at Mizpah
40:14 *G* the son of Ahikam did
40:15 said to *G*, in a place of
40:16 *G* the son of Ahikam said
41:1 *G* the son of Ahikam at
41:2 struck down *G* the son of
41:3 that is, with *G*, in Mizpah
41:4 putting of *G* to death, when
41:6 to *G* the son of Ahikam
41:10 put in the custody of *G*
41:16 *G* the son of Ahikam
41:18 struck down *G* the son of
43:6 *G* the son of Ahikam the
Zep 1:1 *G* the son of Amariah the

Geder
Jos 12:13 the king of *G*, one

Gederah
Jos 15:36 Adithaim and *G* and
1Ch 4:23 inhabitants of Netaim and *G*

Gederathite
1Ch 12:4 Johanan and Jozabad the *G*

Gederite
1Ch 27:28 there was Baal-hanan the *G*

Gederoth
Jos 15:41 *G*, Beth-dagon and Naamah
2Ch 28:18 *G* and Soco and its

Gederothaim
Jos 15:36 Adithaim and Gederah and *G*

Gedor
Jos 15:58 Halhul, Beth-zur and *G*
1Ch 4:4 Penuel the father of *G* and
4:18 Jered the father of *G* and
4:39 to go to the entryway of *G*
8:31 and *G* and Ahio and Zecher
9:37 *G* and Ahio and Zechariah and
12:7 the sons of Jeroham of *G*

Ge-harashim
1Ch 4:14 Joab the father of *G*

Gehazi
2Ki 4:12 he said to *G* his attendant
4:14 *G* now said: For a fact, a son
4:25 said to *G* his attendant
4:27 *G* came near to push her away
4:29 said to *G*: Gird up your loins
2Ki 4:31 *G* himself passed along
4:36 He now called *G* and said
5:20 *G* the attendant of Elisha
5:21 *G* went chasing after Naaman
5:25 Where did you come from, *G*?
8:4 *G* the attendant of the man of
8:5 *G* said: My lord the king

Gehenna
Mt 5:22 will be liable to the fiery *G*
5:29 body to be pitched into *G*
5:30 whole body to land in *G*
10:28 both soul and body in *G*
18:9 two eyes into the fiery *G*
23:15 make him a subject for *G*
23:33 flee from the judgment of *G*
Mr 9:43 to go off into *G*, into the
9:45 two feet to be pitched into *G*
9:47 to be pitched into *G*
Lu 12:5 authority to throw into *G*
Jas 3:6 and it is set aflame by *G*

Geliloth
Jos 18:17 and went out to *G*, which is

Gemalli
Nu 13:12 of Dan, Ammiel the son of *G*

Gemariah
Jer 29:3 *G* the son of Hilkiah, whom
36:10 *G* the son of Shaphan the
36:11 Micaiah the son of *G* the
36:12 *G* the son of Shaphan and
36:25 *G* themselves pleaded with

Genealogical
1Ch 4:33 their *g* enrollments for them
5:7 the *g* enrollment by their
7:5 the *g* enrollment of them all
7:7 and their *g* enrollment was
7:9 their *g* enrollment by their
7:40 their *g* enrollment was in
9:22 by their *g* enrollment
2Ch 12:15 by *g* enrollment
31:16 *g* enrollment of the males
31:17 *g* enrollment of the priests
31:18 *g* enrollment among all
31:19 *g* enrollment among the
Ezr 8:1 *g* enrollment of those going
Ne 7:5 the book of *g* enrollment of

Genealogically
1Ch 5:1 not to be enrolled *g* for the
5:17 enrolled *g* in the days of
9:1 they were enrolled *g*; and
Ne 7:5 get themselves enrolled *g*

Genealogies
1Ti 1:4 *g*, which end up in nothing
Tit 3:9 foolish questionings and *g*

Genealogy
Ezr 2:62 to establish their *g* publicly
Ne 7:64 to establish their *g* publicly
Heb 7:3 motherless, without *g*, having
7:6 did not trace his *g* from

General
1Ki 12:31 from the people in *g*
13:33 from the people in *g*
2Ki 17:32 people in *g* priests of high
Pr 2:15 are devious in their *g* course
Heb 12:23 in *g* assembly, and the

Generally
Isa 28:27 cummin is *g* beaten out
28:28 breadstuff itself *g* crushed

Generation
Ge 7:1 righteous . . . among this *g*
15:16 in the fourth *g* they will
50:23 sons of the third *g*
Ex 1:6 his brothers and all that *g*
3:15, 15 memorial . . . *g* after *g*
17:16, 16 with Amalek from *g* to *g*
20:5 upon the third *g* and upon the
20:5 and upon the fourth *g*, in the
20:6 toward the thousandth *g* in
34:7 upon the third *g* and upon the
34:7 and upon the fourth *g*
Nu 14:18 upon the third *g* and
14:18 and upon the fourth *g*
32:13 until all the *g* that was
De 1:35 these men of this evil *g* will
2:14 the *g* of the men of war had
5:9 upon the third *g* and upon the
5:9 upon the fourth *g*, in the case
5:10 toward the thousandth *g* in
23:2 to the tenth *g* none of his
23:3 to the tenth *g* none of theirs
De 23:8 as the third *g* may come for
29:22 future *g*, your sons who will
32:5 A *g* crooked and twisted!
32:7, 7 the years back from *g* to *g*
32:20 they are a *g* of perverseness
Jg 2:10 that *g* too were gathered to
2:10 another *g* began to rise after
2Ki 10:30 to the fourth *g* will sit
15:12 to the fourth *g* will sit
Es 9:28 and held in each and every *g*
Job 8:8 ask, please, of the former *g*
Ps 10:6, 6 For *g* after *g* I shall be
12:7 preserve each one from this *g*
14:5 among the *g* of the righteous
22:30 concerning Jehovah to the *g*
24:6 the *g* of those seeking him
33:11, 11 to one *g* after another *g*
48:13 recount it to the future *g*
49:11, 11 tabernacles to *g* after *g*
49:19 the *g* of his forefathers
61:6, 6 will be like *g* after *g*
71:18 tell about your arm to the *g*
72:5, 5 the moon for *g* after *g*
73:15 against the *g* of your sons
77:8, 8 to nothing for *g* after *g*
78:4 even to the *g* to come
78:6 In order that the *g* to come
78:8 *g* stubborn and rebellious
78:8 *g* who had not prepared their
79:13, 13 *g* to *g* we shall declare
85:5, 5 your anger to *g* after *g*
89:1, 1 For *g* after *g* I shall make
89:4, 4 your throne to *g* after *g*
90:1, 1 for us During *g* after *g*
95:10 loathing toward that *g*
100:5, 5 faithfulness to *g* after *g*
102:12, 12 will be for *g* after *g*
102:18 written for the future *g*
106:31, 31 For *g* after *g* to time
109:13 following *g* let their name
112:2 *g* of the upright ones, it
119:90, 90 is for *g* after *g*
135:13, 13 is to *g* after *g*
145:4, 4 *G* after *g* will commend
146:10, 10 Zion, for *g* after *g*
Pr 30:11 *g* that calls down evil even
30:12 a *g* that is pure in its own
30:13 a *g* whose eyes have become
30:14 *g* whose teeth are swords and
Ec 1:4 A *g* is going, and a
1:4 is going, and a *g* is coming
Isa 13:20, 20 she reside for *g* after *g*
34:10, 10 From *g* to *g* she will be
34:17, 17 for *g* after *g* they will
53:8 with the details of his *g*
60:15, 15 exultation for *g* after *g*
61:4, 4 desolate for *g* after *g*
Jer 2:31 O *g*, see for yourselves the
7:29 *g* with which he is furious
50:39, 39 she reside for *g* after *g*
La 5:19, 19 throne is for *g* after *g*
Da 4:3, 3 rulership is for *g* after *g*
4:34, 34 kingdom is for *g* after *g*
Joe 1:3 their sons to the following *g*
2:2, 2 to the years of *g* after *g*
3:20, 20 Jerusalem to *g* after *g*
Mt 11:16 whom shall I compare this *g*
12:39 A wicked and adulterous *g*
12:41 in the judgment with this *g*
12:42 in the judgment with this *g*
12:45 be also with this wicked *g*
16:4 A wicked and adulterous *g*
17:17 O faithless and twisted *g*
23:36 will come upon this *g*
24:34 *g* will by no means pass
Mr 8:12 Why does this *g* seek a sign?
8:12 No sign . . . given to this *g*
8:38 this adulterous and sinful *g*
9:19 O faithless *g*, how long must
13:30 *g* will by no means pass
Lu 7:31 compare the men of this *g*
9:41 O faithless and twisted *g*
11:29, 29 This *g* is a wicked *g*
11:30 Son of man be also to this *g*
11:31 with the men of this *g*
11:32 with this *g* and will condemn
11:50 may be required from this *g*
11:51 will be required from this *g*
16:8 toward their own *g* than the
17:25 and be rejected by this *g*
21:32 This *g* will by no means pass
Ac 2:40 saved from this crooked *g*
8:33 tell the details of his *g*
13:36 will of God in his own *g*

Mt 10:41 will *g* a prophet's reward
10:41 *g* a righteous man's reward
16:23 to Peter: *G* behind me, Satan!
Mr 2:9 *G* up and pick up your cot and
2:11 *G* up, pick up your cot, and
5:41 Maiden, I say to you, *G* up!
8:33 *G* behind me, Satan, because
Lu 5:23 or to say, *G* up and walk
5:24 *G* up and pick up your little
7:14 Young man, I say to you, *G* up!
8:54 called, saying: Girl, *g* up!
13:24 *g* in through the narrow door
13:24 seek to *g* in but will not be
13:27 *G* away from me, all you
Ac 2:40 *G* saved from this crooked
4:12 by which we must *g* saved
22:18 *g* out of Jerusalem quickly
Re 18:4 *G* out of her, my people, if

Getaway
Am 9:1 of them will make his *g*

Gether
Ge 10:23 sons of Aram . . . *G* and
1Ch 1:17 and Hul and *G* and Mash

Gethsemane
Mt 26:36 to the spot called *G*, and he
Mr 14:32 they came to a spot named *G*

Gets*
Pr 8:35 and *g* goodwill from Jehovah
12:2 One that is good *g* approval
18:22 one *g* goodwill from Jehovah
31:15 *g* up while it is still night
Ec 12:4 *g* up at the sound of a bird
Ac 10:43 *g* forgiveness of sins through
2Th 2:3 man of lawlessness *g* revealed
Jas 5:7 he *g* the early rain and the

Getting*
Pr 4:18 light that is *g* lighter and
16:16 *g* of wisdom is O how much
16:16 *g* of understanding is to be
Isa 5:11 *g* up early in the morning
Jer 7:13 *g* up early and speaking
7:25 daily *g* up early and
29:19 the prophets, *g* up early
Lu 21:28 your deliverance is *g* near
22:1 Passover, was *g* near
Ac 8:36 prevents me from *g* baptized
Ro 15:22 hindered from *g* to you
Eph 5:18 do not be *g* drunk with wine
5:18 keep *g* filled with spirit

Geuel
Nu 13:15 of Gad, *G* the son of Machi

Gezer
Jos 10:33 Horam the king of *G* went
12:12 the king of *G*, one
16:3 of Lower Beth-horon and *G*
16:10 who were dwelling in *G*
21:21 *G* and its pasture ground
Jg 1:29 who were dwelling in *G*, but
1:29 to dwell in among them in *G*
2Sa 5:25 from Geba to as far as *G*
1Ki 9:15 and Hazor and Megiddo and *G*
9:16 captured *G* and burned it
9:17 Solomon went on to build *G*
1Ch 6:67 *G* with its pasture grounds
7:28 to the west, *G* and its
14:16 from Gibeon to *G*
20:4 war began breaking out at *G*

Giah
2Sa 2:24 front of *G* on the way to the

Gibbar
Ezr 2:20 the sons of *G*, ninety-five

Gibbethon
Jos 19:44 Eltekeh and *G* and Baalath
21:23 *G* and its pasture ground
1Ki 15:27 to strike him down at *G*
15:27 all Israel were besieging *G*
16:15 were encamping against *G*
16:17 now went on up from *G* and

Gibea
1Ch 2:49 and the father of *G*

Gibeah
Jos 15:57 Kain, *G*, and Timnah
18:28 Jerusalem, *G* and Kiriath
Jg 19:12 have to pass on as far as *G*
19:13 either in *G* or in Ramah
19:14 *G*, which belongs to Benjamin
19:15 go in to stay overnight in *G*
19:16 was residing for a time in *G*
Jg 20:4 *G*, which belongs to Benjamin
20:5 landowners of *G* proceeded to
20:9 thing that we shall do to *G*
20:10 going against *G* of Benjamin
20:13 give over the men . . . in *G*
20:14 to *G* to go out to battle
20:15 the inhabitants of *G*, of
20:19 Israel . . . camped against *G*
20:20 formation against them at *G*
20:21 Benjamin came on out from *G*
20:25 Benjamin came on out from *G*
20:29 set men in ambush against *G*
20:30 in formation against *G* the
20:31 to Bethel and the other to *G*
20:33 places in the vicinity of *G*
20:34 Israel came in front of *G*
20:36 that they had set against *G*
20:37 and went dashing toward *G*
20:43 front of *G* toward the rising
1Sa 10:26 he went to his home at *G*
11:4 messengers came to *G* of Saul
13:2 Jonathan at *G* of Benjamin
13:15 Gilgal to *G* of Benjamin
14:2 at the outskirts of *G*
14:16 to Saul in *G* of Benjamin
15:34 his own house at *G* of Saul
22:6 Saul was sitting in *G* under
23:19 up to Saul at *G*, saying
26:1 came to Saul at *G*, saying
2Sa 21:6 expose them to Jehovah in *G*
23:29 Ittai the son of Ribai of *G*
1Ch 11:31 *G* of the sons of Benjamin
2Ch 13:2 daughter of Uriel of *G*
Isa 10:29 *G* of Saul itself has fled
Ho 5:8 Blow a horn in *G*, a trumpet
9:9 ruin, as in the days of *G*
10:9 From the days of *G* you have
10:9 In *G* war against the sons

Gibeath-haaraloth
Jos 5:3 the sons of Israel at *G*

Gibeathite
1Ch 12:3 the sons of Shemaah the *G*

Gibeon
Jos 9:3 inhabitants of *G* heard what
9:17 and their cities were *G* and
10:1 *G* had made peace with Israel
10:2 because *G* was a great city
10:4 let us strike *G*, because it
10:5 camp against *G* and to war
10:6 men of *G* sent to Joshua at
10:10 a great slaughter at *G* and
10:12 Sun, be motionless over *G*
10:41 land of Goshen and up to *G*
11:19 the Hivites inhabiting *G*
18:25 *G* and Ramah and Beeroth
21:17 *G* and its pasture ground
2Sa 2:12 went out from Mahanaim to *G*
2:13 together by the pool of *G*
2:16 which is in *G*
2:24 to the wilderness of *G*
3:30 brother to death at *G* in the
20:8 the great stone that is in *G*
1Ki 3:4 king went to *G* to sacrifice
3:5 In *G* Jehovah appeared to
9:2 he had appeared to him in *G*
1Ch 8:29 it was in *G* . . . Jeiel, dwelt
8:29 father of *G*, Jeiel, dwelt
9:35 in *G* was where the father of
9:35 father of *G*, Jeiel, dwelt
14:16 Philistines from *G* to Gezer
16:39 high place that was at *G*
21:29 on the high place at *G*
2Ch 1:3 the high place that was at *G*
1:13 the high place that was at *G*
Ne 3:7 men of *G* and Mizpah
7:25 the sons of *G*, ninety-five
Isa 28:21 as in the low plain near *G*
Jer 28:1 the prophet who was from *G*
41:12 waters that were in *G*
41:16 he brought back from *G*

Gibeonite
1Ch 12:4 Ishmaiah the *G*, a mighty man
Ne 3:7 Melatiah the *G* and Jadon the

Gibeonites
2Sa 21:1 he put the *G* to death
21:2 the king called the *G* and
21:2 *G* were not of the sons of
21:3 went on to say to the *G*
21:4 the *G* said to him: It is not
21:9 into the hand of the *G*

Giddalti
1Ch 25:4 the sons of Heman . . . *G* and
25:29 the twenty-second, for *G*

Giddel
Ezr 2:47 the sons of *G*
2:56 the sons of *G*
Ne 7:49 the sons of *G*, the sons of
7:58 sons of Darkon, the sons of *G*

Gideon
Jg 6:11 *G* his son was beating out
6:13 *G* said to him: Excuse me, my
6:19 *G* went in and proceeded to
6:22 *G* realized that it was
6:22 *G* said: Alas, Sovereign Lord
6:24 So *G* built an altar there to
6:27 *G* took ten men of his
6:29 *G* the son of Joash is the one
6:34 spirit enveloped *G* so that he
6:36 *G* said to the true God: If
6:39 *G* said to the true God: Do
7:1 *G*, and all the people who were
7:2 said to *G*: The people who are
7:3 *G* put them to the proof
7:4 said to *G*: There are yet too
7:5 said to *G*: Every one that laps
7:7 said to *G*: By the three hundred
7:13 *G* now came, and, look! there
7:14 sword of *G* the son of Joash
7:15 as *G* heard the relating of the
7:19 *G* came with the hundred men
7:24 *G* sent messengers into all
7:25 *G* in the region of the Jordan
8:4 *G* came to the Jordan, crossing
8:7 At this *G* said: That is why
8:11 *G* continued on up by the way
8:13 *G* the son of Joash began his
8:21 *G* got up and killed Zebah and
8:22 said to *G*: Rule over us, you
8:23 But *G* said to them: I myself
8:24 *G* went on to say to them: Let
8:27 *G* proceeded to make it into
8:27 served as a snare to *G* and to
8:28 forty years in the days of *G*
8:30 *G* came to have seventy sons
8:32 *G* the son of Joash died at a
8:33 as soon as *G* had died the sons
8:35 *G*, in return for all the
Heb 11:32 on to relate about *G*, Barak

Gideoni
Nu 1:11 Abidan the son of *G*
2:22 is Abidan the son of *G*
7:60 Abidan the son of *G*
7:65 of Abidan the son of *G*
10:24 Abidan the son of *G*

Gideon's
Jg 7:18 you must say, Jehovah's and *G*!
7:20 Jehovah's sword and *G*!

Gidom
Jg 20:45 after them as far as *G* and

Gift
Ge 32:13 to take a *g* for Esau his
32:18 A *g* it is, sent to my lord
32:20 I may appease him by the *g*
32:21 So the *g* went crossing over
33:10 must take my *g* at my hand
33:11 the *g* conveying my blessing
34:12 the marriage money and *g*
43:11 to the man as a *g*: a little
43:15 the men took this *g*, and
43:25 get the *g* ready for Joseph's
43:26 they brought the *g* that was
Nu 18:6 the Levites . . . as a *g* for you
18:7 As a service of *g* I shall give
18:11 the contribution of their *g*
De 16:17 The *g* of each one's hand
Jos 13:15 Moses made a *g* to the tribe
13:24 a *g* to the tribe of Gad
13:29 a *g* to the half tribe of
22:7 Moses had made a *g* in Bashan
22:7 Joshua made a *g* with their
Jg 6:18 brought out my *g* and set it
Ru 1:9 May Jehovah make a *g* to you
1Sa 9:7 as a *g*, there is nothing to
10:27 did not bring any *g* to him
25:27 *g* blessing that your
30:26 Here is a *g* blessing for
2Sa 11:8 king's courtesy *g* went out
19:42 has a *g* been carried to us?
1Ki 9:16 a parting *g* to his daughter
10:25 were bringing each his *g*
13:7 and let me give you a *g*

2Ki 5:15 accept, please, a blessing g
8:8 Take a g in your hand and go
8:9 and took a g in his hand
20:12 letters and a g to Hezekiah
1Ch 16:29 Carry a g and come in
29:5 today with a g for Jehovah
2Ch 9:24 bringing each his g, articles
28:21 g to the king of Assyria
Ezr 7:16 the g of the people and the
Ps 20:3 remember all your g offerings
45:12 also with a g—The rich ones
72:10 Seba—A g they will present
76:11 Let them bring a g in fear
96:8 Carry a g and come into his
Pr 17:8 g is a stone winning favor in
18:16 g will make a large opening
21:14 A g made in secrecy subdues
25:14 about a g in falsehood
Ec 3:13 It is the g of God
5:19 This is the g of God
7:7 and a g can destroy the heart
Isa 18:7 g will be brought to Jehovah
19:21 render sacrifice and g and
39:1 letters and a g to Hezekiah
43:23 to serve me with a g, nor
57:6 you offered up a g
66:3 The one offering up a g
66:20 nations as a g to Jehovah
66:20 the g in a clean vessel
Eze 27:15 have paid back as g to you
40:43 the flesh of the g offering
46:16 chieftain should give a g
46:17 g from his inheritance to
Da 9:21 of the evening g offering
9:27 and g offering to cease
Ho 2:12 g to me, which my passionate
8:13 As my g sacrifices they kept
10:6 as a g to a great king
Am 5:22 even in your g offerings I
5:25 sacrifices and g offerings
Zep 3:10 will bring a g to me
Mal 1:10 the g offering from your
1:11 to my name, even a clean g
1:13 you have brought it as a g
2:12 a g offering to Jehovah of
2:13 toward the g offering
3:3 presenting a g offering in
3:4 the g offering of Judah and
Mt 5:23 bringing your g to the altar
5:24 leave your g there in front
5:24 come back, offer up your g
8:4 and offer the g that Moses
15:5 is a g dedicated to God
19:11 only those who have the g
23:18 if anyone swears by the g on
23:19 greater, the g or the altar
23:19 altar that sanctifies the g
Mr 7:11 that is, a g dedicated to God
Joh 4:10 had known the free g of God
Ac 2:38 free g of the holy spirit
8:20 of the free g of God
10:45 free g of the holy spirit
11:17 God gave the same free g to
Ro 1:11 may impart some spiritual g
3:24 as a free g that they are
5:15 it is not with the g as it
5:15 God and his free g with the
5:16 it is not with the free g
5:16 the g resulted from many
5:17 free g of righteousness rule
6:23 g God gives is everlasting
1Co 1:7 not fall short in any g at
7:7 has his own g from God, one
13:2 I have the g of prophesying
14:14 it is my g of the spirit
14:15 with the g of the spirit
14:15 with the g of the spirit
14:16 with a g of the spirit, how
16:3 your kind g to Jerusalem
2Co 8:19 kind g to be administered by
9:5 your bountiful g previously
9:5 be ready as a bountiful g and
9:15 for his indescribable free g
Eph 2:8 not owing to you . . . God's g
3:7 the free g of the undeserved
4:7 measured out the free g
Php 4:17 earnestly seeking the g, but
1Ti 4:14 not be neglecting the g in
2Ti 1:6 the g of God which is in you
Heb 6:4 tasted the heavenly free g
Jas 1:17 Every good g and every
1Pe 4:10 each one has received a g

Gifted
1Co 14:37 thinks he is a prophet or g

Gifts
Ge 25:6 Abraham had Abraham gave g
Ex 28:38 all their holy g; and it
Le 23:38 g and besides all your vow
Nu 18:29 From all the g to you, you
1Ki 4:21 g and serving Solomon all
2Ch 21:3 g in silver and in gold and
32:23 many bringing g to Jehovah
Es 9:22 and of g to the poor people
Ps 37:21 favor and is making g
68:18 taken g in the form of men
68:29 Kings will bring g to you
68:31 stretch out its hands with g
Pr 15:27 hater of g . . . keep living
19:6 to the man making g
Isa 1:23 a bribe and a chaser after g
Eze 20:26 become defiled by their g
20:31 lifting up your g by making
20:39 no more profane by your g
Da 2:6 g and a present and much
2:48 many big g he gave to him
5:17 your g prove to be to you
Ho 9:1 You have loved g of hire on
Mic 1:7 all the g made to her as her
1:14 parting g to Moresheth-gath
Mt 2:11 g, gold and frankincense and
6:2 when you go making g of mercy
6:3 when making g of mercy, do
6:4 g of mercy may be in secret
7:11 give good g to your children
Lu 11:13 know how to give good g to
11:41 give as g of mercy the
12:33 and give g of mercy
21:1 rich dropping their g into
21:4 g out of their surplus, but
Ac 3:2 in order to ask g of mercy
3:3 requesting to get g of mercy
3:10 sit for g of mercy at the
9:36 and g of mercy that she was
10:2 he made many g of mercy to
10:4 g of mercy have ascended as
10:31 your g of mercy have been
24:17 g of mercy to my nation
28:10 honored us with many g
Ro 11:29 g and the calling of God
12:6 we have g differing according
1Co 12:1 concerning the spiritual g
12:4 are varieties of g, but there
12:9 to another g of healings by
12:28 then g of healings; helpful
12:30 Not all have g of healings
12:31 seeking the greater g
13:8 g of prophesying, they will
14:1 seeking the spiritual g
14:12 desirous of g of the spirit
14:32 And g of the spirit of the
Eph 4:8 he gave g in men
Heb 5:1 g and sacrifices for sins
8:3 offer both g and sacrifices
8:4 the g according to the Law
9:9 g and sacrifices are offered
11:4 witness respecting his g
Re 11:10 will send g to one another

Gihon
Ge 2:13 name of the second river is G
1Ki 1:33 and lead him down to G
1:38 and then brought him to G
1:45 anointed him as king in G
2Ch 32:30 source of the waters of G
33:14 west of G in the torrent

Gilalai
Ne 12:36 Milalai, G, Maai, Nethanel

Gilboa
1Sa 28:4 and they pitched camp in G
31:1 slain in Mount G
31:8 fallen upon Mount G
2Sa 1:6 chanced to be on Mount G
1:21 mountains of G, let no dew
21:12 struck down Saul on G
1Ch 10:1 falling slain in Mount G
10:8 his sons fallen upon Mount G

Gilead
Ge 31:21 the mountainous region of G
31:23 the mountainous region of G
31:25 the mountainous region of G
37:25 caravan . . . coming from G
Nu 26:29 Machir became father to G
26:29 Of G the family of the
26:30 These were the sons of G
27:1 son of G the son of Machir
32:1 Jazer and the land of G, and
32:26 stay there in the cities of G
Nu 32:29 give them the land of G as a
32:39 march to G and to capture it
32:40 Moses gave G to Machir the
36:1 the family of the sons of G
De 2:36 as far as G, there proved to
3:10 G and all Bashan as far as
3:12 the mountainous region of G
3:13 the rest of G and all Bashan
3:15 And to Machir I have given G
3:16 from G to the torrent valley
4:43 Ramoth in G for the Gadites
34:1 all the land, G as far as Dan
Jos 12:2 half of G as far as Jabbok
12:5 Maacathites, and half of G
13:11 and G and the territory of
13:25 and all the cities of G and
13:31 half of G, and Ashtaroth
17:1 Machir . . . the father of G
17:1 and G and Bashan came to
17:3 Hepher, the son of G
17:5 the land of G and Bashan
17:6 G became the property of the
20:8 G out of the tribe of Gad
21:38 Ramoth in G, and its pasture
22:9 so as to go to the land of G
22:13 in the land of G Phinehas
22:15 Manasseh in the land of G
22:32 land of G to the land of
Jg 5:17 G kept to his residence on the
10:4 they are in the land of G
10:8 land of the Amorites . . . in G
10:17 Ammon . . . pitched camp in G
10:18 the princes of G began to say
10:18 all the inhabitants of G
11:1 G came to be the father of
11:5 older men of G immediately
11:7 said to the older men of G
11:8 the older men of G said to
11:8 all the inhabitants of G
11:9 said to the older men of G
11:10 the older men of G said to
11:11 the older men of G and the
11:29 pass through G and Manasseh
11:29 to pass through Mizpeh of G
11:29 Mizpeh of G he passed along
12:4 collected all the men of G
12:4 the men of G went striking
12:4 G, inside of Ephraim, inside
12:5 G got to capture the fords of
12:5 men of G would say to each
12:7 was buried in his city in G
20:1 along with the land of G, to
1Sa 11:1 and camp against Jabesh in G
11:9 to the men of Jabesh in G
13:7 to the land of Gad and G
2Sa 2:9 king over G and the Ashurites
17:26 camping in the land of G
24:6 they came on to G and the
1Ki 4:13 which are in G; he had the
4:19 land of G, the land of Sihon
17:1 the inhabitants of G
2Ki 10:33 all the land of G, the
10:33 even G and Bashan
15:25 fifty men of the sons of G
15:29 Hazor and G and Galilee
1Ch 2:21 Machir the father of G
2:22 cities in the land of G
2:23 Machir the father of G
5:9 numerous in the land of G
5:10 all the country east of G
5:14 son of G, the son of Michael
5:16 they continued to dwell in G
6:80 Ramoth in G with its pasture
7:14 bore Machir the father of G
7:17 sons of G the son of Machir
10:11 all those of Jabesh in G got
26:31 among them in Jazer in G
27:21 half tribe of Manasseh in G
Ps 60:7 G belongs to me and Manasseh
108:8 G belongs to me; Manasseh
Ca 4:1 the mountainous region of G
6:5 that have hopped down from G
Jer 8:22 Is there no balsam in G?
22:6 You are as G to me, the head
46:11 Go up to G and get some
50:19 of G his soul will be
Eze 47:18 between G and the land of
Ho 6:8 G is a town of practicers of
12:11 With G what is uncanny, also
Am 1:3 account of their threshing G
1:13 the pregnant women of G
Ob 19 must take possession of G
Mic 7:14 feed on Bashan and G as in
Zec 10:10 and to the land of G and

Gileadite
Jg 10:3 Jair the *G* rose up, and he
11:1 Jephthah the *G* had become a
11:40 daughter of Jephthah the *G*
12:7 Jephthah the *G* died and was
2Sa 17:27 Barzillai the *G* from
19:31 Barzillai the *G* himself
1Ki 2:7 the sons of Barzillai the *G*
Ezr 2:61 daughters of Barzillai the *G*
Ne 7:63 Barzillai the *G* and came to

Gileadites
Nu 26:29 Gilead the family of the *G*

Gilead's
Jg 11:2 *G* wife kept bearing sons to

Gilgal
De 11:30 in the Arabah, in front of *G*
Jos 4:19 *G* on the eastern border of
4:20 Joshua set these up at *G*
5:9 to be called *G* until this day
5:10 continued to camp in *G*, and
9:6 Joshua at the camp at *G* and
10:6 to Joshua at the camp at *G*
10:7 So Joshua went on up from *G*
10:9 he had gone up from *G*
10:15 returned to the camp at *G*
10:43 returned to the camp at *G*
12:23 the king of Goiim in *G*, one
14:6 approached Joshua in *G*, and
15:7 turning northward to *G*
Jg 2:1 angel went up from *G* to
3:19 the quarries that were at *G*
1Sa 7:16 circuit of Bethel and *G* and
10:8 go down ahead of me to *G*
11:14 Come and let us go to *G*
11:15 So all the people went to *G*
11:15 king before Jehovah in *G*
13:4 together to follow Saul to *G*
13:7 Saul himself was yet in *G*
13:8 and Samuel did not come to *G*
13:12 come down against me at *G*
13:15 his way up from *G* to Gibeah
15:12 across and descended to *G*
15:21 to Jehovah your God in *G*
15:33 went hacking Agag . . . in *G*
2Sa 19:15 they came to *G* to go and
19:40 the king went across to *G*
2Ki 2:1 Elisha proceeded to go from *G*
4:38 Elisha himself returned to *G*
Ho 4:15 do not you people come to *G*
9:15 All their badness was in *G*
12:11 In *G* they have sacrificed
Am 4:4 At *G* be frequent in
5:5 and to *G* you must not come
5:5 *G* itself will without fail go
Mic 6:5 all the way to *G*, to the

Giloh
Jos 15:51 and Goshen and Holon and *G*
2Sa 15:12 counselor, from his city *G*

Gilonite
2Sa 15:12 Ahithophel the *G*, David's
23:34 the son of Ahithophel the *G*

Gimzo
2Ch 28:18 and *G* and its dependent

Ginath
1Ki 16:21 Tibni the son of *G*
16:22 Tibni the son of *G*

Ginnethoi
Ne 12:4 Iddo, *G*, Abijah

Ginnethon
Ne 10:6 Daniel, *G*, Baruch
12:16 Zechariah; for *G*, Meshullam

Gird
Ex 29:9 *g* them with the sashes, Aaron
Le 16:4 *g* himself with the linen sash
1Sa 2:4 do *g* on vital energy
25:13 *G* on every one his sword
2Sa 22:40 *g* me with vital energy for
2Ki 4:29 *G* up your loins and take my
9:1 *G* up your loins and take this
Job 38:3 *G* up your loins, please, like
40:7 *G* up your loins, please, like
Ps 18:39 *g* me with vital energy for
45:3 *G* your sword upon your thigh
65:12 the very hills *g* themselves
76:10 raging you will *g* upon
Isa 8:9 *G* yourselves, and be shattered
8:9 *G* yourselves, and be shattered
32:11 *g* sackcloth upon the loins
45:5 shall closely *g* you, although
Jer 1:17 *g* up your hips, and you
4:8 *g* on sackcloth, you people
6:26 *g* on sackcloth and wallow
49:3 *G* sackcloth on yourselves
Eze 27:31 and *g* on sackcloth and weep
44:18 *g* themselves with what
Joe 1:13 *G* yourselves, and beat your
Lu 12:37 *g* himself and make them
Joh 21:18 *g* yourself and walk about
21:18 *g* you and bear you where
Ac 12:8 *G* yourself and bind your
1Pe 5:5 *g* yourselves with lowliness

Girded
Ex 12:11 eat it, with your hips *g*
Le 8:7 and *g* him with the sash and
8:7 *g* him with the girdle of the
8:13 and *g* them with sashes and
De 1:41 *g* on, each one, his weapons
Jg 3:16 *g* it underneath his garment
18:11 men *g* with weapons of war
18:16 men *g* with their weapons of
18:17 men *g* with weapons of war
1Sa 2:18 having a linen ephod *g* on
17:39 David *g* his sword on over
25:13 *g* on every one his sword
25:13 David also *g* on his own
2Sa 6:14 David being *g* with an ephod
20:8 Joab was *g*, clothed with a
20:8 *g* a sword attached to his
21:16 was *g* with a new sword
1Ki 18:46 he *g* up his hips and went
20:32 they *g* sackcloth about their
2Ki 1:8 leather belt *g* about his loins
Ne 4:18 the builders were *g*, each one
Ps 30:11 you keep me *g* with rejoicing
65:6 is indeed *g* with mightiness
93:1 strength he has *g* himself
109:19 girdle that he keeps *g* about
Pr 31:17 has *g* her hips with strength
Isa 15:3 they have *g* on sackcloth
La 2:10 They have *g* on sackcloth
Eze 7:18 And they have *g* on sackcloth
23:15 *g* with belts on their hips
Da 10:5 his hips *g* with gold of Uphaz
Joe 1:8 as a virgin *g* with sackcloth
Lu 12:35 Let your loins be *g* and your
Joh 13:4 a towel, he *g* himself
13:5 towel with which he was *g*
21:7 *g* about himself his top
Eph 6:14 loins *g* about with truth
Re 1:13 *g* at the breasts with a
15:6 *g* about their breasts with

Girders
1Ki 7:3 cedarwood above upon the *g*

Girding
1Ki 20:11 not let one *g* on boast about
2Ki 3:21 as many as were *g* on a belt
Ps 18:32 God is the One *g* me closely
Isa 3:24 a *g* of sackcloth; a brand
22:12 and for *g* on sackcloth

Girdle
Ex 28:8 *g*, which is upon it for tying
28:27 above the *g* of the ephod
28:28 above the *g* of the ephod and
29:5 with the *g* of the ephod
39:5 the *g*, which was upon it for
39:20 above the *g* of the ephod
39:21 above the *g* of the ephod and
Le 8:7 the *g* of the ephod and bound
Job 12:21 the *g* of powerful ones he
Ps 109:19 *g* that he keeps girded
Mt 3:4 a leather *g* around his loins
10:9 or copper for your *g* purses
Mr 1:6 a leather *g* around his loins
6:8 copper money in their *g* purses
Ac 21:11 took up the *g* of Paul, bound
21:11 man to whom this *g* belongs
Re 1:13 the breasts with a golden *g*

Girdles
Re 15:6 their breasts with golden *g*

Girgashite
Ge 10:16 and the Amorite and the *G*
1Ch 1:14 the Amorite and the *G*

Girgashites
Ge 15:21 the Canaanites and the *G* and
De 7:1 the *G* and the Amorites and the
Jos 3:10 the *G* and the Amorites and
24:11 the *G*, the Hivites and the
Ne 9:8 and the Jebusites and the *G*

Girl
Ge 21:10 Drive out this slave *g* and
21:10 son of this slave *g* is not
21:12 boy and about your slave *g*
21:13 son of the slave *g*, I shall
30:3 Here is my slave *g* Bilhah
Ex 2:5 she sent her slave *g* that she
20:10 slave man nor your slave *g*
20:17 slave man nor his slave *g*
21:7 sell his daughter as a slave *g*
21:20 his slave man or his slave *g*
21:26 the eye of his slave *g* and he
21:27 the tooth of his slave *g* that
21:32 or a slave *g* that the bull
23:12 son of your slave *g* and the
Le 25:6 slave *g* and your hired laborer
25:44 slave man and your slave *g*
25:44 a slave man and a slave *g*
De 5:14 slave *g* nor your bull nor your
5:14 and your slave *g* may rest the
5:21 his slave *g*, his bull or his
12:18 your slave *g* and the Levite
15:17 to your slave *g* you should
16:11 your slave *g* and the Levite
16:14 your slave *g* and the Levite
22:15 the father of the *g* and her
22:20 was not found in the *g*
22:21 bring the *g* out to the
22:23 a virgin *g* engaged to a man
22:24 the *g* for the reason that she
22:25 found the *g* who was engaged
22:26 to the *g* you must do nothing
22:26 the *g* has no sin deserving
22:27 *g* who was engaged screamed
22:28 In case a man finds a *g*, a
Jg 9:18 the son of his slave *g*, king
11:37 I and my *g* companions
11:38 she with her *g* companions
19:19 and your slave *g* and for the
Ru 3:9 I am Ruth your slave *g*, and
3:9 your skirt over your slave *g*
1Sa 1:11 affliction of your slave *g*
1:11 will not forget your slave *g*
1:11 give to your slave *g* a male
1:16 not make your slave *g* like
25:24 slave *g* speak in your ears
25:24 the words of your slave *g*
25:25 your slave *g*, I did not see
25:28 Pardon . . . your slave *g*
25:31 must remember your slave *g*
25:41 slave *g* as a maidservant to
2Sa 14:15 on the word of his slave *g*
14:16 deliver his slave *g* out of
20:17 the words of your slave *g*
1Ki 1:2 a *g*, a virgin, for my lord
1:3 looking for a beautiful *g*
1:4 the *g* was beautiful in the
1:13 swore to your slave *g*
1:17 swore . . . to your slave *g*
3:20 slave *g* herself was asleep
2Ki 5:2 from . . . Israel a little *g*
5:4 *g* spoke who is from the land
Job 31:13 my slave *g* in their case at
Ps 86:16 save the son of your slave *g*
116:16 the son of your slave *g*
Ca 1:5 A black *g* I am, but comely, O
1:9 you, O *g* companion of mine
1:15 are beautiful, O *g* companion
2:2 so is my *g* companion among
2:10 Rise up, you *g* companion of
2:13 Rise up, come, O *g* companion
4:1 are beautiful, O *g* companion
4:7 beautiful, O *g* companion of
5:2 my *g* companion, my dove, my
6:4 O *g* companion of mine
7:6 pleasant you are, O beloved *g*
Am 2:7 have gone to the same *g*
Mt 9:24 for the little *g* did not die
9:25 and the little *g* got up
26:69 a servant *g* came up to him
26:71 another *g* noticed him and
Mr 14:69 the servant *g*, at the sight
Lu 1:38 Jehovah's slave *g*! May it
1:48 low position of his slave *g*
8:54 called, saying: *G*, get up!
22:56 servant *g* saw him sitting by
Joh 18:17 servant *g*, the doorkeeper
Ac 12:13 servant *g* named Rhoda came
16:16 servant *g* with a spirit, a
16:17 *g* kept following Paul and us
Ga 4:22 sons, one by the servant *g*
4:23 the one by the servant *g* was
4:30 Drive out the servant *g* and

Ga 4:30 son of the servant *g* be an
4:31 children, not of a servant *g*

Girl's
De 22:15 evidence of the *g* virginity
22:16 the *g* father must say to the
22:19 give them to the *g* father
22:29 give the *g* father fifty
Lu 8:51 and the *g* father and mother

Girls
Ge 20:17 slave *g*, and they began
31:33 the tent of the two slave *g*
De 12:12 your slave *g* and the Levite
Jg 21:12 four hundred *g*, virgins, that
1Sa 9:11 *g* going out to draw water
2Sa 6:20 to the eyes of the slave *g*
6:22 slave *g* whom you mentioned
Ezr 2:65 men slaves and their slave *g*
Ne 7:67 men slaves and their slave *g*
Job 19:15 and my slave *g* themselves
41:5 tie it for your young *g*
Pr 27:27 the means of life for your *g*
Na 2:7 her slave *g* will be moaning
Zec 8:5 boys and *g* playing in her
Mr 14:66 servant *g* of the high priest

Girzites
1Sa 27:8 raid the Geshurites and *G*

Gishpa
Ne 11:21 Ziha and *G* were over the

Gittaim
2Sa 4:3 went running away to *G*, and
Ne 11:33 Hazor, Ramah, *G*

Gittite
2Sa 6:10 house of Obed-edom the *G*
6:11 house of Obed-edom the *G*
15:19 the king said to Ittai the *G*
15:22 So Ittai the *G* crossed over
18:2 the hand of Ittai the *G*
21:19 strike down Goliath the *G*
1Ch 13:13 house of Obed-edom the *G*
20:5 the brother of Goliath the *G*

Gittites
Jos 13:3 the *G* and the Ekronites
2Sa 15:18 Pelethites and all the *G*

Gittith
Ps 8:*super* To the director upon the *G*
81:*super* To the director upon the *G*
84:*super* the director upon the *G*

Give
Ge 4:12 will not *g* you back its power
4:23 *G* ear to my saying: A man
9:3 I do *g* it all to you
9:13 My rainbow I do *g* in the
12:7 I am going to *g* this land
13:15 to your seed I am going to *g*
13:17 to you I am going to *g* it
14:21 *G* me the souls, but take the
15:2 what will you *g* me, seeing
15:7 *g* you this land to take it in
15:18 your seed I will *g* this land
16:11 you shall *g* birth to a son
17:2 I will *g* my covenant between
17:8 I will *g* to you and to your
17:16 *g* you a son from her
17:17 woman ninety years old *g*
18:7 and to *g* it to the attendant
18:13 *g* birth although I have
19:32 *g* our father wine to drink
19:34 *g* him wine to drink tonight
20:16 I do *g* a thousand silver
21:19 and to *g* the boy a drink
23:4 *G* me the possession of a
23:9 *g* me the cave of Machpelah
23:9 *g* it to me in the midst of you
23:11 field I do *g* to you, and the
23:11 the cave . . . to you I do *g* it
23:11 I do *g* it to you. Bury your
23:13 I will *g* you the amount of
24:7 To your seed I am going to *g*
24:17 *G* me, please, a little sip
24:36 he will *g* him everything he
24:40 *g* success to your way; and
24:41 they will not *g* her to you
24:45 to her, *G* me a drink, please
24:53 and to *g* them to Rebekah
25:30 please, *g* me a swallow
26:3 to your seed I shall *g* all
26:4 and I will *g* to your seed all
27:28 God *g* you the dews of the
28:4 *g* to you the blessing of
28:13 to you I am going to *g* it
Ge 28:20 *g* me bread to eat and
28:22 everything that you will *g*
28:22 without fail *g* the tenth of
29:19 It is better for me to *g* her
29:19 *g* her to another man
29:21 *G* over my wife, because my
29:26 *g* the younger woman before
30:1 say to Jacob: *G* me children
30:3 she may *g* birth upon my knees
30:9 and to *g* her to Jacob as wife
30:14 *G* me, please, some of your
30:26 *G* over my wives and my
30:28 and I shall *g* them
30:31 What shall I *g* you?
30:31 You will *g* me nothing
31:28 *g* me a chance to kiss my
32:20 he will *g* a kindly reception
34:8 *G* her, please, to him as a
34:9 daughters you are to *g* to us
34:11 say to me I shall *g* it
34:12 and I stand willing to *g*
34:12 only *g* me the young woman
34:14 *g* our sister to a man who
34:15 we *g* consent to you, that
34:16 *g* our daughters to you, and
34:21 daughters we can *g* to them
34:22 the men *g* us their consent
34:23 let us *g* them our consent
35:12 to you I shall *g* it, and to
35:12 I shall *g* the land
35:16 Rachel proceeded to *g* birth
38:9 to *g* offspring to his brother
38:16 What will you *g* me that you
38:17 Will you *g* a security until
38:18 security that I shall *g* you
38:26 I did not *g* her to Shelah
40:13 *g* Pharaoh's cup into his
40:21 *g* the cup into Pharaoh's
42:25 *g* them provisions for the
42:27 opened his sack to *g* fodder
42:34 Your brother I shall *g* back
42:37 *G* him over to my care, and I
43:14 may God Almighty *g* you pity
45:18 *g* you the good of the land
47:15 *G* us bread! And why should
47:16 *g* you bread in exchange for
47:19 *g* us seed that we may live
47:24 *g* a fifth to Pharaoh, but
48:4 *g* this land to your seed
48:22 *g* you one shoulder of land
49:20 *g* the dainties of a king
Ex 1:16 Hebrew women to *g* birth and
2:9 myself shall *g* you your wages
3:16 without fail *g* attention to
3:19 not *g* you permission to go
3:21 *g* this people favor in the
5:7 not gather straw to *g* to the
5:18 *g* the fixed amount of bricks
6:4 to *g* them the land of Canaan
6:8 raised my hand in oath to *g*
6:8 *g* it to you as something to
10:25 *g* into our hands sacrifices
12:25 land that Jehovah will *g* you
13:5 to *g* you, a land flowing with
13:11 when Jehovah . . . does *g* it
13:21 pillar of fire to *g* . . . light
15:26 *g* ear to his commandments
17:2 *G* us water that we may drink
18:25 to *g* them positions as heads
21:4 master should *g* him a wife
21:22 *g* it through the justices
21:23 you must *g* soul for soul
21:30 *g* the redemption price for
21:32 will *g* the price of thirty
22:7 should *g* his fellow money or
22:10 *g* his fellow an ass or bull
22:17 refuses to *g* her to him, he
22:29 you must not *g* hesitantly
22:29 your sons you are to *g* to me
22:30 you are to *g* it to me
23:27 *g* the back of the neck of all
23:31 I shall *g* into your hand the
24:12 *g* you the stone tablets and
25:16 testimony that I shall *g* you
25:21 testimony that I shall *g*
30:12 *g* a ransom for his soul to
30:13 those will *g* who pass over
30:14 *g* Jehovah's contribution
30:15 The rich should not *g* more
30:15 lowly must not *g* less than
30:15 to *g* Jehovah's contribution
30:16 *g* it in behalf of the service
31:18 to *g* Moses two tablets of
32:13 I shall *g* to your seed, that
Ex 32:24 that they may *g* it to me
33:1 To your seed I shall *g* it
33:14 shall certainly *g* you rest
34:7 no means will he *g* exemption
Le 5:16 he must *g* it to the priest
6:5 he will *g* it on the day his
7:32 will *g* the right leg as a
7:34 *g* them to Aaron the priest
7:36 Jehovah had commanded to *g*
14:4 priest must then *g* command
14:5 And the priest must *g* command
14:36 the priest must *g* orders
14:40 *g* orders, and they must tear
14:57 in order to *g* instructions
15:14 and *g* them to the priest
18:20 *g* your emission as semen
18:23 not *g* your emission to any
20:24 shall *g* it to you to take
22:14 *g* the holy thing to the
23:38 you should *g* to Jehovah
25:19 will indeed *g* its fruitage
25:28 find enough to *g* back to him
25:37 *g* him your money on interest
25:37 not *g* your food out on usury
25:38 *g* you the land of Canaan, to
26:4 *g* your showers of rain at
26:4 land will indeed *g* its yield
26:4 the tree . . . will *g* its fruit
26:20 earth will not *g* its yield
26:20 tree of the earth will not *g*
26:26 *g* back your bread by weight
26:31 *g* your cities to the sword
27:9 what he may *g* to Jehovah
27:13 *g* a fifth of it in addition
27:15 *g* a fifth of the money of
27:19 *g* a fifth of the money of
27:23 *g* the estimated value on
27:27 *g* a fifth of it in addition
27:31 *g* a fifth of it in addition
Nu 3:9 *g* the Levites to Aaron and his
3:48 *g* the money to Aaron and his
5:7 *g* it to the one against whom
5:10 one may *g* to the priest, that
7:5 *g* them to the Levites, each
8:19 *g* the Levites as given ones
10:29 Jehovah said, I shall *g* it to
11:4 Who will *g* us meat to eat?
11:13 meat to *g* to all this people
11:13 Do *g* us meat, and let us eat
11:18 Who will *g* us meat to eat
11:18 Jehovah will . . . *g* you meat
11:21 Meat I shall *g* them, and
14:8 into this land and *g* it to us
14:18 *g* exemption from punishment
15:21 should *g* as a contribution to
16:14 *g* us an inheritance of field
18:7 I shall *g* your priesthood
18:12 which they will *g* to Jehovah
18:28 *g* the contribution to Jehovah
19:3 *g* it to Eleazar the priest
20:8 it may indeed *g* its water
20:8 and *g* the assembly and their
20:12 I shall certainly *g* them
20:19 certainly *g* the value of it
20:24 *g* to the sons of Israel, on
21:2 *g* this people into my hand, I
21:16 and let me *g* them water
21:29 *g* his sons as escaped ones
21:34 *g* him and all his people and
22:18 If Balak were to *g* me his
23:18 *g* ear to me, O son of Zippor
24:13 If Balak were to *g* me his
27:4 O *g* us a possession in the
27:7 *g* them the possession of an
27:9 then *g* his inheritance to his
27:10 then *g* his inheritance to his
27:11 then *g* his inheritance to his
27:12 *g* the sons of Israel
31:29 *g* it to Eleazar the priest as
31:30 must *g* them to the Levites
32:7 Jehovah will certainly *g* them
32:9 Jehovah was certain to *g* them
32:29 *g* them the land of Gilead as
33:53 I shall certainly *g* the land
34:13 to *g* to the nine and a half
35:2 *G* the sons of Israel the
35:2 must *g* the Levites cities to
35:2 *g* the Levites the pasture
35:4 which you will *g* the Levites
35:6 you will *g* to the Levites
35:6 *g* for the manslayer to flee
35:6 will *g* forty-two other cities
35:7 cities that you will *g* to the
35:8 cities that you will *g* will

2Ch 20:7 *g* it to the seed of Abraham
20:21 *G* praise to Jehovah, for
20:30 God continued to *g* him rest
21:7 *g* him and his sons a lamp
24:12 king and Jehoiada would *g*
24:19 but they did not *g* ear
25:9 means to *g* you much more
25:18 *g* your daughter to my son
26:8 Ammonites began to *g* tribute
29:11 not *g* yourselves up to rest
30:8 *G* place to Jehovah and come
30:12 *g* them one heart to perform
31:2 *g* thanks and praise in the
31:4 *g* the portion of the priests
31:14 *g* Jehovah's contribution
31:15 *g* to their brothers in the
31:19 *g* portions to every male
32:11 *g* you over to die by famine
34:9 *g* the money that was being
35:12 *g* them to the classes by
Ezr 3:7 to *g* money to the cutters and
4:13 tribute nor toll will they *g*
7:20 it devolves upon you to *g*
7:20 *g* out of the king's house of
9:8 *g* us a little reviving in our
9:9 to *g* us a reviving so as to
9:9 to *g* us a stone wall in Judah
9:12 you people *g* to their sons
Ne 2:8 *g* me trees to build with
4:4 *g* them to the plunder in the
9:8 to *g* him the land of the
9:8 to *g* it to his seed
9:13 to *g* them upright judicial
9:15 in an oath to *g* to them
9:22 *g* them kingdoms and peoples
9:24 to *g* them into their hand
9:27 *g* them saviors who would
9:30 and they did not *g* ear
10:30 not *g* our daughters to the
10:32 commandments to *g*, each of
12:24 to offer praise and *g* thanks
13:25 not *g* your daughters to their
Es 1:19 royal dignity let the king *g*
1:20 will *g* honor to their owners
2:9 haste to *g* her her massages
2:9 to *g* her seven selected young
4:5 to *g* him a command concerning
Job 2:4 will *g* in behalf of his soul
3:20 *g* light to one having trouble
3:23 *g* light to able-bodied man
6:22 I have said, *G* me something
9:16 he would *g* ear to my voice
10:1 I will *g* vent to my concern
20:10 *g* back his valuable things
22:7 not *g* the tired one a drink
32:17 I shall *g* in answer my part
33:1 to all my speaking do *g* ear
34:2 you who know, *g* ear to me
34:16 Do *g* ear to the sound of
35:7 what do you *g* him, Or what
36:6 the afflicted ones he will *g*
37:14 Do *g* ear to this, O Job
39:1 goats of the crag to *g* birth
39:2 time that they *g* birth
39:19 *g* to the horse mightiness
42:10 *g* in addition all that had
42:11 to *g* him a piece of money
42:15 to *g* them an inheritance
Ps 2:8 *g* nations as your inheritance
4:7 *g* a rejoicing in my heart
5:1 To my sayings do *g* ear, O
7:14 bound to *g* birth to falsehood
17:1 Do *g* ear to my prayer without
18:13 began to *g* his voice
18:35 you will *g* me your shield of
18:40 *g* me the back of their neck
20:4 *g* to you according to your
27:12 Do not *g* me over to the soul
28:4 *G* to them according to their
28:4 do you *g* to them
29:11 *g* strength indeed to his
30:4 *G* thanks to his holy memorial
32:8 I will *g* advice with my eye
33:2 *G* thanks to Jehovah on the
37:4 *g* you the requests of your
37:10 *g* attention to his place, and
39:12 to my cry for help do *g* ear
41:2 *g* him over to the soul of his
44:11 You *g* us up like sheep
46:10 *G* in, you people, and know
49:1 *G* ear, all you inhabitants
49:7 Nor *g* to God a ransom for him
50:20 you *g* away a fault
51:16 otherwise I would *g* it

Ps 54:2 Do *g* ear to the sayings of
55:1 *g* ear, O God, to my prayer
60:6 *g* out Shechem as a portion
60:11 Do *g* us assistance from
62:4 they *g* advice so as to allure
65:9 that you may *g* it abundance
67:6 will certainly *g* its produce
69:4 I then proceeded to *g* back
69:27 Do *g* error upon their error
72:1 *g* your own judicial decisions
74:14 *g* it as food to the people
74:19 *g* to the wild beast the
75:1 We *g* thanks to you, O God
75:1 O God; we *g* thanks to you
77:1 he will certainly *g* ear to me
78:1 Do *g* ear, O my people, to my
78:20 able also to *g* bread itself
78:46 *g* to the cockroaches their
78:61 to *g* his strength even to
78:64 own widows did not *g* way to
79:13 *g* thanks to you to time
80:1 Shepherd of Israel, do *g* ear
84:8 Do *g* ear, O God of Jacob
85:7 salvation may you *g* to us
85:12 his part, will *g* what is
85:12 own land will *g* its yield
86:6 *g* ear, O Jehovah, to my
86:9 will *g* glory to your name
86:16 *g* your strength to your
91:11 *g* his own angels a command
92:1 good to *g* thanks to Jehovah
94:13 *g* him quietness from days of
97:12 And *g* thanks to his holy
100:4 *G* thanks to him, bless his
104:11 *g* drink to all the wild
104:27 *g* them their food in its
104:28 you *g* them they pick up
105:1 *G* thanks to Jehovah, call
105:11 shall *g* the land of Canaan
105:39 fire to *g* light by night
106:1 *G* thanks to Jehovah, for he
106:15 to *g* them their request
106:47 *g* thanks to your holy name
107:1 *g* thanks to Jehovah, you
107:8 people *g* thanks to Jehovah
107:15 people *g* thanks to Jehovah
107:21 people *g* thanks to Jehovah
107:31 people *g* thanks to Jehovah
108:7 *g* out Shechem as a portion
108:12 *g* us assistance from
115:1 But to your name *g* glory
115:14 Jehovah will *g* increase
118:1 *G* thanks to Jehovah, you
118:18 not *g* me over to death
118:29 *G* thanks to Jehovah, you
119:62 I get up to *g* thanks to you
120:3 What will one *g* to you
122:4 To *g* thanks to the name of
132:4 will not *g* sleep to my eyes
135:17 can *g* ear to nothing
136:1 *G* thanks to Jehovah, O you
136:2 *G* thanks to the God of the
136:3 *G* thanks to the Lord of the
136:26 *G* thanks to the God of the
140:6 *g* ear, O Jehovah, to the
140:13 will *g* thanks to your name
141:1 *g* ear to my voice when I
143:1 Do *g* ear to my entreaty
Pr 1:4 *g* to the inexperienced ones
2:3 *g* forth your voice for
3:28 back and tomorrow I shall *g*
4:2 I certainly shall *g* to you
4:9 head it will *g* a wreath of
5:9 *g* to others your dignity, nor
6:4 *g* any sleep to your eyes, nor
6:31 of his house he will *g*
9:8 *G* a reproof to a wise person
9:9 *G* to a wise person and he will
10:10 winking his eye will *g* pain
23:26 son, do *g* your heart to me
25:21 hungry, *g* him bread to eat
25:21 he is thirsty, *g* him water
27:1 what a day will *g* birth to
29:15 reproof are what *g* wisdom
29:17 *g* much pleasure to your soul
30:8 *G* me neither poverty nor
30:15, 15 daughters that cry: *G! G!*
31:3 *g* your vital energy to women
31:6 *G* intoxicating liquor, you
31:31 *G* her of the fruitage of her
Ec 1:17 *g* my heart to knowing wisdom
2:26 to *g* to the one that is good
3:6 and a time to *g* up as lost
5:1 to *g* a sacrifice as the stupid

Ec 7:21 do not *g* your heart to all the
11:2 *G* a portion to seven, or even
Ca 7:12 I shall *g* my expressions
8:2 *g* you a drink of spiced wine
8:7 *g* all the valuable things of
Isa 1:2 *g* ear, O earth, for Jehovah
1:10 *G* ear to the law of our God
7:14 *g* you men a sign: Look!
8:9 *g* ear, all you in distant
11:4 *g* reproof in behalf of the
12:4 *G* thanks to Jehovah, you
14:1 *g* them rest upon their soil
14:16 *g* close examination even to
22:21 dominion I shall *g* into his
27:4 *g* me thornbushes and weeds
28:12 *G* rest to the weary one
28:23 *G* ear, you men, and listen
29:11 *g* to someone knowing the
30:20 *g* you people bread in the
30:23 *g* the rain for your seed
32:9 careless daughters, *g* ear to
33:11 *g* birth to stubble
34:2 *g* them to the slaughter
36:8 *g* you two thousand horses
37:3 there is no power to *g* birth
38:1 *G* commands to your household
38:19 *g* knowledge to his own sons
41:2 to *g* before him the nations
41:27 *g* a bringer of good news
42:6 *g* you as a covenant of the
42:8 shall I *g* my own glory
42:23 people will *g* ear to this
43:4 shall *g* men in place of you
43:6 shall say to the north, *G* up!
43:28 will *g* Jacob over as a man
45:3 *g* you the treasures in the
45:4 to *g* you a name of honor
46:13 will *g* in Zion salvation
47:6 to *g* them into your hand
48:11 shall I *g* my own glory
49:8 *g* you as a covenant for the
49:13 *G* a glad cry, you heavens
51:4 group of mine, to me *g* ear
54:1 woman that did not *g* birth
56:5 *g* to them in my house and
56:5 I shall *g* them, one that
60:19 no more *g* you light
61:3 *g* them a headdress instead
61:8 *g* their wages in trueness
62:7 do not *g* him any silence
62:8 no more *g* your grain as food
Jer 2:10 *g* your special consideration
3:8 to *g* the certificate of her
3:15 I will *g* you shepherds in
3:19 *g* you the desirable land
6:10 *g* warning, that they may
8:10 *g* their wives to other men
8:13 things that I *g* to them will
11:5 to *g* them the land flowing
13:15 Hear, you people, and *g* ear
13:16 *G* to Jehovah your God glory
14:10 *g* attention to their sins
14:13 peace is what I shall *g* you
14:22 *g* copious showers
15:4 I will *g* them for a quaking
15:9 I shall *g* the mere remnant
15:13 I shall *g* for mere plunder
16:7 will they *g* them the cup of
16:13 I shall not *g* you any favor
17:3 I shall *g* for mere plunder
17:10 to *g* to each one according
18:21 *g* their sons over to the
19:7 I will *g* their dead bodies
20:4 all Judah I shall *g* into the
20:5 *g* all the stored-up things
20:5 *g* into the hand of their
21:7 I shall *g* Zedekiah the king
22:13 wages he does not *g* him
22:25 *g* you into the hand of those
23:15 *g* them poisoned water to
23:20 *g* your consideration to it
23:39 *g* you people to neglect
24:7 *g* them a heart to know me
24:8 I shall *g* Zedekiah the king
24:9 I will also *g* them over for
25:30 he will *g* forth his voice
25:31 must *g* them to the sword
26:24 *g* him into the hand of the
27:4 you must *g* them a command
28:14 beasts . . . I will *g* him
29:6 *g* your own daughters to
29:6 they may *g* birth to sons
29:11 *g* you a future and a hope
29:18 I will *g* them for a quaking

Jer 30:16 I shall *g* over to plundering
30:24 will *g* your consideration
31:7 *G* praise and say, Save
32:19 *g* to each one according to
32:22 forefathers to *g* to them
32:39 *g* them one heart and one
34:17 *g* you for a quaking to all
34:18 *g* the men sidestepping my
34:20 *g* them into the hand of
34:21 *g* into the hand of their
35:2 must *g* them wine to drink
38:16 *g* you into the hand of these
38:19 *g* me into their hand and
39:10 *g* them vineyards and
39:14 *g* him over to Gedaliah the
42:12 I shall *g* to you mercies
45:5 *g* you your soul as a spoil
46:26 *g* them into the hand of
48:9 *G* a road mark to Moab, you
49:8 Flee! Let yourselves *g* way!
50:31 that I must *g* you attention
50:34 *g* repose to the land and
La 2:18 *G* no numbness to yourself
3:30 Let him *g* his cheek to the
3:64 *g* back to them a treatment
3:65 *g* to them the insolence of
Eze 4:5 *g* to you the years of their
7:21 I will *g* it into the hand of
11:9 and *g* you into the hand of
11:17 *g* you the soil of Israel
11:19 And I will *g* them one heart
11:19 and *g* them a heart of flesh
16:21 you would *g* these to them
16:27 *g* you to the soulful desire
16:33 accustomed to *g* a present
16:38 *g* you the blood of rage and
16:39 will *g* you into their hand
16:41 no more hire will you *g*
16:61 *g* them to you as daughters
17:15 to *g* him horses and a
18:7 hungry one he would *g* his
18:8 *g* on interest and no usury
20:11 to *g* them my statutes
20:28 my hand in an oath to *g*
20:42 to *g* to your forefathers
21:11 *g* it into the hand of a
21:27 and I must *g* it to him
21:31 *g* you into the hand of men
23:4 *g* birth to sons and daughters
23:24 *g* judgment over to them
23:31 to *g* her cup into your hand
25:7 I will *g* you as something to
29:5 I will *g* you for food
29:21 *g* occasion to open the
30:21 in order to *g* it healing by
30:24 *g* my sword into his hand
30:25 *g* my sword into the hand of
31:11 *g* it into the hand of the
33:7 and *g* them warning from me
33:27 certainly *g* him for food
34:27 must *g* its fruitage, and
34:27 land . . . will *g* its yield
36:8 will *g* forth your very own
36:26 I will *g* you a new heart
36:26 *g* you a heart of flesh
39:4 I will *g* you for food
39:11 I shall *g* to Gog a place
43:19 *g* to the Levitical priests
44:28 people *g* them in Israel
44:30 meals you should *g* to the
45:6 *g* five thousand in width
45:8 *g* to the house of Israel
46:5 offering as he is able to *g*
46:11 lambs as he is able to *g*
46:16 chieftain should *g* a gift
46:17 *g* a gift from his
46:18 *g* his sons an inheritance
47:14 to *g* to your forefathers
47:23 you should *g* his inheritance
Da 1:12 *g* us some vegetables that we
2:16 *g* him time expressly to show
4:25 *g* even to you to eat just like
4:32 *g* even to you to eat just like
5:17 presents do you *g* to others
5:21 Vegetation they would *g* him
9:23 *g* consideration to the matter
11:30 *g* consideration to those
11:37 he will *g* no consideration
11:37 he will *g* no consideration
11:38 his position he will *g* glory
11:38 *g* glory by means of gold
Ho 1:6 and to *g* birth to a daughter
1:8 pregnant and *g* birth to a son
2:15 I will *g* her her vineyards

Ho 5:1 O house of the king, *g* ear
5:13 unable to *g* healing to you
9:9 will *g* attention to their sins
9:14 *G* to them, O Jehovah, what you
9:14 Jehovah, what you should *g*
9:14 *G* them a miscarrying womb
11:8 can I *g* you up, O Ephraim
13:10 Do *g* me a king and princes
13:11 to *g* you a king in my anger
14:8 *g* an answer and I shall keep
Joe 1:2 *g* ear, all you inhabitants
1:3 *g* an account to your own sons
2:11 *g* forth his voice before his
2:22 tree will . . . *g* its fruitage
2:22 must *g* their vital energy
2:23 *g* you the autumn rain in
2:30 *g* portents in the heavens
3:3 *g* the male child for a
3:16 he will *g* forth his voice
Am 1:2 he will *g* forth his voice
3:4 maned lion *g* forth its voice
3:13 *g* witness in the house of
5:15 *g* justice a place in the gate
Mic 1:14 you will *g* parting gifts to
5:3 *g* them up until the time
6:7 *g* my firstborn son for my
6:14 I shall *g* to the sword
7:20 *g* the trueness given to
Hab 2:19 It itself will *g* instruction
Zep 1:8 *g* attention to the princes
1:9 *g* attention to everyone that
1:12 *g* attention to the men who
3:9 *g* to peoples the change to a
Hag 2:9 in this place I shall *g* peace
Zec 3:7 *g* you free access among these
8:12 the vine itself will *g* its
8:12 earth . . . will *g* its yield
8:12 heavens . . . *g* their dew
10:6 will *g* them a dwelling
11:12 *g* me my wages; but if not
11:16 he will *g* no attention
Mal 2:2 *g* glory to my name, Jehovah
Mt 1:21 *g* birth to a son, and you
1:23 will *g* birth to a son, and
2:13 stay there until I *g* you word
4:6 He will *g* his angels a charge
4:9 All these things I will *g* you
5:16 and *g* glory to your father
5:31 *g* her a certificate of
5:42 *G* to the one asking you
6:11 *G* us today our bread for this
7:6 Do not *g* what is holy to dogs
7:11 *g* good gifts to your children
7:11 *g* good things to those asking
10:8 You received free, *g* free
14:7 to *g* her whatever she asked
14:8 *G* me here upon a platter the
14:16 you *g* them something to eat
14:31 why did you *g* way to doubt?
15:32 possibly *g* out on the road
16:19 I will *g* you the keys of the
16:26 *g* in exchange for his soul
17:27 *g* it to them for me and you
19:21 *g* to the poor and you will
20:4 whatever is just I will *g*
20:14 *g* to this last one the same
20:21 *G* the word that these my
20:23 is not mine to *g*, but it
20:28 to *g* his soul a ransom in
23:23 you *g* the tenth of the mint
24:24 *g* great signs and wonders
24:29 moon will not *g* its light
24:45 to *g* them their food at the
25:8 *G* us some of your oil
25:28 *g* it to him that has the ten
25:37 and *g* you something to drink
26:15 will you *g* me to betray him
Mr 6:7 to *g* them authority over the
6:22 and I will *g* it to you
6:23 I will *g* it to you, up to
6:25 *g* me right away on a platter
6:37 You *g* them something to eat
6:37 *g* them to the people to eat
8:3 they will *g* out on the road
8:6 *g* them to his disciples to
8:37 *g* in exchange for his soul
10:21 *g* to the poor, and you will
10:40 is not mine to *g*, but it
10:45 to *g* his soul a ransom in
12:9 will *g* the vineyard to others
13:22 *g* signs and wonders to lead
13:24 moon will not *g* its light
14:11 to *g* him silver money
15:23 they tried to *g* him wine

Lu 1:31 and *g* birth to a son, and you
1:32 God will *g* him the throne of
1:57 due for Elizabeth to *g* birth
1:77 to *g* knowledge of salvation
1:79 to *g* light to those sitting
2:6 to the full for her to *g* birth
4:6 will *g* you all this authority
4:6 to whomever I wish I *g* it
4:10 He will *g* his angels a charge
4:22 to *g* favorable witness about
5:36 went on to *g* an illustration
6:30 *G* to everyone asking you, and
6:38 and people will *g* to you
9:13 You *g* them something to eat
9:16 to *g* them to the disciples
9:44 *G* lodgment to these words in
11:3 *G* us our bread for the day
11:7 I cannot rise up and *g* you
11:8 he will not rise up and *g* him
11:8 *g* him what things he needs
11:13 know how to *g* good gifts to
11:13 *g* holy spirit to those asking
11:41 *g* as gifts of mercy the
11:42 you *g* the tenth of the mint
11:48 yet you *g* consent to them
12:33 and *g* gifts of mercy
12:51 to *g* peace on the earth? No
13:15 lead it away to *g* it drink
15:12 Father, *g* me the part of the
15:16 and no one would *g* him
16:12 who will *g* you what is for
16:28 *g* them a thorough witness
17:3 commits a sin *g* him a rebuke
17:5 to the Lord: *G* us more faith
17:18 turned back to *g* glory to God
18:1 to pray and not to *g* up
18:12 I *g* the tenth of all things
19:24 *g* it to him that has the ten
20:10 *g* him some of the fruit of
20:16 *g* the vineyard to others
21:15 I will *g* you a mouth and
22:5 agreed to *g* him silver money
22:32 your faith may not *g* out
23:29 wombs that did not *g* birth
Joh 1:22 that we may *g* an answer to
3:11 not receive the witness we *g*
3:34 not *g* the spirit by measure
4:7 said to her: *G* me a drink
4:10 says to you, *G* me a drink
4:14 water that I will *g* him
4:14 the water that I will *g* him
4:15 Sir, *g* me this water, so
6:27 the Son of man will *g* you
6:32 did not *g* you the bread
6:32 *g* you the true bread from
6:34 Lord, always *g* us this bread
6:51 bread that I shall *g* is my
6:52 man *g* us his flesh to eat
9:24 *G* glory to God; we know that
10:28 I *g* them everlasting life
11:22 God will *g* you
13:26 *g* the morsel that I dip
13:29 *g* something to the poor
14:16 *g* you another helper to be
14:27 I *g* you my peace
14:27 *g* it to you the way that
15:16 he might *g* it to you
16:8 *g* the world convincing
16:23 *g* it to you in my name
17:2 may *g* them everlasting life
19:3 *g* him slaps in the face
Ac 2:14 and *g* ear to my sayings
2:19 *g* portents in heaven above
3:6 what I do have is what I *g* you
4:29 *g* attention to their threats
5:31 *g* repentance to Israel and
7:5 not *g* him any inheritable
7:5 *g* it to him as a possession
7:38 pronouncements to *g* you
8:19 *G* me also this authority
10:42 *g* a thorough witness that
12:23 did not *g* the glory to God
13:34 I will *g* you people the
15:24 not *g* them any instructions
18:4 *g* a talk in the synagogue
20:32 *g* you the inheritance among
21:26 to *g* notice of the days to be
23:35 *g* you a thorough hearing
Ro 1:8 I *g* thanks to my God through
8:32 kindly *g* us all other things
12:20 *g* him something to drink
16:3 *G* my greetings to Prisca and
16:8 *G* my greetings to Ampliatus
1Co 7:10 I *g* instructions, yet not I

1Co 7:25 g my opinion as one who had
7:38 does not g it in marriage
10:30 that for which I g thanks
13:3 if I g all my belongings to
14:7 inanimate things g off sound
14:17 g thanks in a fine way, but
14:21 g heed to me, says Jehovah
2Co 4:1 we do not g up
4:16 we do not g up, but even if
Ga 3:21 that was able to g life
4:27 woman who does not g birth
6:9 g up in doing what is fine
Eph 1:17 g you a spirit of wisdom
3:13 not to g up on account of
4:10 g fullness to all things
Php 2:29 g him the customary welcome
4:21 G my greetings to every holy
Col 4:6 to g an answer to each one
4:15 G my greetings to the
1Th 2:3 the exhortation we g does not
5:13 and to g them more than
5:18 g thanks. For this is the
2Th 1:3 g God thanks always for you
3:10 we used to g you this order
3:12 such persons we g the order
3:13 do not g up in doing right
3:16 g you peace constantly in
1Ti 5:14 to g no inducement to the
6:13 I g you orders
6:17 G orders to those who are
2Ti 2:7 G constant thought to what I
2:7 will really g you discernment
2:25 God may g them repentance
4:8 will g me as a reward in
4:19 G my greetings to Prisca and
Tit 3:15 G my greetings to those who
Heb 11:14 g evidence that they are
12:3 may not get tired and g out
12:5 neither g out when you are
12:9 we used to g them respect
13:24 G my greetings to all those
Jas 2:16 not g them the necessities
4:9 G way to misery and mourn
1Pe 5:1 I g this exhortation, for I
5:12 g encouragement and an
1Jo 5:9 we receive the witness men g
5:16 and he will g life to him
3Jo 12 the witness we g is true
14 G my greetings to the friends
Re 2:10 g you the crown of life
2:17 g some of the hidden manna
2:17 I will g him a white pebble
2:23 I will g to you individually
2:26 g authority over the nations
2:28 will g him the morning star
3:9 g those from the synagogue of
10:9 to g me the little scroll
11:18 g their reward to your
12:2 and in her agony to g birth
12:4 who was about to g birth
12:4 when she did g birth, it
13:15 g breath to the image of the
13:16 g these a mark in their
14:7 Fear God and g him glory
16:9 repent so as to g glory to
16:19 g her the cup of the wine
17:13 they g their power and
18:7 to that extent g her torment
19:7 and let us g him the glory
21:6 I will g from the fountain
22:12 reward I g is with me, to

Given

Ge 1:29 Here I have g to you all
1:30 g all . . . vegetation for food
9:2 Into your hand they are now g
15:3 You have g me no seed, and
21:7 I have g birth to a son in his
24:56 Jehovah has g success to my
26:22 Jehovah has g us ample room
27:37 brothers I have g to him as
28:4 which God has g to Abraham
29:27 g to you also this other
30:18 God has g me a hireling's
30:18 g my maidservant to my
30:25 Rachel had g birth to Joseph
31:15 from the money g for us
35:12 land . . . I have g to Abraham
38:14 not been g as a wife to him
39:8 he has g into my hand
40:22 g them the interpretation
48:9 my sons whom God has g me
Ex 1:19 they have already g birth
5:16 no straw g to your servants
Ex 5:18 no straw will be g to you
16:15 bread that Jehovah has g you
16:29 Jehovah has g you the sabbath
36:1 to whom Jehovah has g wisdom
Le 6:17 I have g it as their share
8:5 Jehovah has g command to do
8:31 just as I was g the command
10:14 been g as your allowance and
10:17 most holy and he has g it to
19:20 nor has freedom been g her
20:3 g some of his offspring to
26:25 g into the hand of an enemy
Nu 3:9, 9 g ones, g to him from the
8:16 For they are g ones
8:16 g to me from among the sons
8:19 Levites as g ones to Aaron and
11:12 I who have g them birth, so
18:6 those g to Jehovah to carry on
18:8 I have g you the custody of
18:8 I have g them to you and to
18:11 I have g them to you and
18:12 I have g them to you
18:19 I have g to you and your
18:21 g every tenth part in Israel
18:24 I have g to the Levites as an
18:26 tenth part that I have g to
26:54 inheritance should be g in
26:62 no inheritance was to be g
32:5 let this land be g to your
De 2:5 I have g Mount Seir to Esau
2:9 to the sons of Lot I have g Ar
2:19 I have g it as a holding
2:24 I have g into your hand Sihon
2:37 Jehovah our God had g command
3:12 I have g to the Reubenites
3:13 I have g to the half tribe of
3:15 And to Machir I have g Gilead
3:16 I have g from Gilead to the
3:18 your God has g you this land
3:19 your cities that I have g you
3:20 holding that I have g you
8:10 good land that he has g you
12:15 blessing . . . that he has g
12:21 that Jehovah has g you
16:17 blessing . . . that he has g
18:14 God has not g you anything
19:8 he has g you all the land
20:14 enemies . . . God has g to you
21:10 God has g them into your
25:2 laid prostrate and g strokes
25:19 God has g you rest from all
26:10 ground that Jehovah has g me
26:11 the good . . . God has g you
26:13 g it to the Levite and the
26:14 g any of it for anyone dead
26:15 the soil that you have g us
28:31 Your sheep g to your enemies
28:32 g to another people and
28:52 land . . . God has g you
28:53 Jehovah your God has g you
29:4 not g you a heart to know and
Jos 1:13 and has g you this land
1:14 land that Moses has g you
1:15 servant of Jehovah has g you
2:24 has g all the land into our
6:2 I have g Jericho and its king
6:16 Jehovah has g you the city
8:1 I have g into your hand the
10:8 into your hand I have g them
10:19 has g them into your hands
13:8 servant of Jehovah had g
14:3 g the inheritance of the two
14:4 not g a share in the land to
15:19 land to the south you have g
17:14 g me as an inheritance one
18:3 your forefathers has g you
18:7 servant of Jehovah has g
21:2 commanded cities to be g us
22:4 God has g your brothers rest
23:1 after Jehovah had g Israel
23:13 ground . . . God has g you
23:15 ground . . . God has g you
23:16 good land that he has g you
24:33 g him in the mountainous
Jg 1:15 land you have g me, and you
3:28 Jehovah has g your enemies
4:6 God of Israel g the command
7:9 for I have g it into your hand
7:14 God has g Midian and all the
7:15 has g the camp of Midian into
8:6 bread has to be g to your army
8:15 bread has to be g to your
16:23 has g into our hand Samson
16:24 our god has g into our hand
Jg 18:10 g it into your hand, a place
Ru 4:15 has g birth to him
1Sa 2:5 barren has g birth to seven
9:23 the portion that I have g to
10:2 father has g up the matter
18:8 g David tens of thousands
18:8 me they have g the thousands
18:19 g to Adriel the Meholathite
25:27 g to the young men that are
25:44 Saul, he had g Michal his
30:23 what Jehovah has g us, in
2Sa 7:1 g him rest from all his
7:19 is the law g for mankind
14:16 the inheritance g by God
17:14 had g command to frustrate
21:6 be g to us seven men of his
1Ki 1:48 g one to sit upon my throne
2:21 Shunammite be g to Adonijah
5:4 God has g me rest all around
5:7 g David a wise son over this
8:15 own hand has g fulfillment
8:36 land that you have g to your
8:56 g a resting-place to his
9:7 ground that I have g to them
9:12 cities that Solomon had g
9:13 you have g me, my brother
13:5 had g by the word of Jehovah
2Ki 5:1 had g salvation to Syria
5:17 be g to your servant some
18:30 city will not be g into the
19:10 be g into the hand of the
22:10 Hilkiah the priest has g me
23:11 g to the sun to cease from
25:30 allowance was constantly g
1Ch 4:9 I have g him birth in pain
5:1 right as firstborn was g to
5:20 were g into their hand, for
6:48 Levites were the ones g for
22:18 has he not g you rest all
22:18 he has g into my hand the
23:25 has g rest to his people
28:5 sons whom Jehovah has g me
29:14 of your own hand we have g
2Ch 1:12 knowledge are being g you
2:12 g to David the king a wise
2:14 device that may be g to him
5:10 two tablets that Moses had g
6:4 own hands has g fulfillment
6:27 g to your people as a
7:20 my ground that I have g them
8:2 that Hiram had g to Solomon
18:14 will be g into your hand
19:2 wicked that help is to be g
24:10 until they all had g
25:9 talents that I have g to the
28:5 the king of Israel he was g
36:23 has g me, and he himself
Ezr 1:2 God of the heavens has g me
4:20 toll were being g to them
5:14 g to Sheshbazzar, the name
6:4 expense be g from the king's
6:8 expense will promptly be g to
6:9 there be g them continually
7:6 the God of Israel had g
7:15 g to the God of Israel
7:19 vessels that are being g to
9:7 we have been g, we ourselves
9:13 g us those who have escaped
10:14 g a dwelling to foreign
10:17 g a dwelling to foreign
10:18 g a dwelling to foreign
Ne 2:7 let letters be g me to the
10:29 been g by the hand of Moses
13:10 portions . . . had not been g them
13:23 g a dwelling to Ashdodite
Es 2:13 would be g her, to come with
3:11 silver is g to you, also the
3:14 g as law in all the different
3:15 law itself was g in Shushan
4:8 law that had been g in Shushan
5:3 let it even be g to you!
7:2 Let it even be g to you
7:3 let there be g me my own soul
8:7 The house of Haman I have g to
8:13 writing was to be g as law
8:14 g out in Shushan the castle
9:12 Let it even be g to you
9:14 a law was g out in Shushan
Job 1:21 Jehovah himself has g, and
9:24 Earth itself has been g into
15:19 them alone the land was g
28:15 Pure gold cannot be g in
34:19 not g more consideration to
37:10 the ice is g And the breadth

Job 39:17 he has not *g* her a share in
41:11 Who has *g* me something
Ps 7:6 *g* command for judgment itself
15:5 His money he has not *g* out
16:7 Jehovah, who has *g* me advice
21:2 desire of his heart you have *g*
60:4 *g* to those fearing you a
61:5 *g* me the possession of those
72:15 of the gold of Sheba be *g*
77:17 cloudy skies have *g* forth
79:2 *g* the dead body of your
111:5 Food he has *g* to those
112:9 he has *g* to the poor ones
115:16 he has *g* to the sons of men
119:4 commandingly *g* your orders
124:6 Jehovah, who has not *g* us
148:6 regulation he has *g*, and it
Pr 6:1 *g* your handshake even to the
7:13 hold of him and *g* him a kiss
18:10 runs and is *g* protection
22:9 *g* of his food to the lowly
22:19 I have *g* you knowledge today
22:24 with anyone *g* to anger
28:5 Men *g* to badness cannot
29:22 A man *g* to anger stirs up
31:24 she has *g* to the tradesmen
Ec 1:13 occupation that God has *g* to
2:21 be *g* the portion of that one
2:26 has *g* wisdom and knowledge
2:26 sinner he has *g* the occupation
3:10 occupation that God has *g* to
5:18 life that the true God has *g*
5:19 the true God has *g* riches and
8:15 God has *g* them under the sun
9:9 vain life that He has *g* you
12:11 been *g* from one shepherd
Ca 1:12 own spikenard has *g* out its
2:13 they have *g* their fragrance
7:13 have *g* their fragrance, and by
Isa 8:18 has *g* me are as signs
9:6 there has been a son *g* to us
10:3 day of being *g* attention
23:4 I have not *g* birth, nor
23:8 *g* this counsel against Tyre
23:9 *g* this counsel, to profane
23:11 *g* a command against
24:22 they will be *g* attention
26:18 we have *g* birth to wind
28:27 cummin is *g* a treading
29:12 *g* to someone that does not
32:7 *g* counsel for acts of loose
32:8 generous things that he has *g*
33:16 bread will certainly be *g*
34:16 Jehovah that has *g* the
35:2 of Lebanon itself must be *g*
36:15 *g* into the hand of the king
37:10 *g* into the hand of the king
42:24 *g* Jacob for mere pillage
43:3 *g* Egypt as a ransom for you
43:20 have *g* water even in the
49:6 *g* you for a light of the
50:4 has *g* me the tongue of the
55:4 I have *g* him, as a leader
55:10 *g* to the sower and bread to
64:4 nor have any *g* ear, nor has
66:8 well as *g* birth to her sons
Jer 2:15 *g* out their voice. And they
4:24 hills . . . all *g* a shaking
8:12 their being *g* attention
10:15 their being *g* attention
11:23 the year of their being *g*
12:7 I have *g* the beloved one
14:5 in the field has *g* birth
15:10 you have *g* birth to me
15:10 I have *g* no loan, and they
15:10 they have *g* me no loan
17:4 possession that I had *g* you
21:10 it will be *g*, and he will
23:12 their being *g* attention
23:18 Who has *g* attention to
23:37 What answer has Jehovah *g*
27:5 *g* it to whom it has proved
27:6 *g* all these lands into the
27:6 I have *g* him to serve him
30:21 *g* his heart in pledge in
32:4 *g* into the hand of the king
32:16 *g* the deed of purchase to
32:24 *g* into the hand of the
32:25 *g* into the hand of the
32:36 *g* into the hand of the king
32:43 *g* into the hand of the
34:3 into his hand you will be *g*
35:15 ground that I have *g* to you
37:17 of Babylon you will be *g*
Jer 38:3 city will be *g* into the hand
38:18 city must also be *g* into
39:17 not be *g* into the hand of
40:11 *g* a remnant to Judah and
44:30 I have *g* Zedekiah the king
46:21 themselves also have *g* way
46:21 of their being *g* attention
46:24 *g* into the hand of the
47:7 himself has *g* a command to
48:34 have *g* forth their voice
48:44 of their being *g* attention
50:15 She has *g* her hand
50:27 for their being *g* attention
51:18 *g* attention they will
51:55 voice will certainly be *g*
52:34 allowance *g* him from the
La 1:11 *g* their desirable things for
1:14 Jehovah has *g* me into the
1:17 Jehovah has *g* a command
3:15 *g* me a sufficiency of bitter
5:6 To Egypt we have *g* the hand
Eze 4:6 for a year, is what I have *g*
4:15 *g* you cattle manure instead
11:15 the land has been *g* us as a
15:6 I have *g* to the fire as fuel
15:6 I have *g* the inhabitants of
16:17 silver that I had *g* to you
16:19 bread that I had *g* to you
16:33 you have *g* your presents to
16:34 no hire has been *g* to you
17:18 he had *g* his hand and has
18:13 On usury he has *g*, and
18:16 to the hungry one he has *g*
20:15 into the land that I had *g*
22:6 each one *g* over to his arm
27:12 lead, your stores were *g*
27:13 articles of exchange were *g*
27:14 which your stores were *g*
27:16 stores were *g* in exchange
27:17 articles of exchange were *g*
27:22 gold, your stores were *g*
29:20 *g* him the land of Egypt
31:14 all of them be *g* to death
32:20 To a sword she has been *g*
33:24 to us the land has been *g*
35:12 they have been *g* for food
36:5 have *g* my land to themselves
38:8 you will be *g* attention
47:11 they will certainly be *g*
Da 2:23 mightiness you have *g* to me
2:37 *g* the kingdom, the might
2:38 into whose hand he has *g*
4:16 heart of a beast be *g* to it
5:28 and *g* to the Medes and the
7:4 *g* to it the heart of a man
7:6 was *g* to it rulership indeed
7:11 it was *g* to the burning fire
7:12 life *g* to them for a time
7:14 *g* rulership and dignity and
7:22 judgment itself was *g* in
7:25 *g* into his hand for a time
7:27 *g* to the people who are the
8:12 army itself was gradually *g*
11:6 and she will be *g* up
11:11 *g* into the hand of that one
11:39 *g* him recognition he will
Ho 2:8 I who had *g* to her the grain
2:12 passionate lovers have *g* to
9:7 The days of being *g* attention
Am 9:15 ground that I have *g* them
Mic 1:7 from the things *g* as the hire
1:7 *g* as the hire of a prostitute
7:4 your being *g* attention, must
7:20 the trueness *g* to Jacob
7:20 loving-kindness *g* to Abraham
Mt 2:12 *g* divine warning in a dream
2:22 *g* divine warning in a dream
7:7 asking, and it will be *g* you
10:19 are to speak will be *g* you
11:19 and *g* to drinking wine, a
12:39 no sign will be *g* it except
13:12 more will be *g* him and he
14:9 king . . . commanded it to be *g*
14:11 head . . . *g* to the maiden
16:4 no sign will be *g* it except
21:43 *g* to a nation producing its
22:30 nor are women *g* in marriage
24:38 women being *g* in marriage
25:29 that has, more will be *g*
26:9 and been *g* to poor people
26:27 having *g* thanks, he gave it
26:48 betrayer had *g* them a sign
27:58 Pilate commanded it to be *g*
28:18 All authority has been *g* me
Mr 4:11 secret of the kingdom . . . *g*
4:12 and forgiveness be *g* them
4:25 he that has will have more *g*
5:43 should be *g* her to eat
6:2 wisdom have been *g* this man
8:12 No sign will be *g* to this
12:25 nor are women *g* in marriage
13:11 *g* you in that hour, speak
14:5 and been *g* to the poor
14:44 had *g* them an agreed sign
Lu 1:1 are *g* full credence among us
1:25 *g* me his attention to take
2:5 Mary, who had been *g* him in
7:34 A man . . . *g* to drinking wine
8:18 whoever has, more will be *g*
8:55 something to be *g* her to eat
10:19 I have *g* you the authority
11:9 asking, and it will be *g* you
11:29 no sign will be *g* it except
12:48 everyone to whom much was *g*
17:27 were being *g* in marriage
19:15 he had *g* the silver money
19:26 that has, more will be *g*
20:34 marry and are *g* in marriage
20:35 marry nor are *g* in marriage
22:19 is to be *g* in your behalf
Joh 1:17 the Law was *g* through Moses
3:27 has been *g* him from heaven
3:35 *g* all things into his hand
4:10 have *g* you living water
5:25 who have *g* heed will live
5:27 has *g* him authority to do
6:23 after the Lord had *g* thanks
6:39 out of all that he has *g* me
7:22 Moses has *g* . . . circumcision
10:29 Father has *g* me is
11:57 Pharisees had *g* orders that
12:5 and *g* to the poor people
12:49 *g* me a commandment as to
13:3 Father had *g* all things into
14:31 *g* me commandment to do
17:2 *g* him authority over all
17:2 number whom you have *g* him
17:4 work you have *g* me to do
17:8 I have *g* to them, and they
17:9 those you have *g* me
17:11 name which you have *g* me
17:12 name which you have *g* me
17:14 I have *g* your word to them
17:22 *g* them the glory that you
17:22 glory that you have *g* me
17:24 as to what you have *g* me
17:24 glory that you have *g* me
18:9 those whom you have *g* me I
18:11 cup that the Father has *g*
Ac 1:2 *g* commandment through holy
3:16 has *g* the man this complete
4:12 *g* among men by which we must
5:32 spirit . . . God has *g* to those
8:18 apostles the spirit was *g*
8:25 *g* the witness thoroughly and
10:22 *g* divine instructions by a
17:22 *g* to the fear of the deities
24:26 money to be *g* him by Paul
27:24 God has freely *g* you all
Ro 5:5 holy spirit, which was *g* us
11:8 God has *g* them a spirit of
11:35 Who has first *g* to him, so
12:3 kindness *g* to me I tell
12:6 undeserved kindness *g* to us
15:15 undeserved kindness *g* to me
1Co 1:4 *g* to you in Christ Jesus
2:12 have been kindly *g* us by God
3:10 kindness of God that was *g*
7:17 as Jehovah has *g* each one a
11:15 her hair is *g* her instead of
12:7 spirit is *g* to each one for a
12:8 to one there is *g* through the
2Co 1:11 thanks may be *g* by many in
1:11 for what is kindly *g* to us
1:22 *g* us the token of what is
2:6 rebuke *g* by the majority is
4:10 treatment *g* to Jesus, that
9:9 he has *g* to the poor ones, his
12:7 *g* me a thorn in the flesh
Ga 2:9 undeserved kindness that was *g*
3:18 *g* it to Abraham through a
3:21 law had been *g* that was
3:22 *g* to those exercising faith
4:15 your eyes and *g* them to me
Eph 3:2 was *g* me with you in view
3:7 undeserved kindness . . . *g* me
3:8 undeserved kindness was *g*
4:7 undeserved kindness was *g*

Eph 6:19 ability to speak may be *g* me
Php 1:29 to you the privilege was *g*
Col 1:25 was *g* me in your interest to
1Th 3:6 *g* us the good news about your
1Ti 4:14 *g* you through a prediction
2Ti 1:9 was *g* us in connection with
Heb 2:6 certain witness has *g* proof
7:11 people were *g* the Law
7:22 become the one *g* in pledge
8:5 was *g* the divine command
11:7 Noah, after being *g* divine
13:9 heart to be *g* firmness by
Jas 1:5 and it will be *g* him
1Pe 1:23 *g* a new birth, not by
2Pe 1:3 divine power has *g* us freely
1:4 freely *g* us the precious and
3:15 according to the wisdom *g*
1Jo 3:1 love the Father has *g* us
5:10 witness *g* in his own case
5:10 his faith in the witness *g*
5:10 which God as witness has *g*
5:11 And this is the witness *g*
5:20 *g* us intellectual capacity
Re 6:2 and a crown was *g* him, and he
6:4 and a great sword was *g* him
6:8 authority was *g* them over the
6:11 white robe was *g* to each of
8:2 seven trumpets were *g* them
8:3 incense was *g* him to offer it
9:1 key . . . of the abyss was *g* him
9:3 authority was *g* them, the
11:1 a rod was *g* me as he said
11:2 it has been *g* to the nations
12:14 wings . . . were *g* the woman
13:5 and blasphemies was *g* it
13:5 act forty-two months was *g*
13:7 authority was *g* it over every
16:6 have *g* them blood to drink
20:4 power of judging was *g* them

Giver
De 8:18 the *g* of power to you to make
2Sa 22:48 *G* of acts of vengeance to
1Ki 5:10 Hiram became a *g* of timbers
Ps 18:47 the *G* of acts of vengeance
Jer 31:35 Jehovah, the *G* of the sun
2Co 9:7 for God loves a cheerful *g*

Givers
1Ch 23:5 *g* of praise to Jehovah on the

Gives
Ex 16:8 Jehovah *g* you in the evening
Le 20:2 *g* any of his offspring to
20:4 he *g* any of his offspring to
20:15 man *g* his seminal emission
De 3:20 Jehovah *g* your brothers rest
20:11 if it *g* a peaceful answer to
21:16 in the day that he *g* as an
Jos 1:15 when Jehovah *g* rest to your
2:14 when Jehovah *g* us the land
Jg 6:13 *g* us into the palm of Midian
8:7 Jehovah *g* Zebah and Zalmunna
21:18 that *g* a wife to Benjamin
1Sa 2:8 throne of glory he *g* to them
2Sa 4:8 Jehovah *g* to my lord the king
16:8 Jehovah *g* the kingship into
1Ch 16:23 the salvation he *g*
2Ch 14:7 and he *g* us rest all around
Job 24:5 desert plain *g* to each one
32:8 that *g* them understanding
36:31 He *g* food in abundance
Ps 1:3 *g* its own fruit in its season
68:11 Jehovah himself *g* the saying
84:11 and glory are what he *g*
111:7 are all the orders he *g*
118:27 And he *g* us light
119:130 of your words *g* light
127:2 *g* sleep even to his beloved
Pr 1:3 discipline that *g* insight
2:6 Jehovah himself *g* wisdom
13:15 Good insight itself *g* favor
21:26 righteous one *g* and holds
23:31 *g* off its sparkle in the cup
31:15 *g* food to her household and
Ec 6:2 a man to whom the true God *g*
Isa 14:3 Jehovah *g* you rest from your
62:11 The reward he *g* is with
Jer 8:14 he *g* us poisoned water to
42:4 every word that Jehovah *g*
Eze 21:11 one *g* it to be polished
Da 4:17 whom he wants to, he *g* it
4:25 one whom he wants to he *g* it
4:32 one whom he wants to he *g* it
Ho 10:12 he comes and *g* instruction
Mic 5:3 actually *g* birth. And the
Zep 2:2 Before the statute *g* birth to
Zec 10:1 *g* a downpour of rain to them
Mt 10:42 *g* one of these little ones
26:73 your dialect *g* you away
Mr 9:41 whoever *g* you a cup of water
Lu 11:36 lamp *g* you light by its rays
Joh 1:9 *g* light to every sort of man
6:33 and *g* life to the world
6:37 Everything the Father *g* me
14:27 way that the world *g* it
21:24 the witness he *g* is true
Ac 17:25 *g* to all persons life and
Ro 6:23 gift God *g* is everlasting
8:2 spirit which *g* life in union
14:6 for he *g* thanks to God
14:6 and yet *g* thanks to God
15:13 May the God who *g* hope fill
15:33 God who *g* peace be with all
16:20 God who *g* peace will crush
1Co 7:38 he also that *g* his virginity
15:38 God *g* it a body just as it
15:57 God, for he *g* us the victory
2Co 9:13 proof that this ministry *g*
Ga 6:6 one who *g* such oral teaching
Eph 3:19 all the fullness that God *g*
4:16 joint that *g* what is needed
Col 2:19 with the growth that God *g*
Jas 1:5 he *g* generously to all and
1:15 fertile, *g* birth to sin; in
4:6 kindness which he *g* is
4:6 *g* undeserved kindness to the
1Pe 5:5 *g* undeserved kindness to the
1Jo 5:9 the witness God *g* is greater
5:9 this is the witness God *g*

Giving
Ge 4:23 Yes, a young man for *g* me a
9:12 covenant that I am *g* between
19:33 *g* their father wine to drink
24:19 *g* him a drink, then she said
24:32 *g* straw and fodder to the
24:35 *g* him sheep and cattle and
24:42 *g* success to my way on which
25:24 came to the full for *g* birth
25:26 at her *g* them birth
29:35 she left off *g* birth
30:9 she had left off *g* birth
31:9 and *g* it to me
32:15 thirty camels *g* suck and
33:13 cattle that are *g* suck are
38:27 in the time of her *g* birth
38:28 when she was *g* birth one
47:17 Joseph kept *g* them bread
49:21 He is *g* words of elegance
49:33 Jacob finished *g* commands to
Ex 5:10 I am *g* you no more straw
16:29 *g* you on the sixth day the
20:12 Jehovah your God is *g* you
Le 14:34 I am *g* you as a possession
23:10 land that I am *g* you, and
25:2 land that I am *g* you, then
Nu 13:2 I am *g* to the sons of Israel
14:1 *g* vent to their voice and
15:2 places, which I am *g* you
17:6 chieftains went *g* him a rod
25:12 *g* him my covenant of peace
De 1:20 Jehovah our God is *g* to us
1:25 land that Jehovah our God is *g*
2:29 Jehovah our God is *g* to us
3:20 Jehovah your God is *g* them
4:1 God of your forefathers is *g*
4:21 God is *g* you as an inheritance
4:40 Jehovah your God is *g* you
5:16 Jehovah your God is *g* you
5:31 the land that I am *g* them to
7:16 Jehovah your God is *g* to you
9:6 God is *g* you this good land
11:17 land that Jehovah is *g* you
11:31 Jehovah your God is *g* you
12:9 Jehovah your God is *g* you
12:10 God is *g* you as a possession
13:12 God is *g* you to dwell there
15:4 *g* you as an inheritance to
15:7 Jehovah your God is *g* you
15:10 not be stingy in your *g* to
16:5 Jehovah your God is *g* you
16:18 Jehovah your God is *g* you
16:20 Jehovah your God is *g* you
17:2 Jehovah your God is *g* you
17:14 Jehovah your God is *g* you
18:9 Jehovah your God is *g* you
19:1 Jehovah your God is *g* you
19:2 land that Jehovah . . . is *g* you
De 19:10 *g* you as an inheritance, and
19:14 the land that . . . God is *g*
20:16 cities . . . God is *g* you as
21:1 the ground . . . God is *g* you
21:17 by *g* him two parts in
21:23 soil . . . God is *g* you
24:4 *g* you as an inheritance
25:15 soil . . . your God is *g* you
25:19 land . . . God is *g* you
26:1 God is *g* you as an inheritance
26:2 the land . . . God is *g* you
27:2 land . . . God is *g* you
27:3 land that . . . God is *g* you
28:8 Jehovah your God is *g* you
32:49 I am *g* to . . . Israel as a
32:52 am *g* to the sons of Israel
Jos 1:2 the land that I am *g* to them
1:11 is *g* you to take possession
1:13 your God is *g* you rest and
1:15 Jehovah your God is *g* them
Jg 20:36 kept *g* ground to Benjamin
21:22 was not you that did the *g*
Ru 1:6 to his people by *g* them bread
1Sa 4:19 was pregnant near to *g* birth
4:19 began *g* birth, because her
6:7 and two cows that are *g* suck
6:10 two cows that were *g* suck
18:19 at the time for *g* Merab
18:27 their foreskins and *g* them
22:13 *g* him bread and a sword
23:4 *g* the Philistines into your
24:4 I am *g* your enemy into your
2Sa 15:3 no one . . . *g* you a hearing
1Ki 4:29 continued *g* Solomon wisdom
5:9 *g* the food for my household
5:11 Solomon kept *g* Hiram year by
8:32 *g* to him according to his
17:14 Jehovah's *g* a downpour upon
20:13 *g* it into your hand today
2Ki 17:20 *g* them into the hand of
1Ch 15:22 *g* instruction in carrying
18:6 Jehovah kept *g* salvation to
23:5 I have made for *g* praise
2Ch 6:23 *g* to him according to his
11:16 *g* their heart to seek
23:13 *g* the signal for offering
25:20 of *g* them into his hand
Ezr 3:11 and *g* thanks to Jehovah
5:2 God's prophets *g* them aid
7:16 *g* to the house of their God
9:8 by *g* us a peg in his holy
Ne 5:2 *g* as security that we may get
5:3 houses we are *g* as security
5:10 *g* money and grain on loan
8:8 *g* understanding in the reading
9:29 kept *g* a stubborn shoulder
12:8 over the *g* of thanks, he and
12:47 *g* the portions of the singers
13:27 *g* a dwelling to foreign
Es 2:3 there be a *g* of their massages
2:18 he kept *g* presents according
Job 4:4 knees *g* way you would make
5:10 *g* rain upon the surface of
15:35 *g* birth to what is hurtful
20:18 *g* back his acquired property
32:11 *g* ear to your reasonings
35:10 One *g* melodies in the night
Ps 48:6 pangs . . . of a woman *g* birth
68:35 *g* strength, even might to
78:71 following the females *g* suck
104:12 they keep *g* forth sound
111:6 *g* them the inheritance of
136:25 One *g* food to all flesh
142:4 one *g* any recognition to me
144:10 The One *g* salvation to kings
145:14 Jehovah is *g* support to all
145:15 *g* them their food in its
146:7 *g* bread to the hungry ones
147:9 beasts he is *g* their food
147:16 He is *g* snow like wool
Pr 1:20 it keeps *g* forth its voice
8:1 discernment keep *g* forth its
9:7 *g* a reproof to someone wicked
17:4 A falsifier is *g* ear to the
21:11 *g* insight to a wise person
21:12 The Righteous One is *g*
22:16 that is *g* to the rich one
25:23 a tongue *g* away a secret, a
26:8 *g* glory to a mere stupid one
26:16 than seven *g* a sensible reply
28:27 *g* to the one of little means
Ca 6:9 of the one *g* birth to her
8:5 she that was *g* birth to you
Isa 7:14 *g* birth to a son, and she

Isa 9:15 prophet *g* false instruction
13:8 woman that is *g* birth they
21:3 of a woman that is *g* birth
26:17 draws near to *g* birth
40:11 *g* suck he will conduct with
40:29 *g* to the tired one power
41:2 kept *g* them like dust to
41:28 no one that was *g* counsel
42:5 One *g* breath to the people
42:14 Like a woman *g* birth I am
47:13 *g* out knowledge at the new
66:9 and not cause the *g* birth
66:9 am I causing a *g* birth and
Jer 4:31 *g* birth to her first child
5:24 *g* the downpour and the
6:24 those of a woman *g* birth
10:13 *g* by him of a turmoil of
13:21 those of a wife *g* birth
15:9 The woman *g* birth to seven
16:3 mothers who are *g* them birth
22:23 of a woman *g* birth
29:21 *g* them into the hand of
30:6 whether a male is *g* birth
30:6 a female that is *g* birth
31:8 one *g* birth, all together
32:3 *g* this city into the hand
32:28 *g* this city into the hand
34:2 *g* this city into the hand of
37:21 *g* of a round loaf of bread
38:20 They will do no such *g*
43:3 *g* us into the hand of the
44:30 *g* Pharaoh Hophra, the king
49:24 a woman that is *g* birth
50:43 just like a woman *g* birth
51:16 *g* by him of a turmoil of
Eze 2:8 and eat what I am *g* you
3:3 this roll that I am *g* you
9:1 *g* their attention to the city
16:34 *g* hire when no hire has
20:28 and *g* there their offensive
23:7 *g* forth her prostitutions
23:28 *g* you into the hand of
25:4 I am *g* you to the Orientals
29:19 *g* to Nebuchadrezzar the king
Da 1:16 and *g* them vegetables
2:21 *g* wisdom to the wise ones
2:23 *g* praise and commendation
6:2 *g* to them the report and the
Ho 2:5 those *g* my bread and my water
9:11 so that there is no *g* birth
13:13 pangs of a woman *g* birth
Joe 3:4 you are *g* me as a reward
3:4 *g* such treatment to me
Am 2:12 *g* the Nazirites wine to drink
Mic 4:9 those of a woman *g* birth
4:10 like a woman *g* birth, for
5:3 time that she who is *g* birth
Hab 2:15 the one *g* his companions
Zep 3:5 *g* his own judicial decision
Zec 7:11 kept *g* a stubborn shoulder
Mal 2:5 *g* them to him, with fear
Mt 10:5 sent . . . *g* them these orders
11:1 *g* instructions to his twelve
19:7 prescribe *g* a certificate of
26:26 *g* it to the disciples, he
27:48 reed and went *g* him a drink
Mr 6:41 began *g* them to the disciples
14:56 *g* false witness against him
15:36 began *g* him a drink, saying
Lu 6:38 Practice *g*, and people will
12:32 Father has approved of *g* you
12:42 to keep *g* them their measure
19:8 I am *g* to the poor, and
Joh 6:11 *g* thanks, he distributed
13:34 *g* you a new commandment
16:21 woman, when she is *g* birth
Ac 4:33 *g* forth the witness
7:25 God was *g* them salvation by
9:41 *G* her his hand, he raised
12:21 *g* them a public address
14:17 *g* you rains from heaven and
15:8 by *g* them the holy spirit
17:23 unknowingly *g* godly devotion
19:8 *g* talks and using persuasion
19:9 daily *g* talks in the school
20:13 *g* instructions to this effect
20:35 is more happiness in *g* than
21:19 *g* in detail an account of the
23:11 been *g* a thorough witness on
Ro 4:20 by his faith, *g* God glory
9:4 *g* of the Law and the sacred
1Co 11:17 while *g* these instructions
11:24 after *g* thanks, he broke it
12:24 *g* honor more abundant to
1Co 14:16 Amen to your *g* of thanks
2Co 5:12 but *g* you an inducement for
6:3 *g* any cause for stumbling
8:4 privilege of kindly *g* and for
8:6 same kind *g* on your part
8:7 you also abound in this kind *g*
Eph 1:16 not cease *g* thanks for you
5:4 but rather the *g* of thanks
5:20 *g* thanks always for all
Php 4:10 you were really *g* thought
4:15 matter of *g* and receiving
2Th 3:6 *g* you orders, brothers, in
1Ti 3:8 not *g* themselves to a lot of
4:6 By *g* these advices to the
4:11 Keep on *g* these commands and
5:7 So keep on *g* these commands
6:2 and *g* these exhortations
Heb 12:25 *g* divine warning upon earth
Re 17:17 *g* their kingdom to the wild

Gizonite
1Ch 11:34 the sons of Hashem the *G*

Glad
Ex 18:9 Jethro felt *g* over all the
De 32:43 Be *g*, you nations, with his
Job 3:6 not feel *g* among the days of
29:13 the widow I would make *g*
Ps 21:6 You make him feel *g* with the
Pr 8:30 *g* before him all the time
8:31 *g* at the productive land of
29:6 cries out joyfully and is *g*
Isa 24:7 *g* at heart have gone to
35:2 joyousness and with *g* crying
49:13 Give a *g* cry, you heavens
49:13 cheerful with a *g* outcry
Da 6:23 king himself became very *g*
Ro 15:10 Be *g*, you nations, with his
Ga 4:27 Be *g*, you barren woman who
Php 2:17 I am *g* and I rejoice with
2:18 be *g* and rejoice with me
Re 12:12 be *g*, you heavens and you
14:6 declare as *g* tidings to those
18:20 Be *g* over her, O heaven

Gladly
Mr 6:20 he continued to hear him *g*
Ac 21:17 the brothers received us *g*
2Co 11:7 I *g* declared the good news
11:19 For you *g* put up with the
12:9 Most *g*, therefore, will I
12:15 I will most *g* spend and be
Heb 11:17 *g* received the promises

Gladness
Isa 35:6 one will cry out in *g*
Lu 1:14 you will have joy and great *g*
1:44 leaped with great *g*

Glance
Pr 23:5 caused your eyes to *g* at it

Glancing
Ca 2:9 *g* through the lattices

Glass
Job 28:17 Gold and *g* cannot be
Re 21:18 was pure gold like clear *g*
21:21 pure gold, as transparent *g*

Glassy
Re 4:6 a *g* sea like crystal
15:2 *g* sea mingled with fire, and
15:2 standing by the *g* sea, having

Glazing
Pr 26:23 As a silver *g* overlaid upon a

Gleam
Ge 31:35 Do not let anger *g* in the

Gleamed
Lu 2:9 Jehovah's glory *g* around them

Gleaming
Ezr 8:27 good copper, *g* red
Eze 1:7 were *g* as with the glow of

Glean
Ru 2:2 and *g* among the ears of grain
2:3 began to *g* in the field behind
2:7 Let me *g*, please, and I shall
2:8 go away to *g* in another field
2:15 she got up to *g*. Boaz now
2:15 *g* also among the cut-off ears
2:16 behind that she may *g* them
2:17 continued to *g* in the field
2:19 Where did you *g* today, and
2:23 to *g* until the harvest of the
Jer 6:9 *g* the remnant of Israel just

Gleaned
Ru 2:17 she beat out what she had *g*
2:18 got to see what she had *g*

Gleaning
Le 19:9 *g* of your harvest you must
23:22 *g* of your harvest you must
Jg 20:45 a *g* of five thousand men of
Isa 17:5 one *g* ears of grain in the
17:6 *g* as when there is a beating
24:13 *g* when the grape gathering
Mic 7:1 the *g* of a grape gathering

Gleanings
Jg 8:2 the *g* of Ephraim better than
Jer 49:9 they not let some *g* remain
Ob 5 they not let some *g* remain

Glede
De 14:13 the *g* according to its kind

Gledes
Isa 34:15 *g* must collect themselves

Glee
Hab 3:14 Their high *g* was as of those

Gleefulness
Job 3:22 Those who are rejoicing to *g*

Gliding
Job 26:13 has pierced the *g* serpent
Isa 27:1 Leviathan, the *g* serpent

Glistening
Mr 9:3 his outer garments became *g*

Glitter
Eze 21:10 purpose of its getting a *g*
21:28 to devour, in order to *g*

Glittering
De 32:41 do indeed sharpen my *g* sword
Job 20:25 a *g* weapon out through his
Eze 21:15 is made for a *g*, polished
Zec 9:16 the stones of a diadem *g*

Glitteringly
Lu 9:29 his apparel became *g* white

Gloom
De 4:11 darkness, cloud and thick *g*
5:22 the cloud and the thick *g*
28:29 gropes about in the *g*
2Sa 22:10 *g* was beneath his feet
1Ki 8:12 was to reside in the thick *g*
2Ch 6:1 was to reside in the thick *g*
Job 3:6 That night—let *g* take it
10:22 the land of obscurity like *g*
10:22 beams no more than *g* does
22:13 Through thick *g* can he judge?
23:17 *g* has covered my own face
28:3 in the *g* and deep shadow
30:26 the light, but *g* came
38:9 *g* as its swaddling band
Ps 11:2 To shoot in the *g* at the ones
18:9 thick *g* was beneath his feet
91:6 that walks in the *g*
97:2 thick *g* are all around him
Pr 4:19 wicked ones is like the *g*
7:9 approach of the night and the *g*
Isa 29:18 out of the *g* and out of
58:10 your *g* will be like midday
59:9 continuous *g* we kept walking
60:2 thick *g* the national groups
Jer 13:16 will turn it into thick *g*
23:12 slippery places in the *g*
Eze 34:12 day of clouds and thick *g*
Joe 2:2 a day of clouds and thick *g*
Am 5:20 have *g*, and not brightness
Zep 1:15 day of clouds and of thick *g*

Gloominess
Ne 2:2 nothing but a *g* of heart
Isa 8:22 and *g* with no brightness
Joe 2:2 a day of darkness and *g*
Zep 1:15 a day of darkness and of *g*

Gloomy
Ge 40:7 what reason are your faces *g*
Ex 10:22 *g* darkness began to occur in
Ne 2:1 I happened to be *g* before him
2:2 Why is your face *g* when you
2:3 face become *g* when the city
Pr 25:20 with songs upon a *g* heart

Gloomy-looking
Mt 16:3 the sky is fire-red, but *g*

Glories
1Pe 1:11 about the *g* to follow these

Glorified
Le 10:3 all the people let me be *g*
2Ch 25:19 has lifted you up to be *g*
Ps 149:8 *g* ones with fetters of iron
Pr 13:18 is the one that is *g*
Isa 26:15 you have *g* yourself
29:13 *g* me merely with their
43:23 you have not *g* me
49:5 *g* in the eyes of Jehovah
58:13 day of Jehovah, one being *g*
66:5 said, May Jehovah be *g!*
Eze 28:22 be *g* in the midst of you
Da 4:34 I praised and *g*, because
5:23 ways belong you have not *g*
Na 3:10 over her *g* men they cast lots
Hag 1:8 I may be *g*, Jehovah has said
Mt 6:2 that they may be *g* by men
9:8 they *g* God, who gave such
15:31 and they *g* the God of Israel
Mr 2:12 *g* God, saying: We never saw
Joh 7:39 Jesus had not yet been *g*
11:4 the Son of God may be *g*
12:16 when Jesus became *g*, then
12:23 the Son of man to be *g*
12:28 both *g* it and will glorify
13:31 Now the Son of man is *g*
13:31 God is *g* in connection with
14:13 the Father may be *g* in
15:8 My Father is *g* in this
17:4 I have *g* you on the earth
17:10 I have been *g* among them
Ac 3:13 has *g* his Servant, Jesus
11:18 they *g* God, saying: Well
Ro 8:17 we may also be *g* together
8:30 are the ones he also *g*
1Co 12:26 if a member is *g*, all the
2Th 1:10 at the time he comes to be *g*
1:12 Lord Jesus may be *g* in you
3:1 being *g* just as it is in fact
Heb 5:5 *g* by him who spoke with
1Pe 1:8 an unspeakable and *g* joy
4:11 God may be *g* through Jesus
Re 18:7 extent that she *g* herself and

Glorifies
Ps 50:23 is the one that *g* me
Joh 8:54 It is my Father that *g* me

Glorify
Jg 9:9 they *g* God and men, and must I
2Sa 6:22 I am determined to *g* myself
Ps 22:23 you the seed of Jacob, *g* him
50:15 rescue you, and you will *g*
86:12 *g* your name to time
91:15 rescue him and *g* him
Pr 4:8 *g* you because you embrace it
Isa 24:15 they must *g* Jehovah, in
25:3 strong people will *g* you
43:20 of the field will *g* me
58:13 *g* it rather than doing your
60:13 *g* the very place of my feet
Eze 39:13 the day that I *g* myself
Lu 5:26 began to *g* God, and they
7:16 they began to *g* God, saying
13:13 and began to *g* God
23:47 army officer began to *g* God
Joh 8:54 If I *g* myself, my glory is
12:28 Father, *g* your name
12:28 and will *g* it again
13:32 God will himself *g* him
13:32 he will *g* him immediately
16:14 one will *g* me, because he
17:1 *g* your son, that your
17:1 that your son may *g* you
17:5 Father, *g* me alongside
21:19 of death he would *g* God
Ac 13:48 to rejoice and to *g* the word
21:20 they began to *g* God, and they
Ro 1:21 they did not *g* him as God nor
11:13 I *g* my ministry
15:6 with one mouth *g* the God and
15:9 nations might *g* God for his
1Co 6:20 *g* God in the body of you
2Co 9:13 they *g* God because you are
Heb 5:5 Christ did not *g* himself by
1Pe 2:12 *g* God in the day for his
Re 15:4 *g* your name, because you

Glorifying
Pr 12:9 one *g* himself but in want of
14:31 favor to the poor . . . *g* Him
Da 4:37 *g* the King of the heavens
Lu 2:20 *g* and praising God for all the
5:25 went off to his home, *g* God
17:15 *g* God with a loud voice
Lu 18:43 to follow him, *g* God
Ac 4:21 *g* God over what had occurred
10:46 with tongues and *g* God
Ga 1:24 began *g* God because of me
1Pe 4:16 keep on *g* God in this name

Glorious
De 28:58 *g* and fear-inspiring name
2Sa 6:20 How *g* the king of Israel
Ne 9:5 And let them bless your *g* name
Es 1:4 riches of his *g* kingdom and
Ps 24:7 That the *g* King may come in
24:8 Who, then, is this *g* King?
24:9 That the *g* King may come in
24:10 is he, this *g* King
24:10 Jehovah . . . he is the *g* King
29:3 *g* God himself has thundered
45:13 The king's daughter is all *g*
66:2 Render his praise *g*
72:19 blessed be his *g* name to
87:3 *G* things are being spoken
145:5 *g* splendor of your dignity
Isa 11:10 must become *g*
Jer 14:21 do not despise your *g* throne
17:12 the *g* throne on high from
Eze 23:41 sat down upon a *g* couch
27:25 very *g* in the heart of the
Mt 19:28 sits down upon his *g* throne
25:31 sit down on his *g* throne
Lu 13:17 rejoice at all the *g* things
Ro 8:21 *g* freedom of the children of
1Co 2:8 not have impaled the *g* Lord
2Co 3:9 condemnation was *g*, much
3:10 once been made *g* has been
4:4 *g* good news about the Christ
4:6 *g* knowledge of God by the
Eph 1:6 his *g* undeserved kindness
1:14 possession, to his *g* praise
1:18 *g* riches are which he holds
Php 3:21 be conformed to his *g* body
Col 1:11 to the extent of his *g* might
1:27 the *g* riches of this sacred
1Ti 1:11 *g* good news of the happy God
Tit 2:13 *g* manifestation of the great
Heb 9:5 the *g* cherubs overshadowing
2Pe 2:10 do not tremble at *g* ones
Jude 8 speaking abusively of *g* ones

Glory
Ge 45:13 about all my *g* in Egypt and
Ex 8:9 said to Pharaoh: You take the *g*
14:4 I shall get *g* for myself by
14:17 get *g* for myself by means of
14:18 get *g* for myself by means of
16:7 will indeed see Jehovah's *g*
16:10 Jehovah's *g* appeared in the
24:16 And Jehovah's *g* continued to
24:17 sight of Jehovah's *g* was
28:2 holy garments . . . for *g* and
28:40 headgears for them for *g* and
29:43 be sanctified by my *g*
33:18 to see, please, your *g*
33:22 while my *g* is passing by I
40:34 *g* filled the tabernacle
40:35 *g* filled the tabernacle
Le 9:6 the *g* of Jehovah may appear
9:23 Jehovah's *g* appeared to all
Nu 14:10 Jehovah's *g* appeared on the
14:21 filled with the *g* of Jehovah
14:22 seeing my *g* and my signs
16:19 Jehovah's *g* appeared to all
16:42 Jehovah's *g* began to appear
20:6 Jehovah's *g* began to appear to
De 5:24 our God has shown us his *g*
Jos 7:19 render, please, *g* to Jehovah
1Sa 2:8 throne of *g* he gives to them
4:21 *G* has gone away from Israel
4:22 *G* has gone away from Israel
6:5 give *g* to the God of Israel
1Ki 3:13 give you, both riches and *g*
8:11 *g* of Jehovah filled the house
1Ch 16:24 among the nations his *g*
16:28 Attribute to Jehovah *g* and
16:29 the *g* of his name
29:12 the *g* are on account of you
29:28 with days, riches and *g*
2Ch 5:14 *g* of Jehovah filled the house
7:1 Jehovah's *g* itself filled the
7:2 Jehovah's *g* had filled the
7:3 *g* of Jehovah was upon the
17:5 riches and *g* in abundance
18:1 riches and *g* in abundance
26:18 *g* to you on the part of
32:27 *g* to a very great amount
Es 5:11 the *g* of his riches and the
Job 19:9 *g* he has stripped from me
29:20 My *g* is fresh with me
Ps 3:3 My *g* and the One lifting up
4:2 must my *g* be for insult
7:5 *g* to reside in the dust itself
8:5 with *g* and splendor you then
16:9 my *g* is inclined to be joyful
19:1 heavens are declaring the *g* of
21:5 *g* is great in your salvation
26:8 the residing of your *g*
29:1 Ascribe to Jehovah *g* and
29:2 to Jehovah the *g* of his name
29:9 each one is saying: *G!*
30:12 my *g* may make melody to you
49:16 the *g* of his house increases
49:17 His *g* will not go down along
57:5 your *g* be above all the earth
57:8 Do awake, O my *g;* Do awake
57:11 Let your *g* be above all the
62:7 are my salvation and my *g*
63:2 your strength and your *g*
66:2 melody to the *g* of his name
72:19 his *g* fill the whole earth
73:24 you will take me even to *g*
79:9 sake of the *g* of your name
84:11 and *g* are what he gives
85:9 For *g* to reside in our land
86:9 will give *g* to your name
96:3 among the nations his *g*
96:7 Ascribe to Jehovah *g* and
96:8 Ascribe to Jehovah the *g*
97:6 the peoples have seen his *g*
102:15 kings of the earth your *g*
102:16 He must appear in his *g*
104:31 *g* of Jehovah will prove to
106:20 they exchanged my *g* For a
108:1 and make melody, Even my *g*
108:5 *g* be above all the earth
112:9 horn will be exalted with *g*
113:4 His *g* is above the heavens
115:1 But to your name give *g*
138:5 the *g* of Jehovah is great
145:11 About the *g* of your kingship
145:12 *g* of the splendor of his
149:5 Let the loyal ones exult in *g*
Pr 3:16 hand there are riches and *g*
8:18 Riches and *g* are with me
11:16 one that takes hold of *g*
15:33 before *g* there is humility
18:12 before *g* there is humility
20:3 a *g* for a man to desist from
21:21 life, righteousness and *g*
22:4 fear . . . is riches and *g*
25:2 *g* of God is the keeping of a
25:2 *g* of kings is the searching
25:27, 27 their own *g*, is it *g*
26:1 *g* is not fitting for a stupid
26:8 giving *g* to a mere stupid one
29:23 humble . . . take hold of *g*
Ec 6:2 and material possessions and *g*
10:1 is precious for wisdom and *g*
Isa 3:8 in the eyes of his *g*
4:2 for decoration and for *g*, and
4:5 over all the *g* there will be
5:13 *g* will be famished men
6:3 all the earth is his *g*
8:7 king of Assyria and all his *g*
10:3 will you leave your *g*
10:16 under his *g* a burning will
10:18 *g* of his forest and of his
14:18 have lain down in *g*, each
16:14 *g* of Moab must also be
17:3 the *g* of the sons of Israel
17:4 *g* of Jacob will become
21:16 *g* of Kedar must even come
22:18 chariots of your *g* will
22:23 throne of *g* to the house of
22:24 *g* of the house of his father
24:23 of his elderly men with *g*
35:2 *g* of Lebanon itself must be
35:2 see the *g* of Jehovah, the
40:5 *g* of Jehovah will certainly
42:8 shall I give my own *g*
42:12 attribute to Jehovah *g*, and
43:7 have created for my own *g*
48:11 shall I give my own *g*
58:8 *g* of Jehovah would be your
59:19 rising of the sun the *g* of
60:1 *g* of Jehovah has shone forth
60:2 his own *g* will be seen
60:13 To you the very *g* of Lebanon
61:6 in their *g* you will speak
62:2 and all kings your *g*
66:11 from the teat of her *g*

Isa 66:12 and the *g* of nations just
66:18 have to come and see my *g*
66:19 have not . . . seen my *g*
66:19 my *g* among the nations
Jer 2:11 people have exchanged my *g*
13:16 Give to Jehovah your God *g*
48:18 Get down from *g*, and sit
Eze 1:28 likeness of the *g* of Jehovah
3:12 Blessed be the *g* of Jehovah
3:23 *g* of Jehovah was standing
3:23 like the *g* that I had seen
8:4 *g* of the God of Israel was
9:3 the *g* of the God of Israel, it
10:4 the *g* of Jehovah proceeded to
10:4 of the *g* of Jehovah
10:18 *g* of Jehovah proceeded to go
10:19 *g* of the God of Israel was
11:22 *g* of the God of Israel was
11:23 *g* of Jehovah went ascending
31:18 in *g* and greatness among
39:21 set my *g* among the nations
43:2 *g* of the God of Israel was
43:2 shone because of his *g*
43:4 *g* of Jehovah itself came
43:5 full of the *g* of Jehovah
44:4 *g* of Jehovah had filled the
Da 11:38 his position he will give *g*
11:38 give *g* by means of gold and
11:39 make abound with *g*, and he
Ho 4:7 My own *g* they have exchanged
9:11 their *g* flies away, so that
10:5 on account of its *g*
Mic 1:15 the *g* of Israel will come
Hab 2:14 knowing of the *g* of Jehovah
2:16 with dishonor instead of *g*
2:16 be disgrace upon your *g*
Hag 2:3 this house in its former *g*
2:7 will fill this house with *g*
2:9 the *g* of this later house
Zec 2:5 a *g* is what I shall become
2:8 Following after the *g* he has
Mal 2:2 give *g* to my name, Jehovah
Mt 4:8 kingdoms . . . and their *g*
5:16 and give *g* to your Father who
6:29 even Solomon in all his *g*
16:27 come in the *g* of his Father
24:30 with power and great *g*
25:31 Son of man arrives in his *g*
Mr 8:38 in the *g* of his Father with
10:37 one at your left, in your *g*
13:26 with great power and *g*
Lu 2:9 Jehovah's *g* gleamed around
2:14 *G* in the heights above to God
2:32 a *g* of your people Israel
4:6 authority and the *g* of them
9:26 when he arrives in his *g*
9:31 These appeared with *g* and
9:32 saw his *g* and the two men
12:27 even Solomon in all his *g*
17:18 turned back to give *g* to God
19:38 and *g* in the highest places
21:27 with power and great *g*
24:26 and to enter into his *g*
Joh 1:14 and we had a view of his *g*
1:14 a *g* such as belongs to an
2:11 he made his *g* manifest
5:41 I do not accept *g* from men
5:44 accepting *g* from one another
5:44 not seeking the *g* that is
7:18 is seeking his own *g*
7:18 seeks the *g* of him that sent
8:50 am not seeking *g* for myself
8:54 my *g* is nothing. It is my
9:24 Give *g* to God; we know that
11:4 but is for the *g* of God, in
11:40 would see the *g* of God
12:41 because he saw his *g*, and
12:43 loved the *g* of men more
12:43 than even the *g* of God
17:5 *g* that I had alongside you
17:22 *g* that you have given me
17:24 *g* that you have given me
Ac 7:2 God of *g* appeared to our
7:55 caught sight of God's *g* and
12:23 did not give the *g* to God
22:11 for the *g* of that light, I
Ro 1:23 *g* of the incorruptible God
2:7 are seeking *g* and honor and
2:10 *g* and honor and peace for
3:7 made more prominent to his *g*
3:23 fall short of the *g* of God
4:20 by his faith, giving God *g*
5:2 based on hope of the *g* of God
6:4 through the *g* of the Father

Ro 8:18 the *g* that is going to be
9:4 adoption as sons and the *g*
9:23 riches of his *g* upon vessels
9:23 he prepared beforehand for *g*
11:36 To him be the *g* forever
15:7 welcomed us, with *g* to God
16:27 the *g* through Jesus Christ
1Co 2:7 systems of things for our *g*
10:31 do all things for God's *g*
11:7 as he is God's image and *g*
11:7 but the woman is man's *g*
11:15 long hair, it is a *g* to her
15:40 but the *g* of the heavenly
15:41 The *g* of the sun is one sort
15:41 *g* of the moon is another
15:41 *g* of the stars is another
15:41 star differs from star in *g*
15:43 it is raised up in *g*
2Co 1:20 said to God for *g* through us
3:7 came about in a *g*, so that
3:7 because of the *g* of his face
3:7 a *g* that was to be done away
3:8 spirit be much more with *g*
3:9 righteousness abound with *g*
3:10 stripped of *g* in this respect
3:10 because of the *g* that excels
3:11 was brought in with *g*
3:11 which remains be with *g*
3:18 reflect . . . *g* of Jehovah
3:18, 18 same image from *g* to *g*
4:15 many more to the *g* of God
4:17 *g* that is of more and more
6:8 through *g* and dishonor
8:19 for the *g* of the Lord and in
8:23 and a *g* of Christ
Ga 1:5 be the *g* forever and ever
Eph 1:12 serve for the praise of his *g*
1:17 Father of *g*, may give you a
3:13 for these mean *g* for you
3:16 the riches of his *g* to be
3:21 to him be the *g* by means
Php 1:11 to God's *g* and praise
2:11 to the *g* of God the Father
3:19 *g* consists in their shame
4:19 extent of his riches in *g* by
4:20 be the *g* forever and ever
Col 1:27 the hope of his *g*
3:4 made manifest with him in *g*
1Th 2:6 been seeking *g* from men, no
2:12 to his kingdom and *g*
2:20 certainly are our *g* and joy
2Th 1:9 from the *g* of his strength
2:14 acquiring the *g* of our Lord
1Ti 1:17 be honor and *g* forever and
3:16 was received up in *g*
2Ti 2:10 along with everlasting *g*
4:18 To him be the *g* forever and
Heb 1:3 He is the reflection of his *g*
2:7 with *g* and honor you crowned
2:9 crowned with *g* and honor for
2:10 bringing many sons to *g*
3:3 worthy of more *g* than Moses
13:21 to whom be the *g* forever
Jas 2:1 Lord Jesus Christ, our *g*
1Pe 1:7 found a cause for praise and *g*
1:21 raised him . . . gave him *g*
1:24 its *g* is like a blossom of
4:11 *g* and the might are his
4:13 the revelation of his *g*
4:14 because the spirit of *g*
5:1 the *g* that is to be revealed
5:4 the unfadable crown of *g*
5:10 everlasting *g* in union with
2Pe 1:3 called us through *g* and virtue
1:17 he received . . . honor and *g*
1:17 to him by the magnificent *g*
3:18 To him be the *g* both now and
Jude 24 in the sight of his *g* with
25 be *g*, majesty, might and
Re 1:6 to him be the *g* and the might
4:9 living creatures offer *g* and
4:11 to receive the *g* and the honor
5:12 and honor and *g* and blessing
5:13 the *g* and the might forever
7:12 blessing and the *g* and the
11:13 gave *g* to the God of heaven
14:7 Fear God and give him *g*
15:8 because of the *g* of God and
16:9 repent so as to give *g* to
18:1 was lighted up from his *g*
19:1 *g* and the power belong to our
19:7 and let us give him the *g*
21:11 and having the *g* of God
21:23 *g* of God lighted it up, and

Re 21:24 will bring their *g* into it
21:26 *g* and the honor of the

Glow
2Sa 14:7 the *g* of my charcoals
Pr 26:21 for causing a quarrel to *g*
Isa 11:15 in the *g* of his spirit
47:14 will be no *g* of charcoals
Eze 1:7 the *g* of burnished copper
1:16 was like the *g* of chrysolite
1:27 like the *g* of electrum, like
8:2 like the *g* of electrum
10:9 the *g* of a chrysolite stone
Joe 2:6 collect a *g* of excitement
Na 2:10 collected a *g* of excitement

Glowing
Ca 6:10 pure like the *g* sun, awesome
Isa 6:6 hand there was a *g* coal that
24:23 *g* sun has become ashamed
30:26 as the light of the *g* sun
30:26 the very light of the *g* sun
54:12 your gates of fiery *g* stones
63:1 garments of *g* colors from
Re 1:15 copper when *g* in a furnace

Glue
Job 14:17 you apply *g* over my error

Glutted
Job 7:4 *g* with restlessness until
10:15 *G* with dishonor and
14:1 Man . . . *g* with agitation
Ps 123:3 have been *g* with contempt
123:4 soul has been *g* with the
Pr 1:31 *g* with their own counsels

Glutting
Job 9:18 *g* me with bitter things

Glutton
De 21:20 being a *g* and a drunkard
Pr 23:21 and a *g* will come to poverty

Gluttonous
Pr 23:20 who are *g* eaters of flesh
Mt 11:19 *g* and given to drinking wine
Lu 7:34 A man *g* and given to drinking

Gluttons
Pr 28:7 having companionship with *g*
Tit 1:12 wild beasts, unemployed *g*

Gnash
Ac 7:54 to *g* their teeth at him

Gnashing
Mt 8:12 and the *g* of their teeth will
13:42 the *g* of their teeth will be
13:50 the *g* of their teeth will be
22:13 the *g* of his teeth will be
24:51 the *g* of his teeth will be
25:30 the *g* of his teeth will be
Lu 13:28 weeping and the *g* of your

Gnat
Isa 51:6 will die like a mere *g*
Mt 23:24 strain out the *g* but gulp

Gnats
Ex 8:16 dust . . . must become *g* in all
8:17 *g* came to be on man and beast
8:17 dust of the earth became *g* in
8:18 bring forth *g*, but they were
8:18 *g* came to be on man and beast
Ps 105:31 *G* in all their territories

Gnaw
Nu 24:8 their bones he will *g*, and he
Eze 23:34 fragments you will *g*, and
Zep 3:3 not *g* bones till the morning
Re 16:10 *g* their tongues for their

Gnawed
Jer 50:17 Babylon has *g* on his bones

Gnawing
Job 30:3 *G* at a waterless region
30:17 pains *g* me do not take any

Go*
Ge 3:14 Upon your belly you will *g*
4:8 Let us *g* over into the field
6:18 and you must *g* into the ark
7:1 *G*, you and all your household
8:16 *G* out of the ark, you and your
12:1 say to Abram: *G* your way out
12:5 to *g* to the land of Canaan
26:2 said: Do not *g* down to Egypt
27:3 *g* out to the field and hunt
27:9 *G*, please, to the herd and
28:2 Get up, *g* to Paddan-aram to

Ge 32:26 Let me *g*, for the dawn has
32:26 I am not going to let you *g*
34:1 *g* out to see the daughters of
37:35 I shall *g* down mourning to
41:55 *G* to Joseph. Whatever he
Ex 1:10 and *g* up out of the country
2:8 *G!* At once the maiden went
4:18 said to Moses: *G* in peace
4:19 *G*, return to Egypt, because
6:11 *G* in, speak to Pharaoh
7:15 *G* to Pharaoh in the morning
8:1 *G* in to Pharaoh, and you must
8:25 Pharaoh . . . said: *G*, sacrifice
10:8 *G*, serve Jehovah your God
10:24 Pharaoh . . . said: *G*, serve
21:2 *g* out as one set free without
23:23 my angel will *g* ahead of you
24:1 *G* up to Jehovah, you and Aaron
28:43 they *g* near to the altar to
30:20 *g* near the altar to minister
32:1 a god who will *g* ahead of
32:8 I have commanded them to *g*
32:23 a god who will *g* ahead of us
Le 6:12 It must not *g* out
9:7 *G* near to the altar and render
25:28 *g* out in the Jubilee, and he
25:30 not *g* out in the Jubilee
25:31 the Jubilee it should *g* out
25:33 also *g* out in the Jubilee
25:54 *g* out in the year of Jubilee
Nu 10:30 I shall *g* to my own country
16:30 to *g* down alive into Sheol
20:15 proceeded to *g* down to Egypt
21:4 to *g* around the land of Edom
22:13 *G* to your country, because
27:21 At his order they will *g* out
De 3:27 *G* up to the top of Pisgah
4:1 *g* in and take possession of the
4:21 *g* into the good land that
4:40 *g* well with you and your sons
5:16 it may *g* well with you on
5:27 *g* near and hear all that
5:29 *g* well with them and their
9:1 to *g* in and dispossess nations
10:11 *g* before the people for a
10:11 *g* in and take possession of
11:31 *g* in and take possession of
13:6 Let us *g* and serve other gods
17:3 *g* and worship other gods and
26:5 *g* down to Egypt and to reside
27:18 causes the blind to *g* astray
28:6 blessed . . . when you *g* out
28:19 cursed . . . when you *g* out
28:41 will *g* off into captivity
29:18 to *g* and serve the gods of
29:26 to *g* and serve other gods
Jg 1:2 Jehovah said: Judah will *g* up
6:14 *G* in this power of yours, and
7:4 Have them *g* down to the water
7:4 This one will *g* with you, he
7:4 one that will *g* with you, but
7:4 will not *g* along with you, he
7:4 is one that will not *g* along
9:38 *G* out now, please, and fight
10:14 *G* and call for aid to the
11:38 *G!* So he sent her away for
11:40 *g* to give commendation to
18:2 *G*, explore the land
18:6 said to them: *G* in peace
19:28 Rise up, and let us *g*
20:8 We shall not *g* any of us to
20:9 Let us *g* up by lot against it
20:14 to Gibeah to *g* out to battle
20:23 Jehovah said: *G* up against
Ru 1:11 Why should you *g* with me?
1:12 Return, my daughters, *g*, for
1:16, 16 for where you *g* I shall *g*
3:1 that it may *g* well with you
1Sa 1:17 *G* in peace, and may the God
3:9 Eli said to Samuel: *G*, lie
8:22 *G* each one to his city
9:19 *G* up before me to the high
10:14 Where did you *g?*
15:3 *g*, and you must strike down
15:6 to the Kenites: *G*, depart
15:18 *G*, and you must devote the
16:2 Samuel said: How can I *g?*
20:42 to David: *G* in peace, since
25:5 *G* up to Carmel, and you must
25:35 *G* up in peace to your house
26:19 saying, *G*, serve other gods!
29:7 *g* in peace that you may not
29:10 rise up early . . . Then *g*
30:8 *G* in chase, for you will
1Sa 30:21 too tired to *g* along with
2Sa 1:15 and said: *G* near. Smite him
2:1 Where shall I *g* up?
13:7 *G*, please, to the house of
13:9 Have everybody *g* out from me!
13:26 Why should he *g* with you?
14:2 *G* in mourning, please, and
14:19 no man can *g* to the right
14:19 or *g* to the left from all
15:7 Let me *g*, please, and pay
15:9 king said to him: *G* in peace
15:14 *G* hurriedly, for fear he
24:1 *G*, take a count of Israel
1Ki 1:13 *G* and enter in to King David
1:53 *G* to your own house
11:10 not to *g* after other gods
11:21 I may *g* to my own land
11:22 to *g* to your own land
12:5 *G* away for three days and
12:24 *G* back each one to his house
12:28 to *g* up to Jerusalem
13:12 Which way, then, did he *g?*
18:21 true God, *g* following him
18:21 if Baal is, *g* following him
18:27 and has to *g* to the privy
18:43 *G* back, for seven times
18:44 *G* up, say to Ahab, Hitch up!
22:6 I *g* against Ramoth-gilead
22:6 *G* up, and Jehovah will give
22:15 *g* to Ramoth-gilead in war
22:15 *G* up and prove successful
22:17 Let them *g* back each one to
22:22 *G* out and do that way
22:48 Tarshish ships to *g* to Ophir
2Ki 1:2 *G*, inquire of Baal-zebub the
2:16 Let them *g*, please, and look
2:18 I not say to you, Do not *g*
2:23, 23 *G* up, you baldhead! *G* up
3:7 Will you *g* with me to Moab
3:13 *G* to the prophets of your
5:19 he said to him: *G* in peace
6:2 *g*, please, as far as the
6:2 So he said: *G*
6:22 drink and *g* to their lord
7:14 Syrians, saying: *G* and see
8:1 *g*, you with your household
9:31 Did it *g* all right with
10:24 will *g* for the other's soul
12:17 to *g* up against Jerusalem
20:5 *g* up to the house of Jehovah
20:8 *g* up on the third day to the
20:9 shadow actually *g* forward
20:9 should it *g* back ten steps
20:10 should *g* backward ten steps
20:11 *g* back on the steps
22:13 *G*, inquire of Jehovah in
1Ch 14:10 *g* up against the Philistines
14:10 Jehovah said to him: *G* up
21:2 *G*, count Israel from
2Ch 6:34 people *g* out to the war
7:19 *g* and serve other gods and
16:3 *G*, break your covenant with
20:36 ships to *g* to Tarshish
25:11 *g* to the Valley of Salt
26:6 *g* out and fight against the
34:21 *G*, inquire of Jehovah in
Ezr 7:13 willing to *g* to Jerusalem
Ne 8:10 *G*, eat the fatty things and
Es 1:19 let a royal word *g* out from
4:16 *G*, gather all the Jews that
Job 11:2 Will . . . words *g* unanswered
12:17 counselors *g* barefoot
12:17 judges themselves *g* crazy
14:5 that he may not *g* beyond
17:16 bars of Sheol they will *g*
34:23 To *g* to God in judgment
Ps 30:9 when I *g* down to the pit
32:8 in the way you should *g*
39:13 Before I *g* away and I am not
44:9 not *g* forth with our armies
45:4 splendor *g* on to success
49:17 His glory will not *g* down
55:7 I would *g* far away in flight
55:10 *g* round about it upon its
55:15 *g* down into Sheol alive
58:7 into waters that *g* their way
59:6 and *g* all around the city
59:14 and *g* all around the city
81:12 *g* in the stubbornness of
90:3 mortal man *g* back to crushed
90:3 say: *G* back, you sons of men
104:14 food to *g* forth from the
104:26 There the ships *g*
104:29 back to their dust they *g*
Ps 107:26 They *g* up to the heavens
107:26 They *g* down to the bottoms
108:11 *g* forth with our armies as
109:7 *g* forth as someone wicked
109:10 his sons *g* wandering about
109:23 I am obliged to *g* away
110:2 *G* subduing in the midst of
118:19 I shall *g* into them
118:20 righteous themselves will *g*
119:10 to *g* astray from your
121:4 not be drowsy nor *g* to sleep
122:1 house of Jehovah let us *g*
125:5 Jehovah will make them *g*
132:3 *g* into the tent of my house
132:3 *g* up on the divan of my
139:7 can I *g* from your spirit
Pr 1:11 Do *g* with us. Do let us lie
1:15 my son, do not *g* in the way
3:28 *G*, and come back and
4:13 discipline; do not let *g*
6:3 *G* humble yourself and storm
6:6 *G* to the ant, you lazy one
10:3 righteous one to *g* hungry
11:21 person will not *g* unpunished
14:7 *G* away from in front of the
14:22 *g* wandering about
15:12 the wise ones he will not *g*
16:29 *g* in a way that is not good
18:8 do *g* down into the innermost
22:10 that contention may *g* out
22:26 who *g* security for loans
25:8 not *g* forth to conduct a legal
26:22 *g* down into the innermost
28:10 to *g* astray into the bad way
29:18 the people *g* unrestrained
30:27 *g* forth all of them divided
31:18 her lamp does not *g* out at
Ec 1:7 are returning so as to *g* forth
5:1 *g* to the house of the true God
5:15 naked will one *g* away again
5:16 has come, so one will *g* away
7:2 to *g* to the house of mourning
7:2 than to *g* to the banquet house
8:10 *g* away from the holy place
9:7 *G*, eat your food with
Ca 3:11 *G* out and look, O you
Isa 2:3 many peoples will certainly *g*
2:3 let us *g* up to the mountain
2:3 out of Zion law will *g* forth
3:16 *g* walking with tripping
6:8 and who will *g* for us?
6:9 *G*, and you must say to this
7:3 *G* out, please, to meet Ahaz
7:6 *g* up against Judah and tear
8:7 and *g* over all his banks
11:1 *g* forth a twig out of the
14:13 To the heavens I shall *g* up
14:14 *g* up above the high places
18:2 *G*, you swift messengers, to
20:2 *G*, and you must loosen the
21:2 *G* up, O Elam! Lay siege
21:6 *G*, post a lookout that he
22:15 *G*, enter in to this steward
23:16 *g* around the city
26:20 *G*, my people, enter into
28:13 *g* and certainly stumble
30:2 to *g* down to Egypt
36:10 *G* up against this land, and
38:10 *g* into the gates of Sheol
38:22 *g* up to the house of Jehovah
41:2 make him *g* subduing even
42:13 Jehovah himself will *g*
45:2 Before you I myself shall *g*
45:13 in exile he will let *g*
46:2 their own soul must *g*
49:10 They will not *g* hungry
49:10 neither will they *g* thirsty
51:4 a law itself will *g* forth
60:3 nations will certainly *g* to
60:14 you must *g*, bowing down
60:20 your moon *g* on the wane
63:12 *g* at the right hand of
65:13 you . . . will *g* hungry
65:13 yourselves will *g* thirsty
66:24 *g* forth and look upon the
Jer 1:7 send you, you should *g*
3:12 *G*, and you must proclaim
6:25 Do not *g* out into the field
7:12 *g*, now, to my place that was
7:23 that it may *g* well with you
9:2 leave my people and *g* away
11:12 *g* and call for aid to the
13:1 *G*, and you must get for
13:4 *g* to the Euphrates, and hide

Jer 13:6 Rise up, *g* to the Euphrates
14:18 *g* out into the field
15:1 that they might *g* out
15:2 Where shall we *g* out to?
16:5 do not *g* to bewail and do
17:19 *G*, and you must stand in
20:6 you will *g* into captivity
25:29 *g* free of punishment
25:29 not *g* free of punishment
31:6 let us *g* up to Zion, to
34:2 *G*, and you must say to
34:14 let *g* each one his brother
34:14 *g* free from being with you
35:2 *G* to the house of the
38:20 it will *g* well with you
40:5, 5 right in your eyes to *g*, *g*
41:15 *g* to the sons of Ammon
41:17 *g* on and enter into Egypt
42:6 *g* well with us because we
42:14 we shall not *g* hungry; and
43:12 *g* out from there in peace
49:3 will *g* even into exile
50:33 refused to let them *g*
51:9 *g* each one to his own land
52:7 *g* forth from the city by
52:21 thread . . . would *g* around it
Eze 1:20 the spirit inclined to *g*
1:20 *g*, the spirit inclining to
1:20 spirit inclining to *g* there
3:1 Eat this roll, and *g*, speak to
3:11 *g*, enter in among the exiled
9:6 is the mark do not *g* near
9:7 *G* forth! And they went forth
10:22 *g* each one straight forward
12:3 *g* into exile in the daytime
12:3 *g* into exile from your place
12:11 into captivity they will *g*
20:39 *G* serve each one of you his
39:9 *g* forth and burn and build
42:14 *g* out from the holy place
46:10 he should *g* out
Da 11:9 and *g* back to his own soil
11:11 *g* forth and fight with him
12:9 *G*, Daniel, because the words
12:13 *g* toward the end; and you
Ho 1:2 *G*, take to yourself a wife of
1:3 *g* and take Gomer the daughter
3:1 *G* once again, love a woman
7:12 Whichever way they *g*, I shall
Joe 2:7 *g* each one in his own ways
Am 1:5 have to *g* as exiles to Kir
1:15 their king must *g* into exile
5:5 without fail *g* into exile
5:27 cause you to *g* into exile
7:11 without fail *g* into exile
7:15 *G*, prophesy to my people
7:17 without fail *g* into exile
8:9 the sun *g* down at high noon
9:2 if they *g* up to the heavens
9:4 if they *g* into captivity
Jon 1:2 *g* to Nineveh the great city
1:3 to *g* with them to Tarshish
3:2 *g* to Nineveh the great city
Mic 2:10 Get up and *g*, because this
4:2 *g* and say: Come, you people
4:2 let us *g* up to the mountain
4:2 out of Zion law will *g* forth
Zec 6:7 *G*, walk about in the earth
8:21 *g* to soften the face of
8:23 We will *g* with you people
14:2 must *g* forth into the exile
14:3 *g* forth and war against
14:8 living waters will *g* forth
14:16 *g* up from year to year to
Mt 2:8 *G* make a careful search for
2:8 may *g* and do it obeisance
4:10 *G* away, Satan! For it is
5:40 a person wants to *g* to court
5:41 *g* with him two miles
6:6 you pray, *g* into your private
7:13 *G* in through the narrow gate
8:4 *g*, show yourself to the priest
8:13 *G*. Just as it has been your
8:19 wherever you are about to *g*
8:32 *G*! They came out and went
9:13 *G*, then, and learn what this
10:5 Do not *g* off into the road of
10:6 *g* continually to the lost
10:7 As you *g*, preach, saying, The
11:4 *G* your way and report to John
11:9 Really, then, why did you *g*
13:30 *g* to gathering the wheat
13:49 the angels will *g* out and
16:21 *g* to Jerusalem and suffer
Mt 18:15 *g* lay bare his fault between
19:21 *g* sell your belongings and
20:17 about to *g* up to Jerusalem
21:28 *g* work today in the vineyard
21:29 I will, sir, but did not *g*
23:13 you yourselves do not *g* in
25:39 or in prison and *g* to you
28:10 *G*, report to my brothers
28:19 *G* therefore and make
Mr 1:12 the spirit impelled him to *g*
1:38 Let us *g* somewhere else
5:34 *G* in peace, and be in good
7:8 Letting *g* the commandment of
7:29 *g*; the demon has gone out of
9:43 to *g* off into Gehenna, into
10:21 *G*, sell what things you have
10:25 to *g* through a needle's eye
10:52 *G*, your faith has made you
11:2 *G* into the village that is
11:6 and they let them *g*
14:42 Get up, let us *g*. Look!
Lu 1:76 *g* in advance before Jehovah
2:41 to *g* from year to year to
7:22 *G* your way, report to John
7:25 What . . . did you *g* out to see?
7:50 *g* your way in peace
8:31 to *g* away into the abyss
8:48 *g* your way in peace
9:60 you *g* away and declare abroad
10:3 *G* forth. Look! I am sending
10:10 *g* out into its broad ways
10:37 *G* your way and be doing the
13:32 *G* and tell that fox, Look!
19:30 *G* into the village that is
21:8 Do not *g* after them
22:8 *G* and get the passover ready
Joh 6:68 whom shall we *g* away to?
7:8 You *g* up to the festival
7:33 I *g* to him that sent me
9:7 *G* wash in the pool of Siloam
9:11 *G* to Siloam and wash
13:33 Where I *g* you cannot come
14:31 Get up, let us *g* from here
16:7 I do *g* my way, I will send
18:8 Jesus answered . . . let these *g*
Ac 18:6 *g* to people of the nations
20:13 was intending to *g* on foot
21:12 him not to *g* up to Jerusalem
22:10 *g* your way into Damascus
25:12 to Caesar you shall *g*
28:26 *G* to this people and say
1Co 1:17 *g* declaring the good news
4:6 Do not *g* beyond the things
6:1 dare to *g* to court before
Ga 5:25 *g* on walking orderly also by
6:2 *G* on carrying the burdens of
Eph 6:3 That it may *g* well with you
6:4 but *g* on bringing them up in
6:10 *g* on acquiring power in the
Php 3:16 let us *g* on walking orderly
Col 1:10 *g* on bearing fruit in every
2:6 *g* on walking in union with
3:1 *g* on seeking the things above
4:5 *G* on walking in wisdom
1Th 2:12 *g* on walking worthily of God
4:6 no one *g* to the point of
4:10 to *g* on doing it in fuller
2Th 2:11 operation of error *g* to them
3:4 will *g* on doing the things we
1Ti 1:3 *g* my way into Macedonia, so
1:18 *g* on waging the fine warfare
2:2 *g* on leading a calm and quiet
2Ti 2:10 I *g* on enduring all things
2:12 if we *g* on enduring, we
3:8 also *g* on resisting the truth
Phm 6 may *g* into action by your
Heb 3:10 *g* astray in their hearts
2Pe 2:10 those who *g* on after flesh
2Jo 6 *g* on walking according to his
6 that you should *g* on walking in
3Jo 3 you *g* on walking in the truth
4 *g* on walking in the truth
Jude 10 *g* on corrupting themselves
Re 10:8 *G*, take the opened scroll that
14:13 they did *g* right with them
16:1 *G* and pour out the seven
16:14 *g* forth to the kings of the
17:8 is to *g* off into destruction
20:8 he will *g* out to mislead
22:14 to *g* to the trees of life

Goad
Jg 3:31 Shamgar . . . with a cattle *g*
Isa 9:11 of that one he will *g* on
Isa 19:2 I will *g* Egyptians against

Goads
Ac 26:14 kicking against the *g* makes

Goah
Jer 31:39 certainly go around to *G*

Goal
Hab 2:5 and he will not reach his *g*
Mt 11:12 *g* toward which men press
Php 3:14 toward the *g* for the prize

Goat
Ge 37:31 slaughtered a male *g* and
Le 3:12 And if his offering is a *g*
4:24 the head of the young *g* and
7:23 not eat any fat of . . . a *g*
9:3 a male *g* for a sin offering
9:15 took the *g* of the sin offering
10:16 the *g* of the sin offering
16:9 the *g* over which the lot came
16:10 *g* over which the lot came up
16:15 slaughter the *g* of the sin
16:20 must also present the live *g*
16:21 live *g* and confess over it
16:21 *g* and send it away by the
16:22 *g* must carry upon itself all
16:22 send the *g* away into the
16:26 one who sent the *g* away for
16:27 *g* of the sin offering, the
17:3 young ram or a *g* in the camp
22:27 or a *g* be born, then it must
Nu 15:27 a female *g* in its first year
18:17 firstborn *g* you should not
28:22 and one *g* of sin offering to
29:22 and one *g* as a sin offering
29:28 and one *g* as a sin offering
29:31 and one *g* as a sin offering
29:34 and one *g* as a sin offering
29:38 and one *g* as a sin offering
De 14:4 the bull, the sheep and the *g*
14:5 wild *g* and antelope and wild
Pr 5:19 and a charming mountain *g*

Goatlike
Isa 14:9 *g* leaders of the earth
Zec 10:3 against the *g* leaders I shall

Goat's
Ex 25:4 and fine linen, and *g* hair
26:7 make cloths of *g* hair for the
35:6 fine linen and *g* hair
35:23 *g* hair and ram skins dyed
35:26 with wisdom spun the *g* hair
36:14 make tent cloths of *g* hair
Le 16:18 some of the *g* blood and put
Nu 31:20 everything made of *g* hair

Goats
Ge 27:9 two kids of the *g*, good ones
27:16 skins of the kids of the *g*
38:17 shall send a kid of the *g*
38:20 send the kid of the *g* by
Ex 12:5 the young rams or from the *g*
Le 1:10 from the young rams or the *g*
4:23 offering a male kid of the *g*
4:28 a female kid of the *g*
5:6 a female kid of the *g*, for a
16:5 of the *g* for a sin offering
16:7 the two *g* and make them stand
16:8 the two *g*, the one lot for
22:19 young rams or among the *g*
23:19 one kid of the *g* as a sin
Nu 7:16 kid of the *g* for a sin
7:22 one kid of the *g* for a sin
7:28 one kid of the *g* for a sin
7:34 one kid of the *g* for a sin
7:40 one kid of the *g* for a sin
7:46 one kid of the *g* for a sin
7:52 one kid of the *g* for a sin
7:58 one kid of the *g* for a sin
7:64 kid . . . *g* for a sin offering
7:70 one kid of the *g* for a sin
7:76 one kid of the *g* for a sin
7:82 one kid of the *g* for a sin
7:87 twelve kids of the *g* for a
15:11 male lambs or among the *g*
15:24 and one kid of the *g* as a
28:15 one kid of the *g* should be
28:30 one kid of the *g* to make
29:5 one male kid of the *g* as a
29:11 one kid of the *g* as a sin
29:16 one kid of the *g* as a sin
29:19 and one kid of the *g* as a sin
29:25 one kid of the *g* as a sin
De 14:26 sheep and *g* and wine and

Jg 6:19 make ready a kid of the *g* and
13:15 and fix up a kid of the *g*
13:19 take the kid of the *g* and the
15:1 with a kid of the *g*
1Sa 16:20 a kid of the *g* and sent
24:2 bare rocks of the mountain *g*
25:2 and a thousand *g*; and he
1Ki 20:27 like two tiny flocks of *g*
2Ch 29:21 seven male *g* . . . offering
29:23 male *g* of the sin offering
Ezr 6:17 twelve male *g*, according to
Job 39:1 *g* of the crag to give birth
Ps 104:18 are for the mountain *g*
Ca 1:8 and pasture your kids of the *g*
4:1 Your hair is like a drove of *g*
6:5 Your hair is like a drove of *g*
Eze 43:22 bring near a buck of the *g*
45:23 a buck of the *g* daily
Da 8:5 male of the *g* coming from the
8:8 male of the *g*, for its part
Mt 25:32 the sheep from the *g*
25:33 but the *g* on his left
Heb 9:12 the blood of *g* and of young
9:13 the blood of *g* and of bulls
9:19 the young bulls and of the *g*
10:4 blood of bulls and of *g* to

Goats'
1Sa 19:13 net of *g* hair she put at
19:16 net of *g* hair at the place
Pr 27:27 a sufficiency of *g* milk for

Goat-shaped
Le 17:7 *g* demons with which they are
2Ch 11:15 and for the *g* demons and
Isa 13:21 *g* demons themselves will go
34:14 *g* demon will call to its

Goatskins
Heb 11:37 in sheepskins, in *g*, while

Gob
2Sa 21:18 with the Philistines at *G*
21:19 with the Philistines at *G*

Goblet
Isa 51:17 The *g*, the cup causing
51:22 The *g*, my cup of rage

Goblets
Jer 35:5 cups full of wine and *g*

God
Ge 1:1 In the beginning *G* created the
1:3 *G* proceeded to say: Let light
1:4 *G* saw that the light was good
1:4 *G* brought about a division
1:5 *G* began calling the light Day
1:6 *G* went on to say: Let an
1:7 *G* proceeded to make the
1:8 *G* began to call the expanse
1:9 And *G* went on to say: Let the
1:10 *G* began calling the dry land
1:10 *G* saw that it was good
1:11 *G* went on to say: Let the
1:12 *G* saw that it was good
1:14 And *G* went on to say: Let
1:16 *G* proceeded to make the two
1:17 *G* put them in the expanse of
1:18 *G* saw that it was good
1:20 And *G* went on to say: Let the
1:21 *G* proceeded to create the
1:21 *G* got to see that it was good
1:22 With that *G* blessed them
1:24 And *G* went on to say: Let the
1:25 *G* proceeded to make the wild
1:25 *G* got to see that it was good
1:26 *G* went on to say: Let us
1:27 *G* proceeded to create the man
1:28, 28 *G* blessed them and *G* said
1:29 *G* went on to say: Here I have
1:31 *G* saw everything he had made
2:2 *G* came to the completion of
2:3 And *G* proceeded to bless the
2:3 work that *G* has created for
2:4 *G* made earth and heaven
2:5 Jehovah *G* had not made it rain
2:7 *G* proceeded to form the man
2:8 Jehovah *G* planted a garden in
2:9 Thus Jehovah *G* made to grow
2:15 Jehovah *G* proceeded to take
2:16 And Jehovah *G* also laid this
2:18 And Jehovah *G* went on to say
2:19 Now Jehovah *G* was forming
2:21 Jehovah *G* had a deep sleep
2:22 *G* proceeded to build the rib
3:1 beasts . . . Jehovah *G* had made
3:1 Is it really so that *G* said
Ge 3:3 *G* has said, You must not eat
3:5 *G* knows that in the very day
3:5 you are bound to be like *G*
3:8 heard the voice of Jehovah *G*
3:8 from the face of Jehovah *G*
3:9 *G* kept calling to the man
3:13 Jehovah *G* said to the woman
3:14 Jehovah *G* proceeded to say to
3:21 Jehovah *G* proceeded to make
3:22 Jehovah *G* went on to say
3:23 Jehovah *G* put him out of the
4:25 *G* has appointed another seed
5:1 made him in the likeness of *G*
5:22 walking with the true *G*
5:24 kept walking with the true *G*
5:24 Enoch . . . was no more, for *G*
6:2 the sons of the true *G* began
6:4 sons of the true *G* continued
6:9 Noah walked with the true *G*
6:11 in the sight of the true *G*
6:12 *G* saw the earth and, look!
6:13 *G* said to Noah: The end of
6:22 all that *G* had commanded him
7:9 just as *G* had commanded Noah
7:16 just as *G* had commanded him
8:1 *G* remembered Noah and every
8:1 *G* caused a wind to pass over
8:15 *G* now spoke to Noah, saying
9:1 *G* went on to bless Noah and
9:8 *G* went on to say to Noah and
9:12 *G* added: This is the sign
9:16 between *G* and every living
9:17 *G* repeated to Noah: This is
9:26 Blessed be Jehovah, Shem's *G*
9:27 Let *G* grant ample space to
14:18 priest of the Most High *G*
14:19 Abram of the Most High *G*
14:20 blessed be the Most High *G*
14:22 Jehovah the Most High *G*
16:13 You are a *G* of sight, for she
17:1 I am *G* Almighty. Walk before
17:3 *G* continued to speak with him
17:7 prove myself *G* to you and to
17:8 I will prove myself *G* to them
17:9 *G* said further to Abraham
17:15 *G* went on to say to Abraham
17:18 Abraham said to the true *G*
17:19 *G* said: Sarah your wife is
17:22 *G* finished speaking with him
17:23 just as *G* had spoken with
19:29 *G* brought the cities of the
19:29 *G* kept Abraham in mind in
20:3 *G* came to Abimelech in a
20:6 true *G* said to him in the
20:11 no fear of *G* in this place
20:13 *G* caused me to wander from
20:17, 17 true *G*; and *G* proceeded
21:2 which *G* had spoken to him
21:4 just as *G* had commanded him
21:6 *G* has prepared laughter for
21:12 *G* said to Abraham: Do not
21:17 *G* heard the voice of the boy
21:17 *G* has listened to the voice
21:19 *G* opened her eyes so that she
21:20 *G* continued to be with the
21:22 *G* is with you in everything
21:23 swear to me here by *G* that
21:33 the indefinitely lasting *G*
22:1 *G* put Abraham to the test
22:3 true *G* designated to him
22:8 *G* will provide himself the
22:9 *G* had designated to him, and
23:6 chieftain of *G* you are in
24:3 *G* of the heavens and the
24:3 Jehovah . . . the *G* of the earth
24:7 *G* of the heavens, who took me
24:12 Jehovah the *G* of my master
24:27 the *G* of my master Abraham
24:42 *G* of my master Abraham, if
24:48 *G* of my master Abraham, who
25:11 *G* continued to bless Isaac
26:24 the *G* of Abraham your father
27:20 your *G* caused it to meet up
27:28 *G* give you the dews of the
28:3 *G* Almighty will bless you and
28:4 which *G* has given to Abraham
28:13 Jehovah the *G* of Abraham
28:13 Jehovah . . . the *G* of Isaac
28:17 the house of *G*
28:20 If *G* will continue with me
28:21 will have proved to be my *G*
28:22 will become a house of *G*
30:2 Am I in the place of *G*
30:6 *G* has acted as my judge and
Ge 30:17 *G* heard and answered Leah
30:18 *G* has given me a hireling's
30:20 *G* has endowed me, yes, me
30:22 *G* remembered Rachel, and
30:22 *G* heard and answered her
30:23 *G* has taken away my reproach
31:5 *G* of my father has proved to
31:7 *G* has not allowed him to do
31:9 *G* kept taking the herd of your
31:11 angel of the true *G* said
31:13 I am the true *G* of Bethel
31:16 riches that *G* has taken
31:16 everything *G* has said to you
31:24 *G* came to Laban the Syrian
31:29 *G* of your father talked to
31:42 If the *G* of my father
31:42 *G* of Abraham and the Dread
31:42 toil of my hands *G* has seen
31:50 *G* is a witness between me
31:53 Let the *g* of Abraham and the
31:53 the *g* of Nahor judge between
31:53 the *g* of their father
32:1 angels of *G* now met up with
32:2 The camp of *G* this is! Hence
32:9 O *G* of my father Abraham and
32:9 *G* of my father Isaac, O
32:28 contended with *G* and with
32:30 I have seen *G* face to face
33:5 *G* has favored your servant
33:11 *G* has favored me and because
33:20, 20 and called it *G* the *G* of
35:1 *G* said to Jacob: Rise, go up
35:1 altar there to the true *G*
35:3 make an altar to the true *G*
35:5 the terror of *G* came to be
35:7 *G* had revealed himself to him
35:9 *G* now appeared to Jacob once
35:10 *G* went on to say to him
35:11 *G* said further to him: I am
35:11 I am *G* Almighty. Be
35:13 *G* went up from above him
35:15 place where *G* had spoken
39:9 and actually sin against *G*
40:8 interpretations belong to *G*
41:16 *G* will announce welfare to
41:25 What the true *G* is doing
41:28 What the true *G* is doing he
41:32 on the part of the true *G*
41:32 true *G* is speeding to do it
41:38 in whom the spirit of *G* is
41:39 *G* has caused you to know all
41:51 *G* has made me forget all my
41:52 *G* has made me fruitful
42:18 I fear the true *G*
42:28 What is this *G* has done
43:14 may *G* Almighty give you pity
43:23, 23 Your *G* and the *G* of your
43:29 May *G* show you his favor
44:16 *G* has found out the error
45:5 *G* has sent me ahead of you
45:7 *G* sent me ahead of you in
45:8 *G*, that he might appoint me
45:9 *G* has appointed me lord for
46:1 sacrifices to the *G* of his
46:2 *G* talked to Israel in visions
46:3, 3 the true *G*, the *G* of your
48:3 *G* Almighty appeared to me at
48:9 my sons whom *G* has given me
48:11 *G* has let me see also your
48:15 The true *G* before whom my
48:15 *G* who has been shepherding
48:20 May *G* constitute you like
48:21 *G* will certainly continue
49:25 from the *G* of your father
50:17 servants of your father's *G*
50:19 for am I in the place of *G*?
50:20 *G* had it in mind for good
50:24 *G* will without fail turn his
50:25 *G* will without fail turn his
Ex 1:17 midwives feared the true *G*
1:20 So *G* dealt well with the
1:21 feared the true *G* he later
2:23 cry . . . up to the true *G*
2:24 time *G* heard their groaning
2:24 *G* remembered his covenant
2:25 *G* looked on the sons of Israel
2:25 *G* took notice
3:1 the mountain of the true *G*
3:4 *G* at once called to him out of
3:6 am the *G* of your father, the
3:6 the *G* of Abraham, the
3:6 of Abraham, the *G* of Isaac and
3:6 of Isaac and the *G* of Jacob
3:6 afraid to look at the true *G*

Ex 3:11 Moses said to the true *G*
3:12 the true *G* on this mountain
3:13 Moses said to the true *G*
3:13 *G* of your forefathers has sent
3:14 *G* said to Moses: I shall
3:15 *G* said once more to Moses
3:15 the *G* of your forefathers, the
3:15 Jehovah . . . the *G* of Abraham
3:15 Jehovah . . . the *G* of Isaac
3:15 Jehovah . . . the *G* of Jacob
3:16 *G* of your forefathers has
3:16 *G* of Abraham, Isaac and Jacob
3:18 Jehovah the *G* of the Hebrews
3:18 to sacrifice to Jehovah our *G*
4:5 the *G* of their forefathers
4:5 forefathers, the *G* of Abraham
4:5 Abraham, the *G* of Isaac and
4:5 *G* of Jacob, has appeared to you
4:16 you will serve as *G* to him
4:20 took the rod of the true *G*
4:27 the mountain of the true *G*
5:1 Jehovah the *G* of Israel has
5:3 *G* of the Hebrews has come in
5:3 and sacrifice to Jehovah our *G*
5:8 we want to sacrifice to our *G*
6:2 *G* went on to speak to Moses
6:3 to appear . . . as *G* Almighty
6:7 indeed prove to be *G* to you
6:7 know that I am Jehovah your *G*
7:1 made you *G* to Pharaoh, and
7:16 Jehovah the *G* of the Hebrews
8:10 no one . . . like Jehovah our *G*
8:19 Pharaoh: It is the finger of *G!*
8:25 Go, sacrifice to your *G* in the
8:26 sacrifice to Jehovah our *G* a
8:27 sacrifice to Jehovah our *G*
8:28 sacrifice to Jehovah your *G*
9:1 Jehovah the *G* of the Hebrews
9:13 Jehovah the *G* of the Hebrews
9:30 fear because of Jehovah *G*
10:3 Jehovah the *G* of the Hebrews
10:7 may serve Jehovah their *G*
10:8 Go, serve Jehovah your *G*
10:16 sinned against Jehovah your *G*
10:17 entreat Jehovah your *G* that
10:25 render them to Jehovah our *G*
10:26 to worship Jehovah our *G*
13:17 *G* did not lead them by the
13:17 for *G* said: It might be the
13:18 *G* made the people go round
13:19 *G* will without fail turn his
14:19 angel of the true *G* who
15:2 This is my *G*, and I shall
15:2 shall laud him; my father's *G*
15:26 the voice of Jehovah your *G*
16:12 that I am Jehovah your *G*
17:9 with the rod of the true *G*
18:1 all that *G* had done for Moses
18:4 *G* of my father is my helper
18:5 the mountain of the true *G*
18:12 sacrifices for *G;* and Aaron
18:12 before the true *G*
18:15 coming to me to inquire of *G*
18:16 decisions of the true *G* and
18:19 *G* will prove to be with you
18:19 before the true *G*, and you
18:19 the cases to the true *G*
18:21 fearing *G*, trustworthy men
18:23 and *G* has commanded you, you
19:3 Moses went up to the true *G*
19:17 to meet the true *G*, and
19:19 the true *G* began to answer
20:1 *G* proceeded to speak all these
20:2 I am Jehovah your *G*, who have
20:5, 5 your *G* am a *G* exacting
20:7 name of Jehovah your *G* in a
20:10 a sabbath to Jehovah your *G*
20:12 Jehovah your *G* is giving you
20:19 let not *G* speak with us for
20:20 the true *G* has come, and
20:21 where the true *G* was
21:6 bring him near to the true *G*
21:13 true *G* lets it occur at his
22:8 brought near to the true *G*
22:9 is to come to the true *G*
22:9 whom *G* will pronounce wicked
22:28 not call down evil upon *G*
23:19 the house of Jehovah your *G*
23:25 must serve Jehovah your *G*
24:10 got to see the *G* of Israel
24:11 got a vision of the true *G*
24:13 the mountain of the true *G*
29:45 I will prove to be their *G*
29:46 Jehovah their *G*, who brought
Ex 29:46 I am Jehovah their *G*
31:3 spirit of *G* in wisdom and in
32:1 for us a *g* who will go ahead
32:4 This is your *G*, O Israel, who
32:8 This is your *G*, O Israel, who
32:11 of Jehovah his *G* and to say
32:16 the workmanship of *G*, and
32:16 writing of *G* engraved upon
32:23 a *g* who will go ahead of us
32:27 Jehovah the *G* of Israel has
32:31 a *g* of gold for themselves
34:6 Jehovah, a *G* merciful and
34:14 prostrate . . . to another *g*
34:14 Jealous, he is a jealous *G*
34:23 Jehovah, the *G* of Israel
34:24 the face of Jehovah your *G*
34:26 house of Jehovah your *G*
35:31 the spirit of *G* in wisdom
Le 2:13 salt of the covenant of your *G*
4:22 that Jehovah his *G* commands
11:44 For I am Jehovah your *G*
11:45 to prove myself *G* to you
18:2 to them, I am Jehovah your *G*
18:4 I am Jehovah your *G*
18:21 profane the name of your *G*
18:30 I am Jehovah your *G*
19:2 because I Jehovah your *G* am
19:3 I am Jehovah your *G*
19:4 I am Jehovah your *G*
19:10 I am Jehovah your *G*
19:12 profane the name of your *G*
19:14 must be in fear of your *G*
19:25 I am Jehovah your *G*
19:31 I am Jehovah your *G*
19:32 must be in fear of your *G*
19:34 I am Jehovah your *G*
19:36 *G* I am, who have brought you
20:7 because I am Jehovah your *G*
20:24 *G* I am, who have divided you
21:6 holy to their *G*, and they
21:6 profane the name of their *G*
21:6 by fire, the bread of their *G*
21:7 because he is holy to his *G*
21:8 presenting the bread of your *G*
21:12 the sanctuary of his *G*
21:12 anointing oil of his *G*, is
21:17 to present the bread of his *G*
21:21 present the bread of his *G*
21:22 eat the bread of his *G* from
22:25 as the bread of your *G*
22:33 Egypt to prove myself *G* to
23:14 the offering of your *G*
23:22 I am Jehovah your *G*
23:28 for you before Jehovah your *G*
23:40 rejoice before Jehovah your *G*
23:43 Egypt. I am Jehovah your *G*
24:15 calls down evil upon his *G*
24:22 because I am Jehovah your *G*
25:17 be in fear of your *G*, because
25:17 because I am Jehovah your *G*
25:36 must be in fear of your *G*
25:38 *G*, who brought you out of
25:38 to prove myself your *G*
25:43 must be in fear of your *G*
25:55 my slaves . . . Jehovah your *G*
26:1 for I am Jehovah your *G*
26:12 and prove myself your *G*, and
26:13 *G*, who brought you out of
26:44 for I am Jehovah their *G*
26:45 prove myself their *G*
Nu 6:7 Naziriteship to his *G* is upon
10:9 remembered before . . . your *G*
10:10 for you before your *G*
10:10 I am Jehovah your *G*
12:13 O *G*, please! Heal her, please!
15:40 prove to be holy to your *G*
15:41 *G*, who have brought you out
15:41 to prove myself your *G*. I am
15:41 I am Jehovah your *G*
16:9 *G* of Israel has separated you
16:22, 22 O *G*, the *G* of the spirits
21:5 speaking against *G* and Moses
22:9 Then *G* came to Balaam and said
22:10 Balaam said to the true *G*
22:12 *G* said to Balaam: You must
22:18 the order of Jehovah my *G*
22:20 *G* came to Balaam by night
22:22 the anger of *G* began to blaze
22:38 word that *G* will place in
23:4 *G* got in touch with Balaam
23:8 whom *G* has not execrated
23:19 *G* is not a man that he
23:21 Jehovah his *G* is with him
23:22 *G* is bringing them out of
Nu 23:23 What has *G* worked out!
23:27 in the eyes of the true *G* so
24:2 spirit of *G* came to be upon
24:4 one hearing the sayings of *G*
24:8 *G* is bringing him out of
24:16 one hearing the sayings of *G*
24:23 survive when *G* causes it
25:13 no rivalry toward his *G* and
27:16 *G* of the spirits of all sorts
De 1:6 Jehovah our *G* spoke to us in
1:10 your *G* has multiplied you
1:11 the *G* of your forefathers
1:17 for the judgment belongs to *G*
1:19 Jehovah our *G* had commanded
1:20 Jehovah our *G* is giving to us
1:21 Jehovah your *G* has abandoned
1:21 the *G* of your forefathers has
1:25 land that Jehovah our *G* is
1:26 the order of Jehovah your *G*
1:30 *G* is the one going before you
1:31 Jehovah your *G* carried you
1:32 faith in Jehovah your *G*
1:41 Jehovah our *G* has commanded
2:7 *G* has blessed you in every deed
2:7 your *G* has been with you
2:29 the land that Jehovah our *G*
2:30 *G* had let his spirit become
2:33 *G* abandoned him to us, so
2:36 *G* abandoned them all to us
2:37 our *G* had given command
3:3 *G* gave into our hand also Og
3:18 *G* has given you this land to
3:20 Jehovah your *G* is giving
3:21 *G* has done to these two kings
3:22 *G* is the One fighting for you
3:24 who is a *g* in the heavens or
4:1 the land that Jehovah the *G* of
4:2 the commandments of . . . *G*
4:3 *G* annihilated from your midst
4:4 cleaving to Jehovah your *G* are
4:5 Jehovah my *G* has commanded me
4:7 the way Jehovah our *G* is in
4:10 stood before Jehovah your *G*
4:19 *G* has apportioned to all the
4:21 land that Jehovah your *G* is
4:23 the covenant of Jehovah your *G*
4:23 Jehovah your *G* has commanded
4:24 your *G* is a consuming fire
4:24 *G* exacting exclusive devotion
4:25 in the eyes of Jehovah your *G*
4:29 look for Jehovah your *G* from
4:30 return to Jehovah your *G* and
4:31, 31 your *G* is a merciful *G*
4:32 the day that *G* created man on
4:33 heard the voice of *G* speaking
4:34 did *G* attempt to come to take
4:34 *G* has done for you in Egypt
4:35 Jehovah is the true *G*
4:39 Jehovah is the true *G* in
4:40 Jehovah your *G* is giving you
5:2 our *G* concluded a covenant
5:6 I am Jehovah your *G*, who
5:9, 9 *G* am a *G* exacting exclusive
5:11 your *G* in a worthless way
5:12 Jehovah your *G* commanded you
5:14 a sabbath to Jehovah your *G*
5:15 *G* proceeded to bring you out
5:15 *G* commanded you to carry on
5:16 your *G* has commanded you; in
5:16 Jehovah your *G* is giving you
5:24 our *G* has shown us his glory
5:24 *G* may speak with man and he
5:25 the voice of Jehovah our *G*
5:26 the voice of the living *G*
5:27 Jehovah our *G* will say
5:27 our *G* will speak to you, and
5:32 your *G* has commanded you
5:33 your *G* has commanded to teach you
6:1 *G* has commanded to teach you
6:2 fear Jehovah your *G* so as to
6:3 the *G* of your forefathers
6:4 Jehovah our *G* is one Jehovah
6:5 you must love Jehovah your *G*
6:10 *G* will bring you into the
6:13 Jehovah your *G* you should fear
6:15 Jehovah your *G* in your midst
6:15 *G* exacting exclusive devotion
6:15 the anger of Jehovah your *G*
6:16 put Jehovah your *G* to the test
6:17 the commandments of . . . *G*
6:20 Jehovah our *G* has commanded
6:24 to fear Jehovah our *G* for our
6:25 before Jehovah our *G*, just as
7:1 *G* at last brings you into the

De 7:2 *G* will certainly abandon them
7:6 holy people to Jehovah your *G*
7:6 you Jehovah your *G* has chosen
7:9, 9 Jehovah your *G* is the true *G*
7:9 the faithful *G*, keeping
7:12 *G* must keep toward you the
7:16 Jehovah your *G* is giving to
7:18 *G* did to Pharaoh and all Egypt
7:19 Jehovah your *G* brought you out
7:19 *G* will do to all the peoples
7:20 *G* will also send the feeling
7:21 your *G* is in your midst
7:21 great and fear-inspiring *G*
7:22 *G* will certainly push these
7:23 *G* will indeed abandon them to
7:25 detestable to Jehovah your *G*
8:2 *G* made you walk these forty
8:5 your *G* was correcting you
8:6 commandments of . . . your *G*
8:7 *G* is bringing you into a good
8:10 bless Jehovah your *G* for the
8:11 not forget Jehovah your *G* so
8:14 indeed forget Jehovah your *G*
8:18 must remember Jehovah your *G*
8:19 forget Jehovah your *G*
8:20 the voice of Jehovah your *G*
9:3 your *G* is crossing before you
9:4 *G* pushes them away from
9:5 *G* is driving them away from
9:6 *G* is giving you this good land
9:7 have provoked Jehovah your *G*
9:16 sinned against Jehovah your *G*
9:23 the order of Jehovah your *G*
10:9 Jehovah your *G* had said to him
10:12 Jehovah your *G* asking of you
10:12 fear Jehovah your *G*, so as to
10:12 serve Jehovah your *G* with
10:14 to Jehovah your *G* belong the
10:17 For Jehovah your *G* is the
10:17 the *G* of gods and the Lord
10:17 the *G* great, mighty and
10:20 your *G* you should fear
10:21 he is your *G*, who has done
10:22 *G* has constituted you like
11:1 you must love Jehovah your *G*
11:2 discipline of Jehovah your *G*
11:12 Jehovah your *G* is caring for
11:12 The eyes of Jehovah your *G*
11:13 so as to love Jehovah your *G*
11:22 to love Jehovah your *G*, to
11:25 *G* will put before the face
11:27 commandments of . . . your *G*
11:28 the commandments of . . . *G*
11:29 *G* brings you into the land
11:31 land that Jehovah your *G* is
12:1 the *G* of your forefathers
12:4 that way to Jehovah your *G*
12:5 Jehovah your *G* will choose
12:7 eat before Jehovah your *G*
12:7 Jehovah your *G* has blessed you
12:9 Jehovah your *G* is giving you
12:10 *G* is giving you as a
12:11 *G* will choose to have his
12:12 rejoice before Jehovah your *G*
12:15 blessing of Jehovah your *G*
12:18 before Jehovah your *G* you
12:18 Jehovah your *G* will choose
12:18 rejoice before Jehovah your *G*
12:20 *G* will widen out your
12:21 *G* will choose to put his
12:27 the altar of Jehovah your *G*
12:27 the altar of Jehovah your *G*
12:28 in the eyes of Jehovah your *G*
12:29 *G* will cut off from before
12:31 that way to Jehovah your *G*
13:3 your *G* is testing you to know
13:3 you are loving Jehovah your *G*
13:4 After Jehovah your *G* you
13:5 revolt against Jehovah your *G*
13:5 *G* has commanded you to walk
13:10 away from Jehovah your *G*
13:12 Jehovah your *G* is giving you
13:16 offering to Jehovah your *G*
13:18 the voice of Jehovah your *G*
13:18 in the eyes of Jehovah your *G*
14:1 Sons you are of Jehovah your *G*
14:2 holy people to Jehovah your *G*
14:21 holy people to Jehovah your *G*
14:23 before Jehovah your *G*, in the
14:23 fear Jehovah your *G* always
14:24 *G* will choose to place his
14:24 your *G* will bless you
14:25 Jehovah your *G* will choose
14:26 before Jehovah your *G* and

De 14:29 *G* may bless you in every
15:4 the land that Jehovah your *G*
15:5 the voice of Jehovah your *G*
15:6 *G* will indeed bless you just
15:7 land that Jehovah your *G* is
15:10 *G* will bless you in every
15:14 your *G* has blessed you
15:15 *G* proceeded to redeem you
15:18 *G* has blessed you in
15:19 sanctify to Jehovah your *G*
15:20 Before Jehovah your *G* you
15:21 not sacrifice it to . . . *G*
16:1 the passover to Jehovah your *G*
16:1 *G* brought you out of Egypt by
16:2 the passover to Jehovah your *G*
16:5 Jehovah your *G* is giving you
16:6 *G* will choose to have his
16:7 the place that Jehovah your *G*
16:8 assembly to Jehovah your *G*
16:10 festival of weeks to . . . *G*
16:10 Jehovah your *G* may bless you
16:11 rejoice before Jehovah your *G*
16:11 *G* will choose to have his
16:15 festival to Jehovah your *G*
16:15 *G* will bless you in all your
16:16 appear before Jehovah your *G*
16:17 blessing of Jehovah your *G*
16:18 Jehovah your *G* is giving
16:20 Jehovah your *G* is giving you
16:21 the altar of Jehovah your *G*
16:22 a thing Jehovah your *G* hates
17:1 sacrifice to Jehovah your *G* a
17:1 detestable to Jehovah your *G*
17:2 Jehovah your *G* is giving you
17:2 in the eyes of Jehovah your *G*
17:8 Jehovah your *G* will choose
17:12 to minister there to . . . *G*
17:14 the land that Jehovah your *G*
17:15 Jehovah your *G* will choose
17:19 learn to fear Jehovah his *G*
18:5 Jehovah your *G* has chosen out
18:7 in the name of Jehovah his *G*
18:9 the land that Jehovah your *G*
18:12 *G* is driving them away from
18:13 faultless with . . . your *G*
18:14 *G* has not given you anything
18:15 *G* will raise up for you
18:16 you asked of Jehovah your *G*
18:16 the voice of Jehovah my *G*
19:1 *G* cuts off the nations whose
19:1 Jehovah your *G* is giving you
19:2 land that . . . *G* is giving
19:3 land that Jehovah your *G*
19:8 *G* widens out your territory
19:9 to love Jehovah your *G* and
19:10 land that . . . *G* is giving
19:14 the land that . . . *G* is giving
20:1 Jehovah your *G* is with you
20:4 *G* is marching with you to
20:13 *G* also will certainly give
20:14 enemies . . . *G* has given to
20:16 cities . . . *G* is giving you
20:17 Jehovah your *G* has commanded
20:18 sin against Jehovah your *G*
21:1 the ground . . . *G* is giving
21:5 *G* has chosen to minister to
21:10 *G* has given them into your
21:23 accursed of *G* is the one hung
21:23 soil . . . *G* is giving you
22:5 detestable to Jehovah your *G*
23:5 *G* did not want to listen to
23:5 *G* in your behalf changed the
23:5 Jehovah your *G* loved you
23:14 *G* is walking about within
23:18 the house of Jehovah your *G*
23:18 detestable to Jehovah your *G*
23:20 *G* may bless you in every
23:21 a vow to Jehovah your *G*
23:21 *G* will without fail require
23:23 vowed to Jehovah your *G* as a
24:4 *G* is giving you as an
24:9 *G* did to Miriam in the way
24:13 for you before Jehovah your *G*
24:18 *G* proceeded to redeem you
24:19 *G* may bless you in every
25:15 soil . . . your *G* is giving you
25:16 detestable to Jehovah your *G*
25:18 and he did not fear *G*
25:19 *G* has given you rest from
25:19 land . . . *G* is giving you
26:1 land that . . . *G* is giving you
26:2 the land . . . *G* is giving you
26:2 *G* will choose to have his
26:3 report today to Jehovah your *G*

De 26:4 the altar of Jehovah your *G*
26:5 say before Jehovah your *G*
26:7 cry out to Jehovah the *G* of
26:10 before Jehovah your *G*
26:10 bow down before . . . *G*
26:11 the good . . . *G* has given you
26:13 say before Jehovah your *G*
26:14 the voice of Jehovah my *G*
26:16 *G* is commanding you to carry
26:17 he will become your *G* while
26:19 people holy to Jehovah your *G*
27:2 land that . . . *G* is giving you
27:3 the land . . . *G* is giving you
27:3 the *G* of your forefathers has
27:5 altar there to Jehovah your *G*
27:6 the altar of Jehovah your *G*
27:6 offerings to Jehovah your *G*
27:7 rejoice before Jehovah your *G*
27:9 the people of Jehovah your *G*
27:10 the voice of Jehovah your *G*
28:1 listen to . . . Jehovah your *G*
28:1 *G* also will certainly put you
28:2 the voice of Jehovah your *G*
28:8 land that . . . *G* is giving you
28:9 the commandments of . . . *G*
28:13 commandments of . . . your *G*
28:15 the voice of Jehovah your *G*
28:45 the voice of Jehovah your *G*
28:47 serve Jehovah your *G* with
28:52 land . . . *G* has given you
28:53 Jehovah your *G* has given you
28:58 name, even Jehovah, your *G*
28:62 the voice of Jehovah your *G*
29:6 know that I am Jehovah your *G*
29:10 stationed today before . . . *G*
29:12 Jehovah your *G* and his oath
29:12 *G* is concluding with you
29:13 prove himself your *G*, just
29:15 today before Jehovah our *G*
29:18 away from Jehovah our *G* to
29:25 the *G* of their forefathers
29:29 belong to Jehovah our *G*
30:1 your *G* has dispersed you
30:2 returned to Jehovah your *G*
30:3 your *G* must also bring back
30:3 your *G* has scattered you
30:4 *G* will collect you and from
30:5 your *G* will indeed bring you
30:6 *G* will have to circumcise
30:6 love Jehovah your *G* with all
30:7 *G* will certainly put all
30:9 *G* will indeed make you have
30:10 your *G* so as to keep his
30:10 return to Jehovah your *G*
30:16 commandments of . . . your *G*
30:16 love Jehovah your *G*, to walk
30:16 *G* must bless you in the land
30:20 loving Jehovah your *G*, by
31:3 *G* is the one crossing before
31:6 *G* is the one marching with
31:11 your *G* in the place that he
31:12 fear Jehovah your *G* and take
31:13 learn to fear Jehovah your *G*
31:17 our *G* is not in our midst
31:26 the ark . . . of Jehovah your *G*
32:3 attribute greatness to our *G*
32:4 A *G* of faithfulness, with
32:12 no foreign *g* along with him
32:15 he forsook *G*, who made him
32:17 sacrificing . . . not to *G*
32:18 to leave *G* out of memory
32:21 jealousy with what is no *g*
33:1 Moses the man of the true *G*
33:26 is none like the true *G* of
33:27 is the *G* of ancient time
Jos 1:9 for Jehovah your *G* is with
1:11 Jehovah your *G* is giving you
1:13 your *G* is giving you rest and
1:15 that Jehovah your *G* is giving
1:17 *G* prove to be with you just
2:11, 11 Jehovah your *G* is *G* in the
3:3 covenant of Jehovah your *G*
3:9 the words of Jehovah your *G*
3:10 a living *G* is in your midst
4:5 the ark of Jehovah your *G*
4:23 *G* dried up the waters of the
4:23 *G* had done to the Red Sea
4:24 fear Jehovah your *G* always
7:13 Jehovah the *G* of Israel has
7:19 glory to Jehovah the *G* of
7:20 sinned against Jehovah the *G*
8:7 your *G* will certainly give it
8:30 an altar to Jehovah the *G* of
9:9 the name of Jehovah your *G*

Jos 9:18 by Jehovah the *G* of Israel
9:19 by Jehovah the *G* of Israel
9:23 house of my *G* will never be
9:24 Jehovah your *G* had commanded
10:19 *G* has given them into your
10:40 Jehovah the *G* of Israel had
10:42 Jehovah the *G* of Israel who
13:14 Jehovah the *G* of Israel
13:33 Jehovah the *G* of Israel is
14:6 Moses the man of the true *G*
14:8 followed Jehovah my *G* fully
14:9 followed Jehovah my *G* fully
14:14 Jehovah the *G* of Israel
18:3 the *G* of your forefathers
18:6 for you before Jehovah our *G*
22:3 commandment of . . . your *G*
22:4 *G* has given your brothers
22:5 by loving Jehovah your *G* and
22:16 against the *G* of Israel in
22:19 the altar of Jehovah our *G*
22:22 *G*, Jehovah, Divine One
22:22 *G*, Jehovah, he is knowing
22:24 Jehovah the *G* of Israel
22:29 the altar of Jehovah our *G*
22:33 Israel proceeded to bless *G*
22:34 Jehovah is the true *G*
23:3 all that Jehovah your *G* did
23:3 Jehovah your *G* was the one
23:5 Jehovah your *G* was the one
23:5 your *G* had promised you
23:8 it is to Jehovah your *G* that
23:10 your *G* is the one who is
23:11 by loving Jehovah your *G*
23:13 *G* will not continue to
23:13 ground . . . *G* has given you
23:14 words that Jehovah your *G*
23:15 word that Jehovah your *G*
23:15 ground . . . *G* has given you
23:16 covenant of . . . your *G*
24:1 stand before the true *G*
24:2 This is what Jehovah the *G*
24:17 our *G* who brought us and
24:18 because he is our *G*
24:19 for he is a holy *G*; he is
24:19 he is a *G* exacting
24:23 to Jehovah the *G* of Israel
24:24 our *G* we shall serve, and
24:27 you may not deny your *G*
Jg 1:7 so *G* has repaid me
2:12 they abandoned Jehovah the *G*
3:7 forgetful of Jehovah their *G*
3:20 A word of *G* I have for you
4:6 the *G* of Israel given the
4:23 *G* subdued Jabin the king of
5:3 melody to Jehovah, Israel's *G*
5:5 the face of Jehovah, Israel's *G*
6:8 the *G* of Israel has said, It
6:10 I am Jehovah your *G*. You must
6:20 angel of the true *G* now
6:26 an altar to Jehovah your *G* at
6:31 If he is *G*, let him make a
6:36 said to the true *G*: If you
6:39 said to the true *G*: Do not
6:40 *G* did that way on that night
7:14 The true *G* has given Midian
8:3 *G* gave Midian's princes Oreb
8:33 Baal-berith as their *g*
8:34 their *G*, who had delivered
9:7 and let *G* listen to you
9:9 they glorify *G* and men, and
9:13 makes *G* and men rejoice, and
9:23 *G* let develop a bad spirit
9:27 house of their *g* and ate and
9:56 *G* made the evil of Abimelech
9:57 *G* made come back upon their
10:10 have left our *G* and we serve
11:21 the *G* of Israel gave Sihon
11:23 the *G* of Israel it was that
11:24 *g* causes you to dispossess
11:24 our *G* has dispossessed from
13:5 a Nazirite of *G* is what the
13:6 man of the true *G* that came
13:6 the angel of the true *G*
13:7 a Nazirite of *G* is what the
13:8 The man of the true *G* that
13:9 *G* listened to the voice of
13:9 the angel of the true *G* came
13:22 it is *G* that we have seen
15:19 *G* split open a mortar-shaped
16:17 I am a Nazirite of *G* from
16:23 sacrifice to Dagon their *g*
16:23 Our *g* has given into our hand
16:24 gave way to praising their *g*
16:24 our *g* has given into our hand

Jg 16:28 you the true *G*, and let me
18:5 Inquire, please, of *G* that we
18:10 *G* has given it into your
18:31 house of the true *G* continued
20:2 of the people of the true *G*
20:18 to Bethel and to inquire of *G*
20:27 the ark . . . of the true *G*
21:2 before the true *G* until the
21:3 O Jehovah the *G* of Israel
Ru 1:16, 16 and your *G* my *G*
2:12 from Jehovah the *G* of Israel
1Sa 1:17 may the *G* of Israel grant
2:2 there is no rock like our *G*
2:3 a *G* of knowledge Jehovah is
2:25 *G* will arbitrate for him
2:27 a man of *G* proceeded to come
2:30 of Jehovah the *G* of Israel
3:3 And the lamp of *G* was not yet
3:3 where the ark of *G* was
3:13 are calling down evil upon *G*
3:17 May *G* do so to you and so
4:4 the ark . . . of the true *G*
4:7 *G* has come into the camp
4:8 the hand of this majestic *G*
4:8 the *G* that was the smiter of
4:11 ark of *G* itself was captured
4:13 over the ark of the true *G*
4:17 ark of the true *G* has been
4:18 the ark of the true *G*
4:19 the ark of the true *G* was
4:22 ark of the true *G* has been
5:1 took the ark of the true *G* and
5:2 take the ark of the true *G* and
5:7 ark of the *G* of Israel dwell
5:7 and against Dagon our *g*
5:8 to the ark of the *G* of Israel
5:8 let the ark of the *G* of Israel
5:8 the ark of the *G* of Israel
5:10 ark of the true *G* to Ekron
5:10 the ark of the true *G* came
5:10 ark of the *G* of Israel around
5:11 ark of the *G* of Israel away
5:11 hand of the true *G* had been
6:3 ark of the *G* of Israel away
6:5 give glory to the *G* of Israel
6:5 off you and your *g* and your
6:20 before Jehovah this holy *G*
7:8 to Jehovah our *G* for aid
9:6 is a man of *G* in this city
9:7 to the man of the true *G*
9:8 to the man of the true *G*
9:9 talked on his going to seek *G*
9:10 the man of the true *G* was
9:27 let you hear the word of *G*
10:3 up to the true *G* at Bethel
10:5 to the hill of the true *G*
10:7 the true *G* is with you
10:9 *G* began changing the heart of
10:10 the spirit of *G* became
10:18 Jehovah the *G* of Israel has
10:19 you have rejected your *G*
10:26 whose heart *G* had touched
11:6 spirit of *G* became operative
12:9 forgetting Jehovah their *G*
12:12 your *G* being your King
12:14 followers of Jehovah your *G*
12:19 to Jehovah your *G*, as we do
13:13 commandment of . . . your *G*
14:15 into a trembling from *G*
14:18 bring the ark of the true *G*
14:18 ark of the true *G* proved to
14:36 approach here to the true *G*
14:37 Saul began to inquire of *G*
14:41 O *G* of Israel, do give
14:44 Saul said: Thus may *G* do
14:45 was with *G* that he worked
15:15 sacrificing to . . . your *G*
15:21 to Jehovah your *G* in Gilgal
15:30 myself to Jehovah your *G*
16:7 is the way *G* sees, because
17:26 battle lines of the living *G*
17:36 battle lines of the living *G*
17:45 the *G* of the battle lines of
17:46 a *G* belonging to Israel
19:20 spirit of *G* came to be upon
19:23 spirit of *G* came to be upon
20:12 *G* of Israel be a witness
22:3 until I know what *G* will do
22:13 an inquiry of *G* for him
22:15 started to inquire of *G* for
23:7 *G* has sold him into my hand
23:10 *G* of Israel, your servant
23:11 *G* of Israel, tell your
23:14 *G* did not give him into his

1Sa 23:16 his hand in regard to *G*
25:22 *G* do to the enemies of
25:29 of life with Jehovah your *G*
25:32 Blessed be Jehovah the *G* of
25:34 *G* of Israel is living, who
26:8 *G* has today surrendered your
28:13 A *g* I saw coming up out of
28:15 *G* himself has departed from
29:9 like an angel of *G*
30:6 by Jehovah his *G*
30:15 swear to me by *G* that you
2Sa 2:27 As the true *G* is living, if
3:9 So may *G* do to Abner and so
3:35 So may *G* do to me and so
5:10 Jehovah the *G* of armies was
6:2 ark of the true *G*, where a
6:3 ark of the true *G* ride upon
6:4 with the ark of the true *G*
6:6 ark of the true *G* and grabbed
6:7 *G* struck him down there for
6:7 by the ark of the true *G*
6:12 of the ark of the true *G*
6:12 bring the ark of the true *G*
7:2 ark of the true *G* is dwelling
7:22 no *G* except you among all of
7:23 *G* went to redeem to himself
7:24 Jehovah, have become their *G*
7:25 *G*, the word that you have
7:26 Jehovah . . . is *G* over Israel
7:27 Jehovah . . . the *G* of Israel
7:28 Jehovah, you are the true *G*
9:3 the loving-kindness of *G*
10:12 of the cities of our *G*
12:7 *G* of Israel has said, I
12:16 seek the true *G* in behalf
14:11 remember Jehovah your *G*
14:13 against the people of *G*
14:14 *G* will not take away a soul
14:16 the inheritance given by *G*
14:17 like an angel of the true *G*
14:17 *G* himself prove to be with
14:20 angel of the true *G* so as
15:24 the covenant of the true *G*
15:24 set the ark of the true *G*
15:25 Take the ark of the true *G*
15:29 took the ark of the true *G*
15:32 used to bow down to *G*
16:23 the word of the true *G*
18:28 Blessed be Jehovah your *G*
19:13 So may *G* do to me and so
19:27 is as an angel of the true *G*
21:14 *G* let himself be entreated
22:3 My *G* is my rock. I shall
22:7 And to my *G* I kept calling
22:22 wickedly departed from my *G*
22:30 By my *G* I can climb a wall
22:31 true *G*, perfect is his way
22:32 who is a *G* besides Jehovah
22:32 who is a rock besides our *G*?
22:33 *G* is my strong fortress
22:47 the *G* of the rock of my
22:48 *G* is the Giver of acts of
23:1 anointed of the *G* of Jacob
23:3 The *G* of Israel said, To me
23:3 Ruling in the fear of *G*
23:5 household like that with *G*
24:3 *G* even add to the people a
24:23 your *G* show pleasure in you
24:24 offer up to Jehovah my *G*
1Ki 1:17 swore by Jehovah your *G*
1:30 Jehovah the *G* of Israel
1:36 *G* of my lord the king say
1:47 May your *G* make Solomon's
1:48 Blessed be Jehovah the *G* of
2:3 obligation to Jehovah your *G*
2:23 So may *G* do to me, and so
3:5 and *G* proceeded to say
3:7 *G*, you yourself have made
3:11 And *G* went on to say to him
3:28 the wisdom of *G* was within
4:29 *G* continued giving Solomon
5:3 a house to the name of . . . *G*
5:4 my *G* has given me rest
5:5 a house to the name of . . . *G*
8:15 Jehovah the *G* of Israel, who
8:17 name of Jehovah the *G* of
8:20 to the name of Jehovah the *G*
8:23 Jehovah the *G* of Israel
8:23 there is no *G* like you in
8:25 O Jehovah the *G* of Israel
8:26 *G* of Israel, let your
8:27 *G* truly dwell upon the earth
8:28 for favor, O Jehovah my *G*
8:57 *G* prove to be with us just

1Ki 8:59 near to Jehovah our *G* by day
8:60 that Jehovah is the true *G*
8:61 complete with Jehovah our *G*
8:65 before Jehovah our *G* seven
9:9 they left Jehovah their *G*
10:9 May Jehovah your *G* come to
10:24 *G* had put in his heart
11:4 complete with Jehovah his *G*
11:9 from Jehovah the *G* of Israel
11:23 *G* proceeded to raise up to
11:31 Jehovah the *G* of Israel has
11:33 to Chemosh the *g* of Moab
11:33 the *g* of the sons of Ammon
12:22 word of the true *G* came to
12:22 man of the true *G*, saying
12:28 Here is your *G*, O Israel
13:1 a man of *G* that had come
13:4 the man of the true *G* that
13:5 the man of the true *G* had
13:6 to the man of the true *G*
13:6 the face of Jehovah your *G*
13:6 man of the true *G* softened
13:7 say to the man of the true *G*
13:8 man of the true *G* said to
13:11 the man of the true *G* had
13:12 man of the true *G* that had
13:14 the man of the true *G* and
13:14 the man of the true *G* who
13:21 the man of the true *G* that
13:21 Jehovah your *G* commanded
13:26 the man of the true *G* that
13:29 of the man of the true *G*
13:31 man of the true *G* is buried
14:7 the *G* of Israel has said
14:9 made for yourself another *g*
14:13 good toward Jehovah the *G*
15:3 Jehovah his *G*, like the
15:4 his *G* gave him a lamp in
15:30 Jehovah the *G* of Israel
16:13 offending . . . the *G* of Israel
16:26 Jehovah the *G* of Israel
16:33 Jehovah the *G* of Israel
17:1 as Jehovah the *G* of Israel
17:12 As Jehovah your *G* is living
17:14 the *G* of Israel has said
17:18 O man of the true *G*
17:20 O Jehovah my *G*, is it also
17:21 my *G*, please, cause the
17:24 you are a man of *G* and that
18:10 As Jehovah your *G* is living
18:21 If Jehovah is the true *G*
18:24 upon the name of your *g*
18:24 true *G* that answers by fire
18:24 by fire is the true *G*
18:25 upon the name of your *g*
18:27 for he is a *g;* for he must
18:36 the *G* of Abraham, Isaac and
18:36 you are *G* in Israel and I
18:37 you, Jehovah, are the true *G*
18:39 Jehovah is the true *G!*
18:39 Jehovah is the true *G!*
19:8 the mountain of the true *G*
19:10 for Jehovah the *G* of armies
19:14 absolutely jealous for . . . *G*
20:23, 23 *G* is a *G* of mountains
20:28 Then the man of the true *G*
20:28 Jehovah is a *G* of mountains
20:28 he is not a *G* of low plains
21:10 have cursed *G* and the king
21:13 has cursed *G* and the king
22:53 offending Jehovah the *G* of
2Ki 1:2 Baal-zebub the *g* of Ekron
1:3 no *G* at all in Israel that
1:3 Baal-zebub the *g* of Ekron
1:6 Is it because there is no *G* at
1:6 Baal-zebub the *g* of Ekron
1:9 Man of the true *G*, the king
1:10 if I am a man of *G*, let fire
1:11 Man of the true *G*, this is
1:12 If I am a man of the true *G*
1:12 fire of *G* came descending
1:13 Man of the true *G*, please
1:16 Baal-zebub the *g* of Ekron
1:16 no *G* at all in Israel of
2:14 is Jehovah the *G* of Elijah
4:7 told the man of the true *G*
4:9 a holy man of *G* that is
4:16 man of the true *G!* Do not
4:21 the man of the true *G* and
4:22 man of the true *G* and return
4:25 man of the true *G* at Mount
4:25 man of the true *G* saw her
4:27 man of the true *G* at the
4:27 the man of the true *G* said
2Ki 4:40 O man of the true *G*
4:42 to the man of the true *G*
5:7 Am I *G*, to put to death and
5:8 Elisha the man of the true *G*
5:11 the name of Jehovah his *G*
5:14 the man of the true *G*
5:15 to the man of the true *G*
5:15 *G* anywhere in the earth but
5:20 Elisha the man of the true *G*
6:6 the man of the true *G* said
6:9 the man of the true *G* sent
6:10 man of the true *G* had said
6:15 man of the true *G* rose
6:31 So may *G* do to me, and so
7:2 the man of the true *G* and
7:17 man of the true *G* had spoken
7:18 man of the true *G* had spoken
7:19 man of the true *G* and said
8:2 word of the man of the true *G*
8:4 the man of the true *G*
8:7 man of the true *G* has come
8:8 meet the man of the true *G*
8:11 man of the true *G* gave way
9:6 Jehovah the *G* of Israel has
10:31 Jehovah the *G* of Israel
13:19 the man of the true *G* grew
14:25 Jehovah the *G* of Israel who
16:2 eyes of Jehovah his *G* like
17:7 against Jehovah their *G*
17:9 toward Jehovah their *G* and
17:14 faith in Jehovah their *G*
17:16 of Jehovah their *G*
17:19 Jehovah their *G*, but they
17:26 religion of the *G* of the
17:26 religion of the *G* of the
17:27 the *G* of the land
17:29 to be a maker of its own *g*
17:39 Jehovah your *G* that you
18:5 In Jehovah the *G* of Israel
18:12 the voice of Jehovah their *G*
18:22 our *G* in whom we have put
19:4 Jehovah your *G* will hear all
19:4 sent to taunt the living *G*
19:4 Jehovah your *G* has heard
19:10 *G* in whom you are trusting
19:15 O Jehovah the *G* of Israel
19:15 *G* of all the kingdoms of
19:16 sent to taunt the living *G*
19:19 Jehovah our *G*, save us
19:19 you, O Jehovah, are *G* alone
19:20 Jehovah the *G* of Israel has
19:37 the house of Nisroch his *g*
20:5 Jehovah the *G* of David your
21:12 Jehovah the *G* of Israel has
21:22 he left Jehovah the *G* of
22:15 Jehovah the *G* of Israel has
22:18 Jehovah the *G* of Israel has
23:16 the man of the true *G* had
23:17 man of the true *G* that came
23:21 passover to Jehovah your *G*
1Ch 4:10 call upon the *G* of Israel
4:10 *G* brought to pass what he
5:20 to *G* that they called for aid
5:22 on the part of the true *G*
5:25 the *G* of their forefathers
5:25 whom *G* had annihilated from
5:26 *G* of Israel stirred up the
6:48 of the house of the true *G*
6:49 the servant of the true *G* had
9:11 of the house of the true *G*
9:13 of the house of the true *G*
9:26 of the house of the true *G*
9:27 the house of the true *G*
10:10 in the house of their *g*, and
11:2 Jehovah your *G* proceeded to
11:19 on my part, as regards my *G*
12:17 let the *G* of our forefathers
12:18 For your *G* has helped you
12:22 like the camp of *G*
13:2 acceptable with . . . our *G*
13:3 let us bring the ark of our *G*
13:5 bring the ark of the true *G*
13:6 ark of the true *G*, Jehovah
13:7 ark of the true *G* ride upon a
13:8 celebrating before the true *G*
13:10 and he died there before *G*
13:12 became afraid of the true *G*
13:12 bring the ark of the true *G*
13:14 the ark of the true *G* kept
14:10 David began to inquire of *G*
14:11 *G* has broken through my
14:14 David inquired again of *G*
14:14 the true *G* now said to him
14:15 *G* will have gone out before
1Ch 14:16 David did just as the true *G*
15:1 for the ark of the true *G* and
15:2 carry the ark of the true *G*
15:12 of Jehovah the *G* of Israel
15:13 Jehovah our *G* broke through
15:14 of Jehovah the *G* of Israel
15:15 carry the ark of the true *G*
15:24 before the ark of the true *G*
15:26 true *G* helped the Levites
16:1 brought the ark of the true *G*
16:1 sacrifices before the true *G*
16:4 Jehovah the *G* of Israel
16:6 of the covenant of the true *G*
16:14 He is Jehovah our *G;* in all
16:35 O *G* of our salvation
16:36 Jehovah the *G* of Israel
16:42 of the song of the true *G*
17:2 for the true *G* is with you
17:3 the word of *G* came to Nathan
17:16 Who am I, O Jehovah *G*, and
17:17 little in your eyes, O *G*
17:17 the ascendancy, O Jehovah *G*
17:20 there is no *G* except you in
17:21 the true *G* went to redeem
17:22 O Jehovah, became their *G*
17:24 of armies, the *G* of Israel
17:24 is *G* to Israel, and let the
17:25 *G*, have revealed to your
17:26 Jehovah, you are the true *G*
19:13 of the cities of our *G*
21:7 bad in the eyes of the true *G*
21:8 David said to the true *G*
21:15 the true *G* sent an angel to
21:17 to the true *G:* Was it not I
21:17 Jehovah my *G*, let your hand
21:30 to go before it to consult *G*
22:1 house of Jehovah the true *G*
22:2 the house of the true *G*
22:6 to Jehovah the *G* of Israel
22:7 to the name of Jehovah my *G*
22:11 the house of Jehovah your *G*
22:12 the law of Jehovah your *G*
22:18 Is not Jehovah your *G* with
22:19 inquire after Jehovah your *G*
22:19 of Jehovah the true *G*, to
22:19 holy utensils of the true *G*
23:14 Moses the man of the true *G*
23:25 Jehovah the *G* of Israel has
23:28 of the house of the true *G*
24:5 chiefs of the true *G* from
24:19 Jehovah the *G* of Israel had
25:5 in the things of the true *G*
25:5 the true *G* proceeded to give
25:6 of the house of the true *G*
26:5 for *G* had blessed him
26:20 of the house of the true *G*
26:32 every matter of the true *G*
28:2 and as the footstool of our *G*
28:3 true *G* himself said to me
28:4 Jehovah the *G* of Israel chose
28:8 in the ears of our *G*, take
28:8 Jehovah your *G*, in order that
28:9 know the *G* of your father
28:12 of the house of the true *G*
28:20, 20 Jehovah *G*, my *G*, is
28:21 of the house of the true *G*
29:1 the one whom *G* has chosen
29:1 castle is . . . for Jehovah *G*
29:2 for the house of my *G* the
29:3 in the house of my *G*
29:3 give it to the house of my *G*
29:7 of the house of the true *G*
29:10 the *G* of Israel our father
29:13 O our *G*, we are thanking
29:16 O Jehovah our *G*, all this
29:17 *G*, that you are an examiner
29:18 the *G* of Abraham, Isaac and
29:20 Bless, now, Jehovah your *G*
29:20 the *G* of their forefathers
2Ch 1:1 Jehovah his *G* was with him
1:3 tent of meeting of the true *G*
1:4 ark of the true *G* David had
1:7 *G* appeared to Solomon and
1:8 Solomon said to *G:* You are
1:9 O Jehovah *G*, let your promise
1:11 *G* said to Solomon: For the
2:4 to the name of Jehovah my *G*
2:4 seasons of Jehovah our *G*
2:5 our *G* is greater than all the
2:12 Blessed be . . . *G* of Israel
3:3 the house of the true *G*
4:11 on the house of the true *G*
4:19 at the house of the true *G*
5:1 of the house of the true *G*

2Ch 5:14 the house of the true *G*
6:4 be Jehovah the *G* of Israel
6:7 Jehovah the *G* of Israel
6:10 Jehovah the *G* of Israel
6:14 O Jehovah the *G* of Israel
6:14 there is no *G* like you in the
6:16 *G* of Israel, keep toward
6:17 *G* of Israel, let your
6:18 *G* truly dwell with mankind
6:19 Jehovah my *G*, by listening
6:40 *G*, please, let your eyes
6:41 Jehovah *G*, into your rest
6:41 O Jehovah *G*, be clothed with
6:42 Jehovah *G*, do not turn back
7:5 the house of the true *G*
7:22 left Jehovah the *G* of their
8:14 David the man of the true *G*
9:8 your *G* come to be blessed
9:8 as king for Jehovah your *G*
9:8 because your *G* loved Israel
9:23 true *G* had put in his heart
10:15 of affairs from the true *G*
11:2 the man of the true *G*
11:16 heart to seek Jehovah the *G*
11:16 sacrifice to Jehovah the *G*
13:5 *G* of Israel himself gave a
13:10 Jehovah is our *G*, and we
13:11 obligation to Jehovah our *G*
13:12 at the head the true *G* with
13:12 do not fight against . . . *G*
13:15 *G* himself defeated Jeroboam
13:16 *G* gave them into their hand
13:18 the *G* of their forefathers
14:2 in the eyes of Jehovah his *G*
14:4 the *G* of their forefathers
14:7 searched for Jehovah our *G*
14:11 call to Jehovah his *G* and
14:11 *G*, for upon you we do lean
14:11 Jehovah, you are our *G*
15:1 spirit of *G* came to be upon
15:3 had been without a true *G*
15:4 *G* of Israel and looked for
15:6 *G* himself kept them in
15:9 saw that Jehovah his *G* was
15:12 the *G* of their forefathers
15:13 search for Jehovah the *G* of
15:18 into the house of the true *G*
16:7 not lean upon Jehovah your *G*
17:4 *G* of his father that he
18:5 true *G* will give it into the
18:13 what my *G* will say, that is
18:31 *G* at once allured them away
19:3 to search for the true *G*
19:4 the *G* of their forefathers
19:7 with Jehovah our *G* there is
20:6 *G* of our forefathers, are you
20:6 are you not *G* in the heavens
20:7 *G* of ours, drive away the
20:12 *G*, will you not execute
20:19 praise Jehovah the *G* of
20:20 Put faith in Jehovah your *G*
20:29 dread of *G* came to be upon
20:30 *G* continued to give him
20:33 the *G* of their forefathers
21:10 the *G* of his forefathers
21:12 *G* of David your forefather
22:7 from *G* that the downfall of
22:12 house of the true *G* hidden
23:3 house of the true *G*, after
23:9 in the house of the true *G*
24:5 repair the house of your *G*
24:7 house of the true *G*, and even
24:9 the servant of the true *G*
24:13 house of the true *G* stand
24:16 the true *G* and His house
24:18 the *G* of their forefathers
24:20 true *G* has said, Why are
24:24 the *G* of their forefathers
24:27 of the house of the true *G*
25:7 man of the true *G* came to
25:8 *G* could cause you to stumble
25:8 power with *G* to help and to
25:9 to the man of the true *G*
25:9 the man of the true *G* said
25:16 *G* has resolved to bring you
25:20 the true *G* for the purpose
25:24 house of the true *G* with
26:5 search for *G* in the days of
26:5 fear of the true *G*
26:5 true *G* made him prosperous
26:7 true *G* continued to help him
26:16 against Jehovah his *G* and
26:18 you on the part of Jehovah *G*
27:6 ways before Jehovah his *G*

2Ch 28:5 *G* gave him into the hand of
28:6 the *G* of their forefathers
28:9 rage of Jehovah the *G* of
28:10 guilt against Jehovah your *G*
28:24 house of the true *G* and cut
28:24 house of the true *G*, and
28:25 the *G* of his forefathers
29:5 the *G* of your forefathers
29:6 in the eyes of Jehovah our *G*
29:7 place to the *G* of Israel
29:10 *G* of Israel, that his
29:36 true *G* had made preparation
30:1 to Jehovah the *G* of Israel
30:5 *G* of Israel at Jerusalem
30:6 *G* of Abraham, Isaac and
30:7 the *G* of their forefathers
30:8 serve Jehovah your *G*, that
30:9 Jehovah your *G* is gracious
30:12 hand of the true *G* proved
30:16 Moses the man of the true *G*
30:19 search for the true *G*
30:19 the *G* of his forefathers
30:22 the *G* of their forefathers
31:6 sanctified to Jehovah their *G*
31:13 of the house of the true *G*
31:14 offerings of the true *G*, to
31:20 before Jehovah his *G*
31:21 of the house of the true *G*
31:21 to search for his *G*, it
32:8 our *G* to help us and to fight
32:11 *G* himself will deliver us
32:14 *G* should be able to deliver
32:15 for no *g* of any nation or
32:15 own *G* deliver you out of my
32:16 against Jehovah the true *G*
32:17 *G* of Israel and to talk
32:17 *G* of Hezekiah will not
32:19 against the *G* of Jerusalem
32:21 house of his *g* and there
32:29 *G* gave him very many goods
32:31 *G* left him to put him to
33:7 in the house of the true *G*
33:7 *G* had said to David and to
33:12 the face of Jehovah his *G*
33:12 of the *G* of his forefathers
33:13 that Jehovah is the true *G*
33:16 serve Jehovah the *G* of
33:17 it was to Jehovah their *G*
33:18 and his prayer to his *G*
33:18 Jehovah the *G* of Israel
34:3 *G* of David his forefather
34:8 the house of Jehovah his *G*
34:9 brought to the house of *G*
34:23 Jehovah the *G* of Israel has
34:26 Jehovah the *G* of Israel has
34:27 because of *G* at your hearing
34:32 to the covenant of *G*
34:32 the *G* of their forefathers
34:33 to serve Jehovah their *G*
34:33 Jehovah the *G* of their
35:3 serve Jehovah your *G* and his
35:8 the house of the true *G* gave
35:21 *G* himself said that I
35:21 because of *G*, who is with
35:22 from the mouth of *G*
36:5 in the eyes of Jehovah his *G*
36:12 in the eyes of Jehovah his *G*
36:13 had made him swear by *G*
36:13 return to Jehovah the *G* of
36:15 Jehovah the *G* of their
36:16 messengers of the true *G*
36:18 the house of the true *G*
36:19 burn the house of the true *G*
36:23 Jehovah the *G* of the heavens
36:23 Jehovah his *G* be with him
Ezr 1:2 Jehovah the *G* of the heavens
1:3 his *G* prove to be with him
1:3 Jehovah the *G* of Israel
1:3 of Israel—he is the true *G*
1:4 for the house of the true *G*
1:5 spirit the true *G* had roused
1:7 then put in the house of his *g*
2:68 to the house of the true *G*
3:2 the altar of the *G* of Israel
3:2 Moses the man of the true *G*
3:8 to the house of the true *G* at
3:9 in the house of the true *G*
4:1 to Jehovah the *G* of Israel
4:2 we search for your *G* and to
4:3 in building a house to our *G*
4:3 to Jehovah the *G* of Israel
4:24 the work on the house of *G*
5:1 name of the *G* of Israel
5:2 to rebuild the house of *G*

Ezr 5:5 eye of their *G* proved to be
5:8 to the house of the great *G*
5:11 the *G* of the heavens and the
5:12 irritated the *G* of the
5:13 to rebuild this house of *G*
5:14 vessels of the house of *G*
5:15 let the house of *G* be rebuilt
5:16 foundations of the house of *G*
5:17 rebuild that house of *G* in
6:3 the house of *G* in Jerusalem
6:5 vessels of the house of *G* that
6:5 be deposited in the house of *G*
6:7 work on that house of *G* alone
6:7 rebuild that house of *G* upon
6:8 for rebuilding that house of *G*
6:9 burnt offerings to the *G* of
6:10 offerings to the *G* of the
6:12 may the *G* who has caused his
6:12 and destroy that house of *G*
6:14 the order of the *G* of Israel
6:16 this house of *G* with joy
6:17 this house of *G* a hundred
6:18 for the service of *G* which
6:21 for Jehovah the *G* of Israel
6:22, 22 true *G*, the *G* of Israel
7:6 Jehovah the *G* of Israel had
7:6 hand of Jehovah his *G* upon
7:9 good hand of his *G* upon him
7:12 law of the *G* of the heavens
7:14 the law of your *G* that is in
7:15 given to the *G* of Israel
7:16 to the house of their *G*
7:17 altar of the house of your *G*
7:18 will of your *G*, you men
7:19 of the house of your *G*
7:19 deliver in full before *G* at
7:20 house of your *G* that it
7:21 law of the *G* of the heavens
7:23 order of the *G* of the heavens
7:23 house of the *G* of the heavens
7:24 workers of this house of *G*
7:25 the wisdom of your *G* that is
7:25 knowing the laws of your *G*
7:26 the law of your *G* and the
7:27 the *G* of our forefathers
7:28 hand of Jehovah my *G* upon me
8:17 for the house of our *G*
8:18 good hand of our *G* upon us
8:21 our *G*, to seek from him the
8:22 The hand of our *G* is over all
8:23 and made request of our *G*
8:25 the house of our *G* that the
8:28 Jehovah the *G* of your
8:30 to the house of our *G*
8:31 hand of our *G* proved to be
8:33 in the house of our *G*
8:35 sacrifices to the *G* of Israel
8:36 and the house of the true *G*
9:4 the words of the *G* of Israel
9:5 my palms to Jehovah my *G*
9:6 O my *G*, I do feel ashamed and
9:6 O my *G*, for our errors
9:8 favor from Jehovah our *G* has
9:8 make our eyes shine, O our *G*
9:9 our *G* has not left us, but he
9:9 raise up the house of our *G*
9:10 what shall we say, O our *G*
9:13 our *G*, have underestimated
9:15 O Jehovah the *G* of Israel
10:1 the house of the true *G*
10:2 unfaithfully against our *G*
10:3 a covenant with our *G* to
10:3 at the commandment of our *G*
10:6 the house of the true *G* and
10:9 the house of the true *G*
10:11 the *G* of your forefathers
10:14 burning anger of our *G* from
Ne 1:4 before the *G* of the heavens
1:5 Jehovah the *G* of the heavens
1:5 the *G* great and fear-inspiring
2:4 prayed to the *G* of the heavens
2:8 the good hand of my *G* upon me
2:12 what my *G* was putting into
2:18 hand of my *G*, how it was
2:20 The *G* of the heavens is the
4:4 O our *G*, for we have become an
4:9 we prayed to our *G* and kept a
4:15 true *G* had frustrated their
4:20 Our *G* himself will fight for
5:9 Is it not in the fear of our *G*
5:13 the true *G* shake out from his
5:15 on account of the fear of *G*
5:19 Do remember for me, O my *G*
6:10 at the house of the true *G*

Ne 6:12 was not *G* that had sent him
6:14 Do remember, O my *G*, Tobiah
6:16 know that it was from our *G*
7:2 feared the true *G* more than
7:5 my *G* put it into my heart that
8:6 Ezra blessed Jehovah the true *G*
8:8 from the law of the true *G*
8:9 day is holy to Jehovah your *G*
8:16 the house of the true *G* and
8:18 book of the law of the true *G*
9:3 the law of Jehovah their *G*
9:3 bowing down to Jehovah their *G*
9:4 a loud voice to Jehovah their *G*
9:5 Rise, bless Jehovah your *G*
9:7 You are Jehovah the true *G*
9:17 a *G* of acts of forgiveness
9:18 *G* who led you up out of Egypt
9:31 are a *G* gracious and merciful
9:32, 32 *G*, the *G* great, mighty
10:28 to the law of the true *G*
10:29 in the law of the true *G*
10:29 the servant of the true *G*
10:32 service of the house of our *G*
10:33 work of the house of our *G*
10:34 bring to the house of our *G*
10:34 the altar of Jehovah our *G*
10:36 to the house of our *G*
10:36 in the house of our *G*
10:37 halls of the house of our *G*
10:38 to the house of our *G* to the
10:39 neglect the house of our *G*
11:11 of the house of the true *G*
11:16 of the house of the true *G*
11:22 of the house of the true *G*
12:24 David the man of the true *G*
12:36 David the man of the true *G*
12:40 at the house of the true *G*
12:43 the true *G* himself caused
12:45 the obligation of their *G*
12:46 praise and thanksgivings to *G*
13:1 the congregation of the true *G*
13:2 our *G* changed the malediction
13:4 hall of the house of our *G*
13:7 of the house of the true *G*
13:9 of the house of the true *G*
13:11 house of the true *G* been
13:14 Do remember me, O my *G*
13:14 the house of my *G* and the
13:18 *G* brought upon us all this
13:22 O my *G*, and do feel sorry
13:25 and make them swear by *G*
13:26 loved of his *G* he happened to
13:26 *G* constituted him king over
13:27 against our *G* by giving
13:29 Do remember them, O my *G*
13:31 remember me, O my *G*, for
Job 1:1 fearing *G* and turning aside
1:5 have cursed *G* in their heart
1:6 sons of the true *G* entered to
1:8 fearing *G* and turning aside
1:9 nothing that Job has feared *G*
1:16 very fire of *G* fell from the
1:22 anything improper to *G*
2:1 sons of the true *G* entered to
2:3 fearing *G* and turning aside
2:9 Curse *G* and die!
2:10 what is good from the true *G*
3:4 Let not *G* look for it from
3:23 And whom *G* hedges in
4:9 Through the breath of *G* they
4:17 be more just than *G* himself
5:8 I myself would apply to *G*
5:8 to *G* I would submit my cause
5:17 is the man whom *G* reproves
6:4 The terrors from *G* range
6:8 *G* would grant even my hope
6:9 *G* would go ahead and crush me
8:3 Will *G* . . . pervert judgment
8:5 If you . . . will look for *G*
8:13 of all those forgetting *G*
8:20 *G* himself will not reject
9:2 in the right in a case with *G*
9:13 *G* himself will not turn back
10:2 say to *G*, Do not pronounce
11:5 only *G* himself would speak
11:6 *G* allows some of your error
11:7 find out the deep things of *G*
12:4 One calling to *G* that he
12:6 the ones enraging *G* have the
12:6 has brought a *g* in his hand
13:3 arguing with *G* I . . . delight
13:7 speak unrighteousness for *G*
13:8 Or for the true *G* will you
15:4 make fear before *G* to have

Job 15:4 of any concern before *G*
15:8 talk of *G* do you listen
15:11 consolations of *G* not enough
15:13 turn your spirit against *G*
15:25 his hand against *G* himself
16:11 *G* hands me over to young
16:20 To *G* my eye has looked
16:21 an able-bodied man and *G*
18:21 of one that has not known *G*
19:6 *G* himself has misled me
19:22 persecuting me as *G* does
19:26 I shall behold *G*
20:15 *G* will drive it out from
20:29 is the share . . . from *G*
20:29 stated inheritance from *G*
21:9 rod of *G* is not upon them
21:14 And they say to the true *G*
21:22 teach knowledge even to *G*
22:2 man be of use to *G* himself
22:12 not *G* the height of heaven
22:13 What does *G* really know?
22:17 are saying to the true *G*
22:26 will raise your face to *G*
23:16 *G* . . . made my heart timid
24:12 And *G* himself considers it
25:4 man be in the right before *G*
27:2 As *G* lives, who has taken
27:3 the spirit of *G* is in my
27:8 In case *G* carries off his
27:9 Will *G* hear an outcry of his
27:10 call to *G* at all times
27:11 you men by the hand of *G*
27:13 the wicked man from *G*
28:23 *G* is the One who has
29:2 days when *G* was guarding me
29:4 intimacy with *G* was at my
31:2 what portion is there from *G*
31:6 *G* will get to know my
31:14 what can I do when *G* rises
31:23 disaster from *G* was a dread
31:28 denied the true *G* above
32:2 soul righteous rather than *G*
32:3 to pronounce *G* wicked
32:13 *G* that drives him away
33:6 I am to the true *G* just what
33:12 *G* is much more than mortal
33:14 *G* speaks once, And twice
33:26 make entreaty to *G* that he
33:29 All these things *G* performs
34:5 *G* himself has turned aside
34:9 By his taking pleasure in *G*
34:10 Far be it from the true *G*
34:12 *G* himself does not act
34:23 To go to *G* in judgment
34:31 actually say to *G* himself
34:37 sayings against the true *G*
35:10 Where is *G* my Grand Maker
35:13 the untruth *G* does not hear
36:2 are yet words to say for *G*
36:5 *G* is mighty and will not
36:22 *G* himself acts exaltedly
36:26 *G* is more exalted than we
37:5 *G* thunders with his voice in
37:10 By the breath of *G* the ice
37:14 to the wonderful works of *G*
37:15 *G* laid an appointment upon
37:22 Upon *G* dignity is
38:7 the sons of *G* began shouting
38:41 young ones cry to *G* for help
39:17 *G* has made her forget
40:2 reprover of *G* himself answer
40:9 arm like that of the true *G*
40:19 beginning of the ways of *G*
Ps 3:2 no salvation for him by *G*
3:7 O Jehovah! Save me, O my *G!*
4:1 answer me, O my righteous *G*
5:2 O my King and my *G*, because to
5:4 are not a *G* taking delight in
5:10 *G* will certainly hold them
7:1 Jehovah my *G*, in you I have
7:3 my *G*, if I have done this
7:9 *G* as righteous is testing out
7:10 The shield for me is upon *G*
7:11 *G* is a righteous Judge
7:11 *G* is hurling denunciations
9:17 all the nations forgetting *G*
10:4 his ideas are: There is no *G*
10:11 in his heart: *G* has forgotten
10:12 O *G*, lift up your hand
10:13 one has disrespected *G*
13:3 answer me, O Jehovah my *G*
16:1 Keep me, O *G*, for I have
17:6 you will answer me, O *G*
18:2 My *G* is my rock. I shall take

Ps 18:6 my *G* I kept crying for help
18:21 wickedly departed from my *G*
18:28 My *G* himself will make my
18:29 by my *G* I can climb a wall
18:30 true *G*, perfect is his way
18:31 who is a *G* besides Jehovah?
18:31 who is a rock except our *G?*
18:32 *G* is the One girding me
18:46 *G* of my salvation be exalted
18:47 *G* is the Giver of acts of
19:1 are declaring the glory of *G*
20:1 the *G* of Jacob protect you
20:5 in the name of our *G* we shall
20:7 our *G* we shall make mention
22:1, 1 My *G*, my *G*, why have you
22:2 O my *G*, I keep calling by day
22:10 you have been my *G*
24:5 righteousness from his *G* of
24:6 for your face, O *G* of Jacob
25:2 *G*, in you have I put my trust
25:5 For you are my *G* of salvation
25:22 O *G*, redeem Israel out of
27:9 O my *G* of salvation
29:3 *G* himself has thundered
30:2 my *G*, I cried to you for help
30:12 *G*, to time indefinite I will
31:5 O Jehovah the *G* of truth
31:14 I have said: You are my *G*
33:12 nation whose *G* is Jehovah
35:23 O my *G*, even Jehovah, to my
35:24 Judge me . . . O Jehovah my *G*
36:1 no dread of *G* in front of his
36:6 is like mountains of *G*
36:7 your loving-kindness is, O *G*
37:31 law of his *G* is in his heart
38:15 to answer, O Jehovah my *G*
38:21 my *G*, do not keep far away
40:3 Praise to our *G*
40:5 *G*, even your wonderful works
40:8 To do your will, O my *G*, I
40:17 O my *G*, do not be too late
41:13 Jehovah the *G* of Israel
42:1 very soul longs for you, O *G*
42:2 My soul indeed thirsts for *G*
42:2 thirsts . . . for the living *G*
42:2 come and appear before *G*
42:3 all day long: Where is your *G?*
42:4 walk . . . to the house of *G*
42:5 Wait for *G*, For I shall yet
42:6 my *G*, within me my very soul
42:8 prayer to the *G* of my life
42:9 I will say to *G* my crag
42:10 Where is your *G?*
42:11 Wait for *G*, For I shall yet
42:11 laud him . . . as my *G*
43:1 Judge me, O *G*, And do conduct
43:2 you are the *G* of my fortress
43:4 I will come to the altar of *G*
43:4 To *G*, my exultant rejoicing
43:4, 4 on the harp, O *G*, my *G*
43:5 Wait for *G*, For I shall yet
43:5 laud him . . . as my *G*
44:1 O *G*, with our ears we have
44:4 You yourself are my King, O *G*
44:8 In *G* we will offer praise
44:20 forgotten the name of our *G*
44:20 our palms to a strange *g*
44:21 *G* himself search this out
45:2 why *G* has blessed you to time
45:6 *G* is your throne to time
45:7, 7 *G*, your *G*, has anointed you
46:1 *G* is for us a refuge and
46:4 make the city of *G* rejoice
46:5 *G* is in the midst of the city
46:5 *G* will help it at the
46:7 The *G* of Jacob is a secure
46:10 Give in . . . know that I am *G*
46:11 The *G* of Jacob is a secure
47:1 Shout in triumph to *G* with
47:5 *G* has ascended with joyful
47:6 Make melody to *G*, make
47:7 For *G* is King of all the earth
47:8 *G* has become king over the
47:8 *G* himself has taken his seat
47:9 people of the *G* of Abraham
47:9 to *G* the shields of the earth
48:1 In the city of our *G*, in his
48:3 *G* himself has become known
48:8 in the city of our *G*
48:8 *G* himself will firmly
48:9 We have pondered, O *G*, over
48:10 Like your name, O *G*, so your
48:14, 14 this *G* is our *G* to time
49:7 give to *G* a ransom for him

Ps 49:15 *G* himself will redeem my
50:1 *G*, Jehovah, has himself
50:2 *G* himself has beamed forth
50:3 *G* will come and cannot
50:6 For *G* himself is Judge
50:7, 7 I am *G*, your *G*
50:14 as your sacrifice to *G*
50:16 to the wicked one *G* will
50:22 please, you forgetters of *G*
50:23 to see salvation by *G*
51:1 Show me favor, O *G*, according
51:10 in me even a pure heart, O *G*
51:14 from bloodguiltiness, O *G*
51:14 the *G* of my salvation
51:17 sacrifices to *G* are a broken
51:17 heart broken and crushed, O *G*
52:1 The loving-kindness of *G* is
52:7 not put *G* as his fortress
52:8 in the loving-kindness of *G*
53:2 As for *G*, he has looked down
53:5 For *G* himself will certainly
54:1 O *G*, by your name save me
54:2 O *G*, hear my prayer
54:3 not set *G* in front of them
54:4 Look! *G* is my helper
55:1 give ear, O *G*, to my prayer
55:14 Into the house of *G* we used
55:16 to *G* I shall call out
55:19 *G* will hear and answer them
55:19 And who have not feared *G*
55:23 *G*, will bring them down to
56:1 Show me favor, O *G*, because
56:4 with *G* I shall praise his
56:4 In *G* I have put my trust
56:7 down even the peoples, O *G*
56:9 I well know, that *G* is for me
56:10 In union with *G* I shall
56:11 In *G* I have put my trust
56:12 O *G*, there are vows to you
56:13 walk about before *G* in the
57:1 Show me favor, O *G*, show me
57:2 I call to *G* the Most High, to
57:2 the true *G* who is bringing
57:3 *G* will send his
57:5 exalted above the heavens, O *G*
57:7 My heart is steadfast, O *G*
57:11 above the heavens, O *G*
58:6 O *G*, knock out their teeth
58:11 exists a *G* that is judging
59:1 from my enemies, O my *G*
59:5 you, O Jehovah *G* of armies
59:5 you . . . are the *G* of Israel
59:9 For *G* is my secure height
59:10 The *G* of loving-kindness to
59:10 *G* himself will cause me to
59:13 *G* is ruling in Jacob to the
59:17 *G* is my secure height, the
59:17 *G* of loving-kindness to me
60:1 O *G*, you have cast us off
60:6 *G* himself has spoken in his
60:10 O *G*, who have cast us off
60:10 with our armies as *G*
60:12 By *G* we shall gain vital
61:1 hear, O *G*, my entreating cry
61:5 *G*, have listened to my vows
61:7 to time indefinite before *G*
62:1 toward *G* is my soul waiting
62:5 toward *G* wait silently, O my
62:7 Upon *G* are my salvation and
62:7 rock, my refuge is in *G*
62:8 *G* is a refuge for us. *Se'lah*
62:11 Once *G* has spoken, twice I
62:11 That strength belongs to *G*
63:1, 1 O *G*, you are my *G*, I keep
63:11 king . . . will rejoice in *G*
64:1 Hear, O *G*, my voice in my
64:7 *G* will shoot at them with an
64:9 tell of the activity of *G*
65:1 silence—, O *G*, in Zion
65:5 O *G* of our salvation
65:9 stream from *G* is full of
66:1 Shout in triumph to *G*, all
66:3 Say to *G*: How fear-inspiring
66:5 and see the activities of *G*
66:8 Bless our *G*, O you peoples
66:10 you have examined us, O *G*
66:16 listen, all you who fear *G*
66:19 Truly *G* has heard: He has
66:20 Blessed be *G*, who has not
67:1 *G* himself will show us favor
67:3 Let peoples laud you, O *G*
67:5 Let peoples laud you, O *G*
67:6, 6 *G*, our *G*, will bless us
67:7 *G* will bless us, And all the

Ps 68:1 Let *G* arise, let his enemies
68:2 perish from before *G*
68:3 Let them be elated before *G*
68:4 Sing you to *G*, make melody
68:5 Is *G* in his holy dwelling
68:6 *G* is causing the solitary
68:7 O *G*, when you went forth
68:8 also dripped because of *G*
68:8, 8 *G*, the *G* of Israel
68:9 you began causing to fall, O *G*
68:10 for the afflicted one, O *G*
68:15 Bashan is a mountain of *G*
68:16 mountain that *G* has desired
68:17 The war chariots of *G* are in
68:18 reside among them, O Jah *G*
68:19 The true *G* of our salvation
68:20 The true *G* is for us a
68:20 is for us a *G* of saving acts
68:21 *G* himself will break the
68:24 seen your processions, O *G*
68:24 The processions of my *G*, my
68:26 congregated throngs bless *G*
68:28 Your *G* has laid command upon
68:28 *G*, you who have acted for us
68:31 its hands with gifts to *G*
68:32 the earth, sing to *G*
68:34 Ascribe strength to *G*
68:35 *G* is fear-inspiring out of
68:35 The *G* of Israel he is, giving
68:35 to the people. Blessed be *G*
69:1 Save me, O *G*, for the waters
69:3 while waiting for my *G*
69:5 O *G*, you yourself have come
69:6 because of me, O *G* of Israel
69:13 At an acceptable time, O *G*
69:29 salvation, O *G*, protect me
69:30 I will praise the name of *G*
69:32 seeking *G*, let your heart
69:35 For *G* himself will save Zion
70:1 O *G*, to deliver me, O Jehovah
70:4 *G* be magnified!—those loving
70:5 O *G*, do act quickly for me
71:4 my *G*, provide me with escape
71:11 *G* himself has left him
71:12 O *G*, do not keep far away
71:12 O my *G*, do hurry to my
71:17 O *G*, you have taught me from
71:18 O *G*, do not leave me
71:19 Your righteousness, O *G*, is
71:19 O *G*, who is like you?
71:22 your trueness, O my *G*
72:1 O *G*, give your own judicial
72:18 Blessed be Jehovah *G*
72:18 Blessed be . . . Israel's *G*
73:1 *G* is indeed good to Israel
73:11 How has *G* come to know?
73:17 into the grand sanctuary of *G*
73:26 *G* is the rock of my heart
73:28 near to *G* is good for me
74:1 O *G*, have you cast off forever
74:8 meeting places of *G* must be
74:10 O *G*, will the adversary keep
74:12 *G* is my King from long ago
74:22 Do arise, O *G*, do conduct
75:1 We give thanks to you, O *G*
75:7 For *G* is the judge. This one
75:9 make melody to the *G* of Jacob
76:1 *G* is known in Judah; In
76:6 your rebuke, O *G* of Jacob
76:9 When *G* rose up to judgment
76:11 and pay to Jehovah your *G*
77:1 I will even cry out to *G*
77:1 my voice to *G*, and he will
77:3 I will remember *G* and be
77:9 *G* forgotten to be favorable
77:13 O *G*, your way is in the holy
77:13, 13 Who is a great *G* like *G*?
77:14 You are the true *G*, doing
77:16 waters have seen you, O *G*
78:7 set their confidence in *G*
78:7 not forget the practices of *G*
78:8 was not trustworthy with *G*
78:10 not keep the covenant of *G*
78:18 to test *G* in their heart
78:19 began to speak against *G*
78:19 *G* able to arrange a table in
78:22 they did not put faith in *G*
78:34 returned and looked for *G*
78:35 that *G* was their Rock
78:35 *G* the Most High was their
78:41 they would put *G* to the test
78:56 rebel against *G* the Most
78:59 *G* heard and got to be furious
79:1 O *G*, the nations have come

Ps 79:9 Help us, O *G* of our salvation
79:10 say: Where is their *G*?
80:3 O *G*, bring us back; And light
80:4 *G* of armies, how long must
80:7 *G* of armies, bring us back
80:10 cedars of *G* with its boughs
80:14 O *G* of armies, return
80:19 *G* of armies, bring us back
81:1 cry out . . . to *G* our strength
81:1 in triumph to the *G* of Jacob
81:4 decision of the *G* of Jacob
81:9 prove to be no strange *g*
81:9 not bow down to a foreign *g*
81:10 I, Jehovah, am your *G*, The
82:1 *G* is stationing himself in
82:8 *G*, do judge the earth
83:1 *G*, let there be no silence
83:12 abiding places of *G* for
83:13 *G*, make them like a thistle
84:2 out joyfully to the living *G*
84:3 of armies, my King and my *G*
84:7 Each one appears to *G* in Zion
84:8 Jehovah *G* of armies, do hear
84:8 Do give ear, O *G* of Jacob
84:9 see, O *G*, And look upon the
84:10 in the house of my *G*
84:11 Jehovah *G* is a sun and a
85:4 O *G* of our salvation, And
85:8 true *G* Jehovah will speak
86:2 your servant—you are my *G*
86:10 You are *G*, you alone
86:12 I laud you, O Jehovah my *G*
86:14 *G*, the presumptuous ones
86:15 Jehovah, are a *G* merciful
87:3 you, O city of the true *G*
88:1 the *G* of my salvation
89:6 Jehovah among the sons of *G*
89:7 *G* is to be held in awe among
89:8 *G* of armies, Who is vigorous
89:26 My *G* and the Rock of my
90:*super* the man of the true *G*
90:2 to time indefinite you are *G*
90:17 of Jehovah our *G* prove to be
91:2 My *G*, in whom I will trust
92:13 courtyards of our *G*, they
94:1 O *G* of acts of vengeance
94:1 *G* of acts of vengeance, beam
94:7 *G* of Jacob does not understand
94:22 my *G* the rock of my refuge
94:23 our *G* will silence them
95:3 For Jehovah is a great *G*
95:7 he is our *G*, and we are the
98:3 seen the salvation by our *G*
99:5 Exalt Jehovah our *G* and bow
99:8 Jehovah our *G*, you yourself
99:8 A *G* granting pardon you proved
99:9 Exalt Jehovah our *G* And bow
99:9 For Jehovah our *G* is holy
100:3 Know that Jehovah is *G*
102:24 O my *G*, Do not take me off
104:1 Jehovah my *G*, you have
104:21 seeking their food from *G*
104:33 melody to my *G* as long as I
105:7 He is Jehovah our *G*
106:14 *G* to the proof in the desert
106:21 They forgot *G* their Savior
106:47 Save us, O Jehovah our *G*
106:48 Blessed be Jehovah the *G* of
107:11 against the sayings of *G*
108:1 My heart is steadfast, O *G*
108:5 above the heavens, O *G*
108:7 *G* himself has spoken in his
108:11 O *G*, who have cast us off
108:11 forth with our armies as *G*
108:13 By *G* we shall gain vital
109:1 *G* of my praise, do not keep
109:26 Help me, O Jehovah my *G*
113:5 Who is like Jehovah our *G*
114:7 Because of the *G* of Jacob
115:2 Where, now, is their *G*?
115:3 But our *G* is in the heavens
116:5 our *G* is One showing mercy
118:28 My *G*—I shall exalt you
119:115 the commandments of my *G*
122:9 the house of Jehovah our *G*
123:2 are toward Jehovah our *G*
135:2 of the house of our *G*
136:2 thanks to the *G* of the gods
136:26 to the *G* of the heavens
139:17 *G*, how much does the grand
139:19 *G*, would slay the wicked
139:23 Search through me, O *G*, and
140:6 to Jehovah: You are my *G*
143:10 your will, For you are my *G*

Ps 144:9 O G, a new song I will sing
144:15 people whose G is Jehovah
145:1 I will exalt you, O my G
146:2 melody to my G as long as I
146:5 has the G of Jacob for his
146:5 hope is in Jehovah his G
146:10 Your G, O Zion, for
147:1 to make melody to our G
147:7 melody to our G on the harp
147:12 Praise your G, O Zion
149:6 songs extolling G be in their
150:1 Praise G in his holy place
Pr 2:5 find the very knowledge of G
2:17 the very covenant of her G
3:4 good insight in the eyes of G
25:2 glory of G is the keeping of a
30:5 Every saying of G is refined
30:9 and assail the name of my G
Ec 1:13 calamitous occupation that G
2:24 from the hand of the true G
2:26 that is good before the true G
3:10 occupation that G has given to
3:11 work that the true G has made
3:13 It is the gift of G
3:14 that the true G makes
3:14 true G himself has made it
3:15 true G himself keeps seeking
3:17 The true G will judge both
3:18 G is going to select them
5:1 go to the house of the true G
5:2 a word before the true G
5:2 the true G is in the heavens
5:4 a vow to G, do not hesitate to
5:6 the true G become indignant on
5:7 But fear the true G himself
5:18 life that the true G has given
5:19 the true G has given riches
5:19 This is the gift of G
5:20 true G is preoccupying him
6:2 man to whom the true G gives
6:2 G does not enable him to eat
7:13 See the work of the true G
7:14 G has made even this exactly
7:18 he that fears G will go forth
7:26 good before the true G if one
7:29 G made mankind upright, but
8:2 out of regard for the oath of G
8:12 with those fearing the true G
8:13 because he is not in fear of G
8:15 G has given them under the
8:17 all the work of the true G
9:1 are in the hand of the true G
9:7 G has found pleasure in your
11:5 true G, who does all things
11:9 true G will bring you into
12:7 returns to the true G who
12:13 Fear the true G and keep his
12:14 G himself will bring every
Isa 1:10 Give ear to the law of our G
2:3 to the house of the G of Jacob
5:16 true G, the Holy One, will
7:11 sign from Jehovah your G
7:13 should also tire out my G
8:10 not stand, for G is with us
8:19 to its G that any people
8:21 upon his king and upon his G
9:6 Mighty G, Eternal Father
10:10 valueless g whose graven
10:21 of Jacob, to the Mighty G
12:2 G is my salvation. I shall
13:19 G overthrew Sodom and
14:13 Above the stars of G I shall
17:6 of Jehovah the G of Israel
17:10 the G of your salvation
21:10 G of Israel, I have reported
21:17 G of Israel, has spoken it
24:15 Jehovah, the G of Israel
25:1 Jehovah, you are my G
25:9 This is our G. We have hoped
26:13 Jehovah our G, other
28:26 His own G instructs him
29:2 me as the altar hearth of G
29:23 G of Israel they will
30:18 Jehovah is a G of judgment
31:3 are earthling men, and not G
35:2 the splendor of our G
35:4 Your own G will come with
35:4 G even with a repayment
36:7 G in whom we have trusted
37:4 Jehovah your G will hear the
37:4 sent to taunt the living G
37:4 that Jehovah your G has heard
37:10 G in whom you are trusting
37:16 G of Israel, sitting upon
Isa 37:16 true G of all the kingdoms
37:17 sent to taunt the living G
37:20 G, save us out of his hand
37:20 you, O Jehovah, are G alone
37:21 G of Israel has said
37:38 the house of Nisroch his g
38:5 Jehovah the G of David your
40:1 says the G of you men
40:3 highway for our G through
40:8 word of our G, it will last
40:9 Judah: Here is your G
40:18 whom can you people liken G
40:27 justice to me eludes my G
40:28 is a G to time indefinite
41:10 I am your G. I will fortify
41:13 For I, Jehovah your G, am
41:17 G of Israel, shall not leave
42:5 true G, Jehovah, has said
43:3 For I am Jehovah your G, the
43:10 Before me there was no G
43:12 was among you no strange g
43:12 of Jehovah, and I am G
44:6 besides me there is no G
44:8 Does there exist a G besides
44:10 Who has formed a g or cast
44:15 a g to which he may bow
44:17 makes into a g itself, into
44:17 Deliver me . . . you are my g
45:3 your name, the G of Israel
45:5 exception of me . . . no G
45:14 G is in union with you, and
45:14 there is no other G
45:15 a G keeping yourself
45:15 G of Israel, a Savior
45:18 He the true G, the Former
45:20 to a g that cannot save
45:21, 21 G; a righteous G and a
45:22 G, and there is no one else
46:6 and he makes it into a g
46:9 and there is no other G
48:1 even of the G of Israel
48:2 upon the G of Israel they
48:17 I, Jehovah, am your G, the
49:4 and my wages with my G
49:5 G will have become my
50:10 support himself upon his G
51:15 But I, Jehovah, am your G
51:20 the rebuke of your G
51:22 G, who contends for his
52:7 Your G has become king!
52:10 see the salvation of our G
52:12 G of Israel will be your
53:4 stricken by G and afflicted
54:5 The G of the whole earth he
54:6 rejected, your G has said
55:5 the sake of Jehovah your G
55:7 G, for he will forgive in a
57:21 no peace, my G has said
58:2 the very justice of their G
58:2 G in whom they had delight
59:2 between you and your G
59:13 a moving back from our G
60:9 the name of Jehovah your G
60:19 and your G your beauty
61:2 on the part of our G
61:6 ministers of our G you will
61:10 soul will be joyful in my G
62:3 turban in the palm of your G
62:5 G will exult even over you
64:4 eye itself seen a G, except
65:11 table for the g of Good Luck
65:11 wine for the g of Destiny
65:16 bless himself by the G of
65:16 swear by the G of faith
66:9 shutting up? your G has said
Jer 2:17 your leaving Jehovah your G
2:19 your leaving Jehovah your G
3:13 against Jehovah your G that
3:21 forgotten Jehovah their G
3:22 for you, O Jehovah, are our G
3:23 G is the salvation of Israel
3:25 toward Jehovah our G that we
3:25 the voice of Jehovah our G
5:4 the judgment of their G
5:5 the judgment of their G
5:7 keep swearing by what is no G
5:14 Jehovah, the G of armies
5:19 our G done to us all these
5:19 have gone serving a foreign g
5:24 fear Jehovah our G, the One
7:3 the G of Israel, has said
7:21 the G of Israel, has said
7:23 and I will become your G
7:28 the voice of Jehovah its G
Jer 8:14 our G has himself put us to
9:15 the G of Israel, has said
10:10 But Jehovah is in truth G
10:10 He is the living G and the
11:3 Jehovah the G of Israel has
11:4 I myself shall become your G
13:12 the G of Israel has said
13:16 to Jehovah your G glory
14:22 the One, O Jehovah our G
15:16 O Jehovah G of armies
16:9 the G of Israel, has said
16:10 sinned against Jehovah our G
19:3 the G of Israel, has said
19:15 the G of Israel, has said
21:4 the G of Israel has said
22:9 covenant of Jehovah their G
23:2 the G of Israel has said
23:23 Am I a G nearby, is the
23:23 and not a G far away
23:36 the words of the living G
23:36 Jehovah of armies, our G
24:5 the G of Israel has said
24:7 shall become their G, for
25:15 the G of Israel said to me
25:27 the G of Israel, has said
26:13 the voice of Jehovah your G
26:16 the name of Jehovah our G
27:4 the G of Israel, has said
27:21 the G of Israel, has said
28:2 the G of Israel, has said
28:14 the G of Israel, has said
29:4 the G of Israel, has said
29:8 the G of Israel, has said
29:21 the G of Israel, has said
29:25 the G of Israel, has said
30:2 the G of Israel has said
30:9 serve Jehovah their G and
30:22 myself shall become your G
31:1 G to all the families of
31:6 up to Zion, to Jehovah our G
31:18 for you are Jehovah my G
31:23 G of Israel, has said
31:33 I will become their G, and
32:14 G of Israel, has said
32:15 G of Israel, has said
32:18 true G, the great One, the
32:27 Jehovah, the G of all flesh
32:36 G of Israel has said
32:38 myself shall become their G
33:4 the G of Israel has said
34:2 the G of Israel has said
34:13 G of Israel has said
35:4 a man of the true G, which
35:13 G of Israel, has said, Go
35:17 Jehovah the G of armies
35:17 G of Israel, has said
35:18 G of Israel, has said
35:19 the G of Israel, has said
37:3 our behalf to Jehovah our G
37:7 G of Israel has said, This
38:17, 17 G of armies, the G of
39:16 the G of Israel, has said
40:2 Jehovah your G himself spoke
42:2 Jehovah your G, in behalf
42:3 Jehovah your G tell us the
42:4 praying to Jehovah your G
42:5 Jehovah your G sends you
42:6 voice of Jehovah our G to
42:6 the voice of Jehovah our G
42:9 Jehovah the G of Israel, to
42:13 voice of Jehovah your G
42:15 G of Israel, has said
42:18 G of Israel, has said
42:20 sent me to Jehovah your G
42:20 our behalf to Jehovah our G
42:20 Jehovah our G says tell us
42:21 voice of Jehovah your G or
43:1 words of Jehovah their G
43:1 Jehovah their G had sent him
43:2 Jehovah our G has not sent
43:10 G of Israel, has said
44:2 G of Israel, has said, You
44:7 Jehovah, the G of armies
44:7 G of Israel, has said, Why
44:11 the G of Israel, has said
44:25 the G of Israel, has said
45:2 Jehovah the G of Israel has
46:25 G of Israel, has said
48:1 G of Israel, has said: Woe
48:35 sacrificial smoke to his g
50:4 their G they will seek
50:18 the G of Israel, has said
50:28 of Jehovah our G, the
51:5 are not widowed from their G

Jer 51:10 the work of Jehovah our G
51:33 G of Israel, has said
51:56 is a G of recompenses
La 3:41 our palms to G in the heavens
Eze 1:1 I began to see visions of G
8:3 in the visions of G, to the
8:4 glory of the G of Israel was
8:14 weeping over the g Tammuz
9:3 the glory of the G of Israel
10:5 like the sound of G Almighty
10:19 the glory of the G of Israel
10:20 seen under the G of Israel
11:20 myself may become their G
11:22 the glory of the G of Israel
11:24 vision by the spirit of G
14:11 myself shall become their G
20:5 saying, I am Jehovah your G
20:7 I am Jehovah your G
20:19 I am Jehovah your G
20:20 that I am Jehovah your G
28:2 you keep saying, I am a g
28:2 In the seat of g I have
28:2 and not a g, and you keep
28:2 heart like the heart of g
28:6 heart like the heart of g
28:9 without fail say, I am g
28:9 earthling man, and not a g
28:13 In Eden, the garden of G
28:14 On the holy mountain of G
28:16 out of the mountain of G
28:26 that I am Jehovah their G
31:8 for it in the garden of G
31:8 other tree in the garden of G
31:9 in the garden of the true G
34:24 Jehovah . . . become their G
34:30 that I, Jehovah their G
34:31 I am your G, is the
36:28 myself shall become your G
37:23 myself shall become their G
37:27 certainly become their G
39:22 that I am Jehovah, their G
39:28 that I am Jehovah, their G
40:2 In the visions of G he
43:2 glory of the G of Israel
44:2 G of Israel, has come in by
Da 1:2 of the house of the true G
1:2 Shinar to the house of his g
1:2 to the treasure-house of his g
1:9 true G gave Daniel over to
1:17 true G gave knowledge and
2:18 part of the G of heaven
2:19 blessed the G of heaven
2:20 name of G become blessed from
2:23 To you, O G of my forefathers
2:28 G in the heavens who is a
2:37 G of heaven has given the
2:44 G of heaven will set up a
2:45 grand G himself has made
2:47, 47 G . . . is a G of gods and
3:15 who is that g that can rescue
3:17 G whom we are serving is
3:26 servants of the Most High G
3:28 Blessed be the G of Shadrach
3:28 not worship any g at all
3:28 except their own G
3:29 against the G of Shadrach
3:29 g that is able to deliver like
4:2 wonders that the Most High G
4:8 according to the name of my g
5:3 the house of G that was in
5:18 Most High G himself gave to
5:21 Most High G is Ruler in the
5:23 G in whose hand your breath
5:26 MENE, G has numbered the days
6:5 in the law of his G
6:7 petition to any g or man for
6:10 offering praise before his G
6:11 imploring favor before his G
6:12 petition from any g or man for
6:16 Your G whom you are serving
6:20 servant of the living G, has
6:20 G whom you are serving with
6:22 My own G sent his angel and
6:23 he had trusted in his G
6:26 fearing before the G of Daniel
6:26 For he is the living G and
9:3 my face to Jehovah the true G
9:4 pray to Jehovah my G and to
9:4 Jehovah the true G, the great
9:9 To . . . G belong the mercies
9:10 Jehovah our G by walking in
9:11 the servant of the true G
9:13 the face of Jehovah our G
9:14 our G is righteous in all his
Da 9:15 our G, you who brought your
9:17 listen, O our G, to the prayer
9:18 Incline your ear, O my G
9:19 G, for your own name has been
9:20 Jehovah my G concerning the
9:20 the holy mountain of my G
10:12 humbling . . . before your G
11:32 who are knowing their G
11:36 the king . . . above every g
11:36 against the G of gods he
11:37 g of his fathers he will
11:37 other g he will give no
11:38 to the g of fortresses, in
11:38 g that his fathers did not
11:39 along with a foreign g
Ho 1:7 save them by Jehovah their G
1:10 The sons of the living G
2:22 Jezreel [=G will sow seed]
2:23 will say: You are my G
3:5 look for Jehovah their G
4:1 nor knowledge of G in the land
4:6 forgetting the law of your G
4:12 go out from under their G
5:4 a returning to their G
6:6 the knowledge of G rather than
7:10 returned to Jehovah their G
8:2 my G, we, Israel, have known
8:6 it is not G; because the calf
9:1 gone from alongside your G
9:8 watchman . . . was with my G
9:8 in the house of his G
9:17 My G will reject them, for
11:9 for I am G and not man, the
11:12 Judah is yet roaming with G
12:3 energy he contended with G
12:5 Jehovah the G of the armies
12:6 to your G you should return
12:6 a hoping in your G constantly
12:9 your G from the land of Egypt
13:4 your G from the land of Egypt
13:4 no G except me that you used
13:16 rebellious against her G
14:1 back . . . to Jehovah your G
14:3 O our G! to the work of our
Joe 1:13 you ministers of my G
1:13 from the house of your G
1:14 the house of Jehovah your G
1:16 from the house of our G
2:13 come back to Jehovah your G
2:14 offering for Jehovah your G
2:17 Where is their G?
2:23 and rejoice in Jehovah your G
2:26 the name of Jehovah your G
2:27 your G and there is no other
3:17 that I am Jehovah your G
Am 3:13 Jehovah, the G of the armies
4:12 get ready to meet your G
4:13 the G of armies is his name
5:14 Jehovah the G of armies may
5:15 the G of armies will show
5:16 what Jehovah the G of armies
5:26 images, the star of your g
5:27 the G of armies has said
6:8 of Jehovah the G of armies
6:14 Jehovah the G of the armies
8:14 As your g is alive, O Dan!
9:15 Jehovah your G has said
Jon 1:5 for aid, each one to his g
1:6 Get up, call out to your g!
1:6 the true G will show himself
1:9 G of the heavens I am fearing
2:1 Jonah prayed to Jehovah his G
2:6 my life, O Jehovah my G
3:3 proved to be a city great to G
3:5 began to put faith in G, and
3:8 call out to G with strength
3:9 the true G may turn back and
3:10 G got to see their works
3:10 G felt regret over the
4:2 you are a G gracious and
4:6 G appointed a bottle-gourd
4:7 the true G appointed a worm
4:8 G also went on to appoint a
4:9 G proceeded to say to Jonah
Mic 3:7 for there is no answer from G
4:2 the house of the G of Jacob
4:5 in the name of its g; but we
4:5 walk in the name of . . G
5:4 the name of Jehovah his G
6:6 I bow myself to G on high
6:8 in walking with your G
7:7 for the G of my salvation
7:7 salvation. My G will hear me
7:10 Where is he, Jehovah your G?
Mic 7:17 To Jehovah our G they will
7:18 Who is a G like you, one
Na 1:2 a G exacting exclusive devotion
Hab 1:11 its power is due to its g
1:12 O my G, my Holy One, you do
3:3 G . . . to come from Teman
3:18 in the G of my salvation
Zep 2:7 G will turn his attention to
2:9 armies, the G of Israel
3:2 To her G she did not draw
3:17 G is in the midst of you
Hag 1:12 the voice of Jehovah their G
1:12 Jehovah their G had sent him
1:14 Jehovah of armies their G
Zec 6:15 the voice of Jehovah your G
8:8 become their G in trueness
8:23 that G is with you people
9:7 be left remaining for our G
9:16 G will certainly save them
10:6 for I am Jehovah their G
11:4 my G has said, Shepherd the
12:5 Jehovah of armies their G
12:8 and the house of David like G
13:9 will say, Jehovah is my G
14:5 my G will certainly come
Mal 1:9 please, soften the face of G
2:10 one G that has created us
2:11 daughter of a foreign g as
2:15 The seed of G. And you
2:16 Jehovah the G of Israel has
2:17 Where is the G of justice?
3:8 Will earthling man rob G?
3:14 It is of no value to serve G
3:15 they have tested G out and
3:18 one serving G and one who
Mt 1:23 translated, With Us Is G
3:9 G is able to raise up children
4:3 If you are a son of G, tell
4:6 If you are a son of G, hurl
4:7 not put Jehovah your G to the
4:10 It is Jehovah your G you must
5:8 pure in heart . . . will see G
5:9 they will be called sons of G
6:8 G your Father knows what
6:24 cannot slave for G and for
6:30 If, now, G thus clothes the
8:29 to do with you, Son of G
9:8 they glorified G, who gave
12:4 entered into the house of G
12:28 the kingdom of G has really
15:3 commandment of G because of
15:4 G said, Honor your father and
15:5 is a gift dedicated to G
15:6 made the word of G invalid
15:31 glorified the G of Israel
16:16 the Son of the living G
19:6 what G has yoked together let
19:24 to get into the kingdom of G
19:26 G all things are possible
21:31 into the kingdom of G
21:43 kingdom of G will be taken
22:16 teach the way of G in truth
22:21 but God's things to G
22:29 nor the power of G
22:31 what was spoken to you by G
22:32 I am the G of Abraham and
22:32 and the G of Isaac and the
22:32 of Isaac and the G of Jacob
22:32 G, not of the dead, but of
22:37 love Jehovah your G with
23:22 swearing by the throne of G
26:61 throw down the temple of G
26:63 By the living G I put you
26:63 are the Christ the Son of G
27:40 If you are a son of G, come
27:43 He has put his trust in G
27:46, 46 My G, my G, why have
Mr 1:14 preaching the good news of G
1:15 kingdom of G has drawn near
1:24 you are, the Holy One of G
2:7 can forgive sins except one, G
2:12 glorified G, saying: We never
2:26 entered into the house of G
3:11 saying: You are the Son of G
3:35 Whoever does the will of G
4:11 secret of the kingdom of G
4:26 kingdom of G is just as when
4:30 we to liken the kingdom of G
5:7 Jesus, Son of the Most High G
5:7 under oath by G not to torment
7:8 the commandment of G, you
7:9 aside the commandment of G
7:11 is, a gift dedicated to G
7:13 make the word of G invalid

r 9:1 they see the kingdom of G
9:47 into the kingdom of G
10:9 what G yoked together let no
10:14 the kingdom of G belongs to
10:15 receive the kingdom of G
10:18 Nobody is good, except . . . G
10:23 enter into the kingdom of G
10:24 enter into the kingdom of G
10:25 enter into the kingdom of G
10:27 but not so with G, for all
10:27 things are possible with G
11:22 said . . . Have faith in G
12:14 you teach the way of G in
12:17 but God's things to G
12:24 Scriptures or the power of G
12:26 G said to him, I am the
12:26 I am the G of Abraham and
12:26 of Abraham and G of Isaac
12:26 Isaac and G of Jacob
12:27 He is a G, not of the dead
12:29 Jehovah our G is one Jehovah
12:30 you must love Jehovah your G
12:34 far from the kingdom of G
13:19 creation which G created
14:25 new in the kingdom of G
15:34, 34 My G, my G, why have
15:43 for the kingdom of G
u 1:6 both were righteous before G
1:8 of his division before G
1:16 turn back to Jehovah their G
1:19 who stands near before G
1:26 was sent forth from G to a
1:30 you have found favor with G
1:32 G will give him the throne
1:37 with G no declaration will be
1:47 from being overjoyed at G
1:64 he began to speak, blessing G
1:68 Blessed be Jehovah the G of
1:78 tender compassion of our G
2:13 heavenly army, praising G and
2:14 Glory . . . to G, and upon earth
2:20 praising G for all the things
2:28 and blessed G and said
2:38 began returning thanks to G
2:52 in favor with G and men
3:6 will see the saving means of G
3:8 G has power to raise up
3:38 Seth, son of Adam, son of G
4:3 If you are a son of G, tell
4:8 your G you must worship
4:9 If you are a son of G, hurl
4:12 put Jehovah your G to the test
4:34 you are, the Holy One of G
4:41 saying: You are the Son of G
4:43 good news of the kingdom of G
5:1 listening to the word of G, he
5:21 Who can forgive sins except G
5:25 off to his home, glorifying G
5:26 and they began to glorify G
6:4 he entered into the house of G
6:12 whole night in prayer to G
6:20 yours is the kingdom of G
7:16 began to glorify G, saying
7:16 G has turned his attention to
7:28 lesser one in the kingdom of G
7:29 declared G to be righteous
7:30 disregarded the counsel of G
8:1 good news of the kingdom of G
8:10 secrets of the kingdom of G
8:11 The seed is the word of G
8:21 hear the word of G and do it
8:28 Jesus Son of the Most High G
8:39 what things G did for you
9:2 to preach the kingdom of G and
9:11 about the kingdom of G
9:20 in reply: The Christ of G
9:27 they see the kingdom of G
9:43 at the majestic power of G
9:60 abroad the kingdom of G
9:62 fitted for the kingdom of G
10:9 kingdom of G has come near
10:11 kingdom of G has come near
10:27 You must love Jehovah your G
11:20 the kingdom of G has really
11:28 the word of G and keeping it
11:42 justice and the love of G
11:49 the wisdom of G also said
12:6 goes forgotten before G
12:8 him before the angels of G
12:9 before the angels of G
12:20 G said to him, Unreasonable
12:21 but is not rich toward G
12:24 and yet G feeds them
12:28 If, now, G thus clothes the

Lu 13:13 and began to glorify G
13:18 is the kingdom of G like
13:20 I compare the kingdom of G
13:28 prophets in the kingdom of G
13:29 table in the kingdom of G
14:15 bread in the kingdom of G
15:10 arises among the angels of G
16:13 be slaves to G and to riches
16:15 but G knows your hearts
16:16 kingdom of G is being
17:15 glorifying G with a loud
17:18 back to give glory to G but
17:20 the kingdom of G was coming
17:20 The kingdom of G is not
17:21 kingdom of G is in your
18:2 judge that had no fear of G
18:4 not fear G or respect a man
18:7 shall not G cause justice to
18:11 O G, I thank you I am not as
18:13 O G, be gracious to me a
18:16 For the kingdom of G belongs
18:17 receive the kingdom of G
18:19 Nobody is good, except one, G
18:24 way into the kingdom of G
18:25 to get into the kingdom of G
18:27 are possible with G
18:29 the sake of the kingdom of G
18:43 to follow him, glorifying G
18:43 seeing it, gave praise to G
19:11 kingdom of G was going to
19:37 praise G with a loud voice
20:21 way of G in line with truth
20:25 but God's things to G
20:37 Jehovah the G of Abraham and
20:37, 37 G of Isaac and G of Jacob
20:38 He is a G, not of the dead
21:31 the kingdom of G is near
22:16 in the kingdom of G
22:18 the kingdom of G arrives
22:69 powerful right hand of G
22:70 Are you . . . the Son of G?
23:35 the Christ of G, the Chosen
23:40 Do you not fear G at all
23:47 officer began to glorify G
23:51 waiting for the kingdom of G
24:19 before G and all the people
24:53 in the temple blessing G
Joh 1:1 and the Word was with G, and
1:1 and the Word was a g
1:2 was in the beginning with G
1:6 as a representative of G
1:13 from man's will, but from G
1:18 No man has seen G at any
1:18 only-begotten g who is in
1:29 Lamb of G that takes away
1:34 this one is the Son of G
1:36 he said: See, the Lamb of G!
1:49 Rabbi, you are the Son of G
1:51 angels of G ascending and
3:2 as a teacher have come from G
3:2 perform unless G is with him
3:3 cannot see the kingdom of G
3:5 enter into the kingdom of G
3:16 G loved the world so much
3:17 G sent forth his Son into
3:18 the only-begotten Son of G
3:21 worked in harmony with G
3:33 seal to it that G is true
3:34 the one whom G sent forth
3:34 speaks the sayings of G
3:36 wrath of G remains upon him
4:10 had known the free gift of G
4:24 G is a Spirit, and those
5:18 calling G his own Father
5:18 making himself equal to G
5:25 the voice of the Son of G
5:42 not have the love of G in you
5:44 glory . . . from the only G
6:27 this one the Father, even G
6:28 to work the works of G
6:29 This is the work of G, that
6:33 the bread of G is the one
6:46 except he who is from G
6:69 you are the Holy One of G
7:17 from G or I speak of my own
8:40 truth that I heard from G
8:41 we have one Father, G
8:42 If G were your Father, you
8:42 from G I came forth and am
8:47 He that is from G listens to
8:47 listens to the sayings of G
8:47 because you are not from G
8:54 he who you say is your G
9:3 the works of G might be made

Joh 9:16 not a man from G, because
9:24 Give glory to G; we know
9:29 know that G has spoken to
9:31 G does not listen to sinners
9:33 If this man were not from G
10:33 a man, make yourself a g
10:35 against whom the word of G
11:4 but is for the glory of G
11:4 Son of G may be glorified
11:22 things as you ask G for
11:22 G will give you
11:27 are the Christ the Son of G
11:40 would see the glory of G
11:52 that the children of G who
12:43 than even the glory of G
13:3 he came forth from G and
13:3 and was going to G
13:31 G is glorified in connection
13:32 G will himself glorify him
14:1 Exercise faith in G
16:2 a sacred service to G
16:30 that you came out from G
17:3 the only true G, and of the
20:17, 17 and to my G and your G
20:28 to him: My Lord and my G!
20:31 is the Christ the Son of G
21:19 death he would glorify G
Ac 1:3 things about the kingdom of G
2:11 the magnificent things of G
2:17 G says, I shall pour out
2:22 man publicly shown by G to
2:22 signs that G did through him
2:23 and foreknowledge of G
2:24 G resurrected him by loosing
2:30 G had sworn to him with an
2:32 Jesus G resurrected, of
2:33 exalted to the right hand of G
2:36 G made him both Lord and
2:39 Jehovah our G may call to him
2:47 praising G and finding favor
3:8 and leaping and praising G
3:9 him walking and praising G
3:13 G of Abraham and of Isaac
3:13 the G of our forefathers, has
3:15 G raised him up from the dead
3:18 G has fulfilled the things he
3:21 G spoke through the mouth
3:22 Jehovah G will raise up for
3:25 G covenanted with your
3:26 G, after raising up his
4:10 G raised up from the dead
4:19 righteous in the sight of G
4:19 listen to you rather than to G
4:21 glorifying G over what had
4:24 raised their voices to G and
4:31 speaking the word of G with
5:4 false, not to men, but to G
5:29 G as ruler rather than men
5:30 G of our forefathers raised
5:31 G exalted this one as Chief
5:32 spirit . . . G has given to
5:39 from G, you will not be able
5:39 fighters actually against G
6:2 us to leave the word of G to
6:7 word of G went on growing
6:11 sayings against Moses and G
7:2 G of glory appeared to our
7:4 G caused him to change his
7:6 G spoke to this effect, that
7:7 I shall judge, G said, and
7:9 But G was with him
7:17 G had openly declared to
7:25 G was giving them salvation
7:32 am the G of your forefathers
7:32 G of Abraham and of Isaac
7:35 G sent off as both ruler and
7:37 G will raise up for you from
7:42 G turned and handed them over
7:43 star of the g Rephan that you
7:45 nations, whom G thrust out
7:46 favor in the sight of G
7:46 habitation for the G of Jacob
8:10 This man is the Power of G
8:12 good news of the kingdom of G
8:14 had accepted the word of G
8:20 of the free gift of G
8:21 straight in the sight of G
9:20 that this One is the Son of G
10:2 fearing G together with all
10:2 made supplication to G
10:3 angel of G come in to him
10:4 as a remembrance before G
10:15 the things G has cleansed
10:22 fearing G and well reported

Ac 10:28 *G* has shown me I should call
10:31 have been remembered before *G*
10:33 we are all present before *G*
10:34 that *G* is not partial
10:38 *G* anointed him with holy
10:38 because *G* was with him
10:40 *G* raised this One up on the
10:41 appointed beforehand by *G*
10:42 One decreed by *G* to be judge
10:46 tongues and glorifying *G*
11:1 also received the word of *G*
11:9 the things *G* has cleansed
11:17 *G* gave the same free gift to
11:17 I should be able to hinder *G*
11:18 they glorified *G*, saying
11:18 *G* has granted repentance for
11:23 the undeserved kindness of *G*
12:5 prayer to *G* for him was being
12:23 did not give the glory to *G*
13:5 publishing the word of *G* in
13:7 sought to hear the word of *G*
13:16 you others that fear *G*, hear
13:17 *G* of this people Israel
13:21 *G* gave them Saul son of
13:23 *G* has brought to Israel a
13:26 others among you who fear *G*
13:30 *G* raised him up from the
13:33 *G* has entirely fulfilled it
13:36 served the express will of *G*
13:37 *G* raised up did not see
13:43 proselytes who worshiped *G*
13:43 the undeserved kindness of *G*
13:46 word of *G* to be spoken first
13:50 women who worshiped *G* and
14:15 to the living *G*, who made
14:22 enter into the kingdom of *G*
14:26 the undeserved kindness of *G*
14:27 things *G* had done by means
15:4 *G* had done by means of them
15:7 *G* made the choice among you
15:8 *G*, who knows the heart, bore
15:10 a test of *G* by imposing upon
15:12 and portents that *G* did
15:14 *G* for the first time turned
15:19 nations who are turning to *G*
16:10 that *G* had summoned us to
16:14 Lydia . . . a worshiper of *G*
16:17 slaves of the Most High *G*
16:25 and praising *G* with song
16:34 now that he had believed *G*
17:4 the Greeks who worshiped *G*
17:13 word of *G* was published also
17:17 other people who worshiped *G*
17:23 inscribed To an Unknown *G*
17:24 *G* that made the world and
17:27 to seek *G*, if they might
17:29 that we are the progeny of *G*
17:30 *G* has overlooked the times
18:7 Justus, a worshiper of *G*
18:11 among them the word of *G*
18:13 persuasion in worshiping *G*
18:26 expounded the way of *G* more
19:8 concerning the kingdom of *G*
19:11 And *G* kept performing
20:21 about repentance toward *G*
20:24 the undeserved kindness of *G*
20:27 all the counsel of *G*
20:28 congregation of *G*, which he
20:32 I commit you to *G* and to the
21:19 account of the things *G* did
21:20 they began to glorify *G*, and
22:3 zealous for *G* just as all of
22:14 The *G* of our forefathers has
23:1 I have behaved before *G* with
23:3 *G* is going to strike you, you
23:4 reviling the high priest of *G*
24:14 sacred service to the *G* of
24:15 I have hope toward *G*, which
24:16 no offense against *G* and men
26:6 promise that was made by *G*
26:8 that *G* raises up the dead
26:18 authority of Satan to *G*, in
26:20 turn to *G* by doing works
26:22 the help that is from *G* I
26:29 Paul said: I could wish to *G*
27:23 of the *G* to whom I belong
27:24 *G* has freely given you all
27:25 I believe *G* that it will be
27:35 gave thanks to *G* before
28:6 and began saying he was a *g*
28:15 Paul thanked *G* and took
28:23 concerning the kingdom of *G*
28:28 means by which *G* saves, has
28:31 preaching the kingdom of *G*

Ro 1:7 peace from *G* our Father and
1:8 I give thanks to my *G* through
1:9 *G*, to whom I render sacred
1:10 prospered in the will of *G*
1:19 what may be known about *G* is
1:19 *G* made it manifest to them
1:21 although they knew *G*, they
1:21 they did not glorify him as *G*
1:23 glory of the incorruptible *G*
1:24 *G*, in keeping with the
1:25 exchanged the truth of *G* for
1:26 *G* gave them up to disgraceful
1:28 holding *G* in accurate
1:28 *G* gave them up to a
1:30 haters of *G*, insolent
1:32 righteous decree of *G*, that
2:2 judgment of *G* is, in accord
2:3 will escape the judgment of *G*
2:4 kindly quality of *G* is trying
2:11 there is no partiality with *G*
2:13 the ones righteous before *G*
2:16 *G* through Christ Jesus judges
2:17 law and taking pride in *G*
2:23 of the Law dishonor *G*
2:24 name of *G* is being blasphemed
2:29 not from men, but from *G*
3:2 sacred pronouncements of *G*
3:3 faithfulness of *G* without
3:4 let *G* be found true, though
3:5 *G* is not unjust when he vents
3:6 will *G* judge the world
3:7 truth of *G* . . . more prominent
3:11 is no one that seeks for *G*
3:18 fear of *G* before their eyes
3:19 may become liable to *G* for
3:23 fall short of the glory of *G*
3:25 *G* set him . . . as an offering
3:25 *G* was exercising forbearance
3:29 is he the *G* of the Jews only?
3:30 if truly *G* is one, who will
4:2 for boasting; but not with *G*
4:6 whom *G* counts righteousness
4:17 *G*, who makes the dead alive
4:20 because of the promise of *G*
4:20 by his faith, giving *G* glory
5:1 enjoy peace with *G* through
5:2 based on hope of the glory of *G*
5:5 love of *G* has been poured out
5:8 *G* recommends his own love to
5:10 reconciled to *G* through the
5:11 exulting in *G* through our
5:15 undeserved kindness of *G* and
6:10 he lives with reference to *G*
6:11 living with reference to *G*
6:13 present yourselves to *G* as
6:13 your members to *G* as weapons
6:17 thanks to *G* that you were the
6:22 but became slaves to *G*, you
6:23 gift *G* gives is everlasting
7:4 we should bear fruit to *G*
7:22 delight in the law of *G*
7:25 Thanks to *G* through Jesus
8:3 *G*, by sending his own Son in
8:7 the flesh means enmity with *G*
8:7 subjection to the law of *G*
8:8 with the flesh cannot please *G*
8:17 heirs indeed of *G*, but joint
8:19 revealing of the sons of *G*
8:21 freedom of the children of *G*
8:27 pleading in accord with *G*
8:28 that *G* makes all his works
8:28 the good of those who love *G*
8:31 If *G* is for us, who will be
8:33 *G* is the One who declares
8:34 who is on the right hand of *G*
9:5 *G*, who is over all, be blessed
9:6 the word of *G* had failed
9:8 not really the children of *G*
9:11 purpose of *G* respecting the
9:14 Is there injustice with *G*?
9:16 but upon *G*, who has mercy
9:20 to be answering back to *G*
9:22 *G*, although having the will
9:26 called sons of the living *G*
10:1 supplication to *G* for them
10:2 have a zeal for *G*; but not
10:3 the righteousness of *G* but
10:3 to the righteousness of *G*
10:9 *G* raised him up from the dead
11:1 *G* did not reject his people
11:2 *G* did not reject his people
11:2 pleads with *G* against Israel
11:8 *G* has given them a spirit of
11:21 *G* did not spare the natural

Ro 11:23 *G* is able to graft them in
11:29 calling of *G* are not things
11:30 once disobedient to *G* but
11:32 *G* has shut them all up
12:1 by the compassions of *G*
12:1 living, holy, acceptable to *G*
12:2 and perfect will of *G*
12:3 as *G* has distributed to him
13:1 no authority except by *G*
13:1 their relative positions by *G*
13:2 against the arrangement of *G*
14:3 for *G* has welcomed that one
14:6 for he gives thanks to *G*; and
14:6 and yet gives thanks to *G*
14:10 the judgment seat of *G*
14:11 open acknowledgement to *G*
14:12 account for himself to *G*
14:17 kingdom of *G* does not mean
14:18 is acceptable to *G* and has
14:20 tearing down the work of *G*
14:22 faith . . . in the sight of *G*
15:5 *G* who supplies endurance and
15:6 glorify the *G* and Father of
15:7 with glory to *G* in view
15:9 might glorify *G* for his mercy
15:13 May the *G* who gives hope
15:15 kindness given to me from *G*
15:16 work of the good news of *G*
15:17 to things pertaining to *G*
15:30 with me in prayers to *G*
15:33 May the *G* who gives peace be
16:20 *G* who gives peace will crush
16:26 of the everlasting *G* to
16:27 to *G*, wise alone, be the
1Co 1:2 congregation of *G* that is in
1:3 peace from *G* our Father and
1:4 thank *G* for you in view of
1:4 the undeserved kindness of *G*
1:9 *G* is faithful, by whom you
1:20 Did not *G* make the wisdom
1:21 in the wisdom of *G*, the
1:21 world . . . not get to know *G*
1:21 *G* saw good through the
1:24 Christ the power of *G* and
1:24 and the wisdom of *G*
1:25 foolish thing of *G* is wiser
1:25 weak thing of *G* is stronger
1:27 *G* chose the foolish things of
1:27 *G* chose the weak things of
1:28 *G* chose the ignoble things of
1:29 boast in the sight of *G*
1:30 become to us wisdom from *G*
2:1 sacred secret of *G* to you
2:7 which *G* foreordained before
2:9 things that *G* has prepared
2:10 *G* has revealed them through
2:10 even the deep things of *G*
2:11 to know the things of *G*
2:11 except the spirit of *G*
2:12 the spirit which is from *G*
2:12 been kindly given us by *G*
2:14 things of the spirit of *G*
3:6 but *G* kept making it grow
3:7 but *G* who makes it grow
3:10 undeserved kindness of *G* that
3:16 spirit of *G* dwells in you
3:17 destroys the temple of *G*
3:17 *G* will destroy him; for the
3:17 for the temple of *G* is holy
3:19 world is foolishness with *G*
3:23 Christ, in turn, belongs to *G*
4:1 of sacred secrets of *G*
4:5 praise come to him from *G*
4:9 *G* has put us the apostles last
4:20 the kingdom of *G* lies not
5:13 while *G* judges those outside
6:11 and with the spirit of our *G*
6:13 but *G* will bring both it and
6:14 *G* both raised up the Lord and
6:19 you, which you have from *G*
6:20 glorify *G* in the body of you
7:7 has his own gift from *G*, one
7:15 but *G* has called you to peace
7:17 so walk as *G* has called him
7:24 in it associated with *G*
8:3 if anyone loves *G*, this one is
8:4 and that there is no *G* but one
8:6 to us one *G* the Father, out of
8:8 will not commend us to *G*
9:9 Is it bulls *G* is caring for?
9:21 not without law toward *G*
10:5 *G* did not express his
10:13 But *G* is faithful, and he
10:20 to demons, and not to *G*

1Co 10:32 and to the congregation of *G*
11:3 the head of the Christ is *G*
11:12 but all things are out of *G*
11:13 to pray uncovered to *G*
11:16 do the congregations of *G*
11:22 the congregation of *G* and
12:6 the same *G* who performs all
12:18 *G* has set the members in
12:24 *G* compounded the body
12:28 And *G* has set the respective
14:2 not to men, but to *G*
14:18 I thank *G*, I speak in more
14:25 and worship *G*, declaring
14:25 *G* is really among you
14:28 speak to himself and to *G*
14:33, 33 *G* is a *G* . . . of peace
14:36 from you that the word of *G*
15:9 the congregation of *G*
15:10 the undeserved kindness of *G*
15:15 found false witnesses of *G*
15:15 witness against *G* that he
15:24 the kingdom to his *G* and
15:25 until *G* has put all enemies
15:27 *G* subjected all things under
15:28 that *G* may be all things to
15:34 are without knowledge of *G*
15:38 *G* gives it a body just as it
15:57 thanks to *G*, for he gives
2Co 1:1 the congregation of *G* that is
1:2 peace from *G* our Father and
1:3 Blessed be the *G* and Father
1:3 and the *G* of all comfort
1:4 being comforted by *G*
1:9 in the *G* who raises up the
1:18 *G* can be relied upon that our
1:19 Son of *G*, Christ Jesus, who
1:20 how many the promises of *G*
1:20 the Amen said to *G* for glory
1:21 he who has anointed us is *G*
1:23 I call upon *G* as a witness
2:14 thanks be to *G* who always
2:15 to *G* we are a sweet odor of
2:17 peddlers of the word of *G*
2:17 yes, as sent from *G*, under
3:3 with spirit of a living *G*
3:4 sort of confidence toward *G*
3:5 qualified issues from *G*
4:2 adulterating the word of *G*
4:2 conscience in the sight of *G*
4:4 *g* of this system of things
4:4 Christ, who is the image of *G*
4:6 *G* is he who said: Let the
4:6 knowledge of *G* by the face
4:15 many more to the glory of *G*
5:1 are to have a building from *G*
5:5 us for this very thing is *G*
5:11 have been made manifest to *G*
5:13 out of our mind . . . for *G*
5:18 *G*, who reconciled us to
5:19 *G* was by means of Christ
5:20 *G* were making entreaty
5:20 Become reconciled to *G*
6:1 undeserved kindness of *G* and
6:16 are a temple of a living *G*
6:16 *G* said: I shall reside among
6:16 I shall be their *G*, and they
7:6 *G*, who comforts those laid
7:12 among you in the sight of *G*
8:1 undeserved kindness of *G* that
8:16 thanks be to *G* for putting
9:7 for *G* loves a cheerful giver
9:8 *G*, moreover, is able to make
9:11 an expression of thanks to *G*
9:12 expressions of thanks to *G*
9:13 they glorify *G* because you
9:14 undeserved kindness of *G* upon
9:15 Thanks be to *G* for his
10:4 weapons . . . powerful by *G*
10:5 against the knowledge of *G*
10:13 territory that *G* apportioned
11:7 declared the good news of *G*
11:11 love you? *G* knows I do
11:31 *G* and Father of the Lord
12:2 *G* knows—was caught away as
12:3 I do not know, *G* knows
12:19 before *G* that we are
12:21 *G* might humiliate me among
13:7 we pray to *G* that you may
13:11 *G* of love and of peace
13:14 love of *G* and the sharing
Ga 1:1 *G* the Father, who raised him
1:3 peace from *G* our Father and
1:4 according to the will of our *G*
1:10 now trying to persuade or *G*
Ga 1:13 the congregation of *G* and
1:15 *G*, who separated me from my
1:20 in the sight of *G*, I am not
1:24 began glorifying *G* because of
2:6 *G* does not go by a man's
2:19 might become alive toward *G*
2:20 the Son of *G*, who loved me
2:21 the undeserved kindness of *G*
3:8 *G* would declare people of the
3:11 declared righteous with *G*
3:17 previously validated by *G*
3:18 *G* has kindly given it to
3:20 but *G* is only one
3:21 against the promises of *G*
3:26 sons of *G* through your faith
4:4 *G* sent forth his Son, who
4:6 *G* has sent forth the spirit
4:7 son, also an heir through *G*
4:8 when you did not know *G*, then
4:9 you have come to know *G*, or
4:9 have come to be known by *G*
4:14 me like an angel of *G*, like
6:7 *G* is not one to be mocked
6:16 even upon the Israel of *G*
Eph 1:2 peace from *G* our Father and
1:3 Blessed be the *G* and Father
1:17 *G* of our Lord Jesus Christ
2:1 it is you *G* made alive though
2:4 But *G*, who is rich in mercy
2:10 which *G* prepared in advance
2:12 were without *G* in the world
2:16 reconcile . . . to *G* through
2:19 of the household of *G*
2:22 for *G* to inhabit by spirit
3:2 undeserved kindness of *G* that
3:7 undeserved kindness of *G* that
3:9 been hidden in *G*, who created
3:10 diversified wisdom of *G*
3:19 all the fullness that *G* gives
4:6 one *G* and Father of all
4:13 knowledge of the Son of *G*
4:18 the life that belongs to *G*
4:32 *G* also by Christ freely
5:1 imitators of *G*, as beloved
5:2 offering and a sacrifice to *G*
5:5 in the kingdom of . . . *G*
5:6 wrath of *G* is coming upon the
5:19 with psalms and praises to *G*
5:20 giving thanks . . . to our *G*
6:6 the will of *G* whole-souled
6:11 suit of armor from *G* that
6:13 suit of armor from *G*, that
6:23 faith from *G* the Father and
Php 1:2 and peace from *G* our Father
1:3 I thank my *G* always upon
1:8 For *G* is my witness of how
1:14 the word of *G* fearlessly
1:28 this indication is from *G*
2:6 that he should be equal to *G*
2:9 *G* exalted him to a superior
2:11 to the glory of *G* the Father
2:13 for *G* is the one that, for
2:15 children of *G* without a
2:27 but *G* had mercy on him
3:9 from *G* on the basis of faith
3:14 upward call of *G* by means of
3:15 *G* will reveal the above
3:19 and their *g* is their belly
4:6 petitions be made known to *G*
4:7 peace of *G* that excels all
4:9 the *G* of peace will be with
4:18 well-pleasing to *G*
4:19 *G* will fully supply all your
4:20 to our *G* and Father be the
Col 1:2 and peace from *G* our Father
1:3 We thank *G* the Father of our
1:6 the undeserved kindness of *G*
1:10 the accurate knowledge of *G*
1:15 the image of the invisible *G*
1:19 *G* saw good for all fullness
1:25 stewardship from *G* which
1:25 preach the word of *G* fully
1:27 *G* has been pleased to make
2:2 sacred secret of *G*, namely
2:12 faith in the operation of *G*
2:13 *G* made you alive together
2:19 with the growth that *G* gives
3:1 seated at the right hand of *G*
3:3 the Christ in union with *G*
3:6 the wrath of *G* is coming
3:16 praises to *G*, spiritual songs
3:17 thanking *G* the Father through
4:3 that *G* may open a door of
4:11 workers for the kingdom of *G*
Col 4:12 in all the will of *G*
1Th 1:1 in union with *G* the Father
1:2 always thank *G* when we make
1:3 before our *G* and Father
1:4 we know, brothers loved by *G*
1:8 faith toward *G* has spread
1:9 turned to *G* from your idols
1:9 slave for a living and true *G*
2:2 boldness by means of our *G* to
2:2 the good news of *G* with a
2:4 we have been proved by *G* as
2:4 pleasing, not men, but *G*
2:5 *G* is witness!
2:8 not only the good news of *G*
2:9 preached the good news of *G*
2:10 You are witnesses, *G* is also
2:12 go on walking worthily of *G*
2:13 also thank *G* incessantly
2:13 as the word of *G*, which is
2:14 congregations of *G* that are
2:15 they are not pleasing *G*, but
3:9 render to *G* concerning you in
3:9 rejoicing . . . before our *G*
3:11 may our *G* and Father himself
3:13 in holiness before our *G*
4:1 ought to walk and please *G*
4:3 *G* wills, the sanctifying of
4:5 nations . . . do not know *G*
4:7 For *G* called us, not with
4:8 *G*, who puts his holy spirit
4:9 taught by *G* to love one
4:14 *G* will bring with him
5:9 *G* assigned us, not to wrath
5:18 For this is the will of *G*
5:23 *G* of peace sanctify you
2Th 1:1 in union with *G* our Father
1:2 peace from *G* the Father and
1:3 give *G* thanks always for you
1:4 among the congregations of *G*
1:5 the righteous judgment of *G*
1:5 worthy of the kingdom of *G*
1:8 those who do not know *G* and
1:11 *G* may count you worthy of
1:12 undeserved kindness of our *G*
2:4 who is called *g* or an object
2:4 in the temple of The *G*
2:4 showing himself to be a *g*
2:11 *G* lets an operation of error
2:13 obligated to thank *G* always
2:13 because *G* selected you from
2:16 *G* our Father, who loved us
3:5 into the love of *G* and into
1Ti 1:1 under command of *G* our Savior
1:2 peace from *G* the Father
1:4 a dispensing of anything by *G*
1:11 good news of the happy *G*
1:17 invisible, the only *G*, be
2:3 in the sight of our Savior, *G*
2:5 is one *G*, and one mediator
2:5 mediator between *G* and men
2:10 professing to reverence *G*
3:15 congregation of the living *G*
4:3 foods which *G* created to be
4:4 every creation of *G* is fine
4:10 our hope on a living *G*
5:5 has put her hope in *G* and
5:21 solemnly charge you before *G*
6:1 that the name of *G* and the
6:11 O man of *G*, flee from these
6:13 *G*, who preserves all things
6:17 on *G*, who furnishes us all
2Ti 1:2 peace from *G* the Father and
1:3 I am grateful to *G*, to whom
1:6 the gift of *G* which is in you
1:7 *G* gave us not a spirit of
1:8 according to the power of *G*
2:9 the word of *G* is not bound
2:14 before *G* as witness, not to
2:15 approved to *G*, a workman
2:19 solid foundation of *G* stays
2:25 *G* may give them repentance
3:4 rather than lovers of *G*
3:16 Scripture is inspired of *G*
3:17 the man of *G* may be fully
4:1 solemnly charge you before *G*
Tit 1:1 Paul, a slave of *G* and an
1:2 which *G*, who cannot lie
1:3 command of our Savior, *G*
1:4 peace from *G* the Father and
1:16 publicly declare they know *G*
2:5 that the word of *G* may not be
2:10 the teaching of our Savior, *G*
2:11 undeserved kindness of *G*
2:13 manifestation of the great *G*

Tit 3:4 on the part of our Savior, *G*
3:8 those who have believed *G* may
Phm 3 and peace from *G* our Father and
4 I always thank my *G* when I
Heb 1:1 *G*, who long ago spoke on
1:8 *G* is your throne forever, and
1:9, 9 *G*, your *G*, anointed you
2:4 *G* joined in bearing witness
2:8 *G* left nothing that is not
2:17 in things pertaining to *G*
3:4 constructed all things is *G*
3:12 away from the living *G*
3:17 did *G* become disgusted for
4:4 *G* rested on the seventh day
4:8 *G* would not afterward have
4:9 resting for the people of *G*
4:10 just as *G* did from his own
4:12 the word of *G* is alive and
4:14 heavens, Jesus the Son of *G*
5:1 the things pertaining to *G*
5:4 when he is called by *G*, just
5:10 called by *G* a high priest
5:12 sacred pronouncements of *G*
6:1 and faith toward *G*
6:3 will do, if *G* indeed permits
6:5 tasted the fine word of *G* and
6:6 impale the Son of *G* afresh
6:7 in return a blessing from *G*
6:10 *G* is not unrighteous so as
6:13 when *G* made his promise to
6:17 *G*, when he purposed to
6:18 is impossible for *G* to lie
7:1 priest of the Most High *G*
7:3 been made like the Son of *G*
7:19 we are drawing near to *G*
7:25 approaching *G* through him
8:10 I will become their *G*, and
9:14 without blemish to *G*
9:14 service to the living *G*
9:20 *G* has laid as a charge upon
9:24 before the person of *G* for us
10:7 to do your will, O *G*
10:12 down at the right hand of *G*
10:21 priest over the house of *G*
10:29 trampled upon the Son of *G*
10:31 the hands of the living *G*
10:36 you have done the will of *G*
11:4 Abel offered *G* a sacrifice
11:4 *G* bearing witness respecting
11:5 *G* had transferred him; for
11:5 that he had pleased *G* well
11:6 he that approaches *G* must
11:10 maker of which city is *G*
11:16 *G* is not ashamed of them
11:16 be called upon as their *G*
11:19 *G* was able to raise him up
11:25 with the people of *G* rather
11:40 *G* foresaw something better
12:2 right hand of the throne of *G*
12:7 *G* is dealing with you as
12:15 undeserved kindness of *G*
12:22 and a city of the living *G*
12:23 *G* the Judge of all, and the
12:28 render *G* sacred service
12:29 *G* is also a consuming fire
13:4 *G* will judge fornicators and
13:7 spoken the word of *G* to you
13:15 to *G* a sacrifice of praise
13:16 *G* is well pleased
13:20 *G* of peace, who brought
Jas 1:1 James, a slave of *G* and of
1:5 let him keep on asking *G*, for
1:13 say: I am being tried by *G*
1:13 *G* cannot be tried nor does
1:27 from the standpoint of our *G*
2:5 *G* chose the ones who are
2:19 believe there is one *G*, do
3:9 in the likeness of *G*
4:4 the world is enmity with *G*
4:4 himself an enemy of *G*
4:6 *G* opposes the haughty ones
4:7 to *G*; but oppose the Devil
4:8 Draw close to *G*, and he will
1Pe 1:2 foreknowledge of *G* the Father
1:3 Blessed be the *G* and Father
1:21 are believers in *G*, the One
1:21 faith and hope might be in *G*
1:23 the living and enduring *G*
2:4 but chosen, precious, with *G*
2:5 sacrifices acceptable to *G*
2:12 glorify *G* in the day for his
2:15 the will of *G* is, that by
2:16 badness, but as slaves of *G*
2:17 be in fear of *G*, have honor
1Pe 2:19 of conscience toward *G*
2:20 is a thing agreeable with *G*
3:4 great value in the eyes of *G*
3:5 women who were hoping in *G*
3:17 if the will of *G* wishes it
3:18 that he might lead you to *G*
3:20 patience of *G* was waiting
3:21 request made to *G* for a good
4:6 from the standpoint of *G*
4:11 sacred pronouncements of *G*
4:11 strength that *G* supplies
4:11 *G* may be glorified through
4:14 spirit of *G*, is resting upon
4:16 glorifying *G* in this name
4:17 start with the house of *G*
4:17 to the good news of *G*
4:19 harmony with the will of *G*
5:2 Shepherd the flock of *G* in
5:5 *G* opposes the haughty ones
5:6 under the mighty hand of *G*
5:10 *G* of all undeserved kindness
5:12 undeserved kindness of *G*
2Pe 1:1 by the righteousness of our *G*
1:2 by an accurate knowledge of *G*
1:17 received from *G* the Father
1:21 men spoke from *G* as they
2:4 *G* did not hold back from
3:5 by the word of *G*
1Jo 1:5 *G* is light and there is no
2:5 love of *G* . . . made perfect
2:14 the word of *G* remains in you
2:17 does the will of *G* remains
3:1 should be called children of *G*
3:2 now we are children of *G*, but
3:8 Son of *G* was made manifest
3:9 been born from *G* does not
3:9 he has been born from *G*
3:10 The children of *G* and the
3:10 does not originate with *G*
3:17 does the love of *G* remain in
3:20 *G* is greater than our hearts
3:21 freeness of speech toward *G*
4:1 whether they originate with *G*
4:2 inspired expression from *G*
4:2 originates with *G*
4:3 does not originate with *G*
4:4 You originate with *G*, little
4:6 We originate with *G*. He that
4:6 that gains the knowledge of *G*
4:6 does not originate with *G*
4:7 because love is from *G*, and
4:7 been born from *G* and gains
4:7 and gains the knowledge of *G*
4:8 has not come to know *G*
4:8 because *G* is love
4:9 love of *G* was made manifest
4:9 *G* sent forth his only-begotten
4:10 not that we have loved *G*
4:11 if this is how *G* loved us
4:12 no time has anyone beheld *G*
4:12 *G* remains in us and his love
4:15 Jesus Christ is the Son of *G*
4:15 *G* remains in union with such
4:15 and he in union with *G*
4:16 love that *G* has in our case
4:16 *G* is love, and he that
4:16 remains in union with *G* and
4:16 *G* remains in union with him
4:20 I love *G*, and yet is hating
4:20 cannot be loving *G*, whom he
4:21 one who loves *G* should be
5:1 has been born from *G*, and
5:2 are loving the children of *G*
5:2 we are loving *G* and doing his
5:3 is what the love of *G* means
5:4 been born from *G* conquers the
5:5 that Jesus is the Son of *G*
5:9 witness *G* gives is greater
5:9 this is the witness *G* gives
5:10 his faith in the Son of *G*
5:10 person not having faith in *G*
5:10 which *G* as witness has given
5:11 that *G* gave us everlasting
5:12 does not have the Son of *G*
5:13 in the name of the Son of *G*
5:18 been born from *G* does not
5:18 One born from *G* watches him
5:19 We know we originate with *G*
5:20 that the Son of *G* has come
5:20 true *G* and life everlasting
2Jo 3 and peace from *G* the Father and
9 does not have *G*. He that does
3Jo 6 in a manner worthy of *G*
11 does good originates with *G*
3Jo 11 that does bad has not seen *G*
Jude 1 loved in relationship with *G*
4 undeserved kindness of our *G*
25 *G* our Savior through Jesus
Re 1:1 A revelation . . . *G* gave him, to
1:2 witness to the word *G* gave
1:6 priests to his *G* and Father
1:8 and the Omega, says Jehovah *G*
1:9 Patmos for speaking about *G*
2:7 which is in the paradise of *G*
2:18 things that the Son of *G* says
3:1 has the seven spirits of *G*
3:2 fully performed before my *G*
3:12 pillar in the temple of my *G*
3:12 upon him the name of my *G*
3:12 name of the city of my *G*
3:12 out of heaven from my *G*
3:14 beginning of the creation by *G*
4:5 mean the seven spirits of *G*
4:8 Holy, holy, holy is Jehovah *G*
4:11 our *G*, to receive the glory
5:6 mean the seven spirits of *G*
5:9 bought persons for *G* out of
5:10 kingdom and priests to our *G*
6:9 because of the word of *G* and
7:2 a seal of the living *G*; and he
7:3 sealed the slaves of our *G* in
7:10 Salvation we owe to our *G*
7:11 the throne and worshiped *G*
7:12 strength be to our *G* forever
7:15 are before the throne of *G*
7:17 *G* will wipe out every tear
8:2 angels that stand before *G*, and
8:4 of the holy ones before *G*
9:4 seal of *G* on their foreheads
9:13 golden altar that is before *G*
10:7 the sacred secret of *G*
11:1 the temple sanctuary of *G*
11:11 spirit of life from *G*
11:13 gave glory to the *G* of heaven
11:16 seated before *G* upon their
11:16 their faces and worshiped *G*
11:17 We thank you, Jehovah *G*
11:19 temple sanctuary of *G* that
12:5 child was caught away to *G*
12:6 has a place prepared by *G*
12:10 and the kingdom of our *G*
12:10 day and night before our *G*
12:17 the commandments of *G* and
13:6 in blasphemies against *G*
14:4 firstfruits to *G* and to the
14:7 Fear *G* and give him glory
14:10 the wine of the anger of *G*
14:12 the commandments of *G*
14:19 winepress of the anger of *G*
15:1 anger of *G* is brought to a
15:2 having harps of *G*
15:3 song of Moses the slave of *G*
15:3 your works, Jehovah *G*, the
15:7 were full of the anger of *G*
15:8 because of the glory of *G*
16:1 seven bowls of the anger of *G*
16:7 Jehovah *G*, the Almighty
16:9 they blasphemed the name of *G*
16:11 blasphemed the *G* of heaven
16:14 the great day of *G* the Almighty
16:19 remembered in the sight of *G*
16:21 men blasphemed *G* due to
17:17 *G* put it into their hearts
17:17 words of *G* will have been
18:5 *G* has called her acts of
18:8 Jehovah *G*, who judged her
18:20 *G* has judicially exacted
19:1 and the power belong to our *G*
19:4 worshiped *G* seated upon the
19:5 Be praising our *G*, all you his
19:6 Jehovah our *G*, the Almighty
19:9 are the true sayings of *G*
19:10 Worship *G*; for the bearing
19:13 is called is The Word of *G*
19:15 the wrath of *G* the Almighty
19:17 the great evening meal of *G*
20:4 and for speaking about *G*, and
20:6 they will be priests of *G*
21:2 down out of heaven from *G*
21:3 The tent of *G* is with mankind
21:3 *G* himself will be with them
21:7 I shall be his *G* and he will
21:10 down out of heaven from *G*
21:11 and having the glory of *G*
21:22 *G* the Almighty is its
21:23 glory of *G* lighted it up
22:1 throne of *G* and of the Lamb
22:3 throne of *G* and of the Lamb

e 22:5 Jehovah *G* will shed light
22:6 *G* of the inspired expressions
22:9 of this scroll. Worship *G*
22:18 *G* will add to him the
22:19 *G* will take his portion

oddess

Ki 11:5 Ashtoreth the *g* of the
11:33 Ashtoreth the *g* of the
c 19:27 temple . . . great *g* Artemis
19:37 nor blasphemers of our *g*

od-fearing

e 22:12 know that you are *G* in that
h 9:31 is *G* and does his will

odlike

s 8:5 a little less than *g* ones

odly

c 3:12 *g* devotion we have made him
17:23 giving *g* devotion to, this
Co 1:12 holiness and *g* sincerity
7:9 you were saddened in a *g* way
7:10 sadness in a *g* way makes
7:11 being saddened in a *g* way
11:2 over you with a *g* jealousy
Ti 2:2 *g* devotion and seriousness
3:16 secret of this *g* devotion is
4:7 with *g* devotion as your aim
4:8 *g* devotion is beneficial for
5:4 to practice *g* devotion in
6:3 that accords with *g* devotion
6:5 thinking that *g* devotion is a
6:6 this *g* devotion along with
6:11 righteousness, *g* devotion
Ti 3:5 having a form of *g* devotion
3:12 to live with *g* devotion
it 1:1 which accords with *g* devotion
2:12 *g* devotion amid this present
eb 5:7 favorably heard for his *g* fear
11:7 showed *g* fear and
12:28 service with *g* fear and awe
Pe 1:3 concern life and *g* devotion
1:6 to your endurance *g* devotion
1:7 to your *g* devotion brotherly
2:9 deliver people of *g* devotion
3:11 and deeds of *g* devotion

od's

e 1:2 *G* active force was moving
1:27 in *G* image he created him
5:1 In the day of *G* creating Adam
9:6 for in *G* image he made man
21:17 *G* angel called to Hagar out
28:12 *G* angels ascending and
33:10 your face as though seeing *G*
x 9:28 occurring of *G* thunders and
31:18 written on by *G* finger
e 9:10 written upon with *G* finger
os 24:26 in the book of *G* law and
Sa 4:21 the ark of the true *G* being
16:15 *G* bad spirit is terrorizing
16:16 when *G* bad spirit comes to
16:23 when *G* spirit came to be
18:10 that *G* bad spirit became
Ch 20:15 battle is not yours, but *G*
24:20 *G* spirit itself enveloped
zr 5:2 *G* prophets giving them aid
ob 19:21 *G* own hand has touched me
33:4 *G* own spirit made me, And
35:2 righteousness is more than *G*
s 52:8 olive tree in *G* house
78:31 *G* wrath itself ascended
er 50:40 *G* overthrow of Sodom and of
m 4:11 like *G* overthrow of Sodom
t 3:16 like a dove *G* spirit coming
5:34 because it is *G* throne
12:28 by means of *G* spirit that I
14:33 saying: You are really *G* Son
16:23 you think, not *G* thoughts
22:21 but *G* things to God
27:43 for he said, I am *G* Son
27:54 Certainly this was *G* Son
r 8:33 not *G* thoughts, but those of
12:17 but *G* things to God
15:39 this man was *G* Son
u 1:35 will be called holy, *G* Son
2:40 *G* favor continued upon him
3:2 *G* declaration came to John the
11:20 by means of *G* finger I expel
16:15 disgusting thing in *G* sight
20:25 but *G* things to God
20:36 and they are *G* children by
oh 1:12 to become *G* children
10:36 I said, I am *G* Son

Joh 19:7 he made himself *G* son
Ac 7:55 caught sight of *G* glory and
7:55 Jesus standing at *G* right hand
7:56 standing at *G* right hand
12:22 A *g* voice, and not a man's
18:27 of *G* undeserved kindness
Ro 1:1 separated to *G* good news
1:4 declared *G* Son according to
1:7 in Rome as *G* beloved ones
1:16 *G* power for salvation to
1:17 *G* righteousness is being
1:18 *G* wrath is being revealed
2:5 of *G* righteous judgment
3:5 *G* righteousness to the fore
3:21 *G* righteousness has been
3:22 *G* righteousness through the
7:25 am a slave to *G* law, but
8:9 *G* spirit truly dwells in you
8:14 all who are led by *G* spirit
8:14 these are *G* sons
8:16 that we are *G* children
8:33 accusation against *G* chosen
8:39 *G* love that is in Christ
11:22 *G* kindness and severity
11:22 *G* kindness, provided you
11:28 reference to *G* choosing they
11:33 depth of *G* riches and wisdom
13:4 *G* minister to you for your
13:4 *G* minister, an avenger to
13:6 *G* public servants constantly
15:8 in behalf of *G* truthfulness
15:32 with joy by *G* will I shall
1Co 1:1 Christ through *G* will, and
1:18 to us . . . it is *G* power
2:5 faith might be . . . *G* power
2:7 speak *G* wisdom in a sacred
3:9 For we are *G* fellow workers
3:9 You people are *G* field under
3:9 You people are . . . *G* building
3:16 that you people are *G* temple
6:9 will not inherit *G* kingdom
6:10 will inherit *G* kingdom
7:19 of *G* commandments does
7:40 think I also have *G* spirit
10:31 do all things for *G* glory
11:7 as he is *G* image and glory
12:3 when speaking by *G* spirit
15:10 by *G* undeserved kindness I
15:50 cannot inherit *G* kingdom
2Co 1:1 apostle . . . through *G* will
1:12 with *G* undeserved kindness
2:17 under *G* view, in company
4:7 *G* and not that out of
5:21 *G* righteousness by means of
6:4 ourselves as *G* ministers, by
6:7 truthful speech, by *G* power
6:16 *G* temple have with idols
7:1 perfecting holiness in *G* fear
8:5 and to us through *G* will
13:4 is alive owing to *G* power
13:4 owing to *G* power toward you
Ga 5:21 will not inherit *G* kingdom
Eph 1:1 through *G* will, to the holy
1:14 ransom *G* own possession, to
2:8 not owing to you . . . *G* gift
4:24 created according to *G* will
4:30 not be grieving *G* holy spirit
6:17 spirit, that is, *G* word
Php 1:11 to *G* glory and praise
2:6 he was existing in *G* form
3:3 sacred service by *G* spirit
Col 1:1 an apostle . . . through *G* will
3:12 as *G* chosen ones, holy and
1Th 2:13 when you received *G* word
3:2 *G* minister in the good news
4:16 and with *G* trumpet, and
2Th 1:6 righteous on *G* part to repay
1Ti 3:5 take care of *G* congregation
3:15 in *G* household, which is the
4:5 sanctified through *G* word and
5:4 this is acceptable in *G* sight
2Ti 1:1 through *G* will according to
Tit 1:1 the faith of *G* chosen ones
1:7 *G* steward, not self-willed
Heb 1:6 all *G* angels do obeisance to
2:9 he by *G* undeserved kindness
4:10 has entered into *G* rest has
11:3 put in order by *G* word, so
Jas 1:20 work out *G* righteousness
1Pe 1:5 by *G* power through faith for
2:10 but are now *G* people; you
3:22 He is at *G* right hand, for he
4:2 he may live . . . for *G* will
4:10 of *G* undeserved kindness

1Pe 5:3 those who are *G* inheritance
Jude 21 keep yourselves in *G* love

Gods

Ge 31:30 have you stolen my *g*
31:32 you may find your *g*, let
35:2 Put away the foreign *g* that
35:4 gave Jacob all the foreign *g*
Ex 12:12 and on all the *g* of Egypt I
15:11 Who among the *g* is like you
18:11 greater than all the other *g*
20:3 You must not have any other *g*
20:23 not make . . . *g* of silver
20:23 must not make *g* of gold for
22:20 to any *g* but Jehovah alone is
23:13 mention the name of other *g*
23:24 not bow down to their *g* or
23:32 with them or their *g*
23:33 case you should serve their *g*
34:15 intercourse with their *g*
34:15 and sacrifice to their *g*, and
34:16 intercourse with their *g* and
34:16 intercourse with their *g*
34:17 not make molten idol *g* for
Le 19:4 to valueless *g*, and you must
19:4 make molten *g* for yourselves
26:1 not make valueless *g* for
Nu 25:2 to the sacrifices of their *g*
25:2 and to bow down to their *g*
33:4 and upon their *g* Jehovah had
De 4:7 *g* near to it the way Jehovah
4:28 you will have to serve *g*, the
5:7 never have any other *g* against
6:14 must not walk after other *g*
6:14 any *g* of the peoples who are
7:4 will certainly serve other *g*
7:16 you must not serve their *g*
7:25 their *g* you should burn in
8:19 walk after other *g* and serve
10:17 the God of *g* and the Lord of
11:16 worship other *g* and bow
11:28 *g* whom you have not known
12:2 have served their *g*, on the
12:3 graven images of their *g*
12:30 inquire respecting their *g*
12:30 nations used to serve their *g*
12:31 they have done to their *g*
12:31 burn in the fire to their *g*
13:2 Let us walk after other *g*
13:6 Let us go and serve other *g*
13:7 *g* of the peoples who are all
13:13 Let us go and serve other *g*
17:3 worship other *g* and bow down
18:20 in the name of other *g*
20:18 they have done to their *g*
28:14 after other *g* to serve them
28:36 will have to serve other *g*
28:64 *g* whom you have not known
29:18 serve the *g* of those nations
29:26 serve other *g* and to bow
29:26 *g* that they had not known
30:17 to other *g* and serve them
31:16 with foreign *g* of the land
31:18 they have turned to other *g*
31:20 grow fat and turn to other *g*
32:16 to jealousy with strange *g*
32:17 *G* whom they had not known
32:37 say, Where are their *g*
32:39 are no *g* together with me
Jos 23:7 the names of their *g* nor
23:16 served other *g* and bowed
24:2 they used to serve other *g*
24:14 and remove the *g* that your
24:15 the *g* that your forefathers
24:15 the *g* of the Amorites in
24:16 so as to serve other *g*
24:20 and you do serve foreign *g*
24:23 remove the foreign *g* that
Jg 2:3 their *g* will serve as a lure
2:12 went following other *g* from
2:12 the *g* of the peoples who
2:17 intercourse with other *g* and
2:19 by walking after other *g* to
3:6 they took up serving their *g*
5:8 They proceeded to choose new *g*
6:10 fear the *g* of the Amorites
10:6 images and the *g* of Syria and
10:6 Syria and the *g* of Sidon and
10:6 and the *g* of Moab and
10:6 the *g* of the sons of Ammon
10:6 the *g* of the Philistines
10:13 and took up serving other *g*
10:14 the *g* whom you have chosen
10:16 to remove the foreign *g* from
17:5 Micah, he had a house of *g*

Jg 18:24 My *g* that I made you have
Ru 1:15 to her people and her *g*
1Sa 7:3 put away the foreign *g* from
8:8 they kept . . . serving other *g*
17:43 evil upon David by his *g*
26:19 saying, Go, serve other *g*
2Sa 7:23 the nations and their *g*
20:1 Every one to his *g*, O Israel!
1Ki 9:6 serve other *g* and bow down to
9:9 other *g* and bow down to
11:2 your heart to follow their *g*
11:4 his heart to follow other *g*
11:8 and sacrificing to their *g*
11:10 not to go after other *g*
12:16 To your *g*, O Israel
19:2 So may the *g* do, and so may
20:10 So may the *g* do to me, and
2Ki 5:17 to any other *g* but to Jehovah
17:7 they began to fear other *g*
17:31 the *g* of Sepharvaim
17:33 own *g* that they proved to
17:35 You must not fear other *g*
17:37 you must not fear other *g*
17:38 you must not fear other *g*
18:33 Have the *g* of the nations
18:34 the *g* of Hamath and Arpad
18:34 the *g* of Sepharvaim, Hena
18:35 all the *g* of the lands that
19:12 Have the *g* of the nations
19:18 consigned their *g* to the
19:18 because they were no *g*
22:17 smoke to other *g*
1Ch 5:25 *g* of the peoples of the land
14:12 they left their *g* there
16:25 more than all other *g*
16:26 all the *g* of the peoples are
16:26 valueless *g*. As for Jehovah
2Ch 2:5 greater than all the other *g*
7:19 serve other *g* and bow down
7:22 other *g* and bow down to
10:16 Each one to your *g*
13:8 Jeroboam made for you as *g*
13:9 priest of what are no *g*
25:14 *g* of the sons of Seir and
25:14 them up for himself as *g*
25:15 searched for the people's *g*
25:20 searched for the *g* of Edom
28:23 to the *g* of Damascus
28:23 *g* of the kings of Syria
28:25 smoke to other *g*, so that
32:13 *g* of the nations of the
32:14 *g* of these nations that my
32:17 Like the *g* of the nations
32:19 *g* of the peoples of the
33:15 remove the foreign *g* and
34:25 smoke to other *g*, in order
Ps 82:1 middle of the *g* he judges
82:6 have said, You are *g*
86:8 none like you among the *g*
95:3 great King over all other *g*
96:4 above all other *g*
96:5 *g* of the peoples are valueless
96:5 of the peoples are valueless *g*
97:7 their boast in valueless *g*
97:7 Bow down to him, all you *g*
97:9 your ascent over all other *g*
135:5 is more than all other *g*
136:2 thanks to the God of the *g*
138:1 In front of other *g* I shall
Isa 2:8 is filled with valueless *g*
2:18 valueless *g* . . . pass away
2:20 worthless *g* of silver and
2:20 valueless *g* of gold that
10:11 and to her valueless *g*, even
19:1 valueless *g* of Egypt will
19:3 resort to the valueless *g* and
21:9 images of her *g* he has
31:7 his worthless *g* of silver
31:7 and his valueless *g* of gold
36:18 *g* of the nations delivered
36:19 the *g* of Hamath and Arpad
36:19 the *g* of Sepharvaim
36:20 *g* of these lands that have
37:12 *g* of the nations that my
37:19 of their *g* to the fire
37:19 no *g*, but the workmanship
41:23 we may know that you are *g*
42:17 molten image: You are our *g*
Jer 1:16 sacrificial smoke to other *g*
2:11 Has a nation exchanged *g*
2:11 even for those that are no *g*
2:28 where are your *g* that you
2:28 your *g* have become, O Judah
7:6 after other *g* you will not
Jer 7:9 *g* whom you had not known
7:18 drink offerings to other *g*
8:19 with their vain foreign *g*
10:11 The *g* that did not make the
11:10 walked after other *g* in
11:12 call for aid to the *g* to
11:13 your *g* have become as many
13:10 keep walking after other *g*
16:11 kept going after other *g*
16:13 serve other *g* day and night
16:20 man make for himself *g*
16:20 when they are no *g*
19:4 *g* whom they had not known
19:13 drink offerings to other *g*
22:9 bow down to other *g* and to
25:6 do not walk after other *g*
32:29 offerings to other *g* for
35:15 walk after other *g* to serve
43:12 houses of the *g* of Egypt
43:13 houses of the *g* of Egypt he
44:3 rendering service to other *g*
44:5 sacrificial smoke to other *g*
44:8 sacrificial smoke to other *g*
44:15 smoke to other *g*, and
46:25 upon Egypt and upon her *g*
Eze 30:13 the valueless *g* to cease
Da 2:11 *g*, whose own dwelling does
2:47 God . . . is a God of *g* and
3:12 are not serving your own *g*
3:14 you are not serving my own *g*
3:18 your *g* are not the ones we
3:25 is resembling a son of the *g*
4:8 is the spirit of the holy *g*
4:9 spirit of the holy *g* is in you
4:18 the spirit of holy *g* is in you
5:4 praised the *g* of gold and of
5:11 is the spirit of holy *g*; and
5:11 wisdom of *g* were found in
5:14 the spirit of *g* is in you, and
5:23 praised mere *g* of silver and
11:8 *g*, with their molten images
11:36 against the God of *g* he will
Ho 3:1 they are turning to other *g* and
Am 2:8 drink at the house of their *g*
Na 1:14 Out of the house of your *g* I
Hab 2:18 *g* that are speechless
Zep 2:11 emaciate all the *g* of the
Joh 10:34 Law, I said: You are *g*
10:35 he called *g* those against
Ac 7:40 to Aaron, Make *g* for us to go
14:11 *g* have become like humans
19:26 are made by hands are not *g*
1Co 8:5 who are called *g*, whether in
8:5 are many *g* and many lords
Ga 4:8 those who by nature are not *g*

Godship

Ro 1:20 even his eternal power and *G*

Goes

Ge 9:2 everything that *g* moving on
24:35 he *g* on making him greater
24:62 way that *g* to Beer-lahai-roi
40:14 as soon as it *g* well with
Ex 28:35 be heard when he *g* into the
Le 11:20 creature that *g* on all fours
11:42 that *g* upon the belly and
11:42 creature that *g* on all fours
13:16 living flesh *g* back and it
16:17 he *g* in to make atonement
22:4 man from whom there *g* out a
27:21 when it *g* out in the Jubilee
Nu 35:26 *g* out of the boundary of
De 5:26 and yet *g* on living
18:6 the Levite *g* out of one of
19:5 *g* with his fellowman into the
Jos 2:19 who *g* out of the doors of
11:17 which *g* up to Seir, and as
12:7 which *g* up to Seir, after
Jg 5:31 when the sun *g* forth in its
8:13 by the pass that *g* up to Heres
20:31 one of which *g* up to Bethel
21:19 *g* up from Bethel to Shechem
1Sa 6:9 to its territory that it *g* up
9:13 *g* up to the high place to eat
1Ki 18:36 the grain offering *g* up
2Ki 11:8 with the king when he *g* out
12:20 way that *g* down to Silla
1Ch 26:16 by the highway that *g* up
2Ch 23:7 comes in and when he *g* out
Ne 3:15 *g* down from the City of David
3:25 *g* out from the King's House
Job 7:4 evening . . . *g* its measure
7:9 cloud . . . to its end and *g*
8:16 in his garden his own twig *g*
Job 14:20 so that he *g* away
16:6 what *g* away from me
28:5 earth, out of it food *g* forth
37:2 growling that *g* forth from
39:21 It *g* forth to meet armor
41:20 Out of its nostrils smoke *g*
41:21 a flame *g* forth out of its
Ps 97:3 Before him a very fire *g*
104:23 Man *g* forth to his activity
126:6 without fail *g* forth, even
146:4 His spirit *g* out, he
146:4 he *g* back to his ground
Pr 5:23 of his foolishness he *g* astray
15:21 is one who *g* straight ahead
19:15 and a slack soul *g* hungry
23:31 when it *g* with a slickness
26:20 is no wood the fire *g* out
Ec 4:15 how it *g* with the child, who
6:4 and in darkness he *g* away, and
Isa 15:5 with weeping each one *g* up
32:19 hail when the forest *g* down
55:11 *g* forth from my mouth
62:1 *g* forth just like the
63:14 *g* down into the valley
Jer 46:22 of a serpent that *g* along
48:5 with weeping that one *g* up
La 1:6 there *g* out all her splendor
1:9 And down she *g* in a wondrous
Eze 40:40 as one *g* up to the entrance
Ho 6:4 like the dew that early *g* away
6:5 be as the light that *g* forth
13:3 the dew that early *g* away
Hab 1:4 and justice never *g* forth
1:4 reason justice *g* forth crooked
Zec 10:4 *g* forth every taskmaster
Mt 12:45 it *g* its way and takes along
13:44 *g* and sells what things he
Mr 14:14 wherever he *g* inside say to
Lu 11:26 it *g* its way and takes along
12:6 not one of them *g* forgotten
12:21 So it *g* with the man that
16:30 if someone from the dead *g*
Joh 10:4 *g* before them, and the sheep
1Co 6:6 but brother *g* to court with
Col 2:19 *g* on growing with the
1Ti 5:6 the one that *g* in for sensual
Jas 1:24 looks at himself . . . off he *g*
1:26 *g* on deceiving his own heart
3Jo 10 his works which he *g* on doing
Re 13:10 he *g* away into captivity
14:4 Lamb no matter where he *g*
17:11 and it *g* off into destruction
19:3 smoke from her *g* on ascending

Gog

1Ch 5:4 Shemaiah his son, *G* his son
Eze 38:2 *G* of the land of Magog, the
38:3 *G*, you head chieftain of
38:14 must say to *G*, This is what
38:16 before their eyes, O *G*
38:18 when *G* comes in upon the
39:1 prophesy against *G*, and you
39:1 I am against you, O *G*, you
39:11 give to *G* a place there
39:11 to bury *G* and all his crowd
Re 20:8 *G* and Magog, to gather them

Gog's

Eze 39:11 the Valley of *G* Crowd
39:15 in the Valley of *G* Crowd

Goiim

Ge 14:1 and Tidal king of *G*
14:9 Tidal king of *G* and
Jos 12:23 king of *G* in Gilgal, one

Going*

Ex 34:12 the land to which you are *g*
Nu 14:14 *g* before them in the pillar
24:14 I am *g* away to my people
34:2 are *g* into the land of Canaan
De 1:30 God is the one *g* before you
7:1 the land to which you are *g*
11:10 the land to which you are *g*
23:4 when you were *g* out of Egypt
23:20 the land to which you are *g*
31:16 the land to which they are *g*
1Sa 18:16 *g* out and coming in before
29:6 your *g* out and your coming
2Sa 3:25 your *g* out and your coming
2Ki 19:27 *g* out and your coming in
Job 7:9 So he that is *g* down to Sheol
33:24 from *g* down into the pit
Ps 22:29 all those *g* down to the dust
28:1 like those *g* down to the pit
78:39 spirit is *g* forth and does

s 88:4 those *g* down to the pit
115:17 do any *g* down into silence
c 1:4 A generation is *g*, and a
9:10 the place to which you are *g*
a 8:6 the Shiloah that are *g* gently
31:1 those *g* down to Egypt for
37:28 your *g* out and your coming
38:18 Those *g* down into the pit
ze 31:14 those *g* down into the pit
31:15 day of its *g* down to Sheol
31:16 those *g* down into the pit
32:24 those *g* down into the pit
32:25 those *g* down into the pit
32:29 those *g* down into the pit
32:30 those *g* down into the pit
t 26:24 the Son of man is *g* away
r 14:21 the Son of man is *g* away
u 22:22 Son of man is *g* his way
h 8:14 I know . . . where I am *g*
8:14 not know . . . where I am *g*
8:21 I am *g* you cannot come
8:22 Where I am *g* you cannot
12:35 not know where he is *g*
13:3 and was *g* to God
13:36 Lord, where are you *g*?
13:36 *g* you cannot follow me now
14:2 *g* my way to prepare a place
14:4 I am *g* you know the way
14:5 do not know where you are *g*
14:12 *g* my way to the Father
14:28 I am *g* away and I am coming
14:28 am *g* my way to the Father
16:28 am *g* my way to the Father
eb 11:8 obeyed in *g* out into a place
11:8 not knowing where he was *g*
o 2:11 does not know where he is *g*

oings
s 65:8 The *g* forth of the morning
r 31:27 the *g* on of her household

olan
e 4:43 and *G* in Bashan for the
s 20:8 *G* in Bashan out of the tribe
21:27 city of refuge . . . *G*, in
h 6:71 *G* in Bashan with its pasture

old
e 2:11 of Havilah, where there is *g*
2:12 And the *g* of that land is
13:2 with herds and silver and *g*
24:22 man took a *g* nose ring of a
24:22 ten shekels of *g* was their
24:35 silver and *g* and menservants
24:53 articles of *g* and garments
41:42 a necklace of *g* about his
44:8 could we steal silver or *g*
x 3:22 articles of *g* and mantles
11:2 of silver and articles of *g*
12:35 articles of *g* and mantles
20:23 must not make gods of *g* for
25:3 to take up from them: *g* and
25:11 must overlay it with pure *g*
25:11 border of *g* round about upon
25:12 cast four rings of *g* for it
25:13 and overlay them with *g*
25:17 must make a cover of pure *g*
25:18 must make two cherubs of *g*
25:24 must overlay it with pure *g*
25:24 a border of *g* round about
25:25 the border of *g* for its rim
25:26 make for it four rings of *g*
25:28 and overlay them with *g*, and
25:29 to make them out of pure *g*
25:31 make a lampstand of pure *g*
25:36 of hammered work, of pure *g*
25:38 fire holders are of pure *g*
25:39 Of a talent of pure *g* he
26:6 fifty hooks of *g* and join
26:29 the panel frames with *g*, and
26:29 rings you will make of *g* as
26:29 must overlay the bars with *g*
26:32 of acacia overlaid with *g*
26:32 Their pegs are of *g*. They are
26:37 and overlay them with *g*
26:37 Their pegs are of *g*
28:5 take the *g* and the blue thread
28:6 ephod of *g*, blue thread and
28:8 materials, of *g*, blue thread
28:11 Set in settings of *g* is how
28:13 you must make settings of *g*
28:14 and two chains of pure *g*
28:15 Of *g*, blue thread and wool
28:20 Sockets of *g* should be in
28:22 in rope work, of pure *g*
28:23 two rings of *g*, and you must

Ex 28:24 must put the two ropes of *g*
28:26 make two rings of *g* and set
28:27 make two rings of *g* and put
28:33 bells of *g* in between them
28:34 bell of *g* and a pomegranate
28:34 bell of *g* and a pomegranate
28:36 a shining plate of pure *g*
30:3 must overlay it with pure *g*
30:3 a border of *g* round about for
30:4 make for it two rings of *g*
30:5 and overlay them with *g*
31:4 devices, for working in *g* and
31:8 lampstand of pure *g* and all
32:2 Tear off the *g* earrings that
32:3 tearing off the *g* earrings
32:4 took the *g* from their hands
32:24 Who have any *g*? They must
32:31 a god of *g* for themselves
35:5 *g* and silver and copper
35:22 all sorts of articles of *g*
35:22 wave offering of *g* to Jehovah
35:32 working in *g* and silver and
36:13 made fifty hooks of *g* and
36:34 the panel frames with *g*, and
36:34 rings of *g* as supports for
36:34 to overlay the bars with *g*
36:36 and overlaid them with *g*
36:36 their pegs being of *g*, and
36:38 tops and their joints with *g*
37:2 with pure *g* inside and outside
37:2 border of *g* round about for it
37:3 he cast four rings of *g* for it
37:4 and overlaid them with *g*
37:6 to make the cover of pure *g*
37:7 made two cherubs of *g*
37:11 overlaid it with pure *g* and
37:11 border of *g* round about for
37:12 border of *g* for its rim
37:13 cast four rings of *g* for it
37:15 overlaid them with *g* for
37:16 be poured, out of pure *g*
37:17 made the lampstand of pure *g*
37:22 of hammered work of pure *g*
37:23 fire holders out of pure *g*
37:24 a talent of pure *g* he made
37:26 he overlaid it with pure *g*
37:26 border of *g* round about for
37:27 made for it two rings of *g*
37:28 and overlaid them with *g*
38:24 All the *g* that was used for
38:24 amount of the *g* of the wave
39:2 ephod of *g*, blue thread and
39:3 plates of *g* to thin sheets
39:5 of *g*, blue thread, and wool
39:6 stones set with settings of *g*
39:8 of the ephod, out of *g*, blue
39:13 set with settings of *g* in
39:15 in rope work, of pure *g*
39:16 they made two settings of *g*
39:16 and two rings of *g* and put
39:17 they put the two ropes of *g*
39:19 made two rings of *g* and set
39:20 made two rings of *g* and put
39:25 made bells of pure *g* and put
39:30 shining plate . . . of pure *g*
39:37 the lampstand of pure *g*, its
39:38 altar of *g* and the anointing
Le 8:9 the shining plate of *g*, the
24:4 lampstand of pure *g* he should
24:6 table of pure *g* before Jehovah
Nu 7:14 *g* cup of ten shekels, full of
7:20 *g* cup of ten shekels, full
7:26 *g* cup of ten shekels, full
7:32 *g* cup of ten shekels, full of
7:38 *g* cup of ten shekels, full of
7:44 *g* cup of ten shekels, full of
7:50 *g* cup of ten shekels, full of
7:56 *g* cup of ten shekels, full
7:62 *g* cup of ten shekels, full of
7:68 one *g* cup of ten shekels, full
7:74 *g* cup of ten shekels, full of
7:80 *g* cup of ten shekels, full of
7:84 twelve *g* cups
7:86 twelve *g* cups full of incense
7:86 all the *g* of the cups being a
8:4 It was hammered work of *g*
22:18 house full of silver and *g*
24:13 house full of silver and *g*
31:22 Only the *g* and the silver
31:50 articles of *g*, ankle
31:51 priest accepted the *g* from
31:52 all the *g* of the contribution
31:54 the *g* from the chiefs of the
De 7:25 desire the silver and the *g*

De 8:13 silver and *g* may increase for
17:17 increase silver and *g* for
29:17 dungy idols . . . silver and *g*
Jos 6:19 all the silver and the *g* and
6:24 the silver and the *g* and the
7:21 one *g* bar, fifty shekels
7:24 the bar of *g* and his sons and
22:8 with silver and *g* and copper
Jg 8:24 For they had nose rings of *g*
8:26 weight of the nose rings of *g*
8:26 *g* shekels, besides the
2Sa 1:24 put ornaments of *g* upon your
8:7 circular shields of *g* that
8:10 and articles of *g* and
8:11 *g* that he had sanctified
12:30 of which was a talent of *g*
21:4 not a matter of silver or *g*
1Ki 6:20 to overlay it with pure *g*
6:21 the house inside with pure *g*
6:21 chainwork of *g* pass across
6:21 and to overlay it with *g*
6:22 house he overlaid with *g*
6:22 altar . . . he overlaid with *g*
6:28 overlaid the cherubs with *g*
6:30 overlaid with *g*, inside and
6:32 and he overlaid them with *g*
6:32 beat the *g* down upon the
6:35 and overlaid *g* foil upon the
7:48 the altar of *g* and the table
7:48 was the showbread, of *g*
7:49 of pure *g*, and the blossoms
7:49 lamps and the snuffers, of *g*
7:50 the fire holders, of pure *g*
7:50 house of the temple, of *g*
7:51 the silver and the *g* and the
9:11 *g* as much as he delighted in
9:14 and twenty talents of *g*
9:28 and twenty talents of *g* and
10:2 much *g* and precious stones
10:10 talents of *g* and a very
10:11 that carried *g* from Ophir
10:14 the weight of the *g* that
10:14 and sixty-six talents of *g*
10:16 large shields of alloyed *g*
10:16 six hundred shekels of *g* he
10:17 bucklers of alloyed *g*
10:17 three minas of *g* he
10:18 overlaid it with refined *g*
10:21 vessels . . . were of *g*
10:21 vessels . . . were of pure *g*
10:22 carrying *g* and silver
10:25 of silver and articles of *g*
14:26 all the *g* shields that
15:15 silver and *g* and articles
15:18 all the silver and the *g*
15:19 a present of silver and *g*
20:3 silver and your *g* are mine
20:5 silver and your *g* and your
20:7 my silver and my *g*, and I
22:48 ships to go to Ophir for *g*
2Ki 5:5 and six thousand pieces of *g*
7:8 silver and *g* and garments and
12:13 any sort of *g* article and
12:18 all the *g* to be found in
14:14 he took all the *g* and silver
16:8 took the silver and the *g*
18:14 and thirty *g* talents
20:13 the silver and the *g* and
23:33 talents and a *g* talent
23:35 the *g* Jehoiakim gave to
23:35 the silver and the *g* from
24:13 to pieces all the *g* utensils
25:15 that were of genuine *g* and
1Ch 18:7 the circular shields of *g*
18:10 articles of *g* and silver and
18:11 the silver and the *g* that he
20:2 a talent of *g* in weight, and
21:25 *g* shekels to the weight of
22:14 thousand talents of *g* and
22:16 The *g*, the silver and the
28:14 for the *g* by weight
28:14 *g* for all the utensils for
28:15 for the lampstands of *g*
28:15 and their lamps of *g*, by
28:16 *g* by weight for the tables
28:17 and the pitchers of pure *g*
28:17 small *g* bowls by weight
28:18 the incense altar refined *g*
28:18 cherubs of *g* for spreading
29:2 the *g* for the goldwork, and
29:3 *g* and silver; I do give it
29:4, 4 of *g* of the *g* of Ophir
29:5 of the *g* for the goldwork
29:7 *g* worth five thousand

2Ch 1:15 silver . . . *g* in Jerusalem
2:7 skillful man to work in *g* and
2:14 to work in *g* and in silver
3:4 overlay it inside with pure *g*
3:5 he covered it with good *g*
3:6 stone for beauty; and the *g*
3:6, 6 was *g* from the *g* country
3:7 walls and its doors with *g*
3:8 he covered it with good *g* to
3:9 the nails was fifty *g* shekels
3:9 chambers he covered with *g*
3:10 two cherubs . . . *g*
4:7 made lampstands of *g*, ten of
4:8 and made a hundred bowls of *g*
4:20 and their lamps of pure *g*
4:21 lamps and the snuffers, of *g*
4:21 it was the purest *g*
4:22 the fire holders, of pure *g*
4:22 house of the temple, of *g*
5:1 silver and the *g* and all the
8:18 and fifty talents of *g* and
9:1 *g* in great quantity, and
9:9 and twenty talents of *g*, and
9:10 *g* from Ophir brought timbers
9:13 *g* that came to Solomon in
9:13 and sixty-six talents of *g*
9:14 in *g* and silver to Solomon
9:15 large shields of alloyed *g*
9:15 hundred shekels of alloyed *g*
9:16 hundred bucklers of alloyed *g*
9:16 three minas of *g* he
9:17 and overlaid it with pure *g*
9:18 footstool in *g* to the throne
9:20 vessels . . . were of *g*
9:20 vessels . . . were of pure *g*
9:21 carrying *g* and silver, ivory
9:24 articles of *g* and garments
12:9 *g* shields that Solomon had
13:11 upon the table of pure *g*
15:18 silver and *g* and utensils
16:2 *g* from the treasures of
16:3 I do send you silver and *g*
21:3 gifts in silver and in *g* and
24:14 utensils of *g* and of silver
25:24 he took all the *g* and the
32:27 *g* and for precious stones
36:3 silver talents and a *g* talent
Ezr 1:4 with silver and with *g* and
1:6 utensils of silver, with *g*
1:9 basket-shaped vessels of *g*
1:10 thirty small bowls of *g*
1:11 utensils of *g* and of silver
2:69 *g* for the working supplies
5:14 also the *g* and silver vessels
6:5 let the *g* and silver vessels
7:15 to bring the silver and the *g*
7:16 all the silver and the *g* that
7:18 the rest of the silver and *g*
8:25 the silver and the *g* and the
8:26 and *g* a hundred talents
8:27 twenty small *g* bowls worth
8:27 red, as desirable as *g*
8:28 the silver and the *g* are a
8:30 silver and the *g* and the
8:33 the silver and the *g* and the
Ne 7:70 a thousand *g* drachmas
7:71 twenty thousand *g* drachmas
7:72 twenty thousand *g* drachmas
Es 1:6 couches of *g* and silver upon a
1:7 wine to drink in *g* vessels
8:15 with a great crown of *g*, and
Job 3:15 Or with princes who have *g*
22:24 *g* of Ophir in the rock of
23:10 I shall come forth as *g*
28:1 place for *g* that they refine
28:6 And it has *g* dust
28:15 Pure *g* cannot be given in
28:16 paid for with *g* of Ophir
28:17 *G* and glass cannot be
28:17 any vessel of refined *g*
28:19 even with *g* in its purity
31:24 put *g* as my confidence, Or
31:24 to *g* I have said, You are
42:11 and each one a *g* ring
Ps 19:10 more to be desired than *g*
19:10 yes, than much refined *g*
21:3 a crown of refined *g*
45:9 her stand . . . in *g* of Ophir
45:13 is with settings of *g*
68:13 with yellowish-green *g*
72:15 of the *g* of Sheba be given
105:37 them out with silver and *g*
115:4 Their idols are silver and *g*
119:72 thousands of pieces of *g*
Ps 119:127, 127 than *g*, even refined *g*
135:15 nations are silver and *g*
Pr 3:14 having it as produce than *g*
8:10 rather than choice *g*
8:19 My fruitage is better than *g*
8:19 even than refined *g*, and my
11:22 *g* nose ring in the snout of
16:16 wisdom is . . . better than *g*
17:3 the furnace for *g*, but Jehovah
20:15 exists *g*, also an abundance
22:1 better than even silver and *g*
25:11 As apples of *g* in silver
25:12 An earring of *g*, and an
25:12 ornament of special *g*, is a
27:21 and the furnace is for *g*
Ec 2:8 accumulated also silver and *g*
Ca 1:11 Circlets of *g* we shall make
3:10 its supports of *g*. Its seat is
5:11, 11 His head is *g*, refined *g*
5:14 His hands are cylinders of *g*
5:15 socket pedestals of refined *g*
Isa 2:7 is filled with silver and *g*
2:20 valueless gods of *g* that
13:12 man rarer than refined *g*
13:12 rarer than the *g* of Ophir
13:17 *g*, take no delight in it
30:22 your molten statue of *g*
31:7 his valueless gods of *g*, that
39:2 the silver and the *g* and the
40:19 with *g* the metalworker
46:6 lavishing out the *g* from
60:6 *G* and frankincense they will
60:9 their silver and their *g*
60:17 I shall bring in *g*, and
Jer 4:30 with ornaments of *g*
10:4 with *g* one makes it pretty
10:9 and *g* from Uphaz, the
52:19 that were of genuine *g*
La 4:1 the *g* that shines becomes dim
4:1 shines becomes dim, the good *g*
4:2 were weighed against refined *g*
Eze 7:19 abhorrent thing their own *g*
7:19 nor their *g* will be able to
16:13 decking yourself with *g* and
16:17 articles from my *g* and
27:22 precious stones and *g*
28:4 you keep getting *g* and silver
28:13 *g* was the workmanship of
38:13 to carry off silver and *g*
Da 2:32 image, its head was of good *g*
2:35 silver and the *g* were, all
2:38 yourself are the head of *g*
2:45 clay, the silver and the *g*
3:1 king made an image of *g*, the
3:5 worship the image of *g* that
3:7 worshiping the image of *g*
3:10 and worship the image of *g*
3:12 image of *g* that you have set
3:14 image of *g* that I have set up
3:18 image of *g* that you have set
5:2 to bring in the vessels of *g*
5:3 vessels of *g* that they had
5:4 praised the gods of *g* and of
5:7 necklace of *g* about his neck
5:16 necklace of *g* around your neck
5:23 mere gods of silver and of *g*
5:29 necklace of *g* about his neck
10:5 hips girded with *g* of Uphaz
11:8 articles of silver and of *g*
11:38 give glory by means of *g*
11:43 hidden treasures of the *g*
Ho 2:8 *g*, which they made use of for
8:4 With their silver and their *g*
Joe 3:5 my own silver and my own *g*
Na 2:9 plunder *g*; as there is no
Hab 2:19 is sheathed in *g* and silver
Zep 1:18 silver nor their *g* will be
Hag 2:8 silver is mine, and the *g* is
Zec 4:2 a lampstand, all of it of *g*
6:11 take silver and *g* and make a
9:3 *g* like the mire of the
13:9 as in the examining of *g*
14:14 *g* and silver and garments
Mal 3:3 must clarify them like *g* and
Mt 2:11 *g* and frankincense and myrrh
10:9 Do not procure *g* or silver or
23:16 by the *g* of the temple, he
23:17 greater, the *g* or the temple
23:17 temple . . . sanctified the *g*
Ac 3:6 Silver and *g* I do not possess
17:29 the Divine Being is like *g* or
20:33 coveted no man's silver or *g*
1Co 3:12 builds on the foundation *g*
1Ti 2:9 hair braiding and *g* or pearls
2Ti 2:20 vessels not only of *g* and
Heb 9:4 overlaid all around with *g*
Jas 2:2 man with *g* rings on his
5:3 Your *g* and silver are rusted
1Pe 1:7 greater value than *g* that
1:18 with silver or *g*, that you
3:3 the putting on of *g* ornaments
Re 3:18 buy from me *g* refined by
9:7 seemed to be crowns like *g*
9:20 the idols of *g* and silver and
17:4 adorned with *g* and precious
18:12 full stock of *g* and silver
18:16 adorned with *g* ornament and
21:18 city was pure *g* like clear
21:21 way of the city was pure *g*

Golden
Ex 40:5 put the *g* altar for incense
40:26 the *g* altar in the tent of
Nu 4:11 over the *g* altar they will
1Sa 6:4 five *g* piles and five
6:4 five *g* jerboas, for every one
6:8 the *g* articles that you must
6:11 the box and the *g* jerboas
6:15 in which the *g* articles were
6:17 *g* piles that the Philistines
6:18 *g* jerboas were to the number
1Ki 12:28 made two *g* calves and said
2Ki 10:29 the *g* calves of which one
2Ch 4:19 the *g* altar and the tables
13:8 *g* calves that Jeroboam made
13:11 *g* lampstands and its lamps
Es 4:11 holds out . . . the *g* scepter
5:2 out to Esther the *g* scepter
8:4 king held the *g* scepter out to
Job 37:22 Out of the north *g* splendor
Ec 12:6 and the *g* bowl gets crushed
Jer 51:7 Babylon has been a *g* cup in
Zec 4:12 two *g* tubes, are pouring
4:12 pouring . . . the *g* liquid
Heb 9:4 a *g* censer and the ark of the
9:4 the *g* jar having the manna
Re 1:12 I saw seven *g* lampstands
1:13 the breasts with a *g* girdle
1:20 of the seven *g* lampstands
2:1 of the seven *g* lampstands
4:4 upon their heads *g* crowns
5:8 each one a harp and *g* bowls
8:3 having a *g* incense vessel; and
8:3 upon the *g* altar that was
9:13 the *g* altar that is before God
14:14 *g* crown on his head and a
15:6 their breasts with *g* girdles
15:7 seven *g* bowls that were full
17:4 *g* cup that was full of
21:15 as a measure a *g* reed, that

Goldsmith
Ne 3:31 a member of the *g* guild

Goldsmiths
Ne 3:8 Uzziel the son of Harhaiah, *g*
3:32 the *g* and the traders did

Goldwork
1Ch 29:2 the gold for the *g*, and the
29:5 of the gold for the *g*, and

Golgotha
Mt 27:33 *G*, that is to say, Skull
Mr 15:22 brought him to the place *G*
Joh 19:17 is called *G* in Hebrew

Goliath
1Sa 17:4 his name being *G*, from Gath
17:23 *G* the Philistine from Gath
21:9 sword of *G* the Philistine
22:10 sword of *G* the Philistine
2Sa 21:19 strike down *G* the Gittite
1Ch 20:5 Lahmi the brother of *G* the

Gomer
Ge 10:2 sons of Japheth were *G* and
10:3 sons of *G* were Ashkenaz
1Ch 1:5 *G* and Magog and Madai and
1:6 sons of *G* were Ashkenaz and
Eze 38:6 *G* and all its bands, the
Ho 1:3 *G* the daughter of Diblaim, so

Gomorrah
Ge 10:19 as far as Sodom and *G* and
13:10 Jehovah brought Sodom and *G*
14:2 Birsha king of *G*, Shinab king
14:8 and also the king of *G* and the
14:10 the kings of Sodom and *G*
14:11 Sodom and *G* and all their
18:20 complaint about Sodom and *G*
19:24 upon Sodom and upon *G*

Ge 19:28 down toward Sodom and *G*
De 29:23 the overthrow of Sodom and *G*
32:32 And from the terraces of *G*
Isa 1:9 we should have resembled *G*
1:10 Give ear . . . you people of *G*
13:19 God overthrew Sodom and *G*
Jer 23:14 inhabitants of her like *G*
49:18 overthrow of Sodom and *G*
50:40 *G* and of her neighbor towns
Am 4:11 overthrow of Sodom and *G*
Zep 2:9 and the sons of Ammon like *G*
Mt 10:15 for the land of Sodom and *G*
Ro 9:29 have been made just like *G*
2Pe 2:6 cities Sodom and *G* to ashes
Jude 7 and *G* and the cities about

Gone

Ge 19:23 sun had *g* forth over the land
20:4 Abimelech had not *g* near her
31:19 Laban had *g* to shear his
31:30 you have actually *g* now
35:3 in the way that I have *g*
37:30 he exclaimed: The child is *g!*
44:4 had not *g* far when Joseph
49:4 have *g* up to your father's bed
Ex 4:21 After you have *g* and returned
14:28 *g* into the sea after them
33:9 as Moses had *g* into the tent
Nu 11:26 had not *g* out to the tent
14:24 into the land where he has *g*
16:46 indignation has *g* out from
30:2 that has *g* out of his mouth
31:21 who had *g* into the battle
32:24 has *g* forth from your mouth
De 2:3 *g* around this mountain long
13:13 men have *g* out from your
Jos 2:5 know where the men have *g*
2:7 chasing after them had *g* out
10:9 he had *g* up from Gilgal
10:24 men of war that had *g* with
23:16 you have *g* and served other
Jg 4:12 had *g* up to Mount Tabor
4:14 Jehovah that has *g* out before
11:36 what has *g* forth from your
18:14 men that had *g* to spy out
18:17 men that had *g* to spy out
19:11 as the daylight had *g* down
20:3 Israel had *g* up to Mizpah
Ru 1:13 Jehovah has *g* out against me
1Sa 4:21 Glory has *g* away from Israel
4:22 Glory has *g* away from Israel
10:2 that you have *g* to look for
14:3 not know that Jonathan had *g*
14:17 see who has *g* out from us
14:21 *g* up with them into the
15:35 Samuel had *g* into mourning
23:15 Saul had *g* out to look for
24:14 the king of Israel *g* out
25:37 wine had *g* out of Nabal
26:20 *g* out to look for a single
30:22 men that had *g* with David
2Sa 5:24 Jehovah will have *g* out
11:10 Why have you not *g* down to
15:11 there had *g* with Absalom
1Ki 1:25 *g* down that he might
2:41 was told: Shimei has *g* out
13:12 had come out of Judah had *g*
20:40 why, he himself was *g*
21:18 *g* down to take possession
22:13 that had *g* to call Micaiah
2Ki 1:4 couch upon which you have *g*
1:6 couch upon which you have *g*
1:16 couch upon which you have *g*
2:9 as soon as they had *g* across
5:2 had *g* out as marauder bands
9:16 had *g* down to see Jehoram
20:4 not yet *g* out to the middle
20:11 shadow that had *g* down
22:17 have *g* making sacrificial
25:11 *g* over to the king of
1Ch 14:15 God will have *g* out before
2Ch 34:25 *g* making sacrificial smoke
Ne 2:16 did not know where I had *g*
4:7 *g* forward, for the gaps had
4:15 all of us *g* back to the wall
Job 1:5 banquet days had *g* round the
24:5 *g* forth in their activity
Ps 19:4 measuring line has *g* out
34:10 little on hand and *g* hungry
122:4 To which the tribes have *g*
Pr 6:1 if you have *g* surety for your
7:19 *g* traveling on a way of
11:15 has *g* surety for a stranger
20:16 has *g* surety for a stranger
27:13 has *g* surety for a stranger
Ec 4:14 *g* forth from the prison house
Ca 2:11 is over, it has *g* its way
4:2 freshly-shorn ewes that have *g*
5:6 My very soul had *g* out of me
6:1 Where has your dear one *g*, O
6:2 My own dear one has *g* down to
6:11 garden of nut trees I had *g*
Isa 15:2 *g* up to The House and to
15:8 outcry has *g* around the
16:8 they had *g* over to the sea
22:1 *g* up in your entirety to the
24:4 land has *g* to mourning, has
24:7 new wine has *g* to mourning
24:7 at heart have *g* to sighing
28:7 wine they have *g* astray and
28:7 *g* astray because of
28:7 *g* astray in their seeing
31:6 have *g* deep in their revolt
33:9 land has *g* mourning, has
38:8 had *g* down on the steps of
38:8 stairs that it had *g* down
45:23 the word has *g* forth
49:21 *g* into exile and taken
59:4 *g* to court in faithfulness
Jer 3:20 a wife has treacherously *g*
4:7 *g* up as a lion out of his
4:7 *g* forth from his place in
4:29 into the rocks they have *g* up
5:19 have *g* serving a foreign god
9:10 they will have *g*
10:20 My own sons have *g* forth
14:2 Judah has *g* mourning, and
14:2 outcry of Jerusalem has *g* up
14:18 *g* around to a land that they
22:11 has *g* forth from this place
23:10 the land has *g* to mourning
23:15 apostasy has *g* forth to all
29:2 had *g* forth from Jerusalem
29:16 *g* forth with you into exile
30:23 rage itself, has *g* forth
44:17 word that has *g* forth from
48:11 into exile they have not *g*
48:15 *g* up against her own cities
48:15 *g* down to the slaughtering
49:7 wisdom *g* to putrefying
50:3 They have *g* away
50:6 to hill they have *g*
La 1:3 Judah has *g* into exile because
1:18 men have *g* into captivity
4:15 For they have *g* homeless
Eze 7:10 The garland has *g* forth
15:7 Out of the fire they have *g*
24:6 rust of which has not *g*
25:3 they have *g* into exile
31:17 also have *g* down to Sheol
32:24 have *g* down uncircumcised
32:27 who have *g* down to Sheol
32:30 *g* down with the slain ones
36:20 from his land they have *g*
37:21 to which they have *g*, and
Da 2:14 *g* out to kill the wise men of
4:31 kingdom itself has *g* away
Ho 4:18 Their wheat beer being *g*
5:2 have *g* deep down, and I was
7:11 to Assyria they have *g*
8:9 have *g* up to Assyria
9:1 *g* from alongside your God
9:9 *g* down deep in bringing ruin
10:5 it will have *g* into exile
Joe 1:10 the ground has *g* to mourning
1:12 exultation has *g* ashamed
Am 2:7 *g* to the same girl, for the
Jon 1:5 Jonah himself had *g* down to
Mic 1:11 Zaanan has not *g* forth
1:16 *g* away from you into exile
Zec 5:3 has *g* free of punishment
5:3 has *g* free of punishment
Mt 9:28 After he had *g* into the house
26:71 had *g* out to the gatehouse
Mr 1:38 this purpose I have *g* out
3:21 He has *g* out of his mind
5:30 that power had *g* out of him
7:29 demon has *g* out of your
7:30 and the demon *g* out
Lu 7:24 the messengers of John had *g*
8:38 the demons had *g* out
Joh 4:8 *g* off into the city to buy
4:45 also had *g* to the festival
7:10 brothers had *g* up to the
11:11 Lazarus our friend has *g* to
11:12 if he has *g* to rest, he
12:19 The world has *g* after him
13:31 when he had *g* out, Jesus
Ac 8:27 *g* to Jerusalem to worship
Ac 11:3 *g* into the house of men that
13:6 *g* through the whole island
13:31 *g* up with him from Galilee
15:38 had not *g* with them to the
1Co 16:5 *g* through Macedonia, for I
2Ti 4:10 he has *g* to Thessalonica
Heb 11:15 from which they had *g* forth
Jas 5:5 have *g* in for sensual pleasure
1Jo 4:1 false prophets have *g* forth
2Jo 7 deceivers have *g* forth into the
Jude 7 *g* out after flesh for unnatural
11 have *g* in the path of Cain

Good

Ge 1:4 God saw that the light was *g*
1:10 God saw that it was *g*
1:12 God saw that it was *g*
1:18 Then God saw that it was *g*
1:21 God got to see that it was *g*
1:25 God got to see that it was *g*
1:31 and, look! it was very *g*
2:9 *g* for food and also the tree
2:9 tree of the knowledge of *g* and
2:12 the gold of that land is *g*
2:17 tree of the knowledge of *g*
2:18 It is not *g* for the man to
3:5 to be like God, knowing *g* and
3:6 woman saw that the tree was *g*
3:22 like one of us in knowing *g*
4:7 If you turn to doing *g*, will
4:7 if you do not turn to doing *g*
15:15 be buried at a *g* old age
16:6 Do to her what is *g* in your
18:7 get a tender and *g* young bull
19:8 do to them as is *g* in your
20:3 you are as *g* as dead because
20:15 Dwell where it is *g* in your
24:10 with every sort of *g* thing
24:50 unable to speak bad or *g* to
25:8 and died in a *g* old age, old
26:8 was Isaac having a *g* time
26:29 just as we have done only *g*
27:9 two kids of the goats, *g* ones
27:46 what *g* is life to me?
30:11 Leah said: With *g* fortune
30:20 with a *g* endowment
31:24 speaking either *g* or bad
31:29 speaking either *g* or bad
34:18 And their words seemed *g* in
35:16 yet a *g* stretch of land
40:16 had interpreted something *g*
41:5 on one stalk, fat and *g*
41:22 up on one stalk, full and *g*
41:24 the seven *g* ears of grain
41:26 The seven *g* cows are seven
41:26 the seven *g* ears of grain are
41:35 foodstuffs of . . . *g* years
41:37 *g* in the eyes of Pharaoh and
44:4 have you repaid bad for *g*
45:16 *g* in the eyes of Pharaoh
45:18 the *g* of the land of Egypt
45:20 *g* of all the land of Egypt
45:23 ten asses carrying *g* things
48:7 a *g* stretch of land before
49:15 the resting-place is *g* and
50:20 God had it in mind for *g* for
Ex 3:8 to a land *g* and spacious, to a
12:33 we are all as *g* as dead
18:9 the *g* that Jehovah had done
18:17 It is not *g* the way you are
32:6 they got up to have a *g* time
Le 5:4 lips to do evil or to do *g*
24:22 decision . . . hold *g* for you
27:10 exchange it with *g* for bad
27:10 or with bad for *g*
27:12 whether it is *g* or bad
27:14 whether it is *g* or bad
27:33 examine whether it is *g* or
Nu 10:29 do *g* to you, because Jehovah
10:29 because Jehovah has spoken *g*
10:32 Jehovah will do *g* with us
10:32 in turn, will do *g* to you
13:19 whether it is *g* or bad, and
14:7 is a very, very *g* land
24:1 was *g* in the eyes of Jehovah
24:13 *g* or bad out of my own heart
36:6 To whom it is *g* in their eyes
De 1:14 have spoken for us to do is *g*
1:23 proved to be *g* in my eyes, so
1:25 land . . . God is giving us is *g*
1:35 see the *g* land that I swore
1:39 do not know *g* or bad, these
3:25 see the *g* land that is across
3:25 *g* mountainous region and
4:9 take *g* care of your soul, that

De 4:15 take *g* care of your souls
4:21 go into the *g* land that
4:22 take possession of this *g* land
6:11 houses full of all *g* things
6:18 right and *g* in Jehovah's eyes
6:18 take possession of the *g* land
6:24 fear Jehovah our God for our *g*
8:7 bringing you into a *g* land
8:10 *g* land that he has given you
8:12 build *g* houses and indeed
8:16 to do you *g* in your afterdays
9:6 God is giving you this *g* land
10:13 commanding . . . for your *g*
11:17 the *g* land that Jehovah is
12:28 do what is *g* and right in
19:13 that you may have *g*
19:15 the matter should stand *g*
24:8 take *g* care and do according
26:11 rejoice over all the *g*
28:12 open up . . . his *g* storehouse
28:63 do you *g* and to multiply you
30:5 do you *g* and multiply you
30:9 again exult over you for *g*
30:15 life and *g*, and death and bad
Jos 9:25 as it is *g* and right in your
21:45 *g* promise that Jehovah had
22:30 came to be *g* in their eyes
22:33 the word came to be *g* in
23:13 this *g* ground that Jehovah
23:14 the *g* words that Jehovah
23:15 the *g* word that Jehovah
23:15 off this *g* ground that
23:16 off the *g* land that he has
24:20 after he has done you *g*
Jg 8:32 died at a *g* old age and was
9:11 sweetness and my *g* produce
10:15 anything . . . *g* in your eyes
17:13 Jehovah will do me *g*
18:9 land, and, look! it is very *g*
19:6 and let your heart feel *g*
19:9 and let your heart feel *g*
19:22 making their hearts feel *g*
19:24 what is *g* in your eyes
Ru 3:7 and his heart was feeling *g*
1Sa 1:23 Do what is *g* in your eyes
2:24 because the report is not *g*
2:32 the *g* that is done to Israel
3:18 What is *g* in his eyes let
9:10 Your word is *g*. Do come, let
11:10 all that is *g* in your eyes
12:23 in the *g* and right way
14:36 that is *g* in your eyes do
14:40 What is *g* in your eyes do
15:9 and upon all that was *g*, and
18:5 seemed *g* in the eyes of all
19:4 have been very *g* toward you
20:13 *g* to my father to do evil
24:4 it may seem *g* in your eyes
24:17 you who have rendered me *g*
24:18 today what *g* you have done
24:19 send him away on a *g* road
24:19 reward you with *g*, due to
25:3 wife was *g* in discretion and
25:8 upon a *g* day that we came
25:15 men were very *g* to us, and
25:21 evil in return for *g*
25:30 *g* toward you according to
25:31 Jehovah will certainly do *g*
25:36 Nabal's heart was feeling *g*
26:16 that you have done is not *g*
29:6 has been *g* in my eyes
29:6 you are not *g*
29:9 been *g* in my own eyes
2Sa 3:13 *G!* I myself shall conclude
3:19 *g* in the eyes of Israel and
3:36 and it was *g* in their eyes
3:36 the eyes of all the people *g*
4:10 like a bringer of *g* news
10:12 what is *g* in his own eyes
11:2 was very *g* in appearance
13:22 with Amnon either bad or *g*
14:17 distinguish what is *g* and
15:3 matters are *g* and straight
15:26 just as it is *g* in his eyes
17:7 is not *g* in this instance
17:14 the counsel . . . although *g*
18:4 *g* in your eyes I shall do
18:27 This is a *g* man, and with
18:27 with *g* news he should come
19:18 do what was *g* in his eyes
19:27 do what is *g* in your eyes
19:35 discern between *g* and bad
19:37 what is *g* in your eyes
19:38 what is *g* in your eyes

2Sa 24:22 offer up what is *g* in
1Ki 1:42 and you bring *g* news
2:18 Bath-sheba said: *G!* I myself
2:38 The word is *g*. Just as my
2:42 *G* is the word that I have
3:9 to discern between *g* and bad
8:36 teach them the *g* way in
8:56 one word of all his *g* promise
12:7 speak to them with *g* words
14:13 something *g* toward Jehovah
14:15 Israel off this *g* ground
18:24 and said: The thing is *g*
21:2 if it is *g* in your eyes, I
22:8 does not prophesy *g* things
22:13 words . . . *g* to the king
22:13 and you must speak *g*
22:18 not *g* things, but bad
2Ki 2:19 situation of the city is *g*
3:19 every *g* tree you should fell
3:19 *g* tract of land you should
3:25 every *g* tract of land, they
3:25 every *g* tree they would fell
5:19 for a *g* stretch of the land
7:9 This day is a day of *g* news!
8:9 every sort of *g* thing of
10:5 What is *g* in your own eyes
20:3 what was *g* in your eyes I
20:13 balsam oil and the *g* oil
20:19 that you have spoken is *g*
25:28 to speak *g* things with him
1Ch 4:40 found fat and *g* pasturage
13:2 If it seems *g* to you and it
16:34 Jehovah . . . for he is *g*
19:13 *g* in his own eyes he will
21:23 what is *g* in his own eyes
28:8 you may possess the *g* land
29:28 he died in a *g* old age
2Ch 3:5 he covered it with *g* gold
3:8 he covered it with *g* gold to
5:13 praising Jehovah, for he is *g*
6:27 *g* way in which they should
7:3 thanked Jehovah, for he is *g*
7:10 feeling *g* at heart over the
10:7 *g* to this people and
10:7 speak *g* words to them, they
12:12 to be *g* things in Judah
14:2 *g* and right in the eyes of
18:7 not for *g*, but all his days
18:12 unanimously of *g* to the
18:12 and you must speak *g*
18:17 not *g* things, but bad
19:3 *g* things that have been found
19:11 prove to be with what is *g*
24:16 he had done *g* in Israel and
30:18 *g* Jehovah himself make
31:20 *g* and right and faithful
Ezr 3:11 Jehovah, for he is *g*, for his
5:17 if to the king it seems *g*
7:9 *g* hand of his God upon him
7:18 whatever it seems *g* to you
8:18 the *g* hand of our God upon us
8:22 all those seeking him for *g*
8:27 and two utensils of *g* copper
9:12 eat the *g* of the land and
Ne 2:5 If to the king it does seem *g*
2:5 if your servant seems *g* before
2:6 it seemed *g* before the king
2:7 If to the king it does seem *g*
2:8 the *g* hand of my God upon me
2:10 had come to seek something *g*
2:18 how it was *g* upon me, and
2:18 their hands for the *g* work
5:9 that you are doing is not *g*
5:19 for *g*, all that I have done
6:19 *g* things about him they were
9:13 laws of truth, *g* regulations
9:20 your *g* spirit you gave to
9:25 houses full of all *g* things
9:35 amid your abundant *g* things
9:36 its fruitage and its *g* things
13:31 O my God, for *g*
Es 1:19 If to the king it does seem *g*
3:9 If to the king it does seem *g*
3:11 what is *g* in your own eyes
5:4 If to the king it does seem *g*
5:8 if to the king it does seem *g*
5:14 thing seemed *g* before Haman
7:3 if to the king it does seem *g*
7:9 spoken *g* concerning the king
8:5 If to the king it does seem *g*
8:5 and I am *g* in his eyes, let it
8:8 what is *g* in your own eyes in
8:17 a banquet and a *g* day
9:13 If to the king it does seem *g*

Es 9:19 and a *g* day and a sending of
9:22 and from mourning to a *g* day
10:3 working for the *g* of his
Job 2:10 we accept merely what is *g*
7:7 my eye will not see *g* again
9:25 my own days . . . not see *g*
10:3 *g* for you . . . do wrong
11:12 will get *g* motive As soon
13:9 be *g* that he sound you out
21:13 spend their days in *g* times
21:25 he has not eaten of *g* things
22:18 their houses with *g* things
22:21 *g* things will come to you
24:21 to whom he does no *g*
30:26 for *g* I waited, yet bad
34:4 among ourselves what is *g*
34:18 You are *g* for nothing
34:33 make *g* for it from your
36:11 their days in what is *g*
Ps 4:6 saying: Who will show us *g?*
14:1 There is no one doing *g*
14:3 There is no one doing *g*
21:3 meet him with blessings of *g*
25:8 *G* and upright is Jehovah
34:8 Jehovah is *g*, O you people
34:10 will not lack anything *g*
34:12 to see what is *g*
34:14 and do what is *g*
35:12 reward me with bad for *g*
36:3 to have insight for doing *g*
36:4 on a way that is not *g*
37:3 Trust in Jehovah and do *g*
37:27 and do what is *g*
38:20 rewarding me with bad for *g*
38:20 for my pursuing what is *g*
39:2 I kept quiet from what is *g*
40:9 the *g* news of righteousness
52:3 bad more than what is *g*
52:9 your name, because it is *g*
53:1 There is no one doing *g*
53:3 There is no one doing *g*
54:6 name, O Jehovah, for it is *g*
68:11 women telling the *g* news
69:16 for your loving-kindness is *g*
73:1 God is indeed *g* to Israel
73:28 near to God is *g* for me
84:11 anything *g* from those
85:12 will give what is *g*
86:5 are *g* and ready to forgive
92:1 *g* to give thanks to Jehovah
96:2 tell the *g* news of salvation
100:5 For Jehovah is *g*
103:5 lifetime with what is *g*
104:28 get satisfied with *g* things
106:1 to Jehovah, for he is *g*
107:1 you people, for he is *g*
107:9 he has filled with *g* things
109:5 they render to me bad for *g*
109:21 loving-kindness is *g*
111:10 doing them have a *g* insight
112:5 man is *g* who is gracious
118:1 you people, for he is *g*
118:29 you people, for he is *g*
119:39 judicial decisions are *g*
119:68, 68 are *g* and are doing *g*
119:71 *g* for me that I have been
119:72 law of your mouth is *g* for
119:122 your servant for what is *g*
122:9 will keep seeking *g* for you
125:4, 4 do *g*, O Jehovah, to the *g*
128:5 See also the *g* of Jerusalem
133:1 How *g* and how pleasant it is
133:2 like the *g* oil upon the head
135:3 Praise Jah, for Jehovah is *g*
136:1 O you people, for he is *g*
143:10 my God. Your spirit is *g*
145:9 Jehovah is *g* to all, And his
147:1 it is *g* to make melody to
Pr 2:9 entire course of what is *g*
2:20 walk in the way of *g* people
3:4 *g* insight in the eyes of God
3:27 *g* from those to whom it is
4:2 *g* instruction is what I
6:31 make it *g* with seven times
11:23 righteous ones is surely *g*
11:27 He that is looking for *g*
12:2 One that is *g* gets approval
12:14 he is satisfied with *g*, and
12:25 *g* word is what makes it
13:2 a man will eat *g*
13:15 *G* insight itself gives favor
13:21 are the ones whom *g* rewards
13:22 One who is *g* will leave an
14:14 *g* man with the results of

Pr 14:19 bow down before the *g* ones
14:22 as regards those devising *g*
15:2 does *g* with knowledge, but
15:3 the bad ones and the *g* ones
15:13 joyful heart has a *g* effect
15:15 is *g* at heart has a feast
15:23 at its right time is O how *g*
15:30 report that is *g* makes the
16:20 showing insight . . . find *g*
16:29 to go in a way that is not *g*
17:13 for anyone repaying bad for *g*
17:20 crooked . . . will not find *g*
17:22 heart that is joyful does *g*
17:26 fine . . . is not *g*
18:5 to the wicked one is not *g*
18:22 Has one found a *g* wife?
18:22 One has found a *g* thing, and
19:2 be without knowledge is not *g*
19:8 is going to find *g*
20:23 cheating . . . scales is not *g*
24:13 son, eat honey, for it is *g*
24:23 partiality . . . is not *g*
24:25 will come the blessing of *g*
25:25 *g* report from a distant land
25:27 too much honey is not *g*
28:10 come into possession of *g*
28:21 partiality is not *g*, nor
31:12 She has rewarded him with *g*
31:18 sensed that her trading is *g*
Ec 2:1 with rejoicing. Also, see *g*
2:3 what *g* there was to the sons
2:24 *g* because of his hard work
2:26 the man that is *g* before him
2:26 to give to the one that is *g*
3:12 and to do *g* during one's life
3:13 see *g* for all his hard work
4:8 my soul to lack in *g* things
4:9 a *g* reward for their hard work
5:11 When *g* things become many
5:18 see *g* for all his hard work
6:3 is not satisfied with *g* things
6:6 yet he has not seen what is *g*
6:12 what *g* a man has in life for
7:1 A name is better than *g* oil
7:11 with an inheritance is *g*
7:14 On a *g* day prove yourself to
7:20 keeps doing *g* and does not sin
7:26 *g* before the true God if one
9:2 the *g* one and the clean one
9:2 The *g* one is the same as the
9:7 drink your wine with a *g* heart
9:18 one sinner can destroy much *g*
11:6 both of them will alike be *g*
11:7 *g* for the eyes to see the sun
11:9 let your heart do you *g* in the
12:14 as to whether it is *g* or bad
Ca 1:3 For fragrance your oils are *g*
Isa 1:17 Learn to do *g*; search for
1:19 *g* of the land you will eat
5:9 houses, though great and *g*
5:20, 20 *g* is bad and bad is *g*
6:5 I am as *g* as brought to
7:15 the bad and choose the *g*
7:16 the bad and choose the *g*
38:3 *g* in your eyes I have done
38:14 Stand *g* for me
39:2 balsam oil and the *g* oil
39:8 word . . . you have spoken is *g*
40:9 bringing *g* news for Zion
40:9 *g* news for Jerusalem
41:7 It is *g*. Finally one
41:23 ought to do *g* or do bad
41:27 give a bringer of *g* news
52:7 the one bringing *g* news
52:7 bringing *g* news of something
55:2 and eat what is *g*, and let
57:4 that you have a jolly *g* time
61:1 tell *g* news to the meek ones
65:2 in the way that is not *g*
65:11 table for the god of *G* Luck
65:14 *g* condition of the heart
Jer 2:7 its fruitage and its *g* things
4:22 for doing *g* they actually
5:25 what is *g* from you people
6:16 where, now, the *g* way is
6:20 *g* cane from the land far
7:3 your ways and your dealings *g*
7:5 your ways and your dealings *g*
8:15 for peace, but no *g* came
10:5 doing of any *g* is not with
12:6 they speak to you *g* things
13:23 would also be able to do *g*
14:11 Do not pray . . . for any *g*
14:19 for peace, but no *g* came

Jer 15:11 will minister to you for *g*
17:6 will not see when *g* comes
18:10 also feel regret over the *g*
18:10 to do for its *g*
18:11 ways and your dealings *g*
18:20 Should bad be repaid for *g*?
18:20 speak *g* even concerning
20:15 the man that brought *g* news
21:10 for calamity and not for *g*
24:2 the figs were very *g*, like
24:3, 3 the *g* figs being very *g*
24:5 Like these *g* figs, so I shall
24:5 Chaldeans, in a *g* way
24:6 upon them in a *g* way
26:13 ways and your dealings *g*
26:14 according to what is *g*
29:10 my *g* word in bringing you
29:32 he will not look upon the *g*
32:39 *g* to them and to their sons
32:40 for me to do them *g*
32:41 over them to do them *g*
33:11 for Jehovah is *g*; for to
33:14 *g* word that I have spoken
35:15 and make your dealings *g*
39:16 calamity and not for *g*
40:4 *g* in your eyes to come with
40:4 *g* and right in your eyes
42:6 Whether *g* or bad, it is
44:27 for calamity and not for *g*
52:32 speak with him *g* things
La 3:17 lost memory of what *g* is
3:25 *G* is Jehovah to the one hoping
3:26 *G* it is that one should wait
3:27 *G* it is for an able-bodied
3:38 and what is *g* do not go forth
4:1 shines becomes dim, the *g* gold
Eze 17:8 a *g* field, by vast waters
18:18 whatever is not *g* he has
20:25 regulations that were not *g*
24:4 every *g* piece, thigh and
34:14 In a *g* pasturage I shall
34:14 in a *g* abiding place, and
36:11 do more *g* than in your
36:31 dealings that were not *g*
Da 1:4 *g* in appearance and having
2:32 image, its head was of *g* gold
4:2 has seemed *g* to me to declare
4:27 may my counsel seem *g* to you
6:1 It seemed *g* to Darius, and he
Ho 4:11 are what take away *g* motive
4:13 because its shade is *g*
8:3 Israel has cast off *g*
10:1 they put up *g* pillars
14:2 accept what is *g*, and we will
Joe 3:5 my own desirable *g* things
Am 5:14 Search for what is *g*, and not
5:15 love what is *g*, and give
9:1 will make *g* his flight, and
9:4 for bad, and not for *g*
Mic 1:12 Maroth has waited for *g*
2:7 Do not my own words do *g* in
3:2 haters of what is *g* and
6:8 O earthling man, what is *g*
Na 1:7 Jehovah is *g*, a stronghold in
1:15 feet of one bringing *g* news
Zep 1:12 Jehovah will not do *g*, and
Zec 1:13 *g* words, comforting words
8:19 and *g* festal seasons
11:12 If it is *g* in your eyes
Mal 2:17 doing bad is *g* in the eyes
Mt 4:23 the *g* news of the kingdom
5:45 rise upon wicked people and *g*
6:1 Take *g* care not to practice
7:11 give *g* gifts to your children
7:11 give *g* things to those asking
7:17 *g* tree produces fine fruit
7:18 *g* tree cannot bear worthless
9:35 the *g* news of the kingdom
11:5 poor are having the *g* news
12:34 how can you speak *g* things
12:35 The *g* man out of his
12:35 out of his *g* treasure sends
12:35 sends out *g* things, whereas
19:16 what *g* must I do in order
19:17 you ask me about what is *g*
19:17 One there is that is *g*
20:15 eye wicked because I am *g*
22:10 found, both wicked and *g*
24:14 *g* news of the kingdom will
25:21 *g* and faithful slave
25:23 *g* and faithful slave
26:13 Wherever this *g* news is
26:16 *g* opportunity to betray him
26:49 *G* day, Rabbi! and kissed him

Mt 26:58 at a *g* distance, as far as
27:24 Seeing that it did no *g* but
27:29 *G* day, you King of the Jews!
28:9 met them and said: *G* day!
Mr 1:1 the *g* news about Jesus Christ
1:14 preaching the *g* news of God
1:15 and have faith in the *g* news
3:4 on the sabbath to do a *g* deed
5:34 and be in *g* health from your
8:35 sake of me and the *g* news
10:17 *G* Teacher, what must I do
10:18 Why do you call me *g*?
10:18 Nobody is *g*, except one, God
10:29 for the sake of the *g* news
13:10 *g* news has to be preached
14:7 you can always do them *g*
14:9 Wherever the *g* news is
14:54 But Peter, from a *g* distance
15:18 *G* day, you King of the Jews!
Lu 1:19 the *g* news of these things to
1:28 *G* day, highly favored one
1:53 hungry ones with *g* things and
2:10 *g* news of a great joy that
3:18 *g* news to the people
4:14 *g* talk concerning him spread
4:18 declare *g* news to the poor
4:43 I must declare the *g* news of
6:9 to do *g* or to do injury, to
6:27 to do *g* to those hating you
6:33 And if you do *g* to those doing
6:33 to those doing *g* to you
6:35 do *g* and to lend without
6:45 A *g* man brings forth
6:45 brings forth *g* out of the
6:45 the *g* treasure of his heart
7:10 found the slave in *g* health
7:22 are being told the *g* news
8:1 and declaring the *g* news of
8:8 other fell upon the *g* soil
8:15 with a fine and *g* heart
9:6 declaring the *g* news and
10:42 Mary chose the *g* portion
11:13 know how to give *g* gifts to
12:18 my grain and all my *g* things
12:19 you have many *g* things laid
13:9 well and *g*; but if not, you
15:27 he got him back in *g* health
16:16 is being declared as *g* news
16:25 *g* things in your lifetime
18:18 *G* Teacher, by doing what
18:19 Why do you call me *g*? Nobody
18:19 Nobody is *g*, except one, God
19:17 Well done, *g* slave! Because
20:1 and declaring the *g* news, the
22:6 seek a *g* opportunity to betray
23:9 with a *g* many words; but he
23:50 a *g* and righteous man
Joh 1:46 Can anything *g* come out of
5:29 *g* things to a resurrection
7:12 would say: He is a *g* man
19:3 *G* day, you king of the Jews!
Ac 2:28 fill me with *g* cheer with
4:9 basis of a *g* deed to an ailing
5:42 declaring the *g* news about
8:4 declaring the *g* news of the
8:12 *g* news of the kingdom of God
8:25 declaring the *g* news to many
8:35 to him the *g* news about Jesus
8:40 declaring the *g* news to all
9:23 *g* many days were coming to
9:36 She abounded in *g* deeds and
10:36 *g* news of peace through
10:38 through the land doing *g*
11:20 *g* news of the Lord Jesus
11:24 he was a *g* man and full of
13:32 *g* news about the promise
14:7 went on declaring the *g* news
14:15 declaring the *g* news to you
14:17 witness in that he did *g*
14:17 full with food and *g* cheer
14:21 after declaring the *g* news
15:7 hear the word of the *g* news
15:29 *G* health to you!
15:35 the *g* news of the word of
16:10 declare the *g* news to them
17:18 the *g* news of Jesus and the
20:24 the *g* news of the undeserved
23:11 Be of *g* courage! For as you
27:13 as *g* as realized their
27:22 be of *g* cheer, for not a
27:25 be of *g* cheer, men; for I
Ro 1:1 separated to God's *g* news
1:9 with the *g* news about his Son
1:15 declare the *g* news also to

Ro 1:16 not ashamed of the *g* news
2:7 endurance in work that is *g*
2:10 everyone who works what is *g*
2:16 to the *g* news I declare
3:8 that the *g* things may come
5:7 for the *g* man, perhaps
7:12 commandment is . . . and *g*
7:13 what is *g* become death to me
7:13 through that which is *g;* that
7:18 there dwells nothing *g*
7:19 *g* that I wish I do not do
8:28 the *g* of those who love God
9:11 practiced anything *g* or vile
10:15 of those who declare *g* news
10:15 news of *g* things
10:16 did not all obey the *g* news
11:28 with reference to the *g* news
12:2 *g* and acceptable and perfect
12:9 cling to what is *g*
12:21 the evil with the *g*
13:3 of fear, not to the *g* deed
13:3 Keep doing *g*, and you will
13:4 minister to you for your *g*
14:16 let the *g* you people do be
15:2 what is *g* for his upbuilding
15:16 work of the *g* news of God
15:19 the *g* news about the Christ
15:20 to declare the *g* news where
16:19 be wise as to what is *g*, but
16:25 with the *g* news I declare
1Co 1:17 to go declaring the *g* news
1:21 God saw *g* through the
4:6 for your *g*, that in our case
4:10 you are in *g* repute, but we
4:15 father through the *g* news
9:12 any hindrance to the *g* news
9:14 proclaiming the *g* news to
9:14 live by means of the *g* news
9:16 I am declaring the *g* news
9:16 I did not declare the *g* news
9:18 while declaring the *g* news I
9:18 the *g* news without cost
9:18 my authority in the *g* news
9:23 for the sake of the *g* news
10:7 they got up to have a *g* time
14:6 what *g* would I do you unless
15:1 the *g* news which I declared
15:2 I declared the *g* news to you
15:32 of what *g* is it to me?
2Co 2:12 the *g* news about the Christ
4:3 *g* news we declare is in fact
4:4 *g* news about the Christ, who
5:6 always of *g* courage and know
5:8 we are of *g* courage and are
5:10 whether it is *g* or vile
6:8 bad report and *g* report
7:16 *g* courage by reason of you
8:18 *g* news has spread through
9:8 have plenty for every *g* work
9:13 the *g* news about the Christ
10:14 the *g* news about the Christ
10:16 to declare the *g* news to
11:4 *g* news other than what you
11:7 declared the *g* news of God
Ga 1:6 over to another sort of *g* news
1:7 pervert the *g* news about the
1:8 *g* news something beyond what
1:8 we declared to you as *g* news
1:9 *g* news something beyond what
1:11 *g* news which was declared by
1:11 *g* news is not something
1:15 But when God . . . thought *g*
1:16 declare the *g* news about him
1:23 the *g* news about the faith
2:2 *g* news which I am preaching
2:5 the truth of the *g* news might
2:7 entrusted to me the *g* news for
2:14 to the truth of the *g* news
3:8 *g* news beforehand to Abraham
4:13 I declared the *g* news to you
6:6 share in all *g* things with
6:10 work what is *g* toward all
Eph 1:5 the *g* pleasure of his will
1:8 in all wisdom and *g* sense
1:9 *g* pleasure which he purposed
1:13 *g* news about your salvation
2:10 for *g* works, which God
2:17 declared the *g* news of peace
3:6 through the *g* news
3:8 *g* news about the unfathomable
4:28 doing . . . what is *g* work
4:29 whatever saying is *g* for
6:7 Be slaves with *g* inclinations
6:8 whatever *g* he may do, will
Eph 6:15 equipment of the *g* news of
6:19 sacred secret of the *g* news
Php 1:5 made to the *g* news from the
1:6 he who started a *g* work in
1:7 establishing of the *g* news
1:12 advancement of the *g* news
1:16 the defense of the *g* news
1:27 worthy of the *g* news about
1:27 for the faith of the *g* news
2:13 the sake of his *g* pleasure
2:22 in furtherance of the *g* news
4:3 with me in the *g* news along
4:15 of declaring the *g* news
Col 1:5 the truth of that *g* news
1:10 fruit in every *g* work and
1:19 God saw *g* for all fullness
1:23 from the hope of that *g* news
1:23 Of this *g* news I Paul became
2:5 beholding your *g* order and
1Th 1:5 the *g* news we preach did not
2:2 speak to you the *g* news of
2:4 be entrusted with the *g* news
2:8 not only the *g* news of God
2:9 we preached the *g* news of God
3:1 saw *g* to be left alone in
3:2 the *g* news about the Christ
3:6 given us the *g* news about
3:6 having *g* remembrance of us
3:10 to make *g* the things that
5:15 pursue what is *g* toward one
2Th 1:8 who do not obey the *g* news
2:14 the *g* news we declare
2:16 comfort and *g* hope by means
2:17 firm in every *g* deed and
1Ti 1:5 and out of a *g* conscience and
1:11 *g* news of the happy God
1:19 faith and a *g* conscience
2:10 through *g* works
5:10 followed every *g* work
6:2 benefit of their *g* service
6:18 to work at *g*, to be rich in
2Ti 1:8 suffering evil for the *g* news
1:10 through the *g* news
2:8 the *g* news I preach
2:21 prepared for every *g* work
3:17 equipped for every *g* work
Tit 1:16 not approved for *g* work of
2:3 teachers of what is *g*
2:5 chaste, workers at home, *g*
2:10 exhibiting *g* fidelity to the
3:1 to be ready for every *g* work
Phm 6 every *g* thing among us as
13 for the sake of the *g* news
14 so that your *g* act may be, not
Heb 4:2 had the *g* news declared to us
4:6 *g* news was first declared did
9:11 high priest of the *g* things
10:1 shadow of the *g* things to
11:12 man, and him as *g* as dead
11:17 as *g* as offered up Isaac
12:10 to what seemed *g* to them
13:6 we may be of *g* courage and
13:16 not forget the doing of *g*
13:21 *g* thing to do his will
Jas 1:17 Every *g* gift and every
3:17 full of mercy and *g* fruits
5:13 Is there anyone in *g* spirits?
1Pe 1:12 declared the *g* news to you
1:25 declared to you as *g* news
2:14 but to praise doers of *g*
2:15 by doing *g* you may muzzle
2:18 fear, not only to the *g* and
2:20 when you are doing *g* and you
3:6 provided you keep on doing *g*
3:10 love life and see *g* days, let
3:11 what is bad and do what is *g*
3:13 become zealous for what is *g*
3:16 Hold a *g* conscience, so that
3:16 *g* conduct in connection with
3:17 because you are doing *g*, if
3:21 request . . . a *g* conscience
4:6 *g* news was declared also to
4:17 obedient to the *g* news of
4:19 while they are doing *g*
3Jo 2 prospering and having *g* health
11 imitator . . . of what is *g*
11 He that does *g* originates
Re 10:7 the *g* news which he declared
14:6 everlasting *g* news to declare

Good-bye
Mr 6:46 after saying *g* to them he
Lu 9:61 first permit me to say *g* to
14:33 say *g* to all his belongings
Ac 18:18 Paul said *g* to the brothers
18:21 said *g* and told them: I will
21:6 said *g* to one another, and we
2Co 2:13 said *g* to them and departed

Good-for-nothing
De 13:13 *G* men have gone out from
Jg 19:22 mere *g* men, surrounded the
20:13 *g* men, that are in Gibeah
1Sa 1:16 slave girl like a *g* woman
2:12 the sons of Eli were *g* men
10:27 As for the *g* men, they said
25:17 is too much of a *g* fellow
25:25 upon this *g* man Nabal
30:22 bad and *g* man out of the
2Sa 16:7 bloodguilty man and *g* man
20:1 *g* man, whose name was Sheba
22:5 flash floods of *g* men that
23:6 *g* persons are chased away
1Ki 21:10 *g* fellows, sit in front of
21:13 *g* fellows, came in and sat
21:13 *g* men began to bear witness
2Ch 13:7 idle men, *g* fellows, kept
Ps 18:4 *g* men also kept terrifying me
41:8 A *g* thing is poured out upon
101:3 front of my eyes any *g* thing
Pr 6:12 A *g* man, a man of hurtfulness
16:27 *g* man is digging up what is
19:28 A *g* witness derides justice
Na 1:15 no more will any *g* person
Mt 25:30 throw the *g* slave out into
Lu 17:10 say, We are *g* slaves

Good-looking
Ge 6:2 daughters of men . . . were *g*
Ex 2:2 When she saw how *g* he was
Nu 24:5 How *g* are your tents, O Jacob
De 6:10 great and *g* cities that you
Jos 7:21 garment from Shinar, a *g* one
1Ki 1:6 he was also very *g* in form
Ho 10:11 passed over her *g* neck

Goodly
Ps 45:1 become astir with a *g* matter

Goodness
Ex 33:19 all my *g* to pass before your
Nu 10:32 *g* Jehovah will do good with
Jg 8:35 the *g* that he had exercised
9:16 *g* that you have exercised
2Sa 2:6 exercise to you this *g* because
7:28 you promise . . . this *g*
16:12 *g* instead of his malediction
1Ki 8:66 all the *g* that Jehovah had
1Ch 17:26 and you promise this *g*
2Ch 6:41 ones themselves rejoice in *g*
7:10 *g* that Jehovah had performed
Ne 9:25 to luxuriate in your great *g*
Ps 16:2 my *g* is, not for your sake
23:6 Surely *g* and loving-kindness
25:7 For the sake of your *g*
25:13 soul will lodge in *g* itself
27:13 in seeing the *g* of Jehovah
31:19 How abundant your *g* is
65:4 with the *g* of your house
65:11 crowned the year with your *g*
68:10 your *g* you proceeded to make
86:17 with me a sign meaning *g*
106:5 the *g* to your chosen ones
119:66 Teach me *g*, sensibleness
145:7 abundance of your *g* they
Pr 11:10 Because of the *g* of the
Ec 7:14 prove yourself to be in *g*, and
Isa 63:7 abundant *g* to the house of
Jer 31:12 over the *g* of Jehovah
31:14 *g* my own people will
32:42 *g* that I am speaking
33:9 the *g* that I am rendering
33:9 on account of all the *g* and
Ho 3:5 *g* in the final part of the
10:1 to the *g* of his land, they
Zec 1:17 will yet overflow with *g*
9:17 O how great his *g* is, and
Ro 15:14 are also full of *g*, as you
Ga 5:22 fruitage of the spirit . . . *g*
Eph 5:9 *g* and righteousness and truth
2Th 1:11 *g* and the work of faith
2Ti 3:3 fierce, without love of *g*
Tit 1:8 a lover of *g*, sound in mind

Goods
Ge 12:5 *g* that they had accumulated
13:6 their *g* had become many and
14:11 victors took all the *g* of
14:12 Lot . . . his *g* and continued
14:16 to recover all the *g*, and he

2Ch 30:9 your God is *g* and merciful
Ne 9:17 *g* and merciful, slow to anger
9:31 you are a God *g* and merciful
Ps 86:15 are a God merciful and *g*
103:8 Jehovah is merciful and *g*
111:4 Jehovah is *g* and merciful
112:4 He is *g* and merciful and
112:5 man is good who is *g* and
116:5 Jehovah is *g* and righteous
145:8 Jehovah is *g* and merciful
Pr 26:25 he makes his voice *g*, do not
Joe 2:13 for he is *g* and merciful
Jon 4:2 a God *g* and merciful, slow to
Lu 18:13 O God, be *g* to me a sinner

Graciously
Le 1:4 must be *g* accepted for him to

Graciousness
Ac 6:8 Stephen, full of *g* and power
7:10 gave him *g* and wisdom in the
Eph 2:7 his *g* toward us in union with
Col 3:16 spiritual songs with *g*
4:6 utterance be always with *g*

Gradually
Ge 11:8 they *g* left off building the
25:24 *G* her days came to the full
41:53 seven years . . . *g* ended
47:18 *G* that year came to its
47:29 *G* the days approached for
Jos 24:12 it *g* drove them out before
24:29 Joshua . . . *g* died at the
Jg 20:5 they raped, and she *g* died
2Sa 6:6 came *g* as far as the
12:18 seventh day . . . child *g* died
1Ki 2:1 days of David *g* drew near for
2:12 *g* his kingship became very
7:22 the pillars was *g* completed
7:40 Hiram *g* made the basins and
7:48 Solomon *g* made all the
11:3 wives *g* inclined his heart
22:35 *g* he died in the evening
2Ki 1:17 he *g* died, according to the
2:8 *g* they were divided this way
2:14 were *g* divided this way
4:20 until noon, and *g* he died
4:34 *g* the child's flesh grew
11:19 *g* by the way of the gate
20:7 after which he *g* revived
20:11 *g* go back on the steps
1Ch 13:9 they came *g* as far as the
29:28 *g* he died in a good old age
2Ch 18:34 *g* he died at the time of
21:19 *g* died in his bad maladies
24:15 *g* died, being a hundred and
24:18 *g* they left the house of
Ezr 10:17 *g* they finished with all
Es 2:12 procedure were *g* fulfilled
Job 32:5 Elihu *g* saw that there was
42:17 *g* Job died, old and
Ps 78:55 *g* drove out the nations
80:11 *g* sent forth its boughs as
105:24 *g* made them mightier than
105:44 *g* he gave them the lands of
106:9 and it was *g* dried up
Isa 5:2 it *g* produced wild grapes
5:4 it *g* produced wild grapes
6:4 itself *g* filled with smoke
12:1 your anger *g* turned back
38:8 sun *g* went back ten steps
44:13 *g* he makes it like the
49:2 *g* made me a polished arrow
51:2 Sarah who *g* brought you
Jer 2:7 I *g* brought you to a land of
43:7 came *g* as far as Tahpanhes
Eze 2:10 he *g* spread it out before me
3:2 he *g* made me eat this roll
8:8 I *g* bored through the wall
10:4 house *g* became filled with
16:13 *g* you became fit for royal
17:6 and *g* became a luxuriantly
17:6 its roots, they *g* came to be
19:3 *g* she brought up one of her
19:6 *g* learned how to tear apart
19:11 its height *g* became tall up
24:18 wife *g* died in the evening
34:5 were *g* scattered because of
40:2 *g* set me down upon a very
40:17 *g* brought me into the outer
40:24 *g* brought me toward the
40:28 *g* brought me into the inner
40:32 *g* brought me into the inner
42:1 *g* brought me forth to the
47:1 *g* he brought me back to the
47:2 *g* brought me forth by the
Da 8:12 army itself was *g* given over
10:10 *g* stirred me up to get upon
Ho 1:8 And she *g* weaned Lo-ruhamah
12:4 with an angel and *g* prevailed
Jon 4:5 *g* he made for himself there a
4:7 plant; and it *g* dried up
Zec 5:9 *g* raised the ephah up between
11:8 my soul *g* became impatient
Mr 4:28 the ground bears fruit *g*

Graft
Ro 11:23 God is able to *g* them in

Grafted
Ro 11:17 wild olive, were *g* in among
11:19 that I might be *g* in
11:23 will be *g* in; for God is
11:24 *g* contrary to nature into
11:24 *g* into their own olive tree

Grain
Ge 27:28 abundance of *g* and new wine
27:37 *g* and new wine I have
41:5 seven ears of *g* coming up on
41:6 seven ears of *g*, thin and
41:7 the thin ears of *g* began to
41:7 seven fat and full ears of *g*
41:22 seven ears of *g* coming up on
41:23 seven ears of *g* shriveled
41:24 thin ears of *g* began to
41:24 the seven good ears of *g*
41:26 the seven good ears of *g* are
41:27 the seven empty ears of *g*
41:35 let them pile up *g* under
41:49 Joseph continued piling up *g*
41:56 open . . . the *g* depositories
42:3 down to buy *g* from Egypt
42:25 their receptacles with *g*
45:23 she-asses carrying *g* and
Ex 22:6 or standing *g* or a field gets
29:41 With a *g* offering like that
30:9 or a *g* offering; and you must
40:29 and the *g* offering upon it
Le 2:1 a *g* offering to Jehovah
2:3 what is left of the *g* offering
2:4 as an offering a *g* offering in
2:5 is a *g* offering from off the
2:6 It is a *g* offering
2:7 *g* offering out of the deep-fat
2:8 bring the *g* offering that was
2:9 some of the *g* offering as a
2:10 left of the *g* offering belongs
2:11 No *g* offering that you will
2:13 *g* offering you will season
2:13 missing upon your *g* offering
2:14 *g* offering of the first ripe
2:14 the grits of new *g*, as the
2:14 *g* offering of your first ripe
2:15 It is a *g* offering
5:13 the same as a *g* offering
6:14 is the law of the *g* offering
6:15 fine flour of the *g* offering
6:15 that is upon the *g* offering
6:20 fine flour as a *g* offering
6:21 the pastries of the *g* offering
6:23 every *g* offering of a priest
7:9 every *g* offering that may be
7:10 *g* offering that is moistened
7:37 the *g* offering and the sin
9:4 a *g* offering moistened with
9:17 presented the *g* offering and
10:12 Take the *g* offering that
14:10 a *g* offering moistened with
14:20 the *g* offering upon the altar
14:21 as a *g* offering and a log
14:31 along with the *g* offering
23:13 *g* offering two tenths of an
23:14 eat no bread nor roasted *g*
23:14 nor new *g* until this very
23:16 present a new *g* offering to
23:18 *g* offering and their drink
23:37 *g* offering of the sacrifice
Nu 4:16 constant *g* offering and the
5:15 is a *g* offering of jealousy
5:15 memorial *g* offering bringing
5:18 the memorial *g* offering
5:18 the *g* offering of jealousy
5:25 the *g* offering of jealousy
5:25 wave the *g* offering to and
5:26 *g* offering as a remembrancer
6:15 and their *g* offering and their
6:17 render up its *g* offering and
7:13 with oil for a *g* offering
7:19 with oil for a *g* offering
7:25 with oil for a *g* offering
7:31 with oil for a *g* offering
Nu 7:37 with oil for a *g* offering
7:43 with oil for a *g* offering
7:49 with oil for a *g* offering
7:55 with oil for a *g* offering
7:61 with oil for a *g* offering
7:67 with oil for a *g* offering
7:73 with oil for a *g* offering
7:79 with oil for a *g* offering
7:87 and their *g* offerings
8:8 young bull and its *g* offering
15:4 a *g* offering of fine flour, a
15:6 a *g* offering of two tenths of
15:9 *g* offering of three tenths of
15:24 its *g* offering and its drink
16:15 to look at their *g* offering
18:9 every *g* offering of theirs and
18:12 and the *g*, their firstfruits
18:27 the *g* of the threshing floor
28:5 *g* offering moistened with
28:8 With the same *g* offering as
28:9 fine flour as a *g* offering
28:12 fine flour as a *g* offering
28:12 fine flour as a *g* offering
28:13 *g* offering moistened with oil
28:20 *g* offerings of fine flour
28:26 present a new *g* offering to
28:28 as their *g* offering of fine
28:31 burnt offering and its *g*
29:3 their *g* offering of fine flour
29:6 burnt offering and its *g*
29:6 *g* offering, together with
29:9 as their *g* offering of fine
29:11 burnt offering and its *g*
29:14 *g* offering of fine flour
29:16 its *g* offering and its drink
29:18 their *g* offering and their
29:19 and its *g* offering, together
29:21 their *g* offering and their
29:22 its *g* offering and its drink
29:24 their *g* offering and their
29:25 its *g* offering and its drink
29:27 their *g* offering and their
29:28 its *g* offering and its drink
29:30 their *g* offering and their
29:31 its *g* offering and its drink
29:33 their *g* offering and their
29:34 its *g* offering and its drink
29:37 their *g* offering and their
29:38 its *g* offering and its drink
29:39 and your *g* offerings and your
De 7:13 your *g* and your new wine and
11:14 gather your *g* and your sweet
12:17 the tenth part of your *g*
14:23 eat the tenth part of your *g*
16:9 first put to the standing *g*
18:4 The first of your *g*, your new
23:25 standing *g* of your fellowman
23:25 standing *g* of your fellowman
28:51 let no *g*, new wine or oil
33:28 a land of *g* and new wine
Jos 22:23 offer up . . . *g* offerings
22:29 altar for . . . *g* offering
Jg 13:19 the *g* offering and to offer
13:23 and *g* offering from our hand
15:5 standing *g* of the Philistines
15:5 standing *g* and the vineyards
Ru 2:2 and glean among the ears of *g*
2:7 among the cut-off ears of *g*
2:14 hold out roasted *g* to her and
2:15 among the cut-off ears of *g*
3:7 at the extremity of the *g* heap
1Sa 17:17 this ephah of roasted *g* and
25:18 seah measures of roasted *g*
26:19 let him smell a *g* offering
2Sa 17:19 heaped up cracked *g* upon it
17:28 roasted *g* and broad beans
17:28 and lentils and parched *g*
1Ki 8:64 *g* offering and the fat pieces
8:64 *g* offering and the fat pieces
18:29 going up of the *g* offering
18:36 that the *g* offering goes up
2Ki 3:20 going up of the *g* offering
4:42 and new *g* in his bread bag
16:13 his *g* offering smoke and
16:15 *g* offering of the evening
16:15 the king and his *g* offering
16:15 and their *g* offering and
18:32 a land of *g* and new wine
19:29 *g* that shoots up of itself
1Ch 21:23 the wheat as a *g* offering
23:29 for the *g* offering and for
2Ch 7:7 and the *g* offering and the fat
31:5 firstfruits of the *g*, new
32:28 for the produce of *g* and

Ezr 7:17 their *g* offerings and their
9:4 the *g* offering of the evening
9:5 *g* offering of the evening
Ne 5:2 get *g* and eat and keep alive
5:3 get *g* during the food shortage
5:10 giving money and *g* on loan
5:11 the *g*, the new wine and the
10:33 the constant *g* offering and
10:39 the contribution of the *g*
13:5 putting the *g* offering
13:5 tenth of the *g*, the new wine
13:9 the *g* offering and the
13:12 tenth of the *g* and of the
13:15 bringing in *g* heaps and
Job 24:24 like the head of an ear of *g*
Ps 4:7 their *g* and their new wine have
65:9 You prepare their *g*, For that
65:13 are enveloped with *g*
72:16 be plenty of *g* on the earth
78:24 *g* of heaven he gave to them
141:2 as the evening *g* offering
Pr 11:26 one holding back *g*—the
27:22 a mortar, in among cracked *g*
Isa 1:13 more valueless *g* offerings
17:5 gathering the standing *g*
17:5 arm harvests the ears of *g*
17:5 gleaning ears of *g* in the
36:17 a land of *g* and new wine
37:30 *g* that shoots up of itself
62:8 no more give your *g* as food
Jer 9:22 like a row of newly cut *g*
14:12 and the *g* offering, I am
17:26 *g* offering and frankincense
23:28 straw have to do with *g*
31:12 over the *g* and over the new
33:18 smoke with a *g* offering
41:5 *g* offering and frankincense
La 2:12 saying: Where are *g* and wine?
Eze 36:29 the *g* and make it abound
42:13 the *g* offering and the sin
44:29 The *g* offering and the sin
45:15 for the *g* offering and for
45:17 *g* offering and the drink
45:17 and the *g* offering and
45:24 as a *g* offering an ephah
45:25 and as the *g* offering and
46:5 *g* offering an ephah for the
46:5 *g* offering as he is able to
46:7 render up as a *g* offering
46:11 *g* offering should prove to
46:14 as a *g* offering you should
46:14 *g* offering to Jehovah is an
46:15 and the *g* offering and
46:20 bake the *g* offering, in
Ho 2:8 I who had given to her the *g*
2:9 take away my *g* in its time
2:22 *g* and the sweet wine and the
7:14 On account of their *g* and
8:7 Nothing has standing *g*
9:1 all the threshing floors of *g*
14:7 They will grow *g*, and will
Joe 1:9 *G* offering and drink offering
1:10 the *g* has been despoiled
1:13 *g* offering and drink offering
1:17 for the *g* has dried up
2:14 a blessing, a *g* offering and
2:19 sending to you the *g* and the
2:24 must be full of cleansed *g*
Am 2:13 with a row of newly cut *g*
5:11 *g* you keep taking from him
8:5 and we may offer *g* for sale
8:6 we may sell mere refuse for *g*
Mic 4:12 like a row of newly cut *g*
Hag 1:11 upon the *g*, and upon the new
2:19 the seed in the *g* pit
Zec 9:17 *G* is what will make the
12:6 in a row of newly cut *g*
Mt 12:1 started to pluck heads of *g*
13:31 kingdom . . . a mustard *g*
17:20 the size of a mustard *g*, you
Mr 2:23 plucking the heads of *g*
4:28 the full *g* in the head
4:31 Like a mustard *g*, which at
Lu 6:1 eating the heads of *g*, rubbing
12:18 I will gather all my *g* and
13:19 is like a mustard *g* that a
17:6 faith the size of a mustard *g*
Joh 12:24 *g* of wheat falls into the
12:24 it remains just one *g*
1Co 9:9 it is threshing out the *g*
15:37 but a bare *g*, it may be, of
1Ti 5:18 when it threshes out the *g*

Grainfields
Mt 12:1 Jesus went through the *g* on
Mr 2:23 through the *g* on the sabbath
Lu 6:1 to be passing through *g*, and

Grains
Ge 22:17 *g* of sand that are on the
32:12 seed like the *g* of sand of
Jos 5:11 and roasted *g*, on this same
11:4 as numerous as the *g* of sand
Jg 7:12 the *g* of sand that are on the
1Sa 13:5 people like the *g* of sand
1Ki 4:20 *g* of sand that are by the sea
Job 29:18 like the *g* of sand I shall
Ps 78:27 like the sand *g* of the seas
139:18 than even the *g* of sand
Isa 10:22 the *g* of sand of the sea
48:19 parts like the *g* of it
Jer 15:8 the sand *g* of the seas
Ho 1:10 *g* of the sand of the sea that

Granaries
Jer 50:26 Open up her *g*. Bank her up

Grand
1Ki 8:62 a *g* sacrifice before Jehovah
2Ch 16:14 *g* burial place that he had
33:6 *g* scale what was bad in the
Job 31:36 around me like a *g* crown
35:10 Where is God my *G* Maker
Ps 28:8 *g* salvation of his anointed
42:5 the *g* salvation of my person
42:11 laud him as the *g* salvation
43:3 and to your *g* tabernacle
43:5 laud him as the *g* salvation
44:4 Command *g* salvation for Jacob
45:8 Out from the *g* ivory palace
46:4 *g* tabernacle of the Most High
48:2 The town of the *g* King
53:6 the *g* salvation of Israel
68:35 out of your *g* sanctuary
71:16 shall come in *g* mightiness
73:17 into the *g* sanctuary of God
74:12 One performing *g* salvation
84:1 How lovely your *g* tabernacle
84:3 Your *g* altar, O Jehovah of
89:7 *g* and fear-inspiring over all
106:7 of your *g* loving-kindness
106:45 of his *g* loving-kindness
114:2 Israel his *g* dominion
116:13 cup of *g* salvation I shall
132:3 on the divan of my *g* lounge
132:5 *g* tabernacle for the
132:7 come into his *g* tabernacle
139:17 *g* sum of them amount to
149:2 rejoice in its *g* Maker
Pr 16:13 are a pleasure to a *g* king
17:8 in the eyes of its *g* owner
30:28 is in the *g* palace of a king
Ec 5:11 is there to the *g* owner of
5:13 being kept for their *g* owner
12:1 Remember . . . your *G* Creator
Ca 1:17 The beams of our *g* house are
Isa 19:20 savior, even a *g* one, who
22:11 look at the *g* maker of it
30:20 *G* Instructor will no longer
30:20 seeing your *G* Instructor
42:5 the *G* One stretching them
54:2 cloths of your *g* tabernacle
54:5 *G* Maker is your husbandly
Jer 29:26 the *g* overseer of the house
50:41 great nation and *g* kings
Da 2:10 *g* king or governor has asked
2:45 *g* God himself has made known
4:3 How *g* his signs are, and how
11:45 between the *g* sea and the
Ho 12:14 *g* Master will repay to him
Zec 6:11 make a *g* crown and put it
6:14 *g* crown itself will come to
Mal 1:6 and a servant, his *g* master
1:6 if I am a *g* master, where is
Lu 14:16 spreading a *g* evening meal
2Pe 1:4 precious and very *g* promises

Grandchildren
1Ti 5:4 any widow has children or *g*

Granddaughter
Ge 36:2 Oholibamah . . . *g* of Zibeon
36:14 *g* of Zibeon, Esau's wife
1Ki 15:2 Maacah the *g* of Abishalom
15:10 Maacah the *g* of Abishalom
2Ki **8:26** Athaliah the *g* of Omri the
2Ch 11:20 Maacah the *g* of Absalom
11:21 Maacah the *g* of Absalom
22:2 Athaliah the *g* of Omri

Grandees
Da 4:36 my *g* began eagerly searching
Da 5:1 feast for a thousand of his *g*
5:2 from them the king and his *g*
5:3 from them the king and his *g*
5:9 and his *g* were perplexed
5:10 words of the king and his *g*
5:23 you yourself and your *g*, your
6:17 the signet ring of his *g*, in

Grandeur
Da **4:22** your *g* has grown great and
7:27 *g* of the kingdoms under all

Grandfather
2Sa **9:7** all the field of Saul your *g*

Grandiose
Da 7:8 was a mouth speaking *g* things
7:11 *g* words that the horn was
7:20 mouth speaking *g* things and

Grandmother
1Ki 15:13 As for even Maacah his *g*
2Ch 15:16 Maacah his *g*, Asa the king
2Ti 1:5 your *g* Lois and your mother

Grandmother's
1Ki 15:10 his *g* name was Maacah the

Grandparents
1Ti 5:4 compensation to their . . . *g*

Grandson
Ge 11:31 Lot, the son of Haran, his *g*
29:5 know Laban the *g* of Nahor
De 6:2 you and your son and your *g*
Jg 8:22 your son and your *g* as well
2Sa 9:9 give to the *g* of your master
9:10 *g* of your master, and they
9:10 *g* of your master, will eat
19:24 Mephibosheth the *g* of Saul
1Ki 19:16 And Jehu the *g* of Nimshi
2Ki 9:20 Jehu the *g* of Nimshi
2Ch 22:7 Jehu the *g* of Nimshi, whom
22:9 *g* of Jehoshaphat, who
Ezr 5:1 Zechariah the *g* of Iddo the
6:14 Zechariah the *g* of Iddo
8:18 Mahli the *g* of Levi the son
Jer 27:7 his *g* until the time even of

Grandsons
Ex 34:7 error of fathers . . . upon *g*
De 4:9 to your sons and to your *g*
4:25 become father to sons and *g*
Jg 12:14 forty sons and thirty *g* who
2Ki 17:41 both their sons and their *g*
1Ch 8:40 and having many sons and *g*
Job 42:16 and his *g*—four generations
Pr 17:6 The crown of old men is the *g*

Grant
Ge **9:27** Let God *g* ample space to
Le 25:24 *g* to the land the right of
Nu 20:21 Edom refused to *g* Israel to
Jg 1:15 Do *g* me a blessing, for it
Ru 4:11 May Jehovah *g* the wife who
1Sa 1:17 may the God of Israel *g* your
1:27 that Jehovah should *g* me my
2Ki 24:4 not consent to *g* forgiveness
Ne 1:11 do *g* success to your servant
2:20 One that will *g* us success
Es 5:8 seem good to *g* my petition and
Job 6:8 that God would *g* even my hope
9:18 not *g* me . . . a fresh breath
24:23 *g* him to become confident
Ps 18:32 will *g* my way to be perfect
106:46 *g* them to be objects of
118:25 Jehovah, do *g* success
140:8 Do not *g*, O Jehovah, the
Isa 58:10 *g* to the hungry one your
Mr 10:37 *G* us to sit down, one at
Lu 1:74 to *g* us, after we have been
Ac 4:29 *g* your slaves to keep speaking
Ro 15:5 *g* you to have among
Eph 3:16 *g* you according to the riches
2Ti 1:16 May the Lord *g* mercy to the
1:18 Lord *g* him to find mercy
Re 2:7 I will *g* to eat of the tree
3:21 *g* to sit down with me on my

Granted
Ex **12:36** these *g* what was asked; and
Ru 4:13 Jehovah *g* her conception and
2Ch 30:27 hearing was *g* to their
33:19 entreaty was *g* him and all
Ezr 3:7 *g* by Cyrus the king of Persia
7:6 so that the king *g* him
Es 2:18 jurisdictional districts he *g*
5:6 Let it even be *g* you
8:11 king *g* to the Jews that were

2Ch 2:5 that I am building will be *g*
2:9 timbers for me in *g* number
2:9 *g*, yes, in a wonderful way
3:5 the *g* house he covered with
4:9 the *g* enclosure and the doors
4:18 utensils in very *g* quantity
6:32 by reason of your *g* name and
7:8 a very *g* congregation from
9:1 gold in *g* quantity, and
9:9 balsam oil in very *g* quantity
9:17 king made a *g* ivory throne
11:12 them to a very *g* degree
14:13 a very *g* deal of spoil
14:15 captive flocks in *g* number
15:9 from Israel in *g* number
15:13 death, whether small or *g*
16:8 *g* military force in
16:14 *g* funeral burning for him
17:12 growing *g* to a superior
18:30 small nor with the *g*, but
21:14 *g* blow to your people and
24:24 force of very *g* number
25:13 and taking a *g* plunder
26:10 *g* deal of livestock that
26:15 shoot arrows and *g* stones
26:15 went out to a *g* distance
27:3 he did a *g* deal of building
28:5 *g* number of captives and
28:5 him with a *g* slaughter
28:8 *g* deal of spoil they took
28:19 *g* unfaithfulness toward
29:35 were in *g* quantity with
30:18 *g* number of the people
30:21 seven days with *g* rejoicing
30:24 themselves in *g* number
30:26 *g* rejoicing in Jerusalem
31:10 left over is this *g* plenty
31:15 equally to *g* and small
32:4 find a *g* deal of water
32:27 glory to a very *g* amount
34:21 *g* is Jehovah's rage that
34:30 the *g* as well as the small
36:18 the utensils, *g* and small
Ezr 3:13 heard even to a *g* distance
4:10 the *g* and honorable Asenappar
5:8 to the house of the *g* God
5:11 a *g* king of Israel built
9:6 guiltiness has grown *g* even
9:7 we have been in *g* guiltiness
9:13 deeds and our *g* guiltiness
10:13 rebelled to a *g* extent in
Ne 1:5 the God *g* and fear-inspiring
1:10 you redeemed by your *g* power
3:27 the *g* protruding tower as
4:10 there is a *g* deal of rubbish
4:14 the *g* and the fear-inspiring
5:1 a *g* outcry of the people and
5:7 a *g* assembly on their account
6:3 It is a *g* work that I am doing
7:4 the city was wide and *g*, and
8:6 the true God, the *g* One
8:12 to carry on a *g* rejoicing
8:17 came to be very *g* rejoicing
9:18 commit *g* acts of disrespect
9:25 luxuriate in your *g* goodness
9:26 acts of *g* disrespect
9:32 the God *g*, mighty and
9:37 and we are in *g* distress
11:14 Zabdiel the son of the *g* ones
12:43 *g* sacrifices and to rejoice
12:43 to rejoice with *g* joy
13:27 commit all this *g* badness in
Es 1:5 the *g* as well as the small
1:7 royal wine was in *g* quantity
1:8 every *g* man of his household
1:20 the *g* as well as the small
2:18 *g* banquet for all his princes
4:3 was *g* mourning among the Jews
6:3 What honor and *g* thing has
8:15 with a *g* crown of gold, and a
9:4 Mordecai was *g* in the king's
10:3 and was *g* among the Jews and
Job 1:19 there came a *g* wind from
2:13 saw that the pain was very *g*
3:19 Small and *g* are there the
5:9 doing *g* things unsearchable
8:7 afterward would grow very *g*
9:10 Doing *g* things unsearchable
12:23 Making the nations grow *g*
19:5 you men do put on *g* airs
35:9 the arm of the *g* ones
37:5 *g* things that we cannot know
Ps 12:3 The tongue speaking *g* things
14:5 were filled with a *g* dread

Ps 18:16 drawing me out of *g* waters
18:35 own humility will make me *g*
18:50 *g* acts of salvation for his
21:5 glory is *g* in your salvation
35:26 assuming *g* airs against me
38:16 assume *g* airs against me
47:2 A *g* King over all the earth
48:1 Jehovah is *g* and much to be
53:5 were filled with a *g* dread
55:12 assumed *g* airs against me
57:10 your loving-kindness is *g*
71:19 *g* things that you have done
76:1 In Israel his name is *g*
77:13 Who is a *g* God like God?
80:5 upon tears in *g* measure
86:10 For you are *g* and are doing
86:13 loving-kindness is *g* toward
92:5 *g* your works are, O Jehovah
95:3 For Jehovah is a *g* God
95:3 *g* King over all other gods
96:4 Jehovah is *g* and very much to
99:2 Jehovah is *g* in Zion
99:3 *G* and fear-inspiring, holy it
104:1 God, you have proved very *g*
104:25 for this sea so *g* and wide
104:25 small as well as *g*
106:21 Doer of *g* things in Egypt
108:4 loving-kindness is *g* up to
111:2 The works of Jehovah are *g*
115:13 as well as the *g* ones
119:107 afflicted to a *g* extent
126:2 Jehovah has done a *g* thing
126:3 Jehovah has done a *g* thing
131:1 I walked in things too *g*
135:5 well know that Jehovah is *g*
136:4 Doer of wonderful, *g* things
136:7 the One making the *g* lights
136:17 One striking down *g* kings
138:5 the glory of Jehovah is *g*
145:3 Jehovah is *g* and very much
145:8 and *g* in loving-kindness
147:5 Our Lord is *g* and is abundant
Pr 13:23 yields a *g* deal of food
18:16 him even before *g* people
19:19 *g* rage will be bearing the
25:6 place of *g* ones do not stand
Ec 1:16 heart saw a *g* deal of wisdom
2:7 cattle and flocks in *g* quantity
5:17 with a *g* deal of vexation
9:13 and it was *g* to me
9:14 and there came to it a *g* king
9:14 built against it *g* strongholds
10:4 calmness itself allays *g* sins
10:18 Through *g* laziness the
Isa 5:9 houses, though *g* and good
5:26 to a *g* nation far away
9:2 have seen a *g* light
9:3 you have made the rejoicing *g*
12:6 *g* in the midst of you is the
27:1 *g* and strong sword, will
27:13 blowing on a *g* horn, and
29:6 quaking and with a *g* sound
34:6 *g* slaughtering in the land
36:4 *g* king, the king of Assyria
36:13 the words of the *g* king
54:7 but with *g* mercies I shall
56:12 *g* in a very much larger way
Jer 2:12 bristle up in very *g* horror
4:6 the north, even a *g* crash
5:5 go my way to the *g* ones and
5:27 *g* and they gain riches
6:1 the north, even a *g* crash
6:22 there is a *g* nation that
10:6 You are *g*, and your name is
10:6 your name is *g* in mightiness
10:22 a *g* pounding from the land
11:16 With sound of the *g* roaring
14:17 with a *g* crash the virgin
16:6 the *g* ones and the small
16:10 this *g* calamity, and what
21:5 rage and with *g* indignation
21:6 *g* pestilence they will die
22:8 do like this to this *g* city
25:14 many nations and *g* kings
25:32 a *g* tempest itself will be
26:19 a *g* calamity against our
27:5 by my *g* power and by my
27:7 *g* kings must exploit him as
28:8 and concerning *g* kingdoms
30:7 For that day is a *g* one
31:8 As a *g* congregation they
32:17 earth by your *g* power and
32:18 the *g* One, the mighty One
32:19 *g* in counsel and abundant

Jer 32:21 and with *g* fearsomeness
32:37 rage and in *g* indignation
32:42 all this *g* calamity
33:3 *g* and incomprehensible
36:7 *g* is the anger and the
40:12 fruits in very *g* quantity
41:9 *g* cistern, the one that
43:9 Take in your hand *g* stones
44:7 *g* calamity to your souls, in
44:15 *g* congregation, and all the
44:26 sworn by my *g* name, Jehovah
45:5 seeking *g* things for yourself
46:16 In *g* numbers they are
48:3 and *g* breaking down
48:26 on *g* airs against Jehovah
48:42 that he has put on *g* airs
50:9 *g* nations from the land of
50:22 the land, and a *g* breakdown
50:41 *g* nation and grand kings
51:54 *g* crash from the land of
51:55 out of her the *g* voice
52:13 every *g* house he burned
La 1:9 the enemy has put on *g* airs
1:16 the enemy has put on *g* airs
2:13 breakdown is just as *g* as the
Eze 1:4 a *g* cloud mass and quivering
3:12 the sound of a *g* rushing
3:13 and the sound of a *g* rushing
8:6 *g* detestable things they are
8:6 see again *g* detestable things
8:13 *g* detestable things that they
8:15 *g* detestable things worse
9:9 The error . . . is very, very *g*
16:7 grow big and become *g* and
16:26 your neighbors *g* of flesh
17:3, 3 *g* eagle, having *g* wings
17:7 came to be another *g* eagle
17:7 eagle, having *g* wings, and
17:9 Neither by a *g* arm nor by a
17:17 by a *g* military force and
21:14 someone slain who is *g*
24:9 also shall make the pile *g*
24:12 the *g* amount of its rust
25:17 *g* acts of vengeance, with
29:3 the *g* sea monster lying
29:18 perform a *g* service against
29:19 do a *g* deal of plundering
30:24 do a *g* deal of groaning
35:13 acting in *g* style against
36:23 sanctify my *g* name, which
37:10 very, very *g* military force
38:13 to get a very *g* spoil
38:15 a *g* congregation, even a
38:19 that day a *g* quaking will
39:17 a *g* sacrifice on the
47:10 fish of the *G* Sea, very
47:15 *G* Sea by the way to Hethlon
47:19 torrent valley to the *G* Sea
47:20 western side is the *G* Sea
48:28 as far as the *G* Sea
Da 2:48 king made Daniel someone *g*
4:1 May your peace grow *g*
4:20 grew *g* and became strong and
4:22 grown *g* and become strong
4:22 your grandeur has grown *g* and
4:30 Babylon the *G*, that I myself
7:28 kept frightening me a *g* deal
8:4 and it put on *g* airs
8:8 put on *g* airs to an extreme
8:8 the *g* horn was broken, and
8:11 it put on *g* airs, and from
8:21 *g* horn that was between its
8:25 heart he will put on *g* airs
9:4 true God, the *g* One and the
9:12 bringing upon us *g* calamity
10:1 was a *g* military service
10:4 *g* river, that is, Hiddekel
10:7 *g* trembling that fell upon
10:8 that I saw this *g* appearance
11:13 with a *g* military force and
11:13 and with a *g* deal of goods
11:25 with a *g* military force; and
11:25 *g* and mighty military force
11:28 with a *g* amount of goods
11:44 *g* rage in order to annihilate
12:1 *g* prince who is standing in
Ho 1:11 *g* will be the day of Jezreel
5:13 and send to a *g* king
10:6 as a gift to a *g* king
Joe 2:11 the day of Jehovah is *g* and
2:20 do a *g* thing in what He does
2:21 do a *g* thing in what He does
2:25 my *g* military force that I
2:31 the *g* and fear-inspiring day

Am 6:11 strike down the *g* house into
8:5 to make the shekel *g* and to
Jon 1:2 go to Nineveh the *g* city, and
1:4 a *g* wind at the sea, and
1:4 to be a *g* tempest on the sea
1:12 this *g* tempest is upon you
1:17 a *g* fish to swallow Jonah
3:2 go to Nineveh the *g* city, and
3:3 proved to be a city *g* to God
3:7 the king and his *g* ones
4:11 sorry for Nineveh the *g* city
Mic 5:4 he will be *g* as far as the
7:3 the *g* one is speaking forth
Na 1:3 slow to anger and *g* in power
3:10 her *g* ones have all been bound
Zep 1:10 a *g* crashing from the hills
1:14 The *g* day of Jehovah is near
2:8 putting on *g* airs against
2:10 putting on *g* airs against
Zec 1:14 for Zion with *g* jealousy
1:15 With *g* indignation I am
4:7 Who are you, O *g* mountain?
7:12 occurred *g* indignation on the
8:2 for Zion with *g* jealousy
8:2 with *g* rage I will be jealous
9:17 O how *g* his goodness is, and
9:17 how *g* his handsomeness is
12:7 not become too *g* over Judah
12:11 wailing . . . will be *g*
14:4 will be a very *g* valley
Mal 1:11 my name will be *g* among
1:11 my name will be *g* among
1:14 I am a *g* King, Jehovah of
4:5 *g* and fear-inspiring day of
Mt 2:16 fell into a *g* rage, and he
4:16 saw a *g* light, and as for
4:25 *g* crowds followed him from
5:12 reward is *g* in the heavens
5:19 *g* in relation to the kingdom
5:35 it is the city of the *g* King
6:23 how *g* that darkness is!
7:27 and its collapse was *g*
8:1 *g* crowds followed him
8:10 have I found so *g* a faith
8:24 *g* agitation arose in the sea
8:26 sea, and a *g* calm set in
9:37 harvest is *g*, but the workers
13:2 and *g* crowds gathered to him
14:14 a *g* crowd; and he felt pity
15:28 O woman, *g* is your faith
15:30 *g* crowds approached him
19:2 *g* crowds followed him, and
19:25 expressed very *g* surprise
20:25 *g* men wield authority over
20:26 wants to become *g* among you
20:29 a *g* crowd followed him
24:21 *g* tribulation such as has
24:24 give *g* signs and wonders so
24:30 with power and *g* glory
24:31 with a *g* trumpet sound, and
26:9 have been sold for a *g* deal
26:47 a *g* crowd with swords and
28:2 *g* earthquake had taken place
28:8 with fear and *g* joy, they ran
Mr 1:45 to proclaim it a *g* deal and
3:7 *g* multitude from Galilee and
3:8 a *g* multitude, on hearing of
4:1 *g* crowd gathered near him, so
4:32 produces *g* branches, so that
4:37 a *g* violent windstorm broke
4:39 abated, and a *g* calm set in
5:11 a *g* herd of swine was there
5:21 a *g* crowd gathered together
5:24 a *g* crowd was following him
5:42 themselves with *g* ecstasy
6:20 was at a *g* loss what to do
6:34 he saw a *g* crowd, but he
9:14 they noticed a *g* crowd about
10:42 their *g* ones wield authority
10:43 whoever wants to become *g*
12:37 the *g* crowd was listening
13:2 behold these *g* buildings
13:26 with *g* power and glory
14:5 feeling *g* displeasure at her
Lu 1:14 will have joy and *g* gladness
1:15 he will be *g* before Jehovah
1:32 This one will be *g* and will
1:44 leaped with *g* gladness
1:49 has done *g* deeds for me, and
2:10 good news of a *g* joy that all
4:25 *g* famine fell upon all the
5:6 enclosed a *g* multitude of fish
5:15 *g* crowds would come together
5:29 *g* crowd of tax collectors and
Lu 6:17 a *g* crowd of his disciples
6:17 a *g* multitude of people from
6:23 your reward is *g* in heaven
6:35 your reward will be *g*, and
6:49 ruin of that house became *g*
7:9 have I found so *g* a faith
7:11 *g* crowd were traveling with
7:16 A *g* prophet has been raised up
8:4 when a *g* crowd had collected
8:37 were in the grip of *g* fear
9:7 and he was in *g* perplexity
9:37 a *g* crowd met him
9:48 lesser . . . the one that is *g*
10:2 The harvest, indeed, is *g*, but
14:25 Now *g* crowds were traveling
16:26 a *g* chasm has been fixed
21:11 there will be *g* earthquakes
21:11 and from heaven *g* signs
21:23 *g* necessity upon the land
21:27 with power and *g* glory
23:27 following him a *g* multitude
24:52 to Jerusalem with *g* joy
Joh 3:23 a *g* quantity of water there
3:29 *g* deal of joy on account of
6:2 a *g* crowd kept following him
6:5 *g* crowd was coming to him
7:37 the *g* day of the festival
12:9 *g* crowd of the Jews got to
12:12 *g* crowd that had come to
19:31 that Sabbath was a *g* one
Ac 2:20 *g* and illustrious day of
2:46 food with *g* rejoicing and
4:33 with *g* power the apostles
5:5 *g* fear came over all those
5:11 *g* fear came over the whole
6:7 *g* crowd of priests began to
6:8 performing *g* portents and
7:11 even a *g* tribulation; and
8:1 *g* persecution arose against
8:2 made a *g* lamentation over him
8:8 *g* deal of joy in that city
8:9 he himself was somebody *g*
8:10 God, which can be called *G*
8:13 at beholding *g* signs and
10:11 *g* linen sheet being let down
10:17 Peter was in *g* perplexity
11:5 *g* linen sheet being let down
11:21 and a *g* number that became
11:28 *g* famine was about to come
14:1 *g* multitude of both Jews and
15:3 *g* joy to all the brothers
16:26 a *g* earthquake occurred, so
17:4 a *g* multitude of the Greeks
19:27 of the *g* goddess Artemis
19:28 saying: *G* is Artemis of the
19:34 *G* is Artemis of the
19:35 keeper of the *g* Artemis and
21:40 When a *g* silence fell, he
22:6 out of heaven a *g* light
23:10 when the dissension grew *g*
24:2 Seeing that we enjoy *g* peace
26:22 witness to both small and *g*
26:24 *G* learning is driving you
27:10 *g* loss not only of the cargo
27:14 After no *g* while, however
Ro 3:2 A *g* deal in every way
9:2 I have *g* grief and unceasing
1Co 9:11 is it something *g* if we
2Co 1:10 From such a *g* thing as death
3:12 using *g* freeness of speech
7:4 I have *g* freeness of speech
7:4 I have *g* boasting in regard
7:11 *g* earnestness it produced in
8:2 a *g* test under affliction
8:22 due to his *g* confidence in
10:15 be made *g* among you with
11:15 nothing *g* if his ministers
Eph 2:4 his *g* love with which he
5:32 This sacred secret is *g*
Col 2:1 to realize how *g* a struggle I
4:13 to *g* effort in behalf of you
1Th 2:2 with a *g* deal of struggling
2:17 see your faces with *g* desire
1Ti 3:13 and *g* freeness of speech in
3:16 devotion is admittedly *g*
6:6 it is a means of *g* gain, this
Tit 2:13 manifestation of the *g* God
Phm 8 I have *g* freeness of speech in
Heb 4:14 *g* high priest who has passed
7:4 how *g* this man was to whom
10:21 *g* priest over the house of
10:32 you endured a *g* contest
10:35 *g* reward to be paid it
12:1 so *g* a cloud of witnesses
Heb 13:20 *g* shepherd of the sheep
Jas 3:5 the tongue . . . makes *g* brags
3:5 set so *g* a woodland on fire
1Pe 1:3 according to his *g* mercy he
3:4 of *g* value in the eyes of God
Jude 6 the judgment of the *g* day
24 of his glory with *g* joy
Re 2:22 with her into *g* tribulation
5:4 to a *g* deal of weeping because
6:4 and a *g* sword was given him
6:12 and a *g* earthquake occurred
6:17 the *g* day of their wrath has
7:9 a *g* crowd, which no man was
7:14 come out of the *g* tribulation
8:8 a *g* mountain burning with fire
8:10 a *g* star burning as a lamp
9:2 the smoke of a *g* furnace
9:14 at the *g* river Euphrates
11:8 the broad way of the *g* city
11:11 and *g* fear fell upon those
11:13 in that hour a *g* earthquake
11:17 taken your *g* power and begun
11:18 the small and the *g*, and to
11:19 an earthquake and a *g* hail
12:1 a *g* sign was seen in heaven
12:3 *g* fiery-colored dragon, with
12:9 down the *g* dragon was hurled
12:12 having *g* anger, knowing he
12:14 two wings of the *g* eagle
13:2 its throne and *g* authority
13:5 mouth speaking *g* things and
13:13 it performs *g* signs, so that
13:16 persons, the small and the *g*
14:8 Babylon the *g* has fallen, she
14:19 *g* winepress of the anger of
15:1 sign, *g* and wonderful, seven
15:3 *G* and wonderful are your
16:9 were scorched with *g* heat
16:12 upon the *g* river Euphrates
16:14 war of the *g* day of God
16:18 *g* earthquake occurred such
16:18 extensive an earthquake, so *g*
16:19 *g* city split into three parts
16:19 and Babylon the *G* was
16:21 *g* hail with every stone
16:21 plague of it was unusually *g*
17:1 judgment upon the *g* harlot
17:5 Babylon the *G*, the mother of
17:6 wondered with *g* wonderment
17:18 woman . . . means the *g* city
18:1 from heaven, with *g* authority
18:2 Babylon the *G* has fallen, and
18:10 too bad, you *g* city, Babylon
18:16 *g* city, clothed with fine
18:17 *g* riches have been devastated
18:18 city is like the *g* city
18:19 *g* city, in which all those
18:21 *g* millstone and hurled it
18:21 Babylon the *g* city be hurled
19:1 voice of a *g* crowd in heaven
19:2 judgment upon the *g* harlot
19:5 the small ones and the *g*
19:6 as a voice of a *g* crowd and
19:17 to the *g* evening meal of God
19:18 and of small ones and *g*
20:1 and a *g* chain in his hand
20:11 I saw a *g* white throne and
20:12 I saw the dead, the *g* and
21:10 to a *g* and lofty mountain
21:12 It had a *g* and lofty wall
21:16 length is as *g* as its breadth

Greater

Ge 1:16 *g* luminary for dominating the
24:35 making him *g* and giving him
39:9 no one *g* in this house than I
41:40 as to the throne shall I be *g*
48:19 brother will become *g* than
Ex 18:11 Jehovah is *g* than all the
Nu 14:12 make you a nation *g* and
22:15 other princes in *g* number
De 1:28 A people *g* and taller than we
4:38 nations *g* and mightier than
9:1 nations *g* and mightier than
11:23 nations *g* and more numerous
Jos 10:2 and because it was *g* than Ai
1Sa 2:33 *g* number of your house will
14:19, 19 go on, getting *g* and *g*
2Sa 5:10, 10 went on getting *g* and *g*
13:15 *g* than the love with which
13:16 sending me away is *g* than
1Ki 1:37 may he make his throne *g*
1:47 make his throne *g* than your
10:23 Solomon was *g* in riches and

1Ch 11:9, 9 went on getting *g* and *g*
12:29 the *g* number of them were
2Ch 2:5 is *g* than all the other gods
9:22 Solomon was *g* than all the
Es 9:4 Mordecai . . . growing *g*
Job 10:17 your vexation with me *g*
15:10 *g* than your father in days
Ps 4:7 *G* than in the time when their
Ec 2:4 I engaged in *g* works. I built
2:9 I became *g* and increased more
La 4:6 *g* than the punishment for the
Da 8:9 very much *g* toward the south
8:10 *g* all the way to the army of
11:2 amass *g* riches than all
11:5 dominion *g* than that one's
Hag 2:9 *G* will the glory of this
Mt 10:37 *g* affection for father or
10:37 has *g* affection for son or
11:11 a *g* than John the Baptist
11:11 lesser one . . . *g* than he is
12:6 *g* than the temple is here
23:17 is *g*, the gold or the temple
23:19 is *g*, the gift or the altar
24:12 love of the *g* number will
Mr 4:32 *g* than all other vegetables
6:2 *g* number of those listening
9:26 the *g* number of them were
9:34 they had argued . . . who is *g*
12:31 no other commandment *g* than
Lu 7:28 there is none *g* than John
7:28 lesser one . . . is *g* than he is
13:4 they were proved *g* debtors
22:27 For which one is *g*, the one
Joh 1:50 will see things *g* than these
4:12 not *g* than our forefather
5:20 show him works *g* than these
5:36 witness *g* than that of John
8:53 *g* than our father Abraham
10:29 *g* than all other things, and
13:16 slave is not *g* than his
13:16 *g* than the one that sent
14:12 he will do works *g* than
14:28 the Father is *g* than I am
15:13 one has love *g* than this
15:20 is not *g* than his master
19:11 man . . . has *g* sin
20:4 with *g* speed and reached
Ac 28:23 *g* numbers to him in his
1Co 12:31 seeking the *g* gifts
14:5 he that prophesies is *g* than
Ga 1:14 making *g* progress in Judaism
Php 2:28 *g* haste I am sending him
Heb 6:13 could not swear by anyone *g*
6:16 For men swear by the one *g*
7:7 the less is blessed by the *g*
9:11 through the *g* and more
11:4 sacrifice of *g* worth than
11:26 riches *g* than the treasures
Jas 4:6 kindness which he gives is *g*
1Pe 1:7 much *g* value than gold that
2Pe 2:11 *g* in strength and power
1Jo 3:20 God is *g* than our hearts and
4:4 *g* than he that is in union
5:9 the witness God gives is *g*
3Jo 4 No *g* cause for thankfulness do

Greatest
Ge 19:11 least to the *g*, so that they
De 28:66 in the *g* peril for your life
1Sa 30:2 from the smallest to the *g*
30:19 from the smallest to the *g*
1Ch 12:14 and the *g* to a thousand
Job 1:3 the *g* of all the Orientals
Ec 1:2 The *g* vanity! the congregator
1:2 the *g* vanity! Everything is
12:8 *g* vanity! said the congregator
Jer 6:13 even to the *g* one of them
8:10 least one even to the *g* one
31:34 even to the *g* one of them
42:1 even to the *g* one, approached
42:8 even to the *g* one
44:12 even to the *g* one
Jon 3:5 from the *g* one of them even
Mt 18:1 really is *g* in the kingdom
18:4 the *g* in the kingdom of the
22:36 which is the *g* commandment
22:38 the *g* and first commandment
23:11 the *g* one among you must be
24:51 with the *g* severity and
Lu 9:46 who would be the *g* of them
12:46 with the *g* severity and
22:24 one of them seemed to be *g*
22:26 the *g* among you become as
Ac 8:10 least to the *g*, would pay
Ac 17:11 with the *g* eagerness of mind
20:19 the *g* lowliness of mind and
24:3 with the *g* thankfulness
28:31 the *g* freeness of speech
1Co 13:13 but the *g* of these is love
Heb 8:11 the least one to the *g* one

Greatly
Ge 3:16 I shall *g* increase the pain
7:18 waters . . . kept increasing *g*
7:19 overwhelmed the earth so *g*
16:10 I shall *g* multiply your seed
Nu 22:17 without fail honor you *g*
Jg 6:6 Israel became *g* impoverished
10:9 and Israel was *g* distressed
1Sa 1:10 she began to . . . weep *g*
12:18 *g* in fear of Jehovah and of
17:11 terrified and were *g* afraid
28:21 he had been *g* disturbed
1Ki 5:7 he began to rejoice *g*, and he
18:3 one *g* fearing Jehovah
2Ki 10:4 became very *g* afraid and
2Ch 33:12 humbling himself *g* because
Ps 79:8 have become *g* impoverished
Ec 1:16 *g* increased in wisdom more
Isa 28:29 *g* in effectual working
66:10 Exult *g* with her, all you
Jon 1:10 the men began to fear *g*
1:16 men began to fear Jehovah *g*
4:6 Jonah began to rejoice *g* over
Lu 22:15 I have *g* desired to eat this
23:8 Herod saw Jesus he rejoiced *g*
Joh 5:35 to rejoice *g* in his light
8:56 rejoiced *g* in the prospect
Ac 2:26 and my tongue rejoiced *g*
16:34 he rejoiced *g* with all his
18:27 he *g* helped those who had
Eph 3:10 *g* diversified wisdom of God
Php 4:10 I do rejoice *g* in the Lord
1Pe 1:6 you are *g* rejoicing, though
1:8 are *g* rejoicing with an
2Pe 2:7 Lot, who was *g* distressed by

Greatness
Ex 15:16 Because of the *g* of your arm
Nu 14:19 the *g* of your loving-kindness
De 3:24 your *g* and your strong arm
5:24 shown us his glory and his *g*
9:26 you redeemed with your *g*
11:2 God, his *g*, his strong hand
32:3 Do you attribute *g* to our God!
1Ch 29:11 Yours, O Jehovah, are the *g*
Es 1:4 honor and the beauty of his *g*
10:2 statement of Mordecai's *g*
Ps 71:21 May you enlarge my *g*
79:11 *g* of your arm preserve those
145:3 And his *g* is unsearchable
145:6 your *g*, I will declare it
150:2 to the abundance of his *g*
Eze 31:2 come to resemble in your *g*
31:7 came to be pretty in its *g*
31:18 glory and *g* among the trees
Da 4:36 *g* extraordinary was added to
5:18 *g* and the dignity and the
5:19 because of the *g* that He gave
Eph 1:19 *g* of his power is toward us
Heb 2:3 a salvation of such *g* in that

Greaves
1Sa 17:6 *g* of copper above his feet

Grecian
Mr 7:26 was a *G*, a Syrophoenician

Greece
Da 8:21 stands for the king of *G*
10:20 the prince of *G* is coming
11:2 against the kingdom of *G*
Zec 9:13 against your sons, O *G*
Ac 20:2 he came into *G*

Greed
Pr 20:21 is being got by *g* at first

Greedily
1Sa 14:32 began darting *g* at the spoil
15:19 darting *g* at the spoil and
Pr 18:8 like things to be swallowed *g*
26:22 things to be swallowed *g*

Greediness
Eph 4:19 uncleanness . . . with *g*
5:3 or *g* not even be mentioned

Greedy
1Co 5:10 *g* persons and extortioners or
5:11 or a *g* person or an idolater
6:10 nor *g* persons, nor drunkards
Eph 5:5 or *g* person—which means
1Ti 3:8 not *g* of dishonest gain
Tit 1:7 not *g* of dishonest gain

Greek
Joh 19:20 in Hebrew, in Latin, in *G*
Ac 16:1 Timothy . . . of a *G* father
16:3 knew that his father was a *G*
17:12 of the reputable *G* women and
21:37 He said: Can you speak *G*?
Ro 1:16 Jew first and also to the *G*
2:9 Jew first and also of the *G*
2:10 Jew first and also for the *G*
10:12 between Jew and *G*, for there
Ga 2:3 Titus . . . although he was a *G*
3:28 There is neither Jew nor *G*
Col 3:11 there is neither *G* nor Jew
Re 9:11 in *G* he has the name Apollyon

Greeks
Joe 3:6 sold to the sons of the *G*
Joh 7:35 Jews dispersed among the *G*
7:35 and teach the *G*, does he
12:20 *G* among those that came up
Ac 14:1 Jews and *G* became believers
17:4 a great multitude of the *G*
18:4 and would persuade Jews and *G*
19:10 both Jews and *G*
19:17 the *G* that dwelt in Ephesus
20:21 both to Jews and to *G* about
21:28 brought *G* into the temple
Ro 1:14 to *G* and to Barbarians, both
3:9 well as *G* are all under sin
1Co 1:22 and the *G* look for wisdom
1:24 the called, both Jews and *G*
10:32 to Jews as well as *G* and to
12:13 one body, whether Jews or *G*

Greek-speaking
Ac 6:1 of the *G* Jews against the
9:29 disputing with the *G* Jews
11:20 talking to the *G* people

Green
Ge 1:30 all *g* vegetation for food
9:3 As in the case of *g* vegetation
Ex 10:15 left nothing *g* on the trees
Le 2:14 should present *g* ears roasted
Nu 22:4 the *g* growth of the field
1Ki 18:5 find *g* grass, that we may
2Ki 19:26 and *g* tender grass
Job 39:8 every . . . *g* plant it seeks
40:15 *G* grass it eats just as a
Ps 37:2 like *g* new grass they will
58:9 The live *g* as well as the
90:5 like *g* grass that changes
103:15 are like those of *g* grass
104:14 *g* grass sprout for the
129:6 like *g* grass of the roofs
147:8 mountains to sprout *g* grass
Pr 27:25 The *g* grass has departed, and
Isa 15:6 *g* grass has dried up, the
15:6 nothing has become *g*
35:7 be *g* grass with reeds and
37:27 field and *g* tender grass
40:6 All flesh is *g* grass, and
40:7 The *g* grass has dried up
40:7 Surely the people are *g* grass
40:8 The *g* grass has dried up
44:4 among the *g* grass, like
51:12 rendered as mere *g* grass
Joe 2:22 wilderness will . . . grow *g*
Mr 6:39 recline . . . on the *g* grass
Re 8:7 the *g* vegetation was burned up
9:4 any *g* thing nor any tree

Greens
Ex 12:8 cakes along with bitter *g*
Nu 9:11 bitter *g* they should eat it

Greet
2Ki 4:29 you must not *g* him
4:29 in case anyone should *g* you
Mt 5:47 if you *g* your brothers only
10:12 *g* the household
Mr 9:15 they began to *g* him
Ro 16:5 *g* the congregation that is in
16:5 *G* my beloved Epaenetus, who
16:6 *G* Mary, who has performed
16:7 *G* Andronicus and Junias my
16:9 *G* Urbanus our fellow worker
16:10 *G* Apelles, the approved one
16:10 *G* those from the household
16:11 *G* Herodion my relative
16:11 *G* those from the household
16:12 *G* Tryphaena and Tryphosa
16:12 *G* Persis our beloved one, for

Ro 16:13 *G* Rufus the chosen one in
16:14 *G* Asyncritus, Phlegon
16:15 *G* Philologus and Julia
16:16 *G* . . . with a holy kiss
16:16 congregations of the Christ *g*
16:22 *g* you in the Lord
1Co 16:19 *g* you heartily in the Lord
16:20 All the brothers *g* you
16:20 *G* . . . with a holy kiss
2Co 13:12 *G* . . . with a holy kiss
1Th 5:26 *G* all the brothers with a
1Pe 5:14 *G* one another with a kiss

Greeted

Lu 1:40 of Zechariah and *g* Elizabeth
Ac 18:22 *g* the congregation, and went
21:7 we *g* the brothers and stayed
21:19 he *g* them and began giving

Greeting

Mr 15:18 *g* him: Good day, you King of
Lu 1:29 what sort of *g* this might be
1:41 Elizabeth heard the *g* of Mary
1:44 as the sound of your *g* fell
10:4 do not embrace anybody in *g*
1Co 16:21 *g*, Paul's, in my own hand
Col 4:18 Here is my *g*, Paul's, in my
2Th 3:17 Here is my *g*, Paul's, in
2Jo 10 or say a *g* to him
11 says a *g* to him is a sharer

Greetings

Ezr 4:17 beyond the River: *G!* And now
Mt 23:7 the *g* in the marketplaces and
Mr 12:38 want *g* in the marketplaces
Lu 11:43 the *g* in the marketplaces
20:46 like *g* in the marketplaces
Ac 15:23 who are from the nations: *G!*
23:26 excellency, Governor Felix: *G!*
Ro 16:3 my *g* to Prisca and Aquila my
16:8 Give my *g* to Ampliatus my
1Co 16:19 of Asia send you their *g*
2Co 13:13 holy ones send you their *g*
Php 4:21 Give my *g* to every holy one
4:21 brothers . . . send you their *g*
4:22 send you their *g*
Col 4:10 sends you his *g*, and so does
4:12 Epaphras . . . sends you his *g*
4:14 his *g*, and so does Demas
4:15 *g* to the brothers at Laodicea
2Ti 4:19 Give my *g* to Prisca and
4:21 Eubulus sends you his *g*, and
Tit 3:15 with me send you their *g*
3:15 Give my *g* to those who have
Phm 23 Sending you *g* is Epaphras
Heb 13:24 Give my *g* to all those who
13:24 in Italy send you their *g*
Jas 1:1 to the twelve tribes . . . *G!*
1Pe 5:13 sends you her *g*, and so does
2Jo 13 send you their *g*
3Jo 14 The friends send you their *g*
14 my *g* to the friends by name

Greets

Ro 16:21 my fellow worker *g* you, and
16:23 all the congregation, *g* you
16:23 steward *g* you, and so does

Grew

Ge 4:5 And Cain *g* hot with great
26:34 Esau *g* to be forty years old
28:17 And he *g* fearful and added
32:7 much afraid and *g* anxious
34:7 and they *g* very angry, because
37:11 brothers *g* jealous of him
39:6 Joseph *g* to be beautiful in
40:2 Pharaoh *g* indignant at his
45:26 his heart *g* numb, because he
47:27 and *g* to be very many
Ex 2:10 And the child *g* up. Then she
4:14 Jehovah's anger *g* hot against
10:15 land *g* dark; and they went
34:30 *g* afraid of coming near to
Le 10:16 he *g* indignant at Eleazar
Nu 11:1 anger *g* hot, and a fire of
31:14 And Moses *g* indignant at the
Jos 7:1 Jehovah's anger *g* hot against
Jg 1:28 Israel *g* strong and proceeded
1Sa 11:11 till the day *g* hot
17:28 anger *g* hot against David
18:12 And Saul *g* afraid of David
20:30 Saul's anger *g* hot against
2Sa 12:5 David's anger *g* very hot
21:15 and David *g* tired
2Ki 4:34 the child's flesh *g* warm
5:11 Naaman *g* indignant and began
13:19 *g* indignant at him
Es 1:12 the king *g* highly indignant
Job 31:18 he *g* up with me as with a
Ps 39:3 My heart *g* hot inside me
Ca 1:6 sons of my own mother *g* angry
Isa 47:6 I *g* indignant at my people
57:17 I *g* indignant, and I
Eze 16:7 your own hair *g* luxuriantly
16:13 *g* to be very, very pretty
31:5 *g* higher in its stature
Da 4:11 tree *g* up and became strong
4:20 *g* great and became strong and
4:33 hair *g* long just like eagles'
Zec 1:2 Jehovah *g* indignant at your
Mt 22:7 king *g* wrathful, and sent
25:25 I *g* afraid and went off and
27:54 *g* very much afraid, saying
Mr 5:15 and they *g* fearful
10:22 he *g* sad at the saying and
Lu 8:7 the thorns that *g* up with it
13:19 it *g* and became a tree
Ac 7:17 *g* and multiplied in Egypt
16:38 *g* fearful when they heard
23:10 when the dissension *g* great
Re 12:17 dragon *g* wrathful at the

Greyhound

Pr 30:31 the *g* or the he-goat, and a

Griddle

Le 2:5 grain offering from off the *g*
6:21 made with oil upon a *g*
7:9 grain offering . . . upon the *g*
1Ch 23:29 for the *g* cakes and for the
Eze 4:3 take to yourself an iron *g*

Grief

Ge 42:38 gray hairs with *g* to Sheol
44:31 our father with *g* to Sheol
Es 9:22 from *g* to rejoicing and from
Ps 13:2 *G* in my heart by day
31:10 with *g* my life has come to
107:39 restraint, calamity and *g*
116:3 Distress and *g* I kept finding
119:28 has been sleepless from *g*
Pr 10:1 son is the *g* of his mother
14:13 *g* is what rejoicing ends up
17:21 a stupid child—it is a *g* to
Isa 35:10 *g* and sighing must flee
51:11 *G* and sighing will certainly
Jer 8:18 A *g* that is beyond curing
20:18 to see hard work and *g*
31:13 rejoice away from their *g*
45:3 Jehovah has added *g* to my
La 1:5 Jehovah himself has brought *g*
1:12 Jehovah has caused *g* in the
3:32 although he has caused *g*, he
Eze 23:33 With drunkenness and *g* you
Mt 11:17 did not beat yourselves in *g*
Lu 8:52 beating themselves in *g* for
22:45 them slumbering from *g*
23:27 beating themselves in *g* and
Joh 16:6 *g* has filled your hearts
16:20 *g* will be turned into joy
16:21 she is giving birth, has *g*
16:22 are now, indeed, having *g*
Ro 9:2 I have great *g* and unceasing
Php 2:27, 27 should not get *g* upon *g*
2:28 may be the more free from *g*
Re 1:7 beat themselves in *g* because
18:9 beat themselves in *g* over

Grief-stricken

La 1:4 Her virgins are *g*, and she
Zep 3:18 ones *g* in absence from your

Grieve

La 3:33 or does he *g* the sons of men

Grieved

Job 30:25 soul has *g* for the poor one
Isa 19:10 wage workers *g* in soul
Mt 14:9 *G* though he was, the king out
17:23 they were very much *g*
18:31 they became very much *g*
19:22 he went away *g*, for he was
26:22 Being very much *g* at this
26:37 he started to be *g* and to be
26:38 My soul is deeply *g*, even to
Mr 3:5 *g* at the insensibility of
6:26 became deeply *g*, yet the king
10:22 *g*, for he was holding many
14:19 started to be *g* and to say to
14:34 My soul is deeply *g*, even to
Lu 18:23 *g*, for he was very rich
Joh 16:20 you will be *g*, but your
21:17 Peter became *g* that he
Ro 14:15 brother is being *g*, you are
1Pe 1:6 have been *g* by various trials

Grieving

Eph 4:30 do not be *g* God's holy spirit

Grievous

Mr 3:10 all those who had *g* diseases
5:29 been healed of the *g* sickness
5:34 health from your *g* sickness
Lu 7:21 of sicknesses and *g* diseases
Heb 12:11 to be joyous, but *g*; yet
1Pe 2:19 bears up under *g* things and

Grind

Ps 112:10 He will *g* his very teeth
Isa 3:15 *g* the very faces of the
47:2 a hand mill and *g* out flour

Grinder

Jg 16:21 a *g* in the prison house

Grinding

De 9:21 *g* it thoroughly until it had
Job 31:10 Let my wife do the *g* for
Ps 35:16 a *g* of their teeth even
37:12 at him he is *g* his teeth
Ec 12:3 *g* women have quit working
12:4 of the *g* mill becomes low
La 2:16 whistled and kept *g* the teeth
Da 2:40 and *g* everything else, so
Mt 24:41 will be *g* at the hand mill
Lu 17:35 two women *g* at the same

Grinds

Job 16:9 *g* his teeth against me
Mr 9:18 he foams and *g* his teeth

Grindstone

De 24:6 or its upper *g* as a pledge

Grip

Ge 41:56 the famine got a strong *g* on
41:57 a strong *g* on all the earth
47:20 famine had got a strong *g* on
Lu 8:37 were in the *g* of great fear
Php 2:16 tight *g* on the word of life

Gripping

Mr 16:8 strong emotion were *g* them

Grits

Le 2:14 the *g* of new grain, as the
2:16 some of its *g* and oil, along

Groan

Pr 5:11 *g* in your future when your
Isa 42:14 going to *g*, pant, and gasp
Jer 51:52 the pierced one will *g*
Eze 24:23 actually *g* over one another
Ro 8:23 *g* within ourselves, while we
2Co 5:2 *g*, earnestly desiring to put
5:4 *g*, being weighed down

Groaned

Mr 8:12 he *g* deeply with his spirit
Joh 11:33 *g* in the spirit and became

Groaning

Ex 2:24 In time God heard their *g* and
6:5 heard the *g* of the sons of
Jg 2:18 feel regret over their *g*
Job 24:12 the dying keep *g*, And the
Ps 32:3 bones wore out through my *g*
38:8 due to the *g* of my heart
Isa 59:11 We keep *g*, all of us, just
Eze 9:4 and *g* over all the detestable
30:24 do a great deal of *g* before
Joh 11:38 Jesus, after *g* again
Ac 7:34 I have heard their *g* and I
Ro 8:22 creation keeps on *g* together

Groanings

Ro 8:26 pleads . . . with *g* unuttered

Groans

Eze 26:15 the fatally wounded one *g*

Groomsman

Jg 14:20 belong to a *g* of his who had
15:2 I gave her to your *g*. Is not
15:6 and then gave her to his *g*

Groomsmen

Jg 14:11 took thirty *g*, that these

Grope

Job 5:14 *g* about at midday as if at
12:25 They *g* in darkness, where
Ac 17:27 *g* for him and really find

Gropes

De 28:29 one who *g* about at midday
28:29 a blind man *g* about in

Groping
Isa 59:10 We keep *g* for the wall just
59:10 keep *g*. We have stumbled

Gross
Ge 13:13 men of Sodom . . . *g* sinners

Ground
Ge 1:25 every moving animal of the *g*
2:5 was no man to cultivate the *g*
2:6 the entire surface of the *g*
2:7 man out of dust from the *g* and
2:9 grow out of the *g* every tree
2:19 God was forming from the *g*
3:17 cursed is the *g* on your
3:19 until you return to the *g*
3:23 Eden to cultivate the *g* from
4:2 became a cultivator of the *g*
4:3 fruits of the *g* as an offering
4:10 crying out to me from the *g*
4:11 in banishment from the *g*
4:12 When you cultivate the *g*, it
4:14 from off the surface of the *g*
5:29 *g* which Jehovah has cursed
6:1 surface of the *g* and daughters
6:7 off the surface of the *g*
6:20 all moving animals of the *g*
7:4 off the surface of the *g*
7:8 everything that moves on the *g*
7:22 all that were on the dry *g*
7:23 surface of the *g*, from man to
8:8 from the surface of the *g*
8:13 surface of the *g* had drained
8:21 I call down evil upon the *g*
9:2 that goes moving on the *g*
12:3 all the families of the *g*
19:25 and the plants of the *g*
28:14 families of the *g* will
28:15 I will return you to this *g*
Ex 3:5 you are standing is holy *g*
8:21 gadfly, and also the *g* upon
10:6 existing upon the *g* until this
14:21 the sea basin into dry *g*
20:12 upon the *g* that Jehovah your
20:24 altar of *g* you are to make
23:19 first ripe fruits of your *g*
32:12 from the surface of the *g*
33:16 are upon the surface of the *g*
Le 20:24 possession of their *g*, and I
20:25 *g* that I have divided off for
25:34 pasture *g* of their cities
Nu 11:8 *g* it in hand mills or pounded
12:3 upon the surface of the *g*
16:30 *g* has to open its mouth and
16:31 *g* that was under them began
20:24 the *g* that you men rebelled
35:2 pasture *g* of the cities all
De 4:18 of anything moving on the *g*
5:16 on the *g* that Jehovah your
6:15 from off the surface of the *g*
7:6 on the surface of the *g*
8:15 thirsty *g* that has no water
11:17 *g* will not give its produce
12:24 pour it out upon the *g* as
14:2 on the surface of the *g*
21:1 found slain on the *g* that
26:10 *g* that Jehovah has given
28:4 the fruit of your *g* and the
28:11 and the fruitage of your *g*
28:11 on the *g* that Jehovah swore
28:18 and the fruitage of your *g*
28:21 the *g* to which you are going
28:33 The fruitage of your *g* and
28:42 the fruitage of your *g*
28:51 the fruitage of your *g*
30:18 on the *g* to which you are
30:20 may dwell upon the *g* that
31:20 to the *g* that I have sworn
32:43 for the *g* of his people
Jos 3:17 standing immovable on dry *g*
3:17 were passing over on dry *g*
4:18 drawn out onto the dry *g*
21:11 its pasture *g* all around it
21:13 Hebron, and its pasture *g*
21:13 Libnah and its pasture *g*
21:14 Jattir and its pasture *g*
21:14 Eshtemoa and its pasture *g*
21:15 and Holon and its pasture *g*
21:15 and Debir and its pasture *g*
21:16 and Ain and its pasture *g*
21:16 and Juttah and its pasture *g*
21:16 Beth-shemesh . . . pasture *g*
21:17 Gibeon and its pasture *g*
21:17 Geba and its pasture *g*
21:18 Anathoth and its pasture *g*
Jos 21:18 Almon and its pasture *g*
21:21 Shechem, and its pasture *g*
21:21 and Gezer and its pasture *g*
21:22 Kibzaim and its pasture *g*
21:22 Beth-horon and its pasture *g*
21:23 Elteke and its pasture *g*
21:23 Gibbethon and its pasture *g*
21:24 Aijalon and its pasture *g*
21:24 Gath-rimmon . . . pasture *g*
21:25 Taanach and its pasture *g*
21:25 Gath-rimmon . . . pasture *g*
21:27 Golan . . . and its pasture *g*
21:27 Beeshterah and its pasture *g*
21:28 Kishion and its pasture *g*
21:28 Daberath and its pasture *g*
21:29 Jarmuth and its pasture *g*
21:29 En-gannim and its pasture *g*
21:30 Mishal and its pasture *g*
21:30 Abdon and its pasture *g*
21:31 Helkath and its pasture *g*
21:31 Rehob and its pasture *g*
21:32 Kedesh . . . and its pasture *g*
21:32 Hammoth-dor . . . pasture *g*
21:32 Kartan and its pasture *g*
21:34 Jokneam and its pasture *g*
21:34 Kartah and its pasture *g*
21:35 Dimnah and its pasture *g*
21:35 Nahalal and its pasture *g*
21:36 Bezer and its pasture *g*
21:36 Jahaz and its pasture *g*
21:37 Kedemoth and its pasture *g*
21:37 Mephaath and its pasture *g*
21:38 Ramoth . . . and its pasture *g*
21:38 Mahanaim and its pasture *g*
21:39 Heshbon and its pasture *g*
21:39 Jazer and its pasture *g*
21:42 its pasture *g* all around it
23:13 this good *g* that Jehovah
23:15 from off this good *g* that
Jg 20:36 kept giving *g* to Benjamin
1Sa 20:15 from the surface of the *g*
20:31 is alive on the *g*, you and
2Sa 7:8 took you from the pasture *g*
9:10 cultivate the *g* for him, you
14:7 on the surface of the *g*
17:12 the dew falls upon the *g*
1Ki 8:34 bring them back to the *g*
8:40 the *g* that you gave to our
9:7 *g* that I have given to them
13:34 off the surface of the *g*
14:15 Israel off this good *g* that
17:14 upon the surface of the *g*
18:1 upon the surface of the *g*
2Ki 2:8 went across on the dry *g*
5:17 given to your servant some *g*
21:8 the *g* that I gave to their
23:6 and *g* it to dust and cast
23:15 he *g* it to dust and burned
1Ch 17:7 took you from the pasture *g*
2Ch 4:17 cast them in the thick *g*
6:25 *g* that you gave to them and
6:31 surface of the *g* that you
7:20 my *g* that I have given them
20:6 hold his *g* against you
31:19 fields of pasture *g* of their
33:8 *g* that I assigned to their
Ne 10:35 first ripe fruits of our *g*
Es 9:2 not a man stood his *g* before
Job 5:6 from mere *g* trouble does not
5:24 to go and see your pasture *g*
31:38 my own *g* would cry for aid
41:10 can hold his *g* before me
Ps 69:2 where there is no standing *g*
73:18 slippery *g* is where you
83:10 became manure for the *g*
89:43 not to gain *g* in the battle
104:30 make the face of the *g* new
105:35 the fruitage of their *g*
107:33 of water into thirsty *g*
137:4 sing . . . Upon foreign *g*
146:4 he goes back to his *g*
Pr 12:11 one cultivating his *g* will
13:23 Plowed *g* of persons of
28:19 is cultivating his own *g*
Isa 1:7 your *g*—right in front of you
6:11 *g* itself is ruined into a
7:16 *g* of whose two kings you
7:25 and a trampling *g* of sheep
15:9 the remaining ones of the *g*
19:17 *g* of Judah must become to
23:17 upon the surface of the *g*
24:21, 21 of the *g* upon the *g*
27:10 pasture *g* will be left to
28:24 loosens and harrows his *g*
Isa 30:23 with which you sow the *g*
30:23 produce of the *g* bread
30:24 asses cultivating the *g*
32:13 *g* of my people merely
35:7 heat-parched *g* will have
35:7 thirsty *g* as springs of
40:4 knobby *g* must become level
40:4 the rugged *g* a valley plain
45:9 fragments of the *g*
65:10 a pasture *g* for sheep and
Jer 7:20 upon the fruitage of the *g*
8:2 manure upon the face of the *g*
12:14 from off their *g*; and the
16:4 upon the surface of the *g*
23:3 back to their pasture *g*
23:8 dwell on their own *g*
24:10 the *g* that I gave to them
25:5 *g* that Jehovah gave to you
25:26 are on the surface of the *g*
25:33 on the surface of the *g*
27:10 far away from off your *g*
27:11 also let it rest upon its *g*
28:16 off the surface of the *g*
33:12 pasture *g* of the shepherds
35:7 surface of the *g* where you
35:15 *g* that I have given to you
50:19 Israel back to his pasture *g*
Eze 25:5 Rabbah a pasture *g* of camels
30:12 make the Nile canals dry *g*
34:19 pasture *g* trampled by your
36:5 the sake of its pasture *g*
38:20 that are creeping on the *g*
38:20 upon the surface of the *g*
43:11 the *g* plan of the House
43:11 all its *g* plans and all its
43:11 and all its *g* plans and
43:11 observe all its *g* plan and
45:2 as pasture *g* on each side
48:15 and for pasture *g*
48:17 come to have a pasture *g*
Da 11:39 *g* he will apportion out for
12:2 those asleep in the *g* of dust
Ho 2:18 creeping thing of the *g*, and
9:13 Tyre planted in a pasture *g*
Joe 1:10 the *g* has gone to mourning
2:21 Do not be fearful, O *g*
Am 3:2 of all the families of the *g*
3:5 Does a trap go up from the *g*
5:2 forsaken upon her own *g*
7:11 into exile from its own *g*
7:17 as regards your *g*, by the
7:17 on unclean *g* you will die
7:17 into exile from its own *g*
9:8 upon the surface of the *g*
9:15 plant them upon their *g*
9:15 be uprooted from their *g*
Jon 4:2 I happened to be on my own *g*
Hab 1:8 its steeds have pawed the *g*
Zep 1:2 off the surface of the *g*
1:3 from the surface of the *g*
Hag 1:11 what the *g* would bring forth
2:6 and the sea and the dry *g*
Zec 2:12 his portion upon the holy *g*
Mal 3:11 for you the fruit of the *g*
4:2 go forth and paw the *g* like
Mt 10:29 will fall to the *g* without
15:35 crowd to recline upon the *g*
19:3 his wife on every sort of *g*
19:9 on the *g* of fornication, and
25:18 and dug in the *g* and hid the
25:25 and hid your talent in the *g*
Mr 4:26 man casts the seed upon the *g*
4:28 Of its own self the *g* bears
4:31 time it was sown in the *g*
8:6 the crowd to recline on the *g*
9:18 it dashes him to the *g*, and
9:20 after falling on the *g* he
9:41 water to drink on the *g* that
14:35 to fall on the *g* and began
Lu 6:49 a house upon the *g* without a
9:42 demon dashed him to the *g*
13:7 should it keep the *g* useless
19:44 will dash you . . . to the *g*
22:44 of blood falling to the *g*
23:14 no *g* for the charges you are
24:5 their faces turned to the *g*
Joh 9:6 he spit on the *g* and made a
12:24 of wheat falls into the *g*
18:6 drew back and fell to the *g*
Ac 4:21 any *g* on which to punish
7:33 you are standing is holy *g*
9:4 he fell to the *g* and heard a
9:8 Saul got up from the *g*, and
22:7 I fell to the *g* and heard a

Ac 26:14 we had all fallen to the *g*
Ro 4:2 *g* for boasting; but not with
Eph 2:9 should have *g* for boasting
Php 2:10 earth and those under the *g*
Heb 6:7 *g* that drinks in the rain

Grounds
Nu 35:3 pasture *g* will serve for
35:4 the pasture *g* of the cities
35:5 as pasture *g* of the cities
35:7 together with their pasture *g*
Jos 14:4 pasture *g* for their livestock
21:2 pasture *g* for our domestic
21:3 cities and their pasture *g*
21:8 cities and their pasture *g*
21:19 cities and their pasture *g*
21:26 cities . . . their pasture *g*
21:33 cities and their pasture *g*
21:41 with their pasture *g*
1Ch 5:16 all the pasture *g* of Sharon
6:55 its pasture *g* all around it
6:57 Libnah with its pasture *g*
6:57 Eshtemoa with its pasture *g*
6:58 and Hilen with its pasture *g*
6:58 Debir with its pasture *g*
6:59 and Ashan with its pasture *g*
6:59 Beth-shemesh . . . pasture *g*
6:60 Geba with its pasture *g* and
6:60 Alemeth with its pasture *g*
6:60 Anathoth with its pasture *g*
6:64 cities with their pasture *g*
6:67 Shechem with its pasture *g*
6:67 and Gezer with its pasture *g*
6:68 Jokmeam with its pasture *g*
6:68 Beth-horon . . . its pasture *g*
6:69 Aijalon with its pasture *g*
6:69 Gath-rimmon . . . pasture *g*
6:70 Aner with its pasture *g* and
6:70 Bileam with its pasture *g*
6:71 Golan in Bashan . . . pasture *g*
6:71 Ashtaroth with its pasture *g*
6:72 Kedesh with its pasture *g*
6:72 Daberath with its pasture *g*
6:73 Ramoth with its pasture *g*
6:73 and Anem with its pasture *g*
6:74 Mashal with its pasture *g*
6:74 and Abdon with its pasture *g*
6:75 and Hukok with its pasture *g*
6:75 and Rehob with its pasture *g*
6:76 Kedesh . . . its pasture *g*
6:76 Hammon with its pasture *g*
6:76 Kiriathaim . . . its pasture *g*
6:77 Rimmono with its pasture *g*
6:77 Tabor with its pasture *g*
6:78 Bezer . . . with its pasture *g*
6:78 and Jahaz with its pasture *g*
6:79 Kedemoth with its pasture *g*
6:79 Mephaath with its pasture *g*
6:80 in Gilead with its pasture *g*
6:80 Mahanaim with its pasture *g*
6:81 Heshbon with its pasture *g*
6:81 and Jazer with its pasture *g*
13:2 their cities with pasture *g*
2Ch 11:14 Levites left their pasture *g*
Ps 65:12 pasture *g* of the wilderness
Pr 24:28 a witness . . . without *g*
Jer 9:10 pasture *g* of the wilderness
23:10 pasture *g* of the wilderness
Joe 1:19 devoured the pasture *g* of
1:20 devoured the pasture *g* of
2:22 pasture *g* of the wilderness
Am 1:2 the pasture *g* of the shepherds
Zep 2:6 sea must become pasture *g*
Mr 14:59 neither on these *g* was their
Php 3:4 do have *g* for confidence also
3:4 *g* for confidence in the flesh

Group
Ge 25:23 one national *g* . . . stronger
25:23 than the other national *g*
47:26 priests as a distinct *g* did
49:6 Into their intimate *g* do not
Ex 14:20 this *g* did not come near
14:20 did not come near that *g* all
Nu 4:3 service *g* to do the work in
4:23 enter into the service *g* to
4:30 enter into the service *g*
4:35 entered into the service *g*
4:39 entered into the service *g* for
4:43 entering into the service *g*
1Sa 10:5 meet a *g* of prophets coming
10:10 a *g* of prophets to meet him
1Ch 26:16 guard *g* corresponding with
26:16 corresponding with guard *g*
27:5 chief of the third service *g*
2Ch 23:6 because they are a holy *g*
Ezr 2:64 entire congregation as one *g*
3:9 one *g* to act as supervisors
6:20 cleansed themselves as one *g*
Ne 7:66 entire congregation as one *g*
12:24 guard *g* corresponding with
12:24 corresponding with guard *g*
12:25 a guard *g* by the stores of
Job 19:19 my intimate *g* detest me
Ps 89:7 the intimate *g* of holy ones
111:1 intimate *g* of upright ones
Isa 51:4 and you national *g* of mine
Jer 6:11 the intimate *g* of young men
15:17 *g* of those playing jokes
23:18 the intimate *g* of Jehovah
23:22 had stood in my intimate *g*
Eze 13:9 the intimate *g* of my people
29:14 bring back the captive *g*
Da 3:29 national *g* or language that
Mt 22:34 they came together in one *g*
Mr 3:14 And he formed a *g* of twelve
3:16 *g* of twelve that he formed

Groups
Ge 25:23 national *g* will be separated
27:29 national *g* bow low to you
1Ch 25:1 the chiefs of the service *g*
27:3 the chiefs of the service *g*
Ps 2:1 the national *g* themselves kept
7:7 national *g* surround you
9:8 judicially try national *g* in
44:2 You went breaking national *g*
44:14 among the national *g*
47:3 And national *g* under our feet
57:9 to you among the national *g*
65:7 turmoil of the national *g*
67:4 Let national *g* rejoice and
67:4 And as for national *g*, on the
105:44 hard work of national *g*
108:3 to you among the national *g*
148:11 and all you national *g*
149:7 Rebukes upon the national *g*
Pr 14:34 disgraceful to national *g*
24:24 national *g* will denounce him
30:27 all of them divided into *g*
Isa 17:12 noise of national *g*, who
17:13 national *g* themselves will
34:1 national *g*, pay attention
41:1 national *g* themselves regain
43:4 national *g* in place of your
43:9 let national *g* be gathered
49:1 you national *g* far away
55:4 a witness to the national *g*
55:4 commander to the national *g*
60:2 thick gloom the national *g*
Jer 51:58 national *g* simply for the
Da 3:4 national *g* and languages
3:7 national *g* and languages were
4:1 national *g* and languages that
5:19 national *g* and languages
6:25 national *g* and the tongues
7:14 national *g* and languages
Hab 2:13 that national *g* will tire
Mr 6:40 *g* of a hundred and of fifty
Lu 9:14 in *g* of about fifty each

Grove
Ex 23:11 vineyard and your olive *g*

Groves
Jos 24:13 olive *g* that you did not
Jg 15:5 the vineyards and the olive *g*
1Sa 8:14 your olive *g*, the best ones
2Ki 5:26 or olive *g* or vineyards or
1Ch 27:28 over the olive *g* and the
Ne 5:11 their olive *g* and their houses
9:25 olive *g* and trees for food

Grow
Ge 2:9 to *g* out of the ground every
3:18 thistles it will *g* for you
6:1 men started to *g* in numbers
18:30 please, not *g* hot with anger
18:32 not *g* hot with anger, but
27:40 when you *g* restless
44:18 do not let your anger *g* hot
Nu 6:5 locks of the hair of his head *g*
De 11:8 order that you may *g* strong
31:20 and be satisfied and *g* fat
32:15 Jeshurun began to *g* fat, then
Jg 3:12 the king of Moab *g* strong
7:11 hands will certainly *g* strong
16:7 must also *g* weak and become
16:11 *g* weak and become like an
16:17 *g* weak and become like all
16:22 hair . . . started to *g*
Ru 1:13 until they could *g* up
1Sa 3:2 his eyes had begun to *g* dim
2Sa 10:5 your beards *g* abundantly
23:5 why he will make it *g*
1Ch 19:5 your beards *g* abundantly
2Ch 28:19 let unrestraint *g* in Judah
Ezr 9:12 *g* strong and certainly eat
Ne 9:25 to *g* fat and to luxuriate in
Job 3:9 stars of its twilight *g* dark
8:7 afterward would *g* very great
8:11 papyrus plant *g* tall without
8:11 a reed *g* big without water
12:23 Making the nations *g* great
15:29 He will not *g* rich and his
15:32 certainly not *g* luxuriantly
18:6 certainly *g* dark in his tent
33:21 And his bones . . . *g* bare
Ps 77:2 hand . . . does not *g* numb
92:12 Lebanon does, he will *g* big
132:17 the horn of David to *g*
Ec 12:2 the moon and the stars *g* dark
Isa 13:10 sun will actually *g* dark
28:22 your bands may not *g* strong
29:22 his own face now *g* pale
40:28 not tire out or *g* weary
40:30 tire out and *g* weary
40:31 will run and not *g* weary
42:4 not *g* dim nor be crushed
57:16 spirit itself would *g*
Eze 16:7 so that you would *g* big and
30:18 day will actually *g* dark
31:4 watery deep caused it to *g*
Da 4:1 May your peace *g* great
6:25 May your peace *g* very much
Ho 14:7 They will *g* grain, and will
Joe 2:22 wilderness will . . . *g* green
Zec 11:17 will without fail *g* dim
Mt 13:30 *g* together until the harvest
Lu 12:27 Mark well how the lilies *g*
Joh 21:18 when you *g* old you will
Ro 4:19 he did not *g* weak in faith
1Co 3:6 but God kept making it *g*
3:7 but God who makes it *g*
16:13 carry on as men, *g* mighty
Eph 4:15 *g* up in all things into him
Heb 1:11 they will all *g* old
1Pe 2:2 you may *g* to salvation

Growing
Ge 21:8 child kept *g* and came to be
21:20 he kept *g* and dwelling in
24:36 to my master after her *g* old
26:13 *g* great until he got very
41:6 grain . . . *g* up after them
41:23 *g* up after them
Ex 1:7 multiplying and *g* mightier at
1:20 people kept *g* more numerous
Nu 11:10 Jehovah's anger began *g* very
1Sa 2:21 Samuel continued *g* up with
2:26 Samuel was *g* bigger and
3:19 Samuel continued *g* up, and
2Sa 12:3 *g* up with him and with his
15:12 people were continually *g*
1Ki 11:4 Solomon's *g* old that his
15:23 time of his *g* old he got
2Ki 4:18 And the child kept on *g* up
2Ch 17:12 *g* great to a superior degree
Es 9:4 Mordecai was steadily *g*
Eze 17:6 luxuriantly *g* vine low in
Jon 1:11 *g* more tempestuous
1:13 *g* more tempestuous against
Mt 6:28 lilies . . . how they are *g*
28:1 *g* light on the first day of
Lu 1:80 the young child went on *g*
2:40 continued *g* and getting strong
Ac 6:7 word of God went on *g*, and
12:24 word of Jehovah went on *g*
19:20 word of Jehovah kept *g* and
Eph 2:21 *g* into a holy temple for
Col 2:19 *g* with the growth that God
2Th 1:3 your faith is *g* exceedingly
Heb 8:13 *g* old is near to vanishing
2Pe 3:18 go on *g* in the undeserved

Growl
Isa 5:29 *g* and grab hold of the prey
5:30 *g* over it in that day as
Jer 51:38 *g* like the whelps of lions

Growling
Job 37:2 the *g* that goes forth from
Pr 19:12 raging of a king is a *g* like
20:2 frightfulness of a king is a *g*
28:15 As a *g* lion and an onrushing
Isa 5:30 as with the *g* of the sea
30:6 the lion and the leopard *g*

Growls
Isa 31:4 Just as the lion *g*, even

Grown
Ge 19:13 against them has *g* loud
26:16 you have *g* far stronger than
38:14 she saw that Shelah had *g* up
Le 13:6 if the plague has *g* dull and
13:37 and black hair has *g* in it
De 32:15 *g* fat, you have become thick
34:7 His eye had not *g* dim, and
Jos 2:24 *g* disheartened because of us
13:1 You yourself have *g* old and
17:13 sons of Israel had *g* strong
23:2 As for me, I have *g* old, I
Ru 1:12 I have *g* too old to get to
1Sa 8:1 as soon as Samuel had *g* old
8:5 Look! You yourself have *g* old
10:27 like one *g* speechless
12:2 I have *g* old and gray, and
1Ki 12:8 young men that had *g* up with
12:10 that had *g* up with him
1Ch 23:1 David himself had *g* old and
2Ch 10:8 young men that had *g* up with
10:10 men that had *g* up with him
Ezr 9:6 guiltiness has *g* great even to
Ne 13:19 *g* shadowy before the sabbath
Job 21:7 Have *g* old, also have become
42:7 My anger has *g* hot against
Ps 6:6 *g* weary with my sighing
6:7 It has *g* old because of all
37:25 I have also *g* old, And yet
38:8 *g* numb and become crushed to
63:1 my flesh has *g* faint with
102:7 I have *g* emaciated, And
109:24 my very flesh has *g* lean
144:12 plants *g* up in their youth
Pr 23:22 just because she has *g* old
Isa 5:25 anger of Jehovah has *g* hot
5:30 light has *g* dark because
43:22 *g* weary of me, O Israel
47:13 *g* weary with the multitude
57:10 is why you have not *g* sick
Jer 5:28 They have *g* fat
8:21 shattered. I have *g* sad
45:3 *g* weary because of my
La 5:5 We have *g* weary. No rest has
5:10 skin has *g* hot just like a
5:17 our eyes have *g* dim
Da 4:22 *g* great and become strong
4:22 your grandeur has *g* great and
Ho 8:5 anger has *g* hot against them
11:8 my compassions have *g* hot
Joe 3:13 for harvest has *g* ripe
Zec 10:3 my anger has *g* hot, and
Mt 13:15 heart . . . has *g* unreceptive
13:32 has *g* it is the largest of
Mr 6:35 now the hour had *g* late
Joh 6:17 had *g* dark and Jesus had not
Ac 28:27 the heart . . . has *g* unreceptive
Heb 11:24 Moses, when *g* up, refused
Re 2:3 and have not *g* weary

Grows
Ge 38:11 until Shelah my son *g* up
Le 13:40 head *g* bald, it is baldness
13:41 his head *g* bald up in front
25:25 *g* poor and has to sell some
25:35 brother *g* poor and so he is
25:39 in case your brother *g* poor
Job 6:17 When it *g* hot they are dried
14:8 its root *g* old in the earth
17:7 vexation my eye *g* dimmer
19:11 anger also *g* hot against me
Ps 61:2 when my heart *g* feeble
102:*super* in case he *g* feeble and
Pr 22:6 *g* old he will not turn aside
26:20 slanderer contention *g* still
Hab 1:4 law *g* numb, and justice never
Mt 24:32 as its young branch *g* tender
Mr 4:27 the seed sprouts and *g* tall
13:28 branch *g* tender and puts

Growth
Le 25:5 *g* from spilled kernels of
25:11 nor reap the land's *g* from
Nu 22:4 the green *g* of the field
2Ki 19:29 the *g* from spilled kernels
Job 38:27 the *g* of grass to sprout
Isa 10:33 those tall in *g* are being
37:30 *g* from spilled kernels
Jon 4:10 a mere *g* of a night and
4:10 as a mere *g* of a night
Lu 2:52 in wisdom and in physical *g*
Eph 4:16 makes for the *g* of the body
Col 2:19 with the *g* that God gives

Grudge
Le 19:18 have a *g* against the sons of
Mr 6:19 But Herodias was nursing a *g*

Grudgingly
2Co 9:7 not *g* or under compulsion

Grumbling
De 1:27 you kept *g* in your tents and
Ps 106:25 they kept *g* in their tents
Isa 29:24 those who are *g* will learn
1Pe 4:9 hospitable . . . without *g*

Guarantee
Ac 17:31 furnished a *g* to all men in
Heb 6:16 as it is a legal *g* to them

Guarantees
2Co 1:21 who *g* that you and we belong

Guard
Ge 3:24 *g* the way to the tree of life
24:6 Be on your *g* that you do not
Ex 19:12 *G* yourselves against going up
21:29 he would not keep it under *g*
21:36 would not keep it under *g*
23:13 And you are to be on your *g*
Nu 10:25 forming the rear *g* for all
De 24:8 Be on your *g* in the plague of
Jos 6:9 rear *g* was following the Ark
6:13 rear *g* was following the ark
10:18 assign men over it to *g*
23:11 you must be on constant *g*
Jg 8:11 the camp happened to be off *g*
1Sa 7:1 to *g* the ark of Jehovah
19:2 And now be on your *g*, please
2Sa 11:16 Joab was keeping *g* over the
20:10 not on *g* against the sword
1Ki 14:28 *g* chamber of the runners
20:39 *G* this man. If he should in
2Ki 6:9 *G* yourself against passing by
9:14 keeping *g* at Ramoth-gilead
1Ch 9:23 of the tent, for *g* service
9:27 for *g* service was upon them
26:16 *g* group corresponding with
26:16 corresponding with *g* group
2Ch 12:11 to the *g* chamber of
Ezr 8:29 Keep awake and be on *g* until
Ne 3:25 to the Courtyard of the *G*
4:9 kept a *g* posted against them
4:22 a *g* by night and workers by
4:23 men of the *g* who were behind
11:19 keeping *g* in the gates
12:9 opposite them for *g* duties
12:24 *g* group corresponding with
12:24 corresponding with *g* group
12:25 keeping *g* as gatekeepers
12:25 a *g* group by the stores of
12:39 a stand at the Gate of the *G*
13:22 keeping *g* of the gates to
Job 7:12 that you should set a *g* over
36:21 *g* that you do not turn to
Ps 12:7 O Jehovah, will *g* them
25:20 Do *g* my soul and deliver me
39:1 I will *g* my ways To keep
39:1 as a *g* to my own mouth
41:2 Jehovah himself will *g* him
86:2 do *g* my soul, for I am loyal
91:11 To *g* you in all your ways
119:9 keeping on *g* according to
121:7 Jehovah himself will *g* you
121:7 He will *g* your soul
121:8 Jehovah himself will *g* your
127:1 that the *g* has kept awake
141:3 set a *g*, O Jehovah, for my
Pr 2:8 *g* the very way of his loyal
2:11 will keep *g* over you
5:2 so as to *g* thinking abilities
6:22 it will stand *g* over you
6:24 *g* you against the bad woman
7:5 *g* you against the woman
14:3 of the wise ones will *g* them
Ec 5:1 *G* your feet whenever you go to
Isa 52:12 will be your rear *g*
58:8 Jehovah would be your rear *g*
Jer 9:4 *G* yourselves each one against
32:2 Courtyard of the *G* that is
32:8 into the Courtyard of the *G*
32:12 in the Courtyard of the *G*
33:1 up in the Courtyard of the *G*
37:21 in the Courtyard of the *G*
37:21 in the Courtyard of the *G*
38:6 in the Courtyard of the *G*
38:13 in the Courtyard of the *G*
38:28 Courtyard of the *G* until the
Jer 39:14 of the Courtyard of the *G*
39:15 up in the Courtyard of the *G*
Eze 38:7 and you must become their *g*
40:7 *g* chamber was one reed in
40:7 between the *g* chambers there
40:10 the *g* chambers of the gate
40:12 in front of the *g* chambers
40:12 *g* chamber was six cubits
40:13 one *g* chamber to the roof
40:16 for the *g* chambers and for
40:21 its *g* chambers were three
40:29 its *g* chambers and its side
40:33 its *g* chambers and its side
40:36 its *g* chambers, its side
Mic 7:5 *g* the openings of your mouth
Hab 2:1 At my *g* post I will keep
Mal 2:15 people must *g* yourselves
2:16 *g* . . . respecting your spirit
Mt 10:17 Be on your *g* against men
27:65 You have a *g*. Go make it as
27:66 grave secure by . . . the *g*
28:11 some of the *g* went into the
Lu 8:29 chains and fetters under *g*
12:15 *g* against . . . covetousness
Ac 12:4 to *g* him, as he intended to
12:10 through the first sentinel *g*
23:35 under *g* in the praetorian
Php 1:13 among all the Praetorian *G*
4:7 will *g* your hearts and your
1Ti 6:20 *g* what is laid up in trust
2Ti 1:12 able to *g* what I have laid
1:14 *g* through the holy spirit
4:15 you too be on *g* against him
2Pe 3:17 be on your *g* that you may
1Jo 5:21 *g* yourselves from idols
Jude 24 able to *g* you from stumbling

Guarded
1Sa 25:21 *g* everything that belongs
Job 10:12 own care has *g* my spirit
Ps 37:28 they will certainly be *g*
Pr 4:23 than all else that is to be *g*
Ho 12:12 and for a wife he *g* sheep
12:13 and by a prophet he was *g*
Ga 3:23 we were being *g* under law

Guardian
Ge 4:9 not know. Am I my brother's *g*?
1Sa 28:2 *g* of my head I shall appoint
Es 2:3 eunuch, the *g* of the women
2:8 of Hegai the *g* of the women
2:14 the *g* of the concubines
2:15 eunuch, the *g* of the women
Da 1:11 Daniel said to the *g* whom
1:16 *g* kept on taking away their

Guardianship
Ne 13:14 house of my God and the *g* of

Guarding
Ge 30:31 I shall continue *g* it
Jos 24:17 who kept *g* us in all the
1Ch 23:32 *g* of the tent of meeting
23:32 and the *g* of the holy place
23:32 the *g* of the sons of Aaron
Job 29:2 the days when God was *g* me
Ps 34:20 *g* all the bones of that one
97:10 *g* the souls of his loyal ones
116:6 *g* the inexperienced ones
121:3 One *g* you cannot possibly
121:4 He that is *g* Israel
121:5 Jehovah is *g* you
145:20 Jehovah is *g* all those
146:9 Jehovah is *g* the alien
Pr 13:3 one *g* his mouth is keeping
19:8 is *g* discernment is going to
22:5 he that is *g* his soul keeps
27:18 *g* his master will be honored
Ac 22:20 and *g* the outer garments of
28:16 with the soldier *g* him
2Co 11:32 *g* the city of the Damascenes

Guardpost
Ne 7:3 each one at his own *g* and each
Isa 21:8 *g* I am stationed all the

Guards
1Sa 2:9 feet of his loyal ones he *g*
1Ki 14:27 the *g* of the entrance of
2Ch 12:10 *g* of the entrance of the
Ne 7:3 station *g* of the inhabitants
Ps 127:1 Jehovah himself *g* the city
Jer 4:17 Like *g* of the open field
5:24 *g* even the prescribed weeks
Lu 11:21 well armed, *g* his palace
23:11 together with his soldier *g*
Ac 5:23 *g* standing at the doors, but

c 12:6 and *g* before the door were
12:19 he examined the *g* and

uardsman
Ir 6:27 dispatched a body *g*

uardsmen
a 3:17 Your *g* are like the locust

udgodah
e 10:7 they pulled away for *G*, and
10:7 from *G* for Jotbathah, a land

uest
s 15:1 who will be a *g* in your tent?
61:4 a *g* in your tent for times
Ir 14:14 Where is the *g* room for me
u 10:38 Martha received him as *g*
19:6 he received him as *g*
22:11 *g* room in which I may eat

uests
It 22:11 came in to inspect the *g* he
u 14:10 front of all your fellow *g*
14:15 one of the fellow *g* said to

uidance
x 38:21 the Levites under the *g* of

uide
s 48:14 will *g* us until we die
u 6:39 A blind man cannot *g* a blind
oh 16:13 *g* you into all the truth
c 1:16 *g* to those who arrested
o 2:19 you are a *g* of the blind, a
e 7:17 will *g* them to fountains of

uided
c 8:31 do so, unless someone *g* me

uides
It 15:14 Blind *g* is what they are
15:14 a blind man *g* a blind man
23:16 Woe to you, blind *g*, who
23:24 Blind *g*, who strain out the

uiding
e 29:5 kept *g* you forty years in the

uild
e 3:31 member of the goldsmith *g*

uileless
o 16:18 seduce the hearts of *g* ones
eb 7:26 loyal, *g*, undefiled

uilt
e 26:10 would have brought *g* upon us
e 5:6 bring his *g* offering to Jehovah
5:7 as his *g* offering for the sin
5:15 bring as his *g* offering to
5:15 holy place, as a *g* offering
5:16 the ram of the *g* offering
5:18 for a *g* offering, to the
5:19 It is a *g* offering
6:5 on the day his *g* is proved
6:6 And as his *g* offering he
6:6 value, for a *g* offering
6:17 and like the *g* offering
7:1 is the law of the *g* offering
7:2 will slaughter the *g* offering
7:5 It is a *g* offering
7:7 so is the *g* offering
7:37 the *g* offering and the
14:12 and offer it for a *g* offering
14:13 the *g* offering belongs to the
14:14 the blood of the *g* offering
14:17 the blood of the *g* offering
14:21 young ram as a *g* offering
14:24 young ram of the *g* offering
14:25 young ram of the *g* offering
14:25 the blood of the *g* offering
14:28 the blood of the *g* offering
19:21 *g* offering to Jehovah to the
19:21 a ram of *g* offering
19:22 ram of the *g* offering before
u 5:7 return the amount of his *g* in
5:8 return the amount of the *g*
5:8 amount of the *g* that is being
6:12 its first year as a *g* offering
18:9 and every *g* offering of theirs
32:22 free from *g* against Jehovah
e 19:13 the *g* of innocent blood out
21:8 put the *g* of innocent blood
21:9 the *g* of innocent blood from
os 2:17 are free from *g* respecting
2:19 we shall be free from *g*
2:20 free from *g* respecting this
g 15:3 I must be free of *g* against
Sa 6:3 return to him a *g* offering
1Sa 6:4 What is the *g* offering that
6:8 return to him as a *g* offering
6:17 as a *g* offering to Jehovah
28:10 *g* for error will not befall
2Ki 7:9 *g* must also catch up with us
12:16 money for *g* offerings and
1Ch 21:3 a cause of *g* to Israel
2Ch 19:10 do that you may not incur *g*
24:18 because of this *g* of theirs
28:10 cases of *g* against Jehovah
28:13 result in *g* against Jehovah
28:13 to our sins and to our *g*
28:13 abundant is the *g* we have
Pr 14:9 who make a derision of *g*
Isa 53:10 set his soul as a *g* offering
Jer 51:5 been full of *g* from the
Eze 40:39 offering and the *g* offering
42:13 and the *g* offering, because
44:29 *g* offering—they are the
46:20 boil the *g* offering and
Ho 5:15 until they bear their *g*
Joe 1:18 the ones made to bear *g*

Guiltiness
Le 4:3 sins so as to bring *g* upon the
6:7 he might do resulting in *g* by
22:16 to bear the punishment of *g*
2Ch 33:23 one that made *g* increase
Ezr 9:6 our *g* has grown great even to
9:7 been in great *g* until this day
9:13 bad deeds and our great *g*
9:15 we are before you in our *g*
10:10 to add to the *g* of Israel
10:19 ram . . . for their *g*
Ps 68:21 walking about in his *g*
69:5 my own *g* has not been hidden
Am 8:14 swearing by the *g* of Samaria

Guiltless
Mt 12:5 as not sacred and continue *g*
12:7 not have condemned the *g* ones
Ac 13:39 not be declared *g* by means
13:39 *g* by means of this One

Guilty
Ge 42:21 *g* with regard to our brother
Le 4:13 be done and so have become *g*
4:22 done, and so has become *g*
4:27 done and he does become *g*
5:2 is unclean and has become *g*
5:3 then he has become *g*
5:4 he has become *g* as respects
5:5 he becomes *g* as respects one
5:17 become *g* and must answer for
5:19 become *g* against Jehovah
6:4 he sins and indeed becomes *g*
Nu 5:6 that soul has also become *g*
Jg 21:22 when you would become *g*
2Sa 14:13 like one that is *g*, in
Ezr 10:19 being *g*, there should be a
Ps 5:10 will certainly hold them *g*
34:21 hating the righteous . . . *g*
34:22 none . . . will be held *g*
Pr 30:10 may not have to be held *g*
Isa 24:6 inhabiting it are held *g*
Jer 2:3 would make themselves *g*
50:7 We shall not become *g*, due
Eze 22:4 have shed you have become *g*
Da 1:10 make my head *g* to the king
Ho 4:15 let not Judah become *g*
10:2 now they will be found *g*
13:1 *g* in regard to Baal and die
13:16 Samaria will be held *g*
Hab 1:11 and will actually become *g*
Zec 11:5 they are not held *g*
Mr 3:29 but is *g* of everlasting sin
1Co 11:27 will be *g* respecting the

Gull
Le 11:16 the owl and the *g* and the
De 14:15 owl and the *g* and the falcon

Gulloth
Jos 15:19, 19 Upper *G* and Lower *G*
Jg 1:15, 15 Upper *G* and Lower *G*

Gulloth-maim
Jos 15:19 and you must give me *G*
Jg 1:15 and you must give me *G*

Gully
2Sa 2:29 through the entire *g* and
Lu 3:5 Every *g* must be filled up, and

Gulp
Ob 16 drink and *g* down and become as
Mt 23:24 but *g* down the camel

Gum
Ge 2:12 also are the bdellium *g* and
Nu 11:7 like the look of bdellium *g*

Gums
Ps 22:15 tongue . . . to stick to my *g*

Guni
Ge 46:24 sons of Naphtali were . . . *G*
Nu 26:48 *G* the family of the Gunites
1Ch 5:15 son of Abdiel, the son of *G*
7:13 sons of Naphtali were . . . *G*

Gunites
Nu 26:48 of Guni the family of the *G*

Gur
2Ki 9:27 chariot on the way up to *G*

Gurbaal
2Ch 26:7 dwelling in *G* and the Meunim

Gushing
Eze 32:2 you kept *g* in your rivers

Gutters
Ge 30:38 in the *g*, in the water
30:41 locate the staffs in the *g*
Ex 2:16 drew water and filled the *g*

Ha
Isa 17:12 *H* for the commotion of
18:1 *H* for the land of the

Haahashtari
1Ch 4:6 Hepher and Temeni and *H*

Habaiah
Ezr 2:61 the sons of *H*
Ne 7:63 the priests: the sons of *H*

Habakkuk
Hab 1:1 that *H* the prophet visioned
3:1 *H* the prophet in dirges

Habazziniah
Jer 35:3 Jeremiah the son of *H* and

Habit
Ex 21:29 formerly in the *h* of goring
21:36 in the *h* of goring formerly
De 28:56 being of dainty *h* and for

Habitation
Ps 107:4 any way to a city of *h*
107:7 to come to a city of *h*
107:36 establish a city of *h*
Isa 38:12 own *h* has been pulled out
Ac 7:46 a *h* for the God of Jacob

Habits
1Co 15:33 associations spoil useful *h*
1Ti 3:2 moderate in *h*, sound in mind
3:11 moderate in *h*, faithful in
Tit 2:2 aged men be moderate in *h*
2Pe 2:18 by loose *h* they entice those

Habor
2Ki 17:6 in *H* at the river Gozan and
18:11 Halah and in *H* at the river
1Ch 5:26 brought them to Halah and *H*

Hacaliah
Ne 1:1 Nehemiah the son of *H*
10:1 the Tirshatha, the son of *H*

Hachilah
1Sa 23:19 on the hill of *H*, which is
26:1 hill of *H*, facing Jeshimon
26:3 camping on the hill of *H*

Hachmoni
1Ch 27:32 and Jehiel the son of *H*

Hachmonite
1Ch 11:11 Jashobeam the son of a *H*

Hacking
1Sa 15:33 Samuel went *h* Agag to

Hadad
Ge 25:15 *H* and Tema, Jetur, Naphish
36:35 *H* son of Bedad, who defeated
36:36 When *H* died, Samlah from
1Ki 11:14 *H* the Edomite of the
11:17 *H* went running away, he and
11:17 while *H* was a young boy
11:19 *H* continued to find favor
11:21 *H* himself heard in Egypt
11:21 So *H* said to Pharaoh
11:25 the injury that *H* did
1Ch 1:30 Dumah, Massa, *H* and Tema
1:46 and *H* the son of Bedad
1:47 *H* died, and Samlah from
1:50 *H* began to reign in place of

1Ch 1:51 Eventually *H* died

Hadadezer
2Sa 8:3 *H* the son of Rehob the king
8:5 to help *H* the king of Zobah
8:7 on the servants of *H* and
8:8 cities of *H*, King David took
8:9 all the military force of *H*
8:10 fought against *H* so that he
8:10 *H* had become trained in
8:12 *H* the son of Rehob the king
10:16 *H* sent and brought out the
10:16 chief of the army of *H*
10:19 servants of *H*, saw that
1Ki 11:23 *H* the king of Zobah his lord
1Ch 18:3 *H* the king of Zobah at
18:5 to help *H* the king of Zobah
18:7 to be on the servants of *H*
18:8 Tibhath and Cun, cities of *H*
18:9 all the military force of *H*
18:10 he had fought against *H* so
18:10 *H* had become trained in
19:16 the chief of the army of *H*
19:19 servants of *H* saw that they

Hadadrimmon
Zec 12:11 like the wailing of *H* in

Hadar
Ge 36:39 *H* began to reign instead of

Hadashah
Jos 15:37 Zenan and *H* and Migdal-gad

Hadassah
Es 2:7 caretaker of *H*, that is, Esther

Hades
Mt 11:23 Down to *H* you will come
16:18 *H* will not overpower it
Lu 10:15 Down to *H* you will come
16:23 in *H* he lifted up his eyes
Ac 2:27 will not leave my soul in *H*
2:31 neither was he forsaken in *H*
Re 1:18 the keys of death and of *H*
6:8 *H* was closely following him
20:13 and *H* gave up those dead in
20:14 *H* were hurled into the lake

Hadid
Ezr 2:33 the sons of Lod, *H* and Ono
Ne 7:37 the sons of Lod, *H* and Ono
11:34 *H*, Zeboim, Neballat

Hadlai
2Ch 28:12 Amasa the son of *H*, rose

Hadoram
Ge 10:27 *H* and Uzal and Diklah
1Ch 1:21 *H* and Uzal and Diklah
18:10 sent *H* his son to King David
2Ch 10:18 *H*, who was over those

Hadrach
Zec 9:1 against the land of *H*, and

Ha-eleph
Jos 18:28 and Zelah, *H* and Jebusi

Hagab
Ezr 2:46 the sons of *H*

Hagabah
Ezr 2:45 the sons of *H*
Ne 7:48 the sons of *H*, the sons of

Hagar
Ge 16:1 and her name was *H*
16:3 Sarai, Abram's wife, took *H*
16:4 he had relations with *H*
16:8 *H*, maidservant of Sarai, just
16:15 *H* bore to Abram a son and
16:15 his son whom *H* bore Ishmael
21:9 son of *H* the Egyptian, whom
21:14 gave it to *H*, setting it upon
21:17 God's angel called to *H* out
21:17 matter with you, *H*? Do not
25:12 *H* the maidservant of Sarah
Ga 4:24 for slavery, and which is *H*
4:25 *H* means Sinai, a mountain

Hagar's
Ge 16:16 *H* bearing Ishmael to Abram

Haggai
Ezr 5:1 *H* the prophet and Zechariah
6:14 prophesying of *H* the prophet
Hag 1:1 by means of *H* the prophet to
1:3 by means of *H* the prophet
1:12 the words of *H* the prophet
1:13 *H* the messenger of Jehovah
2:1 by means of *H* the prophet
Hag 2:10 to *H* the prophet, saying
2:13 *H* went on to say: If someone
2:14 *H* answered and said: That is
2:20 to occur a second time to *H*

Haggi
Ge 46:16 the sons of Gad were . . . *H*
Nu 26:15 of *H* the family of the

Haggiah
1Ch 6:30 *H* his son, Asaiah his son

Haggites
Nu 26:15 of Haggi the family of the *H*

Haggith
2Sa 3:4 was Adonijah the son of *H*
1Ki 1:5 Adonijah the son of *H* was
1:11 the son of *H* has become king
2:13 Adonijah the son of *H* came
1Ch 3:2 Adonijah the son of *H*

Hagri
1Ch 11:38 Mibhar the son of *H*

Hagrite
1Ch 27:31 there was Jaziz the *H*

Hagrites
1Ch 5:10 made war upon the *H*
5:19 make war upon the *H*, and
5:20 the *H* and all those who were
Ps 83:6 Ishmaelites, Moab and the *H*

Hail
Ex 9:18 rain down . . . a very heavy *h*
9:19 *h* will have to come down
9:22 *h* may come on all the land of
9:23 Jehovah gave thunders and *h*
9:23 *h* upon the land of Egypt
9:24 came *h*, and fire quivering in
9:24 fire quivering in among the *h*
9:25 *h* went striking at all the
9:25 *h* struck everything that was
9:26 in the land of Goshen . . . no *h*
9:28 of God's thunders and *h*
9:29 the *h* will not continue any
9:33 *h* began to stop and rain did
9:34 *h* and the thunders had stopped
10:5 left to you people by the *h*
10:12 everything that the *h* has let
10:15 eating up all . . . *h* had left
Job 38:22 the storehouses of the *h*
Ps 18:12 *H* and burning coals of fire
18:13 *H* and burning coals of fire
78:47 their vine even by the *h*
78:48 of burden even to the *h*
105:32 He made their downpours *h*
148:8 *h*, snow and thick smoke
Isa 28:2 Like a thunderous storm of *h*
28:17 *h* must sweep away the
32:19 *h* when the forest goes
Hag 2:17 with mildew and with *h*
Re 8:7 occurred a *h* and fire mingled
11:19 earthquake and a great *h*
16:21 great *h* with every stone
16:21 due to the plague of *h*

Hailing
Nu 23:21 loud *h* of a king is in his

Hailstones
Jos 10:11 more who died from the *h*
Ps 78:47 their sycamore trees by *h*
Isa 30:30 and rainstorm and *h*
Eze 13:11 you, O *h*, will fall, and a
13:13 in rage there will be *h* for
38:22 flooding downpour and *h*

Hair
Ge 25:25 an official garment of *h*
Ex 25:4 and fine linen, and goat's *h*
26:7 make cloths of goat's *h* for
35:6 fine linen and goat's *h*
35:23 goat's *h* and ram skins dyed
35:26 spun the goat's *h*
36:14 make tent cloths of goat's *h*
Le 13:3 the *h* in the plague has turned
13:4 its *h* has not turned white
13:10 has turned the *h* white and
13:20 and its *h* has turned white
13:21 there is no white *h* in it
13:25 if the *h* has been changed
13:26 is no white *h* in the blotch
13:30 the *h* is yellow and scarce
13:30 an abnormal falling off of *h*
13:31 abnormal falling off of *h*
13:31 and there is no black *h* in it
13:31 abnormal falling off of *h*
Le 13:32 falling off of *h* has not
13:32 no yellow *h* has developed in
13:32 of *h* is not deeper than the
13:33 falling off of *h* shaved; and
13:33 falling off of *h* seven days
13:34 abnormal falling off of *h* on
13:34 abnormal falling off of *h*
13:35 abnormal falling off of *h*
13:36 abnormal falling off of *h*
13:36 examination for yellow *h*
13:37 falling off of *h* has stood
13:37 and black *h* has grown in it
13:37 falling off of *h* . . . healed
14:8 shave off all his *h* and bathe
14:9 should shave off all his *h*
14:9 shave off all his *h*, and he
14:54 abnormal falling off of *h*
19:32 Before gray *h* you should rise
Nu 5:18 loosen the *h* of the woman's
6:5 locks of the *h* of his head
6:18 take the *h* of the head of his
31:20 everything made of goat's *h*
Jg 5:2 For letting the *h* hang loose in
16:22 the *h* of his head started to
1Sa 14:45 not as much as a single *h*
19:13 net of goats' *h* she put at
19:16 net of goats' *h* at the
2Sa 14:11 not a single *h* of your son
14:26 weighed the *h* of his head
1Ki 1:52 not fall a single *h* of his
2Ki 1:8 A man possessing a *h* garment
Ezr 9:3 pull out some of the *h* of my
Ne 13:25 and pull out their *h* and
Job 1:20 cut the *h* off his head and
4:15 The *h* of my flesh began to
Ca 1:10 are comely among the *h* braids
4:1 Your *h* is like a drove of goats
5:2 *h* with the drops of the night
5:11 The locks of his *h* are date
5:11 His black *h* is like the raven
6:5 Your *h* is like a drove of goats
Isa 3:24 an artistic *h* arrangement
7:20 and the *h* of the feet, and
50:6 to those plucking off the *h*
Jer 7:29 Shear off your uncut *h* and
9:26 *h* clipped at the temples
25:23 *h* clipped at the temples
49:32 *h* clipped at the temples
Eze 5:1 and divide the *h* in portions
8:3 took me by a tuft of *h* of my
16:7 your own *h* grew luxuriantly
44:20 *h* of the head they should
44:20 clip the *h* of their heads
Da 3:27 not a *h* . . . had been singed
4:33 *h* grew long just like eagles'
7:9 *h* of his head was like clean
Mic 1:16 shear your *h* off on account
Zec 13:4 an official garment of *h*
Mt 3:4 camel's *h* and a leather girdle
5:36 cannot turn one *h* white or
Mr 1:6 was clothed with camel's *h*
Lu 7:38 with the *h* of her head
7:44 wiped them off with her *h*
21:18 not a *h* of your heads will
Joh 11:2 his feet dry with her *h*
12:3 his feet dry with her *h*
Ac 18:18 had the *h* of his head clipped
27:34 not a *h* of the head of one
1Co 11:14 man has long *h*, it is a
11:15 if a woman has long *h*, it
11:15 Because her *h* is given her
1Ti 2:9 not with styles of *h* braiding
1Pe 3:3 external braiding of the *h* and
Re 1:14 his head and his *h* were white
6:12 black as sackcloth of *h*
9:8, 8 they had *h* as women's *h*

Hairbreadth
Jg 20:16 a slinger of stones to a *h*

Hairless
Ge 27:16 upon the *h* part of his neck

Hairs
Ge 42:38 gray *h* with grief to Sheol
44:29 *h* with calamity to Sheol
44:31 bring down the gray *h* of
1Ki 2:6 gray *h* go down in peace to
2:9 gray *h* down to Sheol with
Ps 40:12 more numerous than the *h* of
69:4 more than the *h* of my head
Ho 7:9 gray *h* . . . have become white
Mt 10:30 *h* of your head . . . numbered
Lu 12:7 *h* of your heads . . . numbered

Hairy
Ge 27:11 Esau my brother is a *h* man
27:23 *h* like the hands of Esau
Ps 68:21 The *h* crown of the head of
Da 8:21 *h* he-goat stands for the king

Hakkatan
Ezr 8:12 Johanan the son of *H*, and

Hakkoz
1Ch 24:10 for *H* the seventh, for
Ezr 2:61 the sons of *H*
Ne 3:4 Urijah the son of *H* did
3:21 Urijah the son of *H* repaired
7:63 the sons of *H*, the sons of

Hakupha
Ezr 2:51 the sons of *H*
Ne 7:53 the sons of *H*, the sons of

Halah
2Ki 17:6 dwelling in *H* and in Habor
18:11 in *H* and in Habor at the
1Ch 5:26 brought them to *H* and Habor

Halak
Jos 11:17 from Mount *H*, which goes
12:7 and as far as Mount *H*

Hale
Lu 12:58 never *h* you before the judge

Haled
Mt 10:18 *h* before governors and kings
Lu 21:12 *h* before kings and governors
22:66 *h* him into their Sanhedrin

Half
Ge 24:22 ring of a *h* shekel in weight
Ex 24:6 Moses took *h* the blood and
24:6 *h* the blood he sprinkled upon
25:10 two and a *h* cubits its
25:10 a cubit and a *h* its width
25:10 a cubit and a *h* its height
25:17 two and a *h* cubits its
25:17 a cubit and a *h* its width
25:23 a cubit and a *h* its height
26:12 *H* of the tent cloth that
26:16 a cubit and a *h* is the width
30:13 a *h* shekel by the shekel of
30:13 *h* shekel is the contribution
30:15 give less than the *h* shekel
30:23 sweet cinnamon in *h* that
36:21 one cubit and a *h* the width
37:1 Two cubits and a *h* was its
37:1 and a cubit and a *h* its width
37:1 and a cubit and a *h* its height
37:6 Two cubits and a *h* was its
37:6 and a cubit and a *h* its width
37:10 a cubit and a *h* its height
38:26 *h* shekel for an individual
38:26 *h* of a shekel by the shekel
Le 6:20 *h* of it in the morning and
6:20 and *h* of it in the evening
Nu 12:12 whose flesh . . . is *h* eaten
15:9 moistened with *h* a hin of oil
15:10 *h* a hin, as an offering made
28:14 *h* a hin of wine for a bull
31:29 From their *h* you should take
31:30 the *h* of the sons of Israel
31:36 the *h* that was the share of
31:42 the *h* belonging to the sons
31:43 the *h* of the assembly from
31:47 *h* belonging to the sons of
32:33 to *h* the tribe of Manasseh
34:13 to the nine and a *h* tribes
34:14 the *h* tribe of Manasseh have
34:15 The two and a *h* tribes have
De 3:12 *h* of the mountainous region
3:13 the *h* tribe of Manasseh
29:8 *h* the tribe of the Manassites
Jos 1:12 and the *h* tribe of Manasseh
4:12 and the *h* tribe of Manasseh
8:33 one *h* of them in front of
8:33 other *h* of them in front of
12:2 *h* of Gilead as far as Jabbok
12:5 Maacathites, and *h* of Gilead
12:6 *h* of the tribe of Manasseh
13:7 and the *h* tribe of Manasseh
13:8 other *h* tribe the Reubenites
13:25 and *h* of the land of the
13:29 to the *h* tribe of Manasseh
13:29 the *h* tribe of the sons of
13:31 *h* of Gilead, and Ashtaroth
13:31 to *h* of the sons of Machir
14:2 nine tribes and the *h* tribe
14:3 and the other *h* tribe on the
18:7 and the *h* tribe of Manasseh
Jos 21:5 of the *h* tribe of Manasseh
21:6 the *h* tribe of Manasseh in
21:25 the *h* tribe of Manasseh
21:27 out of the *h* tribe of
22:1 and the *h* tribe of Manasseh
22:7 to the *h* tribe of Manasseh
22:7 to the other *h* of it Joshua
22:9 *h* tribe of Manasseh returned
22:10 *h* tribe of Manasseh built
22:11 *h* tribe of Manasseh have
22:13 the *h* tribe of Manasseh in
22:15 the *h* tribe of Manasseh in
22:21 the *h* tribe of Manasseh
1Sa 14:14 *h* the plowing line in an
2Sa 10:4 shaved off *h* their beards and
10:4 cut their garments in *h* to
18:3 and if *h* of us would die
19:40 also *h* the people of Israel
1Ki 3:25 *h* to the one woman and the
3:25 and the other *h* to the other
7:31 a stand of one and a *h* cubits
7:32 was one and a *h* cubits
7:35 a stand a *h* a cubit in height
10:7 I had not been told the *h*
13:8 If you gave me *h* of your
16:9 the chief of *h* the chariots
1Ch 2:52 Haroeh, *h* of the Menuhoth
2:54 and *h* of the Manahathites
5:18 and the *h* tribe of Manasseh
5:23 of the *h* tribe of Manasseh
5:26 the *h* tribe of Manasseh and
6:61 from the *h* tribe
6:61 the *h* of Manasseh, by the
6:70 *h* of the tribe of Manasseh
6:71 *h* tribe of Manasseh Golan in
12:31 of the *h* tribe of Manasseh
12:37 and the *h* tribe of Manasseh
19:4 cut their garments in *h* to
26:32 *h* tribe of the Manassites
27:20 of the *h* tribe of Manasseh
27:21 the *h* tribe of Manasseh in
2Ch 9:6 *h* of the abundance of your
Ne 3:9 *h* the district of Jerusalem
3:12 *h* the district of Jerusalem
3:16 prince of *h* the district of
3:17 *h* the district of Keilah
3:18 *h* the district of Keilah
4:6 clear to *h* its height, and the
4:16 *h* of my young men were
4:16 *h* of them were holding the
4:21 *h* of them also were holding
12:32 *h* of the princes of Judah
12:38 also *h* of the people, upon
12:40 *h* of the deputy rulers with
13:24 *h* were speaking Ashdodite
Es 5:3 To the *h* of the kingship—let
5:6 To the *h* of the kingship—let
7:2 To the *h* of the kingship—let
Ps 55:23 not live out *h* their days
102:24 at the *h* of my days
Isa 44:16 *H* of it he actually burns
44:16 Upon *h* of it he roasts well
44:19 *h* of it I have burned up in
Jer 17:11 At the *h* of his days he
Eze 16:51 even up to *h* of your sins
40:42 was one cubit and a *h*
40:42 width one cubit and a *h*
43:17 surrounding it is *h* a cubit
Da 7:25 time, and times and *h* a time
9:27 *h* of the week he will cause
12:7 appointed times and a *h*
Zec 14:2 *h* of the city must go forth
14:4 *h* of the mountain will
14:4 and *h* of it to the south
14:8 *h* of them to the eastern sea
14:8 *h* of them to the western sea
Mr 6:23 to you, up to *h* my kingdom
Lu 19:8 *h* of my belongings, Lord, I
Joh 7:14 now the festival was *h* over
Re 8:1 silence . . . for about a *h* hour
11:9 for three and a *h* days, and
11:11 after the three and a *h* days
12:14 time and times and *h* a time

Half-dead
Lu 10:30 and went off, leaving him *h*

Halfhearted
Ps 119:113 The *h* ones I have hated

Half-homer
Ho 3:2 and a *h* of barley

Halhul
Jos 15:58 *H*, Beth-zur and Gedor

Hali
Jos 19:25 *H* and Beten and Achshaph

Hall
1Sa 9:22 brought them to the dining *h*
Ezr 10:6 to the dining *h* of Jehohanan
Ne 3:30 work in front of his own *h*
13:4 a dining *h* of the house of our
13:5 make for him a large dining *h*
13:7 a *h* in the courtyard of the
13:8 outside the dining *h*
Da 5:10 right into the banqueting *h*
Lu 22:66 him into their Sanhedrin *h*
Ac 4:15 go outside the Sanhedrin *h*
5:27 stood them in the Sanhedrin *h*

Hallohesh
Ne 3:12 Shallum the son of *H*
10:24 *H*, Pilha, Shobek

Halls
Ezr 8:29 the dining *h* of the house of
Ne 10:37 dining *h* of the house of our
10:38 dining *h* of the supply house
10:39 the dining *h* that the sons of
12:44 over the *h* for the stores
13:9 they cleansed the dining *h*

Halt
2Sa 2:28 people came to a *h* and did
Isa 10:32 day in Nob to make a *h*
Jon 1:15 sea began to *h* . . . its raging
Ac 8:38 commanded the chariot to *h*

Halted
Nu 25:8 scourge was *h* from upon the
2Sa 24:21 that the scourge may be *h*
24:25 the scourge was *h* from upon
1Ch 21:22 that the scourge may be *h*
Ps 106:30 Then the scourge was *h*

Halter
Ps 32:9 curbed even by bridle or *h*

Ham
Ge 5:32 Noah became father to . . . *H*
6:10 father to three sons, Shem, *H*
7:13 Noah went in, and Shem and *H*
9:18 Noah's sons . . . Shem and *H*
9:18 *H* was the father of Canaan
9:22 Later *H* the father of Canaan
10:1 Noah's sons, Shem, *H* and
10:6 And the sons of *H* were Cush
10:20 sons of *H* according to their
14:5 defeats on . . . the Zuzim in *H*
1Ch 1:4 Noah, Shem, *H* and Japheth
1:8 sons of *H* were Cush and
4:40 in former times were of *H*
Ps 78:51 power in the tents of *H*
105:23 an alien in the land of *H*
105:27 miracles in the land of *H*
106:22 works in the land of *H*

Haman
Es 3:1 *H* the son of Hammedatha the
3:2 prostrating themselves to *H*
3:4 they told *H* to see whether
3:5 *H* kept seeing that Mordecai
3:5 and *H* became filled with rage
3:6 *H* began seeking to annihilate
3:7 before *H* from day to day and
3:8 And *H* proceeded to say to King
3:10 and gave it to *H* the son of
3:11 the king went on to say to *H*
3:12 that *H* commanded the king's
3:15 king and *H*, they sat down to
4:7 money that *H* had said to pay
5:4 let the king with *H* come today
5:5 have *H* act quickly on the word
5:5 king and *H* came to the banquet
5:8 king and *H* come to the banquet
5:9 *H* went out on that day joyful
5:9 but as soon as *H* saw Mordecai
5:9 *H* was immediately filled with
5:10 *H* kept control of himself and
5:11 *H* proceeded to declare to
5:12 *H* went on to say: What is
5:14 thing seemed good before *H*
6:4 *H* himself had come into the
6:5 is *H* standing in the courtyard
6:6 When *H* came in, the king
6:6 *H* said in his heart: To whom
6:7 *H* said to the king: As for the
6:10 At once the king said to *H*
6:11 And *H* proceeded to take the
6:12 *H*, he hurried to his house
6:13 *H* went on to relate to Zeresh
6:14 to bring *H* to the banquet that

Es 7:1 king and *H* came in to banquet
7:6 and enemy, is this bad *H*
7:6 *H*, he became terrified because
7:7 and *H* himself stood up to make
7:8 *H* was fallen upon the couch on
7:9 there is the stake that *H* made
7:10 to hang *H* on the stake that he
8:1 *H*, the one showing hostility
8:2 that he had taken away from *H*
8:2 Mordecai over the house of *H*
8:3 the badness of *H* the Agagite
8:5 *H* the son of Hammedatha the
8:7 The house of *H* I have given to
9:10 the ten sons of *H* the son of
9:12 and the ten sons of *H*
9:13 the ten sons of *H* be hanged
9:14 the ten sons of *H* were hanged
9:24 For *H* the son of Hammedatha

Haman's
Es 7:8 and *H* face they covered
7:9 stake . . . standing in *H* house

Hamath
Nu 13:21 Rehob to the entering in of *H*
34:8 to the entering in of *H*, and
Jos 13:5 to the entering in of *H*
Jg 3:3 far as to the entering in of *H*
2Sa 8:9 Toi the king of *H* got to hear
1Ki 8:65 *H* down to the torrent valley
2Ki 14:25 the entering in of *H* clear
14:28 restored Damascus and *H* to
17:24 Avva and *H* and Sepharvaim
17:30 men of *H*, for their part
18:34 the gods of *H* and Arpad
19:13 the king of *H* and the king
23:33 Riblah in the land of *H*
25:21 Riblah in the land of *H*
1Ch 13:5 as far as the entering of *H*
18:3 the king of Zobah at *H* as he
18:9 Tou the king of *H* heard that
2Ch 7:8 entering in of *H* down to the
8:4 cities that he had built in *H*
Isa 10:9 Is not *H* just like Arpad?
11:11 remnant . . . from *H* and
36:19 are the gods of *H* and Arpad
37:13 Where is the king of *H*
Jer 39:5 Riblah in the land of *H* that
49:23 *H* and Arpad have become
52:9 at Riblah in the land of *H*
52:27 Riblah in the land of *H*
Eze 47:16 *H*, Berothah, Sibraim
47:16 and the boundary of *H*
47:17 and the boundary of *H*
47:20 to the entering in to *H*
48:1 to the entering in to *H*
48:1 on the side of *H*
Am 6:2 go from there to populous *H*
6:14 *H* down to the torrent valley
Zec 9:2 *H* itself will also border

Hamathite
Ge 10:18 and the Zemarite and the *H*
1Ch 1:16 and the Zemarite and the *H*

Hamath-zobah
2Ch 8:3 Solomon went to *H* and

Hamites
1Ch 4:41 tents of the *H* and the

Hammath
Jos 19:35 Zer and *H*, Rakkath and
1Ch 2:55 *H* the father of the house of

Hammedatha
Es 3:1 Haman the son of *H* the Agagite
3:10 the son of *H* the Agagite
8:5 Haman the son of *H* the Agagite
9:10 sons of Haman the son of *H*
9:24 the son of *H*, the Agagite

Hammer
Jg 4:21 to put the *h* into her hand
Isa 41:7 with the forge *h* him that
Jer 23:29 a forge *h* that smashes the
50:23 forge *h* of all the earth

Hammered
Ex 25:18 Of *h* work you are to make
25:31 Of *h* work the lampstand is
25:36 it is one piece of *h* work
37:7 Of *h* work he made them on
37:17 Of *h* work he made the
37:22 piece of *h* work of pure gold
Nu 8:4 It was *h* work of gold
8:4 to its blossoms it was *h* work
10:2 make them of *h* work, and they
Jg 5:26 she *h* Sisera, she pierced his

Hammering
Isa 41:7 is *h* away at the anvil

Hammers
1Ki 6:7 as for *h* and axes or any tools
Isa 44:12 with the *h* he proceeds to
Jer 10:4 with *h* they fasten them

Hammolecheth
1Ch 7:18 sister was *H*. She gave birth

Hammon
Jos 19:28 to Ebron and Rehob and *H*
1Ch 6:76 *H* with its pasture grounds

Hammoth-dor
Jos 21:32 *H* and its pasture ground

Hammuel
1Ch 4:26 sons of Mishma were *H* his

Hamonah
Eze 39:16 of the city will also be *H*

Hamor
Ge 33:19 at the hand of the sons of *H*
34:2 And Shechem the son of *H* the
34:4 Shechem said to *H* his father
34:6 *H*, Shechem's father, went out
34:8 *H* proceeded to speak with
34:13 to answer Shechem and *H* his
34:18 seemed good in the eyes of *H*
34:20 *H* and Shechem his son went
34:24 listened to *H* and to
34:26 *H* and Shechem his son they
Jos 24:32 *H*, Shechem's father, for a
Jg 9:28 men of *H*, Shechem's father
Ac 7:16 from the sons of *H* in Shechem

Hamor's
Ge 34:18 the eyes of Shechem, *H* son

Hampers
La 3:8 help, he actually *h* my prayer

Hamstring
Jos 11:6 Their horses you will *h*
2Sa 8:4 *h* all the chariot horses, but

Hamstrung
Ge 49:6 arbitrariness they *h* bulls
Jos 11:9 their horses he *h*, and
1Ch 18:4 *h* all the chariot horses

Hamul
Ge 46:12 sons of Perez . . . *H*
Nu 26:21 of *H* the family of the
1Ch 2:5 sons of Perez were . . . *H*

Hamulites
Nu 26:21 of Hamul the family of the *H*

Hamutal
2Ki 23:31 *H* the daughter of Jeremiah
24:18 *H* the daughter of Jeremiah
Jer 52:1 *H* the daughter of Jeremiah

Hanamel
Jer 32:7 *H* the son of Shallum your
32:8 *H* the son of my paternal
32:9 buy from *H* the son of my
32:12 eyes of *H* the son of my

Hanan
1Ch 8:23 and Abdon and Zichri and *H*
8:38 and *H* . . . the sons of Azel
9:44 and *H* . . . the sons of Azel
11:43 *H* the son of Maacah, and
Ezr 2:46 the sons of *H*
Ne 7:49 the sons of *H*, the sons of
8:7 *H*, Pelaiah, even the Levites
10:10 Kelita, Pelaiah, *H*
10:22 Pelatiah, *H*, Anaiah
10:26 and Ahijah, *H*, Anan
13:13 *H* the son of Zaccur the son
Jer 35:4 dining room of the sons of *H*

Hananel
Ne 3:1 as far as the Tower of *H*
12:39 and the Tower of *H* and the
Jer 31:38 tower of *H* to the Corner
Zec 14:10 from the Tower of *H* all

Hanani
1Ki 16:1 to Jehu the son of *H*
16:7 Jehu the son of *H* the prophet
1Ch 25:4 the sons of Heman . . . *H*
25:25 for the eighteenth, for *H*
2Ch 16:7 *H* the seer came to Asa the
19:2 son of *H* the visionary now
20:34 words of Jehu the son of *H*
Ezr 10:20 sons of Immer there were *H*
Ne 1:2 *H*, one of my brothers, came in
Ne 7:2 *H* my brother and Hananiah the
12:36 Nethanel and Judah, *H*, with

Hananiah
1Ch 3:19 sons of Zerubbabel . . . *H*
3:21 sons of *H* were Pelatiah
8:24 *H* and Elam and Anthothijah
25:4 the sons of Heman . . . *H*
25:23 for the sixteenth, for *H*
2Ch 26:11 *H* of the king's princes
Ezr 10:28 the sons of Bebai . . . *H*
Ne 3:8 *H* a member of the ointment
3:30 *H* the son of Shelemiah and
7:2 *H* the prince of the Castle
10:23 Hoshea, *H*, Hasshub
12:12 Meraiah; for Jeremiah, *H*
12:41 *H* with the trumpets
Jer 28:1 *H* the son of Azzur, the
28:5 to say to *H* the prophet
28:10 *H* the prophet took the yoke
28:11 *H* went on to say before the
28:12 after *H* the prophet had
28:13 Go, and you must say to *H*
28:15 to say to *H* the prophet
28:15 Listen, please, O *H*!
28:17 So *H* the prophet died in
36:12 Zedekiah the son of *H* and
37:13 Shelemiah the son of *H*, was
Da 1:6 sons of Judah, Daniel, *H*
1:7 and to *H*, Shadrach; and to
1:11 *H*, Mishael and Azariah
1:19 *H*, Mishael and Azariah
2:17 to *H*, Mishael and Azariah his

Hand
Ge 3:22 not put his *h* out and
4:11 brother's blood at your *h*
8:9 he put his *h* out and took it
9:2 Into your *h* they are now given
9:5 From the *h* of every living
9:5 and from the *h* of man
9:5 from the *h* of each one who is
14:20 your oppressors into your *h*
14:22 I do lift up my *h* in an oath
16:9 humble yourself under her *h*
16:12 His *h* will be against
16:12 *h* of everyone will be
19:16 men seized hold of his *h*
19:16 the *h* of his wife and of the
21:18 take hold of him with your *h*
21:30 accept the . . . lambs at my *h*
22:9 bound Isaac his son *h* and foot
22:10 Abraham put out his *h* and
22:12 not put out your *h* against
24:2 Put your *h*, please, under my
24:9 put his *h* under the thigh of
24:10 of his master's in his *h*
24:18 jar upon her *h* and gave him
24:49 may turn to the right *h* or
25:26 *h* was holding onto the heel
27:17 into the *h* of Jacob her son
31:8 If on the one *h* he would say
31:8 on the other *h* he would say
31:29 power of my *h* to do harm to
31:39 a claim for it from my *h*
32:11 from my brother's *h*, from
32:11 Deliver me . . . from Esau's *h*
32:13 And from what came to his *h*
33:10 must take my gift at my *h*
33:19 the *h* of the sons of Hamor
37:21 deliver him out of their *h*
37:22 do not lay a violent *h* upon
37:22 deliver him out of their *h*
37:27 not let our *h* be upon him
38:18 your rod that is in your *h*
38:20 kid of the goats by the *h* of
38:20 security from the *h* of the
38:28 one extended his *h*, and the
38:28 a scarlet piece about his *h*
38:29 soon as he drew back his *h*
38:30 whose *h* the scarlet piece
39:1 from the *h* of the Ishmaelites
39:3 turn out successful in his *h*
39:4 was his he gave into his *h*
39:6 everything . . . in Joseph's *h*
39:8 he has given into my *h*
39:12 left his garment in her *h*
39:13 left his garment in her *h*
39:22 gave over into Joseph's *h*
39:23 nothing that was in his *h*
40:11 Pharaoh's cup was in my *h*
40:11 gave the cup into Pharaoh's *h*
40:13 Pharaoh's cup into his *h*
40:21 the cup into Pharaoh's *h*
41:35 grain under Pharaoh's *h* as

Ge 41:42 signet ring from his own *h*
41:42 put it upon Joseph's *h* and
41:44 no man may lift up his *h*
43:9 Out of my *h* you may exact the
43:12 double the money in your *h*
43:12 you will take back in your *h*
43:15 double the money in their *h*
43:26 the gift that was in their *h*
44:16 in whose *h* the cup was found
44:17 The man in whose *h* the cup
46:4 lay his *h* upon your eyes
47:16 *H* over your livestock and I
47:29 place your *h*, please, under
48:13 Ephraim by his right *h* to
48:13 Manasseh by his left *h* to
48:14 Israel put out his right *h*
48:14 left *h* upon Manasseh's head
48:17 *h* placed on Ephraim's head
48:17 take hold of his father's *h*
48:18 Put your right *h* on his head
48:22 from the *h* of the Amorites
49:8 Your *h* will be on the back of
Ex 2:19 out of the *h* of the shepherds
3:8 deliver them out of the *h* of
3:19 to go except by a strong *h*
3:20 stretch out my *h* and strike
4:2 What is that in your *h?*
4:4 Thrust your *h* out and grab hold
4:4 he thrust his *h* out and grabbed
4:6 Stick your *h*, please, into the
4:6 stuck his *h* into the upper fold
4:6 *h* was stricken with leprosy
4:7 Return your *h* into the upper
4:7 returned his *h* into the upper
4:13 send, please, by the *h* of the
4:17 rod you will take in your *h*
4:20 rod of the true God in his *h*
4:21 I have put in your *h* before
5:21 put a sword in their *h* to
6:1 on account of a strong *h* he
6:1 on account of a strong *h* he
6:8 raised my *h* in oath to give to
7:4 to lay my *h* upon Egypt and
7:5 stretch out my *h* against Egypt
7:15 the rod . . . take in your *h*
7:17 rod that is in my *h* upon the
7:19 stretch your *h* out over the
8:5 Stretch your *h* with your rod
8:6 Aaron stretched his *h* out over
8:17 Aaron stretched out his *h*
9:3 Jehovah's *h* is coming upon
9:15 I could have thrust my *h* out
9:22 Stretch out your *h* toward the
10:12 Stretch your *h* out over the
10:21 Stretch your *h* out toward
10:22 stretched his *h* out toward
11:5 who is at the *h* mill and
12:11 and your staff in your *h*; and
13:3 by strength of *h* Jehovah
13:9 as a sign upon your *h* and as
13:9 by a strong *h* Jehovah brought
13:14 By strength of *h* Jehovah
13:16 serve as a sign upon your *h*
13:16 by strength of *h* Jehovah
14:8 going out with uplifted *h*
14:16 stretch your *h* out over the
14:20 On the one *h* it proved to be
14:20 On the other *h* it kept
14:21 Moses now stretched his *h*
14:22 their right *h* and on their
14:26 Stretch your *h* out over the
14:27 stretched his *h* out over the
14:29 wall on their right *h* and on
14:30 from the *h* of the Egyptians
14:31 *h* that Jehovah put in action
15:6 Your right *h*, O Jehovah, is
15:6 Your right *h*, O Jehovah, can
15:9 My *h* will drive them away
15:12 stretched out your right *h*
15:20 take a tambourine in her *h*
16:3 died by Jehovah's *h* in the
17:5 Take it in your *h* and you
17:9 rod of the true God in my *h*
17:11 as Moses would lift his *h* up
17:11 as he would let down his *h*
17:16 a *h* is against the throne of
18:9 them from the *h* of Egypt
18:10 from the *h* of Egypt and from
18:10 from the *h* of Pharaoh, and
18:10 from under the *h* of Egypt
19:13 No *h* is to touch him
21:13 God lets it occur at his *h*
21:16 in whose *h* he has been found
21:20 actually dies under his *h*

Ex 21:24, 24 *h* for *h*, foot for foot
22:4 found in his *h* what was
22:8 not put his *h* upon the goods
22:11 not put his *h* on the goods of
23:31 into your *h* the inhabitants
24:11 did not put out his *h* against
28:16 a span of the *h* being its
28:16 a span of the *h* its width
28:41 and fill their *h* with power
29:9 you must fill the *h* of Aaron
29:9 the *h* of his sons with power
29:20 the thumb of their right *h*
29:29 fill their *h* with power in
29:33 fill their *h* with power, in
29:35 fill their *h* with power
32:11 power and with a strong *h*
32:15 two tablets . . . in his *h*
32:29 Fill your *h* today with power
34:4 two tablets of stone in his *h*
34:29 the Testimony were in the *h*
39:9 a span of the *h* in its length
Le 1:4 lay his *h* upon the head of the
3:2 must lay his *h* upon the head
3:8 lay his *h* upon the head of his
3:13 must lay his *h* upon its head
4:4 lay his *h* upon the bull's head
4:24 lay his *h* upon the head of
4:29 lay his *h* upon the head of
4:33 lay his *h* upon the head of
6:2 a deposit in *h* or a robbery
8:23 the thumb of his right *h* and
8:24 the thumb of their right *h*
8:33 to fill your *h* with power
9:17 filled his *h* with some of it
14:14 the thumb of his right *h*
14:17 the thumb of his right *h* and
14:25 the thumb of his right *h*
14:28 the thumb of his right *h*
16:21 *h* of a ready man into the
16:32 whose *h* will be filled with
21:10 *h* was filled with power to
21:19 or a fracture of the *h*
22:25 from the *h* of a foreigner
25:14 from your associate's *h*, do
25:26 *h* does make gain and he does
25:28 *h* does not find enough to
25:28 *h* of its purchaser until the
25:47 *h* of the alien resident or
25:49 *h* has become wealthy, he
26:25 given into the *h* of an enemy
Nu 4:28 under the *h* of Ithamar the
4:33 under the *h* of Ithamar the
5:18 *h* of the priest there should
5:25 from the woman's *h* and wave
7:8 under the *h* of Ithamar the son
11:8 ground it in *h* mills or
11:23 *h* of Jehovah is cut short, is
14:21 on the other *h*, as I live
14:30 lifted up my *h* in oath to
20:11 Moses lifted his *h* up and
20:20 many people and a strong *h*
21:2 give this people into my *h*
21:26 all his land out of his *h*
21:34 into your *h* I shall certainly
22:23 his drawn sword in his *h*
22:29 there were a sword in my *h*
22:31 his drawn sword in his *h*
23:25 If, on the one *h*, you cannot
23:25 on the other *h*, you should
25:7 and took a lance in his *h*
27:18 you must lay your *h* upon him
31:6 trumpets . . . were in his *h*
33:1 by the *h* of Moses and Aaron
33:3 went out with uplifted *h*
35:21 he has struck him with his *h*
35:25 the *h* of the avenger of blood
De 1:25 the fruitage . . . in their *h*
1:27 into the *h* of the Amorites
2:7 in every deed of your *h*
2:15 the *h* of Jehovah also proved
2:24 I have given into your *h* Sihon
2:30 give him into your *h* just as
3:2 people and his land into your *h*
3:3 God gave into our *h* also Og
3:8 the land from the *h* of the two
4:34 with war and with a strong *h*
5:15 a strong *h* and an outstretched
6:8 tie them as a sign upon your *h*
6:21 out of Egypt with a strong *h*
7:5 On the other *h*, this is what
7:8 out with a strong *h*, that he
7:8 from the *h* of Pharaoh the king
7:19 the miracles and the strong *h*
7:24 give their kings into your *h*

De 8:17 the full might of my own *h*
9:26 out of Egypt with a strong *h*
10:3 the two tablets were in my *h*
11:2 his greatness, his strong *h*
11:18 as a sign upon your *h*, and
12:6 the contribution of your *h*
12:11 the contribution of your *h*
12:17 the contribution of your *h*
13:9 Your *h* first of all should
13:9 the *h* of all the people
13:17 should stick to your *h*
14:25 wrap the money up in your *h*
14:29 in every deed of your *h* that
15:3 let your *h* release
15:8 generously open your *h* to him
15:11 generously open up your *h* to
16:10 voluntary offering of your *h*
16:15 in every deed of your *h*
16:17 gift of each one's *h* should
17:7 The *h* of the witnesses first
17:7 *h* of all the people afterward
17:9 they must *h* down to you the
17:10 they will *h* down to you
17:11 word that they will *h* down
19:5 *h* has been raised to strike
19:12 into the *h* of the avenger
19:21, 21 *h* for *h*, foot for foot
20:13 certainly give it into your *h*
21:10 given them into your *h* and
23:15 You must not *h* over a slave
23:25 must pluck . . . with your *h*
24:1 put it in her *h* and dismiss
24:3 put it in her *h* and dismissed
24:6 No one should seize a *h* mill
24:19 in every deed of your *h*
25:11 the *h* of the one striking
25:11 she has thrust out her *h*
25:12 you must then amputate her *h*
26:4 take the basket out of your *h*
26:8 out of Egypt with a strong *h*
28:12 bless every deed of your *h*
30:9 in every work of your *h*
32:27 Our *h* has proved superior
32:39 no one snatching out of my *h*
32:40 I raise my *h* to heaven in
32:41 my *h* takes hold on judgment
33:2 At his right *h* warriors
33:3 their holy ones are in your *h*
34:9 Moses had laid his *h* upon him
34:12 the strong *h* and all the
Jos 2:19 if a *h* should come upon him
2:24 all the land into our *h*
4:24 may know Jehovah's *h*, that
5:13 his drawn sword in his *h*
6:2 mighty men, into your *h*
7:7 into the *h* of the Amorites
8:1 I have given into your *h* the
8:18 that is in your *h* toward Ai
8:18 into your *h* I shall give it
8:18 was in his *h* toward the city
8:19 he stretched out his *h*
8:26 did not draw back his *h* with
9:25 now here we are, in your *h*
9:26 deliver them from the *h* of
10:6 Do not let your *h* relax from
10:8 into your *h* I have given
10:30 and its king into Israel's *h*
10:32 gave Lachish into Israel's *h*
11:8 gave them into Israel's *h*
20:5 the manslayer into his *h*
20:9 by the *h* of the avenger of
21:44 Jehovah gave into their *h*
22:31 delivered . . . out of the *h*
24:8 I gave them into your *h*
24:10 delivered you out of his *h*
24:11 I gave them into your *h*
Jg 1:2 give the land into his *h*
1:35 the *h* of the house of Joseph
2:14 to sell them into the *h* of
2:15 the *h* of Jehovah proved to be
2:16 save them out of the *h* of
2:18 out of the *h* of their
2:23 give them into Joshua's *h*
3:8 he sold them into the *h* of
3:10 the king of Syria into his *h*
3:10 so that his *h* overpowered
3:15 tribute by his *h* to Eglon the
3:21 Ehud thrust in his left *h* and
3:28 the Moabites, into your *h*
3:30 subdued . . . under Israel's *h*
4:2 sold them into the *h* of Jabin
4:7 indeed give him into your *h*
4:9 into the *h* of a woman that
4:14 give Sisera into your *h*

Jg 4:21 to put the hammer into her *h*
4:24 the *h* of the sons of Israel
5:26 Her *h* to the tent pin she then
5:26 her right *h* to the mallet of
6:1 gave them into the *h* of Midian
6:2 *h* of Midian came to prevail
6:9 out of the *h* of Egypt and out
6:9 the *h* of all your oppressors
6:21 staff that was in his *h* and
7:2 to give Midian into their *h*
7:2 My *h* it was that saved me
7:6 lapping with their *h* to their
7:7 I will give Midian into your *h*
7:8 people in their *h*, and their
7:9 for I have given it into your *h*
7:14 and all the camp into his *h*
7:15 camp of Midian into your *h*
7:20 torches with their left *h* and
7:20 right *h* on the horns to blow
8:3 was into your *h* that God gave
8:6 in your *h* so that bread has to
8:7 Zebah and Zalmunna into my *h*
8:15 in your *h* so that bread has to
8:22 out of the *h* of Midian
8:34 out of the *h* of all their
9:17 deliver you out of Midian's *h*
9:29 people were in my *h*! Then
9:33 as your *h* finds it possible
9:48 an ax in his *h* and cut down a
10:7 into the *h* of the Philistines
10:7 the *h* of the sons of Ammon
10:12 to save you out of their *h*
11:21 his people into Israel's *h*
11:30 the sons of Ammon into my *h*
11:32 to give them into his *h*
12:2 not save me out of their *h*
12:3 Jehovah gave them into my *h*
13:1 into the *h* of the Philistines
13:5 Israel out of the *h* of the
13:23 grain offering from our *h*
14:6 was nothing at all in his *h*
15:12 into the *h* of the Philistines
15:13 will give you into their *h*
15:15 thrust his *h* out and took it
15:17 the jawbone out of his *h* and
15:18 salvation into the *h* of your
15:18 the *h* of the uncircumcised
16:18 the money in their *h*
16:23 has given into our *h* Samson
16:24 given into our *h* our enemy
16:26 was holding him by his *h*
16:29 the other with his left *h*
17:3 silver to Jehovah from my *h*
17:5 fill the *h* of one of his sons
17:12 filled the *h* of the Levite
18:10 given it into your *h*, a place
18:19 Put your *h* over your mouth
20:28 I shall give him into your *h*
Ru 1:13 the *h* of Jehovah has gone out
4:5 buy the field from Naomi's *h*
4:9 buy . . . from the *h* of Naomi
1Sa 2:13 three-pronged fork in his *h*
4:8 the *h* of this majestic God
5:6 *h* of Jehovah came to be heavy
5:7 his *h* has been hard against us
5:9 *h* of Jehovah came to be upon
5:11 *h* of the true God had been
6:3 his *h* would not turn away
6:5 lighten his *h* from off you
6:9 was not his *h* that touched us
7:3 from the *h* of the Philistines
7:8 from the *h* of the Philistines
7:13 *h* of Jehovah continued to be
7:14 the *h* of the Philistines
9:8 silver found in my *h*, and
9:16 the *h* of the Philistines
10:4 accept them from their *h*
10:7 what your *h* finds possible
10:18 from the *h* of Egypt and
10:18 the *h* of all the kingdoms
11:7 by the *h* of the messengers
12:3 from whose *h* have I accepted
12:4 from the *h* of a single one
12:5 found nothing at all in my *h*
12:9 into the *h* of Sisera the
12:9 into the *h* of the Philistines
12:9 the *h* of the king of Moab
12:10 out of the *h* of our enemies
12:11 deliver you out of the *h* of
12:15 *h* of Jehovah will certainly
13:22 in the *h* of any of the
14:10 give them into our *h*, and
14:12 them into the *h* of Israel
14:19 Withdraw your *h*

1Sa 14:26 putting his *h* to his mouth
14:27 the rod that was in his *h*
14:27 and drew his *h* back to his
14:34 his bull that was in his *h*
14:37 them into the *h* of Israel
14:43 of the rod that is in my *h*
14:48 of the *h* of their pillager
16:1 while I, on the other *h*
16:16 have to play with his *h*
16:20 by the *h* of David his son to
16:23 harp and played with his *h*
17:37 the *h* of this Philistine
17:40 to take his staff in his *h*
17:40 and in his *h* was his sling
17:46 surrender you into my *h*
17:47 give you men into our *h*
17:49 David thrust his *h* into his
17:50 was no sword in David's *h*
17:57 of the Philistine in his *h*
18:10 playing music with his *h*
18:10 the spear was in Saul's *h*
18:17 my *h* come to be upon him
18:17 let the *h* of the Philistines
18:21 *h* of the Philistines may
18:25 by the *h* of the Philistines
19:9 with his spear in his *h*
19:9 playing music with his *h*
20:16 at the *h* of David's enemies
21:3 give them into my *h*, or
21:4 ordinary bread under my *h*
21:8 weapons did I take in my *h*
21:13 acting insane in their *h*
22:6 with his spear in his *h* and
22:17 their *h* also is with David
22:17 *h* to assault the priests of
23:4 the Philistines into your *h*
23:6 that went down in his *h*
23:7 God has sold him into my *h*
23:11 surrender me into his *h*
23:12 and my men into Saul's *h*
23:14 not give him into his *h*
23:16 strengthen his *h* in regard
23:17 *h* of Saul my father will not
23:20 into the *h* of the king
24:4 your enemy into your *h*
24:6 thrusting out my *h* against
24:10 gave you today into my *h*
24:10 not thrust out my *h* against
24:11 sleeveless coat in my *h*
24:11 badness or revolt in my *h*
24:12 own *h* will not come to be
24:13 own *h* will not come to be
24:15 to free me from your *h*
24:18 surrendered me into your *h*
24:20 in your *h* the kingdom of
25:8 whatever your *h* may find
25:26 *h* come to your salvation
25:31 *h* of my lord itself come to
25:33 own *h* come to my salvation
25:34 on the other *h*, as Jehovah
25:35 David accepted from her *h*
25:39 free me from Nabal's *h* and
26:8 your enemy into your *h*
26:9 thrust his *h* out against the
26:11 thrust my *h* out against the
26:18 badness is there in my *h*
26:23 gave you into my *h*, and I
26:23 thrust my *h* out against the
27:1 swept away . . . by Saul's *h*
27:1 certainly escape from his *h*
28:17 kingdom away from your *h*
28:19 the *h* of the Philistines
28:19 the *h* of the Philistines
30:15 into the *h* of my master
30:23 came against us into our *h*
2Sa 1:14 fear to thrust your *h* out to
3:8 in the *h* of David
3:12 my *h* will be with you to
3:18 By the *h* of David my servant
3:18 the *h* of the Philistines
3:18 the *h* of all their enemies
5:19 you give them into my *h*
6:6 Uzzah now thrust his *h* out to
8:1 of the *h* of the Philistines
8:10 in his *h* there proved to be
10:10 *h* of Abishai his brother
11:14 send it by the *h* of Uriah
12:7 you out of the *h* of Saul
13:5 shall have to eat from her *h*
13:6 as a patient from her *h*
13:10 as a patient from your *h*
14:19 *h* of Joab with you in all
15:5 thrust his *h* out and grabbed
16:8 the kingship into the *h* of

2Sa 18:2 people under the *h* of Joab
18:2 under the *h* of Abishai the
18:2 under the *h* of Ittai the
18:12 *h* out against the king's son
18:19 from the *h* of his enemies
18:28 *h* against my lord the king
18:31 *h* of all those rising up
20:9 Joab's right *h* took hold of
20:10 sword that was in Joab's *h*
20:21 his *h* against King David
21:9 into the *h* of the Gibeonites
21:22 fall by the *h* of David and
21:22 and by the *h* of his servants
23:6 by the *h* that they should be
23:10 until his *h* wearied and
23:10 his *h* kept cleaving to the
23:21 in the *h* of the Egyptian
23:21 away from the Egyptian's *h*
24:14 into the *h* of Jehovah, for
24:14 into the *h* of man do not
24:16 angel kept his *h* thrust out
24:16 enough! Now let your *h* drop
24:17 your *h*, please, come upon
1Ki 2:46 in the *h* of Solomon
8:15 own *h* has given fulfillment
8:24 with your own *h* you have
8:42 name and of your strong *h*
11:12 Out of the *h* of your son I
11:26 his *h* against the king
11:27 his *h* against the king
11:31 out of the *h* of Solomon
11:34 entire kingdom out of his *h*
11:35 kingship out of the *h* of his
13:4 his *h* from off the altar
13:4 his *h* that he had thrust out
13:6 my *h* may be restored to me
13:6 the king's *h* was restored to
13:33 fill his *h* with power
14:3 take in your *h* ten loaves of
15:18 in the *h* of his servants
17:11 a bit of bread in your *h*
18:9 *h* of Ahab to put me to death
18:46 *h* of Jehovah proved to be
20:6 put in their *h*, and they
20:13 giving it into your *h* today
20:23 on the other *h*, let us
20:28 great crowd into your *h*
20:42 have let go out of your *h*
22:3 the *h* of the king of Syria
22:6 give it into the king's *h*
22:12 give it into the king's *h*
22:15 give it into the king's *h*
22:34 Turn your *h* around, and take
2Ki 3:10 give them into the *h* of Moab
3:13 give them into the *h* of Moab
3:15 the *h* of Jehovah came to be
3:18 give Moab into your *h*
4:29 take my staff in your *h* and
5:5 take in his *h* ten talents of
5:11 move his *h* to and fro over
5:18 supporting himself upon my *h*
5:20 from his *h* what he brought
5:24 took them from their *h* and
6:7 thrust his *h* out and took it
7:2 upon whose *h* the king was
7:17 adjutant upon whose *h* he was
8:8 Take a gift in your *h* and go
8:9 and took a gift in his *h*
8:20 from under the *h* of Judah
8:22 from under the *h* of Judah
9:1 this flask of oil in your *h*
9:7 at the *h* of Jezebel
9:24 filled his *h* with a bow and
10:15 If it is, do give me your *h*
10:15 So he gave him his *h*
10:18 Ahab, on the one *h*
10:18 Jehu, on the other *h*, will
11:8 with his weapons in his *h*
11:11 with his weapons in his *h*
12:15 the men into whose *h* they
13:3 into the *h* of Hazael the king
13:3 into the *h* of Ben-hadad the
13:5 from under the *h* of Syria
13:16 Put your *h* to the bow
13:16 he put his *h* to it, after
13:25 from the *h* of Ben-hadad
13:25 from the *h* of Jehoahaz
14:5 had become firm in his *h*
14:27 by the *h* of Jeroboam the
15:19 the kingdom in his own *h*
17:7 from under the *h* of Pharaoh
17:20 into the *h* of pillagers
17:39 the *h* of all your enemies
18:29 to deliver you out of my *h*

2Ki 18:30 into the *h* of the king of
18:33 the *h* of the king of Assyria
18:34 Samaria out of my *h*
18:35 their land out of my *h*
18:35 Jerusalem out of my *h*
19:10 *h* of the king of Assyria
19:14 the *h* of the messengers
19:19 out of his *h*, that all the
21:14 into the *h* of their enemies
22:5 *h* of those doing the work
22:7 into whose *h* it is being put
22:9 *h* of the doers of the work
1Ch 4:10 your *h* really proves to be
5:10 came to fall by their *h*
5:20 were given into their *h*, for
6:15 by the *h* of Nebuchadnezzar
6:44 their brothers on the left *h*
11:23 And in the *h* of the Egyptian
11:23 away from the Egyptian's *h*
12:2 using the right *h* and using
12:2 using the left *h* with stones
13:9 Uzzah now thrust his *h* out
13:10 his *h* out upon the Ark
14:10 give them into my *h*
14:10 give them into your *h*
14:11 by my *h* like a gap made by
18:1 of the *h* of the Philistines
19:11 gave into the *h* of Abishai
20:8 to fall by the *h* of David and
20:8 and by the *h* of his servants
21:13 fall into the *h* of Jehovah
21:13 *h* of man do not let me fall
21:15 enough! Now let your *h* drop
21:16 his drawn sword in his *h*
21:17 Jehovah my God, let your *h*
22:18 he has given into my *h* the
24:19 due right by the *h* of Aaron
28:19 the *h* of Jehovah upon me
29:5 by the *h* of the craftsmen
29:5 fill his *h* today with a gift
29:12 in your *h* there are power
29:12 in your *h* is ability to
29:14 out of your own *h* we have
29:16 from your *h* it is, and to
29:17 your people who are on *h*
2Ch 6:15 your own *h* you have made
6:32 great name and your strong *h*
7:6 render praise by their *h*
12:5 left you to the *h* of Shishak
12:7 by the *h* of Shishak
13:8 *h* of the sons of David, when
13:9 filled his *h* with power by
13:16 God gave them into their *h*
16:7 has escaped out of your *h*
16:8 he not give them into your *h*
17:5 firmly established in his *h*
18:5 give it into the king's *h*
18:11 give it into the king's *h*
18:14 be given into your *h*
18:33 Turn your *h* around, and you
20:6 your *h* power and mightiness
21:8 under the *h* of Judah and then
21:10 under the *h* of Judah down
21:10 revolt . . . from under his *h*
23:10 with his missile in his *h*
23:18 *h* of the priests and the
24:11 by the *h* of the Levites, and
24:13 kept advancing by their *h*
24:24 into their *h* a military
25:15 own people out of your *h*
25:20 of giving them into his *h*
26:11 *h* of Jeiel the secretary
26:19 in his *h* there was a censer
28:5 the *h* of the king of Syria
28:5 *h* of the king of Israel he
28:9 gave them into your *h*, so
29:25 by the *h* of Jehovah that
29:31 *h* with power for Jehovah
30:3 enough priests, on the one *h*
30:3 people, on the other *h*, had
30:6 from the *h* of the king
30:12 *h* of the true God proved to
30:16 from the *h* of the Levites
32:13 their land out of my *h*
32:14 his people out of my *h*, so
32:14 to deliver you out of my *h*
32:15 his people out of my *h* and
32:15 of the *h* of my forefathers
32:15 God deliver you out of my *h*
32:17 their people out of my *h*
32:17 his people out of my *h*
32:22 out of the *h* of Sennacherib
32:22 the *h* of all others and
33:8 decisions by the *h* of Moses

2Ch 34:9 *h* of Manasseh and Ephraim
34:10 *h* of the doers of the work
34:14 law by the *h* of Moses
34:16 in the *h* of your servants
34:17 *h* of the appointed men
34:17 *h* of the doers of the work
35:11 the blood from their *h*
36:17 He gave into his *h*
Ezr 5:12 into the *h* of Nebuchadnezzar
6:12 thrusts his *h* out to commit
7:6 the *h* of Jehovah his God upon
7:9 good *h* of his God upon him
7:14 law . . . that is in your *h*
7:25 that is in your *h* appoint
7:28 the *h* of Jehovah my God upon
8:18 good *h* of our God upon us
8:22 The *h* of our God is over all
8:26 into their *h* six hundred and
8:31 *h* of our God proved to be
8:33 into the *h* of Meremoth the
9:2 the *h* of the princes and the
9:7 into the *h* of the kings of the
Ne 1:10 power and by your strong *h*
2:8 the good *h* of my God upon me
2:18 tell them of the *h* of my God
4:17 work with his one *h* while
4:17 the other *h* was holding the
4:23 his missile in his right *h*
5:16 of this wall I took a *h*
6:5 with an open letter in his *h*
8:4 and Maaseiah to his right *h*
9:15 lifted your *h* in an oath to
9:24 and to give them into their *h*
9:27 the *h* of their adversaries
9:27 the *h* of their adversaries
9:28 to the *h* of their enemies
9:30 into the *h* of the peoples of
10:29 been given by the *h* of Moses
10:31 and the debt of every *h*
13:21 a *h* I shall lay on you
Es 2:21 to lay *h* on King Ahasuerus
3:6 to lay *h* upon Mordecai alone
3:10 signet ring from his own *h*
5:2 scepter that was in his *h*
6:2 to lay *h* on King Ahasuerus
8:7 thrust out his *h* against the
8:10 *h* of the couriers on horses
9:2 lay *h* on those seeking their
9:10 they did not lay their *h*
9:15 they did not lay their *h*
9:16 they did not lay their *h*
Job 1:11 thrust out your *h*, please
1:12 that he has is in your *h*
1:12 do not thrust out your *h*
2:5 thrust out your *h*, please, and
2:6 There he is in your *h*
5:15 from the *h* of the strong one
6:9 release his *h* and cut me off
6:23 out of the *h* of an adversary
6:23 out of the *h* of tyrants you
8:4 go into the *h* of their revolt
8:20 hold of the *h* of evildoers
9:24 into the *h* of the wicked one
9:33 put his *h* upon both of us
10:7 delivering out of your own *h*
11:14 is hurtful is in your *h*
12:6 has brought a god in his *h*
12:9 *h* of Jehovah itself has done
12:10 In whose *h* is the soul of
13:4 On the other *h*, you men are
13:21 Put your own *h* far away
15:23 darkness is ready at his *h*
15:25 his *h* against God himself
19:21 God's own *h* has touched me
21:5 put your *h* upon your mouth
23:2 My own *h* is heavy on account
26:13 His *h* has pierced the
27:11 you men by the *h* of God
28:9 he has thrust out his *h*
29:20 my bow in my *h* will shoot
30:12 At my right *h* they rise up
30:21 the full might of your *h*
30:24 no one thrusts his *h* out
31:21 If I waved my *h* to and fro
31:25 *h* had found a lot of things
31:27 my *h* proceeded to kiss my
34:20 powerful ones depart by no *h*
35:7 he receive from your own *h*
37:7 On the *h* of every earthling
40:4 *h* I have put over my mouth
40:14 your right *h* can save you
Ps 10:12 O God, lift up your *h*
10:14 to get them into your *h*
16:8 Because he is at my right *h*

Ps 16:11 pleasantness at your right *h*
17:7 revolters against your right *h*
17:14 men, by your *h*, O Jehovah
18:*super* and out of the *h* of Saul
18:35 right *h* will sustain me
20:6 mighty acts of his right *h*
21:8 Your *h* will find all your
21:8 *h* will find those hating
26:10 right *h* is full of bribery
31:5 Into your *h* . . . my spirit
31:8 into the *h* of the enemy
31:15 My times are in your *h*
31:15 from the *h* of my enemies
32:4 your *h* was heavy upon me
34:10 little on *h* and gone hungry
36:11 the *h* of wicked people
37:24 Jehovah is supporting his *h*
37:33 to the *h* of that one
38:2 upon me your *h* is come down
39:10 to the hostility of your *h*
44:2 *h* drove away even nations
44:3 your right *h* and your arm
45:4 your right *h* will instruct
45:9 at your right *h* in gold of
48:10 *h* is full of righteousness
49:15 my soul from the *h* of Sheol
60:5 O do save with your right *h*
63:8 your right *h* keeps fast hold
71:4 from the *h* of the wicked one
73:23 taken hold of my right *h*
74:11 Why do you keep your *h*
74:11 even your right *h*, withdrawn
75:8 is a cup in the *h* of Jehovah
77:2 *h* has been stretched out and
77:10 the right *h* of the Most High
77:20 By the *h* of Moses and Aaron
78:42 did not remember his *h*
78:48 *h* over their beasts of burden
78:54 that his right *h* acquired
78:61 beauty into the *h* of the
80:15 that your right *h* has planted
80:17 *h* prove to be upon the man
80:17 upon the man of your right *h*
81:14 I would turn my *h*
82:4 Out of the *h* of the wicked
88:5 from your own helping *h*
89:13 Your *h* is strong, Your right
89:13 Your right *h* is exalted
89:21 whom my own *h* will be firm
89:25 on the sea I have put his *h*
89:25 on the rivers his right *h*
89:42 right *h* of his adversaries
89:48 his soul from the *h* of Sheol
91:7 ten thousand at your right *h*
95:4 in whose *h* are the inmost
95:7 and the sheep of his *h*
97:10 Out of the *h* of the wicked
98:1 His right *h*, even his holy
104:28 You open your *h*—they get
106:10 from the *h* of the hater
106:10 from the *h* of the enemy
106:26 raise his *h* in an oath
106:41 into the *h* of the nations
106:42 be subdued under their *h*
107:2 from the *h* of the adversary
108:6 save with your right *h* and
109:6 keep standing at his right *h*
109:27 know that this is your *h*
109:31 at the right *h* of the poor
110:1 Sit at my right *h* Until I
110:5 himself at your right *h*
118:15 The right *h* of Jehovah is
118:16 The right *h* of Jehovah is
118:16 The right *h* of Jehovah is
119:173 your *h* serve to help me
121:5 your shade on your right *h*
123:2 toward the *h* of their master
123:2 toward the *h* of her mistress
125:3 their *h* upon any wrongdoing
127:4 in the *h* of a mighty man
129:7 has not filled his own *h*
136:12 By a strong *h* and by an arm
137:5 Let my right *h* be forgetful
138:7 you will thrust out your *h*
138:7 your right *h* will save me
139:5 you place your *h* upon me
139:10 your own *h* would lead me
139:10 right *h* would lay hold of
142:4 Look to the right *h* and see
144:7 From the *h* of the foreigners
144:8 And whose right *h* is a
144:8 is a right *h* of falsehood
144:11 the *h* of the foreigners
144:11 And whose right *h* is a

Ps 144:11 is a right *h* of falsehood
145:16 You are opening your *h*
149:6 sword be in their *h*
Pr 1:24 stretched out my *h* but there
3:16 of days is in its right *h*
3:16 left *h* there are riches and
3:27 power of your *h* to do it
4:27 incline to the right *h* or to
6:5 like a gazelle from the *h* and
6:5 from the *h* of the birdcatcher
7:20 money he has taken in his *h*
10:4 one working with a slack *h*
10:4 *h* of the diligent one is what
11:21, 21 Though *h* be to *h*, a bad
12:24 *h* of the diligent ones is
12:24 slack *h* will come to be for
13:11 one collecting by the *h* is
16:5, 5 *H* may join to *h*, yet one
17:16 in the *h* of a stupid one the
19:24 lazy one has hidden his *h* in
21:1 water in the *h* of Jehovah
26:6 into the *h* of someone stupid
26:9 up into the *h* of a drunkard
26:15 his *h* in the banquet bowl
27:16 and oil is what his right *h*
30:32 put the *h* to the mouth
Ec 2:24 is from the *h* of the true God
5:14 is nothing at all in his *h*
5:15 he can take along with his *h*
7:18 also do not withdraw your *h*
9:1 are in the *h* of the true God
9:10 All that your *h* finds to do
10:2 of the wise is at his right *h*
10:2 of the stupid at his left *h*
11:6 do not let your *h* rest
Ca 2:6 His left *h* is under my head
2:6 his right *h*—it embraces me
5:4 pulled back his *h* from the
8:3 left *h* would be under my head
8:3 right *h*—it would embrace me
Isa 1:12 required this from your *h*
1:25 will turn back my *h* upon you
3:6 mass should be under your *h*
3:23 *h* mirrors and the
5:25 stretch out his *h* against
5:25 *h* is stretched out still
6:6 *h* there was a glowing coal
8:11 with strongness of the *h*
9:12 his *h* is stretched out still
9:17 his *h* is stretched out still
9:21 his *h* is stretched out still
10:4 his *h* is stretched out still
10:5 stick that is in their *h*
10:10 *h* has reached the kingdoms
10:13 the power of my *h* I shall
10:14 *h* will reach the resources
10:32 waves his *h* threateningly
11:8 child actually put his own *h*
11:11 will again offer his *h*
11:14 will thrust out their *h*
11:15 wave his *h* at the River in
13:2 wave the *h*, that they may
14:26 *h* that is stretched out
14:27 *h* is the one stretched out
19:4 into the *h* of a hard master
19:16 waving of the *h* of Jehovah
20:2 spoke by the *h* of Isaiah
22:21 I shall give into his *h*
23:11 *h* he has stretched out over
25:10 *h* of Jehovah will settle
26:11 Jehovah, your *h* has become
31:3 will stretch out his *h*, and
34:17 *h* has apportioned the place
36:15 *h* of the king of Assyria
36:18 *h* of the king of Assyria
36:19 Samaria out of my *h*
36:20 out of my *h* so that Jehovah
36:20 Jerusalem out of my *h*
37:10 *h* of the king of Assyria
37:14 of the *h* of the messengers
37:20 God, save us out of his *h*
40:2 from the *h* of Jehovah she
40:12 in the mere hollow of his *h*
41:10 my right *h* of righteousness
41:13 am grasping your right *h*
41:20 the very *h* of Jehovah has
42:6 to take hold of your *h*
43:13 deliverance out of my own *h*
44:5 will write upon his *h*
44:20 a falsehood in my right *h*
45:1 right *h* I have taken hold of
47:2 a *h* mill and grind out flour
47:6 to give them into your *h*
48:13 own *h* laid the foundation
Isa 48:13 right *h* extended out the
49:2 In the shadow of his *h* he
49:22 raise up my *h* even to the
50:2 Has my *h* become in fact so
50:11 my *h* you will certainly
51:16 with the shadow of my *h* I
51:17 drunk at the *h* of Jehovah
51:18 taking hold of her *h*
51:22 take away from your *h* the
51:23 *h* of the ones irritating you
53:10 and in his *h* what is the
56:1 my salvation is at *h* to come
56:2 keeping his *h* in order not to
59:1 The *h* of Jehovah has not
62:3 in the *h* of Jehovah, and a
62:8 has sworn with his right *h*
63:12 go at the right *h* of Moses
64:8 are the work of your *h*
66:2 things my own *h* has made
66:14 the *h* of Jehovah will
Jer 1:9 Jehovah thrust his *h* out and
6:9 Put your *h* back like one that
6:12 stretch my *h* out against the
11:21 you may not die at our *h*
15:6 stretch out my *h* against you
15:17 Because of your *h* I have
15:21 the *h* of the bad ones, and
16:21 cause them to know my *h*
18:4 spoiled by the potter's *h*
18:6 clay in the *h* of the potter
18:6 in my *h*, O house of Israel
19:7 the *h* of those seeking for
20:4 into the *h* of the king of
20:5 into the *h* of their enemies
20:13 out of the *h* of evildoers
21:4 in the *h* of you people
21:5 with a stretched-out *h* and
21:7 into the *h* of Nebuchadrezzar
21:7 into the *h* of their enemies
21:7 into the *h* of those who are
21:10 *h* of the king of Babylon
21:12 the *h* of the defrauder
22:3 out of the *h* of the defrauder
22:24 the seal ring on my right *h*
22:25 give you into the *h* of those
22:25 into the *h* of those of whom
22:25 into the *h* of Nebuchadrezzar
22:25 into the *h* of the Chaldeans
25:10 the sound of the *h* mill and
25:15 wine of rage out of my *h*
25:17 cup out of the *h* of Jehovah
25:28 take the cup out of your *h*
26:14 here I am in your *h*
26:24 it was the *h* of Ahikam
26:24 into the *h* of the people
27:3 by the *h* of the messengers
27:6 into the *h* of Nebuchadnezzar
27:8 finished them off by his *h*
29:3 by the *h* of Elasah the son
29:21 into the *h* of Nebuchadrezzar
31:11 *h* of the one stronger than
31:32 hold of their *h* to bring
32:3 *h* of the king of Babylon
32:4 from the *h* of the Chaldeans
32:4 *h* of the king of Babylon
32:21 with a strong *h* and with
32:24 into the *h* of the Chaldeans
32:25 into the *h* of the Chaldeans
32:28 into the *h* of the Chaldeans
32:28 *h* of Nebuchadrezzar the king
32:36 *h* of the king of Babylon
32:43 into the *h* of the Chaldeans
34:1 the dominion under his *h*
34:2 *h* of the king of Babylon
34:3 not escape out of his *h*
34:3 into his *h* you will be given
34:20 into the *h* of their enemies
34:20 *h* of those seeking for their
34:21 into the *h* of their enemies
34:21 *h* of those seeking for their
34:21 *h* of the military forces of
36:14 take it in your *h* and come
36:14 took the roll in his *h* and
37:17 *h* of the king of Babylon
38:3 *h* of the military force of
38:16 *h* of these men who are
38:18 into the *h* of the Chaldeans
38:18 not escape out of their *h*
38:19 give me into their *h* and
38:23 not escape out of their *h*
38:23 *h* of the king of Babylon
39:17 *h* of the men of whom you
41:5 in their *h* to bring to the
42:11 deliver you out of his *h*
Jer 43:3 into the *h* of the Chaldeans
43:9 Take in your *h* great stones
44:30 into the *h* of his enemies
44:30 *h* of those seeking for his
44:30 into the *h* of Nebuchadrezzar
46:24 *h* of the people of the north
46:26 *h* of those seeking for their
46:26 *h* of Nebuchadrezzar the
46:26 into the *h* of his servants
50:15 She has given her *h*
51:7 cup in the *h* of Jehovah
51:25 stretch out my *h* against
La 1:7 into the *h* of the adversary
1:10 spread out his own *h* against
1:14 In his *h* they intertwine one
1:14 *h* of those against whom I am
2:3 turned his right *h* back from
2:4 right *h* has taken its position
2:7 Into the *h* of the enemy he has
2:8 has not turned back his *h* from
3:3 repeatedly turns his *h* all day
5:6 To Egypt we have given the *h*
5:8 tearing us away from their *h*
5:12 been hanged by just their *h*
5:13 lifted up a *h* mill itself
Eze 1:3 in that place the *h* of Jehovah
2:9 was a *h* thrust out to me, and
3:14 the *h* of Jehovah upon me was
3:18 ask back from your own *h*
3:20 ask back from your own *h*
3:22 *h* of Jehovah came to be upon
6:14 stretch out my *h* against
7:21 into the *h* of the strangers
8:1 the *h* of the Sovereign Lord
8:3 the representation of a *h* and
8:11 with his censer in his *h*
9:1 with his weapon in his *h* for
9:2 weapon for smashing in his *h*
10:7 cherub thrust his *h* out from
10:8 the representation of a *h* of
11:3 building of houses close at *h*
11:9 into the *h* of strangers and
12:7 way through the wall by *h*
13:9 my *h* has come to be against
13:21 my people out of your *h*
13:21 in your *h* something caught
13:23 my people out of your *h*
14:9 stretch out my *h* against him
14:13 stretch out my *h* against it
16:27 stretch out my *h* against
16:39 will give you into their *h*
16:49 *h* of the afflicted one and
17:18 he had given his *h* and has
18:8 he would draw back his *h*
18:17 he has drawn back his *h*
20:5 to lift up my *h* in an oath
20:5 to lift up my *h* in an oath
20:6 I lifted up my *h* in an oath
20:15 lifted up my *h* in an oath
20:22 I drew back my *h* and went
20:23 lifted up my *h* in an oath
20:28 lifted up my *h* in an oath
20:33 be with a strong *h* and with
20:34 scattered with a strong *h*
20:42 I lifted up my *h* in an oath
21:11 to wield it with the *h*
21:11 into the *h* of a killer
21:19 an index *h* should be cut out
21:22 his right *h* the divination
21:24 be seized even by the *h*
21:31 give you into the *h* of men
22:13 struck my *h* at your unjust
23:9 the *h* of those passionately
23:9 the *h* of the sons of Assyria
23:28 giving you into the *h* of
23:28 *h* of those from whom your
23:31 to give her cup into your *h*
25:7 stretched out my *h* against
25:13 stretch out my *h* against
25:14 the *h* of my people Israel
25:16 stretching out my *h* against
28:9 the *h* of those profaning you
28:10 die by the *h* of strangers
29:7 took hold of you by the *h*
30:10 by the *h* of Nebuchadrezzar
30:12 into the *h* of bad men, and
30:12 desolated by the *h* of
30:22 sword to fall out of his *h*
30:24 give my sword into his *h*
30:25 *h* of the king of Babylon
31:11 into the *h* of the despot of
33:6 from the *h* of the watchman
33:8 ask back at your own *h*
33:22 *h* of Jehovah had come to be

Eze 34:10 my sheep from their *h* and
34:27 delivered them out of the *h*
35:3 stretch out my *h* against you
36:7 raised my *h* in an oath that
37:1 The *h* of Jehovah proved to
37:17 become just one in your *h*
37:19 is in the *h* of Ephraim
37:19 must become one in my *h*
37:20 must prove to be in your *h*
38:12 in order to turn your *h* back
38:17 by the *h* of my servants the
39:3 your bow out of your left *h*
39:3 out of your own right *h*
39:21 my *h* that I have placed
39:23 the *h* of their adversaries
40:1 *h* of Jehovah proved to be
40:3 was a flax cord in his *h*
40:5 in the *h* of the man there
44:12 raised my *h* against them
47:3 measuring line in his *h*
47:14 I raised my *h* in an oath to
Da 1:2 Jehovah gave into his *h*
2:38 into whose *h* he has given
3:17 and out of your *h*, O king
4:35 no one that can check his *h*
5:5 fingers of a man's *h* came
5:5 back of the *h* that was writing
5:23 God in whose *h* your breath
5:24 being sent the back of a *h*
7:25 given into his *h* for a time
8:4 any delivering out of its *h*
8:7 no deliverer out of its *h*
8:25 deception to succeed in his *h*
8:25 *h* that he will be broken
9:10 *h* of his servants the prophets
9:15 land of Egypt by a strong *h*
10:10 was a *h* that touched me
11:11 given into the *h* of that one
11:16 be extermination in his *h*
11:41 escape out of his *h*, Edom
11:42 out his *h* against the lands
12:7 raise his right *h* and his left
12:7 left *h* to the heavens and to
Ho 2:10 man to snatch her out of my *h*
4:12 *h* staff keeps telling them
7:5 his *h* along with deriders
12:7 in his *h* are the scales of
12:10 by the *h* of the prophets I
13:14 From the *h* of Sheol I
Joe 3:8 into the *h* of the sons of
Am 1:6 exiles to *h* over to Edom
1:8 turn my *h* back upon Ekron
5:19 his *h* against the wall
7:7 there was a plummet in his *h*
9:2 from there my own *h* will
Ob 13 thrust out a *h* upon his wealth
14 not to *h* over his survivors in
Jon 4:11 their right *h* and their left
Mic 2:1 it is in the power of their *h*
3:8 on the other *h*, I myself have
5:9 Your *h* will be high above
5:12 sorceries out of your *h*
7:16 put their *h* upon their mouth
Hab 2:16 cup of the right *h* of Jehovah
3:4 two rays issuing out of his *h*
Zep 1:4 stretch out my *h* against
2:13 stretch out his *h* toward
2:15 whistle; he will wag his *h*
Zec 2:1 and in his *h* a measuring rope
2:9 waving my *h* against them
3:1 Satan standing at his right *h*
4:10 in the *h* of Zerubbabel
8:4 with his staff in his *h*
11:6 in the *h* of his companion
11:6 and in the *h* of his king
11:6 no delivering out of their *h*
12:6 devour on the right *h* and
13:7 turn my *h* back upon those
14:13 of the *h* of his companion
14:13 his *h* will actually come up
14:13 against the *h* of his
Mal 1:9 From your *h* this has occurred
1:10 gift offering from your *h*
1:13 pleasure in it at your *h*
2:13 in anything from your *h*
Mt 3:12 winnowing shovel is in his *h*
5:30 if your right *h* is making you
6:3 do not let your left *h* know
7:9 not *h* him a stone, will he?
7:10 not *h* him a serpent, will he?
8:3 stretching out his *h*, he
8:15 he touched her *h*, and the
9:18 come and lay your *h* upon her
9:25 took hold of her *h*, and the

Mt 12:10 a man with a withered *h*!
12:13 the man: Stretch out your *h*
12:13 sound like the other *h*
12:49 extending his *h* toward his
14:31 stretching out his *h* Jesus
18:8 *h* or your foot is making you
20:21 one at your right *h* and one
20:23 sitting down at my right *h*
22:13 Bind him *h* and foot and
22:44 Sit at my right *h* until I
24:41 be grinding at the *h* mill
25:33 put the sheep on his right *h*
26:23 He that dips his *h* with me
26:51 reached out his *h* and drew
26:64 at the right *h* of power and
27:29 and a reed in his right *h*
Mr 1:31 taking her by the *h*; and the
1:41 he stretched out his *h* and
3:1 was there with a dried-up *h*
3:3 the man with the withered *h*
3:5 to the man: Stretch out your *h*
3:5 it out, and his *h* was restored
5:41 taking the *h* of the young
7:32 to lay his *h* upon him
8:23 took the blind man by the *h*
9:27 Jesus took him by the *h* and
9:43 your *h* makes you stumble
10:37 one at your right *h* and one
12:36 Sit at my right *h* until I
14:62 at the right *h* of power and
Lu 1:66 the *h* of Jehovah was indeed
1:71 the *h* of all those hating us
3:17 winnowing shovel is in his *h*
5:13 stretching out his *h*, he
6:6 whose right *h* was withered
6:8 the man with the withered *h*
6:10 Stretch out your *h*. He did so
6:10 and his *h* was restored
6:49 On the other *h*, he who hears
8:54 he took her by the *h* and
9:62 put his *h* to a plow and looks
10:40 Martha, on the other *h*, was
11:11 *h* him a serpent instead of
11:12 will *h* him a scorpion
15:22 and put a ring on his *h* and
16:2 *H* in the account of your
20:42 my Lord, Sit at my right *h*
22:21 the *h* of my betrayer is
22:69 the powerful right *h* of God
24:30 and began to *h* it to them
Joh 3:35 given all things into his *h*
7:6 your due time is always at *h*
7:30 no one laid a *h* upon him
8:45 I, on the other *h*, tell the
10:28 snatch them out of my *h*
10:29 snatch them out of the *h* of
20:25 my *h* into his side, I will
20:27 *h* and stick it into my side
Ac 2:23 by the *h* of lawless men and
2:25 he is at my right *h* that I
2:33 exalted to the right *h* of God
2:34 to my Lord: Sit at my right *h*
3:7 by the right *h* and raised him
4:28 your *h* and counsel had
4:30 stretch out your *h* for healing
5:31 to his right *h*, to give
7:25 them salvation by his *h*
7:35 *h* of the angel that appeared
7:50 My *h* made all these things
7:55 standing at God's right *h*
7:56 standing at God's right *h*
9:8 they led him by the *h* and
9:41 Giving her his *h*, he raised
11:21 *h* of Jehovah was with them
11:30 by the *h* of Barnabas and Saul
12:11 me out of Herod's *h* and
12:17 motioned to them with his *h*
13:11 Jehovah's *h* is upon you, and
13:11 men to lead him by the *h*
13:16 motioning with his *h*, he
13:36 David, on the one *h*, served
13:37 On the other *h*, he whom God
15:23 and by their *h* they wrote
17:17 who happened to be on *h*
19:33 motioned with his *h* and was
21:40 motioned with his *h* to the
22:11 led by the *h* of those who
23:19 took him by the *h* and
25:11 If, on the one *h*, I am really
25:11 if, on the other *h*, none of
25:11 *h* me over to them as a favor
25:16 to *h* any man over as a favor
26:1 Paul stretched his *h* out and
27:1 *h* both Paul and certain other

Ac 28:3 and fastened itself on his *h*
28:4 creature hanging from his *h*
Ro 4:5 On the other *h*, to the man
8:34 who is on the right *h* of God
1Co 5:5 *h* such a man over to Satan
12:15 Because I am not a *h*, I am
12:21 The eye cannot say to the *h*
13:3 if I *h* over my body, that I
16:21 greeting . . . in my own *h*
2Co 6:7 righteousness on the right *h*
Ga 2:9 the right *h* of sharing together
3:19 by the *h* of a mediator
5:22 On the other *h*, the fruitage
6:11 written you with my own *h*
Eph 1:20 his right *h* in the heavenly
5:33 on the other *h*, the wife
Col 3:1 seated at the right *h* of God
4:18 greeting . . . in my own *h*
1Th 5:14 On the other *h*, we exhort
2Th 3:17 in my own *h*, which is a
1Ti 4:7 On the other *h*, be training
5:11 On the other *h*, turn down
Phm 19 am writing with my own *h*
Heb 1:3 on the right *h* of the Majesty
1:13 Sit at my right *h*, until I
8:1 sat down at the right *h* of
8:9 taking hold of their *h* to
10:12 down at the right *h* of God
12:2 sat down at the right *h* of
1Pe 3:22 He is at God's right *h*, for
5:6 under the mighty *h* of God
Re 1:16 in his right *h* seven stars
1:17 he laid his right *h* upon me
1:20 you saw upon my right *h*
2:1 the seven stars in his right *h*
5:1 the right *h* of the One seated
5:7 right *h* of the One seated on
6:5 had a pair of scales in his *h*
8:4 from the *h* of the angel with
10:2 had in his *h* a little scroll
10:5 raised his right *h* to heaven
10:8 in the *h* of the angel who is
10:10 out of the *h* of the angel
13:16 mark in their right *h* or
14:9 on his forehead or upon his *h*
14:14 and a sharp sickle in his *h*
17:4 in her *h* a golden cup that
19:2 blood of his slaves at her *h*
20:1 and a great chain in his *h*
20:4 mark . . . upon their *h*

Handbreadth
Ex 25:25 make for it a rim of a *h*
37:12 a rim of a *h* round about and
1Ki 7:26 And its thickness was a *h*
2Ch 4:5 And its thickness was a *h*
Eze 40:5 by a cubit and a *h*. And he
40:43 ledges . . . were of one *h*
43:13 cubit being a cubit and a *h*

Handclapping
Job 36:18 allure you into spiteful *h*

Handcuffs
Jer 40:1 he was bound with *h* in the
40:4 loose today from the *h* that

Handed
Ge 32:16 *h* over to his servants one
Le 9:12 Aaron's sons *h* him the blood
9:13 they *h* him the burnt offering
9:18 sons *h* him the blood and he
1Ki 3:28 decision that the king had *h*
Ps 78:50 life he *h* over even to the
Mt 27:2 and *h* him over to Pilate the
27:18 of envy they had *h* him over
27:26 *h* him over to be impaled
Mr 7:13 tradition which you *h* down
15:1 and *h* him over to Pilate
15:10 chief priests had *h* him over
15:15 he *h* him over to be impaled
Lu 4:17 scroll of . . . Isaiah was *h*
4:20 *h* it back to the attendant
24:20 *h* him over to the sentence
24:42 *h* him a piece of broiled
Joh 19:11 why the man that *h* me over
19:16 *h* him over to them to be
Ac 6:14 that Moses *h* down to us
7:42 God turned and *h* them over
15:30 and *h* them the letter
Ro 6:17 teaching to which you were *h*
1Co 11:2 just as I *h* them on to you
11:23 which I also *h* on to you
11:23 he was going to be *h* over
15:3 For I *h* on to you, among the
Ga 2:20 and *h* himself over for me

1Ti 1:20 have *h* them over to Satan

Handful

Le 2:2 his *h* of its fine flour and
5:12 must grasp from it his *h* as
6:15 must lift up by his *h* some
1Ki 17:12 a *h* of flour in the large
Ec 4:6 Better is a *h* of rest than a
4:6 than a double *h* of hard work

Handfuls

Ge 41:47 went on producing by the *h*
1Ki 20:10 *h* for all the people that
Eze 13:19 for the *h* of barley and for

Handing

Ps 78:62 *h* over his people to the
Isa 38:12 you keep *h* me over
38:13 you keep *h* me over
Am 1:9 *h* over a . . . body of exiles
Ac 22:4 *h* over to prisons both men

Handle

Ge 4:21 who *h* the harp and the pipe
Ex 18:22 they . . . will *h* as judges
18:26 themselves would *h* as judges
Le 5:10 one he will *h* as a burnt
Nu 6:11 priest must *h* one as a sin
De 19:5 slipped off from the wooden *h*
Jg 3:22 And the *h* kept going in also
Jer 50:42 Bow and javelin they *h*
Col 2:21 Do not *h*, nor taste, nor

Handled

Le 9:16 and *h* it according to the

Handleless

2Ki 21:13 wipes the *h* bowl clean

Handles

1Ti 1:8 provided one *h* it lawfully

Handling

Jg 5:14 *h* the equipment of a scribe
2Ch 25:5 *h* lance and large shield
Jer 2:8 ones *h* the law did not know
46:9 who are *h* the shield, and
46:9 are *h* and treading the bow
50:16 one *h* the sickle in the
Eze 27:29 those *h* an oar, mariners
38:4 all of them *h* swords
Am 2:15 no one *h* the bow will stand
Lu 16:1 as *h* his goods wastefully
2Ti 2:15 *h* the word of the truth

Handmade

Ac 17:24 does not dwell in *h* temples

Hands

Ge 5:29 from the pain of our *h*
19:10 men thrust out their *h* and
19:16 *h* of his two daughters and
20:5 with innocency of my *h* I
22:6 took in his *h* the fire and the
23:20 at the *h* of the sons of Heth
24:22 and two bracelets for her *h*
24:30 bracelets on the *h* of his
24:47 and the bracelets on her *h*
27:16 skins . . . put upon his *h*
27:22, 22 the *h* are the *h* of Esau
27:23 his *h* proved to be hairy like
27:23 hairy like the *h* of Esau
30:35 over into the *h* of his sons
31:42 toil of my *h* God has seen
35:4 gods that were in their *h*
43:21 return it with our own *h*
43:22 in our *h* to buy food
48:14 He purposely laid his *h* so
49:24 strength of his *h* was supple
49:24 the *h* of the powerful one of
Ex 9:8 Take for yourselves both *h* full
9:29 spread my *h* up to Jehovah
9:33 spread his *h* up to Jehovah
10:25 give into our *h* sacrifices
15:17 that your *h* have established
17:12 the *h* of Moses were heavy
17:12 Aaron and Hur supported his *h*
17:12 his *h* held steady until the
29:10 lay their *h* upon the bull's
29:15 their *h* upon the ram's head
29:19 their *h* upon the ram's head
29:25 must take them off their *h*
30:19 wash their *h* and their feet
30:21 wash their *h* and their feet
32:4 took the gold from their *h*
32:19 threw the tablets from his *h*
35:25 spun with their *h*, and they
40:31 washed their *h* and their
Le 4:15 lay their *h* upon the bull's
7:30 His *h* will bring as Jehovah's
8:14 *h* upon the head of the bull
8:18 *h* upon the head of the ram
8:22 their *h* upon the ram's head
9:22 Aaron raised his *h* toward the
15:11 not rinsed his *h* in water
16:12 hollows of both his *h* full
16:21 Aaron must lay both his *h*
24:14 *h* upon his head, and the
Nu 3:3 anointed priests whose *h* had
8:10 Israel must lay their *h* upon
8:12 Levites will lay their *h* upon
22:7 in their *h* and went to Balaam
24:10 clapped his *h*, and Balak
27:23 laid his *h* upon him and
De 4:28 the product of the *h* of man
9:15 tablets . . . were in both my *h*
9:17 flung . . . from both my *h*
21:6 wash their *h* over the young
21:7 Our *h* did not shed this blood
27:15 manufacture of the *h* of a
28:32 *h* will be without power
31:29 by the works of your *h*
33:11 in the activity of his *h*
Jos 8:7 certainly give it into your *h*
9:11 provisions in your *h* for the
10:19 has given them into your *h*
15:18 clapped her *h* while upon
Jg 1:4 the Perizzites into their *h*
1:6 cut off the thumbs of his *h*
1:7 the thumbs of their *h* and the
1:14 she clapped her *h* while upon
2:14 he gave them into the *h* of
7:11 *h* will certainly grow strong
7:16 horns in the *h* of all of them
7:19 jars that were in their *h*
9:16 as the doing of his *h* deserved
9:24 strengthened his *h* to kill his
15:14 his fetters melted off his *h*
19:27 her *h* upon the threshold
1Sa 5:4 palms of both his *h* cut off
14:13 up on his *h* and his feet
2Sa 2:7 *h* strengthen themselves and
3:34 *h* had not been bound ones
4:1 *h* became feeble and all the
4:11 his blood from your *h*
4:12 cut off their *h* and their
5:19 Philistines into your *h*
13:19 *h* put upon her head and
16:21 the *h* of all those who are
17:2 weary and feeble in both *h*
21:20 six fingers on each of his *h*
22:21 cleanness of my *h* he repays
22:35 teaching my *h* for warfare
1Ki 16:7 with the work of his *h*
2Ki 3:11 water upon the *h* of Elijah
9:23 made a turn with his *h*
9:35 feet and the palms of the *h*
10:24 I am bringing into your *h*
11:12 to clap their *h* and say
11:16 they laid their *h* upon her
12:11 the *h* of doers of the work
13:16, 16 *h* upon the *h* of the king
15:19 his *h* might prove to be
19:18 the workmanship of man's *h*
22:17 all the work of their *h*
2Ch 6:4 own *h* has given fulfillment
15:7 not let your *h* drop down
23:7 with his weapons in his *h*
23:15 they laid their *h* upon her
23:18 song by the *h* of David
29:23 and laid their *h* upon them
32:19 the work of man's *h*
34:25 all the doings of their *h*
Ezr 1:6 strengthened their *h* with
4:4 weakening the *h* of the people
5:8 is making progress in their *h*
6:22 strengthen their *h* in the
10:19 promised by shaking *h* to
Ne 2:18 strengthened their *h* for the
5:5 no power in our *h* while our
6:9 Their *h* will drop down from
6:9 But now strengthen my *h*
8:6 with the lifting up of their *h*
Es 3:9 the *h* of those doing the work
Job 1:10 The work of his *h* you have
4:3 weak *h* you used to strengthen
5:12 *h* do not work with effect
5:18 but his own *h* do the healing
9:30 cleansed my *h* in potash
10:3 reject . . . work of your *h*
10:8 Your own *h* have shaped me so
11:10 moves on and *h* someone over
14:15 For the work of your *h* you
16:11 God *h* me over to young boys
16:11 into the *h* of wicked ones
17:3 shake *h* with me in pledge
17:9 the one with clean *h* keeps
20:10 his own *h* will give back
22:30 for the cleanness of your *h*
27:23 One will clap his *h* at him
30:2 Even the power of their *h*
34:19 are the work of his *h*
34:37 Among us he claps his *h* and
36:32 In his *h* he has covered
41:8 Put your *h* upon it
Ps 7:3 exists any injustice in my *h*
8:6 over the works of your *h*
9:16 By the activity of his own *h*
18:20 cleanness of my *h* he repays
18:24 the cleanness of my *h* in
18:34 is teaching my *h* for warfare
19:1 the work of his *h* the expanse
22:16 they are at my *h* and my feet
24:4 innocent in his *h* and clean
26:6 shall wash my *h* in innocency
26:10 In whose *h* there is loose
28:2 When I raise my *h* to the
28:4 to the work of their *h*
28:5 Nor for the work of his *h*
47:1 All you peoples, clap your *h*
55:20 thrust out his *h* against
58:2 the very violence of your *h*
68:31 stretch out its *h* with gifts
73:13 I wash my *h* in innocence
76:5 men have found their *h*
78:72 skillfulness of his *h* he
81:6 own *h* got to be free even
90:17 work of our *h* do you firmly
90:17 work of our *h*, do you firmly
91:12 Upon their *h* they will carry
92:4 works of your *h* I cry out
95:5 own *h* formed the dry land
98:8 rivers . . . clap their *h*
102:25 are the work of your *h*
111:7 works of his *h* are truth and
115:4 work of the *h* of earthling
115:7 *H* . . . but they cannot feel
119:73 Your own *h* have made me
128:2 eat the toil of your own *h*
134:2 Raise your *h* in holiness
135:15 work of the *h* of earthling
138:8 the works of your own *h*
140:4 from the *h* of the wicked one
143:5 the work of your own *h*
143:6 have spread out my *h* to you
144:1 teaching my *h* for fighting
144:7 Thrust your *h* out from the
Pr 6:10 folding of the *h* in lying
6:17 *h* that are shedding innocent
12:14 doing of a man's *h* will
14:1 tears it down with her own *h*
17:18 is wanting in heart shakes *h*
21:25 his *h* have refused to work
22:26 to be among those striking *h*
24:33 folding of the *h* to lie down
30:4 wind in the hollow of both *h*
30:28 takes hold with its own *h*
31:13 is the delight of her *h*
31:16 from the fruitage of her *h*
31:19 Her *h* she has thrust out to
31:19 *h* take hold of the spindle
31:20 *h* she has thrust out to the
31:31 of the fruitage of her *h*, and
Ec 2:11 works of mine that my *h* had
4:5 stupid one is folding his *h* and
5:6 to wreck the work of your *h*
7:26 and whose *h* are fetters
10:18 the letting down of the *h*
Ca 5:5 my own *h* dripped with myrrh
5:14 His *h* are cylinders of gold
7:1 the work of an artisan's *h*
Isa 1:15 bloodshed your very *h* have
2:8 the work of one's *h* they bow
3:11 rendered by his own *h* will
5:12 work of his *h* they have
13:7 *h* themselves will drop down
17:8 altars, the work of his *h*
19:25 work of my *h*, Assyria, and
25:11 slap out his *h* in the midst
25:11 tricky movements of his *h*
29:23 children, the work of my *h*
31:7 *h* have made for yourselves
33:15 *h* clear from taking hold
35:3 Strengthen the weak *h*, you
37:19 workmanship of man's *h*
45:9 say: He has no *h*
45:11 activity of my *h* you people

Isa 45:12 my own *h* have stretched out
55:12 will all clap their *h*
60:21 the work of my *h*, for me
65:2 I have spread out my *h* all
65:22 the work of their own *h*
Jer 1:16 the works of their own *h*
2:37 with your *h* upon your head
6:24 Our *h* have dropped
10:3 *h* of the craftsman with the
10:9 of the *h* of a metalworker
23:14 the *h* of evildoers in
25:6 with the work of your *h*
25:7 with the work of your *h*
25:14 to the work of their *h*
30:6 *h* upon his loins like a
32:30 by the work of their *h*, is
33:13 *h* of the one taking the
38:4 *h* of the men of war who are
38:4 *h* of all the people, by
38:5 Look! He is in your *h*
40:4 that were upon your *h*
44:8 with the works of your *h*
44:25 with your *h* you people have
47:3 dropping down of their *h*
48:37 Upon all *h* there are cuts
50:43 his *h* have dropped down
La 1:17 Zion has spread out her *h*
2:15 clapped their *h*. They have
3:64 to the work of their *h*
4:2 the work of the *h* of a potter
4:6 to which no *h* turned helpfully
4:10 *h* of compassionate women
Eze 1:8 *h* of a man under their wings
6:11 Clap your *h* and stamp with
7:17 *h*, they keep dropping down
7:27 *h* of the people of the land
10:2 the hollows of both your *h*
10:7 *h* of the one clothed with
10:12 their *h* . . . full of eyes
10:21 of the *h* of earthling man
13:22 *h* of a wicked one strong
16:11 to put bracelets upon your *h*
21:7 and all *h* must drop down
22:14 or your *h* furnish strength
23:37 there is blood on their *h*
23:42 put bracelets on the *h* of
23:45 there is blood on their *h*
25:6 you clapped the *h* and you
Da 2:34 stone was cut out not by *h*
2:45 stone was cut not by *h*, and
3:15 can rescue you out of my *h*
10:10 knees and the palms of my *h*
Ho 14:3 to the work of our *h*
Jon 3:8 violence that was in their *h*
Mic 5:13 down to the work of your *h*
7:3 Their *h* are upon what is bad
Na 3:19 certainly clap their *h* at you
Hab 3:10 On high its *h* it lifted up
Zep 3:16 May your *h* not drop down
Hag 1:11 upon all the toil of the *h*
2:14 all the work of their *h* is
2:17 even all the work of your *h*
Zec 4:9 *h* of Zerubbabel have laid the
4:9 and his own *h* will finish it
8:9 *h* of you people be strong
8:13 May your *h* be strong
13:6 wounds . . . between your *h*
Mt 4:6 will carry you on their *h*
15:2 not wash their *h* when about
15:20 take a meal with unwashed *h*
17:12 to suffer at their *h*
17:22 to be betrayed into men's *h*
18:8 be thrown with two *h* or two
19:13 to put his *h* upon them and
19:15 he put his *h* upon them and
26:45 into the *h* of sinners
26:50 laid *h* on Jesus and took him
27:24 and washed his *h* before the
Mr 5:23 put your *h* upon her that she
6:2 be performed through his *h*
6:5 to lay his *h* upon a few sickly
7:2 eat their meal with defiled *h*
7:3 wash their *h* up to the elbow
7:5 their meal with defiled *h*
8:23 he laid his *h* upon him and
8:25 *h* again upon the man's eyes
9:31 delivered into men's *h*, and
9:43 with two *h* to go off into
10:16 laying his *h* upon them
14:41 into the *h* of sinners
14:46 they laid their *h* upon him
14:58 temple . . . made with *h*
14:58 another not made with *h*
Lu 1:74 rescued from the *h* of enemies
Lu 4:11 will carry you on their *h*
4:40 laying his *h* upon each one
6:1 rubbing them with their *h*
9:44 delivered into the *h* of men
13:13 And he laid his *h* on her
20:19 sought to get their *h* on him
21:12 will lay their *h* upon you
22:53 stretch out your *h* against
23:46 Father, into your *h* I entrust
24:7 into the *h* of sinful men and
24:39 See my *h* and my feet, that
24:40 showed them his *h* and his
24:50 lifted up his *h* and blessed
Joh 7:44 no one did lay his *h* upon
11:44 his feet and *h* bound with
13:3 given all things into his *h*
13:9 but also my *h* and my head
20:20 showed them both his *h*
20:25 his *h* the print of the nails
20:27 and see my *h*, and take
21:18 you will stretch out your *h*
Ac 4:3 they laid their *h* upon them
5:12 *h* of the apostles many signs
5:18 laid *h* upon the apostles
6:6 these laid their *h* upon them
7:41 in the works of their *h*
7:48 dwell in houses made with *h*
7:57 put their *h* over their ears
8:17 laying their *h* upon them
8:18 laying on of the *h* of the
8:19 I lay my *h* may receive holy
9:12 lay his *h* upon him that he
9:17 laid his *h* upon him and said
12:1 applied his *h* to mistreating
12:7 his chains fell off his *h*
13:3 laid their *h* upon them and
14:3 portents . . . through their *h*
17:25 attended to by human *h* as if
19:6 Paul laid his *h* upon them
19:11 through the *h* of Paul
19:26 are made by *h* are not gods
20:34 these *h* have attended to the
21:11 bound his own feet and *h* and
21:11 *h* of people of the nations
21:27 they laid their *h* upon him
27:19 with their own *h*, they
28:8 his *h* upon him and healed
28:17 into the *h* of the Romans
Ro 10:21 spread out my *h* toward a
1Co 4:12 working with our own *h*
15:24 *h* over the kingdom to his
2Co 5:1 a house not made with *h*
11:33 basket and escaped his *h*
Eph 2:11 made in the flesh with *h*
4:28 with his *h* what is good
Col 2:11 performed without *h* by the
1Th 2:14 suffering at the *h* of your
2:14 at the *h* of the Jews
4:11 and work with your *h*, just
1Ti 2:8 prayer, lifting up loyal *h*
4:14 older men laid their *h* upon
5:22 Never lay your *h* hastily
2Ti 1:6 through the laying of my *h*
Heb 1:10 heavens . . . works of your *h*
2:7 over the works of your *h*
6:2 and the laying on of the *h*
9:11 tent not made with *h*, that
9:24 a holy place made with *h*
10:31 into the *h* of the living God
12:12 straighten up the *h* that
Jas 4:8 Cleanse your *h*, you sinners
1Jo 1:1 and our *h* felt, concerning
Re 7:9 were palm branches in their *h*
9:20 of the works of their *h*

Handshake
Pr 6:1 your *h* even to the stranger

Handshaking
Pr 11:15 one hating *h* is keeping

Handsome
1Sa 9:2 name was Saul, young and *h*
16:12 and *h* in appearance
Ps 45:2 more *h* than the sons of men

Handsomeness
Isa 33:17 king in his *h* is what your
Zec 9:17 and how great his *h* is!

Handsomer
1Sa 9:2 no man . . . that was *h* than he

Handstaves
Eze 39:9 the *h* and with the lances

Handwritten
Col 2:14 blotted out the *h* document

Hanes
Isa 30:4 his own envoys reach even *H*

Hang
Ge 40:19 certainly *h* you upon a stake
Ex 26:12 is to *h* over the back of the
De 28:60 the diseases . . . *h* onto you
Jos 10:26 *h* them upon five stakes
Jg 5:2 the hair *h* loose in Israel for
Es 5:14 they should *h* Mordecai on it
6:4 to *h* Mordecai on the stake
7:9 king said: You men, *h* him on
7:10 to *h* Haman on the stake that
Isa 22:24 *h* upon him all the glory
33:23 Your ropes must *h* loose
Eze 15:3 to *h* any kind of utensil
Heb 12:12 the hands that *h* down and

Hanged
Ge 41:13 to my office, but him he *h*
Jos 8:29 he *h* the king of Ai upon a
2Sa 4:12 *h* them by the pool in Hebron
21:12 the Philistines had *h* them
Es 2:23 got to be *h* on a stake
8:7 him they have *h* on the stake
9:13 ten sons of Haman be *h* upon
9:14 the ten sons of Haman were *h*
9:25 *h* him and his sons upon the
La 5:12 have been *h* by just their hand
Mt 27:5 and went off and *h* himself
Ga 3:13 is every man *h* upon a stake

Hanging
Jos 10:26 *h* upon the stakes until the
1Ki 7:29 were wreaths in *h* work
Job 26:7 *H* the earth upon nothing
Lu 19:48 kept *h* onto him to hear him
Ac 5:30 slew, *h* him upon a stake
10:39 by *h* him on a stake
28:4 creature *h* from his hand

Hangings
Ex 27:9 has *h* of fine twisted linen
27:11 *h* being for a hundred cubits
27:12 the *h* are of fifty cubits
27:14 fifteen cubits of *h* to one
27:15 there are fifteen cubits of *h*
35:17 the *h* of the courtyard, its
38:9 the *h* of the courtyard were of
38:12 the *h* were for fifty cubits
38:14 *h* were for fifteen cubits to
38:15 *h* were for fifteen cubits
38:16 the *h* of the courtyard round
38:18 with the *h* of the courtyard
39:40 the *h* of the courtyard, its
Nu 3:26 *h* of the courtyard and the
4:26 *h* of the courtyard and the

Hangs
Mt 22:40 the whole Law *h*, and the

Hannah
1Sa 1:2 the name of the one being *H*
1:2 but *H* had no children
1:5 to *H* he gave one portion
1:5 it was *H* that he loved, and
1:8 *H*, why do you weep, and why
1:9 *H* got up after they had eaten
1:13 As for *H*, she was speaking
1:15 At this *H* answered and said
1:19 intercourse with *H* his wife
1:20 that *H* became pregnant and
1:22 As for *H*, she did not go up
2:1 And *H* went on to pray and say
2:21 turned his attention to *H*, so

Hannathon
Jos 19:14 around it on the north to *H*

Hanniel
Nu 34:23 of Manasseh a chieftain, *H*
1Ch 7:39 of Ulla were Ara and *H* and

Hanoch
Ge 25:4 sons of Midian were . . . *H* and
46:9 sons of Reuben were *H* and
Ex 6:14 sons of Reuben . . . were *H*
Nu 26:5 Reuben's sons: Of *H* the
1Ch 1:33 sons of Midian . . . *H*
5:3 the sons of Reuben . . . *H*

Hanochites
Nu 26:5 Of Hanoch the family of the *H*

Hanun
2Sa 10:1 *H* his son began to reign
10:2 *H* the son of Nahash, just
10:3 said to *H* their lord: Is
10:4 *H* took the servants of David

1Ch 19:2 toward *H* the son of Nahash
19:2 to *H* to comfort him
19:3 said to *H:* Is David honoring
19:4 *H* took the servants of David
19:6 and *H* and the sons of Ammon
Ne 3:13 *H* and the inhabitants of
3:30 *H* the sixth son of Zalaph

Hapharaim
Jos 19:19 *H* and Shion and Anaharath

Happen
Ge 12:12 *h* that the Egyptians will
24:12 cause it to *h*, please, before
49:1 tell you what will *h* to you
Le 16:17 *h* to be in the tent of
Nu 9:10 *h* to be unclean by a soul or
9:13 *h* to be off on a journey and
De 19:11 there should *h* to be a man
Ru 2:13 I myself may not *h* to be like
1Sa 1:28 the days that he does *h* to be
18:30 *h* that as often as they
19:3 see what will *h*, and I shall
20:2 This does not *h*
2Sa 18:22 Let, now, *h* whatever will
18:23 Let, now, *h* whatever will
1Ki 12:31 not *h* to be of the sons of
14:3 is going to *h* to the boy
2Ki 2:10 it will *h* to you that way
2:10 if you do not, it will not *h*
1Ch 24:2 did not *h* to have any sons
26:10 not *h* to be the firstborn
2Ch 16:8 *h* to be a very great
Ne 1:9 should *h* to be at the end of
13:6 did not *h* to be in Jerusalem
Job 38:4 Where did you *h* to be when I
Ec 6:12 what will *h* after him under
Isa 23:15 *h* to Tyre as in the song of
41:22 things that are going to *h*
Jer 14:13 no famine to *h* to you
39:16 *h* before you in that day
Eze 15:2 vine tree *h* to be different
16:16 and it should not *h*
20:32 positively not *h*, in that
Mt 9:29 to your faith let it *h* to you
15:28 let it *h* to you as you wish
21:21 you have faith . . . it will *h*
Mr 13:30 until all these things *h*
Lu 20:16 they said: Never may that *h!*
22:49 saw what was going to *h*
Joh 5:14 something worse does not *h*
Ac 20:22 things that will *h* to me in
28:6 nothing hurtful *h* to him
Ro 3:4 Never may that *h!* But let God
3:6 Never may that *h!*
3:31 Never may that *h!* On the
6:2 Never may that *h!* Seeing that
6:15 Never may that *h!*
7:13 Never may that *h!* But sin did
11:1 Never may that *h!* For I also
11:11 Never may that *h!* But by
1Co 6:15 Never may that *h!*
Ga 2:17 May that never *h!*
3:21 May that never *h!* For if

Happened
Ge 12:14 it *h* that, as soon as Abram
25:20 Isaac *h* to be forty years old
34:5 sons *h* to be with his herd
37:2 *h* to be tending sheep with
38:5 he *h* to be in Achzib at the
38:24 three months later it *h*
39:11 But it *h* that on this day as
41:13 interpreted to us so it *h*
Ex 32:1 not know what has *h* to him
32:23 do not know what has *h* to
Nu 9:6 *h* to be men who had become
19:18 souls that *h* to be there and
36:3 *h* to get them as wives, the
De 22:23 there *h* to be a virgin girl
Jos 2:23 things that had *h* to them
5:13 Joshua *h* to be by Jericho
Jg 7:1 Midian *h* to be on the north of
7:8 it *h* to be down below him in
8:11 the camp *h* to be off guard
9:51 a strong tower *h* to be in the
13:2 there *h* to be a certain man
17:1 there *h* to be a man of the
17:7 there *h* to be a young man of
19:1 it *h* in those days that there
1Sa 1:1 there *h* to be a certain man
2:27 *h* to be in Egypt as slaves to
4:16 What is the thing that has *h*
6:9 accident it was that *h* to us
8:2 firstborn son *h* to be Joel
1Sa 9:1 *h* to be a man of Benjamin
9:2 *h* to have a son whose name
10:11 has *h* to the son of Kish
13:22 *h* on the day of battle that
14:25 honey *h* to be over all the
20:26 *h* so that he is not clean
21:6 *h* to be no bread there but
22:4 that David *h* to be in the
25:7 *h* themselves to be with us
25:7 days they *h* to be in Carmel
25:15 we *h* to be in the field
25:16 that we *h* to be with them
28:20 *h* to be no power in him
29:3 *h* to be with me here a year
2Sa 2:18 sons of Zeruiah *h* to be
4:2 *h* to belong to the son of
4:4 Five years old he *h* to be
5:2 Saul *h* to be king over us
8:7 shields of gold that *h* to be
12:1 that *h* to be in one city
12:2 rich man *h* to have very
13:20 brother that *h* to be with
15:2 *h* to have a legal case to
20:1 Now there *h* to be there a
21:20 there *h* to be a man of
23:11 *h* to be a tract of the field
24:16 angel himself *h* to be close
1Ki 3:12 has not *h* to be before you
3:13 *h* to be any among the kings
10:2 that *h* to be close to her
14:9 who *h* to be prior to you
16:33 that *h* to be prior to him
21:1 that *h* to belong to Naboth
2Ki 7:3 *h* to be at the entrance of the
7:20 it *h* to him like that, when
8:17 *h* to be when he became king
9:14 *h* to be keeping guard at
14:2 he *h* to be when he began to
15:2 *h* to be when he began to
15:33 he *h* to be when he began to
17:2 *h* to be prior to him
18:2 *h* to be when he began to
18:5 *h* to be prior to him
24:7 *h* to belong to the king of
25:16 *h* to be no way to tell the
25:25 *h* to be with him in Mizpah
1Ch 7:23 that she *h* to be in his house
9:20 *h* to be leader over them in
11:2 even while Saul *h* to be king
11:13 that *h* to be with David at
11:13 *h* to be a tract of the field
16:19 you *h* to be few in number
17:13 that *h* to be prior to you
18:7 that *h* to be on the servants
20:6 when there *h* to be a man of
2Ch 1:3 tent of meeting . . . *h* to be
1:12 were prior to you *h* to have
9:1 *h* to be close to her heart
12:12 *h* to be good things in Judah
13:7 *h* to be young and
14:14 *h* to be much to plunder in
21:20 years old he *h* to be when
22:11 *h* to be the sister of
27:8 *h* to be when he began to
28:9 *h* to be a prophet of Jehovah
29:34 *h* to be too few, and they
32:31 portent that had *h* in the
Ne 1:1 *h* to be in Shushan the castle
1:11 *h* to be cupbearer to the king
2:1 never had I *h* to be gloomy
3:26 *h* to be dwellers in Ophel
5:18 *h* to be made ready daily
8:5 he *h* to be above all the people
12:12 *h* to be priests, the heads
13:26 loved of his God he *h* to be
Es 2:5 a Jew, *h* to be in Shushan the
2:12 had *h* to her according to the
2:20 she *h* to be under care by him
Job 1:1 *h* to be a man in the land of
1:14 cattle themselves *h* to be
29:4 *h* to be in the days of my
Ps 63:*super* *h* to be in the wilderness
105:12 they *h* to be few in number
142:*super* he *h* to be in the cave
Ec 1:12 the congregator, *h* to be king
1:16 anyone that *h* to be before me
2:7 those who *h* to be before me in
2:9 *h* to be before me in Jerusalem
3:15 *h* to be, it had already been
4:16 those before whom he *h* to be
7:10 *h* that the former days proved
7:19 ten men in power who *h* to be
12:7 the earth just as it *h* to be
Ca 8:11 that Solomon *h* to have in
Jer 2:10 anything like this has *h*
22:24 *h* to be the seal ring on
26:18 *h* to be prophesying in the
26:20 there also *h* to be a man
28:8 the prophets that *h* to be
32:2 *h* to be under restraint in
32:24 what you have said has *h*
34:5 kings who *h* to be prior to
39:15 *h* to be shut up in the
40:3 this thing has *h* to you
41:2 men that *h* to be with him
41:3 Jews who *h* to be with him
46:2 who *h* to be by the river
52:20 *h* to be no weight taken of
52:25 *h* to be commissioner over
La 1:7 *h* to be from days of long ago
5:1 what has *h* to us. Do look and
Eze 2:5 prophet himself *h* to be in
9:3 cherubs over which it *h* to be
16:22 you *h* to be naked and nude
16:22 in your blood you *h* to be
16:49 *h* to belong to her and her
23:2 one mother, there *h* to be
27:7 your cloth expanse *h* to be
27:8 *h* to be in you; they were
27:9 skilled ones *h* to be in you
27:10 *h* to be in your military
27:11 *h* to be in your own towers
33:24 Abraham *h* to be just one
35:10 *h* to be right there
Da 1:6 *h* to be among them some of
2:31 *h* to be beholding, and
4:4 *h* to be at ease in my house
4:10 *h* to be beholding, and, look!
4:29 *h* to be walking upon the
5:19 Whom he *h* to want to, he
5:19 whom he *h* to want to, he was
5:19 whom he *h* to want to, he was
5:19 whom he *h* to want to, he was
7:2 *h* to be beholding in my
7:13 son of man *h* to be coming
8:2 *h* to be by the watercourse of
10:2 Daniel, *h* to be mourning
10:4 *h* to be on the bank of the
10:7 men that *h* to be with me
10:9 *h* to be fast asleep upon my
Am 1:1 *h* to be among the sheep
Ob 16 as though they had never *h* to be
Jon 4:2 I *h* to be on my own ground
Zep 3:18 absent from you they *h* to be
Hag 2:16 when those things *h* to be
Zec 3:3 *h* to be clothed in befouled
7:7 Jerusalem *h* to be inhabited
Mt 18:31 saw the things that had *h*
18:31 all the things that had *h*
26:6 Jesus *h* to be in Bethany in
28:11 all the things that had *h*
Mr 2:15 he *h* to be reclining at the
2:23 it *h* that he was proceeding
5:14 see what it was that had *h*
5:16 *h* to the demon-possessed man
5:33 knowing what had *h* to her
Lu 1:5 *h* to be a certain priest named
4:23 as having *h* in Capernaum
6:1 on a sabbath he *h* to be passing
8:34 the herders saw what had *h*
8:35 turned out to see what had *h*
8:56 to tell no one what had *h*
Joh 14:22 what has *h* that you intend
Ac 3:10 ecstasy at what had *h* to him
5:7 not knowing what had *h*
7:40 not know what has *h* to him
9:37 she *h* to fall sick and die
13:12 seeing what had *h*, became a
16:16 *h* that as we were going to
17:17 those who *h* to be on hand
28:8 *h* that the father of Publius
Ro 11:25 *h* in part to Israel until
1Co 12:2 just as you *h* to be led
2Co 1:8 tribulation that *h* to us in
1Th 3:4 just as it has also *h* and as
2Ti 1:17 when he *h* to be in Rome, he
3:11 the sort of things that *h*
2Pe 2:22 true proverb has *h* to them

Happening
1Ki 5:4 and there is nothing bad *h*
Ec 8:14 to whom it is *h* as if for the
8:14 wicked ones to whom it is *h*
Mt 27:54 earthquake and the things *h*
Mr 9:21 How long has this been *h*
13:29 when you see these things *h*
Lu 9:7 heard of all the things *h*
Ac 12:9 he did not know what was *h*

1Pe 4:12 is *h* to you for a trial

Happens
Le 15:10 that *h* to be under him will
Nu 5:17 dust that *h* to be on the floor
30:6 *h* to belong to a husband, and
De 20:14 *h* to be in the city, all its
21:16 to his sons what he *h* to
21:18 a man *h* to have a son who is
22:6 a bird's nest *h* to be before
23:10 there *h* to be in you a man
Jos 20:6 high priest who *h* to be in
2Sa 15:4 *h* to have a legal case or
Pr 3:27 *h* to be in the power of your
Eze 15:5 When it *h* to be intact, it
18:5 in case he *h* to be righteous
44:22 *h* to be the widow of a
Zec 14:15 that *h* to be in those camps
Mt 18:13 And if he *h* to find it, I

Happier
1Co 7:40 *h* if she remains as she is

Happiness
Ge 30:13 Leah said: With my *h*
Ac 20:35 is more *h* in giving than
Ro 4:6 David also speaks of the *h*
4:9 Does this *h*, then, come upon
Ga 4:15 Where, then, is that *h* you

Happizzez
1Ch 24:15 for *H* the eighteenth

Happy
Ge 30:13 certainly pronounce me *h*
De 33:29 *H* you are, O Israel! Who is
1Ki 10:8 *H* are your men
10:8 *h* are these servants of yours
2Ch 9:7 *H* are your men, and
9:7 *h* are these servants of yours
Job 5:17 *H* is the man whom God
29:11 proceeded to pronounce me *h*
Ps 1:1 *H* is the man that has not
2:12 *H* are all those taking
32:1 *H* is the one whose revolt is
32:2 *H* is the man to whose account
33:12 *H* is the nation whose God is
34:8 *H* is the able-bodied man that
40:4 *H* is the able-bodied man that
41:1 *H* is anyone acting with
41:2 pronounced *h* in the earth
65:4 *H* is the one you choose and
72:17 all nations pronounce him *h*
84:4 *H* are those dwelling in your
84:5 *H* are the men whose strength
84:12 *h* is the man that is
89:15 *H* are the people knowing the
94:12 *H* is the able-bodied man
106:3 *H* are those observing justice
112:1 *H* is the man in fear of
119:1 *H* are the ones faultless in
119:2 *H* are those observing his
127:5 *H* is the able-bodied man
128:1 *H* is everyone fearing Jehovah
128:2 *H* you will be and it will
137:8 *H* will he be that rewards
137:9 *H* will he be that grabs
144:15 *H* is the people for whom it
144:15 *H* is the people whose God
146:5 *H* is the one who has the God
Pr 3:13 *H* is the man that has found
3:18 those . . . are to be called *h*
8:32 *h* are the ones that keep my
8:34 *H* is the man that is
14:21 *h* is he who is showing favor
16:20 *h* is he that is trusting in
20:7 *H* are his sons after him
28:14 *H* is the man that is feeling
29:18 *h* are they that are keeping
31:28 proceeded to pronounce her *h*
Ec 10:17 *H* are you, O land, when your
Ca 6:9 proceeded to pronounce her *h*
Isa 30:18 *H* are all those keeping in
32:20 *H* are you people who are
56:2 *H* is the mortal man that
Da 12:12 *H* is the one who is keeping
Zep 3:17 joyful over you with *h* cries
Mal 3:12 will have to pronounce you *h*
3:15 presumptuous people *h*
Mt 5:3 *H* are those conscious of their
5:4 *H* are those who mourn, since
5:5 *H* are the mild-tempered ones
5:6 *H* are those hungering and
5:7 *H* are the merciful, since they
5:8 *H* are the pure in heart, since
5:9 *H* are the peaceable, since
Mt 5:10 *H* are those . . . persecuted
5:11 *H* . . . when people reproach
11:6 *h* is he that finds no cause
13:16 *h* are your eyes because they
16:17 *H* you are, Simon son of
24:46 *H* is that slave if his
Lu 1:45 *H* too is she that believed
1:48 will pronounce me *h*
6:20 *H* are you poor, because yours
6:21 *H* are you who hunger now
6:21 *H* are you who weep now
6:22 *H* are you whenever men hate
7:23 *h* is he who has not stumbled
10:23 *H* are the eyes that behold
11:27 *H* is the womb that carried
11:28 *H* are those hearing the word
12:37 *H* are those slaves whom the
12:38 finds them thus, *h* are they
12:43 *H* is that slave, if his
14:14 you will be *h*, because they
14:15 *H* is he who eats bread in
23:29 *H* are the barren women, and
Joh 13:17 *h* you are if you do them
20:29 *H* are those who do not see
Ac 26:2 *h* that it is before you I am
Ro 4:7 *H* are those . . . pardoned
4:8 *h* is the man whose sin Jehovah
14:22 *H* is the man that does not
1Ti 1:11 good news of the *h* God
6:15 the *h* and only Potentate
Tit 2:13 for the *h* hope and glorious
Jas 1:12 *H* is the man that keeps on
1:25 doer of the work, will be *h*
5:11 *h* those who have endured
1Pe 3:14 should suffer . . . you are *h*
4:14 you are *h*, because the
Re 1:3 *H* is he who reads aloud and
14:13 *H* are the dead who die in
16:15 *H* is the one that stays
19:9 *H* are those invited to the
20:6 *H* and holy is anyone having
22:7 *H* is anyone observing the
22:14 *H* are those who wash their

Hara
1Ch 5:26 and *H* and the river Gozan to

Haradah
Nu 33:24 and went camping in *H*
33:25 they pulled away from *H* and

Haran
Ge 11:26 father to Abram, Nahor and *H*
11:27 Terah became father . . . *H*
11:27 and *H* became father to Lot
11:28 *H* died while in company
11:29 Milcah, the daughter of *H*
11:31 Lot, the son of *H*, his
11:31 In time they came to *H* and
11:32 Then Terah died in *H*
12:4 Abram . . . went out from *H*
12:5 whom they had acquired in *H*
27:43 to Laban my brother at *H*
28:10 and kept going to *H*
29:4 they said: We are from *H*
2Ki 19:12 Gozan and *H* and Rezeph and
1Ch 2:46 she gave birth to *H* and Moza
2:46 *H*, he became father to Gazez
23:9 sons of Shimei . . . *H*, three
Isa 37:12 *H* and Rezeph and the sons
Eze 27:23 *H* and Canneh and Eden
Ac 7:2 he took up residence in *H*
7:4 and took up residence in *H*

Hararite
2Sa 23:11 the son of Agee the *H*
23:33 Shammah the *H*, Ahiam the
23:33 the son of Sharar the *H*
1Ch 11:34 the son of Shagee the *H*
11:35 the son of Sacar the *H*

Harass
Ex 23:22, 22 and *h* those who *h* you
Nu 33:55 they will indeed *h* you on
Da 7:25 *h* continually the holy ones
Lu 3:14 Do not *h* anybody or accuse

Harassing
Ge 49:23 *h* him and shot at him and
Nu 10:9 the oppressor who is *h* you
25:17 a *h* of the Midianites, and
25:18 they are *h* you with their

Harbona
Es 1:10 said to Mehuman, Biztha, *H*
7:9 *H*, one of the court officials

Harbor
Job 30:21 you *h* animosity toward me
Ps 55:3 in anger they *h* animosity
Ac 27:12 *h* was inconvenient for
27:12 a *h* of Crete that opens

Harbored
Ge 27:41 Esau *h* animosity for Jacob

Harboring
Ge 49:23 kept *h* animosity against him
50:15 Joseph is *h* animosity

Harbors
Job 16:9 he *h* animosity against me

Hard
Ge 35:16 *h* with her in making the
Ex 1:14 life bitter with *h* slavery at
6:9 and for the *h* slavery
18:26 A *h* case they would bring to
De 1:17 the case that is too *h* for you
2:30 his heart become *h*, in order
15:18 should not be something *h*
26:6 putting *h* slavery upon us
Jg 5:26 the mallet of *h* workers
1Sa 1:15 *h* pressed in spirit I am
5:7 his hand has been *h* against us
13:6 the people were *h* pressed
14:24 were *h* pressed on that day
2Sa 2:17 fighting . . . extremely *h*
5:17 to the place *h* to approach
23:14 in the place *h* to approach
1Ki 11:28 young man was a *h* worker
12:4 made our yoke *h*, and, as for
12:4 the *h* service of your father
1Ch 11:16 in the place *h* to approach
29:2 to be set with *h* mortar
2Ch 10:4 his part, made our yoke *h*
10:4 *h* service of your father and
Job 10:3 of the *h* work of your hands
19:3 that you deal so *h* with me
30:25 the one having a *h* day
37:18 *H* like a molten mirror
Ps 105:44 *h* work of national groups
118:13 You pushed me *h* that I
127:1 builders have worked *h* on it
Pr 1:27 and *h* times come upon you
16:26 The soul of the *h* worker has
16:26 worker has worked *h* for him
16:26 his mouth has pressed him *h*
29:1 but making his neck *h* will
Ec 1:3 a man have in all his *h* work
1:3 which he works *h* under the sun
2:10 because of all my *h* work, and
2:10 portion from all my *h* work
2:11 toward the *h* work that I had
2:11 I had worked *h* to accomplish
2:18 even I, hated all my *h* work
2:18 I was working *h* under the sun
2:19 control over all my *h* work
2:19 work at which I worked *h* and
2:20 despair over all the *h* work
2:20 I had worked *h* under the sun
2:21 *h* work has been with wisdom
2:21 not worked *h* at such a thing
2:22 to have for all his *h* work
2:22 he is working *h* under the sun
2:24 good because of his *h* work
3:9 in what he is working *h* at
3:13 see good for all his *h* work
4:4 have seen all the *h* work and
4:6 a double handful of *h* work and
4:8 is no end to all his *h* work
4:8 And for whom am I working *h*
4:9 a good reward for their *h* work
5:15 one carry away for his *h* work
5:16 keeps working *h* for the wind
5:18 see good for all his *h* work
5:18 he works *h* under the sun for
5:19 and to rejoice in his *h* work
6:7 *h* work of mankind is for their
8:15 in their *h* work for the days
8:17 keep working *h* to seek, yet
9:9 in life and in your *h* work
9:9 are working *h* under the sun
10:15 *h* work of the stupid ones
Isa 8:21 *h* pressed and hungry
8:22 *h* times and gloominess with
14:3 *h* slavery in which you were
19:4 into the hand of a *h* master
21:2 *h* vision that has been told
27:1 *h* and great and strong sword
27:8 blast, a *h* one in the day
30:6 distress and *h* conditions
48:4 knowing that you are *h* and

Isa 53:7 He was *h* pressed, and he
54:11 laying with *h* mortar your
63:17 heart *h* against the fear of
Jer 20:18 to see *h* work and grief
Eze 2:4 of face and *h* of heart
3:8 made your face exactly as *h*
3:8 your forehead exactly as *h* as
Da 5:20 and his own spirit became *h*
Mt 14:24 *h* put to it by the waves
Mr 6:48 *h* put to it in their rowing
Lu 11:46 with loads *h* to be borne
Joh 12:40 made their hearts *h*, that
Ac 26:14 against the goads makes it *h*
Ro 16:12 women who are working *h* in
2Co 8:13 for others, but *h* on you
Eph 4:28 but rather let him do *h* work
Php 2:16 in vain or work *h* in vain
Col 1:29 indeed working *h*, exerting
1Th 5:12 working *h* among you and
1Ti 4:10 are working *h* and exerting
5:17 who work *h* in speaking and
2Ti 3:1 critical times *h* to deal with
Heb 5:11 to say and *h* to be explained
Jas 3:4 big and are driven by *h* winds
1Pe 2:18 but also to those *h* to please
2Pe 3:16 some things *h* to understand
Jude 3 put up a *h* fight for the faith

Harden
De 10:16 not *h* your necks any longer
15:7 you must not *h* your heart or
Ne 9:16 proceeded to *h* their neck
Ps 95:8 *h* your heart as at Meribah
Jer 17:23 *h* their neck in order not
Heb 3:8 do not *h* your hearts as on
3:15 do not *h* your hearts as on
4:7 do not *h* your hearts

Hardened
Ne 9:17 *h* their neck and appointed
9:29 and their neck they *h*, and
Jer 19:15 they have *h* their neck in
Heb 3:13 become *h* by the deceptive

Hardening
2Ki 17:14 kept *h* their necks like the
2Ch 36:13 *h* his heart so as not to
Pr 28:14 *h* his heart will fall into
Jer 7:26 they kept *h* their neck
Ac 19:9 some went on *h* themselves

Harder
Jg 4:24, 24 went on getting *h* and *h*
Jer 5:3 their faces *h* than a crag
Eze 3:9 *h* than flint, I have made

Hardheaded
Eze 3:7 Israel are *h* and hardhearted

Hardhearted
Eze 3:7 Israel are hardheaded and *h*

Hardheartedness
Mt 19:8 out of regard for your *h*
Mr 10:5 Out of regard for your *h*

Hardly
Ca 3:4 *H* had I passed on from them
Ac 27:16 *h* able to get possession
Ro 5:7 For *h* will anyone die for a

Hardness
De 9:27 Do not turn your face to the *h*
Da 2:41 *h* of iron will prove to be in
Ro 2:5 *h* and unrepentant heart you are

Hardship
Ex 18:8 all the *h* that had befallen
Nu 20:14 the *h* that has overtaken us
Ne 9:32 not let all the *h* that has
Job 10:17, 17 *H* after *h* is with me
Ps 60:3 caused your people to see *h*
La 3:5 with poisonous plant and *h*

Hardworking
2Ti 2:6 *h* farmer must be the first to

Hare
Le 11:6 the *h*, because it is a chewer
De 14:7 you must not eat . . . the *h*

Hareph
1Ch 2:51 *H* the father of Beth-gader

Harhaiah
Ne 3:8 Uzziel the son of *H*

Harhas
2Ki 22:14 Tikvah the son of *H*
2Ch 34:22 Tikvah the son of *H*

Harhur
Ezr 2:51 the sons of *H*
Ne 7:53 sons of Hakupha, the sons of *H*

Harim
1Ch 24:8 for *H* the third, for Seorim
Ezr 2:32 sons of *H*, three hundred and
2:39 sons of *H*, a thousand and
10:21 sons of *H*, Maaseiah and
10:31 the sons of *H*, Eliezer
Ne 3:11 Malchijah the son of *H* and
7:35 sons of *H*, three hundred and
7:42 sons of *H*, a thousand and
10:5 *H*, Meremoth, Obadiah
10:27 Malluch, *H*, Baanah
12:15 for *H*, Adna; for Meraioth

Hariph
Ne 7:24 sons of *H*, a hundred and
10:19 *H*, Anathoth, Nebai

Hariphite
1Ch 12:5 and Shephatiah the *H*

Harlot
Ge 38:15 at once took her for a *h*
38:24 Tamar . . . has played the *h*
De 23:18 not bring the hire of a *h*
Ho 4:18 treated woman as a *h*
1Co 6:15 make them members of a *h*
6:16 is joined to a *h* is one body
Heb 11:31 Rahab the *h* did not perish
Jas 2:25 also Rahab the *h* declared
Re 17:1 judgment upon the great *h*
17:15 where the *h* is sitting, mean
17:16 hate the *h* and will make
19:2 judgment upon the great *h*

Harlotry
Ge 38:24 she is also pregnant by her *h*

Harlots
Ho 4:10 actually treat women as *h*
4:14 it is with the *h* that they
5:3 you have treated women like *h*
Mt 21:31 the *h* are going ahead of you
21:32 and the *h* believed him, and
Lu 15:30 your means of living with *h*
Re 17:5 mother of the *h* and of the

Harm
Ge 31:7 not allowed him to do me *h*
31:29 power of my hand to do *h* to
31:52 pillar against me for *h*
43:6 Why did you have to do *h* to
Nu 20:15 Egyptians began doing *h* to us
Ezr 4:22 *h* may not increase to the
Ne 6:2 they were scheming to do me *h*
Isa 11:9 They will not do any *h* or
29:20 those keeping alert to do *h*
65:25 do no *h* nor cause any ruin
Ac 28:5 the fire and suffered no *h*
1Pe 3:13 the man that will *h* you if
Re 6:6 do not *h* the olive oil and the
7:2 to *h* the earth and the sea
7:3 Do not *h* the earth or the sea
9:4 told to *h* no vegetation of
9:19 and with these they do *h*
11:5 if anyone wants to *h* them
11:5 if anyone should want to *h*

Har–Magedon
Re 16:16 that is called in Hebrew *H*

Harmed
Nu 16:15 nor have I *h* one of them
Re 2:11 be *h* by the second death

Harmful
Isa 10:1 are enacting *h* regulations
55:7 and the *h* man his thoughts
Ho 6:8 of practicers of what is *h*
Mic 2:1 who are scheming what is *h*
2Th 3:2 delivered from *h* . . . men, for

Harming
1Th 4:6 go to the point of *h* and

Harmless
Le 13:39 it is a *h* eruption. It has
Pr 13:6 the one who is *h* in his way

Harmon
Am 4:3 certainly be thrown out to *H*

Harmoniously
Eph 2:21 being *h* joined together, is
4:16 being *h* joined together and
Col 2:2 *h* joined together in love and
2:19 *h* joined together by means

Harmony
Ge 33:10 in *h* with its purpose I have
1Sa 2:35 *h* with what is in my heart
11:10 do to us in *h* with all that
23:20 *h* with the craving of your
Joh 3:21 worked in *h* with God
Ro 3:8 judgment . . . in *h* with justice
8:8 who are in *h* with the flesh
8:9 *h*, not with the flesh, but
2Co 6:15 *h* is there between Christ
Eph 2:3 in *h* with the desires of our
Php 1:20 *h* with my eager expectation
1Th 2:11 In *h* with that you well
Heb 2:2 retribution in *h* with justice
1Pe 4:19 suffering in *h* with the will

Harnepher
1Ch 7:36 of Zophah were Suah and *H*

Harness
Jer 46:4 *H* the horses, and mount

Harnessing
Ho 10:10 a *h* of them to their two

Harod
Jg 7:1 camping at the well of *H*; and

Harodite
2Sa 23:25 Shammah the *H*, Elika the
23:25 Elika the *H*

Haroeh
1Ch 2:52 *H*, half of the Menuhoth

Harorite
1Ch 11:27 Shammoth the *H*, Helez the

Harosheth
Jg 4:2 he was dwelling in *H* of the
4:13 out of *H* of the nations to
4:16 as far as *H* of the nations

Harp
Ge 4:21 those who handle the *h* and
31:27 with tambourine and with *h*
1Sa 10:5 tambourine and flute and *h*
16:16 man playing upon the *h*
16:23 David took the *h* and played
1Ch 25:3 prophesying with the *h* for
Job 21:12 with the tambourine and *h*
30:31 my *h* came to be merely for
Ps 33:2 thanks to Jehovah on the *h*
43:4 I will laud you on the *h*
49:4 On a *h* I shall open up my
57:8 you too, O *h*. I will awaken
71:22 make melody to you on the *h*
81:2 pleasant *h* together with the
92:3 resounding music on the *h*
98:5 melody to Jehovah with the *h*
98:5 the *h* and the voice of melody
108:2 instrument; you too, O *h*
147:7 melody to our God on the *h*
149:3 *h* let them make melody to
150:3 instrument and the *h*
Isa 5:12 *h* and stringed instrument
16:11 boisterous just like a *h*
23:16 Take a *h*, go around the
24:8 exultation of the *h* has
Da 3:5 the triangular *h*, the stringed
3:7 the triangular *h*, the stringed
3:10 the triangular *h*, the stringed
3:15 the triangular *h*, the stringed
1Co 14:7 whether a flute or a *h*
14:7 played on the flute or . . . *h*
Re 5:8 each one a *h* and golden bowls
14:2 accompany themselves on the *h*
18:22 accompany . . . on the *h*

Harpoons
Job 41:7 fill its skin with *h*

Harps
2Sa 6:5 and with *h* and with stringed
1Ki 10:12 *h* and stringed instruments
1Ch 13:8 with songs and with *h* and
15:16 and *h* and cymbals, playing
15:21 with *h* tuned to Sheminith
15:28 stringed instruments and *h*
16:5 with *h*, and Asaph with the
25:1 ones prophesying with the *h*
25:6 *h* for the service of the
2Ch 5:12 stringed instruments and *h*
9:11 *h* and stringed instruments
20:28 with *h* and with trumpets
29:25 and with *h*, by the
Ne 12:27 instruments and with *h*
Ps 137:2 We hung our *h*
Isa 30:32 tambourines and with *h*

Eze 26:13 *h* will be heard no more
Re 14:2 playing on their *h*
15:2 having *h* of God

Harrow
Job 39:10 *h* low plains after you

Harrows
Isa 28:24 loosens and *h* his ground
Ho 10:11 Judah plows; Jacob *h* for him

Harsh
1Sa 20:10 father may answer you is *h*
25:3 husband was *h* and bad in his
Da 2:15 *h* order on the part of the
3:22 king's word was *h* and the
Lu 19:21 because you are a *h* man
19:22 that I am a *h* man, taking
2Co 2:5 not to be too *h* in what I say

Harsha
Ezr 2:52 the sons of *H*
Ne 7:54 sons of Mehida, the sons of *H*

Harshly
Ge 42:7 So he spoke *h* with them and
42:30 lord of the country spoke *h*
49:7 fury, because it acts *h*
1Ki 12:13 to answer the people *h*
2Ch 10:13 king began to answer them *h*

Harshness
Jg 4:3 Israel with *h* twenty years
Eze 34:4 with *h* you have had them in

Harum
1Ch 4:8 Aharhel the son of *H*

Harumaph
Ne 3:10 Jedaiah the son of *H*

Haruz
2Ki 21:19 daughter of *H* from Jotbah

Harvest
Ge 8:22 seed sowing and *h*, and cold
30:14 in the days of the wheat *h*
45:6 will be no plowing time or *h*
Ex 23:16 *h* of the first ripe fruits of
34:21 in *h* you will keep sabbath
34:22 ripe fruits of the wheat *h*
Le 19:9 people reap the *h* of your land
19:9 gleaning of your *h* you must
23:10 reaped its *h*, you must also
23:10 the firstfruits of your *h* to
23:22 reap the *h* of your land, you
23:22 *h* you must not pick up
25:5 *h* you must not reap, and the
De 24:19 reap your *h* in your field
Jos 3:15 all the days of *h*
Jg 15:1 in the days of wheat *h*
Ru 1:22 the commencement of barley *h*
2:9 on the field that they will *h*
2:21 finished the entire *h* that I
2:23 until the *h* of the barley and
2:23 *h* of the wheat came to an end
1Sa 6:13 the wheat *h* in the low plain
8:12 plowing and to reap his *h*
12:17 Is it not wheat *h* today?
2Sa 21:9 death in the first days of *h*
21:9 the start of the barley *h*
21:10 the start of *h* until water
23:13 come at the *h*, to David at
Job 24:6 the field its fodder they *h*
Pr 6:8 food supplies even in the *h*
10:5 is fast asleep during the *h*
25:13 snow in the day of *h* is the
Isa 16:9 over your *h* has fallen down
17:11 *h* will certainly flee in
18:4 of dew in the heat of *h*
18:5 before the *h*, when the
23:3 *h* of the Nile, your revenue
Jer 5:17 eat up your *h* and your bread
5:24 prescribed weeks of the *h*
8:20 The *h* has passed, the summer
50:16 sickle in the time of *h*
51:33 the *h* must come for her
Ho 6:11 a *h* has been fixed for you
Joe 1:11 *h* of the field has perished
3:13 for *h* has grown ripe
Am 4:7 yet three months to the *h*
Mt 9:37 *h* is great, but the workers
9:38 beg the Master of the *h* to
9:38 send out workers into his *h*
13:30 grow together until the *h*
13:30 in the *h* season I will tell
13:39 The *h* is a conclusion of a
Lu 10:2 The *h*, indeed, is great, but
10:2 beg the Master of the *h* to
Lu 10:2 send out workers into his *h*
Joh 4:35 months before the *h* comes
Re 14:15 *h* of the earth is thoroughly

Harvested
Jas 5:4 wages due the workers who *h*

Harvester
Isa 17:5 *h* is gathering the standing
Am 9:13 will actually overtake the *h*

Harvesters
Ru 2:3 glean in the field behind the *h*
2:4 and proceeded to say to the *h*
2:5 man who was set over the *h*
2:6 the young man set over the *h*
2:7 gather . . . behind the *h*
2:14 So she sat down beside the *h*

Harvesting
Joh 4:35 that they are white for *h*

Harvests
Job 5:5 What he *h* the hungry one eats
Isa 17:5 arm *h* the ears of grain, he

Harvesttime
Pr 26:1 like rain in *h*, so glory is
Isa 9:3 with the rejoicing in the *h*
18:6 of the earth will pass the *h*
Mr 4:29 because the *h* has come

Has*
Job 1:11 touch everything he *h* and see
1:12 Everything that he *h* is in
2:4 everything that a man *h* he
Mt 13:12 For whoever *h*, more will be
13:12 what he *h* will be taken
13:43 Let him that *h* ears listen
25:29 For to everyone that *h*, more
25:29 what he *h* will be taken
Mr 4:9 Let him that *h* ears to listen
4:23 Whoever *h* ears to listen, let
4:25 that *h* will have more given
4:25 what he *h* will be taken away
Lu 8:8 Let him that *h* ears to listen
8:18 whoever *h*, more will be
8:18 even what he imagines he *h*
12:15 a person *h* an abundance his
14:35 that *h* ears to listen, listen
19:26 everyone that *h*, more will
19:26 what he *h* will be taken
Joh 14:30 And he *h* no hold on me
2Co 8:12 according to what a person *h*

Hasadiah
1Ch 3:20 Berechiah and *H*, Jushab-hesed

Hashabiah
1Ch 6:45 son of *H*, the son of Amaziah
9:14 of *H* from the sons of Merari
25:3 the sons of Jeduthun . . . *H*
25:19 the twelfth for *H*, his sons
26:30 Of the Hebronites, *H* and his
27:17 of Levi, *H* the son of
2Ch 35:9 *H* and Jeiel and Jozabad
Ezr 8:19 and *H* and with him Jeshaiah
8:24 *H*, and with them ten of
Ne 3:17 at his side *H*, a prince of
10:11 Mica, Rehob, *H*
11:15 *H* the son of Bunni
11:22 *H* the son of Mattaniah the
12:21 for Hilkiah, *H*; for Jedaiah
12:24 heads of the Levites were *H*

Hashabnah
Ne 10:25 Rehum, *H*, Maaseiah

Hashabneiah
Ne 3:10 Hattush the son of *H* did
9:5 And the Levites . . . *H*

Hash-baddanah
Ne 8:4 and *H*, Zechariah and Meshullam

Hashem
1Ch 11:34 the sons of *H* the Gizonite

Hashmonah
Nu 33:29 and went camping in *H*
33:30 pulled away from *H* and went

Hashubah
1Ch 3:20 *H* and Ohel and Berechiah

Hashum
Ezr 2:19 sons of *H*, two hundred and
10:33 the sons of *H*, Mattenai
Ne 7:22 sons of *H*, three hundred and
8:4 *H* and Hash-baddanah, Zechariah
10:18 Hodiah, *H*, Bezai

Hassenaah
Ne 3:3 the sons of *H* built

Hassenuah
1Ch 9:7 son of Hodaviah the son of *H*
Ne 11:9 Judah the son of *H* over the

Hasshub
1Ch 9:14 son of *H* the son of Azrikam
Ne 3:11 *H* the son of Pahath-moab
3:23 Benjamin and *H* did repair
10:23 Hoshea, Hananiah, *H*
11:15 *H* the son of Azrikam the son

Haste
Ex 12:11 and you must eat it in *h*
De 16:3 in *h* that you came out of the
32:35 the events . . . do make *h*
1Sa 20:38 In *h*! Act quickly! Do not
Es 2:9 *h* to give her her massages
Ps 22:19 do make *h* to my assistance
38:22 Do make *h* to my assistance
40:13 to my assistance do make *h*
70:1 to my assistance do make *h*
141:1 Do make *h* to me
Isa 5:26 *h* it will swiftly come in
Mr 6:25 went in with *h* to the king
Lu 1:39 with *h*, to a city of Judah
2:16 went with *h* and found Mary
Php 2:28 greater *h* I am sending him

Hasten
Jos 10:13 sun . . . did not *h* to set for
1Sa 23:27 Do *h* and go, for the
Ps 55:8 *h* to a place of escape for me
Isa 5:19 Let his work *h*
Jer 17:16 *h* from being a shepherd
Na 2:5 They will *h* to her wall, and

Hastened
1Sa 25:18 Abigail *h* and took two
25:23 *h* and got down off the ass
25:34 *h* that you might come to
25:42 Abigail *h* and rose up and
2Ch 26:20 himself also *h* to go out

Hastening
Pr 1:16 they keep *h* to shed blood
19:2 is *h* with his feet is sinning
28:20 *h* to gain riches will not
Ac 20:16 he was *h* to get to Jerusalem

Hastens
Job 31:5 my foot *h* to deception
Pr 7:23 as a bird *h* into the trap

Hastily
Es 6:14 *h* to bring Haman to the
Job 24:6 vineyard . . . they *h* despoil
Ps 139:11 darkness . . . will *h* seize me
Pr 25:8 to conduct a legal case *h*
1Ti 5:22 Never lay your hands *h* upon

Hasty
Pr 21:5 *h* surely heads for want
29:20 a man *h* with his words
Ec 5:2 heart, let it not be *h* to bring

Hasupha
Ezr 2:43 the sons of *H*
Ne 7:46 the sons of *H*, the sons of

Hatch
Isa 34:15 eggs, and it must *h* them

Hatched
Isa 59:5 what they have *h*, and they
59:5 would be *h* into a viper
Ac 20:3 a plot was *h* against him by

Hatchet
Ps 74:6 they strike even with *h* and

Hate
Ge 24:60 the gate of those who *h* it
37:4 they began to *h* him, and they
37:5 found further reason to *h* him
37:8 found fresh reason to *h* him
Ex 1:10 those who *h* us and will fight
20:5 in the case of those who *h* me
Le 19:17 not *h* your brother in your
26:17 *h* you will just tread down
Nu 10:35 who intensely *h* you flee
De 5:9 in the case of those who *h* me
7:15 upon all those who *h* you
12:31 he does *h* they have done to
22:13 and has come to *h* her
24:3 latter man has come to *h* her
30:7 enemies and those who *h* you
32:41 to those who intensely *h* me
33:11 those who intensely *h* him

Jg 14:16 You only *h* me, you do, and
15:2 You must unquestionably *h* her
1Ki 22:8 *h* him, for he does not
2Ch 18:7 I myself certainly *h* him
Ps 5:5 *h* all those practicing what is
31:6 I do *h* those paying regard
36:2 his error so as to *h* it
45:7 and you *h* wickedness
68:1 those who intensely *h* him
97:10 *h* what is bad
105:25 heart change to *h* his people
139:21 *h* those who are intensely
139:22 I do *h* them. They have
Pr 6:16 things that Jehovah does *h*
9:8 ridiculer, that he may not *h*
25:17 that he may not . . . *h* you
29:10 Bloodthirsty men *h* anyone
Ec 3:8 a time to love and a time to *h*
9:1 *h* that were all prior to them
9:6 their love and their *h* and
Ho 9:15 for there I had to *h* them
Am 5:15 *H* what is bad, and love what
Mt 5:43 You heard . . . *h* your enemy
6:24 *h* the one and love the other
24:10 and will *h* one another
Lu 6:22 Happy . . . whenever men *h* you
14:26 does not *h* his father and
16:13 *h* the one and love the other
Joh 7:7 world has no reason to *h* you
Ro 7:15 but what I *h* is what I do
Jude 23 *h* even the inner garment that
Re 2:6 *h* the deeds of the sect of
2:6 of Nicolaus, which I also *h*
17:16 *h* the harlot and will make

Hated
Ge 26:27 you yourselves *h* me and so
29:31 to see that Leah was *h*
29:33 I was *h* and so he gave me
De 1:27 It was because Jehovah *h* us
9:28 because he *h* them he brought
21:15 the one loved and the other *h*
21:15 the loved one and the *h* one
21:15 has come to be of the *h* one
21:16 at the expense of the *h* one's
21:17 the firstborn the *h* one's son
Jg 11:7 Was it not you that *h* me so
2Sa 13:15 hatred with which he *h* her
13:22 for Absalom *h* Amnon over
Ps 25:19 they have *h* me
26:5 I have *h* the congregation of
50:17 you—you have *h* discipline
101:3 those who fall away I have *h*
119:104 I have *h* every false path
119:113 halfhearted ones I have *h*
119:128 Every false path I have *h*
119:163 Falsehood I have *h*, and I
Pr 1:29 reason that they *h* knowledge
5:12 I have *h* discipline and my
8:13 the perverse mouth I have *h*
14:17 of thinking abilities is *h*
19:7 little means have all *h* him
30:23 under a *h* woman when she is
Ec 2:17 I *h* life, because the work
2:18 I, even I, *h* all my hard work
Isa 1:14 festal seasons my soul has *h*
60:15 one left entirely and *h*
Jer 12:8 That is why I have *h* her
44:4 sort of thing that I have *h*
Eze 16:37 with all those whom you *h*
23:28 those whom you have *h*
35:6 it was blood that you *h*
Am 5:10 they have *h* a reprover
5:21 I have *h*, I have rejected
6:8 his dwelling towers I have *h*
Zec 8:17 are all things that I have *h*
Mal 1:3 and Esau I have *h*; and I
2:16 For he has *h* a divorcing
Lu 19:14 citizens *h* him and sent out
Joh 15:18 you know that it has *h* me
15:18 me before it *h* you
15:24 *h* me as well as my Father
15:25 They *h* me without cause
17:14 but the world has *h* them
Ro 9:13 I loved Jacob, but Esau I *h*
Eph 5:29 no man ever *h* his own flesh
Heb 1:9 and you *h* lawlessness
Re 18:2 of every unclean and *h* bird

Hateful
2Sa 5:8 *h* to the soul of David

Hater
De 19:4 he was no *h* of him formerly
19:6 he was no *h* of him formerly
Ps 55:12 was not an intense *h* of me

Ps 106:10 from the hand of the *h*
Pr 12:1 *h* of reproof is unreasoning
15:27 *h* of gifts . . . keep living
26:24 With his lips the *h* makes
27:6 kisses of a *h* are things to be

Haters
Ps 120:6 With the *h* of peace
Mic 3:2 *h* of what is good and lovers
Ro 1:30 *h* of God, insolent, haughty

Hates
Ex 23:5 the ass of someone who *h* you
De 7:10 repaying . . . one who *h* him
7:10 toward the one who *h* him
16:22 a thing Jehovah your God *h*
Ps 11:5 His soul certainly *h*
Pr 13:5 what the righteous *h*, but
26:28 A tongue that is false *h* the
Joh 3:20 *h* the light and does not
7:7 but it *h* me, because I bear
12:25 *h* his soul in this world
15:18 If the world *h* you, you
15:19 account the world *h* you
15:23, 23 *h* me *h* also my Father
1Jo 2:9 yet *h* his brother is in the
2:11 he that *h* his brother is in
3:13 that the world *h* you
3:15 *h* his brother is a manslayer

Hathach
Es 4:5 *H*, one of the king's eunuchs
4:6 So *H* went out to Mordecai into
4:9 *H* now came in and told Esther
4:10 Then Esther said to *H* and

Hathath
1Ch 4:13 the sons of Othniel, *H*

Hating
Ex 18:21 men, *h* unjust profit; and
De 4:42 he was not *h* him formerly
19:11 a man *h* his fellowman, and
22:16 and he went *h* her
Jos 20:5 he was not *h* him formerly
2Sa 13:15 Amnon began *h* her with a
19:6 loving those *h* you and by
19:6 and by *h* those loving you
22:18 From those *h* me; because
22:41 Those *h* me intensely—I
2Ch 1:11 for the soul of those *h* you
19:2 those *h* Jehovah that you
Es 9:1 domineered over those *h* them
9:5 went doing to those *h* them
9:16 a killing among those *h* them
Job 8:22 The very ones *h* you will be
31:29 of one intensely *h* me
34:17 will anyone *h* justice
Ps 9:13 my affliction by those *h* me
18:17 And from those *h* me; because
18:40 as for those *h* me intensely
21:8 hand will find those *h* you
34:21 the very ones *h* the righteous
35:19 those *h* me without cause
38:19 those *h* me for no reason
41:7 those *h* me whisper to one
44:7 those intensely *h* us you put
44:10 the very ones intensely *h* us
69:4 Those *h* me without a cause
69:14 delivered from those *h* me
81:15 those intensely *h* Jehovah
83:2 ones intensely *h* you have
86:17 those *h* me may see it and
89:23 those intensely *h* him I kept
106:41 those *h* them might rule
118:7 shall look upon those *h* me
129:5 All those *h* Zion
139:21 intensely *h* you, O Jehovah
Pr 1:22 stupid ones keep *h* knowledge
8:13 Jehovah means the *h* of bad
8:36 all those intensely *h* me are
11:15 one *h* handshaking is keeping
13:24 back his rod is *h* his son
15:10 anyone *h* reproof will die
25:21 If the one *h* you is hungry
28:16 *h* unjust profit will prolong
29:24 partner with a thief is *h*
Isa 61:8 loving justice, *h* robbery
66:5 Your brothers that are *h* you
Eze 16:27 desire of the women *h* you
Da 4:19 dream apply to those *h* you
Lu 1:71 the hand of all those *h* us
6:27 to do good to those *h* you
Tit 3:3 abhorrent, *h* one another
1Jo 4:20 and yet is *h* his brother, he

Hatipha
Ezr 2:54 the sons of *H*
Ne 7:56 sons of Neziah, the sons of *H*

Hatita
Ezr 2:42 the sons of *H*
Ne 7:45 the sons of *H*, the sons of

Hatred
Nu 35:20 if in *h* he was pushing him
2Sa 13:15 with a very great *h*
13:15 *h* with which he hated her
Ps 25:19 with a violent *h* they have
109:3 with words of *h* they have
109:5 And *h* for my love
139:22 With a complete *h* I do hate
Pr 10:12 *H* is what stirs up
10:18 one covering over *h* there
14:20 is an object of *h*, but many
15:17 than a manger-fed bull and *h*
26:26 *H* is covered over by deceit
Eze 23:29 take action against you in *h*
35:11 owing to your feelings of *h*
Mt 10:22 objects of *h* by all people
24:9 you will be objects of *h* by
Mr 13:13 objects of *h* by all people
Lu 21:17 objects of *h* by all people

Hattil
Ezr 2:57 the sons of *H*
Ne 7:59 the sons of *H*, the sons of

Hattush
1Ch 3:22 the sons of Shemaiah, *H*
Ezr 8:2 of the sons of David, *H*
Ne 3:10 *H* the son of Hashabneiah did
10:4 *H*, Shebaniah, Malluch
12:2 Amariah, Malluch, *H*

Haughtily
Ex 9:17 behaving *h* against my people
1Sa 2:3 people speak very *h* so much
Job 10:16 if it acts *h*, like a young
Mic 2:3 so that you will not walk *h*
Zep 3:11 remove . . . *h* exultant ones

Haughtiness
2Ch 32:26 for the *h* of his heart, he
Job 41:15 Furrows of scales are its *h*
Ps 10:2 In his *h* the wicked one hotly
17:10 they have spoken in *h*
31:18 unrestrainedly in *h* and
31:23 anyone showing *h*
36:11 foot of *h* come against me
73:6 *h* has served as a necklace to
Pr 14:3 rod of *h* is in the mouth of
29:23 very *h* of earthling man will
Isa 2:17 *h* of the earthling man must
9:9 because of their *h* and
13:11 *h* of the tyrants I shall
16:6 *h* and his pride and his fury
25:11 its *h* with the tricky
Jer 48:29 of his pride and of his *h*
Mr 7:22 envious eye, blasphemy, *h*

Haughty
2Sa 22:28 your eyes are against the *h*
2Ch 26:16 his heart became *h* even to
32:25 for his heart became *h* and
Job 40:11 see every one *h* and bring
40:12 See every one *h*, humble him
Ps 18:27 the *h* eyes you will abase
94:2 retribution upon the *h* ones
101:5 Anyone of *h* eyes and of
131:1 my heart has not been *h*
Pr 16:18 a *h* spirit before stumbling
21:4 *H* eyes and an arrogant heart
Ec 7:8 than one who is *h* in spirit
Isa 2:11 *h* eyes of earthling man must
3:16 of Zion have become *h* and
Jer 13:15 Do not be *h*, for Jehovah
48:29 Moab—he is very *h*
Eze 16:50 they continued to be *h* and
28:2 your heart has become *h*
28:5 your heart began to be *h*
28:17 Your heart became *h* because
Da 5:20 heart became *h* and his own
Zep 3:11 be *h* in my holy mountain
Lu 1:51 *h* in the intention of their
Ro 1:30 insolent, *h*, self-assuming
2Ti 3:2 *h*, blasphemers, disobedient
Jas 4:6 God opposes the *h* ones, but
1Pe 5:5 God opposes the *h* ones, but

Hauled
Mt 13:48 they *h* it up onto the beach

Haunt
Mr 5:3 He had his *h* among the tombs

Haunters
Isa 13:21 *h* of waterless regions
23:13 her for the desert *h*
34:14 *h* of waterless regions
Jer 50:39 *h* of waterless regions will

Hauran
Eze 47:16 toward the boundary of *H*
47:18 between *H* and Damascus and

Have*
Ps 115:5 A mouth they *h*, but they
115:5 Eyes they *h*, but they cannot
115:6 Ears they *h*, but they cannot
115:6 A nose they *h*, but they
135:16 A mouth they *h*, but they
135:16 Eyes they *h*, but they can
135:17 Ears they *h*, but they can
Isa 65:21 build houses and *h* occupancy
65:22 someone else *h* occupancy
Jer 5:21 They *h* eyes, but they
5:21 they *h* ears, but they cannot
Eze 12:2 that *h* eyes to see but they
12:2 that *h* ears to hear but they
Mr 4:25 he that does not *h*, even what
2Co 8:11 out of what you *h*
8:12 to what a person does not *h*

Haven
Ps 107:30 to the *h* of their delight

Havens
Ac 27:8 place called Fair *H*, near

Havilah
Ge 2:11 the entire land of *H*, where
10:7 sons of Cush . . . *H* and
10:29 *H* and . . . the sons of Joktan
25:18 took up tabernacling from *H*
1Sa 15:7 Amalek from *H* as far as Shur
1Ch 1:9 sons of Cush were . . . *H*
1:23 *H* . . . sons of Joktan

Havvoth-jair
Nu 32:41 and he began to call them *H*
De 3:14 his own name, *H*, to this day
Jg 10:4 to call *H* down to this day
1Ch 2:23 Geshur and Syria took *H* from

Hay
1Co 3:12 wood materials, *h*, stubble

Hazael
1Ki 19:15 anoint *H* as king over Syria
2Ki 8:8 king said to *H*: Take a gift
8:9 *H* went to meet him and took
8:12 *H* said: Why is my lord
8:13 *H* said: What is your servant
8:15 *H* began to reign in place of
8:28 against *H* the king of Syria
8:29 fought *H* the king of Syria
9:14 *H* the king of Syria
9:15 fought *H* the king of Syria
10:32 *H* kept striking them in all
12:17 *H* the king of Syria
12:17 *H* set his face to go up
12:18 to *H* the king of Syria
13:3 hand of *H* the king of Syria
13:3 Ben-hadad the son of *H*
13:22 As for *H* the king of Syria
13:24 *H* the king of Syria died
13:25 Ben-hadad the son of *H*
2Ch 22:5 *H* the king of Syria at
22:6 fought *H* the king of Syria
Am 1:4 a fire onto the house of *H*

Hazael's
1Ki 19:17 one escaping from *H* sword

Hazaiah
Ne 11:5 *H* the son of Adaiah the son

Hazar-addar
Nu 34:4 go out to *H* and pass over to

Hazardous
Ac 27:9 now it was *h* to navigate

Hazar-enan
Nu 34:9 termination must . . . be *H*
34:10 the east from *H* to Shepham
Eze 48:1 *H*, the boundary of Damascus

Hazar-enon
Eze 47:17 *H* the boundary of Damascus

Hazar-gaddah
Jos 15:27 and *H* and Heshmon and

Hazarmaveth
Ge 10:26 Joktan became father . . . *H*
1Ch 1:20 Almodad and Sheleph and *H*

Hazar-shual
Jos 15:28 and *H* and Beer-sheba and
19:3 and *H* and Balah and Ezem
1Ch 4:28 and Moladah and *H*
Ne 11:27 in *H* and in Beer-sheba and

Hazar-susah
Jos 19:5 and Beth-marcaboth and *H*

Hazar-susim
1Ch 4:31 and in *H* and in Beth-biri

Hazazon-tamar
Ge 14:7 who were dwelling in *H*
2Ch 20:2 *H*, that is to say, En-gedi

Hazer-hatticon
Eze 47:16 *H* which is toward the

Hazeroth
Nu 11:35 the people pulled away for *H*
11:35 and they continued in *H*
12:16 people pulled away from *H*
33:17 and went camping in *H*
33:18 pulled away from *H* and went
De 1:1 and Laban and *H* and Dizahab

Haziel
1Ch 23:9 sons of Shimei . . . *H* and

Hazo
Ge 22:22 Chesed and *H* and Pildash and

Hazor
Jos 11:1 Jabin the king of *H* heard of
11:10 at that time and captured *H*
11:10 *H* was before that the head
11:11 he burned *H* in the fire
11:13 Joshua did burn *H* by itself
12:19 the king of *H*, one
15:23 and Kedesh and *H* and Ithnan
15:25 that is to say, *H*
19:36 and Adamah and Ramah and *H*
Jg 4:2 Jabin . . . who reigned in *H*
4:17 Jabin the king of *H* and the
1Sa 12:9 the chief of the army of *H*
1Ki 9:15 and *H* and Megiddo and Gezer
2Ki 15:29 and *H* and Gilead and Galilee
Ne 11:33 *H*, Ramah, Gittaim
Jer 49:28 and the kingdoms of *H*
49:30 O inhabitants of *H*, is the
49:33 *H* must become the lair of

Hazor-hadattah
Jos 15:25 and *H* and Kerioth-hezron

Hazy
1Co 13:12 we see in *h* outline by

Hazzelelponi
1Ch 4:3 name of their sister was *H*

Head
Ge 3:15 He will bruise you in the *h*
28:11 set it as his *h* supporter
28:18 stone . . . as his *h* supporter
40:13 Pharaoh will lift up your *h*
40:16 white bread upon my *h*
40:17 the basket on top of my *h*
40:19 Pharaoh will lift up your *h*
40:20 lift up the *h* of the chief
40:20 *h* of the chief of the bakers
47:31 over the *h* of the couch
48:14 and placed it on Ephraim's *h*
48:14 left hand upon Manasseh's *h*
48:17 hand placed on Ephraim's *h*
48:17 Ephraim's *h* to Manasseh's
48:17 Ephraim's . . . to Manasseh's *h*
48:18 Put your right hand on his *h*
49:26 continue upon the *h* of Joseph
49:26 the *h* of the one singled out
Ex 12:9 *h* together with its shanks
29:6 set the turban upon his *h* and
29:7 pour it upon his *h* and anoint
29:10 their hands upon the bull's *h*
29:15 their hands upon the ram's *h*
29:17 one another and up to its *h*
29:19 their hands upon the ram's *h*
Le 1:4 lay his hand upon the *h* of the
1:8 with the *h* and the suet over
1:12 its parts and its *h* and its
1:15 nip off its *h* and make it
3:2 lay his hand upon the *h* of his
3:8 lay his hand upon the *h* of his
3:13 must lay his hand upon its *h*
4:4 his hand upon the bull's *h*
4:11 its *h* and its shanks and its
4:15 their hands upon the bull's *h*
4:24 lay his hand upon the *h* of
4:29 the *h* of the sin offering
Le 4:33 the *h* of the sin offering and
5:8 nip off its *h* at the front of
8:9 placed the turban upon his *h*
8:12 anointing oil upon Aaron's *h*
8:14 the *h* of the bull of the sin
8:18 hands upon the *h* of the ram
8:20 the *h* and the pieces and the
8:22 their hands upon the ram's *h*
9:13 in its pieces and the *h*
13:12 plague from his *h* to his
13:29 on the *h* or on the chin
13:30 leprosy of the *h* or of the
13:40 his *h* grows bald, it is
13:41 his *h* grows bald up in front
13:44 His plague is on his *h*
13:45 *h* should become ungroomed
14:9 hair on his *h* and his chin
14:18 the *h* of the one cleansing
14:29 the *h* of the one cleansing
16:21 the *h* of the live goat and
16:21 put them upon the *h* of the
21:10 *h* the anointing oil would be
21:10 *h* go ungroomed, and he should
24:14 their hands upon his *h*, and
27:32 the tenth *h* should become
Nu 1:2, 2 all the males, *h* by *h* of
1:4 *h* to the house of his fathers
1:18, 18 *h* by *h* of them
1:20, 20 *h* by *h* of them, all the
1:22, 22 *h* by *h* of them, all the
5:18 the hair of the woman's *h* and
6:5 no razor should pass over his *h*
6:5 locks of the hair of his *h*
6:7 Naziriteship . . . upon his *h*
6:9 the *h* of his Naziriteship, he
6:9 shave his *h* in the day of
6:11 sanctify his *h* on that day
6:18 Nazirite must shave the *h* of
6:18 take the hair of the *h* of his
14:4 appoint a *h*, and let us return
15:11 one *h* among the male lambs
17:3 one rod for the *h* of the house
21:20 at the *h* of Pisgah, and it
24:17 the temples of Moab's *h* And
25:4 all the *h* ones of the people
25:15 a *h* one of the clans of a
De 20:9 at the *h* of the people
21:12 shave her *h* and attend to
28:13 at the *h* and not at the tail
28:23 skies that are over your *h*
28:35 to the crown of your *h*
28:44 He will become the *h*, while
33:16 come upon the *h* of Joseph
33:16 the *h* of the one singled out
33:20 tear . . . the crown of the *h*
Jos 2:19 blood will be upon his own *h*
11:10 the *h* of all these kingdoms
22:14 a *h* of the house of their
Jg 3:27 he being at their *h*
5:26 she pierced his *h* through, And
6:26 at the *h* of this stronghold
7:25 they brought the *h* of Oreb and
8:28 not lift up their *h* anymore
9:39 at the *h* of the landowners of
9:53 Abimelech's *h* and broke his
10:18 the *h* of all the inhabitants
11:8 *h* of all the inhabitants of
11:9 shall become your *h*
11:11 set him over them as *h* and
13:5 and no razor . . . upon his *h*
16:13 the seven braids of my *h*
16:17 has never come upon my *h*
16:19 the seven braids of his *h*
16:22 the hair of his *h* started to
1Sa 1:11 razor will come upon his *h*
4:12 and dirt on his *h*
5:4 *h* of Dagon and the palms of
9:22 at the *h* of those invited
10:1 poured it out upon his *h* and
14:45 single hair of his *h* will
15:17 *h* of the tribes of Israel
17:5 a helmet of copper on his *h*
17:38 a copper helmet upon his *h*
17:46 and remove your *h* off you
17:51 he cut his *h* off with it
17:54 Then David took the *h* of the
17:57 *h* of the Philistine in his
19:13 put at the place of his *h*
19:16 at the place of his *h*
25:39 turned back upon his own *h*
26:7 into the earth at his *h*
26:11 spear that is at his *h* and
26:12 place at Saul's *h*, and then
26:16 jug are that were at his *h*

1Sa 28:2 guardian of my *h* I shall
31:9 cut off his *h* and strip off
2Sa 1:2 and dirt upon his *h*
1:10 diadem that was upon his *h*
1:16 upon your own *h*
2:16 hold of one another by the *h*
3:8 Am I a dog's *h* that belongs
3:29 back upon the *h* of Joab
4:7 which they removed his *h*
4:7 took his *h* and walked on the
4:8 bringing the *h* of Ish-bosheth
4:8 Here is the *h* of Ish-bosheth
4:12 *h* of Ish-bosheth they took
12:30 crown of Malcam off its *h*
12:30 came to be upon David's *h*
13:19 placed ashes upon her *h*
13:19 hands put upon her *h* and
14:25 to the crown of his *h* there
14:26 And when he shaved his *h*
14:26 weighed the hair of his *h*
15:30 David . . . his *h* covered
15:30 covered each one his *h*, and
15:32 and dirt upon his *h*
16:9 Let me . . . take off his *h*
18:9 *h* got caught fast in the big
20:21 His *h* will be pitched to
20:22 cut off the *h* of Sheba the
22:44 safeguard me to be the *h* of
23:8 the *h* of the three
23:13 three of the thirty *h* ones
23:18 he was the *h* of the thirty
1Ki 2:32 his blood upon his own *h*
2:33 come back upon the *h* of Joab
2:33 upon the *h* of his offspring
2:37 come to be upon your own *h*
2:44 by you upon your own *h*
8:32 his way upon his own *h*
19:6 at his *h* was a round cake
21:9 Naboth sit at the *h* of the
21:12 sit at the *h* of the people
2Ki 4:19, 19 My *h*, O my *h*! At last he
6:25 an ass's *h* got to be worth
6:31 if the *h* of Elisha the son
6:32 has sent to take off my *h*
9:3 pour it out upon his *h* and
9:6 pour the oil out upon his *h*
9:30 do her *h* up beautifully and
19:21 Jerusalem has wagged her *h*
25:27 the *h* of Jehoiachin the
1Ch 4:42 the sons of Ishi at their *h*
5:7 as the *h*, Jeiel, and Zechariah
5:12 Joel was the *h*, and Shapham
5:15 *h* of the house of their
9:17 their brother Shallum the *h*
10:9 strip him and take off his *h*
11:6 he will become *h* and prince
11:6 And Joab . . . came to be *h*
11:11 the *h* of the three
11:15 three of the thirty *h* ones
11:20 became *h* of the three
11:42 a *h* of the Reubenites, by
12:3 the *h* Ahi-ezer and Joash the
12:9 Ezer was the *h*, Obadiah the
12:18 Amasai, the *h* of the thirty
12:32 were two hundred *h* ones of
16:5 Asaph the *h*, and second to
20:2 crown of Malcam off its *h*
20:2 it came to be on David's *h*
23:3, 3 number, *h* by *h* of them
23:11 And Jahath came to be the *h*
23:16 Gershom were Shebuel the *h*
23:17 came to be Rehabiah the *h*
23:19 of Hebron were Jeriah the *h*
23:20 of Uzziel were Micah the *h*
23:24, 24 *h* by *h* of them, the
24:21 of Rehabiah, Isshiah the *h*
24:23 sons of Hebron, Jeriah the *h*
24:31 the *h* one was exactly as
26:10 Shimri was the *h*, for he
26:10 father appointed him as *h*
26:31 was the *h* of the Hebronites
27:3 Perez the *h* of all the chiefs
29:11 yourself up as *h* over all
2Ch 6:23 course upon his own *h* and
11:22 in office as *h*, as leader
13:12 at the *h* the true God with
20:27 Jehoshaphat at their *h*, to
24:6 king called Jehoiada the *h*
Ezr 5:10 men that are at their *h*
7:28 out of Israel the *h* ones to
8:16 I sent for . . . *h* ones, and
8:17 Iddo the *h* one in the place
9:3 hair of my *h* and of my beard
9:6 multiplied over our *h* and our

Ne 4:4 return upon their own *h*
9:17 appointed a *h* to return to
Es 2:17 the royal headdress upon her *h*
6:8 on the *h* of which the royal
6:12 and with his *h* covered
9:25 come back upon his own *h*
Job 1:20 cut the hair off his *h* and
2:7 foot to the crown of his *h*
10:15 I may not raise my *h*
12:24 *h* ones of the people of the
16:4 would I wag my *h* against
19:9 takes . . . the crown of my *h*
20:6 very *h* reaches to the clouds
24:24 the *h* of an ear of grain
29:3 his lamp to shine upon my *h*
29:25 and I was sitting as *h*
41:7 Or its *h* with fish spears
Ps 3:3 and the One lifting up my *h*
7:16 will return upon his own *h*
7:16 upon the crown of his *h* his
18:43 the *h* of the nations
21:3 on his *h* a crown of refined
22:7 they keep wagging their *h*
23:5 With oil you . . . greased my *h*
27:6 my *h* will be high above my
38:4 errors have passed over my *h*
40:12 than the hairs of my *h*
44:14 A shaking of the *h* among the
60:7 is the fortress of my *h* one
64:8 will shake their *h*
66:12 man to ride over our *h*
68:21 break the *h* of his enemies
68:21 The hairy crown of the *h* of
69:4 more than the hairs of my *h*
83:2 hating you have raised their *h*
108:8 is the fortress of my *h* one
109:25 begin wagging their *h*
110:6 *h* one over a populous land
110:7 he will raise high his *h*
118:22 become the *h* of the corner
133:2 like the good oil upon the *h*
140:7 screened over my *h* in the
141:5 it would be oil upon the *h*
141:5 *h* would not want to refuse
Pr 1:9 of attractiveness to your *h*
4:9 *h* it will give a wreath of
10:6 for the *h* of the righteous
11:26 *h* of the one letting it be
25:22 raking together upon his *h*
Ec 2:14 wise, his eyes are in his *h*
9:8 oil not be lacking upon your *h*
Ca 2:6 His left hand is under my *h*
5:2 For my *h* is filled with dew
5:11 His *h* is gold, refined gold
7:5 Your *h* upon you is like Carmel
7:5 the tresses of your *h* are like
8:3 left hand would be under my *h*
Isa 1:5 *h* is in a sick condition, and
1:6 sole of the foot even to the *h*
3:17 crown of the *h* of the
7:8 *h* of Syria is Damascus, and
7:8 *h* of Damascus is Rezin
7:9 *h* of Ephraim is Samaria, and
7:9 *h* of Samaria is the son of
7:20 Jehovah will shave the *h* and
9:14 cut off from Israel *h* and
9:15 respected one is the *h*, and
19:15 work that the *h* or the tail
28:1 *h* of the fertile valley of
28:4 *h* of the fertile valley must
35:10 will be upon their *h*
37:22 Jerusalem has wagged her *h*
51:11 will be upon their *h*
51:20 the *h* of all the streets
58:5 bowing down his *h* just like
59:17 of salvation upon his *h*
Jer 2:16 on you at the crown of the *h*
2:37 with your hands upon your *h*
9:1 O that my *h* were waters
14:3 they have covered their *h*
14:4 they have covered their *h*
18:16 stare . . . and shake his *h*
22:6 to me, the *h* of Lebanon
23:19 the *h* of the wicked ones
30:23 *h* of the wicked ones it
31:7 at the *h* of nations
48:37 every *h* there is baldness
48:45 *h* of the sons of uproar
52:31 up the *h* of Jehoiachin
La 1:5 adversaries have become the *h*
2:10 brought up dust upon their *h*
2:10 *h* down to the very earth
2:15 kept wagging their *h* at the
2:19 at the *h* of all the streets

La 3:54 Waters have flowed over my *h*
4:1 at the *h* of all the streets
5:16 The crown of our *h* has fallen
Eze 1:25 expanse . . . over their *h*
1:26 that was over their *h* there
5:1 upon your *h* and upon your
8:3 by a tuft of hair of my *h*
9:10 bring upon their own *h*
10:1 over the *h* of the cherubs
10:11 to which the *h* would face
11:21 upon their *h* I shall
13:18 making veils upon the *h* of
16:12 a beautiful crown on your *h*
16:25 At every *h* of the way you
16:31 mound at the *h* of every way
16:43 own way upon your very *h*
17:19 even bring it upon his *h*
21:19 *h* of the way to the city
21:21 at the *h* of the two ways
22:31 bring upon their own *h*
29:18 Every *h* was one made bald
33:4 come to be upon his own *h*
38:2 the *h* chieftain of Meshech
38:3 Gog, you *h* chieftain of
39:1 you *h* chieftain of Meshech
42:12 at the *h* of the way, the
44:18 prove to be on their *h*, and
44:20 *h* they should not shave
44:20 hair of the *h* they should
Da 1:10 make my *h* guilty to the king
2:28 visions of your *h* upon your
2:32 image, its *h* was of good gold
2:38 yourself are the *h* of gold
3:27 not a hair of their *h* had
4:5 visions of my *h* that began to
4:10 visions of my *h* upon my bed
4:13 visions of my *h* upon my bed
7:1 visions of his *h* upon his bed
7:9 hair of his *h* was like clean
7:15 visions of my *h* began to
7:20 ten horns that were on its *h*
Ho 1:11 set up for themselves one *h*
Am 2:7 on the *h* of lowly persons
6:7 *h* of those going into exile
8:10 and upon every *h* baldness
9:1 Strike the pillar *h*, so that
9:1 And cut them off at the *h*
Ob 15 will return upon your own *h*
Jon 2:5 Weeds . . . around my *h*
4:6 to become a shade over his *h*
4:8 upon the *h* of Jonah, so that
Mic 2:13 Jehovah at the *h* of them
3:9 *h* ones of the house of Jacob
3:11 *h* ones judge merely for a
Na 3:10 at the *h* of all the streets
Hab 3:13 broke to pieces the *h* one
3:14 you pierced the *h* of his
Zec 1:21 no one at all raised his *h*
3:5 put a clean turban upon his *h*
3:5 the clean turban upon his *h*
6:11 put it upon the *h* of Joshua
Mt 5:36 Nor by your *h* must you swear
6:17 when fasting, grease your *h*
8:20 nowhere to lay down his *h*
10:30 hairs of your *h* . . . numbered
14:8 the *h* of John the Baptist
14:11 *h* was brought on a platter
17:25 receive duties or *h* tax
22:17 Is it lawful to pay *h* tax to
22:19 Show me the *h* tax coin
26:7 began pouring it upon his *h*
27:29 put it on his *h* and a reed
27:30 began hitting him upon his *h*
27:37 they posted above his *h* the
Mr 4:28 grass-blade, then the stalk *h*
4:28 the full grain in the *h*
6:24 The *h* of John the baptizer
6:25 the *h* of John the Baptist
6:27 commanded him to bring his *h*
6:28 brought his *h* on a platter
12:4 they struck on the *h* and
12:14 to pay *h* tax to Caesar
14:3 began to pour it upon his *h*
15:19 they would hit him on the *h*
Lu 7:38 with the hair of her *h*
7:46 did not grease my *h* with oil
9:58 nowhere to lay down his *h*
Joh 13:9 but also my hands and my *h*
19:2 thorns and put it on his *h*
19:30 bowing his *h*, he delivered
20:7 that had been upon his *h*
20:12 sitting one at the *h* and
Ac 1:18 and pitching *h* foremost he
2:29 family *h* David, that he both

Ac 4:11 become the *h* of the corner
18:18 had the hair of his *h* clipped
27:15 keep its *h* against the wind
27:34 not a hair of the *h* of one
Ro 12:20 heap fiery coals upon his *h*
1Co 11:3 *h* of every man is the Christ
11:3 the *h* of a woman is the man
11:3 the *h* of the Christ is God
11:4 having something on his *h*
11:4 shames his *h*
11:5 with her *h* uncovered shames
11:5 shames her *h*, for it is one
11:5 a woman with a shaved *h*
11:7 not to have his *h* covered
11:10 sign of authority upon her *h*
12:21 the *h* cannot say to the feet
Eph 1:22 made him *h* over all things
4:15 him who is the *h*, Christ
5:23 a husband is *h* of his wife
5:23 as the Christ also is *h* of
Col 1:18 and he is the *h* of the body
2:10 the *h* of all government and
2:19 is not holding fast to the *h*
Heb 7:4 Abraham, the family *h*, gave
1Pe 2:7 become the *h* of the corner
Re 1:14 his *h* and his hair were white
10:1 and a rainbow was upon his *h*
12:1 *h* was a crown of twelve stars
14:14 golden crown on his *h* and a
19:12 upon his *h* are many diadems

Headbands
Isa 3:18 *h* and the moon-shaped

Headcloth
Ge 24:65 take a *h* and to cover herself

Headdress
Es 1:11 queen in the royal *h* before
2:17 put the royal *h* upon her head
6:8 which the royal *h* has been put
Pr 14:18 will bear knowledge as a *h*
Isa 61:3 a *h* instead of ashes, the
61:10 priestly way, puts on a *h*
Eze 24:17 Your *h* bind on yourself
24:23 *h* will be on your heads
1Co 11:15 is given her instead of a *h*

Headdresses
Isa 3:20 *h* and the step chains and
Eze 44:18 Linen *h* are what should

Headgear
Ex 29:9 must wrap the *h* upon them
Le 8:13 and wrapped the *h* upon them

Headgears
Ex 28:40 *h* for them for glory and
39:28 ornamental *h* of fine linen

Headlong
Nu 22:32 has been *h* against my will
Job 5:13 of astute ones is carried *h*
16:11 wicked ones he throws me *h*
Lu 4:29 in order to throw him down *h*

Headman
1Ch 23:8 of Ladan were Jehiel the *h*
23:18 Izhar were Shelomith the *h*

Headmen
1Ch 8:28 by their descendants, *h*
9:34 by their descendants, *h*
24:4 more numerous in *h* than the
26:12 the *h* had duties exactly as

Heads
Ge 2:10 became, as it were, four *h*
Ex 6:14 the *h* of the house of their
6:25 are the *h* of the . . . Levites
18:25 *h* over the people, as chiefs
38:19 *h* and their joints were of
Le 10:6 not let your *h* go ungroomed
21:5 produce baldness upon their *h*
Nu 1:16 *h* of the thousands of Israel
7:2 *h* of the house of their
8:12 hands upon the *h* of the bulls
10:4 *h* of the thousands of Israel
13:3 All the men were *h* of the
30:1 spoke to the *h* of the tribes
31:26 the *h* of the fathers of the
32:28 the *h* of the fathers of the
36:1 the *h* of the fathers of the
36:1 *h* of the fathers of the sons
De 1:13 I may set them as *h* over you
1:15 I took the *h* of your tribes
1:15 and put them as *h* over you
5:23 the *h* of your tribes and your
29:10 the *h* of your tribes, your
De 32:42 the *h* of the leaders of the
33:5 the *h* of the people gathered
33:21 And the *h* of the people will
Jos 2:19 his blood will be on our *h*
7:6 putting dust upon their *h*
14:1 the *h* of the fathers of the
19:51 *h* of the fathers of the
21:1 *h* of the fathers of the
21:1 the *h* of the fathers of the
22:21 spoke with the *h* of the
22:30 *h* of the thousands of Israel
23:2 its *h* and its judges and its
24:1 Israel and its *h* and its
Jg 9:57 come back upon their own *h*
1Sa 29:4 with the *h* of those our men
1Ki 8:1 all the *h* of the tribes, the
20:31 and ropes upon our *h*, and
20:32 with ropes upon their *h*
2Ki 10:6 *h* of the men that are sons
10:7 put their *h* in baskets and
10:8 *h* of the sons of the king
1Ch 5:24 the *h* of the house of their
5:24 men of fame, *h* of the house
7:2 *h* of the house of their
7:3 five, all of them being *h*
7:7 *h* of the house of their
7:9 respects the *h* of the house
7:11 the *h* of their forefathers
7:40 sons of Asher, *h* of the house
7:40 *h* of the chieftains
8:6 were the *h* of the houses
8:10 his sons, *h* of the houses of
8:13 These were *h* of the houses
8:28 These were *h* of the houses
9:9 *h* of the fathers by the house
9:13 *h* of the house of their
9:33 the *h* of the fathers of the
9:34 the *h* of the fathers of the
11:10 *h* of the mighty men that
12:14 sons of Gad, *h* of the army
12:18 among the *h* of the troops
12:19 At the risk of our own *h*
12:20 *h* of the thousands that
12:23 numbers of the *h* of those
15:12 the *h* of the fathers of the
23:9 *h* of the fathers for Ladan
23:24 the *h* of the fathers, by
24:4 *h* for their paternal houses
24:4 sons of Ithamar, as *h* for
24:6 the *h* of the fathers of the
24:31 *h* of the paternal houses of
26:21 the *h* of the paternal houses
26:26 the *h* of the paternal houses
26:32 *h* of the paternal houses
27:1 the *h* of the paternal houses
2Ch 1:2 the *h* of the paternal houses
5:2 and all the *h* of the tribes
19:8 *h* of the paternal houses of
23:2 *h* of the paternal houses of
26:12 *h* of the paternal houses
28:12 *h* of the sons of Ephraim
Ezr 1:5 the *h* of the fathers of Judah
2:68 *h* of the paternal houses
3:12 the *h* of the paternal houses
4:2 the *h* of the paternal houses
4:3 the *h* of the paternal houses
8:1 *h* of their paternal houses
10:16 the *h* of the fathers for
Ne 7:70 the *h* of the paternal houses
7:71 the *h* of the paternal houses
8:13 the *h* of the fathers of all
10:14 The *h* of the people: Parosh
11:3 the *h* of the jurisdictional
11:13 *h* of paternal houses
11:16 of the *h* of the Levites
12:7 *h* of the priests and their
12:12 *h* of the paternal houses
12:22 as *h* of paternal houses
12:23 as *h* of the paternal houses
12:24 the *h* of the Levites were
12:46 *h* of the singers and the
Job 2:12 toss dust . . . upon their *h*
Ps 24:7 Raise your *h*, O you gates
24:9 Raise your *h*, O you gates
74:13 *h* of the sea monsters in
74:14 crushed . . . *h* of Leviathan
140:9 *h* of those surrounding me
Pr 21:5 hasty surely *h* for want
Isa 15:2 *h* in it there is baldness
29:10 he has covered even your *h*
Jer 13:18 down from your *h* your
Eze 1:22 the *h* of the living creatures
1:22 stretched out over their *h*
7:18 all their *h* there is baldness
Eze 23:15 pendant turbans on their *h*
23:42 crowns upon their *h*
24:23 headdress will be on your *h*
27:30 bring up dust upon their *h*
32:27 their swords under their *h*
44:20 clip the hair of their *h*
Da 7:6 And the beast had four *h*, and
Joe 3:4 your treatment upon your *h*
3:7 treatment upon your own *h*
Mic 3:1 Hear, please, you *h* of Jacob
Mt 12:1 started to pluck *h* of grain
27:39 wagging their *h*
Mr 2:23 plucking the *h* of grain
15:29 wagging their *h* and saying
Lu 6:1 eating the *h* of grain, rubbing
12:7 hairs of your *h* . . . numbered
21:18 not a hair of your *h* will
21:28 lift your *h* up, because your
Ac 7:8 Jacob of the twelve family *h*
7:9 family *h* became jealous of
18:6 your blood be upon your own *h*
21:24 they may have their *h* shaved
Re 4:4 upon their *h* golden crowns
9:7 upon their *h* were what seemed
9:17 the *h* of the horses were as
9:17 horses were as *h* of lions
9:19 are like serpents and have *h*
12:3 dragon, with seven *h* and ten
12:3 and upon its *h* seven diadems
13:1 with ten horns and seven *h*
13:1 upon its *h* blasphemous names
13:3 *h* as though slaughtered to
17:3 had seven *h* and ten horns
17:7 the seven *h* and the ten horns
17:9 seven *h* mean seven mountains
18:19 threw dust upon their *h*

Headship
2Ki 2:3 your master from *h* over you
2:5 your master from *h* over you

Headstone
Zec 4:7 certainly bring forth the *h*

Headstrong
2Ti 3:4 betrayers, *h*, puffed up with

Heal
Ge 20:17 *h* Abimelech and his wife and
Nu 12:13 O God, please! *H* her, please!
De 32:39 wounded, and I—I will *h*
2Ki 20:8 sign that Jehovah will *h* me
2Ch 7:14 and I shall *h* their land
Ps 6:2 *H* me, O Jehovah, for my bones
30:2 and you proceeded to *h* me
41:4 Do *h* my soul, for I have
60:2 *H* its breaches, for it has
107:20 send his word and *h* them
Ec 3:3 a time to kill and a time to *h*
Isa 19:22 by them and must *h* them
57:18 to *h* him and conduct him
57:19 has said, and I will *h* him
Jer 3:22 *h* your renegade condition
6:14 *h* the breakdown of my people
8:11 they try to *h* the breakdown
17:14 *H* me, O Jehovah, and I
30:17 from your strokes I shall *h*
33:6 *h* them and reveal to them
Ho 6:1 in pieces but he will *h* us
14:4 I shall *h* their unfaithfulness
Zec 11:16 broken sheep he will not *h*
Mt 13:15 and turn back, and I *h* them
Lu 9:2 the kingdom of God and to *h*
Joh 4:47 to come down and *h* his son
12:40 around and I should *h* them
Ac 28:27 back, and I should *h* them

Healed
Ex 21:19 he gets him completely *h*
Le 13:18 boil develops . . . does get *h*
13:37 falling off of hair . . . *h*
14:48 because the plague has been *h*
De 28:27 you will not be able to be *h*
28:35 will not be able to be *h*
1Sa 6:3 Then it is that you will be *h*
2Ki 2:22 water continues *h* down to
8:29 returned to get *h* at Jezreel
9:15 to get *h* at Jezreel from the
2Ch 22:6 returned to get *h* at Jezreel
30:20 to Hezekiah and *h* the people
Jer 15:18 It has refused to be *h*
17:14 I shall be *h*. Save me, and
51:8 Perhaps she may be *h*
51:9 We would have *h* Babylon, but
51:9 but she has not been *h*
Eze 34:4 ailing one you have not *h*
47:8 water is also actually *h*

Eze 47:9 and the seawater will be *h*
47:11 and they will not be *h*
Ho 11:3 recognize that I had *h* them
Mt 8:8 and my manservant will be *h*
8:13 manservant . . . *h* in that hour
15:28 And her daughter was *h* from
Mr 5:29 *h* of the grievous sickness
Lu 6:17 and be *h* of their sicknesses
7:7 and let my servant be *h*
8:47 how she was *h* instantly
9:11 he *h* those needing a cure
9:42 *h* the boy and delivered him
14:4 *h* him and sent him away
17:15 he saw he was *h*, turned
22:51 touched the ear and *h* him
Joh 5:13 *h* man did not know who he
Ac 28:8 his hands upon him and *h* him
Heb 12:13 but rather that it may be *h*
Jas 5:16 that you may get *h*
1Pe 2:24 by his stripes you were *h*
Re 13:3 its death-stroke got *h*, and
13:12 whose death-stroke got *h*

Healer
Jer 8:22 Or is there no *h* there?

Healers
2Ch 16:12 searched . . . for the *h*

Healing
Ex 15:26 I am Jehovah who is *h* you
2Ki 20:5 Here I am *h* you
2Ch 21:18 for which there was no *h*
36:16 until there was no *h*
Job 5:18 but his own hands do the *h*
Ps 103:3 Who is *h* all your maladies
147:3 is *h* the brokenhearted ones
Pr 3:8 *h* to your navel and a
6:15 and there will be no *h*
12:18 tongue of the wise . . . a *h*
13:17 a faithful envoy is a *h*
16:24 and a *h* to the bones
29:1 be broken, and that without *h*
Isa 6:10 and get *h* for themselves
19:22 a dealing of a blow and a *h*
53:5 there has been a *h* for us
Jer 8:15 a time of *h*, but, look!
14:19 so that there is no *h* for us
14:19 a time of *h*, and, look!
30:13 no means of *h*, no mending
46:11 multiplied the means of *h*
La 2:13 Who can bring *h* to you?
Eze 30:21 *h* by putting a bandage on
47:12 and their leafage for *h*
Ho 5:13 unable to give *h* to you people
7:1 that I would bring *h* to Israel
Mal 4:2 with *h* in its wings
Lu 5:17 power . . . for him to do *h*
6:19 out of him and *h* them all
13:32 *h* today and tomorrow, and
Ac 4:22 upon whom this sign of *h* had
4:30 stretch out your hand for *h*
10:38 *h* all those oppressed by the

Healings
1Co 12:9 to another gifts of *h* by that
12:28 then gifts of *h*; helpful
12:30 Not all have gifts of *h*, do

Heals
Isa 30:26 *h* even the severe wound
Ac 9:34 Aeneas, Jesus Christ *h* you

Health
Pr 4:22 and *h* to all their flesh
Isa 38:16 you will restore me to *h*
Jer 33:6 for her a recuperation and *h*
Mt 9:12 Persons in *h* do not need a
Mr 5:34 and be in good *h* from your
Lu 7:10 found the slave in good *h*
15:27 he got him back in good *h*
Joh 4:52 in which he got better in *h*
5:6 want to become sound in *h*
5:9 became sound in *h*, and he
5:11 one that made me sound in *h*
5:14 you have become sound in *h*
5:15 that made him sound in *h*
7:23 a man completely sound in *h*
Ac 15:29 will prosper. Good *h* to you!
3Jo 2 be prospering and having good *h*

Healthful
2Ki 2:21 I do make this water *h*
Hab 1:16 oiled, and his food is *h*
1Ti 1:10 opposition to the *h* teaching
6:3 does not assent to *h* words
2Ti 1:13 the pattern of *h* words
4:3 put up with the *h* teaching
Tit 1:9 by the teaching that is *h* and
2:1 are fitting for *h* teaching

Healthy
Lu 5:31 Those who are *h* do not need
Tit 1:13 they may be *h* in the faith
2:2 sound in mind, *h* in faith

Heap
Ge 31:46 taking stones and making a *h*
31:46 they ate there on the *h*
31:48 *h* is a witness between me
31:51 Here is this *h* and here is
31:52 This *h* is a witness, and the
31:52 not pass this *h* against you
31:52 will not pass this *h* and
De 13:16 it must become a *h* of ruins
Jg 15:16 male ass—one *h*, two heaps
Ru 3:7 the extremity of the grain *h*
Job 8:17 In a stone *h* his roots
30:24 against a mere *h* of ruins
Ps 79:1 Jerusalem in a *h* of ruins
Pr 26:8 a stone in a *h* of stones, so
Ca 7:2 Your belly is a *h* of wheat
Isa 17:1 she has become a *h*, a
24:12 crushed to a mere rubble *h*
25:10 straw *h* is trodden down in
Ho 2:6 *h* up a stone wall against her
Mic 1:6 make Samaria a *h* of ruins of
Hab 3:15 through the *h* of vast waters
Hag 2:16 a *h* of twenty measures
Ro 12:20 you will *h* fiery coals upon

Heaped
Ex 15:8 waters were *h* up; They stood
2Sa 17:19 *h* up cracked grain upon it

Heaps
Ex 8:14, 14 piling them up, *h* upon *h*
Jg 15:16 male ass—one heap, two *h*
1Ki 9:8 will become *h* of ruins
2Ki 10:8 in two *h* at the entrance of
2Ch 7:21 become *h* of ruins, everyone
31:6, 6 and so gave *h* upon *h*
31:7 started the *h* by laying the
31:8 came and saw the *h*, they
31:9 inquired . . . concerning the *h*
Ne 4:2 out of the *h* of dusty rubbish
13:15 bringing in grain *h* and
Job 15:28 destined for *h* of stones
Ps 68:13 between the camp ash *h*
Jer 26:18 become mere *h* of ruins
50:26 just like those making *h*
La 4:5 have had to embrace ash *h*
Mic 3:12 become mere *h* of ruins, and

Hear
Ge 4:23 *H* my voice, you wives of
14:14 Abram got to *h* that his
23:6 *H* us, my lord. A chieftain of
31:1 he got to *h* the words of the
35:22 and Israel got to *h* of it
41:15 can *h* a dream and interpret
45:2 the Egyptians got to *h* it
45:2 Pharaoh's house got to *h* it
Ex 2:15 Pharaoh got to *h* of this
15:14 Peoples must *h*, they will be
18:1 *h* about all that God had done
19:9 people may *h* when I speak
22:23 unfailingly *h* his outcry
22:27 I shall certainly *h*, because
32:17 Joshua began to *h* the noise
33:4 people got to *h* this evil
Le 10:20 Moses got to *h* that, then
Nu 7:89 *h* the voice conversing with
9:8 *h* what Jehovah may command
11:1 Jehovah got to *h* it, then his
11:10 Moses got to *h* the people
12:6 *H* my words, please
14:13 Egyptians will be bound to *h*
16:4 When Moses got to *h* it he at
20:10 *H*, now, you rebels! Is it
21:1 got to *h* that Israel had come
22:36 Balak got to *h* that Balaam
33:40 got to *h* about the coming of
De 1:17 *h* the little one the same as
1:17 present to me, and I must *h*
2:25 will *h* the report about you
4:6 *h* of all these regulations, and
4:10 let them *h* my words, that
4:28 cannot see or *h* or eat or
4:36 *h* his voice so as to correct
5:1 *H*, O Israel, the regulations
5:27 *h* all that Jehovah our God
9:1 *H*, O Israel, you are today
13:11 all Israel will *h* and become
De 13:12 *h* it said in one of your
17:13 the people will *h* and become
18:16 *h* again the voice of Jehovah
19:20 those who remain will *h* and
20:3 *H*, O Israel, you are drawing
21:21 *h* and indeed become afraid
26:7 Jehovah proceeded to *h* our
29:4 eyes to see and ears to *h*
30:12 let us *h* it that we may do
30:13 may let us *h* it that we may
32:1 *h* the sayings of my mouth
33:7 *H*, O Jehovah, the voice of
Jos 2:11 got to *h* it, then our hearts
6:5 *h* the sound of the horn, all the
7:9 inhabitants of the land will *h*
9:16 to *h* that they were near to
22:12 sons of Israel got to *h* of
Jg 9:30 got to *h* the words of Gaal
13:23 not as now have let us *h*
14:13 your riddle, and let us *h* it
20:3 sons of Benjamin got to *h*
1Sa 4:6 Philistines also got to *h* the
4:14 Eli got to *h* the sound of the
4:19 she got to *h* the report that
7:7 Philistines came to *h* that
9:27 let you *h* the word of God
13:3 Philistines got to *h* of it
13:3 saying: Let the Hebrews *h*!
17:28 brother got to *h* as he spoke
22:1 house of his father got to *h*
22:6 Saul got to *h* that David and
23:25 Saul got to *h* of it, he
25:4 David got to *h* in the
25:39 David got to *h* that Nabal
31:11 *h* what the Philistines had
2Sa 5:17 Philistines got to *h* that
5:24 *h* the sound of a marching in
8:9 *h* that David had struck down
11:26 *h* that Uriah her husband had
15:10 you *h* the sound of the horn
15:35 *h* from the house of the
15:36 everything that you may *h*
16:21 Israel will certainly *h*
17:5 *h* what is in his mouth
17:9 then be bound to *h* and say
22:45 Ears will be obedient to *h*
1Ki 1:41 Adonijah . . . got to *h* it
1:41 Joab got to *h* the sound of
3:11 understanding to *h* judicial
3:28 *h* of the judicial decision
4:34 to *h* Solomon's wisdom, even
8:30 *h* at the place of your
8:30 and you must *h* and forgive
8:32 *h* from the heavens, and you
8:34 you yourself *h* from heaven
8:36 *h* from the heavens, and you
8:39 *h* from the heavens, your
8:42 *h* of your great name and of
8:45 also *h* from the heavens
8:49 *h* from the heavens, your
10:24 to *h* his wisdom that God
22:19 *h* the word of Jehovah
22:28 added: *H*, all you peoples
2Ki 7:6 *h* the sound of war chariots
18:28 *H* the word of the great
19:4 *h* all the words of Rabshakeh
19:7 must *h* a report and return
19:16 your ear, O Jehovah, and *h*
19:16 *h* the words of Sennacherib
20:16 *H* the word of Jehovah
1Ch 10:11 Jabesh in Gilead got to *h*
14:8 Philistines got to *h* that
14:15 *h* the sound of the marching
28:2 *H* me, my brothers and my
2Ch 6:21 *h* from the place of your
6:21 and you must *h* and forgive
6:23 *h* from the heavens, and you
6:25 *h* from the heavens, and you
6:27 yourself *h* from the heavens
6:30 yourself *h* from the heavens
6:35 *h* from the heavens their
6:39 also *h* from the heavens
7:14 *h* from the heavens and
9:23 Solomon to *h* his wisdom
13:4 *H* me, O Jeroboam and all
15:2 *H* me, O Asa and all Judah
18:18 *h* the word of Jehovah: I
18:27 he added: *H*, all you peoples
20:9 and may you *h* and save
20:20 *H* me, O Judah and you
Ne 2:10 the Ammonite, got to *h* of it
4:4 *H*, O our God, for we have
4:20 you *h* the sound of the horn
9:27 would *h* from the very heavens

Ne 9:28 *h* from the very heavens and
Job 2:11 to *h* of all this calamity
3:18 do not *h* the voice of one
5:27 *H* it, and you—know it for
13:6 *H* . . . my counterarguments
13:17 *H* my word clear through
20:3 exhortation to me I *h*
22:27 and he will *h* you; And your
27:9 Will God *h* an outcry of his
33:1 O Job, please *h* my words
35:13 the untruth God does not *h*
39:7 a stalker it does not *h*
42:4 *H*, please, and I myself
Ps 4:1 Show me favor and *h* my prayer
4:3 will *h* when I call to him
5:3 you will *h* my voice
6:8 *h* the sound of my weeping
6:9 indeed *h* my request for favor
10:17 will certainly *h*, O Jehovah
17:1 Do *h* what is righteous
17:6 your ear to me. *H* my saying
18:6 he proceeded to *h* my voice
27:7 *H*, O Jehovah, when I call
28:2 *H* the voice of my entreaties
30:10 *H*, O Jehovah, and show me
34:2 The meek ones will *h* and
39:12 Do *h* my prayer, O Jehovah
49:1 *H* this, all you peoples
51:8 to *h* exultation and rejoicing
54:2 O God, *h* my prayer
55:19 God will *h* and answer them
61:1 *h*, O God, my entreating cry
64:1 *H*, O God, my voice in my
66:18 Jehovah will not *h* me
81:8 *H*, O my people, and I will
84:8 God of armies, do *h* my prayer
85:8 *h* what the true God Jehovah
92:11 *h* about the very ones who
94:9 planting the ear, can he not *h*?
102:1 O Jehovah, do *h* my prayer
102:20 *h* the sighing of the
115:6 Ears . . . but they cannot *h*
119:149 *h* my own voice according
130:2 O Jehovah, do *h* my voice
143:1 O Jehovah, *h* my prayer
143:8 to *h* your loving-kindness
145:19 cry for help he will *h*
Pr 4:10 *H*, my son, and accept my
22:17 *h* the words of the wise ones
23:19 my son, *h* and become wise
29:24 *h*, but he reports nothing
Ec 5:1 there be a drawing near to *h*
7:5 *h* the rebuke of someone wise
7:21 not *h* your servant calling
Ca 2:14 let me *h* your voice, for your
8:13 to your voice. Let me *h* it
Isa 1:2 *H*, O heavens, and give ear, O
1:10 *H* the word of Jehovah, you
6:8 *h* the voice of Jehovah saying
6:9 *H* again and again, O men
6:10 their ears they may not *h*
18:3 *h* a sound just as when there
21:3 so that I do not *h*
28:12 who were not willing to *h*
28:14 *h* the word of Jehovah, you
29:18 deaf ones will certainly *h*
30:9 unwilling to *h* the law of
30:21 *h* a word behind you saying
33:13 *H*, you men who are far
34:1 up close, you nations, to *h*
36:13 *H* the words of the great
37:4 God will *h* the words of
37:7 *h* a report and return to his
37:17 O Jehovah, and *h*. Open your
37:17 and *h* all the words of
39:5 *H* the word of Jehovah of
40:21 Do you not *h*? Has it not
41:22 to *h* even the things that
41:26 no one causing one to *h*
42:9 I cause you people to *h* them
42:18 *H*, you deaf ones; and look
43:9 to *h* even the first things
43:9 *h* and say, It is the truth!
44:8 caused you individually to *h*
47:8 *h* this, you pleasure-given
48:1 *H* this, O house of Jacob
48:5 I caused you to *h* it, that
48:6 made you *h* new things from
48:14 all you people, and *h*
48:16 you people. *H* this
50:4 to *h* like the taught ones
59:1 too heavy that it cannot *h*
65:24 speaking, I myself shall *h*
66:5 *H* the word of Jehovah, you
Jer 2:4 *H* the word of Jehovah, O
5:15 you cannot *h* understandingly
5:21 *H*, now, this, O unwise
5:21 have ears, but they cannot *h*
6:10 warning, that they may *h*
6:18 Therefore *h*, O you nations
7:2 *H* the word of Jehovah, all
9:10 not *h* the sound of livestock
9:20 *h*, O you women, the word of
10:1 *H* the word that Jehovah has
11:2 *H* the words of this covenant
11:6 *H*, you people, the words of
13:15 *H*, you people, and give ear
13:17 if you will not *h* it, in
17:20 *H* the word of Jehovah
17:23 in order not to *h* and in
18:2 cause you to *h* my words
19:3 *H* the word of Jehovah, O you
20:16 *h* an outcry in the morning
21:11 *h*, O men, the word of
22:2 *H* the word of Jehovah
22:29 *h* the word of Jehovah
23:18 he might see and *h* his word
23:18 his word that he might *h* it
23:22 my people *h* my own words
26:7 people began to *h* Jeremiah
26:10 got to *h* these words, and
26:21 princes got to *h* his words
26:21 When Urijah got to *h* of it
28:7 *h*, please, this word that I
29:20 *h* the word of Jehovah
31:10 *H* the word of Jehovah, O
33:9 *h* of all the goodness that
34:4 *h* the word of Jehovah
36:11 *h* all the words of Jehovah
37:5 *h* the report about them
38:1 *h* the words that Jeremiah
38:7 *h* that they had put Jeremiah
38:25 princes *h* that I have spoken
40:7 *h* that the king of Babylon
41:11 *h* all the bad that Ishmael
42:14 horn we shall not *h* and
42:15 *h* the word of Jehovah, O
44:24 *H* the word of Jehovah, all
44:26 *h* the word of Jehovah, all
49:20 *h*, O men, the counsel of
50:45 *h*, O men, the counsel of
La 3:56 My voice you must *h*. Do not
Eze 1:24 *h* the sound of their wings
1:28 I began to *h* the voice of one
2:2 *h* the One speaking to me
2:5 they will *h* or will refrain
2:7 regardless of whether they *h*
2:8 *h* what I am speaking to you
3:6 you cannot *h* understandingly
3:10 and *h* with your own ears
3:11 regardless of whether they *h*
3:12 I began to *h* behind me the
3:17 must *h* from my mouth speech
3:27 Let the one hearing *h*, and
6:3 *h* the word of the Sovereign
8:18 but I shall not *h* them
12:2 ears to *h* but they actually
12:2 but they actually do not *h*
13:2 *H* the word of Jehovah
16:35 O prostitute, *h* the word of
18:25 *H*, please, O house of Israel
20:47 *H* the word of Jehovah
24:26 one for making the ears *h*
25:3 *H* the word of the Sovereign
33:7 you must *h* the word and give
33:30 *h* what the word is that is
33:31 *h* your words but these they
33:32 will certainly *h* your words
34:7 *h* the word of Jehovah
34:9 *h* the word of Jehovah
36:1 *h* the word of Jehovah
36:4 *h* the word of the Sovereign
37:4 dry bones, *h* the word of
40:4 and with your ears *h*, and
43:6 *h* someone speaking to me
44:5 *h* all that I am speaking
Da 3:5 *h* the sound of the horn, the
3:15 *h* the sound of the horn, the
8:13 *h* a certain holy one speaking
8:16 *h* the voice of an earthling
9:18 your ear, O my God, and *h*
9:19 O Jehovah, do *h*
12:7 *h* the man clothed with the
Ho 4:1 *H* the word of Jehovah, O sons
5:1 *H* this, O priests, and pay
Joe 1:2 *H* this, you older men, and
Am 3:1 *H* this word that Jehovah has
3:13 *H* and give witness in the
Am 4:1 *H* this word, you cows of
5:1 *H* this word that I am taking
5:23 instruments may I not *h*
7:16 now *h* the word of Jehovah
8:4 *H* this, you men snapping at
Mic 1:2 *H*, O you peoples, all of you
3:1 *H*, please, you heads of Jacob
3:9 *H*, please, this, you head
6:1 *H*, please, you people, what
6:1 may the hills *h* your voice
6:2 *H*, O you mountains, the legal
6:9 *H* the rod and who it was
7:7 salvation. My God will *h* me
Hab 1:2 cry for help, and you do not *h*
Zec 3:8 *H*, please, O Joshua the high
7:11 made too unresponsive to *h*
Mt 10:27 you *h* whispered, preach
12:19 nor will anyone *h* his voice
12:42 to *h* the wisdom of Solomon
13:13 and hearing, they *h* in vain
13:14 *h* but by no means get the
13:15 never . . . *h* with their ears
13:16 and your ears because they *h*
13:17 *h* the things you are hearing
13:17 and did not *h* them
14:13 crowds, getting to *h* of it
21:16 you *h* what these are saying
21:33 *H* another illustration: There
24:6 You are going to *h* of wars
27:13 Do you not *h* how many
Mr 4:12 *h* and yet not get the sense
6:11 not receive you nor *h* you
6:20 he continued to *h* him gladly
7:37 He even makes the deaf *h*
8:18 having ears, do you not *h*?
12:29 *H*, O Israel, Jehovah our God
13:7 when you *h* of wars and
Lu 6:17 *h* him and be healed of their
8:13 *h* it, receive the word with
8:21 *h* the word of God and do it
10:24 to *h* the things you are
10:24 but did not *h* them
11:31 to *h* the wisdom of Solomon
15:1 kept drawing near to him to *h*
16:2 What is this I *h* about you?
18:6 *H* what the judge, although
19:48 hanging onto him to *h* him
21:9 *h* of wars and disorders, do
21:38 in the temple to *h* him
Joh 3:8 and you *h* the sound of it
5:25 dead will *h* the voice of the
5:28 tombs will *h* his voice
5:30 just as I *h*, I judge; and
9:27 do you want to *h* it again
11:42 I knew that you always *h* me
Ac 2:11 we *h* them speaking in our
2:22 Men of Israel, *h* these words
2:33 this which you see and *h*
7:2 Men, brothers and fathers, *h*
10:22 *h* the things you have to say
10:33 *h* all the things you have
13:7 sought to *h* the word of God
13:16 you others that fear God, *h*
13:44 to *h* the word of Jehovah
15:7 nations should *h* the word of
15:13 saying: Men, brothers, *h* me
17:32 *h* you about this even another
19:26 *h* how not only in Ephesus
21:22 going to *h* you have arrived
22:1 *h* my defense to you now
22:9 did not *h* the voice of the one
22:14 to *h* the voice of his mouth
24:4 I beseech you to *h* us briefly
25:22 would also like to *h* the man
25:22 he said, you shall *h* him
26:3 I beg you to *h* me patiently
26:29 those who *h* me today would
28:22 proper to *h* from you what
28:26 *h* but by no means understand
28:27 *h* with their ears and
Ro 10:14 *h* without someone to preach
10:18 did not fail to *h*, did they?
11:8 ears so as not to *h*, down
1Co 11:18 I *h* divisions exist among
Ga 1:23 only used to *h*: The man that
4:21 Do you not *h* the Law?
Php 1:27 *h* about the things which
1:30 you now *h* about in my case
2Th 3:11 we *h* certain ones are
2Ti 4:17 all the nations might *h* it
Heb 4:2 with those who did *h*
Re 1:3 *h* the words of this prophecy
2:7 *h* what the spirit says to the
2:11 *h* what the spirit says to the

Re 2:17 *h* what the spirit says to the
2:29 *h* what the spirit says to
3:6 *h* what the spirit says to the
3:13 *h* what the spirit says to
3:22 *h* what the spirit says to
9:20 neither see nor *h* nor walk
13:9 anyone has an ear, let him *h*

Heard

Ge 3:8 Later they *h* the voice of
3:10 he said: Your voice I *h* in the
16:11 Jehovah has *h* your affliction
17:20 as regards Ishmael I have *h*
21:17 God *h* the voice of the boy
21:26 also not *h* of it except today
24:52 Abraham's servant had *h*
27:6 *h* your father speaking to
29:13 *h* the report about Jacob
30:17 God *h* and answered Leah
30:22 God *h* and answered her
34:5 Jacob *h* that he had defiled
34:7 as soon as they *h* of it; and
37:17 I *h* them saying, Let us go
37:21 When Reuben *h* this he tried
39:15 he *h* that I raised my voice
39:19 *h* the words of his wife
41:15 have *h* it said about you
42:2 *h* that there are cereals in
43:25 they had *h* that it was there
45:16 the news was *h* at the house
Ex 2:24 In time God *h* their groaning
3:7 and I have *h* their outcry as a
4:31 *h* that Jehovah had turned his
6:5 *h* the groaning of the sons of
16:7 he has *h* your murmurings
16:8 Jehovah has *h* your murmurings
16:9 he has *h* your murmurings
16:12 I have *h* the murmurings of
23:13 not be *h* upon your mouth
28:35 sound from him must be *h*
Le 5:1 he has *h* public cursing and he
24:14 all those who *h* him must lay
Nu 14:14 *h* that you are Jehovah in
14:15 nations who have *h* of your
14:27 I have *h* the murmurings of
20:16 cried out to Jehovah and he *h*
30:11 husband has *h* it and has kept
De 1:34 Jehovah *h* the voice of your
4:32 or was anything *h* like it?
4:33 *h* the voice of God speaking
4:33 have *h* it, and kept on living
4:36 *h* from the middle of the fire
5:23 *h* the voice out of the middle
5:24 we have *h* his voice out of
5:26 all flesh that has *h* the voice
5:28 Jehovah *h* the voice of your
5:28 *h* the voice of the words of
9:2 you yourself have *h* it said
17:4 told you and you have *h* it
29:19 has *h* the words of this oath
Jos 2:10 have *h* how Jehovah dried up
5:1 *h* that Jehovah had dried up
6:10 nor let your voices be *h*
6:20 *h* the sound of the horn and
9:1 and the Jebusites, *h* of it
9:3 Gibeon *h* what Joshua had done
9:9 we have *h* of his fame and of all
10:1 *h* that Joshua had captured
11:1 the king of Hazor *h* of it
14:12 *h* on that day that there
22:11 sons of Israel *h* it said
22:30 *h* the words that the sons
24:27 it has itself *h* all the
Jg 7:15 Gideon *h* the relating of the
9:46 landowners . . . of Shechem *h* of
18:25 Do not let your voice be *h*
Ru 1:6 she had *h* in the field of Moab
2:8 Boaz said to Ruth: You have *h*
1Sa 1:13 and her voice was not *h*
2:22 *h* of all that his sons kept
7:7 the sons of Israel *h* of it
13:4 And all Israel itself *h* tell
14:22 *h* that the Philistines had
16:2 Once Saul has *h* of it he
17:11 When Saul and all Israel *h*
17:31 David spoke came to be *h*
23:10 *h* that Saul is seeking to
23:11 just as your servant has *h*
25:7 *h* that you have shearers
2Sa 3:28 David *h* of it afterward, he
4:1 son of Saul *h* that Abner had
5:17 David *h* of it, then he went
7:22 we have *h* with our ears
10:7 David *h* of it, then he sent

2Sa 13:21 David himself *h* about all
18:5 *h* when the king commanded
19:2 the people *h* say on that day
22:7 he *h* my voice, With my cry
1Ki 1:11 Have you not *h* that Adonijah
1:45 the noise that you men *h*
2:42 the word that I have *h*
4:34 who had *h* of his wisdom
5:1 *h* that it was he that they
5:7 Hiram *h* the words of Solomon
5:8 I have *h* what you sent to me
6:7 they were not *h* in the house
9:3 *h* your prayer and your request
10:6 I *h* in my own land about
10:7 things *h* to which I listened
11:21 Hadad himself *h* in Egypt
12:2 *h* of it while he was yet in
12:20 Israel *h* that Jeroboam had
13:4 king *h* the word of the man
13:26 the prophet . . . *h* of it
14:6 Ahijah *h* the sound of her
15:21 as soon as Baasha *h* of it
16:16 *h* it said: Zimri has
19:13 that as soon as Elijah *h* it
20:12 as soon as he *h* this word
20:31 *h* that the kings of the
21:15 *h* that Naboth had been
21:16 Ahab *h* that Naboth was dead
21:27 soon as Ahab *h* these words
2Ki 3:21 *h* that the kings had come up
5:8 *h* that the king of Israel had
6:30 king *h* the woman's words
9:30 and Jezebel herself *h* of it
11:13 *h* the sound of the people
19:1 as soon as King Hezekiah *h*
19:4 that Jehovah your God has *h*
19:6 words that you have *h* with
19:8 he had *h* that he had pulled
19:9 He *h* it said respecting
19:11 *h* what the kings of Assyria
19:20 The prayer . . . I have *h*
19:25 Have you not *h*? From remote
20:5 I have *h* your prayer
20:12 *h* that Hezekiah had been
22:11 *h* the words of the book
22:18 the words that you have *h*
22:19 have *h*, is the utterance of
25:23 *h* that the king of Babylon
1Ch 14:8 When David *h* of it, then he
17:20 we have *h* with our ears
18:9 *h* that David had struck
19:8 When David *h* of it, he
2Ch 5:13 causing one sound to be *h* in
7:12 I have *h* your prayer, and I
9:1 queen of Sheba herself *h* the
9:5 True was the word that I *h*
9:6 the report that I have *h*
10:2 *h* of it while he was yet in
15:8 Asa *h* these words and the
16:5 soon as Baasha *h* of it, he
20:29 *h* that Jehovah had fought
23:12 Athaliah *h* the sound of the
33:13 *h* his request for favor and
34:19 king *h* the words of the law
34:26 the words that you have *h*
34:27 have *h*, is the utterance of
Ezr 3:13 *h* even to a great distance
4:1 *h* that the sons of the Exile
9:3 as soon as I *h* of this thing
Ne 1:4 as soon as I *h* these words
2:19 Geshem the Arabian *h* of it
4:1 *h* that we were rebuilding the
4:7 *h* that the repairing of the
4:15 enemies *h* that it had become
5:6 *h* their outcry and these words
6:6 it has been *h*, and Geshem is
6:16 as soon as all our enemies *h*
9:9 outcry at the Red Sea you *h*
12:42 kept making themselves *h*
12:43 of Jerusalem could be *h* far
13:3 as soon as they *h* the law
Es 1:18 have *h* the affair of the queen
1:20 must be *h* in all his realm
2:8 word and his law were *h*
Job 4:16 a calm, and I now *h* a voice
13:1 My ear has *h* and considers
16:2 I have *h* many things like
26:14 a whisper . . . been *h* of him
28:22 we have *h* a report of it
37:4 when his voice is *h*
42:5 In hearsay I have *h* about you
Ps 19:3 voice on their part is being *h*
22:24 cried to him for help he *h*
26:7 thanksgiving to be *h* aloud

Ps 28:6 *h* the voice of my entreaties
31:13 *h* the bad report by many
31:22 *h* the voice of my entreaties
34:6 called, and Jehovah himself *h*
34:17 and Jehovah himself *h*
40:1 and *h* my cry for help
44:1 with our ears we have *h*
48:8 Just as we have *h*, so we have
62:11 twice I have *h* even this
66:8 praise to him to be *h*
66:19 Truly God has *h*; He has paid
76:8 the legal contest to be *h*
78:3 Which we have *h* and know
78:21 Jehovah *h* and began to be
78:59 God *h* and got to be furious
97:8 Zion *h* and began to rejoice
106:2 make all his praise to be *h*
106:44 he *h* their entreating cry
132:6 We have *h* it in Ephrathah
138:4 *h* the sayings of your mouth
141:6 they have *h* my sayings
Pr 13:1 is one that has not *h* rebuke
13:8 has not *h* rebuke
Ec 9:17 more to be *h* than the cry of
12:13 everything having been *h*, is
Ca 2:12 turtledove itself has been *h*
Isa 11:3 to the thing *h* by his ears
15:4 Jahaz their voice has been *h*
16:6 *h* of the pride of Moab, that
21:10 what I have *h* from Jehovah
24:16 are melodies that we have *h*
28:9 understand what has been *h*
28:19 understand what has been *h*
28:22 *h* of from the Sovereign
30:30 dignity of his voice to be *h*
37:1 as soon as King Hezekiah *h*
37:4 that Jehovah your God has *h*
37:6 words that you have *h* with
37:8 *h* that he had pulled away
37:9 *h* it said concerning Tirhakah
37:9 When he *h*, he at once sent
37:11 *h* what the kings of Assyria
37:26 Have you not *h*? From remote
38:5 I have *h* your prayer. I have
39:1 *h* that he had been sick but
40:28 or have you not *h*? Jehovah
42:2 will not let his voice be *h*
43:12 have caused it to be *h*
45:21 be *h* from a long time ago
48:3 and I kept making them *h*
48:6 You have *h*. Behold it all
48:7 before today you have not *h*
48:8 Moreover, you have not *h*
48:20 cause this to be *h*. Make it
52:15 to what they had not *h* they
53:1 faith in the thing *h* by us
58:4 voice to be *h* in the height
60:18 No more will violence be *h*
62:11 *h* to the farthest part of
64:4 time long ago none have *h*
65:19 be *h* in her the sound of
66:8 Who has *h* of a thing like
66:19 not *h* a report about me
Jer 3:21 there has been *h* a sound
4:19 horn is what my soul has *h*
4:31 a sick woman I have *h*
6:7 and despoiling are *h* in her
6:24 have *h* the report about it
8:16 From Dan has been *h* the
9:19 what has been *h* from Zion
18:13 Who has *h* things like these?
18:22 be *h* out of their houses
20:10 I *h* the bad report of many
23:25 I have *h* what the prophets
26:11 have *h* with your own ears
26:12 the words that you have *h*
30:5 sound of trembling we have *h*
31:15 In Ramah a voice is being *h*
31:18 *h* Ephraim bemoaning
33:10 there will yet be *h*
36:13 *h* when Baruch read aloud
36:16 as they *h* all the words
38:27 for the matter was not *h*
40:11 *h* that the king of Babylon
42:4 I have *h*. Here I am praying
46:12 nations have *h* your dishonor
48:4 have caused a cry to be *h*
48:5 breakdown that people have *h*
48:29 *h* of the pride of Moab
49:2 alarm signal of war to be *h*
49:14 that I have *h* from Jehovah
49:21 *h* even at the Red Sea
49:23 bad report that they have *h*
50:43 *h* the report about them

Jer 50:46 an outcry itself be *h*
51:46 report that is to be *h* in
51:51 for we have *h* reproach
La 1:21 *h* how I myself am sighing as
1:21 have *h* of my calamity
3:61 You have *h* their reproach, O
Eze 10:5 *h* to the outer courtyard
19:9 his voice might no more be *h*
26:13 harps will be *h* no more
27:30 be *h* with their voice and
33:5 The sound of the horn he *h*
35:12 *h* all your disrespectful
35:13 words. I myself have *h*
36:15 the nations to be *h*
Da 5:14 *h* concerning you that the
5:16 *h* concerning you, that you are
6:14 king, as soon as he *h* the
10:12 your words have been *h*, and
12:8 I *h*, but I could not
Ob 1 a report that we have *h* from
Jon 2:2 I cried for help. You *h* my
Na 2:13 voice of your messengers be *h*
Hab 3:2 I have *h* the report about you
3:16 I *h*, and my belly began to
Zep 2:8 *h* the reproach by Moab and
Zec 8:23 *h* that God is with you
Mt 2:9 *h* the king, they went their
2:18 A voice was *h* in Ramah
4:12 *h* that John had been arrested
5:21 You *h* that it was said to
5:27 You *h* that it was said, You
5:33 you *h* that it was said to
5:38 *h* that it was said, Eye for
5:43 You *h* that it was said
11:2 John, having *h* in jail about
13:15 they have *h* without response
14:1 Herod, the district ruler, *h*
19:22 the young man *h* this saying
19:25 When the disciples *h* that
20:24 the ten others *h* of this
20:30 *h* that Jesus was passing by
21:45 *h* his illustrations, they
22:22 they *h* that, they marveled
22:34 After the Pharisees *h* that
26:65 you have *h* the blasphemy
Mr 3:21 when his relatives *h* about it
4:15 as they have *h* it Satan comes
4:16 have *h* the word, they accept
4:18 the ones that have *h* the word
5:27 she *h* the things about Jesus
6:16 when Herod *h* it he began to
6:29 When his disciples *h* of it
6:55 to where they *h* he was
7:25 *h* about him and came and
10:41 when the ten others *h* about
10:47 When he *h* that it was Jesus
11:18 priests and the scribes *h* it
12:28 *h* them disputing, knowing
14:11 they *h* it, they rejoiced
14:58 We *h* him say, I will throw
14:64 You *h* the blasphemy
Lu 1:13 supplication . . . favorably *h*
1:41 *h* the greeting of Mary, the
1:58 her relatives *h* that Jehovah
1:66 all that *h* made note of it
2:18 all that *h* marveled over the
2:20 all the things they *h* and saw
4:21 scripture that you just *h* is
4:23 the things we *h* as having
7:3 When he *h* about Jesus, he sent
7:9 when Jesus *h* these things he
7:22 to John what you saw and *h*
7:29 when they *h* this, declared
8:12 are the ones that have *h*
8:14 these are the ones that have *h*
9:7 Herod the district ruler *h* of
12:3 will be *h* in the light, and
15:25 he *h* a music concert and
18:23 he *h* this, he became deeply
18:26 *h* this said: Who possibly
18:36 *h* a crowd moving through
22:71 *h* it out of his own mouth
23:8 because of having *h* about him
Joh 1:37 two disciples *h* him speak
1:40 *h* what John said and
3:32 What he has seen and *h*
4:1 Pharisees had *h* that Jesus
4:42 *h* for ourselves and we know
4:47 *h* that Jesus had come out
5:37 neither *h* his voice at any
6:45 *h* from the Father and has
6:60 when they *h* this, said
7:32 The Pharisees *h* the crowd
7:40 crowd that *h* these words
Joh 7:51 *h* from him and come to know
8:26 the very things I *h* from him
8:38 you have *h* from your father
8:40 the truth that I *h* from God
9:32 *h* that anyone opened the eyes
9:35 Jesus *h* that they had thrown
9:40 *h* these things, and they said
11:4 But when Jesus *h* it he said
11:6 he *h* that he was sick, then
11:20 Martha, when she *h* that
11:29 when she *h* this, got up
11:41 thank you that you have *h*
12:18 *h* he had performed this
12:29 *h* it began to say that it
12:34 *h* from the Law that the
12:38 faith in the thing *h* by us
14:28 You *h* that I said to you
15:15 I have *h* from my Father
18:21 have *h* what I spoke to them
19:8 Pilate *h* this saying, he
Ac 1:4 about which you *h* from me
2:6 *h* them speaking in his own
2:37 *h* this they were stabbed to
4:20 things we have seen and *h*
5:24 chief priests *h* these words
5:33 When they *h* this, they felt
6:11 *h* him speaking blasphemous
6:14 *h* him say that this Jesus the
7:12 Jacob *h* there were foodstuffs
7:34 I have *h* their groaning and
8:14 *h* that Samaria had accepted
8:30 *h* him reading aloud Isaiah
9:4 *h* a voice say to him: Saul
9:13 *h* from many about this man
9:38 *h* that Peter was in this city
10:31 prayer has been favorably *h*
10:46 *h* them speaking with tongues
11:1 *h* that people of the nations
11:7 I also *h* a voice say to me
11:18 when they *h* these things
13:48 those of the nations *h* this
14:14 Barnabas and Paul *h* of it
15:24 we have *h* that some from
16:38 *h* that the men were Romans
17:8 when they *h* these things
17:32 *h* of a resurrection of the
18:8 Corinthians that *h* began to
18:26 Priscilla and Aquila *h* him
19:2 never *h* whether there is a
19:10 Asia *h* the word of the Lord
21:12 when we *h* this, both we and
21:21 *h* it rumored about you that
22:2 *h* he was addressing them in
22:7 *h* a voice say to me, Saul
22:15 of things you have seen and *h*
22:26 when the army officer *h* this
23:16 the son of Paul's sister *h* of
26:14 I *h* a voice say to me in
28:15 *h* the news about us, came
28:27 have *h* without response, and
Ro 10:14 of whom they have not *h*
10:16 faith in the thing *h* by us
10:17 faith follows the thing *h*
10:17 thing *h* is through the word
15:21 those who have not *h* will
1Co 2:9 ear has not *h*, neither have
2Co 6:2 I *h* you, and in a day of
12:4 *h* unutterable words which
Ga 1:13 *h* about my conduct formerly
Eph 1:13 *h* the word of truth, the
1:15 I have *h* of the faith you
3:2 have *h* about the stewardship
4:21 *h* him and were taught by
Php 2:26 you *h* he had fallen sick
4:9 as well as accepted and *h* and
Col 1:4 *h* of your faith in connection
1:5 This hope you *h* of before by
1:6 you *h* and accurately knew the
1:9 from the day we *h* of it, have
1:23 good news which you *h*, and
1Th 2:13 God's word, which you *h*
2Ti 1:13 words that you *h* from me
2:2 the things you *h* from me
Heb 2:1 attention to the things *h* by
2:3 for us by those who *h* him
3:16 *h* and yet provoked to bitter
4:2 word which was *h* did not
5:7 favorably *h* for his godly fear
Jas 5:11 *h* of the endurance of Job and
2Pe 1:18 these words we *h* borne from
2:8 *h* while dwelling among them
1Jo 1:1 which we have *h*, which we
1:3 that which we have seen and *h*
1:5 message which we have *h* from
1Jo 2:7 is the word which you *h*
2:18 *h* that antichrist is coming
2:24 *h* from the beginning remain
2:24 have *h* from the beginning
3:11 message which you have *h*
4:3 which you have *h* was coming
2Jo 6 *h* from the beginning, that you
Re 1:10 I *h* behind me a strong voice
3:3 and how you *h*, and go on
4:1 voice that I *h* was as of a
5:11 I *h* a voice of many angels
5:13 I *h* saying: To the One sitting
6:1 *h* one of the four living
6:3 *h* the second living creature
6:5 *h* the third living creature say
6:6 I *h* a voice as if in the midst
6:7 I *h* the voice of the fourth
7:4 I *h* the number of those who
8:13 I *h* an eagle flying in
9:13 I *h* one voice out of the horns
9:16 I *h* the number of them
10:4 I *h* a voice out of heaven say
10:8 voice that I *h* out of heaven
11:12 they *h* a loud voice out of
12:10 I *h* a loud voice in heaven
14:2 I *h* a sound out of heaven as
14:2 I *h* was as of singers who
14:13 I *h* a voice out of heaven
16:1 I *h* a loud voice out of the
16:5 I *h* the angel over the
16:7 I *h* the altar say: Yes
18:4 I *h* another voice out of
18:22 trumpeters will never be *h*
18:22 will ever be *h* in you again
18:23 will ever be *h* in you again
19:1 I *h* what was as a loud voice
19:6 I *h* what was as a voice of
21:3 I *h* a loud voice from the
22:8 I had *h* and seen, I fell

Hearer

Ps 65:2 O *H* of prayer, even to you
Eze 33:4 *h* actually hears the sound
Jas 1:23 *h* of the word, and not a
1:25 not a forgetful *h*, but a doer

Hearers

Eze 13:19 my people, the *h* of a lie
Ro 2:13 *h* of law are not the ones
Eph 4:29 what is favorable to the *h*
Jas 1:22 and not *h* only, deceiving

Hearing

Ge 21:6 everybody *h* of it will laugh
23:10 *h* of the sons of Heth with
23:13 spoke to Ephron in the *h* of
23:16 spoken in the *h* of the sons
24:30 *h* the words of Rebekah his
27:34 *h* his father's words Esau
44:18 word in the *h* of my master
50:4 in the *h* of Pharaoh, saying
Ex 32:18 other singing that I am *h*
Nu 24:4 the one *h* the sayings of God
24:16 the one *h* the sayings of God
30:5 the day of his *h* all her vows
30:7 day of his *h* it, her vows
30:8 her husband on the day of *h*
30:12 *h* any expression of her lips
30:14 on the day of his *h* them
30:15 annuls them after his *h* them
De 1:16 a *h* between your brothers
4:12 words was what you were *h*
5:25 again *h* the voice of Jehovah
31:11 of all Israel in their *h*
31:28 speak in their *h* these words
31:30 *h* of all the congregation of
32:44 song in the *h* of the people
Jos 20:4 in the *h* of the older men of
Jg 7:3 in the *h* of the people, saying
9:2 in the *h* of all the landowners
9:3 in the *h* of all the landowners
17:2 and also said it in my *h*
1Sa 2:23 the things I am *h* about you
2:24 is not good that I am *h*
8:21 Samuel gave a *h* to all the
11:6 Saul on his *h* these words
15:14 the herd that I am *h*
2Sa 15:3 no one . . . giving you a *h*
17:9 one *h* of it will then be
18:12 in our *h* it was that the
1Ki 10:1 queen of Sheba was *h* the
2Ki 22:19 your *h* what I have spoken
2Ch 30:27 *h* was granted to their
34:27 at your *h* his words
Ne 8:9 were *h* the words of the law
Job 33:8 sound of your words I kept *h*

Ps 38:14 like a man that was not *h*
81:5 that I did not know I kept *h*
Pr 20:12 The *h* ear and the seeing eye
25:12 wise reprover upon the *h* ear
28:9 his ear away from *h* the law
Ec 1:8 is the ear filled from *h*
7:5 *h* the song of the stupid ones
Isa 32:3 those *h* will pay attention
41:26 one that is *h* any sayings
59:2 to keep from *h*
Jer 4:21 keep *h* the sound of the horn
Eze 3:27 Let the one *h* hear, and let
16:56 worth *h* about from your
19:4 And nations kept *h* about him
Da 3:7 *h* the sound of the horn, the
5:23 *h* nothing or knowing nothing
10:9 *h* the sound of his words
10:9 *h* the sound of his words, I
Am 8:11 for *h* the words of Jehovah
Na 3:19 All those *h* the report about
Zec 8:9 *h* in these days these words
Mt 2:3 At *h* this King Herod was
2:22 *h* that Archelaus ruled as
6:7 imagine they will get a *h* for
7:26 *h* these sayings of mine and
8:10 *H* that, Jesus became amazed
9:12 *H* them, he said: Persons in
11:4 report to John what you are *h*
11:5 deaf are *h*, and the dead are
12:24 *h* this, the Pharisees said
13:13 and *h*, they hear in vain
13:14 *h*, you will hear but by no
13:17 hear the things you are *h*
13:20 one *h* the word and at once
13:22 *h* the word, but the anxiety
13:23 one *h* the word and getting
14:13 At *h* this Jesus withdrew
15:12 the Pharisees stumbled at *h*
17:6 At *h* this the disciples fell
22:33 On *h* that, the crowds were
27:47 At *h* this, some of those
Mr 2:17 Upon *h* this Jesus said to them
3:8 *h* of how many things he was
4:12 *h*, they may hear and yet not
4:24 attention to what you are *h*
6:20 And after *h* him he was at a
7:35 his *h* powers were opened
15:35 on *h* it, began to say: See
Lu 4:28 all those *h* these things in
7:1 in the *h* of the people, he
7:22 the deaf are *h*, the dead are
8:10 though *h*, they may not get
8:15 after *h* the word with a fine
8:50 On *h* this, Jesus answered him
9:9 about whom I am *h* such things
10:24 to hear the things you are *h*
11:28 Happy are those *h* the word
14:15 On *h* these things a certain
18:22 *h* that, Jesus said to him
20:16 On *h* this they said: Never
23:6 On *h* that, Pilate asked
Joh 12:12 *h* that Jesus was coming to
14:24 word that you are *h* is not
19:13 Pilate, after *h* these words
21:7 upon *h* that it was the Lord
Ac 2:8 *h*, each one of us, his own
4:24 *h* this they with one accord
5:5 On *h* these words Ananias fell
5:5 fear came over all those *h*
5:11 those *h* about these things
5:21 *h* this, they entered into the
7:54 *h* these things they felt cut
9:7 *h*, indeed, the sound of a
9:21 all those *h* him gave way to
10:44 upon all those *h* the word
16:25 the prisoners were *h* them
19:5 On *h* this, they got baptized
19:28 *H* this and becoming full of
21:20 *h* this they began to glorify
23:35 shall give you a thorough *h*
28:26 By *h*, you will hear but by
1Co 12:17 where would the sense of *h*
12:17 If it were all *h*, where
Ga 3:2 or due to a *h* by faith
3:5 or owing to a *h* by faith
Phm 5 keep *h* of your love and faith
Heb 5:11 have become dull in your *h*
12:19 on *h* which voice the people
Jas 1:19 man must be swift about *h*
3Jo 4 *h* that my children go on
Re 22:8 I John was the one *h* and
22:17 let anyone *h* say: Come!

Hears
Nu 30:4 her father actually *h* her vow
30:7 her husband actually *h* it and
1Sa 3:11 if anyone *h* about, both
2Ki 21:12 *h* both his ears will tingle
Job 34:28 so he *h* the outcry of the
Ps 55:17 I moan, And he *h* my voice
116:1 Jehovah *h* My voice, my
Pr 15:29 of the righteous ones he *h*
18:13 replying . . . before he *h* it
Isa 30:19 soon as he *h* it he will
Jer 19:3 when anyone *h*, his ears will
Eze 33:4 *h* the sound of the horn
Da 3:10 *h* the sound of the horn, the
Mt 7:24 *h* these sayings of mine and
13:19 *h* the word of the kingdom
Lu 6:47 *h* my words and does them
6:49 he who *h* and does not do is
Joh 3:29 when he stands and *h* him
5:24 that *h* my word and believes
12:47 *h* my sayings and does not
16:13 things he *h* he will speak
2Co 12:6 sees I am or he *h* from me
1Jo 5:14 we ask . . . he *h* us
5:15 *h* us respecting whatever
Re 3:20 *h* my voice and opens the
22:18 *h* the words of the prophecy

Hearsay
Job 42:5 In *h* I have heard about you
Ps 18:44 At mere *h* they will be

Heart
Ge 6:5 thoughts of his *h* was only bad
6:6 and he felt hurt at his *h*
8:21 Jehovah said in his *h*: Never
8:21 inclination of the *h* of man
17:17 say in his *h*: Will a man a
20:5 the honesty of my *h* and with
20:6 honesty of your *h* you have
24:45 speaking in my *h*, why, there
27:41 Esau kept saying in his *h*
45:26 But his *h* grew numb, because
Ex 4:14 certainly rejoice in his *h*
4:21 let his *h* become obstinate
7:3 Pharaoh's *h* become obstinate
7:13 Pharaoh's *h* became obstinate
7:14 Pharaoh's *h* is unresponsive
7:22 Pharaoh's *h* . . . obstinate, and
7:23 Pharaoh . . . did not set his *h*
8:15 he made his *h* unresponsive
8:19 But Pharaoh's *h* continued to
8:32 However, Pharaoh made his *h*
9:7 Pharaoh's *h* continued to be
9:12 Pharaoh's *h* become obstinate
9:14 all my blows against your *h*
9:21 whoever did not set his *h* to
9:34 and making his *h* unresponsive
9:35 And Pharaoh's *h* continued
10:1 I have let his *h* and the
10:20 Pharaoh's *h* become obstinate
10:27 Pharaoh's *h* become obstinate
11:10 Pharaoh's *h* become obstinate
14:4 Pharaoh's *h* become obstinate
14:5 *h* of Pharaoh as well as his
14:8 Jehovah let the *h* of Pharaoh
15:8 congealed in the *h* of the sea
25:2 every man whose *h* incites
28:3 *h* that I have filled with the
28:29 over his *h* when he comes
28:30 prove to be over Aaron's *h*
28:30 over his *h* before Jehovah
31:6, 6 the *h* of everyone wise of *h*
35:21 everyone whose *h* impelled
35:25 women who were wise of *h*
35:34 into his *h* that he should
35:35 wisdom of *h* to do all the
36:2 into whose *h* Jehovah had put
36:2 *h* impelled him to approach
Le 19:17 hate your brother in your *h*
26:41 *h* will be humbled, and at
Nu 16:28 that it is not of my own *h*
24:13 good or bad out of my own *h*
De 1:28 caused our *h* to melt, saying
2:30 his *h* become hard, in order
4:9 not depart from your *h* all the
4:29 with all your *h* and with all
4:39 call back to your *h* that
5:29 develop this *h* . . . to fear
6:5 love . . . with all your *h* and
6:6 must prove to be on your *h*
7:17 case you say in your *h*
8:2 as to know what was in your *h*
8:5 know with your own *h* that
De 8:14 your *h* may indeed be lifted
8:17 say in your *h*, My own power
9:4 Do not say in your *h* when
9:5 for the uprightness of your *h*
10:12 with all your *h* and all your
11:13 serve him with all your *h*
11:16 fear your *h* may be enticed
11:18 to your *h* and your soul and
13:3 all your *h* and all your soul
15:7 you must not harden your *h* or
15:9 come to be in your *h*, saying
15:10 your *h* should not be stingy
17:17 his *h* may not turn aside
17:20 his *h* may not exalt itself
18:21 say in your *h*: How shall we
19:6 because his *h* is hot, chase
20:8 to melt as his own *h*
26:16 all your *h* and all your soul
28:28 and bewilderment of *h*
28:47 with rejoicing and joy of *h*
28:65 give you there a trembling *h*
28:67 of the dread of your *h* with
29:4 not given you a *h* to know and
29:18 a tribe whose *h* is turning
29:19 blessed himself in his *h*
29:19 in the stubbornness of my *h*
30:1 brought them back to your *h*
30:2 all your *h* and all your soul
30:6 to circumcise your *h* and the
30:6 the *h* of your offspring
30:6 all your *h* and all your soul
30:10 all your *h* and all your soul
30:14 in your own *h*, that you may
30:17 if your *h* turns away and you
Jos 7:5 the *h* of the people began to
14:7 just as it was in my *h*
14:8 the *h* of the people to melt
22:5 serving him with all your *h*
Jg 5:9 My *h* is for the commanders of
5:15 the searchings of the *h*
5:16 great searchings of the *h*
9:3 *h* inclined toward Abimelech
16:15 when your *h* is not with me
16:17 disclosed to her all his *h*
16:18 disclosed to her all his *h*
16:18 disclosed to me all his *h*
16:25 because their *h* was merry
18:20 *h* of the priest was pleased
19:5 Sustain your *h* with a bit of
19:6 and let your *h* feel good
19:8 take sustenance for your *h*
19:9 and let your *h* feel good
Ru 3:7 and his *h* was feeling good
1Sa 1:8 and why does your *h* feel bad?
1:13 she was speaking in her *h*
2:1 My *h* does exult in Jehovah
2:35 what is in my *h* and in my
4:13 *h* had become atremble over
4:20 and did not set her *h* on it
6:6 make your *h* unresponsive just
6:6 made their *h* unresponsive
7:3 If it is with all your *h* you
7:3 direct your *h* unswervingly to
9:19 in your *h* I shall tell you
9:20 do not set your *h* on them
10:9 God began changing the *h* of
10:26 men whose *h* God had touched
12:20 Jehovah with all your *h*
12:24 in truth with all your *h*
13:14 a man agreeable to his *h*
14:7 Do whatever is in your *h*
14:7 in accord with your *h*
16:7 Jehovah, he sees what the *h*
17:28 and the badness of your *h*
17:32 the *h* of any man collapse
21:12 take these words to his *h*
24:5 David's *h* kept striking him
25:25 my lord set his *h* upon this
25:31 stumbling block to the *h*
25:36 Nabal's *h* was feeling good
25:37 *h* came to be dead inside
27:1 David said in his *h*: Now I
28:5 his *h* began to tremble very
2Sa 6:16 to despise him in her *h*
7:3 Everything that is in your *h*
7:21 agreement with your own *h*
7:27 servant has taken *h* to pray
13:20 not set your *h* on this
13:28 Amnon's *h* is in a merry
13:33 king take to his *h* the word
14:1 king's *h* was toward Absalom
15:13 The *h* of the men of Israel
17:10 valiant man whose *h* is as
17:10 is as the *h* of the lion

Sa 18:3 they would not set *h* upon us
18:3 they would not set *h* upon us
18:14 through the *h* of Absalom
18:14 in the *h* of the big tree
19:7 to the *h* of your servants
19:14 bend the *h* of all the men
19:19 king should lay it to his *h*
24:10 David's *h* began to beat him
Ki 2:4 all their *h* and with all their
2:44 your *h* well knows that you
3:6 uprightness of *h* with you
3:9 an obedient *h* to judge your
3:12 a wise and understanding *h*
4:29 a broadness of *h*, like the
8:17 close to the *h* of David my
8:18 close to your *h* to build a
8:18 proved to be close to your *h*
8:23 before you with all their *h*
8:38 the plague of his own *h*
8:39 you know his *h* (for you
8:39 *h* of all the sons of mankind
8:48 with all their *h* and with
8:58 incline our *h* to himself
8:61 *h* must prove to be complete
8:66 feeling merry of *h* over all
9:3 my *h* will certainly prove to
9:4 with integrity of *h* and with
10:2 happened to be close to her *h*
10:24 that God had put in his *h*
11:2 will incline your *h*
11:3 gradually inclined his *h*
11:4 had inclined his *h* to follow
11:4 *h* did not prove . . . complete
11:4 like the *h* of David his
11:9 his *h* had inclined away from
12:26 began to say in his *h*
12:27 the *h* of this people will
14:8 with all his *h* by doing only
15:3 his *h* did not prove to be
15:3 *h* of David his forefather
15:14 Asa's *h* itself proved to be
18:37 have turned their *h* back
21:7 and let your *h* be merry
2Ki 5:26 Did not my *h* itself go along
6:11 the *h* of the king of Syria
9:24 the arrow came out at his *h*
10:15 Is your *h* upright with me
10:15, 15 my own *h* is with your *h*
10:30 all that was in my *h* you
10:31 of Israel with all his *h*
12:4 the *h* of each one to bring
14:10 your *h* has lifted you up
20:3 and with a complete *h*, and
22:19 *h* was soft so that you
23:3 his statutes with all the *h*
23:25 his *h* and with all his soul
1Ch 12:17 my own *h* will become at
12:33 they were not of a double *h*
12:38 with a complete *h* they
12:38 one *h* for making David king
15:29 to despise him in her *h*
16:10 *h* of those seeking Jehovah
17:2 Everything that is in your *h*
17:19 agreement with your own *h*
22:7 close to my *h* to build a
22:19 set your *h* and your soul to
28:2 was close to my *h* to build a
28:9 serve him with a complete *h*
29:9 with a complete *h* that they
29:17 are an examiner of the *h*
29:17 in the uprightness of my *h*
29:18 thoughts of the *h* of your
29:18 and direct their *h* to you
29:19 my son give a complete *h* to
2Ch 1:11 proved to be close to your *h*
6:7 close to the *h* of David my
6:8 close to your *h* to build a
6:8 proved to be close to your *h*
6:14 before you with all their *h*
6:30 because you know his *h*
6:30 know the *h* of the sons of
6:38 to you with all their *h* and
7:10 feeling good at *h* over the
7:11 Solomon's *h* to do regarding
7:16 *h* will certainly prove to
9:1 happened to be close to her *h*
9:23 true God had put in his *h*
11:16 *h* to seek Jehovah the God
12:14 his *h* to search for Jehovah
15:12 with all their *h* and with
15:15 with all their *h* that they
15:17 Asa's *h* itself proved to
16:9 those whose *h* is complete
17:6 *h* became bold in the ways of

2Ch 19:3 *h* to search for the true God
19:9 and with a complete *h*
20:33 prepared their *h* for the God
22:9 for Jehovah with all his *h*
24:4 close to the *h* of Jehoash
25:2 only not with a complete *h*
25:19 *h* has lifted you up to be
26:16 *h* became haughty even to
29:10 close to my *h* to conclude
29:31 every one willing of *h*
29:34 more upright of *h* for
30:12 them one *h* to perform the
30:19 prepared his *h* to search for
30:22 Hezekiah spoke to the *h* of
31:21 all his *h* that he acted
32:6 and speak to the *h* of them
32:25 *h* became haughty and there
32:26 for the haughtiness of his *h*
32:31 know everything in his *h*
34:27 your *h* was soft so that
34:31 his *h* and with all his soul
36:13 hardening his *h* so as not
Ezr 6:22 the *h* of the king of Assyria
7:10 prepared his *h* to consult the
7:27 into the *h* of the king
Ne 2:2 nothing but a gloominess of *h*
2:12 God was putting into my *h* to
4:6 to have a *h* for working
5:7 my *h* took consideration within
6:8 own *h* that you are inventing
7:5 God put it into my *h* that I
9:8 And you found his *h* faithful
Es 1:10 king's *h* was in a merry mood
5:9 joyful and merry of *h*; but as
6:6 Haman said in his *h*: To whom
Job 1:5 and have cursed God in their *h*
1:8 your *h* upon my servant Job
2:3 set your *h* upon my servant
4:20 anyone's taking it to *h* they
7:17 should set your *h* upon him
8:10 from their *h* will they not
9:4 He is wise in *h* and strong in
10:13 you have concealed in your *h*
11:13 will really prepare your *h*
12:3 I too have a *h* . . . as you
12:24 *h* of the head ones of the
15:12 does your *h* carry you away
17:4 their *h* you have closed to
17:11 The wishes of my *h*
22:22 put his sayings in your *h*
23:16 God . . . made my *h* timid
27:6 My *h* will not taunt me for
29:13 the *h* of the widow I would
31:7 *h* has walked merely after
31:9 *h* has been enticed toward a
31:27 my *h* began to be enticed in
33:3 the uprightness of my *h*
34:10 you men of *h*, listen to me
34:14 If he sets his *h* upon anyone
34:34 Men of *h* themselves will
36:5 He is mighty in power of *h*
36:13 those apostate in *h* will
37:1 my *h* begins to tremble
37:24 who are wise in their own *h*
41:24 Its *h* is cast like stone
Ps 4:4 Have your say in your *h*
4:7 give a rejoicing in my *h*
7:9 is testing out *h* and kidneys
7:10 a Savior of those upright in *h*
9:1 O Jehovah, with all my *h*
10:6 He has said in his *h*: I shall
10:11 has said in his *h*: God has
10:13 He has said in his *h*
10:17 You will prepare their *h*
11:2 at the ones upright in *h*
12:2 speaking even with a double *h*
13:2 Grief in my *h* by day
13:5 Let my *h* be joyful in your
14:1 has said in his *h*
15:2 speaking the truth in his *h*
16:9 my *h* does rejoice, and my
17:3 You have examined my *h*, you
19:8 causing the *h* to rejoice
19:14 and the meditation of my *h*
20:4 to you according to your *h*
21:2 desire of his *h* you have given
22:14 My *h* has become like wax
24:4 in his hands and clean in *h*
25:17 Distresses of my *h* have
26:2 Refine my kidneys and my *h*
27:3 My *h* will not fear
27:8 Concerning you my *h* has said
27:14 and let your *h* be strong
28:7 In him my *h* has trusted

Ps 28:7 helped, so that my *h* exults
31:12 and not in the *h*
31:24 and may your *h* be strong
32:11 all you who are upright in *h*
33:11 The thoughts of his *h* are to
33:21 For in him our *h* rejoices
34:18 those that are broken at *h*
35:25 may they not say in their *h*
36:1 is in the midst of his *h*
36:10 to those upright in *h*
37:4 the requests of your *h*
37:15 will enter into their *h*
37:31 law of his God is in his *h*
38:8 due to the groaning of my *h*
38:10 My own *h* has palpitated
39:3 My *h* grew hot inside me
40:10 not covered over within my *h*
40:12 And my own *h* left me
41:6 untruth is what his *h* will
44:18 *h* has not turned faithlessly
44:21 the secrets of the *h*
45:1 My *h* has become astir with
45:5 In the *h* of the enemies of
46:2 into the *h* of the vast sea
49:3 the meditation of my *h* will
51:10 Create in me even a pure *h*
51:17 A *h* broken and crushed
53:1 said in his *h*: There is no
55:4 *h* is in severe pain within me
55:21 his *h* is disposed to fight
57:7 My *h* is steadfast, O God
57:7 My *h* is steadfast. I will
58:2 with the *h* practice outright
61:2 when my *h* grows feeble
62:8 Before him pour out your *h*
62:10 do not set your *h* on them
64:6 even his *h*, is deep
64:10 the upright in *h* will boast
66:18 anything hurtful in my *h*
69:20 Reproach . . . broken my *h*
69:32 let your *h* also keep alive
73:1 Israel, to those clean in *h*
73:7 the imaginations of the *h*
73:13 that I have cleansed my *h*
73:21 For my *h* was soured And in
73:26 and my *h* have failed
73:26 God is the rock of my *h* and
74:8 said together in their own *h*
76:5 ones powerful in *h* have been
77:6 my *h* I will show concern
78:8 who had not prepared their *h*
78:18 to test God in their *h*
78:37 *h* was not steadfast with
78:72 to the integrity of his *h*
81:12 the stubbornness of their *h*
83:5 *h* they have unitedly
84:2 My own *h* and my very flesh
84:5 In whose *h* are the highways
86:11 Unify my *h* to fear your name
86:12 my God, with all my *h*
90:12 may bring a *h* of wisdom in
94:15 upright in *h* will follow it
95:8 harden your *h* as at Meribah
95:10 are a people wayward at *h*
97:11 for the ones upright in *h*
101:2 integrity of my *h* inside my
101:4 crooked *h* departs from me
101:5 haughty eyes . . . arrogant *h*
102:4 *h* has been struck just like
104:15 *h* of mortal man rejoice
104:15 the very *h* of mortal man
105:3 *h* of those seeking Jehovah
105:25 *h* change to hate his people
107:12 proceeded to subdue their *h*
108:1 My *h* is steadfast, O God
109:16 one dejected at *h*, to put
109:22 *h* itself has been pierced
111:1 laud Jehovah with all my *h*
112:7 His *h* is steadfast, made
112:8 His *h* is unshakable; he
119:2 all the *h* they keep searching
119:7 you in uprightness of *h*
119:10 whole *h* I have searched for
119:11 In my *h* I have treasured
119:32 make my *h* have the room
119:34 keep it with the whole *h*
119:36 Incline my *h* to your
119:58 your face with all my *h*
119:69 all my *h* I shall observe
119:70 *h* has become unfeeling just
119:80 *h* prove faultless in your
119:111 the exultation of my *h*
119:112 I have inclined my *h* to do
119:145 called with my whole *h*

Ps 119:161 *h* has been in dread of
131:1 my *h* has not been haughty
138:1 laud you with all my *h*
139:23 God, and know my *h*
140:2 bad things in their *h*
141:4 incline my *h* to anything bad
143:4 my *h* shows itself numbed
Pr 2:2 incline your *h* to discernment
2:10 wisdom enters into your *h* and
3:1 commandments may your *h*
3:3 them upon the tablet of your *h*
3:5 in Jehovah with all your *h*
4:4 *h* keep fast hold of my words
4:21 them in the midst of your *h*
4:23 safeguard your *h*, for out of
5:12 *h* has disrespected even
6:14 Perverseness is in his *h*
6:18 *h* fabricating hurtful schemes
6:21 upon your *h* constantly
6:25 her prettiness in your *h*
6:32 with a woman is in want of *h*
7:3 upon the tablet of your *h*
7:7 a young man in want of *h*
7:10 prostitute and cunning of *h*
7:25 *h* not turn aside to her ways
8:5 you stupid ones, understand *h*
9:4 Whoever is in want of *h*
9:16 whoever is in want of *h*
10:8 one wise in *h* will accept
10:13 back of one in want of *h*
10:20 *h* of the wicked one is worth
10:21 for want of *h* the foolish
11:12 one in want of *h* has
11:20 crooked at *h* are something
11:29 servant to the one wise in *h*
12:8 one who is twisted at *h* will
12:11 is in want of *h*
12:20 Deception is in the *h* of
12:23 *h* of the stupid ones is one
12:25 Anxious care in the *h* of a
13:12 is making the *h* sick
14:10 *h* is aware of the bitterness
14:13 the *h* may be in pain
14:14 The one faithless at *h* will
14:30 A calm *h* is the life of the
14:33 *h* of the understanding one
15:7 *h* of the stupid ones is not
15:13 joyful *h* has a good effect on
15:13 because of the pain of the *h*
15:14 understanding *h* is one that
15:15 that is good at *h* has a feast
15:21 to one who is in want of *h*
15:28 The *h* of the righteous one
15:30 the eyes makes the *h* rejoice
15:32 to reproof is acquiring *h*
16:1 belong the arrangings of the *h*
16:5 Everyone that is proud in *h* is
16:9 *h* of earthling man may think
16:21 one that is wise in *h* will
16:23 *h* of the wise one causes his
17:16 wisdom, when he has no *h*
17:18 A man that is wanting in *h*
17:20 crooked at *h* will not find
17:22 *h* that is joyful does good as
18:2 his *h* should uncover itself
18:12 Before a crash the *h* of a
18:15 *h* of the understanding one
19:3 his *h* becomes enraged against
19:8 acquiring *h* is loving his own
19:21 Many are the plans in the *h*
20:5 Counsel in the *h* of a man is
20:9 can say: I have cleansed my *h*
21:1 A king's *h* is as streams of
21:4 an arrogant *h*, the lamp of
22:11 The one loving purity of *h*
22:15 tied up with the *h* of a boy
22:17 your very *h* to my knowledge
23:7 his *h* itself is not with you
23:12 Do bring your *h* to discipline
23:15 if your *h* has become wise
23:15 wise, my *h* will rejoice
23:17 *h* not be envious of sinners
23:19 lead your *h* on in the way
23:26 My son, do give your *h* to me
23:33 *h* will speak perverse things
23:34 down in the *h* of the sea
24:2 what their *h* keeps meditating
24:17 may your *h* not be joyful
24:30 of the man in need of *h*
24:32 I began taking it to *h*
25:3 and the *h* of kings, that is
25:20 with songs upon a gloomy *h*
26:23 lips along with a bad *h*
26:25 detestable things in his *h*
Pr 27:9 are what make the *h* rejoice
27:11 make my *h* rejoice, that I
27:19 *h* of a man with that of a
27:23 Set your *h* to your droves
28:14 is hardening his *h* will fall
28:26 trusting . . . own *h* is stupid
30:19 a ship in the *h* of the sea
31:11 *h* of her owner has put trust
Ec 1:13 set my *h* to seek and explore
1:16 I, spoke with my *h*, saying
1:16 *h* saw a great deal of wisdom
1:17 give my *h* to knowing wisdom
2:1 I said, even I, in my *h*
2:3 explored with my *h* by cheering
2:3 was leading my *h* with wisdom
2:10 I did not hold back my *h* from
2:10 my *h* was joyful because of
2:15 And I myself said in my *h*
2:15 I spoke in my *h*: This too is
2:20 *h* despair over all the hard
2:22 and for the striving of his *h*
2:23 his *h* just does not lie down
3:11 he has put in their *h*, that
3:17 said in my *h*: The true God
3:18 I, even I, have said in my *h*
5:2 *h*, let it not be hasty to bring
5:20 with the rejoicing of his *h*
7:2 alive should take it to his *h*
7:3 the face the *h* becomes better
7:4 *h* of the wise ones is in the
7:4 *h* of the stupid ones is in the
7:7 and a gift can destroy the *h*
7:21 do not give your *h* to all the
7:22 your own *h* well knows even
7:25 turned around, even my *h* did
7:26 and whose *h* is dragnets and
8:5 wise *h* will know both time
8:9 applying of my *h* to every work
8:11 the *h* of the sons of men has
8:16 applied my *h* to know wisdom
9:1 I took all this to my *h*, even
9:3 *h* of the sons of men is also
9:3 there is madness in their *h*
9:7 drink your wine with a good *h*
10:2 *h* of the wise is at his right
10:2 *h* of the stupid at his left
10:3 his own *h* is lacking, and he
11:9 let your *h* do you good in the
11:9 walk in the ways of your *h*
11:10 remove vexation from your *h*
Ca 3:11 day of the rejoicing of his *h*
4:9 You have made my *h* beat, O my
4:9 my *h* beat by one of your eyes
5:2 am asleep, but my *h* is awake
8:6 Place me as a seal upon your *h*
Isa 1:5 and the whole *h* is feeble
6:10 *h* of this people unreceptive
6:10 own *h* may not understand
7:2, 2 his *h* . . . *h* of his people
7:4 *h* itself be timid because
9:9 their insolence of *h* in saying
10:7 *h* may not be that way, he
10:7 to annihilate is in his *h*
10:12 *h* of the king of Assyria
13:7 whole *h* itself of mortal
14:13 said in your *h*, To the
15:5 own *h* cries out over Moab
19:1 *h* of Egypt will melt in the
21:4 My *h* has wandered about
24:7 glad at *h* have gone to
29:13 removed their *h* itself far
30:29 rejoicing of *h* like that of
32:4 *h* itself of those who are
32:6 *h* will work at what is
33:18 *h* will comment in low
35:4 those who are anxious at *h*
38:3 and with a complete *h*, and
40:2 Speak to the *h* of Jerusalem
41:22 apply our *h* and know the
42:25 he would lay nothing to *h*
44:18 *h* so as to have no insight
44:19 no one recalls to his *h* or
44:20 *h* that has been trifled
46:8 to *h*, you transgressors
46:12 you the ones powerful at *h*
47:7 take these things to your *h*
47:8 the one saying in her *h*
47:10 you keep saying in your *h*
49:21 for certain say in your *h*
51:7 people in whose *h* is my law
57:1 is no one taking it to *h*
57:11 You took nothing to your *h*
57:15 to revive the *h* of the ones
57:17 in the way of his *h*
Isa 59:13 falsehood from the very *h*
60:5 your *h* will actually quiver
63:4 day of vengeance is in my *h*
63:17 *h* hard against the fear of
65:14 the good condition of the *h*
65:14 because of the pain of *h*
65:17 they come up into the *h*
66:14 *h* will be bound to exult
Jer 3:10 with all her *h*, only falsely
3:15 in agreement with my *h*
3:16 will it come up into the *h*
3:17 stubbornness of their bad *h*
4:9 the *h* of the king will perish
4:9 also the *h* of the princes
4:14 Wash your *h* clean of sheer
4:18 has reached clear to your *h*
4:19 pains in the walls of my *h*
4:19 My *h* is boisterous within me
5:21 people that is without *h*
5:23 stubborn and rebellious *h*
5:24 have not said in their *h*
7:24 stubbornness of their bad *h*
7:31 had not come up into my *h*
8:18 come up into me. My *h* is ill
9:14 the stubbornness of their *h*
9:26 are uncircumcised in *h*
11:8 stubbornness of their bad *h*
11:20 the kidneys and the *h*
12:3 you have examined my *h* in
12:11 man that has taken it to *h*
13:10 the stubbornness of their *h*
13:22 you will say in your *h*
14:14 the trickiness of their *h*
15:16 and the rejoicing of my *h*
16:12 stubbornness of his bad *h*
17:1 on the tablet of their *h*
17:5 *h* turns away from Jehovah
17:9 The *h* is more treacherous
17:10 searching the *h*, examining
18:12 stubbornness of his bad *h*
19:5 had not come up into my *h*
20:9 my *h* it proved to be like a
20:12 seeing the kidneys and the *h*
22:17 your eyes and your *h* are
23:9 my *h* has been broken within
23:16 The vision of their own *h*
23:17 the stubbornness of his *h*
23:20 ideas of his *h* come true
23:26 in the *h* of the prophets
23:26 trickiness of their own *h*
24:7 give them a *h* to know me
24:7 return . . . with all their *h*
29:13 with all your *h*
30:21 given his *h* in pledge in
30:24 the ideas of his *h*
31:21 Fix your *h* upon the highway
31:33 in their *h* I shall write it
32:35 come up into my *h* to do
32:39 give them one *h* and one way
32:40 put in their *h* in order not
32:41 trueness with all my *h* and
44:21 to come up into his *h*
48:29 of the loftiness of his *h*
48:36 *h* will be boisterous for
48:36 *h* will be boisterous, just
48:41 *h* of the mighty men of
48:41 *h* of a wife having
49:16 presumptuousness of your *h*
49:22 *h* of the mighty men of
49:22 *h* of the wife having
51:46 your *h* will be timid, and
51:50 herself come up into your *h*
La 1:20 My *h* has been overturned in
1:22 and my *h* is ill
2:18 *h* has cried out to Jehovah
2:19 Pour out your *h* before the
3:21 I shall bring back to my *h*
3:33 not out of his own *h* has he
3:41 raise our *h* along with our
3:65 to them the insolence of *h*
5:15 exultation of our *h* has ceased
5:17 our *h* has become ill
Eze 2:4 insolent of face and hard of *h*
3:10 take into your *h* and hear
6:9 fornicating *h* that has turned
11:19 And I will give them one *h*
11:19 remove the *h* of stone from
11:19 and give them a *h* of flesh
11:21 whose *h* is walking in their
13:2 out of their own *h*, Hear the
13:17 out of their own *h*, and
13:22 By reason of dejecting the *h*
14:3 dungy idols upon their *h*
14:4 his dungy idols upon his *h*

Eze 14:5 house of Israel by their *h*
14:7 his dungy idols upon his *h*
18:31 make for yourselves a new *h*
20:16 idols that their *h* was
21:7 and every *h* must melt and
21:15 In order for the *h* to melt
22:14 Will your *h* keep enduring
27:4 In the *h* of the seas are
27:25 in the *h* of the open sea
27:26 in the *h* of the open sea
27:27 in the *h* of the open sea
28:2 your *h* has become haughty
28:2 in the *h* of the open sea
28:2, 2 your *h* like the *h* of god
28:5 your *h* began to be haughty
28:6, 6 *h* like the *h* of god
28:8 in the *h* of the open sea
28:17 Your *h* became haughty
31:10 its *h* became exalted
32:9 offend the *h* of many peoples
33:31 is where their *h* is going
36:5 the rejoicing of all the *h*
36:26 a new *h*, and a new spirit
36:26 take away the *h* of stone
36:26 and give you a *h* of flesh
38:10 will come up into your *h*
40:4 set your *h* upon all that I
44:5 Son of man, set your *h* and
44:5 set your *h* upon the entryway
44:7 uncircumcised in *h* and
44:9 uncircumcised in *h* and
Da 1:8 Daniel determined in his *h*
2:30 thoughts of your *h* you may
4:16 its *h* be changed from that
4:16 *h* of a beast be given to it
5:20 *h* became haughty and his own
5:21 *h* was . . . like that of a beast
5:22 you have not humbled your *h*
7:4 was given to it the *h* of a man
7:28 matter . . . I kept in my own *h*
8:25 in his *h* he will put on great
10:12 gave your *h* to understanding
11:12 *h* will become exalted, and
11:25 arouse his power and his *h*
11:27 *h* will be inclined to doing
11:28 *h* will be against the holy
Ho 2:14 and I will speak to her *h*
7:2 do not say to their own *h*
7:6 brought their *h* near as to a
7:11 simple-minded dove without *h*
7:14 did not call . . . with their *h*
10:2 *h* has become hypocritical
11:8 My *h* has changed within me
13:6 their *h* began to be exalted
13:8 the enclosure of their *h*
Am 2:16 as for one strong in his *h*
Ob 3 *h* is what has deceived you
3 saying in his *h*, Who will bring
Jon 2:3 into the *h* of the open sea
Na 2:10 the *h* is melting, and there
Zep 1:12 saying in their *h*, Jehovah
2:15 that was saying in her *h*
3:14 and exult with all the *h*
Hag 1:5 Set your *h* upon your ways
1:7 Set your *h* upon your ways
2:15 please, set your *h* on this
2:18 Set your *h*, please, on this
2:18 set your *h* on this
Zec 7:12 their *h* they set as an emery
10:7 their *h* must rejoice as
10:7 *h* will be joyful in Jehovah
12:5 have to say in their *h*
Mal 2:2 if you will not lay it to *h*
2:2 you are not laying it to *h*
4:6 turn the *h* of fathers back
4:6 *h* of sons back toward fathers
Mt 5:8 Happy are the pure in *h*, since
5:28 adultery with her in his *h*
6:21 treasure is, there your *h*
11:29 lowly in *h*, and you will
12:34 of the abundance of the *h*
12:40 in the *h* of the earth three
13:15 *h* . . . has grown unreceptive
13:19 what has been sown in his *h*
15:8 *h* is far removed from me
15:18 come out of the *h*, and those
15:19 out of the *h* come wicked
22:37 with your whole *h* and with
24:48 slave should say in his *h*
Mr 7:19 it passes, not into his *h*
7:21 out of the *h* of men
9:10 they took the word to *h*
11:23 does not doubt in his *h*
12:30 with your whole *h* and with
Mr 12:33 with one's whole *h* and with
Lu 2:19 drawing conclusions in her *h*
2:51 all these sayings in her *h*
6:45 the good treasure of his *h*
8:15 with a fine and good *h*
10:27 with your whole *h* and with
12:45 slave should say in his *h*
24:25 and slow in *h* to believe on
Joh 13:2 put it into the *h* of Judas
Ac 2:26 my *h* became cheerful and my
2:37 they were stabbed to the *h*
2:46 rejoicing and sincerity of *h*
4:32 had one *h* and soul, and not
5:4 such a deed as this in your *h*
7:23 his *h* to make an inspection
8:21 your *h* is not straight in the
8:22 the device of your *h* may be
13:22 a man agreeable to my *h*
15:8 God, who knows the *h*, bore
16:14 Jehovah opened her *h* wide to
21:13 and making me weak at *h*
28:27 *h* of this people has grown
28:27 understand with their *h* and
Ro 1:21 unintelligent *h* became
2:5 unrepentant *h* you are storing
2:29 circumcision is that of the *h*
6:17 became obedient from the *h*
9:2 and unceasing pain in my *h*
10:1 the goodwill of my *h* and my
10:6 Do not say in your *h*, Who
10:8 and in your own *h*; that is
10:9 exercise faith in your *h* that
10:10 with the *h* one exercises
1Co 2:9 conceived in the *h* of man
7:37 stands settled in his *h*
7:37 this decision in his own *h*
14:25 the secrets of his *h* become
2Co 2:4 anguish of *h* I wrote you with
5:12 appearance but not over the *h*
6:11 our *h* has widened out
8:16 for you in the *h* of Titus
9:7 he has resolved in his *h*, not
Eph 1:18 eyes of your *h* having been
Php 1:7 my having you in my *h*, all
Col 3:22 with sincerity of *h*, with
1Th 2:17 in person, not in *h*, we
1Ti 1:5 love out of a clean *h* and
2Ti 2:22 the Lord out of a clean *h*
Heb 3:12 a wicked *h* lacking faith by
4:12 and intentions of the *h*
13:9 *h* to be given firmness by
Jas 1:26 on deceiving his own *h*
1Pe 1:22 intensely from the *h*
3:4 the secret person of the *h* in
2Pe 2:14 a *h* trained in covetousness
Re 18:7 in her *h* she keeps saying

Hearth
Le 6:9 offering will be on the *h*
Isa 29:2 to me as the altar *h* of God
Eze 43:15 altar *h* is four cubits
43:15 altar *h* and upward there
43:16 altar *h* is twelve cubits

Heartily
Ac 2:41 embraced his word *h* were
1Co 16:19 greet you *h* in the Lord

Heart's
Lu 6:45 out of the *h* abundance his

Hearts
Ge 18:5 and refresh your *h*
42:28 their *h* sank, so that they
Ex 10:1 the *h* of his servants become
14:17 *h* of the Egyptians become
35:26 women whose *h* impelled them
35:29 *h* incited them to bring
Le 26:36 timidity into their *h* in the
Nu 15:39 go about following your *h*
De 10:16 the foreskin of your *h* and
20:3 Do not let your *h* be timid
20:8 the *h* of his brothers to melt
32:46 Apply your *h* to all the
Jos 2:11 our *h* began to melt, and no
5:1 then their *h* began to melt
11:20 let their *h* become stubborn
23:14 with all your *h* and with
24:23 incline your *h* to Jehovah
Jg 19:22 making their *h* feel good
19:30 Set your *h* upon it, take
2Sa 15:6 stealing the *h* of the men of
1Ch 28:9 all *h* Jehovah is searching
Ps 22:26 May your *h* live forever
28:3 in whose *h* is what is bad
33:15 forming their *h* all together
Ps 48:13 Set your *h* upon its rampart
125:4 ones upright in their *h*
Pr 15:11 the *h* of the sons of mankind
17:3 Jehovah is the examiner of *h*
21:2 is making an estimate of *h*
24:12 is making an estimate of *h*
Jer 4:4 the foreskins of your *h*
Joe 2:12 back to me with all your *h*
2:13 rip apart your *h*, and not
Na 2:7 repeatedly upon their *h*
Zec 7:10 against one another in your *h*
8:17 not you scheme up in your *h*
Mt 9:4 wicked things in your *h*
13:15 the sense of it with their *h*
18:35 forgive . . . from your *h*
Mr 2:6 and reasoning in their *h*
2:8 these things in your *h*
3:5 the insensibility of their *h*
6:52 *h* . . . dull of understanding
7:6 *h* are far removed from me
8:17 your *h* dull of understanding
Lu 1:17 turn back the *h* of fathers
1:51 in the intention of their *h*
1:66 made note of it in their *h*
2:35 many *h* may be uncovered
3:15 reasoning in their *h* about
5:22 you reasoning out in your *h*
8:12 the word away from their *h*
9:47 the reasoning of their *h*
12:34 treasure is, there your *h*
16:15 but God knows your *h*
21:14 settle it in your *h* not to
21:34 *h* never become weighed down
24:32 *h* burning as he was speaking
24:38 doubts come up in your *h*
Joh 12:40 made their *h* hard, that
12:40 the thought with their *h*
14:1 not let your *h* be troubled
14:27 not let your *h* be troubled
16:6 grief has filled your *h*
16:22 and your *h* will rejoice
Ac 1:24 Jehovah, who know the *h* of
7:39 in their *h* they turned back
7:51 uncircumcised in *h* and ears
7:54 they felt cut to their *h*
14:17 filling your *h* to the full
15:9 but purified their *h* by faith
Ro 1:24 the desires of their *h*
2:15 law to be written in their *h*
5:5 love . . . poured out into our *h*
8:27 he who searches the *h* knows
16:18 seduce the *h* of guileless
1Co 4:5 make the counsels of the *h*
2Co 1:22 that is, the spirit, in our *h*
3:2 inscribed on our *h* and known
3:3 but on fleshly tablets, on *h*
3:15 a veil lies upon their *h*
4:6 shone on our *h* to illuminate
7:3 you are in our *h* to die and
Ga 4:6 spirit of his Son into our *h*
Eph 3:17 through your faith in your *h*
4:18 the insensibility of their *h*
5:19 with music in your *h* to
6:5 in the sincerity of your *h*
6:22 that he may comfort your *h*
Php 4:7 will guard your *h* and your
Col 2:2 their *h* may be comforted
3:15 control in your *h*, for you
3:16 singing in your *h* to Jehovah
4:8 that he may comfort your *h*
1Th 2:4 who makes proof of our *h*
3:13 he may make your *h* firm
2Th 2:17 comfort your *h* and make you
3:5 directing your *h* successfully
Heb 3:8 do not harden your *h* as on
3:10 always go astray in their *h*
3:15 do not harden your *h* as on
4:7 do not harden your *h*
8:10 in their *h* I shall write
10:16 put my laws in their *h*
10:22 approach with true *h* in
10:22 *h* sprinkled from a wicked
Jas 3:14 contentiousness in your *h*, do
4:8 purify your *h*, you indecisive
5:5 have fattened your *h* on the
5:8 make your *h* firm, because the
1Pe 3:15 the Christ as Lord in your *h*
2Pe 1:19 a daystar rises, in your *h*
1Jo 3:19 assure our *h* before him
3:20 our *h* may condemn us in
3:20 God is greater than our *h*
3:21 if our *h* do not condemn us
Re 2:23 searches the kidneys and *h*
17:17 God put it into their *h* to

Heart-shaped
2Sa 13:6 bake two *h* cakes under my
13:8 and cooked the *h* cakes
13:10 Tamar took the *h* cakes that

Hearty
Ac 11:23 in the Lord with *h* purpose

He-ass
Jer 22:19 With the burial of a *h* he

He-asses
Jg 19:3 and a couple of *h*
19:10 the couple of *h* saddled up
19:19 straw and fodder for our *h*
19:21 and threw mash to the *h*

Heat
Ge 8:22 cold and *h*, and summer and
18:1 about the *h* of the day
30:38 they might get into a *h*
30:39 the flocks would get in *h*
30:41 robust flocks would get in *h*
30:41 might get in *h* by the staffs
31:10 when the flock got in *h*
31:40 by day the *h* consumed me
Ex 11:8 Pharaoh in the *h* of anger
De 28:22 inflammation and feverish *h*
29:24 the *h* of this great anger
1Sa 20:34 in the *h* of anger, and he
2Ch 25:10 in the *h* of anger
Job 24:19 the *h*, snatch away the snow
Ps 19:6 nothing concealed from its *h*
32:4 as in the dry *h* of summer
85:3 back from the *h* of your anger
119:53 raging *h* itself has taken
Isa 4:6 shade by day from the dry *h*
18:4 dazzling *h* along with the
18:4 of dew in the *h* of harvest
25:4 a shade from the *h*, when the
25:5 *h* in a waterless country
25:5 *h* with the shadow of a cloud
49:10 parching *h* or sun strike
Jer 5:8 Horses seized with sexual *h*
17:8 will not see when *h* comes
36:30 thrown out to the *h* by day
La 2:3 In the *h* of anger he has cut
Da 3:19 saying to *h* up the furnace
3:19 it was customary to *h* it up
Na 1:6 up against the *h* of his anger
Mt 20:12 of the day and the burning *h*
Lu 12:55 There will be a *h* wave, and
Ac 28:3 viper came out due to the *h*
Jas 1:11 sun rises with its burning *h*
Re 7:16 upon them nor any scorching *h*
16:9 were scorched with great *h*

Heated
Ex 21:14 becomes *h* against his fellow
Le 26:28 *h* opposition to you, and I
De 1:43 and to get all *h* up, and you
2Sa 4:5 about when the day had *h* up
1Ki 19:6 a round cake upon *h* stones
Ps 37:1 *h* up because of the evildoers
37:7 Do not show yourself *h* up
37:8 *h* up only to do evil
Pr 24:19 yourself *h* up at evildoers
Isa 41:11 getting *h* up against you
45:24 getting *h* up against him
Jer 51:39 When they are *h* I shall
Eze 24:11 its copper must become *h* up
Da 3:22 the furnace was *h* to excess
Lu 22:24 arose a *h* dispute among them

Heat-parched
Isa 35:7 *h* ground will have become as

Heave
Jas 5:9 *h* sighs against one another

Heaven
Ge 1:8 God began to call the expanse *H*
2:4 Jehovah God made earth and *h*
14:19 God, Producer of *h* and earth
14:22 God, Producer of *h* and earth
De 32:40 my hand to *h* in an oath
33:13 choice things of *h*, with dew
33:26 Who rides upon *h* in help of
Jg 5:20 From *h* did the stars fight
2Sa 22:14 From *h* Jehovah began to
1Ki 8:27 *h* of the heavens, themselves
8:34 you yourself hear from *h*
8:35 *h* is shut up so that no rain
2Ch 2:6 the *h* of the heavens cannot
6:18, 18 *H*, yes the *h* of the
Ezr 6:9 offerings to the God of *h*
Ne 9:6 even the *h* of the heavens, and
9:13 and spoke with them out of *h*
Ne 9:15 bread from *h* you gave them
Job 11:8 It is higher than *h*
14:12 Until *h* is no more they
20:6 his excellency ascends to *h*
20:27 *H* will uncover his error
22:12 Is not God the height of *h*?
22:14 on the vault of *h* he walks
26:11 The very pillars of *h* shake
26:13 wind he has polished up *h*
35:5 Look up to *h* and see, And
38:29 as for the hoarfrost of *h*
38:37 water jars of *h*—who can
Ps 8:8 The birds of *h* and the fish of
14:2 looked down from *h* itself
53:2 he has looked down from *h*
57:3 send from *h* and save me
68:8 *H* itself also dripped because
68:33 One riding on the ancient *h*
69:34 Let *h* and earth praise him
76:8 *h* you caused the legal contest
78:23 opened the very doors of *h*
78:24 grain of *h* he gave to them
80:14 Look down from *h* and see
89:11 *H* is yours, the earth also
89:29 his throne as the days of *h*
105:40 with bread from *h* he kept
113:6 to look on *h* and earth
115:15 The Maker of *h* and earth
121:2 The Maker of *h* and earth
124:8 The Maker of *h* and earth
134:3 the Maker of *h* and earth
139:8 ascend to *h*, there you would
146:6 The Maker of *h* and earth
148:13 is above earth and *h*
Pr 30:4 Who has ascended to *h* that he
Isa 13:13 *h* itself to become agitated
14:12 you have fallen from *h*
63:15 Look from *h* and see out of
Jer 33:25 statutes of *h* and earth
La 2:1 thrown down from *h* to earth
3:50 looks down and sees from *h*
Da 2:18 on the part of the God of *h*
2:19 himself blessed the God of *h*
2:37 God of *h* has given the
2:44 the God of *h* will set up a
Joe 3:16 *h* and earth certainly will
Mt 5:18 sooner would *h* and earth pass
5:34 swear at all, neither by *h*
6:10 as in *h*, also upon earth
6:20 store up . . . treasures in *h*
6:26 Observe . . . the birds of *h*
8:20 and birds of *h* have roosts
11:23 you perhaps be exalted to *h*
11:25 Father, Lord of *h* and earth
12:50 of my Father who is in *h*
13:32 the birds of *h* come and find
14:19 looking up to *h*, he said a
16:1 to them a sign from *h*
18:10 their angels in *h* always
18:10 of my Father who is in *h*
18:14 with my Father who is in *h*
18:18 will be things bound in *h*
18:18 will be things loosed in *h*
18:19 due to my Father in *h*
19:21 you will have treasure in *h*
21:25 From *h* or from men?
21:25 If we say, From *h*, he will
22:30 but are as angels in *h*
23:22 and he that swears by *h* is
24:29 the stars will fall from *h*
24:30 will appear in *h*, and then
24:30 coming on the clouds of *h*
24:35 *H* and earth will pass away
26:64 coming on the clouds of *h*
28:2 angel had descended from *h*
28:18 in *h* and on the earth
Mr 4:32 birds of the *h* are able to
6:41 he looked up to *h* and said a
7:34 with a look up into *h* he
8:11 seeking . . . a sign from *h*
10:21 you will have treasure in *h*
11:30 baptism by John from *h* or
11:31 If we say, From *h*, he will
13:25 stars . . . falling out of *h*
13:31 *H* and earth will pass away
13:32 the angels in *h* nor the Son
14:62 coming with the clouds of *h*
Lu 2:15 had departed from them into *h*
3:21 was praying, the *h* opened up
3:22 and a voice came out of *h*
4:25 *h* was shut up three years and
6:23 your reward is great in *h*
8:5 the birds of *h* ate it up
9:16 he looked up to *h*, blessed
Lu 9:54 fire to come down from *h* and
9:58 and birds of *h* have roosts
10:15 you perhaps be exalted to *h*
10:18 fallen like lightning from *h*
10:21 Father, Lord of *h* and earth
11:13 the Father in *h* give holy
11:16 seeking a sign out of *h* from
13:19 birds of *h* took up lodging
15:7 more joy in *h* over one sinner
15:18 sinned against *h* and against
15:21 sinned against *h* and against
16:17 for *h* and earth to pass away
17:24 shines from one part under *h*
17:24 to another part under *h*
17:29 fire and sulphur from *h*
19:38 Peace in *h*, and glory in
20:4 baptism of John from *h* or
20:5 If we say, From *h*, he will
21:11 and from *h* great signs
21:33 *H* and earth will pass away
22:43 angel from *h* appeared to him
24:51 began to be borne up to *h*
Joh 1:32 down as a dove out of *h*
1:51 You will see *h* opened up and
3:13 no man has ascended into *h*
3:13 but he that descended from *h*
3:27 has been given him from *h*
3:31 He that comes from *h* is over
6:31 them bread from *h* to eat
6:32 give you the bread from *h*
6:32 the true bread from *h*
6:33 one who comes down from *h*
6:38 from *h* to do, not my will
6:41 bread that came down from *h*
6:42 I have come down from *h*
6:50 bread . . . down from *h*
6:51 bread that came down from *h*
6:58 bread that came down from *h*
12:28 a voice came out of *h*
17:1 raising his eyes to *h*, he
Ac 2:2 from *h* a noise just like that
2:5 every nation of those under *h*
2:19 I will give portents in *h*
3:21 *h*, indeed, must hold within
4:12 name under *h* that has been
4:24 One who made the *h* and the
7:42 service to the army of *h*
7:49 *h* is my throne, and the
7:55 gazed into *h* and caught sight
9:3 light from *h* flashed around
10:11 *h* opened and some sort of
10:12 of the earth and birds of *h*
10:16 vessel was taken up into *h*
11:5 great linen sheet . . . from *h*
11:6 things and birds of *h*
11:9 voice from *h* answered, You
11:10 was pulled up again into *h*
14:15 living God, who made the *h*
14:17 giving you rains from *h* and
17:24 One is, Lord of *h* and earth
19:35 the image that fell from *h*
22:6 out of *h* a great light flashed
26:13 flash from *h* about me and
Ro 1:18 wrath . . . revealed from *h*
10:6 Who will ascend into *h*?
1Co 8:5 whether in *h* or on earth
15:47 the second man is out of *h*
2Co 5:2 put on the one for us from *h*
12:2 away as such to the third *h*
Ga 1:8 angel out of *h* were to declare
Eph 3:15 to whom every family in *h*
Php 2:10 of those in *h* and those on
Col 1:23 all creation that is under *h*
4:1 you also have a Master in *h*
1Th 4:16 will descend from *h* with a
2Th 1:7 the Lord Jesus from *h* with
Heb 9:24 into *h* itself, now to appear
11:12 stars of *h* for multitude
11:16 that is, one belonging to *h*
12:26 the earth but also the *h*
Jas 5:12 stop swearing . . . by *h* or by
5:18 the *h* gave rain and the land
1Pe 1:12 spirit sent forth from *h*
3:22 for he went his way to *h*
2Pe 1:18 words we heard borne from *h*
Re 3:12 out of *h* from my God, and
4:1 an opened door in *h*, and the
4:2 was in its position in *h*
5:3 neither in *h* nor upon earth nor
5:13 creature that is in *h* and on
6:13 and the stars of *h* fell to
6:14 *h* departed as a scroll that
8:1 a silence occurred in *h* for
8:10 a great star . . . fell from *h*

Re 9:1 star that had fallen from *h*
10:1 angel descending from *h*
10:4 I heard a voice out of *h* say
10:5 raised his right hand to *h*
10:6 who created the *h* and the
10:8 voice that I heard out of *h*
11:6 to shut up *h* that no rain
11:12 a loud voice out of *h* say
11:12 went up into *h* in the cloud
11:13 gave glory to the God of *h*
11:15 loud voices occurred in *h*
11:19 sanctuary of God that is in *h*
12:1 great sign was seen in *h*
12:3 another sign was seen in *h*
12:4 third of the stars of *h*, and
12:7 war broke out in *h*: Michael
12:8 for them any longer in *h*
12:10 I heard a loud voice in *h*
13:6 even those residing in *h*
13:13 fire come down out of *h*
14:2 I heard a sound out of *h* as
14:7 One who made the *h* and the
14:13 I heard a voice out of *h*
14:17 sanctuary that is in *h*
15:1 And I saw in *h* another sign
15:5 tent . . . was opened in *h*
16:11 blasphemed the God of *h* for
16:21 out of *h* upon the men, and
18:1 angel descending from *h*
18:4 another voice out of *h* say
18:5 sins have massed . . . to *h*
18:20 Be glad over her, O *h*, also
19:1 voice of a great crowd in *h*
19:11 I saw the *h* opened, and
19:14 armies that were in *h* were
20:1 angel coming down out of *h*
20:9 fire came down out of *h* and
20:11 earth and the *h* fled away
21:1 I saw a new *h* and a new
21:1 former *h* and the former earth
21:2 down out of *h* from God and
21:10 down out of *h* from God

Heavenly

Mt 5:48 as your *h* Father is perfect
6:14 *h* Father will also forgive
6:26 your *h* Father feeds them
6:32 your *h* Father knows you need
15:13 my *h* Father did not plant
18:35 my *h* Father will also deal
23:9 one is your Father, the *h* One
Lu 2:13 a multitude of the *h* army
Joh 3:12 if I tell you *h* things
Ac 26:19 disobedient to the *h* sight
1Co 15:40 there are *h* bodies, and
15:40 the glory of the *h* bodies
15:48 and as the *h* one is, so
15:48 so those who are *h* are also
15:49 the image of the *h* one
Eph 1:3 *h* places in union with Christ
1:20 right hand in the *h* places
2:6 together in the *h* places in
3:10 authorities in the *h* places
6:12 spirit forces in the *h* places
2Ti 4:18 save me for his *h* kingdom
Heb 3:1 partakers of the *h* calling
6:4 tasted the *h* free gift, and
8:5 a shadow of the *h* things
9:23 *h* things themselves with
12:22 *h* Jerusalem, and myriads of

Heaven's

Mr 13:27 from earth's extremity to *h*

Heavens

Ge 1:1 God created the *h* and the earth
1:9 Let the waters under the *h* be
1:14 to be in the expanse of the *h*
1:15 luminaries in the . . . *h*
1:17 expanse of the *h* to shine upon
1:20 face of the expanse of the *h*
1:26 the flying creatures of the *h*
1:28 the flying creatures of the *h*
1:30 flying creature of the *h*
2:1 Thus the *h* and the earth and
2:4 This is a history of the *h* and
2:19 flying creature of the *h*
2:20 the flying creatures of the *h*
6:7 and to flying creature of the *h*
6:17 ruin all flesh . . . under the *h*
7:3 flying creatures of the *h* by
7:11 floodgates of the *h* were
7:14 flying creature of the *h*
7:19 under the whole *h* came to be
7:23 flying creature of the *h*
Ge 8:2 floodgates of the *h* became
8:2 so the downpour from the *h*
9:2 every flying creature of the *h*
11:4 tower with its top in the *h*
15:5 Look . . . to the *h* and count
19:24 from the *h*, upon Sodom and
21:17 out of the *h* and said to her
22:11 calling to him out of the *h*
22:15 the second time out of the *h*
22:17 seed like the stars of the *h*
24:3 God of the *h* and the God of
24:7 God of the *h*, who took me
26:4 seed like the stars of the *h*
27:28 give you the dews of the *h*
27:39 away from the dew of the *h*
28:12 top reaching up to the *h*
28:17 and this is the gate of the *h*
49:25 the blessings of the *h* above
Ex 9:8 must toss it toward the *h* in
9:10 Moses tossed it toward the *h*
9:22 hand toward the *h*, that hail
9:23 stretched . . . rod toward the *h*
10:21 *h*, that darkness may occur
10:22 his hand out toward the *h*
16:4 bread for you from the *h*; and
17:14 of Amalek from under the *h*
20:4 in the *h* above or that is on
20:11 Jehovah made the *h* and the
20:22 from the *h* I spoke with you
24:10 like the very *h* for purity
31:17 made the *h* and the earth and
32:13 like the stars of the *h*
Le 26:19 *h* like iron and your earth
De 1:10 like the stars of the *h* for
1:28 great and fortified to the *h*
2:25 the peoples beneath all the *h*
3:24 god in the *h* or on the earth
4:17 bird that flies in the *h*
4:19 raise your eyes to the *h* and
4:19 all the army of the *h*, and
4:19 the peoples under the whole *h*
4:26 the *h* and the earth, that you
4:32 one end of the *h* clear to the
4:32 to the other end of the *h*
4:36 Out of the *h* he made you hear
4:39 God in the *h* above and on the
5:8 like anything that is in the *h*
7:24 their names from under the *h*
9:1 great and fortified to the *h*
9:14 name from under the *h*, and
10:14 to . . . your God belong the *h*
10:14, 14 even the *h* of the *h*, the
10:22 like the stars of the *h*
11:11 Of the rain of the *h* it
11:17 shut up the *h* so that no rain
11:21 days of the *h* over the earth
17:3 or all the army of the *h*
25:19 Amalek from under the *h*
26:15 your holy dwelling, the *h*
28:12 his good storehouse, the *h*
28:24 From the *h* it will come
28:26 flying creature of the *h*
28:62 stars of the *h* for multitude
29:20 his name from under the *h*
30:4 the end of the *h*, from there
30:12 It is not in the *h*, so as to
30:12 ascend for us into the *h*
30:19 do take the *h* and the earth
31:28 *h* and the earth as witnesses
32:1 Give ear, O *h*, and let me
33:28 his *h* will let the dew drip
Jos 2:11 God in the *h* above and on the
8:20 smoke . . . ascended to the *h*
10:11 great stones from the *h*
10:13 in the middle of the *h* and
Jg 5:4 *h* also dripped, Clouds also
1Sa 2:10 he will thunder in the *h*
5:12 kept ascending to the *h*
17:44 flesh to the fowls of the *h*
17:46 to the fowls of the *h* and
2Sa 18:9 taken up between the *h* and
21:10 down upon them from the *h*
21:10 allow the fowls of the *h* to
22:8 *h* themselves became agitated
22:10 to bend the *h* down and to
1Ki 8:22 his palms out to the *h*
8:23 no God like you in the *h*
8:27 The *h*, yes, the heaven of
8:27 heaven of the *h*, themselves
8:30 your dwelling, in the *h*
8:32 hear from the *h*, and you
8:36 hear from the *h*, and you
8:39 hear from the *h*, your
8:43 listen from the *h*, your
1Ki 8:45 hear from the *h* their
8:49 also hear from the *h*, your
8:54 palms spread out to the *h*
14:11 the fowls of the *h* will eat
16:4 the fowls of the *h* will eat
18:45 the *h* themselves darkened
21:24 fowls of the *h* will eat up
22:19 army of the *h* standing by
2Ki 1:10 fire come down from the *h*
1:10 descending from the *h* and
1:12 fire come down from the *h*
1:12 descending from the *h* and
1:14 fire came down from the *h*
2:1 windstorm up to the *h*, Elijah
2:11 in the windstorm to the *h*
7:2 making floodgates in the *h*
7:19 making floodgates in the *h*
14:27 Israel from under the *h*
17:16 to all the army of the *h*
19:15 made the *h* and the earth
21:3 to all the army of the *h*
21:5 all the army of the *h* in two
23:4 for all the army of the *h*
23:5 to all the army of the *h*
1Ch 16:26 Jehovah, he made the *h*
16:31 Let the *h* rejoice, let the
21:16 between the earth and the *h*
21:26 fire from the *h* upon the
27:23 many as the stars of the *h*
29:11 *h* and in the earth is yours
2Ch 2:6 the *h* and the heaven of the
2:6 heaven of the *h* cannot contain
2:12 who made the *h* and the earth
6:13 his palms out to the *h*
6:14 no God like you in the *h* or
6:18 *h* themselves, cannot contain
6:21 your dwelling, from the *h*
6:23 hear from the *h*, and you
6:25 hear from the *h*, and you
6:26 *h* are shut up so that no
6:27 yourself hear from the *h*
6:30 yourself hear from the *h*
6:33 yourself listen from the *h*
6:35 hear from the *h* their prayer
6:39 also hear from the *h*, from
7:1 came down from the *h* and
7:13 shut up the *h* that no rain
7:14 hear from the *h* and forgive
18:18 army of the *h* standing at
20:6 are you not God in the *h*
28:9 has reached clear to the *h*
30:27 to his holy dwelling, the *h*
32:20 crying to the *h* for aid
33:3 army of the *h* and serve them
33:5 to all the army of the *h*
36:23 Jehovah the God of the *h*
Ezr 1:2 Jehovah the God of the *h* has
5:11 God of the *h* and the earth
5:12 irritated the God of the *h*
6:10 offerings to the God of the *h*
7:12 the law of the God of the *h*
7:21 the law of the God of the *h*
7:23 the order of the God of the *h*
7:23 house of the God of the *h*
9:6 grown great even to the *h*
Ne 1:4 before the God of the *h*
1:5 Jehovah the God of the *h*
1:9 to be at the end of the *h*
2:4 I prayed to the God of the *h*
2:20 God of the *h* is the One that
9:6 you yourself have made the *h*
9:6 even the heaven of the *h*, and
9:6 army of the *h* are bowing down
9:23 many as the stars of the *h*
9:27 would hear from the very *h*
9:28 would hear from the very *h*
Job 1:16 fire of God fell from the *h*
2:12 toss dust toward the *h* upon
9:8 Stretching out the *h* by
12:7 winged creatures of the *h*
15:15 *h* . . . not clean in his eyes
16:19 in the *h* is one testifying
28:21 flying creatures of the *h*
28:24 Under the whole *h* he sees
35:11 flying creatures of the *h*
37:3 Under the whole *h* he lets it
38:33 know the statutes of the *h*
41:11 the whole *h* it is mine
Ps 2:4 One sitting in the *h* will
8:1 is recounted above the *h*
8:3 *h*, the works of your fingers
11:4 in the *h* is his throne
18:9 bend the *h* down and descend
18:13 in the *h* Jehovah began to

Ps 19:1 The *h* are declaring the glory
19:6 From one extremity of the *h*
20:6 answers him from his holy *h*
33:6 the *h* themselves were made
33:13 From the *h* Jehovah has
36:5 loving-kindness is in the *h*
50:4 He calls to the *h* above and
50:6 *h* tell of his righteousness
57:5 be exalted above the *h*, O God
57:10 is great up to the *h*
57:11 Do be exalted above the *h*
68:33 on the ancient heaven of *h*
73:9 their mouth in the very *h*
73:25 Whom do I have in the *h*?
78:26 wind burst forth in the *h*
79:2 food to the fowls of the *h*
85:11 look down from the very *h*
89:2 *h*, you keep your faithfulness
89:5 *h* will laud your marvelous
96:5 he has made the very *h*
96:11 Let the *h* rejoice, and let
97:6 *h* have told forth his
102:19 From the very *h* Jehovah
102:25 *h* are the work of your
103:11 *h* are higher than the earth
103:19 his throne in the very *h*
104:2 the *h* like a tent cloth
104:12 flying creatures of the *h*
107:26 They go up to the *h*
108:4 is great up to the *h*
108:5 exalted above the *h*, O God
113:4 His glory is above the *h*
115:3 But our God is in the *h*
115:16 As regards the *h*, to Jehovah
115:16 to Jehovah the *h* belong
119:89 word is stationed in the *h*
123:1 who are dwelling in the *h*
135:6 In the *h* and in the earth
136:5 One making the *h* with
136:26 thanks to the God of the *h*
144:5 Jehovah, bend down your *h*
147:8 covering the *h* with clouds
148:1 Praise Jehovah from the *h*
148:4, 4 you *h* of the *h*
148:4 waters that are above the *h*
Pr 3:19 fixed the *h* in discernment
8:27 prepared the *h* I was there
23:5 and flies away toward the *h*
25:3 *h* for height and the earth for
30:19 the way of an eagle in the *h*
Ec 1:13 that has been done under the *h*
2:3 in what they did under the *h*
3:1 for every affair under the *h*
5:2 the true God is in the *h* but
10:20 a flying creature of the *h*
Isa 1:2 Hear, O *h*, and give ear, O
13:5 from the extremity of the *h*
13:10 stars of the *h* and their
14:13 To the *h* I shall go up
34:4 army of the *h* must rot
34:4 *h* must be rolled up, just
34:5 For in the *h* my sword will
37:16 made the *h* and the earth
40:12 the proportions of the *h*
40:22 stretching out the *h* just as
42:5 the Creator of the *h* and the
44:23 Joyfully cry out, you *h*
44:24 stretching out the *h* by
45:8 *h*, cause a dripping from
45:12 have stretched out the *h*
45:18 the Creator of the *h*, He the
47:13 the worshipers of the *h*
48:13 hand extended out the *h*
49:13 Give a glad cry, you *h*, and
50:3 clothe the *h* with obscurity
51:6 Raise your eyes to the *h*
51:6 very *h* must be dispersed in
51:13 the One stretching out the *h*
51:16 in order to plant the *h* and
55:9 *h* are higher than the earth
55:10 and the snow, from the *h*
64:1 you had ripped the *h* apart
65:17 new *h* and a new earth
66:1 The *h* are my throne, and the
66:22 the new *h* and the new earth
Jer 2:12 Stare in amazement, O you *h*
4:23 into the *h*, and their light
4:25 the flying creatures of the *h*
4:28 the *h* above will certainly
7:18 cakes to the queen of the *h*
7:33 the flying creatures of the *h*
8:2 to all the army of the *h*
8:7 Even the stork in the *h*—it
9:10 the flying creature of the *h*
Jer 10:2 even at the signs of the *h*
10:11 make the very *h* and the
10:11 and from under these *h*
10:12 stretched out the *h*
10:13 turmoil of waters in the *h*
14:22 *h* themselves give copious
15:3 flying creatures of the *h*
16:4 flying creatures of the *h*
19:7 flying creatures of the *h*
19:13 to all the army of the *h*
23:24 Is it not the *h* and the
31:37 If the *h* up above could be
32:17 made the *h* and the earth
33:22 army of the *h* cannot be
34:20 flying creatures of the *h*
44:17 to the queen of the *h* and
44:18 smoke to the queen of the *h*
44:19 to the queen of the *h* and
44:25 smoke to the queen of the *h*
49:36 four extremities of the *h*
51:9 to the *h* her judgment has
51:15 stretched out the *h*
51:16 turmoil of waters in the *h*
51:48 *h* and the earth and all that
51:53 should ascend to the *h* and
La 3:41 our palms to God in the *h*
3:66 from under the *h* of Jehovah
4:19 than the eagles of the *h* our
Eze 1:1 *h* were opened and I began to
8:3 between the earth and the *h*
29:5 flying creatures of the *h*
31:6 the flying creatures of the *h*
31:13 flying creatures of the *h*
32:4 flying creatures of the *h* to
32:7 cover the *h* and darken their
32:8 luminaries of light in the *h*
38:20 flying creatures of the *h*
Da 2:28 God in the *h* who is a
2:38 winged creatures of the *h*
4:11 height finally reached the *h*
4:12 birds of the *h* would dwell
4:13 one, coming down from the *h*
4:15 dew of the *h* let it be wet
4:20 reached the *h* and which was
4:21 birds of the *h* would reside
4:22 and reached to the *h*, and your
4:23 coming down from the *h*, who
4:23 with the dew of the *h* let it
4:25 with the dew of the *h* you
4:26 know that the *h* are ruling
4:31 voice that fell from the *h*
4:33 with the dew of the *h* his
4:34 lifted up to the *h* my eyes
4:35 among the army of the *h* and
4:37 glorifying the King of the *h*
5:21 with the dew of the *h* his
5:23 against the Lord of the *h* you
6:27 signs and wonders in the *h*
7:2 the four winds of the *h* were
7:13 with the clouds of the *h*
7:27 kingdoms under all the *h*
8:8 toward the four winds of the *h*
8:10 to the army of the *h*, so
9:12 done under the whole *h* as
11:4 the four winds of the *h*
12:7 left hand to the *h* and to
Ho 2:18 flying creature of the *h* and
2:21 I shall answer the *h*, and
4:3 the flying creature of the *h*
7:12 flying creatures of the *h*
Joe 2:10 agitated, the *h* have rocked
2:30 will give portents in the *h*
Am 9:2 and if they go up to the *h*
9:6 building in the *h* his stairs
Jon 1:9 the God of the *h* I am fearing
Na 3:16 more than the stars of the *h*
Hab 3:3 His dignity covered the *h*
Zep 1:3 the flying creature of the *h*
1:5 to the army of the *h*, and
Hag 1:10 the *h* kept back their dew
2:6 rocking the *h* and the earth
2:21 rocking the *h* and the earth
Zec 2:6 of the four winds of the *h*
5:9 between the earth and the *h*
6:5 four spirits of the *h* that
8:12 *h* . . . will give their dew
12:1 who is stretching out the *h*
Mal 3:10 the floodgates of the *h* and
Mt 3:2 kingdom of the *h* has drawn
3:16 look! the *h* were opened up
3:17 a voice from the *h* that said
4:17 kingdom of the *h* has drawn
5:3 the kingdom of the *h* belongs
5:10 kingdom of the *h* belongs to
Mt 5:12 your reward is great in the *h*
5:16 your Father who is in the *h*
5:19 to the kingdom of the *h*
5:19 to the kingdom of the *h*
5:20 into the kingdom of the *h*
5:45 your Father who is in the *h*
6:1 your Father who is in the *h*
6:9 Our Father in the *h*, let your
7:11 your Father who is in the *h*
7:21 into the kingdom of the *h*
7:21 Father who is in the *h* will
8:11 in the kingdom of the *h*
10:7 kingdom of the *h* has drawn
10:32 my Father who is in the *h*
10:33 my Father who is in the *h*
11:11 one in the kingdom of the *h*
11:12 kingdom of the *h* is the goal
13:11 of the kingdom of the *h*, but
13:24 kingdom of the *h* has become
13:31 kingdom of the *h* is like a
13:33 The kingdom of the *h* is like
13:44 kingdom of the *h* is like a
13:45 kingdom of the *h* is like a
13:47 kingdom of the *h* is like a
13:52 the kingdom of the *h*
16:17 my Father who is in the *h*
16:19 keys of the kingdom of the *h*
16:19 be the thing bound in the *h*
16:19 be the thing loosed in the *h*
18:1 in the kingdom of the *h*
18:3 into the kingdom of the *h*
18:4 in the kingdom of the *h*
18:23 kingdom of the *h* has become
19:12 of the kingdom of the *h*
19:14 kingdom of the *h* belongs to
19:23 into the kingdom of the *h*
20:1 kingdom of the *h* is like a
22:2 kingdom of the *h* has become
23:13 shut up the kingdom of the *h*
24:29 powers of the *h* . . . shaken
24:31 from one extremity of the *h*
24:36 neither the angels of the *h*
25:1 kingdom of the *h* will become
Mr 1:10 he saw the *h* being parted
1:11 and a voice came out of the *h*
11:25 your Father who is in the *h*
12:25 but are as angels in the *h*
13:25 the powers that are in the *h*
Lu 10:20 have been inscribed in the *h*
12:33 treasure in the *h*, where a
18:22 will have treasure in the *h*
21:26 powers of the *h* will be
Ac 2:34 David did not ascend to the *h*
7:56 I behold the *h* opened up
2Co 5:1 everlasting in the *h*
Eph 1:10 things in the *h* and the
4:10 ascended far above all the *h*
6:9 Master . . . is in the *h*, and
Php 3:20 citizenship exists in the *h*
Col 1:5 reserved for you in the *h*
1:16 created in the *h* and upon the
1:20 earth or the things in the *h*
1Th 1:10 wait for his Son from the *h*
Heb 1:10 the *h* are the works of your
4:14 passed through the *h*, Jesus
7:26 become higher than the *h*
8:1 of the Majesty in the *h*
9:23 of the things in the *h*
12:23 have been enrolled in the *h*
12:25 him who speaks from the *h*
1Pe 1:4 It is reserved in the *h* for
2Pe 3:5 there were *h* from of old and
3:7 the *h* and the earth that are
3:10 the *h* will pass away with a
3:12 the *h* being on fire will be
3:13 new *h* and a new earth that
Re 12:12 be glad, you *h* and you who

Heavenward
Jg 13:20 from off the altar *h*
20:40 the whole city went up *h*
Lu 18:13 even to raise his eyes *h*
Joh 11:41 Jesus raised his eyes *h*

Heavier
2Ch 10:14 make your yoke *h*, and I
Job 6:3 *h* even than the sands of the
Pr 27:3 vexation . . . *h* than both of
Mr 12:40 will receive a *h* judgment
Lu 20:47 will receive a *h* judgment
Jas 3:1 we shall receive *h* judgment

Heaviest
2Sa 11:15 of the *h* battle charges

Ieavily
ie 13:2 Abram was *h* stocked with
19:9 they came pressing *h* in on
g 10:8 they shattered and *h* oppressed
's 38:10 own heart has palpitated *h*
'r 8:24 springs *h* charged with water

Ieaviness
'r 27:3 The *h* of a stone and a load of
sa 21:15 because of the *h* of the war

Ieaving
Ki 9:17 the *h* mass of Jehu's men as
9:17 There is a *h* mass of men
ob 22:11 a *h* mass of water itself
38:34 a *h* mass of water itself
sa 60:6 The *h* mass of camels
ze 26:10 to the *h* mass of his horses

Ieavy
e 18:20 sin, yes, it is very *h*
50:10 a very great and *h* wailing
50:11 This is a *h* mourning for the
x 5:9 Let the service be *h* upon the
8:24 *h* swarms of gadflies began to
9:3 will be a very *h* pestilence
9:18 about this time a very *h* hail
9:24 hail. It was very *h*, so that
17:12 the hands of Moses were *h*
19:16 a *h* cloud upon the mountain
'u 11:14 they are too *h* for me
g 1:35 hand . . . got to be so *h* that
20:34 and the fighting was *h*
Sa 4:18 the man was old and *h*
5:6 hand of Jehovah came to be *h*
5:11 had been very *h* there
14:52 warfare continued *h* against
31:3 fighting became *h* against
Sa 14:26 so *h* upon him, he shaved it
Ki 12:4 his *h* yoke that he put upon
12:10 made our yoke *h*, but, as
12:11 loaded upon you a *h* yoke
12:14 his part, made your yoke *h*
Ki 6:14 and a *h* military force there
18:17 with a *h* military force to
Ch 10:3 fighting became *h* against
Ch 10:4 *h* yoke that he put upon us
10:10 made our yoke *h*, but as for
10:11 loaded upon you a *h* yoke
'e 5:15 had made it *h* upon the people
5:18 upon this people was *h*
ob 20:28 A *h* shower will roll his
23:2 My own hand is *h* on account
33:7 no pressure by me will be *h*
s 32:4 your hand was *h* upon me
38:4 Like a *h* load they are too
38:4 they are too *h* for me
r 23:20 be among *h* drinkers of wine
sa 1:4 the people *h* with error, an
24:20 transgression has become *h*
30:27 anger and with *h* clouds
32:2 shadow of a *h* crag in an
36:2 with a *h* military force
47:6 you made your yoke very *h*
59:1 ear become too *h* that it
er 30:19 make them *h* in number
a 3:7 has made my copper fetters *h*
ze 3:5 *h* of tongue that you are being
3:6 or *h* in tongue, whose words
a 2:9 *h* amount of all sorts of
3:3 and the *h* mass of carcasses
3:15 *h* in numbers like the locust
3:15 *h* in numbers like the locust
ab 2:6 making debt *h* against himself
t 23:4 They bind up *h* loads and put
26:43 for their eyes were *h*
u 2:5 at present *h* with child
21:34 overeating and *h* drinking
e 19:6 and as a sound of *h* thunders

Ieber
e 46:17 sons of Beriah were *H* and
u 26:45 Of *H* the family of the
g 4:11 *H* the Kenite had separated
4:17 Jael the wife of *H* the
4:17 the household of *H* the Kenite
4:21 And Jael the wife of *H*
5:24 Jael the wife of *H* the Kenite
Ch 4:18 *H* the father of Soco and
7:31 sons of Beriah were *H* and
7:32 *H* . . . father to Japhlet
8:17 Meshullam and Hizki and *H*

Ieberites
u 26:45 Of Heber the family of the *H*

Hebrew
Ge 14:13 came and told Abram the *H*
39:14 He brought to us a man, a *H*
39:17 The *H* servant whom you
41:12 a *H*, a servant of the chief
Ex 1:15 *H* midwives, the name of one
1:16 the *H* women to give birth and
1:19 *H* women are not like the
2:7 nursing woman from the *H*
2:11 Egyptian striking a certain *H*
2:13 two *H* men struggling with
21:2 buy a *H* slave, he will be a
De 15:12 sold to you your brother, a *H*
Jer 34:9, 9 *H* man and *H* woman, go
34:14 *H* man, who came to be sold
Jon 1:9 I am a *H*, and Jehovah the God
Joh 5:2 pool designated in *H* Bethzatha
19:13 but, in *H*, *Gab'ba·tha*
19:17 is called *Gol'go·tha* in *H*
19:20 written in *H*, in Latin, in
20:16 to him, in *H*: *Rab·bo'ni!*
Ac 21:40 in the *H* language, saying
22:2 was addressing them in the *H*
26:14 say to me in the *H* language
Php 3:5 a *H* born from Hebrews
Re 9:11 In *H* his name is Abaddon, but
16:16 called in *H* Har–Magedon

Hebrewess
De 15:12 a Hebrew or a *H*, and he has

Hebrews
Ge 40:15 from the land of the *H*; and
43:32 to eat a meal with the *H*
Ex 2:6 one of the children of the *H*
3:18 Jehovah the God of the *H* has
5:3 God of the *H* has come in touch
7:16 God of the *H* has sent me to
9:1 Jehovah the God of the *H* has
9:13 Jehovah the God of the *H* has
10:3 Jehovah the God of the *H* has
1Sa 4:6 shouting in the camp of the *H*
4:9 you may not serve the *H* just
13:3 saying: Let the *H* hear!
13:7 *H* even crossed the Jordan to
13:19 *H* may not make a sword or
14:11 are the *H* coming out from
14:21 *H* that had come to belong
29:3 What do these *H* mean?
2Co 11:22 Are they *H*? I am one also
Php 3:5 a Hebrew born from *H*

Hebrew-speaking
Ac 6:1 against the *H* Jews, because

Hebron
Ge 13:18 big trees of Mamre . . . in *H*
23:2 *H*, in the land of Canaan, and
23:19 Mamre, that is to say, *H*, in
35:27 that is to say, *H*, where
37:14 from the low plain of *H*
Ex 6:18 sons of Kohath . . . *H* and
Nu 3:19 sons of Kohath . . . Izhar, *H*
13:22 they then came to *H*
13:22 *H* had been built seven years
Jos 10:3 sent to Hoham the king of *H*
10:5 king of *H*, the king of
10:23 the king of *H*
10:36 went up from Eglon to *H*
10:39 Just as he had done to *H*
11:21 mountainous region, from *H*
12:10 the king of *H*, one
14:13 and gave *H* to Caleb the
14:14 *H* has come to belong to
14:15 name of *H* before that was
15:13 that is to say, *H*
15:54 that is to say, *H*, and Zior
20:7 *H*, in the mountainous region
21:11 *H*, in the mountainous
21:13 *H*, and its pasture ground
Jg 1:10 who were dwelling in *H* (now
1:10 the name of *H* before that
1:20 they gave Caleb *H*, just as
16:3 that is in front of *H*
1Sa 30:31 those in *H*, and to all the
2Sa 2:1 Then he said: To *H*
2:3 dwelling in the cities of *H*
2:11 David proved to be king in *H*
2:32 daylight for them at *H*
3:2 sons were born to David in *H*
3:5 ones born to David in *H*
3:19 of David at *H* all that was
3:20 Abner came to David at *H*
3:22 with David in *H*, for he had
3:27 Abner returned to *H*, Joab
3:32 burial of Abner in *H*
2Sa 4:1 that Abner had died in *H*
4:8 to David at *H* and said to the
4:12 by the pool in *H*
4:12 burial place of Abner in *H*
5:1 Israel came to David at *H* and
5:3 Israel came to the king at *H*
5:3 covenant with them in *H*
5:5 In *H* he ruled as king over
5:13 after he came from *H*
15:7 pay in *H* my vow that I
15:9 he rose up and went to *H*
15:10 Absalom . . . king in *H*
1Ki 2:11 In *H* he had reigned seven
1Ch 2:42 Mareshah the father of *H*
2:43 the sons of *H* were Korah
3:1 that were born to him in *H*
3:4 were six born to him in *H*
6:2 the sons of Kohath were . . . *H*
6:18 sons of Kohath were . . . *H*
6:55 *H* in the land of Judah, with
6:57 gave the cities of refuge, *H*
11:1 to David at *H*, saying: Look!
11:3 came to the king at *H* and
11:3 a covenant . . . in *H* before
12:23 that came to David at *H* to
12:38 to *H* to make David king
15:9 sons of *H*, Eliel the chief
23:12 sons of Kohath . . . *H* and
23:19 sons of *H* were Jeriah the
24:23 sons of *H*, Jeriah the head
29:27 In *H* he reigned for seven
2Ch 11:10 and *H*, fortified cities

Hebronites
Nu 3:27 and the family of the *H*
26:58 family of the *H*, the family
1Ch 26:23 for the *H*, for the
26:30 Of the *H*, Hashabiah and his
26:31 Of the *H*, Jerijah was the
26:31 was the head of the *H* by

Hedge
Job 1:10 put up a *h* about him and
Pr 15:19 lazy one is like a brier *h*
Isa 5:5 be a removing of its *h*
Mic 7:4 is worse than a thorn *h*

Hedges
Job 3:23 concealed, And whom God *h* in

Hedging
Ho 2:6 *h* your way about with thorns

Heed
Job 23:6 himself would pay *h* to me
Pr 29:19 but he is paying no *h*
Isa 41:20 pay *h* and have insight at
Joh 5:25 who have given *h* will live
Ac 5:40 they gave *h* to him, and they
1Co 14:21 give *h* to me, says Jehovah

Heeding
Ac 27:11 officer went *h* the pilot

Heel
Ge 3:15 you will bruise him in the *h*
25:26 holding onto the *h* of Esau
Job 18:9 trap will seize him by the *h*
Ps 41:9 magnified his *h* against me
Ho 12:3 seized his brother by the *h*
Joh 13:18 lifted up his *h* against me

Heels
Ge 49:17 bites the *h* of the horse so
Jer 13:22 your *h* have been treated

Hegai
Es 2:3 charge of *H* the king's eunuch
2:8 in charge of *H*, then Esther
2:8 *H* the guardian of the women
2:15 *H* the king's eunuch, the

He-goat
Pr 30:31 the greyhound or the *h*, and
Eze 43:25 *h* as a sin offering for the
Da 8:5 *h*, there was a conspicuous horn
8:21 hairy *h* stands for the king

He-goats
Ge 30:35 set aside on that day the *h*
31:10 *h* springing upon the flock
31:12 *h* springing upon the flock
32:14 twenty *h*, two hundred
Nu 7:17 five *h*, five male lambs each
7:23 five *h*, five male lambs each
7:29 sacrifice . . . five *h*
7:35 sacrifice . . . five *h*
7:41 sacrifice . . . five *h*
7:47 sacrifice . . . five *h*

Nu 7:53 sacrifice . . . five *h*
7:59 sacrifice . . . five *h*
7:65 sacrifice . . . five *h*
7:71 sacrifice . . . five *h*
7:77 sacrifice . . . five *h*
7:83 sacrifice . . . five *h*
7:88 sacrifice . . . sixty *h*
De 32:14 *h* Together with the kidney
2Ch 17:11 thousand seven hundred *h*
Ezr 8:35 twelve *h* as a sin offering
Ps 50:9 Out of your pens *h*
50:13 the blood of *h* shall I drink?
66:15 render up a bull with *h*
Pr 27:26 *h* are the price of the field
Isa 1:11 and *h* I have taken no delight
34:6 blood of young rams and *h*
Jer 51:40 like rams along with *h*
Eze 27:21 male lambs and rams and *h*
34:17 between the rams and the *h*
39:18 *h*, young bulls, the

Heifer
Ge 15:9 for me a three-year-old *h*
Jer 46:20 Egypt is as a very pretty *h*
50:11 pawing like a *h* in the
Ho 10:11 Ephraim was a trained *h*
Heb 9:13 the ashes of a *h* sprinkled on

Height
Ge 6:15 ark . . . thirty cubits its *h*
Ex 25:10 and a cubit and a half its *h*
25:23 and a cubit and a half its *h*
27:1 and its *h* three cubits
27:18 and the *h* five cubits, of
30:2 and its *h* two cubits
37:1 and a cubit and a half its *h*
37:10 and a cubit and a half its *h*
37:25 and two cubits was its *h*
38:1 and three cubits was its *h*
38:18 the *h* throughout its extent
1Sa 16:7 and at the *h* of his stature
17:4 his *h* being six cubits and a
2Sa 22:3 salvation, my secure *h*
1Ki 6:2 and thirty cubits in its *h*
6:10 five cubits in their *h*, and
6:20 and twenty cubits in its *h*
6:23 ten cubits being the *h* of
6:26 The *h* of the one cherub was
7:2 and thirty cubits in its *h*
7:15 being the *h* of each pillar
7:16 the *h* of the one capital
7:16 the *h* of the other capital
7:23 and its *h* was five cubits
7:27 and three cubits its *h*
7:32 the *h* of each wheel was one
7:35 a stand a half a cubit in *h*
2Ki 19:23 *h* of mountainous regions
25:17 was the *h* of each pillar
25:17 *h* of the capital was three
2Ch 3:4 *h* was a hundred and twenty
4:1 and ten cubits its *h*
4:2 and its *h* was five cubits
6:13 and its *h* three cubits
Ezr 6:3 its *h* being sixty cubits, its
Ne 4:6 together clear to half its *h*
Job 22:12 Is not God the *h* of heaven?
Ps 9:9 a secure *h* for anyone crushed
9:9 secure *h* in times of distress
18:2 salvation, my secure *h*
46:7 God of Jacob is a secure *h*
46:11 God of Jacob is a secure *h*
48:3 become known as a secure *h*
59:9 For God is my secure *h*
59:16 to be a secure *h* for me
59:17 God is my secure *h*, the God
62:2 my salvation, my secure *h*
62:6 my salvation, my secure *h*
71:19 O God, is up to the *h*
93:4 Jehovah is majestic in the *h*
94:22 become a secure *h* for me
102:19 looked down from his holy *h*
144:2 My secure *h* and my Provider
144:7 your hands out from the *h*
Pr 25:3 heavens for *h* and the earth
Isa 22:16 On a *h* he is hewing out
24:21, 21 army of the *h* in the *h*
26:5 low those inhabiting the *h*
33:5 for he is residing in the *h*
33:16 secure *h* will be craggy
37:24 *h* of mountainous regions
37:24 enter its final *h*, the
38:14 languishingly to the *h*
57:15 In the *h* and in the holy
58:4 voice to be heard in the *h*
Jer 31:12 joyfully on the *h* of Zion
Jer 48:1 secure *h* has been put to
49:16 holding the *h* of the hill
51:53 make the *h* of her strength
52:21 eighteen cubits in *h* was
52:22 *h* of the one capital was
La 1:13 From the *h* he has sent fire
Eze 1:18 their rims, they had such *h*
16:24 a *h* in every public square
16:25 you built your *h* and you
16:31 made your own *h* in every
17:6 vine low in *h*, inclined to
17:23 mountain of the *h* of Israel
19:11 its *h* gradually became tall
20:40 mountain of the *h* of Israel
31:10 exalted because of its *h*
31:14 against them in their *h*
40:5 and the *h*, one reed
40:42 and the *h* one cubit
Da 3:1 *h* of which was sixty cubits
4:10 the *h* of which was immense
4:11 *h* finally reached the heavens
4:20 *h* of which finally reached
Am 2:9, 9 *h* was like the *h* of cedars
Ob 3 the *h* where he dwells, saying
Hab 2:9 to set his nest on the *h*
Ro 8:39 *h* nor depth nor any other
Eph 3:18 length and *h* and depth
Re 21:16 length and breadth and *h* are

Heights
Jos 17:11 three of the *h*
Jg 5:18 on the *h* of the field
Job 16:19 And my witness is in the *h*
25:2 He is making peace on his *h*
Ps 78:69 sanctuary just like the *h*
148:1 Praise him in the *h*
Pr 8:2 On top of the *h*, by the way
9:3 on top of the *h* of the town
Isa 33:16 that will reside on the *h*
Eze 16:39 *h* will certainly be pulled
Mt 21:9 Save him, we pray, in the *h*
Mr 11:10 we pray, in the *h* above
Lu 2:14 Glory in the *h* above to God

Heir
Ge 15:3 is succeeding me as *h*
15:4 not succeed you as *h*, but one
15:4 one . . . will succeed you as *h*
21:10 not going to be an *h* with my
2Sa 14:7 let us even annihilate the *h*
Mt 21:38 is the *h*; come, let us kill
Mr 12:7 This is the *h*. Come, let us
Lu 20:14 This is the *h*; let us kill
Ro 4:13 he should be *h* of a world
Ga 4:1 as long as the *h* is a babe he
4:7 son, also an *h* through God
4:30 of the servant girl be an *h*
Heb 1:2 he appointed *h* of all things
11:7 *h* of the righteousness that

Heirs
Ro 4:14 who adhere to law are *h*
8:17 are children, we are also *h*
8:17 *h* indeed of God, but joint
8:17 but joint *h* with Christ
Ga 3:29 *h* with reference to a promise
Eph 1:11 we were also assigned as *h*
3:6 joint *h* and fellow members
Tit 3:7 *h* according to a hope of
Heb 6:17 to the *h* of the promise the
11:9 *h* . . . the very same promise
Jas 2:5 and *h* of the kingdom, which
1Pe 3:7 you are also *h* with them of

Helah
1Ch 4:5 two wives, *H* and Naarah
4:7 the sons of *H* were Zereth

Helam
2Sa 10:16 then they came to *H*, with
10:17 the Jordan and came to *H*

Helbah
Jg 1:31 and *H* and Aphik and Rehob

Helbon
Eze 27:18 the wine of *H* and the wool

Held
Ge 30:2 *h* back the fruit of the belly
Ex 17:12 his hands *h* steady until the
Nu 24:11 Jehovah has *h* you back from
Ru 3:15 So she *h* it open, and he
1Sa 9:6 and the man is *h* in honor
25:26 Jehovah has *h* you back from
25:34 *h* me back from doing injury
2Sa 18:16 Joab had *h* back the people
1Ki 1:9 Adonijah *h* a sacrifice of
2Ki 5:1 *h* in esteem, because it was
19:21 she has *h* you in derision
23:22 had been *h* from the days of
23:23 passover was *h* to Jehovah
2Ch 7:9 *h* a solemn assembly, because
7:9 they had *h* for seven days
30:21 *h* the festival of the
30:23 *h* it for seven days with
35:1 Josiah *h* in Jerusalem a
35:18 never been *h* a passover like
35:18 *h* a passover like that
35:18 inhabitants of Jerusalem *h*
35:19 this passover was *h*
Ezr 3:4 they *h* the festival of booths
6:16 *h* the inauguration of this
Es 1:3 he *h* a banquet for all his
1:5 king *h* a banquet for seven days
1:6 *h* fast in ropes of fine fabric
1:9 *h* a banquet for the women at
5:2 king *h* out to Esther the golden
8:4 king *h* the golden scepter out
9:28 *h* in each and every generation
Job 1:4 his sons went and *h* a banquet
16:6 my own pain is not *h* back
38:15 their light is *h* back
Ps 34:21 will be *h* guilty
34:22 none . . . will be *h* guilty
89:7 God is to be *h* in awe among
103:19 kingship has *h* domination
Pr 30:10 may not have to be *h* guilty
Ca 7:5 The king is *h* bound by the
Isa 24:6 inhabiting it are *h* guilty
37:22 she has *h* you in derision
53:3 we *h* him as of no account
Jer 5:25 *h* back what is good from
6:6 an accounting must be *h*
44:13 I *h* an accounting against
Eze 41:6 order that they might be *h*
41:6 not *h* in in the wall of the
Ho 13:16 Samaria will be *h* guilty
Zec 11:5 they are not *h* guilty
Mt 21:46 these *h* him to be a prophet
27:1 *h* a consultation against
Mr 11:32 *h* that John had really been
Lu 4:15 being *h* in honor by all
8:29 a long time it had *h* him fast
13:16 and whom Satan *h* bound
Ac 2:24 continue to be *h* fast by it
5:2 secretly *h* back some of the
19:38 court days are *h* and there
20:27 not *h* back from telling you
Ro 7:6 by which we were being *h* fast
Jas 5:4 wages . . . are *h* up by you
2Pe 1:1 *h* in equal privilege with

Heldai
1Ch 27:15 was *H* the Netophathite, of
Zec 6:10 from *H* and from Tobijah

Heleb
2Sa 23:29 *H* the son of Baanah the

Heled
1Ch 11:30 *H* the son of Baanah the

Helek
Nu 26:30 of *H* the family of the
Jos 17:2 and the sons of *H* and the

Helekites
Nu 26:30 of Helek the family of the *H*

Helem
1Ch 7:35 sons of *H* his brother were
Zec 6:14 come to belong to *H* and to

Heleph
Jos 19:33 boundary came to be from *H*

Helez
2Sa 23:26 *H* the Paltite, Ira the son
1Ch 2:39 in turn, became father to *H*
2:39 *H*, in turn, became father to
11:27 *H* the Pelonite
27:10 *H* the Pelonite of the sons

Heli
Lu 3:23 of Joseph, son of *H*

Helkai
Ne 12:15 Adna; for Meraioth, *H*

Helkath
Jos 19:25 boundary came to be *H* and
21:31 *H* and its pasture ground

Helkath-hazzurim
2Sa 2:16 place came to be called *H*

Helm
Jas 3:4 of the man at the *h* wishes

Ielmet
Sa 17:5 a *h* of copper on his head
17:38 he put a copper *h* upon his
sa 59:17 *h* of salvation upon his head
er 46:4 yourselves with the *h*
ze 23:24 shield and buckler and *h*
27:10 Shield and *h* they hung up
38:5 with buckler and *h*
ph 6:17 accept the *h* of salvation
Th 5:8 as a *h* the hope of salvation

Ielmets
Ch 26:14 *h* and coats of mail and

Ielon
u 1:9 Eliab the son of *H*
2:7 Eliab the son of *H*
7:24 of Zebulun, Eliab the son of *H*
7:29 of Eliab the son of *H*
10:16 Eliab the son of *H*

Ielp
e 49:25 he will *h* you; and he is
x 1:16 When you *h* the Hebrew women
2:23 their cry for *h* kept going up
u 11:17 *h* you in carrying the load
e 22:4 *h* him raise them up
32:38 Let them get up and *h* you
33:26 rides upon heaven in *h* of you
33:29 The shield of your *h*, And
os 1:14 and you must *h* them
10:4 and *h* me and let us strike
10:6 and *h* us, for all the kings
10:33 went up to *h* Lachish
Sa 5:12 cry of the city for *h* kept
Sa 8:5 came to *h* Hadadezer the king
18:3 to give *h* from the city
21:17 came to his *h* and struck
22:7 my cry for *h* in his ears
22:42 They cry for *h*, but there is
Ki 1:7 offering *h* as followers of
Ch 12:17 you have come to me to *h*
12:19 he did not *h* them, for on
12:21 were of *h* to David against
12:22 coming to David to *h* him
18:5 Syria of Damascus came to *h*
22:17 Israel to *h* Solomon his son
Ch 14:11 *H* us, O Jehovah our God
19:2 wicked that *h* is to be given
25:8 power with God to *h* and to
26:7 true God continued to *h* him
26:13 *h* the king against the
28:16 Assyria for them to *h* him
28:23 that they may *h* me
32:8 our God to *h* us and to fight
zr 8:22 to *h* us against the enemy
ob 7:13 bed will *h* carry my concern
19:7 I keep crying for *h*, but
24:12 wounded ones cries for *h*
26:2 how much *h* you have been to
29:12 afflicted one crying for *h*
30:20 I cry to you for *h*, but you
30:24 a cry for *h* respecting
30:28 I kept crying for *h*
35:9 They keep crying for *h*
36:13 cry for *h* because he has
36:19 your cry for *h* take effect
38:41 young ones cry to God for *h*
s 5:2 to the sound of my cry for *h*
18:6 my God I kept crying for *h*
18:6 my own cry before him for *h*
18:41 They cry for *h*, but there
20:2 your *h* out of the holy place
22:24 cried to him for *h* he heard
28:2 when I cry to you for *h*
30:2 I cried to you for *h*, and you
31:22 when I cried to you for *h*
34:15 are toward their cry for *h*
37:40 Jehovah will *h* them and
39:12 to my cry for *h* do give ear
40:1 and heard my cry for *h*
46:1 *h* that is readily to be found
46:5 *h* it at the appearance of
70:5 You are my *h* and the Provider
72:12 the poor one crying for *h*
79:9 *H* us, O God of our salvation
88:13 I myself have cried for *h*
89:19 placed *h* upon a mighty one
102:1 may my own cry for *h* come
107:13 to Jehovah for *h* in their
107:19 to Jehovah for *h* in their
109:26 *H* me, O Jehovah my God
115:9 is their *h* and their shield
115:10 is their *h* and their shield
115:11 is their *h* and their shield
Ps 119:86 persecuted me. O *h* me
119:147 that I may cry for *h*
119:173 your hand serve to *h* me
119:175 judicial decisions *h* me
121:1 From where will my *h* come?
121:2 My *h* is from Jehovah
124:8 *h* is in the name of Jehovah
145:19 cry for *h* he will hear
146:5 the God of Jacob for his *h*
Isa 30:5 are of no *h* and bring no
30:7 *h* simply for nothing
31:3 offering *h* will have to
41:10 I will really *h* you
41:13 I myself will *h* you
41:14 I myself will *h* you, is the
50:7 Jehovah himself will *h* me
50:9 Jehovah himself will *h* me
58:9 cry for *h*, and he would say
Jer 8:19 the sound of the cry for *h*
La 3:8 I call for aid and cry for *h*
3:56 to my relief, to my cry for *h*
Eze 12:14 are round about him as a *h*
Da 10:13 princes, came to *h* me; and
11:34 be helped with a little *h*
Jon 2:2 Out of . . . Sheol I cried for *h*
Hab 1:2 O Jehovah, must I cry for *h*
Mt 15:25 to him, saying: Lord, *h* me!
Mr 9:22 have pity on us and *h* us
9:24 *H* me out where I need faith
Ac 16:9 over into Macedonia and *h* us
21:28 crying out: Men of Israel, *h!*
26:22 the *h* that is from God I
Ro 8:26 spirit also joins in with *h*
2Co 1:11 *h* along by your supplication
Heb 4:16 for *h* at the right time
Jas 5:4 the calls for *h* on the part
Re 12:16 earth came to the woman's *h*

Helped
Ex 2:17 Moses got up and *h* the women
1Sa 7:12 Till now Jehovah has *h* us
1Ch 5:20 came to be *h* against them
12:18 For your God has *h* you
15:26 the true God *h* the Levites
2Ch 18:31 Jehovah himself *h* him, and
20:23 *h* each one to bring his own
26:15 *h* wonderfully until he was
29:34 Levites *h* them out until
32:3 and so they *h* him
Ezr 10:15 were the ones that *h* them
Ps 28:7 And I have been *h*, so that
86:17 Jehovah, have *h* me and
118:13 But Jehovah himself *h* me
Isa 31:3 he that is being *h* will have
49:8 day of salvation I have *h* you
Da 11:34 be *h* with a little help; and
Zec 1:15 they . . . *h* toward calamity
Ac 18:27 *h* those who had believed on
2Co 6:2 in a day of salvation I *h* you

Helper
Ge 2:18 I am going to make a *h* for
2:20 for man there was found no *h*
Ex 18:4 the God of my father is my *h*
De 33:7 a *h* from his adversaries
2Ki 14:26 was there a *h* for Israel
Job 29:12 and anyone that had no *h*
30:13 Without their having any *h*
Ps 10:14 You . . . have become his *h*
22:11 Because there is no other *h*
30:10 Jehovah, prove yourself my *h*
33:20 Our *h* and our shield he is
54:4 Look! God is my *h*
72:12 and whoever has no *h*
Isa 63:5 looking, but there was no *h*
La 1:7 the adversary and she had no *h*
Da 11:45 there will be no *h* for him
Ho 13:9 me, against your *h*
Joh 14:16 *h* to be with you forever
14:26 the *h*, the holy spirit
15:26 *h* arrives that I will send
16:7 *h* will by no means come to
Heb 13:6 Jehovah is my *h*; I will not
1Jo 2:1 we have a *h* with the Father

Helpers
1Ch 12:1 the *h* in the warfare
Job 9:13 the *h* of a stormer must bow
Eze 30:8 its *h* are actually broken
32:21 even to him, with his *h*

Helpful
1Co 12:28 *h* services, abilities to

Helpfully
La 4:6 and to which no hands turned *h*
Ac 28:2 received all of us *h* because

Helping
1Ki 20:16 kings that were *h* him
1Ch 12:18 and peace to the one *h* you
2Ch 14:11 Jehovah, as to *h*, it does
28:23 of the kings of Syria are *h*
Ps 88:5 severed from your own *h* hand
107:12 and there was no one *h*
118:7 on my side among those *h* me
Isa 41:6 *h* each one his companion
44:2 *h* you even from the belly
Jer 47:4 every survivor that was *h*
Lu 10:40 therefore, to join in *h* me

Helpless
De 32:36 only a *h* and worthless one
1Ki 14:10 a *h* and worthless one in
21:21 the *h* and worthless one in
2Ki 9:8 any *h* and worthless one in
14:26 any *h* one nor any worthless

Helps
Ac 27:17 *h* to undergird the boat

Hem
Ex 28:33 must make upon the *h* of it
28:33 upon its *h* round about, and
28:34 the *h* of the sleeveless coat
39:24 the *h* of the sleeveless coat
39:25 the *h* of the sleeveless coat
39:26 the *h* of the sleeveless coat
De 28:53 your enemy will *h* you in
28:55 your enemy will *h* you in
28:57 your enemy will *h* you in
Jer 19:9 will *h* them in

Hemam
Ge 36:22 sons of Lotan . . . *H*; and

Heman
1Ki 4:31 wiser than . . . *H* and Calcol
1Ch 2:6 the sons of Zerah were . . . *H*
6:33 the Kohathites *H* the singer
15:17 stationed *H* the son of Joel
15:19 singers *H*, Asaph and Ethan
16:41 with them *H* and Jeduthun
16:42 *H* and Jeduthun, to sound
25:1 of Asaph, *H* and Jeduthun the
25:4, 4 Of *H*: the sons of *H*
25:5 *H*, a visionary of the king in
25:5 to give *H* fourteen sons and
25:6 Asaph and Jeduthun and *H*
2Ch 5:12 singers belonging to . . . *H*
29:14 sons of *H*, Jehiel and
35:15 Asaph and of *H* and of
Ps 88:*super* Maskil of *H* the Ezrahite

Hemdan
Ge 36:26 sons of Dishon: *H* and Eshban
1Ch 1:41 sons of Dishon were *H* and

Hemming
Isa 51:13 rage of the one *h* you in
51:13 rage of the one *h* you in
Lu 8:45 the crowds are *h* you in and

Hen
Zec 6:14 to *H* the son of Zephaniah
Mt 23:37 way a *h* gathers her chicks
Lu 13:34 manner that a *h* gathers her

Hena
2Ki 18:34 gods of Sepharvaim, *H* and
19:13 Sepharvaim, *H* and Ivvah
Isa 37:13 of *H* and of Ivvah

Henadad
Ezr 3:9 also the sons of *H*, their
Ne 3:18 Bavvai the son of *H*, a prince
3:24 Binnui the son of *H*
10:9 of the sons of *H*, Kadmiel

Henna
Ca 1:14 As a cluster of *h* my dear one
4:13 *h* plants along with spikenard
7:11 lodge among the *h* plants

Hepher
Nu 26:32 of *H* the family of the
26:33 Now Zelophehad the son of *H*
27:1 son of *H* the son of Gilead the
Jos 12:17 the king of *H*, one
17:2 and the sons of *H* and the
17:3 *H*, the son of Gilead
1Ki 4:10 Socoh and all the land of *H*
1Ch 4:6 *H* and Temeni and Haahashtari
11:36 *H* the Mecherathite

Hepherites
Nu 26:32 Hepher the family of the *H*

Hephzibah
2Ki 21:1 his mother's name was *H*
Herald
Da 3:4 the *h* was crying out loudly
Heralded
Da 5:29 *h* concerning him that he was
Herb
Job 30:4 plucking the salt *h* by the
Herbs
Ca 5:13 of spice, towers of scented *h*
Herd
Ge 18:7 Abraham ran to the *h* and
27:9 Go, please, to the *h* and get
30:29 your *h* has fared with me
31:9 *h* of your father away and
31:18 he began driving all his *h*
31:18 *h* of his acquisition that he
33:17 for his *h* he made booths
34:5 be with his *h* in the field
36:6 Esau took . . . his *h* and all
38:17 kid of the goats from the *h*
47:17 the livestock of the *h* and
Ex 9:3 the *h* and the flock there will
20:24 your flock and your *h*
22:1 compensate with five of the *h*
34:3 no flock or *h* should be
Le 1:2 offering from the *h* and from
1:3 burnt offering from the *h*, a
3:1 is presenting it from the *h*
22:19 male among the *h*, among the
22:21 sound one among the *h* or the
27:32 tenth part of the *h* and flock
Nu 15:3 from the *h* or from the flock
15:8 render up a male of the *h* as
15:9 with the male of the *h* a
31:28 of humankind and of the *h*
31:30 of humankind, of the *h*, of
31:33 thousand of the *h*
31:38 And of the *h* there were
31:44 of the *h*, thirty-six thousand
De 8:13 *h* and your flock may increase
12:6 ones of your *h* and of your
12:17 the firstborn ones of your *h*
12:21 slaughter some of your *h*
14:23 the firstborn ones of your *h*
15:19 born in your *h* and in your
16:2 flock and of the *h*, in the
21:3 take a young cow of the *h*
32:14 Butter of the *h* and milk of
1Sa 11:5 Saul coming after the *h* from
15:9 and the *h* and the fat ones
15:14 the sound of the *h* that I
15:15 upon the best of the . . . *h*
16:2 A young cow of the *h* you
2Ch 32:29 and of the *h* in abundance
Isa 7:21 young cow of the *h* and two
Eze 43:19 bull, the son of the *h*
43:23 young bull, the son of the *h*
43:25 bull, the son of the *h*
45:18 young bull, a son of the *h*
46:6 bull, the son of the *h*
Ho 5:6 with their *h* they proceeded
Jon 3:7 no *h* and no flock, should
Hab 3:17 be no *h* in the enclosures
Mt 8:30 a *h* of many swine was at
8:31 us forth into the *h* of swine
8:32 *h* rushed over the precipice
Mr 5:11 a great *h* of swine was there
5:13 *h* rushed over the precipice
Lu 8:32 a *h* of a considerable number
8:33 *h* rushed over the precipice
15:15 into his fields to *h* swine
Herder
Ge 4:2 Abel came to be a *h* of sheep
46:34 every *h* of sheep is a
Herders
Ge 13:7 a quarrel arose between the *h*
13:7 the *h* of Lot's livestock
47:3 Your servants are *h* of sheep
Mt 8:33 the *h* fled and, going into
Mr 5:14 *h* of them fled and reported
Lu 8:34 when the *h* saw what had
Herds
Ge 13:2 Abram was . . . stocked with *h*
26:14 came to have . . . *h* of cattle
29:7 the time for gathering the *h*
34:28 their *h* and their asses and
36:7 as a result of their *h*
45:10 your flocks and your *h* and
46:6 took along their *h* and their
46:32 their flocks and their *h*
47:1 their *h* and all they have
50:8 *h* they left in the land of
Ex 12:32 both your flocks and your *h*
12:38 as well as flocks and *h*
Nu 11:22 *h* be slaughtered for them
1Sa 8:16 your best *h*, and your asses
27:9 took flocks and *h* and asses
30:20 all the flocks and the *h*
1Ch 27:29 the *h* that were grazing in
27:29 the *h* in the low plains
Ne 10:36 the firstborn of our *h* and
Jer 3:24 their flocks and their *h*
5:17 eat up your flocks and your *h*
Herdsman
Am 7:14 but I was a *h* and a nipper of
Herdsmen
Ge 13:8, 8 between my *h* and your *h*
Hereafter
Ge 30:32 *H* such must be my wages
Hereditary
Jos 14:1 a *h* possession in the land of
1Ki 8:36 land . . . as a *h* possession
21:3 to give the *h* possession of
21:4 not give you the *h* possession
2Ch 6:27 your people as a *h* possession
Ne 11:20 in his own *h* possession
Pr 8:18 *h* values and righteousness
Isa 49:8 the desolated *h* possessions
54:17 *h* possession of the servants
58:14 the *h* possession of Jacob
63:17 tribes of your *h* possession
65:9 *h* possessor of my mountains
Jer 3:18 I gave as a *h* possession to
3:19 land, the *h* possession of
12:14 touching the *h* possession
12:15 each one to his *h* possession
17:4 your *h* possession that I had
32:8 right of *h* possession is
La 5:2 Our own *h* possession has been
Eze 36:12 become a *h* possession to
Mic 2:2 a man and his *h* possession
Heres
Jg 1:35 dwelling in Mount *H* and in
8:13 by the pass that goes up to *H*
Heresh
1Ch 9:15 and Bakbakkar, *H* and Galal
Hereth
1Sa 22:5 came into the forest of *H*
Heretofore
Pr 22:20 Have I not written you *h*
Hermas
Ro 16:14 Patrobas, *H*, and the brothers
Hermes
Ac 14:12 Barnabas Zeus, but Paul *H*
Ro 16:14 Greet Asyncritus, Phlegon, *H*
Hermogenes
2Ti 1:15 Phygelus and *H* are of that
Hermon
De 3:8 Arnon as far as Mount *H*
3:9 used to call *H* Sirion, and the
4:48 Mount Sion, that is to say, *H*
Jos 11:3 of *H* in the land of Mizpah
11:17 at the base of Mount *H*
12:1 Mount *H* and all the Arabah
12:5 and who ruled in Mount *H*
13:5 at the base of Mount *H* as
13:11 Mount *H* and all Bashan as
1Ch 5:23 and Senir and Mount *H*
Ps 42:6 Jordan and the peaks of *H*
89:12 Tabor and *H*—in your name
133:3 It is like the dew of *H*
Ca 4:8 from the top of Senir, even *H*
Herod
Mt 2:1 in the days of *H* the king
2:3 At hearing this King *H* was
2:7 *H* secretly summoned the
2:12 not to return to *H*, they
2:13 *H* is about to search for the
2:15 there until the decease of *H*
2:16 Then *H*, seeing he had been
2:19 When *H* had deceased, look!
2:22 instead of his father *H*
14:1 *H*, the district ruler, heard
14:3 *H* had arrested John and bound
14:6 danced at it and pleased *H* so
22:16 with party followers of *H*
Mr 3:6 with the party followers of *H*
6:14 it got to the ears of King *H*
6:16 when *H* heard it he began to
6:17 *H* himself had sent out and
6:18 John had repeatedly said to *H*
6:20 For *H* stood in fear of John
6:21 *H* spread an evening meal on
6:22 danced and pleased *H* and
8:15 Pharisees and the leaven of *H*
12:13 of the party followers of *H*
Lu 1:5 the days of *H*, king of Judea
3:1 *H* was district ruler of
3:19 *H* the district ruler, for
3:19 the wicked deeds that *H* did
9:7 *H* the district ruler heard
9:9 *H* said: John I beheaded
13:31 because *H* wants to kill you
23:7 from the jurisdiction of *H*
23:7 he sent him on to *H* who was
23:8 When *H* saw Jesus he rejoiced
23:11 *H* together with his soldier
23:12 *H* and Pilate now became
23:15 In fact, neither did *H*, for
Ac 4:27 *H* and Pontius Pilate with
12:1 *H* the king applied his hands
12:6 *H* was about to produce him
12:19 *H* made diligent search for
12:21 *H* clothed himself with royal
13:1 Manaen . . . educated with *H*
23:35 in the praetorian palace of *H*
Herodias
Mt 14:3 *H* the wife of Philip his
14:6 daughter of *H* danced at it
Mr 6:17 of *H* the wife of Philip his
6:19 But *H* was nursing a grudge
6:22 the daughter of this very *H*
Lu 3:19 *H* the wife of his brother and
Herodion
Ro 16:11 Greet *H* my relative. Greet
Herod's
Mt 14:6 when *H* birthday was being
Lu 8:3 Chuza, *H* man in charge, and
Ac 12:11 delivered me out of *H* hand
Heroes
Isa 33:7 *h* have cried out in the
Heron
Le 11:19 the *h* according to its kind
De 14:18 the *h* according to its kind
Hesed
1Ki 4:10 the son of *H*, in Arubboth
Heshbon
Nu 21:25 in *H* and all its dependent
21:26 For *H* was the city of Sihon
21:27 Come to *H*. Let the city of
21:28 a fire has come out of *H*, a
21:30 *H* will certainly perish
21:34 who used to dwell in *H*
32:3 Jazer and Nimrah and *H* and
32:37 sons of Reuben built *H* and
De 1:4 Sihon . . . was dwelling in *H*
2:24 Sihon the king of *H*, the
2:26 king of *H* with words of peace
2:30 Sihon the king of *H* did not
3:2 who was dwelling in *H*
3:6 Sihon the king of *H*, in
4:46 who was dwelling in *H*, whom
29:7 and Sihon the king of *H* and
Jos 9:10 Sihon the king of *H* and Og
12:2 dwelt in *H*, ruling from
12:5 Sihon the king of *H*
13:10 reigned in *H*, up to the
13:17 *H* and all its towns that
13:21 reigned in *H*, and whom
13:26 from *H* to Ramath-mizpeh
13:27 of Sihon the king of *H*
21:39 *H* and its pasture ground
Jg 11:19 the king of *H*, and Israel
11:26 Israel was dwelling in *H*
1Ch 6:81 *H* with its pasture grounds
Ne 9:22 the land of the king of *H*
Ca 7:4 eyes are like the pools in *H*
Isa 15:4 And *H* and Elealeh cry out
16:8 terraces themselves of *H*
16:9 drench you, O *H* and Elealeh
Jer 48:2 *H* they have thought out
48:34 cry in *H* clear to Elealeh
48:45 In the shadow of *H* those
48:45 certainly go forth out of *H*
49:3 Howl, O *H*, for Ai has been
Heshmon
Jos 15:27 and *H* and Beth-pelet

Hesitant
g 18:9 you are *h*. Do not be sluggish

Hesitantly
x 22:29 you must not give *h*

Hesitate
e 7:10 He will not *h* toward the one
c 5:4 a vow to God, do not *h* to pay
c 9:38 not *h* to come on as far as us

Hesitating
Ki 22:3 *h* to take it out of the hand
Ki 7:9 If we are *h*, and we actually

Heth
e 10:15 Canaan became father . . . *H*
23:3 speak to the sons of *H*, saying
23:5 sons of *H* answered Abraham
23:7 the natives, to the sons of *H*
23:10 sitting among the sons of *H*
23:10 hearing of the sons of *H*
23:16 the hearing of the sons of *H*
23:18 eyes of the sons of *H* among
23:20 at the hands of the sons of *H*
25:10 purchased from the sons of *H*
27:46 because of the daughters of *H*
27:46 wife from the daughters of *H*
49:32 were from the sons of *H*
Ch 1:13 Sidon his firstborn and *H*

Hethlon
ze 47:15 Sea by the way to *H*, as
48:1 side by the way of *H* to

Hew
e 6:11 that you did not *h* out
Ch 22:2 hewers to *h* squared stones
er 2:13 to *h* out for themselves
o 6:5 have to *h* them by the prophets

Hewed
Ch 26:10 and *h* out many cisterns
a 5:2 winepress that he *h* out in it
22:16 *h* out for yourself here a

Hewers
Ki 12:12 and to the *h* of stone
Ch 22:2 as stone *h* to hew squared
22:15 stone *h* and workers in

Hewing
s 29:7 *h* with the flames of fire
a 22:16 is *h* out his burial place

Hewn
x 20:25 not build them as *h* stones
e 6:11 cisterns *h* out that you did
Ki 5:17 foundation . . . with *h* stones
6:36 with three rows of *h* stone
7:9 *h*, sawed with stone-saws
7:11 expensive stones . . . *h*
7:12 three rows of *h* stone and a
Ki 12:12 to buy timbers and *h* stones
22:6 to buy timbers and *h* stones
Ch 34:11 builders to buy *h* stones and
e 9:25 cisterns *h* out, vineyards and
ob 19:24 Forever in the rock . . . *h*
r 9:1 it has *h* out its seven pillars
a 9:10 with *h* stone we shall build
22:25 must be *h* down and fall
51:1 rock from which you were *h*
a 3:9 blocked . . . ways with *h* stone
ze 40:42 tables . . . were of *h* stone
m 5:11 houses of *h* stone you have

Hey
a 55:1 *H* there, all you thirsty ones!
ec 2:6, 6 *H* there! *H* there! Flee
2:7 *H* there, Zion! Make your

Hezekiah
Ki 16:20 *H* his son began to reign in
18:1 *H* the son of Ahaz the king
18:9 the fourth year of King *H*
18:10 in the sixth year of *H*
18:13 fourteenth year of King *H*
18:14 *H* the king of Judah sent
18:14 *H* the king of Judah
18:15 *H* gave all the silver that
18:16 *H* cut off the doors of the
18:16 that *H* the king of Judah had
18:17 from Lachish to King *H*
18:19 say to *H*, This is what the
18:22 whose altars *H* has removed
18:29 Do not let *H* deceive you
18:30 do not let *H* cause you to
18:31 Do not listen to *H*; for this
18:32 And do not listen to *H*
18:37 the recorder came to *H*
2Ki 19:1 as soon as King *H* heard
19:3 *H* has said, This day is a
19:5 the servants of King *H* came
19:9 sent messengers again to *H*
19:10 *H* the king of Judah
19:14 *H* took the letters out of
19:14 *H* went up to the house of
19:15 And *H* began to pray before
19:20 send to *H*, saying: This is
20:1 *H* got sick to the point of
20:3 *H* began to weep profusely
20:5 *H* the leader of my people
20:8 *H* said to Isaiah: What is
20:10 *H* said: It is an easy thing
20:12 sent letters and a gift to *H*
20:12 heard that *H* had been sick
20:13 *H* proceeded to listen to
20:13 that *H* did not show them in
20:14 came in to King *H* and said
20:14 *H* said: From a distant land
20:15 *H* said: Everything that is
20:16 Isaiah now said to *H*
20:19 At that *H* said to Isaiah
20:20 *H* and all his mightiness
20:21 Finally *H* lay down with his
21:3 *H* his father had destroyed
1Ch 3:13 *H* his son, Manasseh his son
4:41 *H* the king of Judah
2Ch 28:27 *H* his son began to reign
29:1 *H* himself became king at
29:18 to *H* the king and said: We
29:20 *H* the king proceeded to get
29:27 *H* said to offer up the
29:30 *H* the king and the princes
29:31 *H* answered and said: Now
29:36 *H* and all the people
30:1 *H* proceeded to send to all
30:18 *H* prayed for them, saying
30:20 Jehovah listened to *H* and
30:22 *H* spoke to the heart of all
30:24 *H* the king of Judah
31:2 *H* set the divisions of the
31:8 *H* and the princes came and
31:9 *H* inquired of the priests and
31:11 *H* said to prepare dining
31:13 by the order of *H* the king
31:20 *H* proceeded to do like this
32:2 *H* saw that Sennacherib had
32:8 words of *H* the king of Judah
32:9 to *H* the king of Judah and
32:11 *H* alluring you so as to give
32:12 *H* himself that removed his
32:15 not let *H* deceive you or
32:16 and against *H* his servant
32:17 God of *H* will not deliver
32:20 *H* the king and Isaiah the
32:22 Jehovah saved *H* and the
32:23 *H* the king of Judah, and
32:24 *H* fell sick to the point of
32:25 *H* made no return, for his
32:26 *H* humbled himself for the
32:26 upon them in the days of *H*
32:27 *H* came to have riches and
32:30 *H* was the one that stopped
32:30 and *H* continued to prove
32:32 *H* and his acts of
32:33 *H* lay down with his
33:3 *H* his father had pulled down
Ezr 2:16 sons of Ater, of *H*
Ne 7:21 of Ater, of *H*, ninety-eight
10:17 Ater, *H*, Azzur
Pr 25:1 men of *H* the king of Judah
Isa 1:1 Ahaz and *H*, kings of Judah
36:1 fourteenth year of King *H*
36:2 *H*, with a heavy military
36:4 say to *H*, This is what the
36:7 whose altars *H* has removed
36:14 not let *H* deceive you
36:15 *H* cause you to trust in
36:16 Do not listen to *H*, for
36:18 *H* may not allure you
36:22 to *H* with their garments
37:1 as soon as King *H* heard
37:3 This is what *H* has said
37:5 servants of King *H* came in
37:9 once sent messengers to *H*
37:10 say to *H* the king of Judah
37:14 *H* took the letters out of
37:14 *H* went up to the house of
37:15 *H* began to pray to Jehovah
37:21 send to *H*, saying: This is
38:1 *H* got sick to the point of
38:2 *H* turned his face to the
38:3 *H* began to weep profusely
Isa 38:5 and you must say to *H*
38:9 *H* the king of Judah
38:22 *H* said: What is the sign
39:1 sent letters and a gift to *H*
39:2 *H* began to rejoice over them
39:2 nothing that *H* did not show
39:3 to King *H* and said to him
39:3 *H* said: From a distant land
39:4 *H* said: Everything that is
39:5 Isaiah now said to *H*: Hear
39:8 At that *H* said to Isaiah
Jer 15:4 Manasseh the son of *H*
26:18 in the days of *H* the king
26:19 Did *H* the king of Judah
Ho 1:1 Ahaz and *H*, kings of Judah
Mic 1:1 Jotham, Ahaz, *H*, kings of
Zep 1:1 Amariah the son of *H* in the
Mt 1:9 Ahaz became father to *H*
1:10 *H* became father to Manasseh

Hezion
1Ki 15:18 Tabrimmon the son of *H*

Hezir
1Ch 24:15 for *H* the seventeenth
Ne 10:20 Magpiash, Meshullam, *H*

Hezro
2Sa 23:35 *H* the Carmelite, Paarai the
1Ch 11:37 *H* the Carmelite, Naarai the

Hezron
Ge 46:9 sons of Reuben were . . . *H*
46:12 sons of Perez . . . *H* and
Ex 6:14 The sons of Reuben . . . *H* and
Nu 26:6 of *H* the family of the
26:21 Of *H* the family of the
Jos 15:3 passed over to *H* and went
Ru 4:18 Perez became father to *H*
4:19 and *H* became father to Ram
1Ch 2:5 sons of Perez were *H* and
2:9 sons of *H* that were born to
2:18 As for Caleb the son of *H*
2:21 *H* had relations with the
2:24 death of *H* in Caleb-ephrathah
2:24 Abijah being the wife of *H*
2:25 Jerahmeel the firstborn of *H*
4:1 sons of Judah were Perez, *H*
5:3 the sons of Reuben . . . *H*
Mt 1:3 Perez became father to *H*
1:3 *H* became father to Ram
Lu 3:33 son of Arni, son of *H*, son

Hezronites
Nu 26:6 of Hezron the family of the *H*
26:21 Hezron the family of the *H*

Hid
Ge 3:10 I was naked and so I *h* myself
35:4 Jacob *h* them under the big
Ex 2:12 down and *h* him in the sand
Jos 2:16 must keep *h* there three days
6:17 she *h* the messengers whom we
6:25 she *h* the messengers whom
10:27 the cave where they had *h*
Jg 9:5 left over, because he had *h*
1Ki 18:4 *h* by fifties in a cave
18:13 the prophets of Jehovah *h*
2Ki 6:29 eat him. But she *h* her son
Job 29:8 The boys saw me and *h*
Ps 9:15 In the net that they *h*, their
10:1 *h* in times of distress
35:7 *h* for me their netted pit
35:8 own net that he *h* catch him
Pr 2:4 as for *h* treasures you keep
Jer 13:5 *h* it by the Euphrates, just
13:7 place in which I had *h* it
16:17 their error been *h* from in
18:22 they have *h* for my feet
Mt 5:14 A city cannot be *h* when
13:33 leaven . . . *h* in three large
13:44 treasure . . . man found and *h*
25:18 *h* the silver money of his
25:25 *h* your talent in the ground
Lu 13:21 *h* in three large measures
19:42 have been *h* from your eyes
Joh 8:59 Jesus *h* and went out of the
12:36 went off and *h* from them
1Ti 5:25 otherwise cannot be kept *h*
Heb 11:23 Moses was *h* for three
Re 6:15 *h* themselves in the caves

Hiddai
2Sa 23:30 *H* of the torrent valleys of

Hiddekel
Ge 2:14 name of the third river is *H*
Da 10:4 the great river, that is, *H*

Hidden
Le 4:13 been *h* from the eyes of the
5:2 although it has been *h* from
5:3 although it had been *h* from
5:4 although it had been *h* from
Nu 5:13 *h* from the eyes of her
De 33:19 And the *h* hoards of the sand
Jos 7:21 they are *h* in the earth in
7:22 it was *h* in his tent with
10:17 *h* in the cave at Makkedah
1Sa 10:22 he is, *h* among the luggage
14:11 the holes where they have *h*
14:22 *h* in the mountainous region
19:2 secrecy and keep yourself *h*
2Sa 18:13 not be *h* from the king
1Ki 10:3 no matter *h* from the king
2Ki 4:27 Jehovah himself has *h* it
2Ch 9:2 no matter was *h* from Solomon
22:12 *h* for six years, while
Job 3:16 Or, like a *h* miscarriage, I
3:21 more than for *h* treasures
5:21 you will be *h*, And you will
6:10 not *h* the sayings of the Holy
18:10 A cord for him is *h* on the
24:4 have kept themselves *h*
28:21 *h* even from the eyes of
29:10 voice of the leaders . . . *h*
38:30 waters keep themselves *h*
40:13 faces in the *h* place
Ps 31:4 net that they have *h* for me
40:10 not *h* your loving-kindness
64:6 They have *h* a shrewd device
69:5 own guiltiness has not been *h*
90:8 *h* things before your bright
139:15 bones were not *h* from you
140:5 have *h* a trap for me
142:3 they have *h* a trap for me
Pr 19:24 lazy one has *h* his hand in
26:15 lazy one has *h* his hand in
Ec 12:14 in relation to every *h* thing
Isa 3:9 They have not *h* it
42:22 they have been kept *h*
45:3 the *h* treasures in the
49:2 of his hand he has *h* me
Jer 41:8 our possession *h* treasures
43:10 stones that I have *h*, and
Eze 22:26 they have *h* their eyes
Da 11:43 rule over the *h* treasures
Ho 5:3 Israel itself has not been *h*
Na 3:11 you will become something *h*
Mt 11:25 have *h* these things from the
13:35 things *h* since the founding
13:44 a treasure *h* in the field
Mr 4:22 is nothing *h* except for the
Lu 8:17 nothing *h* that will not
10:21 carefully *h* these things
18:34 this utterance was *h* from
1Co 2:7 sacred secret, the *h* wisdom
Eph 3:9 been *h* in God, who created
Col 1:26 the sacred secret that was *h*
3:3 *h* with the Christ in union
Jude 12 rocks *h* below water in your
Re 2:17 give some of the *h* manna

Hide
Ge 47:18 shall not *h* it from my lord
Le 20:4 *h* their eyes from that man
Jos 7:19 Do not *h* it from me
1Sa 3:17 Do not, please, *h* it from me
3:17 *h* from me a word of all the
3:18 did not *h* anything from him
12:3 should *h* my eyes with it
2Sa 14:18 *h* from me a thing about
1Ki 22:25 the innermost chamber to *h*
2Ki 7:12 went out from the camp to *h*
2Ch 18:24 innermost chamber to *h*
Job 15:18 And which they did not *h*
27:11 I shall not *h*
40:13 *H* them together in the dust
Ps 26:4 those who *h* what they are
27:5 he will *h* me in his covert
31:20 will *h* them in your booth
55:1 *h* yourself from my request
78:4 we do not *h* from their sons
Isa 1:15 I *h* my eyes from you
2:10 and *h* yourself in the dust
26:20 *H* yourself for but a moment
30:20 will no longer *h* himself
58:7 *h* . . . from your own flesh
Jer 13:4 *h* it there in a cleft of the
13:6 that I commanded you to *h*
38:14 Do not *h* from me anything
38:25 not *h* anything from us, and
43:9 *h* them in the mortar in the
Jer 49:10 not be able to *h* oneself
50:2 publish it. *H* nothing, O men
La 3:56 not *h* your ear to my relief
Am 9:3 if they *h* themselves on the
Re 6:16 and *h* us from the face of the

Hides
1Sa 23:23 places where he *h* himself
Job 6:16 Upon them snow *h* itself

Hiding
Ge 3:8 man and his wife went into *h*
De 27:15 who has put it in a *h* place
27:24 strikes . . . from a *h* place
33:27 A *h* place is the God of
Jos 10:16 *h* themselves in the cave at
1Sa 13:6 *h* themselves in the caves
23:23 all the *h* places where he
2Sa 17:9 in *h* in one of the hollows
2Ki 11:3 in *h* for six years, while
1Ch 21:20 four sons with him were *h*
2Ch 22:9 as he was *h* in Samaria, and
Job 31:33 *h* my error in my shirt
37:8 in its *h* places it dwells
38:40 they crouch in the *h* places
Ps 64:5 statements about *h* traps
104:22 down in their own *h* places
Pr 28:27 is *h* his eyes will get many
Isa 4:6 *h* place from the rainstorm
32:2 *h* place from the wind and a
57:11 silent and *h* matters
Da 10:7 running away in *h* themselves
Am 3:4 its voice from its *h* place
Na 2:12 his *h* places with animals
Hab 3:4 the *h* of his strength was

Hiel
1Ki 16:34 In his days *H* the Bethelite

Hierapolis
Col 4:13 Laodicea and of those at *H*

Higgaion
Ps 9:16 has been ensnared. *H. Se'lah*

High
Ge 7:17 ark and it was floating *h*
14:18 he was priest of the Most *H*
14:19 Abram of the Most *H* God
14:20 blessed be the Most *H* God
14:22 Jehovah the Most *H* God
34:12 very *h* the marriage money
Ex 15:2 and I shall raise him on *h*
Le 21:10 *h* priest of his brothers upon
26:30 your sacred *h* places and
Nu 21:28 of the *h* places of the Arnon
24:16 the knowledge of the Most *H*
33:52 all their sacred *h* places you
35:25 the death of the *h* priest
35:28 until the *h* priest's death
35:28 after the *h* priest's death
35:32 the death of the *h* priest
De 2:36 no town that was too *h* up for
3:5 cities fortified with a *h* wall
26:19 *h* above all the other nations
28:1 *h* above all other nations of
28:52 your *h* and fortified walls
32:8 Most *H* gave the nations an
32:13 ride upon earth's *h* places
33:29 *h* places you will tread
Jos 20:6 the death of the *h* priest
Jg 5:3 give ear, you *h* officials: I to
1Sa 9:12 the people on the *h* place
9:13 goes up to the *h* place to eat
9:14 to go up to the *h* place
9:19 up before me to the *h* place
9:25 went down from the *h* place
10:5 down from the *h* place
10:13 and came to the *h* place
22:6 on the *h* place with his
2Sa 1:19 is slain upon your *h* places
1:25 slain upon your *h* places
22:14 the Most *H* himself began to
22:17 He was sending from on *h*
22:34 upon places *h* for me he
23:1 man that was raised up on *h*
1Ki 3:2 sacrificing on the *h* places
3:3 on the *h* places that he was
3:4 that was the great *h* place
11:7 build a *h* place to Chemosh
12:31 to make a house of *h* places
12:32 priests of the *h* places
13:2 the priests of the *h* places
13:32 the houses of the *h* places
13:33 making priests of *h* places
13:33 the priests of *h* places
14:23 *h* places and sacred pillars
1Ki 14:23 poles upon every *h* hill
15:14 *h* places he did not remove
22:43 the *h* places themselves did
22:43 smoke on the *h* places
2Ki 12:3 the *h* places that did not
12:3 smoke on the *h* places
12:10 the *h* priest would come up
14:4 the *h* places that did not
14:4 smoke on the *h* places
15:4 *h* places did not disappear
15:4 smoke on the *h* places
15:35 *h* places did not disappear
15:35 smoke on the *h* places
16:4 smoke on the *h* places and
17:9 *h* places in all their cities
17:10 upon every *h* hill and under
17:11 on all the *h* places they
17:29 the house of the *h* places
17:32 priests of *h* places, and
17:32 in the house of the *h* places
18:4 removed the *h* places and
18:22 the one whose *h* places and
19:22 do you raise your eyes on *h*
21:3 built again the *h* places that
22:4 Go up to Hilkiah the *h* priest
22:8 Hilkiah the *h* priest said to
23:4 Hilkiah the *h* priest and the
23:5 *h* places in the cities of
23:8 for worship the *h* places
23:8 pulled down the *h* places of
23:9 the priests of the *h* places
23:13 the *h* places that were in
23:15 the *h* place that Jeroboam
23:15 that altar and the *h* place
23:15 Then he burned the *h* place
23:19 the houses of the *h* places
23:20 the priests of the *h* places
1Ch 16:39 *h* place that was at Gibeon
21:29 on the *h* place at Gibeon
2Ch 1:3 *h* place that was at Gibeon
1:13 *h* place that was at Gibeon
11:15 priests for the *h* places and
14:3 *h* places and broke up the
14:5 *h* places and the incense
15:17 *h* places themselves did not
17:6 removed the *h* places and the
20:33 *h* places themselves did not
21:11 made *h* places on the
28:4 smoke on the *h* places and
28:25 made *h* places for making
31:1 pull down the *h* places and
32:12 removed his *h* places and
33:3 *h* places that Hezekiah his
33:14 to make it very *h*
33:17 upon the *h* places
33:19 built *h* places and set up
34:3 from the *h* places and the
34:9 Hilkiah the *h* priest and give
Ne 3:1 And Eliashib the *h* priest and
3:20 house of Eliashib the *h* priest
13:28 Eliashib the *h* priest was a
Es 5:14 make a stake fifty cubits *h*
7:9 the stake . . . fifty cubits *h*
Job 5:11 who are low on a *h* place
5:11 sad are *h* up in salvation
9:8 treading upon the *h* waves of
21:22 One himself judges *h* ones
22:12 the stars, that they are *h*
24:24 become *h* up a little while
31:2 from the Almighty from on *h*
38:15 *h* arm itself gets broken
39:18 she flaps her wings on *h*
39:27 that it builds its nest *h* up
41:34 Everything *h* it sees
Ps 2:2 *h* officials themselves have
7:7 against it do you return on *h*
7:17 the name of Jehovah the Most *H*
9:2 melody to your name, O Most *H*
10:5 Your judicial decisions are *h*
18:13 the Most *H* himself began to
18:16 He was sending from on *h*
18:33 upon places *h* for me he
21:7 loving-kindness of the Most *H*
27:5 *H* on a rock he will put me
27:6 *h* above my enemies all around
46:4 tabernacle of the Most *H*
47:2 the Most *H*, is fear-inspiring
47:9 He is very *h* in his ascent
50:14 pay to the Most *H* your vows
57:2 I call to God the Most *H*, to
68:18 You have ascended on *h*
73:11 knowledge in the Most *H*
74:5 axes on *h* against a thicket
75:5 Do not exalt your horn on *h*

's 77:10 the right hand of the Most *H*
78:17 rebelling against the Most *H*
78:35 Most *H* was their Avenger
78:56 rebel against God the Most *H*
78:58 with their *h* places
82:6 you are sons of the Most *H*
83:18 Most *H* over all the earth
87:5 Most *H* himself will firmly
89:27 most *h* of the kings of the
91:1 secret place of the Most *H*
91:9 Most *H* himself your dwelling
92:1 to your name, O Most *H*
92:8 are on *h* to time indefinite
97:9 the Most *H* over all the earth
97:9 *h* in your ascent over all
99:2 he is *h* over all the peoples
104:18 *h* mountains are for the
107:11 counsel of the Most *H* they
110:7 he will raise *h* his head
113:4 Jehovah has become *h* above
113:5 is making his dwelling on *h*
138:6 For Jehovah is *h*, and yet
139:6 so *h* up that I cannot attain
148:13 name alone is unreachably *h*
Pr 8:15 *h* officials themselves keep
9:14 in the *h* places of the town
14:28 is the ruin of a *h* official
17:19 Anyone making his entryway *h*
24:7 true wisdom is too *h*
31:4 or for *h* officials to say
Ec 5:8 *h* one is watching, and there
5:8 are those who are *h* above them
10:6 been put in many *h* positions
12:5 afraid merely at what is *h*
Isa 2:11 Jehovah alone . . . put on *h* in
2:15 upon every *h* tower and upon
2:17 must be put on *h* in that day
5:15 eyes of the *h* ones will
5:16 become *h* through judgment
7:11 it *h* as the upper regions
9:11 of Rezin on *h* against him
10:15 the ones raising it on *h*
10:15 rod raised on *h* the one who
10:33 *h* ones themselves become
12:4 that his name is put on *h*
14:14 the *h* places of the clouds
14:14 myself resemble the Most *H*
15:2 the *h* places, to a weeping
16:12 made weary upon the *h* place
24:4 *h* ones of the people of the
24:18 floodgates on *h* will
25:12 your *h* walls of security
26:11 your hand has become *h*, but
30:25 upon every *h* mountain and
32:15 is poured out from on *h*
33:5 certainly be put on *h*, for
36:7 the one whose *h* places and
37:23 you raise your eyes on *h*
40:9 even onto a *h* mountain
40:23 reducing *h* officials to
40:26 your eyes *h* up and see
52:13 He will be in *h* station and
57:7 Upon a mountain *h* and lifted
57:15 is what the *H* and Lofty One
58:14 the *h* places of the earth
59:10 stumbled at *h* noon just as
Jer 2:20 upon every *h* hill and under
3:6 going upon every *h* mountain
7:31 the *h* places of Topheth
17:2 upon the *h* hills
17:3 your *h* places because of sin
17:12 the glorious throne on *h*
19:5 the *h* places of the Baal
25:30 From on *h* Jehovah himself
26:18 for *h* places of a forest
32:35 built the *h* places of Baal
48:35 offering upon the *h* place
49:16 nest *h* up just like an eagle
51:58 her gates, although *h*
La 2:17 the horn of your adversaries *h*
3:35 before the face of the Most *H*
3:38 From the mouth of the Most *H*
Eze 6:3 destroy your *h* places
6:6 *h* places . . . become desolated
6:13 upon every *h* hill, on all the
10:16 to be *h* above the earth
16:16 *h* places of varied colors
17:22 upon a *h* and lofty mountain
17:24 have abased the *h* tree, have
17:24 have put on *h* the low tree
20:29 What does the *h* place mean
20:29 should be called a *H* Place
21:26 Put on *h* even what is low
21:26 bring low even the *h* one
Eze 31:3 and *h* in stature, so that
31:4 caused it to grow *h*
31:10 you became *h* in stature
31:14 become *h* in their stature
34:6 and on every *h* hill; and
34:14 on Israel's *h* mountains
36:2 the *h* places of old time
40:2 upon a very *h* mountain, on
41:8 a *h* platform for the house
41:22 altar was three cubits *h*
47:5 for the water had got *h*
Da 3:24 to his *h* royal officials
3:26 servants of the Most *H* God
3:27 the *h* officials of the king
4:2 wonders that the Most *H* God
4:17 the Most *H* is Ruler in the
4:24 decree of the Most *H* is that
4:25 the Most *H* is Ruler in the
4:32 the Most *H* is Ruler in the
4:34 I blessed the Most *H* himself
4:36 even my *h* royal officers and
5:18 Most *H* God himself gave to
5:21 Most *H* God is Ruler in the
6:2 three *h* officials, of whom
6:3 over the *h* officials and the
6:4 *h* officials and the satraps
6:6 these *h* officials and satraps
6:7 *h* officials of the kingdom
6:7 the *h* royal officers and the
7:25 even words against the Most *H*
Ho 10:8 the *h* places of Beth-aven
Am 4:13 treading on earth's *h* places
7:9 the *h* places of Isaac will
8:9 the sun go down at *h* noon
Ob 4 your position *h* like the eagle
Mic 1:3 tread upon earth's *h* places
1:5 are the *h* places of Judah
3:12 as the *h* places of a forest
5:9 be *h* above your adversaries
6:6 I bow myself to God on *h*
Hab 1:10 *h* officials are something
3:10 On *h* its hands it lifted up
3:14 Their *h* glee was as of those
3:19 upon my *h* places he will
Zep 1:16 against the *h* corner towers
2:4 at *h* noon they will drive her
Hag 1:1 Jehozadak the *h* priest
1:12 son of Jehozadak the *h* priest
1:14 son of Jehozadak the *h* priest
2:2 Joshua . . . the *h* priest
2:4 son of Jehozadak the *h* priest
Zec 3:1 Joshua the *h* priest standing
3:8 Joshua the *h* priest, you and
6:11 son of Jehozadak the *h* priest
Mt 4:8 to an unusually *h* mountain
13:46 finding one pearl of *h* value
26:3 the courtyard of the *h* priest
26:51 the slave of the *h* priest
26:57 to Caiaphas the *h* priest
26:58 courtyard of the *h* priest
26:62 *h* priest stood up and said
26:63 So the *h* priest said to him
26:65 *h* priest ripped his outer
Mr 5:7 Jesus, Son of the Most *H* God
14:47 the slave of the *h* priest
14:53 Jesus away to the *h* priest
14:54 courtyard of the *h* priest
14:60 the *h* priest rose in their
14:61 *h* priest began to question
14:63 the *h* priest ripped his
14:66 girls of the *h* priest
Lu 1:32 called Son of the Most *H*
1:35 and power of the Most *H* will
1:76 a prophet of the Most *H*, for
1:78 will visit us from on *h*
4:38 distressed with a *h* fever
6:35 will be sons of the Most *H*
8:28 Jesus Son of the Most *H* God
22:50 the slave of the *h* priest
22:54 the house of the *h* priest
24:49 with power from on *h*
Joh 11:49 Caiaphas, who was *h* priest
11:51 he was *h* priest that year
18:10 the slave of the *h* priest
18:13 Caiaphas, who was *h* priest
18:15 was known to the *h* priest
18:15 courtyard of the *h* priest
18:16 was known to the *h* priest
18:24 to Caiaphas the *h* priest
18:26 the slaves of the *h* priest
Ac 5:17 *h* priest and all those with
5:21 *h* priest and those with him
5:27 *h* priest questioned them
7:1 *h* priest said: Are these
Ac 7:48 Most *H* does not dwell in
9:1 Saul . . . went to the *h* priest
16:17 are slaves of the Most *H* God
22:5 *h* priest and all the assembly
23:2 *h* priest Ananias ordered those
23:4 Are you reviling the *h* priest
23:5 did not know he was *h* priest
24:1 the *h* priest Ananias came
Eph 4:8 When he ascended on *h* he
1Ti 2:2 those who are in *h* station
Heb 2:17 *h* priest in things pertaining
3:1 the apostle and *h* priest whom
4:14 great *h* priest who has
4:15 For we have as *h* priest, not
5:1 every *h* priest taken from
5:5 by becoming a *h* priest, but
5:10 called by God a *h* priest
6:20 Jesus . . . become a *h* priest
7:1 priest of the Most *H* God
7:26 such a *h* priest as this was
7:27 as those *h* priests do, to
7:28 Law appoints men *h* priests
8:1 We have such a *h* priest as
8:3 *h* priest is appointed to
9:7 the *h* priest alone enters
9:11 Christ came as a *h* priest of
9:25 *h* priest enters into the
13:11 by the *h* priest for sin are
Re 6:13 fig tree shaken by a *h* wind
14:20 *h* up as the bridles of the

Higher
Nu 24:7 king also will be *h* than Agag
De 28:43, 43 keep ascending *h* and *h*
2Ki 25:28 throne *h* than the thrones
Job 11:8 It is *h* than heaven
35:5 they are indeed *h* than you
Ps 61:2 a rock that is *h* than I am
103:11 heavens are *h* than the earth
Ec 5:8 one that is *h* than the high one
Isa 55:9 heavens are *h* than the earth
55:9 my ways are *h* than your
Jer 52:32 put his throne *h* than the
Eze 31:5 grew *h* in its stature than
Ho 7:16 return, not to anything *h*
Lu 14:10 Friend, go on up *h*. Then you
Heb 7:26 become *h* than the heavens

Highest
Lu 19:38 and glory in the *h* places

Highly
Ex 15:1 for he has become *h* exalted
15:21 for he has become *h* exalted
1Ch 14:2 his kingship was *h* exalted
Ne 4:1 he became angry and *h* offended
Es 1:12 the king grew *h* indignant and
Ps 21:6 constitute him *h* blessed
Pr 4:8 *H* esteem it, and it will exalt
Isa 3:3 and *h* respected man and
9:15 *h* respected one is the head
24:8 noise of the *h* elated ones
30:13 out in a *h* raised wall
32:13 yes, the *h* elated town
Jon 4:1 it was *h* displeasing, and he
Lu 1:28 Good day, *h* favored one

High-minded
1Ti 6:17 not to be *h*, and to rest

High-mindedly
Ps 56:2 many warring against me *h*

Highness
Job 40:10 with superiority and *h*
Jer 48:29 his *h* and of his pride and

Highway
Nu 20:19 By the *h* we shall go up; and
Jg 21:19 *h* that goes up from Bethel
1Sa 6:12 one *h* they went, lowing as
2Sa 20:12 in the middle of the *h*
20:12 he moved Amasa from the *h*
20:13 had removed him from the *h*
2Ki 18:17 *h* of the laundryman's field
1Ch 26:16 gate Shallecheth by the *h*
26:18 four at the *h*, two at the
Pr 16:17 *h* of the upright ones is to
Isa 7:3 *h* of the laundryman's field
11:16 *h* out of Assyria for the
19:23 *h* out of Egypt to Assyria
35:8 *h* there, even a way
36:2 *h* of the laundryman's field
40:3 the *h* for our God through
62:10 Bank up, bank up the *h*
Jer 31:21 Fix your heart upon the *h*

2Ch 2:12 *H* went on to say: Blessed be
4:11 *H* made the cans and the
4:11 *H* finished doing the work
8:2 cities that *H* had given to
8:18 *H* regularly sent to him by
9:10 besides, the servants of *H*
9:21 with the servants of *H*

Hiram-abi
2Ch 2:13 belonging to *H*

Hiram-abiv
2Ch 4:16 *H* made for King Solomon

Hiram's
1Ki 5:18 *H* builders and the Gebalites
10:11 And *H* fleet of ships that
10:22 along with *H* fleet of ships

Hire
Ex 22:15 hired, it must come in its *h*
De 23:18 not bring the *h* of a harlot
Jg 9:4 *h* idle and insolent men, that
18:4 that he might *h* me, and that
1Sa 2:5 *h* themselves out for bread
2Sa 10:6 *h* Syrians of Beth-rehob and
1Ch 19:6 *h* for themselves chariots
Isa 23:17 return to her *h* and commit
23:18 her *h* must become
23:18 *h* will come to be for those
46:6 They *h* a metalworker, and
Eze 16:31 a prostitute in disdaining *h*
16:34 even in your giving *h* when
16:34 no *h* has been given to you
16:41 no more *h* will you give
Ho 9:1 You have loved gifts of *h* on
Mic 1:7 gifts made to her as her *h*
1:7 as the *h* of a prostitute
1:7 as the *h* of a prostitute they
Mt 20:1 to *h* workers for his vineyard

Hired
Ge 30:16 I have *h* you outright with
Ex 12:45 *h* laborer may not eat of it
22:15 If it is *h*, it must come in
Le 19:13 wages of a *h* laborer should
22:10 *h* laborer may eat anything
25:6 *h* laborer and the settler
25:40 be with you like a *h* laborer
25:50 workdays of a *h* laborer
25:53 *h* laborer from year to year
De 15:18 the value of a *h* laborer
23:4 they *h* against you Balaam the
24:14 not defraud a *h* laborer who
2Ki 7:6 *h* against us the kings of the
1Ch 19:7 *h* for themselves thirty-two
2Ch 25:6 *h* from Israel a hundred
Ne 6:12 Sanballat themselves had *h*
6:13 been *h* in order that I might
Job 7:1 like the days of a *h* laborer
7:2 like a *h* laborer he waits for
14:6 as a *h* laborer does in his
Isa 7:20 by means of a *h* razor in the
16:14 the years of a *h* laborer
21:16 to the years of a *h* laborer
Jer 46:21 *h* soldiers in the midst of
Ho 8:9 they have *h* lovers
Mt 20:7 Because nobody has *h* us
Mr 1:20 in the boat with the *h* men
Lu 15:17 How many *h* men of my father
15:19 me as one of your *h* men
15:21 me as one of your *h* men
20:20 sent out men secretly *h* to
Joh 10:12 *h* man, who is no shepherd
10:13 *h* man and does not care for
Ac 28:30 years in his own *h* house

Hireling's
Ge 30:18 God has given me a *h* wages

Hirers
2Ch 24:12 *h* of the stonecutters and

Hiring
Ezr 4:5 *h* counselors against them to
Ne 13:2 went *h* against them Balaam
Pr 26:10 one *h* someone stupid or the
26:10 or the one *h* passersby
Ho 8:10 *h* them among the nations
Hag 1:6 and he that is *h* himself out
1:6 is *h* himself out for a bag

Hissing
2Pe 3:10 pass away with a *h* noise

History
Ge 2:4 This is a *h* of the heavens
5:1 This is the book of Adam's *h*
6:9 This is the *h* of Noah
Ge 10:1 *h* of Noah's sons, Shem, Ham
11:10 This is the *h* of Shem
11:27 And this is the *h* of Terah
25:12 *h* of Ishmael the son of
25:19 And this is the *h* of Isaac
36:1 And this is the *h* of Esau
36:9 And this is the *h* of Esau
37:2 This is the *h* of Jacob
Mt 1:1 book of the *h* of Jesus Christ

Hit
De 19:5 it has *h* his fellowman and he
Mt 26:67 and *h* him with their fists
Mr 14:65 *h* him with their fists and
15:19 would *h* him on the head
Joh 18:23 if rightly, why do you *h* me?

Hitch
1Sa 6:7 must *h* the cows to the wagon
1Ki 18:44 say to Ahab, *H* up! And go
2Ki 9:21 Jehoram said: *H* up!

Hitched
1Sa 6:10 and *h* them to the wagon, and
2Ki 9:21 his war chariot was *h* up

Hither
Ps 73:10 he brings his people back *h*
Eph 4:14 carried *h* and thither by

Hitting
Mt 27:30 began *h* him upon his head
Lu 22:63 to make fun of him, *h* him

Hittite
Ge 23:10 So Ephron the *H* answered
25:9 Zohar the *H* that is in front
26:34 the daughter of Beeri the *H*
26:34 daughter of Elon the *H*
36:2 the daughter of Elon the *H*
49:29 the field of Ephron the *H*
49:30 purchased from Ephron the *H*
50:13 from Ephron the *H* in front
1Sa 26:6 said to Ahimelech the *H* and
2Sa 11:3 the wife of Uriah the *H*
11:6 Send to me Uriah the *H*
11:17 and Uriah the *H* also died
11:21 servant Uriah the *H* died
11:24 servant Uriah the *H* also
12:9 Uriah the *H* you struck down
12:10 wife of Uriah the *H* to
23:39 Uriah the *H*—thirty-seven
1Ki 11:1 loved . . . *H* women
15:5 the matter of Uriah the *H*
1Ch 11:41 Uriah the *H*, Zabad the son
Eze 16:3 and your mother was a *H*
16:45 mother of you . . . was a *H*

Hittites
Ge 15:20 the *H* and the Perizzites and
Ex 3:8 to the locality of . . . the *H*
3:17 to the land of . . . the *H*
13:5 into the land of the . . . *H*
23:23 indeed bring you to the . . . *H*
23:28 the *H* out from before you
33:2 and drive out the . . . *H* and
34:11 driving out . . . the *H*
Nu 13:29 the *H* and the Jebusites and
De 7:1 the *H* and the Girgashites and
20:17 to destruction, the *H* and the
Jos 1:4 all the land of the *H*, and to
3:10 the Canaanites and the *H* and
9:1 the *H* and the Amorites, the
11:3 the Amorites and the *H* and
12:8 the *H*, the Amorites and the
24:11 the *H* and the Girgashites
Jg 1:26 the land of the *H* and built
3:5 dwelt in among . . . the *H* and
1Ki 9:20 the *H*, the Perizzites, the
10:29 all the kings of the *H* and
2Ki 7:6 the kings of the *H* and the
2Ch 1:17 for all the kings of the *H*
8:7 left over of the *H* and the
Ezr 9:1 the *H*, the Perizzites, the
Ne 9:8 land of the Canaanites, the *H*

Hivite
Ge 10:17 *H* and the Arkite and the
34:2 the son of Hamor the *H*, a
36:2 granddaughter of Zibeon the *H*
1Ch 1:15 the *H* and the Arkite and the

Hivites
Ex 3:8 to the locality of . . . the *H*
3:17 to the land of . . . the *H*
13:5 into the land of the . . . *H* and
23:23 indeed bring you to the . . . *H*
23:28 simply drive the *H* . . . out
33:2 and drive out the . . . *H* and
Ex 34:11 driving out . . . the *H* and
De 7:1 the *H* and the Jebusites, seven
20:17 the *H* and the Jebusites
Jos 3:10 the *H* and the Perizzites and
9:1 the *H* and the Jebusites
9:7 men of Israel said to the *H*
11:3 the *H* at the base of Hermon
11:19 the *H* inhabiting Gibeon
12:8 the *H* and the Jebusites
24:11 the *H* and the Jebusites
Jg 3:3 *H* inhabiting Mount Lebanon
3:5 dwelt in among . . . the *H* and
2Sa 24:7 the cities of the *H* and of
1Ki 9:20 the *H* and the Jebusites, who
2Ch 8:7 left over of the . . . *H* and

Hizki
1Ch 8:17 Meshullam and *H* and Heber

Hizkiah
1Ch 3:23 sons of Neariah were . . . *H*

Hoards
De 33:19 And the hidden *h* of the sand

Hoarfrost
Ex 16:14 fine like *h* upon the earth
Job 38:29 And as for the *h* of heaven
Ps 147:16 *H* he scatters just like

Hoarse
Ps 69:3 My throat has become *h*

Hobab
Nu 10:29 Moses said to *H* the son of
Jg 4:11 the Kenites, the sons of *H*

Hobah
Ge 14:15 *H*, which is north of

Hod
1Ch 7:37 Bezer and *H* and Shamma and

Hodaviah
1Ch 3:24 the sons of Elioenai were *H*
5:24 Jeremiah and *H* and Jahdiel
9:7 son of *H* the son of Hassenuah
Ezr 2:40 the sons of *H*, seventy-four

Hodesh
1Ch 8:9 by *H* his wife he came to be

Hodevah
Ne 7:43 sons of *H*, seventy-four

Hodiah
Ne 8:7 *H*, Maaseiah, Kelita, Azariah
9:5 And the Levites . . . *H*
10:10 their brothers Shebaniah, *H*
10:13 *H*, Bani and Beninu
10:18 *H*, Hashum, Bezai

Hodiah's
1Ch 4:19 *H* wife, the sister of Naham

Hoe
Ex 21:18 fellow with a stone or a *h*
Isa 7:25 troublesome plants with a *h*

Hoed
Isa 5:6 be pruned, nor will it be *h*

Hoglah
Nu 26:33 of Zelophehad . . . *H*, Milcah
27:1 daughters of Zelophehad . . . *H*
36:11 Tirzah and *H* and Milcah and
Jos 17:3 Noah, *H*, Milcah and Tirzah

Hoham
Jos 10:3 sent to *H* the king of Hebron

Hoisting
Ac 27:17 *h* it aboard they began
27:40 *h* the foresail to the wind

Hold
Ge 19:16 men seized *h* of his hand and
21:18 take *h* of him with your hand
23:6 *h* back his burial place from
39:12 she grabbed *h* of him by his
48:17 take *h* of his father's hand
Ex 4:4 and grab *h* of it by the tail
4:4 hand out and grabbed *h* of it
9:2 are still keeping *h* of them
15:14 Birth pangs must take *h* on
15:15 trembling will take *h* on
20:8 the sabbath day to *h* it sacred
Le 24:22 decision . . . *h* good for you
Nu 28:25 should *h* a holy convention
28:26 should *h* a holy convention
29:1 you should *h* a holy convention
29:7 you should *h* a holy convention
29:12 should *h* a holy convention
29:35 should *h* a solemn assembly

De 5:12 sabbath day to *h* it sacred
9:17 I took *h* of the two tablets
21:19 take *h* of him and bring him
22:25 grabbed *h* of her and lay
25:11 *h* of him by his privates
32:41 my hand takes *h* on judgment
Jos 8:4 *h* yourselves in readiness
Jg 1:6 and got *h* of him and cut off
7:8 he kept *h* of the three hundred
7:20 took fresh *h* on the torches
12:6 lay *h* of him and slay him at
14:10 to *h* a banquet there; for
16:3 grabbed *h* of the doors of the
16:21 Philistines grabbed *h* of him
19:4 woman's father took *h* of him
19:25 took *h* of his concubine and
19:29 laid *h* of his concubine and
Ru 2:14 *h* out roasted grain to her and
3:15 Bring the cloak . . . *h* it open
1Sa 15:27 grabbed *h* of the skirt of
17:35 I grabbed *h* of its beard and
23:26 his men to grab *h* of them
2Sa 1:11 David took *h* of his garments
2:16 grabbing *h* of one another by
3:29 man taking *h* of the twirling
4:10 took *h* of him and killed him
6:6 grabbed *h* of it, for the
13:11 grabbed *h* of her and said to
15:5 grabbed *h* of him and kissed
18:14 Let me not *h* myself up this
20:9 took *h* of Amasa's beard so
1Ki 1:50 *h* of the horns of the altar
1:51 *h* on the horns of the altar
2:28 *h* fast to the horns of the
6:6 a *h* in the walls of the house
6:10 a *h* on the house by timbers
9:9 to take *h* of other gods and
11:30 took *h* of the new garment
13:4 You men, grab *h* of him!
20:7 not *h* them back from him
2Ki 2:12 took *h* of his own garments
4:3 Do not *h* yourself to a few
4:24 Do not *h* back for my sake
4:27 took *h* of him by his feet
23:21 *H* a passover to Jehovah your
1Ch 13:9 to grab *h* of the Ark, for the
2Ch 7:8 *h* the festival at that time
7:22 take *h* of other gods and bow
13:7 not *h* his own against them
20:6 *h* his ground against you
28:15 took *h* of the captives, and
30:1 *h* the passover to Jehovah the
30:2 resolved to *h* the passover in
30:3 able to *h* it at that time
30:5 *h* the passover to Jehovah
30:13 *h* the festival of the
30:23 *h* it for seven more days
35:16 to *h* the passover and to
35:17 proceeded to *h* the passover
Ezr 6:19 *h* the passover on the
6:22 to *h* the festival of
Ne 9:20 manna you did not *h* back from
Es 2:18 went on to *h* a great banquet
5:8 the banquet that I shall *h* for
9:22 *h* them as days of banqueting
Job 7:11 I shall not *h* back my mouth
8:15 He will take *h* of it, but it
8:20 *h* of the hand of evildoers
9:28 you will not *h* me innocent
10:14 you do not *h* me innocent
16:5 my own lips would *h* back
18:9 A snare keeps *h* upon him
21:6 shuddering has taken *h* of my
22:7 hungry one you *h* back bread
22:19 will *h* them in derision
23:11 steps my foot has laid *h*
27:6 On my justness I have laid *h*
30:10 did not *h* back their spit
30:16 Days of affliction take *h*
31:16 *h* back the lowly ones from
31:23 I could not *h* out
36:17 will themselves take *h*
37:4 he does not *h* them back
38:13 take *h* on the extremities
41:1 can you *h* down its tongue?
41:10 can *h* his ground before me
Ps 2:4 will *h* them in derision
5:10 will certainly *h* them guilty
17:5 steps take *h* on your tracks
19:13 from presumptuous acts *h*
22:7 they *h* me in derision
35:2 Take *h* of buckler and large
48:6 Trembling itself took *h* of
56:*super* Philistines laid *h* of him

Ps 59:8 *h* all the nations in derision
63:8 your right hand keeps fast *h*
64:5 *h* themselves down to bad
73:23 taken *h* of my right hand
77:4 have seized *h* of my eyelids
78:50 *h* back their soul from death
84:11 *h* back anything good from
119:53 heat itself has taken *h* of
139:10 hand would lay *h* of me
Pr 1:15 *H* back your foot from their
3:18 life to those taking *h* of it
3:18 those keeping fast *h* of it
3:27 not *h* back good from those
4:4 heart keep fast *h* of my words
4:13 Take *h* on discipline; do not
5:5 Her very steps take *h* on Sheol
5:22 sin he will be taken *h* of
7:13 grabbed *h* of him and given
11:16 one that takes *h* of glory
11:16 their part, take *h* of riches
23:13 not *h* back discipline from
24:11 O may you *h* them back
26:17 *h* of the ears of a dog is
28:17 Let them not get *h* of him
29:23 humble . . . take *h* of glory
30:28 gecko lizard takes *h* with
31:19 hands take *h* of the spindle
Ec 2:3 lay *h* on folly until I could
2:10 I did not *h* back my heart
7:18 you should take *h* of the one
Ca 2:15 grab *h* of the foxes for us
3:4 I grabbed *h* of him, and I
7:8 take *h* of its fruit stalks of
Isa 2:22 *h* off from the earthling
3:6 lay *h* of his brother in the
4:1 grab *h* of one man in that
5:29 growl and grab *h* of the prey
13:8 pains themselves grab *h*
21:3 have grabbed *h* of me, like
27:5 take *h* of my stronghold
33:14 grabbed *h* of the apostates
33:15 from taking *h* on a bribe
33:23 will not *h* firmly erect
41:9 you, whom I have taken *h* of
41:10 *h* of you with my right hand
42:1 on whom I keep fast *h*
42:6 to take *h* of your hand
45:1 right hand I have taken *h* of
51:18 taking *h* of her hand
54:2 Do not *h* back. Lengthen out
56:2 mankind that lays *h* of it
56:4 are laying *h* of my covenant
56:6 and laying *h* of my covenant
58:1 do not *h* back. Raise your
60:21 *h* possession of the land
64:7 to lay *h* on you; for you
Jer 2:25 *H* your foot back from
5:29 Should I not *h* an accounting
6:15 I must *h* an accounting with
6:23 javelin they will grab *h* of
6:24 seized *h* of us, labor pains
8:5 have taken *h* of trickiness
8:21 astonishment has seized *h*
9:9 *h* an accounting with them
9:25 I will *h* an accounting with
10:10 *h* up under his denunciation
13:21 pangs themselves seize *h*
21:14 *h* an accounting against you
26:8 the people laid *h* of him
31:16 *H* back your voice from
31:32 *h* of their hand to bring
37:13 took *h* of Jeremiah the
37:14 Irijah kept *h* of Jeremiah
42:4 not *h* back from you a word
44:13 *h* an accounting against
49:24 have taken *h* of her, as
50:24 and also taken *h* of, for
50:33 captive have laid *h* on them
50:43 pains have seized *h* of him
Eze 29:7 took *h* of you by the hand
30:21 to take *h* of the sword
31:15 *h* back its streams and that
Da 11:21 take *h* of the kingdom by
Ho 1:4 *h* an accounting for the acts
2:13 *h* an accounting against her
4:9 *h* an accounting against them
4:14 *h* an accounting against your
8:13 *h* an accounting for their sins
12:2 even to *h* an accounting
Joe 2:11 and who can *h* up under it?
Am 3:2 *h* an accounting against you
3:14 *h* an accounting against the
7:5 Lord Jehovah, *h* off, please
Mic 4:9 pangs . . . grabbed *h* of you

Mic 7:18 not *h* onto his anger forever
Na 1:3 Jehovah *h* back from punishing
3:14 grab *h* of the brick mold
Zec 8:23 men . . . will take *h*
8:23 take *h* of the skirt of a man
10:3 I shall *h* an accounting
14:13 grab *h*, each one of the hand
Mt 9:25 took *h* of her hand, and the
12:11 get *h* of it and lift it out
14:31 Jesus caught *h* of him and
21:26 they all *h* John as a prophet
22:6 rest, laying *h* of his slaves
Mr 3:21 went out to lay *h* of him
7:4 traditions . . . to *h* fast
7:8 *h* fast the tradition of men
Lu 14:4 he took *h* of the man, healed
19:17 *h* authority over ten cities
23:26 they laid *h* of Simon, a
Joh 2:6 able to *h* two or three liquid
7:30 seeking to get *h* of him
7:32 officers to get *h* of him
7:44 wanting to get *h* of him
8:20 But no one laid *h* of him
14:30 And he has no *h* on me
Ac 3:7 *h* of him by the right hand
3:21 *h* within itself until the
5:3 *h* back secretly some of the
6:10 *h* their own against the
12:4 laying *h* of him, he put him
16:19 they laid *h* of Paul and Silas
17:19 they laid *h* of him and led
18:17 all laid *h* of Sosthenes the
20:20 did not *h* back from telling
21:30 laid *h* of Paul and dragged
21:33 came near and took *h* of him
Php 3:12 lay *h* on that for which I
3:12 laid *h* on by Christ Jesus
3:13 as having laid *h* on it
1Th 5:21 *h* fast to what is fine
2Th 2:15 and maintain your *h* on the
1Ti 6:12 get a firm *h* on the
6:19 a firm *h* on the real life
Phm 13 like to *h* him back for myself
Heb 3:6 our *h* on our freeness of
3:14 if we make fast our *h* on the
4:14 *h* onto our confessing of him
6:18 lay *h* on the hope set before
8:9 taking *h* of their hand to
10:23 Let us *h* fast the public
1Pe 3:16 *H* a good conscience, so that
2Pe 2:4 did not *h* back from punishing
2:5 not *h* back from punishing
1Jo 5:18 does not fasten his *h* on him
3Jo 3 bore witness to the truth you *h*
Jude 3 the salvation we *h* in common
Re 2:4 I *h* this against you, that you
2:20 I do *h* this against you
2:25 *h* fast what you have until I

Holder
Le 10:1 brought each one his fire *h*
16:12 take the fire *h* full of
Nu 16:17 take each one his fire *h*, and
16:17 his fire *h* before Jehovah
16:17 you and Aaron each his fire *h*
16:18 they took each one his fire *h*
16:46 Take the fire *h* and put fire
Am 1:5 the *h* of the scepter from
1:8 the *h* of the scepter from

Holders
Ex 25:38 its fire *h* are of pure gold
27:3 its forks, and its fire *h*; and
37:23 its fire *h* out of pure gold
38:3 the forks and the fire *h*
Nu 4:9 and its fire *h* and all its
4:14 the fire *h*, the forks and
16:6 Take fire *h* for yourselves
16:17 fire *h*, and you and Aaron
16:37 he should take up the fire *h*
16:38 even the fire *h* of these men
16:39 took the copper fire *h*
1Ki 7:50 the cups and the fire *h*
2Ki 25:15 the fire *h* and the bowls
2Ch 4:22 and the fire *h*, of pure gold
Jer 52:19 fire *h* and the bowls and

Holding
Ge 20:6 *h* you back from sinning
25:26 his hand was *h* onto the heel
De 2:5 Mount Seir to Esau as a *h*
2:9 his land as a *h*, for to the
2:9 I have given Ar as a *h*
2:12 the land that is his *h*, which
2:19 as a *h*, for it is to the sons

De 2:19 I have given it as a *h*
3:20 each one to his *h* that I have
Jos 1:15 the land of your *h* and take
12:6 as a *h* to the Reubenites
12:7 as a *h* by their shares
Jg 16:26 the boy that was *h* him by
1Ki 4:24 *h* in subjection everything
1Ch 11:10 to David, *h* strongly with
2Ch 13:8 *h* your own against the
30:9 before those *h* them captive
Ne 4:16 *h* the lances, the shields and
4:17 other hand was *h* the missile
4:21 were *h* the lances, from the
8:18 *h* the festival seven days
Es 9:21 regularly *h* the fourteenth day
9:27 regularly *h* these two days
Job 2:3 yet he is *h* fast his integrity
2:9 you yet *h* fast your integrity
17:9 righteous one keeps *h* fast to
20:13 *h* it back in the midst of
Ps 16:5 You are *h* fast my lot
106:46 those *h* them captive
118:10 that I kept *h* them off
118:11 that I kept *h* them off
118:12 that I kept *h* them off
137:3 those *h* us captive asked
Pr 10:17 *h* to discipline is a path to
11:26 one *h* back grain—the
13:24 one *h* back his rod is hating
17:5 *h* the one of little means in
17:27 Anyone *h* back his sayings is
Isa 14:2 those *h* them captive
Jer 6:11 have become weary with *h* in
20:7 everyone is *h* me in derision
20:9 I got tired of *h* in, and I
37:13 officer *h* the oversight
48:10 *h* back his sword from blood
49:16 *h* the height of the hill
Da 10:21 one *h* strongly with me in
Am 3:14 my *h* an accounting for the
Mt 19:22 he was *h* many possessions
27:16 were *h* a notorious prisoner
Mr 3:6 began *h* council with the party
7:3 *h* fast the tradition of the
10:22 he was *h* many possessions
Joh 13:29 Judas was *h* the money box
Ac 3:11 *h* onto Peter and John, all
Ro 1:28 *h* God in accurate knowledge
1Co 11:2 are *h* fast the traditions
15:2 if you are *h* it fast, unless
2Co 10:6 *h* ourselves in readiness to
Php 2:2 *h* the one thought in mind
2:29 keep *h* men of that sort dear
Col 2:19 he is not *h* fast to the head
1Ti 1:19 *h* faith and a good conscience
3:9 *h* the sacred secret of the
2Ti 1:13 *h* the pattern of healthful
Tit 1:9 *h* firmly to the faithful word
Jas 2:1 *h* the faith of our Lord Jesus
1Pe 2:16 and yet *h* your freedom, not
Re 2:13 you keep on *h* fast my name
2:14 *h* fast the teaching of
2:15 *h* fast the teaching of the
3:11 on *h* fast what you have
7:1 *h* tight the four winds of the
21:15 *h* as a measure a golden

Holds
Es 4:11 king *h* out to him the golden
Pr 21:26 one gives and *h* nothing back
30:17 that *h* a father in derision
Eph 1:18 *h* as an inheritance for the
1Ti 4:8 as it *h* promise of the life
Re 2:1 he says who *h* the seven stars

Hole
Ge 40:15 put me in the prison *h*
41:14 quickly from the prison *h*
Ex 12:29 prison *h*, and every firstborn
33:22 place you in a *h* in the rock
De 23:13 dig a *h* with it and turn and
2Ki 12:9 bored a *h* in its lid and put
Ps 7:15 he will fall into the *h* that
Ca 5:4 hand from the *h* of the door
Isa 11:8 play upon the *h* of the cobra
Eze 8:7 look! a certain *h* in the wall
Ho 13:3 like smoke from the roof *h*

Holes
1Sa 14:11 coming out from the *h*
Job 30:6 In *h* of the dust and in rocks
Isa 2:19 and into the *h* of the dust
2:21 *h* in the rocks and into the
42:22 being trapped in the *h*, and
60:8 doves to their birdhouse *h*

Na 2:12 kept his *h* filled with prey
Hag 1:6 for a bag having *h*

Holies
Da 9:24 and to anoint the Holy of *H*

Holiest
Ps 46:4 The *h* grand tabernacle of the

Holiness
Ex 15:11 mighty in *h*? The One to be
28:36 seal, *H* belongs to Jehovah
39:30 a seal: *H* belongs to Jehovah
Ps 60:6 has spoken in his *h*
89:35 Once I have sworn in my *h*
93:5 *H* is befitting to your own
108:7 himself has spoken in his *h*
110:3 In the splendors of *h*, from
134:2 Raise your hands in *h*
Isa 35:8 Way of *H* it will be called
63:15 abode of *h* and beauty
64:11 Our house of *h* and beauty
65:5 certainly convey *h* to you
Am 4:2 Jehovah has sworn by his *h*
Zec 14:20 *H* belongs to Jehovah
Mal 2:11 profaned the *h* of Jehovah
Ro 1:4 to the spirit of *h* by means
6:19 righteousness with *h* in view
6:22 your fruit in the way of *h*
2Co 1:12 with *h* and godly sincerity
7:1 perfecting *h* in God's fear
1Th 3:13 unblamable in *h* before our
Heb 12:10 we may partake of his *h*

Hollow
Ex 27:8 A *h* chest of planks you will
38:7 made it a *h* chest of planks
Jg 15:19 mortar-shaped *h* that was in
1Sa 25:29 inside the *h* of the sling
2Sa 18:17 in the forest into a big *h*
Pr 30:4 wind in the *h* of both hands
Isa 24:17 *h* and the trap are upon you
24:18 thing will fall into the *h*
24:18 up from inside the *h* will
40:12 in the mere *h* of his hand
51:1 to the *h* of the pit from
Jer 48:28 of the mouth of the *h*
48:43 *h* and the trap are upon you
48:44 will fall into the *h*
48:44 coming up out of the *h* will
52:21 pillars . . . being *h*
La 3:47 *h* themselves have become ours

Hollow-minded
Job 11:12 *h* man himself will get

Hollows
Le 16:12 *h* of both his hands full of
1Sa 13:6 hiding themselves in . . . *h*
2Sa 17:9 is in hiding in one of the *h*
2Ch 33:11 captured Manasseh in the *h*
Ca 5:5 myrrh, upon the *h* of the lock
Eze 10:2 fill the *h* of both your hands
10:7 into the *h* of the hands of

Holon
Jos 15:51 and Goshen and *H* and Giloh
21:15 *H* and its pasture ground
Jer 48:21 level country, to *H* and to

Holy
Ex 3:5 where you are standing is *h*
12:16 for you a *h* convention, and
12:16 seventh day a *h* convention
15:13 to your *h* abiding place
16:23 a *h* sabbath to Jehovah
19:6 of priests and a *h* nation
22:31 prove yourselves *h* men to me
26:33, 33 *H* and the Most *H*
26:34 the testimony in the Most *H*
28:2 make *h* garments for Aaron
28:4 make the *h* garments for Aaron
28:29 when he comes into the *H* as
28:38 against the *h* objects
28:38 all their *h* gifts; and it
28:43 to minister in the *h* place
29:6 put the *h* sign of dedication
29:21 with him may indeed be *h*
29:29 *h* garments that are Aaron's
29:30 minister in the *h* place will
29:31 boil its flesh in a *h* place
29:33 they are something *h*
29:34 because it is something *h*
29:37 become a most *h* altar
29:37 touches the altar is to be *h*
30:10 It is most *h* to Jehovah
30:13 the shekel of the *h* place
30:24 the shekel of the *h* place

Ex 30:25 *h* anointing oil, an ointment
30:25 is to be a *h* anointing oil
30:29 may indeed become most *h*
30:29 touching them is to be *h*
30:31 continue as a *h* anointing oil
30:32 It is something *h*
30:32 as something *h* for you
30:35 salted, pure, something *h*
30:36 be most *h* to you people
30:37 continue as something *h* to
31:10 the *h* garments for Aaron the
31:14 sabbath . . . is something *h*
31:15 It is something *h* to Jehovah
35:2 become something *h* to you, a
35:19 *h* garments for Aaron the
35:21 and for the *h* garments
36:1 work of the *h* service
36:3 work of the *h* service so as
36:4 were doing all the *h* work
36:6 stuff for the *h* contribution
37:29 *h* anointing oil and the pure
38:24 the work of the *h* place came
38:24 by the shekel of the *h* place
38:25 by the shekel of the *h* place
38:26 by the shekel of the *h* place
38:27 pedestals of the *h* place
39:1 ministering in the *h* place
39:1 *h* garments that were for
39:30 the *h* sign of dedication
39:41 the *h* garments for Aaron the
40:9 so it must become something *h*
40:10 must become a most *h* altar
40:13 Aaron with the *h* garments
Le 2:3 most *h* from Jehovah's
2:10 most *h* of Jehovah's offerings
4:6 the curtain of the *h* place
5:15 the *h* things of Jehovah
5:15 by the shekel of the *h* place
5:16 committed against the *h* place
6:16 be eaten . . . in a *h* place
6:17 It is something most *h*, like
6:18 may touch them will become *h*
6:25 It is a most *h* thing
6:26 In a *h* place it will be eaten
6:27 its flesh will become *h*
6:27 blood upon in a *h* place
6:29 It is something most *h*
6:30 atonement in the *h* place
7:1 It is something most *h*
7:6 In a *h* place it will be eaten
7:6 It is something most *h*
8:9 the *h* sign of dedication
10:4 in front of the *h* place to
10:10 the *h* thing and the profane
10:12 it is something most *h*
10:13 you must eat it in a *h* place
10:17 in the place that is *h*
10:17 it is something most *h* and
10:18 brought into the *h* place
10:18 without fail in the *h* place
11:44 you must prove yourselves *h*
11:44 because I am *h*
11:45 prove yourselves *h*, because
11:45 because I am *h*
12:4 should not touch any *h* thing
12:4 not come into the *h* place
14:13 slaughtered, in a *h* place
14:13 It is something most *h*
16:2 into the *h* place inside the
16:3 should come into the *h* place
16:4 should put on the *h* linen robe
16:4 turban. They are *h* garments
16:16 atonement for the *h* place
16:17 in the *h* place until he
16:20 atonement for the *h* place
16:23 went into the *h* place, and
16:24 in a *h* place and put on his
16:27 atonement in the *h* place
16:32 They are *h* garments
16:33 for the *h* sanctuary, and
19:2 prove yourselves *h*, because I
19:2 I Jehovah your God am *h*
19:8 profaned a *h* thing of Jehovah
19:24 fruit will become a *h* thing
20:3 of defiling my *h* place
20:3 and to profane my *h* name
20:7 prove yourselves *h*, because I
20:26 prove yourselves *h* to me
20:26 I Jehovah am *h*; and I am
21:6 *h* to their God, and they
21:6 they must prove themselves *h*
21:7 because he is *h* to his God
21:8 *h* to you, because I Jehovah
21:8 I Jehovah . . . am *h*

Le 21:22 from the most *h* things and
21:22 and from the *h* things
22:2 separate from the *h* things of
22:2 profane my *h* name in the
22:3 comes near to the *h* things
22:4 eat of the *h* things until he
22:6 eat any of the *h* things, but
22:7 may eat some of the *h* things
22:10 at all may eat anything *h*
22:10 laborer may eat anything *h*
22:12 contribution of the *h* things
22:14 eats a *h* thing by mistake
22:14 give the *h* thing to the
22:15 profane the *h* things of the
22:16 their eating their *h* things
22:32 profane my *h* name, and I
23:2 festivals . . . *h* conventions
23:3 complete rest, a *h* convention
23:4 *h* conventions, which you
23:7 have a *h* convention occur
23:8 there will be a *h* convention
23:20 *h* to Jehovah for the priest
23:21 Jehovah's *h* convention for
23:24 a *h* convention
23:27 *h* convention should take
23:35 first day is a *h* convention
23:36 occur a *h* convention for you
23:37 proclaim as *h* conventions
24:9 eat it in a *h* place, because
24:9 most *h* for him from Jehovah's
25:12 become something *h* to you
27:3 by the shekel of the *h* place
27:9 will become something *h*
27:10 should become something *h*
27:14 his house as something *h* to
27:21 *h* to Jehovah, as a field that
27:23 is something *h* to Jehovah
27:25 in the shekel of the *h* place
27:28 something most *h* to Jehovah
27:30 It is something *h* to Jehovah
27:32 something *h* to Jehovah
27:33 it should become something *h*
Nu 3:28 the obligation to the *h* place
3:31 utensils of the *h* place with
3:32 the obligation to the *h* place
3:47 shekel of the *h* place you
3:50 in the shekel of the *h* place
4:4 It is something most *h*
4:12 minister in the *h* place, and
4:15 finish covering the *h* place
4:15 utensils of the *h* place when
4:15 not touch the *h* place so that
4:16 the *h* place and its utensils
4:19 approaching the most *h* things
4:20 see the *h* things for the least
5:9 of all the *h* things
5:10 *h* things of each one will
5:17 priest must take *h* water
6:5 *h* by letting the locks of the
6:8 Naziriteship he is *h* to Jehovah
6:20 something *h* for the priest
7:9 service of the *h* place was
7:13 by the shekel of the *h* place
7:19 by the shekel of the *h* place
7:25 by the shekel of the *h* place
7:31 by the shekel of the *h* place
7:37 by the shekel of the *h* place
7:43 by the shekel of the *h* place
7:49 by the shekel of the *h* place
7:55 by the shekel of the *h* place
7:61 by the shekel of the *h* place
7:67 by the shekel of the *h* place
7:73 by the shekel of the *h* place
7:79 by the shekel of the *h* place
7:85 by the shekel of the *h* place
7:86 by the shekel of the *h* place
8:19 Israel approach the *h* place
15:40 prove to be *h* to your God
16:3 assembly are all of them *h*
16:5 will make known . . . who is *h*
16:7 Jehovah will choose . . . *h* one
16:37 for they are *h*
16:38 so that they became *h*
18:3 the utensils of the *h* place
18:5 your obligation to the *h* place
18:8 *h* things of the sons of Israel
18:9 out of the most *h* things, out
18:9 is something most *h* for you
18:10 In a most *h* place you should
18:10 become something *h* to you
18:16 by the shekel of the *h* place
18:17 They are something *h*
18:19 All the *h* contributions
18:29 as some *h* thing from them

Nu 18:32 not profane the *h* things of
28:7 Pour out in the *h* place the
28:18 there will be a *h* convention
28:25 should hold a *h* convention
28:26 should hold a *h* convention
29:1 you should hold a *h* convention
29:7 you should hold a *h* convention
29:12 should hold a *h* convention
31:6 *h* utensils and the trumpets
35:25 was anointed with the *h* oil
De 7:6 you are a *h* people to Jehovah
12:26 *h* things that will become
14:2 you are a *h* people to Jehovah
14:21 you are a *h* people to Jehovah
23:14 your camp must prove to be *h*
26:13 cleared away what is *h* from
26:15 your *h* dwelling, the heavens
26:19 people *h* to Jehovah your God
28:9 *h* people to himself, just
33:2 And with him were *h* myriads
33:3 their *h* ones are in your hand
Jos 5:15 which you are standing is *h*
6:19 are something *h* to Jehovah
24:19 for he is a *h* God; he is a
1Sa 2:2 There is no one *h* like Jehovah
6:20 before Jehovah this *h* God
21:4 there is *h* bread; provided
21:5 of the young men continue *h*
21:5 when one becomes *h* in his
21:6 priest gave him what was *h*
2Sa 1:21 be fields of *h* contributions
1Ki 6:16 innermost room, the Most *H*
7:50 house, that is, the Most *H*
7:51 things made *h* by David his
8:4 the *h* utensils that were in
8:6 the Most *H*, to underneath the
8:8 poles were visible from the *H*
8:10 came out from the *h* place
15:15 things made *h* by his father
15:15 things made *h* by himself
2Ki 4:9 it is a *h* man of God that is
12:4 money for the *h* offerings
12:18 *h* offerings that Jehoshaphat
12:18 *h* offerings and all the gold
19:22 against the *H* One of Israel
1Ch 6:49 work of the most *h* things
9:29 over all the *h* utensils and
16:10 your boast in his *h* name
16:29 to Jehovah in *h* adornment
16:35 give thanks to your *h* name
22:19 *h* utensils of the true God
23:13 might sanctify the Most *H*
23:28 the purification of every *h*
23:32 the guarding of the *h* place
24:5 chiefs of the *h* place and
26:20 of the things made *h*
26:26 things made *h*, that David
26:26 of the army had made *h*
26:27 made things *h* to maintain
26:28 son of Zeruiah had made *h*
26:28 What anyone made *h* was
28:12 of the things made *h*
29:3 have prepared for the *h* house
29:16 a house for your *h* name
2Ch 3:8 make the house of the Most *H*
3:10 the Most *H* two cherubs in
4:22 inner doors for the Most *H*
5:1 things made *h* by David his
5:5 *h* utensils that were in the
5:7 the ark . . . into the Most *H*
5:9 were visible at the *H* in
5:11 came out from the *h* place
8:11 has come are something *h*
15:18 things made *h* by his father
15:18 things made *h* by himself
20:21 praise in *h* adornment as
23:6 they are a *h* group, and all
24:7 *h* things of the house of
29:5 thing out from the *h* place
29:7 offer up in the *h* place to
29:33 *h* offerings, six hundred
30:19 purification for what is *h*
30:27 *h* dwelling, the heavens
31:6 the tenth of the *h* things
31:12 *h* things in faithfulness
31:14 and the most *h* things
31:18 sanctify . . . for what was *h*
35:3 those *h* to Jehovah
35:3 Put the *h* Ark in the house
35:5 stand in the *h* place by the
35:13 made *h* they boiled in
Ezr 2:63 the most *h* things until a
8:28 something *h* to Jehovah
8:28 the utensils are something *h*

Ezr 9:2 the *h* seed, have become
9:8 giving us a peg in his *h* place
Ne 7:65 not eat from the most *h*
8:9 day is *h* to Jehovah your God
8:10 this day is *h* to our Lord
8:11 for this day is *h*; and do not
9:14 your *h* sabbath you made known
10:31 on the sabbath or on a *h* day
10:33 for the *h* things and for the
11:1 dwell in Jerusalem the *h* city
11:18 the Levites in the *h* city
Job 5:1 of the *h* ones will you turn
6:10 the sayings of the *H* One
15:15 In his *h* ones he has no
Ps 2:6 Upon Zion, my *h* mountain
3:4 answer me from his *h* mountain
5:7 bow down toward your *h* temple
11:4 Jehovah is in his *h* temple
15:1 reside in your *h* mountain
16:3 *h* ones that are in the earth
20:2 your help out of the *h* place
20:6 answers him from his *h*
22:3 But you are *h*, Inhabiting the
24:3 may rise up in his *h* place
28:2 the innermost room of your *h*
29:2 to Jehovah in *h* adornment
30:4 Give thanks to his *h* memorial
33:21 in his *h* name we have put
34:9 Fear Jehovah, you *h* ones of
43:3 bring me to your *h* mountain
47:8 his seat upon his *h* throne
48:1 city of our God, in his *h*
51:11 *h* spirit O do not take away
63:2 beheld you in the *h* place
65:4 The *h* place of your temple
68:5 Is God in his *h* dwelling
68:17 from Sinai into the *h* place
68:24 my King, into the *h* place
71:22 on the harp, O *H* One of
74:3 treated badly in the *h* place
77:13 way is in the *h* place
78:41 even the *H* One of Israel
78:54 bring . . . to his *h* territory
79:1 have defiled your *h* temple
87:1 is in the *h* mountains
89:5 the congregation of the *h* ones
89:7 intimate group of *h* ones
89:18 to the *H* One of Israel
89:20 my *h* oil I have anointed
96:9 to Jehovah in *h* adornment
97:12 thanks to his *h* memorial
98:1 right hand, even his *h* arm
99:3 your name . . . *h* it is
99:5 Jehovah . . . He is *h*
99:9 bow . . . at his *h* mountain
99:9 For Jehovah our God is *h*
102:19 down from his *h* height
103:1 Bless Jehovah . . . his *h* name
105:3 your boast in his *h* name
105:42 remembered his *h* word with
106:16 Aaron the *h* one of Jehovah
106:47 give thanks to your *h* name
111:9 name is *h* and fear-inspiring
114:2 Judah became his *h* place
138:2 down toward your *h* temple
145:21 all flesh bless his *h* name
150:1 Praise God in his *h* place
Pr 9:10 knowledge of the Most *H* One
20:25 has rashly cried out, *H!* and
30:3 the Most *H* One I do not know
Ec 8:10 go away from the *h* place
Isa 1:4 treated the *H* One of Israel
4:3 will be said to be *h* to him
5:16 the *H* One, will certainly
5:19 counsel of the *H* One of
5:24 *H* One of Israel they have
6:3, 3, 3 *H*, *h*, *h* is Jehovah of
6:13 *h* seed will be the stump of
8:13 whom you should treat as *h*
10:17 and his *H* One a flame
10:20 *H* One of Israel, in trueness
11:9 ruin in all my *h* mountain
12:6 is the *H* One of Israel
17:7 gaze at the *H* One of Israel
23:18 something *h* to Jehovah
27:13 *h* mountain in Jerusalem
29:19 joyful in the *H* One of
29:23 sanctify the *H* One of Jacob
30:11 *H* One of Israel to cease
30:12 *H* One of Israel has said
30:15 *H* One of Israel, has said
31:1 looked to the *H* One of Israel
37:23 against the *H* One of Israel
40:25 his equal? says the *H* One

Isa 41:14 the *H* One of Israel
41:16 In the *H* One of Israel you
41:20 the *H* One of Israel has
43:3 the *H* One of Israel your
43:14 the *H* One of Israel
43:15 I am Jehovah your *H* One
43:28 the princes of the *h* place
45:11 the *H* One of Israel and the
47:4 the *H* One of Israel
48:2 as being from the *h* city
48:17 the *H* One of Israel
49:7 of Israel, his *H* One, has
49:7 the *H* One of Israel, who
52:1 O Jerusalem, the *h* city
52:10 Jehovah has bared his *h* arm
54:5 the *H* One of Israel is your
55:5 and for the *H* One of Israel
56:7 bring them to my *h* mountain
57:13 possession of my *h* mountain
57:15 whose name is *h*, has said
57:15 *h* place is where I reside
58:13 own delights on my *h* day
58:13 exquisite delight, a *h* day
60:9 and to the *H* One of Israel
60:14 Zion of the *H* One of Israel
62:9 drink it in my *h* courtyards
62:12 call them the *h* people
63:10 made his *h* spirit feel hurt
63:11 His own *h* spirit
63:18 your *h* people had possession
64:10 Your own *h* cities have
65:11 forgetting my *h* mountain
65:25 ruin in all my *h* mountain
66:20 my *h* mountain, Jerusalem
Jer 2:3 Israel was something *h* to
11:15 with *h* flesh will they
23:9 because of his *h* words
25:30 from his *h* dwelling he
31:23 place, O *h* mountain
31:40 be something *h* to Jehovah
50:29 against the *H* One of Israel
51:5 of the *H* One of Israel
51:51 *h* places of the house of
La 4:1 *h* stones are poured out at the
Eze 20:39 my *h* name you will no more
20:40 For in my *h* mountain, in
20:40 in all your *h* things
21:2 toward the *h* places, and
22:8 *h* places you have despised
22:26 keep profaning my *h* places
22:26 the *h* thing and the common
28:14 On the *h* mountain of God
36:20 to profane my *h* name in
36:21 compassion on my *h* name
36:22 but for my *h* name, which
36:38 Like a flock of *h* persons
39:7 *h* name I shall make known
39:7 let my *h* name be profaned
39:7 Jehovah, the *H* One in Israel
39:25 devotion for my *h* name
41:4 This is the Most *H*
41:21 in front of the *h* place
41:23 the *h* place had two doors
42:13 they are the *h* dining rooms
42:13 eat the most *h* things
42:13 deposit the most *h* things
42:13 because the place is *h*
42:14 go out from the *h* place
42:14 they are something *h*
42:20 is *h* and what is profane
43:7 Israel, defile my *h* name
43:8 defiled my *h* name by their
43:12 is something most *h*
44:8 obligation of my *h* things
44:13 to any *h* things of mine
44:13 to the most *h* things, and
44:19 in the *h* dining rooms
44:23 a *h* thing and a profane
44:27 coming into the *h* place
44:27 minister in the *h* place
45:1 *h* portion out of the land
45:1 *h* portion in all its
45:2 for the *h* place five hundred
45:3 something most *h*
45:4 *h* portion out of the land it
45:6 exactly as the *h* contribution
45:7 side of the *h* contribution
45:7 beside the *h* contribution
46:19 to the *h* dining rooms
48:10 *h* contribution for the
48:12 land as something most *h*
48:14 is something *h* to Jehovah
48:18 as the *h* contribution, ten
48:18 as the *h* contribution, and
Eze 48:20 as the *h* contribution
48:21 side of the *h* contribution
48:21 *h* contribution and the
Da 4:8 is the spirit of the *h* gods
4:9 spirit of the *h* gods is in you
4:13 watcher, even a *h* one, coming
4:17 and by the saying of *h* ones the
4:18 the spirit of *h* gods is in you
4:23 watcher, even a *h* one
5:11 is the spirit of *h* gods; and
7:18 *h* ones of the Supreme One
7:21 horn made war upon the *h* ones
7:22 given in favor of the *h* ones
7:22 *h* ones took possession of the
7:25 harass continually the *h* ones
7:27 *h* ones of the Supreme One
8:13 *h* one speaking, and another
8:13 *h* one proceeded to say to the
8:13 *h* place and the army things
8:14 *h* place will certainly be
8:24 people made up of the *h* ones
9:16 Jerusalem, your *h* mountain
9:20 the *h* mountain of my God
9:24 upon your *h* city, in order to
9:24 to anoint the *H* of Holies
9:26 *h* place the people of a leader
11:28 be against the *h* covenant
11:30 against the *h* covenant and
11:30 those leaving the *h* covenant
11:45 *h* mountain of Decoration
12:7 power of the *h* people to
Ho 11:9 the *H* One in the midst of you
11:12 the Most *H* One he is
Joe 2:1 a war cry in my *h* mountain
3:17 in Zion my *h* mountain
3:17 must become a *h* place
Am 2:7 of profaning my *h* name
Ob 16 drunk upon my *h* mountain, all
17 and it must become something *h*
Jon 2:4 gaze again upon your *h* temple
2:7 in to you, into your *h* temple
Mic 1:2 Jehovah from his *h* temple
Hab 1:12 my *H* One, you do not die
2:20 Jehovah is in his *h* temple
3:3 a *H* One from Mount Paran
Zep 3:4 profaned what was *h*
3:11 be haughty in my *h* mountain
Hag 2:12 If a man carries *h* flesh in
2:12 of food, will it become *h?*
Zec 2:12 his portion upon the *h* ground
2:13 aroused himself from his *h*
8:3 of armies, the *h* mountain
14:5 the *h* ones being with him
14:21 *h* belonging to Jehovah of
Mt 1:18 to be pregnant by *h* spirit
1:20 begotten . . . by *h* spirit
3:11 baptize . . . with *h* spirit
4:5 took him along into the *h* city
7:6 Do not give what is *h* to dogs
12:32 speaks against the *h* spirit
24:15 standing in a *h* place, (let
27:52 many bodies of the *h* ones
27:53 entered into the *h* city
28:19 the Son and of the *h* spirit
Mr 1:8 baptize you with *h* spirit
1:24 who you are, the *H* One of God
3:29 against the *h* spirit has no
6:20 to be a righteous and *h* man
8:38 his Father with the *h* angels
12:36 By the *h* spirit David
13:11 but the *h* spirit is
Lu 1:15 will be filled with *h* spirit
1:35 *H* spirit will come upon you
1:35 what is born will be called *h*
1:41 Elizabeth was filled with *h*
1:49 and *h* is his name
1:67 filled with *h* spirit, and he
1:70 the mouth of his *h* prophets
1:72 call to mind his *h* covenant
2:23 must be called *h* to Jehovah
2:25 and *h* spirit was upon him
2:26 revealed . . . by the *h* spirit
3:16 baptize . . . with *h* spirit
3:22 the *h* spirit in bodily shape
4:1 Jesus, full of *h* spirit, turned
4:34 you are, the *H* One of God
9:26 the Father and of the *h* angels
10:21 overjoyed in the *h* spirit and
11:13 give *h* spirit to those asking
12:10 against the *h* spirit will
12:12 *h* spirit will teach you in
Joh 1:33 one that baptizes in *h* spirit
6:69 you are the *H* One of God
14:26 the helper, the *h* spirit
Joh 17:11 *H* Father, watch over them
20:22 to them: Receive *h* spirit
Ac 1:2 commandment through *h* spirit
1:5 baptized in *h* spirit not many
1:8 the *h* spirit arrives upon you
1:16 *h* spirit spoke beforehand by
2:4 filled with *h* spirit and
2:33 promised *h* spirit from the
2:38 free gift of the *h* spirit
3:14 that *h* and righteous one
3:21 his *h* prophets of old time
4:8 Peter, filled with *h* spirit
4:25 *h* spirit said by the mouth
4:27 against your *h* servant Jesus
4:30 name of your *h* servant Jesus
4:31 all filled with the *h* spirit
5:3 play false to the *h* spirit and
5:32 *h* spirit . . . to those obeying
6:5 man full of faith and *h* spirit
6:13 against this *h* place and
7:33 you are standing is *h* ground
7:51 always resisting the *h* spirit
7:55 he, being full of *h* spirit
8:15 for them to get *h* spirit
8:17 began to receive *h* spirit
8:19 may receive *h* spirit
9:13 to your *h* ones in Jerusalem
9:17 and be filled with *h* spirit
9:31 the comfort of the *h* spirit
9:32 *h* ones that dwelt in Lydda
9:41 he called the *h* ones and the
10:22 instructions by a *h* angel to
10:38 anointed him with *h* spirit
10:44 *h* spirit fell upon all those
10:45 free gift of the *h* spirit
10:47 the *h* spirit even as we have
11:15 *h* spirit fell upon them just
11:16 will be baptized in *h* spirit
11:24 full of *h* spirit and of faith
13:2 *h* spirit said: Of all persons
13:4 sent out by the *h* spirit
13:9 filled with *h* spirit, looked
13:52 filled with joy and *h* spirit
15:8 by giving them the *h* spirit
15:28 *h* spirit and we ourselves
16:6 forbidden by the *h* spirit to
19:2 Did you receive *h* spirit when
19:2 whether there is a *h* spirit
19:6 the *h* spirit came upon them
20:23 the *h* spirit repeatedly bears
20:28 *h* spirit has appointed you
21:11 says the *h* spirit, The man
21:28 and has defiled this *h* place
26:10 the *h* ones I locked up in
28:25 *h* spirit aptly spoke through
Ro 1:2 prophets in the *h* Scriptures
1:7 beloved ones, called to be *h*
5:5 hearts through the *h* spirit
7:12 the Law is *h*, and the
7:12 commandment is *h* and
8:27 in accord with God for *h* ones
9:1 witness with me in *h* spirit
11:16 as firstfruits is *h*, the
11:16 root is *h*, the branches are
12:1 living, *h*, acceptable to God
12:13 Share with the *h* ones
14:17 peace and joy with *h* spirit
15:13 with power of *h* spirit
15:16 the *h* work of the good news
15:16 sanctified with *h* spirit
15:19 with the power of *h* spirit
15:25 to minister to the *h* ones
15:26 to the poor of the *h* ones in
15:31 be acceptable to the *h* ones
16:2 in a way worthy of the *h* ones
16:15 and all the *h* ones with them
16:16 Greet . . . with a *h* kiss
1Co 1:2 called to be *h* ones, together
3:17 for the temple of God is *h*
6:1 and not before the *h* ones
6:2 *h* ones will judge the world
6:19 the temple of the *h* spirit
7:14 unclean, but now they are *h*
7:34 be *h* both in her body and in
12:3 except by *h* spirit
14:33 congregations of the *h* ones
16:1 collection . . . for the *h* ones
16:15 to minister to the *h* ones
16:20 Greet . . . with a *h* kiss
2Co 1:1 all the *h* ones who are in all
6:6 by kindness, by *h* spirit, by
8:4 destined for the *h* ones
9:1 ministry . . . for the *h* ones
9:12 the wants of the *h* ones but

2Co 13:12 Greet . . . with a *h* kiss
13:13 *h* ones send you their
13:14 sharing in the *h* spirit be
Eph 1:1 *h* ones who are in Ephesus
1:4 *h* and without blemish before
1:13 with the promised *h* spirit
1:15 and toward all the *h* ones
1:18 an inheritance for the *h* ones
2:19 citizens of the *h* ones and
2:21 growing into a *h* temple for
3:5 revealed to his *h* apostles
3:8 than the least of all *h* ones
3:18 with all the *h* ones what is
4:12 readjustment of the *h* ones
4:30 be grieving God's *h* spirit
5:3 just as it befits *h* people
5:27 be *h* and without blemish
6:18 in behalf of all the *h* ones
Php 1:1 to all the *h* ones in union
4:21 greetings to every *h* one in
4:22 the *h* ones, but especially
Col 1:2 to the *h* ones and faithful
1:4 love you have for . . . *h* ones
1:12 inheritance of the *h* ones in
1:22 *h* and unblemished and
1:26 made manifest to his *h* ones
3:12 God's chosen ones, *h* and
1Th 1:5 with power and with *h* spirit
1:6 with joy of *h* spirit
3:13 with all his *h* ones
4:8 who puts his *h* spirit in you
5:26 the brothers with a *h* kiss
2Th 1:10 connection with his *h* ones
1Ti 4:7 which violate what is *h* and
5:10 washed the feet of *h* ones
6:20 that violate what is *h*
2Ti 1:9 called us with a *h* calling
1:14 *h* spirit which is dwelling
2:16 that violate what is *h*
3:15 have known the *h* writings
Tit 3:5 making of us new by *h* spirit
Phm 5 and toward all the *h* ones
7 tender affections of the *h* ones
Heb 2:4 distributions of *h* spirit
3:1 *h* brothers, partakers of the
3:7 just as the *h* spirit says
6:4 become partakers of *h* spirit
6:10 ministered to the *h* ones and
8:2 public servant of the *h* place
9:1 and its mundane *h* place
9:2 and it is called the *H* Place
9:3 called the Most *H*
9:8 the *h* spirit makes it plain
9:8 the way into the *h* place had
9:12 once for all time into the *h*
9:24 a *h* place made with hands
9:25 enters into the *h* place
10:15 *h* spirit also bears witness
10:19 entry into the *h* place by
13:11 into the *h* place by the
13:24 and to all the *h* ones
1Pe 1:12 *h* spirit sent forth from
1:15 the *H* One who called you, do
1:15 become *h* yourselves in all
1:16, 16 be *h*, because I am *h*
2:5 the purpose of a *h* priesthood
2:9 royal priesthood, a *h* nation
3:5 the *h* women who were hoping
2Pe 1:18 with him in the *h* mountain
1:21 were borne along by *h* spirit
2:21 to turn away from the *h*
3:2 spoken by the *h* prophets and
3:11 *h* acts of conduct and deeds
1Jo 2:20 an anointing from the *h* one
Jude 3 time delivered to the *h* ones
14 came with his *h* myriads
20 on your most *h* faith, and
20 and praying with *h* spirit
Re 3:7 he says who is *h*, who is true
4:8, 8, 8 *H*, *h*, *h* is Jehovah God
5:8 the prayers of the *h* ones
6:10 Sovereign Lord *h* and true
8:3 prayers of all the *h* ones upon
8:4 prayers of the *h* ones before
11:2 trample the *h* city underfoot
11:18 reward . . . to the *h* ones
13:7 wage war with the *h* ones and
13:10 and faith of the *h* ones
14:10 sight of the *h* angels and
14:12 endurance for the *h* ones
16:6 poured out the blood of *h* ones
17:6 with the blood of the *h* ones
18:20 you *h* ones and you apostles
18:24 the blood . . . of *h* ones and
Re 19:8 righteous acts of the *h* ones
20:6 Happy and *h* is anyone having
20:9 the camp of the *h* ones and
21:2 the *h* city, New Jerusalem
21:10 *h* city Jerusalem coming
22:11, 11 *h* one be made *h* still
22:19 and out of the *h* city
22:21 Christ be with the *h* ones

Homage
Da 2:46 to Daniel he paid *h*, and he

Homam
1Ch 1:39 sons of Lotan were . . . *H*

Home
Ex 2:18 came *h* to Reuel their father
2:18 How is it you have come *h* so
De 5:30 Return *h* to your tents
22:2 bring it *h* into the midst of
Jos 15:18 when she was going *h*, she
Jg 1:14 while she was going *h*, she
7:8 he sent away each one to his *h*
11:34 came to Mizpah to his *h*, and
14:8 he went on back to take her *h*
1Sa 1:23 Stay at *h* until you wean him
1:23 stayed at *h* and kept nursing
6:7 their young ones go back *h*
6:10 young ones they shut up at *h*
10:26 he went to his *h* at Gibeah
21:15 this one come into my *h*
23:18 himself went to his own *h*
24:22 Saul went to his *h*
2Sa 11:27 took her *h* to his house
18:17 they fled each man to his *h*
19:8 had fled each one to his *h*
20:22 each one to his *h*; and Joab
1Ki 12:24 went back *h* according to
Ps 68:12 at *h*, she shares in the spoil
Isa 13:11 bring *h* its own badness
Mt 1:20 to take Mary your wife *h*
1:24 and he took his wife *h*
9:6 Get up . . . and go to your *h*
9:7 got up and went off to his *h*
13:54 coming into his *h* territory
13:57 except in his *h* territory
26:18 with my disciples at your *h*
Mr 1:29 went into the *h* of Simon and
2:1 and he was reported to be at *h*
2:11 your cot, and go to your *h*
5:19 Go *h* to your relatives, and
5:35 *h* of the presiding officer
6:1 and came into his *h* territory
6:4 except in his *h* territory and
6:10 enter into a *h*, stay there
7:30 to her *h* and found the young
8:26 So he sent him off *h*, saying
Lu 1:23 he went off to his *h*
1:40 into the *h* of Zechariah and
1:56 and returned to her own *h*
4:23 here in your *h* territory
4:24 is accepted in his *h* territory
4:38 he entered into Simon's *h*
5:24 and be on your way *h*
5:25 went off to his *h*, glorifying
8:27 he was staying, not at *h*, but
8:39 Be on your way back *h*, and
9:4 wherever you enter into a *h*
15:6 when he gets *h* he calls his
18:14 This man went down to his *h*
Joh 1:11 He came to his own *h*, but
11:20 but Mary kept sitting at *h*
14:3 receive you *h* to myself
19:27 took her to his own *h*
Ac 7:20 months in his father's *h*
16:40 and went to the *h* of Lydia
18:3 he stayed at their *h*, and they
21:16 man at whose *h* we were to
1Co 11:34 let him eat at *h*, that you
14:35 their own husbands at *h*
2Co 5:6 we have our *h* in the body
5:8 to make our *h* with the Lord
5:9 having our *h* with him or
Tit 2:5 chaste, workers at *h*, good

Homeland
Joh 4:44 own *h* a prophet has no honor

Homeless
Isa 58:7 *h* people into your house
La 1:7 affliction and of her *h* people
3:19 my affliction and my *h* state
4:15 For they have gone *h*
1Co 4:11 we continue . . . to be *h*

Homer
Le 27:16 *h* of barley seed, then at
Isa 5:10 even a *h* measure of seed
Eze 45:11 carry a tenth of a *h* and
45:11 tenth of a *h* an ephah
45:11 with reference to the *h*
45:13 ephah from the *h* of wheat
45:13 ephah from the *h* of barley
45:14 Ten baths are a *h*; because
45:14 because ten baths are a *h*
Ho 3:2 *h* measure of barley and a

Homers
Nu 11:32 least gathered ten *h*, and

Homes
1Ki 5:14 for two months at their *h*
8:66 go to their *h*, rejoicing
2Ki 13:5 dwell in their *h* as formerly
2Ch 7:10 the people away to their *h*
Ne 4:14 your wives and your *h*
Ps 78:55 to reside in their own *h*
Jer 17:22 bring no load out of your *h*
Mr 8:3 send them off to their *h*
Lu 16:4 will receive me into their *h*
Joh 20:10 went back to their *h*
Ac 2:46 their meals in private *h* and
21:6 but they returned to their *h*
2Jo 10 never receive him into your *h*

Homeward
Isa 14:17 open the way *h* even for his

Honest
2Co 8:21 For we make *h* provision, not
Heb 13:18 we have an *h* conscience

Honestly
Heb 13:18 conduct ourselves *h* in all

Honesty
Ge 20:5 In the *h* of my heart and with
20:6 *h* of your heart you have done

Honey
Ge 43:11 balsam, and a little *h*
Ex 3:8 land flowing with milk and *h*
3:17 land flowing with milk and *h*
13:5 land flowing with milk and *h*
16:31 that of flat cakes with *h*
33:3 land flowing with milk and *h*
Le 2:11 and no *h* at all smoke as an
20:24 land flowing with milk and *h*
Nu 13:27 flowing with milk and *h*
14:8 is flowing with milk and *h*
16:13 flowing with milk and *h*
16:14 land flowing with milk and *h*
De 6:3 land flowing with milk and *h*
8:8 a land of oil olives and *h*
11:9 land flowing with milk and *h*
26:9 land flowing with milk and *h*
26:15 flowing with milk and *h*
27:3 flowing with milk and *h*
31:20 which flows with milk and *h*
32:13 suck *h* out of a crag
Jos 5:6 land flowing with milk and *h*
Jg 14:8 in the lion's corpse, and *h*
14:9 that he had scraped the *h*
14:18 What is sweeter than *h*, And
1Sa 14:25 *h* happened to be over all
14:26 there was a dripping of *h*
14:29 tasted this little bit of *h*
14:43 *h* on the tip of the rod
2Sa 17:29 *h* and butter and sheep and
1Ki 14:3 cakes and a flask of *h*
2Ki 18:32 of oil-olive trees and *h*
2Ch 31:5 *h* and all the produce of the
Job 20:17 streams of *h* and butter
Ps 19:10 sweeter than *h* and the
19:10 the flowing *h* of the combs
81:16 shall satisfy you with *h*
119:103 More so than *h* to my
Pr 24:13 son, eat *h*, for it is good
24:13 let sweet comb *h* be upon
25:16 Is it *h* that you have found?
25:27 too much *h* is not good
27:7 will tread down comb *h*, but
Ca 4:11 *h* your lips keep dripping
4:11 *H* and milk are under your
5:1 my honeycomb along with my *h*
Isa 7:15 Butter and *h* he will eat by
7:22 butter and *h* are what
Jer 11:5 flowing with milk and *h*
32:22 flowing with milk and *h*
41:8 and barley and oil and *h*
Eze 3:3 like *h* for sweetness
16:13 *h* and oil were what you ate
16:19 and *h* that I had had you eat
20:6 one flowing with milk and *h*

Eze 20:15 flowing with milk and *h*
27:17 and *h* and oil and balsam
Mt 3:4 insect locusts and wild *h*
Mr 1:6 insect locusts and wild *h*
Re 10:9 it will be sweet as *h*
10:10 my mouth it was sweet as *h*

Honeycomb
1Sa 14:27 and dipped it into the *h* and
Pr 5:3 as a *h* the lips of a strange
16:24 Pleasant sayings are a *h*
Ca 5:1 I have eaten my *h* along with

Honor
Ge 41:43 in the second chariot of *h*
Ex 20:12 *H* your father and your
Nu 22:17 without fail *h* you greatly
22:37 and truly able to *h* you
24:11 without fail going to *h* you
24:11 has held you back from *h*
De 5:16 *H* your father and your mother
Jg 13:17 we shall certainly do you *h*
1Sa 2:30 those honoring me I shall *h*
9:6 and the man is held in *h*
15:30 *h* me, please, in front of
2Ki 14:10 Enjoy your *h* and dwell in
2Ch 1:11 for wealth, riches and *h*
1:12 riches and *h* I shall give you
32:33 *h* was what all Judah and
Es 1:4 *h* and the beauty of his
1:20 wives themselves will give *h*
6:3 What *h* and great thing has
6:6 the man in whose *h* the king
6:6 take delight in rendering an *h*
6:7 the man in whose *h* the king
6:9 the man in whose *h* the king
6:9 to the man in whose *h* the king
6:11 the man in whose *h* the king
8:16 rejoicing and exultation and *h*
Ps 49:12 man, though in *h*, cannot
49:20 man, although in *h*, who does
Pr 3:9 *H* Jehovah with your valuable
3:35 *H* is what the wise ones will
25:6 do yourself *h* before the king
Isa 45:4 to give you a name of *h*
Mal 1:6 am a father, where is the *h*
Mt 15:4 *H* your father and your mother
15:6 must not *h* his father at all
19:19 *H* your father and your
Mr 7:6 *h* me with their lips, but
7:10 *H* your father and your mother
10:19 *H* your father and mother
Lu 4:15 being held in *h* by all
14:10 have *h* in front of all your
18:20 *H* your father and mother
Joh 4:44 homeland a prophet has no *h*
5:23 that all may *h* the Son just
5:23 just as they *h* the Father
5:23 does not *h* the Son does not
5:23 not *h* the Father who sent
8:49 I *h* my Father, and you
12:26 the Father will *h* him
Ro 2:7 are seeking glory and *h* and
2:10 *h* and peace for everyone who
12:10 showing *h* to one another
13:7, 7 who calls for *h*, such *h*
1Co 12:23 with more abundant *h*, and
12:24 giving *h* more abundant to
Eph 6:2 *H* your father and your mother
1Th 4:4 in sanctification and *h*
1Ti 1:17 be *h* and glory forever and
5:3 *H* widows that are actually
5:17 reckoned worthy of double *h*
6:1 worthy of full *h*, that the
6:16 be *h* and might everlasting
2Ti 2:20 for a purpose lacking *h*
Heb 2:7 with glory and *h* you crowned
2:9 crowned with glory and *h* for
3:3 who constructs it has more *h*
5:4 this *h*, not of his own accord
1Pe 1:7 *h* at the revelation of Jesus
2:17 *H* men of all sorts, have
2:17 have *h* for the king
3:7 assigning them *h* as to a
2Pe 1:17 he received . . . *h* and glory
Re 4:9 *h* and thanksgiving to the one
4:11 to receive the glory and the *h*
5:12 and *h* and glory and blessing
5:13 the *h* and the glory and the
7:12 the *h* and the power and the
21:26 *h* of the nations into it

Honorable
Ge 34:19 most *h* of the whole house of
Nu 22:15 and more *h* than the former
1Ch 4:9 Jabez came to be more *h* than
Ezr 4:10 the great and *h* Asenappar
Isa 23:8 the *h* ones of the earth
23:9 all the *h* ones of the earth
43:4 you have been considered *h*
63:1 one who is *h* in his clothing
Ro 9:21 one vessel for an *h* use
1Co 12:23 which we think to be less *h*
2Ti 2:20 some for an *h* purpose but
2:21 a vessel for an *h* purpose
Heb 13:4 Let marriage be *h* among all

Honored
1Sa 22:14 and *h* in your house
Job 14:21 His sons get *h*, but he does
Pr 27:18 guarding his master . . . be *h*
Isa 3:5 against the one to be *h*
9:1 time one caused it to be *h*
La 5:12 even old men have not been *h*
Ac 28:10 *h* us with many gifts and

Honoring
1Sa 2:29 *h* your sons more than me
2:30 those *h* me I shall honor
2Sa 10:3 Is David *h* your father in
1Ch 17:18 as to *h* your servant, when
19:3 Is David *h* your father in
La 1:8 All who were *h* her have

Honors
Ps 15:4 those fearing Jehovah he *h*
Mal 1:6 son, for his part, *h* a father
Mt 15:8 people *h* me with their lips

Hoof
Ex 10:26 Not a *h* will be allowed to
Le 11:3 creature that splits the *h*
11:4 and the splitters of the *h*
11:4 but is no splitter of the *h*
11:5 but does not split the *h*
11:6 it does not have the *h* split
11:7 it is a splitter of the *h* and
11:7 a former of a cleft in the *h*
11:26 is a splitter of the *h* but is
De 14:6 every beast that splits the *h*
14:7 that split the *h*, cloven
14:7 but do not split the *h*
14:8 it is a splitter of the *h* but
Ps 69:31 horns, splitting the *h*

Hoofbeats
Jg 5:28 *h* of his chariots be so late

Hoofs
Le 11:3 a cleft in the *h* and chews
De 14:6 forms a cleft into two *h*
Jg 5:22 then that the *h* of horses pawed
Isa 5:28 *h* of their horses will have
Jer 47:3 of the *h* of his stallions
Eze 26:11 the *h* of his horses he will
32:13 the *h* of a domestic animal
Mic 4:13 *h* I shall change into copper
Zec 11:16 *h* of the sheep he will tear

Hook
2Ki 19:28 put my *h* in your nose and
Isa 37:29 put my *h* in your nose and

Hooks
Ex 26:6 make fifty *h* of gold and join
26:6 join . . . by means of the *h*
26:11 make fifty *h* of copper and
26:11 put the *h* in the loops and
26:33 put the curtain under the *h*
35:11 its *h* and its panel frames
36:13 made fifty *h* of gold and
36:13 joined . . . by the *h*, so that
36:18 fifty *h* of copper for joining
39:33 its *h*, its panel frames, its
Job 5:5 from butcher *h* one takes it
Eze 19:4 bring him by means of *h* to
19:9 in the cage by means of *h*
29:4 I will put *h* in your jaws
38:4 and put *h* in your jaws and
Am 4:2 lift you up with butcher *h*

Hoopoe
Le 11:19 and the *h* and the bat
De 14:18 the *h* and the bat

Hope
Ru 1:12 If I had said I had *h* also
2Ki 4:28 not lead me to a false *h*
1Ch 29:15 and there is no *h*
Ezr 10:2 there exists a *h* for Israel
Job 4:6 your *h* even the integrity of
5:16 there comes to be *h*, But
6:8 God would grant even my *h*
8:13 *h* of an apostate will perish
11:18 trust because there exists *h*
Job 11:20 their *h* will be an expiring
14:7 exists *h* for even a tree
14:19 destroyed . . . *h* of mortal
17:15 So where, then, is my *h*?
17:15 *h*—who is it that beholds
19:10 he pulls my *h* out just like
27:8 what is the *h* of an apostate
Ps 9:18 the *h* of the meek ones ever
27:14 *H* in Jehovah; be courageous
27:14 Yes, *h* in Jehovah
37:34 *H* in Jehovah and keep his
52:9 And I shall *h* in your name
62:5 Because from him is my *h*
71:5 For you are my *h*, O Sovereign
119:116 put me to shame for my *h*
146:5 *h* is in Jehovah his God
Pr 10:28 *h* of the wicked ones will
11:7 man dies, his *h* perishes
11:23 *h* of the wicked ones is fury
19:18 son while there exists *h*
20:22 *H* in Jehovah, and he will
23:18 own *h* will not be cut off
24:14 own *h* will not be cut off
26:12 is more *h* for the stupid one
29:20 is more *h* for someone stupid
Isa 8:17 and I will *h* in him
20:5 Ethiopia their looked-for *h*
20:6 how our looked-for *h* is, to
51:5 islands themselves will *h*
64:3 for which we could not *h*
Jer 13:16 certainly *h* for the light
14:8 O you the *h* of Israel, the
14:22 *h* in you, for you yourself
17:13 Jehovah, the *h* of Israel
29:11 give you a future and a *h*
31:17 exists a *h* for your future
50:7 *h* of their forefathers
La 3:29 Perhaps there exists a *h*
Eze 19:5 and her *h* had perished, then
37:11 and our *h* has perished
Ho 2:15 of Achor as an entrance to *h*
Mic 5:7 that does not *h* for man or
Zec 9:5 *h* will . . . experience shame
9:12 you prisoners of the *h*
Mt 12:21 in his name nations will *h*
Lu 6:34 from whom you *h* to receive
Joh 5:45 in whom you have put your *h*
Ac 2:26 my flesh will reside in *h*
16:19 that their *h* of gain had left
23:6 Over the *h* of resurrection of
24:15 I have *h* toward God, which
24:15 which *h* these . . . entertain
26:6 for the *h* of the promise
26:7 Concerning this *h* I am accused
27:20 all *h* of our being saved
28:20 because of the *h* of Israel
Ro 4:18 Although beyond *h*, yet based
4:18 yet based on *h* he had faith
5:2 based on *h* of the glory of God
5:4 approved condition, in turn, *h*
5:5 and the *h* does not lead to
8:20 subjected it . . . basis of *h*
8:24 For we were saved in this *h*
8:24, 24 *h* that is seen is not *h*
8:24 sees a thing, does he *h* for it
8:25 we *h* for what we do not see
12:12 Rejoice in the *h*
15:4 we might have *h*
15:12 nations will rest their *h*
15:13 God who gives *h* fill you
15:13 may abound in *h* with power
15:24 I *h*, above all, when I am on
1Co 9:10 ought to plow in *h* and the
9:10 in *h* of being a partaker
13:13 remain faith, *h*, love
16:7 I *h* to remain some time
2Co 1:7 our *h* for you is unwavering
1:10 our *h* is in him that he will
1:13 which I *h* you will continue
3:12 as we have such a *h*, we are
5:11 I *h* that we have been made
10:15 entertain *h* that, as your
13:6 *h* you will come to know we
Eph 1:12 first to *h* in the Christ
1:18 *h* to which he called you
2:12 no *h* and were without God
4:4 you were called in the one *h*
Php 1:20 eager expectation and *h* that
Col 1:5 the *h* that is being reserved
1:5 This *h* you heard of before by
1:23 the *h* of that good news
1:27 the *h* of his glory
1Th 1:3 due to your *h* in our Lord
2:19 what is our *h* or joy or

1Th 4:13 also do who have no *h*
5:8 a helmet the *h* of salvation
2Th 2:16 comfort and good *h* by means
1Ti 1:1 and of Christ Jesus, our *h*
4:10 rested our *h* on a living God
5:5 has put her *h* in God and
6:17 *h*, not on uncertain riches
Tit 1:2 a *h* of the everlasting life
2:13 the happy *h* and glorious
3:7 a *h* of everlasting life
Heb 3:6 our boasting over the *h* firm
6:11 the full assurance of the *h*
6:18 hold on the *h* set before us
6:19 This *h* we have as an anchor
7:19 bringing . . . of a better *h*
10:23 public declaration of our *h*
1Pe 1:3 *h* through the resurrection of
1:13 your *h* upon the undeserved
1:21 faith and *h* might be in God
3:15 a reason for the *h* in you
1Jo 3:3 everyone who has this *h* set

Hoped
Ps 25:5 In you I have *h* all day long
25:21 For I have *h* in you
39:7 for what have I *h*, O Jehovah?
40:1 I earnestly *h* in Jehovah
119:166 *h* for your salvation
130:5 I have *h*, O Jehovah, my
130:5 Jehovah, my soul has *h*
Isa 5:4 I *h* for it to produce grapes
25:9 We have *h* in him, and he
25:9 Jehovah. We have *h* in him
26:8 Jehovah, we have *h* in you
33:2 In you we have *h*
La 2:16 is the day that we have *h* for
1Co 15:19 we have *h* in Christ, we are
2Co 8:5 not merely as we had *h*, but
Eph 1:13 *h* in him after you heard the
Heb 11:1 expectation of things *h* for

Hoped-for
Ga 5:5 for the *h* righteousness as

Hopefully
Ps 145:15 the eyes of all look *h*
Isa 38:18 look *h* to your trueness

Hopeless
Isa 57:10 You have not said, It is *h!*
Jer 2:25 proceeded to say, It is *h!*
18:12 And they said: It is *h!*

Hopelessness
Job 7:6 And they come to an end in *h*

Hopes
1Co 13:7 *h* all things, endures all

Hophni
1Sa 1:3 sons of Eli, *H* and Phinehas
2:34 two sons, *H* and Phinehas
4:4 namely, *H* and Phinehas
4:11 *H* and Phinehas, died
4:17 have died—*H* and Phinehas

Hophra
Jer 44:30 Pharaoh *H*, the king of Egypt

Hoping
Ps 25:3 none of those *h* in you will
37:9 those *h* in Jehovah are the
69:6 those *h* in you not be ashamed
69:20 *h* for someone to show
Isa 5:2 *h* for it to produce grapes
5:7 he kept *h* for judgment, but
40:31 *h* in Jehovah will regain
49:23 those *h* in me will not be
59:9 We keep *h* for light, but
59:11 We kept *h* for justice, but
60:9 will keep *h*, the ships of
Jer 8:15 There was a *h* for peace
14:19 *h* for peace, but no good
La 3:25 to the one *h* in him, to the
Ho 12:6 a *h* in your God constantly
Lu 6:35 not *h* for anything back
23:8 *h* to see some sign performed
24:21 *h* that this man was the one
Ac 24:26 he was *h* for money to be
26:7 tribes are *h* to attain to the
Php 2:19 I am *h* in the Lord Jesus to
2:23 is the man I am *h* to send
1Ti 3:14 am *h* to come to you shortly
Phm 22 *h* that through the prayers
1Pe 3:5 holy women who were *h* in God
2Jo 12 I am *h* to come to you and to
3Jo 14 I am *h* to see you directly

Hopped
Ca 4:1 of goats that have *h* down from
6:5 that have *h* down from Gilead

Hor
Nu 20:22 and come to Mount *H*
20:23 Moses and Aaron in Mount *H*
20:25 bring them up into Mount *H*
20:27 they went climbing Mount *H*
21:4 trekking from Mount *H* by the
33:37 and went camping in Mount *H*
33:38 to go up into Mount *H* at the
33:39 at his death on Mount *H*
33:41 pulled away from Mount *H*
34:7 to Mount *H* as a boundary for
34:8 From Mount *H* you will mark
De 32:50 your brother died on Mount *H*

Horam
Jos 10:33 that *H* the king of Gezer

Horeb
Ex 3:1 he came at length . . . to *H*
17:6 standing . . . on the rock in *H*
33:6 from Mount *H* onward
De 1:2 it being eleven days from *H* by
1:6 our God spoke to us in *H*
1:19 pulled away from *H* and went
4:10 before Jehovah your God in *H*
4:15 Jehovah's speaking to you in *H*
5:2 a covenant with us in *H*
9:8 Even in *H* you provoked Jehovah
18:16 in *H* on the day of the
29:1 had concluded with them in *H*
1Ki 8:9 had deposited there in *H*
19:8 mountain of the true God, *H*
2Ch 5:10 that Moses had given at *H*
Ps 106:19 they made a calf in *H*
Mal 4:4 which I commanded him in *H*

Horem
Jos 19:38 *H* and Beth-anath and

Horesh
1Sa 23:15 wilderness of Ziph at *H*
23:16 went to David at *H*, that he
23:18 David kept dwelling in *H*
23:19 difficult to approach at *H*

Hor-haggidgad
Nu 33:32 and went camping in *H*
33:33 pulled away from *H* and went

Hori
Ge 36:22 sons of Lotan . . . *H* and
Nu 13:5 Simeon, Shaphat the son of *H*
1Ch 1:39 sons of Lotan were *H*

Horite
Ge 36:20 the sons of Seir the *H*
36:21 These are the sheiks of the *H*
36:29 sheiks of the *H*: Sheik Lotan
36:30 sheiks of the *H* according to

Horites
Ge 14:6 *H* in their mountain of Seir
De 2:12 the *H* dwelt in Seir in former
2:22 he annihilated the *H* from

Hormah
Nu 14:45 scattering them as far as *H*
21:3 the name of the place *H*
De 1:44 in Seir as far as *H*
Jos 12:14 the king of *H*, one
15:30 Eltolad and Chesil and *H*
19:4 Eltolad and Bethul and *H*
Jg 1:17 the city was called *H*
1Sa 30:30 and to those in *H*, and to
1Ch 4:30 in *H* and in Ziklag

Horn
Ex 19:13 the blowing of the ram's *h*
19:16 and a very loud sound of a *h*
19:19 *h* became continually louder
20:18 the sound of the *h* and the
Le 25:9 the *h* of loud tone to sound
25:9 *h* to sound in all your land
Jos 6:5 sound with the *h* of the ram
6:5 you hear the sound of the *h*
6:20 heard the sound of the *h* and
Jg 3:27 he began blowing the *h* in
6:34 he went blowing the *h*, and
7:18 I have blown the *h*, I and all
1Sa 2:1 My *h* is indeed exalted in
2:10 exalt the *h* of his anointed
13:3 had the *h* blown throughout
16:1 Fill your *h* with oil and go
16:13 Samuel took the *h* of oil
2Sa 2:28 Joab now blew the *h*, and all
2Sa 6:15 shouting and sound of *h*
15:10 you hear the sound of the *h*
18:16 Joab now blew the *h*, that
20:1 he proceeded to blow the *h*
20:22 Upon that he blew the *h*
22:3 my *h* of salvation, my secure
1Ki 1:34 must blow the *h* and say
1:39 the *h* of oil out of the tent
1:39 and they began to blow the *h*
1:41 to hear the sound of the *h*
2Ki 9:13 began to blow the *h* and say
1Ch 15:28 with the sounding of the *h*
25:5 to raise up his *h*; thus the
Ne 4:18 the one to blow the *h* was
4:20 you hear the sound of the *h*
Job 16:15 thrust my *h* in the . . . dust
39:24 it is the sound of a *h*
39:25 as the *h* blows it says Aha!
Ps 18:2 shield and my *h* of salvation
47:5 with the sound of the *h*
75:4 Do not exalt the *h*
75:5 Do not exalt your *h* on high
81:3 On the new moon, blow the *h*
89:17 goodwill our *h* is exalted
89:24 in my name his *h* is exalted
92:10 exalt my *h* like that of a
98:6 and the sound of the *h*
112:9 His own *h* will be exalted
132:17 the *h* of David to grow
148:14 exalt the *h* of his people
150:3 with the blowing of the *h*
Isa 18:3 there is the blowing of a *h*
27:13 blowing on a great *h*, and
58:1 your voice just like a *h*
Jer 4:5 blow a *h* throughout the land
4:19 *h* is what my soul has heard
4:21 hearing the sound of the *h*
6:1 and in Tekoa blow the *h*
6:17 to the sound of the *h*
42:14 *h* we shall not hear and
48:25 *h* of Moab has been cut down
51:27 Blow a *h* among the nations
La 2:3 has cut down every *h* of Israel
2:17 the *h* of your adversaries high
Eze 29:21 shall cause a *h* to sprout
33:3 blows the *h* and warns the
33:4 hears the sound of the *h*
33:5 The sound of the *h* he heard
33:6 does not blow the *h* and the
Da 3:5 hear the sound of the *h*, the
3:7 hearing the sound of the *h*, the
3:10 hears the sound of the *h*, the
3:15 hear the sound of the *h*, the
7:8 another *h*, a small one, came
7:8 the eyes of a man in this *h*
7:11 words that the *h* was speaking
7:20 *h* that came up and before
7:20 *h* that had eyes and a mouth
7:21 *h* made war upon the holy ones
8:5 conspicuous *h* between its eyes
8:8 the great *h* was broken, and
8:9 another *h*, a small one, and it
8:21 great *h* that was between its
Ho 5:8 Blow a *h* in Gibeah, a trumpet
8:1 To your mouth—a *h!* One comes
Joe 2:1 Blow a *h* in Zion, O men, and
2:15 Blow a *h* in Zion, O men
Am 2:2 signal, with the sound of a *h*
3:6 If a *h* is blown in a city, do
Mic 4:13 *h* I shall change into iron
Zep 1:16 day of *h* and of alarm signal
Zec 1:21 a *h* against the land of Judah
9:14 on the *h* the Sovereign Lord
Lu 1:69 raised up a *h* of salvation

Horned
Ge 49:17 a *h* snake at the wayside
Ps 140:3 venom of the *h* viper is

Horns
Ge 22:13 ram caught by its *h* in a
Ex 27:2 its *h* upon its four corners
27:2 Its *h* will proceed out of it
29:12 upon the *h* of the altar, and
30:2 Its *h* extend out of it
30:3 sides round about and its *h*
30:10 atonement upon its *h* once a
37:25 Its *h* proceeded out of it
37:26 sides round about and its *h*
38:2 its *h* upon its four corners
38:2 Its *h* proceeded out of it
Le 4:7 the *h* of the altar of perfumed
4:18 upon the *h* of the altar that
4:25 and put it upon the *h* of the
4:30 put it upon the *h* of the altar

Le 4:34 the *h* of the altar of burnt
8:15 *h* of the altar round about
9:9 put it upon the *h* of the altar
16:18 the *h* of the altar round about
De 33:17, 17 *h* . . . *h* of a wild bull
Jos 6:4 should carry seven rams' *h*
6:4 the priests should blow the *h*
6:6 carry seven rams' *h* before
6:8 carrying seven rams' *h* before
6:8 passed on and blew the *h*, and
6:9 of the priests blowing the *h*
6:9 a continual blowing on the *h*
6:13 carrying seven rams' *h*
6:13 continually blowing the *h*
6:13 a continual blowing on the *h*
6:16 the priests blew the *h*, and
6:20 they proceeded to blow the *h*
Jg 7:8 their *h*, and all the men
7:16 put *h* in the hands of all of
7:18 blow the *h*, you too, round
7:19 blew the *h*, and there was a
7:20 blew the *h* and shattered the
7:20 on the *h* to blow them, and
7:22 continued to blow the *h*, and
1Ki 1:50 hold of the *h* of the altar
1:51 hold on the *h* of the altar
2:28 fast to the *h* of the altar
22:11 *h* of iron and said: This is
2Ch 15:14 the trumpets and with *h*
18:10 made for himself *h* of iron
Ps 22:21 from the *h* of wild bulls
69:31 a young bull displaying *h*
75:10 *h* of the wicked ones I shall
75:10 *h* of the righteous one will
118:27 far as the *h* of the altar
Jer 17:1 on the *h* of their altars
Eze 27:15 *h* of ivory and ebony they
34:21 your *h* you kept shoving
43:15 there are the four *h*
43:20 put it upon its four *h*
Da 7:7 and it had ten *h*
7:8 I kept on considering the *h*
7:8 three of the first *h* that
7:20 ten *h* that were on its head
7:24 ten *h*, out of that kingdom
8:3 ram standing . . . had two *h*
8:3 two *h* were tall, but the one
8:6 ram possessing the two *h*
8:7 ram and to break its two *h*
8:20 possessing the two *h* stands
Am 3:14 the *h* of the altar will
6:13 in our strength taken *h* to
Zec 1:18 look! there were four *h*
1:19 the *h* that dispersed Judah
1:21 the *h* that dispersed Judah
1:21 the *h* of the nations that
Re 5:6 having seven *h* and seven eyes
9:13 heard one voice out of the *h*
12:3 seven heads and ten *h* and
13:1 with ten *h* and seven heads
13:1 and upon its *h* ten diadems
13:11 it had two *h* like a lamb
17:3 had seven heads and ten *h*
17:7 seven heads and the ten *h*
17:12 ten *h* that you saw mean ten
17:16 ten *h* that you saw, and the

Horonaim
Isa 15:5 way to *H* they arouse the
Jer 48:3 sound of an outcry from *H*
48:5 on the way down from *H*
48:34 from Zoar clear to *H*, to

Horonite
Ne 2:10 Sanballat the *H* and Tobiah
2:19 Sanballat the *H* and Tobiah
13:28 of Sanballat the *H*

Horrible
1Ki 15:13 a *h* idol to the sacred pole
15:13 cut down her *h* idol and
2Ch 15:16 made a *h* idol for the
15:16 Asa cut down her *h* idol and
Jer 5:30 a *h* thing, has been brought
18:13 There is a *h* thing that the
23:14 I have seen *h* things
Ho 6:10 I have seen a *h* thing

Horror
Jer 2:12 bristle up in very great *h*
Eze 4:16 in *h* that they will drink
5:15 a *h* to the nations that are
12:19 with *h* . . . they will drink
27:35 will have to shudder in *h*
32:10 will shudder in *h* at you

Horse
Ge 49:17 bites the heels of the *h* so
Ex 15:1 *h* and its rider he has pitched
15:21 The *h* and its rider he has
1Ki 10:28 the *h* drove for a price
10:29 a *h* for a hundred and fifty
20:20 got to escape upon a *h*
20:25, 25 *h* for *h* and chariot
2Ki 9:18 a rider on a *h* went to meet
9:19 a second rider on a *h*
11:16 *h* entry of the king's house
2Ch 1:16 take the *h* drove for a price
1:17 a *h* for a hundred and fifty
23:15 *h* gate of the king's house
Ne 3:28 Above the *H* Gate the priests
Es 6:8 a *h* upon which the king does
6:9 the *h* into the charge of one of
6:9 ride on the *h* in the public
6:10 take the apparel and the *h*
6:11 to take the apparel and the *h*
Job 39:18 laughs at the *h* and at its
39:19 give to the *h* mightiness
Ps 32:9 not make yourselves like a *h*
33:17 The *h* is a deception for
76:6 charioteer and the *h* have
147:10 mightiness of the *h* does he
Pr 21:31 *h* is something prepared for
26:3 A whip is for the *h*, a bridle
Isa 43:17 the war chariot and the *h*
63:13 like a *h* in the wilderness
Jer 8:6 *h* that is dashing into the
31:40 corner of the *H* Gate toward
51:21 dash the *h* and his rider to
Am 2:15 no rider of the *h* . . . escape
Na 3:2 the dashing *h* and the leaping
Zec 1:8 a man riding on a red *h*, and
9:10 and the *h* from Jerusalem
10:3 like his *h* of dignity in
12:4 I shall strike every *h* with
12:4 *h* of the peoples I shall
14:15 scourge of the *h*, the mule
14:20 upon the bells of the *h*
Re 6:2 a white *h*; and the one seated
6:4 came forth, a fiery-colored *h*
6:5 I saw, and, look! a black *h*
6:8 a pale *h*; and the one seated
19:11 and, look! a white *h*
19:19 with the one seated on the *h*
19:21 of the one seated on the *h*

Horseman
Na 3:3 The mounted *h*, and the flame

Horsemen
Ge 50:9 with him both chariots and *h*
1Sa 8:11 Your sons . . . among his *h*
13:5 six thousand *h* and people
2Sa 8:4 one thousand seven hundred *h*
10:18 and forty thousand *h*, and
1Ki 1:5 with *h* and fifty men running
4:26 and twelve thousand *h*
9:19 and the cities for the *h*
9:22 his charioteers and of his *h*
20:20 together with the *h*
2Ki 2:12 chariot of Israel and his *h*
13:7 but fifty *h* and ten chariots
13:14 chariot of Israel and his *h*
18:24 for chariots and for *h*
1Ch 18:4 and seven thousand *h* and
19:6 and *h* from Mesopotamia and
2Ch 8:6 cities for the *h* and every
8:9 charioteers and of his *h*
12:3 and with sixty thousand *h*
16:8 in chariots and in *h*
Ezr 8:22 ask a military force and *h*
Ne 2:9 of the military force and *h*
Isa 36:9 Egypt for chariots and for *h*
Jer 4:29 the sound of the *h* and bow
46:4 mount, O you *h*, and station
Eze 38:4 military force, horses and *h*
Da 11:40 with chariots and with *h*
Ho 1:7 or by war, by horses or by *h*
Ac 23:23 seventy *h* and two hundred
23:32 permitted the *h* to go on
23:33 *h* entered into Caesarea

Horses
Ge 47:17 bread in exchange for their *h*
Ex 9:3 On the *h*, the asses, the
14:9 all the chariot *h* of Pharaoh
14:23 and all the *h* of Pharaoh, his
15:19 Pharaoh's *h* with his war
De 11:4 his *h* and his war chariots
17:16 not increase *h* for himself
17:16 in order to increase *h*
De 20:1 see *h* and war chariots, a
Jos 11:4 very many *h* and war chariots
11:6 Their *h* you will hamstring
11:9 their *h* he hamstrung, and
Jg 5:22 the hoofs of *h* pawed Because
2Sa 8:4 hamstring all the chariot *h*
8:4 hundred chariot *h* of them
15:1 with *h* and with fifty men
1Ki 4:26 forty thousand stalls of *h*
4:28 the straw for the *h* and for
4:28 for the teams of *h* they kept
10:25 balsam oil, *h* and mules as
10:28 *h* that Solomon had from
18:5 may preserve the *h* and mules
20:1 and *h* and chariots, and he
20:21 striking down the *h* and the
22:4 My *h* are the same as your
22:4 are the same as your *h*
2Ki 2:11 war chariot and fiery *h*
3:7, 7 *h* are the same as your *h*
5:9 his *h* and his war chariots
6:14 he sent *h* and war chariots
6:15 city with *h* and war chariots
6:17 full of *h* and war chariots
7:6 war chariots, the sound of *h*
7:7 and their *h* and their asses
7:10 only the *h* tied and the asses
7:13 five of the remaining *h* that
7:14 took two chariots with *h* and
9:33 upon the wall and upon the *h*
10:2 war chariots and the *h* and
14:20 carried him upon *h* and he
18:23 give you two thousand *h* to
23:11 *h* that the kings of Judah
1Ch 18:4 hamstrung all the chariot *h*
18:4 a hundred chariot *h* of them
2Ch 1:16 export of the *h* that Solomon
9:24 *h* and mules as a yearly
9:25 four thousand stalls of *h*
9:28 *h* to Solomon from Egypt and
25:28 they carried him upon *h*
Ezr 2:66 *h* were seven hundred and
Ne 7:68 *h* were seven hundred and
Es 8:10 the hand of the couriers on *h*
8:10 post *h* used in the royal
8:14 *h* used in the royal service
Ps 20:7 and others concerning *h*
Ec 10:7 seen servants on *h* but princes
Isa 2:7 their land is filled with *h*
5:28 hoofs of their *h* will have
30:16 No, but on *h* we shall flee
30:16 on swift *h* we shall ride
31:1 those who rely on mere *h*
31:3 *h* are flesh, and not spirit
36:8 give you two thousand *h* to
66:20 on *h* and in chariots and
Jer 4:13 *h* are swifter than eagles
5:8 *H* seized with sexual heat
6:23 and upon *h* they will ride
8:16 heard the snorting of his *h*
12:5 can you run a race with *h*
17:25 in the chariot and upon *h*
22:4 on *h*, he with his servants
46:4 Harness the *h*, and mount
46:9 Go up, O you *h*; and drive
50:37 sword against their *h* and
50:42 upon *h* they will ride
51:27 *h* come up like bristly
Eze 17:15 for it to give him *h* and a
23:6 cavalrymen riding *h*
23:12 cavalrymen riding *h*
23:20 genital organ of male *h*
23:23 riding on *h*, all of them
26:7 with *h* and war chariots and
26:10 the heaving mass of his *h*
26:11 With the hoofs of his *h* he
27:14 *h* and steeds and mules
38:4 *h* and horsemen, all of them
38:15 all of them riding on *h*
39:20 *h* and charioteers, mighty
Ho 1:7 or by war, by *h* or by horsemen
14:3 Upon *h* we shall not ride
Joe 2:4 is like the appearance of *h*
Am 4:10 the taking captive of your *h*
6:12 On a crag will *h* run, or
Mic 1:13 the chariot to the team of *h*
5:10 I will cut off your *h* from
Hab 1:8 its *h* have proved swifter than
3:8 you went riding upon your *h*
3:15 you trod with your *h* through
Hag 2:22 the *h* and their riders will
Zec 1:8 *h* red, bright red, and white
6:2 chariot there were red *h*
6:2 the second chariot, black *h*

Zec 6:3 chariot there were white *h*
6:3 *h* speckled, parti-colored
6:6 one in which the black *h* are
10:5 riders of *h* will have to
Jas 3:3 bridles in the mouths of *h*
Re 9:7 locusts resembled *h* prepared
9:9 many *h* running into battle
9:17 I saw the *h* in the vision
9:17 the heads of the *h* were as
9:19 the authority of the *h* is in
14:20 up as the bridles of the *h*
18:13 *h* and coaches and slaves and
19:14 following him on white *h*
19:18 fleshy parts of *h* and of

Hosah
Jos 19:29 the boundary went back to *H*
1Ch 16:38 and *H* as gatekeepers
26:10 *H* of the sons of Merari had
26:11 brothers of *H* were thirteen
26:16 *H* had theirs to the west

Hosea
Ho 1:1 *H* the son of Beeri in the days
1:2 the word of Jehovah by *H*, and
1:2 Jehovah proceeded to say to *H*
Ro 9:25 he says also in *H*: Those not

Hoshaiah
Ne 12:32 *H* and half of the princes of
Jer 42:1 Jezaniah the son of *H* and
43:2 Azariah the son of *H* and

Hoshama
1Ch 3:18 Jekamiah, *H* and Nedabiah

Hoshea
Nu 13:8 of Ephraim, *H* the son of Nun
13:16 *H* the son of Nun Jehoshua
De 32:44 he and *H* the son of Nun
2Ki 15:30 Finally *H* the son of Elah
17:1 *H* the son of Elah became
17:3 *H* came to be his servant
17:6 In the ninth year of *H*
18:1 third year of *H* the son of
18:9 *H* the son of Elah the
18:10 ninth year of *H* the king
1Ch 27:20 of Ephraim, *H* the son of
Ne 10:23 *H*, Hananiah, Hasshub

Hoshea's
2Ki 17:4 find conspiracy in *H* case

Hospitable
1Ti 3:2 *h*, qualified to teach
Tit 1:8 *h*, a lover of goodness, sound
1Pe 4:9 Be *h* . . . without grumbling

Hospitably
Mt 25:35 and you received me *h*
25:38 a stranger and receive you *h*
25:43 but you did not receive me *h*
Ac 28:7 and he received us *h* and
Jas 2:25 received the messengers *h*
3Jo 8 to receive such persons *h*, that

Hospitality
Ac 17:7 has received them with *h*
Ro 12:13 Follow the course of *h*
Heb 13:2 Do not forget *h*, for through

Host
Ro 16:23 Gaius, my *h* and that of all

Hostages
2Ki 14:14 the *h* and then returned to
2Ch 25:24 the king's house and the *h*

Hostile
Ex 23:22 *h* to your enemies and harass

Hostility
Es 3:10 the one showing *h* to the Jews
8:1 Haman, the one showing *h* to
8:11 that were showing *h* to them
9:10 the one showing *h* to the Jews
9:24 one showing *h* to all the Jews
Ps 6:7 all those showing *h* to me
7:4 despoiled anyone showing *h* to
7:6 fury of those showing *h* to me
8:2 account of those showing *h* to
10:5 all those showing *h* to him
23:5 of those showing *h* to me
31:11 those showing *h* to me I
39:10 Due to the *h* of your hand
42:10 those showing *h* to me have
69:19 those showing *h* to me are in
74:4 those showing *h* to you have
74:23 those showing *h* to you
129:1 shown *h* to me from my youth
Ps 129:2 shown *h* to me from my youth
143:12 those showing *h* to my soul
Isa 11:13 showing *h* to Judah will be
11:13 Judah show *h* toward
Am 5:12 *h* toward someone righteous

Hot
Ge 4:5 Cain grew *h* with great anger
4:6 said to Cain: Why are you *h*
18:30 not grow *h* with anger
18:32 not grow *h* with anger, but
36:24 Anah who found the *h* springs
44:18 do not let your anger grow *h*
Ex 4:14 anger grew *h* against Moses
16:21 the sun got *h*, it melted
Nu 11:1 anger grew *h*, and a fire of
11:10 anger began growing very *h*
12:9 Jehovah's anger got to be *h*
De 9:19 *h* anger with which Jehovah
19:6 because his heart is *h*
Jos 7:1 Jehovah's anger grew *h*
7:26 turned away from his *h* anger
9:12 bread of ours, it was *h* when
Jg 14:19 his anger continued *h*, and he
1Sa 11:6 and his anger got very *h*
11:9 for you when the sun gets *h*
11:11 till the day grew *h*
17:28 anger grew *h* against David
20:30 Saul's anger grew *h* against
2Sa 12:5 David's anger grew very *h*
24:1 came to be *h* against Israel
2Ki 13:3 became *h* against Israel
2Ch 25:10 anger got very *h* against
25:15 Jehovah's anger became *h*
Ne 7:3 opened until the sun gets *h*
Job 6:17 it grows *h* they are dried up
19:11 His anger also grows *h*
30:30 bones became *h* from dryness
32:2 Elihu . . . came to be *h*
37:17 How your garments are *h*
42:7 My anger has grown *h* against
Ps 2:5 in his *h* displeasure he will
39:3 My heart grew *h* inside me
Isa 5:25 of Jehovah has grown *h*
7:4 *h* anger of Rezin and Syria
La 5:10 skin has grown *h* just like a
Eze 7:12 is *h* feeling against all its
7:14 my *h* feeling is against all
24:10 bones . . . become piping *h*
24:11 in order that it may get *h*
Ho 7:7 They get *h*, all of them, like
8:5 anger has grown *h* against them
11:8 compassions have grown *h*
Jon 4:1 and he got to be *h* with anger
4:4 rightly become *h* with anger
4:9 become *h* with anger over the
4:9 become *h* with anger, to the
Hab 3:8 that your anger has become *h*
Zec 10:3 my anger has grown *h*, and
2Pe 3:10 elements being intensely *h*
3:12 elements being intensely *h*
Re 3:15 you are neither cold nor *h*
3:15 wish you were cold or else *h*
3:16 lukewarm and neither *h* nor

Hotham
1Ch 7:32 Japhlet and Shomer and *H*
11:44 the sons of *H* the Aroerite

Hothir
1Ch 25:4 the sons of Heman . . . *H*
25:28 for the twenty-first, for *H*

Hotly
Ge 31:36 why you have *h* pursued after
1Sa 17:53 *h* pursuing the Philistines
Ps 10:2 *h* pursues the afflicted one
La 4:19 they have *h* pursued us. In the

Hotter
Job 32:5 his anger kept getting *h*

Hour
Mt 8:13 was healed in that *h*
9:22 that *h* the woman became well
10:19 will be given you in that *h*
14:15 *h* is already far advanced
15:28 was healed from that *h* on
17:18 boy was cured from that *h*
18:1 In that *h* the disciples came
20:3 the third *h*, he saw others
20:5 the sixth and the ninth *h* and
20:6 eleventh *h* he went out and
24:36 that day and *h* nobody knows
24:44 an *h* that you do not think
24:50 an *h* that he does not know
25:13 neither the day nor the *h*
Mt 26:40 not so much as watch one *h*
26:45 The *h* has drawn near for the
26:55 In that *h* Jesus said to the
27:45 the sixth *h* on a darkness
27:45 until the ninth *h*
27:46 the ninth *h* Jesus called out
Mr 6:35 now the *h* had grown late
6:35 and the *h* is already late
11:11 as the *h* was already late
13:11 given you in that *h*, speak
13:32 day or the *h* nobody knows
14:35 the *h* might pass away from
14:37 to keep on the watch one *h*
14:41 It is enough! The *h* has come!
15:25 It was now the third *h*, and
15:33 the sixth *h* a darkness fell
15:33 until the ninth *h*
15:34 at the ninth *h* Jesus called
Lu 1:10 at the *h* of offering incense
2:38 in that very *h* she came near
7:21 In that *h* he cured many of
7:45 from the *h* that I came in
10:21 In that very *h* he became
12:12 teach you in that very *h*
12:39 known at what *h* the thief
12:40 at an *h* that you do not think
12:46 an *h* that he does not know
13:31 In that very *h* certain
14:17 at the *h* of the evening meal
20:19 that very *h*, but they feared
22:14 At length when the *h* came
22:53 your *h* and the authority of
22:59 after about an *h* intervened
23:44 it was about the sixth *h*
23:44 darkness . . . the ninth *h*
24:33 in that very *h* they rose and
Joh 1:39 it was about the tenth *h*
2:4 My *h* has not yet come
4:6 The *h* was about the sixth
4:21 The *h* is coming when neither
4:23 *h* is coming, and it is now
4:52 *h* in which he got better in
4:52 the seventh *h* the fever left
4:53 very *h* that Jesus said to
5:25 The *h* is coming, and it is
5:28 *h* is coming in which all
7:30 his *h* had not yet come
8:20 his *h* had not yet come
12:23 *h* has come for the Son of
12:27 save me out of this *h*
12:27 why I have come to this *h*
13:1 *h* had come for him to move
16:2 *h* is coming when everyone
16:4 *h* for them arrives, you may
16:21 because her *h* has arrived
16:25 *h* is coming when I will
16:32 *h* is coming, indeed, it has
17:1 Father, the *h* has come
19:14 it was about the sixth *h*
19:27 from that *h* on the disciple
Ac 2:15 it is the third *h* of the day
3:1 temple for the *h* of prayer
3:1 of prayer, the ninth *h*
10:3 ninth *h* of the day he saw
10:9 about the sixth *h* to pray
10:30 counting from this *h* I was
10:30 in my house at the ninth *h*
16:18 And it came out that very *h*
16:33 in that *h* of the night and
22:13 looked up at him that very *h*
23:23 at the third *h* of the night
Ro 13:11 *h* for you to awake from
1Co 4:11 to this very *h* we continue to
15:30 we also in peril every *h*
Ga 2:5 no, not for an *h*, in order that
Phm 15 he broke away for an *h*, that
1Jo 2:18 children, it is the last *h*
2:18 that it is the last *h*
Re 3:3 what *h* I shall come upon you
3:10 *h* of test, which is to come
8:1 silence . . . for about a half *h*
9:15 prepared for the *h* and day
11:13 in that *h* a great earthquake
14:7 *h* of the judgment by him has
14:15 the *h* has come to reap, for
17:12 authority as kings one *h*
18:10 in one *h* your judgment has
18:17 in one *h* such great riches
18:19 *h* she has been devastated

Hour's
Mt 20:12 These last put in one *h* work

Hours
Joh 11:9 twelve *h* of daylight, are

Ac 5:7 interval of about three *h*
19:34 they shouted for about two *h*

House

Ge 12:1 from the *h* of your father to
12:15 taken to the *h* of Pharaoh
15:2 one who will possess my *h* is
17:12 anyone born in the *h* and
17:13 Every man born in your *h*
17:23 all the men born in his *h*
17:27 anyone born in the *h* and
19:2 turn aside, please, into the *h*
19:3 to him and came into his *h*
19:4 of Sodom, surrounded the *h*
19:10 brought Lot . . . into the *h*
19:11 at the entrance of the *h*
20:13 to wander from the *h* of my
20:18 shut up every womb of the *h*
24:7 took me from my father's *h*
24:23 Is there any room at the *h*
24:27 to the *h* of the brothers of
24:31 made the *h* ready and room
24:32 man came on into the *h*, and
24:38 go to the *h* of my father and
24:40 and from the *h* of my father
27:15 were with her in the *h*
28:2 to the *h* of Bethuel the father
28:17 nothing else but the *h* of God
28:21 to the *h* of my father
28:22 will become a *h* of God
29:13 brought him on into his *h*
30:30 something . . . for my own *h*
31:14 in the *h* of our father
31:30 yearning intensely for the *h*
31:37 of all the goods of your *h*
31:41 twenty years . . . in your *h*
33:17 to build himself a *h* and for
34:19 honorable of the whole *h* of
34:26 took Dinah from Shechem's *h*
34:30 be annihilated, I and my *h*
36:6 all the souls of his *h* and
38:11 in the *h* of your father until
38:11 dwell at her own father's *h*
39:2 be over the *h* of his master
39:4 he appointed him over his *h*
39:5 he appointed him over his *h*
39:5 Jehovah kept blessing the *h*
39:5 all that he had in the *h* and
39:8 what is with me in the *h*
39:9 no one greater in this *h* than
39:11 into the *h* to do his business
39:11 none of the men of the *h*
39:11 there in the *h*
39:14 cry out to the men of her *h*
39:16 his master came to his *h*
39:20 over to the prison *h*, the
39:20 there in the prison *h*
39:21 chief officer of the prison *h*
39:22 officer of the prison *h* gave
39:22 who were in the prison *h*
39:23 chief officer of the prison *h*
40:3 jail of the *h* of the chief
40:3 the prison *h*, the place where
40:5 prisoners in the prison *h*
40:7 the jail of his master's *h*
40:14 must get me out of this *h*
41:10 jail of the *h* of the chief
41:40 will personally be over my *h*
41:51 and all the *h* of my father
42:19 bound in your *h* of custody
43:16 the man who was over his *h*
43:16 Take the men to the *h* and
43:17 took the men to Joseph's *h*
43:18 had been taken to Joseph's *h*
43:19 man who was over Joseph's *h*
43:19 at the entrance of the *h*
43:24 the men into Joseph's *h*
43:26 Joseph went on into the *h*
43:26 to him into the *h*
44:1 the man who was over his *h*
44:4 the man who was over his *h*
44:8 silver or gold from the *h* of
44:14 went on into Joseph's *h*, and
45:2 Pharaoh's *h* got to hear it
45:8 a lord for all his *h* and as
45:11 for fear you and your *h*
45:16 the news was heard at the *h*
46:27 the souls of the *h* of Jacob
47:14 the money into Pharaoh's *h*
50:22 he and the *h* of his father
Ex 2:1 man of the *h* of Levi went
3:22 residing as an alien in her *h*
6:14 the heads of the *h* of their
7:23 Pharaoh . . . went into his *h*
Ex 8:3 frogs . . . enter into your *h*
8:3 frogs . . . into the *h* of your
8:24 gadflies began to invade the *h*
9:19 not gathered into the *h*, the
12:3 a sheep for the ancestral *h*
12:3 take . . . a sheep to a *h*
12:4 must take it into his *h*
12:22 out of the entrance of his *h*
12:30 not a *h* where there was not
12:46 In one *h* it is to be eaten
12:46 out of the *h* to some place
13:3 Egypt, from the *h* of slaves
13:14 out . . . from the *h* of slaves
16:31 *h* of Israel began to call its
19:3 to say to the *h* of Jacob and
20:2 out of the *h* of slaves
20:17 desire your fellowman's *h*
22:7 gets stolen from the man's *h*
22:8 the owner of the *h* must be
23:19 to bring to the *h* of Jehovah
34:26 the *h* of Jehovah your God
40:38 of all the *h* of Israel during
Le 9:7 and in behalf of your *h*; and
10:6 *h* of Israel will do the
14:34 leprosy in a *h* of the land
14:35 one to whom the *h* belongs
14:35 a plague . . . in the *h*
14:36 clear out the *h* before the
14:36 everything that is in the *h*
14:36 will come in to see the *h*
14:37 is in the walls of the *h*
14:38 then go out of the *h* to the
14:38 the entrance of the *h* and he
14:38 quarantine the *h* seven days
14:39 plague . . . walls of the *h*
14:41 the *h* scraped off all around
14:42 must have the *h* plastered
14:43 it does break out in the *h*
14:43 cut off the *h* and plastered
14:44 plague has spread in the *h*
14:44 malignant leprosy in the *h*
14:45 the *h* pulled down with its
14:45 all the clay mortar of the *h*
14:46 comes into the *h* any of the
14:47 whoever lies down in the *h*
14:47 eats in the *h* should wash
14:48 has not spread in the *h*
14:48 after having plastered the *h*
14:48 then pronounce the *h* clean
14:49 to purify the *h* from sin he
14:51 spatter it toward the *h*
14:52 purify the *h* from sin with
14:53 make atonement for the *h*
14:55 leprosy . . . in the *h*
16:6 behalf of himself and his *h*
16:11 behalf of himself and his *h*
16:17 and in behalf of his *h* and
17:3 any man of the *h* of Israel
17:8 man of the *h* of Israel or
17:10 man of the *h* of Israel or
22:11 slaves born in his *h*, they
22:13 father's *h* as in her youth
22:18 *h* of Israel or some alien
25:29 a dwelling *h* in a walled
25:30 *h* that is in the city that
25:33 *h* sold in the city of his
27:14 *h* as something holy to
27:15 buy his *h* back, he must then
Nu 1:2 *h* of their fathers, by the
1:4 head to the *h* of his fathers
1:18 families in the *h* of their
1:20 in the *h* of their fathers
1:22 in the *h* of their fathers
1:24 in the *h* of their fathers
1:26 in the *h* of their fathers
1:28 in the *h* of their fathers
1:30 in the *h* of their fathers
1:32 in the *h* of their fathers
1:34 in the *h* of their fathers
1:36 in the *h* of their fathers
1:38 in the *h* of their fathers by
1:40 in the *h* of their fathers by
1:42 in the *h* of their fathers by
1:44 one each the *h* of his fathers
1:45 according to the *h* of their
2:2 signs for the *h* of their
2:32 according to the *h* of their
2:34 with regard to the *h* of his
3:15 Levi according to the *h* of
3:20 Levites according to the *h* of
3:24 paternal *h* for the Gershonites
3:30 paternal *h* for the families
3:35 paternal *h* for the families
4:2 in the *h* of their fathers
Nu 4:22 *h* of their fathers according
4:29 families in the *h* of their
4:34 and by the *h* of their fathers
4:38 and by the *h* of their fathers
4:40 by the *h* of their fathers
4:42 by the *h* of their fathers
4:46 by the *h* of their fathers
7:2 *h* of their fathers, made a
12:7 entrusted with all my *h*
17:2 one rod for each paternal *h*
17:2 by the *h* of their fathers
17:3 one rod for the head of the *h*
17:6 by the *h* of their fathers
17:8 Aaron's rod for the *h* of Levi
18:1 the *h* of your father with you
18:11 Everyone clean in your *h* may
18:13 Everyone clean in your *h* may
20:29 all the *h* of Israel continued
22:18 his *h* full of silver and gold
24:13 his *h* full of silver and gold
25:14 paternal *h* of the Simeonites
25:15 of a paternal *h* in Midian
26:2 to the *h* of their fathers, all
30:3 *h* of her father in her youth
30:10 in the *h* of her husband that
30:16 youth in the *h* of her father
34:14 by the *h* of their fathers and
34:14 by the *h* of their fathers
De 5:6 Egypt, out of the *h* of slaves
5:21 crave your fellowman's *h*
6:7 when you sit in your *h* and
6:9 upon the doorposts of your *h*
6:12 out of the *h* of slaves
7:8 redeem you from the *h* of
7:26 a detestable thing into your *h*
8:14 out of the *h* of slaves
11:19 when you sit in your *h* and
11:20 upon the doorposts of your *h*
13:5 from the *h* of slaves, to turn
13:10 out of the *h* of slaves
20:5 man that has built a new *h*
20:5 return to his *h*, for fear he
20:6 return to his *h*, for fear he
20:7 return to his *h*, for fear he
20:8 go and return to his *h*
21:12 into the midst of your *h*
21:13 dwell in your *h* and weep for
22:2 home into the midst of your *h*
22:8 In case you build a new *h*
22:8 place bloodguilt upon your *h*
22:21 entrance of her father's *h*
22:21 prostitution in the *h* of her
23:18 a dog into the *h* of Jehovah
24:1 and dismiss her from his *h*
24:2 she must go out of his *h* and
24:3 dismissed her from his *h*
24:5 exempt at his *h* for one year
24:10 not enter into his *h* to take
25:10 the *h* of the one who had
25:14 in your *h* two sorts of
26:13 what is holy from the *h*
28:30 You will build a *h*, but you
Jos 2:1 the *h* of a prostitute woman
2:3 that have come into your *h*
2:15 *h* was on a side of the wall
2:18 gather to yourself into the *h*
2:19 out of the doors of your *h*
2:19 continues with you in the *h*
6:17 who are with her in the *h*
6:22 Go into the *h* of the woman
6:24 the treasure of Jehovah's *h*
9:23 the *h* of my God will never
17:17 to the *h* of Joseph, Ephraim
18:5 the *h* of Joseph will keep
20:6 into his city and into his *h*
21:45 made to the *h* of Israel; it
22:14 each paternal *h* of all the
22:14 a head of the *h* of their
24:17 out of the *h* of slaves
Jg 1:22 the *h* of Joseph itself also
1:23 the *h* of Joseph began to spy
1:35 the hand of the *h* of Joseph
6:8 you out of the *h* of slaves
6:15 the smallest in my father's *h*
8:29 continued to dwell in his *h*
9:1 the *h* of his mother's father
9:4 from the *h* of Baal-berith, and
9:5 the *h* of his father at Ophrah
9:6 all the *h* of Millo gathered
9:20 the *h* of Millo, and let fire
9:20 the *h* of Millo and consume
9:27 the *h* of their god and ate and
9:46 vault of the *h* of El-berith
10:9 the *h* of Ephraim; and Israel

Jg 11:7 drove me out of my father's *h*
11:31 doors of my *h* to meet me
12:1 Your very *h* we shall burn
14:15 *h* of your father with fire
14:19 his way up to his father's *h*
16:21 a grinder in the prison *h*
16:25 Samson out of the prison *h*
16:26 the *h* is firmly established
16:27 the *h* was full of men and
16:29 the *h* was firmly established
16:30 the *h* went falling upon the
17:4 and it got to be in Micah's *h*
17:5 Micah, he had a *h* of gods
17:8 as far as the *h* of Micah
17:12 continue in the *h* of Micah
18:2 *h* of Micah and got to spend
18:3 close by the *h* of Micah, they
18:13 as far as the *h* of Micah
18:15 the *h* of the young man, the
18:15 the *h* of Micah, and began to
18:18 went into the *h* of Micah and
18:19 priest to the *h* of one man
18:22 away from the *h* of Micah
18:22 close by the *h* of Micah were
18:26 and went back to his *h*
18:31 *h* of the true God continued
19:2 *h* of her father at Bethlehem
19:3 him come into her father's *h*
19:15 into the *h* to stay overnight
19:18 to my own *h* that I am going
19:18 taking me on into the *h*
19:21 he brought him into his *h*
19:22 surrounded the *h*, shoving one
19:22 old man, the owner of the *h*
19:22 man that came into your *h*
19:23 the owner of the *h* went on
19:23 this man has come into my *h*
19:26 man's *h* where her master
19:27 opened the doors of the *h*
19:27 at the entrance of the *h*
19:29 he entered his *h* and took the
20:5 surround the *h* against me by
20:8 turn aside any of us to his *h*
Ru 1:8 to the *h* of her mother
1:9 in the *h* of her husband
2:7 in the *h* a little while
4:11 who is coming into your *h*
4:11 built the *h* of Israel
4:12 may your *h* become like the
4:12 become like the *h* of Perez
1Sa 1:7 went up into the *h* of Jehovah
1:19 came into their *h* at Ramah
1:24 the *h* of Jehovah in Shiloh
2:11 went to Ramah to his *h*
2:27 to the *h* of your forefather
2:27 as slaves to the *h* of Pharaoh
2:28 to the *h* of your forefather
2:30 indeed say, As for your *h*
2:30 and the *h* of your forefather
2:31 of the *h* of your forefather
2:31 to be an old man in your *h*
2:32 to be an old man in your *h*
2:33 the greater number of your *h*
2:35 build for him a lasting *h*
2:36 anyone left over in your *h*
3:12 I have said respecting his *h*
3:13 I am judging his *h* to time
3:14 I have sworn to the *h* of Eli
3:14 the error of the *h* of Eli
3:15 the doors of Jehovah's *h*
5:2 bring it into the *h* of Dagon
5:5 going into the *h* of Dagon
7:1 the *h* of Abinadab on the hill
7:2 *h* of Israel went lamenting
7:3 to say to all the *h* of Israel
7:17 Ramah . . . where his *h* was
9:18 where is the *h* of the seer?
9:20 the whole *h* of your father
10:25 away, each one to his *h*
15:34 his own *h* at Gibeah of Saul
17:25 *h* of his father he will set
18:2 to return to his father's *h*
18:10 like a prophet within the *h*
19:9 sitting in his *h* with his
19:11 messengers to David's *h* to
20:16 off from the *h* of David
22:1 *h* of his father got to hear
22:11 *h* of his father, the priests
22:14 and honored in your *h*
22:15 entire *h* of my father, for
22:16 all the *h* of your father
22:22 soul of the *h* of your father
24:21 out of the *h* of my father
25:1 bury him at his *h* in Ramah
1Sa 25:17 against all his *h*, as he is
25:28 for my lord a lasting *h*
25:35 Go up in peace to your *h*
25:36 having a feast in his *h* like
28:24 a fattened calf in the *h*
31:10 *h* of the Ashtoreth images
2Sa 1:12 over the *h* of Israel, because
2:4 as king over the *h* of Judah
2:7 I whom the *h* of Judah have
2:10 *h* of Judah proved themselves
2:11 over the *h* of Judah came to
3:1 war between the *h* of Saul and
3:1 and the *h* of David came to be
3:1 *h* of Saul kept declining more
3:6 war between the *h* of Saul and
3:6 of Saul and the *h* of David
3:6 his position in the *h* of Saul
3:8 toward the *h* of Saul your
3:10 kingdom from the *h* of Saul
3:19 of the whole *h* of Benjamin
3:29 the entire *h* of his father
3:29 cut off from Joab's *h* a man
4:5 to the *h* of Ish-bosheth about
4:6 came into the middle of the *h*
4:7 went into the *h*, he was lying
4:11 in his own *h* upon his bed
5:8 one will not come into the *h*
5:11 began to build a *h* for David
6:3 from the *h* of Abinadab
6:4 carried it from Abinadab's *h*
6:5 David and all the *h* of Israel
6:10 to the *h* of Obed-edom the
6:11 *h* of Obed-edom the Gittite
6:12 *h* of Obed-edom and all that
6:12 out of the *h* of Obed-edom up
6:15 David and all the *h* of Israel
6:19 went each to his own *h*
7:1 king dwelt in his own *h* and
7:2 am dwelling in a *h* of cedars
7:5 build me a *h* for me to dwell
7:6 not dwelt in a *h* from the day
7:7 not build me a *h* of cedars
7:11 *h* is what Jehovah will make
7:13 build a *h* for my name, and
7:16 your *h* and your kingdom will
7:18 what is my *h* that you have
7:19 *h* of your servant down to a
7:25 servant and concerning his *h*
7:26 *h* of your servant David
7:27 A *h* I shall build for you
7:29 bless the *h* of your servant
7:29 *h* of your servant be blessed
9:1 left over of the *h* of Saul
9:2 *h* of Saul had a servant whose
9:3 there nobody of the *h* of Saul
9:4 *h* of Machir the son of
9:5 *h* of Machir the son of
9:9 Saul and to all his *h* I do
9:12 dwelling in the *h* of Ziba
11:2 rooftop of the king's *h*
11:4 Later she returned to her *h*
11:8 Go down to your *h* and bathe
11:8 out from the king's *h*, and
11:9 entrance of the king's *h*
11:9 not go down to his own *h*
11:10 not go down to his own *h*
11:10 not gone down to your own *h*
11:11 go into my own *h* to eat
11:13 to his own *h* he did not go
11:27 took her home to his *h*
12:8 give you the *h* of your lord
12:8 give you the *h* of Israel and
12:10 depart from your own *h* to
12:11 calamity out of your own *h*
12:15 Nathan went to his own *h*
12:17 older men of his *h* stood up
12:20 came to the *h* of Jehovah
12:20 came into his own *h* and
13:7 sent to Tamar at the *h*
13:7 *h* of Amnon your brother and
13:8 went to the *h* of Amnon her
13:20 *h* of Absalom her brother
14:8 Go to your *h*, and I myself
14:9 upon the *h* of my father
14:24 turn toward his own *h*, but
14:24 turned toward his own *h*
14:31 came to Absalom at the *h*
15:16 to take care of the *h*
15:35 hear from the *h* of the king
16:3 *h* of Israel will give back
16:5 of the family of Saul's *h*
16:8 bloodguilt for the *h* of Saul
16:21 to take care of the *h*
17:18 the *h* of a man in Bahurim
2Sa 17:20 came to the woman at her *h*
17:23 to his *h* at his own city
19:5 to the king at the *h* and said
19:11 bring the king back to his *h*
19:11 come to the king at his *h*
19:17 attendant of the *h* of Saul
19:20 first of all the *h* of Joseph
19:30 has come in peace to his *h*
20:3 came to his *h* at Jerusalem
20:3 to take care of the *h*
20:3 in a *h* of confinement
21:1 Upon Saul and upon his *h*
24:17 and upon the *h* of my father
1Ki 1:53 Go to your own *h*
2:24 made a *h* for me just as he
2:27 spoken against the *h* of Eli
2:31 from off the *h* of my father
2:33 for his *h* and for his throne
2:34 buried at his own *h* in the
2:36 Build . . . a *h* in Jerusalem
3:1 finished building his own *h*
3:1 *h* of Jehovah and Jerusalem's
3:2 a *h* had not been built to the
3:17 are dwelling in one *h*, so
3:17 birth close by her in the *h*
3:18 no stranger with us in the *h*
3:18 but the two of us in the *h*
5:3 a *h* to the name of Jehovah
5:5 a *h* to the name of Jehovah my
5:5 will build the *h* to my name
5:17 lay the foundation of the *h*
5:18 and the stones to build the *h*
6:1 to build the *h* to Jehovah
6:2 the *h* that King Solomon built
6:3 front of the temple of the *h*
6:3 front of the width of the *h*
6:3 its depth, in front of the *h*
6:4 for the *h* he went on to make
6:5 against the wall of the *h*
6:5 against the walls of the *h*
6:6 he gave to the *h* all around
6:6 a hold in the walls of the *h*
6:7 *h*, while it was being built
6:7 they were not heard in the *h*
6:8 on the right side of the *h*
6:9 he continued building the *h*
6:9 covered in the *h* with beams
6:10 chambers against the whole *h*
6:10 a hold on the *h* by timbers
6:12 this *h* that you are building
6:14 building the *h* that he might
6:15 build the walls of the *h*
6:15 the floor of the *h* up to the
6:15 overlay the floor of the *h*
6:16 at the rear sides of the *h*
6:17 forty cubits that the *h*
6:18 cedarwood on the *h* inside
6:19 in the interior of the *h*
6:21 overlay the *h* inside with
6:22 *h* he overlaid with gold
6:22 all the *h* was completed
6:27 cherubs inside the inner *h*
6:27 toward the middle of the *h*
6:29 walls of the *h* round about
6:30 floor of the *h* he overlaid
6:37 fourth year the *h* of Jehovah
6:38 the *h* was finished as
7:1 his own *h* Solomon built in
7:1 he finished all his own *h*
7:2 the *H* of the Forest of Lebanon
7:8 *h* of his where he was to
7:8 the *h* belonging to the Porch
7:8 there was a *h* like this Porch
7:12 courtyard of the *h* of Jehovah
7:12 and for the porch of the *h*
7:39 on the right side of the *h*
7:39 on the left side of the *h*
7:39 to the right side of the *h*
7:40 as respects the *h* of Jehovah
7:45 for the *h* of Jehovah
7:48 pertained to the *h* of Jehovah
7:50 inner *h*, that is, the Most
7:50 the doors of the *h* of the
7:51 as regards the *h* of Jehovah
7:51 treasures of the *h* of Jehovah
8:6 the innermost room of the *h*
8:10 cloud itself filled the *h* of
8:11 glory of Jehovah filled the *h*
8:13 a *h* of lofty abode for you
8:16 to build a *h* for my name to
8:17 David my father to build a *h*
8:18 to build a *h* to my name
8:19 you . . . will not build the *h*
8:19 will build the *h* to my name

1Ki 8:20 build the *h* to the name of
8:27 how much less, then, this *h*
8:29 toward this *h* night and day
8:31 before your altar in this *h*
8:33 favor toward you in this *h*
8:38 spread . . . palms to this *h*
8:42 and prays toward this *h*
8:43 upon this *h* that I have built
8:44 the *h* that I have built to
8:48 the *h* that I have built
8:63 inaugurate the *h* of Jehovah
8:64 before the *h* of Jehovah
9:1 finished building the *h* of
9:1 the *h* of the king and every
9:3 I have sanctified this *h* that
9:7 the *h* that I have sanctified
9:8 *h* itself will become heaps
9:8 to this land and this *h*
9:10 the *h* of Jehovah and the
9:10 and the *h* of the king
9:15 to build the *h* of Jehovah
9:15 his own *h* and the Mound and
9:24 her own *h* that he had built
9:25 and he completed the *h*
10:4 and the *h* that he had built
10:5 at the *h* of Jehovah
10:12 for the *h* of Jehovah and
10:12 and for the *h* of the king
10:17 *H* of the Forest of Lebanon
10:21 *H* of the Forest of Lebanon
11:18 who then gave him a *h*
11:20 inside the *h* of Pharaoh
11:20 at the *h* of Pharaoh
11:28 service of the *h* of Joseph
11:38 I will build a lasting *h*
12:16 to your own *h*, O David
12:19 against the *h* of David
12:20 follower of the *h* of David
12:21 all the *h* of Judah and the
12:21 against the *h* of Israel
12:23 and to all the *h* of Judah
12:24 Go back each one to his *h*
12:26 return to the *h* of David
12:27 *h* of Jehovah in Jerusalem
12:31 to make a *h* of high places
13:2 A son born to the *h* of David
13:7 come with me to the *h* and
13:8 gave me half of your *h* I
13:15 Go with me to the *h* and eat
13:18 to your *h* that he may eat
13:19 eat bread in his *h* and
14:4 and came to the *h* of Ahijah
14:8 away from the *h* of David
14:10 upon the *h* of Jeroboam
14:10 behind the *h* of Jeroboam
14:12 rise up, go to your *h*
14:13 in the *h* of Jeroboam
14:14 cut off the *h* of Jeroboam
14:17 at the threshold of the *h*
14:26 of the *h* of Jehovah
14:26 of the *h* of the king
14:27 the entrance of the king's *h*
14:28 came to the *h* of Jehovah
15:15 into the *h* of Jehovah
15:18 of the *h* of Jehovah
15:18 the *h* of the king and put
15:27 Ahijah of the *h* of Issachar
15:29 all the *h* of Jeroboam
16:3 after Baasha and after his *h*
16:3, 3 *h* like the *h* of Jeroboam
16:7 against Baasha and his *h*
16:7 like the *h* of Jeroboam
16:9 drunk at the *h* of Arzah
16:11 all the *h* of Baasha
16:12 the whole *h* of Baasha
16:18 tower of the king's *h* and
16:18 and burned the king's *h*
16:32 *h* of Baal that he built in
17:17 the mistress of the *h*
17:23 the roof chamber into the *h*
18:18 the *h* of your father have
20:6 carefully search your *h* and
20:31 kings of the *h* of Israel
20:43 on his way toward his *h*
21:2 it is close by my *h*
21:4 Ahab came into his *h*, sullen
21:22 constitute your *h* like the
21:22 like the *h* of Jeroboam the
21:22 like the *h* of Baasha the
21:29 the calamity upon his *h*
22:17 each one to his *h* in peace
22:27 in the *h* of detention and
22:39 *h* of ivory that he built
2Ki 4:2 what do you have in the *h*?
2Ki 4:2 has nothing at all in the *h*
4:32 Elisha came into the *h*
4:35 began walking again in the *h*
5:9 entrance of the *h* of Elisha
5:18 into the *h* of Rimmon to bow
5:18 bow down at the *h* of Rimmon
5:18 bow down at the *h* of Rimmon
5:24 deposited them in the *h* and
6:32 Elisha was . . . in his own *h*
7:9 make report at the king's *h*
7:11 reported to the king's *h*
8:3 cry out to the king for her *h*
8:5 for her *h* and for her field
8:18 those of the *h* of Ahab had
8:27 in the way of the *h* of Ahab
8:27 like the *h* of Ahab, for he
8:27 a relative of the *h* of Ahab
9:6 got up and came into the *h*
9:7 strike down the *h* of Ahab
9:8 whole *h* of Ahab must perish
9:9 constitute the *h* of Ahab like
9:9 Ahab like the *h* of Jeroboam
9:9 like the *h* of Baasha the son
9:27 by the way of the garden *h*
10:3 fight for the *h* of your lord
10:5 one who was over the *h* and
10:10 against the *h* of Ahab
10:11 of the *h* of Ahab in Jezreel
10:12 binding *h* of the shepherds
10:14 cistern of the binding *h*
10:21 coming into the *h* of Baal
10:21 *h* of Baal came to be full
10:23 into the *h* of Baal
10:25 the city of the *h* of Baal
10:26 pillars of the *h* of Baal
10:27 pulled down the *h* of Baal
10:30 have done to the *h* of Ahab
11:3 at the *h* of Jehovah in hiding
11:4 *h* of Jehovah and concluded a
11:4 swear at the *h* of Jehovah
11:5 watch over the king's *h*
11:6 watch over the *h* by turns
11:7 watch over the *h* of Jehovah
11:10 were in the *h* of Jehovah
11:11 right side of the *h* clear to
11:11 to the left side of the *h*
11:11 by the altar and by the *h*
11:13 people at the *h* of Jehovah
11:15 in the *h* of Jehovah
11:16 horse entry of the king's *h*
11:18 *h* of Baal and pulled down
11:18 over the *h* of Jehovah
11:19 from the *h* of Jehovah
11:19 the runners to the king's *h*
11:20 the sword at the king's *h*
12:4 brought to the *h* of Jehovah
12:4 to bring to the *h* of Jehovah
12:5 repair the cracks of the *h*
12:6 repaired the cracks of the *h*
12:7 repairing the cracks of the *h*
12:7 of the *h* you should give it
12:8 repair the cracks of the *h*
12:9 comes into the *h* of Jehovah
12:9 brought into the *h* of Jehovah
12:10 found at the *h* of Jehovah
12:11 to the *h* of Jehovah
12:11 working at the *h* of Jehovah
12:12 cracks of the *h* of Jehovah
12:12 was expended upon the *h* to
12:13 as respects the *h* of Jehovah
12:13 brought to the *h* of Jehovah
12:14 repaired the *h* of Jehovah
12:16 brought to the *h* of Jehovah
12:18 of the *h* of Jehovah
12:18 the *h* of the king and sent
12:20 at the *h* of the Mound
13:6 the sin of the *h* of Jeroboam
14:10 and dwell in your own *h*
14:14 found at the *h* of Jehovah
14:14 the *h* of the king and the
15:5 dwelling in his *h* exempt
15:5 king's son was over the *h*
15:25 tower of the king's *h*
15:35 gate of the *h* of Jehovah
16:8 found at the *h* of Jehovah
16:8 the treasures of the king's *h*
16:14 near from in front of the *h*
16:14 altar and the *h* of Jehovah
16:18 the *h* and the king's outer
16:18 from the *h* of Jehovah
17:4 bound in the *h* of detention
17:21 from the *h* of David
17:29 the *h* of the high places
17:32 in the *h* of the high places
2Ki 18:15 found at the *h* of Jehovah
18:15 treasures of the king's *h*
19:1 came into the *h* of Jehovah
19:14 went up to the *h* of Jehovah
19:30 escape of the *h* of Judah
19:37 at the *h* of Nisroch his god
20:5 go up to the *h* of Jehovah
20:8 to the *h* of Jehovah
20:13 *h* and in all his dominion
20:15 What did they see in your *h*?
20:15 Everything that is in my *h*
20:17 all that is in your own *h*
21:4 altars in the *h* of Jehovah
21:5 of the *h* of Jehovah
21:7 in the *h* of which Jehovah
21:7 In this *h* and in Jerusalem
21:13 applied to the *h* of Ahab
21:18 in the garden of his *h*
21:23 king to death in his own *h*
22:3 secretary to the *h* of Jehovah
22:4 brought into the *h* of Jehovah
22:5 in the *h* of Jehovah
22:5 who are in the *h* of Jehovah
22:5 to repair the cracks of the *h*
22:6 hewn stones to repair the *h*
22:8 found in the *h* of Jehovah
22:9 money . . . found in the *h*
22:9 in the *h* of Jehovah
23:2 up to the *h* of Jehovah
23:2 found in the *h* of Jehovah
23:6 from the *h* of Jehovah to the
23:7 were in the *h* of Jehovah
23:11 entering the *h* of Jehovah
23:12 two courtyards of the *h* of
23:24 found at the *h* of Jehovah
23:27 the *h* of which I have said
24:13 of the *h* of Jehovah and the
24:13 treasures of the king's *h*
25:9 to burn the *h* of Jehovah and
25:9 and the king's *h* and all the
25:9 *h* of every great man he
25:13 were in the *h* of Jehovah
25:13 were in the *h* of Jehovah
25:16 made for the *h* of Jehovah
25:27 out of the *h* of detention
1Ch 2:55 the father of the *h* of Rechab
4:21 *h* of the workers of fine
4:21 fabric of the *h* of Ashbea
5:13 to the *h* of their forefathers
5:15 of the *h* of their forefathers
5:24 of the *h* of their forefathers
5:24 of the *h* of their forefathers
6:10 the *h* that Solomon built in
6:31 singing at the *h* of Jehovah
6:32 *h* of Jehovah in Jerusalem
6:48 of the *h* of the true God
7:2 of the *h* of their forefathers
7:4 to the *h* of their forefathers
7:7 of the *h* of their forefathers
7:9 of the *h* of their forefathers
7:23 she happened to be in his *h*
7:40 of the *h* of the forefathers
9:9 by the *h* of their forefathers
9:11 of the *h* of the true God
9:13 of the *h* of their forefathers
9:13 of the *h* of the true God
9:19 *h* of his father the Korahites
9:23 of the *h* of Jehovah, even the
9:23 *h* of the tent, for guard
9:26 of the *h* of the true God
9:27 around the *h* of the true God
10:6 those of his *h* died together
10:10 armor in the *h* of their god
10:10 fastened to the *h* of Dagon
12:28 and the *h* of his forefathers
12:29 watch of the *h* of Saul
12:30 the *h* of their forefathers
13:7 from the *h* of Abinadab, and
13:13 *h* of Obed-edom the Gittite
13:14 Obed-edom, at his *h* three
14:1 to build him a *h*
15:25 from the *h* of Obed-edom
16:43 to go each one to his own *h*
16:43 around to bless his own *h*
17:1 dwelling in his own *h*, David
17:1 am dwelling in a *h* of cedars
17:4 build me the *h* in which to
17:5 I have not dwelt in a *h* from
17:6 not built me a *h* of cedars
17:10 a *h* Jehovah will build for
17:12 one that will build me a *h*
17:14 cause him to stand in my *h*
17:16 what is my *h* that you have
17:17 *h* of your servant down to a

1Ch 17:23 and concerning his *h* prove
17:24 the *h* of David your servant
17:25 purpose to build him a *h*
17:27 bless the *h* of your servant
21:17 upon me and my father's *h*
22:1 the *h* of Jehovah the true God
22:2 the *h* of the true God
22:5 the *h* to be built to Jehovah
22:6 to build a *h* to Jehovah the
22:7 a *h* to the name of Jehovah
22:8 not build a *h* to my name
22:10 will build a *h* to my name
22:11 build the *h* of Jehovah your
22:14 prepared for Jehovah's *h*
22:19 the *h* built to the name of
23:4 the work of the *h* of Jehovah
23:11 paternal *h* for one official
23:24 by the *h* of their fathers
23:24 service of the *h* of Jehovah
23:28 service of the *h* of Jehovah
23:28 of the *h* of the true God
23:32 service of the *h* of Jehovah
24:6 one paternal *h* being picked
24:19 come into the *h* of Jehovah
25:6 in song at the *h* of Jehovah
25:6 of the *h* of the true God
26:6 of the *h* of their father
26:12 to minister at the *h* of
26:20 of the *h* of the true God and
26:22 over the treasures of the *h*
26:27 maintain the *h* of Jehovah
28:2 build a resting *h* for the ark
28:3 not build a *h* to my name
28:4 of all the *h* of my father
28:4 and in the *h* of Judah my
28:4 of Judah my father's *h*, and
28:6 the one that will build my *h*
28:10 to build a *h* as a sanctuary
28:11 *h* of the propitiatory cover
28:12 courtyards of Jehovah's *h*
28:12 of the *h* of the true God and
28:13 the service of Jehovah's *h*
28:13 the service of Jehovah's *h*
28:20 the service of Jehovah's *h*
28:21 of the *h* of the true God
29:2 prepared for the *h* of my God
29:3 pleasure in the *h* of my God
29:3 give it to the *h* of my God
29:3 have prepared for the holy *h*
29:7 gave to the service of the *h*
29:8 treasure of the *h* of Jehovah
29:16 a *h* for your holy name
2Ch 2:1 build a *h* to Jehovah's name
2:1 and a *h* for his kingship
2:3 a *h* in which to dwell
2:4 a *h* to the name of Jehovah my
2:5 *h* that I am building will be
2:6 retain power to build him a *h*
2:6 that I should build him a *h*
2:9 *h* that I am building will be
2:12 will build a *h* to Jehovah
2:12 and a *h* for his kingship
3:1 to build the *h* of Jehovah in
3:3 building the *h* of the true God
3:4 front of the width of the *h*
3:5 *h* he covered with juniper
3:6 overlaid the *h* with precious
3:7 to cover the *h*, the rafters
3:8 make the *h* of the Most Holy
3:8 to the width of the *h* being
3:10 in the *h* of the Most Holy
3:11 to the wall of the *h*, and
3:12 to the wall of the *h*, and
3:15 before the *h* two pillars
4:11 on the *h* of the true God
4:16 for the *h* of Jehovah, of
4:19 utensils that were at the *h*
4:22 and the entrance of the *h*
4:22 doors of the *h* of the temple
5:1 had to do for the *h* of Jehovah
5:1 treasures of the *h* of the true
5:7 the innermost room of the *h*
5:13 *h* itself was filled with a
5:13 the very *h* of Jehovah
5:14 glory of Jehovah filled the *h*
6:2 built a *h* of lofty abode for
6:5 to build a *h* for my name to
6:7 a *h* to the name of Jehovah
6:8 to build a *h* to my name
6:9 not build the *h*, but your son
6:9 the one that will build the *h*
6:10 that I might build the *h* to
6:18 this *h* that I have built
6:20 toward this *h* day and night

2Ch 6:22 before your altar in this *h*
6:24 favor before you in this *h*
6:29 out his palms toward this *h*
6:32 come and pray toward this *h*
6:33 this *h* that I have built
6:34 *h* that I have built to your
6:38 *h* that I have built to your
7:1 glory itself filled the *h*
7:2 enter into the *h* of Jehovah
7:2 had filled the *h* of Jehovah
7:3 of Jehovah was upon the *h*
7:5 inaugurated the *h* of the true
7:7 was before the *h* of Jehovah
7:11 finished the *h* of Jehovah and
7:11 and the *h* of the king
7:11 do regarding the *h* of Jehovah
7:11 own *h* he proved successful
7:12 place . . . as a *h* of sacrifice
7:16 choose and sanctify this *h*
7:20 *h* that I have sanctified for
7:21 *h* that had become heaps of
7:21 to this land and to this *h*
8:1 had built the *h* of Jehovah and
8:1 of Jehovah and his own *h*
8:11 *h* that he had built for her
8:11 not dwell in the *h* of David
8:16 *h* of Jehovah until it was
8:16 *h* of Jehovah was complete
9:3 and the *h* that he had built
9:4 offered up at the *h* of Jehovah
9:11 stairs for the *h* of Jehovah
9:11 and for the king's *h* and
9:16 *H* of the Forest of Lebanon
9:20 *H* of the Forest of Lebanon
10:16 Now see to your own *h*
10:19 against the *h* of David
11:1 congregated the *h* of Judah
11:4 Return each one to his *h*, for
12:9 treasures of the *h* of Jehovah
12:9 treasures of the king's *h*
12:10 entrance of the king's *h*
12:11 came to the *h* of Jehovah
15:18 into the *h* of the true God
16:2 treasures of Jehovah's *h* and
16:2 treasures of . . . the king's *h*
16:10 him in the *h* of the stocks
17:14 *h* of their forefathers
18:16 back each one to his *h* in
18:26 in the *h* of detention and
19:1 to his own *h* at Jerusalem
19:11 leader of the *h* of Judah
20:5 in the *h* of Jehovah before
20:9 stand before this *h* and
20:9 for your name is in this *h*
20:28 to the *h* of Jehovah
21:6 those of the *h* of Ahab had
21:7 bring the *h* of David to ruin
21:13 *h* of Ahab caused the having
21:17 found in the king's *h* and
22:3 ways of the *h* of Ahab, for
22:4 same as the *h* of Ahab, for
22:7 to cut off the *h* of Ahab
22:8 with the *h* of Ahab, he got
22:9 no one of the *h* of Ahaziah
22:10 offspring of the *h* of Judah
22:12 *h* of the true God hidden
23:3 *h* of the true God, after
23:5 be at the *h* of the king
23:5 courtyards of the *h* of
23:6 enter the *h* of Jehovah but
23:7 anyone coming into the *h*, he
23:9 in the *h* of the true God
23:10 right side of the *h* clear
23:10 to the left side of the *h*
23:10 by the *h*, all around near
23:12 people at the *h* of Jehovah
23:14 to death at the *h* of Jehovah
23:15 horse gate of the king's *h*
23:17 *h* of Baal and pulled it
23:18 offices of the *h* of Jehovah
23:18 over the *h* of Jehovah to
23:19 gates of the *h* of Jehovah
23:20 down from the *h* of Jehovah
23:20 upper gate to the king's *h*
24:4 to renovate the *h* of Jehovah
24:5 repair the *h* of your God
24:7 broken into the *h* of the true
24:7 things of the *h* of Jehovah
24:8 gate of the *h* of Jehovah
24:12 service of Jehovah's *h*, and
24:12 renovating Jehovah's *h*, and
24:12 for repairing Jehovah's *h*
24:13 *h* of the true God stand as
24:14 for the *h* of Jehovah

2Ch 24:14 in the *h* of Jehovah
24:16 with the true God and His *h*
24:18 left the *h* of Jehovah the
24:21 the courtyard of Jehovah's *h*
24:27 of the *h* of the true God
25:5 *h* of the forefathers, by
25:19 keep dwelling in your own *h*
25:24 *h* of the true God with
25:24 treasures of the king's *h*
26:19 in the *h* of Jehovah beside
26:21 dwelling in a *h* exempt
26:21 from the *h* of Jehovah
26:21 son was over the king's *h*
27:3 upper gate of Jehovah's *h*
28:21 stripped the *h* of Jehovah
28:21 *h* of the king and of the
28:24 of the true God and cut
28:24 *h* of the true God, and
28:24 doors of the *h* of Jehovah
29:3 doors of the *h* of Jehovah
29:5 sanctify the *h* of Jehovah
29:15 to cleanse the *h* of Jehovah
29:16 *h* of Jehovah to do the
29:16 of the *h* of Jehovah
29:17 sanctified the *h* of Jehovah
29:18 the whole *h* of Jehovah, the
29:20 go up to the *h* of Jehovah
29:25 at the *h* of Jehovah, with
29:31 to the *h* of Jehovah
29:35 service of the *h* of Jehovah
30:1 come to the *h* of Jehovah in
30:15 to the *h* of Jehovah
31:10 priest of the *h* of Zadok
31:10 into the *h* of Jehovah there
31:11 rooms in the *h* of Jehovah
31:13 of the *h* of the true God
31:16 coming to the *h* of Jehovah
31:17 by the *h* of their fathers
31:21 of the *h* of the true God
32:21 *h* of his god and there
33:4 altars in the *h* of Jehovah
33:5 of the *h* of Jehovah
33:7 in the *h* of the true God
33:7 In this *h* and in Jerusalem
33:15 image from the *h* of Jehovah
33:15 of the *h* of Jehovah and in
33:20 buried him at his *h*
33:24 to death in his own *h*
34:8 cleansed the land and the *h*
34:8 repair the *h* of Jehovah his
34:9 brought to the *h* of God
34:10 over the *h* of Jehovah
34:10 active in the *h* of Jehovah
34:10 mending and repairing the *h*
34:14 brought to the *h* of Jehovah
34:15 found in the *h* of Jehovah
34:17 found in the *h* of Jehovah
34:30 up to the *h* of Jehovah
34:30 found at the *h* of Jehovah
35:2 service of the *h* of Jehovah
35:3 Ark in the *h* that Solomon
35:4 by the *h* of your forefathers
35:5 the *h* of the forefathers for
35:5 paternal *h* belonging to the
35:8 leaders of the *h* of the true
35:12 classes by the paternal *h*
35:20 Josiah had prepared the *h*
35:21 against another *h* that my
36:7 utensils of the *h* of Jehovah
36:10 articles of the *h* of Jehovah
36:14 defiled the *h* of Jehovah
36:17 in the *h* of their sanctuary
36:18 of the *h* of the true God
36:18 of the *h* of Jehovah
36:19 burn the *h* of the true God
36:23 build him a *h* in Jerusalem
Ezr 1:2 to build him a *h* in Jerusalem
1:3 rebuild the *h* of Jehovah the
1:4 offering for the *h* of the true
1:5 and rebuild the *h* of Jehovah
1:7 utensils of the *h* of Jehovah
1:7 then put in the *h* of his god
2:36 Jedaiah of the *h* of Jeshua
2:59 tell the *h* of their fathers
2:68 coming to the *h* of Jehovah
2:68 the *h* of the true God
3:8 to the *h* of the true God at
3:8 the work of the *h* of Jehovah
3:9 work in the *h* of the true God
3:11 of the *h* of Jehovah
3:12 that had seen the former *h*
3:12 the foundation of this *h*
4:3 in building a *h* to our God
4:24 the work on the *h* of God

Ezr 5:2 to rebuild the *h* of God
5:3 to build this *h* and to finish
5:8 to the *h* of the great God
5:9 to build this *h* and to finish
5:11 we are rebuilding the *h* that
5:12 demolished this *h* and took
5:13 to rebuild this *h* of God
5:14 vessels of the *h* of God that
5:15 let the *h* of God be rebuilt
5:16 foundations of the *h* of God
5:17 the king's *h* of treasures
5:17 to rebuild that *h* of God in
6:1 in the *h* of the records of
6:3 the *h* of God in Jerusalem
6:3 Let the *h* be rebuilt as the
6:4 be given from the king's *h*
6:5 vessels of the *h* of God that
6:5 be deposited in the *h* of God
6:7 work on that *h* of God alone
6:7 rebuild that *h* of God upon its
6:8 for rebuilding that *h* of God
6:11 be pulled out of his *h* and
6:11 his *h* will be turned into a
6:12 and destroy that *h* of God
6:15 completed this *h* by the
6:16 inauguration of this *h* of God
6:17 inauguration of this *h* of God
6:22 the *h* of the true God
7:16 giving to the *h* of their God
7:17 altar of the *h* of your God
7:19 service of the *h* of your God
7:20 necessities of the *h* of your
7:20 the king's *h* of treasures
7:23 *h* of the God of the heavens
7:24 workers of this *h* of God
7:27 to beautify the *h* of Jehovah
8:17 for the *h* of our God
8:25 to the *h* of our God that
8:29 halls of the *h* of Jehovah
8:30 to the *h* of our God
8:33 utensils in the *h* of our God
8:36 and the *h* of the true God
9:9 to raise up the *h* of our God
10:1 before the *h* of the true God
10:6 before the *h* of the true God
10:9 the *h* of the true God
10:16 fathers for their paternal *h*
Ne 1:6 I and the *h* of my father
2:3 the *h* of the burial places of
2:8 Castle that belongs to the *h*
2:8 the *h* into which I am to enter
3:10 work in front of his own *h*
3:16 the *H* of the Mighty Ones
3:20 entrance of the *h* of Eliashib
3:21 entrance of the *h* of Eliashib
3:21 far as the end of Eliashib's *h*
3:23 work in front of their own *h*
3:23 work close by his own *h*
3:24 *h* of Azariah as far as the
3:25 goes out from the King's *H*
3:28 in front of his own *h*
3:29 work in front of his own *h*
3:31 far as the *h* of the Nethinim
4:16 behind the whole *h* of Judah
5:13 God shake out from his *h* and
6:10 entered the *h* of Shemaiah the
6:10 at the *h* of the true God
7:3 each one in front of his own *h*
7:39 Jedaiah of the *h* of Jeshua
7:61 to tell the *h* of their fathers
8:16 the *h* of the true God and in
10:32 service of the *h* of our God
10:33 the work of the *h* of our God
10:34 bring to the *h* of our God
10:34 the *h* of our forefathers
10:35 year, to the *h* of Jehovah
10:36 to the *h* of our God, to the
10:36 in the *h* of our God
10:37 halls of the *h* of our God
10:38 *h* of our God to the dining
10:38 dining halls of the supply *h*
10:39 not neglect the *h* of our God
11:11 of the *h* of the true God
11:12 doers of the work of the *h*
11:16 of the *h* of the true God
11:22 of the *h* of the true God
12:37 wall above the *H* of David
12:40 at the *h* of the true God
13:4 hall of the *h* of our God
13:7 of the *h* of the true God
13:8 furniture of Tobiah's *h*
13:9 utensils of the *h* of the true
13:11 the *h* of the true God been
13:14 the *h* of my God and the
Es 1:9 royal *h* that belonged to King
1:22 acting as prince in his own *h*
2:3 *h* of the women in charge of
2:8 the king's *h* in charge of Hegai
2:9 young women from the king's *h*
2:9 of the *h* of the women
2:11 *h* of the women to know of
2:13 *h* of the women to the king's
2:13 of the women to the king's *h*
2:14 to the second *h* of the women
2:16 King Ahasuerus at his royal *h*
4:14 as for you and your father's *h*
5:1 inner courtyard of the king's *h*
5:1 opposite the king's *h*, while
5:1 throne in the royal *h* opposite
5:1 opposite the entrance of the *h*
5:10 Haman . . . came into his *h*
6:4 outer courtyard of the king's *h*
6:12 Haman, he hurried to his *h*
7:8 to the *h* of the wine banquet
7:8 of the queen, with me in the *h*
7:9 stake . . . in Haman's *h*
8:1 the *h* of Haman, the one
8:2 Mordecai over the *h* of Haman
8:7 The *h* of Haman I have given to
9:4 was great in the king's *h* and
Job 1:4 banquet at the *h* of each one
1:10 and about his *h* and about
1:13 in the *h* of their brother the
1:18 in the *h* of their brother the
1:19 the four corners of the *h*, so
7:10 not return anymore to his *h*
8:14 whose trust is a spider's *h*
8:15 He will lean upon his *h*, but
8:17 A *h* of stones he beholds
17:13 keep waiting, Sheol is my *h*
19:15 residing as aliens in my *h*
20:19 He has snatched away a *h*
20:28 shower will roll his *h*
21:21 in his *h* after him
21:28 the *h* of the noble one
27:18 his *h* like a mere moth
30:23 *h* of meeting for everyone
38:20 the roadways to its *h*
39:6 *h* I have appointed the desert
42:11 eat bread with him in his *h*
Ps 5:7 I shall come into your *h*
23:6 dwell in the *h* of Jehovah
26:8 loved the dwelling of your *h*
27:4 may dwell in the *h* of Jehovah
30:*super* of inauguration of the *h*
31:2 A *h* of strongholds to save me
36:8 fill of the fatness of your *h*
42:4 walk . . . to the *h* of God
45:10 forget . . . your father's *h*
45:13 is all glorious within the *h*
49:16 the glory of his *h* increases
50:9 not take out of your *h* a bull
52:*super* to the *h* of Ahimelech
52:8 olive tree in God's *h*
55:14 Into the *h* of God we used to
59:*super* they kept watching the *h*
65:4 with the goodness of your *h*
66:13 into your *h* with whole burnt
68:6 solitary ones to dwell in a *h*
69:9 zeal for your *h* has eaten me
84:3 bird itself has found a *h*
84:4 are those dwelling in your *h*
84:10 threshold in the *h* of my God
92:13 planted in the *h* of Jehovah
93:5 to your own *h*, O Jehovah
98:3 to the *h* of Israel
101:2 of my heart inside my *h*
101:7 *h* no worker of trickiness
104:17 juniper trees are its *h*
112:3 and riches are in his *h*
113:9 woman to dwell in a *h*
114:1 *h* of Jacob from a people
115:10 *h* of Aaron, put your trust
115:12 will bless the *h* of Israel
115:12 will bless the *h* of Aaron
116:19 of the *h* of Jehovah
118:3 of the *h* of Aaron now say
118:26 out of the *h* of Jehovah
119:54 *h* of my alien residences
122:1 To the *h* of Jehovah let us
122:5 Thrones for the *h* of David
122:9 sake of the *h* of Jehovah our
127:1 Jehovah himself builds the *h*
128:3 innermost parts of your *h*
132:3 not go into the tent of my *h*
134:1 standing in the *h* of Jehovah
135:2 standing in the *h* of Jehovah
135:2 of the *h* of our God
Ps 135:19 *h* of Israel, do you men
135:19 *h* of Aaron, do you men
135:20 *h* of Levi, do you men bless
Pr 2:18 down to death her *h* does sink
3:33 curse of Jehovah is on the *h*
5:8 near to the entrance of her *h*
5:10 be in the *h* of a foreigner
6:31 valuables of his *h* he will
7:6 at the window of my *h*
7:8 in the way to her *h* he marches
7:11 In her *h* her feet do not keep
7:19 the husband is not in his *h*
7:20 he will come to his *h*
7:27 ways to Sheol her *h* is
9:1 True wisdom has built its *h*
9:14 entrance of her *h*, upon a seat
11:29 ostracism upon his own *h*
12:7 *h* of the righteous ones will
14:1 woman has built up her *h*
14:11 *h* of wicked people will be
15:6 In the *h* of the righteous one
15:25 *h* of the self-exalted ones
15:27 ostracism upon his own *h*
17:1 *h* full of the sacrifices of
17:13 not move away from his *h*
19:14 from fathers is a *h* and
21:9 although in a *h* in common
21:12 to the *h* of the wicked one
25:17 Make your foot rare at the *h*
25:24 although in a *h* in common
27:10 the *h* of your own brother
30:26 is where they put their *h*
Ec 4:14 gone forth from the prison *h*
5:1 you go to the *h* of the true God
7:2 to the *h* of mourning than to
7:2 than to go to the banquet *h*
7:4 ones is in the *h* of mourning
7:4 ones is in the *h* of rejoicing
10:18 of the hands the *h* leaks
12:3 the keepers of the *h* tremble
12:5 walking to his long-lasting *h*
Ca 1:17 The beams of our grand *h* are
2:4 brought me into the *h* of wine
3:4 him into my mother's *h* and
8:2 into the *h* of my mother
8:7 things of his *h* for love
Isa 2:2 mountain of the *h* of Jehovah
2:3 to the *h* of the God of Jacob
2:5 O men of the *h* of Jacob, come
2:6 your people, the *h* of Jacob
3:6 brother in the *h* of his father
3:7 my *h* there is neither bread
5:7 is the *h* of Israel, and the
5:8, 8 ones joining *h* to *h*, and
6:4 *h* itself gradually filled
7:2 made to the *h* of David
7:13 Listen, please, O *h* of David
7:17 against the *h* of your father
8:17 face from the *h* of Jacob
10:20 escaped of the *h* of Jacob
14:1 to the *h* of Jacob
14:2 *h* of Israel must take them
14:18 each one in his own *h*
15:2 He has gone up to The *H* and
22:8 of the *h* of the forest
22:15 Shebna, who is over the *h*
22:18 dishonor of the *h* of your
22:21 and to the *h* of Judah
22:22 key of the *h* of David upon
22:23 glory to the *h* of his father
22:24 glory of the *h* of his father
24:10 *h* has been shut up from
29:22 said to the *h* of Jacob
31:2 against the *h* of evildoers
37:1 came into the *h* of Jehovah
37:14 up to the *h* of Jehovah and
37:31 escape of the *h* of Judah
37:38 the *h* of Nisroch his god
38:20 at the *h* of Jehovah
38:22 go up to the *h* of Jehovah
39:2 *h* and in all his dominion
39:4 What did they see in your *h*?
39:4 Everything that is in my *h*
39:6 all that is in your own *h*
42:7 out of the *h* of detention
44:13 mankind, to sit in a *h*
46:3 Listen to me, O *h* of Jacob
46:3 ones of the *h* of Israel
48:1 Hear this, O *h* of Jacob
56:5 in my *h* and within my walls
56:7 inside my *h* of prayer
56:7 my own *h* will be called
56:7 a *h* of prayer for all the
58:1 the *h* of Jacob their sins

Isa 58:7 homeless people into your *h*
60:7 beautify my own *h* of beauty
63:7 goodness to the *h* of Israel
64:11 Our *h* of holiness and beauty
66:1 *h* that you people can build
66:20 into the *h* of Jehovah
Jer 2:4 O *h* of Jacob, and all you
2:4 families of the *h* of Israel
2:26 *h* of Israel have felt shame
3:18 *h* of Judah alongside the
3:18 alongside the *h* of Israel
3:20 O *h* of Israel, have dealt
5:7 to the *h* of a prostitute
5:11 the *h* of Israel and the
5:11 *h* of Judah have positively
5:15 from far away, O *h* of Israel
5:20 Tell this in the *h* of Jacob
7:2 the gate of the *h* of Jehovah
7:10 stand before me in this *h*
7:11 this *h* upon which my name
7:14 the *h* upon which my name
7:30 disgusting things in the *h*
9:26 all the *h* of Israel are
10:1 you people, O *h* of Israel
11:10 The *h* of Israel and the
11:10 *h* of Judah have broken my
11:15 beloved one have in my *h*
11:17 badness of the *h* of Israel
11:17 Israel and the *h* of Judah
12:7 I have left my *h;* I have
12:14 *h* of Judah I shall uproot
13:11 the whole *h* of Israel and
13:11 *h* of Judah to cling even to
16:5 the *h* of a mourners' feast
16:8 enter no *h* of banqueting
17:26 into the *h* of Jehovah
18:2 down to the *h* of the potter
18:3 down to the *h* of the potter
18:6 to you people, O *h* of Israel
18:6 in my hand, O *h* of Israel
19:14 courtyard of the *h* of
20:1 in the *h* of Jehovah
20:2 was in the *h* of Jehovah
20:6 the inhabitants of your *h*
21:12 O *h* of David, this is what
22:1 Go down to the *h* of the king
22:4 through the gates of this *h*
22:5 this *h* will become a mere
22:6 the *h* of the king of Judah
22:13 to the one building his *h*
22:14 build for myself a roomy *h*
23:8 offspring of the *h* of Israel
23:11 in my own *h* I have found
26:2 courtyard of the *h* of Jehovah
26:2 down at the *h* of Jehovah
26:6 this *h* like that in Shiloh
26:7 words in the *h* of Jehovah
26:9 is how this *h* will become
26:9 Jeremiah in the *h* of Jehovah
26:10 from the *h* of the king
26:10 to the *h* of Jehovah and
26:12 prophesy concerning this *h*
26:18 the mountain of the *H* will
27:16 utensils of the *h* of Jehovah
27:18 over in the *h* of Jehovah
27:18 the *h* of the king of Judah
27:21 over at the *h* of Jehovah
27:21 the *h* of the king of Judah
28:1 in the *h* of Jehovah
28:3 utensils of the *h* of Jehovah
28:5 standing in the *h* of Jehovah
28:6 utensils of the *h* of Jehovah
29:26 the grand overseer of the *h*
31:27 sow the *h* of Israel and
31:27 *h* of Judah with the seed
31:31 with the *h* of Israel and
31:31 *h* of Judah a new covenant
31:33 with the *h* of Israel after
32:2 *h* of the king of Judah
32:34 *h* upon which my own name
33:11 into the *h* of Jehovah, for
33:14 concerning the *h* of Israel
33:14 concerning the *h* of Judah
33:17 throne of the *h* of Israel
34:13 out of the *h* of servants
34:15 *h* upon which my name has
35:2 *h* of the Rechabites, and
35:2 *h* of Jehovah, to one of the
35:4 into the *h* of Jehovah, to
35:5 of the *h* of the Rechabites
35:7 no *h* must you build, and
36:3 *h* of Judah will listen to
36:5 enter into the *h* of Jehovah
36:6 *h* of Jehovah in the day of
Jer 36:8 at the *h* of Jehovah
36:10 at the *h* of Jehovah, in the
36:10 gate of the *h* of Jehovah
36:12 down to the *h* of the king
36:22 sitting in the winter *h*
37:4 him in the *h* of detention
37:15 into the *h* of fetters, in
37:15 the *h* of Jehonathan the
37:15 made the *h* of detention
37:16 into the *h* of the cistern
37:17 *h* in a place of concealment
37:18 into the *h* of detention
37:20 back to the *h* of Jehonathan
38:7 was in the *h* of the king
38:8 out of the *h* of the king and
38:11 into the *h* of the king to
38:14 is in the *h* of Jehovah
38:22 *h* of the king of Judah are
38:26 *h* of Jehonathan to die there
39:8 *h* of the king and the
39:14 bring him forth to his *h*
41:5 bring to the *h* of Jehovah
43:9 *h* of Pharaoh in Tahpanhes
48:13 *h* of Israel have become
51:51 places of the *h* of Jehovah
52:11 put him in the *h* of custody
52:13 burn the *h* of Jehovah and
52:13 and the *h* of the king and
52:13 every great *h* he burned
52:17 belonged to the *h* of Jehovah
52:17 was in the *h* of Jehovah
52:20 made for the *h* of Jehovah
52:31 him forth from the prison *h*
La 1:20 Within the *h* it is the same
2:7 In the *h* of Jehovah they have
Eze 2:5 for they are a rebellious *h*
2:6 for they are a rebellious *h*
2:8 like the rebellious *h*
3:1 go, speak to the *h* of Israel
3:4 in among the *h* of Israel, and
3:5 being sent—to the *h* of Israel
3:7 *h* of Israel, they will not
3:7 *h* of Israel are hardheaded and
3:9 for they are a rebellious *h*
3:17 made you to the *h* of Israel
3:24 be shut up inside your *h*
3:26 they are a rebellious *h*
3:27 they are a rebellious *h*
4:3 is a sign to the *h* of Israel
4:4 error of the *h* of Israel upon
4:5 the error of the *h* of Israel
4:6 error of the *h* of Judah forty
5:4 forth to all the *h* of Israel
6:11 of the *h* of Israel, because
8:1 I was sitting in my *h* and the
8:6 that the *h* of Israel are doing
8:10 idols of the *h* of Israel, the
8:11 ones of the *h* of Israel
8:12 *h* of Israel are doing in the
8:14 the gate of the *h* of Jehovah
8:16 *h* of Jehovah, and, look! at
8:17 light thing to the *h* of Judah
9:3 to the threshold of the *h,* and
9:6 men that were before the *h*
9:7 Defile the *h* and fill the
9:9 error of the *h* of Israel and
10:3 to the right of the *h* when
10:4 to the threshold of the *h*
10:4 *h* gradually became filled
10:18 over the threshold of the *h*
10:19 the gate of the *h* of Jehovah
11:1 gate of the *h* of Jehovah that
11:5 right thing, O *h* of Israel
11:15 all the *h* of Israel, all of
12:2 the midst of a rebellious *h*
12:2 for they are a rebellious *h*
12:3 they are a rebellious *h*
12:6 made you to the *h* of Israel
12:9 *h* of Israel, the rebellious
12:9 of Israel, the rebellious *h*
12:10 all the *h* of Israel who are
12:24 midst of the *h* of Israel
12:25 in your days, O rebellious *h*
12:27 the *h* of Israel are saying
13:5 in behalf of the *h* of Israel
13:9 register of the *h* of Israel
14:4 of the *h* of Israel that
14:5 catching the *h* of Israel by
14:6 say to the *h* of Israel, This
14:7 from the *h* of Israel or from
14:11 *h* of Israel may no more go
17:2 toward the *h* of Israel
17:12 to the rebellious *h,* Do you
18:6 idols of the *h* of Israel, and
Eze 18:15 idols of the *h* of Israel
18:25 Hear, please, O *h* of Israel
18:29 *h* of Israel will certainly
18:29 right, O *h* of Israel
18:30 judge you, O *h* of Israel
18:31 you die, O *h* of Israel
20:5 to the seed of the *h* of Jacob
20:13 the *h* of Israel, rebelled
20:27 speak to the *h* of Israel, O
20:30 say to the *h* of Israel
20:31 you people, O *h* of Israel
20:39 And you, O *h* of Israel
20:40 *h* of Israel in its entirety
20:44 dealings, O *h* of Israel
22:18 the *h* of Israel have
23:39 done in the midst of my *h*
24:3 concerning the rebellious *h*
24:21 Say to the *h* of Israel
25:3 and against the *h* of Judah
25:8 The *h* of Judah is like all
25:12 upon the *h* of Judah
27:14 From the *h* of Togarmah
28:24 to be to the *h* of Israel
28:25 together the *h* of Israel
29:6 a reed to the *h* of Israel
29:16 the *h* of Israel's confidence
29:21 sprout for the *h* of Israel
33:7 to the *h* of Israel, and at
33:10 say to the *h* of Israel
33:11 should die, O *h* of Israel
33:20 judge you, O *h* of Israel
34:30 my people, the *h* of Israel
35:15 of the *h* of Israel because
36:10 the whole *h* of Israel
36:17 *h* of Israel were dwelling
36:21 *h* of Israel have profaned
36:22 say to the *h* of Israel
36:22 doing it, O *h* of Israel
36:32 your ways, O *h* of Israel
36:37 by the *h* of Israel to do
37:11 are the whole *h* of Israel
37:16 the *h* of Israel his partners
38:6 the *h* of Togarmah, of the
39:12 *h* of Israel will have to
39:22 the *h* of Israel will have
39:23 the *h* of Israel, went into
39:25 upon all the *h* of Israel
39:29 spirit upon the *h* of Israel
40:4 Tell . . . to the *h* of Israel
40:5 outside the *h* all round about
40:45 of the obligation of the *h*
40:47 the altar was before the *h*
40:48 into the porch of the *h*
41:5 measure the wall of the *h*
41:5 all around the *h* it was
41:6 wall that belonged to the *h*
41:6 held in in the wall of the *h*
41:7 winding passage of the *h* was
41:7 upward all around the *h*
41:7 a widening to the *h* upward
41:8 a high platform for the *h*
41:9 that belonged to the *h*
41:10 round about the *h,* all
41:13 the *h,* a hundred cubits in
41:14 width of the front of the *h*
41:17 and as far as the inner *h*
41:17 inner *h* and on the outside
41:19 carved on the whole *h* all
41:26 the side chambers of the *h*
42:15 measurements of the inner *h*
43:4 into the *H* by way of the
43:5 *H* had become full of the
43:6 speaking to me out of the *H*
43:7 *h* of Israel, defile my holy
43:10 inform the *h* of Israel about
43:10 inform . . . about the *H*
43:11 the ground plan of the *H*
43:12 This is the law of the *H*
43:12 This is the law of the *H*
43:21 appointed place of the *H*
44:4 north gate to before the *H*
44:4 had filled the *h* of Jehovah
44:5 statutes of the *h* of Jehovah
44:5 entryway of the *H* with all
44:6 to the *h* of Israel, This is
44:6 O *h* of Israel
44:7 to profane it, even my *h*
44:11 over the gates of the *H*
44:11 and ministers at the *H*
44:12 became to the *h* of Israel a
44:14 the obligation of the *H,* as
44:22 offspring of the *h* of Israel
44:30 blessing to rest upon your *h*
45:5 the ministers of the *h*

Eze 45:6 To all the *h* of Israel it
45:8 give to the *h* of Israel
45:17 seasons of the *h* of Israel
45:17 behalf of the *h* of Israel
45:19 upon the doorpost of the *H*
45:20 make atonement for the *H*
46:24 ministers of the *H* boil
47:1 to the entrance of the *H*, and
47:1 under the threshold of the *H*
47:1 front of the *H* was east
47:1 right-hand side of the *H*
48:21 sanctuary of the *H* must
Da 1:2 of the *h* of the true God, so
1:2 Shinar to the *h* of his god
2:17 Daniel went to his own *h*
3:29 *h* should be turned into a
4:4 to be at ease in my *h* and
4:30 built for the royal *h* with
5:3 temple of the *h* of God that
5:23 even the vessels of his *h*; and
6:10 entered into his *h*, and, the
Ho 1:4 Jezreel against the *h* of Jehu
1:4 royal rule of the *h* of Israel
1:6 mercy again to the *h* of Israel
1:7 *h* of Judah I shall show mercy
5:1 pay attention, O *h* of Israel
5:1 O *h* of the king, give ear
5:12 rottenness to the *h* of Judah
5:14 young lion to the *h* of Judah
6:10 In the *h* of Israel I have seen
8:1 eagle against the *h* of Jehovah
9:4 not come into the *h* of Jehovah
9:8 animosity in the *h* of his God
9:15 away from my own *h*
10:14 Shalman of the *h* of Arbel
11:12 deception the *h* of Israel
Joe 1:9 cut off from the *h* of Jehovah
1:13 from the *h* of your God grain
1:14 to the *h* of Jehovah your God
1:16 from the *h* of our God
3:18 out of the *h* of Jehovah
Am 1:4 a fire onto the *h* of Hazael
2:8 drink at the *h* of their gods
3:13 witness in the *h* of Jacob
3:15 strike down the winter *h*
3:15 in addition to the summer *h*
5:1 as a dirge, O *h* of Israel
5:3 ten left, for the *h* of Israel
5:4 *h* of Israel, Search for me
5:6 just like fire, O *h* of Joseph
5:19 he went into the *h* and
5:25 forty years, O *h* of Israel
6:1 the *h* of Israel have come
6:9 be left remaining in one *h*
6:10 the bones from the *h*
6:10 the innermost parts of the *h*
6:11 strike down the great *h* into
6:11 and the small *h* into debris
6:14 against you, O *h* of Israel
7:9 against the *h* of Jeroboam
7:10 right inside the *h* of Israel
7:13 and it is the *h* of a kingdom
7:16 drop against the *h* of Isaac
9:8 annihilate the *h* of Jacob
9:9 I will jiggle the *h* of Israel
Ob 17 *h* of Jacob must take possession
18 the *h* of Jacob must become a
18 and the *h* of Joseph a flame
18 and the *h* of Esau as stubble
18 no survivor to the *h* of Esau
Mic 1:5 the sins of the *h* of Israel
1:10 In the *h* of Aphrah wallow
2:7 being said, O *h* of Jacob
2:9 you drive out from the *h* in
3:1 commanders of the *h* of
3:9 head ones of the *h* of Jacob
3:9 commanders . . . *h* of Israel
3:12 the mountain of the *h* will
4:1 mountain of the *h* of Jehovah
4:2 to the *h* of the God of Jacob
6:4 from the *h* of slaves I
6:10 in the *h* of a wicked one
6:16 the work of the *h* of Ahab
Na 1:14 Out of the *h* of your gods I
Hab 2:9 making evil gain for his *h*
2:10 something shameful to your *h*
3:13 the *h* of the wicked one
Zep 1:9 the *h* of their masters
2:7 ones of the *h* of Judah
Hag 1:2 the time of the *h* of Jehovah
1:4 houses, while this *h* is waste
1:8 lumber. And build the *h*
1:9 you have brought it into the *h*
1:9 reason of my *h* that is waste

Hag 1:9 one in behalf of his own *h*
1:14 work in the *h* of Jehovah of
2:3 this *h* in its former glory
2:7 I will fill this *h* with glory
2:9 the glory of this later *h*
Zec 1:16 My own *h* will be built in
3:7 you that will judge my *h*
4:9 laid the foundation of this *h*
5:4 enter into the *h* of the thief
5:4 into the *h* of the one making
5:4 lodge in the midst of his *h*
5:11 a *h* in the land of Shinar
6:10 come into the *h* of Josiah
7:3 belonged to the *h* of Jehovah
8:9 foundation of the *h* of Jehovah
8:13 O *h* of Judah and
8:13 of Judah and *h* of Israel
8:15 and with the *h* of Judah
8:19 *h* of Judah an exultation
9:8 encamp as an outpost for my *h*
10:3 his drove, the *h* of Judah
10:6 make the *h* of Judah superior
10:6 *h* of Joseph I shall save
11:13 treasury at the *h* of Jehovah
12:4 upon the *h* of Judah I shall
12:7 the beauty of the *h* of David
12:8 the *h* of David like God, like
12:10 pour out upon the *h* of David
12:12 family of the *h* of David by
12:12 family of the *h* of Nathan
12:13 family of the *h* of Levi by
13:1 to the *h* of David and to the
13:6 the *h* of my intense lovers
14:20 pots in the *h* of Jehovah
14:21 in the *h* of Jehovah of
Mal 3:10 may come to be food in my *h*
Mt 2:11 they went into the *h* they
5:15 shines upon all . . . in the *h*
7:24 his *h* upon the rock-mass
7:25 and lashed against that *h*
7:26 who built his *h* upon the sand
7:27 and struck against that *h* and
8:6 laid up in the *h* with
8:14 on coming into Peter's *h*
9:10 at the table in the *h*
9:23 he came into the ruler's *h*
9:28 After he had gone into the *h*
10:6 lost sheep of the *h* of Israel
10:12 you are entering into the *h*
10:13 if the *h* is deserving, let
10:14 on going out of that *h* or
12:4 he entered into the *h* of God
12:25 or *h* divided against itself
12:29 invade the *h* of a strong man
12:29 then he will plunder his *h*
12:44 I will go back to my *h* out
13:1 Jesus, having left the *h*, was
13:36 he went into the *h*. And his
13:57 unhonored . . . in his own *h*
15:24 lost sheep . . . *h* of Israel
17:25 when he entered the *h* Jesus
21:13 My *h* will be called a
21:13 will be called a *h* of prayer
23:38 Your *h* is abandoned to you
24:17 take the goods out of his *h*
24:18 not return to the *h* to pick
24:43 his *h* to be broken into
26:6 in the *h* of Simon the leper
26:58 with the *h* attendants to see
Mr 2:15 at the table in his *h*, and
2:26 he entered into the *h* of God
3:19 And he went into a *h*
3:25 *h* . . . divided against itself
3:25 *h* will not be able to stand
3:27 into the *h* of a strong man
3:27 then he will plunder his *h*
5:38 *h* of the presiding officer of
6:4 his relatives and in his own *h*
7:17 a *h* away from the crowd
7:24 And he entered into a *h* and
9:28 after he entered into a *h*
9:33 when he was inside the *h*
10:10 in the *h* the disciples
10:29 No one has left *h* or
11:17 My *h* will be called a
11:17 be called a *h* of prayer
13:15 take anything out of his *h*
13:34 left his *h* and gave the
13:35 master of the *h* is coming
14:3 at Bethany in the *h* of Simon
14:54 with the *h* attendants and
Lu 1:27 Joseph of David's *h*; and the
1:33 king over the *h* of Jacob
1:69 in the *h* of David his servant

Lu 2:4 of the *h* and family of David
2:49 be in the *h* of my Father
5:29 feast for him in his *h*
6:4 he entered into the *h* of God
6:48 like a man building a *h*
6:48 river dashed against that *h*
6:49 a *h* upon the ground without a
6:49 ruin of that *h* became great
7:6 he was not far from the *h*
7:10 on getting back to the *h*
7:36 into the *h* of the Pharisee
7:37 in the *h* of the Pharisee
7:44 I entered into your *h*; you
8:41 him to enter into his *h*
8:51 When he reached the *h* he did
10:5 Wherever you enter into a *h*
10:5 May this *h* have peace
10:7 stay in that *h*, eating and
10:7, 7 transferring from *h* to *h*
10:38 as guest into the *h*
11:17 a *h* divided against itself
11:24 I will return to my *h* out of
11:51 between the altar and the *h*
12:39 let his *h* be broken into
12:52 be five in one *h* divided
13:35 Your *h* is abandoned to you
14:1 *h* of a certain one of the
14:23 that my *h* may be filled
15:8 light a lamp and sweep her *h*
15:25 he came and got near the *h*
16:2 can no longer manage the *h*
16:13 No *h* servant can be a slave
16:27 him to the *h* of my father
17:31 movable things are in the *h*
18:29 no one who has left *h* or
19:5 today I must stay in your *h*
19:9 salvation has come to this *h*
19:46, 46 *h* will be a *h* of prayer
22:10 Follow him into the *h* into
22:11 say to the landlord of the *h*
22:54 into the *h* of the high priest
Joh 2:16 the *h* of my Father a
2:16 a *h* of merchandise
2:17 The zeal for your *h* will eat
11:31 with her in the *h* and that
12:3 *h* became filled with the
14:2 *h* of my Father there are
16:32 each one to his own *h* and
Ac 2:2 filled the whole *h* in which
2:36 the *h* of Israel know for a
5:42, 42 and from *h* to *h* they
7:10 govern Egypt and his whole *h*
7:42 was it, O *h* of Israel?
7:47 Solomon built a *h* for him
7:49 What sort of *h* will you
8:3 Invading one *h* after another
9:11 at the *h* of Judas look for
9:17 entered into the *h*, and he
10:6 who has a *h* by the sea
10:7 called two of his *h* servants
10:17 made inquiries for Simon's *h*
10:22 for you to come to his *h*
10:30 I was praying in my *h* at
10:32 in the *h* of Simon, a tanner
11:3 the *h* of men that were not
11:11 standing at the *h* in which
11:12 into the *h* of the man
11:13 angel stand in his *h* and say
12:12 *h* of Mary the mother of John
16:15 enter into my *h* and stay
16:32 with all those in his *h*
16:34 he brought them into his *h*
17:5 they assaulted the *h* of Jason
18:7 the *h* of a man named Titius
18:7 *h* was adjoining the synagogue
19:16 fled naked . . . out of that *h*
20:20, 20 publicly and from *h* to *h*
21:8 *h* of Philip the evangelizer
28:30 years in his own hired *h*
Ro 14:4 judge the *h* servant of another
16:5 that is in their *h*. Greet my
1Co 1:11 by those of the *h* of Chloe
16:2 at his own *h* set something
16:19 congregation . . . in their *h*
2Co 5:1 if our earthly *h*, this tent
5:1 a *h* not made with hands
5:2 in this dwelling *h* we do
Col 4:15 to the congregation at her *h*
2Ti 2:20 in a large *h* there are
Phm 2 congregation that is in your *h*
Heb 3:2 in all the *h* of that One
3:3 has more honor than the *h*
3:4 every *h* is constructed by
3:5 in all the *h* of that One as

Heb 3:6 Son over the *h* of that One
3:6 We are the *h* of that One, if we
8:8 conclude with the *h* of Israel
8:8 with the *h* of Judah a new
8:10 with the *h* of Israel after
10:21 priest over the *h* of God
1Pe 2:5 being built up a spiritual *h*
2:18 *h* servants be in subjection
4:17 to start with the *h* of God
Re 3:20 I will come into his *h* and

Household

Ge 7:1 Go, you and all your *h*, into
12:17 touched Pharaoh and his *h*
14:14 slaves born in his *h*, and
15:3 son of my *h* is succeeding me
17:23 the men of the *h* of Abraham
17:27 all the men of his *h*, anyone
18:19 his *h* after him so that they
24:2 the oldest one of his *h*
24:28 telling the *h* of her mother
35:2 Jacob said to his *h* and to all
46:31 to his father's *h*: Let me
46:31 my father's *h* who were in
47:12 the entire *h* of his father
50:4 Joseph spoke to Pharaoh's *h*
50:7 the older men of his *h* and
50:8 Joseph's *h* and his brothers
50:8 and the *h* of his father
Ex 1:1 each man and his *h* came
12:4 the *h* proves to be too small
Le 18:9 born in the same *h* or born
Nu 18:31 you and your *h*, because it is
De 6:22 Pharaoh and upon all his *h*
14:26 rejoice, you and your *h*
15:16 he does love you and your *h*
15:20 eat it . . . you and your *h*
25:9 not build up his brother's *h*
26:11 God has given you and your *h*
Jos 2:12 toward the *h* of my father
2:18 all the *h* of your father you
6:25 the *h* of her father and all
7:14, 14 will come near, *h* by *h*
7:14 the *h* that Jehovah will pick
7:18 he had his *h* come near
24:15 and my *h*, we shall serve
Jg 4:17 the *h* of Heber the Kenite
6:27 he feared the *h* of his father
8:27 snare to Gideon and to his *h*
8:35 the *h* of Jerubbaal, Gideon, in
9:16 toward Jerubbaal and his *h*
9:18 against the *h* of my father
9:19 toward Jerubbaal and his *h*
11:2 no inheritance in the *h* of our
16:31 *h* of his father came on down
18:25 and the soul of your *h*
1Sa 1:21 went up with all his *h* to
20:15 my *h* to time indefinite
25:6 *h* be well and all that you
27:3 each one with his *h*, David
2Sa 2:3 brought up, each with his *h*
6:11 Obed-edom and all his *h*
6:20 to bless his own *h*, and
6:21 your father and all his *h*
15:16 with all his *h* at his feet
16:2 for the *h* of the king to ride
17:23 he gave commands to his *h*
19:18 conduct the *h* of the king
19:28 all the *h* of my father
19:41 bring the king and his *h*
21:4 with Saul and his *h*
23:5 my *h* like that with God
1Ki 4:6 Ahishar was over the *h* and
4:7 king and his *h* with food
5:9 by giving the food for my *h*
5:11 as food supplies for his *h*
13:34 the *h* of Jeroboam and an
16:9 was over the *h* in Tirzah
17:15 him and her *h*, for days
18:3 Obadiah, who was over the *h*
2Ki 8:1 you with your *h*, and reside
8:2 and went, she with her *h*
18:18 who was over the *h*, and
18:37 Eliakim . . . was over the *h*
19:2 who was over the *h*
20:1 Give commands to your *h*
1Ch 4:38 and the *h* itself of their
13:14 with the *h* of Obed-edom
13:14 blessing the *h* of Obed-edom
2Ch 21:13 the *h* of your father
28:7 leader of the *h* and
Es 1:8 for every great man of his *h*
4:13 that the king's *h* will escape
Ps 105:21 set him as master to his *h*
Pr 24:3 By wisdom a *h* will be built
24:27 must also build up your *h*
27:27 for the food of your *h*, and
31:15 gives food to her *h* and the
31:21 She does not fear for her *h*
31:21 *h* are clothed with double
31:27 over the goings on of her *h*
Ec 2:7 I came to have sons of the *h*
Isa 36:3 who was over the *h*, and
36:22 who was over the *h*, and
37:2 Eliakim, who was over the *h*
38:1 Give commands to your *h*
Jer 2:14 or a slave born in the *h*
12:6 the *h* of your own father
21:11 the *h* of the king of Judah
23:34 that man and upon his *h*
35:3 all the *h* of the Rechabites
35:18 to the *h* of the Rechabites
38:17 *h* will certainly keep
Mic 2:2 able-bodied man and his *h*
7:6 enemies are the men of his *h*
Mt 10:12 into the house, greet the *h*
10:25 they call those of his *h* so
10:36 be persons of his own *h*
Lu 9:61 good-bye to those in my *h*
Joh 4:53 and his whole *h* believed
8:35 not remain in the *h* forever
Ac 10:2 together with all his *h*, and
11:14 all your *h* may get saved
16:15 she and her *h* got baptized
16:31 get saved, you and your *h*
16:34 with all his *h* now that he
18:8 so did all his *h*. And many
Ro 16:10 from the *h* of Aristobulus
16:11 from the *h* of Narcissus
1Co 1:16 baptized the *h* of Stephanas
16:15 the *h* of Stephanas is the
Eph 2:19 members of the *h* of God
Php 4:22 those of the *h* of Caesar
1Ti 3:4 man presiding over his own *h*
3:5 how to preside over his own *h*
3:15 conduct yourself in God's *h*
5:4 godly devotion in their own *h*
5:8 who are members of his *h*
5:14 widows . . . to manage a *h*
2Ti 1:16 to the *h* of Onesiphorus
4:19 and the *h* of Onesiphorus
Heb 11:7 ark for the saving of his *h*

Householder

Mt 10:25 have called the *h* Beelzebub
13:27 slaves of the *h* came up and
13:52 like a man, a *h*, who brings
20:1 a *h*, who went out early in
20:11 to murmur against the *h*
21:33 a *h*, who planted a vineyard
24:43 if the *h* had known in what
Mr 14:14 say to the *h*, The Teacher
Lu 12:39 if the *h* had known at what
13:25 the *h* has got up and locked
14:21 *h* became wrathful and said

Households

Ge 45:18 take your father and your *h*
Nu 16:32 swallow up them and their *h*
De 11:6 swallow them up and their *h*
12:7 rejoice . . . you and your *h*
1Ti 3:12 presiding . . . their own *h*
2Ti 3:6 slyly work their way into *h*
Tit 1:11 subverting entire *h* by

Houses

Ge 34:29 plundered all . . . in the *h*
42:19 for the famine in your *h*
42:33 the famine in your *h*
47:24 for those who are in your *h*
Ex 8:9 frogs off from you and your *h*
8:11 your *h* and your servants and
8:13 began to die off from the *h*
8:21 and into your *h* the gadfly
8:21 the gadfly; and the *h* of Egypt
8:24 and the *h* of his servants and
9:20 livestock to flee into the *h*
10:6, 6 your *h* and the *h* of all
10:6 *h* of all Egypt will be filled
12:7 *h* in which they will eat it
12:13 sign upon the *h* where you
12:15 away sour dough from your *h*
12:19 no sour dough . . . in your *h*
12:23 enter into your *h* to plague
12:27 who passed over the *h* of the
12:27 but he delivered our *h*
Le 25:31 *h* of settlements that have
25:32 *h* of the cities of their
25:33 *h* of the cities of the
Nu 32:18 We shall not return to our *h*
De 6:11 *h* full of all good things and
8:12 build good *h* and indeed
19:1 in their cities and their *h*
Jos 9:12 provisions out of our *h* on
Jg 18:14 are in these *h* an ephod and
18:22 the *h* that were close by the
1Sa 31:9 inform the *h* of their idols
1Ki 9:10 Solomon built the two *h*
13:32 all the *h* of the high places
20:6 and the *h* of your servants
2Ki 23:7 the *h* of the male temple
23:19 all the *h* of the high places
25:9 and all the *h* of Jerusalem
1Ch 8:6 *h* of forefathers belonging to
8:10 heads of the *h* of forefathers
8:13 heads of the *h* of forefathers
8:28 These were heads of the *h* of
15:1 building *h* for himself in
24:4 as heads for their paternal *h*
24:4 as heads for their paternal *h*
24:30 Levites by their paternal *h*
24:31 paternal *h* of the priests
24:31 As respects paternal *h*, the
26:13 by their paternal *h*, for the
26:21 the paternal *h* belonging to
26:26 the heads of the paternal *h*
26:32 heads of the paternal *h*
27:1 the heads of the paternal *h*
28:11 of the porch and of its *h*
29:4 coating the walls of the *h*
29:6 the princes of the paternal *h*
2Ch 1:2 the heads of the paternal *h*
5:2 chieftains of the paternal *h*
19:8 of the paternal *h* of Israel
23:2 of the paternal *h* of Israel
26:12 heads of the paternal *h*
34:11 *h* that the kings of Judah
Ezr 2:68 the heads of the paternal *h*
3:12 the heads of the paternal *h*
4:2 the heads of the paternal *h*
4:3 the paternal *h* of Israel
8:1 the heads of their paternal *h*
Ne 5:3 *h* we are giving as security
5:11 their olive groves and their *h*
7:4 and there were no *h* built
7:70 the heads of the paternal *h*
7:71 the heads of the paternal *h*
9:25 *h* full of all good things
11:13 brothers, heads of paternal *h*
12:12 the heads of the paternal *h*
12:22 as heads of paternal *h*
12:23 as heads of the paternal *h*
Job 3:15 who fill their *h* with silver
4:19 those dwelling in *h* of clay
15:28 *h* in which people will not
21:9 Their *h* are peace itself
22:18 filled their *h* with good
24:16 darkness he has dug into *h*
Ps 49:11 *h* may be to time indefinite
Pr 1:13 us fill our *h* with spoil
Ec 2:4 I built *h* for myself
Isa 3:14 afflicted one is in your *h*
3:20 and the *h* of the soul and
5:9 many *h*, though great and
6:11 *h* be without earthling man
8:14 to both the *h* of Israel, as
13:16 *h* will be pillaged, and
13:21 *h* must be filled with eagle
22:10 *h* of Jerusalem you will
22:10 pull down the *h* to make
32:13 all the *h* of exultation
42:22 and in the *h* of detention
65:21 build *h* and have occupancy
Jer 5:27 their *h* are full of deception
6:12 their *h* will certainly be
18:22 cry be heard out of their *h*
19:13 the *h* of Jerusalem and the
19:13 the *h* of the kings of Judah
19:13 the *h* upon the roofs of
29:5 Build *h* and inhabit them
29:28 Build *h* and inhabit them
32:15 *H* and fields and vineyards
32:29 *h* upon the roofs of which
33:4 the *h* of this city and
33:4 *h* of the kings of Judah
35:9 *h* for us to dwell in, so
39:8 *h* of the people the Chaldeans
43:12 *h* of the gods of Egypt
43:13 *h* of the gods of Egypt he
52:13 all the *h* of Jerusalem
La 5:2 our *h* to foreigners
Eze 7:24 take possession of their *h*
11:3 building of *h* close at hand
16:41 must burn your *h* with fire

Eze 23:47 their *h* they will burn
26:12 *h* they will pull down
28:26 build *h* and plant vineyards
33:30 in the entrances of the *h*
45:4 prove to be a place for *h*
46:24 *h* of those doing the boiling
Da 2:5 privies your own *h* will be
Ho 11:11 make them dwell in their *h*
Joe 2:9 On the *h* they go up
Am 3:15 the *h* of ivory will have to
3:15 *h* will have to come to their
5:11 *h* of hewn stone you have
Mic 1:14 The *h* of Achzib were as
2:2 also *h*, and have taken them
Zep 1:13 their *h* for a desolate waste
1:13 build *h*, but they will not
2:7 In the *h* of Ashkelon, in the
Hag 1:4 to dwell in your paneled *h*
Zec 14:2 and the *h* be pillaged, and
Mt 11:8 are in the *h* of kings
19:29 everyone that has left *h* or
Mr 10:30 *h* and brothers and sisters
12:40 the *h* of the widows and for
Lu 7:25 in luxury are in royal *h*
20:47 devour the *h* of the widows
Ac 4:34 possessors of fields or *h*
7:48 Most High does not dwell in *h*
1Co 11:22 you do have *h* for eating and
1Ti 5:13 gadding about to the *h*

Housetop
1Sa 9:25 speaking with Saul on the *h*
9:26 call to Saul on the *h*, saying
Mt 24:17 man on the *h* not come down
Mr 13:15 man on the *h* not come down
Lu 17:31 the person that is on the *h*
Ac 10:9 Peter went up to the *h* about

Housetops
Mt 10:27 preach from the *h*
Lu 12:3 will be preached from the *h*

Hovers
De 32:11 *H* over its fledglings

How
Ge 6:15 this is *h* you will make it
25:27 a man knowing *h* to hunt
26:9 *h* is it that you said, She is
27:20 *H* is it that you have been
28:17 *H* fear-inspiring this place
30:29 know *h* I have served you
30:29 *h* your herd has fared with
39:9 *h* could I commit this great
43:7 *H* could we know for certain
44:8 *H*, then, could we steal
44:16 And *h* can we prove ourselves
44:34 *h* can I go up to my father
47:8 *H* many are the days of the
Ex 2:2 saw *h* good-looking he was
2:18 *H* is it you have come home
6:12 *h* will Pharaoh ever listen to
6:30 *h* will Pharaoh ever listen to
10:2 *h* severely I have dealt with
10:3 *H* long must you refuse to
10:7 *H* long will this man prove to
16:28 *H* long must you people
18:1 *h* Jehovah had brought Israel
18:7 *h* the other was getting along
28:11 is *h* you will make them
36:1 to know *h* to do all the work
Nu 11:5 *H* we remember the fish that
14:11 *H* long will this people
14:11 *h* long will they not put
14:27 *H* long will this evil
23:8 *H* could I execrate those whom
23:8 *h* could I denounce those whom
24:5 *H* good-looking are your tents
24:22 *H* long will it be till
De 1:12 *H* can I carry by myself the
1:31 *h* Jehovah your God carried you
7:17 *H* shall I be able to drive
9:7 *h* you have provoked Jehovah
12:30 *H* was it these nations used
18:21 *H* shall we know the word
25:18 *h* he met you in the way and
29:16 well know *h* we dwelt
29:16 *h* we passed through the
31:27 then *h* much more so after
32:30 *H* could one pursue a
Jos 2:10 heard *h* Jehovah dried up the
9:7 So *h* could we conclude a
18:3 *H* long are you going to be
Jg 7:17 that is *h* you should do
16:15 *H* dare you say, I do love you
18:7 saw *h* the people that were
Jg 18:8 *H* was it with you?
18:15 ask *h* he was getting along
18:24 *H* . . . is it that you can say
20:3 *H* has this bad thing been
Ru 2:10 *H* is it I have found favor in
2:11 *h* you proceeded to leave your
3:18 *h* the matter will turn out
1Sa 1:14 *H* long will you behave drunk?
2:22 *h* they would lie down with
10:27 *H* will this one save us?
14:29 *h* my eyes have beamed
14:30 *H* much more so if the
16:1 *h* long will you be mourning
16:2 But Samuel said: *H* can I go?
16:18 I have seen *h* a son of Jesse
21:5 And *h* much more so today
23:3 *h* much more so in case we
24:10 *h* Jehovah gave you today
28:9 *h* he cut off the spirit
30:21 to ask them *h* they were
2Sa 1:4 *H* did the matter turn out?
1:5 *H* do you really know that
1:14 *H* was it that you did not
1:19 *H* have the mighty men fallen!
1:25 *H* have the mighty ones
1:27 *H* have the mighty ones
2:22 *H*, then, could I raise my
2:26 *H* long, then, will it be
4:11 *h* much more so when wicked
6:9 *H* will the ark of Jehovah
6:20 *H* glorious the king of Israel
11:7 David began to ask *h* Joab
11:7 *h* the people were getting
11:7 *h* the war was getting along
12:18 *h* can we say to him, The
16:11 and *h* much more now a
1Ki 3:7 I do not know *h* to go out and
3:7 to go out and *h* to come in
5:6 no one knowing *h* to cut trees
8:27 *h* much less, then, this
12:6 *H* are you advising to reply
14:5 is *h* you should speak to her
14:19 Jeroboam, *h* he warred and
14:19 he warred and *h* he reigned
18:13 *h* I kept some of the
18:21 *H* long will you be limping
19:1 *h* he had killed all the
20:18 alive is *h* you should seize
21:29 seen *h* Ahab has humbled
22:16 For *h* many times am I
22:45 and *h* he warred, are they
2Ki 3:10 *H* unfortunate that Jehovah
4:43 *H* shall I put this before a
5:7 see *h* he is seeking a quarrel
5:13 *H* much more, then, since he
6:32 *h* this son of a murderer has
8:5 *h* he had revived the dead one
10:4 *h* shall we ourselves stand?
13:12 *h* he fought against Amaziah
14:15 *h* he fought against Amaziah
14:28 mightiness, *h* he fought and
14:28 *h* he restored Damascus and
17:28 *h* they ought to fear Jehovah
18:24 *H*, then, could you turn
20:3 *h* I have walked before you
20:20 *h* he made the pool and the
1Ch 12:32 *h* to discern the times to
13:12 *H* shall I bring the ark of
2Ch 2:7 knowing *h* to cut engravings
6:18 *h* much less, then, this house
10:6 *H* are you advising to reply
18:15 For *h* many times am I
19:9 *h* you should do in the fear
19:10 *h* you should do that you
32:15 *H* much less, then, will
33:19 *h* his entreaty was granted
Ne 2:6 *H* long will your journey come
2:13 *h* they were broken down and
2:17 *h* Jerusalem is devastated and
2:18 *h* it was good upon me
9:33 faithfully is *h* you have acted
13:24 knowing *h* to speak Jewish
Es 5:11 *h* he had exalted him over the
6:9 *h* it is done to the man in
6:11 *h* it is done to the man in
8:6 *h* can I bear it when I must
8:6 *h* can I bear it when I must
Job 4:19 *H* much more so with those
6:27 *H* much more will you cast
8:2 *H* long will you keep uttering
9:2 *h* can . . . man be in the right
9:14 *H* much more so in case I
15:16 *H* much less so when one is
18:2 *H* long will you people be at
Job 19:2 *H* long will you men keep
21:15 *h* do we benefit ourselves
21:17 *H* many times is the lamp
21:17 And *h* many times does their
21:17 *H* many times in his anger
21:34 So *h* vainly you men try to
25:4 *h* can mortal man be in the
25:4 *h* can one born of a woman be
25:6 *H* much less so mortal man
26:2 *h* much help you have been to
26:2 *h* you have saved an arm that
26:3 *H* much you have advised one
31:1 *h* could I show myself
32:22 *h* I can bestow a title
35:14 *H* much less, then, when you
37:17 *H* your garments are hot
Ps 4:2 *h* long must my glory be for
6:3 And you, O Jehovah—*h* long?
8:1 *h* majestic your name is in all
8:9 *h* majestic your name is in all
11:1 *H* dare you men say to my soul
13:1 *H* long, O Jehovah, will you
13:1 *H* long will you conceal your
13:2 *H* long shall I set resistance
13:2 *H* long will my enemy be
21:1 *h* very joyful he wants to be
25:19 See *h* many my enemies have
31:19 *H* abundant your goodness is
35:17 *h* long will you keep seeing
36:7 *H* precious your
39:4 I may know *h* transient I am
46:8 *H* he has set astonishing
58:2 *H* much, rather, do you with
62:3 *H* long will you carry on
66:3 *H* fear-inspiring your works
73:11 *H* has God come to know?
73:19 *h* they have become an object
73:19 *H* they have reached their
74:9 one with us knowing *h* long
74:10 *H* long, O God, will the
78:40 *H* often they would rebel
78:43 *H* he put his signs in Egypt
78:44 *h* he began changing to blood
79:5 *H* long, O Jehovah, will you
79:5 *H* long will your ardor burn
80:4 *h* long must you fume against
82:2 *H* long will you keep on
89:51 *H* your enemies have
89:51 *H* they have reproached the
90:12 *h* to count our days in such
90:13 Jehovah! *H* long will it be?
92:5 *H* great your works are, O
94:3 *H* long are the wicked
94:3 *H* long are the wicked
104:24 *H* many your works are, O
107:25 *H* he says the word and
119:9 *H* will a young man cleanse
119:84 *H* many are the days of your
119:97 *H* I do love your law!
119:103 *H* smooth to my palate your
128:4 *h* the able-bodied man will
132:2 *H* he swore to Jehovah
132:2 *H* he vowed to the Powerful
133:1, 1 *H* good and *h* pleasant it
137:4 *H* can we sing the song of
139:17 *h* precious your thoughts
139:17 God, *h* much does the grand
Pr 1:22 *H* long will you inexperienced
1:22 *h* long must you ridiculers
1:22 *h* long will you stupid ones
5:12 *H* I have hated discipline and
6:9 *H* long, you lazy one, will you
6:35 *h* large you make the present
11:31 *H* much more should the
15:11 *H* much more so the hearts of
15:23 its right time is O *h* good
16:16 wisdom is O *h* much better
17:7 *H* much less so for a noble
19:7 *H* much farther have his
19:10 *H* much less for a servant to
20:24 *h* can he discern his way?
21:27 *H* much more so when one
30:13 eyes have become O *h* lofty!
Ec 2:16 and *h* will the wise one die?
4:10 *h* will it be with just the
4:11 but *h* can just one keep warm?
4:15 *h* it goes with the child, who
6:8 knowing *h* to walk in front of
8:7 just *h* it will come to be
8:10 *h* they came in and
8:10 *h* they would go away from
8:17 *h* mankind are not able to
10:15 know *h* to go to the city
10:16 *H* will it be with you, O

Ca 4:10 *H* beautiful your expressions
4:10 *H* much better your
5:3 robe. *H* can I put it back on?
5:3 my feet. *H* can I soil them?
5:9 *H* is your dear one more than
5:9 *H* is your dear one more than
7:1 *H* beautiful your steps have
7:6 *H* beautiful you are, and
7:6 *h* pleasant you are, O beloved
Isa 1:21 O *h* the faithful town has
6:11 I said: *H* long, O Jehovah?
7:15 *h* to reject the bad and
7:16 *h* to reject the bad and
8:4 *h* to call out, My father!
14:4 *H* has the one driving others
14:12 *h* you have fallen from
14:12 *H* you have been cut down to
19:11 *H* will you men say to
20:6 *h* our looked-for hope is
20:6 *h* shall we ourselves escape?
36:9 *H*, then, could you turn back
38:3 *h* I have walked before you
48:11 *h* could one let oneself be
50:4 know *h* to answer the tired
52:7 *H* comely upon the mountains
56:11 not known *h* to understand
Jer 1:6 do not know *h* to speak, for I
2:21 So *h* have you been changed
2:23 *H* can you say, I have not
3:19 *h* I proceeded to place you
4:14 *H* long will your erroneous
4:21 *H* long shall I keep seeing
5:7 *H* can I forgive you for this
5:13 *h* it will be done to them
6:15 even *h* to feel humiliated
8:8 *H* can you men say: We are
8:12 even *h* to feel humiliated
9:7 *h* otherwise shall I act on
9:19 *H* we have been despoiled!
9:19 *H* much we have felt shame!
12:4 *H* long should the land keep
12:5 *h*, then, can you run a race
12:5 *h* will you act among the
13:27 clean—after *h* much longer
19:12 *h* I shall do to this place
22:23 *h* you will certainly sigh
23:26 *H* long will it exist in the
26:9 is *h* this house will become
31:22 *H* long will you turn this
36:17 *H* did you write all these
38:4 *h* he is weakening the hands
47:5 *h* long will you keep making
47:6 *H* long will you not stay
47:7 *H* can it stay quiet, when
48:14 *H* dare you people say: We
48:17 *h* the rod of strength has
48:39 *h* she has become terrified!
48:39 *h* Moab has turned the back!
49:25 *H* is it that the city of
50:23 O *h* the forge hammer of all
50:23 *h* Babylon has become a mere
51:41 *h* Sheshach has been captured
51:41 *h* the Praise of the whole
51:41 *H* Babylon has become a
51:64 *h* Babylon will sink down
La 1:1 *h* she has come to sit solitary
1:1 *H* she has become like a widow
1:1 *H* she that was a princess
1:21 heard *h* I myself am sighing
2:1 *h* Jehovah in his anger beclouds
3:39 *H* can a living man indulge in
4:1 *h* the gold that shines becomes
4:1 *h* the holy stones are poured
4:2 *h* they have been reckoned as
Eze 1:5 and this was *h* they looked
1:28 *h* the appearance was of the
15:5 *H* much less so, when fire
16:30 *h* I am filled up with rage
18:30 ways is *h* I shall judge you
19:3 to learn *h* to tear apart prey
19:6 learned *h* to tear apart prey
26:17 *H* you have perished, that
33:10 *h*, then, shall we keep
40:49 steps was *h* they would go
44:2 shut is *h* it will continue
45:20 *h* you will do on the
Da 4:3 *H* grand his signs are, and
4:3 and *h* mighty his wonders are
8:13 *H* long will the vision be of
10:17 *h* was the servant of this
12:6 *H* long will it be to the end
Ho 8:5 *H* long will they be incapable
11:8 *H* can I give you up, O
11:8 *H* can I deliver you up, O
Ho 11:8 *H* can I set you as Admah?
11:8 *H* can I place you like
Joe 1:18 *h* the domestic animal has
1:18 *H* the droves of cattle have
Am 2:16 *h* he will flee in that day
3:10 not known *h* to do what is
5:12 known *h* many your revolts
5:12 *h* mighty your sins are
8:5 *H* long will it be before the
Ob 6 *H* his concealed treasures have
Jon 2:4 *H* shall I gaze again upon
Mic 2:4 *H* he removes it from me!
Hab 1:2 *H* long, O Jehovah, must I cry
1:2 *H* long shall I call to you
2:6 what is not his own—O *h* long!
Zep 2:15 *h* she has become an object
Hag 2:3 *h* are you people seeing it
2:14 That is *h* this people is
2:14 is *h* this nation is before
2:14 *h* all the work of their
Zec 1:6 that is *h* he has done with us
1:12 *h* long will you yourself
4:7, 7 *H* charming! *H* charming!
7:3 done these O *h* many years
9:17 O *h* great his goodness is
9:17 *h* great his handsomeness is!
14:15 this is *h* the scourge of the
Mt 2:5 this is *h* it has been written
5:13 *h* will its saltness be
6:23 *h* great that darkness is!
6:28 lilies . . . *h* they are growing
7:4 *h* can you say to your brother
7:5 *h* to extract the straw from
7:11 know *h* to give good gifts to
7:11 *h* much more so will your
10:19 *h* or what you are to speak
10:25 *h* much more will they call
12:4 *H* he entered into the house
12:12 *h* much more worth is a man
12:26 *h*, then, will his kingdom
12:29 Or *h* can anyone invade the
12:34 *h* can you speak good things
12:45 That is *h* it will be also
13:27 *H*, then, does it come to
13:49 That is *h* it will be in the
15:34 *H* many loaves have you?
16:3 You know *h* to interpret the
16:9 *h* many baskets you took up
16:10 *h* many provision baskets you
16:11 *H* is it you do not discern
17:17 *h* long must I continue with
17:17 *H* long must I put up with
18:21 *h* many times is my brother
21:20 *H* is it that the fig tree
22:12 *h* did you get in here not
22:43 *H*, then, is it that David by
22:45 *h* is he his son?
23:33 *h* are you to flee from the
23:37 *h* often I wanted to gather
26:54 *h* would the Scriptures be
27:13 Do you not hear *h* many
27:65 as secure as you know *h*
Mr 2:26 *H* he entered into the house
3:8 of *h* many things he was doing
3:23 *H* can Satan expel Satan?
4:13 *h* will you understand all the
4:27 just *h* he does not know
5:16 *h* this had happened to the
6:38 *H* many loaves have you?
8:5 *H* many loaves have you?
8:19 *h* many baskets full of
8:20 *h* many provision baskets full
9:12 *h* is it that it is written
9:19 *h* long must I continue with
9:19 *H* long must I put up with you?
9:21 *H* long has this been
10:23 *H* difficult a thing it
10:24 *h* difficult a thing it is
11:18 to seek *h* to destroy him
12:12 seeking *h* to seize him, but
12:26 *h* God said to him, I am the
12:35 *H* is it that the scribes
12:37 *h* does it come that he is
12:41 observing *h* the crowd was
14:1 *h* to seize him by crafty
14:11 seeking *h* to betray him
15:4 See *h* many charges they are
Lu 1:18 *H* am I to be sure of this?
1:34 *H* is this to be, since I am
1:43 *h* is it that this privilege is
6:4 *H* he entered into the house of
6:42 *H* can you say to your brother
6:42 *h* to extract the straw that
8:18 pay attention to *h* you listen
Lu 8:36 *h* the demon-possessed man had
8:47 *h* she was healed instantly
9:41 *h* long must I continue with
10:26 in the Law? *H* do you read?
11:1 Lord, teach us *h* to pray
11:13 know *h* to give good gifts to
11:13 *h* much more so will the
11:18 *h* will his kingdom stand?
12:11 anxious about *h* or what you
12:24 *h* much more worth are you
12:27 Mark well *h* the lilies grow
12:28 *h* much rather will he clothe
12:50 *h* I am being distressed
12:56 *h* to examine the outward
12:56 *h* is it you do not know
12:56 not know *h* to examine this
13:34 *h* often I wanted to gather
14:7 *h* they were choosing the most
15:17 *H* many hired men of my
16:5 *H* much are you owing my
16:7 *h* much are you owing?
18:24 *H* difficult a thing it will
20:41 *H* is it they say that the
20:44 Lord; so *h* is he his son?
21:5 temple, *h* it was adorned
21:14 *h* to make your defense
23:55 and *h* his body was laid
24:6 Recall *h* he spoke to you
24:20 *h* our chief priests and
24:35 *h* he became known to them
Joh 1:48 *H* does it come that you know
3:4 *H* can a man be born when he
3:9 *H* can these things come about?
3:12 *h* will you believe if I tell
4:9 *H* is it that you, despite
5:44 *H* can you believe, when you
5:47 *h* will you believe my
6:42 *H* is it that now he says
6:52 *H* can this man give us his
7:15 *H* does this man have a
8:33 *H* is it you say, You will
9:10 *H*, then, were your eyes
9:15 asking him *h* he gained sight
9:16 *H* can a man that is a sinner
9:19 *H*, then, is it he sees at
9:21 *h* it is he now sees we do
9:26 *H* did he open your eyes?
10:24 *H* long are you to keep our
12:34 *h* is it you say that the
14:5 *H* do we know the way?
14:9 *H* is it you say, Show us the
19:12 seeking *h* to release him
Ac 2:8 *h* is it we are hearing, each
8:31 *h* could I ever do so, unless
9:13 *h* many injurious things he
9:16 *h* many things he must suffer
9:27 *h* on the road he had seen the
9:27 *h* in Damascus he had spoken
10:28 *h* unlawful it is for a Jew
10:38 *h* God anointed him with holy
11:13 *h* he saw the angel stand in
11:16 *h* he used to say, John, for
12:17 *h* Jehovah brought him out
15:14 *h* God for the first time
15:36 return . . . to see *h* they are
19:26 hear *h* not only in Ephesus
20:18 *h* from the first day that I
21:20 You behold, brother, *h* many
Ro 1:9 *h* without ceasing I always
3:6 *H*, otherwise, will God judge
6:2 *h* shall we keep on living any
10:14 *h* will they call on him in
10:14 *H*, in turn, will they put
10:14 *H*, in turn, will they hear
10:15 *H*, in turn, will they preach
10:15 *H* comely are the feet of
11:12 *h* much more will the full
11:24 *h* much rather will these
11:33 *H* unsearchable his judgments
1Co 3:10 keep watching *h* he is
7:16 wife, *h* do you know but that
7:16 husband, *h* do you know but
7:32 *h* he may gain the Lord's
7:33 *h* he may gain the approval
7:34 *h* she may gain the approval
14:7 *h* will it be known what is
14:9 *h* will it be known what is
14:16 *h* will the man occupying
15:12 *h* is it some among you say
15:35 *H* are the dead to be raised
2Co 1:20 *h* many the promises of God
7:15 *h* you received him with
Ga 2:14 *h* is it that you are
4:9 *h* is it that you are turning

Eph 3:9 men see *h* the sacred secret
4:7 according to *h* the Christ
5:15 *h* you walk is not as unwise
6:21 affairs, as to *h* I am doing
Php 1:8 *h* I am yearning for all of you
2:23 have seen *h* things stand
4:12 *h* to be low on provisions
4:12 *h* to have an abundance
4:12 secret of both *h* to be full
4:12 to be full and *h* to hunger
4:12 *h* to have an abundance and
4:12 and *h* to suffer want
Col 2:1 realize *h* great a struggle I
4:6 *h* you ought to give an answer
1Th 1:9 *h* you turned to God from your
2:1 *h* our visit to you has not
2:2 but *h*, after we had first
2:10 *h* loyal and righteous and
2:11 *h*, as a father does his
4:1 on *h* you ought to walk and
4:4 *h* to get possession of his
1Ti 3:5 not know *h* to preside over
3:5 *h* will he take care of God's
3:15 know *h* you ought to conduct
Phm 16 *h* much more so to you both
Heb 2:3 *h* shall we escape if we have
7:4 *h* great this man was to
9:14 *h* much more will the blood
10:29 Of *h* much more severe a
13:7 *h* their conduct turns out
Jas 3:5 *H* little a fire it takes to
4:17 knows *h* to do what is right
2Pe 2:9 *h* to deliver people of godly
1Jo 4:6 This is *h* we take note of the
4:11 if this is *h* God loved us
4:17 This is *h* love has been made
Jude 18 *h* they used to say to you
Re 3:3 of *h* you have received and
3:3 *h* you heard, and go on keeping
9:17 *h* I saw the horses in the
17:8 *h* the wild beast was, but is

Howl
Isa 13:6 *H*, you people, for the day
13:22 jackals must *h* in her
14:31 *H*, O gate! Cry out, O city!
16:7 Moab will *h* for Moab; even
16:7 Moab; even all of it will *h*
23:1 *H*, you ships of Tarshish!
23:6 *h*, you inhabitants of the
23:14 *H*, you ships of Tarshish
65:14 will *h* because of sheer
Jer 4:8 Beat your breasts and *h*
25:34 *H*, you shepherds, and cry
47:2 dwelling in the land must *h*
48:20 *H* and cry out. Tell in
48:31 is over Moab that I shall *h*
48:39 *H*, you people! O how Moab
49:3 *H*, O Heshbon, for Ai has been
51:8 *H* over her, you people
Eze 21:12 Cry out and *h*, O son of man
30:2 *H*, you people, Alas for the
Joe 1:5 *h*, all you wine drinkers, on
1:13 *H*, you ministers of the
Mic 1:8 I will wail and *h*; I will
Zep 1:11 *H*, you inhabitants of
Zec 11:2 *H*, O juniper tree, for the
11:2 *H*, you massive trees of

Howled
Joe 1:11 vinedressers have *h*, on

Howling
De 32:10 And in an empty, *h* desert
Isa 15:8 *h* thereof is clear to Eglaim
15:8 *h* . . . is clear to Beer-elim
34:14 meet up with *h* animals
52:5 ones ruling over them kept *h*
Jer 25:36 the *h* of the majestic ones
50:39 dwell with the *h* animals
Ho 7:14 they kept *h* on their beds
Am 8:3 actually be a *h* in that day
Zep 1:10 a *h* from the second quarter
Zec 11:3 *h* of shepherds, for their
Jas 5:1 *h* over your miseries that are

Howls
Isa 15:2 over Medeba Moab itself *h*
15:3 everyone thereof *h*, going

Hubbub
Isa 32:14 *h* of the city has been

Hubs
1Ki 7:33 their spokes and their *h*

Huddle
Job 30:7 they would *h* together

Hug
Job 24:8 they have to *h* a rock

Huge
Da 7:3 four *h* beasts were coming up
7:17 *h* beasts, because they are
Mt 12:40 in the belly of the *h* fish

Hukkok
Jos 19:34 went out from there to *H*

Hukok
1Ch 6:75 *H* with its pasture grounds

Hul
Ge 10:23 sons of Aram were Uz and *H*
1Ch 1:17 *H* and Gether and Mash

Huldah
2Ki 22:14 *H* the prophetess the wife
2Ch 34:22 *H* the prophetess, the wife

Human
Nu 9:6 unclean by a *h* soul so that
9:7 We are unclean by a *h* soul
19:11 the corpse of any *h* soul
31:35 *h* souls from the women who
31:40 And the *h* souls were sixteen
31:46 and *h* souls, sixteen thousand
2Ki 23:14 their places with *h* bones
23:20 burned *h* bones upon them
1Ch 5:21 *h* souls a hundred thousand
Ps 105:14 allow any *h* to defraud them
Ac 17:25 attended to by *h* hands as if
27:3 treated Paul with *h* kindness
28:2 us extraordinary *h* kindness
Ro 6:19 I am speaking in *h* terms
1Co 2:13 words taught by *h* wisdom
4:3 by you or by a *h* tribunal
9:8 speaking these things by *h*
2Co 4:2 *h* conscience in the sight of
Ga 1:11 good news is not something *h*
3:15 with a *h* illustration
Heb 9:16 death of the *h* covenanter
9:17 the *h* covenanter is living
1Pe 2:13 to every *h* creation: whether
Re 18:13 and slaves and *h* souls

Humankind
Nu 16:32 all *h* that belonged to Korah
31:26 captives both of *h* and of
31:28 of *h* and of the herd and of
31:30 of *h*, of the herd, of the
31:47 of *h* and of domestic animals
Jos 11:14 all *h* that they struck with
Ps 49:2 You sons of *h* as well as you
Eze 36:10 will multiply upon you *h*
36:11 multiply upon you *h* and
36:12 will cause *h* to walk
36:13 A devourer of *h* is what
36:14 *h* you will no more devour
Jas 3:7 and has been tamed by *h*

Humans
Nu 31:11 booty in the way of *h* and
Ac 14:11 The gods have become like *h*
14:15 We also are *h* having the

Humble
Ge 16:9 and *h* yourself under her hand
De 8:2 in order to *h* you, to put you
8:16 to *h* you and in order to put
2Sa 22:28 the *h* people you will save
1Ch 17:10 I . . . *h* all your enemies
2Ch 7:14 *h* themselves and pray and
33:23 not *h* himself because of
36:12 not *h* himself on account
Ezr 8:21 to *h* ourselves before our God
Job 30:11 and proceeded to *h* me
40:12 every one haughty, *h* him
Ps 76:12 will *h* the spirit of leaders
138:6 and yet the *h* one he sees
Pr 6:3 *h* yourself and storm your
29:23 haughtiness . . . will *h* him
29:23 *h* in spirit will take hold
Zep 3:12 a people *h* and lowly, and
Zec 9:9 *h*, and riding upon an ass
Mt 18:4 *h* himself like this young
Jas 4:6 kindness to the *h* ones
4:10 *H* yourselves in the eyes of
1Pe 3:8 compassionate, *h* in mind
5:5 undeserved kindness to the *h*
5:6 *H* yourselves, therefore, under

Humbled
Le 26:41 heart will be *h*, and at that
De 8:3 he *h* you and let you go hungry
1Ki 21:29 how Ahab has *h* himself on
21:29 *h* himself because of me
2Ki 22:19 you *h* yourself because of
2Ch 12:6 and the king *h* themselves
12:7 that they had *h* themselves
12:7 They have *h* themselves
12:12 And because he *h* himself
13:18 Israel were *h* at that time
28:19 Jehovah *h* Judah on account
30:11 from Zebulun *h* themselves
32:26 Hezekiah *h* himself for the
33:19 images before he *h* himself
33:23 Manasseh his father *h*
34:27 *h* yourself because of God
34:27 *h* yourself before me and
La 5:11 The wives in Zion they have *h*
Da 5:22 you have not *h* your heart
Mt 23:12 exalts himself will be *h*
Lu 14:11 exalts himself will be *h*
Php 2:8 as a man, he *h* himself and

Humbles
Mt 23:12 whoever *h* himself will be
Lu 14:11 *h* himself will be exalted
18:14 *h* himself will be exalted

Humbling
2Ch 33:12 *h* himself greatly because
Da 10:12 *h* yourself before your God
2Co 11:7 I commit a sin by *h* myself

Humiliate
Ge 16:6 Sarai began to *h* her so that
2Sa 13:12 Do not *h* me; for it is not
1Ki 11:39 *h* the offspring of David
Da 4:37 in pride he is able to *h*
7:24 and three kings he will *h*
2Co 12:21 God might *h* me among you

Humiliated
Nu 12:14 she not be *h* seven days
De 21:14 after you have *h* her
22:24 that he *h* the wife of his
22:29 due to the fact that he *h* her
Ru 1:21 it is Jehovah that has *h* me
1Sa 20:34 his own father had *h* him
2Sa 10:5 men . . . feeling very *h*
13:14 *h* her and lay down with her
13:22 he had *h* Tamar his sister
13:32 that he *h* Tamar his sister
1Ch 19:5 had become men very much *h*
2Ch 30:15 themselves had been *h*, so
Ps 35:4 May those be shamed and *h*
40:14 May those turn back and be *h*
69:6 those seeking you not be *h*
70:2 be *h* who are taking
74:21 crushed one not return *h*
Isa 41:11 become ashamed and be *h*
45:16 ashamed and even be *h*
45:17 *h* for the indefinite times
50:7 I shall not have to feel *h*
54:4 do not feel *h*, for you will
Jer 3:3 You have refused to feel *h*
6:15 to know even how to feel *h*
8:12 know even how to feel *h*
22:22 feel *h* because of all your
31:19 I also felt *h*, for I had
Eze 16:27 *h* on account of your way
16:54 you must feel *h* owing to
16:61 and feel *h* when you receive
22:10 they have *h* in you
22:11 a man has *h* in you
43:10 *h* because of their errors
43:11 feel *h* because of all that
Lu 18:14 exalts himself will be *h*
Php 3:21 will refashion our *h* body

Humiliates
Pr 25:8 your fellowman now *h* you
28:7 with gluttons *h* his father

Humiliating
Ps 44:9 have cast off and keep *h* us
Isa 50:6 not conceal from *h* things
Eze 36:15 cause no further *h* talk
Da 5:19 happened to want to, he was *h*

Humiliation
Ezr 9:5 I stood up from my *h*, with
Job 22:29 *h* when you speak arrogantly
Ps 35:26 clothed with shame and *h*
44:15 my *h* is in front of me
69:7 *H* has covered my face
69:19 and my shame and my *h*
71:13 with reproach and *h* who are
109:29 be clothed with *h*
Pr 18:13 on his part and a *h*
Isa 30:3 of Egypt a cause for *h*
45:16 in *h* the manufacturers of
61:7 instead of *h* they will cry

Jer 3:25 our *h* keeps covering us
20:11 Their indefinitely lasting *h*
23:40 *h* to time indefinite, which
51:51 *H* has covered our faces
Eze 16:52 You also, bear your *h* when
16:52 be ashamed and bear your *h*
16:54 that you may bear your *h*
16:63 because of your *h*, when I
32:24 bear their *h* with those
32:25 bear their *h* with those
32:30 and will bear their *h*
34:29 bear the *h* by the nations
36:6 *h* by nations is what you
36:7 will bear their own *h*
36:32 Be ashamed and feel *h*
39:26 will have borne their *h* and
44:13 they must bear their *h* and
Ac 8:33 During his *h* the judgment
Jas 1:10 and the rich one over his *h*

Humiliations
Ps 132:1 concerning David All his *h*
Mic 2:6 *H* will not move away

Humility
2Sa 22:36 your *h* that makes me great
Ps 18:35 own *h* will make me great
45:4 in the cause of truth and *h*
Pr 15:33 and before glory there is *h*
18:12 and before glory there is *h*
22:4 result of *h* and the fear of
Col 2:18 takes delight in a mock *h*
2:23 form of worship and mock *h*

Humming
Isa 3:20 and the ornamental *h* shells

Humps
Isa 30:6 *h* of camels their supplies

Humtah
Jos 15:54 and *H* and Kiriath-arba

Hunchback
Le 21:20 *h* or thin or diseased in his

Hundred
Ge 5:3 Adam . . . a *h* and thirty years
5:4 Seth came to be eight *h* years
5:5 Adam . . . nine *h* and thirty
5:6 Seth lived on for a *h* and five
5:7 Seth . . . eight *h* and seven years
5:8 Seth . . . nine *h* and twelve
5:10 Enosh . . . eight *h* and fifteen
5:11 Enosh . . . nine *h* and five
5:13 Kenan . . . eight *h* and forty
5:14 Kenan . . . nine *h* and ten
5:16 eight *h* and thirty years
5:17 eight *h* and ninety-five years
5:18 Jared . . . a *h* and sixty-two
5:19 Jared . . . eight *h* years
5:20 Jared . . . nine *h* and sixty-two
5:22 Enoch . . . three *h* years
5:23 three *h* and sixty-five years
5:25 a *h* and eighty-seven years
5:26 seven *h* and eighty-two years
5:27 nine *h* and sixty-nine years
5:28 Lamech lived on for a *h* and
5:30 five *h* and ninety-five years
5:31 seven *h* and seventy-seven
5:32 Noah got to be five *h* years
6:3 amount to a *h* and twenty years
6:15 make it: three *h* cubits the
7:6 Noah was six *h* years old when
7:24 a *h* and fifty days
8:3 the end of a *h* and fifty days
8:13 in the six *h* and first year
9:28 three *h* and fifty years after
9:29 nine *h* and fifty years and he
11:10 Shem was a *h* years old when
11:11 to live five *h* years
11:13 live four *h* and three years
11:15 live four *h* and three years
11:17 four *h* and thirty years
11:19 live two *h* and nine years
11:21 live two *h* and seven years
11:23 to live two *h* years
11:25 live a *h* and nineteen years
11:32 Terah . . . two *h* and five years
14:14 three *h* and eighteen slaves
15:13 afflict . . . four *h* years
17:17 Will a man a *h* years old
21:5 Abraham was a *h* years old
23:1 *h* and twenty-seven years long
23:15 plot worth four *h* silver
23:16 four *h* silver shekels
25:7 a *h* and seventy-five years
25:17 a *h* and thirty-seven years
Ge 26:12 getting up to a *h* measures
32:6 and four *h* men with him
32:14 two *h* she-goats and twenty
32:14 two *h* female sheep and
33:1 and with him four *h* men
33:19 for a *h* pieces of money
35:28 to be a *h* and eighty years
45:22 gave three *h* silver pieces
47:9 a *h* and thirty years. Few and
47:28 a *h* and forty-seven years
50:22 Joseph lived for a *h* and ten
50:26 the age of a *h* and ten years
Ex 6:16 a *h* and thirty-seven years
6:18 a *h* and thirty-three years
6:20 a *h* and thirty-seven years
12:37 six *h* thousand able-bodied
12:40 was four *h* and thirty years
12:41 the four *h* and thirty years
14:7 to take six *h* chosen chariots
27:9 a *h* cubits being the length
27:11 for a *h* cubits of length
27:18 courtyard is a *h* cubits, and
30:23 five *h* units, and sweet
30:23 two *h* and fifty units, and
30:23 two *h* and fifty units
30:24 five *h* units by the shekel
38:9 twisted linen, for a *h* cubits
38:11 side there were a *h* cubits
38:24 seven *h* and thirty shekels by
38:25 a *h* talents and one thousand
38:25 one thousand seven *h* and
38:26 amounting to six *h* and three
38:26 thousand five *h* and fifty
38:27 a *h* talents of silver went
38:27 A *h* socket pedestals equaled
38:27 pedestals equaled a *h* talents
38:28 the thousand seven *h* and
38:29 two thousand four *h* shekels
Le 26:8 five . . . certainly chase a *h*
26:8 a *h* of you will chase
Nu 1:21 forty-six thousand five *h*
1:23 fifty-nine thousand three *h*
1:25 forty-five thousand six *h*
1:27 seventy-four thousand six *h*
1:29 fifty-four thousand four *h*
1:31 fifty-seven thousand four *h*
1:33 forty thousand five *h*
1:35 thirty-two thousand two *h*
1:37 thirty-five thousand four *h*
1:39 sixty-two thousand seven *h*
1:41 forty-one thousand five *h*
1:43 fifty-three thousand four *h*
1:46 six *h* and three thousand
1:46 thousand five *h* and fifty
2:4 seventy-four thousand six *h*
2:6 fifty-four thousand four *h*
2:8 fifty-seven thousand four *h*
2:9 one *h* eighty-six thousand four
2:9 eighty-six thousand four *h*
2:11 forty-six thousand five *h*
2:13 fifty-nine thousand three *h*
2:15 forty-five thousand six *h* and
2:16 one *h* and fifty-one thousand
2:16 thousand four *h* and fifty
2:19 forty thousand five *h*
2:21 thirty-two thousand two *h*
2:23 thirty-five thousand four *h*
2:24 one *h* and eight thousand one
2:24 and eight thousand one *h*
2:26 sixty-two thousand seven *h*
2:28 forty-one thousand five *h*
2:30 fifty-three thousand four *h*
2:31 one *h* fifty-seven thousand
2:31 fifty-seven thousand six *h*
2:32 six *h* and three thousand five
2:32 three thousand five *h* and
3:22 were seven thousand five *h*
3:28 eight thousand six *h*
3:34 were six thousand two *h*
3:43 twenty-two thousand two *h* and
3:46 the two *h* and seventy-three
3:50 thousand three *h* and
4:36 two thousand seven *h* and fifty
4:40 two thousand six *h* and thirty
4:44 three thousand two *h*
4:48 thousand five *h* and eighty
7:13 weight being a *h* and thirty
7:19 a *h* and thirty shekels, one
7:25 a *h* and thirty shekels, one
7:31 a *h* and thirty shekels, one
7:37 *h* and thirty shekels, one
7:43 a *h* and thirty shekels, one
7:49 a *h* and thirty shekels, one
7:55 *h* and thirty shekels, one
Nu 7:61 being a *h* and thirty shekels
7:67 being a *h* and thirty shekels
7:73 being a *h* and thirty shekels
7:79 being a *h* and thirty shekels
7:85 a *h* and thirty shekels to
7:85 two thousand four *h* shekels
7:86 being a *h* and twenty shekels
11:21 six *h* thousand men on foot
16:2 two *h* and fifty men of the
16:17 two *h* and fifty fire holders
16:35 consume the two *h* and fifty
16:49 fourteen thousand seven *h*
26:7 thousand seven *h* and thirty
26:10 consumed two *h* and fifty
26:14 twenty-two thousand two *h*
26:18 Gad . . . forty thousand five *h*
26:22 seventy-six thousand five *h*
26:25 sixty-four thousand three *h*
26:27 sixty thousand five *h*
26:34 fifty-two thousand seven *h*
26:37 thirty-two thousand five *h*
26:41 forty-five thousand six *h*
26:43 sixty-four thousand four *h*
26:47 fifty-three thousand four *h*
26:50 forty-five thousand four *h*
26:51 six *h* and one thousand seven
26:51 thousand seven *h* and thirty
31:28 one soul out of five *h*, of
31:32 to six *h* and seventy-five
31:36 three *h* and thirty-seven
31:36 thirty-seven thousand five *h*
31:37 six *h* and seventy-five
31:39 were thirty thousand five *h*
31:43 to three *h* and thirty-seven
31:43 thirty-seven thousand five *h*
31:45 asses, thirty thousand five *h*
31:52 sixteen thousand seven *h* and
33:39 a *h* and twenty-three years
De 22:19 fine him a *h* silver shekels
31:2 A *h* and twenty years old I am
34:7 a *h* and twenty years old at
Jos 7:21 two *h* shekels of silver and
24:29 Joshua . . . a *h* and ten
24:32 for a *h* pieces of money
Jg 2:8 the age of a *h* and ten years
3:31 Philistines, six *h* men, with
4:3 he had nine *h* war chariots
4:13 the nine *h* war chariots with
7:6 to be three *h* men. As for all
7:7 By the three *h* men who did the
7:8 kept hold of the three *h* men
7:16 he divided the three *h* men up
7:19 the *h* men who were with him
7:22 the three *h* continued to blow
8:4 three *h* men that were with
8:10 a *h* and twenty thousand men
8:26 one thousand seven *h* gold
11:26 dwelling . . . for three *h* years
15:4 to catch three *h* foxes and to
16:5 one thousand one *h* silver
17:2 thousand one *h* silver pieces
17:3 the thousand one *h* pieces of
17:4 took two *h* silver pieces and
18:11 Then six *h* men girded with
18:16 six *h* men girded with their
18:17 the six *h* men girded with
20:2 four *h* thousand men on foot
20:10 ten men out of a *h* of all
20:10 and a *h* out of a thousand
20:15 seven *h* chosen men were
20:16 were seven *h* chosen men
20:17 four *h* thousand men drawing
20:35 twenty-five thousand one *h*
20:47 six *h* men turned and went
21:12 four *h* girls, virgins, that
1Sa 11:8 amounted to three *h* thousand
13:15 with him, about six *h* men
14:2 with him were about six *h*
15:4 two *h* thousand men on foot
17:7 was six *h* shekels of iron
18:25 but in a *h* foreskins of the
18:27 the Philistines two *h* men
22:2 with him about four *h* men
23:13 six *h* men, and they went
25:13 about four *h* men, while two
25:13 two *h* sat by the baggage
25:18 two *h* loaves of bread and
25:18 *h* cakes of raisins and two
25:18 two *h* cakes of pressed figs
27:2 six *h* men that were with
30:9 six *h* men that were with
30:10 he and four *h* men, but two
30:10 two *h* men that were too
30:17 four *h* young men that rode

1Sa 30:21 two *h* men who had been too
2Sa 2:31 three *h* and sixty men that
3:14 for a *h* foreskins of the
8:4 one thousand seven *h* horsemen
8:4 *h* chariot horses of them
10:18 seven *h* charioteers and
14:26 two *h* shekels by the royal
15:11 two *h* men from Jerusalem
15:18 six *h* men that had followed
16:1 two *h* loaves of bread and a
16:1 a *h* cakes of raisins and a
16:1 a *h* loads of summer fruit
21:16 three *h* shekels of copper
23:8 eight *h* slain at one time
23:18 over three *h* slain ones
24:3 add to the people a *h* times
24:9 eight *h* thousand valiant men
24:9 were five *h* thousand men
1Ki 4:23 *h* sheep, besides some stags
5:16 three thousand three *h*
6:1 the four *h* and eightieth year
7:2 a *h* cubits in its length
7:20 two *h* pomegranates in rows
7:42 four *h* pomegranates for the
8:63 *h* and twenty thousand sheep
9:14 a *h* and twenty talents of
9:23 five *h* and fifty, the
9:28 four *h* and twenty talents
10:10 a *h* and twenty talents of
10:14 six *h* and sixty-six talents
10:16 make two *h* large shields
10:16 six *h* shekels of gold he
10:17 three *h* bucklers of alloyed
10:26 a thousand four *h* chariots
10:29 for six *h* silver pieces
10:29 a horse for a *h* and fifty
11:3 came to have seven *h* wives
11:3 and three *h* concubines
12:21 a *h* and eighty thousand
18:4 to take a *h* prophets and keep
18:13 *h* men by fifties in a cave
18:19 four *h* and fifty prophets
18:19 the four *h* prophets of the
18:22 are four *h* and fifty men
20:15 two *h* and thirty-two
20:29 a *h* thousand men on foot in
22:6 about four *h* men, and said
2Ki 3:4 a *h* thousand lambs and a
3:4 *h* thousand unshorn male sheep
3:26 took with him seven *h* men
4:43 put this before a *h* men
14:13 corner gate, four *h* cubits
18:14 three *h* silver talents
19:35 a *h* and eighty-five thousand
23:33 a *h* silver talents and a
1Ch 4:42 to Mount Seir, five *h* men
5:18 thousand seven *h* and sixty
5:21 two *h* and fifty thousand
5:21 and human souls a *h* thousand
7:2 twenty-two thousand six *h*
7:9 was twenty thousand two *h*
7:11 seventeen thousand two *h*
8:40 and grandsons, a *h* and fifty
9:6 and six *h* and ninety brothers
9:9 were nine *h* and fifty-six
9:13 a thousand seven *h* and sixty
9:22 were two *h* and twelve
11:11 over three *h* slain at one
11:20 his spear over three *h* slain
12:14 least one was equal to a *h*
12:24 were six thousand eight *h*
12:25 were seven thousand one *h*
12:26 Levites four thousand six *h*
12:27 were three thousand seven *h*
12:30 twenty thousand eight *h*
12:32 two *h* head ones of theirs
12:35 twenty-eight thousand six *h*
12:37 a *h* and twenty thousand
15:5 of Kohath . . . a *h* and twenty
15:6 Merari . . . two *h* and twenty
15:7 Gershom . . . a *h* and thirty
15:8 sons of Elizaphan . . . two *h*
15:10 Uzziel . . . a *h* and twelve
18:4 a *h* chariot horses of them
21:3 *h* times as many as they are
21:5 a million one *h* thousand men
21:5 four *h* and seventy thousand
21:25 to the weight of six *h*
22:14 a *h* thousand talents of gold
25:7 two *h* and eighty-eight
26:30 a thousand seven *h*, were
26:32 were two thousand seven *h*
29:7 worth a *h* thousand talents
2Ch 1:14 a thousand four *h* chariots

2Ch 1:17 a chariot for six *h* silver
1:17 and a horse for a *h* and fifty
2:2 three thousand six *h*
2:17 *h* and fifty-three thousand
2:17 fifty-three thousand six *h*
2:18 and three thousand six *h*
3:4 its height was a *h* and twenty
3:8 the amount of six *h* talents
3:16 made a *h* pomegranates and
4:8 and made a *h* bowls of gold
4:13 four *h* pomegranates for the
5:12 a *h* and twenty sounding the
7:5 *h* and twenty thousand sheep
8:10 two *h* and fifty, the
8:18 four *h* and fifty talents of
9:9 *h* and twenty talents of gold
9:13 six *h* and sixty-six talents
9:15 two *h* large shields of
9:15 six *h* shekels of alloyed
9:16 three *h* bucklers of alloyed
11:1 *h* and eighty thousand choice
12:3 twelve *h* chariots and with
13:3 four *h* thousand mighty men
13:3 eight *h* thousand chosen men
13:17 five *h* thousand chosen men
14:8 three *h* thousand out of Judah
14:8 two *h* and eighty thousand
14:9 three *h* chariots, and came
15:11 seven *h* cattle and
17:11 seven thousand seven *h* rams
17:11 seven thousand seven *h*
17:14 three *h* thousand valiant
17:15 two *h* and eighty thousand
17:16 two *h* thousand valiant
17:17 two *h* thousand men equipped
17:18 *h* and eighty thousand men
18:5 four *h* men, and said to them
24:15 *h* and thirty years old at
25:5 three *h* thousand choice men
25:6 from Israel a *h* thousand
25:6 for a *h* silver talents
25:9 *h* talents that I have given
25:23 Corner Gate, four *h* cubits
26:12 was two thousand six *h*
26:13 three *h* and seven thousand
26:13 seven thousand five *h* men
27:5 *h* silver talents and ten
28:6 *h* and twenty thousand in
28:8 Israel took two *h* thousand
29:32 seventy cattle, a *h* rams
29:32 two *h* male lambs—all
29:33 six *h* cattle and three
35:8 two thousand six *h*
35:8 and three *h* cattle
35:9 and five *h* cattle
36:3 a *h* silver talents and a gold
Ezr 1:10 four *h* and ten small
1:11 were five thousand four *h*
2:3 two thousand one *h* and
2:4 three *h* and seventy-two
2:5 seven *h* and seventy-five
2:6 two thousand eight *h* and
2:7 thousand two *h* and fifty-four
2:8 nine *h* and forty-five
2:9 seven *h* and sixty
2:10 six *h* and forty-two
2:11 six *h* and twenty-three
2:12 a thousand two *h* and
2:13 six *h* and sixty-six
2:15 four *h* and fifty-four
2:17 three *h* and twenty-three
2:18 of Jorah, a *h* and twelve
2:19 two *h* and twenty-three
2:21 a *h* and twenty-three
2:23 a *h* and twenty-eight
2:25 seven *h* and forty-three
2:26 six *h* and twenty-one
2:27 a *h* and twenty-two
2:28 two *h* and twenty-three
2:30 Magbish, a *h* and fifty-six
2:31 a thousand two *h* and
2:32 three *h* and twenty
2:33 seven *h* and twenty-five
2:34 three *h* and forty-five
2:35 three thousand six *h* and
2:36 nine *h* and seventy-three
2:38 a thousand two *h* and
2:41 a *h* and twenty-eight
2:42 together, a *h* and thirty-nine
2:58 three *h* and ninety-two
2:60 six *h* and fifty-two
2:64 forty-two thousand three *h*
2:65 seven thousand three *h* and
2:65 two *h* male singers and

Ezr 2:66 seven *h* and thirty-six
2:66 mules two *h* and forty-five
2:67 four *h* and thirty-five
2:67 six thousand seven *h* and
2:69 and a *h* robes of priests
6:17, 17 a *h* bulls, two *h* rams
6:17 four *h* lambs, and as a sin
7:22 a *h* talents of silver and a
7:22 a *h* cor measures of wheat
7:22 *h* bath measures of wine
7:22 a *h* bath measures of oil
8:3 a *h* and fifty males
8:4 and with him two *h* males
8:5 and with him three *h* males
8:9 two *h* and eighteen males
8:10 a *h* and sixty males
8:12 with him a *h* and ten males
8:20 two *h* and twenty Nethinim
8:26 six *h* and fifty talents of
8:26 a *h* silver utensils worth
8:26 and gold a *h* talents
Ne 5:17 rulers, a *h* and fifty men
7:8 two thousand one *h* and
7:9 three *h* and seventy-two
7:10 six *h* and fifty-two
7:11 two thousand eight *h* and
7:12 thousand two *h* and fifty-four
7:13 eight *h* and forty-five
7:14 seven *h* and sixty
7:15 six *h* and forty-eight
7:16 six *h* and twenty-eight
7:17 two thousand three *h* and
7:18 six *h* and sixty-seven
7:20 six *h* and fifty-five
7:22 three *h* and twenty-eight
7:23 three *h* and twenty-four
7:24 of Hariph, a *h* and twelve
7:26 a *h* and eighty-eight
7:27 a *h* and twenty-eight
7:29 seven *h* and forty-three
7:30 six *h* and twenty-one
7:31 a *h* and twenty-two
7:32 a *h* and twenty-three
7:34 thousand two *h* and fifty-four
7:35 three *h* and twenty
7:36 three *h* and forty-five
7:37 seven *h* and twenty-one
7:38 three thousand nine *h* and
7:39 nine *h* and seventy-three
7:41 a thousand two *h* and
7:44 of Asaph, a *h* and forty-eight
7:45 a *h* and thirty-eight
7:60 three *h* and ninety-two
7:62 six *h* and forty-two
7:66 forty-two thousand three *h*
7:67 seven thousand three *h* and
7:67 two *h* and forty-five male
7:68 seven *h* and thirty-six
7:68 mules two *h* and forty-five
7:69 four *h* and thirty-five
7:69 six thousand seven *h* and
7:70 five *h* and thirty priests'
7:71 two thousand two *h* silver
11:6 four *h* and sixty-eight
11:8 nine *h* and twenty-eight
11:12 eight *h* and twenty-two
11:13 two *h* and forty-two
11:14 a *h* and twenty-eight
11:18 two *h* and eighty-four
11:19 a *h* and seventy-two
Es 1:1 over a *h* and twenty-seven
1:4 a *h* and eighty days
8:9 a *h* and twenty-seven
9:6 was a destroying of five *h* men
9:12 a destroying of five *h* men
9:15 kill in Shushan three *h* men
9:30 in the one *h* and twenty-seven
Job 1:3 five *h* spans of cattle and
1:3 five *h* she-asses, along with
42:16 a *h* and forty years and
Pr 17:10 striking a stupid one a *h*
Ec 6:3 become a father a *h* times, and
8:12 may be doing bad a *h* times
Ca 8:12 two *h* to those keeping its
Isa 37:36 a *h* and eighty-five thousand
65:20 although a *h* years of age
65:20 sinner, although a *h* years
Jer 52:23 one *h* upon the network
52:29 eight *h* and thirty-two
52:30 seven *h* and forty-five souls
52:30 four thousand and six *h*
Eze 4:5 three *h* and ninety days, and
4:9 three *h* and ninety days you
40:19 Outside it was a *h* cubits

Eze 40:23 gate to gate a *h* cubits
40:27 toward the south a *h* cubits
40:47 The length was a *h* cubits
40:47 the width a *h* cubits
41:13 house, a *h* cubits in length
41:13 a *h* cubits in length
41:14 area . . . was a *h* cubits
41:15 on that side, a *h* cubits
42:2 the length of a *h* cubits
42:8 the temple it was a *h* cubits
42:16 It was five *h* reeds, by
42:17 side, five *h* reeds, by the
42:18 measured, five *h* reeds
42:19 measured five *h* reeds, by
42:20 length of five *h* reeds and
42:20 width of five *h* reeds, to
45:2, 2 five *h* by five *h*, it being
45:15 two *h* from the livestock
48:16 four thousand five *h* cubits
48:16 four thousand five *h*, and
48:16 four thousand five *h*, and
48:16 border four thousand five *h*
48:17 two *h* and fifty cubits, and
48:17 south two *h* and fifty
48:17 east two *h* and fifty
48:17 west two *h* and fifty
48:30 four thousand five *h* cubits
48:32 four thousand five *h* cubits
48:33 four thousand five *h* cubits
48:34 four thousand five *h* cubits
Da 6:1 one *h* and twenty satraps, who
8:14 two thousand three *h* evenings
12:11 two *h* and ninety days
12:12 three *h* and thirty-five days
Am 5:3 thousand will have a *h* left
5:3 the one going forth with a *h*
Jon 4:11 one *h* and twenty thousand
Mt 18:12 man comes to have a *h* sheep
18:28 was owing him a *h* denarii
Mr 4:8 thirtyfold, and sixty and a *h*
4:20 thirtyfold and sixty and a *h*
6:37 buy two *h* denarii worth of
6:40 in groups of a *h* and of fifty
14:5 upward of three *h* denarii
Lu 7:41 in debt for five *h* denarii
15:4 man of you with a *h* sheep
16:6 *h* bath measures of olive oil
16:7 A *h* cor measures of wheat
Joh 6:7 Two *h* denarii worth of loaves
12:5 sold for three *h* denarii and
19:39 aloes, about a *h* pounds of
21:8 about three *h* feet away
21:11 one *h* and fifty-three
Ac 1:15 about one *h* and twenty
5:36 men, about four *h*, joined
7:6 afflict them for four *h* years
13:20 about four *h* and fifty years
23:23 Get two *h* soldiers ready to
23:23 two *h* spearmen, at the third
27:37 two *h* and seventy-six
Ro 4:19 he was about one *h* years old
1Co 15:6 five *h* brothers at one time
Ga 3:17 four *h* and thirty years
Re 7:4 a *h* and forty-four thousand
11:3 a thousand two *h* and sixty
12:6 thousand two *h* and sixty days
13:18 is six *h* and sixty-six
14:1 a *h* and forty-four thousand
14:3 the *h* and forty-four thousand
14:20 of a thousand six *h* furlongs
21:17 one *h* and forty-four cubits

Hundredfold
Mt 13:8 to yield fruit, this one a *h*
13:23 this one a *h*, that one sixty
Mr 10:30 get a *h* now in this period
Lu 8:8 it produced fruit a *h*. As he

Hundreds
Ex 18:21 chiefs over *h*, chiefs over
18:25 thousands, chiefs of *h*, chiefs
Nu 31:14 the chiefs of the *h* who were
31:48 and the chiefs of the *h*
31:52 and the chiefs of the *h*
31:54 the chiefs . . . of the *h* and
De 1:15 chiefs of *h* and chiefs of
1Sa 22:7 thousands and chiefs of *h*
29:2 passing along by *h* and by
2Sa 18:1 over them . . . chiefs of *h*
18:4 out by *h* and by thousands
2Ki 11:4 took the chiefs of *h* of the
11:9 the chiefs of *h* proceeded to
11:10 the chiefs of *h* the spears
11:15 commanded the chiefs of *h*
11:19 took the chiefs of *h* and
1Ch 13:1 with the chiefs of the . . . *h*
26:26 of the *h*, and the chiefs of
27:1 and the chiefs . . . of the *h*
28:1 and the chiefs of *h* and
29:6 chiefs of thousands and of *h*
2Ch 1:2 to the chiefs . . . of the *h*
23:1 chiefs of *h*, namely, Azariah
23:9 gave the chiefs of *h* the
23:14 chiefs of *h*, the appointed
23:20 chiefs of *h* and the lordly
25:5 chiefs of *h* for all Judah
Mt 14:24 *h* of yards away from land

Hundredth
Ge 7:11 six *h* year of Noah's life
Ne 5:11 the *h* of the money and the

Hung
Ge 40:22 chief of the bakers he *h* up
De 21:22 you have *h* him upon a stake
21:23 accursed of God is the one *h*
2Sa 18:10 Absalom *h* in a big tree
Ps 137:2 We *h* our harps
Ca 4:4 which are *h* a thousand shields
Eze 27:10 Shield and helmet they *h* up
27:11 circular shields they *h* up
Mt 18:6 *h* around his neck a millstone
Lu 23:39 one of the *h* evildoers began

Hunger
De 28:48 *h* and thirst and nakedness
32:24 Exhausted from *h* they will
1Sa 2:5 hungry actually cease to *h*
Ne 9:15 you gave them for their *h*
Job 5:22 At . . . *h* you will laugh
30:3 Because of want and *h* they
Isa 51:19 breakdown, and *h* and sword
La 5:10 because of the pangs of *h*
Lu 6:21 Happy are you who *h* now
Ro 8:35 *h* or nakedness or danger or
1Co 4:11 we continue to *h* and also to
2Co 11:27 in *h* and thirst, in
Php 4:12 how to be full and how to *h*
Re 7:16 will *h* no more nor thirst

Hungering
Mt 5:6 Happy are those *h* and

Hungrily
Eze 17:7 vine stretched its roots *h*

Hungry
De 8:3 let you go *h* and fed you with
1Sa 2:5 the *h* actually cease to hunger
2Sa 17:29 The people are *h* and tired
2Ki 7:12 well know that we are *h*
Job 5:5 he harvests the *h* one eats
22:7 the *h* one you hold back bread
24:10 *h*, they have to carry the
Ps 34:10 little on hand and gone *h*
50:12 If I were *h*, I would not say
107:5 They were *h*, also thirsty
107:9 *h* soul he has filled with
107:36 causes the *h* ones to dwell
146:7 giving bread to the *h* ones
Pr 6:30 fill his soul when he is *h*
10:3 the righteous one to go *h*
19:15 and a slack soul goes *h*
25:21 If the one hating you is *h*
27:7 to a *h* soul every bitter thing
Isa 8:21 hard pressed and *h*
8:21 because he is *h* and has made
9:20 and will certainly be *h*
29:8 someone *h* dreams and here
32:6 *h* one to go empty, and he
44:12 Also, he has become *h*
49:10 They will not go *h*, neither
58:7 your bread out to the *h* one
58:10 grant to the *h* one your
65:13 you yourselves will go *h*
Jer 42:14 for bread we shall not go *h*
Eze 18:7 *h* one he would give his own
18:16 to the *h* one he has given
Mt 4:2 fasted . . . then he felt *h*
12:1 disciples got *h* and started
12:3 and the men with him got *h*
21:18 in the morning, he got *h*
25:35 I became *h* and you gave me
25:37 we see you *h* and feed you
25:42 I became *h*, but you gave me
25:44 when did we see you *h* or
Mr 2:25 he fell in need and got *h*, he
11:12 from Bethany, he became *h*
Lu 1:53 he has fully satisfied *h* ones
4:2 were concluded, he felt *h*
6:3 and the men with him got *h*
6:25 because you will go *h*
Joh 6:35 comes to me will not get *h*
Ac 10:10 he became very *h* and wanted
Ro 12:20 your enemy is *h*, feed him
1Co 11:21 that one is *h* but another is
11:34 is *h*, let him eat at home

Hunt
Ge 25:27 a man knowing how to *h*
27:3 go out to the field and *h*
27:5 to *h* game and to bring it in
Job 10:16 you will *h* for me, And you
38:39 Can you *h* prey for a lion
Ps 140:11 let evil itself *h* him with
Jer 16:16 *h* them from every mountain
Eze 13:18 in order to *h* souls! Are the
13:18 the souls that you women *h*
13:21 something caught in the *h*
Mic 7:2 *h*, everyone his own brother
Lu 2:44 began to *h* him up among the

Hunted
Ge 27:33 *h* for game and came bringing
La 3:52 *h* for me just as for a bird
4:18 They have *h* our steps so that
Mr 1:36 those with him *h* him down

Hunter
Ge 10:9 mighty *h* in opposition to
10:9 Just like Nimrod a mighty *h*

Hunters
Jer 16:16 I shall send for many *h*

Hunting
Ge 27:30 brother came back from his *h*
Ex 4:19 men who were *h* for your soul
Le 17:13 *h* catches a wild beast or a
Job 19:6 *h* net he has closed in upon
Ps 35:4 who are *h* for my soul
66:11 have brought us into a *h* net
Ec 7:26 who is herself nets for *h* and
Eze 12:13 must be caught in my *h* net
13:20 you are *h* down the souls as
13:20 souls that you are *h* down
17:20 be caught in my *h* net
19:9 bring him by means of *h* nets
Lu 4:42 the crowds began *h* about for

Hunts
Pr 6:26 *h* even for a precious soul

Hupham
Nu 26:39 of *H* the family of the

Huphamites
Nu 26:39 of Hupham the family of the *H*

Huppah
1Ch 24:13 for *H* the thirteenth, for

Huppim
Ge 46:21 sons of Benjamin were . . . *H*
1Ch 7:12 the *H* were the sons of Ir
7:15 took a wife for *H* and for

Hur
Ex 17:10 Moses, Aaron and *H* went up
17:12 Aaron and *H* supported his
24:14 Aaron and *H* are with you
31:2 Uri the son of *H* of the tribe
35:30 *H* of the tribe of Judah
38:22 the son of Uri the son of *H*
Nu 31:8 kings of Midian . . . Zur and *H*
Jos 13:21 and Zur and *H* and Reba
1Ki 4:8 son of *H*, in the mountainous
1Ch 2:19 who in time bore *H* to him
2:20 *H*, in turn, became father to
2:50 *H* the firstborn of Ephrathah
4:1 sons of Judah were . . . *H*
4:4 *H* the firstborn of Ephrathah
2Ch 1:5 the son of Uri the son of *H*
Ne 3:9 Rephaiah the son of *H*, a prince

Hurai
1Ch 11:32 *H* from the torrent valleys

Huram
1Ch 8:5 Gera and Shephuphan and *H*

Huri
1Ch 5:14 son of *H*, the son of Jaroah

Hurl
1Sa 18:11 *h* the spear and say: I will
Job 27:22 it will *h* itself at him and
Jer 16:13 *h* you out from off this
22:26 *h* you and your mother who
Eze 32:4 the field I shall *h* you
Da 11:30 *h* denunciations against the
Jon 1:12 and *h* me into the sea
Zec 7:14 *h* them throughout all the

It 4:6 son of God, *h* yourself down
u 4:9 *h* yourself down from here
oh 8:59 they picked up stones to *h*

Iurled
os 10:11 Jehovah *h* great stones from
Ie 9:11 *h* into the depths like a stone
ob 41:9 *h* down at the mere sight of
's 37:24 he will not be *h* down
89:44 throne you have *h* to the
er 22:28 his offspring must be *h*
ze 21:12 ones *h* to the sword have
on 1:4 *h* forth a great wind at the
1:15 and *h* him into the sea
e 8:5 altar and *h* it to the earth
8:7 and it was *h* to the earth
8:8 burning with fire was *h* into
12:4 it *h* them down to the earth
12:9 down the great dragon was *h*
12:9 he was *h* down to the earth
12:9 angels were *h* down with him
12:10 *h* down, who accuses them
12:13 it was *h* down to the earth
14:19 he *h* it into the great
18:21 millstone and *h* it into the
18:21 Babylon the great city be *h*
19:20 *h* into the fiery lake that
20:3 he *h* him into the abyss and
20:10 *h* into the lake of fire and
20:14 Hades were *h* into the lake
20:15 was *h* into the lake of fire

Iurling
Sa 20:33 Saul went *h* the spear at
's 7:11 God is *h* denunciations every
sa 22:17 Jehovah is *h* you down with
22:17 down with violent *h*
a 3:53 and they kept *h* stones at me
on 1:5 *h* out the articles that were

Iurried
x 34:8 Moses at once *h* to bow low
os 4:10 people *h* up and passed over
8:19 *h* and set the city on fire
g 13:10 the woman *h* and ran and told
Sa 4:14 *h* that he might go in and
23:26 David became *h* to go away
Sa 19:16 *h* and went down with the
s 6:12 Haman, he *h* to his house
's 119:60 I *h* up, and I did not delay
sa 49:17 Your sons have *h* up
u 4:29 *h* him outside the city, and
19:6 he *h* and got down and with

Iurriedly
x 10:16 Pharaoh *h* called Moses and
Sa 15:14 Go *h*, for fear he may hurry
Ki 20:41 he *h* removed the bandage
Ki 9:13 *h* took each one his garment

Iurry
e 18:6 *H!* Get three seah measures of
19:22 *H!* Escape there, because I
43:30 Joseph was now in a *h*
45:13 must *h* and bring my father
x 32:8 turned aside in a *h* from the
Iu 16:46 go to the assembly in a *h*
e 4:26 perish in a *h* from off the
7:4 certainly annihilate you in a *h*
28:20 and have perished in a *h*
os 8:14 men of the city got in a *h*
23:16 perish in a *h* from off the
g 9:48 seen me do—*h* up, do like me
Sa 9:12 *H* now, because today he has
Sa 15:14 *h* up and actually catch up
zr 4:23 went in a *h* to Jerusalem to
's 16:4 do *h* after him
71:12 God, do *h* to my assistance
79:8 *H!* Let your mercies confront
102:2 day that I call, *h*, answer
143:7 O *h*, answer me, O Jehovah
r 6:18 are in a *h* to run to badness
c 5:2 Do not *h* yourself as regards
7:9 not *h* yourself in your spirit
8:3 not *h* yourself, that you may
sa 59:7 in a *h* to shed innocent blood
er 9:18 that they may *h* and raise up
a 2:25 Arioch, in a *h*, took Daniel
3:24 and he rose up in a *h*
6:19 *h* he went right to the lions'
u 19:5 Zacchaeus, *h* and get down
c 22:18 saying to me, *H* up and get

Hurrying
e 18:6 Abraham went *h* to the tent to
18:7 and he went *h* to get it ready
Sa 17:48 David began *h* and running

2Ki 7:15 thrown away as they were *h*
Jer 48:16 calamity is actually *h* up
Zep 1:14 near, and there is a *h* of it

Hurt
Ge 6:6 and he felt *h* at his heart
34:7 the men became *h* in their
45:5 do not feel *h* and do not be
Ex 21:22 *h* a pregnant woman and her
21:35 bull should *h* another's bull
Jos 9:19 not allowed to *h* them
1Sa 20:3 for fear he may feel *h*
20:34 had been *h* respecting David
24:9 David is seeking your *h*
2Sa 14:10 he will never *h* you again
19:2 king has felt *h* over his son
1Ki 1:6 father did not *h* his feelings
1Ch 4:10 that it may not *h* me
Ne 8:10 do not feel *h*, for the joy
8:11 day is holy; and do not feel *h*
Ps 78:40 him feel *h* in the desert
Ec 10:9 will *h* himself with them
Isa 54:6 left entirely and *h* in spirit
63:10 made his holy spirit feel *h*
Da 3:25 and there is no *h* to them
6:23 was no *h* at all found on him
Lu 10:19 will by any means do you *h*
Ac 16:28 Do not *h* yourself, for we
Re 9:10 to *h* the men five months

Hurtful
Job 4:8 those devising what is *h* And
5:6 does what is *h* go forth, And
11:11 When he sees what is *h*
11:14 what is *h* is in your hand
15:35 a giving birth to what is *h*
22:15 That *h* men have trodden
31:3 those practicing what is *h*
34:8 practicers of what is *h*
34:22 those practicing what is *h*
36:10 turn back from what is *h*
36:21 do not turn to what is *h*
Ps 5:5 those practicing what is *h*
6:8 you practicers of what is *h*
7:14 pregnant with what is *h*
10:7 are trouble and what is *h*
14:4 the practicers of what is *h*
28:3 with practicers of what is *h*
41:6 gather . . . something *h*
53:4 the practicers of what is *h*
55:3 dropping upon me what is *h*
59:2 the practicers of what is *h*
59:5 show favor to any *h* traitors
66:18 anything *h* in my heart
90:10 is on trouble and *h* things
92:7 practicers of what is *h*
92:9 practicers of what is *h* will
94:4 the practicers of what is *h*
101:8 the practicers of what is *h*
119:133 may no kind of *h* thing
125:5 the practicers of what is *h*
141:4 are practicing what is *h*
141:9 those practicing what is *h*
Pr 6:18 heart fabricating *h* schemes
10:29 the practicers of what is *h*
12:21 Nothing *h* will befall the
19:28 swallows down what is *h*
21:15 those practicing what is *h*
22:8 will reap what is *h*, but the
Isa 31:2 those practicing what is *h*
32:6 will work at what is *h*
58:9 the speaking of what is *h*
59:4 a bringing of what is *h* to
59:6 Their works are *h* works
59:7 Their thoughts are *h* thoughts
Jer 4:15 publishing something *h* from
Da 6:22 king, no *h* act have I done
Hab 1:3 you make me see what is *h*
3:7 Under what is *h* I saw the
Ac 28:6 nothing *h* happen to him
Col 3:5 *h* desire, and covetousness
1Ti 6:9 many senseless and *h* desires
Re 16:2 *h* and malignant ulcer came

Hurtfulness
Job 21:19 store up one's *h* for one's
34:36 his replies among men of *h*
Ps 36:3 The words of his mouth are *h*
36:4 *H* is what he keeps scheming
36:12 practicers of *h* have fallen
55:10 *h* and trouble are within it
56:7 On account of their *h* cast
64:2 the tumult of practicers of *h*
94:16 against the practicers of *h*
94:23 turn back upon them their *h*
Pr 6:12 a man of *h*, is walking with

Pr 17:4 attention to the lip of *h*
Eze 11:2 men that are scheming *h* and

Hurting
Ps 56:5 keep *h* my personal affairs
Lu 4:35 demon came out . . . without *h*

Husband
Ge 3:6 she gave some also to her *h*
3:16 craving will be for your *h*
16:3 gave her to Abram her *h* as
29:32 my *h* will begin to love me
29:34 this time my *h* will join
30:15 your having taken my *h*
30:18 my maidservant to my *h*
30:20 my *h* will tolerate me
Le 21:7 woman divorced from her *h*
Nu 5:13 hidden from the eyes of her *h*
5:19 while under your *h* you have
5:20 aside while under your *h*
5:20 emission, besides your *h*
5:27 unfaithfulness toward her *h*
5:29 turn aside while under her *h*
30:6 belong to a *h*, and her vow is
30:7 *h* actually hears it and keeps
30:8 if her *h* on the day of hearing
30:10 in the house of her *h* that
30:11 *h* has heard it and has kept
30:12 if her *h* has totally annulled
30:12 Her *h* has annulled them, and
30:13 her *h* should establish it or
30:13 or her *h* should annul it
30:14 her *h* absolutely keeps silent
30:16 as between a *h* and his wife
De 25:11 deliver her *h* out of the hand
28:56 her cherished *h* and her son
Jg 13:6 said to her *h*: There was a
13:9 Manoah her *h* was not with
13:10 told her *h* and said to him
14:15 Fool your *h* that he may tell
19:3 her *h* got up and went after
20:4 the *h* of the murdered woman
Ru 1:3 Elimelech the *h* of Naomi died
1:5 her two children and her *h*
1:9 each one in the house of her *h*
1:12 old to get to belong to a *h*
2:1 Naomi had a kinsman of her *h*
2:11 after the death of your *h*, and
1Sa 1:8 Elkanah her *h* proceeded to say
1:22 for she had said to her *h*
1:23 Elkanah her *h* said to her
2:19 up with her *h* to sacrifice
4:19 and her *h* had died
4:21 her father-in-law and her *h*
25:3 *h* was harsh and bad in his
25:19 her *h* Nabal she told nothing
2Sa 3:15 from her *h*, Paltiel the son
3:16 *h* kept walking with her
11:26 that Uriah her *h* had died
14:5 now that my *h* is dead
14:7 to my *h* neither a name nor
20:3 widowhood with a living *h*
2Ki 4:1 Your servant, my *h*, is dead
4:9 At length she said to her *h*
4:14 and her *h* is old
4:22 now called her *h* and said
4:26 Is it all right with your *h*?
Es 1:22 for every *h* to be continually
Pr 7:19 *h* is not in his house
Eze 16:32 instead of her own *h*
16:45 abhorring her *h* and her sons
Ho 2:2 and I am not her *h*
2:7 return to my *h*, the first one
2:16 call me My *h* and you will no
Mt 1:16 Joseph the *h* of Mary, of
1:19 Joseph her *h*, because he
Mr 10:12 after divorcing her *h*
Lu 2:36 lived with a *h* for seven
16:18 woman divorced from a *h*
Joh 4:16 call your *h* and come to this
4:17 said: I do not have a *h*
4:17 A *h* I do not have
4:18 the man . . . is not your *h*
Ac 5:9 of those who buried your *h*
5:10 buried her alongside her *h*
Ro 7:2 to her *h* while he is alive
7:2 but if her *h* dies, she is
7:2 from the law of her *h*
7:3 while her *h* is living, she
7:3 But if her *h* dies, she is free
1Co 7:2 each woman have her own *h*
7:3 *h* render to his wife her due
7:3 also do likewise to her *h*
7:4 over her own body, but her *h*
7:4 *h* does not exercise authority

1Co 7:10 should not depart from her *h*
7:11 make up again with her *h*
7:11 *h* should not leave his wife
7:13 has an unbelieving *h*, and
7:13 let her not leave her *h*
7:14 unbelieving *h* is sanctified
7:16 that you will save your *h*
7:16 *h*, how do you know but that
7:34 gain the approval of her *h*
7:39 all the time her *h* is alive
7:39 if her *h* should fall asleep
2Co 11:2 you in marriage to one *h*
Ga 4:27 those of her who has the *h*
Eph 5:23 a *h* is head of his wife as
5:33 have deep respect for her *h*
1Ti 3:2 a *h* of one wife, moderate in
5:9 a wife of one *h*
Tit 1:6 a *h* of one wife, having
Re 21:2 as a bride adorned for her *h*

Husbandly
Isa 54:1 the woman with a *h* owner
54:5 your *h* owner, Jehovah of
Jer 3:14 the *h* owner of you people
31:32 had *h* ownership of them

Husband's
De 25:7 My *h* brother has refused to
Ru 1:12 become a *h* tonight and also
1:13 so as not to become a *h*
Eze 44:25 that has not become a *h*

Husbands
Ru 1:11 they have to become your *h*
Jer 29:6 give your own daughters to *h*
44:19 without asking our *h* make
Eze 16:45 abhorred their *h* and their
Joh 4:18 For you have had five *h*
1Co 14:35 question their own *h* at
Eph 5:22 be in subjection to their *h*
5:24 let wives also be to their *h*
5:25 *H*, continue loving your
5:28 *h* ought to be loving their
Col 3:18 be in subjection to your *h*
3:19 *h*, keep on loving your wives
1Ti 3:12 be *h* of one wife, presiding
Tit 2:4 to love their *h*, to love
2:5 to their own *h*, so that the
1Pe 3:1 in subjection to your own *h*
3:5 subjecting . . . to their own *h*
3:7 You *h*, continue dwelling in

Hush
1Sa 12:3 have I accepted *h* money that
Am 5:12 you who are taking *h* money
8:3 certainly throw them out—*h!*
Mr 4:39 said to the sea: *H!* Be quiet!

Hushah
1Ch 4:4 Ezer the father of *H*

Hushai
2Sa 15:32 *H* the Archite, with his
15:37 *H*, David's companion, came
16:16 *H* the Archite, David's
16:16 *H* proceeded to say to
16:17 At this Absalom said to *H*
16:18 So *H* said to Absalom
17:5 Call, please, *H* the Archite
17:6 So *H* came in to Absalom
17:7 At this *H* said to Absalom
17:8 And *H* went on to say
17:14 The counsel of *H* the Archite
17:15 *H* said to Zadok and Abiathar
1Ki 4:16 Baana the son of *H*, in Asher
1Ch 27:33 and *H* the Archite was the

Husham
Ge 36:34 When Jobab died, *H* from the
36:35 When *H* died, Hadad son of
1Ch 1:45 *H* from the land of the
1:46 *H* died, and Hadad the son of

Hushathite
2Sa 21:18 Sibbecai the *H* struck down
23:27 Mebunnai the *H*
1Ch 11:29 Sibbecai the *H*, Ilai the
20:4 Sibbecai the *H* struck down
27:11 was Sibbecai the *H* of the

Hushim
Ge 46:23 And the sons of Dan were *H*
1Ch 7:12 the *H* were the sons of Aher
8:8 *H* and Baara were his wives
8:11 by *H* he became father to

Hut
Isa 1:8 like a lookout *h* in a field of
24:20 and fro like a lookout *h*

Huts
Isa 65:4 night even in the watch *h*

Hyacinth
Re 21:20 the eleventh *h*, the twelfth

Hyacinth-blue
Re 9:17 and *h* and sulphur-yellow

Hymenaeus
1Ti 1:20 *H* and Alexander belong to
2Ti 2:17 *H* and Philetus are of that

Hypocrisy
Mt 23:28 inside you are full of *h* and
Mr 12:15 Detecting their *h*, he said
Lu 12:1 leaven . . . which is *h*
Ro 12:9 Let your love be without *h*
2Co 6:6 by love free from *h*
1Ti 1:5 and out of faith without *h*
4:2 the *h* of men who speak lies
2Ti 1:5 the faith . . . without any *h*
1Pe 2:1 *h* and envies and all sorts of

Hypocrite
Mt 7:5 *H!* First extract the rafter
Lu 6:42 *H!* First extract the rafter

Hypocrites
Mt 6:2 as the *h* do in the synagogues
6:5 pray, you must not be as the *h*
6:16 sad-faced like the *h*, for
15:7 *h*, Isaiah aptly prophesied
22:18 do you put me to the test, *h*
23:13 scribes and Pharisees, *h*
23:15 scribes and Pharisees, *h*
23:23 scribes and Pharisees, *h*
23:25 scribes and Pharisees, *h*
23:27 scribes and Pharisees, *h*
23:29 scribes and Pharisees, *h*
24:51 his part with the *h*
Mr 7:6 aptly prophesied about you *h*
Lu 12:56 *H*, you know how to examine
13:15 *H*, does not each one of you

Hypocritical
Ho 10:2 Their heart has become *h*
Jas 3:17 partial distinctions, not *h*

Hyssop
Ex 12:22 *h* and dip it into the blood
Le 14:4 coccus scarlet material and *h*
14:6 and the *h*, and he must dip
14:49 scarlet material and *h*
14:51 the cedarwood and the *h* and
14:52 cedarwood and the *h* and the
Nu 19:6 must take cedarwood and *h* and
19:18 *h* and dip it into the water
1Ki 4:33 *h* that is coming forth on
Ps 51:7 purify me from sin with *h*
Joh 19:29 sour wine upon a *h* stalk
Heb 9:19 and *h* and sprinkled the book

Ibhar
2Sa 5:15 *I* and Elishua and Nepheg and
1Ch 3:6 *I* and Elishama and Eliphelet
14:5 and *I* and Elishua and Elpelet

Ibleam
Jos 17:11 *I* and its dependent towns
Jg 1:27 the inhabitants of *I* and its
2Ki 9:27 to Gur, which is by *I*
15:10 struck him down at *I* and

Ibneiah
1Ch 9:8 and *I* the son of Jeroham, and

Ibnijah
1Ch 9:8 the son of Reuel the son of *I*

Ibri
1Ch 24:27 Of Jaaziah . . . Zaccur and *I*

Ibsam
1Ch 7:2 sons of Tola . . . Jahmai and *I*

Ibzan
Jg 12:8 And *I* from Bethlehem began to
12:10 *I* died and was buried in

Ice
Job 6:16 They are dark from *i*, Upon
37:10 By the breath of God the *i*
38:29 does the *i* actually come
Ps 147:17 throwing his *i* like morsels
Eze 1:22 the sparkle of awesome *i*

Ichabod
1Sa 4:21 But she called the boy *I*
14:3 *I*, the son of Phinehas, the

Iconium
Ac 13:51 against them and went to *I*
14:1 in *I* they entered together
14:19 arrived from Antioch and *I*
14:21 returned to Lystra and to *I*
16:2 the brothers in Lystra and *I*
2Ti 3:11 in *I*, in Lystra, the sort

Idalah
Jos 19:15 Shimron and *I* and Bethlehem

Idbash
1Ch 4:3 Jezreel and Ishma and *I*

Iddo
1Ki 4:14 Ahinadab the son of *I*, in
1Ch 6:21 Joah his son, *I* his son
27:21 *I* the son of Zechariah
2Ch 9:29 record of visions of *I*
12:15 words . . . of *I* the visionary by
13:22 exposition of the prophet *I*
Ezr 5:1 *I* the prophet prophesied to
6:14 Zechariah the grandson of *I*
8:17 *I* the head one in the place
8:17 speak to *I* and his brothers
Ne 12:4 *I*, Ginnethoi, Abijah
12:16 for *I*, Zechariah; for
Zec 1:1 the son of *I* the prophet
1:7 son of *I* the prophet, saying

Idea
Ge 48:11 no *i* of seeing your face, but
Job 42:2 no *i* that is unattainable
Ps 139:20 according to their *i*
Jer 51:11 against Babylon that his *i*
51:12 Jehovah . . . formed the *i*
Ro 2:3 do you have this *i*, O man

Ideas
Ps 10:2 *i* that they have thought up
10:4 All his *i* are: There is no God
21:11 *I* that they are unable to
37:7 the man carrying out his *i*
Pr 12:2 but the man of wicked *i* he
24:8 a mere master at evil *i*
Jer 23:20 *i* of his heart come true
30:24 the *i* of his heart
Ro 11:20 Quit having lofty *i*, but

Identical
1Pe 2:7 the *i* stone that the builders

Idle
Jg 5:17 Asher sat *i* at the seashore
9:4 hire *i* and insolent men, that
11:3 And *i* men kept bringing
2Ch 13:7 *i* men, good-for-nothing
1Ti 1:6 been turned aside into *i* talk

Idlers
Ac 17:5 men of the marketplace *i* and

Idol
Ex 34:17 not make molten *i* gods for
1Ki 15:13 *i* to the sacred pole
15:13 her horrible *i* and burned it
2Ch 15:16 made a horrible *i* for the
15:16 Asa cut down her horrible *i*
33:15 *i* image from the house of
Isa 45:16 manufacturers of *i* forms
48:5 My own *i* has done them, and
Jer 2:5 kept walking after the vain *i*
Ho 4:12 Of their wooden *i* my own
10:5 For the calf *i* of Beth-aven
Ac 7:41 sacrifice to the *i* and began
1Co 8:4 we know that an *i* is nothing
8:7 accustomed until now to the *i*
8:7 something sacrificed to an *i*
8:10 at a meal in an *i* temple
10:19 what is sacrificed to an *i*
10:19 or that an *i* is anything

Idolater
1Co 5:11 in company with . . . an *i*
Eph 5:5 greedy person . . . an *i*

Idolaters
1Co 5:10 and extortioners or *i*
6:9 Neither fornicators, nor *i*
10:7 neither become *i*, as some of
Re 21:8 *i* and all the liars, their
22:15 *i* and everyone liking and

Idolatries
1Pe 4:3 proceeded in . . . illegal *i*

Idolatry
1Co 10:14 beloved ones, flee from *i*
Ga 5:20 *i*, practice of spiritism
Col 3:5 and covetousness, which is *i*

Idols
Le 26:30 carcasses of your dungy *i*

De 29:17 their dungy *i*, wood and
32:21 vexed me with their vain *i*
Sa 31:9 inform the houses of their *i*
Sa 5:21 they left their *i* there, and
Ki 15:12 removed all the dungy *i*
16:13 with their vain *i*
16:26 with their vain *i*
21:26 by going after the dungy *i*
Ki 17:12 continued to serve dungy *i*
17:15 went following vain *i* and
21:11 Judah sin with his dungy *i*
21:21 serving the dungy *i* that
23:24 teraphim and the dungy *i*
Ch 10:9 to inform their *i* and the
Ch 24:18 the sacred poles and the *i*
Ps 31:6 regard to worthless, vain *i*
106:36 they kept serving their *i*
106:38 to the *i* of Canaan
115:4 Their *i* are silver and gold
135:15 *i* of the nations are silver
Isa 10:11 to Jerusalem and to her *i*
46:1 *i* have come to be for the
Jer 14:22 the vain *i* of the nations
50:2 dungy *i* have become
Eze 6:4 to fall before your dungy *i*
6:5 before their dungy *i*, and I
6:6 your dungy *i* may be actually
6:9 going . . . after their dungy *i*
6:13 the midst of their dungy *i*
6:13 odor to all their dungy *i*
8:10 the dungy *i* of the house of
14:3 dungy *i* upon their heart
14:4 his dungy *i* upon his heart
14:4 the multitude of his dungy *i*
14:5 through their dungy *i*—all of
14:6 back from your dungy *i* and
14:7 his dungy *i* upon his heart
16:36 all your detestable dungy *i*
18:6 *i* of the house of Israel, and
18:12 *i* he lifted up his eyes
18:15 *i* of the house of Israel
20:7 with the dungy *i* of Egypt do
20:8 *i* of Egypt they did not leave
20:16 *i* that their heart was
20:18 with their dungy *i* do not
20:24 dungy *i* of their forefathers
20:31 dungy *i* down till today
20:39 each . . . his own dungy *i*
20:39 gifts and by your dungy *i*
22:3 has made dungy *i* within
22:4 dungy *i* that you have made
23:7 dungy *i*—she defiled herself
23:30 with their dungy *i*
23:37 with their dungy *i* they
23:39 their sons to their dungy *i*
23:49 the sins of your dungy *i*
30:13 destroy the dungy *i* and
33:25 to your dungy *i*, and blood
36:18 unclean with their dungy *i*
36:25 from all your dungy *i* I
37:23 with their dungy *i* and with
44:10 after their dungy *i*, they
44:12 before their dungy *i* and
Ho 4:17 Ephraim is joined with *i*
8:4 have made for themselves *i*
13:2 *i* according to their own
14:8 to do any longer with the *i*
Jon 2:8 observing the *i* of untruth
Mic 1:7 her *i* I shall make a desolate
Zec 13:2 cut off the names of the *i*
Ac 15:20 from things polluted by *i*
15:29 from things sacrificed to *i*
17:16 that the city was full of *i*
21:25 from what is sacrificed to *i*
Ro 2:22 expressing abhorrence of the *i*
1Co 8:1 concerning foods offered to *i*
8:4 eating of foods offered to *i*
8:10 eating foods offered to *i*
12:2 to those voiceless *i* just as
2Co 6:16 God's temple have with *i*
1Th 1:9 you turned to God from your *i*
1Jo 5:21 guard yourselves from *i*
Re 2:14 eat things sacrificed to *i*
2:20 eat things sacrificed to *i*
9:20 the *i* of gold and silver and

Idumea
Mr 3:8 from Jerusalem and from *I* and

Iezer
Nu 26:30 sons of Gilead: Of *I* the

Iezerites
Nu 26:30 Of Iezer the family of the *I*

Igal
Nu 13:7 *I* the son of Joseph
2Sa 23:36 *I* the son of Nathan of Zobah
1Ch 3:22 Shemaiah, Hattush and *I*

Igdaliah
Jer 35:4 Hanan the son of *I*, a man

Ignited
De 32:22 fire has been *i* in my anger
Jer 15:14 a fire itself has been *i* in
17:4 have been *i* in my anger

Ignites
Isa 64:2 when a fire *i* the brushwood

Igniting
Isa 50:11 All you who are *i* a fire

Ignoble
1Co 1:28 God chose the *i* things of

Ignorance
Ac 3:17 I know that you acted in *i*
17:30 the times of such *i*, yet now
Eph 4:18 the *i* that is in them
Heb 9:7 the sins of *i* of the people
1Pe 1:14 formerly had in your *i*

Ignorant
Ro 11:25 to be *i* of this sacred secret
1Co 10:1 I do not want you to be *i*
12:1 I do not want you to be *i*
14:38, 38 is *i*, he continues *i*
2Co 1:8 we do not wish you to be *i*
2:11 we are not *i* of his designs
1Th 4:13 we do not want you to be *i*
1Ti 1:13 *i* and acted with a lack of
2Ti 2:23 foolish and *i* questionings
Heb 5:2 deal moderately with the *i*
1Pe 2:15 muzzle the *i* talk of the
2Pe 2:12 things of which they are *i*

Ignored
Isa 59:8 the way of peace they have *i*
Jer 5:4 have *i* the way of Jehovah
9:3 and they *i* even me, is the
10:25 the nations who have *i* you

Iim
Jos 15:29 Baalah and *I* and Ezem

Ijon
1Ki 15:20 striking down *I* and Dan
2Ki 15:29 *I* and Abel-beth-maacah
2Ch 16:4 struck *I* and Dan and

Ikkesh
2Sa 23:26 Ira the son of *I* the Tekoite
1Ch 11:28 Ira the son of *I* the Tekoite
27:9 Ira the son of *I* the Tekoite

Ilai
1Ch 11:29 *I* the Ahohite

Ill
Ps 35:13 when they became *i*, my
Jer 5:3 but they did not become *i*
8:18 up into me. My heart is *i*
La 1:13 desolate. All the day I am *i*
1:22 and my heart is *i*
5:17 our heart has become *i*
Mt 14:35 all those who were *i*
17:15 he is an epileptic and is *i*
Mr 1:32 all those who were *i* and
1:34 So he cured many that were *i*
2:17 those who are *i* do. I came
Joh 6:2 upon those who were *i*

Illegal
1Pe 4:3 proceeded in . . . *i* idolatries

Illegitimate
Ex 30:9 not offer upon it *i* incense
Le 10:1 offering before Jehovah *i* fire
Nu 3:4 offered *i* fire before Jehovah
26:61 *i* fire before Jehovah
De 23:2 No *i* son may come into the
Zec 9:6 an *i* son will actually seat
Heb 12:8 you are really *i* children, and

Illicit
Ro 13:13 not in *i* intercourse and

Illness
Ps 41:3 sustain him upon a divan of *i*

Ill-treated
Heb 11:25 *i* with the people of God
13:3 and those being *i*, since you

Ill-treating
Isa 66:4 choose ways of *i* them

Ill-treatment
Heb 11:37 in tribulation, under *i*

Illuminate
2Co 4:6 on our hearts to *i* them with

Illumination
Ex 35:14 the lampstand of *i* and its
35:14 its lamps and the oil for *i*
35:28 oil for *i* and for the
39:37 utensils and the oil of *i*
1Ki 7:4 an *i* opening opposite an
7:4 an *i* opening in three tiers
7:5 the forefront of the *i* opening
7:5 an *i* opening in three tiers
Da 5:11 *i* and insight and wisdom like
5:14 and *i* and insight and wisdom
2Co 4:4 *i* of the glorious good news
Re 8:12 day might not have *i* for a

Illuminators
Php 2:15 shining as *i* in the world

Illustration
Mt 13:18 the *i* of the man that sowed
13:24 Another *i* he set before them
13:31 Another *i* he set before them
13:33 Another *i* he spoke to them
13:34 without an *i* he would not
13:36 *i* of the weeds in the field
15:15 Make the *i* plain to us
21:33 Hear another *i*: There was a
24:32 from the fig tree as an *i*
Mr 4:13 You do not know this *i*, and
4:30 or in what *i* shall we set it
4:34 without an *i* he would not
7:17 question him respecting the *i*
12:12 he spoke the *i* with them
13:28 learn the *i*: Just as soon as
Lu 4:23 will apply this *i* to me
5:36 went on to give an *i* to them
6:39 he also spoke an *i* to them
8:4 he spoke by means of an *i*
8:9 what this *i* might mean
8:11 the *i* means this: The seed
12:16 spoke an *i* to them, saying
12:41 saying this *i* to us or also
13:6 he went on to tell this *i*
14:7 to tell the invited men an *i*
15:3 spoke this *i* to them, saying
18:1 an *i* with regard to the need
18:9 he spoke this *i* also to some
19:11 he spoke in addition an *i*
20:9 *i*: A man planted a vineyard
20:19 this *i* with them in mind
21:29 he spoke an *i* to them
Ga 3:15 I speak with a human *i*
Heb 9:9 *i* for the appointed time that

Illustrations
Mt 13:3 told them many things by *i*
13:10 speak . . . by the use of *i*
13:13 speak . . . by the use of *i*
13:34 spoke to the crowds by *i*
13:35 will open my mouth with *i*
13:53 Jesus had finished these *i*
21:45 Pharisees had heard his *i*
22:1 again spoke to them with *i*
Mr 3:23 began to say to them with *i*
4:2 teach them many things with *i*
4:10 questioning him on the *i*
4:11 outside all things occur in *i*
4:13 understand all the other *i*
4:33 many *i* of that sort he would
12:1 to speak to them with *i*
Lu 8:10 in *i*, in order that, though

Illustrative
Heb 11:19 him also in an *i* way

Illustrious
Ac 2:20 and *i* day of Jehovah arrives

Illyricum
Ro 15:19 in a circuit as far as *I*

Image
Ge 1:26 Let us make man in our *i*
1:27 to create the man in his *i*
1:27 in God's *i* he created him
5:3 in his likeness, in his *i*
9:6 for in God's *i* he made man
Ex 20:4 *i* or a form like anything
Le 26:1 not set up a carved *i* or a
De 4:16 a carved *i*, the form of any
4:23 a carved *i*, the form of
4:25 carved *i*, a form of anything
5:8 a carved *i*, any form like

De 9:12 made themselves a molten *i*
27:15 man who makes a carved *i*
Jg 17:3 carved *i* and a molten statue
17:4 he went making a carved *i* and
18:14 and a carved *i* and a molten
18:17 take the carved *i* and the
18:17 teraphim and the molten *i*
18:18 take the carved *i*, the ephod
18:18 teraphim and the molten *i*
18:20 teraphim and the carved *i*
18:30 stood up the carved *i* for
18:31 kept the carved *i* of Micah
1Sa 19:13 Michal took the teraphim *i*
19:16 teraphim *i* on the couch and
2Ki 21:7 carved *i* of the sacred pole
2Ch 33:7 carved *i* that he had made in
33:15 *i* from the house of Jehovah
Ps 73:20 will despise their very *i*
97:7 serving any carved *i* be
106:19 bowed down to a molten *i*
Isa 40:19 has cast a mere molten *i*
40:20 a carved *i* that may not be
42:17 trust in the carved *i*
42:17 are saying to a molten *i*
44:9 formers of the carved *i* are
44:10 or cast a mere molten *i*
44:15 has made it into a carved *i*
44:17 his carved *i*. He prostrates
45:20 the wood of their carved *i*
48:5 and my own carved *i* and my
48:5 and my own molten *i* have
Jer 10:14 because of the carved *i*
10:14 his molten *i* is a falsehood
44:19 order to make an *i* of her
51:17 because of the carved *i*
51:17 his molten *i* is a falsehood
Da 2:31 look! a certain immense *i*
2:31 *i*, which was large and the
2:32 *i*, its head was of good gold
2:34 struck the *i* on its feet of
2:35 stone that struck the *i*, it
3:1 king made an *i* of gold, the
3:2 *i* that Nebuchadnezzar the king
3:3 *i* that Nebuchadnezzar the king
3:3 standing in front of the *i*
3:5 worship the *i* of gold that
3:7 worshiping the *i* of gold that
3:10 and worship the *i* of gold
3:12 *i* of gold that you have set
3:14 *i* of gold that I have set up
3:15 worship the *i* that I have
3:18 *i* of gold that you have set
Na 1:14 I shall cut off carved *i* and
Hab 2:18 benefit has a carved *i* been
Mt 22:20 Whose *i* and inscription is
Mr 12:16 Whose *i* and inscription is
Lu 20:24 Whose *i* and inscription does
Ac 19:35 the *i* that fell from heaven
Ro 1:23 *i* of corruptible man and of
8:29 after the *i* of his Son, that
1Co 11:7 as he is God's *i* and glory
15:49 *i* of the one made of dust
15:49 the *i* of the heavenly one
2Co 3:18 transformed into the same *i*
4:4 Christ, who is the *i* of God
Col 1:15 the *i* of the invisible God
3:10 *i* of the One who created it
Re 13:14 *i* to the wild beast that
13:15 breath to the *i* of the wild
13:15 *i* of the wild beast should
13:15 worship the *i* of the wild
14:9 the wild beast and its *i*
14:11 the wild beast and its *i*
15:2 wild beast and from its *i*
16:2 that were worshiping its *i*
19:20 who render worship to its *i*
20:4 wild beast nor its *i* and who

Images

Nu 33:52 all their *i* of molten metal
De 7:5 their graven *i* you should burn
7:25 The graven *i* of their gods
12:3 cut down the graven *i* of
Jg 2:13 Baal and the Ashtoreth *i*
10:6 the Ashtoreth *i* and the gods
1Sa 6:5 must make *i* of your piles and
6:5 *i* of your jerboas that are
6:11 and the *i* of their piles
7:3 put away . . . the Ashtoreth *i*
7:4 the Baals and the Ashtoreth *i*
12:10 Baals and the Ashtoreth *i*
31:10 house of the Ashtoreth *i*
1Ki 14:9 and molten *i* to offend me
2Ki 11:18 his *i* they broke up
17:41 their own graven *i* that
2Ch 3:10 in the workmanship of *i*, and
23:17 altars and his *i* they broke
33:19 graven *i* before he humbled
33:22 graven *i* that Manasseh his
34:3 graven *i* and the molten
34:4 graven *i* and the molten
34:7 graven *i* he crushed and
Ps 78:58 graven *i* they kept inciting
Isa 10:10 god whose graven *i* are
21:9 graven *i* of her gods he has
30:22 overlaying of your graven *i*
41:29 their molten *i* are wind and
42:8 my praise to graven *i*
Jer 8:19 with their graven *i*
9:14 and after the Baal *i*
50:2 *i* have been put to shame
50:38 it is a land of graven *i*
51:47 upon the graven *i* of Babylon
51:52 attention upon her graven *i*
Eze 7:20 and their detestable *i*, their
16:17 *i* of a male and prostitute
23:14 *i* of Chaldeans carved in
Da 4:5 mental *i* upon my bed and
11:8 gods, with their molten *i*
Ho 2:13 days of the Baal *i* to which
2:17 names of the Baal *i* from
11:2 To the Baal *i* they took up
11:2 to the graven *i* they began
Am 5:26 Kaiwan, your *i*, the star of
Mic 1:7 graven *i* will all be crushed
5:13 cut off your graven *i* and

Imagination

Pr 18:11 a protective wall in his *i*

Imaginations

Ps 73:7 exceeded the *i* of the heart
Lu 11:17 Knowing their *i* he said to

Imagine

Es 4:13 Do not *i* within your own soul
Mt 6:7 they *i* they will get a hearing
Lu 12:51 Do you *i* I came to give
13:2 Do you *i* that these Galileans
13:4 *i* that they were proved
Joh 16:2 *i* he has rendered a sacred
Ac 17:29 not to *i* that the Divine

Imagined

Jg 20:36 the sons of Benjamin *i* that
Ps 50:21 *i* that I would positively
Joh 11:13 *i* he was speaking about

Imagines

Lu 8:18 even what he *i* he has will be

Imagining

Lu 19:11 *i* that the kingdom of God
24:37 *i* they beheld a spirit
Joh 13:29 *i*, since Judas was holding
20:15 *i* it was the gardener
Ac 14:19 *i* he was dead
16:27 *i* that the prisoners had
21:29 *i* Paul had brought him into

Imitate

2Th 3:7 the way you ought to *i* us
3:9 as an example to you to *i* us
Heb 13:7 turns out *i* their faith

Imitation

2Ki 17:15 even in *i* of the nations

Imitator

3Jo 11 be an *i*, not of what is bad

Imitators

1Co 4:16 therefore, become *i* of me
11:1 Become *i* of me, even as I am
Eph 5:1 *i* of God, as beloved children
Php 3:17 Unitedly become *i* of me
1Th 1:6 you became *i* of us and of
2:14 you became *i*, brothers, of
Heb 6:12 *i* of those who through faith

Imlah

1Ki 22:8 Micaiah the son of *I*
22:9 bring Micaiah the son of *I*
2Ch 18:7 He is Micaiah the son of *I*
18:8 Bring Micaiah the son of *I*

Immanuel

Isa 7:14 certainly call his name *I*
8:8 the breadth of your land, O *I*
Mt 1:23 they will call his name *I*

Immediate

Mr 1:23 at that *i* time there was in

Immediately

Ge 29:10 Jacob *i* approached and rolled
30:25 Jacob *i* said to Laban: Send
32:2 *I* Jacob said, when he saw
42:9 *I* Joseph remembered the
43:17 *I* the man did just as Joseph
Ex 2:5 *I* she sent her slave girl that
5:6 *I* on that day Pharaoh
7:20 *I* Moses and Aaron did so
10:22 Moses *i* stretched his hand
14:5 *I* the heart of Pharaoh as
18:24 *I* Moses listened to the
19:8 *I* Moses took back the words
Le 9:8 Aaron *i* went near to the altar
Nu 12:11 *I* Aaron said to Moses
16:27 *I* they got away from before
23:2 Balak *i* did just as Balaam
Jos 2:7 shut the gate *i* after those
Jg 9:46 they *i* went to the vault of
9:54 *I* his attendant ran him
11:5 older men of Gilead *i* went to
12:4 *I* Jephthah collected all the
13:10 *I* the woman hurried and ran
14:11 they *i* took thirty groomsmen
15:17 he *i* threw the jawbone out
16:18 she *i* sent and called the
1Sa 15:27 *i* grabbed hold of the skirt
17:22 *I* David left the baggage
19:12 *I* Michal had David descend
19:21 *i* sent other messengers
20:34 *I* Jonathan rose up from the
22:18 *I* Doeg the Edomite turned
25:13 *I* David said to his men
25:41 *I* she rose up and bowed
28:10 *I* Saul swore to her by
31:12 *I* all the valiant men rose
2Sa 6:13 *i* sacrificed a bull and a
9:5 *I* King David sent and took
10:17 *i* gathered all Israel and
11:27 David *i* sent and took her
17:22 *I* David rose up and also
1Ki 1:32 *I* King David said: You men
2:25 *I* King Solomon sent by
2:40 *I* Shimei got up and saddled
12:21 he *i* congregated all the
13:4 *I* his hand that he had thrust
13:26 he *i* said: It is the man of
15:21 *i* quit building Ramah and
17:5 *I* he went and did according
18:17 Ahab *i* said to him: Is this
18:39 they *i* fell upon their faces
19:13 he *i* wrapped his face in
20:12 he *i* said to his servants
21:15 Jezebel *i* said to Ahab
22:33 *i* came back from following
2Ki 1:5 he *i* said to them: Why is it
1:8 *I* he said: It was Elijah the
3:24 the Israelites *i* rose up and
4:15 *I* he said: Call her. So he
4:25 he *i* said to Gehazi his
4:29 *I* he said to Gehazi: Gird
5:7 *i* ripped his garments apart
5:24 *i* took them from their hand
5:27 *I* he went out from before
6:6 *I* he cut off a piece of wood
6:14 *I* he sent horses and war
6:17 *I* Jehovah opened the
6:20 *I* Jehovah opened their eyes
6:30 *i* ripped his garments apart
7:7 *I* they got up and went
7:12 *I* the king rose up by night
9:22 he *i* said: Is there peace
9:32 *I* two or three court
10:14 *I* he said: Seize them alive
10:25 Jehu *i* said to the runners
11:14 *I* Athaliah ripped her
13:21 *i* came to life and stood
19:1 he *i* ripped his garments
22:11 he *i* ripped his garments
25:23 they *i* came to Gedaliah at
1Ch 18:10 he *i* sent Hadoram his son
19:8 he *i* sent Joab and all the
19:17 he *i* gathered all Israel
21:21 *i* went out of the threshing
2Ch 7:3 *i* bowed low with their faces
10:2 Jeroboam *i* came back from
11:1 *i* congregated the house of
16:5 *i* quit building Ramah and
18:32 *i* came back from following
23:13 *I* Athaliah ripped her
25:16 king *i* said to him: Was it
26:17 *I* Azariah the priest and
34:19 *i* ripped his garments apart
Ezr 4:2 *i* approached Zerubbabel and
Ne 4:14 *i* rose and said to the nobles
6:2 Geshem *i* sent to me, saying

Ne 13:19 I *i* said the word and the
Es 2:22 and he *i* told Esther the queen
5:9 Haman was *i* filled with rage
Isa 37:1 Hezekiah heard, he *i* ripped
Jer 41:8 who *i* said to Ishmael
Da 6:13 *I* they answered, and they
6:21 *I* Daniel himself spoke even
Mt 3:16 *i* came up from the water
8:3 *i* his leprosy was cleansed
14:31 *I* stretching out his hand
20:34 *i* they received sight, and
21:3 he will *i* send them forth
24:29 *I* after the tribulation of
25:16 *I* the one that received the
26:74 And *i* a cock crowed
27:48 *i* one of them ran and took a
Mr 1:10 And *i* on coming up out of the
1:12 *i* the spirit impelled him to
1:28 report about him spread out *i*
1:29 And *i* they went out of the
1:42 *i* the leprosy vanished from
2:8 Jesus, having discerned *i* by
2:12 and *i* picked up his cot and
3:6 *i* began holding council with
4:5 it *i* sprang up because of not
5:2 *i* after he got out of the boat
5:29 *i* her fountain of blood dried
5:30 *I*, also, Jesus recognized in
5:42 *i* the maiden rose and began
6:25 *I* she went in with haste
6:27 the king *i* dispatched a body
6:50 *I* he spoke with them, and he
7:25 but *i* a woman whose little
8:10 *i* he boarded the boat with
9:24 *I* crying out, the father of
10:52 *i* he recovered sight, and he
14:43 *i*, while he was yet speaking
14:72 *i* a cock crowed a second
15:1 *i* at dawn the chief priests
Lu 5:13 *i* the leprosy vanished from
6:49 *i* it collapsed, and the ruin
14:5 will not *i* pull him out on
21:9 but the end does not occur *i*
Joh 5:9 man *i* became sound in health
13:30 morsel, he went out *i*
13:32 and he will glorify him *i*
18:27 and *i* a cock crowed
19:34 *i* blood and water came out
Ac 9:18 *i* there fell from his eyes
9:20 *i* in the synagogues he began
9:34 And he rose *i*
10:16 *i* the vessel was taken up
12:10 *i* the angel departed from
17:10 *I* by night the brothers sent
17:14 brothers *i* sent Paul off to
21:30 And *i* the doors were closed
22:29 *I*, therefore, the men that
Jas 1:24 *i* forgets what sort of man
Re 4:2 I *i* came to be in the power

Immense
Da 2:31 look! a certain *i* image
4:10 the height of which was *i*

Immer
1Ch 9:12 Meshillemith the son of *I*
24:14 for *I* the sixteenth
Ezr 2:37 sons of *I*, a thousand and
2:59 Addon and *I*, and they proved
10:20 sons of *I* there were Hanani
Ne 3:29 Zadok the son of *I* did
7:40 sons of *I*, a thousand and
7:61 Cherub, Addon and *I*, and they
11:13 Meshillemoth the son of *I*
Jer 20:1 Pashhur the son of *I*, the

Imminent
2Ti 4:6 time for my releasing is *i*

Immoderateness
Mt 23:25 are full of plunder and *i*

Immoral
Ex 34:15 *i* intercourse with their
34:16 *i* intercourse with their gods
34:16 *i* intercourse with their gods
Le 17:7 they are having *i* intercourse
20:5 *i* intercourse along with him
20:5 *i* intercourse with Molech off
20:6 *i* intercourse with them, I
Nu 15:39 following in *i* intercourse
25:1 started to have *i* relations
De 31:16 *i* intercourse with foreign
Jg 2:17 they had *i* intercourse with
8:27 began to have *i* intercourse
8:33 *i* intercourse with the Baals
1Ch 5:25 *i* intercourse with the gods
2Ch 21:11 to have *i* intercourse, and
21:13 *i* intercourse the same way
21:13 having of *i* intercourse
Ps 106:39 *i* intercourse by their
Eze 20:30 you going in *i* intercourse
23:8 their *i* intercourse upon her
23:17 with their *i* intercourse

Immorally
Ps 73:27 every one *i* leaving you

Immortality
1Co 15:53 mortal must put on *i*
15:54 which is mortal puts on *i*
1Ti 6:16 the one alone having *i*, who

Immovable
Jos 3:17 standing *i* on dry ground in
Job 41:23 are as a casting upon it, *i*
Ac 27:41 stuck and stayed *i*, but the

Imna
1Ch 7:35 the sons of Helem . . . *I* and

Imnah
Ge 46:17 the sons of Asher were *I* and
Nu 26:44 *I* the family of the Imnites
1Ch 7:30 The sons of Asher were *I* and
2Ch 31:14 son of *I* the Levite was the

Imnites
Nu 26:44 Of Imnah the family of the *I*

Impale
Mt 20:19 to scourge and to *i*, and the
23:34 them you will kill and *i*
Mr 15:13 they cried out: *I* him!
15:14 cried out all the more: *I*
15:20 they led him out to *i* him
Lu 23:21, 21 yell, saying: *I! I* him!
Joh 19:6, 6 saying: *I* him! *I* him!
19:6 Take him yourselves and *i*
19:10 I have authority to *i* you
19:15 Take him away! *I* him!
19:15 Shall I *i* your king?
Heb 6:6 they *i* the Son of God afresh

Impaled
Ezr 6:11 and he will be *i* upon it
Mt 26:2 is to be delivered up to be *i*
27:22 They all said: Let him be *i!*
27:23 all the more: Let him be *i!*
27:26 and handed him over to be *i*
27:35 had *i* him they distributed
27:38 two robbers were *i* with
27:44 even the robbers that were *i*
28:5 looking for Jesus who was *i*
Mr 15:15 he handed him over to be *i*
15:24 they *i* him and distributed
15:25 third hour, and they *i* him
15:27 they *i* two robbers with him
15:32 those *i* together with him
16:6 the Nazarene, who was *i*
Lu 23:23 demanding that he be *i*; and
23:33 Skull, there they *i* him
24:7 hands of sinful men and be *i*
24:20 sentence of death and *i* him
Joh 19:16 him over to them to be *i*
19:18 there they *i* him, and two
19:20 place where Jesus was *i*
19:23 the soldiers had *i* Jesus
19:32 other man that had been *i*
19:41 place where he was *i* there
Ac 2:36 this Jesus whom you *i*
4:10 the Nazarene, whom you *i*
Ro 6:6 our old personality was *i*
1Co 1:13 Paul was not *i* for you, was
1:23 but we preach Christ *i*, to
2:2 Jesus Christ, and him *i*
2:8 not have *i* the glorious Lord
2Co 13:4 he was *i* owing to weakness
Ga 2:20 I am *i* along with Christ
3:1 Christ was openly portrayed *i*
5:24 *i* the flesh together with
6:14 world has been *i* to me and I
Re 11:8 where their Lord was also *i*

Impaling
Mt 27:31 and led him off for *i*

Impart
Ge 46:28 to Joseph to *i* information
Pr 9:9 *I* knowledge to someone
Da 9:22 to *i* understanding and speak
11:33 *i* understanding to the many
Joh 4:14 bubbling up to *i* everlasting
Ro 1:11 I may *i* some spiritual gift
Eph 4:29 *i* what is favorable to the
1Th 2:8 pleased to *i* to you, not only

Imparted
Ga 2:6 outstanding men *i* nothing new
1Ti 1:12 Lord, who *i* power to me
1Jo 4:13 he has *i* his spirit to us

Impartially
1Pe 1:17 the Father who judges *i*

Imparts
Php 4:13 of him who *i* power to me

Impatient
Jg 10:16 his soul became *i* because of
16:16 his soul got to be *i* to the
Job 21:4 my spirit does not get *i*
Pr 14:29 is *i* is exalting foolishness
Zec 11:8 my soul gradually became *i*

Impediment
Mr 7:32 man deaf and with a speech *i*
7:35 *i* of his tongue was loosed

Impel
Jg 13:25 spirit started to *i* him in

Impelled
Ex 35:21 everyone whose heart *i* him
35:26 women whose hearts *i* them
36:2 *i* him to approach the work in
Mr 1:12 spirit *i* him to go into the

Impending
Jg 20:34 calamity was *i* over them

Impenetrable
Zec 11:2 the *i* forest has come down

Imperial
2Ch 32:9 all his *i* might with him

Impetuous
Hab 1:6 the nation bitter and *i*

Implanting
Jas 1:21 mildness the *i* of the word

Implements
Ge 27:3 your *i*, your quiver and your
De 23:13 a peg . . . along with your *i*
2Sa 24:22 *i* of the cattle for the
1Ki 19:21 with the *i* of the bulls he
Ec 9:18 is better than *i* for fighting
Eze 40:42 also deposit the *i* with
Zec 11:15 *i* of a useless shepherd

Implicitly
Ge 41:40 my people will obey you *i*

Implore
De 3:23 to *i* favor from Jehovah at
2Ki 1:13 began to *i* favor of him and
Es 4:8 to the king and *i* favor of him
Job 8:5 of the Almighty . . . *i* favor
9:15 opponent-at-law I would *i*
Ho 12:4 he might *i* favor for himself

Implored
Ge 42:21 he *i* compassion on our part
Es 8:3 wept and *i* favor of him to
Heb 12:19 people *i* that no word

Imploring
Job 19:16 I keep *i* him for compassion
Da 6:11 and *i* favor before his God

Importance
Mt 18:19 concerning anything of *i*

Important
Jer 50:12 least *i* of the nations
Php 1:10 sure of the more *i* things

Importunities
Pr 6:3 storm your fellowman with *i*

Impose
Ex 5:8 you will further *i* upon them
De 14:1 *i* baldness on your foreheads
2Ki 18:14 Whatever you may *i* upon me
Es 9:21 *i* upon them the obligation to
2Th 3:8 so as not to *i* an expensive

Imposed
Ge 34:12 marriage money and gift *i*
Ex 21:22 damages *i* upon him without
21:30 If a ransom should be *i* upon
21:30 all that may be *i* upon him
De 24:5 anything else be *i* onto him
2Ki 23:33 *i* a fine upon the land of
Ezr 7:24 is allowed to be *i* upon them
Ne 10:32 Also, we *i* upon ourselves
Es 9:27 the Jews *i* and accepted upon
9:31 and Esther the queen had *i*

Es 9:31 had *i* upon their own soul and
Heb 9:10 *i* until the appointed time

Imposing
Ac 15:10 by *i* upon the neck of the

Impossibility
Lu 1:37 no declaration will be an *i*

Impossible
Ezr 9:15 *i* to stand before you on
Mt 17:20 nothing will be *i* for you
19:26 With men this is *i*, but
Mr 10:27 With men it is *i*, but not
Lu 18:27 The things *i* with men are
Heb 6:4 *i* as regards those who have
6:18 it is *i* for God to lie
11:6 faith it is *i* to please him

Impostor
Mt 27:63 that *i* said while yet alive

Impostors
2Ti 3:13 *i* will advance from bad to

Imposture
Mt 27:64 this last *i* will be worse

Impotent
Job 26:5 *i* in death keep trembling
Ps 88:10 those *i* in death themselves
Pr 2:18 down to those *i* in death her
9:18 those *i* in death are there
21:16 of those *i* in death
Isa 14:9 awakened those *i* in death
26:14 *I* in death, they will not
26:19 those *i* in death drop in

Impounded
Ex 7:19 and over all their *i* waters
Le 11:36 and a pit of *i* waters will

Impoverished
Jg 6:6 Israel became greatly *i* due to
Ps 79:8 we have become greatly *i*
116:6 I was *i*, and he proceeded
142:6 I have become very much *i*

Impoverisher
1Sa 2:7 Jehovah is an *I* and an

Impregnates
Job 21:10 His own bull actually *i*

Impressed
Mt 27:32 *i* into service to lift up
Mr 15:21 *i* into service a passerby

Impresses
Mt 5:41 *i* you into service for a mile

Impressive
1Ki 10:2 with a very *i* train, camels
2Ch 9:1 with a very *i* train and

Imprint
Da 9:24 *i* a seal upon vision and

Imprison
Ac 22:19 I used to *i* and flog in one

Imprisonment
Ezr 7:26 for money fine or for *i*

Improper
Job 1:22 or ascribe anything *i* to God
24:12 not as anything *i*

Improperly
1Co 7:36 he is behaving *i* toward his

Impropriety
Jer 23:13 I have seen *i*. They have

Improve
Jer 2:33 *i* your way in order to look

Improvising
Am 6:5 *i* according to the sound of

Impulse
Joh 12:49 spoken out of my own *i*
16:13 speak of his own *i*, but

Impulses
1Ti 5:11 their sexual *i* have come

Impure
Le 19:23 fruitage *i* as its foreskin
2Ch 29:5 *i* thing out from the holy
Ezr 9:11 possession of is an *i* land

Impurities
Eze 36:25 clean; from all your *i* and
36:29 save you from all your *i*

Impurity
Le 12:2 as in the days of the *i* when
14:19 cleansing himself from his *i*
15:19 days in her menstrual *i*
15:20 menstrual *i* will be unclean
15:24 her menstrual *i* comes to be
15:25 time of her menstrual *i*, or
15:25 her menstrual *i*, all the
15:25 menstrual *i*. She is unclean
15:26 the bed of her menstrual *i*
15:26 uncleanness . . . menstrual *i*
18:19 of her *i* to lay her nakedness
Ezr 9:11 the *i* of the peoples of the
Eze 18:6 woman in her *i* he would not

Imrah
1Ch 7:36 sons of Zophah . . . Beri and *I*

Imri
1Ch 9:4 *I* the son of Bani, of the sons
Ne 3:2 Zaccur the son of *I* did

Inaccessible
1Sa 22:4 happened to be in the *i* place
22:5 dwelling in the *i* place
Job 39:28 a crag and an *i* place

Inactive
Ro 6:6 sinful body might be made *i*
Jas 2:20 faith apart from works is *i*
2Pe 1:8 you from being either *i* or

Inanimate
Jer 51:6 rendered *i* through her error
1Co 14:7 the *i* things give off sound

Inasmuch
Nu 27:14 *i* as you men rebelled
1Sa 8:6 *i* as they had said: Do give us
1Ki 16:2 *I* as I raised you up out of
2Ki 17:26 *i* as there are none knowing
2Ch 20:37 *I* as you have had
Ezr 4:14 *i* as we do eat the salt of
7:14 *I* as from before the king
Ro 2:1 *i* as you that judge practice
Heb 3:3 *i* as he who constructs it has

Inaugurate
De 20:5 another man should *i* it
1Ki 8:63 might *i* the house of Jehovah

Inaugurated
De 20:5 a new house and has not *i* it
2Ch 7:5 *i* the house of the true God
Heb 9:18 former covenant *i* without
10:20 he *i* for us as a new and

Inauguration
Nu 7:10 at the *i* of the altar on
7:11 for the *i* of the altar
7:84 *i* offering of the altar on the
7:88 *i* offering of the altar after
2Ch 7:9 *i* of the altar they had held
Ezr 6:16 the *i* of this house of God
6:17 the *i* of this house of God a
Ne 12:27 *i* of the wall of Jerusalem
12:27 carry on an *i* and a rejoicing
Ps 30:*super* A song of *i* of the house
Da 3:2 to the *i* of the image that
3:3 for the *i* of the image that

Incapability
Ro 8:3 an *i* on the part of the Law

Incapable
Ho 8:5 will they be *i* of innocency

Incense
Ex 25:6 and for perfumed *i*
30:1 a place for burning *i*
30:7 perfumed *i* smoke upon it
30:8 *i* constantly before Jehovah
30:9 illegitimate *i* or a burnt
30:27 utensils and the altar of *i*
30:35 make it into an *i*, a spice
30:37 *i* that you will make with
31:8 utensils, and the altar of *i*
31:11 and the perfumed *i* for the
35:8 and for the perfumed *i*
35:15 altar of *i* and its poles
35:15 oil and the perfumed *i*
35:28 for the perfumed *i*
37:25 altar of *i* out of acacia wood
37:29 and the pure, perfumed *i*, the
39:38 perfumed *i* and the screen
40:5 put the golden altar for *i*
40:27 make perfumed *i* smoke upon
Le 4:7 perfumed *i* before Jehovah
10:1 fire in them and placed *i*
16:12 full of fine perfumed *i*, and
Le 16:13 put the *i* upon the fire
16:13 and the cloud of the *i* must
26:30 cut off your *i* stands and lay
Nu 4:16 and the perfumed *i* and the
7:14 cup of ten shekels, full of *i*
7:20 gold cup . . . full of *i*
7:26 cup of ten shekels, full of *i*
7:32 cup of ten shekels, full of *i*
7:38 cup of ten shekels, full of *i*
7:44 cup of ten shekels, full of *i*
7:50 cup of ten shekels, full of *i*
7:56 cup of ten shekels, full of *i*
7:62 cup of ten shekels, full of *i*
7:68 cup of ten shekels, full of *i*
7:74 cup of ten shekels, full of *i*
7:80 cup of ten shekels, full of *i*
7:86 twelve gold cups full of *i*
16:7 place *i* upon them before
16:17 put *i* upon them and present
16:18 placed *i* upon them and stood
16:35 men offering the *i*
16:40 make *i* smoke before Jehovah
16:46 and put on *i* and go to the
16:47 he put the *i* on and began
De 33:10 *i* before your nostrils
1Ch 6:49 and upon the altar of *i* for
28:18 for the *i* altar refined gold
2Ch 2:4 to burn perfumed *i* before him
13:11 and also perfumed *i*; and
14:5 high places and the *i* stands
26:16 burn *i* upon the altar of
26:16 upon the altar of *i*
26:18 burn *i* to Jehovah, but it
26:18 ones sanctified, to burn *i*
26:19 was a censer for burning *i*
26:19 beside the altar of *i*
29:7 *i* they did not burn, and
30:14 *i* altars they removed and
34:4 *i* stands that were up above
34:7 *i* stands he cut down in all
Ps 141:2 prayer be prepared as *i*
Pr 27:9 Oil and *i* are what make the
Isa 1:13 *I* . . . something detestable
17:8 poles or at the *i* stands
27:9 *i* stands will not rise up
Eze 6:4 your *i* stands must be broken
6:6 your *i* stands cut down and
8:11 of the cloud of the *i* was
16:18 my *i* you would actually put
23:41 my *i* and my oil you put
Da 2:46 even a present and *i* to him
Lu 1:9 his turn to offer *i* when he
1:10 at the hour of offering *i*
1:11 right side of the *i* altar
Re 5:8 bowls that were full of *i*
5:8 the *i* means the prayers of the
8:3 having a golden *i* vessel; and
8:3 large quantity of *i* was given
8:4 smoke of the *i* ascended from
8:5 took the *i* vessel, and he
18:13 *i* and perfumed oil and

Incensed
De 1:37 Jehovah got *i* on your account
4:21 Jehovah got *i* at me on your
9:8 Jehovah got *i* at you to the
9:20 Jehovah got very *i* to the
1Ki 8:46 *i* at them and abandon them
11:9 came to be *i* at Solomon
2Ki 17:18 got very *i* against Israel
2Ch 6:36 you have to be *i* at them
Ezr 9:14 not get *i* at us to the limit
Ps 2:12 that He may not become *i*
60:1 You have become *i*. You should
79:5 Jehovah, will you be *i*
85:5 that you will be *i* at us
Isa 12:1 you got *i* at me, your anger
2Co 11:29 is stumbled, and I am not *i*

Incessantly
Jg 5:23 Curse its inhabitants *i*, For
Isa 14:6 in fury with a stroke *i*, the
28:28 one *i* keep treading it out
1Th 1:3 we bear *i* in mind your
2:13 we also thank God *i*, because
5:17 Pray *i*

Incidental
2Ti 2:22 from the desires *i* to youth

Incidentally
Le 24:11 *I*, his mother's name was
Nu 11:7 *I*, the manna was like
13:22 *I*, Hebron had been built
25:14 *I* the name of the fatally
Jg 1:23 *i*, the name of the city

Jg 4:11 *I* Heber the Kenite had
16:27 *I*, the house was full of men
2Sa 21:2 *I*, the Gibeonites were not
Joh 9:14 *I* it was Sabbath on the day
19:41 *I*, at the place where he

Incinerate
Eze 5:4 and *i* them in the fire

Incision
Le 21:5 they should not make an *i*

Incite
De 32:21 shall *i* them to jealousy
1Ch 21:1 to *i* David to number Israel
Job 2:3 although you *i* me against him
Ac 17:13 to *i* and agitate the masses
Ro 10:19 *i* you people to jealousy
10:19 *i* you to violent anger
11:11 to *i* them to jealousy
11:14 *i* those who are my own
Heb 10:24 *i* to love and fine works

Incited
Ex 35:21 everyone whose spirit *i* him
35:29 hearts *i* them to bring
De 32:21 have *i* me to jealousy with
1Sa 26:19 Jehovah that has *i* you
2Sa 24:1 *i* David against them, saying
1Ki 14:22 they *i* him to jealousy more
Jer 23:13 acted as prophets *i* by Baal

Incites
Ex 25:2 From every man whose heart *i*

Inciting
De 32:16 began *i* him to jealousy
Jos 15:18 she kept *i* him to ask a
Jg 1:14 she kept *i* him to ask a
Ps 78:58 they kept *i* him to jealousy
Eze 8:3 symbol . . . that is *i* to jealousy
Lu 23:14 one *i* the people to revolt
1Co 10:22 Or are we *i* Jehovah to

Inclination
Ge 6:5 every *i* of the thoughts of his
8:21 *i* of the heart of man is bad
De 31:21 *i* that they are developing
1Ch 28:9 every *i* of the thoughts he is
29:18 *i* of the thoughts of the
Isa 26:3 *i* that is well supported
Jas 3:4 the *i* of the man at the helm

Inclinations
Eph 6:7 Be slaves with good *i*, as to

Incline
Jos 24:23 *i* your hearts to Jehovah
2Sa 2:19 *i* to go to the right or to
1Ki 8:58 *i* our heart to himself to
11:2 will *i* your heart to follow
2Ki 19:16 *I* your ear, O Jehovah
Ps 17:6 *I* your ear to me. Hear my
17:11 their eyes to *i* to the earth
31:2 *I* to me your ear
45:10 and see, and *i* your ear
49:4 I shall *i* my ear
71:2 *I* to me your ear and save me
78:1 *I* your ear to the sayings of
86:1 *I*, O Jehovah, your ear
88:2 *I* your ear to my entreating
102:2 *I* to me your ear
119:36 *I* my heart to your
141:4 *i* my heart to anything bad
Pr 2:2 *i* your heart to discernment
4:20 To my sayings *i* your ear
4:27 *i* to the right hand or to
5:1 my discernment *i* your ears
22:17 *I* your ear and hear the
Isa 37:17 *I* your ear, O Jehovah, and
55:3 *I* your ear and come to me
Jer 7:24 neither did they *i* their ear
7:26 they did not *i* their ear
11:8 did not listen or *i* their ear
17:23 not listen or *i* their ear
25:4 you *i* your ear to listen
34:14 neither did they *i* their ear
35:15 you did not *i* your ear
44:5 *i* their ear to turn back
Eze 1:12 the spirit would *i* to go
Da 9:18 *I* your ear, O my God, and

Inclined
Jg 9:3 heart *i* toward Abimelech, for
1Sa 8:3 *i* to follow unjust profit and
1Ki 2:28 Joab himself had *i* to follow
2:28 Absalom he had not *i* to
11:3 wives gradually *i* his heart
11:4 had *i* his heart to follow
1Ki 11:9 heart had *i* . . . from Jehovah
Ps 16:9 my glory is *i* to be joyful
40:1 he *i* his ear to me and heard
40:5 *i* to tell and speak of them
71:23 *i* to make melody to you
116:2 he has *i* his ear to me
119:112 *i* my heart to do your
Pr 5:13 teachers I have not *i* my ear
Ca 2:7 love in me until it feels *i*
3:5 love in me until it feels *i*
8:4 love in me until it feels *i*
Isa 10:7 he will feel *i*
Eze 1:20 spirit *i* to go, they would
17:6 *i* to turn its foliage inward
Da 11:27 heart will be *i* to doing
Mr 6:48 but he was *i* to pass them by
Php 3:15 are mentally *i* otherwise in

Inclining
Eze 1:20 go, the spirit *i* to go there

Included
Isa 40:12 *i* in a measure the dust of

Income
Ec 5:10 any lover of wealth with *i*

Incomprehensible
Jer 33:3 tell you great and *i* things

Inconvenient
Ac 27:12 harbor was *i* for wintering

Incorruptible
Ro 1:23 glory of the *i* God into
1Co 9:25 but we an *i* one
15:52 dead will be raised up *i*
1Ti 1:17 the King of eternity, *i*
1Pe 1:4 to an *i* and undefiled and
1:23 by *i* reproductive seed
3:4 in the *i* apparel of the quiet

Incorruptibleness
Ro 2:7 *i* by endurance in work that

Incorruption
1Co 15:42 it is raised up in *i*
15:50 does corruption inherit *i*
15:53 corruptible must put on *i*
15:54 corruptible puts on *i* and
2Ti 1:10 shed light upon life and *i*

Incorruptness
Eph 6:24 our Lord Jesus Christ in *i*

Increase
Ge 3:16 I shall greatly *i* the pain
43:34 *i* Benjamin's portion five
48:16 let them *i* to a multitude in
Le 25:16 *i* its purchase value, and in
Nu 26:54 should *i* one's inheritance
33:54 you should *i* his inheritance
De 1:11 *i* you a thousand times as
8:13 herd and your flock may *i*
8:13 silver and gold may *i* for you
8:13 and all that is yours may *i*
17:16 not *i* horses for himself
17:16 in order to *i* horses
17:17 nor should he *i* silver and
32:23 I shall *i* calamities upon
2Ch 33:23 one that made guiltiness *i*
Ezr 4:22 harm may not *i* to the injury
Job 35:6 if your revolts actually *i*
Ps 72:17 let his name have *i*
115:14 Jehovah will give *i* to you
Pr 9:9 and he will *i* in learning
13:11 is the one that makes *i*
Isa 29:19 *i* their rejoicing in Jehovah
Eze 5:16 famine I shall *i* upon you
Ho 4:10 they will not *i*, because they
Ac 16:5 *i* in number from day to day
2Co 9:10 will *i* the products of your
1Th 3:12 may the Lord cause you to *i*

Increased
Ex 11:9 miracles to be *i* in the land
1Ch 4:38 forefathers *i* in multitude
2Ch 31:5 Israel *i* the firstfruits of
Ps 73:12 *i* their means of maintenance
Pr 11:24 scattering and yet is being *i*
Ec 1:16 *i* in wisdom more than anyone
2:9 I became greater and *i* more
2Co 10:15 as your faith is being *i*
1Pe 1:2 kindness and peace be *i* to you
2Pe 1:2 peace be *i* to you by an
Jude 2 peace and love be *i* to you

Increases
Ps 49:16 the glory of his house *i*
Pr 23:28 she *i* the treacherous ones
Ec 1:18, 18 that *i* knowledge *i* pain

Increasing
Ge 7:17 waters kept *i* and began
7:18 waters . . . kept *i* greatly
30:43 went on *i* more and more
Job 17:9 keeps *i* in strength
Mt 24:12 of the *i* of lawlessness the
Mr 4:8 *i*, they began to yield fruit
Joh 3:30 That one must go on *i*, but
Ac 6:1 days when the disciples were *i*
Col 1:6 and *i* in all the world just
1:10 *i* in the accurate knowledge
2Th 1:3 is *i* one toward the other

Inculcate
De 6:7 you must *i* them in your son

Incumbent
Pr 7:14 sacrifices were *i* upon me

Incur
Ex 28:43 not *i* error and certainly die
Nu 18:22 to *i* sin so as to die
18:32 you must not *i* sin for it
De 15:2 that he may let his fellow *i*
2Ch 19:10 that you may not *i* guilt
1Jo 5:16 sin that does not *i* death
5:16 not sinning so as to *i* death
5:16 is a sin that does *i* death
5:17 a sin that does not *i* death

Incurable
Job 34:6 My severe wound is *i* though
Ps 69:20 my heart, and the wound is *i*
Isa 17:11 of the disease and *i* pain
Jer 15:18 chronic and my stroke *i*
30:15 pain is *i* on account of the

Indebtedness
Eze 18:7 pledge that he took for *i*

Indecent
De 23:14 he may see nothing *i* in you
24:1 found something *i* on her part

Indecently
1Co 13:5 does not behave *i*, does not

Indecisive
Jas 1:8 he is an *i* man, unsteady in
4:8 purify your hearts, you *i*

Indefinite
Ge 3:22 and eat and live to time *i*
9:12 for the generations to time *i*
9:16 the covenant to time *i*
13:15 to give it until time *i*
17:7 covenant to time *i*, to prove
17:8 for a possession to time *i*
17:13 serve as a covenant to time *i*
17:19 covenant to time *i* to his
48:4 give this land . . . to time *i*
Ex 3:15 This is my name to time *i*
12:14 As a statute to time *i* you
12:17 as a statute to time *i*
12:24 you and your sons to time *i*
15:18 king to time *i*, even forever
19:9 they may put faith to time *i*
21:6 must be his slave to time *i*
27:21 It is a statute to time *i*
28:43 It is a statute to time *i*
29:9 theirs as a statute to time *i*
29:28 by a regulation to time *i* to
30:21 regulation to time *i* for them
31:16 It is a covenant to time *i*
31:17 it is a sign to time *i*
32:13 possession of it to time *i*
40:15 as a priesthood to time *i*
Le 3:17 It is a statute to time *i* for
6:18 It is an allowance to time *i*
6:22 It is a regulation to time *i*
7:34 as a regulation to time *i*
7:36 It is a statute to time *i*
10:9 It is a statute to time *i*
10:15 as an allowance to time *i*
16:29 statute to time *i* for you
16:31 It is a statute to time *i*
16:34 serve as a statute to time *i*
17:7 statute to time *i* for you
23:14 time *i* for your generations
23:21 time *i* in all your dwelling
23:31 time *i* for your generations
23:41 statute to time *i* during
24:3 statute to time *i* during your
24:8 covenant to time *i* with the
24:9 as a regulation to time *i*
25:32 to time *i* for the Levites
25:34 possession to time *i* for

Le 25:46 as a possession to time *i*
Nu 10:8 to time *i* during your
15:15 statute to time *i* for your
18:8 as an allowance to time *i*
18:11 as an allowance to time *i*
18:19 as an allowance to time *i*
18:23 It is a statute to time *i*
19:10 as a statute to time *i*
19:21 serve as a statute to time *i*
25:13 priesthood to time *i* for him
De 5:29 their sons to time *i*
12:28 sons after you to time *i*
13:16 a heap of ruins to time *i*
15:17 become your slave to time *i*
23:3 none of theirs . . . to time *i*
23:6 all your days to time *i*
28:46 sign and a portent to time *i*
29:29 and to our sons to time *i*
32:40 As I am alive to time *i*
Jos 4:7 the sons of Israel to time *i*
14:9 an inheritance to time *i*
1Sa 1:22 and dwell there to time *i*
2:30 walk before me to time *i*
3:13 judging his house to time *i*
3:14 or by offering to time *i*
13:13 firm over Israel to time *i*
20:15 my household to time *i*
20:23 me and you to time *i*
20:42 your offspring to time *i*
27:12 my servant to time *i*
2Sa 3:28 innocent for time *i* of
7:13 kingdom firmly to time *i*
7:16 steadfast to time *i* before
7:16 established to time *i*
7:24 as your people to time *i*
7:25 carry out to time *i* and do
7:26 name become great to time *i*
7:29 to time *i* before you
7:29 servant be blessed to time *i*
12:10 your own house to time *i*
22:51 to his seed for time *i*
1Ki 1:31 King David live to time *i*
2:33 his offspring to time *i*
2:33 come to be peace to time *i*
8:13 to dwell in to time *i*
9:3 my name there to time *i*
9:5 kingdom over Israel to time *i*
10:9 loves Israel to time *i*
2Ki 5:27 your offspring to time *i*
21:7 shall put my name to time *i*
1Ch 15:2 minister to him to time *i*
16:15 his covenant even to time *i*
16:34 For to time *i* is his
16:36, 36 from time *i* to time *i*
16:41 *i* is his loving-kindness
17:12 his throne firmly to time *i*
17:14 in my kingship to time *i*
17:14 one lasting to time *i*
17:22 as your people to time *i*
17:23 prove faithful to time *i*
17:24 become great to time *i*
17:27 continue to time *i* before
17:27 and it is blessed to time *i*
22:10 over Israel to time *i*
23:13 he and his sons to time *i*
23:13 in his name to time *i*
23:25 in Jerusalem to time *i*
28:4 king over Israel to time *i*
28:7 kingship firmly to time *i*
28:8 sons after you to time *i*
29:10, 10 from time *i* even to time *i*
29:18 do keep this to time *i* as
2Ch 2:4 To time *i* this will be upon
5:13 is good, for to time *i* is
6:2 for you to dwell in to time *i*
7:3 loving-kindness is to time *i*
7:6 loving-kindness is to time *i*
7:16 be there to time *i*, and
9:8 make it stand to time *i*, so
13:5 kingdom . . . over Israel to time *i*
20:7 your lover, to time *i*
20:21 for to time *i* is his
30:8 he has sanctified to time *i*
33:4 will prove to be to time *i*
33:7 put my name to time *i*
Ezr 3:11 toward Israel is to time *i*
9:12 to time *i* you must not work
9:12 for your sons to time *i*
Ne 2:3 king himself live to time *i*
9:5, 5 God from time *i* to time *i*
13:1 the true God to time *i*
Job 7:16 to time *i* I would not live
41:4 as a slave to time *i*
Ps 5:11 To time *i* they will cry out
Ps 9:5 you have wiped out to time *i*
9:7 Jehovah, he will sit to time *i*
10:16 Jehovah is King to time *i*
12:7 this generation to time *i*
18:50 and to his seed to time *i*
21:4 Length of days to time *i*
25:6 For they are from time *i*
28:9 and carry them to time *i*
29:10 sits as king to time *i*
30:12 to time *i* I will laud you
33:11 To time *i* the very counsel
37:18 continue even to time *i*
37:27 And so reside to time *i*
37:28 To time *i* they will
41:12 before your face to time *i*
41:13, 13 time *i* even to time *i*
44:8 to time *i* your name we shall
45:2 God has blessed you to time *i*
45:6 God is your throne to time *i*
45:17 will laud you to time *i*
48:8 firmly establish it to time *i*
48:14 God is our God to time *i*
49:8 That it has ceased to time *i*
49:11 houses may be to time *i*
52:8 to time *i*, even forever
52:9 I will laud you to time *i*
61:4 in your tent for times *i*
61:7 He will dwell to time *i*
66:7 by his mightiness to time *i*
72:17 name prove to be to time *i*
72:19 his glorious name to time *i*
73:26 and my share to time *i*
75:9 shall tell of it to time *i*
77:5 On the years in the *i* past
77:7 to times *i* that Jehovah keeps
78:66 reproach of *i* duration he
78:69 he has founded to time *i*
79:13 thanks to you to time *i*
81:15 will prove to be to time *i*
85:5 to time *i* that you will be
86:12 glorify your name to time *i*
89:1 sing about even to time *i*
89:2 stay built even to time *i*
89:4 to time *i* I shall firmly
89:28 To time *i* I shall preserve
89:36 prove to be even to time *i*
89:37 established for time *i*
89:52 Blessed be Jehovah to time *i*
90:2 Even from time *i* to
90:2 to time *i* you are God
92:8 on high to time *i*, O Jehovah
93:2 You are from time *i*
100:5 loving-kindness is to time *i*
102:12 Jehovah, to time *i* you will
103:9 to time *i* keep resentful
103:17 of Jehovah is from time *i*
103:17 loving-kindness . . . to time *i*
104:5 totter to time *i*, or forever
104:31 will prove to be to time *i*
105:8 his covenant even to time *i*
106:1 loving-kindness is to time *i*
106:31 after generation to time *i*
106:48, 48 time *i* even to time *i*
107:1 loving-kindness is to time *i*
110:4 a priest to time *i* According
111:5 time *i* he will remember his
111:8 supported forever, to time *i*
111:9 To time *i* he has commanded
112:6 for remembrance to time *i*
113:2 From now on and to time *i*
115:18 From now on and to time *i*
117:2 the trueness . . . is to time *i*
118:1 loving-kindness is to time *i*
118:2 loving-kindness is to time *i*
118:3 loving-kindness is to time *i*
118:4 loving-kindness is to time *i*
118:29 loving-kindness is to time *i*
119:44 To time *i*, even forever
119:52 decisions from time *i*
119:89 To time *i*, O Jehovah, Your
119:93 time *i* I shall not forget
119:98 to time *i* it is mine
119:111 as a possession to time *i*
119:112 time *i*, down to the last
119:142 righteousness to time *i*
119:144 reminders is to time *i*
119:152 to time *i* you have founded
119:160 of yours is to time *i*
121:8 From now on and to time *i*
125:1 but dwells even to time *i*
125:2 From now on and to time *i*
131:3 From now on and to time *i*
133:3 Even life to time *i*
135:13 your name is to time *i*
Ps 136:1 loving-kindness is to time *i*
136:2 loving-kindness is to time *i*
136:3 loving-kindness is to time *i*
136:4 loving-kindness is to time *i*
136:5 loving-kindness is to time *i*
136:6 loving-kindness is to time *i*
136:7 loving-kindness is to time *i*
136:8 loving-kindness is to time *i*
136:9 loving-kindness is to time *i*
136:10 loving-kindness is to time *i*
136:11 loving-kindness is to time *i*
136:12 loving-kindness is to time *i*
136:13 loving-kindness is to time *i*
136:14 loving-kindness is to time *i*
136:15 loving-kindness is to time *i*
136:16 loving-kindness is to time *i*
136:17 loving-kindness is to time *i*
136:18 loving-kindness is to time *i*
136:19 loving-kindness is to time *i*
136:20 loving-kindness is to time *i*
136:21 loving-kindness is to time *i*
136:22 loving-kindness is to time *i*
136:23 loving-kindness is to time *i*
136:24 loving-kindness is to time *i*
136:25 loving-kindness is to time *i*
136:26 loving-kindness is to time *i*
138:8 Jehovah, to time *i* is your
139:24 in the way of time *i*
143:3 like those dead for time *i*
145:1 bless your name to time *i*
145:2 praise your name to time *i*
145:13 kingship for all times *i*
145:21 to time *i*, even forever
146:6 keeping trueness to time *i*
146:10 will be king to time *i*
148:6 standing forever, to time *i*
Pr 8:23 From time *i* I was installed
10:25 is a foundation to time *i*
10:30 to time *i* he will not be
27:24 will not be to time *i*, nor
Ec 1:4 is standing even to time *i*
1:10 had existence for time *i*
2:16 of the stupid one to time *i*
3:11 time *i* he has put in their
3:14 will prove to be to time *i*
9:6 no portion anymore to time *i*
Isa 9:7 from now on and to time *i*
14:20 To time *i* the offspring of
25:2 be rebuilt even to time *i*
26:4 is the Rock of times *i*
30:8 for a witness to time *i*
32:14 for time *i* the exultation
32:17 and security to time *i*
34:10 to time *i* its smoke will
34:17 To time *i* they will take
35:10 rejoicing to time *i* will
40:8 it will last to time *i*
40:28 is a God to time *i*. He does
45:17 a salvation for times *i*
45:17 the *i* times of eternity
47:7 To time *i* I shall prove to
51:6 prove to be even to time *i*
51:8 prove to be even to time *i*
51:11 and rejoicing to time *i*
54:8 loving-kindness to time *i*
55:13 a sign to time *i* that will
56:5 A name to time *i* I shall
57:16 it will not be to time *i*
59:21 from now on even to time *i*
60:15 a thing of pride to time *i*
60:21 to time *i* they will hold
61:7 Rejoicing to time *i* is what
Jer 3:5 stay resentful to time *i*
3:12 not stay resentful to time *i*
7:7, 7 time *i* even to time *i*
10:10 and the King to time *i*
17:4 To time *i* it will keep
17:25 be inhabited to time *i*
18:16 for whistling at to time *i*
20:17 womb be pregnant to time *i*
23:40 reproach to time *i* and
23:40 humiliation to time *i*
25:9 places devastated to time *i*
25:12 desolate wastes to time *i*
31:3 to time *i* I have loved you
31:40 down anymore to time *i*
33:11 for to time *i* is his
35:6 nor your sons, to time *i*
49:13 devastated places to time *i*
49:33 desolate waste to time *i*
51:26 desolate wastes to time *i*
51:62 desolate wastes to time *i*
La 3:31 to time *i* will Jehovah keep
5:19 to time *i* you will sit

Eze 26:21 no more be found to time *i*
27:36 be no more to time *i*
28:19 be no more to time *i*
37:25 their sons' sons to time *i*
37:25 their chieftain to time *i*
37:26 midst of them to time *i*
37:28 midst of them to time *i*
43:7 sons of Israel to time *i*
43:9 reside . . . to time *i*
Da 2:4 live on even for times *i*
2:20 blessed from time *i* even to
2:20 even to time *i*, for wisdom
2:44 itself will stand to times *i*
3:9 king, live on even for times *i*
4:3 kingdom to time *i*, and his
4:34 One living to time *i* I
4:34 is a rulership to time *i*
5:10 keep living even to times *i*
6:6 live on even for times *i*
6:21 live on even to times *i*
6:26 One enduring to times *i*, and
7:18 of the kingdom for time *i*
7:18, 18 for time *i* upon times *i*
9:24 in righteousness for times *i*
12:3 like the stars to time *i*
12:7 One who is alive for time *i*
Ho 2:19 engage you to me for time *i*
Joe 2:2 to exist from the *i* past
2:26 not be ashamed to time *i*
2:27 not be ashamed to time *i*
3:20 to time *i* . . . inhabited
Ob 10 have to be cut off to time *i*
Jon 2:6 bars were upon me for time *i*
Mic 2:9 take my splendor, to time *i*
4:5 Jehovah our God to time *i*
4:7 from now on and into time *i*
5:2 from the days of time *i*
Zep 2:9 waste, even to time *i*
Zec 1:5 time *i* that they continued
Mal 1:4 has denounced to time *i*
Eph 3:9 from the *i* past been hidden

Indefinitely
Ge 6:3 shall not act toward man *i*
21:33 Jehovah the *i* lasting God
49:26 *i* lasting hills. They will
De 33:15 things of the *i* lasting hills
33:27 are the *i* lasting arms
Jos 8:28 to an *i* lasting mound
2Sa 23:5 it is an *i* lasting covenant
1Ch 16:17 an *i* lasting covenant even
Ps 73:12 wicked, who are at ease *i*
105:10 *i* lasting covenant even to
Isa 24:5 broken the *i* lasting covenant
55:3 an *i* lasting covenant
60:19 to you an *i* lasting light
60:20 for you an *i* lasting light
61:8 an *i* lasting covenant I shall
63:12 an *i* lasting name for his
Jer 5:22 *i* lasting regulation that it
20:11 Their *i* lasting humiliation
32:40 an *i* lasting covenant, that
50:5 in an *i* lasting covenant
51:39 *i* lasting sleep, from which
51:57 must sleep an *i* lasting
Eze 16:60 an *i* lasting covenant
25:15 with an *i* lasting enmity
35:5 to have an *i* lasting enmity
35:9 *I* lasting desolate wastes
37:26 an *i* lasting covenant is
46:14 is an *i* lasting statute
Da 7:14 *i* lasting rulership that will
7:27 *i* lasting kingdom, and all
12:2 these to *i* lasting life
12:2 and to *i* lasting abhorrence
Hab 3:6 the *i* lasting hills bowed

Indescribable
2Co 9:15 to God for his *i* free gift

Indestructible
Heb 7:16 the power of an *i* life

Index
Eze 21:19 an *i* hand should be cut out

India
Es 1:1 as king from *I* to Ethiopia
8:9 that were from *I* to Ethiopia

Indian
Re 18:13 cinnamon and *I* spice and

Indicate
Lu 12:5 I will *i* to you whom to fear
Ac 11:28 *i* through the spirit that a

Indicating
1Pe 1:11 the spirit . . . *i* concerning

Indication
Php 1:28 and this *i* is from God

Indications
Pr 6:13 making *i* with his fingers

Indicator
Pr 16:11 just *i* and scales belong to
Isa 40:12 weighed with an *i* the

Indignant
Ge 40:2 Pharaoh grew *i* at his two
41:10 Pharaoh was *i* at his
Ex 16:20 that Moses became *i* at them
Le 10:6 not become *i* against all the
10:16 *i* at Eleazar and Ithamar
Nu 16:22 become *i* against the entire
31:14 And Moses grew *i* at the
De 1:34 became *i* and swore, saying
9:19 Jehovah had got *i* at you
Jos 22:18 Israel that he will be *i*
1Sa 29:4 Philistines became *i* at him
2Ki 5:11 Naaman grew *i* and began to
13:19 the man . . . grew *i* at him
Es 1:12 the king grew highly *i* and
2:21 became *i* and kept seeking to
Ec 5:6 *i* on account of your voice and
Isa 8:21 has made himself feel *i*
47:6 I grew *i* at my people
54:9 not become *i* toward you
57:16 that I shall be *i*
57:17 I grew *i*, and I proceeded
57:17 my face, while I was *i*
64:5 You yourself became *i*
64:9 Do not be *i*, O Jehovah, to
Jer 37:15 princes began to get *i*
La 5:22 been *i* toward us very much
Zec 1:2 Jehovah . . . *i* at your fathers
1:15 feeling *i* against the nations
1:15 *i* to only a little extent
8:14 forefathers' making me *i*
Mt 20:24 *i* at the two brothers
21:15 chief priests . . . became *i*
26:8 disciples became *i* and said
Mr 10:14 Jesus was *i* and said to
10:41 to be *i* at James and John
Lu 13:14 *i* because Jesus did the cure

Indignation
Nu 1:53 no *i* may arise against the
16:46 *i* has gone out from the face
18:5 that no further *i* may occur
De 29:28 and rage and great *i* and
Jos 9:20 that no *i* may come upon us
22:20 there came *i*? And he was
2Ki 3:27 to be great *i* against Israel
1Ch 27:24 came to be *i* against Israel
2Ch 19:2 *i* against you from the
19:10 *i* may not have to take
24:18 to be *i* against Judah and
29:8 Jehovah's *i* came to be
32:25 came to be *i* against him
32:26 Jehovah's *i* did not come
Es 1:18 be plenty of contempt and *i*
Ps 38:1 do not in your *i* reprove me
102:10 denunciation and your *i*
Ec 5:17 on his part and cause for *i*
Isa 34:2 Jehovah has *i* against all
54:8 a flood of *i* I concealed my
60:10 for in my *i* I shall have
Jer 10:10 Because of his *i* the earth
21:5 with rage and with great *i*
32:37 in my rage and in great *i*
50:13 Because of the *i* of Jehovah
Zec 1:15 With great *i* I am feeling
7:12 *i* on the part of Jehovah of
Mr 3:5 looking . . . upon them with *i*
14:4 there were some expressing *i*
2Co 7:11 yes, *i*, yes, fear, yes

Indisposed
Jas 5:15 will make the *i* one well

Indisputable
Ac 19:36 since these things are *i*, it

Indistinct
1Co 14:8 trumpet sounds an *i* call

Individual
Ge 42:25 to each one's *i* sack and to
45:22 he gave *i* changes of mantles
Ex 16:16 an omer measure for each *i*
38:26 The half shekel for an *i* was
Nu 3:47 take five shekels for each *i*
2Ki 12:4 according to *i* valuation
23:35 one's *i* tax rate he exacted
Ezr 10:14 older men of each *i* city
Job 31:35 the *i* in the case at law
Pr 21:17 will be an *i* in want
24:30 by the field of the lazy *i*
27:21 *i* is according to his praise
Isa 7:21 *i* will preserve alive a

Individually
Isa 44:8 caused you *i* to hear and
65:15 put you *i* to death, but his
Eze 20:8 they did not *i* throw away
Ro 12:5 members belonging *i* to one
1Co 4:6 not be puffed up *i* in favor of
12:27 Christ's body . . . members *i*
Eph 5:33 *i* so love his wife as he does
Re 2:23 I will give to you *i*
20:13 judged *i* according to their

Individuals
2Ch 30:11 *i* from Asher and Manasseh

Indoors
De 32:25 bereave them, And *i* fright
Joh 20:26 disciples were again *i*

Induce
Nu 31:16 to *i* the sons of Israel to

Induced
Ex 20:5 nor be *i* to serve them
23:24 or be *i* to serve them, and
De 26:17 Jehovah you have *i* to say
26:18 he has *i* you to say today
Pr 25:15 By patience a commander is *i*
Ac 6:11 they secretly *i* men to say

Inducement
Ro 7:8 sin, receiving an *i* through
7:11 sin, receiving an *i* through
2Co 5:12 *i* for boasting in respect
Ga 5:13 freedom as an *i* for the flesh
1Ti 5:14 to give no *i* to the opposer

Indulge
Jg 21:2 *i* in a great deal of weeping
La 3:39 a living man *i* in complaints
2Co 1:17 I did not *i* in any lightness

Indulgence
2Pe 2:7 *i* of the law-defying people

Indulgent
Ne 9:30 *i* with them for many years

Indulging
Ec 8:8 no escape for those *i* in it
10:11 to the one *i* in the tongue
12:11 *i* in collections of sentences
2Pe 2:13 *i* with unrestrained delight
Jude 8 *i* in dreams, are defiling the

Industriousness
Heb 6:11 show the same *i* so as to

Ineffectiveness
Heb 7:18 of its weakness and *i*

Inexcusable
Ro 1:20 so that they are *i*
2:1 you are *i* . . . if you judge

Inexperience
Pr 1:22 keep loving *i*, and how long

Inexperienced
Ps 19:7 making the *i* one wise
116:6 Jehovah is guarding the *i*
119:130 the *i* ones understand
Pr 1:4 give to the *i* ones shrewdness
1:22 How long will you *i* ones
1:32 renegading of the *i* ones is
7:7 I might peer upon the *i* ones
8:5 *i* ones, understand shrewdness
9:4 Whoever is *i*, let him turn
9:6 Leave the *i* ones and keep
9:16 *i*, let him turn aside here
14:15 *i* puts faith in every word
14:18 *i* ones will certainly take
19:25 the *i* one may become shrewd
21:11 the *i* becomes wise; and by
22:3 *i* have passed along and must
27:12 *i* that have passed along have
Eze 45:20 because of any *i* one

Infamy
Eze 23:10 she came to be *i* to women

Infancy
2Ti 3:15 from *i* you have known the

Infant
Lu 1:41 the *i* in her womb leaped
1:44 the *i* in my womb leaped with
2:12 an *i* bound in cloth bands and
2:16 the *i* lying in the manger

Infants
Lu 18:15 bring him also their *i* for
18:16 Jesus called the *i* to him
Ac 7:19 fathers to expose their *i*
1Pe 2:2 as newborn *i*, form a longing

Inferior
Job 12:3 I am not *i* to you, And with
13:2 I am not *i* to you
Da 2:39 rise another kingdom *i* to you
Joh 2:10 people are intoxicated, the *i*
2Co 11:5 *i* to your superfine apostles
12:11 *i* to your superfine

Infirmities
Ac 14:15 having the same *i* as you do

Infirmity
Mt 4:23 every sort of *i* among the
9:35 curing . . . every sort of *i*
10:1 to cure . . . every sort of *i*

Inflame
Pr 29:8 boastful talk *i* a town

Inflamed
Isa 13:8 Their faces are *i* faces
Ro 1:27 violently *i* in their lust
1Co 7:9 than to be *i* with passion

Inflames
Isa 5:11 that wine itself *i* them

Inflammation
Le 13:23 it is the *i* of the boil
13:28 it is an *i* of the scar
De 28:22 burning fever and *i* and
Ac 28:6 to swell up with *i* or

Inflict
Le 26:21 *i* seven times more blows
2Ki 8:29 Syrians got to *i* upon him
9:15 Syrians got to *i* upon him
2Co 10:6 to *i* punishment for every
1Pe 2:14 to *i* punishment on evildoers

Inflicted
Ge 14:5 they *i* defeats on the Rephaim
2Ch 22:6 wounds that they had *i* upon
Pr 27:6 *i* by a lover are faithful
Lu 10:30 stripped him and *i* blows
Ac 16:23 had *i* many blows upon them

Inflicting
Job 33:22 his life to those *i* death

Influence
Da 5:2 under the *i* of the wine, said
Ga 3:1 that brought you under evil *i*

Influenced
Ac 14:2 wrongly *i* the souls of people

Inform
1Sa 31:9 *i* the houses of their idols
2Sa 15:28 comes from you men to *i*
1Ch 10:9 *i* their idols and the people
Job 38:3 question you, and you *i* me
40:7 question you, and you *i* me
42:4 question you, and you *i* me
Eze 43:10 *i* the house of Israel about

Information
Ge 46:28 to Joseph to impart *i* ahead
Da 7:16 from him reliable *i* on all
Ac 21:31 *i* came up to the commander
24:1 *i* to the governor against Paul
25:2 Jews gave him *i* against Paul
25:15 brought *i* about him, asking

Informed
Jer 11:18 Jehovah himself has *i* me
Ac 14:6 they, on being *i* of it, fled

Informer
2Sa 15:13 an *i* came to David, saying

Infused
2Ti 4:17 near me and *i* power into me

Ingathering
Ex 23:16 festival of *i* at the outgoing
34:22 the festival of *i* at the turn
De 16:13 *i* from your threshing floor

Ingenious
Ex 35:33 to make *i* products of every

Inhabit
Ex 15:17 ready for you to *i*, O Jehovah
Nu 35:2 give the Levites cities to *i*
35:3 must serve for them to *i*
Isa 54:3 *i* even the desolated cities
Jer 29:5 Build houses and *i* them
29:28 Build houses and *i* them
Am 9:14 *i* them, and plant vineyards
Zec 14:11 people will certainly *i* her
Eph 2:22 place for God to *i* by spirit
Re 17:2 those who *i* the earth were

Inhabitant
Isa 5:9 astonishment, without an *i*
6:11 ruins, to be without an *i*
9:9 Ephraim and the *i* of Samaria
20:6 *i* of this coastland will be
22:21 to the *i* of Jerusalem and
24:17 you *i* of the land
26:21 error of the *i* of the land
Jer 2:15 afire, so that there is no *i*
4:7 so that there will be no *i*
9:11 desolate waste, without an *i*
26:9 so as to be without an *i*
33:10 without *i* and without
34:22 desolate waste without an *i*
44:2 in them there is no *i*
44:22 without an *i*, as at this
46:19 so as to be without an *i*
48:43 are upon you, O *i* of Moab
51:29 astonishment, without an *i*
51:37 whistle at, without an *i*
51:62 no *i*, either man or even
Ho 4:3 every *i* in it will have to
Am 1:5 cut off the *i* from Bikath-aven
1:8 cut off the *i* from Ashdod
8:8 every *i* . . . have to mourn
Zep 2:5 that there will be no *i*
3:6 so that there was no *i*

Inhabitants
Ge 19:25 all the *i* of the cities and
34:30 a stench to the *i* of the land
36:20 the *i* of the land: Lotan and
50:11 And the *i* of the land, the
Ex 15:14 hold on the *i* of Philistia
15:15 All the *i* of Canaan will
23:31 give into your hand the *i* of
34:12 not . . . covenant with the *i*
34:15 with the *i* of the land, as
Le 18:25 land will vomit its *i* out
25:10 in the land to all its *i*
Nu 13:32 is a land that eats up its *i*
14:14 tell it to the *i* of this land
32:17 away from the face of the *i*
33:52 drive away all the *i* of the
33:55 drive the *i* of the land away
De 13:13 turn away the *i* of their
13:15 strike the *i* of that city
Jos 2:9 all the *i* of the land have
2:24 all the *i* of the land have
7:9 Canaanites and all the *i* of
8:24 killing of all the *i* of Ai
8:26 the *i* of Ai to destruction
9:3 the *i* of Gibeon heard what
9:11 all the *i* of our land said
9:24 annihilate all the *i* of the
10:1 *i* of Gibeon had made peace
13:6 the *i* of the mountainous
15:15 to the *i* of Debir
17:7 to the *i* of En-Tappuah
17:11 and the *i* of Dor and its
17:11 the *i* of En-dor and its
17:11 the *i* of Taanach and its
17:11 the *i* of Megiddo and its
Jg 1:11 against the *i* of Debir
1:19 dispossess the *i* of the low
1:27 and the *i* of Dor and its
1:27 and the *i* of Ibleam and its
1:27 and the *i* of Megiddo and its
1:30 not drive out the *i* of Kitron
1:30 Kitron and the *i* of Nahalol
1:31 not drive out the *i* of Acco
1:31 the *i* of Sidon and Ahlab and
1:33 the *i* of Beth-shemesh and
1:33 the *i* of Beth-anath, but they
1:33 the *i* of Beth-shemesh and of
2:2 covenant with the *i* of this
5:23 Curse its *i* incessantly, For
10:18 head of all the *i* of Gilead
11:8 head of all the *i* of Gilead
20:15 apart from the *i* of Gibeah
21:9 from the *i* of Jabesh-gilead
21:10 strike the *i* of Jabesh-gilead
21:12 out of the *i* of Jabesh-gilead
Ru 4:4 Buy it in front of the *i* and
1Sa 6:21 to the *i* of Kiriath-jearim
23:5 savior of the *i* of Keilah
31:11 *i* of Jabesh-gilead got to
1Ki 17:1 from the *i* of Gilead
2Ki 19:26 *i* will be feeble-handed
22:16 this place and upon its *i*
22:19 this place and its *i* for
23:2 all the *i* of Jerusalem with
1Ch 4:23 potters and the *i* of Netaim
8:6 belonging to the *i* of Geba
8:13 belonging to the *i* of Aijalon
8:13 chased away the *i* of Gath
9:2 first *i* that were in their
11:4 Jebusites were the *i* of the
11:5 *i* of Jebus began to say to
22:18 given into my hand the *i* of
2Ch 15:5 disorders among all the *i*
19:8 cases of the *i* of Jerusalem
20:7 away the *i* of this land
20:15 you *i* of Jerusalem and King
20:18 *i* of Jerusalem themselves
20:20 and you *i* of Jerusalem
20:23 *i* of the mountainous region
20:23 finished with the *i* of Seir
21:11 *i* of Jerusalem to have
21:13 *i* of Jerusalem to have
22:1 *i* of Jerusalem made Ahaziah
31:4 people, the *i* of Jerusalem
32:22 *i* of Jerusalem out of the
32:26 he and the *i* of Jerusalem
32:33 *i* of Jerusalem rendered to
33:9 *i* of Jerusalem to do worse
34:9 and the *i* of Jerusalem
34:24 this place and its *i*
34:27 this place and its *i*
34:28 upon this place and its *i*
34:30 and the *i* of Jerusalem
34:32 *i* of Jerusalem proceeded
35:18 the *i* of Jerusalem held
Ezr 4:6 against the *i* of Judah and
4:9 the Babylonians, the *i* of Susa
Ne 3:13 the *i* of Zanoah repaired
7:3 guards of the *i* of Jerusalem
9:24 *i* of the land, the Canaanites
Ps 33:8 the *i* of the productive land
49:1 you *i* of the system of things
65:8 the *i* of the uttermost parts
72:9 *i* of waterless regions will
75:3 earth and all its *i* being
83:7 together with the *i* of Tyre
Isa 5:3 *i* of Jerusalem and you men
8:14 snare to the *i* of Jerusalem
10:13 bring down the *i* just like
10:31 *i* of Gebim themselves have
18:3 *i* of the productive land and
21:14 you *i* of the land of Tema
23:2 you *i* of the coastland
23:6 howl, you *i* of the coastland
24:1 and scattered its *i*
24:5 has been polluted under its *i*
24:6 *i* of the land have decreased
26:9 righteousness is what the *i*
26:18 *i* for the productive land
37:27 *i* will be feeble-handed
38:11 *i* of the land of cessation
42:11 Let the *i* of the crag cry
51:6 its *i* themselves will die
Jer 1:14 against all the *i* of the land
4:4 of Judah and *i* of Jerusalem
6:12 out against the *i* of the land
8:1 bones of the *i* of Jerusalem
8:16 fills it, the city and its *i*
10:18 slinging out the *i* of the
11:2 and to the *i* of Jerusalem
11:9 among the *i* of Jerusalem
11:12 the *i* of Jerusalem will
13:13 all the *i* of this land
13:13 all the *i* of Jerusalem
17:20 all you *i* of Jerusalem
17:25 and the *i* of Jerusalem
18:11 and to the *i* of Jerusalem
19:3 and you *i* of Jerusalem
19:12 to the *i* of it, even to
20:6 all the *i* of your house
21:6 strike the *i* of this city
23:14 the *i* of her like Gomorrah
25:2 the *i* of Jerusalem, saying
25:9 against its *i* and against
25:29 all the *i* of the earth
25:30 sing out against all the *i*
26:15 this city and upon her *i*
32:32 and the *i* of Jerusalem
35:13 and to the *i* of Jerusalem

Jer 35:17 all the *i* of Jerusalem
36:31 upon the *i* of Jerusalem and
42:18 upon the *i* of Jerusalem, so
48:28 on the crag, you *i* of Moab
49:8 O *i* of Dedan! For the
49:20 against the *i* of Teman
49:30 dwell, O *i* of Hazor, is
50:21 and against the *i* of Pekod
50:34 to the *i* of Babylon
50:35 against the *i* of Babylon
51:1 against the *i* of Leb-kamai
51:12 against the *i* of Babylon
51:24 to all the *i* of Chaldea all
51:35 upon the *i* of Chaldea
La 4:12 the *i* of the productive land
Eze 11:15 *i* of Jerusalem have said
12:19 said to the *i* of Jerusalem
15:6 given the *i* of Jerusalem
26:17 all the *i* of the earth
27:8 The *i* of Sidon and of Arvad
27:35 All the *i* of the islands
29:6 *i* of Egypt will have to know
32:15 strike down all the *i* in it
33:24 *i* of these devastated places
39:9 the *i* of the cities of Israel
Da 4:35 the *i* of the earth are being
4:35 and the *i* of the earth
9:7 to the *i* of Jerusalem and to
Ho 4:1 case with the *i* of the land
Joe 1:2 all you *i* of the land
1:14 all the *i* of the land, to the
2:1 Let all the *i* of the land
Am 9:5 *i* in it will have to mourn
Mic 6:12 own *i* have spoken falsehood
6:16 her *i* something to be
7:13 waste on account of its *i*
Zep 1:4 all the *i* of Jerusalem
1:11 Howl, you *i* of Maktesh
1:18 of all the *i* of the earth
Zec 8:20 *i* of many cities will come
8:21 the *i* of one city will
11:6 upon the *i* of the land
12:5 The *i* of Jerusalem are a
12:7 beauty of the *i* of Jerusalem
12:8 around the *i* of Jerusalem
12:10 upon the *i* of Jerusalem the
13:1 to the *i* of Jerusalem for
Mr 1:5 all the *i* of Jerusalem made
Joh 7:25 some of the *i* of Jerusalem
Ac 1:19 to all the *i* of Jerusalem
2:9 *i* of Mesopotamia, and Judea
2:14 *i* of Jerusalem, let this be
4:16 to all the *i* of Jerusalem
13:27 *i* of Jerusalem and their

Inhabited
Ex 16:35 their coming to a land *i*
Isa 13:20 will never be *i*, nor will
44:26 She will be *i*, and of the
45:18 formed it even to be *i*
Jer 6:8 desolate waste, a land not *i*
17:6 salt country that is not *i*
17:25 be *i* to time indefinite
22:6 cities, not one will be *i*
50:13 she will not be *i*, and
Eze 12:20 *i* cities . . . be devastated
26:17 used to be *i* from the seas
26:19 that are actually not *i*
26:20 that you may not be *i*
29:11 forty years . . . not be *i*
35:9 own cities will not be *i*
36:10 the cities must become *i*
36:11 to be *i* as in your former
36:33 cause the cities to be *i*
36:35 they have become *i*
Joe 3:20 Judah . . . will be *i*
Zec 2:4 country Jerusalem will be *i*
7:7 Jerusalem happened to be *i*
7:7 and the Shephelah were *i*
9:5 Ashkelon . . . will not be *i*
12:6 Jerusalem must yet be *i* in
14:10 must rise and become *i* in
14:11 Jerusalem . . . *i* in security
Mt 24:14 preached in all the *i* earth
Lu 2:1 all the *i* earth to be registered
4:5 the kingdoms of the *i* earth
21:26 coming upon the *i* earth
Ac 9:35 those who *i* Lydda and the
11:28 upon the entire *i* earth
17:6 have overturned the *i* earth
17:31 purposes to judge the *i* earth
19:27 and the *i* earth worships is
24:5 throughout the *i* earth and a
Ro 10:18 extremities of the *i* earth
Heb 1:6 Firstborn into the *i* earth
Heb 2:5 the *i* earth to come, about
Re 3:10 come upon the whole *i* earth
12:9 misleading the entire *i* earth
16:14 kings of the entire *i* earth

Inhabiter
Eze 7:7 O *i* of the land, the time

Inhabiting
Jos 10:6 *i* the mountainous region
11:19 the Hivites *i* Gibeon
Jg 1:9 Canaanites *i* the mountainous
1:17 Canaanites *i* Zephath and to
1:21 Jebusites *i* Jerusalem; but
1:32 the Canaanites *i* the land
1:33 Canaanites *i* the land; and
3:3 Hivites *i* Mount Lebanon from
11:21 the Amorites *i* that land
1Sa 27:8 *i* the land that extended
2Sa 5:6 Jebusites *i* the land, and
Es 9:19 *i* the cities of the outlying
Ps 22:3 holy, *I* the praises of Israel
74:14 *i* the waterless regions
Isa 24:6 those *i* it are held guilty
26:5 laid low those *i* the height
42:10 you islands and you *i* them
Jer 46:8 destroy the city and those *i*
47:2 the city and those *i* it
Eze 26:17 she and those *i* her, those
39:6 *i* the islands in security
Zep 2:5 those *i* the region of the sea
Mt 23:21 and by him that is *i* it
Lu 13:4 all other men *i* Jerusalem
Ac 19:10 those *i* the district of Asia

Inhabitress
Isa 12:6 *i* of Zion, for great in
Jer 21:13 *i* of the low plain, O rock
46:19 exile, O *i*, the daughter of
48:18 *i* of the daughter of Dibon
48:19 O *i* of Aroer
51:35 *i* of Zion will say
Mic 1:11 O *i* of Shaphir, in shameful
1:11 The *i* of Zaanan has not gone
1:12 the *i* of Maroth has waited
1:13 horses, O *i* of Lachish
1:15 to you, O *i* of Mareshah

Inhabits
Isa 42:11 settlements that Kedar *i*

Inherit
Le 25:46 *i* as a possession to time
De 1:38 he will cause Israel to *i* it
3:28 cause them to *i* the land that
19:14 *i* in the land that Jehovah
Jos 1:6 people to *i* the land that I
13:32 Moses caused them to *i*
14:1 Israel caused them to *i*
Ps 69:36 servants themselves will *i*
Isa 57:13 will *i* the land and will
Eze 47:14 you people must *i* it
Zec 8:12 people to *i* all these things
Mt 5:5 since they will *i* the earth
19:29 and will *i* everlasting life
25:34 *i* the kingdom prepared for
Mr 10:17 do to *i* everlasting life
Lu 10:25 shall I *i* everlasting life
18:18 shall I *i* everlasting life
1Co 6:9 persons will not *i* God's
6:10 will *i* God's kingdom
15:50 cannot *i* God's kingdom
15:50 corruption *i* incorruption
Ga 5:21 will not *i* God's kingdom
Heb 1:14 who are going to *i* salvation
6:12 and patience *i* the promises
12:17 when he wanted to *i* the
1Pe 3:9 that you might *i* a blessing
Re 21:7 Anyone conquering will *i*

Inheritable
Ac 7:5 not give him any *i* possession

Inheritance
Ge 31:14 Is there a share of *i* for us
48:6 will be called in their *i*
Ex 15:17 in the mountain of your *i*
Le 25:46 pass them on as an *i* to your
Nu 16:14 may give us an *i* of field
18:20 you will not have an *i*, and
18:20 I am your share and your *i*
18:21 *i* in return for their service
18:23 not get possession of an *i*
18:24 given to the Levites as an *i*
18:24 not get possession of an *i*
18:26 tenth part . . . for your *i*
26:53 apportioned for an *i* by the
26:54 you should increase one's *i*
Nu 26:54 you should reduce one's *i*
26:54 Each one's *i* should be given
26:55 they should get an *i*
26:56 one's *i* should be apportioned
26:62 no *i* was to be given to them
27:7 an *i* in the midst of their
27:7 father's *i* to pass to them
27:8 his *i* to pass to his daughter
27:9 give his *i* to his brothers
27:10 *i* to his father's brothers
27:11 *i* to his blood relation who
32:18 each with his own *i*
32:19 shall not get an *i* with them
32:19 our *i* has come to us from
32:32 the possession of our *i* will
33:54 you should increase his *i*
33:54 you should reduce his *i*
34:2 that will fall to you by *i*
34:14 have already taken their *i*
34:15 have already taken their *i*
35:2 of the *i* of their possession
35:8 in proportion to his *i* that he
36:2 give the land in *i* by lot to
36:2 to give the *i* of Zelophehad
36:3 the women's *i* must also be
36:3 withdrawn from the *i* of our
36:3 added to the *i* of the tribe
36:3 from the lot of our *i*
36:4 women's *i* must also be added
36:4 added to the *i* of the tribe to
36:4 their *i* would be withdrawn
36:4 *i* of the tribe of our fathers
36:7 And no *i* . . . should circulate
36:7 cleave each one to the *i* of
36:8 getting possession of an *i* out
36:8 of the *i* of his forefathers
36:9 no *i* should circulate from
36:9 cleave each to its own *i*
36:12 *i* might continue together
De 4:21 God is giving you as an *i*
4:38 their land as an *i* as at this
10:9 Levi . . . no share and *i*
10:9 Jehovah is his *i*, just as
12:9 the *i* that Jehovah your God
12:12 has no share or *i* with you
14:27 has no share or *i* with you
14:29 no share or *i* with you
15:4 God is giving you as an *i*
18:1 No share or *i* with Israel
18:1 even his *i*, they should eat
18:2 no *i* should come to belong
18:2 Jehovah is his *i*, just as he
19:10 God is giving you as an *i*
19:14 set the boundaries in your *i*
20:16 God is giving you as an *i*
21:16 gives as an *i* to his sons
21:23 God is giving you as an *i*
24:4 God is giving you as an *i*
25:19 an *i* to take possession of
26:1 God is giving you as an *i*
29:8 an *i* to the Reubenites and the
31:7 will give it to them as an *i*
32:8 gave the nations an *i*
Jos 11:23 gave it as an *i* to Israel
13:6 fall to Israel as an *i*
13:7 *i* to the nine tribes and
13:8 Gadites took their *i* that
13:14 that he did not give an *i*
13:14 offerings . . . are their *i*
13:23 territory was the *i* of the
13:28 the *i* of the sons of Gad by
13:33 Moses did not give an *i*
13:33 God of Israel is their *i*
14:2 *i* was by lot, just as
14:3 *i* of the two other tribes
14:3 Levites he did not give an *i*
14:9 as an *i* to time indefinite
14:13 and gave Hebron . . . as an *i*
14:14 as an *i* down to this day
15:20 *i* of the tribe of the sons
16:5 the boundary of their *i*
16:8 *i* of the tribe of the sons of
16:9 in the midst of the *i*
17:4 give us an *i* in the midst of
17:4 an *i* in the midst of the
17:6 an *i* in the midst of his
17:14 as an *i* one lot and one
18:2 *i* they had not apportioned
18:4 in accord with their *i*, and
18:7 priesthood . . . is their *i*
18:7 *i* on the side of the Jordan
18:20 *i* of the sons of Benjamin
18:28 *i* of the sons of Benjamin
19:1 *i* came to be in the midst of

Jos 19:1 the *i* of the sons of Judah
19:2 have in their *i* Beer-sheba
19:8 *i* of the tribe of the sons of
19:9 *i* of the sons of Simeon was
19:9 in the midst of their *i*
19:10 *i* came to be as far as
19:16 the *i* of the sons of Zebulun
19:23 *i* of the tribe of the sons
19:31 *i* of the tribe of the sons
19:39 *i* of the tribe of the sons
19:41 *i* came to be Zorah and
19:48 *i* of the tribe of the sons
19:49 gave an *i* to Joshua the son
21:3 grounds out of their *i*
23:4 as an *i* for your tribes, and
24:28 each one to his *i*
24:30 the territory of his *i* in
24:32 the sons of Joseph as an *i*
Jg 2:6 each to his *i*, to take
2:9 in the territory of his *i* in
11:2 no *i* in the household of our
18:1 looking for an *i* for itself
18:1 an *i* had not fallen to them
20:6 into every field of Israel's *i*
21:23 returned to their *i* and built
21:24 each one to his own *i*
Ru 4:5 name . . . to rise upon his *i*
4:6 for fear I may ruin my own *i*
4:10 to rise upon his *i* and that
1Sa 10:1 as a leader over his *i*
26:19 attached to the *i* of Jehovah
2Sa 14:16 son from the *i* given by God
20:1 no *i* in the son of Jesse
20:19 swallow up the *i* of Jehovah
21:3 bless the *i* of Jehovah
1Ki 8:51 your people and your *i*, whom
8:53 *i* out of all the peoples of
12:16 no *i* in the son of Jesse
2Ki 21:14 forsake the remnant of my *i*
1Ch 16:18 As the allotment of your *i*
28:8 pass it on as an *i* to your
2Ch 10:16 no *i* in the son of Jesse
Job 20:29 Even his stated *i* from God
27:13 the *i* of the tyrants they
31:2 *i* from the Almighty from on
42:15 *i* in among their brothers
Ps 2:8 I may give nations as your *i*
28:9 your people, and bless your *i*
33:12 whom he has chosen as his *i*
37:18 their very *i* will continue
47:4 He will choose for us our *i*
68:9 *i*, even when it was weary
74:2 that you redeemed as your *i*
78:55 went allotting them an *i*
78:62 against his *i* he became
78:71 And over Israel his *i*
79:1 nations have come into your *i*
94:5 your *i* they keep afflicting
94:14 Nor will he leave his own *i*
105:11 as the allotment of your *i*
106:5 make my boast with your *i*
106:40 he came to detest his *i*
111:6 them the *i* of the nations
127:3 Sons are an *i* from Jehovah
135:12 gave their land as an *i*
135:12 An *i* to Israel his people
136:21 gave their land as an *i*
136:22 *i* to Israel his servant
Pr 13:22 good will leave an *i* to sons
17:2 he will have a share of the *i*
19:14 *i* from fathers is a house
20:21 An *i* is being got by greed at
Ec 7:11 Wisdom along with an *i* is
Isa 19:25 and my *i*, Israel
47:6 I profaned my *i*, and I
Jer 2:7 my own *i* you made something
10:16 Israel is the staff of his *i*
12:7 I have deserted my *i*; I have
12:8 My *i* has become to me like
12:9 My *i* is as a many-colored
16:18 they had filled my *i*
50:11 when pillaging my own *i*
51:19 even the staff of his *i*
Eze 35:15 *i* of the house of Israel
44:28, 28 as an *i*: I am their *i*
45:1 allot the land as an *i*
46:16 one of his sons as his *i*
46:16 It is their possession by *i*
46:17 gift from his *i* to one of
46:17 *i*—as regards his sons
46:18 *i* of the people so as to
46:18 give his sons an *i*, to the
47:13 *i* as the land for the
47:14 fall to you by lot for *i*
Eze 47:22 should allot it for *i* to
47:22 fall by lot into an *i* in
47:23 you should give his *i*
48:29 *i* to the tribes of Israel
Joe 2:17 make your *i* a reproach
3:2 my people and my *i* Israel
Mic 7:14 the flock of your *i*, the one
7:18 of the remnant of his *i*
Mal 1:3 his *i* for the jackals of the
Mt 21:38 kill him and get his *i*
Mr 12:7 and the *i* will be ours
Lu 12:13 brother to divide the *i* with
20:14 that the *i* may become ours
Ac 20:32 *i* among all the sanctified
26:18 *i* among those sanctified by
Ga 3:18 if the *i* is due to law, it
Eph 1:14 token in advance of our *i*
1:18 as an *i* for the holy ones
5:5 has any *i* in the kingdom of
Col 1:12 in the *i* of the holy ones
3:24 the due reward of the *i*
Heb 9:15 of the everlasting *i*
11:8 destined to receive as an *i*
1Pe 1:4 undefiled and unfading *i*
5:3 over those who are God's *i*

Inheritances
Jos 19:51 *i* that Eleazar the priest

Inherited
Heb 1:4 *i* a name more excellent than

Inheritor
Jer 49:1 is there no *i* that he has

Inherits
De 32:9 is the allotment that he *i*

Iniquity
Da 4:27 your *i* by showing mercy to

Initial
Eze 36:11 than in your *i* state

Initiate
2Co 8:6 the one to *i* it among you

Initiated
Mr 6:7 *i* sending them out two by two
2Co 8:10 you *i* not only the doing but

Initiative
Joh 5:19 a single thing of his own *i*
5:30 single thing of my own *i*
7:28 have not come of my own *i*
8:28 I do nothing of my own *i*
8:42 I come of my own *i* at all
10:18 surrender it of my own *i*

Injuries
2Ti 4:14 did me many *i*—Jehovah will

Injurious
Le 26:6 make the *i* wild beast cease
2Ki 4:41 nothing *i* proved to be in the
Job 5:19 nothing *i* will touch you
Ps 144:10 free from the *i* sword
Isa 8:9 Be *i*, O you peoples, and be
Eze 5:16 *i* arrows of the famine upon
5:17 famine and *i* wild beasts
14:15 *i* wild beasts pass through
14:21 my four *i* acts of judgment
14:21 famine and *i* wild beast and
34:25 *i* wild beast to cease
38:10 think up an *i* scheme
Mr 7:21 *i* reasonings issue forth
Lu 16:25 Lazarus correspondingly the *i*
Ac 9:13 *i* things he did to your holy
Ro 1:30 inventors of *i* things
2:9 man who works what is *i*, of
14:20 it is *i* to the man who with
1Co 10:6 persons desiring *i* things
1Ti 6:10 of all sorts of *i* things
Tit 1:12 *i* wild beasts, unemployed
Jas 3:8 tongue . . . An unruly *i* thing

Injuriously
Ac 19:9 speaking *i* about The Way
23:5 must not speak *i* of a ruler
1Ti 6:1 may never be spoken of *i*
Tit 3:2 to speak *i* of no one, not to

Injury
Nu 35:23 and was not seeking his *i*
Jos 24:20 do you *i* and exterminate
Jg 15:3 dealing with them to their *i*
1Sa 25:26 those seeking *i* to my lord
25:34 held me back from doing *i*
26:21 no more do you *i*, in view
2Sa 19:7 worse for you than all the *i*
1Ki 2:44 *i* which your heart well
1Ki 2:44 *i* by you upon your own head
11:25 the *i* that Hadad did
17:20 *i* by putting her son to
2Ki 8:12 *i* you will do to the sons of
Ezr 4:22 increase to the *i* of kings
Es 9:2 hand on those seeking their *i*
Ec 8:9 has dominated man to his *i*
Lu 6:9 to do good or to do *i*, to save
Ac 18:10 so as to do you *i*; for I have
Ro 14:16 be spoken of with *i* to you
1Co 13:5 not keep account of the *i*
Php 3:2 look out for the workers of *i*
1Th 5:15, 15 no one renders *i* for *i* to
1Pe 3:9, 9 not paying back *i* for *i* or

Injustice
Le 19:15 You people must not do *i* in
19:35 not commit *i* in judging, in
De 25:16 every doer of *i*, is
32:4 with whom there is no *i*
Ps 7:3 exists any *i* in my hands
82:2 you keep on judging with *i*
Pr 29:27 *i* is something detestable to
Eze 3:20 actually does *i* and I must
18:8 from *i* he would draw back
18:24 and actually does *i*
18:26 does *i* and dies on account
18:26 for his *i* . . . he will die
28:18 the *i* of your sales goods
33:13 and does *i*, all his own
33:13 his *i* that he has done
33:15 by not doing *i*, he will
33:18 and actually does *i*, he
Ro 9:14 Is there *i* with God?
Re 18:5 called her acts of *i* to mind

Ink
Jer 36:18 writing in the book with *i*
2Co 3:3 inscribed not with *i* but with
2Jo 12 to do so with paper and *i*, but
3Jo 13 writing you with *i* and pen

Inkhorn
Eze 9:2 a secretary's *i* at his hips
9:3 there was the secretary's *i*
9:11 whose hips there was the *i*

Inland
Ac 19:1 Paul went through the *i* parts

Inmost
Ps 95:4 are the *i* depths of the earth
Joh 7:38 from his *i* part streams of

Inn
Lu 10:34 brought him to an *i* and took

Inner
Ex 8:3 frogs . . . your *i* bedroom and
2Sa 4:7 his couch in his *i* bedroom
1Ki 6:27 cherubs inside the *i* house
6:36 build the *i* courtyard with
7:12 for the *i* courtyard of the
7:50 *i* house, that is, the Most
2Ki 6:12 you speak in your *i* bedroom
11:2 the *i* room for the couches
1Ch 28:11 its dark *i* rooms and the
2Ch 4:22 *i* doors for the Most Holy
22:11 the *i* room for the couches
Es 4:11 to the king at the *i* courtyard
5:1 her stand in the *i* courtyard
Eze 8:3 entrance of the *i* gate that is
8:12 the *i* rooms of his showpiece
8:16 *i* courtyard of the house of
10:3 was filling the *i* courtyard
40:15 the porch of the *i* gate was
40:19 the front of the *i* courtyard
40:23 the gate of the *i* courtyard
40:27 the *i* courtyard had a gate
40:28 the *i* courtyard by the gate
40:32 the *i* courtyard by way of
40:44 the outside of the *i* gate
40:44 singers, in the *i* courtyard
40:47 measuring the *i* courtyard
41:15 the temple and the *i* place
41:17 and as far as the *i* house
41:17 *i* house and on the outside
42:3 belonged to the *i* courtyard
42:15 measurements of the *i* house
43:5 me into the *i* courtyard
44:17 gates of the *i* courtyard
44:17 gates of the *i* courtyard
44:21 come into the *i* courtyard
44:27 *i* courtyard, to minister
45:19 gate of the *i* courtyard
46:1 gate of the *i* courtyard that
Mt 5:40 possession of your *i* garment
24:26 He is in the *i* chambers, do

Mr 14:63 priest ripped his *i* garments
Joh 19:23 part, and the *i* garment
19:23 *i* garment was without a
Ac 9:39 exhibiting many *i* garments
16:24 threw them into the *i* prison
Jude 23 hate even the *i* garment that

Innermost
1Ki 6:5 the temple and the *i* room
6:16 the *i* room, the Most Holy
6:19 the *i* room in the interior
6:20 the *i* room was twenty cubits
6:21 in front of the *i* room, and
6:22 altar . . . toward the *i* room
6:23 in the *i* room two cherubs of
6:31 the entrance of the *i* room
7:49 before the *i* room, of pure
8:6 to the *i* room of the house
8:8 Holy in front of the *i* room
20:30 the city into the *i* chamber
22:25 enter the *i* chamber to hide
2Ki 9:2 bring him into the *i* chamber
2Ch 4:20 before the *i* room according
5:7 into the *i* room of the house
5:9 Holy in front of the *i* room
18:24 enter the *i* chamber to hide
Ps 28:2 the *i* room of your holy place
128:3 In the *i* parts of your house
Pr 18:8 into the *i* parts of the belly
20:27 all the *i* parts of the belly
20:30 the *i* parts of the belly
26:22 into the *i* parts of the belly
Eze 32:23 put in the *i* parts of a pit
Am 6:10 in the *i* parts of the house
Jon 1:5 *i* parts of the decked vessel

Innkeeper
Lu 10:35 gave them to the *i*, and said

Innocence
1Ki 22:34 that bent the bow in his *i*
2Ch 18:33 bent the bow in his *i*, but
Ps 73:13 that I wash my hands in *i*
Da 6:22 *i* itself was found in me

Innocency
Ge 20:5 with *i* of my hands I have
Ps 26:6 I shall wash my hands in *i*
Ho 8:5 will they be incapable of *i*

Innocent
Ge 44:10 you . . . will be proved *i*
Ex 23:7 And do not kill the *i* and the
Nu 5:31 man must be *i* of error, but
De 19:10 no *i* blood may be spilled in
19:13 the guilt of *i* blood out of
21:8 *i* blood in the midst of your
21:9 the guilt of *i* blood from
27:25 when it is *i* blood
1Sa 19:5 sin against *i* blood in
26:9 and has remained *i*
2Sa 3:28 *i* for time indefinite of
14:9 king and his throne are *i*
2Ki 21:16 also *i* blood that Manasseh
24:4 the *i* blood that he had shed
24:4 Jerusalem with *i* blood
Job 4:7 that is *i* has ever perished
9:23 At the very despair of the *i*
9:28 that you will not hold me *i*
10:14 error you do not hold me *i*
17:8 *i* one gets excited over the
22:19 *i* one himself will hold
22:30 He will rescue an *i* man
27:17 the *i* would be the one to
Ps 10:8 he will kill someone *i*
15:5 a bribe against the *i* one he
19:12 From . . . sins pronounce me *i*
19:13 *i* from much transgression
24:4 *i* in his hands and clean in
94:21 even the blood of the *i* one
106:38 they kept spilling *i* blood
Pr 1:11 the *i* men without any cause
6:17 that are shedding *i* blood
28:20 riches will not remain *i*
Isa 59:7 in a hurry to shed *i* blood
Jer 2:34 the souls of the *i* poor ones
2:35 you say, I have remained *i*
7:6 *i* blood you will not shed in
19:4 with the blood of the *i* ones
22:3 And do not shed any *i* blood
22:17 upon the blood of the *i* one
26:15 it is *i* blood that you are
Joe 3:19 whose land they shed *i* blood
3:21 will consider *i* their blood
3:21 that I had not considered *i*
Jon 1:14 do not put upon us *i* blood
Mt 10:16 serpents and yet *i* as doves
Mt 27:24 I am *i* of the blood of this
Ro 16:19 but *i* as to what is evil
Php 2:15 come to be blameless and *i*

Innumerable
Heb 11:12 that are by the seaside, *i*

Inquire
Ge 24:57 woman and *i* at her mouth
25:22 she went to *i* of Jehovah
32:29 Why is it that you *i* for my
40:7 *i* of the officers of Pharaoh
Ex 13:14 son should *i* of you later on
18:15 coming to me to *i* of God
Nu 27:21 he must *i* in his behalf by
De 4:29 *i* for him with all your heart
12:30 *i* respecting their gods
13:14 search and investigate and *i*
Jos 9:14 of Jehovah they did not *i*
Jg 1:1 Israel proceeded to *i* of
18:5 *I*, please, of God that we may
20:18 up to Bethel and to *i* of God
1Sa 14:37 And Saul began to *i* of God
17:56 You *i* whose son the lad is
19:22 *i* and say: Where are Samuel
22:10 *i* of Jehovah for him; and
22:15 started to *i* of God for him
23:2 David proceeded to *i* of
28:6 Saul would *i* of Jehovah
28:16 Why, then, do you *i* of me
30:8 David began to *i* of Jehovah
2Sa 2:1 David proceeded to *i* of
5:19 David began to *i* of Jehovah
16:23 *i* of the word of the true
20:18 Let them but *i* in Abel, and
1Ki 22:5 *I*, please, first of all for
22:7 Then let us *i* through him
22:8 through whom to *i* of Jehovah
2Ki 1:2 *i* of Baal-zebub the god of
1:3 going to *i* of Baal-zebub the
1:6 sending to *i* of Baal-zebub
1:16 to *i* of Baal-zebub the god of
1:16 of whose word to *i*
3:11 *i* of Jehovah through him
8:8 must *i* of Jehovah through him
22:13 *i* of Jehovah in my own
22:18 sending you to *i* of Jehovah
1Ch 10:14 And he did not *i* of Jehovah
14:10 And David began to *i* of God
22:19 to *i* after Jehovah your God
2Ch 18:4 *i* first of all for the word
18:6 Then let us *i* through him
18:7 through whom to *i* of Jehovah
20:4 together to *i* of Jehovah
32:31 *i* about the portent that
34:21 *i* of Jehovah in my own
34:26 sending you to *i* of Jehovah
Ezr 10:16 to *i* into the matter
Isa 21:12, 12 If you people would *i*, *i*
Jer 21:2 *i* in our behalf of Jehovah
37:7 sending you to me to *i* of me
Eze 20:1 came in to *i* of Jehovah
20:3 Is it in order to *i* of me
Mt 2:4 *i* of them where the Christ
Lu 18:36 to *i* what this might mean
Joh 4:52 began to *i* of them the hour
21:12 *i* of him: Who are you?
Ac 4:7 *i*: By what power or in whose
10:29 I *i* the reason that you have
21:33 *i* who he might be and what

Inquired
Ge 32:29 Jacob *i* and said: Tell me
37:15 the man *i* of him, saying
43:7 The man directly *i* concerning
43:27 he *i* whether they were
Jg 20:23 and *i* of Jehovah, saying
20:27 sons of Israel *i* of Jehovah
1Sa 10:22 they *i* further of Jehovah
23:4 David *i* yet again of Jehovah
2Sa 5:23 David *i* of Jehovah, but he
11:3 David sent and *i* about the
1Ch 14:14 David *i* again of God, and
2Ch 31:9 Hezekiah *i* of the priests and
Ps 34:4 I *i* of Jehovah, and he
78:34 they also *i* for him
Isa 30:2 not *i* of my own mouth, to
Eze 14:3 Shall I be *i* of at all by
20:3 I will not be *i* of by you
20:31 *i* of by you people, O house
20:31 I will not be *i* of by you
Da 1:20 king *i* about from them, he
Zep 1:6 and have not *i* of him
Lu 15:26 *i* what these things meant
Ac 10:18 *i* whether Simon who was
23:34 he read it and *i* from what

Inquirer
Eze 14:10 error of the *i* will prove

Inquires
De 18:11 anyone who *i* of the dead

Inquiries
Jg 8:14 made *i* of him. So he wrote
Ac 10:17 made *i* for Simon's house and

Inquiring
Ge 38:21 *i* of the men of her place
Ex 33:7 everyone *i* of Jehovah would
Jg 6:29 And they went *i* and seeking
Ps 142:4 is no one *i* for my soul
Ho 4:12 my own people keep *i*
Joh 16:19 *i* among yourselves over
Ac 23:19 *i* privately: What is it you

Inquiringly
Isa 11:10 the nations will turn *i*

Inquiry
De 17:9 you must make *i*, and they
1Sa 22:13 being an *i* of God for him
1Ch 10:13 a spirit medium to make *i*
Eze 14:7 to the prophet to make *i* for
1Co 10:25 making no *i* on account of
10:27 making no *i* on account of
1Pe 1:10 a diligent *i* and a careful

Inroads
Mr 4:19 make *i* and choke the word

Insane
1Sa 21:13 acting *i* in their hand and

Insanity
Ec 2:2 I said to laughter: *I!* and to

Inscribe
Isa 30:8 *i* it even in a book, that

Inscribed
Ex 39:30 and *i* upon it an inscription
Job 19:23 in a book they were even *i*
Da 5:24 and this very writing was *i*
5:25 is the writing that was *i*
Lu 10:20 names have been *i* in the
Ac 17:23 had been *i* To an Unknown God
2Co 3:2 *i* on our hearts and known and
3:3 *i* not with ink but with
Re 21:12 names were *i* which are those

Inscription
Ex 39:30 an *i* with the engravings of a
Mt 22:20 Whose image and *i* is this?
Mr 12:16 Whose image and *i* is this?
15:26 *i* of the charge against him
Lu 20:24 Whose image and *i* does it
23:38 an *i* over him: This is the

Insect
Mt 3:4 *i* locusts and wild honey
Mr 1:6 was eating *i* locusts and wild

Insects
De 28:42 your ground whirring *i* will
Isa 18:1 whirring *i* with wings

Insensibility
Mr 3:5 at the *i* of their hearts, he
Eph 4:18 the *i* of their hearts

Insert
Le 14:42 other stones and *i* them in

Inserted
2Ch 20:34 *i* in the Book of the Kings

Inshore
Ac 27:13 coasting *i* along Crete

Inside
Ge 6:14 you must cover it *i* and
7:9 went in by twos to Noah *i* the
7:15 they kept going to Noah *i*
8:9 it to himself *i* the ark
18:12 Hence Sarah began to laugh *i*
18:24 fifty righteous who are *i*
Ex 20:10 resident who is *i* your gates
25:11 pure gold. *I* and outside
37:2 with pure gold *i* and outside
Le 14:41 scraped off all around *i*
16:2 holy place *i* the curtain
16:12 bring them *i* the curtain
16:15 bring its blood *i* the curtain
Nu 18:7 regards what is *i* the curtain
De 5:14 alien resident who is *i* your
12:12 Levite who is *i* your gates
12:15 *i* all your gates
12:17 not be allowed to eat *i* your
12:18 Levite who is *i* your gates

De 12:21 you must eat *i* your gates
14:21 the alien resident who is *i*
14:27 Levite who is *i* your gates
14:28 deposit it *i* your gates
14:29 who are *i* your gates, must
15:22 *I* your gates you should eat
16:11 Levite who is *i* your gates
16:14 who are *i* your gates
16:18 officers for yourself *i* all
17:8 dispute, *i* your gates
Jg 7:16 torches *i* the large jars
12:4 O Gilead, *i* of Ephraim
12:4 Ephraim, *i* of Manasseh
1Sa 25:29 *i* the hollow of the sling
25:37 heart came to be dead *i* him
2Sa 3:27 led him aside *i* the gate to
6:17 place *i* the tent that David
23:20 lion *i* a waterpit on a day
1Ki 6:15 walls of the house *i* it
6:15 he overlaid it with timber *i*
6:16 *i* the innermost room, the
6:18 cedarwood on the house *i* was
6:19 the house he prepared *i*
6:21 the house *i* with pure gold
6:27 cherubs *i* the inner house
6:29 blossoms, *i* and outside
6:30 with gold, *i* and outside
7:9 *i* and outside, and from the
7:31 from *i* to the supports and
8:51 from *i* the iron furnace
11:20 *i* the house of Pharaoh
2Ki 7:11 to the king's house *i*
11:15 her out from *i* the rows
1Ch 11:22 a lion *i* a waterpit in the
16:1 placed it *i* the tent that
2Ch 3:4 overlay it *i* with pure gold
23:14 her out from *i* the rows
29:16 *i* the house of Jehovah to
29:18 came *i* to Hezekiah the king
Ne 7:4 there were few people *i* it
Ps 39:3 My heart grew hot *i* me
62:4 *i* themselves they call down
94:19 thoughts became many *i* of
101:2 integrity of my heart *i* my
101:7 dwell *i* my house no worker
Pr 26:24 *i* of him he puts deception
Isa 7:6 another king reign *i* it, the
24:18 from *i* the hollow will be
56:7 rejoice *i* my house of prayer
Eze 1:27 of fire all around *i* thereof
3:24 be shut up *i* your house
7:15 and the famine are *i*
11:19 a new spirit I shall put *i*
36:26 new spirit I shall put *i*
36:27 spirit I shall put *i* you
40:16 *i* of the gate all around
40:16 all around toward the *i*
41:3 went *i* and proceeded to
42:4 the *i*, a way of one cubit
44:17 the inner courtyard and *i*
Ho 7:6 heart . . . is burning *i* them
Am 3:9 cases of defrauding *i* her
7:10 right *i* the house of Israel
Zec 12:1 the spirit of man *i* him
Mt 7:15 *i* they are ravenous wolves
12:45 getting *i*, they dwell there
23:25 *i* they are full of plunder
23:26 cleanse first the *i* of the
23:27 but *i* are full of dead men's
23:28 *i* you are full of hypocrisy
26:58 and, after going *i*, he was
Mr 7:21 from *i*, out of the heart of
9:33 when he was *i* the house he
13:15 nor go *i* to take anything
14:14 wherever he goes *i* say to
Lu 11:7 that one from *i* says in reply
11:26 after getting *i*, they dwell
11:39 *i* of you is full of plunder
11:40 made also the *i*, did he not?
11:41 the things that are *i*, and
Ac 5:23 opening up we found no one *i*
12:14 ran *i* and reported that
17:2 he went *i* to them, and for
19:30 Paul was willing to go *i* to
Ro 2:29 Jew who is one on the *i*, and
1Co 5:12 Do you not judge those *i*
2Co 4:16 man we are *i* is being
Eph 3:16 mighty in the man you are *i*

Insight
1Ch 28:19 He gave *i* for the entire
Ne 8:13 gain *i* into the words of the
Job 22:2 That anyone having *i* should
34:35 are without his having *i*
Ps 2:10 And now, O kings, exercise *i*
14:2 there exists anyone having *i*
32:8 I shall make you have *i* and
36:3 to have *i* for doing good
53:2 there exists anyone having *i*
64:9 have *i* into his work
94:8 when will you have any *i*?
106:7 *i* into your wonderful works
111:10 doing them have a good *i*
119:99 More *i* than all my teachers
Pr 1:3 discipline that gives *i*
3:4 good *i* in the eyes of God and
10:5 son acting with *i* is
13:15 Good *i* itself gives favor
14:35 servant who is acting with *i*
15:24 upward to one acting with *i*
16:20 showing *i* in a matter will
16:22 *i* is a well of life
16:23 causes his mouth to show *i*
17:2 A servant that is showing *i*
19:11 *i* . . . slows down his anger
21:11 giving *i* to a wise person
21:16 wandering from the way of *i*
Isa 41:20 pay heed and have *i* at the
44:18 heart so as to have no *i*
52:13 My servant will act with *i*
Jer 3:15 with knowledge and *i*
9:24 the having of *i* and the
10:21 they have not acted with *i*
Da 1:4 having *i* into all wisdom and
1:17 *i* in all writing and wisdom
5:11 *i* and wisdom like the wisdom
5:12 *i* to interpret dreams and
5:14 *i* and wisdom extraordinary
8:25 And according to his *i* he
9:13 showing *i* into your trueness
9:22 you have *i* with understanding
9:25 *i* that from the going forth
11:33 those having *i* among the
11:35 those having *i* will be made
12:3 ones having *i* will shine
12:10 the ones having *i* will
Am 5:13 the very one having *i* will
Ro 3:11 is no one that has any *i*

Insignificant
1Sa 9:21 and my family the most *i* of
Job 14:21 they become *i*, but he does
Ps 119:141 I am *i* and contemptible
Jer 2:36 treat as very *i* the changing
14:3 sent their *i* ones for water
30:19 they will not become *i*
Zec 13:7 back upon those who are *i*
Mt 2:6 by no means the most *i* city

Insinuations
Hab 2:6 an alluding remark, *i* at him

Insist
Isa 22:4 people *i* on comforting me

Insistence
Nu 25:11 my *i* on exclusive devotion
Ps 90:10 Yet their *i* is on trouble
Ca 8:6 *i* on exclusive devotion is as
Eze 5:13 my *i* on exclusive devotion

Insistent
Ge 19:3 he was very *i* with them, so
Lu 23:5 they began to be *i*, saying

Insistently
Ex 21:5 But if the slave should *i* say

Insisting
Lu 22:59 other man began *i* strongly

Insolence
2Ki 19:3 a day of . . . scornful *i*
Isa 9:9 their *i* of heart in saying
10:12 *i* of the heart of the king
37:3 rebuke and of scornful *i*
La 3:65 give to them the *i* of heart

Insolent
Jg 9:4 hire idle and *i* men, that they
Isa 33:19 No *i* people will you see
Eze 2:4 the sons *i* of face and hard of
Zep 3:4 Her prophets were *i*, were
Ro 1:30 *i*, haughty, self-assuming
1Ti 1:13 a persecutor and an *i* man

Insolently
Mt 22:6 treated them *i* and killed
Lu 18:32 be treated *i* and spit upon
Ac 14:5 to treat them *i* and pelt
1Th 2:2 been *i* treated (just as you

Inspect
Ex 3:3 may *i* this great phenomenon
Ex 3:4 saw that he turned aside to *i*
Job 21:29 carefully *i* their very signs
Ps 48:13 *I* its dwelling towers
Mt 22:11 came in to *i* the guests he

Inspected
Lu 19:44 the time of your being *i*

Inspection
Ne 3:31 in front of the *I* Gate and
Ps 17:3 you have made *i* by night
Ac 7:23 *i* of his brothers, the sons
1Pe 2:12 in the day for his *i*

Inspiration
1Ch 28:12 come to be with him by *i*
Mt 22:43 David by *i* calls him Lord
Re 1:10 By *i* I came to be in the

Inspired
Pr 16:10 *I* decision should be upon the
Ho 9:7 the man of *i* expression
1Co 12:10 discernment of *i* utterances
2Th 2:2 through an *i* expression or
1Ti 4:1 *i* utterance says definitely
4:1 misleading *i* utterances and
2Ti 3:16 All Scripture is *i* of God and
1Jo 4:1 not believe every *i* expression
4:1 test the *i* expressions to see
4:2 knowledge of the *i* expression
4:2 *i* expression that confesses
4:3 every *i* expression that does
4:3 the antichrist's *i* expression
4:6 the *i* expression of truth and
4:6 and the *i* expression of error
Re 16:13 three unclean *i* expressions
16:14 expressions *i* by demons and
22:6 God of the *i* expressions of

Inspires
Re 19:10 is what *i* prophesying

Install
Eze 43:26 must cleanse it and *i* it

Installation
Ex 29:22 for it is a ram of *i*
29:26 the breast of the ram of *i*
29:27 from the ram of *i*, from
29:31 take the ram of *i*, and you
29:34 flesh of the *i* sacrifice and
Le 7:37 and the *i* sacrifice and the
8:22 the ram of the *i*, near, and
8:28 an *i* sacrifice for a restful
8:29 From the *i* ram it became the
8:31 bread that is in the *i* basket
8:33 fulfilling the days of your *i*

Installed
Ps 2:6 I, even I, have *i* my king
Pr 8:23 I was *i*, from the start, from

Instance
Ru 3:10 better in the last *i* than in
3:10 better . . . than in the first *i*
2Sa 17:7 is not good in this *i*
1Ki 12:15 at the *i* of Jehovah
12:24 is at the *i* of myself that
2Ch 11:4 at my own *i* that this thing
20:17 not need to fight in this *i*
Pr 20:16 in the *i* of a foreign woman
27:13 in the *i* of a foreign woman
Isa 52:4 in the first *i* to reside
58:12 And at your *i* men will
Jer 50:17 In the first *i* the king
50:17 and in this latter *i*
Mt 9:5 For *i*, which is easier, to say
Lu 4:25 For *i*, I tell you in truth
18:32 For *i*, he will be delivered
Ac 5:36 For *i*, before these days
6:14 For *i*, we have heard him say
17:23 For *i*, while passing along
Ro 2:12 For *i*, all those who sinned
4:2 for *i*, Abraham were declared
7:2 For *i*, a married woman is

Instant
Nu 16:21 exterminate them in an *i*
16:45 exterminate them in an *i*
Jos 3:13 the *i* that the soles of the
3:15 the *i* that the carriers of
8:19 the *i* that he stretched out
Pr 6:15 in an *i* he will be broken
Isa 29:5 must occur in an *i*, suddenly
30:13 come suddenly, in an *i*
Lu 4:5 in an *i* of time
Ac 11:11 that *i* there were three men

Instantly
Ps 6:10 they will be ashamed *i*
Mt 21:19 And the fig tree withered *i*
21:20 that the fig tree withered *i*
Lu 1:64 *I* his mouth was opened and
4:39 *I* she rose and began
5:25 *i* he rose up before them
8:44 *i* her flow of blood stopped
8:47 how she was healed *i*
8:55 she rose *i*, and he ordered
13:13 and *i* she straightened up
18:43 And *i* he recovered sight
19:11 going to display itself *i*
21:34 that day be *i* upon you
22:60 *i*, while he was yet speaking
Ac 3:7 *I* the soles of his feet and
5:10 *I* she fell down at his feet
12:23 *I* the angel of Jehovah struck
13:11 *I* a thick mist and darkness
16:26 all the doors were *i* opened
1Th 5:3 destruction is to be *i* upon

Instigating
Jer 43:3 *i* you against us for the

Instinctively
Pr 30:24 but they are *i* wise

Instruct
De 17:10 according to all that they *i*
24:8 the Levites, will *i* you
33:10 *i* Jacob in your judicial
Jg 13:8 and *i* us as to what we ought
1Sa 12:23 *i* you in the good and right
2Ch 6:27 *i* them regarding the good
Ezr 7:25 known them you men will *i*
Job 6:24 *I* me, and I, for my part
8:10 Will not they . . . *i* you
12:7 domestic animals . . . will *i*
12:8 earth, and it will *i* you
27:11 *i* you men by the hand of
34:32 behold nothing, *i* me
Ps 25:12 He will *i* him in the way
27:11 *I* me, O Jehovah, in your way
32:8 *i* you in the way you should
45:4 your right hand will *i* you
86:11 *I* me, O Jehovah, about your
119:33 *I* me, O Jehovah, in the way
Pr 4:4 he would *i* me and say to me
4:11 *i* you even in the way of
Isa 2:3 he will *i* us about his ways
28:9 will one *i* in knowledge
Eze 44:23 *i* in the difference between
Mic 3:11 priests *i* just for a price
4:2 he will *i* us about his ways
1Co 2:16 that he may *i* him? But we do
14:19 might also *i* others orally

Instructed
2Ki 12:2 Jehoiada the priest *i* him
Ps 119:102 you yourself have *i* me
Mt 28:15 and did as they were *i*
Mr 6:39 *i* all the people to recline
8:6 he *i* the crowd to recline on
Lu 6:40 everyone that is perfectly *i*
8:56 he *i* them to tell no one what
9:21 he *i* them not to be telling
Ac 7:22 Moses was *i* in all the
18:25 been orally *i* in the way of
22:3 *i* according to the strictness
Ro 2:18 are orally *i* out of the Law

Instructing
Ne 8:9 Levites who were *i* the people
Mt 15:35 after *i* the crowd to recline
2Ti 2:25 *i* with mildness those not
Tit 2:12 *i* us to repudiate ungodliness

Instruction
De 32:2 My *i* will drip as the rain
1Ch 15:22 he giving *i* in carrying, for
Job 11:4 Also, you say, My *i* is pure
Pr 1:5 listen and take in more *i*
4:2 good *i* is what I certainly
Isa 9:15 prophet giving false *i* is the
29:24 are grumbling will learn *i*
Ho 10:12 gives *i* in righteousness
Hab 2:19 It itself will give *i*
Ro 15:4 written for our *i*, that
1Th 4:1 *i* from us on how you ought

Instructions
Le 14:57 *i* when something is unclean
Mt 11:1 *i* to his twelve disciples, he
Ac 10:22 divine *i* by a holy angel to
15:24 we did not give them any *i*
20:13 after giving *i* to this effect
1Co 7:10 married people I give *i*, yet
11:17 while giving these *i*, I do

Instructor
2Ch 26:5 Zechariah, the *i* in the fear
Job 36:22 Who is an *i* like him?
Ps 84:6 with blessings the *i* enwraps
Isa 30:20 Grand *I* will no longer hide
30:20 eyes seeing your Grand *I*
Hab 2:18 and an *i* in falsehood
Mt 13:52 every public *i*, when taught
Lu 5:5 *I*, for a whole night we toiled
8:24, 24 *I*, *I*, we are about to
8:45 *I*, the crowds are hemming
9:33 *I*, it is fine for us to be
9:49 *I*, we saw a certain man
17:13 Jesus, *I*, have mercy on us!

Instructors
2Ch 35:3 Levites, the *i* of all Israel
Ezr 8:16 Joiarib and Elnathan, *i*
Pr 5:13 listened to the voice of my *i*
Mt 23:34 and wise men and public *i*

Instructs
Ps 25:8 why he *i* sinners in the way
Isa 28:26 His own God *i* him

Instrument
Nu 35:16 *i* of iron that he has struck
35:18 was with a small *i* of wood
1Sa 10:5 ahead of them a stringed *i*
2Ki 21:13 leveling *i* applied to the
Job 41:30 threshing *i* upon the mire
Ps 33:2 On an *i* of ten strings make
57:8 Do awake, O stringed *i*
71:22 an *i* of a stringed sort
81:2 together with the stringed *i*
92:3 Upon a ten-stringed *i* and
108:2 Do awake, O stringed *i*
144:9 On an *i* of ten strings I
150:3 stringed *i* and the harp
Isa 5:12 be harp and stringed *i*
28:17 righteousness the leveling *i*
28:27 not with a threshing *i*
41:15 a new threshing *i* having
Eze 33:32 and playing a stringed *i*
Da 3:5 the stringed *i*, the bagpipe
3:7 the stringed *i* and all sorts
3:10 the stringed *i*, and the
3:15 the stringed *i*, and the
Am 6:5 the sound of the stringed *i*

Instrumental
La 5:14 young men from their *i* music

Instruments
Ge 49:5 *I* of violence are their
1Sa 8:12 to make his war *i* and his
8:12 to make . . . his chariot *i*
13:21 for the three-toothed *i* and
2Sa 6:5 *i* of juniper wood and with
6:5 and with stringed *i* and with
12:31 sharp *i* of iron and at
1Ki 10:12 harps and stringed *i* for
1Ch 13:8 and with stringed *i* and with
15:16 the *i* of song, stringed
15:16 stringed *i* and harps and
15:20 stringed *i* tuned to Alamoth
15:28 on stringed *i* and harps
16:5 with *i* of the string type
16:42 *i* of the song of the true
20:3 at sharp *i* of iron and at
23:5 praise to Jehovah on the *i*
25:1 with the stringed *i* and with
25:6 stringed *i* and harps for the
2Ch 5:12 with stringed *i* and harps
5:13 and with the *i* of song and
7:6 Levites with the *i* of song to
9:11 stringed *i* for the singers
20:28 stringed *i* and with harps
23:13 singers with the *i* of song
29:25 with stringed *i* and with
29:26 with the *i* of David, and
29:27 *i* of David the king of
30:21 with loud *i*, even to
34:12 expert with the *i* of song
Ne 12:27 stringed *i* and with harps
12:36 the *i* of song of David the
Ps 4:*super* the director on stringed *i*
6:*super* the director on stringed *i*
7:13 must prepare the *i* of death
45:8 stringed *i* themselves have
54:*super* the director on stringed *i*
55:*super* the director on stringed *i*
61:*super* the director on stringed *i*
67:*super* the director on stringed *i*
Ps 68:25 the players on stringed *i*
76:*super* the director on stringed *i*
Isa 14:11 the din of your stringed *i*
32:7 unprincipled man, his *i* are
Da 3:5 and all sorts of musical *i*
3:7 and all sorts of musical *i*
3:10 and all sorts of musical *i*
3:15 and all sorts of musical *i*
6:18 no musical *i* were brought
Am 1:3 even with iron threshing *i*
5:23 sound of your stringed *i*
6:5 devised . . . *i* for song
Hab 3:19 director on my stringed *i*

Insult
Ps 4:2 must my glory be for *i*
Lu 11:45 saying these things . . . *i* us

Insulting
Job 20:3 *i* exhortation to me I hear
Lu 6:28 pray for those who are *i* you

Insults
2Co 12:10 I take pleasure . . . in *i*

Intact
Eze 15:5 When it happens to be *i*, it

Integrity
1Ki 9:4 with *i* of heart and with
Job 2:3 yet he is holding fast his *i*
2:9 you yet holding fast your *i*
4:6 hope even the *i* of your ways
27:5 I shall not take away my *i*
31:6 God will get to know my *i*
Ps 7:8 And according to my *i* in me
25:21 Let *i* . . . safeguard me
26:1 have walked in my own *i*
26:11 in my *i* I shall walk
41:12 my *i* you have upheld me
78:72 to the *i* of his heart
101:2 in the *i* of my heart
Pr 2:7 walking in *i* he is a shield
10:9 He that is walking in *i* will
11:3 *i* of the upright ones is what
14:32 be finding refuge in his *i*
19:1 who is walking in his *i* is
20:7 righteous is walking in his *i*
28:6 who is walking in his *i* than

Intellectual
Mt 11:25 from the wise and *i* ones
Lu 10:21 from wise and *i* ones, and
1Co 1:19 intelligence of the *i* men
1Jo 5:20 has given us *i* capacity that

Intelligence
1Co 1:19 *i* of the intellectual men
Re 13:18 one that has *i* calculate the
17:9 *i* that has wisdom comes in

Intelligent
1Sa 16:18 man of war and an *i* speaker
Ne 8:2 all *i* enough to listen
8:3 and the other *i* ones; and the
Ac 13:7 Sergius Paulus, an *i* man

Intelligently
Job 38:18 Have you *i* considered the
Mr 12:34 discerning he had answered *i*

Intend
Da 7:25 *i* to change times and law
Joh 7:35 Where does this man *i* going
7:35 He does not *i* to go to the
14:22 *i* to show yourself plainly
Ac 5:35 *i* to do respecting these men

Intended
Mt 1:19 *i* to divorce her secretly
Ac 12:4 *i* to produce him for the
23:15 you *i* to determine more

Intending
Ex 2:14 Are you *i* to kill me just as
Da 6:3 king was *i* to elevate him over
Ac 20:13 were *i* to take Paul aboard
20:13 himself was *i* to go on foot
22:26 What are you *i* to do?
23:20 *i* to learn something more
27:30 *i* to let down anchors from
2Co 1:15 was *i* before to come to you

Intense
Ps 55:12 It was not an *i* hater of me
Jer 2:31 or a land of *i* darkness
Zec 13:6 in the house of my *i* lovers
1Pe 4:8 have love for one another

Intensely
Ge 31:30 yearning *i* for the house of

Nu 10:35 those who *i* hate you flee
De 32:41 to those who *i* hate me
33:11 And those who *i* hate him
2Sa 22:41 Those hating me *i*—I shall
Job 31:29 extinction of one *i* hating
Ps 18:40 And as for those hating me *i*
44:7 those *i* hating us you put to
44:10 the very ones *i* hating us
68:1 let those who *i* hate him flee
81:15 those *i* hating Jehovah
83:2 ones *i* hating you have raised
89:23 those *i* hating him I kept
139:21 are *i* hating you, O Jehovah
Pr 8:36 all those *i* hating me are
Jer 6:29 kept refining *i* simply for
22:20 those *i* loving you have
22:22 as for those *i* loving you
30:14 those *i* loving you are the
La 1:19 called to those *i* loving me
Ac 12:5 prayer . . . carried on *i* by
18:5 be *i* occupied with the word
26:7 *i* rendering . . . sacred service
1Pe 1:22 love one another *i* from the
2Pe 3:10 the elements being *i* hot
3:12 the elements being *i* hot

Intensify
2Sa 11:25 *I* your battle against the

Intensity
1Ki 22:35 battle kept rising in *i* on
2Ch 18:34 battle kept rising in *i* on
Ac 18:28 with *i* he thoroughly proved

Intent
Ex 32:12 With evil *i* he brought them
Ec 7:14 to the *i* that mankind may not
Jer 25:7 the *i* that you might offend
42:6 *i* that it may go well with
Eze 4:17 *i* that they may be lacking
Da 2:30 *i* that the interpretation
4:17 *i* that people living may know
Mic 6:5 to the *i* that the righteous
Mt 19:3 *i* on tempting him and saying

Intention
De 29:19 the *i* of sweeping away the
Lu 1:51 in the *i* of their hearts
2Co 1:17 when I had such an *i*, I did

Intentions
Heb 4:12 thoughts and *i* of the heart

Intently
Isa 55:2 Listen *i* to me, and eat what
Mt 6:26 Observe *i* the birds of heaven
Lu 4:20 eyes . . . *i* fixed upon him
Ac 13:9 looked at him *i*
14:9 looking at him *i* and seeing
23:1 Looking *i* at the Sanhedrin
2Co 3:7 not gaze *i* at the face of
3:13 might not gaze *i* at the end
Heb 11:26 *i* toward the payment of
12:2 we look *i* at the Chief Agent

Interbreed
Le 19:19 not *i* your domestic animals

Intercede
Nu 21:7 *I* with Jehovah that he may
Jer 15:11 I will *i* for you in the

Interceding
Nu 21:7 Moses went *i* in behalf of the

Intercessions
1Ti 2:1 supplications, prayers, *i*

Interchange
Ro 1:12 *i* of encouragement among you

Intercourse
Ge 4:1 Adam had *i* with Eve his wife
4:17 Cain had *i* with his wife and
4:25 Adam proceeded to have *i*
19:5 that we may have *i* with them
19:8 who have never had *i*
24:16 no man had had sexual *i* with
38:26 he had no further *i* with her
Ex 34:15 immoral *i* with their gods
34:16 immoral *i* with their gods
34:16 immoral *i* with their gods
Le 17:7 they are having immoral *i*
20:5 immoral *i* along with him in
20:5 immoral *i* with Molech off
20:6 immoral *i* with them, I shall
Nu 15:39 are following in immoral *i*
31:17 every woman who has had *i*
De 31:16 immoral *i* with foreign gods
Jg 2:17 but they had immoral *i* with
Jg 8:27 began to have immoral *i* with
8:33 immoral *i* with the Baals, so
19:22 that we may have *i* with him
19:25 began to have *i* with her
21:12 had not had *i* with a man by
1Sa 1:19 had *i* with Hannah his wife
1Ki 1:4 king . . . had no *i* with her
1Ch 5:25 immoral *i* with the gods of
2Ch 21:11 to have immoral *i*, and that
21:13 immoral *i* the same way
21:13 the having of immoral *i*
Ps 106:39 immoral *i* by their dealings
Eze 20:30 are you going in immoral *i?*
23:8 their immoral *i* upon her
23:17 with their immoral *i*
Mt 1:25 he had no *i* with her until
Lu 1:34 I am having no *i* with a man
Ro 13:13 not in illicit *i* and loose

Interdict
Da 6:7 and to enforce an *i*, that
6:9 signed the writing and the *i*
6:12 concerning the *i* of the king
6:12 *i* that you have signed that
6:13 nor to the *i* that you signed
6:15 any *i* or statute that the king

Interest
Ex 22:25 You must not lay *i* upon him
Le 25:36 not take *i* and usury from
25:37 give him your money on *i*
De 23:19 not make your brother pay *i*
23:19 brother pay . . . *i* on money
23:19 brother pay . . . *i* on food
23:19 *i* on anything on which one
23:19 on which one may claim *i*
23:20 may make a foreigner pay *i*
23:20 you must not make pay *i*
Jg 18:3 and what *i* do you have here?
Ne 5:10 leave off this lending on *i*
5:11 are exacting as *i* from them
Ps 15:5 he has not given out on *i*
Pr 28:8 his valuables by *i* and usury
Isa 22:16 What is there of *i* to you
22:16 who is there of *i* to you
24:2 for the *i* taker as for the
24:2 for the one paying the *i*
52:5 what *i* do I have here?
Eze 18:8 nothing would he give on *i*
18:13 and *i* he has taken, and he
18:17 no usury and *i* has he taken
22:12 *I* and usury you have taken
Hab 2:7 those claiming *i* of you rise
Mt 5:42 borrow from you without *i*
25:27 what is mine with *i*
Lu 6:34 if you lend without *i* to
6:34 Even sinners lend without *i*
6:35 lend without *i*, not hoping
19:23 have collected it with *i*
Ac 27:34 is in the *i* of your safety
Php 2:4 not in personal *i* upon just
2:4 personal *i* upon those of the
Col 1:25 was given me in your *i* to

Interested
Pr 7:7 *i* in discerning among the sons

Interests
2Ch 17:13 many *i* that became his in
1Co 13:5 does not look for its own *i*
2Co 8:23 a fellow worker for your *i*
Php 2:21 are seeking their own *i*, not
1Th 2:15 are against the *i* of all men
Heb 12:3 sinners against their own *i*

Interior
Ge 43:30 he went into an *i* room and
Ex 12:9 its shanks and its *i* parts
Jg 3:24 easing nature in the cool *i*
14:18 he could go into the *i* room
15:1 in to my wife in the *i* room
16:9 sitting in the *i* room of hers
16:12 was sitting in the *i* room
2Sa 13:10 Bring . . . to the *i* room
13:10 her brother in the *i* room
1Ki 1:15 to the king in the *i* room
6:19 room in the *i* of the house
22:35 the *i* of the war chariot
Job 9:9 and the *i* rooms of the South
37:9 Out of the *i* room comes the
Ps 105:30 the *i* rooms of their kings
Pr 7:27 to the *i* rooms of death
24:4 knowledge will the *i* rooms
Ec 10:20 *i* rooms where you lie down
Ca 1:4 brought me into his *i* rooms
3:4 *i* room of her that had been
3:10 *i* being fitted out lovingly by
Isa 26:20 enter into your *i* rooms
Eze 40:7 the gate toward the *i* was
40:8 the gate toward the *i*, one
40:9 the gate was toward the *i*
40:43 firmly fixed on the *i*
Joe 2:16 go forth from his *i* room

Intermeddle
Pr 14:10 no stranger will *i*
24:21 are for a change, do not *i*

Interpose
Isa 53:12 he proceeded to *i*

Interposing
Isa 59:16 that there was no one *i*

Interpret
Ge 41:12 to *i* our dreams to us
41:15 can hear a dream and *i* it
Da 5:12 insight to *i* dreams and the
Mt 16:3 *i* the appearance of the sky
16:3 the signs . . . you cannot *i*

Interpretation
Ge 40:5 his dream with its own *i*
40:12 This is its *i*: The three
40:18 This is its *i*: The three
40:22 Joseph had given them the *i*
41:11 dream with its own *i*
Ec 8:1 there knowing the *i* of a thing
Da 2:4 we shall show the very *i*
2:5 dream known to me, and its *i*
2:6 dream and its *i* you will
2:6 me the very dream and its *i*
2:7 we shall show its very *i*
2:9 can show the very *i* of it
2:16 show the very *i* to the king
2:24 show the *i* itself to the king
2:25 the *i* itself to the king
2:26 that I beheld, and its *i*
2:30 *i* may be made known to the
2:36 dream, and its *i* we shall
2:45 and the *i* of it is trustworthy
4:6 make known . . . *i* of the dream
4:7 *i* they were not making known
4:9 that I have beheld and its *i*
4:18 Belteshazzar, say what the *i*
4:18 known to me the *i* itself
4:19 the *i* themselves frighten you
4:19 and its *i* to your adversaries
4:24 this is the *i*, O king, and the
5:7 and show me its very *i*, with
5:8 make known to the king the *i*
5:12 that he may show the very *i*
5:15 to make known to me its *i*
5:15 show the very *i* of the word
5:16 make known to me its very *i*
5:17 *i* I shall make known to him
5:26 *i* of the word: MENE, God has
7:16 make known to me the very *i*
1Co 12:10 and to another *i* of tongues
14:26 tongue, another has an *i*
2Pe 1:20 springs from any private *i*

Interpretations
Ge 40:8 Do not *i* belong to God?
Da 5:16 that you are able to furnish *i*

Interpreted
Ge 40:16 he had *i* something good, he
41:12 *i* to each according to his
41:13 as he had *i* to us so it
Lu 24:27 *i* to them things pertaining

Interpreter
Ge 40:8 and there is no *i* with us
41:8 no *i* of them for Pharaoh
41:15 a dream, but there is no *i*
42:23 there was an *i* between them

Intertwine
La 1:14 In his hand they *i* one another

Interval
Ge 32:16 an *i* between drove and drove
Ac 5:7 *i* of about three hours his
1Co 14:7 it makes an *i* to the tones

Intervened
Ps 106:30 Phinehas stood up and *i*
Lu 22:59 after about an hour *i* a

Interweave
Mic 7:3 very own; and they *i* it

Interwoven
Job 8:17 his roots become *i*
40:17 sinews of its thighs are *i*
Isa 25:7 is *i* upon all the nations
Na 1:10 *i* even as thorns and they

Intestines
Ex 29:13 all the fat that covers the *i*
29:17 wash its *i* and its shanks
29:22 and the fat that covers the *i*
Le 1:9 its *i* and its shanks will be
1:13 wash the *i* and the shanks
3:3 the fat that covers the *i*
3:3 all the fat that is over the *i*
3:9 and the fat that covers the *i*
3:9 all the fat that is upon the *i*
3:14 the fat that covers the *i*
3:14 all the fat that is upon the *i*
4:8 the fat that covers over the *i*
4:8 all the fat that is over the *i*
4:11 its shanks and its *i* and its
7:3 and the fat that covers the *i*
8:16 the fat that was upon the *i*
8:21 *i* and the shanks he washed
8:25 the fat that was upon the *i*
9:14 washed the *i* and the shanks
Nu 5:22 enter into your *i* to cause
2Sa 20:10 *i* spilled out to the earth
2Ch 21:15 malady of your *i*, until
21:15 *i* have come out because of
21:18 plagued him in his *i*
21:19 *i* came out during his
Job 20:14 be changed in his own *i*
30:27 *i* were made to boil and
Jer 4:19, 19 O my *i*, my *i!* I am in
31:20 *i* have become boisterous
La 1:20 My very *i* are in a ferment
2:11 My *i* are in a ferment
Eze 3:3 fill your very *i* with this
7:19 their *i* they will not fill
Mt 15:17 passes along into the *i* and
Mr 7:19 into his *i*, and it passes out
Ac 1:18 all his *i* were poured out

Intimacy
Job 29:4 *i* with God was at my tent
Ps 25:14 The *i* with Jehovah belongs
55:14 we used to enjoy sweet *i*
Pr 3:32 *i* is with the upright ones

Intimate
Ge 49:6 Into their *i* group do not
Ex 32:27 kill . . . his *i* acquaintance
Job 19:14 *i* acquaintances have ceased
19:19 my *i* group detest me
Ps 15:3 against his *i* acquaintance
89:7 the *i* group of holy ones
111:1 *i* group of upright ones and
Jer 6:11 the *i* group of young men
11:19 like a male lamb, an *i* one
15:17 *i* group of those playing
23:18 in the *i* group of Jehovah
23:22 had stood in my *i* group
Eze 13:9 In the *i* group of my people
Ac 10:24 his relatives and *i* friends

Intimated
Mt 3:7 who has *i* to you to flee from
Lu 3:7 who has *i* to you to flee from

Intoxicate
De 32:42 shall *i* my arrows with blood
Pr 5:19 her own breasts *i* you at all

Intoxicated
Ge 9:21 became *i*, and so he uncovered
Isa 29:9 *i*, but not with wine
Hag 1:6 not to the point of getting *i*
Joh 2:10 and when people are *i*, the
1Co 11:21 is hungry but another is *i*

Intoxicating
Le 10:9 not drink wine or *i* liquor
Nu 6:3 away from wine and *i* liquor
6:3 vinegar of *i* liquor, nor drink
28:7 drink offering of *i* liquor to
De 14:26 goats and wine and *i* liquor
29:6 *i* liquor you did not drink
Jg 13:4 do not drink wine or *i* liquor
13:7 do not drink wine or *i* liquor
13:14 no wine or *i* liquor let her
1Sa 1:15 *i* liquor I have not drunk
Ps 69:12 songs of drinkers of *i* liquor
Pr 20:1 *i* liquor is boisterous, and
31:4 to say: Where is *i* liquor?
31:6 Give *i* liquor, you people, to
Isa 5:11 may seek just *i* liquor
5:22 for mixing *i* liquor
24:9 *i* liquor becomes bitter to
28:7 because of *i* liquor they have
28:7 astray because of *i* liquor
28:7 as a result of the *i* liquor
29:9 not because of *i* liquor
Isa 56:12 drink *i* liquor to the limit
Mic 2:11 and concerning *i* liquor

Intrigues
Pr 16:28 man of *i* keeps sending forth
16:30 with his eyes to scheme up *i*

Introduced
Ge 47:7 *i* him to Pharaoh, and Jacob

Introducing
Ac 17:20 you are *i* some things that

Invade
Ex 8:24 gadflies began to *i* the house
2Ki 7:4 *i* the camp of the Syrians
2Ch 20:10 not allow Israel to *i* when
24:23 to *i* Judah and Jerusalem
27:2 not *i* the temple of Jehovah
32:1 *i* Judah and camp against the
Mt 12:29 *i* the house of a strong man

Invading
Ac 8:3 *I* one house after another and

Invalid
Mt 15:6 have made the word of God *i*
Mr 7:13 you make the word of God *i*

Invalidate
Job 40:8 will you *i* my justice?
Ga 3:17 years later does not *i* it

Invasion
2Ch 24:24 the Syrians made an *i*, and
Mic 5:1 O daughter of an *i;* a siege

Invented
1Ki 12:33 month that he had *i*

Inventing
Ne 6:8 own heart that you are *i* them

Invention
2Ch 26:15 *i* of engineers, that they

Inventoried
Ex 38:21 things *i* of the tabernacle
38:21 *i* at the command of Moses

Inventors
Ro 1:30 *i* of injurious things

Investigate
De 13:14 search and *i* and inquire
Ezr 7:14 *i* concerning Judah and
Ac 7:31 as he was approaching to *i*
7:32 Moses did not dare to *i*

Investigated
Ezr 4:19 they have *i* and found that
Ne 6:12 I *i*, and here it was not God
Job 5:27 Look! This is what we have *i*

Investigating
1Pe 1:11 *i* what particular season or

Investigation
Ezr 4:15 *i* of the book of records of
5:17 an *i* in the king's house of
6:1 *i* in the house of the records
Job 34:24 breaks . . . without any *i*

Invigorate
Isa 58:11 he will *i* your very bones

Invigorates
Pr 31:17 and she *i* her arms

Invisible
Ro 1:20 his *i* qualities are clearly
Col 1:15 He is the image of the *i* God
1:16 visible and the things *i*
1Ti 1:17 *i*, the only God, be honor
Heb 11:27 seeing the One who is *i*

Invite
Ex 34:15 will be certain to *i* you, and
2Sa 13:23 Absalom proceeded to *i* all
1Ki 1:9 *i* all his brothers the king's
1:10 his brother he did not *i*
1:25 *i* all the sons of the king
Mt 22:9 and anyone you find *i* to the
Lu 14:12 also *i* you in return and it
14:13 a feast, *i* poor people

Invited
Ge 31:54 *i* his brothers to eat bread
Jg 14:15 that you people *i* us here
1Sa 9:13 those who are *i* may eat
9:22 place at the head of those *i*
9:24 you may eat with those *i*
1Ki 1:19 *i* all the sons of the king
1:19 Solomon . . . he has not *i*
1:26 your servant he has not *i*
1Ki 1:41 Adonijah and all the ones *i*
1:49 all those *i* that were with
Es 5:12 I am *i* to her with the king
Job 1:4 *i* their three sisters to eat
Zep 1:7 he has sanctified his *i* ones
Mt 22:3 those *i* to the marriage feast
22:4 Tell those *i:* Look! I have
22:8 but those *i* were not worthy
22:14 are many *i*, but few chosen
Lu 7:39 the Pharisee that *i* him said
14:7 went on to tell the *i* men an
14:8 *i* by someone to a marriage
14:8 at the time have been *i* by
14:9 and he that *i* you and him
14:10 *i*, go and recline in the
14:10 the man that has *i* you comes
14:12 also to the man that *i* him
14:16 evening meal, and he *i* many
14:17 to say to the *i* ones, Come
14:24 those men that were *i* shall
Joh 2:2 also *i* to the marriage feast
Ac 10:23 he *i* them in and entertained
Re 19:9 *i* to the evening meal of the

Invites
1Co 10:27 unbelievers *i* you and you

Involved
2Sa 19:9 *i* in dispute in all the
1Ki 1:8 not become *i* with Adonijah
2Ki 6:8 *i* in war against Israel
2Pe 2:20 *i* again with these very

Involves
Pr 7:23 that it *i* his very soul
2Ti 2:4 *i* himself in the commercial

Involving
Nu 5:21 swear with an oath *i* cursing
2Ch 19:10 *i* the shedding of blood
19:10 *i* law and commandment and
Pr 29:24 oath *i* a curse he may hear
Ac 23:15 accurately the matters *i* him
24:22 upon these matters *i* you

Inward
Ge 15:4 come out of your own *i* parts
25:23 separated from your *i* parts
43:30 his *i* emotions were excited
Ex 28:26 the side toward the ephod *i*
39:19 the side toward the ephod *i*
Ru 1:11 still have sons in my *i* parts
2Sa 5:9 around from the Mound and *i*
7:12 come out of your *i* parts
16:11 out of my own *i* parts
1Ki 3:26 her *i* emotions were excited
2Ch 3:13 with their faces *i*
4:4 all their hind parts were *i*
32:21 out of his own *i* parts
Job 20:2 account of my *i* excitement
Ps 5:9 Their *i* part is adversity
22:14 melted deep in my *i* parts
40:8 law is within my *i* parts
49:11 Their *i* wish is that their
51:6 in the *i* parts
64:6 And the *i* part of each one
71:6 the *i* parts of my mother
Ca 5:4 my *i* parts themselves became
Isa 48:19 from your *i* parts like the
49:1 the *i* parts of my mother
63:15 commotion of your *i* parts
Eze 17:6 to turn its foliage *i*
Jon 1:17 in the *i* parts of the fish
2:1 from the *i* parts of the fish
Ro 14:1 decisions on *i* questionings

Inwardly
Ac 10:17 great perplexity *i* over what

Inwards
Isa 16:11 *i* are boisterous just like

Iob
Ge 46:13 sons of Issachar were . . . *I*

Iphdeiah
1Ch 8:25 and *I* . . . the sons of Shashak

Iphtah
Jos 15:43 *I* and Ashnah and Nezib

Iphtah-el
Jos 19:14 to be at the valley of *I*
19:27 valley of *I* to the north

Ir
1Ch 7:12 Huppim were the sons of *I*

Ira
2Sa 20:26 *I* the Jairite also became a
23:26 *I* the son of Ikkesh the

2Sa 23:38 *I* the Ithrite, Gareb the
1Ch 11:28 *I* the son of Ikkesh the
11:40 *I* the Ithrite, Gareb the
27:9 was *I* the son of Ikkesh the

Irad
Ge 4:18, 18 born to Enoch *I*. And *I*

Iram
Ge 36:43 sheik *I* . . . sheiks of Edom
1Ch 1:54 *I* . . . the sheiks of Edom

Iri
1Ch 7:7 the sons of Bela were . . . *I*

Irijah
Jer 37:13 *I* the son of Shelemiah the
37:14 *I* kept hold of Jeremiah

Ir-nahash
1Ch 4:12 Tehinnah the father of *I*

Iron
Ge 4:22 sort of tool of copper and *i*
Le 26:19 heavens like *i* and your earth
Nu 31:22 the *i*, the tin and the lead
35:16 with an instrument of *i* that
De 3:11 His bier was a bier of *i*
4:20 bring you out of the *i* furnace
8:9 the stones of which are *i* and
19:5 the *i* has slipped off from
27:5 not wield an *i* tool upon them
28:23 earth that is beneath you *i*
28:48 put an *i* yoke upon your neck
33:25 *I* and copper are your gate
Jos 6:19 the articles of copper and *i*
6:24 of copper and *i* they gave to
8:31 no *i* tool has been wielded
17:16 war chariots with *i* scythes
17:18 war chariots with *i* scythes
22:8 copper and *i* and garments in
Jg 1:19 war chariots with *i* scythes
4:3 war chariots with *i* scythes
4:13 war chariots with *i* scythes
1Sa 17:7 was six hundred shekels of *i*
2Sa 12:31 sharp instruments of *i* and
12:31 axes of *i*, and he made
23:7 armed with *i* and the shaft
1Ki 6:7 axes or any tools of *i*, they
8:51 from inside the *i* furnace
22:11 horns of *i* and said
1Ch 20:3 at sharp instruments of *i*
22:3 *i* in great quantity for nails
22:14 the *i* there is no means of
22:16 the *i* there is no means of
29:2 the *i* for the ironwork, and
29:7 *i* worth a hundred thousand
2Ch 2:7 and in copper and in *i* and in
2:14 in copper, in *i*, in stones
18:10 made for himself horns of *i*
24:12 workers in *i* and copper for
Job 19:24 With an *i* stylus and with
20:24 run away from armor of *i*
28:2 *I* itself is taken from the
41:27 regards *i* as mere straw
Ps 2:9 break them with an *i* scepter
107:16 cut down even the bars of *i*
149:8 ones with fetters of *i*
Pr 27:17, 17 *i*, *i* itself is sharpened
Ec 10:10 an *i* tool has become blunt
Isa 10:34 forest with an *i* tool
44:12 the carver of *i* with the
45:2 the *i* bars I shall cut down
48:4 that your neck is an *i* sinew
60:17 instead of the *i* I shall
60:17 instead of the stones, *i*
Jer 1:18 an *i* pillar and copper walls
6:28 as slanderers—copper and *i*
11:4 out of the furnace of *i*
15:12 Can one break *i* in pieces
15:12 *i* out of the north, and
17:1 written . . . with an *i* stylus
28:13 have to make yoke bars of *i*
28:14 A yoke of *i* I will put upon
Eze 4:3 take to yourself an *i* griddle
4:3 as an *i* wall between you and
22:18 are copper and tin and *i*
22:20 and *i* and lead and tin into
27:12 its silver, *i*, tin and lead
27:19 *I* in wrought works, cassia
Da 2:33 its legs were of *i*, its feet
2:33 its feet were partly of *i* and
2:34 image on its feet of *i* and
2:35 *i*, the molded clay, the
2:40 prove to be strong like *i*
2:40 *i* is crushing and grinding
2:40 so, like *i* that shatters, it
Da 2:41 and partly of *i*, the kingdom
2:41 hardness of *i* will prove to
2:41 *i* mixed with moist clay
2:42 the feet being partly of *i*
2:43 *i* mixed with moist clay
2:43 *i* is not mixing with molded
2:45 crushed the *i*, the copper
4:15 a banding of *i* and of copper
4:23 banding of *i* and of copper
5:4 praised the gods of . . . *i*
5:23 praised mere gods of . . . *i*
7:7 it had teeth of *i*, big ones
7:19 teeth of which were of *i* and
Am 1:3 with *i* threshing instruments
Mic 4:13 horn I shall change into *i*
Na 2:3 With the fire of *i* fittings
Ac 12:10 *i* gate leading into the city
1Ti 4:2 as with a branding *i*
Re 2:27 people with an *i* rod so that
9:9 like *i* breastplates
12:5 the nations with an *i* rod
18:12 and of *i* and of marble
19:15 shepherd . . . with a rod of *i*

Irons
Ps 105:18 Into *i* his soul came
107:10 in affliction and *i*

Iron-tipped
Ps 74:6 even with hatchet and *i* beams

Ironwork
1Ch 29:2 the iron for the *i*, and the

Irpeel
Jos 18:27 Rekem and *I* and Taralah

Irreprehensible
1Ti 3:2 overseer should therefore be *i*
5:7 commands, that they may be *i*
6:14 in a spotless and *i* way

Irreverent
2Sa 6:7 struck him . . . for the *i* act

Irrigate
Ec 2:6 to *i* with them the forest
Eze 17:7 in order for him to *i* it
Joe 3:18 it must *i* the torrent valley

Irrigating
De 11:10 had to do *i* with your foot

Irritated
Ezr 5:12 our fathers *i* the God of the
Ac 17:16 his spirit . . . came to be *i*

Irritating
Job 19:2 will you men keep *i* my soul
Isa 51:23 the hand of the ones *i* you
Eph 6:4 do not be *i* your children

Ir-shemesh
Jos 19:41 Zorah and Eshtaol and *I*

Iru
1Ch 4:15 sons of Caleb . . . *I*

Isaac
Ge 17:19 you must call his name *I*
17:21 *I*, whom Sarah will bear to
21:3 Sarah had borne to him, *I*
21:4 proceeded to circumcise *I*
21:5 *I* his son was born to him
21:10 heir with my son, with *I*
21:12 by means of *I* that what will
22:2 only son whom you so love, *I*
22:3 attendants with him and *I*
22:6 put it upon *I* his son and took
22:7 *I* began to say to Abraham his
22:9 bound *I* his son hand and foot
24:4 take a wife for my son, for *I*
24:14 assign to your servant, to *I*
24:62 *I* had come from the way that
24:63 *I* was out walking in order
24:64 she caught sight of *I* and she
24:66 servant went relating to *I*
24:67 *I* brought her into the tent
24:67 *I* found comfort after the
25:5 gave everything he had to *I*
25:6 sent them away from *I* his son
25:9 *I* and Ishmael his sons buried
25:11 God continued to bless *I* his
25:11 and *I* was dwelling close by
25:19 And this is the history of *I*
25:19 Abraham became father to *I*
25:20 *I* happened to be forty years
25:21 *I* kept on entreating Jehovah
25:26 *I* was sixty years old at her
25:28 And *I* had love for Esau
26:1 so that *I* directed himself to
Ge 26:6 *I* went on dwelling at Gerar
26:8 there was *I* having a good
26:9 Abimelech called *I* and said
26:9 *I* said to him: I said it for
26:12 *I* began to sow seed in that
26:16 Abimelech said to *I*: Move
26:17 *I* moved from there and
26:18 *I* proceeded to dig again the
26:19 servants of *I* went on digging
26:20 with the shepherds of *I*
26:25 servants of *I* . . . excavating
26:27 *I* said to them: Why have
26:31 *I* sent them away and they
26:32 servants of *I* proceeded to
26:35 bitterness of spirit to *I*
27:1 when *I* was old and his eyes
27:5 while *I* spoke to Esau his son
27:20 *I* said to his son: How is it
27:21 *I* said to Jacob: Come near
27:22 Jacob came near to *I* his
27:26 *I* his father said to him
27:30 *I* had finished blessing Jacob
27:30 from before the face of *I*
27:32 *I* his father said to him
27:33 *I* began to shake with a
27:37 But in answer to Esau *I*
27:39 in answer *I* his father said
27:46 Rebekah kept saying to *I*
28:1 *I* called Jacob and blessed
28:5 So *I* sent Jacob away
28:6 saw that *I* had blessed Jacob
28:8 displeasing in the eyes of *I*
28:13 Jehovah . . . the God of *I*
31:18 to go to *I* his father to the
31:42 Dread of *I*, had not proved
31:53 by the Dread of his father *I*
32:9 God of my father *I*, O Jehovah
35:12 given to Abraham and to *I*
35:27 Jacob came to *I* his father
35:27 Abraham . . . *I* had resided
35:28 And the days of *I* came to be
35:29 *I* expired and died and was
46:1 to the God of his father *I*
48:15 Abraham and *I* walked, The
48:16 my fathers, Abraham and *I*
49:31 they buried *I* and Rebekah
50:24 Abraham, to *I* and to Jacob
Ex 2:24 covenant with Abraham, *I* and
3:6 the God of *I* and the God of
3:15 Jehovah . . . the God of *I*
3:16 God of Abraham, *I* and Jacob
4:5 the God of *I* and the God of
6:3 used to appear to Abraham, *I*
6:8 give to Abraham, *I* and Jacob
32:13 Remember Abraham, *I* and
33:1 swore to Abraham, *I* and Jacob
Le 26:42 and even my covenant with *I*
Nu 32:11 have sworn to Abraham, *I* and
De 1:8 Abraham, *I* and Jacob, to give
6:10 Abraham, *I* and Jacob to
9:5 Abraham, *I* and Jacob
9:27 your servants Abraham, *I* and
29:13 forefathers Abraham, *I* and
30:20 *I* and Jacob to give to them
34:4 sworn to Abraham, *I* and Jacob
Jos 24:3 seed many. So I gave him *I*
24:4 to *I* I gave Jacob and Esau
1Ki 18:36 God of Abraham, *I* and
2Ki 13:23 covenant with Abraham, *I*
1Ch 1:28 sons of Abraham were *I* and
1:34 Abraham . . . father to *I*
1:34 sons of *I* were Esau and
16:16 his sworn statement to *I*
29:18 God of Abraham, *I* and
2Ch 30:6 God of Abraham, *I* and Israel
Ps 105:9 his sworn statement to *I*
Jer 33:26 seed of Abraham, *I* and
Am 7:9 the high places of *I* will
7:16 drop against the house of *I*
Mt 1:2 Abraham became father to *I*
1:2 *I* became father to Jacob
8:11 with Abraham and *I* and Jacob
22:32 the God of *I* and the God of
Mr 12:26 God of *I* and God of Jacob
Lu 3:34 son of Jacob, son of *I*, son of
13:28 when you see Abraham and *I*
20:37 and God of *I* and God of Jacob
Ac 3:13 God of Abraham and of *I* and
7:8 father of *I* and circumcised
7:8 and *I* of Jacob, and Jacob of
7:32 God of . . . *I* and of Jacob
Ro 9:7 your seed will be through *I*
9:10 one man, *I* our forefather
Ga 4:28 promise the same as *I* was

Heb 11:9 in tents with *I* and Jacob
11:17 as good as offered up *I*
11:18 seed will be through *I*
11:20 By faith also *I* blessed
Jas 2:21 offered up *I* his son upon the

Isaac's
Ge 21:8 on the day of *I* being weaned

Isaiah
2Ki 19:2 *I* the prophet the son of
19:5 servants . . . came in to *I*
19:6 Then *I* said to them: This is
19:20 And *I* the son of Amoz
20:1 *I* the son of Amoz the
20:4 *I* himself had not yet gone
20:7 And *I* went on to say
20:8 Hezekiah said to *I:* What is
20:9 *I* said: This is the sign
20:11 *I* the prophet began to call
20:14 *I* the prophet came in to
20:16 *I* now said to Hezekiah
20:19 At that Hezekiah said to *I*
2Ch 26:22 *I* the son of Amoz the
32:20 *I* the son of Amoz, the
32:32 vision of *I* the prophet
Isa 1:1 vision of *I* the son of Amoz
2:1 *I* the son of Amoz visioned
7:3 say to *I:* Go out, please
13:1 *I* the son of Amoz saw in
20:2 spoke by the hand of *I*
20:3 *I* has walked naked and
37:2 *I* the son of Amoz the
37:5 came in to *I*
37:6 *I* said to them: This is
37:21 *I* the son of Amoz proceeded
38:1 *I* the son of Amoz the
38:4 now occurred to *I*, saying
38:21 And *I* proceeded to say
39:3 *I* the prophet came in to
39:5 *I* now said to Hezekiah: Hear
39:8 At that Hezekiah said to *I*
Mt 3:3 the one spoken of through *I*
4:14 spoken through *I* the prophet
8:17 spoken through *I* the prophet
12:17 spoken through *I* the prophet
13:14 of *I* is having fulfillment
15:7 *I* aptly prophesied about you
Mr 1:2 it is written in *I* the prophet
7:6 *I* aptly prophesied about you
Lu 3:4 in the book of the words of *I*
4:17 the scroll of the prophet *I*
Joh 1:23 just as *I* the prophet said
12:38 word of *I* the prophet was
12:39 is that again *I* said
12:41 *I* said these things because
Ac 8:28 reading aloud the prophet *I*
8:30 reading aloud *I* the prophet
28:25 spoke through *I* the prophet
Ro 9:27 *I* cries out concerning Israel
9:29 just as *I* had said aforetime
10:16 *I* says: Jehovah, who put
10:20 *I* becomes very bold and says
15:12 *I* says: There will be the

Iscah
Ge 11:29 Haran . . . father of *I*

Iscariot
Mt 10:4 Judas *I*, who later betrayed
26:14 the one called Judas *I*, went
Mr 3:19 Judas *I*, who later betrayed
14:10 Judas *I*, one of the twelve
Lu 6:16 Judas *I*, who turned traitor
22:3 Judas, the one called *I*, who
Joh 6:71 Judas the son of Simon *I*
12:4 Judas *I*, one of his disciples
13:2 into the heart of Judas *I*
13:26 Judas, the son of Simon *I*
14:22 Judas, not *I*, said to him

Ishbah
1Ch 4:17 *I* the father of Eshtemoa

Ishbak
Ge 25:2 and Midian and *I* and Shuah
1Ch 1:32 Midian and *I* and Shuah

Ishbi-benob
2Sa 21:16 *I*, who was among those

Ish-bosheth
2Sa 2:8 took *I*, Saul's son, and
2:10 *I*, Saul's son, was when he
2:12 servants of *I*, Saul's son
2:15 belonging to Benjamin and *I*
3:7 *I* said to Abner: Why was it
3:8 angry at the words of *I* and
2Sa 3:14 David sent messengers to *I*
3:15 *I* sent and took her from her
4:5 come to the house of *I* about
4:8 bringing the head of *I* to
4:8 Here is the head of *I* the son
4:12 head of *I* they took and then

Ishhod
1Ch 7:18 gave birth to *I* and Abi-ezer

Ishi
1Ch 2:31 the sons of Appaim were *I*
2:31 the sons of *I* were Sheshan
4:20 the sons of *I* were Zoheth and
4:42 the sons of *I* at their head
5:24 Epher and *I* and Eliel and

Ishma
1Ch 4:3 Jezreel and *I* and Idbash

Ishmael
Ge 16:11 must call his name *I*
16:15 his son whom Hagar bore *I*
16:16 Hagar's bearing *I* to Abram
17:18 O that *I* might live before
17:20 as regards *I* I have heard you
17:23 take *I* his son and all the
17:25 *I* his son was thirteen years
17:26 circumcised, and also *I* his
25:9 Isaac and *I* his sons buried
25:12 the history of *I* the son of
25:13 the names of the sons of *I*
25:16 These are the sons of *I*, and
28:9 Esau went to *I* and took as
28:9 Mahalath the daughter of *I*
2Ki 25:23 *I* the son of Nethaniah
25:25 *I* the son of Nethaniah
1Ch 1:28 sons of Abraham . . . *I*
1:31 These were the sons of *I*
8:38 and *I* . . . the sons of Azel
9:44 and *I* . . . the sons of Azel
2Ch 19:11 Zebadiah the son of *I* the
23:1 *I* the son of Jehohanan and
Ezr 10:22 the sons of Pashhur . . . *I*
Jer 40:8 *I* the son of Nethaniah and
40:14 sent *I* the son of Nethaniah
40:15 *I* the son of Nethaniah, as
40:16 are speaking concerning *I*
41:1 *I* the son of Nethaniah the
41:2 *I* the son of Nethaniah and
41:3 men of war, *I* struck down
41:6 *I* the son of Nethaniah went
41:7 *I* the son of Nethaniah went
41:8 immediately said to *I*
41:9 *I* threw all the carcasses
41:9 *I* the son of Nethaniah filled
41:10 *I* took captive all the
41:10 *I* the son of Nethaniah took
41:11 *I* the son of Nethaniah had
41:12 *I* the son of Nethaniah and
41:13 people that were with *I*
41:14 *I* had led captive from
41:15 *I* the son of Nethaniah, he
41:16 *I* the son of Nethaniah
41:18 *I* the son of Nethaniah had

Ishmaelite
1Ch 2:17 of Amasa was Jether the *I*
27:30 camels there was Obil the *I*

Ishmaelites
Ge 37:25 here was a caravan of *I* that
37:27 let us sell him to the *I*
37:28 sold Joseph to the *I* for
39:1 the *I* who had brought him
Jg 8:24 gold, because they were *I*
Ps 83:6 *I*, Moab and the Hagrites

Ishmael's
Ge 25:13 family origins: *I* firstborn
25:17 the years of *I* life, a
36:3 Basemath, *I* daughter, the
1Ch 1:29 *I* firstborn Nebaioth and

Ishmaiah
1Ch 12:4 *I* the Gibeonite, a mighty
27:19 of Zebulun, *I* the son of

Ishmerai
1Ch 8:18 and *I* . . . the sons of Elpaal

Ishpah
1Ch 8:16 *I* . . . the sons of Beriah

Ishpan
1Ch 8:22 and *I* and Eber and Eliel

Ishtob
2Sa 10:6 and *I*, twelve thousand men
10:8 *I* and Maacah by themselves

Ishvah
Ge 46:17 the sons of Asher were . . . *I*
1Ch 7:30 of Asher were Imnah and *I*

Ishvi
Ge 46:17 the sons of Asher were . . . *I*
Nu 26:44 *I* the family of the Ishvites
1Sa 14:49 sons of Saul . . . *I* and
1Ch 7:30 The sons of Asher were . . . *I*

Ishvites
Nu 26:44 of Ishvi the family of the *I*

Island
Jer 25:22 the kings of the *i* that is
47:4 ones from the *i* of Caphtor
Ac 13:6 whole *i* as far as Paphos
21:3 in sight of the *i* of Cyprus
27:16 small *i* called Cauda, and
27:26 cast ashore on a certain *i*
28:1 that the *i* was called Malta
28:7 principal man of the *i*
28:9 people on the *i* who had
28:11 that had wintered in the *i*
Re 6:14 and every *i* were removed
16:20 Also, every *i* fled, and

Islands
Ps 72:10 of Tarshish and of the *i*
97:1 Let the many *i* rejoice
Isa 11:11 from the *i* of the sea
24:15 *i* of the sea the name of
40:15 He lifts the *i* themselves
41:1 to me in silence, you *i*
41:5 The *i* saw and began to fear
42:4 for his law the *i* themselves
42:10 you *i* and you inhabiting
42:12 the *i* let them tell forth
42:15 will turn rivers into *i*
49:1 Listen to me, O you *i*, and
51:5 *i* themselves will hope
59:18 To the *i* he will recompense
60:9 in me the *i* themselves will
66:19 the faraway *i*, who have not
Jer 31:10 tell it among the *i* far
Eze 26:15 will not the *i* rock?
26:18 *i* will tremble in the day
26:18 the *i* that are in the sea
27:3 the peoples for many *i*
27:6 from the *i* of Kittim
27:7 from the *i* of Elishah are
27:15 *i* were merchants in your
27:35 All the inhabitants of the *i*
39:6 inhabiting the *i* in security
Zep 2:11 all the *i* of the nations

Isle
Re 1:9 in the *i* that is called Patmos

Isles
Ge 10:5 population of the *i* of the
Es 10:1 the land and the *i* of the sea

Ismachiah
2Ch 31:13 and *I* . . . commissioners at

Isolated
Le 13:46 dwell *i*. Outside the camp is
Nu 23:9 they keep tabernacling *i*, And
Ps 102:7 like a bird *i* upon a roof
Isa 14:31 getting *i* from his ranks
Ho 8:9 as a zebra *i* to itself
Mr 6:35 The place is *i*, and the hour
8:4 anybody here in an *i* place

Isolating
Pr 18:1 One *i* himself will seek his

Isolation
Mt 14:13 into a lonely place for *i*

Israel
Ge 32:28 no longer . . . Jacob but *I*
32:32 sons of *I* are not accustomed
33:20 called it God the God of *I*
34:7 a disgraceful folly against *I*
35:10 *I* will your name become
35:10 he began to call his name *I*
35:21 *I* pulled away and pitched
35:22 while *I* was tabernacling in
35:22 and *I* got to hear of it
36:31 reigned over the sons of *I*
37:3 *I* loved Joseph more than all
37:13 *I* said to Joseph: Your
43:6 *I* exclaimed: Why did you have
43:8 Judah said to *I* his father
43:11 *I* their father said to them
45:21 the sons of *I* did so, and
45:28 *I* exclaimed: It is enough!
46:1 *I* and all who were his

Ge 46:2 God talked to *I* in visions
46:5 and the sons of *I* continued
46:29 meet *I* his father at Goshen
46:30 *I* said to Joseph: This time
47:27 *I* continued to dwell in the
47:29 days approached for *I* to die
47:31 *I* prostrated himself over
48:2 *I* exerted his strength and
48:8 *I* saw Joseph's sons and said
48:10 eyes of *I* were dull from old
48:11 *I* went on to say to Joseph: I
48:14 *I* put out his right hand and
48:20 let *I* repeatedly pronounce
48:21 *I* said to Joseph: Look, I am
49:2 yes, listen to *I* your father
49:7 and let me scatter them in *I*
49:16 as one of the tribes of *I*
49:24 the shepherd, the stone of *I*
49:28 the twelve tribes of *I*, and
50:2 So the physicians embalmed *I*
50:25 sons of *I* swear, saying: God
Ex 1:7 the sons of *I* became fruitful
1:9 sons of *I* are more numerous
1:12 as a result of the sons of *I*
1:13 sons of *I* slave under tyranny
2:23 sons of *I* continued to sigh
2:25 God looked on the sons of *I*
3:9 the outcry of the sons of *I* has
3:10 the sons of *I* out of Egypt
3:11 bring the sons of *I* out of
3:13 now come to the sons of *I*
3:14 are to say to the sons of *I*
3:15 are to say to the sons of *I*
3:16 gather the older men of *I*
3:18 you and the older men of *I*
4:22 *I* is my son, my firstborn
4:29 older men of the sons of *I*
4:31 his attention to the sons of *I*
5:1 Jehovah the God of *I* has said
5:2 obey his voice to send *I* away
5:2 I am not going to send *I* away
5:14 the officers of the sons of *I*
5:15 officers of the sons of *I*
5:19 officers of the sons of *I*
6:5 the groaning of the sons of *I*
6:6 say to the sons of *I*, I am
6:9 spoke to . . . the sons of *I*
6:11 should send the sons of *I* away
6:12 sons of *I* have not listened
6:13 the sons of *I* and to Pharaoh
6:13 to bring the sons of *I* out
6:26 Bring the sons of *I* out from
6:27 bring the sons of *I* out from
7:2 must send the sons of *I* away
7:4 bring . . . sons of *I*, out from
7:5 bring the sons of *I* out from
9:4 between the livestock of *I* and
9:4 not a thing of . . . sons of *I*
9:6 livestock of the sons of *I*
9:26 Goshen, where the sons of *I*
9:35 not send the sons of *I* away
10:20 not send the sons of *I* away
10:23 *I* there proved to be light in
11:7 against any of the sons of *I*
11:7 Egyptians and the sons of *I*
11:10 not send the sons of *I* away
12:3 to the entire assembly of *I*
12:6 *I* must slaughter it between
12:15 soul must be cut off from *I*
12:19 from the assembly of *I*
12:21 all the older men of *I* and
12:27 the houses of the sons of *I*
12:28 sons of *I* went and did just
12:31 sons of *I*, and go, serve
12:35 sons of *I* did according to
12:37 *I* proceeded to depart from
12:40 dwelling of the sons of *I*
12:42 the part of all the sons of *I*
12:47 All . . . of *I* are to celebrate
12:50 sons of *I* did just as Jehovah
12:51 Jehovah brought the sons of *I*
13:2 among the sons of *I*, among
13:18 sons of *I* went up out of the
13:19 made the sons of *I* solemnly
14:2 Speak to the sons of *I*, that
14:3 sons of *I*, They are wandering
14:5 sent *I* away from slaving for
14:8 chasing after the sons of *I*
14:8 sons of *I* were going out with
14:10 the sons of *I* began to raise
14:10 sons of *I* got quite afraid
14:15 Speak to the sons of *I* that
14:16 *I* may go through the midst
14:19 ahead of the camp of *I*
Ex 14:20 and the camp of *I*
14:22 *I* went through the midst of
14:25 flee from any contact with *I*
14:29 *I*, they walked on dry land
14:30 Jehovah saved *I* from the
14:30 *I* got to see the Egyptians
14:31 *I* also got to see the great
15:1 *I* proceeded to sing this song
15:19 sons of *I* walked on dry land
15:22 Moses caused *I* to depart
16:1 sons of *I* finally came to the
16:2 sons of *I* began to murmur
16:3 the sons of *I* kept saying to
16:6 said to all the sons of *I*: At
16:9 assembly of the sons of *I*
16:10 assembly of the sons of *I*
16:12 murmurings of the sons of *I*
16:15 the sons of *I* got to see it
16:17 the sons of *I* began to do so
16:31 *I* began to call its name
16:35 *I* ate the manna forty years
17:1 *I* proceeded to depart from
17:5 some of the older men of *I*
17:6 eyes of the older men of *I*
17:7 quarreling of the sons of *I*
17:8 fight against *I* in Rephidim
18:1 for *I* his people, how Jehovah
18:1 had brought *I* out of Egypt
18:8 on account of *I*, and all the
18:9 that Jehovah had done for *I*
18:12 all the older men of *I* came
18:25 capable men out of all *I* and
19:1 after the sons of *I* came out
19:2 *I* went camping there in front
19:3 and to tell the sons of *I*
19:6 are to say to the sons of *I*
20:22 are to say to the sons of *I*
24:1 seventy of the older men of *I*
24:4 with the twelve tribes of *I*
24:5 young men of the sons of *I*
24:9 seventy of the older men of *I*
24:10 they got to see the God of *I*
24:11 distinguished men of . . . *I*
24:17 to the eyes of the sons of *I*
25:2 Speak to the sons of *I*, that
25:22 for the sons of *I*
27:20 command the sons of *I* that
27:21 performed by the sons of *I*
28:1 the midst of the sons of *I*
28:9 the names of the sons of *I*
28:11 the names of the sons of *I*
28:12 stones for the sons of *I*
28:21 the names of the sons of *I*
28:29 the names of the sons of *I*
28:30 judgments of the sons of *I*
28:38 the sons of *I* will sanctify
29:28 performed by the sons of *I*
29:28 rendered by the sons of *I*
29:43 myself there to the sons of *I*
29:45 the midst of the sons of *I*
30:12 sum of the sons of *I* as a
30:16 from the sons of *I* and give
30:16 sons of *I*, to make atonement
30:31 speak to the sons of *I*
31:13 speak to the sons of *I*
31:16 the sons of *I* must keep the
31:17 and the sons of *I* it is a
32:4 This is your God, O *I*, who
32:8 your God, O *I*, who led you up
32:13 Isaac and *I* your servants
32:20 made the sons of *I* drink it
32:27 the God of *I* has said
33:5 Say to the sons of *I*, You are
33:6 sons of *I* went stripping their
34:23 Lord, Jehovah, the God of *I*
34:27 covenant with you and *I*
34:30 sons of *I* got to see Moses
34:32 sons of *I* came near to him
34:34 spoke to the sons of *I* what
34:35 sons of *I* saw Moses' face
35:1 sons of *I* together and said to
35:4 assembly of the sons of *I*
35:20 sons of *I* went out from
35:29 sons of *I* brought a voluntary
35:30 Moses said to the sons of *I*
36:3 the sons of *I* had brought for
39:6 the names of the sons of *I*
39:7 stones for the sons of *I*
39:14 the names of the sons of *I*
39:32 the sons of *I* kept doing
39:42 the way the sons of *I* did
40:36 sons of *I* would break camp
40:38 of all the house of *I* during
Le 1:2 Speak to the sons of *I*, and you
Le 4:2 Speak to the sons of *I*, saying
4:13 of *I* makes a mistake and the
7:23 Speak to the sons of *I*
7:29 Speak to the sons of *I*
7:34 I do take from the sons of *I*
7:34 from the sons of *I*
7:36 from among the sons of *I*
7:38 sons of *I* to present their
9:1 his sons and the older men of *I*
9:3 the sons of *I* you will speak
10:6 of *I* will do the weeping over
10:11 to teach the sons of *I* all
10:14 sacrifices of the sons of *I*
11:2 Speak to the sons of *I*, saying
12:2 Speak to the sons of *I*, saying
15:2 sons of *I*, and you must say
15:31 keep the sons of *I* separate
16:5 of the sons of *I* he should
16:16 *I* and concerning their
16:17 entire congregation of *I*
16:19 of the sons of *I*
16:21 the errors of the sons of *I*
16:34 atonement for the sons of *I*
17:2 all the sons of *I*, and you
17:3 any man of the house of *I* who
17:5 *I* may bring their sacrifices
17:8 man of the house of *I* or
17:10 man of the house of *I* or
17:12 *I*: No soul of you must eat
17:13 *I* or some alien resident
17:14 sons of *I*: You must not eat
18:2 Speak to the sons of *I*, and
19:2 sons of *I*, and you must say
20:2 *I*, Any man of the sons of
20:2 Any man of the sons of *I*, and
20:2 in *I*, who gives any of his
21:24 Moses spoke to . . . sons of *I*
22:2 *I* and not profane my holy
22:3 *I* will sanctify to Jehovah
22:15 holy things of the sons of *I*
22:18 *I*, and you must say to them
22:18 *I* or some alien resident in
22:18 in *I* who presents his
22:32 sons of *I*. I am Jehovah who
23:2 sons of *I*, and you must say
23:10 *I*, and you must say to them
23:24 *I*, saying, In the seventh
23:34 *I*, saying, On the fifteenth
23:42 natives in *I* should dwell in
23:43 *I* to dwell when I was
23:44 of Jehovah to the sons of *I*
24:2 *I* that they get for you pure
24:8 covenant . . . sons of *I*
24:10 *I*, and the son of the
24:15 *I*, saying, In case any man
24:23 spoke to the sons of *I*, and
24:23 *I* did just as Jehovah had
25:2 *I*, and you must say to them
25:33 the midst of the sons of *I*
25:46 *I*, you must not tread, the
25:55 the sons of *I* are slaves
26:46 between himself and . . . *I*
27:2 Speak to the sons of *I*, and
27:34 commands to the sons of *I* in
Nu 1:2 *I* according to their families
1:3 going out to the army in *I*
1:16 heads of the thousands of *I*
1:44 Aaron and the chieftains of *I*
1:45 *I* according to the house of
1:45 going out to the army in *I*
1:49 in among the sons of *I*
1:52 *I* must encamp each with
1:53 assembly of the sons of *I*
1:54 *I* proceeded to do according
2:2 *I* should encamp, each man by
2:32 *I* according to the house of
2:33 in among the sons of *I*, just
2:34 *I* proceeded to do according
3:8 obligation of the sons of *I* in
3:9 given . . . from the sons of *I*
3:12 from among the sons of *I*
3:12 the womb of the sons of *I*
3:13 firstborn in *I* from man to
3:38 obligation for the sons of *I*
3:40 *I* from a month old upward
3:41 firstborn among the sons of *I*
3:41 animals of the sons of *I*
3:42 firstborn among the sons of *I*
3:45 firstborn among the sons of *I*
3:46 firstborn of the sons of *I*
3:50 firstborn of the sons of *I*
4:46 chieftains of *I* registered as
5:2 Command the sons of *I* that
5:4 *I* proceeded to do so, even to

Nu 5:4 so the sons of *I* did
5:6 *I*, As for a man or a woman, in
5:9 holy things of the sons of *I*
5:12 Speak to the sons of *I*, and
6:2 Speak to the sons of *I* and you
6:23 bless the sons of *I*, saying
6:27 my name upon the sons of *I*
7:2 chieftains of *I*, the heads of
7:84 part of the chieftains of *I*
8:6 *I*, and you must cleanse them
8:9 the assembly of the sons of *I*
8:10 *I* must lay their hands upon
8:11 offering from the sons of *I*
8:14 from among the sons of *I*
8:16 from among the sons of *I*
8:16 firstborn of the sons of *I*
8:17 among the sons of *I* is mine
8:18 among the sons of *I*
8:19 from among the sons of *I*
8:19 service of the sons of *I* in
8:19 atonement for the sons of *I*
8:19 occur among the sons of *I*
8:19 sons of *I* approach the holy
8:20 assembly of the sons of *I*
8:20 way the sons of *I* did to them
9:2 *I* should prepare the passover
9:4 Moses spoke to the sons of *I*
9:5 so the sons of *I* did
9:7 the midst of the sons of *I*
9:10 Speak to the sons of *I*
9:17 sons of *I* would pull away
9:17 the sons of *I* would encamp
9:18 sons of *I* would pull away
9:19 *I* also kept their obligation
9:22 *I* remained encamped and would
10:4 heads of the thousands of *I*
10:12 *I* began to pull away in the
10:28 departures of the sons of *I*
10:29 spoken good concerning *I*
10:36 myriads of thousands of *I*
11:4 *I* too began to weep again and
11:16 older men of *I*, whom you do
11:30 he and the older men of *I*
13:2 I am giving to the sons of *I*
13:3 were heads of the sons of *I*
13:24 cluster that the sons of *I*
13:26 assembly of the sons of *I*
13:32 to the sons of *I* a bad report
14:2 the sons of *I* began to murmur
14:5 the assembly of the sons of *I*
14:7 the assembly of the sons of *I*
14:10 to all the sons of *I*
14:27 murmurings of the sons of *I*
14:39 words to all the sons of *I*
15:2 Speak to the sons of *I*, and
15:18 Speak to the sons of *I*, and
15:25 assembly of the sons of *I*
15:26 assembly of the sons of *I*
15:29 native among the sons of *I*
15:32 sons of *I* were continuing in
15:38 Speak to the sons of *I*, and
16:2 of the sons of *I*, chieftains
16:9 God of *I* has separated you
16:9 men from the assembly of *I*
16:25 older men of *I* went with
16:38 as a sign to the sons of *I*
16:40 a memorial for the sons of *I*
16:41 sons of *I* began to murmur
17:2 Speak to the sons of *I* and
17:5 murmurings of the sons of *I*
17:6 Moses spoke to the sons of *I*
17:9 to all the sons of *I*, and they
17:12 sons of *I* began to say this
18:5 occur against the sons of *I*
18:6 from among the sons of *I*, as
18:8 holy things of the sons of *I*
18:11 offerings of the sons of *I*
18:14 Every devoted thing in *I*
18:19 sons of *I* will contribute to
18:20 the midst of the sons of *I*
18:21 given every tenth part in *I*
18:22 *I* should no more come near
18:23 the midst of the sons of *I*
18:24 tenth part of the sons of *I*
18:24 the midst of the sons of *I*
18:26 receive from the sons of *I*
18:28 receive from the sons of *I*
18:32 holy things of the sons of *I*
19:2 Speak to the sons of *I* that
19:9 the assembly of the sons of *I*
19:10 serve the sons of *I* and the
19:13 soul must be cut off from *I*
20:1 And the sons of *I*, the entire
20:12 the eyes of the sons of *I*

Nu 20:13 *I* quarreled with Jehovah, so
20:14 what your brother *I* has said
20:19 sons of *I* said to him: By
20:21 Edom refused to grant *I* to
20:21 *I* turned away from him
20:22 *I*, the entire assembly
20:24 give to the sons of *I*, on the
20:29 house of *I* continued weeping
21:1 hear that *I* had come by the
21:1 he began to fight with *I* and
21:2 *I* made a vow to Jehovah and
21:6 so that many people of *I* died
21:10 sons of *I* pulled away and
21:17 *I* proceeded to sing this song
21:21 *I* now sent messengers to
21:23 Sihon did not allow *I* to
21:23 to meet *I* in the wilderness
21:23 and began fighting with *I*
21:24 *I* struck him with the edge
21:25 *I* took all these cities, and
21:25 *I* began dwelling in all the
21:31 *I* began to dwell in the land
22:1 *I* pulled away and encamped on
22:2 *I* had done to the Amorites
22:3 dread of the sons of *I*
23:7 Yes, do come, do denounce *I*
23:10 counted the fourth part of *I*
23:21 trouble has he seen against *I*
23:23 Nor any divination against *I*
23:23 said respecting Jacob and *I*
24:1 the eyes of Jehovah to bless *I*
24:2 *I* tabernacling by his tribes
24:5 your tabernacles, O *I*
24:17 a scepter . . . rise out of *I*
24:18 *I* is displaying his courage
25:1 *I* was dwelling in Shittim
25:3 *I* attached itself to the Baal
25:3 began to blaze against *I*
25:4 may turn back from *I*
25:5 Moses said to the judges of *I*
25:6 a man of the sons of *I* came
25:6 the assembly of the sons of *I*
25:8 he went after the man of *I*
25:8 the man of *I* and the woman
25:8 from upon the sons of *I*
25:11 from upon the sons of *I* by
25:11 not exterminated . . . *I*
25:13 atonement for the sons of *I*
26:2 *I* from twenty years of age
26:2 going out to the army in *I*
26:4 sons of *I* who went out of the
26:51 registered . . . sons of *I*
26:62 in among the sons of *I*
26:62 in among the sons of *I*
26:63 registered the sons of *I* in
26:64 registered the sons of *I* in
27:8 to the sons of *I* you should
27:11 for the sons of *I*, just as
27:12 certainly give the sons of *I*
27:20 sons of *I* may listen to him
27:21 all the sons of *I* with him
28:2 Command the sons of *I*, and
29:40 to talk to the sons of *I*
30:1 of the tribes of the sons of *I*
31:2 vengeance for the sons of *I*
31:4 of all the tribes of *I* you
31:5 from the thousands of *I*
31:9 *I* carried off the women of
31:12 assembly of the sons of *I*
31:16 to induce the sons of *I* to
31:30 the half of the sons of *I*
31:42 belonging to the sons of *I*
31:47 belonging to the sons of *I*
31:54 a memorial for the sons of *I*
32:4 before the assembly of *I*
32:7 dishearten the sons of *I* from
32:9 disheartened the sons of *I*
32:13 anger blazed against *I* and he
32:14 anger of Jehovah against *I*
32:17 before the sons of *I* until
32:18 until the sons of *I* have
32:22 against Jehovah and against *I*
32:28 the tribes of the sons of *I*
33:1 stages of the sons of *I* who
33:3 the sons of *I* went out with
33:5 *I* pulled away from Rameses
33:38 going out of the sons of *I*
33:40 the coming of the sons of *I*
33:51 Speak to the sons of *I*, and
34:2 Command the sons of *I*, and
34:13 commanded the sons of *I*
34:29 sons of *I* landholders in the
35:2 *I* the command that they must
35:8 possession of the sons of *I*

Nu 35:10 Speak to the sons of *I*, and
35:15 For the sons of *I* and for the
35:34 the midst of the sons of *I*
36:1 the fathers of the sons of *I*
36:2 by lot to the sons of *I*; and
36:3 other tribes of the sons of *I*
36:4 takes place for the sons of *I*
36:5 commanded the sons of *I* at
36:7 inheritance of the sons of *I*
36:7 the sons of *I* should cleave
36:8 of the tribes of the sons of *I*
36:8 that the sons of *I* may get
36:9 tribes of the sons of *I* should
36:13 to the sons of *I* on the
De 1:1 that Moses spoke to all *I*
1:3 Moses spoke to the sons of *I*
1:38 he will cause *I* to inherit it
2:12 just the same as *I* must do to
3:18 your brothers, the sons of *I*
4:1 *I*, listen to the regulations
4:44 set before the sons of *I*
4:45 Moses spoke to the sons of *I*
4:46 the sons of *I* defeated on
5:1 call all *I* and to say to them
5:1 Hear, O *I*, the regulations
6:3 listen, O *I*, and take care to
6:4 Listen, O *I*: Jehovah our God is
9:1 *I*, you are today crossing the
10:6 sons of *I* pulled away from
10:12 *I*, what is Jehovah your God
11:6 in the midst of all *I*
13:11 all *I* will hear and become
17:4 thing has been done in *I*
17:12 clear out what is bad from *I*
17:20 his sons in the midst of *I*
18:1 share or inheritance with *I*
18:6 one of your cities of all *I*
19:13 innocent blood out of *I*
20:3 *I*, you are drawing near today
21:8 the account of your people *I*
21:8 in the midst of your people *I*
21:21 all *I* will hear and indeed
22:19 bad name upon a virgin of *I*
22:21 a disgraceful folly in *I*
22:22 what is bad out of *I*
23:17 None of the daughters of *I*
23:17 anyone of the sons of *I*
24:7 his brothers of the sons of *I*
25:6 may not be wiped out of *I*
25:7 his brother's name in *I*
25:10 his name must be called in *I*
26:15 bless your people *I* and the
27:1 the older men of *I* went on to
27:9 the Levites, spoke to all *I*
27:9 Keep silent and listen, O *I*
27:14 say . . . to every man of *I*
29:1 sons of *I* in the land of Moab
29:2 call all *I* and to say to them
29:10 every man of *I*
29:21 the tribes of *I* in accord
31:1 spoke these words to all *I*
31:7 before the eyes of all *I*
31:9 and to all the older men of *I*
31:11 all *I* comes to see the face
31:11 this law in front of all *I*
31:19 teach it to the sons of *I*
31:19 against the sons of *I*
31:22 teach it to the sons of *I*
31:23 the sons of *I* into the land
31:30 the congregation of *I* the
32:8 the number of the sons of *I*
32:45 all these words to all *I*
32:49 to the sons of *I* as a
32:51 *I* at the waters of Meribah
32:51 the middle of the sons of *I*
32:52 am giving to the sons of *I*
33:1 blessed the sons of *I* before
33:5 number of the tribes of *I*
33:10 And *I* in your law. Let them
33:21 judicial decisions with *I*
33:28 *I* will reside in security
33:29 O *I*! Who is there like you
34:8 sons of *I* proceeded to weep
34:9 sons of *I* began to listen to
34:10 a prophet in *I* like Moses
34:12 before the eyes of all *I*
Jos 1:2 to them, to the sons of *I*
2:2 the sons of *I* have come in
3:1 and he and all the sons of *I*
3:7 you great in the eyes of all *I*
3:9 on to say to the sons of *I*
3:12 men from the tribes of *I*
3:17 *I* were passing over on dry
4:4 appointed from the sons of *I*

Jos 4:5 the tribes of the sons of *I*
4:7 a memorial to the sons of *I*
4:8 the sons of *I* did so, just as
4:8 of the tribes of the sons of *I*
4:12 the sight of the sons of *I*
4:14 great in the eyes of all *I*
4:21 on to say to the sons of *I*
4:22 *I* passed over this Jordan
5:1 from before the sons of *I*
5:1 because of the sons of *I*
5:2 and circumcise the sons of *I*
5:3 and circumcised the sons of *I*
5:6 sons of *I* had walked forty
5:10 sons of *I* continued to camp
5:12 anymore for the sons of *I*
6:1 because of the sons of *I*, no
6:18 camp of *I* a thing devoted to
6:23 outside the camp of *I*
6:25 in the midst of *I* down to
7:1 sons of *I* went committing an
7:1 against the sons of *I*
7:6 he and the older men of *I*
7:8 after *I* has turned his back
7:11 *I* has sinned, and they have
7:12 sons of *I* will not be able
7:13 Jehovah the God of *I* has said
7:13 is in your midst, O *I*
7:15 a disgraceful folly in *I*
7:16 had *I* come near, tribe by
7:19 glory to Jehovah the God of *I*
7:20 Jehovah the God of *I*, and
7:23 Joshua and all the sons of *I*
7:24 Joshua, and all *I* with him
7:25 all *I* went pelting him with
8:10 he and the older men of *I*
8:14 went out to meet *I* in battle
8:15 Joshua and all *I* suffered a
8:17 that did not go out after *I*
8:17 and went chasing after *I*
8:21 Joshua and all *I* saw that
8:22 they got to be in between *I*
8:24 *I* was finishing the killing
8:24 all *I* returned to Ai and
8:27 and the spoil of that city *I*
8:30 altar to Jehovah the God of *I*
8:31 had commanded the sons of *I*
8:32 written before the sons of *I*
8:33 all *I* and their older men
8:33 bless the people of *I* first
8:35 of all the congregation of *I*
9:2 make war against Joshua and *I*
9:6 said to him and the men of *I*
9:7 men of *I* said to the Hivites
9:17 the sons of *I* pulled out and
9:18 sons of *I* did not strike
9:18 by Jehovah the God of *I*
9:19 by Jehovah the God of *I*
9:26 the hand of the sons of *I*
10:1 Gibeon had made peace with *I*
10:4 Joshua and the sons of *I*
10:10 into confusion before *I*
10:11 were fleeing from before *I*
10:11 *I* killed with the sword
10:12 Amorites to the sons of *I*
10:12 say before the eyes of *I*
10:14 was fighting for *I*
10:15 all *I* with him returned to
10:20 Joshua and the sons of *I* had
10:21 against the sons of *I*
10:24 to call all the men of *I*
10:29 Joshua and all *I* with him
10:31 Joshua and all *I* with him
10:34 Joshua and all *I* with him
10:36 and all *I* with him went up
10:38 all *I* with him came back
10:40 Jehovah the God of *I* had
10:42 Jehovah the God of *I* who
10:42 who was fighting for *I*
10:43 all *I* with him returned to
11:5 to fight against *I*
11:6 all of them slain to *I*
11:13 that *I* did not burn
11:14 the sons of *I* plundered
11:16 mountainous region of *I* and
11:19 peace with the sons of *I*
11:20 to declare war against *I*
11:21 the mountainous region of *I*
11:22 in the land of the sons of *I*
11:23 as an inheritance to *I*
12:1 whom the sons of *I* defeated
12:6 sons of *I* who defeated them
12:7 the sons of *I* defeated on
12:7 gave it to the tribes of *I* as
13:6 from before the sons of *I*

Jos 13:6 fall to *I* as an inheritance
13:13 sons of *I* did not dispossess
13:13 dwelling in the midst of *I*
13:14 Jehovah the God of *I*
13:22 whom the sons of *I* killed
13:33 the God of *I* is their
14:1 what the sons of *I* took as a
14:1 tribes of the sons of *I*
14:5 so the sons of *I* did; and
14:10 *I* walked in the wilderness
14:14 Jehovah the God of *I*
17:13 sons of *I* had grown strong
18:1 assembly of the sons of *I*
18:2 left among the sons of *I*
18:3 Joshua said to the sons of *I*
18:10 the land to the sons of *I*
19:49 the sons of *I* gave an
19:51 the tribes of the sons of *I*
20:2 Speak to the sons of *I*
20:9 all the sons of *I* and for
21:1 the tribes of the sons of *I*
21:3 sons of *I* gave the Levites
21:8 sons of *I* gave the Levites
21:41 possession of the sons of *I*
21:43 Jehovah gave *I* all the land
21:45 made to the house of *I*; it
22:9 from the other sons of *I*
22:11 the other sons of *I* heard
22:11 belonging to the sons of *I*
22:12 sons of *I* got to hear of it
22:12 assembly of the sons of *I*
22:13 the sons of *I* sent to the
22:14 of all the tribes of *I*, and
22:14 of the thousands of *I*
22:16 against the God of *I* in
22:18 the entire assembly of *I*
22:20 all the assembly of *I* that
22:21 heads of the thousands of *I*
22:22 and *I*, he too will know
22:24 with Jehovah the God of *I*
22:30 heads of the thousands of *I*
22:31 delivered the sons of *I* out
22:32 sons of *I* and brought back
22:33 the eyes of the sons of *I*
22:33 *I* proceeded to bless God
23:1 after Jehovah had given *I*
23:2 to call all *I*, its older
24:1 all the tribes of *I* together
24:1 call the older men of *I* and
24:2 the God of *I* has said, It
24:9 and went fighting against *I*
24:23 to Jehovah the God of *I*
24:31 And *I* continued to serve
24:31 Jehovah that he did for *I*
24:32 which the sons of *I* had
Jg 1:1 the sons of *I* proceeded to
1:28 *I* grew strong and proceeded
2:4 words to all the sons of *I*
2:6 the sons of *I* went their way
2:7 great work that he did for *I*
2:10 work that he had done for *I*
2:11 the sons of *I* fell to doing
2:14 anger blazed against *I*, so
2:20 anger blazed against *I* and
2:22 to test *I*, whether they will
3:1 stay so as by them to test *I*
3:2 *I* to have the experience, so
3:4 serving as agents to test *I*
3:5 the sons of *I* dwelt in among
3:7 sons of *I* did what was bad in
3:8 anger blazed against *I*, so
3:8 sons of *I* continued to serve
3:9 *I* began to call to Jehovah for
3:9 of *I* that he might save them
3:10 and he became the judge of *I*
3:12 *I* went doing what was bad
3:12 Moab grow strong against *I*
3:13 they went and struck *I* and
3:14 sons of *I* continued to serve
3:15 *I* began to call to Jehovah
3:15 *I* sent tribute by his hand to
3:27 sons of *I* began going down
3:31 and he too got to save *I*
4:1 *I* again began to do what was
4:3 *I* began to cry out to Jehovah
4:3 oppressed the sons of *I* with
4:4 Deborah . . . was judging *I* at
4:5 sons of *I* would go up to her
4:6 Jehovah the God of *I* given
4:23 the sons of *I* on that day
4:24 And the hand of the sons of *I*
5:2 hair hang loose in *I* for war
5:7 ceased, in *I* they ceased, Until
5:7 I rose up as a mother in *I*

Jg 5:8 Among forty thousand in *I*
5:9 the commanders of *I*, Who were
5:11 dwellers in open country in *I*
6:1 *I* began to do what was bad in
6:2 Midian came to prevail over *I*
6:2 sons of *I* made for themselves
6:3 if *I* sowed seed, Midian and
6:4 or bull or ass remain in *I*
6:6 *I* became greatly impoverished
6:6 *I* began to call to Jehovah for
6:7 *I* called to Jehovah for aid on
6:8 *I* and to say to them: This is
6:8 God of *I* has said, It was I
6:14 save *I* out of Midian's palm
6:15 With what shall I save *I*?
6:36 saving *I* by means of me, just
6:37 you will save *I* by means of
7:2 Perhaps *I* would brag about
7:8 the men of *I* he sent away each
7:14 man of *I*. The true God has
7:15 returned to the camp of *I* and
7:23 *I* were called together from
8:22 *I* said to Gideon: Rule over us
8:27 all *I* began to have immoral
8:28 subdued before the sons of *I*
8:33 sons of *I* again took up having
8:34 *I* did not remember Jehovah
8:35 he had exercised toward *I*
9:22 kept playing the prince over *I*
9:55 *I* got to see that Abimelech
10:1 to save *I* Tola the son of Puah
10:2 to judge *I* for twenty-three
10:3 judge *I* for twenty-two years
10:6 *I* again proceeded to do what
10:7 anger blazed against *I*, so
10:8 oppressed the sons of *I* in
10:8 *I* that were on the side of
10:9 and *I* was greatly distressed
10:10 *I* began to call to Jehovah
10:11 said to the sons of *I*: Was
10:15 *I* said to Jehovah: We have
10:16 because of the trouble of *I*
10:17 So the sons of *I* gathered
11:4 began to fight against *I*
11:5 did fight against *I*, the older
11:13 because *I* took my land when
11:15 *I* did not take the land of
11:16 *I* went walking through the
11:17 *I* sent messengers to the
11:17 *I* kept dwelling in Kadesh
11:19 *I* sent messengers to Sihon
11:19 *I* said to him: Let us pass
11:20 and fighting against *I*
11:21 God of *I* gave Sihon and all
11:21 *I* took possession of all the
11:23 the God of *I* it was that
11:23 from before his people *I*
11:25 Did he ever contend with *I*
11:26 *I* was dwelling in Heshbon
11:27 *I* and the sons of Ammon
11:33 subdued before the sons of *I*
11:39 came to be a regulation in *I*
11:40 daughters of *I* would go to
12:7 to judge *I* for six years
12:8 Ibzan . . . began to judge *I*
12:9 to judge *I* for seven years
12:11 Elon . . . began to judge *I*
12:11 to judge *I* ten years
12:13 Abdon . . . began to judge *I*
12:14 to judge *I* eight years
13:1 *I* engaged again in doing what
13:5 saving *I* out of the hand of
14:4 were ruling over *I*
15:20 to judge *I* in the days of the
16:31 he had judged *I* twenty years
17:6 there was no king in *I*
18:1 there was no king in *I*
18:1 the midst of the tribes of *I*
18:19 priest to a . . . family in *I*
18:29 Dan, who had been born to *I*
19:1 that there was no king in *I*
19:12 are no part of the sons of *I*
19:29 into every territory of *I*
19:30 the sons of *I* went up out
20:1 all the sons of *I* went out
20:2 and all the tribes of *I* took
20:3 *I* had gone up to Mizpah
20:3 Then the sons of *I* said: Speak
20:6 and disgraceful folly in *I*
20:7 *I*, give your word and counsel
20:10 of all the tribes of *I*, and
20:10 folly that they did in *I*
20:11 the men of *I* were gathered
20:12 tribes of *I* sent men to all

2Sa 19:41 all the men of *I* were
19:42 answered the men of *I*
19:43 the men of *I* answered the
19:43 the word of the men of *I*
20:1 Every one to his gods, O *I!*
20:2 the men of *I* began to go up
20:14 through all the tribes of *I*
20:19 and faithful ones of *I*
20:19 a city and a mother in *I*
20:23 was over all the army of *I*
21:2 were not of the sons of *I*
21:2 sons of *I* themselves had
21:2 jealous for the sons of *I*
21:4 to put a man to death in *I*
21:5 in any of the territory of *I*
21:15 to have war again with *I*
21:17 extinguish the lamp of *I*
21:21 And he kept taunting *I*
23:1 one of the melodies of *I*
23:3 The God of *I* said, To me
23:3 To me the Rock of *I* spoke
23:9 so the men of *I* retreated
24:1 came to be hot against *I*
24:1 take a count of *I* and Judah
24:2 through all the tribes of *I*
24:4 Joab . . . to register the people *I*
24:9 *I* amounted to eight hundred
24:15 gave a pestilence in *I*
24:25 was halted from upon *I*
1Ki 1:3 all the territory of *I*, and
1:20 eyes of all *I* are upon you
1:30 Jehovah the God of *I*, saying
1:34 anoint . . . as king over *I*
1:35 leader over *I* and over Judah
1:48 Jehovah the God of *I*, who
2:4 sitting upon the throne of *I*
2:5 two chiefs of the armies of *I*
2:11 David had reigned over *I*
2:15 all *I* had set their face for
2:32 the chief of the army of *I*
3:28 *I* got to hear of the judicial
4:1 continued king over all *I*
4:7 twelve deputies over all *I*
4:20 Judah and *I* were many, like
4:25 Judah and *I* continued to
5:13 for forced labor out of all *I*
6:1 *I* came out from the land of
6:1 Solomon became king over *I*
6:13 the middle of the sons of *I*
6:13 shall not leave my people *I*
8:1 congregate the older men of *I*
8:1 sons of *I*, to King Solomon
8:2 all the men of *I* congregated
8:3 all the older men of *I* came
8:5 all the assembly of *I*, those
8:9 covenanted with the sons of *I*
8:14 all the congregation of *I*
8:14 all the congregation of *I*
8:15 God of *I*, who spoke by his
8:16 brought my people *I* out from
8:16 out of all the tribes of *I*
8:16 come to be over my people *I*
8:17 name of Jehovah the God of *I*
8:20 sit upon the throne of *I*
8:20 name of Jehovah the God of *I*
8:22 of all the congregation of *I*
8:23 O Jehovah the God of *I*
8:25 O Jehovah the God of *I*
8:25 to sit upon the throne of *I*
8:26 God of *I*, let your promise
8:30 your people *I* with which
8:33 your people *I* are defeated
8:34 the sin of your people *I*
8:36 even of your people *I*
8:38 or of all your people *I*
8:41 no part of your people *I*
8:43 the same as your people *I* do
8:52 for favor of your people *I*
8:55 all the congregation of *I*
8:56 to his people *I* according to
8:59 judgment for his people *I*
8:62 *I* with him were offering a
8:63 *I* might inaugurate the house
8:65 and all *I* with him, a great
8:66 and for *I* his people
9:5 throne of your kingdom over *I*
9:5 sitting upon the throne of *I*
9:7 cut *I* off from upon the
9:7 and *I* will indeed become a
9:20 no part of the sons of *I*
9:21 land whom the sons of *I* had
9:22 none of the sons of *I* that
10:9 you upon the throne of *I*
10:9 Jehovah loves *I* to time

1Ki 11:2 had said to the sons of *I*
11:9 from Jehovah the God of *I*
11:16 Joab and all *I* dwelt there
11:25 came to be a resister of *I*
11:25 he had an abhorrence of *I*
11:31 Jehovah the God of *I* has
11:32 out of all the tribes of *I*
11:37 become king over *I*
11:38 and I will give you *I*
11:42 reigned . . . over all *I*
12:1 to Shechem that all *I* came
12:3 the congregation of *I* came
12:16 all *I* got to see that the
12:16 To your gods, O *I*
12:16 *I* began to go to their tents
12:17 the sons of *I* that were
12:18 *I* pelted him with stones
12:20 *I* heard that Jeroboam had
12:20 made him king over all *I*
12:21 fight against the house of *I*
12:24 your brothers the sons of *I*
12:28 Here is your God, O *I*
12:33 a festival for the sons of *I*
14:7 Jehovah the God of *I* has said
14:7 a leader over my people *I*
14:10 and worthless one in *I*
14:13 *I* will indeed bewail him
14:13 toward Jehovah the God of *I*
14:14 a king over *I* who will cut
14:15 strike *I* down, just as the
14:15 *I* off this good ground that
14:16 give *I* up on account of the
14:16 which he caused *I* to sin
14:18 all *I* went wailing for him
14:19 the days of the kings of *I*
14:21 of *I* to put his name there
14:24 from before the sons of *I*
15:9 Jeroboam the king of *I*
15:16 and Baasha the king of *I*
15:17 Baasha the king of *I* came
15:19 Baasha the king of *I*
15:20 against the cities of *I* and
15:25 he became king over *I* in
15:25 reign over *I* two years
15:26 which he caused *I* to sin
15:27 Nadab and all *I* were
15:30 he caused *I* to sin and by
15:30 Jehovah the God of *I*
15:31 the days of the kings of *I*
15:32 and Baasha the king of *I*
15:33 Baasha . . . king over all *I*
15:34 which he caused *I* to sin
16:2 leader over my people *I*
16:2 caused my people *I* to sin
16:5 the days of the kings of *I*
16:8 Elah . . . became king over *I*
16:13 they caused *I* to sin by
16:13 Jehovah the God of *I* with
16:14 the days of the kings of *I*
16:16 *I* made Omri, the chief of
16:16 king over *I* on that day
16:17 Omri and all *I* with him
16:19 by causing *I* to sin
16:20 the days of the kings of *I*
16:21 people of *I* began to divide
16:23 Omri became king over *I*
16:26 caused *I* to sin by offending
16:26 Jehovah the God of *I*
16:27 the days of the kings of *I*
16:29 Ahab . . . became king over *I*
16:29 to reign over *I* in Samaria
16:33 Jehovah the God of *I*
16:33 than all the kings of *I* that
17:1 as Jehovah the God of *I*
17:14 the God of *I* has said
18:17 bringer of ostracism upon *I*
18:18 brought ostracism upon *I*
18:19 collect together all *I* to
18:20 among all the sons of *I*
18:31 *I* is what your name will
18:36 Abraham, Isaac and *I*
18:36 that you are God in *I* and
19:10 the sons of *I* have left
19:14 the sons of *I* have left
19:16 Jehu . . . as king over *I*
19:18 seven thousand remain in *I*
20:2 Ahab the king of *I* at the
20:4 the king of *I* answered and
20:7 king of *I* called all the
20:11 the king of *I* answered and
20:13 Ahab the king of *I* and then
20:15 sons of *I*, seven thousand
20:20 *I* went in pursuit of them
20:21 king of *I* went out and kept

1Ki 20:22 approached the king of *I* and
20:26 Aphek for battle against *I*
20:27 the sons of *I*, they were
20:27 sons of *I* went into camp
20:28 and said to the king of *I*
20:29 sons of *I* went striking
20:31 kings of the house of *I* are
20:31 go out to the king of *I*
20:32 came in to the king of *I*
20:40 the king of *I* said to him
20:41 king of *I* got to recognize
20:43 king of *I* went on his way
21:7 exercise the kingship over *I*
21:18 Ahab the king of *I*, who is
21:21 and worthless one in *I*
21:22 and then caused *I* to sin
21:26 from before the sons of *I*
22:1 war between Syria and *I*
22:2 to go down to the king of *I*
22:3 king of *I* said to his
22:4 said to the king of *I*
22:5 to say to the king of *I*
22:6 king of *I* collected the
22:8 At that the king of *I* said to
22:9 king of *I* called a certain
22:10 king of *I* and Jehoshaphat
22:18 Then the king of *I* said to
22:26 the king of *I* said: Take
22:29 king of *I* and Jehoshaphat
22:30 The king of *I* now said to
22:30 the king of *I* disguised
22:31 with the king of *I* alone
22:32 Surely it is the king of *I*
22:33 it was not the king of *I*
22:34 got to strike the king of *I*
22:39 the days of the kings of *I*
22:41 Ahab the king of *I*
22:44 with the king of *I*
22:51 king over *I* in Samaria
22:51 Ahaziah . . . reign over *I*
22:52 who had caused *I* to sin
22:53 Jehovah the God of *I*
2Ki 1:1 revolt against *I* after the
1:3 no God at all in *I* that you
1:6 no God at all in *I* that you
1:16 no God at all in *I* of whose
1:18 the days of the kings of *I*
2:12 the war chariot of *I* and his
3:1 Jehoram . . . king over *I* in
3:3 with which he caused *I* to sin
3:4 paid to the king of *I* a
3:5 revolt against the king of *I*
3:6 Samaria and mustered all *I*
3:9 And the king of *I* and the
3:10 At length the king of *I* said
3:11 servants of the king of *I*
3:12 king of *I* and Jehoshaphat
3:13 to say to the king of *I*
3:13 the king of *I* said to him
3:24 came into the camp of *I*
3:27 great indignation against *I*
5:2 captive from the land of *I* a
5:4 who is from the land of *I*
5:5 send a letter to the king of *I*
5:6 the letter to the king of *I*
5:7 the king of *I* read the letter
5:8 the king of *I* had ripped his
5:8 there exists a prophet in *I*
5:12 than all the waters of *I*
5:15 in the earth but in *I*
6:8 involved in war against *I*
6:9 sent to the king of *I*, saying
6:10 king of *I* sent to the place
6:11 is for the king of *I*
6:12 the prophet who is in *I*
6:12 tells the king of *I* the
6:21 king of *I* now said to Elisha
6:23 again into the land of *I*
6:26 king of *I* was passing along
7:6 king of *I* has hired against
7:13 same as all the crowd of *I*
7:13 same as all the crowd of *I*
8:12 you will do to the sons of *I*
8:16 Ahab the king of *I*
8:18 the way of the kings of *I*
8:25 son of Ahab the king of *I*
8:26 Omri the king of *I*
9:3 I do anoint you as king over *I*
9:6 Jehovah the God of *I* has said
9:6 over Jehovah's people . . . *I*
9:8 and worthless one in *I*
9:12 anoint you as king over *I*
9:14 Ramoth-gilead, he with all *I*
9:21 and Jehoram the king of *I*

2Ki 10:21 Jehu sent through all *I*
10:28 annihilated Baal out of *I*
10:29 which he caused *I* to sin
10:30 you upon the throne of *I*
10:31 law of Jehovah the God of *I*
10:31 he caused *I* to sin
10:32 cut off *I* piece by piece
10:32 in all the territory of *I*
10:34 the days of the kings of *I*
10:36 Jehu had reigned over *I*
13:1 king over *I* in Samaria for
13:2 he caused *I* to sin. He did
13:3 anger became hot against *I*
13:4 seen the oppression upon *I*
13:5 Jehovah gave *I* a savior
13:5 sons of *I* continued to dwell
13:6 he caused *I* to sin. In it he
13:8 the days of the kings of *I*
13:10 king over *I* in Samaria
13:11 with which he made *I* sin
13:12 the days of the kings of *I*
13:13 Samaria with the kings of *I*
13:14 Jehoash the king of *I*
13:14 war chariot of *I* and his
13:16 to say to the king of *I*
13:18 he said to the king of *I*
13:22 oppressed *I* all the days of
13:25 to recover the cities of *I*
14:1 Jehoahaz the king of *I*
14:8 Jehu the king of *I*, saying
14:9 Jehoash the king of *I* sent
14:11 Jehoash the king of *I* came
14:12 to be defeated before *I*
14:13 Jehoash the king of *I*
14:15 the days of the kings of *I*
14:16 Samaria with the kings of *I*
14:17 Jehoahaz the king of *I* for
14:23 Jehoash the king of *I*
14:24 which he caused *I* to sin
14:25 restored the boundary of *I*
14:25 Jehovah the God of *I*
14:26 bitter affliction of *I*
14:26 was there a helper for *I*
14:27 *I* from under the heavens
14:28 and Hamath to Judah in *I*
14:28 the days of the kings of *I*
14:29 with the kings of *I*, and
15:1 Jeroboam the king of *I*
15:8 king over *I* in Samaria
15:9 he caused *I* to sin
15:11 the days of the kings of *I*
15:12 upon the throne of *I*
15:15 the days of the kings of *I*
15:17 king over *I* for ten years
15:18 he caused *I* to sin, all his
15:20 silver at the expense of *I*
15:21 the days of the kings of *I*
15:23 king over *I* in Samaria
15:24 he caused *I* to sin
15:26 the days of the kings of *I*
15:27 Pekah . . . king over *I*
15:28 he caused *I* to sin
15:29 days of Pekah the king of *I*
15:31 the days of the kings of *I*
15:32 Remaliah the king of *I*
16:3 the way of the kings of *I*
16:3 because of the sons of *I*
16:5 Remaliah the king of *I*
16:7 the palm of the king of *I*
17:1 king in Samaria over *I* for
17:2 not as the kings of *I* that
17:6 led *I* into exile in Assyria
17:7 sons of *I* had sinned against
17:8 from before the sons of *I*
17:8 statutes of the kings of *I*
17:9 sons of *I* went searching
17:13 Jehovah kept warning *I* and
17:18 got very incensed against *I*
17:19 in the statutes of *I*
17:20 rejected all the seed of *I*
17:21 ripped *I* off from the house
17:21 to part *I* from following
17:22 sons of *I* went walking in
17:23 Jehovah removed *I* from his
17:23 *I* went off its own soil
17:24 instead of the sons of *I*
17:34 whose name he made *I*
18:1 Elah the king of *I*
18:4 sons of *I* had continually
18:5 In Jehovah the God of *I* he
18:9 Elah the king of *I*
18:10 Hoshea the king of *I*
18:11 *I* into exile in Assyria and
19:15 O Jehovah the God of *I*

2Ki 19:20 Jehovah the God of *I* has
19:22 against the Holy One of *I*
21:2 from before the sons of *I*
21:3 just as Ahab the king of *I*
21:7 out of all the tribes of *I*
21:8 the foot of *I* wander from
21:9 from before the sons of *I*
21:12 Jehovah the God of *I* has
22:15 Jehovah the God of *I* has
22:18 Jehovah the God of *I* has
23:13 Solomon the king of *I* had
23:15 caused *I* to sin, had made
23:19 the kings of *I* had built
23:22 the judges that had judged *I*
23:22 the days of the kings of *I*
23:27 just as I have removed *I*
24:13 Solomon the king of *I* had
1Ch 1:34 sons of Isaac were . . . *I*
1:43 reigned over the sons of *I*
2:1 sons of *I*: Reuben, Simeon
2:7 bringer of ostracism upon *I*
4:10 call upon the God of *I*
5:1 Reuben the firstborn of *I*
5:1 Joseph the son of *I*
5:3 Reuben the firstborn of *I*
5:17 Jeroboam the king of *I*
5:26 the God of *I* stirred up the
6:38 the son of Levi, the son of *I*
6:49 and to make atonement for *I*
6:64 sons of *I* gave the Levites
7:29 of Joseph the son of *I* dwelt
9:1 in the Book of the Kings of *I*
10:1 made war upon *I*; and the
10:1 men of *I* went fleeing from
10:7 men of *I* that were in the
11:2 the one leading *I* out and
11:2 will shepherd my people *I*
11:2 leader over my people *I*
11:3 older men of *I* came to the
11:3 anointed David as king over *I*
11:4 David and all *I* went to
11:10 with all *I*, to make him
11:10 Jehovah's word concerning *I*
12:32 to know what *I* ought to do
12:38 make David king over all *I*
12:38 remainder of *I* were of one
12:40 there was rejoicing in *I*
13:2 to all the congregation of *I*
13:2 in all the lands of *I* and
13:5 David congregated all *I* from
13:6 David and all *I* proceeded to
13:8 And David and all *I* were
14:2 as king over *I*, for his
14:2 on account of his people *I*
14:8 anointed as king over all *I*
15:3 David congregated all *I* at
15:12 ark of Jehovah the God of *I*
15:14 ark of Jehovah the God of *I*
15:25 and the older men of *I* and
16:4 praise Jehovah the God of *I*
16:13 O offspring of *I* his servant
16:17 lasting covenant even to *I*
16:36 Jehovah the God of *I* from
16:40 he laid in command upon *I*
17:5 day that I brought *I* up until
17:6 that I walked about in all *I*
17:6 with one of the judges of *I*
17:7 a leader over my people *I*
17:9 a place for my people *I* and
17:10 command over my people *I*
17:21 is like your people *I*, whom
17:22 constitute your people *I* as
17:24, 24 God of *I*, is God to *I*
18:14 to reign over all *I*, and he
19:10 the choice men in *I* and
19:16 had been defeated before *I*
19:17 gathered all *I* together and
19:18 took to flight because of *I*
19:19 had been defeated before *I*
20:7 And he kept taunting *I*
21:1 to stand up against *I* and to
21:1 to incite David to number *I*
21:2 count *I* from Beer-sheba to
21:3 become a cause of guilt to *I*
21:4 and walked through all *I*
21:5 all *I* amounted to a million
21:7 and so he struck down *I*
21:12 in all the territory of *I*
21:14 gave a pestilence in *I*, so
21:14 out of *I* seventy thousand
22:1 for burnt offering for *I*
22:2 that were in the land of *I*
22:6 house to Jehovah the God of *I*
22:9 bestow upon *I* in his days

1Ch 22:10 his kingship firmly over *I*
22:12 commandment concerning *I*
22:13 commanded . . . respecting *I*
22:17 all the princes of *I* to
23:1 Solomon his son king over *I*
23:2 gather all the princes of *I*
23:25 Jehovah the God of *I* has
24:19 as Jehovah the God of *I* had
26:29 and as judges over *I*
26:30 the administration of *I* in
27:1 sons of *I* by their number
27:16 And over the tribes of *I*, of
27:22 princes of the tribes of *I*
27:23 make *I* as many as the stars
27:24 indignation against *I*, and
28:1 all the princes of *I*, the
28:4 God of *I* chose me out of all
28:4 over *I* to time indefinite
28:4 to make me king over all *I*
28:5 kingship of Jehovah over *I*
28:8 before the eyes of all *I*
29:6 princes of the tribes of *I*
29:10 the God of *I* our father
29:18 God of . . . *I* our forefathers
29:21 sacrifices . . . for all *I*
29:25 before the eyes of all *I*
29:25 any king before him over *I*
29:26 David . . . reigned over all *I*
29:27 reigned over *I* were forty
29:30 and over *I* and over all the
2Ch 1:2 to say the word to all *I*, to
1:2 to all the chieftains of all *I*
1:13 and continued to reign over *I*
2:4 this will be upon *I*
2:12 Blessed be . . . the God of *I*
2:17 who were in the land of *I*
5:2 the older men of *I* and all
5:2 houses of the sons of *I*
5:3 all the men of *I* congregated
5:4 all the older men of *I* came
5:10 with the sons of *I* while
6:3 all the congregation of *I*
6:3 of *I* were standing up
6:4 be Jehovah the God of *I*, who
6:5 out of all the tribes of *I* to
6:5 leader over my people *I*
6:6 come to be over my people *I*
6:7 name of Jehovah the God of *I*
6:10 and sit upon the throne of *I*
6:10 name of Jehovah the God of *I*
6:11 concluded with the sons of *I*
6:12 all the congregation of *I*
6:13 all the congregation of *I* and
6:14 O Jehovah the God of *I*, there
6:16 God of *I*, keep toward your
6:16 to sit upon the throne of *I*
6:17 God of *I*, let your promise
6:21 people *I* when they pray
6:24 *I* are defeated before an
6:25 the sin of your people *I* and
6:27 even of your people *I*
6:29 or of all your people *I*
6:32 no part of your people *I* and
6:33 the same as your people *I* do
7:3 sons of *I* were spectators
7:8 all *I* with him, a very great
7:10 and toward *I* his people
7:18 cut off from ruling over *I*
8:2 caused the sons of *I* to dwell
8:7 who were no part of *I*
8:8 *I* had not exterminated
8:9 none out of the sons of *I*
8:11 house of David the king of *I*
9:8 because your God loved *I*
9:30 over all *I* for forty years
10:3 Jeroboam and all *I* came and
10:16 all *I*, because the king did
10:16 to your gods, O *I*!
10:16 *I* began to go to its tents
10:17 *I* that were dwelling in the
10:18 *I* pelted him with stones
11:1 to fight against *I* so as to
11:3 all *I* in Judah and Benjamin
11:13 that were in all *I* took
11:16 *I* those that were giving
11:16 seek Jehovah the God of *I*
12:1 and also all *I* with him
12:6 princes of *I* and the king
12:13 out of all the tribes of *I*
13:4 O Jeroboam and all *I*
13:5 God of *I* himself gave a
13:5 kingdom . . . over *I* to time
13:12 *I*, do not fight against
13:15 *I* before Abijah and Judah

2Ch 13:16 *I* took to flight from
13:17 slain of *I* kept falling
13:18 *I* were humbled at that
15:3 *I* had been without a true
15:4 God of *I* and looked for him
15:9 deserted to him from *I* in
15:13 for Jehovah the God of *I*
15:17 did not disappear from *I*
16:1 Baasha the king of *I* came
16:3 Baasha the king of *I*, that
16:4 against the cities of *I*, so
16:11 the Kings of Judah and of *I*
17:1 his position strong over *I*
17:4 according to the doing of *I*
18:3 Ahab the king of *I* went on
18:4 said to the king of *I*
18:5 king of *I* collected the
18:7 king of *I* said to Jehoshaphat
18:8 king of *I* called a court
18:9 king of *I* and Jehoshaphat
18:17 king of *I* said to
18:19 fool Ahab the king of *I*
18:25 king of *I* said: Take
18:28 king of *I* and Jehoshaphat
18:29 king of *I* now said to
18:29 king of *I* disguised himself
18:30 with the king of *I* alone
18:31 It is the king of *I*
18:32 prove to be the king of *I*
18:33 strike the king of *I*
18:34 king of *I* himself had to be
19:8 of the paternal houses of *I*
20:7 from before your people *I*
20:10 not allow *I* to invade when
20:19 praise Jehovah the God of *I*
20:29 against the enemies of *I*
20:34 Book of the Kings of *I*
20:35 Ahaziah the king of *I*, who
21:2 Jehoshaphat the king of *I*
21:4 some of the princes of *I*
21:6 way of the kings of *I*, just
21:13 way of the kings of *I* and
22:5 Ahab the king of *I* to the
23:2 of the paternal houses of *I*
24:5 collect money from all *I* to
24:6 congregation of *I*, for the
24:9 upon *I* in the wilderness
24:16 he had done good in *I* and
25:6 hired from *I* a hundred
25:7 not let the army of *I* come
25:7 for Jehovah is not with *I*
25:9 given to the troops of *I*
25:17 son of Jehu the king of *I*
25:18 Jehoash the king of *I* sent
25:21 Jehoash the king of *I* went
25:22 to be defeated before *I*
25:23 Jehoash the king of *I* seized
25:25 king of *I* fifteen years
25:26 the Kings of Judah and *I*
27:7 Book of the Kings of *I* and
28:2 ways of the kings of *I*, and
28:3 from before the sons of *I*
28:5 hand of the king of *I* he
28:8 *I* took two hundred thousand
28:13 is burning anger against *I*
28:19 Ahaz the king of *I*, because
28:23 him and all *I* stumble
28:26 Kings of Judah and of *I*
28:27 places of the kings of *I*
29:7 holy place to the God of *I*
29:10 God of *I*, that his burning
29:24 make atonement for all *I*
29:24 for all *I* that the king
29:27 of David the king of *I*
30:1 send to all *I* and Judah, and
30:1 to Jehovah the God of *I*
30:5 call pass through all *I*
30:5 the God of *I* at Jerusalem
30:6 throughout all *I* and Judah
30:6 sons of *I*, return to Jehovah
30:6 God of Abraham, Isaac and *I*
30:21 *I* that were found in
30:25 that came from *I* and
30:25 came from the land of *I* and
30:26 David the king of *I* there
31:1 *I* returned to their cities
31:5 *I* increased the firstfruits
31:6 *I* and of Judah that were
31:8 Jehovah and his people *I*
32:17 God of *I* and to talk against
32:32 of the Kings of Judah and *I*
33:2 from before the sons of *I*
33:7 out of all the tribes of *I*
33:8 not remove the foot of *I*
2Ch 33:9 from before the sons of *I*
33:16 serve Jehovah the God of *I*
33:18 of Jehovah the God of *I*
33:18 affairs of the kings of *I*
34:7 down in all the land of *I*
34:9 from all the rest of *I* and
34:21 what is left in *I* and in
34:23 Jehovah the God of *I* has
34:26 Jehovah the God of *I* has
34:33 belonged to the sons of *I*
34:33 found in *I* take up service
35:3 the instructors of all *I*
35:3 the king of *I* built
35:3 your God and his people *I*
35:4 David the king of *I*
35:17 sons of *I* that were to be
35:18 a passover like it in *I*
35:18 any of the other kings of *I*
35:18 and all Judah and *I* that
35:25 set as a regulation over *I*
35:27 the Kings of *I* and Judah
36:8 Book of the Kings of *I* and
36:13 to Jehovah the God of *I*
Ezr 1:3 Jehovah the God of *I*
2:2 the men of the people of *I*
2:59 whether they were of *I*
2:70 and all *I* in their cities
3:1 the sons of *I* were in their
3:2 the altar of the God of *I*
3:10 David the king of *I*
3:11 loving-kindness toward *I* is
4:1 to Jehovah the God of *I*
4:3 the paternal houses of *I*
4:3 build to Jehovah the God of *I*
5:1 the name of the God of *I*
5:11 a great king of *I* built and
6:14 the order of the God of *I*
6:16 the sons of *I*, the priests
6:17 as a sin offering for all *I*
6:17 number of the tribes of *I*
6:21 sons of *I* that had returned
6:21 for Jehovah the God of *I*
6:22 the true God, the God of *I*
7:6 Jehovah the God of *I* had given
7:7 sons of *I* and of the priests
7:10 teach in *I* regulation and
7:11 his regulations toward *I*
7:13 my realm of the people of *I*
7:15 given to the God of *I*
7:28 out of *I* the head ones to
8:18 of Levi the son of *I*
8:29 princes of the fathers of *I*
8:35 sacrifices to the God of *I*
8:35 twelve bulls for all *I*
9:1 people of *I* and the priests
9:4 the words of the God of *I*
9:15 O Jehovah the God of *I*
10:1 *I* collected themselves
10:2 there exists a hope for *I*
10:5 and all *I* take an oath to do
10:10 add to the guiltiness of *I*
10:25 And of *I*, of the sons of
Ne 1:6 the sons of *I* your servants
1:6 the sins of the sons of *I*
2:10 good for the sons of *I*
7:7 the men of the people of *I*
7:61 whether they were of *I*
7:73 *I* took up dwelling in their
7:73 sons of *I* were then in their
8:1 which Jehovah had commanded *I*
8:14 sons of *I* should dwell in
8:17 the sons of *I* had not done
9:1 sons of *I* gathered themselves
9:2 the seed of *I* proceeded to
10:33 to make atonement for *I* and
10:39 sons of *I* and the sons of
11:3 in their cities, *I*, the
11:20 rest of *I*, of the priests
12:47 all *I* during the days of
13:2 not met the sons of *I* with
13:3 all the mixed company from *I*
13:18 the burning anger against *I*
13:26 Solomon the king of *I* sinned
13:26 him king over all *I*
Ps 14:7 there were the salvation of *I*
14:7 be joyful, let *I* rejoice
22:3 Inhabiting the praises of *I*
22:23 all you the seed of *I*
25:22 O God, redeem *I* out of all
41:13 Jehovah the God of *I*
50:7 O *I*, and I will bear witness
53:6 the grand salvation of *I*
53:6 be joyful, let *I* rejoice
59:5 O Jehovah . . . the God of *I*
Ps 68:8 because of God, the God of *I*
68:26 who are from the Source of *I*
68:34 Over *I* his eminence is and
68:35 The God of *I* he is, giving
69:6 because of me, O God of *I*
71:22 on the harp, O Holy One of *I*
73:1 God is indeed good to *I*, to
76:1 In *I* his name is great
78:5 And a law he set in *I*
78:21 anger . . . ascended against *I*
78:31 men of *I* he made collapse
78:41 even the Holy One of *I*
78:55 *I* to reside in their own
78:59 he contemned *I* very much
78:71 And over *I* his inheritance
80:1 Shepherd of *I*, do give ear
81:4 it is a regulation for *I*
81:8 O *I*, if you will listen to me
81:11 *I* itself has not showed any
81:13 *I* itself would walk in my
83:4 *I* may be remembered no more
89:18 belongs to the Holy One of *I*
98:3 faithfulness to the house of *I*
103:7 even to the sons of *I*
105:10 lasting covenant even to *I*
105:23 *I* proceeded to come into
106:48 Jehovah the God of *I*
114:1 *I* went forth from Egypt
114:2 *I* his grand dominion
115:9 O *I*, trust in Jehovah
115:12 will bless the house of *I*
118:2 Let *I* now say
121:4 He that is guarding *I*
122:4 As a reminder to *I* To give
124:1 Let *I* now say
125:5 There will be peace upon *I*
128:6 May there be peace upon *I*
129:1 Let *I* now say
130:7 *I* keep waiting for Jehovah
130:8 redeem *I* out of all his
131:3 Let *I* wait for Jehovah
135:4 *I* for his special property
135:12 inheritance to *I* his people
135:19 *I*, do you men bless Jehovah
136:11 One bringing *I* out of the
136:14 *I* to pass through the
136:22 inheritance to *I* his servant
147:2 dispersed ones of *I* he brings
147:19 judicial decisions to *I*
148:14 *I*, the people near to him
149:2 *I* rejoice in its grand
Pr 1:1 son of David, the king of *I*
Ec 1:12 be king over *I* in Jerusalem
Ca 3:7 from the mighty men of *I*
Isa 1:3 *I* itself has not known, my
1:4 Holy One of *I* with disrespect
1:24 the Powerful One of *I*, is
4:2 those of *I* who have escaped
5:7 is the house of *I*, and the
5:19 counsel of the Holy One of *I*
5:24 Holy One of *I* they have
7:1 king of *I*, came up to
8:14 to both the houses of *I*, as a
8:18 miracles in *I* from Jehovah
9:8 and it fell upon *I*
9:12 eat up *I* with open mouth
9:14 Jehovah will cut off from *I*
10:20 those remaining over of *I*
10:20 Holy One of *I*, in trueness
10:22 *I*, would prove to be like
11:12 the dispersed ones of *I*
11:16 one for *I* in the day of
12:6 is the Holy One of *I*
14:1 yet certain to choose *I*
14:2 *I* must take them to
17:3 the glory of the sons of *I*
17:6 of Jehovah the God of *I*
17:7 gaze at the Holy One of *I*
17:9 on account of the sons of *I*
19:24 *I* will come to be the third
19:25 and my inheritance, *I*
21:10 God of *I*, I have reported
21:17 God of *I*, has spoken it
24:15 of Jehovah, the God of *I*
27:6 *I* will put forth blossoms
27:12 O sons of *I*
29:19 joyful in the Holy One of *I*
29:23 God of *I* they will regard
30:11 Holy One of *I* to cease
30:12 Holy One of *I* has said
30:15 Holy One of *I*, has said
30:29 Jehovah, to the Rock of *I*
31:1 looked to the Holy One of *I*
31:6 *I* have gone deep in their

Isa 37:16 God of *I*, sitting upon the
37:21 the God of *I* has said
37:23 against the Holy One of *I*
40:27 and do you speak out, O *I*
41:8 you, O *I*, are my servant
41:14 men of *I*. I myself will
41:14 the Holy One of *I*
41:16 In the Holy One of *I* you
41:17 God of *I*, shall not leave
41:20 and the Holy One of *I* has
42:24 and *I* to the plunderers
43:1 and your Former, O *I*
43:3 the Holy One of *I* your Savior
43:14 the Holy One of *I*
43:15 the Creator of *I*, your King
43:22 grown weary of me, O *I*
43:28 *I* over to words of abuse
44:1 you, O *I*, whom I have chosen
44:5 by the name of *I* one will
44:6 King of *I* and the Repurchaser
44:21 O *I*, because you are my
44:21 *I*, you will not be
44:23 on *I* he shows his beauty
45:3 your name, the God of *I*
45:4 and of *I* my chosen one
45:11 the Holy One of *I* and the
45:15 the God of *I*, a Savior
45:17 As for *I*, he will certainly
45:25 seed of *I* will prove to be
46:3 ones of the house of *I*
46:13 to *I* my beauty
47:4 the Holy One of *I*
48:1 by the name of *I* and who
48:1 mention even of the God of *I*
48:2 upon the God of *I* they have
48:12 and you *I* my called one
48:17 the Holy One of *I*
49:3 You are my servant, O *I*
49:5 *I* itself may be gathered
49:6 the safeguarded ones of *I*
49:7 Jehovah, the Repurchaser of *I*
49:7 Holy One of *I*, who chooses
52:12 the God of *I* will be your
54:5 the Holy One of *I* is your
55:5 and for the Holy One of *I*
56:8 the dispersed ones of *I*
60:9 and to the Holy One of *I*
60:14 Zion of the Holy One of *I*
63:7 goodness to the house of *I*
63:16 and *I* himself may not
66:20 sons of *I* bring the gift in
Jer 2:3 *I* was something holy to
2:4 families of the house of *I*
2:14 Is *I* a servant, or a slave
2:26 house of *I* have felt shame
2:31 a mere wilderness to *I* or
3:6 what unfaithful *I* has done
3:8 *I* had committed adultery
3:11 Unfaithful *I* has proved her
3:12 Do return, O renegade *I*, is
3:18 alongside the house of *I*
3:20 O house of *I*, have dealt
3:21 entreaties of the sons of *I*
3:23 God is the salvation of *I*
4:1 If you would return, O *I*
5:11 the house of *I* and the house
5:15 from far away, O house of *I*
6:9 remnant of *I* just like a vine
7:3 the God of *I*, has said
7:12 the badness of my people *I*
7:21 the God of *I*, has said
9:15 the God of *I*, has said
9:26 *I* are uncircumcised in heart
10:1 you people, O house of *I*
10:16 *I* is the staff of his
11:3 Jehovah the God of *I* has said
11:10 The house of *I* and the house
11:17 badness of the house of *I*
12:14 I caused my people, even *I*
13:11 caused the whole house of *I*
13:12 the God of *I* has said
14:8 O you the hope of *I*, the
16:9 the God of *I*, has said
16:14 *I* up out of the land of
16:15 *I* up out of the land of the
17:13 Jehovah, the hope of *I*, all
18:6 to you people, O house of *I*
18:6 in my hand, O house of *I*
18:13 *I* has done to an excess
19:3 the God of *I*, has said
19:15 the God of *I*, has said
21:4 Jehovah the God of *I* has said
23:2 the God of *I* has said against
23:6 *I* itself will reside in
Jer 23:7 *I* up out of the land of Egypt
23:8 offspring of the house of *I*
23:13 my people, even *I*, wander
24:5 Jehovah the God of *I* has said
25:15 the God of *I* said to me
25:27 the God of *I*, has said
27:4 the God of *I*, has said
27:21 the God of *I*, has said
28:2 God of *I*, has said, I will
28:14 the God of *I*, has said
29:4 the God of *I*, has said
29:8 the God of *I*, has said
29:21 the God of *I*, has said
29:23 senselessness in *I*
29:25 the God of *I*, has said
30:2 the God of *I* has said
30:3 my people, *I* and Judah
30:4 Jehovah has spoken to *I* and
30:10 struck with terror, O *I*
31:1 God to all the families of *I*
31:2 *I* was walking to get his
31:4 be rebuilt, O virgin of *I*
31:7 people, the remnant of *I*
31:9 I have become to *I* a Father
31:10 One scattering *I* will
31:21 Come back, O virgin of *I*
31:23 the God of *I*, has said
31:27 sow the house of *I* and the
31:31 with the house of *I* and
31:33 with the house of *I* after
31:36 *I* could likewise cease from
31:37 entire seed of *I* on account
32:14 the God of *I*, has said
32:15 the God of *I*, has said
32:20 and in *I* and among men
32:21 *I* out of the land of Egypt
32:30 *I* and the sons of Judah have
32:30 *I* are even offending me by
32:32 badness of the sons of *I*
32:36 God of *I* has said concerning
33:4 the God of *I* has said
33:7 and the captives of *I*, and
33:14 concerning the house of *I*
33:17 throne of the house of *I*
34:2 Jehovah the God of *I* has said
34:13 the God of *I* has said
35:13 God of *I*, has said, Go, and
35:17 the God of *I*, has said
35:18 the God of *I*, has said
35:19 the God of *I*, has said
36:2 spoken to you against *I* and
37:7 God of *I* has said, This
38:17 the God of *I*, has said
39:16 the God of *I*, has said
41:9 Baasha the king of *I*
42:9 Jehovah the God of *I*, to
42:15 the God of *I*, has said
42:18 the God of *I*, has said
43:10 the God of *I*, has said
44:2 God of *I*, has said, You
44:7 God of *I*, has said, Why
44:11 the God of *I*, has said
44:25 the God of *I*, has said
45:2 Jehovah the God of *I* has
46:25 the God of *I*, has said
46:27 not be terror-stricken, O *I*
48:1 God of *I*, has said: Woe to
48:13 *I* have become ashamed of
48:27 *I* become a mere object of
49:1 there no sons that *I* has
49:2 *I* will actually take
50:4 the sons of *I*, they and the
50:17 *I* is a scattered sheep
50:18 the God of *I*, has said
50:19 I will bring *I* back to
50:20 error of *I* will be searched
50:29 against the Holy One of *I*
50:33 *I* and the sons of Judah are
51:5 *I* and Judah are not widowed
51:5 of the Holy One of *I*
51:33 the God of *I*, has said
51:49 slain ones of *I* to fall
La 2:1 heaven to earth the beauty of *I*
2:3 has cut down every horn of *I*
2:5 Jehovah . . . swallowed down *I*
Eze 2:3 sending you to the sons of *I*
3:1 go, speak to the house of *I*
3:4 enter in among the house of *I*
3:5 being sent—to the house of *I*
3:7 house of *I*, they will not
3:7 house of *I* are hardheaded and
3:17 made you to the house of *I*
4:3 It is a sign to the house of *I*
4:4 error of the house of *I* upon
Eze 4:5 the error of the house of *I*
4:13 *I* will eat their bread
5:4 go forth to all the house of *I*
6:2 toward the mountains of *I*
6:3 O mountains of *I*, hear the
6:5 the carcasses of the sons of *I*
6:11 of the house of *I*, because by
7:2 said to the soil of *I*, An end
8:4 the glory of the God of *I* was
8:6 that the house of *I* are doing
8:10 dungy idols of the house of *I*
8:11 ones of the house of *I*, with
8:12 house of *I* are doing in the
9:3 the glory of the God of *I*, it
9:8 all the remaining ones of *I*
9:9 error of the house of *I* and
10:19 glory of the God of *I* was
10:20 had seen under the God of *I*
11:5 the right thing, O house of *I*
11:10 On the border of *I* I shall
11:11 On the border of *I* I shall
11:13 the remaining ones of *I*
11:15 all the house of *I*, all of
11:17 will give you the soil of *I*
11:22 glory of the God of *I* was
12:6 portent . . . to the house of *I*
12:9 house of *I*, the rebellious
12:10 all the house of *I* who are
12:19 upon the soil of *I*
12:22 on the soil of *I*, saying
12:23 say it as a proverb in *I*
12:24 the midst of the house of *I*
12:27 the house of *I* are saying
13:2 concerning the prophets of *I*
13:4 prophets have become, O *I*
13:5 in behalf of the house of *I*
13:9 register of the house of *I*
13:9 soil of *I* they will not come
13:16 the prophets of *I* that are
14:1 from the elderly ones of *I*
14:4 of the house of *I* that brings
14:5 catching the house of *I* by
14:6 say to the house of *I*, This
14:7 from the house of *I* or from
14:7 that reside as aliens in *I*
14:9 the midst of my people *I*
14:11 house of *I* may no more go
17:2 saying toward the house of *I*
17:23 mountain of the height of *I*
18:2 on the soil of *I*, saying
18:3 this proverbial saying in *I*
18:6 dungy idols of the house of *I*
18:15 idols of the house of *I*
18:25 Hear, please, O house of *I*
18:29 *I* will certainly say: The
18:29 adjusted right, O house of *I*
18:30 judge you, O house of *I*
18:31 should you die, O house of *I*
19:1 the chieftains of *I*
19:9 heard on the mountains of *I*
20:1 the elderly ones of *I* came
20:3 with the elderly men of *I*
20:5 In the day of my choosing *I*
20:13 *I*, rebelled against me in
20:27 speak to the house of *I*, O
20:30 say to the house of *I*
20:31 you people, O house of *I*
20:38 onto the soil of *I* they
20:39 And you, O house of *I*
20:40 mountain of the height of *I*
20:40 house of *I* in its entirety
20:42 onto the soil of *I*, into
20:44 dealings, O house of *I*
21:2 against the soil of *I*
21:3 must say to the soil of *I*
21:12 all the chieftains of *I*
21:25 wicked chieftain of *I*
22:6 chieftains of *I* have proved
22:18 the house of *I* have become
24:21 Say to the house of *I*
25:3 against the soil of *I*
25:6 soul against the soil of *I*
25:14 by the hand of my people *I*
27:17 Judah and the land of *I*
28:24 to be to the house of *I* a
28:25 together the house of *I* out
29:6 a reed to the house of *I*
29:21 sprout for the house of *I*
33:7 to the house of *I*, and at
33:10 say to the house of *I*
33:11 should die, O house of *I*
33:20 judge you, O house of *I*
33:24 concerning the soil of *I*
33:28 *I* must be laid desolate

Eze 34:2 against the shepherds of *I*
34:2 Woe to the shepherds of *I*
34:13 on the mountains of *I*
34:14 upon the mountains of *I*
34:30 my people, the house of *I*
35:5 delivering the sons of *I*
35:12 the mountains of *I*, saying
35:15 house of *I* because it was
36:1 the mountains of *I*, and you
36:1 O mountains of *I*, hear the
36:4 mountains of *I*, hear the
36:6 concerning the soil of *I*
36:8 mountains of *I*, will give
36:8 fruitage for my people *I*
36:10 the whole house of *I*
36:12 even my people *I*, and
36:17 house of *I* were dwelling
36:21 house of *I* have profaned
36:22 say to the house of *I*
36:22 doing it, O house of *I*
36:32 your ways, O house of *I*
36:37 by the house of *I* to do
37:11 are the whole house of *I*
37:12 in upon the soil of *I*
37:16 the sons of *I* his partners
37:16 the house of *I* his partners
37:19 tribes of *I* his partners
37:21 taking the sons of *I* from
37:22 on the mountains of *I*, and
37:28 Jehovah, am sanctifying *I*
38:8 onto the mountains of *I*
38:14 my people *I* are dwelling in
38:16 against my people *I*, like
38:17 servants the prophets of *I*
38:18 comes in upon the soil of *I*
38:19 will occur in the soil of *I*
39:2 upon the mountains of *I*
39:4 On the mountains of *I* you
39:7 in the midst of my people *I*
39:7 Jehovah, the Holy One in *I*
39:9 the cities of *I* will
39:11 a burial place in *I*, the
39:12 house of *I* will have to
39:17 on the mountains of *I*
39:22 the house of *I* will have
39:23 the house of *I*, went into
39:25 upon all the house of *I*
39:29 spirit upon the house of *I*
40:2 brought me to the land of *I*
40:4 Tell . . . to the house of *I*
43:2 glory of the God of *I* was
43:7 midst of the sons of *I* to
43:7 *I*, defile my holy name, they
43:10 inform the house of *I* about
44:2 God of *I*, has come in by it
44:6 to the house of *I*, This is
44:6 O house of *I*
44:9 the midst of the sons of *I*
44:10 *I*, who wandered away from
44:12 the house of *I* a stumbling
44:15 sons of *I* wandered away
44:22 offspring of the house of *I*
44:28 you people give them in *I*
44:29 every devoted thing in *I*
45:6 To all the house of *I* it
45:8 his as a possession in *I*
45:8 give to the house of *I*
45:9 of you, O chieftains of *I*
45:15 from the livestock of *I*
45:16 to the chieftain in *I*
45:17 seasons of the house of *I*
45:17 behalf of the house of *I*
47:13 for the twelve tribes of *I*
47:18 Gilead and the land of *I*
47:21 to the twelve tribes of *I*
47:22 native among the sons of *I*
47:22 midst of the tribes of *I*
48:11 sons of *I* wandered away
48:19 tribes of *I* will cultivate
48:29 to the tribes of *I*
48:31 names of the tribes of *I*
Da 1:3 bring some of the sons of *I*
9:7 *I*, those nearby and those far
9:11 *I* have overstepped your law
9:20 the sin of my people *I* and
Ho 1:1 of Jeroboam . . . king of *I*
1:4 royal rule of the house of *I*
1:5 break the bow of *I* in the low
1:6 mercy again to the house of *I*
1:10 number of the sons of *I* must
1:11 *I* will certainly be collected
3:1 love for the sons of *I* while
3:4 *I* will dwell without a king
3:5 the sons of *I* will come back
Ho 4:1 Hear the word of Jehovah . . . *I*
4:15 O *I*, let not Judah become
4:16 *I* has become stubborn
5:1 pay attention, O house of *I*
5:3 *I* itself has not been hidden
5:3 *I* has defiled itself
5:5 the pride of *I* has testified
5:5 *I* and Ephraim themselves are
5:9 Among the tribes of *I* I have
6:10 In the house of *I* I have seen
6:10 *I* has defiled itself
7:1 I would bring healing to *I*
7:10 the pride of *I* has testified
8:2 my God, we, *I*, have known you
8:3 *I* has cast off good
8:6 from *I* was even this
8:8 *I* must be swallowed down
8:14 *I* began forgetting his Maker
9:1 Do not rejoice, O *I*. Do not
9:7 Those of *I* will know it
9:10 in the wilderness I found *I*
10:1 *I* is a degenerating vine
10:6 *I* will be ashamed of its
10:8 of Beth-aven, the sin of *I*
10:9 you have sinned, O *I*
10:15 the king of *I* will positively
11:1 When *I* was a boy, then I
11:8 How can I deliver you up, O *I?*
11:12 deception the house of *I*
12:12 *I* kept serving for a wife
12:13 brought up *I* out of Egypt
13:1 himself carried weight in *I*
13:9 bring you to ruin, O *I*
14:1 come back, O *I*, to Jehovah
14:5 become like the dew to *I*
Joe 2:27 that I am in the midst of *I*
3:2 people and my inheritance *I*
3:16 a fortress for the sons of *I*
Am 1:1 which he visioned concerning *I*
1:1 Jeroboam . . . the king of *I*
2:6 account of three revolts of *I*
2:11 really not be, O sons of *I*
3:1 concerning you, O sons of *I*
3:12 *I* will be snatched away
3:14 the revolts of *I* against him
4:5 have loved, O sons of *I*
4:12 what I shall do to you, O *I*
4:12 to meet your God, O *I*
5:1 as a dirge, O house of *I*
5:2 The virgin, *I*, has fallen
5:3 ten left, for the house of *I*
5:4 has said to the house of *I*
5:25 forty years, O house of *I*
6:1 the house of *I* have come
6:14 against you, O house of *I*
7:8 in the midst of my people *I*
7:9 *I* will be devastated; and I
7:10 to Jeroboam the king of *I*
7:10 right inside the house of *I*
7:11 *I*, it will without fail go
7:15 Go, prophesy to my people *I*
7:16 must not prophesy against *I*
7:17 *I*, it will without fail go
8:2 end has come to my people *I*
9:7 Cushites to me, O sons of *I*
9:7 *I* itself up out of the land
9:9 I will jiggle the house of *I*
9:14 captive ones of my people *I*
Ob 20 to the sons of *I* will belong
Mic 1:5 the sins of the house of *I*
1:13 the revolts of *I* have been
1:14 deceitful to the kings of *I*
1:15 the glory of *I* will come
2:12 the remaining ones of *I*
3:1 commanders of the house of *I*
3:8 to tell . . . to *I* his sin
3:9 commanders of the house of *I*
5:1 strike . . . the judge of *I*
5:2 who is to become ruler in *I*
5:3 will return to the sons of *I*
6:2 with *I* that he will argue
Na 2:2 like the pride of *I*, because
Zep 2:9 of armies, the God of *I*
3:13 the remaining ones of *I*
3:14 Break out in cheers, O *I!*
3:15 The king of *I*, Jehovah, is
Zec 1:19 horns that dispersed . . . *I*
8:13 of Judah and house of *I*
9:1 and on all the tribes of *I*
11:14 between Judah and *I*
12:1 word of Jehovah concerning *I*
Mal 1:1 concerning *I* by means of
1:5 over the territory of *I*
2:11 been committed in *I* and
Mal 2:16 the God of *I* has said
4:4 concerning all *I*, even
Mt 2:6 will shepherd my people, *I*
2:20 your way into the land of *I*
2:21 entered into the land of *I*
8:10 With no one in *I* have I
9:33 anything like this seen in *I*
10:6 lost sheep of the house of *I*
10:23 circuit of the cities of *I*
15:24 lost sheep of the house of *I*
15:31 they glorified the God of *I*
19:28 the twelve tribes of *I*
27:9 whom some of the sons of *I*
27:42 He is King of *I*; let him
Mr 12:29 Hear, O *I*, Jehovah our God
15:32 the King of *I* now come down
Lu 1:16 many of the sons of *I* will
1:54 He has come to the aid of *I*
1:68 Jehovah the God of *I*, because
1:80 showing himself openly to *I*
2:32 a glory of your people *I*
2:34 the rising again of many in *I*
4:25 There were many widows in *I*
4:27 there were many lepers in *I*
7:9 Not even in *I* have I found so
22:30 judge the twelve tribes of *I*
24:21 the one destined to deliver *I*
Joh 1:31 might be made manifest to *I*
1:49 Son of God, you are King of *I*
3:10 Are you a teacher of *I* and
12:13 even the king of *I*
Ac 1:6 restoring the kingdom to *I* at
2:22 Men of *I*, hear these words
2:36 *I* know for a certainty that
3:12 *I*, why are you wondering over
4:10 and to all the people of *I*
4:27 and with peoples of *I* were
5:21 older men of the sons of *I*
5:31 give repentance to *I* and
5:35 Men of *I*, pay attention to
7:23 his brothers, the sons of *I*
7:37 that said to the sons of *I*
7:42 was it, O house of *I?*
9:15 to kings and the sons of *I*
10:36 *I* to declare to them the
13:17 God of this people *I* chose
13:23 God has brought to *I* a savior
13:24 to all the people of *I*
21:28 crying out: Men of *I*, help!
28:20 because of the hope of *I*
Ro 9:6 not all who spring from *I* are
9:6 are really *I*
9:27 Isaiah cries out concerning *I*
9:27 number of the sons of *I* may
9:31 *I*, although pursuing a law
10:19 *I* did not fail to know, did
10:21 as respects *I* he says: All
11:2 he pleads with God against *I*
11:7 thing *I* is earnestly seeking
11:25 to *I* until the full number
11:26 manner all *I* will be saved
1Co 10:18 which is *I* in a fleshly way
2Co 3:7 the sons of *I* could not gaze
3:13 the sons of *I* might not gaze
Ga 6:16 even upon the *I* of God
Eph 2:12 alienated from . . . *I*
Php 3:5 out of the family stock of *I*
Heb 8:8 conclude with the house of *I*
8:10 covenant with the house of *I*
11:22 exodus of the sons of *I*
Re 2:14 *I*, to eat things sacrificed
7:4 of every tribe of the sons of *I*
21:12 tribes of the sons of *I*

Israelite
Le 24:10 son of an *I* woman, who
24:10 *I* man began to struggle with
24:11 son of the *I* woman began to
Nu 25:14 name of the fatally struck *I*
2Sa 17:25 whose name was Ithra the *I*
Joh 1:47 See, an *I* for a certainty
Ro 11:1 *I*, of the seed of Abraham

Israelites
Ex 17:11 *I* proved superior; but as
Nu 16:34 *I* who were round about them
1Sa 2:14 to all the *I* coming there
4:5 *I* broke out into loud shouting
13:20 the *I* would go down to the
17:3 the *I* were standing on the
29:1 *I* were camping by the spring
2Sa 4:1 *I* themselves were disturbed
15:6 *I* that would come in for
1Ki 12:19 *I* kept up their revolt
22:17 see all the *I* scattered on

2Ki 3:24 the *I* immediately rose up
1Ch 9:1 for all *I*, they were enrolled
9:2 *I*, the priests, the Levites
11:1 the *I* collected themselves
15:28 *I* were bringing up the ark
16:3 he apportioned to all the *I*
29:23 the *I* were obedient to him
2Ch 5:6 all the assembly of *I* that
7:6 while all the *I* were standing
10:1 *I* came to make him king
10:19 *I* kept up their revolt
18:16 see all the *I* scattered
31:1 *I* that were found there went
Ezr 8:25 *I* who were to be found had
Ac 13:16 *I* and you others that fear
Ro 9:4 *I*, to whom belong the adoption
2Co 11:22 Are they *I*? I am one also

Israelitess
Le 24:10 son of the *I* and an Israelite

Israel's
Ge 42:5 *I* sons came along with the
46:8 the names of *I* sons who came
48:13 by his right hand to *I* left
48:13 Manasseh . . . to *I* right, and
Ex 1:1 *I* sons who came into Egypt
6:14 sons of Reuben, *I* firstborn
9:7 look! not so much as one of *I*
Nu 1:20 sons of Reuben, *I* firstborn
21:3 Jehovah listened to *I* voice
26:5 Reuben, *I* firstborn; Reuben's
Jos 10:30 and its king into *I* hand
10:32 gave Lachish into *I* hand
11:8 gave them into *I* hand
Jg 3:30 subdued . . . under *I* hand
5:3 make melody to Jehovah, *I* God
5:5 the face of Jehovah, *I* God
11:20 about *I* crossing through his
11:21 all his people into *I* hand
20:6 every field of *I* inheritance
Ps 72:18 be Jehovah God, *I* God
Isa 10:17 *I* Light must become a fire
Jer 49:1 dwelling in *I* very cities
Eze 29:16 the house of *I* confidence
34:14 on *I* high mountains their
Lu 2:25 waiting for *I* consolation

Issachar
Ge 30:18 So she called his name *I*
35:23 sons by Leah were . . . *I*
46:13 And the sons of *I* were Tola
49:14 *I* is a strong-boned ass
Ex 1:3 *I*, Zebulun and Benjamin
Nu 1:8 of *I*, Nethanel the son of Zuar
1:28 sons of *I*, their births
1:29 registered . . . tribe of *I*
2:5 tribe of *I*, and the chieftain
2:5 chieftain for the sons of *I*
7:18 the chieftain of *I*, made a
10:15 the tribe of the sons of *I*
13:7 of *I*, Igal the son of Joseph
26:23 sons of *I* by their families
26:25 These were the families of *I*
34:26 of *I* a chieftain, Paltiel the
De 27:12 *I* and Joseph and Benjamin
33:18 And, *I*, in your tents
Jos 17:10 and on the east, to *I*
17:11 belong to Manasseh in *I* and
19:17 for *I* that the fourth lot
19:17 sons of *I* by their families
19:23 tribe of the sons of *I*
21:6 families of the tribe of *I*
21:28 And out of the tribe of *I*
Jg 5:15 the princes in *I* were with
5:15 And as *I*, so was Barak
10:1 Dodo, a man of *I*, and he was
1Ki 4:17 the son of Paruah, in *I*
15:27 Ahijah of the house of *I*
1Ch 2:1 sons of Israel . . . *I*
6:62 gave from the tribe of *I* and
6:72 from the tribe of *I*, Kedesh
7:1 sons of *I* were Tola and Puah
7:5 of *I* were valiant, mighty
12:32 of the sons of *I* having a
12:40 as far as *I* and Zebulun and
26:5 *I* the seventh, Peullethai the
27:18 of *I*, Omri the son of
2Ch 30:18 *I* and Zebulun, that had not
Eze 48:25 western border, *I* one
48:26 boundary of *I*, from the
48:33 the gate of *I*, one
Re 7:7 out of . . . *I* twelve thousand

Isshiah
1Ch 7:3 sons of Izrahiah were . . . *I*
12:6 Elkanah and *I* and Azarel and
23:20 of Uzziel . . . *I* the second
24:21 of Rehabiah, *I* the head
24:25 The brother of Micah was *I*
24:25 of the sons of *I*, Zechariah

Isshijah
Ezr 10:31 the sons of Harim . . . *I*

Issue
Ex 6:13 *i* the command by them to the
Jg 12:1 you did not *i* a call to go
Isa 10:6 I shall *i* a command to him
Mr 7:15 things that *i* forth out of a
7:21 injurious reasonings *i* forth
7:23 wicked things *i* forth from

Issued
Ge 12:20 Pharaoh *i* commands to men
24:50 Jehovah this thing has *i*
46:26 *i* out of his upper thigh
Ex 1:5 *i* out of Jacob's upper thigh
Jg 8:30 sons that *i* out of his upper
2Ch 24:9 *i* a call throughout Judah
Isa 13:3 *i* the command to my
Heb 7:5 *i* from the loins of Abraham
Re 9:17 smoke and sulphur *i* forth
9:18 the sulphur which *i* forth
16:17 voice *i* out of the sanctuary
19:5 voice *i* forth from the throne

Issues
Mr 7:20 That which *i* forth out of a
2Co 3:5 qualified *i* from God
Php 3:9 righteousness that *i* from God
Re 11:5 fire *i* forth from their

Issuing
Ge 2:10 Now there was a river *i* out
De 8:7 watery deeps *i* forth in the
Hab 3:4 two rays *i* out of his hand
2Co 2:16 odor *i* from death to death
2:16 an odor *i* from life to life
3:5 to reckon anything as *i* from

Italian
Ac 10:1 army officer of the *I* band

Italy
Ac 18:2 who had recently come from *I*
27:1 for us to sail away to *I*
27:6 that was sailing for *I*, and
Heb 13:24 Those in *I* send you their

Ithai
1Ch 11:31 *I* the son of Ribai of Gibeah

Ithamar
Ex 6:23 Later she bore him . . . *I*
28:1 and *I*, the sons of Aaron
38:21 *I* the son of Aaron the priest
Le 10:6 Eleazar and *I* his other sons
10:12 Eleazar and *I*, his sons that
10:16 Eleazar and *I*, Aaron's sons
Nu 3:2 Aaron's sons . . . Eleazar and *I*
3:4 Eleazar and *I* continued to act
4:28 hand of *I* the son of Aaron the
4:33 *I* the son of Aaron the priest
7:8 *I* the son of Aaron the priest
26:60 were born to Aaron . . . *I*
1Ch 6:3 sons of Aaron were . . . *I*
24:1 The sons of Aaron . . . *I*
24:2 *I* continued to act as priests
24:3 Ahimelech from the sons of *I*
24:4 than the sons of *I*. So they
24:4 sons of *I*, as heads for their
24:5 and from the sons of *I*
24:6 one paternal house . . . for *I*
Ezr 8:2 of the sons of *I*, Daniel

Ithiel
Ne 11:7 *I* the son of Jeshaiah
Pr 30:1, 1 man to *I*, to *I* and Ucal

Ithlah
Jos 19:42 and Aijalon and *I*

Ithmah
1Ch 11:46 and *I* the Moabite

Ithnan
Jos 15:23 and Kedesh and Hazor and *I*

Ithra
2Sa 17:25 a man whose name was *I*

Ithran
Ge 36:26 sons of Dishon . . . *I* and
1Ch 1:41 sons of Dishon were . . . *I*
7:37 and Shilshah and *I* and Beera

Ithream
2Sa 3:5 *I* by Eglah, David's wife
1Ch 3:3 *I*, of Eglah his wife

Ithrite
2Sa 23:38 Ira the *I*, Gareb the
23:38 Gareb the *I*
1Ch 11:40, 40 Ira the *I*, Gareb the *I*

Ithrites
1Ch 2:53 *I* and the Puthites and

Ittai
2Sa 15:19 king said to *I* the Gittite
15:21 *I* answered the king and
15:22 David said to *I*: Go and
15:22 *I* the Gittite crossed over
18:2 under the hand of *I* the
18:5 to command . . . *I*, saying
18:12 you and Abishai and *I*
23:29 *I* the son of Ribai of Gibeah

Ituraea
Lu 3:1 ruler of the country of *I* and

Ivory
1Ki 10:18 king made a great *i* throne
10:22 carrying . . . *i*, and apes
22:39 house of *i* that he built
2Ch 9:17 king made a great *i* throne
9:21 carrying gold and silver, *i*
Ps 45:8 Out from the grand *i* palace
Ca 5:14 His abdomen is an *i* plate
7:4 Your neck is like an *i* tower
Eze 27:6 Your prow they made with *i*
27:15 horns of *i* and ebony they
Am 3:15 houses of *i* will . . . perish
6:4 are lying down on couches of *i*
Re 18:12 every sort of *i* object and

Ivvah
2Ki 18:34 Sepharvaim, Hena and *I*
19:13 Sepharvaim, Hena and *I*
Isa 37:13 of Hena and of *I*

Iye-abarim
Nu 21:11 and encamped in *I*, in the
33:44 in *I* on the border of Moab

Iyim
Nu 33:45 pulled away from *I* and went

Izhar
Ex 6:18 sons of Kohath . . . *I* and
6:21 sons of *I* were Korah and
Nu 3:19 sons of Kohath . . . and *I*
16:1 son of *I*, the son of Kohath
1Ch 4:7 the sons of Helah were . . . *I*
6:2 sons of Kohath were Amram, *I*
6:18 sons of Kohath were . . . *I*
6:38 son of *I*, the son of Kohath
23:12 of Kohath were Amram, *I*
23:18 sons of *I* were Shelomith

Izharites
Nu 3:27 and the family of the *I*
1Ch 24:22 of the *I*, Shelomoth; of the
26:23 for the *I*, for the
26:29 Of the *I*, Chenaniah and his

Izliah
1Ch 8:18 and *I* . . . the sons of Elpaal

Izrahiah
1Ch 7:3 And the sons of Uzzi were *I*
7:3 sons of *I* were Michael and
Ne 12:42 *I* the overseer kept making

Izrahite
1Ch 27:8 was Shamhuth the *I*, and in

Izri
1Ch 25:11 the fourth for *I*, his sons

Izziah
Ezr 10:25 sons of Parosh . . . and *I*

Jaakobah
1Ch 4:36 and *J* and Jeshohaiah and

Jaala
Ne 7:58 the sons of *J*, the sons of

Jaalah
Ezr 2:56 the sons of *J*

Jaare-oregim
2Sa 21:19 Elhanan the son of *J* the

Jaareshiah
1Ch 8:27 and *J* . . . sons of Jeroham

Jaasiel
1Ch 11:47 Obed and *J* the Mezobaite
27:21 of Benjamin, *J* the son of

Jaasu
Ezr 10:37 Mattaniah, Mattenai and *J*

Jaazaniah
2Ki 25:23 *J* the son of the Maacathite
Jer 35:3 *J* the son of Jeremiah the
Eze 8:11 *J* the son of Shaphan standing
11:1 *J* the son of Azzur and

Jaaziah
1Ch 24:26 the sons of *J*, Beno
24:27 Of *J*, Beno and Shoham and

Jaaziel
1Ch 15:18 Zechariah, Ben and *J* and

Jabal
Ge 4:20 In time Adah gave birth to *J*

Jabbed
Joh 19:34 soldiers *j* his side with a

Jabbok
Ge 32:22 crossed over the ford of *J*
Nu 21:24 from the Arnon to the *J*
De 2:37 the torrent valley of *J*, nor
3:16 and as far as *J*, the torrent
Jos 12:2 *J* the torrent valley
Jg 11:13 as far as the *J* and as far as
11:22 as far as the *J* and from the

Jabesh
1Sa 11:1 and camp against *J* in Gilead
11:1 the men of *J* said to Nahash
11:3 older men of *J* said to him
11:5 the words of the men of *J*
11:9 to the men of *J* in Gilead
11:9 came and told the men of *J*
11:10 men of *J* said: Tomorrow we
31:12 came to *J* and burned them
31:13 tamarisk tree in *J*, and
2Ki 15:10 Shallum the son of *J*
15:13 Shallum the son of *J*
15:14 Shallum the son of *J*
1Ch 10:11 all those of *J* in Gilead got
10:12 to *J* and buried their bones
10:12 under the big tree in *J*

Jabesh-gilead
Jg 21:8 from *J* to the congregation
21:9 from the inhabitants of *J*
21:10 strike the inhabitants of *J*
21:12 out of the inhabitants of *J*
21:14 alive from the women of *J*
1Sa 31:11 inhabitants of *J* got to hear
2Sa 2:4 men of *J* were the ones that
2:5 to the men of *J* and said to
21:12 from the landowners of *J*

Jabez
1Ch 2:55 the scribes dwelling at *J*
4:9 *J* came to be more honorable
4:9 called his name *J*, saying
4:10 *J* began to call upon the

Jabin
Jos 11:1 *J* the king of Hazor heard
Jg 4:2 sold them into the hand of *J*
4:17 peace between *J* the king of
4:23 Thus God subdued *J* the king of
4:24 against *J* the king of Canaan
4:24 they had cut off *J* the king of
Ps 83:9 *J* at the torrent valley of

Jabin's
Jg 4:7 Sisera the chief of *J* army

Jabneel
Jos 15:11 Baalah and went out to *J*
19:33 and *J* as far as Lakkum

Jabneh
2Ch 26:6 and the wall of *J* and the

Jacan
1Ch 5:13 and *J* and Zia and Eber, seven

Jachin
Ge 46:10 sons of Simeon were . . . *J*
Ex 6:15 the sons of Simeon . . . *J* and
Nu 26:12 of *J* the family of the
1Ki 7:21 and called its name *J*
1Ch 9:10 And of the priests . . . *J*
24:17 for *J* the twenty-first, for
2Ch 3:17 name of the right-hand one *J*
Ne 11:10 Jedaiah the son of Joiarib, *J*

Jachinites
Nu 26:12 Jachin the family of the *J*

Jackals
Job 30:29 A brother to *j* I became
Ps 44:19 crushed us in the place of *j*
Isa 13:22 *j* must howl in her
34:13 an abiding place of *j*
35:7 In the abiding place of *j*
43:20 the *j* and the ostriches
Jer 9:11 stones, the lair of *j*
10:22 waste, the lair of *j*
14:6 snuffed . . . wind like the *j*
49:33 become the lair of *j*, a
51:37 stones, the lair of *j*
La 4:3 *j* themselves have presented
Mic 1:8 make a wailing like the *j*
Mal 1:3 for the *j* of the wilderness

Jacob
Ge 25:26 so he called his name *J*
25:27 but *J* a blameless man
25:28 Rebekah was a lover of *J*
25:29 Once *J* was boiling up some
25:30 Esau said to *J*: Quick, please
25:31 *J* said: Sell me, first of
25:33 *J* added: Swear to me first
25:33 his right as firstborn to *J*
25:34 *J* gave Esau bread and lentil
27:6 Rebekah said to *J* her son
27:11 *J* proceeded to say to Rebekah
27:15 put them on *J* her younger
27:17 into the hand of *J* her son
27:19 *J* went on to say to his
27:21 Isaac said to *J*: Come near
27:22 *J* came near to Isaac his
27:22 The voice is the voice of *J*
27:30 Isaac had finished blessing *J*
27:30 *J* had barely come out from
27:36 why his name is called *J*
27:41 harbored animosity for *J*
27:41 going to kill *J* my brother
27:42 she at once sent and called *J*
27:46 If *J* ever takes a wife from
28:1 Isaac called *J* and blessed
28:5 So Isaac sent *J* away
28:5 Rebekah, mother of *J* and Esau
28:6 Isaac had blessed *J*
28:7 *J* was obeying his father and
28:10 *J* continued on his way out
28:16 *J* awoke from his sleep
28:18 *J* got up early in the
28:20 *J* went on to vow a vow
29:1 *J* set his feet in motion and
29:4 *J* said to them: My brothers
29:10 when *J* saw Rachel the
29:10 *J* immediately approached and
29:11 Then *J* kissed Rachel and
29:12 *J* began to tell Rachel
29:13 heard the report about *J*
29:15 Laban said to *J*: Are you my
29:18 *J* was in love with Rachel
29:20 *J* proceeded to serve seven
29:21 *J* said to Laban: Give over
29:28 *J* did so and celebrated fully
30:1 she had borne nothing to *J*
30:1 say to *J*: Give me children or
30:4 *J* had relations with her
30:5 and in time bore *J* a son
30:7 bore a second son to *J*
30:9 and to give her to *J* as wife
30:10 Zilpah . . . bore a son to *J*
30:12 bore a second son to *J*
30:16 *J* was coming from the field
30:17 bore to *J* a fifth son
30:19 bore a sixth son to *J*
30:25 *J* immediately said to Laban
30:31 And *J* went on to say
30:36 between himself and *J*
30:36 *J* was shepherding the flocks
30:37 *J* took for his use staffs
30:40 *J* separated the young rams
30:41 *J* would locate the staffs
31:1 *J* has taken everything that
31:2 *J* would look at the face of
31:3 Jehovah said to *J*: Return
31:4 *J* sent and called Rachel
31:11 *J*! to which I said, Here I
31:17 *J* got up and lifted his
31:20 *J* outwitted Laban the Syrian
31:22 told to Laban that *J* had run
31:24 either good or bad with *J*
31:25 So Laban approached *J*
31:25 as *J* had pitched his tent in
31:26 Laban said to *J*: What have
31:29 either good or bad with *J*
31:31 *J* proceeded to say to Laban
31:32 *J* did not know that Rachel
31:33 went on into the tent of *J*
31:36 *J* became angry and began to
31:36 *J* went on to say to Laban
Ge 31:43 Laban in answer said to *J*
31:45 *J* took a stone and set it up
31:46 *J* said to his brothers: Pick
31:47 but *J* called it Galeed
31:51 Laban went on to say to *J*
31:53 *J* swore by the Dread of his
31:54 *J* sacrificed a sacrifice in
32:1 *J*, he got on his way, and
32:2 *J* said, when he saw them
32:3 *J* sent messengers ahead of
32:4 *J* has said: With Laban I have
32:6 the messengers returned to *J*
32:7 *J* became very much afraid and
32:9 *J* said: O God of my father
32:18 To your servant, to *J*. A gift
32:20 Here is your servant *J* behind
32:24 *J* was left by himself
32:27 name? to which he said: *J*
32:28 no longer be called *J* but
32:29 *J* inquired and said: Tell
32:30 *J* called . . . the place Peniel
33:1 *J* raised his eyes and looked
33:10 *J* said: No, please. If, now
33:17 *J* pulled out for Succoth, and
33:18 *J* came safe and sound to the
34:1 whom she had borne to *J*, used
34:3 Dinah the daughter of *J*, and
34:5 *J* heard that he had defiled
34:5 and *J* kept silent until they
34:6 Hamor . . . went out to *J*
34:7 sons of *J* came in from the
34:25 sons of *J*, Simeon and Levi
34:27 other sons of *J* attacked the
34:30 *J* said to Simeon and to Levi
35:1 God said to *J*: Rise, go up to
35:2 *J* said to his household and to
35:4 gave *J* all the foreign gods
35:4 *J* hid them under the big tree
35:5 chase after the sons of *J*
35:6 *J* came to Luz, which is in
35:9 appeared to *J* once again
35:10 Your name is *J*. No longer is
35:10 No longer . . . called *J*, but
35:14 *J* stationed a pillar in the
35:15 *J* continued to call the name
35:20 *J* stationed a pillar over
35:22 came to be twelve sons of *J*
35:27 *J* came to Isaac his father
35:29 Esau and *J* his sons buried
36:6 went to a land away from *J*
37:1 *J* continued to dwell in the
37:2 This is the history of *J*
37:34 *J* ripped his mantles apart
42:1 *J* got to see that there were
42:1 *J* said to his sons: Why do
42:4 *J* did not send Benjamin
42:29 they came to *J* their father
42:36 *J* their father exclaimed to
45:25 into the land of Canaan to *J*
45:27 the spirit of *J* their father
46:2, 2 *J*, *J*! to which he said
46:5 *J* got up out of Beer-sheba
46:5 transporting *J* their father
46:6 *J* and all his offspring with
46:8 sons who came into Egypt: *J*
46:15 bore to *J* in Paddan-aram
46:18 In time she bore these to *J*
46:22 sons . . . who were born to *J*
46:25 In time she bore these to *J*
46:26 All the souls who came to *J*
46:27 the souls of the house of *J*
47:7 Joseph brought in *J* his father
47:7 *J* proceeded to bless Pharaoh
47:8 Pharaoh now said to *J*
47:9 *J* said to Pharaoh: The days of
47:10 *J* blessed Pharaoh and went
47:28 *J* lived on in the land of
48:2 it was reported to *J* and said
48:3 *J* proceeded to say to Joseph
49:1 *J* called his sons and said
49:2 listen, you sons of *J*, yes
49:7 Let me parcel them out in *J*
49:24 the powerful one of *J*, from
49:33 *J* finished giving commands
50:24 Abraham, to Isaac and to *J*
Ex 1:1 came into Egypt with *J*; each
2:24 with Abraham, Isaac and *J*
3:6 God of Isaac and the God of *J*
3:15 Jehovah . . . the God of *J*
3:16 God of Abraham, Isaac and *J*
4:5 God of *J*, has appeared to you
6:3 I used to appear to . . . *J*
6:8 give to Abraham, Isaac and *J*
19:3 to say to the house of *J* and

Ex 33:1 swore to Abraham, Isaac and *J*
Le 26:42 remember my covenant with *J*
Nu 23:7 Do come, do curse *J* for me
23:10 the dust particles of *J*, And
23:21 any uncanny power against *J*
23:23 is no unlucky spell against *J*
23:23 said respecting *J* and Israel
24:5 are your tents, O *J*, your
24:17 A star . . . out of *J*, And a
24:19 And out of *J* one will go
32:11 I have sworn to . . . *J*
De 1:8 Abraham, Isaac and *J*, to give
6:10 Abraham, Isaac and *J* to
9:5 Abraham, Isaac and *J*
9:27 servants Abraham, Isaac and *J*
29:13 Abraham, Isaac and *J*
30:20 Isaac and *J* to give to them
32:9 *J* is the allotment that he
33:4 of the congregation of *J*
33:10 instruct *J* in your judicial
33:28 The fountain of *J* by itself
34:4 sworn to Abraham, Isaac and *J*
Jos 24:4 to Isaac I gave *J* and Esau
24:4 *J* and his sons went down to
24:32 field that *J* had acquired
1Sa 12:8 as *J* had come into Egypt and
2Sa 23:1 The anointed of the God of *J*
1Ki 18:31 the tribes of the sons of *J*
2Ki 13:23 Abraham, Isaac and *J*; and
17:34 commanded the sons of *J*
1Ch 16:13 sons of *J*, his chosen ones
16:17 as a regulation even to *J*
Ps 14:7 Let *J* be joyful, let Israel
20:1 the God of *J* protect you
22:23 the seed of *J*, glorify him
24:6 for your face, O God of *J*
44:4 Command grand salvation for *J*
46:7 God of *J* is a secure height
46:11 God of *J* is a secure height
47:4 pride of *J*, whom he has loved
53:6 Let *J* be joyful, let Israel
59:13 God is ruling in *J* to the
75:9 make melody to the God of *J*
76:6 From your rebuke, O God of *J*
77:15 The sons of *J* and of Joseph
78:5 to raise up a reminder in *J*
78:21 fire . . . kindled against *J*
78:71 a shepherd over *J* his people
79:7 For they have eaten up *J*
81:1 in triumph to the God of *J*
81:4 decision of the God of *J*
84:8 Do give ear, O God of *J*
85:1 the ones taken captive of *J*
87:2 all the tabernacles of *J*
94:7 God of *J* does not understand
99:4 righteousness in *J* are what
105:6 sons of *J*, his chosen ones
105:10 as a regulation even to *J*
105:23 *J* himself resided as an
114:1 house of *J* from a people
114:7 Because of the God of *J*
132:2 to the Powerful One of *J*
132:5 for the Powerful One of *J*
135:4 Jah has chosen even *J* for
146:5 has the God of *J* for his help
147:19 is telling his word to *J*
Isa 2:3 to the house of the God of *J*
2:5 O men of the house of *J*, come
2:6 your people, the house of *J*
8:17 face from the house of *J*
9:8 that Jehovah sent against *J*
10:20 escaped of the house of *J*
10:21 remnant of *J*, to the Mighty
14:1 will show mercy to *J*, and
14:1 to the house of *J*
17:4 glory of *J* will become
27:6 days *J* will take root
27:9 error of *J* will be atoned
29:22 said to the house of *J*
29:22 *J* will not now be ashamed
29:23 sanctify the Holy One of *J*
40:27 O *J*, and do you speak out
41:8 O *J*, whom I have chosen
41:14 not be afraid, you worm *J*
41:21 says the King of *J*
42:24 given *J* for mere pillage
43:1 your Creator, O *J*, and your
43:22 not called even me, O *J*
43:28 *J* over as a man devoted to
44:1 now listen, O *J* my servant
44:2 O my servant *J*, and you
44:5 by the name of *J*, and
44:21 Remember these things, O *J*
44:23 Jehovah has repurchased *J*
Isa 45:4 for the sake of my servant *J*
45:19 nor said I to the seed of *J*
46:3 Listen to me, O house of *J*
48:1 Hear this, O house of *J*
48:12 Listen to me, O *J*, and you
48:20 repurchased his servant *J*
49:5 to bring back *J* to him
49:6 to raise up the tribes of *J*
49:26 the Powerful One of *J*
58:1 the house of *J* their sins
58:14 hereditary possession of *J*
59:20 from transgression in *J*
60:16 the Powerful One of *J* is
65:9 out of *J* an offspring and
Jer 2:4 O house of *J*, and all you
5:20 Tell this in the house of *J*
10:16 The Share of *J* is not like
10:25 For they have eaten up *J*
30:7 the time of distress for *J*
30:10 afraid, O my servant *J*
30:10 *J* will certainly return
30:18 ones of the tents of *J*
31:7 Cry out loudly to *J* with
31:11 redeem *J* and reclaim him
33:26 reject even the seed of *J*
33:26 of Abraham, Isaac and *J*
46:27 afraid, O my servant *J*
46:27 *J* will certainly return
46:28 afraid, O my servant *J*
51:19 Share of *J* is not like these
La 1:17 given a command concerning *J*
2:2 upon any abiding places of *J*
2:3 in *J* he keeps burning like a
Eze 20:5 to the seed of the house of *J*
28:25 I gave to my servant, to *J*
37:25 gave to my servant, to *J*
39:25 the captive ones of *J* and
Ho 10:11 Judah plows; *J* harrows for
12:2 hold an accounting against *J*
12:12 *J* proceeded to run away to
Am 3:13 witness in the house of *J*
6:8 I am detesting the pride of *J*
7:2 Who will rise up of *J*?
7:5 Who will rise up of *J*? For he
8:7 sworn by the Superiority of *J*
9:8 annihilate the house of *J*
Ob 10 the violence to your brother *J*
17 house of *J* must take possession
18 house of *J* must become a fire
Mic 1:5 because of the revolt of *J*
1:5 What is the revolt of *J*?
2:7 being said, O house of *J*
2:12 I shall positively gather *J*
3:1 Hear, please, you heads of *J*
3:8 in order to tell to *J* his
3:9 head ones of the house of *J*
4:2 to the house of the God of *J*
5:7 the remaining ones of *J* must
5:8 the remaining ones of *J* must
7:20 the trueness given to *J*
Na 2:2 certainly gather the pride of *J*
Mal 1:2 Esau the brother of *J*
1:2 But I loved *J*
2:12 from the tents of *J*, and
3:6 And you are sons of *J*
Mt 1:2 Isaac became father to *J*
1:2 *J* became father to Judah and
1:15 Matthan became father to *J*
1:16 *J* became father to Joseph
8:11 with Abraham and Isaac and *J*
22:32 of Isaac and the God of *J*
Mr 12:26 God of Isaac and God of *J*
Lu 1:33 king over the house of *J*
3:34 son of *J*, son of Isaac, son of
13:28 and *J* and all the prophets
20:37 and God of Isaac and God of *J*
Joh 4:5 field that *J* gave to Joseph
4:12 *J*, who gave us the well and
Ac 3:13 and of *J*, the God of our
7:8 and Isaac of *J*, and
7:8 *J* of the twelve family heads
7:12 *J* heard there were foodstuffs
7:14 called *J* his father and all
7:15 *J* went down into Egypt
7:32 God of . . . Isaac and of *J*
7:46 habitation for the God of *J*
Ro 9:13 I loved *J*, but Esau I hated
11:26 ungodly practices from *J*
Heb 11:9 in tents with Isaac and *J*
11:20 Isaac blessed *J* and Esau
11:21 *J*, when about to die

Jacob's
Ge 30:2 *J* anger burned against Rachel
Ge 30:42 but the robust ones *J*
32:25 the socket of *J* thigh joint
32:32 the socket of *J* thigh joint
34:7 lying down with *J* daughter
34:13 *J* sons began to answer
34:19 find delight in *J* daughter
35:23 *J* firstborn Reuben
35:26 These are *J* sons who were
46:8 *J* firstborn was Reuben
46:19 The sons of Rachel, *J* wife
46:26 from the wives of *J* sons
47:28 *J* days, the years of his life
Ex 1:5 issued out of *J* upper thigh
Joh 4:6 In fact, *J* fountain was there

Jada
1Ch 2:28 sons of Onam . . . *J*
2:32 *J* the brother of Shammai

Jaddai
Ezr 10:43 the sons of Nebo . . . *J*

Jaddua
Ne 10:21 Meshezabel, Zadok, *J*
12:11 Jonathan . . . father to *J*
12:22 Joiada and Johanan and *J*

Jade
Ex 28:20 is chrysolite and onyx and *j*
39:13 And the fourth row was . . . *j*
Eze 28:13 chrysolite, onyx and *j*

Jadon
Ne 3:7 and *J* the Meronothite, did

Jael
Jg 4:17 to the tent of *J* the wife of
4:18 *J* came on out to meet Sisera
4:21 And *J* the wife of Heber
4:22 *J* now came on out to meet
5:6 In the days of *J*, pathways had
5:24 *J* the wife of Heber the

Jagur
Jos 15:21 Kabzeel and Eder and *J*

Jah
Ex 15:2 strength and my might is *J*
17:16 is against the throne of *J*
Ps 68:4 As *J*, which is his name
68:18 to reside among them, O *J*
77:11 remember the practices of *J*
89:8 Who is vigorous like you, O *J*?
94:7 keep saying: *J* does not see
94:12 man whom you correct, O *J*
102:18 to be created will praise *J*
104:35 Praise *J*, you people!
105:45 Praise *J*, you people!
106:1 Praise *J*, you people!
106:48 Praise *J*, you people!
111:1 Praise *J*, you people!
112:1 Praise *J*, you people!
113:1 Praise *J*, you people!
113:9 Praise *J*, you people!
115:17 dead . . . do not praise *J*
115:18 we ourselves will bless *J*
115:18 Praise *J*, you people!
116:19 Praise *J*, you people!
117:2 Praise *J*, you people!
118:5 I called upon *J*
118:5 *J* answered and put me into
118:14 *J* is my shelter and my
118:17 may declare the works of *J*
118:18 *J* corrected me severely
118:19 I shall laud *J*
122:4 tribes of *J*, As a reminder
130:3 were what you watch, O *J*
135:1 Praise *J*, you people!
135:3 Praise *J*, for Jehovah is good
135:4 *J* has chosen even Jacob for
135:21 Praise *J*, you people!
146:1 Praise *J*, you people!
146:10 Praise *J*, you people!
147:1 Praise *J*, you people, For it
147:20 Praise *J*, you people!
148:1 Praise *J*, you people!
148:14 Praise *J*, you people!
149:1 Praise *J*, you people! Sing
149:9 Praise *J*, you people!
150:1 Praise *J*, you people!
150:6 thing—let it praise *J*
150:6 Praise *J*, you people!
Ca 8:6 of a fire, the flame of *J*
Isa 12:2 *J* Jehovah is my strength and
26:4 *J* Jehovah is the Rock of
38:11, 11 shall not see *J*, even *J*
Re 19:1 said: Praise *J*, you people!
19:3 said: Praise *J*, you people!

Re 19:4 Amen! Praise *J*, you people!
19:6 said: Praise *J*, you people

Jahath
1Ch 4:2 Reaiah . . . became father to *J*
4:2 *J*, in turn, became father to
6:20 *J* his son, Zimmah his son
6:43 son of *J*, the son of Gershom
23:10 sons of Shimei were *J*, Zina
23:11 And *J* came to be the head
24:22 of the sons of Shelomoth, *J*
2Ch 34:12 appointed *J* and Obadiah the

Jahaz
Nu 21:23 came to *J* and began fighting
De 2:32 to meet us in battle at *J*
Jos 13:18 and *J* and Kedemoth and
21:36 *J* and its pasture ground
Jg 11:20 camping in *J* and fighting
1Ch 6:78 *J* with its pasture grounds
Isa 15:4 far as *J* their voice has
Jer 48:21 to *J* and against Mephaath
48:34 to *J* they have given forth

Jahaziel
1Ch 12:4 Jeremiah and *J* and Johanan
16:6 Benaiah and *J* the priests
23:19 of Hebron . . . *J* the third
24:23 of Hebron . . . *J* the third
2Ch 20:14 *J* the son of Zechariah
Ezr 8:5 Shecaniah the son of *J*, and

Jahdai
1Ch 2:47 the sons of *J* were Regem

Jahdiel
1Ch 5:24 and *J*, men that were valiant

Jahdo
1Ch 5:14 the son of *J*, the son of Buz

Jahleel
Ge 46:14 sons of Zebulun were . . . *J*
Nu 26:26 of *J* the family of the

Jahleelites
Nu 26:26 Jahleel the family of the *J*

Jahmai
1Ch 7:2 sons of Tola . . . *J* and Ibsam

Jahzeel
Ge 46:24 the sons of Naphtali were *J*
Nu 26:48 Of *J* the family of the

Jahzeelites
Nu 26:48 Jahzeel the family of the *J*

Jahzeiah
Ezr 10:15 *J* the son of Tikvah

Jahzerah
1Ch 9:12 *J* the son of Meshullam the

Jahziel
1Ch 7:13 sons of Naphtali were *J* and

Jail
Ge 40:3 *j* of the house of the chief
40:4 continued in *j* for some days
40:7 the *j* of his master's house
41:10 the *j* of the house of the
Mt 11:2 John, having heard in *j* about
Ac 5:21 sent out to the *j* to have
5:23 *j* we found locked with all
16:26 foundations of the *j* were

Jailer
Ac 16:23 the *j* to keep them securely
16:27 The *j*, being awakened out of
16:36 *j* reported their words to

Jailers
Mt 18:34 delivered him to the *j*

Jair
Nu 32:41 And *J* the son of Manasseh
De 3:14 *J* the son of Manasseh took
Jos 13:30 all the tent villages of *J*
Jg 10:3 *J* the Gileadite rose up, and
10:5 *J* died and was buried in
1Ki 4:13 had the tent villages of *J*
1Ch 2:22 in turn, became father to *J*
20:5 Elhanan the son of *J* got to
Es 2:5 Mordecai the son of *J* the son

Jairite
2Sa 20:26 Ira the *J* also became a

Jairus
Mr 5:22 officers of the synagogue, *J*
Lu 8:41 a man named J came, and this

Jakeh
Pr 30:1 words of Agur the son of *J*

Jakim
1Ch 8:19 and *J* and Zichri and Zabdi
24:12 the eleventh, for *J* the twelfth

Jalam
Ge 36:5 Oholibamah bore Jeush and *J*
36:14 she bore to Esau Jeush and *J*
36:18 sons of Oholibamah . . . *J*
1Ch 1:35 sons of Esau were . . . *J*

Jalon
1Ch 4:17 the sons of Ezrah . . . *J*

Jambres
2Ti 3:8 Jannes and *J* resisted Moses

James
Mt 4:21 *J* the son of Zebedee and
10:2 *J* the son of Zebedee and John
10:3 *J* the son of Alphaeus, and
13:55 his brothers *J* and Joseph
17:1 Jesus took Peter and *J* and
27:56 Mary the mother of *J* and
Mr 1:19 he saw *J* the son of Zebedee
1:29 Simon and Andrew with *J* and
3:17 *J* the son of Zebedee and John
3:17 and John the brother of *J*
3:18 and *J* the son of Alphaeus and
5:37 except Peter and *J* and John
5:37 and John the brother of *J*
6:3 the brother of *J* and Joseph
9:2 Jesus took Peter and *J* and
10:35 *J* and John, the two sons of
10:41 be indignant at *J* and John
13:3 *J* . . . began to ask him
14:33 he took Peter and *J* and John
15:40 the mother of *J* the Less and
16:1 Mary the mother of *J*, and
Lu 5:10 *J* and John, Zebedee's sons
6:14 *J* and John, and Philip and
6:15 *J* the son of Alphaeus, and
6:16 Judas the son of *J*, and Judas
8:51 Peter and John and *J* and the
9:28 he took Peter and John and *J*
9:54 *J* and John saw this they said
24:10 and Mary the mother of *J*
Ac 1:13 *J* and Andrew, Philip and
1:13 *J* the son of Alphaeus and
1:13 and Judas the son of *J*
12:2 *J* the brother of John by the
12:17 Report these things to *J*
15:13 *J* answered, saying: Men
21:18 Paul went in with us to *J*
1Co 15:7 he appeared to *J*, then to all
Ga 1:19 only *J* the brother of the Lord
2:9 *J* and Cephas and John, the ones
2:12 arrival of certain men from *J*
Jas 1:1 *J*, a slave of God and of the
Jude 1 brother of *J*, to the called

Jamin
Ge 46:10 sons of Simeon were . . . *J*
Ex 6:15 the sons of Simeon . . . *J* and
Nu 26:12 of *J* the family of the
1Ch 2:27 sons of Ram . . . Maaz and *J*
4:24 sons of Simeon . . . *J*
Ne 8:7 *J*, Akkub, Shabbethai, Hodiah

Jaminites
Nu 26:12 of Jamin the family of the *J*

Jamlech
1Ch 4:34 And Meshobab and *J* and

Janai
1Ch 5:12 and *J* and Shaphat in Bashan

Janim
Jos 15:53 *J* and Beth-tappuah and

Jannai
Lu 3:24 son of Melchi, son of *J*, son

Jannes
2Ti 3:8 *J* and Jambres resisted Moses

Janoah
Jos 16:6 passed over eastward to *J*
16:7 went down from *J* to Ataroth
2Ki 15:29 and *J* and Kedesh and Hazor

Japheth
Ge 5:32 Noah became father to . . . *J*
6:10 three sons, Shem, Ham and *J*
7:13 Noah went in . . . Ham and *J*
9:18 Noah's sons . . . Ham and *J*
9:23 Shem and *J* took a mantle and
9:27 God grant ample space to *J*
10:1 Noah's sons . . . Ham and *J*
10:2 sons of *J* were Gomer and
Ge 10:21 the brother of *J* the oldest
1Ch 1:4 Noah, Shem, Ham and *J*
1:5 sons of *J* were Gomer and

Japhia
Jos 10:3 to *J* the king of Lachish and
19:12 Daberath and went up to *J*
2Sa 5:15 Elishua and Nepheg and *J*
1Ch 3:7 and Nogah and Nepheg and *J*
14:6 and Nogah and Nepheg and *J*

Japhlet
1Ch 7:32 Heber, he became father to *J*
7:33 sons of *J* were Pasach and
7:33 These were the sons of *J*

Japhletites
Jos 16:3 to the boundary of the *J*

Jar
Ge 24:14 Let your water *j* down
24:15 and her water *j* was upon her
24:16 fill her water *j* and then
24:17 sip of water from your *j*
24:18 she quickly lowered her *j*
24:20 emptied her *j* into the
24:43 a little water from your *j*
24:45 with her *j* upon her shoulder
24:46 she quickly lowered her *j*
Ex 16:33 Take a *j* and put in it an
Le 11:35 Whether oven or *j* stand, it
1Sa 1:24 flour and a large *j* of wine
10:3 carrying a large *j* of wine
2Sa 16:1 and a large *j* of wine
1Ki 17:12 flour in the large *j* and
17:12 a little oil in the small *j*
17:14 The large *j* of flour itself
17:14 the small *j* of oil itself
17:16 large *j* of flour itself did
17:16 *j* of oil itself did not fail
2Ki 4:2 but a spouted *j* of oil
Ec 12:6 the *j* at the spring is broken
Isa 30:14 a large *j* of the potters
Jer 13:12 Every large *j* is something
13:12 every large *j* is something
Joh 4:28 left her water *j* and went
Heb 9:4 the golden *j* having the manna

Jarah
1Ch 9:42 Ahaz, he became father to *J*
9:42 *J* . . . father to Alemeth

Jared
Ge 5:15 Then he became father to *J*
5:16 after his fathering *J*
5:18 *J* . . . a hundred and sixty-two
5:19 after his fathering Enoch *J*
5:20 days of *J* amounted to nine
1Ch 1:2 Kenan, Mahalalel, *J*
Lu 3:37 son of Enoch, son of *J*, son of

Jarha
1Ch 2:34 servant whose name was *J*
2:35 his daughter to *J* his servant

Jarib
1Ch 4:24 sons of Simeon . . . *J*
Ezr 8:16 I sent for . . . *J* and Elnathan
10:18 Eliezer and *J* and Gedaliah

Jarmuth
Jos 10:3 to Piram the king of *J* and
10:5 five kings . . . the king of *J*
10:23 five kings . . . the king of *J*
12:11 the king of *J*, one
15:35 *J* and Adullam, Socoh and
21:29 *J* and its pasture ground
Ne 11:29 and in Zorah and in *J*

Jaroah
1Ch 5:14 son of *J*, the son of Gilead

Jars
Jg 7:16 large empty *j*, and torches
7:16 and torches inside the large *j*
7:19 *j* that were in their hands
7:20 shattered the large *j* and took
1Sa 25:18 two large *j* of wine and
1Ki 18:33 four large *j* with water
Job 38:37 Or the water *j* of heaven
Isa 22:24 vessels of the large *j*
Jer 48:12 large *j* they will dash to
La 4:2 as large *j* of earthenware, the
Joh 2:6 six stone water *j* sitting
2:7 Fill the water *j* with water

Jashar
Jos 10:13 written in the book of *J*
2Sa 1:18 written in the book of *J*

Jashen
2Sa 23:32 the sons of *J*, Jonathan

Jashobeam
1Ch 11:11 *J* the son of a Hachmonite
12:6 Joezer and *J*, the Korahites
27:2 was *J* the son of Zabdiel

Jashub
Nu 26:24 of *J* the family of the
1Ch 7:1 sons of Issachar were . . . *J*
Ezr 10:29 the sons of Bani . . . *J* and

Jashubi-lehem
1Ch 4:22 Moabite wives, and *J*

Jashubites
Nu 26:24 Jashub the family of the *J*

Jason
Ac 17:5 they assaulted the house of *J*
17:6 dragged *J* and certain brothers
17:7 and *J* has received them with
17:9 sufficient security from *J*
Ro 16:21 Lucius and *J* and Sosipater

Jasper
Ex 28:18 is turquoise, sapphire and *j*
39:11 the second row was . . . *j*
Eze 28:13 ruby, topaz and *j*
Re 4:3 in appearance, like a *j* stone
21:11 *j* stone shining crystal-clear
21:18 structure of its wall was *j*
21:19 first foundation was *j*, the

Jathniel
1Ch 26:2 Meshelemiah had sons . . . *J*

Jattir
Jos 15:48 Shamir and *J* and Socoh
21:14 *J* and its pasture ground
1Sa 30:27 and to those in *J*
1Ch 6:57 and *J* and Eshtemoa with its

Javan
Ge 10:2 sons of Japheth . . . *J* and
10:4 sons of *J* were Elishah and
1Ch 1:5 sons of Japheth . . . *J* and
1:7 sons of *J* were Elishah and
Isa 66:19 Tubal and *J*, the faraway
Eze 27:13 *J*, Tubal and Meshech
27:19 Vedan and *J* from Uzal

Javelin
Jos 8:18 the *j* that is in your hand
8:18 Joshua stretched out the *j*
8:26 he stretched out the *j* until
1Sa 17:6 a *j* of copper between his
17:45 with a *j*, but I am coming
Job 39:23 blade of a spear and a *j*
41:29 at the rattling of a *j*
Jer 6:23 the *j* they will grab hold of
50:42 Bow and *j* they handle

Jaw
Job 41:13 its double *j* who will enter?
Ps 3:7 strike all my enemies on the *j*

Jawbone
Jg 15:15 moist *j* of a male ass and
15:16 With the *j* of a male ass
15:16 the *j* of a male ass I have
15:17 threw the *j* out of his hand

Jawbones
Job 29:17 the *j* of the wrongdoer
Ps 58:6 very *j* of maned young lions
Pr 30:14 *j* are slaughtering knives
Joe 1:6 and it has the *j* of a lion

Jaws
De 18:3 give to the priest . . . the *j*
Job 41:2 thorn can you bore its *j*
Isa 30:28 be in the *j* of the peoples
Eze 29:4 I will put hooks in your *j*
38:4 and put hooks in your *j* and
Ho 11:4 lifting off a yoke on their *j*

Jazer
Nu 21:24 *J* is the border of the sons
21:32 Moses sent some to spy on *J*
32:1 began to see the land of *J* and
32:3 Ataroth and Dibon and *J* and
32:35 and Atroth-shophan and *J* and
Jos 13:25 territory came to be *J*
21:39 *J* and its pasture ground
2Sa 24:5 toward the Gadites, and to *J*
1Ch 6:81 *J* with its pasture grounds
26:31 among them in *J* in Gilead
Isa 16:8 far as *J* they had reached
16:9 weeping of *J* over the vine
Jer 48:32 more than the weeping for *J*
48:32 to *J*—they have reached

Jaziz
1Ch 27:31 there was *J* the Hagrite

Jealous
Ge 30:1 Rachel got *j* of her sister
37:11 his brothers grew *j* of him
Ex 34:14 Jehovah, whose name is *J*
34:14 Jehovah . . . he is a *j* God
Nu 11:29 Are you feeling *j* for me?
2Sa 21:2 *j* for the sons of Israel and
1Ki 19:10 absolutely *j* for Jehovah
19:14 absolutely *j* for Jehovah
Isa 11:13 will not be *j* of Judah, nor
Zec 1:14 I have been *j* for Jerusalem
8:2 I will be *j* for Zion with
8:2 with great rage I will be *j*
Ac 7:9 became *j* of Joseph and sold
17:5 But the Jews, getting *j*, took
1Co 13:4 Love is not *j*, it does not
2Co 11:2 For I am *j* over you with a

Jealousy
Nu 5:14 spirit of *j* has passed upon
5:14 spirit of *j* has passed upon
5:15 it is a grain offering of *j*
5:18 the grain offering of *j*, and
5:25 grain offering of *j* from the
5:29 law about *j*, where a woman
5:30 spirit of *j* may pass upon him
De 32:16 inciting him to *j* with
32:21 incited me to *j* with what is
32:21 shall incite them to *j* with
1Ki 14:22 they incited him to *j* more
Ps 78:58 they kept inciting him to *j*
Pr 6:34 For the rage of . . . man is *j*
14:30 *j* is rottenness to the bones
27:4 but who can stand before *j*?
Ec 9:6 their *j* have already perished
Isa 11:13 *j* of Ephraim must depart
Eze 8:3 symbol of *j* that is inciting
8:3 symbol . . . that is inciting to *j*
8:5 there was this symbol of *j* in
16:38 the blood of rage and *j*
16:42 my *j* must turn away from
35:11 *j* that you have expressed
Zec 1:14 and for Zion with great *j*
8:2 for Zion with great *j*, and
Ac 5:17 and became filled with *j*
13:45 they were filled with *j* and
Ro 10:19 incite you people to *j*
11:11 to incite them to *j*
11:14 to *j* and save some from
13:13 not in strife and *j*
1Co 3:3 there are *j* and strife among
10:22 we inciting Jehovah to *j*
2Co 11:2 over you with a godly *j*, for
12:20 somehow be strife, *j*
Ga 5:20 enmities, strife, *j*, fits of
Heb 10:27 fiery *j* that is going to
Jas 3:14 But if you have bitter *j* and
3:16 where *j* and contentiousness

Jearim
Jos 15:10 to the slope of Mount *J*

Jeatherai
1Ch 6:21 Zerah his son, *J* his son

Jeberechiah
Isa 8:2 Zechariah the son of *J*

Jebus
Jg 19:10 came as far as in front of *J*
19:11 they were close by *J*, as the
1Ch 11:4 Jerusalem, that is to say, *J*
11:5 inhabitants of *J* began to say

Jebusi
Jos 18:28 and Zelah, Ha-eleph and *J*

Jebusite
Ge 10:16 *J* and the Amorite and the
Jos 15:8 slope of the *J* at the south
18:16 slope of the *J* on the south
2Sa 24:16 floor of Araunah the *J*
24:18 floor of Araunah the *J*
1Ch 1:14 the *J* and the Amorite and
21:15 floor of Ornan the *J*
21:18 floor of Ornan the *J*
21:28 floor of Ornan the *J*
2Ch 3:1 threshing floor of Ornan the *J*
Zec 9:7 and Ekron like the *J*

Jebusites
Ge 15:21 the Girgashites and the *J*
Ex 3:8 to the locality of . . . the *J*
Ex 3:17 to the land of . . . the *J*
13:5 into the land of the . . . *J*
23:23 indeed bring you to the . . . *J*
33:2 and drive out the . . . *J*
34:11 I am driving out . . . the *J*
Nu 13:29 the Hittites and the *J* and
De 7:1 the Hivites and the *J*, seven
20:17 the Hivites and the *J*, just
Jos 3:10 and the Amorites and the *J*
9:1 Hivites and the *J*, heard of it
11:3 the Perizzites and the *J* in
12:8 the Hivites and the *J*
15:63 the *J* who were dwelling in
15:63 *J* continue dwelling with
24:11 Hivites and the *J* began
Jg 1:21 did not drive out the *J*
1:21 *J* keep on dwelling with the
3:5 dwelt in among . . . the *J*
19:11 city of the *J* and stay in it
2Sa 5:6 against the *J* inhabiting the
5:8 striking the *J*, let him, by
1Ki 9:20 the Hivites and the *J*
1Ch 11:4 Jebus, where the *J* were the
11:6 Anyone striking the *J* first
2Ch 8:7 *J*, who were no part of Israel
Ezr 9:1 the *J*, the Ammonites, the
Ne 9:8 the *J* and the Girgashites

Jecoliah
2Ki 15:2 name was *J* of Jerusalem
2Ch 26:3 mother's name was *J* of

Jeconiah
1Ch 3:16 sons of Jehoiakim were *J*
3:17 sons of *J* as prisoner were
Es 2:6 exile with *J* the king of Judah
Jer 24:1 *J* the son of Jehoiakim
27:20 *J* the son of Jehoiakim
28:4 *J* the son of Jehoiakim
29:2 after *J* the king and the
Mt 1:11 Josiah became father to *J*
1:12 *J* became father to Shealtiel

Jedaiah
1Ch 4:37 *J* the son of Shimri
9:10 of the priests there were *J*
24:7 for *J* the second
Ezr 2:36 sons of *J* of the house of
Ne 3:10 *J* the son of Harumaph did
7:39 The priests: The sons of *J* of
11:10 *J* the son of Joiarib, Jachin
12:6 Shemaiah, and Joiarib, *J*
12:7 Sallu, Amok, Hilkiah, *J*
12:19 Mattenai; for *J*, Uzzi
12:21 Hashabiah; for *J*, Nethanel
Zec 6:10 from Tobijah and from *J*
6:14 and to *J* and to Hen the son

Jediael
1Ch 7:6 sons of Benjamin were . . . *J*
7:10 the sons of *J* were Bilhan
7:11 All these were the sons of *J*
11:45 *J* the son of Shimri, and
12:20 from Manasseh . . . *J* and
26:2 Meshelemiah had sons . . . *J*

Jedidah
2Ki 22:1 *J* the daughter of Adaiah

Jedidiah
2Sa 12:25 called his name *J*, for the

Jeduthun
1Ch 9:16 the son of Galal the son of *J*
16:38 Obed-edom the son of *J* and
16:41 with them Heman and *J* and
16:42 and *J*, to sound forth the
16:42 the sons of *J* at the gate
25:1 sons of Asaph, Heman and *J*
25:3, 3 Of *J*: the sons of *J*
25:3 the control of their father *J*
25:6 were Asaph and *J* and Heman
2Ch 5:12 singers belonging to . . . *J*
29:14 sons of *J*, Shemaiah and
35:15 *J* the visionary of the king
Ne 11:17 Galal the son of *J*
Ps 39:*super* To the director of *J*
62:*super* To the director of *J*
77:*super* To the director on *J*

Jeer
2Ki 2:23 and began to *j* him and that
Eze 22:5 will *j* you, O you unclean

Jeering
Ps 44:13 *j* to those all around us
79:4 *j* to those round about us
Jer 20:8 cause for reproach and for *j*

Eze 22:4 and of *j* to all the lands

Jeers

Hab 1:10 for its part, it *j* kings

Jegar-sahadutha

Ge 31:47 Laban began calling it *J*

Jehallelel

1Ch 4:16 sons of *J* were Ziph and
2Ch 29:12 Azariah the son of *J*

Jehdeiah

1Ch 24:20 of the sons of Shubael, *J*
27:30 there was *J* the Meronothite

Jehezkel

1Ch 24:16 for *J* the twentieth

Jehiah

1Ch 15:24 and *J* the gatekeepers for

Jehiel

1Ch 15:18 Shemiramoth and *J* and Unni
15:20 and *J* and Unni and Eliab and
16:5 *J* and Mattithiah and Eliab
23:8 of Ladan were *J* the headman
27:32 and *J* the son of Hachmoni
29:8 control of *J* the Gershonite
2Ch 21:2 Jehoshaphat's sons . . . *J* and
29:14 sons of Heman, *J* and
31:13 And *J* . . . commissioners
35:8 Hilkiah and Zechariah and *J*
Ezr 8:9 Obadiah the son of *J*, and
10:2 Shecaniah the son of *J* of
10:21 sons of Harim . . . *J*
10:26 of the sons of Elam . . . *J*

Jehieli

1Ch 26:21 to Ladan the Gershonite, *J*
26:22 sons of *J*, Zetham and Joel

Jehizkiah

2Ch 28:12 *J* the son of Shallum and

Jehoaddah

1Ch 8:36 Ahaz, he became father to *J*
8:36 *J* . . . father to Alemeth

Jehoaddan

2Ch 25:1 mother's name was *J* of

Jehoaddin

2Ki 14:2 name was *J* of Jerusalem

Jehoahaz

2Ki 10:35 *J* his son began to reign
13:1 *J* the son of Jehu became
13:4 *J* softened the face of
13:7 not left to *J* any people but
13:8 the affairs of *J* and all that
13:9 *J* lay down with his
13:10 Jehoash the son of *J*
13:22 Israel all the days of *J*
13:25 Jehoash the son of *J*
13:25 *J* his father in war
14:1 *J* the king of Israel
14:8 *J* the son of Jehu the king of
14:17 *J* the king of Israel for
23:30 took *J* the son of Josiah
23:31 *J* when he began to reign
23:34 *J* he took and then brought
2Ch 21:17 but *J*, his youngest son
25:17 Jehoash the son of *J* the
25:23 Jehoash the son of *J*, that
25:25 Jehoash the son of *J* the
36:1 *J* the son of Josiah and
36:2 Twenty-three years old was *J*
36:4 *J*, Necho took and brought to

Jehoash

2Ki 11:2 took *J* the son of Ahaziah
11:21 Seven years old *J* was when
12:1 *J* became king, and for forty
12:2 *J* continued doing what was
12:4 *J* proceeded to say to the
12:6 twenty-third year of King *J*
12:7 King *J* called Jehoiada the
12:18 *J* the king of Judah took
12:19 *J* and all that he did
12:20 struck *J* down at the house
13:1 *J* the son of Ahaziah the king
13:9 *J* his son began to reign in
13:10 *J* the king of Judah
13:10 *J* the son of Jehoahaz
13:12 affairs of *J* and all that he
13:13 Finally *J* lay down with his
13:13 *J* was buried in Samaria
13:14 So *J* the king of Israel
13:25 *J* the son of Jehoahaz
13:25 Three times *J* struck him
2Ki 14:1 *J* the son of Jehoahaz the
14:1 *J* the king of Judah became
14:3 that *J* his father had done
14:8 to *J* the son of Jehoahaz
14:9 *J* the king of Israel sent
14:11 *J* the king of Israel came
14:13 *J* the son of Ahaziah
14:13 *J* the king of Israel
14:15 *J*, what he did and his
14:16 Finally *J* lay down with his
14:17 *J* the king of Judah
14:17 *J* the son of Jehoahaz the
14:23 *J* the king of Judah
14:23 *J* the king of Israel
14:27 Jeroboam the son of *J*
1Ch 3:11 Ahaziah his son, *J* his son
2Ch 22:11 *J* the son of Ahaziah and
24:1 Seven years old was *J* when
24:2 *J* kept doing what was right
24:4 close to the heart of *J* to
24:22 *J* the king did not remember
24:24 upon *J* they executed acts
25:17 *J* the son of Jehoahaz the
25:18 *J* the king of Israel sent
25:21 *J* the king of Israel went
25:23 *J* the son of Jehoahaz, that
25:23 *J* the king of Israel seized
25:25 Amaziah the son of *J* the
25:25 *J* the son of Jehoahaz the

Jehohanan

1Ch 26:3 *J* the sixth, Elieho-enai the
2Ch 17:15 there was *J* the chief, and
23:1 Ishmael the son of *J* and
28:12 Azariah the son of *J*
Ezr 10:6 *J* the son of Eliashib
10:28 the sons of Bebai, *J*
Ne 6:18 *J* his son had himself taken
12:13 Meshullam; for Amariah, *J*
12:42 and *J* and Malchijah and

Jehoiachin

2Ki 24:6 and *J* his son began to reign
24:8 Eighteen years old was *J*
24:12 *J* the king of Judah went
24:15 took *J* into exile to Babylon
25:27 exile of *J* the king of Judah
25:27 head of *J* the king of Judah
2Ch 36:8 *J* his son began to reign in
36:9 Eighteen years old was *J*
Jer 52:31 *J* the king of Judah, in
52:31 *J* the king of Judah and
Eze 1:2 year of the exile of King *J*

Jehoiada

2Sa 8:18 Benaiah the son of *J* was
20:23 Benaiah the son of *J* was
23:20 Benaiah the son of *J* the
23:22 Benaiah the son of *J* did
1Ki 1:8 Benaiah the son of *J* and
1:26 Benaiah the son of *J* and
1:32 and Benaiah the son of *J*
1:36 Benaiah the son of *J*
1:38 Benaiah the son of *J* and
1:44 Benaiah the son of *J* and the
2:25 Benaiah the son of *J*
2:29 Benaiah the son of *J*, saying
2:34 Benaiah the son of *J* went on
2:35 Benaiah the son of *J* in place
2:46 Benaiah the son of *J*, who
4:4 Benaiah the son of *J* was over
2Ki 11:4 in the seventh year *J* sent
11:9 *J* the priest had commanded
11:9 came in to *J* the priest
11:15 *J* the priest commanded the
11:17 *J* concluded the covenant
12:2 *J* the priest instructed him
12:7 Jehoash called *J* the priest
12:9 *J* the priest now took a
1Ch 11:22 Benaiah the son of *J*, the
11:24 Benaiah the son of *J* did
12:27 *J* was the leader of the
18:17 Benaiah the son of *J* was
27:5 the son of *J* the chief priest
27:34 *J* the son of Benaiah and
2Ch 22:11 wife of *J* the priest
23:1 *J* showed himself courageous
23:8 *J* the priest had commanded
23:8 *J* the priest had not set the
23:9 *J* the priest gave the chiefs
23:11 *J* and his sons anointed him
23:14 *J* the priest brought out
23:16 *J* concluded a covenant
23:18 *J* put the offices of the
24:2 all the days of *J* the priest
2Ch 24:3 *J* proceeded to get two wives
24:6 king called *J* the head and
24:12 king and *J* would give it to
24:14 king and *J* the rest of the
24:14 all the days of *J*
24:15 And *J* got to be old and
24:20 Zechariah the son of *J* the
24:22 loving-kindness that *J* his
24:25 blood of the sons of *J* the
Jer 29:26 you priest instead of *J*

Jehoiada's

2Ch 24:17 after *J* death the princes of

Jehoiakim

2Ki 23:34 and changed his name to *J*
23:35 the gold *J* gave to Pharaoh
23:36 *J* when he began to reign
24:1 so *J* became his servant
24:5 the rest of the affairs of *J*
24:6 *J* lay down with his
24:19 to all that *J* had done
1Ch 3:15 sons of Josiah . . . second, *J*
3:16 sons of *J* were Jeconiah
2Ch 36:4 changed his name to *J*
36:5 Twenty-five years old was *J*
36:8 *J* and his detestable things
Jer 1:3 days of *J* the son of Josiah
22:18 *J* the son of Josiah, the
22:24 Coniah the son of *J*
24:1 Jeconiah the son of *J*
25:1 in the fourth year of *J*
26:1 rule of *J* the son of Josiah
26:21 *J* and all his mighty men
26:22 King *J* sent men to Egypt
26:23 to bring him to King *J*
27:1 the kingdom of *J* the son of
27:20 Jeconiah the son of *J*, the
28:4 Jeconiah the son of *J*
35:1 *J* the son of Josiah, the
36:1 fourth year of *J* the son
36:9 *J* the son of Josiah, the
36:28 *J* the king of Judah burned
36:29 *J* the king of Judah you
36:30 against *J* the king of Judah
36:32 *J* the king of Judah had
37:1 Coniah the son of *J*, whom
45:1 *J* the son of Josiah, the
46:2 *J* the son of Josiah, the
52:2 to all that *J* had done
Da 1:1 third year . . . of *J* the king
1:2 Jehovah gave into his hand *J*

Jehoiarib

1Ch 9:10 of the priests . . . *J* and
24:7 to come out: the first for *J*

Jehonadab

2Sa 13:3 *J*, the son of Shimeah
13:3 *J* was a very wise man
13:5 *J* said to him: Lie down on
13:32 *J* the son of Shimeah
13:35 *J* said to the king: Look!
2Ki 10:15 *J* the son of Rechab
10:15 To this *J* said: It is
10:23 *J* the son of Rechab into
Jer 35:8 *J* the son of Rechab our
35:14 *J* the son of Rechab, that
35:16 of *J* the son of Rechab have
35:18 commandment of *J* your

Jehonathan

2Ch 17:8 *J* and Adonijah and Tobijah
Ne 12:18 Shammua; for Shemaiah, *J*
Jer 37:15 house of *J* the secretary
37:20 house of *J* the secretary
38:26 the house of *J* to die there

Jehoram

1Ki 22:50 *J* his son began to reign in
2Ki 1:17 *J* began to reign in place of
1:17 in the second year of *J* the
3:1 As for *J* the son of Ahab, he
3:6 King *J* went out on that day
8:16 *J* the son of Ahab the king
8:16 *J* the son of Jehoshaphat the
8:21 *J* passed over to Zair, also
8:23 affairs of *J* and all that he
8:24 Finally *J* lay down with his
8:25 *J* the son of Ahab the king of
8:25 son of *J* the king of Judah
8:28 *J* the son of Ahab to the
8:28 the Syrians struck down *J*
8:29 *J* the king returned to get
8:29 son of *J* the king of Judah
8:29 to see *J* the son of Ahab in
9:14 to conspire against *J*

2Ki 9:14 *J* himself had happened to
9:15 *J* the king returned to get
9:16 for *J* was lying there
9:16 had gone down to see *J*
9:17 *J* said: Take a cavalryman
9:21 At that *J* said: Hitch up!
9:21 and *J* the king of Israel
9:22 as soon as *J* saw Jehu, he
9:23 *J* made a turn with his hands
9:24 to shoot *J* between the arms
9:29 *J* the son of Ahab that
11:2 the daughter of King *J*
12:18 Jehoshaphat and *J* and
1Ch 3:11 *J* his son, Ahaziah his son
2Ch 17:8 Elishama and *J* the priests
21:1 *J* his son began to reign in
21:3 the kingdom he gave to *J*
21:4 *J* rose up over the kingdom
21:5 Thirty-two years old was *J*
21:9 *J* together with his chiefs
21:16 Jehovah aroused against *J*
22:1 Ahaziah the son of *J* began
22:5 with *J* the son of Ahab the
22:5 shooters got to strike *J*
22:6 Azariah the son of *J* the
22:6 see *J* the son of Ahab in
22:7 by his coming to *J*; and
22:7 went out with *J* to Jehu the
22:11 daughter of King *J*, the
Mt 1:8 Jehoshaphat became father to *J*
1:8 *J* became father to Uzziah

Jehoshabeath
2Ch 22:11 *J* the daughter of the king
22:11 *J* the daughter of King

Jehoshaphat
2Sa 8:16 *J* the son of Ahilud was
20:24 *J* the son of Ahilud was the
1Ki 4:3 *J* the son of Ahilud, the
4:17 *J* the son of Paruah, in
15:24 *J* his son began to reign
22:2 third year that *J* the king
22:4 to *J*: Will you go with me
22:4 *J* said to the king of Israel
22:5 *J* went on to say to the king
22:7 *J* said: Is there not here a
22:8 said to *J*: There is still
22:8 *J* said: Do not let the king
22:10 *J* the king of Judah were
22:18 said to *J*: Did I not say to
22:29 king of Israel and *J* the
22:30 said to *J*: There will be a
22:32 chiefs . . . saw *J*
22:32 *J* began to cry for aid
22:41 As for *J* the son of Asa, he
22:42 *J* was thirty-five years old
22:44 *J* kept peaceful relations
22:45 *J* and the mightiness with
22:48 *J*, for his part, made
22:49 said to *J*: Let my servants
22:49 but *J* did not consent
22:50 *J* lay down with his
22:51 in the seventeenth year of *J*
2Ki 1:17 *J* the king of Judah
3:1 the eighteenth year of *J* the
3:7 sent to *J* the king of Judah
3:11 *J* said: Is there not here a
3:12 *J* said: The word of Jehovah
3:12 *J* and the king of Edom went
3:14 face of *J* the king of Judah
8:16 *J* was king of Judah
8:16 *J* the king of Judah
9:2 *J* the son of Nimshi
9:14 *J* the son of Nimshi
12:18 *J* and Jehoram and Ahaziah
1Ch 3:10 Asa his son, *J* his son
18:15 *J* the son of Ahilud was
2Ch 17:1 *J* his son began to reign in
17:3 Jehovah continued with *J*
17:5 give presents to *J*, and he
17:10 did not fight against *J*
17:11 to *J* presents and money as
17:12 *J* continued advancing and
18:1 *J* came to have riches and
18:3 say to *J* the king of Judah
18:4 *J* said to the king of Israel
18:6 *J* said: Is there not here a
18:7 king of Israel said to *J*
18:7 *J* said: Do not let the king
18:9 *J* the king of Judah were
18:17 to *J*: Did I not say to you
18:28 and *J* the king of Judah
18:29 to *J*: There will be a
18:31 saw *J*, they, for their part
2Ch 18:31 and *J* began to cry for aid
19:1 *J* the king of Judah returned
19:2 to King *J*: Is it to the
19:4 *J* continued dwelling in
19:8 *J* stationed some of the
20:1 Ammonim came against *J*
20:2 told *J*, saying: There has
20:3 *J* became afraid and set his
20:5 Then *J* stood up in the
20:15 of Jerusalem and King *J*
20:18 *J* bowed low with his face
20:20 *J* stood up and then said
20:25 *J* and his people came to
20:27 with *J* at their head, to
20:30 realm of *J* had no
20:31 *J* went on reigning over
20:34 affairs of *J*, the first and
20:35 *J* the king of Judah had
20:37 prophetically against *J*
21:1 *J* lay down with his
21:2 of *J* the king of Israel
21:12 ways of *J* your father or in
22:9 grandson of *J*, who searched
Joe 3:2 down to the low plain of *J*
3:12 to the low plain of *J*
Mt 1:8 Asa became father to *J*
1:8 *J* became father to Jehoram

Jehoshaphat's
2Ch 21:2 *J* sons, Azariah and Jehiel

Jehosheba
2Ki 11:2 *J* the daughter of King

Jehoshua
Nu 13:16 call Hoshea the son of Nun *J*
1Ch 7:27 Nun his son, *J* his son

Jehovah
Ge 2:4 *J* God made earth and heaven
2:5 *J* God had not made it rain
2:7 *J* God proceeded to form the
2:8 *J* God planted a garden in Eden
2:9 Thus *J* God made to grow out of
2:15 *J* God proceeded to take the
2:16 *J* God also laid this command
2:18 And *J* God went on to say: It
2:19 Now *J* God was forming from
2:21 *J* God had a deep sleep fall
2:22 *J* God proceeded to build the
3:1 wild beasts . . . *J* God had made
3:8 they heard the voice of *J* God
3:8 hiding from the face of *J* God
3:9 *J* God kept calling to the man
3:13 *J* God said to the woman
3:14 *J* God proceeded to say to the
3:21 *J* God proceeded to make long
3:22 *J* God went on to say: Here
3:23 *J* God put him out of the
4:1 a man with the aid of *J*
4:3 fruits . . . as an offering to *J*
4:4 *J* was looking with favor
4:6 *J* said to Cain: Why are you
4:9 *J* said to Cain: Where is Abel
4:13 At this Cain said to *J*: My
4:15 *J* said to him: For that
4:15 *J* set up a sign for Cain in
4:16 went away from the face of *J*
4:26 of calling on the name of *J*
5:29 the ground which *J* has cursed
6:3 *J* said: My spirit shall not
6:5 *J* saw that the badness of man
6:6 *J* felt regrets that he had
6:7 *J* said: I am going to wipe
6:8 found favor in the eyes of *J*
7:1 *J* said to Noah: Go, you and all
7:5 all that *J* had commanded him
7:16 *J* shut the door behind him
8:20 began to build an altar to *J*
8:21 *J* began to smell a restful
8:21 *J* said in his heart: Never
9:26 Blessed be *J*, Shem's God
10:9 hunter in opposition to *J*
10:9 hunter in opposition to *J*
11:5 *J* proceeded to go down to see
11:6 *J* said: Look! They are one
11:8 *J* scattered them from there
11:9 *J* had confused the language
11:9 *J* had scattered them from
12:1 *J* proceeded to say to Abram
12:4 Abram went just as *J* had
12:7 *J* now appeared to Abram and
12:7 he built an altar there to *J*
12:8 he built an altar there to *J*
12:8 to call on the name of *J*
12:17 *J* touched Pharaoh and his
Ge 13:4 call there on the name of *J*
13:10 *J* brought Sodom and Gomorrah
13:10 like the garden of *J*, like
13:13 were gross sinners against *J*
13:14 *J* said to Abram after Lot
13:18 to build an altar to *J*
14:22 *J* the Most High God
15:1 word of *J* came to Abram in a
15:2 Abram said: Sovereign Lord *J*
15:4 the word of *J* to him was in
15:6 he put faith in *J*; and he
15:7 I am *J*, who brought you out
15:8 *J*, by what shall I know
15:18 *J* concluded with Abram a
16:2 *J* has shut me off from
16:5 May *J* judge between me and
16:11 *J* has heard your affliction
16:13 call the name of *J*, who was
17:1 *J* appeared to Abram and said
18:1 *J* appeared to him among the
18:3 *J*, if, now, I have found
18:13 *J* said to Abraham: Why was
18:14 too extraordinary for *J*
18:17 *J* said: Am I keeping covered
18:19 *J* may certainly bring upon
18:20 *J* said: The cry of complaint
18:22 *J*, he was still standing
18:26 *J* said: If I shall find in
18:27 speak to *J*, whereas I am
18:30 *J*, please, not grow hot with
18:31 upon myself to speak to *J*
18:32 May *J*, please, not grow hot
18:33 *J* went his way when he had
19:13 outcry . . . loud before *J*
19:13 *J* sent us to bring the city
19:14 *J* is bringing the city to
19:16 then in the compassion of *J*
19:18 Not that, please, *J*!
19:24 *J* made it rain sulphur and
19:24 rain sulphur and fire from *J*
19:27 where he had stood before *J*
20:4 *J*, will you kill a nation
20:18 *J* had tightly shut up every
21:1 *J* turned his attention to
21:1 *J* now did to Sarah just as he
21:33 *J* the indefinitely lasting
22:14 In the mountain of *J* it will
22:16 utterance of *J*, that by
24:1 and *J* had blessed Abraham in
24:3 swear by *J*, the God of the
24:7 *J* the God of the heavens, who
24:12 *J* the God of my master
24:21 know whether *J* had made his
24:26 prostrate himself before *J*
24:27 *J* the God of my master
24:27 *J* has led me to the house of
24:31 Come, you blessed one of *J*
24:35 *J* has blessed my master very
24:40 *J*, before whom I have walked
24:42 *J* the God of my master
24:44 woman whom *J* has assigned
24:48 prostrate myself before *J*
24:48 and bless *J* the God of my
24:50 From *J* this thing has issued
24:51 just as *J* has spoken
24:52 on the earth before *J*
24:56 seeing that *J* has given
25:21 Isaac kept on entreating *J*
25:21 so *J* let himself be entreated
25:22 she went to inquire of *J*
25:23 *J* proceeded to say to her
26:2 *J* appeared to him and said
26:12 as *J* was blessing him
26:22 *J* has given us ample room
26:24 *J* proceeded to appear to him
26:25 called on the name of *J*
26:28 *J* has proved to be with you
26:29 You now are the blessed of *J*
27:7 bless you before *J* before my
27:20 *J* your God caused it to meet
27:27 scent of the field which *J*
28:13 there was *J* stationed above
28:13 I am *J* the God of Abraham
28:16 Truly *J* is in this place
28:21 *J* will have proved to be my
29:31 *J* came to see that Leah was
29:32 *J* has looked upon my
29:33 It is because *J* has listened
29:35 This time I shall laud *J*
30:24 *J* is adding another son to
30:27 *J* is blessing me due to you
30:30 *J* blessed you since I stepped
31:3 *J* said to Jacob: Return
31:49 *J* keep watch between me and

Ge 32:9 O *J*, you who are saying to me
38:7 Er . . . bad in the eyes of *J*
38:7 hence *J* put him to death
38:10 was bad in the eyes of *J*
39:2 *J* proved to be with Joseph
39:3 his master got to see that *J*
39:3 *J* was making . . . successful
39:5 *J* kept blessing the house of
39:21 *J* continued with Joseph and
39:23 *J* was with Joseph and what
39:23 *J* was making it turn out
49:18 salvation from you, O *J*
Ex 3:4 *J* saw that he turned aside to
3:7 *J* added: Unquestionably I have
3:15 *J* the God of your forefathers
3:16 *J* the God of your forefathers
3:18 *J* the God of the Hebrews has
3:18 we want to sacrifice to *J* our
4:1 say, *J* did not appear to you
4:2 Then *J* said to him: What is
4:4 *J* now said to Moses: Thrust
4:5 believe that *J* . . . appeared to
4:6 Then *J* said to him once more
4:10 Moses now said to *J*: Excuse
4:10 Excuse me, *J*, but I am not a
4:11 *J* said to him: Who appointed
4:11 Is it not I, *J*?
4:13 said: Excuse me, *J*, but send
4:19 *J* said to Moses in Midian
4:21 *J* went on to say to Moses
4:22 *J* has said: Israel is my son
4:24 *J* got to meet him and kept
4:27 *J* said to Aaron: Go to meet
4:28 tell Aaron all the words of *J*
4:30 words that *J* had spoken to
4:31 *J* had turned his attention to
5:1 *J* the God of Israel has said
5:2 Pharaoh said: Who is *J*, so
5:2 I do not know *J* at all and
5:3 wilderness and sacrifice to *J*
5:17 we want to sacrifice to *J*
5:21 May *J* look upon you and judge
5:22 Moses turned to *J* and said
5:22 *J*, why have you caused evil
6:1 So *J* said to Moses: Now you
6:2 God went on . . . I am *J*
6:3 as respects my name *J* I did
6:6 I am *J*, and I shall certainly
6:7 know that I am *J* your God who
6:8 something to possess. I am *J*
6:10 Then *J* spoke to Moses, saying
6:12 Moses spoke before *J*, saying
6:13 *J* continued to speak to Moses
6:26 Aaron and Moses to whom *J*
6:28 the day that *J* spoke to Moses
6:29 *J* went on to speak to Moses
6:29 to Moses, saying: I am *J*
6:30 Then Moses said before *J*
7:1 *J* said to Moses: See, I have
7:5 Egyptians . . . know that I am *J*
7:6 doing as *J* had commanded them
7:8 *J* now said to Moses and Aaron
7:10 exactly as *J* had commanded
7:13 to them, just as *J* had spoken
7:14 *J* said to Moses: Pharaoh's
7:16 *J* the God of the Hebrews has
7:17 This is what *J* has said: By
7:17 you will know that I am *J*
7:19 *J* said to Moses: Say to Aaron
7:20 just as *J* had commanded
7:22 did not listen . . . just as *J*
8:1 Then *J* said to Moses: Go in to
8:1 *J* has said: Send my people
8:5 *J* said to Moses: Say to Aaron
8:8 Pharaoh . . . said: Entreat *J*
8:8 that they may sacrifice to *J*
8:10 is no one else like *J* our God
8:12 Moses cried out to *J* because
8:13 *J* did according to Moses'
8:15 just as *J* had spoken
8:16 *J* now said to Moses: Say to
8:19 just as *J* had spoken
8:20 *J* said to Moses: Get up early
8:20 *J* has said: Send my people
8:22 you may know that I am *J*
8:24 And *J* proceeded to do so
8:26 sacrifice to *J* our God a thing
8:27 sacrifice to *J* our God just as
8:28 sacrifice to *J* your God in the
8:29 indeed make entreaty to *J*, and
8:29 people away to sacrifice to *J*
8:30 Moses . . . made entreaty to *J*
8:31 *J* did according to Moses'
9:1 *J* said to Moses: Go in to

Ex 9:1 *J* the God of the Hebrews has
9:4 *J* will . . . make a distinction
9:5 *J* set an appointed time
9:5 Tomorrow *J* will do this thing
9:6 *J* did this thing on the next
9:8 that *J* said to Moses and Aaron
9:12 *J* let Pharaoh's heart become
9:12 just as *J* had stated to Moses
9:13 *J* said to Moses: Get up early
9:13 what *J* the God of the Hebrews
9:22 *J* now said to Moses: Stretch
9:23 *J* gave thunders and hail, and
9:23 *J* kept making it rain down
9:27 *J* is righteous, and I and my
9:28 Entreat *J* that this may be
9:29 shall spread my hands up to *J*
9:29 that the earth belongs to *J*
9:30 show fear because of *J* God
9:33 spread his hands up to *J*, and
9:35 as *J* had stated by means of
10:1 *J* said to Moses: Go in to
10:2 certainly know that I am *J*
10:3 This is what *J* the God of the
10:7 they may serve *J* their God
10:8 Go, serve *J* your God. Who in
10:9 for we have a festival to *J*
10:10 *J* is with you when I shall
10:11 serve *J*, because that is
10:12 *J* now said to Moses: Stretch
10:13 *J* caused an east wind to
10:16 I have sinned against *J* your
10:17 entreat *J* your God that he
10:18 and made entreaty to *J*
10:19 *J* made a shift to a very
10:20 *J* let Pharaoh's heart become
10:21 *J* then said to Moses
10:24 Go, serve *J*. Only your sheep
10:25 render them to *J* our God
10:26 take some to worship *J* our
10:26 render in worship to *J* until
10:27 *J* let Pharaoh's heart become
11:1 *J* proceeded to say to Moses
11:3 *J* gave the people favor in the
11:4 *J* has said, About midnight I
11:7 that *J* can make a distinction
11:9 *J* said to Moses: Pharaoh will
11:10 *J* would let Pharaoh's heart
12:1 *J* now said to Moses and Aaron
12:12 execute judgments. I am *J*
12:14 festival to *J* throughout your
12:23 *J* does pass through to plague
12:23 *J* will certainly pass over
12:25 land that *J* will give you
12:27 passover to *J*, who passed
12:28 as *J* had commanded Moses
12:29 *J* struck every firstborn in
12:31 serve *J*, just as you have
12:36 *J* gave the people favor in
12:41 armies of *J* went out of the
12:42 observance with regard to *J*
12:42 With regard to *J* this night
12:43 *J* went on to say to Moses
12:48 celebrate the passover to *J*
12:50 did just as *J* had commanded
12:51 *J* brought the sons of Israel
13:1 And *J* spoke further to Moses
13:3 *J* brought you out from here
13:5 when *J* will have brought you
13:6 seventh day is a festival to *J*
13:8 that which *J* has done to me
13:9 *J* brought you out of Egypt
13:11 *J* brings you into the land of
13:12 that opens the womb to *J*
13:12 The males belong to *J*
13:14 *J* brought me out of Egypt
13:15 *J* proceeded to kill every
13:15 I am sacrificing to *J* all
13:16 *J* brought us out of Egypt
13:21 *J* was going ahead of them in
14:1 *J* now spoke to Moses, saying
14:4 certainly know that I am *J*
14:8 *J* let the heart of Pharaoh the
14:10 and began to cry out to *J*
14:13 and see the salvation of *J*
14:14 *J* will himself fight for you
14:15 *J* now said to Moses: Why do
14:18 certainly know that I am *J*
14:21 *J* began making the sea go
14:24 *J* began to look out upon the
14:25 *J* certainly fights for them
14:26 *J* said to Moses: Stretch
14:27 *J* shook the Egyptians off
14:30 *J* saved Israel from the hand
14:31 hand that *J* put in action

Ex 14:31 the people began to fear *J*
14:31 put faith in *J* and in Moses
15:1 to sing this song to *J* and to
15:1 Let me sing to *J*, for he has
15:3 *J* is a manly person of war
15:3 *J* is his name
15:6 Your right hand, O *J*, is
15:6 Your right hand, O *J*, can
15:11 Who . . . is like you, O *J*?
15:16 your people pass by, O *J*
15:17 ready for you to inhabit, O *J*
15:17 A sanctuary, O *J*, that your
15:18 *J* will rule as king to time
15:19 *J* brought back the waters of
15:21 Sing to *J*, for he has become
15:25 Then he cried out to *J*
15:25 So *J* directed him to a tree
15:26 listen to the voice of *J* your
15:26 I am *J* who is healing you
16:4 *J* said to Moses: Here I am
16:6 it is *J* who has brought you
16:7 your murmurings against *J*
16:8 *J* gives you in the evening
16:8 *J* has heard your murmurings
16:8 not against us, but against *J*
16:9 Come near before *J*, because
16:11 And *J* spoke further to Moses
16:12 know that I am *J* your God
16:15 bread that *J* has given you
16:16 *J* has commanded, Pick up
16:23 It is what *J* has spoken
16:23 a holy sabbath to *J*
16:25 today is a sabbath to *J*
16:28 *J* said to Moses: How long
16:29 *J* has given you the sabbath
16:32 *J* has commanded, Fill an
16:33 and deposit it before *J* as
16:34 as *J* had commanded Moses
17:1 according to the order of *J*
17:2 keep putting *J* to the test
17:4 Moses cried out to *J*, saying
17:5 *J* said to Moses: Pass in
17:7 their putting *J* to the test
17:7 Is *J* in our midst or not?
17:14 *J* now said to Moses: Write
17:16 *J* will have war with Amalek
18:1 *J* had brought Israel out of
18:8 all that *J* had done to Pharaoh
18:8 and yet *J* was delivering them
18:9 all the good that *J* had done
18:10 said: Blessed be *J*, who has
18:11 *J* is greater than all the
19:3 *J* began to call to him out of
19:7 words that *J* had commanded
19:8 All that *J* has spoken we are
19:8 the words of the people to *J*
19:9 this *J* said to Moses: Look!
19:9 the words of the people to *J*
19:10 *J* went on to say to Moses
19:11 *J* will come down before the
19:18 *J* came down upon it in fire
19:20 So *J* came down upon Mount
19:20 *J* called Moses to the top of
19:21 *J* now said to Moses: Go
19:21 break through to *J* to take a
19:22 who regularly come near to *J*
19:22 *J* may not break out upon
19:23 Moses said to *J*: The people
19:24 *J* said to him: Go, descend
19:24 to come up to *J*, that he may
20:2 I am *J* your God, who have
20:5 *J* your God am a God exacting
20:7 not take up the name of *J*
20:7 for *J* will not leave the one
20:10 seventh day is a sabbath to *J*
20:11 six days *J* made the heavens
20:11 *J* blessed the sabbath day and
20:12 the ground that *J* your God is
20:22 *J* went on to say to Moses
22:11 an oath by *J* is to take place
22:20 sacrifices to any gods but *J*
23:17 face of the true Lord, *J*
23:19 to bring to the house of *J*
23:25 must serve *J* your God, and
24:1 Go up to *J*, you and Aaron
24:2 And Moses . . . must approach *J*
24:3 all the words of *J* and all
24:3 words that *J* has spoken we
24:4 wrote . . . all the words of *J*
24:5 as communion sacrifices to *J*
24:7 All that *J* has spoken we are
24:8 covenant that *J* has concluded
24:12 *J* now said to Moses: Come
25:1 *J* proceeded to speak to Moses

Ex 27:21 set it in order . . . before J
28:12 carry their names before J
28:29 memorial before J constantly
28:30 comes in before J; and Aaron
28:30 over his heart before J
28:35 into the sanctuary before J
28:36 seal, Holiness belongs to J
28:38 approval for them before J
29:11 slaughter the bull before J
29:18 It is a burnt offering to J
29:18 offering made by fire to J
29:23 basket . . . that is before J
29:24 as a wave offering before J
29:25 as a restful odor before J
29:25 offering made by fire to J
29:26 as a wave offering before J
29:28 their sacred portion for J
29:41 offering made by fire to J
29:42 the tent of meeting before J
29:46 J their God, who brought
29:46 I am J their God
30:8 incense constantly before J
30:10 It is most holy to J
30:11 J went on to speak to Moses
30:12 a ransom for his soul to J
30:13 is the contribution to J
30:16 a memorial before J for the
30:17 J spoke further to Moses
30:20 made by fire smoke to J
30:22 J continued to speak to
30:34 J went on to say to Moses
30:37 as something holy to J
31:1 J continued to speak to Moses
31:12 And J said further to Moses
31:13 that I J am sanctifying you
31:15 It is something holy to J
31:17 in six days J made the heavens
32:5 is a festival to J tomorrow
32:7 J now said to Moses: Go
32:9 J went on to say to Moses
32:11 soften the face of J his
32:11 Why, O J, should your anger
32:14 J began to feel regret over
32:27 J the God of Israel has said
32:29 today with power for J
32:30 and now I shall go up to J
32:31 Moses returned to J and said
32:33 J said to Moses: Whoever has
32:35 J began plaguing the people
33:1 J said further to Moses: Go
33:5 J went on to say to Moses
33:7 everyone inquiring of J would
33:11 J spoke to Moses face to
33:12 Now Moses said to J
33:17 J went on to say to Moses
33:19 will declare the name of J
33:21 J said further: Here is a
34:1 J said to Moses: Carve out
34:4 just as J had commanded him
34:5 J proceeded to come down in
34:5 and declare the name of J
34:6 J went passing by before his
34:6, 6 J, J, a God merciful and
34:9 found favor in your eyes, O J
34:9 let J, please, go along in the
34:10 indeed see the work of J
34:14 J, whose name is Jealous, he
34:23 Lord, J, the God of Israel
34:24 to see the face of J your God
34:26 to the house of J your God
34:27 J went on to say to Moses
34:28 continued there with J forty
34:32 that J had spoken with him
34:34 go in before J to speak with
35:1 words that J has commanded
35:2 sabbath of complete rest to J
35:4 word that J has commanded
35:5 take up a contribution for J
35:10 all that J has commanded
35:22 wave offering of gold to J
35:29 work that J had commanded
35:29 a voluntary offering to J
35:30 J has called by name Bezalel
36:1 to whom J has given wisdom
36:1 all that J has commanded
36:2 whose heart J had put wisdom
36:5 J has commanded to be done
38:22 that J had commanded Moses
39:1 just as J had commanded Moses
39:5 just as J had commanded Moses
39:7 just as J had commanded Moses
39:21 as J had commanded Moses
39:26 just as J had commanded Moses
39:29 as J had commanded Moses
Ex 39:30 a seal: Holiness belongs to J
39:31 as J had commanded Moses
39:32 all that J had commanded
39:42 all that J had commanded
39:43 just as J had commanded
40:1 Then J spoke to Moses, saying
40:16 all that J had commanded him
40:19 as J had commanded Moses
40:21 as J had commanded Moses
40:23 row of bread upon it before J
40:23 as J had commanded Moses
40:25 lit up the lamps before J
40:25 as J had commanded Moses
40:27 as J had commanded Moses
40:29 as J had commanded Moses
40:32 as J had commanded Moses
Le 1:1 J proceeded to call Moses and
1:2 present an offering to J from
1:3 of his own free will before J
1:5 must be slaughtered before J
1:9 by fire of a restful odor to J
1:11 altar to the north before J
1:13 by fire of a restful odor to J
1:14 as a burnt offering to J is
1:17 by fire of a restful odor to J
2:1 a grain offering to J
2:2 by fire of a restful odor to J
2:8 to J; and it must be presented
2:9 by fire of a restful odor to J
2:11 that you will present to J
2:11 offering made by fire to J
2:12 you will present them to J
2:14 the first ripe fruits to J
2:16 an offering made by fire to J
3:1 what he will present before J
3:3 an offering made by fire to J
3:5 by fire of a restful odor to J
3:6 for a communion sacrifice to J
3:7 he must present it before J
3:9 an offering made by fire to J
3:11 an offering made by fire to J
3:12 he must present it before J
3:14 an offering made by fire to J
3:16 All the fat belongs to J
4:1 J went on to speak to Moses
4:2 that J commands should not be
4:3 bull to J as a sin offering
4:4 the tent of meeting before J
4:4 slaughter the bull before J
4:6 the blood seven times before J
4:7 perfumed incense before J
4:13 J commands should not be done
4:15 before J, and the bull must
4:15 must be slaughtered before J
4:17 seven times before J in front
4:18 the altar that is before J
4:22 all the things that J his God
4:24 regularly slaughtered before J
4:27 that J commands should not be
4:31 as a restful odor to J; and
5:6 guilt offering to J for his sin
5:7 or two male pigeons to J
5:14 J continued to speak to Moses
5:15 against the holy things of J
5:15 as his guilt offering to J
5:17 the things that J commands
5:19 become guilty against J
6:1 J went on to speak to Moses
6:2 behave unfaithfully toward J
6:6 bring to J a sound ram from
6:7 atonement for him before J
6:8 J continued to speak to Moses
6:14 present it before J in front
6:15 a remembrancer of it to J
6:19 J went on speaking to Moses
6:20 present to J on the day of
6:21 as a restful odor to J
6:24 J spoke further to Moses
6:25 will be slaughtered before J
7:5 an offering made by fire to J
7:11 anyone will present to J
7:14 as a sacred portion to J
7:20 sacrifice, which is for J
7:21 sacrifice, which is for J
7:22 And J continued to speak to
7:25 an offering made by fire to J
7:28 J went on to speak to Moses
7:29 communion sacrifice to J
7:29 his offering to J from his
7:30 as a wave offering before J
7:35 them to act as priests to J
7:36 just as J had commanded to
7:38 as J had commanded Moses in
7:38 present their offerings to J
Le 8:1 J proceeded to speak to Moses
8:4 Then Moses did just as J had
8:5 J has given command to do
8:9 just as J had commanded Moses
8:13 as J had commanded Moses
8:17 just as J had commanded Moses
8:21 an offering made by fire to J
8:21 just as J had commanded Moses
8:26 cakes that was before J
8:27 as a wave offering before J
8:28 an offering made by fire to J
8:29 as a wave offering before J
8:29 as J had commanded Moses
8:34 J has commanded to be done
8:35 the obligatory watch of J
8:36 J had commanded by means of
9:2 and present them before J
9:4 to sacrifice them before J
9:4 J will certainly appear to you
9:5 came near and stood before J
9:6 J has commanded you should
9:6 glory of J may appear to you
9:7 just as J has commanded
9:10 just as J had commanded Moses
9:21 as a wave offering before J
9:24 fire came out from before J
10:1 they began offering before J
10:2 from before J and consumed
10:2 so that they died before J
10:3 This is what J has spoken
10:6 which J has made burn
10:8 J proceeded to speak to Aaron
10:11 the regulations that J has
10:15 offering to and fro before J
10:15 just as J has commanded
10:17 atonement for them before J
10:19 their burnt offering before J
11:1 J proceeded to speak to Moses
11:44 For I am J your God; and you
11:45 I am J who is leading you up
12:1 J went on to speak to Moses
12:7 must present it before J and
13:1 J proceeded to speak to Moses
14:1 J continued to speak to Moses
14:11 before J at the entrance of
14:12 as a wave offering before J
14:16 finger seven times before J
14:18 atonement for him before J
14:23 the tent of meeting before J
14:24 as a wave offering before J
14:27 seven times before J
14:29 atonement for him before J
14:31 cleansing himself before J
14:33 J proceeded to speak to
15:1 J continued to speak to Moses
15:14 he must come before J to the
15:15 atonement for him before J
15:30 atonement for her before J
16:1 J proceeded to speak to Moses
16:1 before J so that they died
16:2 J proceeded to say to Moses
16:7 before J at the entrance of
16:8 the one lot for J and the
16:9 which the lot came up for J
16:10 before J to make atonement
16:12 from off the altar before J
16:13 upon the fire before J
16:18 the altar, which is before J
16:30 from all your sins before J
16:34 as J had commanded Moses
17:1 J went on to speak to Moses
17:2 thing that J has commanded
17:4 an offering to J before the
17:4 before the tabernacle of J
17:5 them to J to the entrance
17:5 as communion sacrifices to J
17:6 smoke as a restful odor to J
17:9 to render it to J, that man
18:1 J continued to speak to Moses
18:2 say to them, I am J your God
18:4 I am J your God
18:5 keep my statutes . . . I am J
18:6 I am J
18:21 not profane . . . I am J
18:30 I am J your God
19:1 J spoke further to Moses
19:2 because I J your God am holy
19:3 I am J your God
19:4 I am J your God
19:5 a communion sacrifice to J
19:8 profaned a holy thing of J
19:10 I am J your God
19:12 must not swear . . . I am J
19:14 fear of your God. I am J

Le 19:16 I am *J*
19:18 love your fellow . . . I am *J*
19:21 his guilt offering to *J* to
19:22 before *J* for his sin that he
19:24 of festal exultation to *J*
19:25 eat its fruit . . . I am *J*
19:28 I am *J*
19:30 stand in awe . . . I am *J*
19:31 I am *J* your God
19:32 be in fear . . . I am *J*
19:34 love him . . . I am *J* your God
19:36 *J* your God I am, who have
19:37 and you must do them. I am *J*
20:1 *J* went on speaking to Moses
20:7 holy, because I am *J* your God
20:8 *J* who is sanctifying you
20:24 *J* your God I am, who have
20:26 holy to me, because I *J* am
21:1 *J* went on to say to Moses
21:8 *J*, who am sanctifying you
21:12 not profane . . . I am *J*
21:15 I am *J* who is sanctifying
21:16 *J* continued to speak to
21:23 I am *J* who is sanctifying
22:1 *J* spoke further to Moses
22:2 I am *J*
22:3 Israel will sanctify to *J*
22:3 must be cut off . . . I am *J*
22:8 unclean by it. I am *J*
22:9 *J* who is sanctifying them
22:15 they may contribute to *J*
22:16 *J* who is sanctifying them
22:17 And *J* continued to speak to
22:18 may present to *J* for a burnt
22:21 to *J* in order to pay a vow
22:22 these must you present to *J*
22:22 you put upon the altar for *J*
22:24 not present to *J*, and in your
22:26 And *J* spoke further to Moses
22:27 offering made by fire to *J*
22:29 thanksgiving sacrifice to *J*
22:30 I am *J*
22:31 my commandments . . . I am *J*
22:32 I am *J* who is sanctifying
22:33 myself God to you. I am *J*
23:1 *J* went on speaking to Moses
23:2 festivals of *J* that you should
23:3 sabbath to *J* in all places
23:4 seasonal festivals of *J*, holy
23:5 is the passover to *J*
23:6 of unfermented cakes to *J*
23:8 offering made by fire to *J*
23:9 *J* continued to speak to Moses
23:11 sheaf to and fro before *J* to
23:12 for a burnt offering to *J*
23:13 offering made by fire to *J*
23:16 a new grain offering to *J*
23:17 as first ripe fruits to *J*
23:18 burnt offering to *J* along
23:18 of a restful odor to *J*
23:20 wave offering before *J*
23:20 holy to *J* for the priest
23:22 leave them . . . I am *J* your
23:23 *J* went on speaking to Moses
23:25 offering made by fire to *J*
23:26 *J* spoke further to Moses
23:27 offering made by fire to *J*
23:28 atonement for you before *J*
23:33 *J* continued to speak to
23:34 booths for seven days to *J*
23:36 offering made by fire to *J*
23:36 offering made by fire to *J*
23:37 seasonal festivals of *J* that
23:37 offering made by fire to *J*
23:38 sabbaths of *J* and besides
23:38 which you should give to *J*
23:39 celebrate the festival of *J*
23:40 rejoice before *J* your God
23:41 festival to *J* seven days in
23:43 the land of Egypt. I am *J*
23:44 festivals of *J* to the sons of
24:1 *J* proceeded to speak to Moses
24:3 before *J* constantly
24:4 the lamps in order before *J*
24:6 the table of pure gold before *J*
24:7 offering made by fire to *J*
24:8 in order before *J* constantly
24:12 according to the saying of *J*
24:13 *J* proceeded to speak to
24:22 native, because I am *J* your
24:23 as *J* had commanded Moses
25:1 *J* spoke further to Moses in
25:2 must observe a sabbath to *J*
25:4 for the land, a sabbath to *J*

Le 25:17 not wrong anyone . . . I am *J*
25:38 *J* your God, who brought you
25:55 my slaves . . . I am *J* your
26:1 for I am *J* your God
26:2 stand in awe . . . I am *J*
26:13 *J* your God, who brought you
26:44 for I am *J* their God
26:45 I am *J*
26:46 *J* set between himself and
27:1 *J* continued to speak to Moses
27:2 offering of souls to *J*
27:9 one presents in offering to *J*
27:9 what he may give to *J* will
27:11 in offering to *J*, he must
27:14 as something holy to *J*, the
27:16 man would sanctify to *J*, the
27:21 holy to *J*, as a field that
27:22 if he sanctifies to *J* a field
27:23 It is something holy to *J*
27:26 firstborn for *J*, no man
27:26 or sheep, it belongs to *J*
27:28 devote to *J* for destruction
27:28 is something most holy to *J*
27:30 fruit . . . belongs to *J*
27:30 It is something holy to *J*
27:32 become something holy to *J*
27:34 *J* gave Moses as commands to
Nu 1:1 *J* proceeded to speak to Moses
1:19 *J* had commanded Moses; and
1:48 *J* spoke to Moses, saying
1:54 that *J* had commanded Moses
2:1 *J* now spoke to Moses and Aaron
2:33 just as *J* had commanded Moses
2:34 that *J* had commanded Moses
3:1 *J* spoke with Moses in Mount
3:4 Nadab and Abihu died before *J*
3:4 fire before *J* in the
3:5 *J* proceeded to speak to Moses
3:11 *J* continued to speak to Moses
3:13 firstborn is mine . . . I am *J*
3:14 *J* spoke further to Moses in
3:16 at the order of *J*, just
3:39 registered at the order of *J*
3:40 *J* said to Moses: Register all
3:41 Levites for me—I am *J*—in
3:42 as *J* had commanded him, to
3:44 *J* continued to speak to Moses
3:45 must become mine. I am *J*
3:51 according to the order of *J*
3:51 just as *J* had commanded Moses
4:1 *J* now spoke to Moses and Aaron
4:17 *J* spoke further to Moses and
4:21 *J* spoke to Moses, saying
4:37 registered at the order of *J*
4:41 registered at the order of *J*
4:45 order of *J* by means of Moses
4:49 At the order of *J* they were
4:49 just as *J* had commanded Moses
5:1 *J* spoke further to Moses
5:4 *J* had spoken to Moses, so the
5:5 *J* continued speaking to Moses
5:6 unfaithfulness against *J*, that
5:8 returned to *J* belongs to the
5:11 *J* went on to speak to Moses
5:16 make her stand before *J*
5:18 woman stand before *J* and
5:21 May *J* set you for a cursing
5:25 offering to and fro before *J*
5:30 wife stand before *J*, and the
6:1 And *J* spoke further to Moses
6:2 vow to live as a Nazirite to *J*
6:5 he should be separated to *J*
6:6 separate to *J* he may not come
6:8 Naziriteship he is holy to *J*
6:12 Nazirite to *J* for the days of
6:14 offering to *J* one sound young
6:16 present them before *J* and
6:17 communion sacrifice to *J*
6:20 as a wave offering before *J*
6:21 his offering to *J* over his
6:22 *J* spoke to Moses, saying
6:24 May *J* bless you and keep you
6:25 *J* make his face shine toward
6:26 *J* lift up his face toward you
7:3 their offering before *J*
7:4 At this *J* said to Moses
7:11 *J* said to Moses: One
8:1 *J* proceeded to speak to Moses
8:3 just as *J* had commanded Moses
8:4 vision that *J* had shown Moses
8:5 *J* spoke further to Moses
8:10 present the Levites before *J*
8:11 before *J* as a wave offering
8:11 carrying on the service of *J*

Nu 8:12 burnt offering to *J* to make
8:13 as a wave offering to *J*
8:20 that *J* had commanded Moses
8:21 as a wave offering before *J*
8:22 Just as *J* had commanded Moses
8:23 *J* now spoke to Moses, saying
9:1 *J* proceeded to speak to Moses
9:5 that *J* had commanded Moses
9:7 offering to *J* at its appointed
9:8 let me hear what *J* may command
9:9 Then *J* spoke to Moses, saying
9:10 passover sacrifice to *J*
9:13 offering of *J* he did not
9:14 the passover sacrifice to *J*
9:18 order of *J* the sons of Israel
9:18 order of *J* they would encamp
9:19 obligation to *J* that they
9:20 order of *J* they would remain
9:20 order of *J* they would pull
9:23 order of *J* they would encamp
9:23 order of *J* they would pull
9:23 kept their obligation to *J* at
9:23 order of *J* by means of Moses
10:1 *J* proceeded to speak to Moses
10:9 remembered before *J* your God
10:10 I am *J* your God
10:13 order of *J* by means of
10:29 *J* said, I shall give it to
10:29 *J* has spoken good concerning
10:32 *J* will do good with us, we
10:33 from the mountain of *J* for
10:35 arise, O *J*, and let your
10:36 return, O *J*, to the myriads
11:1 in the ears of *J*
11:1 *J* got to hear it, then his
11:1 fire of *J* began to blaze
11:2 made supplication to *J*, and
11:3 fire of *J* had blazed against
11:11 Moses said to *J*: Why have
11:16 *J* said to Moses: Gather for
11:18 have wept in the ears of *J*
11:18 *J* will certainly give you
11:20 because you rejected *J*, who
11:23 *J* said to Moses: The hand of
11:23 hand of *J* is cut short, is it?
11:24 to the people the words of *J*
11:25 *J* came down in a cloud and
11:29 *J* would put his spirit upon
11:31 wind burst forth from *J* and
11:33 *J* began striking at the
12:2 Moses alone that *J* has spoken
12:2 And *J* was listening
12:4 *J* suddenly said to Moses and
12:5 *J* came down in the pillar of
12:6 a prophet of yours for *J*
12:8 appearance of *J* is what he
12:13 Moses began to cry out to *J*
12:14 *J* said to Moses: Were her
13:1 *J* now spoke to Moses, saying
13:3 at the order of *J*. All the
14:3 why is *J* bringing us to this
14:8 If *J* has found delight in us
14:9 Only against *J* do not rebel
14:9 *J* is with us. Do not fear
14:11 *J* said to Moses: How long
14:13 Moses said to *J*: Then the
14:14 heard that you are *J* in
14:14 You are *J*, and your cloud is
14:17 your power become great, O *J*
14:18 *J*, slow to anger and
14:20 Then *J* said: I do forgive
14:21 filled with the glory of *J*
14:26 *J* went on to speak to Moses
14:28 utterance of *J*, if I shall
14:35 I *J* have spoken if this is
14:37 die by the scourge before *J*
14:40 the place that *J* mentioned
14:41 beyond the order of *J*
14:42 *J* is not in your midst, that
14:43 turned back from following *J*
14:43 *J* will not continue with you
15:1 And *J* spoke further to Moses
15:3 render up an offering . . . to *J*
15:3 to make a restful odor to *J*
15:4 present to *J* a grain offering
15:7 as a restful odor to *J*
15:8 or communion sacrifices to *J*
15:10 fire, of a restful odor to *J*
15:13 of a restful odor to *J*
15:14 of a restful odor to *J*, just
15:15 be the same as you before *J*
15:17 *J* went on to speak to Moses
15:19 make a contribution to *J*
15:21 contribution to *J* throughout

Nu 15:22 commandments, which *J* has
15:23 all that *J* has commanded you
15:23 the day that *J* commanded
15:24 for a restful odor to *J*, and
15:25 offering made by fire to *J*
15:25 sin offering before *J* for
15:28 sin unintentionally before *J*
15:30 he speaking abusively of *J*
15:35 *J* said to Moses: Without
15:36 as *J* had commanded Moses
15:37 And *J* went on to say this to
15:39 all the commandments of *J*
15:41 I am *J* your God, who have
15:41 I am *J* your God
16:3 and *J* is in their midst
16:3 above the congregation of *J*
16:5 In the morning *J* will make
16:7 incense upon them before *J*
16:7 the man whom *J* will choose
16:11 together are against *J*
16:15 Moses . . . said to *J:* Do not
16:16 be present before *J*, you and
16:17 his fire holder before *J*
16:20 *J* now spoke to Moses and
16:23 In turn *J* spoke to Moses
16:28 know that *J* has sent me to
16:29 then it is not *J* that has
16:30 created that *J* will create
16:30 treated *J* disrespectfully
16:35 a fire came out from *J* and
16:36 *J* now spoke to Moses, saying
16:38 they presented them before *J*
16:40 make incense smoke before *J*
16:40 just as *J* had spoken to him
16:44 *J* spoke to Moses, saying
16:46 gone out from the face of *J*
17:1 *J* now spoke to Moses, saying
17:7 deposited the rods before *J*
17:9 all the rods from before *J*
17:10 *J* said to Moses: Put Aaron's
17:11 just as *J* had commanded him
18:1 *J* proceeded to say to Aaron
18:6 those given to *J* to carry on
18:8 *J* spoke further to Aaron: As
18:12 which they will give to *J*, I
18:13 which they will bring to *J*
18:15 which they will present to *J*
18:17 fire for a restful odor to *J*
18:19 Israel will contribute to *J*
18:19 covenant of salt before *J* for
18:20 *J* went on to say to Aaron
18:24 will contribute to *J* as a
18:25 *J* spoke to Moses, saying
18:26 to *J* a tenth part of the
18:28 to *J* from all your tenth
18:28 the contribution to *J*
18:29 will contribute . . . to *J*
19:1 *J* proceeded to speak to Moses
19:2 the law that *J* has commanded
20:3 our brothers expired before *J*
20:7 Then *J* spoke to Moses, saying
20:9 took the rod from before *J*
20:12 *J* said to Moses and Aaron
20:13 Israel quarreled with *J*, so
20:16 we cried out to *J* and he
20:23 *J* said this to Moses and
20:27 did just as *J* had commanded
21:2 Israel made a vow to *J* and
21:3 *J* listened to Israel's voice
21:6 So *J* sent poisonous serpents
21:7 we have spoken against *J* and
21:7 Intercede with *J* that he may
21:8 *J* said to Moses: Make for
21:14 the book of the Wars of *J*
21:16 well about which *J* said to
21:34 *J* now said to Moses: Do not
22:8 just as *J* may speak to me
22:13 *J* has refused to let me go
22:18 to pass beyond the order of *J*
22:19 what . . . *J* will speak with
22:28 *J* opened the mouth of the
22:31 And *J* proceeded to uncover
23:3 Perhaps *J* will get in touch
23:5 *J* put a word in the mouth of
23:8 whom *J* has not denounced
23:12 whatever *J* may put in my
23:16 *J* got in touch with Balaam
23:17 What has *J* spoken?
23:21 *J* his God is with him, And
23:26 All that *J* will speak is
24:1 good in the eyes of *J* to bless
24:6 aloe plants that *J* has planted
24:11 *J* has held you back from
24:13 to pass beyond the order of *J*

Nu 24:13 Whatever *J* may speak is
25:3 the anger of *J* began to blaze
25:4 *J* said to Moses: Take all the
25:4 expose them to *J* toward the
25:4 that the burning anger of *J*
25:10 *J* spoke to Moses, saying
25:16 *J* spoke to Moses, saying
26:1 after the scourge, that *J*
26:4 as *J* had commanded Moses
26:9 in a struggle against *J*
26:52 *J* spoke to Moses, saying
26:61 illegitimate fire before *J*
26:65 *J* had said concerning them
27:3 ranged themselves against *J*
27:5 presented their case before *J*
27:6 *J* then said this to Moses
27:11 as *J* has commanded Moses
27:12 *J* said to Moses: Go up into
27:15 Moses spoke to *J*, saying
27:16 *J* the God of the spirits of
27:18 *J* said to Moses: Take for
27:21 the Urim before *J*
27:22 just as *J* had commanded him
27:23 commissioned him, just as *J*
28:1 And *J* spoke further to Moses
28:3 will present to *J:* two sound
28:6 an offering made by fire to *J*
28:7 the drink offering . . . to *J*
28:8 of a restful odor to *J*
28:11 as a burnt offering to *J* two
28:13 offering made by fire to *J*
28:15 sin offering to *J* in addition
28:19 a burnt offering to *J*, two
28:24 of a restful odor to *J*
28:26 a new grain offering to *J*
28:27 for a restful odor to *J* two
29:2 for a restful odor to *J* one
29:6 an offering made by fire to *J*
29:8 as a burnt offering to *J*, as a
29:12 celebrate a festival to *J*
29:13 of a restful odor to *J*
29:36 restful odor to *J*, one bull
29:39 you will render up to *J* at
29:40 that *J* had commanded Moses
30:1 This is the word that *J* has
30:2 case a man makes a vow to *J*
30:3 a woman makes a vow to *J*
30:5 *J* will forgive her, because
30:8 and *J* will forgive her
30:12 and *J* will forgive her
30:16 regulations that *J* commanded
31:1 *J* then spoke to Moses, saying
31:7 as *J* had commanded Moses
31:16 unfaithfulness toward *J* over
31:16 came upon the assembly of *J*
31:21 law that *J* commanded Moses
31:25 *J* proceeded to say this to
31:28 as a tax for *J* you must take
31:31 as *J* had commanded Moses
31:37 the tax for *J* from the flock
31:38 the tax on them for *J* was
31:39 the tax on them for *J* was
31:40 the tax on them for *J* was
31:41 as *J* had commanded Moses
31:47 as *J* had commanded Moses
31:50 make atonement . . . before *J*
31:52 contributed to *J* amounted to
31:54 as a memorial . . . before *J*
32:4 land that *J* defeated before
32:7 land that *J* will certainly
32:9 land that *J* was certain to
32:12 they have followed *J* wholly
32:13 doing evil in the eyes of *J*
32:14 anger of *J* against Israel
32:20 equip yourselves before *J* for
32:21 pass over the Jordan before *J*
32:22 is actually subdued before *J*
32:22 free from guilt against *J*
32:22 as a possession before *J*
32:23 also certainly sin against *J*
32:27 pass over . . . before *J* for
32:29 pass with you . . . before *J*
32:31 What *J* has spoken to your
32:32 pass over equipped before *J*
33:2 their stages at the order of *J*
33:4 those whom *J* had struck
33:4 *J* had executed judgments
33:38 at the order of *J* and to die
33:50 And *J* proceeded to speak to
34:1 And *J* spoke further to Moses
34:13 as *J* has commanded to give
34:16 And *J* spoke further to Moses
34:29 ones whom *J* commanded to
35:1 *J* went on to speak to Moses

Nu 35:9 *J* continued to speak to Moses
35:34 I *J* am residing in the midst
36:2 *J* commanded my lord to give
36:2 commanded by *J* to give the
36:5 at the order of *J*, saying
36:6 word that *J* has commanded
36:10 as *J* had commanded Moses
36:13 *J* commanded by means of
De 1:3 all that *J* had commanded him
1:6 *J* our God spoke to us in Horeb
1:8 land about which *J* swore to
1:10 *J* your God has multiplied you
1:11 *J* the God of your forefathers
1:19 as *J* our God had commanded
1:20 *J* our God is giving to us
1:21 *J* your God has abandoned the
1:21 *J* the God of your forefathers
1:25 land that *J* our God is giving
1:26 against the order of *J* your
1:27 was because *J* hated us that
1:30 *J* your God is the one going
1:31 *J* your God carried you just as
1:32 were not putting faith in *J*
1:34 *J* heard the voice of your
1:36 he has followed *J* fully
1:37 *J* got incensed on your account
1:41 We have sinned against *J*
1:41 *J* our God has commanded us
1:42 *J* said to me, Say to them
1:45, 45 weep before *J*, but *J* did
2:1 just as *J* had spoken to me
2:2 Finally *J* said this to me
2:7 *J* your God has blessed you in
2:7 forty years *J* your God has been
2:9 *J* then said to me, Do not
2:12 *J* will certainly give to them
2:14 just as *J* had sworn to them
2:15 the hand of *J* also proved to
2:17 *J* spoke further to me, saying
2:21 *J* went annihilating them from
2:29 land that *J* our God is giving
2:30 *J* your God had let his spirit
2:31 *J* said to me, See, I have
2:33 *J* our God abandoned him to us
2:36 *J* our God abandoned them all
2:37 *J* our God had given command
3:2 *J* said to me, Do not be afraid
3:3 *J* our God gave into our hand
3:18 *J* your God has given you this
3:20 *J* gives your brothers rest
3:20 land that *J* your God is giving
3:21 all that *J* your God has done
3:21 *J* will do to all the kingdoms
3:22 *J* your God is the One fighting
3:23 implore favor from *J* at that
3:24 *J*, you yourself have started
3:26 *J* continued to be furious
3:26 *J* said to me, That is enough
4:1 the land that *J* the God of
4:2 the commandments of *J* your
4:3 saw what *J* did in the case of
4:3 *J* your God annihilated from
4:4 cleaving to *J* your God are all
4:5 as *J* my God has commanded me
4:7 gods near to it the way *J* our
4:10 you stood before *J* your God in
4:10 *J* said to me, Congregate the
4:12 *J* began to speak to you out of
4:14 it was I whom *J* commanded
4:19 *J* your God has apportioned
4:20 the ones *J* took that he might
4:21 *J* got incensed at me on your
4:21 land that *J* your God is giving
4:23 not forget the covenant of *J*
4:23 *J* your God has commanded you
4:24 *J* your God is a consuming
4:25 commit evil in the eyes of *J*
4:27 *J* will certainly scatter you
4:27 *J* will drive you away
4:29 If you do look for *J* your God
4:30 return to *J* your God and to
4:31 *J* your God is a merciful God
4:34 all that *J* your God has done
4:35 *J* is the true God; there is
4:39 *J* is the true God in the
4:40 *J* your God is giving you
5:2 *J* our God concluded a covenant
5:3 *J* concluded this covenant, but
5:4 Face to face *J* spoke with you
5:5 standing between *J* and you at
5:5 to tell you the word of *J*
5:6 I am *J* your God, who brought
5:9 I *J* your God am a God exacting
5:11 *J* your God in a worthless way

De 5:11 *J* will not leave anyone
5:12 *J* your God commanded you
5:14 seventh day is a sabbath to *J*
5:15 *J* your God proceeded to bring
5:15 *J* your God commanded you to
5:16 *J* your God has commanded you
5:16 *J* your God is giving you
5:22 These Words *J* spoke to all
5:24 *J* our God has shown us his
5:25 again hearing the voice of *J*
5:27 all that *J* our God will say
5:27 all that *J* our God will speak
5:28 *J* heard the voice of your
5:28 *J* went on to say to me, I
5:32 *J* your God has commanded you
5:33 all the way that *J* your God
6:1 decisions that *J* your God has
6:2 fear *J* your God so as to keep
6:3 *J* the God of your forefathers
6:4, 4 Israel: *J* our God is one *J*
6:5 you must love *J* your God with
6:10 *J* your God will bring you
6:12 that you may not forget *J*
6:13 *J* your God you should fear
6:15 *J* your God in your midst is a
6:15 the anger of *J* your God may
6:16 not put *J* your God to the test
6:17 commandments of *J* your God
6:18 land about which *J* has
6:19 just as *J* has promised
6:20 *J* our God has commanded you
6:21 *J* proceeded to bring us out of
6:22 *J* kept putting signs and
6:24 *J* commanded us to carry out
6:24 to fear *J* our God for our good
6:25 before *J* our God, just as he
7:1 When *J* your God at last brings
7:2 *J* your God will certainly
7:6 you are a holy people to *J*
7:6 you *J* your God has chosen to
7:7 *J* showed affection for you so
7:8 *J* brought you out with a
7:9 *J* your God is the true God
7:12 *J* your God must keep toward
7:15 *J* will certainly remove from
7:16 whom *J* your God is giving to
7:18 remember what *J* your God did
7:19 *J* your God brought you out
7:19 the way *J* your God will do to
7:20 *J* your God will also send
7:21 *J* your God is in your midst
7:22 *J* your God will certainly
7:23 *J* your God will indeed
7:25 it is a thing detestable to *J*
8:1 *J* swore to your forefathers
8:2 *J* your God made you walk these
8:5 *J* your God was correcting you
8:6 keep the commandments of *J*
8:7 *J* your God is bringing you into
8:10 bless *J* your God for the good
8:11 not forget *J* your God so as
8:14 may indeed forget *J* your God
8:18 you must remember *J* your God
8:19 if you should at all forget *J*
8:20 nations that *J* is destroying
8:20 not listen to the voice of *J*
9:3 *J* your God is crossing before
9:3 just as *J* has spoken to you
9:4 *J* your God pushes them away
9:4 *J* has brought me in to take
9:4 *J* is driving them away from
9:5 *J* your God is driving them
9:5 *J* swore to your forefathers
9:6 *J* your God is giving you this
9:7 you have provoked *J* your God
9:7 in your behavior with *J*
9:8 you provoked *J* to anger so that
9:8 *J* got incensed at you to the
9:9 covenant that *J* had concluded
9:10 *J* gave me the two tablets of
9:10 the words that *J* had spoken
9:11 *J* gave me the two tablets of
9:12 *J* proceeded to say to me
9:13 *J* went on to say this to me
9:16 you had sinned against *J* your
9:16 which *J* had commanded you
9:18 prostrate myself before *J*
9:18 doing evil in the eyes of *J*
9:19 *J* had got indignant at you
9:19 *J* listened to me also that
9:20 *J* got very incensed to the
9:22 provokers of *J* to anger
9:23 when *J* sent you out of
9:23 against the order of *J*
De 9:24 rebellious in behavior with *J*
9:25 prostrating myself before *J*
9:25 *J* talked of annihilating you
9:26 to make supplication to *J*
9:26 Lord *J*, do not bring to ruin
9:28 *J* was unable to bring them
10:1 *J* said to me, Carve for
10:4 the Ten Words, which *J* had
10:4 tablets . . . *J* gave them to me
10:5 just as *J* had commanded me
10:8 *J* separated the tribe of Levi
10:8 before *J* for ministering
10:9 *J* is his inheritance, just
10:9 just as *J* your God had said
10:10 *J* proceeded to listen to me
10:10 *J* did not want to bring you
10:11 *J* said to me, Get up, go
10:12 what is *J* your God asking of
10:12 fear *J* your God, so as to
10:12 serve *J* your God with all
10:13 keep the commandments of *J*
10:14 to *J* your God belong the
10:15 did *J* get attached so as to
10:17 *J* your God is the God of
10:20 *J* your God you should fear
10:22 *J* your God has constituted
11:1 love *J* your God and keep your
11:2 not seen the discipline of *J*
11:4 *J* proceeded to destroy them
11:7 all the great deeds of *J*
11:9 the soil that *J* swore to
11:12 *J* your God is caring for
11:12 The eyes of *J* your God are
11:13 love *J* your God and to serve
11:17 land that *J* is giving you
11:21 *J* swore to your forefathers
11:22 to love *J* your God, to walk
11:23 *J* also must drive away all
11:25 the fear of you *J* your God
11:27 obey the commandments of *J*
11:28 commandments of *J* your God
11:29 when *J* your God brings you
11:31 the land that *J* your God is
12:1 in the land that *J* the God of
12:4 that way to *J* your God
12:5 *J* your God will choose out of
12:7 eat before *J* your God and
12:7 *J* your God has blessed you
12:9 *J* your God is giving you
12:10 the land that *J* your God is
12:11 the place that *J* your God
12:11 that you will vow to *J*
12:12 rejoice before *J* your God
12:14 the place that *J* will choose
12:15 the blessing of *J* your God
12:18 before *J* your God you will
12:18 in the place that *J* your God
12:18 rejoice before *J* your God
12:20 When *J* your God will widen
12:21 the place that *J* your God
12:21 flock that *J* has given you
12:26 the place that *J* will choose
12:27 upon the altar of *J* your God
12:27 against the altar of *J* your
12:28 right in the eyes of *J* your
12:29 *J* your God will cut off from
12:31 must not do that way to *J*
12:31 everything detestable to *J*
13:3 *J* your God is testing you to
13:3 whether you are loving *J*
13:4 After *J* your God you should
13:5 spoken of revolt against *J*
13:5 *J* your God has commanded you
13:10 to turn you away from *J*
13:12 *J* your God is giving you to
13:16 a whole offering to *J* your
13:17 *J* may turn from his burning
13:18 listen to the voice of *J*
13:18 right in the eyes of *J* your
14:1 Sons you are of *J* your God
14:2 you are a holy people to *J*
14:2 *J* has chosen you to become
14:21 you are a holy people to *J*
14:23 before *J* your God, in the
14:23 fear *J* your God always
14:24 the place that *J* your God
14:24 *J* your God will bless you
14:25 travel to the place that *J*
14:26 eat there before *J* your God
14:29 that *J* your God may bless
15:2 a release to *J* must be called
15:4 *J* will without fail bless you
15:4 the land that *J* your God is
15:5 listen to the voice of *J*
De 15:6 *J* your God will indeed bless
15:7 your land that *J* your God is
15:9 call out to *J* against you
15:10 on this account *J* your God
15:14 *J* your God has blessed you
15:15 *J* your God proceeded to
15:18 *J* your God has blessed you
15:19 should sanctify to *J* your God
15:20 Before *J* your God you should
15:20 the place that *J* will choose
15:21 must not sacrifice it to *J*
16:1 celebrate the passover to *J*
16:1 *J* your God brought you out of
16:2 sacrifice the passover to *J*
16:2 the place that *J* will choose
16:5 any one of your cities that *J*
16:6 *J* your God will choose to
16:7 the eating in the place that *J*
16:8 a solemn assembly to *J* your
16:10 festival of weeks to *J* your
16:10 *J* your God may bless you
16:11 must rejoice before *J* your
16:11 the place that *J* your God
16:15 celebrate the festival to *J*
16:15 the place that *J* will choose
16:15 *J* your God will bless you
16:16 should appear before *J* your
16:16 appear before *J* empty-handed
16:17 the blessing of *J* your God
16:18 *J* your God is giving you by
16:20 possession of the land that *J*
16:21 near the altar of *J* your
16:22 a thing *J* your God hates
17:1 You must not sacrifice to *J*
17:1 a thing detestable to *J* your
17:2 *J* your God is giving you
17:2 bad in the eyes of *J* your God
17:8 the place that *J* your God
17:10 place which *J* will choose
17:12 to minister there to *J* your
17:14 the land that *J* your God is
17:15 a king whom *J* your God will
17:16 *J* has said to you, You must
17:19 learn to fear *J* his God so as
18:1 the offerings made by fire of *J*
18:2 *J* is his inheritance, just as
18:5 the one whom *J* your God has
18:5 minister in the name of *J*
18:6 the place that *J* will choose
18:7 minister in the name of *J*
18:7 are standing there before *J*
18:9 the land that *J* your God is
18:12 something detestable to *J*
18:12 *J* your God is driving them
18:13 faultless with *J* your God
18:14 *J* your God has not given you
18:15 *J* your God will raise up
18:16 all that you asked of *J* your
18:16 hear again the voice of *J*
18:17 *J* said to me, They have done
18:21 the word that *J* has not
18:22 speaks in the name of *J* and
18:22 word that *J* did not speak
19:1 When *J* your God cuts off
19:1 *J* your God is giving you
19:2 land that *J* . . . is giving
19:3 your land that *J* your God
19:8 *J* your God widens out your
19:9 love *J* your God and to walk
19:10 land that *J* . . . is giving
19:14 the land that *J* . . . is giving
19:17 must also stand before *J*
20:1 *J* your God is with you, who
20:4 *J* your God is marching with
20:13 *J* your God also will
20:14 *J* your God has given to you
20:16 *J* your God is giving you as
20:17 *J* your God has commanded
20:18 sin against *J* your God
21:1 the ground that *J* your God is
21:5 the ones *J* your God has chosen
21:5 to bless in the name of *J*
21:8 Israel . . . you redeemed, O *J*
21:10 *J* your God has given them
21:23 soil, which *J* . . . is giving
22:5 detestable to *J* your God
23:1 into the congregation of *J*
23:2 into the congregation of *J*
23:2 into the congregation of *J*
23:3 into the congregation of *J*
23:3 into the congregation of *J*
23:5 *J* your God did not want to
23:5 *J* your God in your behalf
23:5 because *J* your God loved you

De 23:8 into the congregation of J
23:14 J your God is walking about
23:18 into the house of J your God
23:18 something detestable to J
23:20 J your God may bless you in
23:21 you vow a vow to J your God
23:21 J your God will without fail
23:23 vowed to J your God as a
24:4 something detestable before J
24:4 the land that J your God is
24:9 what J your God did to
24:13 for you before J your God
24:15 cry out to J against you
24:18 J your God proceeded to
24:19 J your God may bless you
25:15 that J your God is giving
25:16 detestable to J your God
25:19 J your God has given you rest
25:19 land that J . . . is giving
26:1 land that J your God is giving
26:2 the land of yours that J your
26:2 go to the place that J your
26:3 I must report today to J your
26:3 the land that J swore to our
26:4 before the altar of J
26:5 say before J your God
26:7 we began to cry out to J
26:7 J proceeded to hear our voice
26:8 J brought us out of Egypt
26:10 the ground that J has given
26:10 deposit it before J your
26:10 bow down before J your God
26:11 the good that J your God
26:13 you must say before J
26:14 listened to the voice of J
26:16 J your God is commanding you
26:17 J you have induced to say
26:18 As for J, he has induced you
26:19 a people holy to J your God
27:2 land that J your God is giving
27:3 land that J . . . is giving you
27:3 J the God of your forefathers
27:5 build an altar there to J
27:6 build the altar of J your God
27:6 offer burnt offerings to J
27:7 rejoice before J your God
27:9 the people of J your God
27:10 listen to the voice of J
27:15 a thing detestable to J
28:1 listen to the voice of J
28:1 J your God also will
28:2 listening to the voice of J
28:7 J will cause your enemies
28:8 J will decree for you the
28:8 land that J . . . is giving you
28:9 J will establish you as a
28:9 keep the commandments of J
28:11 J will also make you
28:11 the ground that J swore to
28:12 J will open up to you his
28:13 J will indeed put you at the
28:13 commandments of J your God
28:15 not listen to the voice of J
28:20 J will send upon you the
28:21 J will cause the pestilence
28:22 J will strike you with
28:24 J will give powder and dust
28:25 J will cause you to be
28:27 J will strike you with the
28:28 J will strike you with
28:35 J will strike you with a
28:36 J will march you and your
28:37 J will lead you away
28:45 listen to the voice of J
28:47 serve J your God with
28:48 J will send against you
28:49 J will raise up against you
28:52 J your God has given you
28:53 J your God has given you
28:58 name, even J, your God
28:59 J also will certainly make
28:61 J will bring them upon you
28:62 listen to the voice of J your
28:63 J exulted over you to do you
28:63 J will exult over you to
28:64 J will certainly scatter you
28:65 J will indeed give you there
28:68 J will certainly bring you
29:1 covenant that J commanded
29:2 that J did before your eyes
29:4 J has not given you a heart to
29:6 know that I am J your God
29:10 stationed today before J
29:12 enter into the covenant of J

De 29:12 J your God is concluding
29:15 with us today before J
29:18 turning today away from J
29:20 J will not want to forgive
29:20 J will indeed wipe out his
29:21 J will have to separate him
29:22 maladies with which J has
29:23 J overthrew in his anger and
29:24 Why did J do like this to
29:25 abandoned the covenant of J
29:28 J uprooted them from off
29:29 things concealed belong to J
30:1 J your God has dispersed you
30:2 you have returned to J your
30:3 J your God must also bring
30:3 J your God has scattered you
30:4 J your God will collect you
30:5 J your God will indeed bring
30:6 And J your God will have to
30:6 love J your God with all your
30:7 J your God will certainly put
30:8 voice of J and do all his
30:9 J your God will indeed make
30:9 J will again exult over you
30:10 listen to the voice of J
30:10 return to J your God with
30:16 commandments of J your God
30:16 so as to love J your God
30:16 J your God must bless you in
30:20 by loving J your God, by
30:20 upon the ground that J swore
31:2 J has said to me, You will
31:3 J your God is the one crossing
31:3 crossing before you, just as J
31:4 J will certainly do to them
31:5 J has abandoned them to you
31:6 J . . . is the one marching
31:7 into the land that J swore to
31:8 J is the one marching before
31:11 comes to see the face of J
31:12 fear J your God and take care
31:13 learn to fear J your God all
31:14 J said to Moses: Look! The
31:15 Then J appeared at the tent
31:16 J now said to Moses: Look!
31:26 ark of the covenant of J your
31:27 rebellious . . . toward J
31:29 what is bad in the eyes of J
32:3 I shall declare the name of J
32:6 Is it to J that you keep doing
32:12 J alone kept leading him
32:19 J saw it, then he came to
32:27 not J who worked all this
32:30 And J had surrendered them
32:36 For J will judge his people
32:48 J proceeded to speak to
33:2 J—from Sinai he came, And he
33:7 Hear, O J, the voice of Judah
33:11 Bless, O J, his vital energy
33:12 beloved one of J reside in
33:13 continually blessed from J
33:21 The righteousness of J will
33:23 And full of the blessing of J
33:29 enjoying salvation in J
34:1 J went showing him all the
34:4 And J went on to say to him
34:5 Moses the servant of J died
34:5 at the order of J
34:9 just as J had commanded Moses
34:10 Moses, whom J knew face to
34:11 miracles that J sent him to
Jos 1:1 Moses the servant of J that
1:1 J proceeded to say to Joshua
1:9 for J your God is with you
1:11 land that J your God is
1:13 that Moses the servant of J
1:13 J your God is giving you rest
1:15 when J gives rest to your
1:15 the land that J your God is
1:15 servant of J has given you on
1:17 may J your God prove to be
2:9 J will certainly give you the
2:10 how J dried up the waters of
2:11 J your God is God in the
2:12 please, swear to me by J
2:14 when J gives us the land, we
2:24 J has given all the land into
3:3 the ark of the covenant of J
3:5 J will do wonderful things
3:7 J proceeded to say to Joshua
3:9 listen to the words of J your
3:13 priests carrying the ark of J
4:1 J proceeded to say to Joshua
4:5 Pass ahead of the ark of J

Jos 4:8 just as J had stated to Joshua
4:10 that J had commanded Joshua
4:11 then the ark of J passed over
4:13 passed over before J for the
4:14 J made Joshua great in the
4:15 Then J said to Joshua
4:18 the ark of the covenant of J
4:23 when J your God dried up the
4:23 just as J your God had done
4:24 fear J your God always
5:1 J had dried up the waters
5:2 J said to Joshua: Make for
5:6 not listen to the voice of J
5:6 to whom J swore that he would
5:6 the land that J had sworn to
5:9 J said to Joshua: Today I
5:14 as prince of the army of J
5:15 prince of the army of J said
6:2 J went on to say to Joshua
6:6 horns before the ark of J
6:7 pass on ahead of the ark of J
6:8 seven rams' horns before J
6:8 the ark of the covenant of J
6:11 ark of J go marching round
6:12 went carrying the ark of J
6:13 horns before the ark of J
6:13 was following the ark of J
6:16 J has given you the city
6:17 that is in it belongs to J
6:19 are something holy to J
6:19 Into the treasure of J it
6:26 may the man be before J who
6:27 J proved to be with Joshua
7:6 before the ark of J until the
7:7 Sovereign Lord J, why did you
7:8 Excuse me, O J, but what can
7:10 In turn J said to Joshua
7:13 J the God of Israel has said
7:14 the tribe that J will pick
7:14 the family that J will pick
7:14 household that J will pick
7:15 overstepped the covenant of J
7:19 render, please, glory to J
7:20 sinned against J the God of
7:23 and poured them out before J
7:25 J will bring ostracism upon
7:26 At this J turned away from
8:1 Then J said to Joshua: Do not
8:7 J your God will certainly
8:18 J now said to Joshua
8:30 build an altar to J the God
8:31 Moses the servant of J had
8:31 burnt offerings upon it to J
8:33 the ark of the covenant of J
8:33 Moses the servant of J had
9:9 the name of J your God
9:14 of J they did not inquire
9:18 had sworn to them by J the
9:19 have sworn to them by J the
9:24 J your God had commanded
10:8 Then J said to Joshua: Do not
10:10 J went throwing them into
10:11 J hurled great stones from
10:12 to speak to J on the day of
10:14 J listened to the voice of
10:14 J himself was fighting for
10:19 J your God has given them
10:25 that J will do to all your
10:30 J gave it also and its king
10:32 J gave Lachish into Israel's
10:40 J the God of Israel had
10:42 J the God of Israel who was
11:6 J said to Joshua: Do not be
11:8 J gave them into Israel's
11:9 did to them just as J had said
11:12 Moses the servant of J had
11:15 as J had commanded Moses
11:15 all that J had commanded
11:20 as J had commanded Moses
11:23 that J had promised Moses
12:6 Moses the servant of J and
12:6 Moses the servant of J gave
13:1 J said to him: You yourself
13:8 Moses the servant of J had
13:14 of J the God of Israel are
13:33 J the God of Israel is
14:2 just as J had commanded by
14:5 as J had commanded Moses
14:6 word that J spoke to Moses
14:7 Moses the servant of J sent
14:8 I followed J my God fully
14:9 have followed J my God fully
14:10 J has preserved me alive
14:10 since J made this promise

Jos 14:12 that J promised on that day
14:12 Likely J will be with me
14:12 just as J promised
14:14 he followed J the God of
15:13 the order of J to Joshua
17:4 J it was who commanded
17:4 gave them, at the order of J
17:14 J has blessed me until now
18:3 J the God of your forefathers
18:6 for you before J our God
18:7 the priesthood of J is their
18:7 Moses the servant of J has
18:8 before J in Shiloh
18:10 in Shiloh before J
19:50 order of J they gave him
19:51 by lot in Shiloh before J
20:1 J spoke to Joshua, saying
21:2 J by means of Moses
21:3 at the order of J, these
21:8 J had commanded by means of
21:43 J gave Israel all the land
21:44 J gave them rest all around
21:44 All their enemies J gave
21:45 promise that J had made to
22:2 Moses the servant of J
22:3 commandment of J your God
22:4 J your God has given your
22:4 Moses the servant of J gave
22:5 servant of J commanded you
22:5 by loving J your God and by
22:9 settled at the order of J by
22:16 assembly of J have said
22:16 from following J by your
22:16 rebel today against J
22:17 upon the assembly of J
22:18 today from following J
22:18 rebel today against J, then
22:19 tabernacle of J has resided
22:19 against J do not you rebel
22:19 the altar of J our God
22:22 God, J, Divine One, God
22:22 God, J, he is knowing, and
22:22 unfaithfulness against J
22:23 turn back from following J
22:23 J himself will search out
22:24 with J the God of Israel
22:25 a boundary that J has put
22:25 You have no share in J
22:25 sons desist from fearing J
22:27 render the service of J
22:27 You have no share in J
22:29 to rebel . . . against J and
22:29 from following J by
22:29 besides the altar of J our
22:31 know that J is in our midst
22:31 not perpetrated against J
22:31 Israel out of the hand of J
22:34 that J is the true God
23:1 after J had given Israel
23:3 you have seen all that J
23:3 J your God was the one who
23:5 J your God was the one who
23:5 as J your God had promised
23:8 it is to J your God that you
23:9 J will drive away great and
23:10 J your God is the one who
23:11 souls by loving J your God
23:13 know that J your God will
23:13 ground that J your God has
23:14 good words that J your God
23:15 good word that J your God
23:15 J will bring upon you all
23:15 ground that J your God has
23:16 the covenant of J your God
24:2 This is what J the God of
24:7 they began to cry out to J
24:14 fear J and serve him in
24:14 and in Egypt, and serve J
24:15 to serve J, choose for
24:15 we shall serve J
24:16 to leave J so as to serve
24:17 J our God who brought us
24:18 J proceeded to drive out
24:18 we shall serve J, because
24:19 serve J, for he is a holy
24:20 leave J and you do serve
24:21 No, but J we shall serve
24:22 you . . . have chosen J
24:23 incline your hearts to J
24:24 J our God we shall serve
24:26 by the sanctuary of J
24:27 all the sayings of J that
24:29 Joshua . . . the servant of J
24:31 continued to serve J all

Jos 24:31 known all the work of J
Jg 1:1 proceeded to inquire of J
1:2 J said: Judah will go up
1:4 J gave the Canaanites and the
1:19 J continued with Judah, so
1:22 and J was with them
2:5 to sacrifice there to J
2:7 people continued to serve J
2:8 Joshua . . . the servant of J, died
2:10 that did not know J or the
2:11 bad in the eyes of J and
2:12 they abandoned J the God of
2:12 so that they offended J
2:13 they abandoned J and took up
2:15 the hand of J proved to be
2:15 just as J had spoken and just
2:15 just as J had sworn to them
2:16 J would raise up judges, and
2:17 the commandments of J
2:18 when J did raise up judges
2:18 J proved to be with the
2:18 for J would feel regret over
2:23 J let these nations stay by
3:1 nations that J let stay so as
3:7 and they were forgetful of J
3:9 Israel began to call to J for
3:9 J raised a savior up for the
3:10 The spirit of J now came
3:10 J gave Cushan-rishathaim the
3:12 J let Eglon the king of Moab
3:15 began to call to J for aid
3:15 So J raised up for them a
3:28 J has given your enemies
4:2 J sold them into the hand of
4:3 Israel began to cry out to J
4:6 Has not J the God of Israel
4:9 hand of a woman that J will
4:14 J will certainly give Sisera
4:14 J that has gone out before
4:15 J began to throw Sisera and
5:2 people's volunteering, Bless J
5:3 I to J, yes, I, will sing
5:3 I shall make melody to J
5:4 J, at your going forth from
5:5 from the face of J, This Sinai
5:5 the face of J, Israel's God
5:9 among the people. Bless J
5:11 the righteous acts of J, The
5:23 said the angel of J, Curse
5:23 come to the assistance of J
5:23 the assistance of J with the
5:31 all your enemies perish, O J
6:1 what was bad in the eyes of J
6:1 J gave them into the hand of
6:6 began to call to J for aid
6:7 Israel called to J for aid on
6:8 J proceeded to send a man, a
6:8 J the God of Israel has said
6:10 I am J your God. You must not
6:12 J is with you, you valiant
6:13 if J is with us, then why has
6:13 Egypt that J brought us up
6:13 now J has deserted us, and he
6:14 J faced him and said: Go in
6:15 Excuse me, J. With what shall
6:16 But J said to him: Because I
6:22 J, for the reason that I have
6:23 J said to him: Peace be yours
6:24 built an altar there to J, and
6:25 J went on to say to him: Take
6:26 build an altar to J your God
6:27 just as J had spoken to him
7:2 J now said to Gideon: The
7:4 J said to Gideon: There are yet
7:5 J said to Gideon: Every one
7:7 J now said to Gideon: By the
7:9 J proceeded to say to him
7:15 for J has given the camp of
7:22 J proceeded to set the sword
8:7 J gives Zebah and Zalmunna
8:19 As J lives, if you had
8:23 J is the one who will rule
8:34 did not remember J their God
10:6 bad in the eyes of J, and they
10:6 they left J and did not serve
10:10 to call to J for aid, saying
10:11 J said to the sons of Israel
10:15 Israel said to J: We have
10:16 and to serve J, so that his
11:9 J does abandon them to me
11:10 J prove to be the listener
11:11 his words before J in Mizpah
11:21 J the God of Israel gave
11:23 J the God of Israel it was

Jg 11:24 J our God has dispossessed
11:27 Let J the Judge judge today
11:30 Jephthah made a vow to J and
11:32 J proceeded to give them
11:35 I have opened my mouth to J
11:36 opened your mouth to J, do
11:36 since J has executed acts of
12:3 J gave them into my hand
13:1 J gave them into the hand of
13:8 Manoah began to entreat J and
13:8 and say: Excuse me, J
13:16 a burnt offering to J, you
13:19 offer it upon the rock to J
13:23 If J had been delighted only
13:24 and J continued to bless him
14:4 that was from J, that he was
15:18 he began to call on J and say
16:20 J that had departed from him
16:28 Samson now called to J and
16:28 J, remember me, please, and
17:2 Blessed may my son be of J
17:3 sanctify the silver to J from
17:13 J will do me good, because
18:6 before J that your way is in
20:1 to J at Mizpah
20:18 J said: Judah in the lead
20:23 and wept before J until the
20:23 and inquired of J, saying
20:23 J said: Go up against him
20:26 sat there before J and fasted
20:26 communion offerings before J
20:27 sons of Israel inquired of J
20:28 J said: Go up, because
20:35 And J proceeded to defeat
21:3 Why, O J the God of Israel
21:5 up in the congregation to J
21:5 not come up to J at Mizpah
21:7 sworn by J not to give them
21:8 not come up to J at Mizpah
21:15 J had made a rupture between
21:19 There is a festival of J
Ru 1:6 J had turned his attention to
1:8 May J exercise loving-kindness
1:9 May J make a gift to you, and
1:13 hand of J has gone out against
1:17 May J do so to me and add to
1:21 empty-handed that J has made
1:21 is J that has humiliated me
2:4 J be with you
2:4 would say to him: J bless you
2:12 May J reward the way you act
2:12 a perfect wage for you from J
2:20 Blessed be he of J, who has
3:10 Blessed may you be of J, my
3:13 I myself, as sure as J lives
4:11 May J grant the wife who is
4:12 offspring that J will give
4:13 J granted her conception and
4:14 Blessed be J, who has not let
1Sa 1:3 sacrifice to J of armies in
1:3 sons of Eli . . . priests to J
1:5 J, he had closed up her womb
1:6 J had closed up her womb
1:7 went up into the house of J
1:9 doorpost of the temple of J
1:10 she began to pray to J and to
1:11 O J of armies, if you will
1:11 give him to J all the days
1:12 prayed extendedly before J
1:15 I pour out my soul before J
1:19 prostrated . . . before J
1:19 and J began remembering her
1:20 from J that I have asked him
1:21 to sacrifice to J the yearly
1:22 he must appear before J and
1:23 may J carry out his word
1:24 the house of J in Shiloh
1:26 in this place to pray to J
1:27 I prayed that J should grant
1:28 I . . . have lent him to J
1:28 he is one requested for J
1:28 to bow down there to J
2:1 My heart does exult in J
2:1 horn is indeed exalted in J
2:2 There is no one holy like J
2:3 For a God of knowledge J is
2:6 J is a Killer and a Preserver
2:7 J is an Impoverisher and an
2:8 to J belong earth's supports
2:10 As for J, those contending
2:10 J himself will judge the
2:11 a minister of J before Eli
2:12 they did not acknowledge J
2:17 sin . . . very great before J

2Sa 2:1 *J* said to him: Go up
2:5 Blessed may you be of *J*
2:6 may *J* exercise toward you
3:9 just as *J* swore to David
3:18 *J* himself said to David
3:28 standpoint of *J*, are innocent
3:39 *J* repay the doer of what is
4:8 *J* gives to my lord the king
4:9 As *J* who redeemed my soul
5:2 *J* proceeded to say to you
5:3 with them in Hebron before *J*
5:10 *J* the God of armies was
5:12 *J* had firmly established him
5:19 David began to inquire of *J*
5:19 *J* said to David: Go up, for
5:20 *J* has broken through my
5:23 David inquired of *J*, but he
5:24 *J* will have gone out ahead
5:25 as *J* had commanded him, and
6:2 name of *J* of armies, sitting
6:5 were celebrating before *J*
6:8 *J* had broken through in a
6:9 David became afraid of *J* on
6:9 How will the ark of *J* come to
6:10 remove the ark of *J* to him
6:11 ark of *J* kept dwelling at
6:11 *J* kept blessing Obed-edom
6:12 *J* has blessed the house of
6:13 carriers of the ark of *J* had
6:14 dancing around before *J* with
6:15 bringing up the ark of *J*
6:16 ark of *J* came into the city
6:16 and dancing around before *J*
6:17 ark of *J* in and set it in
6:17 sacrifices before *J*
6:18 in the name of *J* of armies
6:21 *J*, who chose me rather than
6:21 I will celebrate before *J*
7:1 *J* himself had given him rest
7:3 because *J* is with you
7:4 word of *J* came to Nathan
7:5 *J* has said: Should you
7:8 *J* of armies has said: I
7:11 *J* has told you that a house
7:11 house is what *J* will make
7:18 sat down before *J* and said
7:18 am I, O Sovereign Lord *J*
7:19 *J*, yet you also speak
7:19 mankind, O Sovereign Lord *J*
7:20 know your servant . . . Lord *J*
7:22 great, O Sovereign Lord *J*
7:24 *J*, have become their God
7:25 *J* God, the word that you
7:26 *J* of armies is God over
7:27 *J* of armies the God of
7:28 O Sovereign Lord *J*, you are
7:29 Sovereign Lord *J* . . . promised
8:6 *J* continued to save David
8:11 King David sanctified to *J*
8:14 *J* kept saving David wherever
10:12 *J*, he will do what is good
11:27 bad in the eyes of *J*
12:1 *J* proceeded to send Nathan
12:5 As *J* is living, the man
12:7 *J* the God of Israel has said
12:9 despise the word of *J* by
12:11 *J* has said, Here I am
12:13 I have sinned against *J*
12:13 *J*, in turn, does let your
12:14 treated *J* with disrespect
12:15 *J* proceeded to deal a blow
12:20 came to the house of *J* and
12:22 *J* may show me favor, and
12:24 *J* himself did love him
12:25 Jedidiah, for the sake of *J*
14:11 remember *J* your God, that
14:11 As *J* is living, not a single
14:17 *J* your God himself prove to
15:7 my vow that I . . . made to *J*
15:8 If *J* will without fail bring
15:8 also render service to *J*
15:20 may *J* exercise toward you
15:21 *J* is living and as my lord
15:25 favor in the eyes of *J*
15:31 into foolishness, O *J*
16:8 *J* has brought back upon you
16:8 *J* gives the kingship into the
16:10 *J* himself has said to him
16:11 for *J* has said so to him
16:12 *J* will see with his eye
16:12 *J* will actually restore to
16:18 the one whom *J* has chosen
17:14 *J* himself had given
17:14 *J* might bring calamity upon

2Sa 18:19 *J* has judged him to free
18:28 Blessed be *J* your God, who
18:31 *J* has judged you today to
19:7 by *J*, I do swear that, in
19:21 down upon the anointed of *J*
20:19 the inheritance of *J*
21:1 consult the face of *J*
21:1 *J* said: Upon Saul and upon
21:3 bless the inheritance of *J*
21:6 expose them to *J* in Gibeah
21:6 Saul, the chosen one of *J*
21:7 on account of the oath of *J*
21:9 on the mountain before *J*
22:1 speak to *J* the words of this
22:1 *J* had delivered him out of
22:2 *J* is my crag and my
22:4 *J*, I shall call, And from
22:7 I kept calling upon *J*, And
22:14 *J* began to thunder, And the
22:16 At the rebuke of *J*, from the
22:19 But *J* became my support
22:21 *J* rewards me according to
22:22 I have kept the ways of *J*
22:25 let *J* repay me according
22:29 For you are my lamp, O *J*
22:29 *J* that makes . . . shine
22:31 The saying of *J* is a refined
22:32 For who is a God besides *J*
22:42 They cry for help . . . To *J*
22:47 *J* is living; and blessed be
22:50 I shall thank you, O *J*
23:2 spirit of *J* it was that
23:10 *J* performed a great
23:12 so that *J* performed a great
23:16 but poured it out to *J*
23:17 unthinkable on my part, O *J*
24:1 anger of *J* came to be hot
24:3 *J* your God even add to the
24:10 David said to *J*: I have
24:10 *J*, let your servant's error
24:12 This is what *J* has said
24:14 into the hand of *J*, for
24:15 *J* gave a pestilence in
24:16 *J* began to feel regret over
24:17 David proceeded to say to *J*
24:18 set up for *J* an altar on
24:19 what *J* had commanded
24:21 for building an altar to *J*
24:23 *J* your God show pleasure
24:24 offer up to *J* my God burnt
24:25 build there an altar to *J*
24:25 *J* began letting himself
1Ki 1:17 it was you that swore by *J*
1:29 As *J* is living who redeemed
1:30 I have sworn to you by *J*
1:36 may *J* the God of my lord the
1:37 *J* proved to be with my lord
1:48 Blessed be *J* the God of
2:3 keep the obligation to *J*
2:4 *J* may carry out his word that
2:8 I swore to him by *J*, saying
2:15 from *J* that it became his
2:23 Solomon swore by *J*, saying
2:24 as *J* is living who has
2:26 ark of the Sovereign Lord *J*
2:27 serving as a priest of *J*
2:28 fleeing to the tent of *J*
2:29 has fled to the tent of *J*
2:30 came to the tent of *J*
2:32 *J* will certainly bring back
2:33 come to be peace . . . from *J*
2:42 put you under oath by *J*
2:43 not keep the oath of *J* and
2:44 *J* will certainly return the
2:45 established before *J* forever
3:1 house of *J* and Jerusalem's
3:2 been built to the name of *J*
3:3 Solomon continued to love *J*
3:5 *J* appeared to Solomon in a
3:7 *J* my God, you yourself have
3:10 pleasing in the eyes of *J*
3:15 ark of the covenant of *J*
5:3 a house to the name of *J*
5:3 *J* put them under the soles of
5:4 *J* my God has given me rest
5:5 a house to the name of *J*
5:5 just as *J* promised to David
5:7 Blessed is *J* today in that he
5:12 And *J*, for his part, gave
6:1 to build the house to *J*
6:2 house . . . Solomon built to *J*
6:11 word of *J* came to Solomon
6:19 the ark of the covenant of *J*
6:37 fourth year the house of *J*

1Ki 7:12 courtyard of the house of *J*
7:40 as respects the house of *J*
7:45 for the house of *J*
7:48 pertained to the house of *J*
7:51 as regards the house of *J*
7:51 treasures of the house of *J*
8:1 the ark of the covenant of *J*
8:4 bringing up the ark of *J*
8:6 ark of the covenant of *J* to
8:9 *J* had covenanted with the
8:10 filled the house of *J*
8:11 glory of *J* filled the house
8:11 filled the house of *J*
8:12 *J* himself said he was to
8:15 Blessed is *J* the God of
8:17 a house to the name of *J*
8:18 *J* said to David my father
8:20 *J* proceeded to carry out his
8:20 just as *J* had spoken, and
8:20 the house to the name of *J*
8:21 Ark where the covenant of *J*
8:22 the altar of *J* in front of
8:23 *J* the God of Israel, there
8:25 O *J* the God of Israel, keep
8:28 his request for favor, O *J*
8:44 pray to *J* in the direction of
8:53 Egypt, O Sovereign Lord *J*
8:54 finished praying to *J* with
8:54 from before the altar of *J*
8:56 Blessed be *J*, who has given
8:57 *J* our God prove to be with
8:59 request for favor before *J*
8:59 near to *J* our God by day and
8:60 know that *J* is the true God
8:61 prove to be complete with *J*
8:62 a grand sacrifice before *J*
8:63 that he had to offer to *J*
8:63 inaugurate the house of *J*
8:64 that is before the house of *J*
8:64 copper altar that is before *J*
8:65 before *J* our God seven days
8:66 goodness that *J* had performed
9:1 building the house of *J* and
9:2 *J* appeared to Solomon the
9:3 *J* went on to say to him
9:8 *J* do like that to this land
9:9 the reason that they left *J*
9:9 *J* brought upon them all this
9:10 the house of *J* and the house
9:15 to build the house of *J* and
9:25 altar that he had built for *J*
9:25 altar, which was before *J*
10:1 with the name of *J*
10:5 offered up at the house of *J*
10:9 May *J* your God come to be
10:9 *J* loves Israel to time
10:12 supports for the house of *J*
11:2 *J* had said to the sons of
11:4 not . . . complete with *J*
11:6 was bad in the eyes of *J*
11:6 did not follow *J* fully like
11:9 *J* came to be incensed at
11:9 had inclined away from *J*
11:10 which *J* had commanded
11:11 *J* now said to Solomon
11:14 And *J* began to raise up a
11:31 *J* the God of Israel has
12:15 at the instance of *J*
12:15 word that *J* had spoken by
12:24 This is what *J* has said
12:24 obeyed the word of *J*, and
12:24 according to the word of *J*
12:27 sacrifices in the house of *J*
13:1 by the word of *J*
13:2 by the word of *J* and said
13:2 *J* has said, Look! A son born
13:3 the portent of which *J* has
13:5 had given by the word of *J*
13:6 Soften, please, the face of *J*
13:6 softened the face of *J*, so
13:9 by the word of *J*, saying
13:17 to me by the word of *J*
13:18 by the word of *J*, saying
13:20 the word of *J* came to the
13:21 This is what *J* has said
13:21 against the order of *J* and
13:21 *J* your God commanded you
13:26 against the order of *J*
13:26 so *J* gave him to the lion
13:26 the word of *J* that he spoke
13:32 word of *J* against the altar
14:5 *J* himself had said to Ahijah
14:7 *J* the God of Israel has said
14:11 *J* himself has spoken it

1Ki 14:13 good toward *J* the God of
14:14 *J* will certainly raise up
14:15 *J* will indeed strike Israel
14:15 sacred poles, so offending *J*
14:21 the city that *J* had chosen
14:22 was bad in the eyes of *J*
14:24 whom *J* had driven out from
14:26 treasures of the house of *J*
14:28 king came to the house of *J*
15:3 heart . . . complete with *J*
15:4 *J* his God gave him a lamp in
15:5 was right in the eyes of *J*
15:11 right in the eyes of *J*
15:14 heart . . . complete with *J*
15:15 into the house of *J*
15:18 treasures of the house of *J*
15:26 was bad in the eyes of *J*
15:30 he offended *J* the God of
15:34 was bad in the eyes of *J*
16:1 word of *J* now came to Jehu
16:7 committed in the eyes of *J*
16:12 the word of *J* that he had
16:13 sin by offending *J* the God
16:19 was bad in the eyes of *J*
16:25 was bad in the eyes of *J*
16:26 *J* the God of Israel
16:30 do worse in the eyes of *J*
16:33 offend *J* the God of Israel
17:1 as *J* the God of Israel
17:2 word of *J* now came to him
17:5 according to the word of *J*
17:8 word of *J* now came to him
17:12 As *J* your God is living, I
17:14 *J* the God of Israel has said
17:20 calling to *J* and saying
17:20 O *J* my God, is it also upon
17:21 and call to *J* and say
17:21 O *J* my God, please, cause
17:22 *J* listened to Elijah's voice
18:3 to be one greatly fearing *J*
18:10 As *J* your God is living
18:12 the spirit of *J* itself will
18:12 has feared *J* from his youth
18:13 killed the prophets of *J*
18:13 the prophets of *J* hid
18:15 As *J* of armies before whom
18:18 left the commandments of *J*
18:21 If *J* is the true God, go
18:22 been left as a prophet of *J*
18:24 call upon the name of *J*
18:30 to mend the altar of *J* that
18:32 in the name of *J* and to
18:36 O *J*, the God of Abraham
18:37 O *J*, answer me, that this
18:37 you, *J*, are the true God
18:38 fire of *J* came falling and
18:39 *J* is the true God!
18:39 *J* is the true God!
18:46 hand of *J* proved to be upon
19:4 O *J*, take my soul away, for
19:7 the angel of *J* came back a
19:10 absolutely jealous for *J*
19:11 on the mountain before *J*
19:11 And, look! *J* was passing by
19:11 and breaking crags before *J*
19:11 *J* was not in the wind
19:11 *J* was not in the quaking
19:12 *J* was not in the fire
19:14 absolutely jealous for *J*
19:15 *J* now said to him: Go
20:13 This is what *J* has said
20:13 certainly know that I am *J*
20:14 This is what *J* has said
20:28 This is what *J* has said
20:28 *J* is a God of mountains
20:28 certainly know that I am *J*
20:35 *J*: Strike me, please
20:36 not listen to the voice of *J*
20:42 This is what *J* has said
21:19 *J* has said: Have you
21:19 This is what *J* has said
21:20 is bad in the eyes of *J*
21:23 regards Jezebel *J* has spoken
21:25 was bad in the eyes of *J*
21:26 whom *J* drove out from
22:5 for the word of *J*
22:6 Go up, and *J* will give it
22:7 here a prophet of *J* still
22:8 through whom to inquire of *J*
22:11 This is what *J* has said
22:12 *J* will certainly give it
22:14 As *J* is living, what
22:14 what *J* will say to me
22:15 *J* will certainly give it

1Ki 22:16 truth in the name of *J*
22:17 *J* went on to say: These
22:19 hear the word of *J*
22:19 *J* sitting upon his throne
22:20 *J* proceeded to say, Who
22:21 stood before *J* and said
22:21 At that *J* said to him
22:23 *J* has put a deceptive spirit
22:23 *J* himself has spoken
22:24 did the spirit of *J* pass
22:28 *J* has not spoken with me
22:43 was right in the eyes of *J*
22:53 kept offending *J* the God of
2Ki 1:3 angel of *J*, he spoke to Elijah
1:4 *J* has said: As regards the
1:6 This is what *J* has said
1:15 angel of *J* spoke to Elijah
1:16 This is what *J* has said
1:17 word of *J* that Elijah had
2:1 *J* was to take Elijah in a
2:2 *J* himself has sent me clear
2:2 Elisha said: As *J* is living
2:3 today *J* is taking your master
2:4 *J* himself has sent me to
2:4 As *J* is living and as your
2:5 *J* is taking your master from
2:6 *J* himself has sent me to the
2:6 As *J* is living and as your
2:14 Where is *J* the God of Elijah
2:16 spirit of *J* has lifted him
2:21 *J* has said, I do make this
2:24 evil . . . in the name of *J*
3:10 *J* has called these three
3:11 not here a prophet of *J*
3:11 inquire of *J* through him
3:12 word of *J* exists with him
3:13 *J* has called these three
3:14 As *J* of armies before whom
3:15 hand of *J* came to be upon
3:16 *J* has said, Let there be a
3:17 this is what *J* has said
3:18 trivial . . . in the eyes of *J*
4:1 continually feared *J*, and the
4:27 *J* himself has hidden it from
4:30 As *J* is living and as your
4:33 and began to pray to *J*
4:43 for this is what *J* has said
4:44 according to the word of *J*
5:1 *J* had given salvation to Syria
5:11 call upon the name of *J* his
5:16 As *J* before whom I do stand
5:17 to any other gods but to *J*
5:18 may *J* forgive your servant
5:18 may *J*, please, forgive your
5:20 As *J* is living, I will run
6:17 O *J*, open his eyes, please
6:17 *J* opened the attendant's eyes
6:18 Elisha went on to pray to *J*
6:20 O *J*, open the eyes of these
6:20 *J* opened their eyes, and they
6:27 If *J* does not save you
6:33 this is the calamity from *J*
6:33 I wait any longer for *J*
7:1 word of *J*. This is what
7:1 what *J* has said, Tomorrow
7:2 If *J* were making floodgates
7:6 *J* himself had caused the camp
7:16 according to the word of *J*
7:19 if *J* were making floodgates
8:1 *J* has called for a famine
8:8 must inquire of *J* through him
8:10 and *J* has shown me that he
8:13 *J* has shown me you as king
8:19 *J* did not want to bring
9:3 This is what *J* has said
9:6 *J* the God of Israel has said
9:7 blood of all the servants of *J*
9:12 This is what *J* has said
9:25 *J* himself lifted up this
9:26 is the utterance of *J*
9:26 is the utterance of *J*
9:26 according to the word of *J*
9:36 It is the word of *J* that
10:10 *J* has spoken against the
10:10 *J* himself has done what he
10:16 of no rivalry toward *J*
10:23 none of the worshipers of *J*
10:30 *J* said to Jehu: For the
10:31 law of *J* the God of Israel
10:32 *J* started to cut off Israel
11:3 at the house of *J* in hiding
11:4 house of *J* and concluded a
11:4 swear at the house of *J*
11:7 watch over the house of *J*

2Ki 11:10 were in the house of *J*
11:13 people at the house of *J*
11:15 in the house of *J*
11:17 between *J* and the king and
11:17 themselves the people of *J*
11:18 over the house of *J*
11:19 from the house of *J*
12:4 is brought to the house of *J*
12:4 to bring to the house of *J*
12:9 comes into the house of *J*
12:9 brought into the house of *J*
12:10 found at the house of *J*
12:11 appointed to the house of *J*
12:11 working at the house of *J*
12:12 the cracks of the house of *J*
12:13 as respects the house of *J*
12:13 brought to the house of *J*
12:14 they repaired the house of *J*
12:16 brought to the house of *J*
12:18 treasures of the house of *J*
13:4 softened the face of *J*
13:4 so that *J* listened to him
13:5 *J* gave Israel a savior
13:23 *J* showed them favor and had
14:6 *J* gave in command, saying
14:14 found at the house of *J*
14:25 word of *J* the God of Israel
14:26 *J* had seen the very bitter
14:27 *J* had promised not to wipe
15:5 Finally *J* plagued the king
15:35 gate of the house of *J*
15:37 *J* started to send against
16:2 eyes of *J* his God like David
16:3 whom *J* drove out because of
16:8 found at the house of *J*
16:14 altar that was before *J*
16:14 altar and the house of *J*
16:18 from the house of *J*
17:7 Israel had sinned against *J*
17:8 whom *J* had driven out from
17:9 not right toward *J* their God
17:11 *J* had taken into exile
17:11 bad things to offend *J*
17:12 which *J* had said to them
17:13 *J* kept warning Israel and
17:14 not exercised faith in *J*
17:15 *J* had commanded them not
17:16 commandments of *J* their God
17:17 was bad in the eyes of *J*
17:18 *J* got very incensed against
17:19 commandments of *J* their God
17:20 *J* rejected all the seed of
17:21 Israel from following *J*
17:23 *J* removed Israel from his
17:25 that they did not fear *J*
17:25 *J* sent lions among them
17:28 how they ought to fear *J*
17:32 came to be fearers of *J*
17:33 *J* that they became fearers
17:34 none fearing *J* and none
17:34 *J* had commanded the sons
17:35 *J* concluded a covenant with
17:36 *J*, who brought you up out
17:39 *J* your God that you should
17:41 came to be fearers of *J*
18:5 In *J* the God of Israel he
18:6 And he kept sticking to *J*
18:6 that *J* had commanded Moses
18:7 *J* proved to be with him
18:12 the voice of *J* their God
18:12 Moses the servant of *J* had
18:15 found at the house of *J*
18:16 doors of the temple of *J*
18:22 It is *J* our God in whom we
18:25 authorization from *J*
18:25 *J* himself said to me, Go up
18:30 cause you to trust in *J*
18:30 *J* will deliver us, and this
18:32 *J* himself will deliver us
18:35 *J* should deliver Jerusalem
19:1 came into the house of *J*
19:4 Perhaps *J* your God will hear
19:4 words that *J* your God has
19:6 *J* has said: Do not be afraid
19:14 went up to the house of *J*
19:14 and spread it out before *J*
19:15 to pray before *J* and say
19:15 say: O *J* the God of Israel
19:16 Incline your ear, O *J*, and
19:16 Open your eyes, O *J*, and see
19:17 It is a fact, O *J*, the kings
19:19 O *J* our God, save us, please
19:19 that you, O *J*, are God alone
19:20 *J* the God of Israel has said

2Ki 19:21 *J* has spoken against him
19:23 you have taunted *J* and you
19:31 very zeal of *J* of armies
19:32 this is what *J* has said
19:33 is the utterance of *J*
19:35 the angel of *J* proceeded to
20:1 *J* has said, Give commands
20:2 began to pray to *J*, saying
20:3 I beseech you, O *J*, remember
20:5 *J* the God of David your
20:5 will go up to the house of *J*
20:8 the sign that *J* will heal me
20:8 third day to the house of *J*
20:9 is the sign for you from *J*
20:9 *J* will perform the word
20:11 began to call out to *J*
20:16 Hear the word of *J*
20:17 Nothing will be left, *J* has
20:19 The word of *J* that you have
21:2 nations that *J* had driven
21:4 altars in the house of *J*
21:4 respecting which *J* had said
21:5 courtyards of the house of *J*
21:7 in the house of which *J* had
21:9 whom *J* had annihilated
21:10 *J* kept speaking by means
21:12 *J* the God of Israel has said
21:16 was bad in the eyes of *J*
21:22 he left *J* the God of his
21:22 not walk in the way of *J*
22:3 secretary to the house of *J*
22:4 brought into the house of *J*
22:5 in the house of *J*
22:5 house of *J* to repair the
22:8 found in the house of *J*
22:9 appointed, in the house of *J*
22:13 inquire of *J* in my own
22:15 *J* the God of Israel has said
22:16 This is what *J* has said
22:18 sending you to inquire of *J*
22:18 *J* the God of Israel has said
22:19 humbled . . . because of *J*
22:19 heard, is the utterance of *J*
23:2 went up to the house of *J*
23:2 found in the house of *J*
23:3 the covenant before *J*
23:3 to walk after *J* and to keep
23:4 out from the temple of *J*
23:6 from the house of *J* to the
23:7 were in the house of *J*
23:9 altar of *J* in Jerusalem
23:11 entering the house of *J*
23:12 the house of *J*, the king
23:21 Hold a passover to *J* your
23:23 this passover was held to *J*
23:24 found at the house of *J*
23:25 to *J* with all his heart and
23:26 *J* did not turn back from
23:27 *J* said: Judah, too, I shall
24:2 *J* began to send against him
24:3 only by the order of *J* that
24:4 *J* did not consent to grant
24:13 treasures of the house of *J*
24:13 made in the temple of *J*
24:13 just as *J* had spoken
24:20 on account of the anger of *J*
25:9 to burn the house of *J* and
25:13 were in the house of *J*
25:13 were in the house of *J*
25:16 made for the house of *J*
1Ch 2:3 to be bad in the eyes of *J*
6:15 went away when *J* took Judah
6:31 the singing at the house of *J*
6:32 the house of *J* in Jerusalem
9:19 fathers over the camp of *J*
9:20 Phinehas . . . *J* was with him
9:23 gatekeepers of the house of *J*
10:13 acted faithlessly against *J*
10:13 word of *J* that he had not
10:14 And he did not inquire of *J*
11:2 *J* your God proceeded to say
11:3 a covenant . . . before *J*
11:9 *J* of armies was with him
11:14 *J* saved with a great
11:18 but poured it out to *J*
13:2 is acceptable with *J* our God
13:6 *J*, sitting on the cherubs
13:11 *J* had broken through in
13:14 and *J* kept blessing the
14:2 *J* had firmly established him
14:10 *J* said to him: Go up, and I
14:17 *J* himself put the dread of
15:2 *J* has chosen to carry the ark
15:2 chosen to carry the ark of *J*

1Ch 15:3 to bring the ark of *J* up to
15:12 you must bring the ark of *J*
15:13 *J* our God broke through
15:14 to bring up the ark of *J* the
15:25 the ark of the covenant of *J*
15:26 the ark of the covenant of *J*
15:28 the ark of the covenant of *J*
15:29 the ark of the covenant of *J*
16:2 bless . . . in the name of *J*
16:4 he put before the ark of *J*
16:4 to thank and praise *J* the God
16:7 to thank *J* by means of Asaph
16:8 Give thanks to *J*, you people
16:10 of those seeking *J* rejoice
16:11 Search after *J* and his
16:14 He is *J* our God; in all the
16:23 Sing to *J*, all you of the
16:25 *J* is great and very much to
16:26 *J*, he made the heavens
16:28 Attribute to *J*, O families
16:28 Attribute to *J* glory and
16:29 Attribute to *J* the glory of
16:29 Bow down to *J* in holy
16:31 *J* himself has become king
16:33 joyfully on account of *J*
16:34 Give thanks to *J*, you
16:36 Blessed be *J* the God of
16:36 Amen! and a praise to *J*
16:37 the ark of the covenant of *J*
16:39 before the tabernacle of *J*
16:40 burnt offerings to *J* on the
16:40 is written in the law of *J*
16:41 thank *J*, because to time
17:1 the ark of the covenant of *J*
17:4 *J* has said: It will not be
17:7 is what *J* of armies has said
17:10 house *J* will build for you
17:16 sat down before *J* and said
17:16 Who am I, O *J* God, and
17:17 in the ascendancy, O *J* God
17:19 O *J*, for the sake of your
17:20 O *J*, there is none like you
17:22 O *J*, became their God
17:23 O *J*, let the word that you
17:24 *J* of armies, the God of
17:26 O *J*, you are the true God
17:27 yourself, O *J*, have blessed
18:6 *J* kept giving salvation to
18:11 King David sanctified to *J*
18:13 And *J* kept saving David
19:13 as for *J*, what is good in
21:3 May *J* add to his people a
21:9 *J* proceeded to speak to Gad
21:10 *J* has said: There are three
21:11 *J* has said, Take your pick
21:12 sword of *J*, even pestilence
21:13 me fall into the hand of *J*
21:14 Then *J* gave a pestilence in
21:15 *J* saw it and began to feel
21:17 O *J* my God, let your hand
21:18 altar to *J* on the threshing
21:19 had spoken in the name of *J*
21:22 build in it an altar to *J*
21:24 carry what is yours to *J*
21:26 built there an altar to *J*
21:26 to call upon *J*, who now
21:27 *J* said the word to the
21:28 when David saw that *J* had
21:29 tabernacle of *J* that Moses
22:1 the house of *J* the true God
22:5 the house to be built to *J*
22:6 house to *J* the God of Israel
22:7 a house to the name of *J*
22:11 may *J* prove to be with you
22:11 build the house of *J* your
22:12 may *J* give you discretion
22:12 keep the law of *J* your God
22:13 judicial decisions that *J*
22:16 may *J* prove to be with you
22:18 Is not *J* your God with you
22:18 has been subdued before *J*
22:19 to inquire after *J* your God
22:19 build the sanctuary of *J* the
22:19 the ark of the covenant of *J*
22:19 built to the name of *J*
23:4 the work of the house of *J*
23:5 givers of praise to *J* on the
23:13 sacrificial smoke before *J*
23:24 service of the house of *J*
23:25 *J* the God of Israel has
23:28 service of the house of *J*
23:30 to thank and praise *J*, and
23:31 the burnt sacrifices to *J* at
23:31 constantly before *J*

1Ch 23:32 service of the house of *J*
24:19 to come into the house of *J*
24:19 as *J* the God of Israel had
25:3 for thanking and praising *J*
25:6 in song at the house of *J*
25:7 trained in song to *J*, all
26:12 minister at the house of *J*
26:22 treasures of the house of *J*
26:27 to maintain the house of *J*
26:30 for all the work of *J* and
27:23 *J* had promised to make
28:2 the ark of the covenant of *J*
28:4 *J* the God of Israel chose me
28:5 sons whom *J* has given me
28:5 throne of the kingship of *J*
28:8 commandments of *J* your God
28:9 for all hearts *J* is searching
28:10 *J* himself has chosen you to
28:18 the ark of the covenant of *J*
28:19 from the hand of *J* upon me
28:20 *J* God, my God, is with you
29:1 not for man, but for *J* God
29:5 today with a gift for *J*
29:8 treasure of the house of *J*
29:9 voluntary offerings to *J*
29:10 David blessed *J* before the
29:10 Blessed may you be, O *J* the
29:11 O *J*, are the greatness and
29:11 Yours is the kingdom, O *J*
29:16 O *J* our God, all this
29:18 *J* the God of Abraham, Isaac
29:20 Bless, now, *J* your God
29:20 to bless *J* the God of their
29:20 prostrate themselves to *J*
29:21 sacrifice sacrifices to *J*
29:21 burnt offerings to *J* on the
29:22 eating and drinking before *J*
29:22 anoint him to *J* as leader
29:25 *J* continued to make Solomon
2Ch 1:1 *J* his God was with him and
1:3 Moses the servant of *J* had
1:5 put before the tabernacle of *J*
1:6 made offerings there before *J*
1:9 O *J* God, let your promise
2:4 house to the name of *J* my God
2:4 festival seasons of *J* our God
2:11 Because *J* loved his people he
2:12 Blessed be *J* the God of
2:12 who will build a house to *J*
3:1 the house of *J* in Jerusalem
3:1 where *J* had appeared to David
4:16 for the house of *J*, of
5:1 had to do for the house of *J*
5:2 the ark of the covenant of *J*
5:7 the ark of the covenant of *J*
5:10 *J* covenanted with the sons
5:13 in praising and thanking *J*
5:13 with praising *J*, for he is
5:13 the very house of *J*
5:14 glory of *J* filled the house
6:1 Solomon said: *J* himself said
6:4 Blessed be *J* the God of Israel
6:7 house to the name of *J* the
6:8 But *J* said to David my father
6:10 *J* proceeded to carry out his
6:10 just as *J* had spoken, and
6:10 the house to the name of *J*
6:11 ark where the covenant of *J*
6:12 before the altar of *J* in
6:14 O *J* the God of Israel, there
6:16 O *J* the God of Israel, keep
6:17 O *J* the God of Israel, let
6:19 O *J* my God, by listening
6:41 *J* God, into your rest, you
6:41 priests themselves, O *J* God
6:42 *J* God, do not turn back the
7:2 enter into the house of *J*
7:2 had filled the house of *J*
7:3 glory of *J* was upon the house
7:3 thanked *J*, for he is good, for
7:4 offering sacrifice before *J*
7:6 the instruments of song to *J*
7:6 the king had made to thank *J*
7:7 was before the house of *J*
7:10 goodness that *J* had
7:11 finished the house of *J* and
7:11 do regarding the house of *J*
7:12 *J* now appeared to Solomon
7:21 reason did *J* do like that to
7:22 reason that they left *J* the
8:1 had built the house of *J* and
8:11 which the ark of *J* has come
8:12 sacrifices to *J* upon the
8:12 upon the altar of *J* that he

2Ch 8:16 house of *J* until it was
8:16 the house of *J* was complete
9:4 offered up at the house of *J*
9:8 May *J* your God come to be
9:8 upon his throne as king for *J*
9:11 stairs for the house of *J*
10:15 *J* might carry out his word
11:2 word of *J* came to Shemaiah
11:4 *J* has said: You must not go
11:4 they obeyed the word of *J*
11:14 from acting as priests to *J*
11:16 heart to seek *J* the God of
11:16 sacrifice to *J* the God of
12:1 left the law of *J*, and also
12:2 unfaithfully toward *J*
12:5 *J* has said, You, for your
12:6 and said: *J* is righteous
12:7 *J* saw that they had humbled
12:7 word of *J* came to Shemaiah
12:9 treasures of the house of *J*
12:11 came to the house of *J*
12:13 city that *J* had chosen out
12:14 his heart to search for *J*
13:5 *J* the God of Israel himself
13:8 against the kingdom of *J*
13:10 *J* is our God, and we have
13:10 are ministering to *J*
13:11 burnt offerings smoke to *J*
13:11 obligation to *J* our God
13:12 fight against *J* the God of
13:14 began to cry out to *J*
13:18 because they leaned upon *J*
13:20 *J* dealt him a blow, so that
14:2 right in the eyes of *J* his
14:4 Judah to search for *J* the
14:6 for *J* gave him rest
14:7 have searched for *J* our God
14:11 Asa began to call to *J* his
14:11 *J*, as to helping, it does
14:11 *J* our God, for upon you we
14:11 *J*, you are our God. Do not
14:12 *J* defeated the Ethiopians
14:13 broken to pieces before *J*
14:14 dread of *J* had come to be
15:2 *J* is with you as long as you
15:4 distress they returned to *J*
15:8 was before the porch of *J*
15:9 saw that *J* his God was with
15:11 sacrificed to *J* on that day
15:12 covenant to search for *J*
15:13 not search for *J* the God of
15:14 swore to *J* with a loud
15:15 *J* continued to give them
16:7 not lean upon *J* your God, for
16:8 leaning upon *J* did he not
16:9 *J*, his eyes are roving about
16:12 searched not for *J* but for
17:3 *J* continued with Jehoshaphat
17:5 *J* kept the kingdom firmly
17:6 became bold in the ways of *J*
17:10 dread of *J* came to be upon
17:16 volunteer for *J*, and with
18:4 of all for the word of *J*
18:6 here a prophet of *J* still
18:7 through whom to inquire of *J*
18:10 This is what *J* has said
18:11 *J* will certainly give it
18:13 As *J* is living, what my God
18:15 truth in the name of *J*
18:16 *J* went on to say: These
18:18 hear the word of *J*
18:18 *J* sitting upon his throne
18:19 *J* proceeded to say, Who
18:20 stood before *J* and said
18:20 *J* said to him, By what
18:22 *J* has put a deceptive spirit
18:22 *J* himself has spoken
18:23 spirit of *J* pass along from
18:27 *J* has not spoken with me
18:31 *J* himself helped him, and
19:2 those hating *J* that you
19:2 from the person of *J*
19:4 back to *J* the God of their
19:6 you judge but it is for *J*
19:7 dread of *J* come to be upon
19:7 with *J* our God there is no
19:8 judgment of *J* and for the
19:9 fear of *J* with faithfulness
19:10 not do wrong against *J* and
19:11 for every matter of *J*
19:11 *J* prove to be with what is
20:3 his face to search for *J*
20:4 together to inquire of *J*
20:4 Judah they came to consult *J*

2Ch 20:5 in the house of *J* before the
20:6 *J* the God of our forefathers
20:13 were standing before *J*
20:14 spirit of *J* came to be
20:15 *J* has said to you, Do not
20:17 see the salvation of *J* in
20:17 and *J* will be with you
20:18 fell down before *J* to do
20:18 to do obeisance to *J*
20:19 praise *J* the God of Israel
20:20 Put faith in *J* your God that
20:21 stationed singers to *J* and
20:21 Give praise to *J*, for to
20:22 *J* set men in ambush against
20:26 for there they blessed *J*
20:27 *J* had made them rejoice
20:28 trumpets to the house of *J*
20:29 *J* had fought against the
20:37 *J* will certainly break down
21:7 *J* did not want to bring the
21:10 left *J* the God of his
21:12 *J* the God of David your
21:14 *J* is dealing a great blow
21:16 *J* aroused against Jehoram
21:18 *J* plagued him in his
22:7 *J* had anointed to cut off the
22:9 searched for *J* with all his
23:3 *J* promised concerning the
23:5 courtyards of the house of *J*
23:6 house of *J* but the priests
23:6 keep the obligation to *J*
23:12 people at the house of *J*
23:14 to death at the house of *J*
23:16 continue as the people of *J*
23:18 offices of the house of *J*
23:18 house of *J* to offer up
23:18 the burnt sacrifices of *J*
23:19 gates of the house of *J*
23:20 down from the house of *J*
24:4 to renovate the house of *J*
24:6 Moses the servant of *J*, even
24:7 things of the house of *J*
24:8 gate of the house of *J*
24:9 bring to *J* the sacred tax
24:14 utensils for the house of *J*
24:14 in the house of *J*
24:18 left the house of *J* the God
24:19 bring them back to *J*
24:20 commandments of *J*, so that
24:20 left *J*, he will, in turn
24:22 *J* see to it and ask it back
24:24 *J* himself gave into their
24:24 left *J* the God of their
25:4 *J* commanded, saying: Fathers
25:7 for *J* is not with Israel
25:9 with *J* the means to give you
25:27 aside from following *J*
26:5 searching for *J*, the true
26:16 unfaithfully against *J* his
26:16 temple of *J* to burn incense
26:17 priests of *J*, eighty valiant
26:18 burn incense to *J*, but it
26:18 to you on the part of *J* God
26:19 in the house of *J* beside
26:20 because *J* had smitten him
26:21 severed from the house of *J*
27:2 not invade the temple of *J*
27:6 his ways before *J* his God
28:3 nations that *J* had driven
28:5 *J* his God gave him into the
28:6 leaving *J* the God of their
28:9 prophet of *J* there whose
28:9 rage of *J* the God of your
28:10 cases of guilt against *J*
28:13 guilt against *J* on our
28:19 *J* humbled Judah on account
28:19 unfaithfulness toward *J*
28:21 stripped the house of *J*
28:22 unfaithfully . . . toward *J*
28:24 doors of the house of *J*, and
28:25 offended *J* the God of his
29:3 doors of the house of *J*
29:5 sanctify the house of *J* the
29:6 bad in the eyes of *J* our God
29:6 from the tabernacle of *J*
29:10 conclude a covenant with *J*
29:11 *J* has chosen to stand before
29:15 in the words of *J*, to
29:15 to cleanse the house of *J*
29:16 house of *J* to do the
29:16 found in the temple of *J*
29:16 courtyard of the house of *J*
29:17 came to the porch of *J*
29:17 sanctified the house of *J*

2Ch 29:18 the whole house of *J*, the
29:19 are before the altar of *J*
29:20 go up to the house of *J*
29:21 them up upon the altar of *J*
29:25 at the house of *J*, with
29:25 by the hand of *J* that the
29:27 song of *J* started and also
29:30 Levites to praise *J* in the
29:31 your hand with power for *J*
29:31 sacrifices to the house of *J*
29:32 as a burnt offering to *J*
29:35 service of the house of *J*
30:1 come to the house of *J* in
30:1 passover to *J* the God of
30:5 passover to *J* the God of
30:6 Israel, return to *J* the God
30:7 unfaithfully toward *J* the
30:8 Give place to *J* and come
30:8 serve *J* your God, that his
30:9 when you return to *J*, your
30:9 *J* your God is gracious and
30:12 in the matter of *J*
30:15 offerings to the house of *J*
30:17 to sanctify them to *J*
30:18 good *J* himself make
30:19 search for the true God, *J*
30:20 *J* listened to Hezekiah and
30:21 were offering praise to *J*
30:21 instruments, even to *J*
30:22 fine discretion toward *J*
30:22 making confession to *J* the
31:2 gates of the camps of *J*
31:3 is written in the law of *J*
31:4 strictly to the law of *J*
31:6 sanctified to *J* their God
31:8 bless *J* and his people Israel
31:10 into the house of *J* there
31:10 *J* himself has blessed his
31:11 rooms in the house of *J*
31:16 coming to the house of *J*
31:20 faithful before *J* his God
32:8 with us there is *J* our God
32:11 *J* our God himself will
32:16 against *J* the true God and
32:17 he wrote to reproach *J* the
32:21 *J* proceeded to send an angel
32:22 *J* saved Hezekiah and the
32:23 many bringing gifts to *J* at
32:24 and he began to pray to *J*
33:2 nations that *J* had driven out
33:4 altars in the house of *J*
33:4 *J* had said: In Jerusalem my
33:5 courtyards of the house of *J*
33:6 bad in the eyes of *J*, to
33:9 that *J* had annihilated
33:10 *J* kept speaking to Manasseh
33:11 *J* brought against them the
33:12 softened the face of *J* his
33:13 know that *J* is the true God
33:15 image from the house of *J*
33:15 of the house of *J* and in
33:16 prepared the altar of *J* and
33:16 say to Judah to serve *J*
33:17 only it was to *J* their God
33:18 name of *J* the God of Israel
33:23 because of *J* the same as
34:8 repair the house of *J* his God
34:10 over the house of *J*
34:10 active in the house of *J*
34:14 brought to the house of *J*
34:15 found in the house of *J*
34:17 found in the house of *J*
34:21 inquire of *J* in my own
34:21 did not keep the word of *J*
34:23 *J* the God of Israel has
34:24 *J* has said, Here I am
34:26 sending you to inquire of *J*
34:26 *J* the God of Israel has
34:27 heard, is the utterance of *J*
34:30 up to the house of *J*
34:30 found at the house of *J*
34:31 the covenant before *J*
34:31 to go following *J* and to
34:33 to serve *J* their God
34:33 *J* the God of their
35:1 in Jerusalem a passover to *J*
35:2 service of the house of *J*
35:3 those holy to *J*: Put the holy
35:3 serve *J* your God and his
35:6 word of *J* by means of Moses
35:12 to make a presentation to *J*
35:16 service of *J* was prepared
35:16 upon the altar of *J*
35:26 written in the law of *J*

2Ch 36:5 bad in the eyes of J his God
36:7 utensils of the house of J
36:10 articles of the house of J
36:12 was bad in the eyes of J
36:12 at the order of J
36:13 not to return to J the God
36:14 defiled the house of J
36:15 J the God of their
36:16 until the rage of J came
36:18 treasures of the house of J
36:22 J roused the spirit of Cyrus
36:23 J the God of the heavens
36:23 J his God be with him
Ezr 1:1 J roused the spirit of Cyrus
1:2 J the God of the heavens has
1:3 rebuild the house of J the God
1:5 and rebuild the house of J
1:7 utensils of the house of J
2:68 coming to the house of J
3:3 burnt sacrifices to J upon it
3:5 festival seasons of J and for
3:5 a voluntary offering to J
3:6 offer up burnt sacrifices to J
3:8 the work of the house of J
3:10 the temple of J, then the
3:10 stood up to praise J
3:11 giving thanks to J, for he is
3:11 a loud shout in praising J
3:11 foundation of the house of J
4:1 building a temple to J the
4:3 build to J the God of Israel
6:21 to search for J the God of
6:22 J caused them to rejoice
7:6 J the God of Israel had given
7:6 hand of J his God upon him
7:10 to consult the law of J and
7:11 the commandments of J
7:27 Blessed be J the God of our
7:27 to beautify the house of J
7:28 the hand of J my God upon me
8:28 You are something holy to J
8:28 a voluntary offering to J
8:29 halls of the house of J
8:35 as a burnt offering to J
9:5 spread out my palms to J my
9:8 favor from J our God has come
9:15 O J the God of Israel
10:3 according to the counsel of J
10:11 make confession to J the
Ne 1:5 J the God of the heavens
1:11 J, please, let your ear
4:14 J the great and the
5:13 And they began to praise J
8:1 J had commanded Israel
8:6 Ezra blessed J the true God
8:6 to J with their faces to the
8:9 very day is holy to J your God
8:10 joy of J is your stronghold
8:14 law that J had commanded by
9:3 book of the law of J their God
9:3 and bowing down to J their God
9:4 with a loud voice to J their
9:5 Rise, bless J your God from
9:6 You are J alone; you yourself
9:7 You are J the true God, who
10:29 commandments of J our Lord
10:34 upon the altar of J our God
10:35 year, to the house of J
Job 1:6 to take their station before J
1:7 J said to Satan: Where do you
1:7 Satan answered J and said
1:8 And J went on to say to Satan
1:9 Satan answered J and said
1:12 J said to Satan: Look!
1:12 away from the person of J
1:21 J himself has given, and
1:21 and J himself has taken away
1:21 name of J continue to be
2:1 to take their station before J
2:1 to take his station before J
2:2 J said to Satan: Just where
2:2 Satan answered J and said
2:3 And J went on to say to Satan
2:4 But Satan answered J and said
2:6 J said to Satan: There he is
2:7 out away from the person of J
12:9 hand of J itself has done
28:28 fear of J—that is wisdom
38:1 J proceeded to answer Job
40:1 J proceeded to answer Job
40:3 Job went on to answer J
40:6 J went on to answer Job out
42:1 Job proceeded to answer J
42:7 J had spoken these words to

Job 42:7 J proceeded to say to Eliphaz
42:9 did just as J had spoken to
42:9 and so J accepted Job's face
42:10 J himself turned back the
42:10 J began to give in addition
42:11 calamity that J had let
42:12 As for J, he blessed the end
Ps 1:2 his delight is in the law of J
1:6 J is taking knowledge of the
2:2 Against J and against his
2:4 J himself will hold them in
2:7 refer to the decree of J
2:11 Serve J with fear And be
3:1 O J, why have my adversaries
3:3 you, O J, are a shield about
3:4 I shall call to J himself
3:5 J himself keeps supporting me
3:7 arise, O J! Save me, O my God!
3:8 Salvation belongs to J
4:3 So take knowledge that J will
4:3 J himself will hear when I
4:5 And trust in J
4:6 light of your face upon us, O J
4:8 J, make me dwell in security
5:1 To my sayings do give ear, O J
5:3 O J, in the morning you will
5:6 and deception J detests
5:8 O J, lead me in your
5:12 bless anyone righteous, O J
6:1 O J, do not in your anger
6:2 Show me favor, O J, for I am
6:2 Heal me, O J, for my bones
6:3 And you, O J—how long?
6:4 return, O J, do rescue my soul
6:8 J will certainly hear the
6:9 J will indeed hear my request
6:9 J himself will accept my
7:*super* of David that he sang to J
7:1 O J my God, in you I have
7:3 J my God, if I have done this
7:6 Do arise, O J, in your anger
7:8 J himself will pass sentence
7:8 Judge me, O J, according to
7:17 I shall laud J according to
7:17 make melody to the name of J
8:1 J our Lord, how majestic your
8:9 J our Lord, how majestic your
9:1 I will laud you, O J, with all
9:7 As for J, he will sit to time
9:9 J will become a secure height
9:10 those looking for you, O J
9:11 Make melody, you people, to J
9:13 Show me favor, O J; see my
9:16 J is known by the judgment
9:19 O J! Let not mortal man prove
9:20 Do put fear into them, O J
10:1 J, do you keep standing afar
10:3 He has disrespected J
10:12 arise, O J. O God, lift up
10:16 J is King to time indefinite
10:17 you will certainly hear, O J
11:1 In J I have taken refuge
11:4 J is in his holy temple
11:4 J—in the heavens is his
11:5 J himself examines the
11:7 J is righteous; he does love
12:1 save me, O J, for the loyal
12:3 J will cut off all smooth
12:5 at this time arise, says J
12:6 The sayings of J are pure
12:7 You yourself, O J, will guard
13:1 O J, will you forget me
13:3 answer me, O J my God
13:6 I will sing to J, for he has
14:1 in his heart: There is no J
14:2 As for J, he has looked down
14:2 insight, anyone seeking J
14:4 have not called even upon J
14:5 For J is among the generation
14:6 Because J is his refuge
14:7 J gathers back the captive
15:1 O J, who will be a guest in
15:4 But those fearing J he honors
16:2 I have said to J: You are
16:2 You are J; my goodness is
16:5 J is the portion of my
16:7 J, who has given me advice
16:8 have placed J in front of me
17:1 hear what is righteous, O J
17:13 rise up, O J; do confront
17:14 From men, by your hand, O J
18:*super* of David, who spoke to J
18:*super* day that J had delivered
18:1 affection for you, O J my

Ps 18:2 J is my crag and my
18:3 to be praised, J, I shall call
18:6 I kept calling upon J
18:13 in the heavens J began to
18:15 From your rebuke, O J, from
18:18 J came to be as a support
18:20 J rewards me according to
18:21 I have kept the ways of J
18:24 J repay me according to my
18:28 will light my lamp, O J
18:30 The saying of J is a refined
18:31 For who is a God besides J?
18:41 To J, but he actually does
18:46 J is living, and blessed be
18:49 among the nations, O J
19:7 The law of J is perfect
19:7 reminder of J is trustworthy
19:8 The orders from J are upright
19:8 commandment of J is clean
19:9 fear of J is pure, standing
19:9 The judicial decisions of J
19:14 O J my Rock and my Redeemer
20:1 J answer you in the day of
20:5 J fulfill all your requests
20:6 J certainly saves his anointed
20:7 J our God we shall make
20:9 J, do save the king! He will
21:1 O J, in your strength the
21:7 For the king is trusting in J
21:9 J in his anger will swallow
21:13 exalted in your strength, O J
22:8 He committed himself to J
22:19 O J, O do not keep far off
22:23 You fearers of J, praise him!
22:26 Those seeking . . . praise J
22:27 remember and turn back to J
22:28 For the kingship belongs to J
22:30 be declared concerning J to
23:1 J is my Shepherd. I shall
23:6 will dwell in the house of J
24:1 To J belong the earth and
24:3 ascend into the mountain of J
24:5 carry away blessing from J
24:8 J strong and mighty
24:8 J mighty in battle
24:10 J of armies—he is the
25:1 To you, O J, I raise my very
25:4 know your own ways, O J
25:6 Remember your mercies, O J
25:7 the sake of your goodness, O J
25:8 Good and upright is J
25:10 All the paths of J are
25:11 For your name's sake, O J
25:12 the man fearful of J
25:14 intimacy with J belongs to
25:15 eyes are constantly toward J
26:1 Judge me, O J, for I myself
26:1 And in J I have trusted
26:2 Examine me, O J, and put me
26:6 march around your altar, O J
26:8 J, I have loved the dwelling
26:12 I shall bless J
27:1 J is my light and my
27:1 J is the stronghold of my
27:4 One thing I have asked from J
27:4 I may dwell in the house of J
27:4 behold the pleasantness of J
27:6 sing and make melody to J
27:7 Hear, O J, when I call with
27:8 Your face, O J, I shall seek
27:10 J himself would take me up
27:11 Instruct me, O J, in your
27:13 the goodness of J in the land
27:14 Hope in J; be courageous and
27:14 Yes, hope in J
28:1 To you, O J, I keep calling
28:5 regard for the activities of J
28:6 Blessed be J, for he has heard
28:7 J is my strength and my
28:8 J is a strength to his people
29:1 Ascribe to J, O you sons of
29:1 to J glory and strength
29:2 Ascribe to J the glory of his
29:2 Bow . . . to J in holy adornment
29:3 voice of J is over the waters
29:3 J is over many waters
29:4 The voice of J is powerful
29:4 The voice of J is splendid
29:5 voice of J is breaking the
29:5 J breaks the cedars of Lebanon
29:7 The voice of J is hewing with
29:8 voice of J itself makes the
29:8 J makes the wilderness of
29:9 The voice of J itself makes

Ps 29:10 Upon the deluge J has seated
29:10 J sits as king to time
29:11 J himself will give strength
29:11 J himself will bless his
30:1 I shall exalt you, O J, for
30:2 O J my God, I cried to you
30:3 O J, you have brought up my
30:4 Make melody to J, O you
30:7 O J, in your goodwill you
30:8 To you, O J, I kept calling
30:8 J I kept making entreaty for
30:10 Hear, O J, and show me favor
30:10 J, prove yourself my helper
30:12 J my God, to time indefinite
31:1 you, O J, have I taken refuge
31:5 You have redeemed me, O J the
31:6 as for me, in J I do trust
31:9 Show me favor, O J, for I am
31:14 I have put my trust, O J
31:17 O J, may I not be ashamed
31:21 Blessed be J, For he has
31:23 love J, all you loyal ones
31:23 J is safeguarding
31:24 you who are waiting for J
32:2 J does not put error
32:5 over my transgressions to J
32:10 as for the one trusting in J
32:11 Rejoice in J and be joyful
33:1 Cry out . . . because of J
33:2 Give thanks to J on the harp
33:4 For the word of J is upright
33:5 With the loving-kindness of J
33:6 By the word of J the heavens
33:8 Let all . . . be in fear of J
33:10 J himself has broken up the
33:11 very counsel of J will stand
33:12 the nation whose God is J
33:13 From the heavens J has
33:18 J is toward those fearing
33:20 has been in expectation of J
33:22 your loving-kindness, O J
34:1 I will bless J at all times
34:2 In J my soul will make its
34:3 O magnify J with me, you
34:4 I inquired of J, and he
34:6 called, and J himself heard
34:7 The angel of J is camping all
34:8 Taste and see that J is good
34:9 Fear J, you holy ones of his
34:10 as for those seeking J
34:11 The fear of J is what I
34:15 The eyes of J are toward the
34:16 The face of J is against
34:17 cried out, and J . . . heard
34:18 J is near to those that are
34:19 out of them all J delivers
34:22 J is redeeming the soul of
35:1 Do conduct my case, O J
35:9 my own soul be joyful in J
35:10 O J, who is there like you
35:17 J, how long will you keep
35:22 You have seen, O J. Do not
35:22 O J, do not keep yourself far
35:23 J, to my case at law
35:24 Judge me . . . O J my God
35:27 Let J be magnified, who
36:5 O J, your loving-kindness is
36:6 Man and beast you save, O J
37:3 Trust in J and do good
37:4 take exquisite delight in J
37:5 Roll upon J your way
37:7 Keep silent before J
37:9 those hoping in J are the ones
37:13 J himself will laugh at him
37:17 J will be supporting the
37:18 J is aware of the days of
37:20 enemies of J will be like
37:23 By J the very steps of an
37:24 J is supporting his hand
37:28 For J is a lover of justice
37:33 J, he will not leave him to
37:34 Hope in J and keep his way
37:39 salvation . . . is from J
37:40 J will help them and provide
38:1 J, do not in your indignation
38:9 O J, in front of you is all
38:15 For on you, O J, I waited
38:15 to answer, O J my God
38:21 Do not leave me, O J
38:22 O J my salvation
39:4 Cause me, O J, to know my
39:7 for what have I hoped, O J?
39:12 Do hear my prayer, O J
40:1 I earnestly hoped in J, And so

Ps 40:3 And they will trust in J
40:4 that has put J as his trust
40:5 O J my God, even your
40:9 O J, you yourself know that
40:11 O J, do not restrain your
40:13 pleased, O J, to deliver me
40:13 O J, to my assistance do
40:16 May J be magnified
40:17 J himself takes account of
41:1 J will provide escape for him
41:2 J himself will guard him and
41:3 J himself will sustain him
41:4 O J, show me favor
41:10 O J, show me favor and cause
41:13 Blessed be J the God of
42:8 By day J will command his
44:23 do you keep sleeping, O J
46:7 J of armies is with us
46:8 behold the activities of J
46:11 J of armies is with us
47:2 For J, the Most High, is
47:5 J with the sound of the horn
48:1 J is great and much to be
48:8 In the city of J of armies
50:1 God, J, has himself spoken
51:15 O J, may you open these lips
53:1 in his heart: There is no J
53:2 insight, anyone seeking J
53:4 have not called even upon J
53:5 J himself has rejected them
53:6 J gathers back the captive
54:4 J is among those supporting
54:6 I shall laud your name, O J
55:9 O J, divide their tongue
55:16 And J himself will save me
55:22 Throw your burden upon J
56:10 In union with J I shall
57:9 among the peoples, O J
58:6 maned young lions, O J
59:3 nor any sin on my part, O J
59:5 you, O J God of armies, are
59:8 you yourself, O J, will laugh
59:11 down, O our shield J
62:12 belongs to you, O J
64:10 will rejoice in J and will
66:18 J will not hear me
68:11 J himself gives the saying
68:16 J himself will reside there
68:17 J himself has come from
68:19 J, who daily carries the
68:20 to J the Sovereign Lord
68:22 J has said: From Bashan I
68:26 bless God, J, O you who are
68:32 Make melody to J—*Se'lah*
69:6 Sovereign Lord, J of armies
69:13 my prayer was to you, O J
69:16 Answer me, O J, for your
69:31 more pleasing to J than a
69:33 J is listening to the poor
70:1 O J, to my assistance do make
70:5 O J, do not be too late
71:1 J, I have taken refuge
71:5 J, my confidence from my
71:16 O Sovereign Lord J
72:18 Blessed be J God, Israel's
73:20 dream after awaking, O J
73:28 J I have placed my refuge
74:18 enemy . . . reproached, O J
75:8 is a cup in the hand of J
76:11 Vow and pay to J your God
77:2 I have searched for J himself
77:7 that J keeps casting off
78:4 praises of J and his strength
78:21 J heard and began to be
78:65 J began to awake as from
79:5 O J, will you be incensed
79:12 have reproached you, O J
80:4 O J God of armies, how long
80:19 J God of armies, bring us
81:10 I, J, am your God, The One
81:15 those intensely hating J
83:16 search for your name, O J
83:18 that you, whose name is J
84:1 tabernacle is, O J of armies
84:2 for the courtyards of J
84:3 Your grand altar, O J of
84:8 J God of armies, do hear
84:11 J God is a sun and a shield
84:11 J himself will not hold back
84:12 J of armies, happy is the
85:1 taken pleasure, O J, in your
85:7 Show us, O J, your
85:8 the true God J will speak
85:12 J, for his part, will give

Ps 86:1 Incline, O J, your ear
86:3 Show me favor, O J
86:4 For to you, O J, I lift up
86:5 O J, are good and ready to
86:6 give ear, O J, to my prayer
86:8 like you among the gods, O J
86:9 bow down before you, O J
86:11 Instruct me, O J, about your
86:12 laud you, O J my God, with
86:15 J, are a God merciful and
86:17 O J, have helped me and
87:2 J is more in love with the
87:6 J himself will declare, when
88:1 J, the God of my salvation
88:9 called on you, O J, all day
88:13 O J, I myself have cried for
88:14 J, that you cast off my soul
89:5 laud your marvelous act, O J
89:6 skies can be compared to J
89:6 Who can resemble J among the
89:8 O J God of armies, Who is
89:15 J, in the light of your face
89:18 For our shield belongs to J
89:46 J, will you keep yourself
89:49 acts of loving-kindness, O J
89:50 Remember, O J, the reproach
89:51 enemies have reproached, O J
89:52 Blessed be J to time
90:1 J, you yourself have proved
90:13 Do return, O J! How long
90:17 pleasantness of J our God
91:2 say to J: You are my refuge
91:9 you said: J is my refuge
92:1 good to give thanks to J
92:4 you have made me rejoice, O J
92:5 great your works are, O J
92:8 high to time indefinite, O J
92:9 For, look! your enemies, O J
92:13 planted in the house of J
92:15 To tell that J is upright
93:1 J himself has become king!
93:1 J is clothed—with strength
93:3 The rivers have raised, O J
93:4 J is majestic in the height
93:5 to your own house, O J
94:1 God of acts of vengeance, J
94:3 How long are the wicked, O J
94:5 Your people, O J, they keep
94:11 J is knowing the thoughts
94:14 J will not forsake his
94:17 J had been of assistance to
94:18 loving-kindness, O J, kept
94:22 J will become a secure
94:23 J our God will silence them
95:1 us cry out joyfully to J
95:3 For J is a great God
95:6 kneel before J our Maker
96:1 Sing to J a new song
96:1 Sing to J, all you people of
96:2 Sing to J, bless his name
96:4 J is great and very much to
96:5 J, he has made the very
96:7 Ascribe to J, O you families
96:7 Ascribe to J glory and
96:8 Ascribe to J the glory
96:9 Bow down to J in holy
96:10 J himself has become king
96:13 Before J. For he has come
97:1 J himself has become king!
97:5 like wax on account of J
97:8 your judicial decisions, O J
97:9 O J, are the Most High over
97:10 lovers of J, hate what is
97:12 Rejoice in J, O you righteous
98:1 Sing to J a new song
98:2 J has made his salvation
98:4 Shout in triumph to J, all
98:5 Make melody to J with the
98:6 in triumph before the King, J
98:9 J, for he has come to judge
99:1 J himself has become king
99:2 J is great in Zion
99:5 Exalt J our God and bow down
99:6 calling to J, and he himself
99:8 J our God, you yourself
99:9 Exalt J our God And bow down
99:9 For J our God is holy
100:1 Shout in triumph to J, all
100:2 Serve J with rejoicing
100:3 Know that J is God
100:5 For J is good
101:1 To you, O J, I will make
101:8 cut off from the city of J
102:*super* his concern before J

Pr 3:7 Fear *J* and turn away from
3:9 Honor *J* with your valuable
3:11 discipline of *J*, O my son
3:12 one whom *J* loves he reproves
3:19 *J* himself in wisdom founded
3:26 *J* himself will prove to be
3:32 detestable thing to *J*, but
3:33 curse of *J* is on the house of
5:21 are in front of the eyes of *J*
6:16 six things that *J* does hate
8:13 fear of *J* means the hating of
8:22 *J* himself produced me as the
8:35 and gets goodwill from *J*
9:10 fear of *J* is the start of
10:3 *J* will not cause the soul of
10:22 blessing of *J* . . . makes rich
10:27 fear of *J* will add days, but
10:29 way of *J* is a stronghold for
11:1 something detestable to *J*
11:20 something detestable to *J*
12:2 good gets approval from *J*
12:22 something detestable to *J*
14:2 uprightness is fearing *J*
14:26 In the fear of *J* there is
14:27 fear of *J* is a well of life
15:3 eyes of *J* are in every place
15:8 is something detestable to *J*
15:9 is something detestable to *J*
15:11 Sheol . . . in front of *J*
15:16 is a little in the fear of *J*
15:25 ones *J* will tear down, but
15:26 detestable to *J*, but pleasant
15:29 *J* is far . . . from the wicked
15:33 fear of *J* is a discipline
16:1 from *J* is the answer of the
16:2 *J* is making an estimate of
16:3 Roll your works upon *J*
16:4 *J* has made for his purpose
16:5 is something detestable to *J*
16:6 in the fear of *J* one turns
16:7 *J* takes pleasure in the ways
16:9 *J* himself does the directing
16:11 and scales belong to *J*
16:20 is he that is trusting in *J*
16:33 decision by it is from *J*
17:3 *J* is the examiner of hearts
17:15 something detestable to *J*
18:10 name of *J* is a strong tower
18:22 and one gets goodwill from *J*
19:3 becomes enraged against *J*
19:14 a discreet wife is from *J*
19:17 is lending to *J*, and his
19:21 counsel of *J* . . . will stand
19:23 fear of *J* tends toward life
20:10 something detestable to *J*
20:12 *J* himself has made even both
20:22 Hope in *J*, and he will save
20:23 something detestable to *J*
20:24 From *J* are the steppings of
20:27 breath . . . is the lamp of *J*
21:1 water in the hand of *J*
21:2 *J* is making an estimate of
21:3 preferable to *J* than sacrifice
21:30 counsel in opposition to *J*
21:31 but salvation belongs to *J*
22:2 The Maker of them all is *J*
22:4 fear of *J* is riches and glory
22:12 The eyes of *J* himself have
22:14 one denounced by *J* will fall
22:19 confidence . . . in *J* himself
22:23 *J* himself will plead their
23:17 be in the fear of *J* all day
24:18 that *J* may not see and it be
24:21 My son, fear *J* and the king
25:22 *J* himself will reward you
28:5 are seeking *J* can understand
28:25 relying upon *J* will be made
29:13 *J* is lighting up the eyes of
29:25 in *J* will be protected
29:26 judgment of a man is from *J*
30:9 deny you and say: Who is *J*?
31:30 woman that fears *J* is the
Isa 1:2 *J* himself has spoken: Sons I
1:4 They have left *J*, they have
1:9 Unless *J* of armies himself
1:10 Hear the word of *J*, you
1:11 says *J*. I have had enough of
1:18 straight between us, says *J*
1:20 mouth of *J* has spoken it
1:24 *J* of armies, the Powerful
1:28 those leaving *J* will come to
2:2 mountain of the house of *J*
2:3 us go up to the mountain of *J*
2:3 word of *J* out of Jerusalem

Isa 2:5 let us walk in the light of *J*
2:10 the dreadfulness of *J*, and
2:11 *J* alone must be put on high
2:12 day belonging to *J* of armies
2:17 *J* alone must be put on high
2:19 the dreadfulness of *J* and
2:21 of the dreadfulness of *J*
3:1 *J* of armies, is removing
3:8 dealings are against *J*
3:13 *J* is stationing himself to
3:14 *J* himself will enter into
3:15 Sovereign Lord, *J* of armies
3:16 *J* says: For the reason that
3:17 *J* also will actually make the
3:17 *J* himself will lay their
3:18 *J* will take away the beauty
4:2 *J* makes sprout will come to
4:4 *J* will have washed away the
4:5 *J* will also certainly create
5:7 vineyard of *J* of armies is
5:9 *J* of armies has sworn that
5:12 activity of *J* they do not
5:16 *J* of armies will become
5:24 rejected the law of *J* of
5:25 anger of *J* has grown hot
6:1 see *J*, sitting on a throne
6:3 holy is *J* of armies
6:5 seen the King, *J* of armies
6:8 *J* saying: Whom shall I send
6:11 I said: How long, O *J*?
6:12 *J* actually removes earthling
7:3 *J* proceeded to say to Isaiah
7:7 *J* has said: It will not stand
7:10 *J* went on speaking some more
7:11 sign from *J* your God, making
7:12 shall I put *J* to the test
7:14 *J* himself will give you men
7:17 *J* will bring against you
7:18 *J* will whistle for the flies
7:20 *J* will shave the head and
8:1 *J* proceeded to say to me
8:3 *J* now said to me: Call his
8:5 *J* proceeded to speak yet
8:7 *J* is bringing up against them
8:11 what *J* has said to me with
8:13 *J* of armies—he is the One
8:17 keep in expectation of *J*
8:18 children whom *J* has given
8:18 miracles in Israel from *J*
9:7 zeal of *J* of armies will
9:8 word that *J* sent against
9:11 *J* will set the adversaries
9:13 *J* of armies they have not
9:14 *J* will cut off from Israel
9:17 *J* will not rejoice even over
9:19 fury of *J* of armies the
10:12 *J* terminates all his work
10:16 *J* of armies, will keep
10:20 support themselves upon *J*
10:23 Sovereign Lord, *J* of armies
10:24 *J* of armies, has said
10:26 *J* of armies will certainly
10:33 *J* of armies, is lopping off
11:2 spirit of *J* must settle down
11:2 and of the fear of *J*
11:3 by him in the fear of *J*
11:9 knowledge of *J* as the waters
11:11 *J* will again offer his hand
11:15 *J* will certainly cut off
12:1 I shall thank you, O *J*, for
12:2 Jah *J* is my strength and my
12:4 Give thanks to *J*, you people!
12:5 Make melody to *J*, for he
13:4 *J* of armies is mustering the
13:5 *J* and the weapons of his
13:6 for the day of *J* is near
13:9 day of *J* itself is coming
13:13 fury of *J* of armies and
14:1 *J* will show mercy to Jacob
14:2 upon the soil of *J* as
14:3 day when *J* gives you rest
14:5 *J* has broken the rod of the
14:22 utterance of *J* of armies
14:22 is the utterance of *J*
14:23 utterance of *J* of armies
14:24 *J* of armies has sworn
14:27 *J* of armies himself has
14:32 *J* himself has laid the
16:13 *J* spoke concerning Moab
16:14 now *J* has spoken, saying
17:3 utterance of *J* of armies
17:6 utterance of *J* the God of
18:4 is what *J* has said to me
18:7 gift will be brought to *J* of

Isa 18:7 the name of *J* of armies
19:1 *J* is riding on a swift cloud
19:4 true Lord, *J* of armies
19:12 *J* of armies has counseled
19:14 *J* himself has mingled in
19:16 waving of the hand of *J* of
19:17 counsel of *J* of armies
19:18 swearing to *J* of armies
19:19 altar to *J* in the midst of
19:19 pillar to *J* beside its
19:20 a witness to *J* of armies
19:20 cry out to *J* because of the
19:21 *J* will certainly become
19:21 Egyptians must know *J* in
19:21 make a vow to *J* and pay it
19:22 *J* will certainly deal Egypt
19:22 and they must return to *J*
19:25 *J* of armies will have
20:2 *J* spoke by the hand of Isaiah
20:3 *J* went on to say: Just as
21:6 what *J* has said to me
21:8 Upon the watchtower, O *J*, I
21:10 heard from *J* of armies, the
21:16 what *J* has said to me
21:17 *J* himself, the God of
22:5 *J* of armies, has in the
22:12 *J* of armies, will call in
22:14 *J* of armies has revealed
22:14 *J* of armies, has said
22:15 *J* of armies, has said: Go
22:17 *J* is hurling you down with
22:25 utterance of *J* of armies
22:25 *J* himself has spoken it
23:9 *J* of armies himself has
23:11 *J* himself has given a
23:17 *J* will turn his attention
23:18 become something holy to *J*
23:18 for those dwelling before *J*
24:1 *J* is emptying the land and
24:3 *J* himself has spoken this
24:14 In the superiority of *J*
24:15 they must glorify *J*, in
24:15 name of *J*, the God of
24:21 *J* will turn his attention
24:23 *J* of armies has become king
25:1 *J*, you are my God. I exalt
25:6 *J* of armies will certainly
25:8 *J* will certainly wipe the
25:8 *J* himself has spoken it
25:9 This is *J*. We have hoped
25:10 hand of *J* will settle down
26:4 Trust in *J*, you people, for
26:4 Jah *J* is the Rock of times
26:8 path of your judgments, O *J*
26:10 not see the eminence of *J*
26:11 *J*, your hand has become
26:12 *J*, you will adjudge peace
26:13 *J* our God, other masters
26:15 *J*, you have added to the
26:16 *J*, during distress they
26:17 become because of you, O *J*
26:21 *J* is coming forth from his
27:1 *J*, with his hard and great
27:3 I, *J*, am safeguarding her
27:12 *J* will beat off the fruit
27:13 bow down to *J* in the holy
28:2 *J* has someone strong and
28:5 *J* of armies will become as
28:13 word of *J* will certainly
28:14 hear the word of *J*, you
28:16 *J* has said: Here I am
28:21 *J* will rise up just as at
28:22 Sovereign Lord, *J* of armies
28:29 forth from *J* of armies
29:6 From *J* of armies you will
29:10 *J* has poured a spirit of
29:13 *J* says: For the reason that
29:15 concealing counsel from *J*
29:19 their rejoicing in *J*
29:22 *J* has said to the house of
30:1 is the utterance of *J*, those
30:9 to hear the law of *J*
30:15 Sovereign Lord *J*, the Holy
30:18 *J* will keep in expectation
30:18 *J* is a God of judgment
30:20 *J* will certainly give you
30:26 *J* binds up the breakdown of
30:27 name of *J* is coming from
30:29 into the mountain of *J*
30:30 *J* will certainly make the
30:31 voice of *J* Assyria will
30:32 *J* will cause to settle down
30:33 breath of *J*, like a torrent
31:1 not searched for *J* himself

Isa 31:3 *J* himself will stretch out
31:4 what *J* has said to me
31:4 *J* of armies will come down
31:5 *J* of armies will in the
31:9 *J*, whose light is in Zion
32:6 speak against *J* what is
33:2 *J*, show us favor. In you
33:5 *J* will certainly be put on
33:6 fear of *J*, which is his
33:10 Now I will rise up, says *J*
33:21 Majestic One, *J*, will be
33:22 For *J* is our Judge
33:22 *J* is our Statute-giver
33:22 *J* is our King; he himself
34:2 *J* has indignation against
34:6 *J* has a sword; it must be
34:6 *J* has a sacrifice in Bozrah
34:8 *J* has a day of vengeance
34:16 book of *J* and read out loud
34:16 mouth of *J* that has given
35:2 see the glory of *J*, the
35:10 ones redeemed by *J* will
36:7 *J* our God in whom we have
36:10 authorization from *J*
36:10 *J* himself said to me
36:15 cause you to trust in *J*
36:15 *J* will deliver us
36:18 *J* himself will deliver us
36:20 *J* should deliver Jerusalem
37:1 came into the house of *J*
37:4 *J* your God will hear the
37:4 that *J* your God has heard
37:6 *J* has said: Do not be afraid
37:14 up to the house of *J* and
37:14 and spread it out before *J*
37:15 Hezekiah began to pray to *J*
37:16 *J* of armies, the God of
37:17 Incline your ear, O *J*, and
37:17 Open your eyes, O *J*, and
37:18 *J*, that the kings of Assyria
37:20 *J* our God, save us out of
37:20 you, O *J*, are God alone
37:21 *J* the God of Israel has
37:22 *J* has spoken against him
37:24 you have taunted *J* and you
37:32 zeal of *J* of armies will do
37:33 *J* has said concerning the
37:34 is the utterance of *J*
37:36 angel of *J* proceeded to go
38:1 This is what *J* has said
38:2 and began to pray to *J*
38:3 to say: I beseech you, O *J*
38:4 word of *J* now occurred to
38:5 *J* the God of David your
38:7 is the sign for you from *J*
38:7 *J* will perform this word
38:14 O *J*, I am under oppression
38:16 O *J*, on that account they
38:20 O *J*, undertake to save me
38:20 life at the house of *J*
38:22 go up to the house of *J*
39:5 Hear the word of *J* of armies
39:6 Nothing will be left, *J* has
39:8 word of *J* that you have
40:2 from the hand of *J* she has
40:3 Clear up the way of *J*, you
40:5 glory of *J* will certainly
40:5 mouth of *J* has spoken it
40:7 spirit of *J* has blown upon
40:10 The Sovereign Lord *J*
40:13 the spirit of *J*, and who
40:27 has been concealed from *J*
40:28 *J*, the Creator of the
40:31 hoping in *J* will regain
41:4 I, *J*, the First One; and
41:13 For I, *J* your God, am
41:14 is the utterance of *J*
41:16 will be joyful in *J*
41:17 *J*, shall answer them
41:20 the very hand of *J* has done
41:21 says *J*. Produce your
42:5 the true God, *J*, has said
42:6 I myself, *J*, have called you
42:8 I am *J*. That is my name
42:10 Sing to *J* a new song, his
42:12 attribute to *J* glory, and
42:13 *J* himself will go forth
42:19 or blind as the servant of *J*
42:21 *J* himself for the sake of
42:24 *J*, the One against whom we
43:1 this is what *J* has said
43:3 For I am *J* your God, the
43:10 is the utterance of *J*, even
43:11 I—I am *J*, and besides me
Isa 43:12 is the utterance of *J*, and I
43:14 This is what *J* has said
43:15 I am *J* your Holy One, the
43:16 This is what *J* has said
44:2 This is what *J* has said
44:5 one will say: I belong to *J*
44:5 upon his hand: Belonging to *J*
44:6 This is what *J* has said, the
44:6 *J* of armies, I am the first
44:23 for *J* has taken action
44:23 *J* has repurchased Jacob, and
44:24 *J* has said, your Repurchaser
44:24 I, *J*, am doing everything
45:1 *J* has said to his anointed
45:3 you may know that I am *J*
45:5 *J*, and there is no one else
45:6 I am *J*, and there is no one
45:7 *J*, am doing all these things
45:8 myself, *J*, have created it
45:11 *J* has said, the Holy One
45:13 *J* of armies has said
45:14 *J* has said: The unpaid
45:17 be saved in union with *J*
45:18 this is what *J* has said
45:18 I am *J*, and there is no one
45:19 I am *J*, speaking what is
45:21 Is it not I, *J*, besides
45:24 Surely in *J* there are full
45:25 In *J* all the seed of Israel
47:4 One repurchasing us. *J* of
48:1 swearing by the name of *J*
48:2 *J* of armies being his name
48:14 *J* himself has loved him
48:16 now the Sovereign Lord *J*
48:17 This is what *J* has said
48:17 I, *J*, am your God, the One
48:20 *J* has repurchased his
48:22 no peace, *J* has said, for
49:1 *J* himself has called me even
49:4 Truly my judgment is with *J*
49:5 *J*, the One forming me from
49:5 glorified in the eyes of *J*
49:7 *J*, the Repurchaser of Israel
49:7 *J*, who is faithful, the Holy
49:8 This is what *J* has said
49:13 *J* has comforted his people
49:14 saying: *J* has left me, and
49:14 *J* himself has forgotten me
49:18 is the utterance of *J*
49:22 *J* has said: Look! I shall
49:23 have to know that I am *J*
49:25 this is what *J* has said
49:26 I, *J*, am your Savior and
50:1 This is what *J* has said
50:4 The Sovereign Lord *J* himself
50:5 The Sovereign Lord *J* himself
50:7 *J* himself will help me
50:9 *J* himself will help me
50:10 you people is in fear of *J*
50:10 trust in the name of *J* and
51:1 who are seeking to find *J*
51:3 *J* will certainly comfort
51:3 plain like the garden of *J*
51:9 with strength, O arm of *J*
51:11 Then the redeemed ones of *J*
51:13 should forget *J* your Maker
51:15 But I, *J*, am your God
51:15 *J* of armies is his name
51:17 the hand of *J* his cup of
51:20 full of the rage of *J*, the
51:22 your Lord, *J*, even your God
52:3 For this is what *J* has said
52:4 *J* has said: It was to Egypt
52:5 the utterance of *J*. For my
52:5 is the utterance of *J*, and
52:8 see when *J* gathers back Zion
52:9 *J* has comforted his people
52:10 *J* has bared his holy arm
52:11 carrying the utensils of *J*
52:12 *J* will be going even before
53:1 And as for the arm of *J*, to
53:6 *J* himself has caused the
53:10 *J* himself took delight in
53:10 delight of *J* will succeed
54:1 husbandly owner, *J* has said
54:5 your husbandly owner, *J*
54:6 *J* called you as if you were
54:8 your Repurchaser, *J*, has said
54:10 *J*, the One having mercy
54:13 will be persons taught by *J*
54:17 the servants of *J*, and their
54:17 is the utterance of *J*
55:5 for the sake of *J* your God
55:6 Search for *J*, you people
Isa 55:7 and let him return to *J*
55:8 is the utterance of *J*
55:13 for *J* something famous, a
56:1 *J* has said: Keep justice
56:3 has joined himself to *J*
56:3 *J* will divide me off from
56:4 *J* has said to the eunuchs
56:6 joined themselves to *J* to
56:6 and to love the name of *J*
56:8 Lord *J*, who is collecting
57:19 *J* has said, and I will heal
58:5 and a day acceptable to *J*
58:8 glory of *J* would be your
58:9 and *J* himself would answer
58:11 *J* will be bound to lead you
58:13 a holy day of *J*, one being
58:14 your exquisite delight in *J*
58:14 mouth of *J* . . . spoken it
59:1 The hand of *J* has not become
59:13 and a denying of *J*
59:15 And *J* got to see, and it
59:19 begin to fear the name of *J*
59:19 spirit of *J* has driven along
59:20 is the utterance of *J*
59:21 covenant with them, *J* has
59:21 your offspring, *J* has said
60:1 glory of *J* has shone forth
60:2 upon you *J* will shine forth
60:6 the praises of *J* they will
60:9 to the name of *J* your God
60:14 to call you the city of *J*
60:16 I, *J*, am your Savior, and
60:19 *J* must become to you an
60:20 *J* himself will become for
60:22 *J*, shall speed it up in its
61:1 the Sovereign Lord *J* is
61:1 *J* has anointed me to tell
61:2 goodwill on the part of *J*
61:3 the planting of *J*, for him
61:6 the priests of *J* you will be
61:8 I, *J*, am loving justice
61:9 offspring whom *J* has blessed
61:10 I shall exult in *J*. My soul
61:11 in like manner *J* himself
62:2 mouth of *J* will designate
62:3 beauty in the hand of *J*
62:4 *J* will have taken delight
62:6 are making mention of *J*
62:8 *J* has sworn with his right
62:9 be certain to praise *J*
62:11 *J* himself has caused it to
62:12 those repurchased by *J*
63:7 The loving-kindnesses of *J*
63:7 mention, the praises of *J*
63:7 all that *J* has rendered to us
63:14 spirit of *J* proceeded to
63:16 you, O *J*, are our Father
63:17 Why do you, O *J*, keep
64:8 O *J*, you are our Father
64:9 Do not be indignant, O *J*
64:12 O *J*? Will you stay still
65:7 *J* has said. Because they
65:8 This is what *J* has said
65:11 men are those leaving *J*
65:13 *J* has said: Look! My own
65:15 *J* will actually put you
65:23 the chosen ones of *J*
65:25 holy mountain, *J* has said
66:1 *J* has said: The heavens are
66:2 to be, is the utterance of *J*
66:5 Hear the word of *J*, you men
66:5 said, May *J* be glorified!
66:6 *J* repaying what is deserved
66:9 the giving birth? says *J*
66:12 this is what *J* has said
66:14 hand of *J* will certainly be
66:15 *J* himself comes as a very
66:16 *J* himself will for a fact
66:16 slain of *J* will certainly
66:17 end, is the utterance of *J*
66:20 nations as a gift to *J*
66:20 *J* has said, just as when
66:20 vessel into the house of *J*
66:21 for the Levites, *J* has said
66:22 is the utterance of *J*
66:23 bow down before me, *J* has
Jer 1:2 the word of *J* occurred in
1:4 the word of *J* began to occur
1:6 *J*! Here I actually do not
1:7 *J* went on to say to me
1:8 is the utterance of *J*
1:9 *J* thrust his hand out and
1:9 Then *J* said to me: Here I
1:11 word of *J* continued to occur

Jer 1:12 *J* went on to say to me
1:13 the word of *J* proceeded to
1:14 At this *J* said to me: Out
1:15 north, is the utterance of *J*
1:19 utterance of *J*, to deliver
2:1 the word of *J* proceeded to
2:2 This is what *J* has said
2:3 was something holy to *J*
2:3 was the utterance of *J*
2:4 Hear the word of *J*, O house
2:5 This is what *J* has said
2:6 Where is *J*, the One bringing
2:8 did not say, Where is *J?*
2:9 is the utterance of *J*, and
2:12 is the utterance of *J*
2:17 your leaving *J* your God
2:19 your leaving *J* your God is
2:19 Sovereign Lord, *J* of armies
2:22 the Sovereign Lord *J*
2:29 is the utterance of *J*
2:31 the word of *J*
2:37 *J* has rejected the objects
3:1 is the utterance of *J*
3:6 *J* proceeded to say to me
3:10 is the utterance of *J*
3:11 *J* went on to say to me
3:12 is the utterance of *J*
3:12 is the utterance of *J*
3:13 against *J* your God that you
3:13 is the utterance of *J*
3:14 is the utterance of *J*
3:16 is the utterance of *J*
3:16 The ark of the covenant of *J!*
3:17 Jerusalem the throne of *J*
3:17 the name of *J* at Jerusalem
3:20 is the utterance of *J*
3:21 have forgotten *J* their God
3:22 for you, O *J*, are our God
3:23 *J* our God is the salvation of
3:25 toward *J* our God that we
3:25 not obeyed the voice of *J*
4:1 is the utterance of *J*
4:2 As *J* is alive in truth
4:3 *J* has said to the men of
4:4 Get . . . circumcised to *J*
4:8 anger of *J* has not turned back
4:9 is the utterance of *J*, that
4:10 Alas, O Sovereign Lord *J!*
4:17 is the utterance of *J*
4:26 It was because of *J*, because
4:27 this is what *J* has said
5:2 As *J* is alive! they would
5:3 O *J*, are not those eyes of
5:4 have ignored the way of *J*
5:5 taken note of the way of *J*
5:9 is the utterance of *J*
5:10 for they do not belong to *J*
5:11 is the utterance of *J*
5:12 They have denied *J*, and
5:14 *J*, the God of armies, has
5:15 is the utterance of *J*
5:18 is the utterance of *J*
5:19 Due to what fact has *J* our
5:22 is the utterance of *J*
5:24 fear *J* our God, the One who
5:29 is the utterance of *J*
6:6 what *J* of armies has said
6:9 *J* of armies has said: They
6:10 very word of *J* has become
6:11 with the rage of *J* I have
6:12 is the utterance of *J*
6:15 they will stumble, *J* has
6:16 This is what *J* has said
6:21 this is what *J* has said
6:22 *J* has said: Look! A people
6:30 for *J* has rejected them
7:1 to Jeremiah from *J*, saying
7:2 the gate of the house of *J*
7:2 Hear the word of *J*, all you
7:2 to bow down to *J*
7:3 This is what *J* of armies
7:4 The temple of *J*, the temple
7:4, 4 of *J*, the temple of *J*
7:11 is the utterance of *J*
7:13 is the utterance of *J*
7:19 is the utterance of *J*
7:20 *J* has said, Look! My anger
7:21 This is what *J* of armies
7:28 not obeyed the voice of *J*
7:29 *J* has rejected and will
7:30 is the utterance of *J*
7:32 is the utterance of *J*
8:1 is the utterance of *J*
8:3 the utterance of *J* of armies

Jer 8:4 This is what *J* has said
8:7 to know the judgment of *J*
8:8 and the law of *J* is with us
8:9 rejected the very word of *J*
8:12 they will stumble, *J* has
8:13 is the utterance of *J*
8:14 *J* our God has himself put us
8:14 we have sinned against *J*
8:17 is the utterance of *J*
8:19 Is *J* not in Zion? Or is her
9:3 is the utterance of *J*
9:6 is the utterance of *J*
9:7 what *J* of armies has said
9:9 is the utterance of *J*
9:12 the mouth of *J* has spoken
9:13 And *J* proceeded to say
9:15 *J* of armies, the God of
9:17 *J* of armies has said
9:20 O you women, the word of *J*
9:22 what the utterance of *J* is
9:23 This is what *J* has said
9:24 I am *J*, the One exercising
9:24 is the utterance of *J*
9:25 is the utterance of *J*
10:1 *J* has spoken against you
10:2 This is what *J* has said
10:6 anyone like you, O *J*
10:10 But *J* is in truth God
10:16 *J* of armies is his name
10:18 this is what *J* has said
10:21 have not looked even for *J*
10:23 I well know, O *J*, that to
10:24 Correct me, O *J*, however
11:1 to Jeremiah from *J*, saying
11:3 *J* the God of Israel has said
11:5 answer and say: Amen, O *J*
11:6 *J* went on to say to me
11:9 *J* said to me: Conspiracy has
11:11 this is what *J* has said
11:16 what *J* has called your name
11:17 And *J* of armies himself
11:18 *J* himself has informed me
11:20 *J* of armies is judging with
11:21 *J* has said against the men
11:21 prophesy in the name of *J*
11:22 what *J* of armies has said
12:1 You are righteous, O *J*, when
12:3 you yourself, O *J*, know me
12:12 the sword belonging to *J* is
12:13 the burning anger of *J*
12:14 This is what *J* has said
12:16 As *J* is alive! just as they
12:17 is the utterance of *J*
13:1 This is what *J* has said to
13:2 in accord with the word of *J*
13:3 the word of *J* proceeded to
13:5 just as *J* had commanded me
13:6 *J* proceeded to say to me
13:8 the word of *J* occurred to me
13:9 This is what *J* has said
13:11 is the utterance of *J*
13:12 *J* the God of Israel has said
13:13 *J* has said: Here I am
13:14 is the utterance of *J*
13:15 for *J* himself has spoken
13:16 Give to *J* your God glory
13:17 the drove of *J* will have
13:25 is the utterance of *J*
14:1 the word of *J* to Jeremiah
14:7 O *J*, act for the sake of your
14:9 in the midst of us, O *J*
14:10 what *J* has said concerning
14:10 *J* himself has taken no
14:11 *J* proceeded to say to me
14:13 Alas, O Sovereign Lord *J!*
14:14 *J* went on to say to me
14:15 this is what *J* has said
14:20 We do acknowledge, O *J*, our
14:22 the One, O *J* our God
15:1 *J* proceeded to say to me
15:2 This is what *J* has said
15:3 is the utterance of *J*
15:6 is the utterance of *J*
15:9 is the utterance of *J*
15:11 *J* has said: Surely I will
15:15 O *J*, remember me and turn
15:16 O *J* God of armies
15:19 this is what *J* has said
15:20 is the utterance of *J*
16:1 the word of *J* continued to
16:3 this is what *J* has said
16:5 For this is what *J* has said
16:5 is the utterance of *J*
16:9 this is what *J* of armies

Jer 16:10 has *J* spoken against us all
16:10 sinned against *J* our God
16:11 is the utterance of *J*
16:14 is the utterance of *J*
16:14 As *J* is alive who brought
16:15 As *J* is alive who brought
16:16 is the utterance of *J*
16:19 O *J* my strength and my
16:21 to know that my name is *J*
17:5 This is what *J* has said
17:5 heart turns away from *J*
17:7 man who puts his trust in *J*
17:7 whose confidence *J* has
17:10 I, *J*, am searching the
17:13 *J*, the hope of Israel, all
17:13 source of living water, *J*
17:14 Heal me, O *J*, and I shall
17:15 Where is the word of *J?*
17:19 what *J* has said to me
17:20 Hear the word of *J*, you
17:21 This is what *J* has said
17:24 is the utterance of *J*
17:26 into the house of *J*
18:1 to Jeremiah from *J*, saying
18:5 word of *J* continued to occur
18:6 is the utterance of *J*
18:11 This is what *J* has said
18:13 this is what *J* has said
18:19 pay attention to me, O *J*
18:23 you yourself, O *J*, well
19:1 This is what *J* said
19:3 Hear the word of *J*, O you
19:3 This is what *J* of armies
19:6 is the utterance of *J*
19:11 what *J* of armies has said
19:12 is the utterance of *J*
19:14 *J* had sent him to prophesy
19:14 courtyard of the house of *J*
19:15 *J* of armies, the God of
20:1 in the house of *J*, kept
20:2 was in the house of *J*
20:3 *J* has called your name
20:4 this is what *J* has said
20:7 You have fooled me, O *J*, so
20:8 the word of *J* became for me
20:11 *J* was with me like a
20:12 you, O *J* of armies, are
20:13 Sing to *J*, you people!
20:13 Praise *J!* For he has
20:16 that *J* has overthrown
21:1 occurred to Jeremiah from *J*
21:2 inquire in our behalf of *J*
21:2 Perhaps *J* will do with us
21:4 *J* the God of Israel has said
21:7 is the utterance of *J*
21:8 This is what *J* has said
21:10 is the utterance of *J*
21:11 hear, O men, the word of *J*
21:12 this is what *J* has said
21:13 is the utterance of *J*
21:14 is the utterance of *J*
22:1 This is what *J* has said
22:2 Hear the word of *J*, O king
22:3 is what *J* has said: Render
22:5 is the utterance of *J*
22:6 this is what *J* has said
22:8 did *J* do like this to this
22:9 they left the covenant of *J*
22:11 this is what *J* has said
22:16 is the utterance of *J*
22:18 this is what *J* has said
22:24 is the utterance of *J*
22:29 earth, hear the word of *J*
22:30 This is what *J* has said
23:1 is the utterance of *J*
23:2 what *J* the God of Israel has
23:2 is the utterance of *J*
23:4 is the utterance of *J*
23:5 is the utterance of *J*, and I
23:6 *J* Is Our Righteousness
23:7 is the utterance of *J*
23:7 *J* is alive who brought the
23:8 *J* is alive who brought up and
23:9 *J* and because of his holy
23:11 is the utterance of *J*
23:12 is the utterance of *J*
23:15 what *J* of armies has said
23:16 what *J* of armies has said
23:16 not from the mouth of *J*
23:17 *J* has spoken: Peace is what
23:18 in the intimate group of *J*
23:19 The windstorm of *J*, rage
23:20 The anger of *J* will not
23:23 is the utterance of *J*

Jer 23:24 is the utterance of *J*
23:24 is the utterance of *J*
23:28 is the utterance of *J*
23:29 is the utterance of *J*
23:30 is the utterance of *J*
23:31 is the utterance of *J*
23:32 is the utterance of *J*
23:32 is the utterance of *J*
23:33 What is the burden of *J*?
23:33 is the utterance of *J*
23:34 who say, The burden of *J*!
23:35 What has *J* answered?
23:35 And what has *J* spoken?
23:36 the burden of *J* you people
23:36 *J* of armies, our God
23:37 What answer has *J* given you?
23:37 And what has *J* spoken?
23:38 And if The burden of *J*! is
23:38 this is what *J* has said
23:38 is the very burden of *J*
23:38 not say: The burden of *J*!
24:1 *J* showed me, and, look! two
24:1 set before the temple of *J*
24:3 *J* proceeded to say to me
24:4 the word of *J* occurred to me
24:5 *J* the God of Israel has said
24:7 to know me, that I am *J*
24:8 *J* has said: So I shall give
25:3 the word of *J* has occurred
25:4 And *J* sent to you all his
25:5 the ground that *J* gave to you
25:7 is the utterance of *J*
25:8 what *J* of armies has said
25:9 is the utterance of *J*
25:12 is the utterance of *J*
25:15 *J* the God of Israel said
25:17 the cup out of the hand of *J*
25:17 to whom *J* had sent me
25:27 *J* of armies, the God of
25:28 what *J* of armies has said
25:29 utterance of *J* of armies
25:30 *J* himself will roar, and
25:31 a controversy that *J* has
25:31 is the utterance of *J*
25:32 This is what *J* of armies
25:33 And those slain by *J* will
25:36 for *J* is despoiling their
25:37 the burning anger of *J*
26:1 this word occurred from *J*
26:2 This is what *J* has said
26:2 courtyard of the house of *J*
26:2 bow down at the house of *J*
26:4 This is what *J* has said
26:7 words in the house of *J*
26:8 all that *J* had commanded
26:9 prophesied in the name of *J*
26:9 Jeremiah in the house of *J*
26:10 to the house of *J* and
26:10 of the new gate of *J*
26:12 *J* that sent me to prophesy
26:13 obey the voice of *J* your
26:13 *J* will feel regret for the
26:15 *J* did send me to you to
26:16 in the name of *J* our God
26:18 what *J* of armies has said
26:19 Did he not fear *J* and
26:19 soften the face of *J*
26:19 *J* got to feeling regret
26:20 in the name of *J*
27:1 to Jeremiah from *J*, saying
27:2 *J* has said to me, Make for
27:4 This is what *J* of armies
27:8 is the utterance of *J*
27:11 is the utterance of *J*
27:13 *J* has spoken to the nation
27:15 is the utterance of *J*
27:16 This is what *J* has said
27:16 utensils of the house of *J*
27:18 if the word of *J* does exist
27:18 please, beseech *J* of armies
27:18 over in the house of *J*
27:19 this is what *J* of armies
27:21 this is what *J* of armies
27:21 over at the house of *J*
27:22 is the utterance of *J*
28:1 said to me in the house of *J*
28:2 This is what *J* of armies
28:3 utensils of the house of *J*
28:4 is the utterance of *J*
28:5 standing in the house of *J*
28:6 Amen! Thus may *J* do!
28:6 May *J* establish your words
28:6 utensils of the house of *J*
28:9 the prophet whom *J* has sent

Jer 28:11 This is what *J* has said
28:12 the word of *J* occurred to
28:13 This is what *J* has said
28:14 this is what *J* of armies
28:15 *J* has not sent you, but you
28:16 this is what *J* has said
28:16 outright revolt against *J*
29:4 This is what *J* of armies
29:7 and pray in its behalf to *J*
29:8 For this is what *J* of armies
29:9 is the utterance of *J*
29:10 this is what *J* has said
29:11 is the utterance of *J*
29:14 is the utterance of *J*
29:14 is the utterance of *J*
29:15 *J* has raised up for us
29:16 *J* has said to the king
29:17 what *J* of armies has said
29:19 is the utterance of *J*
29:19 is the utterance of *J*
29:20 hear the word of *J*, all you
29:21 This is what *J* of armies
29:22 *J* make you like Zedekiah
29:23 is the utterance of *J*
29:25 This is what *J* of armies
29:26 *J* himself has made you
29:26 overseer of the house of *J*
29:30 the word of *J* occurred to
29:31 This is what *J* has said
29:32 this is what *J* has said
29:32 is the utterance of *J*
29:32 outright revolt against *J*
30:1 to Jeremiah from *J*, saying
30:2 This is what *J* the God of
30:3 is the utterance of *J*
30:3 *J* has said, and I will bring
30:4 words that *J* has spoken to
30:5 this is what *J* has said
30:8 the utterance of *J* of armies
30:9 serve *J* their God and David
30:10 is the utterance of *J*
30:11 is the utterance of *J*
30:12 this is what *J* has said
30:17 is the utterance of *J*
30:18 is what *J* has said
30:21 is the utterance of *J*
30:23 windstorm of *J*, rage itself
30:24 burning anger of *J* will
31:1 time, is the utterance of *J*
31:2 This is what *J* has said
31:3 *J* himself appeared to me
31:6 go up to Zion, to *J* our God
31:7 what *J* has said: Cry out
31:7 Save, O *J*, your people, the
31:10 Hear the word of *J*, O you
31:11 *J* will actually redeem
31:12 over the goodness of *J*
31:14 is the utterance of *J*
31:15 This is what *J* has said
31:16 This is what *J* has said
31:16 is the utterance of *J*, and
31:17 is the utterance of *J*
31:18 for you are *J* my God
31:20 is the utterance of *J*
31:22 *J* has created a new thing
31:23 *J* of armies, the God of
31:23 *J* bless you, O righteous
31:27 is the utterance of *J*
31:28 is the utterance of *J*
31:31 is the utterance of *J*, and
31:32 is the utterance of *J*
31:33 is the utterance of *J*
31:34 Know *J*! for they will all
31:34 is the utterance of *J*
31:35 *J*, the Giver of the sun for
31:35 whose name is *J* of armies
31:36 utterance of *J*, those who
31:37 *J* has said: If the heavens
31:37 is the utterance of *J*
31:38 utterance of *J*, and the city
31:38 be built to *J* from the
31:40 be something holy to *J*
32:1 to Jeremiah from *J* in the
32:3 is what *J* has said: Here I
32:5 is the utterance of *J*
32:6 word of *J* has occurred to me
32:8 according to the word of *J*
32:8 had been the word of *J*
32:14 *J* of armies, the God of
32:15 *J* of armies, the God of
32:16 pray to *J* after my having
32:17 Alas, O Sovereign Lord *J*!
32:18 *J* of armies being his name
32:25 Sovereign Lord *J*, Buy for

Jer 32:26 word of *J* occurred to
32:27 *J*, the God of all flesh
32:28 this is what *J* has said
32:30 is the utterance of *J*
32:36 *J* the God of Israel has said
32:42 *J* has said, Just as I have
32:44 is the utterance of *J*
33:1 word of *J* proceeded to
33:2 *J* the Maker of earth has
33:2 *J* the Former of it to
33:2 *J* being his name
33:4 *J* the God of Israel has said
33:10 *J* has said, In this place
33:11 Laud *J* of armies, for
33:11 for *J* is good; for to time
33:11 into the house of *J*, for
33:11 at the start, *J* has said
33:12 *J* of armies has said, In
33:13 the count, *J* has said
33:14 utterance of *J*, and I shall
33:16 *J* Is Our Righteousness
33:17 *J* has said, There will not
33:19 word of *J* came further to
33:20 *J* has said, If you people
33:23 word of *J* continued to
33:24 families whom *J* has chosen
33:25 *J* has said, If it was not
34:1 occurred to Jeremiah from *J*
34:2 *J* the God of Israel has said
34:2 *J* has said, Here I am
34:4 However, hear the word of *J*
34:4 *J* has said concerning you
34:5 is the utterance of *J*
34:8 to Jeremiah from *J* after
34:12 word of *J* occurred to
34:12 to Jeremiah from *J*, saying
34:13 *J* the God of Israel has
34:17 *J* has said, You yourselves
34:17 utterance of *J*, to the
34:22 utterance of *J*, and I shall
35:1 to Jeremiah from *J* in the
35:2 house of *J*, to one of the
35:4 into the house of *J*, to
35:12 word of *J* proceeded to
35:13 *J* of armies, the God of
35:13 is the utterance of *J*
35:17 *J* the God of armies, the
35:18 *J* of armies, the God of
35:19 *J* of armies, the God of
36:1 to Jeremiah from *J*, saying
36:4 words of *J* that He had
36:5 enter into the house of *J*
36:6 words of *J* in the ears of
36:6 house of *J* in the day of
36:7 fall before *J* and they
36:7 *J* has spoken against this
36:8 words of *J* at the house of
36:8 at the house of *J*
36:9 proclaimed a fast before *J*
36:10 at the house of *J*, in the
36:10 gate of the house of *J*, in
36:11 hear all the words of *J*
36:26 *J* kept them concealed
36:27 the word of *J* occurred
36:29 *J* has said: You yourself
36:30 what *J* has said against
37:2 words of *J* that he spoke
37:3 in our behalf to *J* our God
37:6 word of *J* occurred to
37:7 *J* the God of Israel has said
37:9 *J* has said: Do not deceive
37:17 there exist a word from *J*
38:2 what *J* has said, The one
38:3 *J* has said, Without fail
38:14 is in the house of *J*, and
38:16 As *J* is alive, who has
38:17 *J*, the God of armies, the
38:20 voice of *J* in what I am
38:21 *J* has caused me to see
39:15 to Jeremiah the word of *J*
39:16 *J* of armies, the God of
39:17 is the utterance of *J*
39:18 me, is the utterance of *J*
40:1 to Jeremiah from *J* after
40:2 *J* your God himself spoke
40:3 *J* might bring it true and
40:3 people have sinned against *J*
41:5 bring to the house of *J*
42:2 pray in our behalf to *J*
42:3 *J* your God tell us the way
42:4 I am praying to *J* your God
42:4 every word that *J* gives in
42:5 *J* prove to be a true and
42:5 *J* your God sends you to us

Jer 42:6 voice of *J* our God to
42:6 obey the voice of *J* our God
42:7 word of *J* proceeded to occur
42:9 *J* the God of Israel, to
42:11 is the utterance of *J*, for
42:13 disobey the voice of *J* your
42:15 word of *J*, O remnant of
42:15 *J* of armies, the God of
42:18 *J* of armies, the God of
42:19 *J* has spoken against you
42:20 sent me to *J* your God
42:20 Pray in our behalf to *J*
42:20 *J* our God says tell us that
42:21 not obey the voice of *J*
43:1 words of *J* their God with
43:1 *J* their God had sent him
43:2 *J* our God has not sent you
43:4 not obey the voice of *J*, to
43:7 did not obey the voice of *J*
43:8 word of *J* occurred to
43:10 what *J* of armies, the God
44:2 is what *J* of armies, the God
44:7 is what *J*, the God of armies
44:11 this is what *J* of armies
44:16 to us in the name of *J*
44:21 this that *J* remembered and
44:22 *J* was no longer able to put
44:23 sinned against *J* and did
44:23 did not obey the voice of *J*
44:24 Hear the word of *J*, all
44:25 is what *J* of armies, the
44:26 hear the word of *J*, all
44:26 great name, *J* has said
44:26 Sovereign Lord *J* is alive
44:29 utterance of *J*, that I am
44:30 is what *J* has said: Here I
45:2 *J* the God of Israel has
45:3 *J* has added grief to my pain!
45:4 *J* has said: Look! What I
45:5 utterance of *J*, and I will
46:1 word of *J* to Jeremiah the
46:5 is the utterance of *J*
46:10 *J* of armies, the day of
46:10 *J* of armies, has a
46:13 *J* spoke to Jeremiah the
46:15 *J* himself has pushed them
46:18 whose name is *J* of armies
46:23 utterance of *J*, for it could
46:25 *J* of armies, the God of
46:26 is the utterance of *J*
46:28 utterance of *J*, for I am
47:1 word of *J* to Jeremiah the
47:2 This is what *J* has said
47:4 For *J* is despoiling the
47:6 Aha, the sword of *J*!
47:7 *J* himself has given a
48:1 *J* of armies, the God of
48:8 a thing that *J* has said
48:10 mission of *J* neglectfully
48:12 utterance of *J*, and I will
48:15 whose name is *J* of armies
48:25 is the utterance of *J*
48:26 put on great airs against *J*
48:30 fury, is the utterance of *J*
48:35 Moab, is the utterance of *J*
48:38 is the utterance of *J*
48:40 *J* has said, Look! Just like
48:42 against *J* that he has put
48:43 Moab, is the utterance of *J*
48:44 is the utterance of *J*
48:47 is the utterance of *J*
49:1 *J* has said: Are there no
49:2 utterance of *J*, and I will
49:2 *J* has said
49:5 Sovereign Lord, *J* of armies
49:6 Ammon, is the utterance of *J*
49:7 what *J* of armies has said
49:12 *J* has said: Look! Although
49:13 is the utterance of *J*
49:14 that I have heard from *J*
49:16 is the utterance of *J*
49:18 *J* has said, no man will
49:20 counsel of *J* that he has
49:26 utterance of *J* of armies
49:28 *J* has said: Rise up, go up
49:30 Hazor, is the utterance of *J*
49:31 is the utterance of *J*
49:32 is the utterance of *J*
49:34 the word of *J* to Jeremiah
49:35 *J* of armies has said, Here
49:37 is the utterance of *J*
49:38 is the utterance of *J*
49:39 is the utterance of *J*
50:1 *J* spoke concerning Babylon

Jer 50:4 utterance of *J*, the sons of
50:4 *J* their God they will seek
50:5 us join ourselves to *J* in an
50:7 they have sinned against *J*
50:7 hope of their forefathers, *J*
50:10 is the utterance of *J*
50:13 of the indignation of *J*
50:14 against *J* that she has
50:15 it is the vengeance of *J*
50:18 *J* of armies, the God of
50:20 utterance of *J*, the error
50:21 is the utterance of *J*
50:24 against *J* that you excited
50:25 *J* has opened his storehouse
50:25 *J* of armies, has in the
50:28 vengeance of *J* our God
50:29 against *J* that she has acted
50:30 day, is the utterance of *J*
50:31 *J* of armies, for your day
50:33 *J* of armies has said
50:34 *J* of armies being his name
50:35 utterance of *J*, and against
50:40 utterance of *J*, no man will
50:45 counsel of *J* that he has
51:1 *J* has said: Here I am
51:5 their God, from *J* of armies
51:6 of vengeance belonging to *J*
51:7 golden cup in the hand of *J*
51:10 *J* has brought forth deeds
51:10 the work of *J* our God
51:11 *J* has aroused the spirit of
51:11 For it is the vengeance of *J*
51:12 *J* both has formed the idea
51:14 *J* of armies has sworn by
51:19 *J* of armies is his name
51:24 is the utterance of *J*
51:25 utterance of *J*, you ruiner
51:26 is the utterance of *J*
51:29 thoughts of *J* have risen up
51:33 *J* of armies, the God of
51:36 *J* has said: Here I am
51:39 is the utterance of *J*
51:45 the burning anger of *J*
51:48 is the utterance of *J*
51:50 From far away remember *J*
51:51 places of the house of *J*
51:52 utterance of *J*, and I will
51:53 is the utterance of *J*
51:55 *J* is despoiling Babylon
51:56 *J* is a God of recompenses
51:57 whose name is *J* of armies
51:58 *J* of armies has said
51:62 *J*, you yourself have spoken
52:2 was bad in the eyes of *J*
52:3 account of the anger of *J*
52:13 burn the house of *J* and
52:17 belonged to the house of *J*
52:17 was in the house of *J*
52:20 had made for the house of *J*
La 1:5 *J* himself has brought grief to
1:9 O *J*, see my affliction, for
1:11 See, O *J*, and do look, for I
1:12 *J* has caused grief in the day
1:14 *J* has given me into the hand
1:15 my powerful ones *J* has tossed
1:15 *J* has trodden the very
1:17 *J* has given a command
1:18 *J* is righteous, for it is
1:20 O *J*, for I am in sore straits
2:1 *J* in his anger beclouds the
2:2 *J* has swallowed up, he has
2:5 *J* has become like an enemy
2:6 *J* has caused to be forgotten in
2:7 *J* has cast off his altar
2:7 In the house of *J* they have let
2:8 *J* has thought of bringing the
2:9 have found no vision from *J*
2:17 *J* has done what he had in
2:18 Their heart has cried out to *J*
2:19 heart before the face of *J*
2:20 See, O *J*, and do look to the
2:20 in the sanctuary of *J* should
2:22 in the day of the wrath of *J*
3:18 and my expectation from *J*
3:22 acts of loving-kindness of *J*
3:24 *J* is my share, my soul has
3:25 Good is *J* to the one hoping in
3:26 for the salvation of *J*
3:31 will *J* keep on casting off
3:36 *J* . . . has had no countenance
3:37 *J* himself has not commanded
3:40 do let us return clear to *J*
3:50 Until *J* looks down and sees
3:55 called out your name, O *J*

La 3:58 taken up, O *J*, the contests of
3:59 You have seen, O *J*, the wrong
3:61 have heard their reproach, O *J*
3:64 back to them a treatment, O *J*
3:66 from under the heavens of *J*
4:11 *J* has accomplished his rage
4:16 face of *J* has divided them up
4:20 the anointed one of *J*, has
5:1 Remember, O *J*, what has
5:19 O *J*, to time indefinite you
5:21 us back, O *J*, to yourself
Eze 1:3 the word of *J* occurred
1:3 in that place the hand of *J*
1:28 likeness of the glory of *J*
2:4 the Sovereign Lord *J* has said
3:11 the Sovereign Lord *J* has said
3:12 Blessed be the glory of *J*
3:14 hand of *J* upon me was strong
3:16 word of *J* proceeded to occur
3:22 hand of *J* came to be upon me
3:23 the glory of *J* was standing
3:27 the Sovereign Lord *J* has said
4:13 *J* went on to say: Just like
4:14 Alas, O Sovereign Lord *J*!
5:5 the Sovereign Lord *J* has said
5:7 the Sovereign Lord *J* has said
5:8 the Sovereign Lord *J* has said
5:11 of the Sovereign Lord *J*
5:13 myself, *J*, have spoken in my
5:15 I myself, *J*, have spoken
5:17 I myself, *J*, have spoken
6:1 word of *J* continued to occur
6:3 word of the Sovereign Lord *J*
6:3 *J* has said to the mountains
6:7 have to know that I am *J*
6:10 have to know that I am *J*
6:11 *J* has said, Clap your hands
6:13 have to know that I am *J*
6:14 have to know that I am *J*
7:1 word of *J* continued to occur
7:2 Lord *J* has said to the soil of
7:4 have to know that I am *J*
7:5 *J* has said, A calamity, a
7:9 have to know that I am *J*
7:27 have to know that I am *J*
8:1 hand of the Sovereign Lord *J*
8:12 saying, *J* is not seeing us
8:12 *J* has left the land
8:14 the gate of the house of *J*
8:16 courtyard of the house of *J*
8:16 entrance of the temple of *J*
8:16 backs to the temple of *J* and
9:4 *J* went on to say to him: Pass
9:8 Alas, O Sovereign Lord *J*!
9:9 have said, *J* has left the land
9:9 the land, and *J* is not seeing
10:4 glory of *J* proceeded to rise
10:4 brightness of the glory of *J*
10:18 glory of *J* proceeded to go
10:19 the gate of the house of *J*
11:1 gate of the house of *J* that
11:5 the spirit of *J* fell upon me
11:5 Say, This is what *J* has said
11:7 the Sovereign Lord *J* has said
11:8 of the Sovereign Lord *J*
11:10 have to know that I am *J*
11:12 have to know that I am *J*
11:13 Alas, O Sovereign Lord *J*!
11:14 the word of *J* continued to
11:15 said, Get far away from *J*
11:16 Sovereign Lord *J* has said
11:17 Sovereign Lord *J* has said
11:21 of the Sovereign Lord *J*
11:23 glory of *J* went ascending
11:25 the things of *J* that he had
12:1 word of *J* continued to occur
12:8 word of *J* continued to occur
12:10 Sovereign Lord *J* has said
12:15 have to know that I am *J*
12:16 have to know that I am *J*
12:17 the word of *J* continued to
12:19 Sovereign Lord *J* has said
12:20 have to know that I am *J*
12:21 word of *J* occurred further
12:23 Lord *J* has said: I shall
12:25 *J*, shall speak what word I
12:25 of the Sovereign Lord *J*
12:26 the word of *J* continued to
12:28 Sovereign Lord *J* has said
12:28 of the Sovereign Lord *J*
13:1 word of *J* continued to occur
13:2 Hear the word of *J*
13:3 Lord *J* has said: Woe to the
13:5 in the battle in the day of *J*

Eze 13:6 saying, The utterance of *J* is
13:6 *J* himself has not sent them
13:7 saying, The utterance of *J* is
13:8 the Sovereign Lord *J* has said
13:8 of the Sovereign Lord *J*
13:9 I am the Sovereign Lord *J*
13:13 *J* has said, I will also
13:14 have to know that I am *J*
13:16 of the Sovereign Lord *J*
13:18 Lord *J* has said: Woe to the
13:20 Sovereign Lord *J* has said
13:21 have to know that I am *J*
13:23 have to know that I am *J*
14:2 the word of *J* occurred to me
14:4 *J* has said: Any man at all
14:4 I, *J*, I will let myself be
14:6 *J* has said: Come back and
14:7 I, *J*, I am letting myself be
14:8 have to know that I am *J*
14:9 *J*, have fooled that prophet
14:11 of the Sovereign Lord *J*
14:12 word of *J* continued to come
14:14 of the Sovereign Lord *J*
14:16 of the Sovereign Lord *J*
14:18 of the Sovereign Lord *J*
14:20 of the Sovereign Lord *J*
14:21 Sovereign Lord *J* has said
14:23 of the Sovereign Lord *J*
15:1 word of *J* continued to occur
15:6 *J* has said, Just like the
15:7 know that I am *J*, when I
15:8 of the Sovereign Lord *J*
16:1 word of *J* came further to
16:3 Lord *J* has said to Jerusalem
16:8 of the Sovereign Lord *J*, and
16:14 of the Sovereign Lord *J*
16:19 of the Sovereign Lord *J*
16:23 of the Sovereign Lord *J*
16:30 of the Sovereign Lord *J*
16:35 hear the word of *J*
16:36 *J* has said, For the reason
16:43 of the Sovereign Lord *J*
16:48 of the Sovereign Lord *J*
16:58 is the utterance of *J*
16:59 Sovereign Lord *J* has said
16:62 have to know that I am *J*
16:63 of the Sovereign Lord *J*
17:1 word of *J* continued to occur
17:3 *J* has said: The great eagle
17:9 the Sovereign Lord *J* has said
17:11 the word of *J* continued to
17:16 of the Sovereign Lord *J*
17:19 *J* has said: As I am alive
17:21 I myself, *J*, have spoken it
17:22 Sovereign Lord *J* has said
17:24 *J*, have abased the high tree
17:24 *J*, have spoken and have done
18:1 word of *J* continued to occur
18:3 of the Sovereign Lord *J*
18:9 of the Sovereign Lord *J*
18:23 of the Sovereign Lord *J*
18:25 way of *J* is not adjusted
18:29 way of *J* is not adjusted
18:30 of the Sovereign Lord *J*
18:32 of the Sovereign Lord *J*
20:1 came in to inquire of *J*
20:2 the word of *J* occurred to me
20:3 the Sovereign Lord *J* has said
20:3 of the Sovereign Lord *J*
20:5 the Sovereign Lord *J* has said
20:5 saying, I am *J* your God
20:7 I am *J* your God
20:12 I am *J* who is sanctifying
20:19 I am *J* your God. Walk in
20:20 know that I am *J* your God
20:26 might know that I am *J*
20:27 Sovereign Lord *J* has said
20:30 Sovereign Lord *J* has said
20:31 the Sovereign Lord *J*
20:33 the Sovereign Lord *J*
20:36 the Sovereign Lord *J*
20:38 have to know that I am *J*
20:39 *J* has said, Go serve each
20:40 the Sovereign Lord *J*
20:42 have to know that I am *J*
20:44 have to know that I am *J*
20:44 the Sovereign Lord *J*
20:45 word of *J* continued to
20:47 Hear the word of *J*
20:47 *J* has said: Here I am
20:48 *J*, have set it afire
20:49 Alas, O Sovereign Lord *J!*
21:1 word of *J* continued to occur
21:3 This is what *J* has said

Eze 21:5 *J* have brought forth my
21:7 the Sovereign Lord *J*
21:8 word of *J* continued to occur
21:9 *J* has said: Say, A sword
21:13 the Sovereign Lord *J*
21:17 I myself, *J*, have spoken
21:18 word of *J* continued to
21:24 *J* has said, By reason of
21:26 *J* has said, Remove the
21:28 Sovereign Lord *J* has said
21:32 I myself, *J*, have spoken
22:1 the word of *J* continued to
22:3 Sovereign Lord *J* has said
22:12 the Sovereign Lord *J*
22:14 I myself, *J*, have spoken
22:16 have to know that I am *J*
22:17 word of *J* continued to come
22:19 Sovereign Lord *J* has said
22:22 *J*, have poured out my rage
22:23 the word of *J* continued to
22:28 Sovereign Lord *J* has said
22:28 *J* himself has not spoken
22:31 the Sovereign Lord *J*
23:1 word of *J* proceeded to come
23:22 the Sovereign Lord *J* has
23:28 the Sovereign Lord *J* has
23:32 the Sovereign Lord *J* has
23:34 the Sovereign Lord *J*
23:35 the Sovereign Lord *J*
23:36 *J* went on to say to me
23:46 the Sovereign Lord *J* has
23:49 I am the Sovereign Lord *J*
24:1 the word of *J* continued to
24:3 the Sovereign Lord *J* has said
24:6 the Sovereign Lord *J* has said
24:9 the Sovereign Lord *J* has said
24:14 I myself, *J*, have spoken
24:14 the Sovereign Lord *J*
24:15 the word of *J* continued to
24:20 word of *J* has occurred to
24:21 Sovereign Lord *J* has said
24:24 I am the Sovereign Lord *J*
24:27 have to know that I am *J*
25:1 the word of *J* continued to
25:3 word of the Sovereign Lord *J*
25:3 the Sovereign Lord *J* has said
25:5 have to know that I am *J*
25:6 the Sovereign Lord *J* has said
25:7 have to know that I am *J*
25:8 the Sovereign Lord *J* has said
25:11 have to know that I am *J*
25:12 the Sovereign Lord *J* has
25:13 Sovereign Lord *J* has said
25:14 the Sovereign Lord *J*
25:15 Sovereign Lord *J* has said
25:16 the Sovereign Lord *J* has
25:17 have to know that I am *J*
26:1 word of *J* occurred to me
26:3 the Sovereign Lord *J* has said
26:5 the Sovereign Lord *J*
26:6 have to know that I am *J*
26:7 the Sovereign Lord *J* has said
26:14 I myself, *J*, have spoken
26:14 the Sovereign Lord *J*
26:15 Sovereign Lord *J* has said
26:19 Sovereign Lord *J* has said
26:21 the Sovereign Lord *J*
27:1 word of *J* continued to occur
27:3 Sovereign Lord *J* has said
28:1 word of *J* continued to occur
28:2 the Sovereign Lord *J* has said
28:6 Sovereign Lord *J* has said
28:10 the Sovereign Lord *J*
28:11 word of *J* continued to
28:12 Sovereign Lord *J* has said
28:20 word of *J* continued to
28:22 Sovereign Lord *J* has said
28:22 have to know that I am *J*
28:23 have to know that I am *J*
28:24 I am the Sovereign Lord *J*
28:25 Sovereign Lord *J* has said
28:26 know that I am *J* their God
29:1 word of *J* occurred to me
29:3 the Sovereign Lord *J* has said
29:6 have to know that I am *J*
29:8 the Sovereign Lord *J* has said
29:9 have to know that I am *J*
29:13 Sovereign Lord *J* has said
29:16 I am the Sovereign Lord *J*
29:17 word of *J* occurred to me
29:19 Sovereign Lord *J* has said
29:20 the Sovereign Lord *J*
29:21 have to know that I am *J*
30:1 the word of *J* continued to

Eze 30:2 the Sovereign Lord *J* has said
30:3 a day belonging to *J* is near
30:6 This is what *J* has said
30:6 the Sovereign Lord *J*
30:8 have to know that I am *J*
30:10 Sovereign Lord *J* has said
30:12 I myself, *J*, have spoken
30:13 Sovereign Lord *J* has said
30:19 have to know that I am *J*
30:20 word of *J* occurred to me
30:22 Sovereign Lord *J* has said
30:25 have to know that I am *J*
30:26 have to know that I am *J*
31:1 word of *J* occurred to me
31:10 Sovereign Lord *J* has said
31:15 Sovereign Lord *J* has said
31:18 the Sovereign Lord *J*
32:1 word of *J* occurred to me
32:3 the Sovereign Lord *J* has said
32:8 the Sovereign Lord *J*
32:11 Sovereign Lord *J* has said
32:14 the Sovereign Lord *J*
32:15 have to know that I am *J*
32:16 the Sovereign Lord *J*
32:17 word of *J* occurred to me
32:31 the Sovereign Lord *J*
32:32 the Sovereign Lord *J*
33:1 word of *J* proceeded to occur
33:11 the Sovereign Lord *J*
33:17 way of *J* is not adjusted
33:20 way of *J* is not adjusted
33:22 hand of *J* had come to be
33:23 word of *J* began to occur
33:25 Sovereign Lord *J* has said
33:27 Sovereign Lord *J* has said
33:29 have to know that I am *J*
33:30 that is going forth from *J*
34:1 word of *J* continued to occur
34:2 Sovereign Lord *J* has said
34:7 hear the word of *J*
34:8 the Sovereign Lord *J*
34:9 hear the word of *J*
34:10 Sovereign Lord *J* has said
34:11 Sovereign Lord *J* has said
34:15 the Sovereign Lord *J*
34:17 Sovereign Lord *J* has said
34:20 Sovereign Lord *J* has said
34:24 *J*, will become their God
34:24 I myself, *J*, have spoken
34:27 have to know that I am *J*
34:30 know that I, *J* their God
34:30 the Sovereign Lord *J*
34:31 the Sovereign Lord *J*
35:1 word of *J* continued to occur
35:3 Sovereign Lord *J* has said
35:4 have to know that I am *J*
35:6 the Sovereign Lord *J*
35:9 have to know that I am *J*
35:10 *J* himself happened to be
35:11 the Sovereign Lord *J*
35:12 know that I myself, *J*, have
35:14 Sovereign Lord *J* has said
35:15 have to know that I am *J*
36:1 Israel, hear the word of *J*
36:2 Sovereign Lord *J* has said
36:3 Sovereign Lord *J* has said
36:4 the Sovereign Lord *J*
36:4 Sovereign Lord *J* has said
36:5 Sovereign Lord *J* has said
36:6 Sovereign Lord *J* has said
36:7 Sovereign Lord *J* has said
36:11 have to know that I am *J*
36:13 Sovereign Lord *J* has said
36:14 the Sovereign Lord *J*
36:15 the Sovereign Lord *J*
36:16 word of *J* continued to
36:20 These are the people of *J*
36:22 Sovereign Lord *J* has said
36:23 have to know that I am *J*
36:23 the Sovereign Lord *J*
36:32 the Sovereign Lord *J*
36:33 Sovereign Lord *J* has said
36:36 *J*, have built the things
36:36 *J*, have spoken and I have
36:37 Sovereign Lord *J* has said
36:38 have to know that I am *J*
37:1 The hand of *J* proved to be
37:1 in the spirit of *J* and set
37:3 I said: Sovereign Lord *J*
37:4 bones, hear the word of *J*
37:5 Sovereign Lord *J* has said
37:6 have to know that I am *J*
37:9 Sovereign Lord *J* has said
37:12 Sovereign Lord *J* has said

Eze 37:13 have to know that I am *J*
37:14 I myself, *J*, have spoken
37:14 is the utterance of *J*
37:15 word of *J* continued to
37:19 Sovereign Lord *J* has said
37:21 Sovereign Lord *J* has said
37:28 I, *J*, am sanctifying Israel
38:1 word of *J* continued to occur
38:3 the Sovereign Lord *J* has said
38:10 Sovereign Lord *J* has said
38:14 Sovereign Lord *J* has said
38:17 Sovereign Lord *J* has said
38:18 the Sovereign Lord *J*
38:21 the Sovereign Lord *J*
38:23 have to know that I am *J*
39:1 the Sovereign Lord *J* has said
39:5 the Sovereign Lord *J*
39:6 have to know that I am *J*
39:7 have to know that I am *J*
39:8 the Sovereign Lord *J*
39:10 the Sovereign Lord *J*
39:13 the Sovereign Lord *J*
39:17 Sovereign Lord *J* has said
39:20 the Sovereign Lord *J*
39:22 have to know that I am *J*
39:25 Sovereign Lord *J* has said
39:28 have to know that I am *J*
39:29 the Sovereign Lord *J*
40:1 the hand of *J* proved to be
40:46 approaching *J* to minister
41:22 the table that is before *J*
42:13 who are approaching *J*
43:4 glory of *J* itself came into
43:5 full of the glory of *J*
43:18 Sovereign Lord *J* has said
43:19 Sovereign Lord *J*, to
43:24 bring them near before *J*
43:24 whole burnt offering to *J*
43:27 of the Sovereign Lord *J*
44:2 *J* said to me: As regards
44:2 *J* himself, the God of Israel
44:3 order to eat bread before *J*
44:4 glory of *J* had filled the
44:4 had filled the house of *J*
44:5 *J* said to me: Son of man
44:5 statutes of the house of *J*
44:6 Sovereign Lord *J* has said
44:9 Sovereign Lord *J* has said
44:12 Sovereign Lord *J*, and
44:15 of the Sovereign Lord *J*
44:27 of the Sovereign Lord *J*
45:1 offer a contribution to *J*
45:4 approaching to minister to *J*
45:9 Sovereign Lord *J* has said
45:9 of the Sovereign Lord *J*
45:15 of the Sovereign Lord *J*
45:18 Sovereign Lord *J* has said
45:23 whole burnt offering to *J*
46:1 Sovereign Lord *J* has said
46:3 on the new moons, before *J*
46:4 chieftain should present to *J*
46:9 before *J* in the festal
46:12 voluntary offering to *J*
46:13 burnt offering daily to *J*
46:14 grain offering to *J* is an
46:16 Sovereign Lord *J* has said
47:13 Sovereign Lord *J* has said
47:23 of the Sovereign Lord *J*
48:9 you should contribute to *J*
48:10 sanctuary of *J* must prove
48:14 it is something holy to *J*
48:29 of the Sovereign Lord *J*
48:35 will be *J* Himself Is There
Da 1:2 *J* gave into his hand Jehoiakim
9:2 word of *J* . . . to Jeremiah
9:3 set my face to *J* the true God
9:4 pray to *J* my God and to make
9:4 *J* the true God, the great One
9:7 *J*, there belongs the
9:8 *J*, to us belongs the shame of
9:9 To *J* . . . belong the mercies
9:10 obeyed the voice of *J* our
9:13 softened the face of *J* our God
9:14 *J* kept alert to the calamity
9:14 *J* our God is righteous in all
9:15 *J* our God, you who brought
9:16 *J*, according to all your acts
9:17 for the sake of *J*
9:19 O *J*, do hear
9:19 O *J*, do forgive
9:19 *J*, do pay attention and act
9:20 *J* my God concerning the holy
Ho 1:1 The word of *J* . . . to Hosea
1:2 the word of *J* by Hosea, and
Ho 1:2 *J* proceeded to say to Hosea
1:2 turns from following *J*
1:4 *J* went on to say to him: Call
1:7 will save them by *J* their God
2:13 is the utterance of *J*
2:16 utterance of *J*, that you
2:20 and you will certainly know *J*
2:21 utterance of *J*, I shall
3:1 And *J* went on to say to me
3:5 certainly look for *J* their God
3:5 come quivering to *J* and to his
4:1 Hear the word of *J*, O sons of
4:1 *J* has a legal case with the
4:10 left off paying regard to *J*
4:15 nor swear As *J* is alive!
4:16 *J* will shepherd them like a
5:4 *J* himself they have not
5:6 to go and look for *J*, but they
5:7 With *J* himself they have dealt
6:1 do let us return to *J*
6:3 we will pursue to know *J*
7:10 not returned to *J* their God
8:1 an eagle against the house of *J*
8:13 *J* himself took no pleasure in
9:3 dwelling in the land of *J*
9:4 continue pouring out wine to *J*
9:4 not come into the house of *J*
9:5 the day of the festival of *J*
9:14 Give to them, O *J*, what you
10:3 for we have not feared *J*
10:12 time for searching for *J*
11:10 After *J* they will walk
11:11 is the utterance of *J*
12:2 *J* has a legal case with Judah
12:5 And *J* the God of the armies
12:5 *J* is his memorial
12:9 I am *J* your God from the land
12:13 *J* brought up Israel out of
13:4 I am *J* your God from the land
13:15 an east wind, the wind of *J*
14:1 come back, O Israel, to *J*
14:2 words and come back to *J*
14:9 the ways of *J* are upright
Joe 1:1 The word of *J* that occurred
1:9 cut off from the house of *J*
1:9 ministers of *J*, have mourned
1:14 to the house of *J* your God
1:14 and cry to *J* for aid
1:15 because the day of *J* is near
1:19 To you, O *J*, I shall call
2:1 the day of *J* is coming
2:11 *J* himself will certainly
2:11 the day of *J* is great and
2:12 the utterance of *J* is, come
2:13 come back to *J* your God
2:14 a drink offering for *J* your
2:17 priests, the ministers of *J*
2:17 feel sorry, O *J*, for your
2:18 *J* will be zealous for his
2:19 *J* will answer and say to his
2:21 for *J* will actually do a
2:23 be joyful and rejoice in *J*
2:26 praise the name of *J* your
2:27 I am *J* your God and there is
2:31 fear-inspiring day of *J*
2:32 who calls on the name of *J*
2:32 just as *J* has said, and in
2:32 survivors, whom *J* is calling
3:8 for *J* himself has spoken it
3:11 To that place, O *J*, bring
3:14 for the day of *J* is near
3:16 *J* himself will roar, and out
3:16 *J* will be a refuge for his
3:17 know that I am *J* your God
3:18 out of the house of *J* there
3:21 *J* will be residing in Zion
Am 1:2 *J*—out of Zion he will roar
1:3 This is what *J* has said
1:5 go as exiles . . . *J* has said
1:6 This is what *J* has said
1:8 the Sovereign Lord *J* has said
1:9 This is what *J* has said
1:11 This is what *J* has said
1:13 This is what *J* has said
1:15 into exile . . . *J* has said
2:1 This is what *J* has said
2:3 kill with him, *J* has said
2:4 This is what *J* has said
2:4 their rejecting the law of *J*
2:6 This is what *J* has said
2:11 is the utterance of *J*
2:16 is the utterance of *J*
3:1 word that *J* has spoken
3:6 not also *J* who has acted
Am 3:7 *J* will not do a thing unless
3:8 Lord *J* himself has spoken
3:10 is the utterance of *J*
3:11 *J* has said, There is an
3:12 This is what *J* has said
3:13 the Sovereign Lord *J*, the God
3:15 is the utterance of *J*
4:2 *J* has sworn by his holiness
4:3 is the utterance of *J*
4:5 utterance of . . . Lord *J*
4:6 is the utterance of *J*
4:8 is the utterance of *J*
4:9 is the utterance of *J*
4:10 is the utterance of *J*
4:11 is the utterance of *J*
4:13 *J* the God of armies is his
5:3 Sovereign Lord *J* has said
5:4 *J* has said to the house of
5:6 Search for *J*, and keep living
5:8 —*J* is his name
5:14 *J* the God of armies may come
5:15 *J* the God of armies will
5:16 what *J* the God of armies
5:16 God of armies, *J*, has said
5:17 the midst of you, *J* has said
5:18 who are craving the day of *J*
5:18 the day of *J* mean to you
5:20 the day of *J* be darkness
5:27 *J* the God of armies has said
6:8 *J* has sworn by his own soul
6:8 the utterance of *J* the God of
6:10 any mention of the name of *J*
6:11 For here is *J* commanding
6:14 the utterance of *J* the God
7:1 *J* caused me to see, and, look!
7:2 Lord *J*, forgive, please
7:3 *J* felt regret over this
7:3 It shall not occur, *J* said
7:4 *J* caused me to see, and, look!
7:4 *J* was calling for a contention
7:5 Lord *J*, hold off, please
7:6 *J* felt regret over this
7:6 the Sovereign Lord *J* said
7:7 *J* was stationed on a wall
7:8 Then *J* said to me: What are
7:8 And *J* went on to say: Here I
7:15 *J* proceeded to take me from
7:15 *J* went on to say to me
7:16 now hear the word of *J*
7:17 this is what *J* has said
8:1 *J* caused me to see, and, look!
8:2 *J* went on to say to me
8:3 the Sovereign Lord *J*
8:7 *J* has sworn by the Superiority
8:9 of the Sovereign Lord *J*
8:11 the Sovereign Lord *J*
8:11 for hearing the words of *J*
8:12 searching for the word of *J*
9:1 *J* stationed above the altar
9:5 Lord, *J* of the armies
9:6 of the earth—*J* is his name
9:7 is the utterance of *J*
9:8 eyes of the Sovereign Lord *J*
9:8 is the utterance of *J*
9:12 is the utterance of *J*, who is
9:13 is the utterance of *J*, and
9:15 *J* your God has said
Ob 1 Lord *J* has said regarding Edom
1 report that we have heard from *J*
4 is the utterance of *J*
8 is the utterance of *J*
15 the day of *J* against all the
18 for *J* himself has spoken it
Jon 1:1 the word of *J* began to occur
1:3 to Tarshish from before *J*
1:3 to Tarshish from before *J*
1:4 *J* himself hurled forth a
1:9 *J* the God of the heavens I am
1:10 from before *J* that he was
1:14 to call out to *J* and to say
1:14 *J*, may we, please, not
1:14 since you yourself, O *J*, have
1:16 men began to fear *J* greatly
1:16 they offered a sacrifice to *J*
1:17 *J* appointed a great fish to
2:1 Then Jonah prayed to *J* his God
2:2 I called out to *J*, and he
2:6 bring up my life, O *J* my God
2:7 *J* was the One whom I
2:9 Salvation belongs to *J*
2:10 *J* commanded the fish, so
3:1 the word of *J* occurred to
3:3 accord with the word of *J*
4:2 he prayed to *J* and said

Jon 4:2 *J*, was not this an affair of
4:3 *J*, take away, please, my soul
4:4 In turn *J* said: Have you
4:6 *J* God appointed a bottle-gourd
4:10 *J* said: You, for your part
Mic 1:1 The word of *J* that occurred
1:2 the Sovereign Lord *J* serve
1:2 *J* from his holy temple
1:3 *J* is going forth from his
1:12 bad has come down from *J*
2:3 this is what *J* has said
2:5 in the congregation of *J*
2:7 Has the spirit of *J* become
2:13 with *J* at the head of them
3:4 they will call to *J* for aid
3:5 what *J* has said against the
3:8 power, with the spirit of *J*
3:11 upon *J* they keep supporting
3:11 Is not *J* in the midst of us?
4:1 mountain of the house of *J*
4:2 go up to the mountain of *J*
4:2 the word of *J* out of
4:4 *J* of armies has spoken it
4:5 in the name of *J* our God to
4:6 is the utterance of *J*
4:7 *J* will actually rule as king
4:10 *J* will buy you back out of
4:12 to know the thoughts of *J*
4:13 devote to *J* their unjust
5:4 in the strength of *J*, in the
5:4 superiority of the name of *J*
5:7 peoples like dew from *J*
5:10 is the utterance of *J*
6:1 Hear . . . what *J* is saying
6:2 the legal case of *J*, also
6:2 for *J* has a legal case with
6:5 that the righteous acts of *J*
6:6 With what shall I confront *J?*
6:7 Will *J* be pleased with
6:8 what is *J* asking back from
6:9 the very voice of *J* calls out
7:7 for *J* that I shall keep on
7:8 *J* will be a light to me
7:9 The raging of *J* I shall bear
7:10 Where is he, *J* your God?
7:17 To *J* our God they will come
Na 1:2 *J* is a God exacting exclusive
1:2 *J* is taking vengeance and is
1:2 *J* is taking vengeance against
1:3 *J* is slow to anger and great
1:3 *J* hold back from punishing
1:7 *J* is good, a stronghold in the
1:9 you men think up against *J*
1:11 thinking up against *J* what is
1:12 This is what *J* has said
1:14 *J* has commanded, Nothing of
2:2 *J* will certainly gather the
2:13 the utterance of *J* of armies
3:5 the utterance of *J* of armies
Hab 1:2 How long, O *J*, must I cry for
1:12 you not from long ago, O *J*
1:12 O *J*, for a judgment you have
2:2 *J* proceeded to answer me and
2:13 Is it not from *J* of armies
2:14 knowing of the glory of *J*
2:16 cup of the right hand of *J*
2:20 *J* is in his holy temple
3:2 *J*, I have heard the report
3:2 I have become afraid, O *J*
3:8 O *J*, is it against the rivers
3:18 I will exult in *J* himself
3:19 *J* the Sovereign Lord is my
Zep 1:1 word of *J* that occurred to
1:2 is the utterance of *J*
1:3 is the utterance of *J*
1:5 making sworn oaths to *J*
1:6 back from following *J*
1:6 have not sought *J* and have
1:7 before the Sovereign Lord *J*
1:7 for the day of *J* is near
1:7 *J* has prepared a sacrifice
1:10 is the utterance of *J*, the
1:12 *J* will not do good, and he
1:14 The great day of *J* is near
1:14 the day of *J* is bitter
1:17 against *J* that they have
2:2 the burning anger of *J*
2:3 seek *J*, all you meek ones of
2:5 The word of *J* is against you
2:7 *J* their God will turn his
2:9 the utterance of *J* of armies
2:10 the people of *J* of armies
2:11 *J* will be fear-inspiring
3:2 In *J* she did not trust
Zep 3:5 *J* was righteous in the midst
3:8 is the utterance of *J*, till
3:9 to call upon the name of *J*
3:12 take refuge in the name of *J*
3:15 *J* has removed the judgments
3:15 The king of Israel, *J*, is
3:17 *J* your God is in the midst
3:20 before your eyes, *J* has said
Hag 1:1 word of *J* occurred by means
1:2 what *J* of armies has said
1:2 the time of the house of *J*
1:3 word of *J* continued to come
1:5 *J* of armies has said, Set
1:7 *J* of armies has said, Set
1:8 may be glorified, *J* has said
1:9 the utterance of *J* of armies
1:12 the voice of *J* their God
1:12 *J* their God had sent him
1:12 began to fear because of *J*
1:13 Haggai the messenger of *J*
1:13 commission from *J*, saying
1:13 is the utterance of *J*
1:14 *J* proceeded to rouse up the
1:14 the house of *J* of armies
2:1 word of *J* occurred by means
2:4 is the utterance of *J*, and be
2:4 the utterance of *J*, and work
2:4 the utterance of *J* of armies
2:6 what *J* of armies has said
2:7 *J* of armies has said
2:8 the utterance of *J* of armies
2:9 *J* of armies has said
2:9 the utterance of *J* of armies
2:10 word of *J* occurred to Haggai
2:11 what *J* of armies has said
2:14 is the utterance of *J*, and
2:15 a stone in the temple of *J*
2:17 is the utterance of *J*
2:18 foundation . . . temple of *J*
2:20 word of *J* proceeded to occur
2:23 the utterance of *J* of armies
2:23 is the utterance of *J*; and
2:23 the utterance of *J* of armies
Zec 1:1 the word of *J* occurred to
1:2 *J* grew indignant at your
1:3 what *J* of armies has said
1:3 the utterance of *J* of armies
1:3 *J* of armies has said
1:4 *J* of armies has said, Return
1:4 is the utterance of *J*
1:6 what *J* of armies had in mind
1:7 the word of *J* occurred to
1:10 ones whom *J* has sent forth
1:11 answer the angel of *J* who
1:12 angel of *J* answered and
1:12 *J* of armies, how long will
1:13 *J* proceeded to answer the
1:14 what *J* of armies has said
1:16 this is what *J* has said
1:16 the utterance of *J* of armies
1:17 what *J* of armies has said
1:17 *J* will yet certainly feel
1:20 *J* showed me four craftsmen
2:5 is the utterance of *J*
2:6 is the utterance of *J*
2:6 is the utterance of *J*
2:8 what *J* of armies has said
2:9 know that *J* of armies
2:10 is the utterance of *J*
2:11 joined to *J* in that day
2:11 to know that *J* of armies
2:12 And *J* will certainly take
2:13 silence, all flesh, before *J*
3:1 standing before the angel of *J*
3:2 the angel of *J* said to Satan
3:2 *J* rebuke you, O Satan, yes
3:2 *J* rebuke you, he who is
3:5 angel of *J* was standing by
3:6 the angel of *J* began to bear
3:7 what *J* of armies has said
3:9 the utterance of *J* of armies
3:10 the utterance of *J* of armies
4:6 the word of *J* to Zerubbabel
4:6 *J* of armies has said
4:8 word of *J* continued to occur
4:9 have to know that *J* of armies
4:10 These seven are the eyes of *J*
5:4 the utterance of *J* of armies
6:8 caused the spirit of *J* to rest
6:9 word of *J* continued to occur
6:12 what *J* of armies has said
6:12 build the temple of *J*
6:13 will build the temple of *J*
6:14 memorial in the temple of *J*
Zec 6:15 build in the temple of *J*
6:15 to know that *J* of armies
6:15 listen to the voice of *J* your
7:1 word of *J* occurred to
7:2 men to soften the face of *J*
7:3 belonged to the house of *J*
7:4 the word of *J* of armies
7:7 *J* called out by means of the
7:8 word of *J* continued to occur
7:9 what *J* of armies has said
7:12 words that *J* of armies sent
7:12 indignation on the part of *J*
7:13 *J* of armies has said
8:1 word of *J* of armies continued
8:2 what *J* of armies has said
8:3 This is what *J* has said
8:3 the mountain of *J* of armies
8:4 what *J* of armies has said
8:6 what *J* of armies has said
8:6 the utterance of *J* of armies
8:7 what *J* of armies has said
8:9 what *J* of armies has said
8:9 foundation of the house of *J*
8:11 the utterance of *J* of armies
8:14 what *J* of armies has said
8:14 *J* of armies has said, and I
8:17 is the utterance of *J*
8:18 the word of *J* of armies
8:19 what *J* of armies has said
8:20 what *J* of armies has said
8:21 go to soften the face of *J*
8:21 and to seek *J* of armies
8:22 come to seek *J* of armies in
8:22 and to soften the face of *J*
8:23 what *J* of armies has said
9:1 word of *J* is against the land
9:1 *J* has an eye on earthling man
9:4 *J* himself will dispossess her
9:14 *J* himself will be seen
9:14 the horn the Sovereign Lord *J*
9:15 *J* of armies himself will
9:16 *J* their God will certainly
10:1 Make your requests of *J* for
10:1 *J* who is making the storm
10:3 *J* of armies has turned his
10:5 in battle, for *J* is with
10:6 for I am *J* their God, and I
10:7 heart will be joyful in *J*
10:12 make them superior in *J*
10:12 is the utterance of *J*
11:4 *J* my God has said, Shepherd
11:5 May *J* be blessed, while I
11:6 is the utterance of *J*
11:11 that it was the word of *J*
11:13 *J* said to me: Throw it to
11:13 treasury at the house of *J*
11:15 *J* went on to say to me
12:1 word of *J* concerning Israel
12:1 is the utterance of *J*, the
12:4 is the utterance of *J*
12:5 *J* of armies their God
12:7 *J* will certainly save the
12:8 *J* will be a defense around
13:2 the utterance of *J* of armies
13:3 spoken in the name of *J*
13:7 the utterance of *J* of armies
13:8 is the utterance of *J*
13:9 will say, *J* is my God
14:1 a day coming, belonging to *J*
14:3 *J* will certainly go forth
14:5 *J* my God will certainly come
14:7 is known as belonging to *J*
14:9 *J* must become king over all
14:9 *J* will prove to be one, and
14:12 *J* will scourge all the
14:13 confusion from *J* will
14:16 the King, *J* of armies
14:17 bow down to the King, *J* of
14:18 *J* scourges the nations that
14:20 Holiness belongs to *J!*
14:20 pots in the house of *J* must
14:21 holy belonging to *J* of
14:21 in the house of *J* of armies
Mal 1:1 word of *J* concerning Israel
1:2 loved you people, *J* has said
1:2 is the utterance of *J*
1:4 what *J* of armies has said
1:4 people whom *J* has denounced
1:5 May *J* be magnified over the
1:6 *J* of armies has said to you
1:7 table of *J* . . despised
1:8 *J* of armies has said
1:9 *J* of armies has said
1:10 *J* of armies has said, and

Mal 1:11 *J* of armies has said
1:12 table of *J* is something
1:13 *J* of armies has said
1:13 at your hand? *J* has said
1:14 a ruined one to *J*
1:14 I am a great King, *J* of
2:2 *J* of armies has said
2:4 *J* of armies has said
2:7 the messenger of *J* of armies
2:8 *J* of armies has said
2:11 profaned the holiness of *J*
2:12 *J* will cut off each one that
2:12 a gift offering to *J* of
2:13 with tears the altar of *J*
2:14 *J* himself has borne witness
2:16 *J* the God of Israel has said
2:16 *J* of armies has said
2:17 made *J* weary by your words
2:17 bad is good in the eyes of *J*
3:1 *J* of armies has said
3:3 to *J* people presenting a gift
3:4 be gratifying to *J*, as in the
3:5 *J* of armies has said
3:6 I am *J*; I have not changed
3:7 *J* of armies has said
3:10 *J* of armies has said
3:11 *J* of armies has said
3:12 *J* of armies has said
3:13 against me, *J* has said
3:14 dejectedly on account of *J*
3:16 those in fear of *J* spoke
3:16 *J* kept paying attention and
3:16 for those in fear of *J* and
3:17 mine, *J* of armies has said
4:1 *J* of armies has said
4:3 *J* of armies has said
4:5 and fear-inspiring day of *J*
Mt 1:22 was spoken by *J* through his
1:24 angel of *J* had directed him
2:15 spoken by *J* through his
3:3 Prepare the way of *J*, you
4:7 not put *J* your God to the test
4:10 It is *J* your God you must
5:33 must pay your vows to *J*
21:42 From *J* this has come to be
22:37 love *J* your God with your
22:44 *J* said to my Lord: Sit at
27:10 to what *J* had commanded me
Mr 1:3 Prepare the way of *J*, you
5:19 the things *J* has done for you
12:11 From *J* this has come to be
12:29, 29 *J* our God is one *J*
12:30 you must love *J* your God
12:36 *J* said to my Lord: Sit at
13:20 unless *J* had cut short the
Lu 1:6 and legal requirements of *J*
1:9 into the sanctuary of *J*
1:15 for he will be great before *J*
1:16 turn back to *J* their God
1:17 ready for *J* a prepared people
1:25 the way *J* has dealt with me
1:28 favored one, *J* is with you
1:32 *J* God will give him the
1:45 things spoken to her from *J*
1:46 My soul magnifies *J*
1:58 *J* had magnified his mercy to
1:66 the hand of *J* was indeed with
1:68 Blessed be *J* the God of Israel
1:76 will go in advance before *J*
2:15 *J* has made known to us
2:22 Jerusalem to present him to *J*
2:23 must be called holy to *J*
2:24 what is said in the law of *J*
2:26 he had seen the Christ of *J*
2:39 according to the law of *J*
3:4 Prepare the way of *J*, you
4:8 It is *J* your God you must
4:12 not put *J* your God to the test
10:27 You must love *J* your God
20:37 calls *J* the God of Abraham
20:42 *J* said to my Lord, Sit at my
Joh 1:23 Make the way of *J* straight
6:45 they will all be taught by *J*
12:38 *J*, who has put faith in the
12:38 arm of *J*, to whom has it
Ac 1:24 *J*, who know the hearts of all
2:20 illustrious day of *J* arrives
2:21 who calls on the name of *J*
2:25 *J* constantly before my eyes
2:34 *J* said to my Lord: Sit at my
2:39 *J* our God may call to him
2:47 *J* continued to join to them
3:19 come from the person of *J*
3:22 *J* God will raise up for you
Ac 4:26 together as one against *J*
4:29 *J*, give attention to their
5:9 a test of the spirit of *J*
7:33 *J* said to him, Take the
7:49 you build for me? *J* says
7:60 *J*, do not charge this sin
8:22 supplicate *J* that, if
8:24 supplication for me to *J*
8:25 had spoken the word of *J*
9:31 it walked in the fear of *J*
10:33 been commanded by *J* to say
11:21 hand of *J* was with them
12:11 *J* sent his angel forth and
12:17 *J* brought him out of the
12:23 the angel of *J* struck him
12:24 word of *J* went on growing
13:2 publicly ministering to *J*
13:10 the right ways of *J*
13:12 at the teaching of *J*
13:44 to hear the word of *J*
13:47 *J* has laid commandment upon
13:48 and to glorify the word of *J*
13:49 the word of *J* went on being
14:3 by the authority of *J*, who
14:23 they committed them to *J* in
15:17 the men may earnestly seek *J*
15:17 called by my name, says *J*
15:35 good news of the word of *J*
15:36 we published the word of *J*
15:40 the undeserved kindness of *J*
16:14 *J* opened her heart wide to
16:15 judged me . . . faithful to *J*
16:32 spoke the word of *J* to him
18:21 return . . . if *J* is willing
18:25 in the way of *J* and, as he
19:20 word of *J* kept growing and
21:14 Let the will of *J* take place
Ro 4:3 Abraham exercised faith in *J*
4:8 sin *J* will by no means take
9:28 *J* will make an accounting on
9:29 *J* of armies had left a seed
10:13 who calls on the name of *J*
10:16 *J*, who put faith in the
11:3 *J*, they have killed your
12:11 Slave for *J*
12:19 I will repay, says *J*
14:4 for *J* can make him stand
14:6 He . . . observes it to *J*
14:6 he who eats, eats to *J*
14:6 does not eat to *J*, and yet
14:8 we live to *J*, and if
14:8 and if we die, we die to *J*
14:8 if we die, we belong to *J*
14:11 As I live, says *J*, to me
15:11 Praise *J*, all you nations
1Co 1:31 let him boast in *J*
2:16 come to know the mind of *J*
3:20 *J* knows that the reasonings
4:4 but he that examines me is *J*
4:19 if *J* wills, and I shall get
7:17 as *J* has given each one a
10:9 put *J* to the test, as some
10:21 drinking the cup of *J* and
10:21 partaking of the table of *J*
10:22 we inciting *J* to jealousy
10:26 to *J* belong the earth and
11:32 we are disciplined by *J*
14:21 give heed to me, says *J*
16:7 time with you, if *J* permits
16:10 is performing the work of *J*
2Co 3:16 when there is a turning to *J*
3:17 *J* is the Spirit; and where
3:17 and where the spirit of *J* is
3:18 mirrors the glory of *J*, are
3:18 as done by *J* the Spirit
6:17 separate yourselves, says *J*
6:18 you will be sons . . . says *J*
8:21 not only in the sight of *J*
10:17 let him boast in *J*
10:18 the man whom *J* recommends
Ga 3:6 Abraham put faith in *J*, and it
Eph 2:21 into a holy temple for *J*
5:17 what the will of *J* is
5:19 music in your hearts to *J*
6:4 and mental-regulating of *J*
6:7 Be slaves . . . as to *J*, and not
6:8 will receive this back from *J*
Col 1:10 to walk worthily of *J* to the
3:13 Even as *J* freely forgave you
3:16 singing in your hearts to *J*
3:22 with fear of *J*
3:23 at it whole-souled as to *J*
3:24 you know that it is from *J*
1Th 1:8 the word of *J* sounded forth
1Th 4:6 *J* is one who exacts
2Th 2:2 that the day of *J* is here
2:13 you, brothers loved by *J*
3:1 that the word of *J* may keep
2Ti 1:18 mercy from *J* in that day
2:19 *J* knows those who belong to
2:19 naming the name of *J*
4:14 *J* will repay him according
Heb 2:13 children, whom *J* gave me
7:21 *J* has sworn (and he will
8:2 true tent, which *J* put up
8:8 days coming, says *J*, and I
8:9 I stopped caring . . . says *J*
8:10 after those days, says *J*
8:11 Know *J*! For they will all
10:16 says *J*. I will put my laws
10:30 *J* will judge his people
12:5 the discipline from *J*
12:6 whom *J* loves he disciplines
13:6 *J* is my helper; I will not
Jas 1:7 will receive anything from *J*
1:12 *J* promised to those who
2:23 Abraham put faith in *J*, and
3:9 With it we bless *J*, even the
4:10 Humble . . . in the eyes of *J*
4:15 you ought to say: If *J* wills
5:4 entered into the ears of *J*
5:10 who spoke in the name of *J*
5:11 have seen the outcome *J* gave
5:11 *J* is very tender in affection
5:14 with oil in the name of *J*
5:15 and *J* will raise him up
1Pe 1:25 saying of *J* endures forever
3:12 For the eyes of *J* are upon
3:12 but the face of *J* is against
2Pe 2:9 *J* knows how to deliver people
2:11 out of respect for *J*
3:8 one day is with *J* as a
3:9 *J* is not slow respecting his
3:12 the presence of the day of *J*
Jude 5 *J*, although he saved a people
9 but said: May *J* rebuke you
14 *J* came with his holy myriads
Re 1:8 Alpha and the Omega, says *J*
4:8 Holy, holy, holy is *J* God, the
4:11 You are worthy, *J*, even our
11:17 We thank you, *J* God, the
15:3 wonderful are your works, *J*
15:4 will not really fear you, *J*
16:7 *J* God, the Almighty, true
18:8 *J* God, who judged her, is
19:6 *J* . . . begun to rule as king
21:22 *J* God the Almighty is its
22:5 *J* God will shed light upon
22:6 *J* the God of the inspired

Jehovah-jireh
Ge 22:14 the name of that place *J*

Jehovah-nissi
Ex 17:15 altar and to call its name *J*

Jehovah's
Ge 16:7 Later *J* angel found her at a
16:9 *J* angel went on to say to her
16:10 *J* angel said to her: I shall
16:11 *J* angel added to her: Here
18:19 they shall keep *J* way to do
22:11 *J* angel began calling to him
22:15 *J* angel proceeded to call to
39:5 *J* blessing came to be upon
Ex 3:2 *J* angel appeared to him in a
4:14 *J* anger . . . against Moses
7:25 *J* striking the Nile River
9:3 *J* hand is coming upon your
9:20 Anyone who feared *J* word
9:21 to have any regard for *J* word
12:11 eat it . . . It is *J* passover
13:9 in order that *J* law may prove
16:3 died by *J* hand in the land of
16:7 you will indeed see *J* glory
16:10 *J* glory appeared in the cloud
24:16 *J* glory continued to reside
24:17 sight of *J* glory was like
30:14 will give *J* contribution
30:15 give *J* contribution so as
32:26 Who is on *J* side?
35:5 bring it as *J* contribution
35:21 *J* contribution for the work
35:24 brought *J* contribution
40:34 *J* glory filled the tabernacle
40:35 *J* glory filled the tabernacle
40:38 For *J* cloud was over the
Le 2:3 from *J* offerings made by fire
2:10 most holy of *J* offerings by

Le 4:35 upon *J* offerings made by fire
5:12 upon *J* offerings made by fire
6:18 from *J* offerings made by fire
7:30 as *J* offerings made by fire
7:35 *J* offerings made by fire
9:23 *J* glory appeared to all the
10:7 *J* anointing oil is upon you
10:12 left over from *J* offerings
10:13 *J* offerings made by fire
10:19 prove satisfactory in *J* eyes
17:6 blood upon *J* altar at the
21:6 *J* offerings made by fire, the
21:21 present *J* offerings made by
23:21 *J* holy convention for
24:9 *J* offerings made by fire, as
24:16 abuser of *J* name should be
Nu 5:21 *J* letting your thigh fall
10:33 ark of *J* covenant was
10:34 *J* cloud was over them by day
11:10 *J* anger began growing very
11:29 *J* people were prophets
11:33 *J* anger blazed against the
12:9 *J* anger got to be hot against
14:10 *J* glory appeared on the tent
14:16 Because of *J* not being able
14:44 ark of *J* covenant and Moses
15:31 *J* word that he has despised
16:9 service of *J* tabernacle and to
16:19 *J* glory appeared to all the
16:41 have put *J* people to death
16:42 and *J* glory began to appear
17:13 coming near to *J* tabernacle
19:13 has defiled *J* tabernacle, and
19:20 *J* sanctuary that he has
20:4 brought *J* congregation into
20:6 and *J* glory began to appear to
22:22 *J* angel proceeded to station
22:23 the ass got to see *J* angel
22:24 *J* angel kept standing in the
22:25 she-ass kept seeing *J* angel
22:26 *J* angel now passed by again
22:27 the ass got to see *J* angel
22:31 saw *J* angel stationed in the
22:32 *J* angel said to him: Why
22:34 Balaam said to *J* angel: I
22:35 *J* angel said to Balaam: Go
27:17 *J* assembly may not become
28:16 will be *J* passover
31:3 execute *J* vengeance upon Midian
31:29 give it . . . as *J* contribution
31:30 obligation of *J* tabernacle
31:41 the tax as *J* contribution to
31:47 obligation of *J* tabernacle
31:50 as *J* offering, articles of
32:10 *J* anger blazed on that day so
32:13 *J* anger blazed against Israel
De 1:43 rebelliously against *J* order
4:15 *J* speaking to you in Horeb
6:18 right and good in *J* eyes
7:4 *J* anger will indeed blaze
7:8 it was because of *J* loving you
8:3 every expression of *J* mouth
10:8 carry the ark of *J* covenant
11:17 *J* anger does blaze against
12:25 do what is right in *J* eyes
21:9 do what is right in *J* eyes
28:10 *J* name has been called upon
29:20 *J* anger and his ardor will
29:27 *J* anger blazed against that
31:9 of the ark of *J* covenant
31:25 of the ark of *J* covenant
32:9 For *J* share is his people
Jos 3:17 the ark of *J* covenant kept
4:7 before the ark of *J* covenant
4:24 earth may know *J* hand, that
6:24 to the treasure of *J* house
7:1 *J* anger grew hot against the
8:8 According to *J* word you
8:27 according to *J* word that he
9:27 and for *J* altar, down to
10:12 the day of *J* abandoning the
11:20 proved to be *J* course to let
22:19 to the land of *J* possession
22:28 representation of *J* altar
23:16 And *J* anger will certainly
Jg 2:1 *J* angel went up from Gilgal
2:4 as *J* angel had spoken these
2:7 all of *J* great work that he
2:14 *J* anger blazed against Israel
2:20 *J* anger blazed against Israel
2:22 keepers of *J* way by walking
3:4 obey *J* commandments that he
3:7 did what was bad in *J* eyes
3:8 *J* anger blazed against Israel
Jg 3:12 what was bad in *J* eyes
3:12 did what was bad in *J* eyes
4:1 to do what was bad in *J* eyes
5:11 *J* people made their way down
5:13 *J* people came down to me
6:11 *J* angel came and sat under
6:12 *J* angel appeared to him and
6:21 *J* angel thrust out the tip of
6:21 *J* angel, he vanished from his
6:22 realized that it was *J* angel
6:22 have seen *J* angel face to face
6:34 *J* spirit enveloped Gideon so
7:18 you must say, *J* and Gideon's!
7:20 *J* sword and Gideon's!
10:7 *J* anger blazed against Israel
11:29 *J* spirit now came upon
11:31 must also become *J*, and I
13:1 doing what was bad in *J* eyes
13:3 *J* angel appeared to the woman
13:13 So *J* angel said to Manoah
13:15 Manoah now said to *J* angel
13:16 But *J* angel said to Manoah
13:16 not know that he was *J* angel
13:17 Then Manoah said to *J* angel
13:18 *J* angel said to him
13:20 then *J* angel ascended in the
13:21 And *J* angel did not repeat
13:21 he had been *J* angel
13:25 *J* spirit started to impel
14:6 *J* spirit became operative
14:19 *J* spirit became operative
15:14 *J* spirit became operative
1Sa 2:26 from *J* standpoint and from
3:15 opened the doors of *J* house
4:3 the ark of *J* covenant, that it
19:9 *J* bad spirit came to be upon
24:6 from *J* standpoint, that I
26:11 from *J* standpoint, to
30:26 from the spoil of *J* enemies
2Sa 6:7 *J* anger blazed against Uzzah
6:21 leader over *J* people Israel
24:11 *J* word itself came to Gad
24:16 *J* angel himself happened to
1Ki 2:27 to fulfill *J* word that he
14:18 *J* word that he had spoken
15:29 *J* word that he had spoken
16:7 *J* word itself had come
16:34 according to *J* word that he
17:14 *J* giving a downpour upon
17:16 according to *J* word that
17:24 *J* word in your mouth is
18:1 *J* own word came to Elijah
18:4 Jezebel cut off *J* prophets
18:31 *J* word had come, saying
19:9 there was *J* word for him
21:3 from *J* standpoint, for me
21:17 *J* word came to Elijah the
21:28 *J* word came to Elijah the
22:38 *J* word that he had spoken
22:52 what was bad in *J* eyes
2Ki 3:2 doing what was bad in *J* eyes
8:18 doing what was bad in *J* eyes
8:27 doing what was bad in *J* eyes
9:6 as king over *J* people
10:10 nothing of *J* word will fall
10:17 *J* word that he had spoken
12:2 what was right in *J* eyes
13:2 do what was bad in *J* eyes
13:3 *J* anger became hot against
13:11 do what was bad in *J* eyes
13:17 *J* arrow of salvation, even
14:3 what was upright in *J* eyes
14:24 do what was bad in *J* eyes
15:3 what was upright in *J* eyes
15:9 what was bad in *J* eyes
15:12 *J* word that he had spoken
15:18 what was bad in *J* eyes
15:24 what was bad in *J* eyes
15:28 what was bad in *J* eyes
15:34 what was right in *J* eyes
17:2 do what was bad in *J* eyes
18:3 what was right in *J* eyes
20:4 *J* word itself came to him
21:2 do what was bad in *J* eyes
21:6 what was bad in *J* eyes
21:20 what was bad in *J* eyes
22:2 was right in *J* eyes and
22:13 for great is *J* rage that
23:16 *J* word that the man of the
23:32 what was bad in *J* eyes
23:37 what was bad in *J* eyes
24:2 *J* word that he had spoken by
24:9 do what was bad in *J* eyes
24:19 what was bad in *J* eyes
1Ch 11:3 *J* word by means of Samuel
11:10 king according to *J* word
12:23 to him according to *J* order
13:10 *J* anger blazed against Uzzah
15:15 had commanded by *J* word
21:12 *J* angel bringing ruin in all
21:15 *J* angel was standing close
21:16 got to see *J* angel standing
21:18 *J* angel, for his part, said
21:30 the sword of *J* angel
22:8 But *J* word came against me
22:14 I have prepared for *J* house
28:8 all Israel, *J* congregation
28:12 the courtyards of *J* house
28:13 the service of *J* house and
28:13 of the service of *J* house
28:20 the service of *J* house is
29:23 to sit upon *J* throne as king
2Ch 2:1 to build a house to *J* name
7:1 *J* glory itself filled the
7:2 *J* glory had filled the house
12:12 *J* anger turned back from
13:9 driven out *J* priests, the
15:8 renew *J* altar that was
16:2 treasures of *J* house and the
17:9 was the book of *J* law
20:32 what was right in *J* eyes
21:6 to do what was bad in *J* eyes
22:4 what was bad in *J* eyes, the
24:2 what was right in *J* eyes
24:12 service of *J* house, and
24:12 renovating *J* house, and
24:12 copper for repairing *J* house
24:21 courtyard of *J* house
25:2 what was right in *J* eyes
25:15 *J* anger became hot against
26:4 what was right in *J* eyes
27:2 what was right in *J* eyes
27:3 the upper gate of *J* house
28:1 what was right in *J* eyes
28:11 *J* burning anger is against
29:2 what was right in *J* eyes
29:8 *J* indignation came to be
31:14 give *J* contribution and the
32:26 *J* indignation did not come
33:2 do what was bad in *J* eyes
33:22 do what was bad in *J* eyes
34:2 right in *J* eyes and walk in
34:14 book of *J* law by the hand
34:21 *J* rage that must be poured
36:9 what was bad in *J* eyes
36:21 to fulfill *J* word by the
36:22 *J* word by the mouth of
Ezr 1:1 *J* word from the mouth of
3:6 the foundation of *J* temple
Ps 18:*super* Of *J* servant, of David
35:5 let *J* angel be pushing them
35:6 let *J* angel be pursuing them
36:*super* Of *J* servant, David
89:1 *J* expressions of
107:43 *J* acts of loving-kindness
113:2 May *J* name become blessed
113:3 *J* name is to be praised
Eze 7:19 day of *J* fury. Their souls
Ho 3:1 *J* love for the sons of Israel
Ob 21 and the kingship must become *J*
Zep 1:8 on the day of *J* sacrifice
1:18 in the day of *J* fury
2:2 upon you the day of *J* anger
2:3 in the day of *J* anger
Zec 12:8 like *J* angel before them
Mt 1:20 *J* angel appeared to him in
2:13 *J* angel appeared in a dream
2:19 *J* angel appeared in a dream
4:4 coming forth through *J* mouth
21:9 is he that comes in *J* name
23:39 is he that comes in *J* name
28:2 *J* angel had descended from
Mr 11:9 he that comes in *J* name
Lu 1:11 To him *J* angel appeared
1:38 *J* slave girl! May it take
2:9 suddenly *J* angel stood by them
2:9 *J* glory gleamed around them
2:23 as it is written in *J* law
4:18 *J* spirit is upon me, because
4:19 to preach *J* acceptable year
5:17 *J* power was there for him to
13:35 is he that comes in *J* name
19:38 coming as the King in *J* name
Joh 12:13 is he that comes in *J* name
Ac 5:19 *J* angel opened the doors of
7:31 investigate, *J* voice came
8:26 *J* angel spoke to Philip
8:39 *J* spirit quickly led Philip

Ac 12:7 *J* angel stood by, and a light
13:11 *J* hand is upon you, and you
Ro 11:34 has come to know *J* mind
1Th 4:15 what we tell you by *J* word
5:2 *J* day is coming exactly as a
Jas 2:23 came to be called *J* friend
2Pe 3:10 *J* day will come as a thief

Jehovah-shalom
Jg 6:24 called *J* down to this day

Jehozabad
2Ki 12:21 *J* the son of Shomer, his
1Ch 26:4 Obed-edom had sons . . . *J* the
2Ch 17:18 under his control . . . was *J*
24:26 *J* the son of Shimrith the

Jehozadak
1Ch 6:14 Seraiah . . . father to *J*
6:15 *J* it was that went away
Ezr 3:2 And Jeshua the son of *J* and
3:8 and Jeshua the son of *J* and
5:2 Jeshua the son of *J* got up
10:18 Jeshua the son of *J* and
Hag 1:1 the son of *J* the high priest
1:12 son of *J* the high priest
1:14 son of *J* the high priest
2:2 Joshua the son of *J* the
2:4 the son of *J* the high priest
Zec 6:11 son of *J* the high priest

Jehu
1Ki 16:1 came to *J* the son of Hanani
16:7 *J* the son of Hanani the
16:12 by means of *J* the prophet
19:16 *J* the grandson of Nimshi
19:17 *J* will put to death
2Ki 9:2 *J* the son of Jehoshaphat the
9:5 *J* said: For which one of all
9:11 As for *J*, he went out to the
9:13 and say: *J* has become king!
9:14 And *J* the son of Jehoshaphat
9:15 *J* now said: If your soul
9:16 *J* began to ride and go to
9:18 But *J* said: What do you have
9:19 *J* said: What do you have to
9:20 *J* the grandson of Nimshi
9:21 continued on out to meet *J*
9:22 as soon as Jehoram saw *J*, he
9:22 said: Is there peace, *J?*
9:24 *J* himself filled his hand
9:27 *J* went in pursuit of him and
9:30 At length *J* came to Jezreel
9:31 And *J* himself came in by
10:1 *J* wrote letters and sent
10:5 caretakers sent to *J*, saying
10:11 *J* went on to strike down
10:13 *J* himself encountered the
10:18 *J* collected all the people
10:18 *J*, on the other hand, will
10:19 As for *J*, he acted slyly
10:20 *J* went on to say: Sanctify
10:21 *J* sent through all Israel
10:23 *J* entered with Jehonadab
10:24 *J* himself stationed eighty
10:25 *J* immediately said to the
10:28 *J* annihilated Baal out of
10:29 *J* did not turn aside from
10:30 Jehovah said to *J*: For the
10:31 *J* himself did not take care
10:34 affairs of *J* and all that he
10:35 Finally *J* lay down with his
10:36 *J* had reigned over Israel
12:1 In the seventh year of *J*
13:1 Jehoahaz the son of *J*
14:8 *J* the king of Israel, saying
15:12 that he had spoken to *J*
1Ch 2:38 in turn, became father to *J*
2:38 *J*, in turn, became father to
4:35 *J* the son of Joshibiah the
12:3 Beracah and *J* the Anathothite
2Ch 19:2 *J* the son of Hanani the
20:34 of *J* the son of Hanani
22:7 *J* the grandson of Nimshi
22:8 *J* had entered into
22:9 they . . . brought him to *J*
25:17 son of *J* the king of Israel
Ho 1:4 Jezreel against the house of *J*

Jehubbah
1Ch 7:34 sons of Shemer were . . . *J*

Jehucal
Jer 37:3 *J* the son of Shelemiah and

Jehud
Jos 19:45 *J* and Bene-berak and

Jehudi
Jer 36:14 *J* the son of Nethaniah the
36:21 sent *J* out to get the roll
36:21 *J* began to read it aloud
36:23 *J* had read three or four

Jehu's
1Ki 19:17 one escaping from *J* sword
2Ki 9:17 the heaving mass of *J* men

Jeiel
1Ch 5:7 as the head, *J*, and Zechariah
8:29 father of Gibeon, *J*, dwelt
9:35 father of Gibeon, *J*, dwelt
11:44 and *J*, the sons of Hotham
15:18 and *J* the gatekeepers
15:21 *J* and Azaziah with harps
16:5 and *J* and Shemiramoth and
16:5 and *J*, with instruments of
2Ch 20:14 *J* the son of Mattaniah the
26:11 hand of *J* the secretary and
35:9 *J* and Jozabad, the chiefs of
Ezr 8:13 sons of Adonikam . . . *J*
10:43 the sons of Nebo, *J*

Jekabzeel
Ne 11:25 in *J* and its settlements

Jekameam
1Ch 23:19 of Hebron . . . *J* the fourth
24:23 of Hebron . . . *J* the fourth

Jekamiah
1Ch 2:41 in turn, became father to *J*
2:41 *J*, in turn, became father to
3:18 *J*, Hoshama and Nedabiah

Jekuthiel
1Ch 4:18 *J* the father of Zanoah

Jemimah
Job 42:14 name of the first *J* and

Jemuel
Ge 46:10 sons of Simeon were *J* and
Ex 6:15 sons of Simeon were *J* and

Jephthah
Jg 11:1 *J* the Gileadite had become a
11:1 came to be the father of *J*
11:2 to drive *J* out and to say to
11:3 So *J* ran away because of his
11:3 to *J*, and they would go out
11:5 take *J* out of the land of Tob
11:6 said to *J*: Do come and serve
11:7 *J* said to the older men of
11:8 said to *J*: That is why now
11:9 So *J* said to the older men of
11:10 men of Gilead said to *J*: Let
11:11 *J* went with the older men
11:11 *J* proceeded to speak all his
11:12 *J* sent messengers to the
11:13 said to the messengers of *J*
11:14 *J* sent once more messengers
11:15 what *J* has said, Israel did
11:28 words of *J* that he had sent
11:29 spirit now came upon *J*, and
11:30 *J* made a vow to Jehovah and
11:32 *J* passed along to the sons of
11:34 *J* came to Mizpah to his
11:40 daughter of *J* the Gileadite
12:1 said to *J*: Why is it that you
12:2 *J* said to them: I became a
12:4 *J* collected all the men of
12:7 *J* continued to judge Israel
12:7 *J* the Gileadite died and was
1Sa 12:11 *J* and Samuel and deliver
Heb 11:32 go on to relate about . . . *J*

Jephunneh
Nu 13:6 of Judah, Caleb the son of *J*
14:6 and Caleb the son of *J*, who
14:30 except Caleb the son of *J* and
14:38 and Caleb the son of *J* will
26:65 except Caleb the son of *J* and
32:12 except Caleb the son of *J* the
34:19 of Judah, Caleb the son of *J*
De 1:36 except Caleb the son of *J*
Jos 14:6 *J* the Kenizzite said to him
14:13 Caleb the son of *J*
14:14 Caleb the son of *J*
15:13 to Caleb the son of *J* he
21:12 Caleb the son of *J* as his
1Ch 4:15 Caleb the son of *J*
6:56 gave to Caleb the son of *J*
7:38 sons of Jether were *J* and

Jerah
Ge 10:26 Joktan became father . . . *J*
1Ch 1:20 and Hazarmaveth and *J*

Jerahmeel
1Ch 2:9 the sons of Hezron . . . *J*
2:25 *J* the firstborn of Hezron
2:26 *J* came to have another wife
2:27 Ram the firstborn of *J*
2:33 became the sons of *J*
2:42 Caleb the brother of *J*
24:29 the sons of Kish were *J*
Jer 36:26 *J* the son of the king and

Jerahmeelites
1Sa 27:10 south of the *J* and upon
30:29 in the cities of the *J*

Jerboa
Le 11:29 and the *j* and the lizard

Jerboas
1Sa 6:4 five golden *j*, for every one
6:5 *j* that are bringing the land
6:11 also the box and the golden *j*
6:18 golden *j* were to the number

Jered
1Ch 4:18 *J* the father of Gedor and

Jeremai
Ezr 10:33 the sons of Hashum . . . *J*

Jeremiah
2Ki 23:31 Hamutal the daughter of *J*
24:18 Hamutal the daughter of *J*
1Ch 5:24 Eliel and Azriel and *J* and
12:4 *J* and Jahaziel and Johanan
12:10 the fourth, *J* the fifth
12:13 *J* the tenth, Machbannai the
2Ch 35:25 *J* began to chant over Josiah
36:12 on account of *J* the prophet
36:21 word by the mouth of *J*
36:22 word by the mouth of *J*
Ezr 1:1 word from the mouth of *J*
Ne 10:2 Seraiah, Azariah, *J*
12:1 Seraiah, *J*, Ezra
12:12 Meraiah; for *J*, Hananiah
12:34 Benjamin and Shemaiah and *J*
Jer 1:1 words of *J* the son of Hilkiah
1:11 What are you seeing, *J?*
7:1 The word that occurred to *J*
11:1 The word that occurred to *J*
14:1 the word of Jehovah to *J*
18:1 The word that occurred to *J*
18:18 think out against *J* some
19:14 *J* proceeded to come from
20:1 kept listening to *J* while
20:2 Pashhur struck *J* the prophet
20:3 let *J* out from the stocks
20:3 and *J* now said to him
21:1 The word that occurred to *J*
21:3 *J* proceeded to say to them
24:3 What are you seeing, *J?*
25:1 The word that occurred to *J*
25:2 which *J* the prophet spoke
25:13 written in this book that *J*
26:7 the people began to hear *J*
26:8 *J* had completed speaking
26:9 congregating . . . about *J*
26:12 *J* said to all the princes
26:20 with all the words of *J*
26:24 that proved to be with *J*
27:1 this word occurred to *J*
28:5 *J* the prophet proceeded to
28:6 yes, *J* the prophet proceeded
28:10 bar from off the neck of *J*
28:11 *J* the prophet proceeded to
28:12 the word . . . occurred to *J*
28:12 bar from off the neck of *J*
28:15 *J* the prophet went on to
29:1 the letter that *J* the prophet
29:27 why have you not rebuked *J*
29:29 this letter in the ears of *J*
29:30 occurred to *J*, saying
30:1 The word that occurred to *J*
32:1 to *J* from Jehovah in the
32:2 *J* the prophet, he happened
32:6 *J* proceeded to say: The word
32:26 occurred to *J*, saying
33:1 to *J* the second time, while
33:19 further to *J*, saying
33:23 to occur to *J*, saying
34:1 word that occurred to *J* from
34:6 *J* the prophet proceeded to
34:8 word that occurred to *J*
34:12 word . . . occurred to *J*
35:1 to *J* from Jehovah in the
35:3 Jaazaniah the son of *J* the
35:12 to occur to *J*, saying
35:18 *J* said: This is what Jehovah

Jer 36:1 to *J* from Jehovah, saying
36:4 *J* proceeded to call Baruch
36:4 write at the mouth of *J* all
36:5 *J* commanded Baruch, saying
36:8 *J* the prophet had commanded
36:10 words of *J* at the house of
36:19 conceal yourself, you and *J*
36:26 and *J* the prophet
36:27 to *J* after the king had
36:27 at the mouth of *J*, saying
36:32 *J* himself took another roll
36:32 mouth of *J* all the words
37:2 by means of *J* the prophet
37:3 to *J* the prophet, saying
37:4 *J* was coming in and going
37:6 occurred to *J* the prophet
37:12 *J* began to go forth from
37:13 hold of *J* the prophet
37:14 *J* said: It is false!
37:14 Irijah kept hold of *J* and
37:15 get indignant at *J*, and
37:16 *J* came into the house of
37:16 *J* continued dwelling there
37:17 *J* said: There does exist!
37:18 *J* said to King Zedekiah
37:21 put *J* in custody in the
37:21 *J* continued dwelling in
38:1 *J* was speaking to all the
38:6 take *J* and throw him into
38:6 let *J* down by means of ropes
38:6 *J* began to sink down into
38:7 had put *J* into the cistern
38:9 done to *J* the prophet, whom
38:10 get *J* the prophet up out of
38:11 to *J* into the cistern by
38:12 said to *J*: Put, please . . . rags
38:12 *J* now did so
38:13 drew out *J* by means of the
38:13 *J* continued to dwell in
38:14 take *J* the prophet to him
38:14 king said to *J*: I am asking
38:15 At this *J* said to Zedekiah
38:16 King Zedekiah swore to *J*
38:17 *J* now said to Zedekiah
38:19 King Zedekiah said to *J*
38:20 But *J* said: They will do
38:24 say to *J*: May no man at all
38:27 princes came in to *J* and
38:28 *J* continued to dwell in
39:11 gave command concerning *J*
39:14 take *J* out of the Courtyard
39:15 to *J* the word of Jehovah
40:1 word that occurred to *J*
40:2 took *J* and said to him
40:6 *J* came to Gedaliah the son
42:2 and said to *J* the prophet
42:4 *J* the prophet said to them
42:5 said to *J*: May Jehovah prove
42:7 proceeded to occur to *J*
43:1 *J* finished speaking to all
43:2 say to *J*: It is a falsehood
43:6 *J* the prophet and Baruch
43:8 word . . . occurred to *J*
44:1 word that occurred to *J* for
44:15 to answer *J*, saying
44:20 *J* said to all the people
44:24 *J* continued on to say
45:1 *J* the prophet spoke to Baruch
45:1 from the mouth of *J* in
46:1 word of Jehovah to *J* the
46:13 Jehovah spoke to *J* the
47:1 of Jehovah to *J* the prophet
49:34 word of Jehovah to *J* the
50:1 by means of *J* the prophet
51:59 *J* the prophet commanded
51:60 *J* proceeded to write in one
51:61 *J* said to Seraiah
51:64 point are the words of *J*
52:1 Hamutal the daughter of *J*
Da 9:2 word of Jehovah . . . to *J*
Mt 2:17 spoken through *J* the prophet
16:14 *J* or one of the prophets
27:9 spoken through *J* the prophet

Jeremoth
1Ch 7:8 sons of Becher . . . Omri and *J*
8:14 were Ahio, Shashak and *J*
23:23 sons of Mushi . . . *J*, three
25:22 for the fifteenth, for *J*
Ezr 10:26 of the sons of Elam . . . *J*
10:27 the sons of Zattu . . . *J*
10:29 the sons of Bani . . . *J*

Jeriah
1Ch 23:19 of Hebron were *J* the head
24:23 sons of Hebron, *J* the head

Jeribai
1Ch 11:46 *J* and Joshaviah the sons of

Jericho
Nu 22:1 across the Jordan from *J*
26:3 by the Jordan at *J*, saying
26:63 by the Jordan at *J*
31:12 which are by the Jordan at *J*
33:48 of Moab by the Jordan at *J*
33:50 by the Jordan at *J*, saying
34:15 the region of the Jordan by *J*
35:1 of Moab by the Jordan at *J*
36:13 of Moab by the Jordan at *J*
De 32:49 which fronts toward *J*, and
34:1 Pisgah, which fronts toward *J*
34:3 the valley plain of *J*, the
Jos 2:1 take a look at the land and *J*
2:2 was said to the king of *J*
2:3 the king of *J* sent to Rahab
3:16 passed over in front of *J*
4:13 onto the desert plains of *J*
4:19 on the eastern border of *J*
5:10 on the desert plains of *J*
5:13 Joshua happened to be by *J*
6:1 *J* was tightly shut up because
6:2 I have given *J* and its king
6:25 Joshua sent out to spy on *J*
6:26 does build this city, even *J*
7:2 sent men out from *J* to Ai
8:2 as you did to *J* and its king
9:3 what Joshua had done to *J* and
10:1 just as he had done to *J* and
10:28 he had done to the king of *J*
10:30 had done to the king of *J*
12:9 The king of *J*, one
13:32 at *J*, toward the east
16:1 from the Jordan at *J* to the
16:1 to the waters of *J* eastward
16:1 wilderness going up from *J*
16:7 and reached to *J* and went
18:12 the slope of *J* on the north
18:21 *J* and Beth-hoglah and
20:8 region of the Jordan, at *J*
24:11 and came to *J*. And the
24:11 the landowners of *J*, the
2Sa 10:5 Dwell in *J* until your beards
1Ki 16:34 Hiel the Bethelite built *J*
2Ki 2:4 Jehovah . . . has sent me to *J*
2:4 So they came on to *J*
2:5 prophets that were at *J*
2:15 prophets that were at *J* saw
2:18 he was dwelling in *J*
25:5 in the desert plains of *J*
1Ch 6:78 region of the Jordan at *J*
19:5 Dwell in *J* until your beards
2Ch 28:15 *J*, the city of palm trees
Ezr 2:34 sons of *J*, three hundred and
Ne 3:2 the men of *J* did building
7:36 the sons of *J*, three hundred
Jer 39:5 in the desert plains of *J*
52:8 in the desert plains of *J*
Mt 20:29 as they were going out of *J*
Mr 10:46 they came into *J*. But as he
10:46 crowd were going out of *J*
Lu 10:30 down from Jerusalem to *J*
18:35 as he was getting near to *J*
19:1 he entered *J* and was going
Heb 11:30 the walls of *J* fell down

Jeriel
1Ch 7:2 sons of Tola . . . *J* and Jahmai

Jerijah
1Ch 26:31 Of the Hebronites, *J* was

Jerimoth
1Ch 7:7 sons of Bela . . . Uzziel and *J*
12:5 Eluzai and *J* and Bealiah and
24:30 the sons of Mushi . . . *J*
25:4 the sons of Heman . . . *J*
27:19 of Naphtali, *J* the son of
2Ch 11:18 Mahalath the daughter of *J*
31:13 and *J* . . . commissioners at

Jerioth
1Ch 2:18 by Azubah his wife and by *J*

Jeroboam
1Ki 11:26 *J* the son of Nebat an
11:28 *J* was a valiant, mighty
11:29 *J* himself went out from
11:31 he went on to say to *J*
11:40 seeking to put *J* to death
11:40 *J* got up and went running
12:2 *J* the son of Nebat heard of
1Ki 12:2 that *J* might dwell in Egypt
12:3 *J* and all the congregation
12:12 And *J* and all the people
12:15 to *J* the son of Nebat
12:20 heard that *J* had returned
12:25 And *J* proceeded to build
12:26 *J* began to say in his heart
12:32 And *J* went on to make a
13:1 *J* was standing by the altar
13:4 *J* at once thrust out his hand
13:33 this thing *J* did not turn
13:34 the household of *J* and an
14:1 Abijah the son of *J* fell sick
14:2 *J* said to his wife: Rise up
14:2 that you are the wife of *J*
14:4 wife of *J* proceeded to do so
14:5 wife of *J* coming to apply
14:6 Come in, you wife of *J*
14:7 say to *J*, This is what
14:10 upon the house of *J*
14:10 certainly cut off from *J*
14:10 behind the house of *J*
14:13 in him in the house of *J*
14:14 cut off the house of *J* the
14:16 sins of *J* with which he
14:19 the rest of the affairs of *J*
14:20 the days that *J* reigned
14:30 between Rehoboam and *J*
15:1 King *J* the son of Nebat
15:6 between Rehoboam and *J* all
15:7 between Abijam and *J*
15:9 twentieth year of *J* the king
15:25 Nadab the son of *J*
15:29 all the house of *J*
15:30 on account of the sins of *J*
15:34 walking in the way of *J*
16:2 walking in the way of *J*
16:3 *J* the son of Nebat
16:7 become like the house of *J*
16:19 walking in the way of *J*
16:26 *J* the son of Nebat and
16:31 *J* the son of Nebat
21:22 house of *J* the son of Nebat
22:52 *J* the son of Nebat, who had
2Ki 3:3 stuck to the sins of *J* the
9:9 *J* the son of Nebat and like
10:29 sins of *J* the son of Nebat
10:31 from the sins of *J* with
13:2 sin of *J* the son of Nebat
13:6 the sin of the house of *J*
13:11 sins of *J* the son of Nebat
13:13 *J* himself sat upon his
14:16 *J* his son began to reign in
14:23 *J* the son of Jehoash the
14:24 sins of *J* the son of Nebat
14:27 *J* the son of Jehoash
14:28 affairs of *J* and all that
14:29 *J* lay down with his
15:1 *J* the king of Israel
15:8 Zechariah the son of *J*
15:9 *J* the son of Nebat
15:18 sins of *J* the son of Nebat
15:24 *J* the son of Nebat
15:28 *J* the son of Nebat
17:21 to make *J* the son of Nebat
17:21 *J* proceeded to part Israel
17:22 in all the sins of *J* that
23:15 *J* the son of Nebat
1Ch 5:17 days of *J* the king of Israel
2Ch 9:29 concerning *J* the son of Nebat
10:2 *J* the son of Nebat heard of
10:2 *J* immediately came back
10:3 *J* and all Israel came and
10:12 *J* and all the people
10:15 Ahijah the Shilonite to *J*
11:4 from going against *J*
11:14 because *J* and his sons had
12:15 between Rehoboam and *J* all
13:1 eighteenth year of King *J* it
13:2 war . . . between Abijah and *J*
13:3 *J* himself drew up in battle
13:4 O *J* and all Israel
13:6 *J* the son of Nebat, the
13:8 golden calves that *J* made
13:13 *J*, for his part, dispatched
13:15 true God himself defeated *J*
13:19 chasing after *J* and got to
13:20 *J* did not retain any more
Ho 1:1 days of *J* the son of Joash, the
Am 1:1 *J* the son of Joash, the king
7:9 rise up against the house of *J*
7:10 send to *J* the king of Israel
7:11 By the sword *J* will die; and

2Ch 32:2 face set for war against J
32:9 sent his servants to J
32:9 the Judeans that were in J
32:10 quiet under siege in J
32:12 said to Judah and to J
32:18 to the people of J that
32:19 against the God of J
32:22 J out of the hand of
32:23 gifts to Jehovah at J and
32:25 and against Judah and J
32:26 he and the inhabitants of J
32:33 J rendered to him at his
33:1 Manasseh . . . he reigned in J
33:4 In J my name will prove to
33:7 J, which I have chosen out
33:9 J to do worse than the
33:13 restored him to J to his
33:15 and in J and then had them
33:21 Amon . . . he reigned in J
34:1 Josiah . . . reigned in J
34:3 cleanse Judah and J from the
34:5 Thus he cleansed Judah and J
34:7 after which he returned to J
34:9 and the inhabitants of J
34:22 she was dwelling in J in
34:29 older men of Judah and of J
34:30 the inhabitants of J and
34:32 found in J and Benjamin to
34:32 inhabitants of J proceeded
35:1 in J a passover to Jehovah
35:18 and the inhabitants of J
35:24 and brought him to J
35:24 all Judah and J were
36:1 the place of his father in J
36:2 Jehoahaz . . . he reigned in J
36:3 removed him in J and fined
36:4 Eliakim . . . over Judah and J
36:5 Jehoiakim . . . reigned in J
36:9 Jehoiachin . . . he reigned in J
36:10 king over Judah and J
36:11 Zedekiah . . . he reigned in J
36:14 he had sanctified in J
36:19 and pull down the wall of J
36:23 to build him a house in J
Ezr 1:2 to build him a house in J
1:3 up to J, which is in Judah
1:3 which was in J
1:4 which was in J
1:5 the house . . . which was in J
1:7 had brought out from J and
1:11 people out of Babylon to J
2:1 returned to J and Judah
2:68 the house of Jehovah . . . in J
3:1 gather . . . as one man to J
3:8 house of the true God at J
3:8 out of the captivity to J
4:6 inhabitants of Judah and J
4:8 letter against J to Artaxerxes
4:12 the Jews . . . have come to J
4:20 strong kings over J and
4:23 to J to the Jews and stopped
4:24 which was in J, stopped
5:1 were in Judah and in J
5:2 house of God, which was in J
5:14 the temple, which was in J
5:15 in the temple that is in J
5:16 house of God, which is in J
5:17 that house of God in J
6:3 the house of God in J
6:5 the temple that was in J
6:5 temple that is in J at its
6:9 as the priests that are in J
6:12 house of God, which is in J
6:18 service of God which is in J
7:7 the Nethinim went up to J in
7:8 came to J in the fifth month
7:9 fifth month he came to J
7:13 willing to go to J with you
7:14 concerning Judah and J in
7:15 whose residence is in J
7:16 house of their God . . . in J
7:17 of your God, which is in J
7:19 in full before God at J
7:27 house of Jehovah . . . in J
8:29 fathers of Israel in J
8:30 to J to the house of our God
8:31 to go to J, and the very
8:32 J and dwelt there three days
9:9 stone wall in Judah and in J
10:7 throughout Judah and J for
10:7 themselves together at J
10:9 at J within three days
Ne 1:2 the captivity, and also about J
1:3 the wall of J is broken down
Ne 2:11 At length I came to J, and I
2:12 into my heart to do for J
2:13 examining the walls of J
2:17 J is devastated and its gates
2:17 let us rebuild the wall of J
2:20 claim, nor memorial in J
3:8 J as far as the Broad Wall
3:9 half the district of J
3:12 half the district of J, did
4:7 repairing of the walls of J
4:8 come and fight against J and
4:22 in the midst of J, and they
6:7 throughout J, saying, There is
7:2 in command of J Hanani my
7:3 gates of J should not be opened
7:3 guards of the inhabitants of J
7:6 returned to J and to Judah
8:15 and throughout J, saying
11:1 had their dwelling in J
11:1 to dwell in J the holy city
11:2 volunteered to dwell in J
11:3 heads . . . who dwelt in J
11:4 in J there dwelt some of the
11:6 who were dwelling in J were
11:22 overseer of the Levites in J
12:27 of the wall of J
12:27 to J to carry on an
12:28 from all around J and from
12:29 for themselves all around J
12:43 rejoicing of J could be heard
13:6 I did not happen to be in J
13:7 came to J and got to notice
13:15 into J on the sabbath day
13:16 the sons of Judah and in J
13:19 the gates of J had grown
13:20 spent the night outside J
Es 2:6 taken into exile from J with
Ps 51:18 May you build the walls of J
68:29 Because of your temple at J
79:1 laid J in a heap of ruins
79:3 All around J, and there is
102:21 And his praise in J
116:19 In the midst of you, O J
122:2 Within your gates, O J
122:3 J is one that is built like
122:6 for the peace of J
125:2 J—as mountains are all
128:5 See also the good of J all
135:21 Who is residing in J
137:5 If I should forget you, O J
137:6 I were not to make J ascend
137:7 the day of J, Who were
147:2 Jehovah is building J
147:12 Commend Jehovah, O J
Ec 1:1 the son of David the king in J
1:12 to be king over Israel in J
1:16 happened to be before me in J
2:7 happened to be before me in J
2:9 happened to be before me in J
Ca 1:5 comely, O you daughters of J
2:7 under oath, O daughters of J
3:5 under oath, O daughters of J
3:10 lovingly by the daughters of J
5:8 under oath, O daughters of J
5:16 companion, O daughters of J
6:4 comely like J, awesome as
8:4 under oath, O daughters of J
Isa 1:1 concerning Judah and J in the
2:1 concerning Judah and J
2:3 the word of Jehovah out of J
3:1 removing from J and from
3:8 J has stumbled, and Judah
4:3 ones left over in J will be
4:3 written down for life in J
4:4 even the bloodshed of J from
5:3 J and you men of Judah
7:1 came up to J for war against
8:14 snare to the inhabitants of J
10:10 those at J and at Samaria
10:11 do to J and to her idols
10:12 in Mount Zion and in J
10:32 of Zion, the hill of J
22:10 houses of J you will
22:21 to the inhabitant of J and
24:23 king in Mount Zion and J
27:13 in the holy mountain in J
28:14 this people who are in J
30:19 in Zion will dwell in J
31:5 in the same way defend J
31:9 and whose furnace is in J
33:20 J an undisturbed abiding
36:2 Rabshakeh from Lachish to J
36:7 he says to Judah and J
36:20 deliver J out of my hand
Isa 37:10 J will not be given into
37:22 J has wagged her head
37:32 out of J a remnant will
40:2 Speak to the heart of J and
40:9 bringing good news for J
41:27 to J I shall give a bringer
44:26 the One saying of J
44:28 J, She will be rebuilt
51:17 rise up, O J, you who have
52:1 O J, the holy city
52:2 rise up, take a seat, O J
52:9 you devastated places of J
52:9 he has repurchased J
62:1 for the sake of J I shall not
62:6 Upon your walls, O J, I have
62:7 J as a praise in the earth
64:10 J a desolate waste
65:18 J a cause for joyfulness and
65:19 be joyful in J and exult in
66:10 Rejoice with J and be
66:13 in the case of J you will
66:20 up to my holy mountain, J
Jer 1:3 J went into exile in the
1:15 entrance of the gates of J
2:2 call out in the ears of J
3:17 call J the throne of Jehovah
3:17 to the name of Jehovah at J
4:3 to the men of Judah and to J
4:4 Judah and inhabitants of J
4:5 publish it even in J, and say
4:10 deceived this people and J
4:11 to this people and to J
4:14 clean of sheer badness, O J
4:16 Publish it against J
5:1 about in the streets of J
6:1 from the midst of J
6:6 against J a siege rampart
6:8 Be corrected, O J, that my
7:17 and in the streets of J
7:34 and from the streets of J
8:1 bones of the inhabitants of J
8:5 this people, J, is unfaithful
9:11 will make J piles of stones
11:2 and to the inhabitants of J
11:6 and in the streets of J
11:9 among the inhabitants of J
11:12 the inhabitants of J will
11:13 as the streets of J
13:9 the abundant pride of J
13:13 all the inhabitants of J
13:27 Woe to you, O J! You cannot
14:2 the outcry of J has gone up
14:16 out into the streets of J
15:4 for what he did in J
15:5 compassion upon you, O J
17:19 and in all the gates of J
17:20 all you inhabitants of J
17:21 in through the gates of J
17:25 and the inhabitants of J
17:26 and from round about J
17:27 through the gates of J on
17:27 the dwelling towers of J
18:11 and to the inhabitants of J
19:3 and you inhabitants of J
19:7 the counsel of Judah and of J
19:13 the houses of J and the
22:19 beyond the gates of J
23:14 the prophets of J I have
23:15 from the prophets of J
24:1 from J that he might bring
24:8 the remnant of J who are
25:2 the inhabitants of J, saying
25:18 J and the cities of Judah
26:18 J herself will become mere
27:3 coming to J to Zedekiah
27:18 the king of Judah and in J
27:20 exile from J to Babylon
27:20 the nobles of Judah and J
27:21 the king of Judah and J
29:1 sent from J to the remainder
29:1 into exile from J to Babylon
29:2 the princes of Judah and J
29:2 had gone forth from J
29:4 into exile from J to Babylon
29:20 sent away from J to Babylon
29:25 all the people who are in J
32:2 laying siege to J
32:32 and the inhabitants of J
32:44 in the surroundings of J
33:10 streets of J that are
33:13 in the surroundings of J
33:16 J itself will reside in
34:1 fighting against J and
34:6 all these words in J

Jer 34:7 fighting against *J* and
34:8 people who were in *J* to
34:19 and the princes of *J*, the
35:11 and let us enter into *J*
35:11 and let us dwell in *J*
35:13 to the inhabitants of *J*
35:17 all the inhabitants of *J*
36:9 people in *J* and all the
36:9 into *J* proclaimed a fast
36:31 upon the inhabitants of *J*
37:5 that were laying siege to *J*
37:5 withdrew from against *J*
37:11 from against *J* because of
37:12 to go forth from *J* to
38:28 the day that *J* was captured
38:28 just when *J* was captured
39:1 *J* and began to lay siege
39:8 walls of *J* they pulled down
40:1 exiles of *J* and of Judah
42:18 upon the inhabitants of *J*
44:2 I have brought in upon *J*
44:6 and in the streets of *J*
44:9 and in the streets of *J*
44:13 an accounting against *J*
44:17 and in the streets of *J*
44:21 and in the streets of *J*
51:35 of Chaldea! *J* will say
51:50 *J* herself come up into your
52:1 Zedekiah . . . he reigned in *J*
52:3 occurred in *J* and Judah
52:4 military force, against *J*
52:12 Nebuzaradan . . . came into *J*
52:13 and all the houses of *J*
52:14 walls of *J*, round about
52:29 from *J* there were eight
La 1:7 *J* has remembered in the days
1:8 *J* has committed outright sin
1:17 *J* has become an abhorrent
2:10 The virgins of *J* have brought
2:13 liken to you, O daughter of *J*
2:15 at the daughter of *J*, saying
4:12 come into the gates of *J*
Eze 4:1 engrave upon it a city, even *J*
4:7 to the siege of *J* you will
4:16 loaves are suspended, in *J*
5:5 Jehovah has said, This is *J*
8:3 to *J* in the visions of God, to
9:4 through the midst of *J*, and
9:8 pouring out your rage upon *J*
11:15 inhabitants of *J* have said
12:10 pronouncement against *J*
12:19 said to the inhabitants of *J*
13:16 prophesying to *J* and that
14:21 send upon *J* in order to cut
14:22 I shall have brought upon *J*
15:6 given the inhabitants of *J*
16:2 known to *J* her detestable
16:3 Jehovah has said to *J*: Your
17:12 king of Babylon came to *J*
21:2 set your face toward *J* and
21:20 against Judah, against *J*
21:22 proved to be for *J*
22:19 into the midst of *J*
23:4 and Oholibah is *J*
24:2 thrown himself against *J*
26:2 Tyre has said against *J*, Aha!
33:21 the escaped one from *J*
36:38 *J* in her festal seasons
Da 1:1 Nebuchadnezzar . . . came to *J*
5:2 from the temple that was in *J*
5:3 the house of God that was in *J*
6:10 being open for him toward *J*
9:2 the devastations of *J*
9:7 to the inhabitants of *J* and to
9:12 what has been done in *J*
9:16 turn back from your city *J*
9:16 *J* and your people are an
9:25 restore and to rebuild *J* until
Joe 2:32 for in Mount Zion and in *J*
3:1 captive ones of Judah and *J*
3:6 the sons of *J* you have sold
3:16 out of *J* he will give forth
3:17 *J* must become a holy place
3:20 and *J* to generation after
Am 1:2 out of *J* he will give forth
2:5 the dwelling towers of *J*
Ob 11 and over *J* they cast lots
20 the exiles of *J*, who were in
Mic 1:1 concerning Samaria and *J*
1:5 Are they not *J*?
1:9 my people, as far as *J*
1:12 Jehovah to the gate of *J*
3:10 and *J* with unrighteousness
3:12 *J* herself will become mere
Mic 4:2 word of Jehovah out of *J*
4:8 to the daughter of *J*
Zep 1:4 all the inhabitants of *J*
1:12 carefully search *J* with
3:14 Rejoice . . . O daughter of *J*!
3:16 day it will be said to *J*
Zec 1:12 not show mercy to *J* and to
1:14 jealous for *J* and for Zion
1:16 return to *J* with mercies
1:16 will be stretched out over *J*
1:17 and yet actually choose *J*
1:19 dispersed Judah, Israel and *J*
2:2 To measure *J*, in order to see
2:4 country *J* will be inhabited
2:12 and he must yet choose *J*
3:2 he who is choosing *J*
7:7 *J* happened to be inhabited
8:3 and reside in the midst of *J*
8:3 *J* will certainly be called
8:4 in the public squares of *J*
8:8 must reside in the midst of *J*
8:15 deal well with *J* and with
8:22 seek Jehovah of armies in *J*
9:9 in triumph, O daughter of *J*
9:10 and the horse from *J*
12:2 making *J* a bowl causing
12:2 the siege, even against *J*
12:3 *J* a burdensome stone to all
12:5 The inhabitants of *J* are a
12:6 *J* must yet be inhabited in
12:6 in her own place, in *J*
12:7 of the inhabitants of *J*
12:8 around the inhabitants of *J*
12:9 that are coming against *J*
12:10 upon the inhabitants of *J*
12:11 wailing in *J* will be great
13:1 to the inhabitants of *J* for
14:2 all the nations against *J*
14:4 front of *J*, on the east
14:8 waters will go forth from *J*
14:10 Rimmon to the south of *J*
14:11 *J* must be inhabited in
14:12 military service against *J*
14:14 Judah . . . warring at *J*
14:16 that are coming against *J*
14:17 families of the earth to *J*
14:21 cooking pot in *J* and in
Mal 2:11 in Israel and in *J*
3:4 gift offering of Judah and of *J*
Mt 2:1 from eastern parts came to *J*
2:3 and all *J* along with him
3:5 Then *J* and all Judea and all
4:25 and *J* and Judea and from the
5:35 nor by *J*, because it is the
15:1 to Jesus from *J* Pharisees and
16:21 that he must go to *J* and
20:17 about to go up to *J*, Jesus
20:18 We are going up to *J*, and
21:1 when they got close to *J* and
21:10 Now when he entered into *J*
23:37, 37 *J*, *J*, the killer of the
Mr 1:5 all the inhabitants of *J* made
3:8 from *J* and from Idumea and
3:22 that came down from *J* were
7:1 scribes that had come from *J*
10:32 on the road up to *J*, and
10:33 we are, advancing up to *J*
11:1 they were getting near to *J*
11:11 into *J*, into the temple; and
11:15 they came to *J*. There he
11:27 And they came again to *J*
15:41 up together with him to *J*
Lu 2:22 they brought him up to *J* to
2:25 a man in *J* named Simeon, and
2:41 from year to year to *J* for
2:43 Jesus remained behind in *J*
2:45 they returned to *J*, making a
4:9 led him into *J* and stationed
5:17 Galilee and Judea and *J*
6:17 from all of Judea and *J* and
9:31 was destined to fulfill at *J*
9:51 set his face to go to *J*
9:53 face was set for going to *J*
10:30 down from *J* to Jericho and
13:4 all other men inhabiting *J*
13:22 on his journey to *J*
13:33 to be destroyed outside of *J*
13:34, 34 *J*, *J*, the killer of the
17:11 while he was going to *J* he
18:31 We are going up to *J*, and
19:11 he was near *J* and they were
19:28 go on ahead, going up to *J*
21:20 *J* surrounded by encamped
21:24 *J* will be trampled on by the
Lu 23:7 Herod . . . in *J* in these days
23:28 Daughters of *J*, stop weeping
24:13 seven miles distant from *J*
24:18 an alien by yourself in *J*
24:33 they rose and returned to *J*
24:47 starting out from *J*
24:52 returned to *J* with great joy
Joh 1:19 Levites from *J* to him to
2:13 and Jesus went up to *J*
2:23 was in *J* at the passover
4:20 *J* is the place where persons
4:21 in this mountain nor in *J*
4:45 all the things he did in *J*
5:1 and Jesus went up to *J*
5:2 in *J* at the sheepgate there
7:25 some of the inhabitants of *J*
10:22 dedication took place in *J*
11:18 Bethany was near *J* at a
11:55 to *J* before the passover
12:12 that Jesus was coming to *J*
Ac 1:4 Do not withdraw from *J*, but
1:8 witnesses of me both in *J* and
1:12 they returned to *J* from a
1:12 which is near *J*, being a
1:19 to all the inhabitants of *J*
2:5 dwelling in *J* Jews, reverent
2:14 inhabitants of *J*, let this be
4:5 in *J* the gathering together of
4:16 to all the inhabitants of *J*
5:16 from the cities around *J*
5:28 filled *J* with your teaching
6:7 kept multiplying in *J*
8:1 congregation that was in *J*
8:14 apostles in *J* heard that
8:25 they turned back to *J*, and
8:26 road that runs down from *J*
8:27 He had gone to *J* to worship
9:2 he might bring bound to *J* any
9:13 did to your holy ones in *J*
9:21 man that ravaged those in *J*
9:26 in *J* he made efforts to join
9:28 walking in and out at *J*
10:39 country of the Jews and in *J*
11:2 when Peter came up to *J*, the
11:22 congregation that was in *J*
11:27 prophets came down from *J*
12:25 relief ministration in *J*
13:13 But John . . . returned to *J*
13:27 inhabitants of *J* and their
13:31 with him from Galilee to *J*
15:2 apostles and older men in *J*
15:4 On arriving in *J* they were
16:4 and older men who were in *J*
19:21 would journey to *J*, saying
20:16 he was hastening to get to *J*
20:22 am journeying to *J*, although
21:4 told Paul not to set foot in *J*
21:11 bind in this manner in *J* and
21:12 him not to go up to *J*
21:13 but also to die at *J* for the
21:15 and began going up to *J*
21:17 When we got into *J*, the
21:31 that all *J* was in confusion
22:5 bound to *J* to be punished
22:17 I had returned to *J* and was
22:18 get out of *J* quickly, because
23:11 things about me in *J*, so you
24:11 I went up to worship in *J*
25:1 three days later to *J* from
25:3 send for him to come to *J*
25:7 that had come down from *J*
25:9 Do you wish to go up to *J*
25:15 when I was in *J* the chief
25:20 go to *J* and there be judged
25:24 to me both in *J* and here
26:4 among my nation and in *J*
26:10 I did in *J*, and many of the
26:20 and to those in *J*, and over
28:17 prisoner from *J* into the
Ro 15:19 from *J* and in a circuit as
15:25 journey to *J* to minister to
15:26 poor of the holy ones in *J*
15:31 ministry which is for *J* may
1Co 16:3 to carry your kind gift to *J*
Ga 1:17 go up to *J* to those who were
1:18 went up to *J* to visit Cephas
2:1 went up to *J* with Barnabas
4:25 she corresponds with the *J*
4:26 *J* above is free, and she is
Heb 12:22 heavenly *J*, and myriads of
Re 3:12 new *J* which descends out of
21:2 New *J*, coming down out of
21:10 *J* coming down out of heaven

Jerusalem's
1Ki 3:1 finished building . . . *J* wall
Lu 2:38 waiting for *J* deliverance

Jerusha
2Ki 15:33 *J* the daughter of Zadok

Jerushah
2Ch 27:1 mother's name was *J* the

Jeshaiah
1Ch 3:21 sons of Hananiah were . . . *J*
3:21 the sons of *J* Rephaiah
25:3 the sons of Jeduthun . . . *J*
25:15 the eighth for *J*, his sons
26:25 *J* his son and Joram his son
Ezr 8:7 *J* the son of Athaliah, and
8:19 *J* from the sons of Merari
Ne 11:7 Ithiel the son of *J*

Jeshanah
1Sa 7:12 set it between Mizpah and *J*
2Ch 13:19 *J* and its dependent towns

Jesharelah
1Ch 25:14 the seventh for *J*, his sons

Jeshebeab
1Ch 24:13 for *J* the fourteenth

Jesher
1Ch 2:18 *J* and Shobab and Ardon

Jeshimon
Nu 21:20 over toward the face of *J*
23:28 Peor, which looks toward *J*
1Sa 23:19 is to the right side of *J*
23:24 Arabah to the south of *J*
26:1 hill of Hachilah, facing *J*
26:3 Hachilah, which faces *J*

Jeshishai
1Ch 5:14 son of *J*, the son of Jahdo

Jeshohaiah
1Ch 4:36 and *J* and Asaiah and Adiel

Jeshua
1Ch 24:11 for *J* the ninth, for
2Ch 31:15 and *J* . . . in office of trust
Ezr 2:2 came with Zerubbabel, *J*
2:6 the sons of *J* and Joab
2:36 Jedaiah of the house of *J*
2:40 The sons of *J* and Kadmiel
3:2 And *J* the son of Jehozadak and
3:8 and *J* the son of Jehozadak
3:9 *J*, his sons and his brothers
4:3 Zerubbabel and *J* and the rest
5:2 and *J* the son of Jehozadak
8:33 Jozabad the son of *J* and
10:18 *J* the son of Jehozadak and
Ne 3:19 And Ezer the son of *J*
7:7 came in with Zerubbabel, *J*
7:11 of the sons of *J* and Joab
7:39 Jedaiah of the house of *J*
7:43 The Levites: The sons of *J*
8:7 *J* and Bani and Sherebiah
9:4 And *J* and Bani, Kadmiel
9:5 the Levites *J* and Kadmiel
10:9 *J* the son of Azaniah
11:26 in *J* and in Moladah and in
12:1 *J*: Seraiah, Jeremiah, Ezra
12:7 brothers in the days of *J*
12:8 the Levites were *J*, Binnui
12:10 *J* himself became father to
12:24 and *J* the son of Kadmiel and
12:26 *J* the son of Jozadak

Jeshurun
De 32:15 *J* began to grow fat, then he
33:5 And he came to be king in *J*
33:26 none like the true God of *J*
Isa 44:2 *J*, whom I have chosen

Jesimiel
1Ch 4:36 and Adiel and *J* and Benaiah

Jesse
Ru 4:17 father of *J*, David's father
4:22 and Obed became father to *J*
4:22 and *J* became father to David
1Sa 16:1 you to *J* the Bethlehemite
16:3 must call *J* to the sacrifice
16:5 he sanctified *J* and his sons
16:8 *J* called Abinadab and had
16:9 Next *J* had Shammah pass by
16:10 *J* had seven of his sons pass
16:10 still Samuel said to *J*
16:11 said to *J*: Are these all the
16:11 Samuel said to *J*: Do send
16:18 son of *J* the Bethlehemite
1Sa 16:19 Saul sent messengers to *J*
16:20 *J* took an ass, bread and a
16:22 Saul sent to *J*, saying
17:12 David was the son of . . . *J*
17:13 the three oldest sons of *J*
17:17 Then *J* said to David his son
17:20 as *J* had commanded him
17:58 The son of your servant *J*
20:27 son of *J* come to the meal
20:30 choosing the son of *J* to
20:31 son of *J* is alive on the
22:7 son of *J* also give to all of
22:8 covenant with the son of *J*
22:9 I saw the son of *J* come to
22:13 you and the son of *J*, by
25:10 and who is the son of *J*?
2Sa 20:1 inheritance in the son of *J*
23:1 David the son of *J*, And the
1Ki 12:16 inheritance in the son of *J*
1Ch 2:12 in turn, became father to *J*
2:13 *J*, in turn, became father to
10:14 over to David the son of *J*
12:18 with you we are, O son of *J*
29:26 As for David the son of *J*
2Ch 10:16 inheritance in the son of *J*
11:18 of Eliab the son of *J*
Ps 72:20 David, the son of *J*, have
Isa 11:1 twig out of the stump of *J*
11:10 root of *J* that will be
Mt 1:5 Obed became father to *J*
1:6 *J* became father to David the
Lu 3:32 son of *J*, son of Obed, son of
Ac 13:22 David the son of *J*, a man
Ro 15:12 There will be the root of *J*

Jest
2Ch 36:16 *j* at the messengers of the

Jesting
Eph 5:4 foolish talking nor obscene *j*

Jesus
Mt 1:1 *J* Christ, son of David, son
1:16 Mary, of whom *J* was born
1:18 birth of *J* Christ was in this
1:21 you must call his name *J*
1:25 and he called his name *J*
2:1 *J* had been born in Bethlehem
3:13 *J* came from Galilee to the
3:15 *J* said to him: Let it be
3:16 *J* immediately came up from
4:1 *J* was led by the spirit up
4:7 *J* said to him: Again it is
4:10 *J* said to him: Go away
4:17 *J* commenced preaching and
7:28 when *J* finished these sayings
8:4 Then *J* said to him: See that
8:10 *J* became amazed and said to
8:13 *J* said to the army officer
8:14 *J*, on coming into Peter's
8:18 When *J* saw a crowd around
8:20 *J* said to him: Foxes have
8:22 *J* said to him: Keep
8:34 city turned out to meet *J*
9:2 *J* said to the paralytic: Take
9:4 *J*, knowing their thoughts
9:9 *J* caught sight of a man named
9:10 reclining with *J* and his
9:15 *J* said to them: The friends
9:19 Then *J*, getting up, began to
9:22 *J* turned around and, noticing
9:24 *J* began to say: Leave the
9:27 As *J* was passing along from
9:28 *J* asked them: Do you have
9:30 *J* sternly charged them
9:35 *J* set out on a tour of all
10:5 These twelve *J* sent forth
11:1 when *J* had finished giving
11:4 *J* said to them: Go your way
11:7 *J* started to say to the
11:25 that time *J* said in response
12:1 At that season *J* went through
12:15 *J* withdrew from there
13:1 *J*, having left the house, was
13:34 All these things *J* spoke to
13:53 when *J* had finished these
13:57 *J* said to them: A prophet is
14:1 heard the report about *J*
14:12 and came and reported to *J*
14:13 At hearing this *J* withdrew
14:16 *J* said to them: They do not
14:27 *J* spoke to them with the
14:29 Peter . . . went toward *J*
14:31 *J* caught hold of him and
15:1 came to *J* from Jerusalem
Mt 15:21 *J* now withdrew into the
15:28 Then *J* said in reply to her
15:29 *J* next came near the sea of
15:32 *J* called his disciples to
15:34 *J* said to them: How many
16:6 *J* said to them: Keep your
16:8 *J* said: Why are you doing
16:13 *J* went asking his disciples
16:17 *J* said to him: Happy you are
16:21 *J* Christ commenced showing
16:24 Then *J* said to his disciples
17:1 *J* took Peter and James and
17:4 Peter said to *J*: Lord, it is
17:7 *J* came near and, touching
17:8 saw no one but *J* himself
17:9 *J* commanded them, saying
17:17 *J* said: O faithless and
17:18 *J* rebuked it, and the demon
17:19 the disciples came up to *J*
17:22 in Galilee that *J* said to
17:25 *J* got ahead of him by saying
17:26 *J* said to him: Really, then
18:1 disciples came near to *J* and
18:22 *J* said to him: I say to you
19:1 *J* had finished these words
19:14 *J*, however, said: Let the
19:18 *J* said: Why, You must not
19:21 *J* said to him: If you want
19:23 But *J* said to his disciples
19:26 *J* said to them: With men
19:28 *J* said to them: Truly I say
20:17 *J* took the twelve disciples
20:22 *J* said in answer: You men
20:25 But *J*, calling them to him
20:30 heard that *J* was passing by
20:32 *J* stopped, called them and
20:34 *J* touched their eyes, and
21:1 *J* sent forth two disciples
21:6 did just as *J* ordered them
21:11 *J*, from Nazareth of Galilee
21:12 *J* entered into the temple
21:16 *J* said to them: Yes. Did you
21:21 *J* said to them: Truly I say
21:24 *J* said to them: I, also
21:27 So in answer to *J* they said
21:31 *J* said to them: Truly I say
21:42 *J* said to them: Did you
22:1 *J* again spoke to them with
22:18 *J*, knowing their wickedness
22:29 In reply *J* said to them: You
22:41 the Pharisees . . . *J* asked
23:1 *J* spoke to the crowds and to
24:1 *J* was on his way from the
24:4 *J* said to them: Look out that
26:1 when *J* had finished all these
26:4 to seize *J* by crafty device
26:6 *J* happened to be in Bethany
26:10 Aware of this, *J* said to
26:17 the disciples came up to *J*
26:19 disciples did as *J* ordered
26:26 *J* took a loaf and, after
26:31 *J* said to them: All of you
26:34 *J* said to him: Truly I say
26:36 *J* came with them to the
26:49 going straight up to *J* he
26:50 *J* said to him: Fellow, for
26:50 laid hands on *J* and took him
26:51 one of those with *J* reached
26:52 *J* said to him: Return your
26:55 *J* said to the crowds: Have
26:57 who took *J* into custody led
26:59 for false witness against *J*
26:63 *J* kept silent. So the high
26:64 *J* said to him: You yourself
26:69 were with *J* the Galilean
26:71 man was with *J* the Nazarene
26:75 the saying *J* spoke, namely
27:1 held a consultation against *J*
27:11 *J* now stood before the
27:11 *J* replied: You yourself say
27:17 or *J* the so-called Christ
27:20 but to have *J* destroyed
27:22 with *J* the so-called Christ
27:26 he had *J* whipped and handed
27:27 *J* into the governor's palace
27:37 is *J* the King of the Jews
27:46 the ninth hour *J* called out
27:50 Again *J* cried out with a
27:54 with him watching over *J*
27:55 accompanied *J* from Galilee
27:57 Joseph . . . a disciple of *J*
27:58 and asked for the body of *J*
28:5 I know you are looking for *J*
28:9 *J* met them and said: Good

Mt 28:10 J said to them: Have no fear
28:16 where J had arranged for
28:18 J approached and spoke to
Mr 1:1 the good news about J Christ
1:9 J came from Nazareth of
1:14 J went into Galilee
1:17 J said to them: Come after
1:24 do with you, J you Nazarene
1:25 But J rebuked it, saying: Be
1:45 J was no longer able to enter
2:4 to bring him right to J on
2:5 J saw their faith he said to
2:8 But J, having discerned
2:15 sinners . . . reclining with J
2:17 hearing this J said to them
2:19 J said to them: While the
3:7 J with his disciples withdrew
5:6 on catching sight of J from a
5:7 What have I to do with you, J
5:15 So they came to J, and they
5:20 all the things J did for him
5:21 J had crossed back again in
5:27 she heard the things about J
5:30 J recognized in himself that
5:36 J, overhearing the word being
6:4 J went on to say to them: A
6:14 the name of J became public
6:30 gathered together before J
8:27 J and his disciples now left
9:2 J took Peter and James and
9:4 they were conversing with J
9:5 Peter said to J: Rabbi, it is
9:8 no one . . . except J alone
9:23 J said to him
9:25 J, now noticing that a crowd
9:27 J took him by the hand and
9:39 But J said: Do not try to
10:5 J said to them: Out of regard
10:14 J was indignant and said to
10:18 J said to him: Why do you
10:21 J looked upon him and felt
10:23 J said to his disciples
10:24 In response J again said
10:27 J said: With men it is
10:29 J said: Truly I say to you
10:32 J was going in front of
10:38 But J said to them: You do
10:39 J said to them: The cup
10:42 J, after calling them to
10:47 When he heard that it was J
10:47 J, have mercy on me!
10:49 J stopped and said: Call him
10:50 he leaped . . . and went to J
10:51 And in answer to him J said
10:52 J said . . . Go, your faith has
11:6 just as J had said; and they
11:7 they brought the colt to J
11:22 J said to them: Have faith
11:29 J said to them: I will ask
11:33 in reply to J they said
11:33 J said to them: Neither am
12:17 J then said: Pay back
12:24 J said to them: Is not this
12:29 J answered: The first is
12:34 J, discerning he had
12:35 J began to say as he taught
13:2 J said to him: Do you behold
13:5 J started to say to them
14:6 But J said: Let her alone
14:18 J said: Truly I say to you
14:27 J said to them: You will
14:30 J said to him: Truly I say
14:48 J said to them: Did you
14:53 led J . . . to the high priest
14:55 testimony against J to put
14:60 questioned J, saying: Do you
14:62 J said: I am; and you
14:67 with the Nazarene, this J
14:72 saying that J spoke to him
15:1 they bound J and led him off
15:5 J made no further answer, so
15:15 after having J whipped, he
15:34 J called out with a loud
15:37 But J let out a loud cry and
15:43 and asked for the body of J
16:6 looking for J the Nazarene
Lu 1:31 you are to call his name J
2:21 his name was also called J
2:27 brought the young child J in
2:43 the boy J remained behind in
2:52 J went on progressing in
3:21 J also was baptized and, as
3:23 J himself, when he commenced
3:29 son of J, son of Eliezer

Lu 4:1 J, full of holy spirit, turned
4:4 But J replied to him: It is
4:8 In reply J said to him: It is
4:12 In answer J said to him
4:14 Now J returned in the power
4:34 do with you, J you Nazarene
4:35 But J rebuked it, saying
5:8 fell down at the knees of J
5:10 J said to Simon: Stop being
5:12 When he caught sight of J he
5:19 among those in front of J
5:22 J, discerning their reasonings
5:31 In reply J said to them
5:34 J said to them: You cannot
6:3 J said in reply to them
6:9 J said to them: I ask you men
6:11 what they might do to J
7:3 When he heard about J, he sent
7:4 came up to J began to entreat
7:6 J started off with them
7:9 when J heard these things he
7:40 But in reply J said to him
8:28 At the sight of J he cried
8:28 What have I to do with you, J
8:30 J asked him: What is your
8:35 they came to J and found the
8:35 sitting at the feet of J
8:39 what things J did for him
8:40 When J got back, the crowd
8:41 he fell at the feet of J and
8:45 So J said: Who . . . touched me?
8:46 J said: Someone touched me
8:50 J answered him: Have no fear
9:33 Peter said to J: Instructor
9:36 J was found alone
9:41 response J said: O faithless
9:42 J rebuked the unclean spirit
9:47 J, knowing the reasoning of
9:50 But J said to him: Do not
9:58 J said to him: Foxes have
9:62 J said to him: No man that
10:29 the man said to J
10:30 J said: A certain man was
10:37 J then said to him: Go your
13:12 J addressed her and said to
13:14 J did the cure on the sabbath
14:3 J spoke to those versed in the
14:16 J said to him: A certain man
17:13 J, Instructor, have mercy
17:17 In reply J said: The ten
18:16 J called the infants to him
18:19 J said to him: Why do you
18:22 J said to him: There is yet
18:24 J looked at him and said
18:37 J the Nazarene is passing by!
18:38 J, Son of David, have mercy
18:40 J stood still and commanded
18:40 he got near, J asked him
18:42 J said to him: Recover your
19:3 seeking to see who this J was
19:5 when J got to the place, he
19:9 J said to him: This day
19:35 they led it to J, and they
19:35 the colt and set J upon it
20:8 And J said to them: Neither
20:34 J said to them: The children
22:47 he approached J to kiss him
22:48 J said to him: Judas, do you
22:51 in reply J said: Let it go
22:52 J then said to the chief
23:8 When Herod saw J he rejoiced
23:20 he wanted to release J
23:25 surrendered J to their will
23:26 him to bear it behind J
23:28 J turned to the women and
23:34 J was saying: Father
23:42 J, remember me when you get
23:46 J called with a loud voice
23:52 and asked for the body of J
24:3 find the body of the Lord J
24:15 J himself approached and
24:19 The things concerning J the
Joh 1:17 came to be through J Christ
1:29 beheld J coming toward him
1:36 as he looked at J walking he
1:37 and they followed J
1:38 J turned and, getting a view
1:40 John said and followed J
1:42 He led him to J
1:42 J looked upon him he said
1:43 J found Philip and said to
1:45 J, the son of Joseph, from
1:47 J saw Nathanael coming
1:48 J in answer said to him

Joh 1:50 J in answer said to him
2:1 and the mother of J was there
2:2 J and his disciples were also
2:3 the mother of J said to him
2:4 J said to her: What have I
2:7 J said to them: Fill the
2:11 J performed this in Cana of
2:13 J went up to Jerusalem
2:19 In answer J said to them
2:22 and the saying that J said
2:24 J himself was not entrusting
3:3 In answer J said to him
3:5 J answered: Most truly I say
3:10 In answer J said to him
3:22 J and his disciples went
4:1 J was making and baptizing
4:2 J himself did no baptizing
4:6 J, tired out from the journey
4:7 J said . . . Give me a drink
4:10 In answer J said to her
4:13 In answer J said to her
4:17 J said to her: You said well
4:21 J said to her: Believe me
4:26 J said to her: I who am
4:34 J said to them: My food is
4:44 J . . . bore witness that in
4:47 heard that J had come out
4:48 J said to him: Unless you
4:50 J said to him: Go your way
4:50 the word that J spoke to him
4:53 hour that J said to him
4:54 second sign J performed when
5:1 and J went up to Jerusalem
5:6 J said to him: Do you want to
5:8 J said to him: Get up, pick
5:13 for J had turned aside
5:14 J found him in the temple
5:15 J that made him sound in
5:16 the Jews went persecuting J
5:19 J went on to say to them
6:1 J departed across the sea of
6:3 So J went up into a mountain
6:5 J raised his eyes and observed
6:10 J said: Have the men recline
6:11 So J took the loaves and
6:15 J, knowing they were about
6:17 J had not yet come to them
6:19 J walking upon the sea and
6:22 J had not entered into the
6:24 neither J was there nor his
6:24 to Capernaum to look for J
6:26 J answered them and said
6:29 J said . . . exercise faith in
6:32 J said to them: Most truly
6:35 J said . . . I am the bread of
6:42 Is this not J the son of
6:43 J said . . . Stop murmuring
6:53 J said . . . Unless you eat
6:61 J, knowing in himself that
6:64 J knew who were the ones
6:67 J said to the twelve
6:70 J answered them: I chose
7:1 J continued walking about in
7:6 J said to them: My due time
7:14 J went up into the temple
7:16 J, in turn, answered them
7:21 In answer J said to them
7:28 J cried out as he was
7:33 J said: I continue a little
7:37 J was standing up and he
7:39 J had not yet been glorified
8:12 J spoke . . . I am the light
8:14 J said to them: Even if I
8:19 J answered: You know neither
8:25 J said to them: Why am I
8:28 J said: When once you have
8:31 J went on to say to the Jews
8:34 J answered them: Most truly
8:39 J said to them: If you are
8:42 J said to them: If God were
8:49 J answered: I do not have a
8:54 J answered: If I glorify
8:58 J said to them: Most truly I
8:59 J hid and went out of the
9:3 J answered: Neither this man
9:11 man called J made a clay and
9:14 J made the clay and opened
9:35 J heard that they had thrown
9:37 J said to him: You have seen
9:39 J said: For this judgment
9:41 J said to them: If you were
10:6 J spoke this comparison to
10:7 J said again: Most truly I
10:23 J was walking in the

Joh 10:25 J answered them: I told you
10:32 J replied to them: I
10:34 J answered them: Is it not
11:4 when J heard it he said
11:5 J loved Martha and her
11:9 J answered: There are twelve
11:13 J had spoken, however
11:14 J said to them outspokenly
11:17 J arrived, he found he had
11:20 heard that J was coming
11:21 Martha therefore said to J
11:23 J said to her: Your brother
11:25 J said to her: I am the
11:30 J had not yet, in fact
11:32 arrived where J was and
11:33 J, therefore, when he saw
11:35 J gave way to tears
11:38 J, after groaning again
11:39 J said: Take the stone away
11:40 J said to her: Did I not
11:41 Now J raised his eyes
11:44 J said to them: Loose him
11:46 told them the things J did
11:51 J was destined to die for
11:54 J no longer walked about
11:56 they went looking for J
12:1 J, six days before the
12:1 J had raised up from the
12:3 greased the feet of J and
12:7 J said: Let her alone, that
12:9 not on account of J only
12:11 and putting faith in J
12:12 J was coming to Jerusalem
12:14 J had found a young ass, he
12:16 when J became glorified
12:21 Sir, we want to see J
12:22 and Philip came and told J
12:23 J answered them, saying
12:30 J said: This voice has
12:35 J therefore said to them
12:36 J spoke these things and
12:44 J cried out and said
13:1 J, having loved his own that
13:7 J said to him: What I am
13:8 J answered him: Unless I
13:10 J said to him: He that has
13:21 J became troubled in spirit
13:23 disciples, and J loved him
13:25 upon the breast of J and
13:26 J answered: It is that one
13:27 J, therefore, said to him
13:29 that J was telling him: Buy
13:31 J said: Now the Son of man
13:36 J answered: Where I am
13:38 J answered: Will you
14:6 J said to him: I am the way
14:9 J said to him: Have I been
14:23 J said . . . If anyone loves
16:19 J knew they were wanting to
16:31 J answered them: Do you
17:1 J spoke these things, and
17:3 one whom you sent forth, J
18:1 J went out with his
18:2 J had many times met there
18:4 J, therefore, knowing all
18:5 J the Nazarene. He said to
18:7 They said: J the Nazarene
18:8 J answered: I told you I am
18:11 J, however, said to Peter
18:12 seized J and bound him
18:15 disciple was following J
18:15 he went in with J into the
18:19 chief priest questioned J
18:20 J answered him: I have
18:22 gave J a slap in the face
18:23 J answered him: If I spoke
18:28 they led J from Caiaphas
18:32 the word of J might be
18:33 called J and said to him
18:34 J answered: Is it of your
18:36 J answered: My kingdom is
18:37 J answered: You yourself
19:1 Pilate took J and scourged
19:5 J came outside, wearing the
19:9 to J: Where are you from?
19:9 But J gave him no answer
19:11 J answered him: You would
19:13 brought J outside, and he
19:16 they took charge of J
19:18 but J in the middle
19:19 J the Nazarene the King
19:20 where J was impaled was
19:23 the soldiers had impaled J
19:25 By the torture stake of J

Joh 19:26 J, seeing his mother and
19:28 J knew that by now all
19:30 J said: It has been
19:33 coming to J, as they saw
19:38 disciple of J but a secret
19:38 take away the body of J
19:40 took the body of J and
19:42 they laid J, because the
20:2 for whom J had affection
20:12 body of J had been lying
20:14 and viewed J standing, but
20:14 did not discern it was J
20:15 J said to her: Woman, why
20:16 J said to her: Mary! Upon
20:17 J said to her: Stop clinging
20:19 J came and stood in their
20:21 J, therefore, said . . . peace
20:24 not with them when J came
20:26 J came, although the doors
20:29 J said to him: Because you
20:30 J performed many other
20:31 J is the Christ the Son of
21:1 J manifested himself again
21:4 J stood on the beach, but
21:4 discern that it was J
21:5 J said to them: Young
21:7 disciple whom J used to love
21:10 J said to them: Bring some
21:12 J said to them: Come, take
21:13 J came and took the bread
21:14 third time that J appeared
21:15 J said to Simon Peter
21:17 J said to him: Feed my
21:20 whom J used to love
21:21 Peter said to J: Lord
21:22 J said to him: If it is my
21:23 J did not say to him that
21:25 things also which J did
Ac 1:1 J started both to do and to
1:11 J who was received up from
1:14 and Mary the mother of J and
1:16 guide to those who arrested J
1:21 Lord J went in and out
2:22 J the Nazarene, a man
2:32 J God resurrected, of which
2:36 this J whom you impaled
2:38 baptized in the name of J
3:6 name of J Christ the Nazarene
3:13 glorified his Servant, J
3:20 Christ appointed for you, J
4:2 resurrection . . . the case of J
4:10 name of J Christ the Nazarene
4:13 that they used to be with J
4:18 the basis of the name of J
4:27 against your holy servant J
4:30 name of your holy servant J
4:33 resurrection of the Lord J
5:30 raised up J, whom you slew
5:42 good news about the Christ, J
6:14 J the Nazarene will throw
7:55 J standing at God's right
7:59 Lord J, receive my spirit
8:12 and of the name of J Christ
8:16 in the name of the Lord J
8:35 to him the good news about J
9:5 J, whom you are persecuting
9:17 J that appeared to you on the
9:20 preach J, that this One is
9:27 boldly in the name of J
9:34 Aeneas, J Christ heals you
10:36 of peace through J Christ
10:38 J who was from Nazareth
10:48 baptized in the name of J
11:17 believed upon the Lord J
11:20 the good news of the Lord J
13:23 brought to Israel a savior, J
13:33 in that he resurrected J
15:11 kindness of the Lord J in
15:26 name of our Lord J Christ
16:7 spirit of J did not permit
16:18 I order you in the name of J
16:31 Believe on the Lord J and you
17:3 This is the Christ, this J
17:7 there is another king, J
17:18 the good news of J and the
18:5 to prove that J is the Christ
18:25 the things about J, but being
18:28 that J was the Christ
19:4 one coming after him . . . J
19:5 in the name of the Lord J
19:13 name the name of the Lord J
19:13 I solemnly charge you by J
19:15 I know J and I am acquainted
19:17 name of the Lord J went on

Ac 20:21 and faith in our Lord J
20:24 that I received of the Lord J
20:35 mind the words of the Lord J
21:13 for the name of the Lord J
22:8 I am J the Nazarene, whom
24:24 on the belief in Christ J
25:19 J who was dead but who Paul
26:9 the name of J the Nazarene
26:15 J, whom you are persecuting
28:23 J from both the law of
28:31 concerning the Lord J Christ
Ro 1:1 Paul, a slave of J Christ and
1:4 from the dead—yes, J Christ
1:6 called to belong to J Christ
1:7 Father and the Lord J Christ
1:8 thanks to my God through J
2:16 God through Christ J judges
3:22 through the faith in J Christ
3:24 the ransom paid by Christ J
3:26 the man that has faith in J
4:24 believe on him who raised J
5:1 peace . . . through our Lord J
5:11 God through our Lord J Christ
5:15 kindness by the one man J
5:17 the one person, J Christ
5:21 life in view through J Christ
6:3 were baptized into Christ J
6:11 reference to God by Christ J
6:23 everlasting life by Christ J
7:25 Thanks to God through J
8:1 those in union with Christ J
8:2 life in union with Christ J
8:11 of him that raised up J
8:11 raised up Christ J from the
8:34 Christ J is the one who died
8:39 God's love that is in Christ J
10:9 that J is Lord, and exercise
13:14 put on the Lord J Christ
14:14 in the Lord J that nothing
15:5 attitude that Christ J had
15:6 Father of our Lord J Christ
15:16 a public servant of Christ J
15:17 exulting in Christ J when
15:30 through our Lord J Christ and
16:3 fellow workers in Christ J
16:20 kindness of our Lord J be
16:25 and the preaching of J Christ
16:27 be the glory through J Christ
1Co 1:1 to be an apostle of J Christ
1:2 union with Christ J, called
1:2 name of our Lord, J Christ
1:3 our Father and the Lord J
1:4 given to you in Christ J
1:7 the revelation of our Lord J
1:8 the day of our Lord J Christ
1:9 sharing with his Son J Christ
1:10 name of our Lord J Christ
1:30 are in union with Christ J
2:2 except J Christ, and him
3:11 foundation . . . which is J
4:15 in Christ J I have become
4:17 in connection with Christ J
5:4 in the name of our Lord J
5:4 with the power of our Lord J
6:11 in the name of our Lord J
8:6 and there is one Lord, J
9:1 Have I not seen J our Lord?
11:23 the Lord J in the night in
12:3 says: J is accursed! and
12:3 can say: J is Lord! except
15:31 I have in Christ J our Lord
15:57 victory through our Lord J
16:23 kindness of the Lord J be
16:24 in union with Christ J
2Co 1:1 an apostle of Christ J
1:2 and the Lord J Christ
1:3 Father of our Lord J Christ
1:14 in the day of our Lord J
1:19 Christ J, who was preached
4:5 preaching . . . Christ J as Lord
4:10 treatment given to J, that
4:10 life of J may also be made
4:11 life of J may also be made
4:14 he who raised J up will
4:14 us up also together with J
8:9 kindness of our Lord J Christ
11:4 preaches a J other than the
11:31 and Father of the Lord J
13:5 J Christ is in union with
13:14 kindness of the Lord J
Ga 1:1 but through J Christ and God
1:3 Father and the Lord J Christ
1:12 revelation by J Christ
2:4 we have in union with Christ J

Ga 2:16 through faith toward Christ J
2:16 have put our faith in Christ J
3:1 before whose eyes J Christ was
3:14 by means of J Christ for the
3:22 from faith toward J Christ
3:26 through your faith in Christ J
3:28 person in union with Christ J
4:14 angel of God, like Christ J
5:6 as regards Christ J neither
5:24 those who belong to Christ J
6:12 torture stake of the Christ, J
6:14 torture stake of our Lord J
6:17 brand marks of a slave of J
6:18 kindness of our Lord J Christ
Eph 1:1 Paul, an apostle of Christ J
1:1 ones in union with Christ J
1:2 Father and the Lord J Christ
1:3 Father of our Lord J Christ
1:5 adoption through J Christ as
1:15 faith you have in the Lord J
1:17 God of our Lord J Christ
2:6 in union with Christ J
2:7 in union with Christ J
2:10 in union with Christ J
2:13 now in union with Christ J
2:20 J himself is the foundation
3:1 Paul, the prisoner of Christ J
3:6 union with Christ J through
3:11 the Christ, J our Lord
3:21 by means of Christ J to all
4:21 just as truth is in J
5:20 in the name of our Lord J
6:23 Father and the Lord J Christ
6:24 all those loving our Lord J
Php 1:1 slaves of Christ J, to all
1:1 in union with Christ J who
1:2 Father and the Lord J Christ
1:6 until the day of J Christ
1:8 tender affection as Christ J
1:11 which is through J Christ
1:19 a supply of the spirit of J
1:26 overflow in Christ J by
2:5 that was also in Christ J
2:10 in the name of J every knee
2:11 J Christ is Lord to the glory
2:19 I am hoping in the Lord J
2:21 not those of Christ J
3:3 have our boasting in Christ J
3:8 knowledge of Christ J my Lord
3:12 laid hold on by Christ J
3:14 of God by means of Christ J
3:20 a savior, the Lord J Christ
4:7 by means of Christ J
4:19 glory by means of Christ J
4:21 one in union with Christ J
4:23 the Lord J Christ be with
Col 1:1 Paul, an apostle of Christ J
1:3 Father of our Lord J Christ
1:4 in connection with Christ J
2:6 as you have accepted Christ J
3:17 in the name of the Lord J
4:11 and J who is called Justus
4:12 a slave of Christ J, sends
1Th 1:1 and the Lord J Christ
1:3 hope in our Lord J Christ
1:10 from the dead, namely, J
2:14 in union with Christ J
2:15 who killed even the Lord J
2:19 our Lord J at his presence
3:11 our Lord J direct our way
3:13 at the presence of our Lord J
4:1 and exhort you by the Lord J
4:2 gave you through the Lord J
4:14 J died and rose again, so
4:14 asleep in death through J
5:9 salvation through our Lord J
5:18 in union with Christ J
5:23 presence of our Lord J Christ
5:28 Lord J Christ be with you
2Th 1:1 and the Lord J Christ
1:2 and the Lord J Christ
1:7 the revelation of the Lord J
1:8 good news about our Lord J
1:12 Lord J may be glorified in
1:12 and of the Lord J Christ
2:1 presence of our Lord J Christ
2:8 Lord J will do away with by
2:14 glory of our Lord J Christ
2:16 may our Lord J Christ
3:6 in the name of the Lord J
3:12 exhortation in the Lord J
3:18 J Christ be with all of you
1Ti 1:1 Paul, an apostle of Christ J
1:1 and of Christ J, our hope
1Ti 1:2 and Christ J our Lord
1:12 grateful to Christ J our Lord
1:14 in connection with Christ J
1:15 Christ J came into the world
1:16 Christ J might demonstrate
2:5 a man, Christ J
3:13 in connection with Christ J
4:6 a fine minister of Christ J
5:21 before God and Christ J
6:3 those of our Lord J Christ
6:13 Christ J, who as a witness
6:14 manifestation of our Lord J
2Ti 1:1 Paul, an apostle of Christ J
1:1 is in union with Christ J
1:2 and Christ J our Lord
1:9 in connection with Christ J
1:10 our Savior, Christ J, who
1:13 in connection with Christ J
2:1 in connection with Christ J
2:3 As a fine soldier of Christ J
2:8 J Christ was raised up from
2:10 is in union with Christ J
3:12 in association with Christ J
3:15 in connection with Christ J
4:1 before God and Christ J, who
Tit 1:1 Paul . . . apostle of J Christ
1:4 and Christ J our Savior
2:13 the Savior of us, Christ J
3:6 through J Christ our Savior
Phm 1 prisoner for . . . Christ J
3 peace from . . . Lord J Christ
5 have toward the Lord J and
9 prisoner for . . . Christ J
25 the Lord J Christ be with the
Heb 2:9 J, who has been made a
3:1 priest whom we confess—J
4:14 passed through the heavens, J
6:20 J who has become a high
7:22 J has become the one given
8:6 now J has obtained a more
10:10 offering of the body of J
10:19 place by the blood of J
12:2 and Perfecter of our faith, J
12:24 J the mediator of a new
13:8 J Christ is the same
13:12 J also, that he might
13:20 covenant, our Lord J
13:21 performing in us through J
Jas 1:1 slave of God and of the Lord J
2:1 faith of our Lord J Christ
1Pe 1:1 Peter, an apostle of J Christ
1:2 with the blood of J Christ
1:3 Father of our Lord J Christ
1:3 the resurrection of J Christ
1:7 at the revelation of J Christ
1:13 the revelation of J Christ
2:5 acceptable to God through J
3:21 through the resurrection of J
4:11 God . . . glorified through J
2Pe 1:1 apostle of J Christ, to those
1:1 and the Savior J Christ
1:2 accurate knowledge of . . . J
1:8 knowledge of our Lord J
1:11 kingdom of . . . J Christ
1:14 J Christ signified to me
1:16 presence of our Lord J
2:20 Lord and Savior J Christ
3:18 our Lord and Savior J Christ
1Jo 1:3 and with his Son J Christ
1:7 blood of J his Son cleanses
2:1 J Christ, a righteous one
2:22 denies that J is the Christ
3:23 in the name of his Son J
4:2 confesses J Christ as having
4:3 that does not confess J does
4:15 J Christ is the Son of God
5:1 believing that J is the Christ
5:5 faith that J is the Son of God
5:6 water and blood, J Christ
5:20 by means of his Son J Christ
2Jo 3 J Christ the Son of the Father
7 J Christ as coming in the flesh
Jude 1 Jude, a slave of J Christ, but
1 and preserved for J Christ
4 only Owner and Lord, J Christ
17 apostles of our Lord J Christ
21 mercy of our Lord J Christ
25 through J Christ our Lord
Re 1:1 revelation by J Christ, which
1:2 to the witness J Christ gave
1:5 J Christ, the Faithful Witness
1:9 endurance in company with J
1:9 God and bearing witness to J
12:17 of bearing witness to J
Re 14:12 of God and the faith of J
17:6 blood of the witnesses of J
19:10 the work of witnessing to J
19:10 bearing witness to J is
20:4 witness they bore to J and
22:16 I, J, sent my angel to bear
22:20 Amen! Come, Lord J
22:21 kindness of the Lord J

Jesus'
Lu 17:16 fell upon his face at J feet
Joh 13:23 in front of J bosom one of
Ac 5:40 upon the basis of J name
2Co 4:5 as your slaves for J sake
4:11 death for J sake, that the

Jether
Jg 8:20 he said to J his firstborn
1Ki 2:5 Amasa the son of J, when he
2:32 J the chief of the army of
1Ch 2:17 J the Ishmaelite
2:32 sons of Jada . . . J and
2:32 But J died without sons
4:17 the sons of Ezrah were J
7:38 sons of J were Jephunneh and

Jetheth
Ge 36:40 sheiks of Esau . . . shiek J
1Ch 1:51 sheiks of Edom . . . J

Jethro
Ex 3:1 a shepherd of the flock of J
4:18 Moses went and returned to J
4:18 So J said to Moses: Go in
18:1 Now J the priest of Midian
18:2 J, Moses' father-in-law, took
18:5 J, Moses' father-in-law, and
18:6 I, your father-in-law, J, am
18:9 J felt glad over all the good
18:10 J said: Blessed be Jehovah
18:12 Then J, Moses' father-in-law

Jetur
Ge 25:15 J, Naphish and Kedemah
1Ch 1:31 J . . . sons of Ishmael
5:19 began to make war upon . . . J

Jeuel
1Ch 9:6 And of the sons of Zerah, J
2Ch 29:13 of Elizaphan, Shimri and J

Jeush
Ge 36:5 Oholibamah bore J and Jalam
36:14 she bore to Esau J and Jalam
36:18 sons of Oholibamah . . . J
1Ch 1:35 sons of Esau were . . . J
7:10 sons of Bilhan were J and
8:39 of Eshek . . . J the second
23:10 sons of Shimei . . . J and
23:11 J and Beriah, they did not
2Ch 11:19 J and Shemariah and Zaham

Jeuz
1Ch 8:10 and J and Sachia and Mirmah

Jew
Es 2:5 a J, happened to be in Shushan
3:4 had told them that he was a J
5:13 Mordecai the J sitting in the
6:10 do that way to Mordecai the J
8:7 queen and to Mordecai the J
9:29 Mordecai the J proceeded to
9:31 as Mordecai the J and Esther
10:3 Mordecai the J was second to
Jer 34:9 a J, who is his brother
Zec 8:23 skirt of a man who is a J
Joh 3:25 a J concerning purification
4:9 despite being a J, ask me
18:35 I am not a J, am I?
Ac 10:28 J to join himself to or
13:6 J whose name was Bar-Jesus
18:2 J named Aquila, a native of
18:24 J named Apollos, a native of
19:34 recognized that he was a J
21:39 am, in fact, a J, of Tarsus
22:3 I am a J, born in Tarsus of
Ro 1:16 having faith, to the J first
2:9 of the J first and also of the
2:10 J first and also for the Greek
2:17 J in name and are resting
2:28 not a J who is one on the
2:29 J who is one on the inside
3:1 is the superiority of the J
10:12 no distinction between J and
1Co 9:20 to the Jews I became as a J
Ga 2:14 though you are a J, live as
3:28 There is neither J nor Greek
Col 3:11 there is neither Greek nor J

Jewelry
Nu 31:51 priest accepted . . . all the *j*

Jewess
Ac 24:24 Drusilla . . . who was a *J*

Jewish
1Ch 4:18 his *J* wife, she gave birth
Ne 5:1 against their *J* brothers
5:8 *J* brothers who were sold to
13:24 knowing how to speak *J*
Jer 43:9 the eyes of the *J* men
Ac 16:1 son of a believing *J* woman
19:14 Sceva, a *J* chief priest
Ga 2:14 live according to *J* practice
Tit 1:14 no attention to *J* fables

Jews
2Ki 16:6 cleared out the *J* from Elath
25:25 also the *J* and the Chaldeans
Ezr 4:12 the *J* who came up here from
4:23 to the *J* and stopped them by
5:1 *J* who were in Judah and in
5:5 upon the older men of the *J*
6:7 The governor of the *J* and the
6:7 and the older men of the *J*
6:8 with these older men of the *J*
6:14 the older men of the *J* were
Ne 1:2 the *J*, those who had escaped
2:16 and to the *J* and the priests
4:1 and he kept deriding the *J*
4:2 What are the feeble *J* doing?
4:12 the *J* dwelling close by them
5:17 the *J* and the deputy rulers
6:6 the *J* are scheming to rebel
13:23 *J* that had given a dwelling
Es 3:6 seeking to annihilate all the *J*
3:10 showing hostility to the *J*
3:13 kill and to destroy all the *J*
4:3 great mourning among the *J*
4:7 against the *J*, to destroy them
4:13 any more than all the other *J*
4:14 for the *J* from another place
4:16 the *J* that are to be found in
6:13 seed of the *J* that Mordecai
8:1 one showing hostility to the *J*
8:3 he had schemed against the *J*
8:5 he wrote to destroy the *J* that
8:7 his hand against the *J*
8:8 write in behalf of the *J*
8:9 to the *J* and to the satraps and
8:9 to the *J* in their own style of
8:11 king granted to the *J* that
8:13 *J* should become ready for
8:16 For the *J* there occurred light
8:17 and exultation for the *J*, a
8:17 declaring themselves *J*, for
8:17 dread of the *J* had fallen upon
9:1 enemies of the *J* had waited to
9:1 *J* themselves domineered over
9:2 *J* congregated themselves in
9:3 were assisting the *J*, for the
9:5 *J* went striking down all their
9:6 the *J* killed and there was a
9:10 showing hostility to the *J*
9:12 the *J* have killed, and there
9:13 to the *J* that are in Shushan
9:15 the *J* that were in Shushan
9:16 As for the rest of the *J* that
9:18 *J* that were in Shushan, they
9:19 the country *J*, inhabiting the
9:20 documents to all the *J* that
9:22 the *J* had rested from their
9:23 the *J* accepted what they had
9:24 hostility to all the *J*
9:24 schemed against the *J* to
9:25 he has schemed against the *J*
9:27 the *J* imposed and accepted
9:28 from the midst of the *J* and
9:30 documents to all the *J* in
10:3 and was great among the *J* and
Jer 32:12 eyes of all the *J* who were
38:19 I am in fright of the *J*
40:11 *J* that were in Moab and
40:12 *J* began to return from all
41:3 *J* who happened to be with
44:1 *J* that were dwelling in the
52:28 thousand and twenty-three *J*
52:30 took *J* into exile, seven
Da 3:8 approached and accused the *J*
3:12 *J* whom you appointed over the
Mt 2:2 is the one born king of the *J*
27:11 Are you the king of the *J*?
27:29 Good day, you King of the *J*!
27:37 is Jesus the King of the *J*
Mt 28:15 spread abroad among the *J*
Mr 7:3 the *J* do not eat unless they
15:2 Are you the king of the *J*?
15:9 release . . . the king of the *J*
15:12 you call the king of the *J*
15:18 Good day, you King of the *J*!
15:26 The King of the *J*
Lu 7:3 sent forth older men of the *J*
23:3 Are you the king of the *J*?
23:37 If you are the king of the *J*
23:38 This is the king of the *J*
Joh 1:19 the *J* sent forth priests and
2:6 purification rules of the *J*
2:13 passover of the *J* was near
2:18 in answer, the *J* said to
2:20 the *J* said: This temple was
3:1 Nicodemus . . . ruler of the *J*
4:9 For *J* have no dealings with
4:22 originates with the *J*
5:1 there was a festival of the *J*
5:10 *J* began to say to the cured
5:15 told the *J* it was Jesus that
5:16 *J* went persecuting Jesus
5:18 *J* began seeking all the more
6:4 festival of the *J*, was near
6:41 *J* began to murmur at him
6:52 *J* began contending with one
7:1 *J* were seeking to kill him
7:2 the festival of the *J*, the
7:11 the *J* began looking for him
7:13 because of the fear of the *J*
7:15 the *J* fell to wondering
7:35 the *J* said among themselves
7:35 *J* dispersed among the Greeks
8:22 the *J* began to say: He will
8:31 to the *J* that had believed
8:48 In answer the *J* said to him
8:52 The *J* said to him: Now we
8:57 *J* said to him: You are not
9:18 *J* did not believe concerning
9:22 they were in fear of the *J*
9:22 *J* had already come to an
10:19 division . . . among the *J*
10:24 *J* encircled him and began
10:31 *J* lifted up stones to stone
10:33 *J* answered him: We are
11:19 *J* had come to Martha and
11:31 *J* that were with her in the
11:33 *J* that came with her
11:36 *J* began to say: See, what
11:45 *J* that had come to Mary
11:54 walked about . . . among the *J*
11:55 passover of the *J* was near
12:9 *J* got to know he was there
12:11 *J* were going there and
13:33 just as I said to the *J*
18:12 *J* seized Jesus and bound
18:14 counseled the *J* that it was
18:20 all the *J* come together
18:31 *J* said to him: It is not
18:33 Are you the king of the *J*?
18:36 be delivered up to the *J*
18:38 he went out again to the *J*
18:39 to you the king of the *J*
19:3 Good day, you king of the *J*!
19:7 *J* answered him: We have a
19:12 *J* shouted . . . If you release
19:14 said to the *J*: See! Your
19:19 Nazarene the King of the *J*
19:20 *J* read this title, because
19:21 chief priests of the *J*
19:21 write The King of the *J*
19:21 said, I am King of the *J*
19:31 *J*, since it was Preparation
19:38 out of his fear of the *J*
19:40 *J* have the custom of
19:42 of the preparation of the *J*
20:19 were for fear of the *J*
Ac 2:5 *J*, reverent men, from every
2:10 both *J* and proselytes
6:1 Greek-speaking *J* against the
6:1 against the Hebrew-speaking *J*
9:22 confounding the *J* that dwelt
9:23 *J* took counsel together to do
9:29 with the Greek-speaking *J*
10:22 the whole nation of the *J*
10:39 in the country of the *J*
11:19 word to no one except to *J*
12:3 it was pleasing to the *J*
12:11 of the *J* were expecting
13:5 in the synagogues of the *J*
13:43 many of the *J* and of the
13:45 *J* got sight of the crowds
13:50 *J* stirred up the reputable
Ac 14:1 into the synagogue of the *J*
14:1 *J* and Greeks became believers
14:2 the *J* that did not believe
14:4 and some were for the *J* but
14:5 people of the nations and *J*
14:19 *J* arrived from Antioch and
16:3 because of the *J* that were in
16:20 very much, they being *J*
17:1 was a synagogue of the *J*
17:5 the *J*, getting jealous, took
17:10 into the synagogue of the *J*
17:13 *J* from Thessalonica learned
17:17 in the synagogue with the *J*
18:2 all the *J* to depart from Rome
18:4 would persuade *J* and Greeks
18:5 witnessing to the *J* to prove
18:12 *J* rose up with one accord
18:14 Gallio said to the *J*: If it
18:14 O *J*, I would with reason put
18:19 and reasoned with the *J*
18:28 proved the *J* to be wrong
19:10 both *J* and Greeks
19:13 roving *J* who practiced the
19:17 both the *J* and the Greeks
19:33 the *J* thrusting him up front
20:3 hatched against him by the *J*
20:19 by the plots of the *J*
20:21 witness both to *J* and to
21:11 *J* will bind in this manner
21:20 believers . . . among the *J*
21:21 all the *J* among the nations
21:27 *J* from Asia on beholding him
22:12 reported on by all the *J*
22:30 was being accused by the *J*
23:12 the *J* formed a conspiracy
23:20 The *J* have agreed to request
23:27 man was seized by the *J* and
24:5 seditions among all the *J*
24:9 the *J* also joined in the
24:18 *J* from the district of Asia
24:27 to gain favor with the *J*
25:2 the *J* gave him information
25:7 the *J* that had come down
25:8 against the Law of the *J*
25:9 to gain favor with the *J*
25:10 have done no wrong to the *J*
25:15 the older men of the *J*
25:24 *J* together have applied to
26:2 of which I am accused by *J*
26:3 as the controversies among *J*
26:4 and in Jerusalem, all the *J*
26:7 I am accused by *J*, O king
26:21 *J* seized me in the temple
28:17 principal men of the *J*
28:19 *J* kept speaking against it
Ro 3:9 *J* as well as Greeks are all
3:29 is he the God of the *J* only?
9:24 not only from among *J* but
1Co 1:22 both the *J* ask for signs and
1:23 to the *J* a cause for
1:24 called, both *J* and Greeks
9:20 And so to the *J* I became as
9:20 that I might gain *J*; to
10:32 to *J* as well as Greeks and
12:13 whether *J* or Greeks
2Co 11:24 By *J* I five times received
Ga 2:13 rest of the *J* also joined him
2:14 the nations do, and not as *J*
2:15 We who are *J* by nature, and
1Th 2:14 at the hands of the *J*
Re 2:9 say they themselves are *J*
3:9 who say they are *J*, and yet

Jews'
2Ki 18:26 *J* language in the ears of
18:28 loud voice in the *J* language
2Ch 32:18 in the *J* language to the
Isa 36:11 not speak . . . *J* language
36:13 voice in the *J* language

Jezaniah
Jer 40:8 *J* the son of the Maacathite
42:1 *J* the son of Hoshaiah and

Jezebel
1Ki 16:31 *J* the daughter of Ethbaal
18:4 *J* cut off Jehovah's prophets
18:13 when *J* killed the prophets
18:19 eating at the table of *J*
19:1 Ahab told *J* all that Elijah
19:2 *J* sent a messenger to Elijah
21:5 *J* his wife came in to him
21:7 Then *J* his wife said to him
21:11 did just as *J* had sent to
21:14 They now sent to *J*, saying
21:15 as soon as *J* heard that

1Ki 21:15 *J* immediately said to Ahab
21:23 as regards *J* Jehovah has
21:23 dogs will eat up *J* in the
21:25 whom *J* his wife egged on
2Ki 9:7 at the hand of *J*
9:10 *J* the dogs will eat up in
9:22 fornications of *J* your
9:30 and *J* herself heard of it
9:36 dogs will eat the flesh of *J*
9:37 And the dead body of *J* will
9:37 they may not say: This is *J*
Re 2:20 you tolerate that woman *J*

Jezer
Ge 46:24 sons of Naphtali were . . . *J*
Nu 26:49 of *J* the family of the
1Ch 7:13 sons of Naphtali were . . . *J*

Jezerites
Nu 26:49 of Jezer the family of the *J*

Jeziel
1Ch 12:3 and *J* and Pelet the sons of

Jezreel
Jos 15:56 *J* and Jokdeam and Zanoah
17:16 in the low plain of *J*
19:18 boundary came to be to *J*
Jg 6:33 camp in the low plain of *J*
1Sa 25:43 taken Ahinoam from *J*; and
29:1 by the spring that was in *J*
29:11 Philistines . . . went up to *J*
2Sa 2:9 king over . . . *J* and over
4:4 report . . . came from *J*
1Ki 4:12 Zarethan below *J*, from
18:45 and made his way to *J*
18:46 and went running . . . to *J*
21:1 in *J*, beside the palace of
21:23 in the plot of land of *J*
2Ki 8:29 to get healed at *J* from the
8:29 Jehoram the son of Ahab in *J*
9:10 in the tract of land at *J*
9:15 returned to get healed at *J*
9:15 go and make report in *J*
9:16 began to ride and go to *J*
9:17 standing upon the tower in *J*
9:30 At length Jehu came to *J*
9:36 In the tract of land of *J*
9:37 in the tract of land of *J*
10:1 Samaria to the princes of *J*
10:6 tomorrow at this time at *J*
10:7 and sent them to him at *J*
10:11 of the house of Ahab in *J*
1Ch 4:3 *J* and Ishma and Idbash
2Ch 22:6 healed at *J* from the wounds
22:6 son of Ahab in *J*, for he was
Ho 1:4 Call his name *J*, for yet a
1:4 acts of bloodshed of *J* against
1:5 Israel in the low plain of *J*
1:11 great will be the day of *J*
2:22 answer *J* [=God will sow seed]

Jezreelite
1Ki 21:1 to belong to Naboth the *J*
21:4 Naboth the *J* had spoken to
21:6 to speak to Naboth the *J* and
21:7 vineyard of Naboth the *J*
21:15 vineyard of Naboth the *J*
21:16 vineyard of Naboth the *J*
2Ki 9:21 tract of land of Naboth the *J*
9:25 the field of Naboth the *J*

Jezreelitess
1Sa 27:3 two wives, Ahinoam the *J*
30:5 Ahinoam the *J* and Abigail
2Sa 2:2 Ahinoam the *J* and Abigail the
3:2 Amnon by Ahinoam the *J*
1Ch 3:1 Ahinoam the *J*

Jidlaph
Ge 22:22 Pildash and *J* and Bethuel

Jiggle
Am 9:9 I will *j* the house of Israel

Jiggles
Am 9:9 just as one *j* the sieve, so

Joab
1Sa 26:6 Abishai . . . the brother of *J*
2Sa 2:13 *J* the son of Zeruiah and
2:14 Abner said to *J*: Let the
2:14 *J* said: Let them rise up
2:18 *J* and Abishai and Asahel
2:22 my face to *J* your brother
2:24 *J* and Abishai went chasing
2:26 Abner began to call to *J*
2:27 *J* said: As the true God is
2:28 *J* now blew the horn, and all
2Sa 2:30 *J*, he turned back from
2:32 *J* and his men went marching
3:22 David's servants and *J* were
3:23 *J* and all the army that was
3:23 reported to *J*, saying: Abner
3:24 *J* went in to the king and
3:26 *J* went out from David and
3:27 *J* now led him aside inside
3:29 back upon the head of *J*
3:30 *J* and Abishai his brother
3:31 David said to *J* and all the
8:16 *J* the son of Zeruiah was
10:7 sent *J* and all the army and
10:9 *J* saw that the battle
10:13 *J* and the people that were
10:14 *J* returned from the sons of
11:1 David proceeded to send *J*
11:6 David sent to *J*, saying
11:6 So *J* sent Uriah to David
11:7 ask how *J* was getting along
11:11 my lord *J* and the servants
11:14 letter to *J* and send it by
11:16 *J* was keeping guard over
11:17 fighting against *J*, then
11:18 *J* now sent that he might
11:22 about which *J* had sent him
11:25 say to *J*, Do not let this
12:26 *J* continued to fight against
12:27 *J* sent messengers to David
14:1 *J* the son of Zeruiah came to
14:2 *J* sent to Tekoa and took
14:3 *J* put the words in her mouth
14:19 hand of *J* with you in all
14:19 servant *J* that commanded
14:20 *J* has done this thing, but
14:21 king said to *J*: Here, now
14:22 *J* fell upon his face to the
14:22 *J* went on to say: Today
14:23 *J* rose up and went to
14:29 Absalom sent for *J* to send
14:31 *J* rose up and came to
14:32 Absalom said to *J*: Look! I
14:33 *J* came in to the king and
17:25 place of *J* over the army
18:2 people under the hand of *J*
18:5 king went on to command *J*
18:10 saw it and told *J* and said
18:11 *J* said to the man who was
18:12 But the man said to *J*
18:14 To this *J* said: Let me not
18:16 *J* now blew the horn, that
18:16 *J* had held back the people
18:20 But *J* said to him: You are
18:21 Then *J* said to the Cushite
18:21 the Cushite bowed to *J* and
18:22 now said once again to *J*
18:22 *J* said: Why is it that you
18:29 *J* sent the king's servant
19:1 Later it was reported to *J*
19:5 *J* came in to the king at
19:13 army chief . . . instead of *J*
20:7 men of *J* and the Cherethites
20:8 *J* was girded, clothed with a
20:9 *J* proceeded to say to Amasa
20:10 *J* and Abishai his brother
20:11 has found delight in *J* and
20:11 let him follow *J*
20:13 following *J* to chase after
20:15 the people that were with *J*
20:16 Say, please, to *J*, Come
20:17 Are you *J*? to which he said
20:20 To this *J* answered and said
20:21 Then the woman said to *J*
20:22 and pitch it to *J*. Upon that
20:22 and *J* himself returned to
20:23 *J* was over all the army of
23:18 Abishai the brother of *J*
23:24 Asahel the brother of *J* was
23:37 armor-bearers of *J* the son
24:2 the king said to *J* the chief
24:3 But *J* said to the king
24:4 king's word prevailed upon *J*
24:4 *J* and the chiefs of the
24:9 *J* now gave the number of the
1Ki 1:7 came to have dealings with *J*
1:19 *J* the chief of the army
1:41 *J* got to hear the sound of
2:5 what *J* the son of Zeruiah did
2:22 and for *J* the son of Zeruiah
2:28 report itself came clear to *J*
2:28 *J* himself had inclined to
2:28 *J* went fleeing to the tent
2:29 *J* has fled to the tent of
2:30 This is what *J* spoke, and
1Ki 2:31 the blood . . . that *J* spilled
2:33 come back upon the head of *J*
11:15 *J* the chief of the army
11:16 *J* and all Israel dwelt
11:21 *J* the chief of the army had
1Ch 2:16 sons of Zeruiah were . . . *J*
4:14 *J* the father of Ge-harashim
11:6 *J* the son of Zeruiah got to
11:8 *J* himself brought to life
11:20 Abishai the brother of *J*
11:26 Asahel the brother of *J*
11:39 the armor-bearer of *J* the
18:15 *J* the son of Zeruiah was
19:8 sent *J* and all the army and
19:10 When *J* saw that the battle
19:14 *J* and the people that were
19:15 Later *J* came into Jerusalem
20:1 that *J* proceeded to lead the
20:1 *J* went on to strike Rabbah
21:2 So David said to *J* and the
21:3 *J* said: May Jehovah add to
21:4 prevailed over *J*, so that
21:4 *J* went out and walked
21:5 *J* now gave the number of the
21:6 had been detestable to *J*
26:28 *J* the son of Zeruiah had
27:24 *J* the son of Zeruiah had
27:34 *J* was chief of the army
Ezr 2:6 the sons of Jeshua and *J*
8:9 of the sons of *J*, Obadiah the
Ne 7:11 of the sons of Jeshua and *J*
Ps 60:*super* *J* proceeded to return and

Joab's
2Sa 3:29 cut off from *J* house a man
14:30 *J* tract of land beside mine
17:25 Zeruiah, *J* mother
18:2 son of Zeruiah, *J* brother
18:15 carrying *J* weapons
20:9 *J* right hand took hold of
20:10 sword that was in *J* hand
20:11 one of *J* young men stood
1Ch 27:7 was Asahel, *J* brother, and

Joah
2Ki 18:18 *J* the son of Asaph the
18:26 and *J* said to Rabshakeh
18:37 and *J* the son of Asaph the
1Ch 6:21 *J* his son, Iddo his son
26:4 Obed-edom had sons . . . *J* the
2Ch 29:12 *J* the son of Zimmah and
29:12 and Eden the son of *J*
34:8 *J* the son of Joahaz the
Isa 36:3 *J* the son of Asaph the
36:11 and *J* said to Rabshakeh
36:22 *J* the son of Asaph the

Joahaz
2Ch 34:8 Joah the son of *J* the

Joanan
Lu 3:27 son of *J*, son of Rhesa

Joanna
Lu 8:3 *J* the wife of Chuza, Herod's
24:10 Magdalene Mary, and *J*, and

Joash
Jg 6:11 belonged to *J* the Abi-ezrite
6:29 the son of *J* is the one that
6:30 said to *J*: Bring your son out
6:31 *J* said to all those who stood
7:14 the son of *J*, a man of Israel
8:13 the son of *J* began his return
8:29 the son of *J* went his way and
8:32 the son of *J* died at a good
8:32 burial place of *J* his father
1Ki 22:26 and to *J* the king's son
1Ch 4:22 and *J* and Saraph, who
7:8 of Becher were Zemirah and *J*
12:3 and *J* the sons of Shemaah
27:28 oil supplies there was *J*
2Ch 18:25 and to *J* the king's son
Ho 1:1 days of Jeroboam the son of *J*
Am 1:1 Jeroboam the son of *J*, the

Job
Job 1:1 *J* . . . proved to be blameless
1:5 *J* would send and sanctify
1:5 said *J*, maybe my sons have
1:5 is the way *J* would do always
1:8 your heart upon my servant *J*
1:9 nothing that *J* has feared God
1:14 there came a messenger to *J*
1:20 *J* proceeded to get up and rip
1:22 *J* did not sin or ascribe
2:3 *J*, that there is no one like

Job 2:7 and struck *J* with a malignant
2:10 *J* did not sin with his lips
2:11 three companions of *J* got to
3:1 *J* opened his mouth and began
3:2 *J* now answered and said
6:1 *J* proceeded to answer and say
9:1 *J* proceeded to answer and say
12:1 *J* proceeded to answer and
16:1 *J* proceeded to answer and
19:1 *J* proceeded to answer and
21:1 *J* proceeded to answer and
23:1 *J* proceeded to answer and
26:1 *J* proceeded to answer and
27:1 *J* proceeded again to lift up
29:1 *J* proceeded again to lift up
31:40 words of *J* have come to an
32:1 men ceased from answering *J*
32:2 Against *J* his anger blazed
32:4 had waited for *J* with words
32:12 there is no one reproving *J*
33:1 O *J*, please hear my words
33:31 Pay attention, O *J*! Listen
34:5 For *J* has said, I certainly
34:7 able-bodied man is like *J*
34:35 *J* himself speaks without
34:36 let *J* be tested out to the
35:16 *J* himself opens his mouth
37:14 Do give ear to this, O *J*
38:1 to answer *J* out of the
40:1 proceeded to answer *J*
40:3 *J* went on to answer Jehovah
40:6 Jehovah went on to answer *J*
42:1 *J* proceeded to answer Jehovah
42:7 had spoken these words to *J*
42:7 truthful as has my servant *J*
42:8 rams and go to my servant *J*
42:8 *J* my servant will himself
42:8 as has my servant *J*
42:10 the captive condition of *J*
42:12 he blessed the end of *J*
42:16 *J* continued living after
42:17 *J* died, old and satisfied
Eze 14:14 Noah, Daniel and *J*, they
14:20 were Noah, Daniel and *J* in
Jas 5:11 heard of the endurance of *J*

Jobab
Ge 10:29 and *J* . . . sons of Joktan
36:33 When Bela died, *J* son of
36:34 When *J* died, Husham from
Jos 11:1 to *J* the king of Madon
1Ch 1:23 *J* . . . the sons of Joktan
1:44 *J* the son of Zerah from
1:45 *J* died, and Husham from the
8:9 father to *J* and Zibia and
8:18 and *J*, the sons of Elpaal

Job's
Job 42:9 so Jehovah accepted *J* face
42:10 all that had been *J*
42:15 as pretty as *J* daughters

Jochebed
Ex 6:20 Amram took *J* his father's
Nu 26:59 Amram's wife was *J*, Levi's

Joda
Lu 3:26 son of Josech, son of *J*

Joed
Ne 11:7 *J* the son of Pedaiah the son

Joel
1Sa 8:2 firstborn son happened to be *J*
1Ch 4:35 and *J* and Jehu the son of
5:4 The sons of *J* were Shemaiah
5:8 son of Shema the son of *J*
5:12 *J* was the head, and Shapham
6:28 of Samuel . . . firstborn *J*
6:33 son of *J*, the son of Samuel
6:36 son of *J*, the son of Azariah
7:3 sons of Izrahiah were . . . *J*
11:38 *J* the brother of Nathan
15:7 of the sons of Gershom, *J*
15:11 Levites Uriel, Asaiah and *J*
15:17 Heman the son of *J* and, of
23:8 sons of Ladan . . . *J*, three
26:22 of Jehieli, Zetham and *J*
27:20 half tribe of Manasseh, *J*
2Ch 29:12 *J* the son of Azariah of the
Ezr 10:43 the sons of Nebo . . . *J* and
Ne 11:9 and *J* the son of Zichri
Joe 1:1 to *J* the son of Pethuel
Ac 2:16 said through the prophet *J*

Joelah
1Ch 12:7 *J* and Zebadiah the sons of

Joezer
1Ch 12:6 Azarel and *J* and Jashobeam

Jogbehah
Nu 32:35 and Jazer and *J*
Jg 8:11 to the east of Nobah and *J* and

Jogli
Nu 34:22 Bukki the son of *J*

Joha
1Ch 8:16 and *J*, the sons of Beriah
11:45 and *J* his brother the Tizite

Johanan
2Ki 25:23 and *J* the son of Kareah
1Ch 3:15 sons of Josiah were . . . *J*
3:24 sons of Elioenai were . . . *J*
6:9 Azariah . . . father to *J*
6:10 *J* . . . father to Azariah
12:4 Jahaziel and *J* and Jozabad
12:12 *J* the eighth, Elzabad the
Ezr 8:12 *J* the son of Hakkatan, and
Ne 12:22 Joiada and *J* and Jaddua
12:23 *J* the son of Eliashib
Jer 40:8 *J* and Jonathan, the sons of
40:13 *J* the son of Kareah and
40:15 *J* the son of Kareah himself
40:16 *J* the son of Kareah
41:11 *J* the son of Kareah and
41:13 saw *J* the son of Kareah
41:14 go to *J* the son of Kareah
41:15 men from before *J*, that
41:16 *J* the son of Kareah and
42:1 *J* the son of Kareah and
42:8 *J* the son of Kareah and for
43:2 *J* the son of Kareah and all
43:4 *J* the son of Kareah and all
43:5 *J* the son of Kareah and all

John
Mt 3:1 In those days *J* the Baptist
3:4 *J* had his clothing of camel's
3:13 to *J*, in order to be baptized
4:12 that *J* had been arrested
4:21 of Zebedee and *J* his brother
10:2 James . . . and *J* his brother
11:2 *J*, having heard in jail about
11:4 Go your way and report to *J*
11:7 respecting *J*: What did you go
11:11 a greater than *J* the Baptist
11:12 days of *J* the Baptist until
11:13 the Law, prophesied until *J*
11:18 *J* came neither eating nor
14:2 *J* the Baptist. He was raised
14:3 For Herod had arrested *J* and
14:4 For *J* had been saying to him
14:8 the head of *J* the Baptist
14:10 had *J* beheaded in the prison
16:14 said: Some say *J* the Baptist
17:1 and James and *J* his brother
17:13 to them about *J* the Baptist
21:25 The baptism by *J*, from what
21:26 they all hold *J* as a prophet
21:32 *J* came to you in a way of
Mr 1:4 *J* the baptizer turned up in
1:6 *J* was clothed with camel's
1:9 baptized in the Jordan by *J*
1:14 after *J* was put under arrest
1:19 James . . . and *J* his brother
1:29 and Andrew with James and *J*
2:18 Why is it the disciples of *J*
3:17 and *J* the brother of James
5:37 and *J* the brother of James
6:14 saying: *J* the baptizer has
6:16 The *J* that I beheaded, this
6:17 had sent out and arrested *J*
6:18 For *J* had repeatedly said to
6:20 For Herod stood in fear of *J*
6:24 The head of *J* the baptizer
6:25 the head of *J* the Baptist
8:28 *J* the Baptist, and others
9:2 took Peter and James and *J*
9:38 *J* said to him: Teacher, we
10:35 James and *J*, the two sons
10:41 be indignant at James and *J*
11:30 baptism by *J* from heaven or
11:32 *J* had really been a prophet
13:3 *J* . . . began to ask him
14:33 took Peter and James and *J*
Lu 1:13 you are to call his name *J*
1:60 but he shall be called *J*
1:63 and wrote: *J* is its name
3:2 God's declaration came to *J*
3:15 reasoning . . . about *J*
3:16 *J* gave the answer, saying to
Lu 3:20 he locked *J* up in prison
5:10 James and *J*, Zebedee's sons
5:33 The disciples of *J* fast
6:14 James and *J*, and Philip and
7:19 *J* summoned a certain two of
7:20 *J* the Baptist dispatched us
7:22 report to *J* what you saw and
7:24 the messengers of *J* had gone
7:24 to the crowds concerning *J*
7:28 there is none greater than *J*
7:29 with the baptism of *J*
7:33 *J* the Baptist has come
8:51 Peter and *J* and James and the
9:7 said by some that *J* had been
9:9 Herod said: *J* I beheaded
9:19 *J* the Baptist; but others
9:28 he took Peter and *J* and James
9:49 *J* said: Instructor, we saw a
9:54 James and *J* saw this they
11:1 as *J* also taught his disciples
16:16 the Prophets were until *J*
20:4 the baptism of *J* from heaven
20:6 that *J* was a prophet
22:8 dispatched Peter and *J*, saying
Joh 1:6 his name was *J*
1:15 *J* bore witness about him
1:19 this is the witness of *J*
1:26 *J* answered them, saying
1:28 where *J* was baptizing
1:32 *J* also bore witness, saying
1:35 *J* was standing with two of
1:40 heard what *J* said and
1:42 You are Simon the son of *J*
3:23 But *J* also was baptizing in
3:24 *J* had not yet been thrown
3:25 part of the disciples of *J*
3:26 So they came to *J* and said
3:27 *J* said: A man cannot receive
4:1 more disciples than *J*
5:33 You have dispatched men to *J*
5:36 witness greater than . . . *J*
10:40 where *J* was baptizing at
10:41 *J*, indeed, did not perform
10:41 *J* said about this man were
21:15 Simon son of *J*, do you love
21:16 Simon son of *J*, do you love
21:17 Simon son of *J*, do you have
Ac 1:5 *J*, indeed, baptized with water
1:13 *J* and James and Andrew
1:22 with his baptism by *J* and
3:1 Peter and *J* were going up
3:3 sight of Peter and *J* about to
3:4 Peter, together with *J*, gazed
3:11 holding onto Peter and *J*, all
4:6 *J* and Alexander and as many as
4:13 outspokenness of Peter and *J*
4:19 Peter and *J* said to them
8:14 dispatched Peter and *J* to
10:37 the baptism that *J* preached
11:16 *J*, for his part, baptized
12:2 James the brother of *J* by the
12:12 *J* who was surnamed Mark
12:25 *J*, the one surnamed Mark
13:5 had *J* also as an attendant
13:13 *J* withdrew from them and
13:24 *J*, in advance of the entry of
13:25 *J* was fulfilling his course
15:37 also *J*, who was called Mark
18:25 with only the baptism of *J*
19:4 *J* baptized with the baptism
Ga 2:9 James and Cephas and *J*, the
Re 1:1 through him to his slave *J*
1:4 *J* to the seven congregations
1:9 I *J*, your brother and a sharer
22:8 I *J* was the one hearing and

John's
Mt 9:14 *J* disciples came to him and
Mr 2:18 *J* disciples and the Pharisees
Lu 7:18 *J* disciples reported to him
Ac 19:3 They said: In *J* baptism

Joiada
Ne 3:6 *J* the son of Paseah and
12:10 and Eliashib to *J*
12:11 *J* . . . father to Jonathan
12:22 *J* and Johanan and Jaddua
13:28 *J* the son of Eliashib the

Joiakim
Ne 12:10 Jeshua . . . father to *J*
12:10 *J* . . . father to Eliashib
12:12 days of *J* there happened to
12:26 days of *J* the son of Jeshua

Joiarib
Ezr 8:16 J and Elnathan, instructors
Ne 11:5 J the son of Zechariah the
11:10 Jedaiah the son of J, Jachin
12:6 Shemaiah, and J, Jedaiah
12:19 for J, Mattenai; for Jedaiah

Join
Ge 29:34 husband will j himself to me
Ex 26:6 j the tent cloths one to the
26:9 must j five tent cloths by
26:11 loops and j the tent together
Pr 16:5 Hand may j to hand, yet one
Jer 50:5 us j ourselves to Jehovah
Da 11:34 and many will certainly j
Lu 10:40 to j in helping me
Ac 2:47 j to them daily those being
5:13 courage to j himself to them
8:29 j yourself to this chariot
9:26 to j himself to the disciples
10:28 Jew to j himself to or

Joined
Ex 26:3 the one j to the other, and
26:3 with the one j to the other
26:17 has two tenons j one to the
28:7 be j at its two extremities
28:7 extremities, and it must be j
36:10 j five tent cloths one to
36:10 cloths he j one to another
36:13 j the tent cloths to one
36:16 j five tent cloths together
36:17 tent cloth that j with it
38:28 tops and j them together
39:4 shoulder pieces . . . were j
39:4 was j at its two extremities
Nu 18:2 be j to you and may minister
18:4 And they must be j to you and
Ne 4:6 wall came to be j together
Ps 83:8 Assyria itself has become j
122:3 been j together in oneness
Ec 9:4 whoever is j to all the living
Isa 14:1 alien resident must be j to
56:3 has j himself to Jehovah
56:6 j themselves to Jehovah to
Ho 4:17 Ephraim is j with idols
Zec 2:11 j to Jehovah in that day
Ac 5:36 four hundred, j his party
17:33 some men j themselves to
24:9 the Jews also j in the attack
1Co 6:16 he who is j to a harlot is
6:17 he who is j to the Lord is
Ga 2:13 also j him in putting on this
Eph 2:21 harmoniously j together
4:16 harmoniously j together and
Php 2:2 being j together in soul
Col 2:2 j together in love and with a
2:19 body . . . j together by means
Heb 2:4 God j in bearing witness with

Joining
Ex 28:27 near its place of j, above
36:18 j the tent together to
39:20 near its place of j, above
Es 9:27 those j themselves to them
Isa 5:8 Woe to the ones j house to
Eze 1:9 wings were j one to the other
1:11 Each one had two j to each
41:8 reed of six cubits to the j

Joinings
Ex 38:17 silver j for all the pillars

Joins
Ro 8:26 spirit also j in with help

Joint
Ge 32:25 the socket of his thigh j
32:25 the socket of Jacob's thigh j
32:32 on the socket of the thigh j
32:32 the socket of Jacob's thigh j
Ro 8:17 but j heirs with Christ
Eph 3:6 j heirs and fellow members
4:16 j that gives what is needed
Heb 12:13 not be put out of j, but

Jointly
Ps 71:10 have j exchanged counsel

Joints
Ex 27:10 and their j are of silver
27:11 and their j being of silver
36:38 tops and their j with gold
38:10 of the pillars and their j
38:11 and their j were of silver
38:12 and their j were of silver
38:17 and their j were of silver
38:19 and their j were of silver
Da 5:6 his hip j were loosening and
Col 2:19 by means of its j and
Heb 4:12 and of j and their marrow

Jokdeam
Jos 15:56 Jezreel and J and Zanoah

Jokes
Jer 15:17 group of those playing j

Jokim
1Ch 4:22 J and the men of Cozeba

Joking
Ge 19:14 like a man who was j

Jokmeam
1Ki 4:12 to the region of J
1Ch 6:68 J with its pasture grounds

Jokneam
Jos 12:22 king of J in Carmel, one
19:11 that is in front of J
21:34 J and its pasture ground

Jokshan
Ge 25:2 she bore him Zimran and J
25:3 J became father to Sheba and
1Ch 1:32 J and Medan and Midian and
1:32 sons of J were Sheba and

Joktan
Ge 10:25 name of his brother was J
10:26 J became father to Almodad
10:29 these were the sons of J
1Ch 1:19 name of his brother was J
1:20 J, he became father to
1:23 these were the sons of J

Joktheel
Jos 15:38 Dilean and Mizpeh and J
2Ki 14:7 called J down to this day

Jolly
Isa 57:4 that you have a j good time

Jonadab
Jer 35:6 J the son of Rechab, our
35:10 J our forefather commanded
35:19 J the son of Rechab a man

Jonah
2Ki 14:25 J the son of Amittai
Jon 1:1 occur to J the son of Amittai
1:3 J proceeded to get up and run
1:5 J himself had gone down to
1:7 finally the lot fell upon J
1:15 lifted up J and hurled him
1:17 a great fish to swallow J
1:17 J came to be in the inward
2:1 J prayed to Jehovah his God
2:10 vomited out J onto the dry
3:1 occurred to J the second time
3:3 J got up and went to Nineveh
3:4 J started to enter into the
4:1 To J, though, it was highly
4:5 J went out of the city and
4:6 come up over J, in order to
4:6 J began to rejoice greatly
4:8 upon the head of J, so that
4:9 God proceeded to say to J
Mt 12:39 the sign of J the prophet
12:40 just as J was in the belly
12:41 repented at what J preached
12:41 more than J is here
16:4 given it except the sign of J
16:17 Simon son of J, because
Lu 11:29 except the sign of J
11:30 just as J became a sign to
11:32 repented at what J preached
11:32 more than J is here

Jonam
Lu 3:30 son of Joseph, son of J, son

Jonathan
Jg 18:30 J the son of Gershom, Moses'
1Sa 13:2 thousand proved to be with J
13:3 J struck down the garrison
13:16 Saul and J his son and the
13:22 that were with Saul and J
13:22 to Saul and to J his son
14:1 J the son of Saul proceeded
14:3 did not know that J had gone
14:4 passages that J looked for
14:6 So J said to the attendant
14:8 J said: Here we are crossing
14:12 So the men . . . answered J
14:12 J said to his armor-bearer
14:13 J kept going up on his hands
14:13 they began to fall before J
1Sa 14:14 slaughter with which J
14:17 J and his armor-bearer were
14:21 who was with Saul and J
14:27 As for J, he had not been
14:29 J said: My father has
14:39 even if it is in J my son
14:40 I and J my son—we will
14:41 Then J and Saul were taken
14:42 decide between me and J my
14:42 And J got to be taken
14:43 Saul said to J: Do tell me
14:43 J told him and said: I did
14:44 you do not positively die, J
14:45 Is J to die, who has
14:45 the people redeemed J, and
14:49 sons of Saul came to be J
18:1 J began to love him as his
18:3 And J and David proceeded to
18:4 J stripped himself of the
19:1 Saul spoke to J his son and
19:2 J, Saul's son, he took great
19:2 J told David, saying: Saul
19:4 J spoke well of David to
19:6 Saul obeyed the voice of J
19:7 J called David and
19:7 J told him all these words
19:7 J brought David to Saul, and
20:1 said in front of J: What
20:3 not let J know this for fear
20:4 J went on to say to David
20:5 At this David said to J
20:9 J said: That is unthinkable
20:10 David said to J: Who will
20:11 J said to David: Just come
20:12 J went on to say to David
20:13 So may Jehovah do to J
20:16 name of J be cut off from
20:17 So J swore again to David
20:18 J went on to say to him
20:25 J was facing him, and Abner
20:27 Saul said to J his son
20:28 J answered Saul: David
20:30 anger grew hot against J
20:32 J answered Saul his father
20:33 J came to know that it had
20:34 J rose up from the table
20:35 J made his way out to the
20:37 the arrow that J had shot
20:37 J began to call from behind
20:38 J went on calling from
20:38 attendant of J went picking
20:39 J and David themselves knew
20:40 J gave his weapons to the
20:42 J went on to say to David
20:42 J himself came into the
23:16 J the son of Saul now rose
23:18 J himself went to his own
31:2 struck down J and Abinadab
2Sa 1:4 Saul and J his son have died
1:5 has died and also J his son
1:12 and over J his son and
1:17 dirge over Saul and J his son
1:22 bow of J did not turn back
1:23 Saul and J, the lovable ones
1:25 J slain upon your high places
1:26 my brother J, Very pleasant
4:4 J, the son of Saul, had a son
4:4 report about Saul and J came
9:1 for the sake of J
9:3 a son of J, lame in the feet
9:6 Mephibosheth the son of J the
9:7 for the sake of J your father
15:27 and J the son of Abiathar
15:36 J belonging to Abiathar
17:17 As J and Ahimaaz were
17:20 Where are Ahimaaz and J?
21:7 Mephibosheth the son of J
21:7 between David and J the son
21:12 the bones of J his son from
21:13 and the bones of J his son
21:14 the bones of Saul and of J
21:21 J the son of Shimei
23:32 the sons of Jashen, J
1Ki 1:42 J the son of Abiathar the
1:43 J answered and said to
1Ch 2:32 sons of Jada . . . J
2:33 the sons of J were Peleth
8:33 Saul . . . became father to J
9:39 Saul . . . became father to J
9:40 the son of J was Merib-baal
10:2 got to strike down J and
11:34 J the son of Shagee the
20:7 Finally J the son of Shimea
27:25 was J the son of Uzziah

1Ch 27:32 *J*, David's nephew, was a
Ezr 8:6 Ebed the son of *J*, and with
10:15 *J* the son of Asahel and
Ne 12:11 Joiada . . . father to *J*
12:11 *J* . . . father to Jaddua
12:14 for Malluchi, *J*; for
12:35 *J* the son of Shemaiah the
Jer 40:8 *J*, the sons of Kareah, and

Jonathan's
1Sa 18:1 *J* very soul became bound up
1Ch 8:34 And *J* son was Merib-baal

Joppa
Jos 19:46 the border in front of *J*
2Ch 2:16 to you as rafts by sea to *J*
Ezr 3:7 from Lebanon to the sea at *J*
Jon 1:3 he finally came down to *J* and
Ac 9:36 in *J* there was a certain
9:38 as Lydda was near *J*, when
9:42 known throughout all *J*, and
9:43 in *J* with a certain Simon
10:5 send men to *J* and summon a
10:8 and dispatched them to *J*
10:23 brothers that were from *J*
10:32 to *J* and call for Simon
11:5 in the city of *J* praying, and
11:13 Dispatch men to *J* and send

Jorah
Ezr 2:18 sons of *J*, a hundred and

Jorai
1Ch 5:13 Sheba and *J* and Jacan and Zia

Joram
2Sa 8:10 Toi sent *J* his son to King
1Ch 26:25 *J* his son and Zichri his son

Jordan
Ge 13:10 the whole District of the *J*
13:11 whole District of the *J*
32:10 I crossed this *J* and now I
50:10 in the region of the *J*
50:11 in the region of the *J*
Nu 13:29 sea and by the side of the *J*
22:1 across the *J* from Jericho
26:3 by the *J* at Jericho, saying
26:63 by the *J* at Jericho
31:12 are by the *J* at Jericho
32:5 Do not make us cross the *J*
32:19 the side of the *J* and beyond
32:19 the *J* toward the sunrising
32:21 actually pass over the *J*
32:29 pass with you over the *J*
32:32 on this side of the *J*
33:48 of Moab by the *J* at Jericho
33:49 continued camping by the *J*
33:50 by the *J* at Jericho, saying
33:51 You are crossing the *J* into
34:12 border must go down to the *J*
34:15 region of the *J* by Jericho
35:1 of Moab by the *J* at Jericho
35:10 You are crossing the *J* to the
35:14 on this side of the *J*, and
36:13 of Moab by the *J* at Jericho
De 1:1 in the region of the *J* in the
1:5 In the region of the *J* in the
2:29 I shall pass over the *J* into
3:8 were in the region of the *J*
3:17 the Arabah and the *J* and the
3:20 giving them across the *J*
3:25 land that is across the *J*
3:27 will not pass over this *J*
4:21 I should not cross the *J* or
4:22 I am not crossing the *J*, but
4:26 crossing the *J* to take
4:41 cities on the side of the *J*
4:46 in the region of the *J* in
4:47 in the region of the *J* toward
4:49 Arabah in the region of the *J*
9:1 crossing the *J* to go in and
11:30 the side of the *J* toward the
11:31 you are crossing the *J* to go
12:10 cross the *J* and dwell in the
27:2 cross the *J* into the land
27:4 when you have crossed the *J*
27:12 when you have crossed the *J*
30:18 *J* to go to take possession
31:2 You will not cross this *J*
31:13 you are crossing the *J* to
32:47 you are crossing the *J* to take
Jos 1:2 cross this *J*, you and all this
1:11 you are crossing this *J* to go
1:14 this side of the *J*; but you
1:15 *J* toward the rising of the
2:7 direction of the *J* at the
Jos 2:10 other side of the *J*, namely
3:1 and to come as far as the *J*
3:8 edge of the waters of the *J*
3:8 should stand still in the *J*
3:11 passing before you into the *J*
3:13 rest in the waters of the *J*
3:13 waters of the *J* will be cut
3:14 before passing over the *J*
3:15 came as far as the *J* and the
3:15 *J* overflows all its banks
3:17 in the middle of the *J* as
3:17 completed passing over the *J*
4:1 completed passing over the *J*
4:3 from the very middle of the *J*
4:5 to the middle of the *J*, and
4:7 waters of the *J* were cut off
4:7 When it passed through the *J*
4:7 waters of the *J* were cut off
4:8 from the middle of the *J*
4:9 set up in the middle of the *J*
4:10 in the middle of the *J* until
4:16 that they go up out of the *J*
4:17 Go up out of the *J*
4:18 out of the middle of the *J*
4:18 the waters of the *J* began
4:19 people came up out of the *J*
4:20 they had taken out of the *J*
4:22 Israel passed over this *J*
4:23 dried up the waters of the *J*
5:1 side of the *J* to the west
5:1 dried up the waters of the *J*
7:7 all the way across the *J*
7:7 on the other side of the *J*
9:1 of the *J* in the mountainous
9:10 on the other side of the *J*
12:1 the side of the *J* toward the
12:7 side of the *J* toward the
13:8 the *J* toward the east
13:23 came to be the *J*; and this
13:27 the *J* being the border as
13:27 side of *J* toward the east
13:32 Moab on the side of the *J*
14:3 on the other side of the *J*
15:5 eastern boundary . . . the *J*
15:5 at the end of the *J*
16:1 from the *J* at Jericho to the
16:7 and went out to the *J*
17:5 on the other side of the *J*
18:7 the *J* toward the east
18:12 northern corner from the *J*
18:19 the southern end of the *J*
18:20 *J* served as its boundary
19:22 border proved to be at the *J*
19:33 came to be at the *J*
19:34 to Judah at the *J* toward
20:8 region of the *J*, at Jericho
22:4 on the other side of the *J*
22:7 side of the *J* to the west
22:10 to the regions of the *J*
22:10 built . . . an altar by the *J*
22:11 regions of the *J* on the side
22:25 namely, the *J*. You have no
23:4 from the *J* to the Great Sea
24:8 on the other side of the *J*
24:11 you went crossing the *J*
Jg 3:28 capture the fords of the *J*
5:17 on the other side of the *J*
7:24 Beth-barah and the *J*. So all
7:24 as far as Beth-barah and the *J*
7:25 Gideon in the region of the *J*
8:4 Gideon came to the *J*, crossing
10:8 on the side of the *J* in the
10:9 would cross the *J* to fight
11:13 as far as the *J*. And now do
11:22 wilderness as far as the *J*
12:5 to capture the fords of the *J*
12:6 at the fords of the *J*
1Sa 13:7 Hebrews even crossed the *J*
31:7 in the region of the *J* saw
2Sa 2:29 went crossing the *J* and
10:17 Israel and crossed the *J* and
17:22 they kept crossing the *J*
17:22 had not passed over the *J*
17:24 crossed the *J*, he and all
19:15 come as far as the *J*
19:15 the king across the *J*
19:17 successfully to the *J* before
19:18 he was about to cross the *J*
19:31 to the *J* with the king
19:31 to escort him to the *J*
19:36 bring the king . . . to the *J*
19:39 now began to cross the *J*
19:41 with him over the *J*
20:2 from the *J* to Jerusalem
2Sa 24:5 they crossed the *J* and took
1Ki 2:8 down to meet me at the *J*
7:46 In the District of the *J* it
17:3 that is east of the *J*
17:5 that is east of the *J*
2Ki 2:6 has sent me to the *J*
2:7 they stood by the *J*
2:13 stood by the shore of the *J*
5:10 bathe seven times in the *J*
5:14 plunge into the *J* seven
6:2 as far as the *J* and take from
6:4 they finally came to the *J*
7:15 as far as the *J*
10:33 the *J* toward the rising of
1Ch 6:78 region of the *J* at Jericho
6:78 Jericho to the east of the *J*
12:15 the ones that crossed the *J*
12:37 And from across the *J* of
19:17 crossed the *J* and came to
26:30 region of the *J* to the west
2Ch 4:17 In the District of the *J* the
Ne 3:22 men of the *J* District, did
Job 40:23 although the *J* should burst
Ps 42:6 From the land of *J* and the
114:3 the *J*, it began to turn back
114:5 *J*, that you began to turn
Isa 9:1 region of the *J*, Galilee of
Jer 12:5 proud thickets along the *J*
49:19 proud thickets along the *J*
50:44 proud thickets along the *J*
Eze 47:18 *J*, from the boundary to
Zec 11:3 proud thickets along the *J*
Mt 3:5 all the country around the *J*
3:6 baptized by him in the *J* River
3:13 from Galilee to the *J* to John
4:15 on the other side of the *J*
4:25 from the other side of the *J*
19:1 of Judea across the *J*
Mr 1:5 baptized by him in the *J* River
1:9 was baptized in the *J* by John
3:8 from across the *J* and around
10:1 Judea and across the *J*, and
Lu 3:3 all the country around the *J*
4:1 turned away from the *J*, and he
Joh 1:28 in Bethany across the *J*
3:26 was with you across the *J*
10:40 across the *J* to the place

Jorim
Lu 3:29 son of *J*, son of Matthat, son

Jorkeam
1Ch 2:44 Raham the father of *J*

Josech
Lu 3:26 son of Semein, son of *J*, son

Joseph
Ge 30:24 So she called his name *J*
30:25 Rachel had given birth to *J*
33:2 Rachel and *J* to the rear of
33:7 *J* came forward, and Rachel
35:24 sons by Rachel were *J* and
37:2 *J*, when seventeen years old
37:2 *J* brought a bad report about
37:3 Israel loved *J* more than all
37:5 *J* had a dream and told it to
37:13 Israel said to *J*: Your
37:17 *J* kept on after his brothers
37:23 as *J* came to his brothers
37:23 stripping *J* of his long
37:28 lifted up *J* out of the
37:28 sold *J* to the Ishmaelites
37:28 these brought *J* into Egypt
37:29 *J* was not in the waterpit
37:33 *J* is surely torn to pieces!
39:1 As for *J*, he was brought down
39:2 Jehovah proved to be with *J*
39:4 *J* kept finding favor in his
39:5 due to *J*, and Jehovah's
39:6 *J* grew to be beautiful in
39:7 raise her eyes toward *J* and
39:10 as she spoke to *J* day after
39:21 Jehovah continued with *J* and
39:23 Jehovah was with *J* and what
40:3 place where *J* was a prisoner
40:4 assigned *J* to be with them
40:6 When *J* came in to them in
40:8 So *J* said to them: Do not
40:9 to relate his dream to *J*
40:12 *J* said to him: This is its
40:16 he, in turn, said to *J*: I too
40:18 *J* answered and said: This is
40:22 just as *J* had given them the
40:23 did not remember *J* and went
41:14 to send and to call *J*, that

Jos 4:14 made *J* great in the eyes of
4:15 Then Jehovah said to *J*
4:17 So *J* commanded the priests
4:20 *J* set these up at Gilgal
5:2 said to *J:* Make for yourself
5:3 *J* made flint knives for
5:4 why *J* did the circumcising
5:7 These *J* circumcised, because
5:9 said to *J:* Today I have rolled
5:13 *J* happened to be by Jericho
5:13 *J* walked up to him and said
5:14 *J* fell on his face to the
5:15 said to *J:* Draw your sandals
5:15 At once *J* did so
6:2 to say to *J:* See, I have given
6:6 *J* the son of Nun called the
6:8 just as *J* said to the people
6:10 *J* had commanded the people
6:12 Then *J* got up early in the
6:16 *J* proceeded to say to the
6:22 *J* said: Go into the house of
6:25 Rahab . . . *J* preserved alive
6:25 whom *J* sent out to spy on
6:26 Then *J* had an oath pronounced
6:27 Jehovah proved to be with *J*
7:2 *J* sent men out from Jericho
7:3 they returned to *J* and said to
7:6 *J* ripped his mantles and fell
7:7 And *J* went on to say: Alas
7:10 In turn Jehovah said to *J*
7:16 *J* rose early in the morning
7:19 *J* said to Achan: My son
7:20 Achan answered *J* and said
7:22 At once *J* sent messengers
7:23 brought them to *J* and all
7:24 *J*, and all Israel with him
7:25 *J* said: Why have you brought
8:1 Jehovah said to *J:* Do not be
8:3 *J* and all the people of war
8:3 *J* proceeded to choose thirty
8:9 that *J* sent them out and they
8:9 *J* kept lodging on that night
8:10 Then *J* rose up early in the
8:13 *J* proceeded to go during
8:15 *J* and all Israel suffered a
8:16 they went chasing after *J*
8:18 Jehovah now said to *J*
8:18 *J* stretched out the javelin
8:21 *J* and all Israel saw that
8:23 to bring him near to *J*
8:26 *J* did not draw back his hand
8:27 had laid in command upon *J*
8:28 *J* burned Ai and reduced it to
8:29 *J* gave the command, and then
8:30 *J* proceeded to build an altar
8:35 that *J* did not read aloud in
9:2 make war against *J* and Israel
9:3 what *J* had done to Jericho
9:6 went to *J* at the camp at
9:8 they said to *J:* We are your
9:8 *J* said to them: Who are you
9:15 *J* went making peace with
9:22 *J* now called them and spoke
9:24 they answered *J* and said
9:27 *J* constituted them on that
10:1 *J* had captured Ai and then
10:4 made peace with *J* and the
10:6 to *J* at the camp at Gilgal
10:7 So *J* went on up from Gilgal
10:8 Jehovah said to *J:* Do not be
10:9 *J* proceeded to come against
10:12 *J* proceeded to speak to
10:15 *J* and all Israel with him
10:17 the report was made to *J*
10:18 *J* said: Roll great stones
10:20 *J* and the sons of Israel had
10:21 return to the camp, to *J*
10:22 *J* said: Open the mouth of
10:24 brought out these kings to *J*
10:24 *J* proceeded to call all the
10:25 *J* went on to say to them
10:26 *J* proceeded to strike them
10:27 *J* commanded, and they went
10:28 *J* captured Makkedah on that
10:29 *J* and all Israel with him
10:31 *J* and all Israel with him
10:33 *J* struck him and his people
10:34 *J* and all Israel with him
10:36 Then *J* and all Israel with
10:38 *J* and all Israel with him
10:40 *J* proceeded to strike all
10:41 *J* went striking them from
10:42 *J* captured all these kings
10:43 *J* and all Israel with him
Jos 11:6 said to *J:* Do not be afraid
11:7 *J* and all the people of war
11:9 *J* did to them just as
11:10 *J* turned about at that time
11:12 all their kings *J* captured
11:13 *J* did burn Hazor by itself
11:15 so Moses commanded *J*, and
11:15 and so *J* did
11:16 *J* proceeded to take all
11:18 that *J* waged war with all
11:21 *J* went and cut off the
11:21 their cities *J* devoted them
11:23 So *J* took all the land
11:23 and *J* then gave it as an
12:7 *J* and the sons of Israel
12:7 *J* gave it to the tribes of
13:1 *J* was old, being advanced in
14:1 and *J* the son of Nun
14:6 sons of Judah approached *J*
14:13 *J* blessed him and gave
15:13 the order of Jehovah to *J*
17:4 and *J* the son of Nun and the
17:14 to speak with *J*, saying
17:15 At this *J* said to them
17:17 *J* said this to the house of
18:3 *J* said to the sons of Israel
18:8 *J* proceeded to command those
18:9 *J* at the camp in Shiloh
18:10 *J* went drawing lots for
18:10 *J* there apportioned the land
19:49 gave an inheritance to *J*
19:51 and *J* the son of Nun and
20:1 Jehovah spoke to *J*, saying
21:1 and *J* the son of Nun and the
22:1 *J* proceeded to call the
22:6 *J* blessed them and sent them
22:7 *J* made a gift with their
22:7 *J* sent them away to their
23:1 *J* was old and advanced in
23:2 *J* proceeded to call all
24:1 *J* proceeded to assemble all
24:2 *J* went on to say to all the
24:19 *J* said to the people
24:21 the people said to *J*
24:22 *J* said to the people
24:24 the people said to *J*
24:25 *J* proceeded to conclude a
24:26 *J* wrote these words in the
24:27 *J* went on to say to all
24:28 *J* sent the people away
24:29 *J* the son of Nun, the
24:31 all the days of *J* and all
24:31 extended their days after *J*
Jg 1:1 after the death of *J* it came
2:6 *J* sent the people away, then
2:7 Jehovah all the days of *J* and
2:7 after *J* and who had seen all
2:8 *J* the son of Nun, the servant
2:21 nations that *J* left behind
1Sa 6:14 field of *J* the Beth-shemite
6:18 field of *J* the Beth-shemite
1Ki 16:34 *J* the son of Nun
2Ki 23:8 the entrance of the gate of *J*
Ne 8:17 the days of *J* the son of Nun
Hag 1:1 *J* the son of Jehozadak the
1:12 and *J* the son of Jehozadak
1:14 *J* the son of Jehozadak the
2:2 *J* the son of Jehozadak the
2:4 *J* the son of Jehozadak the
Zec 3:1 *J* the high priest standing
3:3 *J*, he happened to be clothed
3:6 to bear witness to *J*, saying
3:8 please, O *J* the high priest
3:9 stone that I have put before *J*
6:11 *J* the son of Jehozadak the
Ac 7:45 brought it in with *J* into
Heb 4:8 *J* had led them into a place

Joshua's
Ex 17:14 and propound it in *J* ears
Jg 2:23 did not give them into *J*

Josiah
1Ki 13:2 A son . . . whose name is *J*
2Ki 21:24 made *J* his son king in
21:26 *J* his son began to reign
22:1 Eight years old was *J* when
22:3 eighteenth year of King *J*
23:16 When *J* turned, he got to
23:19 to cause offense *J* removed
23:23 eighteenth year of King *J*
23:24 *J* cleared out, in order
23:28 the rest of the affairs of *J*
23:29 King *J* proceeded to go to
23:30 Jehoahaz the son of *J*
2Ki 23:34 Eliakim the son of *J* king
23:34 king in place of *J* his
1Ch 3:14 Amon his son, *J* his son
3:15 sons of *J* were the firstborn
2Ch 33:25 *J* his son king in place of
34:1 Eight years old was *J* when
34:33 *J* removed all the
35:1 *J* held in Jerusalem a
35:7 *J* now contributed to the
35:16 the commandment of King *J*
35:18 *J* and the priests and the
35:20 *J* had prepared the house
35:20 *J* went out to an encounter
35:22 *J* did not turn his face
35:23 got to shoot at King *J*
35:24 were mourning over *J*
35:25 began to chant over *J*
35:25 talking about *J* in their
35:26 rest of the affairs of *J* and
36:1 Jehoahaz the son of *J*
Jer 1:2 days of *J* the son of Amon
1:3 Jehoiakim the son of *J*
1:3 *J*, the king of Judah
3:6 in the days of *J* the king
22:11 Shallum the son of *J*
22:11 is reigning instead of *J*
22:18 Jehoiakim the son of *J*
25:1 Jehoiakim the son of *J*
25:3 the thirteenth year of *J*
26:1 Jehoiakim the son of *J*
27:1 Jehoiakim the son of *J*
35:1 Jehoiakim the son of *J*
36:1 Jehoiakim the son of *J*
36:2 since the days of *J*, clear
36:9 Jehoiakim the son of *J*, the
37:1 King Zedekiah the son of *J*
45:1 Jehoiakim the son of *J*, the
46:2 Jehoiakim the son of *J*, the
Zep 1:1 days of *J* the son of Amon the
Zec 6:10 *J* the son of Zephaniah
Mt 1:10 Amon became father to *J*
1:11 *J* became father to Jeconiah

Josiah's
2Ch 35:19 eighteenth year of *J* reign

Josiphiah
Ezr 8:10 Shelomith the son of *J*

Jotbah
2Ki 21:19 daughter of Haruz from *J*

Jotbathah
Nu 33:33 and went camping in *J*
33:34 pulled away from *J* and went
De 10:7 *J*, a land of torrent valleys

Jotham
Jg 9:5 *J* the youngest son of Jerubbaal
9:7 to *J* he at once went and stood
9:21 *J* took to flight and went
9:57 the malediction of *J* the son
2Ki 15:5 *J* the king's son was over
15:7 and *J* his son began to reign
15:30 *J* the son of Uzziah
15:32 *J* the son of Uzziah
15:36 the rest of the affairs of *J*
15:38 *J* lay down with his
16:1 *J* the king of Judah
1Ch 2:47 sons of Jahdai were . . . *J*
3:12 Azariah his son, *J* his son
5:17 days of *J* the king of Judah
2Ch 26:21 *J* his son was over the
26:23 *J* his son began to reign
27:1 *J* when he began to reign
27:6 *J* kept strengthening himself
27:7 affairs of *J* and all his
27:9 *J* lay down with his
Isa 1:1 days of Uzziah, *J*, Ahaz and
7:1 *J* the son of Uzziah, the
Ho 1:1 in the days of Uzziah, *J*, Ahaz
Mic 1:1 in the days of *J*, Ahaz
Mt 1:9 Uzziah became father to *J*
1:9 *J* became father to Ahaz

Journey
Ge 30:36 a distance of three days' *j*
31:23 a distance of seven days' *j*
33:14 continue the *j* at my leisure
42:25 provisions for the *j*
Ex 3:18 a *j* of three days into the
5:3 please, a *j* of three days into
8:27 *j* of three days into the
40:36 during all their stages of *j*
40:38 during all their stages of *j*
Nu 9:10 or off on a distant *j*, he too
9:13 off on a *j* and neglected to

Nu 10:33 for a *j* of three days, and
10:33 *j* of three days to search
11:31 about a day's *j* this way
11:31 about a day's *j* that way
33:8 three-day *j* in the wilderness
De 14:24 the *j* should be too long for
Jos 9:11 for the *j* and go to meet
9:13 the great length of the *j*
Jg 19:9 must get up early for your *j*
2Sa 11:10 from a *j* that you have come
1Ki 19:4 the wilderness a day's *j*
19:7 the *j* is too much for you
Ne 2:6 long will your *j* come to be
Pr 12:28 *j* in its pathway means no
Lu 11:6 has just come to me on a *j*
13:22 on his *j* to Jerusalem
15:18 rise and *j* to my father
Joh 4:6 Jesus, tired out from the *j*
Ac 1:12 being a sabbath day's *j* away
10:9 they were pursuing their *j*
19:21 would *j* to Jerusalem, saying
20:1 forth to *j* into Macedonia
21:15 we prepared for the *j* and
Ro 15:24 when I am on the *j* there, to
15:25 *j* to Jerusalem to minister
Jas 4:13 we will *j* to this city and

Journeyed
Lu 13:22 *j* through from city to city
Ac 12:17 and *j* to another place
17:1 They now *j* through Amphipolis

Journeying
Ge 11:2 in their *j* eastward they
Ps 139:3 My *j* and my lying
Lu 8:1 *j* from city to city and from
24:13 *j* to a village about seven
24:28 village where they were *j*
24:28 as if he was *j* on farther
Joh 11:11 *j* there to awaken him from
Ac 9:7 men that were *j* with him
20:22 am *j* to Jerusalem, although
22:6 I was *j* and drawing close to
26:12 as I was *j* to Damascus
26:13 and about those *j* with me

Journeys
2Co 11:26 in *j* often, in dangers

Joy
De 28:47 rejoicing and *j* of heart
1Ki 1:40 rejoicing with great *j*, so
1Ch 16:27 Strength and *j* are at his
29:9 rejoiced with great *j*
Ezr 3:12 the voice in shouting for *j*
6:16 this house of God with *j*
Ne 8:10 the *j* of Jehovah is your
12:43 to rejoice with great *j*
Job 6:10 leap for *j* at my labor pains
Isa 12:6 out shrilly and shout for *j*
42:11 of the crag cry out in *j*
Mt 5:12 Rejoice and leap for *j*, since
13:20 at once accepting it with *j*
13:44 for the *j* he has he goes and
25:21 into the *j* of your master
25:23 into the *j* of your master
28:8 with fear and great *j*, they
Mr 4:16 word, they accept it with *j*
Lu 1:14 you will have *j* and great
2:10 good news of a great *j* that
8:13 receive the word with *j*
10:17 the seventy returned with *j*
15:7 more *j* in heaven over one
15:10 *j* arises among the angels of
24:41 sheer *j* and were wondering
24:52 to Jerusalem with great *j*
Joh 3:29 a great deal of *j* on account
3:29 *j* of mine has been made full
15:11 that my *j* may be in you and
15:11 your *j* may be made full
16:20 grief will be turned into *j*
16:21 *j* that a man has been born
16:22 *j* no one will take from you
16:24 your *j* may be made full
17:13 they may have my *j* in
Ac 8:8 great deal of *j* in that city
12:14 out of *j* she did not open
13:52 filled with *j* and holy spirit
15:3 great *j* to all the brothers
Ro 14:17 peace and *j* with holy
15:13 fill you with all *j* and
15:32 to you with *j* by God's will
2Co 1:15 have a second occasion for *j*
1:24 are fellow workers for your *j*
2:3 *j* I have is that of all of you
7:4 I am overflowing with *j* in
7:13 due to the *j* of Titus
8:2 their abundance of *j* and their
Ga 5:22 fruitage of the spirit . . . *j*
Php 1:4 offer my supplication with *j*
1:25 *j* that belongs to your faith
2:2 make my *j* full in that you
2:29 in the Lord with all *j*; and
4:1 my *j* and crown, stand firm
Col 1:11 and be long-suffering with *j*
1Th 1:6 tribulation with *j* of holy
2:19 what is our hope or *j* or
2:20 are our glory and *j*
3:9 in return for all the *j* with
2Ti 1:4 that I may get filled with *j*
Phm 7 I got much *j* and comfort over
Heb 12:2 the *j* that was set before
13:17 they may do this with *j*
Jas 1:2 Consider it all *j*, my
4:9 and your *j* into dejection
1Pe 1:8 unspeakable and glorified *j*
1Jo 1:4 our *j* may be in full measure
2Jo 12 your *j* may be in full measure
Jude 24 of his glory with great *j*

Joyful
De 16:15 become nothing but *j*
2Sa 6:15 *j* shouting and sound of horn
1Ch 15:28 with *j* shouting and with
16:31 let the earth be *j*, And let
2Ch 7:10 *j* and feeling good at heart
15:14 voice and with *j* shouting
20:22 started off with the *j* cry
Es 5:9 *j* and merry of heart; but as
5:14 to the banquet *j*. So the thing
8:15 cried out shrilly and was *j*
Job 3:7 Let no *j* cry come in it
8:21 your lips with *j* shouting
20:5 *j* cry of wicked . . . is short
33:26 see his face with *j*
Ps 2:11 And be *j* with trembling
9:14 I may be *j* in your salvation
13:4 may not be *j* because I am
13:5 heart be *j* in your salvation
14:7 Let Jacob be *j*, let Israel
16:9 my glory is inclined to be *j*
21:1 how very *j* he wants to be
27:6 sacrifices of *j* shouting
30:5 the morning there is a *j* cry
31:7 I will be *j* and rejoice in
32:7 *j* cries at providing escape
32:11 Rejoice in Jehovah and be *j*
33:3 along with *j* shouting
35:9 my own soul be *j* in Jehovah
35:26 Who are *j* at my calamity
42:4 With the voice of a *j* cry and
47:1 with the sound of a *j* cry
47:5 has ascended with *j* shouting
48:11 towns of Judah be *j*
51:8 bones . . . may be *j*
53:6 Let Jacob be *j*, let Israel
63:5 with lips of *j* cries my
89:15 knowing the *j* shouting
89:16 In your name they are *j* all
96:11 and let the earth be *j*
97:1 Let the earth be *j*
97:8 towns of Judah began to be *j*
100:2 in before him with a *j* cry
105:43 ones even with a *j* cry
107:22 his works with a *j* cry
113:9 As a *j* mother of sons
118:15 voice of a *j* cry and
118:24 will be *j* and rejoice in it
126:2 And our tongue with a *j* cry
126:3 We have become *j*
126:5 Will reap even with a *j* cry
126:6 come in with a *j* cry
149:2 them be *j* in their King
Pr 2:14 *j* in the perverse things of
11:10 ones perish there is a *j* cry
15:13 *j* heart has a good effect on
17:5 *j* at another's disaster will
17:22 heart that is *j* does good as
23:24 will without fail be *j*
23:25 gave birth to you will be *j*
24:17 may your heart not be *j*
Ec 2:10 my heart was *j* because of all
Ca 1:4 let us be *j* and rejoice in you
Isa 9:3 are *j* when they divide up the
14:7 become cheerful with *j* cries
16:10 there is no *j* crying out
25:9 Let us be *j* and rejoice in
29:19 *j* in the Holy One of Israel
35:1 desert plain will be *j* and
35:2 it will really be *j* with
35:10 come to Zion with a *j* cry
41:16 will be *j* in Jehovah
44:23 with *j* outcry, you forest
48:20 with the sound of a *j* cry
49:13 and be *j*, you earth
51:11 to Zion with a *j* outcry
54:1 cheerful with a *j* outcry and
55:12 with a *j* outcry, and the
61:10 soul will be *j* in my God
65:18 exult, you people, and be *j*
65:19 be *j* in Jerusalem and exult
66:10 Jerusalem and be *j* with her
Ho 9:1 Do not act *j* like the peoples
10:5 priests who used to be *j*
Joe 2:21 Be *j* and rejoice; for Jehovah
2:23 Zion, be *j* and rejoice in
Hab 1:15 why he rejoices and is *j*
3:18 *j* in the God of my salvation
Zep 3:17 *j* over you with happy cries
Zec 9:9 Be very *j*, O daughter of Zion
10:7 heart will be *j* in Jehovah

Joyfully
1Ch 16:33 the forest break out *j*
Job 38:7 morning stars *j* cried out
Ps 5:11 they will cry out *j*
20:5 We will cry out *j* because
32:11 cry out *j*, all you who are
33:1 Cry out *j*, O you righteous
35:27 cry out *j* and rejoice
51:14 my tongue may *j* tell about
59:16 I shall *j* tell about your
63:7 I cry out *j*
65:8 you cause to cry out *j*
67:4 groups rejoice and cry out *j*
71:23 My lips will cry out *j* when
81:1 cry out *j*, you people, to
84:2 cry out *j* to the living God
89:12 your name they cry out *j*
90:14 cry out *j* and may rejoice
92:4 of your hands I cry out *j*
95:1 let us cry out *j* to Jehovah
96:12 the forest break out *j*
98:4 cry out *j* and make melody
98:8 the very mountains cry out *j*
132:9 own loyal ones cry out *j*
132:16 without fail cry out *j*
145:7 they will cry out *j*
149:5 cry out *j* on their beds
Pr 29:6 righteous cries out *j* and is
Isa 24:14 they will cry out *j*
26:19 cry out *j*, you residents
44:23 *J* cry out, you heavens
52:8 unison they keep crying out *j*
52:9 cry out *j* in unison, you
54:1 Cry out *j*, you barren woman
61:7 cry out *j* over their share
65:14 servants will cry out *j*
Jer 31:12 cry out *j* on the height of
51:48 cry out *j*, for out of the
Zep 3:14 *J* cry out, O daughter of
Heb 10:34 *j* took the plundering of

Joyfulness
Ps 45:15 brought with rejoicing and *j*
65:12 with *j* the very hills gird
Isa 16:10 *j* have been taken away
65:18 Jerusalem a cause for *j* and
Jer 48:33 *j* have been taken away from
Joe 1:16 rejoicing and *j*

Joyous
Heb 12:11 no discipline seems . . . *j*

Joyously
Job 39:13 female ostrich flapped *j*

Joyousness
Isa 35:2 with *j* and with glad crying

Jozabad
1Ch 12:4 and *J* the Gederathite
12:20 *J* and Jediael and Michael
12:20 Michael and *J* and Elihu and
2Ch 31:13 and *J* . . . commissioners at
35:9 *J*, the chiefs of the Levites
Ezr 8:33 *J* the son of Jeshua and
10:22 the sons of Pashhur . . . *J*
10:23 of the Levites, *J* and
Ne 8:7 *J*, Hanan, Pelaiah, even the
11:16 and *J*, of the heads of the

Jozacar
2Ki 12:21 *J* the son of Shimeath and

Jozadak
Ne 12:26 Jeshua the son of *J*

Jubal
Ge 4:21 name of his brother was *J*
Jubilate
Ps 68:4 his name; and *j* before him
Jubilee
Le 25:10 *J* for you, and you must
25:11 *J* is what that fiftieth year
25:12 For it is a *J*. It should
25:13 *J* you should return each one
25:15 years after the *J* you should
25:28 until the *J* year
25:28 go out in the *J*, and he must
25:30 it should not go out in the *J*
25:31 and in the *J* it should go out
25:33 must also go out in the *J*
25:40 serve with you till the *J*
25:50 till the *J* year, and the
25:52 years until the *J* year, he
25:54 go out in the year of *J*
27:17 from the year of *J* on, it
27:18 after the *J* . . . he sanctifies
27:18 until the next year of *J*, and
27:21 it goes out in the *J* must
27:23 up till the year of *J*, and
27:24 year of *J* the field will
Nu 36:4 if the *J* takes place for the
Jucal
Jer 38:1 *J* the son of Shelemiah and
Judah
Ge 29:35 therefore called his name *J*
35:23 sons by Leah were . . . *J*
37:26 *J* said to his brothers: What
38:1 when *J* went down from his
38:2 *J* got to see a daughter of
38:6 *J* took a wife for Er his
38:8 *J* said to Onan: Have relations
38:11 So *J* said to Tamar his
38:12 *J* kept the period of
38:15 When *J* caught sight of her
38:20 *J* proceeded to send the kid
38:22 returned to *J* and said: I
38:23 *J* said: Let her take them
38:24 it was told to *J*: Tamar your
38:24 *J* said: Bring her out and let
38:26 *J* examined them and said
43:3 Then *J* said to him: The man
43:8 *J* said to Israel his father
44:14 *J* and his brothers went on
44:16 *J* exclaimed: What can we
44:18 *J* now came near to him and
46:12 the sons of *J* were Er and
46:28 he sent *J* in advance of him
49:8 *J*, your brothers will laud
49:9 A lion cub *J* is. From the
49:10 will not turn aside from *J*
Ex 1:2 Reuben, Simeon, Levi and *J*
31:2 son of Hur of the tribe of *J*
35:30 Hur of the tribe of *J*
38:22 Hur of the tribe of *J* did all
Nu 1:7 of *J*, Nahshon the son of
1:26 sons of *J*, their births
1:27 registered . . . tribe of *J*
2:3 camp of *J* in their armies
2:3 for the sons of *J* is Nahshon
2:9 of the camp of *J* are one
7:12 Amminadab of the tribe of *J*
10:14 camp of the sons of *J* pulled
13:6 of the tribe of *J*, Caleb the
26:19 sons of *J* were Er and Onan
26:20 the sons of *J* came to be
26:22 These were the families of *J*
34:19 Of the tribe of *J*, Caleb the
De 27:12 *J* and Issachar and Joseph
33:7 O Jehovah, the voice of *J*
34:2 the land of *J* as far as the
Jos 7:1 Zerah, of the tribe of *J*, took
7:16 tribe of *J* got to be picked
7:17 the families of *J* come near
7:18 tribe of *J*, got to be picked
11:21 mountainous region of *J*
14:6 sons of *J* approached Joshua
15:1 the tribe of the sons of *J*
15:12 sons of *J* by their families
15:13 the midst of the sons of *J*
15:20 the tribe of the sons of *J*
15:21 the tribe of the sons of *J*
15:63 sons of *J* were not able to
15:63 the sons of *J* in Jerusalem
18:5 *J* will keep standing on his
18:11 the sons of *J* and the sons
18:14 a city of the sons of *J*
19:1 inheritance of the sons of *J*
Jos 19:9 allotment of the sons of *J*
19:9 the share of the sons of *J*
19:34 to *J* at the Jordan toward
20:7 the mountainous region of *J*
21:4 out of the tribe of *J* and
21:9 tribe of the sons of *J* and
21:11 the mountainous region of *J*
Jg 1:2 Jehovah said: *J* will go up
1:3 *J* said to Simeon his brother
1:4 *J* went on up and Jehovah gave
1:8 the sons of *J* carried on war
1:9 sons of *J* went down to fight
1:10 So *J* marched against the
1:16 with the sons of *J* to the
1:16 wilderness of *J*, which is to
1:17 *J* marched on with Simeon his
1:18 *J* captured Gaza and its
1:19 Jehovah continued with *J*, so
10:9 against *J* and Benjamin and
15:9 and camped in *J* and went
15:10 men of *J* said: Why have you
15:11 men of *J* went down to the
17:7 young man of Bethlehem in *J*
17:7 man . . . of the family of *J*
17:8 Bethlehem in *J* to reside for
17:9 a Levite from Bethlehem in *J*
18:12 at Kiriath-jearim in *J*
19:1 from Bethlehem in *J*
19:2 her father at Bethlehem in *J*
19:18 from Bethlehem in *J* to the
19:18 but I went to Bethlehem in *J*
20:18 Jehovah said: *J* in the lead
Ru 1:1 from Bethlehem in *J* to reside
1:2 from Bethlehem in *J*
1:7 to return to the land of *J*
4:12 Perez, whom Tamar bore to *J*
1Sa 11:8 the men of *J* thirty thousand
15:4 and ten thousand men of *J*
17:1 at Socoh, which belongs to *J*
17:12 from Bethlehem of *J* whose
17:52 men of Israel and of *J* rose
18:16 Israel and *J* were lovers of
22:5 yourself into the land of *J*
23:3 are afraid while here in *J*
23:23 all the thousands of *J*
27:6 belong to the kings of *J*
27:10 Upon the south of *J* and
30:14 that which belongs to *J* and
30:16 and the land of *J*
30:26 spoil to the older men of *J*
2Sa 1:18 sons of *J* should be taught
2:1 one of the cities of *J*
2:4 men of *J* came and anointed
2:4 as king over the house of *J*
2:7 I whom the house of *J* have
2:10 house of *J* proved themselves
2:11 over the house of *J* came to
3:8 dog's head that belongs to *J*
3:10 *J* from Dan to Beer-sheba
5:5 king over *J* for seven years
5:5 over all Israel and *J*
11:11 Israel and *J* are dwelling
12:8 house of Israel and of *J*
19:11 Speak to the older men of *J*
19:14 heart of all the men of *J*
19:15 As for *J*, they came to
19:16 men of *J* to meet King David
19:40 also all the people of *J*
19:41 the men of *J* steal you that
19:42 all the men of *J* answered
19:43 answered the men of *J* and
19:43 the word of the men of *J*
20:2 the men of *J*, they stuck to
20:4 Call the men of *J* together
20:5 Amasa went to call *J*
21:2 for the sons of Israel and *J*
24:1 take a count of Israel and *J*
24:7 the Negeb of *J* at Beer-sheba
24:9 men of *J* were five hundred
1Ki 1:9 men of *J* the king's servants
1:35 leader over Israel and over *J*
2:32 the chief of the army of *J*
4:20 *J* and Israel were many, like
4:25 *J* and Israel continued to
12:17 dwelling in the cities of *J*
12:20 except the tribe of *J* by
12:21 all the house of *J* and the
12:23 Solomon the king of *J* and
12:23 and to all the house of *J*
12:27 Rehoboam the king of *J*
12:27 Rehoboam the king of *J*
12:32 the festival that was in *J*
13:1 out of *J* by the word of
13:12 had come out of *J* had gone
1Ki 13:14 who has come out of *J*
13:21 that had come out of *J*
14:21 he had become king in *J*
14:22 *J* went on doing what was
14:29 the times of the kings of *J*
15:1 Abijam became king over *J*
15:7 the days of the kings of *J*
15:9 Asa reigned as king of *J*
15:17 came up against *J* and began
15:17 to Asa the king of *J*
15:22 Asa . . . summoned all *J*
15:23 the days of the kings of *J*
15:25 Asa the king of *J*
15:28 Asa the king of *J*
15:33 Asa the king of *J*
16:8 Asa the king of *J*
16:10 Asa the king of *J*
16:15 Asa the king of *J*
16:23 Asa the king of *J*
16:29 Asa the king of *J*
19:3 Beer-sheba . . . belongs to *J*
22:2 Jehoshaphat the king of *J*
22:10 Jehoshaphat the king of *J*
22:29 Jehoshaphat the king of *J*
22:41 Jehoshaphat . . . king over *J*
22:45 the days of the kings of *J*
22:51 Jehoshaphat the king of *J*
2Ki 1:17 Jehoshaphat the king of *J*
3:1 Jehoshaphat the king of *J*
3:7 Jehoshaphat the king of *J*
3:9 and the king of *J* and the king
3:14 Jehoshaphat the king of *J*
8:16 Jehoshaphat was king of *J*
8:16 Jehoshaphat the king of *J*
8:19 not want to bring *J* to ruin
8:20 from under the hand of *J*
8:22 from under the hand of *J*
8:23 of the days of the kings of *J*
8:25 Jehoram the king of *J*
8:29 Jehoram the king of *J*
9:16 Ahaziah the king of *J*
9:21 and Ahaziah the king of *J*
9:27 And Ahaziah the king of *J*
9:29 Ahaziah . . . king over *J*
10:13 Ahaziah the king of *J*
12:18 Jehoash the king of *J* took
12:18 kings of *J*, had sanctified
12:19 the days of the kings of *J*
13:1 Ahaziah the king of *J*
13:10 Jehoash the king of *J*
13:12 Amaziah the king of *J*
14:1 Jehoash the king of *J*
14:9 Amaziah the king of *J*
14:10 to fall, you and *J* with you
14:11 and Amaziah the king of *J*
14:11 which belongs to *J*
14:12 *J* came to be defeated
14:13 was Amaziah the king of *J*
14:15 Amaziah the king of *J*
14:17 Jehoash the king of *J*
14:18 the days of the kings of *J*
14:21 people of *J* took Azariah
14:22 and got to restore it to *J*
14:23 Jehoash the king of *J*
14:28 Damascus and Hamath to *J* in
15:1 Amaziah the king of *J*
15:6 the days of the kings of *J*
15:8 Azariah the king of *J*
15:13 Uzziah the king of *J*
15:17 Azariah the king of *J*
15:23 Azariah the king of *J*
15:27 Azariah the king of *J*
15:32 Uzziah the king of *J*
15:36 the days of the kings of *J*
15:37 started to send against *J*
16:1 Jotham the king of *J*
16:19 the days of the kings of *J*
17:1 Ahaz the king of *J*
17:13 warning Israel and *J* by
17:18 remain but the tribe of *J*
17:19 *J* itself did not keep the
18:1 Ahaz the king of *J*
18:5 among all the kings of *J*
18:13 the fortified cities of *J*
18:14 Hezekiah the king of *J*
18:14 Hezekiah the king of *J*
18:16 Hezekiah the king of *J* had
18:22 he says to *J* and Jerusalem
19:10 Hezekiah the king of *J*
19:30 escape of the house of *J*
20:20 the days of the kings of *J*
21:11 Manasseh the king of *J*
21:11 *J* sin with his dungy idols
21:12 upon Jerusalem and *J*

2Ki 21:16 caused *J* to sin by doing
21:17 the days of the kings of *J*
21:25 the days of the kings of *J*
22:13 in behalf of all *J*
22:16 that the king of *J* has read
22:18 king of *J* who is sending
23:1 all the older men of *J* and
23:2 all the men of *J* and all
23:5 whom the kings of *J* had put
23:5 places in the cities of *J*
23:8 priests from the cities of *J*
23:11 horses that the kings of *J*
23:12 the kings of *J* had made
23:17 that came from *J* and
23:22 of Israel and the kings of *J*
23:24 appeared in the land of *J*
23:26 his anger burned against *J*
23:27 *J*, too, I shall remove from
23:28 the days of the kings of *J*
24:2 kept sending them against *J*
24:3 it took place against *J*
24:5 the days of the kings of *J*
24:12 Jehoiachin the king of *J*
24:20 place in Jerusalem and in *J*
25:21 *J* went into exile from off
25:22 left behind in the land of *J*
25:27 Jehoiachin the king of *J*
25:27 Jehoiachin the king of *J*
1Ch 2:1 sons of Israel . . . *J*
2:3 sons of *J* were Er and Onan
2:3 Er the firstborn of *J* came
2:4 All the sons of *J* were five
2:10 chieftain of the sons of *J*
4:1 sons of *J* were Perez, Hezron
4:21 Shelah the son of *J*
4:27 as many as the sons of *J*
4:41 Hezekiah the king of *J*
5:2 *J* himself proved to be
5:17 days of Jotham the king of *J*
6:15 *J* and Jerusalem into exile
6:55 Hebron in the land of *J*
6:65 the tribe of the sons of *J*
9:1 *J* itself was taken into exile
9:3 dwelt some of the sons of *J*
9:4 the sons of Perez the son of *J*
12:16 the sons of Benjamin and *J*
12:24 the sons of *J* carrying the
13:6 which belongs to *J*, to bring
21:5 *J* four hundred and seventy
27:18 of *J*, Elihu, one of David's
28:4 *J* that he chose as leader
28:4 and in the house of *J* my
2Ch 2:7 in *J* and in Jerusalem, whom
9:11 seen before in the land of *J*
10:17 dwelling in the cities of *J*
11:1 congregated the house of *J*
11:3 king of *J* and to all Israel
11:3 Israel in *J* and Benjamin
11:5 build fortified cities in *J*
11:10 cities, which were in *J*
11:12 *J* and Benjamin continued
11:14 came to *J* and Jerusalem
11:17 the kingship of *J* and
11:23 lands of *J* and of Benjamin
12:4 cities that belonged to *J*
12:5 and the princes of *J* who
12:12 to be good things in *J*
13:1 Abijah began to reign over *J*
13:13 front of *J* and the ambush
13:14 *J* turned around, why, there
13:15 men of *J* broke out shouting
13:15 men of *J* shouted a war cry
13:15 Israel before Abijah and *J*
13:16 to flight from before *J*
13:18 *J* proved superior because
14:4 *J* to search for Jehovah the
14:5 from all the cities of *J*
14:6 build fortified cities in *J*
14:7 said to *J*: Let us build these
14:8 hundred thousand out of *J*
14:12 before Asa and before *J*
15:2 Hear me, O Asa and all *J* and
15:8 from all the land of *J*
15:9 collect together all *J* and
15:15 *J* gave way to rejoicing
16:1 of Israel came up against *J*
16:1 come in to Asa the king of *J*
16:6 Asa the king, he took all *J*
16:7 Asa the king of *J* and then
16:11 Book of the Kings of *J* and
17:2 the fortified cities of *J*
17:2 garrisons in the land of *J*
17:5 *J* continued to give presents
17:6 and the sacred poles from *J*
2Ch 17:7 teach in the cities of *J*
17:9 they began teaching in *J*, and
17:9 through all the cities of *J*
17:10 that were all around *J*
17:12 and storage cities in *J*
17:13 his in the cities of *J*
17:14 Of *J* the chiefs of thousands
17:19 cities throughout all *J*
18:3 to Jehoshaphat the king of *J*
18:9 Jehoshaphat the king of *J*
18:28 Jehoshaphat the king of *J*
19:1 Jehoshaphat the king of *J*
19:5 fortified cities of *J*, city
19:11 leader of the house of *J* for
20:3 proclaimed a fast for all *J*
20:4 *J* were collected together to
20:4 all the cities of *J* they
20:5 congregation of *J* and of
20:13 *J* were standing before
20:15 Pay attention, all *J* and
20:17 *J* and Jerusalem, do not be
20:18 *J* and the inhabitants of
20:20 Hear me, O *J* and you
20:22 who were coming into *J*
20:24 *J*, it came to the
20:27 *J* and Jerusalem returned
20:31 went on reigning over *J*
20:35 Jehoshaphat the king of *J*
21:3 with fortified cities in *J*
21:8 from under the hand of *J* and
21:10 under the hand of *J* down
21:11 on the mountains of *J*
21:11 that he might drive *J* away
21:12 ways of Asa the king of *J*
21:13 cause *J* and the inhabitants
21:17 into *J* and forced it open
22:1 to reign as king of *J*
22:6 Jehoram the king of *J*, he
22:8 find the princes of *J* and
22:10 offspring of the house of *J*
23:2 throughout *J* and collected
23:2 from all the cities of *J* and
23:8 Levites and all *J* proceeded
24:5 Go out to the cities of *J*
24:6 for bringing in from *J* and
24:9 issued a call throughout *J*
24:17 princes of *J* came in and
24:18 indignation against *J* and
24:23 to invade *J* and Jerusalem
25:5 collect *J* together and to
25:5 chiefs of hundreds for all *J*
25:10 got very hot against *J*, so
25:12 sons of *J* captured alive
25:13 raids upon the cities of *J*
25:17 Amaziah the king of *J* took
25:18 to Amaziah the king of *J*
25:19 to fall, you and *J* with you
25:21 and Amaziah the king of *J*
25:21 which belongs to *J*
25:22 *J* came to be defeated
25:23 Amaziah the king of *J*, the
25:25 king of *J* continued to live
25:26 the Kings of *J* and Israel
25:28 forefathers in the city of *J*
26:1 people of *J* took Uzziah
26:2 restored it to *J* after the
27:4 the mountainous region of *J*
27:7 Kings of Israel and of *J*
28:6 killed in *J* a hundred and
28:9 against *J* that he gave them
28:10 *J* and of Jerusalem you are
28:17 striking down *J* and
28:18 and the Negeb of *J* and got
28:19 Jehovah humbled *J* on
28:19 let unrestraint grow in *J*
28:25 even the cities of *J*, he
28:26 Book of the Kings of *J* and
29:8 against *J* and Jerusalem, so
29:21 the sanctuary and for *J*
30:1 send to all Israel and *J*
30:6 throughout all Israel and *J*
30:12 God proved to be also in *J*
30:24 For Hezekiah the king of *J*
30:25 congregation of *J* and the
30:25 those dwelling in *J*
31:1 went out to the cities of *J*
31:1 altars out of all *J* and
31:6 of *J* that were dwelling in
31:6 dwelling in the cities of *J*
31:20 do like this in all *J*, and
32:1 invade *J* and camp against
32:8 of Hezekiah the king of *J*
32:9 to Hezekiah the king of *J* and
32:12 said to *J* and to Jerusalem
2Ch 32:23 Hezekiah the king of *J*, and
32:25 and against *J* and Jerusalem
32:32 Book of the Kings of *J* and
32:33 honor was what all *J* and
33:9 Manasseh kept seducing *J* and
33:14 fortified cities in *J*
33:16 say to *J* to serve Jehovah
34:3 cleanse *J* and Jerusalem from
34:5 he cleansed *J* and Jerusalem
34:9 from all *J* and Benjamin and
34:11 houses that the kings of *J*
34:21 is left in Israel and in *J*
34:24 read before the king of *J*
34:26 king of *J*, who is sending
34:29 all the older men of *J* and
34:30 *J* and the inhabitants of
35:18 all *J* and Israel that
35:21 to do with you, O king of *J*
35:24 all *J* and Jerusalem were
35:27 the Kings of Israel and *J*
36:4 Eliakim . . . king over *J* and
36:8 the Kings of Israel and *J*
36:10 Zedekiah . . . king over *J* and
36:23 Jerusalem, which is in *J*
Ezr 1:2 in Jerusalem, which is in *J*
1:3 to Jerusalem, which is in *J*
1:5 fathers of *J* and of Benjamin
1:8 Sheshbazzar the chieftain of *J*
2:1 returned to Jerusalem and *J*
3:9 the sons of *J*, stood up as one
4:1 adversaries of *J* and Benjamin
4:4 the hands of the people of *J*
4:6 the inhabitants of *J* and
5:1 Jews who were in *J* and in
5:8 jurisdictional district of *J*
7:14 investigate concerning *J* and
9:9 a stone wall in *J* and in
10:7 throughout *J* and Jerusalem
10:9 the men of *J* and Benjamin
10:23 of the Levites . . . *J* and
Ne 1:2 he and other men from *J*
2:5 *J*, to the city of the burial
2:7 let me pass until I come to *J*
4:10 *J* began to say: The power of
4:16 behind the whole house of *J*
5:14 governor in the land of *J*
6:7 saying, There is a king in *J!*
6:17 the nobles of *J* were making
6:18 many in *J* were sworn to him
7:6 returned to Jerusalem and to *J*
11:3 in the cities of *J* there
11:4 dwelt some of the sons of *J*
11:4 sons of *J* there were Athaiah
11:9 *J* the son of Hassenuah over
11:20 in all the other cities of *J*
11:24 Zerah the son of *J* was at
11:25 sons of *J* that dwelt in
11:36 divisions of *J* for Benjamin
12:8 Sherebiah, *J*, Mattaniah
12:31 princes of *J* upon the wall
12:32 half of the princes of *J*
12:34 *J* and Benjamin and Shemaiah
12:36 Nethanel and *J*, Hanani
12:44 the rejoicing of *J* was
13:12 *J*, for their part, brought
13:15 saw in *J* people treading
13:16 sons of *J* and in Jerusalem
13:17 fault with the nobles of *J*
Es 2:6 with Jeconiah the king of *J*
Ps 48:11 towns of *J* be joyful
60:7 *J* is my commander's staff
63:*super* be in the wilderness of *J*
68:27 The princes of *J* with their
69:35 will build the cities of *J*
76:1 God is known in *J*; In Israel
78:68 he chose the tribe of *J*
97:8 towns of *J* began to be joyful
108:8 *J* is my commander's staff
114:2 *J* became his holy place
Pr 25:1 men of Hezekiah the king of *J*
Isa 1:1 that he visioned concerning *J*
1:1 Ahaz and Hezekiah, kings of *J*
2:1 visioned concerning *J* and
3:1 from *J* support and stay
3:8 and *J* itself has fallen
5:3 men of *J*, please judge
5:7 men of *J* are the plantation
7:1 Uzziah, the king of *J*, that
7:6 against *J* and tear it apart
7:17 away from alongside *J*
8:8 and move on through *J*
9:21 they will be against *J*
11:12 scattered ones of *J* he
11:13 hostility to *J* will be cut

Isa 11:13 will not be jealous of *J*
11:13 *J* show hostility toward
19:17 ground of *J* must become to
22:8 will remove the screen of *J*
22:21 and to the house of *J*
26:1 sung in the land of *J*
36:1 the fortified cities of *J*
36:7 he says to *J* and Jerusalem
37:10 to Hezekiah the king of *J*
37:31 escape of the house of *J*
38:9 Hezekiah the king of *J*
40:9 Say to the cities of *J*
44:26 and of the cities of *J*
48:1 from the very waters of *J*
65:9 out of *J* the hereditary
Jer 1:2 Amon, the king of *J*
1:3 Josiah, the king of *J*
1:3 Josiah, the king of *J*
1:15 against all the cities of *J*
1:18 toward the kings of *J*
2:28 your gods have become, O *J*
3:7 and *J* kept looking at her
3:8 *J* her sister did not become
3:10 *J* did not return to me with
3:11 than treacherously dealing *J*
3:18 the house of *J* alongside the
4:3 said to the men of *J* and to
4:4 men of *J* and inhabitants
4:5 Tell it in *J*, you men, and
4:16 against the very cities of *J*
5:11 house of *J* have positively
5:20 and publish it in *J*, saying
7:2 you of *J*, who are entering
7:17 are doing in the cities of *J*
7:30 the sons of *J* have done what
7:34 cease from the cities of *J*
8:1 the bones of the kings of *J*
9:11 *J* I shall make a desolate
9:26 upon Egypt and upon *J* and
10:22 *J* a desolate waste, the
11:2 speak them to the men of *J*
11:6 words in the cities of *J*
11:9 found among the men of *J*
11:10 and the house of *J* have
11:12 And the cities of *J* and the
11:13 many as your cities, O *J*
11:17 Israel and the house of *J*
12:14 house of *J* I shall uproot
13:9 bring to ruin the pride of *J*
13:11 house of *J* to cling even to
13:19 *J* in its entirety has been
14:2 *J* has gone mourning, and
14:19 you absolutely rejected *J*
15:4 Hezekiah, the king of *J*
17:1 The sin of *J* is written down
17:19 the kings of *J* enter in
17:20 you kings of *J* and all
17:20 *J* and all you inhabitants
17:25 the men of *J* and the
17:26 come from the cities of *J*
18:11 to the men of *J* and to the
19:3 you kings of *J* and you
19:4 the kings of *J*; and they have
19:7 make void the counsel of *J*
19:13 the houses of the kings of *J*
20:4 all *J* I shall give into the
20:5 treasures of the kings of *J*
21:7 give Zedekiah the king of *J*
21:11 household of the king of *J*
22:1 the house of the king of *J*
22:2 O king of *J* who are sitting
22:6 the house of the king of *J*
22:11 Josiah, the king of *J*
22:18 Josiah, the king of *J*
22:24 Jehoiakim, the king of *J*
22:30 and ruling anymore in *J*
23:6 In his days *J* will be saved
24:1 Jehoiakim, the king of *J*
24:1 the princes of *J* and the
24:5 shall regard the exiles of *J*
24:8 give Zedekiah the king of *J*
25:1 all the people of *J*
25:1 Josiah, the king of *J*
25:2 all the people of *J*
25:3 son of Amon, the king of *J*
25:18 the cities of *J* and her
26:1 Josiah, the king of *J*
26:2 all the cities of *J* that are
26:10 the princes of *J* got to hear
26:18 Hezekiah the king of *J*
26:18 say to all the people of *J*
26:19 Hezekiah the king of *J*
26:19 all those of *J* by any means
27:1 Josiah, the king of *J*

Jer 27:3 Zedekiah the king of *J*
27:12 Zedekiah the king of *J*
27:18 the house of the king of *J*
27:20 Jehoiakim, the king of *J*
27:20 nobles of *J* and Jerusalem
27:21 the house of the king of *J*
28:1 Zedekiah the king of *J*
28:4 Jehoiakim, the king of *J*
28:4 all the exiles of *J* who have
29:2 princes of *J* and Jerusalem
29:3 Zedekiah the king of *J* sent
29:22 entire body of exiles of *J*
30:3 my people, Israel and *J*
30:4 has spoken to Israel and to *J*
31:23 this word in the land of *J*
31:24 *J* and all his cities will
31:27 house of *J* with the seed of
31:31 house of *J* a new covenant
32:1 of Zedekiah the king of *J*
32:2 house of the king of *J*
32:3 Zedekiah the king of *J* had
32:4 king of *J*, will not escape
32:30 *J* have proved to be mere
32:32 *J* that they have done to
32:32 prophets, and the men of *J*
32:35 purpose of making *J* sin
32:44 and in the cities of *J*
33:4 houses of the kings of *J*
33:7 bring back the captives of *J*
33:10 in the cities of *J* and in
33:13 in the cities of *J* flocks
33:14 concerning the house of *J*
33:16 *J* will be saved and
34:2 Zedekiah the king of *J*, yes
34:4 Zedekiah king of *J*, This is
34:6 to Zedekiah the king of *J*
34:7 against all the cities of *J*
34:7 over among the cities of *J*
34:19 the princes of *J* and the
34:21 Zedekiah the king of *J* and
34:22 cities of *J* I shall make
35:1 the king of *J*, saying
35:13 say to the men of *J* and
35:17 I am bringing upon *J* and
36:1 king of *J*, that this word
36:2 against Israel and against *J*
36:3 house of *J* will listen to
36:6 ears of all *J* who are coming
36:9 king of *J*, in the ninth
36:9 in from the cities of *J*
36:28 king of *J* burned up
36:29 Jehoiakim the king of *J* you
36:30 Jehoiakim the king of *J*
36:31 and upon the men of *J* all
36:32 Jehoiakim the king of *J* had
37:1 made king in the land of *J*
37:7 say to the king of *J*, the
38:22 house of the king of *J* are
39:1 Zedekiah the king of *J*, in
39:4 Zedekiah the king of *J* and
39:6 nobles of *J* the king of
39:10 remain in the land of *J*
40:1 exiles of Jerusalem and of *J*
40:5 over the cities of *J*, and
40:11 given a remnant to *J* and
40:12 into the land of *J* to
40:15 *J* who are being collected
40:15 and the remnant of *J* perish
42:15 Jehovah, O remnant of *J*
42:19 against you, O remnant of *J*
43:4 dwelling in the land of *J*
43:5 took all the remnant of *J*
43:5 for a while in the land of *J*
44:2 upon all the cities of *J*
44:6 burned in the cities of *J*
44:7 out of the midst of *J*, so
44:9 bad deeds of the kings of *J*
44:9 in the land of *J* and in
44:11 and for cutting off all *J*
44:12 remnant of *J* who set their
44:14 for the remnant of *J* who
44:14 return to the land of *J* to
44:17 did in the cities of *J* and
44:21 in the cities of *J* and in
44:24 *J* who are in the land of
44:26 *J* who are dwelling in the
44:26 mouth of any man of *J*
44:27 men of *J* that are in the
44:28 to the land of *J*, few in
44:28 those of the remnant of *J*
44:30 Zedekiah the king of *J* into
45:1 the king of *J*, saying
46:2 of Josiah, the king of *J*
49:34 Zedekiah the king of *J*

Jer 50:4 they and the sons of *J*
50:20 and the sins of *J*, and they
50:33 of *J* are being oppressed
51:5 Israel and *J* are not widowed
51:59 Zedekiah the king of *J* to
52:3 occurred in Jerusalem and *J*
52:10 princes of *J* he slaughtered
52:27 *J* went into exile from off
52:31 Jehoiachin the king of *J*
52:31 Jehoiachin the king of *J*
La 1:3 *J* has gone into exile because
1:15 to the virgin daughter of *J*
2:2 places of the daughter of *J*
2:5 in the daughter of *J* he makes
5:11 the virgins in the cities of *J*
Eze 4:6 error of the house of *J* forty
8:1 older men of *J* were sitting
8:17 light thing to the house of *J*
9:9 of the house of Israel and *J*
21:20 one against *J*, against
25:3 and against the house of *J*
25:8 The house of *J* is like all
25:12 upon the house of *J*
27:17 *J* and the land of Israel
37:16 For *J* and for the sons of
37:19 the stick of *J*, and I shall
48:7 the western border, *J* one
48:8 on the boundary of *J*, from
48:22 Between the boundary of *J*
48:31 the gate of *J*, one
Da 1:1 Jehoiakim the king of *J*
1:2 Jehoiakim the king of *J* and
1:6 sons of *J*, Daniel, Hananiah
2:25 man of the exiles of *J* who
5:13 that is of the exiles of *J*
5:13 my father brought out of *J*
6:13 who is of the exiles of *J*
9:7 to the men of *J* and to the
Ho 1:1 Ahaz and Hezekiah, kings of *J*
1:7 house of *J* I shall show mercy
1:11 And the sons of *J* and the
4:15 let not *J* become guilty
5:5 *J* has also stumbled with them
5:10 The princes of *J* have become
5:12 rottenness to the house of *J*
5:13 his sickness, and *J* his ulcer
5:14 young lion to the house of *J*
6:4 What shall I do to you, O *J*
6:11 O *J*, a harvest has been fixed
8:14 *J*, for his part, multiplied
10:11 *J* plows; Jacob harrows for
11:12 *J* is yet roaming with God
12:2 has a legal case with *J*
Joe 3:1 the captive ones of *J* and
3:6 the sons of *J* and the sons of
3:8 into the hand of the sons of *J*
3:18 the very stream beds of *J*
3:19 violence to the sons of *J*
3:20 as for *J*, to time indefinite
Am 1:1 days of Uzziah the king of *J*
2:4 account of three revolts of *J*
2:5 And I will send a fire into *J*
7:12 your way off to the land of *J*
Ob 12 not to rejoice at the sons of *J*
Mic 1:1 Ahaz, Hezekiah, kings of *J*
1:5 what are the high places of *J*?
1:9 for it has come as far as *J*
5:2 among the thousands of *J*
Na 1:15 O *J*, celebrate your festivals
Zep 1:1 son of Amon the king of *J*
1:4 stretch out my hand against *J*
2:7 ones of the house of *J*
Hag 1:1 Zerubbabel . . . the governor of *J*
1:14 Zerubbabel . . . the governor of *J*
2:2 Zerubbabel . . . governor of *J*
2:21 Zerubbabel the governor of *J*
Zec 1:12 and to the cities of *J*, whom
1:19 the horns that dispersed *J*
1:21 the horns that dispersed *J* to
1:21 a horn against the land of *J*
2:12 take possession of *J* as his
8:13 O house of *J* and house of
8:15 and with the house of *J*
8:19 house of *J* an exultation
9:7 become like a sheik in *J*
9:13 I will tread as my bow *J*
10:3 his drove, the house of *J*
10:6 make the house of *J* superior
11:14 between *J* and Israel
12:2 against *J* he will come to be
12:4 upon the house of *J* I shall
12:5 sheiks of *J* will have to say
12:6 shall make the sheiks of *J*
12:7 save the tents of *J* first

Zec 12:7 not become too great over *J*
14:5 days of Uzziah the king of *J*
14:14 *J* itself also will be
14:21 in Jerusalem and in *J* must
Mal 2:11 *J* has dealt treacherously
2:11 *J* has profaned the holiness
3:4 the gift offering of *J* and
Mt 1:2 Jacob became father to *J* and
1:3 *J* became father to Perez and
2:6 O Bethlehem of the land of *J*
2:6 city among the governors of *J*
Lu 1:39 with haste, to a city of *J*
3:33 son of Perez, son of *J*
Heb 7:14 Lord has sprung up out of *J*
8:8 with the house of *J* a new
Re 5:5 Lion that is of the tribe of *J*
7:5 Out of the tribe of *J* twelve

Judah's
Ge 38:7 Er, *J* firstborn, proved to be
38:12 daughter of Shua, *J* wife
De 33:7 this was *J* blessing, as he

Judaism
Ga 1:13 my conduct formerly in *J*
1:14 greater progress in *J* than

Judas
Mt 10:4 and *J* Iscariot, who later
13:55 his brothers . . . Simon and *J*
26:14 the one called *J* Iscariot
26:25 *J*, who was about to betray
26:47 *J*, one of the twelve, came
27:3 *J*, who betrayed him, seeing
Mr 3:19 and *J* Iscariot, who later
6:3 the brother of . . . *J* and Simon
14:10 *J* Iscariot, one of the
14:43 *J*, one of the twelve
Lu 3:30 son of Symeon, son of *J*, son
6:16 *J* the son of James, and
6:16 *J* Iscariot, who turned
22:3 Satan entered into *J*, the one
22:47 the man called *J*, one of
22:48 *J*, do you betray the Son of
Joh 6:71 *J* the son of Simon Iscariot
12:4 But *J* Iscariot, one of his
13:2 into the heart of *J* Iscariot
13:26 *J*, the son of Simon
13:29 *J* was holding the money box
14:22 *J*, not Iscariot, said to
18:2 *J*, his betrayer, also knew
18:3 *J* took the soldier band and
18:5 *J*, his betrayer, was also
Ac 1:13 and *J* the son of James
1:16 *J*, who became a guide to
1:25 *J* deviated to go to his own
5:37 *J* the Galilean rose in the
9:11 at the house of *J* look for
15:22 *J* who was called Barsabbas
15:27 dispatching *J* and Silas
15:32 And *J* and Silas, since they

Jude
Jude 1 *J*, a slave of Jesus Christ

Judea
Mt 2:1 born in Bethlehem of *J* in the
2:5 In Bethlehem of *J*; for this
2:22 Archelaus ruled as king of *J*
3:1 in the wilderness of *J*
3:5 Jerusalem and all *J* and all
4:25 and Jerusalem and *J* and from
19:1 came to the frontiers of *J*
24:16 let those in *J* begin fleeing
Mr 1:5 all the territory of *J* and all
3:7 Galilee and from *J* followed
10:1 came to the frontiers of *J*
13:14 let those in *J* begin fleeing
Lu 1:5 the days of Herod, king of *J*
1:65 mountainous country of *J*
2:4 into *J*, to David's city
3:1 Pilate was governor of *J*
4:44 in the synagogues of *J*
5:17 every village of Galilee and *J*
6:17 from all of *J* and Jerusalem and
7:17 spread out into all *J* and
21:21 let those in *J* begin fleeing
23:5 by teaching throughout all *J*
Joh 4:3 left *J* and departed again for
4:47 Jesus had come out of *J* into
4:54 came out of *J* into Galilee
7:1 not want to walk about in *J*
7:3 and go into *J*, in order that
11:7 Let us go into *J* again
Ac 1:8 *J* and Samaria and to the most
2:9 *J* and Cappadocia, Pontus and
Ac 2:14 Men of *J* and all you
8:1 the regions of *J* and Samaria
9:31 throughout the whole of *J*
10:37 throughout the whole of *J*
11:1 brothers that were in *J*
11:29 the brothers dwelling in *J*
12:19 he went down from *J* to
15:1 certain men came down from *J*
21:10 Agabus came down from *J*
26:20 over all the country of *J*
28:21 concerning you from *J*
Ro 15:31 unbelievers in *J* and that my
2Co 1:16 conducted part way . . . to *J*
Ga 1:22 to the congregations of *J* that
1Th 2:14 congregations . . . in *J*

Judean
Joh 3:22 went into *J* country, and

Judeans
2Ch 32:9 *J* that were in Jerusalem
Lu 23:51 Arimathea, a city of the *J*
Joh 11:8 *J* were seeking to stone you

Judge
Ge 16:5 May Jehovah *j* between me and
18:25 *J* of all the earth not going
19:9 he would actually play the *j*
30:6 God has acted as my *j* and
31:53 god of Nahor *j* between us
49:16 Dan will *j* his people as one
Ex 2:14 Who appointed you as a . . . *j*
5:21 Jehovah look upon you and *j*
18:13 to serve as *j* for the people
18:16 I must *j* between the one
18:22 And they must *j* the people
Le 19:15 With justice you should *j*
Nu 35:24 *j* between the striker and
De 1:16 *j* with righteousness between
16:18 *j* the people with righteous
17:9 to the *j* who will be acting
17:12 not listening . . . to the *j*
25:1 they must also *j* them and
25:2 the *j* must also have him laid
32:36 Jehovah will *j* his people
Jg 2:18 proved to be with the *j*, and
2:18 all the days of the *j*; for
2:19 when the *j* died they would
3:10 he became the *j* of Israel
10:2 to *j* Israel for twenty-three
10:3 to *j* Israel for twenty-two
11:27, 27 Let Jehovah the *J* *j* today
12:7 to *j* Israel for six years
12:8 Ibzan . . . began to *j* Israel
12:9 to *j* Israel for seven years
12:11 Elon . . . began to *j* Israel
12:11 to *j* Israel ten years
12:13 Abdon . . . began to *j* Israel
12:14 to *j* Israel eight years
15:20 to *j* Israel in the days of
1Sa 2:10 Jehovah himself will *j* the
8:5 appoint for us a king to *j* us
8:6 Do give us a king to *j* us
8:20 our king must *j* us and go
12:7 I will *j* you before Jehovah
24:12 Jehovah *j* between me and
24:15 Jehovah must become *j*, and
24:15 must *j* between me and you
24:15 *j* me to free me from your
2Sa 15:4 O that I were appointed *j*
1Ki 3:9 heart to *j* your people
3:9 to *j* this difficult people
8:32 act and *j* your servants by
1Ch 16:33 he has come to *j* the earth
2Ch 1:10 *j* this great people of yours
1:11 that you may *j* my people
6:23 *j* your servants so as to pay
19:6 not for man that you *j* but
Ezr 7:25 continually *j* all the people
Job 19:29 men may know there is a *j*
22:13 Through . . . gloom can he *j*?
23:7 go safe forever from my *j*
Ps 7:8 *J* me, O Jehovah, according to
7:11 God is a righteous *J*, And God
9:8 will *j* the productive land in
10:18 To *j* the fatherless boy and
26:1 *J* me, O Jehovah, for I myself
35:24 *J* me according to your
43:1 *J* me, O God, And do conduct
50:6 For God himself is *J*. *Se'lah*
51:4 be in the clear when you *j*
58:1 Can you *j* in uprightness
67:4 you will *j* the peoples with
68:5 a *j* of widows Is God in his
72:4 Let him *j* the afflicted ones
Ps 75:7 For God is the *j*. This one
82:8 O God, do *j* the earth
94:2 yourself up, O *J* of the earth
96:13 he has come to *j* the earth
96:13 *j* the productive land with
98:9 Jehovah, for he has come to *j*
98:9 *j* the productive land with
Pr 31:9 *j* righteously and plead the
Ec 3:17 true God will *j* both the
Isa 3:2 *j* and prophet, and practicer
5:3 *j* between me and my vineyard
11:3 *j* by any mere appearance to
11:4 he must *j* the lowly ones
33:22 For Jehovah is our *J*
51:5 will *j* even the peoples
Eze 7:3 *j* you according to your ways
7:8 *j* you according to your ways
7:27 I shall *j* them; and they
11:10 I shall *j* you people
11:11 Israel I shall *j* you
16:38 *j* you with the judgments of
18:30 ways is how I shall *j* you
20:4 Will you *j* them? Will you
20:4 Will you *j* them, O son of
21:30 I shall *j* you
22:2 O son of man, will you *j*
22:2 *j* the bloodguilty city and
23:24 *j* you with their judgments
23:36 *j* Oholah and Oholibah and
23:45 ones that will *j* her with
24:14 they will certainly *j* you
33:20 *j* you, O house of Israel
34:20 *j* between a plump sheep and
34:22 *j* between a sheep and a
35:11 among them when I *j* you
44:24 should stand in order to *j*
44:24 they must also *j* it
Joe 3:12 in order to *j* all the nations
Am 2:3 cut off the *j* from the midst
Ob 21 to *j* the mountainous region of
Mic 3:11 *j* merely for a bribe, and
5:1 strike upon the cheek the *j*
Zec 3:7 you that will *j* my house
Mt 5:25 not turn you over to the *j*
5:25 *j* to the court attendant
Lu 12:14 Man, who appointed me *j* or
12:57 *j* also for yourselves what
12:58 never hale you before the *j*
12:58 *j* deliver you to the court
18:2 *j* that had no fear of God
18:6 *j*, although unrighteous, said
19:22 I *j* you, wicked slave
22:30 to *j* the twelve tribes of
Joh 3:17 not for him to *j* the world
5:30 just as I hear, I *j*; and
7:24 *j* with righteous judgment
7:51 Our law does not *j* a man
8:15 You *j* according to the flesh
8:15 I do not *j* any man at all
8:16 if I do *j*, my judgment is
12:47 I do not *j* him; for I came
12:47 not to *j* the world, but to
12:48 has one to *j* him
12:48 will *j* him in the last day
18:31 *j* him according to your law
Ac 4:19 than to God, *j* for yourselves
7:7 I shall *j*, God said, and after
7:27 appointed you ruler and *j*
7:35 appointed you ruler and *j*
10:42 *j* of the living and the dead
13:46 do not *j* yourselves worthy
17:31 to *j* the inhabited earth in
17:34 Dionysius, a *j* of the court
18:15 I do not wish to be a *j* of
23:3 *j* me in accord with the Law
24:10 had you as *j* for many years
Ro 2:1 are inexcusable . . . if you *j*
2:1 thing in which you *j* another
2:1 you that *j* practice the same
2:3 *j* those who practice such
2:27 *j* you who with its written
3:6 will God *j* the world
14:3 not *j* the one eating, for
14:4 *j* the house servant of another
14:10 why do you *j* your brother?
1Co 4:5 do not *j* anything before the
5:12 Do you not *j* those inside
6:2 holy ones will *j* the world
6:3 know that we shall *j* angels
6:5 will be able to *j* between his
10:15 *j* for yourselves what I say
11:13 *J* for your own selves: Is
Col 2:16 let no man *j* you in eating
2Ti 4:1 to *j* the living and the dead

2Ti 4:8 the Lord, the righteous *j*
Heb 10:30 Jehovah will *j* his people
12:23 God the *J* of all, and the
13:4 God will *j* fornicators and
Jas 4:11 if you *j* law, you are, not a
4:11 not a doer of law, but a *j*
4:12 that is lawgiver and *j*, he
5:9 The *J* is standing before the
1Pe 4:5 one ready to *j* those living

Judged
Ex 18:26 And they *j* the people on
Jg 16:31 he had *j* Israel twenty years
1Sa 4:18 had *j* Israel forty years
7:16 *j* Israel at all these places
7:17 Ramah . . . there he *j* Israel
2Sa 18:19 Jehovah has *j* him to free
18:31 Jehovah has *j* you today
2Ki 23:22 the judges that had *j* Israel
Ps 9:19 nations be *j* before your face
37:33 wicked when he is being *j*
109:7 When he is *j*, let him go
Eze 36:19 to their dealings I *j* them
Da 9:12 against our judges who *j* us
Mt 7:1 judging that you may not be *j*
7:2 you are judging, you will be *j*
Lu 6:37 you will by no means be *j*
7:43 said to him: You *j* correctly
Joh 3:18 faith in him is not to be *j*
3:18 has been *j* already, because
16:11 ruler of this world . . . *j*
Ac 16:15 have *j* me to be faithful to
23:6 I am being *j*
24:21 today being *j* before you
25:9 *j* there before me concerning
25:10 where I ought to be *j*
25:20 *j* concerning these matters
26:8 it *j* unbelievable among you
Ro 2:12 under law will be *j* by law
3:4 win when you are being *j*
3:7 also yet being *j* as a sinner
1Co 5:3 *j* already, as if . . . present
6:2 if the world is to be *j* by
10:29 my freedom is *j* by another
11:31 we would not be *j*
11:32 are *j*, we are disciplined
2Co 5:14 *j*, that one man died for all
2Th 2:12 that they all may be *j*
Jas 2:12 by the law of a free
5:9 so that you do not get *j*
1Pe 4:6 *j* as to the flesh from the
Re 11:18 time for the dead to be *j*
18:8 Jehovah God, who *j* her, is
20:12 dead were *j* out of those
20:13 *j* individually according to

Judges
Ex 18:22 they . . . will handle as *j*
18:26 themselves would handle as *j*
Nu 25:5 Moses said to the *j* of Israel
De 1:16 I went on to command your *j*
16:18 set *j* and officers for
19:17 before the priests and the *j*
19:18 the *j* must search thoroughly
21:2 your older men and your *j*
Jos 8:33 and the officers and their *j*
23:2 its *j* and its officers, and
24:1 its *j* and its officers, and
Jg 2:16 So Jehovah would raise up *j*
2:17 even to their *j* they did not
2:18 raise up *j* for them, Jehovah
Ru 1:1 the *j* administered justice
1Sa 8:1 appointments of his sons as *j*
2Sa 7:11 put *j* in command over my
2Ki 23:22 *j* that had judged Israel
1Ch 17:6 with one of the *j* of Israel
17:10 I put *j* in command over my
23:4 officers and *j* six thousand
26:29 and as *j* over Israel
2Ch 1:2 *j* and to all the chieftains
19:5 station *j* throughout the land
19:6 say to the *j*: See what you
Ezr 4:9 the *j* and the lesser governors
7:25 appoint magistrates and *j*
10:14 individual city and its *j*
Job 9:24 The face of its *j* he covers
12:17 makes *j* themselves go crazy
21:22 One himself *j* high ones
Ps 2:10 corrected, O *j* of the earth
82:1 middle of the gods he *j*
82:3 Be *j* for the lowly one and
141:6 *j* have been thrown down by
148:11 all you *j* of the earth
Isa 1:26 bring back again *j* for you as
40:23 *j* of the earth as a mere
Da 3:2 *j*, the police magistrates and
3:3 the *j*, the police magistrates
9:12 against our *j* who judged us
Ho 7:7 they actually devour their *j*
13:10 all your cities, and your *j*
Zep 3:3 Her *j* were evening wolves
Mt 12:27 why they will be *j* of you
Lu 11:19 they will be *j* of you
Joh 5:22 the Father *j* no one at all
Ac 13:20 *j* until Samuel the prophet
13:27 acting as *j*, they fulfilled
Ro 2:16 God through Christ Jesus *j*
14:5 *j* one day as above another
14:5 man *j* one day as all others
1Co 5:13 while God *j* those outside
6:4 that you put in as *j*
Jas 2:4 *j* rendering wicked decisions
4:11 *j* his brother speaks against
4:11 speaks against law and *j* law
1Pe 1:17 the Father who *j* impartially
2:23 to the one who *j* righteously
Re 19:11 he *j* and carries on war in

Judging
Ge 15:14 I am *j*, and after that they
Le 19:35 not commit injustice in *j*
Jg 4:4 Deborah . . . was *j* Israel at
1Sa 3:13 I am *j* his house to time
7:6 Samuel took up *j* the sons of
7:15 Samuel kept on *j* Israel all
8:2 they were *j* in Beer-sheba
1Ki 7:7 Throne where he would do *j*
2Ki 15:5 *j* the people of the land
2Ch 26:21 *j* the people of the land
Ps 9:4 have sat on the throne *j* with
58:11 a God that is *j* in the earth
75:2 began *j* with uprightness
82:2 keep on *j* with injustice
109:31 from those *j* his soul
Pr 8:16 and nobles are all *j* in
29:14 *j* the lowly ones in trueness
Isa 16:5 *j* and seeking justice and
Jer 11:20 Jehovah of armies is *j*
Eze 34:17 *j* between a sheep and a
Mic 7:3 *j* does so for the reward
Zec 7:9 With true justice do your *j*
8:16 do your *j* in your gates
Mt 7:1 Stop *j* that you may not be
7:2 you are *j*, you will be judged
19:28 *j* the twelve tribes of
Lu 6:37 stop *j*, and you will by no
Joh 5:22 all the *j* to the Son
5:27 given him authority to do *j*
7:24 Stop *j* from the outward
8:50 is One that is seeking and *j*
12:31 there is a *j* of this world
Ro 14:13 not be *j* one another any
1Co 5:12 to do with *j* those outside
Jas 4:12 are you to be *j* your neighbor?
Re 6:10 from *j* and avenging our blood
20:4 power of *j* was given them

Judgment
Ge 18:19 to do righteousness and *j*
Ex 15:25 a case for *j* and there he put
28:15 make the breastpiece of *j*
28:29 on the breastpiece of *j* over
28:30 into the breastpiece of *j*
Le 19:15 not do injustice in the *j*
Nu 27:21 *j* of the Urim before Jehovah
35:12 before the assembly for *j*
35:29 as a statute of *j* for you
De 1:17 You must not be partial in *j*
1:17 for the *j* belongs to God; and
10:18 *j* for the fatherless boy
16:18 judge . . . with righteous *j*
16:19 You must not pervert *j*
24:17 pervert the *j* of the alien
25:1 presented . . . for the *j*
27:19 perverts the *j* of an alien
32:41 And my hand takes hold on *j*
Jos 20:6 before the assembly for *j*
Jg 4:5 would go up to her for *j*
1Sa 8:3 accept a bribe and pervert *j*
2Sa 15:2 to come to the king for *j*
15:4 have a legal case or *j*
15:6 come in for *j* to the king
1Ki 7:7 he made the porch of *j*
8:45 you must execute *j* for them
8:49 you must execute *j* for them
8:59 execute *j* for his servant
8:59 *j* for his people Israel as it
20:40 Thus your own *j* is
2Ch 6:35 you must execute *j* for them
6:39 execute *j* for them and
2Ch 19:6 with you in the matter of *j*
19:8 *j* of Jehovah and for the
20:9 sword, adverse *j*, or
20:12 God, will you not execute *j*
24:24 they executed acts of *j*
Ezr 7:26 let *j* be promptly executed
Job 8:3 Will God himself pervert *j*
9:32 we should come together in *j*
14:3 me you bring into *j* with you
22:4 he come with you into the *j*
27:2 who has taken away my *j*
31:13 refuse the *j* of my slave
32:9 old that understand *j*
34:4 *J* let us choose for ourselves
34:5 has turned aside the *j* of me
34:6 Against my own *j* do I tell
34:12 Almighty . . . not pervert *j*
34:23 To go to God in *j*
34:33 because you do refuse *j*
36:6 the *j* of the afflicted ones
Ps 1:5 will not stand up in the *j*
7:6 given command for *j* itself
9:4 executed my *j* and my cause
9:7 establishing his throne for *j*
9:16 Jehovah is known by the *j*
17:2 before you may my *j* go forth
35:23 awake to my *j*, O my God
50:4 to execute *j* on his people
76:9 When God rose up to *j*
89:14 *j* are the established place
97:2 *j* are the established place
99:4 *j* he has loved
99:4 *J* and righteousness in Jacob
101:1 and *j* I will sing
110:6 execute *j* among the nations
111:7 works . . . are truth and *j*
119:84 *j* against those persecuting
119:121 I have executed *j* and
122:5 thrones for *j* have been
140:12 the *j* of the poor ones
143:2 not enter into *j* with your
146:7 *j* for the defrauded ones
Pr 1:3 and *j* and uprightness
2:8 observing the paths of *j*, and
2:9 understand righteousness and *j*
8:20 middle of the roadways of *j*
12:5 righteous ones are *j*; the
13:23 swept away for lack of *j*
16:10 in *j* his mouth should not
17:23 to bend the paths of *j*
18:5 of the righteous one in *j*
20:8 sitting upon the throne of *j*
21:3 carry on righteousness and *j*
24:23 partiality in *j* is not good
28:5 badness cannot understand *j*
29:9 into *j* with a foolish man
29:26 *j* of a man is from Jehovah
Ec 5:8 the violent taking away of *j*
8:5 will know both time and *j*
8:6 a time and *j* even for every
11:9 God will bring you into *j*
12:14 sort of work into the *j*
Isa 1:17 *j* for the fatherless boy
1:23 boy they do not render *j*
2:4 render *j* among the nations
3:14 *j* with the elderly ones of
4:4 by the spirit of *j* and by
5:7 he kept hoping for *j*, but
5:16 become high through *j*
28:6 the one sitting in the *j*
30:18 Jehovah is a God of *j*
41:1 together for the *j* itself
43:26 put ourselves on *j* together
49:4 Truly my *j* is with Jehovah
53:8 Because of restraint and of *j*
54:17 in the *j* you will condemn
Jer 5:4 the *j* of their God
5:5 the *j* of their God
5:28 the *j* of the poor ones
8:7 to know the *j* of Jehovah
10:24 Correct me . . . with *j*
12:1 even about matters of *j*
25:31 put himself in *j* with all
26:11 the *j* of death belongs
26:16 There is no *j* of death
48:21 *j* itself has come to the
48:47 is the *j* upon Moab
51:9 heavens her *j* has reached
La 3:35 For turning aside the *j* of an
3:59 O do conduct the *j* for me
Eze 5:10 execute in you acts of *j* and
5:15 in you acts of *j* in anger and
7:23 full of bloodstained *j* and
11:9 execute upon you acts of *j*

Eze 14:21 my four injurious acts of *j*
16:41 and execute in you acts of *j*
17:20 put myself on *j* with him
20:35 put myself on *j* with you
20:36 Just as I put myself on *j*
20:36 put myself on *j* with you
23:10 *j* were what they executed
23:24 I will give *j* over to them
23:45 the *j* for adulteresses and
23:45 *j* for female shedders of
25:11 I shall execute acts of *j*
28:22 execute acts of *j* in her
28:26 execute acts of *j* upon all
30:14 execute acts of *j* in No
30:19 execute acts of *j* in Egypt
34:16 shall feed that one with *j*
38:22 bring myself into *j* with
39:21 will have to see my *j* that
Da 7:22 *j* itself was given in favor
Ho 5:1 with you people the *j* has to
10:4 *j* has sprouted like a
Joe 3:2 I will put myself on *j*
Mic 4:3 render *j* among many peoples
Hab 1:12 for a *j* you have set it
Zec 8:16 truth and the *j* of peace
Mal 3:5 near to you people for *j*, and
Mt 7:2 what *j* you are judging, you
10:15 Sodom and Gomorrah on *J* Day
11:22 for Tyre and Sidon on *J* Day
11:24 the land of Sodom on *J* Day
12:36 concerning it on *J* Day
12:41 will rise up in the *j* with
12:42 the *j* with this generation
23:33 flee from the *j* of Gehenna
27:19 was sitting on the *j* seat
Mr 12:40 will receive a heavier *j*
Lu 10:14 Tyre and Sidon in the *j*
11:31 will be raised up in the *j*
11:32 Nineveh will rise in the *j*
20:47 will receive a heavier *j*
23:40 that you are in the same *j*
Joh 3:19 Now this is the basis for *j*
5:24 does not come into *j* but has
5:29 to a resurrection of *j*
5:30 *j* that I render is righteous
7:24 but judge with righteous *j*
8:16 my *j* is truthful, because I
8:26 and to pass *j* upon
9:39 For this *j* I came into this
16:8 evidence . . . concerning *j*
16:11 concerning *j*, because the
19:13 *j* seat in a place called
Ac 8:33 *j* was taken away from him
12:21 sat down upon the *j* seat and
18:12 and led him to the *j* seat
18:16 them away from the *j* seat
18:17 him in front of the *j* seat
24:25 and the *j* to come, Felix
25:6 sat down on the *j* seat and
25:10 standing before the *j* seat
25:15 asking a *j* of condemnation
25:17 I sat down on the *j* seat
26:6 I stand called to *j*
Ro 2:2 *j* of God is, in accord with
2:3 you will escape the *j* of God
2:5 revealing of God's righteous *j*
3:8 *j* against those men is in
5:16 *j* resulted from one trespass
13:2 will receive *j* to themselves
14:10 all stand before the *j* seat
14:22 not put himself on *j* by
1Co 11:29 eats and drinks *j* against
11:34 may not come together for *j*
2Co 5:10 the *j* seat of the Christ
Ga 5:10 will bear his *j*, no matter
2Th 1:5 is a proof of the righteous *j*
1Ti 3:6 the *j* passed upon the Devil
5:12 having a *j* because they have
5:24 leading directly to *j*, but
Heb 6:2 of the dead and everlasting *j*
9:27 all time, but after this a *j*
10:27 fearful expectation of *j*
Jas 2:13 have his *j* without mercy
2:13 Mercy exults . . . over *j*
3:1 we shall receive heavier *j*
5:12 you do not fall under *j*
1Pe 4:17 *j* to start with the house
2Pe 2:3 the *j* from of old is not
2:4 to be reserved for *j*
2:9 the day of *j* to be cut off
3:7 being reserved to the day of *j*
1Jo 4:17 in the day of *j*, because
Jude 4 by the Scriptures to this *j*
6 for the *j* of the great day
Jude 9 not dare to bring a *j* against
15 to execute *j* against all, and
Re 14:7 the hour of the *j* by him has
17:1 *j* upon the great harlot who
18:10 one hour your *j* has arrived
19:2 *j* upon the great harlot who

Judgments
Ex 6:6 reclaim you . . . with great *j*
7:4 the land of Egypt with great *j*
12:12 I shall execute *j*. I am
28:30 Aaron must carry the *j* of
Nu 33:4 Jehovah had executed *j*
35:24 according to these *j*
Pr 19:29 *J* have been firmly
Isa 26:8 for the path of your *j*
26:9 *j* from you for the earth
58:2 asking me for righteous *j*
Jer 1:16 my *j* over all their badness
4:12 speak forth the *j* with them
Eze 7:27 with their *j* I shall judge
11:12 and my *j* you did not do
11:12 *j* of the nations that are
16:38 with the *j* of adulteresses
20:18 and their *j* do not you keep
23:24 judge you with their *j*
Ho 6:5 the *j* upon you will be as the
Zep 3:15 Jehovah has removed the *j*
Ro 11:33 How unsearchable his *j* are
Re 19:2 his *j* are true and righteous

Judicial
Ex 21:1 these are the *j* decisions that
21:31 according to this *j* decision
23:6 *j* decision of your poor man
24:3 and all the *j* decisions, and
Le 18:4 My *j* decisions you should
18:5 keep my statutes and my *j*
18:26 *j* decisions, and you must
19:37 *j* decisions, and you must do
20:22 my *j* decisions and do them
24:22 One *j* decision should hold
25:18 keep my *j* decisions and you
26:15 abhor my *j* decisions so as
26:43 rejected my *j* decisions, and
26:46 *j* decisions and the laws
Nu 15:16 one *j* decision for you and
27:11 as a statute by *j* decision
36:13 the *j* decisions that Jehovah
De 4:1 *j* decisions that I am teaching
4:5 regulations and *j* decisions
4:8 *j* decisions like all this law
4:14 regulations and *j* decisions
4:45 *j* decisions that Moses spoke
5:1 the *j* decisions that I am
5:31 the *j* decisions that you
6:1 the *j* decisions that Jehovah
6:20 What . . . the *j* decisions mean
7:11 keep . . . the *j* decisions
7:12 listening to these *j* decisions
8:11 *j* decisions and his statutes
11:1 his *j* decisions and his
11:32 the *j* decisions that I am
12:1 the *j* decisions that you
17:8 a matter for *j* decision
17:9 the word of the *j* decision
17:11 according to the *j* decision
26:16 regulations and *j* decisions
26:17 his *j* decisions and listen
30:16 statutes and his *j* decisions
33:10 Jacob in your *j* decisions
33:21 his *j* decisions with Israel
Jos 24:25 and *j* decision in Shechem
1Sa 30:25 *j* decision for Israel down
2Sa 8:15 rendering *j* decision and
22:23 his *j* decisions are in front
1Ki 2:3 his *j* decisions and his
3:11 understanding to hear *j* cases
3:28 *j* decision that the king
3:28 to execute *j* decision
6:12 perform my *j* decisions and
8:58 and his *j* decisions, which
9:4 and my *j* decisions
10:9 as king to render *j* decision
11:33 my *j* decisions like David
2Ki 17:34 statutes and his *j* decisions
17:37 the *j* decisions and the law
25:6 pronounce a *j* decision upon
1Ch 16:12 *j* decisions of his mouth
16:14 are his *j* decisions
18:14 rendering *j* decision and
22:13 the *j* decisions that Jehovah
28:7 and my *j* decisions, as at
2Ch 7:17 and my *j* decisions
9:8 king to execute *j* decision
2Ch 19:10 *j* decisions, you must warn
33:8 *j* decisions by the hand of
Ne 1:7 regulations and the *j* decisions
9:13 upright *j* decisions and laws
9:29 against your own *j* decisions
10:29 his *j* decisions and his
Job 36:17 the *j* sentence upon the
36:17 *J* sentence and justice will
Ps 10:5 Your *j* decisions are high up
18:22 For all his *j* decisions are
19:9 The *j* decisions of Jehovah are
25:9 to walk in his *j* decision
36:6 *j* decision is a vast watery
48:11 account of your *j* decisions
72:1 give your own *j* decisions to
72:2 afflicted ones with *j*
81:4 *j* decision of the God of Jacob
89:30 my *j* decisions they do not
94:15 *j* decision will return even
97:8 your *j* decisions, O Jehovah
103:6 *j* decisions for all those
105:5 the *j* decisions of his mouth
105:7 *j* decisions are in all the
119:7 your righteous *j* decisions
119:13 *j* decisions of your mouth
119:20 For your *j* decisions all
119:30 your *j* decisions I have
119:39 your *j* decisions are good
119:43 for your own *j* decision
119:52 remembered your *j* decisions
119:62 your righteous *j* decisions
119:75 that your *j* decisions are
119:91 to your *j* decisions they
119:102 From your *j* decisions I
119:106 your righteous *j* decisions
119:108 your own *j* decisions
119:120 *j* decisions I have been
119:132 your *j* decision toward
119:137 *j* decisions are upright
119:149 *j* decision preserve me
119:156 to your *j* decisions
119:160 righteous *j* decision of
119:164 your righteous *j* decisions
119:175 your own *j* decisions help
147:19 his *j* decisions to Israel
147:20 *j* decisions, they have not
149:9 the *j* decision written
Isa 50:8 Who is my *j* antagonist?
51:4 and my *j* decision I shall
Jer 39:5 upon him *j* decisions
52:9 pronounce . . . *j* decisions
Eze 5:6 against my *j* decisions in
5:6 my *j* decisions they rejected
5:7 my *j* decisions you did not
5:7 *j* decisions of the nations
5:8 will execute . . . *j* decisions
11:20 keep my own *j* decisions and
18:9 and my *j* decisions he kept
18:17 *j* decisions he has carried
20:11 *j* decisions I made known to
20:13 *j* decisions they rejected
20:16 rejected my own *j* decisions
20:19 keep my own *j* decisions and
20:21 my *j* decisions they did not
20:24 my own *j* decisions and they
20:25 *j* decisions by which they
36:27 *j* decisions you will keep
37:24 *j* decisions they will walk
44:24 with my *j* decisions they
Da 9:5 and from your *j* decisions
Zep 2:3 practiced His own *j* decision
3:5 giving his own *j* decision
3:8 my *j* decision is to gather
Mal 4:4 regulations and *j* decisions
Ac 25:26 *j* examination has taken
2Th 1:9 undergo the *j* punishment of
Jude 7 *j* punishment of everlasting
Re 16:7 righteous are your *j* decisions

Judicially
Ps 9:8 will *j* try national groups in
Re 18:20 God has *j* exacted punishment

Judith
Ge 26:34 *J* the daughter of Beeri the

Jug
1Sa 26:11 and the water *j*, and let us
26:12 the water *j* from the place
26:16 water *j* are that were at
1Ki 19:6 at his head . . . a *j* of water

Juice
Job 6:6 the slimy *j* of marshmallow
Ca 8:2 fresh *j* of pomegranates

Julia
Ro 16:15 Greet Philologus and *J*

Julius
Ac 27:1 officer named *J* of the band
27:3 *J* treated Paul with human

Jumping
Isa 66:17 even the *j* rodent, they

Junction
Ex 26:4 at the other place of *j*
26:5 is at the other place of *j*
26:10 cloth at the other place of *j*
36:11 tent cloth at the *j* end
36:11 at the other place of *j*
36:12 at the other place of *j*
36:17 at the place of *j*, and

Junias
Ro 16:7 Greet Andronicus and *J* my

Juniper
2Sa 6:5 instruments of *j* wood and
1Ki 5:8 and timbers of *j* trees
5:10 *j* trees to Solomon according
6:15 with boards of *j*
6:34 two doors were of *j* wood
9:11 and timbers of *j* trees and
2Ki 19:23 its choice *j* trees
2Ch 2:8 *j* and almug from Lebanon, for
3:5 house he covered with *j* wood
Ps 104:17 the *j* trees are its house
Ca 1:17 cedars, our rafters *j* trees
Isa 14:8 *j* trees have also rejoiced
37:24 its choice *j* trees
41:19 I shall place the *j* tree
55:13 the *j* tree will come up
60:13 the *j* tree, the ash tree and
Jer 48:6 *j* tree in the wilderness
Eze 27:5 Out of *j* timbers from Senir
31:8 As for *j* trees, they bore
Ho 14:8 I am like a luxuriant *j* tree
Na 2:3 the *j* tree spears have been
Zec 11:2 Howl, O *j* tree, for the

Jurisdiction
Lu 23:7 from the *j* of Herod, he sent
Ac 1:7 has placed in his own *j*

Jurisdictional
1Ki 20:14 princes of the *j* districts
20:15 princes of the *j* districts
20:17 princes of the *j* districts
20:19 princes of the *j* districts
Ezr 2:1 the sons of the *j* district
4:15 to kings and *j* districts
5:8 to the *j* district of Judah
6:2 in the *j* district of Media
7:16 the *j* district of Babylon
Ne 1:3 there in the *j* district
7:6 the sons of the *j* district
11:3 the heads of the *j* district
Es 1:1 and twenty-seven *j* districts
1:3 princes of the *j* districts
1:16 *j* districts of King Ahasuerus
1:22 to all the king's *j* districts
1:22 to each *j* district in its own
2:3 the *j* districts of his realm
2:18 amnesty for the *j* districts
3:8 the *j* districts of your realm
3:12 over the different *j* districts
3:12 each *j* district, in its own
3:13 to all the king's *j* districts
3:14 all the different *j* districts
4:3 all the different *j* districts
4:11 king's *j* districts are aware
8:5 in all the king's *j* districts
8:9 the princes of the *j* districts
8:9 and twenty-seven *j* districts
8:9 to each *j* district in its own
8:11 *j* district that were showing
8:12 *j* districts of King Ahasuerus
8:13 throughout all the different *j*
8:17 all the different *j* districts
9:2 *j* districts of King Ahasuerus
9:3 the princes of the *j* districts
9:4 throughout all the *j* districts
9:12 In the rest of the *j* districts
9:16 in the *j* districts of the king
9:20 *j* districts of King Ahasuerus
9:28 each *j* district and each city
9:30 hundred and twenty-seven *j*
Ec 2:8 to kings and the *j* districts
5:8 righteousness in a *j* district
La 1:1 princess among the *j* districts
Eze 19:8 around from the *j* districts
Da 2:48 ruler over all the *j* district
2:49 *j* district of Babylon
3:1 in the *j* district of Babylon
3:2 of the *j* districts to come to
3:3 of the *j* districts were
3:12 the *j* district of Babylon
3:30 in the *j* district of Babylon
8:2 is in Elam the *j* district
11:24 *j* district he will enter in

Jushab-hesed
1Ch 3:20 Berechiah and Hasadiah, *J*

Just*
Ge 6:22 Noah . . . did *j* so
7:16 *j* as God had commanded him
21:4 *j* as God had commanded him
Ex 7:6 Moses and Aaron . . . did *j* so
7:22 *j* as Jehovah had spoken
8:15 *j* as Jehovah had spoken
8:19 *j* as Jehovah had spoken
12:28 *j* as Jehovah had commanded
12:28 and Aaron. They did *j* so
12:50 *j* as Jehovah had commanded
12:50 sons of Israel . . . did *j* so
17:10 Joshua did *j* as Moses had
39:5 *j* as Jehovah had commanded
39:21 *j* as Jehovah had commanded
39:26 *j* as Jehovah had commanded
39:29 *j* as Jehovah had commanded
39:31 *j* as Jehovah had commanded
39:32 They did *j* so
39:43 *j* as Jehovah had commanded
40:16 He did *j* so
40:21 *j* as Jehovah had commanded
40:23 *j* as Jehovah had commanded
40:25 *j* as Jehovah had commanded
40:27 *j* as Jehovah had commanded
40:29 *j* as Jehovah had commanded
Le 7:38 *j* as Jehovah had commanded
8:4 Moses did *j* as Jehovah had
8:9 *j* as Jehovah had commanded
8:13 *j* as Jehovah had commanded
8:17 *j* as Jehovah had commanded
8:21 *j* as Jehovah had commanded
8:29 *j* as Jehovah had commanded
9:7 *j* as Jehovah has commanded
9:10 *j* as Jehovah had commanded
16:34 *j* as Jehovah had commanded
Nu 17:11 Moses did *j* as Jehovah had
17:11 Moses . . . did *j* so
20:27 Moses did *j* as Jehovah had
26:4 *j* as Jehovah had commanded
27:11 *j* as Jehovah has commanded
27:22 *j* as Jehovah had commanded
27:23 *j* as Jehovah had spoken by
31:7 *j* as Jehovah had commanded
31:31 *j* as Jehovah had commanded
31:41 *j* as Jehovah had commanded
31:47 *j* as Jehovah had commanded
34:13 *j* as Jehovah has commanded
De 6:19 *j* as Jehovah has promised
10:5 *j* as Jehovah had commanded
10:9 *j* as Jehovah your God had said
11:25 *j* as he has promised you
12:20 *j* as he has promised you
12:21 *j* as I have commanded you
13:17 *j* as he has sworn to your
16:10 *j* as Jehovah your God may
18:2 *j* as he has spoken to him
20:17 *j* as Jehovah your God has
23:23 must do *j* as you have vowed
24:8 *J* as I have commanded them
25:15 A weight accurate and *j*
25:15 An ephah accurate and *j*
26:15 *j* as you swore to our
26:18 *j* as he has promised you
34:9 *j* as Jehovah had commanded
Jos 4:23 *j* as Jehovah your God had
6:22 *j* as you have sworn to her
8:2 *j* as you did to Jericho and
11:20 *j* as Jehovah had commanded
14:5 *J* as Jehovah had commanded
14:10 *j* as he promised
14:12 *j* as Jehovah promised
21:8 *j* as Jehovah had commanded
22:4 rest, *j* as he promised them
23:10 *j* as he has promised you
23:15 *j* as all the good word
Jg 1:20 *j* as Moses had promised
2:15 *j* as Jehovah had spoken and
2:15 *j* as Jehovah had sworn to
2:22 *j* as their fathers kept it
6:27 went doing *j* as Jehovah had
6:37 *j* as you have promised
2Sa 3:9 *j* as Jehovah swore to David
1Ki 11:38 *j* as David my servant did
Job 42:9 did *j* as Jehovah had spoken
Ps 22:15 dried up *j* like a fragment
39:11 consume . . . *j* as a moth does
48:8 *J* as we have heard, so we
64:3 their tongue *j* like a sword
Pr 16:11 *j* indicator and scales belong
Jer 13:5 *j* as Jehovah had commanded
Mt 20:4 whatever is *j* I will give

Justice
Ex 23:2 turn aside . . . to pervert *j*
Le 19:15 With *j* you should judge your
De 16:20, 20 *J*—*j* you should pursue
32:4 For all his ways are *j*. A God
Ru 1:1 when the judges administered *j*
2Sa 15:4 should certainly do *j* to him
Ezr 7:10 in Israel regulation and *j*
Job 9:19 And if in *j* anyone is strong
13:18 have presented a case of *j*
19:7 but there is no *j*
23:4 before him a case of *j*
29:14 My *j* was like a sleeveless
34:17 will anyone hating *j*
35:2 what you have regarded as *j*
36:17 Judicial sentence and *j*
37:23 *j* . . . he will not belittle
40:8 will you invalidate my *j*?
Ps 33:5 a lover of righteousness and *j*
37:6 And your *j* as the midday
37:28 For Jehovah is a lover of *j*
82:3 one of little means do *j*
106:3 Happy are those observing *j*
112:5 sustains his affairs with *j*
Pr 16:8 of products without *j*
19:28 witness derides *j*, and the
21:7 for they have refused to do *j*
21:15 for the righteous one to do *j*
29:4 By *j* a king makes a land keep
Ec 3:16 *j* where there was wickedness
Isa 1:17 search for *j*; set right the
1:21 was full of *j*; righteousness
1:27 With *j* Zion herself will be
9:7 sustain it by means of *j* and
10:2 away *j* from the afflicted
16:5 judging and seeking *j* and
28:6 *j* to the one sitting in the
28:17 *j* the measuring line and
32:1 will rule as princes for *j*
32:16 *j* will certainly reside
33:5 fill Zion with *j* and
34:5 by me to destruction in *j*
40:14 him in the path of *j*
40:27 and *j* to me eludes my God
42:1 *J* to the nations is what he
42:3 he will bring forth *j*
42:4 until he sets *j* in the earth
56:1 said: Keep *j*, you people, and
58:2 the very *j* of their God
59:8 there is no *j* in their tracks
59:9 *j* has come to be far away
59:11 We kept hoping for *j*, but
59:14 *j* was forced to move back
59:15 that there was no *j*
61:8 I, Jehovah, am loving *j*
Jer 4:2 in *j* and in righteousness
5:1 there exists anyone doing *j*
7:5 will positively carry out *j*
9:24 *j* and righteousness in the
17:11 riches, but not with *j*
21:12 render sentence in *j*, and
22:3 Render *j* and righteousness
22:13 but not with *j*, by use of
22:15 execute *j* and righteousness
23:5 execute *j* and righteousness
33:15 *j* and righteousness in the
Eze 18:5 executed *j* and righteousness
18:8 true *j* he would execute
18:19 as regards the son, *j* and
18:21 execute *j* and righteousness
18:27 execute *j* and righteousness
22:29 have defrauded without *j*
33:14 on *j* and righteousness
33:16 *J* and righteousness are
33:19 *j* and righteousness
45:9 do *j* and righteousness
Da 4:37 are truth and his ways are *j*
Ho 2:19 in *j* and in loving-kindness
5:11 Ephraim is . . . crushed in *j*
12:6 keeping loving-kindness and *j*
Am 5:7 turning *j* into mere wormwood
5:15 give *j* a place in the gate
5:24 *j* roll forth just like waters

De 11:1 *k* your obligation to him and
11:8 *k* the whole commandment that
11:22 *k* all this commandment that
13:4 commandments you should *k*
16:20 you may *k* alive and may
17:19 *k* all the words of this law
19:9 *k* all this commandment
23:9 *k* yourself from every bad
23:16 *k* on dwelling in among you
23:23 utterance of your lips . . . *k*
27:9 *K* silent and listen, O Israel
28:2 *k* listening to the voice of
28:9 *k* the commandments of
28:13 *k* obeying the commandments
28:43 *k* ascending higher and higher
28:43 *k* descending lower and lower
29:9 *k* the words of this covenant
30:10 so as to *k* his commandments
30:16 and to *k* his commandments
30:16 will be bound to *k* alive and
30:19 order that you may *k* alive
32:6 that you *k* doing this way
Jos 2:16 must *k* hid there three days
6:17 prostitute may *k* on living
6:18 only *k* away from the
13:13 *k* dwelling in the midst of
18:5 Judah will *k* standing on his
18:5 *k* standing on their territory
23:6 courageous to *k* and to do
Jg 1:21 Jebusites *k* on dwelling with
3:19 So he said: *K* silence!
6:18 shall *k* sitting here until you
13:13 she should *k* herself
13:14 have commanded her let her *k*
14:11 that these should *k* with him
Ru 1:13 would you *k* waiting for them
1:13 you *k* yourselves secluded for
2:8 *k* close by my young women
2:21 *k* until they have finished the
2:23 *k* close by the young women of
3:13 *K* lying down until the
1Sa 2:23 you *k* doing things like these
2:29 *k* kicking at my sacrifice
2:29 *k* honoring your sons more
7:8 Do not *k* silent for our sakes
9:17 *k* my people within bounds
10:8 *k* waiting until my coming
13:14 you did not *k* what Jehovah
16:22 David, please, *k* attending
19:2 and *k* yourself hidden
22:5 not *k* dwelling in the
2Sa 3:8 *k* exercising loving-kindness
13:20 now, my sister, *k* silent
14:7 *k* saying, Give over the
18:18 *k* my name in remembrance
19:29 Why do you yet *k* speaking
22:24 I will *k* myself from error
1Ki 1:25 *k* saying, Let King Adonijah
2:3 *k* the obligation to Jehovah
2:43 not *k* the oath of Jehovah and
6:12 *k* all my commandments by
8:25 *k* toward your servant David
8:58 to *k* his commandments and
9:4 *k* my regulations and my
9:6 not *k* my commandments and
13:21 did not *k* the commandment
18:4 *k* them hid by fifties in a
2Ki 10:19 missing will not *k* living
11:6 *k* strict watch over the
11:7 must *k* strict watch over the
17:13 and *k* my commandments
17:19 not *k* the commandments of
18:32 *k* living that you may not
22:9 *k* putting it into the hand
23:3 *k* his commandments and his
23:33 to *k* him from reigning in
1Ch 22:12 to *k* the law of Jehovah
29:18 *k* this to time indefinite
29:19 to *k* your commandments
2Ch 6:16 *k* toward your servant David
7:17 *k* my regulations and my
13:9 *k* making priests for
23:6 *k* the obligation to Jehovah
25:19 *k* dwelling in your own
34:21 not *k* the word of Jehovah
34:31 to *k* his commandments and
35:25 *k* talking about Josiah in
Ezr 6:6 *k* your distance from there
8:29 *K* awake and be on guard
Ne 4:14 *k* in your mind; and fight for
5:2 get grain and eat and *k* alive
8:11 *K* quiet! for this day is holy
10:29 to *k* and to perform all the
Job 3:21 *k* digging for it more than
Job 6:11 that I should *k* waiting
6:11 should *k* prolonging my soul
6:15 torrents that *k* passing away
8:2 you *k* uttering these things
8:15 but it will not *k* standing
10:6 my sin you should *k* looking
11:3 will you *k* deriding without
13:5 would absolutely *k* silent
13:13 *K* silent before me, that I
13:25 *k* chasing after mere dry
13:26 *k* writing against me bitter
13:27 *k* my feet put in the stocks
14:2 and does not *k* existing
14:13 *k* me secret until your
14:16 *k* counting my very steps
14:22 own flesh . . . will *k* aching
14:22 his own soul . . . *k* mourning
15:24 anguish *k* terrifying him
15:28 people will not *k* dwelling
17:12 Night they *k* putting for day
17:13 If I *k* waiting, Sheol is my
19:2 you men *k* irritating my soul
19:2 *k* crushing me with words
19:7 I *k* crying out, Violence! but
19:7 I *k* crying for help, but
19:16 I *k* imploring him for
19:22 you men *k* persecuting me as
19:28 Why do we *k* persecuting
21:7 wicked themselves *k* living
21:11 *k* sending out their young
21:12 *k* rejoicing at the sound of
22:15 Will you *k* to the very way
22:21 and *k* peace; Thereby good
22:23 *k* unrighteousness far from
24:12 the dying *k* groaning, And
24:16 must *k* themselves locked in
26:5 in death *k* trembling
29:21 *k* silent for my counsel
30:27 to boil and did not *k* silent
31:34 I would *k* silent, I would
33:31 *K* silent, and I myself
33:33 *K* silent, and I shall teach
35:9 they *k* calling for aid
35:9 They *k* crying for help
35:12 they *k* crying out, but he
38:30 waters *k* themselves hidden
38:40 *k* lying in the covert for an
38:41 *k* wandering about because
39:29 distance its eyes *k* looking
39:30 young . . . *k* sipping up blood
40:22 lotus trees *k* it blocked off
41:12 I shall not *k* silent about
Ps 4:2 you *k* loving empty things
4:2 you *k* seeking to find a lie
4:4 upon your bed, and *k* silent
8:4 man that you *k* him in mind
10:1 do you *k* standing afar off
10:1 *k* yourself hid in times of
10:5 His ways *k* prospering all the
10:14 You *k* looking on, to get
12:2 Untruth they *k* speaking one
12:2 they *k* speaking even with a
16:1 *K* me, O God, for I have taken
17:8 *K* me as the pupil of the
17:9 enemies . . . *k* closing in
18:23 *k* myself from error on my
22:2 O my God, I *k* calling by day
22:7 *k* opening their mouths wide
22:7 they *k* wagging their head
22:11 Do not *k* far off from me
22:19 Jehovah, O do not *k* far off
28:1 To you, O Jehovah, I *k* calling
28:1 may not *k* still toward me
30:11 *k* me girded with rejoicing
30:12 glory may . . . not *k* silent
31:17 May they *k* silent in Sheol
35:15 and did not *k* silent
35:17 how long will you *k* seeing
35:20 deception they *k* scheming
35:22 O Jehovah. Do not *k* silent
35:22 do not *k* yourself far from
37:7 *K* silent before Jehovah
37:34 Hope in Jehovah and *k* his
37:37 *k* the upright one in sight
38:11 they *k* standing away from my
38:12 deceptions they *k* muttering
38:21 my God, do not *k* far away
39:1 To *k* from sinning with my
39:12 At my tears do not *k* silent
41:7 Against me they *k* scheming
44:9 cast off and *k* humiliating us
44:10 You *k* making us turn back
44:23 Why do you *k* sleeping, O
44:23 do not *k* casting off forever
Ps 44:24 *k* your very face concealed
45:5 under you peoples *k* falling
49:6 *k* boasting about the abundance
49:12 in honor, cannot *k* lodging
50:3 and cannot possibly *k* silent
50:17 *k* throwing my words behind
50:19 your tongue you *k* attached to
55:3 they *k* dropping upon me what
55:6 *k* saying: O that I had wings
56:5 *k* hurting my personal affairs
56:6 *k* observing my very steps
59:6 *k* returning at eveningtime
59:6 They *k* barking like a dog
59:9 toward you I will *k* watch
63:1 my God, I *k* looking for you
63:9 those who *k* seeking my soul
64:6 *k* searching out unrighteous
65:12 grounds of the wilderness *k*
66:7 nations his own eyes *k* watch
68:16 *k* watching enviously
69:26 they *k* recounting
69:32 let your heart also *k* alive
71:12 do not *k* far away from me
71:17 I *k* telling about your
74:1 anger *k* smoking against the
74:10 the adversary *k* reproaching
74:10 enemy *k* treating your name
74:11 Why do you *k* your hand
77:10 I *k* saying: This is what
78:10 not *k* the covenant of God
78:56 reminders they did not *k*
80:5 *k* making them drink tears
80:6 enemies *k* deriding as they
80:13 *k* feeding upon it
81:16 *k* feeding him off the fat
82:2 *k* on judging with injustice
82:5 In darkness they *k* walking
83:1 Do not *k* speechless, and do
84:4 They still *k* on praising you
86:3 you I *k* calling all day long
88:14 *k* your face concealed from
89:2 *k* your faithfulness firmly
89:15 your face they *k* walking
89:31 not *k* my own commandments
89:38 and you *k* contemning
89:46 *k* yourself concealed? For all
89:46 rage *k* on burning just like
92:14 still *k* on thriving during
93:3 rivers *k* raising their
94:4 *k* bubbling forth, they keep
94:4 *k* speaking unrestrained
94:4 *k* bragging about themselves
94:5 Jehovah, they *k* crushing
94:5 inheritance they *k* afflicting
94:7 *k* saying: Jah does not see
102:26 yourself will *k* standing
103:9 for all time *k* finding fault
103:9 time indefinite *k* resentful
104:10 springs . . . *k* going on
104:12 they *k* giving forth sound
104:27 for you they *k* waiting To
105:45 might *k* his regulations
107:29 waves of the sea *k* quiet
109:1 my praise, do not *k* silent
109:3 *k* fighting against me
109:4 For my love they *k* resisting
109:6 *k* standing at his right hand
118:17 *k* living, That I may
119:2 the heart they *k* searching
119:5 To *k* your regulations
119:8 regulations I continue to *k*
119:17 And that I may *k* your word
119:34 *k* it with the whole heart
119:44 will *k* your law constantly
119:55 That I may *k* your law
119:57 promised to *k* your words
119:60 To *k* your commandments
119:77 that I may *k* living
119:88 *k* the reminder of your
119:90 that it may *k* standing
119:95 *k* showing myself attentive
119:101 that I may *k* your word
119:106 *k* your righteous judicial
119:116 that I may *k* living
119:134 And I will *k* your orders
119:144 that I may *k* living
119:146 I will *k* your reminders
119:163 and I do *k* detesting it
119:175 soul *k* living and praising
122:9 I will *k* seeking good for
125:3 *k* resting upon the lot of the
130:7 Israel *k* waiting for Jehovah
132:12 sons will *k* my covenant
140:2 all day long *k* attacking as

Ps 140:4 *K* me, O Jehovah, from the
141:9 *K* me from the clutches of
147:9 young ravens that *k* calling
Pr 1:11 *k* saying: Do go with us
1:16 *k* hastening to shed blood
1:22 ones *k* loving inexperience
1:22 stupid ones *k* hating
1:24 called out but you *k* refusing
1:25 *k* neglecting all my counsel
1:28 time they will *k* calling me
1:28 *k* looking for me, but they
2:4 *k* seeking for it as for silver
2:4 treasures you *k* searching for
2:11 will *k* guard over you
2:20 righteous ones you may *k*
3:20 skies *k* dripping down light
3:26 *k* your foot against capture
4:4 heart *k* fast hold of my words
4:4 *K* my commandments and
4:6 not leave it, and it will *k*
4:19 at what they *k* stumbling
4:21 *K* them in the midst of your
5:3 the lips of a strange woman *k*
5:8 *K* your way far off from
6:9 lazy one, will you *k* lying
7:1 son, *k* my sayings, and may
7:2 *K* my commandments and
7:11 her feet do not *k* residing
8:1 Does not wisdom *k* calling out
8:1 discernment *k* giving forth its
8:15 kings themselves *k* reigning
8:15 *k* decreeing righteousness
8:16 princes themselves *k* ruling
8:21 their storehouses I *k* filled
8:32 the ones that *k* my very ways
9:6 inexperienced ones and *k* living
10:21 righteous one *k* pasturing
10:21 foolish themselves *k* dying
10:30 not *k* residing on the earth
11:27 will *k* seeking goodwill
12:7 righteous ones will *k*
15:7 The lips of the wise ones *k*
15:27 hater of gifts . . . *k* living
19:19 *k* doing it again and again
22:18 should *k* them in your belly
24:2 their own lips *k* speaking
29:4 king makes a land *k* standing
29:10 *k* seeking for the soul of
Ec 2:10 I did not *k* away from them
3:5 time to *k* away from embracing
3:6 time to *k* and a time to throw
3:7 a time to *k* quiet and a time
4:11 but how can just one *k* warm?
8:2 *K* the very order of the king
8:17 *k* working hard to seek, yet
10:6 the rich ones themselves *k*
10:16 princes *k* eating even in the
12:13 God and *k* his commandments
Ca 1:6 my vineyard . . . I did not *k*
4:11 honey your lips *k* dripping
Isa 1:12 *k* coming in to see my face
5:6 *k* from precipitating any rain
7:4 *k* undisturbed. Do not be
8:12 people *k* saying, A conspiracy!
8:17 *k* in expectation of Jehovah
8:20 *k* saying what is according
10:4 people *k* falling under those
10:16 *k* sending upon his fat ones
10:16 will *k* burning away like
15:4 Moab themselves *k* shouting
15:7 *k* carrying them away right
18:4 *k* undisturbed and look upon
26:9 *k* looking for you; because
28:28 incessantly *k* treading it
30:18 will *k* in expectation of
34:10 its smoke will *k* ascending
36:21 *k* silent and did not answer
38:12 you *k* handing me over
38:13 you *k* handing me over
38:14 the bulbul, so I *k* chirping
38:14 I *k* cooing like the dove
38:15 I *k* walking solemnly all
38:16 that account they *k* living
41:10 really *k* fast hold of you
42:1 on whom I *k* fast hold
42:4 islands . . . will *k* waiting
42:20 but you did not *k* watching
42:20 but you did not *k* listening
43:6 to the south, Do not *k* back
44:15 for man to *k* a fire burning
46:4 I myself shall *k* bearing up
47:10 you *k* saying in your heart
48:13 may *k* standing together
52:8 In unison they *k* crying out
Isa 52:11 *k* yourselves clean, you who
55:2 people *k* paying out money
55:3 and your soul will *k* alive
56:1 said: *K* justice, you people
56:4 eunuchs that *k* my sabbaths
57:4 you *k* opening wide the mouth
57:4 *k* sticking out the tongue
57:20 *k* tossing up seaweed and
58:4 *k* fasting as in the day for
59:2 to *k* from hearing
59:7 own feet *k* running to sheer
59:9 We *k* hoping for light, but
59:10 We *k* groping for the wall
59:10 *k* groping. We have stumbled
59:11 We *k* groaning, all of us
59:11 we mournfully *k* cooing
60:4 your own sons *k* coming, and
60:9 will *k* hoping, the ships of
62:1 Zion I shall not *k* still
62:6 let them not *k* still
63:17 *k* making us wander from
64:5 *k* remembering you in your
65:5 saying, *K* close to yourself
65:6 I shall not *k* still, but I
66:13 *k* comforting you people
66:22 you people will *k* standing
Jer 1:16 they *k* making sacrificial
2:29 people *k* contending against
3:2 you *k* polluting the land with
3:5 *k* watching something forever
4:3 do not *k* sowing among thorns
4:19 I cannot *k* silent, for the
4:21 shall I *k* seeing the signal
4:21 *k* hearing the sound of the
4:30 *k* seeking for your very soul
5:7 they *k* swearing by what is no
5:12 they *k* saying, He is not
5:23 *k* walking in their course
5:26 They *k* peering, as when
6:4 shadows of evening *k*
7:3 *k* you people residing in this
7:7 *k* you residing in this place
9:5 *k* trifling each one with his
10:25 they *k* at exterminating him
12:2 They *k* going ahead; they
12:4 the land *k* withering away
13:10 *k* walking after other gods
13:14 *k* from bringing them to
13:25 you *k* putting your trust in
14:17 and let them not *k* still
15:6 is the way you *k* walking
16:11 my law they did not *k*
17:4 it will *k* kindled
21:9 will *k* living, and his soul
23:13 they *k* making my people
23:27 *k* relating each one to the
23:35 This is what you *k* saying
23:38 is what you *k* on saying
27:12 his people and *k* on living
27:17 of Babylon and *k* on living
29:23 they *k* committing adultery
29:23 *k* speaking falsely in my
30:14 for whom they *k* searching
31:10 *k* him as a shepherd does
31:28 *k* alert toward them to
32:5 men *k* warring against the
33:24 *k* treating with disrespect
35:7 *k* living many days upon the
35:8 *k* obeying the voice of
35:10 *k* dwelling in tents and
35:15 *k* dwelling on the ground
38:2 one that will *k* living and
38:17 certainly *k* living and this
38:17 will certainly *k* living
39:12 *k* your own eyes set upon
40:4 I shall *k* my eye upon you
42:10 *k* dwelling in this land
43:4 *k* on dwelling in the land of
45:5 *k* seeking great things for
45:5 Do not *k* on seeking
46:16 *k* saying one to the other
47:5 *k* making cuts upon yourself
47:6 Take your repose and *k* silent
48:2 Madmen, should *k* silent
49:23 not able to *k* undisturbed
50:5 they will *k* asking the way
50:38 visions they *k* acting crazy
51:7 the nations *k* acting crazed
51:50 from the sword, *k* going
La 1:6 they *k* walking without power
2:10 earth, where they *k* silence
2:18 pupil of your eye not *k* quiet
2:20 the women *k* eating their own
3:18 I *k* saying: My excellency has
La 3:28 sit solitary and *k* silent
3:31 will Jehovah *k* on casting off
3:43 and you *k* pursuing us
3:49 will not *k* still, so that
4:17 eyes *k* pining away in vain
Eze 3:21 without fail *k* on living
7:17 hands, they *k* dropping down
7:17 they *k* dripping with water
11:20 *k* my own judicial decisions
13:23 will not *k* on visioning
16:6 *K* living! yes, to say to you
16:6 to say to you . . . *K* living!
18:9 He will positively *k* living
18:13 will not *k* living
18:17 He will positively *k* living
18:19 He will positively *k* living
18:21 actually *k* all my statutes
18:21 he will positively *k* living
18:22 he will *k* living
18:23 and actually *k* living
18:28 he will positively *k* living
18:32 a turning back and *k* living
20:11 might also *k* living by them
20:13 should the man *k* doing, he
20:13 will also *k* living by them
20:17 *k* me from bringing them to
20:18 judgments do not you *k*
20:19 *k* my own judicial decisions
20:21 decisions they did not *k*
20:21 should the man *k* doing, he
20:21 will also *k* living by them
20:25 they could not *k* living
22:12 *k* making gain of your
22:14 Will your heart *k* enduring
22:25 things they *k* taking
22:26 *k* profaning my holy places
23:43 *k* on committing her
28:2 and you *k* saying, I am a god
28:2 you *k* making your heart like
28:4 you *k* getting gold and silver
33:10 shall we *k* living
33:12 *k* living because of it in
33:13 will positively *k* living
33:15 he will positively *k* living
33:16 He will positively *k* living
33:19 he himself will *k* living
33:25 With the blood you *k* eating
33:25 eyes you *k* lifting to your
33:25 blood you *k* pouring out
36:27 decisions you will *k*
37:24 my statutes they will *k*
39:14 they will *k* making search
44:7 *k* breaking my covenant
44:24 festal seasons they should *k*
Da 5:10 king, *k* living even to times
8:26 *k* secret the vision, because
9:27 *k* the covenant in force for
11:15 be no power to *k* standing
11:27 is what they will *k* speaking
11:42 *k* thrusting out his hand
Ho 4:6 *k* forgetting the law of your
4:8 sin . . . they *k* devouring
4:8 they *k* lifting up their soul
4:12 my own people *k* inquiring
8:2 To me they *k* crying, O my God
8:7 it is wind that they *k* sowing
8:10 they *k* hiring them among the
13:7 by the way I shall *k* looking
14:8 and I shall *k* looking on him
Joe 1:20 *k* longing for you, because
2:4 is the way they *k* running
2:5 they *k* skipping about, as
2:8 they *k* going; and should some
2:20 stench . . . will *k* ascending
Am 2:4 did not *k* his own regulations
5:4 Search for me, and *k* living
5:6 for Jehovah, and *k* living
5:11 grain you *k* taking from him
5:11 will not *k* dwelling in them
5:11 will not *k* drinking the wine
5:13 will in that time *k* silent
5:14 that you people may *k* living
6:10 will have to say, *K* silence!
8:12 *k* roving about while
Ob 16 nations will *k* drinking
Mic 3:11 upon Jehovah they *k*
4:9 that you *k* shouting loudly
5:4 will certainly *k* dwelling
7:7 that I shall *k* on the lookout
Na 2:4 war chariots *k* driving madly
2:4 They *k* rushing up and down
2:4 the lightnings they *k* running
3:3 *k* stumbling among their dead
Hab 1:3 *k* looking upon mere trouble

Hab 1:13 you *k* silent when someone
2:1 At my guard post I will *k*
2:1 *k* myself stationed upon the
2:1 *k* watch, to see what he will
2:3 should delay, *k* in expectation
2:4 faithfulness he will *k* living
2:20 *K* silence before him, all
Zep 1:7 *K* silence before the Sovereign
2:14 A voice will *k* singing in
3:8 *k* yourselves in expectation
Zec 2:13 *K* silence, all flesh, before
3:7 my obligation that you will *k*
3:7 and also *k* my courtyards
6:7 and *k* seeking where to go
7:12 to *k* from obeying the law
10:2 are what they *k* speaking
11:9 I shall not *k* shepherding you
Mal 2:7 ones that should *k* knowledge
3:15 and *k* getting away
Mt 6:33 *K* on, then, seeking first the
7:7 *K* on asking, and it will be
7:7 *k* on seeking, and you will
7:7 *k* on knocking, and it will be
8:22 *K* following me, and let the
15:9 vain that they *k* worshiping
16:6 *K* your eyes open and watch
20:31 told them to *k* silent
24:20 *K* praying that your flight
24:42 *K* on the watch, therefore
25:13 *K* on the watch, therefore
26:38 and *k* on the watch with me
26:41 *K* on the watch and pray
Mr 7:7 in vain that they *k* worshiping
8:15 *K* your eyes open, look out
9:50 *k* peace between one another
13:18 *K* praying that it may not
13:33, 33 *K* looking, *k* awake, for you
13:34 doorkeeper to *k* on the watch
13:35 *k* on the watch, for you do
13:37 I say to all, *K* on the watch
14:34 Stay here and *k* on the watch
14:37 to *k* on the watch one hour
14:38 *k* on the watch and praying
Lu 1:47 my spirit cannot *k* from being
6:37 *K* on releasing, and you will
8:39 *k* on relating what things God
10:11 *k* this in mind, that the
10:28 *k* on doing this and you will
11:9 *K* on asking, and it will be
11:9 *k* on seeking, and you will
11:9 *k* on knocking, and it will be
12:15 *K* your eyes open and guard
12:40 *k* ready, because at an hour
12:42 to *k* giving them their
13:7 should it *k* the ground useless
17:33 seeks to *k* his soul safe for
18:5 not *k* coming and pummeling
18:39 tell him sternly to *k* quiet
21:36 *K* awake, then, all the time
22:19 *K* doing this in remembrance
Joh 4:15 nor *k* coming over to this
5:17 until now, and I *k* working
10:24 to *k* our souls in suspense
12:7 *k* this observance in view
12:47 sayings and does not *k* them
15:8 you *k* bearing much fruit
15:16 and *k* bearing fruit and that
Ac 1:4 *k* waiting for what the Father
4:29 *k* speaking your word with
5:20 *k* on speaking to the people
5:28 *k* teaching upon the basis of
12:8 on and *k* following me
15:29 to *k* abstaining from things
15:29 *k* yourselves from these
16:23 jailer to *k* them securely
18:9 but *k* on speaking and do not
18:9 speaking and do not *k* silent
19:36 becoming for you to *k* calm
20:31 *k* awake, and bear in mind
21:25 *k* themselves from what is
26:14 To *k* kicking against the
27:15 *k* its head against the wind
28:4 permit him to *k* on living
Ro 1:32 not only *k* on doing them but
6:2 *k* on living any longer in it
6:16 *k* presenting yourselves to
8:25 we *k* on waiting for it with
12:14 *K* on blessing those who
12:21 *k* conquering the evil with
13:3 *K* doing good, and you will
16:17 *k* your eye on those who cause
1Co 3:10 let each one *k* watching how
5:8 let us *k* the festival, not
7:5 that Satan may not *k* tempting
1Co 7:37 to *k* his own virginity, he
8:9 But *k* watching that this
10:24 Let each one *k* seeking, not
10:25 *k* eating, making no inquiry
10:32 *K* from becoming causes for
11:24 *K* doing this in remembrance
11:25 *K* doing this, as often as
11:26 you *k* proclaiming the death
12:31 But *k* zealously seeking the
13:5 not *k* account of the injury
14:1 *k* zealously seeking the
14:28 *k* silent in the congregation
14:30 let the first one *k* silent
14:34 let the women *k* silent in
14:39 *k* zealously seeking the
16:16 *k* submitting yourselves to
2Co 4:18 *k* our eyes, not on the
5:11 we *k* persuading men, but
11:9 and will *k* myself so
11:15 *k* transforming themselves
12:7 of Satan, to *k* slapping me
13:5 *K* testing whether you are in
13:5 *k* proving what you
Ga 2:10 we should *k* the poor in mind
5:15 you *k* on biting and devouring
5:16 *K* walking by spirit and you
6:1 *k* an eye on yourself, for fear
6:13 circumcised *k* the Law
Eph 2:11 *k* bearing in mind that
5:10 *K* on making sure of what is
5:15 *k* strict watch that how you
5:18 *k* getting filled with spirit
6:9 masters, *k* doing the same
6:18 *k* awake with all constancy
Php 1:18 I will also *k* on rejoicing
2:5 *K* this mental attitude in you
2:12 *K* working out your own
2:14 *K* doing all things free from
2:29 *k* holding men of that sort
3:17 *k* your eye on those who are
4:3 *k* assisting these women who
Col 3:2 *K* your minds fixed on the
3:16 *K* on teaching and
3:19 *k* on loving your wives and
4:1 *k* dealing out what is
4:17 *K* watching the ministry
1Th 1:9 *k* reporting about the way we
4:1 *k* on doing it more fully
4:18 *k* comforting one another
5:6 stay awake and *k* our senses
5:8 let us *k* our senses and have
5:11 *k* comforting one another and
2Th 3:1 word . . . *k* moving speedily
3:3 and *k* you from the wicked one
3:14 *k* this one marked, stop
1Ti 4:11 *K* on giving these commands
5:4 *k* paying a due compensation
5:7 So *k* on giving these commands
5:21 to *k* these things without
6:1 *k* on considering their owners
6:2 *K* on teaching these things
2Ti 1:13 *K* holding the pattern of
2:1 *k* on acquiring power in the
2:14 *K* reminding them of these
4:5 *k* your senses in all things
Tit 1:11 men *k* on subverting entire
1:13 *k* on reproving them with
2:1 *k* on speaking what things are
2:6 *k* on exhorting the younger
2:15 *K* on speaking these things
3:8 *k* their minds on maintaining
Phm 5 *k* hearing of your love and
13 might *k* on ministering to me
18 *k* this charged to my account
Heb 2:6 man that you *k* him in mind
3:13 *k* on exhorting one another
10:32 *k* on remembering the
12:13 *k* making straight paths for
13:3 *K* in mind those in prison
Jas 1:5 let him *k* on asking God, for
1:6 him *k* on asking in faith
1:27 *k* oneself without spot from
2:3 You *k* standing, or: Take that
2:12 *K* on speaking in such a way
2:12 *k* on doing in such a way as
2:16 *k* warm and well fed, but you
5:4 *k* crying out, and the calls
1Pe 1:13 *k* your senses completely
2:11 *k* abstaining from fleshly
3:6 provided you *k* on doing good
4:16 *k* on glorifying God in this
4:19 *k* on commending their souls
5:8 *K* your senses, be watchful
2Pe 1:10 you *k* on doing these things
Jude 6 angels that did not *k* their
21 *k* yourselves in God's love
Re 2:10 Devil will *k* on throwing
2:13 *k* on holding fast my name
3:10 *k* you from the hour of test
3:11 *K* on holding fast what you
6:16 *k* saying to the mountains and
7:10 they *k* on crying with a loud
14:4 *k* following the Lamb no
22:17 and the bride *k* on saying

Keeper
1Sa 17:22 care of the *k* of the baggage
Ne 2:8 to Asaph the *k* of the park
3:29 the *k* of the East Gate
Ca 1:6 me the *k* of the vineyards
Ac 19:35 is the temple *k* of the great

Keeper's
1Sa 17:20 the sheep to the *k* charge

Keepers
Nu 31:30 the *k* of the obligation of
31:47 the *k* of the obligation of
Jg 2:22 be *k* of Jehovah's way by
1Ch 9:19 the *k* of the entryway
Ec 12:3 the *k* of the house tremble
Ca 8:11 the vineyard over to the *k*

Keeping
Ge 18:17 Am I *k* covered from Abraham
24:21 *k* silent to know whether
47:30 shall do in *k* with your word
Ex 9:2 you are still *k* hold of them
Le 26:3 *k* my commandments and you
Nu 6:6 *k* separate to Jehovah he may
De 5:12 *K* the sabbath day to hold it
7:8 his *k* the sworn statement that
7:9 *k* covenant and loving-kindness
13:18 by *k* all his commandments
28:45 by *k* his commandments and
Jos 22:5 by *k* his commandments and
Jg 6:37 here I am *k* a fleece of wool
8:4 tired but *k* up the pursuit
2Sa 11:16 Joab was *k* guard over the
22:27 the one *k* clean you will
1Ki 2:3 by *k* his statutes, his
3:6 *k* toward him this great
3:14 *k* my regulations and my
8:5 those *k* their appointment
8:23 *k* the covenant and the
8:61 *k* his commandments as at
11:38 by *k* my statutes and my
15:4 and *k* Jerusalem in existence
18:42 *k* his face put between his
2Ki 9:14 be *k* guard at Ramoth-gilead
11:5 and *k* strict watch over the
18:6 *k* his commandments that
1Ch 12:8 *k* the large shield and the
12:29 *k* strict watch of the house
2Ch 2:18 for *k* the people in service
5:6 *k* their appointment with him
6:14 *k* the covenant and the
13:11 *k* the obligation to Jehovah
Ne 1:5 *k* the covenant and
1:5 and *k* his commandments
9:32 *k* the covenant and
11:19 were *k* guard in the gates
12:25 were *k* guard as gatekeepers
13:22 *k* guard of the gates to
Ps 18:26 the one *k* clean you will
19:11 In the *k* of them there is a
37:32 wicked one is *k* on the watch
50:23 as for the one *k* a set way
71:10 ones *k* watch for my soul
73:27 *k* away from you will perish
103:18 Toward those *k* his covenant
119:9 *k* on guard according to your
119:63 And of those *k* your orders
146:6 One *k* trueness to time
Pr 3:18 those *k* fast hold of it are
8:34 *k* awake at my doors day by
10:19 one *k* his lips in check is
11:15 handshaking is *k* carefree
11:24 *k* back from what is right
13:3 his mouth is *k* his soul
13:18 the one *k* a reproof is the
15:3 *k* watch upon the bad ones and
16:17 his way is *k* his soul
17:28 foolish, when *k* silent, will
19:16 that is *k* the commandment
19:16 commandment is *k* his soul
21:23 He that is *k* his mouth and
21:23 *k* his soul from distresses
25:2 is the *k* of a matter secret
28:4 *k* the law excite themselves

Pr 29:18 are they that are *k* the law
Ec 8:5 He that is *k* the commandment
Ca 8:12 to those *k* its fruitage
Isa 26:2 *k* faithful conduct may enter
29:20 *k* alert to do harm must be
30:15 in *k* undisturbed and in
30:18 those *k* in expectation of
40:16 for *k* a fire burning, and
45:15 a God *k* yourself concealed
56:2 *k* the sabbath in order not
56:2 *k* his hand in order not to
56:6 *k* the sabbath in order not to
57:11 *k* silent and hiding matters
64:12 continue *k* yourself in check
66:10 *k* yourselves in mourning
Jer 1:12 I am *k* awake concerning my
5:6 a leopard is *k* awake at their
34:17 *k* on proclaiming liberty
35:18 *k* all his commandments and
44:27 *k* alert toward them for
48:11 *k* undisturbed on their
Eze 16:49 *k* undisturbed were what
17:14 by *k* his covenant it might
Da 9:4 *k* the covenant and the
9:4 to those *k* his commandments
12:12 one who is *k* in expectation
Ho 12:6 *k* loving-kindness and justice
Mal 2:9 you were not *k* my ways, but
Mr 6:20 Herod . . . was *k* him safe
Lu 2:8 *k* watches in the night over
11:28 the word of God and *k* it
Ac 12:6 guards . . . were *k* the prison
21:24 you yourself also *k* the Law
Ro 1:24 God, in *k* with the desires
Ga 5:7 from *k* on obeying the truth
Php 2:4 *k* an eye, not in personal
2:16 *k* a tight grip on the word
2Ti 2:24 *k* himself restrained under
Heb 9:9 in *k* with it both gifts and
13:17 *k* watch over your souls as
2Pe 3:12 *k* close in mind the presence
Re 3:3 and go on *k* it, and repent

Keeps
Ge 21:12 that Sarah *k* saying to you be
31:15 he *k* eating continually even
Nu 24:7 Water *k* trickling from his
30:7 hears it and *k* silent toward
30:14 husband absolutely *k* silent
2Sa 22:34 he *k* me standing
1Ki 2:24 *k* me seated upon the throne
2Ki 17:26 he *k* sending lions among
Job 9:18 *k* glutting me with bitter
16:14 He *k* breaking through me
17:9 righteous one *k* holding fast
17:9 *k* increasing in strength
18:9 A snare *k* hold upon him
19:11 And he *k* reckoning me as an
20:13 if he *k* holding it back in
33:18 He *k* his soul back from the
36:25 man himself *k* looking from
39:14 in the dust she *k* them
Ps 3:5 Jehovah himself *k* supporting
10:9 He *k* lying in wait in the
10:9 He *k* lying in wait to carry
18:33 high for me he *k* me standing
24:2 he *k* it firmly established
36:4 he *k* scheming upon his bed
56:1 all day long, he *k* oppressing
63:8 your right hand *k* fast hold
77:7 Jehovah *k* casting off
80:13 *k* eating it away
88:13 prayer *k* confronting you
103:5 youth *k* renewing itself just
109:19 girdle that he *k* girded
147:14 wheat he *k* satisfying you
148:6 *k* them standing forever
Pr 1:20 True wisdom itself *k* crying
1:20 *k* giving forth its voice
6:14 He *k* sending out merely
8:3 entrances it *k* crying loudly
11:12 is one that *k* silent
16:28 *k* sending forth contention
17:9 that *k* talking about a matter
17:11 what the bad one *k* seeking
22:5 guarding his soul *k* far away
24:2 what their heart *k* meditating
26:14 door *k* turning upon its pivot
29:11 wise *k* it calm to the last
Ec 3:15 true God himself *k* seeking
5:16 *k* working hard for the wind
7:20 *k* doing good and does not sin
Isa 38:13 he *k* breaking all my bones
44:12 *k* busy at it with his
Isa 44:13 compass he *k* tracing it out
44:14 rain itself *k* making it get
64:4 one that *k* in expectation of
66:13 own mother *k* comforting
Jer 3:25 humiliation *k* covering us
4:31 who *k* gasping for breath
4:31 *k* spreading out her palms
5:6 a wolf . . . *k* despoiling them
6:7 a cistern *k* its waters cool
9:8 what a person *k* speaking
La 2:3 *k* burning like a flaming fire
3:25 soul that *k* seeking for him
3:48 water my eye *k* running down
Eze 18:14 *k* seeing all the sins of his
18:19 statutes . . . he *k* doing
18:24 he *k* doing and he is living
20:11 man who *k* doing them might
33:11 and actually *k* living
Ho 4:12 own hand staff *k* telling
10:1 Fruit he *k* putting forth for
12:8 Ephraim *k* saying, Indeed, I
Am 1:11 anger *k* tearing away forever
Hab 2:3 it *k* panting on to the end
2:5 he *k* gathering to himself all
Mal 1:4 Edom *k* saying, We have been
Mt 5:28 *k* on looking at a woman so
12:39 *k* on seeking for a sign, but
15:23 she *k* crying out after us
16:4 *k* on seeking for a sign, but
Ro 2:26 *k* the righteous requirements
8:22 creation *k* on groaning
2Co 11:14 for Satan himself *k*
2Ti 2:21 *K* clear of the latter ones
Jas 1:12 that *k* on enduring trial
4:5 that the spirit . . . *k* longing
5:7 the farmer *k* waiting for the
Re 9:6 death *k* fleeing from them
16:15 and *k* his outer garments
18:7 in her heart she *k* saying

Kehelathah
Nu 33:22 and went camping in *K*
33:23 pulled away from *K* and went

Keilah
Jos 15:44 *K* and Achzib and Mareshah
1Sa 23:1 are warring against *K*
23:2 Go . . . and save *K*
23:3 to *K* against the battle lines
23:4 go down to *K*, because I am
23:5 to *K* and fought against the
23:5 of the inhabitants of *K*
23:6 ran away to David at *K*
23:7 David had come to *K*
23:8 to *K*, to besiege David and
23:10 to *K* to lay the city in ruin
23:11 landowners of *K* surrender
23:12 landowners of *K* surrender
23:13 they went out of *K* and
23:13 David had escaped from *K*
1Ch 4:19 father of *K* the Garmite and
Ne 3:17 half the district of *K*, did
3:18 half the district of *K*

Kelaiah
Ezr 10:23 and *K* (that is, Kelita)

Kelita
Ezr 10:23 and Kelaiah (that is, *K*)
Ne 8:7 *K*, Azariah, Jozabad, Hanan
10:10 *K*, Pelaiah, Hanan

Kemuel
Ge 22:21 and *K* the father of Aram
Nu 34:24 of Ephraim a chieftain, *K*
1Ch 27:17 Hashabiah the son of *K*; of

Kenan
Ge 5:9 Enosh . . . became father to *K*
5:10 after his fathering *K* Enosh
5:12 *K* lived on for seventy years
5:13 his fathering Mahalalel *K*
5:14 all the days of *K* amounted
1Ch 1:2 *K*, Mahalalel, Jared

Kenath
Nu 32:42 marched and went capturing *K*
1Ch 2:23 *K* and its dependent towns

Kenaz
Ge 36:11 sons of Eliphaz . . . *K*
36:15 sons of Eliphaz . . . sheik *K*
36:42 sheik *K*, sheik Teman, sheik
Jos 15:17 Othniel the son of *K*
Jg 1:13 And Othniel the son of *K*
3:9 Othniel the son of *K*, the
3:11 Othniel the son of *K* died
1Ch 1:36 sons of Eliphaz . . . *K* and
1Ch 1:53 sheik *K*, sheik Teman
4:13 the sons of *K* were Othniel
4:15 and the sons of Elah, *K*

Kenite
Jg 1:16 And the sons of the *K*, whose
4:11 Heber the *K* had separated
4:17 Jael the wife of Heber the *K*
4:17 the household of Heber the *K*
5:24 the wife of Heber the *K* will

Kenites
Ge 15:19 the *K* and the Kenizzites and
Nu 24:21 When he got to see the *K*, he
Jg 4:11 had separated from the *K*
1Sa 15:6 Meanwhile Saul said to the *K*
15:6 *K* departed from . . . Amalek
27:10 upon the south of the *K*
30:29 in the cities of the *K*
1Ch 2:55 *K* that came from Hammath

Kenizzite
Nu 32:12 son of Jephunneh the *K* and
Jos 14:6 Jephunneh the *K* said to him
14:14 Jephunneh the *K*

Kenizzites
Ge 15:19 the Kenites and the *K* and the

Kept
Ge 3:9 God *k* calling to the man
5:24 Enoch *k* walking with the true
7:15 they *k* going to Noah inside
7:17 the waters *k* increasing and
7:18 waters . . . *k* increasing
7:18 ark *k* going on the surface
7:23 with him in the ark *k* on
8:5 waters *k* on progressively
14:15 *k* in pursuit of them up to
15:11 Abram *k* driving them away
18:8 *k* standing by them under the
19:5 they *k* calling out to Lot and
19:14 he *k* on saying: Get up! Get
19:16 he *k* lingering, then in
19:29 God *k* Abraham in mind in
19:33 they *k* giving their father
21:8 child *k* growing and came to
21:9 Sarah *k* noticing the son of
21:20 he *k* growing and dwelling
24:20 *k* drawing for all his camels
25:21 Isaac *k* on entreating Jehovah
26:7 the men of the place *k* asking
27:41 Esau *k* saying in his heart
27:46 Rebekah *k* saying to Isaac
28:10 and *k* going to Haran
31:9 God *k* taking the herd of your
31:34 and she *k* sitting upon them
31:41 you *k* changing my wages
32:13 *k* lodging there on that night
34:3 *k* speaking persuasively to the
34:5 and Jacob *k* silent until they
37:17 Joseph *k* on after his
37:35 *k* rising up to comfort him
37:35 *k* refusing to take comfort
38:12 *k* the period of mourning
38:21 they *k* saying: No temple
39:4 Joseph *k* finding favor in his
39:5 Jehovah *k* blessing the house
39:16 she *k* his garment laid up
39:20 prisoners of the king were *k*
39:21 *k* extending loving-kindness
41:48 he *k* collecting all the
42:19 one of your brothers be *k*
43:31 *k* control of himself and
43:33 *k* looking at one another in
43:34 he *k* having portions carried
47:12 Joseph *k* supplying his father
47:14 Joseph *k* bringing the money
47:17 Joseph *k* giving them bread
47:17 *k* providing them with bread
48:17 his father *k* his right hand
48:19 But his father *k* refusing and
48:20 he *k* putting Ephraim before
49:23 the archers *k* harassing him
49:23 *k* harboring animosity
50:10 *k* up the mourning rites for
Ex 1:7 *k* on multiplying and growing
1:12 more they *k* spreading abroad
1:14 *k* making their life bitter
1:20 people *k* growing more
2:2 she *k* him concealed for three
2:23 their cry for help *k* going up
3:2 As he *k* looking, why, here the
4:24 *k* looking for a way to put
5:13 them to work *k* urging them
9:16 *k* you in existence, for the

Ex 9:23 *k* making it rain down hail
14:20 it *k* lighting up the night
14:25 he *k* taking wheels off their
14:28 And the waters *k* coming back
15:21 Miriam *k* responding to the
16:3 the sons of Israel *k* saying
16:23 something to be *k* until the
16:32 *k* throughout your generations
16:33 *k* throughout your generations
16:34 as something to be *k*
17:3 *k* murmuring against Moses
18:13 *k* standing before Moses from
19:18 smoke *k* ascending like the
20:21 the people *k* standing at a
35:22 *k* coming, the men along with
35:25 *k* bringing as yarn the blue
39:32 the sons of Israel *k* doing
Le 6:12 the altar will be *k* burning
6:13 *k* constantly burning on the
10:3 And Aaron *k* silent
Nu 9:19 Israel also *k* their obligation
9:23 *k* their obligation to Jehovah
11:32 and *k* gathering the quail
11:32 *k* spreading them extensively
12:2 *k* saying: Is it just by Moses
13:32 And they *k* on bringing forth
14:22 *k* testing me these ten times
14:24 *k* following wholly after me
16:48 *k* standing between the dead
17:10 to be *k* for a sign to the
19:9 *k* for the water for cleansing
21:5 people *k* speaking against God
21:6 they *k* biting the people, so
21:9 he then *k* alive
22:24 Jehovah's angel *k* standing in
22:25 she-ass *k* seeing Jehovah's
22:27 *k* beating the ass with his
30:11 has heard it and has *k* silent
30:14 he *k* silent toward her on
33:2 *k* recording the departure
33:8 and *k* marching a three-day
De 1:27 you *k* grumbling in your tents
1:46 So you *k* dwelling in Kadesh
3:3 we *k* striking him until he had
4:33 heard it, and *k* on living
6:22 Jehovah *k* putting signs and
9:9 I *k* dwelling in the mountain
9:25 I *k* prostrating myself before
29:5 I *k* guiding you forty years in
32:12 Jehovah alone *k* leading him
32:13 He *k* making him ride upon
32:13 *k* making him suck honey out
32:14 grape you *k* drinking as wine
32:16 they *k* offending him
33:9 For they *k* your saying, And
Jos 2:6 and she *k* them out of sight
2:22 *k* dwelling there three days
3:17 *k* standing immovable on dry
5:8 they *k* sitting in their place
7:6 *k* putting dust upon their
7:11 stolen and also *k* it secret
8:9 Joshua *k* lodging on that night
8:24 they *k* falling, all of them
10:13 the sun *k* motionless, and
10:13 And the sun *k* standing still
11:8 they *k* striking them until
15:18 she *k* inciting him to ask
22:2 you have *k* all that Moses
22:3 you have *k* the obligation of
23:5 the one who *k* pushing them
24:17 who *k* guarding us in all
Jg 1:14 she *k* inciting him to ask a
1:34 Amorites *k* pressing the sons
2:22 just as their fathers *k* it
3:4 they *k* serving as agents to
3:22 the handle *k* going in also
3:25 they *k* waiting until they
5:17 Gilead *k* to his residence on
5:17 landing places he *k* residing
5:28 and *k* watching for him, The
7:8 he *k* hold of the three hundred
7:21 they *k* standing each one in
7:22 the camp *k* up their flight as
7:25 *k* on pursuing Midian, and
9:22 *k* playing the prince over
9:40 slain *k* falling in numbers
11:2 Gilead's wife *k* bearing sons
11:3 And idle men *k* bringing
11:17 Israel *k* dwelling in Kadesh
11:38 she *k* going, she with her
13:24 and the boy *k* getting bigger
14:17 she *k* weeping over him the
16:2 they *k* quiet the whole night
16:3 Samson *k* lying till midnight
Jg 16:16 *k* urging him, his soul got
16:19 his power *k* departing from
16:23 they *k* saying: Our god has
18:23 they *k* crying out to the sons
18:26 sons of Dan *k* going on their
18:27 they *k* going toward Laish
18:31 they *k* the carved image of
19:7 father-in-law *k* begging him
19:8 And both of them *k* eating
19:14 *k* on their way, and the sun
19:22 they *k* saying to the old man
19:25 *k* on abusing her all night
20:36 *k* giving ground to Benjamin
20:45 and they *k* following closely
21:2 came to Bethel and *k* sitting
Ru 1:7 they *k* walking on the road to
1:10 *k* saying to her: No, but with
1:19 *k* saying: Is this Naomi?
2:7 *k* on her feet from that time
2:23 she *k* on dwelling with her
3:14 she *k* lying at his feet until
1Sa 1:23 *k* nursing her son until she
2:22 all that his sons *k* doing to
5:12 *k* ascending to the heavens
6:14 and *k* standing there, where
7:2 days *k* multiplying, so that
7:6 and *k* a fast on that day
7:11 *k* striking them down as far
7:14 *k* coming back to Israel from
7:15 Samuel *k* on judging Israel
8:8 they *k* leaving me and serving
10:14 we *k* on going to see, but
12:9 they *k* fighting against them
12:12 *k* saying to me, No, but a
13:13 have not *k* the commandment
14:13 Jonathan *k* going up on his
14:31 they *k* striking down the
15:11 he *k* crying out to Jehovah
17:16 Philistine *k* coming forward
17:48 rose and *k* coming and
17:52 Philistines *k* falling on the
18:7 *k* responding and saying
18:15 Saul *k* seeing that he was
19:23 he *k* on his way from there
21:4 *k* themselves from womankind
21:5 womankind has been *k* away
21:11 *k* responding with dances
21:13 *k* making cross marks on the
23:14 *k* dwelling in the
23:14 Saul *k* looking for him
23:18 David *k* dwelling in Horesh
24:5 David's heart *k* striking him
24:7 and *k* going on his way
25:39 *k* his servant back from
28:23 the woman *k* urging him
29:5 *k* responding in the dances
30:10 David *k* up the chase, he
30:21 *k* sitting by the torrent
30:22 *k* saying: For the reason
30:25 *k* it set as a regulation
31:1 *k* falling down slain in
31:2 Philistines *k* in close range
2Sa 2:13 *k* sitting, these on this side
2:23 *k* refusing to turn aside
2:25 *k* standing upon the top of
3:1 David *k* getting stronger
3:1 house of Saul *k* declining
3:6 the war . . . *k* up
3:16 husband *k* walking with her
5:18 *k* tramping about in the low
6:11 ark of Jehovah *k* dwelling at
6:11 Jehovah *k* blessing Obed-edom
8:14 *k* garrisons placed in Edom
8:14 Jehovah *k* saving David
8:15 David *k* reigning over all
11:12 Uriah *k* dwelling in
11:16 *k* Uriah put in the place
11:23 *k* pressing them right up
11:24 *k* shooting at your servants
12:21 you fasted and *k* weeping
12:22 I did fast and I *k* weeping
13:19 *k* her hands put upon her
13:20 *k* from association with
13:25 *k* urging him, he did not
15:6 Absalom *k* doing a thing like
15:6 *k* stealing the hearts of
15:12 the conspiracy *k* getting
16:13 David and his men *k* going
16:13 he *k* throwing stones while
17:20 they *k* on searching, and
17:22 they *k* crossing the Jordan
18:4 the king *k* standing at the
18:25 *k* coming, steadily getting
18:30 and *k* standing still
2Sa 20:3 *k* on supplying food to them
20:11 stood over him and *k* saying
21:21 And he *k* taunting Israel
22:5 men that *k* terrifying me
22:7 I *k* calling upon Jehovah
22:7 And to my God I *k* calling
22:8 they *k* shaking back and forth
22:9 fire itself . . . *k* devouring
22:15 he *k* sending out arrows
22:19 They *k* confronting me in
22:22 have *k* the ways of Jehovah
23:10 rose up and *k* striking down
23:10 his hand *k* cleaving to the
23:12 and *k* striking down the
24:16 angel *k* his hand thrust out
1Ki 1:4 *k* waiting upon him, and the
2:38 Shimei *k* dwelling in
3:22 *k* on speaking before the king
4:28 they *k* bringing to wherever
4:34 they *k* coming from all the
5:11 Solomon *k* giving Hiram year
5:13 Solomon *k* bringing up those
5:18 they *k* preparing the timbers
8:7 cherubs *k* the Ark and its
8:24 *k* toward your servant David
8:33 they *k* sinning against you
8:35 they *k* sinning against you
8:35 you *k* afflicting them
9:21 Solomon *k* levying them for
9:27 Hiram *k* sending in the fleet
10:26 *k* gathering more chariots
10:26 he *k* them stationed in the
11:10 not *k* that which Jehovah
11:11 have not *k* my covenant and
11:24 he *k* collecting men to his
11:34 he *k* my commandments and
12:19 Israelites *k* up their revolt
13:30 and they *k* wailing over him
14:8 who *k* my commandments and
14:23 *k* building for themselves
15:26 *k* doing what was bad in the
15:34 he *k* doing what was bad in
16:25 Omri *k* doing what was bad
17:6 torrent valley he *k* drinking
18:13 *k* some of the prophets of
18:13 *k* supplying them bread and
18:26 *k* calling upon the name
18:26 *k* limping around the altar
18:45 Ahab *k* riding and made his
19:8 he *k* going in the power of
20:21 *k* striking down the horses
20:38 he *k* himself disguised with
21:4 *k* his face turned, and he did
21:27 *k* lying down in sackcloth
22:35 battle *k* rising in intensity
22:35 *k* in a standing position in
22:35 blood . . . *k* pouring out
22:43 *k* walking in all the way of
22:44 *k* peaceful relations with
22:52 he *k* doing what was bad in
22:53 *k* offending Jehovah the God
2Ki 2:7 and *k* standing in view at a
2:17 they *k* urging him until he
2:17 they *k* looking for three days
2:23 *k* saying to him: Go up, you
2:25 *k* going from there to Mount
3:2 *k* on doing what was bad in
3:9 they *k* going their way around
4:15 and she *k* standing at the
4:18 And the child *k* on growing
4:19 he *k* saying to his father
4:20 he *k* sitting upon her knees
4:34 and *k* bent over him, and
5:16 accept it, but he *k* refusing
5:23 he *k* urging him and finally
6:10 he *k* away from there, not
7:7 they *k* fleeing for their soul
7:17 people *k* trampling him in
7:20 people *k* trampling him in
8:11 And he *k* a fixed look and
8:11 *k* it set to the point of
8:18 *k* doing what was bad in
8:22 Edom *k* up its revolt from
8:27 *k* doing what was bad in
10:16 they *k* him riding with
10:21 they *k* coming into the
10:25 *k* going as far as the city
10:27 *k* it set aside for privies
10:32 Hazael *k* striking them in
11:2 *k* him concealed from the
11:11 runners *k* standing each one
15:5 *k* dwelling in his house
16:4 he *k* sacrificing and making
16:6 entered Elath and *k* dwelling

2Ki 17:4 and *k* him bound in the house
17:6 *k* them dwelling in Halah and
17:8 *k* walking in the statutes of
17:9 *k* building themselves high
17:10 *k* setting up for themselves
17:11 *k* doing bad things to offend
17:13 Jehovah *k* warning Israel
17:14 *k* hardening their necks
17:16 And they *k* leaving all the
17:17 *k* selling themselves to do
17:20 *k* afflicting them and
18:6 he *k* sticking to Jehovah
18:12 *k* overstepping his covenant
18:36 people *k* silent and did not
21:9 Manasseh *k* seducing them to
21:10 Jehovah *k* speaking by means
21:21 he *k* walking in all the
23:3 king *k* standing by the pillar
24:2 *k* sending them against Judah
1Ch 6:32 they *k* attending upon their
7:22 his brothers *k* coming in to
10:1 *k* falling slain in Mount
10:2 *k* in close range of Saul and
10:13 that he had not *k* and also
11:14 and *k* striking down the
12:22 people *k* coming to David to
13:14 the ark of the true God *k*
13:14 *k* blessing the household of
14:9 *k* making raids in the low
16:17 statement he *k* standing as
16:20 they *k* walking about from
18:6 Jehovah *k* giving salvation to
18:13 And Jehovah *k* saving David
20:3 *k* them employed at sawing
20:7 And he *k* taunting Israel
2Ch 1:1 and *k* making him surpassingly
1:14 Solomon *k* gathering chariots
1:14 *k* them stationed in chariot
2:3 *k* sending him cedarwood to
6:13 and he *k* standing upon it
6:15 *k* toward your servant David
6:24 *k* sinning against you, and
6:26 they *k* sinning against you
6:26 because you *k* afflicting
8:8 Solomon *k* levying men for
9:25 *k* them stationed in the
10:19 Israelites *k* up their revolt
11:17 *k* strengthening the kingship
12:13 in Jerusalem and *k* reigning
13:7 *k* collecting themselves
13:17 slain of Israel *k* falling
13:19 Abijah *k* chasing after
14:13 *k* pursuing them as far as
15:6 *k* them in disorder with
17:5 Jehovah *k* the kingdom firmly
17:9 *k* going around through all
18:34 battle *k* rising in intensity
18:34 *k* in a standing position in
20:32 *k* walking in the way of his
21:10 Edom *k* up its revolt from
22:11 *k* him concealed because of
24:2 Jehoash *k* doing . . . right
24:10 *k* bringing and casting it
24:13 repair work *k* advancing by
24:19 *k* sending prophets among
24:19 *k* bearing witness against
26:4 *k* doing what was right in
26:21 *k* dwelling in a house
27:2 *k* doing what was right in
27:6 Jotham *k* strengthening
29:2 *k* doing what was right in
29:7 *k* the lamps extinguished
29:26 Levites *k* standing with the
29:30 they *k* bending down and
30:16 *k* standing at their place
30:24 priests *k* sanctifying
31:12 they *k* bringing in the
32:1 *k* thinking of making them
32:18 *k* calling with a loud voice
32:20 *k* praying over this and
32:30 *k* them directed straight
33:9 Manasseh *k* seducing Judah
33:10 Jehovah *k* speaking to
33:12 *k* humbling himself greatly
33:13 *k* praying to Him, so that
33:18 visionaries that *k* speaking
34:31 king *k* standing in his place
35:10 priests *k* standing at their
36:13 *k* stiffening his neck and
36:15 *k* sending against them by
36:21 lying desolated it *k* sabbath
Ezr 8:15 *k* encamped there three days
9:3 and I *k* sitting stunned
10:9 *k* sitting in the open place

Ne 1:7 not *k* the commandments and
1:9 and *k* my commandments and
2:15 *k* on ascending in the torrent
2:15 *k* on examining the wall
4:1 and he *k* deriding the Jews
4:6 we *k* building the wall
4:9 *k* a guard posted against them
4:11 our adversaries *k* saying
4:13 I *k* men posted at the lowest
4:13 *k* the people posted by
5:15 *k* taking from them for bread
6:4 I *k* replying to them with the
8:4 Ezra the copyist *k* standing
9:26 *k* casting your law behind
9:27 who *k* causing them distress
9:29 *k* giving a stubborn shoulder
9:30 *k* bearing witness against
12:42 *k* making themselves heard
Es 1:12 But Queen Vashti *k* refusing to
2:18 he *k* giving presents according
2:21 *k* seeking to lay hand on King
3:5 Haman *k* seeing that Mordecai
5:10 Haman *k* control of himself
7:4 I should have *k* silent
Job 2:13 *k* sitting with him on the
10:14 and you have *k* watching me
21:16 has *k* far from me
21:24 his bones is being *k* moist
21:32 a tomb a vigil will be *k*
22:18 counsel . . . *k* far from me
23:11 His way I have *k*, and I do
24:4 have *k* themselves hidden
29:6 *k* pouring out streams of oil
30:10 *k* themselves far from me
30:26 I *k* awaiting the light, but
30:28 I *k* crying for help
31:9 I *k* lying in wait at the
31:18 I *k* leading her
31:32 doors I *k* open to the path
32:5 his anger *k* getting hotter
32:11 I *k* giving ear to your
32:12 to you I *k* my attention
33:8 your words I *k* hearing
38:23 *k* back for the time of
42:11 there *k* coming to him all
Ps 2:1 *k* muttering an empty thing
18:4 men also *k* terrifying me
18:6 I *k* calling upon Jehovah
18:6 to my God I *k* crying for help
18:7 they *k* shaking back and forth
18:8 fire itself from his mouth *k*
18:14 he *k* sending out his arrows
18:18 They *k* confronting me in the
18:21 I have *k* the ways of Jehovah
22:4 *k* providing them with escape
30:3 You have *k* me alive, that I
30:8 To you, O Jehovah, I *k* calling
30:8 I *k* making entreaty for favor
32:3 When I *k* silent my bones
33:22 we have *k* waiting for you
37:36 I *k* seeking him, and he was
38:20 *k* resisting me in return for
39:2 I *k* quiet from what is good
39:3 During my sighing the fire *k*
39:9 I *k* speechless; I could not
44:6 in my bow that I *k* trusting
49:18 he *k* blessing his own soul
50:21 have done, and I *k* silent
56:2 My foes have *k* snapping
59:*super* they *k* watching the house
68:13 *k* lying between the camp ash
69:20 I *k* hoping for someone to
73:16 *k* considering so as to know
76:8 itself feared and *k* quiet
78:17 *k* sinning still more against
78:24 *k* raining upon them manna
78:28 *k* making them fall in the
78:39 *k* remembering that they
78:53 *k* leading them in security
78:57 *k* turning back and acting
78:58 *k* offending him with their
78:58 *k* inciting him to jealousy
78:62 *k* handing over his people
80:8 *k* driving out the nations
81:5 I did not know I *k* hearing
89:23 hating him I *k* dealing out
94:18 Jehovah, *k* sustaining me
95:10 *k* feeling a loathing toward
99:6 he himself *k* answering them
99:7 *k* his reminders and the
105:10 statement he *k* standing as
105:13 *k* walking about from nation
105:24 *k* making his people very
105:40 from heaven he *k* satisfying

Ps 105:44 *k* taking possession of the
106:25 *k* grumbling in their tents
106:36 they *k* serving their idols
106:38 *k* spilling innocent blood
106:39 And *k* having immoral
107:6 *k* crying out to Jehovah in
109:16 *k* pursuing the afflicted
109:17 *k* loving the malediction
116:3 and grief I *k* finding
118:10 that I *k* holding them off
118:11 that I *k* holding them off
118:12 that I *k* holding them off
119:4 orders To be carefully *k*
119:67 I have *k* your very saying
119:136 they have not *k* your law
119:158 not *k* your own saying
119:167 soul has *k* your reminders
119:168 I have *k* your orders and
127:1 that the guard has *k* awake
139:13 *k* me screened off in the
142:2 I *k* pouring out my concern
143:5 willingly *k* myself concerned
Pr 19:7 friends *k* away from him
Ec 5:13 riches being *k* for their grand
Isa 5:2 *k* hoping for it to produce
5:7 *k* hoping for judgment, but
6:2 two he *k* his face covered
6:2 two he *k* his feet covered
25:6 of wine *k* on the dregs, of
25:6 of wine *k* on the dregs
38:17 soul and *k* it from the pit
41:2 *k* giving them like dust to
41:3 Who *k* pursuing them
41:3 *k* peacefully passing along
41:5 drew near and *k* coming
41:28 *k* seeing, and there was not
41:28 *k* asking them, that they
42:14 *k* quiet for a long time
42:14 I *k* exercising self-control
42:22 they have been *k* hidden
42:25 He *k* pouring out upon him
42:25 *k* consuming him all around
42:25 *k* blazing up against him
44:2 *k* helping you even from the
47:7 you *k* saying: To time
47:10 *k* trusting in your badness
48:3 I *k* making them heard
48:5 I also *k* telling you from
48:6 even things *k* in reserve
48:8 you *k* dealing treacherously
49:8 I *k* safeguarding you that I
49:14 Zion *k* saying: Jehovah has
52:5 ruling over them *k* howling
57:9 and *k* making your ointments
57:17 he *k* walking as a renegade
58:2 I whom they *k* seeking, and
58:2 *k* asking me for righteous
58:3 that you *k* driving to work
59:3 tongue *k* muttering sheer
59:5 *k* weaving the mere cobweb
59:9 gloom we *k* walking
59:11 We *k* hoping for justice
59:14 *k* standing simply far off
60:11 be *k* open constantly
63:3 *k* treading them in my anger
63:3 *k* trampling them down in my
63:3 blood *k* spattering upon my
63:5 *k* looking, but there was no
63:6 *k* stamping down peoples in
64:5 we *k* sinning—in them a
65:12 *k* doing what was bad in my
66:4 *k* on doing what was bad in
Jer 1:3 it *k* on occurring in the days
2:5 *k* walking after the vain idol
2:16 *k* feeding on you at the
3:7 I *k* saying that she should
3:7 Judah *k* looking at her own
3:9 she *k* polluting the land and
5:7 And I *k* satisfying them, but
6:7 she has *k* her badness cool
6:16 they *k* saying: We are not
6:17 they *k* saying: We are not
6:19 law—they also *k* rejecting
6:29 *k* refining intensely simply
7:13 you *k* doing all these works
7:13 I *k* speaking to you, getting
7:13 I *k* calling you, but you did
7:25 I *k* sending to you all my
7:26 they *k* hardening their neck
8:6 attention, and I *k* listening
8:6 the way they *k* speaking
9:14 they *k* on walking after the
11:8 they *k* walking each one in
14:10 they have not *k* in check

Jer 16:11 *k* going after other gods
20:1 *k* listening to Jeremiah
23:2 and you *k* dispersing them
23:38 I *k* sending to you, saying
25:3 I *k* speaking to you people
26:9 all the people *k* congregating
26:20 he *k* prophesying against
31:28 *k* alert toward them to
32:33 *k* turning to me the back
35:15 *k* sending to you all my
35:17 *k* calling to them but they
36:18 *k* declaring to me all these
36:26 Jehovah *k* them concealed
37:14 Irijah *k* hold of Jeremiah
39:4 *k* going out by the way of
40:12 *k* coming into the land of
44:4 *k* sending to you all my
50:11 For you men *k* rejoicing
50:11 *k* exulting when pillaging
50:11 *k* pawing like a heifer in
50:11 *k* neighing like stallions
51:30 *k* sitting in the strong
52:7 *k* going by the way of the
La 1:14 *k* himself alert against my
2:4 *k* killing all those desirable
2:12 *k* saying: Where are grain and
2:14 *k* visioning for you worthless
2:15 and *k* wagging their head at
2:16 and *k* grinding the teeth
3:53 they *k* hurling stones at me
3:57 the day that I *k* calling you
Eze 1:15 *k* seeing the living creatures
3:15 I *k* dwelling there for seven
16:13 you *k* decking yourself with
16:28 *k* prostituting yourself
16:29 *k* making your prostitution
16:51 *k* making your detestable
18:9 in my statutes he *k* walking
18:9 my judicial decisions he *k*
18:19 statutes of mine he has *k*
19:4 nations *k* hearing about him
22:30 I *k* looking for a man from
23:5 and *k* lusting after those
23:8 *k* pouring out their immoral
23:14 *k* adding to her acts of
23:17 sons of Babylon *k* coming
23:19 *k* multiplying her acts of
23:20 *k* lusting in the style of
23:44 they *k* on coming in to her
24:19 the people *k* saying to me
25:6 *k* rejoicing with all scorn
25:12 *k* doing wrong extensively
25:15 *k* avenging themselves with
31:5 its boughs *k* multiplying
31:9 other trees . . . *k* envying it
32:2 *k* gushing in your rivers
32:2 *k* muddying the waters with
34:6 sheep *k* straying on all the
34:8 the shepherds *k* feeding
34:21 you *k* pushing and with
34:21 your horns you *k* shoving
35:5 *k* delivering the sons of
35:13 *k* acting in great style
36:17 *k* making it unclean with
39:23 *k* falling, all of them
39:24 I *k* concealing my face from
44:12 *k* ministering to them
Da 1:8 *k* requesting of the principal
1:16 guardian *k* on taking away
2:34 *k* on looking until a stone
6:14 *k* on striving to deliver him
7:4 I *k* on beholding until its
7:6 *k* on beholding, and, see there!
7:7 *k* on beholding in the visions
7:8 *k* on considering the horns
7:9 I *k* on beholding until there
7:10 thousands that *k* ministering
7:10 *k* standing right before him
7:11 *k* on beholding at that time
7:11 I *k* on beholding until the
7:13 *k* on beholding in the visions
7:21 I *k* on beholding when that
7:28 my own thoughts *k* frightening
7:28 matter . . . *k* in my own heart
8:4 no wild beasts *k* standing
8:5 *k* on considering, and, look!
8:6 *k* coming all the way to the
8:9 *k* getting very much greater
8:10 *k* getting greater all the way
8:12 *k* throwing truth to the earth
8:27 I *k* showing myself numbed on
9:14 Jehovah *k* alert to the
10:17 *k* standing in me no power
Ho 2:13 *k* making sacrificial smoke
Ho 2:13 *k* decking herself with her
2:13 *k* going after her passionate
6:1 He *k* striking, but he will
7:14 they *k* howling on their beds
7:14 they *k* loafing about
7:14 they *k* turning against me
7:15 they *k* scheming what was bad
8:13 they *k* sacrificing flesh
8:13 *k* eating what Jehovah himself
11:4 I *k* drawing them, with the
12:4 he *k* contending with an angel
12:10 I *k* making likenesses
12:12 Israel *k* serving for a wife
Joe 3:3 they *k* casting lots
Am 1:11 fury—he has *k* it perpetually
2:4 lies . . . *k* making them wander
2:10 I *k* making you walk through
2:11 I *k* raising up some of your
2:12 you *k* giving the Nazirites
4:10 I *k* making the stink of your
Jon 1:5 *k* hurling out the articles
1:7 they *k* casting lots, and
2:5 the watery deep itself *k*
3:4 he *k* proclaiming and saying
4:8 sun *k* striking upon the head
4:8 he *k* asking that his soul
Na 2:12 *k* his holes filled with prey
Hab 3:5 Before him pestilence *k* going
3:11 your own arrows *k* going
Zep 2:8 *k* putting on great airs
2:10 *k* putting on great airs
3:5 he *k* giving his own judicial
Hag 1:10 heavens *k* back their dew
1:10 earth itself *k* back its yield
1:11 *k* calling for dryness upon
Zec 7:11 *k* refusing to pay attention
7:11 *k* giving a stubborn shoulder
8:10 I *k* thrusting all mankind
Mal 2:5 I *k* giving them to him, with
3:7 regulations and have not *k*
3:14 have *k* the obligation to him
3:16 Jehovah *k* paying attention
Mt 9:21 she *k* saying to herself
19:20 I have *k* all these; what yet
21:9 *k* crying out: Save, we pray
21:11 crowds *k* telling: This is
24:43 he would have *k* awake and
26:5 *k* saying: Not at the festival
26:16 *k* seeking a good opportunity
26:58 Peter *k* following him at a
26:63 Jesus *k* silent. So the high
27:23 *k* crying out all the more
Mr 1:45 *k* coming to him from all
2:13 the crowd *k* coming to him
3:4 kill a soul? But they *k* silent
4:37 waves *k* dashing into the boat
5:28 she *k* saying: If I touch just
7:26 she *k* asking him to expel
9:20 he *k* rolling about, foaming
9:34 They *k* silent, for on the
10:20 I have *k* from my youth on
10:48 *k* shouting that much more
11:9 those coming behind *k* crying
11:17 he *k* teaching and saying
14:61 *k* silent and made no reply
Lu 1:22 he *k* making signs to them
1:24 *k* herself secluded for five
2:51 *k* all these sayings in her
4:37 *k* going out into every corner
7:36 *k* asking him to dine with
8:31 they *k* entreating him not to
8:38 *k* begging to continue with
9:36 they *k* quiet and did not
10:39 and *k* listening to his word
12:39 he would have *k* watching and
14:4 they *k* silent. With that he
15:1 *k* drawing near to him to hear
15:2 scribes *k* muttering, saying
18:3 she *k* going to him, saying
18:13 *k* beating his breast, saying
18:21 I have *k* from youth on
18:39 that much more he *k* shouting
19:20 mina . . . *k* laid away in a
19:36 *k* spreading their outer
19:48 *k* hanging onto him to hear
23:10 *k* standing up and vehemently
23:27 and of women who *k* beating
24:5 *k* their faces turned to the
24:16 eyes were *k* from recognizing
Joh 3:23 people *k* coming and being
5:17 My Father has *k* working
6:2 great crowd *k* following him
11:20 but Mary *k* sitting at home
12:17 crowd . . . *k* bearing witness
Joh 17:12 I have *k* them, and not one
19:12 Pilate *k* on seeking how to
20:11 *k* standing outside near the
Ac 2:40 and *k* exhorting them, saying
5:14 *k* on being added, multitudes
5:16 *k* coming together, bearing
6:7 disciples *k* multiplying in
7:53 by angels but have not *k* it
8:39 *k* going on his way rejoicing
8:40 *k* on declaring the good news
9:22 Saul *k* on acquiring power
9:31 it *k* on multiplying
12:5 Peter was being *k* in the
12:9 *k* following him, but he did
12:15 she *k* on strongly asserting
16:17 girl *k* following Paul and us
16:18 she *k* doing for many days
18:6 *k* on opposing and speaking
18:20 *k* requesting him to remain
19:11 And God *k* performing
19:20 word of Jehovah *k* growing
20:9 sleep while Paul *k* talking on
21:36 people *k* following, crying
22:2 they *k* all the more silent
22:22 they *k* listening to him down
23:35 he be *k* under guard in the
24:23 *k* and have some relaxation
25:4 Paul was to be *k* in Caesarea
25:19 Paul *k* asserting was alive
25:21 when Paul appealed to be *k*
25:21 *k* until I should send him
28:19 Jews *k* speaking against it
Ro 16:25 *k* in silence for long-lasting
1Co 3:6 but God *k* making it grow
6:9 men *k* for unnatural purposes
2Co 8:4 *k* begging us with much
11:9 I *k* myself unburdensome to
Ga 1:13 of excess I *k* on persecuting
1Th 2:11 we *k* exhorting each one of
1Ti 2:15 *k* safe through childbearing
5:25 otherwise cannot be *k* hid
Heb 11:15 *k* remembering that place
1Pe 1:11 They *k* on investigating what
2:23 *k* on committing himself to
2Pe 2:5 but *k* Noah, a preacher of
Re 3:8 you *k* my word and did not
3:10 *k* the word about my endurance
12:4 dragon *k* standing before the

Keren-happuch
Job 42:14 and the name of the third *K*

Kerioth
Jer 48:24 against *K* and against Bozrah
Am 2:2 the dwelling towers of *K*

Kerioth-hezron
Jos 15:25 *K*, that is to say, Hazor

Kernels
Le 25:5 growth from spilled *k* of your
25:11 from spilled *k* nor gather
2Ki 19:29 the growth from spilled *k*
Isa 37:30 growth from spilled *k*

Keros
Ezr 2:44 the sons of *K*
Ne 7:47 sons of *K*, the sons of Sia

Kesil
Job 9:9 the *K* constellation, And the
38:31 cords of the *K* constellation
Isa 13:10 their constellations of *K*
Am 5:8 the *K* constellation, and the

Kettle
Le 2:7 offering out of the deep-fat *k*
7:9 one made in the deep-fat *k* and

Keturah
Ge 25:1 a wife, and her name was *K*
25:4 All these were the sons of *K*
1Ch 1:32 *K*, Abraham's concubine
1:33 these were the sons of *K*

Key
Jg 3:25 they took the *k* and opened
1Ch 9:27 charge of the *k*, even to open
Isa 22:22 *k* of the house of David
Lu 11:52 took away the *k* of knowledge
Re 3:7 who has the *k* of David, who
9:1 *k* of the pit of the abyss was
20:1 *k* of the abyss and a great

Keyman
Zec 10:4 Out of him is the *k*, out of

Keymen
Jg 20:2 the *k* of all the people and

1Sa 14:38 all you *k* of the people, and
Isa 19:13 *k* of her tribes have caused

Keys
Mt 16:19 the *k* of the kingdom of the
Re 1:18 I have the *k* of death and

Keziah
Job 42:14 the name of the second *K*

Kibroth-hattaavah
Nu 11:34 place came to be called *K*
11:35 From *K* the people pulled
33:16 and went camping at *K*
33:17 Then they pulled away from *K*
De 9:22 at *K* you proved yourselves

Kibzaim
Jos 21:22 *K* and its pasture ground

Kicked
De 32:15 began to grow fat, then he *k*

Kicking
1Sa 2:29 men keep *k* at my sacrifice
Eze 16:6 *k* about in your blood, and I
16:22 *k* about in your blood you
Ac 26:14 *k* against the goads makes

Kid
Ge 38:17 shall send a *k* of the goats
38:20 Judah proceeded to send the *k*
38:23 I have sent this *k*, but you
Ex 23:19 not boil a *k* in its mother's
34:26 must not boil a *k* in its
Le 4:23 his offering a male *k* of the
4:28 a female *k* of the goats
5:6 or a female *k* of the goats
23:19 one *k* of the goats as a sin
Nu 7:16 *k* of the goats for a sin
7:22 one *k* of the goats for a sin
7:28 one *k* of the goats for a sin
7:34 one *k* of the goats for a sin
7:40 one *k* of the goats for a sin
7:46 one *k* of the goats for a sin
7:52 one *k* of the goats for a sin
7:58 one *k* of the goats for a sin
7:64 one *k* . . . for a sin offering
7:70 one *k* of the goats for a sin
7:76 one *k* . . . for a sin offering
7:82 one *k* . . . for a sin offering
15:24 and one *k* of the goats as a
28:15 one *k* of the goats should be
28:30 one *k* of the goats to make
29:5 one male *k* of the goats as a
29:11 *k* . . . as a sin offering
29:16 one *k* . . . as a sin offering
29:19 one *k* . . . as a sin offering
29:25 one *k* . . . as a sin offering
De 14:21 You must not boil a *k* in its
Jg 6:19 make ready a *k* of the goats
13:15 and fix up a *k* of the goats
13:19 take the *k* of the goats and
14:6 tears a male *k* in two, and
15:1 with a *k* of the goats
1Sa 16:20 and a *k* of the goats and
Isa 11:6 with the *k* the leopard
Lu 15:29 never once gave a *k* for me

Kidnapped
Ge 40:15 I was in fact *k* from the

Kidnapper
De 24:7 that *k* must also die. And you

Kidnappers
1Ti 1:10 *k*, liars, false swearers

Kidnapping
De 24:7 found *k* a soul of his brothers

Kidnaps
Ex 21:16 *k* a man and who . . . sells

Kidney
De 32:14 with the *k* fat of wheat; And

Kidneys
Ex 29:13 the two *k* and the fat that is
29:22 the two *k* and the fat that
Le 3:4 the two *k* and the fat that is
3:4 remove it along with the *k*
3:10 the two *k* and the fat that is
3:10 remove it along with the *k*
3:15 two *k* and the fat that is
3:15 remove it along with the *k*
4:9 two *k* and the fat that is upon
4:9 remove it along with the *k*
7:4 two *k* and the fat that is upon
7:4 remove it along with the *k*
8:16 the two *k* and their fat and
Le 8:25 the two *k* and their fat and
9:10 the *k* and the appendage of
9:19 the *k* and the appendage of the
Job 16:13 He splits open my *k* and
19:27 My *k* have failed deep
Ps 7:9 is testing out heart and *k*
16:7 my *k* have corrected me
26:2 Refine my *k* and my heart
73:21 my *k* I was sharply pained
139:13 yourself produced my *k*
Pr 23:16 my *k* will exult when your
Isa 34:6 the fat of the *k* of rams
Jer 11:20 examining the *k* and the
12:2 but far away from their *k*
17:10 examining the *k*, even to
20:12 seeing the *k* and the heart
La 3:13 He has brought into my *k* the
Re 2:23 who searches the *k* and hearts

Kidron
2Sa 15:23 by the torrent valley of *K*
1Ki 2:37 the torrent valley of *K*
15:13 the torrent valley of *K*
2Ki 23:4 on the terraces of *K*, and he
23:6 to the torrent valley of *K*
23:6 in the torrent valley of *K*
23:12 the torrent valley of *K*
2Ch 15:16 in the torrent valley of *K*
29:16 torrent valley of *K* outside
30:14 into the torrent valley of *K*
Jer 31:40 torrent valley of *K*, clear
Joh 18:1 winter torrent of *K* to where

Kids
Ge 27:9 get me from there two *k* of
27:16 skins of the *k* of the goats
Le 16:5 two male *k* of the goats for a
Nu 7:87 twelve *k* of the goats for a
1Sa 10:3 one carrying three *k* and one
2Ch 35:7 male lambs and male *k*
Ca 1:8 and pasture your *k* of the goats

Kill
Ge 4:8 assault Abel his brother and *k*
4:14 anyone finding me will *k* me
12:12 they will certainly *k* me
20:4 Jehovah, will you *k* a nation
20:11 *k* me because of my wife
22:10 knife to *k* his son
26:7 *k* me because of Rebekah
27:41 going to *k* Jacob my brother
27:42 in regard to you—to *k* you
34:25 to the city and to *k* every
37:20 come and let us *k* him and
Ex 2:14 Are you intending to *k* me
2:15 he attempted to *k* Moses
5:21 a sword in their hand to *k* us
13:15 *k* every firstborn in the land
22:24 *k* you with the sword, and
23:7 do not *k* the innocent and the
32:12 order to *k* . . . exterminate
32:27 *k* each one his brother and
Le 14:50 must *k* the one bird in an
20:15 and you should *k* the beast
20:16 *k* the woman and the beast
Nu 11:15 please *k* me off altogether
25:5 Each one of you *k* his men who
31:7 proceeded to *k* every male
31:17 now *k* every male among the
31:17 *k* every woman who has had
De 13:9 you should *k* him without fail
Jos 9:26 and they did not *k* them
Jg 7:25 to *k* Oreb on the rock of Oreb
8:17 to *k* the men of the city
8:19 I would not have to *k* you
8:20 *k* them. And the young men did
9:18 *k* his sons, seventy men, upon
9:24 his hands to *k* his brothers
16:2 we must also *k* him
1Sa 16:2 Saul . . . will certainly *k* me
24:10 someone said to *k* you but
24:11 I did not *k* you
24:18 and you did not *k* me
2Sa 10:18 David got to *k* of the
1Ki 2:32 to *k* them with the sword
12:27 *k* me and return to Rehoboam
18:12 he will be bound to *k* me
18:14 he will be bound to *k* me
2Ki 8:12 choice men you will *k* with
10:9 my lord, and I got to *k* him
2Ch 22:8 and he proceeded to *k* them
24:25 *k* him upon his own couch
36:17 *k* their young men with the
Ne 4:11 *k* them and put a stop to the
6:10 they are coming in to *k* you
Ne 6:10 they are coming in to *k* you
Es 3:13 *k* and to destroy all the Jews
8:11 *k* and destroy all the force of
9:15 *k* in Shushan three hundred
Job 5:2 foolish one vexation will *k*
20:16 tongue of a viper will *k*
Ps 10:8 he will *k* someone innocent
59:11 Do not *k* them, that my
94:6 and the alien resident they *k*
136:18 to *k* majestic kings
Pr 1:32 is what will *k* them, and
Ec 3:3 a time to *k* and a time to heal
Isa 27:1 *k* the sea monster that is in
Jer 15:3 the sword to *k*, and the dogs
Eze 9:6 and women you should *k* off
23:47 their daughters they will *k*
26:8 will *k* even with the sword
26:11 people he will *k* even with
Da 2:14 *k* the wise men of Babylon
Ho 6:5 to *k* them by the sayings of
Am 2:3 all her princes I shall *k* with
9:1 I shall *k* with the sword
9:4 sword, and it must *k* them
Hab 1:17 to *k* nations constantly
Zec 11:5 proceed to *k* them although
Mt 10:28 of those who *k* the body but
10:28 body but cannot *k* the soul
14:5 although he wanted to *k* him
17:23 will *k* him, and the third
21:38 is the heir; come, let us *k*
23:34 Some of them you will *k* and
24:9 to tribulation and will *k* you
26:4 to seize Jesus . . . and *k* him
Mr 3:4 to save or to *k* a soul
6:19 and was wanting to *k* him
9:31 they will *k* him, but
10:34 scourge him and *k* him, but
12:7 Come, let us *k* him, and the
14:1 by crafty device and *k* him
Lu 11:49 will *k* and persecute some of
12:4 those who *k* the body and
13:31 Herod wants to *k* you
18:33 *k* him, but on the third day
20:14 is the heir; let us *k* him
Joh 5:18 all the more to *k* him
7:1 Jews were seeking to *k* him
7:19 Why are you seeking to *k* me?
7:20 Who is seeking to *k* you?
7:25 man they are seeking to *k*
8:22 He will not *k* himself, will
8:37 but you are seeking to *k* me
8:40 now you are seeking to *k* me
11:53 they took counsel to *k* him
12:10 took counsel to *k* Lazarus
18:31 lawful for us to *k* anyone
Ac 21:31 they were seeking to *k* him
27:42 soldiers to *k* the prisoners
Re 2:23 her children I will *k* with
6:8 to *k* with a long sword and
9:5 granted the locusts, not to *k*
9:15 to *k* a third of the men
11:7 and conquer them and *k* them
13:10 *k* with the sword, he must

Killed
Ge 4:23 A man I have *k* for wounding
4:25 place of Abel, because Cain *k*
34:26 Shechem his son they *k* with
37:26 in case we *k* our brother and
49:6 in their anger they *k* men
Ex 2:14 just as you *k* the Egyptian
Le 14:5 the one bird must be *k* in an
14:6 blood of the bird that was *k*
14:51 blood of the bird that was *k*
Nu 22:29 for now I should have *k* you
22:33 even you I should have *k*, but
31:8 they *k* the kings of Midian
31:8 *k* Balaam the son of Beor with
31:19 Everyone who has *k* a soul
Jos 10:11 Israel *k* with the sword
13:22 whom the sons of Israel *k*
Jg 7:25 they *k* Zeeb at the wine vat
8:18 they whom you *k* in Tabor? To
8:21 Gideon got up and *k* Zebah and
9:5 and *k* his brothers, the sons of
9:24 because he *k* them, and upon
9:45 he *k* the people that were in
9:54 It was a woman that *k* him
1Sa 22:21 Saul has *k* the priests of
2Sa 3:30 *k* Abner over the fact that
4:10 *k* him in Ziklag when it
4:11 *k* a righteous man in his
4:12 *k* them and cut off their
12:9 *k* by the sword of the sons

2Sa 14:7 brother whom he *k*, and let
23:21 *k* him with his own spear
1Ki 2:5 *k* them and placed the blood
9:16 in the city he had *k*
11:24 when David *k* them
18:13 when Jezebel *k* the prophets
19:1 he had *k* all the prophets
19:10 your prophets they have *k*
19:14 your prophets they have *k*
2Ki 11:18 priest of Baal they *k* before
1Ch 7:21 *k* them because they came
11:23 *k* him with his own spear
2Ch 21:4 *k* all his brothers with the
21:13 own brothers . . . you have *k*
22:1 had *k* all the older ones
23:17 they *k* before the altars
24:22 so that he *k* his son, who
25:3 promptly *k* his servants
28:6 *k* in Judah a hundred and
28:7 *k* Maaseiah the son of the
Ne 9:26 and your own prophets they *k*
Es 7:4 be annihilated, *k* and destroyed
9:6 the Jews *k* and there was a
9:10 ten sons of Haman . . . they *k*
9:11 those *k* in Shushan the castle
9:12 the Jews have been *k*, and there
Ps 44:22 we have been *k* all day long
78:34 As often as he *k* them, they
135:10 And *k* potent kings
Pr 7:26 being *k* by her are numerous
Isa 10:4 under those who have been *k*
14:19 clothed with *k* men stabbed
14:20 you *k* your own people
14:30 over of you will be *k*
26:21 longer cover over her *k* ones
27:7 the slaughter of his *k* ones
27:7 does he have to be *k*?
Jer 18:21 those *k* with deadly plague
La 2:20 should priest and prophet be *k*?
2:21 *k* in the day of your anger
3:43 You have *k*; you have shown no
Eze 23:10 her they *k* even with sword
26:6 by the sword they will be *k*
37:9 blow upon these *k* people
Da 2:13 wise men were about to be *k*
2:13 for them to be *k*
3:22 ones that the fiery flame *k*
5:30 the Chaldean king was *k*
7:11 beast was *k* and its body was
Am 4:10 the sword I *k* your young men
Mt 16:21 be *k*, and on the third day
21:35 another they *k*, another they
21:39 out of the vineyard and *k*
22:6 treated them insolently and *k*
Mr 8:31 *k*, and rise three days later
9:31 despite being *k*, he will rise
12:5 that one they *k*; and many
12:5 and some of whom they *k*
12:8 they took him and *k* him, and
Lu 9:22 be *k*, and on the third day
11:47 but your forefathers *k* them
11:48 these *k* the prophets but you
20:15 outside the vineyard and *k*
Ac 3:15 you *k* the Chief Agent of life
7:52 they *k* those who made
23:12 until they had *k* Paul
23:14 of food until we have *k* Paul
Ro 7:11 and *k* me through it
11:3 they have *k* your prophets
Eph 2:16 *k* off the enmity by means of
1Th 2:15 who *k* even the Lord Jesus
Re 2:13 who was *k* by your side
6:11 who were about to be *k*
9:18 a third of the men were *k*
9:20 were not *k* by these plagues
11:5 in this manner he must be *k*
11:13 were *k* by the earthquake
13:10 he must be *k* with the sword
13:15 cause to be *k* all those who
19:21 *k* off with the long sword

Killer
1Sa 2:6 Jehovah is a *K* and a Preserver
2Ki 9:31 Zimri the *k* of his lord
Eze 21:11 give it into the hand of a *k*
Ho 9:13 his sons even to a *k*
Mt 23:37 Jerusalem, the *k* of the
Lu 13:34 Jerusalem, the *k* of the

Killers
2Ki 17:25 came to be *k* among them
Jer 4:31 my soul is tired of the *k*

Killing
Ge 4:15 anyone *k* Cain must suffer
Ex 4:23 *k* your son, your firstborn
21:14 of *k* him with craftiness
Jos 8:24 *k* of all the inhabitants of
Jg 9:56 by *k* his seventy brothers
20:5 was I that they figured on *k*
1Ch 19:18 David went *k* of the Syrians
2Ch 28:9 you did a *k* among them
Es 9:5 and with a *k* and destruction
9:16 a *k* among those hating them
Ps 78:31 *k* among their stout ones
78:47 *k* their vine even by the hail
Isa 22:13 the *k* of cattle and the
Jer 7:32 but the valley of the *k*
12:3 apart for the day of *k*
19:6 but the valley of the *k*
La 2:4 kept *k* all those desirable to
Eze 26:15 a *k* with slaughter in the
28:9 before the one *k* you
Da 5:19 happened to want to, he was *k*
Ob 9 region of Esau, because of a *k*
Zec 11:4 the flock meant for the *k*
11:7 the flock meant for the *k*
Lu 12:5 Fear him who after *k* has
13:4 fell, thereby *k* them, do

Kills
Joh 16:2 *k* you will imagine he has

Kiln
Ge 19:28 like the thick smoke of a *k*
Ex 9:8 hands full of soot from a *k*
9:10 took the soot of a *k* and stood
19:18 like the smoke of a *k*, and

Kimah
Job 9:9 And the *K* constellation and
38:31 bonds of the *K* constellation
Am 5:8 Maker of the *K* constellation

Kinah
Jos 15:22 *K* and Dimonah and Adadah

Kind
Ge 1:12 seed according to its *k*
1:12 seed . . . according to its *k*
1:21 creature according to its *k*
1:24 beast . . . according to its *k*
1:25 beast . . . according to its *k*
1:25 animal according to its *k*
1:25 animal . . . according to its *k*
7:14 wild beast according to its *k*
7:14 animal according to its *k*
7:14 animal . . . according to its *k*
7:14 flying creature . . . to its *k*
Ex 18:14 What *k* of business is this
31:3 in every *k* of craftsmanship
31:5 to make products of every *k*
Le 11:14 black kite according to its *k*
11:15 raven according to its *k*
11:16 the falcon according to its *k*
11:19 the heron according to its *k*
11:22 locust according to its *k*
11:22 the edible locust after its *k*
11:22 cricket according to its *k*
11:22 according to its *k*
11:29 lizard according to its *k*
De 14:13 the glede according to its *k*
14:14 raven according to its *k*
14:15 the falcon according to its *k*
14:18 the heron according to its *k*
Ne 10:31 wares and every *k* of cereal
Ps 119:133 may no *k* of hurtful thing
Pr 14:23 By every *k* of toil there
Isa 56:2 not to do any *k* of badness
Eze 15:3 to hang any *k* of utensil
Mt 13:47 gathering up fish of every *k*
16:22 Be *k* to yourself, Lord
Mr 9:29 This *k* cannot get out by
Lu 6:35 he is *k* toward the unthankful
7:39 who and what *k* of woman it
1Co 13:4 Love is long-suffering and *k*
14:10 no *k* is without meaning
16:3 your *k* gift to Jerusalem
16:16 to persons of that *k* and to
2Co 8:6 same *k* giving on your part
8:7 also abound in this *k* giving
8:19 *k* gift to be administered by
11:28 things of an external *k*
Eph 4:32 become *k* to one another
1Pe 2:3 have tasted that the Lord is *k*

Kindle
Eze 24:10 *K* the fire. Boil the flesh

Kindled
Le 6:9 fire of the altar will be *k* in
Ps 58:9 Before your pots feel the *k*
Ps 78:21 fire itself was *k* against
Jer 15:14 Against you people it is *k*
17:4 it will keep *k*
Ac 28:2 *k* a fire and received all of

Kindliness
Ac 24:4 hear us briefly in your *k*

Kindling
Eze 20:47 The *k* flame will not be

Kindly
Ge 32:20 he will give a *k* reception
Pr 22:9 *k* in eye will be blessed
Isa 47:3 I shall not meet any man *k*
Mal 1:8 or will he receive you *k*?
1:9 he receive any of you men *k*
Mt 11:30 my yoke is *k* and my load is
Lu 8:40 the crowd received him *k*, for
9:11 he received them *k* and began
Ac 15:4 they were *k* received by the
18:27 to receive him *k*. So when he
28:30 *k* receive all those who
Ro 2:4 *k* quality of God is trying to
8:32 *k* give us all other things
1Co 2:12 have been *k* given us by God
2Co 1:11 for what is *k* given to us
2:7 should *k* forgive and comfort
2:10 Anything you *k* forgive anyone
2:10 whatever I have *k* forgiven
2:10 if I have *k* forgiven anything
8:4 privilege of *k* giving and for
12:13 *K* forgive me this wrong
Ga 3:18 God has *k* given it to
Eph 1:6 he *k* conferred upon us by
Php 2:9 *k* gave him the name that is
Col 2:13 He *k* forgave us all our
Phm 17 receive him *k* the way you

Kindness
Jg 1:24 certainly exercise *k* toward
Mic 6:8 justice and to love *k* and
Joh 1:14 full of undeserved *k* and
1:16 even undeserved *k* upon
1:16 upon undeserved *k*
1:17 undeserved *k* and the truth
Ac 4:33 undeserved *k* in large measure
11:23 saw the undeserved *k* of God
13:43 in the undeserved *k* of God
14:3 the word of his undeserved *k*
14:26 to the undeserved *k* of God
15:11 undeserved *k* of the Lord
15:40 the undeserved *k* of Jehovah
18:27 account of God's undeserved *k*
20:24 of the undeserved *k* of God
20:32 the word of his undeserved *k*
27:3 treated Paul with human *k*
28:2 us extraordinary human *k*
Ro 1:5 we received undeserved *k* and
1:7 undeserved *k* and peace from
2:4 despise the riches of his *k*
3:12 there is no one that does *k*
3:24 righteous by his undeserved *k*
4:4 not as an undeserved *k*, but as
4:16 according to undeserved *k*
5:2 undeserved *k* in which we now
5:15 undeserved *k* of God and his
5:15 undeserved *k* by the one man
5:17 abundance of the undeserved *k*
5:20 undeserved *k* abounded still
5:21 undeserved *k* might rule as
6:1 that undeserved *k* may abound
6:14 law but under undeserved *k*
6:15 law but under undeserved *k*
11:5 choosing due to undeserved *k*
11:6 if it is by undeserved *k*, it
11:6 undeserved *k* no longer proves
11:6 no longer . . . undeserved *k*
11:22 God's *k* and severity
11:22 God's *k*, provided you
11:22 provided you remain in his *k*
12:3 undeserved *k* given to me I
12:6 the undeserved *k* given to us
15:15 because of the undeserved *k*
16:20 the undeserved *k* of our Lord
1Co 1:3 undeserved *k* and peace from
1:4 undeserved *k* of God given to
3:10 the undeserved *k* of God that
15:10 by God's undeserved *k* I am
15:10 undeserved *k* that was
15:10 the undeserved *k* of God that
16:23 the undeserved *k* of the Lord
2Co 1:2 undeserved *k* and peace from
1:12 but with God's undeserved *k*
4:15 the undeserved *k* which was
6:1 accept the undeserved *k* of

2Co 6:6 by *k,* by holy spirit, by love
8:1 undeserved *k* of God that has
8:9 undeserved *k* of our Lord
9:8 undeserved *k* abound toward
9:14 undeserved *k* of God upon you
10:1 mildness and *k* of the Christ
12:9 undeserved *k* is sufficient
13:14 undeserved *k* of the Lord
Ga 1:3 May you have undeserved *k* and
1:6 you with Christ's undeserved *k*
1:15 through his undeserved *k*
2:9 undeserved *k* that was given
2:21 shove aside the undeserved *k*
5:4 away from his undeserved *k*
5:22 fruitage of the spirit . . . *k*
6:18 undeserved *k* of our Lord Jesus
Eph 1:2 undeserved *k* and peace from
1:6 his glorious undeserved *k*
1:7 the riches of his undeserved *k*
2:5 by undeserved *k* you have been
2:7 riches of his undeserved *k* in
2:8 By this undeserved *k,* indeed
3:2 undeserved *k* of God that was
3:7 free gift of the undeserved *k*
3:8 this undeserved *k* was given
4:7 undeserved *k* was given
6:24 May the undeserved *k* be with
Php 1:2 May you have undeserved *k* and
1:7 sharers . . . the undeserved *k*
4:23 The undeserved *k* of the Lord
Col 1:2 undeserved *k* and peace from
1:6 undeserved *k* of God in truth
3:12 clothe yourselves with . . . *k*
4:18 The undeserved *k* be with you
1Th 1:1 May you have undeserved *k* and
5:28 The undeserved *k* of our Lord
2Th 1:2 May you have undeserved *k* and
1:12 the undeserved *k* of our God
2:16 by means of undeserved *k*
3:18 The undeserved *k* of our Lord
1Ti 1:2 May there be undeserved *k*
1:14 undeserved *k* of our Lord
6:21 undeserved *k* be with you
2Ti 1:2 May there be undeserved *k*
1:9 own purpose and undeserved *k*
2:1 power in the undeserved *k*
4:22 His undeserved *k* be with you
Tit 1:4 undeserved *k* and peace from
2:11 undeserved *k* of God which
3:4 when the *k* and the love for
3:7 by virtue of the undeserved *k*
3:15 undeserved *k* be with all of
Phm 3 undeserved *k* and peace from God
25 undeserved *k* of the Lord Jesus
Heb 2:9 by God's undeserved *k* might
4:16 the throne of undeserved *k*
4:16 find undeserved *k* for help at
10:29 the spirit of undeserved *k*
12:15 deprived of the undeserved *k*
12:28 to have undeserved *k*
13:9 firmness by undeserved *k*
13:25 undeserved *k* be with all
Jas 4:6 undeserved *k* which he gives
4:6 undeserved *k* to the humble
1Pe 1:2 undeserved *k* and peace be
1:10 undeserved *k* meant for you
1:13 hope upon the undeserved *k*
4:10 stewards of . . . undeserved *k*
5:5 undeserved *k* to the humble
5:10 the God of all undeserved *k*
5:12 the true undeserved *k* of God
2Pe 1:2 undeserved *k* and peace be
3:18 undeserved *k* and knowledge
2Jo 3 undeserved *k,* mercy and peace
Jude 4 undeserved *k* of our God into
Re 1:4 undeserved *k* and peace from
22:21 undeserved *k* of the Lord

Kinds

Ge 1:11 fruit according to their *k*
1:21 forth according to their *k*
1:24 souls according to their *k*
6:20 creatures according to their *k*
6:20 animals according to their *k*
6:20 according to their *k,* two of
Eze 47:10 In their *k* their fish will
1Co 14:10 so many *k* of speech sounds

King

Ge 14:1 days of Amraphel *k* of Shinar
14:1 Arioch *k* of Ellasar
14:1 Chedorlaomer *k* of Elam, and
14:1 and Tidal *k* of Goiim
14:2 war with Bera *k* of Sodom and
14:2 Birsha *k* of Gomorrah, Shinab
Ge 14:2 Shinab *k* of Admah, and
14:2 Shemeber *k* of Zeboiim, and
14:2 *k* of Bela (that is to say
14:8 *k* of Sodom went on the march
14:8 and also the *k* of Gomorrah
14:8 on the march . . . *k* of Admah
14:8 on the march . . . *k* of Zeboiim
14:8 on the march . . . *k* of Bela
14:9 Chedorlaomer *k* of Elam
14:9 Tidal *k* of Goiim and
14:9 Amraphel *k* of Shinar and
14:9 and Arioch *k* of Ellasar
14:17 *k* of Sodom went out to meet
14:18 Melchizedek *k* of Salem
14:21 *k* of Sodom said to Abram
14:22 Abram said to the *k* of Sodom
20:2 Abimelech *k* of Gerar sent and
26:1 *k* of the Philistines, to Gerar
26:8 *k* of the Philistines, was
36:31 before any *k* reigned over the
37:8 Are you going to be *k* over us
39:20 where the prisoners of the *k*
40:1 cupbearer of the *k* of Egypt
40:1 their lord the *k* of Egypt
40:5 belonged to the *k* of Egypt
41:46 before Pharaoh the *k* of Egypt
49:20 give the dainties of a *k*
Ex 1:8 there arose over Egypt a new *k*
1:15 the *k* of Egypt said to the
1:17 did not do as the *k* of Egypt
1:18 *k* of Egypt called the
2:23 the *k* of Egypt finally died
3:18 come . . . to the *k* of Egypt
3:19 *k* of Egypt will not give you
5:4 the *k* of Egypt said to them
6:11 speak to Pharaoh, Egypt's *k*
6:13 Pharaoh, Egypt's *k,* in order
6:27 speaking to Pharaoh, Egypt's *k*
6:29 Speak to Pharaoh *k* of Egypt
14:5 reported to the *k* of Egypt
14:8 *k* of Egypt become obstinate
15:18 Jehovah will rule as *k* to
Nu 20:14 from Kadesh to the *k* of Edom
21:1 the Canaanite the *k* of Arad
21:21 Sihon the *k* of the Amorites
21:26 He was the *k* of the Amorites
21:26 fought with the *k* of Moab
21:29 the *k* of the Amorites, Sihon
21:33 Og the *k* of Bashan came out
21:34 Sihon, the *k* of the Amorites
22:4 son of Zippor was *k* of Moab
22:10 the *k* of Moab, has sent to
23:7 Balak the *k* of Moab tried to
23:21 loud hailing of a *k* is in his
24:7 His *k* also will be higher
32:33 Sihon the *k* of the Amorites
32:33 of Og the *k* of Bashan, the
33:40 the Canaanite, the *k* of Arad
De 1:4 Sihon the *k* of the Amorites
1:4 Og the *k* of Bashan, who was
2:24 Sihon the *k* of Heshbon, the
2:26 Sihon the *k* of Heshbon
2:30 Sihon the *k* of Heshbon did not
3:1 Og the *k* of Bashan came on
3:2 Sihon the *k* of the Amorites
3:3 Og the *k* of Bashan and all his
3:6 Sihon the *k* of Heshbon, in
3:11 Og the *k* of Bashan remained
4:46 Sihon the *k* of the Amorites
4:47 land of Og the *k* of Bashan
7:8 from the hand of Pharaoh the *k*
11:3 Pharaoh the *k* of Egypt and
17:14 Let me set a *k* over myself
17:15 set over yourself a *k* whom
17:15 set a *k* over yourself
28:36 your *k* whom you will set up
29:7 and Sihon the *k* of Heshbon
29:7 Og the *k* of Bashan proceeded
33:5 he came to be *k* in Jeshurun
Jos 2:2 was said to the *k* of Jericho
2:3 the *k* of Jericho sent to Rahab
6:2 I have given Jericho and its *k*
8:1 into your hand the *k* of Ai
8:2 do to Ai and to its *k* just as
8:2 you did to Jericho and its *k*
8:14 soon as the *k* of Ai saw it
8:23 the *k* of Ai they caught alive
8:29 hanged the *k* of Ai upon a
9:10 Sihon the *k* of Heshbon and Og
9:10 Og the *k* of Bashan, who was
10:1 Adoni-zedek the *k* of
10:1 had done to Jericho and its *k*
10:1 he had done to Ai and its *k*
10:3 the *k* of Jerusalem sent to
Jos 10:3 to Hoham the *k* of Hebron and
10:3 to Piram the *k* of Jarmuth
10:3 Japhia the *k* of Lachish and
10:3 Debir the *k* of Eglon, saying
10:5 the *k* of Jerusalem, the
10:5 the *k* of Hebron, the
10:5 the *k* of Jarmuth
10:5 the *k* of Lachish
10:5 the *k* of Eglon, these and all
10:23 the *k* of Jerusalem, the
10:23 the *k* of Hebron
10:23 the *k* of Jarmuth
10:23 the *k* of Lachish
10:23 the *k* of Eglon
10:28 As for its *k,* he devoted
10:28 did to the *k* of Makkedah
10:28 had done to the *k* of Jericho
10:30 its *k* into Israel's hand
10:30 they did to its *k* just as
10:30 had done to the *k* of Jericho
10:33 Horam the *k* of Gezer went
10:37 went striking it and its *k*
10:39 got to capture it and its *k*
10:39 so he did to Debir and its *k*
10:39 had done to Libnah and its *k*
11:1 Jabin the *k* of Hazor heard of
11:1 to Jobab the *k* of Madon and
11:1 and to the *k* of Shimron
11:1 and the *k* of Achshaph
11:10 and its *k* he struck down
12:2 Sihon the *k* of the Amorites
12:4 Og the *k* of Bashan
12:5 Sihon the *k* of Heshbon
12:9 The *k* of Jericho, one
12:9 *k* of Ai, which was beside
12:10 the *k* of Jerusalem, one
12:10 the *k* of Hebron, one
12:11 the *k* of Jarmuth, one
12:11 the *k* of Lachish, one
12:12 the *k* of Eglon, one
12:12 the *k* of Gezer, one
12:13 the *k* of Debir, one
12:13 the *k* of Geder, one
12:14 the *k* of Hormah, one
12:14 the *k* of Arad, one
12:15 the *k* of Libnah, one
12:15 the *k* of Adullam, one
12:16 the *k* of Makkedah, one
12:16 the *k* of Bethel, one
12:17 the *k* of Tappuah, one
12:17 the *k* of Hepher, one
12:18 the *k* of Aphek, one
12:18 the *k* of Lassharon, one
12:19 the *k* of Madon, one
12:19 the *k* of Hazor, one
12:20 the *k* of Shimron-meron, one
12:20 the *k* of Achshaph, one
12:21 the *k* of Taanach, one
12:21 the *k* of Megiddo, one
12:22 the *k* of Kedesh, one
12:22 the *k* of Jokneam in Carmel
12:23 *k* of Dor on the mountain
12:23 *k* of Goiim in Gilgal, one
12:24 the *k* of Tirzah, one
13:10 Sihon the *k* of the Amorites
13:21 Sihon the *k* of the Amorites
13:27 of Sihon the *k* of Heshbon
13:30 realm of Og the *k* of Bashan
24:9 Zippor, the *k* of Moab, got
Jg 3:8 of Cushan-rishathaim the *k* of
3:10 the *k* of Syria into his hand
3:12 let Eglon the *k* of Moab grow
3:14 to serve Eglon the *k* of Moab
3:15 to Eglon the *k* of Moab
3:17 tribute to Eglon the *k* of
3:19 a secret word for you, O *k*
4:2 Jabin the *k* of Canaan, who
4:17 Jabin the *k* of Hazor and the
4:23 God subdued Jabin the *k* of
4:24 against Jabin the *k* of Canaan
4:24 cut off Jabin the *k* of Canaan
8:18 like the sons of a *k* in form
9:6 Abimelech reign as *k,* close by
9:8 trees went to anoint a *k* over
9:8 the olive tree, Do be *k* over us
9:14 the bramble, You come, be *k*
9:15 anointing me as *k* over you
9:16 went making Abimelech *k,* and
9:18 *k* over the landowners of
11:12 the *k* of the sons of Ammon
11:13 the *k* of the sons of Ammon
11:14 the *k* of the sons of Ammon
11:17 messengers to the *k* of Edom
11:17 the *k* of Edom did not listen

Jg 11:17 the *k* of Moab they sent
11:19 Sihon the *k* of the Amorites
11:19 the *k* of Heshbon, and Israel
11:25 Balak . . . the *k* of Moab
11:28 the *k* of the sons of Ammon
17:6 there was no *k* in Israel
18:1 there was no *k* in Israel
19:1 that there was no *k* in Israel
21:25 there was no *k* in Israel
1Sa 2:10 may give strength to his *k*
8:5 appoint for us a *k* to judge us
8:6 Do give us a *k* to judge us
8:7 rejected from being *k* over
8:9 the rightful due of the *k* who
8:10 people who were asking a *k*
8:11 rightful due of the *k* that
8:18 that day by reason of your *k*
8:19 a *k* is what will come to be
8:20 our *k* must judge us and go
8:22 you must cause a *k* to reign
10:19 a *k* is what you should put
10:24 and say: Let the *k* live!
11:12 Saul—is he to be *k* over us?
11:15 make Saul *k* before Jehovah
12:1 cause a *k* to reign over you
12:2 here is the *k* walking before
12:9 the hand of the *k* of Moab
12:12 Nahash the *k* of the sons of
12:12 a *k* is what should reign
12:12 your God being your *K*
12:13 the *k* whom you have chosen
12:13 Jehovah has put over you a *k*
12:14 *k* who must reign over you
12:17 in asking for yourselves a *k*
12:19 in asking for ourselves a *k*
12:25 both you and your *k*
15:1 as *k* over his people Israel
15:8 catch Agag the *k* of Amalek
15:11 caused Saul to reign as *k*
15:17 anoint you as *k* over Israel
15:20 Agag the *k* of Amalek
15:23 rejects you from being *k*
15:26 Jehovah rejects you . . . as *k*
15:32 Bring Agag the *k* of Amalek
15:35 had made Saul *k* over Israel
16:1 from ruling as *k* over Israel
16:1 among his sons a *k* for
17:25 the *k* will enrich him with
17:55 the life of your soul, O *k*
17:56 *k* said: You inquire whose
18:6 dances to meet Saul the *k*
18:18 become son-in-law to the *k*
18:22 *k* has found delight in you
18:22 alliance with the *k*
18:23 alliance with the *k*, when I
18:25 The *k* has delight, not in
18:25 on the enemies of the *k*
18:26 alliance with the *k*, and
18:27 in full number to the *k*
18:27 alliance with the *k*
19:4 *k* sin against his servant
20:5 sitting with the *k* to eat
20:24 *k* took his seat at the meal
20:25 *k* was sitting in his seat
21:2 *k* himself commanded me as
21:10 to Achish the *k* of Gath
21:11 this David the *k* of the land
21:12 of Achish the *k* of Gath
22:3 said to the *k* of Moab: Let
22:4 before the *k* of Moab, and
22:11 *k* sent to call Ahimelech the
22:11 all of them came to the *k*
22:14 Ahimelech answered the *k*
22:14 son-in-law of the *k* and a
22:15 *k* lay anything against his
22:16 *k* said: You will positively
22:17 *k* said to the runners
22:17 servants of the *k* did not
22:18 *k* said to Doeg: You turn and
23:17 will be *k* over Israel
23:20 craving of your soul, O *k*
23:20 into the hand of the *k*
24:8 My lord the *k*! At this Saul
24:14 has the *k* of Israel gone out
24:20 without fail, rule as *k*
25:36 like the feast of the *k*; and
26:14 have called out to the *k*
26:15 watch over your lord the *k*
26:15 bring the *k* your lord to
26:17 is my voice, my lord the *k*
26:19 lord the *k*, please, listen
26:20 *k* of Israel has gone out
26:22 Here is the spear of the *k*
27:2 Achish . . . the *k* of Gath
1Sa 28:13 *k* said to her: Do not be
29:3 servant of Saul *k* of Israel
29:8 the enemies of my lord the *k*
2Sa 2:4 David there as *k* over the
2:7 Judah have anointed as *k* over
2:9 make him *k* over Gilead and
2:10 when he became *k* over Israel
2:10 for two years he ruled as *k*
2:11 David proved to be *k* in
3:3 of Talmai the *k* of Geshur
3:17 seeking David as *k* over you
3:21 together to my lord the *k*
3:21 *k* over all that your soul
3:23 son of Ner came to the *k*
3:24 Joab went in to the *k* and
3:31 Even *K* David was walking
3:32 *k* began to raise his voice
3:33 *k* went on to chant over
3:36 everything that the *k* did
3:37 not originated with the *k* to
3:38 *k* went on to say to his
3:39 weak although anointed as *k*
4:8 said to the *k*: Here is the
4:8 to my lord the *k* revenge this
5:2 Saul happened to be *k* over us
5:3 came to the *k* at Hebron
5:3 *K* David concluded a covenant
5:3 anointed David as *k* over
5:4 was David when he became *k*
5:4 For forty years he ruled as *k*
5:5 *k* over Judah for seven years
5:5 in Jerusalem he ruled as *k*
5:6 the *k* and his men went to
5:11 Hiram the *k* of Tyre
5:12 firmly established him as *k*
5:17 David as *k* over Israel
6:12 report was made to *K* David
6:16 *K* David leaping and dancing
6:20 How glorious the *k* of Israel
7:1 *k* dwelt in his own house and
7:2 *k* said to Nathan the prophet
7:3 Nathan said to the *k*
7:18 *K* David came in and sat down
8:3 *k* of Zobah as he was going
8:5 help Hadadezer the *k* of Zobah
8:8 *K* David took copper in very
8:9 Toi the *k* of Hamath got to
8:10 son to *K* David to ask him
8:11 *K* David sanctified to Jehovah
8:12 Hadadezer . . . *k* of Zobah
9:2 *k* then said to him: Are you
9:3 *k* went on to say: Is there
9:3 Ziba said to the *k*: There is
9:4 *k* said to him: Where is he?
9:4 Ziba said to the *k*: Look! He
9:5 *K* David sent and took him
9:9 *k* now called Ziba, Saul's
9:11 Ziba said to the *k*: In accord
9:11 *k* commands for his servant
9:11 like one of the sons of the *k*
9:13 table of the *k* that he was
10:1 *k* of the sons of Ammon came
10:5 *k* went on to say: Dwell in
10:6 *k* of Maacah, a thousand men
11:19 speaking to the *k* about all
11:20 rage of the *k* comes up and
11:24 servants of the *k* died
12:7 anointed you as *k* over Israel
13:4 son of the *k*, so downcast
13:6 so the *k* came in to see him
13:6 Amnon said to the *k*: Please
13:13 speak, please, to the *k*
13:18 way the daughters of the *k*
13:21 *K* David himself heard about
13:23 invite all the sons of the *k*
13:24 Absalom came in to the *k*
13:24 Let the *k* go, please, and
13:25 *k* said to Absalom: No, my
13:26 *k* said to him: Why should
13:27 and all the sons of the *k*
13:29 other sons of the *k* began
13:30 all the sons of the *k*
13:31 *k* got up and ripped his
13:32 young men the sons of the *k*
13:33 *k* take to his heart the
13:35 Jehonadab said to the *k*
13:36 *k* and all his servants wept
13:37 Ammihud the *k* of Geshur
13:39 soul of David the *k* longed
14:3 come in to the *k* and speak
14:4 come in to the *k* and fall
14:4 Do save, O *k*!
14:5 *k* said to her: What is the
14:8 *k* said to the woman: Go to
2Sa 14:9 Tekoite woman said to the *k*
14:9 my lord the *k*, be the error
14:9 *k* and his throne are innocent
14:10 *k* went on to say: If there
14:11 *k*, please, remember Jehovah
14:12 a word to my lord the *k*
14:13 *k* is speaking this word he
14:13 *k* does not bring back his
14:15 speak this word to the *k*
14:15 me speak, please, to the *k*
14:15 *k* will act on the word of
14:16 *k* proceeded to listen so
14:17 word of my lord the *k* serve
14:17 way my lord the *k* is, to
14:18 *k* now answered and said to
14:18 Let my lord the *k* speak
14:19 *k* went on to say: Is the
14:19 lord the *k*, no man can go
14:19 my lord the *k* has spoken
14:21 *k* said to Joab: Here, now
14:22 and blessed the *k*; and Joab
14:22 your eyes, O my lord the *k*
14:22 *k* has acted on the word of
14:24 *k* said: Let him turn toward
14:24 face of the *k* he did not see
14:28 face of the *k* he did not see
14:29 to send him to the *k*, and
14:32 let me send you to the *k*
14:32 see the face of the *k* and
14:33 Joab came in to the *k* and
14:33 now came in to the *k* and
14:33 to the earth before the *k*
14:33 the *k* kissed Absalom
15:2 legal case to come to the *k*
15:3 no one from the *k* giving you
15:6 in for judgment to the *k*
15:7 proceeded to say to the *k*
15:9 the *k* said to him: Go in
15:10 Absalom has become *k* in
15:15 servants said to the *k*
15:15 my lord the *k* may choose
15:16 So the *k* went out with all
15:16 and the *k* left ten women
15:17 the *k* continued on his way
15:19 *k* said to Ittai the Gittite
15:19 dwell with the *k*; for you
15:21 Ittai answered the *k* and
15:21 as my lord the *k* is living
15:21 my lord the *k* may come to
15:23 the *k* was standing by the
15:25 But the *k* said to Zadok
15:27 *k* went on to say to Zadok
15:34 I am your servant, O *K*
15:35 from the house of the *k*
16:2 Then the *k* said to Ziba
16:2 household of the *k* to ride
16:3 The *k* now said: And where is
16:3 At this Ziba said to the *k*
16:4 The *k* then said to Ziba
16:4 in your eyes, my lord the *k*
16:5 And *K* David came as far as
16:6 all the servants of *K* David
16:8 you have ruled as *k*
16:9 son of Zeruiah said to the *k*
16:9 evil upon my lord the *k*
16:10 the *k* said: What do I have
16:14 the *k* and all the people
16:16, 16 *k* live! Let the *k* live!
17:2 strike down the *k* by himself
17:16 for fear that the *k* and all
17:17 as they had to tell *K* David
17:21 went on and told *K* David
18:2 the *k* said to the people
18:4 So the *k* said to them
18:4 the *k* kept standing at the
18:5 *k* went on to command Joab
18:5 *k* commanded all the chiefs
18:12 *k* commanded you and Abishai
18:13 not be hidden from the *k*
18:18 in the Low Plain of the *K*
18:19 and break the news to the *k*
18:21 tell the *k* what you have
18:25 told the *k*, at which the
18:25 the *k* said: If he is by
18:26 the *k* said: This one also
18:27 *k* said: This is a good man
18:28 said to the *k*: It is well!
18:28 he bowed to the *k* with his
18:28 hand against my lord the *k*
18:29 the *k* said: Is it well with
18:30 the *k* said: Step aside, take
18:31 my lord the *k* accept news
18:32 the *k* said to the Cushite
18:32 enemies of my lord the *k*

2Sa 18:33 the *k* became disturbed and
19:1 The *k* is weeping, and he
19:2 *k* has felt hurt over his son
19:4 the *k* himself covered up his
19:4 the *k* continued crying out
19:5 Joab came in to the *k* at
19:8 *k* rose up and seated himself
19:8 the *k* sitting in the gate
19:8 began to come before the *k*
19:9 It was the *k* that delivered
19:10 nothing to bring the *k* back
19:11 As for *K* David, he sent to
19:11 the *k* back to his house
19:11 come to the *k* at his house
19:12 ones to bring the *k* back
19:14 they sent word to the *k*
19:15 the *k* began to go back and
19:15 to go and meet the *k*
19:15 the *k* across the Jordan
19:16 hurried . . . to meet *K* David
19:17 to the Jordan before the *k*
19:18 the household of the *k*
19:18 he fell down before the *k*
19:19 now said to the *k*: Do not
19:19 the *k* went out of Jerusalem
19:19 *k* should lay it to his heart
19:20 to meet my lord the *k*
19:22 today I am *k* over Israel
19:23 Then the *k* said to Shimei
19:23 *k* went on to swear to him
19:24 he came down to meet the *k*
19:24 day that the *k* went away
19:25 to Jerusalem to meet the *k*
19:25 then the *k* said to him
19:26 My lord the *k*, it was my
19:26 and go with the *k*, for your
19:27 to my lord the *k*
19:27 lord the *k* is as an angel
19:28 to my lord the *k*
19:28 crying out further to the *k*
19:29 However, the *k* said to him
19:30 Mephibosheth said to the *k*
19:30 the *k* has come in peace
19:31 to the Jordan with the *k*
19:32 supplied the *k* with food
19:33 the *k* said to Barzillai
19:34 But Barzillai said to the *k*
19:34 with the *k* to Jerusalem
19:35 burden . . . to my lord the *k*
19:36 the *k* along to the Jordan
19:36 the *k* repay me with this
19:37 cross over with . . . the *k*
19:38 *k* said: With me Chimham
19:39 and the *k* himself crossed
19:39 the *k* kissed Barzillai and
19:40 the *k* went across to Gilgal
19:40 might bring the *k* across
19:41 coming to the *k*, and they
19:41 proceeded to say to the *k*
19:41 the *k* and his household and
19:42 the *k* is closely related to
19:43 We have ten parts in the *k*
19:43 for us to bring our *k* back
20:2 they stuck to their *k* from
20:3 the *k* took the ten women
20:4 The *k* now said to Amasa
20:21 his hand against *K* David
20:22 to Jerusalem to the *k*
21:2 the *k* called the Gibeonites
21:5 At this they said to the *k*
21:6 the *k* said: I myself shall
21:7 the *k* felt compassion upon
21:8 the *k* took the two sons of
21:14 the *k* had commanded
22:51 acts of salvation for his *k*
24:2 the *k* said to Joab the chief
24:3 But Joab said to the *k*
24:3 eyes of my lord the *k* are
24:3 But as for my lord the *k*
24:4 went out from before the *k*
24:9 gave the number . . . to the *k*
24:20 saw the *k* and his servants
24:20 bowed down to the *k* with
24:21 Why has my lord the *k*
24:22 the *k* take it and offer up
24:23 Everything Araunah, O *k*
24:23 does give to the *k*
24:23 went on to say to the *k*
24:24 the *k* said to Araunah
1Ki 1:1 *K* David was old, advanced in
1:2 a virgin, for my lord the *k*
1:2 have to attend upon the *k*
1:2 *k* will certainly feel warm
1:3 then brought her in to the *k*

1Ki 1:4 *k* himself had no intercourse
1:5 am going to rule as *k*
1:11 of Haggith has become *k*
1:13 Go and enter in to *K* David
1:13 my lord the *k*, that swore to
1:13 the one that will become *k*
1:13 why has Adonijah become *k*?
1:14 speaking there with the *k*
1:15 Bath-sheba went in to the *k*
1:15 and the *k* was very old, and
1:15 was waiting upon the *k*
1:16 prostrated herself to the *k*
1:16 upon which the *k* said
1:17 the one that will become *k*
1:18 Adonijah . . . has become *k*
1:18 the *k* himself does not know
1:19 invited all the sons of the *k*
1:20 my lord the *k*—the eyes of
1:20 the throne of my lord the *k*
1:21 my lord the *k* lies down
1:22 was yet speaking with the *k*
1:23 they told the *k*, saying
1:23 he came in before the *k* and
1:23 prostrated himself to the *k*
1:24 My lord the *k*, did you
1:24 the one that will become *k*
1:25 invite all the sons of the *k*
1:25 saying, Let *K* Adonijah live!
1:27 If it is from my lord the *k*
1:27 the throne of my lord the *k*
1:28 *K* David now answered and
1:28 she came in before the *k*
1:28 and stood before the *k*
1:29 the *k* proceeded to swear
1:30 the one that will become *k*
1:31 prostrated herself to the *k*
1:31 Let my lord *K* David live to
1:32 *K* David said: You men, call
1:32 So they came in before the *k*
1:33 the *k* went on to say to them
1:34 anoint him there as *k* over
1:34 and say, Let *K* Solomon live!
1:35 will be *k* in place of me
1:36 Benaiah . . . answered the *k*
1:36 the God of my lord the *k* say
1:37 with my lord the *k*, so let
1:37 throne of my lord *K* David
1:38 upon the she-mule of *K* David
1:39 saying: Let *K* Solomon live!
1:43 *K* David himself has made
1:43 David . . . has made Solomon *k*
1:44 the *k* sent with him Zadok
1:44 upon the she-mule of the *k*
1:45 anointed him as *k* in Gihon
1:47 the servants of the *k* have
1:47 wish our lord *K* David well
1:47 *k* bowed down upon the bed
1:48 this is what the *k* said
1:51 become afraid of *K* Solomon
1:51 *K* Solomon first of all swear
1:53 So *K* Solomon sent and they
1:53 and bowed down to *K* Solomon
2:15 for me to become *k*
2:17 Please, say to Solomon the *k*
2:18 speak for you to the *k*
2:19 in to *K* Solomon to speak
2:19 the *k* rose to meet her and
2:19 for the mother of the *k*
2:20 the *k* said to her: Make it
2:22 *K* Solomon answered and said
2:23 *K* Solomon swore by Jehovah
2:25 *K* Solomon sent by means of
2:26 the *k* said: Go to Anathoth
2:29 *K* Solomon was told: Joab has
2:30 the *k* has said, Come on out!
2:30 brought word back to the *k*
2:31 Then the *k* said to him
2:35 the *k* put Benaiah the son of
2:35 Zadok the priest the *k* put in
2:36 the *k* sent and called Shimei
2:38 At this Shimei said to the *k*
2:38 my lord the *k* has spoken
2:39 Maacah the *k* of Gath
2:42 the *k* sent and called Shimei
2:44 *k* went on to say to Shimei
2:45 *K* Solomon will be blessed
2:46 the *k* commanded Benaiah the
3:1 alliance with Pharaoh the *k*
3:4 *k* went to Gibeon to sacrifice
3:7 *k* in the place of David my
3:16 to the *k* and stand before
3:22 kept on speaking before the *k*
3:23 the *k* said: This one is
3:24 And the *k* went on to say

1Ki 3:24 the sword before the *k*
3:25 And the *k* proceeded to say
3:26 said to the *k* (for her
3:27 the *k* answered and said
3:28 decision that the *k* had
3:28 fearful because of the *k*
4:1, 1 *K* Solomon continued *k* over
4:5 a priest, the friend of the *k*
4:7 provided the *k* and his
4:19 Sihon the *k* of the Amorites
4:19 Og the *k* of Bashan, and there
4:27 supplied food to *K* Solomon
4:27 the table of *K* Solomon
5:1 Hiram the *k* of Tyre proceeded
5:1 as *k* in place of his father
5:13 *K* Solomon kept bringing up
5:17 the *k* commanded that they
6:1 Solomon became *k* over Israel
6:2 house that *K* Solomon built
7:13 *K* Solomon proceeded to send
7:14 he came to *K* Solomon and
7:40 that he did for *K* Solomon
7:45 for *K* Solomon for the house
7:46 the *k* cast them in the clay
7:51 the work that *K* Solomon had
8:1 to *K* Solomon at Jerusalem
8:2 congregated . . . to *K* Solomon
8:5 *K* Solomon and with him all
8:14 the *k* turned his face and
8:62 the *k* and all Israel with
8:63 *k* and all the sons of Israel
8:64 the *k* had to sanctify the
8:66 bless the *k* and to go to
9:1 the house of the *k* and every
9:10 and the house of the *k*
9:11 Hiram the *k* of Tyre had
9:11 *K* Solomon proceeded to give
9:14 sent to the *k* a hundred and
9:15 *K* Solomon levied to build
9:16 Pharaoh the *k* of Egypt
9:26 of ships that *K* Solomon
9:28 and bring it in to *K* Solomon
10:3 no matter hidden from the *k*
10:6 said to the *k*: True has the
10:9 appointed you as *k* to render
10:10 she gave the *k* a hundred and
10:10 Sheba gave to *K* Solomon
10:12 the *k* proceeded to make
10:12 and for the house of the *k*
10:13 *K* Solomon himself gave the
10:13 openhandedness of *K* Solomon
10:16 *K* Solomon went on to make
10:17 the *k* put them in the House
10:18 *k* made a great ivory throne
10:21 vessels of *K* Solomon were
10:22 the *k* had a fleet of ships
10:23 *K* Solomon was greater in
10:26 close by the *k* in Jerusalem
10:27 *k* came to make the silver
11:1 *K* Solomon himself loved
11:14 of the offspring of the *k*
11:18 to Pharaoh the *k* of Egypt
11:23 Hadadezer the *k* of Zobah
11:26 his hand against the *k*
11:27 his hand against the *k*
11:37 become *k* over Israel
11:40 to Shishak the *k* of Egypt
12:1 Israel came to make him *k*
12:2 on account of *K* Solomon
12:6 And *K* Rehoboam began to take
12:12 just as the *k* had spoken
12:13 the *k* began to answer the
12:15 the *k* did not listen to the
12:16 that the *k* had not listened
12:16 the people replied to the *k*
12:18 *K* Rehoboam sent Adoram
12:18 *K* Rehoboam himself managed
12:20 made him *k* over all Israel
12:23 Rehoboam . . . the *k* of Judah
12:27 Rehoboam the *k* of Judah
12:27 Rehoboam the *k* of Judah
12:28 the *k* took counsel and made
13:4 *k* heard the word of the man
13:6 *k* now answered and said to
13:7 *k* went on to say to the man
13:8 said to the *k*: If you gave
13:11 that he had spoken to the *k*
14:2 becoming *k* over this people
14:14 a *k* over Israel who will
14:21 he had become *k* in Judah
14:25 fifth year of *K* Rehoboam
14:25 Shishak the *k* of Egypt came
14:26 of the house of the *k*
14:27 *K* Rehoboam made in place of

1Ki 14:28 the *k* came to the house of
15:1 *K* Jeroboam the son of Nebat
15:1 Abijam became *k* over Judah
15:9 Jeroboam the *k* of Israel
15:9 Asa reigned as *k* of Judah
15:16 and Baasha the *k* of Israel
15:17 Baasha the *k* of Israel came
15:17 to Asa the *k* of Judah
15:18 of the house of the *k*
15:18 and *K* Asa now sent them to
15:18 the *k* of Syria, who was
15:19 Baasha the *k* of Israel
15:20 Ben-hadad listened to *K* Asa
15:22 *K* Asa, for his part
15:22 and *K* Asa began to build
15:25 he became *k* over Israel in
15:25 Asa the *k* of Judah
15:28 Asa the *k* of Judah
15:29 as soon as he became *k*
15:32 and Baasha the *k* of Israel
15:33 of Asa the *k* of Judah
15:33 Baasha . . . *k* over all Israel
16:8 Asa the *k* of Judah
16:8 Elah . . . *k* over Israel
16:10 Asa the *k* of Judah
16:15 Asa the *k* of Judah
16:15 *k* for seven days in Tirzah
16:16 and also struck down the *k*
16:16 Omri . . . *k* over Israel on
16:21 of Ginath, to make him *k*
16:23 Asa the *k* of Judah
16:23 Omri became *k* over Israel
16:29 Ahab . . . became *k* over
16:29 Asa the *k* of Judah
16:31 the *k* of the Sidonians
19:15 Hazael as *k* over Syria
19:16 Jehu . . . as *k* over Israel
20:1 Ben-hadad the *k* of Syria
20:2 Ahab the *k* of Israel at the
20:4 the *k* of Israel answered and
20:4 your word, my lord the *k*
20:7 the *k* of Israel called all
20:9 Say to my lord the *k*, All
20:11 the *k* of Israel answered
20:13 Ahab the *k* of Israel and
20:20 *k* of Syria got to escape
20:21 *k* of Israel went out and
20:22 approached the *k* of Israel
20:22 the *k* of Syria is coming up
20:23 servants of the *k* of Syria
20:28 and said to the *k* of Israel
20:31 go out to the *k* of Israel
20:32 came in to the *k* of Israel
20:38 for the *k* by the road, and
20:39 as the *k* was passing by, he
20:39 he cried out to the *k* and
20:40 the *k* of Israel said to him
20:41 *k* of Israel got to recognize
20:43 At that the *k* of Israel
21:1 Ahab the *k* of Samaria
21:10 have cursed God and the *k*
21:13 has cursed God and the *k*
21:18 Ahab the *k* of Israel, who
22:2 Jehoshaphat the *k* of Judah
22:2 go down to the *k* of Israel
22:3 *k* of Israel said to his
22:3 the hand of the *k* of Syria
22:4 said to the *k* of Israel
22:5 to say to the *k* of Israel
22:6 the *k* of Israel collected
22:8 At that the *k* of Israel said
22:8 Do not let the *k* say a thing
22:9 *k* of Israel called a certain
22:10 *k* of Israel and Jehoshaphat
22:10 Jehoshaphat the *k* of Judah
22:13 words . . . good to the *k*
22:15 he came in to the *k*, and
22:15 *k* proceeded to say to him
22:16 *k* said to him: For how
22:18 Then the *k* of Israel said
22:26 *k* of Israel said: Take
22:27 This is what the *k* has said
22:29 And the *k* of Israel and
22:29 Jehoshaphat the *k* of Judah
22:30 The *k* of Israel now said
22:30 the *k* of Israel disguised
22:31 As for the *k* of Syria, he
22:31 with the *k* of Israel alone
22:32 it is the *k* of Israel
22:33 it was not the *k* of Israel
22:34 to strike the *k* of Israel
22:35 *k* himself had to be kept
22:37 Thus the *k* died. When he
22:37 buried the *k* in Samaria

1Ki 22:41 Jehoshaphat . . . *k* over Judah
22:41 fourth year of Ahab the *k* of
22:44 with the *k* of Israel
22:47 regards a *k*, there was none
22:47 in Edom; a deputy was *k*
22:51 *k* over Israel in Samaria
22:51 Jehoshaphat the *k* of Judah
2Ki 1:3 the *k* of Samaria and say to
1:6 return to the *k* who sent you
1:9 the *k* himself has spoken
1:11 *k* has said, Do come down
1:15 went down with him to the *k*
1:17 Jehoshaphat the *k* of Judah
3:1 Jehoram . . . *k* over Israel
3:1 Jehoshaphat the *k* of Judah
3:4 Mesha the *k* of Moab, he
3:4 he paid to the *k* of Israel a
3:5 the *k* of Moab began to revolt
3:5 revolt against the *k* of Israel
3:6 *K* Jehoram went out on that
3:7 Jehoshaphat the *k* of Judah
3:7 The *k* of Moab himself has
3:9 the *k* of Israel and the
3:9 and the *k* of Judah and the
3:9 and the *k* of Edom proceeded
3:10 the *k* of Israel said: How
3:11 servants of the *k* of Israel
3:12 *k* of Israel and Jehoshaphat
3:12 *k* of Edom went down to him
3:13 to say to the *k* of Israel
3:13 the *k* of Israel said to him
3:14 Jehoshaphat the *k* of Judah
3:26 the *k* of Moab saw that the
3:26 through to the *k* of Edom
4:13 to speak to the *k* or to the
5:1 the army of the *k* of Syria
5:5 *k* of Syria said: Get going!
5:5 a letter to the *k* of Israel
5:6 the letter to the *k* of Israel
5:7 *k* of Israel read the letter
5:8 *k* of Israel had ripped his
5:8 at once sent to the *k*, saying
6:8 the *k* of Syria, for his part
6:9 sent to the *k* of Israel
6:10 *k* of Israel sent to the place
6:11 the heart of the *k* of Syria
6:11 is for the *k* of Israel
6:12 None, my lord the *k*, but it
6:12 tells the *k* of Israel the
6:21 The *k* of Israel now said to
6:24 Ben-hadad the *k* of Syria
6:26 the *k* of Israel was passing
6:26 Do save, O my lord the *k*!
6:28 the *k* went on to say to her
6:30 *k* heard the woman's words
6:33 and the *k* proceeded to say
7:2 the *k* was supporting himself
7:6 *k* of Israel has hired against
7:12 the *k* rose up by night and
7:14 *k* sent them out after the
7:15 and reported to the *k*
7:17 the *k* himself had appointed
7:17 the *k* came down to him
7:18 had spoken to the *k*, saying
8:3 cry out to the *k* for her house
8:4 *k* was speaking to Gehazi the
8:5 relating to the *k* how he had
8:5 crying out to the *k* for her
8:5 My lord the *k*, this is the
8:6 the *k* asked the woman, and
8:6 *k* gave her a court official
8:7 Ben-hadad the *k* of Syria was
8:8 *k* said to Hazael: Take a gift
8:9 Ben-hadad, the *k* of Syria, has
8:13 shown me you as *k* over Syria
8:16 son of Ahab the *k* of Israel
8:16 Jehoshaphat was *k* of Judah
8:16 Jehoshaphat the *k* of Judah
8:16 Jehoram . . . became *k*
8:17 when he became *k*, and for
8:20 made a *k* reign over them
8:25 son of Ahab the *k* of Israel
8:25 Jehoram the *k* of Judah
8:25 Ahaziah . . . became *k*
8:26 Omri the *k* of Israel
8:28 Hazael the *k* of Syria
8:29 Jehoram the *k* returned to
8:29 Hazael the *k* of Syria
8:29 Jehoram the *k* of Judah
9:3 anoint you as *k* over Israel
9:6 as *k* over Jehovah's people
9:12 anoint you as *k* over Israel
9:13 and say: Jehu has become *k*!
9:14 Hazael the *k* of Syria

2Ki 9:15 Jehoram the *k* returned to
9:15 fought Hazael the *k* of Syria
9:16 Ahaziah the *k* of Judah
9:18 *k* has said, Is there peace?
9:19 *k* has said, Is there peace?
9:21 and Jehoram the *k* of Israel
9:21 and Ahaziah the *k* of Judah
9:27 And Ahaziah the *k* of Judah
9:29 Ahaziah . . . *k* over Judah
9:34 she is the daughter of a *k*
10:5 We shall not make anyone *k*
10:6 sons of the *k*, seventy men
10:7 taking the sons of the *k* and
10:8 heads of the sons of the *k*
10:13 Ahaziah the *k* of Judah
10:13 well with the sons of the *k*
11:2 daughter of *K* Jehoram
11:2 sons of the *k* that were to
11:4 showed them the son of the *k*
11:7 in behalf of the *k*
11:8 encircle the *k* all around
11:8 with the *k* when he goes out
11:10 had belonged to *K* David
11:11 all around near the *k*
11:12 brought the son of the *k* out
11:12 made him *k* and anointed
11:12 and say: Let the *k* live!
11:14 the *k* was standing by the
11:14 and the trumpets by the *k*
11:17 Jehovah and the *k* and the
11:17 the *k* and the people
11:19 bring the *k* down from the
12:1 Jehoash became *k*, and for
12:6 year of *K* Jehoash
12:7 *K* Jehoash called Jehoiada
12:10 secretary of the *k* and the
12:17 Hazael the *k* of Syria
12:18 Jehoash the *k* of Judah took
12:18 and the house of the *k* and
12:18 to Hazael the *k* of Syria
13:1 Ahaziah the *k* of Judah
13:1 *k* over Israel in Samaria for
13:3 Hazael the *k* of Syria and
13:4 *k* of Syria had oppressed
13:7 *k* of Syria had destroyed
13:10 Jehoash the *k* of Judah
13:10 *k* over Israel in Samaria
13:12 Amaziah the *k* of Judah
13:14 Jehoash the *k* of Israel
13:16 to say to the *k* of Israel
13:16 upon the hands of the *k*
13:18 he said to the *k* of Israel
13:22 Hazael the *k* of Syria
13:24 Hazael the *k* of Syria died
14:1 Jehoahaz the *k* of Israel
14:1 Jehoash the *k* of Judah
14:1 Amaziah . . . became *k*
14:5 struck down the *k* his father
14:8 Jehu the *k* of Israel, saying
14:9 Jehoash the *k* of Israel
14:9 Amaziah the *k* of Judah
14:11 So Jehoash the *k* of Israel
14:11 and Amaziah the *k* of Judah
14:13 was Amaziah the *k* of Judah
14:13 Jehoash the *k* of Israel
14:14 the house of the *k* and the
14:15 Amaziah the *k* of Judah
14:17 Jehoash the *k* of Judah
14:17 Jehoahaz the *k* of Israel
14:21 they made him *k* in place of
14:22 the *k* lay down with his
14:23 Jehoash the *k* of Judah
14:23 Jehoash the *k* of Israel
14:23 *k* in Samaria for forty-one
15:1 Jeroboam the *k* of Israel
15:1 Amaziah the *k* of Judah
15:1 Azariah . . . became *k*
15:5 Jehovah plagued the *k*, and he
15:8 Azariah the *k* of Judah
15:8 *k* over Israel in Samaria
15:13 *k* in the thirty-ninth year
15:13 Uzziah the *k* of Judah
15:17 Azariah the *k* of Judah
15:17 *k* over Israel for ten years
15:19 Pul the *k* of Assyria came
15:20 to give to the *k* of Assyria
15:20 the *k* of Assyria turned back
15:23 Azariah the *k* of Judah
15:23 *k* over Israel in Samaria
15:27 Azariah the *k* of Judah
15:27 Pekah . . . *k* over Israel
15:29 Pekah the *k* of Israel
15:29 Tiglath-pileser the *k* of
15:32 Remaliah the *k* of Israel

2Ki 15:32 Uzziah the *k* of Judah
15:32 Jotham . . . became *k*
15:37 Rezin the *k* of Syria
16:1 Jotham the *k* of Judah
16:1 Ahaz . . . became *k*
16:5 Rezin the *k* of Syria and
16:5 Remaliah the *k* of Israel
16:6 Rezin the *k* of Syria restored
16:7 Tiglath-pileser the *k*
16:7 the palm of the *k* of Syria
16:7 the palm of the *k* of Israel
16:8 sent the *k* of Assyria a bribe
16:9 the *k* of Assyria listened to
16:9 the *k* of Assyria went up to
16:10 Then *K* Ahaz went to meet
16:10 Tiglath-pileser the *k* of
16:10 *K* Ahaz sent Urijah the
16:11 that *K* Ahaz had sent from
16:11 the time that *K* Ahaz came
16:12 the *k* came from Damascus
16:12 the *k* got to see the altar
16:12 the *k* began to go near to
16:15 *K* Ahaz went on to command
16:15 the burnt offering of the *k*
16:16 that *K* Ahaz had commanded
16:17 *K* Ahaz cut the sidewalls of
16:18 because of the *k* of Assyria
17:1 twelfth year of Ahaz the *k*
17:1 Hoshea . . . became *k* in
17:3 Shalmaneser the *k* of Assyria
17:4 *k* of Assyria got to find
17:4 to So the *k* of Egypt and
17:4 up to the *k* of Assyria
17:4 the *k* of Assyria shut him up
17:5 *k* of Assyria proceeded to
17:6 the *k* of Assyria captured
17:7 Pharaoh the *k* of Egypt
17:21 Jeroboam the son of Nebat *k*
17:24 the *k* of Assyria brought
17:26 word to the *k* of Assyria
17:27 the *k* of Assyria commanded
18:1 Elah the *k* of Israel
18:1 Ahaz the *k* of Judah
18:1 Hezekiah . . . became *k*
18:7 against the *k* of Assyria
18:9 the fourth year of *K* Hezekiah
18:9 Elah the *k* of Israel
18:9 Shalmaneser the *k* of Assyria
18:10 ninth year of Hoshea the *k*
18:11 *k* of Assyria took Israel
18:13 year of *K* Hezekiah
18:13 Sennacherib the *k* of Assyria
18:14 Hezekiah the *k* of Judah
18:14 the *k* of Assyria at Lachish
18:14 the *k* of Assyria laid upon
18:14 Hezekiah the *k* of Judah
18:16 Hezekiah the *k* of Judah had
18:16 gave . . . to the *k* of Assyria
18:17 *k* of Assyria proceeded to
18:17 from Lachish to *K* Hezekiah
18:18 began to call out to the *k*
18:19, 19 *k*, the *k* of Assyria
18:21 way Pharaoh the *k* of Egypt
18:23 my lord the *k* of Assyria
18:28, 28 *k*, the *k* of Assyria
18:29 the *k* has said, Do not let
18:30 the hand of the *k* of Assyria
18:31 the *k* of Assyria has said
18:33 the hand of the *k* of Assyria
18:36 *k* was, saying: You must not
19:1 as soon as *K* Hezekiah heard
19:4 the *k* of Assyria his lord
19:5 servants of *K* Hezekiah came
19:6 *k* of Assyria spoke abusively
19:8 the *k* of Assyria fighting
19:9 Tirhakah the *k* of Ethiopia
19:10 Hezekiah the *k* of Judah
19:10 the hand of the *k* of Assyria
19:13 the *k* of Hamath and the
19:13 and the *k* of Arpad and the
19:13 the *k* of the cities of
19:20 Sennacherib the *k* of Assyria
19:32 concerning the *k* of Assyria
19:36 Sennacherib the *k* of Assyria
20:6 the palm of the *k* of Assyria
20:12 *k* of Babylon sent letters
20:14 came in to *K* Hezekiah and
20:18 palace of the *k* of Babylon
21:3 just as Ahab the *k* of Israel
21:11 Manasseh the *k* of Judah
21:23 *k* to death in his own house
21:24 conspirators against *K* Amon
21:24 Josiah his son *k* in place
22:3 eighteenth year of *K* Josiah

2Ki 22:3 the *k* sent Shaphan the son
22:9 came in to the *k* and replied
22:9 replied to tell the *k* and said
22:10 on to tell the *k*, saying
22:10 to read it before the *k*
22:11 *k* heard the words of the
22:12 the *k* commanded Hilkiah
22:16 that the *k* of Judah has read
22:18 *k* of Judah who is sending
22:20 to bring the *k* the reply
23:1 *k* sent and they gathered
23:2 the *k* went up to the house of
23:3 *k* kept standing by the pillar
23:4 the *k* went on to command
23:12 the *k* pulled down, after
23:13 Solomon the *k* of Israel had
23:13 *k* made unfit for worship
23:21 The *k* now commanded all
23:23 eighteenth year of *K* Josiah
23:25 not prove to be a *k* prior
23:29 Pharaoh Nechoh the *k* of
23:29 came up to the *k* of Assyria
23:29 *K* Josiah proceeded to go to
23:30 *k* in place of his father
23:34 *k* in place of Josiah his
24:1 Nebuchadnezzar the *k* of
24:7 *k* of Egypt come out from his
24:7 *k* of Babylon had taken all
24:7 to belong to the *k* of Egypt
24:10 Nebuchadnezzar the *k* of
24:11 Nebuchadnezzar the *k* of
24:12 Jehoiachin the *k* of Judah
24:12 out to the *k* of Babylon
24:12 *k* of Babylon got to take
24:12 eighth year of his being *k*
24:13 Solomon the *k* of Israel
24:16 *k* of Babylon proceeded to
24:17 *k* of Babylon made Mattaniah
24:17 his uncle *k* in place of him
24:20 against the *k* of Babylon
25:1 ninth year of his being *k*
25:1 Nebuchadnezzar the *k* of
25:2 eleventh year of *K* Zedekiah
25:4 the *k* began to go in the
25:5 went chasing after the *k*
25:6 seized the *k* and brought him
25:6 *k* of Babylon at Riblah
25:8 *K* Nebuchadnezzar the
25:8 Nebuchadnezzar the *k* of
25:8 servant of the *k* of Babylon
25:11 over to the *k* of Babylon
25:19 having access to the *k*
25:20 the *k* of Babylon at Riblah
25:21 the *k* of Babylon proceeded
25:22 Nebuchadnezzar the *k* of
25:23 heard that the *k* of Babylon
25:24 and serve the *k* of Babylon
25:27 Jehoiachin the *k* of Judah
25:27 Evil-merodach the *k* of
25:27 the year of his becoming *k*
25:27 Jehoiachin the *k* of Judah
25:30 given him from the *k*, daily
1Ch 1:43 *k* reigned over the sons of
3:2 Talmai the *k* of Geshur
4:23 the *k* in his work that they
4:41 Hezekiah the *k* of Judah
5:6 Tilgath-pilneser the *k* of
5:17 Jotham the *k* of Judah
5:17 Jeroboam the *k* of Israel
5:26 of Pul the *k* of Assyria
5:26 Tilgath-pilneser the *k* of
11:2 while Saul happened to be *k*
11:3 came to the *k* at Hebron and
11:3 they anointed David as *k* over
11:10 *k* according to Jehovah's
12:31 to come to make David *k*
12:38 to Hebron to make David *k*
12:38 heart for making David *k*
14:1 And Hiram the *k* of Tyre
14:2 established him as *k* over
14:8 David had been anointed as *k*
15:29 see *K* David skipping about
16:31 Jehovah . . . has become *k*
17:16 *K* David came in and sat
18:3 Hadadezer the *k* of Zobah at
18:5 help Hadadezer the *k* of Zobah
18:9 Tou the *k* of Hamath heard
18:9 of Hadadezer the *k* of Zobah
18:10 Hadoram his son to *K* David
18:11 *K* David sanctified to
18:17 at the side of the *k*
19:1 Nahash the *k* of the sons of
19:5 *k* went on to say: Dwell in
19:7 *k* of Maacah and his people

1Ch 21:3 Do they not, O my lord the *k*
21:23 let my lord the *k* do what
21:24 *K* David said to Ornan
23:1 made Solomon his son *k* over
24:6 before the *k* and the princes
24:31 before David the *k* and Zadok
25:2 under the control of the *k*
25:5 Heman, a visionary of the *k*
25:6 Under the control of the *k*
26:26 David the *k* and the heads of
26:32 David the *k* assigned them
26:32 and matter of the *k*
27:1 ministering to the *k* in
27:24 of the days of *K* David
27:25 over the treasures of the *k*
27:31 that belonged to *K* David
27:33 was a counselor of the *k*
27:34 chief of the army of the *k*
28:1 those ministering to the *k*
28:1 goods and livestock of the *k*
28:2 David the *k* rose to his feet
28:4 to become *k* over Israel to
28:4 to make me *k* over all Israel
29:1 David the *k* now said to all
29:6 of the business of the *k*
29:9 David the *k* himself rejoiced
29:20 to Jehovah and to the *k*
29:22 to make Solomon . . . *k* and
29:23 as *k* in place of David his
29:24 also all the sons of *K* David
29:24 to Solomon the *k*
29:25 upon any *k* before him over
29:29 the affairs of David the *k*
2Ch 1:8 made me *k* in place of him
1:9 *k* over a people as numerous
1:11 over whom I have made you *k*
1:14 close by the *k* at Jerusalem
1:15 *k* came to make the silver
2:3 sent to Hiram the *k* of Tyre
2:11 Hiram the *k* of Tyre said the
2:11 constituted you *k* over them
2:12 to David the *k* a wise son
4:11 that he did for *K* Solomon
4:16 made for *K* Solomon for the
4:17 the *k* cast them in the thick
5:3 to the *k* at the festival, that
5:6 And *K* Solomon and all the
6:3 *k* turned his face and began to
7:4 *k* and all the people were
7:5 *K* Solomon went on offering
7:5 *k* and all the people
7:6 David the *k* had made to thank
7:11 and the house of the *k*
8:10 that belonged to *K* Solomon
8:11 of David the *k* of Israel
8:18 and bring it to *K* Solomon
9:5 she said to the *k*: True was
9:8 his throne as *k* for Jehovah
9:8 *k* to execute judicial decision
9:9 she gave the *k* a hundred and
9:9 of Sheba gave to *K* Solomon
9:11 *k* proceeded to make out of
9:12 *K* Solomon himself gave the
9:12 she brought to the *k*
9:15 *K* Solomon went on to make
9:16 *k* put them in the House of
9:17 *k* made a great ivory throne
9:20 vessels of *K* Solomon were
9:21 ships belonging to the *k*
9:22 *K* Solomon was greater than
9:25 close by the *k* in Jerusalem
9:27 *k* made the silver in
10:1 came to make him *k*
10:2 on account of Solomon the *k*
10:6 *K* Rehoboam began to take
10:12 just as the *k* had spoken
10:13 *k* began to answer them
10:13 *K* Rehoboam left the counsel
10:15 *k* did not listen to the
10:16 *k* did not listen to them
10:16 people now replied to the *k*
10:18 *K* Rehoboam sent Hadoram
10:18 *K* Rehoboam himself managed
11:3 *k* of Judah and to all Israel
11:22 he thought of making him *k*
12:2 fifth year of *K* Rehoboam
12:2 Shishak the *k* of Egypt came
12:6 and the *k* humbled themselves
12:9 Shishak the *k* of Egypt came
12:10 *K* Rehoboam made in their
12:11 *k* came to the house of
12:13 *K* Rehoboam continued to
13:1 eighteenth . . . of *K* Jeroboam
15:16 Asa the *k* himself removed

2Ch 16:1 Baasha the *k* of Israel came
16:1 in to Asa the *k* of Judah
16:2 to Ben-hadad the *k* of Syria
16:3 Baasha the *k* of Israel, that
16:4 Ben-hadad listened to *K* Asa
16:6 Asa the *k*, he took all Judah
16:7 Asa the *k* of Judah and then
16:7 leaned upon the *k* of Syria
16:7 force of the *k* of Syria has
17:19 ones ministering to the *k*
17:19 *k* put in the fortified
18:3 Ahab the *k* of Israel went on
18:3 to Jehoshaphat the *k* of Judah
18:4 said to the *k* of Israel
18:5 *k* of Israel collected the
18:7 *k* of Israel said to
18:7 the *k* say a thing like that
18:8 *k* of Israel called a court
18:9 *k* of Israel and Jehoshaphat
18:9 Jehoshaphat the *k* of Judah
18:12 words . . . of good to the *k*
18:14 came in to the *k*, and the
18:14 *k* proceeded to say to him
18:15 *k* said to him: For how
18:17 *k* of Israel said to
18:19 fool Ahab the *k* of Israel
18:25 *k* of Israel said: Take
18:26 *k* has said: Put this fellow
18:28 *k* of Israel and Jehoshaphat
18:28 Jehoshaphat the *k* of Judah
18:29 *k* of Israel now said to
18:29 *k* of Israel disguised
18:30 *k* of Syria, he had
18:30 with the *k* of Israel alone
18:31 It is the *k* of Israel
18:32 prove to be the *k* of Israel
18:33 strike the *k* of Israel
18:34 *k* of Israel himself had to
19:1 Jehoshaphat the *k* of Judah
19:2 to *K* Jehoshaphat: Is it to
19:11 for every matter of the *k*
20:15 Jerusalem and *K* Jehoshaphat
20:35 Jehoshaphat the *k* of Judah
20:35 Ahaziah the *k* of Israel
21:2 Jehoshaphat the *k* of Israel
21:8 made a *k* to reign over them
21:12 ways of Asa the *k* of Judah
22:1 Ahaziah his youngest son *k*
22:1 to reign as *k* of Judah
22:5 Ahab the *k* of Israel to the
22:5 Hazael the *k* of Syria at
22:6 fought Hazael the *k* of Syria
22:6 Jehoram the *k* of Judah, he
22:11 daughter of the *k* took
22:11 sons of the *k* that were to
22:11 daughter of *K* Jehoram, the
23:3 covenant with the *k* in the
23:3 son of the *k* himself will
23:5 be at the house of the *k*
23:7 Levites must encircle the *k*
23:7 *k* when he comes in and when
23:9 that had belonged to *K* David
23:10 all around near the *k*
23:11 and made him *k*, and so
23:11 said: Let the *k* live!
23:12 and praising the *k*, she
23:13 *k* standing by his pillar at
23:13 and the trumpets by the *k*
23:16 and all the people and the *k*
23:20 *k* down from the house of
23:20 seated the *k* upon the throne
24:6 *k* called Jehoiada the head
24:8 *k* said the word, and so they
24:11 care of the *k* by the hand
24:11 secretary of the *k* and the
24:12 *k* and Jehoiada would give
24:14 *k* and Jehoiada the rest of
24:17 to bow down to the *k*
24:17 the *k* listened to them
24:22 Jehoash the *k* did not
24:23 sent to the *k* of Damascus
25:1 Amaziah became *k*, and for
25:3 struck down the *k* his father
25:7 O *k*, do not let the army of
25:16 *k* immediately said to him
25:16 counselor of the *k* that we
25:17 Amaziah the *k* of Judah
25:17 son of Jehu the *k* of Israel
25:18 Jehoash the *k* of Israel
25:18 to Amaziah the *k* of Judah
25:21 Jehoash the *k* of Israel
25:21 and Amaziah the *k* of Judah
25:23 Amaziah the *k* of Judah
25:23 Jehoash the *k* of Israel
2Ch 25:25 *k* of Judah continued to live
25:25 *k* of Israel fifteen years
26:1 Uzziah . . . *k* in place of his
26:2 *k* had lain down with his
26:13 to help the *k* against the
26:18 up against Uzziah the *k* and
26:21 Uzziah the *k* continued to
27:5 *k* of the sons of Ammon and
28:5 the hand of the *k* of Syria
28:5 hand of the *k* of Israel he
28:7 Maaseiah the son of the *k*
28:7 Elkanah the one next to the *k*
28:16 *K* Ahaz sent to the kings
28:19 of Ahaz the *k* of Israel
28:20 Tilgath-pilneser the *k* of
28:21 house of the *k* and of the
28:21 gift to the *k* of Assyria
28:22 that is, *K* Ahaz did
29:1 Hezekiah himself became *k*
29:18 to Hezekiah the *k* and said
29:19 utensils that *K* Ahaz
29:20 Hezekiah the *k* proceeded to
29:23 near before the *k* and the
29:24 *k* said the burnt offering
29:27 of David the *k* of Israel
29:29 *k* and all those found with
29:30 Hezekiah the *k* and the
30:2 *k* and his princes and all the
30:4 right in the eyes of the *k*
30:6 from the hand of the *k* and
30:6 to the commandment of the *k*
30:12 the commandment of the *k*
30:24 For Hezekiah the *k* of Judah
30:26 David the *k* of Israel there
31:3 portion of the *k* from his
31:13 order of Hezekiah the *k*
32:1 Sennacherib the *k* of Assyria
32:7 because of the *k* of Assyria
32:8 of Hezekiah the *k* of Judah
32:9 Sennacherib the *k* of Assyria
32:9 to Hezekiah the *k* of Judah
32:10 Sennacherib the *k* of Assyria
32:11 palm of the *k* of Assyria
32:20 Hezekiah the *k* and Isaiah
32:21 camp of the *k* of Assyria
32:22 Sennacherib the *k* of Assyria
32:23 Hezekiah the *k* of Judah
33:11 belonged to the *k* of Assyria
33:25 conspirators against *K* Amon
33:25 Josiah his son *k* in place
34:16 brought the book to the *k*
34:16 replied further to the *k*
34:18 to report to the *k*, saying
34:18 read out of it before the *k*
34:19 *k* heard the words of the
34:20 the *k* commanded Hilkiah and
34:22 *k* had said went to Huldah
34:24 read before the *k* of Judah
34:26 the *k* of Judah, who is
34:28 brought the reply to the *k*
34:29 *k* proceeded to send and
34:30 *k* now went up to the house
34:31 *k* kept standing in his place
35:3 the *k* of Israel built
35:4 David the *k* of Israel
35:7 were from the goods of the *k*
35:15 the visionary of the *k*
35:16 commandment of *K* Josiah
35:20 Necho the *k* of Egypt came
35:21 do with you, O *k* of Judah
35:23 got to shoot at *K* Josiah
35:23 *k* said to his servants
36:1 made him *k* in the place of
36:3 the *k* of Egypt removed him
36:4 the *k* of Egypt made Eliakim
36:4 Eliakim . . . *k* over Judah and
36:6 Nebuchadnezzar the *k* of
36:10 *K* Nebuchadnezzar sent and
36:10 Zedekiah . . . *k* over Judah
36:13 against *K* Nebuchadnezzar
36:17 the *k* of the Chaldeans
36:18 treasures of the *k* and of
36:22 Cyrus the *k* of Persia
36:22 Cyrus the *k* of Persia
36:23 Cyrus the *k* of Persia has
Ezr 1:1 Cyrus the *k* of Persia
1:1 Cyrus the *k* of Persia
1:2 what Cyrus the *k* of Persia
1:7 *K* Cyrus himself brought forth
1:8 Cyrus the *k* of Persia
2:1 Nebuchadnezzar the *k* of
3:7 by Cyrus the *k* of Persia
3:10 David the *k* of Israel
4:2 Esar-haddon the *k* of Assyria
Ezr 4:3, 3 *K* Cyrus the *k* of Persia has
4:5 days of Cyrus the *k* of Persia
4:5 Darius the *k* of Persia
4:7 Artaxerxes the *k* of Persia
4:8 Artaxerxes the *k*, as follows
4:11 To Artaxerxes the *k* your
4:12 become known to the *k* that
4:13 become known to the *k* that
4:14 to see the denuding of the *k*
4:14 and made it known to the *k*
4:16 making known to the *k* that
4:17 The *k* sent word to Rehum
4:23 document of Artaxerxes the *k*
4:24 Darius the *k* of Persia
5:6 sent to Darius the *k*
5:7 To Darius the *k*: All peace!
5:8 Let it become known to the *k*
5:11 a great *k* of Israel built
5:12 Nebuchadnezzar the *k* of
5:13 Cyrus the *k* of Babylon
5:13 Cyrus the *k* put an order
5:14 Cyrus the *k* took out of the
5:17 if to the *k* it seems good
5:17 from Cyrus the *k* an order
5:17 decision of the *k* concerning
6:1 Darius the *k* put an order
6:3 the first year of Cyrus the *k*
6:3 Cyrus the *k* put an order
6:10 praying for the life of the *k*
6:12 overthrow any *k* and people
6:13 Darius the *k* had sent word
6:14 Artaxerxes the *k* of Persia
6:15 the reign of Darius the *k*
6:22 heart of the *k* of Assyria
7:1 Artaxerxes the *k* of Persia
7:6 so that the *k* granted him
7:7 year of Artaxerxes the *k*
7:8 in the seventh year of the *k*
7:11 letter that *K* Artaxerxes
7:12 Artaxerxes, the *k* of kings
7:14 *k* and his seven counselors
7:15 that the *k* and his counselors
7:21 Artaxerxes the *k*, an order
7:26 and the law of the *k*, let
7:27 into the heart of the *k*
7:28 the *k* and his counselors
7:28 the mighty princes of the *k*
8:1 the reign of Artaxerxes the *k*
8:22 from the *k* to help us
8:22 because we had said to the *k*
8:25 the *k* and his counselors and
8:36 gave the laws of the *k* to
8:36 to the satraps of the *k* and
Ne 1:11 to be cupbearer to the *k*
2:1 year of Artaxerxes the *k*
2:1 the wine and gave it to the *k*
2:2 So the *k* said to me: Why is
2:3 I said to the *k*: Let the
2:3 Let the *k* himself live to time
2:4 In turn the *k* said to me
2:5 I said to the *k*: If to the
2:5 If to the *k* it does seem good
2:6 *k* said to me, as his queenly
2:6 it seemed good before the *k*
2:7 And I went on to say to the *k*
2:7 If to the *k* it does seem good
2:8 the park that belongs to the *k*
2:8 So the *k* gave them to me
2:9 gave them the letters of the *k*
2:9 *k* sent with me chiefs of the
2:19 Is it against the *k* that you
5:14 Artaxerxes the *k*, twelve
6:6 you are becoming a *k* to them
6:7 saying, There is a *k* in Judah!
6:7 these will be told to the *k*
7:6 Nebuchadnezzar the *k* of Babylon
9:22 the land of the *k* of Heshbon
9:22 the land of Og the *k* of Bashan
11:23 commandment of the *k* in
11:24 at the side of the *k* for
13:6 Artaxerxes the *k* of Babylon
13:6 I came to the *k*, and
13:6 leave of absence from the *k*
13:26 Solomon the *k* of Israel
13:26 proved to be no *k* like him
13:26 him *k* over all Israel
Es 1:1 Ahasuerus who was ruling as *k*
1:2 as *K* Ahasuerus was sitting
1:5 *k* held a banquet for seven days
1:7 to the means of the *k*
1:8 *k* had arranged for every great
1:9 that belonged to *K* Ahasuerus
1:10 to the person of *K* Ahasuerus
1:11 bring Vashti . . . before the *k*

Es 1:12 the *k* grew highly indignant
1:13 the *k* proceeded to say to the
1:14 having access to the *k*, and
1:15 the saying of *K* Ahasuerus by
1:16 Memucan said before the *k* and
1:16 It is not against the *k* alone
1:16 districts of *K* Ahasuerus
1:17 *K* Ahasuerus himself said to
1:18 to all the princes of the *k*
1:19 If to the *k* it does seem good
1:19 come in before *K* Ahasuerus
1:19 royal dignity let the *k* give
1:20 decree of the *k* that he will
1:21 pleasing in the eyes of the *k*
1:21 *k* proceeded to do according to
2:1 the rage of *K* Ahasuerus had
2:2 seek young women . . . for the *k*
2:3 the *k* appoint commissioners
2:6 with Jeconiah the *k* of Judah
2:6 Nebuchadnezzar the *k* of Babylon
2:12 go in to *K* Ahasuerus after it
2:13 woman . . . came in to the *k*
2:14 not come in anymore to the *k*
2:14 the *k* had taken delight in her
2:15 Esther . . . come in to the *k*
2:16 taken to *K* Ahasuerus at his
2:17 *k* came to love Esther more
2:18 the *k* went on to hold a great
2:18 the means of the *k*
2:21 two court officials of the *k*
2:21 to lay hand on *K* Ahasuerus
2:22 In turn Esther talked to the *k*
2:23 of the days before the *k*
3:1 *K* Ahasuerus magnified Haman
3:2 the *k* had commanded respecting
3:7 twelfth year of *K* Ahasuerus
3:8 to say to *K* Ahasuerus: There is
3:8 for the *k* it is not appropriate
3:9 If to the *k* it does seem good
3:10 the *k* removed his signet ring
3:11 the *k* went on to say to Haman
3:12 in the name of *K* Ahasuerus it
3:15 *k* and Haman, they sat down to
4:8 in to the *k* and implore favor
4:11 that comes in to the *k* at the
4:11 only in case the *k* holds out
4:11 called to come in to the *k*
4:16 I shall come in to the *k*
5:1 the *k* was sitting on his royal
5:2 as soon as the *k* saw Esther
5:2 *k* held out to Esther the golden
5:3 *k* said to her: What do you
5:4 If to the *k* it does seem good
5:4 let the *k* with Haman come
5:5 *k* said: You men, have Haman
5:5 the *k* and Haman came to the
5:6 In time the *k* said to Esther
5:8 if to the *k* it does seem good
5:8 let the *k* and Haman come to
5:11 the *k* had magnified him
5:11 and the servants of the *k*
5:12 in with the *k* to the banquet
5:12 am invited to her with the *k*
5:14 say to the *k* that they should
5:14 in with the *k* to the banquet
6:1 a reading of them before the *k*
6:2 two court officials of the *k*
6:2 to lay hand on *K* Ahasuerus
6:3 *k* said: What honor and great
6:4 the *k* said: Who is in the
6:4 say to the *k* to hang Mordecai
6:5 So the *k* said: Let him come in
6:6 When Haman came in, the *k*
6:6 *k* himself has taken a delight
6:6 *k* take delight in rendering an
6:7 Haman said to the *k*: As for
6:7 the man in whose honor the *k*
6:8 with which the *k* does clothe
6:8 upon which the *k* does ride
6:9 *k* himself has taken a delight
6:9 *k* himself has taken a delight
6:10 At once the *k* said to Haman
6:11 *k* himself has taken a delight
7:1 the *k* and Haman came in to
7:2 *k* now said to Esther also on
7:3 found favor in your eyes, O *k*
7:3 if to the *k* it does seem good
7:4 when with damage to the *k*
7:5 *K* Ahasuerus now said, yes, he
7:6 because of the *k* and the queen
7:7 *k*, he rose up in his rage from
7:7 against him by the *k*
7:8 *k* himself returned from the
7:8 *k* said: Is there also to be a
Es 7:9 court officials before the *k*
7:9 spoken good concerning the *k*
7:9 *k* said: You men, hang him on
8:1 *K* Ahasuerus gave to Esther the
8:1 came in before the *k*, because
8:2 the *k* removed his signet ring
8:3 Esther spoke again before the *k*
8:4 *k* held the golden scepter out
8:4 rose and stood before the *k*
8:5 If to the *k* it does seem good
8:5 thing is proper before the *k*
8:7 So *K* Ahasuerus said to Esther
8:9 secretaries of the *k* were
8:10 in the name of *K* Ahasuerus
8:11 *k* granted to the Jews that
8:12 districts of *K* Ahasuerus, on
8:15 went forth from before the *k*
8:17 the word of the *k* and his law
9:2 districts of *K* Ahasuerus to lay
9:3 business that belonged to the *k*
9:11 number . . . came before the *k*
9:12 *k* proceeded to say to Esther
9:12 districts of the *k* what have
9:13 If to the *k* it does seem good
9:14 *k* said for it to be done that
9:16 districts of the *k*, they
9:20 districts of *K* Ahasuerus, the
9:25 Esther came in before the *k*
10:1 *K* Ahasuerus proceeded to lay
10:2 which the *k* magnified him
10:3 was second to *K* Ahasuerus and
Job 15:24 like a *k* in readiness for
18:14 to the *k* of terrors
29:25 as a *k* among his troops
34:18 say to a *k*, You are good
41:34 *k* over all majestic wild
Ps 2:6 I, even I, have installed my *k*
5:2 O my *K* and my God, because to
10:16 Jehovah is *K* to time
18:50 acts of salvation for his *k*
20:9 O Jehovah, do save the *k*!
21:1 your strength the *k* rejoices
21:7 the *k* is trusting in Jehovah
24:7 the glorious *K* may come in
24:8 Who, then, is this glorious *K*?
24:9 the glorious *K* may come in
24:10 is he, this glorious *K*
24:10 Jehovah . . . is the glorious *K*
29:10 Jehovah sits as *k* to time
33:16 no *k* saved by the abundance
44:4 You yourself are my *K*, O God
45:1 My works are concerning a *k*
45:5 heart of the enemies of the *k*
45:11 the *k* will long for your
45:14 she will be brought to the *k*
45:15 into the palace of the *k*
47:2 A great *K* over all the earth
47:6 Make melody to our *K*, make
47:7 For God is *K* of all the earth
47:8 God has become *k* over the
48:2 The town of the grand *K*
61:6 add to the days of the *k*
63:11 the *k* himself will rejoice
68:24 processions of my God, my *K*
72:1 judicial decisions to the *k*
72:1 to the son of the *k*
74:12 God is my *K* from long ago
84:3 Jehovah of armies, my *K* and
89:18 *k* belongs to the Holy One of
93:1 Jehovah himself has become *k*!
95:3 great *K* over all other gods
96:10 Jehovah himself has become *k*
97:1 Jehovah himself has become *k*!
98:6 Shout in triumph before the *K*
99:1 Jehovah himself has become *k*
99:4 with the strength of a *k*
105:20 *k* sent that he might
135:11 Sihon the *k* of the Amorites
135:11 And Og the *k* of Bashan
136:19 Sihon the *k* of the Amorites
136:20 And Og the *k* of Bashan
145:1 exalt you, O my God the *K*
146:10 Jehovah will be *k* to time
149:2 them be joyful in their *K*
Pr 1:1 David, the *k* of Israel
14:28 there is an adornment of a *k*
14:35 The pleasure of a *k* is in the
16:10 be upon the lips of a *k*
16:13 are a pleasure to a grand *k*
16:14 rage of a *k* means messengers
19:12 raging of a *k* is a growling
20:2 The frightfulness of a *k* is a
20:8 *k* is sitting upon the throne
20:26 wise *k* is scattering wicked
Pr 20:28 they safeguard the *k*
22:11 the *k* will be his companion
23:1 to feed yourself with a *k*
24:21 son, fear Jehovah and the *k*
25:1 of Hezekiah the *k* of Judah
25:5 the wicked one before the *k*
25:6 do yourself honor before the *k*
29:4 By justice a *k* makes a land
29:14 *k* is judging the lowly ones
30:22 a slave when he rules as *k*
30:27 locusts have no *k*, and yet
30:28 is in the grand palace of a *k*
30:31 *k* of a band of soldiers of
31:1 The words of Lemuel the *k*
Ec 1:1 of David the *k* in Jerusalem
1:12 be *k* over Israel in Jerusalem
2:12 do who comes in after the *k*
4:13 child than an old but stupid *k*
4:14 house itself to become *k*
5:9 the *k* himself has been served
8:2 Keep the very order of the *k*
8:4 word of the *k* is the power of
9:14 there came to it a great *k*
10:16 when your *k* is a boy and
10:17 *k* is the son of noble ones
10:20 call down evil upon the *k*
Ca 1:4 The *k* has brought me into his
1:12 as the *k* is at his round table
3:9 litter that *K* Solomon has made
3:11 on *K* Solomon with the wreath
7:5 The *k* is held bound by the
Isa 6:1 year that *K* Uzziah died I
6:5 seen the *K*, Jehovah of armies
7:1 Uzziah, the *k* of Judah, that
7:1 Rezin the *k* of Syria and
7:1 *k* of Israel, came up to
7:6 make another *k* reign inside
7:17 namely, the *k* of Assyria
7:20 by means of the *k* of Assyria
8:4 before the *k* of Assyria
8:7 *k* of Assyria and all his glory
8:21 call down evil upon his *k*
10:12 heart of the *k* of Assyria
14:4 against the *k* of Babylon
14:28 year that *K* Ahaz died this
19:4 *k* that will rule over them
20:1 Sargon the *k* of Assyria sent
20:4 *k* of Assyria will lead the
20:6 because of the *k* of Assyria
23:15 same as the days of one *k*
24:23 *k* in Mount Zion and
30:33 prepared for the *k* himself
32:1 *k* will reign for
33:17 *k* in his handsomeness is
33:22 Jehovah is our *K*
36:1 fourteenth year of *K* Hezekiah
36:1 Sennacherib the *k* of Assyria
36:2 *k* of Assyria finally sent
36:2 *K* Hezekiah, with a heavy
36:4, 4 great *k*, the *k* of Assyria
36:6 *k* of Egypt is to all those
36:8 my lord the *k* of Assyria
36:13 the words of the great *k*
36:13 the *k* of Assyria
36:14 *k* has said, Do not let
36:15 hand of the *k* of Assyria
36:16 *k* of Assyria has said
36:18 hand of the *k* of Assyria
36:21 the commandment of the *k*
37:1 soon as *K* Hezekiah heard
37:4 *k* of Assyria his lord sent
37:5 servants of *K* Hezekiah came
37:6 of the *k* of Assyria spoke
37:8 *k* of Assyria fighting against
37:9 Tirhakah the *k* of Ethiopia
37:10 to Hezekiah the *k* of Judah
37:10 hand of the *k* of Assyria
37:13 Where is the *k* of Hamath
37:13 Hamath and the *k* of Arpad
37:13 and the *k* of the city of
37:21 Sennacherib the *k* of Assyria
37:33 *k* of Assyria: He will not
37:37 Sennacherib the *k* of Assyria
38:6 the *k* of Assyria I shall
38:9 Hezekiah the *k* of Judah
39:1 Baladan the *k* of Babylon sent
39:3 to *K* Hezekiah and said to
39:7 palace of the *k* of Babylon
41:21 says the *K* of Jacob
43:15 Creator of Israel, your *K*
44:6 the *K* of Israel and the
52:7 Your God has become *k*!
Jer 1:2 Amon, the *k* of Judah
1:3 Josiah, the *k* of Judah

Jer 1:3 Josiah, the *k* of Judah
3:6 in the days of Josiah the *k*
4:9 heart of the *k* will perish
8:19 Or is her *k* not in her?
10:7 fear you, O *K* of the nations
10:10 the living God and the *K*
13:18 Say to the *k* and to the lady
15:4 Hezekiah, the *k* of Judah
20:4 the hand of the *k* of Babylon
21:1 *K* Zedekiah sent to him
21:2 *k* of Babylon is making war
21:4 fighting the *k* of Babylon
21:7 Zedekiah the *k* of Judah and
21:7 Nebuchadrezzar the *k* of
21:10 the hand of the *k* of Babylon
21:11 household of the *k* of Judah
22:1 the house of the *k* of Judah
22:2 O *k* of Judah who are sitting
22:6 the house of the *k* of Judah
22:11 Josiah, the *k* of Judah
22:18 Josiah, the *k* of Judah
22:24 Jehoiakim, the *k* of Judah
22:25 Nebuchadrezzar the *k* of
23:5 a *k* will certainly reign and
24:1 the *k* of Babylon had
24:1 Jehoiakim, the *k* of Judah
24:8 Zedekiah the *k* of Judah
25:1 Josiah, the *k* of Judah
25:1 Nebuchadrezzar the *k* of
25:3 son of Amon, the *k* of Judah
25:9 Nebuchadrezzar the *k* of
25:11 to serve the *k* of Babylon
25:12 against the *k* of Babylon
25:19 Pharaoh the *k* of Egypt and
25:26 the *k* of Sheshach himself
26:1 Josiah, the *k* of Judah
26:10 from the house of the *k*
26:18 Hezekiah the *k* of Judah
26:19 Hezekiah the *k* of Judah
26:21 *K* Jehoiakim and all his
26:21 the *k* began seeking to put
26:22 *K* Jehoiakim sent men to
26:23 to bring him to *K* Jehoiakim
27:1 Josiah, the *k* of Judah
27:3 send them to the *k* of Edom
27:3 to the *k* of Moab and to the
27:3 the *k* of the sons of Ammon
27:3 to the *k* of Tyre and to the
27:3 to the *k* of Sidon by the hand
27:3 Zedekiah the *k* of Judah
27:6 Nebuchadnezzar the *k* of
27:8 Nebuchadnezzar the *k* of
27:8 the yoke of the *k* of Babylon
27:9 you men will not serve the *k*
27:11 the yoke of the *k* of Babylon
27:12 Zedekiah the *k* of Judah
27:12 the yoke of the *k* of Babylon
27:13 not serve the *k* of Babylon
27:14 not serve the *k* of Babylon
27:17 Serve the *k* of Babylon and
27:18 the house of the *k* of Judah
27:20 Nebuchadnezzar the *k* of
27:20 Jehoiakim, the *k* of Judah
27:21 the house of the *k* of Judah
28:1 Zedekiah the *k* of Judah
28:2 the yoke of the *k* of Babylon
28:3 the *k* of Babylon took from
28:4 Jehoiakim, the *k* of Judah
28:4 the yoke of the *k* of Babylon
28:11 Nebuchadnezzar the *k* of
28:14 Nebuchadnezzar the *k* of
29:2 after Jeconiah the *k* and the
29:3 Zedekiah the *k* of Judah sent
29:3 Nebuchadnezzar the *k* of
29:16 Jehovah has said to the *k*
29:21 Nebuchadrezzar the *k* of
29:22 the *k* of Babylon roasted in
30:9 and David their *k*, whom I
32:1 of Zedekiah the *k* of Judah
32:2 forces of the *k* of Babylon
32:2 house of the *k* of Judah
32:3 Zedekiah the *k* of Judah had
32:3 hand of the *k* of Babylon
32:4 *k* of Judah, will not escape
32:4 hand of the *k* of Babylon
32:28 Nebuchadrezzar the *k* of
32:36 hand of the *k* of Babylon
33:21 son ruling as *k* upon his
34:1 *k* of Babylon and all his
34:2 Zedekiah the *k* of Judah, yes
34:2 hand of the *k* of Babylon, and
34:3 the eyes of the *k* of Babylon
34:4 Zedekiah the *k* of Judah, This is
34:6 to Zedekiah the *k* of Judah

Jer 34:7 forces of the *k* of Babylon
34:8 *K* Zedekiah concluded a
34:21 Zedekiah the *k* of Judah and
34:21 forces of the *k* of Babylon
35:1 the *k* of Judah, saying
35:11 Nebuchadrezzar the *k* of
36:1 *k* of Judah, that this word
36:9 *k* of Judah, in the ninth
36:12 down to the house of the *k*
36:16 tell the *k* all these words
36:20 came in to the *k*, to the
36:20 words in the ears of the *k*
36:21 *k* sent Jehudi out to get
36:21 in the ears of the *k*
36:21 princes standing by the *k*
36:22 *k* was sitting in the winter
36:24 the *k* and all his servants
36:25 pleaded with the *k* not to
36:26 *k* commanded Jerahmeel the
36:26 Jerahmeel the son of the *k*
36:27 *k* had burned up the roll
36:28 *k* of Judah burned up
36:29 Jehoiakim the *k* of Judah
36:29 *k* of Babylon will come
36:30 Jehoiakim the *k* of Judah
36:32 Jehoiakim the *k* of Judah
37:1 *K* Zedekiah the son of Josiah
37:1 Nebuchadrezzar the *k* of
37:1 made *k* in the land of Judah
37:3 *K* Zedekiah proceeded to
37:7 say to the *k* of Judah, the
37:17 *K* Zedekiah proceeded to
37:17 *k* began asking him
37:17 hand of the *k* of Babylon
37:18 Jeremiah said to *K* Zedekiah
37:19 *k* of Babylon will not come
37:20 my lord the *k*. May my
37:21 *K* Zedekiah commanded, and
38:3 force of the *k* of Babylon
38:4 princes began to say to the *k*
38:5 *K* Zedekiah said: Look!
38:5 *k* himself can prevail
38:6 Malchijah the son of the *k*
38:7 was in the house of the *k*
38:7 *k* was sitting in the gate of
38:8 out of the house of the *k*
38:8 and spoke to the *k*, saying
38:9 my lord the *k*, these men
38:10 *k* commanded Ebed-melech the
38:11 into the house of the *k*
38:14 *K* Zedekiah proceeded to
38:14 *k* said to Jeremiah: I am
38:16 *K* Zedekiah swore to
38:17 princes of the *k* of Babylon
38:18 princes of the *k* of Babylon
38:19 *K* Zedekiah said to Jeremiah
38:22 house of the *k* of Judah are
38:22 princes of the *k* of Babylon
38:23 hand of the *k* of Babylon
38:25 you speak about to the *k*
38:25 the *k* speak about to you
38:26 for favor fall before the *k*
38:27 that the *k* had commanded
39:1 Zedekiah the *k* of Judah, in
39:1 Nebuchadrezzar the *k* of
39:3 princes of the *k* of Babylon
39:3 princes of the *k* of Babylon
39:4 Zedekiah the *k* of Judah and
39:4 way of the garden of the *k*
39:5 *k* of Babylon at Riblah in
39:6 *k* of Babylon proceeded to
39:6 *k* of Babylon slaughtered
39:8 house of the *k* and the
39:11 Nebuchadrezzar the *k* of
39:13 men of the *k* of Babylon
40:5 *k* of Babylon has
40:7 *k* of Babylon had
40:9 serve the *k* of Babylon, and
40:11 *k* of Babylon had given a
40:14 Baalis, the *k* of the sons
41:1 principal men of the *k* and
41:2 one whom the *k* of Babylon
41:9 one that *K* Asa had made
41:9 Baasha the *k* of Israel
41:10 daughters of the *k* and all
41:18 *k* of Babylon had
42:11 because of the *k* of Babylon
43:6 daughters of the *k* and every
43:10 Nebuchadrezzar the *k* of
44:30 Hophra, the *k* of Egypt
44:30 Zedekiah the *k* of Judah into
44:30 Nebuchadrezzar the *k* of
45:1 the *k* of Judah, saying
46:2 Pharaoh Necho the *k* of Egypt

Jer 46:2 *k* of Babylon defeated in the
46:2 of Josiah, the *k* of Judah
46:13 Nebuchadrezzar the *k* of
46:17 Pharaoh the *k* of Egypt is
46:18 *K*, whose name is Jehovah of
46:26 Nebuchadrezzar the *k* of
48:15 *K*, whose name is Jehovah of
49:28 Nebuchadrezzar the *k* of
49:30 Nebuchadrezzar the *k* of
49:34 Zedekiah the *k* of Judah
49:38 destroy out of there the *k*
50:17 *k* of Assyria has devoured
50:17 Nebuchadrezzar the *k* of
50:18 *k* of Babylon and upon his
50:18 upon the *k* of Assyria
50:43 *k* of Babylon has heard
51:31 report to the *k* of Babylon
51:34 Nebuchadrezzar the *k* of
51:57 *K*, whose name is Jehovah
51:59 Zedekiah the *k* of Judah to
51:59 fourth year of his being *k*
52:3 against the *k* of Babylon
52:4 ninth year of his being *k*
52:4 Nebuchadrezzar the *k* of
52:5 eleventh year of *K* Zedekiah
52:8 went chasing after the *k*
52:9 seized the *k* and brought him
52:9 up to the *k* of Babylon
52:10 *k* of Babylon proceeded to
52:11 *k* of Babylon bound him with
52:12 year of *K* Nebuchadrezzar
52:12 Nebuchadrezzar, the *k* of
52:12 before the *k* of Babylon
52:13 and the house of the *k* and
52:15 away to the *k* of Babylon
52:20 that *K* Solomon had made for
52:25 having access to the *k*
52:26 to the *k* of Babylon at
52:27 And these the *k* of Babylon
52:31 Jehoiachin the *k* of Judah
52:31 Evil-merodach the *k* of
52:31 year of his becoming *k*
52:31 Jehoiachin the *k* of Judah
52:34 from the *k* of Babylon
La 2:6 no respect for *k* and priest
2:9 Her *k* and her princes are
Eze 1:2 of the exile of *K* Jehoiachin
7:27 *k* . . . will go into mourning
17:12 The *k* of Babylon came to
17:12 take its *k* and its princes
17:16 in the place of the *k* who
17:16 as *k* the one that despised
19:9 to the *k* of Babylon
20:33 rule as *k* over you people
21:19 sword of the *k* of Babylon
21:21 the *k* of Babylon stood still
24:2 The *k* of Babylon has thrown
26:7 Nebuchadrezzar the *k* of
26:7 a *k* of kings, with horses
28:12 concerning the *k* of Tyre
29:2 Pharaoh the *k* of Egypt and
29:3 Pharaoh, *k* of Egypt, the
29:18 Nebuchadrezzar . . . the *k* of
29:19 Nebuchadrezzar the *k* of
30:10 Nebuchadrezzar the *k* of
30:21 Pharaoh the *k* of Egypt
30:22 Pharaoh the *k* of Egypt
30:24 arms of the *k* of Babylon
30:25 arms of the *k* of Babylon
30:25 hand of the *k* of Babylon
31:2 say to Pharaoh the *k* of Egypt
32:2 Pharaoh the *k* of Egypt, and
32:11 sword of the *k* of Babylon
37:22 one *k* is what all of them
37:22 will come to have as *k*
37:24 my servant David will be *k*
Da 1:1 Jehoiakim the *k* of Judah
1:1 Nebuchadnezzar the *k* of Babylon
1:2 Jehoiakim the *k* of Judah and
1:3 *k* said to Ashpenaz his chief
1:4 stand in the palace of the *k*
1:5 *k* appointed a daily allowance
1:5 from the delicacies of the *k*
1:5 they might stand before the *k*
1:8 with the delicacies of the *k*
1:10 in fear of my lord the *k*, who
1:10 make my head guilty to the *k*
1:13 the delicacies of the *k*
1:15 eating the delicacies of the *k*
1:18 *k* had said to bring them in
1:19 *k* began to speak with them
1:19 to stand before the *k*
1:20 *k* inquired about from them

Da 1:21 first year of Cyrus the *k*
2:2 So the *k* said to call the
2:2 to tell the *k* his dreams
2:2 and to stand before the *k*
2:3 *k* said to them: There is a
2:4 Chaldeans spoke to the *k* in the
2:4 *k*, live on even for times
2:5 *k* was answering and saying to
2:7 *k* say what the dream is to
2:8 *k* was answering and saying
2:10 answered before the *k*
2:10 to show the matter of the *k*
2:10 grand *k* or governor has asked
2:11 *k* himself is asking is
2:11 show it before the *k* except
2:12 *k* himself became angry and
2:15 to Arioch the officer of the *k*
2:15 order on the part of the *k*
2:16 asked from the *k* that he
2:16 very interpretation to the *k*
2:23 the very matter of the *k*
2:24 *k* had appointed to destroy
2:24 Take me in before the *k*
2:24 interpretation itself to the *k*
2:25 took Daniel in before the *k*
2:25 interpretation itself to the *k*
2:26 *k* was answering and saying
2:27 before the *k* and saying
2:27 secret that the *k* himself is
2:27 unable to show to the *k*
2:28 known to *K* Nebuchadnezzar
2:29 *k*, on your bed your own
2:30 be made known to the *k*
2:31 You, O *k*, happened to be
2:36 we shall say before the *k*
2:37, 37 You, O *k*, the *k* of kings
2:45 known to the *k* what is to
2:46 *K* Nebuchadnezzar himself fell
2:47 *k* was answering Daniel and
2:48 *k* made Daniel someone great
2:49 made a request of the *k*, and
2:49 was in the court of the *k*
3:1 Nebuchadnezzar the *k* made an
3:2 *k* sent to assemble the satraps
3:2 Nebuchadnezzar the *k* had set
3:3 Nebuchadnezzar the *k* had set
3:5 Nebuchadnezzar the *k* has set
3:7 Nebuchadnezzar the *k* had set
3:9 saying to Nebuchadnezzar the *k*
3:9 O *k*, live on even for times
3:10 O *k*, set forth the command
3:12 paid no regard to you, O *k*
3:13 were brought in before the *k*
3:16 and they were saying to the *k*
3:17 and out of your hand, O *k*, he
3:18 O *k*, that your gods are not
3:24 *k* himself became frightened
3:24, 24 saying to the *k*: Yes, O *k*
3:27 the high officials of the *k*
3:28 the very word of the *k* and
3:30 *k* himself caused Shadrach
4:1 Nebuchadnezzar the *k*, to all
4:18 *K* Nebuchadnezzar, beheld
4:19 *k* was answering and saying
4:22 *k*, because you have grown
4:23 *k* beheld a watcher, even a
4:24 interpretation, O *k*, and the
4:24 must befall my lord the *k*
4:27 O *k*, may my counsel seem good
4:28 befell Nebuchadnezzar the *k*
4:30 *k* was answering and saying
4:31 O Nebuchadnezzar the *k*
4:37 *K* of the heavens, because all
5:1 Belshazzar the *k*, he made a
5:2 the *k* and his grandees
5:3 the *k* and his grandees, his
5:5 wall of the palace of the *k*
5:5 *k* was beholding the back of
5:6 *k*, his very complexion was
5:7 *k* was calling out loudly to
5:7 *k* was answering and saying to
5:8 wise men of the *k* were coming
5:8 to the *k* the interpretation
5:9 *K* Belshazzar was very much
5:10 because of the words of the *k*
5:10 *k*, keep living even to times
5:11 *K* Nebuchadnezzar your father
5:11 even your father, O *k*
5:12 *k* himself named Belteshazzar
5:13 was brought in before the *k*
5:13 *k* was speaking up and saying
5:13 *k* my father brought out of
5:17 before the *k*: Let your gifts
5:17 the writing itself to the *k*

Da 5:18 As for you, O *k*, the Most
5:30 Belshazzar the Chaldean *k* was
6:2 *k* himself might not become the
6:3 *k* was intending to elevate him
6:6 entered as a throng to the *k*
6:6 Darius the *k*, live on even for
6:7 thirty days except to you, O *k*
6:8 O *k*, may you establish the
6:9 *K* Darius himself signed the
6:12 saying before the *k* concerning
6:12 the interdict of the *k*: Is
6:12 except from you, O *k*, he
6:12 *k* was answering and saying
6:13 saying before the *k*: Daniel
6:13 paid no regard to you, O *k*
6:14 *k*, as soon as he heard the
6:15 entered as a throng to the *k*
6:15 saying to the *k*: Take note
6:15 Take note, O *k*, that the law
6:15 statute that the *k* himself
6:16 *k* himself commanded, and
6:16 *k* was answering and saying to
6:17 *k* sealed it with his signet
6:18 *k* went to his palace and
6:19 the *k* himself, at dawn
6:20 *k* was speaking up and saying
6:21 himself spoke even with the *k*
6:21 O *k*, live on even to times
6:22 *k*, no hurtful act have I done
6:23 *k* himself became very glad
6:24 *k* commanded, and they brought
6:25 Darius the *k* himself wrote to
7:1 first year of Belshazzar the *k*
8:1 of Belshazzar the *k*, there was
8:21 stands for the *k* of Greece
8:21 it stands for the first *k*
8:23 *k* fierce in countenance and
8:27 and did the work of the *k*
9:1 made *k* over the kingdom of
10:1 year of Cyrus the *k* of Persia
11:3 mighty *k* will certainly stand
11:5 *k* of the south will become
11:6 daughter of the *k* of the south
11:6 come to the *k* of the north in
11:7 fortress of the *k* of the north
11:8 off from the *k* of the north
11:9 kingdom of the *k* of the south
11:11 *k* of the south will embitter
11:11 with the *k* of the north; and
11:13 *k* of the north must return
11:14 against the *k* of the south
11:15 *k* of the north will come and
11:25 against the *k* of the south
11:25 *k* of the south, for his part
11:36 *k* will actually do according
11:40 *k* of the south will engage
11:40 *k* of the north will storm
Ho 1:1 of Jeroboam . . . *k* of Israel
3:4 Israel will dwell without a *k*
3:5 and for David their *k*
5:1 O house of the *k*, give ear
5:13 and send to a great *k*
7:3 they make the *k* rejoice
7:5 On the day of our *k*, princes
8:10 the burden of *k* and princes
10:3 We have no *k*, for we have not
10:3 the *k*, what will he do for us?
10:6 as a gift to a great *k*
10:7 Samaria and her *k* will
10:15 the *k* of Israel . . . silenced
11:5 but Assyria will be his *k*
13:10 Where, then, is your *k*
13:10 Do give me a *k* and princes
13:11 to give you a *k* in my anger
Am 1:1 days of Uzziah the *k* of Judah
1:1 Jeroboam . . . the *k* of Israel
1:15 their *k* must go into exile
2:1 the bones of the *k* of Edom
5:26 carry Sakkuth your *k* and
7:1 the mown grass of the *k*
7:10 to Jeroboam the *k* of Israel
7:13 it is the sanctuary of a *k*
Jon 3:6 word reached the *k* of Nineveh
3:7 by the decree of the *k* and his
Mic 2:13 their *k* will pass through
4:7 Jehovah will . . . rule as *k*
4:9 Is there no *k* in you, or has
6:5 Balak the *k* of Moab counseled
Na 3:18 become drowsy, O *k* of Assyria
Zep 1:1 son of Amon the *k* of Judah
1:8 and to the sons of the *k*
3:15 The *k* of Israel, Jehovah
Hag 1:1 second year of Darius the *k*
1:15 second year of Darius the *k*

Zec 7:1 fourth year of Darius the *k*
9:5 a *k* will certainly perish
9:9 Your *k* himself comes to you
11:6 and in the hand of his *k*
14:5 of Uzziah the *k* of Judah
14:9 Jehovah must become *k* over
14:10 to the press vats of the *k*
14:16 bow down to the *K*, Jehovah
14:17 bow down to the *K*, Jehovah
Mal 1:14 I am a great *K*, Jehovah of
Mt 1:6 became father to David the *k*
2:1 in the days of Herod the *k*
2:2 is the one born *k* of the Jews
2:3 At hearing this *K* Herod was
2:9 heard the *k*, they went their
2:22 Archelaus ruled as *k* of Judea
5:35 it is the city of the great *K*
14:9 *k* out of regard for his oaths
18:23 a *k*, that wanted to settle
21:5 Look! Your *K* is coming to you
22:2 a *k*, that made a marriage
22:7 *k* grew wrathful, and sent
22:11 the *k* came in to inspect the
22:13 *k* said to his servants, Bind
25:34 *k* will say to those on his
25:40 the *k* will say to them
27:11 Are you the *k* of the Jews?
27:29 Good day, you *K* of the Jews!
27:37 is Jesus the *K* of the Jews
27:42 He is *K* of Israel; let him
Mr 6:14 it got to the ears of *K* Herod
6:22 The *k* said to the maiden
6:25 went in with haste to the *k*
6:26 *k* did not want to disregard
6:27 the *k* immediately dispatched
15:2 Are you the *k* of the Jews?
15:9 release . . . the *k* of the Jews
15:12 you call the *k* of the Jews
15:18 Good day, you *K* of the Jews!
15:26 The *K* of the Jews
15:32 the Christ the *K* of Israel
Lu 1:5 the days of Herod, *k* of Judea
1:33 *k* over the house of Jacob
14:31 Or what *k*, marching to meet
14:31 to meet another *k* in war
19:14 want this man to become *k*
19:27 did not want me to become *k*
19:38 as the *K* in Jehovah's name
23:2 saying he . . . is Christ a *k*
23:3 Are you the *k* of the Jews?
23:37 *k* of the Jews, save yourself
23:38 This is the *k* of the Jews
Joh 1:49 Son of God . . . *K* of Israel
4:46 attendant of the *k* whose son
4:49 attendant of the *k* said to
6:15 and seize him to make him *k*
12:13 even the *k* of Israel
12:15 Your *k* is coming, seated
18:33 Are you the *k* of the Jews?
18:37 Well, then, are you a *k*?
18:37 are saying that I am a *k*
18:39 to you the *k* of the Jews
19:3 Good day, you *k* of the Jews!
19:12 making himself a *k* speaks
19:14 to the Jews: See! Your *k*!
19:15 Shall I impale your *k*?
19:15 We have no *k* but Caesar
19:19 Nazarene the *K* of the Jews
19:21 write The *K* of the Jews
19:21 said, I am *K* of the Jews
Ac 7:10 sight of Pharaoh *k* of Egypt
7:18 different *k* over Egypt, who
12:1 Herod the *k* applied his hands
12:20 of the bedchamber of the *k*
12:20 with food from that of the *k*
13:21 then on they demanded a *k*
13:22 up for them David as *k*
17:7 there is another *k*, Jesus
25:13 Agrippa the *k* and Bernice
25:14 Festus laid before the *k* the
25:24 *K* Agrippa and all you men
25:26 before you, *K* Agrippa, in
26:2 *K* Agrippa, I count myself
26:7 I am accused by Jews, O *k*
26:13 I saw . . . O *k*, a light
26:19 *K* Agrippa, I did not become
26:26 *k* to whom I am speaking
26:27 Do you, *K* Agrippa, believe
26:30 *k* rose and so did the
Ro 5:14 death ruled as *k* from Adam
5:17 death ruled as *k* through
5:21 as sin ruled as *k* with death
5:21 kindness might rule as *k*
6:12 sin continue to rule as *k*

1Co 15:25 he must rule as *k* until God
2Co 11:32 under Aretas the *k* was
1Ti 1:17 *K* of eternity, incorruptible
6:15 *K* of those who rule as kings
Heb 7:1 Melchizedek, *k* of Salem
7:2 *K* of Righteousness, and
7:2 and is then also *k* of Salem
7:2 Salem, that is, *K* of Peace
11:23 not fear the order of the *k*
11:27 fearing the anger of the *k*
1Pe 2:13 to a *k* as being superior
2:17 of God, have honor for the *k*
Re 9:11 a *k*, the angel of the abyss
11:15 rule as *k* forever and ever
11:17 and begun ruling as *k*
15:3 are your ways, *K* of eternity
17:11 is also itself an eighth *k*
17:14 *K* of kings, the Lamb will
19:6 has begun to rule as *k*
19:16 *K* of kings and Lord of lords

Kingdom
Ge 10:10 his *k* came to be Babel and
20:9 upon me and my *k* a great sin
Ex 19:6 *k* of priests and a holy nation
Nu 24:7 And his *k* will be lifted up
32:33 *k* of Sihon the king of the
32:33 *k* of Og the king of Bashan
De 3:4 the *k* of Og in Bashan
3:10 the cities of the *k* of Og in
3:13 Bashan of the *k* of Og I have
17:18 seat on the throne of his *k*
17:20 lengthen his days upon his *k*
1Sa 13:13 your *k* firm over Israel to
13:14 now your *k* will not last
24:20 in your hand the *k* of Israel
28:17 Jehovah will rip the *k* away
2Sa 3:10 transfer the *k* from the
3:28 my *k*, from the standpoint
5:12 exalted his *k* for the sake
7:12 firmly establish his *k*
7:13 throne of his *k* firmly to
7:16 your *k* will certainly be
12:26 capture the city of the *k*
1Ki 2:46 the *k* was firmly established
9:5 throne of your *k* over Israel
10:20 no other *k* had any made
11:11 rip the *k* away from off you
11:13 it will not be all the *k*
11:31 ripping the *k* out of the
11:34 the entire *k* out of his
12:26 *k* will return to the house
14:8 to rip the *k* away from the
18:10 not a nation or *k* where my
18:10 the *k* and the nation swear
2Ki 11:1 all the offspring of the *k*
14:5 *k* had become firm in his
15:19 strengthen the *k* in his own
1Ch 16:20 one *k* to another people
29:11 Yours is the *k*, O Jehovah
2Ch 9:19 No other *k* had any made just
11:1 bring the *k* back to Rehoboam
13:5 *k* to David over Israel to
13:8 against the *k* of Jehovah
14:5 and the *k* continued without
17:5 Jehovah kept the *k* firmly
21:3 *k* he gave to Jehoram, for
21:4 Jehoram rose up over the *k* of
22:9 to retain power for the *k*
23:20 upon the throne of the *k*
25:3 *k* had become strong upon him
29:21 offering for the *k* and for
32:15 god of any nation or *k* was
36:22 to pass through all his *k*
Ne 9:35 during their *k* and amid your
Es 1:4 the riches of his glorious *k*
1:14 were sitting first in the *k*
Ps 105:13 From one *k* to another
Isa 9:7 *k* in order to establish it
17:3 and the *k* out of Damascus
19:2, 2 *k* against *k*
60:12 any *k* that will not serve
Jer 18:7 against a *k* to uproot it and
18:9 a *k* to build it up and to
27:1 the *k* of Jehoiakim the son
27:8 *k* that will not serve him
28:1 the *k* of Zedekiah the king
La 2:2 profaned the *k* and her princes
Eze 17:14 the *k* might become low
29:14 they must become a lowly *k*
Da 2:37 given the *k*, the might, and
2:39 rise another *k* inferior to you
2:39 another *k*, a third one, of
2:40 fourth *k*, it will prove to be

Da 2:41 *k* itself will prove to be
2:42 *k* will partly prove to be
2:44 God . . . will set up a *k* that
2:44 *k* itself will not be passed
4:3, 3 His *k* is a *k* to time
4:17 Most High is Ruler in the *k*
4:18 wise men of my *k* are unable
4:25 Ruler in the *k* of mankind
4:26 *k* will be sure to you after
4:31 *k* itself has gone away from
4:32 is Ruler in the *k* of mankind
4:34 and his *k* is for generation
4:36 for the dignity of my *k* my
4:36 reestablished upon my own *k*
5:7 as the third one in the *k* he
5:11 capable man in your *k* in whom
5:16 as the third one in the *k* you
5:18 *k* and the greatness and the
5:20 down from the throne of his *k*
5:21 Ruler in the *k* of mankind
5:26 numbered the days of your *k*
5:28 *k* has been divided and given
5:29 the third ruler in the *k*
5:31 Mede himself received the *k*
6:1 set up over the *k* one hundred
6:1 were to be over the whole *k*
6:3 to elevate him over all the *k*
6:4 against Daniel respecting the *k*
6:7 All the high officials of the *k*
6:26 in every dominion of my *k*
6:26 his *k* is one that will not
6:28 prospered in the *k* of Darius
6:28 in the *k* of Cyrus the Persian
7:14 rulership and dignity and *k*
7:14 his *k* one that will not be
7:18 will receive the *k*, and they
7:18 possession of the *k* for time
7:22 ones took possession of the *k*
7:23 fourth *k* that will come to be
7:24 ten horns, out of that *k* there
7:27 *k* and the rulership and the
7:27 *k* is an indefinitely lasting
7:27 indefinitely lasting *k*, and
8:23 final part of their *k*, as the
9:1 over the *k* of the Chaldeans
11:2 against the *k* of Greece
11:4 his *k* will be broken and be
11:4 his *k* will be uprooted, even
11:9 *k* of the king of the south
11:17 forcefulness of his entire *k*
11:20 pass through the splendid *k*
11:21 the dignity of the *k*
11:21 take hold of the *k* by means
Am 7:13 and it is the house of a *k*
9:8 are upon the sinful *k*
Mic 4:8 *k* belonging to the daughter
Mt 3:2 the *k* of the heavens has drawn
4:17 *k* of the heavens has drawn
4:23 the good news of the *k* and
5:3 the *k* of the heavens belongs
5:10 *k* of the heavens belongs to
5:19 least in relation to the *k* of
5:19 great in relation to the *k* of
5:20 by no means enter into the *k*
6:10 Let your *k* come. Let your
6:33 seeking first the *k* and his
7:21 will enter into the *k* of the
8:11 in the *k* of the heavens
8:12 sons of the *k* will be thrown
9:35 the good news of the *k* and
10:7 *k* of the heavens has drawn
11:11 lesser one in the *k* of the
11:12 *k* of the heavens is the goal
12:25 *k* divided against itself
12:26 how, then, will his *k* stand?
12:28 *k* of God . . . overtaken you
13:11 sacred secrets of the *k* of
13:19 hears the word of the *k* but
13:24 *k* of the heavens has become
13:31 *k* of the heavens is like a
13:33 *k* . . . is like leaven, which
13:38 fine seed . . . sons of the *k*
13:41 collect out from his *k* all
13:43 sun in the *k* of their Father
13:44 *k* . . . like a treasure hidden
13:45 *k* of the heavens is like a
13:47 the *k* . . . is like a dragnet
13:52 taught respecting the *k* of
16:19 give you the keys of the *k*
16:28 Son of man coming in his *k*
18:1 greatest in the *k* of the
18:3 by no means enter into the *k*
18:4 the greatest in the *k* of the
18:23 *k* of the heavens has become

Mt 19:12 eunuchs on account of the *k*
19:14 *k* of the heavens belongs to
19:23 rich man to get into the *k*
19:24 rich man to get into the *k*
20:1 *k* of the heavens is like a
20:21 one at your left, in your *k*
21:31 ahead of you into the *k* of
21:43 *k* of God will be taken from
22:2 *k* of the heavens has become
23:13 you shut up the *k* of the
24:7, 7 and *k* against *k*, and there
24:14 good news of the *k* will be
25:1 *k* . . . become like ten virgins
25:34 inherit the *k* prepared for
26:29 in the *k* of my Father
Mr 1:15 the *k* of God has drawn near
3:24 *k* . . . divided against itself
3:24 divided . . . *k* cannot stand
4:11 sacred secret of the *k* of God
4:26 *k* of God is just as when a
4:30 are we to liken the *k* of God
6:23 to you, up to half my *k*
9:1 until first they see the *k* of
9:47 enter one-eyed into the *k* of
10:14 for the *k* of God belongs to
10:15 receive the *k* of God like a
10:23 to enter into the *k* of God
10:24 to enter into the *k* of God
10:25 to enter into the *k* of God
11:10 the coming *k* of our father
12:34 not far from the *k* of God
13:8, 8 nation and *k* against *k*
14:25 drink it new in the *k* of God
15:43 waiting for the *k* of God
Lu 1:33 there will be no end of his *k*
4:43 the good news of the *k* of God
6:20 because yours is the *k* of God
7:28 lesser one in the *k* of God is
8:1 the good news of the *k* of God
8:10 the sacred secrets of the *k* of
9:2 to preach the *k* of God and to
9:11 speak to them about the *k*
9:27 first they see the *k* of God
9:60 declare abroad the *k* of God
9:62 well fitted for the *k* of God
10:9 The *k* of God has come near to
10:11 the *k* of God has come near
11:2 Let your *k* come
11:17 Every *k* divided against
11:18 how will his *k* stand?
11:20 the *k* of God has really
12:31 seek continually his *k*, and
12:32 approved of giving you the *k*
13:18 What is the *k* of God like
13:20 shall I compare the *k* of God
13:28 the prophets in the *k* of God
13:29 at the table in the *k* of God
14:15 eats bread in the *k* of God
16:16 *k* of God is being declared
17:20 when the *k* of God was
17:20 *k* of God is not coming with
17:21 *k* of God is in your midst
18:16 *k* of God belongs to suchlike
18:17 receive the *k* of God like a
18:24 their way into the *k* of God
18:25 rich man to get into the *k*
18:29 for the sake of the *k* of God
19:11 imagining that the *k* of God
21:10, 10 and *k* against *k*
21:31 that the *k* of God is near
22:16 fulfilled in the *k* of God
22:18 until the *k* of God arrives
22:29 a covenant with me, for a *k*
22:30 drink at my table in my *k*
23:42 when you get into your *k*
23:51 was waiting for the *k* of God
Joh 3:3 he cannot see the *k* of God
3:5 cannot enter into the *k* of God
18:36 My *k* is no part of this
18:36 *k* were part of this world
18:36 *k* is not from this source
Ac 1:3 the things about the *k* of God
1:6 restoring the *k* to Israel at
8:12 good news of the *k* of God
14:22 must enter into the *k* of God
19:8 persuasion concerning the *k* of
20:25 whom I went preaching the *k*
28:23 concerning the *k* of God and
28:31 preaching the *k* of God to
Ro 14:17 the *k* of God does not mean
1Co 4:20 For the *k* of God lies not in
6:9 will not inherit God's *k*
6:10 will inherit God's *k*
15:24 hands over the *k* to his God

1Co 15:50 blood cannot inherit God's *k*
Ga 5:21 will not inherit God's *k*
Eph 5:5 has any inheritance in the *k*
Col 1:13 the *k* of the Son of his love
4:11 workers for the *k* of God
1Th 2:12 God . . . calling you to his *k*
2Th 1:5 counted worthy of the *k* of
2Ti 4:1 his manifestation and his *k*
4:18 save me for his heavenly *k*
Heb 1:8 the scepter of your *k* is the
12:28 *k* that cannot be shaken
Jas 2:5 and heirs of the *k*, which he
2Pe 1:11 everlasting *k* of our Lord
Re 1:6 made us to be a *k*, priests
1:9 in the tribulation and *k* and
5:10 a *k* and priests to our God
11:15 *k* of the world did become
11:15 become the *k* of our Lord and
12:10 power and the *k* of our God
16:10 its *k* became darkened, and
17:12 have not yet received a *k*
17:17 giving their *k* to the wild
17:18 *k* over the kings of the

Kingdoms
De 3:21 Jehovah will do to all the *k*
28:25 to all the earth's *k*
Jos 11:10 the head of all these *k*
1Sa 10:18 *k* that were oppressing you
1Ki 4:21 ruler over all the *k* from
2Ki 19:15 true God of all the *k* of
19:19 all the *k* of the earth may
1Ch 29:30 over all the *k* of the lands
2Ch 12:8 service of the *k* of the lands
17:10 *k* of the lands that were
20:6 all the *k* of the nations
20:29 *k* of the lands when they
36:23 *k* of the earth Jehovah the
Ezr 1:2 All the *k* of the earth Jehovah
Ne 9:22 to give them *k* and peoples
Ps 46:6 boisterous, the *k* tottered
68:32 *k* of the earth, sing to God
79:6 *k* that have not called upon
102:22 And the *k* to serve Jehovah
135:11 And all the *k* of Canaan
Isa 10:10 *k* of the valueless god
13:4 Listen! The uproar of *k*
13:19 the decoration of *k*, the
14:16 that was making *k* rock
23:11 caused *k* to be agitated
23:17 all the *k* of the earth upon
37:16 God of all the *k* of the
37:20 *k* of the earth may know
47:5 people call you Mistress of *K*
Jer 1:10 the nations and over the *k*
1:15 of the *k* of the north
15:4 to all the *k* of the earth
24:9 in all the *k* of the earth
25:26 all the other *k* of the earth
28:8 and concerning great *k*
29:18 to all the *k* of the earth
34:1 and all the *k* of the earth
34:17 to all the *k* of the earth
49:28 Kedar and the *k* of Hazor
51:20 will bring *k* to ruin
51:27 *k* of Ararat, Minni and
Eze 29:15 Lower than the other *k* it
37:22 any longer into two *k*
Da 2:44 put an end to all these *k*, and
7:23 different from . . . other *k*
7:27 grandeur of the *k* under
8:22 four *k* from his nation that
Am 6:2 Are they better than these *k*
Na 3:5 and *k* your dishonor
Zep 3:8 to collect together *k*, in
Hag 2:22 overthrow the throne of *k*
2:22 of the *k* of the nations
Mt 4:8 all the *k* of the world and
Lu 4:5 showed him all the *k* of the
Heb 11:33 through faith defeated *k* in

Kingly
Isa 62:3 a *k* turban in the palm of
Lu 19:12 secure *k* power for himself
19:15 having secured the *k* power
Jas 2:8 carrying out the *k* law

King's
Ge 14:17 that is, the *k* Low Plain
Nu 20:17 On the *k* road we shall march
21:22 On the *k* road we shall march
1Sa 20:29 not come to the *k* table
21:8 *k* matter proved to be urgent
26:16 where the *k* spear and the
2Sa 11:2 rooftop of the *k* house
2Sa 11:8 out from the *k* house, and
11:8 *k* courtesy gift went out
11:9 entrance of the *k* house
13:33 *k* sons themselves have died
13:35 *k* sons themselves have come
13:36 *k* sons themselves came in
14:1 *k* heart was toward Absalom
15:15 *k* servants said to the king
15:18 crossing before the *k* face
18:12 hand out against the *k* son
18:20 the *k* own son has died
18:29 Joab sent the *k* servant and
19:42 at the *k* expense, or has a
24:4 *k* word prevailed upon Joab
1Ki 1:4 she came to be the *k* nurse
1:9 all his brothers the *k* sons
1:9 men of Judah the *k* servants
10:28 company of the *k* merchants
13:6 the *k* hand was restored to
14:27 the entrance of the *k* house
16:18 tower of the *k* house and
16:18 and burned the *k* house
22:6 give it into the *k* hand
22:12 give it into the *k* hand
22:15 give it into the *k* hand
22:26 and to Joash the *k* son
2Ki 7:9 make report at the *k* house
7:11 reported to the *k* house
11:5 watch over the *k* house
11:16 horse entry of the *k* house
11:19 the runners to the *k* house
11:20 the sword at the *k* house
15:5 Jotham the *k* son was over
15:25 tower of the *k* house
16:8 treasures of the *k* house
16:18 the *k* outer entryway he
18:15 treasures of the *k* house
22:12 and Asaiah the *k* servant
24:13 treasures of the *k* house
24:15, 15 *k* mother and the *k* wives
25:4 wall that is by the *k* garden
25:9 and the *k* house and all the
1Ch 9:18 in the *k* gate to the east
21:4 *k* word, however, prevailed
21:6 *k* word had been detestable
26:30 and for the *k* service
27:32 Jehiel . . . with the *k* sons
27:33 Hushai . . . the *k* companion
2Ch 1:16 company of the *k* merchants
8:15 *k* commandment to the
9:11 and for the *k* house and also
12:9 treasures of the *k* house
12:10 entrance of the *k* house
16:2 treasures of . . . the *k* house
18:5 will give it into the *k* hand
18:11 give it into the *k* hand
18:25 and to Joash the *k* son
21:17 found in the *k* house and
23:11 *k* son out and put upon him
23:15 horse gate of the *k* house
23:20 upper gate to the *k* house
24:21 at the *k* commandment
25:24 treasures of the *k* house
26:11 Hananiah of the *k* princes
26:21 son was over the *k* house
29:15 to the *k* commandment
29:25 Gad the *k* visionary and of
34:20 Asaiah the *k* servant, saying
35:10 to the *k* commandment
Ezr 5:17 the *k* house of treasures
6:4 be given from the *k* house
7:20 the *k* house of treasures
7:23 the *k* realm and his sons
Ne 2:14 Gate and to the *K* Pool
2:18 also of the *k* words that he
3:15 to the *K* Garden and as far
3:25 goes out from the *K* House
5:4 money for the *k* tribute on our
Es 1:5 the garden of the *k* palace
1:10 *k* heart was in a merry mood
1:12 to come at the *k* word that
1:13 the *k* matter came before all
1:22 the *k* jurisdictional districts
2:2 *k* attendants, his ministers
2:3 in charge of Hegai the *k* eunuch
2:4 seems pleasing in the *k* eyes
2:4 was pleasing in the *k* eyes
2:8 *k* word and his law were heard
2:8 the *k* house in charge of Hegai
2:9 young women from the *k* house
2:13 of the women to the *k* house
2:14 Shaashgaz the *k* eunuch, the
2:15 what Hegai the *k* eunuch, the
2:19 was sitting in the *k* gate
Es 2:21 was sitting in the *k* gate
3:2 *k* servants that were in the
3:2 in the *k* gate were bowing low
3:3 the *k* servants who were in the
3:3 in the *k* gate began to say to
3:3 Why are you sidestepping the *k*
3:8 the *k* own laws they are not
3:9 bringing it into the *k* treasury
3:12 The *k* secretaries were then
3:12 *k* satraps and the governors
3:12 sealed with the *k* signet ring
3:13 the *k* jurisdictional districts
3:15 speed because of the *k* word
4:2 far as in front of the *k* gate
4:2 come into the *k* gate in
4:3 wherever the *k* word and his
4:5 Hathach, one of the *k* eunuchs
4:6 that was before the *k* gate
4:7 said to pay to the *k* treasury
4:11 All the *k* servants and the
4:11 the *k* jurisdictional districts
4:13 the *k* household will escape
5:1 inner courtyard of the *k* house
5:1 opposite the *k* house, while
5:8 have found favor in the *k* eyes
5:8 do according to the *k* word
5:9 saw Mordecai in the *k* gate and
5:13 the Jew sitting in the *k* gate
6:1 that night the *k* sleep fled
6:3 *k* attendants, his ministers
6:4 outer courtyard of the *k* house
6:5 the *k* attendants said to him
6:9 of one of the *k* noble princes
6:10 who is sitting in the *k* gate
6:12 returned to the *k* gate
6:14 *k* court officials themselves
7:8 went out of the *k* mouth, and
7:10 and the *k* rage itself subsided
8:5 the *k* jurisdictional districts
8:8 in the *k* name and seal it with
8:8 seal it with the *k* signet ring
8:8 that is written in the *k* name
8:8 sealed with the *k* signet ring
8:10 with the *k* signet ring and
8:14 with speed by the *k* word
9:1 *k* word and his law came due
9:4 was great in the *k* house and
Ps 45:13 *k* daughter is all glorious
Pr 16:15 In the light of the *k* face
21:1 A *k* heart is as streams of
Jer 52:7 wall that is by the *k* garden
Da 2:14 chief of the *k* bodyguard, who
3:22 *k* word was harsh and the
4:31 word was yet in the *k* mouth

Kings
Ge 14:5 *k* who were with him, and they
14:9 four *k* against the five
14:10 the *k* of Sodom and Gomorrah
14:17 *k* that were with him, to the
17:6 make you . . . nations, and *k*
17:16 *k* of peoples will come from
35:11 *k* will come out of your
36:31 *k* . . . in the land of Edom
Nu 31:8 they killed the *k* of Midian
31:8 the five *k* of Midian; and
De 3:8 the two *k* of the Amorites who
3:21 God has done to these two *k*
4:47 the two *k* of the Amorites
7:24 give their *k* into your hand
31:4 the *k* of the Amorites, and to
Jos 2:10 two *k* of the Amorites who
5:1 *k* of the Amorites, who were
5:1 all the *k* of the Canaanites
9:1 *k* who were on the side of the
9:10 to the two *k* of the Amorites
10:5 five *k* of the Amorites, the
10:6 all the *k* of the Amorites
10:16 these five *k* fled and went
10:17 The five *k* have been found
10:22 bring out these five *k* from
10:23 from the cave these five *k*
10:24 brought . . . *k* to Joshua
10:24 back of the necks of these *k*
10:40 the slopes and all their *k*
10:42 Joshua captured all these *k*
11:2 the *k* that were to the north
11:5 all these *k* met together by
11:12 all the cities of these *k*
11:12 all their *k* Joshua captured
11:17 he captured all their *k* and
11:18 waged war with all these *k*
12:1 the *k* of the land whom the
12:7 these are the *k* of the land

Jos 12:24 all the *k* being thirty-one
24:12 two *k* of the Amorites—not
Jg 1:7 There have been seventy *k*
5:3 Listen, you *k;* give ear, you
5:19 *K* came, they fought; It was
5:19 then that the *k* of Canaan fought
8:5 and Zalmunna, the *k* of Midian
8:12 got to capture Midian's two *k*
8:26 were upon the *k* of Midian and
1Sa 14:47 and against the *k* of Zobah
27:6 belong to the *k* of Judah
2Sa 10:19 all the *k*, the servants of
11:1 time that *k* sally forth
1Ki 3:13 any among the *k* like you
4:24 the *k* this side of the River
4:34 from all the *k* of the earth
10:15 and all the *k* of the Arabs
10:23 the other *k* of the earth
10:29 the *k* of the Hittites and
10:29 and the *k* of Syria
14:19 the days of the *k* of Israel
14:29 the times of the *k* of Judah
15:7 the days of the *k* of Judah
15:23 the days of the *k* of Judah
15:31 the days of the *k* of Israel
16:5 the days of the *k* of Israel
16:14 the days of the *k* of Israel
16:20 the days of the *k* of Israel
16:27 the days of the *k* of Israel
16:33 than all the *k* of Israel
20:1 also thirty-two *k* with him
20:12 the *k* were drinking in the
20:16 he together with the *k*
20:16 the thirty-two *k* that were
20:24 Remove the *k* each one from
20:31 the *k* of the house of Israel
20:31 *k* of loving-kindness
22:39 the days of the *k* of Israel
22:45 the days of the *k* of Judah
2Ki 1:18 the days of the *k* of Israel
3:10 three *k* to give them into
3:13 three *k* to give them into
3:21 the *k* had come up to fight
3:23 *k* have unquestionably been
7:6 the *k* of the Hittites and the
7:6 *k* of Egypt to come against us
8:18 the way of the *k* of Israel
8:23 of the days of the *k* of Judah
10:4 Two *k* themselves did not
10:34 the days of the *k* of Israel
11:19 upon the throne of the *k*
12:18 *k* of Judah, had sanctified
12:19 the days of the *k* of Judah
13:8 the days of the *k* of Israel
13:12 the days of the *k* of Israel
13:13 with the *k* of Israel
14:15 the days of the *k* of Israel
14:16 with the *k* of Israel
14:18 the days of the *k* of Judah
14:28 the days of the *k* of Israel
14:29 with the *k* of Israel, and
15:6 the days of the *k* of Judah
15:11 the days of the *k* of Israel
15:15 the days of the *k* of Israel
15:21 the days of the *k* of Israel
15:26 the days of the *k* of Israel
15:31 the days of the *k* of Israel
15:36 the days of the *k* of Judah
16:3 the way of the *k* of Israel
16:19 the days of the *k* of Judah
17:2 not as the *k* of Israel that
17:8 statutes of the *k* of Israel
18:5 among all the *k* of Judah
19:11 what the *k* of Assyria did
19:17 the *k* of Assyria have
20:20 the days of the *k* of Judah
21:17 the days of the *k* of Judah
21:25 the days of the *k* of Judah
23:5 whom the *k* of Judah had put
23:11 horses that the *k* of Judah
23:12 the *k* of Judah had made
23:19 *k* of Israel had built to
23:22 the days of the *k* of Israel
23:22 and the *k* of Judah
23:28 the days of the *k* of Judah
24:5 the days of the *k* of Judah
25:28 *k* that were with him in
1Ch 1:43 *k* that reigned in the land
9:1 the Book of the *K* of Israel
16:21 their account he reproved *k*
19:9 the *k* that had come were by
20:1 time that *k* sally forth
2Ch 1:12 as no *k* that were prior to
1:17 for all the *k* of the Hittites
2Ch 1:17 Hittites and the *k* of Syria
9:14 all the *k* of the Arabs and
9:22 all the other *k* of the earth
9:23 *k* of the earth were seeking
9:26 ruler over all the *k* from
16:11 Book of the *K* of Judah and
20:34 Book of the *K* of Israel
21:6 way of the *k* of Israel, just
21:13 way of the *k* of Israel and
21:20 the burial places of the *k*
24:16 along with the *k*, because
24:25 the burial places of the *k*
24:27 of the Book of the *K*
25:26 the *K* of Judah and Israel
26:23 that belonged to the *k*
27:7 Book of the *K* of Israel and
28:2 ways of the *k* of Israel, and
28:16 sent to the *k* of Assyria
28:23 gods of the *k* of Syria are
28:26 Book of the *K* of Judah and
28:27 places of the *k* of Israel
30:6 palm of the *k* of Assyria
32:4 *k* of Assyria come and
32:32 Book of the *K* of Judah and
33:18 affairs of the *k* of Israel
34:11 houses that the *k* of Judah
35:18 the other *k* of Israel
35:27 Book of the *K* of Israel and
36:8 Book of the *K* of Israel and
Ezr 4:13 to the treasuries of the *k*
4:15 and causing loss to *k*
4:19 one rising up against *k* and
4:20 strong *k* over Jerusalem and
4:22 increase to the injury of *k*
7:12 Artaxerxes, the king of *k*
9:7 our *k*, our priests, into the
9:7 the hand of the *k* of the lands
9:9 before the *k* of Persia, to
Ne 9:24 *k* and the peoples of the land
9:32 our *k*, our princes and our
9:32 days of the *k* of Assyria
9:34 our *k*, our princes, our
9:37 *k* that you have put over us
Es 10:2 of the *k* of Media and Persia
Job 3:14 *k* and counselors of the earth
12:18 bonds of *k* he . . . loosens
36:7 Even *k* on the throne
Ps 2:2 The *k* of earth take their stand
2:10 now, O *k*, exercise insight
45:9 The daughters of *k* are among
48:4 the *k* themselves have met by
68:12 Even the *k* of armies flee
68:14 scattered abroad the *k* in it
68:29 *K* will bring gifts to you
72:10 The *k* of Tarshish and of the
72:10 *k* of Sheba and of Seba
72:11 him all the *k* will prostrate
76:12 he is to the *k* of the earth
89:27 most high of the *k* of the
102:15 *k* of the earth your glory
105:14 their account he reproved *k*
105:30 interior rooms of their *k*
110:5 break *k* to pieces on the day
119:46 your reminders in front of *k*
135:10 And killed potent *k*
136:17 One striking down great *k*
136:18 to kill majestic *k*
138:4 *k* of the earth will laud
144:10 One giving salvation to *k*
148:11 *k* of the earth and all you
149:8 bind their *k* with shackles
Pr 8:15 *k* themselves keep reigning
16:12 is something detestable to *k*
22:29 Before *k* is where he will
25:2 glory of *k* is the searching
25:3 and the heart of *k*, that is
31:3 to what leads to wiping out *k*
31:4 It is not for *k*, O Lemuel, it
31:4 it is not for *k* to drink wine
Ec 2:8 and property peculiar to *k* and
Isa 1:1 Ahaz and Hezekiah, *k* of Judah
7:16 whose two *k* you are feeling
10:8 princes at the same time *k*
14:9 all the *k* of the nations get
14:18 All other *k* of the nations
19:11 son of *k* of ancient time
24:21 *k* of the ground upon the
37:11 *k* of Assyria did to all the
37:18 *k* of Assyria have devastated
41:2 make him go subduing even *k*
45:1 ungird even the hips of *k*
49:7 *K* themselves will see and
49:23 *k* must become caretakers
52:15 *k* will shut their mouth
Isa 60:3 and *k* to the brightness of
60:10 *k* will minister to you
60:11 *k* will be taking the lead
60:16 breast of *k* you will suck
62:2 and all *k* your glory
Jer 1:18 toward the *k* of Judah
2:26 their *k*, their princes and
8:1 the bones of the *k* of Judah
13:13 the *k* that are sitting for
17:19 the *k* of Judah enter in and
17:20 you *k* of Judah and all
17:25 *k* with princes, sitting on
19:3 you *k* of Judah and you
19:4 and the *k* of Judah; and they
19:13 the houses of the *k* of Judah
20:5 treasures of the *k* of Judah
22:4 the *k* sitting for David upon
25:14 many nations and great *k*
25:18 cities of Judah and her *k*
25:20 all the *k* of the land of Uz
25:20 all the *k* of the land of the
25:22 all the *k* of Tyre and all
25:22 all the *k* of Sidon and the
25:22 the *k* of the island that is
25:24 all the *k* of the Arabs and
25:24 the *k* of the mixed company
25:25 all the *k* of Zimri and
25:25 all the *k* of Elam and all
25:25 and all the *k* of the Medes
25:26 all the *k* of the north who
27:7 *k* must exploit him as a
32:32 offend me, they, their *k*
33:4 houses of the *k* of Judah
34:5 former *k* who happened to be
44:9 bad deeds of the *k* of Judah
44:17 our *k* and our princes did
44:21 your *k* and your princes
46:25 her *k*, even upon Pharaoh
50:41 great nation and grand *k*
51:11 of the *k* of the Medes
51:28 nations, the *k* of Media
52:32 thrones of the other *k*
La 4:12 The *k* of the earth and all the
Eze 26:7 a king of *k*, with horses and
27:33 you made earth's *k* rich
27:35 *k* themselves will have to
28:17 Before *k* I will set you
32:10 *k* themselves will shudder
32:29 Edom, her *k* and all her
43:7 *k*, by their fornication and
43:7 carcasses of their *k* at
43:9 carcasses of their *k* far
Da 2:21 removing *k* and setting up
2:21 and setting up *k*, giving
2:37 the king of *k*, you to whom
2:44 days of those *k* the God of
2:47 a Lord of *k* and a Revealer of
7:17 four *k* that will stand up
7:24 ten *k* that will rise up; and
7:24 three *k* he will humiliate
8:20 stands for the *k* of Media and
9:6 spoken in your name to our *k*
9:8 shame of face, to our *k*, to
10:13 there beside the *k* of Persia
11:2 three *k* standing up for Persia
11:27 two *k*, their heart will be
Ho 1:1 Ahaz and Hezekiah, *k* of Judah
7:7 Their own *k* have all fallen
8:4 have set up *k*, but not because
Mic 1:1 Ahaz, Hezekiah, *k* of Judah
1:14 deceitful to the *k* of Israel
Hab 1:10 it jeers *k* themselves, and
Mt 10:18 haled before governors and *k*
11:8 are in the houses of *k*
17:25 the *k* of the earth receive
Mr 13:9 before governors and *k* for
Lu 10:24 Many prophets and *k* desired
21:12 haled before *k* and governors
22:25 The *k* of the nations lord it
Ac 4:26 *k* of the earth took their
9:15 to *k* and the sons of Israel
Ro 5:17 rule as *k* in life through
1Co 4:8 begun ruling as *k* without us
4:8 that you had begun ruling as *k*
4:8 also might rule with you as *k*
1Ti 2:2 concerning *k* and all those
6:15 King of those who rule as *k*
2Ti 2:12 also rule together as *k*
Heb 7:1 from the slaughter of the *k*
Re 1:5 Ruler of the *k* of the earth
5:10 to rule as *k* over the earth
6:15 the *k* of the earth and the
10:11 and tongues and many *k*
16:12 *k* from the rising of the sun

De 19:4 without *k* it and he was no
Jos 20:3 unintentionally without *k* it
20:5 without *k* it that he struck
22:22 God, Jehovah, he is *k*, and
1Sa 10:11 those *k* him formerly saw
2Sa 12:22 *k* whether Jehovah may show
1Ki 5:6 no one *k* how to cut trees
2Ki 17:26 none *k* the religion of the
2Ch 2:7 and *k* how to cut engravings
Ezr 7:25 those *k* the laws of your God
Ne 13:24 none of them *k* how to speak
Es 4:14 who is there *k* whether it is
Job 19:13 ones *k* me have even turned
24:1 ones *k* him have not beheld
42:11 all those formerly *k* him
Ps 9:10 those *k* your name will trust
35:8 ruin come . . . without his *k*
36:10 loving-kindness to those *k*
74:9 no one with us *k* how long
87:4 Babylon as among those *k* me
89:15 people *k* the joyful shouting
90:11 *k* the strength of your anger
94:11 Jehovah is *k* the thoughts
119:79 Those also *k* your reminders
Pr 29:7 is *k* the legal claim of the
Ec 1:17 give my heart to *k* wisdom
1:17 wisdom and to *k* madness, and
2:19 who is there *k* whether he
3:21 Who is there *k* the spirit of
6:8 *k* how to walk in front of the
6:12 *k* what good a man has in life
8:1 *k* the interpretation of a thing
8:7 no one *k* what will come to be
11:6 not *k* where this will have
Isa 29:11 to someone *k* the writing
29:15 and who is *k* of us?
48:4 *k* that you are hard and that
51:7 you the ones *k* righteousness
Jer 22:16 Was not that a case of *k* me?
29:23 I am the One *k* and am a
44:15 *k* that their wives had
48:17 even all those *k* their name
Eze 28:19 *k* you among the peoples
Da 2:21 to those *k* discernment
2:22 *k* what is in the darkness
5:23 hearing nothing or *k* nothing
11:32 people who are *k* their God
Joe 2:14 *k* whether he will turn back
Jon 3:9 *k* whether the true God may
Hab 2:14 the *k* of the glory of Jehovah
Zep 3:5 one was *k* no shame
Mt 9:4 Jesus, *k* their thoughts, said
12:25 *K* their thoughts, he said to
16:8 *K* this, Jesus said: Why are
22:18 Jesus, *k* their wickedness
Mr 5:33 *k* what had happened to her
6:20 *k* him to be a righteous and
12:24 not *k* either the Scriptures
12:28 *k* that he had answered
Lu 9:47 Jesus, *k* the reasoning of
11:17 *K* their imaginations he said
18:34 were not *k* the things said
21:25 nations, not *k* the way out
22:34 three times denied *k* me
Joh 2:24 because of his *k* them all
6:15 *k* they were about to come
6:61 Jesus, *k* in himself that
10:38 *k* that the Father is in
13:3 *k* that the Father had given
18:4 *k* all the things coming upon
Ac 5:2 his wife also *k* about it
5:7 not *k* what had happened
20:22 not *k* the things that will
24:10 *K* well that this nation has
24:22 Felix, *k* quite accurately
Ro 10:3 not *k* the righteousness of God
1Co 15:58 *k* that your labor is not in
2Co 1:7 *k* as we do that, just as you
4:14 *k* that he who raised Jesus
5:11 *K*, therefore, the fear of
Ga 2:16 *k* as we do that a man is
Col 4:1 *k* that you also have a Master
4:8 *k* the things having to do
2Ti 2:23 *k* they produce fights
3:14 *k* from what persons you
Tit 3:11 *k* that such a man has been
Phm 21 *k* you will even do more than
Heb 10:34 *k* you yourselves have a
11:8 not *k* where he was going
Jas 1:3 *k* as you do that this tested
3:1 *k* that we shall receive
1Pe 5:9 *k* that the same things in
2Pe 1:14 *k* as I do that the putting
2:21 after *k* it accurately to
Jude 5 *k* all things once for all
Re 12:12 *k* he has a short period of

Knowledge

Ge 2:9 tree of the *k* of good and bad
2:17 tree of the *k* of good and bad
Ex 31:3 in understanding and in *k* and
35:31 in understanding and in *k*
Nu 24:16 the *k* of the Most High
1Sa 2:3 For a God of *k* Jehovah is
23:17 Saul my father also has *k*
1Ki 7:14 the *k* for doing every sort
9:27 having a *k* of the sea
1Ch 12:32 a *k* of how to discern the
2Ch 1:10 Give me now wisdom and *k*
1:11 you ask for wisdom and *k* for
1:12 and the *k* are being given you
8:18 servants having a *k* of the
Ne 10:28 having *k* and understanding
Es 1:13 men having *k* of the times
4:1 And Mordecai himself got *k* of
Job 10:7 *k* that I am not in the wrong
15:2 answer with windy *k*
21:14 in the *k* of your ways we
21:22 Will he teach *k* even to God
32:6 declare my *k* to you men
32:10 I shall declare my *k*, even
32:17 shall declare my *k*, even I
33:3 *k* is what my lips do utter
34:35 Job . . . speaks without *k*
35:16 Without *k* he multiplies
36:3 carry my *k* from far off
36:4 One perfect in *k* is with you
36:12 they will expire without *k*
37:16 the One perfect in *k*
38:2 By words without *k*
42:3 obscuring counsel without *k*
Ps 1:6 *k* of the way of righteous ones
4:3 So take *k* that Jehovah will
14:4 Have none . . . hurtful got *k*
19:2 another night shows forth *k*
53:4 of what is hurtful got *k*
73:11 exist *k* in the Most High
94:10 Even the One teaching men *k*
119:66 Teach me goodness . . . and *k*
139:6 Such *k* is too wonderful for
Pr 1:4 to a young man *k* and thinking
1:7 Jehovah is the beginning of *k*
1:22 stupid ones keep hating *k*
1:29 reason that they hated *k*
2:5 find the very *k* of God
2:6 out of his mouth there are *k*
2:10 *k* itself becomes pleasant to
3:20 By his *k* the watery deeps
5:2 may your own lips safeguard *k*
8:9 upright to the ones finding *k*
8:10 *k* rather than choice gold
8:12 the *k* of thinking abilities
9:9 Impart *k* to someone righteous
9:10 *k* of the Most Holy One is
10:14 the ones that treasure up *k*
11:9 by *k* are the righteous rescued
12:1 is a lover of *k*, but a hater
12:23 shrewd man is covering *k*
13:16 shrewd will act with *k*
14:6 *k* is an easy thing
14:7 take note of the lips of *k*
14:18 will bear *k* as a headdress
15:2 of wise ones does good with *k*
15:7 wise ones keep scattering *k*
15:14 is one that searches for *k*
17:27 his sayings is possessed of *k*
18:15 understanding one acquires *k*
18:15 wise ones seeks to find *k*
19:2 be without *k* is not good, and
19:25 that he may discern *k*
19:27 stray from the sayings of *k*
20:15 the lips of *k* are precious
21:11 to a wise person he gets *k*
22:12 have safeguarded *k*, but he
22:17 your very heart to my *k*
22:19 I have given you *k* today
22:20 with counselings and *k*
23:12 your ear to the sayings of *k*
24:4 by *k* will the interior rooms
24:5 man of *k* is reinforcing power
28:2 man having *k* of right
29:7 does not consider such *k*
30:3 *k* of the Most Holy One I do
Ec 1:16 a great deal of wisdom and *k*
1:18 increases *k* increases pain
2:21 with *k* and with proficiency
2:26 he has given wisdom and *k* and
7:12 advantage of *k* is that wisdom
Ec 9:10 nor *k* nor wisdom in Sheol
9:11 those having *k* have the favor
12:9 he also taught the people *k*
Isa 5:13 into exile for lack of *k*
6:9 but do not get any *k*
11:2 spirit of *k* and of the fear
11:9 *k* of Jehovah as the waters
28:9 will one instruct in *k*, and
32:4 overhasty will consider *k*
33:6 *k*, the fear of Jehovah
38:19 can give *k* to his own sons
40:14 or teaches him *k*, or makes
44:19 or has *k* or understanding
44:25 their *k* into foolishness
45:20 have not come to any *k*
47:10 Your wisdom and your *k*
47:13 *k* at the new moons
53:11 By means of his *k* the
58:2 in the *k* of my ways that
Jer 3:15 feed you with *k* and insight
4:22 good they actually have no *k*
9:24 and the having of *k* of me
Da 1:4 being acquainted with *k*, and
1:17 God gave *k* and insight in all
2:21 and *k* to those knowing
5:12 *k* and insight to interpret
12:4 true *k* will become abundant
Ho 4:1 nor *k* of God in the land
4:6 because there is no *k*
4:6 *k* is what you . . . rejected
6:6 in the *k* of God rather than
Mal 2:7 the ones that should keep *k*
Mt 10:29 without your Father's *k*
Lu 1:77 *k* of salvation to his people
11:52 you took away the key of *k*
Joh 7:15 man have a *k* of letters
17:3 their taking in *k* of you
17:23 *k* that you sent me forth
Ac 1:7 *k* of the times or seasons
Ro 1:28 holding God in accurate *k*
2:20 framework of the *k* and of the
3:20 law is the accurate *k* of sin
10:2 not according to accurate *k*
11:33 riches and wisdom and *k*
15:14 been filled with all *k*, and
1Co 1:5 to speak and in full *k*
8:1 we know we all have *k*
8:1 *K* puffs up, but love builds up
8:2 thinks he has acquired *k* of
8:7 not this *k* in all persons; but
8:10 the one having *k*, reclining
8:11 by your *k*, the man that is
12:8 to another speech of *k*
13:2 am acquainted with . . . all *k*
13:8 whether there is *k*, it will
13:9 we have partial *k* and we
14:6 a revelation or with *k* or
15:34 some are without *k* of God
2Co 2:14 makes the odor of the *k* of
4:6 glorious *k* of God by the
6:6 by purity, by *k*, by
8:7 *k* and all earnestness and in
10:5 against the *k* of God; and we
11:6 I am unskilled . . . not in *k*
Eph 1:17 in the accurate *k* of him
3:19 which surpasses *k*, that you
4:13 the accurate *k* of the Son of
Php 1:9 with accurate *k* and full
1:13 bonds have become public *k*
3:8 *k* of Christ Jesus my Lord
Col 1:9 the accurate *k* of his will
1:10 in the accurate *k* of God
2:2 *k* of the sacred secret of God
2:3 treasures of wisdom and of *k*
3:10 through accurate *k* is being
1Ti 1:9 in the *k* of this fact, that
2:4 to an accurate *k* of truth
6:20 of the falsely called *k*
6:21 For making a show of such *k*
2Ti 2:25 to an accurate *k* of truth
3:7 to an accurate *k* of truth
Tit 1:1 the accurate *k* of the truth
Heb 10:26 accurate *k* of the truth
1Pe 3:7 according to *k*, assigning
2Pe 1:2 by an accurate *k* of God and
1:3 accurate *k* of the one who
1:5 to your virtue *k*
1:6 to your *k* self-control, to
1:8 accurate *k* of our Lord Jesus
2:20 an accurate *k* of the Lord
3:17 having this advance *k*, be
3:18 and *k* of our Lord and Savior
1Jo 2:3 have the *k* that we have come
2:5 *k* that we are in union with

1Jo 2:18 *k* that it is the last hour
2:20 all of you have *k*
2:29 you gain the *k* that everyone
3:1 world does not have a *k* of us
3:24 *k* that he is remaining in
4:2 *k* of the inspired expression
4:6 gains the *k* of God listens to
4:7 and gains the *k* of God
4:13 *k* that we are remaining in
5:2 gain the *k* that we are loving
5:20 gain the *k* of the true one

Known

Ge 20:6 I too have *k* that in the
41:21 could not be *k* that they had
41:31 will not be *k* as a result
45:1 Joseph made himself *k* to his
Ex 2:14 the thing has become *k*
6:3 did not make myself *k* to them
18:16 I must make *k* the decisions
18:20 make *k* to them the way in
21:36 was *k* that a bull was in the
23:9 have *k* the soul of the alien
33:16 will it be *k* that I have
Le 4:14 sin . . . has become *k*
4:23 has been made *k* to him, then
4:28 sin . . . been made *k* to him
Nu 12:6 I would make myself *k*
16:5 make *k* who belongs to him
31:18 not *k* the act of lying with
31:35 women who had not *k* the act
De 4:9 make them *k* to your sons and
7:15 evil diseases . . . you have *k*
8:3 neither you had *k* nor your
8:3 nor your fathers had *k*; in
8:16 which your fathers had not *k*
9:2 whom you yourself have *k* and
11:2 your sons who have not *k* and
11:28 gods whom you have not *k*
13:2 gods, whom you have not *k*
13:6 gods, whom you have not *k*
13:13 gods, whom you have not *k*
21:1 *k* who struck him fatally
28:33 whom you have not *k*; and you
28:36 a nation whom you have not *k*
28:64 gods whom you have not *k*
29:26 gods that they had not *k*
31:13 who have not *k* should listen
32:17 Gods whom they had not *k*
Jos 24:31 *k* all the work of Jehovah
Jg 16:9 his power did not become *k*
Ru 2:11 a people whom you had not *k*
3:3 Do not make yourself *k* to the
3:14 not let it be *k* that a woman
1Sa 3:13 for the error that he has *k*
6:3 must become *k* to you why his
16:3 shall make *k* to you what you
2Sa 17:19 not a thing became *k* of it
22:44 A people that I have not *k*
1Ki 2:32 David himself had not *k* of
18:36 be *k* that you are God in
2Ki 17:26 not *k* the religion of the
1Ch 16:8 Make his deeds *k* among the
17:19 the great achievements *k*
Ezr 4:12 let it become *k* to the king
4:13 let it become *k* to the king
4:14 and made it *k* to the king
4:16 making *k* to the king that
5:8 Let it become *k* to the king
7:24 made *k* that, as respects
7:25 anyone that has not *k* them
Ne 4:15 that it had become *k* to us
8:12 had been made *k* to them
9:14 your holy sabbath you made *k*
Es 2:22 came to be *k* to Mordecai, and
Job 18:21 of one that has not *k* God
19:14 And those *k* by me have
20:4 Have you at all times *k* this
24:16 They have not *k* daylight
26:3 practical wisdom itself *k* to
28:7 no bird of prey has *k* it
28:23 he himself has *k* its place
32:7 what should make wisdom *k*
Ps 9:16 Jehovah is *k* by the judgment
18:43 A people that I have not *k*
31:7 have *k* about the distresses
35:11 What I have not *k* they ask
48:3 become *k* as a secure height
67:2 way may be *k* in the earth
76:1 God is *k* in Judah; In Israel
77:14 have made your strength *k*
77:19 have not come to be *k*
78:5 make them *k* to their sons
79:6 nations that have not *k* you
Ps 79:10 there be *k* before our eyes
82:5 They have not *k*, and they do
88:12 be *k* in the darkness itself
89:1 faithfulness *k* with my mouth
98:2 has made his salvation *k*
103:7 made *k* his ways to Moses
105:1 Make *k* among the peoples his
106:8 to make his mightiness *k*
119:152 *k* some of your reminders
143:8 *k* to me the way in which I
145:12 *k* to the sons of men his
147:20 decisions, they have not *k*
Pr 1:23 will make my words *k* to you
4:19 *k* at what they keep stumbling
7:23 not *k* that it involves his
10:9 crooked will make himself *k*
12:16 *k* his vexation in the same
14:33 it becomes *k*
31:23 Her owner is someone *k* in
Ec 6:5 he has not seen, neither *k*
6:10 it has become *k* what man is
Isa 1:3 Israel itself has not *k*, my
5:5 *k* to you men what I am doing
12:4 Make *k* among the peoples his
12:5 is made *k* in all the earth
19:21 become *k* to the Egyptians
42:16 way that they have not *k*
42:16 that they have not *k*
45:5 although you have not *k* me
48:6 reserve, that you have not *k*
48:7 Look! I have already *k* them
48:8 not heard, neither have you *k*
55:5 a nation who have not *k* you
56:11 they have *k* no satisfaction
56:11 not *k* how to understand
61:9 be *k* even among the nations
63:16 may not have *k* us and
64:2 order to make your name *k*
66:14 be made *k* to his servants
Jer 7:9 gods whom you had not *k*
9:16 nor their fathers have *k*
14:18 land that they have not *k*
15:14 a land that you have not *k*
15:15 You yourself have *k*
16:13 land that you . . . have not *k*
17:4 land that you have not *k*
17:16 *k* the expression of my lips
19:4 gods whom they had not *k*
22:28 land that they have not *k*
28:9 prophet . . . will become *k*
33:3 things that you have not *k*
44:3 themselves had not *k*
48:30 I myself have *k* his fury
Eze 11:5 I myself have *k* it
16:2 make *k* to Jerusalem her
20:5 to make myself *k* to them in
20:9 I had made myself *k* to them
20:11 decisions I made *k* to them
22:26 they have made nothing *k*
32:9 to lands that you have not *k*
35:11 make myself *k* among them
36:32 let it be *k* to you
38:23 *k* before the eyes of many
39:7 holy name I shall make *k*
43:11 laws do you make *k* to them
Da 1:4 discernment of what is *k*
2:5 make the dream *k* to me, and
2:9 make *k* to me the very dream
2:15 Arioch made *k* the matter
2:17 he made *k* the matter
2:23 you have made *k* to me what
2:23 *k* to us the very matter of
2:25 make *k* the interpretation
2:26 make *k* to me the dream that
2:28 *k* to King Nebuchadnezzar what
2:29 *k* to you what is to occur
2:30 interpretation may be made *k*
2:45 God himself has made *k* to the
3:18 *k* to you, O king, that your
4:6 might make *k* to me the very
4:7 they were not making *k* to me
4:18 *k* to me the interpretation
5:8 to make *k* to the king the
5:15 *k* to me its interpretation
5:16 to make *k* to me its very
5:17 I shall make *k* to him
7:16 to make *k* to me the very
Ho 5:3 I personally have *k* Ephraim
5:9 made *k* trustworthy words
8:2 God, we, Israel, have *k* you
Am 3:2 You people only have I *k* out
3:10 not *k* how to do what is
5:12 *k* how many your revolts are
Mic 6:5 acts of Jehovah might be *k*
Hab 3:2 may you make it *k*
Zec 7:14 nations that they had not *k*
14:7 day that is *k* as belonging
Mt 10:26 that will not become *k*
12:33 by its fruit the tree is *k*
24:43 if the householder had *k* in
Mr 3:12 them not to make him *k*
Lu 2:15 Jehovah has made *k* to us
2:17 they made *k* the saying that
6:44 tree is *k* by its own fruit
7:37 *k* in the city to be a sinner
8:17 that will never become *k* and
12:2 secret that will not become *k*
12:39 had *k* at what hour the thief
24:35 how he became *k* to them by
Joh 4:10 If you had *k* the free gift
7:4 seeking to be *k* publicly
8:55 yet you have not *k* him
14:7 If you men had *k* me, you
14:7 would have *k* my Father also
15:15 I have made *k* to you
17:26 made your name *k* to them
17:26 and will make it *k*, in
18:15 disciple was *k* to the high
18:16 was *k* to the high priest
Ac 1:19 *k* to all the inhabitants of
2:14 let this be *k* to you and give
2:28 made life's ways *k* to me
4:10 *k* to all of you and to all
7:13 Joseph was made *k* to his
9:23 became *k* to Saul
9:42 *k* throughout all Joppa, and
13:38 therefore be *k* to you
15:18 *k* from of old
19:17 This became *k* to all, both
28:22 sect it is *k* to us that
28:28 *k* to you that this, the
Ro 1:19 be *k* about God is manifest
3:17 have not *k* the way of peace
7:7 not have *k* covetousness if the
9:22 and to make his power *k*
9:23 *k* the riches of his glory
16:26 has been made *k* through the
1Co 2:8 if they had *k* it they would
8:3 this one is *k* by him
13:12 even as I am accurately *k*
14:7 *k* what is being played on
14:9 be *k* what is being spoken
15:1 I make *k* to you, brothers
2Co 3:2 *k* and being read by all
5:16 Even if we have *k* Christ
Ga 4:9 you have come to be *k* by God
Eph 1:9 *k* to us the sacred secret
3:3 sacred secret was made *k* to
3:5 this secret was not made *k* to
3:10 *k* through the congregation
6:19 make *k* the sacred secret of
6:21 make everything *k* to you
Php 1:22 to select I do not make *k*
4:5 reasonableness become *k* to
4:6 petitions be made *k* to God
Col 1:27 been pleased to make *k* what
4:7 will make *k* to you
4:9 they will make *k* to you
2Ti 3:15 you have *k* the holy writings
2Pe 2:21 *k* the path of righteousness

Knows

Ge 3:5 God *k* that in the very day of
De 2:7 *k* of your walking through this
2Sa 19:20 well *k* that I am the one
1Ki 2:44 your heart well *k* that you
Job 11:11 well *k* men who are untrue
15:23 *k* that the day of darkness
23:10 he well *k* the way I take
Ps 103:14 well *k* the formation of us
104:19 sun itself *k* well where it
138:6 lofty one he *k* only from a
Ec 7:22 your own heart well *k* even
Isa 1:3 A bull well *k* its buyer, and
7:15 *k* how to reject the bad and
Jer 8:7 it well *k* its appointed times
Mt 6:8 your Father *k* what things you
6:32 heavenly Father *k* you need
11:27 no one fully *k* the Son but
24:36 that day and hour nobody *k*
Mr 13:32 day or the hour nobody *k*
Lu 10:22 who the Son is no one *k*
10:22 who the Father is, no one *k*
12:30 *k* you need these things
16:15 but God *k* your hearts
Joh 10:15 the Father *k* me and I know
14:17 neither beholds it nor *k* it
19:35 man *k* he tells true things

Ac 15:8 God, who k the heart, bore
26:26 well k about these things
Ro 8:27 k what the meaning of the
1Co 2:11 who among men k the things
3:20 Jehovah k that the reasonings
2Co 11:11 not love you? God k I do
11:31 God . . . k I am not lying
12:2 God k—was caught away as
12:3 body, I do not know, God k
2Ti 2:19 Jehovah k those who belong
Jas 4:17 k how to do what is right
2Pe 2:9 Jehovah k how to deliver
1Jo 3:20 because God . . . k all things
Re 2:17 name written which no one k
7:14 lord, you are the one that k
19:12 name written that no one k

Koa
Eze 23:23 and K, all the sons of

Kohath
Ge 46:11 sons of Levi were . . . K
Ex 6:16 sons of Levi . . . K and Merari
6:18 sons of K were Amram and
Nu 3:17 sons of Levi . . . Gershon and K
3:19 sons of K by their families
3:27 of K there were the family of
3:29 sons of K were encamped on
4:2 sons of K from among the
4:4 service of the sons of K in
4:15 sons of K will come in to
4:15 load of the sons of K in the
7:9 to the sons of K he gave none
16:1 the son of K, the son of Levi
26:57 of K the family of the
26:58 K became father to Amram
Jos 21:5 for the sons of K that were
21:20 sons of K, the Levites who
21:20 left out of the sons of K
21:26 sons of K who were left
1Ch 6:1 sons of Levi were Gershon, K
6:2 the sons of K were Amram
6:16 sons of Levi were Gershom, K
6:18 sons of K were Amram and
6:22 sons of K were Amminadab
6:38 son of K, the son of Levi
6:61 to the sons of K that were
6:66 families of the sons of K
6:70 sons of K that were left
15:5 of the sons of K, Uriel the
23:6 sons of Levi, to Gershon, K
23:12 The sons of K were Amram

Kohathites
Nu 3:27 were the families of the K
3:30 for the families of the K was
4:18 K be cut off from among the
4:34 register the sons of the K
4:37 families of the K, all those
10:21 K as carriers of the
26:57 Kohath the family of the K
Jos 21:4 for the families of the K
21:10 of the families of the K
1Ch 6:33 of the K Heman the singer
6:54 to the family of the K, for
9:32 some of the sons of the K
2Ch 20:19 Levites of the sons of the K
29:12 Azariah of the sons of the K
34:12 from the sons of the K, to

Kohath's
Ex 6:18 the years of K life were a

Kolaiah
Ne 11:7 K the son of Maaseiah the son
Jer 29:21 Ahab the son of K and

Korah
Ge 36:5 Oholibamah bore . . . K
36:14 she bore to Esau . . . K
36:16 sheik K . . . of Edom
36:18 sons of Oholibamah . . . K
Ex 6:21 sons of Izhar were K and
6:24 sons of K were Assir and
Nu 16:1 K the son of Izhar, the son of
16:5 Then he spoke to K and to his
16:6 K and his entire assembly
16:8 Moses went on to say to K
16:16 Moses said to K: You and all
16:19 When K got all the assembly
16:24 tabernacles of K, Dathan and
16:27 tabernacle of K, Dathan and
16:32 humankind that belonged to K
16:40 like K and his assembly
16:49 those dead on account of K
26:9 in the assembly of K, when
Nu 26:10 As for K, he died at the
26:11 the sons of K did not die
27:3 in the assembly of K, but for
1Ch 1:35 sons of Esau were . . . K
2:43 the sons of Hebron were K
6:22 Amminadab his son, K his son
6:37 son of Ebiasaph, the son of K
9:19 son of Ebiasaph the son of K
Ps 42:*super* Maskil for the sons of K
44:*super* Of the sons of K. Maskil
45:*super* Of the sons of K. Maskil
46:*super* Of the sons of K upon The
47:*super* Of the sons of K
48:*super* A melody of the sons of K
49:*super* Of the sons of K
84:*super* Of the sons of K
85:*super* the sons of K. A melody
87:*super* the sons of K. A melody
88:*super* a melody of the sons of K
Jude 11 in the rebellious talk of K

Korahite
1Ch 9:31 firstborn of Shallum the K

Korahites
Ex 6:24 were the families of the K
Nu 26:58 the family of the K
1Ch 9:19 the house of his father the K
12:6 Joezer and Jashobeam, the K
26:1 Of the K, Meshelemiah
26:19 of the sons of the K and of
2Ch 20:19 sons of the K rose up to

Kore
1Ch 9:19 son of K the son of Ebiasaph
26:1 Meshelemiah the son of K of
2Ch 31:14 K the son of Imnah the

Koz
1Ch 4:8 K, he became father to Anub

Kushaiah
1Ch 15:17 Ethan the son of K

Laadah
1Ch 4:21 L the father of Mareshah and

Laban
Ge 24:29 brother and his name was L
24:29 L went running to the man
24:50 L and Bethuel answered and
25:20 the sister of L the Syrian
27:43 run away to L my brother
28:2 wife from the daughters of L
28:5 for L the son of Bethuel the
29:5 know L the grandson of Nahor
29:10 saw Rachel the daughter of L
29:10 and the sheep of L
29:10 watered the sheep of L
29:13 soon as L heard the report
29:13 relate to L all these things
29:14 L said to him: You are
29:15 L said to Jacob: Are you my
29:16 L had two daughters
29:19 L said: It is better for me
29:21 Jacob said to L: Give over
29:22 L gathered all the men of
29:24 L gave to her Zilpah his
29:25 said to L: What is this you
29:26 L said: It is not customary
29:29 L gave Bilhah his
30:25 Jacob immediately said to L
30:27 Then L said to him: If, now
30:34 L said: Why, that is fine!
30:36 shepherding the flocks of L
30:40 among the flocks of L
30:40 set them by the flocks of L
31:1 the words of the sons of L
31:2 would look at the face of L
31:12 seen all that L is doing
31:19 L had gone to shear his sheep
31:20 Jacob outwitted L the Syrian
31:22 told to L that Jacob had run
31:24 God came to L the Syrian
31:25 L approached Jacob, as Jacob
31:25 L had encamped his brothers
31:26 L said to Jacob: What have
31:31 Jacob proceeded to say to L
31:33 L went on into the tent of
31:34 L went feeling through the
31:36 began to quarrel with L
31:36 Jacob went on to say to L
31:43 L in answer said to Jacob
31:47 And L began calling it
31:48 L proceeded to say: This heap
31:51 L went on to say to Jacob
31:55 L got up early in the
Ge 31:55 L got on his way that he
32:4 With L I have resided as an
46:18 Zilpah, whom L gave to his
46:25 Bilhah, whom L gave to his
De 1:1 between Paran and Tophel and L

Laban's
Ge 30:42 feeble ones . . . came to be L

Labdanum
Ge 37:25 camels were carrying l and
43:11 honey, l and resinous bark

Labor
Ge 49:15 subject to slavish forced l
Ex 1:11 chiefs of forced l for the
34:21 Six days you are to l, but on
De 20:11 become yours for forced l
Jos 16:10 subject to slavish forced l
17:13 the Canaanites at forced l
Jg 1:28 Canaanites to forced l, and
1:30 to be subject to forced l
1:33 became theirs for forced l
2Sa 20:24 conscripted for forced l
1Ki 4:6 those conscripted for forced l
5:13 conscripted for forced l
5:13 conscripted for forced l
5:14 conscripted for forced l
9:15 conscripted for forced l
9:21 for slavish forced l until
12:18 conscripted for forced l
2Ch 8:8 men for forced l until this
10:18 conscripted for forced l
Es 10:1 forced l upon the land and
Job 6:10 leap for joy at my l pains
7:1 compulsory l for mortal man
15:7 brought forth with l pains
Ps 90:2 as with l pains the earth
Pr 8:24 forth as with l pains, when
8:25 brought forth as with l pains
12:24 come to be for forced l
25:23 as with l pains a downpour
Isa 13:8 birth they have l pains
26:17 has l pains, cries out in
26:18 had l pains; as it were, we
31:8 come to be for forced l
66:7 into l pains she gave birth
66:8 with l pains in one day
66:8 Zion has come into l pains
Jer 6:24 l pains like those of a
22:23 the l pains like those of a
La 1:1 has come to be for forced l
Ho 13:13 The l pangs of a woman
Joh 4:38 what you have spent no l on
4:38 into the benefit of their l
1Co 3:8 according to his own l
15:58 your l is not in vain in
2Co 11:27 in l and toil, in sleepless
1Th 1:3 loving l and your endurance
2:9 brothers, our l and toil
3:5 our l might have turned out
2Th 3:8 by l and toil night and day
Re 2:2 I know your deeds, and your l

Labored
Joh 4:38 Others have l, and you have
1Co 15:10 I l in excess of them all

Laborer
Ex 12:45 a hired l may not eat of it
Le 19:13 wages of a hired l should not
22:10 nor a hired l may eat anything
25:6 hired l and the settler with
25:40 be with you like a hired l
25:50 workdays of a hired l are
25:53 with him like a hired l from
De 15:18 the value of a hired l
24:14 not defraud a hired l who is
Job 7:1 like the days of a hired l
7:2 l he waits for his wages
14:6 as a hired l does in his day
Isa 16:14 the years of a hired l
21:16 to the years of a hired l

Laborers
2Ki 25:12 and compulsory l
Isa 45:14 The unpaid l of Egypt and
Jer 52:16 and as compulsory l

Laboring
Ac 20:35 by thus l you must assist
1Co 16:16 everyone cooperating and l

Laborious
Le 23:7 No sort of l work may you do
23:8 No sort of l work may you do
23:21 No sort of l work may you do
23:25 No sort of l work may you do

Le 23:35 No sort of *l* work may you do
23:36 No sort of *l* work may you do
Nu 4:47 render the *l* service and the
28:18 No sort of *l* work must you
28:25 No sort of *l* work must you
28:26 No sort of *l* work must you
29:1 No sort of *l* work must you do
29:12 No sort of *l* work must you
29:35 No sort of *l* work must you

Labors
Ex 23:16 first ripe fruits of your *l*
23:16 gather in your *l* from the
Ro 16:6 Mary . . . performed many *l* for
16:12 performed many *l* in the Lord
2Co 6:5 by *l*, by sleepless nights, by
10:15 in the *l* of someone else
11:23 in *l* more plentifully, in
Re 14:13 them rest from their *l*

Lace
Ge 14:23 from a thread to a sandal *l*
Lu 3:16 the *l* of whose sandals I am
Joh 1:27 *l* of whose sandal I am not

Laces
Isa 5:27 *l* of their sandals be torn
Mr 1:7 and untie the *l* of his sandals

Lachish
Jos 10:3 Japhia the king of *L* and
10:5 the king of *L*
10:23 the king of *L*
10:31 passed on from Libnah to *L*
10:32 gave *L* into Israel's hand
10:33 Gezer went up to help *L*
10:34 passed on from *L* to Eglon
10:35 all that they had done to *L*
12:11 the king of *L*, one
15:39 *L* and Bozkath and Eglon
2Ki 14:19 and he went fleeing to *L*
14:19 in pursuit of him to *L* and
18:14 the king of Assyria at *L*
18:17 from *L* to King Hezekiah
19:8 had pulled away from *L*
2Ch 11:9 and Adoraim and *L* and Azekah
25:27 At length he fled to *L*
25:27 sent after him to *L* and
32:9 at *L* and all his imperial
Ne 11:30 *L* and its fields
Isa 36:2 Rabshakeh from *L* to
37:8 he had pulled away from *L*
Jer 34:7 against *L* and against Azekah
Mic 1:13 horses, O inhabitress of *L*

Lack
De 8:9 in which you will *l* nothing
Jg 18:10 is no *l* of any sort of thing
19:19 is no *l* of a single thing
19:20 let any *l* of yours be upon me
Job 4:21 They die for *l* of wisdom
Ps 23:1 I shall *l* nothing
34:9 there is no *l* to those fearing
34:10 will not *l* anything good
Pr 13:23 away for *l* of judgment
14:28 *l* of population is the ruin
Ec 4:8 my soul to *l* in good things
Isa 5:13 exile for *l* of knowledge
La 4:9 *l* of the produce of the open
Mt 13:58 account of their *l* of faith
Mr 6:6 wondered at their *l* of faith
Ro 3:3 their *l* of faith perhaps make
4:20 not waver in a *l* of faith
11:20 For their *l* of faith they
11:23 remain in their *l* of faith
1Co 7:5 for your *l* of self-regulation
12:24 to the part which had a *l*
1Ti 1:13 acted with a *l* of faith
Tit 3:13 that they may not *l* anything
Heb 3:19 because of *l* of faith

Lacked
De 2:7 You have not *l* a thing
Ne 9:21 They *l* nothing. Their very
Jer 44:18 to her we have *l* everything
Php 4:10 but you *l* opportunity

Lacking
Ge 8:3 fifty days the waters were *l*
18:28 righteous should be *l* five
1Sa 30:19 nothing of theirs *l*, from
2Sa 17:22 until not a one was *l* that
1Ki 4:27 They left nothing *l*
Pr 31:11 and there is no gain *l*
Ec 9:8 let oil not be *l* upon your head
10:3 his own heart is *l*, and he
Ca 7:2 Let not the mixed wine be *l*
Isa 51:14 his bread may not be *l*
Eze 4:17 may be *l* bread and water and
Zep 3:5 At daylight it did not prove *l*
Mt 19:20 what yet am I *l*?
Lu 18:22 yet one thing *l* about you
Col 1:24 am filling up what is *l* of
1Th 3:10 that are *l* about your faith
1Ti 1:9 *l* loving-kindness, and
2Ti 2:20 others for a purpose *l* honor
Heb 3:12 a wicked heart *l* faith by
Jas 1:4 respects, not *l* in anything
1:5 *l* in wisdom, let him keep on
2:15 *l* the food sufficient for the

Lad
1Sa 17:56 inquire whose son the *l* is
20:22 way I should say to the *l*

Ladan
1Ch 7:26 *L* his son, Ammihud his son
23:7 Gershonites, *L* and Shimei
23:8 sons of *L* were Jehiel the
23:9 heads of the fathers for *L*
26:21 The sons of *L*, the sons of
26:21 Gershonite belonging to *L*
26:21 to *L* the Gershonite, Jehieli

Ladder
Ge 28:12 *l* stationed upon the earth

Ladies
Jg 5:29 her noble *l* would answer her
Ru 4:17 the neighbor *l* gave it a name
Ec 2:8 of mankind, a lady, even *l*
12:3 *l* seeing at the windows have

Lady
Ge 24:61 Rebekah and her *l* attendants
34:4 Get me this young *l* as a wife
1Ki 11:19 the sister of Tahpenes the *l*
15:13 to remove her from being *l*
2Ki 10:13 and the sons of the *l*
2Ch 15:16 removed her from being *l*
Pr 9:3 sent forth its *l* attendants
Ec 2:8 of mankind, a *l*, even ladies
Jer 13:18 Say to the king and to the *l*
29:2 the *l* and the court officials
2Jo 1 The older man to the chosen *l*
5 now I request you, *l*, as a

Lael
Nu 3:24 Eliasaph the son of *L*

Lahad
1Ch 4:2 father to Ahumai and *L*

Lahmam
Jos 15:40 Cabbon and *L* and Chitlish

Lahmi
1Ch 20:5 *L* the brother of Goliath the

Laid
Ge 2:16 And Jehovah God also *l* this
28:6 he *l* the command upon him
39:16 garment *l* up beside her
47:19 our land not be *l* desolate
48:14 He purposely *l* his hands so
Le 8:14 *l* their hands upon the head of
8:18 *l* their hands upon the head
8:22 *l* their hands upon the ram's
20:11 *l* bare the nakedness of his
20:17 sister that he has *l* bare
20:18 has *l* bare the source of her
20:20 *l* bare the nakedness of his
20:21 brother that he has *l* bare
Nu 27:23 *l* his hands upon him and
De 25:2 *l* prostrate and given strokes
32:34 Is it not *l* up with me
33:4 Moses *l* as a command upon us
34:9 Moses had *l* his hand upon him
Jos 2:6 stalks of flax *l* in rows for
7:11 that I *l* as a command upon
8:27 that he had *l* in command
Jg 19:29 *l* hold of his concubine and
1Ki 2:43 that I solemnly *l* upon you
3:20 *l* him in her own bosom, and
3:20 dead son she *l* in my bosom
6:37 had its foundation *l*, in the
7:10 stones *l* as a foundation
11:11 that I *l* in command upon
16:34 he *l* the foundation of it
17:19 *l* him upon his own couch
2Ki 4:21 *l* him upon the couch of the
4:32 dead, being *l* upon his couch
11:16 they *l* their hands upon her
13:16 Elisha *l* his hands upon
16:5 *l* siege against Ahaz
18:14 *l* upon Hezekiah the king of
1Ch 16:40 he *l* in command upon Israel
2Ch 3:3 Solomon *l* as a foundation for
16:14 *l* him in the bed that had
19:9 he *l* a command upon them
23:15 they *l* their hands upon her
29:23 and *l* their hands upon them
Ezr 3:6 foundation . . . not yet been *l*
3:10 builders *l* the foundation of
4:15 that city has been *l* waste
5:8 timbers are being *l* in the
5:16 came he *l* the foundations of
Es 2:10 had *l* the command upon her
2:20 Mordecai had *l* the command
4:17 Esther had *l* in command upon
Job 23:11 steps my foot has *l* hold
27:6 On my justness I have *l* hold
37:15 God *l* an appointment upon
38:6 Or who *l* its cornerstone
Ps 56:*super* *l* hold of him in Gath
62:9 When *l* upon the scales they
68:28 Your God has *l* command upon
79:1 *l* Jerusalem in a heap of
81:5 reminder he *l* it upon Joseph
89:40 *l* his fortifications in ruin
102:25 *l* the foundations of the
141:9 trap that they have *l* for me
Isa 14:32 *l* the foundation of Zion
23:18 stored up, nor be *l* up
26:5 *l* low those inhabiting the
44:28 will have your foundation *l*
48:13 own hand *l* the foundation
Jer 17:11 what it has not *l* is the
26:8 the people *l* hold of him
35:6 one that *l* the command upon
50:24 I have *l* a snare for you
50:33 captive have *l* hold on them
La 1:4 All her gates are *l* desolate
1:13 made me a woman *l* desolate
1:16 have become those *l* desolate
3:11 He has made me one *l* desolate
3:28 he has *l* something upon him
Eze 12:19 land may be *l* desolate of
19:7 the land was *l* desolate and
25:3 it has been *l* desolate
32:19 be *l* with the uncircumcised
32:32 must be *l* in the midst of
33:28 Israel must be *l* desolate
35:12 They have been *l* desolate
35:15 because it was *l* desolate
36:4 places that were *l* desolate
36:35 which was *l* desolate has
36:35 and that were *l* desolate
36:36 what has been *l* desolate
Joe 1:17 have been *l* desolate
Am 2:12 you *l* a command, saying
7:9 will certainly be *l* desolate
Mic 5:1 a siege he has *l* against us
Na 2:10 voidness, and a city *l* waste
Zep 3:6 Their cities were *l* waste
Hag 2:18 the temple of Jehovah was *l*
Zec 4:9 *l* the foundation of this house
8:9 foundation of the house . . . *l*
Mt 8:6 my manservant is *l* up in the
26:50 *l* hands on Jesus and took
27:60 *l* it in his new memorial
Mr 6:29 and *l* it in a memorial tomb
6:40 they *l* themselves down in
7:30 child *l* on the bed and the
8:23 he *l* his hands upon him and
8:25 he *l* his hands again upon the
14:46 they *l* their hands upon him
15:46 *l* him in a tomb which was
15:47 at where he had been *l*
16:6 The place where they *l* him
Lu 2:7 *l* him in a manger, because
2:34 This one is *l* for the fall
6:48 down deep and *l* a foundation
12:19 good things *l* up for many
13:13 And he *l* his hands on her
19:20 mina . . . kept *l* away in a
23:26 they *l* hold of Simon, a
23:53 he *l* him in a tomb carved in
23:55 and how his body was *l*
Joh 7:30 no one *l* a hand upon him
8:20 no one *l* hold of him
11:34 said: Where have you *l* him?
13:4 *l* aside his outer garments
13:12 *l* himself down at the table
19:41 no one had ever yet been *l*
19:42 they *l* Jesus, because the
20:2 know where they have *l* him
20:13 know where they have *l* him
20:15 where you have *l* him, and
Ac 4:3 *l* their hands upon them and

Ge 41:34 appoint overseers over the *l*
41:34 one fifth of the *l* of Egypt
41:36 as a supply for the *l* for
41:36 develop in the *l* of Egypt
41:36 the *l* may not be cut off by
41:41 you over all the *l* of Egypt
41:43 over all the *l* of Egypt
41:44 in all the *l* of Egypt
41:45 to go out over the *l* of Egypt
41:46 toured about in all the *l* of
41:47 the *l* went on producing by
41:48 came upon the *l* of Egypt and
41:52 in the *l* of my wretchedness
41:53 obtained in the *l* of Egypt
41:54 but in all the *l* of Egypt
41:55 *l* of Egypt became famished
41:56 strong grip on the *l* of Egypt
42:5 existed in the *l* of Canaan
42:6 the man in power over the *l*
42:7 From the *l* of Canaan to buy
42:9 the exposed condition of the *l*
42:12 exposed condition of the *l*
42:13 sons of but one man in the *l*
42:29 to the *l* of Canaan and told
42:32 our father in the *l* of Canaan
42:34 carry on business in the *l*
43:1 famine was severe in the *l*
43:11 the finest products of the *l*
44:8 to you from the *l* of Canaan
45:8 dominating over all the *l* of
45:10 must dwell in the *l* of Goshen
45:17 go enter the *l* of Canaan
45:18 the good of the *l* of Egypt
45:18 eat the fat part of the *l*
45:19 wagons from the *l* of Egypt
45:20 good of all the *l* of Egypt
45:25 came into the *l* of Canaan
45:26 over all the *l* of Egypt
46:6 in the *l* of Canaan
46:12 Onan died in the *l* of Canaan
46:20 born to Joseph in the *l* of
46:28 came into the *l* of Goshen
46:31 were in the *l* of Canaan
46:34 dwell in the *l* of Goshen
47:1 come from the *l* of Canaan
47:1 they are in the *l* of Goshen
47:4 reside as aliens in the *l*
47:4 famine is severe in the *l*
47:4 dwell . . . in the *l* of Goshen
47:6 The *l* of Egypt is at your
47:6 in the very best of the *l*
47:6 dwell in the *l* of Goshen
47:11 possession in the *l* of Egypt
47:11 in the very best of the *l*
47:11 in the *l* of Rameses
47:13 no bread in all the *l*
47:13 and the *l* of Egypt
47:13 *l* of Canaan became exhausted
47:14 found in the *l* of Egypt
47:14 *l* of Canaan for the cereals
47:15 money from the *l* of Egypt
47:15 the *l* of Canaan was spent
47:18 but our bodies and our *l*
47:19 both we and our *l*
47:19 Buy us and our *l* for bread
47:19 we together with our *l* will
47:19 our *l* not be laid desolate
47:20 Joseph bought all the *l* of
47:20 the *l* came to be Pharaoh's
47:22 *l* of the priests he did not
47:22 they did not sell their *l*
47:23 you and your *l* for Pharaoh
47:23 you must sow the *l* with it
47:26 Only the *l* of the priests as
47:27 to dwell in the *l* of Egypt
47:27 in the *l* of Goshen; and
47:28 lived on in the *l* of Egypt
48:3 Luz in the *l* of Canaan
48:4 will give this *l* to your seed
48:5 born to you in the *l* of Egypt
48:7 in the *l* of Canaan on the way
48:7 a good stretch of *l* before
48:21 return you to the *l* of your
48:22 one shoulder of *l* more
49:15 the *l* is pleasant; and he
49:30 Mamre in the *l* of Canaan
50:5 in the *l* of Canaan is where
50:7 older men of the *l* of Egypt
50:8 they left in the *l* of Goshen
50:11 And the inhabitants of the *l*
50:13 sons carried him into the *l*
50:24 bring you up out of this *l*
50:24 *l* about which he swore to
Ex 1:7 *l* got to be filled with them

Ex 2:15 dwell in the *l* of Midian
2:22 come to be in a foreign *l*
3:8 bring them up out of that *l* to
3:8 to a *l* good and spacious, to a
3:8 to a *l* flowing with milk and
3:17 to the *l* of the Canaanites
3:17 to a *l* flowing with milk and
4:9 and pour it out on the dry *l*
4:9 become blood on the dry *l*
4:20 to return to the *l* of Egypt
5:5 people of the *l* are now many
5:12 over all the *l* of Egypt
6:1 will drive them out of his *l*
6:4 to give them the *l* of Canaan
6:4 Canaan, the *l* of their alien
6:8 bring you into the *l* that I
6:11 Israel away out of his *l*
6:13 out from the *l* of Egypt
6:26 Israel out from the *l* of
6:28 to Moses in the *l* of Egypt
7:2 sons of Israel away from his *l*
7:3 my miracles in the *l* of Egypt
7:4 out from the *l* of Egypt with
7:19 be blood in all the *l* of Egypt
7:21 blood came to be in all the *l*
8:5 frogs come up over the *l* of
8:6 frogs . . . cover the *l* of Egypt
8:7 frogs . . . over the *l* of Egypt
8:14 and the *l* began to stink
8:16 gnats in all the *l* of Egypt
8:17 gnats in all the *l* of Egypt
8:22 the *l* of Goshen . . . distinct
8:24 and all the *l* of Egypt
8:24 *l* came to ruin as a result of
8:25 sacrifice to your God in the *l*
9:5 will do this thing in the *l*
9:9 powder upon all the *l* of Egypt
9:9 and beast in all the *l* of Egypt
9:22 hail . . . on all the *l* of Egypt
9:22 of the field in the *l* of Egypt
9:23 hail upon the *l* of Egypt
9:24 hail . . . in all the *l* of Egypt
9:25 striking at all the *l* of Egypt
9:26 Only in the *l* of Goshen
10:12 hand out over the *l* of Egypt
10:12 come up over the *l* of Egypt
10:12 all the vegetation of the *l*
10:13 rod out over the *l* of Egypt
10:13 east wind to blow upon the *l*
10:14 locusts . . . over all the *l*
10:15 surface of the entire *l*
10:15 *l* grew dark; and they went
10:15 all the vegetation of the *l*
10:15 in all the *l* of Egypt
10:21 *l* of Egypt and the darkness
10:22 occur in all the *l* of Egypt
11:3 very great in the *l* of Egypt
11:5 firstborn in the *l* of Egypt
11:6 outcry in all the *l* of Egypt
11:9 increased in the *l* of Egypt
11:10 Israel away from his *l*
12:1 and Aaron in the *l* of Egypt
12:12 pass through the *l* of Egypt
12:12 firstborn in the *l* of Egypt
12:13 I strike at the *l* of Egypt
12:17 out from the *l* of Egypt
12:19 or a native of the *l*, that
12:25 *l* that Jehovah will give you
12:29 firstborn in the *l* of Egypt
12:33 away quickly out of the *l*
12:41 went out of the *l* of Egypt
12:42 out of the *l* of Egypt
12:48 like a native of the *l*
12:51 armies out of the *l* of Egypt
13:5 into the *l* of the Canaanites
13:5 *l* flowing with milk and honey
13:11 into the *l* of the Canaanites
13:15 firstborn in the *l* of Egypt
13:17 of the *l* of the Philistines
13:18 up out of the *l* of Egypt
14:3 in confusion in the *l*
14:16 midst of the sea on dry *l*
14:22 midst of the sea on dry *l*
14:29 walked on dry *l* in the midst
15:19 Israel walked on dry *l*
16:1 coming out of the *l* of Egypt
16:3 in the *l* of Egypt while we
16:6 you out from the *l* of Egypt
16:32 you out of the *l* of Egypt
16:35 coming to a *l* inhabited
16:35 frontier of the *l* of Canaan
18:3 come to be in a foreign *l*
18:27 and he went his way to his *l*
19:1 came out of the *l* of Egypt

Ex 20:2 out of the *l* of Egypt, out of
22:21 residents in the *l* of Egypt
23:9 residents in the *l* of Egypt
23:10 to sow your *l* with seed and
23:26 woman will exist in your *l*
23:29 that the *l* may not become a
23:30 take possession of the *l*
23:31 the inhabitants of the *l*, and
23:33 should not dwell in your *l*
29:46 out of the *l* of Egypt that
32:1 out of the *l* of Egypt, we
32:4 led you up out of the *l* of
32:7 out of the *l* of Egypt have
32:8 led you up out of the *l* of
32:11 you brought out of the *l*
32:13 *l* that I have designated I
32:23 out of the *l* of Egypt, we
33:1 led up out of the *l* of Egypt
33:1 to the *l* about which I swore
33:3 a *l* flowing with milk and
34:12 the *l* to which you are going
34:15 the inhabitants of the *l*
34:24 nobody will desire your *l*
Le 4:27 people of the *l* sins
11:45 out of the *l* of Egypt to
14:34 come into the *l* of Canaan
14:34 of the *l* of your possession
16:22 errors into a desert *l*, and
18:3 The way the *l* of Egypt does
18:3 the way the *l* of Canaan does
18:25 *l* is unclean, and I shall
18:25 *l* will vomit its inhabitants
18:27 men of the *l* who were
18:27 so that the *l* is unclean
18:28 *l* will not vomit you out for
19:9 reap the harvest of your *l*
19:23 people come into the *l*, and
19:29 that the *l* may not commit
19:29 *l* actually be filled with
19:33 alien in your *l*, you must
19:34 residents in the *l* of Egypt
19:36 you out of the *l* of Egypt
20:2 people of the *l* should pelt
20:4 And if the people of the *l*
20:22 *l* to which I am bringing you
20:24 a *l* flowing with milk and
22:24 and in your *l* you should not
22:33 *l* of Egypt to prove myself
23:10 *l* that I am giving you, and
23:22 reap the harvest of your *l*
23:39 gathered the produce of the *l*
23:43 out of the *l* of Egypt. I am
25:2 *l* that I am giving you, then
25:2 *l* must observe a sabbath to
25:4 complete rest for the *l*, a
25:5 of complete rest for the *l*
25:6 sabbath of the *l* must serve
25:7 wild beast that is in your *l*
25:9 horn to sound in all your *l*
25:10 liberty in the *l* to all its
25:12 may eat what the *l* produces
25:18 dwell on the *l* in security
25:19 the *l* will indeed give its
25:23 the *l* should not be sold in
25:23 because the *l* is mine
25:24 *l* of your possession you
25:24 grant to the *l* the right of
25:38 *l* of Egypt to give you the
25:38 to give you the *l* of Canaan
25:42 brought out of the *l* of Egypt
25:45 had born to them in your *l*
25:55 brought out of the *l* of Egypt
26:1 as a showpiece in your *l*
26:4 *l* will indeed give its yield
26:5 dwell in security in your *l*
26:6 put peace in the *l*, and you
26:6 wild beast cease out of the *l*
26:6 will not pass through your *l*
26:13 you out of the *l* of Egypt
26:32 lay the *l* desolate, and your
26:33 *l* must become a desolation
26:34 *l* will pay off its sabbaths
26:34 in the *l* of your enemies
26:34 *l* will keep sabbath, as it
26:38 *l* of your enemies must eat
26:41 into the *l* of their enemies
26:42 and the *l* I shall remember
26:43 *l* was left abandoned by them
26:44 in the *l* of their enemies
26:45 out of the *l* of Egypt under
27:24 possession of the *l* belongs
27:30 tenth part of the *l*, out of
27:30 seed of the *l* and the fruit
Nu 1:1 coming out of the *l* of Egypt

Nu 3:13 firstborn in the *l* of Egypt
8:17 firstborn in the *l* of Egypt
9:1 coming out of the *l* of Egypt
9:14 and for the native of the *l*
10:9 war in your *l* against the
13:2 may spy out the *l* of Canaan
13:16 Moses sent to spy out the *l*
13:17 to spy out the *l* of Canaan
13:18 you must see what the *l* is
13:19 what the *l* is in which they
13:20 what the *l* is, whether it
13:20 the fruitage of the *l*
13:21 went up and spied out the *l*
13:25 from spying out the *l*
13:26 the fruitage of the *l*
13:27 We entered into the *l* to
13:28 dwell in the *l* are strong
13:29 in the *l* of the Negeb, and
13:32 a bad report of the *l* that
13:32 *l*, which we passed through
13:32 is a *l* that eats up its
14:2 died in the *l* of Egypt, or if
14:3 bringing us to this *l* to fall
14:6 of those who spied out the *l*
14:7 The *l* that we passed through
14:7 is a very, very good *l*
14:8 bring us into this *l* and give
14:8 *l* that is flowing with milk
14:9 you fear the people of the *l*
14:14 to the inhabitants of this *l*
14:16 *l* about which he swore to
14:23 the *l* about which I swore to
14:24 bring him into the *l* where
14:30 will not enter into the *l*
14:31 the *l* that you have rejected
14:34 days that you spied out the *l*
14:36 Moses sent to spy out the *l*
14:36 a bad report against the *l*
14:37 the bad report about the *l*
14:38 who went to spy out the *l*
15:2 the *l* of your dwelling places
15:18 *l* where I am bringing you
15:19 eat any of the bread of the *l*
15:41 you out of the *l* of Egypt
16:13 out of a *l* flowing with
16:14 any *l* flowing with milk and
18:13 of all that is on their *l*
18:20 In their *l* you will not have
20:12 this congregation into the *l*
20:17 pass, please, through your *l*
20:23 the border of the *l* of Edom
20:24 he will not enter into the *l*
21:4 to go around the *l* of Edom
21:22 Let me pass through your *l*
21:24 and took possession of his *l*
21:26 taking all his *l* out of his
21:31 in the *l* of the Amorites
21:34 and all his people and his *l*
21:35 taking possession of his *l*
22:5 *l* of the sons of his people
22:6 I may drive them out of the *l*
26:4 went out of the *l* of Egypt
26:19 Onan died in the *l* of Canaan
26:53 *l* should be apportioned for
26:55 should the *l* be apportioned
27:12 and see the *l* that I shall
32:1 began to see the *l* of Jazer
32:1 Jazer and the *l* of Gilead, and
32:4 *l* that Jehovah defeated before
32:4 is a *l* for livestock, and your
32:5 let this *l* be given to your
32:7 from crossing into the *l* that
32:8 Kadesh-barnea to see the *l*
32:9 Eshcol and saw the *l*, then
32:9 so as not to go into the *l*
32:17 of the inhabitants of the *l*
32:22 *l* is actually subdued before
32:22 this *l* must become yours as
32:29 and the *l* is actually subdued
32:29 give them the *l* of Gilead as
32:30 in the *l* of Canaan
32:32 to the *l* of Canaan, and the
32:33 *l* belonging to its cities in
32:33 cities of the *l* round about
33:1 went out of the *l* of Egypt in
33:37 frontier of the *l* of Edom
33:38 Israel from the *l* of Egypt
33:40 the Negeb, in the *l* of Canaan
33:51 into the *l* of Canaan
33:52 inhabitants of the *l* from
33:53 take possession of the *l* and
33:53 I shall certainly give the *l*
33:54 apportion the *l* to yourselves
33:55 inhabitants of the *l* away

Nu 33:55 harass you on the *l* in which
34:2 are going into the *l* of Canaan
34:2 the *l* that will fall to you
34:2 the *l* of Canaan according to
34:12 *l* according to its boundaries
34:13 *l* that you will apportion
34:17 divide the *l* to you people
34:18 of each tribe to divide the *l*
34:29 in the *l* of Canaan
35:10 to the *l* of Canaan
35:14 will give in the *l* of Canaan
35:28 to the *l* of his possession
35:32 to resume dwelling in the *l*
35:33 must not pollute the *l* in
35:33 is blood that pollutes the *l*
35:33 *l* there may be no atonement
35:34 not defile the *l* in which
36:2 the *l* in inheritance by lot
De 1:5 in the *l* of Moab Moses
1:7 the *l* of the Canaanites, and
1:8 I do put the *l* before you
1:8 and take possession of the *l*
1:21 God has abandoned the *l* to you
1:22 may search out the *l* for us
1:25 some of the fruitage of the *l*
1:25 *l* . . . God is giving us is good
1:27 out of the *l* of Egypt to give
1:35 *l* that I swore to give to
1:36 to his sons I shall give the *l*
2:5 I shall not give you of their *l*
2:9 shall not give you any of his *l*
2:12 as Israel must do to the *l*
2:19 the *l* of the sons of Ammon as
2:20 As the *l* of the Rephaim it
2:24 take possession of his *l*, and
2:27 Let me pass through your *l*
2:29 the *l* that Jehovah our God is
2:31 abandon Sihon and his *l* to you
2:31 take possession of his *l*
2:37 the *l* of the sons of Ammon
3:2 people and his *l* into your hand
3:8 the *l* from the hand of the two
3:12 we took possession of this *l*
3:13 called the *l* of the Rephaim
3:18 your God has given you this *l*
3:20 taken possession of the *l*
3:25 *l* that is across the Jordan
3:28 cause them to inherit the *l*
4:1 take possession of the *l* that
4:5 the *l* to which you are going
4:14 *l* to which you are passing
4:21 the good *l* that Jehovah your
4:22 For I am dying in this *l*
4:22 take possession of this good *l*
4:25 a long time in the *l* and do
4:26 *l* to which you are crossing
4:38 their *l* as an inheritance as
4:46 in the *l* of Sihon the king of
4:47, 47 his *l* and of the *l* of Og
5:6 out of the *l* of Egypt, out of
5:15 a slave in the *l* of Egypt and
5:31 the *l* that I am giving them
5:33 lengthen your days in the *l*
6:1 in the *l* to which you are
6:3 *l* flowing with milk and honey
6:10 God will bring you into the *l*
6:12 out of the *l* of Egypt, out of
6:18 take possession of the good *l*
6:23 *l* about which he had sworn to
7:1 at last brings you into the *l*
8:1 and take possession of the *l*
8:7 bringing you into a good *l*
8:7 a *l* of torrent valleys of
8:8 a *l* of wheat and barley and
8:8 a *l* of oil olives and honey
8:9 a *l* in which you will not eat
8:9 a *l* the stones of which are
8:10 good *l* that he has given you
8:14 out of the *l* of Egypt, out of
9:4 to take possession of this *l*
9:5 to take possession of their *l*
9:6 God is giving you this good *l*
9:7 you went out of the *l* of Egypt
9:23 take possession of the *l* that
9:28 the *l* out of which you brought
9:28 bring them into the *l* that he
10:7 a *l* of torrent valleys running
10:11 take possession of the *l* that
10:19 residents in the *l* of Egypt
11:3 king of Egypt and to all his *l*
11:8 take possession of the *l*
11:9 *l* flowing with milk and honey
11:10 the *l* to which you are going
11:10 not like the *l* of Egypt out

De 11:11 *l* to which you are crossing
11:11 it is a *l* of mountains and
11:12 a *l* that Jehovah your God is
11:14 give rain for your *l* at its
11:17 *l* that Jehovah is giving you
11:25 *l* on which you will tread
11:29 the *l* to which you are going
11:30 in the *l* of the Canaanites
11:31 take possession of the *l*
12:1 in the *l* that Jehovah the God
12:10 dwell in the *l* that Jehovah
12:29 and dwell in their *l*
13:5 out of the *l* of Egypt and has
13:7 from one end of the *l* to the
13:7 to the other end of the *l*
13:10 out of the *l* of Egypt, out
15:4 the *l* that Jehovah your God
15:7 in your *l* that Jehovah your
15:11 to be in the midst of the *l*
15:11 poor brother in your *l*
15:15 a slave in the *l* of Egypt
16:3 came out of the *l* of Egypt
16:3 coming out of the *l* of Egypt
16:20 take possession of the *l*
17:14 the *l* that Jehovah your God
18:9 the *l* that Jehovah your God
19:1 the nations whose *l* Jehovah
19:2 in the midst of your *l* that
19:3 your *l* that Jehovah your God
19:8 he has given you all the *l*
19:10 in the midst of your *l* that
19:14 *l* that Jehovah . . . is giving
20:1 up out of the *l* of Egypt
23:20 the *l* to which you are going
24:4 you must not lead the *l* that
24:14 residents who are in your *l*
24:22 a slave in the *l* of Egypt
25:19 enemies round about in the *l*
26:1 enter into the *l* that Jehovah
26:2 the *l* of yours that Jehovah
26:3 I have come into the *l* that
26:9 and gave us this *l*
26:9 a *l* flowing with milk and
26:15 *l* flowing with milk and
27:2 cross the Jordan into the *l*
27:3 the *l* . . . . God is giving you
27:3 a *l* flowing with milk and
28:8 *l* that Jehovah your God is
28:12 to give the rain on your *l*
28:24 dust as the rain of your *l*
28:52 fall in all your *l*
28:52 your gates in all your *l*
29:1 Israel in the *l* of Moab
29:2 the *l* of Egypt to Pharaoh and
29:2 all his servants and all his *l*
29:8 took their *l* and gave it as an
29:16 dwelt in the *l* of Egypt and
29:22 will come from a distant *l*
29:22 the plagues of that *l* and its
29:23 its whole *l* will not be sown
29:24 do like this to this *l*? Why
29:25 out of the *l* of Egypt
29:27 anger blazed against that *l*
29:28 threw them into another *l* as
30:5 the *l* of which your fathers
30:16 the *l* to which you are going
31:4 the Amorites, and to their *l*
31:7 into the *l* that Jehovah swore
31:16 *l* to which they are going
31:21 *l* about which I have sworn
31:23 *l* about which I have sworn
32:10 find him in a wilderness *l*
32:49 which is in the *l* of Moab
32:49 see the *l* of Canaan, which I
32:52 distance you will see the *l*
32:52 will not go there into the *l*
33:13 May his *l* be continually
33:28 a *l* of grain and new wine
34:1 showing him all the *l*, Gilead
34:2 Naphtali and the *l* of Ephraim
34:2 the *l* of Judah as far as the
34:4 *l* about which I have sworn to
34:5 died there in the *l* of Moab
34:6 bury him . . . in the *l* of Moab
34:11 in the *l* of Egypt to Pharaoh
34:11 his servants and all his *l*
Jos 1:2 into the *l* that I am giving
1:4 all the *l* of the Hittites
1:6 people to inherit the *l* that
1:11 take possession of the *l* that
1:13 and has given you this *l*
1:14 the *l* that Moses has given
1:15 taken possession of the *l*
1:15 to the *l* of your holding and

Jos 2:1 a look at the l and Jericho
2:2 tonight to search out the l
2:3 search out all the l that they
2:9 give you the l, and that the
2:9 the inhabitants of the l have
2:14 when Jehovah gives us the l
2:18 coming into the l. This cord
2:24 given all the l into our
2:24 inhabitants of the l have
4:22 dry l it was that Israel
5:6 the l that Jehovah had sworn
5:6 a l flowing with milk and
5:11 the yield of the l the day
5:12 some of the yield of the l
5:12 produce of the l of Canaan
6:22 had done the spying on the l
7:2 Go up and spy on the l
7:9 the inhabitants of the l will
8:1 people and his city and his l
9:6 from a distant l that we have
9:9 from a very distant l that
9:11 the inhabitants of our l said
9:24 to give you all the l and to
9:24 all the inhabitants of the l
10:40 l of the mountainous region
10:41 Gaza and all the l of Goshen
10:42 and their l at one time
11:3 Hermon in the l of Mizpah
11:16 l, the mountainous region
11:16 and all the l of Goshen
11:22 No Anakim . . . in the l
11:23 So Joshua took all the l
11:23 l had no disturbance from
12:1 kings of the l whom the sons
12:1 and whose l they then took
12:7 kings of the l whom Joshua
13:1 l yet remains to be taken
13:2 This is the l yet remaining
13:4 all the l of the Canaanites
13:5 the l of the Gebalites and
13:7 this l as an inheritance
13:21 who were dwelling in the l
13:25 half of the l of the sons of
14:1 in the l of Canaan, which
14:4 not given a share in the l to
14:5 proceeded to apportion the l
14:7 to spy out the l, and I came
14:9 The l upon which your foot
14:15 the l had no disturbance
15:19 a piece of l to the south
16:4 to take possession of l
17:5 apart from the l of Gilead
17:6 the l of Gilead became the
17:8 The l of Tappuah became
17:12 in dwelling in this l
17:15 in the l of the Perizzites
17:16 in the l of the low plain
18:1 the l was now subdued before
18:3 the l that Jehovah the God
18:4 in the l and map it out in
18:6 map out the l into seven
18:8 were going to map out the l
18:8 in the l and map it out and
18:9 the l and mapped it out by
18:10 the l to the sons of Israel
19:49 finished dividing the l for
19:51 from apportioning the l
21:2 in Shiloh in the l of Canaan
21:43 gave Israel all the l that
22:4 go . . . to your tents in the l
22:9 Shiloh . . . in the l of Canaan
22:9 to go to the l of Gilead, to
22:9 to the l of their possession
22:10 in the l of Canaan, then the
22:11 frontier of the l of Canaan
22:13 in the l of Gilead Phinehas
22:15 Manasseh in the l of Gilead
22:19 the l of your possession is
22:19 l of Jehovah's possession
22:32 Gad in the l of Gilead to
22:32 l of Canaan to the other
22:33 against them to ruin the l
23:5 took possession of their l
23:16 good l that he has given
24:3 through all the l of Canaan
24:8 the l of the Amorites who
24:8 take possession of their l
24:13 I gave you a l for which
24:15 Amorites in whose l you
24:17 out of the l of Egypt, out
24:18 in the l from before us
Jg 1:2 I shall certainly give the l
1:15 it is a southern piece of l
Jg 1:26 to the l of the Hittites and
1:27 in dwelling in this l
1:32 Canaanites inhabiting the l
1:33 Canaanites inhabiting the l
2:1 you into the l about which I
2:2 the inhabitants of this l
2:6 to take possession of the l
2:12 out of the l of Egypt and
3:11 the l had no disturbance for
3:30 and the l had no further
5:31 l had no further disturbance
6:5 come into the l to ruin it
6:9 before you and gave you their l
6:10 in whose l you are dwelling
8:28 l had no further disturbance
9:37 out of the center of the l
10:4 they are in the l of Gilead
10:8 in the l of the Amorites that
11:3 dwelling in the l of Tob
11:5 Jephthah out of the l of Tob
11:12 against me to fight in my l
11:13 Israel took my l when they
11:15 did not take the l of Moab
11:15 the l of the sons of Ammon
11:17 through your l, and the king
11:18 around the l of Edom and the
11:18 the l of Moab, so that they
11:18 the l of Moab and took up
11:19 through your l to my own
11:21 all the l of the Amorites
11:21 Amorites inhabiting that l
12:12 Aijalon in the l of Zebulun
12:15 Pirathon in the l of Ephraim
16:24 devastator of our l and the
18:2 spy out the l and to explore
18:2 Go, explore the l
18:7 molesting a thing in the l
18:9 we have seen the l, and, look!
18:9 to take possession of the l
18:10 and the l is quite wide
18:14 to spy out the l of Laish
18:17 had gone to spy out the l
19:30 up out of the l of Egypt
20:1 along with the l of Gilead
21:12 which is in the l of Canaan
21:21 must go to the l of Benjamin
Ru 1:1 a famine arose in the l, and a
1:7 to return to the l of Judah
2:11 and the l of your relatives
1Sa 2:8 upon them the productive l
6:5 are bringing the l to ruin
6:5 you and your god and your l
9:4 on through the l of Shalishah
9:4 on through the l of Shaalim
9:4 the l of the Benjaminites
9:5 came into the l of Zuph
9:16 man from the l of Benjamin
12:6 up out of the l of Egypt
13:3 blown throughout all the l
13:7 to the l of Gad and Gilead
13:17 Ophrah, to the l of Shual
13:19 found in all the l of Israel
14:25 all those of the l came
14:29 ostracism upon the l
21:11 this David the king of the l
22:5 yourself into the l of Judah
23:23 if he is in the l, I will
23:27 have made a raid on the l
27:1 to the l of the Philistines
27:8 l that extended from Telam
27:8 and down to the l of Egypt
27:9 David struck the l, but he
28:3 foretellers . . . from the l
28:9 cut off . . . from the l
29:11 the l of the Philistines
30:16 over . . . all the l
30:16 l of the Philistines and
30:16 and the l of Judah
31:9 l of the Philistines all
2Sa 3:12 To whom does the l belong?
5:6 Jebusites inhabiting the l
10:2 the l of the sons of Ammon
14:30 Joab's tract of l beside
14:30 set the tract of l ablaze
14:31 l that is mine ablaze with
15:4 appointed judge in the l
15:23 the people of the l were
17:26 camping in the l of Gilead
18:8 spread out over all the l
19:9 out of the l from Absalom
21:14 the l of Benjamin in Zela
21:14 be entreated for the l
22:16 productive l . . . uncovered
24:6 and the l of Tahtim-hodshi
2Sa 24:8 about through all the l
24:13 years of famine in your l
24:13 pestilence in your l
24:25 be entreated for the l, so
1Ki 4:10 Socoh and all the l of Hepher
4:19 in the l of Gilead, the
4:19 the l of Sihon the king of
4:19 deputies that were in the l
4:21 to the l of the Philistines
6:1 came out from the l of Egypt
8:9 out from the l of Egypt
8:21 out from the l of Egypt
8:36 must give rain upon your l
8:37 a famine occurs in the l
8:37 in the l of their gates
8:41 comes from a distant l
8:46 to the l of the enemy
8:47 l where they have been
8:47 in the l of their captors
8:48 in the l of their enemies
8:48 in the direction of their l
9:8 Jehovah do like that to this l
9:9 out from the l of Egypt
9:11 cities in the l of Galilee
9:13 called the L of Cabul down
9:18 the wilderness, in the l
9:19 in all the l of his dominion
9:21 l whom the sons of Israel
9:26 Red Sea in the l of Edom
10:6 I heard in my own l about
10:13 and went to her own l
10:15 and the governors of the l
11:18 and l he gave him
11:21 that I may go to my own l
11:22 seeking to go to your own l
12:28 out of the l of Egypt
14:24 proved to be in the l
15:12 pass out of the l and
15:20 all the l of Naphtali
18:5 through the l to all the
18:6 the l through which to pass
20:7 all the older men of the l
20:23 against them on the level l
20:25 against them on the level l
21:23 in the plot of l of Jezreel
22:36 and everyone to his l!
22:46 he cleared out from the l
2Ki 2:19 l is causing miscarriages
3:19 tract of l you should mar
3:20 l came to be filled with the
3:25 every good tract of l, they
3:27 and returned to their l
4:38 there was famine in the l
5:2 captive from the l of Israel
5:4 who is from the l of Israel
5:19 for a good stretch of the l
6:23 again into the l of Israel
8:1 upon the l for seven years
8:2 l of the Philistines for seven
8:3 from the l of the Philistines
8:6 the day of her leaving the l
9:10 the tract of l at Jezreel
9:21 tract of l of Naboth the
9:26 repay you in this tract of l
9:26 into the tract of l
9:36 In the tract of l of Jezreel
9:37 the tract of l of Jezreel
10:33 all the l of Gilead
11:3 was reigning over the l
11:14 people of the l rejoicing
11:18 the people of the l came
11:19 and all the people of the l
11:20 people of the l continued to
13:20 into the l at the coming in
15:5 judging the people of the l
15:19 of Assyria came into the l
15:20 did not stay there in the l
15:29 all the l of Naphtali
16:15 the people of the l and
17:5 to come up against all the l
17:7 out of the l of Egypt from
17:26 religion of the God of the l
17:26 religion of the God of the l
17:27 religion of the God of the l
17:36 out of the l of Egypt with
18:25 Go up against this l, and
18:32, 32 a l like your own l
18:32 a l of grain and new wine
18:32 a l of bread and vineyards
18:32 a l of oil-olive trees and
18:33 l out of the hand of the
18:35 their l out of my hand
19:7 and return to his own l
19:7 by the sword in his own l

2Ki 19:17 the nations and their *l*
19:37 escaped to the *l* of Ararat
20:14 From a distant *l* they came
21:24 people of the *l* struck down
21:24 people of the *l* made Josiah
23:24 appeared in the *l* of Judah
23:30 the people of the *l* took
23:33 Riblah in the *l* of Hamath
23:33 imposed a fine upon the *l*
23:35 he taxed the *l*, to give the
23:35 from the people of the *l*
24:7 come out from his *l*
24:14 of the people of the *l*
24:15 the foremost men of the *l*
25:3 bread for the people of the *l*
25:12 the lowly people of the *l*
25:19 the people of the *l*
25:19 men of the people of the *l*
25:21 Riblah in the *l* of Hamath
25:22 behind in the *l* of Judah
25:24 Dwell in the *l* and serve
1Ch 1:43 reigned in the *l* of Edom
1:45 the *l* of the Temanites began
2:22 cities in the *l* of Gilead
4:40 *l* was quite wide and having
5:9 numerous in the *l* of Gilead
5:11 dwelt in the *l* of Bashan as
5:23 dwelt in the *l* from Bashan
5:25 gods of the peoples of the *l*
6:55 Hebron in the *l* of Judah
7:21 Gath that were born in the *l*
10:9 into the *l* of the Philistines
11:4 the inhabitants of the *l*
16:18 I shall give the *l* of Canaan
16:30 *l* is firmly established
19:2 the *l* of the sons of Ammon
19:3 for spying out the *l* that his
20:1 the *l* of the sons of Ammon
21:12 even pestilence, in the *l*
22:2 that were in the *l* of Israel
22:18 the inhabitants of the *l*
22:18 *l* has been subdued before
28:8 you may possess the good *l*
2Ch 2:17 who were in the *l* of Israel
6:5 people out from the *l* of
6:27 *l* that you have given to your
6:28 a famine occurs in the *l*
6:28 in the *l* of their gates
6:32 comes from a distant *l* by
6:36 captive to a *l* distant or
6:37 *l* where they have been
6:37 *l* where they are captives
6:38 *l* where they are captives
6:38 in the direction of their *l*
7:13 grasshoppers to eat up the *l*
7:14 and I shall heal their *l*
7:21 do like that to this *l*
7:22 out of the *l* of Egypt, and
8:6 in all the *l* of his dominion
8:8 left behind them in the *l*
8:17 of the sea in the *l* of Edom
9:5 that I heard in my own *l*
9:11 seen before in the *l* of Judah
9:12 went to her own *l*, she
9:14 governors of the *l* who were
9:26 to the *l* of the Philistines
13:9 like the peoples of the *l*
14:1 *l* had no disturbance for ten
14:6 *l* had no disturbance
14:7 *l* is yet available, because
15:8 from all the *l* of Judah
17:2 garrisons in the *l* of Judah
19:3 sacred poles from the *l* and
19:5 judges throughout the *l* in
20:7 inhabitants of this *l* from
20:10 out of the *l* of Egypt, but
22:12 ruling as queen over the *l*
23:13 people of the *l* were
23:20 all the people of the *l*
23:21 people of the *l* continued
26:21 judging the people of the *l*
30:9 allowed to return to this *l*
30:10 *l* of Ephraim and Manasseh
30:25 came from the *l* of Israel
32:4 through the middle of the *l*
32:13 deliver their *l* out of my
32:21 shame of face to his own *l*
32:31 had happened in the *l*, the
33:25 people of the *l* struck down
33:25 people of the *l* then made
34:7 in all the *l* of Israel
34:8 cleansed the *l* and the house
36:1 the people of the *l* took
36:3 fined the *l* a hundred silver
2Ch 36:21 *l* had paid off its sabbaths
Ezr 4:4 the people of the *l* were
6:21 of the nations of the *l*
9:11 The *l* that you people are
9:11 an impure *l* because of the
9:12 eat the good of the *l* and
10:2 from the peoples of the *l*
10:11 from the peoples of the *l*
Ne 4:4 plunder in the *l* of captivity
5:14 governor in the *l* of Judah
9:8 the *l* of the Canaanites
9:10 and all the people of his *l*
9:11 midst of the sea on the dry *l*
9:15 enter and possess the *l* that
9:22 possession of the *l* of Sihon
9:22 the *l* of the king of Heshbon
9:22 the *l* of Og the king of Bashan
9:23 the *l* that you had promised
9:24 and took the *l* in possession
9:24 the inhabitants of the *l*, the
9:24 kings and the peoples of the *l*
9:35 the broad and fat *l* that you
9:36 as for the *l* that you gave to
10:30 to the peoples of the *l*, and
10:31 the peoples of the *l* who
Es 8:17 many of the peoples of the *l*
10:1 lay forced labor upon the *l*
Job 1:1 a man in the *l* of Uz whose
10:21 To the *l* of darkness and
10:22 *l* of obscurity like gloom
12:24 of the people of the *l*
15:19 them alone the *l* was given
18:18 from the productive *l* they
22:8 of strength, the *l* is his
24:18 tract of *l* will be cursed
28:13 in the *l* of those living
30:8 scourged out of the *l*
34:13 productive *l*, even all of it
37:12 productive *l* of the earth
37:13 for a rod or for his *l*
38:26 To make it rain upon the *l*
42:15 in all the *l*
Ps 9:8 judge the productive *l* in
18:15 *l* became uncovered
19:4 extremity of the productive *l*
24:1 *l* and those dwelling in it
27:13 goodness of Jehovah in the *l*
33:8 productive *l* be frightened
42:6 From the *l* of Jordan and the
44:3 they took possession of the *l*
50:12 to me the productive *l* and
52:5 out of the *l* of the living
63:1 In a *l* dry and exhausted
66:6 changed the sea into dry *l*
68:6 to reside in a scorched *l*
74:8 must be burned in the *l*
77:18 lighted up the productive *l*
78:12 In the *l* of Egypt, the field
80:9 take root and fill the *l*
81:5 forth over the *l* of Egypt
81:10 up out of the *l* of Egypt
85:1 pleasure, O Jehovah, in your *l*
85:9 For glory to reside in our *l*
85:12 own *l* will give its yield
88:12 in the *l* of oblivion
89:11 productive *l* and what fills
90:2 earth and the productive *l*
93:1 productive *l* also becomes
95:5 own hands formed the dry *l*
96:10 productive *l* also becomes
96:13 judge the productive *l* with
97:4 lighted up the productive *l*
98:7 *l* and those dwelling in it
98:9 judge the productive *l* with
105:11 shall give the *l* of Canaan
105:16 for a famine upon the *l*
105:23 as an alien in the *l* of Ham
105:27 miracles in the *l* of Ham
105:30 *l* swarmed with frogs
105:32 A flaming fire on their *l*
105:35 the vegetation in their *l*
105:36 every firstborn in their *l*
106:22 works in the *l* of Ham
106:24 contemning the desirable *l*
106:38 *l* came to be polluted with
107:34 Fruitful *l* into salt country
107:35 *l* of a waterless region
110:6 head one over a populous *l*
119:19 an alien resident in the *l*
135:12 their *l* as an inheritance
136:21 their *l* as an inheritance
142:5 share in the *l* of the living
143:6 soul is like an exhausted *l*
143:10 in the *l* of uprightness
Pr 8:26 masses of the productive *l*
8:31 productive *l* of his earth
21:19 to dwell in a wilderness *l*
25:25 good report from a distant *l*
28:2 of the transgression of a *l*
29:4 By justice a king makes a *l*
30:16 *l* that has not been satisfied
31:23 with the older men of the *l*
Ec 10:16 will it be with you, O *l*
10:17 Happy are you, O *l*, when
Ca 2:12 have appeared in the *l*
2:12 turtledove . . . heard in our *l*
Isa 1:7 Your *l* is a desolation, your
1:19 good of the *l* you will eat
2:7 *l* is filled with silver and
2:7 their *l* is filled with horses
2:8 *l* is filled with valueless
4:2 fruitage of the *l* will be
5:8 in the midst of the *l*
5:30 actually gaze at the *l*, and
6:12 in the midst of the *l*
7:18 that are in the *l* of Assyria
7:22 the midst of the *l* will eat
7:24 *l* will become mere
8:8 fill the breadth of your *l*
8:21 pass through the *l* hard
9:1 as when the *l* had stress
9:1 the *l* of Zebulun and the
9:1 and the *l* of Naphtali and
9:2 in the *l* of deep shadow
9:19 the *l* has been set afire, and
10:23 in the midst of the whole *l*
11:16 up out of the *l* of Egypt
13:5 coming from the *l* far away
13:9 *l* an object of astonishment
13:11 upon the productive *l*
13:14 flee, each one to his own *l*
14:17 productive *l* like the
14:20 brought your own *l* to ruin
14:21 productive *l* with cities
14:25 break the Assyrian in my *l*
16:1 to the ruler of the *l*, from
18:1 *l* of the whirring insects
18:2 *l* the rivers have washed
18:3 of the productive *l* and
18:7 *l* the rivers have washed
19:18 cities in the *l* of Egypt
19:19 midst of the *l* of Egypt
19:20 in the *l* of Egypt; for they
21:1 from a fear-inspiring *l*
21:14 of the *l* of Tema, confront
22:18 like a ball for a wide *l*
23:1 *l* of Kittim it has been
23:10 Cross over your *l* like the
23:13 The *l* of the Chaldeans
24:1 Jehovah is emptying the *l*
24:3 the *l* will be emptied, and
24:4 *l* has gone to mourning, has
24:4 productive *l* has withered
24:4 of the people of the *l* have
24:5 *l* has been polluted under
24:6 itself has eaten up the *l*
24:6 inhabitants of the *l* have
24:11 exultation of the *l* has
24:13 in the midst of the *l*
24:16 From the extremity of the *l*
24:17 you inhabitant of the *l*
24:18 foundations of the *l* will
24:19 *l* has absolutely burst apart
24:19 *l* has absolutely been shaken
24:19 *l* has absolutely been sent
24:20 *l* absolutely moves
26:1 sung in the *l* of Judah
26:9 of the productive *l* will
26:10 *l* of straightforwardness
26:15 all the borders of the *l*
26:18 accomplish as regards the *l*
26:18 for the productive *l* proceed
26:21 of the inhabitant of the *l*
26:21 *l* will certainly expose her
27:6 productive *l* with produce
27:13 in the *l* of Assyria and
27:13 dispersed in the *l* of Egypt
28:22 decided upon . . . all the *l*
30:6 *l* of distress and hard
32:2 heavy crag in an exhausted *l*
33:9 *l* has gone mourning, has
33:17 will see a *l* far away
33:24 that are dwelling in the *l*
34:1 productive *l* and all its
34:6 in the *l* of Edom
34:7 *l* must be drenched with
34:9 *l* must become as burning

Isa 36:10 this *l* to bring it to ruin
36:10 Go up against this *l*, and
36:17, 17 to a *l* like your own *l*
36:17 a *l* of grain and new wine
36:17 a *l* of bread and vineyards
36:18 own *l* out of the hand of
36:20 delivered their *l* out of my
37:7 and return to his own *l*
37:7 by the sword in his own *l*
37:18 the lands, and their own *l*
37:38 escaped to the *l* of Ararat
38:11 in the *l* of the living ones
38:11 of the *l* of cessation
39:3 From a distant *l* they came
40:4 ground must become level *l*
41:18 waterless *l* into sources of
42:16 rugged terrain into level *l*
45:2 *l* I shall straighten out
46:11 from a distant *l* the man to
49:8 to rehabilitate the *l*, to
49:12 these from the *l* of Sinim
49:19 and the *l* of your ruins
53:2 a root out of waterless *l*
53:8 the *l* of the living ones
57:13 will inherit the *l* and will
58:11 even in a scorched *l*, and
60:18 violence be heard in your *l*
60:21 hold possession of the *l*
61:7 in their *l* they will take
62:4 your own *l* will no more be
62:4 and your *l* Owned as a Wife
62:4 *l* will be owned as a wife
66:8 a *l* be brought forth with
Jer 1:1 Anathoth in the *l* of Benjamin
1:14 all the inhabitants of the *l*
1:18 walls against all the *l*
1:18 toward the people of the *l*
2:2 in a *l* not sown with seed
2:6 up out of the *l* of Egypt
2:6 through a *l* of desert plain
2:6 a *l* of no water and of deep
2:6 a *l* through which no man
2:7 to a *l* of the orchard, to eat
2:7 you came in and defiled my *l*
2:15 *l* an object of astonishment
2:31 or a *l* of intense darkness
3:1 Has that *l* not positively
3:2 you keep polluting the *l* with
3:9 she kept polluting the *l* and
3:16 bear fruit in the *l* in those
3:18 out of the *l* of the north
3:18 into the *l* that I gave as a
3:19 to give you the desirable *l*
4:3 Plow for yourselves arable *l*
4:5 blow a horn throughout the *l*
4:7 render your *l* as an object of
4:16 coming from a *l* far away
4:20 whole *l* has been despoiled
4:23 I saw the *l*, and, look! it
4:27 waste is what the whole *l*
4:28 the *l* will mourn, and the
5:19 a foreign god in your *l*
5:19 serve strangers in a *l* that
5:30 been brought to be in the *l*
6:8 waste, a *l* not inhabited
6:12 the inhabitants of the *l*
6:20 cane from the *l* far away
6:22 people is coming from the *l*
7:7 in the *l* that I gave to your
7:22 out from the *l* of Egypt
7:25 out of the *l* of Egypt until
7:34 the *l* will become nothing
8:16 whole *l* has begun to rock
8:16 come in and eat up the *l*
8:19 my people from a *l* far away
9:3 they proved mighty in the *l*
9:12 should the *l* actually perish
9:19 For we have left the *l*
10:12 the productive *l*
10:22 a great pounding from the *l*
11:4 out of the *l* of Egypt
11:5 *l* flowing with milk and
11:7 up out of the *l* of Egypt and
11:19 from the *l* of the living
12:4 the *l* keep withering away
12:5 in the *l* of peace are you
12:11 *l* has been made desolate
12:12 from one end of the *l* even
12:12 to the other end of the *l*
12:15 and each one to his *l*
13:13 the inhabitants of this *l*
14:4 no downpour upon the *l*
14:8 an alien resident in the *l*
14:15 famine will occur in this *l*
Jer 14:18 gone around to a *l* that
15:7 in the gates of the *l*
15:14 a *l* that you have not known
16:3 their birth in this *l*
16:6 the small ones, in this *l*
16:13 from off this *l* into the
16:13 into the *l* . . . not known
16:14 up out of the *l* of Egypt
16:15 out of the *l* of the north
16:18 their profaning my *l*
17:4 *l* that you have not known
17:26 and from the *l* of Benjamin
18:16 *l* an object of astonishment
21:13 O rock of the level *l*
22:10 see the *l* of his relatives
22:12 this *l* he will see no more
22:26 into another *l* in which you
22:27 the *l* to which they will be
22:28 *l* that they have not known
23:5 righteousness in the *l*
23:7 up out of the *l* of Egypt
23:8 out of the *l* of the north
23:10 that the *l* has become full
23:10 the *l* has gone to mourning
23:15 has gone forth to all the *l*
24:5 to the *l* of the Chaldeans
24:6 to return to this *l*
24:8 remaining over in this *l*
24:8 dwelling in the *l* of Egypt
25:9 bring them against this *l*
25:11 all this *l* must become a
25:12 the *l* of the Chaldeans
25:13 upon that *l* all my words
25:20 the kings of the *l* of Uz
25:20 the *l* of the Philistines
25:38 *l* has become an object of
26:17 the older men of the *l* rose
26:20 city and against this *l*
27:7 his own *l* comes, and many
30:3 bring them back to the *l*
30:10 the *l* of their captivity
31:8 them from the *l* of the north
31:16 from the *l* of the enemy
31:23 this word in the *l* of Judah
31:32 forth out of the *l* of Egypt
32:8 is in the *l* of Benjamin, for
32:15 yet be bought in this *l*
32:20 miracles in the *l* of Egypt
32:21 out of the *l* of Egypt
32:22 you gave them this *l* that
32:22 *l* flowing with milk and
32:41 plant them in this *l* in
32:43 *l* of which you people will
32:44 in the *l* of Benjamin and
33:11 captives of the *l* just as
33:13 in the *l* of Benjamin and
33:15 and righteousness in the *l*
34:13 out of the *l* of Egypt, out
34:19 people of the *l* who went
35:11 came up against the *l* that
36:29 bring this *l* to ruin and
37:1 made king in the *l* of Judah
37:2 people of the *l* did not
37:7 go back to their *l*, Egypt
37:12 go to the *l* of Benjamin
37:19 men and against this *l*
39:5 Riblah in the *l* of Hamath
39:10 remain in the *l* of Judah
40:4 The entire *l* is before you
40:6 were left remaining in the *l*
40:7 over the *l* and that he had
40:7 lowly people of the *l*, who
40:9 Continue dwelling in the *l*
40:12 into the *l* of Judah to
41:2 had commissioned over the *l*
41:18 had commissioned over the *l*
42:10 keep dwelling in this *l*
42:13 going to dwell in this *l*
42:14 *l* of Egypt we shall enter
42:16 with you in the *l* of Egypt
43:4 dwelling in the *l* of Judah
43:5 a while in the *l* of Judah
43:7 came into the *l* of Egypt
43:11 and strike the *l* of Egypt
43:12 up in the *l* of Egypt, just
43:13 which is in the *l* of Egypt
44:1 dwelling in the *l* of Egypt
44:1 and in the *l* of Pathros
44:8 other gods in the *l* of Egypt
44:9 in the *l* of Judah and in
44:12 the *l* of Egypt to reside
44:12 finish in the *l* of Egypt
44:13 dwelling in the *l* of Egypt
44:14 aliens, in the *l* of Egypt
Jer 44:14 return to the *l* of Judah
44:15 the *l* of Egypt, in Pathros
44:21 and the people of the *l*
44:22 *l* came to be a devastated
44:24 who are in the *l* of Egypt
44:26 dwelling in the *l* of Egypt
44:26 in all the *l* of Egypt
44:27 that are in the *l* of Egypt
44:28 return from the *l* of Egypt
44:28 to the *l* of Judah, few in
44:28 the *l* of Egypt to reside
45:4 uprooting, even all the *l*
46:10 *l* of the north by the river
46:12 own outcry has filled the *l*
46:13 strike down the *l* of Egypt
46:16 to the *l* of our relatives
46:27 the *l* of their captivity
47:2 flood the *l* and what fills
47:2 everyone dwelling in the *l*
48:8 the level *l* be annihilated
48:21 *l* of level country, to Holon
48:24 cities of the *l* of Moab
48:33 and from the *l* of Moab
50:1 the *l* of the Chaldeans, by
50:3 *l* an object of astonishment
50:8 out of the *l* of the Chaldeans
50:9 from the *l* of the north
50:16 flee each one to his own *l*
50:18 Babylon and upon his *l*
50:21 Against the *l* of Merathaim
50:22 sound of war in the *l*, and
50:25 in the *l* of the Chaldeans
50:28 from the *l* of Babylon to
50:34 give repose to the *l* and
50:38 is a *l* of graven images
50:45 the *l* of the Chaldeans
51:2 who will make her *l* empty
51:4 in the *l* of the Chaldeans
51:5 *l* of those has been full of
51:9 us go each one to his own *l*
51:15 productive *l* by his wisdom
51:27 Lift up a signal in the *l*
51:28 *l* of each one's dominion
51:29 *l* of Babylon an object of
51:43 waterless *l* and a desert
51:43 As a *l*, in them no man
51:46 to be heard in the *l*
51:47 own *l* will become ashamed
51:52 throughout all her *l* the
51:54 from the *l* of the Chaldeans
52:6 bread for the people of the *l*
52:9 at Riblah in the *l* of Hamath
52:16 the lowly ones of the *l*
52:25 the people of the *l*, and
52:25 men of the people of the *l*
52:27 Riblah in the *l* of Hamath
La 4:12 of the productive *l* had not
4:21 as you do in the *l* of Uz
Eze 1:3 in the *l* of the Chaldeans by
6:14 make the *l* a desolate waste
7:2 the four extremities of the *l*
7:7 O inhabiter of the *l*, the
7:23 *l* itself has become full of
7:27 hands of the people of the *l*
8:12 Jehovah has left the *l*
8:17 to fill the *l* with violence
9:9 *l* is filled with bloodshed
9:9 said, Jehovah has left the *l*
11:15 the *l* has been given us as a
12:13 to the *l* of the Chaldeans
12:19 say to the people of the *l*
12:19 *l* may be laid desolate of
12:20 the *l* itself will become a
14:13 as regards a *l*, in case it
14:15 beasts pass through the *l*
14:16 the *l* itself would become a
14:17 I should bring upon that *l*
14:17 sword . . . through the *l*
14:19 I should send upon that *l*
15:8 make the *l* a desolate waste
16:3 from the *l* of the Canaanite
16:29 toward the *l* of Canaan
17:4 to the *l* of Canaan; in a city
17:5 some of the seed of the *l*
17:13 men of the *l* he took away
19:4 hooks to the *l* of Egypt
19:7 the *l* was laid desolate and
19:13 a waterless and thirsty *l*
20:5 to them in the *l* of Egypt
20:6 forth from the *l* of Egypt
20:6 *l* that I had spied out for
20:8 the midst of the *l* of Egypt
20:9 forth from the *l* of Egypt
20:10 forth from the *l* of Egypt

Eze 20:15 into the *l* that I had given
20:28 bring them into the *l* that
20:36 wilderness of the *l* of
20:38 *l* of their alien residence
20:40 will serve me, in the *l*
20:42 into the *l* that I lifted
21:19 From the one *l* both of them
21:30 in the *l* of your origin
21:32 to be in the midst of the *l*
22:24 are a *l* not being cleansed
22:29 people of the *l* themselves
22:30 in behalf of the *l*, in order
23:15 the *l* of their birth
23:19 in the *l* of Egypt
23:27 carried from the *l* of Egypt
23:48 to cease out of the *l*
25:9 the decoration of the *l*
26:20 to dwell in the lowest *l*
26:20 in the *l* of those alive
27:17 Judah and the *l* of Israel
27:29 upon the *l* they will stand
29:9 *l* of Egypt must become a
29:10 *l* of Egypt devastated places
29:12 *l* of Egypt a desolate waste
29:14 back to the *l* of Pathros
29:14 to the *l* of their origin
29:19 the *l* of Egypt, and he
29:20 given him the *l* of Egypt
30:5 sons of the *l* of the covenant
30:11 to reduce the *l* to ruin
30:11 fill the *l* with the slain
30:12 sell the *l* into the hand of
30:12 cause the *l* and its fullness
30:13 out of the *l* of Egypt
30:13 put fear in the *l* of Egypt
30:25 against the *l* of Egypt
31:14 to the *l* down below, in the
31:16 *l* down below all the trees
31:18 to the *l* down below. In the
32:4 must abandon you on the *l*
32:6 cause the *l* to drink up your
32:8 put darkness upon your *l*
32:15 make the *l* of Egypt a
32:15 *l* is desolated of its
32:18 to the *l* down below
32:23 in the *l* of those alive
32:24 to the *l* down below
32:24 terror in the *l* of those
32:25 in the *l* of those alive
32:26 terror in the *l* of those
32:27 terror in the *l* of those
32:32 in the *l* of those alive
33:2 As regards a *l*, in case I
33:2 the people of the *l*, one
33:3 the sword coming upon the *l*
33:24 he took possession of the *l*
33:24 to us the *l* has been given
33:25 So should you possess the *l*?
33:26 So should you possess the *l*?
33:28 make the *l* a desolate waste
33:29 make the *l* a desolate waste
34:13 dwelling places of the *l*
34:25 beast to cease out of the *l*
34:27 *l* itself will give its
34:29 by famine in the *l*, and
35:10 take possession of each *l*
36:5 who have given my *l* to
36:13 a *l* bereaving your nations
36:18 had poured out upon the *l*
36:18 *l* they had made unclean
36:20 from his *l* they have gone
36:28 dwell in the *l* that I gave
36:34 *l* itself will be cultivated
36:35 *l* yonder which was laid
37:22 one nation in the *l*, on the
37:25 actually dwell upon the *l*
38:2 Gog of the *l* of Magog, the
38:8 *l* of people brought back
38:8 a *l* that has been brought
38:9 Like clouds to cover the *l*
38:11 the *l* of open rural country
38:16 like clouds to cover the *l*
38:16 bring you against my *l*
39:12 cleansing the *l*, for seven
39:13 people of the *l* will have
39:14 passing along through the *l*
39:15 pass along through the *l*
39:16 will have to cleanse the *l*
40:2 to the *l* of Israel and
45:1 allot the *l* as an inheritance
45:1 holy portion out of the *l*
45:4 holy portion out of the *l* it
45:8 as regards the *l*, it will
45:8 *l* they will give to the

Eze 45:16 all the people of the *l*
45:22 of all the people of the *l*
46:3 people of the *l* must bow
46:9 people of the *l* come in
47:13 *l* for the twelve tribes of
47:14 which *l* I raised my hand in
47:14 *l* must fall to you by lot
47:15 boundary of the *l* to the
47:18 Gilead and the *l* of Israel
47:21 you must apportion this *l*
48:12 the contribution of the *l*
48:14 choicest of the *l* to pass
48:29 *l* that you people should
Da 1:2 them to the *l* of Shinar to the
2:10 not exist a man on the dry *l*
9:6 and to all the people of the *l*
9:15 out from the *l* of Egypt
11:16 in the *l* of the Decoration
11:19 the fortresses of his own *l*
11:28 back to his *l* with a great
11:28 certainly go back to his *l*
11:41 into the *l* of the Decoration
11:42 and as regards the *l* of Egypt
Ho 1:2 *l* positively turns from
1:11 go up out of the *l*, because
2:3 place her like a waterless *l*
2:15 up out of the *l* of Egypt
2:18 I shall break out of the *l*
4:1 with the inhabitants of the *l*
4:1 nor knowledge of God in the *l*
4:3 That is why the *l* will mourn
7:16 derision in the *l* of Egypt
9:3 dwelling in the *l* of Jehovah
10:1 to the goodness of his *l*
10:12 Till for yourselves arable *l*
11:5 not return to the *l* of Egypt
11:11 out of the *l* of Assyria
12:9 your God from the *l* of Egypt
13:4 your God from the *l* of Egypt
13:5 in the *l* of fevers
Joe 1:2 all you inhabitants of the *l*
1:6 that has come up into my *l*
1:14 all the inhabitants of the *l*
2:1 the inhabitants of the *l*
2:3 the *l* is ahead of it
2:10 the *l* has become agitated
2:18 will be zealous for his *l*
2:20 to a waterless *l* and
3:2 apportioned out my own *l*
3:19 in whose *l* they shed innocent
Am 2:10 up out of the *l* of Egypt
2:10 of the *l* of the Amorite
3:1 up out of the *l* of Egypt
3:9 towers in the *l* of Egypt
3:11 even round about the *l*
4:7 *l* that would be rained on
4:7 *l* on which I would not make
7:2 the vegetation of the *l*
7:4 and ate up the tract of *l*
7:10 The *l* is not able to put up
7:12 off to the *l* of Judah
8:8 that the *l* will be agitated
8:9 cause darkness for the *l* on a
8:11 send a famine into the *l*
9:5 is the One touching the *l*
9:7 Israel itself up out of the *l*
Jon 1:9 made the sea and the dry *l*
1:13 the ship back to the dry *l*
2:10 out Jonah onto the dry *l*
Mic 5:5 Assyrian . . . comes into our *l*
5:6 shepherd the *l* of Assyria
5:6 *l* of Nimrod in its entrances
5:6 Assyrian . . . comes into our *l*
5:11 cut off the cities of your *l*
6:4 you up out of the *l* of Egypt
7:13 *l* must become a desolate
7:15 from the *l* of Egypt I shall
Na 1:5 the productive *l* also, and all
3:13 the gates of your *l* must
Hab 3:7 cloths of the *l* of Midian
Zep 2:5 the *l* of the Philistines
3:19 in all the *l* of their shame
Hag 2:4 all you people of the *l*, is
Zec 1:21 a horn against the *l* of Judah
2:6 from the *l* of the north
3:9 take away the error of that *l*
4:7 you will become a level *l*
5:11 a house in the *l* of Shinar
6:6 forth to the *l* of the north
6:6 forth to the *l* of the south
6:8 forth to the *l* of the north
6:8 to rest in the *l* of the north
7:5 to all the people of the *l*
7:14 the *l* itself has been left

Zec 7:14 *l* an object of astonishment
8:7 from the *l* of the sunrise and
8:7 *l* of the setting of the sun
9:1 against the *l* of Hadrach, and
10:10 back from the *l* of Egypt
10:10 and to the *l* of Gilead and
11:6 upon the inhabitants of the *l*
11:6 crush to pieces the *l*, and I
11:16 a shepherd rise up in the *l*
12:12 the *l* will certainly wail
13:2 the idols out of the *l*, and
13:2 cause to pass out of the *l*
13:8 it must occur in all the *l*
14:10 whole *l* will be changed
Mal 3:12 will become a *l* of delight
Mt 2:6 O Bethlehem of the *l* of Judah
2:20 your way into the *l* of Israel
2:21 entered into the *l* of Israel
4:15 O *l* of Zebulun and
4:15 of Zebulun and *l* of Naphtali
5:30 body to *l* in Gehenna
10:15 the *l* of Sodom and Gomorrah
11:24 *l* of Sodom on Judgment Day
14:24 yards away from *l*, being
14:34 and came to *l* in Gennesaret
23:15 you traverse sea and dry *l*
27:45 darkness fell over all the *l*
Mr 6:47 but he was alone on the *l*
6:53 when they got across to *l*
15:33 over the whole *l* until the
Lu 4:25 famine fell upon all the *l*
4:26 in the *l* of Sidon to a widow
5:3 to pull away a bit from *l*
5:11 brought the boats back to *l*
8:27 as he got out onto *l* a certain
12:16 The *l* of a certain rich man
19:12 traveled to a distant *l* to
21:23 be great necessity upon the *l*
Joh 6:21 *l* to which they were trying
21:8 were not a long way from *l*
21:9 when they disembarked onto *l*
21:11 drew the net to *l* full of
Ac 4:37 possessing a piece of *l*, sold
7:3 Go out from your *l* and from
7:3 into the *l* I shall show you
7:4 from the *l* of the Chaldeans
7:4 *l* in which you now dwell
7:6 residents in a foreign *l* and
7:29 in the *l* of Midian, where
7:40 led us out of the *l* of Egypt
7:45 *l* possessed by the nations
8:4 through the *l* declaring the
10:38 through the *l* doing good
13:17 residence in the *l* of Egypt
13:19 nations in the *l* of Canaan
13:19 the *l* of them by lot
27:27 drawing near to some *l*
27:39 could not recognize the *l*
27:43 and make it to *l* first
27:44 were brought safely to *l*
Heb 8:9 forth out of the *l* of Egypt
11:9 in the *l* of the promise
11:9 as in a foreign *l*, and dwelt
11:13 temporary . . . in the *l*
11:29 Red Sea as on dry *l*, but on
Jas 5:17 it did not rain upon the *l*
5:18 and the *l* put forth its fruit
Jude 5 people out of the *l* of Egypt

Landed

Ge 47:26 over the *l* estate of Egypt
Nu 32:18 *l* property, each with his
33:54 yourselves with *l* property
Ps 49:11 called their *l* estates by
Lu 8:6 other *l* upon the rock-mass
Ac 21:3 on to Syria, and *l* at Tyre
27:3 we *l* at Sidon, and Julius

Landholders

Nu 34:29 *l* in the land of Canaan

Landing

Jg 5:17 And by his *l* places he kept

Landlord

Lu 22:11 say to the *l* of the house

Landowners

Jos 24:11 And the *l* of Jericho, the
Jg 9:2 all the *l* of Shechem, Which is
9:3 all the *l* of Shechem so that
9:6 the *l* of Shechem and all the
9:7 you *l* of Shechem, and let God
9:18 king over the *l* of Shechem
9:20 consume the *l* of Shechem and
9:20 *l* of Shechem and the house

Jg 9:23 and the l of Shechem, and the
9:23 the l of Shechem proceeded to
9:24 the l of Shechem because they
9:25 l of Shechem set ambush men
9:26 l of Shechem began to trust
9:39 head of the l of Shechem and
9:46 the l of the tower of Shechem
9:47 the l of the tower of Shechem
9:51 l of the city went fleeing
20:5 l of Gibeah proceeded to rise
1Sa 23:11 l of Keilah surrender me
23:12 l of Keilah surrender me
2Sa 21:12 from the l of Jabesh-gilead

Land's
Le 25:3 you must gather the l produce
25:11 nor reap the l growth from
Jg 18:30 the l being taken into exile
Isa 13:9 annihilate the l sinners out

Lands
Ge 10:5 was spread about in their l
10:20 in their l, by their nations
10:31 their tongues, in their l
26:3 seed I shall give all these l
26:4 give to your seed all these l
41:54 famine . . . in all the l, but
Le 26:36 in the l of their enemies
26:39 in the l of your enemies
2Ki 18:35 all the gods of the l that
19:11 Assyria did to all the l by
1Ch 13:2 in all the l of Israel and
14:17 to go out into all the l
22:5 distinction to all the l
29:30 all the kingdoms of the l
2Ch 9:28 and from all the other l
11:23 l of Judah and of Benjamin
12:8 of the kingdoms of the l
15:5 the inhabitants of the l
17:10 l that were all around
20:29 kingdoms of the l when they
32:13 to all the peoples of the l
32:13 gods of the nations of the l
32:17 nations of the l who did
34:33 l that belonged to the sons
Ezr 3:3 the peoples of the l
9:1 peoples of the l as regards
9:2 with the peoples of the l
9:7 the hand of the kings of the l
9:11 of the peoples of the l
Ne 9:30 hand of the peoples of the l
10:28 from the peoples of the l to
Ps 105:44 them the l of the nations
106:27 scatter them among the l
107:3 together even from the l
116:9 in the l of those living
Isa 36:20 gods of these l that have
37:11 Assyria did to all the l
37:18 devastated all the l, and
Jer 16:15 l to which he had dispersed
23:3 l to which I had dispersed
23:8 l to which I have dispersed
27:6 given all these l into the
28:8 prophesy concerning many l
32:37 together out of all the l
40:11 were in all the other l
Eze 5:5 set her, with l all around
5:6 more than the l that are all
6:8 get scattered among the l
11:16 scattered them among the l
11:16 l to which they have come
11:17 gather you from the l among
12:15 scatter them among the l
20:6 the decoration of all the l
20:15 the decoration of all the l
20:23 disperse them among the l
20:32 like the families of the l
20:34 l to which you have been
20:41 l to which you have been
22:4 and of jeering to all the l
22:5 l nearby and those far away
22:15 disperse you among the l
25:7 and destroy you from the l
29:12 in the midst of desolated l
29:12 disperse them among the l
30:7 in the midst of desolated l
30:23 disperse them among the l
30:26 disperse them among the l
32:9 to l that you have not known
34:13 together from the l and
35:10 two nations and these two l
36:19 were dispersed among the l
36:24 together out of all the l
39:27 the l of their enemies
Da 9:7 l to which you dispersed them
Da 11:40 enter into the l and flood
11:41 many l that will be made
11:42 out his hand against the l
Mt 19:29 children or l for the sake
Ac 28:7 named Publius, had l; and

Lanes
Lu 14:21 and the l of the city, and

Language
Ge 11:1 one l and of one set of words
11:6 there is one l for them all
11:7 confuse their l that they may
11:7 not listen to one another's l
11:9 Jehovah had confused the l
2Ki 18:26 Syrian l, for we can listen
18:26 Jews' l in the ears of the
18:28 a loud voice in the Jews' l
2Ch 32:18 the Jews' l to the people
Ezr 4:7 translated into the Aramaic l
Ps 81:5 l that I did not know I kept
Isa 19:18 speaking the l of Canaan
33:19 too deep in l to listen to
36:11 in the Syrian l, for we are
36:11 speak to us in the Jews' l
36:13 loud voice in the Jews' l
Jer 5:15 nation whose l you do not
Eze 3:5 unintelligible in l or heavy
3:6 peoples unintelligible in l or
Da 2:4 to the king in the Aramaic l
3:29 national group or l that
Zep 3:9 the change to a pure l
Ac 1:19 called in their l *A·kel'da·ma*
2:6 speaking in his own l
2:8 own l in which we were born
21:40 in the Hebrew l, saying
22:2 in the Hebrew l, they kept
26:14 say to me in the Hebrew l

Languages
Da 3:4 national groups and l
3:7 national groups and l were
4:1 and l that are dwelling in all
5:19 and l proved to be quaking
7:14 l should all serve even him
Zec 8:23 ten men out of all the l of

Languish
Jer 31:12 no more will they l again

Languished
Ps 88:9 own eye has l because of my

Languishing
Jer 31:25 every l soul I will fill

Languishingly
Isa 38:14 have looked l to the height

Laodicea
Col 2:1 behalf of you and those at L
4:13 of those at L and of those
4:15 to the brothers at L and
4:16 also read the one from L
Re 1:11 the seven congregations . . . L
3:14 angel of the congregation in L

Laodiceans
Col 4:16 in the congregation of the L

Lap
Pr 16:33 Into the l the lot is cast

Lappidoth
Jg 4:4 the wife of L, was judging

Lapping
Jg 7:6 of those l with their hand to
7:7 men who did the l I shall save

Laps
Jg 7:5 that l up some of the water
7:5 just as a dog l, you will set
Lu 6:38 into your l a fine measure

Large
Ge 26:14 and a l body of servants, so
Le 11:30 the l lizard and the newt
Jos 19:9 proved to be too l for them
Jg 5:25 l banquet bowl of majestic
6:38 to fill a l banquet bowl with
7:16 and l empty jars, and torches
7:16 and torches inside the l jars
7:19 the l water jars that were in
7:20 shattered the l jars and took
1Sa 1:24 flour and a l jar of wine
6:14 where there was a l stone
6:15 to put it upon the l stone
10:3 one carrying a l jar of wine
17:7 bearer of the l shield was
17:41 man carrying the l shield
1Sa 25:18 two l jars of wine and
2Sa 16:1 and a l jar of wine
22:37 room l enough for my steps
1Ki 4:13 sixty l cities with wall and
10:16 make two hundred l shields
10:16 to lay upon each l shield
17:12 flour in the l jar and a
17:14 The l jar of flour itself
17:16 The l jar of flour itself
18:33 fill four l jars with water
2Ki 4:38 Put the l cooking pot on and
21:6 on a l scale what was bad
1Ch 12:8 l shield and the lance ready
12:24 carrying the l shield and
12:34 with the l shield and the
2Ch 9:15 two hundred l shields of
9:15 to lay upon each l shield
11:12 l shields and lances
13:8 when you are a l crowd and
14:8 force bearing the l shield
20:2 l crowd from the region of
20:12 l crowd that is coming
20:15 because of this l crowd
25:5 handling lance and l shield
36:14 unfaithfulness on a l scale
Ezr 10:1 a very l congregation, men
Ne 4:19 The work is l and extensive
12:31 two l thanksgiving choirs
13:5 make for him a l dining hall
Es 5:11 the l number of his sons and
Job 1:3 a very l body of servants
16:10 In l number they mass
31:34 suffer a shock at a l crowd
36:18 let not a l ransom itself
Ps 5:12 As with a l shield, with
18:36 room l enough for my steps
19:11 there is a l reward
22:25 be in the l congregation
35:2 hold of buckler and l shield
68:11 The women . . . are a l army
88:6 In dark places, in a l abyss
91:4 trueness will be a l shield
Pr 6:35 how l you make the present
18:16 gift will make a l opening
Isa 3:23 the turbans and the l veils
8:1 l tablet and write upon it
22:24 the vessels of the l jars
30:14 of a l jar of the potters
55:7 he will forgive in a l way
Jer 2:22 l quantities of lye, your
13:12 Every l jar is something
13:12 every l jar is something
46:3 and l shield, and approach
48:12 l jars they will dash to
La 4:2 as l jars of earthenware, the
4:20 been captured in their l pit
Eze 17:7 wings, and having l pinions
23:24 with l shield and buckler
26:8 against you a l shield
38:4 with l shield and buckler
39:9 and bucklers and l shields
Da 2:31 image, which was l and the
2:35 l mountain and filled the
11:10 crowd of l military forces
11:11 a l crowd stand up, and the
Mt 13:33 in three l measures of flour
Mr 14:15 show you a l upper room
16:4 although it was very l
Lu 13:21 in three l measures of flour
22:12 a l upper room furnished
Ac 4:33 kindness in l measure was
22:28 citizen for a l sum of money
1Co 16:9 l door that leads to activity
Ga 6:11 l letters I have written you
Eph 6:16 take up the l shield of faith
2Ti 2:20 in a l house there are
Re 8:3 a l quantity of incense was

Larger
Isa 56:12 great in a very much l way
Da 11:13 crowd l than the first; and

Largest
Mt 13:32 the l of the vegetables and

Lasea
Ac 27:8 near which was the city L

Lasha
Ge 10:19 Admah and Zeboiim, near L

Lashed
Mt 7:25 winds blew and l against

Lashings
Ac 27:40 l of the rudder oars and

Laughable
Hab 1:10 officials are something *l*

Laughed
Ge 18:13 Why was it that Sarah *l*
Job 30:1 now they have *l* at me
Pr 29:9 become excited and has also *l*
La 1:7 They *l* over her collapse

Laughing
Jer 30:19 sound of those who are *l*
31:4 dance of those who are *l*
Lu 6:25 Woe, you who are *l* now

Laughingstock
Ge 39:14 a Hebrew, to make us a *l*
39:17 came to me to make me a *l*
Job 12:4 a *l* to his fellowman I
12:4 A *l* is the righteous

Laughs
Job 39:7 *l* at the turmoil of a town
39:18 She *l* at the horse and at
39:22 It *l* at dread, and is not
41:29 it *l* at the rattling of a
Pr 31:25 and she *l* at a future day
Hab 1:10 it *l* even at every fortified

Laughter
Ge 21:6 God has prepared *l* for me
Job 8:21 he fills your mouth with *l*
Ps 126:2 came to be filled with *l*
Pr 14:13 *l* the heart may be in pain
Ec 2:2 I said to *l*: Insanity! and to
7:3 Better is vexation than *l*, for
7:6 so is the *l* of the stupid one
10:19 Bread is for the *l* of the
Jer 20:7 an object of *l* all day long
La 3:14 I have become an object of *l*
Eze 23:32 an object of *l* and derision
Jas 4:9 *l* be turned into mourning

Launches
Ps 27:12 And he who *l* forth violence
Pr 6:19 witness that *l* forth lies
12:17 He that *l* forth faithfulness
14:5 witness *l* forth mere lies
14:25 one *l* forth mere lies
19:5 *l* forth lies will not escape
19:9 that *l* forth lies will perish

Laundryman's
2Ki 18:17 highway of the *l* field
Isa 7:3 the highway of the *l* field
36:2 highway of the *l* field

Laundrymen
Mal 3:2 and like the lye of *l*

Laurel
Isa 44:14 He planted the *l* tree, and

Lavishing
Isa 46:6 *l* out the gold from the

Law
Ex 12:49 One *l* is to exist for the
13:9 that Jehovah's *l* may prove to
16:4 they will walk in my *l* or
24:12 the *l* and the commandment
24:14 Whoever has a case at *l*, let
Le 6:9 is the *l* of the burnt offering
6:14 is the *l* of the grain offering
6:25 is the *l* of the sin offering
7:1 is the *l* of the guilt offering
7:7 There is one *l* for them
7:11 is the *l* of the communion
7:37 is the *l* concerning the burnt
11:46 is the *l* about the beast
12:7 is the *l* about her who bears
13:59 *l* of the plague of leprosy
14:2 become the *l* of the leper
14:32 the *l* for the one in whom
14:54 the *l* respecting any plague
14:57 This is the *l* about leprosy
15:32 the *l* about the man having a
Nu 5:29 *l* about jealousy, where a
5:30 carry out . . . all this *l*
6:13 *l* about the Nazirite: On the
6:21 *l* about the Nazirite who
6:21 the *l* of his Naziriteship
15:16 should prove to be one *l*
15:29 prove to be one *l* for you as
19:2 This is a statute of the *l*
19:14 *l* in case a man should die
31:21 This is the statute of the *l*
De 1:5 undertook to explain this *l*
4:8 *l* that I am putting before you
4:44 the *l* that Moses set before
De 17:11 In accordance with the *l*
17:18 a copy of this *l* from that
17:19 keep all the words of this *l*
27:3 all the words of this *l*
27:8 all the words of this *l*
27:26 the words of this *l* in force
28:58 all the words of this *l* that
28:61 in the book of this *l*
29:21 in this book of the *l*
29:29 all the words of this *l*
30:10 this book of the *l*, because
31:9 Moses wrote this *l* and gave
31:11 read this *l* in front of all
31:12 all the words of this *l*
31:24 words of this *l* in a book
31:26 this book of the *l*, you must
32:46 do all the words of this *l*
33:4 laid as a command upon us a *l*
33:10 And Israel in your *l*
Jos 1:7 the *l* that Moses my servant
1:8 book of the *l* should not
8:31 the book of the *l* of Moses
8:32 a copy of the *l* of Moses
8:34 words of the *l*, the blessing
8:34 written in the book of the *l*
22:5 the *l* that Moses the servant
23:6 the book of the *l* of Moses
24:26 in the book of God's *l* and
2Sa 7:19 is the *l* given for mankind
1Ki 2:3 written in the *l* of Moses
2Ki 10:31 walk in the *l* of Jehovah
14:6 Moses' *l* that Jehovah gave
17:13 the *l* that I commanded your
17:34 the *l* and the commandment
17:37 judicial decisions and the *l*
21:8 the *l* that my servant Moses
22:8 book of the *l* I have found
22:11 words of the book of the *l*
23:24 the words of the *l* that
23:25 to all the *l* of Moses
1Ch 16:40 written in the *l* of Jehovah
22:12 to keep the *l* of Jehovah
2Ch 6:16 by walking in my *l*, just as
12:1 left the *l* of Jehovah, and
14:4 the *l* and the commandment
15:3 teaching and without *L*
17:9 was the book of Jehovah's *l*
19:10 involving *l* and
23:18 written in the *l* of Moses
25:4 what is written in the *l*
30:16 *l* of Moses the man of the
31:3 written in the *l* of Jehovah
31:4 strictly to the *l* of Jehovah
31:21 *l* and in the commandment
33:8 all the *l* and the regulations
34:14 *l* by the hand of Moses
34:15 book of the *l* I have found
34:19 heard the words of the *l*
35:26 written in the *l* of Jehovah
Ezr 3:2 written in the *l* of Moses the
7:6 copyist in the *l* of Moses
7:10 consult the *l* of Jehovah and
7:12 copyist of the *l* of the God
7:14 *l* of your God that is in your
7:21 *l* of the God of the heavens
7:26 the *l* of your God and the
7:26 the *l* of the king
10:3 be done according to the *l*
Ne 8:1 the book of the *l* of Moses
8:2 the *l* before the congregation
8:3 to the book of the *l*
8:7 explaining the *l* to the people
8:8 from the *l* of the true God
8:9 hearing the words of the *l*
8:13 into the words of the *l*
8:14 *l* that Jehovah had commanded
8:18 book of the *l* of the true God
9:3 book of the *l* of Jehovah their
9:14 a *l* you commanded them by
9:26 casting your *l* behind their
9:29 to bring them back to your *l*
9:34 have not performed your *l*
10:28 to the *l* of the true God
10:29 to walk in the *l* of the true
10:34 to what is written in the *l*
10:36 to what is written in the *l*
12:44 called for by the *l* for the
13:3 as soon as they heard the *l*
Es 1:8 drinking according to the *l*
1:13 versed in *l* and legal cases
1:15 According to the *l* what is to
2:8 king's word and his *l* were
3:14 writing to be given as *l* in
3:15 *l* itself was given in Shushan
Es 4:3 the king's word and his *l* were
4:8 a copy of the writing of the *l*
4:11 *l* is to have him put to death
4:16 is not according to the *l*
8:13 writing was to be given as *l*
8:14 the *l* itself was given out in
8:17 word of the king and his *l*
9:1 king's word and his *l* came due
9:13 do according to the *l* of today
9:14 *l* was given out in Shushan
Job 13:8 will you contend at *l*?
22:22 the *l* from his own mouth
31:13 in their case at *l* with me
31:35 in the case at *l* with me
Ps 1:2 delight is in the *l* of Jehovah
1:2 *l* he reads in an undertone
19:7 The *l* of Jehovah is perfect
35:23 Jehovah, to my case at *l*
37:31 *l* of his God is in his heart
40:8 *l* is within my inward parts
74:22 conduct your own case at *l*
78:1 give ear . . . people, to my *l*
78:5 And a *l* he set in Israel
78:10 his *l* they refused to walk
89:30 If his sons leave my *l*
94:12 you teach out of your own *l*
119:1 walking in the *l* of Jehovah
119:18 things out of your *l*
119:29 favor me with your own *l*
119:34 that I may observe your *l*
119:44 will keep your *l* constantly
119:51 your *l* I have not deviated
119:53 Who are leaving your *l*
119:55 That I may keep your *l*
119:61 Your *l* I did not forget
119:70 been fond of your own *l*
119:72 *l* of your mouth is good for
119:77 your *l* is what I am fond of
119:85 not in accord with your *l*
119:92 *l* had not been what I am
119:97 How I do love your *l*!
119:109 your *l* I have not forgotten
119:113 But your *l* I have loved
119:126 They have broken your *l*
119:136 they have not kept your *l*
119:142 And your *l* is truth
119:150 far away from your own *l*
119:153 not forgotten your own *l*
119:163 Your *l* I have loved
119:165 to those loving your *l*
119:174 And your *l* I am fond of
Pr 1:8 forsake the *l* of your mother
3:1 My son, my *l* do not forget
4:2 My *l* do not leave
6:20 forsake the *l* of your mother
6:23 and a light the *l* is, and
7:2 *l* like the pupil of your eyes
13:14 *l* of the wise one is a
28:4 Those who are leaving the *l*
28:4 who are keeping the *l* excite
28:7 son is observing the *l*, but
28:9 ear away from hearing the *l*
29:18 they that are keeping the *l*
31:26 *l* of loving-kindness is upon
Isa 1:10 Give ear to the *l* of our God
2:3 out of Zion *l* will go forth
5:7 the breaking of *l*
5:24 rejected the *l* of Jehovah
8:16 put a seal about the *l* among
8:20 To the *l* and to the attestation!
30:9 to hear the *l* of Jehovah
42:4 for his *l* the islands
42:21 the *l* and make it majestic
42:24 whose *l* they did not listen
51:4 a *l* itself will go forth
51:7 in whose heart is my *l*
Jer 2:8 ones handling the *l* did not
6:19 *l*—they also kept rejecting
8:8 the *l* of Jehovah is with us
9:13 their leaving my *l* that I
11:20 have revealed my case at *l*
16:11 my *l* they did not keep
18:18 the *l* will not perish from
20:12 have revealed my case at *l*
26:4 *l* that I have put before you
31:33 put my *l* within them
32:23 your *l* they did not walk
44:10 nor did they walk in my *l*
44:23 Jehovah and in his *l* and in
La 2:9 There is no *l*. Her own
Eze 7:26 *l* itself will perish from a
22:26 have done violence to my *l*
43:12 This is the *l* of the House
43:12 This is the *l* of the House

Da 6:5 in the *l* of his God
6:8 *l* of the Medes and the
6:12 *l* of the Medes and the
6:15 *l* belonging to the Medes and
7:25 intend to change times and *l*
9:11 Israel have overstepped your *l*
9:11 written in the *l* of Moses
9:13 written in the *l* of Moses
Ho 4:6 forgetting the *l* of your God
8:1 my *l* they have transgressed
8:12 many things of my *l*
Am 2:4 rejecting the *l* of Jehovah
Mic 4:2 out of Zion *l* will go forth
Hab 1:4 *l* grows numb, and justice
Zep 3:4 they did violence to the *l*
Hag 2:11 the priests as to the *l*
Zec 7:12 to keep from obeying the *l*
Mal 2:6 *l* of truth proved to be in
2:7 *l* is what people should seek
2:8 many to stumble in the *l*
2:9 showing partiality in the *l*
4:4 the *l* of Moses my servant
Mt 5:17 destroy the *L* or the Prophets
5:18 to pass away from the *L* by
5:25 complaining against you at *l*
7:12 the *L* and the Prophets mean
11:13 all, the Prophets and the *L*
12:5 in the *L* that on the sabbaths
22:35 one of them, versed in the *L*
22:36 greatest . . . in the *L*
22:40 the whole *L* hangs, and the
23:23 weightier matters of the *L*
Lu 2:22 according to the *l* of Moses
2:23 it is written in Jehovah's *l*
2:24 said in the *l* of Jehovah
2:27 customary practice of the *l*
2:39 according to the *l* of Jehovah
5:17 teachers of the *l* who had
7:30 and those versed in the *L*
10:25 man versed in the *L* rose up
10:26 What is written in the *L*?
11:45 one of those versed in the *L*
11:46 you who are versed in the *L*
11:52 you who are versed in the *L*
12:58 with your adversary at *l* to
14:3 spoke to those versed in the *L*
16:16 *L* and the Prophets were
16:17 particle of a letter of the *L*
18:3 from my adversary at *l*
24:44 written in the *l* of Moses
Joh 1:17 *L* was given through Moses
1:45 in the *L*, and the Prophets
7:19 Moses gave you the *L*, did he
7:19 not one of you obeys the *L*
7:23 *l* of Moses may not be broken
7:49 crowd . . . not know the *L*
7:51 Our *l* does not judge a man
8:17 in your own *L* it is written
10:34 it not written in your *L*
12:34 We heard from the *L* that
15:25 *L* may be fulfilled, They
18:31 him according to your *l*
19:7 We have a *l*, and according
19:7 according to the *l* he ought
Ac 5:34 Gamaliel, a *L* teacher
6:13 and against the *L*
7:53 *L* as transmitted by angels
13:15 public reading of the *L* and
13:39 by means of the *l* of Moses
15:5 to observe the *l* of Moses
18:13 Contrary to the *l* this person
18:15 speech and names and the *l*
21:20 are all zealous for the *L*
21:24 yourself also keeping the *L*
21:28 against the people and the *L*
22:3 strictness of the ancestral *L*
22:12 reverent according to the *L*
23:3 judge me in accord with the *L*
23:3 transgressing the *L*, command
23:29 about questions of their *L*
24:14 set forth in the *L* and
25:8 against the *L* of the Jews
28:23 from both the *l* of Moses
Ro 2:12 those who sinned without *l*
2:12 will also perish without *l*
2:12 sinned under *l* will be
2:12 will be judged by *l*
2:13 hearers of *l* are not the ones
2:13 doers of *l* will be declared
2:14 nations that do not have *l*
2:14 by nature the things of the *l*
2:14 people, although not having *l*
2:14 are a *l* to themselves
2:15 *l* to be written in their
Ro 2:17 resting upon *l* and taking
2:18 orally instructed out of the *L*
2:20 and of the truth in the *L*
2:23 You, who take pride in *l*, do
2:23 transgressing of the *L*
2:25 benefit only if you practice *l*
2:25 if you are a transgressor of *l*
2:26 requirements of the *L*, his
2:27 by carrying out the *L*, judge
2:27 are a transgressor of *l*
3:19 things the *L* says it addresses
3:19 addresses to those under the *L*
3:20 by works of *l* no flesh will
3:20 *l* is the accurate knowledge
3:21 But now apart from *l* God's
3:21 borne witness to by the *L*
3:27 Through what *l*? That of works?
3:27 but through the *l* of faith
3:28 faith apart from works of *l*
3:31 abolish *l* by means of our
3:31 the contrary, we establish *l*
4:13 through *l* that Abraham or
4:14 who adhere to *l* are heirs
4:15 the *L* produces wrath, but
4:15 no *l*, neither is there any
4:16 that which adheres to the *L*
5:13 until the *L* sin was in the
5:13 anyone when there is no *l*
5:20 *L* came in beside in order
6:14 you are not under *l* but under
6:15 because we are not under *l*
7:1 speaking to those who know *l*
7:1 *L* is master over a man as long
7:2 married woman is bound by *l*
7:2 discharged from the *l* of her
7:3 she is free from his *l*, so
7:4 dead to the *L* through the body
7:5 that were excited by the *L*
7:6 been discharged from the *L*
7:7 Is the *L* sin? Never may that
7:7 if it had not been for the *L*
7:7 *L* had not said: You must not
7:8 apart from *l* sin was dead
7:9 I was once alive apart from *l*
7:12 the *L* is holy, and the
7:14 know that the *L* is spiritual
7:16 I agree that the *L* is fine
7:21 this *l* in my case: that when
7:22 delight in the *l* of God
7:23 another *l* warring against
7:23 against the *l* of my mind and
7:23 captive to sin's *l* that is in
7:25 am a slave to God's *l*, but
7:25 but with my flesh to sin's *l*
8:2 *l* of that spirit which gives
8:2 free from the *l* of sin and of
8:3 on the part of the *L*, while
8:4 righteous requirement of the *L*
8:7 subjection to the *l* of God
9:4 giving of the *L* and the sacred
9:31 pursuing a *l* of righteousness
9:31 did not attain to the *l*
10:4 Christ is the end of the *L*
10:5 righteousness of the *L* will
13:8 that loves . . . fulfilled the *l*
13:9 *l* code, You must not commit
1Co 9:8 does not the *L* also say these
9:9 For in the *l* of Moses it is
9:20 to those under *l* I became as
9:20 I became as under *l*, though
9:20 I myself am not under *l*
9:20 I might gain those under *l*
9:21 To those without *l* I became
9:21 I became as without *l*
9:21 although I am not without *l*
9:21 but under *l* toward Christ
9:21 I might gain those without *l*
14:21 In the *L* it is written
14:34 even as the *L* says
15:56 the power for sin is the *L*
Ga 2:16 not due to works of *l*, but
2:16 and not due to works of *l*
2:16 due to works of *l* no flesh
2:19, 19 through *l* I died toward *l*
2:21 if righteousness is through *l*
3:2 due to works of *l* or due to a
3:5 he do it owing to works of *l*
3:10 depend upon works of *l* are
3:10 in the scroll of the *L* in
3:11 that by *l* no one is declared
3:12 *L* does not adhere to faith
3:13 us from the curse of the *L*
3:17 *L* that has come into being
3:18 the inheritance is due to *l*
Ga 3:19 Why, then, the *L*? It was
3:21 *L*, therefore, against the
3:21 *l* had been given that was
3:21 have been by means of *l*
3:23 were being guarded under *l*
3:24 *L* has become our tutor
4:4 and who came to be under *l*
4:5 by purchase those under *l*
4:21 you who want to be under *l*
4:21 Do you not hear the *L*?
5:3 to perform the whole *L*
5:4 righteous by means of *l*; you
5:14 entire *L* stands fulfilled in
5:18 spirit, you are not under *l*
5:23 such things there is no *l*
6:2 fulfill the *l* of the Christ
6:13 circumcised keep the *L*
Eph 2:15 the *L* of commandments
Php 3:5 as respects *l*, a Pharisee
3:6 righteousness . . . means of *l*
3:9 which results from *l*, but
1Ti 1:7 wanting to be teachers of *l*
1:8 we know that the *L* is fine
1:9 that *l* is promulgated, not
Tit 3:9 strife and fights over the *L*
3:13 Zenas . . . is versed in the *L*
Heb 7:5 according to the *L*, that is
7:11 people were given the *L*
7:12 a change also of the *l*
7:16 to the *l* of a commandment
7:19 *L* made nothing perfect, but
7:28 *L* appoints men high priests
7:28 oath . . . after the *L* appoints
8:4 the gifts according to the *L*
9:19 *L* had been spoken by Moses
9:22 blood according to the *L*
10:1 *L* has a shadow of the good
10:8 offered according to the *L*
10:28 disregarded the *l* of Moses
Jas 1:25 perfect *l* that belongs to
2:6 they drag you before *l* courts
2:8 carrying out the kingly *l*
2:9 you are reproved by the *l* as
2:10 whoever observes all the *L*
2:11 become a transgressor of *l*
2:12 judged by the *l* of a free
4:11 speaks against *l* and judges
4:11 and judges *l*. Now if you
4:11 if you judge *l*, you are, not
4:11 not a doer of *l*, but a judge

Law-defying
2Pe 2:7 indulgence of the *l* people
3:17 by the error of the *l* people

Lawful
Mt 12:2 is not *l* to do on the sabbath
12:4 it was not *l* for him to eat
12:10 it *l* to cure on the sabbath
12:12 *l* to do a fine thing on the
14:4 is not *l* for you to be having
19:3 Is it *l* for a man to divorce
20:15 *l* for me to do what I want
22:17 *l* to pay head tax to Caesar
27:6 not *l* to drop them into the
Mr 2:24 on the sabbath what is not *l*
2:26 is not *l* for anybody to eat
3:4 *l* on the sabbath to do a good
6:18 is not *l* for you to be having
10:2 *l* for a man to divorce a
12:14 Is it *l* to pay head tax to
Lu 6:2 what is not *l* on the sabbath
6:4 it is *l* for no one to eat but
6:9 Is it *l* on the sabbath to do
14:3 Is it *l* on the sabbath to cure
20:22 Is it *l* for us to pay tax
Joh 5:10 not *l* for you to carry the
18:31 not *l* for us to kill anyone
Ac 16:21 customs that it is not *l* for
22:25 *l* for you men to scourge a
1Co 6:12 All things are *l* for me; but
6:12 All things are *l* for me; but
10:23 All things are *l*; but not
10:23 All things are *l*; but not
2Co 12:4 not *l* for a man to speak

Lawfully
1Ti 1:8 provided one handles it *l*

Lawgiver
Jas 4:12 One there is that is *l* and

Lawless
Lu 22:37 was reckoned with *l* ones
Ac 2:23 by the hand of *l* men and did
Ro 4:7 *l* deeds have been pardoned

2Th 2:8 *l* one will be revealed, whom
2:9 But the *l* one's presence is
1Ti 1:9 for persons *l* and unruly
Heb 10:17 *l* deeds to mind anymore
2Pe 2:8 by reason of their *l* deeds

Lawlessness
Mt 7:23 Get away . . . you workers of *l*
13:41 and persons who are doing *l*
23:28 are full of hypocrisy and *l*
24:12 of the increasing of *l* the
Ro 6:19 slaves to uncleanness and *l*
6:19 with *l* in view, so now
2Co 6:14 do righteousness and *l* have
2Th 2:3 the man of *l* gets revealed
2:7 the mystery of this *l* is
Tit 2:14 from every sort of *l* and
Heb 1:9 and you hated *l*
1Jo 3:4 sin is also practicing *l*
3:4 and so sin is *l*

Law's
Ro 13:10 love is the *l* fulfillment

Laws
Ge 26:5 my statutes, and my *l*
Ex 16:28 my commandments and my *l*
18:16 of the true God and his *l*
18:20 the regulations and the *l* are
Le 26:46 *l* that Jehovah set between
Ezr 7:25 knowing the *l* of your God
8:36 gave the *l* of the king to
Ne 9:13 decisions and *l* of truth
Es 1:19 the *l* of Persia and Media
3:8 their *l* are different from all
3:8 the king's own *l* they are not
Ps 105:45 And observe his own *l*
Isa 24:5 they have bypassed the *l*
Eze 43:11 *l* do you make known to
44:5 and regarding all its *l*
44:24 my *l* and my statutes in
Da 9:10 by walking in his *l* that he
Heb 8:10 will put my *l* in their mind
10:16 put my *l* in their hearts

Lawsuits
1Co 6:7 are having *l* with one another

Lay
Ge 19:33 firstborn went in and *l* down
19:33 he did not know when she *l*
19:34 I *l* down with my father
19:35 younger got up and *l* down
19:35 not know when she *l* down
28:11 and *l* down in that place
30:16 *l* down with her that night
34:2 *l* down with her and violated
35:22 Reuben went and *l* down with
37:22 do not *l* a violent hand upon
46:4 *l* his hand upon your eyes
Ex 7:4 to *l* my hand upon Egypt and
21:22 *l* upon him; and he must give
22:25 must not *l* interest upon him
29:10 *l* their hands upon the bull's
29:15 *l* their hands upon the ram's
29:19 *l* their hands upon the ram's
Le 1:4 must *l* his hand upon the head
3:2 must *l* his hand upon the head
3:8 *l* his hand upon the head of
3:13 *l* his hand upon its head
4:4 *l* his hand upon the bull's head
4:15 *l* their hands upon the bull's
4:24 *l* his hand upon the head of
4:29 *l* his hand upon the head of
4:33 *l* his hand upon the head of
16:21 Aaron must *l* both his hands
16:23 he must *l* them down there
18:6 relative of his to *l* bare
18:7 mother you must not *l* bare
18:7 You must not *l* bare her
18:8 wife you must not *l* bare
18:9 not *l* bare their nakedness
18:10 not *l* bare their nakedness
18:11 you must not *l* bare her
18:12 sister you must not *l* bare
18:13 sister you must not *l* bare
18:14 brother you must not *l* bare
18:15 you must not *l* bare. She is
18:15 not *l* her nakedness bare
18:16 wife you must not *l* bare
18:17 daughter you must not *l* bare
18:17 order to *l* her nakedness bare
18:19 impurity to *l* her nakedness
20:18 *l* bare her nakedness, he has
20:19 nakedness . . . not *l* bare
24:14 *l* their hands upon his head

Le 26:30 *l* your own carcasses upon
26:31 *l* your sanctuaries desolate
26:32 *l* the land desolate, and your
Nu 8:10 Israel must *l* their hands
8:12 Levites will *l* their hands
22:27 she now *l* down under Balaam
24:9 he *l* down like the lion, And
27:18 must *l* your hand upon him
De 20:19 *l* siege to a city many days
22:23 and *l* down with her
22:25 and *l* down with her
22:25 the man who *l* down with her
22:29 the man who *l* down with her
Jos 6:26 let him *l* the foundation of
Jg 5:27 he *l* down; Between her feet
12:6 they would *l* hold of him and
16:2 *l* in wait for him all night
Ru 3:7 at his feet and *l* down
1Sa 3:5 So he went and *l* down
3:9 Samuel went and *l* down in
19:24 he *l* fallen naked all that
22:15 king *l* anything against his
23:10 Keilah to *l* the city in ruin
2Sa 11:1 *l* siege to Rabbah, while
11:4 and he *l* down with her
11:9 Uriah *l* down at the entrance
12:16 and *l* down on the earth
12:24 to her and *l* down with her
13:6 Amnon *l* down and played sick
13:14 humiliated her and *l* down
13:31 and *l* upon the earth, and
19:19 should *l* it to his heart
19:38 you may choose to *l* upon
20:15 *l* siege against him in Abel
1Ki 2:10 Then David *l* down with his
3:19 because she *l* upon him
5:17 to *l* the foundation of the
10:16 to *l* upon each large shield
10:17 gold . . . to *l* upon each
11:43 Solomon *l* down with his
14:20 *l* down with his forefathers
14:31 Rehoboam *l* down with his
15:8 Abijam *l* down with his
15:24 Asa *l* down with his
16:6 *l* down with his forefathers
16:17 began to *l* siege to Tirzah
16:28 Finally Omri *l* down with
19:5 he *l* down and fell asleep
19:6 after which he *l* down again
20:1 and *l* siege to Samaria and
21:4 he *l* down upon his couch and
22:40 Ahab *l* down with his
22:50 *l* down with his forefathers
2Ki 4:11 roof chamber and *l* down
4:34 and *l* down upon the child
8:24 *l* down with his forefathers
10:35 *l* down with his forefathers
13:9 *l* down with his forefathers
13:13 Jehoash *l* down with his
14:16 Jehoash *l* down with his
14:22 the king *l* down with his
14:29 *l* down with his forefathers
15:7 *l* down with his forefathers
15:22 Menahem *l* down with his
15:38 Jotham *l* down with his
16:20 Ahaz *l* down with his
17:5 to Samaria and *l* siege
18:9 and began to *l* siege to it
20:21 Hezekiah *l* down with his
21:18 Manasseh *l* down with his
24:6 *l* down with his forefathers
1Ch 20:1 *l* the land of the sons of
2Ch 9:15 *l* upon each large shield
9:16 to *l* upon each buckler
9:31 Solomon *l* down with his
12:16 Rehoboam *l* down with his
14:1 Abijah *l* down with his
16:13 Asa *l* down with his
21:1 Jehoshaphat *l* down with his
26:23 Uzziah *l* down with his
27:9 Jotham *l* down with his
28:27 Ahaz *l* down with his
32:33 Hezekiah *l* down with his
33:20 Manasseh *l* down with his
Ne 13:21 a hand I shall *l* on you
Es 2:21 to *l* hand on King Ahasuerus
3:6 to *l* hand upon Mordecai alone
4:8 to *l* the command upon her to
6:2 to *l* hand on King Ahasuerus
9:2 *l* hand on those seeking their
9:10 they did not *l* their hand
9:15 they did not *l* their hand
9:16 they did not *l* their hand
10:1 *l* forced labor upon the land

Job 36:13 will themselves *l* up anger
Ps 17:14 do *l* up for their children
38:12 seeking my soul *l* out traps
109:11 usurer *l* out traps for all
137:7, 7 *L* it bare! *L* it bare to
139:10 right hand would *l* hold of
Ec 2:3 *l* hold on folly until I could
Isa 3:6 *l* hold of his brother in the
3:17 *l* their very forehead bare
5:6 clouds I shall *l* a command
21:2 *L* siege, O Media!
25:12 security, he must *l* low
29:3 *l* siege to you with a
29:21 and those who *l* bait even
42:25 would *l* nothing to heart
46:8 *L* it to heart, you
51:16 and *l* the foundation of the
54:11 *l* your foundation with
64:7 to *l* hold on you; for you
65:15 *l* up your name for an oath
Jer 39:1 and began to *l* siege to it
Eze 4:2 *l* siege against it and build a
4:4 *l* the error of the house of
19:2 *l* down in among maned young
Da 1:1 proceeded to *l* siege to it
Ho 2:12 *l* desolate her vine and her
Mic 1:6 foundations I shall *l* bare
Zep 2:14 *l* bare the very wainscoting
Mal 2:2 if you will not *l* it to heart
Mt 8:20 nowhere to *l* down his head
9:18 come and *l* your hand upon her
18:15 go *l* bare his fault between
Mr 3:21 went out to *l* hold of him
6:5 *l* his hands upon a few sickly
7:32 to *l* his hand upon him
Lu 9:58 nowhere to *l* down his head
14:29 he might *l* its foundation
21:12 people will *l* their hands
Joh 7:44 no one did *l* his hands upon
Ac 8:19 I *l* my hands may receive holy
9:12 *l* his hands upon him that he
1Co 3:11 For no man can *l* any other
2Co 12:14 to *l* up for their parents
Php 3:12 to see if I may also *l* hold
1Ti 5:22 Never *l* your hands hastily
Heb 6:18 *l* hold on the hope set before

Layer
Ex 16:13 a *l* of dew round about the
16:14 *l* of dew evaporated and here
Le 24:6 six to the *l* set, upon the
24:7 frankincense upon each *l* set
1Ch 9:32 in charge of the *l* bread
23:29 even for the *l* bread and for
28:16 the tables of the *l* bread
2Ch 2:4 with the constant *l* bread and
29:18 table of the *l* bread and all
31:7 heaps by laying the lowest *l*
Ezr 6:4 and one *l* of timbers; and let
Ne 10:33 the *l* bread and the constant

Layers
Le 24:6 place them in two sets of *l*
2Ch 13:11 *l* of bread are upon the
Ezr 6:4 three *l* of stones rolled into
Job 36:29 can understand the cloud *l*
38:36 put wisdom in the cloud *l*

Laying
Ge 30:37 *l* bare white places which
2Sa 24:12 Three things I am *l* upon
2Ki 24:11 were *l* siege against it
2Ch 31:7 heaps by *l* the lowest layer
Ezr 3:11 *l* of the foundation of the
3:12 *l* of the foundation of this
Ps 136:6 One *l* out the earth above
Pr 17:26 the *l* of a fine upon the
21:11 *l* of a fine on the ridiculer
Isa 24:1 land and *l* it waste
28:16 *l* as a foundation in Zion
42:5 the One *l* out the earth and
44:24 by myself, *l* out the earth
51:13 *l* the foundation of the
54:11 *l* with hard mortar your
56:4 are *l* hold of my covenant
56:6 and *l* hold of my covenant
Jer 21:4 *l* siege against you outside
21:9 Chaldeans who are *l* siege
32:2 *l* siege to Jerusalem
37:5 Chaldeans that were *l* siege
Hab 3:13 a *l* of the foundation bare
Zec 12:1 *l* the foundation of the earth
Mal 2:2 you are not *l* it to heart
Mt 22:6 rest, *l* hold of his slaves
Mr 10:16 *l* his hands upon them

Ac 2:27 will not l my soul in Hades
6:2 us to l the word of God to
14:17 l himself without witness
1Co 7:11 husband should not l his
7:12 with him, let him not l her
7:13 let her not l her husband
Eph 5:31 l his father and his mother
2Ti 1:3 never l off remembering you
Heb 13:5 I will by no means l you

Leaven
Mt 13:33 kingdom . . . like l, which
16:6 the l of the Pharisees and
16:11 for the l of the Pharisees
16:12 not for the l of the loaves
Mr 8:15 the l of the Pharisees and
8:15 Pharisees and the l of Herod
Lu 12:1 the l of the Pharisees, which
13:21 like l, which a woman took
1Co 5:6 a little l ferments the whole
5:7 Clear away the old l, that
5:8 not with old l, neither with
5:8 neither with l of badness and
Ga 5:9 A little l ferments the whole

Leavened
Ex 12:15 anyone eating what is l
12:19 anyone tasting what is l
12:20 Nothing l are you to eat
12:34 dough before it was l, with
12:39 because it had not l, for
13:3 So nothing l may be eaten
13:7 nothing l is to be seen with
23:18 not sacrifice . . . what is l
34:25 along with what is l the
Le 2:11 should be made a l thing
6:17 not be baked with anything l
7:13 ring-shaped cakes of l bread
23:17 baked l, as first ripe fruits
De 16:3 eat nothing l along with it
Ho 7:4 kneading dough until it is l
Am 4:5 from what is l make a

Leaves
Ge 3:7 they sewed fig l together
1Ki 6:34 two l of the one door turned
6:34 two l of the other door
Ne 8:15 and bring in olive l and the
8:15 and the l of oil trees and
8:15, 15 myrtle l and palm l
8:15 the l of branchy trees to
Job 39:14 she l her eggs to the earth
Isa 33:9 are shaking off their l
Eze 41:24 two door l belonged to the
41:24 One door had two door l
41:24 the other had two door l
Ho 12:14 he l upon his own self
Mt 21:19 nothing on it except l only
24:32 it puts forth l, you know
Mr 11:13 a fig tree that had l
11:13 he found nothing but l, for
12:19 dies and l a wife behind
13:28 tender and puts forth its l
Re 22:2 l of the trees were for the

Leaving
Ex 23:5 you must refrain from l him
Jg 13:5 will become on l the belly
13:7 will become on l the belly
1Sa 8:8 l me and serving other gods
1Ki 20:39 a man was l the line, and
2Ki 7:7 l their tents and their horses
8:6 the day of her l the land
17:16 l all the commandments of
2Ch 28:6 l Jehovah the God of their
Ezr 8:22 against all those l him
9:8 by l over for us those who
Ps 73:27 every one immorally l you
119:53 Who are l your law
Pr 2:13 l the paths of uprightness
2:17 l the confidential friend of
10:17 l reproof is causing to
15:10 is bad to the one l the path
28:4 l the law praise the wicked
28:13 confessing and l them will
Isa 1:28 those l Jehovah will come to
65:11 men are those l Jehovah
Jer 2:17 your l Jehovah your God
2:19 your l Jehovah your God is
9:13 On account of their l my law
14:5 has given birth, but l it
17:13 those who are l you will
Da 11:30 to those l the holy covenant
Zec 11:17 shepherd . . . l the flock
Mt 4:13 after l Nazareth, he came
4:22 l the boat and their father
Mt 9:32 Now when they were l, look!
15:21 L there, Jesus now withdrew
16:4 he went away, l them behind
21:17 And l them behind he went
22:22 they marveled, and l him
26:44 So l them, he again went
28:8 quickly l the memorial tomb
Mr 12:21 died without l offspring
Lu 5:28 l everything behind he rose
10:30 went off, l him half-dead
Joh 16:28 I am l the world and am
1Pe 2:21 l you a model for you to

Lebanah
Ezr 2:45 the sons of L
Ne 7:48 the sons of L, the sons of

Lebanon
De 1:7 and L, up to the great river
3:25 mountainous region and L
11:24 From the wilderness up to L
Jos 1:4 this L to the great river
9:1 Great Sea and in front of L
11:17 the valley plain of L at
12:7 in the valley plain of L and
13:5 L toward the rising of the
13:6 from L to Misrephoth-maim
Jg 3:3 Hivites inhabiting Mount L
9:15 and consume the cedars of L
1Ki 4:33 from the cedar that is in L
5:6 they cut for me cedars from L
5:9 down out of L to the sea
5:14 to L in shifts of ten
5:14 they would continue in L
7:2 the House of the Forest of L
9:19 build in Jerusalem and in L
10:17 House of the Forest of L
10:21 House of the Forest of L
2Ki 14:9 was in L sent to the cedar
14:9 the cedar that was in L
14:9 wild beast . . . in L passed by
19:23 The remotest parts of L
2Ch 2:8 juniper and almug from L, for
2:8 cutting down the trees of L
2:16 shall cut down trees from L
8:6 in L and in all the land of
9:16 House of the Forest of L
9:20 House of the Forest of L
25:18 weed itself that was in L
25:18 to the cedar that was in L
25:18 wild beast . . . that was in L
Ezr 3:7 bring cedar timbers from L to
Ps 29:5 breaks the cedars of L in
29:6 L and Sirion like the sons
72:16 His fruit will be as in L
92:12 As a cedar in L does, he
104:16 cedars of L that he planted
Ca 3:9 from the trees of L
4:8 With me from L, O bride, with
4:8 with me from L may you come
4:11 is like the fragrance of L
4:15 and trickling streams from L
5:15 His appearance is like L
7:4 nose is like the tower of L
Isa 2:13 cedars of L that are lofty
10:34 by a powerful one L itself
14:8 the cedars of L, saying
29:17 L must be turned into an
33:9 L has become abashed; it has
35:2 glory of L itself must be
37:24 The remotest parts of L
40:16 Even L is not sufficient
60:13 very glory of L will come
Jer 18:14 Will the snow of L go away
22:6 Gilead to me, the head of L
22:20 Go on up onto L and cry out
22:23 you who are dwelling in L
Eze 17:3 great eagle . . . came to L
27:5 A cedar from L they took to
31:3 An Assyrian, a cedar in L
31:15 I shall darken L, and on
31:16 choicest and the best of L
Ho 14:5 strike his roots like L
14:6 will be like that of L
14:7 will be like the wine of L
Na 1:4 very blossom of L has withered
Hab 2:17 the violence done to L is
Zec 10:10 to the land of Gilead and L
11:1 Open up your doors, O L

Lebaoth
Jos 15:32 L and Shilhim and Ain and

Leb-kamai
Jer 51:1 the inhabitants of L

Lebonah
Jg 21:19 and toward the south of L

Lecah
1Ch 4:21 Er the father of L and Laadah

Led
Ge 24:27 Jehovah has l me to the
24:48 l me in the true way to take
Ex 15:13 have l the people whom you
22:10 maimed or gets l off while
32:1 l us up out of the land of
32:4 who l you up out of the land
32:7 people whom you l up out of
32:8 l you up out of the land of
32:23 Moses, the man who l us up
33:1 people whom you l up out of
Le 8:14 he l up the bull of the sin
Nu 14:13 have l this people up out of
De 5:9 be l to serve them, because I
1Sa 30:16 he l him down, and there
2Sa 3:27 Joab now l him aside inside
2Ki 16:9 l its people into exile at
17:6 l Israel into exile in
17:27 whom you l into exile from
17:28 l into exile from Samaria
17:33 they had l them into exile
24:15 he l away as exiled people
Ne 9:12 by a pillar of cloud you l
9:18 God who l you up out of Egypt
Job 15:31 being l astray, For mere
Ps 77:20 l your people just like a
Isa 9:16 of them who are being l on
44:20 has l him astray. And he
47:10 this is what has l you away
63:14 l your people in order to
Jer 31:19 after my being l to know I
41:14 Ishmael had l captive from
50:6 they have l them away
La 3:2 It is I whom he has l and
Eze 13:10 have l my people astray
Mt 4:1 Jesus was l by the spirit up
26:57 l him away to Caiaphas the
27:2 they l him off and handed
27:31 and l him off for impaling
Mr 14:53 l Jesus away to the high
15:1 bound Jesus and l him off
15:16 l him off into the courtyard
15:20 l him out to impale him
Lu 4:1 l about by the spirit in the
4:9 he l him into Jerusalem and
4:29 l him to the brow of the
18:40 the man to be l to him
19:35 they l it to Jesus, and they
21:24 be l captive into all the
22:54 arrested him and l him off
23:1 and all, and l him to Pilate
23:26 as they l him away, they
23:32 l to be executed with him
24:50 l them out as far as Bethany
Joh 1:42 He l him to Jesus
9:13 l the once-blind man himself
18:13 they l him first to Annas
18:28 they l Jesus from Caiaphas
Ac 6:12 and l him to the Sanhedrin
7:36 l them out after doing
7:40 Moses, who l us out of the
8:39 spirit quickly l Philip away
9:8 they l him by the hand and
9:27 l him to the apostles, and
9:39 l him up into the upper
12:19 to be l off to punishment
17:19 and l him to the Areopagus
18:12 l him to the judgment seat
21:37 l into the soldiers' quarters
21:38 l the four thousand dagger
22:11 arrived in Damascus, being l
23:18 and l him to the military
26:4 I l from the beginning among
Ro 8:14 all who are l by God's spirit
12:16 l along with the lowly
1Co 12:2 you were being l away to
12:2 just as you happened to be l
2Co 8:6 This l us to encourage Titus
Ga 2:13 Barnabas was l along with
5:18 if you are being l by spirit
Php 2:17 to which faith has l you
1Ti 1:18 predictions that l directly
6:10 l astray from the faith and
2Ti 3:6 l by various desires
Heb 4:8 l them into a place of rest
2Pe 3:17 may not be l away with them

Ledge
Eze 43:14 the lower surrounding l

Eze 43:14 the small surrounding *l* to
43:14 to the big surrounding *l*
43:17 surrounding *l* is fourteen
43:20 corners of the surrounding *l*
45:19 *l* belonging to the altar

Ledges

Eze 40:43 *l* for setting down things

Leeches

Pr 30:15 *l* have two daughters that

Leeks

Nu 11:5 eat in Egypt . . . *l* and the

Left

Ge 11:8 *l* off building the city
13:9 If you go to the *l*, then I
13:9 then I will go to the *l*
24:27 not *l* his loving-kindness and
24:49 the right hand or to the *l*
29:35 she *l* off giving birth
30:9 she had *l* off giving birth
32:24 Jacob was *l* by himself
39:6 he *l* everything that was his
39:12 he *l* his garment in her hand
39:13 he had *l* his garment in her
39:15 he then *l* his garment beside
39:18 *l* his garment beside me and
42:38 he has been *l* by himself
44:20 he alone is *l* of his mother
48:13 his right hand to Israel's *l*
48:13 Manasseh by his *l* hand to
48:14 *l* hand upon Manasseh's head
50:8 they *l* in the land of Goshen
Ex 2:20 you have *l* the man behind
8:9 the Nile River will they be *l*
8:11 the Nile River will they be *l*
8:31 gadflies . . . Not one was *l*
9:21 *l* his servants and his
10:5 *l* to you people by the hail
10:15 eating up all . . . hail had *l*
10:15 *l* nothing green on the trees
12:10 what is *l* over of it till
14:22 right hand and on their *l*
14:29 right hand and on their *l*
23:11 what is *l* over by them the
29:34 bread should be *l* over until
29:34 burn what is *l* over with
Le 2:3 is *l* of the grain offering
2:10 what is *l* of the grain
6:16 And what is *l* of it Aaron and
7:16 what is *l* of it also may be
7:17 what is *l* of the flesh of the
8:32 what is *l* over of the flesh
10:12 his sons that were *l*
10:12 grain offering that was *l*
10:16 Aaron's sons that were *l*
14:15 upon the priest's *l* palm
14:16 oil that is upon his *l* palm
14:18 And what is *l* over of the oil
14:26 oil upon the priest's *l* palm
14:27 oil that is upon his *l* palm
14:29 what is *l* over of the oil
19:6 what is *l* over till the third
26:43 land was *l* abandoned by them
27:18 years that are *l* over until
Nu 20:17 toward the right or the *l*
22:26 aside to the right or the *l*
26:65 not *l* of them a man except
De 2:27 turn to the right or to the *l*
2:34 We *l* no survivor
3:11 what was *l* of the Rephaim
5:32 turn to the right or to the *l*
17:11 to the right or to the *l*
17:20 to the right or to the *l*
28:14 to the right or to the *l*
28:62 be *l* with very few in number
Jos 1:7 to the right or to the *l*
8:17 they *l* the city wide open
11:11 no breathing thing . . . *l*
11:22 No Anakim were *l* in the
12:4 was *l* over of the Rephaim
13:12 what was *l* of the Rephaim
17:2 *l* over according to their
17:6 sons of Manasseh who were *l*
18:2 *l* among the sons of Israel
19:27 went out to Cabul on the *l*
19:51 *l* off from apportioning the
21:5 sons of Kohath that were *l*
21:20 Levites who were *l* out of
21:26 sons of Kohath who were *l*
21:34 the Levites who were *l* out
21:40 who were *l* out from the
22:3 You have not *l* your brothers
23:6 to the right or to the *l*
Jos 23:12 do cleave to what is *l* of
Jg 2:21 nations that Joshua *l* behind
3:21 Ehud thrust in his *l* hand and
7:20 torches with their *l* hand and
8:10 *l* over out of the entire camp
9:5 was *l* over, because he had hid
10:6 So they *l* Jehovah and did not
10:10 have *l* our God and we serve
16:29 the other with his *l* hand
21:7 who are *l* over as to wives
21:16 that are *l* over as to wives
Ru 1:18 then she *l* off speaking to her
2:14 and yet had something *l* over
2:18 took out what food she had *l*
2:20 has not *l* his loving-kindness
1Sa 2:36 anyone *l* over in your house
5:4 Only the fish part had been *l*
6:12 to the right or to the *l*
11:11 to be some that were *l* over
11:11 not *l* over among them two
12:10 for we have *l* Jehovah that
15:15 what was *l* over we have
16:11 one has till now been *l* out
17:20 *l* the sheep to the keeper's
17:22 David *l* the baggage from
30:9 men that were to be *l* behind
30:13 master *l* me because I took
2Sa 2:19 the *l* from following Abner
2:21 or to your *l* and seize one
5:21 *l* their idols there, and so
9:1 *l* over of the house of Saul
13:30 not one . . . has been *l* over
14:19 or go to the *l* from all
15:16 and the king *l* ten women
16:6 at his right and at his *l*
16:21 *l* behind to take care of the
17:12 not be *l* even a single one
20:3 concubines whom he had *l*
1Ki 4:27 They *l* nothing lacking
7:39 on the *l* side of the house
7:47 Solomon *l* all the utensils
7:49 the right and five to the *l*
9:9 they *l* Jehovah their God
9:21 sons who had been *l* over
11:33 *l* me and begun to bow down
12:8 he *l* the counsel of the older
15:18 were *l* in the treasures of
17:17 was no breath *l* in him
18:18 *l* the commandments of
18:22 *l* as a prophet of Jehovah
19:3 he *l* his attendant behind
19:10 Israel have *l* your covenant
19:10 I only am *l*; and they begin
19:14 Israel have *l* your covenant
19:14 I only am *l*; and they begin
19:20 he *l* the bulls and went
20:30 those . . . *l* went fleeing
20:30 thousand men that were *l*
22:19 to his right and to his *l*
22:46 prostitutes that had been *l*
2Ki 3:25 they *l* only the stones of
4:7 should live from what is *l*
10:11 all who were *l* over of the
10:17 *l* over of Ahab's in Samaria
10:21 not a single one was *l* over
11:11 to the *l* side of the house
13:7 not *l* to Jehoahaz any people
19:30 of Judah, those who are *l*
20:17 Nothing will be *l*, Jehovah
21:22 he *l* Jehovah the God of his
22:2 to the right or to the *l*
22:17 they have *l* me and have
23:8 was at the *l* as a person
24:14 No one had been *l* behind
25:11 were *l* behind in the city
25:22 people *l* behind in the land
25:22 king of Babylon had *l*
1Ch 6:44 their brothers on the *l* hand
6:61 sons of Kohath that were *l*
6:70 sons of Kohath that were *l*
6:77 sons of Merari that were *l*
12:2 using the *l* hand with stones
13:2 our brothers that are *l* over
14:12 they *l* their gods there
16:37 he *l* there before the ark of
24:20 sons of Levi that were *l*
2Ch 3:17 to the right and one to the *l*
4:6 ten basins . . . five to the *l*
4:7 lampstands . . . five to the *l*
4:8 ten tables . . . five to the *l*
7:22 reason that they *l* Jehovah
8:7 people that were *l* over of
8:8 sons that had been *l* behind
10:8 *l* the counsel of the older
2Ch 10:13 Rehoboam *l* the counsel of
11:14 Levites *l* their pasture
12:1 *l* the law of Jehovah, and
12:5 for your part, have *l* me
12:5 *l* you to the hand of Shishak
13:10 God, and we have not *l* him
13:11 you yourselves have *l* him
18:18 at his right and his *l*
21:10 *l* Jehovah the God of his
21:17 *l* to him a son but Jehoahaz
23:10 to the *l* side of the house
24:18 *l* the house of Jehovah the
24:20 *l* Jehovah, he will, in turn
24:24 *l* Jehovah the God of their
24:25 *l* him with many diseases
28:14 armed men *l* the captives
29:6 *l* him and turned around
30:6 escaped ones that are *l* of
31:10 *l* over is this great plenty
32:31 God *l* him to put him to the
34:2 to the right or to the *l*
34:21 what is *l* in Israel and in
34:25 have *l* me and gone making
Ezr 1:4 anyone that is *l* from all the
9:9 our God has not *l* us, but he
9:10 we have *l* your commandments
9:15 we have been *l* over as an
Ne 1:2 been *l* over of the captivity
1:3 Those *l* over, who have been
1:3 been *l* over from the captivity
6:1 had not been *l* in it a gap
8:4 at his *l* Pedaiah and Mishael
Job 20:19 he has *l* lowly ones
20:21 nothing *l* over . . . to devour
22:20 And what is *l* of them a
23:9 To the *l* where he is working
30:11 the bridle they *l* loose on
Ps 22:1 my God, why have you *l* me?
37:25 not seen anyone righteous *l*
38:10 my power has *l* me
40:12 And my own heart *l* me
71:11 Saying: God himself has *l* him
106:11 Not one of them was *l*
Pr 2:21 ones that will be *l* over in
3:16 *l* hand there are riches and
4:27 to the right hand or to the *l*
Ec 10:2 heart of the stupid at his *l*
Ca 2:6 His *l* hand is under my head
8:3 *l* hand would be under my head
Isa 1:4 They have *l* Jehovah, they have
1:8 daughter of Zion has been *l*
1:9 *l* remaining to us just a few
4:3 ones *l* over in Jerusalem
7:16 dread will be *l* entirely
7:22 *l* remaining in the midst of
9:20 one will eat on the *l*, and
10:14 eggs that have been *l*
16:8 had been *l* to luxuriate
17:2 *l* behind become mere places
17:9 place *l* entirely in the
17:9 branch that they have *l*
18:6 *l* all together for the bird
24:12 condition has been *l* behind
27:10 pasture ground will be *l*
30:21 case you should go to the *l*
37:31 those who are *l* remaining
39:6 Nothing will be *l*, Jehovah
49:14 saying: Jehovah has *l* me
49:21 had been *l* behind alone
54:3 to the right and to the *l* you
54:6 wife *l* entirely and hurt in
54:7 I *l* you entirely, but with
58:2 not *l* the very justice of
60:15 one *l* entirely and hated
62:4 to be a woman *l* entirely
62:12 a City Not *L* Entirely
Jer 1:16 have *l* me and they keep
2:13 They have *l* even me, the
4:29 Every city is *l*, and there is
5:7 Your own sons have *l* me
5:19 *l* me and have gone serving
9:19 For we have *l* the land
12:7 I have *l* my house; I have
16:11 fact that your fathers *l* me
16:11 But me they *l*, and my law
17:13 *l* the source of living
19:4 reason that they have *l* me
22:9 *l* the covenant of Jehovah
25:38 *l* his covert just like a
32:11 and the one *l* open
32:14 and the other deed *l* open
34:7 Judah that were *l* remaining
38:4 the men of war who are *l*
38:22 *l* remaining in the house

Jer 39:9 people who were *l* remaining
39:9 people who were *l* remaining
40:6 *l* remaining in the land
42:2 we have been *l* remaining
49:12 be absolutely *l* unpunished
49:12 will not be *l* unpunished
52:15 people that were *l*
La 5:5 No rest has been *l* for us
Eze 1:10 had a bull's face on the *l*
4:4 lie upon your *l* side, and you
6:12 that has been *l* remaining
8:12 Jehovah has *l* the land
9:8 were striking and I was *l*
9:9 said, Jehovah has *l* the land
14:22 be *l* remaining in it an
16:46 who is dwelling on your *l*
17:21 ones *l* remaining will be
21:16 your position; go to the *l!*
24:21 you people have *l* behind
34:18 ones *l* over you should foul
36:36 the nations that will be *l*
39:3 your bow out of your *l* hand
39:14 *l* remaining on the surface
41:9 was a space *l* open by the
41:11 was to the space *l* open
41:11 space *l* open was five
48:15 *l* remaining in width
48:18 *l* remaining over in length
48:21 *l* over will belong to the
Da 7:7 what was *l* it was treading
7:19 what was *l* with its feet
10:8 I was *l* remaining by myself
10:8 *l* remaining in me no power
10:17 no breath at all was *l*
12:7 *l* hand to the heavens and to
Ho 4:10 *l* off paying regard to Jehovah
Joe 1:4 What was *l* by the caterpillar
1:4 and what was *l* by the locust
1:4 unwinged locust has *l*, the
Am 5:3 thousand will have a hundred *l*
5:3 a hundred will have ten *l*
6:9 if ten men should be *l*
9:12 what is *l* remaining of Edom
Jon 4:11 their right hand and their *l*
Zec 4:3 bowl and one on its *l* side
4:11 and on its *l* side mean
7:14 has been *l* desolate behind
9:7 be *l* remaining for our God
11:9 as for the ones *l* remaining
12:6 on the *l* all the peoples
12:14 the families that are *l*
13:8 it will be *l* remaining in it
14:16 *l* remaining out of all the
Mt 4:11 the Devil *l* him, and, look!
6:3 do not let your *l* hand know
8:15 and the fever *l* her, and she
13:1 Jesus, having *l* the house
13:25 in among the wheat, and *l*
19:27 We have *l* all things and
19:29 everyone that has *l* houses
20:21 and one at your *l*, in your
20:23 my right hand and at my *l*
22:25 *l* his wife for his brother
24:2 no means will a stone be *l*
25:33 but the goats on his *l*
25:41 to those on his *l*, Be on
27:38 two robbers . . . one on his *l*
27:60 of the memorial tomb, he *l*
Mr 1:20 they *l* their father Zebedee
1:31 fever *l* her, and she began
1:35 and *l* for a lonely place, and
8:13 he *l* them, got aboard again
8:27 now *l* for the villages of
10:28 We *l* all things and have
10:29 No one has *l* house or
10:37 and one at your *l*, in your
10:40 down at my right or at my *l*
12:12 So they *l* him and went away
12:20 died he *l* no offspring
13:2 stone be *l* here upon a stone
13:34 *l* his house and gave the
14:52 *l* his linen garment behind
15:27 his right and one on his *l*
Lu 4:39 rebuked the fever, and it *l*
10:40 my sister has *l* me alone to
18:28 have *l* our own things and
18:29 no one who has *l* house or
21:6 stone upon a stone will be *l*
23:33 on his right and one on his *l*
Joh 4:3 he *l* Judea and departed again
4:28 *l* her water jar and went
4:43 he *l* there for Galilee
4:52 seventh hour the fever *l* him
6:13 *l* over by those who had
Joh 6:22 only his disciples had *l*
Ac 10:7 angel that spoke to him had *l*
14:20 he *l* with Barnabas for Derbe
16:19 that their hope of gain had *l*
18:19 at Ephesus, and he *l* them
19:12 and the diseases *l* them, and
21:3 Cyprus we *l* it behind on the
21:3 Cyprus . . . on the *l* side
24:27 Felix . . . *l* Paul bound
25:14 man *l* prisoner by Felix
Ro 1:27 males *l* the natural use of
9:29 had *l* a seed to us, we should
11:3 I alone am *l*, and they are
11:4 I have *l* seven thousand men
1Co 7:29 the time *l* is reduced
2Co 4:9 persecuted, but not *l* in the
6:7 on the right hand and on the *l*
1Th 3:1 to be *l* alone in Athens
1Ti 5:5 a widow and *l* destitute has
2Ti 4:13 bring the cloak I *l* at Troas
4:20 *l* Trophimus sick at Miletus
Tit 1:5 this reason I *l* you in Crete
Heb 2:8 *l* nothing that is not subject
4:1 promise is *l* of entering into
6:1 *l* the primary doctrine about
10:26 any sacrifice for sins *l*
11:27 By faith he *l* Egypt, but
Re 2:4 *l* the love you had at first
10:2 but his *l* one upon the earth

Left-hand
1Ki 7:21 set up the *l* pillar and
2Ch 3:17 the name of the *l* one Boaz

Left-handed
Jg 3:15 Gera, a Benjamite, a *l* man
20:16 seven hundred chosen men *l*

Leftovers
Le 19:10 not gather the *l* of your
De 24:21 you must not gather the *l*
2Ki 4:43 an eating and a having of *l*
4:44 began to eat, and they had *l*
Isa 15:7 *l* and their stored goods that

Leg
Ex 29:22 the right *l*, for it is a ram
29:27 *l* of the sacred portion that
Le 7:32 give the right *l* as a sacred
7:33 the right *l* will become his
7:34 the *l* of the sacred portion
8:25 and their fat and the right *l*
8:26 fatty pieces and the right *l*
9:21 right *l* Aaron waved to and
10:14 the *l* of the sacred portion
10:15 the *l* of the sacred portion
Nu 6:20 and the *l* of the contribution
18:18 like the right *l*, it should
1Sa 9:24 the cook lifted off the *l* and
Isa 47:2 Uncover the *l*. Cross over the

Legal
De 17:8 a *l* claim has been raised
Jg 6:31 make a *l* defense for Baal to
6:31 Whoever makes a *l* defense for
6:31 let him make a *l* defense for
6:32 make a *l* defense in his own
21:22 conduct a *l* case against us
1Sa 24:15 conduct the *l* case for me
25:39 *l* case of my reproach to
2Sa 15:2 a *l* case to come to the king
15:4 have a *l* case or judgment
2Ch 19:8 *l* cases of the inhabitants
19:10 every *l* case that will come
Es 1:13 versed in law and *l* cases
Job 29:16 the *l* case of one whom I
35:14 The *l* case is before him
Ps 43:1 *l* case against a nation not
76:8 the *l* contest to be heard
119:154 do conduct my *l* case and
140:12 *l* claim of the afflicted
Pr 18:17 one first in his *l* case is
22:10 *l* contest and dishonor may
25:8 to conduct a *l* case hastily
29:7 the *l* claim of the lowly ones
Isa 1:23 *l* case of a widow does not
10:2 lowly ones from a *l* case and
34:8 for the *l* case over Zion
Jer 5:28 No *l* case have they pleaded
5:28 *l* case of the fatherless boy
22:16 *l* claim of the afflicted
50:34 conduct their *l* case, in
51:36 I am conducting your *l* case
La 3:36 a man crooked in his *l* case
Eze 21:27 comes who has the *l* right
44:24 And in a *l* case they
Ho 2:2 Carry on a *l* case with your
Ho 2:2 carry on a *l* case, for she is
4:1 Jehovah has a *l* case with the
12:2 has a *l* case with Judah
Mic 6:1 conduct a *l* case with the
6:2 the *l* case of Jehovah, also
6:2 Jehovah has a *l* case with
7:9 until he conducts my *l* case
Lu 1:6 and *l* requirements of Jehovah
Heb 6:16 it is a *l* guarantee to them
9:10 *l* requirements pertaining to

Legally
Php 1:7 *l* establishing of the good
Heb 8:6 been *l* established upon better

Legion
Mr 5:9 My name is *L*, because there
5:15 this man that had had the *l*
Lu 8:30 What is your name? He said: *L*

Legions
Mt 26:53 than twelve *l* of angels

Legs
Le 11:21 leaper *l* above their feet
11:23 four *l* is a loathsome thing
De 28:35 upon both knees and both *l*
28:57 out from between her *l*
Jg 15:8 piling *l* upon thighs with a
Ps 147:10 in the *l* of the man does he
Pr 26:7 *l* of the lame one drawn up
Ca 5:15 His *l* are pillars of marble
Da 2:33 *l* were of iron, its feet
Joh 19:31 to have their *l* broken and
19:32 broke the *l* of the first
19:33 they did not break his *l*

Lehabim
Ge 10:13 Mizraim became father . . . *L*
1Ch 1:11 Ludim and Anamim and *L*

Lehi
Jg 15:9 and went tramping about in *L*
15:14 came as far as *L*, and the
15:19 hollow that was in *L*, and
15:19 in *L* down to this day
2Sa 23:11 to gather themselves to *L*

Leisure
Ge 33:14 continue the journey at my *l*
Mr 6:31 no *l* time even to eat a meal
Ac 17:21 their *l* time at nothing but

Leisurely
De 33:25 to your days is your *l* walk

Lemuel
Pr 31:1 The words of *L* the king, the
31:4 O *L*, it is not for kings to

Lend
Ex 22:25 *l* money to my people, to the
De 15:6 *l* on pledge to many nations
15:8 *l* him on pledge as much as he
24:10 In case you *l* your fellowman
28:12 certainly *l* to many nations
28:44 He will be the one to *l* to you
28:44 you will not *l* to him
Joe 3:11 *L* your aid and come, all
Lu 6:34 if you *l* without interest to
6:34 sinners *l* without interest
6:35 *l* without interest, not

Lender
Isa 24:2 the *l* as for the borrower
Lu 7:41 were debtors to a certain *l*

Lending
Ne 5:10 leave off this *l* on interest
Ps 37:26 he is showing favor and *l*
112:5 who is gracious and is *l*
Pr 19:17 is *l* to Jehovah, and his
22:7 to the man doing the *l*

Length
Ge 6:15 three hundred cubits the *l*
13:17 land through its *l* and
35:27 At *l* Jacob came to Isaac his
42:29 At *l* they came to Jacob
45:25 at *l* came into the land of
50:24 At *l* Joseph said to his
Ex 3:1 he came at *l* to the mountain
14:22 At *l* the sons of Israel went
24:16 At *l* on the seventh day he
25:10 two and a half cubits its *l*
25:17 two and a half cubits its *l*
25:23 two cubits its *l* and a cubit
26:2 The *l* of each tent cloth is
26:8 *l* of each tent cloth is thirty
26:13 *l* of the cloths of the tent
26:16 is the *l* of a panel frame

Ex 27:1 five cubits its *l* and five
27:9 a hundred cubits being the *l*
27:11 it is for the north side in *l*
27:11 for a hundred cubits of *l*
27:18 The *l* of the courtyard is a
28:16 being its *l* and a span of the
30:2 A cubit in *l* and a cubit in
36:9 *l* of each tent cloth was
36:15 *l* of each tent cloth was
36:21 was the *l* of a panel frame
37:1 cubits and a half was its *l*
37:6 cubits and a half was its *l*
37:10 Two cubits was its *l*, and a
37:25 A cubit was its *l* and a
38:1 Five cubits was its *l*, and
38:18 and twenty cubits was the *l*
39:9 a span of the hand in its *l*
De 3:11 Nine cubits is its *l*, and four
30:20 life and the *l* of your days
34:8 At *l* the days of weeping of
Jos 9:13 the great *l* of the journey
Jg 3:16 its *l* being a cubit. Then he
17:8 At *l* while going his way he
18:8 At *l* they came to their
1Sa 10:13 At *l* he finished speaking as
15:13 At *l* Samuel came to Saul
19:1 At *l* Saul spoke to Jonathan
21:10 at *l* came to Achish the
24:3 At *l* he came to the stone
28:20 his full *l* to the earth
30:21 At *l* David came to the two
2Sa 2:20 At *l* Abner looked behind
16:14 At *l* the king and all the
18:24 At *l* he raised his eyes and
21:11 At *l* it was reported to
1Ki 6:2 was sixty cubits in its *l*
6:3 was twenty cubits in its *l*
6:20 was twenty cubits in *l*, and
7:2 a hundred cubits in its *l*
7:6 made fifty cubits in its *l*
7:27 being the *l* of each carriage
7:40 At *l* Hiram finished doing
18:30 At *l* Elijah said to all the
19:4 at *l* came and sat down
2Ki 3:10 At *l* the king of Israel said
4:9 At *l* she said to her husband
9:30 At *l* Jehu came to Jezreel
14:19 At *l* they leagued against
15:7 At *l* Azariah lay down with
24:12 At *l* Jehoiachin the king of
2Ch 3:3 the *l* in cubits by the former
3:4 that was in front of the *l*
3:8 *l* in relation to the width
3:11 their *l* was twenty cubits
3:15 thirty-five cubits in *l*, and
4:1 twenty cubits being its *l*
6:13 Its *l* was five cubits, and
9:1 At *l* she came in to Solomon
25:27 At *l* he fled to Lachish
Ezr 7:8 At *l* he came to Jerusalem in
10:10 At *l* Ezra the priest rose
Ne 2:11 At *l* I came to Jerusalem
6:15 At *l* the wall came to
12:40 At *l* the two thanksgiving
Es 6:2 At *l* there was found written
Job 12:12 understanding in *l* of days
Ps 21:4 *L* of days to time indefinite
23:6 I will dwell . . . to the *l* of days
91:16 *l* of days I shall satisfy
93:5 Jehovah, for *l* of days
Pr 3:2 *l* of days and years of life
3:16 *L* of days is in its right
Jer 52:31 At *l* it came about in the
La 5:20 you leave us for the *l* of days
Eze 31:7 in the *l* of its foliage
33:21 At *l* it occurred in the
40:7 chamber was one reed in *l*
40:11 *l* of the gate, thirteen
40:18 as the *l* of the gates
40:20 its *l* and its width
40:21 Fifty cubits was its *l*
40:25 Fifty cubits was the *l*
40:29 Fifty cubits was the *l*
40:30 *l* was twenty-five cubits
40:33 The *l* was fifty cubits
40:36 The *l* was fifty cubits, and
40:42 *l* was one cubit and a half
40:47 The *l* was a hundred cubits
40:49 *l* of the porch was twenty
41:2 he went measuring its *l*
41:4 its *l*, twenty cubits
41:12 and its *l* was ninety cubits
41:13 house, a hundred cubits in *l*
41:13 a hundred cubits in *l*
Eze 41:15 the *l* of the building
41:22 its *l* was two cubits
41:22 *l* and its walls were of
42:2 the *l* of a hundred cubits
42:7 Its *l* was fifty cubits
42:8 the *l* of the dining rooms
42:11 so their *l* was and so their
42:20 *l* of five hundred reeds and
43:16 hearth is twelve cubits in *l*
43:17 is fourteen cubits in *l*
45:1 out of the land; as to *l*
45:1 thousand cubits in *l*
45:3 *l* of twenty-five thousand
45:5 twenty-five thousand in *l*
45:6 *l* of twenty-five thousand
45:7 *l* will be exactly as one
46:22 forty cubits in *l* and
48:8 *l* according to one of the
48:9 *l* will be twenty-five
48:10 south a *l* of twenty-five
48:13 thousand cubits in *l*, and
48:13 *l* being twenty-five thousand
48:18 left remaining over in *l*
Jon 1:6 At *l* the ship captain came
Zec 2:2 and what her *l* amounts to
5:2 *l* of which is twenty cubits
11:9 At *l* I said: I shall not keep
Lu 22:14 At *l* when the hour came
22:66 At *l* when it became day, the
Joh 19:23 the top throughout its *l*
Ac 20:11 he at *l* departed
Eph 3:18 what is the breadth and *l*
1Th 2:16 his wrath has at *l* come upon
Re 21:16 *l* is as great as its breadth
21:16 *l* and breadth and height are

Lengthen
De 4:26 You will not *l* your days on
4:40 may *l* your days on the soil
5:33 *l* your days in the land of
11:9 *l* your days on the soil that
17:20 that he may *l* his days upon
22:7 you may indeed *l* your days
30:18 You will not *l* your days on
32:47 you may *l* your days upon the
1Ki 3:14 I will also *l* your days
Isa 54:2 *L* out your tent cords, and

Lengthened
Ps 129:3 They have *l* their furrows

Lengthening
Da 4:27 occur a *l* of your prosperity
7:12 *l* in life given to them for

Lent
1Sa 1:28 I . . . have *l* him to Jehovah
2:20 in place of the thing *l*, that
2:20 that was *l* to Jehovah

Lentil
Ge 25:34 Jacob gave Esau bread and *l*

Lentils
2Sa 17:28 and *l* and parched grain
23:11 tract of the field full of *l*
Eze 4:9 *l* and millet and spelt, and

Leopard
Isa 11:6 kid the *l* itself will lie
30:6 the lion and the *l* growling
Jer 5:6 a *l* is keeping awake at their
13:23 his skin? or a *l* its spots
Da 7:6 beast, one like a *l*, but it
Ho 13:7 Like a *l* by the way I shall
Re 13:2 beast that I saw was like a *l*

Leopards
Ca 4:8 from the mountains of *l*
Hab 1:8 have proved swifter than *l*

Leper
Le 13:44 he is a *l*. He is unclean
14:2 law of the *l* in the day for
2Sa 3:29 or a *l* or a man taking hold
2Ki 5:1 mighty man, though a *l*
5:11 actually give the *l* recovery
5:27 a *l* white as snow
15:5 *l* until the day of his death
2Ch 26:21 *l* until the day of his death
26:21 exempt from duties, as a *l*
26:23 they said: He is a *l*
Mt 26:6 in the house of Simon the *l*
Mr 1:40 There also came to him a *l*
14:3 in the house of Simon the *l*

Lepers
2Ki 7:3 And there were four men, *l*
7:8 these *l* came as far as the
Mt 10:8 make *l* clean, expel demons
11:5 the *l* are being cleansed and
Lu 4:27 there were many *l* in Israel
7:22 the *l* are being cleansed and

Leprosy
Ex 4:6 his hand was stricken with *l*
Le 13:2 flesh into the plague of *l*
13:3 it is the plague of *l*
13:8 scab has spread . . . It is *l*
13:9 plague of *l* develops in a man
13:11 it is chronic *l* in the skin
13:12 *l* unquestionably breaks out
13:12 the *l* does cover all the skin
13:13 *l* has covered all his flesh
13:15 flesh is unclean. It is *l*
13:20 It is the plague of *l*. It has
13:25 deeper than the skin, it is *l*
13:25 It is the plague of *l*
13:27 It is the plague of *l*
13:30 is *l* of the head or of the
13:42 it is *l* breaking out in the
13:43 *l* in the skin of the flesh
13:47 plague of *l* develops in it
13:49 it is the plague of *l*, and
13:51 the plague is malignant *l*
13:52 it is malignant *l*. It should
13:59 plague of *l* in a garment of
14:3 plague of *l* has been cured in
14:7 cleansing himself from the *l*
14:32 in whom the plague of *l* was
14:34 plague of *l* in a house of
14:44 is malignant *l* in the house
14:54 respecting any plague of *l*
14:55 *l* of the garment and in the
14:57 This is the law about *l*
Nu 12:10 Miriam was struck with *l* as
12:10 look! she was struck with *l*
De 24:8 guard in the plague of *l* to
2Ki 5:3 recover him from his *l*
5:6 may recover him from his *l*
5:7 to recover a man from his *l*
5:27 *l* of Naaman will stick to
2Ch 26:19 *l* itself flashed up in his
26:20 with *l* in his forehead
Mt 8:3 his *l* was cleansed away
Mr 1:42 immediately the *l* vanished
Lu 5:12 look! a man full of *l*
5:13 the *l* vanished from him

Leprous
Le 13:45 As for the *l* one in whom the
14:3 has been cured in the *l* one
22:4 *l* or has a running discharge
Nu 5:2 out of the camp every *l* person
Mt 8:2 a *l* man came up and began
Lu 17:12 ten *l* men met him, but

Leshem
Ex 28:19 the third row is *l* stone
39:12 third row was *l* stone, agate
Jos 19:47 to go up and war against *L*
19:47 they began to call *L* Dan

Less
Ex 30:15 give *l* than the half shekel
1Ki 8:27 how much *l*, then, this house
2Ch 6:18 much *l*, then, this house
32:15 How much *l*, then, will your
Job 15:16 *l* so when one is detestable
25:6 How much *l* so mortal man
35:14 How much *l*, then, when you
Ps 8:5 a little *l* than godlike ones
Pr 17:7 How much *l* so for a noble the
19:10 *l* for a servant to rule over
Eze 15:5 How much *l* so, when fire
Mr 15:40 the mother of James the *L*
1Co 12:23 we think to be *l* honorable
2Co 11:24 forty strokes *l* one
12:13 you became *l* than the rest
12:15 am I to be loved the *l*?
Eph 3:8 a man *l* than the least of
1Ti 5:9 not *l* than sixty years old
Heb 7:7 *l* is blessed by the greater

Lessening
Ge 8:5 waters kept on progressively *l*

Lesser
Ge 1:16 *l* luminary for dominating the
Ezr 4:9 the judges and the *l* governors
5:6 the *l* governors that were
6:6 *l* governors that are beyond
Mt 11:11 *l* one in the kingdom of the
Lu 7:28 a *l* one in the kingdom of God
9:48 conducts himself as a *l* one

Lesson
Mt 6:28 Take a *l* from the lilies of

Let
Ge 1:3 *L* light come to be. Then there
1:6 *L* an expanse come to be in
1:6 *l* a dividing occur between
1:9 *L* the waters under the heavens
1:9 and *l* the dry land appear
1:11 *L* the earth cause grass to
1:14 *L* luminaries come to be in
1:20 *L* the waters swarm forth a
1:20 *l* flying creatures fly over
1:22 *l* the flying creatures become
1:24 *L* the earth put forth living
1:26 *L* us make man in our image
1:26 *l* them have in subjection
1:29 To you *l* it serve as food
4:8 *L* us go over into the field
9:25 *L* him become the lowest
9:26 *l* Canaan become a slave to
9:27 *L* God grant ample space to
9:27 *l* him reside in the tents of
9:27 *L* Canaan become a slave to
11:3 *L* us make bricks and bake
11:4 *L* us build ourselves a city
11:4 *l* us make a celebrated name
11:7 Come now! *L* us go down and
13:8 not *l* any quarreling continue
14:24 *l* them take their share
18:4 *L* a little water be taken
18:5 *l* me get a piece of bread
18:30 but *l* me go on speaking
18:32 *l* me speak just this once
19:8 *l* me bring them out to you
19:32 *l* us give our father wine to
19:32 *l* us lie down with him and
19:34 *L* us give him wine to drink
19:34 *l* us preserve offspring from
21:12 Do not *l* anything that Sarah
21:16 *L* me not see it when the
23:9 *l* him give it to me in the
24:14 *L* your water jar down
24:14 *l* me know that you have
24:43 *l* me drink a little water
24:51 *l* her become a wife to the
24:55 *L* the young woman stay with
24:57 *L* us call the young woman
24:60 *l* your seed take possession
25:21 *l* himself be entreated for
26:28 *L*, please, an oath of
26:28 *l* us conclude a covenant
27:4 ah, *l* me eat, in order that
27:7 *l* me eat, that I may bless
27:29 *L* peoples serve you and
27:29 *l* national groups bow low to
27:29 *l* the sons of your mother
27:31 *L* my father get up and eat
29:21 *l* me have relations with her
30:34 *L* it be according to your
31:32 *l* him not live. Before our
31:35 Do not *l* anger gleam in the
31:37 *l* them decide between us
31:44 *l* us conclude a covenant, I
31:49 *L* Jehovah keep watch between
31:53 *L* the god of Abraham and the
32:26 After that he said: *L* me go
32:26 I am not going to *l* you go
33:9 *L* continue yours what is
33:12 *L* us pull out and go, and
33:12 *l* me go in advance of you
33:14 *L* my lord, please, pass on
33:15 Esau said: *L* me, please, put
33:15 *L* me find favor in the eyes
34:11 *L* me find favor in your eyes
34:21 *l* them dwell in the land and
34:23 *l* us give them our consent
35:3 *l* us rise and go up to Bethel
37:13 *l* me send you to them
37:17 *L* us go to Dothan. So Joseph
37:20 come and *l* us kill him and
37:20 *l* us see what will become
37:21 *L* us not strike his soul
37:27 *l* us sell him to the
37:27 do not *l* our hand be upon
38:23 *L* her take them for herself
38:24 and *l* her be burned
41:33 *l* Pharaoh look for a man
41:34 *L* Pharaoh act and appoint
41:35 And *l* them collect all the
41:35 *l* them pile up grain under
42:19 *l* one of your brothers be
44:9 *L* the one of your slaves with
44:9 *l* us ourselves also become
Ge 44:10 he said: *L* it be now exactly
44:11 *l* down each one his bag to
44:18 *l* your slave speak a word
44:18 do not *l* your anger grow hot
44:33 *l* your slave stay instead
45:20 do not *l* your eye feel sorry
45:28 *l* me go and see him before I
46:31 *L* me go up and report to
47:4 *l* your servants dwell, please
47:6 *L* them dwell in the land of
47:25 *L* us find favor in the eyes
48:11 *l* me see also your offspring
48:16 *l* my name be called upon
48:16 And *l* them increase to a
48:20 *l* Israel repeatedly pronounce
49:7 *L* me parcel them out in Jacob
49:7 *l* me scatter them in Israel
49:17 *L* Dan prove to be a serpent
50:5 *l* me go up and bury my father
Ex 1:10 *L* us deal shrewdly with them
3:3 Moses said: *L* me just turn
3:10 *l* me send you to Pharaoh, and
4:21 *l* his heart become obstinate
4:26 Consequently he *l* go of him
5:7 *L* them . . . go and gather straw
5:9 *L* the service be heavy upon the
5:9 and *l* them work at it
5:9 *l* them not pay attention to
7:3 shall *l* Pharaoh's heart become
8:29 *l* not Pharaoh trifle again in
9:12 Jehovah *l* Pharaoh's heart
10:1 I have *l* his heart and the
10:10 *L* it prove to be so, that
10:12 that the hail has *l* remain
10:19 Not a single locust was *l*
10:20 Jehovah *l* Pharaoh's heart
10:27 Jehovah *l* Pharaoh's heart
11:10 *l* Pharaoh's heart become
12:48 *l* there be a circumcising of
13:3 *L* there be a remembering of
14:4 *l* Pharaoh's heart become
14:8 Jehovah *l* the heart of Pharaoh
14:12 *L* us alone, that we may
14:25 *L* us flee from any contact
14:28 among them was *l* remain
15:1 *L* me sing to Jehovah, for he
16:19 *L* nobody leave any of it
16:29 *L* nobody go out from his
17:11 as he would *l* down his hand
19:22 And *l* the priests also who
19:24 but *l* not the priests and the
20:19 speak . . . and *l* us listen
20:19 *l* not God speak with us for
23:11 and you must *l* it lie fallow
24:14 at law, *l* him approach them
32:10 now *l* me be, that my anger
32:10 *l* me make you into a great
32:22 not *l* the anger of my lord
32:25 *l* them go unrestrained for a
33:12 have not *l* me know whom you
34:3 *l* nobody else be seen in all
34:9 *l* Jehovah, please, go along
35:5 *L* every willing-hearted one
35:10 *l* all the wise-hearted ones
Le 10:3 to me *l* me be sanctified
10:3 the people *l* me be glorified
10:6 not *l* your heads go ungroomed
21:10 *l* his head go ungroomed, and
26:23 not *l* yourselves be corrected
Nu 4:18 not *l* the tribe of the
9:8 *l* me hear what Jehovah may
9:12 not *l* any of it remain until
10:35 *l* your enemies be scattered
10:35 *l* those who intensely hate
11:13 give us meat, and *l* us eat!
11:15 *l* me not look upon my
12:12 do not *l* her continue like
12:14 *L* her be quarantined seven
12:14 *l* her be received in
13:30 *L* us go up directly, and we
14:4 *L* us appoint a head, and
14:4 and *l* us return to Egypt!
14:12 *L* me strike them with
14:12 *l* me make you a nation
14:17 *l* your power become great, O
20:17 *L* us pass, please, through
21:16 and *l* me give them water
21:22 *L* me pass through your land
21:27 *L* the city of Sihon be built
21:30 So *l* us shoot at them
22:13 refused to *l* me go with you
22:34 *l* me go my way back
23:3 Station yourself . . . *l* me go
23:10 *L* my soul die the death of
Nu 23:10 *l* my end turn out afterward
23:15 *l* me get in touch with him
23:27 *L* me take you to still
24:14 *l* me advise you what this
25:17 *L* there be a harassing of the
27:16 *L* Jehovah the God of the
31:50 *l* us present each one what
32:5 *l* this land be given to your
32:15 *l* them stay longer in the
32:16 *L* us build here stone flock
De 1:22 Do *l* us send men ahead of us
2:27 *L* me pass through your land
2:28 *l* me pass through on my feet
2:30 king of Heshbon did not *l* us
2:30 *l* his spirit become obstinate
3:25 *L* me pass over, please, and
4:10 *l* them hear my words, that
4:27 be *l* remain few in number
5:31 *l* me speak to you all the
7:20 who were *l* remain and who
8:3 *l* you go hungry and fed you
9:14 *L* me alone that I may
9:14 and *l* me make you a nation
12:20 *L* me eat meat, because your
13:2 *L* us walk after other gods
13:2 and *l* us serve them
13:6 *L* us go and serve other gods
13:13 *L* us go and serve other gods
15:2 debt that he may *l* his fellow
15:3 *l* your hand release
16:1 *L* there be an observing of
17:14 *L* me set a king over myself
18:16 Do not *l* me hear again the
18:16 fire do not *l* me see anymore
20:3 Do not *l* your hearts be timid
20:5 *L* him go and return to his
20:6 *L* him go and return to his
20:7 *L* him go and return to his
20:8 *L* him go and return to his
28:51 *l* no grain, new wine or oil
30:12 he may *l* us hear it that we
30:13 that he may *l* us hear it
31:28 *l* me speak in their hearing
31:28 *l* me take the heavens
32:1 O heavens, and *l* me speak
32:1 *l* the earth hear the sayings
32:20 *L* me conceal my face from
32:20 *L* me see what their end will
32:38 *L* them get up and help you
32:38 *L* them become a concealment
33:6 *L* Reuben live and not die off
33:6 And *l* his men not become few
33:10 *L* them instruct Jacob in
33:10 *L* them render up incense
33:12 *L* the beloved one of Jehovah
33:24 *L* him become one approved by
33:28 his heavens will *l* the dew
Jos 1:13 *L* there be a remembering of
2:21 to your words so *l* it be
3:4 *l* there prove to be a distance
4:22 *l* your sons know, saying
5:6 never *l* them see the land
6:10 nor *l* your voices be heard
6:26 *l* him lay the foundation of
6:26 *l* him put up its doors
7:3 *L* not all the people go up
7:3 *L* about two thousand men or
9:15 covenant with them to *l* them
9:21 said to them: *L* them live
9:21 *l* them become gatherers of
10:4 *l* us strike Gibeon, because
10:6 not *l* your hand relax from
10:28 He *l* no survivor remain
10:30 did not *l* a survivor remain
10:33 *l* not a survivor of his
10:37 did not *l* a survivor remain
10:39 did not *l* a survivor remain
10:40 did not *l* a survivor remain
11:8 not *l* a survivor of theirs
11:14 not *l* anyone that breathed
11:20 to *l* their hearts become
18:4 *l* me send them out, that
18:4 and *l* them come to me
22:26 *L* us take action in our
Jg 1:3 and *l* us fight against the
1:25 all his family they *l* go
2:23 Jehovah *l* these nations stay
3:1 that Jehovah *l* stay so as by
3:12 Jehovah *l* Eglon the king of
5:31 *l* all your enemies perish, O
5:31 *l* your lovers be as when the
6:4 would not *l* any sustenance or
6:31 *l* him make a legal defense
6:32 *L* Baal make a legal defense

Jg 6:39 Do not *l* your anger blaze
6:39 but *l* me speak just once more
6:39 *L* me, please, make a test
6:39 *L*, please, dryness occur to
6:39 earth *l* there come to be dew
7:3 *L* him retire. So Gideon put
7:7 *l* them go each one to his
8:24 *L* me make a request of you
9:7 and *l* God listen to you
9:15 if not, *l* fire come out of
9:19 *l* him too rejoice over you
9:20 *l* fire come out of Abimelech
9:20 and *l* fire come out of the
9:23 God *l* develop a bad spirit
10:14 *L* them be the ones to save
10:18 *L* him become the head of all
11:6 *l* us fight against the sons of
11:10 *L* Jehovah prove to be the
11:17 *L* me pass, please, through
11:19 *L* us pass, please, through
11:27 *L* Jehovah the Judge judge
11:37 *L* this thing be done to me
11:37 *L* me alone for two months
11:37 *l* me go, and I will descend
11:37 *l* me weep over my virginity
12:5 *L* me pass over, then the men
13:8 *l* him, please, come again to
13:12 Now *l* your words come true
13:14 no wine . . . *l* her drink, and
13:14 of any sort *l* her eat
13:14 commanded her *l* her keep
13:15 *L* us, please, detain you and
13:23 not as now have *l* us hear
14:12 *L* me, please, propound a
14:13 your riddle, and *l* us hear it
15:2 *L* her, please, become yours
16:26 and *l* me lean against them
16:28 *l* me avenge myself upon the
16:30 *L* my soul die with the
18:9 *l* us go up against them
18:25 Do not *l* your voice be heard
19:6 and *l* your heart feel good
19:9 and *l* your heart feel good
19:11 *l* us turn aside to this city
19:12 *L* us not turn aside to a city
19:13 and *l* us approach one of the
19:20 *l* any lack of yours be upon
19:24 *L* me bring them out, please
19:28 Rise up, and *l* us go
20:9 *L* us go up by lot against it
20:13 *l* us clear out what is bad
20:32 *L* us flee, and we shall
21:5 *L* him be put to death without
Ru 2:2 *L* me go, please, to the field
2:7 *L* me glean, please, and I
2:9 *L* your eyes be on the field
2:13 *L* me find favor in your eyes
2:15 *L* her glean also among the
3:13 *L* him do the repurchasing
3:14 Do not *l* it be known that a
4:14 not *l* a repurchaser fail for
1Sa 1:18 *L* your maidservant find
2:3 *L* nothing go forth
2:16 *L* them be sure to make the
3:18 is good in his eyes *l* him do
4:3 *L* us take to ourselves from
5:7 not *l* the ark of the God of
5:8 Toward Gath *l* the ark of the
6:2 *L* us know with what we
9:5 *l* us return, that my father
9:6 *L* us go there now. Perhaps he
9:9 Come, and *l* us go to the seer
9:10 Do come, *l* us go. And they
9:27 *l* you hear the word of God
10:8 *l* you know what you should
10:24 and say: *L* the king live!
11:14 Come and *l* us go to Gilgal
13:3 saying: *L* the Hebrews hear!
14:1 come and *l* us cross over to
14:6 come and *l* us cross over to
14:8 *l* us expose ourselves to
14:12 we will *l* you know a thing
14:36 Saul said: *L* us go down
14:36 *l* us not leave a single one
14:36 *L* us approach here to the
14:43 Here I am! *L* me die!
16:16 *L* our lord, please, command
16:22 *L* David, please, keep
17:8 and *l* him come down to me
17:10 and *l* us fight together
17:32 not *l* the heart of any man
18:17 Do not *l* my hand come to be
18:17 but *l* the hand of the
19:4 not *l* the king sin against
1Sa 20:3 not *l* Jonathan know this for
20:11 *l* us go out into the field
20:29 *l* me slip away, please
21:2 *L* no one know anything at
21:13 *l* his saliva run down upon
22:3 *L* my father and my mother
22:15 Do not *l* the king lay
25:22 *l* anyone of all who are his
25:24 *l* your slave girl speak in
25:25 *l* my lord set his heart
25:26 *l* your enemies and those
25:31 *l* this not become to you a
26:8 *l* me, please, pin him to the
26:11 and *l* us get on our way
26:19 *l* my lord the king, please
26:19 *l* him smell a grain
26:20 not *l* my blood fall to the
26:22 *l* one of the young men come
27:5 *l* them give me a place in
28:15 calling you to *l* me know
28:22 *l* me set before you a piece
29:4 *l* him go back to his place
29:4 *l* him go down with us into
29:9 *L* him not go up with us
30:22 *l* them lead them and go
2Sa 1:21 *l* no dew . . . be upon you
1:21 *l* no rain be upon you, nor
1:21 nor *l* there be fields of holy
2:7 now *l* your hands strengthen
2:14 *L* the young men rise up
2:14 *l* them put on a combat
2:14 Joab said: *L* them rise up
3:8 *l* you find yourself in the
3:21 *L* me rise up and go and
3:29 *l* there not be cut off from
5:8 *l* him, by means of the water
5:24 *l* it occur that, when you
7:26 *l* your own name become
7:26 *l* the very house of your
7:28 *l* them prove to be truth
7:29 *l* the house of your servant
8:4 *l* a hundred chariot horses of
11:25 *l* this matter appear bad
12:13 does *l* your sin pass by
13:5 *l* Tamar my sister come in
13:6 *l* Tamar my sister come in
13:24 *L* the king go, please, and
13:25 not *l* all of us go, please
13:26 *l* Amnon my brother go
13:32 *l* my lord think that it is
13:33 *l* my lord the king take to
14:7 and *l* us even annihilate the
14:11 *L* the king, please
14:12 *L* your maidservant, please
14:15 *L* me speak, please, to the
14:17 *L* the word of my lord the
14:18 *L* my lord the king speak
14:24 *L* him turn toward his own
14:32 *l* me send you to the king
14:32 *l* me see the face of the
15:7 *L* me go, please, and pay
15:14 Get up, and *l* us run away
15:25 *l* me see it and its abiding
15:26 *l* him do to me just as it
16:4 *L* me find favor in your eyes
16:9 *L* me go over, please, and
16:10 Thus *l* him call down evil
16:11 *L* him alone that he may
16:16, 16 *L* the king live! *L* the
17:1 *L* me choose, please, twelve
17:3 *l* me bring all the people
17:5 *l* us hear what is in his
17:11 *L* all Israel without fail
18:14 *L* me not hold myself up
18:19 *L* me run, please, and break
18:22 *L*, now, happen whatever
18:22 *l* me also myself, please
18:23 *L*, now, happen whatever
18:23 whatever will, *l* me run
18:31 *L* my lord the king accept
19:19 Do not *l* my lord attribute
19:26 *L* me saddle the female ass
19:30 *L* him even take the whole
19:37 *L* your servant return
19:37 *l* me die in my city close
19:37 *L* him cross over with my
20:11 *l* him follow Joab
20:16 and *l* me speak to you
20:18 *L* them but inquire in Abel
21:6 *l* there be given to us seven
21:14 God *l* himself be entreated
22:25 And *l* Jehovah repay me
22:47 *l* the God of the rock of
24:10 *l* your servant's error pass
2Sa 24:14 *L* us fall, please, into the
24:14 do not *l* me fall
24:16 Now *l* your hand drop
24:17 *L* your hand, please, come
24:22 *L* my lord the king take it
1Ki 1:2 *L* them look for a girl, a
1:12 *l* me, please, solemnly
1:25 saying, *L* King Adonijah live!
1:31 *L* my lord King David live to
1:34 say, *L* King Solomon live!
1:37 *l* him . . . be with Solomon
1:39 saying: *L* King Solomon live!
1:51 *L* King Solomon first of all
2:6 *l* his gray hairs go down in
2:21 *L* Abishag the Shunammite be
8:26 *l* your promise that you
13:7 and *l* me give you a gift
13:33 *l* him become one of the
15:29 not *l* anyone breathing
16:11 not *l* anyone of his remain
18:23 *l* them give us two young
18:23 and *l* them choose for
18:36 *l* it be known that you are
18:40 Do not *l* a single one of
19:18 *l* seven thousand remain
19:20 *L* me, please, kiss my
20:11 not *l* one girding on boast
20:23 *l* us fight against them on
20:25 *l* us fight against them on
20:31 *l* us carry sackcloth upon
20:31 and *l* us go out to the king
20:32 Please, *l* my soul live
20:42 have *l* go out of your hand
21:2 *l* me give you in place of it
21:6 if you prefer, *l* me give you
21:7 and *l* your heart be merry
21:10 *l* them bear witness against
22:7 *l* us inquire through him
22:8 Do not *l* the king say a thing
22:13 *L* your word, please
22:17 *L* them go back each one to
22:49 *L* my servants go with your
2Ki 1:10 *l* fire come down from the
1:12 *l* fire come down from the
1:13 please *l* my soul and the
1:14 *l* my soul be precious in
2:16 *L* them go, please, and look
3:11 *l* us inquire of Jehovah
3:16 *L* there be a making of this
4:10 *l* us make a little roof
4:22 *l* me run as far as the man
4:27 *L* her alone, for her soul is
5:5 *l* me send a letter to the
5:8 *L* him come, please, to me
5:17 *l* there be given to your
6:2 *L* us go, please, as far as the
6:19 *l* me conduct you to the man
7:4 *L* us enter the city, when the
7:4 *l* us invade the camp of the
7:9 *l* us enter and make report at
7:12 *L* me tell you, please, what
7:13 *L* them take, please, five of
7:13 And *l* us send out and see
9:15 do not *l* anyone go out in
9:17 *l* him say, Is there peace?
9:33 *L* her drop! Then they
9:33 Then they *l* her drop, and
10:11 had *l* no survivor of his
10:14 not *l* a single one of them
10:19 Do not *l* a single one be
10:25 not *l* a single one go out
11:12 and say: *L* the king live!
11:15 *l* there be an execution of
11:15 Do not *l* her be put to death
12:5 *l* the priests take for
12:5 *l* them, for their part
14:8 *L* us look each other in the
17:18 not *l* any remain but the
18:23 *l* me give you two thousand
18:29 Do not *l* Hezekiah deceive
18:30 do not *l* Hezekiah cause you
19:10 Do not *l* your God in whom
22:4 *l* him complete the money
22:5 *l* them put it into the hand
23:18 So he said: *L* him rest
23:18 Do not *l* anyone disturb his
23:18 they *l* his bones alone along
25:12 *l* remain as vinedressers
1Ch 5:20 he *l* himself be entreated in
12:17 *l* the God of our forefathers
13:2 *l* us send to our brothers
13:3 *l* us bring the ark of our
14:15 *l* it occur that, when you
16:10 *L* the heart of those seeking

1Ch 16:31 L the heavens rejoice
16:31 l the earth be joyful, And
16:31 And l them say among the
16:32 L the sea thunder and also
16:32 L the field exult and all
16:33 l the trees of the forest
17:23 l the word that you have
17:24 l your name prove faithful
17:24 l the house of David your
18:4 he l a hundred chariot horses
21:13 l me fall into the hand of
21:13 of man do not l me fall
21:15 Now l your hand drop
21:17 Jehovah my God, l your hand
21:23 l my lord the king do what
22:5 L me, then, make preparation
28:9 l himself be found by you
2Ch 1:9 l your promise with David my
2:15 l him send to his servants
6:17 l your promise that you have
6:40 l your eyes prove to be
6:41 L your priests themselves
6:41 l your loyal ones themselves
10:5 L there be yet three days
14:7 L us build these cities and
14:11 not l mortal man retain
15:2 l himself be found by you
15:4 l himself be found by them
15:7 l your hands drop down
15:15 l himself be found by them
18:6 l us inquire through him
18:7 l the king say a thing like
18:12 l your word, please, become
18:16 L them go back each one
19:7 l the dread of Jehovah come
19:11 l Jehovah prove to be with
20:9 l us stand before this house
23:6 l anyone enter the house of
23:11 said: L the king live!
24:22 L Jehovah see to it and ask
25:7 king, do not l the army of
25:17 L us look each other in the
28:19 l unrestraint grow in Judah
32:15 not l Hezekiah deceive you
33:13 l himself be entreated by
35:21 not l him bring you to ruin
36:23 So l him go up
Ezr 1:3 So l him go up to Jerusalem
1:4 l the men of his place assist
4:2 L us build along with you
4:12 l it become known to the
4:13 l it become known to the
5:8 L it become known to the king
5:10 so as to l you know, that
5:15 l the house of God be rebuilt
5:17 l there be an investigation
5:17 concerning this l him send
6:3 L the house be rebuilt as the
6:4 l the expense be given from
6:5 l the gold and silver vessels
6:7 L the work on that house of
6:9 l there be given them
6:12 order. L it be done promptly
7:23 L all that is by the order of
7:26 l judgment be promptly
8:23 l himself be entreated by us
10:3 l us conclude a covenant
10:14 please, l our princes act
10:14 l them come at the times
Ne 1:6 l your ear become attentive
1:11 l your ear become attentive
2:3 L the king himself live to
2:7 l letters be given me to the
2:7 l me pass until I come to
2:17 l us rebuild the wall of
2:18 L us get up, and we must
4:5 L it not be wiped out, for
4:22 L the men spend the night
5:10 L us, please, leave off this
6:2 and l us meet together by
6:7 and l us consult together
6:10 L us meet by appointment at
6:10 l us close the doors of the
9:5 l them bless your glorious
9:32 do not l all the hardship
Es 1:19 l a royal word go out from
1:19 and l it be written among the
1:19 royal dignity l the king give
2:2 said: L them seek young women
2:3 and l the king appoint
2:3 l them collect together all
2:3 l there be a giving of their
3:8 appropriate to l them alone
3:9 l there be a writing that they
Es 5:3 l it even be given to you
5:4 l the king with Haman come
5:6 L it even be granted you!
5:6 kingship—l it even be done!
5:8 l the king and Haman come to
5:14 L them make a stake fifty
6:5 the king said: L him come in
6:8 l them bring royal apparel
6:9 And l there be a putting of the
6:10 not l anything go unfulfilled
7:2 L it even be given to you
7:2 the kingship—l it even be done!
7:3 l there be given me my own
8:5 l it be written to undo the
9:12 L it even be given to you
9:12 request? L it even be done
9:13 l it be granted tomorrow also
9:13 l the ten sons of Haman be
9:25 L his bad scheme that he has
Job 1:21 L the name of Jehovah
3:3 L the day perish on which I
3:4 day, l it become darkness
3:4 L not God look for it from
3:4 Nor l daylight beam upon it
3:5 L darkness and deep shadow
3:5 L a rain cloud reside over it
3:5 L the things that darken a day
3:6 That night—l gloom take it
3:6 L it not feel glad among the
3:6 lunar months l it not enter
3:7 night—l it become sterile
3:7 L no joyful cry come in it
3:8 L curses of the day execrate
3:9 L the stars of its twilight
3:9 L it wait for the light and
3:9 And l it not see the beams of
6:29 l no unrighteousness arise
7:19 l me alone until I swallow
9:27 said, L me forget my concern
9:27 L me alter my countenance
9:34 L him remove his rod from
9:34 l it not terrify me
9:35 L me speak and not be afraid
10:20 L him leave off
10:20 L him turn his gaze from
11:14 l no unrighteousness dwell
13:13 l come upon me whatever it
13:17 l my declaration be in your
15:17 beheld, so l me relate it
15:31 L him put no faith in
16:18 l there prove to be no place
18:8 l go into a net by his feet
19:18 L me but rise up, and they
20:23 L it occur that, to fill his
21:2 And l this become your
27:6 and I shall not l it go
27:7 L my enemy become in every
30:12 My feet they have l go
31:8 L me sow seed and someone
31:8 l my own descendants be
31:10 L my wife do the grinding
31:10 over her l other men kneel
31:22 L my own shoulder blade
31:22 l my own arm be broken
31:40 l the thorny weed go forth
32:20 L me speak that it may be
32:21 L me not, please, show
33:24 L him off from going down
33:25 L his flesh become fresher
33:25 L him return to the days
34:4 l us choose for ourselves
34:4 L us know among ourselves
34:36 l Job be tested out to the
36:18 l not a large ransom itself
37:19 L us know what we should
37:24 Therefore l men fear him
38:3 l me question you, and you
40:2 L the reprover of God
40:11 L flow the furious outburst
42:11 Jehovah had l come upon him
Ps 2:3 L us tear their bands apart
2:7 L me refer to the decree of
2:10 L yourselves be corrected, O
5:10 l there be a dispersing of
7:5 L an enemy pursue my soul
7:5 l him overtake and trample
7:7 l the very assembly of
9:19 L not mortal man prove
9:19 L the nations be judged
13:5 L my heart be joyful in your
14:7 L Jacob be joyful
14:7 be joyful, l Israel rejoice
17:5 L my steps take hold on your
18:24 l Jehovah repay me according
Ps 18:46 l the God of my salvation be
19:13 Do not l them dominate me
19:14 L the sayings of my mouth
22:8 L Him provide him with
22:8 L him deliver him, since he
25:21 L integrity and uprightness
27:14 and l your heart be strong
30:1 l my enemies rejoice over me
33:8 L all those of the earth be
33:8 l all the inhabitants of the
33:22 L your loving-kindness
34:3 l us exalt his name together
35:5 l Jehovah's angel be pushing
35:6 L their way become darkness
35:6 l Jehovah's angel be pursuing
35:8 L ruin come upon him without
35:8 l his own net that he hid
35:8 With ruin l him fall into it
35:9 l my own soul be joyful in
35:9 L it exult in his salvation
35:10 L all my bones themselves
35:19 l them not wink the eye
35:26 L those be ashamed and
35:26 L those be clothed with
35:27 L those cry out joyfully
35:27 And l them say constantly
35:27 L Jehovah be magnified, who
35:28 l my own tongue utter in an
36:11 l it not make me a wanderer
37:8 L anger alone and leave rage
40:11 L your loving-kindness and
40:15 L those stare in amazement
40:16 L those exult and rejoice in
40:16 L those say constantly
50:19 Your mouth you have l loose to
53:6, 6 L Jacob be joyful, l Israel
55:15 L them go down into Sheol
57:5 L your glory be above all the
57:11 L your glory be above all the
59:14 l them return at eveningtime
59:14 L them bark like a dog and
59:15 L those very ones wander
59:15 L them not be satisfied or
66:7 l them not be exalted in
67:3 L peoples laud you, O God
67:3 L the peoples, all of them
67:4 L national groups rejoice and
67:5 L peoples laud you, O God
67:5 L peoples, all of them, laud
68:1, 1 L God arise, l his enemies
68:1 l those who intensely hate
68:2 L the wicked ones perish from
68:3 the righteous, l them rejoice
68:3 L them be elated before God
68:3 l them exult with rejoicing
69:22 L their table before them
69:23 L their eyes become darkened
69:25 L their walled camp become
69:28 L them be wiped out of the
69:32 l your heart also keep alive
69:34 L heaven and earth praise
72:3 L the mountains carry peace
72:4 L him judge the afflicted
72:4 L him save the sons of the
72:4 l him crush the defrauder
72:15 And l him live, and to him
72:15 l some of the gold of Sheba
72:15 l prayer be made constantly
72:15 day long l him be blessed
72:17 L his name prove to be to
72:17 l his name have increase
72:17 means of him l them bless
72:17 L all nations pronounce him
72:19 l his glory fill the whole
76:11 L them bring a gift in fear
78:13 he might l them pass over
79:8 L your mercies confront us
79:10 l there be known before our
80:17 L your hand prove to be upon
81:12 so I l them go in the
83:1 God, l there be no silence
83:4 l us efface them from being
83:12 L us take possession of the
85:8 But l them not return to
90:17 l the pleasantness of Jehovah
95:1 l us cry out joyfully to
95:1 L us shout in triumph to our
95:2 L us come before his person
95:2 L us with melodies shout in
95:6 l us worship and bow down
95:6 L us kneel before Jehovah our
96:11 L the heavens rejoice, and
96:11 and l the earth be joyful
96:11 L the sea thunder and that

Ps 96:12 *L* the open field exult and
96:12 *l* all the trees of the forest
97:1 *L* the earth be joyful
97:1 *L* the many islands rejoice
97:7 *L* all those serving any carved
98:7 *L* the sea thunder and that
98:8 *L* the rivers themselves clap
98:8 *l* the very mountains cry out
99:1 *L* the peoples be agitated
99:1 *L* the earth quiver
99:3 *L* them laud your name
104:34 *L* my musing about him be
105:3 *L* the heart of those seeking
105:20 that he might *l* him loose
105:25 *l* their heart change to hate
107:2 *L* the reclaimed ones of
107:8 *l* people give thanks to
107:15 *l* people give thanks to
107:21 *l* people give thanks to
107:22 *l* them offer the sacrifices
107:31 *l* people give thanks to
107:32 *l* them extol him in the
107:32 elderly men *l* them praise
107:38 *l* their cattle become few
108:5 *l* your glory be above all
109:7 *l* him go forth as someone
109:7 *l* his very prayer become a
109:8 *L* his days prove to be few
109:8 oversight *l* someone else
109:9 *L* his sons become fatherless
109:10 *l* his sons go wandering
109:11 *L* the usurer lay out traps
109:11 *l* strangers make plunder of
109:13 *L* his posterity be for
109:13 *l* their name be wiped out
109:14 *L* the error of his
109:15 *L* them prove to be in front
109:28 *L* them, for their part
109:28 but *l* them be ashamed
109:28 *l* your own servant rejoice
109:29 *L* those resisting me be
109:29 *l* them enwrap themselves
118:2 *L* Israel now say
118:3 *L* those of the house of Aaron
118:4 *L* those fearing Jehovah now
119:77 *L* your mercies come to me
119:78 *L* the presumptuous ones be
119:79 *L* those fearing you turn
119:80 *L* my heart prove faultless
122:1 house of Jehovah *l* us go
124:1 *L* Israel now say
129:1 *L* Israel now say
130:7 *L* Israel keep waiting for
131:3 *L* Israel wait for Jehovah
132:7 *L* us come into his grand
132:7 *L* us bow down at his
132:9 *L* your priests themselves be
132:9 *l* your own loyal ones cry
137:5 *L* my right hand be forgetful
137:6 *L* my tongue stick to my
140:10 *L* them be made to fall into
140:11 big talker—*l* him not be
140:11 *l* evil itself hunt him
142:7 Around me *l* the righteous
145:21 *l* all flesh bless his holy
148:5 *L* them praise the name of
148:13 *L* them praise the name of
149:2 *L* Israel rejoice in its grand
149:2 *l* them be joyful in their
149:3 *L* them praise his name
149:3 *l* them make melody to him
149:5 *L* the loyal ones exult in
149:5 *L* them cry out joyfully on
149:6 *L* the songs extolling God be
150:6 thing—*l* it praise Jah
Pr 1:11 *l* us lie in ambush for blood
1:11 *l* us lie in concealment for
1:12 *L* us swallow them down alive
1:13 *L* us find all sorts of
1:13 *L* us fill our houses with
1:14 *L* there come to be just one
4:13 on discipline; do not *l* go
5:17 *L* them prove to be for you
5:18 *L* your water source prove to
5:19 *L* her own breasts intoxicate
7:18 *l* us drink our fill of love
7:18 *l* us enjoy each other with
9:4 *l* him turn aside here
9:16 *l* him turn aside here
17:12 *L* there be an encountering by
23:17 *L* your heart not be envious
24:13 *l* sweet comb honey be upon
25:4 *L* there be a removing of
25:5 *L* there be the removing of

Pr 28:17 *L* them not get hold of him
29:15 a boy *l* on the loose will be
29:19 not *l* himself be corrected
30:8 *L* me devour the food
31:7 *L* one drink and forget one's
31:7 and *l* one remember one's own
31:31 *l* her works praise her even
Ec 2:1 Do come now, *l* me try you out
5:1 *l* there be a drawing near to
5:2 heart, *l* it not be hasty to
9:8 *l* your garments prove to be
9:8 *l* oil not be lacking upon your
11:6 do not *l* your hand rest
11:8 in all of them *l* him rejoice
11:8 *l* him remember the days of
11:9 *l* your heart do you good in
Ca 1:4 Draw me with you; *l* us run
1:4 *l* us be joyful and rejoice in
1:4 *l* us mention your expressions
2:14 *l* me hear your voice, for
3:2 *L* me rise up, please, and go
3:2 *l* me seek the one whom my
3:4 I would not *l* go of him, until
4:16 *L* its perfumes trickle
4:16 *L* my dear one come into his
7:2 *L* not the mixed wine be
7:11 *l* us go forth to the field
7:11 *l* us lodge among the henna
7:12 *l* us rise early and go to the
8:13 to your voice. *L* me hear it
Isa 1:18 *l* us set matters straight
2:3 *l* us go up to the mountain of
2:5 and *l* us walk in the light of
5:1 *L* me sing, please, to my
5:19 *L* his work hasten
5:19 *l* it come quickly, in order
5:19 *l* the counsel of the Holy One
7:4 *l* your heart itself be timid
7:6 *L* us go up against Judah and
7:6 *l* us make another king reign
8:2 *l* me have attestation for
10:30 *L* your voice out in shrill
13:20 shepherds will *l* their
19:22 *l* himself be entreated by
21:5 *L* there be a setting of the
22:13 *L* there be eating and
25:9 *L* us be joyful and rejoice
26:19 *l* even those impotent in
27:5 *l* him take hold of my
27:5 *l* him make peace with me
27:5 peace *l* him make with me
29:1 *l* the festivals run the
34:1 *L* the earth and that which
36:8 *l* me give you two thousand
36:14 not *l* Hezekiah deceive you
36:15 *l* Hezekiah cause you to
37:10 *l* your God in whom you are
38:21 *L* them take a cake of
40:4 *L* every valley be raised up
41:1 *l* national groups themselves
41:1 *L* them approach. At that
41:1 At that time *l* them speak
41:1 *L* us come up close together
42:2 not *l* his voice be heard
42:11 *L* the wilderness and its
42:11 *L* the inhabitants of the
42:11 *l* people cry aloud
42:12 *L* them attribute to Jehovah
42:12 *l* them tell forth even his
42:13 he will *l* out a war cry
43:9 *L* the nations all be
43:9 *l* national groups be gathered
43:9 *L* them furnish their
43:9 *l* them hear and say, It is
43:26 *l* us put ourselves on
44:7 *L* him call out, that he may
44:7 *l* them tell on their part
45:8 and *l* the cloudy skies
45:8 *L* the earth open up, and
45:8 and *l* it be fruitful with
45:8 *l* it cause righteousness
45:13 in exile he will *l* go, not
45:21 *l* them consult together in
47:13 *L* them stand up, now, and
48:11 one *l* oneself be profaned
49:13 *L* the mountains become
50:8 *L* us stand up together
50:8 *L* him approach me
50:10 *L* him trust in the name of
54:2 *l* them stretch out the tent
55:2 and *l* your soul find its
55:7 *L* the wicked man leave his
55:7 and *l* him return to Jehovah
56:3 *l* not the foreigner that has

Isa 56:3 Neither *l* the eunuch say
56:12 *L* me take some wine
56:12 and *l* us drink intoxicating
62:6 *l* them not keep still
62:6 *l* there be no silence on
64:12 and *l* us be afflicted to
65:1 I have *l* myself be searched
65:1 have *l* myself be found by
Jer 2:28 *L* them rise up if they can
4:5 *l* us enter into the fortified
4:16 *l* out their voice against the
5:24 *L* us, now, fear Jehovah our
6:4 and *l* us go up at midday
6:5 *l* us go up during the night
8:14 and *l* us enter into the
9:23 *L* not the wise man brag
9:23 *l* not the mighty man brag
9:23 *L* not the rich man brag
9:24 *l* the one bragging about
11:19 *L* us bring to ruin the tree
11:19 *l* us cut him off from the
12:8 She has *l* loose her voice
14:9 Do not *l* us down
14:17 *L* my eyes run down with
14:17 and *l* them not keep still
17:4 you *l* loose, even of your
17:15 *L* it come in, please
17:18 *L* my persecutors be put to
17:18 *l* me personally be put to
17:18 *L* them be the ones to be
17:18 *l* me personally not be
18:18 *l* us think out against
18:18 *l* us strike him with the
18:18 *l* us pay no attention to
18:22 *L* a cry be heard out of
18:23 *l* them become those who are
20:3 *l* Jeremiah out from the
22:20 on Bashan *l* your voice out
23:28 *l* him relate the dream
23:28 *l* him speak forth my word
27:11 *l* it rest upon its ground
27:18 *l* them, please, beseech
29:8 *L* not your prophets who are
29:14 *l* myself be found by you
31:6 *l* us go up to Zion, to
34:9 *l* each one his manservant
34:10 *l* each one his manservant
34:10 to obey and *l* them go
34:11 whom they had *l* go free
34:14 *l* go each one his brother
34:14 *l* him go free from being
34:16 *l* go free agreeably to
35:11 *l* us enter into Jerusalem
35:11 *l* us dwell in Jerusalem
38:4 *L* this man, please, be put
38:6 *l* Jeremiah down by means of
38:11 *l* them down to Jeremiah
39:10 *l* remain in the land of
40:4 I have *l* you loose today
40:5 and a present and *l* him go
43:6 *l* stay with Gedaliah the son
46:6 *L* not the swift one try to
46:6 *l* not the mighty man try to
46:9 *l* the mighty men go forth
46:16 *l* us return to our people
46:17 *l* the festal time pass by
48:2 *l* us cut her off from being
49:8 Flee! *L* yourselves give way!
49:9 not *l* some gleanings remain
50:5 *l* us join ourselves to
50:20 those whom I *l* remain
50:21 *L* there be a massacre and
50:33 have refused to *l* them go
51:3 *L* the one treading his bow
51:3 *l* no one raise himself up
51:9 *l* us go each one to his own
51:10 *l* us recount in Zion the
51:29 *l* the earth rock and be in
52:16 *l* remain as vinedressers
La 2:7 have *l* out their own voice
3:28 *L* him sit solitary and keep
3:29 *L* him put his mouth in the
3:30 *L* him give his cheek to the
3:30 *L* him have his sufficiency of
3:40 *L* us search out our ways and
3:40 *l* us return clear to Jehovah
3:41 *L* us raise our heart along
Eze 1:24 would *l* their wings down
1:25 would *l* their wings down
3:27 *L* the one hearing hear, and
3:27 *l* the one refraining refrain
6:8 *l* you have as a remnant the
7:12 the buyer, *l* him not rejoice
7:12 *l* him not go into mourning

Eze 9:5 *L* not your eye feel sorry, and
13:20 *l* go the souls that you are
14:4 will *l* myself be brought to
14:17 say: *L* a sword itself pass
18:30 *l* nothing prove to be for
20:25 *l* them have regulations
20:26 *l* them become defiled by
20:32 *L* us become like the
23:48 *l* themselves be corrected
24:5 *L* there be a taking of the
24:10 *l* the bones themselves
24:11 *L* its rust get consumed
27:30 *l* themselves be heard with
32:7 will not *l* its light shine
36:32 *l* it be known to you
36:37 *l* myself be searched for by
38:7 *l* there be preparation on
39:7 no more *l* my holy name be
43:9 Now *l* them remove their
Da 1:12 *l* them give us some
1:13 *l* our countenances and the
2:7 *L* the king say what the dream
2:20 *L* the name of God become
3:18 *l* it become known to you
4:14 *L* the beast flee from under
4:15 of the heavens *l* it be wet
4:15 *l* its portion be among the
4:16 *L* its heart be changed from
4:16 and *l* the heart of a beast be
4:16 *l* seven times pass over it
4:19 do not *l* the dream and the
4:23 *l* it become wet, and with
4:23 of the field *l* its portion be
5:10 not *l* your thoughts frighten
5:10 *l* your complexion be changed
5:12 *l* Daniel himself be called
5:17 *L* your gifts prove to be to
10:19 *L* my lord speak, because you
Ho 4:4 *l* no man contend, neither
4:4 neither *l* a man reprove, as
4:15 *l* not Judah become guilty
4:17 *L* him be to himself
6:1 do *l* us return to Jehovah
8:3 *L* one who is an enemy pursue
12:6 *l* there be a hoping in your
13:2 *L* the sacrificers who are men
Joe 2:1 *L* all the inhabitants of the
2:14 *l* remain after it a blessing
2:16 *L* the bridegroom go forth
2:17 *l* the priests, the ministers
3:9 men! *L* them draw near!
3:9 *L* them come up, all the men
3:10 the weak one, *l* him say
3:12 *L* the nations be aroused
Am 4:1 Do bring, and *l* us drink!
5:24 *l* justice roll forth just
7:16 *l* no word drop against the
Ob 1 *l* us rise up against her in
5 not *l* some gleanings remain
Jon 1:7 *l* us cast lots, that we may
3:8 *l* them cover themselves with
3:8 *l* them call out to God with
Mic 1:2 *l* the Sovereign Lord Jehovah
2:6 you people *l* words drop
2:6 They *l* words drop. They will
2:6 They will not *l* words drop
2:11 I shall *l* words drop to you
4:2 *l* us go up to the mountain of
4:11 *L* her be polluted, and may
7:14 *L* them feed on Bashan and
Na 2:1 *L* there be a safeguarding of
Zep 3:12 *l* remain in the midst of
Zec 3:5 *L* them put a clean turban
6:10 *L* there be a taking of
8:9 *L* the hands of you people be
8:21 *L* us earnestly go to soften
11:9 one that is dying, *l* her die
11:9 effaced, *l* her be effaced
11:9 *l* them devour, each one the
13:7 *l* those of the flock be
Mt 3:15 *L* it be, this time, for in
5:16 *l* your light shine before men
5:31 *l* him give her a certificate
5:37 *l* your word *Yes* mean Yes
5:40 *l* your outer garment also go
6:3 do not *l* your left hand know
6:9 *l* your name be sanctified
6:10 *L* your kingdom come
6:10 *L* your will take place, as
8:13 so *l* it come to pass for you
8:22 *l* the dead bury their dead
9:29 to your faith *l* it happen to
10:13 *l* the peace you wish it come
10:13 *l* the peace from you return
Mt 11:15 *L* him that has ears listen
13:9 *L* him that has ears listen
13:30 *L* both grow together until
13:43 *L* him that has ears listen
13:47 dragnet *l* down into the sea
15:4 *L* him that reviles father or
15:14 *L* them be. Blind guides is
15:28 *l* it happen to you as you
16:24 *l* him disown himself and
18:17 *l* him be to you just as a
18:27 *l* him off and canceled his
19:6 *l* no man put apart
19:12 *L* him that can make room
19:14 *L* the young children alone
20:33 Lord, *l* our eyes be opened
21:19 *L* no fruit come from you
21:33 *l* it out to cultivators, and
21:38 is the heir; come, *l* us kill
21:41 *l* out the vineyard to other
24:15 *l* the reader use discernment
24:16 then *l* those in Judea begin
24:17 *L* the man on the housetop
24:18 *l* the man in the field not
26:39 *l* this cup pass away from
26:42 *l* your will take place
26:46 *l* us go. Look! My betrayer
27:22 all said: *L* him be impaled!
27:23 *L* him be impaled!
27:42 *l* him now come down off
27:43 *l* Him now rescue him if He
27:49 rest of them said: *L* him be!
27:49 *L* us see whether Elijah
Mr 1:34 would not *l* the demons speak
1:38 *L* us go somewhere else, into
4:9 *L* him that has ears to listen
4:23 ears to listen, *l* him listen
4:35 *L* us cross to the other shore
5:19 he did not *l* him, but said to
5:37 he did not *l* anyone follow
5:43 *l* no one learn of this, and
7:10 *L* him that reviles father or
7:12 *l* him do a single thing for
7:27 *l* the children be satisfied
8:34 *l* him disown himself and
9:5 *l* us erect three tents, one
10:9 *l* no man put apart
10:14 *L* the young children come to
10:51 *l* me recover sight
11:6 and they *l* them go
11:14 *L* no one eat fruit from you
11:16 not *l* anyone carry a utensil
12:1 and *l* it out to cultivators
12:7 Come, *l* us kill him, and the
13:14 *l* the reader use discernment
13:14 *l* those in Judea begin
13:15 *L* the man on the housetop
13:16 *l* the man in the field not
14:6 But Jesus said: *L* her alone
14:42 Get up, *l* us go. Look!
15:32 *L* the Christ the King of
15:36, 36 *L* him be! *L* us see
15:37 Jesus *l* out a loud cry and
Lu 2:15 *L* us by all means go clear to
3:11 *L* the man that has two
3:11 *l* him that has things to eat
5:4 *l* down your nets for a catch
5:19 through the tiling they *l* him
7:7 and *l* my servant be healed
8:8 *L* him that has ears to listen
8:22 *L* us cross to the other side
8:51 he did not *l* anyone go in
9:23 *l* him disown himself and
9:33 so *l* us erect three tents
9:60 *L* the dead bury their dead
11:2 *l* your name be sanctified
11:2 *L* your kingdom come
12:35 *L* your loins be girded and
12:39 not have *l* his house be
13:8 *l* it alone also this year
14:9 *L* this man have the place
14:35 *L* him that has ears to
15:23 *l* us eat and enjoy ourselves
16:29 *l* them listen to these
17:31 On that day *l* the person
17:31 *l* him likewise not return
18:16 *L* the young children come
18:41 Lord, *l* me recover sight
20:9 and *l* it out to cultivators
20:14 This is the heir; *l* us kill
21:21 *l* those in Judea begin
21:21 *l* those in the midst of her
21:21 *l* those in the country places
22:26 *l* him that is the greatest
22:36 now *l* the one that has a
Lu 22:36 *l* the one having no sword
22:42 *l*, not my will, but yours
22:51 *L* it go as far as this
23:35 *l* him save himself, if this
Joh 7:37 *l* him come to me and drink
11:7 *L* us go into Judea again
11:15 But *l* us go to him
11:16 *L* us also go, that we may
11:44 Loose him and *l* him go
11:48 *l* him alone this way, they
12:7 Jesus said: *L* her alone
12:26 *l* him follow me, and
14:1 not *l* your hearts be troubled
14:27 *l* your hearts be troubled
14:27 nor *l* them shrink for fear
14:31 Get up, *l* us go from here
18:8 Jesus answered . . . *l* these go
19:24 *L* us not tear it, but
19:24 *l* us determine by lots over
Ac 1:20 *L* his lodging place become
1:20 *l* there be no dweller in it
1:20 oversight *l* someone else take
2:14 *l* this be known to you and
2:36 *l* all the house of Israel
2:38 *l* each one of you be baptized
4:10 *l* it be known to all of you
4:17 *l* us tell them with threats
5:38 these men, but *l* them alone
5:40 Jesus' name, and *l* them go
9:25 *l* him down by night through
10:11 sheet being *l* down by its
11:5 sheet being *l* down by its
13:3 upon them and *l* them go
13:38 *L* it therefore be known to
15:30 when these men were *l* go
15:33 they were *l* go in peace by
15:36 *l* us return and visit the
16:37 *l* them come themselves and
17:9 and the others they *l* them go
18:6 *L* your blood be upon your own
19:38 *l* them bring charges against
21:14 *L* the will of Jehovah take
22:30 *l* him loose and commanded
23:21 do not *l* them persuade you
23:22 *l* the young man go after
24:20 *l* the men here say for
25:5 *l* those who are in power
27:7 wind did not *l* us get on, we
27:30 *l* down anchors from the
27:32 skiff and *l* it fall off
27:40 anchors, they *l* them fall
28:28 *l* it be known to you that
Ro 3:4 *l* God be found true, though
3:8 *L* us do the bad things that
5:1 *l* us enjoy peace with God
5:2 *l* us exult, based on hope of
5:3 but *l* us exult while in
6:12 do not *l* sin continue to rule
9:17 cause I have *l* you remain
11:9 *L* their table become for
11:10 *l* their eyes become
12:6 *l* us prophesy according to
12:7 *l* us be at this ministry
12:7 *l* him be at his teaching
12:8 *l* him be at his exhortation
12:8 *l* him do it with liberality
12:8 *l* him do it in real earnest
12:8 *l* him do it with cheerfulness
12:9 *L* your love be without
12:21 not *l* yourself be conquered
13:1 *L* every soul be in subjection
13:12 *L* us therefore put off the
13:12 *l* us put on the weapons of
13:13 *l* us walk decently, not in
14:3 *L* the one eating not look
14:3 *l* the one not eating not
14:5 *l* each man be fully convinced
14:13 *l* us not be judging one
14:16 *l* the good you people do be
14:19 *l* us pursue the things
15:2 *L* each of us please his
15:11 *l* all the peoples praise
1Co 1:31 *l* him boast in Jehovah
3:10 *l* each one keep watching how
3:18 *L* no one be seducing himself
3:18 *l* him become a fool, that he
3:21 *l* no one be boasting in men
4:1 *L* a man so appraise us as
5:8 *l* us keep the festival, not
6:7 do you not rather *l* yourselves
6:7 *l* yourselves be defrauded
6:12 will not *l* myself be brought
7:2 *l* each man have his own wife
7:3 *L* the husband render to his

1Co 7:3 *l* the wife also do likewise
7:9 *l* them marry, for it is
7:11 *l* her remain unmarried or
7:12 with him, *l* him not leave
7:13 *l* her not leave her husband
7:15 *l* him depart; a brother or a
7:17 *l* each one so walk as God
7:18 circumcised? *L* him not
7:18 *L* him not get circumcised
7:20 called, *l* him remain in it
7:21 Do not *l* it worry you; but
7:24 brothers, *l* him remain in it
7:29 *l* those who have wives be as
7:36 *l* him do what he wants; he
7:36 does not sin. *L* them marry
10:8 Neither *l* us practice
10:9 Neither *l* us put Jehovah to
10:12 *l* him that thinks he is
10:13 not *l* you be tempted beyond
10:24 *L* each one keep seeking, not
11:6 *l* her also be shorn; but if
11:6 or shaved, *l* her be covered
11:28 *l* a man approve himself
11:28 *l* him eat of the loaf and
11:34 *l* him eat at home, that you
14:13 *l* the one who speaks in a
14:26 *L* all things take place for
14:27 *l* it be limited to two or
14:27 and *l* someone translate
14:28 *l* him keep silent in the
14:29 *l* two or three prophets
14:29 *l* the others discern the
14:30 *l* the first one keep silent
14:34 *l* the women keep silent in
14:34 *l* them be in subjection
14:35 *l* them question their own
14:37 *l* him acknowledge the
14:40 But *l* all things take place
15:32 *l* us eat and drink, for
16:2 *l* each of you at his own
16:11 *L* no one, therefore, look
16:14 *L* all your affairs take
16:22 *l* him be accursed. O our
2Co 4:6 *L* the light shine out of
7:1 *l* us cleanse ourselves of
8:1 we *l* you know, brothers
9:7 *L* each one do just as he has
10:7 *l* him again take this fact
10:11 *L* such a man take this into
10:17 *l* him boast in Jehovah
11:16 *L* no man think I am
Ga 1:8 *l* him be accursed
1:9 *l* him be accursed
5:1 *l* yourselves be confined again
5:25 *l* us go on walking orderly
5:26 *L* us not become egotistical
6:4 *l* him prove what his own work
6:6 *l* anyone who is being orally
6:9 *l* us not give up in doing
6:10 *l* us work what is good
6:17 *l* no one be making trouble
Eph 4:15 *l* us by love grow up in all
4:26 *l* the sun not set with you
4:28 *L* the stealer steal no more
4:28 rather *l* him do hard work
4:29 *L* a rotten saying not proceed
4:31 *L* all malicious bitterness
5:3 *L* fornication and uncleanness
5:6 *L* no man deceive you with
5:22 *L* wives be in subjection to
5:24 so *l* wives also be to their
5:33 also, *l* each one of you
Php 3:15 *L* us, then, as many of us
3:16 *l* us go on walking orderly
4:5 *L* your reasonableness become
4:6 *l* your petitions be made
Col 2:16 *l* no man judge you in eating
2:18 *L* no man deprive you of the
3:15 *l* the peace of the Christ
3:16 *L* the word of the Christ
4:6 *L* your utterance be always
1Th 5:6 *l* us not sleep on as the rest
5:6 *l* us stay awake and keep our
5:8 *l* us keep our senses and have
2Th 2:3 *L* no one seduce you in any
3:10 to work, neither *l* him eat
1Ti 2:11 *L* a woman learn in silence
3:10 *l* these be tested as to
3:10 *l* them serve as ministers
3:12 *L* ministerial servants be
4:12 *L* no man ever look down on
5:4 *l* these learn first to
5:9 *L* a widow be put on the list
5:16 widows, *l* her relieve them
1Ti 5:16 *l* the congregation not be
5:17 *L* the older men who preside
6:1 *L* as many as are slaves under
6:2 *l* those having believing
6:2 *l* them the more readily be
2Ti 2:19 *L* everyone naming the name
Tit 2:2 *L* the aged men be moderate in
2:3 *l* the aged women be reverent
2:9 *L* slaves be in subjection to
2:15 *L* no man ever despise you
3:14 *l* our people also learn to
Heb 1:6 *l* all God's angels do
4:1 *l* us fear that sometime
4:11 *L* us therefore do our utmost
4:14 *l* us hold onto our confessing
4:16 *L* us, therefore, approach
6:1 *l* us press on to maturity
10:22 *l* us approach with true
10:23 *L* us hold fast the public
10:24 *l* us consider one another
12:1 *l* us also put off every
12:1 *l* us run with endurance the
12:28 *l* us continue to have
13:1 *L* your brotherly love
13:4 *L* marriage be honorable
13:5 *L* your manner of life be
13:13 *L* us, then, go forth to
13:15 *l* us always offer to God
Jas 1:4 *l* endurance have its work
1:5 *l* him keep on asking God, for
1:6 *l* him keep on asking in
1:7 *l* not that man suppose that
1:9 *l* the lowly brother exult
1:13 under trial, *l* no one say
3:13 *L* him show out of his fine
4:9 *L* your laughter be turned into
5:12 *l* your *Yes* mean Yes, and
5:13 *L* him carry on prayer
5:13 *L* him sing psalms
5:14 *L* him call the older men of
5:14 and *l* them pray over him
1Pe 2:18 *L* house servants be in
3:3 do not *l* your adornment be
3:4 *l* it be the secret person of
3:10 *l* him restrain his tongue
3:11 *l* him turn away from what
3:11 *l* him seek peace and pursue
4:11 *l* him speak as it were the
4:11 *l* him minister as dependent
4:15 *l* none of you suffer as a
4:16 *l* him not feel shame, but
4:16 *l* him keep on glorifying
4:19 *l* those who are suffering in
2Pe 3:8 *l* this one fact not be
1Jo 2:24 *l* that which you have heard
3:7 *l* no one mislead you; he
3:18 *l* us love, neither in word
4:7 *l* us continue loving one
Re 2:7 *L* the one who has an ear hear
2:11 *L* the one who has an ear
2:17 *L* the one who has an ear hear
2:29 *L* the one who has an ear
3:6 *L* the one who has an ear hear
3:13 *L* the one who has an ear
3:22 *L* the one who has an ear
11:9 do not *l* their corpses be laid
13:9 anyone has an ear, *l* him hear
13:18 *L* the one that has
14:13 *l* them rest from their
19:7 *L* us rejoice and be overjoyed
19:7 and *l* us give him the glory
20:3 be *l* loose for a little while
20:7 Satan will be *l* loose out of
22:11 *l* him do unrighteousness
22:11 *l* the filthy one be made
22:11 *l* the righteous one do
22:11 *l* the holy one be made holy
22:17 *l* anyone hearing say: Come!
22:17 *l* anyone thirsting come
22:17 *l* anyone that wishes take

Lets

Ex 21:13 God *l* it occur at his hand
Job 8:4 *l* them go into the hand of
37:3 whole heavens he *l* it loose
Pr 29:11 is what a stupid one *l* out
Isa 44:14 he *l* it become strong for
Ro 9:18 wishes he *l* become obstinate
2Th 2:11 God *l* an operation of error

Letter

2Sa 11:14 *l* to Joab and send it by
11:15 wrote in the *l*, saying
2Ki 5:5 send a *l* to the king of Israel
5:6 the *l* to the king of Israel
2Ki 5:6 time that this *l* comes to you
5:7 the king of Israel read the *l*
10:2 time that this *l* comes to
10:6 he wrote them a second *l*
10:7 as soon as the *l* came to
Ezr 4:7 the *l* was written in Aramaic
4:8 a *l* against Jerusalem to
4:11 this is a copy of the *l* that
5:6 copy of the *l* that Tattenai
7:11 this is a copy of the *l* that
Ne 2:8 *l* to Asaph the keeper of the
6:5 with an open *l* in his hand
Es 9:26 all the words of this *l* and
9:29 second *l* concerning Purim
Jer 29:1 the *l* that Jeremiah the
29:29 read this *l* in the ears of
Mt 5:18 than for one smallest *l* or
5:18 one particle of a *l* to pass
Lu 16:17 one particle of a *l* of the
Ac 15:30 and handed them the *l*
23:25 wrote a *l* having this form
23:33 the *l* to the governor
Ro 16:22 done the writing of this *l*
1Co 5:9 In my *l* I wrote you to quit
2Co 3:2 You yourselves are our *l*
3:3 a *l* of Christ written by us
7:8 if I saddened you by my *l*
7:8 I see that that *l* saddened you
Col 4:16 when this *l* has been read
1Th 5:27 this *l* to be read to all the
2Th 2:2 through a *l* as though from us
2:15 or through a *l* of ours
3:14 through this *l*, keep this
3:17 which is a sign in every *l*
Heb 13:22 *l* to you in few words
2Pe 3:1 second *l* I am writing you

Letters

1Ki 21:8 she wrote *l* in Ahab's name
21:8 sent the *l* to the older men
21:9 she wrote in the *l*, saying
21:11 the *l* that she had sent to
2Ki 10:1 Jehu wrote *l* and sent them
19:14 the *l* out of the hand of the
20:12 *l* and a gift to Hezekiah
2Ch 30:1 *l* he wrote to Ephraim and
30:6 *l* from the hand of the king
32:17 *l* he wrote to reproach
Ne 2:7 let *l* be given me to the
2:9 gave them the *l* of the king
6:17 *l* that were going to Tobiah
6:19 *l* that Tobiah sent to make me
Es 3:13 sending of the *l* by means of
Isa 37:14 Hezekiah took the *l* out of
39:1 sent *l* and a gift to Hezekiah
Jer 29:25 sent in your name *l* to all
Joh 7:15 man have a knowledge of *l*
Ac 9:2 for *l* to the synagogues in
22:5 *l* to the brothers in Damascus
28:21 Neither have we received *l*
1Co 16:3 men you approve of by *l*
2Co 3:1 need *l* of recommendation to
3:7 was engraved in *l* in stones
10:9 want to terrify you by my *l*
10:10 his *l* are weighty and
10:11 our word by *l* when absent
Ga 6:11 large *l* I have written you
2Pe 3:16 as he does also in all his *l*

Letting

Ex 14:17 *l* the hearts of the Egyptians
Nu 5:21 Jehovah's *l* your thigh fall
6:5 holy by *l* the locks of the hair
11:31 *l* them fall above the camp
Jos 9:20 to them while *l* them live
Jg 5:2 For *l* the hair hang loose in
1Sa 19:11 *l* your soul escape tonight
2Sa 24:25 Jehovah began *l* himself be
Pr 11:26 of the one *l* it be bought
17:14 is as one *l* out waters
Ec 10:18 the *l* down of the hands
Isa 7:25 place for *l* bulls loose and
53:7 was *l* himself be afflicted
Jer 38:26 *l* my request for favor
Eze 14:7 I am *l* myself be brought to
Da 9:18 *l* our entreaties fall before
9:20 *l* my request for favor fall
Mic 2:11 *l* words drop for this
Zep 1:14 a mighty man is *l* out a cry
Zec 11:16 *l* a shepherd rise up in the
Mt 4:18 *l* down a fishing net into the
Mr 5:38 weeping and *l* out many wails
7:8 *L* go the commandment of God
Lu 2:29 you are *l* your slave go free
Eph 6:9 *l* up on the threatening, for

Letup
Ac 5:42 without *l* teaching and

Letushim
Ge 25:3 sons of Dedan . . . *L* and

Leummim
Ge 25:3 sons of Dedan became . . . *L*

Level
1Ki 20:23 against them on the *l* land
20:25 against them on the *l* land
Ps 26:12 certainly stand on a *l* place
Isa 40:4 ground must become *l* land
42:16 rugged terrain into *l* land
Jer 21:13 O rock of the *l* land
48:8 the *l* land be annihilated
48:21 land of *l* country, to Holon
Zec 4:7 you will become a *l* land
Lu 6:17 took his station on a *l* place

Leveled
Lu 3:5 every mountain and hill *l* down

Leveling
2Ki 21:13 *l* instrument applied to the
Ps 65:10 a *l* off of its clods
Isa 28:17 the *l* instrument
Ac 25:7 *l* against him many and

Levi
Ge 29:34 name was therefore called *L*
34:25 sons of Jacob, Simeon and *L*
34:30 said to Simeon and to *L*
35:23 sons by Leah were . . . *L*
46:11 the sons of *L* were Gershon
49:5 Simeon and *L* are brothers
Ex 1:2 Reuben, Simeon, *L* and Judah
2:1 man of the house of *L* went
2:1 man . . . took a daughter of *L*
6:16 the names of the sons of *L*
32:26 sons of *L* began gathering
32:28 sons of *L* proceeded to do as
Nu 1:49 the tribe of *L* you must not
3:6 Bring the tribe of *L* near, and
3:15 Register the sons of *L*
3:17 sons of *L* by their names
4:2 from among the sons of *L*
16:1 son of Kohath, the son of *L*
16:7 enough of you, you sons of *L*
16:8 Listen, please, you sons of *L*
16:10 your brothers the sons of *L*
17:8 Aaron's rod for the house of *L*
18:2 brothers of the tribe of *L*
18:21 And to the sons of *L*, look!
26:59 his wife bore to *L* in Egypt
De 10:8 tribe of *L* to carry the ark
10:9 *L* has come to have no share
18:1 the entire tribe of *L*
21:5 the sons of *L* must approach
27:12 Simeon and *L* and Judah and
31:9 to the priests the sons of *L*
33:8 And as to *L* he said: Your
Jos 21:10 the sons of *L*, because the
1Ki 12:31 to be of the sons of *L*
1Ch 2:1 sons of Israel . . . *L* and
6:1 The sons of *L* were Gershon
6:16 The sons of *L* were Gershom
6:38 son of *L*, the son of Israel
6:43 son of Gershom, the son of *L*
6:47 son of Merari, the son of *L*
9:18 the camps of the sons of *L*
21:6 *L* and Benjamin he did not
23:6 sons of *L*, to Gershon, Kohath
23:24 sons of *L* by the house of
23:27 the number of the sons of *L*
24:20 sons of *L* that were left
27:17 of *L*, Hashabiah the son of
Ezr 8:15 none of the sons of *L* did I
8:18 *L* the son of Israel
Ne 12:23 sons of *L* as heads of the
Ps 135:20 *L*, do you men bless Jehovah
Eze 40:46 from the sons of *L*, are
48:31 the gate of *L*, one
Zec 12:13 family of the house of *L* by
Mal 2:4 covenant with *L* may continue
2:8 have ruined the covenant of *L*
3:3 must cleanse the sons of *L*
Mr 2:14 *L* the son of Alphaeus sitting
Lu 3:24 son of Matthat, son of *L*, son
3:29 son of Matthat, son of *L*
5:27 a tax collector named *L*
5:29 *L* spread a big reception feast
Heb 7:5 the men from the sons of *L*
7:9 *L* who receives tithes has
Re 7:7 out of . . . *L* twelve thousand

Leviathan
Job 3:8 Those ready to awaken *L*
41:1 draw out *L* with a fishhook
Ps 74:14 to pieces the heads of *L*
104:26 *L*, him you have formed to
Isa 27:1 will turn his attention to *L*
27:1 *L*, the crooked serpent, and

Levied
1Ki 9:15 that King Solomon *l* to build

Levi's
Ex 6:16 the years of *L* life were a
Nu 17:3 you will write upon *L* rod
26:59 Jochebed, *L* daughter, whom

Levite
Ex 4:14 Aaron the *L* your brother
De 12:12 *L* who is inside your gates
12:18 *L* who is inside your gates
12:19 you may not abandon the *L*
14:27 *L* who is inside your gates
14:29 the *L*, because he has no
16:11 *L* who is inside your gates
16:14 the *L* and the alien resident
18:6 the *L* goes out of one of your
26:11 you and the *L* and the alien
26:12 must also give it to the *L*
26:13 I have also given it to the *L*
Jg 17:7 of Judah, and he was a *L*
17:9 I am a *L* from Bethlehem in
17:10 Accordingly the *L* went in
17:11 the *L* took it upon himself
17:12 the hand of the *L* with power
17:13 *L* has become priest for me
18:3 voice of the young man, the *L*
18:15 the young man, the *L*, at the
19:1 a certain *L* was residing for
20:4 the *L*, the husband of the
2Ch 20:14 Mattaniah the *L* of the sons
31:12 Conaniah the *L* was in
31:14 son of Imnah the *L* was the
Lu 10:32 a *L* also, when he got down
Ac 4:36 a *L*, a native of Cyprus

Levites
Ex 6:19 were the families of the *L*
6:25 heads of the fathers of the *L*
38:21 the *L* under the guidance of
Le 25:32 cities of the *L* with the
25:32 time indefinite for the *L*
25:33 property of the *L* is not
25:33 the cities of the *L* are
Nu 1:47 *L* according to the tribe of
1:50 appoint the *L* over the
1:51 *L* should take it down; and
1:51 *L* should set it up; and any
1:53 *L* should encamp around the
1:53 *L* must keep the service due
2:17 camp of the *L* will be in the
2:33 *L* did not get registered in
3:9 give the *L* to Aaron and his
3:12 take the *L* from among the
3:12 and the *L* must become mine
3:20 families of the *L* according
3:32 of the *L* was Eleazar the son
3:39 registered ones of the *L*
3:41 *L* for me—I am Jehovah—in
3:41 domestic animals of the *L* in
3:45 Take the *L* in place of all
3:45 domestic animals of the *L* in
3:45 and the *L* must become mine
3:46 who are in excess of the *L*
3:49 the ransom price of the *L*
4:18 be cut off from among the *L*
4:46 registered as *L* by their
7:5 give them to the *L*, each one
7:6 cattle and gave them to the *L*
8:6 *L* from among the sons of
8:9 present the *L* before the tent
8:10 present the *L* before Jehovah
8:10 lay their hands upon the *L*
8:11 *L* to move to and fro before
8:12 *L* will lay their hands upon
8:12 make atonement for the *L*
8:13 *L* stand before Aaron and his
8:14 separate the *L* from among the
8:14 and the *L* must become mine
8:15 *L* will come in to serve at
8:18 take the *L* in place of all
8:19 *L* as given ones to Aaron and
8:20 proceeded to do so to the *L*
8:20 Moses as regards the *L*, that
8:21 *L* purified themselves and
8:22 *L* came in to carry on their
8:22 respecting the *L*, so they did
Nu 8:24 This is what applies to the *L*
8:26 the *L* in their obligations
18:6 the *L* . . . as a gift for you
18:23 *L* themselves must carry on
18:24 to the *L* as an inheritance
18:26 you should speak to the *L*
18:30 be reckoned to the *L* as the
26:57 the registered ones of the *L*
26:58 were the families of the *L*
31:30 you must give them to the *L*
31:47 and gave them to the *L*, the
35:2 give the *L* cities to inhabit
35:2 give the *L* the pasture ground
35:4 which you will give the *L*
35:6 to the *L*: six cities of refuge
35:7 *L* will be forty-eight cities
35:8 some of his cities to the *L*
De 17:9 go to the priests, the *L*, and
17:18 charge of the priests, the *L*
18:1 belong to the priests, the *L*
18:7 all his brothers, the *L*, who
24:8 the *L*, will instruct you
27:9 the *L*, spoke to all Israel
27:14 the *L* must answer and say
31:25 began to command the *L*, the
Jos 3:3 the priests, the *L*, carrying
8:33 the *L*, carrying the ark of
13:14 the tribe of the *L* that he
13:33 the tribe of the *L* Moses
14:3 to the *L* he did not give an
14:4 not given . . . to the *L*
18:7 *L* have no share in among
21:1 heads of the fathers of the *L*
21:3 sons of Israel gave the *L*
21:4 Aaron the priest, of the *L*
21:8 sons of Israel gave the *L*
21:20 the *L* who were left out of
21:27 of the families of the *L*
21:34 sons of Merari, the *L* who
21:40 from the families of the *L*
21:41 All the cities of the *L* in
1Sa 6:15 *L* themselves took the ark of
2Sa 15:24 the *L* carrying the ark of
1Ki 8:4 the *L* came bringing them up
1Ch 6:19 families of the *L* by their
6:48 *L* were the ones given for
6:64 sons of Israel gave the *L*
9:2 Israelites, the priests, the *L*
9:14 of the *L* there were Shemaiah
9:26 the gatekeepers. They were *L*
9:31 Mattithiah of the *L*, who
9:33 heads of the fathers of the *L*
9:34 heads of the fathers of the *L*
12:26 Of the sons of the *L* four
13:2 to the priests and the *L* in
15:2 but the *L*, for they are the
15:4 the sons of Aaron and the *L*
15:11 *L* Uriel, Asaiah and Joel
15:12 of the fathers of the *L*
15:14 priests and the *L* sanctified
15:15 *L* began to carry the ark of
15:16 said to the chiefs of the *L*
15:17 *L* stationed Heman the son
15:22 chief of the *L* in carrying
15:26 the true God helped the *L*
15:27 all the *L* carrying the Ark
16:4 some of the *L* as ministers
23:2 and the priests and the *L*
23:3 *L* were numbered from the
23:14 among the tribe of the *L*
23:26 *L* will not have to carry
24:6 the secretary of the *L* wrote
24:6 of the priests and of the *L*
24:30 *L* by their paternal houses
24:31 of the priests and of the *L*
26:17 the east there were six *L*
26:20 As regards the *L*, Ahijah
28:13 of the priests and of the *L*
28:21 of the priests and of the *L*
2Ch 5:4 the *L* began to carry the Ark
5:5 priests the *L* brought them up
5:12 and the *L* that were singers
7:6 *L* with the instruments of
8:14 *L* at their posts of duty, to
8:15 *L* concerning any matter and
11:13 *L* themselves that were in
11:14 *L* left their pasture grounds
13:9 sons of Aaron, and the *L*
13:10 and also the *L* in the work
17:8 *L*, Shemaiah and Nethaniah
17:8 the *L*, and with them
19:8 stationed some of the *L* and
19:11 *L* are available for you
20:19 *L* of the sons of the

2Ch 23:2 collected together the *L*
23:4 of the priests and of the *L*
23:6 those of the *L* ministering
23:7 *L* must encircle the king all
23:8 *L* and all Judah proceeded to
23:18 priests and the *L*, whom
24:5 *L* together and said to them
24:5 *L* did not act quickly
24:6 required an account of the *L*
24:11 by the hand of the *L*, and
29:4 brought the priests and the *L*
29:5 Listen to me, you *L*
29:12 *L* rose up, Mahath the son
29:16 *L* received it to take it
29:25 *L* stationed at the house of
29:26 *L* kept standing with the
29:30 *L* to praise Jehovah in the
29:34 *L* helped them out until the
29:34 *L* were more upright of
30:15 *L* themselves had been
30:16 from the hand of the *L*
30:17 *L* were in charge of
30:21 *L* and the priests were
30:22 heart of all the *L* who were
30:25 *L* and all the congregation
30:27 *L*, stood up and blessed the
31:2 *L* in their divisions, each
31:2 for the *L* as regards the
31:4 of the priests and of the *L*
31:9 and the *L* concerning the
31:17 *L*, from the age of twenty
31:19 enrollment among the *L*
34:9 *L* the doorkeepers had
34:12 Jahath and Obadiah the *L*
34:12 *L*, each of whom was expert
34:13 *L* there were secretaries
34:30 the priests and the *L* and
35:3 *L*, the instructors of all
35:5 house belonging to the *L*
35:8 for the priests and for the *L*
35:9 the chiefs of the *L*
35:9 to the *L* for passover
35:10 and the *L* by their divisions
35:11 *L* were stripping the skins
35:14 and the *L*, for their part
35:15 their brothers the *L*
35:18 the priests and the *L* and
Ezr 1:5 the priests and the *L* rose up
2:40 The *L*: The sons of Jeshua
2:70 the priests and the *L* and
3:8 the priests and the *L*, and
3:8 *L* from twenty years of age
3:9 and their brothers, the *L*
3:10 and the *L* the sons of Asaph
3:12 the priests and the *L* and
6:16 the priests and the *L* and
6:18 the *L* in their divisions
6:20 the priests and the *L* had
7:7 and the *L* and the singers
7:13 and their priests and *L* that
7:24 the priests and the *L*, the
8:20 gave to the service of the *L*
8:29 the *L* and the princes of the
8:30 priests and the *L* received
8:33 the son of Binnui the *L*
9:1 the priests and the *L* have not
10:5 the *L* and all Israel take an
10:15 *L* were the ones that helped
10:23 of the *L*, Jozabad and
Ne 3:17 the *L* did repair work
7:1 and the singers and the *L*
7:43 The *L*: The sons of Jeshua
7:73 the priests and the *L* and the
8:7 even the *L*, were explaining
8:9 *L* who were instructing the
8:11 the *L* were ordering all the
8:13 the priests and the *L*
9:4 on the platform of the *L* and
9:5 the *L* Jeshua and Kadmiel
9:38 princes, our *L* and our priests
10:9 the *L*: Jeshua the son of
10:28 the priests, the *L*, the
10:34 *L* and the people should bring
10:37 tenth from our soil to the *L*
10:37 the *L*, are the ones receiving
10:38 must prove to be with the *L*
10:38 when the *L* receive a tenth
10:38 *L* themselves should offer up
10:39 sons of the *L* should bring
11:3 the priests and the *L*, and
11:15 And of the *L*: Shemaiah the
11:16 of the heads of the *L*
11:18 the *L* in the holy city were
11:20 the priests and of the *L*
Ne 11:22 the overseer of the *L* in
11:36 the *L* there were divisions
12:1 priests and the *L* that went
12:8 the *L* were Jeshua, Binnui
12:22 The *L* in the days of Eliashib
12:24 the heads of the *L* were
12:27 looked for the *L*, to bring
12:30 the priests and the *L*
12:44 for the priests and the *L*
12:44 the priests and of the *L*
12:47 sanctifying them to the *L*
12:47 *L* were sanctifying them to
13:5 the *L* and the singers and the
13:10 portions of the *L* had not
13:10 *L* and the singers doing the
13:13 Pedaiah of the *L* in charge
13:22 to say to the *L* that they
13:29 the priesthood and of the *L*
13:30 the priests and to the *L*
Isa 66:21 for the priests, for the *L*
Jer 33:18 *L*, there will not be cut
33:21 *L*, the priests, my
33:22 *L* who are ministering to
Eze 44:10 *L* who got far away from me
48:11 just as the *L* wandered away
48:12 on the boundary of the *L*
48:13 *L* should have, right next
48:22 possession of the *L* and
Joh 1:19 sent forth priests and *L*

Levites'
Eze 45:5 It will become the *L*

Levitical
Eze 43:19 give to the *L* priests, who
44:15 *L* priests, the sons of Zadok
Heb 7:11 through the *L* priesthood

Levying
1Ki 9:21 *l* them for slavish forced
2Ch 8:8 Solomon kept *l* men for forced

Liability
1Ki 8:31 under *l* to the curse
2Ch 6:22 him under *l* to the curse
Ne 10:29 coming into *l* to a curse

Liable
Mt 5:22 be *l* to the fiery Gehenna
26:66 answer: He is *l* to death
Mr 14:64 condemned . . . *l* to death
Ro 3:19 world may become *l* to God

Liar
Job 24:25 who will make me out a *l*
Ps 116:11 Every man is a *l*
Pr 30:6 may not have to be proved a *l*
Joh 8:44 *l* and the father of the lie
8:55 I should be like you, a *l*
Ro 3:4 every man be found a *l*, even
1Jo 1:10 we are making him a *l*, and
2:4 is a *l*, and the truth is not
2:22 Who is the *l* if it is not
4:20 hating his brother, he is a *l*
5:10 has made him a *l*, because

Liars
1Ti 1:10 *l*, false swearers and
Tit 1:12 said: Cretans are always *l*
Re 2:2 and you found them *l*
21:8 and idolaters and all the *l*

Libation
Isa 30:1 and to pour out a *l*, but

Libations
Ex 25:29 with which they will pour *l*
37:16 which *l* would be poured

Liberal
2Co 8:20 with this *l* contribution to
1Ti 6:18 to be *l*, ready to share

Liberality
Ro 12:8 let him do it with *l*; he that

Liberty
Le 25:10 *l* in the land to all its
Isa 61:1 *l* to those taken captive
Jer 34:8 to proclaim to them *l*
34:15 proclaiming *l* each one to
34:17 proclaiming *l* each one to
34:17 proclaiming to you a *l*, is
Eze 46:17 his until the year of *l*
Phm 22 I shall be set at *l* for you

Libnah
Nu 33:20 and went camping in *L*
33:21 pulled away from *L* and went
Jos 10:29 from Makkedah to *L* and
Jos 10:29 and warred against *L*
10:31 passed on from *L* to Lachish
10:32 all that they had done to *L*
10:39 just as he had done to *L*
12:15 the king of *L*, one
15:42 *L* and Ether and Ashan
21:13 *L* and its pasture ground
2Ki 8:22 *L* began to revolt at that
19:8 Assyria fighting against *L*
23:31 daughter of Jeremiah from *L*
24:18 daughter of Jeremiah from *L*
1Ch 6:57 *L* with its pasture grounds
2Ch 21:10 *L* began to revolt at the
Isa 37:8 Assyria fighting against *L*
Jer 52:1 daughter of Jeremiah of *L*

Libni
Ex 6:17 sons of Gershon were *L* and
Nu 3:18 Gershon by their families: *L*
1Ch 6:17 of Gershom: *L* and Shimei
6:20 Of Gershom, *L* his son
6:29 *L* his son, Shimei his son

Libnites
Nu 3:21 family of the *L* and the
26:58 the family of the *L*, the

Libya
Ac 2:10 *L*, which is toward Cyrene

Libyans
2Ch 12:3 out of Egypt—*L*, Sukkiim and
16:8 *L* themselves happen to be a
Da 11:43 *L* and the Ethiopians will be
Na 3:9 Put and the *L* themselves

License
Ge 49:4 With reckless *l* like waters

Lick
Nu 22:4 *l* up all our surroundings
1Ki 21:19 dogs will *l* up your blood
Ps 72:9 enemies will *l* the dust
Isa 49:23 the dust . . . they will *l* up
Mic 7:17 *l* up dust like the serpents
Lu 16:21 would come and *l* his ulcers

Licked
1Ki 18:38 was in the trench it *l* up
21:19 dogs *l* up the blood of

Licking
Nu 22:4 bull *l* up the green growth of
1Ki 22:38 dogs went *l* up his blood

Lid
Nu 19:15 upon which there is no *l*
2Ki 12:9 bored a hole in its *l* and
Zec 5:7 circular *l* of lead was lifted

Lie
Ge 19:4 Before they could *l* down, the
19:32 us *l* down with him and
19:34 you go in, *l* down with him
30:15 to *l* down with you tonight
39:7 and say: *L* down with me
39:10 never listened to her to *l*
39:12 *L* down with me! But he left
39:14 came to me to *l* down with
47:30 I must *l* with my fathers
49:13 where the ships *l* anchored
Ex 21:13 where one does not *l* in wait
22:27 In what will he *l* down?
23:11 and you must let it *l* fallow
Le 15:4 may *l* down will be unclean
15:18 may *l* down with an emission
15:20 upon which she may *l* down in
15:24 upon which he might *l* down
15:26 bed upon which she may *l* any
18:22 not *l* down with a male the
18:22 the same as you *l* down with
19:12 not swear in my name to a *l*
26:6 *l* down, with no one making
Nu 23:24 not *l* down until it may eat
De 6:7 when you *l* down and when you
11:19 when you *l* down and when
Jos 2:8 before they could *l* down, she
Jg 9:32 and *l* in wait in the field
9:34 began to *l* in wait against
9:43 to *l* in wait in the field
21:20 *l* in wait in the vineyards
Ru 3:4 uncover . . . his feet and *l*
3:7 Then he went to *l* down at the
1Sa 2:22 *l* down with the women that
3:5 I did not call. *L* down again
3:6 not call, my son. *L* down
3:9 said to Samuel: Go, *l* down
15:5 *l* in ambush by the torrent
2Sa 7:12 *l* down with your forefathers

2Sa 8:2 l down on the earth
11:11 and to l down with my wife
11:13 l down on his bed with the
12:3 and in his bosom it would l
12:11 l down with your wives
13:5 L down on your bed and play
13:11 l down with me, my sister
1Ki 1:2 she must l in your bosom, and
Job 6:28 see whether I shall l to
7:21 now in dust I shall l down
11:18 in security you will l down
14:12 Man also has to l down and
20:11 will l down in mere dust
21:26 in the dust they will l
27:19 Rich he will l down, but
Ps 3:5 will l down that I may sleep
4:2 you keep seeking to find a l
4:8 I will both l down and sleep
5:6 destroy those speaking a l
23:2 pastures he makes me l down
57:4 I cannot but l down among
62:4 They take pleasure in a l
62:9 The sons of mankind are a l
78:36 they tried to l to him
104:22 l down in their own hiding
Pr 1:11 let us l in ambush for blood
1:11 l in concealment for the
1:18 l in ambush for the very
1:18 l in concealment for their
3:24 l down you will feel no dread
3:24 l down, and your sleep must
6:22 l down, it will stand guard
14:5 is one that will not l
24:15 l in wait for the abiding
24:33 of the hands to l down
Ec 2:23 heart just does not l down
4:11 if two l down together, they
10:20 rooms where you l down do
Ca 1:7 the flock l down at midday
Isa 11:6 the leopard itself will l
11:7 their young ones will l
13:20 let their flocks l down
13:21 will certainly l down, and
14:30 themselves will l down
17:2 where they actually l down
27:10 there it will l down
28:15 made a l our refuge and in
28:17 away the refuge of a l
43:17 They will l down
50:11 In sheer pain you will l
58:11 waters of which do not l
Jer 3:25 We l down in our shame
33:12 making the flock l down
La 3:11 and he makes me to l fallow
Eze 4:4 l upon your left side, and you
4:4 days that you will l upon it
4:6 l upon your right side in the
6:6 that they may l devastated
6:6 your altars may l desolated
13:8 and you have visioned a l
13:9 and that are divining a l
13:19 by your l to my people, the
13:19 people, the hearers of a l
21:29 their divining for you a l
22:28 and divining for them a l
31:18 l down with those slain by
32:21 l down as the uncircumcised
32:27 not l down with mighty ones
32:28 l down with those slain by
32:29 will l down even with the
32:30 l down uncircumcised with
34:14 l down in a good abiding
34:15 shall make them l down
Da 11:27 l is what they will keep
Ho 2:18 make them l down in security
Jon 1:5 to l down and go fast asleep
Mic 2:11 If a man . . . has told the l
7:2 for bloodshed they l in wait
Hab 2:3 and it will not tell a l
Zep 2:7 they will l stretched out
2:14 certainly l stretched out
2:15 wild animals to l stretched
3:13 nor speak a l, nor will
3:13 actually l stretched out
Lu 5:25 what he used to l on and went
14:8 do not l down in the most
Joh 8:44 When he speaks the l, he
8:44 liar and the father of the l
Ro 1:25 the truth of God for the l
3:7 by reason of my l the truth
1Co 6:9 nor men who l with men
2Th 2:11 may get to believing the l
1Ti 1:10 men who l with males
Tit 1:2 God, who cannot l, promised
Heb 6:18 is impossible for God to l
1Jo 2:21 no l originates with the
2:27 and is true and is no l, and
Re 21:27 l will in no way enter into
22:15 liking and carrying on a l

Lier

1Sa 22:8 against me as a l in ambush
22:13 l in ambush the way it is

Lies

Ex 22:16 he actually l down with her
Le 14:47 whoever l down in the house
15:24 if a man l down with her at
15:33 who l down with an unclean
19:20 man l down with a woman and
20:11 a man who l down with his
20:12 where a man l down with his
20:13 man l down with a male the
20:13 as one l down with a woman
20:18 where a man l down with a
20:20 l down with his uncle's
Nu 5:13 man actually l down with her
23:19 a man that he should tell l
De 22:28 seizes her and l down with
27:20 l down with his father's
27:21 who l down with any beast
27:22 who l down with his sister
27:23 Cursed is the one who l down
Jg 16:10 that you might speak l to me
16:13 that you might speak l to me
Ru 3:4 when he l down, you must also
3:4 of the place where he l down
1Ki 1:21 l down with his forefathers
2Ki 4:16 Do not tell l in connection
Job 14:10 man dies and l vanquished
34:6 my own judgment do I tell l
40:21 Under . . . lotus trees it l
Ps 40:4 to those falling away to l
58:3 They are speaking l
89:35 To David I will not tell l
Pr 6:19 witness that launches forth l
7:12 every corner she l in wait
14:5 witness launches forth mere l
14:25 one launches forth mere l
19:5 forth l will not escape
19:9 launches forth l will perish
23:3 as it is the food of l
23:28 like a robber, l in wait
Ho 7:13 spoken l even against me
Am 2:4 l . . . kept making them wander
1Co 4:20 kingdom of God l not in
2Co 3:15 a veil l upon their hearts
1Ti 4:2 hypocrisy of men who speak l
Re 21:16 the city l foursquare, and

Life

Ge 1:30 there is l as a soul I have
2:7 his nostrils the breath of l
2:9 tree of l in the middle of the
3:14 eat all the days of your l
3:17 eat . . . all the days of your l
3:22 from the tree of l and eat
3:24 the way to the tree of l
6:17 flesh in which the force of l
7:11 six hundredth year of Noah's l
7:15 flesh in which the force of l
7:22 breath of the force of l
23:1 Sarah's l got to be a hundred
23:1 were the years of Sarah's l
25:7 Abraham's l which he lived, a
25:17 Ishmael's l, a hundred and
27:46 I have come to abhor this l
27:46 what good is l to me?
45:5 for the preservation of l God
47:8 days of the years of your l
47:9 the days of the years of my l
47:28 Jacob's . . . l, came to be a
Ex 1:14 l bitter with hard slavery at
6:16 the years of Levi's l were a
6:18 the years of Kohath's l were
6:20 And the years of Amram's l
Nu 22:30 ridden upon all your l long
De 4:9 all the days of your l; and you
6:2 all the days of your l, and in
16:3 all the days of your l
17:19 all the days of his l
28:66 greatest peril for your l
28:66 will not be sure of your l
30:6 for the sake of your l
30:15 put before you today l and
30:19 have put l and death before
30:19 choose l in order that you
30:20 your l and the length of your
32:47 but it means your l, and by
Jos 1:5 all the days of your l
4:14 Moses all the days of his l
Jg 13:12 child's mode of l and his
1Sa 1:11 all the days of his l, and no
1:26 By the l of your soul, my
2:6 a Killer and a Preserver of l
7:15 judging Israel all . . . his l
17:55 By the l of your soul, O
25:29 wrapped up in the bag of l
2Sa 1:23 pleasant ones during their l
15:21 whether for death or for l
19:34 days of the years of my l
1Ki 4:21 all the days of his l
11:34 for all the days of his l
15:5 all the days of his l, only
15:6 all the days of his l
17:22 the child . . . came to l
2Ki 13:21 came to l and stood upon
25:29 all the days of his l
25:30 all the days of his l
1Ch 11:8 to l the rest of the city
Ezr 6:10 praying for the l of the king
Ne 4:2 they bring the stones to l
Job 3:20 And l to those bitter of soul
7:7 Remember that my l is wind
9:21 I would refuse my l
10:1 feels a loathing toward my l
10:12 L and loving-kindness you
24:22 and not be sure of his l
33:4 proceeded to bring me to l
33:18 his l from passing away
33:20 his l certainly makes bread
33:22 his l to those inflicting
33:28 l itself will see the light
36:14 their l among male temple
Ps 7:5 trample my l down to the very
16:11 to know the path of l
17:14 whose share is in this l
21:4 L he asked of you. You gave it
23:6 all the days of my l
26:9 my l along with bloodguilty
27:1 is the stronghold of my l
27:4 all the days of my l
31:10 with grief my l has come to
34:12 man that is delighting in l
36:9 with you is the source of l
42:8 prayer to the God of my l
63:3 is better than l
64:1 may you safeguard my l
66:9 He is setting our soul in l
74:19 l of your afflicted ones
78:50 l he handed over even to the
88:3 l has come in touch even with
89:47 of what duration of l I am
103:4 reclaiming your l from the
104:33 to Jehovah throughout my l
128:5 all the days of your l
133:3 Even l to time indefinite
143:3 crushed my l to the very
Pr 3:2 years of l and peace will be
3:18 tree of l to those taking
3:22 l to your soul and charm
4:10 years of l will become many
4:13 for it itself is your l
4:22 l to those finding them and
4:23 of it are the sources of l
5:6 path of l she does not
6:23 discipline are the way of l
8:35 will certainly find l, and
9:11 years of l will be added
10:11 one is a source of l
10:16 righteous one results in l
10:17 discipline is a path to l
11:19 is in line for l, but the
11:30 is a tree of l, and he that
12:28 path of righteousness . . . l
13:12 thing desired is a tree of l
13:14 wise one is a source of l
14:27 The fear . . . is a well of l
14:30 l of the fleshly organism
15:4 of the tongue is a tree of l
15:24 path of l is upward to one
15:31 listening to the reproof of l
16:15 of the king's face there is l
16:22 insight is a well of l
18:21 Death and l are in the power
19:23 fear . . . tends toward l
21:21 will find l, righteousness
22:4 the fear of Jehovah is . . . l
27:27 means of l for your girls
29:21 later l he will even become
31:12 all the days of her l
Ec 2:3 number of the days of their l
2:17 I hated l, because the work

Ec 3:12 and to do good during one's l
5:18 l that the true God has given
5:20 he remember the days of his l
6:12 what good a man has in l for
6:12 of the days of his vain l
8:15 l, which the true God has
9:9 l with the wife whom you love
9:9 all the days of your vain l
9:9 that is your portion in l and
10:19 wine itself makes l rejoice
11:10 the prime of l are vanity
Isa 4:3 down for l in Jerusalem
38:12 rolled up my l just like a
38:16 is the l of my spirit
38:20 All the days of our l at
Jer 8:3 chosen rather than l
21:8 the way of l and the way of
52:33 all the days of his l
52:34 all the days of his l
La 3:53 have silenced my l in the pit
3:58 You have repurchased my l
Eze 7:13 l is yet among the living
7:13 his own l by his own error
33:15 the very statutes of l by
37:3 can these bones come to l?
37:5 and you must come to l
37:6 and you must come to l
37:9 that they may come to l
37:14 and you must come to l
47:9 torrent comes, will get l
Da 7:12 lengthening in l given to
12:2 to indefinitely lasting l
Jon 2:6 proceeded to bring up my l
Hab 3:2 O bring it to l! In the midst
Mal 2:5 one of l and of peace, and
Mt 7:14 the road leading off into l
9:18 and she will come to l
18:8 enter into l maimed or lame
18:9 to enter one-eyed into l than
19:16 order to get everlasting l
19:17 to enter into l, observe the
19:29 will inherit everlasting l
25:46 ones into everlasting l
Mr 9:43 finer for you to enter into l
9:45 enter into l lame than with
10:17 do to inherit everlasting l
10:30 coming system . . . everlasting l
Lu 8:14 riches and pleasures of this l
10:25 shall I inherit everlasting l
10:28 and you will get l
12:15 his l does not result from
15:13 by living a debauched l
15:24 son was dead and came to l
15:32 was dead and came to l, and
18:18 shall I inherit everlasting l
18:30 of things everlasting l
21:34 and anxieties of l, and
Joh 1:4 by means of him was l, and
1:4 the l was the light of men
3:15 may have everlasting l
3:16 but have everlasting l
3:36 has everlasting l; he that
3:36 will not see l, but the
4:14 to impart everlasting l
4:36 fruit for everlasting l, so
5:24 has everlasting l, and he
5:24 passed over from death to l
5:26 the Father has l in himself
5:26 the Son to have l in himself
5:29 to a resurrection of l
5:39 you will have everlasting l
5:40 to me that you may have l
6:27 food . . . for l everlasting
6:33 and gives l to the world
6:35 I am the bread of l. He that
6:40 should have everlasting l
6:47 believes has everlasting l
6:48 I am the bread of l
6:51 behalf of the l of the world
6:53 you have no l in yourselves
6:54 my blood has everlasting l
6:63 sayings . . . spirit and are l
6:68 have sayings of everlasting l
8:12 will possess the light of l
10:10 l and . . . in abundance
10:28 I give them everlasting l
11:25 the resurrection and the l
11:25 he dies, will come to l
12:25 it for everlasting l
12:50 means everlasting l
14:6 way and the truth and the l
17:2 may give them everlasting l
17:3 This means everlasting l
20:31 have l by means of his name
Ac 3:15 killed the Chief Agent of l
5:20 all the sayings about this l
8:33 l is taken away from the
11:18 l to people of the nations
13:46 worthy of everlasting l
13:48 disposed for everlasting l
17:25 to all persons l and breath
17:28 by him we have l and move
26:4 manner of l from youth up
Ro 2:7 everlasting l to those who are
5:10 we shall be saved by his l
5:17 l through the one person
5:18 of them righteous for l
5:21 l in view through Jesus
6:4 walk in a newness of l
6:10 l that he lives, he lives
6:22 and the end everlasting l
6:23 God gives is everlasting l
7:9 sin came to l again, but I
7:10 commandment which was to l
8:2 spirit which gives l in union
8:6 minding of the spirit means l
8:10 l on account of righteousness
8:38 death nor l nor angels nor
11:15 mean but l from the dead
14:9 Christ died and came to l
1Co 3:22 or l or death or things now
6:3 then, not matters of this l
6:4 have matters of this l to be
15:19 in this l only we have
2Co 2:16, 16 odor issuing from l to l
4:10 l of Jesus may also be made
4:11 l of Jesus may also be made
4:12 at work in us, but l in you
5:4 may be swallowed up by l
Ga 2:20 l that I now live in flesh I
3:21 that was able to give l
6:8 everlasting l from the spirit
Eph 4:18 the l that belongs to God
Php 1:20 through l or through death
2:16 tight grip on the word of l
4:3 names are in the book of l
Col 3:3 your l has been hidden with
3:4 the Christ, our l, is made
1Ti 1:16 faith . . . for everlasting l
2:2 leading a calm and quiet l
4:8 holds promise of the l now
6:12 hold on the everlasting l
6:19 a firm hold on the real l
2Ti 1:1 promise of the l that is in
1:10 has shed light upon l and
2:4 commercial businesses of l
3:10 my course of l, my purpose
Tit 1:2 a hope of the everlasting l
3:5 the bath that brought us to l
3:7 to a hope of everlasting l
Heb 7:3 nor an end of l, but having
7:16 power of an indestructible l
12:9 of our spiritual l and live
13:5 manner of l be free of the
Jas 1:11 fade away in his ways of l
1:12 will receive the crown of l
3:6 wheel of natural l aflame and
4:14 know what your l will be
1Pe 3:7 of the undeserved favor of l
3:10 he that would love l and see
2Pe 1:3 things that concern l and
1Jo 1:1 concerning the word of l
1:2 the l was made manifest, and
1:2 everlasting l which was with
2:16 display of one's means of l
2:25 the l everlasting
3:14 passed over from death to l
3:15 manslayer has everlasting l
3:17 means for supporting l and
4:9 we might gain l through him
5:11 God gave us everlasting l
5:11 and this l is in his Son
5:12 that has the Son has this l
5:12 does not have this l
5:13 that you have l everlasting
5:16 and he will give l to him
5:20 true God and l everlasting
Jude 16 complainers about . . . l
21 with everlasting l in view
Re 2:7 grant to eat of the tree of l
2:8 became dead and came to l
2:10 will give you the crown of l
3:5 his name from the book of l
7:17 to fountains of waters of l
11:11 spirit of l from God entered
13:8 written in the scroll of l
17:8 written upon the scroll of l
20:4 came to l and ruled as kings
Re 20:5 dead did not come to l until
20:12 opened; it is the scroll of l
20:15 written in the book of l
21:6 of the water of l free
21:27 in the Lamb's scroll of l
22:1 river of water of l, clear
22:2 trees of l producing twelve
22:14 to go to the trees of l may
22:19 away from the trees of l

Life-giving
Joh 6:63 It is the spirit that is l
1Co 15:45 last Adam became a l spirit

Lifeless
Jer 25:37 rendered l because of the

Life's
Job 11:17 will your l duration arise
Ps 32:4 l moisture has been changed
39:5 my l duration is as nothing
Ac 2:28 made l ways known to me
Re 22:17 wishes take l water free

Life-span
Mt 6:27 can add one cubit to his l
Lu 12:25 can add a cubit to his l

Lifetime
Le 18:18 besides her during her l
Jg 16:30 had put to death during his l
Ps 30:5 under his goodwill is for a l
49:18 during his l he kept blessing
63:4 shall bless you during my l
103:5 satisfying your l with what
146:2 praise Jehovah during my l
Ec 9:3 in their heart during their l
Lu 16:25 your good things in your l

Lift
Ge 14:22 I do l up my hand in an oath
21:18 l up the boy and take hold of
40:13 Pharaoh will l up your head
40:19 Pharaoh will l up your head
40:20 l up the head of the chief
41:44 no man may l up his hand or
45:19 you must l your father on
Ex 14:16 l up your rod and stretch
17:11 as Moses would l his hand up
40:37 if the cloud did not l itself
Le 2:9 priest must l off some of the
4:8 he will l up from it the fat
4:19 will l up all its fat from
6:10 he must l up the fatty ashes
6:15 must l up by his handful some
Nu 6:26 Jehovah l up his face toward
16:3 should you l yourselves up
23:24 the lion it will l itself up
Jos 4:5 l up for yourselves each one
Jg 8:28 they did not l up their head
2Sa 22:49 you will l me up; From the
1Ki 11:26 to l up his hand against
13:29 l up the dead body of the
2Ki 4:36 Then he said: L up your son
6:7 said: L it up for yourself
9:25 L him up; throw him into
9:26 l him up; throw him into
19:4 must l up prayer in behalf
Job 27:1 l up his proverbial utterance
29:1 l up his proverbial utterance
30:22 You l me to the wind, you
Ps 4:6 L up the light of your face
7:6 L yourself up at the outbursts
10:12 O God, l up your hand
18:48 you will l me up
20:5 we shall l our banners
74:3 l up your steps to the
86:4 I l up my very soul
Pr 19:18 not l up your soulful desire
Isa 2:4 Nation will not l up sword
10:24 l up his own staff against
10:26 l it up in the way that he
13:2 L up the voice to them, wave
14:13 I shall l up my throne
33:10 now I will l myself up
37:4 l up prayer in behalf of the
49:22 I shall l up my signal
63:9 to l them up and carry them
Jer 11:14 do not l up in their behalf
13:26 l up your skirts over your
50:2 l up a signal; publish it
51:12 of Babylon l up a signal
51:27 L up a signal in the land
Eze 11:1 a spirit proceeded to l me
17:14 unable to l itself up, that
20:5 l up my hand in an oath to
20:5 to l up my hand in an oath

Eze 21:26 and *l* off the crown
27:32 *l* up a dirge and chant over
28:12 Son of man, *l* up a dirge
29:15 no more *l* itself up over
32:2 Son of man, *l* up a dirge
45:9 *L* your expropriations off
Am 4:2 *l* you up with butcher hooks
Jon 1:12 *L* me up and hurl me into the
Mic 4:3 not *l* up sword, nation
Hab 2:6 *l* up against him a proverbial
Mt 12:11 get hold of it and *l* it out
27:32 to *l* up his torture stake
Mr 15:21 *l* up his torture stake
Lu 21:28 *l* your heads up, because
Joh 4:35 *L* up your eyes and view the

Lifted

Ge 31:17 Then Jacob got up and *l* his
37:28 they drew and *l* up Joseph
44:13 *l* each one his load back onto
Ex 7:20 *l* up the rod and struck the
40:36 cloud *l* itself up from over
40:37 the day when it *l* itself up
Le 4:10 as what is *l* up of a bull of
Nu 9:21 cloud *l* itself in the morning
9:21 by night that the cloud *l*
9:22 when it *l* itself they would
10:11 cloud *l* itself from over
14:30 I *l* up my hand in oath to
20:11 Moses *l* his hand up and
24:7 And his kingdom will be *l* up
De 8:14 your heart may indeed be *l* up
Jg 9:48 and *l* it up and put it on his
16:31 *l* him up and brought him up
1Sa 9:24 the cook *l* off the leg and
2Sa 18:28 *l* up their hand against my
20:21 *l* up his hand against King
1Ki 11:27 reason why he *l* up his hand
2Ki 2:16 spirit of Jehovah has *l* him
4:37 she *l* up her son and went
9:25 *l* up this pronouncement
14:10 your heart has *l* you up
19:22 have you *l* up your voice
2Ch 5:13 they *l* up the sound with the
24:11 *l* it up and returned it to
25:19 heart has *l* you up to be
Ne 9:15 *l* your hand in an oath to give
Ps 102:10 you have *l* me up, that you
143:8 to you I have *l* up my soul
Pr 30:13 whose beaming eyes are *l* up
Ca 5:7 *l* my wide wrap off me
Isa 2:2 be *l* up above the hills
2:12 upon everyone *l* up or low
2:13 that are lofty and *l* up and
2:14 all the hills that are *l* up
6:1 on a throne lofty and *l* up
37:23 have you *l* up your voice
57:7 a mountain high and *l* up
Jer 51:9 been *l* up to the cloudy skies
La 5:13 men have *l* up a hand mill
Eze 1:19 living creatures were *l* up
1:19 the wheels would be *l* up
1:20 be *l* up close alongside them
1:21 were *l* up from the earth
1:21 wheels would be *l* up close
10:16 cherubs *l* up their wings to
10:19 the cherubs now *l* up their
11:22 the cherubs now *l* up their
11:24 a spirit itself *l* me up and
17:9 to be *l* up from its roots
18:12 dungy idols he *l* up his eyes
18:15 eyes he has not *l* up to the
20:6 I *l* up my hand in an oath to
20:15 *l* up my hand in an oath to
20:23 *l* up my hand in an oath to
20:28 *l* up my hand in an oath to
20:42 I *l* up my hand in an oath
Da 4:34 *l* up to the heavens my eyes
6:23 to be *l* up out of the pit
6:23 was *l* up out of the pit
7:4 was *l* up from the earth and
Jon 1:15 they *l* up Jonah and hurled
Mic 4:1 be *l* up above the hills; and
Hab 3:10 On high its hands it *l* up
Zec 5:7 circular lid of lead was *l* up
Mt 21:21 say to this mountain, Be *l*
Mr 11:23 Be *l* up and thrown into the
Lu 6:20 he *l* up his eyes upon his
16:23 in Hades he *l* up his eyes
24:50 *l* up his hands and blessed
Joh 3:14 as Moses *l* up the serpent in
3:14 the Son of man must be *l* up
8:28 have *l* up the Son of man
10:31 Jews *l* up stones to stone
Joh 12:32 if I am *l* up from the earth
12:34 the Son of man must be *l* up
13:18 *l* up his heel against me
Ac 1:9 *l* up and a cloud caught him
10:26 Peter *l* him up, saying: Rise
27:13 *l* anchor and began coasting
Re 18:21 strong angel *l* up a stone

Lifting

De 24:15 *l* up his soul to his wages
1Ki 1:5 was *l* himself up, saying
1Ch 29:11 *l* yourself up as head over
Ne 8:6 with the *l* up of their hands
Ps 3:3 and the One *l* up my head
9:13 *l* me up from the gates of
Pr 30:32 senselessly by *l* yourself up
Jer 22:27 be *l* up their soul to return
44:14 *l* up their soulful desire
Eze 20:31 *l* up your gifts by making
33:25 eyes you keep *l* to your
Ho 4:8 they keep *l* up their soul
11:4 *l* off a yoke on their jaws
Zec 1:21 *l* up a horn against the land
12:3 All those *l* it will without
1Ti 2:8 prayer, *l* up loyal hands

Lifts

1Sa 2:8 *l* up a poor one, To make them
Ps 107:25 So that it *l* up its waves
Isa 40:15 He *l* the islands themselves
2Th 2:4 *l* himself up over everyone

Ligaments

Col 2:19 by means of its joints and *l*

Light

Ge 1:3 Let *l* come to be. Then there
1:3 Then there came to be *l*
1:4 God saw that the *l* was good
1:4 division between the *l* and the
1:5 God began calling the *l* Day
1:18 make a division between the *l*
44:3 The morning had become *l*
Ex 10:23 to be *l* in their dwellings
13:21 fire to give them *l* to go in
27:20 *l* up the lamps constantly
35:3 not *l* a fire in any of your
40:4 lampstand and *l* up its lamps
Le 24:2 to *l* up the lamp constantly
Nu 8:2 *l* up the lamps, the seven
Jg 16:2 the morning gets *l*, we must
1Sa 25:34 until the morning *l* anyone
25:36 until the morning *l*
29:10 it has become *l* for you
2Sa 17:22 until the morning became *l*
23:4 it is as the *l* of morning
2Ki 7:9 wait until the morning *l*
2Ch 4:20 to *l* them up before the
13:11 lamps to *l* up evening by
Ne 9:12 to *l* up for them the way in
9:19 pillar of fire by night to *l*
Es 8:16 For the Jews there occurred *l*
Job 3:9 Let it wait for the *l* and
3:16 children that have seen no *l*
3:20 give *l* to one having trouble
3:23 he give *l* to able-bodied man
12:22 forth to the *l* deep shadow
12:25 where there is no *l*
17:12 *L* is near on account of
18:5 *l* also of wicked ones will
18:6 *l* . . . grow dark in his tent
18:18 will push him out of the *l*
22:28 And upon your ways *l* will
24:13 among the rebels against *l*
25:3 whom does his *l* not rise
26:10 To where *l* ends in darkness
28:11 he brings forth to the *l*
29:3 through darkness by his *l*
29:24 the *l* of my face they would
30:26 I kept awaiting the *l*, but
31:26 *l* when it would flash forth
33:28 life itself will see the *l*
33:30 with the *l* of those living
36:30 has spread out over it his *l*
37:11 His *l* scatters the cloud
37:15 the *l* of his cloud to beam
37:21 do not really see the *l*
38:15 their *l* is held back
38:19 the way to where *l* resides
38:24 the *l* distributes itself
41:18 sneezings flash forth *l*
Ps 4:6 Lift up the *l* of your face
18:28 you yourself will *l* my lamp
27:1 Jehovah is my *l* and my
36:9, 9 By *l* from you we can see *l*
37:6 righteousness as the *l* itself
Ps 38:10 the *l* of my own eyes also is
43:3 Send out your *l* and your
44:3 and the *l* of your face
49:19 will they see the *l*
56:13 in the *l* of those alive
76:4 You are enveloped with *l*
78:14 whole night with a *l* of fire
80:3 *l* up your face, that we may
80:7 And *l* up your face, that we
80:19 *L* up your face, that we may
89:15 in the *l* of your face they
97:11 *L* itself has flashed up for
104:2 Enwrapping yourself with *l*
105:39 fire to give *l* by night
112:4 as a *l* to the upright ones
118:27 And he gives us *l*
119:105 And a *l* to my roadway
119:130 of your words gives *l*
139:11 night would be *l* about me
139:12 just as well be the *l*
148:3 all you stars of *l*
Pr 3:20 keep dripping down *l* rain
4:18 bright *l* that is getting
6:23 and a *l* the law is, and the
13:9 *l* of the righteous ones will
16:15 In the *l* of the king's face
Ec 2:13 more advantage for *l* than for
11:7 The *l* is also sweet, and it
12:2 before the sun and the *l* and
Isa 2:5 us walk in the *l* of Jehovah
5:20 putting darkness for *l* and
5:20 and *l* for darkness, those
5:30 even the *l* has grown dark
8:20 will have no *l* of dawn
9:2 have seen a great *l*
9:2 *l* itself has shone upon them
10:17 Israel's *L* must become a
11:8 *l* aperture of a poisonous
13:10 not flash forth their *l*
13:10 not cause its *l* to shine
18:4 heat along with the *l*, like
24:15 in the region of *l* they
30:26 *l* of the full moon must
30:26 as the *l* of the glowing sun
30:26 *l* of the glowing sun will
30:26 like the *l* of seven days
31:9 Jehovah, whose *l* is in Zion
42:6 as a *l* of the nations
42:16 place before them into *l*
45:7 Forming *l* and creating
49:6 you for a *l* of the nations
50:11 making sparks *l* up, walk in
50:11 walk in the *l* of your fire
51:4 even as a *l* to the peoples
58:8 your *l* would break forth
58:10 your *l* also will certainly
59:9 We keep hoping for *l*, but
60:1 Arise, O woman, shed forth *l*
60:1 for your *l* has come and
60:3 go to your *l*, and kings to
60:19 prove to be a *l* by day, and
60:19 will no more give you *l*
60:19 an indefinitely lasting *l*
60:20 an indefinitely lasting *l*
Jer 4:23 and their *l* was no more
13:16 certainly hope for the *l*
25:10 and the *l* of the lamp
31:35 Giver of the sun for *l* by
31:35 the stars for *l* by night
La 3:2 walk in darkness and not in *l*
Eze 8:17 *l* thing to the house of Judah
32:7 will not let its *l* shine
32:8 luminaries of *l* in the
39:9 have to *l* fires seven years
39:10 the armor they will *l* fires
Da 2:22 with him the *l* does dwell
Ho 6:5 be as the *l* that goes forth
Joe 2:2 like *l* of dawn spread out
Am 5:18 will be darkness, and no *l*
5:20 be darkness, and not *l*
Mic 2:1 By the *l* of the morning they
7:8 Jehovah will be a *l* to me
7:9 will bring me forth to the *l*
Hab 3:4 it got to be just like the *l*
3:11 Like *l* your own arrows kept
Zec 14:6 prove to be no precious *l*
14:7 evening . . . will become *l*
Mal 1:10 you men will not *l* my altar
Mt 4:16 saw a great *l*, and as for
4:16 shadow, *l* rose upon them
5:14 You are the *l* of the world
5:15 People *l* a lamp and set it
5:16 let your *l* shine before men
6:23 *l* that is in you is darkness

Mt 10:27 say in the l; and what you
11:30 is kindly and my load is l
17:2 became brilliant as the l
24:29 moon will not give its l
28:1 growing l on the first day of
Mr 13:24 moon will not give its l
Lu 1:79 to give l to those sitting
2:32 a l for removing the veil
8:16 stepping in may behold the l
11:33 stepping in may behold the l
11:35 l that is in you is darkness
11:36 lamp gives you l by its rays
12:3 will be heard in the l, and
15:8 l a lamp and sweep her house
16:8 than the sons of the l are
23:54 evening l of the sabbath was
Joh 1:4 the life was the l of men
1:5 l is shining in the darkness
1:7 to bear witness about the l
1:8 He was not that l, but he
1:8 to bear witness about that l
1:9 The true l that gives
1:9 gives l to every sort of man
3:19 l has come into the world
3:19 darkness rather than the l
3:20 hates the l and does not
3:20 does not come to the l
3:21 what is true comes to the l
5:35 to rejoice greatly in his l
8:12 I am the l of the world
8:12 will possess the l of life
9:5 I am the world's l
11:9 he sees the l of this world
11:10 because the l is not in him
12:35 l will be among you a
12:35 Walk while you have the l
12:36 While you have the l
12:36 exercise faith in the l, in
12:36 to become sons of l
12:46 come as a l into the world
Ac 9:3 l from heaven flashed around
12:7 l shone in the prison cell
13:47 as a l of nations, for you
22:6 out of heaven a great l
22:9 beheld, indeed, the l but did
22:11 for the glory of that l, I
26:13 l beyond the brilliance of
26:18 them from darkness to l and
26:23 publish l both to this people
Ro 2:19 a l for those in darkness
13:12 put on the weapons of the l
1Co 4:5 things of darkness to l and
2Co 4:6 l shine out of darkness, and
4:17 the tribulation is . . . l
6:14 does l have with darkness
11:14 Satan . . . into an angel of l
Eph 5:8 l in connection with the Lord
5:8 walking as children of l
5:9 the fruitage of the l consists
5:13 are made manifest by the l
5:13 being made manifest is l
Col 1:12 of the holy ones in the l
1Th 5:5 you are all sons of l and sons
1Ti 6:16 dwells in unapproachable l
2Ti 1:10 has shed l upon life and
1Pe 2:9 into his wonderful l
2Pe 1:9 shutting his eyes to the l
1Jo 1:5 God is l and there is no
1:7 if we are walking in the l as
1:7 as he himself is in the l
2:8 the true l is already shining
2:9 He that says he is in the l
2:10 remains in the l, and there
Re 18:23 no l of a lamp will ever
21:24 walk by means of its l
22:5 God will shed l upon them

Lighted
Ru 2:3 she l on the tract of the field
Ps 77:18 Lightnings have l up the
97:4 lightnings l up the productive
Lu 12:49 if it has already been l
Ac 27:41 l upon a shoal washed on
Re 18:1 earth was l up from his glory
21:23 glory of God l it up, and

Lighten
1Sa 6:5 will l his hand from off you
Ps 144:6 L with lightning that you
Jon 1:5 to the sea, in order to l it
Ac 27:18 they began to l the ship
27:38 l the boat by throwing the

Lightens
1Sa 14:36 until the morning l up

Lighter
Ex 18:22 make it l for yourself, and
1Ki 12:4 yoke that he put upon us l
12:9 Make the yoke . . . l
12:10 you, make it l upon us
2Ch 10:4 yoke that he put upon us l
10:9 your father put upon us l
10:10 for you, make it l upon us
Ps 62:9 together l than an exhalation
Pr 4:18, 18 l and l until the day is

Lighting
Ex 14:20 it kept l up the night
Pr 29:13 Jehovah is l up the eyes of
Isa 27:11 break them off, l them up
Jer 7:18 the fathers are l the fire
Lu 8:16 No one, after l a lamp
11:33 After l a lamp, a person

Lightly
1Sa 18:23 little means and l esteemed
2Sa 6:22 even more l esteemed than
Pr 12:9 one l esteemed but having a
Isa 3:5 l esteemed one against the
Jer 6:14 l, saying, There is peace!
8:11 l, saying: There is peace!

Lightness
2Co 1:17 I did not indulge in any l

Lightning
Ex 20:18 the l flashes and the sound
2Sa 22:15 L, that he might throw
Job 36:32 he has covered over the l
37:3 his l is to the extremities
41:19 there go l flashes
Ps 144:6 Lighten with l that you may
Eze 1:13 out of the fire there was l
1:14 with the appearance of the l
Da 10:6 face like the appearance of l
Na 3:3 and the l of the spear, and the
Hab 3:11 The l of your spear served
Zec 9:14 go forth just like l
Mt 24:27 l comes out of eastern parts
28:3 outward appearance was as l
Lu 10:18 fallen like l from heaven
17:24 l, by its flashing, shines

Lightnings
Ex 19:16 that thunders and l began
Job 38:35 send forth l that they may
Ps 18:14 And l he shot out, that he
77:18 L have lighted up the
97:4 l lighted up the productive
Na 2:4 Like the l they keep running
Re 4:5 l and voices and thunders
8:5 voices and l and an earthquake
11:19 occurred l and voices and

Lights
Ex 30:8 when Aaron l up the lamps
Ps 136:7 the One making the great l
Ac 16:29 he asked for l and leaped in
Jas 1:17 Father of the celestial l

Likable
1Sa 2:26 growing bigger and more l

Like*
Ex 15:11 Who is l you, proving
1Ch 29:15 L a shadow our days are
2Ch 32:17 L the gods of the nations
Mt 6:5 they l to pray standing in the
11:16 l young children sitting in
23:6 l the most prominent place
Lu 20:46 in robes and l greetings

Likely
Jos 14:12 L Jehovah will be with me
Lu 12:40 hour that you do not think l
20:13 L they will respect this one

Like-minded
1Pe 3:8 all of you be l, showing

Liken
Isa 40:18 whom can you people l God
40:25 whom can you people l me
46:5 whom will you people l me
La 2:13 What shall I l to you, O
Mr 4:30 we to l the kingdom of God

Likened
Ca 1:9 I have l you, O girl companion
Mt 7:24 will be l to a discreet man
7:26 will be l to a foolish man

Likeness
Ge 1:26 according to our l, and let
5:1 he made him in the l of God
5:3 father to a son in his l
2Ch 4:3 l of gourd-shaped ornaments
Ps 17:12 His l is that of a lion that
Isa 40:18 l can you put alongside him
Eze 1:5 the l of four living creatures
1:5 had the l of earthling man
1:10 as for the l of their faces
1:13 the l of the living creatures
1:16 the four of them had one l
1:22 the l of an expanse like the
1:26 stone, the l of a throne
1:26 And upon the l of the throne
1:26 l of someone in appearance
1:28 the l of the glory of Jehovah
8:2 a l similar to the appearance
10:1 the l of a throne, appearing
10:10 the four of them had one l
10:21 l of the hands of earthling
10:22 as for the l of their faces
23:15 l of the sons of Babylon
Da 10:16 l of the sons of mankind was
Ro 5:14 l of the transgression by
6:5 in the l of his death, we
6:5 in the l of his resurrection
8:3 Son in the l of sinful flesh
Php 2:7 came to be in the l of men
Jas 3:9 into existence in the l of God

Likenesses
Ho 12:10 prophets I kept making l
Re 9:7 the l of the locusts resembled

Likes
De 23:16 one of your cities . . . he l
3Jo 9 l to have the first place

Likhi
1Ch 7:19 sons of Shemida . . . L and

Liking
1Sa 18:20 and the matter was to his l
18:26 the matter was to David's l
Ne 9:24 according to their l
9:37 according to their l, and we
Es 1:8 do according to the l of each
9:5 doing . . . according to their l
Re 22:15 l and carrying on a lie

Lilies
Ps 45:*super* To the director upon The L
69:*super* To the director on The L
80:*super* To the director upon The L
Ca 2:16 He is shepherding among the l
4:5 that are feeding among the l
5:13 His lips are l, dripping with
6:2 the gardens, and to pick l
6:3 He is shepherding among the l
7:2 wheat, fenced about with l
Mt 6:28 a lesson from the l of the
Lu 12:27 Mark well how the l grow

Lily
1Ki 7:19 the porch were of l work
7:22 upon the top . . . l work
7:26 brim of a cup, a l blossom
2Ch 4:5 brim of a cup, a l blossom
Ps 60:*super* on The L of Reminder
Ca 2:1 I am, a l of the low plains
2:2 Like a l among thorny weeds
Ho 14:5 He will blossom like the l

Limbs
Job 18:13 will eat his l

Lime
De 27:2 and whitewash them with l
27:4 must whitewash them with l
Isa 33:12 as the burnings of l
Am 2:1 burning the bones . . . for l

Limit
Nu 16:13 the prince over us to the l
23:11 have blessed them to the l
24:10 have blessed them to the l
Ezr 7:22 oil, and salt without l
9:14 get incensed at us to the l
Job 11:7 the very l of the Almighty
14:13 time l for me and remember
15:8 do you l wisdom to yourself?
28:3 every l he is searching out
34:36 Job be tested out to the l
Isa 2:7 is no l to their treasures
2:7 is no l to their chariots
56:12 intoxicating liquor to the l
Na 2:9 there is no l to the things
3:9 Egypt; and that without l
Ga 4:4 full l of the time arrived
Eph 1:10 l of the appointed times
Heb 11:11 she was past the age l

Limited
Job 38:11 here your proud waves are *l*
1Co 14:27 let it be *l* to two or three

Limits
Ac 17:26 set *l* of the dwelling of men

Limp
Job 18:12 stands ready to make him *l*
Ps 38:17 For I was ready to *l*, And my

Limping
Ge 32:31 but he was *l* upon his thigh
1Ki 18:21 *l* upon two different
18:26 kept *l* around the altar
Ps 35:15 But at my *l* they rejoiced
Jer 20:10 they are watching for my *l*
Mic 4:6 I will gather her that was *l*
4:7 her that was *l* a remnant
Zep 3:19 I will save her that is *l*

Line
1Sa 4:2 closed battle *l* in the field
4:12 running from the battle *l* so
4:16 one coming from the battle *l*
4:16 from the battle *l* that I
14:14 half the plowing *l* in an
17:20 going out to the battle *l*
17:21 began drawing up battle *l*
17:21 to meet battle *l*
17:22 running to the battle *l*
17:48 running toward the battle *l*
2Sa 8:2 and measure them with a *l*
8:2 full *l* to preserve them alive
1Ki 7:23 *l* of thirty cubits to circle
20:39 a man was leaving the *l*
2Ki 21:13 measuring *l* applied to
1Ch 12:38 together in battle *l*
2Ch 4:2 *l* of thirty cubits to circle
Job 13:27 you mark your own *l*
38:5 upon it the measuring *l*
Ps 19:4 measuring *l* has gone out
37:26 are in *l* for a blessing
78:55 by the measuring *l* he went
Pr 11:19 is in *l* for life, but
11:19 is in *l* for his own death
Isa 28:10, 10 *l* upon measuring *l*
28:10, 10 *l* upon measuring *l*
28:13, 13 *l* upon measuring *l*
28:13, 13 *l* upon measuring *l*
28:17 justice the measuring *l* and
34:11 measuring *l* of emptiness
34:17 to them by the measuring *l*
44:13 out the measuring *l*
Jer 31:39 *l* for measurement will yet
La 2:8 stretched out the measuring *l*
Eze 47:3 measuring *l* in his hand
Zec 1:16 a measuring *l* itself will be
Mr 12:14 way of God in *l* with truth
12:32 well said in *l* with truth
Lu 12:47 or do in *l* with his will
20:21 way of God in *l* with truth
1Co 1:10 and in the same *l* of thought
Jude 14 seventh one in *l* from Adam

Linen
Ge 41:42 with garments of fine *l* and
Ex 25:4 and fine *l*, and goat's hair
26:1 cloths, of fine twisted *l* and
26:31 material and fine twisted *l*
26:36 material and fine twisted *l*
27:9 hangings of fine twisted *l*
27:16 fine twisted *l*, the work of
27:18 of fine twisted *l*, and their
28:5 material and the fine *l*
28:6 material and fine twisted *l*
28:8 material and fine twisted *l*
28:15 and fine twisted *l* you will
28:39 the robe of fine *l* and make
28:39 and make a turban of fine *l*
28:42 make drawers of *l* for them
35:6 and fine *l* and goat's hair
35:23 fine *l* and goat's hair and
35:25 kept bringing . . . fine *l*
35:35 scarlet material and fine *l*
36:8 tent cloths of fine twisted *l*
36:35 material and fine twisted *l*
36:37 material and fine twisted *l*
38:9 fine twisted *l*, for a hundred
38:16 hangings . . . fine twisted *l*
38:18 material and fine twisted *l*
38:23 scarlet material and fine *l*
39:2 material and fine twisted *l*
39:3 material and the fine *l*
39:5 and fine twisted *l*, just as
39:8 material and fine twisted *l*
Ex 39:27 made the robes of fine *l*
39:28 the turban of fine *l* and the
39:28 headgears of fine *l* and
39:28 *l* drawers of fine twisted
39:28 drawers of fine twisted *l*
39:29 the sash of fine twisted *l*
Le 6:10 with his official dress of *l*
6:10 *l* drawers on over his flesh
13:47 garment or in a *l* garment
13:48 in the woof of the *l* and of
13:52 or in the *l*, or any article
13:59 a garment of wool or of *l*
16:4 should put on the holy *l* robe
16:4 *l* drawers should come upon
16:4 gird himself with the *l* sash
16:4 wrap . . . with the *l* turban
16:23 strip off the *l* garments
16:32 must put on the *l* garments
De 22:11 mixed stuff of wool and *l*
Jg 15:14 came to be like *l* threads
1Sa 2:18 having a *l* ephod girded on
22:18 men bearing an ephod of *l*
2Sa 6:14 girded with an ephod of *l*
1Ch 15:27 there was an ephod of *l*
Es 1:6 There were *l*, fine cotton and
8:15 in royal apparel of blue and *l*
Pr 7:16 divan, with . . . *l* of Egypt
31:13 She has sought wool and *l*
31:22 Her clothing is of *l* and
Jer 13:1 get for yourself a *l* belt
Eze 9:2 in among them clothed with *l*
9:3 the man . . . clothed with the *l*
9:11 the man clothed with the *l*
10:2 the man clothed with the *l*
10:6 the man clothed with the *l*
10:7 the one clothed with the *l*
16:10 to wrap you in fine *l* and
16:13 your attire was fine *l* and
27:7 *L* in various colors from
44:17 *l* garments they should wear
44:18 *L* headdresses are what
44:18 *l* drawers are what should
Da 10:5 man clothed in *l*, with his
12:6 the man clothed with the *l*
12:7 the man clothed with the *l*
Ho 2:5 and my *l*, my oil and my drink
2:9 snatch away my wool and my *l*
Mt 27:59 wrapped . . . in clean fine *l*
Mr 14:51 wearing a fine *l* garment
14:52 he left his *l* garment behind
15:46 he bought fine *l* and took
15:46 wrapped him in the fine *l*
Lu 16:19 himself with purple and *l*
23:53 and wrapped it up in fine *l*
Ac 10:11 great *l* sheet being let down
11:5 great *l* sheet being let down
Re 15:6 clothed with clean, bright *l*
18:12 fine *l* and purple and silk
18:16 city, clothed with fine *l*
19:8 in bright, clean, fine *l*
19:8 *l* stands for the righteous
19:14 in white, clean, fine *l*

Lines
1Sa 17:8 to the battle *l* of Israel
17:10 taunt the battle *l* of Israel
17:23 battle *l* of the Philistines
17:26 battle *l* of the living God
17:36 he has taunted the battle *l*
17:45 the God of the battle *l* of
23:3 battle *l* of the Philistines
2Sa 8:2 measure two *l* to put them to
Ps 16:6 measuring *l* themselves have

Linger
Ex 12:39 and had not been able to *l*
Isa 29:9 *L*, you men, and be amazed

Lingered
Ge 43:10 if we had not *l* around, we
Jg 19:8 they *l* until the fading away

Lingering
Ge 19:16 he kept *l*, then in the
Jg 3:26 he escaped while they were *l*
2Sa 15:28 I am *l* by the fords of the
Isa 5:11 *l* till late in the evening

Lingers
Ex 21:21 if he *l* for a day or two

Linus
2Ti 4:21 Pudens and *L* and Claudia and

Lion
Ge 49:9 A *l* cub Judah is. From the
49:9 he stretched . . . like a *l* and
Ge 49:9 *l*, who dares rouse him?
Nu 23:24 people will get up like a *l*
23:24 And like the *l* it will lift
24:9 he lay down like the *l*, And
24:9 like a *l*, who dares rouse
De 33:20 As a *l* he must reside, And
33:22 he said: Dan is a *l* cub
Jg 14:5 a maned young *l* roaring upon
14:8 look at the carcass of the *l*
14:9 out of the corpse of the *l*
14:18 what is stronger than a *l*?
1Sa 17:34 there came a *l*, and also a
17:36 Both the *l* and the bear your
17:37 from the paw of the *l* and
2Sa 17:10 is as the heart of the *l*
23:20 struck down a *l* inside a
1Ki 13:24 a *l* found him on the road
13:24 the *l* was standing beside
13:25 *l* standing beside the dead
13:26 Jehovah gave him to the *l*
13:28 *l* standing beside the dead
13:28 *l* had not eaten the dead
20:36 a *l* will certainly strike
20:36 the *l* got to find him and
1Ch 11:22 struck down a *l* inside a
Job 4:10 There is the roaring of a *l*
4:10 and the voice of a young *l*
4:11 A *l* is perishing from there
4:11 the cubs of a *l* are separated
10:16 like a young *l* you will
28:8 young *l* has not paced over it
38:39 Can you hunt prey for a *l*
Ps 7:2 tear my soul to pieces as a *l*
10:9 like a *l* in his covert
17:12 His likeness is that of a *l*
17:12 *l* sitting in concealed places
22:13 As a *l* tearing in pieces
22:16 Like a *l* they are at my
22:21 from the mouth of the *l*
91:13 Upon the young *l* and the
91:13 trample . . . the maned young *l*
Pr 19:12 like that of a maned young *l*
20:2 like that of a maned young *l*
22:13 said: There is a *l* outside
26:13 is a young *l* in the way, a
26:13 a *l* in among the public
28:1 righteous are like a young *l*
28:15 As a growling *l* and an
30:30 *l*, which is the mightiest
Ec 9:4 dog is better off than a dead *l*
Isa 5:29 roaring . . . like that of a *l*
11:6 calf and the maned young *l*
11:7 even the *l* will eat straw
15:9 *l* for the escapees of Moab
21:8 call out like a *l*
30:6 *l* and the leopard growling
31:4 Just as the *l* growls, even
31:4 even the maned young *l*, over
35:9 *l* will prove to be there
38:13 Like a *l*, so he keeps
65:25 *l* will eat straw just like
Jer 2:30 like a *l* that is causing ruin
4:7 as a *l* out of his thicket
5:6 a *l* out of the forest has
12:8 like a *l* in the forest
25:38 just like a maned young *l*
49:19 *l* from the proud thickets
50:44 *l* from the proud thickets
La 3:10 a *l* in places of concealment
Eze 10:14 third was the face of a *l*
19:3 A maned young *l* is what he
19:5 As a maned young *l* she put
19:6 A maned young *l* is what he
22:25 like the roaring *l*, tearing
32:2 a maned young *l* of nations
41:19 face of a maned young *l*
Da 7:4 first one was like a *l*, and it
Ho 5:14 be like a young *l* to Ephraim
5:14 like a maned young *l* to the
11:10 Like a *l* he will roar
13:7 become to them like a young *l*
13:8 devour them there like a *l*
Joe 1:6 teeth are the teeth of a *l*
1:6 it has the jawbones of a *l*
Am 3:4 Will a *l* roar in the forest
3:4 maned *l* give forth its voice
3:8 There is a *l* that has roared
3:12 from the mouth of the *l*
5:19 a man flees because of the *l*
Mic 5:8 a *l* among the beasts of a
5:8 young *l* among droves of sheep
Na 2:11 the *l* walked and entered
2:12 The *l* was tearing to pieces
1Pe 5:8 walks about like a roaring *l*

Re 4:7 living creature is like a l
5:5 L that is of the tribe of Judah
10:3 just as when a l roars

Lioness
Eze 19:2 your mother? A l among lions

Lionesses
Na 2:12 and was strangling for his l

Lion's
Jg 14:8 bees in the l corpse, and
Eze 1:10 with a l face to the right
Na 2:11 where the l cub was, and no
2Ti 4:17 delivered from the l mouth
Re 13:2 its mouth was as a l mouth

Lions
2Sa 1:23 Mightier than the l they
1Ki 7:29 were l, bulls and cherubs
7:29 beneath the l and the bulls
7:36 l and palm-tree figures
10:19 two l were standing beside
10:20 twelve l standing there
2Ki 17:25 Jehovah sent l among them
17:26 keeps sending l among them
1Ch 12:8 faces were the faces of l
2Ch 9:18 two l were standing beside
9:19 twelve l standing there upon
Job 4:10 teeth of maned young l do
38:39 lively appetite of young l
Ps 34:10 l themselves have had little
35:17 from the maned young l
57:4 My soul is in the middle of l
58:6 jawbones of maned young l
104:21 maned young l are roaring
Ca 4:8 from the lairs of l, from the
Isa 5:29 they roar like maned young l
Jer 2:15 maned young l roar
50:17 L themselves have done the
51:38 just like maned young l
51:38 growl like the whelps of l
Eze 19:2 A lioness among l. She lay
19:2 down in among maned young l
19:6 walk about in the midst of l
38:13 all its maned young l
Da 6:16 him into the pit of the l
6:20 able to rescue you from the l
6:22 and shut the mouth of the l
6:24 l had got the mastery over
6:27 Daniel from the paw of the l
Na 2:11 Where is the lair of l, and
2:11 belongs to the maned young l
2:13 devour your own maned young l
Zep 3:3 midst of her were roaring l
Zec 11:3 roaring of maned young l
Heb 11:33 stopped the mouths of l
Re 9:8 their teeth were as those of l
9:17 horses were as heads of l

Lions'
Da 6:7 should be thrown to the l pit
6:12 should be thrown to the l pit
6:19 went right to the l pit
6:24 the l pit they threw them

Lip
Ps 12:2 With a smooth l they keep
Pr 12:19 l of truth that will be
17:4 to the l of hurtfulness
17:7 the l of uprightness is not
17:7 for a noble the l of falsehood
Eze 43:13 border is upon its l round

Lips
Ex 6:12 as I am uncircumcised in l
6:30 I am uncircumcised in l, so
Le 5:4 with his l to do evil or to do
Nu 30:6 thoughtless promise of her l
30:8 thoughtless promise of her l
30:12 expression of her l as her
De 23:23 The utterance of your l you
1Sa 1:13 only her l were quivering
2Ki 18:20 but it is the word of l
19:28 my bridle between your l
Job 2:10 Job did not sin with his l
8:21 your l with joyful shouting
11:5 And open his l with you
13:6 to the pleadings of my l pay
15:6 own l answer against you
16:5 the consolation of my own l
23:12 the commandment of his l
27:4 My l will speak no
32:20 shall open my l that I may
33:3 knowledge . . . my l do utter
Ps 12:3 will cut off all smooth l
12:4 Our l are with us
Ps 16:4 carry their names upon my l
17:1 prayer without l of deception
17:4 By the word of your l I
21:2 wish of his l you have not
31:18 false l become speechless
34:13 l against speaking deception
40:9 Look! My l I do not restrain
45:2 been poured out upon your l
51:15 may you open these l of mine
59:7 Swords are on their l, For
59:12 the word of their l
63:3 My own l will commend you
63:5 with l of joyful cries my
66:14 my l have opened up to say
71:23 My l will cry out joyfully
89:34 expression out of my l I
106:33 to speak rashly with his l
119:13 With my l I have declared
119:171 my l bubble forth praise
120:2 deliver my soul from false l
140:3 venom . . . is under their l
140:9 trouble of their own l cover
141:3 watch over the door of my l
Pr 4:24 deviousness of l put far away
5:2 own l safeguard knowledge
5:3 l of a strange woman keep
7:21 smoothness of her l she
8:6 opening of my l is about
8:7 something detestable to my l
10:8 foolish with his l will be
10:10 one foolish with his l will
10:13 l of the understanding person
10:18 there are l of falsehood
10:19 one keeping his l in check
10:21 l of the righteous one keep
10:32 l of the righteous one
12:13 transgression of the l the
12:22 False l are something
13:3 one opening wide his l
14:3 l of the wise ones will guard
14:7 note of the l of knowledge
14:23 word of the l tends to want
15:7 The l of the wise ones keep
16:10 be upon the l of a king
16:13 The l of righteousness are a
16:21 he that is sweet in his l
16:23 his l it adds persuasiveness
16:27 upon his l . . . scorching fire
16:30 Pinching his l together, he
17:28 anyone closing up his own l
18:6 l of one who is stupid enter
18:7 his l are a snare for his soul
18:20 with the produce of his l
19:1 than the one crooked in his l
20:15 l of knowledge are precious
20:19 that is enticed with his l
22:11 for the charm of his l the
22:18 together upon your l
23:16 your l speak uprightness
24:2 trouble is what their own l
24:26 L will he kiss who is
24:28 to be foolish with your l
26:23 fervent l along with a bad
26:24 With his l the hater makes
27:2 foreigner, and not your own l
Ec 10:12 l of the stupid one swallow
Ca 4:3 Your l are just like a scarlet
4:11 honey your l keep dripping
5:13 His l are lilies, dripping
7:9 over the l of sleeping ones
Isa 6:5 man unclean in l I am, and
6:5 people unclean in l I am
6:7 touched your l, and your
11:4 spirit of his l he will put
28:11 stammering with their l
29:13 merely with their l
30:27 l, they have become full
36:5 but it is the word of l
37:29 my bridle between your l
57:19 creating the fruit of the l
59:3 own l have spoken falsehood
Jer 17:16 the expression of my l
La 3:62 l of those rising up against
Da 10:16 was touching my l, and I
Ho 14:2 the young bulls of our l
Hab 3:16 at the sound my l quivered
Mal 2:6 no unrighteousness . . . his l
2:7 the l of a priest are the
Mt 15:8 honors me with their l, yet
Mr 7:6 honor me with their l, but
Ro 3:13 Poison . . . is behind their l
1Co 14:21 and with the l of strangers
Heb 13:15 fruit of l which make
1Pe 3:10 l from speaking deception

Liquefied
Eze 22:21 be l in the midst of her
22:22 you people will be l in the
24:11 uncleanness must be l in

Liquefy
Eze 22:20 and cause you people to l

Liquefying
Eze 22:20 with fire to cause a l
22:22 l of silver in the midst of

Liquid
Nu 6:3 drink any l made from grapes
Ca 5:5 and my fingers with l myrrh
5:13 lilies, dripping with l myrrh
Zec 4:12 pouring . . . the golden l
Joh 2:6 hold two or three l measures

Liquids
Le 19:35 weighing or in measuring l

Liquor
Le 10:9 Do not drink . . . l
Nu 6:3 from wine and intoxicating l
6:3 vinegar of intoxicating l, nor
28:7 offering of intoxicating l
De 14:26 wine and intoxicating l and
29:6 intoxicating l you did not
Jg 13:4 or intoxicating l, and do not
13:7 or intoxicating l, and do not
13:14 no wine or intoxicating l
1Sa 1:15 intoxicating l I have not
Ps 69:12 drinkers of intoxicating l
Pr 20:1 intoxicating l is boisterous
31:4 Where is intoxicating l?
31:6 Give intoxicating l, you
Isa 5:11 seek just intoxicating l
5:22 for mixing intoxicating l
24:9 intoxicating l becomes
28:7 because of intoxicating l
28:7 because of intoxicating l
28:7 result of the intoxicating l
29:9 not because of intoxicating l
56:12 intoxicating l to the limit
Mic 2:11 concerning intoxicating l

List
1Ch 11:11 l of the mighty men that
1Ti 5:9 Let a widow be put on the l

Listen
Ge 4:10 L! Your brother's blood is
11:7 may not l to one another's
21:12 L to her voice, because it is
23:8 l to me and urge Ephron the
23:11 L to me. The field I do give
23:13 l to me! I will give you the
23:15 l to me. A land plot worth
27:8 now, my son, l to my voice
27:13 l to my voice and go, get
27:43 l to my voice and get up
34:17 if you do not l to us to get
37:6 L, please, to this dream that
42:21 but we did not l. That is
42:22 you did not l
49:2 Assemble yourselves and l, you
49:2 yes, l to Israel your father
Ex 3:18 they will certainly l to
4:1 suppose they . . . do not l to
4:8 and will not l to the voice
4:9 and will not l to your voice
6:9 they did not l to Moses out of
6:12 how will Pharaoh ever l to
6:30 how will Pharaoh ever l to
7:4 Pharaoh will not l to you men
7:13 and he did not l to them
7:22 and he did not l to them
8:15 Pharaoh . . . did not l to them
8:19 and he did not l to them
9:12 he did not l to them, just as
11:9 Pharaoh will not l to you men
15:26 l to the voice of Jehovah
16:20 But they did not l to Moses
18:19 Now l to my voice. I shall
20:19 speak with us, and let us l
Le 26:14 not l to me nor do all these
26:18 not l to me, I shall then
26:21 not wishing to l to me, I
26:27 l to me and you just must
Nu 16:8 say to Korah: L, please, you
23:18 said: Get up, Balak, and l
27:20 sons of Israel may l to him
De 1:43 you did not l but began to
1:45 Jehovah did not l to your
3:26 and did not l to me; but
4:1 Israel, l to the regulations

De 4:30 and to *l* to his voice
5:27 we shall certainly *l* and do
6:3 *l*, O Israel, and take care to
6:4 *L*, O Israel: Jehovah our God
8:20 not *l* to the voice of Jehovah
9:23 did not *l* to his voice
10:10 Jehovah proceeded to *l* to me
13:3 you must not *l* to the words
13:4 to his voice you should *l*
13:8 accede to his wish or *l* to
13:18 *l* to the voice of Jehovah
15:5 *l* to the voice of Jehovah your
18:14 *l* to those practicing magic
18:15 to him you people should *l*
18:19 the man who will not *l* to
21:18 but he will not *l* to them
23:5 did not want to *l* to Balaam
26:17 and *l* to his voice
27:9 Keep silent and *l*, O Israel
27:10 *l* to the voice of Jehovah
28:1 *l* to the voice of Jehovah
28:15 not *l* to the voice of Jehovah
28:45 *l* to the voice of Jehovah
28:62 did not *l* to the voice of
30:8 *l* to the voice of Jehovah and
30:10 you will *l* to the voice of
30:16 will *l* to the commandments
30:17 and you do not *l*, and you
31:12 in order that they may *l* and
31:13 *l*, and they must learn to
34:9 sons of Israel began to *l* to
Jos 1:17 so we shall *l* to you
1:18 does not *l* to your words in
3:9 and *l* to the words of Jehovah
5:6 that did not *l* to the voice of
24:10 And I did not want to *l* to
24:24 to his voice we shall *l*
Jg 2:17 they did not *l*, but they had
5:3 *L*, you kings; give ear, you
5:16 To *l* to the pipings for the
6:10 And you did not *l* to my voice
7:11 you must *l* to what they will
9:7 *L* to me, you landowners of
9:7 and let God *l* to you
11:17 the king of Edom did not *l*
11:28 did not *l* to the words of
19:25 the men did not want to *l*
20:13 not want to *l* to the voice
1Sa 2:25 not *l* to the voice of their
8:7 *L* to the voice of the people
8:9 And now *l* to their voice
8:19 refused to *l* to . . . Samuel
8:22 *L* to their voice, and you
15:1 *l* to the voice of the words
17:23 and David got to *l* in
22:7 *L*, please, you Benjaminites
22:12 *L*, please, you son of
24:9 Why do you *l* to the words of
25:24 *l* to the words of your
26:19 *l* to the words of his
30:24 who will *l* to you as to this
2Sa 12:18 he did not *l* to our voice
13:14 not consent to *l* to her voice
13:16 did not consent to *l* to her
14:16 *l* so as to deliver his slave
19:35 *l* anymore to the voice of
20:16, 16 *L*, men, *l*! Say, please
20:17 *L* to the words of your
1Ki 8:28 *l* to the entreating cry and
8:29 *l* to the prayer with which
8:30 *l* to the request for favor
8:43 *l* from the heavens, your
12:15 king did not *l* to the people
20:36 did not *l* to the voice of
2Ki 7:1 *L*, you men, to the word of
14:11 And Amaziah did not *l*
17:14 did not *l* but kept hardening
18:26 for we can *l*; and do not
18:31 Do not *l* to Hezekiah; for
18:32 And do not *l* to Hezekiah
20:13 to *l* to them and show them
21:9 did not *l*, but Manasseh
22:13 did not *l* to the words of
2Ch 6:21 *l* to the entreaties of your
6:33 *l* from the heavens, from
10:15 king did not *l* to the people
10:16 the king did not *l* to them
25:20 Amaziah did not *l*
28:11 *l* to me and return the
29:5 *L* to me, you Levites
35:22 not *l* to the words of Necho
Ne 1:6 to *l* to the prayer of your
8:2 all intelligent enough to *l*
9:16 not *l* to your commandments
Ne 9:17 they refused to *l*, and they
9:29 not *l* to your commandments
9:29 hardened, and they did not *l*
Es 3:4 and he did not *l* to them, then
Job 15:8 talk of God do you *l*
15:17 *L* to me! Even this I have
21:2 *L*, you men, attentively to
32:10 Do *l* to me. I shall declare
33:31 O Job! *L* to me! Keep silent
33:33 you yourself *l* to me
34:2 *L*, you wise ones, to my
34:10 you men of heart, *l* to me
34:16 have understanding, do *l*
37:2 *L* attentively, you men, to
Ps 34:11 Come, you sons, *l* to me
38:13 someone deaf, I would not *l*
45:10 *L*, O daughter, and see, and
50:7 Do *l*, O my people, and I will
58:5 *l* to the voice of charmers
66:16 *l*, all you who fear God
81:8 Israel, if you will *l* to me
95:7 people *l* to his own voice
106:25 *l* to the voice of Jehovah
Pr 1:5 wise person will *l* and take
1:8 *L*, my son, to the discipline
4:1 *L*, O sons, to the discipline
5:7 sons, *l* to me and do not turn
7:24 sons, *l* to me and pay
8:6 *L*, for it is about the
8:32 sons, *l* to me; yes, happy
8:33 *L* to discipline and become
19:20 *L* to counsel and accept
19:27 to *l* to discipline and it
23:22 *L* to your father who caused
Isa 1:19 show willingness and do *l*
7:13 *L*, please, O house of David
13:4 *L*! A crowd in the mountains
13:4 *L*! The uproar of kingdoms
28:23 and *l* to my voice
28:23 and *l* to my saying
32:9 rise up, *l* to my voice!
33:19 too deep in language to *l*
34:1 and that which fills it *l*
36:16 Do not *l* to Hezekiah, for
40:3 *L*! Someone is calling out in
40:6 *L*! Someone is saying: Call
42:23 and *l* for later times
42:24 to whose law they did not *l*
44:1 now *l*, O Jacob my servant
46:3 *L* to me, O house of Jacob
46:12 *L* to me, you the ones
48:12 *L* to me, O Jacob, and you
49:1 *L* to me, O you islands, and
51:1 *L* to me, you people who are
51:7 *L* to me, you the ones
51:21 *l* to this, please, O woman
52:8 *L*! Your own watchmen have
55:2 *L* intently to me, and eat
55:3 *L*, and your soul will keep
65:12 I spoke, but you did not *l*
Jer 3:13 you people did not *l*
6:19 *L*, O earth! Here I am
7:13 speaking, but you did not *l*
7:24 they did not *l*, neither did
7:26 But they did not *l* to me
7:27 but they will not *l* to you
10:22 *L*! A report! Here it has
11:3 the man that does not *l* to
11:8 they did not *l* or incline
11:11 but I shall not *l* to them
17:23 they did not *l* or incline
18:19 *l* to the voice of my
23:16 Do not *l* to the words of
25:3 speaking, but you did not *l*
25:4 you did not *l*, neither did
25:4 you incline your ear to *l*
25:7 But you did not *l* to me
25:36 *L*! The outcry of the
26:3 they will *l* and return
26:4 *l* to me by walking in my
27:9 do not *l* to your prophets
27:14 do not *l* to the words of
27:16 Do not *l* to the words of
27:17 Do not *l* to them. Serve the
28:15 *L*, please, O Hananiah
29:8 do not you *l* to their dreams
29:12 pray to me, and I will *l*
34:14 forefathers did not *l* to me
35:15 nor did you *l* to me
35:17 to them but they did not *l*
36:3 *l* to all the calamity that I
36:25 but he did not *l* to them
36:31 and they did not *l*
37:2 *l* to the words of Jehovah
Jer 37:14 But he did not *l* to him
37:20 *l*, please, O my lord the
38:15 you will not *l* to me
44:5 they did not *l*, nor did
51:54 *L*! There is an outcry from
La 1:18 *L*, now, all you peoples, and
Eze 3:6 very ones would *l* to you
3:7 will not want to *l* to you
3:7 are not wanting to *l* to me
20:8 did not consent to *l* to me
Da 9:17 *l*, O our God, to the prayer
Zep 3:2 She did not *l* to a voice
Hag 1:12 to *l* to the voice of Jehovah
Zec 1:4 But they did not *l*, and they
6:15 *l* to the voice of Jehovah
7:13 he called and they did not *l*
7:13 call and I would not *l*
11:3 *L*! The howling of shepherds
11:3 *L*! The roaring of maned
Mal 2:2 If you will not *l*, and if
Mt 3:3 *L*! Someone is crying out in
10:14 or *l* to your words, on going
11:15 Let him that has ears *l*
13:9 Let him that has ears *l*
13:18 *l* to the illustration of the
13:43 Let him that has ears *l*
15:10 *L* and get the sense of it
17:5 I have approved; *l* to him
18:16 if he does not *l*, take along
18:17 If he does not *l* to them
18:17 *l* even to the congregation
Mr 1:3 *l*! someone is crying out in
4:3 *L*. Look! The sower went out
4:9, 9 him that has ears to *l* *l*
4:20 *l* to the word and favorably
4:23, 23 has ears to *l*, let him *l*
4:33 as far as they were able to *l*
7:14 *L* to me, all of you, and get
9:7 my Son, the beloved; *l* to him
Lu 3:4 *L*! Someone is crying out in
5:15 come together to *l* and to be
8:8, 8 that has ears to *l*, *l*
8:18 pay attention to how you *l*
9:35 has been chosen. *L* to him
14:35, 35 that has ears to *l*, *l*
16:29 let them *l* to these
16:31 If they do not *l* to Moses
Joh 6:60 shocking; who can *l* to it?
8:43 you cannot *l* to my word
8:47 This is why you do not *l*
9:27 and yet you did not *l*
9:31 God does not *l* to sinners
10:3 sheep *l* to his voice, and
10:16 they will *l* to my voice
10:20 Why do you *l* to him?
10:27 My sheep *l* to my voice
Ac 3:22 *l* to him according to all the
3:23 not *l* to that Prophet will
4:19 *l* to you rather than to God
15:12 to *l* to Barnabas and Paul
28:28 they will certainly *l* to it
1Ti 4:16 and those who *l* to you
Heb 3:7 you people *l* to his own voice
3:15 people *l* to his own voice
4:7 you people *l* to his own voice
Jas 2:5 *L*, my beloved brothers
1Jo 4:6 does not *l* to us. This is how

Listened

Ge 3:17 Because you *l* to your wife's
16:2 Abram *l* to the voice of Sarai
21:17 God has *l* to the voice of the
22:18 fact that you have *l* to my
23:16 Abraham *l* to Ephron, and
26:5 the fact that Abraham *l* to my
29:33 It is because Jehovah has *l*
30:6 and has also *l* to my voice
34:24 *l* to Hamor and to Shechem
37:27 So they *l* to their brother
39:10 he never *l* to her to lie
Ex 6:12 sons of Israel have not *l* to
18:24 Moses *l* to the voice of his
Nu 14:22 and have not *l* to my voice
21:3 Jehovah *l* to Israel's voice
De 9:19 Jehovah *l* to me also that
26:14 *l* to the voice of Jehovah
30:2 and *l* to his voice according
Jos 1:17 we *l* to Moses in everything
10:14 *l* to the voice of a man
Jg 2:2 you have not *l* to my voice
2:20 and have not *l* to my voice
13:9 God *l* to the voice of Manoah
1Sa 12:1 I have *l* to your voice as
25:35 I have *l* to your voice that

1Ki 10:7 things heard to which I *l*
12:16 king had not *l* to them
15:20 Ben-hadad *l* to King Asa and
17:22 Jehovah *l* to Elijah's voice
20:25 he *l* to their voice and did
2Ki 13:4 so that Jehovah *l* to him
16:9 the king of Assyria *l* to him
18:12 not *l* to the voice of
18:12 neither *l* nor performed
2Ch 16:4 Ben-hadad *l* to King Asa and
24:17 the king *l* to them
25:16 have not *l* to my counsel
30:20 Jehovah *l* to Hezekiah and
Job 29:11 ear itself *l* and proceeded
29:21 they *l*; and they waited
Ps 61:5 God, have *l* to my vows
81:11 people has not *l* to my voice
Pr 5:13 not *l* to the voice of my
Ec 9:16 and his words are not *l* to
Isa 66:4 but there were none that *l*
Jer 26:5 whom you have not *l* to
29:19 they have not *l* to my words
29:19 you have not *l*, is the
35:16 this people, they have not *l*
Da 1:14 he *l* to them as regards this
9:6 *l* to your servants the prophets
Ho 9:17 for they have not *l* to him
Joh 10:8 sheep have not *l* to them
Ac 4:4 had *l* to the speech believed
8:6 *l* and looked at the signs he
24:24 he sent for Paul and *l* to

Listener

Jg 11:10 Let Jehovah prove to be the *l*

Listening

Ge 18:10 Now Sarah was *l* at the tent
27:5 Rebekah was *l* while Isaac
42:23 not know that Joseph was *l*
Nu 12:2 And Jehovah was *l*
De 7:12 continue *l* to these judicial
17:12 in not *l* to the priest who
21:18 not *l* to the voice of his
21:20 he is not *l* to our voice
28:2 keep *l* to the voice of Jehovah
30:20 by *l* to his voice and by
1Sa 3:9 your servant is *l*. So Samuel
3:10 Speak, for your servant is *l*
14:27 not been *l* when his father
2Sa 20:17 In turn he said: I am *l*
1Ki 8:52 by *l* to them in all for
10:8 *l* to your wisdom
2Ch 6:19 *l* to the entreating cry and
6:20 *l* to the prayer with which
9:7 and *l* to your wisdom
Job 31:35 that I had someone *l* to me
34:34 able-bodied man that is *l*
Ps 59:7 For who is *l*?
69:33 Jehovah is *l* to the poor
81:13 my people were *l* to me
103:20 *l* to the voice of his word
Pr 1:33 one *l* to me, he will reside
8:34 is the man that is *l* to me
12:15 one *l* to counsel is wise
15:31 is *l* to the reproof of life
15:32 one *l* to reproof is acquiring
21:28 man that is *l* will speak
25:10 that the one *l* may not put
Isa 1:15 many prayers, I am not *l*
33:15 ear from *l* to bloodshed
36:11 for we are *l*
42:20 ears, but you did not keep *l*
50:10 *l* to the voice of his
Jer 7:16 for I shall not be *l* to you
8:6 paid attention, and I kept *l*
11:14 I shall not be *l* in the
14:12 *l* to their entreating cry
20:1 kept *l* to Jeremiah while
26:5 by *l* to the words of my
32:33 *l* to receive discipline
36:24 servants, who were *l* to
44:16 we are not *l* to you
Eze 20:39 if you are not *l* to me
Mal 3:16 kept paying attention and *l*
Mr 6:2 those *l* were astounded and
11:14 And his disciples were *l*
12:37 *l* to him with pleasure
Lu 2:46 *l* to them and questioning
2:47 all those *l* to him were in
5:1 and *l* to the word of God, he
6:27 I say to you who are *l*
10:39 and kept *l* to his word
16:14 *l* to all these things, and
19:11 *l* to these things he spoke
20:45 people were *l* he said to the
Ac 14:9 This man was *l* to Paul speak
16:14 Lydia . . . was *l*, and Jehovah
17:21 or *l* to something new
22:22 they kept *l* to him down to
2Ti 2:14 because it overturns those *l*

Listens

Mt 18:15 If he *l* to you, you have
Lu 10:16, 16 *l* to you *l* to me too
Joh 8:47 *l* to the sayings of God
9:31 he *l* to this one
18:37 *l* to my voice
1Co 14:2 no one *l*, but he speaks
1Jo 4:5 and the world *l* to them
4:6 knowledge of God *l* to us

Lit

Ex 25:37 and the lamps must be *l* up
40:25 *l* up the lamps before Jehovah
Nu 8:3 He *l* up its lamps for the area
Lu 22:55 *l* a fire in the midst of the

Literally

Ex 11:1 *l* drive you out from here

Litter

Ca 3:9 *l* that King Solomon has made

Little

Ge 18:4 Let a *l* water be taken
24:17 *l* sip of water from your jar
24:43 let me drink a *l* water from
26:10 A *l* more and certainly one
30:15 Is this a *l* thing, your
30:30 it was *l* that you actually
34:29 *l* children and their wives
43:2 Return, buy a *l* food for us
43:8 you and our *l* children
43:11, 11 *l* balsam, and a *l* honey
44:25 buy a *l* food for us
45:19 your *l* ones and your wives
46:5 their *l* ones and their wives
47:12 the number of the *l* ones
47:24 and for your *l* ones to eat
50:8 *l* children and their flocks
50:21 your *l* children with food
Ex 10:10 send you and your *l* ones
10:24 Your *l* ones also may go with
12:37 men on foot, besides *l* ones
16:17 much and some gathering *l*
16:18 gathered *l* had no shortage
17:4 *l* longer and they will stone
23:30, 30 *L* by *l* I shall drive
Le 11:17 the *l* owl and the cormorant
Nu 14:3 *l* ones will become plunder
14:31 And your *l* ones who you said
16:9 Is it such a *l* thing for you
16:13 Is it so *l* a thing that you
16:27 their sons and their *l* ones
31:9 of Midian and their *l* ones
31:17 every male among the *l* ones
31:18 *l* ones among the women who
32:16 and cities for our *l* ones
32:17 our *l* ones must dwell in the
32:24 cities for your *l* ones and
32:26 Our *l* ones, our wives, our
De 1:17 hear the *l* one the same as
1:39 your *l* ones of whom you said
2:34 men and women and *l* children
3:6 men, women and *l* children
3:19 your wives and your *l* ones
7:22, 22 from before you *l* by *l*
14:16 the *l* owl and the long-eared
20:14 the women and the *l* children
28:38 but *l* will you gather
29:11 your *l* ones, your wives, and
31:12 the women and the *l* ones and
Jos 1:14 wives, your *l* ones and your
8:35 the women and the *l* ones and
Jg 4:19 Give me, please, a *l* water
18:21 and put the *l* ones and the
21:10 the women and the *l* ones
Ru 2:7 in the house a *l* while
1Sa 2:19 *l* sleeveless coat his mother
2:30 will be of *l* account
14:29 I tasted this *l* bit of honey
14:43 taste a *l* honey on the tip
15:17 you were *l* in your own eyes
18:23 man of *l* means and lightly
20:2 or a *l* thing and not disclose
2Sa 7:19 be something *l* in your eyes
12:1 and the other of *l* means
12:3 man of *l* means had nothing
12:4 lamb of the man of *l* means
15:22 his men and all the *l* ones
16:1 over a *l* beyond the summit
2Sa 19:36 For it is just a *l* way that
1Ki 2:20 *l* request that I am making
3:7 and I am but a *l* boy
12:10 My *l* finger itself will
17:12 a *l* oil in the small jar
2Ki 4:10 make a *l* roof chamber on the
5:2 from . . . Israel a *l* girl
5:14 like the flesh of a *l* boy
10:18 Ahab . . . worshiped Baal a *l*
1Ch 17:17 *l* in your eyes, O God, yet
25:8 the *l* being just the same as
2Ch 10:10 My own *l* finger will
12:7 and in a *l* while I shall
20:13 even their *l* ones, their
31:18 among all their *l* ones
Ezr 8:21 for us and for our *l* ones
9:8 for a *l* moment favor from
9:8 a *l* reviving in our servitude
Ne 9:32 this day, seem *l* before you
Es 3:13 *l* ones and women, on one day
8:11 *l* ones and women, and to
Job 10:20 that I may brighten up a *l*
24:24 become high up a *l* while
36:2 patience with me a *l*
40:4 I have become of *l* account
Ps 8:5 a *l* less than godlike ones
34:10 had *l* on hand and gone hungry
37:10 just a *l* while longer, and
37:16 the *l* of the righteous one
42:6 From the *l* mountain
68:27 There is *l* Benjamin subduing
82:3 one of *l* means do justice
94:17 *l* while my soul would have
102:6 become like a *l* owl of
119:87 In a *l* while they would
144:12 sons are like *l* plants
Pr 6:10 A *l* more sleep, a
6:10 sleep, a *l* more slumbering
6:10 *l* more folding of the hands
10:4 slack hand will be of *l* means
10:20 the wicked one is worth *l*
13:7 pretending to be of *l* means
13:8 one of *l* means has not heard
13:23 ground of persons of *l* means
14:20 one who is of *l* means is an
15:16 is a *l* in the fear of Jehovah
16:8 a *l* with righteousness than
17:5 one of *l* means in derision
18:23 one of *l* means speaks out
19:1 Anyone of *l* means who is
19:7 brothers of one of *l* means
19:22 and one of *l* means is better
22:2 The rich one and the one of *l*
22:7 rules over those of *l* means
24:33 A *l* sleeping, a
24:33 sleeping, a *l* slumbering, a
24:33 a *l* folding of the hands to
28:3 man that is of *l* means and
28:6 Better is the one of *l* means
28:27 giving to the one of *l* means
29:13 The one of *l* means and the
Ec 4:14 been born as one of *l* means
5:8 oppression of the one of *l*
5:12 it is *l* or much that he eats
9:14 There was a *l* city, and the
10:1 So a *l* foolishness does to one
Ca 2:15 *l* foxes that are making spoil
8:8 We have a *l* sister that does
Isa 7:13 *l* thing for you to tire out
10:25 yet a very *l* while—and
11:6 *l* boy will be leader over
28:10, 10 here a *l*, there a *l*
28:13, 13 here a *l*, there a *l*
29:17 very *l* time and Lebanon
54:7 For a *l* moment I left you
60:22 *l* one himself will become
63:18 a *l* while your holy people
Jer 40:7 *l* children and some of the
41:16 wives and the *l* children
43:6 wives and the *l* children
48:4 *l* ones have caused a cry to
49:20 *l* ones of the flock will be
50:45 *l* ones of the flock will be
51:33 Yet a *l* while and the time
Eze 9:6 *l* child and women you should
11:16 a sanctuary for a *l* while
16:47 In a very *l* while you even
34:18 such a *l* thing for you men
Da 11:23 by means of a *l* nation
11:34 will be helped with a *l* help
Ho 1:4 *l* while and I must hold an
8:10 a *l* while in severe pains
Mic 5:2 too *l* to get to be among the
Hag 1:6 there is a bringing of *l* in

Hag 1:9 but here there was just a l
2:6 it is a l while—and I am
Zec 1:15 indignant to only a l extent
Mt 5:26 last coin of very l value
6:30 clothe you, you with l faith
8:26 you with l faith
9:24 for the l girl did not die
9:25 and the l girl got up
10:42 gives one of these l ones
14:31 You with l faith, why did
15:26 and throw it to l dogs
15:27 l dogs do eat of the crumbs
15:34 Seven, and a few l fishes
16:8 no loaves, you with l faith
17:20 Because of your l faith
18:6 stumbles one of these l ones
18:10 not despise one of these l
18:14 of these l ones to perish
26:39 going a l way forward, he
26:73 After a l while those
Mr 1:19 a l farther he saw James the
3:9 have a l boat continually at
5:23 saying: My l daughter is in
7:25 l daughter had an unclean
7:27 and throw it to the l dogs
7:28 the l dogs underneath the
7:28 the crumbs of the l children
8:7 They also had a few l fishes
9:42 these l ones that believe
12:42 which have very l value
14:35 going a l way forward he
14:70 after a l while those
Lu 5:19 let him down with the l bed
5:24 pick up your l bed and be on
7:47, 47 forgiven l, loves l
12:28 clothe you, you with l faith
12:32 Have no fear, l flock
12:59 small coin of very l value
17:2 stumble one of these l ones
21:2 coins of very l value there
Joh 6:7 so that each one may get a l
6:9 l boy that has five barley
6:22 no boat there except a l one
6:24 boarded their l boats and
7:33 a l while longer with you
12:35 among you a l while longer
13:33 L children, I am with you
13:33 I am with you a l longer
14:19 A l longer and the world
16:16 l while you will behold me
16:16 l while you will see me
16:17 l while you will not behold
16:17 l while you will see me
16:18 that he says, a l while
16:19 l while you will not behold
16:19 l while you will see me
21:8 came in the l boat, for
21:16 Shepherd my l sheep
21:17 to him: Feed my l sheep
Ac 5:15 laid them there upon l beds
5:34 men outside for a l while
12:18 no l stir among the soldiers
14:28 So they spent not a l time
15:2 had occurred no l dissension
19:23 there arose no l disturbance
19:24 the craftsmen no l gain
27:20 no l tempest was lying upon
1Co 5:6 a l leaven ferments the whole
2Co 7:8 saddened . . . for a l while
8:15 person with l did not have
8:15 did not have too l
11:1 in some l unreasonableness
11:16 may do some l boasting
Ga 4:19 my l children, with whom
5:9 A l leaven ferments the whole
1Ti 4:8 training is beneficial for a l
5:23 use a l wine for the sake of
Heb 2:7 him a l lower than angels
2:9 made a l lower than angels
10:37 yet a very l while, and
Jas 3:5 the tongue is a l member and
3:5 How l a fire it takes to set
4:14 a mist appearing for a l
1Pe 1:6 for a l while at present
5:10 you have suffered a l while
1Jo 2:1 My l children, I am writing
2:12 am writing you, l children
2:28 l children, remain in union
3:7 L children, let no one
3:18 L children, let us love
4:4 with God, l children
5:21 L children, guard yourselves
Re 3:8 that you have a l power, and
6:11 told to rest a l while longer
Re 10:2 in his hand a l scroll opened
10:9 to give me the l scroll
10:10 I took the l scroll out of
20:3 be let loose for a l while

Live

Ge 3:22 tree of life and eat and l
5:7 Seth continued to l eight
5:10 Enosh continued to l eight
5:13 Kenan continued to l eight
5:16 Mahalalel continued to l
5:19 Jared continued to l eight
5:26 Methuselah continued to l
5:30 Lamech continued to l five
9:28 Noah continued to l three
11:11 Shem continued to l five
11:13 Arpachshad continued to l
11:15 Shelah continued to l four
11:17 Eber continued to l four
11:19 Peleg continued to l two
11:21 Reu continued to l two
11:23 Serug continued to l two
11:25 Nahor continued to l a
12:13 soul will be certain to l
13:18 So Abram continued to l in
17:18 O that Ishmael might l
19:20 and my soul will l on
27:40 by your sword you will l
31:32 let him not l. Before our
47:19 give us seed that we may l
Ex 1:16 a daughter, it must also l
19:13 beast or man, he will not l
21:35 sell the l bull and divide
33:20 no man may see me and yet l
Le 14:4 two l clean birds and
14:51 the l bird and dip them in
14:52 the l bird and the cedarwood
14:53 send the l bird away outside
16:20 must also present the l goat
16:21 l goat and confess over it
18:5 man will do, he must also l
Nu 6:2 l as a Nazirite to Jehovah
6:12 l as a Nazirite to Jehovah for
14:21 as I l, all the earth will
14:28 As I l, is the utterance of
14:38 will certainly l on, of
De 4:1 you may l and may indeed go in
4:37 l, because he loved your
4:42 to one of these cities and l
5:33 that you may l and it may be
8:3 not by bread alone does man l
8:3 of Jehovah's mouth does man l
19:4 may flee there and has to l
19:5 flee to . . . cities and must l
33:6 Let Reuben l and not die off
Jos 9:15 with them to let them l
9:20 while letting them l, that
9:21 said to them: Let them l
1Sa 10:24 and say: Let the king l!
2Sa 1:10 he could not l after he had
12:22 the child will certainly l
16:16, 16 king l! Let the king l!
1Ki 1:25 saying, Let King Adonijah l!
1:31 David l to time indefinite
1:34 and say, Let King Solomon l!
1:39 saying: Let King Solomon l!
20:32 Please, let my soul l
2Ki 4:7 should l from what is left
7:4 preserve us alive, we shall l
11:12 and say: Let the king l!
14:17 continued to l after the
20:1 indeed die and will not l
2Ch 23:11 said: Let the king l!
25:25 l after the death of Jehoash
Ne 2:3 king himself l to time
6:11 enter into the temple and l
9:29 must also l by means of them
Job 5:23 made to l at peace with you
7:16 to time indefinite . . . not l
14:14 man dies can he l again?
Ps 22:26 May your hearts l forever
49:9 l forever and not see the pit
55:23 not l out half their days
58:9 The l green as well as the
72:15 And let him l, and to him
119:17 your servant, that I may l
Ec 6:3 and he should l many years, so
9:4 l dog is better off than a dead
11:8 man should l even many years
Isa 26:14 they will not l. Impotent
26:19 Your dead ones will l
38:1 indeed die and will not l
Jer 38:20 soul will continue to l
La 4:20 In his shade we shall l among
Eze 13:19 souls that ought not to l
37:10 began to l and stand upon
Da 2:4 l on even for times indefinite
3:9 king, l on even for times
6:6 Darius the king, l on even for
6:21 l on even to times indefinite
Ho 6:2 and we shall l before him
Zec 1:5 that they continued to l
13:3 You will not l, because
Mt 4:4 Man must l, not on bread
Mr 5:23 that she may get well and l
Lu 4:4 Man must not l by bread alone
Joh 5:25 who have given heed will l
6:51 bread he will l forever
6:57 I l because of the Father
6:57 one will l because of me
6:58 on this bread will l forever
14:19, 19 I l and you will l
Ac 22:22 for he was not fit to l
25:24 he ought not to l any longer
Ro 1:17 by means of faith he will l
6:8 we shall also l with him
8:12 l in accord with the flesh
8:13 l in accord with the flesh
8:13 by the spirit, you will l
10:5 of the Law will l by it
14:8, 8 if we l, we l to Jehovah
14:8 both if we l and if we die
14:11 As I l, says Jehovah, to me
1Co 9:14 l by means of the good news
2Co 4:11 we who l are ever being
5:15 for all that those who l
5:15 l no longer for themselves
6:9 as dying and yet, look! we l
7:3 to die and to l with us
13:4 we shall l together with
13:11 agreement, to l peaceably
Ga 2:14 l as the nations do, and not
2:14 to l according to Jewish
2:20 no longer I that l, but it is
2:20 life that I now l in flesh I
2:20 I l by the faith that is
3:11 one will l by reason of faith
3:12 shall l by means of them
Php 1:21 in my case to l is Christ
1:22 if it be to l on in the flesh
Col 3:7 when you used to l in them
1Th 3:8 we l if you stand firm in the
4:11 your aim to l quietly and to
5:10 should l together with him
2Ti 2:11 we shall also l together
3:12 to l with godly devotion
Tit 2:12 to l with soundness of mind
Heb 10:38 righteous one will l by
12:9 of our spiritual life and l
Jas 4:15 we shall l and also do this
1Pe 2:24 and l to righteousness
4:2 l the remainder of his time
4:6 l as to the spirit from the

Lived

Ge 5:3 Adam l on for a hundred and
5:5 the days of Adam that he l
5:6 Seth l on for a hundred and
5:9 And Enosh l on for ninety
5:12 Kenan l on for seventy years
5:15 Mahalalel l on for sixty-five
5:18 Jared l on for a hundred and
5:21 Enoch l on for sixty-five
5:25 Methuselah l on for a hundred
5:28 Lamech l on for a hundred
11:12 Arpachshad l thirty-five
11:14 And Shelah l thirty years
11:16 And Eber l on for thirty-four
11:18 Peleg l on for thirty years
11:20 Reu l on for thirty-two years
11:22 Serug l on for thirty years
11:24 Nahor l on for twenty-nine
11:26 Terah l on for seventy years
25:7 Abraham's life which he l
47:28 Jacob l on in the land of
50:22 l for a hundred and ten years
Ec 6:6 l a thousand years twice over
Lu 2:36 l with a husband for seven
Ac 26:5 of worship I l a Pharisee
Jas 5:5 l in luxury upon the earth
Re 18:7 l in shameless luxury, to
18:9 l in shameless luxury will

Lively

Ex 1:19 Hebrew women . . . are l
Job 38:39 l appetite of young lions

Liver

Ex 29:13 and the appendage upon the l

Ex 29:22 the appendage of the *l*, and
Le 3:4 as for the appendage upon the *l*
3:10 for the appendage upon the *l*
3:15 for the appendage upon the *l*
4:9 as for the appendage upon the *l*
7:4 as for the appendage upon the *l*
8:16 the appendage of the *l* and
8:25 the appendage of the *l* and
9:10 the appendage of the *l* from
9:19 and the appendage of the *l*
Pr 7:23 arrow cleaves open his *l*
La 2:11 My *l* has been poured out to
Eze 21:21 he has looked into the *l*

Lives

Ge 42:15 As Pharaoh *l*, you will not
42:16 as Pharaoh *l*, you are spies
47:9 the days of the years of the *l*
47:25 You have preserved our *l*
Jg 8:19 As Jehovah *l*, if you had
Ru 3:13 as sure as Jehovah *l*
Job 27:2 As God *l*, who has taken
27:2 as the Almighty *l*, who has
Joh 4:50 Go your way; your son *l*
4:53 said to him: Your son *l*
Ro 6:10 but the life that he *l*, he
6:10 he *l* with reference to God
7:1 over a man as long as he *l*
14:7 *l* with regard to himself
2Co 1:8 very uncertain even of our *l*
Heb 2:15 slavery all through their *l*
7:8 it is witnessed that he *l*
12:23 spiritual *l* of righteous
Re 4:9 the one that *l* forever and ever
4:10 the One that *l* forever and
10:6 the One who *l* forever and
15:7 God, who *l* forever and ever

Livestock

Ge 4:20 dwell in tents and have *l*
13:7 the herders of Abram's *l* and
13:7 and the herders of Lot's *l*
33:14 the pace of the *l* that is
34:23 *l*, will they not be ours
47:16 Hand over your *l* and I shall
47:16 bread in exchange for your *l*
47:17 bringing their *l* to Joseph
47:17 and the *l* of the flock
47:17 *l* of the herd and the asses
47:17 in exchange for all their *l*
Ex 9:3 coming upon your *l* that is in
9:4, 4 *l* of Israel . . . *l* of Egypt
9:6 *l* of Egypt began to die; but
9:6 not one of the *l* of the sons
9:7 so much as one of Israel's *l*
9:19 bring all your *l* and all that
9:20 his *l* to flee into the houses
9:21 and his *l* in the field
10:26 our *l* will also go with us
17:3 and our *l* to death by thirst
34:19 your *l*, the male firstling of
Nu 20:19 my *l* should drink your water
31:9 all their *l* and all their
32:1 had come to have numerous *l*
32:1 the place was a place for *l*
32:4 is a land for *l*, and your
32:4 and your servants have *l*
32:16 stone flock pens for our *l*
32:26 our *l* and all our domestic
De 3:19 your little ones and your *l*
3:19 you have a great deal of *l*
Jos 1:14 and your *l* will dwell in the
14:4 pasture grounds for their *l*
22:8 riches and with very much *l*
Jg 6:5 they and their *l* would come up
18:21 the *l* and the valuable things
1Sa 23:5 and drove off with their *l*
30:20 drove before that other *l*
2Ki 3:17 your *l* and your domestic
1Ch 5:9 *l* itself had become numerous
5:21 got to take captive their *l*
7:21 came down to take their *l*
28:1 goods and *l* of the king and
2Ch 14:15 tents with *l* they struck so
26:10 great deal of *l* that became
32:29 *l* of the flock and of the
Job 1:3 his *l* got to be seven thousand
1:10 and his *l* itself has spread
36:33 The *l* also concerning the
Ps 78:48 *l* to the flaming fever
Ec 2:7 *l*, cattle and flocks in great
Isa 30:23 *l* will graze in that day
Jer 9:10 will not hear the sound of *l*
49:32 their *l* a spoil
Eze 45:15 from the *l* of Israel, for

Living

Ge 1:20 a swarm of *l* souls and let
1:21 every *l* soul that moves about
1:24 the earth put forth *l* souls
1:28 every *l* creature that is
2:7 the man came to be a *l* soul
2:19 each *l* soul, that was its
3:20 the mother of everyone *l*
6:19 every *l* creature of every sort
8:17 Every *l* creature that is with
8:19 Every *l* creature . . . went out
8:21 deal every *l* thing a blow
9:2 every *l* creature of the earth
9:5 From the hand of every *l*
9:10 every *l* soul that is with you
9:10 all *l* creatures of the earth
9:10 every *l* creature of the earth
9:12 every *l* soul that is with you
9:15 and you and every *l* soul
9:16 every *l* soul among all flesh
20:7 So keep *l*. But if you are not
Le 11:2 the *l* creature that you may
11:10 *l* soul that is in the waters
11:27 *l* creatures that go on all
11:46 every *l* soul that moves
11:47 *l* creature that is eatable
11:47 the *l* creature that may not
13:10 the *l* flesh is in the
13:14 the day the *l* flesh appears
13:15 priest must see the *l* flesh
13:15 The *l* flesh is unclean
13:16 *l* flesh goes back and it does
14:6 the *l* bird, he should take it
14:6 the *l* bird in the blood of the
14:7 the *l* bird over the open field
Nu 16:48 between the dead and the *l*
De 4:33 heard it, and kept on *l*
5:24 and he may actually keep *l*
5:26 heard the voice of the *l* God
5:26 and yet goes on *l*
8:1 continue *l* and indeed multiply
31:13 you are *l* upon the soil to
Jos 3:10 know that a *l* God is in your
6:17 the prostitute may keep on *l*
Ru 2:20 loving-kindness toward the *l*
1Sa 17:26 battle lines of the *l* God
17:36 battle lines of the *l* God
19:6 As Jehovah is *l*, he will not
20:3 as Jehovah is *l* and as your
20:3 as your soul is *l*, there is
20:21 as Jehovah is *l*
25:26 as Jehovah is *l* and as your
25:26 and as your soul is *l*
25:34 God of Israel is *l*, who has
26:10 As Jehovah is *l*
26:16 As Jehovah is *l*, you men
29:6 As Jehovah is *l*, you are
2Sa 2:27 As the true God is *l*, if you
4:9 As Jehovah . . . is *l*
11:11 As you are *l* and as your
11:11 as your soul is *l*, I shall
12:5 As Jehovah is *l*, the man
14:11 As Jehovah is *l*, not a
14:19 As your soul is *l*, O my
15:21 Jehovah is *l* and as my lord
15:21 as my lord the king is *l*
20:3 widowhood with a *l* husband
22:47 Jehovah is *l*; and blessed be
1Ki 1:29 As Jehovah is *l* who redeemed
2:24 as Jehovah is *l* who has
3:22 my son is the *l* one and your
3:22 and my son is the *l* one
3:23 This is my son, the *l* one
3:23 and my son is the *l* one
3:25 sever the *l* child in two
3:26 whose son was the *l* one
3:26 men, give her the *l* child
3:27 men, give her the *l* child
17:1 before whom I do stand is *l*
17:12 As Jehovah your God is *l*
18:10 As Jehovah your God is *l*
18:15 As Jehovah . . . is *l*, today
22:14 As Jehovah is *l*, what
2Ki 2:2 As Jehovah is *l* and as your
2:2 and as your soul is *l*, I
2:4 As Jehovah is *l* and as your
2:4 as your soul is *l*, I will not
2:6 As Jehovah is *l* and as your
2:6 as your soul is *l*, I will not
3:14 before whom I do stand is *l*
4:30 As Jehovah is *l* and as your
4:30 as your soul is *l*, I will
5:16 As Jehovah . . . is *l*, I will
5:20 As Jehovah is *l*, I will run
2Ki 10:19 missing will not keep *l*
18:32 keep *l* that you may not die
19:4 sent to taunt the *l* God
19:16 sent to taunt the *l* God
2Ch 18:13 As Jehovah is *l*, what my
Job 21:7 the wicked themselves keep *l*
28:13 found in the land of those *l*
30:23 meeting for everyone *l*
33:30 with the light of those *l*
42:16 Job continued *l* after this a
Ps 18:46 Jehovah is *l*, and blessed be
42:2 thirsts . . . for the *l* God
52:5 out of the land of the *l* ones
69:28 the book of the *l* ones
84:2 cry out joyfully to the *l* God
104:25 *L* creatures, small as well
116:9 in the lands of those *l*
118:17 keep *l*, That I may declare
119:77 that I may keep *l*
119:116 that I may keep *l*
119:144 that I may keep *l*
119:175 soul keep *l* and praising
142:5 share in the land of the *l*
145:16 desire of every *l* thing
Pr 2:19 regain the paths of those *l*
4:4 commandments and continue *l*
7:2 commandments and continue *l*
9:6 inexperienced ones and keep *l*
15:27 hater of gifts . . . keep *l*
Ec 4:2 the *l* who were still alive
6:8 to walk in front of the *l* ones
9:4 whoever is joined to all the *l*
9:5 *l* are conscious that they will
Isa 8:19 in behalf of *l* persons
37:4 sent to taunt the *l* God
37:17 has sent to taunt the *l* God
38:11 in the land of the *l* ones
38:16 on that account they keep *l*
38:19, 19 The *l*, the *l*, he is the
49:18 As I am *l*, is the utterance
53:8 from the land of the *l* ones
Jer 2:13 the source of *l* water, in
10:10 He is the *l* God and the King
11:19 from the land of the *l* ones
17:13 source of *l* water, Jehovah
21:9 will keep *l*, and his soul
23:36 the words of the *l* God
27:12 his people and keep on *l*
27:17 of Babylon and keep on *l*
35:7 *l* many days upon the surface
38:2 one that will keep *l* and
38:17 certainly keep *l* and this
38:17 will certainly keep *l*
La 3:39 a *l* man indulge in complaints
Eze 1:5 likeness of four *l* creatures
1:13 likeness of the *l* creatures
1:13 between the *l* creatures, and
1:14 the part of the *l* creatures
1:15 I kept seeing the *l* creatures
1:15 earth beside the *l* creatures
1:19 when the *l* creatures went
1:19 *l* creatures were lifted up
1:20 spirit of the *l* creature was
1:21 spirit of the *l* creature was
1:22 the heads of the *l* creatures
3:13 the wings of the *l* creatures
3:21 will without fail keep on *l*
7:13 life is yet among the *l* ones
10:15 same *l* creature that I had
10:17 the spirit of the *l* creature
10:20 *l* creature that I had seen
16:6 Keep *l*! yes, to say to you in
16:6 to say to you . . . Keep *l*!
18:9 He will positively keep *l*
18:13 positively will not keep *l*
18:17 He will positively keep *l*
18:19 He will positively keep *l*
18:21 he will positively keep *l*
18:22 he will keep *l*
18:23 and actually keep *l*
18:24 he keeps doing and he is *l*
18:28 he will positively keep *l*
18:32 a turning back and keep *l*
20:11 might also keep *l* by them
20:13 he will also keep *l* by them
20:21 he will also keep *l* by them
20:25 which they could not keep *l*
33:10 how, then, shall we keep *l*?
33:11 and actually keeps *l*
33:12 keep *l* because of it in the
33:13 You will positively keep *l*
33:15 he will positively keep *l*
33:16 He will positively keep *l*
33:19 he himself will keep *l*

Eze 47:9 every *l* soul that swarms, in
Da 4:17 people *l* may know that the
4:34 One *l* to time indefinite I
5:10 O king, keep *l* even to times
6:20 Daniel, servant of the *l* God
6:26 For he is the *l* God and One
Ho 1:10 The sons of the *l* God
Am 5:4 Search for me, and keep *l*
5:6 Search for Jehovah, and keep *l*
5:14 that you people may keep *l*
Hab 2:4 faithfulness he will keep *l*
Zec 14:8 *l* waters will go forth from
Mt 16:16 Christ, the Son of the *l* God
22:32 He is the God . . . of the *l*
26:63 By the *l* God I put you under
Mr 12:27 He is a God . . . of the *l*
12:44 what she had, her whole *l*
Lu 1:65 fear fell upon all those *l*
2:8 shepherds *l* out of doors and
15:12 divided his means of *l* to
15:13 by *l* a debauched life
15:30 ate up your means of *l* with
20:38 not of the dead, but of the *l*
20:38 for they are all *l* to him
21:4 all the means of *l* she had
24:5 for the *l* One among the dead
Joh 4:10 would have given you *l* water
4:11 do you have this *l* water
4:51 to say that his boy was *l*
6:51 I am the *l* bread that came
6:57 Just as the *l* Father sent me
7:38 streams of *l* water will
11:26 *l* and exercises faith in me
Ac 7:38 *l* sacred pronouncements to
10:42 judge of the *l* and the dead
14:15 to the *l* God, who made the
28:4 not permit him to keep on *l*
Ro 6:2 we keep on *l* any longer in it
6:11 *l* with reference to God by
7:3 while her husband is *l*, she
9:26 be called sons of the *l* God
12:1 *l*, holy, acceptable to God
14:9 over both the dead and the *l*
1Co 15:45 man Adam became a *l* soul
2Co 3:3 with spirit of a *l* God, not
6:16 we are a temple of a *l* God
Ga 2:20 is Christ that is *l* in union
5:25 If we are *l* by spirit, let us
Col 2:20 you, as if *l* in the world
1Th 1:9 to slave for a *l* and true God
4:15 we the *l* who survive to the
4:17 we the *l* who are surviving
1Ti 3:15 the congregation of the *l* God
4:10 rested our hope on a *l* God
5:6 is dead though she is *l*
2Ti 4:1 to judge the *l* and the dead
Heb 3:12 drawing away from the *l* God
9:14 sacred service to the *l* God
9:17 the human covenanter is *l*
10:20 *l* way through the curtain
10:31 into the hands of the *l* God
12:22 and a city of the *l* God
1Pe 1:3 new birth to a *l* hope through
1:23 the *l* and enduring God
2:4 Coming to him as to a *l* stone
2:5 *l* stones are being built up a
4:5 judge those *l* and those dead
2Pe 2:13 luxurious *l* in the daytime
Re 1:18 *l* one; and I became dead
1:18 I am *l* forever and ever, and
4:6 four *l* creatures that are full
4:7 first *l* creature is like a lion
4:7 *l* creature is like a young bull
4:7 third *l* creature has a face
4:7 fourth *l* creature is like a
4:8 as for the four *l* creatures
4:9 *l* creatures offer glory and
5:6 four *l* creatures and in the
5:8 the four *l* creatures and the
5:11 *l* creatures and the elders
5:14 And the four *l* creatures went
6:1 one of the four *l* creatures say
6:3 heard the second *l* creature say
6:5 heard the third *l* creature say
6:6 midst of the four *l* creatures
6:7 voice of the fourth *l* creature
7:2 having a seal of the *l* God; and
7:11 and the four *l* creatures, and
14:3 before the four *l* creatures
15:7 one of the four *l* creatures
16:3 every *l* soul died, yes, the
18:17 who make a *l* by the sea
19:4 four *l* creatures fell down

Lizard
Le 11:29 the *l* according to its kind
11:30 the large *l* and the newt
11:30 the sand *l* and the chameleon
Pr 30:28 gecko *l* takes hold with its

Lo
Ps 68:33 *L!* He sounds with his voice
Isa 8:22 *l!* distress and darkness

Load
Ge 44:13 lifted each one his *l* back
45:17 *L* your beasts of burden and
Ex 18:18 is too big a *l* for you
18:22 must carry the *l* with you
23:5 lying down under its *l*, then
Nu 4:15 *l* of the sons of Kohath in
4:19 to his service and to his *l*
4:31 their obligation, their *l*
4:32 they are obligated, as their *l*
4:49 to his service and his *l*
11:11 *l* of all this people upon
11:17 carrying the *l* of the people
De 1:12 *l* of you and your quarreling
2Sa 15:33 become a *l* upon me
16:2 the *l* of summer fruit are
2Ki 5:17 the *l* of a pair of mules
8:9 the *l* of forty camels, and
Ne 4:17 the burden of *l* bearers
Ps 38:4 Like a heavy *l* they are too
68:19 daily carries the *l* for us
Pr 27:3 of a stone and a *l* of sand
Isa 9:4 yoke of their *l* and the rod
10:27 *l* will depart from upon
14:25 *l* may depart from upon
22:25 *l* that is upon it must be
Jer 10:17 from the earth your pack *l*
17:21 any *l* that you must bring
17:22 no *l* out of your homes on
17:24 to bring in no *l* through the
17:27 and not carrying a *l*, but
Mt 11:30 is kindly and my *l* is light
Lu 11:46 you *l* men with loads hard to
Ga 6:5 each one will carry his own *l*

Loaded
Ge 42:26 they *l* their cereals upon
1Ki 12:11 *l* upon you a heavy yoke
2Ch 10:11 *l* upon you a heavy yoke
Ps 144:14 Our cattle *l* down, without
Mt 11:28 who are toiling and *l* down
Ac 28:10 they *l* us with things for
2Ti 3:6 *l* down with sins, led by

Loading
Ne 13:15 *l* them upon asses, and also

Loads
Nu 4:27 regards all their *l* and all
4:27 assign all their *l* to them by
4:47 service of carrying *l* in the
2Sa 16:1 a hundred *l* of summer fruit
Isa 46:1 their *l*, pieces of luggage
Mt 23:4 They bind up heavy *l* and put
Lu 11:46 with *l* hard to be borne
11:46 do not touch the *l* with one

Loaf
Ex 29:23 also a round *l* of bread and a
1Sa 2:36 money and a round *l* of bread
1Ch 16:3 a round *l* of bread and a date
Pr 6:26 down to a round *l* of bread
Jer 37:21 round *l* of bread to him
Mt 26:26 Jesus took a *l* and, after
Mr 8:14 except for one *l* they had
14:22 he took a *l*, said a blessing
Lu 4:3 tell this stone to become a *l*
22:19 took a *l*, gave thanks, broke
24:30 the *l*, blessed it, broke
24:35 by the breaking of the *l*
Ac 27:35 took a *l*, gave thanks to
1Co 10:16 The *l* which we break, is it
10:17 Because there is one *l*, we
10:17 all partaking of that one *l*
11:23 the Lord Jesus . . . took a *l*
11:26 eat this *l* and drink this
11:27 whoever eats the *l* or
11:28 eat of the *l* and drink of

Loafing
Ho 7:14 they kept *l* about

Lo-ammi
Ho 1:9 Call his name *L*, because you

Loan
De 24:10 a *l* of any sort, you must
24:11 to whom you are making a *l*
Ne 5:10 giving money and grain on *l*
Jer 15:10 I have given no *l*, and they
15:10 they have given me no *l*
Lu 11:5 Friend, *l* me three loaves

Loans
Pr 22:26 those who go security for *l*

Loathe
Le 11:11 you are to *l* their dead body
11:13 these are what you will *l*
De 7:26 *l* it and absolutely detest it

Loathed
Ps 22:24 Nor *l* the affliction of the

Loathing
Nu 11:20 become a *l* to you, just
Job 10:1 feels a *l* toward my life
Ps 95:10 feeling a *l* toward that
119:158 I do feel a *l*, because
139:21 *l* for those revolting against
Eze 6:9 feel a *l* in their faces at the
20:43 feel a *l* at your own faces
36:31 feel a *l* at your own person
Zec 11:8 their own soul felt a *l*

Loathsome
Le 7:21 beast or any unclean *l* thing
11:10 they are a *l* thing for you
11:11 will become a *l* thing to you
11:12 scales is a *l* thing to you
11:13 are a *l* thing: the eagle and
11:20 is a *l* thing to you
11:23 four legs is a *l* thing to
11:41 upon the earth is a *l* thing
11:42 because they are a *l* thing
11:43 *l* with any swarming creature
20:25 souls *l* with the beast and
Job 19:17 My breath . . . *l* to my wife
33:20 certainly makes bread *l*
Isa 66:17 and the *l* thing, even the
Eze 8:10 creeping things and *l* beasts

Loaves
Le 23:17 bring two *l* as a wave
23:18 with the *l* seven sound male
23:20 *l* of the first ripe fruits
26:26 ring-shaped *l* are suspended
Jg 8:5 give round *l* of bread to the
1Sa 10:3 one carrying three round *l* of
10:4 and give you two *l*, and you
17:17 and these ten *l* of bread
21:3 five *l* of bread at your
25:18 two hundred *l* of bread and
2Sa 16:1 two hundred *l* of bread and
1Ki 14:3 in your hand ten *l* of bread
2Ki 4:42 twenty barley *l*, and new
Ps 105:16 ring-shaped *l* were
Eze 4:16 ring-shaped *l* are suspended
5:16 around which ring-shaped *l*
14:13 ring-shaped *l* are suspended
Mt 4:3 stones to become *l* of bread
12:4 ate the *l* of presentation
14:17 but five *l* and two fishes
14:19 and took the five *l* and two
14:19 and, after breaking the *l*
15:33 *l* to satisfy a crowd of this
15:34 How many *l* have you?
15:36 the seven *l* and the fishes
16:5 and forgot to take *l* along
16:7 We did not take any *l* along
16:8 because you have no *l*, you
16:9 the five *l* in the case of the
16:10 seven *l* in the case of the
16:11 did not talk to you about *l*
16:12 not for the leaven of the *l*
Mr 2:26 and ate the *l* of presentation
6:37 *l* and give them to the people
6:38 How many *l* have you? Go see!
6:41 the five *l* and the two fishes
6:41 broke the *l* up and began
6:44 those who ate of the *l* were
6:52 grasped the meaning of the *l*
8:4 to satisfy these people with *l*
8:5 How many *l* have you?
8:6 took the seven *l*, gave thanks
8:14 they forgot to take *l* along
8:16 the fact that they had no *l*
8:17 argue over your having no *l*
8:19 I broke the five *l* for the
Lu 6:4 received the *l* of presentation
9:13 five *l* and two fishes, unless
9:16 five *l* and the two fishes
11:5 Friend, loan me three *l*
Joh 6:5 we buy *l* for these to eat
6:7 hundred denarii worth of *l*

Joh 6:9 boy that has five barley *l*
6:11 So Jesus took the *l* and
6:13 from the five barley *l*
6:26 ate from the *l* and were
Heb 9:2 and the display of the *l*

Lobe
Ex 29:20 the *l* of Aaron's right ear
29:20 the *l* of his sons' right ear
Le 8:23 upon the *l* of Aaron's right
8:24 the *l* of their right ear and
14:14 the *l* of the right ear of the
14:17 the *l* of the right ear of the
14:25 upon the *l* of the right ear
14:28 upon the *l* of the right ear

Local
Mt 10:17 deliver you up to *l* courts
Mr 13:9 deliver you up to *l* courts
Ac 13:1 teachers in the *l* congregation

Locality
Ex 3:8 to the *l* of the Canaanites and
16:29 nobody go out from his *l* on

Locate
Ge 30:41 Jacob would *l* the staffs
30:42 he would not *l* them there
Jos 18:1 *l* the tent of meeting there
1Ki 8:21 *l* a place there for the Ark

Location
Isa 21:5 arranging of the *l* of seats

Locations
2Ch 33:19 *l* in which he built high

Lock
2Sa 13:17 and *l* the door behind her
Ca 5:5 upon the hollows of the *l*

Locked
Jg 3:23 closed the doors . . . *l* them
3:24 of the roof chamber were *l*
2Sa 13:18 he *l* the door behind her
Job 24:16 must keep themselves *l* in
Lu 3:20 he *l* John up in prison
11:7 The door is already *l*, and my
13:25 has got up and *l* the door
Joh 20:19 doors were *l* where the
20:26 the doors were *l*, and he
Ac 5:23 *l* with all security and the
26:10 holy ones I *l* up in prisons

Locks
Nu 6:5 letting the *l* of the hair of
De 33:25 and copper are your gate *l*
Ca 5:2 *l* of my hair with the drops
5:11 The *l* of his hair are date

Locust
Ex 10:12 the land of Egypt for the *l*
10:19 Not a single *l* was let
Le 11:22 the migratory *l* according to
11:22 the edible *l* after its kind
De 28:38 because the *l* will devour it
Job 39:20 cause it to leap like a *l*
Ps 105:34 species of *l*, even without
109:23 been shaken off like a *l*
Isa 33:4 onrush of *l* swarms that is
Jer 46:23 more numerous than the *l*
Joe 1:4 What was left . . . *l* has eaten
1:4 and what was left by the *l*
1:4 unwinged *l* has eaten
1:4 unwinged *l* has left, the
2:25 for the years that the *l*
2:25 the creeping, unwinged *l*
Am 7:1 he was forming a *l* swarm at
Na 3:15 devour you like the *l* species
3:15 heavy in numbers like the *l*
3:15 heavy in numbers like the *l*
3:16 As for the *l* species, it
3:17 Your guardsmen are like the *l*
3:17 officers like the *l* swarm

Locusts
Ex 10:4 *l* within your boundaries
10:13 the east wind carried the *l*
10:14 *l* began to come up over all
10:14 never . . . *l* like them
10:19 carried the *l* away and drove
Jg 6:5 come as numerous as the *l*, and
7:12 as numerous as *l*; and their
1Ki 8:37 scorching, mildew, *l*
2Ch 6:28 *l* and cockroaches occur; in
Ps 78:46 And their toil to the *l*
105:34 that the *l* should come in
Pr 30:27 *l* have no king, and yet they
Jer 51:14 you with men, like the *l*
Jer 51:27 horses . . . like bristly *l*
Mt 3:4 was insect *l* and wild honey
Mr 1:6 eating insect *l* and wild honey
Re 9:3 out of the smoke *l* came forth
9:5 granted the *l*, not to kill
9:7 *l* resembled horses prepared

Lod
1Ch 8:12 Shemed, who built Ono and *L*
Ezr 2:33 sons of *L*, Hadid and Ono
Ne 7:37 the sons of *L*, Hadid and Ono
11:35 *L* and Ono, the valley of the

Lo-debar
2Sa 9:4 the son of Ammiel at *L*
9:5 the son of Ammiel at *L*
17:27 the son of Ammiel from *L*

Lodge
Nu 22:8 *L* here tonight, and I shall
Jos 4:3 in which you will *l* tonight
Ru 3:13 *L* here tonight, and it must
2Sa 17:16 Do not *l* in the desert
19:7 not a man will *l* with you
Job 19:4 that my mistake will *l*
Ps 25:13 soul will *l* in goodness
55:7 I would *l* in the wilderness
Ca 7:11 *l* among the henna plants
Isa 1:21 righteousness . . . used to *l*
Jer 4:14 erroneous thoughts *l* within
Zec 5:4 *l* in the midst of his house
Lu 19:7 sinner he went in to *l*
21:37 go out and *l* on the mountain

Lodged
Ge 32:21 *l* that night in the camp

Lodges
Job 17:2 my eye *l*
41:22 In its neck *l* strength
Pr 15:31 *l* right in among wise people

Lodging
Ge 32:13 kept *l* there on that night
42:27 at the *l* place, he got to
43:21 when we came to the *l* place
Ex 4:24 on the road at the *l* place
Jos 2:1 and they took up *l* there
4:3 deposit them in the *l* place
4:8 with them to the *l* place and
8:9 Joshua kept *l* on that night
2Ki 19:23 enter its final *l* place
Ps 30:5 weeping may take up *l*, but
49:12 in honor, cannot keep *l*
91:1 *l* under the very shadow of
Jer 9:2 a *l* place of travelers
41:17 *l* place of Chimham that
Mt 13:32 find *l* among its branches
Mr 4:32 to find *l* under its shadow
Lu 2:7 place for them in the *l* room
9:12 procure *l* and find provisions
13:19 took up *l* in its branches
Ac 1:20 his *l* place become desolate
28:23 to him in his *l* place
Phm 22 also get *l* ready for me

Lodgment
Lu 9:44 Give *l* to these words in your

Loftiness
Ps 48:2 Pretty for *l*, the exultation
Isa 2:11 the *l* of men must bow down
2:17 *l* of men must become low
10:12 of his *l* of eyes
Jer 48:29 of the *l* of his heart

Lofty
1Ki 8:13 a house of *l* abode for you
2Ki 19:23 shall cut down its *l* cedars
2Ch 6:2 built a house of *l* abode for
Ps 49:14 Sheol rather than a *l* abode
131:1 Nor have my eyes been *l*
138:6 *l* one he knows only from a
Pr 6:17 *l* eyes, a false tongue, and
18:12 the heart of a man is *l*
30:13 eyes have become O how *l*
Isa 2:12 everyone self-exalted and *l*
2:13 cedars of Lebanon that are *l*
2:14 upon all the *l* mountains and
6:1 Jehovah, sitting on a throne *l*
37:24 cut down its *l* cedars, its
57:15 the High and *L* One, who is
63:15 see out of your *l* abode
Eze 17:22 the *l* treetop of the cedar
17:22 upon a high and *l* mountain
Hab 3:11 stood still, in the *l* abode
Mt 17:1 up into a *l* mountain by
Mr 9:2 up into a *l* mountain to
Lu 16:15 *l* among men is a disgusting
Ro 11:20 Quit having *l* ideas, but
12:16 do not be minding *l* things
2Co 10:5 every *l* thing raised up
Heb 1:3 of the Majesty in *l* places
Re 21:10 to a great and *l* mountain
21:12 It had a great and *l* wall

Log
Le 14:10 and one *l* measure of oil
14:12 the *l* measure of oil and
14:15 some of the *l* measure of oil
14:21 and a *l* measure of oil
14:24 and the *l* measure of oil, and
1Ki 5:9 put them in *l* rafts to go by
Am 4:11 a *l* snatched out of the
Zec 3:2 a *l* snatched out of the fire

Logical
Lu 1:3 to write them in *l* order to

Logically
Ac 9:22 proved *l* that this is the

Logs
Ec 10:9 He that is splitting *l* will
Isa 7:4 tail-ends of these smoking *l*
Eze 24:5 stack the *l* in a circle under
24:10 Make the *l* many. Kindle the

Loin
Ge 3:7 and made *l* coverings for

Loins
Ge 35:11 will come out of your *l*
Le 3:4 the same as that upon the *l*
3:10 the same as that upon the *l*
3:15 the same as that upon the *l*
4:9 the same as that upon the *l*
7:4 the same as that upon the *l*
1Ki 8:19 is coming forth from your *l*
20:31 carry sackcloth upon our *l*
20:32 sackcloth about their *l*
2Ki 1:8 belt girded about his *l*
4:29 Gird up your *l* and take my
9:1 Gird up your *l* and take this
2Ch 6:9 is coming forth from your *l*
Job 15:27 he puts on fat upon his *l*
31:20 If his *l* did not bless me
38:3 Gird up your *l*, please, like
40:7 Gird up your *l*, please, like
Ps 38:7 *l* have become full of burning
Isa 5:27 belt around their *l* will
11:5 the belt of his *l*
32:11 gird sackcloth upon the *l*
Jer 30:6 hands upon his *l* like a
Mt 3:4 a leather girdle around his *l*
Mr 1:6 a leather girdle around his *l*
Lu 12:35 Let your *l* be girded and
Ac 2:30 from the fruitage of his *l*
Eph 6:14 *l* girded about with truth
Heb 7:5 issued from the *l* of Abraham
7:10 in the *l* of his forefather

Lois
2Ti 1:5 your grandmother *L* and your

Loiter
Ro 12:11 Do not *l* at your business

Lone
Ge 19:9 *l* man came here to reside
2Sa 14:16 *l* son from the inheritance

Lonely
Mt 14:13 into a *l* place for isolation
14:15 The place is *l* and the hour
15:33 in this *l* place going to get
Mr 1:35 and left for a *l* place, and
1:45 continued outside in *l* places
6:31 privately into a *l* place and
6:32 for a *l* place to themselves
Lu 4:42 out and proceeded to a *l* place
8:29 driven . . . into the *l* places
9:12 out here we are in a *l* place

Long
Ge 3:21 to make *l* garments of skin
23:1 and twenty-seven years *l*
32:4 stayed for a *l* time till now
37:3 he had a *l*, striped shirtlike
37:23 stripping Joseph of his *l*
37:23 the *l* striped garment that
37:31 they took Joseph's *l* garment
37:31 dipped the *l* garment in the
37:32 sent the *l* striped garment
37:32 it is your son's *l* garment
37:33 It is my son's *l* garment
Ex 10:3 How *l* must you refuse to
10:7 How *l* will this man prove to
14:20 near that group all night *l*

Ex 14:21 strong east wind all night *l*
16:28 How *l* must you people refuse
20:12 your days may prove *l* upon
27:16 is a screen twenty cubits *l*
32:1 Moses was taking a *l* time
Le 6:9 upon the altar all night *l*
21:18 or with one member too *l*
22:23 member too *l* or too short
Nu 14:11 How *l* will this people treat
14:11 how *l* will they not put
14:27 How *l* will this evil
22:30 ridden upon all your life *l*
24:6 they have extended a *l* way
24:22 How *l* will it be till
De 1:6 You have dwelt *l* enough in
2:3 around this mountain *l* enough
4:25 a *l* time in the land and do
5:16 your days may prove *l* and it
6:2 that your days may prove *l*
14:24 the journey should be too *l*
25:15 that your days may become *l*
Jos 10:9 All night *l* he had gone up
18:3 How *l* are you going to be
24:2 a *l* time ago, Terah the
Jg 16:2 all night *l* in the city gate
19:25 abusing her all night *l* until
1Sa 1:14 How *l* will you behave drunk?
15:11 crying out . . . all night *l*
16:1 how *l* will you be mourning
31:12 all night *l* and took the
2Sa 2:26 How *l*, then, will it be
2:32 went marching on all night *l*
3:1 came to be *l* drawn out
4:7 road to the Arabah all night *l*
1Ki 8:8 But the poles proved to be *l*
18:21 How *l* will you be limping
2Ki 9:22 peace could there be as *l* as
2Ch 5:9 the poles were *l*, so that the
15:2 Jehovah is with you as *l* as
20:20 yourselves of *l* duration
Ne 2:6 How *l* will your journey come
Es 5:13 as *l* as I am seeing Mordecai
Job 8:2 How *l* will you keep uttering
18:2 How *l* will you people be at
19:2 How *l* will you men keep
22:15 to the very way of *l* ago
29:2 in the lunar months of *l* ago
30:18 the collar of my *l* garment
Ps 4:2 how *l* must my glory be for
6:3 And you, O Jehovah—how *l?*
6:6 All night *l* I make my couch
13:1 How *l*, O Jehovah, will you
13:1 How *l* will you conceal your
13:2 How *l* shall I set resistance
13:2 How *l* will my enemy be
25:5 In you I have hoped all day *l*
32:3 through my groaning all day *l*
35:17 how *l* will you keep seeing
35:28 All day *l* your praise
37:26 All day *l* he is showing
38:6 All day *l* I have walked about
38:12 keep muttering all day *l*
39:1 As *l* as anyone wicked is in
42:3 they say to me all day *l*
42:10 they say to me all day *l*
44:1 In the days of *l* ago
44:8 will offer praise all day *l*
44:15 All day *l* my humiliation
44:22 we have been killed all day *l*
45:11 will *l* for your prettiness
52:1 loving-kindness . . . all day *l*
56:1 Warring all day *l*, he keeps
56:2 have kept snapping all day *l*
56:5 All day *l* they keep hurting
62:3 How *l* will you carry on
71:8 All day *l* with your beauty
71:15 All day *l* your salvation
71:24 all day *l*, will utter in
72:5 as *l* as there is a sun
72:15 All day *l* let him be blessed
73:14 to be plagued all day *l*
74:2 that you acquired *l* ago
74:9 no one with us knowing how *l*
74:10 How *l*, O God, will the
74:12 God is my King from *l* ago
74:22 the senseless one all day *l*
77:5 thought upon the days of *l* ago
77:11 marvelous doing of *l* ago
78:2 riddles of *l* ago to bubble
79:5 How *l*, O Jehovah, will you
79:5 How *l* will your ardor burn
80:4 how *l* must you fume against
82:2 How *l* will you keep on
86:3 I keep calling all day *l*
Ps 88:9 on you, O Jehovah, all day *l*
88:17 like waters all day *l*
89:16 they are joyful all day *l*
89:46 How *l*, O Jehovah, will you
90:13 Jehovah! How *l* will it be?
93:2 firmly established from *l* ago
94:3 How *l* are the wicked
94:3 How *l* are the wicked
102:8 All day *l* my enemies have
102:25 *L* ago you laid the
104:33 to my God as *l* as I am
119:97 All day *l* it is my concern
119:152 *L* ago I have known some
120:6 For too *l* a time my soul has
129:1 *L* enough they have shown
129:2 *L* enough they have shown
140:2 all day *l* keep attacking
143:5 remembered days of *l* ago
145:2 All day *l* I will bless you
146:2 to my God as *l* as I am
Pr 1:22 How *l* will you inexperienced
1:22 how *l* must you ridiculers
1:22 how *l* will you stupid ones
6:9 How *l*, you lazy one, will you
8:22 his achievements of *l* ago
12:19 be only as *l* as a moment
22:28 a boundary of *l* ago, which
23:10 back the boundary of *l* ago
23:17 the fear of Jehovah all day *l*
23:30 a *l* time with the wine
28:2 the prince will remain *l*
Ec 7:15 continuing *l* in his badness
8:12 a *l* time as he pleases, yet I
Ca 1:12 As *l* as the king is at his
Isa 6:11 I said: How *l*, O Jehovah?
7:9 case not be of *l* duration
22:11 one forming it *l* ago you
23:7 exultant from days of *l* ago
28:24 all day *l* that the plower
42:14 kept quiet for a *l* time
44:7 appointed the people of *l* ago
45:21 be heard from a *l* time ago
46:9 first things of a *l* time ago
46:10 from *l* ago the things that
51:9 as in the days of *l* ago
51:9 generations of times *l* past
51:13 the whole day *l* on account
52:5 all day *l*, my name was
58:12 places devastated a *l* time
62:6, 6 All day *l* and all night *l*
63:9 all the days of *l* ago
63:11 remember the days of *l* ago
63:16 Repurchaser of *l* ago is
63:19 for a *l* time become as
64:4 from time *l* ago none have
64:5 sinning—in them a *l* time
65:2 all day *l* to a stubborn
65:5 a fire burning all day *l*
Jer 2:20 For *l* ago I broke your yoke
4:14 How *l* will your erroneous
4:21 How *l* shall I keep seeing
5:15 It is a nation of *l* ago, a
6:16 for the roadways of *l* ago
12:4 How *l* should the land keep
18:15 the paths of *l* ago, to walk
20:7 object of laughter all day *l*
20:8 and for jeering all day *l*
23:26 How *l* will it exist in the
25:5 your forefathers from *l* ago
25:5 and to a *l* time to come
28:8 prior to you from *l* ago
29:28 saying: It is *l* drawn out
31:22 How *l* will you turn this
47:5 how *l* will you keep making
47:6 How *l* will you not stay
La 1:7 to be from days of *l* ago
2:17 from the days of *l* ago
3:3 turns his hand all day *l*
3:6 sit like men dead for a *l* time
3:14 theme of their song all day *l*
3:62 against me all day *l*
5:21 days for us as in the *l* ago
Eze 17:3 *l* pinions, full of plumage
26:20 to the people of *l* ago
26:20 devastated for a *l* time
Da 4:33 hair grew *l* just like eagles'
8:13 How *l* will the vision be of
12:6 How *l* will it be to the end
Ho 7:6 All night *l* their baker is
8:5 How *l* will they be incapable
12:1 after the east wind all day *l*
Am 8:5 How *l* will it be before the
9:11 as in the days of *l* ago
Mic 7:14 in the days of a *l* time ago
Mic 7:20 from the days of *l* ago
Hab 1:2 How *l*, O Jehovah, must I cry
1:2 How *l* shall I call to you
1:12 Are you not from *l* ago, O
2:6 what is not his own—O how *l!*
3:6 The walkings of *l* ago are his
Zec 1:12 Jehovah of armies, how *l*
Mal 3:4 as in the days of *l* ago and
Mt 8:30 a *l* way off from them a
9:15 as *l* as the bridegroom is
11:21 would *l* ago have repented in
17:17 how *l* must I continue with
17:17 How *l* must I put up with
25:19 After a *l* time the master
Mr 2:19 *l* as they have the bridegroom
9:19 how *l* must I continue with
9:19 How *l* must I put up with
9:21 How *l* has this been happening
12:40 pretext making *l* prayers
Lu 2:35 a *l* sword will be run through
8:29 a *l* time it had held him fast
9:41 how *l* must I continue with
10:13 would *l* ago have repented
15:20 he was yet a *l* way off
20:47 for a pretext make *l* prayers
Joh 5:6 already been sick a *l* time
9:5 As *l* as I am in the world, I
10:24 How *l* are you to keep our
14:9 with you men so *l* a time
21:8 were not a *l* way from land
Ac 5:4 As *l* as it remained with you
26:29 short time or in a *l* time
27:21 *l* abstinence from food
28:6 they waited for a *l* while
Ro 7:1 master over a man as *l* as he
8:36 being put to death all day *l*
10:21 All day *l* I have spread out
1Co 11:14 man has *l* hair, it is a
11:15 if a woman has *l* hair, it
2Co 9:14 they *l* for you because of the
Ga 4:1 as *l* as the heir is a babe
6:10 *l* as we have time favorable
Eph 6:3 endure a *l* time on the earth
2Ti 1:9 before times *l* lasting
Tit 1:2 before times *l* lasting
Heb 1:1 God, who *l* ago spoke on many
3:13 *l* as it may be called Today
4:7 after so *l* a time in David's
2Pe 1:9 from his sins of *l* ago
1:13 as *l* as I am in this
Jude 4 *l* ago been appointed by the
Re 1:16 *l* two-edged sword was
2:12 the sharp, *l* two-edged sword
2:16 with the *l* sword of my mouth
6:8 to kill with a *l* sword and
19:15 protrudes a sharp *l* sword
19:21 *l* sword of the one seated

Long-eared
Le 11:17 the cormorant and the *l* owl
De 14:16 the *l* owl and the swan
Isa 34:11 and *l* owls and ravens

Longed
Ge 3:6 to be *l* for to the eyes, yes
2Sa 13:39 David the king *l* to go out
Ps 119:40 I have *l* for your orders
119:131 commandments I have *l*
119:174 I have *l* for your salvation
132:13 *l* for it as a dwelling for
132:14 dwell, for I have *l* for it
Php 4:1 my brothers beloved and *l* for

Longer
Ge 32:28 no *l* be called Jacob but
35:10 No *l* is your name to be
45:1 no *l* able to control himself
Ex 2:3 was no *l* able to conceal him
9:28 and you will not stay any *l*
9:29 hail will not continue any *l*
17:4 little *l* and they will stone
Le 15:25 a flow *l* than her menstrual
17:7 no *l* sacrifice their
Nu 8:25 company and serve no *l*
32:15 stay *l* in the wilderness
De 10:16 not harden your necks any *l*
Jg 2:14 they were no *l* able to stand
1Sa 27:1 looking for me any *l* in all
1Ki 21:15 Naboth is no *l* alive but
2Ki 6:33 I wait any *l* for Jehovah
Ne 2:17 no *l* continue to be a reproach
Job 11:9 *l* than the earth in measure
Ps 37:10 just a little while *l*, and
88:5 you have remembered no *l*
104:35 wicked, they will be no *l*

Ec 4:13 enough to be warned any *l*
Isa 23:10 There is no shipyard any *l*
26:21 no *l* cover over her killed
30:20 Instructor will no *l* hide
32:5 no *l* be called generous
Jer 13:27 clean—after how much *l*
44:22 no *l* able to put up with it
49:7 no *l* any wisdom in Teman
Eze 13:23 you will divine no *l*
24:27 speak and be mute no *l*
31:5 branches continued getting *l*
33:22 proved to be speechless no *l*
34:10 shepherds will no *l* feed
34:22 no *l* become something for
34:28 no *l* become something to
34:29 no *l* bear the humiliation
37:22 no *l* continue to be two
37:22 divided any *l* into two
37:23 will no *l* defile themselves
39:28 remaining there any *l*
39:29 no *l* conceal my face from
Ho 2:16 will no *l* call me My owner
2:17 no *l* remember them by their
14:8 to do any *l* with the idols
Am 7:13 at Bethel you must no *l* do
Mt 5:13 no *l* usable for anything but
19:6 they are no *l* two, but one
Mr 1:45 was no *l* able to enter openly
5:35 Why bother the teacher any *l*?
7:12 no *l* let him do a single
9:8 no one with them any *l*
10:8 are no *l* two, but one flesh
Lu 8:49 not bother the teacher any *l*
15:19 no *l* worthy of being called
15:21 no *l* worthy of being called
16:2 can no *l* manage the house
20:40 no *l* did they have the
Joh 4:42 not believe any *l* on account
6:66 would no *l* walk with him
7:33 a little while *l* with you
11:54 Jesus no *l* walked about
12:35 among you a little while *l*
13:33 I am with you a little *l*
14:19 A little *l* and the world
15:15 I no *l* call you slaves
16:10 you will behold me no *l*
16:16 you will behold me no *l*
17:11 I am no *l* in the world
21:6 no *l* able to draw it in
Ac 18:18 staying quite some days *l*
18:20 to remain for a *l* time, he
25:24 he ought not to live any *l*
Ro 6:2 we keep on living any *l* in it
6:6 no *l* go on being slaves to sin
7:17 no *l* I, but sin that resides
7:20 one working it out is no *l* I
11:6 it is no *l* due to works
11:6 no *l* proves to be undeserved
14:13 judging one another any *l*
14:15 no *l* walking in accord with
15:23 no *l* have untouched territory
16:7 in union with Christ *l* than I
2Co 5:15 live no *l* for themselves
Ga 2:20 no *l* I that live, but it is
3:18 it is no *l* due to promise
3:25 we are no *l* under a tutor
4:7 you are no *l* a slave but a son
Eph 2:19 no *l* strangers and alien
4:14 we should no *l* be babes
4:17 no *l* go on walking just as
1Th 3:1 when we could bear it no *l*
3:5 when I could bear it no *l*, I
1Ti 5:23 Do not drink water any *l*
Phm 16 no *l* as a slave but as more
Heb 10:18 no *l* an offering for sin
10:26 no *l* any sacrifice for sins
Re 6:11 told to rest a little while *l*
10:6 There will be no delay any *l*
12:8 for them any *l* in heaven

Longing
Nu 11:4 expressed selfish *l*, and the
Ps 10:3 the selfish *l* of his soul
63:1 flesh has grown faint with *l*
119:20 My soul is crushed with *l*
Pr 18:1 will seek his own selfish *l*
Ec 6:2 that he shows himself *l* for
Eze 24:25 the *l* of their soul
Joe 1:20 keep *l* for you, because the
Ro 1:11 I am *l* to see you, that I
15:23 having had a *l* to get to you
2Co 7:7 us word again of your *l*
7:11 yes, *l*, yes, zeal, yes
Php 2:26 he is *l* to see all of you
2Ti 1:4 *l* to see you, as I remember
Jas 4:5 spirit . . . within us keeps *l*
1Pe 2:2 *l* for the unadulterated milk

Longingly
Ps 37:7 And wait *l* for him

Long-lasting
De 28:59 great and *l* plagues, and
28:59 malignant and *l* sicknesses
Ps 24:7 O you *l* entrances
24:9 O you *l* entrances
74:3 steps to the *l* desolations
Ec 12:5 man is walking to his *l* house
Isa 33:14 with *l* conflagrations
Ro 16:25 kept in silence for *l* times

Longs
Ps 42:1 the hind that *l* for the water
42:1 my very soul *l* for you, O God

Long-standing
Isa 61:4 rebuild the *l* devastated

Long-suffering
Lu 18:7 even though he is *l* toward
Ro 2:4 do you despise the . . . *l*
9:22 tolerated with much *l* vessels
1Co 13:4 Love is *l* and kind. Love is
2Co 6:6 by *l*, by kindness, by holy
Ga 5:22 fruitage of the spirit . . . *l*
Eph 4:2 mildness, with *l*, putting up
Col 1:11 fully and be *l* with joy
3:12 clothe yourselves with . . . *l*
1Th 5:14 support the weak, be *l*
1Ti 1:16 demonstrate all his *l* for
2Ti 3:10 have closely followed . . . my *l*
4:2 all *l* and art of teaching

Look
Ge 1:31 and, *l!* it was very good
3:6 tree was desirable to *l* upon
4:5 he did not *l* with any favor
6:12 earth and, *l!* it was ruined
8:11 *l!* there was an olive leaf
8:13 *l*, and here the surface of
11:6 Jehovah said: *L!* They are one
13:14 *l* from the place where you
15:3 Abram added: *L!* You have
15:3 *l!* a son of my household is
15:4 *l!* the word of Jehovah to him
15:5 *L* up, please, to the heavens
15:12 *l!* a frightfully great
15:17 *l!* a smoking furnace and a
16:6 Abram said to Sarai: *L!* Your
17:4 *l!* my covenant is with you
17:20 *L!* I will bless him and will
18:10 *l!* Sarah your wife will have
19:17 Do not *l* behind you and do
19:26 wife began to *l* around from
25:24 *l!* twins were in her belly
27:42 *L!* Esau your brother is
28:12 he began to dream, and, *l!*
28:12 *l!* there were God's angels
28:13 And, *l!* there was Jehovah
30:33 may come to *l* over my wages
31:2 would *l* at the face of Laban
32:18 *l!* he himself is also behind
37:19 *L!* Here comes that dreamer
37:25 took a *l*, why, here was a
39:14 *L!* He brought to us a man
41:33 let Pharaoh *l* for a man
44:34 I may *l* upon the calamity
48:1 *L*, your father is becoming
48:21 *L*, I am dying, but God will
50:5 *L!* I am dying. In my burial
Ex 1:9 *L!* The people of the sons of
2:11 might *l* at the burdens they
3:6 afraid to *l* at the true God
3:9 *l!* the outcry of the sons of
5:5 *L!* The people of the land are
5:21 May Jehovah *l* upon you and
6:12 *L!* The sons of Israel have not
6:30 *L!* I am uncircumcised in
7:15 *L!* He is going out to the
8:20 Pharaoh. *L!* He is coming out
9:3 *l!* Jehovah's hand is coming
9:7 Pharaoh sent, and, *l!* not so
14:24 Jehovah began to *l* out upon
16:10 *l!* Jehovah's glory appeared
17:6 *L!* I am standing before you
19:9 *L!* I am coming to you in a
19:21 to take a *l* and many of them
24:14 *l!* Aaron and Hur are with
31:6 *l!* I do put with him Oholiab
32:34 *L!* My angel will go ahead of
34:30 *l!* the skin of his face
Ex 39:43 and, *l!* they had done it
Le 10:16 and, *l!* it had been burned up
10:18 *L!* Its blood has not been
10:19 *L!* Today they have presented
13:3 priest must *l* at the plague
13:3 the priest must *l* at it, and
13:5 *l* at him on the seventh day
13:6 *l* at him on the seventh day
13:8 and the priest must take a *l*
13:10 the priest must take a *l*
13:17 And the priest must *l* at him
13:20 And the priest must *l*, and
13:25 the priest must then *l* at it
13:27 priest must *l* at him on the
13:31 *l!* its appearance is not
13:32 must *l* at the plague on the
13:34 *l* at the abnormal falling
13:37 if in its *l* the abnormal
13:39 priest must then take a *l*
13:43 And the priest must *l* at him
13:53 if the priest takes a *l*, and
13:55 priest must *l* at the plague
13:55 plague has not changed its *l*
13:56 priest has taken a *l*, and
14:3 must *l*; and if the plague of
14:39 take a *l*; and if the plague
14:44 *l*; and if the plague has
14:48 and he does take a *l*, and
19:26 not *l* for omens, and you
Nu 3:12 *l!* I do take the Levites
11:7, 7 *l* . . . the *l* of bdellium
11:15 not *l* upon my calamity
12:10 *l!* Miriam was struck with
12:10 *l!* she was struck with
16:15 not turn to *l* at their grain
16:42 *l!* the cloud covered it, and
16:47 *l!* the plague had started
17:8 *l!* Aaron's rod for the house
18:6 *l!* I have taken your brothers
18:8 *l!* I have given you the
18:21 *l!* I have given every tenth
21:8 bitten, he then has to *l* at it
22:5 *L!* A people has come out of
22:5 *L!* They have covered the earth
22:11 *L!* The people who are coming
22:32 *L!* I—I have come out to
23:6 *l!* he and all the princes of
23:17 *l!* he was stationed by his
23:20 *L!* I have been taken to bless
24:10 *l!* you have blessed them to
24:11 *l!* Jehovah has held you back
25:6 But, *l!* a man of the sons of
31:16 *L!* They are the ones who, by
32:1 *l!* the place was a place for
De 3:11 *L!* His bier was a bier of iron
4:29 If you do *l* for Jehovah your
9:13 *l!* it is a stiff-necked people
17:4 *l!* the thing is established
26:7 *l* on our affliction and our
26:15 *l* down from your holy
31:14 *L!* The days have drawn near
31:16 *L!* You are lying down with
Jos 2:1 Go, take a *l* at the land and
2:2 *L!* Men from the sons of
2:18 *L!* We are coming into the
3:11 *L!* The ark of the covenant of
5:13 to raise his eyes and *l*, and
7:21 *l!* they are hidden in the
7:22 *l!* it was hidden in his tent
8:20 began to turn back and *l*, and
9:12 *l!* it is dry and has become
9:13 and, *l!* they have burst, and
22:11 *L!* The sons of Reuben and
23:14 *l!* I am going today in the
24:27 *L!* This stone is what will
Jg 1:2 *L!* I shall certainly give the
3:25 *l!* there was no one opening
3:25 *l!* their lord was fallen to
4:22 *l!* there was Barak pursuing
4:22 *l!* there was Sisera fallen
6:15 *L!* My thousand is the least
6:28 *l!* the altar of Baal had been
7:13 *l!* there was a man relating a
7:13 *l!* there was a round cake of
9:31 *L!* Gaal the son of Ebed and
9:36 *L!* People coming down from
9:37 *L!* People coming down out of
11:34 *l!* his daughter coming out
13:3 *L*, now, you are barren and
13:5 *l!* you will be pregnant, and
13:7 *L!* You will be pregnant, and
13:10 *L!* The man that came the
14:5 *l!* a maned young lion roaring
14:8 to *l* at the carcass of the

Jg 16:10 *L!* You have trifled with me
17:2 *l!* the silver is with me
18:9 land, and, *l!* it is very good
18:12 *L!* It is west of
19:9 *L,* now! The day has declined
19:16 *l!* an old man coming in
19:22 *l!* the men of the city, mere
19:27 *l!* the woman, his concubine
20:7 *L!* All you sons of Israel
20:40 *l!* the whole city went up
21:8 *l!* no one had come into the
21:9 *l!* there was not a man there
21:19 *L!* There is a festival of
21:21 And you must *l,* and, there
Ru 1:15 So she said: *L!* Your widowed
2:4 *l!* Boaz came from Bethlehem
3:1 *l* for a resting-place for you
3:2 *L!* He is winnowing barley at
3:8 *l!* a woman lying at his feet
4:1 *l!* the repurchaser was passing
1Sa 1:11 *l* upon the affliction of your
2:31 *L!* Days are coming when I
2:32 *l* upon an adversary in my
3:11 *L!* I am doing something in
6:9 you must *l:* if it is the road
8:5 *L!* You yourself have grown
9:3 go, *l* for the she-asses
9:6 *L,* please! There is a man of
9:8 *L!* There is a quarter of a
9:12 He is. *L!* He is ahead of you
10:2 that you have gone to *l* for
10:8 *l!* I am going down to you to
10:11 *l!* it was with prophets
10:14 To *l* for the she-asses, and
14:16 *l!* the turmoil swayed this
14:17 why, *l!* Jonathan and his
14:26 *l!* there was a dripping of
14:33 *L!* The people are sinning
15:12 Saul came to Carmel, and, *l!*
15:22 *L!* To obey is better than a
16:7 Do not *l* at his appearance
16:11 *l!* he is pasturing the sheep
16:16 *l* for a skilled man playing
16:18 *L!* I have seen how a son of
17:18 *l* after your own brothers
18:22 *L!* The king has found
19:19 *L!* David is in Naioth in
20:2 *L!* My father will not do a
20:5 *L!* Tomorrow is new moon, and
20:21 *l!* I shall send the
20:21 *L!* The arrows are on this
20:22 *L!* The arrows are farther
23:3 *L!* We are afraid while here
23:15 Saul had gone out to *l* for
23:25 with his men to *l* for him
24:1 *L!* David is in the
24:4 *L!* I am giving your enemy
24:9 *L!* David is seeking your hurt
24:20 *l!* I well know that you
25:14 *L!* David sent messengers
25:19 *L!* I am coming after you
25:29 and *l* for your soul
26:2 to *l* for David in the
26:7 *l!* Saul was lying asleep in
26:20 out to *l* for a single flea
26:21 *L!* I have acted foolishly
26:24 *l!* just as your soul was
28:7 *L!* There is a woman who is
2Sa 1:2 *l!* a man was coming from the
1:6 *l!* the charioteers and the
1:18 *L!* It is written in the book
3:12 *l!* my hand will be with you
3:24 *L!* Abner has come to you
5:1 *L!* We ourselves are your bone
5:17 Philistines came up to *l* for
9:4 *L!* He is in the house of
12:18 *L!* While the child
13:34 *l!* there were many people
13:35 *L!* The king's sons
14:32 *L!* I sent to you, saying
15:36 *L!* There with them are
16:4 *L!* Yours is everything that
16:5 *l!* coming out from there
17:9 *L!* Now he is in hiding in
18:10 *L!* I have seen Absalom hung
18:24 *l!* there was a man running
18:26 *L!* Another man running by
19:1 *L!* The king is weeping, and
19:41 *l!* all the men of Israel
20:21 *L!* His head will be pitched
1Ki 1:2 *l* for a girl, a virgin, for
1:14 *L!* While you are yet
1:18 *l!* Adonijah himself has
1:22 *l!* while she was yet

1Ki 2:39 *L!* Your slaves are at Gath
2:40 to Achish to *l* for his slaves
3:12 *l!* I shall certainly do
3:12 *L!* I shall certainly give you
3:21 *l!* he did not prove to be
8:27 *L!* The heavens, yes, the
10:7 *l!* I had not been told the
13:2 *L!* A son born to the house of
13:3 *L!* The altar is ripped apart
14:2 *L!* There is where Ahijah
17:9 *L!* I shall certainly command
17:10 *l!* a woman, a widow, was
18:10 has not sent to *l* for you
18:43 *L* in the direction of the
18:44 *L!* There is a small cloud
19:5 *l!* now an angel was
19:9 *l!* there was Jehovah's word
19:11 *l!* Jehovah was passing by
19:13 and, *l!* there was a voice
20:13 And, *l!* a certain prophet
20:39 *l!* a man was leaving the
22:13 *L,* now! The words of the
22:25 *L!* You are seeing which way
2Ki 2:11 *l!* a fiery war chariot and
2:16 and *l* for your master
3:14 would not *l* at you or see
3:20 *l!* water was coming from
4:25 *L!* The Shunammite woman
5:22 *L!* Just now there have come
6:1 *L,* now! The place where we
6:17 *l!* the mountainous region
6:19 to the man you *l* for
6:25 *l!* they were besieging it
6:30 *l!* sackcloth was underneath
7:5 and, *l!* nobody was there
7:6 *L!* The king of Israel has
7:10 *l!* there was nobody there
7:13 *L!* They are the same as all
7:13 *L!* They are the same as all
7:15 *l!* all the way was full of
8:11 kept a fixed *l* and kept it
9:30 *l* down through the window
10:4 *L!* Two kings themselves did
10:16 *l* upon my toleration of no
14:8 *l* each other in the face
14:11 to *l* each other in the face
17:17 to *l* for omens
17:26 *l!* they are putting them to
18:21 *l!* you have put your trust
19:11 *L!* You yourself have heard
20:17 *L!* Days are coming, and all
22:20 not *l* upon all the calamity
1Ch 4:39 to *l* for pasturage for their
11:1 *L!* We are your bone and your
14:8 came up to *l* for David
22:9 *L!* There is a son being born
2Ch 2:10 *l!* to the gatherers of wood
6:18 *L!* Heaven, yes, the heaven
9:6 *l!* there has not been told me
13:12 *l!* with us there is at the
16:11 *l!* the affairs of Asa, the
18:12 *L!* The words of the
18:24 *L!* You are seeing which way
21:14 *l!* Jehovah is dealing a
23:3 *L!* The son of the king
25:17 us *l* each other in the face
25:21 *l* each other in the face
25:26 *l!* are they not written in
28:9 *L!* It was because of the
34:28 not *l* upon all the calamity
Ne 2:19 and *l* on us despisingly and
9:36 *L!* We are today slaves
9:36 *l!* we are slaves upon it
Es 8:6 I must *l* upon the calamity
8:6 I must *l* upon the destruction
8:7 *L!* The house of Haman I have
Job 1:12 *L!* Everything that he has is
1:19 *l!* there came a great wind
3:4 Let not God *l* for it from
3:7 *L!* That night—let it become
4:3 *L!* You have corrected many
4:18 *L!* In his servants he has no
5:17 *L!* Happy is the man whom
5:27 *L!* This is what we have
7:21 *l* for me, and I shall not be
8:5 If you . . . will *l* for God
8:19 *L!* That is the dissolving of
8:20 *L!* God himself will not
9:11 *L!* He passes by me and I do
9:12 *L!* He snatches away. Who can
11:18 certainly *l* carefully around
12:14 *L!* He tears down, that
12:15 *L!* He puts a restraint upon
13:1 *L!* All this my eye has seen

Job 13:18 *L!* Please, I have presented
15:15 *L!* In his holy ones he has
16:19 *l!* in the heavens is one
19:7 *L!* I keep crying out
21:16 *L!* Their well-being is not
21:27 *L!* I well know the thoughts
23:8 *L!* To the east I go, and he
24:5 *L!* As zebras in the
25:5 *L!* There is even the moon
26:14 *L!* These are the fringes of
27:12 *L!* You yourselves have all
28:28 *L!* The fear of Jehovah
32:11 *L!* I have waited for the
32:19 *L!* My belly is like wine
33:2 *L,* please! I have to open my
33:6 *L!* I am to the true God just
33:7 *L!* No frightfulness in me
33:10 *L!* Occasions for opposition
33:12 *L!* In this you have not
33:29 *L!* All these things God
35:5 *L* up to heaven and see
36:5 *L!* God is mighty and will
36:22 *L!* God himself acts
36:30 *L!* He has spread out over
40:4 *L!* I have become of little
41:9 *L!* One's expectation about
Ps 7:14 *L!* There is one . . . pregnant
11:2 For, *l!* the wicked ones
13:3 Do *l* upon me; answer me, O
22:17 They themselves *l,* they gaze
27:4 It is what I shall *l* for
27:4 *l* with appreciation upon his
33:18 *L!* The eye of Jehovah is
39:5 *L!* You have made my days just
39:13 *L* away from me, that I may
40:9 *L!* My lips I do not restrain
48:4 *l!* the kings themselves have
51:5 *L!* With error I was brought
51:6 *L!* You have taken delight in
54:4 *L!* God is my helper
55:7 *L!* I would go far away in
59:3 *l!* they have lain in wait for
59:7 *L!* They make a bubbling forth
59:10 cause me to *l* upon my foes
73:12 *L!* These are the wicked, who
73:15 *L!* against the generation of
73:27 *l!* the very ones keeping
74:20 Take a *l* at the covenant
78:20 *L!* He struck a rock That
80:14 *L* down from heaven and see
80:15 *l* upon the son whom you have
83:2 *l!* your very enemies are in
84:9 *l* upon the face of your
85:11 *l* down from the very heavens
91:8 with your eyes will you *l* on
92:9 *l!* your enemies, O Jehovah
92:9 *l!* your own enemies will
92:11 my eye will *l* on my foes
94:9 forming the eye, can he not *l?*
109:10 *l* for food from their
113:6 to *l* on heaven and earth
118:7 shall *l* upon those hating me
119:6 *l* to all your commandments
119:15 And I will *l* to your paths
119:18 my eyes, that I may *l*
119:40 *L!* I have longed for your
119:176 O *l* for your servant
121:4 *L!* He will not be drowsy
123:2 *L!* As the eyes of servants
127:3 *L!* Sons are an inheritance
128:4 *L!* That is how the
132:6 *L!* We have heard it in
133:1 *L!* How good and how pleasant
139:4 *l!* O Jehovah, you already
139:8 Sheol, *l!* you would be there
142:4 *L* to the right hand and see
145:15 the eyes of all *l* hopefully
Pr 4:25 straight ahead they should *l*
7:10 *l!* there was a woman to meet
7:15 meet you, to *l* for your face
11:31 *L!* The righteous one—in the
13:24 *l* for him with discipline
23:31 Do not *l* at wine when it
24:12 *L!* We did not know of this
24:31 *l!* all of it produced weeds
29:16 righteous will *l* on their
Ec 1:14 *l!* everything was vanity and
1:16 *L!* I myself have greatly
2:1 And, *l!* that too was vanity
2:11 *l!* everything was vanity and
3:22 who will bring him in to *l*
4:1 *l!* the tears of those being
5:18 *L!* The best thing that I
Ca 1:6 *l* at me because I am swarthy

Ca 1:15 *L!* You are beautiful, O girl
1:15 *L!* You are beautiful
1:16 *L!* You are beautiful, my dear
2:8 *L!* This one is coming
2:9 *L!* This one is standing behind
2:11 *l!* the rainy season itself has
3:7 *L!* It is his couch, the one
3:11 Go out and *l*, O you daughters
4:1 *L!* You are beautiful, O girl
4:1 *L!* You are beautiful. Your eyes
Isa 3:1 *l!* the true Lord, Jehovah of
5:7 *l!* the breaking of law
5:7 but, *l!* an outcry
5:12 of Jehovah they do not *l* at
5:26 *l!* in haste it will swiftly
5:30 *l!* there is distressing
6:7 *L!* This has touched your lips
7:14 *L!* The maiden herself will
8:7 *l!* Jehovah is bringing up
8:18 *L!* I and the children whom
8:22 to the earth he will *l*, and
10:33 *L!* The true Lord, Jehovah
12:2 *L!* God is my salvation
13:8 *l* at each other in amazement
13:9 *L!* The day of Jehovah itself
17:1 *L!* Damascus removed from
17:7 man will *l* up to his Maker
17:8 he will not *l* to the altars
17:14 *l!* there is sudden terror
18:4 *l* upon my established place
19:1 *L!* Jehovah is riding on a
22:8 *l* in that day toward the
22:11 *l* at the grand maker of it
22:13 *l!* exultation and rejoicing
22:17 *L!* Jehovah is hurling you
23:13 *L!* The land of the
24:1 *L!* Jehovah is emptying the
25:9 *L!* This is our God. We have
26:21 *l!* Jehovah is coming forth
28:2 *L!* Jehovah has someone
30:27 *L!* The name of Jehovah is
32:1 *L!* A king will reign for
33:7 *L!* Their very heroes have
34:5 *L!* Upon Edom it will descend
35:4 *L!* Your own God will come
36:6 *L!* You have trusted in the
37:11 *L!* You yourself have heard
38:11 shall no more *l* on mankind
38:17 *L!* For peace I had what
38:18 cannot *l* hopefully to your
39:6 *L!* Days are coming, and all
40:10 *L!* The Sovereign Lord
40:10 *L!* His reward is with him
40:15 *L!* The nations are as a drop
40:15 *L!* He lifts the islands
41:11 *L!* All those getting heated
41:15 *L!* I have made you a
41:24 *L!* You are something
41:27 *L!* Here they are! and to
41:29 *L!* All of them are
42:1 *L!* My servant, on whom I
42:18 and *l* forth to see, you
43:19 *L!* I am doing something
44:11 *L!* All his partners
47:14 *L!* They have become like
48:7 *L!* I have already known them
48:10 *L!* I have refined you, but
49:12 *L!* These will come even
49:12 *l!* these from the north and
49:16 *L!* Upon my palms I have
49:21 *L!* I myself had been left
49:22 *L!* I shall raise up my hand
50:1 *L!* Because of your own
50:2 *L!* With my rebuke I dry up
50:9 *L!* The Sovereign Lord Jehovah
50:9 *L!* All of them, like a
50:11 *L!* All you who are igniting
51:1 *L* to the rock from which you
51:2 *L* to Abraham your father and
51:6 and *l* at the earth beneath
51:22 *L!* I will take away from
52:6 that is speaking. *L!* It is I
52:13 *L!* My servant will act
54:16 *L!* I myself have created
55:4 *L!* As a witness to the
55:5 *L!* A nation that you do not
56:3 say, *L!* I am a dry tree
59:1 *L!* The hand of Jehovah has
59:9 light, but, *l!* darkness
60:2 For, *l!* darkness itself will
62:11 *L!* Jehovah himself has
62:11 *L!* Your salvation is coming
62:11 *L!* The reward he gives is
63:15 *L* from heaven and see out
Isa 64:5 *L!* You yourself became
64:9 *L*, now, please: we are all
65:6 *L!* It is written before me
65:13 *L!* My own servants will
65:13 *L!* My own servants will
65:13 *L!* My own servants will
65:14 *L!* My own servants shall
66:2 To this one, then, I shall *l*
66:24 and *l* upon the carcasses of
Jer 2:33 in order to *l* for love
3:5 *L!* You have spoken, and you
4:13 *L!* Like rain clouds he will
4:23 the land, and, *l!* it was
4:24 I saw the mountains, and, *l!*
4:25 *l!* there was not an
4:26 *l!* the orchard itself was a
6:10 *L!* Their ear is
6:10 *L!* The very word of Jehovah
6:22 *L!* A people is coming from
7:20 *L!* My anger and my rage are
7:32 *l!* days are coming, is the
8:9 *L!* They have rejected the
8:15 healing, but, *l!* terror!
9:25 *L!* Days are coming, is the
13:7 *l!* the belt had been ruined
14:18 *l*, now, those slain by the
14:18 *l*, also, the maladies from
14:19 healing, and, *l!* terror!
16:14 *l!* days are coming, is the
17:15 *L!* There are those saying
18:6 *L!* As the clay in the hand
19:6 *l!* there are days coming
23:5 *L!* There are days coming
23:7 *l!* there are days coming is
23:19 *L!* The windstorm of Jehovah
24:1 *l!* two baskets of figs set
25:29 *l!* it is upon the city upon
25:32 *L!* A calamity is going
27:16 *L!* The utensils of the house
28:16 *L!* I am sending you away
29:32 he will not *l* upon the good
30:3 *l!* there are days coming
30:23 *L!* A windstorm of Jehovah
31:27 *L!* There are days coming
31:31 *L!* There are days coming
31:38 *L!* There are days coming
32:24 *L!* With siege ramparts men
33:14 *L!* There are days coming
36:12 *l!* there is where all the
37:7 *L!* The military force of
38:5 *L!* He is in your hands
38:22 *l!* all the women that have
40:4 *l!* I have let you loose
45:4 *L!* What I have built up I am
47:2 *L!* Waters are coming up
48:12 *l!* there are days coming
48:19 *l* out for the way itself
48:40 *L!* Just like an eagle that
49:2 *l!* there are days coming, is
49:12 *L!* Although it is not their
49:15 *l!* I have made you small
49:19 *L!* Someone will come up
49:22 *L!* Just like an eagle
50:12 *L!* She is the least
50:31 *L!* I am against you
50:41 *L!* A people is coming in
50:44 *L!* Someone will come up
51:47 *l!* there are days coming
51:52 *l!* there are days coming
La 1:11 See, O Jehovah, and do *l*, for
1:12 *L* and see. Does there exist
1:19 had to *l* for something to eat
2:20 *l* to the one to whom you have
3:63 *l* at their very sitting down
4:16 He will not *l* upon them again
5:1 Do *l* and see our reproach
Eze 1:4 *l!* there was a tempestuous
1:4 like the *l* of electrum, out
1:15 *l!* there was one wheel on
2:9 *l!* there was a hand thrust
2:9 *l!* in it there was the roll
3:8 *L!* I have made your face
3:23 *l!* the glory of Jehovah was
3:25 *l!* they will certainly put
4:8 *l!* I will put cords upon you
4:14 *L!* My soul is not a defiled
4:17 *l* astonished at one another
7:5 calamity, *l!* it is coming
7:6 *L!* It is coming
7:10, 10 *L!* The day! *L!* It is
8:2 *l!* a likeness similar to the
8:4 *l!* the glory of the God of
8:5 *l!* to the north of the gate of
8:7 *l!* a certain hole in the wall
Eze 8:8 and, *l!* there was a certain
8:10 and began to see, and, *l!*
8:14 *l!* there the women were
8:16 *l!* at the entrance of the
9:2 *l!* there were six men coming
9:11 *l!* the man clothed with the
10:1 *l!* upon the expanse that was
10:9 *l!* there were four wheels
11:1 *l!* in the entrance of the
12:27 *l!* those of the house of
13:12 And, *l!* the wall must fall
14:22 *l!* there will certainly be
15:4 *L!* Into the fire is where it
15:5 *L!* When it happens to be
16:8 *l!* your time was the time
16:27 *l!* I shall certainly stretch
16:44 *L!* Everyone using a proverb
16:49 *L!* This is what proved to
17:7 *l!* this very vine stretched
17:10 *l!* although transplanted
17:12 *L!* The king of Babylon came
17:18 *l!* he had given his hand and
18:4 *L!* All the souls—to me they
18:14 *l!* one has become father to
18:18 *l!* then he must die for his
21:7 *L!* It will certainly come
22:6 *L!* The chieftains of Israel
22:13 *l!* I have struck my hand
23:39 *l!* that is what they have
23:40 *l!* they came, for whom
25:8 *L!* The house of Judah is
28:3 *l!* you are wiser than Daniel
28:17 for them to *l* upon you
30:9 for, *l!* it must come
30:21 *l!* it will not be bound up
31:3 *L!* An Assyrian, a cedar in
33:32 *l!* you are to them like a
33:33 *l!* it must come true
36:6 *L!* I myself in my zeal and
37:2 *l!* there were very many on
37:2 *l!* they were very dry
37:8 *l!* upon them sinews
39:8 *L!* It must come and it must
40:3 and, *l!* there was a man
40:5 *l!* there was a wall outside
40:17 *l!* there were dining rooms
40:24 *l!* there was a gate toward
42:8 and, *l!* before the temple it
43:2 *l!* the glory of the God of
43:5 *l!* the House had become full
43:12 *L!* This is the law of the
44:4 *l!* the glory of Jehovah had
46:19 *l!* there was a place there
46:21 *l!* there was a courtyard
47:1 *l!* there was water going
47:2 *l!* water was trickling from
47:7 *l!* on the bank of the torrent
Da 2:31 *l!* a certain immense image
3:25 *L!* I am beholding four
4:10 *l!* a tree in the midst of the
4:13 *l!* a watcher, even a holy one
7:8 *l!* another horn, a small one
7:8 *l!* there were eyes like the
8:3 *l!* a ram standing before the
8:5 *l!* there was a male of the
8:15 *l!* there was standing in
10:10 *l!* there was a hand that
10:13 *l!* Michael, one of the
10:16 *l!* one similar to the
10:20 *l!* also the prince of Greece
11:2 *L!* There will yet be three
12:5 *l!* there were two others
Ho 2:7 *l* for them, but she will not
3:5 *l* for Jehovah their God
5:6 to go and *l* for Jehovah
9:6 *l!* they will have to go
Joe 3:1 *l!* in those days and in that
Am 4:2 *L!* There are days coming upon
4:13 For, *l!* the Former of the
5:22 I shall not *l*
6:14 *L!* I am raising up against
7:1 *l!* . . . forming a locust swarm
7:1 *l!* it was the later sowing
7:4 *l!* the Sovereign Lord Jehovah
7:7 *L!* Jehovah was stationed on a
8:1 *l!* there was a basket of
8:11 *L!* There are days coming, is
9:8 *L!* The eyes of the Sovereign
9:9 *l!* I am commanding, and I
9:13 *L!* There are days coming, is
Ob 2 *L!* Small is what I have made
Mic 1:3 *l!* Jehovah is going forth
4:11 may our eyes *l* upon Zion
7:9 *l* upon his righteousness

Mic 7:10 My own eyes will *l* upon her
Na 1:15 *L!* Upon the mountains the
2:13 *L!* I am against you, is the
3:5 *L!* I am against you, is the
3:13 *L!* Your people are women in
Hab 1:5 *l* on, and stare in amazement
1:13 *l* on trouble you are not able
1:13 you *l* on those dealing
2:4 *L!* His soul has been swelled
2:13 *L!* Is it not from Jehovah of
2:19 *L!* It is sheathed in gold
Zec 1:8 and, *l!* a man riding on a red
1:11 and, *l!* the whole earth is
1:18 *l!* there were four horns
2:1 *l!* there was a man, and in
2:3 *l!* the angel who was speaking
3:9 *l!* the stone that I have put
4:2 *l!* there is a lampstand, all
5:1 and, *l!* a flying scroll
5:7 *l!* the circular lid of lead
6:1 *l!* there were four chariots
9:4 *L!* Jehovah himself will
9:9 *L!* Your king himself comes
12:10 *l* to the One whom they
14:1 *L!* There is a day coming
Mal 1:13 *L!* What a weariness!
2:3 *L!* I am rebuking on your
3:1 *L!* I am sending my messenger
3:1 *L!* He will certainly come
4:1 *l!* the day is coming that
4:5 *L!* I am sending to you people
Mt 1:20 *l!* Jehovah's angel appeared
1:23 *L!* The virgin will become
2:1 *l!* astrologers from eastern
2:9 *l!* the star they had seen
2:13 *l!* Jehovah's angel appeared
2:19 *l!* Jehovah's angel appeared
3:16 *l!* the heavens were opened up
3:17 *L!* Also, there was a voice
4:11 *l!* angels came and began to
7:3 do you *l* at the straw in your
7:4 *l!* a rafter is in your own eye
8:2 *l!* a leprous man came up and
8:24 *l!* a great agitation arose
8:29 *l!* they screamed, saying
8:32 *l!* the entire herd rushed
8:34 *l!* all the city turned out
9:2 *l!* they were bringing him a
9:3 *l!* certain of the scribes said
9:10 *l!* many tax collectors and
9:18 *l!* a certain ruler who had
9:20 *l!* a woman suffering twelve
9:32 *l!* people brought him a dumb
10:16 *L!* I am sending you forth as
11:10 *L!* I myself am sending
11:19 say, *L!* A man gluttonous and
12:2 *L!* Your disciples are doing
12:10 *l!* a man with a withered
12:18 *L!* My servant whom I chose
12:41 but, *l!* something more than
12:42 but, *l!* something more than
12:46 *l!* his mother and brothers
12:47 said to him: *L!* Your mother
12:49 he said: *L!* My mother and
13:3 *L!* A sower went out to sow
13:13 looking, they *l* in vain, and
13:14 will *l* but by no means see
15:22 *l!* a Phoenician woman from
17:3 *l!* there appeared to them
17:5 speaking, *l!* a bright cloud
17:5 *l!* a voice out of the cloud
19:16 *l!* a certain one came up to
19:27 *L!* We have left all things
20:18 *L!* We are going up to
20:30 *l!* two blind men sitting
21:5 *L!* Your King is coming to you
22:4 *L!* I have prepared my dinner
22:16 do not *l* upon men's outward
23:38 *L!* Your house is abandoned
24:4 *L* out that nobody misleads
24:23 *L!* Here is the Christ, or
24:25 *L!* I have forewarned you
24:26 *L!* He is in the wilderness
24:26 *L!* He is in the inner
25:43 but you did not *l* after me
26:45 *L!* The hour has drawn near
26:46 *L!* My betrayer has drawn
26:47 *l!* Judas, one of the twelve
26:51 *l!* one of those with Jesus
27:51 And, *l!* the curtain of the
28:7 *l!* he is going ahead of you
28:7 see him. *L!* I have told you
28:9 *l!* Jesus met them and said
28:11 *l!* some of the guard went
Mt 28:20 *l!* I am with you all the
Mr 1:2 *L!* I am sending forth my
2:24 *L* here! Why are they doing on
3:32 said to him: *L!* Your mother
4:3 *L!* The sower went out to sow
4:12 they may *l* and yet not see
7:34 with a *l* up into heaven he
8:15 *l* out for the leaven of the
10:28 *L!* We left all things and
12:14 do not *l* upon men's outward
12:15 Bring me a denarius to *l* at
12:38 *L* out for the scribes that
13:5 *L* out that nobody misleads
13:9 *l* out for yourselves; people
14:41 *L!* The Son of man is
14:42 *L!* My betrayer has drawn
Lu 1:20 *l!* you will be silent and not
1:31 *l!* you will conceive in your
1:36 *l!* Elizabeth your relative
1:38 *L!* Jehovah's slave girl!
1:44 For, *l!* as the sound of your
1:48 For, *l!* from now on all
2:10 *l!* I am declaring to you good
2:25 And, *l!* there was a man in
2:34 *L!* This one is laid for the
5:12 *l!* a man full of leprosy
5:18 *l!* men carrying on a bed a
6:23 *l!* your reward is great in
6:41 *l* at the straw that is in
7:12 *l!* there was a dead man being
7:27 *L!* I am sending forth my
7:34 *L!* A man gluttonous and given
7:37 *l!* a woman who was known in
8:10 they may *l* in vain and
8:41 *l!* a man named Jairus came
9:30 *l!* two men were conversing
9:38 *l!* a man cried out from the
9:38 beg you to take a *l* at my son
9:39 *l!* a spirit takes him, and
10:3 *L!* I am sending you forth as
10:19 *L!* I have given you the
10:25 *l!* a certain man versed in
11:31 *l!* something more than
11:32 *l!* something more than Jonah
11:41 *l!* all other things are clean
13:11 *l!* a woman with a spirit of
13:16 bound, *l!* eighteen years
13:30 *l!* there are those last who
13:32 *L!* I am casting out demons
13:35 *L!* Your house is abandoned
14:2 *l!* there was before him a
17:21 *l!* the kingdom of God is in
18:28 *L!* We have left our own
18:31 *L!* We are going up to
19:8 *L!* The half of my belongings
20:46 *L* out for the scribes who
21:8 *L* out that you are not misled
22:10 *L!* When you enter into the
22:21 *l!* the hand of my betrayer
22:31 *l!* Satan has demanded to
22:38 Lord, *l!* here are two swords
22:47 *l!* a crowd, and the man
23:14 *l!* I examined him in front
23:15 *l!* nothing deserving of death
23:29 *l!* days are coming in which
23:50 *l!* a man named Joseph, who
23:55 took a *l* at the memorial
24:4 *l!* two men in flashing
24:13 *l!* on that very day two of
24:49 *l!* I am sending forth upon
Joh 4:35 *L!* I say to you: Lift up
6:24 to Capernaum to *l* for Jesus
7:34 will *l* for me, but you will
7:36 *l* for me, but you will not
8:21 you will *l* for me, and yet
12:15 *L!* Your king is coming
13:22 disciples began to *l* at one
13:33 You will *l* for me; and just
16:32 *L!* The hour is coming
19:5 said to them: *L!* The man!
19:37 *l* to the One whom they
20:11 *l* into the memorial tomb
Ac 1:10 *l!* two men in white garments
3:4 and said: Take a *l* at us
5:9 *L!* The feet of those who
5:25 *L!* The men you put in the
5:28 *l!* you have filled Jerusalem
7:56 *L!* I behold the heavens
8:27 *l!* an Ethiopian eunuch, a man
8:36 *L!* A body of water; what
9:11 *l* for a man named Saul, from
9:11 For, *l!* he is praying
10:17 *l!* the men dispatched by
10:19 *L!* Three men are seeking
Ac 10:21 *L!* I am the one you are
10:30 *l!* a man in bright raiment
11:11 *l!* at that instant there
12:7 *l!* Jehovah's angel stood by
13:11 *l!* Jehovah's hand is upon
13:25 *l!* one is coming after me
13:46 *l!* we turn to the nations
16:1 *l!* a certain disciple was
20:22 *l!* bound in the spirit, I am
20:25 *l!* I know that all of you
27:24 *l!* God has freely given you
28:26 will *l* but by no means see
Ro 9:33 *L!* I am laying in Zion a
14:3 one eating not *l* down on the
14:10 *l* down on your brother
15:24 to get a *l* at you and to be
1Co 1:22 and the Greeks *l* for wisdom
10:18 *L* at that which is Israel
13:5 not *l* for its own interests
15:51 *L!* I tell you a sacred
16:11 no one . . . *l* down upon him
2Co 5:17 *l!* new things have come into
6:2 *L!* Now is the especially
6:2 *L!* Now is the day of
6:9 as dying and yet, *l!* we live
7:11 *l!* this very thing, your
10:7 You *l* at things according to
12:14 *L!* This is the third time
Ga 1:20 *l!* in the sight of God, I am
5:15 *l* out that you do not get
Php 3:2 *L* out for the dogs
3:2 *l* out for the workers of
3:2 *l* out for those who mutilate
Col 2:8 *L* out: perhaps there may be
1Ti 4:12 Let no man ever *l* down on
6:2 not *l* down on them, because
Heb 2:13 *L!* I and the young children
8:8 *L!* There are days coming
10:7 *L!* I am come (in the roll
10:9 *L!* I am come to do your
12:2 we *l* intently at the Chief
Jas 1:27 *l* after orphans and widows
2:3 *l* with favor upon the one
3:4 *L!* Even boats, although they
3:5 *L!* How little a fire it takes
5:4 *L!* The wages due the workers
5:7 *L!* the farmer keeps waiting
5:9 *L!* The Judge is standing
5:11 *L!* We pronounce happy those
1Pe 2:6 *L!* I am laying in Zion a
2Pe 2:10 who *l* down on lordship
2Jo 8 *L* out for yourselves, that you
Jude 14 *L!* Jehovah came with his
Re 1:7 *L!* He is coming with the
1:18 *l!* I am living forever and
2:10 *L!* The Devil will keep on
2:22 *L!* I am about to throw her
3:8 *l!* I have set before you an
3:9 *L!* I will give those from the
3:9 *l!* I will make them come and
3:20 *L!* I am standing at the door
4:1 *l!* an opened door in heaven
4:2 *l!* a throne was in its position
5:3 open the scroll or to *l* into it
5:4 open the scroll or to *l* into it
5:5 *L!* The Lion that is of the
6:2 I saw, and, *l!* a white horse
6:5 I saw, and, *l!* a black horse
6:8 I saw, and, *l!* a pale horse
7:9 I saw, and, *l!* a great crowd
9:12 *L!* Two more woes are coming
11:9 will *l* at their corpses
11:14 *L!* The third woe is coming
12:3 *l!* a great fiery-colored
14:1 *l!* the Lamb standing upon
14:14 *l!* a white cloud, and upon
16:15 *L!* I am coming as a thief
16:15 *l* upon his shamefulness
18:9 *l* at the smoke from the
19:11 *l!* a white horse. And the
21:3 *L!* The tent of God is with
21:5 *L!* I am making all things
22:7 *l!* I am coming quickly
22:12 *L!* I am coming quickly, and

Looked

Ge 16:13 *l* upon him who sees me
18:2 he *l* and there three men were
18:16 *l* down toward Sodom, and
19:28 he *l* down toward Sodom and
22:13 and *l* and there, deep in the
24:63 *l*, why, there camels were
29:2 *l*, and here there was a well
29:32 has *l* upon my wretchedness

Ge 33:1 Jacob raised his eyes and *l*
43:30 he *l* for a place to weep
Ex 2:25 God *l* on the sons of Israel
32:9 I have *l* at this people and
Le 13:13 *l* and there the leprosy has
Nu 23:21 not *l* upon any uncanny power
De 9:16 I *l*, and there you had sinned
Jg 5:28 woman *l* out and kept watching
9:43 he *l*, and there the people
1Sa 6:19 had *l* upon the ark of Jehovah
14:4 passages that Jonathan *l* for
17:42 Philistine *l* and saw David
24:8 Saul *l* behind him, and David
2Sa 2:20 Abner *l* behind him and said
4:8 enemy who *l* for your soul
6:16 *l* down through the window
24:20 Araunah *l* down and saw the
1Ki 18:43 went up and *l* and then said
19:6 he *l*, why, there at his head
2Ki 9:32 officials *l* down at him
21:6 magic and *l* for omens
1Ch 15:29 *l* down through the window
17:17 you have *l* on me according
21:21 When Ornan *l* and saw David
2Ch 15:4 God of Israel and *l* for him
15:15 that they had *l* for him
Ezr 2:62 that *l* for their register
Ne 7:64 that *l* for their register
12:27 *l* for the Levites, to bring
Job 6:19 The caravans of Tema have *l*
16:20 To God my eye has *l*
Ps 14:2 he has *l* down from heaven
33:13 the heavens Jehovah has *l*
34:5 *l* to him and became radiant
53:2 he has *l* down from heaven
54:7 my enemies my eye has *l*
78:34 they returned and *l* for God
86:14 have *l* for my soul
102:19 *l* down from his holy height
102:19 has *l* even at the earth
Pr 7:6 through my lattice I *l* down
Isa 31:1 *l* to the Holy One of Israel
38:14 have *l* languishingly to the
65:1 those who had not *l* for me
65:10 people who will have *l* for
Jer 6:1 calamity itself has *l* down
10:21 have not *l* even for Jehovah
18:4 it *l* right in the eyes of
36:16 *l* at one another in dread
La 4:17 *l* out to a nation that can
Eze 1:5 and this was how they *l*: they
21:21 he has *l* into the liver
Da 2:13 they *l* for Daniel and his
Ho 7:10 nor have they *l* for him
Mt 25:36 fell sick and you *l* after me
Mr 3:34 And having *l* about upon those
6:41 he *l* up to heaven and said a
8:24 the man *l* up and began saying
8:33 *l* at his disciples and
9:8 they *l* around and saw no one
10:21 Jesus *l* upon him and felt
11:11 he *l* around upon all things
14:67 she *l* straight at him and
16:4 when they *l* up, they beheld
Lu 1:48 has *l* upon the low position
9:16 he *l* up to heaven, blessed
18:24 Jesus *l* at him and said
19:5 he *l* up and said to him
20:17 he *l* upon them and said
21:1 he *l* up he saw the rich
22:56 and *l* him over and said
22:61 Lord turned and *l* upon Peter
Joh 1:36 he *l* at Jesus walking he
1:42 Jesus *l* upon him he said
Ac 8:6 they *l* at the signs he was
9:18 his eyes what *l* like scales
13:9 *l* at him intently
22:13 I *l* up at him that very hour
1Co 1:28 and the things *l* down upon
4:2 what is *l* for in stewards is
6:4 is it the men *l* down upon in
2Ti 1:17 *l* for me and found me
Heb 11:26 he *l* intently toward the
Re 16:13 that *l* like frogs come out
18:18 *l* at the smoke from the

Looked-for
Isa 20:5 Ethiopia their *l* hope and
20:6 how our *l* hope is, to which
Zec 9:5 her *l* hope will have to

Lookers
Isa 47:13 the *l* at the stars, those

Looking
Ge 4:4 Jehovah was *l* with favor upon
13:15 land at which you are *l*, to
26:8 *l* out of the window and
31:43 everything you are *l* at is
37:15 What are you *l* for?
37:16 It is my brothers I am *l* for
39:23 *l* after absolutely nothing
40:6 here they were *l* dejected
42:1 do you keep *l* at one another
43:33 kept *l* at one another in
Ex 3:2 As he kept *l*, why, here the
4:24 *l* for a way to put him to
22:10 led off while nobody is *l*
Nu 17:9 they went *l* and taking each
De 28:32 your eyes *l* on and yearning
Jos 2:22 pursuers were *l* for them on
Jg 3:24 servants came and began *l*
4:22 the man you are *l* for
13:19 Manoah and his wife were *l*
13:20 Manoah and his wife were *l*
14:4 he was *l* for an opportunity
16:27 *l* on while Samson offered
18:1 was *l* for an inheritance for
1Sa 10:21 And they went *l* for him
18:9 *l* suspiciously at David from
23:14 Saul kept *l* for him
24:2 *l* for David and his men upon
27:1 *l* for me any longer in all
27:4 *l* for him still another time
2Sa 16:11 own son . . . *l* for my soul
1Ki 1:3 went *l* for a beautiful girl
19:10 *l* for my soul to take it
19:14 they begin *l* for my soul to
20:3 sons, the best *l*, are mine
2Ki 2:17 they kept *l* for three days
2Ch 22:9 *l* for Ahaziah, and they
Job 10:6 for my sin you should keep *l*
24:5 in their activity, *l* for food
36:25 keeps *l* from far off
39:29 the distance its eyes keep *l*
Ps 9:10 not leave those *l* for you
9:12 when *l* for bloodshed, he will
10:14 You keep *l* on, to get them
37:25 Nor his offspring *l* for bread
63:1 my God, I keep *l* for you
64:8 those *l* upon them will shake
104:32 He is *l* at the earth, and
Pr 1:28 they will keep *l* for me
8:17 those *l* for me are the ones
11:27 He that is *l* for good, will
Ec 5:11 *l* at them with his eyes
11:4 *l* at the clouds will not reap
Ca 6:10 that is *l* down like the dawn
7:4 is *l* out toward Damascus
Isa 26:9 I keep *l* for you; because
63:5 *l*, but there was no helper
Jer 2:24 those who are *l* for her will
3:7 *l* at her own treacherous
20:4 your eyes will be *l* on
La 1:11 sighing; they are *l* for bread
4:17 During our *l* about we have
Eze 22:30 I kept *l* for a man from
Da 2:34 *l* until a stone was cut out
Ho 13:7 by the way I shall keep *l*
14:8 and I shall keep *l* on him
Hab 1:3 you keep *l* upon mere trouble
2:15 *l* upon their parts of shame
Hag 1:9 There was a *l* for much, but
Mt 5:28 *l* at a woman so as to have a
6:4 Father who is *l* on in secret
6:18 your Father who is *l* on in
13:13 *l*, they look in vain, and
13:14 *l*, you will look but by no
14:19 *l* up to heaven, he said a
14:30 *l* at the windstorm, he got
19:26 *L* them in the face, Jesus
26:59 *l* for false witness against
28:5 I know you are *l* for Jesus
Mr 1:37 to him: All are *l* for you
3:5 after *l* around upon them with
4:12 *l*, they may look and yet not
5:32 he was *l* around to see her
10:23 After *l* around Jesus said to
10:27 *L* straight at them Jesus
13:33 Keep *l*, keep awake, for you
14:55 *l* for testimony against
15:47 *l* at where he had been laid
16:6 You are *l* for Jesus the
Lu 2:48 distress have been *l* for you
2:49 did you have to go *l* for me
6:10 after *l* around at them all
6:42 not *l* at the rafter in that
8:10 though *l*, they may look in
13:6 *l* for fruit on it, but found
13:7 *l* for fruit on this fig tree
23:35 And the people stood *l* on
24:5 *l* for the living One among
Joh 1:38 What are you *l* for?
4:23 Father is *l* for suchlike ones
4:27 What are you *l* for? or
6:26 are *l* for me, not because
7:11 the Jews began *l* for him at
11:56 went *l* for Jesus and they
18:4 Whom are you *l* for?
18:7 again: Whom are you *l* for?
18:8 it is I you are *l* for, let
20:15 Whom are you *l* for?
Ac 1:9 *l* on, he was lifted up and
1:11 do you stand *l* into the sky
4:14 *l* at the man that had been
14:9 *l* at him intently and seeing
23:1 *L* intently at the Sanhedrin
28:26 *l*, you will look but by no
Ro 11:3 and they are *l* for my soul
Ga 3:23 *l* to the faith that was
Heb 9:28 earnestly *l* for him for
Jas 1:23 *l* at his natural face in a
1Pe 1:8 not *l* upon him at present

Lookout
Ps 10:8 the *l* for someone unfortunate
Isa 1:8 *l* hut in a field of cucumbers
21:6 *l* that he may tell just what
24:20 to and fro like a *l* hut
Mic 7:7 that I shall keep on the *l*

Lookouts
Jer 31:6 *l* in the mountainous region

Looks
Le 13:5 the way it *l* the plague has
13:21 But if the priest *l* at it
13:26 But if the priest *l* at it
Nu 23:28 which *l* toward Jeshimon
De 18:10 anyone who *l* for omens or a
1Sa 13:18 boundary that *l* toward the
22:23 for whoever *l* for my soul
22:23 *l* for your soul, for you are
Job 28:24 *l* to the very ends of the
Ps 112:8 Until he *l* on his adversaries
La 3:50 Until Jehovah *l* down and sees
Mt 6:6 your Father who *l* on in secret
Lu 9:62 and *l* at the things behind
11:29 it *l* for a sign. But no sign
Jas 1:24 he *l* at himself, and off he

Loom
Ex 28:32 the product of a *l* worker
35:35 and of a *l* worker, men doing
39:22 workmanship of a *l* worker
39:27 workmanship of a *l* worker
Jg 16:14 pulled out the *l* pin and the
1Sa 17:7 like the beam of *l* workers
2Sa 21:19 like the beam of *l* workers
1Ch 11:23 like the beam of *l* workers
20:5 like the beam of *l* workers
Isa 19:9 *l* workers on white fabrics
38:12 life just like a *l* worker

Loops
Ex 26:4 make *l* of blue thread upon
26:5 fifty *l* on the one tent cloth
26:5 fifty *l* you will make on the
26:5 *l* being opposite one to the
26:10 fifty *l* upon the edge of the
26:10 fifty *l* upon the edge of the
26:11 put the hooks in the *l* and
36:11 made *l* of blue thread upon
36:12 fifty *l* on the one tent cloth
36:12 fifty *l* on the . . . cloth
36:12 *l* being opposite one another
36:17 made fifty *l* upon the edge
36:17 made fifty *l* upon the edge

Loose
Ex 23:5 are without fail to get it *l*
Le 18:17 It is *l* conduct
19:29 be filled with *l* morals
20:14 her mother, it is *l* conduct
20:14 *l* conduct may not continue
Jg 5:2 the hair hang *l* in Israel for
20:6 they had carried on *l* conduct
Job 30:11 the bridle they left *l* on
31:11 For that would be *l* conduct
37:3 whole heavens he lets it *l*
Ps 26:10 hands there is *l* conduct
50:19 Your mouth you have let *l*
78:57 turned around like a *l* bow
105:20 that he might let him *l*

Ps 119:150 pursuit of *l* conduct have
Pr 10:23 carrying on of *l* conduct is
21:27 along with *l* conduct
24:9 *l* conduct of foolishness is
29:15 a boy let on the *l* will be
Isa 7:25 place for letting bulls *l*
32:7 counsel for acts of *l* conduct
33:23 Your ropes must hang *l*
Jer 12:8 She has let *l* her voice even
13:27 *l* conduct in prostitution
17:4 you let *l*, even of your own
40:4 I have let you *l* today from
Eze 16:27 way as regards *l* conduct
16:43 not carry on any *l* conduct
16:58 Your *l* conduct and your
22:9 *L* conduct they have carried
22:11 defiled with *l* conduct
23:21 the *l* conduct of your youth
23:27 *l* conduct to cease from you
23:29 your *l* conduct and your
23:35 also bear your *l* conduct
23:44 as women of *l* conduct
23:48 cause *l* conduct to cease
23:48 according to your *l* conduct
23:49 bring your *l* conduct upon
24:13 was *l* conduct in your
44:20 they should not wear *l*
Ho 6:9 nothing but *l* conduct
7:16 had become like a *l* bow
Mt 16:19 whatever you may *l* on earth
18:18 things you may *l* on earth
Mr 7:22 *l* conduct, an envious eye
11:2 *l* it and bring it
Lu 19:30 colt tied . . . *L* it and bring
Joh 11:44 *L* him and let him go
Ac 22:30 he let him *l* and commanded
Ro 13:13 and *l* conduct, not in strife
2Co 12:21 *l* conduct that they have
Ga 5:19 of the flesh . . . *l* conduct
Eph 4:19 gave . . . over to *l* conduct
1Pe 4:3 in deeds of *l* conduct, lusts
2Pe 2:2 their acts of *l* conduct
2:7 people in *l* conduct
2:18 by *l* habits they entice those
Jude 4 into an excuse for *l* conduct
Re 5:2 open the scroll and *l* its seals
20:3 be let *l* for a little while
20:7 Satan will be let *l* out of

Loosed
Mt 16:19 the thing *l* in the heavens
18:18 will be things *l* in heaven
Mr 7:35 his tongue was *l*, and he
11:4 found the colt . . . they *l* it
Lu 1:64 his tongue *l* and he began to
13:16 *l* from this bond on the
1Co 7:27 Are you *l* from a wife? Stop
Re 1:5 *l* us from our sins by means

Loosen
Nu 5:18 *l* the hair of the woman's
Job 38:31 *l* the very cords of the
Ps 102:20 *l* those appointed to death
Isa 20:2 *L* the sackcloth from off
52:2 *L* for yourself the bands on
58:6 *l* the fetters of wickedness

Loosened
Job 30:11 he *l* my own bowstring and
39:5 *l* the very bands of the wild
Ps 30:11 You have *l* my sackcloth, and
116:16 You have *l* my bands
Isa 51:14 chains will certainly be *l*
Jer 1:14 calamity will be *l* against
Ac 16:26 and the bonds of all were *l*

Loosening
Da 5:6 his hip joints were *l* and his

Loosens
Job 12:18 bonds of kings he actually *l*
Isa 28:24 *l* and harrows his ground

Loosing
Mr 11:5 What are you doing *l* the colt?
Lu 19:31 Why is it you are *l* it?
19:33 as they were *l* the colt the
19:33 Why are you *l* the colt?
Ac 2:24 by *l* the pangs of death
27:40 *l* the lashings of the

Lop
Isa 18:5 tendrils, must *l* them off

Lopped
Ro 11:22 you also will be *l* off

Lopping
Isa 10:33 *l* off boughs with a

Lord
Ge 15:2 Abram said: Sovereign *L*
15:8 *L* Jehovah, by what shall I
18:12 my *l* being old besides
23:6 my *l*. A chieftain of God you
23:11 No, my *l*! Listen to me
23:15 My *l*, listen to me. A land
24:18 Drink, my *l*. With that she
31:35 gleam in the eyes of my *l*
32:4 say to my *l*, to Esau, This is
32:5 like to send to notify my *l*
32:18 sent to my *l*, to Esau, and
33:8 favor in the eyes of my *l*
33:13 My *l* is aware that the
33:14 Let my *l*, please, pass on
33:14 I shall come to my *l* at Seir
33:15 favor in the eyes of my *l*
40:1 baker sinned against their *l*
42:10 No, my *l*, but your servants
42:30 the *l* of the country spoke
42:33 the *l* of the country said to
43:20 Excuse us, my *l*! We surely
44:7 Why does my *l* speak with such
45:8 a *l* for all his house and as
45:9 appointed me *l* for all Egypt
47:18 shall not hide it from my *l*
47:18 have been spent to my *l*
47:18 remains nothing before my *l*
47:25 favor in the eyes of my *l*
Ex 23:17 the face of the true *L*
32:22 the anger of my *l* blaze
34:23 appear before the true *L*
Nu 11:28 My *l* Moses, restrain them
12:11 Excuse me, my *l*! Do not
32:25 just as my *l* is commanding
32:27 just as my *l* is speaking
36:2 Jehovah commanded my *l* to
36:2 *l* was commanded by Jehovah
De 3:24 *L* Jehovah, you yourself have
9:26 *L* Jehovah, do not bring to
10:17 the *L* of lords, the God great
Jos 3:11 ark of the covenant of the *L*
3:13 the *L* of the whole earth
5:14 What is my *l* saying to his
7:7 Sovereign *L* Jehovah, why did
Jg 3:25 their *l* was fallen to the
4:18 to him: Turn this way, my *l*
6:13 my *l*, but if Jehovah is with
6:22 Sovereign *L* Jehovah, for the
16:28 *L* Jehovah, remember me
Ru 2:13 find favor in your eyes, my *l*
1Sa 1:15 answered and said: No, my *l*!
1:26 Excuse me, my *l*! By the life
1:26 my *l*, I am the woman that
16:16 Let our *l*, please, command
22:12 he said: Here I am, my *l*
24:6 do this thing to my *l*, the
24:8 My *l* the king! At this Saul
24:10 my hand against my *l*
25:24 O my *l*, be the error; and
25:25 my *l* set his heart upon
25:26 my *l*, as Jehovah is living
25:26 seeking injury to my *l*
25:27 has brought to my *l*, it
25:27 in the steps of my *l*
25:28 for my *l* a lasting house
25:28 are what my *l* is fighting
25:29 soul of my *l* will certainly
25:30 Jehovah will do to my *l* the
25:31 to the heart of my *l*
25:31 hand of my *l* itself come to
25:31 do good to my *l*, and you
25:41 of the servants of my *l*
26:15 you not watch over your *l*
26:15 the king your *l* to ruin
26:16 not watched over your *l*
26:17 is my voice, my *l* the king
26:18 my *l* is chasing after his
26:19 *l* the king, please, listen
29:4 himself in favor with his *l*
29:8 against the enemies of my *l*
29:10 servants of your *l* that
2Sa 1:10 I might bring them to my *l*
2:5 loving-kindness toward your *l*
2:7 your *l* Saul is dead, and it
3:21 Israel together to my *l* the
4:8 Jehovah gives to my *l* the
7:18 am I, O Sovereign *L* Jehovah
7:19 *L* Jehovah, yet you also speak
7:19 O Sovereign *L* Jehovah
7:20 O Sovereign *L* Jehovah
7:22 great, O Sovereign *L* Jehovah
7:28 O Sovereign *L* Jehovah, you
2Sa 7:29 *L* Jehovah, have promised
9:11 my *l* the king commands for
10:3 said to Hanun their *l*: Is
11:9 other servants of his *l*, and
11:11 my *l* Joab and the servants
11:11 servants of my *l* are
11:13 with the servants of his *l*
12:8 give you the house of your *l*
12:8 wives of your *l* into your
13:32 my *l* think that it is all
13:33 my *l* the king take to his
14:9 my *l* the king, be the error
14:12 speak a word to my *l* the
14:15 word to the king my *l*
14:17 word of my *l* the king serve
14:17 way my *l* the king is, to
14:18 Let my *l* the king speak
14:19 my *l* the king, no man can
14:19 my *l* the king has spoken
14:20 my *l* is wise as with the
14:22 your eyes, O my *l* the king
15:15 my *l* the king may choose
15:21 as my *l* the king is living
15:21 where my *l* the king may
16:4 favor in your eyes, my *l*
16:9 call down evil upon my *l*
18:28 hand against my *l* the king
18:31 my *l* the king accept news
18:32 May the enemies of my *l*
19:19 Do not let my *l* attribute
19:19 my *l* the king went out of
19:20 to meet my *l* the king
19:26 My *l* the king, it was my
19:27 slandered . . . to my *l*
19:27 *l* the king is as an angel
19:28 to my *l* the king
19:30 my *l* the king has come in
19:35 a burden anymore to my *l*
19:37 cross over with my *l* the
20:6 take the servants of your *l*
24:3 eyes of my *l* the king are
24:3 But as for my *l* the king
24:21 Why has my *l* the king come
24:22 Let my *l* the king take it
1Ki 1:2 a virgin, for my *l* the king
1:2 my *l* the king will certainly
1:11 our *l* David does not know of
1:13 my *l* the king, that swore
1:17 *l*, it was you that swore
1:18 my *l* the king himself does
1:20 my *l* the king—the eyes of
1:20 the throne of my *l* the king
1:21 my *l* the king lies down
1:24 My *l* the king, did you
1:27 If it is from my *l* the king
1:27 the throne of my *l* the king
1:31 Let my *l* King David live to
1:33 the servants of your *l*, and
1:36 the God of my *l* the king say
1:37 proved to be with my *l* the
1:37 throne of my *l* King David
1:43 Our *l* King David himself has
1:47 wish our *l* King David well
2:26 the ark of the Sovereign *L*
2:38 my *l* the king has spoken
3:17 Excuse me, my *l*, I and this
3:26 Excuse me, my *l*! You men
8:53 from Egypt, O Sovereign *L*
11:23 the king of Zobah his *l*
12:27 bound to return to their *l*
18:7 Is this you, my *l* Elijah?
18:8 say to your *l*, Here is Elijah
18:10 where my *l* has not sent to
18:11 say to your *l*: Here is
18:13 Has not my *l* been told what
18:14 to your *l*: Here is Elijah
20:4 your word, my *l* the king
20:9 Say to my *l* the king, All
2Ki 4:28 I ask for a son through my *l*
5:1 a great man before his *l*
5:3 If only my *l* were before the
5:4 reported to his *l*, saying
5:18 my *l* comes into the house of
6:12 None, my *l* the king, but it
6:22 and drink and go to their *l*
6:23 and they went to their *l*
6:26 Do save, O my *l* the king!
6:32 sound of the feet of his *l*
8:5 My *l* the king, this is the
8:12 Why is my *l* weeping?
8:14 came to his own *l*, who then
9:7 the house of Ahab your *l*
9:11 to the servants of his *l*
9:31 Zimri the killer of his *l*

2Ki 10:2 with you the sons of your *l*
10:3 upright of the sons of your *l*
10:3 fight for the house of your *l*
10:6 are sons of your *l* and come
10:9 conspired against my *l*, and
18:23 my *l* the king of Assyria
18:24 smallest servants of my *l*
18:27 Is it to your *l* and to you
18:27 my *l* has sent me to speak
19:4 his *l* sent to taunt the
19:6 you should say to your *l*
1Ch 12:19 will desert to his *l* Saul
21:3 Do they not, O my *l* the king
21:3 belong to my *l* as servants
21:3 Why does my *l* seek this?
21:23 let my *l* the king do what
2Ch 2:14 of my *l* David your father
2:15 wine that my *l* has promised
13:6 and rebel against his *l*
Ne 8:10 this day is holy to our *L*
10:29 Jehovah our *L* and his
Ps 8:1 *L*, how majestic your name is
8:9 *L*, how majestic your name is
45:11 For he is your *l*, So bow
68:20 to Jehovah the Sovereign *L*
69:6 *L*, Jehovah of armies
71:5 *L* Jehovah, my confidence from
71:16 O Sovereign *L* Jehovah
73:28 *L* Jehovah I have placed my
97:5 of the *L* of the whole earth
109:21 Jehovah the Sovereign *L*
110:1 utterance of Jehovah to my *L*
114:7 Because of the *L* be in severe
135:5 *L* is more than all other
136:3 thanks to the *L* of the lords
140:7 Jehovah the Sovereign *L*, the
141:8 O Jehovah the Sovereign *L*
147:5 *L* is great and is abundant
Isa 1:24 true *L*, Jehovah of armies
3:1 true *L*, Jehovah of armies
3:15 Sovereign *L*, Jehovah of
7:7 Sovereign *L* Jehovah has said
10:16 true *L*, Jehovah of armies
10:23 Sovereign *L*, Jehovah of
10:24 Sovereign *L*, Jehovah of
10:33 true *L*, Jehovah of armies
19:4 true *L*, Jehovah of armies
22:5 Sovereign *L*, Jehovah of
22:12 Sovereign *L*, Jehovah of
22:14 Sovereign *L*, Jehovah of
22:15 Sovereign *L*, Jehovah of
25:8 Sovereign *L* Jehovah will
28:16 Sovereign *L* Jehovah has
28:22 the Sovereign *L*, Jehovah
30:15 Sovereign *L* Jehovah, the
36:8 my *l* the king of Assyria
36:9 smallest servants of my *l*
36:12 Is it to your *l* and to you
36:12 my *l* has sent me to speak
37:4 king of Assyria his *l* sent
37:6 you should say to your *l*
40:10 The Sovereign *L* Jehovah
48:16 now the Sovereign *L* Jehovah
49:22 the Sovereign *L* Jehovah has
50:4 The Sovereign *L* Jehovah
50:5 The Sovereign *L* Jehovah
50:7 the Sovereign *L* Jehovah
50:9 Look! The Sovereign *L* Jehovah
51:22 your *L*, Jehovah, even your
52:4 the Sovereign *L* Jehovah has
56:8 the Sovereign *L* Jehovah, who
61:1 the Sovereign *L* Jehovah is
65:13 the Sovereign *L* Jehovah has
65:15 the Sovereign *L* Jehovah
Jer 1:6 Sovereign *L* Jehovah! Here I
2:19 *L*, Jehovah of armies
2:22 the Sovereign *L* Jehovah
4:10 Alas, O Sovereign *L* Jehovah!
7:20 Sovereign *L* Jehovah has said
14:13 O Sovereign *L* Jehovah
32:17 O Sovereign *L* Jehovah
32:25 Sovereign *L* Jehovah, Buy for
37:20 my *l* the king. May my
38:9 my *l* the king, these men
44:26 Sovereign *L* Jehovah is alive
46:10 Sovereign *L*, Jehovah of
46:10 Sovereign *L*, Jehovah of
49:5 Sovereign *L*, Jehovah of
50:25 Sovereign *L*, Jehovah of
50:31 Sovereign *L*, Jehovah of
Eze 2:4 Sovereign *L* Jehovah has said
3:11 Sovereign *L* Jehovah has said
3:27 Sovereign *L* Jehovah has said
4:14 Alas, O Sovereign *L* Jehovah
Eze 5:5 Sovereign *L* Jehovah has said
5:7 Sovereign *L* Jehovah has said
5:8 Sovereign *L* Jehovah has said
5:11 of the Sovereign *L* Jehovah
6:3 of the Sovereign *L* Jehovah
6:3 Sovereign *L* Jehovah has said
6:11 *L* Jehovah has said, Clap your
7:2 *L* Jehovah has said to the soil
7:5 Sovereign *L* Jehovah has said
8:1 the hand of the Sovereign *L*
9:8 Alas, O Sovereign *L* Jehovah!
11:7 Sovereign *L* Jehovah has said
11:8 utterance of the Sovereign *L*
11:13 Alas, O Sovereign *L* Jehovah!
11:16 Sovereign *L* Jehovah has said
11:17 Sovereign *L* Jehovah has said
11:21 of the Sovereign *L* Jehovah
12:10 Sovereign *L* Jehovah has said
12:19 Sovereign *L* Jehovah has said
12:23 Sovereign *L* Jehovah has said
12:25 of the Sovereign *L* Jehovah
12:28 Sovereign *L* Jehovah has said
12:28 of the Sovereign *L* Jehovah
13:3 *L* Jehovah has said: Woe to
13:8 Sovereign *L* Jehovah has said
13:8 of the Sovereign *L* Jehovah
13:9 I am the Sovereign *L* Jehovah
13:13 *L* Jehovah has said, I will
13:16 of the Sovereign *L* Jehovah
13:18 *L* Jehovah has said: Woe to
13:20 Sovereign *L* Jehovah has said
14:4 *L* Jehovah has said: Any man
14:6 *L* Jehovah has said: Come
14:11 of the Sovereign *L* Jehovah
14:14 of the Sovereign *L* Jehovah
14:16 of the Sovereign *L* Jehovah
14:18 of the Sovereign *L* Jehovah
14:20 of the Sovereign *L* Jehovah
14:21 Sovereign *L* Jehovah has said
14:23 of the Sovereign *L* Jehovah
15:6 *L* Jehovah has said, Just like
15:8 of the Sovereign *L* Jehovah
16:3 Sovereign *L* Jehovah has said
16:8 of the Sovereign *L* Jehovah
16:14 of the Sovereign *L* Jehovah
16:19 of the Sovereign *L* Jehovah
16:23 of the Sovereign *L* Jehovah
16:30 of the Sovereign *L* Jehovah
16:36 Sovereign *L* Jehovah has said
16:43 utterance of the Sovereign *L*
16:48 utterance of the Sovereign *L*
16:59 Sovereign *L* Jehovah has said
16:63 utterance of the Sovereign *L*
17:3 *L* Jehovah has said: The great
17:9 Sovereign *L* Jehovah has said
17:16 utterance of the Sovereign *L*
17:19 *L* Jehovah has said: As I am
17:22 Sovereign *L* Jehovah has said
18:3 utterance of the Sovereign *L*
18:9 utterance of the Sovereign *L*
18:23 utterance of the Sovereign *L*
18:30 utterance of the Sovereign *L*
18:32 utterance of the Sovereign *L*
20:3 Sovereign *L* Jehovah has said
20:3 utterance of the Sovereign *L*
20:5 Sovereign *L* Jehovah has said
20:27 Sovereign *L* Jehovah has said
20:30 Sovereign *L* Jehovah has said
20:31 the Sovereign *L* Jehovah
20:33 the Sovereign *L* Jehovah
20:36 the Sovereign *L* Jehovah
20:39 the Sovereign *L* Jehovah
20:40 the Sovereign *L* Jehovah
20:44 the Sovereign *L* Jehovah
20:47 *L* Jehovah has said
20:49 Alas, O Sovereign *L* Jehovah!
21:7 the Sovereign *L* Jehovah
21:13 the Sovereign *L* Jehovah
21:24 Sovereign *L* Jehovah has said
21:26 Sovereign *L* Jehovah has said
21:28 Sovereign *L* Jehovah has said
22:3 Sovereign *L* Jehovah has said
22:12 the Sovereign *L* Jehovah
22:19 Sovereign *L* Jehovah has said
22:28 Sovereign *L* Jehovah has said
22:31 the Sovereign *L* Jehovah
23:22 Sovereign *L* Jehovah has said
23:28 the Sovereign *L* Jehovah has
23:32 the Sovereign *L* Jehovah has
23:34 the Sovereign *L* Jehovah
23:35 the Sovereign *L* Jehovah
23:46 Sovereign *L* Jehovah has said
23:49 the Sovereign *L* Jehovah
24:3 Sovereign *L* Jehovah has said
Eze 24:6 Sovereign *L* Jehovah has said
24:9 Sovereign *L* Jehovah has said
24:14 the Sovereign *L* Jehovah
24:21 Sovereign *L* Jehovah has said
24:24 the Sovereign *L* Jehovah
25:3 the Sovereign *L* Jehovah
25:3 the Sovereign *L* Jehovah has
25:6 Sovereign *L* Jehovah has said
25:8 Sovereign *L* Jehovah has said
25:12 Sovereign *L* Jehovah has said
25:13 Sovereign *L* Jehovah has said
25:14 the Sovereign *L* Jehovah
25:15 Sovereign *L* Jehovah has said
25:16 Sovereign *L* Jehovah has said
26:3 the Sovereign *L* Jehovah has
26:5 the Sovereign *L* Jehovah
26:7 Sovereign *L* Jehovah has said
26:14 the Sovereign *L* Jehovah
26:15 Sovereign *L* Jehovah has said
26:19 Sovereign *L* Jehovah has said
26:21 the Sovereign *L* Jehovah
27:3 Sovereign *L* Jehovah has said
28:2 Sovereign *L* Jehovah has said
28:6 Sovereign *L* Jehovah has said
28:10 the Sovereign *L* Jehovah
28:12 Sovereign *L* Jehovah has said
28:22 Sovereign *L* Jehovah has said
28:24 am the Sovereign *L* Jehovah
28:25 Sovereign *L* Jehovah has said
29:3 Sovereign *L* Jehovah has said
29:8 the Sovereign *L* Jehovah has
29:13 Sovereign *L* Jehovah has said
29:16 the Sovereign *L* Jehovah
29:19 Sovereign *L* Jehovah has said
29:20 the Sovereign *L* Jehovah
30:2 Sovereign *L* Jehovah has said
30:6 the Sovereign *L* Jehovah
30:10 Sovereign *L* Jehovah has said
30:13 Sovereign *L* Jehovah has said
30:22 Sovereign *L* Jehovah has said
31:10 Sovereign *L* Jehovah has said
31:15 Sovereign *L* Jehovah has said
31:18 the Sovereign *L* Jehovah
32:3 Sovereign *L* Jehovah has said
32:8 the Sovereign *L* Jehovah
32:11 Sovereign *L* Jehovah has said
32:14 the Sovereign *L* Jehovah
32:16 the Sovereign *L* Jehovah
32:31 the Sovereign *L* Jehovah
32:32 of the Sovereign *L* Jehovah
33:11 the Sovereign *L* Jehovah
33:25 Sovereign *L* Jehovah has said
33:27 Sovereign *L* Jehovah has said
34:2 Sovereign *L* Jehovah has said
34:8 the Sovereign *L* Jehovah
34:10 Sovereign *L* Jehovah has said
34:11 Sovereign *L* Jehovah has said
34:15 the Sovereign *L* Jehovah
34:17 Sovereign *L* Jehovah has said
34:20 Sovereign *L* Jehovah has said
34:30 the Sovereign *L* Jehovah
34:31 the Sovereign *L* Jehovah
35:3 Sovereign *L* Jehovah has said
35:6 the Sovereign *L* Jehovah
35:11 the Sovereign *L* Jehovah
35:14 the Sovereign *L* Jehovah has
36:2 Sovereign *L* Jehovah has said
36:3 Sovereign *L* Jehovah has said
36:4 the Sovereign *L* Jehovah
36:4 Sovereign *L* Jehovah has said
36:5 Sovereign *L* Jehovah has said
36:6 Sovereign *L* Jehovah has said
36:7 Sovereign *L* Jehovah has said
36:13 Sovereign *L* Jehovah has said
36:14 the Sovereign *L* Jehovah
36:15 the Sovereign *L* Jehovah
36:22 Sovereign *L* Jehovah has said
36:23 the Sovereign *L* Jehovah
36:32 the Sovereign *L* Jehovah
36:33 Sovereign *L* Jehovah has said
36:37 Sovereign *L* Jehovah has said
37:3 I said: Sovereign *L* Jehovah
37:5 Sovereign *L* Jehovah has said
37:9 Sovereign *L* Jehovah has said
37:12 Sovereign *L* Jehovah has said
37:19 Sovereign *L* Jehovah has said
37:21 Sovereign *L* Jehovah has said
38:3 Sovereign *L* Jehovah has said
38:10 Sovereign *L* Jehovah has said
38:14 Sovereign *L* Jehovah has said
38:17 Sovereign *L* Jehovah has said
38:18 the Sovereign *L* Jehovah
38:21 the Sovereign *L* Jehovah
39:1 Sovereign *L* Jehovah has said

ze 39:5 the Sovereign *L* Jehovah
39:8 the Sovereign *L* Jehovah
39:10 the Sovereign *L* Jehovah
39:13 the Sovereign *L* Jehovah
39:17 Sovereign *L* Jehovah has said
39:20 the Sovereign *L* Jehovah
39:25 Sovereign *L* Jehovah has said
39:29 the Sovereign *L* Jehovah
43:18 Sovereign *L* Jehovah has said
43:19 Sovereign *L* Jehovah, to
43:27 of the Sovereign *L* Jehovah
44:6 Sovereign *L* Jehovah has said
44:9 Sovereign *L* Jehovah has said
44:12 Sovereign *L* Jehovah, and
44:15 of the Sovereign *L* Jehovah
44:27 of the Sovereign *L* Jehovah
45:9 Sovereign *L* Jehovah has said
45:9 of the Sovereign *L* Jehovah
45:15 of the Sovereign *L* Jehovah
45:18 Sovereign *L* Jehovah has
46:1 Sovereign *L* Jehovah has said
46:16 Sovereign *L* Jehovah has said
47:13 Sovereign *L* Jehovah has said
47:23 of the Sovereign *L* Jehovah
48:29 of the Sovereign *L* Jehovah
a 1:10 in fear of my *l* the king, who
2:47 a *L* of kings and a Revealer
4:19 my *l*, may the dream apply to
4:24 must befall my *l* the king
5:23 against the *L* of the heavens
10:16 *l*, because of the appearance
10:17 servant of this my *l* able to
10:17 able to speak with this my *l*
10:19 Let my *l* speak, because you
12:8 *l*, what will be the final
m 1:8 Sovereign *L* Jehovah has said
3:7 the Sovereign *L* Jehovah will
3:8 The Sovereign *L* Jehovah
3:11 Sovereign *L* Jehovah has said
3:13 utterance of the Sovereign *L*
4:2 *L* Jehovah has sworn by his
4:5 utterance of the Sovereign *L*
5:3 what the Sovereign *L* Jehovah
6:8 *L* Jehovah has sworn by his own
7:1 *L* Jehovah caused me to see
7:2 *L* Jehovah, forgive, please
7:4 *L* Jehovah caused me to see
7:4 *L* Jehovah was calling for a
7:5 *L* Jehovah, hold off, please
7:6 the Sovereign *L* Jehovah said
8:1 *L* Jehovah caused me to see
8:3 utterance of the Sovereign *L*
8:9 utterance of the Sovereign *L*
8:11 utterance of the Sovereign *L*
9:5 Sovereign *L*, Jehovah of the
9:8 the Sovereign *L* Jehovah
b 1 *L* Jehovah has said regarding
ic 1:2 let the Sovereign *L* Jehovah
4:13 resources to the true *L* of
ab 3:19 Jehovah the Sovereign *L* is
ep 1:7 before the Sovereign *L* Jehovah
ec 1:9 I said: Who are these, my *l*?
4:4 do these things mean, my *l*
4:5 In turn I said: No, my *l*
4:13 In turn I said: No, my *l*
4:14 the *L* of the whole earth
6:4 What are these, my *l*?
6:5 the *L* of the whole earth
9:14 the Sovereign *L* Jehovah
al 3:1 the true *L*, whom you people
t 7:21, 21 saying to me, *L*, *L*, will
7:22, 22 *L*, *L*, did we not prophesy
8:2 *L*, if you just want to, you
8:21 *L*, permit me first to leave
8:25 *L*, save us, we are about to
9:28 They answered him: Yes, *L*
10:24 nor a slave above his *l*
10:25 and the slave as his *l*
11:25 *L* of heaven and earth
12:8 *L* of the sabbath is what the
14:28 *L*, if it is you, command me
14:30 he cried out: *L*, save me!
15:22 Have mercy on me, *L*, Son of
15:25 to him, saying: *L*, help me!
15:27 said: Yes, *L*; but really the
16:22 Be kind to yourself, *L*
17:4 *L*, it is fine for us to be
17:15 *L*, have mercy on my son
18:21 *L*, how many times is my
20:25 rulers of the nations *l* it
20:30 *L*, have mercy on us, Son of
20:31 *L*, have mercy on us, Son of
20:33 *L*, let our eyes be opened
21:3 must say, The *L* needs them
Mt 22:43 by inspiration calls him *L*
22:44 Jehovah said to my *L*: Sit at
22:45 David calls him *L*, how is
24:42 what day your *L* is coming
25:37 *L*, when did we see you
25:44 *L*, when did we see you
26:22 *L*, it is not I, is it?
Mr 2:28 is *L* even of the sabbath
10:42 *l* it over them and their
11:3 The *L* needs it, and will at
12:36 Jehovah said to my *L*
12:37 David himself calls him *L*
Lu 1:43 mother of my *L* come to me
2:11 a Savior, who is Christ the *L*
2:29 Sovereign *L*, you are letting
5:8 because I am a sinful man, *L*
5:12 *L*, if you just want to, you
6:5 *L* of the sabbath is what the
6:46, 46 Why . . . call me *L*! *L*!
7:13 the *L* caught sight of her
7:19 sent them to the *L* to say
9:54 *L*, do you want us to tell
9:61 I will follow you, *L*; but
10:1 the *L* designated seventy
10:17 *L*, even the demons are made
10:21 Father, *L* of heaven and earth
10:39 down at the feet of the *L*
10:40 *L*, does it not matter to you
10:41 In answer the *L* said to her
11:1 *L*, teach us how to pray, just
11:39 the *L* said to him: Now you
12:41 Peter said: *L*, are you saying
12:42 the *L* said: Who really is
13:15 the *L* answered him and said
13:23 *L*, are those who are being
17:5 to the *L*: Give us more faith
17:6 the *L* said: If you had faith
17:37 Where, *L*? He said to them
18:6 *L* said: Hear what the judge
18:41 *L*, let me recover sight
19:8 stood up and said to the *L*
19:8 half of my belongings, *L*, I
19:16 *L*, your mina gained ten
19:18 Your mina, *L*, made five
19:20 *L*, here is your mina, that I
19:25 *L*, he has ten minas!
19:31 this way, The *L* needs it
19:34 They said: The *L* needs it
20:42 Jehovah said to my *L*, Sit at
20:44 *L*; so how is he his son?
22:25 kings of the nations *l* it
22:33 *L*, I am ready to go with
22:38 *L*, look! here are two swords
22:49 *L*, shall we strike with the
22:61 *L* turned and looked upon
22:61 the utterance of the *L*
24:3 find the body of the *L* Jesus
24:34 For a fact the *L* was raised
Joh 4:1 the *L* became aware that the
4:49 *L*, come down before my
6:23 after the *L* had given thanks
6:34 *L*, always give us this bread
6:68 *L*, whom shall we go away to?
9:38 I do put faith in him, *L*
11:2 Mary that greased the *L* with
11:3 *L*, see! the one for whom you
11:12 *L*, if he has gone to rest
11:21 *L*, if you had been here my
11:27 Yes, *L*; I have believed that
11:32 *L*, if you had been here
11:34 *L*, come and see
11:39 *L*, by now he must smell
13:6 *L*, are you washing my feet?
13:9 *L*, not my feet only, but
13:13 address me, Teacher, and, *L*
13:14 I, although *L* and Teacher
13:25 said to him: *L*, who is it?
13:36 *L*, where are you going?
13:37 *L*, why is it I cannot
14:5 *L*, we do not know where you
14:8 *L*, show us the Father, and
14:22 *L*, what has happened that
20:2 *L* out of the memorial tomb
20:13 They have taken my *L* away
20:18 I have seen the *L*! and that
20:20 rejoiced at seeing the *L*
20:25 We have seen the *L*! But he
20:28 to him: My *L* and my God!
21:7 said to Peter: It is the *L*!
21:7 hearing that it was the *L*
21:12 they knew it was the *L*
21:15 Yes, *L*, you know I have
21:16 Yes, *L*, you know I have
21:17 *L*, you know all things
Joh 21:20 *L*, who is the one betraying
21:21 *L*, what will this man do?
Ac 1:6 *L*, are you restoring the
1:21 *L* Jesus went in and out
2:34 Jehovah said to my *L*: Sit at
2:36 God made him both *L* and
4:24 Sovereign *L*, you are the One
4:33 resurrection of the *L* Jesus
5:14 believers in the *L* kept on
7:59 *L* Jesus, receive my spirit
8:16 in the name of the *L* Jesus
9:1 against the disciples of the *L*
9:5 He said: Who are you, *L*?
9:10 the *L* said to him in a vision
9:10 He said: Here I am, *L*
9:11 *L* said to him: Rise, go to
9:13 *L*, I have heard from many
9:15 *L* said to him: Be on your
9:17 the *L*, the Jesus that appeared
9:27 on the road he had seen the *L*
9:28 boldly in the name of the *L*
9:35 and these turned to the *L*
9:42 became believers on the *L*
10:4 What is it, *L*? He said to him
10:14 Peter said: Not at all, *L*
10:36 this One is *L* of all others
11:8 Not at all, *L*, because a
11:16 saying of the *L*, how he
11:17 believed upon the *L* Jesus
11:20 good news of the *L* Jesus
11:21 believers turned to the *L*
11:23 in the *L* with hearty purpose
11:24 crowd was added to the *L*
15:11 kindness of the *L* Jesus in
15:26 name of our *L* Jesus Christ
16:31 Believe on the *L* Jesus and
17:24 One is, *L* of heaven and earth
18:8 became a believer in the *L*
18:9 by night the *L* said to Paul
19:5 baptized in the name of the *L*
19:10 Asia heard the word of the *L*
19:13 name the name of the *L* Jesus
19:17 name of the *L* Jesus went on
20:19 slaving for the *L* with the
20:21 and faith in our *L* Jesus
20:24 I received of the *L* Jesus
20:35 in mind the words of the *L*
21:13 for the name of the *L* Jesus
22:8 I answered, Who are you, *L*?
22:10 I said, What shall I do, *L*?
22:10 The *L* said to me, Rise, go
22:19 I said, *L*, they themselves
23:11 the *L* stood by him and said
25:26 certain to write to my *L*
26:15 I said, Who are you, *L*?
26:15 *L* said, I am Jesus, whom
28:31 concerning the *L* Jesus
Ro 1:4 yes, Jesus Christ our *L*
1:7 Father and the *L* Jesus Christ
4:24 raised Jesus our *L* up from
5:1 peace . . . through our *L* Jesus
5:11 God through our *L* Jesus
5:21 through Jesus Christ our *L*
6:23 life by Christ Jesus our *L*
7:25 God through Jesus Christ our *L*
8:39 love . . . in Christ Jesus our *L*
10:9 that Jesus is *L*, and exercise
10:12 same *L* over all, who is rich
13:14 put on the *L* Jesus Christ
14:9 he might be *L* over both the
14:14 in the *L* Jesus that nothing
15:6 Father of our *L* Jesus Christ
15:30 through our *L* Jesus Christ
16:2 welcome her in the *L* in a
16:8 Ampliatus my beloved in the *L*
16:11 Narcissus who are in the *L*
16:12 are working hard in the *L*
16:12 many labors in the *L*
16:13 Rufus the chosen one in the *L*
16:18 slaves, not of our *L* Christ
16:20 undeserved kindness of our *L*
16:22 greet you in the *L*
1Co 1:2 name of our *L*, Jesus Christ
1:2 Christ, their *L* and ours
1:3 our Father and the *L* Jesus
1:7 revelation of our *L* Jesus
1:8 in the day of our *L* Jesus
1:9 his Son Jesus Christ our *L*
1:10 name of our *L* Jesus Christ
2:8 have impaled the glorious *L*
3:5 even as the *L* granted each
4:5 until the *L* comes, who will
4:17 and faithful child in the *L*
5:4 in the name of our *L* Jesus

Loss
Ge 24:67 comfort after the *l* of his
31:39 myself would stand the *l* of
De 28:28 *l* of sight and bewilderment
Ezr 4:13 cause *l* to the treasuries of
4:15 and causing *l* to kings
Isa 47:8 not know the *l* of children
47:9 *l* of children and widowhood
Zec 12:4 shall strike with *l* of sight
Mr 6:20 was at a great *l* what to do
Joh 13:22 at a *l* as to which one he
Ac 27:10 *l* not only of the cargo
27:21 sustained this damage and *l*
1Co 3:15 he will suffer *l*, but he
Php 3:7 *l* on account of the Christ
3:8 to be *l* on account of the
3:8 taken the *l* of all things and

Lost
Ex 21:19 time *l* from that one's work
22:9 anything *l* of which he may
Le 6:3 he does find something *l* and
6:4 the thing *l* that he has found
De 22:3 anything *l* of your brother's
22:3 which gets *l* from him and
1Sa 9:3 And the she-asses . . . got *l*
9:20 she-asses that were *l* to you
2Sa 17:8 bear that has *l* her cubs in
Ps 119:176 wandered like a *l* sheep
Ec 3:6 and a time to give up as *l*
Ca 4:2 having *l* its young ones
6:6 none among them having *l* its
Jer 49:24 Damascus has *l* courage
La 3:17 *l* memory of what good is
Eze 34:4 the *l* one you have not sought
34:16 The *l* one I shall search
Ho 13:8 a bear that has *l* its cubs
Mt 5:29 one of your members to be *l* to
5:30 to be *l* to you than for your
10:6 the *l* sheep of the house of
15:24 to the *l* sheep . . . of Israel
Mr 2:22 the wine is *l* as well as the
Lu 15:4 for the *l* one until he finds
15:6 found my sheep that was *l*
15:9 the drachma coin that I *l*
15:24 he was *l* and was found
15:32 and he was *l* and was found
19:10 seek and to save what was *l*
Joh 18:9 I have not *l* a single one
Ac 27:22 not a soul of you will be *l*

Lot
Ge 11:27 and Haran became father to *L*
11:31 Abram his son and *L*, the son
12:4 and *L* went with him
12:5 *L* the son of his brother and
13:1 Abram . . . and *L* with him
13:5 *L*, who was going along with
13:8 Abram said to *L:* Please, do
13:10 *L* raised his eyes and saw
13:11 *L* chose for himself the
13:11 *L* moved his camp to the east
13:12 *L* dwelt among the cities
13:14 *L* had separated from him
14:12 They also took *L* the son of
14:16 he recovered also *L* his
19:1 *L* was sitting in the gate of
19:1 *L* caught sight of them, then
19:5 they kept calling out to *L* and
19:6 *L* went out to them to the
19:9 heavily in on the man, on *L*
19:10 brought *L* in to them, into
19:12 men said to *L:* Do you have
19:14 *L* went on out and began to
19:15 angels became urgent with *L*
19:18 *L* said to them: Not that
19:23 land when *L* arrived at Zoar
19:29 he took steps to send *L* out
19:29 cities among which *L* had
19:30 *L* went up from Zoar and
19:36 the daughters of *L* became
Le 16:8 the one *l* for Jehovah and the
16:8 and the other *l* for Azazel
16:9 the *l* came up for Jehovah
16:10 *l* came up for Azazel should
Nu 26:55 Only by the *l* should the land
26:56 the determination of the *l*
33:54 apportion the land . . . by *l*
33:54 where the *l* will come out
34:13 as a possession by *l*, just as
36:2 the land in inheritance by *l*
36:3 from the *l* of our inheritance
De 2:9 the sons of *L* I have given Ar
2:19 to the sons of *L* that I have
28:38 A *l* of seed you will take
Jos 14:2 Their inheritance was by *l*
15:1 the *l* of the tribe of the
16:1 the *l* came out for the sons
17:1 the *l* came to be for the
17:2 a *l* for the sons of Manasseh
17:14 one *l* and one allotment
17:17 You ought not to get one *l*
18:11 *l* came up of the tribe of
18:11 their *l* went out between
19:1 the second *l* came out for
19:10 third *l* came up for the
19:17 the fourth *l* came out
19:24 fifth *l* came out for the
19:32 sixth *l* came out, for the
19:40 that the seventh *l* came out
19:51 possession by *l* in Shiloh
21:4 the *l* came out for the
21:4 by *l*, out of the tribe of
21:5 there were by *l* ten cities
21:6 by *l* thirteen cities out of
21:8 pasture grounds by *l*, just
21:10 the first *l* became theirs
21:20 came to be by their *l* cities
21:40 as their *l*, twelve cities
23:4 I assigned to you by *l* these
Jg 1:3 Come up with me into my *l* and
1:3 will go with you into your *l*
20:9 Let us go up by *l* against it
2Sa 16:13 and he threw a *l* of dust
1Ch 6:54 the *l* had come to be theirs
6:61 by the *l* ten cities
6:63 by the *l* twelve cities
6:65 by the *l* they gave from the
24:7 the *l* proceeded to come out
25:9 the *l* proceeded to come out
26:14 the *l* to the east fell to
26:14 his *l* got to come out to
Es 3:7 cast Pur, that is, the *L*
9:24 had Pur, that is, the *L*, cast
Job 31:25 had found a *l* of things
Ps 16:5 You are holding fast my *l*
83:8 an arm to the sons of *L*
125:3 upon the *l* of the righteous
Pr 1:14 Your *l* you ought to cast in
16:33 Into the lap the *l* is cast
18:18 The *l* puts even contentions
Isa 17:14 *l* belonging to those
34:17 has cast for them the *l*
57:6 They—they were your *l*
Jer 13:25 This is your *l*, your
Eze 24:6 no *l* must be cast over it
47:14 land must fall to you by *l*
47:22 they will fall by *l* into an
48:29 fall by *l* for inheritance
Da 12:13 stand up for your *l* at the
Jon 1:7 finally the *l* fell upon Jonah
Mic 2:5 casting out the cord, by *l*
Mt 27:19 I suffered a *l* today in a
Mr 15:24 casting the *l* over them as
Lu 17:28 it occurred in the days of *L*
17:29 on the day that *L* came out
17:32 Remember the wife of *L*
Joh 6:10 a *l* of grass in the place
7:12 a *l* of subdued talk about
Ac 1:26 and the *l* fell upon Matthias
8:21 part nor *l* in this matter
13:19 the land of them by *l*
Php 3:8 consider . . . as a *l* of refuse
1Ti 3:8 not giving . . . to a *l* of wine
Tit 2:3 enslaved to a *l* of wine
2Pe 2:7 he delivered righteous *L*, who
Jude 16 complainers about their *l* in

Lotan
Ge 36:20 sons of Seir . . . *L* and Shobal
36:22 sons of *L* came to be Hori
36:29 sheiks of the Horite . . . *L*
1Ch 1:38 sons of Seir were *L* and
1:39 sons of *L* were Hori and

Lotan's
Ge 36:22 and *L* sister was Timna
1Ch 1:39 And *L* sister was Timna

Lot's
Ge 13:7 the herders of *L* livestock

Lots
Le 16:8 draw *l* over the two goats
Jos 18:6 cast *l* here for you before
18:8 I shall draw *l* for you
18:10 drawing *l* for them in
1Sa 14:42 Cast *l* to decide between me
1Ch 24:5 they distributed them by *l*
24:31 to cast *l* exactly as their
25:8 cast *l* as to the things to be
1Ch 26:13 cast *l* for the small the
26:14 they cast the *l*, and his lot
Ne 10:34 *l* we cast concerning the
11:1 they cast *l* to bring in one
Job 6:27 *l* even over . . . fatherless
Ps 22:18 upon my clothing they cast *l*
Joe 3:3 they kept casting *l*
Ob 11 over Jerusalem they cast *l*
Jon 1:7 let us cast *l*, that we may
1:7 they kept casting *l*, and
Na 3:10 they cast *l*, and her great
Mt 27:35 outer garments by casting *l*
Lu 23:34 his garments, they cast *l*
Joh 19:24 by *l* over it whose it will
19:24 my apparel they cast *l*
Ac 1:26 So they cast *l* over them

Lotus
Job 40:21 Under the thorny *l* trees it
40:22 *l* trees keep it blocked off

Loud
Ge 18:20 it is *l*, and their sin, yes
19:13 against them has grown *l*
27:34 *l* and bitter manner and to
Ex 19:16 and a very *l* sound of a horn
Le 25:9 the horn of *l* tone to sound
Nu 23:21 *l* hailing of a king is in his
De 5:22 with a *l* voice, and he added
1Sa 4:5 broke out into *l* shouting, so
4:6 the sound of this *l* shouting
7:10 to thunder with a *l* noise on
2Sa 15:23 weeping with a *l* voice
19:4 crying out with a *l* voice
1Ki 8:55 with a *l* voice, saying
2Ki 18:28 and call out in a *l* voice
2Ch 15:14 to Jehovah with a *l* voice
20:19 an extraordinarily *l* voice
30:21 with *l* instruments, even to
32:18 with a *l* voice in the
Ezr 3:11 *l* shout in praising Jehovah
3:12 weeping with a *l* voice at
3:13 were shouting with a *l* shout
10:12 and said with a *l* voice
Ne 9:4 cry out with a *l* voice to
Es 4:1 with a *l* and bitter outcry
Pr 27:14 *l* voice early in the morning
Isa 29:11 Read this out *l*, please
29:12 Read this out *l*, please
34:16 of Jehovah and read out *l*
36:13 in a *l* voice in the Jews'
Eze 8:18 in my ears with a *l* voice
9:1 with a *l* voice, saying: Have
11:13 cry with a *l* voice and say
Mt 27:46 with a *l* voice, saying: *E'li*
27:50 cried out with a *l* voice
Mr 5:7 had cried out with a *l* voice
15:34 called out with a *l* voice
15:37 Jesus let out a *l* cry and
Lu 1:42 called out with a *l* cry and
4:33 he shouted with a *l* voice
8:28 and with a *l* voice he said
17:15 glorifying God with a *l*
19:37 praise God with a *l* voice
23:23 to be urgent, with *l* voices
23:46 Jesus called with a *l* voice
Joh 11:43 cried out with a *l* voice
Ac 8:7 cry out with a *l* voice and
14:10 said with a *l* voice: Stand
16:28 called out with a *l* voice
23:9 there broke out a *l* screaming
26:24 Festus said in a *l* voice
Re 5:2 proclaiming with a *l* voice
5:12 with a *l* voice: The Lamb that
6:10 cried with a *l* voice, saying
7:2 he cried with a *l* voice to the
7:10 crying with a *l* voice, saying
8:13 say with a *l* voice: Woe, woe
10:3 he cried out with a *l* voice
11:12 a *l* voice out of heaven say
11:15 *l* voices occurred in heaven
12:10 I heard a *l* voice in heaven
14:2 and as the sound of *l* thunder
14:7 saying in a *l* voice: Fear God
14:9 *l* voice: If anyone worships
14:15 with a *l* voice to the one
14:18 with a *l* voice to the one
16:1 I heard a *l* voice out of the
16:17 *l* voice issued out of the
19:1 *l* voice of a great crowd in
19:17 he cried out with a *l* voice
21:3 *l* voice from the throne say

Louder
Ex 19:19, 19 continually *l* and *l*

Mt 20:31 yet they cried all the *l*

Loudly

1Ch 15:24 *l* sounding the trumpets
2Ch 7:6 *l* sounding the trumpets in
13:14 *l* sounding the trumpets
Pr 8:3 entrances it keeps crying *l*
Jer 4:5 Call out *l* and say: Gather
12:6 called out *l* behind you
31:7 Cry out *l* to Jacob with
Da 3:4 the herald was crying out *l*
4:14 He was calling out *l*, and
5:7 king was calling out *l* to
Mic 4:9 that you keep shouting *l*
Zec 2:10 Cry out *l* and rejoice, O

Lounge

Ge 49:4 that time you profaned my *l*
1Ch 5:1 profaning the *l* of his father
Job 17:13 have to spread out my *l*
Ps 63:6 remembered you upon my *l*
132:3 on the divan of my grand *l*

Lovable

2Sa 1:23 Saul and Jonathan, the *l* ones
Pr 5:19 a *l* hind and a charming
Php 4:8 whatever things are *l*

Love

Ge 21:23 loyal *l* with which I have
22:2 only son whom you so *l*, Isaac
24:14 loyal *l* with my master
24:67 he fell in *l* with her, and
25:28 And Isaac had *l* for Esau
29:18 Jacob was in *l* with Rachel
29:20 days because of his *l* for her
29:30 more *l* for Rachel than for
29:32 husband will begin to *l* me
34:3 he fell in *l* with the young
44:20 and his father does *l* him
Ex 20:6 in the case of those who *l* me
21:5 I really *l* my master, my
Le 19:18 *l* your fellow as yourself
19:34 you must *l* him as yourself
De 5:10 in the case of those who *l* me
6:5 you must *l* Jehovah your God
7:9 in the case of those who *l* him
7:13 certainly *l* you and bless you
10:12 to *l* him and to serve
10:15 get attached so as to *l* them
10:19 must *l* the alien resident
11:1 *l* Jehovah your God and keep
11:13 so as to *l* Jehovah your God
11:22 to *l* Jehovah your God, to
15:16 he does *l* you and your
19:9 to *l* Jehovah your God and to
30:6 that you may *l* Jehovah your
30:16 so as to *l* Jehovah your God
Jg 14:16 and you do not *l* me
16:4 fell in *l* with a woman in the
16:15 I do *l* you, when your heart
Ru 4:15 does *l* you, who is better to
1Sa 18:1 to *l* him as his own soul
18:20 Michal . . . in *l* with David
18:22 have fallen in *l* with you
20:17 to David because of his *l*
2Sa 1:26 More wonderful was your *l* to
1:26 than the *l* from women
12:24 Jehovah himself did *l* him
13:1 son of David fell in *l* with
13:4 With Tamar . . . I am in *l*
13:15 *l* with which he had loved
1Ki 3:3 Solomon continued to *l*
11:2 Solomon clung to *l* them
2Ch 11:21 Rehoboam was more in *l*
19:2 that you should have *l*
Es 2:17 king came to *l* Esther more
Ps 11:7 he does *l* righteous acts
31:23 O *l* Jehovah, all you loyal
87:2 Jehovah is more in *l* with
109:4 For my *l* they keep resisting
109:5 And hatred for my *l*
116:1 I do *l*, because Jehovah hears
119:97 How I do *l* your law!
119:167 And I *l* them exceedingly
Pr 4:6 *L* it, and it will safeguard
5:19 With her *l* may you be in an
7:18 drink our fill of *l* until the
7:18 each other with *l* expressions
8:17 Those loving me I myself *l*
8:36 the ones that do *l* death
9:8 wise person and he will *l* you
10:12 *l* covers over *even* all
15:12 does not *l* the one reproving
15:17 vegetables where there is *l*
17:9 one covering . . . is seeking *l*
Pr 20:13 Do not *l* sleep, that you may
27:5 reproof than a concealed *l*
Ec 3:8 a time to *l* and a time to hate
9:1 not aware of either the *l* or
9:6 their *l* and their hate and
9:9 life with the wife whom you *l*
Ca 2:4 and his banner over me was *l*
2:7 try not to awaken or arouse *l*
3:5 not to awaken or arouse *l* in
8:4 not to awaken or arouse *l* in
8:6 *l* is as strong as death is
8:7 are not able to extinguish *l*
8:7 things of his house for *l*
Isa 56:6 and to *l* the name of Jehovah
63:9 his *l* and in his compassion
Jer 2:2 the *l* during your being
2:25 fallen in *l* with strangers
2:33 in order to look for *l*
31:3 *l* to time indefinite I have
Eze 23:17 the bed of expressions of *l*
Ho 3:1 *l* a woman loved by a
3:1 Jehovah's *l* for the sons of
9:10 like the thing of their *l*
11:4 with the cords of *l*, so that
14:4 *l* them of my own free will
Am 5:15 *l* what is good, and give
Mic 6:8 justice and to *l* kindness
Zep 3:17 will become silent in his *l*
Zec 8:17 and do not *l* any false oath
8:19 So *l* truth and peace
Mt 5:43 You must *l* your neighbor and
5:44 to *l* your enemies and to pray
5:46 if you *l* those loving you
6:24 hate the one and *l* the other
19:19 *l* your neighbor as yourself
22:37 *l* Jehovah your God with your
22:39 *l* your neighbor as yourself
24:12 the *l* of the greater number
Mr 10:21 felt *l* for him and said to
12:30 you must *l* Jehovah your God
12:31 *l* your neighbor as yourself
Lu 6:27 Continue to *l* your enemies
6:32 if you *l* those loving you, of
6:32 sinners *l* those loving them
6:35 continue to *l* your enemies
7:42 which of them will *l* him the
10:27 You must *l* Jehovah your God
11:42 the justice and the *l* of God
11:43 you *l* the front seats in the
16:13 hate the one and *l* the other
Joh 5:42 not have the *l* of God in you
8:42 you would *l* me, for from
13:34 *l* one another; just as I
13:34 that you also *l* one another
13:35 you have *l* among yourselves
14:15 you *l* me, you will observe
14:21 I will *l* him and will
14:23 and my Father will *l* him
14:24 He that does not *l* me does
14:31 know that I *l* the Father
15:9 loved you, remain in my *l*
15:10 you will remain in my *l*
15:10 Father and remain in his *l*
15:12 *l* one another just as I have
15:13 No one has *l* greater than
15:17 that you *l* one another
17:26 *l* with which you loved me
21:7 whom Jesus used to *l* said
21:15 you *l* me more than these
21:16 son of John, do you *l* me?
21:20 whom Jesus used to *l*
Ro 5:5 *l* of God has been poured out
5:8 God recommends his own *l* to
8:28 the good of those who *l* God
8:35 us from the *l* of the Christ
8:39 God's *l* that is in Christ
12:9 your *l* be without hypocrisy
12:10 In brotherly *l* have tender
13:8 except to *l* one another; for
13:9 You must *l* your neighbor as
13:10 *L* does not work evil to
13:10 *l* is the law's fulfillment
14:15 walking in accord with *l*
15:30 through the *l* of the spirit
1Co 2:9 prepared for those who *l* him
4:21 Shall I come . . . with *l* and
8:1 puffs up, but *l* builds up
13:1 but do not have *l*, I have
13:2 do not have *l*, I am nothing
13:3 do not have *l*, I am not
13:4 *L* is long-suffering and kind
13:4 *L* is not jealous, it does not
13:8 *L* never fails. But whether
13:13 faith, hope, *l*, these three
1Co 13:13 the greatest of these is *l*
14:1 Pursue *l*, yet keep zealously
16:14 affairs take place with *l*
16:24 my *l* be with all of you in
2Co 2:4 *l* that I have more especially
2:8 to confirm your *l* for him
5:14 the *l* the Christ has compels
6:6 by *l* free from hypocrisy
8:7 and in this *l* of ours to you
8:8 of the genuineness of your *l*
8:24 the proof of your *l* and of
11:11 Because I do not *l* you?
12:15 I *l* you the more abundantly
13:11 God of *l* and of peace will
13:14 *l* of God and the sharing in
Ga 5:6 faith operating through *l* is
5:13 through *l* slave for one
5:14 You must *l* your neighbor as
5:22 fruitage of the spirit is *l*
Eph 1:4 before him in *l*
2:4 great *l* with which he loved
3:17 faith in your hearts with *l*
3:19 to know the *l* of the Christ
4:2 with one another in *l*
4:15 let us by *l* grow up in all
4:16 building up of itself in *l*
5:2 go on walking in *l*, just as
5:33 *l* his wife as he does
6:23 have peace and *l* with faith
Php 1:9 that your *l* may abound yet
1:16 publicizing . . . out of *l*
2:1 if any consolation of *l*, if
2:2 and have the same *l*, being
Col 1:4 *l* you have for all the holy
1:8 your *l* in a spiritual way
1:13 kingdom of the Son of his *l*
2:2 joined together in *l* and with
3:14 clothe yourselves with *l*
1Th 3:6 your faithfulness and *l*
3:12 abound, in *l* to one another
4:9 with reference to brotherly *l*
4:9 to *l* one another
5:8 breastplate of faith and *l*
5:13 consideration in *l* because
2Th 1:3 the *l* of each and all of you
2:10 not accept the *l* of the truth
3:5 into the *l* of God and into
1Ti 1:5 *l* out of a clean heart and
1:14 along with faith and *l* that
2:15 continue in faith and *l* and
4:12 in conduct, in *l*, in faith
6:10 the *l* of money is a root of
6:10 by reaching out for this *l*
6:11 faith, *l*, endurance
2Ti 1:7 that of power and of *l* and of
1:13 the faith and *l* that are in
2:22 faith, *l*, peace, along with
3:3 fierce, without *l* of goodness
3:10 closely followed . . . my *l*
Tit 2:2 in faith, in *l*, in endurance
2:4 to *l* their husbands, to
2:4 to *l* their children
3:4 *l* for man on the part of our
Phm 5 hearing of your *l* and faith
7 joy and comfort over your *l*
9 on the basis of *l*, seeing that
Heb 6:10 *l* you showed for his name
10:24 incite to *l* and fine works
13:1 your brotherly *l* continue
13:5 be free of the *l* of money
Jas 2:5 promised to those who *l* him
2:8 You must *l* your neighbor as
1Pe 1:8 you never saw him, you *l* him
1:22 unhypocritical brotherly *l*
1:22 *l* one another intensely
2:17 *l* for the whole association
3:10 he that would *l* life and see
4:8 intense *l* for one another
4:8 *l* covers a multitude of sins
5:2 for *l* of dishonest gain
5:14 Greet . . . with a kiss of *l*
2Pe 1:7 to your brotherly affection *l*
1Jo 2:5 *l* of God . . . made perfect
2:15 the *l* of the Father is not
3:1 *l* the Father has given us
3:10 who does not *l* his brother
3:11 should have *l* for one another
3:14 because we *l* the brothers
3:14 does not *l* remains in death
3:16 we have come to know *l*
3:17 does the *l* of God remain in
3:18 let us *l*, neither in word
4:7 because *l* is from God, and
4:8 He that does not *l* has not

1Jo 4:8 because God is *l*
4:9 *l* of God was made manifest
4:10 The *l* is in this respect
4:11 obligation to *l* one another
4:12 his *l* is made perfect in us
4:16 *l* that God has in our case
4:16 God is *l*, and he that
4:16 he that remains in *l* remains
4:17 how *l* has been made perfect
4:18 There is no fear in *l*, but
4:18 perfect *l* throws fear
4:18 not been made perfect in *l*
4:19 we *l*, because he first loved
4:20 I *l* God, and yet is hating
4:20 who does not *l* his brother
5:3 is what the *l* of God means
2Jo 1 her children, whom I truly *l*
3 the Father, with truth and *l*
5 that we *l* one another
6 And this is what *l* means, that
3Jo 1 the beloved, whom I truly *l*
6 have borne witness to your *l*
Jude 2 and *l* be increased to you
12 in your *l* feasts while they
21 keep yourselves in God's *l*
Re 2:4 left the *l* you had at first
2:19 deeds, and your *l* and faith
12:11 *l* their souls even in the

Loved
Ge 37:3 Israel *l* Joseph more than all
37:4 their father *l* him more than
De 4:37 he *l* your forefathers so that
21:15 the one *l* and the other hated
21:15 the *l* one and the hated one
21:16 constitute the son of the *l*
23:5 because Jehovah your God *l* you
1Sa 1:5 it was Hannah that he *l*, and
18:28 Saul's daughter, she *l* him
20:17 as he *l* his own soul
20:17 Jonathan . . . *l* him
2Sa 13:15 love with which he had *l*
1Ki 11:1 *l* many foreign wives along
2Ch 2:11 Because Jehovah *l* his people
9:8 because your God *l* Israel
Ne 13:26 *l* of his God he happened to
Job 19:19 those whom I *l* have turned
Ps 26:8 *l* the dwelling of your house
45:7 *l* righteousness and you hate
47:4 pride of Jacob, whom he has *l*
52:3 *l* what is bad more than what
52:4 have *l* all devouring words
78:68 Mount Zion, which he *l*
99:4 judgment he has *l*
119:47 That I have *l*
119:48 commandments that I have *l*
119:113 But your law I have *l*
119:119 I have *l* your reminders
119:127 have *l* your commandments
119:159 I have *l* your own orders
119:163 Your law I have *l*
Ca 1:3 maidens themselves have *l* you
1:4 Deservedly they have *l* you
1:7 O you whom my soul has *l*
3:1 the one whom my soul has *l*
3:2 the one whom my soul has *l*
3:3 whom my soul has *l* have you
3:4 the one whom my soul has *l*
Isa 5:1 song of my *l* one concerning
43:4 and I myself have *l* you
48:14 Jehovah himself has *l* him
57:8 You *l* a bed with them
Jer 5:31 people have *l* it that way
8:2 the heavens that they have *l*
14:10 they have *l* to wander about
31:3 time indefinite I have *l* you
Eze 16:37 all those whom you *l* along
Ho 3:1 love a woman *l* by a companion
4:18 have positively *l* dishonor
9:1 You have *l* gifts of hire on
11:1 I *l* him, and out of Egypt I
12:7 to defraud is what he has *l*
Am 4:5 that is the way you have *l*
Mal 1:2 I have *l* you people, Jehovah
1:2 In what way have you *l* us?
1:2 But I *l* Jacob
2:11 of Jehovah, which He has *l*
Lu 7:47 forgiven, because she *l* much
Joh 3:16 God *l* the world so much that
3:19 but men have *l* the darkness
11:5 Jesus *l* Martha and her
12:43 *l* the glory of men more
13:1 Jesus, having *l* his own
13:1 *l* them to the end
Joh 13:23 disciples, and Jesus *l* him
13:34 just as I have *l* you, that
14:21 will be *l* by my Father
14:28 If you *l* me, you would
15:9 Father has *l* me and I have
15:9 I have *l* you, remain in my
15:12 just as I have *l* you
17:23, 23 *l* them just as you *l* me
17:24 *l* me before the founding
17:26 love with which you *l* me
19:26 disciple whom he *l* standing
Ac 15:25 *l* ones, Barnabas and Paul
Ro 8:37 through him that *l* us
9:13 I *l* Jacob, but Esau I hated
2Co 12:15 am I to be *l* the less?
Ga 2:20 who *l* me and handed himself
Eph 1:6 upon us by means of his *l* one
2:4 great love with which he *l* us
5:2 just as the Christ also *l* you
5:25 just as the Christ also *l* the
Col 3:12 chosen ones, holy and *l*
1Th 1:4 we know, brothers *l* by God
2Th 2:13 you, brothers *l* by Jehovah
2:16 God our Father, who *l* us and
2Ti 4:8 who have *l* his manifestation
4:10 he *l* the present system of
Heb 1:9 You *l* righteousness, and you
2Pe 2:15 *l* the reward of wrongdoing
1Jo 4:10 not that we have *l* God, but
4:10 *l* us and sent forth his Son
4:11 if this is how God *l* us
4:19 we love, because he first *l*
Jude 1 *l* in relationship with God
Re 3:9 make them know I have *l* you

Loveliness
Es 1:11 her *l*; for she was beautiful

Lovely
Ps 84:1 How *l* your grand tabernacle

Lover
Ge 25:28 Rebekah was a *l* of Jacob
1Ki 5:1 a *l* of David Hiram had always
2Ch 20:7 Abraham, your *l*, to time
26:10 *l* of agriculture he proved
Ps 33:5 He is a *l* of righteousness
37:28 For Jehovah is a *l* of justice
Pr 12:1 A *l* of discipline is a
12:1 is a *l* of knowledge, but a
27:6 inflicted by a *l* are faithful
Ec 5:10 mere *l* of silver will not be
5:10 any *l* of wealth with income
Isa 1:23 *l* of a bribe and a chaser
1Ti 3:3 not a *l* of money
Tit 1:8 hospitable, a *l* of goodness

Lovers
Jg 5:31 let your *l* be as when the sun
1Sa 18:16 and Judah were *l* of David
Ps 38:11 for my *l* and my companions
97:10 *l* of Jehovah, hate what is
Isa 66:10 all you *l* of her. Exult
Jer 20:4 to yourself and to all your *l*
20:6 be buried with all your *l*
La 1:2 from among all her *l*
Eze 23:22 your passionate *l* against
Ho 2:7 chase after her passionate *l*
2:10 the eyes of her passionate *l*
2:12 passionate *l* have given to me
2:13 going after her passionate *l*
8:9 they have hired *l*
Mic 3:2 *l* of badness, tearing off
Zec 13:6 in the house of my intense *l*
Lu 16:14 Pharisees, who were money *l*
2Ti 3:2 men will be *l* of themselves
3:2 *l* of money, self-assuming
3:4 *l* of pleasures rather than
3:4 pleasures rather than *l* of God

Love's
Eze 16:8 the time for *l* expressions

Loves
1Ki 10:9 Jehovah *l* Israel to time
Ps 119:140 And your own servant *l* it
Pr 3:12 whom Jehovah *l* he reproves
15:9 pursuing righteousness he *l*
16:13 of upright things he *l*
Eze 33:32 like a song of sensuous *l*
Lu 7:5 he *l* our nation and he himself
7:47 is forgiven little, *l* little
Joh 3:35 The Father *l* the Son and has
10:17 Father *l* me, because I
14:21 that one is he who *l* me
14:21 he that *l* me will be loved
14:23 If anyone *l* me, he will
Ro 13:8 he that *l* his fellowman has
1Co 8:3 if anyone *l* God, this one is
2Co 9:7 for God *l* a cheerful giver
Eph 5:28, 28 *l* his wife *l* himself
Heb 12:6 Jehovah *l* he disciplines
1Jo 2:10 He that *l* his brother
2:15 If anyone *l* the world, the
4:7 everyone who *l* has been born
4:21 the one who *l* God should be
5:1 everyone who *l* the one that
5:1 *l* him who has been born from
Re 1:5 To him that *l* us and that

Lovesick
Ca 2:5 sustain me . . . for I am *l*
5:8 should tell him that I am *l*

Loving
De 7:8 because of Jehovah's *l* you
10:18 *l* the alien resident so as to
13:3 whether you are *l* Jehovah
30:20 by *l* Jehovah your God, by
Jos 22:5 by *l* Jehovah your God and by
23:11 souls by *l* Jehovah your God
1Sa 16:21 he got to *l* him very much
18:3 his *l* him as his own soul
2Sa 19:6 *l* those hating you and by
19:6 and by hating those *l* you
Ne 1:5 loving-kindness toward those *l*
Ps 4:2 While you keep *l* empty things
5:11 those *l* your name will exult
11:5 anyone *l* violence His soul
34:12 *l* enough days to see what is
40:16 Those who are *l* salvation
69:36 those *l* his name will be the
70:4 those *l* your salvation
109:17 kept *l* the malediction, so
119:132 toward those *l* your name
119:165 to those *l* your law
122:6 Those *l* you, O city, will
145:20 guarding all those *l* him
146:8 Jehovah is *l* the righteous
Pr 1:22 ones keep *l* inexperience
8:17 Those *l* me I myself love, and
8:21 those *l* me to take possession
13:24 one *l* him is he that does
17:17 companion is *l* all the time
17:19 Anyone *l* transgression is
17:19 transgression is *l* a struggle
18:21 *l* it will eat its fruitage
19:8 acquiring heart is *l* his own
21:17 He that is *l* merriment will
21:17 *l* wine and oil will not gain
22:11 The one *l* purity of heart
29:3 is *l* wisdom makes his father
Isa 56:10 lying down, *l* to slumber
61:8 I, Jehovah, am *l* justice
Jer 22:20 those intensely *l* you have
22:22 as for those intensely *l* you
30:14 those intensely *l* you are
La 1:19 to those intensely *l* me
Eze 16:33 all those passionately *l* you
16:36 those passionately *l* you
16:37 all those passionately *l* you
23:5 those passionately *l* her
23:9 those passionately *l* her
Da 9:4 loving-kindness to those *l* him
Ho 2:5 go after those passionately *l*
3:1 and are *l* raisin cakes
9:15 will not continue on *l* them
10:11 a trained heifer *l* to thresh
Mt 5:46 if you love those *l* you, what
Mr 12:33 *l* him with one's whole
12:33 *l* one's neighbor as oneself
Lu 6:32 if you love those *l* you, of
6:32 the sinners love those *l* them
Eph 5:25 continue *l* your wives, just
5:28 *l* their wives as their own
6:24 all those *l* our Lord Jesus
Col 3:19 keep on *l* your wives and do
1Th 1:3 *l* labor and your endurance
Jas 1:12 to those who continue *l* him
1Jo 2:15 Do not be *l* either the world
3:23 and be *l* one another, just
4:7 let us continue *l* one another
4:12 If we continue *l* one another
4:20 cannot be *l* God, whom he has
4:21 should be *l* his brother also
5:2 we are *l* the children of God
5:2 we are *l* God and doing his

Loving-kindness
Ge 19:19 *l*, which you may have exercised
20:13 *l* which you may exercise
24:12 perform *l* with my master

Ge 24:27 has not left his *l* and his
24:49 exercising *l* and
39:21 *l* to him and granting him to
40:14 you must, please, perform *l*
47:29 and you must exercise *l*
Ex 15:13 You in your *l* have led the
20:6 but exercising *l* toward the
34:6 abundant in *l* and truth
34:7 preserving *l* for thousands
Nu 14:18 abundant in *l*, pardoning
14:19 the greatness of your *l*, and
De 5:10 *l* toward the thousandth
7:9 keeping covenant and *l* in the
7:12 the *l* about which he swore to
Jos 2:12 have exercised *l* toward you
2:12 *l* toward the household of my
2:14 shall certainly exercise *l*
Jg 8:35 did not exercise *l* toward
Ru 1:8 May Jehovah exercise *l* toward
2:20 his *l* toward the living and
3:10 expressed your *l* better in
1Sa 15:6 you exercised *l* with all the
20:8 render *l* toward your servant
20:14 exercise the *l* of Jehovah
20:15 cut off your own *l* from
2Sa 2:5 *l* toward your lord, toward
2:6 Jehovah exercise toward you *l*
3:8 *l* toward the house of Saul
7:15 my *l* . . . not depart from
9:1 *l* toward him for the sake of
9:3 may exercise . . . the *l* of God
9:7 *l* toward you for the sake of
10:2 *l* toward Hanun the son of
10:2 his father exercised *l*
15:20 exercise toward you *l*
16:17 This is the *l* of yours
22:51 exercising *l* to his anointed
1Ki 2:7 you should exercise *l*, and
3:6 *l* toward your servant David
3:6 toward him this great *l*
8:23 *l* toward your servants who
20:31 kings . . . are kings of *l*
1Ch 16:34 to time indefinite is his *l*
16:41 to time indefinite is his *l*
17:13 my *l* I shall not remove
19:2 exercise *l* toward Hanun the
19:2 father exercised *l* toward me
2Ch 1:8 the One that exercised great *l*
5:13 to time indefinite is his *l*
6:14 *l* toward your servants who
7:3 his *l* is to time indefinite
7:6 thank Jehovah, for his *l* is to
20:21 to time indefinite is his *l*
24:22 *l* that Jehoiada his father
32:32 Hezekiah and his acts of *l*
35:26 Josiah and his acts of *l*
Ezr 3:11 his *l* toward Israel is to
7:28 extended *l* before the king
9:9 but he extends toward us *l*
Ne 1:5 *l* toward those loving him and
9:17 and abundant in *l*, and you
9:32 keeping the covenant and *l*
13:14 not wipe out my acts of *l*
13:22 the abundance of your *l*
Es 2:9 she gained *l* before him and he
2:17 she gained more favor and *l*
Job 6:14 withholds *l* from his own
10:12 *l* you have worked with me
37:13 Or for *l*, he makes it
Ps 5:7 in the abundance of your *l*
6:4 Save me for the sake of your *l*
13:5 in your *l* I have trusted
18:50 *l* to his anointed one
21:7 Even in the *l* of the Most High
23:6 goodness and *l* themselves
25:7 According to your *l* do you
25:10 paths of Jehovah are *l* and
26:3 your *l* is in front of my eyes
31:7 joyful and rejoice in your *l*
31:16 Save me in your *l*
31:21 rendered wonderful *l* to me
32:10 *l* itself surrounds him
33:5 With the *l* of Jehovah the
33:18 To those waiting for his *l*
33:22 Let your *l*, O Jehovah, prove
36:5 your *l* is in the heavens
36:7 How precious your *l* is, O God
36:10 Continue your *l* to those
40:10 I have not hidden your *l*
40:11 Let your *l* and your trueness
42:8 Jehovah will command his *l*
44:26 for the sake of your *l*
48:9 pondered, O God, over your *l*
51:1 O God, according to your *l*
Ps 52:1 The *l* of God is all day long
52:8 I do trust in the *l* of God
57:3 God will send his *l* and his
57:10 *l* is great up to the heavens
59:10 The God of *l* to me will
59:16 joyfully tell about your *l*
59:17 the God of *l* to me
61:7 assign *l* and trueness, that
62:12 *l* belongs to you, O Jehovah
63:3 your *l* is better than life
66:20 prayer, Nor his *l* from me
69:13 the abundance of your *l*
69:16 Jehovah, for your *l* is good
77:8 Has his *l* terminated forever?
85:7 Show us, O Jehovah, your *l*
85:10 *l* and trueness, they have
86:5 *l* to all those calling upon
86:13 your *l* is great toward me
86:15 abundant in *l* and trueness
88:11 *l* be declared in the burial
89:1 Jehovah's expressions of *l*
89:2 *L* will stay built even to
89:14 *L* and trueness themselves
89:24 and my *l* are with him
89:28 preserve my *l* toward him
89:33 my *l* I shall not break off
89:49 former acts of *l*, O Jehovah
90:14 in the morning with your *l*
92:2 in the morning about your *l*
94:18 Your own *l*, O Jehovah, kept
98:3 He has remembered his *l* and
100:5 His *l* is to time indefinite
101:1 *l* and judgment I will sing
103:4 crowning you with *l* and
103:8 to anger and abundant in *l*
103:11 *l* is superior toward those
103:17 *l* of Jehovah is from time
106:1 his *l* is to time indefinite
106:7 abundance of your grand *l*
106:45 abundance of his grand *l*
107:1 his *l* is to time indefinite
107:8 thanks to Jehovah for his *l*
107:15 thanks to Jehovah for his *l*
107:21 thanks to Jehovah for his *l*
107:31 thanks to Jehovah for his *l*
107:43 toward Jehovah's acts of *l*
108:4 your *l* is great up to the
109:12 have no one extending *l*
109:16 not remember to exercise *l*
109:21 your *l* is good, deliver me
109:26 Save me according to your *l*
115:1 glory According to your *l*
117:2 his *l* has proved mighty
118:1 his *l* is to time indefinite
118:2 his *l* is to time indefinite
118:3 his *l* is to time indefinite
118:4 his *l* is to time indefinite
118:29 his *l* is to time indefinite
119:64 Your *l*, O Jehovah, has
119:76 *l* serve, please, to comfort
119:88 According to your *l* preserve
119:124 servant according to your *l*
119:149 voice according to your *l*
119:159 according to your *l*
130:7 For there is *l* with Jehovah
136:1 his *l* is to time indefinite
136:2 his *l* is to time indefinite
136:3 his *l* is to time indefinite
136:4 his *l* is to time indefinite
136:5 his *l* is to time indefinite
136:6 his *l* is to time indefinite
136:7 his *l* is to time indefinite
136:8 his *l* is to time indefinite
136:9 his *l* is to time indefinite
136:10 his *l* is to time indefinite
136:11 his *l* is to time indefinite
136:12 his *l* is to time indefinite
136:13 his *l* is to time indefinite
136:14 his *l* is to time indefinite
136:15 his *l* is to time indefinite
136:16 his *l* is to time indefinite
136:17 his *l* is to time indefinite
136:18 his *l* is to time indefinite
136:19 his *l* is to time indefinite
136:20 his *l* is to time indefinite
136:21 his *l* is to time indefinite
136:22 his *l* is to time indefinite
136:23 his *l* is to time indefinite
136:24 his *l* is to time indefinite
136:25 his *l* is to time indefinite
136:26 his *l* is to time indefinite
138:2 Because of your *l* and
138:8 to time indefinite is your *l*
141:5 strike me, it would be a *l*
Ps 143:8 cause me to hear your *l*
143:12 in your *l* may you silence
144:2 My *l* and my stronghold
145:8 and great in *l*
147:11 In those waiting for his *l*
Pr 3:3 *l* and trueness themselves not
11:17 man of *l* is dealing
14:22 are *l* and trueness as regards
16:6 By *l* and trueness error is
19:22 desirable thing . . . is his *l*
20:6 proclaim each one his own *l*
20:28 *L* and trueness—they
20:28 *l* he has sustained his throne
21:21 pursuing righteousness and *l*
31:26 law of *l* is upon her tongue
Isa 16:5 in *l* a throne will certainly
40:6 *l* is like the blossom of the
54:8 with *l* to time indefinite
54:10 my *l* itself will not be
57:1 men of *l* are being gathered
Jer 2:2 the *l* of your youth
9:24 the One exercising *l*, justice
16:5 even *l* and mercies
31:3 I have drawn you with *l*
32:18 One exercising *l* toward
33:11 to time indefinite is his *l*
La 3:22 *l* of Jehovah that we have not
3:32 to the abundance of his *l*
Da 1:9 God gave Daniel over to *l*
9:4 keeping the covenant and the *l*
Ho 2:19 and in *l* and in mercies
4:1 no truth nor *l* nor knowledge
6:4 the *l* of you people is like
6:6 For in *l* I have taken delight
10:12 reap in accord with *l*
12:6 keeping *l* and justice
Joe 2:13 to anger and abundant in *l*
Jon 2:8 they leave their own *l*
4:2 abundant in *l*, and feeling
Mic 7:18 for he is delighting in *l*
7:20 the *l* given to Abraham
Zec 7:9 with one another *l* and
1Ti 1:9 lacking *l*, and profane

Loving-kindnesses
Ge 32:10 I am unworthy of all the *l*
2Ch 6:42 remember the *l* to David your
Ps 17:7 Make your acts of *l* wonderful
25:6 Remember . . . your *l*
119:41 *l* come to me, O Jehovah
Isa 55:3 respecting the *l* to David
63:7 *l* of Jehovah I shall mention
63:7 the abundance of his *l*
Ac 13:34 I will give you people the *l*

Lovingly
Ca 3:10 interior being fitted out *l* by

Low
Ge 14:3 *L* Plain of Siddim, that is
14:8 in the *L* Plain of Siddim
14:10 Now the *L* Plain of Siddim
14:17 *L* Plain of Shaveh, that is
14:17 that is, the king's *L* Plain
27:29 national groups bow *l* to you
27:29 sons of your mother bow *l*
37:14 from the *l* plain of Hebron
42:6 bowed *l* to him with their
Ex 12:27 bowed *l* and prostrated
34:8 to bow *l* to the earth and
Le 13:55 *l* spot in a threadbare patch
Nu 14:25 are dwelling in the *l* plain
22:31 he bowed *l* and prostrated
Jos 7:24 up to the *l* plain of Achor
7:26 been called *L* Plain of Achor
8:13 the middle of the *l* plain
10:12 over the *l* plain of Aijalon
13:19 the mountain of the *l* plain
13:27 in the *l* plain Beth-haram
15:7 Debir at the *l* plain of Achor
15:8 the *l* plain of Rephaim to
17:16 in the land of the *l* plain
17:16 in the *l* plain of Jezreel
18:16 in the *l* plain of Rephaim
Jg 1:19 inhabitants of the *l* plain
1:34 come down into the *l* plain
5:14 their origin in the *l* plain
5:15 Into the *l* plain he was sent
6:33 in the *l* plain of Jezreel
7:1 hill of Moreh, in the *l* plain
7:8 down below him in the *l* plain
7:12 were plumped in the *l* plain
18:28 the *l* plain that belonged to
1Sa 6:13 wheat harvest in the *l* plain
17:2 in the *l* plain of Elah

1Sa 17:19 were in the *l* plain of Elah
21:9 *l* plain of Elah—here it
24:8 David proceeded to bow *l*
28:14 bow *l* with his face to the
31:7 region of the *l* plain and
2Sa 5:18 in the *l* plain of Rephaim
5:22 in the *l* plain of Rephaim
6:22 I will become *l* in my eyes
18:18 in the *L* Plain of the King
22:28 that you may bring them *l*
23:13 the *l* plain of the Rephaim
1Ki 1:16 Bath-sheba bowed *l* and
1:31 Bath-sheba bowed *l* with her
19:12 there was a calm, *l* voice
20:28 he is not a God of *l* plains
1Ch 10:7 that were in the *l* plain saw
11:15 in the *l* plain of Rephaim
12:15 all those of the *l* plains
14:9 in the *l* plain of Rephaim
14:13 made a raid in the *l* plain
27:29 the herds in the *l* plains
29:20 and bow *l* and prostrate
2Ch 7:3 bowed *l* with their faces to
20:18 Jehoshaphat bowed *l* with
20:26 at the *l* plain of Beracah
20:26 *L* Plain of Beracah—until
29:29 bowed *l* and prostrated
Ne 8:6 bowed *l* and prostrated
Es 3:2 were bowing *l* and prostrating
3:2 neither bow *l* nor prostrate
3:5 Mordecai was not bowing *l* and
Job 5:11 who are *l* on a high place
6:5 Or a bull *l* over its fodder
24:24 And they have been brought *l*
39:10 harrow *l* plains after you
39:21 It paws in the *l* plain and
40:11 haughty and bring him *l*
Ps 38:6 I have bowed *l* to an extreme
60:6 the *l* plain of Succoth I shall
65:13 the *l* plains themselves are
84:6 *l* plain of the baca bushes
106:43 brought *l* for their error
108:7 *l* plain of Succoth I shall
136:23 Who during our *l* condition
Pr 8:7 palate in *l* tones utters truth
9:18 are in the *l* places of Sheol
Ec 10:6 merely in a *l* condition
12:4 the grinding mill becomes *l*
12:4 the daughters of song sound *l*
Ca 2:1 I am, a lily of the *l* plains
Isa 2:9 man becomes *l*, and you cannot
2:11 earthling man must become *l*
2:12 upon everyone lifted up or *l*
2:17 loftiness . . . must become *l*
5:15 and man will become *l*, and
5:15 high ones will become *l*
8:19 making utterances in *l* tones
10:33 ones themselves become *l*
17:5 in the *l* plain of Rephaim
19:6 must become *l* and parched
22:7 choicest of your *l* plains
25:12 security, he must lay *l*
26:5 laid *l* those inhabiting the
28:21 in the *l* plain near Gibeon
29:4 you must become *l* so that
29:4 your saying will sound *l*
32:19 city becomes *l* in an abased
33:18 will comment in *l* tones
40:4 mountain and hill be made *l*
65:10 the *l* plain of Achor a
Jer 5:4 Surely they are of *l* class
21:13 inhabitress of the *l* plain
31:40 *l* plain of the carcasses
47:5 O remnant of their *l* plain
48:8 *l* plain will certainly
49:4 brag about the *l* plains
49:4 your flowing *l* plain
La 3:20 remember and bow *l* over me
Eze 17:6 growing vine *l* in height
17:14 the kingdom might become *l*
17:24 have put on high the *l* tree
21:26 Put on high even what is *l*
21:26 bring *l* even the high one
Ho 1:5 in the *l* plain of Jezreel
2:15 *l* plain of Achor as an
Joe 3:2 the *l* plain of Jehoshaphat
3:12 to the *l* plain of Jehoshaphat
3:14 the *l* plain of the decision
3:14 the *l* plain of the decision
Mic 1:4 the *l* plains themselves will
Mal 2:9 to be despised and *l* to all
Lu 1:48 *l* position of his slave girl
1Co 10:5 laid *l* in the wilderness
2Co 7:6 who comforts those laid *l*
Php 4:12 how to be *l* on provisions
1Pe 4:4 same *l* sink of debauchery

Lower
Ge 6:16 will make it with a *l* story
Le 13:20 appearance is *l* than the skin
13:26 it is not *l* than the skin
14:37 is *l* than the wall surface
De 28:43, 43 keep descending *l* and *l*
Jos 15:19 Upper Gulloth and *L* Gulloth
16:3 the boundary of *L* Beth-horon
18:13 the south of *L* Beth-horon
Jg 1:15 Upper Gulloth and *L* Gulloth
1Ki 9:17 build Gezer and *L* Beth-horon
1Ch 7:24 Beth-horon, the *l* and the
2Ch 8:5 *L* Beth-horon, fortified cities
Job 41:24 cast like a *l* millstone
Ps 6:*super* on the *l* octave
12:*super* director on the *l* octave
Isa 22:9 the waters of the *l* pool
Jer 13:18 Seat yourselves in a *l* place
Eze 29:15 *L* than the other kingdoms
40:18 the *l* pavement
40:19 in front of the *l* gate to
43:14 *l* surrounding ledge there
Lu 5:5 I will *l* the nets
Eph 4:9 descended into the *l* regions
Heb 2:7 him a little *l* than angels
2:9 made a little *l* than angels

Lowered
Ge 24:18 she quickly *l* her jar upon
24:46 she quickly *l* her jar from
Isa 57:9 you *l* matters to Sheol
Mr 2:4 they *l* the cot on which the
Ac 27:17 *l* the gear and thus were
27:30 *l* the skiff into the sea
2Co 11:33 I was *l* in a wicker basket

Lowering
Ac 9:25 the wall, *l* him in a basket

Lowest
Ge 9:25 Let him become the *l* slave to
De 32:22 down to Sheol, the *l* place
1Ki 6:6 The *l* side chamber was five
6:8 entrance of the *l* side
2Ch 31:7 heaps by laying the *l* layer
Ne 4:13 *l* parts of the place behind
Ps 55:23 bring them down to the *l* pit
63:9 into the *l* parts of the earth
86:13 out of Sheol, its *l* place
88:6 in a pit of the *l* depths
139:15 in the *l* parts of the earth
Isa 44:23 you *l* parts of the earth
La 3:55 from a pit of the *l* sort
Eze 26:20 to dwell in the *l* land
41:7 from the *l* story one could
42:5 more than the *l* ones and
42:6 the *l* ones and from the
Lu 14:9 to occupy the *l* place
14:10 and recline in the *l* place

Lowing
1Sa 6:12 *l* as they went, and they did

Lowland
Jer 17:26 from the *l* and from the
32:44 in the cities of the *l* and
33:13 cities of the *l* and in the

Lowliest
Da 4:17 even the *l* one of mankind

Lowliness
Ac 20:19 with the greatest *l* of mind
Eph 4:2 with complete *l* of mind and
Php 2:3 with *l* of mind considering
Col 3:12 *l* of mind, mildness, and
1Pe 5:5 *l* of mind toward one another

Lowly
Ex 23:3 As for the *l* one, you must
30:15 the *l* must not give less
Le 14:21 *l* and does not have enough
19:15 not treat the *l* with
Ru 3:10 young fellows whether *l* or
1Sa 2:8 A Raiser of a *l* one from the
2Ki 24:14 the *l* class of the people
25:12 the *l* people of the land
Job 5:16 for the *l* one there comes to
20:10 seek the favor of *l* people
20:19 he has left *l* ones
31:16 hold back the *l* ones from
34:19 noble one than to the *l* one
34:28 the outcry of the *l* one
Ps 41:1 consideration toward the *l*
72:13 feel sorry for the *l* one
82:3 Be judges for the *l* one and
82:4 Provide escape for the *l* one
113:7 Raising up the *l* one from
Pr 10:15 ruin of the *l* ones is their
14:31 that is defrauding the *l* one
16:19 be *l* in spirit with the meek
19:4 *l* gets separated even from
19:17 showing favor to the *l* one
21:13 complaining cry of the *l* one
22:9 given of his food to the *l* one
22:16 is defrauding the *l* one to
22:22 Do not rob the *l* one because
22:22 not rob . . . because he is *l*
28:3 defrauding the *l* ones is as
28:8 one showing favor to the *l*
28:11 the *l* one who is discerning
28:15 wicked ruler over a *l* people
29:7 the legal claim of the *l* ones
29:14 king is judging the *l* ones in
Isa 10:2 push away the *l* ones from
11:4 he must judge the *l* ones
14:30 *l* ones will certainly feed
17:4 glory of Jacob will become *l*
25:4 a stronghold to the *l* one
26:6 the steps of the *l* ones
57:15 one crushed and *l* in spirit
57:15 revive the spirit of the *l*
Jer 39:10 *l* ones who had nothing at
40:7 *l* people of the land, who
52:15 *l* ones of the people and
52:16 of the *l* ones of the land
Eze 29:14 must become a *l* kingdom
Am 2:7 on the head of *l* persons
4:1 who are defrauding the *l* ones
5:11 farm rent from someone *l*
8:6 buy *l* people for mere silver
Zep 3:12 a people humble and *l*, and
Mt 11:29 and *l* in heart, and you will
Lu 1:52 thrones and exalted *l* ones
Ro 12:16 led along with the *l* things
2Co 10:1 *l* though I am in appearance
Jas 1:9 *l* brother exult over his

Loyal
Ge 21:23 *l* love with which I have
24:14 *l* love with my master
De 33:8 belong to the man *l* to you
1Sa 2:9 feet of his *l* ones he guards
2Sa 22:26 With someone *l* you will act
2Ch 6:41 *l* ones themselves rejoice in
Ps 4:3 certainly distinguish his *l* one
12:1 the *l* one has come to an end
16:10 your *l* one to see the pit
18:25 With someone *l* you will act
30:4 Make melody . . . O you *l* ones
31:23 love Jehovah, all you *l* ones
32:6 every *l* one will pray to you
37:28 he will not leave his *l* ones
43:1 case against a nation not *l*
50:5 Gather to me my *l* ones, Those
52:9 in front of your *l* ones
79:2 *l* ones to the wild beasts of
85:8 his people and to his *l* ones
86:2 do guard my soul, for I am *l*
89:19 in a vision to your *l* ones
97:10 the souls of his *l* ones
116:15 Is the death of his *l* ones
132:9 own *l* ones cry out joyfully
132:16 *l* ones will without fail
145:10 your *l* ones will bless you
145:17 And *l* in all his works
148:14 The praise of all his *l* ones
149:1 congregation of *l* ones
149:5 Let the *l* ones exult in glory
149:9 splendor belongs to all his *l*
Pr 2:8 the very way of his *l* ones
Jer 3:12 you people, for I am *l*
Mic 7:2 The *l* one has perished from
Ac 2:27 your *l* one to see corruption
13:35 your *l* one to see corruption
1Th 2:10 how *l* and righteous and
1Ti 2:8 prayer, lifting up *l* hands
Tit 1:8 sound in mind, righteous, *l*
Heb 7:26 *l*, guileless, undefiled
Re 15:4 because you alone are *l*
16:5 the *l* One, are righteous

Loyalty
2Sa 22:26 you will act in *l*
Ps 18:25 loyal you will act in *l*
Lu 1:75 with *l* and righteousness
Eph 4:24 in true righteousness and *l*

Lucius
Ac 13:1 and *L* of Cyrene, and Manaen
Ro 16:21 and so do *L* and Jason and

Luck
Isa 65:11 table for the god of Good *L*
Lud
Ge 10:22 sons of Shem . . . *L* and
1Ch 1:17 sons of Shem were . . . *L*
Isa 66:19 to Tarshish, Pul, and *L*
Eze 30:5 Ethiopia and Put and *L* and
Ludim
Ge 10:13 Mizraim became father to *L*
1Ch 1:11 Mizraim . . . father to *L*
Jer 46:9 the *L*, who are handling and
Eze 27:10 Persians and *L* and men of
Luggage
1Sa 10:22 he is, hidden among the *l*
Isa 46:1 their loads, pieces of *l*
Eze 12:3 *l* for exile and go into exile
12:4 you must bring out your *l*
12:4 like *l* for exile in the
12:7 My *l* I brought out, just
12:7 just like the *l* for exile, in
Luhith
Isa 15:5 on the ascent of *L*—with
Jer 48:5 on the way up to *L* it is
Luke
Col 4:14 *L* the beloved physician sends
2Ti 4:11 *L* alone is with me
Phm 24 Demas, *L*, my fellow workers
Lukewarm
Re 3:16 because you are *l* and neither
Lumber
Hag 1:8 bring in *l*. And build the
Luminaries
Ge 1:14 *l* come to be in the expanse
1:15 they must serve as *l* in the
1:16 to make the two great *l*
Eze 32:8 the *l* of light in the heavens
Luminary
Ge 1:16 greater *l* for dominating the
1:16 lesser *l* for dominating the
Ex 25:6 oil for the *l*, balsam oil for
27:20 beaten olive oil for the *l*
35:8 oil for the *l* and balsam oil
Le 24:2 oil for the *l*, to light up the
Nu 4:9 cover the lampstand of the *l*
4:16 over the oil of the *l* and
Ps 74:16 yourself prepared the *l*
Lump
Ro 9:21 from the same *l* one vessel
11:16 firstfruits is holy, the *l* is
1Co 5:6 leaven ferments the whole *l*
5:7 that you may be a new *l*
Ga 5:9 leaven ferments the whole *l*
Lumps
Job 7:5 with maggots and *l* of dust
Lunar
Ex 2:2 concealed for three *l* months
De 21:13 weep . . . a whole *l* month
33:14 the yield of the *l* months
1Ki 6:37 laid, in the *l* month of Ziv
6:38 in the *l* month of Bul, that
8:2 in the *l* month of Ethanim in
2Ki 15:13 to reign for a full *l* month
Ezr 6:15 day of the *l* month Adar
Job 3:6 the *l* months let it not enter
7:3 to possess worthless *l* months
29:2 in the *l* months of long ago
39:2 *l* months that they fulfill
Da 4:29 end of twelve *l* months he
Zec 11:8 shepherds in one *l* month
Lurch
2Co 4:9 but not left in the *l*; we
Lure
Jg 2:3 their gods will serve as a *l*
Lurking
Re 18:2 *l* place of every unclean
18:2 *l* place of every unclean and
Lust
Eze 23:16 to *l* after them at the
Ro 1:27 violently inflamed in their *l*
2Pe 1:4 is in the world through *l*
Lusted
Eze 23:7 all those after whom she *l*
23:9 toward whom she had *l*
23:12 the sons of Assyria she *l*

Luster
Ge 29:17 the eyes of Leah had no *l*
Ps 89:44 him cease from his *l*
Lustful
Eze 33:31 are expressing *l* desires and
Lustfulness
Eze 16:36 your *l* has been poured out
Lusting
Jer 4:30 Those *l* after you have
Eze 23:5 and kept *l* after those
23:20 kept *l* in the style of
Lustrous
Pr 6:25 not take you with her *l* eyes
Lusts
1Pe 4:3 when you proceeded in . . . *l*
Lute
Ps 92:3 instrument and upon the *l*
Lutes
1Sa 18:6 with rejoicing and with *l*
Luxuriant
De 12:2 hills and under every *l* tree
1Ki 14:23 and under every *l* tree
2Ki 16:4 and under every *l* tree
17:10 and under every *l* tree
2Ch 28:4 under every sort of *l* tree
Ps 37:35 as a *l* tree in native soil
52:8 *l* olive tree in God's house
Isa 57:5 under every *l* tree
Jer 2:20 under every *l* tree you
3:6 and underneath every *l* tree
3:13 strangers under every *l* tree
11:16 A *l* olive tree, pretty with
17:2 sacred poles beside a *l* tree
17:8 will actually prove to be *l*
Eze 6:13 under every *l* tree and under
Ho 14:8 I am like a *l* juniper tree
Luxuriantly
Jg 16:22 started to grow *l* as soon as
Job 15:32 his shoot . . . not grow *l*
Eze 16:7 and your own hair grew *l*
17:6 *l* growing vine low in height
Luxuriate
Ne 9:25 to *l* in your great goodness
Isa 16:8 shoots had been left to *l*
Luxuriating
Jer 5:10 Take away her *l* shoots
Luxurious
2Pe 2:13 consider *l* living in the
Luxury
Pr 19:10 *L* is not fitting for anyone
Lu 7:25 and existing in *l* are in royal
Jas 5:5 lived in *l* upon the earth and
Re 18:3 the power of her shameless *l*
18:7 and lived in shameless *l*, to
18:9 and lived in shameless *l*
Luz
Ge 28:19 *L* was the city's name
35:6 Jacob came to *L*, which is in
48:3 Almighty appeared to me at *L*
Jos 16:2 from Bethel belonging to *L*
18:13 passed over from there to *L*
18:13 at the southern slope of *L*
Jg 1:23 the city before that was *L*
1:26 and called its name *L*
Lycaonia
Ac 14:6 cities of *L*, Lystra and Derbe
Lycaonian
Ac 14:11 saying in the *L* tongue: The
Lycia
Ac 27:5 put into port at Myra in *L*
Lydda
Ac 9:32 holy ones that dwelt in *L*
9:35 those who inhabited *L* and the
9:38 as *L* was near Joppa, when
Lydia
Ac 16:14 *L*, a seller of purple, of
16:40 and went to the home of *L*
Lye
Isa 1:25 your scummy dross as with *l*
Jer 2:22 large quantities of *l*, your
Mal 3:2 and like the *l* of laundrymen
Lying
Ge 28:13 land upon which you are *l*

Ge 29:2 droves of sheep were *l* down
34:7 *l* down with Jacob's daughter
49:14 *l* down between the two
49:25 watery deep *l* down below
Ex 22:19 Anyone *l* down with a beast
23:5 ass . . . *l* down under its load
Le 26:34 the days of its *l* desolated
26:35 days of its *l* desolated it
26:43 *l* desolated without them and
Nu 31:17 by *l* with a male
31:18 the act of *l* with a male
31:35 the act of *l* with a male
35:20 at him while *l* in wait that
35:22 without *l* in wait
De 22:22 *l* down with a woman owned
22:22 man *l* down with the woman
31:16 *l* down with your forefathers
33:13 the watery deep *l* down below
Jos 8:4 *l* in ambush against the city
Jg 16:3 Samson kept *l* till midnight
21:11 experienced *l* with a male
21:12 by *l* with a male
Ru 3:8 look! a woman *l* at his feet
3:13 Keep *l* down until the morning
3:14 she kept *l* at his feet until
1Sa 3:2 Eli was *l* in his place, and
3:3 Samuel was *l* in the temple
3:15 Samuel continued *l* down
24:11 *l* in wait for my soul to
26:5 and Saul was *l* in the camp
26:7 Saul was *l* asleep in the
26:7 people were *l* all around him
2Sa 4:7 he was *l* upon his couch in
13:8 brother while he was *l* down
1Ki 21:27 kept *l* down in sackcloth
2Ki 9:16 for Jehoram was *l* there
2Ch 36:21 All the days of *l* desolated
Ezr 10:1 *l* prostrate before the house
Job 31:9 I kept *l* in wait at the very
38:40 keep *l* in the covert for an
Ps 10:9 *l* in wait in the concealed
10:9 *l* in wait to carry off some
68:13 *l* between the camp ash heaps
88:5 slain ones *l* in the burial
139:3 my *l* outstretched you have
Pr 6:9 lazy one, will you keep *l* down
6:10 of the hands in *l* down
12:6 are a *l* in wait for blood
19:22 is better than a *l* man
21:28 A *l* witness will perish, but
23:34 *l* down in the heart of the
23:34 *l* down at the top of a mast
30:8 *l* word put far away from me
Isa 56:10 *l* down, loving to slumber
57:11 so that you took up *l*
Jer 2:20 *l* sprawled out, prostituting
51:12 ready those *l* in ambush
La 3:10 a bear *l* in wait he is to me
Eze 4:9 days that you are *l* upon your
13:6 is untrue and a *l* divination
13:7 *l* divination that you have
29:3 sea monster *l* stretched out
36:3 been a *l* desolate and a
Da 2:9 it is a *l* and wrong word that
9:27 also upon the one *l* desolate
Ho 6:9 as in the *l* in wait for a man
11:12 With *l*, Ephraim has
12:1 *L* and despoiling are what he
Am 6:4 *l* down on couches of ivory
Mic 7:5 her who is *l* in your bosom
Mt 3:10 ax is *l* at the root of the
8:14 *l* down and sick with fever
9:2 a paralyzed man *l* on a bed
28:6 see the place where he was *l*
Mr 1:30 was *l* down sick with a fever
2:4 on which the paralytic was *l*
Lu 2:12 an infant . . . *l* in a manger
2:16 the infant *l* in the manger
11:54 *l* in wait for him, to catch
Joh 5:3 a multitude . . . was *l* down
5:6 Seeing this man *l* down, and
11:38 a stone was *l* against it
20:5 he beheld the bandages *l*
20:6 he viewed the bandages *l*
20:7 not *l* with the bandages but
20:12 body of Jesus had been *l*
21:9 *l* there a charcoal fire and
21:9 fire and fish *l* upon it and
Ac 9:33 *l* flat on his cot for eight
23:16 heard of their *l* in wait
23:21 *l* in wait for him, and they
27:20 tempest was *l* upon us
28:8 *l* down distressed with fever
Ro 9:1 truth in Christ; I am not *l*

2Co 11:31 God . . . knows I am not *l*
Ga 1:20 the sight of God, I am not *l*
Col 3:9 Do not be *l* to one another
2Th 2:9 and *l* signs and portents
1Ti 2:7 telling the truth, I am not *l*
Jas 3:14 do not be bragging and *l*
1Jo 1:6 are *l* and are not practicing
5:19 world is *l* in the power of
Re 3:9 yet they are not but are *l*

Lyingly
Mt 5:11 *l* say every sort of wicked

Lysanias
Lu 3:1 *L* was district ruler of

Lysias
Ac 23:26 Claudius *L* to his excellency
24:22 *L* the military commander

Lystra
Ac 14:6 Lycaonia, *L* and Derbe and the
14:8 Now in *L* there was sitting a
14:21 returned to *L* and to Iconium
16:1 arrived at Derbe and also at *L*
16:2 the brothers in *L* and Iconium
2Ti 3:11 in Iconium, in *L*, the sort

Maacah
Ge 22:24 and Gaham and Tahash and *M*
2Sa 3:3 Absalom the son of *M* the
10:6 king of *M*, a thousand men
10:8 Ishtob and *M* by themselves
1Ki 2:39 Achish the son of *M* the king
15:2 *M* the granddaughter of
15:10 *M* the granddaughter of
15:13 even *M* his grandmother
1Ch 2:48 As for Caleb's concubine *M*
3:2 *M* the daughter of Talmai the
7:15 name of his sister was *M*
7:16 *M*, Machir's wife, bore a
8:29 and his wife's name was *M*
9:35 And his wife's name was *M*
11:43 Hanan the son of *M*, and
19:7 the king of *M* and his people
27:16 Shephatiah the son of *M*
2Ch 11:20 he took *M* the granddaughter
11:21 was more in love with *M*
11:22 Abijah the son of *M* in
15:16 *M* his grandmother, Asa the

Maacath
Jos 13:13 Geshur and *M* keep dwelling

Maacathite
2Sa 23:34 Ahasbai the son of the *M*
2Ki 25:23 Jaazaniah the son of the *M*
1Ch 4:19 and Eshtemoa the *M*
Jer 40:8 Jezaniah the son of the *M*

Maacathites
De 3:14 the Geshurites and the *M*
Jos 12:5 of the Geshurites and the *M*
13:11 and the *M* and all of Mount
13:13 the Geshurites and the *M*

Maadai
Ezr 10:34 sons of Bani, *M*, Amram

Maadiah
Ne 12:5 Mijamin, *M*, Bilgah

Maai
Ne 12:36 *M*, Nethanel and Judah

Maarath
Jos 15:59 *M* and Beth-anoth and

Maasai
1Ch 9:12 and *M* the son of Adiel the

Maaseiah
1Ch 15:18 Eliab and Benaiah and *M* and
15:20 and Eliab and *M* and Benaiah
2Ch 23:1 *M* the son of Adaiah and
26:11 *M* the officer under the
28:7 *M* the son of the king
34:8 *M* the chief of the city and
Ezr 10:18 his brothers, *M* and Eliezer
10:21 sons of Harim, *M* and Elijah
10:22 the sons of Pashhur . . . *M*
10:30 sons of Pahath-moab . . . *M*
Ne 3:23 *M* the son of Ananiah did
8:4 and *M* to his right hand
8:7 *M*, Kelita, Azariah, Jozabad
10:25 Rehum, Hashabnah, *M*
11:5 *M* the son of Baruch the son
11:7 *M* the son of Ithiel the son
12:41 the priests Eliakim, *M*
12:42 and *M* and Shemaiah, and
Jer 21:1 Zephaniah the son of *M*, the
29:21 Zedekiah the son of *M*, who
29:25 Zephaniah the son of *M*
35:4 above the dining room of *M*
37:3 Zephaniah the son of *M* the

Maath
Lu 3:26 son of *M*, son of Mattathias

Maaz
1Ch 2:27 sons of Ram . . . *M* and Jamin

Maaziah
1Ch 24:18 for *M* the twenty-fourth
Ne 10:8 *M*, Bilgai and Shemaiah

Macedonia
Ac 16:9 Step over into *M* and help us
16:10 we sought to go forth into *M*
16:12 city of the district of *M*
18:5 Timothy came down from *M*
19:21 going through *M* and Achaia
19:22 So he dispatched to *M* two of
20:1 went forth to journey into *M*
20:3 to return through *M*
Ro 15:26 those in *M* and Achaia have
1Co 16:5 when I have gone through *M*
16:5 for I am going through *M*
2Co 1:16 to go to *M*, and to come back
1:16 to come back from *M* to you
2:13 to them and departed for *M*
7:5 when we arrived in *M*, our
8:1 upon the congregations of *M*
11:9 brothers that came from *M*
Php 4:15 when I departed from *M*, not
1Th 1:7 to all the believers in *M* and
1:8 sounded forth from you in *M*
4:10 all the brothers in all of *M*
1Ti 1:3 about to go my way into *M*, so

Macedonian
Ac 16:9 a certain *M* man was standing
27:2 with us Aristarchus a *M* from

Macedonians
Ac 19:29 Gaius and Aristarchus, *M*
2Co 9:2 boasting to the *M* about you
9:4 if *M* should come with me and

Machbannai
1Ch 12:13 the tenth, *M* the eleventh

Machbenah
1Ch 2:49 Sheva the father of *M*

Machi
Nu 13:15 of Gad, Geuel the son of *M*

Machinations
Eph 6:11 against the *m* of the Devil

Machir
Ge 50:23 sons of *M*, Manasseh's son
Nu 26:29 Of *M* the family of the
26:29 *M* became father to Gilead
27:1 son of *M* the son of Manasseh
32:39 of *M* the son of Manasseh
32:40 Moses gave Gilead to *M* the
36:1 Gilead the son of *M* the son
De 3:15 And to *M* I have given Gilead
Jos 13:31 *M* the son of Manasseh
13:31 sons of *M* by their families
17:1 *M* the firstborn of Manasseh
17:3 *M*, the son of Manasseh
Jg 5:14 Out of *M* the commanders went
2Sa 9:4 house of *M* the son of Ammiel
9:5 *M* the son of Ammiel at
17:27 *M* the son of Ammiel from
1Ch 2:21 *M* the father of Gilead
2:23 *M* the father of Gilead
7:14 bore *M* the father of Gilead
7:15 *M* himself took a wife for
7:17 son of *M* the son of Manasseh

Machirites
Nu 26:29 Machir the family of the *M*

Machir's
1Ch 7:16 Maacah, *M* wife, bore a son

Machnadebai
Ezr 10:40 *M*, Shashai, Sharai

Machpelah
Ge 23:9 give me the cave of *M*, which
23:17 *M*, which is in front of
23:19 field of *M* in front of Mamre
25:9 cave of *M* in the field of
49:30 in the field of *M* that is
50:13 the cave of the field of *M*

Mad
Pr 26:18 Just like someone *m* that is
Joh 10:20 He has a demon and is *m*
Ac 12:15 They said to her: You are *m*
26:11 I was extremely *m* against
26:24 You are going *m*, Paul!
26:25 Paul said: I am not going *m*
1Co 14:23 they not say that you are *m*
2Pe 2:16 the prophet's *m* course

Madai
Ge 10:2 sons of Japheth . . . *M* and
1Ch 1:5 sons of Japheth . . . *M* and

Maddened
De 28:34 *m* at the sight of your eyes
Jer 29:26 any man *m* and behaving like
Ho 9:7 *m* on account of the abundance

Made
Ge 1:31 God saw everything he had *m*
2:2 of his work that he had *m*
2:2 all his work that he had *m*
2:4 Jehovah God *m* earth and heaven
2:5 God had not *m* it rain upon the
2:9 God *m* to grow out of the
3:1 beasts . . . Jehovah God had *m*
3:7 and *m* loin coverings for
4:26 At that time a start was *m* of
5:1 he *m* him in the likeness of
6:6 regrets that he had *m* men in
6:7 do regret that I have *m* them
7:4 I have *m* off the surface of
8:6 of the ark that he had *m*
9:6 for in God's image he *m* man
10:8 He *m* the start in becoming
12:10 Abram *m* his way down toward
13:3 he *m* his way from encampment
13:4 altar that he had *m* there
14:2 these *m* war with Bera king
14:23 not say, It was I who *m*
19:3 he *m* a feast for them, and he
19:24 Jehovah *m* it rain sulphur
19:27 Abraham *m* his way early in
24:16 and she *m* her way down to the
24:21 Jehovah had *m* his trip
24:31 *m* the house ready and room
24:37 master *m* me swear, saying
24:45 she *m* her way down to the
26:22 *m* us fruitful in the earth
26:30 he *m* a feast for them and
26:31 and they *m* sworn statements
27:14 his mother *m* a tasty dish
27:17 bread that she had *m* into
29:22 and *m* a feast
33:17 for his herd he *m* booths
37:3 shirtlike garment *m* for him
41:51 God has *m* me forget all my
41:52 God has *m* me fruitful
42:7 he *m* himself unrecognizable
45:1 Joseph *m* himself known to
46:29 had his chariot *m* ready
50:5 My father *m* me swear, saying
50:6 just as he *m* you swear
50:25 *m* the sons of Israel swear
Ex 1:13 *m* the sons of Israel slave
4:20 and *m* them ride on an ass
5:21 you have *m* us smell offensive
7:1 I have *m* you God to Pharaoh
8:7 priests . . . *m* the frogs come
8:15 he *m* his heart unresponsive
8:30 and *m* entreaty to Jehovah
8:32 However, Pharaoh *m* his heart
10:18 and *m* entreaty to Jehovah
10:19 Jehovah *m* a shift to a very
13:18 God *m* the people go round
13:19 he had *m* the sons of Israel
15:17 place that you have *m* ready
16:32 the bread that I *m* you eat
20:11 Jehovah *m* the heavens and
25:31 the lampstand is to be *m*
29:18 is an offering *m* by fire to
29:25 It is an offering *m* by fire
29:33 atonement has been *m* to fill
29:41 offering *m* by fire to
30:20 offering *m* by fire smoke
31:17 Jehovah *m* the heavens and
32:8 *m* a molten statue of a calf
32:20 the calf that they had *m*
32:20 and *m* the sons of Israel
32:31 they *m* a god of gold for
32:35 because they had *m* the calf
32:35 the calf, which Aaron had *m*
33:16 your people . . . *m* distinct
36:8 with cherubs . . . he *m* them
36:11 *m* loops of blue thread upon
36:12 *m* fifty loops on the one

Ex 36:12 he *m* fifty loops on the
36:13 *m* fifty hooks of gold and
36:14 cloths were what he *m*
36:17 *m* fifty loops upon the edge
36:17 *m* fifty loops upon the edge
36:18 *m* fifty hooks of copper for
36:20 *m* the panel frames for the
36:23 *m* the panel frames for the
36:24 *m* forty socket pedestals of
36:25 he *m* twenty panel frames
36:27 he *m* six panel frames
36:28 *m* two panel frames as
36:33 he *m* the middle bar to run
36:34 *m* their rings of gold as
36:35 he *m* it with cherubs
36:36 *m* for it four acacia pillars
37:1 now *m* the Ark of acacia wood
37:2 *m* a border of gold round
37:4 next *m* poles of acacia wood
37:7 *m* two cherubs of gold
37:7 Of hammered work he *m* them
37:8 *m* the cherubs on the cover on
37:11 and *m* a border of gold round
37:12 Next he *m* for it a rim of a
37:12 *m* a border of gold for its
37:15 *m* the poles of acacia wood
37:16 *m* the utensils that are upon
37:17 *m* the lampstand of pure gold
37:17 he *m* the lampstand
37:23 he *m* its seven lamps and its
37:24 a talent of pure gold he *m*
37:25 *m* the altar of incense out
37:26 he *m* a border of gold round
37:27 *m* for it two rings of gold
37:28 *m* the poles of acacia wood
37:29 He *m* additionally the holy
38:2 *m* its horns upon its four
38:3 *m* all the utensils of the
38:3 its utensils he *m* of copper
38:4 *m* for the altar a grating
38:6 *m* the poles of acacia wood and
38:7 *m* it a hollow chest of planks
38:8 *m* the basin of copper and its
38:28 he *m* pegs for the pillars
39:1 *m* garments of knitted work
39:1 they *m* the holy garments that
39:2 he *m* the ephod of gold, blue
39:4 *m* shoulder pieces for it that
39:6 *m* the onyx stones set with
39:8 he *m* the breastpiece with the
39:9 They *m* the breastpiece, when
39:16 they *m* two settings of gold
39:19 *m* two rings of gold and set
39:20 *m* two rings of gold and put
39:22 *m* the sleeveless coat of the
39:24 they *m* upon the hem of the
39:25 *m* bells of pure gold and put
39:27 *m* the robes of fine linen
39:30 they *m* the shining plate, the
Le 1:9 offering *m* by fire of a restful
1:13 *m* by fire of a restful odor
1:17 an offering *m* by fire of a
2:2 an offering *m* by fire of a
2:3 Jehovah's offerings *m* by fire
2:7 be *m* of fine flour with oil
2:8 grain offering that was *m* of
2:9 an offering *m* by fire of a
2:11 should be *m* a leavened thing
2:11 as an offering *m* by fire
2:16 offering *m* by fire to Jehovah
3:3 offering *m* by fire to Jehovah
3:5 an offering *m* by fire of a
3:9 offering *m* by fire to Jehovah
3:11 offering *m* by fire to Jehovah
3:14 offering *m* by fire to Jehovah
3:16 an offering *m* by fire for a
4:23 has been *m* known to him, then
4:28 sin . . . been *m* known to him
4:35 Jehovah's offerings *m* by fire
5:12 Jehovah's offerings *m* by fire
6:17 out of my offerings *m* by fire
6:18 Jehovah's offerings *m* by fire
6:21 It will be *m* with oil upon a
6:22 whole offering it will be *m*
7:5 offering *m* by fire to Jehovah
7:9 one *m* in the deep-fat kettle
7:25 offering *m* by fire to Jehovah
7:30 Jehovah's offerings *m* by fire
7:35 Jehovah's offerings *m* by fire
8:16 *m* them smoke upon the altar
8:21 *m* the entire ram smoke upon
8:21 offering *m* by fire to Jehovah
8:28 *m* them smoke upon the altar
8:28 offering *m* by fire to Jehovah

Le 9:10 he *m* the fat and the kidneys
9:14 *m* them smoke upon the burnt
9:15 *m* an offering for sin with it
9:17 *m* it smoke upon the altar
9:20 *m* the fatty pieces smoke upon
10:6 which Jehovah has *m* burn
10:12 offerings *m* by fire and eat
10:13 Jehovah's offerings *m* by
10:15 with the offerings *m* by fire
11:32 of which some use is *m*
13:48 or in anything *m* of skin
13:51 for which the skin may be *m*
16:30 atonement will be *m* for you
18:24 have *m* themselves unclean
21:6 offerings *m* by fire, the
21:21 Jehovah's offerings *m* by
22:22 and no offering *m* by fire
22:27 offering *m* by fire to
23:8 offering *m* by fire to Jehovah
23:13 as an offering *m* by fire to
23:18 offering *m* by fire, of a
23:25 *m* by fire to Jehovah
23:27 offering *m* by fire to
23:36 offering *m* by fire to
23:36 offering *m* by fire to
23:37 offering *m* by fire to
23:43 I *m* the sons of Israel to
24:7 offering *m* by fire to Jehovah
24:9 Jehovah's offerings *m* by fire
25:27 man to whom he *m* the sale
27:18 deduction should be *m* from
Nu 5:27 *m* her drink the water, it
5:28 be *m* pregnant with semen
6:3 any liquid *m* from grapes
6:4 *m* from the wine vine, from the
7:2 chieftains . . . *m* a presentation
7:10 *m* their presentation at the
7:18 of Issachar, *m* a presentation
8:4 so he had *m* the lampstand
8:21 Aaron *m* an atonement for
11:2 *m* supplication to Jehovah
11:8 *m* it into round cakes, and
15:3 offering *m* by fire to Jehovah
15:10 as an offering *m* by fire, of
15:13 an offering *m* by fire, of a
15:14 an offering *m* by fire, of a
15:25 an offering *m* by fire to
15:28 the soul who *m* a mistake
18:8 of the contributions *m* to me
18:9 out of the offering *m* by fire
18:17 as an offering *m* by fire for
21:2 Israel *m* a vow to Jehovah and
21:9 Moses at once *m* a serpent of
28:2 my offerings *m* by fire as a
28:3 the offering *m* by fire that
28:6 offering *m* by fire to Jehovah
28:8 an offering *m* by fire, of a
28:13 an offering *m* by fire to
28:19 as an offering *m* by fire, a
28:24 bread, an offering *m* by fire
29:6 an offering *m* by fire to
29:13 an offering *m* by fire, of a
29:36 an offering *m* by fire, of a
31:20 everything *m* of goat's hair
32:13 *m* them wander about in the
De 1:38 Him he has *m* strong, because
4:36 he *m* you hear his voice so as
4:36 he *m* you see his great fire
8:2 God *m* you walk these forty
8:17 own hand have *m* this wealth
9:12 *m* themselves a molten image
9:16 *m* yourselves a molten calf
9:20 I *m* supplication also in
9:21 your sin that you had *m*
10:3 I *m* an ark of acacia wood
10:5 in the ark that I had *m*
11:4 *m* the waters of the Red Sea
13:17 the thing *m* sacred by ban
18:1 The offerings *m* by fire of
26:19 other nations that he has *m*
32:6 He who *m* you and proceeded to
32:15 So he forsook God, who *m* him
Jos 2:17 that you have *m* us swear
2:20 that you have *m* us swear
4:14 Jehovah *m* Joshua great in
5:3 Joshua *m* flint knives for
10:1 Gibeon had *m* peace with
10:4 it has *m* peace with Joshua
10:17 the report was *m* to Joshua
11:19 no city that *m* peace
13:14 The offerings *m* by fire of
13:15 Moses *m* a gift to the tribe
13:24 *m* a gift to the tribe of
13:29 *m* a gift to the half tribe

Jos 14:10 Jehovah *m* this promise to
21:45 promise that Jehovah had *m*
22:7 Moses had *m* a gift in Bashan
22:7 Joshua *m* a gift with their
22:28 altar that our fathers *m*
24:3 and *m* his seed many. So I
Jg 3:16 Ehud *m* a sword for himself
3:26 and *m* his escape to Seirah
5:11 people *m* their way down to the
6:2 Israel *m* for themselves the
7:11 *m* their descent to the edge
8:14 and *m* inquiries of him. So he
9:6 and *m* Abimelech reign as king
9:21 and *m* his way to Beer, and he
9:44 *m* a dash that they might
9:44 two bands *m* a dash against
9:52 Abimelech *m* his way to the
9:56 God *m* the evil of Abimelech
9:57 God *m* come back upon their
11:30 Jephthah *m* a vow to Jehovah
11:35 You have indeed *m* me bend
11:39 *m* her return to her father
11:39 vow that he had *m* toward
16:2 report was *m* to the Gazites
18:24 My gods that I *m* you have
18:27 they took what Micah had *m*
18:31 image . . . which he had *m*
20:41 Israel *m* an about-face, and
20:45 they *m* a gleaning of five
21:15 Jehovah had *m* a rupture
Ru 1:20 has *m* it very bitter for me
1:21 that Jehovah has *m* me return
1:22 Thus Naomi *m* her return, Ruth
2:11 The report was fully *m* to me
1Sa 2:14 *m* a thrust into the basin or
2:28 offerings *m* by fire of the
6:6 *m* their heart unresponsive
7:16 *m* the circuit of Bethel and
8:1 *m* appointments of his sons
11:11 they *m* their way into the
13:13 *m* your kingdom firm over
15:12 But report was *m* to Samuel
15:35 had *m* Saul king over Israel
17:35 and *m* the rescue from its
19:18 *m* his escape and got to
20:35 Jonathan *m* his way out to
21:2 *m* an appointment with the
22:1 *m* their way down there to
22:20 Abiathar, *m* his escape and
23:7 report was *m* to Saul: David
23:27 Philistines have *m* a raid
23:29 David *m* his way up from
26:7 David *m* his way with Abishai
27:4 report was *m* to Saul that
30:1 Amalekites *m* a raid on the
30:14 *m* a raid on the south of
2Sa 5:20 like a gap *m* by waters
6:12 report was *m* to King David
6:20 king of Israel *m* himself
7:27 have *m* a revelation to your
10:17 report was *m* to David, he
10:19 *m* peace with Israel and
12:31 *m* them serve at
13:8 *m* the cakes under his eyes
13:10 cakes that she had *m* and
13:38 *m* his way to Geshur
14:15 the people *m* me afraid
15:1 have a chariot *m* for himself
15:7 my vow that I solemnly *m* to
15:8 your servant *m* a solemn vow
15:31 to David the report was *m*
16:21 *m* yourself foul-smelling to
19:8 they *m* the report, saying
19:17 they *m* it successfully to
1Ki 1:5 have a chariot *m* for himself
1:43 David . . . has *m* Solomon king
1:44 they *m* him ride upon the
1:51 the report was *m* to Solomon
2:24 *m* a house for me just as he
3:7 have *m* your servant king in
6:5 *m* side chambers all around
6:23 *m* in the innermost room two
6:31 *m* with doors of oil-tree
6:33 *m* for the entrance of the
7:6 the Porch of Pillars he *m*
7:7 he *m* the porch of judgment
7:16 two capitals he *m* to put
7:37 that he *m* the ten carriages
7:40 Hiram gradually *m* the basins
7:45 Hiram *m* of polished copper
7:48 *m* all the utensils that
7:51 things *m* holy by David his
8:24 you *m* the promise with your
8:24 you have *m* the fulfillment

1Ki 8:59 *m* request for favor before
9:26 Solomon *m* in Ezion-geber
10:18 king *m* a great ivory throne
10:20 had any *m* just like it
10:27 cedarwood he *m* like the
12:4 *m* our yoke hard, and, as for
12:10 *m* our yoke heavy, but, as
12:14 *m* your yoke heavy, but I
12:20 *m* him king over all Israel
12:28 *m* two golden calves and
12:32 that he had *m* in Bethel
12:32 to the calves that he had *m*
12:32 high places that he had *m*
12:33 that he had *m* in Bethel
14:9 *m* for yourself another god
14:15 they *m* their sacred poles
14:26 shields that Solomon had *m*
14:27 *m* in place of them copper
15:12 that his forefathers had *m*
15:13 she had *m* a horrible idol
15:15 things *m* holy by his father
15:15 things *m* holy by himself
16:16 *m* Omri, the chief of the
18:10 *m* the kingdom and the
18:26 the altar that they had *m*
18:45 and *m* his way to Jezreel
22:48 *m* Tarshish ships to go to
2Ki 3:2 pillar . . . his father had *m*
6:6 and *m* the axhead float
6:13 the report was *m* to him
8:7 report was *m* to him, saying
8:20 *m* a king reign over them
9:23 *m* a turn with his hands
10:15 he *m* him get up into the
11:4 *m* them swear at the house
11:12 *m* him king and anointed
12:13 were not *m* basins of silver
13:11 with which he *m* Israel sin
14:13 *m* a breach in the wall of
14:21 they *m* him king in place of
16:3 he *m* pass through the fire
16:11 Urijah the priest *m* it
17:8 of Israel that they had *m*
17:19 of Israel that they had *m*
17:29 that the Samaritans had *m*
17:30 *m* Succoth-benoth, and the
17:30 men of Cuth . . . *m* Nergal
17:30 men of Hamath . . . *m* Ashima
17:31 Avvites, they *m* Nibhaz and
17:34 whose name he *m* Israel
18:4 serpent that Moses had *m*
19:15 *m* the heavens and the earth
19:20 The prayer that you have *m*
20:11 *m* the shadow that had gone
20:20 how he *m* the pool and the
21:3 *m* a sacred pole, just as
21:6 *m* his own son pass through
21:6 *m* spirit mediums and
21:7 sacred pole that he had *m* in
21:24 *m* Josiah his son king in
23:4 all the utensils *m* for Baal
23:8 had *m* sacrificial smoke
23:10 *m* unfit for worship Topheth
23:12 the kings of Judah had *m*
23:12 altars that Manasseh had *m*
23:13 king *m* unfit for worship
23:15 place that Jeroboam . . . *m*
23:26 Manasseh had *m* them offend
23:30 *m* him king in place of his
23:34 Pharaoh Nechoh *m* Eliakim
24:13 *m* in the temple of Jehovah
24:17 *m* Mattaniah his uncle king
25:16 *m* for the house of Jehovah
1Ch 1:10 *m* the start in becoming a
5:10 *m* war upon the Hagrites
10:1 *m* war upon Israel; and the
12:39 had *m* preparation for them
14:11 like a gap *m* by waters
14:13 *m* a raid in the low plain
16:7 David *m* a contribution for
16:26 Jehovah, he *m* the heavens
16:30 will it be *m* to totter
18:8 Solomon *m* the copper sea and
19:17 the report was *m* to David
19:19 *m* peace with David
21:29 that Moses had *m* in the
22:5 David *m* preparation in great
23:1 *m* Solomon his son king over
23:5 I have *m* for giving praise
26:20 of the things *m* holy
26:26 things *m* holy, that David
26:26 of the army had *m* holy
26:27 *m* things holy to maintain
26:28 son of Zeruiah had *m* holy
1Ch 26:28 What anyone *m* holy was
28:2 I had *m* preparation to build
28:12 of the things *m* holy
29:9 *m* voluntary offerings to
29:19 which I have *m* preparation
2Ch 1:3 had *m* in the wilderness
1:5 altar that Bezalel . . . had *m*
1:6 Solomon now *m* offerings
1:8 *m* me king in place of him
1:9 *m* me king over a people as
1:11 over whom I have *m* you king
1:15 he *m* like the sycamore trees
2:12 *m* the heavens and the earth
2:18 *m* seventy thousand of them
3:10 *m* in the house of the Most
3:14 *m* the curtain of blue thread
3:15 he *m* before the house two
3:16 *m* chains in necklace style
3:16 *m* a hundred pomegranates and
4:1 *m* the copper altar, twenty
4:6 he *m* ten basins, and put five
4:7 *m* lampstands of gold, ten of
4:8 *m* ten tables, and stationed
4:8 and *m* a hundred bowls of gold
4:9 Then he *m* the courtyard of
4:11 Hiram *m* the cans and the
4:16 *m* for King Solomon for the
4:18 Solomon *m* all these utensils
5:1 things *m* holy by David his
6:13 Solomon had *m* a platform of
6:15 *m* the promise with your
6:15 *m* fulfillment as at this day
7:6 David the king had *m* to thank
7:7 altar that Solomon had *m* was
9:17 king *m* a great ivory throne
9:19 kingdom had any *m* just like
9:27 king *m* the silver in
9:27 *m* like the sycamore trees
10:4 his part, *m* our yoke hard
10:10 *m* our yoke heavy, but as
11:15 the calves that he had *m*
12:9 shields that Solomon had *m*
12:10 Rehoboam *m* in their place
13:8 calves that Jeroboam *m*
15:16 *m* a horrible idol for the
15:18 things *m* holy by his father
15:18 things *m* holy by himself
16:14 *m* an extraordinarily great
18:10 *m* for himself horns of iron
20:27 Jehovah had *m* them rejoice
20:36 *m* him a partner with
20:36 *m* ships in Ezion-geber
21:8 *m* a king to reign over them
21:11 *m* high places on the
22:1 *m* Ahaziah his youngest son
23:11 and *m* him king, and so
24:8 *m* a chest and put it outside
24:13 *m* the house of the true God
24:13 and *m* it strong
24:24 Syrians *m* an invasion, and
25:23 *m* a breach in the wall of
26:1 Uzziah . . . they *m* him king
26:5 true God *m* him prosperous
26:9 Buttress, and *m* them strong
26:15 *m* in Jerusalem engines of
28:2 statues he *m* of the Baals
28:3 *m* sacrificial smoke in the
28:4 *m* sacrificial smoke on the
28:18 Philistines, they *m* a raid
28:21 *m* a gift to the king of
28:24 *m* altars for himself at
28:25 *m* high places for making
29:24 *m* a sin offering with their
29:36 true God had *m* preparation
32:5 *m* missiles in abundance and
32:25 Hezekiah *m* no return, for
32:27 storehouses he *m* for
33:3 *m* sacred poles, and he began
33:6 *m* his own sons pass through
33:6 *m* spiritistic mediums and
33:7 image that he had *m* in the
33:22 Manasseh his father had *m*
33:23 that *m* guiltiness increase
33:25 *m* Josiah his son king in
35:8 *m* a contribution as a
35:13 things *m* holy they boiled
36:1 *m* him king in the place of
36:4 *m* Eliakim his brother king
36:10 *m* Zedekiah his father's
36:13 *m* him swear by God
Ezr 2:68 *m* voluntary offerings to the
4:14 and *m* it known to the king
5:14 the one whom he *m* governor
6:1 *m* an investigation in the
Ezr 7:24 *m* known that, as respects
8:23 and *m* request of our God
10:1 *m* confession while weeping
Ne 3:16 the pool that had been *m* and
5:12 *m* them swear to do according
5:15 *m* it heavy upon the people
5:18 happened to be *m* ready daily
5:18 were *m* ready for me, and
8:4 they had *m* for the occasion
8:12 words that had been *m* known
8:17 *m* booths and took up dwelling
9:6 yourself have *m* the heavens
9:14 your holy sabbath you *m* known
9:18 *m* for themselves a molten
9:23 sons you *m* as many as the
9:35 land that you *m* available for
Es 2:9 and he *m* haste to give her her
4:5 he had *m* to attend upon her
5:4 banquet that I have *m* for him
5:5 the banquet that Esther had *m*
5:12 to the banquet that she had *m*
5:14 proceeded to have the stake *m*
6:14 banquet that Esther had *m*
7:9 that Haman *m* for Mordecai
Job 1:17 Chaldeans *m* up three bands
5:23 *m* to live at peace with you
7:3 *m* to possess . . . lunar months
10:8 shaped me so that they *m* me
10:9 out of clay you have *m* me
12:5 It is *m* ready for those of
14:5 A decree for him you have *m*
16:7 Only now he has *m* me weary
16:7 has *m* all those assembling
16:21 decision is to be *m* between
19:4 that I have *m* a mistake
23:16 God . . . *m* my heart timid
26:3 *m* practical wisdom itself
27:2 who has *m* my soul bitter
27:18 that a watchman has *m*
28:26 *m* for the rain a regulation
30:27 intestines were *m* to boil
33:4 God's own spirit *m* me, And
39:17 For God has *m* her forget
40:15 Behemoth that I have *m* as
41:33 one *m* to be without terror
Ps 9:15 the pit that they have *m*
10:6 I shall not be *m* to totter
13:4 because I am *m* to stagger
15:5 will never be *m* to totter
16:8 I shall not be *m* to totter
17:3 have *m* inspection by night
17:5 certainly not be *m* to totter
18:11 *m* darkness his concealment
22:15 tongue is *m* to stick to my
30:6 Never shall I be *m* to totter
30:7 *m* my mountain to stand in
31:8 You have *m* my feet stand in
33:6 the heavens themselves were *m*
37:23 have been *m* ready
39:5 have *m* my days just a few
44:12 *m* no wealth by the price for
45:8 instruments . . . *m* you rejoice
46:5 it will not be *m* to totter
60:3 *m* us drink wine sending us
62:2 not be *m* to totter very much
62:6 I shall not be *m* to totter
66:12 *m* mortal man to ride over
69:11 I *m* sackcloth my clothing
71:20 *m* me see many distresses
72:15 let prayer be *m* constantly
73:2 had nearly been *m* to slip
73:18 have *m* them fall to ruins
77:14 have *m* your strength known
78:31 men of Israel he *m* collapse
78:38 *m* his anger turn back
80:5 *m* them eat the bread of tears
80:9 *m* a clearing before it, that
80:15 son whom you have *m* strong
80:17 mankind whom you have *m*
82:5 of the earth are *m* to totter
86:9 nations whom you have *m* will
89:44 *m* him cease from his
91:9 *m* the Most High himself your
92:4 have *m* me rejoice, O Jehovah
93:1 it cannot be *m* to totter
95:5 sea, which he himself *m*
96:5 Jehovah, he has *m* the very
96:10 it cannot be *m* to totter
98:2 Jehovah has *m* his salvation
100:3 It is he that has *m* us, and
102:3 bones have been *m* red-hot
103:7 *m* known his ways to Moses
104:5 *m* to totter to time
104:19 *m* the moon for appointed

Mt 19:12 have *m* themselves eunuchs
20:12 *m* them equal to us who bore
22:2 *m* a marriage feast for his
27:12 he *m* no answer
27:29 they *m* fun of him, saying
27:31 when they had *m* fun of him
27:64 grave to be *m* secure until
27:66 went and *m* the grave secure
Mr 1:5 *m* their way out to him, and
1:41 I want to. Be *m* clean
5:34 your faith has *m* you well
6:25 and *m* her request, saying
6:56 as did touch it were *m* well
10:6 He *m* them male and female
10:52 your faith has *m* you well
11:17 have *m* it a cave of robbers
14:58 this temple . . . *m* with hands
14:58 another not *m* with hands
14:61 kept silent and *m* no reply
15:5 Jesus *m* no further answer
15:20 when they had *m* fun of him
Lu 1:66 *m* note of it in their hearts
2:15 Jehovah has *m* known to us
2:17 they *m* known the saying that
2:31 you have *m* ready in the sight
4:38 they *m* request of him for her
5:13 I want to. Be *m* clean
8:36 man had been *m* well
8:48 your faith has *m* you well
10:17 the demons are *m* subject to
10:20 spirits are *m* subject to you
10:36 *m* himself neighbor to the
11:40, 40 *m* the outside *m* also the
17:19 your faith has *m* you well
18:32 will be *m* fun of and be
18:42 your faith has *m* you well
19:18 mina, Lord, *m* five minas
19:46 you *m* it a cave of robbers
22:29 my Father has *m* a covenant
22:32 I have *m* supplication for
23:9 but he *m* him no answer
23:11 *m* fun of him by clothing
23:36 the soldiers *m* fun of him
24:28 *m* as if he was journeying
Joh 1:31 be *m* manifest to Israel
2:11 he *m* his glory manifest
3:21 works may be *m* manifest
3:29 joy of mine has been *m* full
5:11 that *m* me sound in health
5:15 Jesus that *m* him sound in
7:23 I *m* a man completely sound
9:3 be *m* manifest in his case
9:6 and *m* a clay with the saliva
9:11 Jesus *m* a clay and smeared
9:14 Jesus *m* the clay and opened
12:40 *m* their hearts hard, that
15:11 and your joy may be *m* full
15:15 I have *m* known to you
16:24 your joy may be *m* full
17:6 *m* your name manifest to the
17:26 *m* your name known to them
19:7 he *m* himself God's son
19:23 garments and *m* four parts
21:1 he *m* the manifestation in
Ac 2:14 *m* this utterance to them
2:28 *m* life's ways known to me
2:36 God *m* him both Lord and
3:7 ankle bones were *m* firm
3:12 we have *m* him walk
3:16 *m* this man strong whom you
4:9 this man has been *m* well
4:24 One who *m* the heaven and the
4:31 they had *m* supplication, the
4:35 *m* to each one, just as he
5:22 they returned and *m* report
7:13 Joseph was *m* known to his
7:41 they *m* a calf in those days
7:43 figures . . . you *m* to worship
7:48 dwell in houses *m* with hands
7:50 My hand *m* all these things
7:52 those who *m* announcement in
7:59 Stephen as he *m* appeal and
8:2 *m* a great lamentation over
9:26 he *m* efforts to join himself
9:29 *m* attempts to do away with
10:2 he *m* many gifts of mercy to
10:2 and *m* supplication to God
10:17 *m* inquiries for Simon's
11:6 I *m* observations and saw
12:19 Herod *m* diligent search for
13:32 promise *m* to the forefathers
14:9 he had faith to be *m* well
14:15 God, who *m* the heaven and
15:7 God *m* the choice among you
Ac 15:9 he *m* no distinction at all
16:5 to be *m* firm in the faith and
16:7 *m* efforts to go into Bithynia
16:15 And she just *m* us come
16:24 and *m* their feet fast in the
17:24 The God that *m* the world and
17:26 he *m* out of one man every
19:26 are *m* by hands are not gods
20:3 he *m* up his mind to return
22:26 *m* report, saying: What are
23:22 *m* these things clear to me
25:17 I *m* no delay, but the next
26:6 promise that was *m* by God
26:16 I have *m* myself visible to
27:6 and he *m* us board it
27:9 Paul *m* a recommendation
27:28 *m* a sounding and found it
27:40 they *m* for the beach
28:1 we had *m* it to safety, then
28:4 *m* it to safety from the sea
28:13 we *m* it into Puteoli on
28:25 Paul *m* this one comment
Ro 1:11 in order for you to be *m* firm
1:19 God *m* it manifest to them
1:20 perceived by the things *m*
3:7 truth . . . *m* more prominent
3:9 *m* the charge that Jews as
3:21 righteousness has been *m*
4:14 faith has been *m* useless and
6:6 body might be *m* inactive
7:4 *m* dead to the Law through the
9:22 vessels of wrath *m* fit for
9:29 been *m* just like Gomorrah
14:4 be *m* to stand, for Jehovah
15:8 verify the promises He *m* to
15:20 *m* it my aim not to declare
15:21 no announcement has been *m*
16:26 now been *m* manifest and has
16:26 has been *m* known through the
1Co 1:11 disclosure was *m* to me about
1:17 should not be *m* useless
7:37 *m* this decision in his own
9:12 we have not *m* use of this
9:15 not *m* use of a single one of
9:19 I have *m* myself the slave to
12:13 all *m* to drink one spirit
15:22 all will be *m* alive
15:36 is not *m* alive unless first
15:47 of the earth and *m* of dust
15:48 As the one *m* of dust is
15:48 so those *m* of dust are also
15:49 image of the one *m* of dust
16:17 *m* up for your not being
2Co 2:2 the one that is *m* sad by me
3:10 once been *m* glorious has
4:10 be *m* manifest in our body
4:11 *m* manifest in our mortal
5:1 a house not *m* with hands
5:10 *m* manifest before the
5:11 have been *m* manifest to God
5:11 *m* manifest also to your
5:21 he *m* to be sin for us, that
7:12 *m* manifest among you
7:14 if we have *m* any boast to
8:2 poverty *m* the riches of their
10:15 may be *m* great among you
12:9 my power is being *m* perfect
Ga 3:19 the promise had been *m*
Eph 1:9 *m* known to us the sacred
1:22 *m* him head over all things
2:1 it is you God *m* alive though
2:5 *m* us alive together with the
2:11 *m* in the flesh with hands
2:14 who *m* the two parties one
3:3 sacred secret was *m* known to
3:5 this secret was not *m* known
3:10 might be *m* known through
3:16 to be *m* mighty in the man
4:16 being *m* to cooperate through
4:23 *m* new in the force actuating
5:13 are *m* manifest by the light
5:13 being *m* manifest is light
Php 1:5 contribution you have *m* to
3:12 or am already *m* perfect, but
3:16 extent we have *m* progress
4:6 petitions be *m* known to God
Col 1:11 being *m* powerful with all
1:17 other things were *m* to exist
1:26 *m* manifest to his holy ones
2:13 God *m* you alive together
3:4 is *m* manifest, then you also
3:4 you also will be *m* manifest
3:10 *m* new according to the image
1Ti 2:1 offerings of thanks, be *m*
1Ti 3:16 He was *m* manifest in flesh
6:13 *m* the fine public
2Ti 1:10 *m* clearly evident through
Tit 1:3 *m* his word manifest in the
Heb 1:2 he *m* the systems of things
1:3 *m* a purification for our sins
2:7 *m* him a little lower than
2:9 *m* a little lower than angels
3:2 to the One that *m* him such
3:9 *m* a test of me with a trial
5:9 after he had been *m* perfect
6:13 when God *m* his promise to
7:3 been *m* like the Son of God
7:19 the Law *m* nothing perfect
8:9 the covenant that I *m* with
8:13 *m* the former one obsolete
8:13 that which is *m* obsolete
9:8 *m* manifest while the first
9:11 tent not *m* with hands, that
9:24 a holy place *m* with hands
10:14 offering that he has *m*
11:16 has *m* a city ready for them
11:22 *m* mention of the exodus of
11:34 were *m* powerful, became
11:40 not be *m* perfect apart from
12:23 who have been *m* perfect
12:27 as things that have been *m*
1Pe 1:10 careful search were *m* by the
1:20 *m* manifest at the end of the
3:18 being *m* alive in the spirit
3:21 request *m* to God for a good
3:22 powers were *m* subject to him
5:4 shepherd has been *m* manifest
2Pe 1:19 prophetic word *m* more sure
1Jo 1:2 the life was *m* manifest, and
1:2 and was *m* manifest to us
2:5 love of God . . . *m* perfect
2:28 when he is *m* manifest we
3:2 not been *m* manifest what we
3:2 whenever he is *m* manifest
3:5 *m* manifest to take away
3:8 Son of God was *m* manifest
4:9 love of God was *m* manifest
4:12 his love is *m* perfect in us
4:17 how love has been *m* perfect
4:18 not been *m* perfect in love
5:10 has *m* him a liar, because
Re 1:6 *m* us to be a kingdom, priests
5:10 you *m* them to be a kingdom
7:14 *m* them white in the blood of
8:11 these had been *m* bitter
10:10 my belly was *m* bitter
14:7 One who *m* the heaven and the
14:8 *m* all the nations drink of
15:4 decrees have been *m* manifest
17:2 *m* drunk with the wine of her
21:21 gates was *m* of one pearl
22:11 filthy one be *m* filthy still
22:11 let the holy one be *m* holy

Madly
Jer 46:9 drive *m*, O you chariots!
Na 2:4 war chariots keep driving *m*

Madman
2Co 11:23 I reply like a *m*, I am

Madmannah
Jos 15:31 Ziklag and *M* and Sansannah
1Ch 2:49 Shaaph the father of *M*

Madmen
Jer 48:2 too, O *M*, should keep silent

Madmenah
Isa 10:31 *M* has run away

Madness
De 28:28 strike you with *m* and loss
2Ki 9:20 it is with *m* that he drives
Ec 1:17 wisdom and to knowing *m*
2:12 turned to see wisdom and *m*
7:25 and the foolishness of *m*
9:3 and there is *m* in their heart
10:13 his mouth is calamitous *m*
Zec 12:4 and its rider with *m*
Lu 6:11 they became filled with *m*
Ac 26:24 is driving you into *m*
2Ti 3:9 their *m* will be very plain to
3:9 even as the *m* of those two

Madon
Jos 11:1 to Jobab the king of *M* and
12:19 the king of *M*, one

Magadan
Mt 15:39 came into the regions of *M*

Magbish
Ezr 2:30 the sons of *M*, a hundred and
Magdalene
Mt 27:56 among whom was Mary *M*
27:61 Mary *M* and the other Mary
28:1 Mary *M* and the other Mary
Mr 15:40 among them Mary *M* as well
15:47 Mary *M* and Mary the mother
16:1 Mary *M*, and Mary the mother
Lu 8:2 Mary the so-called *M*, from
24:10 *M* Mary, and Joanna, and
Joh 19:25 stake of Jesus . . . Mary *M*
20:1 Mary *M* came to the
20:18 Mary *M* came and brought
Magdiel
Ge 36:43 sheik *M* . . . sheiks of Edom
1Ch 1:54 *M* . . . the sheiks of Edom
Maggot
Job 17:14 To the *m*, My mother and my
24:20 *m* will sweetly suck him
25:6 mortal man, who is a *m*
Mr 9:48 where their *m* does not die
Maggots
Ex 16:24 nor did *m* develop in it
Job 7:5 My flesh . . . clothed with *m*
21:26 *m* themselves will form a
Isa 14:11 *m* are spread out as a couch
Magic
Ex 7:11 same thing with their *m* arts
Le 19:26 and you must not practice *m*
De 18:10 a practicer of *m* or anyone
18:14 those practicing *m* and to
2Ki 21:6 he practiced *m* and looked
2Ch 33:6 practiced *m* and used
Isa 2:6 they are practicers of *m* like
Jer 27:9 your practicers of *m* and to
Mic 5:12 no practicers of *m* will you
Magical
Isa 3:3 and expert in *m* arts, and
Ac 8:9 practicing *m* arts and amazing
8:11 quite a while by his *m* arts
19:19 who practiced *m* arts brought
Magic-practicing
Ge 41:8 all the *m* priests of Egypt
41:24 I stated it to the *m* priests
Ex 7:11 *m* priests of Egypt themselves
7:22 *m* priests of Egypt proceeded
8:7 *m* priests did the same thing
8:18 *m* priests tried to do the
8:19 the *m* priests said to Pharaoh
9:11 *m* priests were unable to
9:11 boils . . . on the *m* priests
Da 1:20 better than all the *m* priests
2:2 said to call the *m* priests
2:10 asked . . . of any *m* priest
2:27 *m* priests and the astrologers
4:7 *m* priests, the conjurers, the
4:9 the chief of the *m* priests
5:11 as chief of the *m* priests
Magistrates
Ezr 7:25 appoint *m* and judges that
Da 3:2 the police *m* and all the
3:3 the police *m* and all the
Ac 16:20 up to the civil *m*, they said
16:22 civil *m*, after tearing the
16:35 the civil *m* dispatched the
16:36 civil *m* have dispatched men
16:38 these sayings to the civil *m*
Magnificence
Lu 16:19 from day to day with *m*
Ac 19:27 even her *m* which the whole
2Pe 1:16 eyewitnesses of his *m*
Magnificent
1Ch 22:5 surpassingly *m* for beauteous
Ac 2:11 about the *m* things of God
2Pe 1:17 borne to him by the *m* glory
Magnified
Es 3:1 King Ahasuerus *m* Haman the
5:11 which the king had *m* him
10:2 with which the king *m* him
Ps 35:27 Let Jehovah be *m*, who takes
40:16 May Jehovah be *m*
41:9 has *m* his heel against me
70:4 God be *m!*—those loving your
138:2 *m* your saying even above
Mal 1:5 May Jehovah be *m* over the
Lu 1:58 Jehovah had *m* his mercy to
Ac 19:17 Lord Jesus went on being *m*
Php 1:20 be *m* by means of my body
Magnifies
Lu 1:46 Mary said: My soul *m* Jehovah
Magnify
Job 36:24 you should *m* his activity
Ps 34:3 O *m* Jehovah with me, you
69:30 will *m* him with thanksgiving
Isa 10:15 saw *m* itself over the one
42:21 *m* the law and make it
Eze 38:23 *m* myself and sanctify
Da 11:36 *m* himself above every god
11:37 over everyone he will *m*
Magnifying
Ge 19:19 *m* your loving-kindness
Magog
Ge 10:2 sons of Japheth . . . *M* and
1Ch 1:5 sons of Japheth . . . *M* and
Eze 38:2 Gog of the land of *M*, the
39:6 I will send fire upon *M* and
Re 20:8 Gog and *M*, to gather them
Magpiash
Ne 10:20 *M*, Meshullam, Hezir
Mahalaleel
Lu 3:37 son of *M*, son of Cainan
Mahalalel
Ge 5:12 Kenan . . . became father to *M*
5:13 after his fathering *M* Kenan
5:15 *M* lived on for sixty-five
5:16 *M* continued to live eight
5:17 all the days of *M* amounted to
1Ch 1:2 Kenan, *M*, Jared
Ne 11:4 *M* of the sons of Perez
Mahalath
Ge 28:9 Esau . . . took as wife *M*
2Ch 11:18 *M* the daughter of Jerimoth
Ps 53:*super* To the director over *M*
88:*super* To the director over *M*
Mahanaim
Ge 32:2 the name of that place *M*
Jos 13:26 *M* to the border of Debir
13:30 from *M* all of Bashan
21:38 *M* and its pasture ground
2Sa 2:8 to bring him across to *M*
2:12 went out from *M* to Gibeon
2:29 and finally came to *M*
17:24 he came to *M*, and Absalom
17:27 as soon as David came to *M*
19:32 while he was dwelling in *M*
1Ki 2:8 day that I was going to *M*
4:14 the son of Iddo, in *M*
1Ch 6:80 *M* with its pasture grounds
Mahaneh-dan
Jg 13:25 *M* between Zorah and Eshtaol
18:12 have called that place *M*
Maharai
2Sa 23:28 *M* the Netophathite
1Ch 11:30 *M* the Netophathite
27:13 *M* the Netophathite of the
Mahath
1Ch 6:35 son of *M*, the son of Amasai
2Ch 29:12 *M* the son of Amasai and
31:13 and *M* . . . commissioners at
Mahavite
1Ch 11:46 Eliel the *M*, and Jeribai
Mahazioth
1Ch 25:4 the sons of Heman . . . *M*
25:30 for the twenty-third, for *M*
Maher-shalal-hash-baz
Isa 8:1 stylus of mortal man, *M*
8:3 said to me: Call his name *M*
Mahlah
Nu 26:33 of Zelophehad were *M* and
27:1 daughters of Zelophehad . . . *M*
36:11 *M*, Tirzah and Hoglah and
Jos 17:3 *M* and Noah, Hoglah, Milcah
1Ch 7:18 to Ishhod and Abi-ezer and *M*
Mahli
Ex 6:19 sons of Merari were *M* and
Nu 3:20 sons of Merari . . . *M* and
1Ch 6:19 sons of Merari were *M* and
6:29 The sons of Merari were *M*
6:47 son of *M*, the son of Mushi
23:21 of Merari were *M* and Mushi
23:21 sons of *M* were Eleazar and
23:23 sons of Mushi were *M* and
1Ch 24:26 sons of Merari were *M* and
24:28 Of *M*, Eleazar, who did not
24:30 sons of Mushi were *M* and
Ezr 8:18 *M* the grandson of Levi the
Mahlites
Nu 3:33 family of the *M* and the
26:58 family of the *M*, the family
Mahlon
Ru 1:2 two sons were *M* and Chilion
1:5 *M* and Chilion, also died, so
4:9 that belonged to Chilion and *M*
4:10 the wife of *M*, I do buy for
Mahol
1Ki 4:31 and Darda the sons of *M*
Mahseiah
Jer 32:12 Neriah the son of *M* before
51:59 Neriah the son of *M* when
Maid
1Sa 20:30 son of a rebellious *m*, do I
Maiden
Ge 24:43 *m* coming out to draw water
Ex 2:8 At once the *m* went and called
Pr 30:19 an able-bodied man with a *m*
Isa 7:14 *m* herself will actually
Mt 14:11 head was . . . given to the *m*
Mr 5:41 *M*, I say to you, Get up!
5:42 the *m* rose and began walking
6:22 The king said to the *m*
6:28 and he gave it to the *m*
6:28 the *m* gave it to her mother
Maidens
Ps 46:*super* sons of Korah upon The *M*
68:25 the *m* beating tambourines
Ca 1:3 *m* themselves have loved you
6:8 and *m* without number
Maids
1Sa 25:42 with five *m* of hers walking
Maidservant
Ge 16:1 she had an Egyptian *m* and her
16:2 have relations with my *m*
16:3 took Hagar, her Egyptian *m*
16:5 gave my *m* over to your bosom
16:6 Your *m* is at your disposal
16:8 Hagar, *m* of Sarai, just where
25:12 *m* of Sarah bore to Abraham
29:24 gave to her Zilpah his *m*
29:24 his daughter, as a *m*
29:29 Laban gave Bilhah his *m*
29:29 Rachel his daughter as her *m*
30:4 she gave him Bilhah her *m*
30:7 Rachel's *m*, became pregnant
30:9 take Zilpah her *m* and to give
30:10 Leah's *m*, bore a son to
30:12 Leah's *m*, bore a second son
30:18 have given my *m* to my husband
35:25 sons by Bilhah, Rachel's *m*
35:26 sons by Zilpah, Leah's *m*
Ex 11:5 firstborn of the *m* who is at
Le 19:20 when she is a *m* designated
Ru 2:13 spoken reassuringly to your *m*
1Sa 1:18 Let your *m* find favor in
25:27 *m* has brought to my lord
25:41 *m* to wash the feet of the
28:21 *m* has obeyed your voice
28:22 obey the voice of your *m*
2Sa 14:6 *m* had two sons, and the two
14:7 risen up against your *m* and
14:12 Let your *m*, please, speak
14:15 *m* said, Let me speak
14:17 *m* said, Let the word of my
14:19 in the mouth of your *m* all
17:17 a *m* went off and told them
2Ki 4:2 Your *m* has nothing at all in
4:16 in connection with your *m*
Ps 123:2 eyes of a *m* are toward the
Pr 30:23 *m* when she dispossesses her
Isa 24:2 the *m* as for her mistress
Jer 34:9 and each one his *m*
34:10 each one his *m* go free
34:16 each one his *m*, whom you
Maidservants
Ge 12:16 *m* and she-asses and camels
20:14 *m* and gave them to Abraham
24:35 and *m* and camels and asses
30:43 flocks and *m* and menservants
32:5 sheep, and menservants and *m*
32:22 two wives and his two *m* and
33:1 children . . . to the two *m*
33:2 *m* and their children foremost

Ge 33:6 the *m* came forward, they and
De 28:68 as slave men and *m*
Ru 2:13 to be like one of your *m*
1Sa 8:16 your menservants and your *m*
2Ki 5:26 cattle or menservants or *m*
2Ch 28:10 and *m* for yourselves
Es 7:4 for mere *m*, I should have kept
Ec 2:7 I acquired menservants and *m*
Isa 14:2 as *m*; and they must become
Jer 34:11 *m* whom they had let go
34:11 as menservants and as *m*
34:16 your menservants and *m*
Joe 2:29 the menservants and on the *m*
Lu 12:45 start to beat the . . . *m*

Mail
Ex 28:32 the opening of a coat of *m*
39:23 the opening of a coat of *m*
1Sa 17:5 coat of *m*, of overlapping
17:5 weight of the coat of *m* was
17:38 with a coat of *m*
1Ki 22:34 and the coat of *m*
2Ch 18:33 and the coat of *m*, so that
26:14 coats of *m* and bows and
Ne 4:16 the bows and the coats of *m*
Isa 59:17 as a coat of *m*, and the
Jer 46:4 Clothe . . . with coats of *m*
51:3 himself up in his coat of *m*

Maimed
Ex 22:10 and it does die or get *m* or
22:14 and it does get *m* or die
Mt 15:30 people that were lame, *m*
18:8 to enter into life *m* or lame
Mr 9:43 enter into life *m* than with

Main
Jos 8:13 the people set the *m* camp
Da 11:41 *m* part of the sons of
Heb 8:1 this is the *m* point: We have

Maintain
1Ch 26:27 to *m* the house of Jehovah
Ob 12 ought not to *m* a big mouth in
2Th 2:15 stand firm and *m* your hold
Tit 3:14 also learn to *m* fine works
1Pe 2:12 *M* your conduct fine among

Maintaining
Tit 3:8 their minds on *m* fine works

Maintenance
Ge 34:29 And all their means of *m*
Nu 31:9 means of *m* they plundered
Job 5:5 snaps at their means of *m*
Ps 49:6 trusting in their means of *m*
49:10 to others their means of *m*
62:10 the means of *m* should thrive
73:12 increased their means of *m*

Majestic
Ex 15:10 sank like lead in *m* waters
Jg 5:13 came down to the *m* ones
5:25 bowl of *m* ones she presented
1Sa 4:8 from the hand of this *m* God
Ne 3:5 their *m* ones themselves did
10:29 brothers, their *m* ones
Job 28:8 The *m* wild beasts have not
41:34 king over all *m* wild beasts
Ps 8:1 how *m* your name is in all the
8:9 how *m* your name is in all the
16:3 the *m* ones, are the ones in
76:4 more *m* than the mountains of
93:4 *m* breaking waves of the sea
93:4 Jehovah is *m* in the height
136:18 proceeded to kill *m* kings
Isa 33:21 *M* One, Jehovah, will be for
33:21 no *m* ship will pass over it
42:21 the law and make it *m*
Jer 14:3 their *m* ones themselves have
25:34 wallow about, you *m* ones
25:35 escape from the *m* ones
25:36 the howling of the *m* ones
30:21 *m* one will certainly come
Eze 17:8 fruit, to become a *m* vine
17:23 fruit and become a *m* cedar
32:18 the daughters of *m* nations
Mic 2:8 strip off the *m* ornament
Na 2:5 He will remember his *m* ones
3:18 your *m* ones stay in their
Zec 11:2 the *m* ones themselves have
11:13 the *m* value with which I
Lu 9:43 at the *m* power of God

Majesty
Da 4:30 and for the dignity of my *m*
4:36 my *m* and my brightness
5:18 and the dignity and the *m*
Zec 11:3 their *m* has been despoiled
Heb 1:3 on the right hand of the *M*
8:1 of the *M* in the heavens
Jude 25 *m*, might and authority for

Majority
1Ki 18:25 because you are the *m*
Ac 19:32 *m* of them did not know the
27:12 *m* advised setting sail from
2Co 2:6 This rebuke given by the *m* is
9:2 has stirred up the *m* of them

Makaz
1Ki 4:9 the son of Deker, in *M* and in

Make
Ge 1:7 God proceeded to *m* the expanse
1:7 *m* a division between the waters
1:14 *m* a division between the day
1:16 God proceeded to *m* the two
1:18 to *m* a division between the
1:25 God proceeded to *m* the wild
1:26 Let us *m* man in our image
2:3 seventh day and *m* it sacred
2:18 I am going to *m* a helper for
3:21 God proceeded to *m* long
6:14 *M* for yourself an ark out of
6:14 *m* compartments in the ark
6:15 And this is how you will *m* it
6:16 You will *m* a *tso'har* [roof
6:16 you will *m* it with a lower
9:7 *m* the earth swarm with you
11:3 Come on! Let us *m* bricks and
11:4 let us *m* a celebrated name
12:2 and I shall *m* a great nation out
12:2 I will *m* your name great
17:5 of nations I will *m* you
17:6 And I will *m* you very, very
17:6 *m* you become nations, and
17:20 bless him and will *m* him
17:20 I will *m* him become a great
18:6 the dough and *m* round cakes
20:7 he will *m* supplication for
20:17 And Abraham began to *m*
22:2 and *m* a trip to the land of
27:4 *m* me a tasty dish such as I
27:7 *m* me a tasty dish and, ah
27:9 may *m* them up into a tasty
28:3 *m* you fruitful and multiply
32:8 remaining to *m* an escape
35:1 *m* an altar there to the
35:3 *m* an altar to the true God
39:14 to *m* us a laughingstock
39:17 to *m* me a laughingstock
40:20 *m* a feast for all his
43:16 animals and *m* preparation
47:26 *m* it a decree down to this
48:4 I will *m* you many and I will
Ex 5:5 you indeed *m* them desist from
5:7 people to *m* bricks as formerly
5:8 not *m* any reduction for them
5:16 are saying to us, *M* bricks
6:3 not *m* myself known to them
8:5 *m* the frogs come up over the
8:9 say when I shall *m* entreaty
8:22 *m* the land of Goshen upon
8:28 do not *m* it quite so far away
8:28 *M* entreaty in my behalf
8:29 indeed *m* entreaty to Jehovah
9:4 Jehovah . . . *m* a distinction
11:7 Jehovah can *m* a distinction
14:6 to *m* his war chariots ready
18:16 *m* known the decisions of the
18:20 *m* known to them the way in
18:22 So *m* it lighter for yourself
19:23 mountain and *m* it sacred
20:4 not *m* for yourself a carved
20:11 and proceeded to *m* it sacred
20:23 not *m* along with me gods of
20:23 must not *m* gods of gold for
20:24 you are to *m* for me, and you
20:25 *m* an altar of stones for me
21:19 *m* compensation only for the
21:34 is to *m* compensation
21:36 *m* compensation with bull
22:3 *m* compensation without fail
22:4 is to *m* double compensation
22:5 *m* compensation with the best
22:6 *m* compensation without fail
22:7 is to *m* double compensation
22:9 *m* double compensation to his
22:11 is not to *m* compensation
22:12 to *m* compensation to their
22:13 he is not to *m* compensation
22:14 *m* compensation without fail
Ex 22:15 he is not to *m* compensation
23:24 not *m* anything like their
23:26 *m* the number of your days
25:8 must *m* a sanctuary for me
25:9 is the way you are to *m* it
25:10 *m* an Ark of acacia wood
25:11 *m* a border of gold round
25:13 *m* poles of acacia wood and
25:17 must *m* a cover of pure gold
25:18 must *m* two cherubs of gold
25:18 *m* them on both ends of the
25:19 *m* one cherub on this end and
25:19 *m* the cherubs at its two
25:23 *m* a table of acacia wood
25:24 *m* for it a border of gold
25:25 must *m* for it a rim of a
25:25 *m* the border of gold for its
25:26 *m* for it four rings of gold
25:28 *m* the poles of acacia wood
25:29 *m* its dishes and its cups
25:29 to *m* them out of pure gold
25:31 *m* a lampstand of pure gold
25:37 *m* seven lamps for it; and
25:39 of pure gold he should *m* it
25:40 *m* them after their pattern
26:1 tabernacle you are to *m* of
26:1 embroiderer, you will *m* them
26:4 *m* loops of blue thread upon
26:5 *m* fifty loops on the one tent
26:5 fifty loops you will *m* on the
26:6 *m* fifty hooks of gold and
26:7 *m* cloths of goat's hair for
26:7 You will *m* eleven tent cloths
26:10 *m* fifty loops upon the edge
26:11 *m* fifty hooks of copper and
26:14 *m* a covering for the tent of
26:15 *m* the panel frames for the
26:18 *m* the panel frames for the
26:19 *m* forty socket pedestals of
26:22 you will *m* six panel frames
26:23 will *m* two panel frames as
26:26 must *m* bars of acacia wood
26:29 rings you will *m* of gold as
26:31 *m* a curtain of blue thread
26:31 He will *m* it with cherubs
26:33 curtain must *m* a division
26:36 *m* a screen for the entrance
26:37 must *m* for the screen five
27:1 *m* the altar of acacia wood
27:2 *m* its horns upon its four
27:3 *m* its cans for clearing away
27:3 *m* all its utensils of copper
27:4 *m* a grating for it, a network
27:4 *m* upon the net four rings of
27:6 must *m* poles for the altar
27:8 chest of planks you will *m* it
27:8 hollow chest . . . they will *m*
27:9 must *m* the courtyard of the
28:2 *m* holy garments for Aaron
28:3 must *m* Aaron's garments for
28:4 garments that they will *m*
28:4 *m* the holy garments for Aaron
28:6 *m* the ephod of gold, blue
28:11 gold is how you will *m* them
28:13 you must *m* settings of gold
28:14 As cords you will *m* them
28:15 must *m* the breastpiece of
28:15 of the ephod you will *m* it
28:15 twisted linen you will *m* it
28:22 must *m* upon the breastpiece
28:23 must *m* upon the breastpiece
28:26 *m* two rings of gold and set
28:27 *m* two rings of gold and put
28:31 *m* the sleeveless coat of the
28:33 must *m* upon the hem of it
28:36 *m* a shining plate of pure
28:39 and *m* a turban of fine linen
28:39 *m* a sash, the work of a
28:40 for Aaron's sons you will *m*
28:40 you must *m* sashes for them
28:40 *m* headgears for them for
28:42 *m* drawers of linen for them
29:2 wheat flour you will *m* them
29:13 *m* them smoke upon the altar
29:18 *m* the entire ram smoke upon
29:25 *m* them smoke upon the altar
29:37 seven days to *m* atonement
30:1 *m* an altar as a place for
30:1 acacia wood you will *m* it
30:3 must *m* a border of gold
30:4 also *m* for it two rings of
30:4 two of its sides you will *m*
30:5 must *m* the poles of acacia
30:7 *m* perfumed incense smoke

Ex 30:7 he will *m* it smoke
30:8 he will *m* it smoke
30:10 Aaron must *m* atonement
30:10 he will *m* atonement for it
30:15 so as to *m* atonement for
30:16 to *m* atonement for your
30:18 must *m* a basin of copper and
30:20 in order to *m* an offering
30:25 *m* out of it a holy anointing
30:32 you must not *m* any like it
30:35 must *m* it into an incense
30:37 incense that you will *m*
30:37 you must not *m* for
31:5 to *m* products of every kind
31:6 indeed *m* everything I have
32:1 *m* for us a god who will go
32:4 to *m* it into a molten statue
32:10 let me *m* you into a great
32:23 *M* for us a god who will go
32:30 can *m* amends for your sin
33:13 *m* me know, please, your
34:16 and *m* your sons have immoral
34:17 not *m* molten idol gods for
34:24 *m* your territory spacious
35:10 come and *m* all that Jehovah
35:29 Jehovah had commanded to *m*
35:33 to *m* ingenious products of
36:14 *m* tent cloths of goat's hair
36:19 *m* a covering for the tent
36:31 *m* bars of acacia wood, five
36:35 *m* a curtain of blue thread
36:37 *m* a screen for the entrance
37:6 to *m* the cover of pure gold
37:10 *m* the table of acacia wood
38:1 *m* the altar of burnt offering
38:9 proceeded to *m* the courtyard
38:30 *m* the socket pedestals of the
39:15 to *m* upon the breastpiece
40:27 might *m* perfumed incense
Le 1:4 for him to *m* atonement for
1:9 priest must *m* all of it smoke
1:13 and *m* it smoke on the altar
1:15 nip off its head and *m* it
1:17 must *m* it smoke on the altar
2:2 *m* it smoke as a remembrancer
2:9 must *m* it smoke on the altar
2:11 must *m* no sour dough and no
2:16 must *m* the remembrancer of
3:5 must *m* it smoke on the altar
3:11 *m* it smoke on the altar as
3:16 priest must *m* them smoke upon
4:10 *m* them smoke upon the altar
4:19 must *m* it smoke on the altar
4:20 priest must *m* an atonement
4:26 *m* all its fat smoke on the
4:26 priest must *m* an atonement
4:31 priest must *m* it smoke on the
4:31 priest must *m* an atonement
4:35 *m* them smoke on the altar
4:35 priest must *m* an atonement
5:6 priest must *m* an atonement
5:10 priest must *m* an atonement
5:12 must *m* it smoke on the altar
5:13 priest must *m* an atonement
5:16 *m* compensation for the sin
5:16 priest may *m* an atonement
5:18 priest must *m* an atonement
6:5 *m* compensation for it in its
6:7 priest must *m* an atonement
6:12 *m* the fatty pieces of the
6:15 *m* it smoke upon the altar as
6:22 one anointed . . . will *m* it
6:30 to *m* atonement in the holy
7:5 *m* them smoke on the altar as
7:7 priest who will *m* atonement
7:31 *m* the fat smoke upon the
8:3 *m* all the assembly congregate
8:15 sanctify it to *m* atonement
8:20 *m* the head and the pieces
8:34 so as to *m* atonement for you
9:7 *m* atonement in your own
9:7 *m* atonement in their behalf
9:13 *m* them smoke upon the altar
10:10 in order to *m* a distinction
10:17 *m* atonement for them before
11:24 would *m* yourselves unclean
11:43 not *m* your souls loathsome
11:43 not *m* yourselves unclean by
11:44 not *m* your souls unclean by
11:47 in order to *m* a distinction
12:7 *m* atonement for her, and she
12:8 the priest must *m* atonement
13:36 not *m* examination for
14:18 the priest must *m* atonement
Le 14:19 and *m* atonement for the one
14:20 priest must *m* atonement for
14:21 in order to *m* atonement for
14:29 in order to *m* atonement for
14:31 priest must *m* atonement for
14:53 *m* atonement for the house
15:15 *m* atonement for him before
15:30 *m* the one a sin offering and
15:30 *m* atonement for her before
16:6 must *m* atonement in behalf of
16:7 *m* them stand before Jehovah
16:9 he must *m* it a sin offering
16:10 to *m* atonement for it, so as
16:11 *m* an atonement in behalf of
16:16 *m* atonement for the holy
16:17 *m* atonement in the holy
16:17 he must *m* atonement in
16:18 *m* atonement for it, and he
16:24 *m* atonement in his own
16:25 *m* the fat of the sin
16:27 *m* atonement in the holy
16:32 *m* an atonement and must put
16:33 *m* atonement for the holy
16:33 altar he will *m* atonement
16:33 he will *m* atonement
16:34 *m* atonement for the sons of
17:6 *m* the fat smoke as a restful
17:11 *m* atonement for your souls
18:24 not *m* yourselves unclean by
18:30 not *m* yourselves unclean by
19:4 *m* molten gods for yourselves
19:22 priest must *m* atonement for
19:28 not *m* cuts in your flesh for
20:25 *m* a distinction between the
20:25 *m* your souls loathsome with
21:4 so as to *m* himself profane
21:5 they should not *m* an incision
21:9 should *m* herself profane by
22:23 you may *m* it a voluntary
23:28 *m* atonement for you before
24:18 *m* compensation for it, soul
24:21 *m* compensation for it, but
25:26 hand does *m* gain and he does
25:52 *m* a calculation for himself
26:1 not *m* valueless gods for
26:6 *m* the injurious wild beast
26:9 *m* you fruitful and multiply
26:13 bars of your yoke and *m* you
26:19 *m* your heavens like iron and
27:14 priest must then *m* a
Nu 5:8 with which he will *m* atonement
5:16 *m* her stand before Jehovah
5:18 priest must *m* the woman stand
5:19 priest must *m* her swear, and
5:21 must now *m* the woman swear
5:24 *m* the woman drink the bitter
5:26 *m* it smoke upon the altar
5:26 *m* the woman drink the water
5:30 *m* the wife stand before
6:11 *m* atonement for him, since he
6:21 vow that he may *m*, so he
6:25 Jehovah *m* his face shine
8:12 *m* atonement for the Levites
8:19 *m* atonement for the sons of
10:2 *M* for yourself two trumpets
10:2 *m* them of hammered work, and
12:6 I would *m* myself known
14:12 *m* you a nation greater and
14:25 *m* a turn tomorrow and pull
15:3 *m* a restful odor to Jehovah
15:19 *m* a contribution to Jehovah
15:20 should *m* a contribution of
15:22 case you should *m* a mistake
15:25 priest must *m* atonement for
15:28 *m* atonement for the soul
15:28 so as to *m* atonement for it
15:38 *m* for themselves fringed
16:5 *m* known who belongs to him
16:38 *m* them into thin metal
16:40 to *m* incense smoke before
16:46 and *m* atonement for them
17:5 *m* subside from against me
18:17 their fat you should *m* smoke
21:8 *M* for yourself a fiery snake
23:1 *m* ready for me on this spot
23:29 *m* ready for me on this spot
25:13 *m* atonement for the sons of
28:22 sin offering to *m* atonement
28:30 one kid . . . to *m* atonement
29:5 sin offering to *m* atonement
31:50 to *m* atonement for our souls
32:5 Do not *m* us cross the Jordan
34:29 to *m* the sons of Israel
De 2:13 *m* your way across the torrent
De 3:24 *m* your servant see your
4:9 *m* them known to your sons and
4:16 *m* for yourselves a carved
4:23 not *m* for yourselves a carved
4:25 *m* a carved image, a form of
5:8 *m* for yourself a carved image
8:3 *m* you know that not by bread
8:18 power to you to *m* wealth
9:2 Who can *m* a firm stand before
9:14 *m* you a nation mightier and
9:26 to *m* supplication to Jehovah
10:1 you must *m* an ark of wood
10:20 should *m* sworn statements
11:25 No man will *m* a firm stand
14:1 You must not *m* cuttings upon
15:1 you should *m* a release
16:13 when you *m* an ingathering
16:21 that you will *m* for yourself
17:9 you must *m* inquiry, and they
17:16 nor *m* the people go back
20:12 does not *m* peace with you
22:8 *m* a parapet for your roof
22:12 *m* tassels for yourself on
23:19 must not *m* your brother pay
23:20 *m* a foreigner pay interest
23:20 you must not *m* pay interest
24:1 and does *m* her his possession
24:5 *m* his wife whom he has taken
28:11 *m* you overflow indeed with
28:26 no one to *m* them tremble
28:29 not *m* your ways successful
28:59 *m* your plagues and the
29:9 *m* everything you will do turn
30:9 *m* you have more than enough
32:26 *m* the mention of them cease
32:35 the events . . . do *m* haste
32:39 put to death, and I *m* alive
32:43 *m* atonement for the ground
Jos 1:8 *m* your way successful and
3:7 start to *m* you great in the
5:2 *M* for yourself flint knives
7:19 *m* confession to him, and
9:2 to *m* war against Joshua and
13:6 Only *m* it fall to Israel as
22:19 *m* your way across to the
22:19 do not *m* us the ones to
22:25 your sons will certainly *m*
Jg 5:3 I shall *m* melody to Jehovah
6:19 to *m* ready a kid of the goats
6:31 ones to *m* a legal defense for
6:31 let him *m* a legal defense for
6:32 Let Baal *m* a legal defense in
6:39 *m* a test only once more with
8:24 Let me *m* a request of you
8:27 to *m* it into an ephod and to
9:18 *m* Abimelech, the son of his
9:29 *M* your army numerous and
9:33 you must *m* a dash against the
16:19 *m* him sleep upon her knees
16:25 might *m* sport before them
17:3 to *m* a carved image and a
17:5 *m* an ephod and teraphim and
20:38 *m* a smoke signal go up from
Ru 1:9 May Jehovah *m* a gift to you
1:17 *m* a separation between me
3:3 Do not *m* yourself known to the
4:11 and *m* a notable name in
1Sa 1:11 she went on to *m* a vow and
1:16 not *m* your slave girl like
2:8 To *m* them sit with nobles
2:15 they could *m* the fat smoke
2:16 *m* the fat smoke first of all
2:19 his mother would *m* for him
2:28 *m* sacrificial smoke billow
2:33 and to *m* your soul pine away
6:5 must *m* images of your piles
6:6 you *m* your heart unresponsive
6:7 now take and *m* a new wagon
6:7 *m* their young ones go back
8:12 to *m* his war instruments
11:14 there *m* the kingship anew
11:15 *m* Saul king before Jehovah
12:3 I shall *m* restoration to you
12:22 to *m* you his people
13:19 Hebrews may not *m* a sword
14:9 until we *m* contact with you
16:3 shall *m* known to you what
20:36 shot the arrow to *m* it pass
25:28 *m* for my lord a lasting
27:10 Where did you men *m* a raid
28:1 army to *m* war against Israel
29:4 *M* the man go back, and let
30:8 without fail *m* a deliverance
2Sa 2:9 *m* him king over Gilead and

2Sa 3:20 David proceeded to *m* a feast
5:8 *m* contact with both the lame
6:22 *m* myself even more lightly
7:9 *m* for you a great name
7:11 what Jehovah will *m* for you
8:13 David proceeded to *m* a name
12:6 *m* compensation with four
13:5 *m* the bread of consolation
13:7 *m* the bread of consolation
15:20 today shall I *m* you wander
21:3 what shall I *m* atonement
22:37 *m* room large enough for my
22:40 *m* those rising against me
22:50 your name I shall *m* melody
23:5 why he will *m* it grow
1Ki 1:33 *m* Solomon my son ride upon
1:37 *m* his throne greater than
1:38 *m* Solomon ride upon the
1:47 God *m* Solomon's name more
1:47 *m* his throne greater than
2:20 *M* it, my mother; for I shall
6:4 *m* windows of narrowing
6:21 *m* chainwork of gold pass
7:18 to *m* the pomegranates and
7:23 *m* the molten sea ten cubits
7:27 *m* the ten carriages of
7:38 to *m* ten basins of copper
8:33 pray and *m* request for favor
8:47 *m* request to you for favor
8:50 must *m* them objects of pity
10:12 to *m* out of the timbers of
10:16 *m* two hundred large shields
10:27 *m* the silver in Jerusalem
11:28 to *m* him overseer over all
12:1 Israel came to *m* him king
12:4 *m* the hard service of your
12:9 *M* the yoke that your father
12:10 *m* it lighter upon us
12:31 to *m* a house of high places
12:31 *m* priests from the people
12:32 *m* a festival in the eighth
12:32 might *m* offerings upon the
12:33 began to *m* offerings upon
12:33 *m* a festival for the sons
12:33 *m* offerings upon the altar
12:33 to *m* sacrificial smoke
13:1 altar to *m* sacrificial smoke
14:10 *m* a clean sweep behind the
16:21 to *m* him king, and the other
16:33 to *m* the sacred pole
17:12 and *m* something for myself
17:13 *m* me a small round cake
17:13 can *m* something afterward
18:32 and to *m* a trench, of about
19:2 *m* your soul like the soul of
21:10 *m* two men, good-for-nothing
21:21 *m* a clean sweep after you
2Ki 2:11 *m* a separation between them
2:21 I do *m* this water healthful
4:10 *m* a little roof chamber
6:2 *m* for ourselves there a
7:9 *m* report at the king's house
9:2 must come in and *m* him get
9:15 go and *m* report in Jezreel
10:5 We shall not *m* anyone king
13:7 *m* them like the dust at
16:12 the altar and *m* offerings
16:13 *m* his burnt offering and
16:15 altar *m* the burnt offering
17:11 to *m* sacrificial smoke the
17:16 *m* for themselves molten
17:16 and to *m* a sacred pole
17:17 to *m* their sons and their
17:21 to *m* Jeroboam the son of
18:23 *m* a wager, please, with my
18:31 *M* a capitulation to me
19:25 serve to *m* fortified cities
21:8 not again *m* the foot of
21:11 *m* even Judah sin with his
23:5 *m* sacrificial smoke on the
23:8 *m* unfit for worship the high
23:10 no one might *m* his son or
23:16 *m* it unfit for worship
1Ch 5:19 *m* war upon the Hagrites, and
6:49 to *m* atonement for Israel
10:13 spirit medium to *m* inquiry
11:10 to *m* him king according to
12:31 to come to *m* David king
12:38 to Hebron to *m* David king
16:8 *M* his deeds known among the
16:9 Sing to him, *m* melody to
16:10 *M* your boast in his holy
17:8 *m* for you a name like the
21:17 *m* a numbering of the people
1Ch 21:24 I shall *m* the purchase for
22:5 Let me, then, *m* preparation
22:14 you will *m* additions
23:13 *m* sacrificial smoke before
24:3 to *m* divisions of them for
27:23 to *m* Israel as many as the
28:4 to *m* me king over all Israel
29:12 ability to *m* great and to
29:14 to *m* voluntary offerings
29:17 *m* offerings voluntarily to
29:22 second time to *m* Solomon
29:23 and to *m* a success of it
29:25 *m* Solomon surpassingly
2Ch 1:15 king came to *m* the silver
3:8 *m* the house of the Most Holy
4:2 *m* the molten sea ten cubits
4:19 to *m* all the utensils that
6:24 *m* request for favor before
6:37 *m* request to you for favor
7:20 *m* it a proverbial saying and
8:13 *m* offerings according to the
9:8 *m* it stand to time indefinite
9:11 *m* out of the timbers of the
9:15 Solomon went on to *m* two
10:1 Israelites came to *m* him
10:4 *m* the hard service of your
10:9 *M* the yoke that your father
10:10 you, *m* it lighter upon us
10:14 *m* your yoke heavier, and
12:13 *m* his position strong in
14:7 *m* walls around and towers
16:14 in an ointment of special *m*
17:1 *m* his position strong over
21:4 to *m* his position strong
21:19 *m* a burning for him like
24:14 *m* utensils for the house of
25:14 to *m* sacrificial smoke
29:24 *m* atonement for all Israel
30:18 himself *m* allowance for
32:12 should *m* sacrificial smoke
32:18 *m* them afraid and to
33:14 to *m* it very high
35:4 *m* preparation by the house
35:6 *m* preparation for your
35:12 *m* a presentation to Jehovah
Ezr 9:8 to *m* our eyes shine, O our
10:11 *m* confession to Jehovah the
Ne 1:11 *m* him an object of pity
4:4 and *m* their reproach return
5:12 We shall *m* restoration, and
6:9 trying to *m* us afraid, saying
6:14 trying to *m* me afraid
6:19 Tobiah sent to *m* me afraid
8:15 *m* proclamation and cause a
8:15 branchy trees to *m* booths
8:16 *m* booths for themselves
9:2 *m* confession of their own sins
9:10 to *m* a name for yourself as
9:20 you gave to *m* them prudent
9:31 did not *m* an extermination
10:33 sin offerings to *m* atonement
13:5 *m* for him a large dining hall
13:25 and *m* them swear by God
Es 1:20 decree . . . that he will *m*
2:17 *m* her queen instead of Vashti
4:8 *m* request directly before him
5:14 *m* a stake fifty cubits high
6:9 *m* him ride on the horse in the
6:11 and *m* him ride in the public
7:7 to *m* request for his soul from
Job 4:4 giving way you would *m* firm
6:22 *m* a present in my behalf
6:24 mistake . . . *m* me understand
7:14 you *m* me start up in fright
10:9 to dust you . . . *m* me return
10:17 *m* your vexation with me
11:19 no one to *m* you tremble
12:24 *m* them wander about in an
12:25 *m* them wander about like a
13:11 *m* you start up with fright
13:23 *M* me to know my own
13:25 *m* a mere leaf . . . quiver
13:26 And you *m* me possess the
15:4 *m* fear before God to have no
18:11 *m* him start up in fright
18:12 stands ready to *m* him limp
22:3 you *m* your way blameless
22:27 You will *m* entreaty to him
24:25 who will *m* me out a liar
28:25 To *m* a weight for the wind
29:13 the widow I would *m* glad
30:23 you will *m* me turn back
31:15 One making me . . . *m* him
32:7 what should *m* wisdom known
Job 33:5 *m* reply to me, Array words
33:26 *m* entreaty to God that he
33:32 *m* reply to me; Speak, for I
34:33 *m* good for it from your
38:26 *m* it rain upon the land
40:9 can you *m* it thunder?
41:3 *m* many entreaties to you
41:19 fire *m* their escape
42:6 That is why I *m* a retraction
Ps 4:1 you must *m* broad space for me
4:8 *m* me dwell in security
5:8 *M* your way smooth before me
6:6 I *m* my couch swim
6:6 With my tears I *m* my own
7:12 will *m* it ready for shooting
7:13 arrows he will *m* flaming
7:17 *m* melody to the name of
8:2 *m* the enemy and the one taking
8:5 *m* him a little less than
8:6 *m* him dominate over the works
9:2 I will *m* melody to your name
9:11 *M* melody, you people, to
11:2 *m* ready their arrow upon the
13:3 *m* my eyes shine, that I may
17:7 *M* your acts . . . wonderful
17:13 *M* him bow down; do provide
18:28 will *m* my darkness shine
18:35 humility will *m* me great
18:36 *m* room large enough for my
18:39 *m* those rising against me
18:49 your name I will *m* melody
20:7 our God we shall *m* mention
21:6 You *m* him feel glad with the
21:12 *m* them turn their backs in
21:12 bowstrings that you *m* ready
21:13 *m* melody to your mightiness
22:19 do *m* haste to my assistance
25:4 *M* me know your own ways
25:5 *M* me walk in your truth
27:6 sing and *m* melody to Jehovah
30:4 *M* melody to Jehovah, O you
30:12 glory may *m* melody to you
32:5 I shall *m* confession over my
32:8 I shall *m* you have insight
32:9 not *m* yourselves like a horse
33:2 *m* melody to him
34:2 my soul will *m* its boast
36:11 let it not *m* me a wanderer
38:22 Do *m* haste to my assistance
40:13 to my assistance do *m* haste
45:17 will *m* mention of your name
46:4 *m* the city of God rejoice
47:6, 6 *M* melody to God, *m* melody
47:6 *M* melody to our King
47:6 melody to our King, *m* melody
47:7 *M* melody, acting with
52:1 Why do you *m* your boast over
57:7 I will sing and *m* melody
57:9 *m* melody to you among the
59:3 Strong ones *m* an attack upon
59:7 *m* a bubbling forth with their
59:11 *m* them wander about, And
59:17 to you I will *m* melody
61:8 will *m* melody to your name
64:5 *m* statements about hiding
66:2 *M* melody to the glory of his
66:4 they will *m* melody to you
66:4 will *m* melody to your name
67:1 He will *m* his face shine upon
68:4 to God, *m* melody to his name
68:10 *m* it ready for the afflicted
68:32 *M* melody to Jehovah—*Se'lah*
69:21 tried to *m* me drink vinegar
70:1 to my assistance do *m* haste
71:22 *m* melody to you on the harp
71:23 inclined to *m* melody to you
74:11 to *m* an end of us
75:9 *m* melody to the God of Jacob
78:5 *m* them known to their sons
78:27 *m* sustenance rain upon them
78:40 *m* him feel hurt in the
80:8 *m* a vine depart from Egypt
83:11 nobles, *m* these like Oreb
83:13 *m* them like a thistle whirl
85:13 *m* a way by his steppings
86:4 *M* the soul of your servant
87:4 *m* mention of Rahab and
89:1 *m* your faithfulness known
89:22 enemy will *m* exactions upon
90:3 *m* mortal man go back to
90:15 *M* us rejoice correspondingly
92:1 *m* melody to your name
94:21 *m* sharp attacks on the soul
98:4 out joyfully and *m* melody

Ps 98:5 *M* melody to Jehovah with the
101:1 O Jehovah, I will *m* melody
104:15 *m* the face shine with oil
104:17 birds themselves *m* nests
104:30 *m* the face of the ground
104:33 *m* melody to my God as long
105:1 *M* known among the peoples
105:2 to him, *m* melody to him
105:3 *M* your boast in his holy
106:2 *m* all his praise to be heard
106:5 I may *m* my boast with your
106:8 to *m* his mightiness known
106:26 *m* them fall in the
106:27 *m* their offspring fall
108:1 I will sing and *m* melody
108:3 *m* melody to you among the
109:11 let strangers *m* plunder of
113:8 To *m* him sit with nobles
119:27 *M* me understand the way of
119:32 *m* my heart have the room
119:34 *M* me understand, that I may
119:37 *M* my eyes pass on from
119:39 *M* my reproach pass away
119:73 *M* me understand, that I
119:125 servant. *M* me understand
119:135 *M* your own face shine upon
119:144 *M* me understand, that I
119:169 word, O *m* me understand
125:5 Jehovah will *m* them go away
135:3 *M* melody to his name, for
137:6 not to *m* Jerusalem ascend
138:1 I shall *m* melody to you
138:3 *m* me bold in my soul with
141:1 Do *m* haste to me
143:8 *M* known to me the way in
144:9 I will *m* melody to you
145:5 works I will *m* my concern
145:12 *m* known to the sons of men
146:2 *m* melody to my God as long
147:1 good to *m* melody to our God
147:7 *M* melody to our God on the
149:3 harp let them *m* melody to
Pr 1:23 *m* my words known to you
3:6 will *m* your paths straight
6:22 itself will *m* you its concern
6:31 *m* it good with seven times as
6:35 how large you *m* the present
10:4 is what will *m* one rich
10:9 crooked will *m* himself known
11:5 will *m* his way straight, but
14:9 who *m* a derision of guilt
18:16 gift will *m* a large opening
20:25 is disposed to *m* examination
21:5 surely *m* for advantage
24:27 *m* it ready for yourself in
25:17 *M* your foot rare at the
27:1 Do not *m* your boast about the
27:9 are what *m* the heart rejoice
27:11 *m* my heart rejoice, that I
27:11 that I may *m* a reply to him
Ec 4:12 two together could *m* a stand
7:7 may *m* a wise one act crazy
7:13 for who is able to *m* straight
Ca 1:7 where you *m* the flock lie
1:11 Circlets of gold we shall *m*
8:14 *m* yourself like a gazelle or
Isa 1:15 though you *m* many prayers, I
1:16 *m* yourselves clean; remove
3:4 *m* boys their princes, and
3:16 feet they *m* a tinkling sound
3:17 *m* the crown of the head of
5:5 *m* known to you men what I
6:10 *M* the heart of this people
6:10 *m* their very ears
7:6 *m* another king reign inside
8:11 *m* me turn aside from walking
9:10 cedars we shall *m* replacement
10:6 *m* it a trampling place like
10:12 *m* an accounting for the
10:32 day in Nob to *m* a halt
12:4 *M* known among the peoples
12:4 *M* mention that his name is
12:5 *M* melody to Jehovah, for he
13:9 *m* the land an object of
13:12 *m* mortal man rarer than
14:14 *m* myself resemble the Most
14:21 *M* ready, you men, a
14:23 *m* her a possession of
16:3 *M* your shadow just like the
17:2 no one to *m* them tremble
17:12 *m* a din just like the noise
17:13 *m* a din just like the noise
19:21 *m* a vow to Jehovah and pay
22:10 to *m* the wall unattainable
Isa 22:11 basin that you must *m*
23:16 *m* your songs many, in order
25:6 *m* for all the peoples, in
26:13 *m* mention of your name
27:5 let him *m* peace with me
27:5 peace let him *m* with me
28:9 *m* understand what has been
28:17 *m* justice the measuring
28:19 *m* others understand what
29:2 to *m* things tight for Ariel
29:16 its maker: He did not *m* me
30:30 *m* the dignity of his voice
30:30 *m* the descending of his arm
32:11 *m* yourselves naked, and
35:3 *m* the knees that are
36:8 *m* a wager, please, with my
36:16 *M* a capitulation to me and
37:26 *m* fortified cities become
40:3 *M* the highway for our God
40:9 *M* your way up even onto a
40:13 can *m* him know anything
40:14 one might *m* him understand
41:2 to *m* him go subduing even
41:15 the hills you will *m* just
41:18 *m* the wilderness into a
41:28 that they might *m* a reply
42:16 *m* the blind ones walk in a
42:21 the law and *m* it majestic
44:19 *m* into a mere detestable
45:9 its former: What do you *m?*
45:21 *M* your report and your
46:5 *m* me equal or compare me
48:1 *m* mention even of the God of
48:20 *M* it to go forth to the
49:2 *m* my mouth like a sharp
49:11 *m* all my mountains a way
49:20 Do *m* room for me, that I
49:24 the tyrant *m* their escape
49:25 will *m* their escape
49:26 will *m* those maltreating
50:2 I *m* rivers a wilderness
50:3 I *m* sackcloth itself their
51:2 bless him and to *m* him many
51:3 *m* her wilderness like Eden
51:23 used to *m* your back just
53:9 *m* his burial place even with
54:2 *M* the place of your tent
54:2 *m* those tent pins of yours
54:12 *m* your battlements of
54:15 should at all *m* an attack
56:7 *m* them rejoice inside my
57:18 and *m* compensation with
58:14 *m* you ride upon the high
61:4 *m* anew the devastated cities
63:6 *m* them drunk with my rage
63:12 *m* an indefinitely lasting
63:14 proceeded to *m* them rest
63:14 to *m* a beautiful name for
63:17 *m* our heart hard against
64:2 order to *m* your name known
65:14 *m* outcries because of the
Jer 2:3 would *m* themselves guilty
4:6 *M* provision for shelter
4:16 *M* mention of it, you people
4:30 used to *m* yourself pretty
5:10 *m* an actual extermination
6:26 *M* your mourning that for
7:3 *M* your ways and your dealings
7:5 *m* your ways and your dealings
7:18 *m* sacrificial cakes to the
7:33 nobody to *m* them tremble
9:11 *m* Jerusalem piles of stones
9:11 cities of Judah I shall *m*
9:15 *m* them drink poisoned water
10:11 gods that did not *m* the
10:22 to *m* the cities of Judah
11:13 *m* sacrificial smoke to Baal
11:15 *m* it pass over from upon
12:1 I *m* my complaint to you
13:16 actually *m* it deep shadow
16:6 anyone *m* cuts upon himself
16:6 or *m* himself bald for them
16:20 man *m* for himself gods
17:4 *m* you serve your enemies in
18:4 it looked right . . . to *m*
18:11 *m* your ways and your
18:15 they *m* sacrificial smoke to
18:15 *m* men stumble in their
18:16 *m* their land an object of
19:4 *m* this place unrecognizable
19:4 to *m* sacrificial smoke in it
19:7 *m* void the counsel of Judah
19:8 I will *m* this city an object
19:9 I will *m* them eat the flesh
Jer 19:12 to *m* this city like Topheth
20:9 not going to *m* mention of
22:6 I shall *m* you a wilderness
25:9 and *m* them an object of
25:12 I will *m* it desolate wastes
25:15 you must *m* all the nations
25:17 *m* all the nations drink to
25:18 *m* them a devastated place
26:6 *m* this house like that in
26:6 and this city I shall *m* a
26:13 now *m* your ways and your
27:2 *M* for yourself . . . yoke bars
28:13 have to *m* yoke bars of iron
29:17 *m* them like the burst-open
29:22 Jehovah *m* you like Zedekiah
29:31 to *m* you trust in falsehood
30:11 I shall *m* an extermination
30:11 I shall *m* no extermination
30:19 *m* them heavy in number
31:9 *m* them walk to torrent
31:13 *m* them rejoice away from
32:20 *m* a name for your own self
32:35 *m* their sons and their
32:37 *m* them dwell in security
33:15 *m* sprout for David a
33:18 to *m* smoke with a grain
34:5 *m* a burning for you, and
34:22 *m* a desolate waste without
35:15 and *m* your dealings good
44:17 *m* sacrificial smoke to the
44:18 *m* sacrificial smoke to the
44:19 *m* for her sacrificial cakes
44:19 order to *m* an image of her
44:25 to *m* sacrificial smoke to
46:19 *M* for yourself mere baggage
46:28 *m* an extermination among
46:28 I shall *m* no extermination
48:8 city that can *m* its escape
48:26 *M* him drunk, O men, for he
49:19 I will *m* him run away from
49:20 *m* their dwelling place
50:44 *m* them run away from her
51:2 *m* her land empty; for they
51:12 *M* strong the watch
51:12 *M* ready those lying in
51:25 *m* you a burnt-out mountain
51:27 *M* the horses come up like
51:29 *m* the land of Babylon an
51:36 and I will *m* her wells dry
51:39 and I will *m* them drunk
51:53 *m* the height of her
51:57 *m* her princes and her wise
La 2:13 What shall I *m* equal to you
3:45 You *m* us mere offscouring and
Eze 3:26 tongue I will *m* stick to the
4:9 and *m* them into bread for you
4:15 must *m* your bread upon it
5:1 *m* it pass along upon your
5:14 *m* you a devastated place and
6:14 *m* the land a desolate waste
7:16 *m* their escape and become on
7:20 *m* it to them an abhorrent
7:23 *M* the chain, for the land
12:3 *m* up for yourself luggage
14:7 to the prophet to *m* inquiry
14:15 *m* injurious wild beasts
15:8 *m* the land a desolate waste
16:2 *m* known to Jerusalem her
16:8 *m* a sworn statement to you
16:16 *m* for yourself high places
16:17 *m* for yourself images of a
16:25 began to *m* your prettiness
16:52 you *m* your sisters appear
16:63 I *m* an atonement for you
17:9 and *m* its very fruit scaly
17:17 *m* him effective in the war
17:18 He will not *m* his escape
18:31 and *m* for yourselves a new
20:5 *m* myself known to them in
20:17 did not *m* an extermination
20:26 I might *m* them desolate
20:37 I will *m* you pass under the
21:12 *m* a slap on the thigh
21:15 *m* a slaughter by the sword
21:27 a ruin, a ruin I shall *m* it
22:4 *m* you an object of reproach
24:9 also shall *m* the pile great
24:10 *M* the logs many. Kindle the
24:17 no mourning should you *m*
25:5 *m* Rabbah a pasture ground
25:10 *m* it something to possess
25:13 I will *m* it a devastated
26:4 *m* her a shining, bare
26:8 *m* against you a siege wall

Eze 26:14 *m* you a shining, bare
26:19 I *m* you a devastated city
26:21 terrors are what I shall *m*
27:5 took to *m* a mast upon you
27:31 have to *m* themselves bald
28:6 *m* your heart like the heart
28:18 *m* you ashes upon the earth
29:10 *m* the land of Egypt
29:12 *m* the land of Egypt a
29:15 I will *m* them so few as
29:19 and *m* a big spoil of it
30:12 *m* the Nile canals dry
32:14 *m* their waters clear up
32:14 shall *m* go just like oil
32:15 *m* the land of Egypt a
33:28 *m* the land a desolate waste
33:29 *m* the land a desolate waste
34:10 *m* them cease from feeding
34:15 shall *m* them lie down
34:26 *m* them and the surroundings
34:28 no one to *m* them tremble
35:3 *m* you a desolate waste, even
35:7 *m* the mountainous region of
35:9 are what I shall *m* you
35:11 *m* myself known among them
35:14 waste is what I shall *m*
35:15 same thing I shall *m* of you
36:29 the grain and *m* it abound
36:30 *m* the fruitage of the tree
37:19 actually *m* them one stick
37:22 actually *m* them one nation
38:23 *m* myself known before the
39:7 holy name I shall *m* known
39:10 *m* spoil of those who had
39:26 no one to *m* them tremble
42:20 *m* a division between what
43:11 laws do you *m* known to
43:20 and *m* atonement for it
43:26 *m* atonement for the altar
44:14 *m* them caretakers of the
44:25 may *m* themselves unclean
45:15 to *m* atonement for them
45:17 *m* atonement in behalf of
45:20 *m* atonement for the House
46:21 *m* me pass along to the four
47:3 *m* me pass through the water
48:14 should one *m* an exchange
Da 1:10 *m* my head guilty to the king
2:5 men do not *m* the dream known
2:9 *m* known to me the very dream
2:25 *m* known the interpretation
2:26 *m* known to me the dream
4:5 and it began to *m* me afraid
4:6 *m* known to me the very
4:18 *m* known to me the
5:8 or to *m* known to the king the
5:15 even to *m* known to me its
5:16 to *m* known to me its very
5:17 interpretation I shall *m*
7:16 to *m* known to me the very
7:19 to *m* certain concerning the
8:13 *m* both the holy place and the
8:16 *m* that one there understand
9:4 and to *m* confession and to say
9:15 *m* a name for yourself as at
9:22 *m* you have insight with
9:23 come to *m* report, because
9:24 *m* atonement for error, and to
11:6 *m* an equitable arrangement
11:18 *m* the reproach from him
11:18 *m* it turn back upon that one
11:39 *m* abound with glory, and
11:39 *m* them rule among many; and
12:4 Daniel, *m* secret the words
Ho 2:18 *m* them lie down in security
4:13 they *m* sacrificial smoke
6:2 *m* us alive after two days
6:2 third day he will *m* us get up
7:3 they *m* the king rejoice
10:11 I *m* someone ride Ephraim
11:6 *m* an end of his bars and
11:11 *m* them dwell in their
12:9 *m* you dwell in the tents as
13:2 *m* for themselves a molten
Joe 2:17 do not *m* your inheritance a
2:19 not *m* you anymore a reproach
2:25 will *m* compensation to you
Am 4:5 *m* a thanksgiving sacrifice
4:7 I would not *m* it rain
4:7 which I would not *m* it rain
6:2 *M* your way over to Calneh
8:5 in order to *m* the ephah small
8:5 to *m* the shekel great and to
8:9 I will *m* the sun go down at

Am 8:10 I will *m* the situation like
9:1 will *m* good his flight
9:1 no one . . . will *m* his getaway
9:14 *m* gardens and eat the fruit
Ob 4 *m* your position high like the
Jon 4:10 not toil upon or *m* get big
Mic 1:6 *m* Samaria a heap of ruins of
1:7 I shall *m* a desolate waste
1:8 *m* a wailing like the jackals
1:11 *M* your way across, O
3:9 ones who *m* even everything
4:7 *m* her that was limping a
5:1 you *m* cuttings upon yourself
6:13 *m* you sick by striking you
6:16 *m* . . . object of astonishment
Na 1:8 *m* an outright extermination
1:14 *m* a burial place for you
3:6 and I will *m* you despicable
3:15 *M* yourself heavy in numbers
3:15 *m* yourself heavy in numbers
Hab 1:3 you *m* me see what is hurtful
1:14 why do you *m* earthling man
2:15 in order to *m* them drunk
3:2 may you *m* it known
3:19 *m* my feet like those of the
Zep 1:18 he will *m* an extermination
2:13 *m* Nineveh a desolate waste
3:20 *m* you people to be a name
Zec 2:7 Zion! *M* your escape, you who
6:11 *m* a grand crown and put it
7:14 *m* the desirable land an
9:13 *m* you as the sword of a
9:17 *m* the young men thrive
10:1 *M* your requests of Jehovah
10:6 will *m* the house of Judah
10:12 *m* them superior in Jehovah
12:3 *m* Jerusalem a burdensome
12:6 shall *m* the sheiks of Judah
Mal 2:9 *m* you to be despised and low
Mt 1:19 not want to *m* her a public
2:8 *m* a careful search for the
3:3 *M* his roads straight
4:19 I will *m* you fishers of men
5:24 first *m* your peace with your
6:8 do not *m* yourselves like them
8:2 Lord . . . you can *m* me clean
10:8 *m* lepers clean, expel demons
12:16 not to *m* him manifest
12:18 justice is he will *m* clear
12:33 people *m* the tree fine and
12:33 or *m* the tree rotten and its
15:15 *M* the illustration plain to
19:11 Not all men *m* room for the
19:12 Let him that can *m* room for
19:12 Let him that can . . . *m* room
20:19 to *m* fun of and to scourge
23:15 *m* one proselyte, and when
23:15 *m* him a subject for Gehenna
26:10 to *m* trouble for the woman
27:65 *m* it as secure as you know
28:19 *m* disciples of people of all
Mr 1:3 people, *m* his roads straight
1:40 want to, you can *m* me clean
2:23 to *m* their way plucking the
3:12 them not to *m* him known
4:19 *m* inroads and choke the word
7:13 *m* the word of God invalid by
9:6 what response he should *m*
10:34 they will *m* fun of him and
14:6 Why do you try to *m* trouble
15:4 Have you no reply to *m?*
15:8 *m* petition according to what
Lu 1:76 to *m* his ways ready
3:4 people, *m* his roads straight
5:12 want to, you can *m* me clean
5:14 *m* an offering in connection
5:34 You cannot *m* the friends of
9:52 to *m* preparation for him
12:33 *M* purses for yourselves that
12:37 and *m* them recline at the
15:19 *M* me as one of your hired
15:21 *M* me as one of your hired
16:9 *M* friends for yourselves by
18:24 to *m* their way into the
20:47 for a pretext *m* long prayers
21:14 how to *m* your defense
22:29 I *m* a covenant with you
22:63 to *m* fun of him, hitting
Joh 1:23 *M* the way of Jehovah
6:15 and seize him to *m* him king
10:33 a man, *m* yourself a god
14:23 and *m* our abode with him
16:26 *m* request of the Father
17:9 I *m* request concerning them

Joh 17:9 I *m* request, not concerning
17:20 I *m* request, not concerning
17:26 and will *m* it known, in
Ac 2:4 granting them to *m* utterance
4:18 *m* any utterance or to teach
5:9 *m* a test of the spirit of
7:23 to *m* an inspection of his
7:40 to Aaron, *M* gods for us to
7:44 *m* it according to the pattern
8:24 *m* supplication for me to
9:34 Rise and *m* up your bed
9:39 Dorcas used to *m* while she
11:25 *m* a thorough search for
19:33 *m* his defense to the people
20:24 not *m* my soul of any account
23:15 *m* it clear to the military
26:2 to *m* my defense this day
26:11 force . . . to *m* a recantation
26:16 things I shall *m* you see
27:12 *m* it to Phoenix to winter
27:43 sea and *m* it to land first
Ro 1:9 *m* mention of you in my
3:3 *m* the faithfulness of God
8:11 *m* your mortal bodies alive
9:20 Why did you *m* me this way?
9:21 *m* from the same lump one
9:22 and to *m* his power known
9:23 *m* known the riches of his
9:28 Jehovah will *m* an accounting
14:1 not to *m* decisions on inward
14:4 for Jehovah can *m* him stand
14:11 every tongue will *m* open
14:13 *m* this your decision, not
15:9 to your name I will *m* melody
16:25 to him who can *m* you firm
1Co 1:8 He will also *m* you firm to
1:19 I will *m* the wisdom of the
1:20 Did not God *m* the wisdom
4:5 *m* the counsels of the hearts
6:15 *m* them members of a harlot
7:11 *m* up again with her husband
8:13 not *m* my brother stumble
9:15 *m* my reason for boasting
10:13 *m* the way out in order for
11:22 *m* those who have nothing
15:1 I *m* known to you, brothers
2Co 1:6 to *m* you endure the same
2:2 if I *m* you sad, who indeed is
5:8 *m* our home with the Lord
8:8 *m* a test of the genuineness
8:21 For we *m* honest provision
9:8 God, moreover, is able to *m*
10:5 *m* it obedient to the Christ
Ga 3:19 *m* transgressions manifest
6:12 *m* a pleasing appearance in
Eph 2:15 into one new man and *m* peace
3:9 *m* men see how the sacred
6:19 *m* known the sacred secret
6:21 *m* everything known to you
Php 1:10 may *m* sure of the more
1:22 to select I do not *m* known
2:2 *m* my joy full in that you are
2:30 *m* up for your not being here
Col 1:27 to *m* known what are the
4:4 I shall *m* it manifest as I
4:7 will *m* known to you
4:9 they will *m* known to you
1Th 1:2 *m* mention concerning all of
3:2 in order to *m* you firm and
3:10 *m* more than extraordinary
3:10 to *m* good the things that
3:12 *m* you abound, in love to one
3:13 he may *m* your hearts firm
4:11 to *m* it your aim to live
5:21 *M* sure of all things; hold
2Th 1:6 who *m* tribulation for you
2:17 and *m* you firm in every good
3:3 he will *m* you firm and keep
2Ti 3:9 will *m* no further progress
3:15 to *m* you wise for salvation
Tit 1:5 *m* appointments of older men
3:8 *m* firm assertions constantly
Phm 4 when I *m* mention of you in my
Heb 2:10 to *m* the Chief Agent of
3:6 if we *m* fast our hold on our
3:14 only if we *m* fast our hold
5:3 to *m* offerings for sins as
8:5 to *m* the tent in completion
8:5 *m* all things after their
9:9 able to *m* the man doing
10:1 *m* those who approach perfect
13:15 *m* public declaration to his
Jas 4:13 in business and *m* profits
5:8 patience; *m* your hearts firm

Jas 5:15 *m* the indisposed one well
1Pe 3:15 ready to *m* a defense before
4:18 and the sinner *m* a showing
5:10 he will *m* you firm, he
5:10 he will *m* you strong
2Pe 1:10 *m* the calling and choosing
1:15 *m* mention of these things
1Jo 1:6 If we *m* the statement: We
1:8 If we *m* the statement: We
1:10 If we *m* the statement
5:16 do not tell him to *m* request
Jude 19 the ones that *m* separations
Re 3:5 I will *m* acknowledgment of
3:9 I will *m* them come and do
3:9 *m* them know I have loved you
3:12 *m* him a pillar in the temple
10:9 it will *m* your belly bitter
11:7 *m* war with them and conquer
13:13 *m* fire come down out of
13:14 *m* an image to the wild
17:16 *m* her devastated and naked
18:17 who *m* a living by the sea

Maker
Ex 30:25 the work of an ointment *m*
30:35 work of an ointment *m*
37:29 the work of an ointment *m*
2Ki 17:29 to be a *m* of its own god
Job 4:17 be cleaner than his own *M*
32:22 my *M* would carry me away
35:10 Where is God my Grand *M*
40:19 *M* can bring near his sword
Ps 95:6 kneel before Jehovah our *M*
115:15 The *M* of heaven and earth
121:2 The *M* of heaven and earth
124:8 The *M* of heaven and earth
134:3 the *M* of heaven and earth
146:6 The *M* of heaven and earth
149:2 rejoice in its grand *M*
Pr 14:31 has reproached his *M*, but
17:5 has reproached his *M*
22:2 The *M* of them all is Jehovah
Ec 10:1 the oil of the ointment *m* to
Isa 17:7 man will look up to his *M*
22:11 look at the grand *m* of it
27:11 *M* will show it no mercy
29:16 made say respecting its *m*
44:2 your *M* and your Former
45:18 the earth and the *M* of it
51:13 Jehovah your *M*, the One
54:5 Grand *M* is your husbandly
Jer 10:12 *M* of the earth by his power
33:2 Jehovah the *M* of earth has
51:15 *M* of the earth by his power
Ho 8:14 Israel began forgetting his *M*
Am 5:8 *M* of the Kimah constellation
Heb 11:10 and *m* of which city is God

Makers
1Ch 9:30 *m* of the ointment mixture
2Ch 29:11 and *m* of sacrificial smoke

Makes
Ge 31:41 *m* twenty years for me in
Ex 30:33 who *m* an ointment like it
30:38 Whoever *m* any like it to
Le 4:13 Israel *m* a mistake and the
17:11 blood that *m* atonement by
27:2 man *m* a special vow offering
27:14 valuation the priest *m* of it
Nu 30:2 a man *m* a vow to Jehovah or
30:3 a woman *m* a vow to Jehovah
De 18:10 anyone who *m* his son or his
20:12 it actually *m* war with you
27:15 man who *m* a carved image
Jg 6:31 Whoever *m* a legal defense for
9:13 new wine that *m* God and men
2Sa 22:29 that *m* my darkness shine
22:36 your humility that *m* me
Job 9:17 *m* my wounds many for no
12:14 He *m* it shut to man, that
12:17 he *m* judges . . . go crazy
33:20 certainly *m* bread loathsome
34:3 the ear itself *m* a test of
34:24 *m* others stand up instead
35:11 he *m* us wiser than even
37:13 he *m* it produce effects
38:30 deep *m* itself compact
41:31 It *m* the very sea like an
41:32 it *m* a pathway shine
Ps 10:4 wicked one . . . *m* no search
23:2 grassy pastures he *m* me lie
29:6 he *m* them skip about like a
29:8 *m* the wilderness writhe
29:8 *m* the wilderness of Kadesh
Ps 29:9 *m* the hinds writhe with
104:15 wine that *m* the heart of
107:40 *m* them wander about in a
119:98 your commandment *m* me
146:9 wicked ones he *m* crooked
Pr 10:1 one that *m* a father rejoice
10:22 blessing . . . *m* rich
12:16 *m* known his vexation in the
12:25 word is what *m* it rejoice
13:11 is the one that *m* increase
15:1 word causing pain *m* anger to
15:20 one that *m* a father rejoice
15:30 the eyes *m* the heart rejoice
15:30 that is good *m* the bones fat
17:22 a spirit that is stricken *m*
20:11 a boy *m* himself recognized
23:5 *m* wings for itself like those
26:24 his lips the hater *m* himself
26:25 *m* his voice gracious, do not
29:3 wisdom *m* his father rejoice
29:4 a king *m* a land keep standing
Ec 3:14 that the true God *m*, it will
10:15 stupid ones *m* them weary
10:19 wine itself *m* life rejoice
Isa 4:2 Jehovah *m* sprout will come
27:9 *m* all the stones of the
40:14 *m* him know the very way of
40:29 he *m* full might abound
44:13 gradually he *m* it like the
44:17 actually *m* into a god
44:25 *m* diviners themselves act
46:6 and he *m* it into a god
55:10 and *m* it produce and sprout
61:11 *m* the things that are sown
64:2 fire *m* the very water boil
Jer 10:4 with gold one *m* it pretty
17:5 actually *m* flesh his arm
48:28 dove that *m* its nest in the
50:3 *m* her land an object of
La 2:5 he *m* mourning and lamentation
3:2 *m* to walk in darkness and not
3:11 and he *m* me to lie fallow
3:16 he *m* my teeth get broken
Da 6:7 *m* a petition to any god or man
Ho 7:1 *m* a dash on the outside
Na 1:4 rivers he actually *m* run dry
Hab 1:16 *m* sacrificial smoke to his
Mt 5:32 *m* her a subject for adultery
5:45 *m* his sun rise upon wicked
5:45 and *m* it rain upon righteous
Mr 7:37 He even *m* the deaf hear and
9:43 ever your hand *m* you stumble
9:45 if your foot *m* you stumble
9:47 if your eye *m* you stumble
Lu 24:21 this *m* the third day since
Joh 5:21 dead up and *m* them alive
5:21 Son also *m* those alive whom
8:37 my word *m* no progress among
Ac 26:14 against the goads *m* it hard
Ro 4:17 God, who *m* the dead alive
8:28 that God *m* all his works
10:10 one *m* public declaration
1Co 3:7 but God who *m* it grow
4:7 who *m* you to differ from
8:13 food *m* my brother stumble
14:7 *m* an interval to the tones
2Co 2:14 *m* the odor of the knowledge
3:6 but the spirit *m* alive
7:10 godly way *m* for repentance
Ga 2:6 *m* no difference to me—God
Eph 4:16 *m* for the growth of the body
1Th 2:4 who *m* proof of our hearts
Heb 1:7 he *m* his angels spirits, and
9:8 the holy spirit *m* it plain
Jas 2:10 *m* a false step in one point
3:5 the tongue . . . *m* great brags
1Jo 4:15 *m* the confession that Jesus
4:20 If anyone *m* the statement
Re 13:12 it *m* the earth and those
22:18 *m* an addition to these

Makheloth
Nu 33:25 and went camping in *M*
33:26 pulled away from *M* and went

Making
Ge 2:3 created for the purpose of *m*
7:4 I am *m* it rain upon the earth
24:35 *m* him greater and giving
27:12 like one *m* a mockery, and I
27:31 went about *m* a tasty dish
31:46 taking stones and *m* a heap
34:30 *m* me a stench to the
35:16 with her in *m* the delivery
35:17 difficulty in *m* the delivery
Ge 39:3 Jehovah was *m* turn out
39:23 Jehovah was *m* it turn out
48:4 Here I am *m* you fruitful, and
Ex 1:14 they kept *m* their life bitter
5:8 of bricks that they were *m*
5:14 task in *m* bricks as formerly
9:23 kept *m* it rain down hail upon
9:34 and *m* his heart unresponsive
14:21 Jehovah began *m* the sea go
29:36 your *m* atonement over it
36:8 went *m* the tabernacle, the
Le 16:20 *m* atonement for the holy
19:29 *m* her a prostitute, in order
26:6 no one *m* you tremble; and I
26:16 *m* the soul pine away
Nu 14:36 *m* the whole assembly
16:47 *m* atonement for the people
De 20:20 city that is *m* war with you
23:22 in case you omit *m* a vow
24:11 to whom you are *m* a loan
27:8 *m* them quite clear
32:13 *m* him ride upon earth's high
32:13 *m* him suck honey out of a
Jos 9:15 Joshua went *m* peace with
Jg 9:16 went *m* Abimelech king, and
17:4 he went *m* a carved image and
19:22 *m* their hearts feel good
20:33 were *m* a charge out of their
1Sa 1:6 *m* her feel disconcerted
21:13 *m* cross marks on the doors
2Sa 8:2 *m* them lie down on the earth
22:34 *M* my feet like those of the
1Ki 2:16 one request that I am *m* of
2:20 request that I am *m* of you
3:3 sacrificing and *m* offerings
9:1 that he took delight in *m*
9:25 *m* of sacrificial smoke on
11:8 *m* sacrificial smoke and
13:2 *m* sacrificial smoke upon
13:33 *m* priests of high places
14:5 be *m* herself unrecognizable
14:6 *m* yourself unrecognizable
16:3 I am *m* a clean sweep after
22:43 *m* sacrificial smoke on the
2Ki 3:16 *m* of this torrent valley
7:2 *m* floodgates in the heavens
7:19 *m* floodgates in the heavens
12:3 *m* sacrificial smoke on the
14:4 *m* sacrificial smoke on the
15:4 *m* sacrificial smoke on the
15:35 *m* sacrificial smoke on the
16:4 *m* sacrificial smoke on the
17:32 *m* for themselves from the
18:4 been *m* sacrificial smoke to
22:17 *m* sacrificial smoke to
23:5 *m* sacrificial smoke to Baal
1Ch 6:49 *m* sacrificial smoke upon the
12:38 one heart for *m* David king
14:9 *m* raids in the low plain
17:19 by *m* all the great
19:3 sake of *m* a thorough search
29:9 their *m* voluntary offerings
2Ch 1:1 kept *m* him surpassingly great
2:6 *m* sacrificial smoke before
11:22 he thought of *m* him king
13:9 *m* priests for yourselves
13:11 *m* burnt offerings smoke to
20:36 *m* ships to go to Tarshish
24:14 and for *m* offerings and
25:13 *m* raids upon the cities of
28:23 *m* him and all Israel
28:25 *m* sacrificial smoke to
30:22 *m* confession to Jehovah the
32:1 *m* them his by a breakthrough
34:25 *m* sacrificial smoke to
36:16 *m* jest at the messengers
Ezr 4:16 *m* known to the king that
5:8 is *m* progress in their hands
6:14 building and *m* progress
Ne 1:6 *m* confession concerning the
6:17 *m* numerous their letters
9:3 *m* confession and bowing down
12:42 kept *m* themselves heard
13:7 *m* for him a hall in the
13:16 *m* sales on the sabbath to
Es 9:17 a *m* of it a day of banqueting
9:18 a *m* of it a day of banqueting
9:19 *m* the fourteenth day of the
Job 1:15 Sabeans came *m* a raid and
9:6 He is *m* the earth go quaking
9:9 *M* the Ash constellation, the
12:16 belong the one *m* a mistake
12:17 is *m* counselors go barefoot
12:19 is *m* priests walk barefoot

Job 12:23 *M* the nations grow great
25:2 He is *m* peace on his heights
31:15 the One *m* me in the belly
Ps 7:15 into the hole that he went *m*
10:3 the one *m* undue profit has
18:33 *M* my feet like those of the
19:7 *m* the inexperienced one wise
19:8 clean, *m* the eyes shine
22:9 The One *m* me trust while
30:8 I kept *m* entreaty for favor
37:7 anyone *m* his way successful
37:21 showing favor and is *m* gifts
44:10 You keep *m* us turn back from
46:9 He is *m* wars to cease to the
78:26 *m* an east wind burst forth
78:26 *m* a south wind blow by his
78:28 *m* them fall in the middle
80:5 keep *m* them drink tears upon
88:*super* Mahalath for *m* responses
97:7 *m* their boast in valueless
102:8 Those *m* a fool of me have
104:3 *M* the clouds his chariot
104:4 *M* his angels spirits, His
104:14 *m* green grass sprout for
105:24 *m* his people very fruitful
113:5 is *m* his dwelling on high
115:8 *m* them will become just
119:130 *M* the inexperienced ones
135:18 Those *m* them will become
136:5 One *m* the heavens with
136:7 the One *m* the great lights
136:16 One *m* his people walk
147:8 One *m* the mountains to
Pr 1:19 everyone *m* unjust profit
6:13 *m* signs with his foot
6:13 *m* indications with his
10:9 *m* his ways crooked will make
11:18 wicked one is *m* false wages
13:12 is *m* the heart sick
15:27 The one *m* unjust profit is
16:2 Jehovah is *m* an estimate of
17:19 Anyone *m* his entryway high
19:6 companion to the man *m* gifts
21:2 is *m* an estimate of hearts
24:12 is *m* an estimate of hearts
29:1 reproved but *m* his neck hard
Ec 2:20 *m* my heart despair over all
12:12 *m* of many books there is no
Ca 2:15 foxes that are *m* spoil of our
Isa 7:11 *m* it as deep as Sheol or
7:11 *m* it high as the upper
8:19 *m* utterances in low tones
14:16 that was *m* kingdoms rock
29:7 those *m* things tight for her
38:8 I am *m* the shadow of the
43:16 the One *m* a way through the
44:14 keeps *m* it get big
44:26 *m* the word of his servant
45:7 *m* peace and creating
48:3 and I kept *m* them heard
48:15 a *m* of his way successful
48:21 he was *m* them walk even
50:11 *m* sparks light up, walk in
54:15 is *m* an attack upon you
57:9 *m* your ointments abundant
58:4 *m* your voice to be heard in
62:6 are *m* mention of Jehovah
63:12 *m* His beautiful arm go at
63:13 One *m* them walk through
63:17 *m* us wander from your ways
65:3 and *m* sacrificial smoke upon
65:16 *m* a sworn statement in the
66:22 the new earth that I am *m*
Jer 1:16 keep *m* sacrificial smoke to
2:15 went *m* his land an object of
5:14 *m* my words in your mouth
6:13 *m* for himself unjust gain
6:27 one *m* a thorough search
7:9 *m* sacrificial smoke to Baal
8:10 each one is *m* unjust gain
9:15 I am *m* them, that is, this
11:12 are *m* sacrificial smoke
11:17 *m* sacrificial smoke to Baal
17:11 the one *m* riches, but not
18:4 the vessel that he was *m*
18:4 *m* it into another vessel
20:4 I am *m* you a fright to
21:2 Babylon is *m* war against us
23:13 they keep *m* my people
23:15 I am *m* them eat wormwood
23:16 They are *m* you become vain
23:27 thinking of *m* my people
32:35 purpose of *m* Judah sin
33:12 are *m* the flock lie down
Jer 44:3 *m* sacrificial smoke and
44:5 *m* sacrificial smoke to other
44:8 *m* sacrificial smoke to other
44:15 their wives had been *m*
44:19 *m* sacrificial smoke to the
46:14 *m* preparation also for
47:5 keep *m* cuts upon yourself
48:19 her that is *m* her escape
48:35 *m* sacrificial smoke to his
50:10 those *m* spoil of her will
50:26 just like those *m* heaps
51:7 she *m* all the earth drunk
51:13 measure of your profit *m*
La 3:36 *m* a man crooked in his legal
Eze 13:18 *m* veils upon the head of
13:22 *m* the hands of a wicked one
16:21 by *m* them pass through the
16:24 *m* for yourself a height in
16:26 *m* your prostitution abound
16:29 *m* your prostitution abound
16:51 *m* your detestable things
20:31 *m* your sons pass through
21:14 is *m* an encirclement of
22:12 *m* gain of your companions
22:27 purpose of *m* unjust gain
23:46 a *m* of them a frightful
24:26 one for *m* the ears hear
28:2 keep *m* your heart like
34:6 with no one *m* a search and
36:17 kept *m* it unclean with
39:10 had been *m* spoil of them
39:14 they will keep *m* search
43:23 *m* an end of the purifying
45:20 of any man *m* a mistake
Da 4:7 they were not *m* known to me
6:13 in a day he is *m* his petition
8:4 the ram *m* thrusts to the west
11:6 one *m* her strong in those
11:14 try *m* a vision come true
Ho 2:13 she kept *m* sacrificial smoke
10:4 *m* false oaths, concluding a
11:2 began *m* sacrificial smoke
12:10 prophets I kept *m* likenesses
Am 2:4 lies . . . kept *m* them wander
2:10 I kept *m* you walk through
2:13 *m* what is under you sway
4:10 *m* the stink of your camps
4:13 One *m* dawn into obscurity
6:10 *m* any mention of the name of
Mic 2:13 one *m* a breakthrough will
4:4 no one *m* them tremble
Na 2:11 no one was *m* them tremble
Hab 2:6 *m* debt heavy against himself
2:9 is *m* evil gain for his house
2:18 *m* valueless gods that are
Zep 1:5 *m* sworn oaths to Jehovah and
1:5 *m* sworn oaths by Malcam
3:7 *m* all their dealings ruinous
3:13 be no one *m* them tremble
Zec 5:3 everyone *m* a sworn oath
5:4 the one *m* a sworn oath in
8:14 forefathers' *m* me indignant
10:1 Jehovah who is *m* the storm
12:2 *m* Jerusalem a bowl causing
Mal 1:14 *m* a vow and sacrificing a
Mt 5:29 *m* you stumble, tear it out
5:30 hand is *m* you stumble, cut
6:2 when you go *m* gifts of mercy
6:3 when *m* gifts of mercy, do not
18:8 your foot is *m* you stumble
18:9 if your eye is *m* you stumble
21:13 are *m* it a cave of robbers
27:41 *m* fun of him and saying
Mr 8:32 he was *m* that statement
12:35 when *m* a reply, Jesus began
12:40 a pretext *m* long prayers
15:31 chief priests were *m* fun
15:45 after *m* certain from the
Lu 1:22 he kept *m* signs to them, but
2:45 *m* a diligent search for him
11:7 Quit *m* me trouble
18:5 continually *m* me trouble
21:36 all the time *m* supplication
Joh 2:15 *m* a whip of ropes, he drove
2:16 Stop *m* the house of my
4:1 Jesus was *m* and baptizing
5:18 *m* himself equal to God
19:12 *m* himself a king speaks
Ac 14:21 and *m* quite a few disciples
15:10 *m* a test of God by imposing
19:24 *m* silver shrines of Artemis
21:13 and *m* me weak at heart
28:18 after *m* an examination
Ro 12:2 by *m* your mind over, that you
Ro 14:19 things *m* for peace and the
1Co 3:6 but God kept *m* it grow
7:31 those *m* use of the world as
10:25 *m* no inquiry on account of
10:27 *m* no inquiry on account of
12:11 *m* a distribution to each
2Co 4:2 but by *m* the truth manifest
5:9 we are also *m* it our aim
5:20 God were *m* entreaty through
6:10 as poor but *m* many rich, as
10:13 *m* it reach even as far as
12:19 been *m* our defense to you
Ga 1:14 *m* greater progress in Judaism
6:17 no one be *m* trouble for me
Eph 5:10 Keep on *m* sure of what is
Col 1:20 by *m* peace through the blood
1Ti 1:7 they are *m* strong assertions
6:21 *m* a show of such knowledge
Tit 3:5 *m* of us new by holy spirit
Heb 3:8 *m* the test in the wilderness
12:13 keep *m* straight paths for
Jas 3:17 not *m* partial distinctions
3:18 for those who are *m* peace
2Pe 2:16 *m* utterance with the voice
1Jo 1:10 we are *m* him a liar, and
Jude 3 *m* every effort to write you
Re 21:5 Look! I am *m* all things new

Makkedah
Jos 10:10 as far as Azekah and *M*
10:16 hiding . . . in the cave at *M*
10:17 hidden in the cave at *M*
10:21 to Joshua, at *M* in peace
10:28 Joshua captured *M* on that
10:28 So he did to the king of *M*
10:29 passed on from *M* to Libnah
12:16 the king of *M*, one
15:41 Beth-dagon and Naamah and *M*

Maktesh
Zep 1:11 Howl, you inhabitants of *M*

Malachi
Mal 1:1 The word . . . by means of *M*

Maladies
Ex 15:26 put none of the *m* upon you
De 29:22 of that land and its *m* with
2Ch 21:19 gradually died in his bad *m*
Ps 103:3 Who is healing all your *m*
Jer 14:18 the *m* from the famine
16:4 deaths from *m* they will die

Malady
Ex 23:25 turn *m* away from your midst
1Ki 8:37 plague, any sort of *m*
2Ch 6:28 and any sort of *m*
21:15 *m* of your intestines, until
Pr 18:14 a man can put up with his *m*

Malcam
2Sa 12:30 crown of *M* off its head
1Ch 8:9 and Zibia and Mesha and *M*
20:2 David took the crown of *M*
Jer 49:1 *M* has taken possession of
49:3 *M* himself will go even into
Zep 1:5 making sworn oaths by *M*

Malchiah
Jer 21:1 Pashhur the son of *M* and

Malchiel
Ge 46:17 sons of Beriah were . . . *M*
Nu 26:45 of *M* the family of the
1Ch 7:31 of Beriah were Heber and *M*

Malchielites
Nu 26:45 the family of the *M*

Malchijah
1Ch 6:40 of Baaseiah, the son of *M*
9:12 son of Pashhur the son of *M*
24:9 for *M* the fifth, for
Ezr 10:25 Izziah and *M* and Mijamin
10:25 Eleazar and *M* and Benaiah
10:31 the sons of Harim . . . *M*
Ne 3:11 *M* the son of Harim and
3:14 *M* the son of Rechab, a prince
3:31 *M*, a member of the goldsmith
8:4 Mishael and *M* and Hashum
10:3 Pashhur, Amariah, *M*
11:12 Pashhur the son of *M*
12:42 and *M* and Elam and Ezer
Jer 38:1 Pashhur the son of *M* got to
38:6 cistern of *M* the son of the

Malchiram
1Ch 3:18 and *M* and Pedaiah and

Malchi-shua
1Sa 14:49 the sons of Saul . . . *M*, and
31:2 Abinadab and *M*, Saul's sons
1Ch 8:33 father to Jonathan and *M* and
9:39 father to Jonathan and *M* and
10:2 Abinadab and *M*, sons of Saul

Malchus
Joh 18:10 name of the slave was *M*

Male
Ge 1:27 *m* and female he created them
5:2 *M* and female he created them
6:19 *M* and female they will be
7:3 *m* and female, to preserve
7:9 inside the ark, *m* and female
7:16 *m* and female of every sort of
17:10 Every *m* of yours must get
17:12 every *m* of yours eight days
17:14 *m* who will not get the
17:23 every *m* among the men of
34:15 become like us, by every *m*
34:22 every *m* . . . gets circumcised
34:25 to go . . . and to kill every *m*
37:31 slaughtered a *m* goat and
Ex 1:17 preserve the *m* children
1:18 that you preserved the *m*
12:5 sound, a *m*, a year old, for
12:48 a circumcising of every *m* of
13:2 Sanctify to me every *m*
23:17 every *m* of yours will appear
34:19 the *m* firstling of bull and
34:23 every *m* of yours is to appear
Le 1:3 offering from the herd, a *m*
1:10 the goats, a *m*, a sound one
1:14 turtledoves or the *m* pigeons
3:1 herd, whether a *m* or a female
3:6 a *m* or a female, a sound one
4:23 offering a *m* kid of the goats
5:7 or two *m* pigeons to Jehovah
5:11 turtledoves or two *m* pigeons
6:18 Every *m* among the sons of
6:29 Every *m* among the priests
7:6 Every *m* among the priests
9:3 a *m* goat for a sin offering
12:2 seed and does bear a *m*, she
12:6 a *m* pigeon or a turtledove
12:7 bears either a *m* or a female
12:8 two *m* pigeons, one for a
14:22 turtledoves or two *m* pigeons
14:30 or of the *m* pigeons for
15:14 or two *m* pigeons, and he
15:29 or two *m* pigeons, and she
15:33 whether a *m* or a female, and
16:5 two *m* kids of the goats for a
18:22 not lie down with a *m* the
20:13 man lies down with a *m* the
22:19 must be sound, a *m* among the
23:18 seven sound *m* lambs, each a
23:19 two *m* lambs, each a year old
23:20 two *m* lambs. They should
27:3 *m* from twenty years old up to
27:5 value of the *m* must then
27:6 value of the *m* must then
27:7 *m*, the estimated value must
Nu 3:15 Every *m* from a month old
5:3 *m* or a female you should send
6:10 *m* pigeons to the priest to
7:15 one *m* lamb in its first year
7:17 five *m* lambs each a year old
7:21 one *m* lamb in its first year
7:23 five *m* lambs each a year old
7:27 *m* lamb in its first year, for
7:29 sacrifice . . . five *m* lambs
7:33 *m* lamb . . . burnt offering
7:35 sacrifice . . . five *m* lambs
7:39 *m* lamb . . . burnt offering
7:41 sacrifice . . . five *m* lambs
7:45 *m* lamb . . . burnt offering
7:47 sacrifice . . . five *m* lambs
7:51 *m* lamb . . . burnt offering
7:53 sacrifice . . . five *m* lambs
7:57 *m* lamb . . . burnt offering
7:59 sacrifice . . . five *m* lambs
7:63 *m* lamb . . . burnt offering
7:65 sacrifice . . . five *m* lambs
7:69 *m* lamb . . . burnt offering
7:71 sacrifice . . . five *m* lambs
7:75 *m* lamb . . . burnt offering
7:77 sacrifice . . . five *m* lambs
7:81 *m* lamb . . . burnt offering
7:83 sacrifice . . . five *m* lambs
7:87 burnt offering . . . *m* lambs
7:88 sacrifice . . . sixty *m* lambs
Nu 11:12 as the *m* nurse carries the
15:5 the sacrifice of each *m* lamb
15:8 render up a *m* of the herd as
15:9 with the *m* of the herd a
15:11 one head among the *m* lambs
16:15 Not one *m* ass have I taken
18:10 Every *m* should eat it
18:17 or firstborn *m* lamb or
28:3 two sound year-old *m* lambs a
28:4 one *m* lamb you will render
28:4 other *m* lamb you will render
28:7 a hin to each *m* lamb
28:8 render up the other *m* lamb
28:9 two sound year-old *m* lambs
28:11 seven sound *m* lambs each a
28:13 offering . . . for each *m* lamb
28:14 fourth of a hin for a *m* lamb
28:19 seven *m* lambs each a year
28:21 for each *m* lamb of the seven
28:21 lamb of the seven *m* lambs
28:27 seven *m* lambs each a year
28:29 for each *m* lamb of the seven
28:29 lamb of the seven *m* lambs
29:2 seven *m* lambs each a year old
29:4 for each *m* lamb of the seven
29:4 lamb of the seven *m* lambs
29:5 one *m* kid of the goats as a
29:8 seven *m* lambs each a year old
29:10 for each *m* lamb of the seven
29:10 of the seven *m* lambs
29:13 fourteen *m* lambs each a year
29:15 measure for each *m* lamb of
29:15 of the fourteen *m* lambs
29:17 fourteen *m* lambs each a year
29:18 offerings for . . . *m* lambs
29:20 fourteen *m* lambs each a year
29:21 the *m* lambs by their number
29:23 fourteen *m* lambs each a year
29:24 offerings for . . . *m* lambs
29:26 fourteen *m* lambs each a year
29:27 offerings for . . . *m* lambs
29:29 fourteen *m* lambs each a year
29:30 offerings for . . . *m* lambs
29:32 fourteen *m* lambs each a year
29:33 offerings for . . . *m* lambs
29:36 seven *m* lambs each a year
29:37 the *m* lambs by their number
31:7 proceeded to kill every *m*
31:17 now kill every *m* among the
31:17 by lying with a *m*
31:18 the act of lying with a *m*
31:35 the act of lying with a *m*
De 4:16 representation of *m* or female
7:14 a *m* or a female without
15:19 Every *m* firstborn that will
16:16 every *m* of yours should
20:13 you must strike every *m* in
23:1 having his *m* member cut off
32:14 And *m* sheep, the breed of
Jg 14:6 someone tears a *m* kid in two
15:15 a moist jawbone of a *m* ass
15:16 jawbone of a *m* ass—one heap
15:16 jawbone of a *m* ass I have
21:11 Every *m* and every woman
21:11 experienced lying with a *m*
21:12 by lying with a *m*
1Sa 1:11 give to your slave girl a *m*
2Sa 19:35 *m* and female singers
1Ki 11:15 strike down every *m* in Edom
11:16 cut off every *m* in Edom
14:24 the *m* temple prostitute
15:12 the *m* temple prostitutes
22:46 the *m* temple prostitutes
2Ki 3:4 thousand unshorn *m* sheep
23:7 the *m* temple prostitutes
1Ch 29:21 a thousand *m* lambs and
2Ch 29:21 seven *m* lambs . . . offering
29:21 seven *m* goats . . . offering
29:22 slaughtered the *m* lambs and
29:23 *m* goats of the sin offering
29:32 two hundred *m* lambs
31:19 every *m* among the priests
35:7, 7 *m* lambs and *m* kids
35:25 *m* singers and female
Ezr 2:65 two hundred *m* singers and
6:17 twelve *m* goats, according to
8:35 seventy-seven *m* lambs
Ne 7:67 *m* singers and female singers
Job 21:11 own *m* children go skipping
24:3 the *m* ass of fatherless boys
36:14 among *m* temple prostitutes
Ec 2:8 I made *m* singers and female
Isa 1:11 *m* lambs and he-goats I have
5:17 *m* lambs will actually graze
Isa 11:6 for a while with the *m* lamb
57:8 The *m* organ you beheld
60:6 young *m* camels of Midian
66:7 deliverance to a *m* child
Jer 11:19 I was like a *m* lamb, an
20:15 born to you a son, a *m*
30:6 whether a *m* is giving birth
51:40 them down like *m* sheep
Eze 16:17 for yourself images of a *m*
23:20 fleshly member of *m* asses
23:20 genital organ of *m* horses
27:21 In *m* lambs and rams and
39:18 rams, young *m* sheep, and
46:4 six sound *m* lambs and a
46:5 for the *m* lambs a grain
46:6 and six *m* lambs and a ram
46:7 *m* lambs according to what
46:11 *m* lambs as he is able to
46:13 sound *m* lamb, in its first
46:15 provide the *m* lamb and the
Da 8:5 *m* of the goats coming from the
8:8 *m* of the goats, for its part
Joe 3:3 the *m* child for a prostitute
Zec 14:15 the camel, and the *m* ass
Mal 1:14 in his drove a *m* animal
Mt 19:4 made them *m* and female
Mr 10:6 He made them *m* and female
Lu 2:23 Every *m* opening a womb must
Ga 3:28 is neither *m* nor female; for
Re 12:5 *m*, who is to shepherd all
12:13 gave birth to the *m* child

Malediction
Ge 27:12 bring upon myself a *m* and
27:13 Upon me be the *m* meant for
De 11:26 blessing and *m*
11:28 *m*, if you will not obey the
11:29 and the *m* upon Mount Ebal
23:5 changed the *m* into a blessing
27:13 for the *m* on Mount Ebal
29:27 whole *m* written in this book
30:1 the blessing and the *m*, which
30:19 the blessing and the *m*; and
Jos 8:34 the blessing and the *m*
Jg 9:57 the *m* of Jotham the son of
2Sa 16:12 goodness instead of his *m*
1Ki 2:8 upon me with a painful *m*
2Ki 22:19 of astonishment and a *m*
Ne 13:2 the *m* into a benediction
Ps 109:17 he kept loving the *m*, so
109:18 clothed with *m* as his
109:28 their part, pronounce a *m*
Pr 26:2 *m* itself does not come
27:14 as a *m* it will be accounted
Jer 24:9 for a taunt and for a *m*
25:18 to whistle at and a *m*
26:6 this city I shall make a *m*
29:22 a *m* will certainly be taken
42:18 *m* and a reproach, and you
44:8 your becoming a *m* and a
44:12 and a *m* and a reproach
44:22 and a *m*, without an
49:13 *m* will Bozrah become
Zec 8:13 a *m* among the nations

Maledictions
De 28:15 all these *m* must also come
28:45 these *m* will certainly come

Males
Ge 34:24 all the *m* got circumcised
Ex 13:12 The *m* belong to Jehovah
13:15 the *m* that open the womb
Nu 1:2 all the *m*, head by head of
1:20 *m* from twenty years old
1:22 *m* from twenty years old
3:22 all *m* from a month old upward
3:28 all the *m* from a month old
3:34 the *m* from a month old upward
3:39 *m* from a month old upward
3:40 firstborn *m* of the sons of
3:43 firstborn *m* by the number of
26:62 all *m* from a month old and
Jos 5:4 the *m*, all the men of war, had
17:2 the *m* according to their
2Ch 31:16 enrollment of the *m* from
Ezr 8:3 a hundred and fifty *m*
8:4 and with him two hundred *m*
8:5 and with him three hundred *m*
8:6 and with him fifty *m*
8:7 and with him seventy *m*
8:8 and with him eighty *m*
8:9 two hundred and eighteen *m*
8:10 a hundred and sixty *m*
8:11 and with him twenty-eight *m*

Ezr 8:12 a hundred and ten *m*
8:13 and with them sixty *m*
8:14 and with them seventy *m*
Ro 1:27 *m* left the natural use of the
1:27, 27 *m* with *m*, working what
1Ti 1:10 men who lie with *m*

Malicious
Ro 1:29 deceit, *m* disposition, being
Eph 4:31 Let all *m* bitterness and

Malignant
Le 13:51 the plague is *m* leprosy
13:52 it is *m* leprosy. It should
14:44 it is *m* leprosy in the house
De 28:35 strike you with a *m* boil
28:59 *m* and long-lasting sicknesses
Job 2:7 and struck Job with a *m* boil
Eze 28:24 a *m* prickle or a painful
Re 16:2 hurtful and *m* ulcer came to

Mallet
Jg 5:26 to the *m* of hard workers

Mallothi
1Ch 25:4 the sons of Heman . . . *M*
25:26 for the nineteenth, for *M*

Mallows
2Ki 4:39 to the field to pick *m*
Isa 26:19 dew is as the dew of *m*

Malluch
1Ch 6:44 son of Abdi, the son of *M*
Ezr 10:29 the sons of Bani . . . *M*
10:32 Benjamin, *M* and Shemariah
Ne 10:4 Hattush, Shebaniah, *M*
10:27 *M*, Harim, Baanah
12:2 Amariah, *M*, Hattush

Malluchi
Ne 12:14 for *M*, Jonathan; for

Malta
Ac 28:1 that the island was called *M*

Maltreat
Ex 22:21 not *m* an alien resident or
De 23:16 You must not *m* him
Jer 22:3 do not *m* any alien resident
Eze 18:7 and no man would he *m*
45:8 my chieftains *m* my people

Maltreated
Eze 18:12 and poor one he has *m*
18:16 no man has he *m*, no pledge
22:7 and widow they have *m* in
22:29 the poor one they have *m*

Maltreating
Pr 19:26 He that is *m* a father and
Isa 49:26 make those *m* you eat their
Jer 25:38 because of the *m* sword and
46:16 because of the *m* sword
50:16 Because of the *m* sword they

Mamre
Ge 13:18 among the big trees of *M*
14:13 big trees of *M* the Amorite
14:24 Eshcol and *M*—let them
18:1 among the big trees of *M*
23:17 which is in front of *M*
23:19 of Machpelah in front of *M*
25:9 that is in front of *M*
35:27 to *M*, to Kiriath-arba, that
49:30 *M* in the land of Canaan, the
50:13 the field . . . in front of *M*

Man
Ge 1:26 Let us make *m* in our image
1:27 God proceeded to create the *m*
2:5 no *m* to cultivate the ground
2:7 God proceeded to form the *m*
2:7 the *m* came to be a living soul
2:8 there he put the *m* whom he
2:15 God proceeded to take the *m*
2:16 laid this command upon the *m*
2:18 It is not good for the *m* to
2:19 began bringing them to the *m*
2:19 whatever the *m* would call it
2:20 *m* was calling the names of
2:20 for *m* there was found no
2:21 a deep sleep fall upon the *m*
2:22 the rib . . . taken from the *m*
2:22 and to bring her to the *m*
2:23 Then the *m* said: This is at
2:23 Because from *m* this one was
2:24 That is why a *m* will leave
2:25 continued to be naked, the *m*
3:8 *m* and his wife went . . . hiding
Ge 3:9 God kept calling to the *m* and
3:12 *m* went on to say: The woman
3:22 Here the *m* has become like
3:24 he drove the *m* out and
4:1 I have produced a *m* with the
4:23 A *m* I have killed for
4:23 Yes, a young *m* for giving me
5:2 called their name *M* in the
6:3 spirit shall not act toward *m*
6:5 badness of *m* was abundant in
6:7 from *m* to domestic animal
6:9 Noah was a righteous *m*
7:23 *m* to beast, to moving animal
8:21 inclination of the heart of *m*
9:5 from the hand of *m*, from the
9:5 shall I ask back the soul of *m*
9:6 shedding man's blood, by *m*
9:6 for in God's image he made *m*
13:16 *m* could be able to count the
14:13 a *m* who had escaped came
15:2 is a *m* of Damascus, Eliezer
15:4 This *m* will not succeed you
16:12 will become a zebra of a *m*
17:13 Every *m* born in your house
17:13 *m* purchased with money of
17:17 Will a *m* a hundred years old
18:10 and it was behind the *m*
18:25 put to death the righteous *m*
18:25 righteous *m* as it does with
19:4 from boy to old *m*, all the
19:8 had intercourse with a *m*
19:9 lone *m* came here to reside as
19:9 in on the *m*, on Lot, and were
19:14 like a *m* who was joking
19:31 not a *m* in the land to have
24:16 and no *m* had had sexual
24:21 *m* was gazing at her in wonder
24:22 *m* took a gold nose ring of a
24:26 *m* proceeded to bow down and
24:29 the *m* who was outside at the
24:30 *m* spoke to me, then he came
24:30 then he came to the *m* and
24:32 *m* came on into the house
24:58 Will you go with this *m?*
24:61 and following the *m;* and the
24:65 Who is that *m* there walking
25:27 Esau became a *m* knowing how
25:27 a *m* of the field, but Jacob
25:27 Jacob a blameless *m*, dwelling
26:11 Anybody touching this *m* and
26:13 the *m* became great and went
27:11 Esau my brother is a hairy *m*
27:11 and I am a smooth *m*
29:19 to give her to another *m*
30:43 the *m* went on increasing
31:50 there is no *m* with us
32:24 a *m* began to grapple with
34:14 give our sister to a *m* who
34:19 the young *m* did not delay to
37:15 a *m* found him and here he
37:15 the *m* inquired of him
37:17 the *m* continued: They have
38:1 he pitched his tent near a *m*
38:25 the *m* to whom these belong
39:2 turned out a successful *m* and
39:14 He brought to us a *m*, a
41:12 a young *m*, a Hebrew, a
41:33 a *m* discreet and wise and
41:38 Can another *m* be found like
41:44 no *m* may lift up his hand or
42:6 Joseph was the *m* in power
42:11 all of us sons of but one *m*
42:13 We are the sons of but one *m*
42:30 The *m* who is the lord of the
42:33 the *m* who is the lord of the
43:3 The *m* unmistakably bore
43:5 the *m* did say to us, You must
43:6 by telling the *m* you had
43:7 The *m* directly inquired
43:11 to the *m* as a gift: a little
43:13 get up, return to the *m*
43:14 give you pity before the *m*
43:16 the *m* who was over his house
43:17 the *m* did just as Joseph had
43:17 *m* took the men to Joseph's
43:19 the *m* who was over Joseph's
43:24 the *m* brought the men into
43:27 Is your father, the aged *m*
44:1 the *m* who was over his house
44:4 the *m* who was over his house
44:15 a *m* as I am can expertly
44:17 The *m* in whose hand the cup
Ex 1:1 each *m* and his household came
2:1 a certain *m* of the house of
Ex 2:20 you have left the *m* behind
2:21 to dwell with the *m*, and he
4:11 Who appointed a mouth for *m*
8:17 gnats came to be on *m* and
8:18 gnats came to be on *m* and
9:9 boils . . . upon *m* and beast in
9:10 breaking out on *m* and beast
9:19 any *m* and beast that will be
9:22 hail . . . upon *m* and beast and
9:25 from *m* to beast, and all
10:7 *m* prove to be as a snare to
11:2 ask every *m* of his companion
11:3 *m* Moses too was very great
11:7 from *m* to beast; in order
12:12 firstborn . . . *m* to beast
12:44 any slave *m* purchased with
12:48 no uncircumcised *m* may eat
13:13 redeem . . . firstborn of *m*
13:15 from the firstborn of *m* to
19:13 beast or *m*, he will not live
20:10 your slave *m* nor your slave
20:17 nor his slave *m* nor his
21:7 in case a *m* should sell his
21:12 One who strikes a *m* so that
21:14 *m* becomes heated against his
21:16 And one who kidnaps a *m* and
21:20 case a *m* strikes his slave
21:20 strikes his slave *m* or his
21:26 in case a *m* should strike
21:26 of his slave *m* or the eye of
21:27 the tooth of his slave *m* or
21:28 bull should gore a *m* or a
21:29 put a *m* or a woman to death
21:32 If it was a slave *m* or a
21:33 case a *m* should open a pit
21:33 a *m* should excavate a pit
22:1 case a *m* should steal a bull
22:5 If a *m* causes a field or a
22:7 In case a *m* should give his
22:10 In case a *m* should give his
22:16 *m* seduces a virgin who is
23:6 poor *m* in his controversy
25:2 every *m* whose heart incites
32:1 Moses, the *m* who led us up
32:23 Moses, the *m* who led us up
33:11 just as a *m* would speak to
33:20 no *m* may see me and yet live
35:29 *m* and woman whose hearts
36:1 every wise-hearted *m* to whom
36:2 wise-hearted *m* into whose
36:4 come, one *m* after another
38:26 every *m* who was passing over
Le 1:2 In case some *m* of you would
5:3 touches the uncleanness of a *m*
5:4 *m* might speak thoughtlessly
6:3 the *m* might do to sin by them
7:8 the burnt offering of any *m*
7:21 the uncleanness of a *m* or an
13:2 a *m* develops in the skin of
13:9 leprosy develops in a *m*
13:29 As for a *m* or a woman, in
13:38 As for a *m* or a woman, in
13:40 As for a *m*, in case his head
14:11 the *m* who is cleansing
15:2 any *m* has a running discharge
15:5 And a *m* who may touch his bed
15:16 *m* has an emission of semen
15:18 whom a *m* may lie down with
15:24 if a *m* lies down with her at
15:32 *m* having a running discharge
15:32 *m* from whom an emission of
15:33 a *m* who lies down with an
16:17 no other *m* should happen to
16:21 hand of a ready *m* into the
17:3 any *m* of the house of Israel
17:4 will be counted to that *m*
17:4 *m* must be cut off from among
17:8 any *m* of the house of Israel
17:9 that *m* must be cut off from
17:10 *m* of the house of Israel or
17:13 any *m* of the sons of Israel
18:5 which if a *m* will do, he must
18:6 not come near, any *m* of you
19:14 call down evil upon a deaf *m*
19:14 before a blind *m* you must not
19:20 *m* lies down with a woman
19:20 designated for another *m*
19:32 for the person of an old *m*
20:2 Any *m* of the sons of Israel
20:3 set my face against that *m*
20:4 *m* when he gives any of his
20:5 my face against that *m* and
20:9 *m* who calls down evil upon
20:10 *m* who commits adultery with

Le 20:11 a *m* who lies down with his
20:12 where a *m* lies down with his
20:13 *m* lies down with a male the
20:14 *m* takes a woman and her
20:15 *m* gives his seminal emission
20:17 a *m* takes his sister, the
20:18 where a *m* lies down with a
20:20 a *m* who lies down with his
20:21 *m* takes his brother's wife
20:27 *m* or woman in whom there
21:17 No *m* of your seed throughout
21:18 *m* in whom there is a defect
21:18 *m* blind or lame or with his
21:19 *m* in whom there proves to be
21:21 *m* of the seed of Aaron the
22:3 *m* of all your offspring who
22:4 No *m* of Aaron's offspring
22:4 *m* from whom there goes out a
22:5 *m* who touches any swarming
22:5 *m* who is unclean for him as
22:14 *m* eats a holy thing by
22:18 *m* of the house of Israel or
22:21 case a *m* should present a
24:10 son of an Egyptian *m*, went
24:10 *m* began to struggle with
24:15 *m* calls down evil upon his
24:17 case a *m* strikes any soul of
24:19 *m* should cause a defect in
24:20 defect he may cause in the *m*
24:21 striker of a *m* should be put
25:6 slave *m* and your slave girl
25:27 *m* to whom he made the sale
25:29 *m* should sell a dwelling
25:44 slave *m* and your slave girl
25:44 slave *m* and a slave girl
27:2 *m* makes a special vow
27:14 *m* should sanctify his house
27:16 *m* would sanctify to Jehovah
27:20 field is sold to another *m*
27:26 no *m* should sanctify it
27:28 *m* might devote to Jehovah for
27:31 *m* wants to buy any of his
Nu 1:4 one *m* to a tribe; each is a
1:52 each *m* by his three-tribe
2:2 each *m* by his three-tribe
3:13 firstborn in Israel from *m* to
5:6 *m* or a woman, in case they do
5:13 another *m* actually lies down
5:15 *m* must bring his wife to the
5:19 If no *m* has lain down with
5:20 some *m* has put in you his
5:30 case of a *m* where the spirit
5:31 *m* must be innocent of error
6:2 *m* or a woman takes a special
8:17 mine, among *m* and among beast
9:10 any *m* of you or of your
9:13 *m* was clean or did not happen
9:13 his sin that *m* will answer
11:10 each *m* at the entrance of
11:27 *m* went running and reporting
12:3 *m* Moses was by far the
13:2 send out one *m* for each tribe
14:15 people to death as one *m*
15:32 *m* collecting pieces of wood
15:35 the *m* should be put to death
16:7 *m* whom Jehovah will choose
16:22 will just one *m* sin and you
16:40 no strange *m* who is not of
17:5 *m* whom I shall choose, his
17:9 and taking each *m* his own rod
18:15 among *m* and among beast
19:9 a clean *m* must gather up the
19:13 soul of whatever *m* may die
19:14 a *m* should die in a tent
19:16 or a bone of a *m* or a burial
19:18 a clean *m* must take hyssop
19:20 *m* who may be unclean and
21:9 if a serpent had bitten a *m*
23:19 God is not a *m* that he
24:3 able-bodied *m* with the eye
24:15 the *m* with the eye unsealed
25:6 *m* of the sons of Israel came
25:8 he went after the *m* of Israel
25:8 *m* of Israel and the woman
25:14 fatally struck Israelite *m*
26:64 a *m* of those registered by
26:65 not left of them a *m* except
27:8 case any *m* should die without
27:16 over the assembly a *m*
27:18 a *m* in whom there is spirit
30:2 a *m* makes a vow to Jehovah
31:17 intercourse with *m* by lying
De 1:16 between a *m* and his brother
1:17 frightened because of a *m*

De 1:31 just as a *m* carries his son
3:11 width, by the cubit of a *m*
4:3 *m* who walked after the Baal
4:28 the product of the hands of *m*
4:32 the day that God created *m* on
5:14 slave *m* nor your slave girl
5:14 in order that your slave *m*
5:21 his field or his slave *m* or
5:24 God may speak with *m* and he
8:3 not by bread alone does *m* live
8:3 of Jehovah's mouth does *m* live
8:5 just as a *m* corrects his son
11:25 No *m* will make a firm stand
12:12 daughters and your *m* slaves
12:18 daughter and your *m* slave
16:11 daughter and your *m* slave
16:14 daughter and your *m* slave
17:2 a *m* or a woman who should
17:5 bring that *m* or that woman
17:5 the *m* or the woman, and you
17:12 the *m* who will behave with
17:12 that *m* must die; and you
18:19 the *m* who will not listen to
19:11 a *m* hating his fellowman
19:11 the *m* has fled to one of
19:15 rise up against a *m*
19:16 rise up against a *m* to bring
20:5 *m* that has built a new house
20:5 another *m* should inaugurate
20:6 who is the *m* that has planted
20:6 another *m* should begin to use
20:7 the *m* that has become engaged
20:7 and another *m* should take her
20:8 Who is the *m* that is fearful
20:19 is the tree of the field a *m*
21:15 a *m* comes to have two wives
21:18 a *m* happens to have a son
21:22 in a *m* a sin deserving the
22:5 No garb of an able-bodied *m*
22:5 *m* wear the mantle of a
22:13 In case a *m* takes a wife and
22:16 I gave my daughter to this *m*
22:18 take the *m* and discipline
22:22 a *m* is found lying down
22:22 the *m* lying down with the
22:23 a virgin girl engaged to a *m*
22:23 a *m* actually found her in
22:24 the *m* for the reason that he
22:25 the *m* found the girl who
22:25 the *m* grabbed hold of her
22:25 the *m* who lay down with her
22:26 when a *m* rises up against
22:28 In case a *m* finds a girl, a
22:29 the *m* who lay down with her
22:30 No *m* should take his
23:1 No *m* castrated by crushing
23:10 a *m* who does not continue
24:1 a *m* takes a woman and does
24:3 latter *m* has come to hate
24:3 *m* who took her as his wife
24:5 In case a *m* takes a new wife
24:7 a *m* is found kidnapping a
24:11 the *m* to whom you are
24:12 And if the *m* is in trouble
25:7 if the *m* finds no delight in
25:9 the *m* who will not build up
27:14 say . . . to every *m* of Israel
27:15 Cursed is the *m* who makes a
28:29 a blind *m* gropes about in
28:30 but another *m* will rape her
28:50 not be partial to an old *m*
28:50 show favor to a young *m*
28:54 dainty *m* among you
29:10 every *m* of Israel
29:18 not be among you a *m* or a
29:20 will smoke against that *m*
32:25 Of both young *m* and virgin
32:25 together with gray-haired *m*
33:1 Moses the *m* of the true God
33:8 belong to the *m* loyal to you
33:9 The *m* who said to his father
Jos 1:18 *m* that behaves rebelliously
3:12 Israel, one *m* for each tribe
4:2 one *m* from each tribe
4:4 Israel, one *m* from each tribe
5:13 a *m* standing in front of him
6:21 from *m* to woman, from young
6:21, 21 from young *m* to old *m* and
6:26 Cursed may the *m* be before
7:14, 14 *m* by able-bodied *m*
7:17 come near, able-bodied *m* by
7:17 by able-bodied *m*, and Zabdi
7:18, 18 *m* by able-bodied *m*, and
8:17 not a *m* remaining in Ai and

Jos 8:25 from *m* to woman, amounted to
10:8 Not a *m* of them will stand
10:14 to the voice of a *m*
10:21 Not a *m* moved his tongue
14:6 Moses the *m* of the true God
14:15 Arba was the great *m* among
17:1 proved to be a *m* of war
22:20 not the only *m* to expire
23:9 not a *m* has stood before
23:10 one *m* of you will chase a
Jg 1:24 the watchers got to see a *m*
1:25 the *m* showed them the way to
1:25 but the *m* and all his family
1:26 the *m* went to the land of
3:15 a Benjamite, a left-handed *m*
3:17 Now Eglon was a very fat *m*
3:29 every one a valiant *m*; and
4:20 Is there a *m* here? you must
4:22 the *m* you are looking for
5:30 every able-bodied *m*, Spoil
6:8 to send a *m*, a prophet, to the
6:16 down Midian as if one *m*
7:13 a *m* relating a dream to his
7:14 a *m* of Israel. The true God
8:14 captured a young *m* of the men
8:20 the young *m* did not draw his
8:20 for he was yet a young *m*
8:21 for as a *m* is, so is his
9:2 for one *m* to rule over you
10:1 Dodo, a *m* of Issachar, and he
10:18 Who is the *m* that will take
11:1 a mighty, valiant *m*, and he
11:39 never had relations with a *m*
13:2 *m* of Zorah of the family of
13:6 a *m* of the true God that came
13:8 The *m* of the true God that
13:10 The *m* that came the other
13:11 came to the *m* and said to
13:11 Are you the *m* that spoke to
16:7 and become like an ordinary *m*
16:11 become like an ordinary *m*
16:19 she called the *m* and had him
17:1 a *m* of the mountainous region
17:5 the *m* Micah, he had a house
17:7 young *m* of Bethlehem in Judah
17:8 the *m* proceeded to go from
17:11 to dwell with the *m*, and
17:11 young *m* got to be as one of
17:12 the young *m* might serve as a
18:3 the voice of the young *m*
18:15 house of the young *m*, the
18:19 priest to the house of one *m*
19:6 said to the *m*: Come on
19:7 When the *m* rose to go, his
19:9 The *m* now rose to go, he and
19:10 *m* did not consent to stay
19:16 an old *m* coming in from his
19:16 *m* was from the mountainous
19:17 see the *m*, the traveler, in
19:17 So the old *m* said: Where are
19:20 the old *m* said: May you have
19:22 kept saying to the old *m*
19:22 Bring out the *m* that came
19:23 *m* has come into my house
19:24 to this *m* you must not do
19:25 the *m* took hold of his
19:28 the *m* took her upon the ass
20:1 congregated . . . as one *m*
20:4 *m*, the Levite, the husband
20:8 the people rose up as one *m*
20:11 against the city as one *m*
20:17 Every one . . . a *m* of war
21:1 Not a *m* of us will give his
21:9 was not a *m* there from the
21:12 not had intercourse with a *m*
Ru 1:1 and a *m* proceeded to go from
2:1 a *m* mighty in wealth, of the
2:5 Boaz said to the young *m* who
2:6 *m* set over the harvesters
2:19 name of the *m* with whom I
2:20 The *m* is related to us
3:3 make yourself known to the *m*
3:8 that the *m* began to tremble
3:16 that the *m* had done to her
3:18 *m* will have no rest unless
4:5 the wife of the dead *m*, that
4:5 the name of the dead *m* to rise
4:7 A *m* had to draw his sandal off
4:10 name of the dead *m* to rise
4:10 name of the dead *m* may not
1Sa 1:1 *m* of Ramathaim-zophim of the
1:3 that *m* went up out of his
1:21 the *m* Elkanah went up with
2:9 does a *m* prove superior

1Sa 2:13 *m* was offering a sacrifice
2:15 said to the *m* sacrificing
2:16 When the *m* would say to him
2:25 If a *m* should sin against a
2:25 sin against a *m*, God will
2:25 that a *m* should sin, who is
2:27 a *m* of God proceeded to come
2:31 to be an old *m* in your house
2:32 to be an old *m* in your house
2:33 there is a *m* of yours that I
4:12 *m* of Benjamin went running
4:13 *m* himself went in to report
4:14 *m* himself hurried that he
4:16 *m* proceeded to say to Eli
4:18 the *m* was old and heavy
9:1 *m* of Benjamin, and his name
9:1 a *m* mighty in wealth
9:2 no *m* of the sons of Israel
9:6 is a *m* of God in this city
9:6 and the *m* is held in honor
9:7 what shall we bring to the *m*?
9:7 to the *m* of the true God
9:8 to the *m* of the true God
9:9 way the *m* would have talked
9:10 the *m* of the true God was
9:16 *m* from the land of Benjamin
9:17 the *m* of whom I said to you
10:6 be changed into another *m*
10:12 a *m* from there answered
10:22 Has the *m* come here as yet?
11:7 that they came out as one *m*
11:13 Not a *m* should be put to
13:14 a *m* agreeable to his heart
14:24 Cursed is the *m* that eats
14:28 Cursed is the *m* that eats
14:52 When Saul saw any mighty *m*
15:3 to death, *m* as well as
15:29 He is not an earthling *m* so
16:7 not the way *m* sees is the
16:7 *m* sees what appears to the
16:12 he was ruddy, a young *m*
16:16 *m* playing upon the harp
16:17 a *m* doing well at playing
16:18 he is a valiant, mighty *m*
16:18 *m* of war and an intelligent
16:18 well-formed *m*, and Jehovah
17:8 Choose a *m* for yourselves
17:10 Give me a *m*, and let us
17:12 the *m* was already old
17:24 on their seeing the *m*, why
17:25 Have you seen this *m* that
17:25 the *m* who strikes him down
17:26 to the *m* that strikes down
17:27 to the *m* that strikes him
17:32 the heart of any *m* collapse
17:33 *m* of war from his boyhood
17:41 *m* carrying the large shield
18:23 I am a *m* of little means
19:11 will be a *m* put to death
21:14 see a *m* behaving crazy
22:19 *m* as well as woman, child
24:9 you listen to the words of *m*
24:19 *m* finds his enemy, will he
25:2 *m* in Maon, and his work was
25:2 *m* was very great, and he had
25:25 good-for-nothing *m* Nabal
25:29 *m* rises up to pursue you
26:15 to Abner: Are you not a *m*?
26:19 But if it is the sons of *m*
27:9 preserved neither *m* nor
27:11 As for *m* and woman, David
28:14 It is an old *m* coming up
29:4 Make the *m* go back, and let
30:11 find a *m*, an Egyptian, in
30:13 slave of an Amalekite *m*
30:17 not a *m* of them escaped
30:22 and good-for-nothing *m* out
2Sa 1:2 *m* was coming from the camp
1:5 David said to the young *m*
1:6 young *m* that was telling him
1:13 now said to the young *m* that
3:29 *m* with a running discharge
3:29 *m* taking hold of the
3:38 great *m* that has fallen this
4:11 killed a righteous *m* in his
6:19 Israel, *m* as well as woman
12:2 rich *m* happened to have very
12:3 *m* of little means had
12:4 visitor came to the rich *m*
12:4 of the *m* of little means
12:4 ready for the *m* that had
12:5 grew very hot against the *m*
12:5 *m* doing this deserves to die
12:7 You yourself are the *m*!
2Sa 13:3 Jehonadab was a very wise *m*
13:34 young *m*, the watchman
14:16 *m* seeking to annihilate me
14:19 no *m* can go to the right or
14:21 bring the young *m* Absalom
14:25 no *m* so beautiful in all
15:2 when any *m* happened to have
15:4 to me every *m* might come
15:5 a *m* drew near to bow down
16:5 a *m* of the family of Saul's
16:7 get out, you bloodguilty *m*
16:7 and good-for-nothing *m*
16:8 you are a bloodguilty *m*
16:23 as when a *m* would inquire
17:3 the *m* whom you are seeking
17:10 valiant *m* whose heart is as
17:10 your father is a mighty *m*
17:18 a young *m* got to see them
17:18 the house of a *m* in Bahurim
17:25 a *m* whose name was Ithra
18:5 with the young *m* Absalom
18:10 a certain *m* saw it and told
18:11 the *m* who was telling him
18:12 But the *m* said to Joab
18:12 the young *m*, over Absalom
18:17 fled each *m* to his home
18:20 not a *m* of news this day
18:24 a *m* running by himself
18:26 now saw another *m* running
18:26 Another *m* running by
18:27 This is a good *m*, and with
18:29 with the young *m* Absalom
18:32 with the young *m* Absalom
18:32 become as the young *m*
19:7 not a *m* will lodge with you
19:14 the men of Judah as one *m*
19:32 for he was a very great *m*
20:1 a good-for-nothing *m*, whose
20:12 *m* saw that all the people
20:13 each *m* passed by following
20:21 a *m* from the mountainous
21:4 put a *m* to death in Israel
21:5 The *m* that exterminated us
21:20 a *m* of extraordinary size
22:49 From the *m* of violent deeds
23:1 *m* that was raised up on high
23:7 When a *m* touches them He
23:20 the son of a valiant *m*, who
23:21 struck down the Egyptian *m*
24:14 into the hand of *m* do not
1Ki 1:42 a valiant *m*, and you bring
1:52 he will become a valiant *m*
2:2 prove yourself to be a *m*
2:4 there will not be cut off a *m*
2:9 you are a wise *m* and you
4:31 was wiser than any other *m*
7:14 his father was a Tyrian *m*
8:25 will not be cut off a *m* of
8:31 When a *m* sins against his
8:38 any *m* or of all your people
8:46 no *m* that does not sin
9:5 Not a *m* of yours will be cut
11:28 *m* Jeroboam was a valiant
11:28 was a valiant, mighty *m*
11:28 young *m* was a hard worker
12:22 the *m* of the true God
13:1 a *m* of God that had come
13:4 the *m* of the true God that
13:5 the *m* of the true God had
13:6 to the *m* of the true God
13:6 *m* of the true God softened
13:7 say to the *m* of the true God
13:8 *m* of the true God said to
13:11 work that the *m* of the true
13:12 way that the *m* of the true
13:14 following the *m* of the true
13:14 Are you the *m* of the true
13:21 the *m* of the true God that
13:26 is the *m* of the true God
13:29 of the *m* of the true God
13:31 *m* of the true God is buried
17:18 O *m* of the true God
17:24 that you are a *m* of God and
20:20 strike down each one his *m*
20:28 Then the *m* of the true God
20:35 *m* of the sons of the
20:35 the *m* refused to strike him
20:37 went on to find another *m*
20:37 *m* struck him, striking
20:39 a *m* was leaving the line
20:39 he came bringing a *m* to me
20:39 Guard this *m*. If he should
20:42 the *m* devoted to me for
22:8 *m* through whom to inquire
1Ki 22:34 a *m* that bent the bow in
2Ki 1:6 a *m* that came up to meet us
1:7 *m* that came up to meet you
1:8 A *m* possessing a hair garment
1:9 *M* of the true God, the king
1:10 if I am a *m* of God, let fire
1:11 *M* of the true God, this is
1:12 If I am a *m* of the true God
1:13 *M* of the true God, please
4:7 told the *m* of the true God
4:9 it is a holy *m* of God that is
4:16 O *m* of the true God! Do not
4:21 couch of the *m* of the true
4:22 the *m* of the true God and
4:25 come to the *m* of the true
4:25 *m* of the true God saw her
4:27 to the *m* of the true God
4:27 the *m* of the true God said
4:40 O *m* of the true God
4:42 was a *m* that came from
4:42 to the *m* of the true God
5:1 a great *m* before his lord
5:1 *m* himself had proved to be
5:1 mighty *m*, though a leper
5:7 recover a *m* from his leprosy
5:8 Elisha the *m* of the true God
5:14 word of the *m* of the true
5:15 to the *m* of the true God
5:20 Elisha the *m* of the true God
5:26 as the *m* turned to get down
6:6 the *m* of the true God said
6:9 the *m* of the true God sent
6:10 *m* of the true God had said
6:15 the *m* of the true God
6:19 to the *m* you look for
6:32 he sent a *m* from before him
7:2 the *m* of the true God and
7:10 nor sound of a *m*, but only
7:17 *m* of the true God had spoken
7:18 *m* of the true God had spoken
7:19 *m* of the true God and said
8:2 word of the *m* of the true God
8:4 the *m* of the true God
8:7 *m* of the true God has come
8:8 meet the *m* of the true God
8:11 *m* of the true God gave way
9:11 Why did this crazy *m* come
9:11 the *m* and his sort of talk
10:24 the *m* that escapes from the
13:19 *m* of the true God grew
13:21 as they were burying a *m*
13:21 the *m* into Elisha's burial
13:21 *m* touched the bones of
15:20 silver shekels for each *m*
18:21 if a *m* should brace himself
22:15 the *m* that has sent you
23:16 the *m* of the true God had
23:17 *m* of the true God that
25:9 house of every great *m* he
1Ch 11:22 the son of a valiant *m*, who
11:23 struck down the Egyptian *m*
11:23 a *m* of extraordinary size
12:4 a mighty *m* among the thirty
12:28 Zadok a young *m*, mighty in
16:3 *m* as well as woman, to each
17:17 of the *m* in the ascendancy
20:6 a *m* of extraordinary size
21:13 into the hand of *m* do not
22:9 will prove to be a restful *m*
23:3 able-bodied *m* by able-bodied
23:3 by able-bodied *m*, came to be
23:14 Moses the *m* of the true God
27:6 Benaiah was a mighty *m* of
27:32 a *m* of understanding, he
28:1 even every valiant, mighty *m*
28:3 for a *m* of wars you are, and
29:1 the castle is not for *m*, but
2Ch 2:7 skillful *m* to work in gold
2:13 now I do send a skillful *m*
2:14 father was a *m* of Tyre
6:5 a *m* to become leader over my
6:16 not be cut off a *m* of yours
6:22 *m* sins against his
6:29 on the part of any *m* or of
6:36 is no *m* that does not sin
7:18 *m* of yours be cut off from
8:14 David the *m* of the true God
11:2 Shemaiah the *m* of the true
14:11 mortal *m* retain strength
15:13 whether *m* or woman
17:17 valiant, mighty *m* Eliada
18:7 *m* through whom to inquire
18:33 *m* that bent the bow in his
19:6 not for *m* that you judge but

2Ch 25:7 *m* of the true God came to
25:9 to the *m* of the true God
25:9 *m* of the true God said
28:7 Zichri, a mighty *m* of
30:16 Moses the *m* of the true God
32:21 mighty *m* and leader and
34:23 Say to the *m* that sent you
36:17 compassion for young *m* or
Ezr 3:1 as one *m* to Jerusalem
3:2 Moses the *m* of the true God
8:18 a *m* of discretion from the
Ne 1:11 object of pity before this *m*
2:10 very bad that a *m* had come to
2:12 did not tell a *m* what my God
5:13 every *m* that does not carry
6:11 Should a *m* like me run away?
7:2 trustworthy *m* and feared the
8:1 as one *m* at the public square
9:29 sinned, which, if a *m* will
12:24 David the *m* of the true God
12:36 David the *m* of the true God
Es 1:8 every great *m* of his household
2:5 A certain *m*, a Jew, happened
3:13, 13 young *m* as well as old *m*
4:11 any *m* or woman that comes in
6:6 the *m* in whose honor the king
6:7 the *m* in whose honor the king
6:9 the *m* in whose honor the king
6:9 the *m* in whose honor the king
6:11 the *m* in whose honor the king
7:6 Then Esther said: The *m*, the
9:2 and not a *m* stood his ground
9:4 the *m* Mordecai was steadily
Job 1:1 a *m* in the land of Uz whose
1:1 that *m* proved to be blameless
1:3 *m* came to be the greatest
1:8 a *m* blameless and upright
2:3 a *m* blameless and upright
2:4 everything that a *m* has he
3:3 An able-bodied *m* has been
3:23 give light to able-bodied *m*
4:17 Mortal *m*—can he be more
4:17 can able-bodied *m* be cleaner
5:7 *m* himself is born for trouble
5:17 Happy is the *m* whom God
7:1 labor for mortal *m* on earth
7:17 What is mortal *m* that you
9:2 can mortal *m* be in the right
9:32 he is not a *m* like me that I
10:4 is it as a mortal *m* sees
10:5 like the days of mortal *m*
10:5 the days of an able-bodied *m*
11:12 hollow-minded *m* himself
11:12 asinine zebra be born a *m*
12:10 spirit of all flesh of *m*
12:14 He makes it shut to *m*, that
12:25 wander . . . like a drunken *m*
13:9 one trifles with mortal *m*
14:1 *M*, born of woman, Is
14:10 *m* dies and lies vanquished
14:10 *m* expires, and where is he?
14:12 *M* also has to lie down and
14:14 *m* dies can he live again?
14:19 the very hope of mortal *m*
15:7 the very first *m* to be born
15:14 *m* that he should be clean
15:16 A *m* who is drinking in
16:21 an able-bodied *m* and God
16:21 between a son of *m* and his
20:4 Since *m* was put upon the
20:29 share of the wicked *m* from
21:4 is my concern expressed to *m*?
22:2 *m* be of use to God himself
22:8 *m* of strength, the land is
22:30 will rescue an innocent *m*
25:4 *m* be in the right before God
25:6 mortal *m*, who is a maggot
25:6 a son of *m*, who is a worm
27:7 in every way a wicked *m*
27:13 the share of the wicked *m*
28:13 *m* has not come to know its
28:28 And he went on to say to *m*
31:10 the grinding for another *m*
31:13 the judgment of my slave *m*
31:33 If like an earthling *m* I
32:13 drives him away, not a *m*
32:21 show partiality to a *m*
32:21 *m* I shall not bestow a
33:12 much more than mortal *m*
33:17 turn aside a *m* from his
33:17 from an able-bodied *m*
33:23 tell to *m* his uprightness
33:26 righteousness to mortal *m*
33:29 case of an able-bodied *m*
Job 34:7 able-bodied *m* is like Job
34:9 An able-bodied *m* does not
34:11 the way earthling *m* acts
34:11 the path of *m* he will cause
34:15 *m* himself will return to
34:21 eyes are upon the ways of *m*
34:23 no appointed time for any *m*
34:29 a nation or toward a *m*
34:30 an apostate *m* may not reign
34:34 a wise able-bodied *m* that
35:8 may be against a *m* like you
35:8 to a son of earthling *m*
36:25 Mortal *m* himself keeps
37:7 On the hand of every . . . *m*
37:7 mortal *m* to know his work
37:20 has any *m* said that it will
38:3 like an able-bodied *m*
38:26 land where there is no *m*
38:26 there is no earthling *m*
40:7 like an able-bodied *m*
Ps 1:1 Happy is the *m* that has not
5:6 A *m* of bloodshed and deception
8:4 What is mortal *m* that you keep
8:4 *m* that you take care of him
9:19 *m* prove superior in strength
10:18 *m* who is of the earth
18:25 the faultless, able-bodied *m*
18:48 From the *m* of violence you
19:5 exults as a mighty *m* does to
22:6 I am a worm, and not a *m*
25:12 the *m* fearful of Jehovah
32:2 *m* to whose account Jehovah
33:16 *m* himself is not delivered
34:8 *m* that takes refuge in him
34:12 *m* that is delighting in life
36:6 *M* and beast you save, O
37:7 the *m* carrying out his ideas
37:23 steps of an able-bodied *m*
37:25 A young *m* I used to be
37:37 the future of that *m* will be
38:14 a *m* that was not hearing
39:5 *m*, though standing firm, is
39:6 in a semblance *m* walks about
39:11 you have corrected *m*
39:11 earthling *m* is an exhalation
40:4 Happy is the able-bodied *m*
41:9 Also the *m* at peace with me
43:1 From the *m* of deception and
49:2 as well as you sons of *m*
49:12 *m*, though in honor, cannot
49:16 because some *m* gains riches
49:20 *m*, although in honor, who
52:7 *m* that does not put God as
55:13 *m* who was as my equal
56:1 mortal *m* has snapped at me
56:11 can earthling *m* do to me
60:11 salvation by earthling *m* is
62:3 the *m* whom you would murder
62:9 the sons of earthling *m* are
66:12 *m* to ride over our head
73:5 in the trouble of mortal *m*
76:10 rage of *m* will laud you
80:17 hand prove to be upon the *m*
84:12 *m* that is trusting in you
88:4 able-bodied *m* without
89:48 able-bodied *m* is there alive
90:*super* the *m* of the true God
90:3 mortal *m* go back to crushed
92:6 No unreasoning *m* himself can
94:12 Happy is the able-bodied *m*
103:15 mortal *m*, his days are like
104:15 heart of mortal *m* rejoice
104:15 the very heart of mortal *m*
104:23 *M* goes forth to his
105:17 He sent ahead of them a *m*
107:27 unsteadily like a drunken *m*
108:12 salvation by earthling *m* is
109:16 the afflicted and poor *m*
112:1 Happy is the *m* in fear of
112:5 *m* is good who is gracious
115:4 the hands of earthling *m*
116:11 Every *m* is a liar
118:6 can earthling *m* do to me
118:8 Than to trust in earthling *m*
119:9 young *m* cleanse his path
120:4 arrows of a mighty *m*
127:4 in the hand of a mighty *m*
127:5 *m* that has filled his quiver
128:4 able-bodied *m* will be
135:8 of Egypt, Both *m* and beast
135:15 of the hands of earthling *m*
140:1 the *m* of deeds of violence
140:4 the *m* of deeds of violence
140:11 *m* of violence—let evil
Ps 144:3 *m* that you should notice
144:3 mortal *m* that you should
144:4 *M* himself bears resemblance
146:3 *m*, to whom no salvation
147:10 in the legs of the *m* does
Pr 1:4 to a young *m* knowledge and
1:5 *m* of understanding is the one
2:12 *m* speaking perverse things
3:4 eyes of God and of earthling *m*
3:13 *m* that has found wisdom
3:13 *m* that gets discernment
3:30 quarrel with a *m* without
3:31 envious of the *m* of violence
5:21 ways of *m* are in front of
6:11 your want like an armed *m*
6:12 A good-for-nothing *m*, a
6:12 *m* of hurtfulness, is walking
6:27 *m* rake together fire into his
6:28 *m* walk upon the coals and his
6:34 rage of an able-bodied *m* is
7:7 a young *m* in want of heart
7:22 discipline of a foolish *m*
8:34 *m* that is listening to me
10:15 valuable things of a rich *m*
10:23 for the *m* of discernment
10:26 lazy *m* is to those sending
11:7 wicked *m* dies, his hope
11:12 *m* of broad discernment is
11:17 *m* of loving-kindness is
12:2 *m* of wicked ideas he
12:3 *m* will be firmly established
12:8 discretion a *m* will be
12:23 shrewd *m* is covering
12:25 care in the heart of a *m* is
13:2 a *m* will eat good
14:7 in front of the stupid *m*, for
14:12 that is upright before a *m*
14:14 good *m* with the results of
14:17 *m* of thinking abilities is
15:18 An enraged *m* stirs up
15:20 a stupid *m* is despising his
15:21 *m* of discernment is one who
15:23 A *m* has rejoicing in the
16:1 *m* belong the arrangings of
16:2 ways of a *m* are pure in his
16:7 pleasure in the ways of a *m*
16:9 *m* may think out his way, but
16:14 wise *m* is one that averts it
16:25 that is upright before a *m*
16:27 A good-for-nothing *m* is
16:28 *m* of intrigues keeps sending
16:29 A *m* of violence will seduce his
16:32 is better than a mighty *m*
17:12 an encountering by a *m* of a
17:18 A *m* that is wanting in heart
17:27 *m* of discernment is cool of
18:12 the heart of a *m* is lofty
18:14 The spirit of a *m* can put up
19:3 *m* that distorts his way, and
19:6 to the *m* making gifts
19:11 The insight of a *m* certainly
19:21 plans in the heart of a *m*
19:22 desirable . . . in earthling *m*
19:22 is better than a lying *m*
20:3 glory for a *m* to desist from
20:5 Counsel in the heart of a *m*
20:5 *m* of discernment is one that
20:6 a faithful *m* who can find?
20:17 is pleasurable to a *m*, but
20:24 of an able-bodied *m*
20:24 *m*, how can he discern his
20:25 *m* has rashly cried out, Holy
20:27 breath of earthling *m* is the
21:2 way of a *m* is upright in his
21:8 A *m*, even a stranger, is
21:16 *m* wandering from the way of
21:20 the *m* that is stupid will
21:28 the *m* that is listening will
21:29 wicked *m* has put on a bold
22:7 to the *m* doing the lending
22:24 with a *m* having fits of rage
22:29 a *m* skillful in his work
24:5 strength is an able-bodied *m*
24:5 *m* of knowledge is reinforcing
24:12 pay back to earthling *m*
24:30 of the *m* in need of heart
24:34 your neediness as an armed *m*
25:14 *m* boasting himself about a
25:18 a *m* testifying against his
25:28 *m* that has no restraint for
26:12 a *m* wise in his own eyes
26:19 the *m* that has tricked his
26:21 contentious *m* for causing a
27:8 is a *m* fleeing away from his

Pr 27:17 one *m* sharpens the face of
27:19 heart of a *m* with that of a
27:19 with that of a *m*
27:20 eyes of a *m* get satisfied
28:2 discerning *m* having knowledge
28:3 *m* that is of little means and
28:11 A rich *m* is wise in his own
28:12 a *m* disguises himself
28:14 the *m* that is feeling dread
28:17 A *m* burdened with the
28:20 *m* of faithful acts will get
28:21 nor that an able-bodied *m*
28:22 A *m* of envious eye is
28:23 He that is reproving a *m*
28:24 of a *m* causing ruination
28:28 wicked rise up, a *m* conceals
29:1 A *m* repeatedly reproved but
29:3 A *m* that is loving wisdom
29:4 a *m* out for bribes tears it
29:5 *m* that is flattering his
29:6 the transgression of a bad *m*
29:9 A wise *m* having entered into
29:9 judgment with a foolish *m*
29:13 and the *m* of oppressions
29:20 a *m* hasty with his words
29:22 A *m* given to anger stirs up
29:23 haughtiness of earthling *m*
29:26 the judgment of a *m* is from
29:27 *m* of injustice is something
30:1 the able-bodied *m* to Ithiel
30:19 able-bodied *m* with a maiden
Ec 1:3 What profit does a *m* have in
2:12 what can the earthling man do
2:18 *m* who would come to be after
2:21 *m* whose hard work has been
2:21 a *m* that has not worked hard
2:22 what does a *m* come to have
2:24 a *m* there is nothing better
2:26 to the *m* that is good before
3:13 every *m* should eat and indeed
3:19 no superiority of the *m* over
3:22 *m* should rejoice in his works
5:19 every *m* to whom the true God
6:2 *m* to whom the true God gives
6:3 If a *m* should become a father
6:10 has become known what *m* is
6:11 what advantage does a *m* have?
6:12 what good a *m* has in life for
6:12 can tell *m* what will happen
7:5 *m* hearing the song of the
7:20 no *m* righteous in the earth
7:28 One *m* out of a thousand I
8:1 wisdom of a *m* itself causes
8:8 *m* having power over the spirit
8:9, 9 that *m* has dominated *m* to
9:12 For *m* also does not know his
9:15 in it a *m*, needy but wise
9:15 no *m* remembered that needy
9:15 remembered that needy *m*
10:14 *M* does not know what will
11:8 *m* should live even many years
11:9 Rejoice, young *m*, in your
12:5 because *m* is walking to his
12:13 is the whole obligation of *m*
Ca 8:7 If a *m* would give all the
Isa 1:31 vigorous *m* will certainly
2:9 And earthling *m* bows down
2:9 and *m* becomes low, and you
2:11 haughty eyes of earthling *m*
2:17 earthling *m* must bow down
2:20 *m* will throw his worthless
2:22 earthling *m*, whose breath is
3:2 mighty *m* and warrior, judge
3:2 of divination and elderly *m*
3:3 and highly respected *m* and
3:5 the boy against the old *m*
4:1 grab hold of one *m* in that
5:15 earthling *m* will bow down
5:15 and *m* will become low, and
6:5 *m* unclean in lips I am, and
6:11 be without earthling *m*
8:1 with the stylus of mortal *m*
13:7 heart itself of mortal *m*
13:12 make mortal *m* rarer than
13:12 *m* rarer than the gold of
14:16 *m* that was agitating the
17:7 *m* will look up to his Maker
22:6 war chariot of earthling *m*
22:17 hurling, O able-bodied *m*
24:20 unsteadily like a drunken *m*
29:21 bringing a *m* into sin by
31:8 sword, not that of a *m*
31:8 of earthling *m*, will devour
32:5 unprincipled *m*, he will not
Isa 32:7 unprincipled *m*, his
33:8 taken no account of mortal *m*
36:6 *m* should brace himself upon
40:13 who as his *m* of counsel can
41:28 and there was not a *m*
42:13 Like a mighty *m* Jehovah
43:28 a *m* devoted to destruction
44:13 the representation of a *m*
44:15 *m* to keep a fire burning
45:12 have created even *m* upon it
46:11 the *m* to execute my counsel
47:3 shall not meet any *m* kindly
47:6 Upon the old *m* you made your
49:24 be taken from a mighty *m*
49:25 captives of the mighty *m*
51:12 a mortal *m* that will die
52:14 than that of any other *m*
53:3 a *m* meant for pains and for
54:16 ruinous *m* for wrecking
55:7 the wicked *m* leave his way
55:7 the harmful *m* his thoughts
56:2 Happy is the mortal *m* that
58:5 *m* to afflict his soul
59:16 saw that there was no *m*
62:5 young *m* takes ownership of a
63:3 was no *m* with me from the
65:20 old *m* that does not fulfill
66:3 is as one striking down a *m*
66:13 a *m* whom his own mother
Jer 2:6 through which no *m* passed and
2:6 which no earthling *m* dwelt
3:1 If a *m* should send away his
4:25 there was not an earthling *m*
4:29 no *m* dwelling in them
5:1 whether you can find a *m*
6:11 a *m* along with his wife, an
6:11 an old *m* along with one that
6:23 battle order like a *m* of war
7:5 between a *m* and his companion
8:6 There was not a *m* repenting
9:10 there is no *m* passing
9:12 Who is the *m* that is wise
9:23 Let not the wise *m* brag
9:23 let not the mighty *m* brag
9:23 Let not the rich *m* brag
10:14 Every *m* has behaved so
10:23 to earthling *m* his way does
10:23 to *m* who is walking even
11:3 the *m* that does not listen
12:11 no *m* that has taken it to
13:11 clings to the hips of a *m*
14:9 become like a *m* astounded
14:9 like a mighty *m* that is
15:8 young *m*, the despoiler at
15:10 a *m* subject to quarrel and
15:10 a *m* subject to strife with
16:20 *m* make for himself gods
17:5 *m* who puts his trust in
17:5 his trust in earthling *m*
17:7 Blessed is the able-bodied *m*
20:10 mortal *m* bidding me Peace!
20:15 *m* that brought good news
20:16 *m* must become like cities
21:6 this city, both *m* and beast
22:28 Is this *m* Coniah a mere
22:30 this *m* as childless, as an
22:30 an able-bodied *m* who will
23:9 like a *m* that is drunk
23:9 *m* whom wine has overcome
23:24 Or can any *m* be concealed
23:34 my attention upon that *m*
26:11 To this *m* the judgment of
26:16 death belonging to this *m*
26:20 a *m* prophesying in the name
29:26 any *m* maddened and behaving
29:32 a *m* dwelling in the midst
30:6 *m* with his hands upon his
31:22 around an able-bodied *m*
31:27 Judah with the seed of *m*
31:30 *m* eating the unripe grape
32:43 desolate waste without *m*
33:10 waste without *m* and
33:10 desolated without *m* and
33:12 waste place without *m* and
33:17 *m* to sit upon the throne
33:18 *m* from before me to offer
34:9 Hebrew *m* and Hebrew woman
34:14 Hebrew *m*, who came to be
35:4 a *m* of the true God, which
35:19 *m* to stand before me
36:29 cause *m* and beast to cease
38:4 *m*, please, be put to death
38:4 *m* is one seeking not for the
38:7 *m* who was a eunuch and who
Jer 38:24 no *m* at all get to know
44:7 *m* and woman, child and
44:26 mouth of any *m* of Judah
46:6 the mighty *m* try to escape
46:12 stumbled, mighty *m* against
46:12 against mighty *m*
49:18 no *m* will dwell there, and
49:33 No *m* will dwell there, and
50:3 *m* and domestic animal have
50:9 of a mighty *m* causing
50:40 no *m* will dwell there, nor
50:42 in array as one *m* for war
51:17 Every *m* has behaved so
51:22 dash *m* and woman to pieces
51:22 dash old *m* and boy to
51:22 dash young *m* and virgin to
51:43 in them no *m* will dwell
51:62 either *m* or even domestic
La 2:21 Boy and old *m* have lain down
3:1 I am the able-bodied *m* that
3:27 it is for an able-bodied *m*
3:35 judgment of an able-bodied *m*
3:36 For making a *m* crooked in his
3:39 *m* indulge in complaints, an
3:39 an able-bodied *m* on account
Eze 1:5 the likeness of earthling *m*
1:8 the hands of a *m* under their
1:26 like an earthling *m* upon it
2:1 Son of *m*, stand up upon your
2:3 Son of *m*, I am sending you to
2:6 son of *m*, do not be afraid of
2:8 O son of *m*, hear what I am
3:1 Son of *m*, what you find, eat
3:3 Son of *m*, you should cause
3:4 Son of *m*, go, enter in among
3:10 Son of *m*, all my words that
3:17 Son of *m*, a watchman is
3:25 son of *m*, look! they will
3:26 a *m* administering reproof
4:1 son of *m*, take for yourself a
4:16 Son of *m*, here I am breaking
5:1 son of *m*, take for yourself a
6:2 Son of *m*, set your face
7:2 And as for you, O son of *m*
8:5 Son of *m*, please, raise your
8:6 Son of *m*, are you seeing what
8:8 Son of *m*, bore, please
8:12 Have you seen, O son of *m*
8:15 you seen this, O son of *m*
8:17 you seen this, O son of *m*
9:2 one *m* in among them clothed
9:3 the *m* that was clothed with
9:6, 6 Old *m*, young *m* and virgin
9:6 any *m* upon whom there is the
9:11 the *m* clothed with the linen
10:2 the *m* clothed with the linen
10:3 the *m* entered, and the cloud
10:6 the *m* clothed with the linen
10:8 a hand of earthling *m* under
10:14 was the face of earthling *m*
10:21 hands of earthling *m* was
11:2 Son of *m*, these are the men
11:4 Prophesy, O son of *m*
11:15 Son of *m*, as regards your
12:2 Son of *m*, in the midst of a
12:3 As for you, O son of *m*, make
12:9 Son of *m*, did not those of
12:18 Son of *m*, with quaking your
12:22 Son of *m*, what is this
12:27 Son of *m*, look! those of
13:2 Son of *m*, prophesy
13:17 O son of *m*, set your face
14:3 Son of *m*, as regards these
14:4 Any *m* at all of the house of
14:7 any *m* at all from the house
14:8 set my face against that *m*
14:13 Son of *m*, as regards a land
14:13 cut off from it earthling *m*
14:17 cut off from it earthling *m*
14:19 cut off from it earthling *m*
14:21 cut off from it earthling *m*
15:2 Son of *m*, in what way does
16:2 Son of *m*, make known to
17:2 Son of *m*, propound a riddle
18:5 as regards a *m*, in case he
18:7 and no *m* would he maltreat
18:8, 8 execute between *m* and *m*
18:16 and no *m* has he maltreated
19:3 He devoured even earthling *m*
19:6 He devoured even earthling *m*
20:3 Son of *m*, speak with the
20:4 you judge them, O son of *m*
20:11 the *m* who keeps doing them
20:13 should the *m* keep doing, he

Eze 20:21 should the *m* keep doing, he
20:27 son of *m*, and you must say
20:46 Son of *m*, set your face in
21:2 Son of *m*, set your face
21:6 son of *m*, sigh with shaking
21:9 Son of *m*, prophesy, and you
21:12 and howl, O son of *m*
21:14 you, O son of *m*—prophesy
21:19 son of *m*, set for yourself
21:28 you, O son of *m*, prophesy
22:2 O son of *m*, will you judge
22:11 a *m* has done a detestable
22:11 daughter-in-law a *m* has
22:11 a *m* has humiliated in you
22:18 Son of *m*, to me those of
22:24 Son of *m*, say to her
22:30 I kept looking for a *m* from
23:2 Son of *m*, two women, the
23:36 Son of *m*, will you judge
24:2 Son of *m*, write down for
24:16 Son of *m*, here I am taking
24:25 O son of *m*, will it not be
25:2 Son of *m*, set your face
25:13 cut off from it *m* and
26:2 Son of *m*, for the reason
27:2 you, O son of *m*, raise up
28:2 Son of *m*, say to the leader
28:2 earthling *m* is what you are
28:9 you are a mere earthling *m*
28:12 Son of *m*, lift up a dirge
28:21 Son of *m*, set your face
29:2 Son of *m*, set your face
29:8 cut off from you earthling *m*
29:11 the foot of earthling *m*
29:18 Son of *m*, Nebuchadrezzar
30:2 Son of *m*, prophesy, and you
30:21 Son of *m*, the arm of
31:2 Son of *m*, say to Pharaoh the
32:2 Son of *m*, lift up a dirge
32:13 *m* will no more muddy
32:18 Son of *m*, lament over the
33:2 Son of *m*, speak to the sons
33:2 take a *m* and set him as
33:7 O son of *m*, a watchman is
33:10 as regards you, O son of *m*
33:12 son of *m*, say to the sons
33:24 Son of *m*, the inhabitants
33:30 O son of *m*, the sons of
34:2 Son of *m*, prophesy against
35:2 Son of *m*, set your face
36:1 you, O son of *m*, prophesy
36:17 Son of *m*, the house of
37:3 Son of *m*, can these bones
37:9 Prophesy, O son of *m*, and
37:11 Son of *m*, as regards these
37:16 O son of *m*, take for
38:2 Son of *m*, set your face
38:14 prophesy, O son of *m*, and
39:1 as regards you, O son of *m*
39:15 see the bone of a *m*
39:17 as regards you, O son of *m*
40:3 a *m*. His appearance was like
40:4 the *m* began to speak to me
40:4 Son of *m*, see with your eyes
40:5 in the hand of the *m* there
41:19 the face of a *m* was toward
43:6 *m* himself had come to be
43:7 Son of *m*, this is the place
43:10 son of *m*, inform the house
43:18 Son of *m*, this is what the
44:2 mere *m* will come in by it
44:5 Son of *m*, set your heart
45:20 any *m* making a mistake and
47:3 *m* went forth eastward with
47:6 seen this, O son of *m*
Da 2:10 not exist a *m* on the dry land
2:25 able-bodied *m* of the exiles
3:10 every *m* that hears the sound
5:7 Any *m* that will read this
5:11 capable *m* in your kingdom in
6:7 petition to any god or *m* for
6:12 *m* that asks a petition from
6:12 petition from any god or *m*
7:4 up on two feet just like a *m*
7:4 given to it the heart of a *m*
7:8 the eyes of a *m* in this horn
7:13 son of *m* happened to be
8:15 like an able-bodied *m*
8:16 voice of an earthling *m* in
8:17 Understand, O son of *m*, that
9:21 *m* Gabriel, whom I had seen
10:5 certain *m* clothed in linen
10:11 Daniel, you very desirable *m*
10:18 appearance of an earthling *m*
Da 10:19 afraid, O very desirable *m*
12:6 *m* clothed with the linen
12:7 the *m* clothed with the linen
Ho 2:10 *m* to snatch her out of my
3:3 come to belong to another *m*
4:4 let no *m* contend, neither let
4:4 neither let a *m* reprove, as
6:7 like earthling *m*, have
6:9 in the lying in wait for a *m*
9:7 the *m* of inspired expression
9:12 so that there will be no *m*
11:4 With the ropes of earthling *m*
11:9 for I am God and not *m*
Joe 2:8 As an able-bodied *m* in his
3:10 I am a powerful *m*
Am 2:7 a *m* and his own father have
2:14 no mighty *m* will provide his
4:13 One telling to earthling *m*
5:19 a *m* flees because of the lion
Jon 1:14 of the soul of this *m*
3:7 No *m* and no domestic animal
3:8 sackcloth, *m* and domestic
Mic 2:2 defrauded an able-bodied *m*
2:2 a *m* and his hereditary
2:11 If a *m*, walking by wind and
5:7 does not hope for *m* or wait
5:7 for the sons of earthling *m*
6:8 has told you, O earthling *m*
Hab 1:14 *m* like the fishes of the sea
2:5 *m* is self-assuming; and he
Zep 1:3 finish off earthling *m* and
1:14 *m* is letting out a cry
3:6 so that there was no *m*
Hag 1:11 and upon earthling *m*, and
2:12 If a *m* carries holy flesh in
Zec 1:8 a *m* riding on a red horse
1:10 *m* who was standing still
2:1 a *m*, and in his hand a
2:4 speak to the young *m* over
4:1 like a *m* that is awakened
6:12 the *m* whose name is Sprout
8:23 hold of the skirt of a *m*
9:1 has an eye on earthling *m* and
9:13 as the sword of a mighty *m*
10:7 become just like a mighty *m*
12:1 the spirit of *m* inside him
13:3 in case a *m* should prophesy
13:5 am a *m* cultivating the soil
13:5 earthling *m* himself acquired
13:7 *m* who is my associate
Mal 3:8 Will earthling *m* rob God?
3:17 as a *m* shows compassion
Mt 4:4 *M* must live, not on bread
7:9 who is the *m* among you whom
7:24 be likened to a discreet *m*
7:26 be likened to a foolish *m*
8:2 a leprous *m* came up and began
8:8 I am not a fit *m* for you to
8:9 a *m* placed under authority
8:20 Son of *m* has nowhere to lay
9:2 a paralyzed *m* lying on a bed
9:6 the Son of *m* has authority on
9:9 a *m* named Matthew seated at
9:32 dumb *m* possessed of a demon
9:33 expelled the dumb *m* spoke
10:23 until the Son of *m* arrives
10:35 with a *m* against his father
10:41 that receives a righteous *m*
10:41 because he is a righteous *m*
11:8 A *m* dressed in soft garments?
11:19 Son of *m* did come eating
11:19 A *m* gluttonous and given to
12:8 is what the Son of *m* is
12:10 a *m* with a withered hand!
12:11 *m* among you that has one
12:12 how much more worth is a *m*
12:13 said to the *m*: Stretch out
12:22 a demon-possessed *m*, blind
12:22 the dumb *m* spoke and saw
12:29 the house of a strong *m* and
12:29 first he binds the strong *m*
12:32 a word against the Son of *m*
12:35 The good *m* out of his good
12:35 wicked *m* out of his wicked
12:40 so the Son of *m* will be in
12:43 spirit comes out of a *m*, it
12:45 circumstances of that *m*
13:18 of the *m* that sowed
13:24 *m* that sowed fine seed in
13:28 An enemy, a *m*, did this
13:31 a *m* took and planted in his
13:37 sower . . . is the Son of *m*
13:41 Son of *m* will send forth
13:44 which a *m* found and hid
Mt 13:52 is like a *m*, a householder
13:54 did this *m* get this wisdom
13:56 Where, then, did this *m* get
15:11 defiles a *m*; but it is what
15:11 that defiles a *m*
15:14 If, then, a blind *m* guides a
15:14 guides a blind *m*, both will
15:18 and those things defile a *m*
15:20 are the things defiling a *m*
15:20 does not defile a *m*
16:13 men saying the Son of *m* is
16:26 benefit will it be to a *m*
16:26 *m* give in exchange for his
16:27 the Son of *m* is destined to
16:28 see the Son of *m* coming in
17:9 until the Son of *m* is raised
17:12 the Son of *m* is destined to
17:14 *m* approached him, kneeling
17:22 Son of *m* is destined to be
18:7 woe to the *m* through whom
18:12 *m* comes to have a hundred
18:17 just as a *m* of the nations
18:23 has become like a *m*, a king
18:24 brought in a *m* who owed
19:3 it lawful for a *m* to divorce
19:5 *m* will leave his father and
19:6 let no *m* put apart
19:10 of a *m* with his wife, it is
19:20 young *m* said to him: I have
19:22 young *m* heard this saying
19:23 difficult thing for a rich *m*
19:24 than for a rich *m* to get
19:28 when the Son of *m* sits down
20:1 like a *m*, a householder, who
20:8 said to his *m* in charge, Call
20:18 Son of *m* will be delivered
20:28 Son of *m* came, not to be
21:28 A *m* had two children
21:33 was a *m*, a householder, who
22:2 like a *m*, a king, that made
22:11 of a *m* not clothed with a
22:24 any *m* dies without having
24:17 Let the *m* on the housetop
24:18 *m* in the field not return to
24:27 the presence of the Son of *m*
24:30 sign of the Son of *m* will
24:30 see the Son of *m* coming on
24:37 the presence of the Son of *m*
24:39 the presence of the Son of *m*
24:44 the Son of *m* is coming
25:14 a *m*, about to travel abroad
25:24 exacting *m*, reaping where
25:31 the Son of *m* arrives in his
26:2 Son of *m* is to be delivered
26:24 the Son of *m* is going away
26:24 woe to that *m* through whom
26:24 the Son of *m* is betrayed
26:24 if that *m* had not been born
26:45 Son of *m* to be betrayed into
26:61 This *m* said, I am able to
26:64 you will see the Son of *m*
26:71 This *m* was with Jesus the
26:72 oath: I do not know the *m*!
26:74 swear: I do not know the *m*!
27:9 the price upon the *m* that
27:19 to do with that righteous *m*
27:24 of the blood of this *m*
27:32 This *m* they impressed into
27:47 This *m* is calling Elijah
27:49 *m* took a spear and pierced
27:57 came a rich *m* of Arimathea
27:58 This *m* went up to Pilate
Mr 1:23 a *m* under the power of an
1:45 *m* started to proclaim it a
2:7 this *m* talking in this manner
2:10 the Son of *m* has authority to
2:27 sabbath . . . for the sake of *m*
2:27 not *m* for the . . . sabbath
2:28 Son of *m* is Lord even of the
3:1 a *m* was there with a dried-up
3:2 cure the *m* on the sabbath, in
3:3 the *m* with the withered hand
3:5 he said to the *m*: Stretch out
3:27 into the house of a strong *m*
3:27 first he binds the strong *m*
4:26 as when a *m* casts the seed
5:2 a *m* under the power of an
5:8 telling it: Come out of the *m*
5:15 beheld the demon-possessed *m*
5:15 *m* that had had the legion
5:16 to the demon-possessed *m* and
5:18 the *m* that had been
6:2 did this *m* get these things
6:2 wisdom have been given this *m*

Mr 6:20 to be a righteous and holy *m*
7:11 If a *m* says to his father
7:15 nothing from outside a *m*
7:15 that issue forth out of a *m*
7:15 the things that defile a *m*
7:18 passes into a *m* can defile
7:20 issues forth out of a *m*
7:20 is what defiles a *m*
7:23 from within and defile a *m*
7:32 a *m* deaf and with a speech
8:22 people brought him a blind *m*
8:23 took the blind *m* by the hand
8:24 the *m* looked up and began
8:25 the *m* saw clearly, and he
8:31 the Son of *m* must undergo
8:36 a *m* to gain the whole world
8:37 a *m* give in exchange for his
8:38 the Son of *m* will also be
9:9 the Son of *m* had risen from
9:12 the Son of *m* that he must
9:31 Son of *m* is to be delivered
9:38 a certain *m* expelling demons
10:2 lawful for a *m* to divorce
10:7 a *m* will leave his father and
10:9 let no *m* put apart
10:17 a certain *m* ran up and fell
10:20 The *m* said to him: Teacher
10:25 a rich *m* to enter into the
10:33 Son of *m* will be delivered
10:45 even the Son of *m* came, not
10:49 they called the blind *m*
10:51 The blind *m* said to him
12:1 A *m* planted a vineyard, and
13:15 Let the *m* on the housetop
13:16 let the *m* in the field not
13:26 Son of *m* coming in clouds
13:34 like a *m* traveling abroad
14:13 a *m* carrying an earthenware
14:21 the Son of *m* is going away
14:21 woe to that *m* through whom
14:21 the Son of *m* is betrayed
14:21 finer for that *m* if he had
14:41 The Son of *m* is betrayed
14:51 *m* wearing a fine linen
14:62 see the Son of *m* sitting at
14:71 I do not know this *m* of
15:39 this *m* was God's Son
16:5 they saw a young *m* sitting
Lu 1:27 a *m* named Joseph of David's
1:34 no intercourse with a *m*
2:25 *m* in Jerusalem named Simeon
2:25 and this *m* was righteous and
3:11 *m* that has two undergarments
3:11 share with the *m* that has
4:4 *M* must not live by bread alone
4:27 but Naaman the *m* of Syria
4:33 a *m* with a spirit, an unclean
4:35 after throwing the *m* down in
5:8 because I am a sinful *m*, Lord
5:12 look! a *m* full of leprosy!
5:14 he gave the *m* orders to tell
5:18 a *m* who was paralyzed, and
5:20 *M*, your sins are forgiven you
5:24 the Son of *m* has authority on
5:24 he said to the paralyzed *m*
6:5 is what the Son of *m* is
6:6 a *m* present whose right hand
6:8 the *m* with the withered hand
6:10 he said to the *m*: Stretch out
6:22 for the sake of the Son of *m*
6:39 A blind *m* cannot guide a
6:39 cannot guide a blind *m*, can
6:45 A good *m* brings forth good
6:45 a wicked *m* brings forth what
6:48 like a *m* building a house
6:49 is like a *m* who built a house
7:8 am a *m* placed under authority
7:12 a dead *m* being carried out
7:14 Young *m*, I say to you, Get up!
7:15 the dead *m* sat up and started
7:25 A *m* dressed in soft outer
7:34 the Son of *m* has come eating
7:34 A *m* gluttonous and given to
7:39 This *m*, if he were a prophet
7:49 this *m* who even forgives sins
8:3 Chuza, Herod's *m* in charge
8:27 a certain *m* from the city
8:29 spirit to come out of the *m*
8:33 the demons went out of the *m*
8:35 the *m* from whom the demons
8:36 *m* had been made well
8:38 the *m* from whom the demons
8:38 he dismissed the *m*, saying
8:41 a *m* named Jairus came, and
Lu 8:41 this *m* was a presiding officer
9:22 The Son of *m* must undergo
9:25 what does a *m* benefit himself
9:26 Son of *m* will be ashamed of
9:38 a *m* cried out from the crowd
9:44 the Son of *m* is destined to
9:49 a certain *m* expelling demons
9:58 the Son of *m* has nowhere to
9:59 The *m* said: Permit me first
9:62 No *m* that has put his hand to
10:25 certain *m* versed in the Law
10:29 the *m* said to Jesus
10:30 A certain *m* was going down
10:36 the *m* that fell among the
11:14 came out, the dumb *m* spoke
11:21 When a strong *m*, well armed
11:24 spirit comes out of a *m*, it
11:26 circumstances of that *m*
11:30 same way will the Son of *m*
12:8 Son of *m* will also confess
12:10 a word against the Son of *m*
12:14 *M*, who appointed me judge
12:16 The land of a certain rich *m*
12:21 the *m* that lays up treasure
12:40 the Son of *m* is coming
13:6 A certain *m* had a fig tree
13:19 mustard grain that a *m* took
13:23 *m* said to him: Lord, are
14:2 a certain *m* who had dropsy
14:4 took hold of the *m*, healed
14:9 Let this *m* have the place
14:10 the *m* that has invited you
14:12 to the *m* that invited him
14:16 A certain *m* was spreading
14:30 This *m* started to build but
15:2 This *m* welcomes sinners and
15:4 What *m* of you with a hundred
15:11 A certain *m* had two sons
16:1 A certain *m* was rich and he
16:19 *m* was rich, and he used to
16:21 from the table of the rich *m*
16:22 rich *m* died and was buried
17:18 but this *m* of another nation
17:22 the days of the Son of *m*
17:24 so the Son of *m* will be
17:26 in the days of the Son of *m*
17:30 Son of *m* is to be revealed
18:2 and had no respect for *m*
18:4 not fear God or respect a *m*
18:8 when the Son of *m* arrives
18:14 This *m* went down to his
18:14 more righteous than that *m*
18:25 for a rich *m* to get into
18:31 as to the Son of *m* will be
18:35 blind *m* was sitting beside
18:40 the *m* to be led to him
19:2 *m* called . . . Zacchaeus
19:7 With a *m* that is a sinner he
19:10 the Son of *m* came to seek
19:12 *m* of noble birth traveled to
19:14 not want this *m* to become
19:21 because you are a harsh *m*
19:22 that I am a harsh *m*, taking
20:9 A *m* planted a vineyard and
21:27 Son of *m* coming in a cloud
21:36 standing before the Son of *m*
22:10 a *m* carrying an earthenware
22:12 *m* will show you a large
22:22 Son of *m* is going his way
22:22 woe to that *m* through whom
22:47 the *m* called Judas, one of
22:48 betray the Son of *m* with a
22:57 This *m* also was with him
22:58 But Peter said: *M*, I am not
22:59 *m* began insisting strongly
22:59 this *m* also was with him
22:60 Peter said: *M*, I do not know
22:69 Son of *m* will be sitting at
23:2 This *m* we found subverting
23:4 I find no crime in this *m*
23:6 whether the *m* was a Galilean
23:14 You brought this *m* to me as
23:14 found in this *m* no ground
23:19 *m* had been thrown into
23:22 what bad thing did this *m* do?
23:25 he released the *m* that had
23:41 this *m* did nothing out of
23:47 Really this *m* was righteous
23:50 a *m* named Joseph, who was
23:50 a good and righteous *m*
23:51 *m* had not voted in support
23:52 *m* went to Pilate and asked
23:53 in which no *m* had yet lain
24:7 Son of *m* must be delivered
Lu 24:21 hoping that this *m* was the
Joh 1:6 arose a *m* that was sent forth
1:7 This *m* came for a witness
1:9 light to every sort of *m*
1:18 No *m* has seen God at any
1:30 a *m* who has advanced in
1:51 descending to the Son of *m*
2:10 Every other *m* puts out the
2:25 anyone bear witness about *m*
2:25 knew what was in *m*
3:1 was a *m* of the Pharisees
3:4 How can a *m* be born when he
3:13 no *m* has ascended into
3:13 from heaven, the Son of *m*
3:14 Son of *m* must be lifted up
3:26 Rabbi, the *m* that was with
3:27 A *m* cannot receive a single
3:32 but no *m* is accepting his
4:18 *m* you now have is not your
4:29 a *m* that told me all the
4:42 this *m* is for a certainty
4:47 *m* heard that Jesus had come
4:50 *m* believed the word that
5:5 *m* was there who had been in
5:6 Seeing this *m* lying down, and
5:7 The sick *m* answered him
5:7 *m* to put me into the pool
5:9 *m* immediately became sound
5:10 began to say to the cured *m*
5:12 Who is the *m* that told you
5:13 healed *m* did not know who
5:15 *m* went away and told the
5:27 because Son of *m* he is
5:34 accept the witness from *m*
5:35 That *m* was a burning and
6:27 the Son of *m* will give you
6:44 No *m* can come to me unless
6:46 Not that any *m* has seen the
6:52 How can this *m* give us his
6:53 the flesh of the Son of *m*
6:62 the Son of *m* ascending to
7:11 and saying: Where is that *m*?
7:12 would say: He is a good *m*
7:15 this *m* have a knowledge of
7:22 circumcise a *m* on a sabbath
7:23 If a *m* receives circumcision
7:23 I made a *m* completely sound
7:25 *m* they are seeking to kill
7:27 know where this *m* is from
7:31 more signs than this *m* has
7:35 does this *m* intend going
7:46 Never has another *m* spoken
7:51 does not judge a *m* unless
8:15 I do not judge any *m* at all
8:28 have lifted up the Son of *m*
8:40 a *m* that has told you the
9:1 he saw a *m* blind from birth
9:2 sinned, this *m* or his parents
9:3 this *m* sinned nor his parents
9:4 is coming when no *m* can work
9:8 *m* that used to sit and beg
9:9 The *m* would say: I am he
9:11 *m* called Jesus made a clay
9:12 to him: Where is that *m*?
9:13 They led the once-blind *m*
9:16 not a *m* from God, because
9:16 How can a *m* that is a sinner
9:17 said to the blind *m* again
9:17 The *m* said: He is a prophet
9:18 of the *m* that gained sight
9:24 the *m* that had been blind
9:24 know that this *m* is a sinner
9:28 You are a disciple of that *m*
9:29 this *m*, we do not know
9:30 *m* said to them: This
9:33 If this *m* were not from God
9:35 faith in the Son of *m*
9:36 *m* answered: And who is he
10:12 hired *m*, who is no shepherd
10:13 hired *m* and does not care
10:18 No *m* has taken it away
10:21 sayings of a demonized *m*
10:33 a *m*, make yourself a god
10:41 John said about this *m* were
11:1 *m* sick, Lazarus of Bethany
11:37 *m* that opened the eyes of
11:37 the eyes of the blind *m*
11:44 *m* that had been dead came
11:47 this *m* performs many signs
11:50 one *m* to die in behalf of
12:23 Son of *m* to be glorified
12:34 Son of *m* must be lifted up
12:34 Who is this Son of *m*?
13:11 the *m* betraying him

Joh 13:31 Son of *m* is glorified, and
16:21 *m* has been born into the
18:14 *m* to die in behalf of the
18:26 *m* whose ear Peter cut off
18:29 you bring against this *m*
18:30 this *m* were not a wrongdoer
18:39 release a *m* to you at the
18:40 Not this *m*, but Barabbas!
19:5 said to them: Look! The *m!*
19:11 *m* that handed me over to
19:12 If you release this *m*
19:12 *m* making himself a king
19:32 the legs of the first *m*
19:32 *m* that had been impaled
19:35 that *m* knows he tells true
19:39 *m* that came to him in the
21:18 *m* will gird you and bear
21:21 Lord, what will this *m* do?
Ac 1:18 very *m*, therefore, purchased
2:22 a *m* publicly shown by God to
2:23 this *m*, as one delivered up
3:2 *m* that was lame from his
3:10 *m* that used to sit for gifts
3:11 *m* was holding onto Peter and
3:14 asked for a *m*, a murderer, to
3:16 made this *m* strong whom you
3:16 has given the *m* this complete
4:9 of a good deed to an ailing *m*
4:9 this *m* has been made well
4:10 *m* stand here sound in front
4:14 the *m* that had been cured
4:17 this name to any *m* at all
4:22 *m* upon whom this sign of
5:1 *m*, Ananias by name, together
5:25 *m* arrived and reported to
5:28 blood of this *m* upon us
5:34 *m* rose in the Sanhedrin, a
5:37 yet that *m* perished, and all
6:5 Stephen, a *m* full of faith and
6:13 *m* does not stop speaking
7:35 *m* God sent off as both ruler
7:36 *m* led them out after doing
7:56 Son of *m* standing at God's
7:58 of a young *m* called Saul
8:9 *m* named Simon, who, prior to
8:10 This *m* is the Power of God
8:27 *m* in power under Candace
8:34 or about some other *m*
9:7 voice, but not beholding any *m*
9:11 look for a *m* named Saul
9:12 *m* named Ananias come in and
9:13 heard from many about this *m*
9:15 this *m* is a chosen vessel to
9:21 the *m* that ravaged those in
9:33 *m* named Aeneas, who had been
10:1 *m* named Cornelius, an army
10:2 devout *m* and one fearing God
10:4 *m* gazed at him and, becoming
10:6 *m* is being entertained by a
10:22 *m* righteous and fearing God
10:26 Rise; I myself am also a *m*
10:28 approach a *m* of another race
10:28 call no *m* defiled or unclean
10:30 *m* in bright raiment stood
10:32 *m* is being entertained in
10:35 *m* that fears him and works
11:12 into the house of the *m*
11:24 he was a good *m* and full of
13:6 certain *m*, a sorcerer, a
13:7 Paulus, an intelligent *m*
13:7 *m* earnestly sought to hear
13:10 O *m* full of every sort of
13:21 *m* of the tribe of Benjamin
13:22 a *m* agreeable to my heart
13:23 the offspring of this *m*
14:8 *m* disabled in his feet, lame
14:9 This *m* was listening to Paul
16:3 this *m* to go out with him
16:9 Macedonian *m* was standing
17:26 he made out of one *m* every
17:29 the art and contrivance of *m*
17:31 a *m* whom he has appointed
18:7 of a *m* named Titius Justus, a
18:10 no *m* will assault you so as
18:24 Apollos . . . an eloquent *m*
18:25 *m* had been orally instructed
18:26 *m* started to speak boldly in
19:16 *m* in whom the wicked spirit
19:24 a certain *m* named Demetrius
20:9 young *m* named Eutychus fell
21:9 This *m* had four daughters
21:11 The *m* to whom this girdle
21:16 *m* at whose home we were to
21:28 This is the *m* that teaches
Ac 22:12 Now Ananias, a certain *m*
22:22 Take such a *m* away from the
22:25 scourge a *m* that is a Roman
22:26 Why, this *m* is a Roman
23:9 find nothing wrong in this *m*
23:17 Lead this young *m* off to the
23:18 this *m* took him and led him
23:18 to lead this young *m* to you
23:22 let the young *m* go after
23:27 *m* was seized by the Jews
23:30 plot . . . against the *m*
24:5 found this *m* a pestilent
24:23 that the *m* be kept and have
25:3 as a favor against the *m* that
25:5 out of the way about the *m*
25:11 no *m* can hand me over to
25:14 *m* left prisoner by Felix
25:16 to hand any *m* over as a favor
25:16 before the accused *m* meets
25:17 the *m* to be brought in
25:22 also like to hear the *m*
25:24 *m* concerning whom all the
25:25 *m* himself appealed to the
26:31 This *m* practices nothing
26:32 *m* could have been released
28:4 Surely this *m* is a murderer
28:7 principal *m* of the island
Ro 1:23 image of corruptible *m* and
2:1 you are inexcusable, O *m*
2:3 do you have this idea, O *m*
2:9 *m* who works what is injurious
3:4 every *m* be found a liar, even
3:5 I am speaking as a *m* does
3:10 not a righteous *m*, not even
3:26 the *m* that has faith in Jesus
3:28 *m* is declared righteous by
4:4 the *m* that works the pay is
4:5 *m* that does not work but puts
4:6 happiness of the *m* to whom
4:8 happy is the *m* whose sin
5:7 anyone die for a righteous *m*
5:7 for the good *m*, perhaps
5:12 through one *m* sin entered
5:15 kindness by the one *m* Jesus
5:16 through the one *m* that sinned
5:17 by the trespass of the one *m*
5:19 disobedience of the one *m*
7:1 Law is master over a *m* as
7:22 according to the *m* I am
7:24 Miserable *m* that I am!
8:24 *m* sees a thing, does he hope
9:10 from the one *m*, Isaac our
9:20 O *m*, who, then, really are
10:5 Moses writes that the *m* that
14:1 *m* having weaknesses in his
14:2 *m* has faith to eat everything
14:2 but the *m* who is weak eats
14:5 One *m* judges one day as
14:5 another *m* judges one day as
14:5 let each *m* be fully convinced
14:14 *m* considers something to be
14:20 is injurious to the *m* who
14:22 Happy is the *m* that does
1Co 1:20 Where is the wise *m?*
2:9 conceived in the heart of *m*
2:11 knows the things of a *m*
2:11 spirit of *m* that is in him
2:14 physical *m* does not receive
2:15 spiritual *m* examines indeed
2:15 is not examined by any *m*
3:11 For no *m* can lay any other
4:1 Let a *m* so appraise us as
4:2 for a *m* to be found faithful
5:1 a certain *m* has of his father
5:2 *m* that committed this deed
5:3 the *m* who has worked in such
5:5 hand such a *m* over to Satan
5:11 even eating with such a *m*
5:13 Remove the wicked *m* from
6:5 not one wise *m* among you
6:18 sin that a *m* may commit is
7:1 for a *m* not to touch a woman
7:2 let each *m* have his own wife
7:18 any *m* called circumcised
7:18 Has any *m* been called in
7:22 was called when a free *m* is
7:26 is well for a *m* to continue
7:32 unmarried *m* is anxious for
7:33 married *m* is anxious for the
8:11 the *m* that is weak is being
9:10 *m* who plows ought to plow
9:10 the *m* who threshes ought to
9:15 no *m* is going to make my
9:25 every *m* taking part in a
1Co 11:3 the head of every *m* is the
11:3 head of a woman is the *m*
11:4 Every *m* that prays or
11:7 For a *m* ought not to have
11:8 For *m* is not out of woman
11:8 but woman out of *m*
11:9 *m* was not created for the
11:9 woman for the sake of the *m*
11:11 neither is woman without *m*
11:11 nor *m* without woman
11:12 the woman is out of the *m*
11:12 so also the *m* is through
11:14 if a *m* has long hair, it is
11:16 if any *m* seems to dispute
11:28 let a *m* approve himself
13:11 that I have become a *m*
14:16 *m* occupying the seat of the
14:17 *m* is not being built up
15:21 since death is through a *m*
15:21 is also through a *m*
15:45 The first *m* Adam became a
15:47 first *m* is out of the earth
15:47 second *m* is out of heaven
2Co 2:6 is sufficient for such a *m*
2:7 *m* may not be swallowed up by
4:16 *m* we are outside is wasting
4:16 *m* we are inside is being
5:14 one *m* died for all; so
5:16 no *m* according to the flesh
8:20 having any *m* find fault with
10:11 Let such a *m* take this into
10:18 *m* whom Jehovah recommends
11:16 *m* think I am unreasonable
12:2 *m* in union with Christ who
12:3 I know such a *m*—whether in
12:4 not lawful for a *m* to speak
12:5 Over such a *m* I will boast
Ga 1:1 nor through a *m*, but through
1:12 did I receive it from *m*
1:23 *m* that formerly persecuted us
2:16 a *m* is declared righteous
3:13 every *m* hanged upon a stake
5:3 to every *m* getting circumcised
6:1 *m* takes some false step before
6:1 readjust such a *m* in a spirit
6:7 whatever a *m* is sowing, this
Eph 2:9 no *m* should have ground for
2:15 into one new *m* and make
3:8 a *m* less than the least of
3:16 in the *m* you are inside
4:13 to a full-grown *m*, to the
5:6 Let no *m* deceive you with
5:29 no *m* ever hated his own
5:31 *m* will leave his father and
Php 2:8 as a *m*, he humbled himself
2:23 is the *m* I am hoping to send
3:4 *m* thinks he has grounds for
Col 1:28 admonishing every *m* and
1:28 and teaching every *m* in all
1:28 present every *m* complete in
2:4 that no *m* may delude you with
2:16 let no *m* judge you in eating
2:18 Let no *m* deprive you of the
1Th 4:8 the *m* that shows disregard is
4:8 disregarding, not *m*, but God
2Th 2:3 *m* of lawlessness . . . revealed
1Ti 1:9 not for a righteous *m*, but
1:13 persecutor and an insolent *m*
2:5 a *m*, Christ Jesus
2:12 exercise authority over a *m*
3:1 If any *m* is reaching out for
3:4 a *m* presiding over his own
3:5 *m* does not know how to
3:6 not a newly converted *m*, for
4:12 Let no *m* ever look down on
5:1 severely criticize an older *m*
5:19 against an older *m*, except
5:22 hands hastily upon any *m*
6:3 any *m* teaches other doctrine
6:11 O *m* of God, flee from these
2Ti 2:4 No *m* serving as a soldier
3:17 the *m* of God may be fully
Tit 1:6 any *m* free from accusation
2:8 the *m* on the opposing side
2:15 Let no *m* ever despise you
3:4 love for *m* on the part of our
3:10 a *m* that promotes a sect
3:11 such a *m* has been turned out
Phm 9 Paul an aged *m*, yes, now also
Heb 2:6 What is *m* that you keep him
2:6 son of *m* that you take care
2:9 might taste death for every *m*
4:10 the *m* that has entered into
5:4 *m* takes this honor, not of

Heb 7:4 how great this *m* was to
7:6 *m* who did not trace his
7:13 the *m* respecting whom these
8:2 Jehovah put up, and not *m*
9:9 the *m* doing sacred service
10:12 *m* offered one sacrifice
10:28 *m* that has disregarded the
10:29 *m* be counted worthy who
11:12 from one *m*, and him as
11:17 *m* that had gladly received
12:14 without which no *m* will
13:6 What can *m* do to me?
Jas 1:7 *m* suppose that he will
1:8 is an indecisive *m*, unsteady
1:11 rich *m* will fade away in
1:12 Happy is the *m* that keeps
1:19 *m* must be swift about
1:23 *m* looking at his natural
1:24 forgets what sort of *m* he is
1:25 this *m*, because he has
1:26 *m* seems to himself to be a
2:2 *m* with gold rings on his
2:2 poor *m* in filthy clothing
2:6 have dishonored the poor *m*
2:20 know, O empty *m*, that faith
2:24 that a *m* is to be declared
3:2 this one is a perfect *m*, able
3:4 of the *m* at the helm wishes
5:17 Elijah . . . a *m* with feelings
1Pe 3:13 who is the *m* that will harm
4:18 righteous *m* is being saved
4:18 where will the ungodly *m*
5:1 I too am an older *m* with
2Pe 2:8 that righteous *m* by what he
2:16 with the voice of a *m*
2Jo 1 The older *m* to the chosen lady
3Jo 1 older *m* to Gaius, the beloved
Re 1:13 son of *m*, clothed with a
7:9 crowd, which no *m* was able to
9:5 scorpion when it strikes a *m*
14:14 seated like a son of *m*
16:3 became blood as of a dead *m*
18:17 *m* that voyages anywhere

Manaen
Ac 13:1 *M* who was educated with

Manage
Lu 16:2 you can no longer *m* the house
1Ti 5:14 widows . . . to *m* a household
Jas 3:3 we *m* also their whole body

Managed
1Ki 12:18 Rehoboam himself *m* to get
2Ch 10:18 *m* to get up into his

Managing
Ge 24:2 who was *m* all he had: Put

Manahath
Ge 36:23 sons of Shobal . . . *M* and
1Ch 1:40 sons of Shobal were . . . *M*
8:6 to take them into exile at *M*

Manahathites
1Ch 2:54 and half of the *M*

Manasseh
Ge 41:51 the name of the firstborn *M*
46:20 *M* and Ephraim, whom Asenath
48:1 his two sons *M* and Ephraim
48:5 Ephraim and *M* will become
48:13 *M* . . . to Israel's right, and
48:14 since *M* was the firstborn
48:20 you like Ephraim and like *M*
48:20 putting Ephraim before *M*
Nu 1:10 of *M*, Gamaliel the son of
1:34 sons of *M*, their births
1:35 registered . . . tribe of *M*
2:20 will be the tribe of *M*, and
2:20 chieftain for the sons of *M*
7:54 chieftain for the sons of *M*
10:23 tribe of the sons of *M*
13:11 for the tribe of *M*, Gaddi
26:28 by their families were *M* and
26:29 sons of *M* were: Of Machir
26:34 were the families of *M*
27:1 Machir the son of *M*, of the
27:1 of *M* the son of Joseph
32:33 and to half the tribe of *M*
32:39 sons of Machir the son of *M*
32:40 to Machir the son of *M*, and
32:41 Jair the son of *M* marched
34:14 half tribe of *M* have already
34:23 of the sons of *M* a chieftain
36:1 Machir the son of *M* of the
36:12 families of the sons of *M*
De 3:13 given to the half tribe of *M*
De 3:14 Jair the son of *M* took all
33:17 they are the thousands of *M*
34:2 the land of Ephraim and *M*
Jos 1:12 half tribe of *M* Joshua said
4:12 and the half tribe of *M*
12:6 and half of the tribe of *M*
13:7 and the half tribe of *M*
13:29 gift to the half tribe of *M*
13:29 half tribe of the sons of *M*
13:31 of Machir the son of *M*
14:4 two tribes, *M* and Ephraim
16:4 sons of Joseph, *M* and
16:9 inheritance of the sons of *M*
17:1 to be for the tribe of *M*
17:1 Machir the firstborn of *M*
17:2 a lot for the sons of *M*
17:2 *M* the son of Joseph
17:3 Machir, the son of *M*
17:5 ten allotments falling to *M*
17:6 the daughters of *M* came into
17:6 the property of the sons of *M*
17:7 the boundary of *M* came to be
17:8 boundary of *M* belonged to
17:9 the midst of the cities of *M*
17:9 the boundary of *M* was on the
17:11 belong to *M* in Issachar and
17:12 sons of *M* did not prove
17:17 Joshua said this to . . . *M*
18:7 the half tribe of *M* have
20:8 out of the tribe of *M*
21:5 out of the half tribe of *M*
21:6 half tribe of *M* in Bashan
21:25 from the half tribe of *M*
21:27 out of the half tribe of *M*
22:1 and the half tribe of *M*
22:7 the half tribe of *M* Moses
22:9 the half tribe of *M* returned
22:10 the half tribe of *M* built
22:11 half tribe of *M* have built
22:13 half tribe of *M* in the land
22:15 half tribe of *M* in the land
22:21 half tribe of *M* answered
22:30 the sons of *M* spoke, it
22:31 said to . . . the sons of *M*
Jg 1:27 *M* did not take possession of
6:15 My thousand is the least in *M*
6:35 messengers through all of *M*
7:23 Asher and all of *M*, and they
11:29 pass through Gilead and *M*
12:4 Ephraim, inside of *M*
1Ki 4:13 Jair the son of *M*, which are
2Ki 20:21 *M* his son began to reign
21:1 Twelve years old was *M* when
21:9 *M* kept seducing them to do
21:11 *M* the king of Judah has
21:16 blood that *M* shed in very
21:17 affairs of *M* and all that
21:18 *M* lay down with his
21:20 as *M* his father had done
23:12 the altars that *M* had made
23:26 *M* had made them offend
24:3 for the sins of *M*
1Ch 3:13 Hezekiah his son, *M* his son
5:18 and the half tribe of *M*
5:23 half tribe of *M*, they dwelt
5:26 half tribe of *M* and brought
6:61 the half of *M*, by the lot
6:62 the tribe of *M* in Bashan
6:70 from half of the tribe of *M*
6:71 the half tribe of *M* Golan in
7:14 The sons of *M* were Asriel
7:17 son of Machir the son of *M*
7:29 by the side of the sons of *M*
9:3 the sons of Ephraim and of *M*
12:19 of *M* that deserted to David
12:20 deserted to him from *M*
12:20 that belonged to *M*
12:31 And of the half tribe of *M*
12:37 and the half tribe of *M*
27:20 the half tribe of *M*, Joel
27:21 half tribe of *M* in Gilead
2Ch 15:9 from Ephraim and *M* and
30:1 he wrote to Ephraim and *M*
30:10 land of Ephraim and *M*, even
30:11 from Asher and *M* and
30:18 many from Ephraim and *M*
31:1 *M* until they had finished
32:33 *M* his son began to reign in
33:1 Twelve years old was *M* when
33:9 *M* kept seducing Judah and
33:10 Jehovah kept speaking to *M*
33:11 captured *M* in the hollows
33:13 *M* came to know that Jehovah
33:18 *M* and his prayer to his God
2Ch 33:20 *M* lay down with his
33:22 as *M* his father had done
33:22 images that *M* his father
33:23 the same as *M* his father
34:6 cities of *M* and Ephraim and
34:9 the hand of *M* and Ephraim
Ezr 10:30 sons of Pahath-moab . . . *M*
10:33 the sons of Hashum . . . *M*
Ps 60:7 and *M* belongs to me
80:2 and *M* do rouse up your
108:8 *M* belongs to me
Isa 9:21 *M* Ephraim, and Ephraim
9:21 and Ephraim *M*. Together they
Jer 15:4 *M* the son of Hezekiah, the
Eze 48:4 to the western border, *M* one
48:5 on the boundary of *M*, from
Mt 1:10 Hezekiah became father to *M*
1:10 *M* became father to Amon
Re 7:6 out of . . . *M* twelve thousand

Manasseh's
Ge 48:14 his left hand upon *M* head
48:17 from Ephraim's head to *M*
50:23 the sons of Machir, *M* son
Jos 17:8 land of Tappuah became *M*
17:10 and to the north, *M*

Manassites
De 4:43 and Golan in Bashan for the *M*
29:8 and half the tribe of the *M*
2Ki 10:33 the Reubenites and the *M*
1Ch 26:32 and the half tribe of the *M*

Mandate
1Ti 1:5 objective of this *m* is love
1:18 This *m* I commit to you

Mandrakes
Ge 30:14 got to find *m* in the field
30:14 please, some of your son's *m*
30:15 taking also my son's *m*
30:15 exchange for your son's *m*
30:16 with my son's *m*
Ca 7:13 *m* themselves have given their

Mane
Job 39:19 its neck with a rustling *m*

Maned
Jg 14:5 a *m* young lion roaring upon
Job 4:10 teeth of *m* young lions do
Ps 34:10 The *m* young lions themselves
35:17 from the *m* young lions
58:6 jawbones of *m* young lions
91:13 trample . . . the *m* young lion
104:21 *m* young lions are roaring
Pr 19:12 like that of a *m* young lion
20:2 like that of a *m* young lion
Isa 5:29 they roar like *m* young lions
11:6 calf and the *m* young lion
31:4 even the *m* young lion, over
Jer 2:15 *m* young lions roar
25:38 just like a *m* young lion
51:38 just like *m* young lions
Eze 19:2 down in among *m* young lions
19:3 A *m* young lion is what he
19:5 As a *m* young lion she put
19:6 A *m* young lion is what he
32:2 As a *m* young lion of nations
38:13 all its *m* young lions
41:19 face of a *m* young lion
Ho 5:14 like a *m* young lion to the
Am 3:4 *m* lion give forth its voice
Mic 5:8 like a *m* young lion among
Na 2:11 belongs to the *m* young lions
2:13 devour your own *m* young lions
Zec 11:3 The roaring of *m* young lions

Maneh
Eze 45:12 prove to be the *m* for you

Manger
Job 39:9 spend the night by your *m*
Pr 14:4 are no cattle the *m* is clean
Isa 1:3 the ass the *m* of its owner
Lu 2:7 laid him in a *m*, because there
2:12 an infant . . . lying in a *m*
2:16 and the infant lying in the *m*

Manger-fed
Pr 15:17 *m* bull and hatred along with

Manhood
Nu 11:28 of Moses from his young *m*
Ec 11:9 in the days of your young *m*
12:1 days of your young *m*, before

Manifest
Mt 12:16 not to make him *m*
Lu 8:17 that will not become *m*

Joh 1:31 might be made *m* to Israel
2:11 and he made his glory *m*
3:21 his works may be made *m*
7:4 *m* yourself to the world
9:3 might be made *m* in his case
17:6 name *m* to the men you gave
Ac 4:16 *m* to all the inhabitants of
7:13 Joseph became *m* to Pharaoh
10:40 granted him to become *m*
Ro 1:19 God is *m* among them, for
1:19 for God made it *m* to them
3:21 righteousness has been made *m*
10:20 *m* to those who were not
16:26 been made *m* and has been
1Co 3:13 work will become *m*, for the
4:5 the counsels of the hearts *m*
11:19 also become *m* among you
14:25 secrets of his heart . . . *m*
2Co 4:2 but by making the truth *m*
4:10 Jesus may also be made *m*
4:11 made *m* in our mortal flesh
5:10 *m* before the judgment seat
5:11 we have been made *m* to God
5:11 *m* also to your consciences
7:12 *m* among you in the sight of
Ga 3:19 to make transgressions *m*
5:19 works of the flesh are *m*
Eph 5:13 are made *m* by the light
5:13 is being made *m* is light
Col 1:26 been made *m* to his holy ones
3:4 Christ, our life, is made *m*
3:4 be made *m* with him in glory
4:4 make it *m* as I ought to speak
1Ti 3:16 He was made *m* in flesh
4:15 advancement may be *m* to all
5:24 sins of some . . . publicly *m*
5:24 sins also become *m* later
5:25 fine works are publicly *m*
Tit 1:3 word *m* in the preaching with
Heb 4:13 not a creation that is not *m*
9:8 made *m* while the first tent
1Pe 1:20 *m* at the end of the times
5:4 shepherd has been made *m*
1Jo 1:2 yes, the life was made *m*
1:2 and was made *m* to us
2:28 when he is made *m* we may
3:2 not been made *m* what we
3:2 whenever he is made *m* we
3:5 made *m* to take away our sins
3:8 Son of God was made *m*
4:9 the love of God was made *m*
Re 15:4 decrees have been made *m*

Manifestation
Joh 21:1 he made the *m* in this way
1Co 12:7 the *m* of the spirit is given
2Th 2:8 by the *m* of his presence
1Ti 6:14 until the *m* of our Lord
6:15 This *m* the happy and only
2Ti 1:10 *m* of our Savior, Christ
4:1 by his *m* and his kingdom
4:8 those who have loved his *m*
Tit 2:13 *m* of the great God and of

Manifested
Joh 21:1 Jesus *m* himself again to the
2Co 11:6 we *m* it to you in all things
Tit 2:11 undeserved kindness . . . *m*
3:4 kindness and the love . . . *m*
Heb 9:26 *m* himself once for all time
Re 3:18 nakedness may not become *m*

Manifold
Job 11:6 of practical wisdom are *m*

Mankind
Ge 7:21 upon the earth, and all *m*
Ex 30:32 rubbed in the flesh of *m*
Le 24:17 soul of *m* fatally, he should
27:28 from *m* or beasts or from the
27:29 to destruction from among *m*
Nu 5:6 sins of *m* in committing an act
16:29 the death of all *m* that
16:29 the punishment of all *m* that
18:15 redeem the firstborn of *m*
23:19 Neither a son of *m* that he
Jg 18:7 they had nothing to do with *m*
18:28 nothing at all to do with *m*
2Sa 7:19 is the law given for *m*
23:3 When one ruling over *m* is
1Ki 8:39 heart of all the sons of *m*
2Ch 6:18 God truly dwell with *m* upon
6:30 heart of the sons of *m*
Job 7:20 against . . . Observer of *m*
21:33 after him . . . drag all *m*
36:25 All *m* themselves have gazed
Job 36:28 They drip upon *m* abundantly
Ps 58:11 And *m* will say: Surely there
62:9 The sons of *m* are a lie
80:17 *m* whom you have made strong
104:14 for the service of *m*
119:134 from any defrauder of *m*
Pr 15:11 the hearts of the sons of *m*
24:9 ridiculer . . . detestable to *m*
30:2 have the understanding of *m*
30:14 the poor ones from among *m*
Ec 1:13 has given to the sons of *m*
2:3 the sons of *m* in what they did
2:8 delights of the sons of *m*, a
3:10 of *m* in which to be occupied
3:11 that *m* may never find out the
3:18 with regard to the sons of *m*
3:19 as respects the sons of *m* and
3:21 the spirit of the sons of *m*
6:1 and it is frequent among *m*
6:7 work of *m* is for their mouth
7:2 that is the end of all *m*
7:14 *m* may not discover anything
7:29 God made *m* upright, but they
8:6 calamity of *m* is abundant upon
8:15 *m* have nothing better under
8:17 *m* are not able to find out
8:17 *m* keep working hard to seek
9:1 *M* are not aware of either the
Isa 29:19 poor ones of *m* will be
38:11 I shall no more look on *m*
44:13 like the beauty of *m*, to
51:12 a son of *m* that will be
52:14 than that of the sons of *m*
56:2 the son of *m* that lays hold
Jer 7:20 upon *m* and upon domestic
9:22 The dead bodies of *m* must
27:5 *m* and the beasts that are
49:15 despised among *m*
49:18 *m* will reside in her as an
49:33 *m* will reside as an alien
50:40 *m* reside in her as an alien
51:43 no son of *m* will pass
Eze 4:12 cakes of the excrement of *m*
4:15 dung cakes of *m*, and you
23:42 men out of the mass of *m*
27:13 For the souls of *m* and
31:14 midst of the sons of *m*
38:20 *m* that are upon the surface
44:25 to a dead person of *m* he
Da 2:38 the sons of *m* are dwelling
2:43 with the offspring of *m*
4:16 be changed from that of *m*
4:17 Ruler in the kingdom of *m*
4:17 even the lowliest one of *m*
4:25 Ruler in the kingdom of *m*
4:32 from *m* they are driving even
4:32 is Ruler in the kingdom of *m*
4:33 from *m* he was being driven
5:21 sons of *m* he was driven away
5:21 Ruler in the kingdom of *m*
10:16 likeness of the sons of *m*
Joe 1:12 away from the sons of *m*
Mic 5:5 yes, eight dukes of *m*
7:2 among *m* there is no upright
Hab 2:8 the shedding of blood of *m*
2:17 the shedding of blood of *m*
Zep 1:3 cut off *m* from the surface
1:17 will cause distress to *m*
Zec 8:10 wages for *m* made to exist
8:10 all *m* against one another
11:6 causing *m* to find themselves
Mt 5:19 and teaches *m* to that effect
Mr 11:2 which none of *m* has yet sat
Lu 19:30 on which none of *m* ever sat
Ac 17:30 he is telling *m* that they
19:35 who really is there of *m*
Ro 2:16 judges the secret things of *m*
1Co 15:39 but there is one of *m*
2Co 3:2 known and being read by all *m*
Jas 3:8 tongue, not one of *m* can get
Re 13:13 earth in the sight of *m*
14:4 were bought from among *m*
21:3 The tent of God is with *m*

Manly
Ex 15:3 Jehovah is a *m* person of war

Manna
Ex 16:31 began to call its name *m*
16:33 put in it an omerful of *m*
16:35 Israel ate the *m* forty years
16:35 *m* was what they ate until
Nu 11:6 nothing at all except the *m*
11:7 *m* was like coriander seed
11:9 the *m* would descend upon it
De 8:3 fed you with the *m*, which
8:16 with *m* in the wilderness
Jos 5:12 *m* ceased on the following
5:12 *m* did not occur anymore for
Ne 9:20 *m* you did not hold back from
Ps 78:24 raining upon them *m* to eat
Joh 6:31 ate the *m* in the wilderness
6:49 ate the *m* in the wilderness
Heb 9:4 the golden jar having the *m*
Re 2:17 give some of the hidden *m*

Manner
Ge 18:25 acting in this *m* to put to
27:34 extremely loud and bitter *m*
Nu 10:12 *m* of their departures from
10:28 *m* were the departures of
De 15:2 this is the *m* of the release
Jos 6:15 in this *m* seven times
Jg 8:8 in this same *m*, but the men of
Ezr 5:7 writing in it was in this *m*
Ne 5:13 In this *m* may the true God
5:13 this *m* may he become shaken
Ps 110:4 to the *m* of Melchizedek
Ec 11:5 in like *m* you do not know the
Isa 29:14 people, in a wonderful *m*
61:11 in like *m* Jehovah himself
La 1:9 down she goes in a wondrous *m*
2:20 have dealt severely in this *m*
Eze 23:44 in that *m* they came in to
Mt 18:35 like *m* my heavenly Father
27:41 In like *m* also the chief
Mr 2:7 is this man talking in this *m*
15:31 In like *m* also the chief
Lu 13:34 in the *m* that a hen gathers
Joh 5:19 the Son also does in like *m*
Ac 1:11 come thus in the same *m* as
7:28 same *m* that you did away
13:18 up with their *m* of action
14:1 and spoke in such a *m* that a
21:11 Jews will bind in this *m* in
24:14 in this *m* I am rendering
26:4 *m* of life from youth up that
Ro 8:26 In like *m* the spirit also
10:6 from faith speaks in this *m*
11:26 in this *m* all Israel will
2Co 7:5 to be afflicted in every *m*
Ga 4:23 born in the *m* of flesh, the
4:29 one born in the *m* of flesh
4:29 one born in the *m* of spirit
Php 1:27 in a *m* worthy of the good
1Th 5:23 preserved in a blameless *m*
2Th 2:3 no one seduce you in any *m*
1Ti 3:4 own household in a fine *m*
3:12 presiding in a fine *m* over
3:13 who minister in a fine *m*
Heb 5:6 to the *m* of Melchizedek
5:10 to the *m* of Melchizedek
6:17 In this *m* God, when he
6:20 *m* of Melchizedek forever
7:11 to the *m* of Melchizedek
7:11 according to the *m* of Aaron
7:17 to the *m* of Melchizedek
13:5 *m* of life be free of the
Jas 2:25 In the same *m* was not also
1Pe 3:1 In like *m*, you wives, be in
3:7 dwelling in like *m* with them
5:5 In like *m*, you younger men
3Jo 6 in a *m* worthy of God
Jude 7 same *m* as the foregoing ones
8 In like *m*, notwithstanding
Re 11:5 in this *m* he must be killed

Manoah
Jg 13:2 his name was *M*. And his wife
13:8 *M* began to entreat Jehovah
13:9 listened to the voice of *M*
13:9 *M* her husband was not with
13:11 *M* got up and accompanied his
13:12 *M* said: Now let your words
13:13 So Jehovah's angel said to *M*
13:15 *M* now said to Jehovah's
13:16 said to *M*: If you detain me
13:16 *M* did not know that he was
13:17 *M* said to Jehovah's angel
13:19 *M* proceeded to take the kid
13:19 *M* and his wife were looking
13:20 *M* and his wife were looking
13:21 appearing to *M* and his wife
13:21 *M* knew that he had been
13:22 *M* said to his wife: We
16:31 burial place of *M* his father

Man's
Ge 8:21 evil upon the ground on *m*
9:6 Anyone shedding *m* blood, by

Ge 20:7 return the *m* wife, for he is
44:26 not able to see the *m* face
Ex 21:35 in case a *m* bull should hurt
22:7 gets stolen from the *m* house
Le 20:10 adultery with another *m* wife
21:3 become a *m*, for her he may
22:12 *m* who is a stranger, she as
Nu 5:12 *m* wife turns aside in that
De 24:2 go and become another *m*
25:5 should not become a strange *m*
Jg 19:26 *m* house where her master
Ru 1:2 And the *m* name was Elimelech
1Sa 25:3 *m* name was Nabal, and his
1Ki 18:44 small cloud like a *m* palm
2Ki 19:18 workmanship of *m* hands
2Ch 32:19 the work of *m* hands
Pr 6:26 another *m* wife, she hunts
12:14 fruitage of a *m* mouth he is
12:14 doing of a *m* hands will
12:27 is a *m* precious wealth
13:8 ransom for a *m* soul is his
18:4 words of a *m* mouth are deep
18:16 A *m* gift will make a large
18:20 the fruitage of a *m* mouth
Isa 37:19 workmanship of *m* hands
Jer 3:1 and become another *m*, should
Eze 1:10 four of them had a *m* face
Da 5:5 fingers of a *m* hand came forth
Mic 7:6 a *m* enemies are the men of
Mt 10:36 a *m* enemies will be persons
10:41 get a righteous *m* reward
Mr 7:33 his fingers into the *m* ears
8:25 hands again upon the *m* eyes
Lu 20:28 If a *m* brother dies having a
Joh 1:13 fleshly will or from *m* will
9:6 put his clay upon the *m* eyes
18:17 one of this *m* disciples
Ac 12:22 A god's voice, and not a *m*
20:33 I have coveted no *m* silver
Ro 5:15 by one *m* trespass many died
7:3 if she became another *m*
7:3 if she becomes another *m*
15:20 on another *m* foundation
1Co 11:7 but the woman is *m* glory
Ga 2:6 God does not go by a *m* outward
3:15 covenant, though it is a *m*
Jas 1:20 *m* wrath does not work out
1:26 *m* form of worship is futile
5:16 A righteous *m* supplication
2Pe 1:21 no time brought by *m* will
Re 4:7 creature has a face like a *m*
13:18 for it is a *m* number; and
21:17 according to a *m* measure

Manservant
Jer 34:9 to let each one his *m* and
34:10 to let each one his *m*
34:16 bring back each one his *m*
Mt 8:6 my *m* is laid up in the house
8:8 and my *m* will be healed
8:13 *m* was healed in that hour

Manslayer
Nu 35:6 give for the *m* to flee there
35:11 the *m* must flee there who
35:12 that the *m* may not die until
35:25 deliver the *m* out of the
35:26 *m* without fail goes out of
35:27 does slay the *m*, he has no
35:28 *m* may return to the land of
De 4:42 *m* to flee there who slays his
19:3 be for any *m* to flee there
19:4 the *m* who may flee there and
19:6 chase after the *m* and
Jos 20:3 *m* who fatally strikes a soul
20:5 not surrender the *m* into his
20:6 then that the *m* may return
21:13 city of refuge for the *m*
21:21 city of refuge for the *m*
21:27 city of refuge for the *m*
21:32 city of refuge for the *m*
21:38 city of refuge for the *m*
Joh 8:44 was a *m* when he began, and
1Jo 3:15 who hates his brother is a *m*
3:15 no *m* has everlasting life

Manslayers
1Ti 1:9 and murderers of mothers, *m*

Mantle
Ge 9:23 Shem and Japheth took a *m* and
Ex 22:27 It is his *m* for his skin
De 8:4 Your *m* did not wear out upon
10:18 give him bread and a *m*
21:13 the *m* of her captivity from
22:3 way you will do with his *m*
De 22:5 man wear the *m* of a woman
22:17 spread out the *m* before the
Jg 8:25 they spread out a *m* and went
1Sa 21:9 wrapped up in a *m*, behind the
Pr 30:4 wrapped up the waters in a *m*
Isa 3:6 You have a *m*. A dictator you
3:7 is neither bread nor a *m*
9:5 *m* rolled in blood have even
61:3 the *m* of praise instead of

Mantles
Ge 35:2 Jacob said . . . change your *m*
37:34 Jacob ripped his *m* apart and
41:14 changed his *m* and went in to
44:13 they ripped their *m* apart
45:22 gave individual changes of *m*
45:22 and five changes of *m*
Ex 3:22 and articles of gold and *m*
12:34 wrapped up in their *m* upon
12:35 and articles of gold and *m*
19:10 and they must wash their *m*
19:14 engaged in washing their *m*
Jos 7:6 Joshua ripped his *m* and fell
Ru 3:3 put your *m* upon you and go
2Sa 12:20 changed his *m* and came to
Isa 4:1 and wear our own *m*
Da 3:21 men were bound in their *m*
3:27 *m* had not been changed and

Manufacture
De 27:15 the *m* of the hands of a

Manufacturers
Isa 45:16 the *m* of idol forms will

Manure
2Ki 9:37 *m* upon the face of the field
Job 20:7 Like his *m* cakes he perishes
Ps 83:10 became *m* for the ground
Isa 25:10 trodden down in a *m* place
Jer 8:2 *m* upon the face of the ground
9:22 *m* upon the face of the field
16:4 As *m* upon the surface of the
25:33 As *m* on the surface of the
Eze 4:15 given you cattle *m* instead
Lu 13:8 dig around it and put on *m*
14:35 neither for soil nor for *m*

Many
Ge 1:22 Be fruitful and become *m* and
1:22 flying creatures become *m*
1:28 Be fruitful and become *m* and
8:17 be fruitful and become *m*
9:1 Be fruitful and become *m* and
9:7 become *m*, make the earth swarm
9:7 swarm with you and become *m*
13:6 their goods had become *m* and
15:14 will go out with *m* goods
21:34 of the Philistines *m* days
33:9 I have a great *m*, my brother
35:11 Be fruitful and become *m*
37:34 mourning over his son for *m*
38:12 the days became *m* and the
47:8 How *m* are the days of the
47:27 and grew to be very *m*
48:4 I will make you *m* and I will
50:3 this *m* days they customarily
50:20 to preserve *m* people alive
Ex 2:23 about during those *m* days
5:5 people of the land are now *m*
19:21 and *m* of them have to fall
Le 15:25 flowing *m* days when it is
25:51 If there are yet *m* years
Nu 9:19 over the tabernacle *m* days
13:18 whether they are few or *m*
20:15 to dwell in Egypt *m* days
20:20 with a great *m* people and a
21:6 that *m* people of Israel died
22:3 people . . . were *m*
24:7 And his seed is by *m* waters
26:56 between the *m* and the few
32:1 numerous livestock, very *m*
35:8, 8 From the *m* . . . take *m*
De 1:11 a thousand times as *m* as you
1:46, 46 *m* days, as *m* days as you
2:1 were *m* days in going around
3:5 aside from very *m* rural towns
6:3 that you may become very *m*
11:21 days of your sons may be *m*
15:6 lend on pledge to *m* nations
15:6 must dominate over *m* nations
20:19 lay siege to a city *m* days
25:3 *m* strokes in addition to
28:12 certainly lend to *m* nations
31:17 *m* calamities and distresses
31:21 *m* calamities and distresses
Jos 11:4 *m* horses and war chariots
11:18 *M* days it was that Joshua
22:3 *m* days down to this day
22:8 to your tents with *m* riches
23:1 *m* days after Jehovah had
24:3 and made his seed *m*. So I
24:7 in the wilderness *m* days
Jg 7:2 too *m* for me to give Midian
7:4 There are yet too *m* people
8:30 for he came to have *m* wives
1Sa 14:6 to save by *m* or by few
25:10 have become *m*
2Sa 1:4 *m* of the people have fallen
12:2 have very *m* sheep and cattle
13:34 *m* people coming from the
14:2 mourning *m* days over
23:20 who did *m* deeds in Kabzeel
24:3 a hundred times as *m* as
24:14 for *m* are his mercies; but
1Ki 2:38 in Jerusalem *m* days
3:11 not requested . . . *m* days
4:20 Judah and Israel were *m*
11:1 loved *m* foreign wives along
18:1 after *m* days that Jehovah's
22:16 how *m* times am I putting
2Ki 3:21 as *m* as were girding on a
4:35 boy began to sneeze as *m* as
9:22 mother and her *m* sorceries
1Ch 4:27 brothers did not have *m* sons
4:27 as *m* as the sons of Judah
5:22 were *m* that had fallen slain
7:4 for they had *m* wives and sons
7:22 mourning for *m* days, and his
8:40 having *m* sons and grandsons
11:22 who did *m* deeds in Kabzeel
21:3 a hundred times as *m* as they
21:13 for very *m* are his mercies
23:11 they did not have *m* sons
23:17 become exceedingly *m*
27:23 Israel as *m* as the stars of
28:5 *m* are the sons whom Jehovah
2Ch 1:11 *m* days that you have asked
14:11 whether there are *m* or
15:3 *m* were the days that Israel
15:5 *m* disorders among all the
17:13 *m* interests that became his
18:15 *m* times am I putting you
21:3 father gave them *m* gifts in
21:15 will be with *m* sicknesses
24:25 left him with *m* diseases
26:10 and hewed out *m* cisterns
30:17 *m* in the congregation that
30:18 people, *m* from Ephraim and
32:4 *m* people were collected
32:23 *m* bringing gifts to Jehovah
32:29 God gave him very *m* goods
Ezr 3:12 *m* of the priests and the
3:12 *m* others were raising the
5:11 built *m* years before this
10:13 the people are *m*, and it is
Ne 6:18 *m* in Judah were sworn to him
7:2 more than *m* others
9:23 as *m* as the stars of the
9:30 with them for *m* years
13:26 among the *m* nations there
Es 1:4 his greatness for *m* days
2:8 *m* young women were collected
4:3 spread out as a couch for *m*
8:17 *m* of the peoples of the land
Job 4:3 You have corrected *m*, And the
5:25 that your offspring are *m*
9:17 my wounds *m* for no reason
11:19 *m* people will certainly put
16:2 heard *m* things like these
21:17 How *m* times is the lamp of
21:17 And how *m* times does their
21:17 How *m* times in his anger
23:14 things like these are *m*
27:14 If his sons become *m*, it
38:21 in number your days are *m*
41:3 make *m* entreaties to you
Ps 3:1 have my adversaries become *m*
3:1 Why are *m* rising up against
3:2 *M* are saying of my soul
4:6 There are *m* saying: Who will
16:4 Pains become *m* to those who
22:12 *M* young bulls have
25:19 See how *m* my enemies have
29:3 Jehovah is over *m* waters
31:13 heard the bad report by *m*
32:6 As for the flood of *m* waters
32:10 *M* are the pains that the
34:19 *M* are the calamities of the
37:16 abundance of the *m* wicked

Ps 38:19 those hating me . . . *m*
40:3 *M* will see it and will fear
40:5 *M* things you yourself have
56:2 there are *m* warring against
71:7 like a miracle to *m* people
71:20 made me see *m* distresses
77:19 path was through *m* waters
78:38 *m* times he made his anger
89:50 of all the *m* peoples
94:19 thoughts became *m* inside of
97:1 Let the *m* islands rejoice
104:24 *m* your works are, O Jehovah
106:43 *M* times he would deliver
107:38 that they become very *m*
109:30 in among *m* people I shall
119:84 How *m* are the days of your
119:156 *M* are your mercies, O
119:157 and my adversaries are *m*
135:10 who struck down *m* nations
144:7 from the *m* waters
Pr 4:10 years of life will become *m*
7:26 *m* are the ones she has caused
9:11 your days will become *m*
10:21 keep pasturing *m*, but for
13:7 yet he has *m* valuable things
14:20 *m* are the friends of the
19:4 Wealth . . . adds *m* companions
19:6 *M* are those who soften the
19:21 *M* are the plans in the heart
22:16 supply *m* things to himself
28:2 *m* are its successive princes
28:20 will get *m* blessings
28:27 hiding his eyes . . . *m* curses
28:28 the righteous become *m*
29:2 When the righteous become *m*
29:16 When the wicked become *m*
29:22 rage has *m* a transgression
29:26 *M* are those seeking the face
31:29 *m* daughters that have shown
Ec 5:11 When good things become *m*
5:11 those eating . . . become *m*
6:3 and he should live *m* years, so
6:11 *m* things that are causing
7:22 *m* times that you, even you
7:29 have sought out *m* plans
10:6 been put in *m* high positions
10:14 foolish one speaks *m* words
11:1 *m* days you will find it again
11:8 man should live even *m* years
11:8 though they could be *m*
12:9 arrange *m* proverbs in order
12:12 making of *m* books there is
Ca 8:7 *M* waters themselves are not
Isa 1:15 though you make *m* prayers, I
2:3 *m* peoples will certainly go
2:4 straight respecting *m* peoples
5:9 *m* houses, though great and
8:7 and the *m* waters of the River
8:15 *m* among them will be certain
17:12 commotion of *m* peoples
17:13 like the noise of *m* waters
22:9 for they will actually be *m*
23:3 *m* waters has been the seed
23:16 make your songs *m*, in order
42:20 a case of seeing *m* things
51:2 bless him and to make him *m*
52:14 *m* have stared at him in
52:15 likewise startle *m* nations
53:11 to *m* people; and their
53:12 a portion among the *m*, and
53:12 carried the very sin of *m*
59:12 revolts have become *m* in
66:16 slain . . . become *m*
Jer 3:1 prostitution with *m*
3:16 that you will become *m* and
5:6 transgressions have become *m*
11:13 become as *m* as your cities
11:13 as *m* altars as the streets
11:15 *m* of them should do this
12:10 *M* shepherds themselves have
13:6 at the end of *m* days that
14:7 acts of unfaithfulness . . . *m*
16:16 I am sending for *m* fishers
16:16 I shall send for *m* hunters
20:10 I heard the bad report of *m*
22:8 *m* nations will actually
23:3 be fruitful and become *m*
25:14 *m* nations and great kings
27:7 *m* nations and great kings
28:8 prophesy concerning *m* lands
29:6 become *m* there, and do not
32:14 they may last for *m* days
35:7 living *m* days upon the
36:32 to them *m* more words like
Jer 37:16 dwelling there *m* days
42:2 remaining, a few out of *m*
51:55 be boisterous like *m* waters
La 1:22 my sighs are *m*, and my heart
Eze 11:6 your slain ones . . . to be *m*
12:27 visioning is *m* days off
16:41 before the eyes of *m* women
17:17 in order to cut off *m* souls
24:10 Make the logs *m*. Kindle the
26:3 against you *m* nations, just
27:3 the peoples for *m* islands
27:15 *m* islands were merchants
27:33 you satisfied *m* peoples
31:7 proved to be over *m* waters
31:15 *m* waters may be restrained
32:3 a congregation of *m* peoples
32:9 offend the heart of *m*
32:10 *m* peoples to be awestruck
32:13 from beside *m* waters, and
33:24 we are *m*; to us the land
37:2 *m* on the surface of the
38:6 bands, *m* peoples with you
38:8 After *m* days you will be
38:8 together out of *m* peoples
38:9 bands and *m* peoples with you
38:15 and *m* peoples with you, all
38:22 upon the *m* peoples that
38:23 the eyes of *m* nations
39:27 the eyes of *m* nations
47:7 there were very *m* trees
47:9 there will be very *m* fish
47:10 of the Great Sea, very *m*
Da 2:48 *m* big gifts he gave to him
8:25 he will bring *m* to ruin
8:26 because it is yet for *m* days
9:18 according to your *m* mercies
9:27 covenant in force for the *m*
11:14 *m* who will stand up against
11:18 and will actually capture *m*
11:26 *m* will certainly fall down
11:33 understanding to the *m*
11:34 and *m* will certainly join
11:39 make them rule among *m*; and
11:40 and with *m* ships; and he
11:41 *m* lands that will be made
11:44 to devote *m* to destruction
12:2 *m* of those asleep in the
12:3 the *m* to righteousness, like
12:4 *M* will rove about, and the
12:10 *M* will cleanse themselves
Ho 3:3 *m* days you will dwell as mine
3:4 for *m* days the sons of Israel
8:12 for him *m* things of my law
Am 3:9 the *m* disorders in the midst
3:15 *m* houses will have to come
5:12 known how *m* your revolts are
8:3 There will be *m* a carcass
Jon 4:11 besides *m* domestic animals
Mic 4:2 *m* nations will certainly go
4:3 judgment among *m* peoples
4:11 against you *m* nations
4:13 pulverize *m* peoples; and by
5:7 in the midst of *m* peoples
5:8 in the midst of *m* peoples
Na 1:12 there were *m* in that state
Hab 2:8 despoiled *m* nations, all the
2:10 the cutting off of *m* peoples
Zec 2:11 *m* nations will certainly
7:3 have done these O how *m* years
8:20 inhabitants of *m* cities will
8:22 *m* peoples and mighty nations
10:8 become *m*, just like those
10:8 those who have become *m*
Mal 2:6 *m* were those whom he turned
2:8 *m* to stumble in the law
Mt 3:7 sight of *m* of the Pharisees
6:7 for their use of *m* words
7:13 and *m* are the ones going in
7:22 *M* will say to me in that day
7:22 perform *m* powerful works in
8:11 *m* from eastern parts and
8:16 *m* demon-possessed persons
8:30 a herd of *m* swine was at
9:10 *m* tax collectors and sinners
10:31 worth more than *m* sparrows
12:15 *M* also followed him, and he
13:3 *m* things by illustrations
13:17 *M* prophets and righteous
13:58 did not do *m* powerful works
14:24 *m* hundreds of yards away
15:30 dumb, and *m* otherwise, and
15:34 How *m* loaves have you?
16:9 how *m* baskets you took up
16:10 how *m* provision baskets you
Mt 16:21 suffer *m* things from the
18:21 how *m* times is my brother
19:22 was holding *m* possessions
19:29 will receive *m* times more
19:30 *m* that are first will be
20:28 a ransom in exchange for *m*
22:14 *m* invited, but few chosen
24:5 *m* will come on the basis of
24:5 and will mislead *m*
24:10 *m* will be stumbled and will
24:11 *m* false prophets will arise
24:11 will arise and mislead *m*
25:21 appoint you over *m* things
25:23 appoint you over *m* things
26:28 be poured out in behalf of *m*
26:60 although *m* false witnesses
27:13 *m* things they are testifying
27:52 *m* bodies of the holy ones
27:53 became visible to *m* people
27:55 *m* women were there viewing
Mr 1:34 So he cured *m* that were ill
1:34 he expelled *m* demons, but
2:2 *m* gathered, so much so that
2:15 *m* tax collectors and sinners
2:15 there were *m* of them and
3:8 of how *m* things he was doing
3:10 he cured *m*, with the result
3:12 *m* times he sternly charged
4:2 to teach them *m* things with
4:33 *m* illustrations of that sort
5:9 Legion, because there are *m* of
5:10 he entreated him *m* times not
5:23 and entreated him *m* times
5:26 she had been put to *m* pains
5:26 pains by *m* physicians and had
5:38 and letting out *m* wails
6:13 they would expel *m* demons
6:13 grease *m* sickly people with
6:31 *m* coming and going, and they
6:33 *m* got to know it, and from
6:34 to teach them *m* things
6:38 How *m* loaves have you?
6:56 as *m* as did touch it were
7:4 there are *m* other traditions
7:13 *m* things similar to this you
8:5 How *m* loaves have you?
8:19 *m* baskets full of fragments
8:20 how *m* provision baskets full
8:31 must undergo *m* sufferings
9:12 he must undergo *m* sufferings
9:13 did to him as *m* things as
9:26 going through *m* convulsions
10:22 was holding *m* possessions
10:31 *m* . . . first will be last
10:45 a ransom in exchange for *m*
10:48 *m* began sternly telling him
11:8 Also, *m* spread their outer
12:5 *m* others, some of whom they
12:41 *m* rich people were dropping
12:41 were dropping in *m* coins
13:6 *M* will come on the basis of
13:6 I am he, and will mislead *m*
14:24 be poured out in behalf of *m*
14:56 *M*, indeed, were giving
15:3 to accuse him of *m* things
15:4 See how *m* charges they are
15:41 *m* other women who had come
Lu 1:1 *m* have undertaken to compile
1:14 *m* will rejoice over his birth
1:16 *m* of the sons of Israel will
2:34 rising again of *m* in Israel
2:35 *m* hearts may be uncovered
3:18 gave *m* other exhortations and
4:25 There were *m* widows in Israel
4:27 there were *m* lepers in Israel
4:41 come out of *m*, crying out and
7:21 he cured *m* of sicknesses and
7:21 granted *m* blind persons the
7:47 her sins, *m* though they are
8:3 Susanna and *m* other women
8:30 Legion, because *m* demons had
9:22 must undergo *m* sufferings and
10:24 *M* prophets and kings desired
10:40 with attending to *m* duties
10:41 disturbed about *m* things
12:1 in so *m* thousands that they
12:7 worth more than *m* sparrows
12:19 Soul, you have *m* good things
12:19 things laid up for *m* years
12:47 be beaten with *m* strokes
13:24 *m*, I tell you, will seek to
14:16 meal, and he invited *m*
15:13 Later, after not *m* days
15:17 How *m* hired men of my

Lu 15:29 *m* years I have slaved for
17:25 must undergo *m* sufferings
18:30 get *m* times more in this
21:8 *m* will come on the basis of
22:65 *m* other things in blasphemy
23:9 with a good *m* words; but he
Joh 1:12 as *m* as did receive him
2:12 did not stay there *m* days
2:23 *m* people put their faith in
4:39 *m* of the Samaritans out of
4:41 *m* more believed on account
6:9 what are these among so *m?*
6:60 *m* of his disciples, when
6:66 *m* of his disciples went off
7:31 *m* of the crowd put faith in
8:26 I have *m* things to speak
8:30 *m* put faith in him
10:20 *M* of them were saying: He
10:32 *m* fine works from the
10:41 *m* people came to him, and
10:41 *m* things as John said about
10:42 *m* put faith in him there
11:19 *m* of the Jews had come to
11:22 *m* things as you ask God for
11:45 *m* of the Jews that had
11:47 this man performs *m* signs
11:55 *m* people went up out of the
12:11 *m* of the Jews were going
12:37 performed so *m* signs before
12:42 *m* even of the rulers
14:2 there are *m* abodes
16:12 I have *m* things yet to say
18:2 Jesus had *m* times met there
19:20 *m* of the Jews read this
20:30 performed *m* other signs
21:11 so *m* the net did not burst
21:25 *m* other things also which
Ac 1:3 also by *m* positive proofs he
1:5 spirit not *m* days after this
2:39 *m* as Jehovah our God may call
2:40 with *m* other words he bore
2:43 *m* portents and signs began
3:24 just as *m* as have spoken
4:4 *m* of those who had listened
4:6 *m* as were of the chief
5:12 *m* signs and portents
8:7 *m* that had unclean spirits
8:7 *m* that were paralyzed and
8:25 *m* villages of the Samaritans
9:13 heard from *m* about this man
9:13 how *m* injurious things he did
9:16 how *m* things he must suffer
9:23 *m* days were coming to a close
9:39 exhibiting *m* inner garments
9:42 *m* became believers on the
10:2 he made *m* gifts of mercy to
10:27 found *m* people assembled
13:31 *m* days he became visible to
13:43 *m* of the Jews and of the
14:22 through *m* tribulations
14:27 relate the *m* things God had
15:4 recounted the *m* things God
15:12 *m* signs and portents that
15:32 brothers with *m* a discourse
15:35 and declaring, with *m* others
16:18 she kept doing for *m* days
16:23 inflicted *m* blows upon them
17:12 *m* of them became believers
18:8 And *m* of the Corinthians that
18:10 I have *m* people in this city
19:18 *m* of those who had become
20:2 the ones there with *m* a word
21:20 how *m* thousands of believers
24:10 had you as judge for *m* years
25:7 *m* and serious charges for
26:9 commit *m* acts of opposition
26:10 *m* of the holy ones I locked
26:11 punishing them *m* times in
27:20 stars appeared for *m* days
28:10 honored us with *m* gifts
Ro 1:13 I *m* times purposed to come
4:17 you a father of *m* nations
4:18 the father of *m* nations in
5:15 by one man's trespass *m* died
5:15 abounded much more to *m*
5:16 resulted from *m* trespasses
5:19 *m* were constituted sinners
5:19 *m* will be constituted
8:29 firstborn among *m* brothers
12:4 have in one body *m* members
12:5 although *m*, are one body in
15:22 I was *m* times hindered from
16:2 a defender of *m*, yes, of me
16:6 Mary . . . performed *m* labors
Ro 16:12 she performed *m* labors in the
1Co 1:26 not *m* wise in a fleshly way
1:26 called, not *m* powerful, not
1:26 not *m* of noble birth
4:15 do not have *m* fathers; for
8:5, 5 are *m* gods and *m* lords
10:17 we, although *m*, are one body
10:33 but that of the *m*, in order
11:30 *m* among you are weak and
12:12 the body . . . has *m* members
12:12 although being *m*, are one
12:14 is not one member, but *m*
12:20 But now they are *m* members
14:10 so *m* kinds of speech sounds
16:9 but there are *m* opposers
2Co 1:11 thanks may be given by *m* in
1:11 us due to *m* prayerful faces
1:20 how *m* the promises of God
2:4 wrote you with *m* tears, not
2:17 not peddlers . . . as *m* men
4:15 thanksgiving of *m* more to
6:10 as poor but making *m* rich
8:22 often proved in *m* things to
9:12 *m* expressions of thanks to
11:18 *m* are boasting according to
11:27 from food *m* times, in cold
12:21 *m* of those who formerly
Ga 1:14 in Judaism than *m* of my own
3:4 undergo so *m* sufferings to no
3:16 seeds, as in the case of *m*
Php 3:15 as *m* of us as are mature, be
3:18 *m*, I used to mention them
1Ti 6:1 Let as *m* as are slaves under
6:9 *m* senseless and hurtful
6:10 stabbed . . . with *m* pains
6:12 in front of *m* witnesses
2Ti 2:2 the support of *m* witnesses
4:14 did me *m* injuries—Jehovah
Tit 1:10 For there are *m* unruly men
Heb 1:1 long ago spoke on *m* occasions
1:1 in *m* ways to our forefathers
2:10 bringing *m* sons to glory
7:23 *m* had to become priests in
9:28 to bear the sins of *m;* and
12:15 *m* may not be defiled by it
Jas 3:1 Not *m* of you should become
3:2 For we all stumble *m* times
2Pe 2:2 *m* will follow their acts of
1Jo 2:18 come to be *m* antichrists
4:1 *m* false prophets have gone
2Jo 7 For *m* deceivers have gone forth
12 I have *m* things to write you
3Jo 13 I had *m* things to write you
Re 1:15 was as the sound of *m* waters
5:11 I heard a voice of *m* angels
8:11 *m* of the men died from the
9:9 sound of chariots of *m* horses
10:11 and tongues and *m* kings
14:2 as the sound of *m* waters and
17:1 harlot who sits on *m* waters
19:6 as a sound of *m* waters and
19:12 upon his head are *m* diadems

Many-colored
Pr 7:16 with *m* things, linen of Egypt
Jer 12:9 as a *m* bird of prey to me

Maoch
1Sa 27:2 Achish the son of *M*, the

Maon
Jos 15:55 *M*, Carmel and Ziph and
1Sa 23:24 wilderness of *M* in the
23:25 in the wilderness of *M*
23:25 into the wilderness of *M*
25:2 man in *M*, and his work was
1Ch 2:45 the son of Shammai was *M*
2:45 *M* was the father of Beth-zur

Map
Jos 18:4 *m* it out in accord with
18:6 you will *m* out the land
18:8 going to *m* out the land
18:8 the land and *m* it out and

Mapped
Jos 18:9 *m* it out by cities in seven

Mar
2Ki 3:19 you should *m* with stones

Mara
Ru 1:20 Call me *M*, for the Almighty

Marah
Ex 15:23 In time they came to *M*, but
15:23 to drink the water from *M*
15:23 is why he called its name *M*
Nu 33:8 and took up camping at *M*
33:9 pulled away from *M* and came

Marauder
Ge 49:19 Gad, a *m* band will raid him
1Sa 30:8 chase after this *m* band
30:15 down to this *m* band
30:15 lead you . . . to this *m* band
30:23 *m* band that came against us
2Sa 22:30 I can run against a *m* band
1Ki 11:24 to be chief of a *m* band
2Ki 5:2 had gone out as *m* bands, and
24:2 *m* bands of Chaldeans and
24:2 and *m* bands of Syrians
24:2 and *m* bands of Moabites
24:2 *m* bands of the sons of
1Ch 12:21 to David against the *m* band
2Ch 22:1 *m* band that came with the
Ps 18:29 I can run against a *m* band
Jer 18:22 upon them suddenly a *m* band
Ho 7:1 a *m* band actually makes a

Marauding
2Sa 4:2 chiefs of the *m* bands, that
2Ki 6:23 *m* bands of the Syrians come
13:20 *m* bands of the Moabites
13:21 here they saw the *m* band
Ho 6:9 priests are *m* bands

Marble
Es 1:6 silver rings and pillars of *m*
1:6 pavement of porphyry and *m* and
1:6 and pearl and black *m*
Ca 5:15 His legs are pillars of *m*
Re 18:12 copper and of iron and of *m*

March
Ge 14:8 king of Sodom went on the *m*
Nu 14:25 *m* to the wilderness by way
20:17 the king's road we shall *m*
21:22 the king's road we shall *m*
32:39 *m* to Gilead and to capture
De 28:36 *m* you and your king whom
Jos 6:3 must *m* round the city, going
6:4 *m* round the city seven times
6:7 Pass on and *m* round the city
Job 18:14 will *m* him to the king of
Ps 26:6 I will *m* around your altar
48:12 *M* around Zion, you people
Ac 23:23 soldiers ready to *m* clear to

Marched
Ge 14:3 these *m* as allies to the Low
Ex 15:22 and *m* on for three days in
Nu 32:41 *m* and went capturing their
32:42 Nobah *m* and went capturing
Jos 6:15 *m* round the city seven times
8:9 they *m* to the place of ambush
Jg 1:10 So Judah *m* against the
1:11 they *m* on from there against
1:17 Judah *m* on with Simeon his
2Sa 2:29 *m* through the Arabah all
6:13 had *m* six steps, he
Ps 68:7 When you *m* through the desert
Ec 12:5 wailers have *m* around in the

Marches
Pr 7:8 in the way to her house he *m*

Marching
Ex 14:10 Egyptians were *m* after them
Nu 10:33 *m* from the mountain of
10:33 *m* before them for a journey
10:34 *m* out from the encampment
33:8 *m* a three-day journey in the
De 1:19 *m* through all that great and
20:4 God is *m* with you to fight
31:6 God is the one *m* with you
31:8 Jehovah is the one *m* before
Jos 6:11 go *m* round the city, going
6:14 went *m* round the city on the
6:15 went *m* round the city in
Jg 5:4 At your *m* out of the field of
1Sa 17:7 was *m* ahead of him
2Sa 2:29 *m* through the entire gully
2:32 Joab and his men went *m*
5:24 sound of *m* in the tops of
1Ch 14:15 sound of the *m* in the tops
Isa 63:1 *m* in the abundance of his
Hab 3:12 went *m* through the earth
Lu 14:31 king, *m* to meet another king

Mare
Ca 1:9 To a *m* of mine in the chariots

Mareal
Jos 19:11 went up westward also to *M*

Mares
Es 8:10 sons of speedy *m*
Maresha
2Ch 20:37 son of Dodavahu of *M*
Mareshah
Jos 15:44 Keilah and Achzib and *M*
1Ch 2:42 *M* the father of Hebron
4:21 Laadah the father of *M*
2Ch 11:8 and Gath and *M* and Ziph
14:9 and came as far as *M*
14:10 valley of Zephathah at *M*
Mic 1:15 to you, O inhabitress of *M*
Marine
Eze 32:2 the *m* monster in the seas
Mariners
Eze 27:9 *m* themselves proved to be
27:27 your *m* and your sailors
27:29 those handling an oar, *m*
Jon 1:5 the *m* began to fear and to
Maritime
Lu 6:17 the *m* country of Tyre and
Mark
Ex 16:29 *M* the fact that Jehovah has
Nu 34:7 you will *m* out to Mount Hor
34:8 *m* out the boundary to the
34:10 must *m* . . . as your boundary
De 27:17 boundary *m* of his fellowman
Job 13:27 you *m* your own line
Isa 3:24 a brand *m* instead of
Jer 48:9 Give a road *m* to Moab, you
Eze 9:4 put a *m* on the foreheads of
9:6 man upon whom there is the *m*
Lu 12:24 *M* well that the ravens
12:27 *M* well how the lilies grow
Ac 12:12 John who was surnamed *M*
12:25 John, the one surnamed *M*
15:37 also John, who was called *M*
15:39 Barnabas took *M* along and
Col 4:10 *M* the cousin of Barnabas
2Ti 4:11 Take *M* and bring him with
Phm 24 also *M*, Aristarchus, Demas
1Pe 5:13 and so does *M* my son
Re 13:16 *m* in their right hand or
13:17 except a person having the *m*
14:9 receives a *m* on his forehead
14:11 receives the *m* of its name
16:2 had the *m* of the wild beast
19:20 *m* of the wild beast and
20:4 *m* upon their forehead and
Marked
Jos 15:9 was *m* out from the top of
15:9 boundary was *m* out to Baalah
15:11 *m* out to Shikkeron and
18:14 the boundary was *m* out and
18:17 was *m* out northward and
19:13 and was *m* out to Neah
Lu 14:7 he *m* how they were choosing
22:22 according to what is *m* out
2Th 3:14 letter, keep this one *m*
1Ti 4:2 *m* in their conscience as with
Marker
Eze 39:15 also build beside it a *m*
Market
Mr 7:4 when back from *m*, they do not
1Co 10:25 is sold in a meat *m* keep
Marketplace
Mt 20:3 standing unemployed in the *m*
Lu 7:32 children sitting in a *m* and
Ac 16:19 dragged them into the *m* to
17:5 wicked men of the *m* idlers
17:17 and every day in the *m* with
28:15 *M* of Appius and Three
Marketplaces
Mt 11:16 children sitting in the *m*
23:7 the greetings in the *m* and to
Mr 6:56 place the sick ones in the *m*
12:38 and want greetings in the *m*
Lu 11:43 and the greetings in the *m*
20:46 and like greetings in the *m*
Marking
Le 19:28 must not put tattoo *m* upon
Marks
De 19:14 not move back the boundary *m*
1Sa 21:13 making cross *m* on the doors
Job 24:2 who move back boundary *m*
Jer 2:34 the blood *m* of the souls of
31:21 Set up road *m* for yourself

Ga 6:17 brand *m* of a slave of Jesus
Heb 4:7 *m* off a certain day by saying
Maroth
Mic 1:12 *M* has waited for good, but
Marriage
Ge 34:9 and form *m* alliances with us
34:12 the *m* money and gift imposed
38:8 perform brother-in-law *m* with
Ex 21:10 and her *m* due are not to be
De 7:3 form no *m* alliance with them
25:5 perform brother-in-law *m*
25:7 perform brother-in-law *m*
Jos 23:12 you do form *m* alliances
1Sa 18:21 *m* alliance with me today
18:22 a *m* alliance with the king
18:23 a *m* alliance with the king
18:25 has delight, not in *m* money
18:26 a *m* alliance with the king
18:27 a *m* alliance with the king
1Ki 3:1 *m* alliance with Pharaoh the
2Ki 8:27 of the house of Ahab by *m*
2Ch 18:1 a *m* alliance with Ahab
Ezr 9:14 forming *m* alliances with the
Ca 3:11 on the day of his *m* and on
Mt 1:18 Mary was promised in *m* to
22:2 a king, that made a *m* feast
22:3 those invited to the *m* feast
22:4 Come to the *m* feast
22:8 The *m* feast indeed is ready
22:9 invite to the *m* feast
22:11 clothed with a *m* garment
22:12 not having on a *m* garment
22:24 must take his wife in *m*
22:30 nor are women given in *m*
24:38 and women being given in *m*
25:10 in with him to the *m* feast
Mr 12:25 nor are women given in *m*
Lu 1:27 a virgin promised in *m* to a
2:5 given him in *m* as promised
12:36 when he returns from the *m*
14:8 are invited by someone to a *m*
17:27 women were being given in *m*
20:34 marry and are given in *m*
20:35 marry nor are given in *m*
Joh 2:1 a *m* feast took place in Cana
2:2 also invited to the *m* feast
1Co 7:38 gives his virginity in *m*
7:38 give it in *m* will do better
2Co 11:2 personally promised you in *m*
Heb 13:4 Let *m* be honorable among all
13:4 and the *m* bed be without
Re 19:7 *m* of the Lamb has arrived
19:9 evening meal of the Lamb's *m*
Married
Mt 22:25 and the first *m* and deceased
Mr 6:17 because he had *m* her
Lu 14:20 I just *m* a wife and for this
Ro 7:2 *m* woman is bound by law to
1Co 7:10 To the *m* people I give
7:28 if a virgin person *m*, such
7:33 the *m* man is anxious for the
7:34 the *m* woman is anxious for
7:39 is free to be *m* to whom she
Marries
Mt 5:32 *m* a divorced woman commits
19:9 *m* another commits adultery
Mr 10:11 divorces his wife and *m*
10:12 *m* another, she commits
Lu 16:18 divorces his wife and *m*
16:18 he that *m* a woman divorced
Marrow
Job 21:24 *m* of his bones . . . moist
Isa 25:6 dishes filled with *m*, of
Heb 4:12 and of joints and their *m*
Marry
Jer 2:2 your being engaged to *m*
Mt 19:10 it is not advisable to *m*
22:30 neither do men *m* nor are
Mr 12:25 neither do men *m* nor are
Lu 20:34 *m* and are given in marriage
20:35 *m* nor are given in marriage
1Co 7:9 let them *m*, for it is better
7:9 for it is better to *m* than to
7:28 even if you did *m*, you would
7:36 he does not sin. Let them *m*
1Ti 4:3 forbidding to *m*, commanding
5:11 they want to *m*
5:14 the younger widows to *m*
Marrying
Mt 24:38 men *m* and women being
Lu 17:27 men were *m*, women were

Marsena
Es 1:14 *M* . . . seven princes of Persia
Marshmallow
Job 6:6 taste in the slimy juice of *m*
Marshy
Isa 30:14 skim water from a *m* place
Eze 47:11 *m* places, and they will not
Martha
Lu 10:38 woman named *M* received him
10:40 *M* . . . was distracted with
10:41, 41 *M*, *M*, you are anxious
Joh 11:1 of Mary and of *M* her sister
11:5 Jesus loved *M* and her
11:19 Jews had come to *M* and
11:20 *M*, when she heard that
11:21 *M* therefore said to Jesus
11:24 *M* said to him: I know he
11:30 the place where *M* met him
11:39 *M*, the sister of the
12:2 and *M* was ministering, but
Marvel
Ps 88:10 are dead will you do a *m*
88:12 *m* by you be known in the
Mr 12:17 they began to *m* at him
15:5 so that Pilate began to *m*
Lu 4:22 to *m* at the winsome words
Joh 3:7 Do not *m* because I told you
5:20 in order that you may *m*
5:28 Do not *m* at this, because
9:30 This certainly is a *m*, that
Ga 1:6 I *m* that you are being so
1Jo 3:13 Do not *m*, brothers, that the
Marveled
Mt 22:22 they heard that, they *m*
Lu 1:63 its name. At this they all *m*
2:18 all that heard *m* over the
7:9 he *m* at him, and he turned
8:25 they *m*, saying to one another
11:14 man spoke. And the crowds *m*
Ac 7:31 Moses saw it he *m* at the
Marveling
Lu 9:43 *m* at all the things he was
Marvelous
Job 10:16 show yourself *m* in my case
Ps 77:11 remember your *m* doing of
89:5 heavens will laud your *m* act
Da 11:36 he will speak *m* things
Mt 21:15 saw the *m* things he did and
21:42 and it is *m* in our eyes
Mr 12:11 and it is *m* in our eyes
Marvelously
Ps 77:14 are the true God, doing *m*
78:12 forefathers he had done *m*
Marvels
Ex 15:11 the One doing *m*
Mary
Mt 1:16 Joseph the husband of *M*, of
1:18 *M* was promised in marriage
1:20 to take *M* your wife home
2:11 child with *M* its mother
13:55 Is not his mother called *M*
27:56 among whom was *M* Magdalene
27:56 *M* the mother of James and
27:61 *M* Magdalene and the other
27:61 the other *M* continued there
28:1 *M* Magdalene and the other
28:1 *M* came to view the grave
Mr 6:3 is the carpenter the son of *M*
15:40 among them *M* Magdalene
15:40 *M* the mother of James the
15:47 But *M* Magdalene and
15:47 and *M* the mother of Joses
16:1 *M* Magdalene, and
16:1 *M* the mother of James, and
Lu 1:27 the name of the virgin was *M*
1:30 Have no fear, *M*, for you have
1:34 *M* said to the angel: How is
1:38 *M* said: Look! Jehovah's slave
1:39 *M* rose in these days and went
1:41 heard the greeting of *M*, the
1:46 *M* said: My soul magnifies
1:56 *M* remained with her about
2:5 to get registered with *M*, who
2:16 found *M* as well as Joseph
2:19 *M* began to preserve all these
2:34 but said to *M* its mother
8:2 *M* the so-called Magdalene
10:39 also had a sister called *M*
10:42 *M* chose the good portion

Lu 24:10 the Magdalene *M*, and Joanna
24:10 and *M* the mother of James
Joh 11:1 village of *M* and of Martha
11:2 *M* that greased the Lord with
11:19 Jews had come to . . . *M*
11:20 but *M* kept sitting at home
11:28 called *M* her sister, saying
11:31 *M* rise quickly and go out
11:32 *M*, when she arrived where
11:45 Jews that had come to *M*
12:3 *M*, therefore, took a pound
19:25 *M* the wife of Clopas, and
19:25 and *M* Magdalene
20:1 *M* Magdalene came to the
20:11 *M*, however, kept standing
20:16 Jesus said to her: *M!* Upon
20:18 *M* Magdalene came and
Ac 1:14 and *M* the mother of Jesus
12:12 of *M* the mother of John who
Ro 16:6 Greet *M*, who has performed

Mash
Ge 10:23 sons of Aram . . . *M*
Jg 19:21 and threw *m* to the he-asses
1Ch 1:17 and Hul and Gether and *M*

Mashal
1Ch 6:74 from the tribe of Asher, *M*

Maskil
Ps 32:*super* Of David. *M*
42:*super* *M* for the sons of Korah
44:*super* Of the sons of Korah. *M*
45:*super* Of the sons of Korah. *M*
52:*super* *M*. Of David, when Doeg
53:*super* *M*. Of David
54:*super* *M*. Of David. When the
55:*super* *M*. Of David
74:*super* A *m*. Of Asaph
78:*super* *M*. Of Asaph
88:*super* *M* of Heman the Ezrahite
89:*super* *M*. Of Ethan the Ezrahite
142:*super* *M*. Of David, when he

Masons
2Ki 12:12 to the *m* and to the hewers
22:6 and the builders and the *m*

Masrekah
Ge 36:36 Samlah from *M* began to
1Ch 1:47 Samlah from *M* began to reign

Mass
Ex 20:21 near to the dark cloud *m*
2Ki 9:17 heaving *m* of Jehu's men as
9:17 There is a heaving *m* of men
Job 16:10 *m* themselves against me
22:11 *m* of water itself covers
26:8 cloud *m* is not split under
37:11 light scatters the cloud *m*
38:34 *m* of water itself may cover
38:38 out as into a molten *m*
Ps 31:13 they *m* together as one
Isa 3:6 overthrown *m* should be under
44:22 sins just as with a cloud *m*
60:6 The heaving *m* of camels
La 3:44 cloud *m*, that prayer may not
Eze 1:4 a great cloud *m* and quivering
1:28 bow that occurs in a cloud *m*
23:42 out of the *m* of mankind
26:10 the heaving *m* of his horses
Na 1:3 the cloud *m* is the powder of
3:3 and the heavy *m* of carcasses
Mt 13:33 the whole *m* was fermented
Lu 13:21 the whole *m* was fermented

Massa
Ge 25:14 and Mishma and Dumah and *M*
1Ch 1:30 Dumah, *M*, Hadad and Tema

Massacre
Jer 50:21 Let there be a *m* and a
50:27 *M* all her young bulls

Massage
Es 2:12 the days of their *m* procedure

Massages
Es 2:3 there be a giving of their *m*
2:9 her *m* and her appropriate food
2:12 and with the *m* of the women

Massah
Ex 17:7 *M* and Meribah, because of the
De 6:16 you put him to the test at *M*
9:22 at Taberah and at *M* and at
33:8 you put to the test at *M*
Ps 95:8 day of *M* in the wilderness

Massed
Ps 2:2 have *m* together as one
Ac 4:26 rulers *m* together as one
Re 18:5 sins have *m* together clear

Masses
Pr 8:26 dust *m* of the productive land
8:28 made firm the cloud *m* above
Ac 17:13 to incite and agitate the *m*

Massing
Jg 9:31 they are *m* the city against
Lu 11:29 the crowds were *m* together

Massive
Ge 35:8 foot of Bethel under a *m* tree
Jos 24:26 the *m* tree that is by the
2Sa 18:9 boughs of a *m* big tree
Isa 2:13 all the *m* trees of Bashan
6:13 *m* tree in which, when there
44:14 a *m* tree, and he lets it
Eze 27:6 Out of *m* trees from Bashan
Ho 4:13 under *m* tree and storax
Am 2:9 was vigorous like the *m* trees
Zec 11:2 Howl, you *m* trees of Bashan

Mast
Pr 23:34 lying down at the top of a *m*
Isa 30:17 *m* on the top of a mountain
33:23 *m* they will not hold
Eze 27:5 took to make a *m* upon you

Master
Ge 24:9 Abraham his *m* and swore to
24:10 from the camels of his *m* and
24:12 Jehovah the God of my *m*
24:12 loving-kindness with my *m*
24:14 loyal love with my *m*
24:27 the God of my *m* Abraham
24:27 trustworthiness toward my *m*
24:27 of the brothers of my *m*
24:35 Jehovah has blessed my *m*
24:36 Sarah the wife of my *m* bore
24:36 bore a son to my *m* after her
24:37 my *m* made me swear, saying
24:39 I said to my *m*, What if the
24:42 God of my *m* Abraham, if you
24:44 assigned for the son of my *m*
24:48 God of my *m* Abraham, who
24:48 the brother of my *m* for his
24:49 trustworthiness toward my *m*
24:51 wife to the son of your *m*
24:54 said: Send me off to my *m*
24:56 that I may go to my *m*
24:65 servant said: It is my *m*
27:29 Become *m* over your brothers
27:37 appointed him *m* over you
39:2 be over the house of his *m*
39:3 his *m* got to see that Jehovah
39:7 the wife of his *m* began to
39:8 my *m* does not know what is
39:16 his *m* came to his house
39:19 *m* heard the words of his
39:20 Joseph's *m* took him and gave
44:5 thing that my *m* drinks from
44:8 from the house of your *m*
44:9 become slaves to my *m*
44:16 What can we say to my *m?*
44:16 Here we are slaves to my *m*
44:18 my *m*, please let your slave
44:18 word in the hearing of my *m*
44:19 My *m* asked his slaves
44:20 So we said to my *m*, We do
44:22 But we said to my *m*, The boy
44:24 told him the words of my *m*
44:33 as a slave to my *m*, that the
Ex 21:4 his *m* should give him a wife
21:5 I really love my *m*, my wife
21:6 *m* must bring him near to the
21:6 *m* must pierce his ear through
21:8 in the eyes of her *m* so that
21:32 shekels to that one's *m*, and
De 23:15 hand over a slave to his *m*
23:15 escapes from his *m* to you
Jg 16:5 to tie him so as to *m* him
16:6 you be tied for one to *m* you
19:11 said to his *m:* O come, now
19:12 his *m* said to him: Let us
19:26 man's house where her *m* was
19:27 her *m* rose up in the morning
1Sa 20:38 and then came to his *m*
25:10 each one from before his *m*
25:14 to wish our *m* well, but he
25:17 determined against our *m*
30:13 *m* left me because I took
30:15 into the hand of my *m*, and

2Sa 9:9 to the grandson of your *m*
9:10 grandson of your *m*, and they
9:10 grandson of your *m*, will eat
16:3 where is the son of your *m?*
1Ki 16:24 *m* of the mountain, Samaria
2Ki 2:3 Jehovah is taking your *m* from
2:5 Jehovah is taking your *m* from
2:16 please, and look for your *m*
2:19 just as my *m* is seeing
4:16 No, my *m*, O man of the true
5:20 my *m* has spared Naaman this
5:22 My *m* himself has sent me
5:25 stood by his *m*. Elisha now
6:5 my *m*, for it was borrowed!
6:15 my *m!* What shall we do?
Job 3:19 slave is set free from his *m*
Ps 12:4 Who will be a *m* to us?
105:21 him as *m* to his household
123:2 toward the hand of their *m*
Pr 8:30 be beside him as a *m* worker
24:8 called a mere *m* at evil ideas
27:18 is guarding his *m* will be
30:10 slander a servant to his *m*
Isa 19:4 into the hand of a hard *m*
22:18 of the house of your *m*
24:2 for the servant as for his *m*
Jer 22:18 wail for him: Alas, O *m!*
34:5 Alas, O *m!* is what they
52:15 the rest of the *m* workmen
Ho 12:14 grand *M* will repay to him
Mal 1:6 and a servant, his grand *m*
1:6 if I am a grand *m*, where is
Mt 9:38 beg the *M* of the harvest to
13:27 *M*, did you not sow fine
18:25 *m* ordered him and his wife
18:27 *m* of that slave let him off
18:31 made clear to their *m* all
18:32 *m* summoned him and said to
18:34 his *m*, provoked to wrath
20:8 *m* of the vineyard said to his
24:45 slave whom his *m* appointed
24:46 Happy is that slave if his *m*
24:48 My *m* is delaying
24:50 *m* of that slave will come
25:18 the silver money of his *m*
25:19 *m* of those slaves came and
25:20 *M*, you committed five
25:21 *m* said to him, Well done
25:21 Enter into the joy of your *m*
25:22 *M*, you committed to me two
25:23 *m* said to him, Well done
25:23 Enter into the joy of your *m*
25:24 said, *M*, I knew you to be
25:26 *m* said to him, Wicked and
Mr 13:35 the *m* of the house is coming
Lu 10:2 beg the *M* of the harvest to
12:36 men waiting for their *m*
12:37 *m* on arriving finds watching
12:42 his *m* will appoint over his
12:43 if his *m* on arriving finds
12:45 My *m* delays coming, and
12:46 the *m* of that slave will
12:47 understood the will of his *m*
13:8 *M*, let it alone also this
14:21 reported . . . to his *m*
14:22 *M*, what you ordered has
14:23 the *m* said to the slave, Go
16:3 seeing that my *m* will take
16:5 one of the debtors of his *m*
16:5 How much are you owing my *m?*
16:8 his *m* commended the steward
Joh 13:16 is not greater than his *m*
15:15 not know what his *m* does
15:20 is not greater than his *m*
Ro 6:9 death is *m* over him no more
6:14 sin must not be *m* over you
7:1 Law is *m* over a man as long
14:4 To his own *m* he stands or
Eph 6:9 you know that the *M* of both
Col 3:24 Slave for the *M*, Christ
4:1 you also have a *M* in heaven
Re 14:3 *m* that song but the hundred

Master's
Ge 24:10 good thing of his *m* in his
39:8 and would say to his *m* wife
40:7 in the jail of his *m* house
Ex 21:4 children will become her *m*

Masters
1Ki 22:17 These have no *m*
2Ch 18:16 These have no *m*. Let them
Ne 3:5 into the service of their *m*
Pr 25:13 the very soul of his *m*
Isa 26:13 *m* besides you have acted as

Jer 27:4 a command for their *m*
27:4 you should say to your *m*
Am 4:1 who are saying to their *m*
Zep 1:9 filling the house of their *m*
Mt 6:24 No one can slave for two *m*
15:27 from the table of their *m*
Lu 16:13 slave to two *m;* for, either
Ac 16:16 to furnish her *m* with much
16:19 her *m* saw that their hope
2Co 1:24 Not that we are the *m* over
Eph 6:5 are your *m* in a fleshly sense
6:9 you *m*, keep doing the same
Col 3:22 your *m* in a fleshly sense
4:1 You *m*, keep dealing out what

Mastery
Ge 4:7 you, for your part, get the *m*
Jg 16:19 to show the *m* of him
Da 6:24 lions had got the *m* over them
Ac 19:16 the *m* of one after the other

Match
Ge 15:10 each part of them so as to *m*
1Sa 17:9 if I myself am a *m* for him
Eze 28:3 that have proved a *m* for you
31:8 Other cedars were no *m* for
Lu 5:36 patch . . . does not *m* the old

Matches
1Pe 4:3 revelries, drinking *m*, and

Mate
Ge 7:2 by sevens, the sire and its *m*
7:2 just two, the sire and its *m*
Isa 34:15 each one with her *m*
34:16 to have each one her *m*

Material
Ex 25:4 and coccus scarlet *m*, and
26:1 purple and coccus scarlet *m*
26:31 and coccus scarlet *m* and
26:36 coccus scarlet *m* and fine
27:16 and coccus scarlet *m* and
28:5 and coccus scarlet *m* and the
28:6 coccus scarlet *m* and fine
28:8 and coccus scarlet *m* and fine
28:15 and coccus scarlet *m* and
28:33 and coccus scarlet *m*, upon
35:6 and coccus scarlet *m* and fine
35:23 coccus scarlet *m* and fine
35:25 coccus scarlet *m* and the
35:35 coccus scarlet *m* and fine
36:8 coccus scarlet *m;* with
36:35 coccus scarlet *m* and fine
36:37 coccus scarlet *m* and fine
38:18 coccus scarlet *m* and fine
38:23 coccus scarlet *m* and fine
39:1 and coccus scarlet *m* they made
39:2 and coccus scarlet *m* and
39:3 and the coccus scarlet *m* and
39:5 was of the same *m* according
39:5 and coccus scarlet *m* and fine
39:8 and coccus scarlet *m* and fine
39:24 coccus scarlet *m*, twisted
39:29 coccus scarlet *m*, the work
Le 14:4 coccus scarlet *m* and hyssop
14:6 the coccus scarlet *m* and the
14:49 coccus scarlet *m* and hyssop
14:51 coccus scarlet *m* and the
14:52 and the coccus scarlet *m*
Nu 19:6 coccus scarlet *m* and throw it
Ec 5:19 riches and *m* possessions
6:2 riches and *m* possessions and
Isa 41:25 tramples down the moist *m*
Eze 16:10 to cover you with costly *m*
16:13 fine linen and costly *m* and
23:6 clothed with blue *m*
27:16 and *m* of various colors and
27:20 garments of woven *m* for
27:24 in wraps of blue *m* and
27:24 *m* of various colors and in

Materials
Ex 28:8 *m*, of gold, blue thread and
1Co 3:12 stones, wood *m*, hay, stubble

Matred
Ge 36:39 *M* the daughter of Mezahab
1Ch 1:50 *M*, the daughter of Mezahab

Matrites
1Sa 10:21 family of the *M* came to be

Mattan
2Ki 11:18 and *M* the priest of Baal
2Ch 23:17 *M* the priest of Baal they
Jer 38:1 Shephatiah the son of *M*

Mattanah
Nu 21:18 from the wilderness on to *M*
21:19 And from *M* on to Nahaliel

Mattaniah
2Ki 24:17 made *M* his uncle king in
1Ch 9:15 and *M* the son of Mica the
25:4 of Heman, Bukkiah, *M*, Uzziel
25:16 the ninth for *M*, his sons
2Ch 20:14 *M* the Levite of the sons of
29:13 of Asaph, Zechariah and *M*
Ezr 10:26 sons of Elam, *M*, Zechariah
10:27 of the sons of Zattu . . . *M*
10:30 sons of Pahath-moab . . . *M*
10:37 *M*, Mattenai and Jaasu
Ne 11:17 *M* himself, the son of Micah
11:22 *M* the son of Mica of the
12:8 Sherebiah, Judah, *M*
12:25 *M* and Bakbukiah, Obadiah
12:35 *M* the son of Micaiah the son
13:13 Zaccur the son of *M*, for

Mattatha
Lu 3:31 son of Menna, son of *M*

Mattathias
Lu 3:25 son of *M*, son of Amos, son of
3:26 son of *M*, son of Semein

Mattattah
Ezr 10:33 the sons of Hashum . . . *M*

Mattenai
Ezr 10:33 the sons of Hashum . . . *M*
10:37 Mattaniah, *M* and Jaasu
Ne 12:19 for Joiarib, *M;* for Jedaiah

Matter
Ge 21:17 What is the *m* with you
24:9 to him concerning this *m*
Le 4:13 the *m* has been hidden from
De 3:26 speak to me further on this *m*
17:8 a *m* for judicial decision
19:15 the *m* should stand good
Jos 2:14 not tell about this *m* of
2:20 if you should report this *m*
4:10 whole *m* had been completed
Jg 3:22 fecal *m* began to come out
18:23 What is the *m* with you that
18:24 What is the *m* with you?
Ru 3:18 know how the *m* will turn out
3:18 brought the *m* to an end today
1Sa 10:2 the *m* of the she-asses and
10:16 And the *m* of the kingship
11:5 is the *m* with the people
18:20 and the *m* was to his liking
18:26 the *m* was to David's liking
20:2 father conceal this *m* from
20:21 and there is nothing the *m*
20:39 knew about the *m*
21:2 commanded me as to a *m*, and
21:2 *m* concerning which I am
21:8 king's *m* proved to be urgent
28:10 not befall you in this *m*
2Sa 1:4 How did the *m* turn out?
11:25 not let this *m* appear bad
13:20 set your heart on this *m*
14:5 What is the *m* with you?
14:20 altering the face of the *m*
18:5 chiefs over the *m* of Absalom
18:13 *m* itself would not be
19:43 *m* become first for us to
20:18 will certainly end the *m*
20:21 The *m* is not that way, but
21:4 It is not a *m* of silver or
1Ki 2:14 There is a *m* I have for you
5:8 *m* of timbers of cedar trees
10:3 no *m* hidden from the king
10:25 as a yearly *m* of course
15:5 the *m* of Uriah the Hittite
18:27 must be concerned with a *m*
2Ki 6:11 became enraged over this *m*
6:28 What is the *m* with you?
1Ch 26:32 for every *m* of the true God
26:32 and *m* of the king
27:1 every *m* of the divisions of
2Ch 8:13 daily *m* of course to make
8:14 as a daily *m* of course, and
8:15 the Levites concerning any *m*
9:2 no *m* was hidden from Solomon
9:24 as a yearly *m* of course
14:11 not *m* with you whether
19:6 you in the *m* of judgment
19:11 for every *m* of Jehovah
19:11 for every *m* of the king
24:5 should act quickly in the *m*
30:12 in the *m* of Jehovah
2Ch 31:16 as a daily *m* of course
Ezr 10:4 for the *m* devolves upon you
10:9 shivering because of the *m*
10:13 to a great extent in this *m*
10:14 on account of this *m*
10:16 to inquire into the *m*
Ne 11:24 for every *m* of the people
Es 1:13 the king's *m* came before all
2:23 So the *m* was sought out and
Job 19:28 root of the *m* is found in
26:14 a whisper of a *m* has been
41:12 the *m* of its mightiness
Ps 45:1 become astir with a goodly *m*
90:3 man go back to crushed *m*
114:5 What was the *m* . . . O sea
Pr 6:35 no *m* how large you make the
11:13 spirit is covering over a *m*
16:20 showing insight in a *m* will
17:9 that keeps talking about a *m*
18:13 is replying to a *m* before he
25:2 is the keeping of a *m* secret
25:2 is the searching through a *m*
Ec 7:8 is the end afterward of a *m*
10:20 will tell the *m*
12:13 The conclusion of the *m*
Isa 22:1 What is the *m* with you
47:7 the finale of the *m*
49:6 been more than a trivial *m*
Jer 6:20 What does this *m* to me that
32:17 whole *m* is not too
32:27 any *m* at all too wonderful
38:27 for the *m* was not heard
Eze 12:23 and the *m* of every vision
14:4 to answer him in the *m*
32:6 drink up your discharged *m*
39:13 a *m* of fame in the day that
Da 1:14 listened . . . as regards this *m*
1:20 *m* of wisdom and understanding
2:10 to show the *m* of the king
2:15 Arioch made known the *m*
2:17 he made known the *m*
2:23 to us the very *m* of the king
6:12 The *m* is well established
7:28 point is the end of the *m*
7:28 *m* . . . I kept in my own heart
9:23 give consideration to the *m*
10:1 was a *m* revealed to Daniel
10:1 and the *m* was true, and there
10:1 And he understood the *m*, and
Am 3:7 confidential *m* to his servants
Jon 1:6 What is the *m* with you
Mt 6:28 Also, on the *m* of clothing
18:16 every *m* may be established
Mr 3:28 sons of men, no *m* what sins
Lu 10:40 Lord, does it not *m* to you
19:17 very small *m* you have proved
Joh 8:26 As a *m* of fact, he that sent
15:16 *m* what you ask the Father
Ac 8:21 part nor lot in this *m*, for
11:28 for that *m*, did take place
28:23 he explained the *m* to them
Ro 2:15 *m* of the law to be written
16:2 assist her in any *m* where she
1Co 4:3 to me it is a very trivial *m*
2Co 1:20 no *m* how many the promises
7:11 to be chaste in this *m*
8:10 this *m* is of benefit to you
13:1 every *m* must be established
Ga 5:10 no *m* who he may be
Php 3:8 for that *m*, I do indeed also
4:15 *m* of giving and receiving
Col 1:16 no *m* whether they are
1:20 no *m* whether they are the
1Th 4:6 of his brother in this *m*
1Ti 2:7 in the *m* of faith and truth
1Jo 5:14 no *m* what it is that we ask
Re 14:4 Lamb no *m* where he goes

Matters
Ge 24:33 I have spoken about my *m*
De 17:8 *m* of dispute, inside your
2Sa 11:18 all the *m* of the war
11:19 about all the *m* of the war
15:3 *m* are good and straight
1Ki 10:3 to tell her all her *m*
10:6 your *m* and about your wisdom
2Ch 9:2 tell her all her *m*, and no
9:5 your *m* and about your wisdom
Es 9:31 *m* of the fasts and their cry
9:32 confirmed these *m* of Purim
Job 23:7 set *m* straight with him
Ps 105:27 the *m* of his signs
145:5 *m* of your wonderful works
Pr 26:6 thrusting *m* into the hand of

Isa 1:18 set *m* straight between us
2:4 and set *m* straight respecting
57:9 you lowered *m* to Sheol
57:11 keeping silent and hiding *m*
Jer 7:22 the *m* of whole burnt
12:1 *m* of judgment with you
14:1 the *m* of the droughts
Da 7:1 complete account of the *m* he
7:16 very interpretation of the *m*
Mic 4:3 *m* straight respecting mighty
Mt 5:25 Be about settling *m* quickly
23:23 disregarded the weightier *m*
Lu 24:17 *m* that you are debating
Ac 5:24 quandary over these *m* as to
5:32 we are witnesses of these *m*
10:44 speaking about these *m* the
13:42 for these *m* to be spoken to
23:15 accurately the *m* involving
24:18 While I was at these *m* they
24:22 the *m* concerning this Way
24:22 shall decide upon these *m*
25:14 *m* respecting Paul, saying
25:20 the dispute over these *m*
25:20 judged concerning these *m*
1Co 2:13 we combine spiritual *m* with
6:2 unfit to try very trivial *m*
6:3 Why, then, not *m* of this life?
6:4 do have *m* of this life to be
11:34 remaining *m* I will set in
Php 2:4 upon just your own *m*, but
1Pe 4:15 busybody in other people's *m*

Matthan
Mt 1:15 Eleazar became father to *M*
1:15 *M* became father to Jacob

Matthat
Lu 3:24 son of *M*, son of Levi, son of
3:29 son of Jorim, son of *M*, son

Matthew
Mt 9:9 *M* seated at the tax office
10:3 and *M* the tax collector
Mr 3:18 *M* and Thomas and James the
Lu 6:15 *M* and Thomas, and James the
Ac 1:13 *M*, James the son of Alphaeus

Matthias
Ac 1:23 So they put up two . . . and *M*
1:26 and the lot fell upon *M*

Mattithiah
1Ch 9:31 *M* of the Levites, who was
15:18 and *M* and Eliphelehu and
15:21 and *M* and Eliphelehu and
16:5 *M* and Eliab and Benaiah and
25:3 the sons of Jeduthun . . . *M*
25:21 for the fourteenth, *M*, his
Ezr 10:43 the sons of Nebo . . . *M*
Ne 8:4 were standing alongside him *M*

Mattock
1Sa 13:20 plowshare or his *m* or his

Mattocks
1Sa 13:21 a pim . . . for the *m* and for

Mature
Ca 2:13 a *m* color for its early figs
1Co 2:6 among those who are *m*, but
Php 3:15 as many of us as are *m*, be
Heb 5:14 solid food . . . to *m* people

Maturity
Heb 6:1 let us press on to *m*, not

Maybe
Ge 43:12 *M* it was a mistake
1Ki 18:27 Or *m* he is asleep and ought
Job 1:5 *m* my sons have sinned and
Da 4:27 *M* there will occur a

Mazzaroth
Job 38:32 the *M* constellation in its

Meah
Ne 3:1 as far as the Tower of *M* they
12:39 the Tower of *M* and on to the

Meal
Ge 43:31 and said: Set on the *m*
43:32 eat a *m* with the Hebrews
Nu 15:20 firstfruits of your coarse *m*
15:21 firstfruits of your coarse *m*
1Sa 16:11 not sit down to *m* until
20:24 king took his seat at the *m*
20:27 son of Jesse come to the *m*
Ne 10:37 firstfruits of our coarse *m*
Mt 15:2 hands when about to eat a *m*
15:20 a *m* with unwashed hands
Mr 3:20 not able even to eat a *m*
6:21 Herod spread an evening *m* on
6:31 leisure time even to eat a *m*
7:2 eat their *m* with defiled
7:5 their *m* with defiled hands
14:3 as he was reclining at the *m*
Lu 5:29 with them reclining at the *m*
7:37 at a *m* in the house of the
14:1 on the sabbath to eat a *m*
14:12 dinner or evening *m*, do not
14:16 spreading a grand evening *m*
14:17 at the hour of the evening *m*
14:24 have a taste of my evening *m*
17:8 for me to have my evening *m*
22:20 after they had the evening *m*
24:30 at the *m* he took the loaf
Joh 6:10 Have the men recline as at *m*
12:2 they spread an evening *m* for
13:2 the evening *m* was going on
13:4 got up from the evening *m*
21:20 who at the evening *m* had
Ac 20:7 gathered together to have a *m*
20:11 began the *m* and took food
1Co 8:10 at a *m* in an idol temple
11:20 to eat the Lord's evening *m*
11:21 takes his own evening *m*
11:25 after he had the evening *m*
Heb 12:16 in exchange for one *m* gave
Re 3:20 take the evening *m* with him
19:9 the evening *m* of the Lamb's
19:17 the great evening *m* of God

Meals
Eze 44:30 coarse *m* you should give to
Mt 23:6 prominent place at evening *m*
Mr 12:39 places at evening *m*
Lu 9:14 recline as at *m*, in groups of
20:46 places at evening *m*
Ac 2:42 taking of *m* and to prayers
2:46 their *m* in private homes and

Mealtime
Ru 2:14 proceeded to say to her at *m*

Mean
Ge 33:8 What do you *m* by all this
37:10 What does this dream . . . *m*?
38:29 What do you *m* by this, that
Ex 12:26 What does this service *m* to
13:14 What does this *m*? then you
De 6:20 the judicial decisions *m* that
6:25 will *m* righteousness for us
24:13 will *m* righteousness for you
Jos 4:21 What do these stones *m*?
Jg 15:11 what does this *m* that you
1Sa 4:6 What does the sound . . . *m*?
4:14 the sound of this turmoil *m*
15:14 what does this sound . . . *m*
16:4 Does your coming *m* peace?
29:3 What do these Hebrews *m*?
2Sa 12:21 thing *m* that you have done
16:2 What do these things *m* on
1Ki 1:41 What does the noise . . . *m*?
Pr 19:27 *m* to stray from the sayings
Ec 10:12 of the wise one *m* favor
Isa 3:15 *m* in that you crush my
Eze 17:12 know what these things *m*
18:2 What does it *m* to you people
20:29 What does the high place *m*
37:18 tell us what these things *m*
Am 5:18 the day of Jehovah *m* to you
Zec 4:4 What do these things *m*, my
4:5 know what these things *m*
4:11 and on its left side *m*
4:13 know what these things *m*
Mt 5:37 word *Yes m* Yes, your *No*, No
6:25 soul *m* more than food and
7:12 the Law and the Prophets *m*
Lu 8:9 this illustration might *m*
18:36 inquire what this might *m*
20:17 does this that is written *m*
Joh 7:36 What does this saying *m* that
16:17 does this *m* that he says
16:18 does this *m* that he says
Ac 10:17 vision he had seen might *m*
Ro 11:12 full number of them *m* it
11:15 receiving of them *m* but life
14:17 kingdom of God does not *m*
1Co 1:12 What I *m* is this, that each
7:19 Circumcision does not *m* a
2Co 8:13 not *m* for it to be easy for
Ga 4:24 these women *m* two covenants
Eph 3:13 for these *m* glory for you
4:9 he ascended, what does it *m*
Jas 5:12 let your *Yes m* Yes, and your
Re 1:20 seven stars *m* the angels of
1:20 *m* seven congregations
4:5 *m* the seven spirits of God
5:6 eyes *m* the seven spirits of
17:9 seven heads *m* seven mountains
17:12 ten horns . . . *m* ten kings
17:15 The waters . . . *m* peoples and

Meaning
Ge 21:29 What is the *m* here of these
Ne 8:8 being a putting of *m* into it
Ps 86:17 with me a sign *m* goodness
Mr 6:52 grasped the *m* of the loaves
7:14 all of you, and get the *m*
8:17 yet perceive and get the *m*
8:21 Do you not yet get the *m*?
Lu 8:10 they may not get the *m*
18:34 did not get the *m* of any of
24:45 the *m* of the Scriptures
Ro 8:27 what the *m* of the spirit is
1Co 5:10 not *m* entirely with the
14:10 yet no kind is without *m*
14:29 the others discern the *m*

Means
Ge 12:3 bless themselves by *m* of you
18:18 must bless themselves by *m*
21:12 by *m* of Isaac that what will
22:18 *m* of your seed all nations
26:4 by *m* of your seed all nations
28:14 and by *m* of you and by
28:14 by *m* of your seed all the
34:29 their *m* of maintenance and
41:32 *m* that the thing is firmly
44:5 by *m* of which he expertly
48:20 By *m* of you let Israel
Ex 5:23 by no *m* delivered your people
9:35 had stated by *m* of Moses
14:4 by *m* of Pharaoh and all his
14:17 by *m* of Pharaoh and all his
14:18 glory . . . by *m* of Pharaoh
26:6 join . . . by *m* of the hooks
34:7 no *m* will he give exemption
35:29 commanded to make by *m* of
Le 5:11 if he does not have the *m* for
8:36 commanded by *m* of Moses
10:11 spoken to them by *m* of Moses
14:21 and does not have enough *m*
14:22 as he may have the *m*
14:30 for which he may have the *m*
14:31 he may have the *m* as a sin
14:32 who may not have the *m* when
18:5 must also live by *m* of them
19:17 should by all *m* reprove your
26:46 Mount Sinai by *m* of Moses
Nu 4:37 of Jehovah by *m* of Moses
4:45 Jehovah by *m* of Moses
4:49 registered by *m* of Moses
9:23 Jehovah by *m* of Moses
10:13 of Jehovah by *m* of Moses
14:18 no *m* will he give exemption
14:34 what my being estranged *m*
15:23 commanded you by *m* of Moses
16:40 spoken to him by *m* of Moses
27:7 By all *m* you should give them
27:23 had spoken by *m* of Moses
31:9 all their *m* of maintenance
36:13 commanded by *m* of Moses to
De 6:17 You should by all *m* keep the
7:18 by all *m* remember what
15:8 by all *m* lend him on pledge
15:10 You should by all *m* give
21:14 by no *m* sell her for money
21:23 by all *m* bury him on that
22:1 by all *m* lead them back to
22:4 by all *m* help him raise them
22:7 by all *m* send the mother
24:13 by all *m* return the pledge
32:47 but it *m* your life, and by
Jos 14:2 commanded by *m* of Moses for
20:2 I spoke to you by *m* of Moses
21:2 Jehovah by *m* of Moses
21:8 had commanded by *m* of Moses
22:9 at the order of Jehovah by *m*
Jg 3:4 commanded their fathers by *m*
6:36 are saving Israel by *m* of me
6:37 save Israel by *m* of me, just
15:13 by no *m* put you to death
1Sa 6:3 by all *m* return to him a
16:5 It *m* peace. To sacrifice to
18:23 man of little *m* and lightly
20:7 it *m* peace to your servant
20:21 for it *m* peace for you and
28:15 either by *m* of the prophets
28:17 just as he spoke by *m* of me
2Sa 5:8 by *m* of the water tunnel

2Sa 10:2 sent by *m* of his servants
12:1 and the other of little *m*
12:3 man of little *m* had nothing
12:4 lamb of the man of little *m*
12:25 sent by *m* of Nathan the
15:36 by *m* of them you men must
1Ki 2:25 sent by *m* of Benaiah the son
3:26 Do not by any *m* put him to
3:27 by no *m* put him to death
8:53 spoken by *m* of Moses your
8:56 promised by *m* of Moses his
10:29 was by *m* of them that they
12:15 had spoken by *m* of Ahijah
14:18 by *m* of his servant Ahijah
15:29 by *m* of his servant Ahijah
16:7 by *m* of Jehu the son of
16:12 by *m* of Jehu the prophet
16:34 spoke by *m* of Joshua the
17:16 had spoken by *m* of Elijah
22:21 said to him, By what *m?*
2Ki 9:36 by *m* of his servant Elijah
10:10 by *m* of his servant Elijah
14:25 by *m* of his servant Jonah
17:13 by *m* of all his prophets
17:13 by *m* of my servants the
17:23 by *m* of all his servants
19:23 By *m* of your messengers you
21:10 by *m* of his servants the
24:2 spoken by *m* of his servants
1Ch 11:3 Jehovah's word by *m* of
16:7 thank Jehovah by *m* of Asaph
22:14 there is no *m* of weighing
22:16 there is no *m* of numbering
2Ch 1:17 by *m* of them that they did
8:18 to him by *m* of his servants
10:15 *m* of Ahijah the Shilonite
13:9 power by *m* of a young bull
18:20 said to him, By what *m?*
25:9 *m* to give you much more
29:25 was by *m* of his prophets
35:6 of Jehovah by *m* of Moses
36:15 by *m* of his messengers
Ezr 9:11 by *m* of your servants the
Ne 8:14 commanded by *m* of Moses that
9:14 by *m* of Moses your servant
9:29 must also live by *m* of them
9:30 spirit by *m* of your prophets
Es 1:7 according to the *m* of the king
1:12 by *m* of the court officials
1:15 by *m* of the court officials
2:18 the *m* of the king
3:13 the letters by *m* of couriers
Job 5:5 at their *m* of maintenance
19:29 sword *m* a raging against
20:20 *m* of his desirable things
Ps 49:6 are trusting in their *m* of
49:7 any *m* redeem even a brother
49:10 their *m* of maintenance
62:10 In case the *m* of maintenance
72:17 by *m* of him let them bless
73:12 their *m* of maintenance
82:3 one of little *m* do justice
Pr 8:13 Jehovah *m* the hating of bad
10:4 hand will be of little *m*
12:28 in its pathway *m* no death
13:7 pretending to be of little *m*
13:8 one of little *m* has not heard
13:23 of persons of little *m*
14:20 one who is of little *m* is an
15:4 distortion in it *m* a breaking
16:14 rage of a king *m* messengers
17:5 one of little *m* in derision
18:23 one of little *m* speaks out
19:1 Anyone of little *m* who is
19:7 brothers of one of little *m*
19:13 stupid son *m* adversities to
19:22 one of little *m* is better
22:2 the one of little *m* have met
22:7 rules over those of little *m*
27:27 the *m* of life for your girls
28:3 man that is of little *m* and
28:6 Better is the one of little *m*
28:27 to the one of little *m*
29:13 The one of little *m* and the
Ec 2:23 his occupation *m* pains and
4:4 it *m* the rivalry of one toward
4:14 been born as one of little *m*
5:8 of the one of little *m* and the
10:10 of wisdom to success *m*
Isa 7:20 by *m* of a hired razor in the
7:20 by *m* of the king of Assyria
9:7 sustain it by *m* of justice
9:7 *m* of righteousness, from now
18:2 envoys by *m* of the sea

Isa 18:2 by *m* of vessels of papyrus
27:9 this *m* the error of Jacob
30:19 you will by no *m* weep
37:24 *m* of your servants you have
53:11 By *m* of his knowledge the
Jer 22:4 by all *m* perform this word
23:27 by *m* of their dreams that
23:27 forgot my name by *m* of
23:32 by no *m* benefit this people
25:35 a *m* of escape from the
26:15 by all *m* know that, if you
26:19 by any *m* put him to death
30:11 no *m* leave you unpunished
30:13 no *m* of healing, no mending
31:20 By all *m* I shall have pity
37:2 spoke by *m* of Jeremiah the
38:6 Jeremiah down by *m* of ropes
38:11 cistern by *m* of the ropes
38:13 Jeremiah by *m* of the ropes
39:11 *m* of Nebuzaradan the chief
46:11 multiplied the *m* of healing
50:1 by *m* of Jeremiah the prophet
Eze 16:4 no *m* had you been swaddled
19:4 bring him by *m* of hooks to
19:9 in the cage by *m* of hooks
19:9 by *m* of hunting nets, in
21:21 asked by *m* of the teraphim
32:3 by *m* of a congregation of
44:20 by all *m* clip the hair of
Da 11:21 kingdom by *m* of smoothness
11:23 by *m* of a little nation
11:32 apostasy by *m* of smooth
11:34 to them by *m* of smoothness
11:38 give glory by *m* of gold
11:38 and by *m* of silver and by
11:38 by *m* of precious stone and
11:38 by *m* of desirable things
Am 7:4 for a contention by *m* of fire
Na 1:3 by no *m* will Jehovah hold back
Hag 1:1 by *m* of Haggai the prophet to
1:3 by *m* of Haggai the prophet
2:1 by *m* of Haggai the prophet
Zec 4:12 by *m* of the two golden tubes
7:7 by *m* of the former prophets
7:12 by *m* of the former prophets
Mal 1:1 The word . . . by *m* of Malachi
Mt 1:23 which *m*, when translated
2:6 no *m* the most insignificant
5:18 from the Law by any *m* and
5:20 by no *m* enter into the
9:13 learn what this *m*, I want
10:23 no *m* complete the circuit
10:42 by no *m* lose his reward
11:2 by *m* of his own disciples
12:7 had understood what this *m*
12:24 except by *m* of Beelzebub
12:27 if I expel the demons by *m*
12:27 by *m* of whom do your sons
12:28 by *m* of God's spirit that I
13:14 by no *m* get the sense of it
13:14 will look but by no *m* see
18:3 will by no *m* enter into the
18:25 have the *m* to pay it back
23:39 You will by no *m* see me
24:2 By no *m* will a stone be left
24:34 generation . . . by no *m* pass
24:35 my words will by no *m* pass
26:26 Take, eat. This *m* my body
26:28 *m* my blood of the covenant
26:29 by no *m* drink henceforth any
26:35 I will by no *m* disown you
Mr 3:17 which *m* Sons of Thunder
3:22 *m* of the ruler of the demons
5:41 *m:* Maiden, I say to you, Get
9:41 by no *m* lose his reward
10:15 will by no *m* enter into it
13:2 By no *m* will a stone be left
13:30 generation . . . by no *m* pass
14:22 Take it, this *m* my body
14:24 This *m* my blood of the
14:25 by no *m* drink any more of
14:31 I will by no *m* disown you
15:22 Golgotha, which *m*, when
15:34 *m*, when translated: My God
Lu 2:15 Let us by all *m* go clear to
2:30 have seen your *m* of saving
3:6 will see the saving *m* of God
6:37 you will by no *m* be judged
6:37 will by no *m* be condemned
8:4 spoke by *m* of an illustration
8:11 Now the illustration *m* this
10:19 will by any *m* do you hurt
11:15 by *m* of Beelzebub the ruler
11:18 the demons by *m* of Beelzebub

Lu 11:19 If it is by *m* of Beelzebub
11:20 if it is by *m* of God's
13:35 by no *m* see me until you say
15:12 divided his *m* of living to
15:30 ate up your *m* of living with
16:9 *m* of the unrighteous riches
18:17 will by no *m* get into it
18:31 written by *m* of the prophets
20:25 By all *m*, then, pay back
21:4 all the *m* of living she had
21:18 will by any *m* perish
21:32 by no *m* pass away until all
21:33 my words will by no *m* pass
22:19 This *m* my body which is to
22:20 This cup *m* the new covenant
Joh 1:4 by *m* of him was life, and
1:38 Rabbi, (which *m* . . . Teacher
1:41 Messiah (which *m* . . . Christ)
4:48 you will by no *m* believe
5:39 you think that by *m* of them
6:37 I will by no *m* drive away
8:12 by no *m* walk in darkness
10:5 no *m* follow but will flee
10:28 by no *m* ever be destroyed
12:50 commandment *m* everlasting
13:38 A cock will by no *m* crow
16:7 helper will by no *m* come to
16:33 by *m* of me you may have
17:3 This *m* everlasting life
17:17 Sanctify them by *m* of the
17:19 sanctified by *m* of truth
18:11 I not by all *m* drink it
20:16 *Rab·bo'ni* . . . *m* Teacher
20:31 have life by *m* of his name
Ac 4:36 *m*, when translated, Son of
9:36 when translated, *m* Dorcas
13:39 by *m* of the law of Moses
13:39 guiltless by *m* of this One
13:41 you will by no *m* believe
14:27 God had done by *m* of them
15:4 God had done by *m* of them
28:26 hear but by no *m* understand
28:26 will look but by no *m* see
28:28 *m* by which God saves, has
Ro 1:4 by *m* of resurrection from the
1:17 by *m* of faith he will live
3:30 righteous by *m* of their faith
3:31 abolish law by *m* of our faith
4:8 by no *m* take into account
8:6 minding of the flesh *m* death
8:6 minding of the spirit *m* life
8:7 minding of the flesh *m* enmity
11:12 their false step *m* riches
11:12 their decrease *m* riches to
11:14 by any *m* incite those who
11:15 *m* reconciliation for the
14:17 but *m* righteousness and
1Co 3:13 be revealed by *m* of fire
6:7 *m* altogether a defeat for you
6:20 By all *m*, glorify God in the
7:19 uncircumcision *m* not a thing
7:35 which *m* constant attendance
9:14 live by *m* of the good news
9:22 that I might by all *m* save
10:2 by *m* of the cloud and of the
11:24 This *m* my body which is in
11:25 This cup *m* the new covenant
13:12 by *m* of a metal mirror
2Co 1:20 have become Yes by *m* of him
3:14 is done away with by *m* of
5:19 by *m* of Christ reconciling
5:21 God's righteousness by *m* of
8:14 by *m* of an equalizing your
Ga 2:17 declared righteous by *m* of
3:8 By *m* of you all the nations
3:12 shall live by *m* of them
3:14 by *m* of Jesus Christ for the
3:21 have been by *m* of law
4:25 Hagar *m* Sinai, a mountain
4:30 by no *m* shall the son of the
5:4 declared righteous by *m* of law
Eph 1:6 upon us by *m* of his loved one
1:7 *m* of him we have the release
1:13 by *m* of him also, after you
2:15 *m* of his flesh he abolished
2:16 the enmity by *m* of himself
3:12 by *m* of whom we have this
3:21 by *m* of the congregation
3:21 by *m* of Christ Jesus to all
4:14 by *m* of the trickery of men
4:14 by *m* of cunning in
4:21 and were taught by *m* of him
5:5 which *m* being an idolater
5:26 by *m* of the word

Php 1:20 magnified by *m* of my body
3:6 righteousness . . . by *m* of law
3:11 if I may by any *m* attain
3:14 of God by *m* of Christ Jesus
4:7 by *m* of Christ Jesus
4:19 glory by *m* of Christ Jesus
Col 1:14 by *m* of whom we have our
1:16 by *m* of him all other things
1:17 by *m* of him all other things
1:22 by *m* of that one's fleshly
2:10 by *m* of him, who is the
2:15 procession by *m* of it
2:19 by *m* of its joints and
1Th 2:2 boldness by *m* of our God to
5:3 and they will by no *m* escape
2Th 2:16 by *m* of undeserved kindness
1Ti 1:16 by *m* of me as the foremost
6:5 devotion is a *m* of gain
6:6 it is a *m* of great gain, this
Heb 1:1 spoke . . . *m* of the prophets
1:2 spoken to us by *m* of a Son
2:14 having the *m* to cause death
8:11 by no *m* teach each one his
8:12 by no *m* call their sins to
9:23 cleansed by these *m*, but
10:17 no *m* call their sins and
11:2 by *m* of this the men of old
13:5 I will by no *m* leave you
13:5 nor by any *m* forsake you
1Pe 2:6 any *m* come to disappointment
2Pe 1:10 you will by no *m* ever fail
3:6 by those *m* the world of that
1Jo 2:16 display of one's *m* of life
3:17 world's *m* for supporting
5:3 is what the love of God *m*
5:6 came by *m* of water and blood
5:20 by *m* of his Son Jesus Christ
2Jo 6 And this is what love *m*, that
Re 1:5 by *m* of his own blood
2:11 by no *m* be harmed by the
3:5 no *m* blot out his name from
3:12 by no *m* go out from it
5:8 incense *m* the prayers of the
9:6 death but will by no *m* find it
13:10 *m* the endurance and faith
14:12 *m* endurance for the holy
15:1 by *m* of them the anger of
17:18 woman . . . *m* the great city
20:14 This *m* the second death, the
21:8 This *m* the second death
21:24 walk by *m* of its light

Meant
Ge 25:28 it *m* game in his mouth
27:13 malediction *m* for you, my
27:35 get the blessing *m* for you
2Ki 13:19 *m* to strike five or six
Es 4:5 to know what this *m* and what
Isa 53:3 a man *m* for pains and for
53:5 chastisement *m* for our peace
Eze 19:11 rods, *m* for the scepters of
Na 3:10 She, too, was *m* for exile
Zec 11:4 the flock *m* for the killing
11:7 the flock *m* for the killing
Mr 9:10 this rising from the dead *m*
Lu 15:26 inquired what these things *m*
Joh 1:8 he was *m* to bear witness
10:6 *m* that he was speaking to
1Co 10:4 that rock-mass *m* the Christ
1Pe 1:10 kindness *m* for you
Re 13:10 anyone is *m* for captivity

Mearah
Jos 13:4 *M*, which belongs to the

Measure
Ge 27:33 trembling in extreme *m*
Ex 16:16 omer *m* for each individual
16:18 would *m* it by the omer, he
16:32 Fill an omer *m* of it as
16:36 is a tenth of an ephah *m*
26:2 one *m* for all the tent cloths
26:8 is one *m* for the eleven tent
29:40 a tenth part of an ephah *m*
36:9 one *m* for all the tent cloths
36:15 *m* for the eleven tent cloths
Le 14:10 and one log *m* of oil
14:12 the log *m* of oil and must
14:15 the log *m* of oil and pour it
14:21 take . . . a log *m* of oil
14:24 and the log *m* of oil, and
Nu 28:13 and a tenth *m* of fine flour
28:21 a tenth *m* respectively for
28:29 a tenth *m* respectively for
29:4 tenth *m* for each male lamb
Nu 29:10 a tenth *m* respectively for
29:15 tenth *m* for each male lamb
35:5 *m* outside the city on the
De 21:2 *m* to the cities that are all
Jos 3:4 two thousand cubits by *m*
Ru 3:15 *m* out six measures of barley
2Sa 8:2 Moabites and *m* them with a
8:2 *m* two lines to put them to
1Ki 4:29 wisdom . . . in very great *m*
6:25 two cherubs had the same *m*
7:15 twelve cubits would *m*
7:37 one cast, one *m*, one shape
2Ki 6:25 cab *m* of dove's dung was
7:1 a seah *m* of fine flour will
7:16 seah *m* of fine flour came to
7:18 seah *m* of fine flour worth
Job 7:4 evening actually goes its *m*
11:9 longer than the earth in *m*
28:25 waters themselves by a *m*
Ps 39:4 the *m* of my days—what it is
60:6 plain of Succoth I shall *m*
80:5 upon tears in great *m*
108:7 of Succoth I shall *m* off
Isa 5:10 produce but one bath *m*
5:10 homer *m* of seed will
5:10 produce but an ephah *m*
40:12 a *m* the dust of the earth
47:9 In their complete *m* they
65:7 *m* out their wages first of
Jer 51:13 *m* of your profit making
Eze 4:11 you will drink merely by *m*
4:16 by *m* and in horror that they
40:5 *m* the breadth of the thing
40:6 *m* the threshold of the gate
40:8 *m* the porch of the gate
40:13 *m* the gate from the roof
40:19 *m* the width from in front
40:23 to *m* from gate to gate a
40:28 *m* the gate of the south as
40:32 *m* the gate as of the same
41:3 *m* the side pillar of the
41:5 *m* the wall of the house
43:10 they must *m* the pattern
45:3 *m* the length of twenty-five
45:10 accurate bath *m* you men
45:11 bath *m*, there should come
45:14 is the bath *m* of the oil
47:3 *m* a thousand in cubits and
47:18 you people should *m*
Ho 3:2 homer *m* of barley and a
Joe 2:23 autumn rain in right *m*
Mic 6:10 ephah *m* that is denounced
Zec 2:2 To *m* Jerusalem, in order to
5:6 ephah *m* that is going forth
Mt 7:2 the *m* that you are measuring
7:2 they will *m* out to you
23:32 the *m* of your forefathers
Mr 4:24 *m* that you are measuring out
Lu 6:38 pour into your laps a fine *m*
6:38 with the *m* that you are
6:38 will *m* out to you in return
12:42 their *m* of food supplies at
Joh 3:34 not give the spirit by *m*
Ac 4:33 kindness in large *m* was upon
20:12 and were comforted beyond *m*
Ro 12:3 to him a *m* of faith
15:24 in some *m* been satisfied
15:29 a full *m* of blessing from
1Co 11:18 and in some *m* I believe it
2Co 10:13 God apportioned to us by *m*
Eph 4:13 to the *m* of stature that
4:16 in due *m*, makes for the
1Th 2:16 fill up the *m* of their sins
4:10 go on doing it in fuller *m*
1Jo 1:4 that our joy may be in full *m*
2Jo 12 that your joy may be in full *m*
Re 11:1 *m* the temple sanctuary of God
11:2 do not *m* it, because it has
21:15 as a *m* a golden reed, that
21:15 *m* the city and its gates
21:17 according to a man's *m*, at

Measured
Ne 3:11 Another *m* section was what
3:19 repair another *m* section in
3:20 repaired another *m* section
3:21 repaired another *m* section
3:24 repaired another *m* section
3:27 repaired another *m* section
3:30 repaired another *m* section
Ps 139:3 outstretched you have *m* off
Isa 40:12 has *m* the waters in the
Jer 13:25 your *m* portion from me
31:37 heavens up above could be *m*
Jer 33:22 the sand of the sea be *m*
Eze 40:9 *m* the porch of the gate
40:11 he *m* the width of the
40:20 *m* its length and its width
40:24 *m* its side pillars and its
40:27 *m* from gate to gate toward
40:35 the north gate, and he *m*
41:13 *m* the house, a hundred
41:15 he *m* the length of the
42:15 and he *m* it all around
42:16 *m* the eastern side with the
42:17 *m* the northern side, five
42:18 southern side he *m*, five
42:19 *m* five hundred reeds, by
42:20 the four sides he *m* it
Ho 1:10 cannot be *m* or numbered
Mr 4:24 will have it *m* out to you
Eph 4:7 Christ *m* out the free gift
Re 21:16 *m* the city with the reed
21:17 he *m* its wall, one hundred

Measurement
2Ch 3:3 former *m* being sixty cubits
Jer 31:39 the line for *m* will yet
Eze 40:10 were of the same *m*, and
40:10 pillars were of the same *m*
40:21 the *m* of the first gate
40:22 the same *m* as those of the
45:3 out of this *m* you should
46:22 structures had the same *m*
48:30 cubits will be the *m*
48:33 hundred cubits as to *m*

Measurements
Job 38:5 Who set its *m*, in case you
Eze 40:24 of the same *m* as these
40:28 of the same *m* as these
40:29 of the same *m* as these
40:32 of the same *m* as these
40:33 of the same *m* as these
40:35 with the same *m* as these
41:17 the outside, there were *m*
42:15 *m* of the inner house, and
43:13 *m* of the altar in cubits
48:16 these are the city's *m*

Measures
Ge 18:6 three seah *m* of fine flour
26:12 getting up to a hundred *m*
Ex 16:22 two omer *m* for one person
Nu 28:9 two tenth *m* of fine flour as
28:12 three tenth *m* of fine flour
28:12 two tenth *m* of fine flour
28:20 three tenth *m* for a bull and
28:20 and two tenth *m* for the ram
28:28 three tenth *m* for each bull
28:28 two tenth *m* for the one ram
29:3 three tenth *m* for the bull
29:3 two tenth *m* for the ram
29:9 three tenth *m* for the bull
29:9 two tenth *m* for the one ram
29:14 three tenth *m* for each bull
29:14 two tenth *m* for each ram of
Ru 3:15 measure out six *m* of barley
3:17 six *m* of barley he gave me
1Sa 25:18 five seah *m* of roasted
1Ki 4:22 thirty cor *m* of fine flour
4:22 sixty cor *m* of flour
5:11 twenty thousand cor *m* of
5:11 twenty cor *m* of beaten-out
7:9 stones according to *m*, hewn
7:11 stones according to *m*, hewn
7:26 Two thousand bath *m* were
7:38 Forty bath *m* were what each
18:32 with two seah *m* of seed
2Ki 7:1 two seah *m* of barley worth
7:16 two seah *m* of barley worth
7:18 Two seah *m* of barley worth
1Ch 23:29 all *m* of quantity and size
2Ch 4:5 three thousand bath *m* were
27:5 ten thousand cor *m* of wheat
Ezr 7:22 a hundred cor *m* of wheat and
7:22 hundred bath *m* of wine
7:22 a hundred bath *m* of oil, and
Pr 20:10 and two sorts of ephah *m*
Hag 2:16 came to a heap of twenty *m*
2:16 fifty *m* of the wine trough
Mt 13:33 in three large *m* of flour
Lu 13:21 in three large *m* of flour
16:6 A hundred bath *m* of olive oil
16:7 A hundred cor *m* of wheat
Joh 2:6 hold two or three liquid *m*
2Co 10:2 taking bold *m* against some

Measuring
Le 19:35 injustice in judging, in *m*

2Ki 1:6 a man that came up to *m* us
1:7 man that came up to *m* you
2:15 came to *m* him and bowed
4:26 Now run, please, to *m* her
4:31 he went back to *m* him and
5:21 from his chariot to *m* him
5:26 off his chariot to *m* you
8:8 and *m* the man of the true God
8:9 Hazael went to *m* him and
9:17 and send him to *m* them
9:18 rider on a horse went to *m*
9:21 continued on out to *m* Jehu
10:15 Jehonadab . . . to *m* him
16:10 Then King Ahaz went to *m*
23:29 proceeded to go to *m* him
1Ch 19:5 he at once sent to *m* them
19:10 formation to *m* the Syrians
19:11 to *m* the sons of Ammon
19:17 formation to *m* the Syrians
Ne 6:2 *m* together by appointment
6:10 Let us *m* by appointment at
Job 39:21 It goes forth to *m* armor
Ps 21:3 *m* him with blessings of good
35:3 ax to *m* those pursuing me
Pr 7:10 there was a woman to *m* him
7:15 I have come out to *m* you, to
Isa 7:3 Go out, please, to *m* Ahaz
14:9 order to *m* you on coming in
21:14 *m* the thirsty one bring
34:14 *m* up with howling animals
47:3 shall not *m* any man kindly
53:6 all to *m* up with that one
Jer 41:6 out from Mizpah to *m* them
51:31 runs to *m* another runner
51:31 one reporter to *m* another
Am 4:12 get ready to *m* your God
Zec 2:3 angel going forth to *m* him
Mt 8:34 city turned out to *m* Jesus
25:1 went out to *m* the bridegroom
25:6 Be on your way out to *m* him
Lu 14:31 king, marching to *m* another
22:10 will *m* you. Follow him into
Joh 12:13 and went out to *m* him
Ac 28:15 came to *m* us as far as the
1Co 11:17 for the worse that you *m*
1Th 4:17 to *m* the Lord in the air
Tit 3:14 to *m* their pressing needs
Jas 1:2 you *m* with various trials

Meeting
Ex 27:21 In the tent of *m*, outside
28:43 they come into the tent of *m*
29:4 the entrance of the tent of *m*
29:10 bull before the tent of *m*
29:11 entrance of the tent of *m*
29:30 comes into the tent of *m* to
29:32 entrance of the tent of *m*
29:42 entrance of the tent of *m*
29:44 will sanctify the tent of *m*
30:16 service of the tent of *m*
30:18 between the tent of *m* and
30:20 they go into the tent of *m*
30:26 the tent of *m* and the ark of
30:36 in the tent of *m*, where I
31:7 tent of *m* and the Ark for the
33:7 he called it a tent of *m*
33:7 go out to the tent of *m*
35:21 work of the tent of *m*
38:8 the entrance of the tent of *m*
38:30 entrance of the tent of *m*
39:32 tabernacle of the tent of *m*
39:40 for the tent of *m*
40:2 tabernacle of the tent of *m*
40:6 tabernacle of the tent of *m*
40:7 basin between the tent of *m*
40:12 entrance of the tent of *m*
40:22 the table in the tent of *m*
40:24 the tent of *m* in front of
40:26 tent of *m* before the curtain
40:29 tabernacle of the tent of *m*
40:30 the tent of *m* and the altar
40:32 they went into the tent of *m*
40:34 began to cover the tent of *m*
40:35 to go into the tent of *m*
Le 1:1 out of the tent of *m*, saying
1:3 the entrance of the tent of *m*
1:5 the entrance of the tent of *m*
3:2 the entrance of the tent of *m*
3:8 before the tent of *m*
3:13 before the tent of *m*
4:4 entrance of the tent of *m*
4:5 bring it into the tent of *m*
4:7 which is in the tent of *m*
4:7 the entrance of the tent of *m*
Le 4:14 bring it before the tent of *m*
4:16 blood into the tent of *m*
4:18 which is in the tent of *m*
4:18 the entrance of the tent of *m*
6:16 courtyard of the tent of *m*
6:26 courtyard of the tent of *m*
6:30 be brought into the tent of *m*
8:3 the entrance of the tent of *m*
8:4 the entrance of the tent of *m*
8:31 the entrance of the tent of *m*
8:33 the entrance of the tent of *m*
8:35 the entrance of the tent of *m*
9:5 before the tent of *m*
9:23 Aaron went into the tent of *m*
10:7 the entrance of the tent of *m*
10:9 you come into the tent of *m*
12:6 entrance of the tent of *m* to
14:11 entrance of the tent of *m*
14:23 the tent of *m* before Jehovah
15:14 entrance of the tent of *m*
15:29 entrance of the tent of *m*
16:7 the entrance of the tent of *m*
16:16 tent of *m*, which is residing
16:17 be in the tent of *m* from
16:20 tent of *m* and the altar, he
16:23 come into the tent of *m* and
16:33 tent of *m* and for the altar
17:4 tent of *m* to present it as an
17:5 tent of *m* to the priest, and
17:6 tent of *m*, and he must make
17:9 entrance of the tent of *m* to
19:21 entrance of the tent of *m*
24:3 tent of *m* Aaron should set it
Nu 1:1 tent of *m*, on the first day of
2:2 front of the tent of *m* they
2:17 the tent of *m* must set out
3:7 before the tent of *m* in
3:8 utensils of the tent of *m*
3:25 in the tent of *m* was the
3:25 the entrance of the tent of *m*
3:38 before the tent of *m* toward
4:3 to do the work in the tent of *m*
4:4 Kohath in the tent of *m*
4:15 of Kohath in the tent of *m*
4:23 service in the tent of *m*
4:25 tabernacle and the tent of *m*
4:25 the entrance of the tent of *m*
4:28 Gershonites in the tent of *m*
4:30 the service of the tent of *m*
4:31 service in the tent of *m*
4:33 service in the tent of *m*
4:35 service in the tent of *m*
4:37 serving in the tent of *m*
4:39 the service in the tent of *m*
4:41 serving in the tent of *m*
4:43 the service in the tent of *m*
4:47 loads in the tent of *m*
6:10 the entrance of the tent of *m*
6:13 the entrance of the tent of *m*
6:18 the entrance of the tent of *m*
7:5 service of the tent of *m*, and
7:89 tent of *m* to speak with him
8:9 Levites before the tent of *m*
8:15 to serve at the tent of *m*
8:19 in the tent of *m* and to make
8:22 service in the tent of *m*
8:24 service of the tent of *m*
8:26 tent of *m* in taking care of
10:3 entrance of the tent of *m*
11:16 take them to the tent of *m*
12:4 Go . . . to the tent of *m*
14:10 appeared on the tent of *m*
16:2 summoned ones of the *m*, men
16:18 entrance of the tent of *m*
16:19 entrance of the tent of *m*
16:42 turned toward the tent of *m*
16:43 to come before the tent of *m*
16:50 entrance of the tent of *m*
17:4 deposit them in the tent of *m*
18:4 obligation to the tent of *m*
18:6 the service of the tent of *m*
18:21 the service of the tent of *m*
18:22 come near to the tent of *m*
18:23 the service of the tent of *m*
18:31 service in the tent of *m*
19:4 the front of the tent of *m*
20:6 the entrance of the tent of *m*
25:6 the entrance of the tent of *m*
27:2 the entrance of the tent of *m*
31:54 into the tent of *m* as a
De 31:14 yourselves in the tent of *m*
31:14 themselves in the tent of *m*
Jos 18:1 locate the tent of *m* there
19:51 entrance of the tent of *m*
Jg 14:5 young lion roaring upon *m* him
15:14 shouted exultantly at *m* him
1Sa 2:22 entrance of the tent of *m*
16:4 began to tremble at *m* him
21:1 tremble at *m* David and then
1Ki 8:4 the tent of *m* and all the
1Ch 6:32 tabernacle of the tent of *m*
9:21 entrance of the tent of *m*
23:32 guarding of the tent of *m*
2Ch 1:3 the tent of *m* of the true God
1:6 belonged to the tent of *m*
1:13 from before the tent of *m*
5:5 the Ark and the tent of *m* and
Job 30:23 *m* for everyone living
Ps 74:4 in the middle of your *m* place
74:8 the *m* places of God must be
Isa 14:13 upon the mountain of *m*, in
La 1:15 He has called against me a *m*
Ho 9:5 you people do in the day of *m*
Ac 1:4 *m* with them he gave them

Meets
Ec 10:19 money is what *m* a response
Am 5:19 and the bear actually *m* him
Ac 25:16 *m* his accusers face to face

Megiddo
Jos 12:21 the king of *M*, one
17:11 *M* and its dependent towns
Jg 1:27 the inhabitants of *M* and its
5:19 In Taanach by the waters of *M*
1Ki 4:12 in Taanach and *M* and all
9:15 and Hazor and *M* and Gezer
2Ki 9:27 he continued his flight to *M*
23:29 he put him to death at *M*
23:30 dead in a chariot from *M*
1Ch 7:29 *M* and its dependent towns
2Ch 35:22 in the valley plain of *M*
Zec 12:11 in the valley plain of *M*

Mehetabel
Ge 36:39 the name of his wife was *M*
1Ch 1:50 *M*, the daughter of Matred
Ne 6:10 Delaiah the son of *M* while

Mehida
Ezr 2:52 the sons of *M*
Ne 7:54 the sons of *M*, the sons of

Mehir
1Ch 4:11 *M*, who was the father of

Meholathite
1Sa 18:19 to Adriel the *M* as a wife
2Sa 21:8 the son of Barzillai the *M*

Mehujael
Ge 4:18 Irad became father to *M*
4:18 *M* . . . father to Methushael

Mehuman
Es 1:10 said to *M*, Biztha, Harbona

Me-jarkon
Jos 19:46 and *M* and Rakkon, with the

Melatiah
Ne 3:7 *M* the Gibeonite and Jadon the

Melchi
Lu 3:24 son of *M*, son of Jannai, son
3:28 son of *M*, son of Addi, son of

Melchizedek
Ge 14:18 *M* king of Salem brought out
Ps 110:4 According to the manner of *M*
Heb 5:6 according to the manner of *M*
5:10 according to the manner of *M*
6:20 according to the manner of *M*
7:1 For this *M*, king of Salem
7:10 forefather when *M* met him
7:11 according to the manner of *M*
7:15 with a similarity to *M*
7:17 according to the manner of *M*

Melea
Lu 3:31 son of *M*, son of Menna, son

Melech
1Ch 8:35 of Micah were Pithon and *M*
9:41 of Micah were Pithon and *M*
Isa 57:9 descend toward *M* with oil

Melodies
2Sa 23:1 one of the *m* of Israel
Job 35:10 One giving *m* in the night
Ps 95:2 with *m* shout in triumph to
119:54 *M* your regulations have
Isa 24:16 are *m* that we have heard

Melodious
Ps 150:5 the cymbals of *m* sound

Am 5:23 the *m* sound of your stringed

Melody

Jg 5:3 I shall make *m* to Jehovah
2Sa 22:50 your name I shall make *m*
1Ch 16:9 Sing to him, make *m* to him
Ps 3:*super* A *m* of David when he was
4:*super* A *m* of David
5:*super* for Nehiloth. A *m* of David
6:*super* A *m* of David
7:17 make *m* to the name of Jehovah
8:*super* A *m* of David
9:*super* A *m* of David
9:2 I will make *m* to your name
9:11 Make *m*, you people, to
12:*super* A *m* of David
13:*super* Director. A *m* of David
15:*super* A *m* of David
18:49 to your name I will make *m*
19:*super* director. A *m* of David
20:*super* director. A *m* of David
21:*super* director. A *m* of David
21:13 make *m* to your mightiness
22:*super* A *m* of David
23:*super* A *m* of David
24:*super* Of David. A *m*
27:6 sing and make *m* to Jehovah
29:*super* A *m* of David
30:*super* *m*. A song of inauguration
30:4 Make *m* to Jehovah, O you
30:12 *m* to you and not keep silent
31:*super* director. A *m* of David
33:2 make *m* to him
38:*super* A *m* of David, to bring to
39:*super* of Jeduthun. A *m* of David
40:*super* Of David, a *m*
41:*super* A *m* of David
47:*super* Of the sons of Korah. A *m*
47:6, 6 Make *m* to God, make *m*
47:6 Make *m* to our King, make
47:6 to our King, make *m*
47:7 Make *m*, acting with
48:*super* A *m* of the sons of Korah
49:*super* Of the sons of Korah. A *m*
50:*super* A *m* of Asaph
51:*super* A *m* of David. When Nathan
57:7 I will sing and make *m*
57:9 *m* to you among the national
59:17 to you I will make *m*
61:8 make *m* to your name forever
62:*super* of Jeduthun. A *m* of David
63:*super* A *m* of David, when he
64:*super* director. A *m* of David
65:*super* A *m* of David. A song
66:*super* the director. A song, a *m*
66:2 *m* to the glory of his name
66:4 And they will make *m* to you
66:4 will make *m* to your name
67:*super* A *m*, a song
68:*super* Of David. A *m*, a song
68:4 to God, make *m* to his name
68:32 Make *m* to Jehovah—*Se'lah*
71:22 make *m* to you on the harp
71:23 inclined to make *m* to you
73:*super* A *m* of Asaph
75:*super* A *m*. Of Asaph. A song
75:9 make *m* to the God of Jacob
76:*super* A *m*. Of Asaph. A song
77:*super* Of Asaph. A *m*
79:*super* A *m* of Asaph
80:*super* A reminder. Of Asaph. A *m*
81:2 Strike up a *m* and take a
82:*super* A *m* of Asaph
83:*super* A song. A *m* of Asaph
84:*super* Of the sons of Korah. A *m*
85:*super* Of the sons of Korah. A *m*
87:*super* Of the sons of Korah. A *m*
88:*super* *m* of the sons of Korah
92:*super* A *m*, a song, for the
92:1 And to make *m* to your name
98:*super* A *m*
98:4 cry out joyfully and make *m*
98:5 Make *m* to Jehovah with the
98:5 the harp and the voice of *m*
100:*super* A *m* of thanksgiving
101:*super* Of David. A *m*
101:1 O Jehovah, I will make *m*
104:33 *m* to my God as long as I
105:2 Sing to him, make *m* to him
108:*super* A song. A *m* of David
108:1 I will sing and make *m*
108:3 make *m* to you among the
109:*super* Of David. A *m*
110:*super* Of David. A *m*
Ps 135:3 Make *m* to his name, for it
138:1 I shall make *m* to you
139:*super* Of David. A *m*
140:*super* A *m* of David
141:*super* A *m* of David
143:*super* A *m* of David
144:9 I will make *m* to you
146:2 make *m* to my God as long
147:1 good to make *m* to our God
147:7 *m* to our God on the harp
149:3 harp let them make *m* to him
Isa 12:5 Make *m* to Jehovah, for he
25:5 *m* itself of the tyrannical
51:3 and the voice of *m*
Ro 15:9 to your name I will make *m*

Melt

De 1:28 caused our heart to *m*, saying
20:8 to *m* as his own heart
Jos 2:11 our hearts began to *m*, and
5:1 then their hearts began to *m*
7:5 the heart . . . began to *m* and
14:8 the heart of the people to *m*
Job 20:12 to *m* away under his tongue
Ps 46:6 the earth proceeded to *m*
97:5 mountains . . . proceeded to *m*
112:10 wicked . . . actually *m* away
Isa 13:7 itself of mortal man will *m*
19:1 Egypt will *m* in the midst of
34:3 mountains must *m* because of
64:7 *m* by the power of our error
Eze 21:7 and every heart must *m* and
21:15 In order for the heart to *m*
Mic 1:4 the mountains must *m* under
2Pe 3:12 being intensely hot will *m*

Melted

Ex 16:21 When the sun got hot, it *m*
Jg 15:14 his fetters *m* off his hands
Ps 22:14 *m* deep in my inward parts

Melting

Ps 58:8 Like a snail *m* away he walks
107:26 very soul finds itself *m*
Isa 10:18 *m* away of one that is
Am 9:13 will all find themselves *m*
Na 1:5 very hills found themselves *m*
2:10 the heart is *m*, and there

Melts

Ps 68:2 As wax *m* because of the fire
147:18 forth his word and *m* them
Am 9:5 the land, so that it *m*

Member

Le 21:18 or with one *m* too long
22:23 *m* too long or too short, you
25:47 *m* of the family of the alien
De 23:1 or having his male *m* cut off
Ne 3:8 a *m* of the ointment mixers
3:31 a *m* of the goldsmith guild
Eze 23:20 those whose fleshly *m* is
23:20 fleshly *m* of male asses
Mr 15:43 reputable *m* of the Sanhedrin
Lu 2:4 a *m* of the house and family of
23:50 who was a *m* of the Council
1Co 12:14 the body . . . is not one *m*
12:19 If they were all one *m*
12:26 if one *m* suffers, all the
12:26 if a *m* is glorified, all
Eph 4:16 each respective *m* in due
Heb 7:13 been a *m* of another tribe
Jas 3:5 the tongue is a little *m* and

Members

2Ch 25:13 the *m* of the troop whom
Job 17:7 my *m* are all of them like
Mt 5:29 one of your *m* to be lost to you
5:30 one of your *m* to be lost to
Joh 5:3 and those with withered *m*
Ro 6:13 presenting your *m* to sin as
6:13 your *m* to God as weapons of
6:19 presented your *m* as slaves
6:19 *m* as slaves to righteousness
7:5 at work in our *m* that we
7:23 I behold in my *m* another law
7:23 sin's law that is in my *m*
12:4 in one body many *m*, but the
12:4 *m* do not all have the same
12:5 *m* belonging individually to
1Co 6:15 your bodies are *m* of Christ
6:15 take the *m* of the Christ
6:15 and make them *m* of a harlot
12:12 body is one but has many *m*
12:12 and all the *m* of that body
12:18 God has set the *m* in the
12:20 But now they are many *m*
1Co 12:22 the *m* of the body which
12:25 its *m* should have the same
12:26 all the other *m* suffer with
12:26 all the other *m* rejoice
12:27 and *m* individually
Eph 2:19 *m* of the household of God
3:6 *m* of the body and partakers
4:25 *m* belonging to one another
5:30 because we are *m* of his body
Col 3:5 Deaden . . . your body *m* that
1Ti 5:8 who are *m* of his household
Jas 3:6 unrighteousness among our *m*
4:1 carry on a conflict in your *m*

Memorable

Job 13:12 *m* sayings are proverbs of

Memorandum

Ezr 6:2 *m* to this effect was written

Memorial

Ex 3:15 *m* of me to generation after
12:14 this day must serve as a *m*
13:9 as a *m* between your eyes, in
17:14 Write this as a *m* in the
28:12 *m* stones for the sons of
28:12 two shoulder pieces as a *m*
28:29 *m* before Jehovah constantly
30:16 serve as a *m* before Jehovah
39:7 as *m* stones for . . . Israel
Le 23:24 *m* by the trumpet blast, a
Nu 5:15 *m* grain offering bringing
5:18 palms the *m* grain offering
10:10 use must serve as a *m* for
16:40 a *m* for the sons of Israel
31:54 a *m* for the sons of Israel
Jos 4:7 as a *m* to the sons of Israel
Ne 2:20 claim, nor *m* in Jerusalem
Ps 30:4 Give thanks to his holy *m*
97:12 give thanks to his holy *m*
102:12 *m* will be for generation
111:4 *m* he has made for his
135:13 Jehovah, your *m* is to
Isa 26:8 your *m* the desire of the
57:8 doorpost you set your *m*
66:3 a *m* of frankincense is as
Ho 12:5 Jehovah is his *m*
14:7 His *m* will be like the wine
Zec 6:14 a *m* in the temple of Jehovah
Mt 8:28 from among the *m* tombs
23:29 decorate the *m* tombs of the
27:52 the *m* tombs were opened and
27:53 out from among the *m* tombs
27:60 laid it in his new *m* tomb
27:60 to the door of the *m* tomb
28:8 quickly leaving the *m* tomb
Mr 5:2 from among the *m* tombs
6:29 and laid it in a *m* tomb
15:46 to the door of the *m* tomb
16:2 they came to the *m* tomb
16:3 the door of the *m* tomb for
16:5 they entered into the *m* tomb
16:8 they fled from the *m* tomb
Lu 11:44 you are as those *m* tombs
11:47 the *m* tombs of the prophets
23:55 took a look at the *m* tomb
24:2 rolled away from the *m* tomb
24:9 returned from the *m* tomb and
24:12 rose and ran to the *m* tomb
24:22 had been early to the *m* tomb
24:24 went off to the *m* tomb
Joh 5:28 all those in the *m* tombs
11:17 four days in the *m* tomb
11:31 the *m* tomb to weep there
11:38 came to the *m* tomb
12:17 Lazarus out of the *m* tomb
19:41 new *m* tomb, in which no
19:42 the *m* tomb was nearby
20:1 came to the *m* tomb early
20:1 taken away from the *m* tomb
20:2 the Lord out of the *m* tomb
20:3 started for the *m* tomb
20:4 reached the *m* tomb first
20:6 he entered into the *m* tomb
20:8 reached the *m* tomb first
20:11 outside near the *m* tomb
20:11 to look into the *m* tomb
Ac 13:29 and laid him in a *m* tomb

Memory

De 32:18 began to leave God out of *m*
La 3:17 I have lost *m* of what good is

Memphis

Ho 9:6 *M*, for its part, will bury

Memucan
Es 1:14 *M*, seven princes of Persia
1:16 *M* said before the king and
1:21 do according to the word of *M*

Men
Ge 6:1 it came about that when *m*
6:2 to notice the daughters of *m*
6:4 with the daughters of *m* and
6:4 mighty ones . . . the *m* of fame
6:6 regrets that he had made *m* in
6:7 I am going to wipe *m* whom I
9:7 you *m*, be fruitful and become
9:9 my covenant with you *m* and
11:5 tower that the sons of *m* had
12:20 Pharaoh issued commands to *m*
13:8 for we *m* are brothers
13:13 *m* of Sodom were bad and were
14:14 he mustered his trained *m*
14:24 Only what the young *m* have
14:24 share of the *m* who went with
17:10 covenant that you *m* will
17:10 between me and you *m*, even
17:13 in the flesh of you *m*
17:23 his son and all the *m* born
17:23 every male among the *m* of
17:27 all the *m* of his household
18:2 three *m* were standing some
18:16 the *m* got up from there and
18:22 At this point the *m* turned
18:24 fifty righteous *m* in the
18:26 fifty righteous *m* in the
19:4 the *m* of the city
19:4 the *m* of Sodom, surrounded
19:5 Where are the *m* who came in
19:8 to these *m* do not do a thing
19:10 *m* thrust out their hands and
19:11 struck with blindness the *m*
19:12 *m* said to Lot: Do you have
19:16 *m* seized hold of his hand
20:8 the *m* got very much afraid
24:13 daughters of the *m* of the
24:32 feet of the *m* who were
24:54 *m* who were with him, and
24:59 Abraham's servant and his *m*
26:7 *m* of the place kept asking
26:7 to quote him, the *m* of the
29:22 Laban gathered all the *m* of
32:6 and four hundred *m* with him
32:28 with God and with *m* so that
33:1 and with him four hundred *m*
34:7 the *m* became hurt in their
34:20 speak to the *m* of their city
34:21 These *m* are peace-loving
34:22 the *m* give us their consent
34:27 the fatally wounded *m* and
37:28 *m*, Midianite merchants
38:21 inquiring of the *m* of her
38:22 the *m* of the place said, No
39:11 none of the *m* of the house
39:14 to cry out to the *m* of her
41:8 all her wise *m*, and Pharaoh
42:11 We are upright *m*
42:25 return the money of the *m* to
42:30 *m* spying on the country
42:31 We are upright *m*. We do not
42:38 will not go down with you *m*
43:15 the *m* took this gift, and
43:16 Take the *m* to the house and
43:16 *m* are to eat with me at noon
43:17 took the *m* to Joseph's house
43:18 the *m* got afraid because
43:24 brought the *m* into Joseph's
43:33 the *m* kept looking at one
44:1 Fill the bags of the *m* with
44:3 the *m* were sent away, both
44:4 Chase after the *m* and be
45:7 a remnant for you *m* in the
46:32 the *m* are shepherds, because
47:2 took five *m*, that he might
47:6 among them courageous *m*
49:6 in their anger they killed *m*
50:7 the older *m* of his household
50:7 older *m* of the land of Egypt
Ex 2:13 two Hebrew *m* struggling
3:16 gather the older *m* of Israel
3:18 you and the older *m* of Israel
3:18 and you *m* must say to him
4:15 I will teach you *m* what you
4:19 *m* who were hunting for your
4:21 see that you *m* actually
4:29 older *m* of the sons of Israel
5:9 service be heavy upon the *m*
7:4 will not listen to you *m*
Ex 7:11 the wise *m* and the sorcerers
10:7 Send the *m* away that they may
10:11 are able-bodied *m*, and serve
11:9 will not listen to you *m*, in
12:21 all the older *m* of Israel
12:37 able-bodied *m* on foot
13:2 among *m* and beasts. It is
15:21 kept responding to the *m*
16:20 some *m* would leave some of
17:5 some of the older *m* of Israel
17:6 eyes of the older *m* of Israel
17:9 Choose *m* for us and go out
18:12 and all the older *m* of Israel
18:21 of all the people capable *m*
18:21 fearing God, trustworthy *m*
18:25 capable *m* out of all Israel
19:7 the older *m* of the people and
19:15 not you *m* come near a woman
21:7 the way that the slave *m* go
21:18 in case *m* should get into a
21:22 in case *m* should struggle
22:31 yourselves holy *m* to me
23:8 bribe blinds clear-sighted *m*
23:8 the words of righteous *m*
24:1 and seventy of the older *m* of
24:5 sent young *m* of the sons of
24:9 seventy of the older *m* of
24:11 distinguished *m* of the sons
24:14 to the older *m* he had said
32:28 about three thousand *m*
35:22 the *m* along with the women
35:35 *m* doing every sort of work
36:6 *M* and women, do not produce
Le 4:15 the older *m* of the assembly
9:1 his sons and the older *m* of Israel
18:27 *m* of the land who were
Nu 1:4 *m* should be with you, one man
1:5 *m* who will stand with you
1:17 Moses and Aaron took these *m*
1:44 chieftains . . . twelve *m*
9:6 *m* who had become unclean by a
9:7 *m* said to him: We are unclean
10:5 *m* must blow a fluctuating
10:8 statute for you *m* to time
11:1 *m* having something evil to
11:16 Gather for me seventy *m* of
11:16 older *m* of Israel, whom you
11:16 know that they are older *m*
11:21 hundred thousand *m* on foot
11:24 gathering seventy *m* from the
11:24 the older *m* of the people
11:25 each of the seventy older *m*
11:26 two of the *m* remaining in
11:30 he and the older *m* of Israel
12:3 far the meekest of all the *m*
13:2 *m* that they may spy out the
13:3 All the *m* were heads of the
13:16 *m* whom Moses sent to spy
13:23 with a bar on two of the *m*
13:31 *m* who went up with him said
13:32 are *m* of extraordinary size
14:22 *m* who have been seeing my
14:36 *m* whom Moses sent to spy
14:37 the *m* bringing forth the bad
14:38 of those *m* who went to spy
16:2 two hundred and fifty *m* of
16:2 sons of Israel . . . *m* of fame
16:9 little thing for you *m* that
16:9 separated you *m* from the
16:10 must you *m* also try to
16:11 that you *m* should murmur
16:14 Is it the eyes of those *m*
16:17 you *m* must put incense upon
16:25 older *m* of Israel went with
16:26 the tents of these wicked *m*
16:30 these *m* have treated Jehovah
16:35 *m* offering the incense
16:38 *m* who sinned against their
16:41 You *m*, you have put
16:45 You *m*, rise up from the
18:3 neither they nor you *m*
18:4 may come near to you *m*
18:7 you *m* must render service
20:4 And why have you *m* brought
20:24 you *m* rebelled against my
21:30 the *m* up to Medeba
22:4 say to the older *m* of Midian
22:7 So the older *m* of Moab and
22:7 older *m* of Midian traveled
22:9 Who are these *m* with you?
22:19 you *m* also stay here, please
22:20 to call you that the *m* have
22:35 Go with the *m*; and nothing
25:5 Each one of you kill his *m*
Nu 25:17 and you *m* must strike them
26:10 two hundred and fifty *m*
27:14 you *m* rebelled against my
31:3 Equip *m* from among you for
31:14 appointed *m* of the combat
31:21 said to the *m* of the army
31:28 *m* of war who went out on
31:42 to the *m* who waged war
31:48 appointed *m* . . . of the army
31:49 the sum of the *m* of war who
31:53 The *m* of the army had taken
32:11 *m* who came up out of Egypt
32:14 as the brood of sinful *m* in
34:17 *m* who will divide the land
34:19 these are the names of the *m*
De 1:13 experienced *m* of your tribes
1:15 *m* wise and experienced, and
1:22 Do let us send *m* ahead of us
1:23 I took twelve *m* of yours, one
1:35 *m* of this evil generation
2:14 *m* of war had come to their
2:16 all the *m* of war had finished
2:34 to destruction, *m* and women
3:6 city to destruction, *m*, women
3:18 So I commanded you *m* at that
3:18 Israel, all the valiant *m*
3:22 You *m* must not be afraid of
5:23 your tribes and your older *m*
13:13 Good-for-nothing *m* have gone
19:12 the older *m* of his city must
19:17 two *m* who have the dispute
21:2 your older *m* and your judges
21:3 the older *m* of that city must
21:4 the older *m* of that city must
21:6 the older *m* of that city who
21:19 bring him out to the older *m*
21:20 say to the older *m* of his
21:21 the *m* of his city must pelt
22:15 to the older *m* of the city
22:16 say to the older *m*, I gave
22:17 mantle before the older *m*
22:18 the older *m* of that city
22:21 the *m* of her city must pelt
25:1 a dispute arises between *m*
25:7 to the older *m* and say, My
25:8 the older *m* of his city must
25:9 the eyes of the older *m*
25:11 In case *m* struggle together
27:1 older *m* of Israel went on to
28:68 as slave *m* and maidservants
29:10 older *m* and your officers
31:9 to all the older *m* of Israel
31:12 the *m* and the women and the
31:28 the older *m* of your tribes
32:7 Your old *m* . . . can say it to
32:26 of them cease from mortal *m*
32:51 that you *m* acted undutifully
32:51 you *m* did not sanctify me in
33:6 And let his *m* not become few
Jos 1:14 *m* . . . in battle formation
1:14 all the valiant mighty *m*, and
2:1 sent two *m* out secretly from
2:2 *M* from the sons of Israel
2:3 Bring out the *m* that came to
2:4 took the two *m* and concealed
2:4 *m* did come to me, and I did
2:5 by dark that the *m* went out
2:5 not know where the *m* have
2:7 *m* chased after them in the
2:9 she went on to say to the *m*
2:14 *m* said to her: Our souls are
2:17 the *m* said to her: We are
2:23 two *m* proceeded to descend
3:12 twelve *m* from the tribes of
4:2 twelve *m* from the people, one
4:4 Joshua called twelve *m* whom
5:4 all the *m* of war, had died in
5:6 nation of the *m* of war who
6:2 mighty *m*, into your hand
6:3 *m* of war must march round
6:22 the two *m* who had done the
6:23 *m* who had done the spying
7:2 sent *m* out from Jericho
7:2 the *m* went up and spied on Ai
7:3 Let about two thousand *m* or
7:3 three thousand *m* go up and
7:4 three thousand *m* of the
7:4 flight before the *m* of Ai
7:5 *m* of Ai got to strike down
7:5 about thirty-six *m* of them
7:6 he and the older *m* of Israel
8:3 to choose thirty thousand *m*
8:10 he and the older *m* of Israel
8:12 took about five thousand *m*

Jos 8:14 *m* of the city got in a hurry
8:20 *m* of Ai began to turn back
8:21 striking the *m* of Ai down
8:33 all Israel and their older *m*
9:6 to him and the *m* of Israel
9:7 the *m* of Israel said to the
9:11 our older *m* and all the
9:14 the *m* took some of their
10:2 all its *m* were mighty ones
10:6 *m* of Gibeon sent to Joshua
10:7 and all the valiant mighty *m*
10:18 assign *m* over it to guard
10:19 you *m*, do not stand still
10:24 to call all the *m* of Israel
10:24 commanders of the *m* of war
18:4 three *m* of each tribe and
18:8 the *m* got up that they might
18:9 *m* went and passed through
20:4 the older *m* of that city
23:2 its older *m* and its heads
24:1 older *m* of Israel and its
24:31 the days of the older *m*
Jg 1:4 in Bezek, ten thousand *m*
2:7 all the days of the older *m*
3:29 striking . . . ten thousand *m*
3:31 Philistines, six hundred *m*
4:6 take with you ten thousand *m*
4:10 Kedesh, and ten thousand *m*
4:14 with ten thousand *m* behind
5:30 the necks of *m* of spoil
6:27 took ten *m* of his servants
6:27 the *m* of the city too much to
6:28 *m* of the city got up early
6:30 *m* of the city said to Joash
7:6 to be three hundred *m*. As for
7:7 By the three hundred *m* who did
7:8 the *m* of Israel he sent away
7:8 hold of the three hundred *m*
7:16 divided the three hundred *m*
7:19 the hundred *m* who were with
7:23 the *m* of Israel were called
7:24 the *m* of Ephraim were called
8:1 the *m* of Ephraim said to him
8:4 the three hundred *m* that were
8:5 he said to the *m* of Succoth
8:8 the *m* of Penuel answered him
8:8 just as the *m* of Succoth had
8:9 said also to the *m* of Penuel
8:10 hundred and twenty thousand *m*
8:14 young man of the *m* of Succoth
8:14, 14 older *m*, seventy-seven *m*
8:15 went to the *m* of Succoth and
8:15 be given to your tired-out *m*
8:16 took the older *m* of the city
8:16 put the *m* of Succoth through
8:17 to kill the *m* of the city
8:18 What sort of *m* were they
8:22 *m* of Israel said to Gideon
9:2 for seventy *m*, all the sons of
9:4 hire idle and insolent *m*, that
9:5 sons of Jerubbaal, seventy *m*
9:9 glorify God and *m*, and must I
9:13 makes God and *m* rejoice, and
9:18 kill his sons, seventy *m*
9:25 set ambush *m* for him upon
9:28 *m* of Hamor, Shechem's father
9:36 seeing as though they were *m*
9:49 *m* of the tower of Shechem
9:49 about a thousand *m* and women
9:51 the *m* and women and all the
9:55 *m* of Israel got to see that
9:57 the evil of the *m* of Shechem
11:3 And idle *m* kept bringing
11:5 the older *m* of Gilead
11:7 said to the older *m* of Gilead
11:8 the older *m* of Gilead said to
11:9 said to the older *m* of Gilead
11:10 the older *m* of Gilead said
11:11 the older *m* of Gilead and
12:1 the *m* of Ephraim were called
12:4 collected all the *m* of Gilead
12:4 the *m* of Gilead went striking
12:4 *M* escaped from Ephraim is
12:5 escaping *m* of Ephraim would
12:5 the *m* of Gilead would say to
14:18 So the *m* of the city said to
14:19 struck down thirty *m* of
15:10 *m* of Judah said: Why have
15:11 So three thousand *m* of Judah
15:15 striking down a thousand *m*
15:16 struck down a thousand *m*
16:17 and become like all other *m*
16:27 full of *m* and women and all
16:27 three thousand *m* and women

Jg 18:2 sent five *m* of their family
18:2 *m* from among them
18:2 *m* who were valiant fellows
18:7 five *m* went on and came to
18:11 six hundred *m* girded with
18:14 five *m* that had gone to spy
18:16 *m* girded with their weapons
18:17 five *m* that had gone to spy
18:17 six hundred *m* girded with
18:22 *m* who were in the houses
18:25 *m* bitter of soul may assault
19:16 the *m* . . . were Benjamites
19:22 look! the *m* of the city
19:22 mere good-for-nothing *m*
19:25 the *m* did not want to listen
20:2 hundred thousand *m* on foot
20:10 ten *m* out of a hundred of
20:11 *m* of Israel were gathered
20:12 tribes of Israel sent *m* to
20:13 And now give over the *m*, the
20:13 the good-for-nothing *m*, that
20:15 twenty-six thousand *m*
20:15 seven hundred chosen *m* were
20:16 hundred chosen *m* left-handed
20:17 *m* of Israel were mustered
20:17 four hundred thousand *m*
20:20 *m* of Israel now went out to
20:20 the *m* of Israel proceeded to
20:21 twenty-two thousand *m* in
20:22 the people, the *m* of Israel
20:25 eighteen thousand *m* among
20:29 Then Israel set *m* in ambush
20:31 about thirty *m* in Israel
20:33 the *m* of Israel rose up from
20:34 ten thousand chosen *m* out of
20:35 thousand one hundred *m*, all
20:36 the *m* of Israel faced defeat
20:38 *m* of Israel had come to the
20:39 thirty *m* mortally wounded
20:39 among the *m* of Israel
20:41 And the *m* of Israel made an
20:41 and the *m* of Benjamin were
20:42 before the *m* of Israel in
20:42 the *m* from out of the cities
20:44 fell eighteen thousand *m* of
20:44 all of these being valiant *m*
20:45 gleaning of five thousand *m*
20:45 two thousand more *m* of them
20:46 to twenty-five thousand *m*
20:46 all these being valiant *m*
20:47 six hundred *m* turned and
20:48 the *m* of Israel came back
20:48 from *m* to domestic animal
21:1 the *m* of Israel had sworn in
21:10 of the most valiant *m* there
21:16 older *m* of the assembly said
21:16 *m* that are left over as to
Ru 1:4 *m* took wives for themselves
1:8 toward the *m* now dead and
2:9 the young *m* not to touch you
2:9 what the young *m* will draw
2:15 now commanded his young *m*
4:2 After that he took ten *m* of
4:2 of the older *m* of the city and
4:4 and the older *m* of my people
4:9 Boaz said to the older *m* and
4:11 the older *m* said: Witnesses!
1Sa 2:4 The mighty *m* of the bow are
2:12 were good-for-nothing *m*
2:17 *m* treated the offering of
2:26 and from that of *m*
2:29 Why do you *m* keep kicking at
2:33 all die by the sword of *m*
4:2 about four thousand *m* in
4:3 older *m* of Israel began to
4:9 and prove yourselves *m*, you
4:9 prove yourselves *m* and fight
4:10 thirty thousand *m* on foot
5:7 *m* of Ashdod came to see that
5:9 striking the *m* of the city
5:12 *m* that did not die had been
6:10 And the *m* proceeded to do
6:15 *m* of Beth-shemesh, for their
6:19 the *m* of Beth-shemesh
6:19 among the people seventy *m*
6:19 fifty thousand *m*—and the
6:20 the *m* of Beth-shemesh said
7:1 *m* of Kiriath-jearim came and
7:11 *m* of Israel sallied forth
8:4 older *m* of Israel collected
8:22 said to the *m* of Israel
9:13 as you *m* come into the city
9:19 you *m* must eat with me
9:22 and they were about thirty *m*

1Sa 10:2 two *m* close by the tomb of
10:2 become anxious about you *m*
10:3 three *m* going up to the true
10:15 did Samuel say to you *m*
10:26 valiant *m* whose heart God
10:27 for the good-for-nothing *m*
11:1 *m* of Jabesh said to Nahash
11:3 older *m* of Jabesh said to
11:5 the words of the *m* of Jabesh
11:8 *m* of Judah thirty thousand
11:9 to the *m* of Jabesh in Gilead
11:9 and told the *m* of Jabesh
11:10 the *m* of Jabesh said
11:12 Give the *m* over, that we
11:15 and all the *m* of Israel
13:2 three thousand *m* out of
13:6 *m* of Israel themselves saw
13:15 about six hundred *m*
14:2 were about six hundred *m*
14:6 of these uncircumcised *m*
14:8 are crossing over to the *m*
14:12 *m* of the outpost answered
14:14 about twenty *m* within
14:22 *m* of Israel also that were
14:24 *m* of Israel themselves
15:4 two hundred thousand *m* on
15:4 and ten thousand *m* of Judah
15:30 the older *m* of my people
16:4 older *m* of the city began
17:2 Saul and the *m* of Israel
17:12 was already old among *m*
17:19 all the other *m* of Israel
17:24 As for all the *m* of Israel
17:25 *m* of Israel began to say
17:26 David began to say to the *m*
17:28 hear as he spoke to the *m*
17:47 he must give you *m* into our
17:52 *m* of Israel and of Judah
18:5 placed . . . over the *m* of war
18:25 you *m* will say to David
18:27 and he and his *m* went and
18:27 Philistines two hundred *m*
21:2 appointment with the young *m*
21:4 young *m* have at least kept
21:5 of the young *m* continue holy
22:2 all *m* in distress and all
22:2 all *m* who had a creditor and
22:2 all *m* bitter in soul began
22:2 about four hundred *m*
22:6 David and the *m* that were
22:13 *m* conspired against me, you
22:18 eighty-five *m* bearing an
23:3 *m* of David said to him
23:5 David went with his *m* to
23:8 to besiege David and his *m*
23:12 and my *m* into Saul's hand
23:13 David rose up with his *m*
23:13 six hundred *m*, and they
23:19 *m* of Ziph went up to Saul
23:24 David and his *m* were in the
23:25 Saul came with his *m* to
23:26 David and his *m* were on
23:26 Saul and his *m* were closing
23:26 on David and his *m* to grab
24:2 three thousand chosen *m* out
24:2 looking for David and his *m*
24:3 David and his *m* were in the
24:4 David's *m* began to say to
24:6 he said to his *m*: It is
24:7 David dispersed his *m* with
24:22 David and his *m*, they went
25:5 David sent ten young *m* and
25:5 David said to the young *m*
25:8 Ask your own young *m*, and
25:8 my young *m* may find favor in
25:9 David's young *m* came and
25:11 give it to *m* of whom I do
25:12 David's young *m* turned
25:13 David said to his *m*: Gird
25:13 about four hundred *m*, while
25:14 one of the young *m* reported
25:15 *m* were very good to us, and
25:19 said to her young *m*: Pass
25:20 David and his *m* coming down
25:25 see my lord's young *m* that
25:27 given to the young *m* that
26:1 *m* of Ziph came to Saul at
26:2 with him three thousand *m*
26:16 you *m* deserve to die
26:22 one of the young *m* come on
27:2 six hundred *m* that were
27:3 he and his *m*, each one with
27:8 with his *m* that they might
27:10 Where did you *m* make a raid

1Sa 28:1 the camp, you and your *m*
28:8 went, he and two *m* with him
29:2 David and his *m* were passing
29:4 the heads of those our *m*
29:10 *m* must rise up early in the
29:11 David . . . and his *m*, to go
30:1 David and his *m* were coming
30:3 David came with his *m* to
30:9 six hundred *m* that were
30:9 *m* that were to be left
30:10 he and four hundred *m*, but
30:10 two hundred *m* that were too
30:17 young *m* that rode upon
30:21 two hundred *m* who had been
30:22 *m* that had gone with David
30:26 to the older *m* of Judah
30:31 walked about, he and his *m*
31:1 *m* of Israel took to flight
31:4 uncircumcised *m* may not
31:6 all his *m*, came to die
31:7 *m* of Israel that were in
31:7 *m* of Israel had fled, and
31:12 valiant *m* rose up and went
2Sa 1:6 mounted *m* had caught up with
1:11 so did all the *m* also that
1:15 called one of the young *m*
1:19 How have the mighty *m* fallen!
1:20 uncircumcised *m* may exult
2:3 *m* that were with him David
2:4 *m* of Judah came and anointed
2:4 *m* of Jabesh-gilead were the
2:5 to the *m* of Jabesh-gilead
2:7 prove yourselves valiant *m*
2:14 Let the young *m* rise up
2:17 Abner and the *m* of Israel
2:21 seize one of the young *m* as
2:29 Abner and his *m*, they
2:30 nineteen *m* and Asahel
2:31 *m* of Abner—there were three
2:31 three hundred and sixty *m*
2:32 Joab and his *m* went marching
3:17 with the older *m* of Israel
3:20 with him twenty *m*, David
3:20 for Abner and for the *m* that
3:39 these *m*, the sons of Zeruiah
4:2 two *m*, chiefs of the
4:6 the house as *m* fetching wheat
4:11 wicked *m* themselves have
4:12 David commanded the young *m*
5:3 older *m* of Israel came to
5:6 the king and his *m* went to
5:21 David and his *m* took them
6:1 all the choice *m* in Israel
6:20 empty-headed *m* uncovers
7:14 with the rod of *m*
8:4 twenty thousand *m* on foot
8:5 Syrians twenty-two thousand *m*
10:5 *m* had come to feeling very
10:6 twenty thousand *m* on foot
10:6 king of Maacah, a thousand *m*
10:6 Ishtob, twelve thousand *m*
10:7 the army and the mighty *m*
10:9 all the choice *m* in Israel
11:15 *m* must retreat from behind
11:16 that there were valiant *m*
11:17 *m* of the city came on out
11:20 *m* not know that they would
11:21 *m* have to go so close to
11:23 *m* proved superior to us
12:1 two *m* that happened to be in
12:17 older *m* of his house stood
13:13 senseless *m* in Israel
13:28 yourselves to be valiant *m*
13:32 young *m* the sons of the
15:1 fifty *m* running before him
15:6 stealing the hearts of the *m*
15:11 with Absalom two hundred *m*
15:13 heart of the *m* of Israel
15:18 six hundred *m* that had
15:22 *m* and all the little ones
15:27 the two sons of you *m*
15:28 from you *m* to inform me
15:36 you *m* must send to me
16:2 fruit are for the young *m* to
16:6 mighty *m* were at his right
16:10 you *m*, you sons of Zeruiah
16:13 David and his *m* kept going
16:15 *m* of Israel, they entered
16:18 and all the *m* of Israel
16:20 You *m*, give counsel on your
17:1 choose . . . twelve thousand *m*
17:4 all the older *m* of Israel
17:8 know your father and the *m*
17:10 valiant *m* that are with him
2Sa 17:12 the *m* that are with him
17:14 all the *m* of Israel said
17:15 and the older *m* of Israel
17:24 the *m* of Israel with him
18:7 of twenty thousand *m*
18:28 *m* that lifted up their hand
19:11 Speak to the older *m* of
19:14 the heart of all the *m*
19:16 *m* of Judah to meet King
19:17 a thousand *m* from Benjamin
19:22 you *m*, you sons of Zeruiah
19:41 all the *m* of Israel were
19:41 the *m* of Judah steal you
19:41 the *m* of David with him
19:42 all the *m* of Judah answered
19:42 answered the *m* of Israel
19:43 the *m* of Israel answered
19:43 answered the *m* of Judah
19:43 the word of the *m* of Judah
19:43 the word of the *m* of Israel
20:2 all the *m* of Israel began to
20:2 *m* of Judah, they stuck to
20:4 Call the *m* of Judah together
20:7 the *m* of Joab and the
20:7 mighty *m* went out after him
20:11 one of Joab's young *m* stood
20:16 *m*, listen! Say, please, to
21:6 seven *m* of his sons
21:13 gathered the bones of the *m*
21:17 the *m* of David swore to
22:5 floods of good-for-nothing *m*
23:8 *m* that belonged to David
23:9 three mighty *m* with David
23:9 so the *m* of Israel retreated
23:16 three mighty *m* forced their
23:17 *m* going at the risk of
23:17 the three mighty *m* did
23:22 like the three mighty *m*
24:2 you *m* register the people
24:9 valiant *m* drawing sword
24:9 the *m* of Judah were five
24:9 five hundred thousand *m*
1Ki 1:5 fifty *m* running before him
1:8 the mighty *m* that belonged to
1:9 the *m* of Judah the king's
1:10 the mighty *m* and Solomon
1:28 *m*, call Bath-sheba for me
1:32 You *m*, call for me Zadok the
1:45 the noise that you *m* heard
2:32 upon two *m* more righteous
3:24 You *m*, get me a sword
3:25 *m*, sever the living child in
3:26 You *m*, give her the living
3:26 You *m*, do the severing!
3:27 *m*, give her the living child
5:13 to thirty thousand *m*
8:1 congregate the older *m* of
8:2 the *m* of Israel congregated
8:3 the older *m* of Israel came
9:6 that I have put before you *m*
10:8 Happy are your *m*; happy are
10:15 apart from the *m* of travel
11:17 Edomite *m* of the servants
11:18 took *m* with them from Paran
11:24 collecting *m* to his side
12:6 counsel with the older *m*
12:8 the counsel of the older *m*
12:8 counsel with the young *m*
12:10 young *m* that had grown up
12:13 the counsel of the older *m*
12:14 the counsel of the young *m*
12:21 *m* able-bodied for war
13:4 You *m*, grab hold of him!
13:25 there were *m* passing by, so
18:13 a hundred *m* by fifties in a
18:18 because you *m* have left the
18:22 four hundred and fifty *m*
20:7 all the older *m* of the land
20:8 older *m* and all the people
20:11 You *m*, speak to him, Do not
20:14 the young *m* of the princes
20:15 the count of the young *m* of
20:17 young *m* of the princes of
20:17 *m* that have come out from
20:19 young *m* of the princes of
20:28 you *m* will certainly know
20:29 hundred thousand *m* on foot
20:30 twenty-seven thousand *m*
20:33 the *m* themselves took it as
21:8 the letters to the older *m*
21:10 two *m*, good-for-nothing
21:11 So the *m* of his city
21:11 older *m* and the nobles that
21:13 *m*, good-for-nothing fellows
1Ki 21:13 *m* began to bear witness
22:6 about four hundred *m*, and
2Ki 2:7 fifty *m* of the sons of the
2:16 fifty *m*, valiant persons
2:17 sent fifty *m*; and they kept
2:19 *m* of the city said to Elisha
3:15 And now you *m* fetch me a
3:17 You *m* will not see a wind
3:17 you *m* will certainly drink
3:21 called together *m* from as
3:26 with him seven hundred *m*
4:40 poured it out for the *m* to
4:43 put this before a hundred *m*
5:7 just take note, please, you *m*
5:22 have come to me two young *m*
5:24 sent the *m* away. So off they
6:13 You *m* go and see where he is
6:32 the older *m* were sitting
6:32 to the older *m*: Have you
7:1 Listen, you *m*, to the word of
7:3 And there were four *m*, lepers
8:12 their choice *m* you will kill
9:17 heaving mass of Jehu's *m* as
9:17 There is a heaving mass of *m*
9:34 You *m*, please, take care of
10:1 older *m* and the caretakers
10:5 older *m* and the caretakers
10:6 take the heads of the *m* that
10:6 sons of the king, seventy *m*
10:6 distinguished *m* of the city
10:7 slaughtering them, seventy *m*
10:11 all his distinguished *m* and
10:14 Seize them alive, you *m*!
10:14 forty-two *m*, and he did not
10:24 stationed eighty *m* outside
10:24 *m* whom I am bringing into
11:9 took each one his *m* that
12:15 *m* into whose hand they
13:7 and ten thousand *m* on foot
14:7 ten thousand *m*, and got to
15:20 all the valiant, mighty *m*
15:25 fifty *m* of the sons of
17:30 the *m* of Babylon, for their
17:30 *m* of Cuth, for their part
17:30 *m* of Hamath, for their part
18:22 in case you *m* should say to
18:27 the *m* sitting upon the wall
18:27 their own urine with you *m*
19:2 the older *m* of the priests
19:10 *m* should say to Hezekiah
20:7 *m*, take a cake of pressed
20:14 What did these *m* say and
22:15 that has sent you *m* to me
23:1 all the older *m* of Judah and
23:2 all the *m* of Judah and all
23:17 the *m* of the city said to
24:14 all the valiant, mighty *m*
24:15 foremost *m* of the land he
24:16 valiant *m*, seven thousand
24:16 mighty *m* carrying on war
25:4 the *m* of war fled by night
25:19 command over the *m* of war
25:19 five *m* from those having
25:19 sixty *m* of the people of
25:23 forces, they and their *m*
25:23 they and their *m*
25:24 swore to them and their *m*
25:25 and also ten *m* with him
1Ch 4:12 These were the *m* of Recah
4:22 Jokim and the *m* of Cozeba
4:42 Mount Seir, five hundred *m*
5:18 *m* carrying shield and sword
5:24 *m* that were valiant, mighty
5:24 *m* of fame, heads of the
7:2 there were valiant, mighty *m*
7:5 were valiant, mighty *m*
7:7 valiant, mighty *m*; and their
7:9 valiant, mighty *m*, was
7:11 valiant, mighty *m*, seventeen
7:21 *m* of Gath that were born in
7:40 select, valiant, mighty *m*
7:40 was twenty-six thousand *m*
8:40 mighty *m*, bending the bow
9:9 *m* that were heads of the
9:13 mighty *m* of ability for the
9:26 there were four mighty *m* of
9:29 were *m* appointed over the
10:1 *m* of Israel went fleeing
10:4 uncircumcised *m* may not
10:7 When all the *m* of Israel
10:12 the valiant *m* rose up and
11:3 older *m* of Israel came to
11:10 *m* that belonged to David
11:11 mighty *m* that belonged to

1Ch 11:12 among the three mighty *m*
11:19 Is it the blood of these *m*
11:19 that the three mighty *m* did
11:24 among the three mighty *m*
11:26 mighty *m* of the military
12:1 were among the mighty *m*
12:8, 8 mighty *m*, army *m* for the
12:21 were mighty *m* of valor
12:25 mighty *m* of valor of the
12:30 mighty *m* of valor
12:30 *m* of fame, by the house of
12:38 All these were *m* of war
15:25 and the older *m* of Israel
16:22 not you *m* touch my anointed
16:41 *m* that were designated by
17:6 Why have you *m* not built me
18:4 twenty thousand *m* on foot
18:5 twenty-two thousand *m*
19:5 and told David about the *m*
19:5 *m* very much humiliated
19:8 the army and the mighty *m*
19:10 the choice *m* in Israel and
19:18 forty thousand *m* on foot
21:5 thousand *m* drawing sword
21:5 thousand *m* drawing sword
21:16 and David and the older *m*
25:1 official *m* for their service
26:6 they were capable, mighty *m*
26:7 brothers were capable *m*
26:8 capable *m* with the power
26:9 capable *m*, eighteen
26:30 capable *m*, a thousand seven
26:31 mighty *m* came to be found
26:32 his brothers, capable *m*
28:1 and the mighty *m*, even every
29:24 princes and the mighty *m*
2Ch 2:2 *m* as burden bearers and
2:2 *m* as cutters in the mountain
2:14 with your own skillful *m*
2:14 skillful *m* of my lord David
2:17 *m* that were alien residents
5:2 the older *m* of Israel and all
5:3 the *m* of Israel congregated
5:4 the older *m* of Israel came
8:8 Solomon kept levying *m* for
9:7 Happy are your *m*, and
9:14 aside from the *m* of travel
10:6 counsel with the older *m* that
10:8 the counsel of the older *m*
10:8 counsel with the young *m*
10:10 young *m* that had grown up
10:13 the counsel of the older *m*
10:14 counsel of the young *m*
11:1 choice *m* able-bodied for war
13:3 hundred thousand mighty *m*
13:3 of war, chosen *m*
13:3 chosen *m*, valiant, mighty
13:3 valiant, mighty *m*
13:7 idle *m*, good-for-nothing
13:8 *m* are thinking of holding
13:15 *m* of Judah broke out
13:15 *m* of Judah shouted a war
13:17 hundred thousand chosen *m*
14:8 were valiant, mighty *m*
14:9 force of a million *m* and
17:13 mighty *m*, were in
17:14 thousand valiant, mighty *m*
17:16 thousand valiant, mighty *m*
17:17 two hundred thousand *m*
17:18 *m* outfitted for the army
18:5 four hundred *m*, and said to
18:26 *m* must say, This is what
20:21 out ahead of the armed *m*
20:22 Jehovah set *m* in ambush
20:27 *m* of Judah and Jerusalem
23:8 *m* that were coming in on
24:24 small number of *m* that the
25:5 choice *m* going out to the
25:6 mighty *m* for a hundred
26:12 of the valiant, mighty *m*
26:13 *m* engaging in war with the
26:17 eighty valiant *m*, came in
28:6 all valiant *m*, because of
28:12 *m* of the heads of the sons
28:14 armed *m* left the captives
28:15 *m* that were designated by
31:19 *m* that had been designated
32:3 mighty *m* to stop up the
34:12 And the *m* were acting in
34:17 hand of the appointed *m*
34:29 all the older *m* of Judah
34:30 all the *m* of Judah and the
36:17 kill their young *m* with the
Ezr 1:4 *m* of his place assist him
Ezr 2:2 *m* of the people of Israel
2:22 *m* of Netophah, fifty-six
2:23 the *m* of Anathoth, a hundred
2:27 the *m* of Michmas, a hundred
2:28 the *m* of Bethel and Ai, two
2:65 *m* slaves and their slave
3:12 the old *m* that had seen the
4:11 the *m* beyond the River
4:21 these able-bodied *m* to stop
5:4 the able-bodied *m* that are
5:5 upon the older *m* of the Jews
5:9 Then we asked these older *m*
5:10 names of the able-bodied *m*
6:7 and the older *m* of the Jews
6:8 these older *m* of the Jews
6:8 given to these able-bodied *m*
6:14 the older *m* of the Jews
7:18 of your God, you *m* will do
7:21 requests of you *m* it will be
7:24 to you *m* it is being made
7:25 you *m* will instruct
10:1 large congregation, *m* and
10:8 the princes and the older *m*
10:9 the *m* of Judah and Benjamin
10:14 older *m* of each individual
10:16 Ezra the priest and the *m*
10:17 *m* that had given a dwelling
Ne 1:2 he and other *m* from Judah
2:12 I and a few *m* with me, and
3:2 their side the *m* of Jericho
3:7 *m* of Gibeon and Mizpah
3:22 *m* of the Jordan District
4:13 kept *m* posted at the lowest
4:16 *m* were active in the work
4:22 Let the *m* spend the night
4:23 the *m* of the guard who were
5:17 rulers, a hundred and fifty *m*
7:7 the *m* of the people of Israel
7:26 *m* of Bethlehem and Netophah
7:27 the *m* of Anathoth, a hundred
7:28 the *m* of Beth-azmaveth
7:29 the *m* of Kiriath-jearim
7:30 the *m* of Ramah and Geba, six
7:31 the *m* of Michmas, a hundred
7:32 the *m* of Bethel and Ai, a
7:33 the *m* of the other Nebo
7:67 apart from their *m* slaves and
8:2 *m* as well as of women and of
8:3 front of the *m* and the women
11:2 *m* who volunteered to dwell
11:6 and sixty-eight, capable *m*
11:14 brothers, mighty *m* of valor
12:44 *m* over the halls for the
13:25 and strike some *m* of them
Es 1:13 wise *m* having knowledge of
5:5 You *m*, have Haman act quickly
6:13 wise *m* and Zeresh his wife
7:4 been sold for mere *m* slaves
7:9 king said: You *m*, hang him on
9:6 a destroying of five hundred *m*
9:12 destroying of five hundred *m*
9:15 in Shushan three hundred *m*
Job 4:13 When deep sleep falls upon *m*
6:21 *m* have amounted to nothing
6:22 some of the power of you *m*
6:23 you *m* should redeem me
6:25 reproving . . . of you *m*
6:26 that you *m* scheme, When the
11:3 talk itself put *m* to silence
11:11 knows *m* who are untrue
12:2 you *m* are the people, And
12:20 the sensibleness of old *m*
13:2 What you *m* know I . . . know
13:4 *m* are smearers of falsehood
13:7 you *m* speak unrighteousness
16:4 could well speak as you *m* do
17:10 *m* may all of you resume
19:2 *m* keep irritating my soul
19:5 you *m* do put on great airs
19:19 the *m* of my intimate group
19:22 you *m* keep persecuting me
19:28 you *m* say, Why do we keep
19:29 you *m* may know there is a
21:2 Listen, you *m*, attentively
21:27 know the thoughts of you *m*
21:34 vainly you *m* try to comfort
22:15 That hurtful *m* have trodden
22:16 *M* who have been snatched
27:5 declare you *m* righteous
27:11 instruct you *m* by the hand
28:4 mortal *m* have swung down
31:5 walked with *m* of untruth
31:10 over her let other *m* kneel
31:31 *m* of my tent did not say
Job 32:1 three *m* ceased from
32:5 in the mouth of the three *m*
32:6 you *m* are aged. That is why
32:6 my knowledge to you *m*
32:8 it is the spirit in mortal *m*
32:11 for the words of you *m*
32:14 with the sayings of you *m*
33:15 deep sleep falls upon *m*
33:16 he uncovers the ear of *m*
33:27 He will sing to *m* and say
34:8 with *m* of wickedness
34:10 *m* of heart, listen to me
34:34 *M* of heart themselves will
34:36 among *m* of hurtfulness
36:24 Of which *m* have sung
37:2 Listen attentively, you *m*
37:24 Therefore let *m* fear him
42:7 you *m* have not spoken
42:8 you *m* must offer up a burnt
Ps 4:2 You sons of *m*, how long must
9:20 that they are but mortal *m*
11:1 dare you *m* say to my soul
11:4 eyes examine the sons of *m*
12:1 vanished from the sons of *m*
12:8 exalted among the sons of *m*
14:2 upon the sons of *m*
17:4 As for the activities of *m*
17:14 From *m*, by your hand, O
17:14 *m* of this system of things
18:4 floods of good-for-nothing *m*
21:10 offspring from the sons of *m*
22:6 reproach to *m* and despicable
26:4 not sat with *m* of untruth
26:9 along with bloodguilty *m*
31:19 In front of the sons of *m*
31:20 the banding together of *m*
33:13 has seen all the sons of *m*
36:7 *m* themselves take refuge
45:2 handsome than the sons of *m*
53:2 upon the sons of *m*, To see
55:23 deceitful *m*, they will not
57:4 devourers, even the sons of *m*
58:1 O you sons of *m*
59:2 from bloodguilty *m* save me
64:9 *m* will become afraid
66:5 dealing with the sons of *m*
68:13 *m* kept lying between the
68:18 taken gifts in the form of *m*
73:5 plagued the same as other *m*
75:1 *M* have to declare your
76:5 valiant *m* have found their
78:25 *M* ate the very bread of
78:31 young *m* of Israel he made
78:60 resided among earthling *m*
78:63 His young *m* a fire ate up
82:7 you will die just as *m* do
84:5 *m* whose strength is in you
89:47 created all the sons of *m*
90:3 say: Go back, you sons of *m*
94:10 One teaching *m* knowledge
94:11 is knowing the thoughts of *m*
105:15 not you *m* touch my anointed
105:22 to even his elderly *m*
107:8 works to the sons of *m*
107:15 works to the sons of *m*
107:21 works to the sons of *m*
107:31 works to the sons of *m*
107:32 elderly *m* let them praise
110:3 young *m* just like dewdrops
115:16 earth . . . to the sons of *m*
119:24 As *m* of my counsel
119:100 than older *m* I behave
124:2 When *m* rose up against us
127:2 you *m* that you are rising up
129:8 of Jehovah be upon you *m*
135:19 do you *m* bless Jehovah
135:19 do you *m* bless Jehovah
135:20 do you *m* bless Jehovah
139:19 bloodguilty *m* will
140:1 Rescue me . . . from bad *m*
141:4 *m* who are practicing what
145:12 known to the sons of *m* his
148:12 young *m* and also you
148:12 old *m* together with boys
Pr 1:11 innocent *m* without any cause
8:4 To you, O *m*, I am calling
8:4 my voice is to the sons of *m*
8:31 were with the sons of *m*
12:12 the netted prey of bad *m*
17:6 The crown of old *m* is the
20:6 *m* will proclaim each one his
20:29 beauty of young *m* is their
20:29 splendor of old *m* is their
21:22 even the city of mighty *m*

Pr 22:29 before commonplace *m*
23:28 among *m* she increases the
24:1 Do not be envious of bad *m*
25:1 the *m* of Hezekiah the king of
28:5 *M* given to badness cannot
29:8 *M* of boastful talk inflame a
29:10 Bloodthirsty *m* hate anyone
29:25 Trembling at *m* is what lays
31:23 sits down with the older *m*
Ec 7:19 than ten *m* in power who
8:11 heart of the sons of *m* has
9:3 heart of the sons of *m* is also
9:12 sons of *m* . . . being ensnared
9:14 and the *m* in it were few
12:3 *m* of vital energy have bent
Ca 3:3 soul has loved have you *m* seen?
3:7 Sixty mighty *m* are all around
3:7 from the mighty *m* of Israel
4:4 shields of the mighty *m*
Isa 2:5 *m* of the house of Jacob, come
2:11 the loftiness of *m* must bow
2:17 loftiness of *m* must become
3:7 *m* must not set me as
3:10 Say, you *m*, that it will be
3:15 *m* mean in that you crush my
3:25 sword your own *m* will fall
5:3 *m* of Judah, please judge
5:5 known to you *m* what I am
5:7 *m* of Judah are the plantation
5:8 *m* have been made to dwell
5:13 glory will be famished *m*
5:22 *m* with vital energy for
6:9 Hear again and again, O *m*
6:12 removes earthling *m* far
7:13 for you to tire out *m*, that
7:14 will give you *m* a sign
8:12 *m* must not say, A conspiracy!
8:12 you *m* must not fear, nor
9:17 even over their young *m*
10:3 *m* do at the day of being
13:2 raise up a signal, you *m*
13:18 dash even young *m* to pieces
14:19 clothed with killed *m*
14:21 Make ready, you *m*, a
15:4 why the armed *m* of Moab
16:1 Send a ram, you *m*, to the
16:3 Bring in counsel, you *m*
19:11 will you *m* say to Pharaoh
19:12 the wise *m* of yours
20:4 old *m*, naked and barefoot
21:9 war chariot of *m*, with a
21:13 caravans of *m* of Dedan
21:17 *m* of the sons of Kedar
23:4 brought up young *m*, raised
24:6 few mortal *m* have remained
24:23 front of his elderly *m* with
26:2 Open the gates, you *m*
28:15 Because you *m* have said
28:19 it will take you *m* away
28:23 Give ear, you *m*, and listen
29:9 Linger, you *m*, and be amazed
29:10 upon you *m* Jehovah has
29:11 for you *m* the vision of
29:14 wisdom of their wise *m*
29:14 of their discreet *m* will
29:16 The perversity of you *m*!
30:3 for you *m* a reason for shame
30:12 *m* trust in defrauding and
31:3 are earthling *m*, and not God
31:8 young *m* will come to be for
33:13 you *m* who are far away
36:12 *m* sitting upon the wall
36:12 their own urine with you *m*
37:2 older *m* of the priests
37:10 *m* should say to Hezekiah
39:3 What did these *m* say, and
40:1 says the God of you *m*
40:30 young *m* themselves will
41:11 *m* in a quarrel with you
41:12 those *m* in a struggle with
41:12 those *m* at war with you
41:14 you *m* of Israel. I myself
41:26 any sayings of you *m*
42:10 *m* that are going down to
43:4 shall give *m* in place of you
44:11 are from earthling *m*
44:25 turning wise *m* backwards
45:14 and the Sabeans, tall *m*
51:7 the reproach of mortal *m*
53:3 and was avoided by *m*
56:12 Come, *m*! Let me take some
57:1 *m* of loving-kindness are
57:3 you *m*, come up close here
58:12 *m* will certainly build up

Isa 59:10 just like blind *m*, and like
62:10 through the gates, you *m*
62:12 *m* will certainly call them
65:11 you *m* are those leaving
65:12 destine you *m* to the sword
65:15 *m* will certainly lay up
66:5 *m* who are trembling at his
66:24 *m* that were transgressing
Jer 4:3 said to the *m* of Judah and to
4:4 *m* of Judah and inhabitants
4:5 Tell it in Judah, you *m*, and
5:10 do not you *m* make an actual
5:14 you *m* are saying this thing
5:15 bringing in upon you *m* a
5:16 all of them are mighty *m*
5:17 The *m* will eat up your sons
5:18 an extermination of you *m*
5:26 have been found wicked *m*
5:26 It is *m* that they catch
5:31 what will you *m* do in the
6:11 intimate group of young *m*
6:28 are the most stubborn *m*
8:8 How can you *m* say: We are
8:10 give their wives to other *m*
9:21 *m* from the public squares
10:11 what you *m* will say to
11:2 Hear the words . . . you *m*!
11:2 speak them to the *m* of Judah
11:9 found among the *m* of Judah
11:21 against the *m* of Anathoth
11:22 *m* themselves will die
11:23 upon the *m* of Anathoth
17:25 the *m* of Judah and the
18:11 to the *m* of Judah and to
18:15 make *m* stumble in their
18:18 Come, *m*, and let us think
18:21 *m* become those killed with
18:21 *m* those struck down with
19:1 the older *m* of the people
19:1 the older *m* of the priests
19:10 *m* who are going with you
21:11 hear, O *m*, the word of
25:16 act like crazed *m* because
26:17 older *m* of the land rose
26:21 and all his mighty *m*
26:22 Jehoiakim sent *m* to Egypt
26:22 other *m* with him to Egypt
27:9 as for you *m*, do not listen
27:9 You *m* will not serve the
27:14 saying to you *m*, You will
27:15 perish, you *m* and the
29:1 older *m* of the exiled people
30:6 Ask, please, O *m*, and see
31:6 call out, Rise up, O *m*
31:13 dance, also the young *m* and
31:13 and the old *m*, all together
32:5 *m* keep warring against the
32:19 the ways of the sons of *m*
32:20 and in Israel and among *m*
32:24 *m* have come to the city to
32:32 and the *m* of Judah
33:5 *m* whom I have struck down
34:14 you *m* should let go each
34:18 *m* sidestepping my covenant
34:21 from against you *m*
35:13 say to the *m* of Judah and
35:14 spoken to you *m*, rising up
36:19 know where you *m* are
36:31 and upon the *m* of Judah
37:7 you *m* should say to the king
37:10 *m* had struck down all the
37:10 *m* pierced through, they
37:18 *m* have put me into the house
37:19 not come against you *m* and
38:4 the *m* of war who are left
38:9 *m* have done bad in all that
38:10 from this place thirty *m*
38:11 took the *m* in his charge
38:16 *m* who are seeking for your
38:22 *m* at peace with you have
39:4 all the *m* of war saw them
39:13 principal *m* of the king of
39:17 *m* of whom you yourself are
40:7 and their *m*, got to hear
40:7 over the *m* and women and
40:8 they and their *m*
40:9 to them and to their *m*
41:1 principal *m* of the king and
41:1 ten other *m* with him came
41:2 ten *m* that happened to be
41:3 *m* of war, Ishmael struck
41:5 came *m* from Shechem, from
41:5 eighty *m* with their beards
41:7 the *m* that were with him

Jer 41:8 ten *m* that were found among
41:9 *m* that he had struck down
41:12 took all the *m* and went off
41:15 escaped with eight *m* from
41:16, 16 able-bodied *m*, *m* of
42:17 *m* that have set their faces
43:2 presumptuous *m* proceeded to
43:6 able-bodied *m* and the wives
43:9 the eyes of the Jewish *m*
44:15 *m* who were knowing that
44:20 to the able-bodied *m* and to
44:25 As for you *m* and your wives
44:27 *m* of Judah that are in the
46:3 Set in array, O *m*, buckler
46:5 mighty *m* themselves are
46:9 let the mighty *m* go forth
46:14 Tell it in Egypt, O *m*
46:22 vital energy *m* will go
47:2 *m* will certainly cry out
48:2 Come, *m*, and let us cut her
48:14, 14 mighty *m* and *m* of vital
48:15 choicest young *m* themselves
48:20 Tell in Arnon, O *m*, that
48:26 Make him drunk, O *m*, for he
48:31 *m* of Kir-heres one shall
48:36 for the *m* of Kir-heres my
48:41 mighty *m* of Moab must
49:20 hear, O *m*, the counsel
49:22 of the mighty *m* of Edom
49:26 young *m* will fall in her
49:26 *m* of war themselves will
49:28 Kedar, O *m*, and despoil
49:31 Rise up, O *m*, go up against
50:2 Hide nothing, O *m*
50:11 For you *m* kept rejoicing
50:11 *m* kept exulting when
50:12 mother of you *m* has become
50:30 young *m* will fall in her
50:30 *m* of war will be brought
50:36 sword against her mighty *m*
50:45 hear, O *m*, the counsel of
51:3 *m* show any compassion for
51:3 compassion for her young *m*
51:11 the circular shields, O *m*
51:14 I will fill you with *m*
51:27 signal in the land, O *m*
51:30 mighty *m* of Babylon have
51:32 *m* of war themselves have
51:56 mighty *m* will certainly be
51:57 and her mighty *m* drunk
52:7 as regards all the *m* of war
52:25 over the *m* of war, and
52:25 seven *m* of those having
52:25 sixty *m* of the people of
La 1:15 to break my young *m* to pieces
1:18 my own young *m* have gone
1:19 my own old *m* have expired
2:10 older *m* of the daughter of
2:21 My virgins and my young *m*
3:6 like *m* dead for a long time
3:33 does he grieve the sons of *m*
4:16 *M* will certainly show no
4:16 no favor even to the old *m*
5:12 old *m* have not been honored
5:13 young *m* have lifted up a hand
5:14 Old *m* themselves have ceased
5:14 young *m* from their . . . music
Eze 7:26 and counsel from elderly *m*
8:1 older *m* of Judah were sitting
8:11 And seventy *m* of the elderly
8:16 twenty-five *m* with their
9:2 were six *m* coming from the
9:4 the *m* that are sighing and
9:6 started with the old *m* that
11:1 twenty-five *m*, and I got to
11:2 are the *m* that are scheming
11:15 *m* concerned with your right
12:16 a few *m* from the sword
13:5 You *m* will certainly not go
13:7 untrue vision that you *m*
13:8 you *m* have spoken untruth
13:12 said to you *m*, Where is the
13:14 that you *m* have plastered
13:15 say to you *m*: The wall is
14:1 *m* from the elderly ones of
14:3 as regards these *m*, they
14:14 had these three *m* proved to
14:16 three *m* in the midst of it
14:18 three *m* in the midst of it
17:13 *m* of the land he took away
20:1 *m* from the elderly ones of
20:3 with the elderly *m* of Israel
20:3 that you *m* are coming
21:29 wicked *m* whose day has

Eze 21:31 give you into the hand of *m*
23:6 desirable young *m* all of
23:12 desirable young *m* all of
23:14 *m* in carvings upon the wall
23:23 desirable young *m*
23:40 *m* coming from far away
23:42 *m* out of the mass of
23:45 as regards righteous *m*
24:17 bread of *m* you should not
24:22 bread of *m* you will not eat
27:9 Even old *m* of Gebal and her
27:10 and *m* of Put—they happened
27:10 force, your *m* of war
27:11 valorous *m* were the ones
27:27 and all your *m* of war
30:12 into the hand of bad *m*
30:17 young *m* of On and Pibeseth
32:20 and all her crowds, you *m*
32:21 *m* of the mighty ones
34:18 a little thing for you *m*
34:31 you are earthling *m*. I am
36:37 like a flock with *m*
36:38 become full of a flock of *m*
39:14 *m* for continual employment
45:10 *m* should come to have
Da 2:5 *m* do not make the dream known
2:8 time is what you *m* are trying
2:12 destroy all the wise *m* of
2:13 wise *m* were about to be
2:14 kill the wise *m* of Babylon
2:18 of the wise *m* of Babylon
2:24 destroy the wise *m* of Babylon
2:24 destroy any wise *m* of Babylon
2:27 wise *m*, the conjurers, the
2:47 Truly the God of you *m* is a
2:48 all the wise *m* of Babylon
3:12 able-bodied *m* have paid no
3:13 *m* were brought in before the
3:20 *m* of vital energy who were
3:21 *m* were bound in their mantles
3:22 *m* that took up Shadrach
3:23 *m*, the three of them
3:24 able-bodied *m* that we threw
3:25 *m* walking about free in the
3:27 *m*, that the fire had had no
4:6 bring . . . wise *m* of Babylon
4:18 wise *m* of my kingdom are
4:25 will be driving away from *m*
5:7 to the wise *m* of Babylon
5:8 wise *m* of the king were coming
5:15 in before me the wise *m*
6:5 able-bodied *m* were saying: We
6:11 *m* themselves crowded in and
6:15 *m* themselves entered as a
6:24 *m* who had accused Daniel, and
9:7 to the *m* of Judah and to the
10:7 *m* that happened to be with me
Ho 1:9 you *m* are not my people and
1:10 You *m* are not my people, it
4:14 as to the *m*, it is with the
13:2 Let the sacrificers who are *m*
Joe 1:2 Hear this, you older *m*, and
1:14 Gather together the older *m*
2:1 Blow a horn in Zion, O *m*
2:7 Like powerful *m* they run
2:7 *m* of war they go up a wall
2:15 Blow a horn in Zion, O *m*
2:16 Collect the old *m* together
2:28 As for your old *m*, dreams
2:28 As for your young *m*, visions
3:5 *m* have taken my own silver
3:8 sell them to the *m* of Sheba
3:9 Arouse the powerful *m*!
3:9 come up, all the *m* of war
Am 2:11 your young *m* as Nazirites
2:16 among the mighty *m*
4:10 I killed your young *m*, along
6:4 You *m* that are lying down on
6:9 if ten *m* should be left
8:4 *m* snapping at someone poor
8:13 *m*, because of the thirst
Ob 7 *m* in covenant with you have
7 The *m* at peace with you have
9 mighty *m* must become terrified
Jon 1:10 the *m* began to fear greatly
1:10 the *m* had come to know that
1:13 *m* tried to work their way
1:16 the *m* began to fear Jehovah
3:5 the *m* of Nineveh began to
4:11 *m* who do not at all know
Mic 1:10 In Gath do not you *m* tell it
2:8 you *m* strip off the majestic
2:12 they will be noisy with *m*
3:6 you *m* will have night, so
Mic 3:12 on account of you *m* Zion
6:12 rich *m* have become full of
6:16 reproach . . . you *m* will bear
7:6 are the *m* of his household
Na 1:9 What will you *m* think up
2:3 The shield of his mighty *m* is
2:3 his *m* of vital energy are
2:8 Stand still, you *m*! Stand
2:9 Plunder silver, you *m*; plunder
3:10 over her . . . *m* they cast lots
Zep 1:12 *m* who are congealing upon
1:17 walk like blind *m*
3:4 insolent, were *m* of treachery
Zec 2:4 multitude of *m* and domestic
3:8 are *m* serving as portents
7:2 his *m* to soften the face of
8:4 old *m* and old women in the
8:23 *m* out of all the languages
9:17 make the young *m* thrive
10:5 like mighty *m* stamping down
Mal 1:9 receive any of you *m* kindly
1:10 *m* will not light my altar
1:12 *m* are profaning me by your
2:8 you *m*—you have turned aside
Mt 4:19 I will make you fishers of *m*
5:13 to be trampled on by *m*
5:16 let your light shine before *m*
6:1 in front of *m* in order to be
6:2 they may be glorified by *m*
6:5 to be visible to *m*. Truly I
6:14 forgive *m* their trespasses
6:15 if you do not forgive *m* their
6:16 appear to *m* to be fasting
6:18 to be fasting, not to *m*, but
7:12 that you want *m* to do to you
7:20 you will recognize those *m*
8:27 *m* became amazed and said
8:28 demon-possessed *m* coming out
8:33 of the demon-possessed *m*
9:8 who gave such authority to *m*
9:27 two blind *m* followed him
9:28 the blind *m* came to him, and
10:17 Be on your guard against *m*
10:32 union with me before *m*, I
10:33 whoever disowns me before *m*
11:12 goal toward which *m* press
12:3 the *m* with him got hungry
12:31 will be forgiven *m*, but the
12:36 *m* speak, they will render
12:41 *M* of Nineveh will rise up
13:17 righteous *m* desired to see
13:25 *m* were sleeping, his enemy
14:21 were about five thousand *m*
14:35 *m* of that place sent forth
15:2 of the *m* of former times
15:9 they teach commands of *m* as
15:38 four thousand *m*, besides
16:13 *m* saying the Son of man is
16:21 older *m* and chief priests
16:23 thoughts, but those of *m*
17:24 the *m* collecting the two
18:10 you *m* do not despise one of
18:18 I say to you *m*, Whatever
19:11 Not all *m* make room for the
19:12 that were made eunuchs by *m*
19:26 With *m* this is impossible
20:9 the eleventh-hour *m* came
20:19 to *m* of the nations to make
20:22 You *m* do not know what you
20:25 the great *m* wield authority
20:30 two blind *m* sitting beside
21:23 older *m* of the people came
21:25 From heaven or from *m*?
21:26 If, though, we say, From *m*
22:30 neither do *m* marry nor are
23:4 upon the shoulders of *m*, but
23:5 they do to be viewed by *m*
23:7 and to be called Rabbi by *m*
23:13 of the heavens before *m*
23:28 appear righteous to *m*, but
23:34 prophets and wise *m* and
24:38 *m* marrying and women being
24:40 two *m* will be in the field
26:3 chief priests and the older *m*
26:40 Could you *m* not so much as
26:47 and older *m* of the people
26:57 the older *m* were gathered
26:64 Yet I say to you *m*, From
27:1 older *m* of the people held a
27:3 the chief priests and older *m*
27:12 chief priests and older *m*
27:20 and the older *m* persuaded
27:41 older *m* began making fun of
28:4 watchmen . . . as dead *m*
Mt 28:12 together with the older *m*
Mr 1:17 you to become fishers of *m*
1:20 in the boat with the hired *m*
2:3 And *m* came bringing him a
2:10 you *m* to know that the Son
2:25 hungry, he and the *m* with
2:26 gave some also to the *m* who
3:28 be forgiven the sons of *m*, no
5:35 some *m* from the home of the
6:21 for his top-ranking *m* and the
6:44 were five thousand *m*
7:3 of the *m* of former times
7:5 tradition of the *m* of former
7:7 as doctrines commands of *m*
7:8 hold fast the tradition of *m*
7:11 you *m* say, If a man says to
7:12 you *m* no longer let him do a
7:21 out of the heart of *m*
8:9 were about four thousand *m*
8:19 for the five thousand *m*
8:20 for the four thousand *m*
8:24 I see *m*, because I observe
8:27 Who are *m* saying that I am?
8:31 rejected by the older *m* and
8:33 thoughts, but those of *m*
10:27 With *m* it is impossible
10:29 Truly I say to you *m*, No one
10:33 deliver him to *m* of the
11:27 and the older *m* came to him
11:30 from heaven or from *m*
11:32 But dare we say, From *m*?
12:25 neither do *m* marry nor are
14:38 *M*, keep on the watch and
14:43 the scribes and the older *m*
14:53 the older *m* and the scribes
15:1 the older *m* and the scribes
Lu 1:25 away my reproach among *m*
1:52 has brought down *m* of power
2:14 peace among *m* of goodwill
2:52 and in favor with God and *m*
5:4 *m* let down your nets for a
5:10 you will be catching *m* alive
5:18 *m* carrying on a bed a man
6:3 the *m* with him got hungry
6:4 gave some to the *m* with him
6:9 I ask you *m*, Is it lawful on
6:22 Happy . . . whenever *m* hate you
6:26 whenever all *m* speak well of
6:31 just as you want *m* to do to
7:3 sent forth older *m* of the Jews
7:20 the *m* said: John the Baptist
7:31 the *m* of this generation
7:41 Two *m* were debtors to a
9:14 about five thousand *m*
9:22 be rejected by the older *m*
9:30 two *m* were conversing with
9:32 the two *m* standing with him
9:44 delivered into the hands of *m*
9:50 Do not you *m* try to prevent
11:31 the *m* of this generation
11:32 *m* of Nineveh will rise in
11:44 *m* walk upon them and do not
11:46 you load *m* with loads hard
12:8 union with me before *m*, the
12:9 disowns me before *m* will be
12:36 like *m* waiting for their
13:4 other *m* inhabiting Jerusalem
14:7 to tell the invited *m* an
14:24 None of those *m* that were
15:17 hired *m* of my father are
15:19 me as one of your hired *m*
15:21 me as one of your hired *m*
16:15 righteous before *m*, but God
16:15 what is lofty among *m* is a
17:12 ten leprous *m* met him, but
17:27 *m* were marrying, women
17:34 In that night two *m* will be
18:10 Two *m* went up into the
18:11 I am not as the rest of *m*
18:27 things impossible with *m*
18:32 delivered up to *m* of the
20:1 scribes with the older *m* came
20:4 from heaven or from *m*
20:6 if we say, From *m*, the
20:20 sent out *m* secretly hired to
21:26 *m* become faint out of fear
22:31 to have you *m* to sift you as
22:52 older *m* that had come there
22:63 *m* that had him in custody
22:66 the assembly of older *m* of
23:32 But two other *m*, evildoers
24:4 two *m* in flashing clothing
24:5 the *m* said to them: Why are
24:7 into the hands of sinful *m*

Joh 1:4 the life was the light of *m*
1:51 Most truly I say to you *m*
3:19 *m* have loved the darkness
4:28 into the city and told the *m*
5:33 have dispatched *m* to John
5:41 I do not accept glory from *m*
6:10 the *m* recline as at meal
6:10 the *m* reclined, about
6:14 the *m* saw the signs he
8:17 The witness of two *m* is true
12:32 draw *m* of all sorts to me
12:43 loved the glory of *m* more
13:10 you *m* are clean, but not
14:7 If you *m* had known me
14:9 with you *m* so long a time
14:10 things I say to you *m* I do
15:6 *m* gather those branches up
16:2 *M* will expel you from the
17:6 *m* you gave me out of the
19:18 and two other *m* with him
Ac 1:10 two *m* in white garments
1:11 *M* of Galilee, why do you
1:16 *M*, brothers, it was necessary
1:21 *m* that assembled with us
1:22 *m* should become a witness
1:24 which one of these two *m* you
2:5 Jews, reverent *m*, from every
2:14 *M* of Judea and all you
2:17 young *m* will see visions and
2:17 old *m* will dream dreams
2:18 even upon my *m* slaves and
2:22 *M* of Israel, hear these
2:23 by the hand of lawless *m* and
2:29 *M*, brothers, it is allowable
2:37 *M*, brothers, what shall we
3:12 *M* of Israel, why are you
4:4 number of the *m* became about
4:5 and older *m* and scribes
4:8 of the people and older *m*
4:12 given among *m* by which we
4:13 *m* unlettered and ordinary
4:16 shall we do with these *m*
4:23 older *m* had said to them
4:27 Pilate with *m* of nations and
5:4 played false, not to *m*, but
5:6 younger *m* rose, wrapped him
5:10 young *m* came in they found
5:14 multitudes both of *m* and of
5:21 older *m* of the sons of Israel
5:25 *m* you put in the prison are
5:29 God as ruler rather than *m*
5:34 put the *m* outside for a
5:35 *M* of Israel, pay attention
5:35 to do respecting these *m*
5:36 *m*, about four hundred, joined
5:38 Do not meddle with these *m*
5:38 work is from *m*, it will be
6:3 seven certified *m* from among
6:9 *m* rose up of those from the
6:11 secretly induced *m* to say
6:12 older *m* and the scribes, and
7:2 *M*, brothers and fathers, hear
7:26 *M*, you are brothers. Why do
7:51 Obstinate *m* and uncircumcised
8:2 reverent *m* carried Stephen to
8:3 dragging out both *m* and women
8:12 baptized, both *m* and women
8:24 You *m*, make supplication for
9:2 to The Way, both *m* and women
9:7 *m* that were journeying with
9:38 two *m* to him to entreat him
10:5 send *m* to Joppa and summon
10:17 *m* dispatched by Cornelius
10:19 Three *m* are seeking you
10:21 downstairs to the *m* and
11:3 *m* that were not circumcised
11:11 three *m* standing at the
11:13 Dispatch *m* to Joppa and send
11:20 *m* of Cyprus and Cyrene that
11:30 to the older *m* by the hand
13:4 *m*, sent out by the holy
13:11 *m* to lead him by the hand
13:13 *m*, together with Paul, now
13:15 *M*, brothers, if there is
13:16 *M*, Israelites and you
13:26 *M*, brothers, you sons of
13:50 the principal *m* of the city
14:15 *M*, why are you doing these
14:23 they appointed older *m* for
15:1 *m* came down from Judea and
15:2 and older *m* in Jerusalem
15:3 these *m* continued on their
15:4 the apostles and the older *m*
15:6 older *m* gathered together to
Ac 15:7 *M*, brothers, you well know
15:13 saying: *M*, brothers, hear me
15:17 those who remain of the *m*
15:22 the apostles and the older *m*
15:22 favored sending chosen *m*
15:22 leading *m* among the
15:23 The apostles and the older *m*
15:25 favored choosing *m* to send
15:26 *m* that have delivered up
15:30 when these *m* were let go
16:4 the apostles and older *m* who
16:15 If you *m* have judged me to
16:17 These *m* are slaves of the
16:20 These *m* are disturbing our
16:35 to say: Release those *m*
16:36 have dispatched *m* that you
16:37 *m* who are Romans, and threw
16:38 that the *m* were Romans
17:5 wicked *m* of the marketplace
17:6 *m* that have overturned the
17:7 these *m* act in opposition to
17:12 Greek women and of the *m*
17:22 *M* of Athens, I behold that
17:26 one man every nation of *m*
17:26 limits of the dwelling of *m*
17:31 a guarantee to all *m* in that
17:33 some *m* joined themselves to
18:13 *m* to another persuasion in
19:7 there were about twelve *m*
19:25 *M*, you well know that from
19:28 *m* began crying out, saying
19:35 *M* of Ephesus, who really is
19:37 *m* who are neither robbers of
20:17 older *m* of the congregation
20:26 from the blood of all *m*
20:30 *m* will rise and speak
21:8 who was one of the seven *m*
21:18 all the older *m* were present
21:23 have four *m* with a vow upon
21:24 Take these *m* along and
21:26 Paul took the *m* along the
21:28 *M* of Israel, help! This is
21:38 the four thousand dagger *m*
22:1 *M*, brothers and fathers, hear
22:4 to prisons both *m* and women
22:5 all the assembly of older *m*
22:9 *m* that were with me beheld
22:15 a witness for him to all *m*
22:25 lawful for you *m* to scourge
22:29 therefore, the *m* that were
23:1 *M*, brothers, I have behaved
23:6 *M*, brothers, I am a Pharisee
23:13 were more than forty *m* that
23:14 priests and the older *m* and
23:21 more than forty *m* of theirs
24:1 older *m* and a public speaker
24:15 which hope these *m*
24:16 no offense against God and *m*
24:20 let the *m* here say for
24:22 to put the *m* off and said
25:2 the principal *m* of the Jews
25:11 of which these *m* accuse me
25:15 the older *m* of the Jews
25:23 *m* of eminence in the city
25:24 *m* who are present with us
26:8 unbelievable among you *m*
26:29 become *m* such as I also am
26:30 and the *m* seated with them
27:10 *M*, I perceive that
27:21 *M*, you certainly ought to
27:25 be of good cheer, *m*; for I
27:31 *m* remain in the boat, you
28:17 principal *m* of the Jews
28:17 *M*, brothers, although I had
Ro 1:18 *m* . . . suppressing the truth
2:29 not from *m*, but from God
3:8 as some *m* state that we say
3:8 judgment against those *m* is in
3:12 All *m* have deflected, all of
5:6 Christ . . . died for ungodly *m*
5:12 death spread to all *m*
5:18 result to *m* of all sorts was
5:18 result to *m* of all sorts is
11:4 left seven thousand *m* over
11:4 *m* who have not bent the knee
12:17 in the sight of all *m*
12:18 be peaceable with all *m*
14:18 and has approval with *m*
16:7 *m* of note among the apostles
16:18 *m* of that sort are slaves
1Co 1:19 wisdom of the wise *m* perish
1:19 intellectual *m* I will shove
1:25 of God is wiser than *m*, and
1:25 of God is stronger than *m*
1Co 1:27 put the wise *m* to shame
2:11 who among *m* knows the
3:1 to you as to spiritual *m*, but
3:1 as to fleshly *m*, as to babes
3:3 are you not walking as *m* do?
3:4 are you not simply *m*?
3:20 reasonings of the wise *m* are
3:21 let no one be boasting in *m*
4:8 You *m* already have your fill
4:9 on exhibition as *m* appointed
4:9 and to angels, and to *m*
6:1 before unrighteous *m*, and not
6:4 is it the *m* looked down upon
6:9 *m* . . . for unnatural purposes
6:9, 9 nor *m* who lie with *m*
7:7 But I wish all *m* were as I
7:23 stop becoming slaves of *m*
9:12 If other *m* partake of this
9:13 that the *m* performing sacred
10:13 except what is common to *m*
10:15 *m* with discernment; judge
13:1 speak in the tongues of *m*
14:2 not to *m*, but to God, for
14:3 consoles *m* by his speech
15:19 of all *m* most to be pitied
15:32 like *m*, I have fought with
16:3 *m* you approve of by letters
16:13 carry on as *m*, grow mighty
16:18 recognize *m* of that sort
2Co 2:17 not peddlers . . . as many *m*
3:1 like some *m*, need letters of
5:11 we keep persuading *m*, but
8:21 but also in the sight of *m*
11:13 such *m* are false apostles
Ga 1:1 apostle, neither from *m* nor
1:10 *m* I am now trying to
1:10 Or am I seeking to please *m*?
1:10 yet pleasing *m*, I would not
2:2 those who were outstanding *m*
2:6 sort of *m* they formerly were
2:6 outstanding *m* imparted nothing
2:12 the arrival of certain *m* from
4:2 under *m* in charge and under
5:12 *m* who are trying to overturn
Eph 3:5 made known to the sons of *m*
3:9 *m* see how the sacred secret
4:8 he gave gifts in *m*
4:14 means of the trickery of *m*
6:6 eyeservice as *m* pleasers, but
6:7 as to Jehovah, and not to *m*
Php 2:7 to be in the likeness of *m*
2:29 holding *m* of that sort dear
4:5 become known to all *m*
Col 2:8 to the tradition of *m*
2:22 commands and teachings of *m*
3:22 eyeservice, as *m* pleasers
3:23 as to Jehovah, and not to *m*
1Th 1:5 what sort of *m* we became to
2:4 pleasing, not *m*, but God
2:6 been seeking glory from *m*, no
2:13 not as the word of *m*, but
2:15 the interests of all *m*
2Th 3:2 delivered from . . . wicked *m*
1Ti 1:10 *m* who lie with males
2:1 concerning all sorts of *m*
2:4 all sorts of *m* should be
2:5 mediator between God and *m*
2:8 the *m* carry on prayer
3:13 For the *m* who minister in a
4:2 hypocrisy of *m* who speak lies
4:10 a Savior of all sorts of *m*
4:14 older *m* laid their hands
5:1 younger *m* as brothers
5:17 Let the older *m* who preside
5:24 sins of some *m* are publicly
5:24 as for other *m* their sins
6:5 *m* corrupted in mind and
6:9 plunge *m* into destruction
6:16 not one of *m* has seen or can
2Ti 1:15 *m* in the district of Asia
2:2 things commit to faithful *m*
2:18 *m* have deviated from the
3:2 For *m* will be lovers of
3:6 *m* who slyly work their way
3:8 *m* completely corrupted in
3:9 madness of those two *m* became
3:13 wicked *m* and impostors will
Tit 1:5 appointments of older *m* in
1:10 For there are many unruly *m*
1:10 those *m* who adhere to the
1:11 very *m* keep on subverting
1:14 and commandments of *m*
2:2 Let the aged *m* be moderate in
2:6 younger *m* to be sound in mind

Tit 2:11 salvation to all sorts of *m*
3:2 all mildness toward all *m*
3:8 are fine and beneficial to *m*
Heb 5:1 priest taken from among *m*
5:1 is appointed in behalf of *m*
6:16 *m* swear by the one greater
7:5 the *m* from the sons of Levi
7:8 *m* who are dying that receive
7:21 *m* that have become priests
7:28 Law appoints *m* high priests
8:4 being *m* who offer the gifts
8:5 *m* are rendering sacred
9:27 *m* to die once for all time
10:1 *m* can never with the same
11:2 *m* of old times had witness
11:35 but other *m* were tortured
Jas 3:9 with it we curse *m* who have
5:1 Come, now, you rich *m*, weep
5:14 Let him call the older *m*
1Pe 2:4 rejected, it is true, by *m*
2:15 talk of the unreasonable *m*
2:17 Honor *m* of all sorts, have
4:2 no more for the desires of *m*
4:6 from the standpoint of *m* but
5:1 older *m* among you I give
5:5 younger *m*, be in subjection
5:5 in subjection to the older *m*
2Pe 1:21 *m* spoke from God as they
2:12 these *m*, like unreasoning
3:7 destruction of the ungodly *m*
1Jo 2:13 I am writing you, young *m*
2:14 write you, young *m*, because
5:9 receive the witness *m* give
Jude 4 *m* have slipped in who have
4 ungodly *m*, turning the
8 *m* too indulging in dreams
10 *m* are speaking abusively of
16 *m* are murmurers, complainers
19 animalistic *m*, not having
Re 2:2 that you cannot bear bad *m*
8:11 many of the *m* died from the
9:4 only those *m* who do not have
9:6 the *m* will seek death but will
9:10 to hurt the *m* five months
9:15 to kill a third of the *m*
9:18 a third of the *m* were killed
9:20 the rest of the *m* who were
16:2 *m* that had the mark of the
16:8 to scorch the *m* with fire
16:9 *m* were scorched with great
16:18 *m* came to be on the earth
16:21 out of heaven upon the *m*
16:21 *m* blasphemed God due to the
18:23 top-ranking *m* of the earth
19:18 fleshy parts of strong *m*

Menahem
2Ki 15:14 *M* the son of Gadi came
15:16 *M* proceeded to strike down
15:17 *M* the son of Gadi became
15:19 *M* gave Pul a thousand
15:20 *M* brought forth the silver
15:21 the affairs of *M* and all
15:22 Finally *M* lay down with
15:23 Pekahiah the son of *M*

Mend
1Ki 18:30 to *m* the altar of Jehovah

Mending
2Ch 34:10 applied it to *m* and
Jer 30:13 no means of healing, no *m*
46:11 There is no *m* for you
Mt 4:21 *m* their nets, and he called
Mr 1:19 in their boat *m* their nets

Mene
Da 5:25, 25 *M*, *M*, TEKEL and PARSIN
5:26 *M*, God has numbered the days

Menna
Lu 3:31 son of Melea, son of *M*, son

Men's
1Ki 13:2 *m* bones he will burn upon
Isa 29:13 becomes *m* commandment that
Mt 17:22 to be betrayed into *m* hands
22:16 upon *m* outward appearance
23:27 full of dead *m* bones and of
Mr 9:31 delivered into *m* hands, and
12:14 do not look upon *m* outward
1Co 2:5 not in *m* wisdom, but in
Re 9:7 their faces were as *m* faces

Menservants
Ge 12:16 *m* and maidservants and
20:14 *m* and maidservants and gave
24:35 and gold and *m* and
Ge 30:43 *m* and camels and asses
32:5 bulls and asses, sheep, and *m*
1Sa 8:16 your *m* and your maidservants
2Ki 5:26 cattle or *m* or maidservants
2Ch 28:10 reducing to *m* and
Ec 2:7 I acquired *m* and maidservants
Isa 14:2 the soil of Jehovah as *m*
Jer 34:11 bring back the *m* and the
34:11 subjecting them as *m* and
34:16 them to become your *m*
Joe 2:29 *m* and on the maidservants
Lu 12:45 start to beat the *m* and the

Menstrual
Le 15:19 seven days in her *m* impurity
15:20 her *m* impurity will be
15:24 *m* impurity comes to be upon
15:25 time of her *m* impurity, or
15:25 her *m* impurity, all the days
15:25 *m* impurity. She is unclean
15:26 as the bed of her *m* impurity
15:26 uncleanness . . . *m* impurity

Menstruating
Le 12:2 she is *m* she will be unclean
15:33 *m* woman in her uncleanness
20:18 lies down with a *m* woman
Isa 30:22 Like a *m* woman, you will

Menstruation
Ge 18:11 Sarah had stopped having *m*
Le 12:5 unclean . . . as during her *m*
18:19 *m* of her impurity to lay her
Isa 64:6 a garment for periods of *m*
Eze 22:10 a woman unclean in her *m*
36:17 the uncleanness of *m* their

Mental
Da 4:5 *m* images upon my bed and
Am 4:13 man what his *m* concern is
Lu 2:48 in *m* distress have been
Ro 1:28 to a disapproved *m* state, to
15:5 the same *m* attitude that
2Co 3:14 their *m* powers were dulled
Php 2:5 Keep this *m* attitude in you
3:15 be of this *m* attitude
4:7 your hearts and your *m* powers
1Pe 4:1 with the same *m* disposition

Mentally
Eph 3:18 thoroughly able to grasp *m*
4:18 they are in darkness *m*, and
Php 3:15 are *m* inclined otherwise in
1Ti 6:4 *m* diseased over questionings

Mental-regulating
Eph 6:4 discipline and *m* of Jehovah

Mention
Ge 40:14 *m* me to Pharaoh, and you
Ex 23:13 not *m* the name of other gods
De 25:19 wipe out the *m* of Amalek
32:26 the *m* of them cease from
Jos 23:7 you must not *m* the names
Es 2:13 Everything that she would *m*
2:15 what Hegai . . . proceeded to *m*
Ps 6:5 in death there is no *m* of you
9:6 very *m* of them will certainly
20:7 our God we shall make *m*
34:16 cut off the *m* of them from
45:17 I will make *m* of your name
71:16 I shall *m* your righteousness
87:4 *m* of Rahab and Babylon as
145:7 *m* of the abundance of your
Ca 1:4 let us *m* your expressions of
Isa 12:4 Make *m* that his name is put
26:13 we make *m* of your name
26:14 and destroy all *m* of them
48:1 *m* even of the God of Israel
49:1 he has made *m* of my name
62:6 are making *m* of Jehovah
63:7 *m*, the praises of Jehovah
Jer 4:16 Make *m* of it, you people
20:9 not going to make *m* of him
Am 6:10 any *m* of the name of Jehovah
Ro 1:9 make *m* of you in my prayers
Php 3:18 I used to *m* them often but
3:18 I *m* them also with weeping
1Th 1:2 make *m* concerning all of you
Phm 4 make *m* of you in my prayers
Heb 11:22 *m* of the exodus of the sons
2Pe 1:15 to make *m* of these things

Mentioned
Nu 14:40 to the place that Jehovah *m*
Jg 13:13 that I *m* to the woman
Ru 4:1 whom Boaz had *m*
1Sa 4:18 moment that he *m* the ark of
2Sa 6:22 slave girls whom you *m*
Job 28:18 Coral . . . will not be *m*
Eph 5:3 greediness not even be *m*

Mentioning
Ge 41:9 saying: My sins I am *m* today
Job 18:17 *m* of him will . . . perish
Eph 1:16 *m* you in my prayers

Mentions
Isa 19:17 whom one *m* it is in dread

Menuhoth
1Ch 2:52 Haroeh, half of the *M*

Meonenim
Jg 9:37 the way of the big tree of *M*

Meonothai
1Ch 4:14 *M*, he became father to

Mephaath
Jos 13:18 Jahaz and Kedemoth and *M*
21:37 *M* and its pasture ground
1Ch 6:79 *M* with its pasture grounds
Jer 48:21 to Jahaz and against *M*

Mephibosheth
2Sa 4:4 And his name was *M*
9:6 *M* the son of Jonathan the son
9:6 David said: *M!* to which he
9:10 *M* himself, the grandson of
9:11 *M* is eating at my table like
9:12 *M* had a young son whose
9:12 were servants to *M*
9:13 *M* himself was dwelling in
16:1 Ziba the attendant of *M* to
16:4 everything that belongs to *M*
19:24 *M* the grandson of Saul
19:25 did you not go with me, *M*
19:30 *M* said to the king: Let him
21:7 king felt compassion upon *M*
21:8 Armoni and *M*, and the five

Merab
1Sa 14:49 the one born first was *M*
18:17 is my oldest daughter *M*
18:19 giving *M*, Saul's daughter

Meraiah
Ne 12:12 *M*; for Jeremiah, Hananiah

Meraioth
1Ch 6:6 Zerahiah . . . father to *M*
6:7 *M* . . . father to Amariah
6:52 *M* his son, Amariah his son
9:11 son of *M* the son of Ahitub
Ezr 7:3 Azariah the son of *M*
Ne 11:11 *M* the son of Ahitub
12:15 Adna; for *M*, Helkai

Merari
Ge 46:11 sons of Levi were . . . *M*
Ex 6:16 sons of Levi . . . Kohath and *M*
6:19 sons of *M* were Mahli and
Nu 3:17 sons of Levi . . . Kohath and *M*
3:20 sons of *M* by their families
3:33 Of *M* there were the family of
3:33 These were the families of *M*
3:35 for the families of *M* was
3:36 sons of *M* were obligated
4:29 sons of *M*, you will register
4:33 families of the sons of *M*
4:42 sons of *M* by their families
4:45 families of the sons of *M*
7:8 he gave to the sons of *M* in
10:17 *M* as carriers of the
26:57 of *M* the family of the
Jos 21:7 sons of *M* by their families
21:34 sons of *M*, the Levites who
21:40 sons of *M* by their families
1Ch 6:1 The sons of Levi were . . . *M*
6:16 The sons of Levi were . . . *M*
6:19 sons of *M* were Mahli and
6:29 The sons of *M* were Mahli
6:44 sons of *M* their brothers on
6:47 son of *M*, the son of Levi
6:63 To the sons of *M* by their
6:77 sons of *M* that were left
9:14 Hashabiah from the sons of *M*
15:6 of the sons of *M*, Asaiah the
15:17 and, of the sons of *M* their
23:6 to the sons of Levi . . . *M*
23:21 of *M* were Mahli and Mushi
24:26 sons of *M* were Mahli and
24:27 sons of *M*: Of Jaaziah, Beno
26:10 Hosah of the sons of *M* had
26:19 and of the sons of *M*
2Ch 29:12 and from the sons of *M*
34:12 from the sons of *M*, and

Ezr 8:19 Jeshaiah from the sons of *M*

Merarites
Nu 26:57 Merari the family of the *M*

Merathaim
Jer 50:21 Against the land of *M*

Merchandise
Le 25:14 sell *m* to your associate or
Ne 13:16 every sort of *m* and making
13:20 sellers of every sort of *m*
Eze 27:9 to exchange articles of *m*
27:27 your articles of *m* and
Joh 2:16 of my Father a house of *m*

Merchant
Pr 31:14 to be like the ships of a *m*
Eze 27:12 Tarshish was your *m* because
27:16 Edom was your *m* because of
27:18 Damascus was your *m* in the
Mt 13:45 like a traveling *m* seeking

Merchants
Ge 23:16 shekels current with the *m*
37:28 Midianite *m*, went passing
1Ki 10:28 company of the king's *m*
2Ch 1:16 the company of the king's *m*
9:14 *m* who were bringing in and
Isa 23:2 *m* from Sidon, the ones
23:8 whose *m* were princes
45:14 and the *m* of Ethiopia and
Eze 27:15 were *m* in your employ
27:21 *m* in your employ. In male
27:21 in them they were your *m*
27:36 As for *m* among the peoples
38:13 and the *m* of Tarshish and
Re 18:3 traveling *m* of the earth
18:11 traveling *m* of the earth
18:15 traveling *m* of these things
18:23 *m* were the top-ranking men

Mercies
2Sa 24:14 for many are his *m*
1Ch 21:13 for very many are his *m*
Ps 25:6 Remember your *m*, O Jehovah
51:1 *m* wipe out my transgressions
69:16 the multitude of your *m* turn
77:9 he shut off his *m* in anger
79:8 Let your *m* confront us
103:4 with loving-kindness and *m*
119:77 Let your *m* come to me
119:156 Many are your *m*, O Jehovah
145:9 *m* are over all his works
Pr 12:10 *m* of the wicked ones are
Isa 47:6 You showed them no *m*
54:7 with great *m* I shall collect
63:7 according to his *m* and
63:15 your *m*? Toward me they
Jer 16:5 even loving-kindness and *m*
42:12 I shall give to you *m*, and
La 3:22 his *m* . . . not come to an end
Da 2:18 ask for *m* on the part of the
9:9 our God belong the *m* and the
9:18 according to your many *m*
Ho 2:19 in loving-kindness and in *m*
Zec 1:16 return to Jerusalem with *m*
7:9 loving-kindness and *m*
2Co 1:3 Father of tender *m* and the

Merciful
Ex 34:6 Jehovah, a God *m* and gracious
De 4:31 Jehovah your God is a *m* God
2Ch 30:9 your God is gracious and *m*
Ne 9:17 gracious and *m*, slow to anger
9:31 you are a God gracious and *m*
Ps 78:38 But he was *m*; he would cover
86:15 Jehovah, are a God *m* and
103:8 Jehovah is *m* and gracious
111:4 Jehovah is gracious and *m*
112:4 He is gracious and *m* and
145:8 Jehovah is gracious and *m*
Joe 2:13 for he is gracious and *m*
Am 1:11 ruined his own *m* qualities
Jon 4:2 a God gracious and *m*, slow to
Mt 5:7 Happy are the *m*, since they
Lu 6:36 *m*, just as your Father is
6:36 just as your Father is *m*
Heb 2:17 a *m* and faithful high priest
8:12 I shall be *m* to their
Jas 5:11 tender in affection and *m*

Mercifully
Lu 10:37 The one that acted *m* toward

Merciless
Ro 1:31 no natural affection, *m*

Mercy
Ex 33:19 I will show *m* to the one to
33:19 to whom I may show *m*
De 13:17 and may indeed give you *m*
13:17 he may certainly show you *m*
30:3 show you *m* and collect you
2Ki 13:23 had *m* upon them and turned
2Ch 30:9 sons will be objects of *m*
Ne 9:19 abundant *m* did not leave them
9:27 accord with your abundant *m*
9:28 accord with your abundant *m*
9:31 your abundant *m* you did not
Ps 102:13 you will have *m* on Zion
103:13 father shows *m* to his sons
103:13 Jehovah has shown *m* to
116:5 our God is One showing *m*
Pr 28:13 will be shown *m*
Isa 9:17 widows he will have no *m*
14:1 Jehovah will show *m* to
27:11 Maker will show it no *m*
30:18 rise up to show you *m*
54:8 I will have *m* upon you, your
54:10 Jehovah, the One having *m*
55:7 Jehovah, who will have *m*
60:10 certainly have *m* upon you
Jer 12:15 have *m* upon them and will
13:14 I shall not have the *m* to
21:7 compassion or have any *m*
42:12 have *m* upon you and return
50:42 cruel and will show no *m*
La 3:32 will also certainly show *m*
Eze 39:25 *m* upon all the house of
Da 1:9 *m* before the principal court
4:27 showing *m* to the poor ones
Ho 1:6 I shall no more show *m* again
1:7 house of Judah I shall show *m*
2:1 sisters, O woman shown *m*
2:4 her sons I shall not show *m*
2:23 I will show *m* to her who
2:23 her who was not shown *m*
14:3 fatherless boy is shown *m*
Mic 7:19 He will again show us *m*
Hab 3:2 to show *m* may you remember
Zec 1:12 not show *m* to Jerusalem and
10:6 for I will show them *m*
Mt 5:7 since they will be shown *m*
6:2 when you go making gifts of *m*
6:3 when making gifts of *m*, do
6:4 gifts of *m* may be in secret
9:13 I want *m*, and not sacrifice
9:27 Have *m* on us, Son of David
12:7 I want *m*, and not sacrifice
15:22 Have *m* on me, Lord, Son of
17:15 Lord, have *m* on my son
18:33 had *m* on your fellow slave
18:33 as I also had *m* on you
20:30 have *m* on us, Son of David!
20:31 have *m* on us, Son of David!
23:23 namely, justice and *m* and
Mr 5:19 and the *m* he had on you
10:47 Jesus, have *m* on me!
10:48 Son of David, have *m* on me!
Lu 1:50 his *m* is upon those who fear
1:54 to call to mind *m*
1:58 Jehovah had magnified his *m*
1:72 the *m* in connection with our
11:41 as gifts of *m* the things
12:33 and give gifts of *m*
16:24 *m* on me and send Lazarus
17:13 Instructor, have *m* on us!
18:38 Son of David, have *m* on me!
18:39 Son of David, have *m* on me
Ac 3:2 in order to ask gifts of *m*
3:3 requesting to get gifts of *m*
3:10 sit for gifts of *m* at the
9:36 and gifts of *m* that she was
10:2 he made many gifts of *m* to
10:4 gifts of *m* have ascended as
10:31 your gifts of *m* have been
24:17 gifts of *m* to my nation
Ro 9:15 I will have *m* upon whomever
9:15 upon whomever I do have *m*
9:16 but upon God, who has *m*
9:18 upon whom he wishes he has *m*
9:23 his glory upon vessels of *m*
11:30 shown *m* because of their
11:31 with *m* resulting to you
11:31 also may now be shown *m*
11:32 might show all of them *m*
12:8 he that shows *m*, let him do
15:9 might glorify God for his *m*
1Co 7:25 had *m* shown him by the Lord
2Co 4:1 to the *m* that was shown us
Ga 6:16 upon them be peace and *m*
Eph 2:4 God, who is rich in *m*, for
Php 2:27 but God had *m* on him, in
1Ti 1:2 undeserved kindness, *m*, peace
1:13 I was shown *m*, because I
1:16 reason why I was shown *m*
2Ti 1:2 *m*, peace from God the Father
1:16 May the Lord grant *m* to the
1:18 the Lord grant him to find *m*
Tit 3:5 according to his *m* he saved
Heb 4:16 that we may obtain *m* and
Jas 2:13 not practice *m* will have his
2:13 have his judgment without *m*
2:13 *M* exults triumphantly over
3:17 full of *m* and good fruits
1Pe 1:3 according to his great *m* he
2:10 who had not been shown *m*
2:10 those who have been shown *m*
2Jo 3 undeserved kindness, *m* and
Jude 2 May *m* and peace and love be
21 waiting for the *m* of our Lord
22 *m* to some that have doubts
23 continue showing *m* to others

Mere
Jg 19:22 *m* good-for-nothing men
1Sa 16:7 *m* man sees what appears to
2Ki 8:13 your servant, who is a *m* dog
Es 7:4 had been sold for *m* men slaves
7:4 for *m* maidservants, I should
Job 5:6 not from *m* dust does what is
5:6 from *m* ground trouble does
6:26 sayings . . . are for *m* wind
11:2 a *m* boaster be in the right
13:25 make a *m* leaf . . . quiver
13:25 chasing after *m* dry stubble
15:3 *m* utterances will be of no
15:31 *m* worthlessness will prove
20:11 it will lie down in *m* dust
27:18 his house like a *m* moth
30:24 against a *m* heap of ruins
35:16 he multiplies *m* words
41:9 down at the *m* sight of it
41:27 It regards iron as *m* straw
41:27 Copper as *m* rotten wood
41:28 for it into *m* stubble
41:29 regarded by it as *m* stubble
Ps 18:44 At *m* hearsay they will be
63:10 become a *m* portion for foxes
73:22 as *m* beasts from your
78:33 an end as if a *m* exhalation
90:5 they become a *m* sleep
102:11 dried up like *m* vegetation
103:16 *m* wind has to pass over it
144:4 to a *m* exhalation
Pr 1:7 are what *m* fools have despised
14:5 witness launches forth *m* lies
14:25 one launches forth *m* lies
23:13 discipline from the *m* boy
23:21 will clothe one with *m* rags
24:8 called a *m* master at evil
26:6 that is drinking *m* violence
26:8 giving glory to a *m* stupid
28:21 over a *m* piece of bread
29:5 a *m* net for his steps
29:19 be corrected by *m* words, for
Ec 2:23 This too is *m* vanity
5:10 *m* lover of silver will not be
6:2 although a *m* foreigner may eat
7:7 *m* oppression may make a wise
10:17 not for *m* drinking
Ca 2:1 *m* saffron of the coastal plain
Isa 3:4 *m* arbitrary power will rule
3:12 *m* women actually rule over
5:24 *m* dried grass sinks down
7:24 become *m* thornbushes and
10:19 *m* boy will be able to
10:21 *m* remnant will return, the
10:22 *m* remnant among them will
11:3 judge by any *m* appearance to
11:6 *m* little boy will be leader
17:2 become *m* places for droves
24:12 crushed to a *m* rubble heap
30:7 Egyptians are *m* vanity, and
30:22 you will say to it: *M* dirt!
31:1 those who rely on *m* horses
32:6 speak *m* senselessness, and
40:12 in the *m* hollow of his hand
40:12 with a *m* span and included
40:15 as *m* fine dust
40:19 cast a *m* molten image, and
40:23 judges . . . as a *m* unreality
41:2 driven about like *m* stubble
42:24 given Jacob for *m* pillage

Isa 44:10 or cast a *m* molten image
44:19 into a *m* detestable thing
50:9 A *m* moth will eat them up
51:6 will die like a *m* gnat
51:12 rendered as *m* green grass
58:5 *m* sackcloth and ashes as his
59:5 the *m* cobweb of a spider
59:6 *m* cobweb will not serve as
65:20 for one will die as a *m* boy
Jer 2:31 I become a *m* wilderness to
7:11 a *m* cave of robbers in your
9:4 walk around as a *m* slanderer
10:3 a *m* tree out of the forest
10:8 A tree is a *m* exhortation of
15:9 I shall give the *m* remnant
15:13 I shall give for *m* plunder
17:3 I shall give for *m* plunder
20:18 to their end in *m* shame
22:5 become a *m* devastated place
22:28 Coniah a *m* form despised
26:18 plowed up as a *m* field
26:18 become *m* heaps of ruins
31:22 *m* female will press around
32:30 *m* doers of what was bad in
46:17 king of Egypt is a *m* noise
46:19 Make for yourself *m* baggage
46:19 *m* object of astonishment
48:9 *m* object of astonishment
48:27 *m* object of ridicule to you
48:34 will become *m* desolations
50:23 *m* object of astonishment
51:41 *m* object of astonishment
51:62 *m* desolate wastes to time
La 1:8 has become a *m* abhorrent thing
3:45 You make us *m* offscouring and
5:3 *m* orphans without a father
5:8 *M* servants have ruled over us
5:13 *m* boys have stumbled
5:15 been changed into *m* mourning
Eze 12:20 become a *m* desolate waste
28:9 you are a *m* earthling man
44:2 no *m* man will come in by it
Da 5:23 praised *m* gods of silver and
Ho 4:7 exchanged for *m* dishonor
5:9 a *m* object of astonishment
8:6 A *m* craftsman made it, and it
8:6 will become *m* splinters
13:2 sacrificers . . . kiss *m* calves
Am 2:6 righteous for *m* silver
5:7 justice into *m* wormwood, and
8:6 buy lowly people for *m* silver
8:6 we may sell *m* refuse of grain
Jon 4:10 a *m* growth of a night and
4:10 as a *m* growth of a night
Mic 3:12 be plowed up as a *m* field
3:12 become *m* heaps of ruins, and
Hab 1:3 keep looking upon *m* trouble
1:9 it comes for *m* violence
1:15 brought up with a *m* fishhook

Mered
1Ch 4:17 the sons of Ezrah . . . *M*
4:18 Bithiah . . . whom *M* took

Merely
De 12:26 *M* your holy things that will
Jg 15:13 we shall *m* tie you, and we
Job 2:10 accept *m* what is good from
9:29 is it that I toil *m* in vain
15:3 *M* reproving with a word
15:28 *m* resides in cities that
30:31 came to be *m* for mourning
31:7 has walked *m* after my eyes
32:9 not those *m* abundant in days
Pr 6:14 sending out *m* contentions
14:23 *m* the word of the lips tends
28:8 *m* for the one showing favor
Ec 2:26 bringing together *m* to give
9:18 *m* one sinner can destroy much
10:6 *m* in a low condition
12:5 afraid *m* at what is high, and
Isa 3:24 to be *m* a musty smell
29:13 *m* with their lips, and
32:13 of my people *m* thorns
Jer 9:5 tired . . . *m* in doing wrong
Eze 4:11 you will drink *m* by measure
Da 4:35 considered as *m* nothing, and
Mic 3:11 judge *m* for a bribe, and
Hab 2:13 tire . . . out *m* for nothing
2Co 8:5 not *m* as we had hoped, but

Meremoth
Ezr 8:33 *M* the son of Urijah the
10:36 Vaniah, *M*, Eliashib
Ne 3:4 *M* the son of Urijah the son of
3:21 *M* the son of Urijah the son
Ne 10:5 Harim, *M*, Obadiah
12:3 Shecaniah, Rehum, *M*

Meres
Es 1:14 *M* . . . seven princes of Persia

Meribah
Ex 17:7 *M*, because of the quarreling
Nu 20:13 These are the waters of *M*
20:24 respecting the waters of *M*
27:14 These are the waters of *M*
De 32:51 the waters of *M* of Kadesh
33:8 with him by the waters of *M*
Ps 81:7 at the waters of *M*
95:8 harden your heart as at *M*
106:32 at the waters of *M*

Meribath-kadesh
Eze 47:19 to the waters of *M*, the
48:28 to the waters of *M*, to

Merib-baal
1Ch 8:34 And Jonathan's son was *M*
8:34 *M* . . . father to Micah
9:40 the son of Jonathan was *M*
9:40 As for *M*, he became father

Merit
1Pe 2:20 For what *m* is there in it if

Merodach
Jer 50:2 *M* has become terrified

Merodach-baladan
Isa 39:1 *M* the son of Baladan the

Merom
Jos 11:5 at the waters of *M* to fight
11:7 along the waters of *M* by

Meronothite
1Ch 27:30 there was Jehdeiah the *M*
Ne 3:7 Jadon the *M*, did repair work

Meroz
Jg 5:23 Curse *M*, said the angel of

Merriment
Pr 21:17 He that is loving *m* will be

Merry
Jg 16:25 because their heart was *m*
2Sa 13:28 heart is in a *m* mood with
1Ki 8:66 feeling *m* of heart over all
21:7 and let your heart be *m*
Es 1:10 king's heart was in a *m* mood
5:9 joyful and *m* of heart; but as

Mesha
Ge 10:30 from *M* as far as Sephar
2Ki 3:4 As regards *M* the king of Moab
1Ch 2:42 sons of Caleb . . . *M*
8:9 and Zibia and *M* and Malcam

Meshach
Da 1:7 and to Mishael, *M*; and to
2:49 appointed . . . Shadrach, *M* and
3:12 whom you appointed . . . *M*
3:13 said to bring in . . . *M* and
3:14 Is it really so, O . . . *M*
3:16 *M* . . . saying to the king
3:19 Shadrach, *M* and Abednego
3:20 said to bind Shadrach, *M* and
3:22 men that took up Shadrach, *M*
3:23 *M* . . . fell down bound in the
3:26 *M* . . . step out and come here
3:26 Shadrach, *M* and Abednego were
3:28 God of Shadrach, *M* and
3:29 the God of Shadrach, *M* and
3:30 *M* . . . to prosper in the

Meshech
Ge 10:2 sons of Japheth . . . *M* and
1Ch 1:5 sons of Japheth . . . *M* and
Ps 120:5 resided as an alien in *M*
Eze 27:13 *M* themselves were your
32:26 *M* and Tubal and all her
38:2 head chieftain of *M* and
38:3 Gog, you head chieftain of *M*
39:1 Gog, you head chieftain of *M*

Meshelemiah
1Ch 9:21 Zechariah the son of *M* was
26:1 Of the Korahites, *M* the son
26:2 *M* had sons: Zechariah the
26:9 And *M* had sons and brothers

Meshezabel
Ne 3:4 Berechiah the son of *M* did
10:21 *M*, Zadok, Jaddua
11:24 *M* of the sons of Zerah the

Meshillemith
1Ch 9:12 son of *M* the son of Immer

Meshillemoth
2Ch 28:12 Berechiah the son of *M*
Ne 11:13 *M* the son of Immer

Meshobab
1Ch 4:34 And *M* and Jamlech and

Meshullam
2Ki 22:3 Azaliah the son of *M*
1Ch 3:19 sons of Zerubbabel were *M*
5:13 *M* and Sheba and Jorai and
8:17 and *M* and Hizki and Heber
9:7 son of *M* the son of Hodaviah
9:8 *M* the son of Shephatiah the
9:11 *M* the son of Zadok the son
9:12 *M* the son of Meshillemith
2Ch 34:12 *M*, from the sons of the
Ezr 8:16 I sent for . . . *M*, head ones
10:15 and *M* and Shabbethai the
10:29 of the sons of Bani, *M*
Ne 3:4 *M* the son of Berechiah the
3:6 *M* the son of Besodeiah
3:30 *M* the son of Berechiah
6:18 *M* the son of Berechiah
8:4 Hash-baddanah, Zechariah and *M*
10:7 *M*, Abijah, Mijamin
10:20 Magpiash, *M*, Hezir
11:7 *M* the son of Joed the son of
11:11 *M* the son of Zadok the son
12:13 for Ezra, *M*; for Amariah
12:16 Zechariah; for Ginnethon, *M*
12:25 *M*, Talmon, Akkub were
12:33 Azariah, Ezra and *M*

Meshullemeth
2Ki 21:19 *M* the daughter of Haruz

Mesopotamia
Ge 24:10 to *M* to the city of Nahor
De 23:4 son of Beor from Pethor of *M*
Jg 3:8 the king of *M*; and the sons
1Ch 19:6 and horsemen from *M* and
Ac 2:9 inhabitants of *M*, and Judea
7:2 Abraham while he was in *M*

Message
1Ki 14:6 sent to you with a severe *m*
Pr 30:1 son of Jakeh, the weighty *m*
31:1 weighty *m* that his mother
Lu 1:2 the *m* delivered these to us
Ac 26:20 *m* that they should repent
2Th 2:2 or through a verbal *m* or
2:15 through a verbal *m* or
1Jo 1:5 *m* which we have heard from
3:11 *m* which you have heard from

Messenger
1Sa 23:27 *m* that came to Saul, saying
2Sa 11:19 command the *m*, saying
11:22 *m* went and came and told
11:23 *m* went on to say to David
11:25 David said to the *m*: This
1Ki 19:2 Jezebel sent a *m* to Elijah
22:13 the *m* that had gone to call
2Ki 5:10 Elisha sent a *m* to him
6:32 Before the *m* could come in
6:32 as soon as the *m* comes
6:33 the *m* coming down to him
9:18 The *m* came as far as to
10:8 the *m* came in and told him
2Ch 18:12 *m* that went to call
Job 1:14 *m* to Job, and he proceeded
33:23 If there exists for him a *m*
Pr 13:17 *m* that is wicked will fall
17:11 cruel is the *m* that is sent
Isa 42:19 who is deaf as my *m* whom
63:9 own personal *m* saved them
Eze 23:40 there was sent a *m*, then
Hag 1:13 And Haggai the *m* of Jehovah
Mal 2:7 the *m* of Jehovah of armies
3:1 I am sending my *m*, and he
3:1 the *m* of the covenant in
Mt 11:10 am sending forth my *m*
Mr 1:2 Look! I am sending forth my *m*
Lu 7:27 I am sending forth my *m*

Messenger's
2Sa 4:10 me to give him the *m* fee
Hag 1:13 *m* commission from Jehovah

Messengers
Ge 32:3 Jacob sent *m* ahead of him to
32:6 the *m* returned to Jacob
Nu 20:14 Moses sent *m* from Kadesh to
21:21 Israel now sent *m* to Sihon

Nu 22:5 sent *m* to Balaam the son of
24:12 to your *m* whom you sent to
De 2:26 sent *m* from the wilderness
Jos 6:17 hid the *m* whom we sent out
6:25 she hid the *m* whom Joshua
7:22 At once Joshua sent *m*, and
Jg 6:35 *m* through all of Manasseh
6:35 *m* through Asher and Zebulun
7:24 Gideon sent *m* into all the
9:31 So he sent *m* by subterfuge to
11:12 Jephthah sent *m* to the king
11:13 said to the *m* of Jephthah
11:14 sent once more *m* to the king
11:17 Israel sent *m* to the king of
11:19 Israel sent *m* to Sihon the
1Sa 6:21 sent *m* to the inhabitants of
11:3 *m* into all the territory of
11:4 *m* came to Gibeah of Saul and
11:7 by the hand of the *m*, saying
11:9 said to the *m* that had come
11:9 *m* came and told the men of
16:19 Saul sent *m* to Jesse and
19:11 Saul sent *m* to David's
19:14 Saul now sent *m* to take
19:15 Saul sent the *m* to see
19:16 *m* came in, why, there was
19:20 Saul sent *m* to take David
19:20 came to be upon Saul's *m*
19:21 immediately sent other *m*
19:21 Saul sent *m* again, the
25:14 David sent *m* from the
25:42 accompanying the *m* of David
2Sa 2:5 David sent *m* to the men of
3:12 Abner sent *m* to David on
3:14 David sent *m* to Ish-bosheth
3:26 sent *m* after Abner, and
5:11 send *m* to David, and also
11:4 David sent *m* that he might
12:27 Joab sent *m* to David and
1Ki 20:2 he sent *m* to Ahab the king
20:5 the *m* came back and said
20:9 said to the *m* of Ben-hadad
20:9 the *m* went off and brought
2Ki 1:2 he sent *m* and said to them
1:3 the *m* of the king of Samaria
1:5 the *m* came back to him, he
1:16 *m* to inquire of Baal-zebub
7:15 *m* returned and reported to
14:8 Amaziah sent *m* to Jehoash
16:7 sent *m* to Tiglath-pileser
17:4 *m* to So the king of Egypt
19:9 he sent *m* again to Hezekiah
19:14 out of the hand of the *m*
19:23 By means of your *m* you have
1Ch 14:1 *m* to David and cedar timbers
19:2 David sent *m* to comfort him
19:16 send *m* and bring out the
2Ch 35:21 sent *m* to him, saying
36:15 by means of his *m*, sending
36:16 jest at the *m* of the true
Ne 6:3 So I sent *m* to them, saying
Job 4:18 *m* he charges with faultiness
Pr 16:14 means *m* of death, but the
Isa 14:32 to the *m* of the nation
18:2 Go, you swift *m*, to a nation
33:7 *m* of peace will weep
37:9 at once sent *m* to Hezekiah
37:14 out of the hand of the *m*
44:26 the counsel of his own *m*
Jer 27:3 by the hand of the *m* who
Eze 17:15 in sending his *m* to Egypt
23:16 send *m* to them in Chaldea
30:9 In that day *m* will go forth
Na 2:13 the voice of your *m* be heard
Lu 7:24 the *m* of John had gone away
9:52 he sent forth *m* in advance of
Jas 2:25 received the *m* hospitably

Messiah
Da 9:25 until *M* the Leader, there
9:26 *M* will be cut off, with
Joh 1:41 We have found the *M*
4:25 I know that *M* is coming

Met
Ge 32:1 angels of God now *m* up with
33:8 travelers that I have *m*
Ex 4:27 *m* him in the mountain of the
De 25:18 he *m* you in the way and
Jos 11:5 all these kings *m* together
2Sa 2:13 *m* together by the pool of
1Ki 16:22 Tibni *m* death, and Omri
Ne 13:2 not *m* the sons of Israel with
Job 2:11 *m* together by appointment
Ps 48:4 have *m* by appointment
Ps 85:10 trueness they have *m* each
Pr 22:2 one of little means have *m*
29:13 man of oppressions have *m*
Isa 64:5 *m* up with the one exulting
Am 3:3 they have *m* by appointment
Mt 8:28 *m* him two demon-possessed
28:9 Jesus *m* them and said: Good
Mr 5:2 a man . . . *m* him from among
Lu 8:27 man . . . had demons *m* him
9:37 a great crowd *m* him
17:12 ten leprous men *m* him, but
23:24 for their demand to be *m*
Joh 4:51 slaves *m* him to say that his
11:20 Jesus was coming, *m* him
11:30 place where Martha *m* him
12:18 crowd . . . also *m* him
18:2 Jesus had many times *m* there
Ac 10:25 Cornelius *m* him, fell down
13:6 *m* up with a certain man, a
16:16 girl with a spirit . . . *m* us
2Th 1:10 *m* with faith among you
Heb 7:1 *m* Abraham returning from the
7:10 when Melchizedek *m* him

Metal
Nu 16:38 into thin *m* plates as an
33:52 their images of molten *m*
Jer 6:27 I have made you a *m* tester
1Co 13:12 by means of a *m* mirror

Metalworker
Isa 40:19 with gold the *m* overlays it
41:7 went strengthening the *m*
46:6 They hire a *m*, and he makes
Jer 10:9 and of the hands of a *m*
10:14 Every *m* will certainly feel
51:17 Every *m* will feel ashamed

Metheg-ammah
2Sa 8:1 David got to take *M* out of

Methods
1Co 4:17 put you in mind of my *m* in

Methuselah
Ge 5:21 Enoch . . . became father to *M*
5:22 after his fathering *M* Enoch
5:25 *M* lived on for a hundred and
5:26 after his fathering Lamech *M*
5:27 all the days of *M* amounted
1Ch 1:3 Enoch, *M*, Lamech
Lu 3:37 son of *M*, son of Enoch, son

Methushael
Ge 4:18 Mehujael became father to *M*
4:18 *M* became father to Lamech

Meting
Lu 21:22 are days for *m* out justice

Meunim
1Ch 4:41 the *M* that were to be found
2Ch 26:7 in Gurbaal and the *M*
Ezr 2:50 the sons of *M*
Ne 7:52 the sons of *M*, the sons of

Mezahab
Ge 36:39 Matred the daughter of *M*
1Ch 1:50 Matred, the daughter of *M*

Mezobaite
1Ch 11:47 and Obed and Jaasiel the *M*

Mibhar
1Ch 11:38 *M* the son of Hagri

Mibsam
Ge 25:13 Kedar and Adbeel and *M*
1Ch 1:29 Kedar and Adbeel and *M*
4:25 Shallum his son, *M* his son

Mibzar
Ge 36:42 sheik Teman, sheik *M*
1Ch 1:53 sheik Teman, sheik *M*

Mica
2Sa 9:12 young son whose name was *M*
1Ch 9:15 son of *M* the son of Zichri
Ne 10:11 *M*, Rehob, Hashabiah
11:22 *M* of the sons of Asaph

Micah
Jg 17:1 whose name was *M*
17:5 *M*, he had a house of gods
17:8 as far as the house of *M*
17:9 *M* said to him: Where do you
17:10 So *M* said to him: Do dwell
17:12 *M* filled the hand of the
17:12 continue in the house of *M*
17:13 *M* said: Now I do know that
18:2 house of *M* and got to spend
18:3 close by the house of *M*, they
Jg 18:4 *M* did for me that he might
18:13 as far as the house of *M*
18:15 the house of *M*, and began to
18:18 went into the house of *M* and
18:22 away from the house of *M*
18:22 close by the house of *M* were
18:23 to *M*: What is the matter
18:26 *M* got to see that they were
18:27 they took what *M* had made
18:31 kept the carved image of *M*
1Ch 5:5 *M* his son, Reaiah his son
8:34 Merib-baal . . . father to *M*
8:35 sons of *M* were Pithon and
9:40 Merib-baal . . . father to *M*
9:41 sons of *M* were Pithon and
23:20 of Uzziel were *M* the head
24:24 The sons of Uzziel, *M*; of
24:24 of the sons of *M*, Shamir
24:25 brother of *M* was Isshiah
2Ch 34:20 Abdon the son of *M*
Ne 11:17 *M* the son of Zabdi the son
Jer 26:18 *M* of Moresheth himself
Mic 1:1 of Jehovah that occurred to *M*

Micah's
Jg 17:4 and it got to be in *M* house

Micaiah
1Ki 22:8 *M* the son of Imlah
22:9 bring *M* the son of Imlah
22:13 that had gone to call *M*
22:14 *M* said: As Jehovah is
22:15 *M*, shall we go to
22:24 struck *M* upon the cheek
22:25 At that *M* said: Look! You
22:26 Take *M* and turn him back to
22:28 *M* said: If you return at all
2Ki 22:12 Achbor the son of *M*
2Ch 13:2 *M* the daughter of Uriel of
17:7 *M*, to teach in the cities
18:7 He is *M* the son of Imlah
18:8 Bring *M* the son of Imlah
18:12 that went to call *M*
18:13 *M* said: As Jehovah is
18:14 *M*, shall we go to
18:23 struck *M* on the cheek and
18:24 *M* said: Look! You are
18:25 Take *M* and turn him back
18:27 *M* said: If you return at
Ne 12:35 *M* the son of Zaccur the son
12:41 *M*, Elioenai, Zechariah
Jer 36:11 *M* the son of Gemariah the
36:13 *M* proceeded to tell them

Michael
Nu 13:13 Sethur the son of *M*
1Ch 5:13 *M* and Meshullam and Sheba
5:14 of *M*, the son of Jeshishai
6:40 of *M*, the son of Baaseiah
7:3 sons of Izrahiah were *M* and
8:16 *M* . . . the sons of Beriah
12:20 from Manasseh . . . *M* and
27:18 Issachar, Omri the son of *M*
2Ch 21:2 Jehoshaphat's sons . . . *M* and
Ezr 8:8 Zebadiah the son of *M*
Da 10:13 *M*, one of the foremost
10:21 *M*, the prince of you people
12:1 *M* will stand up, the great
Jude 9 when *M* the archangel had a
Re 12:7 *M* and his angels battled with

Michal
1Sa 14:49 name of the younger one *M*
18:20 *M*, Saul's daughter, was in
18:27 In turn Saul gave him *M* his
18:28 As for *M*, Saul's daughter
19:11 *M* his wife told David
19:12 *M* had David descend through
19:13 *M* took the teraphim image
19:17 Saul said to *M*: Why did you
19:17 *M* said to Saul: He himself
25:44 Saul, he had given *M* his
2Sa 3:13 bring *M*, Saul's daughter
3:14 give over my wife *M*, whom
6:16 *M*, Saul's daughter, herself
6:20 *M*, Saul's daughter, came on
6:21 David said to *M*: It was
6:23 *M*, Saul's daughter, she came
21:8 and the five sons of *M*
1Ch 15:29 *M*, Saul's daughter, herself

Michmas
Ezr 2:27 the men of *M*, a hundred and
Ne 7:31 the men of *M*, a hundred and

Michmash
1Sa 13:2 came to be with Saul at *M*

1Sa 13:5 *M* to the east of Beth-aven
13:11 collected together at *M*
13:16 they had encamped in *M*
13:23 to the ravine pass of *M*
14:5 pillar on the north facing *M*
14:31 from *M* to Aijalon, and the
Ne 11:31 *M* and Aija and Bethel and
Isa 10:28 *M* he deposits his articles

Michmethath
Jos 16:6 *M* was on the north, and the
17:7 came to be from Asher to *M*

Michri
1Ch 9:8 son of Uzzi the son of *M*, and

Midday
De 28:29 one who gropes about at *m*
Ne 8:3 from daybreak till *m*, in front
Job 5:14 grope about at *m* as if at
11:17 brighter than *m* will your
Ps 37:6 And your justice as the *m*
91:6 that despoils at *m*
Ca 1:7 make the flock lie down at *m*
Isa 58:10 your gloom will be like *m*
Jer 6:4 and let us go up at *m*
15:8 the despoiler at *m*. I will
20:16 signal at the time of *m*
Ac 22:6 close to Damascus, about *m*
26:13 I saw at *m* on the road

Middin
Jos 15:61 wilderness Beth-arabah, *M*

Middle
Ge 2:9 tree of life in the *m* of the
3:3 tree that is in the *m* of the
37:7 sheaves in the *m* of the field
Ex 2:5 the ark in the *m* of the reeds
26:28 *m* bar at the center of the
28:32 at its top in the *m* of it
36:33 *m* bar to run through at the
36:33 the *m* of the panel frames
39:23 sleeveless coat was in the *m*
Nu 2:17 Levites will be in the *m* of
35:5 with the city in the *m*
De 3:16 the *m* of the torrent valley
4:12 out of the *m* of the fire
4:15 out of the *m* of the fire
4:33 out of the *m* of the fire the
4:36 heard from the *m* of the fire
5:4 out of the *m* of the fire
5:22 out of the *m* of the fire, the
5:23 out of the *m* of the darkness
5:24 out of the *m* of the fire
5:26 out of the *m* of the fire as
9:10 out of the *m* of the fire
10:4 out of the *m* of the fire
13:16 the *m* of its public square
32:51 in the *m* of the sons of
32:51 the *m* of the sons of Israel
Jos 3:17 in the *m* of the Jordan as
4:3 from the very *m* of the Jordan
4:5 to the *m* of the Jordan, and
4:8 from the *m* of the Jordan
4:9 set up in the *m* of the Jordan
4:10 in the *m* of the Jordan until
4:18 out of the *m* of the Jordan
8:13 into the *m* of the low plain
10:13 in the *m* of the heavens
12:2 the *m* of the torrent valley
13:9 the *m* of the torrent valley
13:16 the *m* of the torrent valley
Jg 7:19 start of the *m* night watch
9:51 in the *m* of the city, there
15:4 right in the *m*
16:29 two *m* pillars upon which
1Sa 9:14 into the *m* of the city, why
9:18 in the *m* of the gate and
10:10 a prophet in the *m* of them
10:23 in the *m* of the people, he
11:11 into the *m* of the camp
2Sa 4:6 came into the *m* of the house
7:2 in the *m* of tent cloths
20:12 in the *m* of the highway
23:12 stand in the *m* of the tract
24:5 the *m* of the torrent valley
1Ki 3:8 in the *m* of your people
3:20 got up in the *m* of the night
6:6 the *m* one was six cubits in
6:8 they would go up to the *m* one
6:8 the *m* one up to the third
6:13 the *m* of the sons of Israel
6:27 toward the *m* of the house
8:64 the *m* of the courtyard that
14:7 out of the *m* of your people
2Ki 6:20 were in the *m* of Samaria
2Ki 20:4 the *m* court when Jehovah's
1Ch 11:14 stand in the *m* of the tract
2Ch 6:13 in the *m* of the enclosure
7:7 *m* of the courtyard that was
20:14 the *m* of the congregation
32:4 through the *m* of the land
Es 4:1 into the *m* of the city and cry
Job 34:20 even in the *m* of the night
Ps 22:22 In the *m* of the congregation
57:4 My soul is in the *m* of lions
74:4 the *m* of your meeting place
78:28 fall in the *m* of his camp
82:1 *m* of the gods he judges
136:14 pass through the *m* of it
Pr 8:20 *m* of the roadways of
Isa 5:2 build a tower in the *m* of it
Jer 21:4 into the *m* of this city
39:3 and sit down in the *M* Gate
Eze 15:4 *m* of it does get scorched
41:7 by the *m* story
42:5 than the *m* ones, as regards
42:6 the *m* ones from the floor
Zec 14:4 must be split at its *m*
Mt 25:6 in the *m* of the night there
Lu 23:45 curtain . . . rent down the *m*
Joh 19:18 but Jesus in the *m*
Ac 16:25 the *m* of the night Paul and
Heb 2:12 in the *m* of the congregation
Re 22:2 down the *m* of its broad way

Midheaven
De 4:11 burning with fire up to *m*
Re 8:13 I heard an eagle flying in *m*
14:6 angel flying in *m*, and he
19:17 all the birds that fly in *m*

Midian
Ge 25:2 and *M* and Ishbak and Shuah
25:4 sons of *M* were Ephah and
Ex 2:15 dwell in the land of *M*
2:16 the priest of *M* had seven
3:1 Jethro, the priest of *M*, whose
4:19 Jehovah said to Moses in *M*
18:1 Now Jethro the priest of *M*
Nu 22:4 to say to the older men of *M*
22:7 the older men of *M* traveled
25:15 of a paternal house in *M*
25:18 daughter of a chieftain of *M*
31:3 that they may serve against *M*
31:3 Jehovah's vengeance upon *M*
31:7 went waging war against *M*
31:8 they killed the kings of *M*
31:8 the five kings of *M*; and they
31:9 carried off the women of *M*
Jos 13:21 chieftains of *M*, Evi and
Jg 6:1 gave them into the hand of *M*
6:2 hand of *M* came to prevail over
6:2 Due to *M* the sons of Israel
6:3 if Israel sowed seed, *M* and
6:6 impoverished due to *M*; and the
6:7 for aid on account of *M*
6:11 out of the sight of *M*
6:13 gives us into the palm of *M*
6:16 strike down *M* as if one man
6:33 And all *M* and Amalek and the
7:1 camp of *M* happened to be on
7:2 to give *M* into their hand
7:7 I will give *M* into your hand
7:8 camp of *M*, it happened to be
7:12 Now *M* and Amalek and all the
7:13 the camp of *M*. Then it came
7:14 God has given *M* and all the
7:15 the camp of *M* into your hand
7:23 and they went chasing after *M*
7:24 meet *M* and capture ahead of
7:25 princes of *M*, namely, Oreb
7:25 pursuing *M*, and they brought
8:1 to fight against *M*? And they
8:5 and Zalmunna, the kings of *M*
8:22 saved us out of the hand of *M*
8:26 the kings of *M* and besides
8:28 *M* was subdued before the sons
10:12 *M*, when they oppressed you
1Ki 11:18 rose up out of *M* and came
1Ch 1:32 *M* and Ishbak and Shuah
1:33 sons of *M* were Ephah and
1:46 defeated *M* in the field of
Ps 83:9 Do to them as to *M*, as to
Isa 9:4 to pieces as in the day of *M*
10:26 defeat of *M* by the rock
60:6 young male camels of *M* and
Hab 3:7 tent cloths of the land of *M*
Ac 7:29 resident in the land of *M*

Midianite
Ge 37:28 *M* merchants, went passing
Nu 10:29 Hobab the son of Reuel the *M*
25:6 a *M* woman before Moses' eyes
25:15 *M* woman fatally struck was

Midianites
Ge 36:35 Hadad . . . defeated the *M* in
37:36 the *M* sold him into Egypt
Nu 25:17 a harassing of the *M*, and
31:2 Take vengeance . . . upon the *M*

Midianitess
Nu 25:14 fatally struck with the *M*

Midian's
Jg 6:14 save Israel out of *M* palm
8:3 *M* princes Oreb and Zeeb, and
8:12 got to capture *M* two kings
9:17 deliver you out of *M* hand

Midnight
Ex 11:4 Jehovah has said, About *m* I
12:29 at *m* Jehovah struck every
Jg 16:3 Samson kept lying till *m* and
16:3 rose at *m* and grabbed hold of
Ru 3:8 at *m* that the man began to
Ps 119:62 At *m* I get up to give
Mr 13:35 late in the day or at *m*
Lu 11:5 go to him at *m* and say to
Ac 20:7 prolonged his speech until *m*
27:27 at *m* the sailors began to

Midst
Ge 9:21 uncovered himself in the *m* of
18:24 fifty righteous men in the *m*
18:26 men in the *m* of the city
19:29 send Lot out of the *m* of the
23:6 of God you are in the *m* of us
23:9 *m* of you for the possession of
35:2 gods that are in the *m* of you
40:20 in the *m* of his servants
41:48 he put in the *m* of it
45:6 famine in the *m* of the earth
48:16 a multitude in the *m* of the
Ex 3:2 fire in the *m* of a thornbush
3:4 out of the *m* of the thornbush
3:20 acts that I shall do in the *m*
7:5 Israel out from their *m*
8:22 Jehovah in the *m* of the earth
11:4 going out into the *m* of Egypt
12:31 out from the *m* of my people
12:49 as an alien in your *m*
14:16 go through the *m* of the sea
14:22 the *m* of the sea on dry land
14:23 into the *m* of the sea
14:27 off into the *m* of the sea
14:29 land in the *m* of the seabed
15:19 through the *m* of the sea
17:7 Is Jehovah in our *m* or not?
23:25 malady away from your *m*
24:16 from the *m* of the cloud
24:18 into the *m* of the cloud and
25:8 tabernacle in the *m* of them
28:1 the *m* of the sons of Israel
29:45 I will tabernacle in the *m*
29:46 tabernacle in the *m* of them
31:14 be cut off from the *m* of his
33:3 shall not go up in the *m* of
33:5 into the *m* of you and
33:11 withdraw from the *m* of the
34:9 go along in the *m* of us
34:10 people in the *m* of whom you
34:12 itself a snare in your *m*
Le 15:31 tabernacle . . . in their *m*
16:16 *m* of their uncleannesses
16:29 as an alien in your *m*
17:8 as an alien in your *m* who
17:10 alien in their *m* who eats
17:12 alien in your *m* should eat
17:13 alien in your *m* who in
18:26 as an alien in your *m*
20:14 may not continue in your *m*
22:32 the *m* of the sons of Israel
24:10 *m* of the sons of Israel, and
25:33 possession in the *m* of the
26:11 tabernacle in the *m* of you
26:12 walk in the *m* of you and
26:25 pestilence into the *m* of you
Nu 5:3 *m* of whom I am tabernacling
5:21 oath in the *m* of your people
9:7 *m* of the sons of Israel
11:4 crowd that was in the *m* of
11:20 Jehovah, who is in your *m*
11:21 people in the *m* of whom I am
13:32 saw in the *m* of it are men

Nu 14:13 people up out of their *m*
14:42 Jehovah is not in your *m*
14:44 away from the *m* of the camp
15:14 in your *m* for generations of
15:26 as an alien in their *m*
15:29 as an alien in their *m*
16:3 and Jehovah is in their *m*
16:21 from the *m* of this assembly
16:33 the *m* of the congregation
16:45 from the *m* of this assembly
16:47 the *m* of the congregation
18:20 no share . . . in their *m*
18:20 the *m* of the sons of Israel
18:23 the *m* of the sons of Israel
18:24 the *m* of the sons of Israel
19:6 *m* of the burning of the cow
19:10 as an alien in their *m* as a
19:20 the *m* of the congregation
23:21 loud hailing . . . is in his *m*
25:7 from the *m* of the assembly
25:11 no rivalry . . . in the *m* of
27:4 from the *m* of his family
27:4 *m* of our father's brothers
27:7 *m* of their father's brothers
32:30 then be settled in your *m*
33:8 through the *m* of the sea to
35:15 the settler in the *m* of them
35:34 *m* of which I am residing
35:34 the *m* of the sons of Israel
De 1:42 because I am not in your *m*
2:14 from the *m* of the camp, just
2:15 out of the *m* of the camp
2:16 from the *m* of the people
4:3 God annihilated from your *m*
4:5 in the *m* of the land to which
4:34 the *m* of another nation
6:15 Jehovah your God in your *m* is
7:21 Jehovah your God is in your *m*
11:3 did in the *m* of Egypt
11:6 in the *m* of all Israel
13:1 arises in your *m* and does
13:5 clear . . . evil from your *m*
13:11 bad thing again in your *m*
13:13 gone out from your *m* that
13:14 has been done in your *m*
15:11 to be in the *m* of the land
16:11 in your *m*, in the place
17:2 found in your *m* in one of
17:7 what is bad from your *m*
17:20 his sons in the *m* of Israel
18:2 in the *m* of his brothers
18:15 A prophet from your own *m*
18:18 from the *m* of their brothers
19:2 in the *m* of your land that
19:10 in the *m* of your land that
19:19 what is bad from your *m*
19:20 bad like this in your *m*
21:8 innocent blood in the *m* of
21:9 innocent blood from your *m*
21:12 into the *m* of your house
21:21 what is bad from your *m*
22:2 home into the *m* of your house
22:21 what is bad from your *m*
22:24 what is evil from your *m*
23:10 come into the *m* of the camp
23:11 come into the *m* of the camp
24:7 what is bad from your *m*
26:11 resident who is in your *m*
28:43 resident who is in your *m*
29:11 who is in the *m* of your camp
29:16 through the *m* of the nations
31:16 in their very *m*, and they
31:17 our God is not in our *m* that
Jos 1:11 through the *m* of the camp
3:2 through the *m* of the camp
3:5 do wonderful things in your *m*
3:10 a living God is in your *m*
4:6 may serve as a sign in your *m*
6:25 dwells in the *m* of Israel
7:12 to destruction out of your *m*
7:13 is in your *m*, O Israel
7:13 to destruction from your *m*
7:21 in the *m* of my tent with the
7:23 from the *m* of the tent and
8:9 in the *m* of the people
8:35 who walked in their *m*
9:22 are dwelling in our very *m*
10:1 were continuing in their *m*
13:13 dwelling in the *m* of Israel
14:3 an inheritance in their *m*
15:13 the *m* of the sons of Judah
16:9 in the *m* of the inheritance
17:4 in the *m* of our brothers
17:4 in the *m* of the brothers of
Jos 17:6 inheritance in the *m* of his
17:9 *m* of the cities of Manasseh
19:1 *m* of the inheritance of the
19:9 the *m* of their inheritance
19:49 the son of Nun in their *m*
20:9 as an alien in their *m*
21:41 in the *m* of the possession
22:19 and get settled in our *m*
22:31 that Jehovah is in our *m*
24:5 what I did in its *m*; and
24:17 peoples through the *m* of
Jg 10:16 foreign gods from their *m*
18:1 *m* of the tribes of Israel
18:20 into the *m* of the people
20:42 down to ruin in their *m*
1Sa 4:3 come into our *m* and may save
7:3 the foreign gods from your *m*
15:6 the *m* of the Amalekites
15:6 from the *m* of Amalek
16:13 in the *m* of his brothers
2Sa 1:25 fallen in the *m* of battle
2Ki 9:2 from the *m* of his brothers
Ne 4:22 in the *m* of Jerusalem
9:11 through the *m* of the sea on
Es 9:28 from the *m* of the Jews and
Job 15:19 through the *m* of them
20:13 back in the *m* of his palate
Ps 36:1 is in the *m* of his heart
46:5 God is in the *m* of the city
48:9 In the *m* of your temple
57:6 have fallen into the *m* of it
74:11 *m* of your bosom to make an
74:12 in the *m* of the earth
109:18 waters into the *m* of him
110:2 in the *m* of your enemies
116:19 the *m* of you, O Jerusalem
135:9 into the *m* of you, O Egypt
136:11 Israel out of the *m* of them
137:2 poplar trees in the *m* of her
138:7 walk in the *m* of distress
143:4 *m* of me my heart shows
147:13 your sons in the *m* of you
Pr 4:21 them in the *m* of your heart
5:14 in the *m* of the congregation
5:15 of the *m* of your own well
14:33 in the *m* of stupid ones
22:13 the *m* of the public squares
Isa 5:8 in the *m* of the land
5:25 in the *m* of the streets
6:12 in the *m* of the land
7:22 the *m* of the land will eat
10:23 in the *m* of the whole land
12:6 great in the *m* of you is the
16:3 night in the *m* of noontime
16:11 *m* of me over Kir-hareseth
19:1 Egypt will melt in the *m* of
19:3 bewildered in the *m* of it
19:14 *m* of her the spirit of
19:19 *m* of the land of Egypt
19:24 in the *m* of the earth
24:13 become in the *m* of the land
25:11 his hands in the *m* of it
29:23 in the *m* of him, they will
38:10 In the *m* of my days I will
41:18 in the *m* of the valley
52:11 get out from the *m* of her
58:9 remove from your *m* the yoke
Jer 6:1 from the *m* of Jerusalem
6:6 oppression in the *m* of her
9:6 is in the *m* of deception
12:14 uproot from the *m* of them
12:16 in the *m* of my people
14:9 in the *m* of us, O Jehovah
29:32 in the *m* of this people
30:21 from the *m* of him his own
37:4 into the *m* of the people
37:12 in the *m* of the people
39:14 in the *m* of the people
40:1 *m* of all the exiles of
40:5 in the *m* of the people; or
40:6 *m* of the people who were
41:7 came into the *m* of the city
41:7 into the *m* of the cistern
41:8 in the *m* of their brothers
44:7 out of the *m* of Judah, so
46:21 soldiers in the *m* of her
48:45 flame from the *m* of Sihon
50:8 out of the *m* of Babylon
50:37 company that are in the *m*
51:6 Flee out of the *m* of Babylon
51:45 Get out of the *m* of her
51:47 will fall in the *m* of her
51:63 the *m* of the Euphrates
52:25 found in the *m* of the city
La 1:15 aside from the *m* of me
1:20 overturned in the *m* of me
3:45 in the *m* of the peoples
4:13 in the *m* of her those pouring
Eze 1:1 in the *m* of the exiled people
1:4 out of the *m* of it there was
1:4 out of the *m* of the fire
1:5 out of the *m* of it there was
1:16 to be in the *m* of a wheel
2:5 prophet . . . in the *m* of them
3:15 stunned in the *m* of them
3:25 go forth in the *m* of them
5:2 fire in the *m* of the city as
5:4 into the *m* of the fire and
5:5 *m* of the nations I have set
5:8 *m* of you judicial decisions
5:10 eat sons in the *m* of you
5:12 to their end in the *m* of you
6:7 fall in the *m* of you, and you
6:13 the *m* of their dungy idols
7:4 *m* of you your own detestable
7:9 to be right in the *m* of you
9:4 through the *m* of the city
9:4 through the *m* of Jerusalem
9:4 are being done in the *m* of it
10:10 to be in the *m* of a wheel
11:1 in the *m* of them Jaazaniah
11:7 have put in the *m* of her
11:7 out of the *m* of her
11:9 out of the *m* of her and give
11:11 to be flesh in the *m* of her
11:23 from over the *m* of the city
12:2 the *m* of a rebellious house
12:10 who are in the *m* of them
12:12 chieftain who is in the *m*
12:24 *m* of the house of Israel
13:14 to an end in the *m* of her
14:8 off from the *m* of my people
14:9 the *m* of my people Israel
14:14 *m* of it, Noah, Daniel and
14:16 three men in the *m* of it
14:18 three men in the *m* of it
14:20 Daniel and Job in the *m* of
16:53 captive ones in the *m* of
17:16 *m* of Babylon he will die
18:18 in the *m* of his peoples
19:6 walk about in the *m* of lions
20:8 the *m* of the land of Egypt
21:32 to be in the *m* of the land
22:3 her *m* till her time comes
22:7 defrauding in the *m* of you
22:9 carried on in the *m* of you
22:13 proved to be in the *m* of
22:18 lead in the *m* of a furnace
22:19 into the *m* of Jerusalem
22:20 into the *m* of a furnace
22:21 liquefied in the *m* of her
22:22 in the *m* of a furnace
22:22 liquefied in the *m* of her
22:25 prophets in the *m* of her
22:25 multiplied in the *m* of her
22:26 profaned in the *m* of them
22:27 princes in the *m* of her are
23:39 done in the *m* of my house
24:5 cook its bones in the *m* of
24:7 come to be right in the *m* of
24:11 liquefied in the *m* of it
26:5 in the *m* of the sea
26:12 in the very *m* of the water
26:15 slaughter in the *m* of you
27:27 who are in the *m* of you
27:32 silence in the *m* of the sea
27:34 *m* of you they have fallen
28:14 *m* of fiery stones you
28:16 the *m* of you with violence
28:16 the *m* of the fiery stones
28:18 a fire from the *m* of you
28:22 glorified in the *m* of you
28:23 must fall in the *m* of her
29:3 in the *m* of his Nile canals
29:4 the *m* of your Nile canals
29:12 in the *m* of desolated lands
29:12 *m* of devastated cities for
29:21 in the *m* of them
30:7 in the *m* of desolated lands
30:7 the *m* of devastated cities
31:14 *m* of the sons of mankind
31:17 in the *m* of nations
31:18 the *m* of the uncircumcised
32:20 In the *m* of those slain by
32:21 speak out of the *m* of Sheol
32:25 In the *m* of slain ones they
32:25 In the *m* of slain ones he
32:28 the *m* of uncircumcised ones

Eze 32:32 the *m* of the uncircumcised
33:33 proved to be in the *m* of
34:12 in the *m* of his sheep that
34:24 chieftain in the *m* of them
36:23 profaned in the *m* of them
37:1 the *m* of the valley plain
37:26 sanctuary in the *m* of them
37:28 in the *m* of them to time
39:7 in the *m* of my people Israel
43:7 *m* of the sons of Israel to
43:9 reside in the *m* of them to
44:9 the *m* of the sons of Israel
46:10 the chieftain in their *m*
47:22 as aliens in your *m*, who
47:22 to sons in the *m* of you
47:22 *m* of the tribes of Israel
48:8 prove to be in the *m* of it
48:10 prove to be in the *m* of it
48:15 come to be in the *m* of it
48:21 prove to be in the *m* of it
Da 3:23 *m* of the burning . . . furnace
3:24 bound into the *m* of the fire
3:25 free in the *m* of the fire
3:26 out from the *m* of the fire
4:10 a tree in the *m* of the earth
8:16 man in the *m* of the Ulai, and
Ho 5:4 fornication in the *m* of them
11:9 the Holy One in the *m* of you
Joe 2:27 that I am in the *m* of Israel
Am 2:3 from the *m* of her, and all
3:9 disorders in the *m* of her
5:17 pass through the *m* of you
7:8 in the *m* of my people Israel
Mic 2:12 in the *m* of its pasture
3:3 in the *m* of a cooking pot
3:11 Jehovah in the *m* of us
5:7 in the *m* of many peoples
5:8 in the *m* of many peoples
5:10 horses from the *m* of you
5:13 pillars from the *m* of you
5:14 sacred poles from the *m* of
6:14 emptiness will be in the *m*
7:14 in the *m* of an orchard
Na 3:13 are women in the *m* of you
Hab 2:19 no breath at all in the *m* of
3:2 In the *m* of the years O bring
3:2 In the *m* of the years may
Zep 2:14 And in the *m* of her, droves
3:3 princes in the *m* of her were
3:5 was righteous in the *m* of her
3:11 remove from the *m* of you
3:12 let remain in the *m* of you a
3:15 Jehovah, is in the *m* of you
3:17 your God is in the *m* of you
Zec 2:4 animals in the *m* of her
2:5 glory . . . in the *m* of her
2:10 will reside in the *m* of you
2:11 will reside in the *m* of you
5:4 lodge in the *m* of his house
5:7 sitting in the *m* of the ephah
5:8 back into the *m* of the ephah
8:3 reside in the *m* of Jerusalem
8:8 reside in the *m* of Jerusalem
14:1 apportioned out in the *m* of
Mt 18:2 he set it in their *m*
18:20 there I am in their *m*
Mr 6:47 boat was in the *m* of the sea
7:31 *m* of the regions of Decapolis
9:36 child, stood it in their *m*
14:60 high priest rose in their *m*
Lu 2:46 in the *m* of the teachers and
4:30 went through the *m* of them
4:35 the man down in their *m*
17:11 through the *m* of Samaria and
17:21 kingdom of God is in your *m*
21:21 let those in the *m* of her
22:27 I am in your *m* as the one
22:55 in the *m* of the courtyard
24:36 stood in their *m* and said to
Joh 1:26 In the *m* of you one is
20:19 stood in their *m* and said
20:26 he stood in their *m* and
Ac 1:15 in the *m* of the brothers and
1:18 he noisily burst in his *m*
2:22 did through him in your *m*
4:7 stood them in their *m* and
17:22 in the *m* of the Areopagus
17:33 Paul went out from their *m*
23:10 and snatch him from their *m*
27:21 Paul stood up in the *m* of
1Co 5:2 be taken away from your *m*
1Th 2:7 became gentle in the *m* of you
2Pe 3:5 and in the *m* of water by
Re 1:13 in the *m* of the lampstands
2:1 in the *m* of the seven golden
4:6 in the *m* of the throne and
5:6 in the *m* of the throne and
5:6 in the *m* of the elders a lamb
6:6 voice as if in the *m* of the
7:17 Lamb, who is in the *m* of the

Midwife
Ge 35:17 the *m* said to her: Do not be
38:28 the *m* at once took and tied
Ex 1:19 birth before the *m* can come

Midwives
Ex 1:15 Hebrew *m*, the name of one of
1:17 the *m* feared the true God
1:18 king of Egypt called the *m*
1:19 the *m* said to Pharaoh
1:20 God dealt well with the *m*
1:21 *m* had feared the true God

Migdal-el
Jos 19:38 and *M*, Horem and Beth-anath

Migdal-gad
Jos 15:37 Zenan and Hadashah and *M*

Migdol
Ex 14:2 between *M* and the sea in
Nu 33:7 they went camping before *M*
Jer 44:1 ones dwelling in *M* and in
46:14 publish it in *M*, and
Eze 29:10 from *M* to Syene and to the
30:6 From *M* to Syene they will

Might*
Ex 15:2 My strength and my *m* is Jah
De 8:17 the full *m* of my own hand
2Ch 32:9 all his imperial *m* with him
Job 30:21 the full *m* of your hand
Ps 68:35 giving . . . *m* to the people
118:14 Jah is my shelter and my *m*
Isa 12:2 is my strength and my *m*
40:29 he makes full *m* abound
47:9 the full *m* of your spells
63:15 your zeal and your full *m*
Da 2:37 given the kingdom, the *m*
4:30 with the strength of my *m*
Na 3:9 Ethiopia was her full *m*, also
Col 1:11 the extent of his glorious *m*
1Ti 6:16 be honor and *m* everlasting
1Pe 4:11 *m* are his forever and ever
5:11 To him be the *m* forever
Jude 25 *m* and authority for all past
Re 1:6 to him be the glory and the *m*
5:13 the glory and the *m* forever

Mightier
Ex 1:7 multiplying and growing *m* at
1:9 more numerous and *m* than we
Nu 14:12 greater and *m* than they are
22:6 for they are *m* than I am
De 4:38 nations greater and *m* than
9:1 nations greater and *m* than you
9:14 a nation *m* and more populous
2Sa 1:23 *M* than the lions they were
Ps 65:3 have proved *m* than I am
105:24 *m* than their adversaries
Isa 42:13 he will show himself *m*

Mightiest
Pr 30:30 lion, which is the *m* among

Mightily
Lu 1:51 has performed *m* with his arm

Mightiness
Jg 5:31 the sun goes forth in its *m*
8:21 for as a man is, so is his *m*
1Ki 15:23 Asa and all his *m* and all
16:5 Baasha and . . . his *m*
16:27 Omri, what he did and his *m*
22:45 *m* with which he acted and
2Ki 10:34 that he did and all his *m*
13:8 all that he did and his *m*
13:12 Jehoash . . . and his *m*
14:15 Jehoash . . . and his *m*
14:28 Jeroboam . . . and his *m*
18:20 counsel and *m* for the war
20:20 Hezekiah and all his *m* and
1Ch 29:11 the *m* and the beauty and
29:12 there are power and *m*, and
29:30 all his kingship and his *m*
2Ch 20:6 in your hand power and *m*
Es 10:2 his energetic work and his *m*
Job 12:13 there are wisdom and *m*
39:19 Can you give to the horse *m*?
41:12 Or the matter of its *m*
Ps 21:13 and make melody to your *m*
54:1 with your *m* may you plead my
65:6 He is indeed girded with *m*
66:7 He is ruling by his *m* to time
71:16 I shall come in grand *m*
71:18 are to come, about your *m*
80:2 do rouse up your *m*
89:13 An arm with *m* is yours
90:10 special *m* they are eighty
106:8 So as to make his *m* known
145:11 your *m* they will speak
147:10 *m* of the horse does he take
150:2 for his works of *m*
Pr 8:14 I—understanding; I have *m*
Ec 9:16 Wisdom is better than *m*; yet
10:17 for *m*, not for mere drinking
Isa 3:25 fall, and your *m* by war
11:2 spirit of counsel and of *m*
28:6 *m* to those turning away the
30:15 *m* will prove to be simply
33:13 who are nearby, my *m*
36:5 counsel and *m* for the war
Jer 9:23 because of his *m*
10:6 your name is great in *m*
16:21 to know my hand and my *m*
23:10 and their *m* is not right
49:35 the beginning of their *m*
51:30 Their *m* has run dry
Eze 32:29 in their *m*, were put with
32:30 because of their *m*, ashamed
Da 2:20 wisdom and *m*—for they belong
2:23 and *m* you have given to me
Mic 3:8 justice and *m*, in order to
7:16 ashamed of all their *m*
Eph 1:19 operation of the *m* of his
6:10 and in the *m* of his strength

Mighty
Ge 6:4 the *m* ones who were of old
10:8 start in becoming a *m* one in
10:9 displayed himself a *m* hunter
10:9 Just like Nimrod a *m* hunter in
18:18 become a nation great and *m*
Ex 1:20 people . . . becoming very *m*
15:11 *m* in holiness? The One to be
32:18 singing over *m* performance
De 3:24 *m* performances like yours
7:1 nations more populous and *m*
10:17 great, *m* and fear-inspiring
26:5 great nation, *m* and numerous
Jos 1:14 all the valiant *m* men, and
6:2 valiant *m* men, into your hand
8:3 men, valiant *m* ones, and to
10:2 and all its men were *m* ones
10:7 and all the valiant *m* men
23:9 *m* nations from before you
Jg 5:13 down to me against the *m* ones
5:23 Jehovah with the *m* ones
6:12 with you, you valiant, *m* one
11:1 had become a *m*, valiant man
Ru 2:1 a man *m* in wealth, of the
1Sa 2:4 The *m* men of the bow are
9:1 a man *m* in wealth
14:52 When Saul saw any *m* man or
16:18 he is a valiant, *m* man and
17:51 that their *m* one had died
2Sa 1:19 How have the *m* men fallen!
1:21 shield of *m* ones was
1:22 from the fat of *m* ones
1:25 *m* ones fallen in the midst
1:27 *m* ones fallen And the
10:7 all the army and the *m* men
16:6 the *m* men were at his right
17:8 men of his, that they are *m*
17:10 your father is a *m* man and
20:7 *m* men went out after him
22:26 With the faultless, *m* one
23:8 *m* men that belonged to David
23:9 the three *m* men with David
23:16 three *m* men forced their
23:17 things the three *m* men did
23:22 like the three *m* men
1Ki 1:8 *m* men that belonged to David
1:10 the *m* men and Solomon his
11:28 was a valiant, *m* man
2Ki 5:1 proved to be a valiant, *m* man
15:20 all the valiant, *m* men
24:14 and all the valiant, *m* men
24:16 the *m* men carrying on war
1Ch 1:10 a *m* one in the earth
5:24 *m* fellows, men of fame
7:2 Of Tola there were valiant, *m*
7:5 of Issachar were valiant, *m*
7:7 valiant, *m* men; and their
7:9 valiant, *m* men, was twenty
7:11 valiant, *m* men, seventeen

1Ch 7:40 select, valiant, *m* men
8:40 valiant, *m* men, bending the
9:13 *m* men of ability for the
9:26 there were four *m* men of
11:10 heads of the *m* men that
11:11 the *m* men that belonged to
11:12 was among the three *m* men
11:19 that the three *m* men did
11:24 name among the three *m* men
11:26 the *m* men of the military
12:1 they were among the *m* men
12:4 a *m* man among the thirty
12:8 *m* men, army men for the
12:21 were *m* men of valor, and
12:25 the *m* men of valor of the army
12:28 a young man, *m* in valor
12:30 *m* men of valor, men of
19:8 all the army and the *m* men
26:6 they were capable, *m* men
26:31 *m* men came to be found
27:6 Benaiah was a *m* man of the
28:1 and the *m* men, even every
28:1 even every valiant, *m* man
29:24 the princes and the *m* men
2Ch 13:3 four hundred thousand *m* men
13:3 chosen men, valiant, *m*
14:8 these were valiant, *m* men
17:13 *m* men, were in Jerusalem
17:14 thousand valiant, *m* men
17:16 thousand valiant, *m* men
17:17 valiant, *m* man Eliada, and
25:6 *m* men for a hundred silver
26:12 of the valiant, *m* men, was
28:7 Zichri, a *m* man of Ephraim
32:3 *m* men to stop up the waters
32:21 efface every valiant, *m* man
Ezr 7:28 the *m* princes of the king
Ne 3:16 as the House of the *M* Ones
9:32 the God great, *m* and
11:14 brothers, *m* men of valor
Job 16:14 He runs at me like a *m* one
26:14 of his *m* thunder who can
36:5 God is *m* and will not reject
36:5 He is *m* in power of heart
Ps 19:5 It exults as a *m* man does to
20:6 *m* acts of his right hand
24:8 Jehovah strong and *m*
24:8 Jehovah *m* in battle
33:16 A *m* man himself is not
38:19 my enemies . . . became *m*
45:3 upon your thigh, O *m* one
52:1 what is bad, O you *m* one
78:65 *m* one sobering up from wine
89:19 placed help upon a *m* one
103:20 *m* in power, carrying out
106:2 *m* performances of Jehovah
112:2 *M* in the earth his offspring
117:2 loving-kindness has proved *m*
120:4 Sharpened arrows of a *m* man
127:4 in the hand of a *m* man
145:4 your *m* acts they will tell
145:12 sons of men his *m* acts
Pr 16:32 is better than a *m* man, and
18:18 lot . . . separates even the *m*
21:22 scaled . . . the city of *m* men
30:26 badgers are a people not *m*
Ec 9:11 nor the *m* ones the battle
Ca 3:7 Sixty *m* men are all around it
3:7 from the *m* men of Israel
4:4 circular shields of the *m* men
Isa 1:29 ashamed of the *m* trees that
3:2 *m* man and warrior, judge and
5:22 who are *m* in drinking wine
8:7 *m* and the many waters of the
9:6 *M* God, Eternal Father, Prince
10:21 of Jacob, to the *M* God
13:3 called my *m* ones for
16:14 be a trifling few, not *m*
17:12 like the noise of *m* waters
21:17 *m* men of the sons of Kedar
31:1 because they are very *m*
42:13 Like a *m* man Jehovah
49:24 be taken from a *m* man
49:25 captives of the *m* man will
53:12 with the *m* ones that he
60:22 the small one a *m* nation
Jer 5:16 all of them are *m* men
9:3 they proved *m* in the land
9:23 let not the *m* man brag about
14:9 like a *m* man that is unable
20:11 like a terrible *m* one
26:21 Jehoiakim and . . . *m* men
32:18 the *m* One, Jehovah of
46:5 *m* men themselves are
Jer 46:6 not the *m* man try to escape
46:9 And let the *m* men go forth
46:12, 12 *m* man against *m* man
48:14 We are *m* men and men of
48:41 *m* men of Moab must become
49:22 of the *m* men of Edom will
50:9 *m* man causing bereavement
50:36 sword against her *m* men
51:30 *m* men of Babylon have
51:56 *m* men will certainly be
51:57 and her *m* men drunk, and
Eze 32:12 the very swords of *m* ones
32:21 foremost men of the *m* ones
32:27 not lie down with *m* ones
32:27 *m* ones were a terror in the
39:18 flesh of *m* ones you will
39:20 *m* persons and all sorts of
Da 4:3 and how *m* his wonders are
8:8 as soon as it became *m*, the
8:24 his power must become *m*, but
8:24 bring *m* ones to ruin, also
11:3 *m* king will certainly stand
11:23 *m* by means of a little
11:25 great and *m* military force
Ho 10:13 the multitude of your *m* ones
Joe 1:6 a nation . . . *m* and without
2:2 a people numerous and *m*
2:5 *m* people, drawn up in battle
2:11 carrying out his word is *m*
Am 2:14 *m* man will provide his soul
2:16 strong . . . among the *m* men
5:12 how *m* your sins are, O you
Ob 9 *m* men must become terrified
Mic 4:3 *m* nations far away
4:7 removed far off a *m* nation
Na 2:3 The shield of his *m* men is
Zep 1:14 a *m* man is letting out a
3:17 As a *m* One, he will save
Zec 8:22 many peoples and *m* nations
9:13 as the sword of a *m* man
10:5 like *m* men stamping down in
10:7 become just like a *m* man
Ac 19:20 a *m* way the word of Jehovah
1Co 16:13 carry on as men, grow *m*
Eph 3:16 to be made *m* in the man you
1Pe 5:6 under the *m* hand of God

Migratory
Le 11:22 the *m* locust according to

Migron
1Sa 14:2 pomegranate tree . . . in *M*
Isa 10:28 passed along through *M*

Mijamin
1Ch 24:9 the fifth, for *M* the sixth
Ezr 10:25 of the sons of Parosh . . . *M*
Ne 10:7 Meshullam, Abijah, *M*
12:5 *M*, Maadiah, Bilgah

Mikloth
1Ch 8:32 *M* . . . father to Shimeah
9:37 and Ahio and Zechariah and *M*
9:38 *M* . . . father to Shimeam
27:4 and *M* was the leader, and in

Mikneiah
1Ch 15:18 *M*, and Obed-edom and Jeiel
15:21 *M* and Obed-edom and Jeiel

Miktam
Ps 16:*super* A *m* of David
56:*super* Of David. *M*. When the
57:*super* Of David. *M*. When he ran
58:*super* Of David. *M*
59:*super* Of David. *M*. When Saul
60:*super* *M*. Of David. For teaching

Milalai
Ne 12:36 *M*, Gilalai, Maai, Nethanel

Milcah
Ge 11:29 name of Nahor's wife was *M*
11:29 Haran, the father of *M* and
22:20 *M* herself has also borne
22:23 eight *M* bore to Nahor the
24:15 Bethuel the son of *M* the
24:24 Bethuel the son of *M*, whom
24:47 whom *M* bore to him
Nu 26:33 of Zelophehad . . . *M* and
27:1 daughters of Zelophehad . . . *M*
36:11 *M* and Noah, the daughters of
Jos 17:3 Noah, Hoglah, *M* and Tirzah

Milcom
1Ki 11:5 *M* the disgusting thing of
11:33 to *M* the god of the sons of
2Ki 23:13 *M* the detestable thing of

Mild
Pr 15:1 answer, when *m*, turns away
25:15 *m* tongue itself can break a
1Pe 3:4 of the quiet and *m* spirit
3:15 with a *m* temper and deep

Mildew
De 28:22 sword and scorching and *m*
1Ki 8:37 *m*, locusts, cockroaches
2Ch 6:28 in case scorching and *m*
Am 4:9 people with scorching and *m*
Hag 2:17 with *m* and with hail

Mildness
1Co 4:21 come . . . and *m* of spirit
2Co 10:1 *m* and kindness of the Christ
Ga 5:23 *m*, self-control. Against such
6:1 such a man in a spirit of *m*
Eph 4:2 lowliness of mind and *m*
Col 3:12 clothe yourselves with . . . *m*
1Ti 6:11 love, endurance, *m* of temper
2Ti 2:25 instructing with *m* those not
Tit 3:2 reasonable, exhibiting all *m*
Jas 1:21 with *m* the implanting of
3:13 a *m* that belongs to wisdom

Mild-tempered
Mt 5:5 Happy are the *m* ones, since
11:29 I am *m* and lowly in heart
21:5 King is coming to you, *m*

Mile
Mt 5:41 into service for a *m*, go

Miles
Mt 5:41 a mile, go with him two *m*
Lu 24:13 a village about seven *m*
Joh 6:19 rowed about three or four *m*
11:18 distance of about two *m*

Miletus
Ac 20:15 day we arrived at *M*
20:17 from *M* he sent to Ephesus
2Ti 4:20 I left Trophimus sick at *M*

Military
Ex 14:4 Pharaoh and all his *m* forces
14:9 cavalrymen and his *m* forces
14:17 Pharaoh and all his *m* forces
14:28 all of Pharaoh's *m* forces
15:4 *m* forces he has cast into the
Nu 31:14 in from the *m* expedition
De 11:4 to the *m* forces of Egypt, to
Jos 22:12 for *m* action against them
1Sa 17:20 the *m* forces were going out
2Sa 8:9 all the *m* force of Hadadezer
24:2 Joab the chief of the *m*
24:4 the chiefs of the *m* forces
24:4 the chiefs of the *m* forces
1Ki 15:20 the chiefs of the *m* forces
20:1 collected all his *m* forces
20:19 and the *m* forces that were
20:25 number a *m* force for
20:25 equal to the *m* force that
2Ki 6:14 and a heavy *m* force there
6:15 *m* force was surrounding the
7:6 the sound of a great *m* force
9:5 chiefs of the *m* force were
11:15 ones of the *m* force
18:17 heavy *m* force to Jerusalem
25:1 *m* force, against Jerusalem
25:5 a *m* force of Chaldeans
25:5 *m* force was scattered
25:10 entire *m* force of Chaldeans
25:23 the chiefs of the *m* forces
25:26 the chiefs of the *m* forces
1Ch 11:26 mighty men of the *m* forces
12:37 the weapons of the *m* army
18:9 all the *m* force of Hadadezer
2Ch 13:3 *m* force of four hundred
14:8 Asa came to have a *m* force
14:9 *m* force of a million men
16:4 chiefs of the *m* forces that
16:7 *m* force of the king of Syria
16:8 great *m* force in multitude
17:2 put *m* forces in all the
23:14 appointed ones of the *m*
24:23 *m* force of Syria came up
24:24 *m* force of the Syrians made
24:24 *m* force of very great
26:11 on *m* service in troops, by
26:13 power of a *m* force to help
28:12 from the *m* campaign
32:6 put *m* chiefs over the people
33:14 chiefs of the *m* force in
Ezr 8:22 ask a *m* force and horsemen
Ne 2:9 chiefs of the *m* force and

Ne 4:2 the *m* force of Samaria, yes
Es 1:3 *m* force of Persia and Media
Ps 33:16 by the abundance of *m* forces
110:3 on the day of your *m* force
136:15 Pharaoh and his *m* force
Isa 36:2 with a heavy *m* force
40:2 *m* service has been fulfilled
43:17 the *m* force and the strong
Jer 32:2 *m* forces of the king of
34:1 Babylon and all his *m* force
34:7 *m* forces of the king of
34:21 *m* forces of the king of
35:11 *m* force of the Chaldeans
35:11 *m* force of the Syrians, and
37:5 *m* force of Pharaoh that came
37:7 *m* force of Pharaoh that is
37:10 *m* force of the Chaldeans
37:11 *m* force of the Chaldeans
37:11 of the *m* force of Pharaoh
38:3 *m* force of the king of
39:1 *m* force came to Jerusalem
39:5 *m* force of the Chaldeans
40:7 chiefs of the *m* forces who
40:13 chiefs of the *m* forces who
41:11 chiefs of the *m* forces
41:13 chiefs of the *m* forces who
41:16 chiefs of the *m* forces who
42:1 chiefs of the *m* forces and
42:8 chiefs of the *m* forces who
43:4 chiefs of the *m* forces and
43:5 chiefs of the *m* forces took
46:2 *m* force of Pharaoh Necho
52:4 he and all his *m* force
52:8 *m* force of the Chaldeans
52:8 own *m* force was scattered
52:14 *m* forces of the Chaldeans
Eze 12:14 all his *m* bands, I shall
17:17 by a great *m* force and by
27:10 to be in your *m* force
27:11 even your *m* force, were
29:18 *m* force perform a great
29:18 his *m* force from Tyre for
29:19 wages for his *m* force
32:31 Pharaoh and all his *m* force
37:10 a very, very great *m* force
38:4 your *m* force, horses and
38:15 even a numerous *m* force
Da 3:20 who were in his *m* force he
10:1 there was a great *m* service
11:7 will come to the *m* force and
11:10 crowd of large *m* forces
11:13 with a great *m* force and
11:25 with a great *m* force; and
11:25 great and mighty *m* force
11:26 *m* force, it will be flooded
Joe 2:11 his voice before his *m* force
2:25 *m* force that I have sent
Ob 11 strangers took his *m* force
Zec 4:6 Not by a *m* force, nor by
9:4 strike down her *m* force
14:12 *m* service against Jerusalem
Mr 6:21 and the *m* commanders and the
Lu 3:14 those in *m* service would ask
Joh 18:12 *m* commander and the
Ac 21:32 sight of the *m* commander
21:33 *m* commander came near and
21:37 said to the *m* commander
22:24 *m* commander ordered him to
22:26 he went to the *m* commander
22:27 *m* commander approached and
22:28 The *m* commander responded
22:29 *m* commander became afraid
23:10 *m* commander became afraid
23:15 clear to the *m* commander
23:17 man off to the *m* commander
23:18 led him to the *m* commander
23:19 The *m* commander took him
23:22 the *m* commander let the
24:22 Lysias the *m* commander
25:23 with *m* commanders as well
Re 6:15 and the *m* commanders and the
19:18 may eat . . . *m* commanders

Milk
Ge 18:8 He then took butter and *m* and
49:12 of his teeth is from *m*
Ex 3:8 land flowing with *m* and honey
3:17 a land flowing with *m* and
13:5 land flowing with *m* and
23:19 boil a kid in its mother's *m*
33:3 a land flowing with *m* and
34:26 a kid in its mother's *m*
Le 20:24 land flowing with *m* and
Nu 13:27 flowing with *m* and honey
14:8 is flowing with *m* and honey
16:13 a land flowing with *m* and
16:14 any land flowing with *m* and
De 6:3 land flowing with *m* and honey
11:9 land flowing with *m* and honey
14:21 boil a kid in its mother's *m*
26:9 a land flowing with *m* and
26:15 land flowing with *m* and
27:3 a land flowing with *m* and
31:20 which flows with *m* and honey
32:14 the herd and *m* of the flock
Jos 5:6 land flowing with *m* and honey
Jg 4:19 opened a skin bottle of *m*
5:25 Water he asked, *m* she gave
5:25 she presented curdled *m*
1Sa 17:18 these ten portions of *m* you
Job 10:10 to pour me out as *m* itself
Pr 27:27 sufficiency of goats' *m* for
30:33 churning of *m* is what brings
Ca 4:11 and *m* are under your tongue
5:1 my wine along with my *m*
5:12 are bathing themselves in *m*
Isa 7:22 of the producing of *m*
28:9 been weaned from the *m*
55:1 Yes, come, buy wine and *m*
60:16 suck the *m* of nations, and
Jer 11:5 land flowing with *m* and
32:22 flowing with *m* and honey
La 4:7 Nazirites . . . whiter than *m*
Eze 20:6 flowing with *m* and honey
20:15 flowing with *m* and honey
25:4 will drink your *m*
Joe 3:18 hills will flow with *m*
1Co 3:2 fed you *m*, not something to
9:7 some of the *m* of the flock
Heb 5:12 need *m*, not solid food
5:13 everyone that partakes of *m*
1Pe 2:2 *m* belonging to the word, that

Mill
Ex 11:5 who is at the hand *m* and
De 24:6 No one should seize a hand *m*
Ec 12:4 the sound of the grinding *m*
Isa 47:2 a hand *m* and grind out flour
Jer 25:10 the sound of the hand *m*
La 5:13 men have lifted up a hand *m*
Mt 24:41 be grinding at the hand *m*
Lu 17:35 grinding at the same *m*

Millet
Isa 28:25 *m*, and barley in the
Eze 4:9 lentils and *m* and spelt, and

Million
1Ch 21:5 *m* one hundred thousand
22:14 and a *m* talents of silver
2Ch 14:9 military force of a *m* men
Mt 18:24 [=*60,000,000* denarii]

Millo
Jg 9:6 house of *M* gathered together
9:20 the house of *M*, and let fire
9:20 the house of *M* and consume

Mills
Nu 11:8 ground it in hand *m* or

Millstone
Jg 9:53 woman pitched an upper *m*
2Sa 11:21 pitched an upper *m* upon
Job 41:24 Yes, cast like a lower *m*
Mt 18:6 *m* such as is turned by an ass
Mr 9:42 finer for him if a *m* such as
Lu 17:2 if a *m* were suspended from
Re 18:21 great *m* and hurled it into
18:22 no sound of a *m* will ever

Mina
Lu 19:16 Lord, your *m* gained ten
19:18 Your *m*, Lord, made five
19:20 your *m*, that I kept laid
19:24 Take the *m* from him and

Minas
1Ki 10:17 three *m* of gold he
2Ch 9:16 three *m* of gold he
Ezr 2:69 five thousand *m*, and a
Ne 7:71 thousand two hundred silver *m*
7:72 two thousand silver *m* and
Lu 19:13 gave them ten *m* and told
19:16 Lord, your mina gained ten *m*
19:18 mina, Lord, made five *m*
19:24 to him that has the ten *m*
19:25 Lord, he has ten *m*!

Mind
Ge 11:6 nothing they may have in *m*
19:29 God kept Abraham in *m* in
50:20 you had evil in *m* against me
50:20 God had it in *m* for good
Jg 18:14 have in *m* what you ought to
1Ki 17:18 to bring my error to *m* and
Ne 4:14 keep in your *m*; and fight for
Job 23:13 he is in one *m*, and who can
Ps 8:4 man that you keep him in *m*
Isa 65:17 will not be called to *m*
La 2:17 has done what he had in *m*
Eze 23:19 calling to *m* the days of
Da 6:14 set his *m* in order to rescue
Am 6:3 Are you putting out of your *m*
Zec 1:6 Jehovah of armies had in *m*
8:14 had in *m* to do what was
8:15 have in *m* in these days to
Mt 22:37 soul and with your whole *m*
26:75 Peter called to *m* the saying
27:63 we have called to *m* that
Mr 3:21 He has gone out of his *m*
5:15 clothed and in his sound *m*
12:12 illustration with them in *m*
12:30 with your whole *m* and with
Lu 1:54 to call to *m* mercy
1:72 call to *m* his holy covenant
8:35 clothed and in his sound *m*
10:11 keep this in *m*, that the
10:27 with your whole *m*, and
20:19 illustration with them in *m*
24:8 they called his sayings to *m*
Joh 2:17 disciples called to *m* that
2:22 disciples called to *m* that
12:16 they called to *m* that these
15:20 Bear in *m* the word I said
Ac 10:19 was going over in his *m*
11:16 I called to *m* the saying of
17:11 the greatest eagerness of *m*
20:3 he made up his *m* to return
20:19 greatest lowliness of *m* and
20:31 and bear in *m* that for three
20:35 bear in *m* the words of the
26:25 truth and of soundness of *m*
28:6 they changed their *m* and
Ro 7:23 against the law of my *m* and
7:25 with my *m* I myself am a
11:34 come to know Jehovah's *m*
12:2 by making your *m* over, that
12:3 think so as to have a sound *m*
14:5 fully convinced in his own *m*
1Co 1:10 fitly united in the same *m*
2:16 to know the *m* of Jehovah
2:16 we do have the *m* of Christ
4:17 put you in *m* of my methods
11:2 you have me in *m* and you are
14:14 but my *m* is unfruitful
14:15 I will also pray with my *m*
14:15 also sing praise with my *m*
14:19 speak five words with my *m*
2Co 5:13 if we were out of our *m*
5:13 if we are sound in *m*, it is
7:15 he calls to *m* the obedience
8:19 and in proof of our ready *m*
9:2 I know your readiness of *m* of
Ga 2:10 we should keep the poor in *m*
6:3 he is deceiving his own *m*
Eph 2:11 keep bearing in *m* that
4:2 with complete lowliness of *m*
4:23 the force actuating your *m*
Php 2:2 in that you are of the same *m*
2:2 holding the one thought in *m*
2:3 but with lowliness of *m*
4:2 be of the same *m* in the Lord
Col 2:18 by his fleshly frame of *m*
3:12 lowliness of *m*, mildness
4:18 bearing my prison bonds in *m*
1Th 1:3 in *m* your faithful work and
2:9 bear in *m*, brothers, our
4:11 and to *m* your own business
1Ti 2:9 modesty and soundness of *m*
2:15 along with soundness of *m*
3:2 sound in *m*, orderly
6:5 men corrupted in *m* and
2Ti 1:7 of love and of soundness of *m*
3:8 completely corrupted in *m*
Tit 1:8 sound in *m*, righteous, loyal
1:10 and deceivers of the *m*
2:2 sound in *m*, healthy in faith
2:5 to be sound in *m*, chaste
2:6 younger men to be sound in *m*
2:12 to live with soundness of *m*
Heb 2:6 man that you keep him in *m*
8:10 will put my laws in their *m*
8:12 call their sins to *m* anymore
10:17 lawless deeds to *m* anymore
12:17 sought a change of *m* with
13:3 Keep in *m* those in prison
1Pe 3:8 compassionate, humble in *m*

1Pe 4:7 Be sound in *m*, therefore
5:5 lowliness of *m* toward one
2Pe 3:12 close in *m* the presence of
Jude 17 call to *m* the sayings that
Re 18:5 her acts of injustice to *m*

Minded
Ro 12:16 Be *m* the same way toward

Mindful
Re 3:3 *m* of how you have received

Minding
Lu 17:7 slave plowing or *m* the flock
Ro 8:6 the *m* of the flesh means death
8:6 *m* of the spirit means life
8:7 *m* of the flesh means enmity
12:16 do not be *m* lofty things

Minds
Lu 24:45 opened up their *m* fully to
Joh 14:26 bring back to your *m* all
Ro 8:5 set their *m* on the things of
2Co 4:4 blinded the *m* . . . unbelievers
11:3 your *m* might be corrupted
Eph 4:17 unprofitableness of their *m*
Php 3:19 *m* upon things on the earth
Col 1:21 your *m* were on the works
3:2 *m* fixed on the things above
Tit 1:15 *m* and their consciences are
3:8 keep their *m* on maintaining
Heb 10:16 in their *m* I shall write
1Pe 1:13 brace up your *m* for activity

Mine*
De 8:9 of which you will *m* copper

Mingled
Ezr 9:2 *m* with the peoples of the
Ps 102:9 drink I have *m* even with
Isa 19:14 has *m* in the midst of her
Re 8:7 a hail and fire *m* with blood
15:2 glassy sea *m* with fire, and

Mingles
Ho 7:8 peoples that he personally *m*

Mingling
Ps 106:35 went *m* with the nations

Miniamin
2Ch 31:15 *M* . . . in office of trust
Ne 12:17 Abijah, Zichri; for *M*
12:41 *M*, Micaiah, Elioenai

Minister
Ex 24:13 Moses and Joshua his *m* got
28:35 be upon Aaron that he may *m*
28:43 go near to the altar to *m* in
29:30 into the tent of meeting to *m*
30:20 go near the altar to *m* in
33:11 his *m* Joshua, the son of Nun
Nu 1:50 they themselves will *m* at it
3:6 and they must *m* to him
3:31 with which they would *m* and
4:9 with which they regularly *m* to
4:12 regularly *m* in the holy place
4:14 with which they regularly *m*
8:26 *m* to his brothers in the tent
11:28 *m* of Moses from his young
16:9 before the assembly to *m* to
18:2 and may *m* to you, to both you
De 17:12 to *m* there to Jehovah your
18:5 *m* in the name of Jehovah
18:7 *m* in the name of Jehovah his
21:5 God has chosen to *m* to him
Jos 1:1 Joshua the son of Nun, the *m*
1Sa 2:11 a *m* of Jehovah before Eli
1Ki 19:21 Elijah and began to *m* to
2Ki 6:15 the *m* of the man of the true
25:14 which they used to *m* they
1Ch 15:2 *m* to him to time indefinite
16:37 *m* before the Ark constantly
23:13 *m* to him and to pronounce
26:12 *m* at the house of Jehovah
2Ch 5:14 were not able to stand to *m*
8:14 *m* in front of the priests
29:11 *m* to him and to continue
31:2 *m* and to give thanks and
Ps 101:6 He it is who will *m* to me
Isa 56:6 to Jehovah to *m* to him and
60:7 they will *m* to you
60:10 own kings will *m* to you
Jer 15:11 I will *m* to you for good
52:18 with which they used to *m*
Eze 40:46 Jehovah to *m* to him
42:14 which they customarily *m*
43:19 to *m* to me, a young bull
44:11 before them to *m* to them
Eze 44:15 come near to *m* to me, and
44:16 to my table to *m* to me
44:17 *m* in the gates of the inner
44:27 *m* in the holy place, he
45:4 approaching to *m* to Jehovah
Mt 4:11 angels came and began to *m*
20:26 great . . . must be your *m*
20:28 to *m* and to give his soul a
23:11 greatest . . . must be your *m*
25:44 in prison and did not *m* to
27:55 from Galilee to *m* to him
Mr 9:35 be last of all and *m* of all
10:43 among you must be your *m*
10:45 to *m* and to give his soul
15:41 *m* to him when he was in
Lu 12:37 will come alongside and *m*
17:8 put on an apron and *m* to me
Joh 12:26 *m* to me, let him follow
12:26 there my *m* will be also
12:26 *m* to me, the Father will
Ro 13:4 God's *m* to you for your good
13:4 God's *m*, an avenger to
15:8 Christ actually became a *m*
15:25 to *m* to the holy ones
15:27 also owe it to *m* publicly to
16:1 sister, who is a *m* of the
1Co 16:15 to *m* to the holy ones
2Co 11:8 provisions in order to *m* to
Ga 2:17 is Christ . . . sin's *m*?
Eph 3:7 a *m* of this according to the
6:21 and faithful *m* in the Lord
Col 1:7 a faithful *m* of the Christ
1:23 I Paul became a *m*
1:25 a *m* of this congregation
4:7 faithful *m* and fellow slave
1Th 3:2 God's *m* in the good news
1Ti 3:13 men who *m* in a fine manner
4:6 will be a fine *m* of Christ
Heb 1:14 sent forth to *m* for those
1Pe 4:11 him *m* as dependent on the

Ministered
Mt 20:28 came, not to be *m* to, but
Mr 10:45 not to be *m* to, but to
Ac 19:22 two of those who *m* to him
Heb 6:10 *m* to the holy ones and

Ministerial
Eph 4:12 for *m* work, for the building
Php 1:1 overseers and *m* servants
1Ti 3:8 *M* servants should likewise
3:12 Let *m* servants be husbands

Ministering
Ex 35:19 for *m* in the sanctuary
39:1 for *m* in the holy place
39:26 for *m*, just as Jehovah had
39:41 for *m* in the sanctuary, the
De 10:8 stand before Jehovah for *m*
1Sa 2:18 Samuel was *m* before Jehovah
3:1 boy Samuel was *m* to Jehovah
1Ki 8:11 to stand to do their *m*
1Ch 27:1 officers that were *m* to the
28:1 those *m* to the king and the
2Ch 13:10 priests are *m* to Jehovah
17:19 ones *m* to the king apart
23:6 and those of the Levites *m*
Ne 10:36 priests that were *m* in the
10:39 and the priests that were *m*
Es 1:10 were *m* to the person of King
Jer 33:22 Levites who are *m* to me
Eze 20:32 in *m* to wood and stone
44:12 *m* to them before their
44:19 in which they were *m*
Da 7:10 thousands that kept *m* to him
Mt 8:15 got up and began *m* to him
Mr 1:13 but the angels were *m* to him
1:31 and she began *m* to them
Lu 4:39 she rose and began *m* to them
8:3 women, who were *m* to them
22:26 acting as chief as the one *m*
22:27 at the table or the one *m*
22:27 in your midst as the one *m*
Joh 2:5 His mother said to those *m*
2:9 although those *m* who had
12:2 Martha was *m*, but Lazarus
Ac 13:2 publicly *m* to Jehovah and
2Ti 4:11 he is useful to me for *m*
Phm 13 *m* to me in the prison bonds
Heb 6:10 the holy ones and continue *m*
1Pe 1:12 they were *m* the things that
4:10 use it in *m* to one another

Ministers
1Ch 6:32 *m* in the singing before the
16:4 some of the Levites as *m*
2Ch 22:8 *m* of Ahaziah, and he
29:11 continue as his *m* and
Ezr 8:17 *m* for the house of our God
Es 2:2 king's attendants, his *m*, said
6:3 king's attendants, his *m*, said
Ps 103:21 *m* of his, doing his will
104:4 His *m* a devouring fire
Isa 61:6 the *m* of our God you will be
Jer 33:21 Levites, the priests, my *m*
Eze 44:11 *m* at posts of oversight
44:11 and *m* at the House
45:4 the *m* of the sanctuary
45:5 the *m* of the house
46:24 *m* of the House boil the
Joe 1:9 *m* of Jehovah, have mourned
1:13 Howl, you *m* of the altar
1:13 sackcloth, you *m* of my God
2:17 priests, the *m* of Jehovah
1Co 3:5 *M* through whom you became
2Co 3:3 written by us as *m*, inscribed
3:6 us to be *m* of a new covenant
6:4 God's *m*, by the endurance of
11:15 *m* also keep transforming
11:15 into *m* of righteousness
11:23 Are they *m* of Christ?
1Ti 3:10 then let them serve as *m*
1Pe 4:11 if anyone *m*, let him

Ministration
Ac 11:29 relief *m* to the brothers
12:25 the relief *m* in Jerusalem

Ministries
1Co 12:5 and there are varieties of *m*

Ministry
Nu 4:12 *m* with which they regularly
2Ch 24:14 utensils for the *m* and for
Ac 1:17 he obtained a share in this *m*
1:25 to take the place of this *m*
6:4 and to the *m* of the word
20:24 the *m* that I received of the
21:19 God did . . . through his *m*
Ro 11:13 I glorify my *m*
12:7 or a *m*, let us be at this
12:7 let us be at this *m*; or he
15:31 *m* which is for Jerusalem
2Co 4:1 *m* according to the mercy
5:18 the *m* of the reconciliation
6:3 *m* might not be found fault
8:4 share in the *m* destined for
9:1 *m* that is for the holy ones
9:12 the *m* of this public service
9:13 the proof that this *m* gives
Col 4:17 Keep watching the *m* which
1Ti 1:12 by assigning me to a *m*
2Ti 4:5 fully accomplish your *m*
Re 2:19 your love and faith and *m* and

Minni
Jer 51:27 kingdoms of Ararat, *M* and

Minnith
Jg 11:33 from Aroer all the way to *M*
Eze 27:17 the wheat of *M* and special

Mint
Mt 23:23 you give the tenth of the *m*
Lu 11:42 you give the tenth of the *m*

Miracle
Ex 7:9 Produce a *m* for yourselves
Ps 71:7 like a *m* to many people

Miracles
Ex 4:21 perform all the *m* that I have
7:3 multiply my signs and my *m* in
11:9 *m* to be increased in the land
11:10 all these *m* before Pharaoh
De 4:34 with signs and with *m* and
6:22 kept putting signs and *m*
7:19 the signs and the *m* and the
26:8 out of Egypt with . . . *m*
29:3 those great signs and *m*
34:11 the signs and the *m* that
1Ch 16:12 His *m* and the judicial
Ne 9:10 signs and *m* against Pharaoh
Ps 78:43 his *m* in the field of Zoan
105:5 His *m* and the judicial
105:27 *m* in the land of Ham
135:9 *m* into the midst of you
Isa 8:18 *m* in Israel from Jehovah of
Jer 32:20 *m* in the land of Egypt
32:21 with *m* and with a strong

Mire
2Sa 22:43 Like the *m* of the streets I
Job 41:30 instrument upon the *m*

Ps 18:42 Like the *m* of the streets
40:2 Out of the *m* of the sediment
69:2 I have sunk down in deep *m*
69:14 Deliver me from the *m*, that
Isa 57:20 tossing up seaweed and *m*
Jer 38:6 was no water, but *m*
38:6 to sink down into the *m*
Mic 7:10 like the *m* of streets
Na 3:14 Get into the *m*, and trample
Zec 9:3 gold like the *m* of the
10:5 stamping down in the *m* of
2Pe 2:22 sow . . . to rolling in the *m*

Miriam
Ex 15:20 *M* the prophetess, Aaron's
15:21 *M* kept responding to the men
Nu 12:1 *M* and Aaron began to speak
12:4 said to Moses and Aaron and *M*
12:5 and called Aaron and *M*
12:10 *M* was struck with leprosy
12:10 Aaron turned toward *M*, and
12:15 *M* was quarantined outside
12:15 not pull away until *M* was
20:1 It was there that *M* died and
26:59 and Moses and *M* their sister
De 24:9 God did to *M* in the way when
1Ch 4:17 she got to conceive *M* and
6:3 of Amram . . . there was *M*
Mic 6:4 Moses, Aaron and *M*

Mirmah
1Ch 8:10 and Jeuz and Sachia and *M*

Mirror
Job 37:18 skies Hard like a molten *m*
1Co 13:12 by means of a metal *m*
Jas 1:23 at his natural face in a *m*

Mirrors
Ex 38:8 the *m* of the women servants
Isa 3:23 hand *m* and the undergarments
2Co 3:18 reflect like *m* the glory of

Miscarriage
Job 3:16 like a hidden *m*, I should
Ps 58:8 Like a *m* of a woman they

Miscarriages
2Ki 2:19 and the land is causing *m*
2:21 causing of *m* result from it

Miscarrying
Ho 9:14 Give them a *m* womb and

Mischief
1Sa 23:9 Saul was fabricating *m*
Pr 12:20 heart of those fabricating *m*
14:22 devising *m* go wandering
16:30 brings *m* to completion

Misconstrue
De 32:27 their adversaries might *m* it

Miserable
Ro 7:24 *M* man that I am! Who will
Re 3:17 you do not know you are *m*

Miseries
Jas 5:1 howling over your *m* that are

Misery
Ro 3:16 Ruin and *m* are in their ways
Jas 4:9 Give way to *m* and mourn and

Misfortune
Job 20:22 the power of *m* itself will
31:3 *m* for those practicing what
Ob 12 in the day of his *m*; and you

Mishael
Ex 6:22 sons of Uzziel were *M* and
Le 10:4 *M* and Elzaphan, the sons of
Ne 8:4 at his left Pedaiah and *M* and
Da 1:6 Hananiah, *M* and Azariah
1:7 and to *M*, Meshach; and to
1:11 Hananiah, *M* and Azariah
1:19 Hananiah, *M* and Azariah
2:17 Hananiah, *M* and Azariah his

Mishal
Jos 19:26 Allammelech and Amad and *M*
21:30 *M* and its pasture ground

Misham
1Ch 8:12 of Elpaal were Eber and *M*

Mishma
Ge 25:14 and *M* and Dumah and Massa
1Ch 1:30 *M* and Dumah, Massa, Hadad
4:25 Mibsam his son, *M* his son
4:26 sons of *M* were Hammuel

Mishmannah
1Ch 12:10 *M* the fourth, Jeremiah the

Mishraites
1Ch 2:53 Shumathites and the *M*

Mislead
Mt 24:5 and will *m* many
24:11 prophets will arise and *m*
24:24 *m* . . . even the chosen ones
Mr 13:6 saying, I am he, and will *m*
1Jo 2:26 who are trying to *m* you
3:7 let no one *m* you; he who
Re 20:3 not *m* the nations anymore
20:8 *m* those nations in the four

Misleading
La 2:14 and *m* pronouncements
1Ti 4:1 *m* inspired utterances and
2Ti 3:13 *m* and being misled
1Jo 1:8 We have no sin, we are *m*
Re 12:9 *m* the entire inhabited earth
20:10 Devil who was *m* them was

Misleads
Mt 24:4 Look out that nobody *m* you
Mr 13:5 Look out that nobody *m* you
Joh 7:12 is not, but he *m* the crowd
Re 2:20 she teaches and *m* my slaves
13:14 it *m* those who dwell on

Misled
Job 19:6 that God himself has *m* me
Ps 119:78 without cause they have *m*
Pr 7:21 *m* him by the abundance of
Lu 21:8 Look out that you are not *m*
Joh 7:47 not been *m* also, have you?
1Co 6:9 not be *m*. Neither fornicators
15:33 not be *m*. Bad associations
Ga 6:7 Do not be *m*: God is not one
2Ti 3:13 misleading and being *m*
Tit 3:3 being *m*, being slaves to
Jas 1:16 Do not be *m*, my beloved
5:19 is *m* from the truth and
2Pe 2:15 they have been *m*. They have
Re 18:23 all the nations were *m*
19:20 signs with which he *m* those

Mispar
Ezr 2:2 *M*, Bigvai, Rehum, Baanah

Mispereth
Ne 7:7 *M*, Bigvai, Nehum, Baanah

Misrephoth-maim
Jos 11:8 *M* and the valley plain of
13:6 from Lebanon to *M*, all the

Miss
Jg 20:16 slinger of stones . . . not *m*
1Sa 20:6 father should *m* me at all
25:15 we did not *m* a single thing
Job 5:24 and you will *m* nothing
Jer 3:16 they remember it or *m* it
2Co 6:1 of God and *m* its purpose

Missed
1Sa 20:18 you will certainly be *m*
20:19 third day you will be *m*

Missile
2Ch 23:10 with his *m* in his hand
Ne 4:17 other hand was holding the *m*
4:23 his *m* in his right hand
Job 20:25 A *m* itself will even go out
33:18 from passing away by a *m*
36:12 pass away even by a *m*

Missiles
2Ch 32:5 made *m* in abundance and
Pr 26:18 mad that is shooting fiery *m*
Joe 2:8 some fall even among the *m*
Eph 6:16 the wicked one's burning *m*

Missing
Le 2:13 to be *m* upon your grain
Nu 31:49 not one has been reported *m*
Jg 21:3 for one tribe to be *m* today
1Sa 25:7 nothing at all showed up *m*
25:21 to him showed up *m*, and
2Sa 2:30 *m* from the servants of David
1Ki 20:39 in any way be *m*, your soul
2Ki 10:19 not let a single one be *m*
10:19 is *m* will not keep living
Pr 8:36 one *m* me is doing violence to
Isa 34:16 one has been *m* of them
40:26 not one of them is *m*
59:15 the truth proves to be *m*
Jer 23:4 and none will be *m*, is the
Mr 10:21 One thing is *m* about you
Lu 2:37 was never *m* from the temple

Mission
1Sa 15:18 Jehovah sent you on a *m* and
15:20 *m* on which Jehovah had sent
21:5 the *m* itself is ordinary
Jer 48:10 the *m* of Jehovah

Mist
Ge 2:6 *m* would go up from the earth
Job 36:27 filter as rain for his *m*
Ac 2:19 blood and fire and smoke *m*
13:11 thick *m* and darkness fell
Jas 4:14 you are a *m* appearing for a

Mistake
Ge 43:12 Maybe it was a *m*
Le 4:2 In case a soul sins by *m* in
4:13 assembly of Israel makes a *m*
5:15 sins by *m* against the holy
5:18 for his *m* that he committed
22:14 eats a holy thing by *m*, he
Nu 15:22 in case you should make a *m*
15:24 if it has been done . . . by *m*
15:25 because it was a *m*, and they
15:25 before Jehovah for their *m*
15:26 by *m* on the part of all the
15:27 if any soul should sin by *m*
15:28 *m* by a sin unintentionally
Job 6:24 *m* I have committed make me
12:16 belong the one making a *m*
19:4 granted that I have made a *m*
19:4 that my *m* will lodge
Ps 119:67 I was sinning by *m*
Ec 5:6 neither say . . . it was a *m*
10:5 *m* going forth on account of
Eze 45:20 any man making a *m* and

Mistaken
1Sa 26:21 and am very much *m*
Mt 22:29 You are *m*, because you know
Mr 12:24 why you are *m*, your not
12:27 You are much *m*

Mistakes
Ps 19:12 *M*—who can discern?

Mistreat
Le 19:33 you must not *m* him

Mistreating
Ac 12:1 to *m* . . . the congregation

Mistress
Ge 16:4 her *m* began to be despised in
16:8 from Sarai my *m* I am running
16:9 Return to your *m* and humble
1Sa 28:7 *m* of spirit mediumship, and
28:7 *m* of spirit mediumship in
1Ki 17:17 woman, the *m* of the house
2Ki 5:3 In time she said to her *m*
Ps 123:2 toward the hand of her *m*
Pr 30:23 when she dispossesses her *m*
Isa 24:2 maidservant as for her *m*
47:5 call you *M* of Kingdoms
47:7 shall prove to be *M*, forever
Na 3:4 a *m* of sorceries, she who is

Mists
2Pe 2:17 *m* driven by a violent storm

Mithkah
Nu 33:28 and went camping in *M*
33:29 pulled away from *M* and went

Mithnite
1Ch 11:43 and Joshaphat the *M*

Mithredath
Ezr 1:8 control of *M* the treasurer
4:7 Bishlam, *M*, Tabeel and the

Mitylene
Ac 20:14 him aboard and went to *M*

Mixed
Ex 12:38 a vast *m* company also went
Le 6:21 You will bring it well *m*
19:19 two sorts of thread, *m*
Nu 11:4 *m* crowd that was in the midst
De 22:11 *m* stuff of wool and linen
1Ch 23:29 for the *m* dough and for all
2Ch 16:14 *m* in an ointment of special
Ne 13:3 separate all the *m* company
Pr 9:2 it has *m* its wine; more than
9:5 the wine that I have *m*
23:30 in to search out *m* wine
Ca 7:2 Let not the *m* wine be lacking
Isa 65:11 *m* wine for the god of
Jer 25:20 all the *m* company, and all
25:24 the kings of the *m* company

Jer 50:37 against all the *m* company
Eze 30:5 all the *m* company and Chub
Da 2:41 the iron *m* with moist clay
2:43 iron *m* with moist clay
2:43 *m* with the offspring of
Mt 27:34 gave him wine *m* with gall
Lu 13:1 *m* with their sacrifices

Mixers
1Sa 8:13 for ointment *m* and cooks and
Ne 3:8 a member of the ointment *m*

Mixing
Isa 5:22 for *m* intoxicating liquor
Da 2:43 iron is not *m* with molded
1Co 5:9 to quit *m* in company with
5:11 to quit *m* in company with

Mixture
Ex 30:25 a *m* that is the work of an
30:35 a spice *m*, the work of an
1Ch 9:30 the ointment *m* of balsam
Ps 75:8 is foaming, it is full of *m*
Re 18:6 cup in which she put a *m*
18:6 twice as much of the *m* for

Mizpah
Jos 11:3 Hermon in the land of *M*
Jg 10:17 and pitched camp in *M*
11:11 words before Jehovah in *M*
11:34 Jephthah came to *M* to his
20:1 to Jehovah at *M*
20:3 Israel had gone up to *M*
21:1 men of Israel had sworn in *M*
21:5 not come up to Jehovah at *M*
21:8 not come up to Jehovah at *M*
1Sa 7:5 all Israel together at *M*
7:6 were collected together at *M*
7:6 the sons of Israel in *M*
7:7 together at *M*, and the axis
7:11 Israel sallied forth from *M*
7:12 between *M* and Jeshanah
7:16 of Bethel and Gilgal and *M*
10:17 together to Jehovah at *M*
1Ki 15:22 Geba in Benjamin, and *M*
2Ki 25:23 came to Gedaliah at *M*
25:25 to be with him in *M*
2Ch 16:6 build with them Geba and *M*
Ne 3:7 men of Gibeon and *M*, belonging
3:15 a prince of the district of *M*
3:19 a prince of *M*, proceeded at
Jer 40:6 at *M* and took up dwelling
40:8 they came to Gedaliah at *M*
40:10 I am dwelling in *M*, in
40:12 of Judah to Gedaliah at *M*
40:13 came to Gedaliah at *M*
40:15 place of concealment in *M*
41:1 the son of Ahikam at *M*
41:1 eat bread together in *M*
41:3 that is, with Gedaliah, in *M*
41:6 out from *M* to meet them
41:10 people who were in *M*, the
41:10 remaining over in *M*
41:14 had led captive from *M*
41:16 from *M*, after he had struck
Ho 5:1 is what you have become to *M*

Mizpeh
Jos 11:8 valley plain of *M* to the
15:38 Dilean and *M* and Joktheel
18:26 *M* and Chephirah and Mozah
Jg 11:29 to pass through *M* of Gilead
11:29 *M* of Gilead he passed along
1Sa 22:3 David went from there to *M*

Mizraim
Ge 10:6 sons of Ham . . . *M* and
10:13 *M* became father to Ludim
1Ch 1:8 sons of Ham were . . . *M*
1:11 *M*, he became father to

Mizzah
Ge 36:13 the sons of Reuel . . . *M*
36:17 sons of Reuel . . . sheik *M*
1Ch 1:37 sons of Reuel were . . . *M*

Mnason
Ac 21:16 *M* of Cyprus, an early

Moab
Ge 19:37 a son and called his name *M*
19:37 He is the father of *M*, to
36:35 Midianites in the field of *M*
Ex 15:15 despots of *M*, trembling
Nu 21:11 is toward the front of *M*
21:13 Arnon is the boundary of *M*
21:13 between *M* and the Amorites
21:15 against the border of *M*
Nu 21:20 that is in the field of *M*
21:26 fought with the king of *M*
21:28 It has consumed Ar of *M*, the
21:29 Woe to you, *M!* You will
22:1 desert plains of *M* across the
22:3 *M* became very frightened at
22:3 *M* began to feel a sickening
22:4 And *M* proceeded to say to the
22:4 son of Zippor was king of *M*
22:7 So the older men of *M* and the
22:8 princes of *M* stayed with
22:10 the king of *M*, has sent to
22:14 princes of *M* got up and came
22:21 went with the princes of *M*
22:36 meet him at the city of *M*
23:6 princes of *M* were stationed
23:7 Balak the king of *M* tried to
23:17 the princes of *M* with him
25:1 with the daughters of *M*
26:3 in the desert plains of *M* by
26:63 in the desert plains of *M* by
31:12 to the desert plains of *M*
33:44 on the border of *M*
33:48 on the desert plains of *M* by
33:49 on the desert plains of *M*
33:50 on the desert plains of *M* by
35:1 on the desert plains of *M* by
36:13 desert plains of *M* by the
De 1:5 land of *M* Moses undertook to
2:8 way of the wilderness of *M*
2:9 Do not molest *M* or engage in
2:18 territory of *M*, that is, Ar
29:1 Israel in the land of *M*
32:49 which is in the land of *M*
34:1 from the desert plains of *M*
34:5 died there in the land of *M*
34:6 bury him . . . in the land of *M*
34:8 on the desert plains of *M*
Jos 13:32 on the desert plains of *M*
24:9 Zippor, the king of *M*, got
Jg 3:12 let Eglon the king of *M* grow
3:14 to serve Eglon the king of *M*
3:15 to Eglon the king of *M*
3:17 to Eglon the king of *M*
3:29 they went striking down *M*
3:30 *M* came to be subdued on that
10:6 the gods of *M* and the gods of
11:15 did not take the land of *M*
11:17 the king of *M* they sent
11:18 the land of *M*, so that they
11:18 the land of *M* and took up
11:18 within the boundary of *M*
11:18 Arnon was the boundary of *M*
11:25 Balak . . . the king of *M*
Ru 1:1 as an alien in the fields of *M*
1:2 they came to the fields of *M*
1:6 to return from the fields of *M*
1:6 had heard in the field of *M*
1:22 from the fields of *M*
2:6 Naomi from the field of *M*
4:3 returned from the field of *M*
1Sa 12:9 the hand of the king of *M*
14:47 against *M* and against the
22:3 to Mizpeh in *M* and said to
22:3 said to the king of *M:* Let
22:4 before the king of *M*, and
2Sa 8:12 from *M* and from the sons of
23:20 two sons of Ariel of *M;* and
1Ki 11:7 the disgusting thing of *M*
11:33 to Chemosh the god of *M*
2Ki 1:1 *M* began to revolt against
3:4 Mesha the king of *M*, he
3:5 king of *M* began to revolt
3:7 the king of *M* himself has
3:7 go with me to *M* in war
3:10 give them into the hand of *M*
3:13 give them into the hand of *M*
3:18 give *M* into your hand
3:23 So now, to the spoil, O *M!*
3:24 came into *M*, striking the
3:26 the king of *M* saw that the
23:13 the disgusting thing of *M*
1Ch 1:46 Midian in the field of *M*
8:8 to children in the field of *M*
11:22 the two sons of Ariel of *M*
18:2 Then he struck *M* down, and
18:11 from Edom and from *M* and
2Ch 20:1 that the sons of *M* and the
20:10 sons of Ammon, and *M* and
20:22 *M* and the mountainous
20:23 *M* proceeded to stand up
Ps 60:8 *M* is my washing pot
83:6 Ishmaelites, *M* and the
108:9 *M* is my washing pot
Isa 11:14 Edom and *M* will be those
15:1 The pronouncement against *M*
15:1 Ar of *M* itself has been
15:1 Kir of *M* itself has been
15:2 over Medeba *M* itself howls
15:4 why the armed men of *M*
15:5 own heart cries out over *M*
15:8 around the territory of *M*
15:9 lion for the escapees of *M*
16:2 daughters of *M* will become
16:4 aliens even in you, O *M*
16:6 heard of the pride of *M*
16:7, 7 *M* will howl for *M;* even
16:11 like a harp even over *M*
16:12 *M* was made weary upon the
16:13 Jehovah spoke concerning *M*
16:14 glory of *M* must also be
25:10 *M* must be trodden down in
Jer 9:26 sons of Ammon and upon *M*
25:21 *M* and the sons of Ammon
27:3 to the king of *M* and to the
40:11 Jews that were in *M* and
48:1 For *M* this is what Jehovah
48:2 is there any praise of *M*
48:4 *M* has been broken down
48:9 Give a road mark to *M*, you
48:15 *M* has been despoiled, and
48:18 despoiler of *M* has come up
48:20 *M* has been put to shame
48:20 that *M* has been despoiled
48:24 cities of the land of *M*
48:25 horn of *M* has been cut down
48:26 *M* has slapped around in his
48:28 crag, you inhabitants of *M*
48:29 heard of the pride of *M*
48:31 over *M* that I shall howl
48:31 for *M* in his entirety I
48:33 and from the land of *M*
48:35 cause to cease from *M*, is
48:36 be boisterous for *M* himself
48:38 On all the roofs of *M* and
48:38 I have broken *M* just like
48:39 how *M* has turned the back!
48:39 *M* has become an object of
48:40 spread his wings over *M*
48:41 mighty men of *M* must
48:42 *M* will certainly be
48:43 upon you, O inhabitant of *M*
48:44 bring upon her, upon *M*
48:45 devour the temples of *M*
48:46 Woe to you, O *M!* The
48:47 the captive ones of *M* in
48:47 is the judgment upon *M*
Eze 25:8 the reason that *M* and Seir
25:9 I am opening the slope of *M*
25:11 in *M* I shall execute acts
Da 11:41 *M* and the main part of the
Am 2:1 account of three revolts of *M*
2:2 I will send a fire into *M*
2:2 and with noise *M* must die
Mic 6:5 Balak the king of *M* counseled
Zep 2:8 heard the reproach by *M* and
2:9 *M* herself will become just

Moabite
De 23:3 No Ammonite or *M* may come
Ru 1:4 wives for themselves, *M* women
1:22 Ruth the *M* woman, her
2:2 Ruth the *M* woman said to
1Ki 11:1 foreign wives . . . *M*
1Ch 4:22 became owners of *M* wives
11:46 and Ithmah the *M*
Ne 13:1 the *M* should not come into
13:23 Ammonite and *M* wives

Moabites
De 2:11 *M* used to call them Emim
2:29 and the *M* dwelling in Ar did
Jg 3:28 your enemies, the *M*, into
3:28 against the *M*, and they did
2Sa 8:2 strike down the *M* and
8:2 *M* came to be David's servants
2Ki 3:21 *M*, they heard that the kings
3:22 the *M* from the opposite side
3:24 began striking the *M* down so
3:24 striking the *M* down as they
13:20 marauding bands of the *M*
24:2 and marauder bands of *M*
1Ch 18:2 the *M* came to be David's
Ezr 9:1 the *M*, the Egyptians and the
Jer 48:11 *M* have been at ease since
48:13 *M* will have to be ashamed
48:16 The disaster on the *M* is near

Moabitess
Ru 2:6 The young woman is a *M*, who
2:21 Ruth the *M* said: He also said
4:5 it is also from Ruth the *M*
4:10 also Ruth the *M*, the wife of
2Ch 24:26 the son of Shimrith the *M*

Moab's
Nu 24:17 the temples of *M* head And

Moadiah
Ne 12:17 for *M*, Piltai

Moan
Ps 55:17 but show concern and I *m*
Isa 16:7 stricken ones indeed will *m*
Jer 48:31 of Kir-heres one shall *m*

Moaning
Eze 2:10 written in it dirges and *m*
7:16 *m*, each one in his own error
Na 2:7 her slave girls will be *m*

Moat
Da 9:25 with a public square and a *m*

Mob
Ge 19:4 all the people in one *m*
Ac 17:5 formed a *m* and proceeded to
19:40 reason for this disorderly *m*
24:12 causing a *m* to rush together

Mock
Nu 21:27 sayers of *m* verses would say
1Ki 18:27 Elijah began to *m* them and
Job 9:23 despair . . . he would *m*
Pr 1:26 *m* when what you dread comes
Ac 17:32 some began to *m*, while
Col 2:18 delight in a *m* humility and
2:23 of worship and *m* humility

Mocked
Ac 2:13 *m* at them and began to say
Ga 6:7 God is not one to be *m*

Mockers
Ps 35:16 Among the apostate *m* for a

Mockery
Ge 27:12 like one making a *m*, and I
2Ch 30:10 speaking in *m* of them and
Job 17:2 Certainly there is *m* at me
Jer 10:15 vanity, a work of *m*
51:18 are vanity, a work of *m*

Mocking
2Ch 36:16 and *m* at his prophets
Ps 137:3 those *m* us—for rejoicing

Mockings
Heb 11:36 trial by *m* and scourgings

Mode
Jg 13:12 child's *m* of life and his

Model
1Pe 2:21 leaving you a *m* for you to

Moderate
1Ti 3:2 *m* in habits, sound in mind
3:11 not slanderous, *m* in habits
Tit 2:2 aged men be *m* in habits

Moderately
Heb 5:2 deal *m* with the ignorant and

Modest
Pr 11:2 wisdom is with the *m* ones
Mic 6:8 *m* in walking with your God

Modesty
1Ti 2:9 with *m* and soundness of mind

Moist
Ge 30:37 staffs still *m* of the storax
Jg 15:15 *m* jawbone of a male ass and
Job 21:24 marrow of his bones . . . *m*
Isa 41:25 tramples . . . the *m* material
Da 2:41 the iron mixed with *m* clay
2:43 iron mixed with *m* clay
Lu 23:31 when the tree is *m*, what

Moisten
Ps 92:10 *m* myself with fresh oil

Moistened
Ex 29:2 ring-shaped cakes *m* with oil
29:40 fine flour *m* with the fourth
Le 2:4 cakes *m* with oil or
2:5 to be of fine flour *m* with oil
7:10 that is *m* with oil or dry
7:12 ring-shaped cakes *m* with oil
7:12 ring-shaped cakes *m* with oil
9:4 a grain offering *m* with oil
Le 14:10 a grain offering *m* with oil
14:21 fine flour *m* with oil as a
23:13 fine flour *m* with oil, as an
Nu 6:15 of fine flour, *m* with oil
7:13 flour *m* with oil for a grain
7:19 flour *m* with oil for a grain
7:25 flour *m* with oil for a grain
7:31 flour *m* with oil for a grain
7:37 flour *m* with oil for a grain
7:43 fine flour *m* with oil for a
7:49 fine flour *m* with oil for a
7:55 flour *m* with oil for a grain
7:61 flour *m* with oil for a grain
7:67 fine flour *m* with oil for a
7:73 fine flour *m* with oil for a
7:79 fine flour *m* with oil for a
8:8 flour *m* with oil, and you
15:4 *m* with a fourth of a hin of
15:6 fine flour, *m* with a third of
15:9 *m* with half a hin of oil
28:5 grain offering *m* with the
28:9 a grain offering *m* with oil
28:12 grain offering *m* with oil
28:12 grain offering *m* with oil
28:13 a grain offering *m* with oil
28:20 fine flour *m* with oil you
28:28 offering of fine flour *m*
29:3 fine flour *m* with oil, three
29:9 fine flour *m* with oil three
29:14 offering of fine flour *m*

Moisture
Job 37:11 with *m* he burdens the cloud
Ps 32:4 My life's *m* has been changed
Lu 8:6 because of not having *m*

Moladah
Jos 15:26 Amam and Shema and *M*
19:2 Beer-sheba with Sheba, and *M*
1Ch 4:28 to dwell in Beer-sheba and *M*
Ne 11:26 in Jeshua and in *M* and in

Mold
1Ki 7:46 king cast them in the clay *m*
Na 3:14 grab hold of the brick *m*

Molded
Da 2:33 iron and partly of *m* clay
2:34 feet of iron and of *m* clay
2:35 *m* clay, the copper, the
2:41 toes to be partly of *m* clay
2:42 and partly of *m* clay, the
2:43 is not mixing with *m* clay
2:45 *m* clay, the silver and the
Ro 9:20 thing *m* say to him that
9:20 to him that *m* it, Why did

Molder
Isa 19:6 the rush themselves must *m*

Moldered
Isa 33:9 has become abashed; it has *m*

Mole
Le 11:29 the *m* rat and the jerboa and

Molech
Le 18:21 any of your offspring to *M*
20:2 offspring to *M*, should be put
20:3 some of his offspring to *M*
20:4 to *M* by not putting him to
20:5 immoral intercourse with *M*
1Ki 11:7 to *M* the disgusting thing of
2Ki 23:10 pass through the fire to *M*
Jer 32:35 through the fire to *M*

Molest
De 2:9 Do not *m* Moab or engage in
2:19 Do not *m* them or engage in
Ru 2:15 and you must not *m* her
1Sa 25:7 We did not *m* them, and
25:15 they did not *m* us, and we

Molesting
Jg 18:7 conqueror that was *m* a thing

Molid
1Ch 2:29 bore him Ahban and *M*

Moloch
Ac 7:43 it was the tent of *M* and the

Molten
Ex 32:4 into a *m* statue of a calf
32:8 made a *m* statue of a calf for
34:17 not make *m* idol gods for
Le 19:4 make *m* gods for yourselves
Nu 33:52 all their images of *m* metal
De 9:12 made themselves a *m* image
9:16 made yourselves a *m* calf
27:15 a carved image or a *m* statue
Jg 17:3 a carved image and a *m* statue
17:4 went making . . . a *m* statue
18:14 carved image and a *m* statue
18:17 teraphim and the *m* image
18:18 teraphim and the *m* image
1Ki 7:23 make the *m* sea ten cubits
14:9 and *m* images to offend me
2Ki 17:16 *m* statues, two calves
2Ch 4:2 *m* sea ten cubits from its one
28:2 *m* statues he made of the
34:3 images and the *m* statues
34:4 *m* statues he broke in pieces
Ne 9:18 *m* statue of a calf and began
Job 37:18 skies Hard like a *m* mirror
38:38 pours out as into a *m* mass
Ps 106:19 bowed down to a *m* image
Isa 30:22 of your *m* statue of gold
40:19 has cast a mere *m* image
41:29 *m* images are wind and
42:17 are saying to a *m* image
44:10 or cast a mere *m* image
48:5 and my own *m* image have
Jer 10:14 his *m* image is a falsehood
51:17 his *m* image is a falsehood
Da 11:8 gods, with their *m* images
Ho 13:2 a *m* statue from their silver
Na 1:14 I shall cut off . . . *m* statue
Hab 2:18 carved it, a *m* statue, and

Moment
Ex 33:5 one *m* I could go up into the
Nu 4:20 for the least *m* of time, and
1Sa 4:18 *m* that he mentioned the ark
17:55 the *m* that Saul saw David
24:16 *m* that David finished
Ezr 9:8 for a little *m* favor from
Job 7:18 every *m* you should test him
20:5 rejoicing . . . is for a *m*
21:13 in a *m* down to Sheol they
34:20 In a *m* they die, even in
Ps 30:5 under his anger is for a *m*
73:19 astonishment as in a *m*
Pr 12:19 will be only as long as a *m*
Isa 26:20 Hide yourself for but a *m*
27:3 Every *m* I shall water her
54:7 For a little *m* I left you
54:8 for but a *m*, but with
Jer 4:20 in a *m* my tent cloths
18:7 At any *m* that I may speak
18:9 at any *m* that I may speak
49:19 in a *m* I will make him run
50:44 in a *m* I shall make them
La 4:6 was overthrown as in a *m*
Eze 26:16 certainly tremble every *m*
32:10 have to tremble every *m*
Da 3:6 at the same *m* be thrown into
3:15 same *m* you will be thrown
4:19 was astonished for a *m*, and
4:33 At that *m* the word itself
5:5 At that *m* the fingers of a
Mt 26:53 to supply me at this *m* more
Joh 13:19 From this *m* on I am telling
14:7 this *m* on you know him and
1Co 15:52 in a *m*, in the twinkling of
Php 1:5 the first day until this *m*

Momentary
2Co 4:17 tribulation is *m* and light

Money
Ge 17:12 anyone purchased with *m*
17:13 man purchased with *m* of
17:23 everyone purchased with *m* of
17:27 anyone purchased with *m*
20:16 pieces of *m* to your brother
31:15 from the *m* given for us
33:19 for a hundred pieces of *m*
34:12 high the marriage *m* and gift
42:25 return the *m* of the men to
42:27 he got to see his *m*, and
42:28 My *m* has been returned and
42:35 each one's bundle of *m* in
42:35 to see their bundles of *m*
43:12 double the *m* in your hand
43:12 the *m* that was returned in
43:15 took double the *m* in their
43:18 It is because of the *m* that
43:21 here was the *m* of each one
43:21 our *m* in full weight. So we
43:22 more *m* we have brought down
43:22 who placed our *m* in our bags
43:23 Your *m* came first to me
44:1 place the *m* of each one in
44:2 and the *m* for his cereals
44:8 the *m* that we found in the

Ge 47:14 picking up all the *m* that
47:14 Joseph kept bringing the *m*
47:15 the *m* from the land of Egypt
47:15 because *m* has run out
47:16 livestock, if *m* has run out
47:18 the *m* and the stock of
Ex 12:44 slave man purchased with *m*
21:11 out for nothing, without *m*
21:21 because he is his *m*
22:7 give his fellow *m* or articles
22:17 he is to pay over the *m* at
22:17 of purchase *m* for virgins
22:25 lend *m* to my people, to the
30:16 silver *m* of the atonement
Le 22:11 as a purchase with his *m*, he
25:27 return what *m* remains over
25:37 give him your *m* on interest
25:50 the *m* of his sale must
25:51 from the *m* of his purchase
27:15 fifth of the *m* of the
27:19 give a fifth of the *m* of the
Nu 3:48 give the *m* to Aaron and his
3:49 So Moses took the *m* of the
3:50 took the *m*, a thousand three
3:51 Moses gave the *m* of the
De 2:6 you may buy from them for *m*
2:6 may purchase from them for *m*
2:28 food you will sell me for *m*
2:28 water you will give me for *m*
14:25 must then turn it into *m*
14:25 wrap the *m* up in your hand
14:26 give the *m* for whatever your
21:14 by no means sell her for *m*
23:19 pay . . . interest on *m*
Jos 7:21 with the *m* underneath it
7:22 with the *m* underneath it
24:32 for a hundred pieces of *m*
Jg 16:18 bring up the *m* in their hand
1Sa 2:36 for the payment of *m* and a
12:3 have I accepted hush *m* that
18:25 delight, not in marriage *m*
1Ki 21:2 give you *m* as the price of
21:6 give me your vineyard for *m*
21:15 refused to give you for *m*
2Ki 12:4 the *m* for the holy offerings
12:4 the *m* at which each one is
12:4 *m* for the souls according
12:4 all the *m* that it comes up
12:7 do not take any more *m* from
12:8 not to take any more *m* from
12:9 put all the *m* that was being
12:10 great deal of *m* in the
12:10 count the *m* that was being
12:11 gave the *m* that had been
12:13 *m* that was being brought to
12:15 *m* to give to the doers of
12:16 *m* for guilt offerings and
12:16 and the *m* for sin offerings
22:4 complete the *m* that is being
22:7 be taken of the *m* with them
22:9 *m* that was to be found in
1Ch 21:22 For the *m* in full give it
21:24 purchase for the *m* in full
2Ch 17:11 Jehoshaphat presents and *m*
24:5 collect *m* from all Israel to
24:11 there was plenty of *m*
24:11 gathered *m* in abundance
24:14 rest of the *m*, and they
34:9 *m* that was being brought to
34:14 *m* that was being brought to
34:17 *m* that was found in the
Ezr 3:7 to give *m* to the cutters and
7:17 buy with this *m* bulls, rams
7:26 *m* fine or for imprisonment
Ne 5:4 *m* for the king's tribute on
5:10 giving *m* and grain on loan
5:11 the hundredth of the *m* and
Es 4:7 *m* that Haman had said to pay
Job 31:39 I have eaten without *m*
42:11 to give him a piece of *m*
Ps 15:5 His *m* he has not given out
Pr 7:20 bag of *m* he has taken in his
Ec 7:12 same as *m* is for a protection
10:19 *m* is what meets a response
Isa 43:24 no sweet cane with any *m*
52:3 without *m* that you will be
55:1 no *m!* Come, buy and eat
55:1 without *m* and without price
55:2 people keep paying out *m* for
Jer 32:9 to weigh out to him the *m*
32:10 weighing the *m* in the
32:25 the field with *m* and take
32:44 With *m* people will buy
La 5:4 For *m* we have had to drink
Am 5:12 you who are taking hush *m*
Mic 3:11 divination simply for *m*
Mt 21:12 the tables of the *m* changers
25:18 and hid the silver *m* of his
Mr 6:8 no copper *m* in their girdle
10:23 those with *m* to enter into
11:15 the tables of the *m* changers
12:41 dropping *m* into the treasury
12:43 *m* into the treasury chests
14:11 to give him silver *m*. So he
Lu 9:3 nor bread nor silver *m*
16:14 Pharisees . . . were *m* lovers
18:24 for those having *m* to make
19:15 he had given the silver *m*
19:23 put my silver *m* in a bank
22:5 agreed to give him silver *m*
Joh 2:14 the *m* brokers in their seats
2:15 the coins of the *m* changers
12:6 thief and had the *m* box and
13:29 Judas was holding the *m* box
Ac 4:37 brought the *m* and deposited
7:16 with silver *m* from the sons
8:18 he offered them *m*
8:20 through *m* to get possession
22:28 citizen for a large sum of *m*
24:26 *m* to be given him by Paul
1Ti 3:3 not a lover of *m*
6:10 the love of *m* is a root of
2Ti 3:2 lovers of *m*, self-assuming
Heb 13:5 be free of the love of *m*

Monies

Mt 25:27 deposited my silver *m* with
Joh 12:6 carry off the *m* put in it

Monster

Job 7:12 Am I a sea or a sea *m*, That
Isa 27:1 kill the sea *m* that is in
51:9 that pierced the sea *m*
Eze 29:3 great sea *m* lying stretched
32:2 the marine *m* in the seas

Monsters

Ge 1:21 to create the great sea *m* and
Ps 74:13 heads of the sea *m* in the
148:7 You sea *m* and all you watery

Month

Ge 7:11 Noah's life, in the second *m*
7:11 seventeenth day of the *m*
8:4 And in the seventh *m*, on the
8:4 the seventeenth day of the *m*
8:5 lessening until the tenth *m*
8:5 In the tenth *m*, on the first
8:5 first of the *m*, the tops of
8:13 the first *m*, on the first day
8:13 on the first day of the *m*
8:14 second *m* . . . earth had dried
8:14 twenty-seventh day of the *m*
29:14 he dwelt with him a full *m*
Ex 12:2 This *m* will be the start of
12:3 On the tenth day of this *m*
12:6 the fourteenth day of this *m*
12:18 first *m*, on the fourteenth
12:18 the fourteenth day of the *m*
12:18 twenty-first day of the *m*
13:4 going out in the *m* of Abib
13:5 render this service in this *m*
16:1 fifteenth day of the second *m*
19:1 In the third *m* after the sons
23:15 in the *m* of Abib, because
34:18 appointed time in the *m* of
34:18 it was in the *m* of Abib
40:2 On the day of the first *m*, on
40:2 on the first of the *m*, you
40:17 about that in the first *m*
40:17 on the first day of the *m*
Le 16:29 In the seventh *m* on the
16:29 on the tenth of the *m* you
23:5 first *m*, on the fourteenth
23:5 on the fourteenth day of the *m*
23:6 fifteenth day of this *m* is
23:24 seventh *m*, on the first of
23:24 first of the *m*, there should
23:27 tenth of this seventh *m* is
23:32 ninth of the *m* in the
23:34 seventh *m* is the festival of
23:39 of the seventh *m*, when you
23:41 it in the seventh *m*
25:9 seventh *m* on the tenth of the
25:9 on the tenth of the *m;* on the
27:6 age is from a *m* old up to
Nu 1:1 first day of the second *m* in
1:18 first day of the second *m*
3:15 male from a *m* old upward
3:22 males from a *m* old upward
Nu 3:28 males from a *m* old upward
3:34 the males from a *m* old upward
3:39 males from a *m* old upward
3:40 Israel from a *m* old upward
3:43 from a *m* old upward of their
9:1 second year . . . the first *m*
9:3 fourteenth day in this *m*
9:5 first *m*, on the fourteenth day
9:5 fourteenth day of the *m*
9:11 second *m*, on the fourteenth
9:22 or a *m* or more days during
10:11 second *m*, on the twentieth
10:11 twentieth day in the *m*, the
11:20 up to a *m* of days, until it
11:21 eat for a *m* of days
18:16 from a *m* old onward you
20:1 the first *m*, and the people
26:62 from a *m* old and upward
28:14 burnt offering in its *m* for
28:16 first *m*, on the fourteenth
28:16 the fourteenth day of the *m*
28:17 the fifteenth day of this *m*
29:1 the seventh *m*, on the first
29:1 on the first of the *m*, you
29:7 the tenth of this seventh *m*
29:12 seventh *m* you should hold a
33:3 first *m*, on the fifteenth day
33:3 fifteenth day of the first *m*
33:38 in the fifth *m*, on the first
33:38 on the first of the *m*
De 1:3 eleventh *m*, on the first of
1:3 on the first of the *m*, Moses
16:1 an observing of the *m* of Abib
16:1 in the *m* of Abib Jehovah your
21:13 weep . . . a whole lunar *m*
Jos 4:19 on the tenth of the first *m*
5:10 the fourteenth day of the *m*
1Ki 4:7 the food one *m* in the year
4:27 each one in his *m*
5:14 shifts of ten thousand a *m*
5:14 For a *m* they would continue
6:1 fourth year, in the *m* of Ziv
6:1 Ziv, that is, the second *m*
6:37 laid, in the lunar *m* of Ziv
6:38 in the lunar *m* of Bul, that
6:38 Bul, that is, the eighth *m*
8:2 *m* of Ethanim in the festival
8:2 that is, the seventh *m*
12:32 eighth *m* on the fifteenth
12:32 the fifteenth day of the *m*
12:33 day in the eighth *m*
12:33 *m* that he had invented
2Ki 15:13 to reign for a full lunar *m*
25:1 tenth *m* on the tenth day of
25:1 on the tenth day of the *m*
25:3 ninth day of the fourth *m*
25:8 the fifth *m* on the seventh
25:8 on the seventh day of the *m*
25:25 the seventh *m* that Ishmael
25:27 in the twelfth *m*, on the
25:27 twenty-seventh day of the *m*
1Ch 12:15 the Jordan in the first *m*
27:1, 1 that went out *m* by *m* for
27:2 division of the first *m*
27:3 were for the first *m*
27:4 the division of the second *m*
27:5 third *m* was Benaiah the son
27:7 for the fourth *m* was Asahel
27:8 fifth chief for the fifth *m*
27:9 for the sixth *m* was Ira the
27:10 for the seventh *m* was Helez
27:11 the eighth *m* was Sibbecai
27:12 the ninth *m* was Abi-ezer
27:13 the tenth *m* was Maharai
27:14 the eleventh *m* was Benaiah
27:15 the twelfth *m* was Heldai
2Ch 3:2 second *m* on the second day
5:3 that of the seventh *m*
7:10 day of the seventh *m* he
15:10 third *m* of the fifteenth
29:3 in the first *m*, opened the
29:17 the first *m* at sanctifying
29:17 eighth day of the *m* they
29:17 day of the first *m* they
30:2 passover in the second *m*
30:13 in the second *m*, a
30:15 fourteenth day . . . second *m*
31:7 third *m* they started the
31:7 the seventh *m* they finished
35:1 fourteenth day . . . first *m*
Ezr 3:1 the seventh *m* arrived the
3:6 first day of the seventh *m*
3:8 at Jerusalem, in the second *m*
6:15 day of the lunar *m* Adar

Monthly

Months

Monument

Mood

Moon

Moons

Moon-shaped

Moral

Morally

Morals

Mordecai

Es 3:6 to lay hand upon *M* alone, for
4:1 *M* himself got knowledge of
4:1 and *M* proceeded to rip his
4:4 she sent garments to clothe *M*
4:5 a command concerning *M*, to
4:6 Hathach went out to *M* into
4:7 Then *M* told him about all the
4:10 commanded him concerning *M*
4:12 to tell *M* the words of Esther
4:13 *M* said to reply to Esther
4:15 Esther said to reply to *M*
4:17 *M* passed along and proceeded
5:9 but as soon as Haman saw *M* in
5:9 filled with rage against *M*
5:13 as long as I am seeing *M* the
5:14 that they should hang *M* on it
6:2 was found written what *M* had
6:3 has been done to *M* for this
6:4 to hang *M* on the stake that he
6:10 do that way to *M* the Jew who
6:11 clothe *M* and make him ride
6:12 *M* returned to the king's gate
6:13 seed of the Jews that *M* is
7:9 stake that Haman made for *M*
7:10 that he had prepared for *M*
8:1 *M* himself came in before the
8:2 gave it to *M*; and Esther went
8:2 *M* over the house of Haman
8:7 the queen and to *M* the Jew
8:9 all that *M* commanded to the
8:15 *M*, he went forth from before
9:3 the dread of *M* had fallen upon
9:4 For *M* was great in the king's
9:4 *M* was steadily growing
9:20 *M* proceeded to write these
9:23 what *M* had written to them
9:29 *M* the Jew proceeded to write
9:31 as *M* the Jew and Esther the
10:3 *M* the Jew was second to King

Mordecai's

Es 2:22 talked to the king in *M* name
3:4 whether *M* affairs would stand
3:6 had told him about *M* people
3:6 realm of Ahasuerus, *M* people
4:9 and told Esther *M* words
10:2 statement of *M* greatness

More

Ge 5:24 Enoch . . . was no *m*, for God
7:4 in just seven days *m* I am
9:11 No *m* will all flesh be cut
9:11 no *m* will there occur a
9:15 no *m* will the waters become
26:10 A little *m* and certainly one
26:13, 13 went on advancing *m* and *m*
29:27 with me for seven years *m*
29:30 also expressed *m* love for Rachel
29:30 for yet seven years *m*
29:35 she became pregnant once *m*
30:7 Bilhah . . . pregnant once *m*
30:19 Leah became pregnant once *m*
30:43, 43 increasing *m* and *m*, and
37:3 Israel loved Joseph *m* than
37:4 father loved him *m* than all
37:9 I have had a dream once *m*
38:26 She is *m* righteous than I
42:13 the other one is no *m*
42:32 One is no *m*, and the
42:36 Joseph is no *m* and Simeon
42:36 Simeon is no *m*, and
43:22 *m* money we have brought
48:22 one shoulder of land *m*
Ex 1:9 *m* numerous and mightier than
1:12 the *m* they would oppress them
1:12 the *m* they would multiply and
1:12 *m* they kept spreading abroad
1:20 kept growing *m* numerous
3:15 Then God said once *m* to Moses
4:6 Jehovah said to him once *m*
5:2 what is *m*, I am not going to
5:10 I am giving you no *m* straw
11:1 One plague *m* I am going to
25:35 knob under two *m* branches
30:15 The rich should not give *m*
34:3 What is *m*, no flock or herd
36:5 *m* than what the service needs
36:6 any *m* stuff for the holy
36:7 proved to be . . . *m* than enough
37:21 knob under two *m* branches
Le 12:4 thirty-three days *m* she will
12:5 sixty-six days *m* she will
26:21 inflict seven times *m* blows
Nu 9:22 or a month or *m* days during
18:22 no *m* come near to the tent
Nu 20:19 want nothing *m* than to pass
22:15 *m* honorable than the former
22:25 he went beating her some *m*
De 7:1 seven nations *m* populous and
9:14 mightier and *m* populous than
11:23 greater and *m* numerous than
20:1 a people *m* numerous than you
30:5 and multiply you *m* than your
30:9 make you have *m* than enough
31:2 no *m* be allowed to go out and
31:27 how much *m* so after my death
Jos 10:11 were *m* who died from the
11:10 *M* than that, Joshua
Jg 2:19 act *m* ruinously than their
6:39 let me speak just once *m*
6:39 a test only once *m* with the
9:37 spoke once *m* and said: Look!
11:14 sent once *m* messengers to
16:30 *m* than those he had put to
20:45 two thousand *m* men of them
Ru 1:14 and wept some *m*, after which
1Sa 1:18 became self-concerned no *m*
2:26 growing bigger and *m* likable
2:29 honoring your sons *m* than me
9:8 answered Saul once *m* and said
14:30 much *m* so if the people had
18:29 *m* fear because of David
21:5 how much *m* so today, when
23:3 *m* so in case we should go to
23:22 persevere some *m* and
24:17 You are *m* righteous than I
26:21 no *m* do you injury, in view
28:15 and has answered me no *m*
2Sa 1:26 *M* wonderful was your love
3:1, 1 kept declining *m* and *m*
3:11 one word *m* in reply to Abner
4:11 how much *m* so when wicked
5:13 went on taking *m* concubines
5:13 *m* sons and daughters
6:22 even *m* lightly esteemed than
7:10 no *m* will they be disturbed
7:20 what *m* can David add and
16:11 and how much *m* now a
18:8 the forest did *m* in eating
19:43 in David we are *m* than you
19:43 *m* severe than the word of
21:18 war arose once *m* with the
23:19 *m* than the rest of the
23:23 even *m* than the thirty
1Ki 1:47 Solomon's name *m* splendid
2:32 upon two men *m* righteous and
10:5 no *m* spirit in her
10:26 gathering *m* chariots and
14:22 incited him to jealousy *m*
16:33 Ahab came to do *m* to offend
22:22 what is *m*, you will come
2Ki 2:21 No *m* will death or any
5:13 How much *m*, then, since he
5:17 will no *m* render up a burnt
6:16 are *m* who are with us than
12:7 not take any *m* money from
12:8 not to take any *m* money
21:9 *m* than the nations whom
21:11 has acted *m* wickedly than
1Ch 4:9 Jabez came to be *m* honorable
11:21 *m* distinguished than the
11:25 *m* distinguished than the
14:3 take *m* wives in Jerusalem
14:3 David came to be father to *m*
16:25 feared *m* than all other
17:9 no *m* will they be disturbed
17:18 What *m* could David say to
24:4 *m* numerous in headmen than
2Ch 9:4 to be no *m* spirit in her
11:21 Rehoboam was *m* in love
13:20 retain any *m* power in the
18:21 what is *m*, you will come
20:25 until they could carry no *m*
25:9 means to give you much *m*
28:22 unfaithfully still *m*
29:34 Levites were *m* upright of
30:23 hold it for seven *m* days
32:7 with us there are *m* than
Ne 5:16 what is *m*, in the work of
7:2 true God *m* than many others
Es 2:17 king came to love Esther *m*
2:17 *m* favor and loving-kindness
4:13 any *m* than all the other Jews
5:12 What is *m*, Esther the queen
6:6 rendering an honor *m* than me
Job 3:21 *m* than for hidden treasures
4:17 be *m* just than God himself
4:19 How much *m* so with those
4:19 crushes them *m* quickly than
Job 6:27 much *m* will you cast lots
9:14 How much *m* so in case I
10:22 beams no *m* than gloom does
14:12 Until heaven is no *m* they
20:9 no *m* will his place behold
23:12 *m* than what is prescribed
24:20 He will be remembered no *m*
24:24 then they are no *m*, And
28:18 wisdom is worth *m* than one
32:15 they have answered no *m*
32:16 they answered no *m*
33:12 much *m* than mortal man
34:19 *m* consideration to the
35:2 My righteousness is *m* than
35:3 *m* than by my sinning
35:11 One teaching us *m* than the
36:26 God is *m* exalted than we
42:12 *m* than his beginning
Ps 10:15 until you find no *m*
10:18 may no *m* cause trembling
19:10 *m* to be desired than gold
37:10 the wicked one will be no *m*
40:5 *m* numerous than I can recount
40:12 *M* errors of mine overtook
40:12 *m* numerous than the hairs of
45:2 *m* handsome than the sons of
45:7 of exultation *m* than your
52:3 bad *m* than what is good
52:3 *m* than speaking righteousness
69:4 *m* than the hairs of my head
69:31 *m* pleasing to Jehovah than
72:7 peace until the moon is no *m*
76:4 *m* majestic than the
77:7 he no *m* be pleased again
78:17 kept sinning still *m* against
78:32 they sinned some *m* And did
83:4 may be remembered no *m*
87:2 Jehovah is *m* in love with the
89:43 What is *m*, you again treat
103:16 and it is no *m*
119:72 *M* so than thousands of
119:99 *M* insight than all my
119:100 *m* understanding than older
119:103 *M* so than honey to my
119:127 *M* than gold, even refined
130:6 *M* than watchmen for the
135:5 Lord is *m* than all other
139:18 *m* than even the grains of
Pr 1:5 and take in *m* instruction
3:15 *m* precious than corals, and
4:23 *M* than all else that is to be
6:10 A little *m* sleep, a little
6:10 sleep, a little *m* slumbering
6:10 little *m* folding of the hands
9:2 *m* than that, it has set in
10:25 so the wicked one is no *m*
11:31 much *m* should the wicked
12:7 wicked ones and they are no *m*
15:11 How much *m* so the hearts of
16:16 to be chosen *m* than silver
18:19 is *m* than a strong town
21:3 *m* preferable to Jehovah than
21:27 *m* so when one brings it
23:35 I shall seek it yet some *m*
26:12 is *m* hope for the stupid one
28:23 will afterward find *m* favor
29:20 is *m* hope for someone stupid
30:2 am *m* unreasoning than anyone
31:7 one's own trouble no *m*
31:10 Her value is far *m* than that
Ec 1:16 in wisdom *m* than anyone that
2:7 I came to have, *m* so than all
2:9 increased *m* than anyone that
2:13 *m* advantage for wisdom than
2:13 is *m* advantage for light than
2:16 no *m* remembrance of the wise
6:10 that is *m* powerful than he is
7:26 *M* bitter than death I found
9:17 *m* to be heard than the cry of
Ca 1:4 of endearment *m* than wine
5:9 How is your dear one *m* than
5:9 *m* than any other dear one
Isa 1:5 will you be struck still *m*
1:5 in that you add *m* revolt
1:13 in any *m* valueless grain
5:8 until there is no *m* room and
7:10 speaking some *m* to Ahaz
10:10 *m* than those at Jerusalem
17:14 Before morning—it is no *m*
19:7 and it will be no *m*
38:11 shall no *m* look on mankind
49:6 been *m* than a trivial matter
52:1 no *m* will there come again
52:14 appearance *m* than that of

Isa 52:14 stately form *m* than that of
54:1 *m* numerous than the sons of
54:2 your tent *m* spacious
54:4 you will remember no *m*
54:9 no *m* pass over the earth
60:18 No *m* will violence be heard
60:19 no *m* prove to be a light by
60:19 no *m* give you light
60:20 No *m* will your sun set, nor
62:4 No *m* will you be said to be
62:4 no *m* be said to be desolate
62:8 no *m* give your grain as
65:19 no *m* will there be heard in
65:20 No *m* will there come to be
Jer 2:31 We shall come to you no *m*
3:11 to be *m* righteous than
3:16 No *m* will they say, The ark
3:16 and no *m* will it be made
3:17 will no *m* walk after the
4:23 and their light was no *m*
7:32 no *m* be said to be Topheth
10:5 what is *m*, the doing of any
10:20 and they are no *m*
11:19 his very name may no *m* be
15:8 *m* numerous than the sand
16:14 when it will no *m* be said
17:9 The heart is *m* treacherous
19:6 will be called no *m* Topheth
19:11 no *m* able to be repaired
19:11 there is no *m* place to bury
20:9 shall speak no *m* in his name
22:10 for he will return no *m* and
22:11 He will return there no *m*
22:12 this land he will see no *m*
23:4 and they will be afraid no *m*
23:7 and they will no *m* say
23:36 you people remember no *m*
28:3 years *m* I am bringing back
28:11 within two full years *m*
30:8 no *m* will strangers exploit
31:12 no *m* will they languish
31:15 because they are no *m*
31:29 no *m* say, The fathers were
31:34 no *m* teach each one his
31:34 sin I shall remember no *m*
33:24 no *m* . . . being a nation
34:10 use them no *m* as servants
36:32 to them many *m* words like
42:18 will no *m* see this place
44:26 name will no *m* prove to be
46:23 *m* numerous than the locust
48:2 No *m* is there any praise
48:32 *m* than the weeping for
51:44 nations will stream no *m*
La 4:7 in fact *m* ruddy than corals
5:7 have sinned. They are no *m*
Eze 5:6 wickedness *m* than the nations
5:6 against my statutes *m* than
5:7 you people were *m* turbulent
12:23 no *m* say it as a proverb in
12:24 will no *m* prove to be any
13:15 The wall is no *m*, and those
13:15 plastering it are no *m*
13:21 no *m* prove to be in your
14:11 no *m* go wandering off from
14:11 no *m* go defiling themselves
16:41 no *m* hire will you give
16:42 I shall no *m* feel offended
16:47 act *m* ruinously than they
16:51 detestable things abound *m*
16:52 acted *m* detestably than
16:52 are *m* righteous than you
16:63 no *m* come to have any
18:3 no *m* continue to be yours
19:9 voice might no *m* be heard
20:39 name you will no *m* profane
21:5 No *m* will it go back
23:11 sensual desire *m* ruinously
23:11 *m* than the fornication of
23:27 you will remember no *m*
23:38 What is *m*, this is what
24:13 You will become clean no *m*
26:13 harps will be heard no *m*
26:21 no *m* be found to time
27:36 be no *m* to time indefinite
28:19 be no *m* to time indefinite
28:24 no *m* will there prove to be
29:15 no *m* lift itself up over
29:16 no *m* prove to be the house
30:13 will no *m* prove to be a
32:13 man will no *m* muddy them
32:19 whom are you *m* pleasant
34:29 no *m* become those taken
36:11 do *m* good than in your

Eze 36:12 again of any *m* children
36:14 you will no *m* devour, and
36:14 no *m* bereave of children
36:15 reproach . . . bear no *m*
36:15 no *m* cause to stumble
36:30 no *m* receive among the
39:7 no *m* let my holy name be
42:5 *m* than the lowest ones and
42:6 *m* room was taken away than
43:7 no *m* will they, the house
45:8 no *m* will my chieftains
Da 2:30 in me *m* than in any others
3:19 furnace seven times *m* than it
Ho 1:6 I shall no *m* show mercy again
14:3 And no *m* shall we say
Joe 3:17 will no *m* pass through her
Am 6:10 Are there any *m* with you?
7:8 no *m* do any further excusing
8:2 no *m* do any further excusing
8:14 and they will rise up no *m*
9:15 no *m* be uprooted from their
Jon 1:11 growing *m* tempestuous
1:13 *m* tempestuous against them
3:4 forty days *m*, and Nineveh
4:11 *m* than one hundred and
Mic 5:13 no *m* bow down to the work
Na 1:15 Pay your vows; because no *m*
2:13 no *m* will the voice of your
3:16 multiplied your tradesmen *m*
Hab 1:13 someone *m* righteous than he
Zep 3:15 You will fear calamity no *m*
Zec 9:8 no *m* pass through them a
11:6 show compassion no *m* upon
13:2 will no *m* be remembered
14:11 occur no *m* any banning to
14:21 no *m* prove to be a
Mal 2:13 no *m* a turning toward the
3:10 until there is no *m* want
Mt 2:18 because they are no *m*
5:20 does not abound *m* than that
5:29 *m* beneficial to you for one
5:30 *m* beneficial for one of your
6:25 the soul mean *m* than food
6:26 Are you not worth *m* than
7:11 much *m* so will your Father
10:15 *m* endurable for the land of
10:25 how much *m* will they call
10:31 worth *m* than many sparrows
11:9 and far *m* than a prophet
11:22 be *m* endurable for Tyre and
11:24 *m* endurable for the land of
12:12 much *m* worth is a man than
12:41 *m* than Jonah is here
12:42 *m* than Solomon is here
12:45 different spirits *m* wicked
13:12 *m* will be given him and he
18:6 *m* beneficial for him to have
18:13 he rejoices *m* over it than
18:16 along with you one or two *m*
19:29 will receive many times *m*
20:10 they would receive *m*; but
21:36 slaves, *m* than the first
25:16 with them and gained five *m*
25:17 the two gained two *m*
25:20 see, I gained five talents *m*
25:22 see, I gained two talents *m*
25:29 that has, *m* will be given
26:44 saying once *m* the same word
26:53 *m* than twelve legions of
27:23 kept crying out all the *m*
Mr 2:2 so that there was no *m* room
3:20 Once *m* the crowd gathered
4:24 you will have *m* added to you
4:25 that has will have *m* given
7:36 the *m* he would charge them
7:36 *m* they would proclaim it
9:25 and enter into him no *m*
10:26 became still *m* astounded
10:48 kept shouting that much *m*
12:6 One *m* he had, a beloved son
12:33 worth far *m* than all the
12:43 *m* than all those dropping
14:25 by no means drink any *m* of
14:70 once *m* after a little while
15:13 Once *m* they cried out
15:14 cried out all the *m*: Impale
Lu 3:13 Do not demand anything *m*
5:15 word . . . was spreading the *m*
7:26 and far *m* than a prophet
7:42 will love him the *m*
7:43 whom he freely forgave the *m*
8:18 whoever has, *m* will be given
9:13 nothing *m* than five loaves
10:12 *m* endurable for Sodom in

Lu 10:14 *m* endurable for Tyre and
11:13 much *m* so will the Father
11:26 spirits *m* wicked than itself
11:31 something *m* than Solomon is
11:32 something *m* than Jonah is
12:4 are not able to do anything *m*
12:7 worth *m* than many sparrows
12:23 soul is worth *m* than food
12:24 how much *m* worth are you
12:48 demand *m* than usual of him
12:49 what *m* is there for me to
14:8 someone *m* distinguished than
15:7 *m* joy in heaven over one
17:2 *m* advantage to him if a
17:5 to the Lord: Give us *m* faith
18:14 *m* righteous than that man
18:30 get many times *m* in this
18:39 that much *m* he kept shouting
19:26 that has, *m* will be given
21:3 dropped in *m* than they all
22:44 praying *m* earnestly
Joh 4:1 *m* disciples than John
4:41 many *m* believed on account
5:18 seeking all the *m* to kill
7:31 not perform *m* signs than
10:31 Once *m* the Jews lifted up
12:43 glory of men *m* than even
13:10 have *m* than his feet washed
13:27 get done *m* quickly
14:19 world will behold me no *m*
15:2 that it may bear *m* fruit
16:21 tribulation no *m* because of
16:25 I will speak to you no *m*
19:8 he became *m* fearful
21:15 you love me *m* than these
Ac 4:22 was *m* than forty years old
5:14 *M* than that, believers in the
9:22 acquiring power all the *m*
13:34 no *m* to return to corruption
17:11 latter were *m* noble-minded
17:22 *m* given to the fear of the
18:26 way of God *m* correctly to
20:25 will see my face no *m*
20:35 *m* happiness in giving than
20:38 to behold his face no *m*
21:28 what is *m*, he even brought
22:2 they kept all the *m* silent
23:13 were *m* than forty men that
23:15 determine something *m* accurately the
23:20 something *m* accurate about
23:21 *m* than forty men of theirs
24:11 not been *m* than twelve days
24:26 he sent for him even *m*
25:6 not *m* than eight or ten days
Ro 3:7 truth . . . made *m* prominent
5:9 Much *m*, therefore, since we
5:10 *m*, now that we have become
5:15 abounded much *m* to many
5:17 much *m* will those who
5:20 kindness abounded still *m*
6:9 Christ . . . dies no *m*; death is
6:9 death is master over him no *m*
7:13 might become far *m* sinful
11:12 much *m* will the full number
12:3 not to think *m* of himself
15:15 *m* outspokenly on some
1Co 9:12 over you, do we not much *m*
11:9 what is *m*, man was not
12:23 we surround with *m* abundant
12:23 parts have the *m* abundant
12:24 giving honor *m* abundant to
14:18 speak in *m* tongues than all
2Co 1:12 but *m* especially toward you
2:4 love that I have *m* especially
3:8 spirit be much *m* with glory
3:9 glorious, much *m* does the
3:11 much *m* would that which
4:15 thanksgiving of many *m* to
4:17, 17 glory that is of *m* and *m*
5:16 we now know him so no *m*
7:7 so that I rejoiced yet *m*
7:13 we rejoiced still *m*
7:15 affections are *m* abundant
8:22 much *m* earnest due to his
10:15 we will abound still *m*
11:23 I am *m* outstandingly one
11:23 in labors *m* plentifully
11:23 in prisons *m* plentifully
12:6 *m* than what he sees I am
12:15 I love you the *m* abundantly
Ga 1:14 I was far *m* zealous for the
4:27 *m* numerous than those of her
Eph 3:20 do *m* than superabundantly
4:28 Let the stealer steal no *m*

Php 1:9, 9 love . . . yet *m* and *m*
1:10 sure of the *m* important
1:14 *m* courage to speak the word
1:24 *m* necessary on your account
2:8 *M* than that, when he found
2:12 *m* readily during my absence
2:28 be the *m* free from grief
3:4 in the flesh, I the *m* so
4:4 Once *m* I will say, Rejoice!
4:17 *m* credit to your account
1Th 2:17 far *m* than is usual to see
3:10 make *m* than extraordinary
4:1 keep on doing it *m* fully
5:13 *m* than extraordinary
1Ti 6:2 *m* readily be slaves, because
2Ti 2:16, 16 to *m* and *m* ungodliness
Phm 16 but as *m* than a slave, as a
16 how much *m* so to you both in
21 do *m* than the things I say
Heb 1:4 name *m* excellent than theirs
1:9 *m* than your partners
2:1 *m* than the usual attention
3:3 worthy of *m* glory than Moses
3:3 constructs it has *m* honor
6:17 demonstrate *m* abundantly to
7:15 still *m* abundantly clear
8:6 obtained a *m* excellent public
9:11 *m* perfect tent not made
9:14 much *m* will the blood of
10:25 *m* so as you behold the day
10:29 *m* severe a punishment, do
11:32 And what *m* shall I say? For
11:36 *m* than that, by bonds and
12:9 much *m* subject ourselves to
12:25 much *m* shall we not if we
12:26 Yet once *m* I will set in
12:27 Yet once *m* signifies the
13:19 I exhort you *m* especially
1Pe 4:2 no *m* for the desires of men
2Pe 1:10 all the *m* do your utmost
1:19 prophetic word made *m* sure
Re 2:19 are *m* than those formerly
7:16 will hunger no *m* nor thirst
9:12 Two *m* woes are coming after
21:1 and the sea is no *m*
21:4 death will be no *m*, neither
22:3 no *m* will there be any curse
22:5 Also, night will be no *m*

Moreh
Ge 12:6 near the big trees of *M*
De 11:30 beside the big trees of *M*
Jg 7:1 hill of *M*, in the low plain

Moresheth
Jer 26:18 Micah of *M* . . . prophesying
Mic 1:1 that occurred to Micah of *M*

Moresheth-gath
Mic 1:14 give parting gifts to *M*

Moriah
Ge 22:2 a trip to the land of *M* and
2Ch 3:1 in Jerusalem on Mount *M*

Morning
Ge 1:5 there came to be *m*, a first day
1:8 came to be *m*, a second day
1:13 came to be *m*, a third day
1:19 came to be *m*, a fourth day
1:23 came to be *m*, a fifth day
1:31 came to be *m*, a sixth day
19:27 early in the *m* to the place
20:8 got up early in the *m* and
21:14 early in the *m* and took
22:3 Abraham got up early in the *m*
24:54 there and got up in the *m*
26:31 Next *m* they were early in
28:18 Jacob got up early in the *m*
29:25 it followed in the *m* that
31:55 Laban got up early in the *m*
40:6 came in to them in the *m* and
41:8 in the *m* that his spirit
44:3 The *m* had become light when
49:27 In the *m* he will eat the
Ex 7:15 Go to Pharaoh in the *m*
8:20 Moses: Get up early in the *m*
9:13 Get up early in the *m* and
10:13 *m* came and the east wind
12:10 leave any of it over till *m*
12:10 left over of it till *m* you
12:22 of his house until *m*
14:24 during the *m* watch that
14:27 at the approaching of *m*
16:7 in the *m* you will indeed see
16:8 the *m* bread to satisfaction
Ex 16:12 the *m* you will be satisfied
16:13 in the *m* there had developed
16:19 leave any of it until the *m*
16:20 leave some of it until the *m*
16:21, 21 would pick it up *m* by *m*
16:23 to be kept until the *m*
16:24 they saved it up until the *m*
18:13 from the *m* till the evening
18:14 you from *m* till evening
19:16 when it became *m* it came
23:18 not stay overnight until *m*
24:4 he got up early in the *m* and
27:21 from evening till *m* before
29:34 be left over until the *m*
29:39 will offer . . . ram in the *m*
29:41 offering like that of the *m*
30:7, 7 *M* by *m*, when he dresses
34:2 get ready for the *m*, as you
34:2 in the *m* into Mount Sinai
34:4 got up early in the *m* and
34:25 stay overnight until the *m*
36:3, 3 offering *m* after *m*
Le 6:9 all night long until the *m*
6:12, 12 burn wood on it *m* by *m*
6:20 half of it in the *m* and half
7:15 not save up any of it until *m*
9:17 the burnt offering of the *m*
19:13 all night with you until *m*
22:30 not leave any of it until *m*
24:3 from evening to *m* before
Nu 9:12 let any of it remain until *m*
9:15 over the tabernacle until *m*
9:21 evening to *m*; and the cloud
9:21 cloud lifted itself in the *m*
14:40 they got up early in the *m*
16:5 In the *m* Jehovah will make
22:13 Balaam got up in the *m* and
22:21 Balaam got up in the *m* and
22:41 in the *m* that Balak went
28:4 you will render up in the *m*
28:8 grain offering as of the *m*
28:23 the *m* burnt offering, which
De 16:4 stay all night until the *m*
16:7 in the *m* you must turn around
28:67 In the *m* you will say, If it
28:67 will say, If it only were *m*!
Jos 3:1 Joshua got up early in the *m*
6:12 Joshua got up early in the *m*
7:14 present yourselves in the *m*
7:16 Joshua rose early in the *m*
8:10 rose up early in the *m* and
Jg 6:28 early in the *m* as usual, why
6:31 put to death even this *m*
9:33 in the *m* that as soon as the
16:2 As soon as the *m* gets light
19:5 they got up early in the *m* as
19:8 he got up early in the *m* on
19:25 all night long until the *m*
19:26 came as it was turning to *m*
19:27 her master rose up in the *m*
20:19 Israel rose up in the *m* and
Ru 2:7 from that time in the *m* until
3:13 it must occur in the *m* that
3:13 Keep lying down until the *m*
3:14 lying at his feet until the *m*
1Sa 1:19 they got up early in the *m*
3:15 lying down until the *m*
5:4 in the *m* the very day after
9:19 must send you away in the *m*
11:11 during the *m* watch and
14:36 until the *m* lightens up
15:12 early to meet Saul in the *m*
17:16 at early *m* and at evening
17:20 got up early in the *m* and
19:2 your guard, please, in the *m*
19:11 put to death in the *m*; but
20:35 in the *m* that Jonathan made
25:22 remain until the *m*
25:34 until the *m* light anyone
25:36 until the *m* light
25:37 came about in the *m*, when
29:10 rise up early in the *m*
29:10 rise up early in the *m* when
29:11 go in the *m* and return to
30:17 from the *m* darkness until
2Sa 2:27 by the *m* would the people
11:14 in the *m* that David
13:4, 4 downcast as this, *m* by *m*
17:22 until the *m* became light
23:4 Then it is as the light of *m*
23:4 A *m* without clouds
24:11 to rise up in the *m*
24:15 from the *m* until the time
1Ki 3:21 got up in the *m* to nurse my
1Ki 3:21 examined him . . . in the *m*
17:6 bread and meat in the *m* and
18:26 from *m* till noon, saying
2Ki 3:20 came about in the *m*, at the
3:22 early in the *m*, the sun
7:9 wait until the *m* light
10:8 entrance of the gate until *m*
10:9 in the *m* that he proceeded
16:15 offering of the *m* smoke
19:35 rose up early in the *m*
1Ch 9:27, 27 open up from *m* to *m*
16:40 constantly *m* and evening
23:30, 30 *m* by *m* to thank and
2Ch 2:4 burnt offerings in the *m* and
13:11, 11 offerings . . . *m* by *m*
20:20 rise early in the *m* and go
31:3 burnt offerings of the *m* and
Ezr 3:3 burnt sacrifices of the *m* and
Es 2:14 in the *m* she herself returned
5:14 Then in the *m* say to the king
Job 1:5 and he got up early in the *m*
4:20 From *m* to evening they are
7:4 restlessness until *m* twilight
7:18 pay attention to him every *m*
11:17 Darkness . . . like the *m*
24:17 *m* . . . same as deep shadow
38:7 *m* stars joyfully cried out
38:12 that you commanded the *m*
Ps 5:3 in the *m* you will hear my
5:3 In the *m* I shall address
30:5 the *m* there is a joyful cry
46:5 at the appearance of *m*
49:14 in subjection in the *m*
55:17 Evening and *m* and noontime
59:16 in the *m* I shall joyfully
65:8 goings forth of the *m* and
73:14 And my correction is every *m*
88:13 in the *m* my own prayer
90:5 In the *m* they are just like
90:6 *m* it puts forth blossoms
90:14 Satisfy us in the *m* with
92:2 To tell in the *m* about your
101:8 Every *m* I shall silence all
119:147 up early in the *m* twilight
130:6 than watchmen for the *m*
130:6 Watching for the *m*
143:8 In the *m* cause me to hear
Pr 7:18 our fill of love until the *m*
27:14 a loud voice early in the *m*
Ec 10:16 keep eating even in the *m*
11:6 In the *m* sow your seed and
Isa 5:11 early in the *m* that they
17:11 *m* you may cause the seed of
17:14 Before *m*—it is no more
21:12 *m* has to come, and also the
28:19, 19 *m* by *m* it will pass
33:2 Become our arm every *m*
37:36 rose up early in the *m*
38:13 soothed myself until the *m*
50:4, 4 He awakens *m* by *m*; he
Jer 20:16 hear an outcry in the *m*
21:12 Every *m* render sentence in
La 2:19 at the start of the *m* watches
3:23 They are new each *m*
Eze 12:8 occur to me in the *m*, saying
24:18 to the people in the *m*
24:18 in the *m* just as I had been
33:22 coming to me in the *m*, and
46:13, 13 *M* by *m* you should
46:14, 14 provide with it *m* by *m*
46:15, 15 *m* by *m* as a constant
Da 8:26 the evening and the *m*
Ho 6:4 is like the *m* clouds and like
7:6 by *m* the furnace is burning as
13:3 become like the clouds of *m*
Am 4:4 bring your sacrifices in the *m*
5:8 deep shadow into the *m*
Mic 2:1 By the light of the *m* they
Zep 3:3 did not gnaw bones till the *m*
3:5, 5 *M* by *m* he kept giving his
Mt 16:3 and at *m*, It will be wintry
20:1 went out early in the *m* to
21:18 in the *m*, he got hungry
27:1 When it had become *m*, all
Mr 1:35 early in the *m*, while it was
11:20 passing by early in the *m*
13:35 or early in the *m*
Joh 21:4 as it was getting to be *m*
Ac 28:23 from *m* till evening
Re 2:28 I will give him the *m* star
22:16 and the bright *m* star

Mornings
Da 8:14 three hundred evenings and *m*

Morsel
2Sa 12:3 From his *m* it would eat, and
Job 31:17 used to eat my *m* by myself
Pr 23:8 Your *m* that you have eaten
Joh 13:26 shall give the *m* that I dip
13:26 dipped the *m*, he took and
13:27 after the *m* then Satan
13:30 after he received the *m*, he

Morsels
Ps 147:17 throwing his ice like *m*
Eze 13:19 and for the *m* of bread, in

Mortal
De 32:26 of them cease from *m* men
2Ch 14:11 *m* man retain strength
Job 4:17 *M* man—can he be more just
7:1 compulsory labor for *m* man
7:17 What is *m* man that you
9:2 can *m* man be in the right in
10:4 as a *m* man sees that you see
10:5 like the days of *m* man
13:9 as one trifles with *m* man
14:19 destroyed . . . hope of *m* man
15:14 What is *m* man that he
25:4 how can *m* man be in the
25:6 *m* man, who is a maggot
28:4 *m* men have swung down
28:13 *M* man has not come to know
32:8 it is the spirit in *m* men
33:12 much more than *m* man
33:26 righteousness to *m* man
36:25 *M* man himself keeps
37:7 *m* man to know his work
Ps 8:4 What is *m* man that you keep
9:19 Let not *m* man prove superior
9:20 know that they are but *m* men
10:18 *m* man who is of the earth
55:13 *m* man who was as my equal
56:1 *m* man has snapped at me
66:12 *m* man to ride over our head
73:5 in the trouble of *m* man
90:3 make *m* man go back to crushed
103:15 *m* man, his days are like
104:15 the heart of *m* man rejoice
104:15 the very heart of *m* man
144:3 *m* man that you should take
Isa 8:1 with the stylus of *m* man
13:7 heart itself of *m* man will
13:12 make *m* man rarer than
24:6 few *m* men have remained
33:8 taken no account of *m* man
51:7 the reproach of *m* men, and
51:12 a *m* man that will die
56:2 Happy is the *m* man that does
Jer 20:10 *m* man bidding me Peace!
Ro 6:12 rule as king in your *m* bodies
8:11 make your *m* bodies alive
1Co 15:53 this which is *m* must put
15:54 is *m* puts on immortality
2Co 4:11 manifest in our *m* flesh
5:4 *m* may be swallowed up by

Mortally
Jg 20:31 *m* wounded on the highways
20:39 thirty men *m* wounded among

Mortar
Ge 11:3 bitumen served as *m* for them
Ex 1:14 slavery at clay *m* and bricks
Le 14:41 the clay *m* that they cut off
14:42 have different clay *m* taken
14:45 all the clay *m* of the house
Nu 11:8 pounded it in a *m*, and they
1Ch 29:2 stones to be set with hard *m*
Pr 27:22 fine with a pestle in a *m*
Isa 54:11 with hard *m* your stones
Jer 43:9 *m* in the terrace of bricks

Mortar-shaped
Jg 15:19 a *m* hollow that was in Lehi

Mosaic
1Ch 29:2 and *m* pebbles, and every

Moserah
De 10:6 for *M*. There Aaron died, and

Moseroth
Nu 33:30 and went camping in *M*
33:31 pulled away from *M* and went

Moses
Ex 2:10 call his name *M* and to say
2:11 as *M* was becoming strong
2:14 *M* now got afraid and said
2:15 and he attempted to kill *M*
2:15 *M* ran away from Pharaoh that
Ex 2:17 *M* got up and helped the
2:21 *M* showed willingness to
2:21 Zipporah his daughter to *M*
3:1 *M* became a shepherd of the
3:3 At this *M* said: Let me just
3:4, 4 thornbush and said: *M! M!*
3:6 Then *M* concealed his face
3:11 *M* said to the true God
3:13 *M* said to the true God
3:14 God said to *M:* I shall prove
3:15 Then God said once more to *M*
4:1 However, *M* in answering said
4:3 serpent; and *M* began to flee
4:4 Jehovah now said to *M:* Thrust
4:10 *M* now said to Jehovah: Excuse
4:14 anger grew hot against *M*
4:18 *M* went and returned to Jethro
4:18 Jethro said to *M:* Go in peace
4:19 Jehovah said to *M* in Midian
4:20 *M* took his wife and his sons
4:20 *M* took the rod of the true
4:21 Jehovah went on to say to *M*
4:27 said to Aaron: Go to meet *M*
4:28 *M* proceeded to tell Aaron all
4:29 *M* and Aaron went and gathered
4:30 that Jehovah had spoken to *M*
5:1 afterward *M* and Aaron went in
5:4 Why is it, *M* and Aaron, that
5:20 they encountered *M* and Aaron
5:22 *M* turned to Jehovah and said
6:1 Jehovah said to *M:* Now you
6:2 God went on to speak to *M* and
6:9 *M* spoke to this effect to the
6:9 they did not listen to *M* out
6:10 Jehovah spoke to *M*, saying
6:12 *M* spoke before Jehovah
6:13 continued to speak to *M* and
6:20 she bore him Aaron and *M*
6:26 Aaron and *M* to whom Jehovah
6:27 This is the *M* and Aaron
6:28 day that Jehovah spoke to *M*
6:29 Jehovah went on to speak to *M*
6:30 Then *M* said before Jehovah
7:1 Jehovah said to *M:* See, I have
7:6 *M* and Aaron went ahead doing
7:7 And *M* was eighty years old and
7:8 Jehovah now said to *M* and
7:10 *M* . . . went on in to Pharaoh
7:14 Jehovah said to *M:* Pharaoh's
7:19 Jehovah said to *M:* Say to
7:20 *M* and Aaron did so, just as
8:1 Jehovah said to *M:* Go in to
8:5 Jehovah said to *M:* Say to
8:8 Pharaoh called *M* and Aaron and
8:9 *M* said to Pharaoh: You take
8:12 *M* and Aaron went out from
8:12 and *M* cried out to Jehovah
8:16 Jehovah now said to *M:* Say to
8:20 Jehovah said to *M:* Get up
8:25 Pharaoh called *M* and Aaron
8:26 *M* said: It is not admissible
8:29 *M* said: Here I am going forth
8:30 *M* went out from Pharaoh and
9:1 Jehovah said to *M:* Go in to
9:8 Jehovah said to *M* and Aaron
9:8 and *M* must toss it toward the
9:10 and *M* tossed it toward the
9:11 unable to stand before *M*
9:12 as Jehovah had stated to *M*
9:13 Jehovah said to *M:* Get up
9:22 Jehovah now said to *M*
9:23 So *M* stretched out his rod
9:27 Pharaoh sent and called *M* and
9:29 *M* said to him: As soon as I
9:33 *M* now went out of the city
9:35 had stated by means of *M*
10:1 Jehovah said to *M:* Go in to
10:3 *M* . . . went in to Pharaoh and
10:8 *M* and Aaron were brought back
10:9 *M* said: With our young people
10:12 Jehovah now said to *M*
10:13 *M* stretched his rod out over
10:16 Pharaoh hurriedly called *M*
10:21 Jehovah then said to *M*
10:22 *M* immediately stretched his
10:24 Pharaoh called *M* and said
10:25 *M* said: You yourself will
10:29 *M* said: That is the way you
11:1 say to *M:* One plague more I
11:3 *M* too was very great in the
11:4 *M* went on to say: This is
11:9 Jehovah said to *M:* Pharaoh
11:10 *M* and Aaron performed all
12:1 Jehovah now said to *M* and
Ex 12:21 *M* called all the older men
12:28 as Jehovah had commanded *M*
12:31 called *M* and Aaron by night
12:35 according to the word of *M*
12:43 Jehovah went on to say to *M*
12:50 as Jehovah had commanded *M*
13:1 Jehovah spoke further to *M*
13:3 And *M* went on to say to the
13:19 *M* was taking Joseph's bones
14:1 Jehovah now spoke to *M*
14:11 to say to *M:* Is it because
14:13 *M* said to the people: Do not
14:15 Jehovah now said to *M:* Why
14:21 *M* now stretched his hand out
14:26 Jehovah said to *M:* Stretch
14:27 *M* at once stretched his hand
14:31 faith in Jehovah and in *M*
15:1 *M* and the sons of Israel
15:22 *M* caused Israel to depart
15:24 began to murmur against *M*
16:2 murmur against *M* and Aaron
16:4 Jehovah said to *M:* Here I am
16:6 *M* and Aaron said to all the
16:8 *M* continued: It will be when
16:9 *M* went on to say to Aaron
16:11 Jehovah spoke further to *M*
16:15 *M* said to them: It is the
16:19 *M* said to them: Let nobody
16:20 But they did not listen to *M*
16:20 so that *M* became indignant
16:22 came and reported it to *M*
16:24 just as *M* had commanded
16:25 Then *M* said: Eat it today
16:28 Jehovah said to *M:* How long
16:32 *M* said: This is the word
16:33 *M* said to Aaron: Take a jar
16:34 as Jehovah had commanded *M*
17:2 quarreling with *M* and saying
17:2 *M* said to them: Why are you
17:3 kept murmuring against *M* and
17:4 *M* cried out to Jehovah
17:5 Jehovah said to *M:* Pass in
17:6 *M* did so under the eyes of
17:9 *M* said to Joshua: Choose men
17:10 Joshua did just as *M* had
17:10 *M*, Aaron and Hur went up to
17:11 as *M* would lift his hand up
17:12 the hands of *M* were heavy
17:14 Jehovah now said to *M*
17:15 *M* proceeded to build an
18:1 done for *M* and for Israel his
18:5 and his wife came to *M* into
18:6 Then he sent word to *M:* I
18:7 *M* went on out to meet his
18:8 And *M* went to relating to his
18:13 *M* sat down as usual to serve
18:13 kept standing before *M* from
18:15 *M* said to his father-in-law
18:24 *M* listened to the voice of
18:25 *M* proceeded to choose
18:26 they would bring to *M*, but
18:27 *M* saw his father-in-law off
19:3 *M* went up to the true God
19:7 *M* came and called the older
19:8 *M* took back the words of the
19:9 Jehovah said to *M:* Look! I am
19:9 *M* reported the words of the
19:10 Jehovah went on to say to *M*
19:14 Then *M* went down from the
19:17 *M* now brought the people out
19:19 *M* began to speak, and the
19:20 Jehovah called *M* to the top
19:20 and *M* went on up
19:21 Jehovah now said to *M:* Go
19:23 At this *M* said to Jehovah
19:25 *M* descended to the people
20:19 say to *M:* You speak with us
20:20 *M* said to the people: Do not
20:21 *M* went near to the dark
20:22 Jehovah went on to say to *M*
24:1 And to *M* he said: Go up to
24:2 *M* by himself must approach
24:3 *M* came and related to the
24:4 *M* wrote down all the words
24:6 *M* took half the blood and put
24:8 *M* took the blood and
24:9 *M* and Aaron, Nadab and Abihu
24:12 Jehovah now said to *M:* Come
24:13 So *M* and Joshua his minister
24:13 *M* went up into the mountain
24:15 *M* went up into the mountain
24:16 called to *M* from the midst
24:18 *M* entered into the midst of
24:18 *M* continued in the mountain

Ex 25:1 speak to *M*, saying
30:11 to speak to *M*, saying
30:17 Jehovah spoke further to *M*
30:22 continued to speak to *M*
30:34 say to *M:* Take to yourself
31:1 continued to speak to *M*
31:12 Jehovah said further to *M*
31:18 to give *M* two tablets of the
32:1 that *M* was taking a long
32:1 *M*, the man who led us up out
32:7 Jehovah now said to *M:* Go
32:9 Jehovah went on to say to *M*
32:11 *M* proceeded to soften the
32:15 *M* turned and went down from
32:17 proceeded to say to *M:* There
32:21 After that *M* said to Aaron
32:23 as regards this *M*, the man
32:25 *M* got to see that the people
32:26 *M* took his stand in the gate
32:28 to do as *M* had said, so that
32:29 *M* went on to say: Fill your
32:30 *M* proceeded to say to the
32:31 *M* returned to Jehovah and
32:33 to *M:* Whoever has sinned
33:1 Jehovah said further to *M:* Go
33:5 Jehovah went on to say to *M*
33:7 As for *M*, he proceeded to
33:8 as *M* went out to the tent
33:8 they gazed after *M* until he
33:9 as soon as *M* had gone into
33:9 and he spoke with *M*
33:11 spoke to *M* face to face
33:12 Now *M* said to Jehovah
33:17 went on to say to *M:* This
34:1 Jehovah said to *M:* Carve out
34:4 *M* carved out two tablets of
34:8 *M* at once hurried to bow
34:27 Jehovah went on to say to *M*
34:29 when *M* came down from Mount
34:29 in the hand of *M* when he
34:29 *M* did not know that the skin
34:30 got to see *M*, why, look! the
34:31 And *M* proceeded to call them
34:31 *M* began to speak to them
34:33 *M* would finish speaking with
34:34 *M* would go in before Jehovah
34:35 *M* put the veil back over his
35:1 *M* called the entire assembly
35:4 *M* went on to say to the
35:20 went out from before *M*
35:29 to make by means of *M*
35:30 *M* said to the sons of Israel
36:2 *M* proceeded to call Bezalel
36:3 took from before *M* all the
36:5 say to *M:* The people are
36:6 *M* commanded that they should
38:21 at the command of *M*, as the
38:22 that Jehovah had commanded *M*
39:1 as Jehovah had commanded *M*
39:5 as Jehovah had commanded *M*
39:7 as Jehovah had commanded *M*
39:21 as Jehovah had commanded *M*
39:26 as Jehovah had commanded *M*
39:29 as Jehovah had commanded *M*
39:31 as Jehovah had commanded *M*
39:32 that Jehovah had commanded *M*
39:33 to bring the tabernacle to *M*
39:42 that Jehovah had commanded *M*
39:43 *M* got to see all the work
39:43 Consequently *M* blessed them
40:1 Jehovah spoke to *M*, saying
40:16 *M* proceeded to do according
40:18 When *M* proceeded to set up
40:19 as Jehovah had commanded *M*
40:21 as Jehovah had commanded *M*
40:23 as Jehovah had commanded *M*
40:25 as Jehovah had commanded *M*
40:27 as Jehovah had commanded *M*
40:29 as Jehovah had commanded *M*
40:31 *M* and Aaron and his sons
40:32 as Jehovah had commanded *M*
40:33 So *M* finished the work
40:35 *M* was not able to go into the
Le 1:1 to call *M* and speak to him out
4:1 Jehovah went on to speak to *M*
5:14 continued to speak to *M*
6:1 Jehovah went on to speak to *M*
6:8 continued to speak to *M*
6:19 went on speaking to *M*
6:24 Jehovah spoke further to *M*
7:22 continued to speak to *M*
7:28 Jehovah went on to speak to *M*
7:38 Jehovah had commanded *M* in
8:1 to speak to *M*, saying

Le 8:4 Then *M* did just as Jehovah had
8:5 *M* now said to the assembly
8:6 *M* brought Aaron and his sons
8:9 as Jehovah had commanded *M*
8:10 *M* now took the anointing oil
8:13 *M* then brought Aaron's sons
8:13 as Jehovah had commanded *M*
8:15 *M* proceeded to slaughter it
8:16 *M* made them smoke upon the
8:17 as Jehovah had commanded *M*
8:19 *M* slaughtered it and
8:20 *M* proceeded to make the head
8:21 *M* then made the entire ram
8:21 as Jehovah had commanded *M*
8:23 *M* slaughtered it and took
8:24 *M* brought Aaron's sons near
8:24 *M* sprinkled the rest of the
8:28 *M* took them off their palms
8:29 *M* proceeded to take the
8:29 it became the portion for *M*
8:29 as Jehovah had commanded *M*
8:30 *M* took some of the anointing
8:31 Then *M* said to Aaron and his
8:36 commanded by means of *M*
9:1 *M* called Aaron and his sons
9:5 took what *M* had commanded
9:6 *M* went on to say: This is the
9:7 Then *M* said to Aaron: Go near
9:10 as Jehovah had commanded *M*
9:21 just as *M* had commanded
9:23 *M* and Aaron went into the
10:3 Then *M* said to Aaron: This
10:4 *M* called Mishael and Elzaphan
10:5 just as *M* had spoken
10:6 *M* said to Aaron and to
10:11 to them by means of *M*
10:12 Then *M* spoke to Aaron and
10:16 And *M* searched thoroughly
10:19 At this Aaron spoke to *M*
10:20 When *M* got to hear that
11:1 to speak to *M* and Aaron
12:1 Jehovah went on to speak to *M*
13:1 proceeded to speak to *M* and
14:1 continued to speak to *M*
14:33 to speak to *M* and Aaron
15:1 speak to *M* and Aaron, saying
16:1 speak to *M* after the death of
16:2 to say to *M:* Speak to Aaron
16:34 as Jehovah had commanded *M*
17:1 Jehovah went on to speak to *M*
18:1 continued to speak to *M*
19:1 Jehovah spoke further to *M*
20:1 on speaking to *M*, saying
21:1 to *M:* Talk to the priests
21:16 continued to speak to *M*
21:24 *M* spoke to Aaron and his
22:1 Jehovah spoke further to *M*
22:17 to speak to *M*, saying
22:26 Jehovah spoke further to *M*
23:1 Jehovah went on speaking to *M*
23:9 continued to speak to *M*
23:23 went on speaking to *M*
23:26 Jehovah spoke further to *M*
23:33 continued to speak to *M*
23:44 *M* spoke of the seasonal
24:1 to speak to *M*, saying
24:11 So they brought him to *M*
24:13 to speak to *M*, saying
24:23 *M* spoke to the sons of
24:23 as Jehovah had commanded *M*
25:1 Jehovah spoke further to *M* in
26:46 in Mount Sinai by means of *M*
27:1 to speak to *M*, saying
27:34 Jehovah gave *M* as commands
Nu 1:1 *M* in the wilderness of Sinai
1:17 *M* and Aaron took these men
1:19 Jehovah had commanded *M;* and
1:44 *M* registered, together with
1:48 Jehovah spoke to *M*, saying
1:54 that Jehovah had commanded *M*
2:1 Jehovah now spoke to *M* and
2:33 as Jehovah had commanded *M*
2:34 that Jehovah had commanded *M*
3:1 generations of Aaron and *M* in
3:1 Jehovah spoke with *M* in Mount
3:5 to speak to *M*, saying
3:11 continued to speak to *M*
3:14 Jehovah spoke further to *M*
3:16 *M* began to register them at
3:38 *M* and Aaron and his sons
3:39 *M* and Aaron registered at the
3:40 Jehovah said to *M:* Register
3:42 *M* proceeded, just as Jehovah
3:44 continued to speak to *M*

Nu 3:49 So *M* took the money of the
3:51 *M* gave the money of the
3:51 as Jehovah had commanded *M*
4:1 Jehovah now spoke to *M* and
4:17 Jehovah spoke further to *M*
4:21 Jehovah spoke to *M*, saying
4:34 *M* and Aaron and the
4:37 *M* and Aaron registered at the
4:37 of Jehovah by means of *M*
4:41 *M* and Aaron registered at the
4:45 *M* and Aaron registered at the
4:45 Jehovah by means of *M*
4:46 whom *M* and Aaron and the
4:49 registered by means of *M*
4:49 as Jehovah had commanded *M*
5:1 Jehovah spoke further to *M*
5:4 Jehovah had spoken to *M*, so
5:5 continued speaking to *M*
5:11 Jehovah went on to speak to *M*
6:1 And Jehovah spoke further to *M*
6:22 Jehovah spoke to *M*, saying
7:1 *M* finished setting up the
7:4 At this Jehovah said to *M*
7:6 *M* accepted the wagons and the
7:11 So Jehovah said to *M:* One
7:89 *M* went into the tent of
8:1 to speak to *M*, saying
8:3 as Jehovah had commanded *M*
8:4 that Jehovah had shown *M*
8:5 Jehovah spoke further to *M*
8:20 *M* and Aaron and all the
8:20 Jehovah had commanded *M* as
8:22 Jehovah had commanded *M*
8:23 Jehovah now spoke to *M*
9:1 speak to *M* in the wilderness of
9:4 *M* spoke to the sons of Israel
9:5 that Jehovah had commanded *M*
9:6 before *M* and Aaron on that day
9:8 *M* said to them: Stand there
9:9 Jehovah spoke to *M*, saying
9:23 Jehovah by means of *M*
10:1 proceeded to speak to *M*
10:13 of Jehovah by means of *M*
10:29 *M* said to Hobab the son of
10:29 Hobab . . . father-in-law of *M*
10:35 *M* would say: Do arise
11:2 people began to cry out to *M*
11:10 *M* got to hear the people
11:10 in the eyes of *M* it was bad
11:11 *M* said to Jehovah: Why have
11:16 Jehovah said to *M:* Gather for
11:21 *M* said: The people in the
11:23 Jehovah said to *M:* The hand
11:24 *M* went out and spoke to the
11:27 reporting to *M* and saying
11:28 minister of *M* from his young
11:28 My lord *M*, restrain them!
11:29 *M* said to him: Are you
11:30 *M* withdrew to the camp
12:1 speak against *M* on account of
12:2 by *M* alone that Jehovah has
12:3 *M* was by far the meekest of
12:4 Jehovah suddenly said to *M*
12:7 Not so my servant *M!*
12:8 fear to speak . . . against *M*
12:11 Aaron said to *M:* Excuse me
12:13 And *M* began to cry out to
12:14 Jehovah said to *M:* Were her
13:1 Jehovah now spoke to *M*
13:3 So *M* sent them out from the
13:16 men whom *M* sent to spy out
13:16 *M* continued to call Hoshea
13:17 *M* was sending them to spy
13:26 they walked and came to *M*
13:30 still the people toward *M*
14:2 murmur against *M* and Aaron
14:5 *M* and Aaron fell upon their
14:11 Jehovah said to *M:* How long
14:13 *M* said to Jehovah: Then the
14:26 went on to speak to *M* and
14:36 men whom *M* sent to spy out
14:39 *M* proceeded to speak these
14:41 *M* said: Why is it that you
14:44 *M* did not move away from
15:1 Jehovah spoke further to *M*
15:17 went on to speak to *M*
15:22 Jehovah has spoken to *M*
15:23 commanded you by means of *M*
15:33 brought him up to *M* and
15:35 Jehovah said to *M:* Without
15:36 as Jehovah had commanded *M*
15:37 went on to say this to *M*
16:2 to rise up before *M*, they and
16:3 against *M* and Aaron and said

Nu 16:4 When *M* got to hear it he at
16:8 *M* went on to say to Korah
16:12 *M* sent to call Dathan and
16:15 *M* became very angry and said
16:16 *M* said to Korah: You and all
16:18 together with *M* and Aaron
16:20 Jehovah now spoke to *M* and
16:23 Jehovah spoke to *M*, saying
16:25 *M* got up and went to Dathan
16:28 *M* said: By this you will
16:36 Jehovah now spoke to *M*
16:40 spoken to him by means of *M*
16:41 murmur against *M* and Aaron
16:42 together against *M* and Aaron
16:43 And *M* and Aaron proceeded to
16:44 Jehovah spoke to *M*, saying
16:46 *M* said to Aaron: Take the
16:47 just as *M* had spoken, and
16:50 at last Aaron returned to *M*
17:1 Jehovah now spoke to *M*
17:6 *M* spoke to the sons of Israel
17:7 *M* deposited the rods before
17:8 *M* went into the tent of the
17:9 *M* then brought out all the
17:10 Jehovah said to *M*: Put
17:11 *M* did just as Jehovah had
17:12 began to say this to *M*: Now
18:25 Jehovah spoke to *M*, saying
19:1 to speak to *M* and Aaron
20:2 against *M* and Aaron
20:3 went quarreling with *M* and
20:6 *M* and Aaron came from before
20:7 Jehovah spoke to *M*, saying
20:9 So *M* took the rod from before
20:10 *M* and Aaron called the
20:11 *M* lifted his hand up and
20:12 Jehovah said to *M* and Aaron
20:14 *M* sent messengers from
20:23 Jehovah said this to *M* and
20:27 So *M* did just as Jehovah had
20:28 Then *M* stripped Aaron of his
20:28 *M* and Eleazar came on down
21:5 speaking against God and *M*
21:7 the people came to *M* and said
21:7 *M* went interceding in behalf
21:8 Jehovah said to *M*: Make for
21:9 *M* at once made a serpent of
21:16 Jehovah said to *M*: Gather
21:32 *M* sent some to spy on Jazer
21:34 Jehovah now said to *M*: Do
25:4 Jehovah said to *M*: Take all
25:5 Then *M* said to the judges of
25:10 Jehovah spoke to *M*, saying
25:16 Jehovah spoke to *M*, saying
26:1 to say this to *M* and Eleazar
26:3 And *M* and Eleazar the priest
26:4 as Jehovah had commanded *M*
26:9 struggle against *M* and Aaron
26:52 Jehovah spoke to *M*, saying
26:59 bore to Amram Aaron and *M*
26:63 registered by *M* and Eleazar
26:64 registered by *M* and Aaron
27:2 to stand before *M* and before
27:5 *M* presented their case before
27:6 Jehovah then said this to *M*
27:11 as Jehovah has commanded *M*
27:12 Jehovah said to *M*: Go up
27:15 *M* spoke to Jehovah, saying
27:18 Jehovah said to *M*: Take for
27:22 *M* proceeded to do just as
27:23 had spoken by means of *M*
28:1 Jehovah spoke further to *M*
29:40 *M* proceeded to talk to the
29:40 Jehovah had commanded *M*
30:1 *M* spoke to the heads of the
30:16 that Jehovah commanded *M* as
31:1 Jehovah then spoke to *M*
31:3 *M* spoke to the people, saying
31:6 *M* sent them out, a thousand
31:7 as Jehovah had commanded *M*
31:12 bringing to *M* and Eleazar
31:13 *M* and Eleazar the priest and
31:14 And *M* grew indignant at the
31:15 *M* said to them: Have you
31:21 that Jehovah commanded *M*
31:25 proceeded to say this to *M*
31:31 And *M* and Eleazar the priest
31:31 as Jehovah had commanded *M*
31:41 *M* gave the tax as Jehovah's
31:41 as Jehovah had commanded *M*
31:42 which *M* divided from that
31:47 Then *M* took from the half
31:47 as Jehovah had commanded *M*
31:48 proceeded to approach *M*

Nu 31:49 to say to *M*: Your servants
31:51 *M* and Eleazar the priest
31:54 So *M* and Eleazar the priest
32:2 said this to *M* and Eleazar
32:6 *M* said to the sons of Gad and
32:20 *M* said to them: If you will
32:25 said this to *M*: Your
32:28 *M* gave a command respecting
32:29 *M* said to them: If the sons
32:33 At this *M* gave to them, that
32:40 *M* gave Gilead to Machir the
33:1 by the hand of *M* and Aaron
33:2 And *M* kept recording the
33:50 to speak to *M* on the desert
34:1 Jehovah spoke further to *M*
34:13 So *M* commanded the sons of
34:16 Jehovah spoke further to *M*
35:1 Jehovah went on to speak to *M*
35:9 continued to speak to *M*
36:1 come near and speak before *M*
36:5 Then *M* commanded the sons of
36:10 as Jehovah had commanded *M*
36:13 commanded by means of *M* to
De 1:1 that *M* spoke to all Israel
1:3 *M* spoke to the sons of Israel
1:5 *M* undertook to explain this
4:41 *M* proceeded to set apart
4:44 the law that *M* set before the
4:45 decisions that *M* spoke to the
4:46 *M* and the sons of Israel
5:1 *M* proceeded to call all
27:1 *M* together with the older
27:9 *M* and the priests
27:11 *M* went on to command the
29:1 Jehovah commanded *M* to
29:2 *M* proceeded to call all Israel
31:1 *M* went and spoke these words
31:7 *M* proceeded to call Joshua
31:9 *M* wrote this law and gave it
31:10 *M* went on to command them
31:14 Jehovah said to *M*: Look! The
31:14 So *M* and Joshua went and
31:16 *M*: Look! You are lying down
31:22 *M* wrote this song in that
31:24 *M* had finished writing the
31:25 *M* began to command the
31:30 *M* proceeded to speak in the
32:44 *M* came and spoke all the
32:45 After *M* finished speaking
32:48 speak to *M* on this same day
33:1 *M* the man of the true God
33:4 *M* laid as a command upon us
34:1 *M* proceeded to go up from the
34:5 *M* the servant of Jehovah died
34:7 *M* was a hundred and twenty
34:8 to weep for *M* on the desert
34:8 the mourning period for *M*
34:9 for *M* had laid his hand upon
34:9 as Jehovah had commanded *M*
34:10 a prophet in Israel like *M*
34:12 that *M* exercised before the
Jos 1:1 *M* the servant of Jehovah that
1:1 of Nun, the minister of *M*
1:2 *M* my servant is dead; and now
1:3 just as I promised to *M*
1:5 proved to be with *M* I shall
1:7 that *M* my servant commanded
1:13 *M* the servant of Jehovah
1:14 land that *M* has given you
1:15 *M* the servant of Jehovah
1:17 listened to *M* in everything
1:17 as he proved to be with *M*
3:7 as I proved to be with *M* I
4:10 that *M* had commanded Joshua
4:12 just as *M* had stated to them
4:14 feared *M* all the days of his
8:31 as *M* the servant of Jehovah
8:31 in the book of the law of *M*
8:32 a copy of the law of *M* that
8:33 as *M* the servant of Jehovah
8:35 not a word of all that *M* had
9:24 had commanded *M* his servant
11:12 *M* the servant of Jehovah
11:15 commanded *M* his servant
11:15 so *M* commanded Joshua, and
11:15 Jehovah had commanded *M*
11:20 as Jehovah had commanded *M*
11:23 that Jehovah had promised *M*
12:6 It was *M* the servant of
12:6 *M* the servant of Jehovah
13:8 inheritance that *M* gave them
13:8 *M* the servant of Jehovah had
13:12 and *M* went striking them
13:15 *M* made a gift to the tribe

Jos 13:21 Heshbon, and whom *M* struck
13:24 *M* made a gift to the tribe
13:29 *M* made a gift to the half
13:32 *M* caused them to inherit
13:33 *M* did not give an
14:2 commanded by means of *M* for
14:3 *M* had given the inheritance
14:5 as Jehovah had commanded *M*
14:6 spoke to *M* the man of the
14:7 when *M* the servant of
14:9 *M* swore on that day, saying
14:10 made this promise to *M*
17:4 commanded *M* to give us an
18:7 *M* the servant of Jehovah has
20:2 I spoke to you by means of *M*
21:2 Jehovah by means of *M*
21:8 had commanded by means of *M*
22:2 all that *M* . . . commanded you
22:4 possession, which *M* the
22:5 law that *M* . . . commanded
22:7 *M* had made a gift in Bashan
22:9 by means of *M*
23:6 in the book of the law of *M*
24:5 I sent *M* and Aaron, and I
Jg 1:16 whose son-in-law *M* was
1:20 just as *M* had promised, then
3:4 their fathers by means of *M*
4:11 Hobab, whose son-in-law *M*
1Sa 12:6 who used *M* and Aaron and
12:8 send *M* and Aaron, that they
1Ki 2:3 is written in the law of *M*
8:9 two stone tablets which *M*
8:53 spoken by means of *M* your
8:56 promised by means of *M* his
2Ki 18:4 serpent that *M* had made
18:6 Jehovah had commanded *M*
18:12 *M* the servant of Jehovah
21:8 my servant *M* commanded
23:25 to all the law of *M*
1Ch 6:3 sons of Amram were . . . *M*, and
6:49 according to all that *M* the
15:15 just as *M* had commanded by
21:29 tabernacle . . . *M* had made
22:13 that Jehovah commanded *M*
23:13 of Amram were Aaron and *M*
23:14 *M* the man of the true God
23:15 sons of *M* were Gershom and
26:24 son of Gershom the son of *M*
2Ch 1:3 *M* the servant of Jehovah had
5:10 two tablets that *M* had given
8:13 commandment of *M* for the
23:18 written in the law of *M*
24:6 sacred tax ordered by *M* the
24:9 sacred tax ordered by *M* the
25:4 the law, in the book of *M*
30:16 the law of *M* the man
33:8 decisions by the hand of *M*
34:14 law by the hand of *M*
35:6 Jehovah by means of *M*
35:12 written in the book of *M*
Ezr 3:2 *M* the man of the true God
6:18 of the book of *M*
7:6 copyist in the law of *M*
Ne 1:7 in command to *M* your servant
1:8 you commanded *M* your servant
8:1 the book of the law of *M*
8:14 commanded by means of *M* that
9:14 by means of *M* your servant
10:29 *M* the servant of the true
13:1 reading from the book of *M*
Ps 77:20 By the hand of *M* and Aaron
90:*super* A prayer of *M*, the man of
99:6 *M* and Aaron were among his
103:7 He made known his ways to *M*
105:26 He sent *M* his servant
106:16 began to envy *M* in the camp
106:23 been for *M* his chosen one
106:32 badly with *M* by reason of
Isa 63:11 long ago, *M* his servant
63:12 go at the right hand of *M*
Jer 15:1 *M* and Samuel were standing
Da 9:11 written in the law of *M* the
9:13 written in the law of *M*
Mic 6:4 send before you *M*, Aaron and
Mal 4:4 the law of *M* my servant
Mt 8:4 the gift that *M* appointed
17:3 there appeared to them *M* and
17:4 three tents . . . one for *M* and
19:7 Why, then, did *M* prescribe
19:8 *M*, out of regard for your
22:24 *M* said, If any man dies
23:2 themselves in the seat of *M*
Mr 1:44 the things *M* directed, for a
7:10 *M* said, Honor your father and

Mr 9:4 Elijah with *M* appeared to
9:5 one for *M* and one for Elijah
10:3 What did *M* command you?
10:4 *M* allowed the writing of a
12:19 Teacher, *M* wrote us that if
12:26 read in the book of *M*, in
Lu 2:22 according to the law of *M*
5:14 as *M* directed, for a witness
9:30 who were *M* and Elijah
9:33 one for *M* and one for Elijah
16:29 They have *M* and the Prophets
16:31 do not listen to *M* and the
20:28 *M* wrote us, If a man's
20:37 even *M* disclosed, in the
24:27 *M* and all the Prophets he
24:44 written in the law of *M* and
Joh 1:17 the Law was given through *M*
1:45 found the one of whom *M*
3:14 as *M* lifted up the serpent
5:45 one that accuses you, *M*
5:46 if you believed *M* you would
6:32 *M* did not give you the bread
7:19 *M* gave you the Law, did he
7:22 For this reason *M* has given
7:22 not that it is from *M*, but
7:23 law of *M* may not be broken
9:28 but we are disciples of *M*
9:29 that God has spoken to *M*
Ac 3:22 *M* said, Jehovah God will
6:11 sayings against *M* and God
6:14 customs that *M* handed down
7:20 time *M* was born, and he was
7:22 *M* was instructed in all the
7:29 *M* took to flight and became
7:31 *M* saw it he marveled at the
7:32 *M* did not dare to investigate
7:35 *M*, whom they disowned
7:37 *M* that said to the sons of
7:40 *M*, who led us out of the land
7:44 when speaking to *M* to make
13:39 by means of the law of *M*
15:1 according to the custom of *M*
15:5 to observe the law of *M*
15:21 *M* has had in city after city
21:21 an apostasy from *M*, telling
26:22 *M* stated were going to take
28:23 from both the law of *M* and
Ro 5:14 from Adam down to *M*, even
9:15 he says to *M*: I will have
10:5 *M* writes that the man that
10:19 First *M* says: I will incite
1Co 9:9 For in the law of *M* it is
10:2 got baptized into *M* by means
2Co 3:7 not gaze . . . at the face of *M*
3:13 as when *M* would put a veil
3:15 whenever *M* is read, a veil
2Ti 3:8 Jannes and Jambres resisted *M*
Heb 3:2 *M* was also in all the house
3:3 worthy of more glory than *M*
3:5 And *M* as an attendant was
3:16 went out of Egypt under *M*
7:14 *M* spoke nothing concerning
8:5 just as *M*, when about to
9:19 Law had been spoken by *M* to
10:28 disregarded the law of *M*
11:23 *M* was hid for three months
11:24 *M*, when grown up, refused
12:21 so fearsome that *M* said: I
Re 15:3 are singing the song of *M*

Moses'
Ex 8:13 did according to *M* word, and
8:31 Jehovah did according to *M*
18:1 *M* father-in-law, got to hear
18:2 Jethro, *M* father-in-law, took
18:2 took Zipporah, *M* wife, after
18:5 Jethro, *M* father-in-law, and
18:12 Then Jethro, *M* father-in-law
18:12 *M* father-in-law, before the
18:14 *M* father-in-law got to see
18:17 *M* father-in-law said to him
32:19 *M* anger began to blaze, and
34:35 sons of Israel saw *M* face
34:35 skin of *M* face emitted rays
Le 10:7 they did according to *M* word
Nu 25:6 before *M* eyes and before the
Jos 14:11 the day of *M* sending me out
Jg 18:30 Gershom, *M* son, he and his
2Ki 14:6 book of *M* law that Jehovah
Jude 9 and was disputing about *M* body

Mosquito
Jer 46:20 *m* itself will certainly

Most
Ge 3:1 serpent proved to be the *m*
14:18 he was priest of the *M* High
14:19 Abram of the *M* High God
14:20 blessed be the *M* High God
14:22 Jehovah the *M* High God
27:15 *m* desirable ones which were
34:19 the *m* honorable of the whole
Ex 26:33 the Holy and the *M* Holy
26:34 the testimony in the *M* Holy
29:37 become a *m* holy altar
30:10 It is *m* holy to Jehovah
30:29 may indeed become *m* holy
30:36 It should be *m* holy to you
40:10 must become a *m* holy altar
Le 2:3 *m* holy from Jehovah's
2:10 *m* holy of Jehovah's offerings
6:17 It is something *m* holy, like
6:25 It is a *m* holy thing
6:29 It is something *m* holy
7:1 It is something *m* holy
7:6 It is something *m* holy
10:12 it is something *m* holy
10:17 it is something *m* holy and
14:13 It is something *m* holy
21:22 *m* holy things and from the
24:9 *m* holy for him from Jehovah's
27:28 something *m* holy to Jehovah
Nu 4:4 It is something *m* holy
4:19 approaching the *m* holy things
18:9 out of the *m* holy things, out
18:9 is something *m* holy for you
18:10 In a *m* holy place you should
24:16 the knowledge of the *M* High
De 7:7 *m* populous of all the peoples
7:14 *m* blessed of all the peoples
32:8 *M* High gave the nations an
Jg 5:24 Jael . . . will be *m* blessed
5:24 she will be *m* blessed
21:10 of the *m* valiant men there
1Sa 9:21 family the *m* insignificant
15:33 be *m* bereaved of children
18:30 David acted *m* prudently of
20:41 David had done it the *m*
2Sa 14:27 *m* beautiful in appearance
22:14 the *M* High himself began to
1Ki 6:16 innermost room, the *M* Holy
7:50 house, that is, the *M* Holy
8:6 the *M* Holy, to underneath the
16:31 the *m* trivial thing for him
2Ki 10:3 *m* upright of the sons of
1Ch 6:49 work of the *m* holy things
23:13 might sanctify the *M* Holy
2Ch 3:8 make the house of the *M* Holy
3:10 the *M* Holy two cherubs in
4:22 inner doors for the *M* Holy
5:7 the ark . . . into the *M* Holy
31:14 and the *m* holy things
Ezr 2:63 the *m* holy things until a
Ne 7:65 not eat from the *m* holy
Ps 7:17 the name of Jehovah the *M* High
9:2 melody to your name, O *M* High
18:13 the *M* High himself began to
21:7 loving-kindness of the *M* High
46:4 tabernacle of the *M* High
47:2 the *M* High, is fear-inspiring
50:14 pay to the *M* High your vows
57:2 I call to God the *M* High, to
73:11 knowledge in the *M* High
77:10 the right hand of the *M* High
78:17 rebelling against the *M* High
78:35 *M* High was their Avenger
78:56 rebel against God the *M* High
82:6 you are sons of the *M* High
83:18 alone are the *M* High over
87:5 *M* High himself will firmly
89:27 *m* high of the kings of the
91:1 secret place of the *M* High
91:9 *M* High himself your dwelling
92:1 to your name, O *M* High
97:9 the *M* High over all the earth
107:11 counsel of the *M* High they
139:9 reside in the *m* remote sea
Pr 9:10 knowledge of the *M* Holy One
30:3 the *M* Holy One I do not know
Ca 1:8 *m* beautiful one among women
5:9 *m* beautiful one among women
5:10 *m* conspicuous of ten thousand
6:1 O *m* beautiful one among women
Isa 14:14 myself resemble the *M* High
Jer 6:28 are the *m* stubborn men
La 3:35 before the face of the *M* High
3:38 From the mouth of the *M* High
Eze 41:4 This is the *M* Holy
Eze 42:13 eat the *m* holy things
42:13 deposit the *m* holy things
43:12 is something *m* holy
44:13 to the *m* holy things, and
45:3 something *m* holy
48:12 land as something *m* holy
Da 3:26 servants of the *M* High God
4:2 wonders that the *M* High God
4:17 the *M* High is Ruler in the
4:24 decree of the *M* High is that
4:25 the *M* High is Ruler in the
4:32 the *M* High is Ruler in the
4:34 I blessed the *M* High himself
5:18 *M* High God himself gave to
5:21 *M* High God is Ruler in the
7:25 even words against the *M* High
11:39 the *m* fortified strongholds
Ho 11:12 the *M* Holy One he is
Mic 7:4 their *m* upright one is worse
Mt 2:6 the *m* insignificant city
11:20 *m* of his powerful works had
21:8 *M* of the crowd spread their
23:6 like the *m* prominent place
Mr 5:7 Jesus, Son of the *M* High God
7:37 in a *m* extraordinary way
12:39 *m* prominent places at
Lu 1:3 to you, *m* excellent Theophilus
1:32 called Son of the *M* High
1:35 and power of the *M* High will
1:76 a prophet of the *M* High, for
6:35 will be sons of the *M* High
8:28 Jesus Son of the *M* High God
14:7 the *m* prominent places for
14:8 in the *m* prominent place
20:46 and *m* prominent places at
Joh 1:51 *M* truly I say to you men
3:3 *M* truly I say to you, Unless
3:5 *M* truly I say to you, Unless
3:11 *M* truly I say to you, What
5:19 *M* truly I say to you, The
5:24 *M* truly I say to you, He
5:25 *M* truly I say to you, The
6:26 *M* truly I say to you, You
6:32 *M* truly I say to you, Moses
6:47 *M* truly I say to you, He
6:53 *M* truly I say to you, Unless
8:34 *M* truly I say to you
8:51 *M* truly I say to you, If
8:58 *M* truly I say to you, Before
10:1 *M* truly I say to you, He
10:7 *M* truly I say to you, I am
12:24 *M* truly I say to you
13:16 *M* truly I say to you
13:20 *M* truly I say to you
13:21 *M* truly I say to you
13:38 *M* truly I say to you
14:12 *M* truly I say to you, He
16:20 *M* truly I say to you, You
16:23 *M* truly I say to you, If
21:18 *M* truly I say to you, When
Ac 1:8 *m* distant part of the earth
7:48 *M* High does not dwell in
16:17 are slaves of the *M* High God
1Co 9:2 I *m* certainly am to you, for
9:19 I may gain the *m* persons
10:5 on *m* of them God did not
14:27 to two or three at the *m*
15:6 the *m* of whom remain to the
15:19 of all men *m* to be pitied
2Co 12:9 *M* gladly, therefore, will I
12:15 I will *m* gladly spend and
Php 1:14 and *m* of the brothers in the
Heb 7:1 priest of the *M* High God
9:3 called the *M* Holy
Jude 20 on your *m* holy faith, and
Re 18:12 out of *m* precious wood
21:11 like a *m* precious stone, as

Moth
Job 4:19 more quickly than a *m*
13:28 garment that a *m* . . . eats
27:18 his house like a mere *m*
Ps 39:11 consume . . . just as a *m* does
Isa 50:9 A mere *m* will eat them up
51:8 the *m* will eat them up just
51:8 clothes *m* will eat them up
Ho 5:12 I was like the *m* to Ephraim
Mt 6:19 where *m* and rust consume
6:20 neither *m* nor rust consumes
Lu 12:33 get near nor *m* consumes

Moth-eaten
Jas 5:2 outer garments have become *m*

Mother

Ge 2:24 leave his father and his *m*
3:20 she had to become the *m* of
19:37 firstborn became *m* to a son
20:12 not the daughter of my *m*
21:21 his *m* proceeded to take a
24:28 the household of her *m* about
24:53 to her brother and to her *m*
24:55 her *m* said: Let the young
24:67 into the tent of Sarah his *m*
24:67 after the loss of his *m*
27:11 to say to Rebekah his *m*
27:13 his *m* said to him: Upon me
27:14 and brought them to his *m*
27:14 his *m* made a tasty dish
27:29 the sons of your *m* bow low
28:2 Bethuel the father of your *m*
28:2 Laban the brother of your *m*
28:5 Rebekah, *m* of Jacob and Esau
28:7 obeying his father and his *m*
30:14 brought them to Leah his *m*
32:11 *m* together with children
37:10 Am I and also your *m* and
43:29 the son of his *m*, he went
44:20 he alone is left of his *m*
Ex 2:8 went and called the child's *m*
20:12 Honor your father and your *m*
21:15 strikes his father and his *m*
21:17 upon his father and his *m*
22:30 it will continue with its *m*
Le 18:7 nakedness of your *m* you must
18:7 She is your *m*. You must not
18:9 or the daughter of your *m*
18:13 a blood relation of your *m*
19:3 fear each one his *m* and his
20:9 upon his father and his *m*
20:9 *m* upon whom he has called
20:14 woman and her *m*, it is loose
20:17 daughter of his *m*, and he
21:2 close to him, for his *m* and
21:11 *m* he may not defile himself
22:27 under its *m* seven days, but
Nu 6:7 even for his father or his *m*
De 5:16 Honor your father and your *m*
13:6 the son of your *m*, or your
21:13 for her father and her *m*
21:18 the voice of his *m*, and
21:19 his father and his *m* must
22:6 the *m* is sitting upon the
22:6 *m* along with the offspring
22:7 send the *m* away, but you may
22:15 father of the girl and her *m*
27:16 his *m* with contempt
27:22 or the daughter of his *m*
33:9 said to his father and his *m*
Jos 2:13 my father and my *m* and my
2:18 your father and your *m* and
6:23 her father and her *m* and her
Jg 5:7 I rose up as a *m* in Israel
5:28 *m* of Sisera from the lattice
8:19 brothers, the sons of my *m*
9:1 brothers of his *m* and began
9:3 So the brothers of his *m* began
14:2 told his father and his *m* and
14:3 his father and his *m* said to
14:4 father and his *m*, they did
14:5 with his father and his *m* to
14:6 not tell his father or his *m*
14:9 rejoined his father and his *m*
14:16 my own *m* I have not told
17:2 In time he said to his *m*
17:2 his *m* said: Blessed may my
17:3 pieces of silver to his *m*
17:3 his *m* went on to say: I must
17:4 returned the silver to his *m*
17:4 his *m* took two hundred silver
Ru 1:8 each one to the house of her *m*
2:11 leave your father and your *m*
1Sa 2:19 his *m* would make for him
15:33 *m* will be most bereaved
20:30 the secret parts of your *m*
22:3 Let my father and my *m*
2Sa 17:25 sister of Zeruiah, Joab's *m*
19:37 burial place of . . . my *m*
20:19 put to death a city and a *m*
1Ki 1:6 his *m* had borne him after
1:11 to Bath-sheba, Solomon's *m*
2:13 to Bath-sheba, Solomon's *m*
2:19 a throne set for the *m* of
2:20 Make it, my *m*; for I shall
2:22 answered and said to his *m*
3:27 She is his *m*
17:23 and gave him to his *m*
19:20 kiss my father and my *m*
1Ki 22:52 and in the way of his *m*
2Ki 3:2 like his father or like his *m*
3:13 to the prophets of your *m*
4:19 Carry him to his *m*
4:20 and brought him to his *m*
4:30 the *m* of the boy said
9:22 Jezebel your *m* and her many
11:1 Athaliah the *m* of Ahaziah
24:12 with his *m* and his servants
24:15 the king's *m* and the king's
1Ch 2:26 Atarah . . . *m* of Onam
4:9 *m* that called his name Jabez
2Ch 22:3 *m* herself became his
22:10 Athaliah the *m* of Ahaziah
Es 2:7 she had neither father nor *m*
2:7 death of her father and her *m*
Job 17:14 To the maggot, My *m* and my
31:18 from the belly of my *m* I
Ps 22:9 upon the breasts of my *m*
22:10 From the belly of my *m* you
27:10 and my own *m* did leave me
35:14 like one mourning for a *m*
50:20 Against the son of your *m*
51:5 And in sin my *m* conceived me
69:8 foreigner to the sons of my *m*
71:6 the inward parts of my *m*
109:14 sin of his *m*—may it not
113:9 As a joyful *m* of sons
131:2 Like a weanling upon his *m*
139:13 in the belly of my *m*
Pr 1:8 not forsake the law of your *m*
4:3 the only one before my *m*
6:20 not forsake the law of your *m*
10:1 son is the grief of his *m*
15:20 stupid . . . despising his *m*
19:26 that chases a *m* away is a
20:20 upon his father and his *m*
23:22 do not despise your *m* just
23:25 and your *m* will rejoice, and
28:24 robbing his father and his *m*
29:15 will be causing his *m* shame
30:11 does not bless even its *m*
30:17 despises obedience to a *m*
31:1 message that his *m* gave to
Ca 1:6 sons of my own *m* grew angry
3:11 wreath that his *m* wove for
6:9 there is who belongs to her *m*
8:1 sucking the breasts of my *m*
8:2 into the house of my *m*
8:5 *m* was in birth pangs with you
Isa 8:4 and My *m*! one will carry
49:1 the inward parts of my *m* he
50:1 the *m* of you people, whom
50:1 your *m* has been sent away
66:13 his own *m* keeps comforting
Jer 15:8 upon *m*, young man, the
15:10 Woe to me, O my *m*, because
16:7 and on account of one's *m*
20:14 the day that my *m* gave me
20:17 my *m* should become to me
22:26 hurl you and your *m* who
50:12 *m* of you men has become
52:1 name of his *m* was Hamutal
Eze 16:3 and your *m* was a Hittite
16:44 Like *m* is her daughter
16:45 are the daughter of your *m*
16:45 The *m* of you women was a
19:2 What was your *m*? A lioness
19:10 Your *m* was like a vine in
22:7 Father and *m* they have
23:2 the daughters of one *m*
44:25 for *m* or for son or for
Ho 2:2 on a legal case with your *m*
2:5 *m* has committed fornication
4:5 I will put your *m* to silence
10:14 a *m* herself was dashed to
Mic 7:6 is rising up against her *m*
Zec 13:3 his father and his *m*, the
13:3 father and his *m*, the ones
Mt 1:18 his *m* Mary was promised in
2:11 young child with Mary its *m*
2:13 the young child and its *m*
2:14 the young child and its *m*
2:20 the young child and its *m*
2:21 the young child and its *m*
10:35 and a daughter against her *m*
10:37 affection for father or *m*
12:46 his *m* and brothers took up a
12:47 Your *m* and your brothers are
12:48 Who is my *m*, and who are
12:49 Look! My *m* and my brothers!
12:50 brother, and sister, and *m*
13:55 Is not his *m* called Mary
14:11 and she brought it to her *m*
Mt 15:4 Honor your father and your *m*
15:4 him that reviles father or *m*
15:5 says to his father or *m*
19:5 leave his father and his *m*
19:19 Honor your father and your *m*
19:29 everyone that has left . . . *m*
20:20 the *m* of the sons of Zebedee
27:56 Mary the *m* of James and
27:56 the *m* of the sons of Zebedee
Mr 3:31 his *m* and his brothers came
3:32 said to him: Look! Your *m*
3:33 said to them: Who are my *m*
3:34 See, my *m* and my brothers!
3:35 my brother and sister and *m*
5:40 young child's father and *m*
6:24 said to her *m*: What should I
6:28 the maiden gave it to her *m*
7:10 Honor your father and your *m*
7:10 reviles father or *m* end up
7:11 man says to his father or *m*
7:12 thing for his father or his *m*
10:7 will leave his father and *m*
10:19 Honor your father and *m*
10:29 *m* or father or children or
15:40 Mary the *m* of James the
15:47 and Mary the *m* of Joses
16:1 Mary the *m* of James, and
Lu 1:13 Elizabeth will become *m* to a
1:43 the *m* of my Lord come to me
1:57 and she became *m* to a son
1:60 But its *m* answered and said
2:33 its father and *m* continued
2:34 but said to Mary its *m*
2:48 and his *m* said to him
2:51 his *m* carefully kept all
7:12 only-begotten son of his *m*
7:15 and he gave him to his *m*
8:19 Now his *m* and brothers came
8:20 Your *m* and your brothers are
8:21 My *m* and my brothers are
8:51 and the girl's father and *m*
12:53 *m* against daughter and
12:53 and daughter against her *m*
14:26 hate his father and *m* and
18:20 Honor your father and *m*
24:10 and Mary the *m* of James
Joh 2:1 and the *m* of Jesus was there
2:3 the *m* of Jesus said to him
2:5 *m* said to those ministering
2:12 his *m* and brothers and his
3:4 womb of his *m* a second time
6:42 whose father and *m* we know
19:25 his *m* and the sister of
19:25 and the sister of his *m*
19:26 Jesus, seeing his *m* and
19:26 said to his *m*: Woman, see!
19:27 the disciple: See! Your *m*!
Ac 1:14 and Mary the *m* of Jesus and
12:12 house of Mary the *m* of John
Ro 16:13 Greet Rufus . . . and his *m* and
Ga 4:26 Jerusalem above is . . . our *m*
Eph 5:31 leave his father and his *m*
6:2 Honor your father and your *m*
1Th 2:7 as when a nursing *m* cherishes
2Ti 1:5 and your *m* Eunice, but which
Re 17:5 *m* of the harlots and of the

Mother-in-law

De 27:23 who lies down with his *m*
Ru 1:14 Orpah kissed her *m*
2:11 that you have done to your *m*
2:18 her *m* got to see what she had
2:19 *m* now said to her: Where did
2:19 told her *m* with whom she had
2:23 kept on dwelling with her *m*
3:1 Naomi her *m* now said to her
3:6 that her *m* had commanded her
3:16 she went her way to her *m*
3:17 come empty-handed to your *m*
Mic 7:6 against her *m*; a man's
Mt 8:14 *m* lying down and sick with
10:35 a young wife against her *m*
Mr 1:30 Simon's *m* was lying down
Lu 4:38 Simon's *m* was distressed
12:53 *m* against her
12:53 against her *m*

Motherless

Heb 7:3 being fatherless, *m*, without

Mother's

Ge 29:10 of Laban his *m* brother
29:10 sheep of Laban his *m* brother
29:10 Laban his *m* brother
Ex 23:19 not boil a kid in its *m* milk

Ex 34:26 not boil a kid in its *m*
Le 18:13 nakedness of your *m* sister
20:19 nakedness of your *m* sister
24:11 *m* name was Shelomith, the
Nu 12:12 coming out of his *m* womb
De 14:21 not boil a kid in its *m* milk
Jg 9:1 house of his *m* father, saying
16:17 from my *m* belly
1Ki 11:26 his *m* name was Zeruah
14:21 his *m* name was Naamah the
14:31 *m* name was Naamah the
15:2 his *m* name was Maacah the
22:42 his *m* name was Azubah the
2Ki 8:26 his *m* name was Athaliah the
12:1 his *m* name was Zibiah from
14:2 his *m* name was Jehoaddin
15:2 his *m* name was Jecoliah of
15:33 his *m* name was Jerusha
18:2 his *m* name was Abi the
21:1 his *m* name was Hephzibah
21:19 *m* name was Meshullemeth
22:1 his *m* name was Jedidah
23:31 his *m* name was Hamutal the
23:36 his *m* name was Zebidah
24:8 his *m* name was Nehushta
24:18 his *m* name was Hamutal
2Ch 12:13 *m* name was Naamah the
13:2 *m* name was Micaiah the
20:31 *m* name was Azubah the
22:2 *m* name was Athaliah the
24:1 *m* name was Zibiah from
25:1 *m* name was Jehoaddan of
26:3 *m* name was Jecoliah of
27:1 *m* name was Jerushah the
29:1 his *m* name was Abijah the
Job 1:21 I came out of my *m* belly
3:10 the doors of my *m* belly
19:17 to the sons of my *m* belly
Ec 5:15 come forth from his *m* belly
Ca 3:4 brought him into my *m* house
Mt 14:8 under her *m* coaching, said
19:12 such from their *m* womb
Lu 1:15 right from his *m* womb
Ac 3:2 was lame from his *m* womb
14:8 lame from his *m* womb, and
Ga 1:15 separated me from my *m* womb

Mothers
Jer 16:3 *m* who are giving them birth
La 2:12 To their *m* they kept saying
2:12 out into the bosom of their *m*
5:3 Our *m* are like widows
Mr 10:30 brothers and sisters and *m*
1Ti 1:9 murderers of *m*, manslayers
5:2 older women as *m*

Motion
Ge 29:1 Jacob set his feet in *m* and
Isa 28:28 roller of his wagon in *m*

Motioned
Lu 5:7 they *m* to their partners in
Ac 12:17 he *m* to them with his hand
19:33 Alexander *m* with his hand
21:40 *m* with his hand to the

Motioning
Ac 13:16 *m* with his hand, he said

Motionless
Ex 15:16 they will be *m* like a stone
Jos 4:3 the priests' feet stood *m*
10:12 Sun, be *m* over Gibeon
10:13 sun kept *m*, and the moon

Motive
Job 11:12 will get good *m* As soon as
Ho 4:11 are what take away good *m*
Php 1:17 not with a pure *m*, for they

Mound
Jos 8:28 to an indefinitely lasting *m*
2Sa 5:9 build all around from the *M*
1Ki 9:15 the *M* and the wall of
9:24 was then that he built the *M*
11:27 himself had built the *M*
2Ki 12:20 at the house of the *M*
1Ch 11:8 from the *M* even to the parts
2Ch 32:5 the *M* of the city of David
Jer 30:18 be rebuilt upon her *m*
49:2 a *m* of desolate waste
Eze 16:24 building for yourself a *m*
16:31 *m* at the head of every way
16:39 tear down your *m* and your
Mic 4:8 the *m* of the daughter of Zion

Mounds
Jos 11:13 standing on their own *m*

Mount
Ex 19:11 all the people upon *M* Sinai
19:18 *M* Sinai smoked all over, due
19:20 came down upon *M* Sinai to
19:23 able to come up to *M* Sinai
24:16 to reside upon *M* Sinai, and
31:18 speaking with him on *M* Sinai
33:6 from *M* Horeb onward
34:2 in the morning into *M* Sinai
34:4 went on up into *M* Sinai
34:29 came down from *M* Sinai
34:32 spoken with him on *M* Sinai
Le 7:38 commanded Moses in *M* Sinai
25:1 to Moses in *M* Sinai, saying
26:46 Israel in *M* Sinai by means
27:34 sons of Israel in *M* Sinai
Nu 3:1 spoke with Moses in *M* Sinai
20:22 and come to *M* Hor
20:23 Moses and Aaron in *M* Hor by
20:25 and bring them up into *M* Hor
20:27 they went climbing *M* Hor
21:4 trekking from *M* Hor by the
28:6 rendered up at *M* Sinai as a
33:23 went camping in *M* Shepher
33:24 pulled away from *M* Shepher
33:37 camping in *M* Hor, on the
33:38 to go up into *M* Hor at the
33:39 at his death on *M* Hor
33:41 pulled away from *M* Hor and
34:7 to *M* Hor as a boundary for
34:8 From *M* Hor you will mark out
De 1:2 way of *M* Seir to Kadesh-barnea
2:1 days in going around *M* Seir
2:5 I have given *M* Seir to Esau
3:8 Arnon as far as *M* Hermon
4:48 *M* Sion, that is to say
11:29 the blessing upon *M* Gerizim
11:29 the malediction upon *M* Ebal
27:4 commanding you . . . in *M* Ebal
27:12 bless . . . on *M* Gerizim
27:13 the malediction on *M* Ebal
32:49 mountain of Abarim, *M* Nebo
32:50 your brother died on *M* Hor
34:1 into *M* Nebo, to the top of
Jos 8:30 build an altar . . . in *M* Ebal
8:33 in front of *M* Gerizim and
8:33 in front of *M* Ebal, (just as
11:17 from *M* Halak, which goes
11:17 at the base of *M* Hermon
12:1 *M* Hermon and all the Arabah
12:5 and who ruled in *M* Hermon
12:7 and as far as *M* Halak
13:5 at the base of *M* Hermon as
13:11 *M* Hermon and all Bashan as
15:9 the cities of *M* Ephron
15:10 Baalah westward to *M* Seir
15:10 to the slope of *M* Jearim
15:11 passed over to *M* Baalah and
24:4 Esau I gave *M* Seir to take
24:30 Ephraim, north of *M* Gaash
Jg 1:35 dwelling in *M* Heres and in
2:9 on the north of *M* Gaash
3:3 Hivites inhabiting *M* Lebanon
3:3 from *M* Baal-hermon as far as
4:6 spread yourself out on *M* Tabor
4:12 had gone up to *M* Tabor
4:14 descending from *M* Tabor
9:7 top of *M* Gerizim and raised
9:48 Abimelech went up *M* Zalmon
1Sa 31:1 slain in *M* Gilboa
31:8 fallen upon *M* Gilboa
2Sa 1:6 chanced to be on *M* Gilboa
13:29 *m* each one his mule and
1Ki 18:19 Israel to me at *M* Carmel
18:20 together at *M* Carmel
2Ki 2:25 going from there to *M* Carmel
4:25 of the true God at *M* Carmel
19:31 who escape from *M* Zion
23:13 right of the *M* of Ruination
1Ch 4:42 went to *M* Seir, five hundred
5:23 and Senir and *M* Hermon
10:1 falling slain in *M* Gilboa
10:8 sons fallen upon *M* Gilboa
2Ch 3:1 in Jerusalem on *M* Moriah
13:4 *M* Zemaraim, which is in the
Ne 9:13 upon *M* Sinai you came down
Job 15:29 his wealth will not *m* up
Ps 48:2 Is *M* Zion on the remote sides
48:11 May *M* Zion rejoice, May the
74:2 *M* Zion in which you have
78:68 *M* Zion, which he loved
125:1 like *M* Zion, which cannot
Ec 10:4 ruler should *m* up against you
Isa 4:5 established place of *M* Zion
Isa 8:18 who is residing in *M* Zion
10:12 his work in *M* Zion and in
18:7 of Jehovah of armies, *M* Zion
24:23 king in *M* Zion and
28:21 just as at *M* Perazim
29:8 waging war against *M* Zion
31:4 to wage war over *M* Zion and
37:32 who escape out of *M* Zion
40:31 *m* up with wings like eagles
Jer 46:4 Harness the horses, and *m*
Joe 2:32 in *M* Zion and in Jerusalem
Ob 17 *M* Zion is where those escaping
21 come up onto *M* Zion, in order
Mic 4:7 as king over them in *M* Zion
Hab 3:3 Holy One from *M* Paran. *Se'lah*
Mt 21:1 Bethphage on the *M* of Olives
24:3 sitting upon the *M* of Olives
26:30 went out to the *M* of Olives
Mr 11:1 Bethany at the *M* of Olives
13:3 sitting on the *M* of Olives
14:26 went out to the *M* of Olives
Lu 19:29 mountain called *M* of Olives
19:37 road down the *M* of Olives
21:37 called the *M* of Olives
22:39 went . . . to the *M* of Olives
Ac 1:12 *M* of Olives, which is near
7:30 in the wilderness of *M* Sinai
7:38 spoke to him on *M* Sinai and
Ga 4:24 the one from *M* Sinai, which
Heb 12:22 have approached a *M* Zion
Re 14:1 Lamb . . . upon the *M* Zion

Mountain
Ge 14:6 Horites in their *m* of Seir
22:14 In the *m* of Jehovah it will
31:25 pitched his tent in the *m*
31:54 a sacrifice in the *m* and
31:54 passed the night in the *m*
Ex 3:1 to the *m* of the true God, to
3:12 serve the true God on this *m*
4:27 in the *m* of the true God
15:17 in the *m* of your inheritance
18:5 at the *m* of the true God
19:2 there in front of the *m*
19:3 to call to him out of the *m*
19:12 going up into the *m*, and do
19:12 Anybody touching the *m* will
19:13 may come up to the *m*
19:14 went down from the *m* to the
19:16 a heavy cloud upon the *m* and
19:17 stand at the base of the *m*
19:18 *m* was trembling very much
19:20 Sinai to the top of the *m*
19:20 Moses to the top of the *m*
19:23 Set bounds for the *m* and
20:18 the horn and the *m* smoking
24:4 built at the foot of the *m* an
24:12 Come up to me in the *m* and
24:13 Moses went up into the *m* of
24:15 Moses went up into the *m*
24:15 the cloud was covering the *m*
24:18 went on up the *m*. And Moses
24:18 And Moses continued in the *m*
25:40 was shown to you in the *m*
26:30 you have been shown in the *m*
27:8 as he showed you in the *m*
32:1 about coming down from the *m*
32:15 down from the *m* with the
32:19 shattered them at . . . the *m*
34:2 there on the top of the *m*
34:3 else be seen in all the *m*
34:3 pasturing in front of that *m*
34:29 he came down from the *m*
Nu 10:33 from the *m* of Jehovah for
14:40 to go up to the top of the *m*
14:44 to go up to the top of the *m*
14:45 who were dwelling in that *m*
20:28 there on the top of the *m*
20:28 came on down from the *m*
27:12 Go up into this *m* of Abarim
De 1:41 easy to go up into the *m*
1:43 you tried to go up into the *m*
1:44 Amorites . . . in that *m*
2:3 gone around this *m* long enough
4:11 stood at the base of the *m*
4:11 the *m* was burning with fire
5:4 spoke with you in the *m* out of
5:5 did not go up into the *m*
5:22 your congregation in the *m*
5:23 the *m* was burning with fire
9:9 went up the *m* to receive the
9:9 in the *m* forty days and forty
9:10 spoken with you in the *m*
9:15 and went down from the *m*

De 9:15 the *m* was burning with fire
9:21 was descending from the *m*
10:1 come up to me into the *m*
10:3 and went up into the *m*, and
10:4 had spoken to you in the *m*
10:5 went down from the *m* and
10:10 I stayed in the *m* the same as
32:49 this *m* of Abarim, Mount Nebo
32:50 *m* into which you are going
33:19 to the *m* they will call
Jos 11:2 the *m* ridges of Dor to the
12:23 on the *m* ridge of Dor, one
13:19 in the *m* of the low plain
15:8 the *m* that faces the valley
15:9 the *m* to the spring of the
18:12 went up on the *m* westward
18:13 the *m* that is on the south
18:14 the *m* that faces Beth-horon
18:16 *m* that faces the valley of
Jg 12:15 in the *m* of the Amalekite
16:3 *m* that is in front of Hebron
1Sa 17:3 standing on the *m* on this
17:3 standing on the *m* on that
23:26 came to this side of the *m*
23:26 were on that side of the *m*
24:2 bare rocks of the *m* goats
25:20 secretly going down the *m*
26:13 stood upon the top of the *m*
2Sa 16:13 on the side of the *m*
21:9 expose them on the *m* before
1Ki 4:11 all the *m* ridge of Dor
5:15 thousand cutters in the *m*
11:7 the *m* that was in front of
16:24 buy the *m* of Samaria from
16:24 to build on the *m* and call
16:24 master of the *m*, Samaria
19:8 *m* of the true God, Horeb
19:11 on the *m* before Jehovah
2Ki 1:9 sitting upon the top of the *m*
4:27 at the *m*, she at once took
23:16 burial places . . . in the *m*
2Ch 2:2 men as cutters in the *m*, and
2:18 thousand cutters in the *m*
33:15 *m* of the house of Jehovah
Job 14:18 a *m* itself, falling, will
39:1 *m* goats of the crag to give
Ps 2:6 Upon Zion, my holy *m*
3:4 answer me from his holy *m*
11:1 Flee as a bird to your *m!*
15:1 will reside in your holy *m*
24:3 ascend into the *m* of Jehovah
30:7 my *m* to stand in strength
42:6 From the little *m*
43:3 bring me to your holy *m* and
48:1 In the city . . . his holy *m*
68:15 Bashan is a *m* of God
68:15 Bashan is a *m* of peaks
68:16 The *m* that God has desired
99:9 bow down . . . at his holy *m*
104:18 are for the *m* goats
Pr 5:19 hind and a charming *m* goat
Ca 4:6 go my way to the *m* of myrrh
Isa 2:2 the *m* of the house of Jehovah
2:3 us go up to the *m* of Jehovah
10:32 *m* of the daughter of Zion
11:9 any ruin in all my holy *m*
13:2 Upon a *m* of bare rocks raise
14:13 upon the *m* of meeting, in
16:1 *m* of the daughter of Zion
22:5 and the cry to the *m*
25:6 all the peoples, in this *m*
25:7 *m* he will certainly swallow
25:10 will settle down on this *m*
27:13 in the holy *m* in Jerusalem
30:17 a mast on the top of a *m*
30:25 upon every high *m* and
30:29 enter into the *m* of Jehovah
40:4 *m* and hill be made low
40:9 way up even onto a high *m*
56:7 bring them to my holy *m*
57:7 Upon a *m* high and lifted up
57:13 possession of my holy *m*
65:11 those forgetting my holy *m*
65:25 any ruin in all my holy *m*
66:20 up to my holy *m*, Jerusalem
Jer 3:6 going upon every high *m* and
16:16 hunt them from every *m* and
26:18 the *m* of the House will be
31:23 dwelling place, O holy *m*
50:6 From *m* to hill they have
51:25 against you, O ruinous *m*
51:25 and make you a burnt-out *m*
La 5:18 Zion's *m* that is desolated
Eze 11:23 *m* that is to the east of
Eze 17:22 upon a high and lofty *m*
17:23 *m* of the height of Israel I
20:40 For in my holy *m*, in the
20:40 *m* of the height of Israel
28:14 On the holy *m* of God you
28:16 out of the *m* of God, and
40:2 upon a very high *m*, on
43:12 On the top of the *m* its
Da 2:35 large *m* and filled the whole
2:45 of the *m* a stone was cut not
9:16 city Jerusalem, your holy *m*
9:20 the holy *m* of my God
11:45 the holy *m* of Decoration
Joe 2:1 shout a war cry in my holy *m*
3:17 residing in Zion my holy *m*
Am 4:1 who are on the *m* of Samaria
6:1 trusting in the *m* of Samaria
Ob 16 have drunk upon my holy *m*, all
Mic 3:12 the *m* of the house will be
4:1 the *m* of the house of Jehovah
4:2 go up to the *m* of Jehovah
7:12, 12 and from *m* to the *m*
Zep 3:11 be haughty in my holy *m*
Hag 1:8 Go up to the *m*, and you must
Zec 4:7 Who are you, O great *m?*
8:3 the *m* of Jehovah of armies
8:3 Jehovah of armies, the holy *m*
14:4 the *m* of the olive trees
14:4 the *m* of the olive trees
14:4 half of the *m* will actually
Mt 4:8 along to an unusually high *m*
5:1 he went up into the *m*
5:14 hid when situated upon a *m*
8:1 he had come down from the *m*
14:23 up into the *m* by himself
15:29 after going up into the *m*
17:1 into a lofty *m* by themselves
17:9 descending from the *m*, Jesus
17:20 say to this *m*, Transfer
21:21 say to this *m*, Be lifted up
28:16 *m* where Jesus had arranged
Mr 3:13 he ascended a *m* and summoned
5:11 of swine was there at the *m*
6:46 he went off into a *m* to pray
9:2 up into a lofty *m* to
9:9 were coming down out of the *m*
11:23 tells this *m*, Be lifted up
Lu 3:5 every *m* and hill leveled down
4:29 led him to the brow of the *m*
6:12 went out into the *m* to pray
8:32 was feeding there on the *m*
9:28 climbed up into the *m* to pray
9:37 they got down from the *m*
19:29 *m* called Mount of Olives
21:37 *m* called the Mount of Olives
Joh 4:20 worshiped in this *m;* but you
4:21 in this *m* nor in Jerusalem
6:3 Jesus went up into a *m*, and
6:15 withdrew again into the *m*
Ac 1:12 *m* called the Mount of Olives
Ga 4:25 Sinai, a *m* in Arabia, and
Heb 8:5 was shown to you in the *m*
12:20 if a beast touches the *m*
2Pe 1:18 were with him in the holy *m*
Re 6:14 every *m* and every island
8:8 great *m* burning with fire was
21:10 to a great and lofty *m*, and

Mountainous

Ge 10:30 Sephar, the *m* region of the
12:8 *m* region . . . east of Bethel
14:10 fled to the *m* region
19:17 Escape to the *m* region for
19:19 not able to escape to the *m*
19:30 dwelling in the *m* region
31:21 directed his face to the *m*
31:23 in the *m* region of Gilead
31:25 in the *m* region of Gilead
36:8 in the *m* region of Seir. Esau
36:9 in the *m* region of Seir
Nu 13:17 go up into the *m* region
13:29 are dwelling in the *m* region
De 1:6 dwelt . . . in this *m* region
1:7 the *m* region of the Amorites
1:7 the Arabah, the *m* region and
1:19 the *m* region of the Amorites
1:20 the *m* region of the Amorites
1:24 went up into the *m* region and
2:37 the cities of the *m* region
3:12 the *m* region of Gilead, and
3:25 good *m* region and Lebanon
8:7 and in the *m* region
33:2 from the *m* region of Paran
Jos 2:16 Go to the *m* region, that
Jos 2:22 came to the *m* region and
2:23 the *m* region and to cross
9:1 the Jordan in the *m* region
10:6 inhabiting the *m* region have
10:40 land of the *m* region and
11:2 in the *m* region and in the
11:3 Jebusites in the *m* region
11:16 *m* region and all the Negeb
11:16 *m* region of Israel and its
11:21 Anakim from the *m* region
11:21 the *m* region of Judah and
11:21 the *m* region of Israel
12:8 in the *m* region and in the
13:6 inhabitants of the *m* region
14:12 give me this *m* region that
15:48 the *m* region Shamir and
16:1 the *m* region of Bethel
17:15 the *m* region of Ephraim has
17:16 *m* region is not enough for
17:18 the *m* region should become
19:50 in the *m* region of Ephraim
20:7 in the *m* region of Naphtali
20:7 in the *m* region of Ephraim
20:7 in the *m* region of Judah
21:11 in the *m* region of Judah
21:21 the *m* region of Ephraim
24:30 in the *m* region of Ephraim
24:33 in the *m* region of Ephraim
Jg 1:9 the *m* region and the Negeb
1:19 possession of the *m* region
1:34 Dan into the *m* region, for
2:9 in the *m* region of Ephraim
3:27 in the *m* region of Ephraim
3:27 out of the *m* region, he
4:5 in the *m* region of Ephraim
7:24 all the *m* region of Ephraim
10:1 in the *m* region of Ephraim
17:1 of the *m* region of Ephraim
17:8 *m* region of Ephraim as far
18:2 the *m* region of Ephraim as
18:13 the *m* region of Ephraim and
19:1 of the *m* region of Ephraim
19:16 the *m* region of Ephraim, and
19:18 the *m* region of Ephraim
1Sa 1:1 of the *m* region of Ephraim
9:4 the *m* region of Ephraim and
13:2 in the *m* region of Bethel
14:22 in the *m* region of Ephraim
23:14 *m* region in the wilderness
2Sa 20:21 the *m* region of Ephraim
1Ki 4:8 the *m* region of Ephraim
12:25 the *m* region of Ephraim
2Ki 5:22 the *m* region of Ephraim
6:17 *m* region was full of horses
19:23 the height of *m* regions
1Ch 6:67 in the *m* region of Ephraim
2Ch 13:4 *m* region of Ephraim, and
15:8 *m* region of Ephraim, and to
19:4 *m* region of Ephraim, that he
20:10 the *m* region of Seir, whom
20:22 *m* region of Seir who were
20:23 *m* region of Seir to devote
27:4 in the *m* region of Judah
Ne 8:15 Go out to the *m* region and
Ps 68:15 The *m* region of Bashan is a
68:15 The *m* region of Bashan is a
78:54 *m* region that his right hand
Ca 4:1 from the *m* region of Gilead
Isa 37:24 the height of *m* regions
Jer 4:15 the *m* region of Ephraim
17:26 from the *m* region and from
31:6 in the *m* region of Ephraim
32:44 cities of the *m* region and
33:13 the cities of the *m* region
50:19 *m* region of Ephraim and
Eze 35:2 the *m* region of Seir
35:3 O *m* region of Seir
35:7 *m* region of Seir a desolate
35:15 O *m* region of Seir, even
38:21 all my *m* region a sword
Ob 8 out of the *m* region of Esau
9 from the *m* region of Esau
19 even of the *m* region of Esau
21 to judge the *m* region of Esau
Lu 1:39 went into the *m* country with
1:65 the whole *m* country of Judea

Mountains

Ge 7:19 all the tall *m* that were
7:20 and the *m* became covered
8:4 ark came to rest on the *m* of
8:5 the tops of the *m* appeared
22:2 on one of the *m* that I shall
49:26 blessings of the eternal *m*

Ex 32:12 kill them among the *m* and to
Nu 23:7 From the *m* of the east: Do
33:47 the *m* of Abarim before Nebo
33:48 away from the *m* of Abarim
De 8:9 the *m* of which you will mine
11:11 land of *m* and valley plains
12:2 on the tall *m* and the hills
32:22 ablaze the foundations of *m*
33:15 from the *m* of the east
Jg 5:5 *M* flowed away from the face of
6:2 places that were in the *m*, and
9:25 tops of the *m*, and they would
9:36 from the tops of the *m*
9:36 The shadows of the *m* are
11:37 I will descend upon the *m*
11:38 and weeping . . . upon the *m*
1Sa 26:20 a partridge upon the *m*
2Sa 1:21 *m* of Gilboa, let no dew
1Ki 19:11 wind was rending *m* and
20:23 Their God is a God of *m*
20:28 Jehovah is a God of *m*, and
22:17 scattered on the *m*, like
2Ki 2:16 *m* or in one of the valleys
1Ch 12:8 like the gazelles upon the *m*
2Ch 18:16 scattered upon the *m*, like
21:11 places on the *m* of Judah
26:10 vinedressers in the *m* and
Job 9:5 He is moving *m* away, so that
24:8 From the rainstorm of the *m*
28:9 overthrown *m* from their
39:8 explores *m* for its pasturage
40:20 the *m* themselves bear their
Ps 18:7 *m* themselves became agitated
36:6 is like *m* of God
46:2 *m* totter into the heart of
46:3 the *m* rock at its uproar
50:10 beasts upon a thousand *m*
50:11 winged creature of the *m*
65:6 establishing the *m* with his
68:16 O you *m* of peaks, keep
72:3 Let the *m* carry peace to the
72:16 top of the *m* there will be
76:4 more majestic than the *m* of
80:10 *m* were covered with its
83:14 flame that scorches the *m*
87:1 foundation is in the holy *m*
90:2 the *m* themselves were born
95:4 the peaks of the *m* belong
97:5 *m* . . . proceeded to melt just
98:8 very *m* cry out joyfully
104:6 standing above the very *m*
104:8 *M* proceeded to ascend
104:10 Between the *m* they keep
104:13 watering the *m* from his
104:18 The high *m* are for the
104:32 He touches the *m*, and they
114:4 *m* themselves skipped about
114:6 *m*, that you went skipping
121:1 raise my eyes to the *m*
125:2 Jerusalem—as *m* are all
133:3 upon the *m* of Zion
144:5 Touch the *m* that they may
147:8 the *m* to sprout green grass
148:9 You *m* and all you hills
Pr 8:25 Before the *m* themselves had
27:25 vegetation of the *m* has been
Ca 2:8 coming, climbing upon the *m*
2:17 upon the *m* of separation
4:8 from the *m* of leopards
8:14 stags upon the *m* of spices
Isa 2:2 above the top of the *m*, and
2:14 upon all the lofty *m* and
5:25 *m* will be agitated, and
7:25 *m* that used to be cleared of
13:4 Listen! A crowd in the *m*
14:25 tread him down on my own *m*
17:13 like the chaff of the *m*
18:3 a signal upon the *m*, and
18:6 bird of prey of the *m* and
34:3 *m* must melt because of
40:12 with an indicator the *m*
41:15 tread down the *m* and crush
42:11 From the top of the *m* let
42:15 shall devastate *m* and hills
44:23 Become cheerful, you *m*
49:11 make all my *m* a way, and
49:13 Let the *m* become cheerful
52:7 How comely upon the *m* are the
54:10 *m* themselves may be
55:12 *m* and the hills themselves
64:1 the very *m* had quaked
64:3 the *m* themselves quaked
65:7 sacrificial smoke upon the *m*
65:9 hereditary possessor of my *m*
Jer 3:23 turmoil on the *m* belong to
4:24 I saw the *m*, and, look!
9:10 Over the *m* I shall raise a
13:16 on the *m* at dusk. And you
17:3 on the *m* in the field
31:5 in the *m* of Samaria
46:18 like Tabor among the *m* and
50:6 On the *m* they have led them
La 4:19 Upon the *m* they have hotly
Eze 6:2 face toward the *m* of Israel
6:3 O *m* of Israel, hear the word
6:3 Jehovah has said to the *m* and
6:13 on all the tops of the *m* and
7:7 and not the shouting of the *m*
7:16 on the *m* like the doves
18:6 on the *m* he did not eat and
18:11 has eaten also upon the *m*
18:15 On the *m* he has not eaten
19:9 be heard on the *m* of Israel
22:9 *m* they have eaten in you
31:12 will abandon it upon the *m*
32:5 put your flesh upon the *m*
32:6 upon the *m*; and stream beds
33:28 and the *m* of Israel must
34:6 straying on all the *m* and
34:13 on the *m* of Israel, by
34:14 on Israel's high *m* their
34:14 feed upon the *m* of Israel
35:8 fill its *m* with its slain
35:12 the *m* of Israel, saying
36:1 concerning the *m* of Israel
36:1 say, O *m* of Israel, hear the
36:4 *m* of Israel, hear the word
36:4 to the *m* and to the hills
36:6 to the *m* and to the hills
36:8 *m* of Israel, will give forth
37:22 on the *m* of Israel, and
38:8 onto the *m* of Israel, that
38:20 *m* will actually be thrown
39:2 upon the *m* of Israel
39:4 On the *m* of Israel you will
39:17 sacrifice on the *m* of
Ho 4:13 On . . . *m* they sacrifice
10:8 say to the *m*, Cover us!
Joe 2:2 dawn spread out upon the *m*
2:5 chariots on the tops of the *m*
3:18 *m* will drip with sweet wine
Am 3:9 against the *m* of Samaria
4:13 the Former of the *m* and
9:13 *m* must drip with sweet wine
Jon 2:6 To the bottoms of the *m* I
Mic 1:4 the *m* must melt under him
4:1 above the top of the *m*, and
6:1 a legal case with the *m*, and
6:2 Hear, O you *m*, the legal
Na 1:5 *M* themselves have rocked
1:15 Upon the *m* the feet of one
3:18 been scattered upon the *m*
Hab 3:6 eternal *m* got to be smashed
3:10 *M* saw you; they got to be
Hag 1:11 the earth, and upon the *m*
Zec 6:1 from between two *m*, and the
6:1, 1 and the *m* were copper *m*
14:5 flee to the valley of my *m*
14:5 valley of the *m* will reach
Mal 1:3 his *m* a desolated waste and
Mt 18:12 the ninety-nine upon the *m*
24:16 Judea begin fleeing to the *m*
Mr 5:5 in the tombs and in the *m* and
13:14 begin fleeing to the *m*
Lu 21:21 begin fleeing to the *m*
23:30 say to the *m*, Fall over us!
1Co 13:2 faith so as to transplant *m*
Heb 11:38 wandered about in . . . *m*
Re 6:15 in the rock-masses of the *m*
6:16 they keep saying to the *m* and
16:20 and *m* were not found
17:9 seven heads mean seven *m*

Mountainside
2Sa 13:34 road behind him by the *m*

Mountaintop
Ex 24:17 a devouring fire on the *m*

Mounted
2Sa 1:6 *m* men had caught up with
Na 3:3 The *m* horseman, and the flame
Mt 21:5 *m* upon an ass, yes, upon a
Lu 10:34 Then he *m* him upon his own

Mourn
Ex 33:4 evil word, they began to *m*
Nu 14:39 began to *m* a great deal
2Sa 13:37 David continued to *m* over
Ne 1:4 began to weep and *m* for days
Ne 8:9 day is holy . . . Do not *m*
Isa 3:26 her entrances will have to *m*
19:8 the fishers will have to *m*
Jer 4:28 the land will *m*, and the
Ho 4:3 That is why the land will *m*
10:5 its people will certainly *m*
Am 8:8 every inhabitant . . . have to *m*
9:5 will have to *m*; and it will
Mt 5:4 Happy are those who *m*, since
9:15 no reason to *m* as long as
Lu 6:25 because you will *m* and weep
1Co 5:2 and did you not rather *m*, in
2Co 12:21 *m* over many of those who
Jas 4:9 Give way to misery and *m* and
Re 18:15 merchants . . . weep and *m*

Mourned
Joe 1:9 ministers of Jehovah, have *m*

Mourners
Job 29:25 As one who comforts the *m*

Mourners'
Jer 16:5 into the house of a *m* feast

Mournfully
Isa 59:11 like doves we *m* keep cooing

Mourning
Ge 27:41 period of *m* for my father
37:34 carried on *m* over his son
37:35 I shall go down *m* to my son
38:12 Judah kept the period of *m*
50:10 *m* rites for his father seven
50:11 got to see the *m* rites in
50:11 a heavy *m* for the Egyptians
De 26:14 not eaten of it during my *m*
34:8 the *m* period for Moses were
1Sa 6:19 *m* because Jehovah had struck
15:35 Samuel had gone into *m* for
16:1 long will you be *m* for Saul
2Sa 11:27 *m* period was past, David
14:2 Go in *m*, please, and dress
14:2 with garments of *m*, and do
14:2 *m* many days over someone
19:1 carries on *m* over Absalom
19:2 an occasion of *m* on the part
1Ch 7:22 carried on *m* for many days
2Ch 35:24 were *m* over Josiah
Ezr 10:6 *m* over the unfaithfulness
Es 4:3 was great *m* among the Jews
6:12 *m* and with his head covered
9:22 and from *m* to a good day
Job 14:22 own soul . . . will keep *m*
30:31 came to be merely for *m*
Ps 30:11 changed my *m* into dancing
35:14 like one *m* for a mother
Ec 7:2 to the house of *m* than to go to
7:4 wise ones is in the house of *m*
Ca 1:7 like a woman wrapped in *m*
Isa 22:12 and for *m* and for baldness
24:4 the land has gone to *m*, has
24:7 new wine has gone to *m*
29:2 to be *m* and lamentation
33:9 The land has gone *m*, has
57:18 to him and to his *m* ones
60:20 days of your *m* will have
61:2 to comfort all the *m* ones
61:3 assign to those *m* over Zion
61:3 exultation instead of *m*
66:10 keeping yourselves in *m*
Jer 6:26 *m* that for an only son
14:2 Judah has gone *m*, and its
16:7 on account of *m* to comfort
23:10 the land has gone to *m*
31:13 change their *m* into
La 1:4 ways of Zion are *m*, because
2:5 *m* and lamentation abound
2:8 rampart and wall to go *m*
5:15 has been changed into mere *m*
Eze 7:12 let him not go into *m*, for
7:27 king himself will go into *m*
24:17 no *m* should you make
31:15 shall certainly cause a *m*
Da 10:2 Daniel, happened to be *m* for
Ho 9:4 the bread of times of *m*
Joe 1:10 the ground has gone to *m*
Am 1:2 shepherds must go to *m*
5:16 call a farmer to *m*, and to
8:10 turn your festivals into *m*
8:10 like the *m* for an only son
Mic 1:8 a *m* like female ostriches
2Co 7:7 your *m*, your zeal for me; so
Jas 4:9 laughter be turned into *m*
Re 18:7 give her torment and *m*
18:7 and I shall never see *m*

Jer 1:9 and caused it to touch my *m*
1:9 have put my words in your *m*
1:13 *m* is away from the north
5:14 my words in your *m* a fire
7:28 been cut off from their *m*
9:8 With his *m*, peace is what
9:12 the *m* of Jehovah has spoken
9:20 ear take the word of his *m*
12:2 You are near in their *m*
15:19 will become like my own *m*
23:16 not from the *m* of Jehovah
32:4 his *m* will actually speak
32:4 speak with the *m* of that one
34:3 his own *m* will speak even
34:3 speak even with your *m*, and
36:4 write at the *m* of Jeremiah
36:6 written at my *m* the words
36:17 all these words from his *m*
36:18 Out of his *m* he kept
36:27 at the *m* of Jeremiah
36:32 *m* of Jeremiah all the
44:17 gone forth from our *m*
44:26 *m* of any man of Judah
45:1 from the *m* of Jeremiah in
48:28 of the *m* of the hollow
51:44 bring forth out of his *m*
La 1:18 it is against his *m* that I
2:16 enemies have opened their *m*
3:29 put his *m* in the very dust
3:38 From the *m* of the Most High
3:46 enemies have opened their *m*
Eze 2:8 Open your *m* and eat what I
3:2 opened my *m*, and he gradually
3:3 to be in my *m* like honey for
3:17 must hear from my *m* speech
3:26 stick to the roof of your *m*
3:27 I shall open your *m*, and you
4:14 into my *m* there has come no
16:56 hearing about from your *m*
16:63 any reason to open your *m*
21:22 open one's *m* for a slaying
24:27 your *m* will be opened to
29:21 give occasion to open the *m*
33:7 at my *m* you must hear the
33:22 to open my *m* prior to that
33:22 my *m* was opened and I
33:31 *m* they are expressing
34:10 my sheep out of their *m*
Da 4:31 word was yet in the king's *m*
6:17 placed on the *m* of the pit
6:22 and shut the *m* of the lions
7:5 three ribs in its *m* between
7:8 *m* speaking grandiose things
7:20 horn that had eyes and a *m*
10:3 or wine entered into my *m*
10:16 open my *m* and speak and say
Ho 2:17 Baal images from her *m*, and
6:5 by the sayings of my *m*
8:1 To your *m*—a horn! One comes
Am 3:12 from the *m* of the lion
Ob 12 ought not to maintain a big *m*
Mic 4:4 *m* of Jehovah of armies has
6:12 tongue is tricky in their *m*
7:5 guard the openings of your *m*
7:16 put their hand upon their *m*
Na 3:12 fall into the *m* of an eater
Zec 5:8 the lead weight upon its *m*
8:9 from the *m* of the prophets
9:7 things from his *m* and
14:12 will rot away in one's *m*
Mal 2:6 truth proved to be in his *m*
2:7 seek from his *m*; for he
Mt 4:4 forth through Jehovah's *m*
5:2 he opened his *m* and began
12:34 of the heart the *m* speaks
13:35 I will open my *m* with
15:11 Not what enters into his *m*
15:11 what proceeds out of his *m*
15:17 entering into the *m* passes
15:18 proceeding out of the *m*
17:27 open its *m*, you will find a
18:16 *m* of two or three witnesses
21:16 Out of the *m* of babes and
Lu 1:64 *m* was opened and his tongue
1:70 the *m* of his holy prophets
4:22 words proceeding out of his *m*
6:45 abundance his *m* speaks
11:54 catch something out of his *m*
19:22 Out of your own *m* I judge
21:15 give you a *m* and wisdom
22:71 heard it out of his own *m*
Joh 19:29 and brought it to his *m*
Ac 1:16 by David's *m* about Judas, who
3:18 *m* of all the prophets, that
Ac 3:21 *m* of his holy prophets of
4:25 holy spirit said by the *m*
8:32 so he does not open his *m*
8:35 Philip opened his *m* and
10:34 Peter opened his *m* and said
11:8 has never entered into my *m*
15:7 through my *m* people of the
18:14 Paul was going to open his *m*
22:14 to hear the voice of his *m*
23:2 to strike him on the *m*
Ro 3:14 *m* is full of cursing and
3:19 every *m* may be stopped and
10:8 in your own *m* and in your
10:9 word in your own *m*, that
10:10 the *m* one makes public
15:6 with one *m* glorify the God
2Co 6:11 Our *m* has been opened to you
13:1 At the *m* of two witnesses
Eph 4:29 not proceed out of your *m*
6:19 with the opening of my *m*
Col 3:8 obscene talk out of your *m*
2Th 2:8 by the spirit of his *m* and
2Ti 4:17 delivered from the lion's *m*
Jas 3:10 Out of the same *m* come
1Pe 2:22 was deception found in his *m*
Re 1:16 out of his *m* a sharp, long
2:16 with the long sword of my *m*
3:16 to vomit you out of my *m*
10:9 *m* it will be sweet as honey
10:10 in my *m* it was sweet as
12:15 like a river from its *m*
12:16 the earth opened its *m* and
12:16 dragon disgorged from its *m*
13:2, 2 its *m* was as a lion's *m*
13:5 *m* speaking great things and
13:6 opened its *m* in blasphemies
16:13 out of the *m* of the dragon
16:13 of the *m* of the wild beast
16:13 the *m* of the false prophet
19:15 out of his *m* there protrudes
19:21 sword proceeded out of his *m*

Mouthed
Jg 9:38 saying of yours that you *m*

Mouthings
Ps 49:13 pleasure in their very *m*

Mouths
De 31:19 Place it in their *m* in order
Jos 6:10 no word . . . out of your *m*
Ps 22:7 keep opening their *m* wide
Jer 44:25 also speak with your *m*
Eze 35:13 against me with your *m*
Joe 1:5 cut off from your *m*
Mic 3:5 put something into their *m*
Zep 3:13 in their *m* a tricky tongue
Tit 1:11 necessary to shut the *m* of
Heb 11:33 stopped the *m* of lions
Jas 3:3 bridles in the *m* of horses
Jude 16 *m* speak swelling things
Re 9:17 out of their *m* fire and smoke
9:18 issued forth from their *m*
9:19 in their *m* and in their tails
11:5 issues forth from their *m*
14:5 no falsehood . . . in their *m*

Movable
Mt 12:29 seize his *m* goods, unless
Mr 3:27 able to plunder his *m* goods
Lu 17:31 *m* things are in the house

Move
Ge 8:17 the moving animals that *m*
26:16 *M* from our neighborhood
Ex 11:7 no dog *m* eagerly its tongue
13:22 pillar of cloud would not *m*
33:1 Go, *m* up from here, you and
Nu 8:11 Levites to *m* to and fro
8:13 *m* to and fro as a wave
8:15 *m* to and fro as a wave
8:21 Aaron caused them to *m* to and
14:44 Moses did not *m* away from
De 19:14 *m* back the boundary marks
32:35 their foot will *m* unsteadily
Jg 6:18 Do not . . . *m* away from here
2Sa 24:2 *M* about, please, through all
2Ki 5:11 *m* his hand to and fro over
Job 18:4 rock *m* away from its place
23:12 I do not *m* away
24:2 who *m* back boundary marks
Ps 84:10 *m* around in the tents of
94:18 My foot will certainly *m*
104:20 animals of the forest *m*
107:27 *m* unsteadily like a drunken
Pr 17:13 bad will not *m* away from
22:28 Do not *m* back a boundary of
Pr 23:10 not *m* back the boundary of
Isa 8:8 and *m* on through Judah
46:7 place it does not *m* away
59:14 justice was forced to *m*
Mic 2:6 Humiliations will not *m*
Hab 1:11 *m* onward like wind and will
Mt 8:34 *m* out from their districts
Joh 13:1 *m* out of this world to the
Ac 17:28 by him we have life and *m*
1Co 6:5 am speaking to *m* you to shame
7:35 but to *m* you to that which is
15:34 speaking to *m* you to shame

Moved
Ge 12:8 he *m* from there to the
13:11 Lot *m* his camp to the east
20:1 Abraham *m* camp from there to
26:17 Isaac *m* from there and
26:22 Later he *m* away from there
Jos 10:21 Not a man *m* his tongue
16:8 boundary *m* on westward to
17:7 boundary *m* to the right to
2Sa 20:12 *m* Amasa from the highway
Es 3:15 *m* to speed because of the
8:14 *m* with speed by the king's
Job 9:26 have *m* on like reed boats
14:18 And even a rock will be *m*
32:15 Words have *m* away from
Ps 38:16 When my foot *m* unsteadily
55:11 deception have not *m* away
Isa 10:15 staff *m* back and forth the
28:9 *m* away from the breasts
29:9 they have *m* unsteadily, but
Hab 3:14 *m* tempestuously to scatter
Zec 14:4 actually be *m* to the north
Mt 12:44 my house out of which I *m*
18:27 *M* to pity at this, the
20:34 *M* with pity, Jesus touched
Mr 1:41 At that he was *m* with pity
6:34 he was *m* with pity for them
Lu 7:13 he was *m* with pity for her
10:33 he was *m* with pity
11:24 my house out of which I *m*
15:20 and was *m* with pity, and he
19:36 As he *m* along they kept

Movement
2Co 4:8 but not cramped beyond *m*

Movements
Isa 25:11 tricky *m* of his hands

Movers
Ezr 4:15 *m* of revolt from the days

Moves
Ge 1:21 every living soul that *m*
7:8 everything that *m* on the
7:14 moving animal that *m* on the
8:19 everything that *m* on the
Le 11:44 creature that *m* upon the
11:46 soul that *m* about in the
20:25 *m* on the ground that I have
De 27:17 *m* back the boundary mark of
Job 9:11 he *m* on and I do not discern
11:10 *m* on and hands someone over
Isa 24:20 land absolutely *m*

Moving
Ge 1:2 God's active force was *m* to
1:24 domestic animal and *m* animal
1:25 every *m* animal of the ground
1:26, 26 *m* animal that is *m*
1:28 living creature that is *m*
1:30 everything *m* upon the earth
6:7 to *m* animal and to flying
6:20 all *m* animals of the ground
7:14 every *m* animal that moves on
7:21 all flesh that was *m* upon
7:23 wiped out . . . *m* animal and
8:17 all the *m* animals that move
8:19 every *m* animal . . . went out
9:2 everything that goes *m* on the
9:3 *m* animal that is alive may
De 4:18 anything *m* on the ground, the
2Sa 24:8 *m* about through all the land
1Ki 4:33 about the *m* things and about
Job 9:5 He is *m* mountains away, so
Ps 69:34 seas and everything *m* about
104:25 *m* things without number
Pr 30:29 do well in their *m* along
Isa 10:15 one *m* it back and forth
21:1 south in *m* onward, from
59:13 was a *m* back from our God
Eze 1:13 appearance of torches was *m*
Ho 5:10 like those *m* back a boundary
Lu 18:36 he heard a crowd *m* through

2Th 3:1 word . . . keep *m* speedily and
2Pe 2:3 judgment . . . is not *m* slowly

Mown

Ps 72:6 the rain upon the *m* grass
Am 7:1 the *m* grass of the king

Moza

1Ch 2:46 gave birth to Haran and *M*
8:36 Zimri . . . father to *M*
8:37 *M* . . . became father to Binea
9:42 Zimri . . . father to *M*
9:43 *M*, he became father to Binea

Mozah

Jos 18:26 Mizpeh and Chephirah and *M*

Much

Ge 17:2 multiply you very, very *m*
17:20 multiply him very, very *m*
20:8 the men got very *m* afraid
24:25 straw and *m* fodder with us
24:35 blessed my master very *m* in
32:7 Jacob became very *m* afraid
Ex 9:7 not so *m* as one of Israel's
14:28 Not so *m* as one among them
16:17 some gathering *m* and some
16:18 gathered *m* had no surplus
16:22 picked up twice as *m* bread
19:18 was trembling very *m*
36:5 people are bringing *m* more
Le 26:18 seven times as *m* for your
27:14 so *m* it should cost
Nu 20:11 *m* water began to come out
De 2:5 so *m* as the width of the sole
15:8 on pledge as *m* as he needs
17:17 gold for himself very *m*
31:27 then how *m* more so after
Jos 9:24 very *m* afraid for our souls
10:2 he became very *m* afraid
22:8 and with very *m* livestock
Jg 4:16 Not as *m* as one remained
6:27 too *m* to do it by day, he
1Sa 2:3 speak very haughtily so *m*
14:30 *m* more so if the people had
14:45 not as *m* as a single hair
15:22 Jehovah have as *m* delight
16:21 he got to loving him very *m*
17:24 and were very *m* afraid
20:19 you will be missed very *m*
21:5 how *m* more so today, when
21:12 very *m* afraid on account of
23:3 *m* more so in case we should
25:17 too *m* of a good-for-nothing
26:21 and am very *m* mistaken
28:5 began to tremble very *m*
28:20 became very *m* afraid
31:4 because he was very *m* afraid
2Sa 4:11 how *m* more so when wicked
12:30 the spoil . . . was very *m*
14:25 as to be praised so *m*
16:11 and how *m* more now a
24:10 sinned very *m* in what I
1Ki 8:27 how *m* less, then, this house
9:11 gold as *m* as he delighted in
10:2 *m* gold and precious stones
11:19 so *m* that he gave him a
12:28 too *m* for you to go up to
19:7 the journey is too *m* for you
2Ki 5:13 How *m* more, then, since he
1Ch 10:4 because he was very *m* afraid
16:25 and very *m* to be praised
18:8 David took very *m* copper
19:5 men very *m* humiliated
20:2 spoil of the city . . . very *m*
21:8 I have sinned very *m* in that
2Ch 6:18 *m* less, then, this house that
14:14 to be *m* to plunder in them
25:9 means to give you *m* more
32:15 How *m* less, then, will
Ne 2:2 At this I became very *m* afraid
6:16 very *m* in their own eyes
Es 4:4 the queen was very *m* pained
Job 4:19 How *m* more so with those
6:27 *m* more will you cast lots
9:14 How *m* more so in case I
15:16 How *m* less so when one is
22:5 own badness too *m* already
25:6 How *m* less so mortal man
26:2 how *m* help you have been to
26:3 How *m* you have advised one
31:25 because my property was *m*
33:12 *m* more than mortal man
35:14 How *m* less, then, when you
Ps 6:3 soul has been very *m* disturbed
6:10 my enemies . . . *m* ashamed
Ps 19:10 yes, than *m* refined gold
19:13 from *m* transgression
31:11 to my neighbors very *m* so
48:1 is great and *m* to be praised
58:2 How *m*, rather, do you with
62:2 not be made to totter very *m*
65:9 You enrich it very *m*
78:29 satisfying themselves very *m*
78:59 he contemned Israel very *m*
88:15 things from you very *m*
96:4 and very *m* to be praised
109:30 laud Jehovah very *m* with
112:1 he has taken very *m* delight
116:10 was very *m* afflicted
119:140 saying is very *m* refined
119:162 does when finding *m* spoil
139:17 God, how *m* does the grand
142:6 become very *m* impoverished
145:3 and very *m* to be praised
Pr 6:31 good with seven times as *m*
11:31 *m* more should the wicked
15:11 How *m* more so the hearts of
16:16 wisdom is O how *m* better
17:7 How *m* less so for a noble the
19:7 *m* farther have his personal
19:10 *m* less for a servant to rule
21:27 *m* more so when one brings
25:16 that you may not take too *m*
25:27 too *m* honey is not good
29:17 give *m* pleasure to your soul
Ec 5:12 is little or *m* that he eats
6:11 that are causing *m* vanity
8:17 however *m* mankind keep
9:18 one sinner can destroy *m* good
12:12 and *m* devotion to them is
Ca 4:10 How *m* better your expressions
Isa 10:6 to take *m* spoil and to
10:6 take *m* plunder and to make
16:14 disgraced with *m* commotion
21:7 with *m* attentiveness
30:26 become seven times as *m*
42:17 will be very *m* ashamed
52:13 elevated and exalted very *m*
52:14 *m* was the disfigurement as
56:12 great in a very *m* larger
Jer 9:19 How *m* we have felt shame!
13:27 clean—after how *m* longer
17:18 with twice as *m* breakdown
20:11 certainly be put to *m* shame
48:16 hurrying up very *m*
49:9 as *m* ruin as they wanted
50:12 has become very *m* ashamed
La 5:22 indignant toward us very *m*
Eze 15:5 How *m* less so, when fire
20:13 they profaned very *m*, so
22:18 *M* scummy dross, that of
22:19 become as *m* scummy dross
23:32 the cup containing *m*
31:5 *m* water in its watercourses
38:12 and to do *m* plundering
38:13 Is it to do *m* plundering
Da 2:6 *m* dignity you will receive on
5:9 was very *m* frightened and his
6:25 May your peace grow very *m*!
7:5 to it, Get up, eat *m* flesh
8:9 *m* greater toward the south
Ob 2 You are despised very *m*
5 steal as *m* as they wanted
Na 2:1 Reinforce power very *m*
Zep 1:14 a hurrying of it very *m*
Hag 1:6 You have sown *m* seed, but
1:9 There was a looking for *m*
Zec 1:2 indignant . . . very *m* so
Mt 2:10 they rejoiced very *m* indeed
2:18 weeping and *m* wailing
6:30 he not *m* rather clothe you
7:11 how *m* more so will your
10:25 how *m* more will they call
12:12 *m* more worth is a man than
13:5 they did not have *m* soil
14:6 and pleased Herod so *m*
17:6 and became very *m* afraid
17:23 they were very *m* grieved
18:31 they became very *m* grieved
23:15 for Gehenna twice as *m* so
26:22 Being very *m* grieved at this
26:40 not so *m* as watch one hour
27:14 governor wondered very *m*
27:54 grew very *m* afraid, saying
Mr 2:2 many gathered, so *m* so that
4:5 did not have *m* soil, and it
6:51 they were very *m* amazed
7:36 *m* more they would proclaim
10:48 kept shouting that *m* more
Mr 12:27 You are *m* mistaken
Lu 6:34 that they may get back as *m*
7:47 forgiven, because she loved *m*
11:13 how *m* more so will the
12:24 how *m* more worth are you
12:28 *m* rather will he clothe you
12:48 to whom *m* was given
12:48 *m* will be demanded of him
12:48 people put in charge of *m*
16:5 How *m* are you owing my
16:7 you, how *m* are you owing?
16:10 least is faithful also in *m*
16:10 is unrighteous also in *m*
18:39 that *m* more he kept shouting
Joh 3:16 God loved the world so *m*
6:11 as *m* of the small fishes as
12:24 it then bears *m* fruit
14:30 I shall not speak *m* with
15:5 this one bears *m* fruit
15:8 you keep bearing *m* fruit and
Ac 5:8 sell the field for so *m*
5:8 She said: Yes, for so *m*
6:7 in Jerusalem very *m*
15:7 *m* disputing had taken place
16:16 *m* gain by practicing the art
16:20 disturbing our city very *m*
25:23 came with *m* pompous show
Ro 3:12 there is not so *m* as one
5:9 *M* more, therefore, since we
5:10 *m* more, now that we have
5:15 abounded *m* more to many
5:17 *m* more will those who
9:22 with *m* long-suffering
11:12 *m* more will the full number
11:24 how *m* rather will these who
1Co 2:3 fear and with *m* trembling
9:12 over you, do we not *m* more
12:22 But *m* rather is it the case
16:12 I entreated him very *m* to
2Co 2:4 *m* tribulation and anguish of
3:8 spirit be *m* more with glory
3:9 glorious, *m* more does the
3:11 *m* more would that which
6:4 by the endurance of *m*, by
8:4 *m* entreaty for the privilege
8:15 person with *m* did not have
8:15 did not have too *m*, and the
8:22 but now *m* more earnest due
10:8 boast a bit too *m* about the
Php 2:12 but now *m* more readily
1Th 1:6 under *m* tribulation with joy
Phm 7 I got *m* joy and comfort over
16 how *m* more so to you both in
Heb 5:3 as *m* for himself as for the
5:11 have *m* to say and hard to be
9:14 *m* more will the blood of
10:29 *m* more severe a punishment
12:9 *m* more subject ourselves to
12:25 *m* more shall we not if we
Jas 5:16 it is at work, has *m* force
1Pe 1:7 *m* greater value than gold
2Jo 4 I rejoiced very *m* because I have
3Jo 3 I rejoiced very *m* when brothers
Re 18:6 and do to her twice as *m*
18:6 twice as *m* of the mixture

Muddy

Eze 32:13 man will no more *m* them
32:13 a domestic animal *m* them

Muddying

Eze 32:2 *m* the waters with your feet

Mulberry

Lu 17:6 to this black *m* tree, Be

Mule

2Sa 13:29 mount each one his *m* and
18:9 Absalom was riding upon a *m*
18:9 the *m* got to come under the
18:9 the *m* itself that was under
Ps 32:9 or *m* without understanding
Zec 14:15 scourge of the horse, the *m*

Mules

1Ki 10:25 balsam oil, horses and *m*
18:5 preserve the horses and *m*
2Ki 5:17 the load of a pair of *m*
1Ch 12:40 upon *m* and upon cattle
2Ch 9:24 and *m* as a yearly matter of
Ezr 2:66 *m* two hundred and forty-five
Ne 7:68 their *m* two hundred and
Isa 66:20 *m* and on swift she-camels
Eze 27:14 horses and steeds and *m*

Multiplied

De 1:10 Jehovah your God has *m* you

Musical
Da 3:5 and all sorts of *m* instruments
3:7 and all sorts of *m* instruments
3:10 all sorts of *m* instruments
3:15 all sorts of *m* instruments
6:18 *m* instruments were brought

Musicians
Ezr 7:24 the *m*, the doorkeepers, the
Re 18:22 of *m* and of flutists and of

Musing
Ps 104:34 *m* about him be pleasurable

Must*
Ge 2:17 you *m* not eat from it, for
2:24 he *m* stick to his wife and
2:24 and they *m* become one flesh
3:1 God said you *m* not eat from
3:3 You *m* not eat from it, no, you
3:3 you *m* not touch it that you
3:17 You *m* not eat from it
3:18 *m* eat the vegetation of the
9:4 —its blood—you *m* not eat
9:16 rainbow *m* occur in the cloud
17:10 Every male of yours *m* get
17:11 you *m* get circumcised in the
17:11 it *m* serve as a sign of the
17:12 *m* be circumcised, according
17:13 *m* without fail get
17:13 *m* serve as a covenant to
17:14 *m* be cut off from his people
18:18 nations of the earth *m* bless
Ex 12:19 that soul *m* be cut off from
20:3 You *m* not have any other gods
20:13 You *m* not murder
20:14 You *m* not commit adultery
20:15 You *m* not steal
20:16 You *m* not testify falsely as
20:17 You *m* not desire your
20:17 You *m* not desire your
20:23 *m* not make along with me
20:23 *m* not make gods of gold for
22:25 *m* not become like a usurer
22:25 *m* not lay interest upon him
22:28 *m* not call down evil upon
Nu 35:31 you *m* take no ransom for the
35:32 *m* not take a ransom for one
35:33 *m* not pollute the land in
De 1:17 *m* not be partial in judgment
4:40 you *m* keep his regulations
5:7 *m* never have any other gods
5:8 You *m* not make for yourself a
5:11 You *m* not take up the name of
5:13 *m* do all your work six days
5:14 You *m* not do any work, you
5:15 *m* remember that you became
5:17 You *m* not murder
5:18 *m* you commit adultery
5:19 Neither *m* you steal
5:20 *m* you testify to a falsehood
5:21 Neither *m* you desire your
5:21 Neither *m* you selfishly
5:32 *m* not turn to the right or to
6:3 you *m* listen, O Israel, and
6:5 you *m* love Jehovah your God
6:6 *m* prove to be on your heart
6:7 *m* inculcate them in your son
6:8 *m* tie them as a sign upon your
6:8 *m* serve as a frontlet band
6:9 and you *m* write them upon the
6:14 *m* not walk after other gods
6:15 he *m* annihilate you from off
6:16 *m* not put Jehovah your God
7:16 Your eye *m* not feel sorry for
7:16 you *m* not serve their gods
7:18 you *m* not be afraid of them
7:21 You *m* not suffer a shock
7:24 you *m* destroy their names
7:25 You *m* not desire the silver
7:26 *m* not bring a detestable
8:6 you *m* keep the commandments
8:18 you *m* remember Jehovah your
12:4 *m* not do that way to Jehovah
12:12 you *m* rejoice before Jehovah
12:16 Only the blood you *m* not eat
12:18 you *m* rejoice before Jehovah
12:23 you *m* not eat the soul with
12:24 You *m* not eat it. You should
12:25 You *m* not eat it, in order
14:10 you *m* not eat. It is unclean
14:12 ones of which you *m* not eat
14:21 *m* not eat any body already
15:7 you *m* not harden your heart
15:23 its blood you *m* not eat
De 16:1 you *m* celebrate the passover
16:2 you *m* sacrifice the passover
16:8 You *m* do no work
16:19 You *m* not pervert judgment
16:19 You *m* not be partial or
17:12 you *m* clear out what is bad
19:12 and he *m* die
19:13 you *m* clear away the guilt
19:14 You *m* not move back the
23:21 *m* not be slow about paying
25:4 *m* not muzzle a bull while
Jos 23:6 you *m* be very courageous to
Jg 2:2 you *m* not conclude a covenant
1Sa 12:20 *m* serve Jehovah with all
14:34 *m* not sin against Jehovah
1Ki 8:61 heart *m* prove to be complete
2Ki 9:8 whole house of Ahab *m* perish
9:8 *m* cut off from Ahab anyone
17:35 You *m* not fear other gods
17:35 *m* not bow down to them
17:37 you *m* not fear other gods
17:38 you *m* not forget
17:38 you *m* not fear other gods
Isa 14:24 have figured, so it *m* occur
Mt 4:10 your God you *m* worship, and
4:10 you *m* render sacred service
19:18 Why, You *m* not murder, You
19:18 You *m* not commit adultery
19:18 You *m* not steal, You
19:18 *m* not bear false witness
19:19 You *m* love your neighbor as
20:26 *m* be your minister
20:27 first . . . *m* be your slave
22:37 You *m* love Jehovah your God
22:39 You *m* love your neighbor as
Mr 10:43 *m* be your minister
10:44 *m* be the slave of all
12:30 you *m* love Jehovah your God
12:31 You *m* love your neighbor as
13:7 these things *m* take place
Lu 4:4 Man *m* not live by bread alone
4:8 Jehovah your God you *m* worship
4:12 You *m* not put Jehovah your
4:43 I *m* declare the good news of
10:27 You *m* love Jehovah your God
22:7 passover . . . *m* be sacrificed
24:7 Son of man *m* be delivered
Joh 3:30 That one *m* go on increasing
3:30 but I *m* go on decreasing
10:16 those also I *m* bring, and
12:34 Son of man *m* be lifted up
Ac 3:22 *m* listen to him according
5:29 We *m* obey God as ruler rather
14:22 We *m* enter into the kingdom
20:35 *m* assist those who are weak
Ro 7:7 You *m* not covet
13:9 You *m* not commit adultery
13:9 You *m* not murder, You
13:9 You *m* not steal, You
13:9 You *m* not covet, and whatever
13:9 You *m* love your neighbor as
1Co 9:9 *m* not muzzle a bull when it
11:19 there *m* also be sects among
Ga 5:14 You *m* love your neighbor as
Heb 11:6 *m* believe that he is and
Jas 2:8 You *m* love your neighbor as
2:11 You *m* not commit adultery
2:11 said also: You *m* not murder
Re 4:1 the things that *m* take place

Mustache
Le 13:45 should cover over the *m* and
2Sa 19:24 had he attended to his *m*
Eze 24:17 not cover over the *m*, and
Mic 3:7 have to cover over the *m*

Mustaches
Eze 24:22 *M* you will not cover over

Mustard
Mt 13:31 kingdom . . . like a *m* grain
17:20 faith the size of a *m* grain
Mr 4:31 Like a *m* grain, which at the
Lu 13:19 It is like a *m* grain that a
17:6 faith the size of a *m* grain

Muster
1Ki 20:26 to *m* the Syrians and to go
Isa 46:8 you people may *m* up courage

Mustered
Ge 14:14 he *m* his trained men, three
Jg 20:15 sons of Benjamin got to be *m*
20:15 hundred chosen men were *m*
20:17 were *m* apart from Benjamin
1Ki 20:27 Israel, they were *m* and
2Ki 3:6 and *m* all Israel
1Th 2:2 we *m* up boldness by means of

Mustering
2Ki 25:19 the one *m* the people of the
Isa 13:4 Jehovah of armies is *m* the
Jer 52:25 *m* the people of the land

Musty
Isa 3:24 to be merely a *m* smell
5:24 just like a *m* smell, and

Mute
Isa 53:7 become *m*, he also would not
Eze 3:26 you will certainly become *m*
24:27 speak and be *m* no longer

Muth-labben
Ps 9:*super* To the director upon *M*

Mutilate
Php 3:2 for those who *m* the flesh

Mutilating
Pr 26:6 As one that is *m* his feet, as

Mutter
Job 27:4 tongue will *m* no deceit

Muttering
Ps 2:1 kept *m* an empty thing
38:12 deceptions they keep *m* all
Isa 59:3 *m* sheer unrighteousness
59:13 *m* of words of falsehood
Lu 15:2 the scribes kept *m*, saying
19:7 they all fell to *m*, saying

Mutual
1Co 7:5 except by *m* consent for an

Muzzle
De 25:4 You must not *m* a bull while
Ps 39:1 set a *m* as a guard to my
1Co 9:9 must not *m* a bull when it is
1Ti 5:18 must not *m* a bull when it
1Pe 2:15 *m* the ignorant talk of the

Myra
Ac 27:5 put into port at *M* in Lycia

Myriads
Nu 10:36 *m* of thousands of Israel
De 33:2 And with him were holy *m*
Heb 12:22 Jerusalem, and *m* of angels
Jude 14 Jehovah came with his holy *m*
Re 5:11, 11 many angels . . . *m* of *m*
9:16, 16 cavalry was two *m* of *m*

Myrrh
Ex 30:23 *m* in congealed drops five
Es 2:12 six months with oil of *m* and
Ps 45:8 garments are *m* and aloeswood
Pr 7:17 besprinkled my bed with *m*
Ca 1:13 As a bag of *m* my dear one is
3:6 being perfumed with *m* and
4:6 my way to the mountain of *m*
4:14 frankincense, *m* and aloes
5:1 I have plucked my *m* along
5:5 my own hands dripped with *m*
5:5 and my fingers with liquid *m*
5:13 dripping with liquid *m*
Mt 2:11 gold and frankincense and *m*
Mr 15:23 wine drugged with *m*, but
Joh 19:39 a roll of *m* and aloes

Myrtle
Ne 8:15 and *m* leaves and palm leaves
Isa 41:19 the acacia and the *m* and
55:13 the *m* tree will come up
Zec 1:8 *m* trees that were in the deep
1:10 still among the *m* trees
1:11 standing among the *m* trees

Mysia
Ac 16:7 when getting down to *M* they
16:8 passed *M* by and came down to

Mystery
2Th 2:7 the *m* of this lawlessness is
Re 17:5 written a name, a *m*: Babylon
17:7 I will tell you the *m* of

Naam
1Ch 4:15 sons of Caleb . . . Elah and *N*

Naamah
Ge 4:22 sister of Tubal-cain was *N*
Jos 15:41 Gederoth, Beth-dagon and *N*
1Ki 14:21 *N* the Ammonitess
14:31 was *N* the Ammonitess
2Ch 12:13 mother's name was *N* the

Naaman
Ge 46:21 sons of Benjamin were . . . *N*
Nu 26:40 of Bela came to be Ard and *N*
26:40 of *N* the family of the
2Ki 5:1 *N*, the chief of the army of
5:6 I do send to you *N* my servant
5:9 So *N* came with his horses and
5:11 *N* grew indignant and began
5:17 *N* said: If not, please, let
5:20 spared *N* this Syrian by not
5:21 Gehazi went chasing after *N*
5:21 *N* saw someone running after
5:23 *N* said: Go on, take two
5:27 leprosy of *N* will stick to
1Ch 8:4 and Abishua and *N* and Ahoah
8:7 And *N* and Ahijah; and Gera
Lu 4:27 but *N* the man of Syria

Naaman's
2Ki 5:2 she came to be before *N* wife

Naamathite
Job 2:11 the Shuhite and Zophar the *N*
11:1 Zophar the *N* proceeded to
20:1 Zophar the *N* proceeded to
42:9 Zophar the *N* went and did

Naamites
Nu 26:40 Naaman the family of the *N*

Naarah
Jos 16:7 from Janoah to Ataroth and *N*
1Ch 4:5 two wives, Helah and *N*
4:6 *N* bore to him Ahuzzam and
4:6 These were the sons of *N*

Naarai
1Ch 11:37 *N* the son of Ezbai

Naaran
1Ch 7:28 to the east, *N* and, to the

Nabal
1Sa 25:3 man's name was *N*, and his
25:4 *N* was shearing his sheep
25:5 come to *N* and ask him in my
25:9 spoke to *N* in accord with
25:10 *N* answered David's servants
25:19 husband *N* she told nothing
25:25 good-for-nothing man *N*
25:25 *N* is his name, and
25:26 to my lord become like *N*
25:34 remained to *N* until the
25:36 Abigail came in to *N*, and
25:37 wine had gone out of *N*
25:38 Jehovah struck *N*, so that he
25:39 hear that *N* had died, and
25:39 badness of *N* Jehovah has
30:5 Abigail the wife of *N* the
2Sa 2:2 Abigail the wife of *N* the
3:3 Abigail the wife of *N* the

Nabal's
1Sa 25:14 to Abigail, *N* wife, one of
25:36 *N* heart was feeling good
25:39 free me from *N* hand and has
27:3 and Abigail, *N* wife, the

Naboth
1Ki 21:1 belong to *N* the Jezreelite
21:2 So Ahab spoke to *N*, saying
21:3 But *N* said to Ahab: It is
21:4 word that *N* the Jezreelite
21:6 to speak to *N* the Jezreelite
21:7 vineyard of *N* the Jezreelite
21:8 in his city dwelling with *N*
21:9 have *N* sit at the head of the
21:12 *N* sit at the head of the
21:13 against him, that is, *N*
21:13 *N* has cursed God and the
21:14 *N* has been stoned so that
21:15 *N* had been stoned so that
21:15 vineyard of *N* the Jezreelite
21:15 for *N* is no longer alive
21:16 Ahab heard that *N* was dead
21:16 vineyard of *N* the Jezreelite
21:18 he is in the vineyard of *N*
21:19 licked up the blood of *N*
2Ki 9:21 land of *N* the Jezreelite
9:25 the field of *N* the Jezreelite
9:26 the blood of *N* and the blood

Nacon
2Sa 6:6 as the threshing floor of *N*

Nadab
Ex 6:23 she bore him *N* and Abihu
24:1 you and Aaron, *N* and Abihu
24:9 Moses and Aaron, *N* and Abihu
Ex 28:1 act as priest to me, Aaron, *N*
Le 10:1 Aaron's sons *N* and Abihu took
Nu 3:2 Aaron's sons: the firstborn *N*
3:4 *N* and Abihu died before Jehovah
26:60 born to Aaron *N* and Abihu
26:61 *N* and Abihu died for their
1Ki 14:20 *N* his son began to reign in
15:25 *N* the son of Jeroboam
15:27 *N* and all Israel were
15:31 the rest of the affairs of *N*
1Ch 2:28 sons of Shammai were *N* and
2:30 the sons of *N* were Seled
6:3 the sons of Aaron were *N* and
8:30 Zur and Kish and Baal and *N*
9:36 Kish and Baal and Ner and *N*
24:1 The sons of Aaron were *N* and
24:2 *N* and Abihu died before their

Naggai
Lu 3:25 son of Esli, son of *N*

Nahalal
Jos 19:15 Kattath and *N* and Shimron
21:35 *N* and its pasture ground

Nahaliel
Nu 21:19 And from Mattanah on to *N*
21:19 and from *N* on to Bamoth

Nahalol
Jg 1:30 the inhabitants of *N*, but

Naham
1Ch 4:19 the sister of *N*

Nahamani
Ne 7:7 *N*, Mordecai, Bilshan

Naharai
2Sa 23:37 *N* the Beerothite
1Ch 11:39 *N* the Berothite, the

Nahash
1Sa 11:1 *N* the Ammonite proceeded to
11:1 the men of Jabesh said to *N*
11:2 *N* the Ammonite said to them
12:12 *N* the king of the sons of
2Sa 10:2 Hanun the son of *N*, just
17:25 Abigail the daughter of *N*
17:27 Shobi the son of *N* from
1Ch 19:1 *N* the king of the sons of
19:2 toward Hanun the son of *N*

Nahath
Ge 36:13 the sons of Reuel: *N* and
36:17 sons of Reuel . . . Sheik *N*
1Ch 1:37 sons of Reuel were *N*
6:26 Zophai his son and *N* his son
2Ch 31:13 and *N* . . . commissioners at

Nahbi
Nu 13:14 *N* the son of Vophsi

Nahor
Ge 11:22 Serug . . . became father to *N*
11:23 after his fathering *N* Serug
11:24 *N* lived on for twenty-nine
11:25 *N* continued to live a hundred
11:26 Terah . . . father to Abram, *N*
11:27 Terah . . . father to Abram, *N*
11:29 Abram and *N* proceeded to
22:20 borne sons to *N* your brother
22:23 eight Milcah bore to *N* the
24:10 Mesopotamia to the city of *N*
24:15 son of Milcah the wife of *N*
24:24 Milcah, whom she bore to *N*
24:47 of Bethuel the son of *N*
29:5 know Laban the grandson of *N*
31:53 god of *N* judge between us
Jos 24:2 Terah . . . the father of *N*
1Ch 1:26 Serug, *N*, Terah
Lu 3:34 son of Terah, son of *N*

Nahor's
Ge 11:29 name of *N* wife was Milcah

Nahshon
Ex 6:23 Elisheba . . . the sister of *N*
Nu 1:7 *N* the son of Amminadab
2:3 for the sons of Judah is *N*
7:12 *N* the son of Amminadab of the
7:17 *N* the son of Amminadab
10:14 *N* the son of Amminadab was
Ru 4:20 Amminadab became father to *N*
4:20 and *N* became father to Salmon
1Ch 2:10 *N* the chieftain of the sons
2:11 *N*, in turn, became father
Mt 1:4 Amminadab became father to *N*
1:4 *N* became father to Salmon
Lu 3:32 son of Salmon, son of *N*

Nahum
Na 1:1 The book of the vision of *N* the
Lu 3:25 son of Amos, son of *N*, son of

Nailing
Col 2:14 by *n* it to the torture stake

Nails
De 21:12 and attend to her *n*
1Ch 22:3 iron in great quantity for *n*
2Ch 3:9 weight for the *n* was fifty
Ec 12:11 like *n* driven in are those
Isa 41:7 one fastened it with *n* that
Jer 10:4 With *n* and with hammers
Da 4:33 and his *n* like birds' claws
Joh 20:25 his hands the print of the *n*
20:25 into the print of the *n* and

Nain
Lu 7:11 he traveled to a city called *N*

Naioth
1Sa 19:18 they took up dwelling in *N*
19:19 David is in *N* in Ramah
19:22 There in *N* in Ramah
19:23 from there to *N* in Ramah
19:23 he came into *N* in Ramah
20:1 running away from *N* in Ramah

Naked
Ge 2:25 continued to be *n*, the man and
3:7 to realize that they were *n*
3:10 I was afraid because I was *n*
3:11 Who told you that you were *n*?
Ex 28:42 them to cover the *n* flesh
1Sa 19:24 lay fallen *n* all that day
2Ch 28:15 *n* ones they clothed from
Job 1:21 *N* I came out of my mother's
1:21 And *n* shall I return there
22:6 the garments of *n* people
24:7 *N*, they pass the night
24:10 *N*, they have to go about
26:6 Sheol is *n* in front of him
Ec 5:15 *n* will one go away again
Isa 20:2 walking about *n* and barefoot
20:3 Isaiah has walked about *n*
20:4 old men, *n* and barefoot, and
32:11 make yourselves *n*, and
58:7 someone *n*, you must cover
Eze 16:7 when you had been *n* and nude
16:22 happened to be *n* and nude
16:39 leave you behind *n* and nude
18:7 *n* one he would cover with a
18:16 *n* one he has covered with a
23:29 and leave you *n* and nude
Ho 2:3 strip her *n* and actually place
Am 2:16 *n* is how he will flee in that
Mic 1:8 I will walk barefoot and *n*
Mt 25:36 *n*, and you clothed me
25:38 or *n*, and clothe you
25:43 *n*, but you did not clothe me
25:44 or *n* or sick or in prison
Mr 14:51 garment over his *n* body
14:52 and got away *n*
Joh 21:7 top garment, for he was *n*
Ac 19:16 they fled *n* and wounded out
2Co 5:3 we shall not be found *n*
Heb 4:13 all things are *n* and openly
Jas 2:15 in a *n* state and lacking the
Re 3:17 and poor and blind and *n*
16:15 that he may not walk *n* and
17:16 make her devastated and *n*

Nakedness
Ge 9:22 saw his father's *n* and went
9:23 they covered their father's *n*
9:23 did not see their father's *n*
Le 18:6 relative of his to lay bare *n*
18:7 The *n* of your father and the
18:7 *n* of your mother you must not
18:7 You must not lay bare her *n*
18:8 *n* of your father's wife you
18:8 It is your father's *n*
18:9 *n* of your sister, the daughter
18:9 you must not lay bare their *n*
18:10 *n* of the daughter of your son
18:10 must not lay bare their *n*
18:10 because they are your *n*
18:11 *n* of the daughter of your
18:11 you must not lay bare her *n*
18:12 *n* of your father's sister you
18:13 *n* of your mother's sister
18:14 *n* of your father's brother
18:15 *n* of your daughter-in-law
18:15 must not lay her *n* bare
18:16 *n* of your brother's wife
18:16 It is your brother's *n*

Le 18:17 *n* of a woman and her
18:17 in order to lay her *n* bare
18:18 rival to uncover her *n*, that
18:19 impurity to lay her *n* bare
20:11 laid bare the *n* of his father
20:17 and he does see her *n*, and
20:17 sees his *n*, it is shame
20:17 *n* of his sister that he has
20:18 *n*, he has exposed her source
20:19 *n* of your mother's sister
20:20 bare the *n* of his uncle
20:21 *n* of his brother that he has
De 28:48 with hunger and thirst and *n*
Isa 20:4 stripped, the *n* of Egypt
47:3 You ought to uncover your *n*
La 1:8 cheap, for they have seen her *n*
4:21 drunk and show yourself in *n*
Eze 22:10 *n* of a father they have
23:10 ones that uncovered her *n*
23:18 and uncovering her *n*
Ho 2:9 my linen for covering her *n*
Na 3:5 cause nations to see your *n*
Hab 3:9 its *n* your bow comes to be
Ro 8:35 hunger or *n* or danger or
2Co 11:27 in cold and *n*
Re 3:18 shame of your *n* may not

Name

Ge 2:11 The first one's *n* is Pishon
2:13 And the *n* of the second river
2:14 And the *n* of the third river
2:19 that was its *n*
3:20 Adam called his wife's *n* Eve
4:17, 17 the city's *n* by the *n*
4:19 The *n* of the first was Adah
4:19 the *n* of the second was Zillah
4:21 *n* of his brother was Jubal
4:25 a son and called his *n* Seth
4:26 he proceeded to call his *n*
4:26 calling on the *n* of Jehovah
5:2 and called their *n* Man
5:3 and called his *n* Seth
5:29 proceeded to call his *n* Noah
10:25 The *n* of the one was Peleg
10:25 *n* of his brother was Joktan
11:4 let us make a celebrated *n*
11:9 why its *n* was called Babel
11:29 *n* of Abram's wife was Sarai
11:29 *n* of Nahor's wife was Milcah
12:2 and I will make your *n* great
12:8 to call on the *n* of Jehovah
13:4 call there on the *n* of Jehovah
16:1 and her *n* was Hagar
16:11 must call his *n* Ishmael
16:13 call the *n* of Jehovah, who
16:15 Abram called the *n* of his
17:5 *n* will not be called Abram
17:5 your *n* must become Abraham
17:15 must not call her *n* Sarai
17:15 because Sarah is her *n*
17:19 you must call his *n* Isaac
19:22 called the *n* of the city Zoar
19:37 a son and called his *n* Moab
19:38 called his *n* Ben-ammi
21:3 Abraham called the *n* of his
21:33 *n* of Jehovah the indefinitely
22:14 to call the *n* of that place
22:24 whose *n* was Reumah
24:29 brother and his *n* was Laban
25:1 wife, and her *n* was Keturah
25:25 so they called his *n* Esau
25:26 so he called his *n* Jacob
25:30 is why his *n* was called Edom
26:20 the *n* of the well Esek
26:21 Hence he called its *n* Sitnah
26:22 he called its *n* Rehoboth
26:25 called on the *n* of Jehovah
26:33 Hence he called its *n* Shibah
26:33 *n* of the city is Beer-sheba
27:36 why his *n* is called Jacob
28:19 the *n* of that place Bethel
28:19 Luz was the city's *n*
29:16 The *n* of the older was Leah
29:16 the *n* of the younger Rachel
29:32 then called his *n* Reuben
29:33 she called his *n* Simeon
29:34 *n* was therefore called Levi
29:35 therefore called his *n* Judah
30:6 why she called his *n* Dan
30:8 So she called his *n* Naphtali
30:11 So she called his *n* Gad
30:13 So she called his *n* Asher
30:18 So she called his *n* Issachar
30:20 So she called his *n* Zebulun
Ge 30:21 then called her *n* Dinah
30:24 So she called his *n* Joseph
31:48 why he called its *n* Galeed
32:2 the *n* of that place Mahanaim
32:27 What is your *n*? to which he
32:28 *n* will no longer be called
32:29 Tell me, please, your *n*
32:29 Why . . . inquire for my *n*?
32:30 the *n* of the place Peniel
33:17 the *n* of the place Succoth
35:8 he called its *n* Allon-bacuth
35:10 Your *n* is Jacob. No longer is
35:10 No longer is your *n* to be
35:10 Israel will your *n* become
35:10 he began to call his *n* Israel
35:15 *n* of the place where God had
35:18 she called his *n* Ben-oni
36:32 *n* of his city was Dinhabah
36:35 the *n* of his city was Avith
36:39 and the *n* of his city was Pau
36:39 *n* of his wife was Mehetabel
38:1 and his *n* was Hirah
38:2 and his *n* was Shua
38:3 a son and he called his *n* Er
38:4 a son and called his *n* Onan
38:5 and then called his *n* Shelah
38:6 and her *n* was Tamar
38:29 Hence his *n* was called Perez
38:30 *n* came to be called Zerah
41:45 Pharaoh called Joseph's *n*
41:51 Joseph called the *n* of the
41:52 *n* of the second . . . Ephraim
48:6 the *n* of their brothers they
48:16 let my *n* be called upon them
48:16 *n* of my fathers, Abraham and
50:11 *n* was called Abel-mizraim
Ex 1:15 *n* of one of whom was Shiphrah
1:15 the *n* of the other Puah
2:10 call his *n* Moses and to say
2:22 and he called his *n* Gershom
3:13 say to me, What is his *n*?
3:15 is my *n* to time indefinite
5:23 to speak in your *n*, he has
6:3 as respects my *n* Jehovah I did
9:16 order to have my *n* declared
15:3 Jehovah is his *n*
15:23 is why he called its *n* Marah
16:31 began to call its *n* manna
17:7 the *n* of the place Massah and
17:15 to call its *n* Jehovah-nissi
18:3 *n* of one of whom was Gershom
18:4 *n* of the other was Eliezer
20:7 not take up the *n* of Jehovah
20:7 takes up his *n* in a worthless
20:24 cause my *n* to be remembered
23:13 mention the *n* of other gods
23:21 because my *n* is within him
28:21 each one according to its *n*
31:2 do call by *n* Bezalel the son
33:12 said, I do know you by *n* and
33:17 and I know you by *n*
33:19 declare the *n* of Jehovah
34:5 and declare the *n* of Jehovah
34:14 Jehovah, whose *n* is Jealous
35:30 called by *n* Bezalel the son
39:14 its *n* for the twelve tribes
Le 18:21 profane the *n* of your God
19:12 not swear in my *n* to a lie
19:12 do profane the *n* of your God
20:3 and to profane my holy *n*
21:6 not profane the *n* of their God
22:2 profane my holy *n* in the
22:32 profane my holy *n*, and I
24:11 abuse the *N* and to call down
24:11 mother's *n* was Shelomith
24:16 abuser of Jehovah's *n* should
24:16 death for his abusing the *N*
Nu 6:27 place my *n* upon the sons of
11:3 *n* of that place got to be
11:26 *n* of the one was Eldad, and
11:26 *n* of the other was Medad
11:34 *n* of that place came to be
17:2 the *n* of each one upon his rod
17:3 Aaron's *n* you will write upon
21:3 the *n* of the place Hormah
25:14 the *n* of the fatally struck
25:15 *n* of the Midianite woman
26:46 *n* of Asher's daughter was
26:59 the *n* of Amram's wife was
27:4 *n* of our father be taken away
32:42 call it Nobah by his own *n*
De 3:14 by his own *n*, Havvoth-jair
5:11 *n* of Jehovah your God in a
5:11 his *n* in a worthless way
De 6:13 and by his *n* you should swear
9:14 wipe out their *n* from under
10:8 bless in his *n* until this day
10:20 by his *n* you should make
12:5 to place his *n* there
12:11 to have his *n* reside there
12:21 God will choose to put his *n*
14:23 to have his *n* reside there
14:24 will choose to place his *n*
16:2 choose to have his *n* reside
16:6 choose to have his *n* reside
16:11 choose to have his *n* reside
18:5 minister in the *n* of Jehovah
18:7 minister in the *n* of Jehovah
18:19 that he will speak in my *n*
18:20 presumes to speak in my *n*
18:20 speaks in the *n* of other gods
18:22 speaks in the *n* of Jehovah
21:5 to bless in the *n* of Jehovah
22:14 a bad *n* upon her and has
22:19 a bad *n* upon a virgin of
25:6 the *n* of his dead brother
25:6 *n* may not be wiped out of
25:7 preserve his brother's *n* in
25:10 *n* must be called in Israel
26:2 to have his *n* reside there
28:10 Jehovah's *n* has been called
28:58 fear this glorious . . . *n*
29:20 his *n* from under the heavens
32:3 shall declare the *n* of Jehovah
Jos 2:1 woman whose *n* was Rahab
5:9 the *n* of that place came to
7:9 cut our *n* off from the earth
7:9 will you do for your great *n*
7:26 the *n* of that place has been
9:9 in regard to the *n* of Jehovah
14:15 The *n* of Hebron before that
15:15 the *n* of Debir before that
19:47 *n* of Dan their forefather
21:9 cities that were called by *n*
22:34 of Gad began to *n* the altar
Jg 1:10 the *n* of Hebron before that
1:11 the *n* of Debir before that
1:17 the *n* of the city was called
1:23 the *n* of the city before that
1:26 and called its *n* Luz
1:26 Luz . . . its *n* down to this
2:5 they called the *n* of that
13:2 and his *n* was Manoah
13:6 neither did he tell me his *n*
13:17 What is your *n*, that when
13:18 should you ask about my *n*
13:24 and called his *n* Samson
15:19 he called its *n* En-hakkore
16:4 and her *n* was Delilah
17:1 whose *n* was Micah
18:29 called the *n* of the city Dan
18:29 Dan by the *n* of their father
18:29 Laish was the city's *n* at
Ru 1:2 And the man's *n* was Elimelech
1:2 and his wife's *n* Naomi
1:4 The *n* of the one was Orpah
1:4 and the *n* of the other Ruth
2:1 and his *n* was Boaz
2:19 The *n* of the man with whom I
4:5 *n* of the dead man to rise upon
4:10 the *n* of the dead man to rise
4:10 *n* of the dead man may not be
4:11 make a notable *n* in Bethlehem
4:14 *n* may be proclaimed in Israel
4:17 neighbor ladies gave it a *n*
4:17 they began to call his *n* Obed
1Sa 1:1 and his *n* was Elkanah, the
1:2 the *n* of the one being Hannah
1:2 *n* of the other being Peninnah
1:20 to call his *n* Samuel
7:12 began to call its *n* Ebenezer
8:2 the *n* of his firstborn son
8:2 and the *n* of his second Abijah
9:1 *n* was Kish, the son of Abiel
9:2 have a son whose *n* was Saul
12:22 for the sake of his great *n*
14:4 the *n* of the one was Bozez
14:4 the *n* of the other was Seneh
14:49 *n* of the one born first was
14:49 *n* of the younger one Michal
14:50 the *n* of Saul's wife was
14:50 *n* of the chief of his army
17:4 his *n* being Goliath, from
17:12 *n* was Jesse. And he had
17:23 his *n* being Goliath the
17:45 the *n* of Jehovah of armies
18:30 *n* came to be very precious
20:16 *n* of Jonathan be cut off

1Sa 20:42 in the *n* of Jehovah, saying
21:7 *n* was Doeg the Edomite, the
22:20 *n* was Abiathar, made his
24:21 annihilate my *n* out of the
25:3 man's *n* was Nabal, and his
25:3 his wife's *n* was Abigail
25:5 ask him in my *n* about his
25:9 words in the *n* of David and
25:25 for as his *n* is, so is he
25:25 Nabal is his *n*, and
2Sa 3:7 concubine whose *n* was Rizpah
4:2 *n* of the one being Baanah
4:2 *n* of the other being Rechab
4:4 And his *n* was Mephibosheth
5:20 *n* of that place Baal-perazim
6:2 where a *n* is called on, the
6:2 *n* of Jehovah of armies
6:18 the *n* of Jehovah of armies
7:9 make for you a great *n*, like
7:9 like the *n* of the great ones
7:13 build a house for my *n*, and
7:23 assign himself a *n* and to do
7:26 let your own *n* become great
8:13 David proceeded to make a *n*
9:2 servant whose *n* was Ziba
9:12 young son whose *n* was Mica
12:24 *n* came to be called Solomon
12:25 called his *n* Jedidiah, for
12:28 my *n* should not have to be
13:1 sister whose *n* was Tamar
13:3 whose *n* was Jehonadab
14:7 neither a *n* nor a remnant
14:27 daughter whose *n* was Tamar
16:5 and his *n* was Shimei, the
17:25 a man whose *n* was Ithra
18:18 keep my *n* in remembrance
18:18 the pillar by his own *n*
20:1 whose *n* was Sheba, the son
20:21 whose *n* is Sheba the son of
22:50 your *n* I shall make melody
1Ki 1:47 Solomon's *n* more splendid
1:47 more splendid than your *n*
3:2 built to the *n* of Jehovah
5:3 a house to the *n* of Jehovah
5:5 a house to the *n* of Jehovah
5:5 will build the house to my *n*
7:21 and called its *n* Jachin
7:21 and called its *n* Boaz
8:16 a house for my *n* to continue
8:17 a house to the *n* of Jehovah
8:18 to build a house to my *n*
8:19 will build the house to my *n*
8:20 the house to the *n* of Jehovah
8:29 My *n* will prove to be there
8:33 laud your *n* and pray and
8:35 laud your *n*, and from their
8:41 land by reason of your *n*
8:42 hear of your great *n* and of
8:43 get to know your *n* so as to
8:43 your *n* itself has been called
8:44 that I have built to your *n*
8:48 that I have built to your *n*
9:3 my *n* there to time indefinite
9:7 I have sanctified to my *n*
10:1 with the *n* of Jehovah
11:26 his mother's *n* was Zeruah
11:36 myself to put my *n* there
13:2 A son . . . whose *n* is Josiah
14:21 Israel to put his *n* there
14:21 mother's *n* was Naamah the
14:31 mother's *n* was Naamah the
15:2 mother's *n* was Maacah the
15:10 *n* was Maacah the
16:24 call the *n* of the city that
16:24 by the *n* of Shemer the
18:24 call upon the *n* of your god
18:24 call upon the *n* of Jehovah
18:25 call upon the *n* of your god
18:26 calling upon the *n* of Baal
18:31 Israel is what your *n* will
18:32 in the *n* of Jehovah and to
21:8 wrote letters in Ahab's *n*
22:16 truth in the *n* of Jehovah
22:42 his mother's *n* was Azubah
2Ki 2:24 evil . . . in the *n* of Jehovah
5:11 call upon the *n* of Jehovah
8:26 his mother's *n* was Athaliah
12:1 his mother's *n* was Zibiah
14:2 his mother's *n* was Jehoaddin
14:7 *n* came to be called Joktheel
14:27 the *n* of Israel from under
15:2 his mother's *n* was Jecoliah
15:33 his mother's *n* was Jerusha
17:34 whose *n* he made Israel
2Ki 18:2 his mother's *n* was Abi the
21:1 his mother's *n* was Hephzibah
21:4 Jerusalem I shall put my *n*
21:7 put my *n* to time indefinite
21:19 mother's *n* was Meshullemeth
22:1 his mother's *n* was Jedidah
23:27 My *n* will continue there
23:31 his mother's *n* was Hamutal
23:34 changed his *n* to Jehoiakim
23:36 his mother's *n* was Zebidah
24:8 his mother's *n* was Nehushta
24:17 he changed his *n* to Zedekiah
24:18 his mother's *n* was Hamutal
1Ch 1:19 *n* of the one was Peleg
1:19 *n* of his brother was Joktan
1:43 *n* of whose city was Dinhabah
1:46 *n* of his city was Avith
1:50 *n* of his city was Pau, and
1:50 *n* of his wife was Mehetabel
2:26 wife, whose *n* was Atarah
2:29 *n* of Abishur's wife was
2:34 servant whose *n* was Jarha
4:3 and the *n* of their sister was
4:9 that called his *n* Jabez
7:15 *n* of his sister was Maacah
7:15 And the *n* of the second was
7:16 son and called his *n* Peresh
7:16 *n* of his brother was Sheresh
7:23 But he called his *n* Beriah
8:29 and his wife's *n* was Maacah
9:35 And his wife's *n* was Maacah
11:24 he had a *n* among the three
12:31 designated by *n* to come to
13:6 where his *n* is called on
14:11 called the *n* of that place
16:2 bless . . . in the *n* of Jehovah
16:8 call upon his *n*, Make his
16:10 your boast in his holy *n*
16:29 the glory of his *n*
16:35 give thanks to your holy *n*
17:8 certainly make for you a *n*
17:8 like the *n* of the great ones
17:21 a *n* of great achievements
17:24 let your *n* prove faithful
21:19 spoken in the *n* of Jehovah
22:7 a house to the *n* of Jehovah
22:8 not build a house to my *n*
22:9 Solomon is what his *n* will
22:10 will build a house to my *n*
22:19 built to the *n* of Jehovah
23:13 pronounce blessing in his *n*
28:3 not build a house to my *n*
29:13 praising your beauteous *n*
29:16 a house for your holy *n*
2Ch 2:1 build a house to Jehovah's *n*
2:4 house to the *n* of Jehovah my
3:17 the *n* of the right-hand one
3:17 *n* of the left-hand one Boaz
6:5 for my *n* to prove to be there
6:6 choose Jerusalem for my *n* to
6:7 a house to the *n* of Jehovah
6:8 to build a house to my *n*, you
6:9 will build the house to my *n*
6:10 the house to the *n* of Jehovah
6:20 said you would put your *n*
6:24 laud your *n* and pray and
6:26 laud your *n* and from their
6:32 by reason of your great *n* and
6:33 the earth may know your *n*
6:33 know that your *n* has been
6:34 that I have built to your *n*
6:38 that I have built to your *n*
7:14 whom my *n* has been called
7:16 my *n* may prove to be there
7:20 I have sanctified for my *n*
12:13 Israel to put his *n* there
12:13 mother's *n* was Naamah the
13:2 mother's *n* was Micaiah the
14:11 in your *n* we have come
18:15 truth in the *n* of Jehovah
20:8 a sanctuary for your *n*
20:9 for your *n* is in this house
20:26 *n* of that place Low Plain
20:31 mother's *n* was Azubah the
22:2 mother's *n* was Athaliah the
24:1 mother's *n* was Zibiah from
25:1 mother's *n* was Jehoaddan of
26:3 mother's *n* was Jecoliah of
27:1 mother's *n* was Jerushah the
28:9 there whose *n* was Oded
29:1 his mother's *n* was Abijah
33:4 In Jerusalem my *n* will
33:7 put my *n* to time indefinite
33:18 *n* of Jehovah the God of
2Ch 36:4 changed his *n* to Jehoiakim
Ezr 2:61 came to be called by their *n*
5:1 in the *n* of the God of Israel
5:14 the *n* of the one whom he
6:12 God who has caused his *n* to
Ne 1:9 to have my *n* reside there
1:11 take delight in fearing your *n*
7:63 came to be called by their *n*
9:5 let them bless your glorious *n*
9:7 and constituted his *n* Abraham
9:10 to make a *n* for yourself as
Es 2:5 *n* was Mordecai the son of Jair
2:14 and she had been called by *n*
2:22 to the king in Mordecai's *n*
3:12 in the *n* of King Ahasuerus it
8:8 in the king's *n* and seal it
8:8 is written in the king's *n*
8:10 in the *n* of King Ahasuerus
9:26 Purim, by the *n* of the Pur
Job 1:1 *n* was Job; and that man
1:21 *n* of Jehovah continue to be
18:17 have no *n* out in the street
42:14 *n* of the first Jemimah and
42:14 *n* of the second Keziah
42:14 *n* of the third Keren-happuch
Ps 5:11 those loving your *n* will
7:17 melody to the *n* of Jehovah
8:1 how majestic your *n* is in all
8:9 how majestic your *n* is in all
9:2 I will make melody to your *n*
9:5 Their *n* you have wiped out to
9:10 those knowing your *n* will
18:49 your *n* I will make melody
20:1 *n* of the God of Jacob protect
20:5 in the *n* of our God we shall
20:7 the *n* of Jehovah our God we
22:22 your *n* to my brothers
29:2 to Jehovah the glory of his *n*
31:3 for the sake of your *n* you
33:21 in his holy *n* we have put
34:3 let us exalt his *n* together
41:5 die and his *n* actually perish
44:5 In your *n* we shall tread down
44:8 your *n* we shall laud. *Se'lah*
44:20 forgotten the *n* of our God
45:17 will make mention of your *n*
48:10 Like your *n*, O God, so your
52:9 And I shall hope in your *n*
54:1 O God, by your *n* save me
54:6 shall laud your *n*, O Jehovah
61:5 of those fearing your *n*
61:8 melody to your *n* forever
63:4 In your *n* I shall raise my
66:2 melody to the glory of his *n*
66:4 will make melody to your *n*
68:4 to God, make melody to his *n*
68:4 As Jah, which is his *n*
69:30 I will praise the *n* of God
69:36 those loving his *n* will be
72:17 his *n* prove to be to time
72:17 let his *n* have increase
72:19 blessed be his glorious *n*
74:7 tabernacle of your *n* to the
74:10 your *n* with disrespect
74:18 your *n* with disrespect
74:21 the poor one praise your *n*
75:1 And your *n* is near
76:1 In Israel his *n* is great
79:6 not called upon your own *n*
79:9 sake of the glory of your *n*
79:9 sins on account of your *n*
80:18 we may call upon your own *n*
83:4 *n* of Israel may be
83:16 people may search for your *n*
83:18 that you, whose *n* is Jehovah
86:9 will give glory to your *n*
86:11 my heart to fear your *n*
86:12 glorify your *n* to time
89:12 in your *n* they cry out
89:16 In your *n* they are joyful
89:24 in my *n* his horn is exalted
91:14 he has come to know my *n*
92:1 to make melody to your *n*
96:2 Sing to Jehovah, bless his *n*
96:8 glory belonging to his *n*
99:3 Let them laud your *n*
99:6 those calling upon his *n*
100:4 thanks to him, bless his *n*
102:15 will fear the *n* of Jehovah
102:21 *n* of Jehovah to be declared
103:1 Bless Jehovah . . . his holy *n*
105:1 to Jehovah, call upon his *n*
105:3 your boast in his holy *n*
106:8 for the sake of his *n*

Ps 106:47 give thanks to your holy *n*
109:13 let their *n* be wiped out
109:21 for the sake of your *n*
111:9 *n* is holy and fear-inspiring
113:1 Praise the *n* of Jehovah
113:2 Jehovah's *n* become blessed
113:3 Jehovah's *n* is to be praised
115:1 But to your *n* give glory
116:4 *n* of Jehovah I proceeded to
116:13 *n* of Jehovah I shall call
116:17 on the *n* of Jehovah I shall
118:10 *n* of Jehovah that I kept
118:11 in the *n* of Jehovah that
118:12 in the *n* of Jehovah that I
118:26 coming in the *n* of Jehovah
119:55 your *n*, O Jehovah
119:132 toward those loving your *n*
122:4 thanks to the *n* of Jehovah
124:8 help is in the *n* of Jehovah
129:8 you in the *n* of Jehovah
135:1 Praise the *n* of Jehovah
135:3 Make melody to his *n*, for
135:13 Jehovah, your *n* is to time
138:2 I shall laud your *n*
138:2 saying even above all your *n*
139:20 your *n* in a worthless way
140:13 will give thanks to your *n*
142:7 To laud your *n*
143:11 sake of your *n*, O Jehovah
145:1 bless your *n* to time
145:2 I will praise your *n* to time
145:21 all flesh bless his holy *n*
148:5 them praise the *n* of Jehovah
148:13 praise the *n* of Jehovah
148:13 *n* alone is unreachably high
149:3 praise his *n* with dancing
Pr 10:7 *n* of the wicked ones will rot
18:10 The *n* of Jehovah is a strong
21:24 braggart is the *n* of the one
22:1 A *n* is to be chosen rather
30:4 What is his *n* and what the
30:4 and what the *n* of his son
30:9 and assail the *n* of my God
Ec 6:4 with darkness his own *n* will
6:10 *n* has already been pronounced
7:1 A *n* is better than good oil
Ca 1:3 Like an oil . . . is your *n*
Isa 4:1 called by your *n* to take away
7:14 call his *n* Immanuel
8:3 his *n* Maher-shalal-hash-baz
9:6 *n* will be called Wonderful
12:4 Call upon his *n*. Make known
12:4 that his *n* is put on high
14:22 cut off from Babylon *n* and
18:7 *n* of Jehovah of armies
24:15 *n* of Jehovah, the God of
25:1 I exalt you, I laud your *n*
26:8 your *n* and for your memorial
26:13 we make mention of your *n*
29:23 they will sanctify my *n*
30:27 *n* of Jehovah is coming from
40:26 whom he calls even by *n*
41:25 he will call upon my *n*
42:8 I am Jehovah. That is my *n*
43:1 I have called you by your *n*
43:7 that is called by my *n*
44:5 by the *n* of Jacob, and
44:5 by the *n* of Israel one will
45:3 One calling you by your *n*
45:4 to call you by your *n*
45:4 to give you a *n* of honor
47:4 Jehovah of armies is his *n*
48:1 by the *n* of Israel and who
48:1 swearing by the *n* of Jehovah
48:2 Jehovah of armies . . . his *n*
48:9 for the sake of my *n* I shall
48:19 One's *n* would not be cut
49:1 he has made mention of my *n*
50:10 trust in the *n* of Jehovah
51:15 Jehovah of armies is his *n*
52:5 my *n* was being treated with
52:6 my people will know my *n*
54:5 Jehovah . . . being his *n*
56:5 a monument and a *n*
56:5 A *n* to time indefinite
56:6 and to love the *n* of Jehovah
57:15 whose *n* is holy, has said
59:19 to fear the *n* of Jehovah
60:9 to the *n* of Jehovah your God
62:2 be called by a new *n*, which
63:12 lasting *n* for his own self
63:14 beautiful *n* for your own
63:16 Our Repurchaser . . . your *n*
63:19 your *n* had not been called
Isa 64:2 order to make your *n* known
64:7 no one calling upon your *n*
65:1 was not calling upon my *n*
65:15 lay up your *n* for an oath
65:15 he will call by another *n*
66:5 by reason of my *n*, said
66:22 *n* of you people will keep
Jer 3:17 *n* of Jehovah at Jerusalem
7:10 this house upon which my *n*
7:11 this house upon which my *n*
7:12 I caused my *n* to reside at
7:14 the house upon which my *n*
7:30 house upon which my *n* has
10:6 *n* is great in mightiness
10:16 Jehovah of armies is his *n*
10:25 not called even upon your *n*
11:16 Jehovah has called your *n*
11:19 his very *n* may no more be
11:21 prophesy in the *n* of Jehovah
12:16 in swearing by my *n*, As
13:11 to me a people and a *n*
14:7 act for the sake of your *n*
14:9 your own *n* has been called
14:14 are prophesying in my *n*
14:15 who are prophesying in my *n*
14:21 for the sake of your *n*
15:16 your *n* has been called
16:21 know that my *n* is Jehovah
20:3 Jehovah has called your *n*
20:9 shall speak no more in his *n*
23:6 this is his *n* with which he
23:25 falsehood in my own *n*
23:27 forget my *n* by means of
23:27 fathers forgot my *n* by
25:29 city upon which my *n* is
26:9 in the *n* of Jehovah, saying
26:16 in the *n* of Jehovah our God
26:20 in the *n* of Jehovah
27:15 prophesying in my *n* falsely
29:9 prophesying to you in my *n*
29:21 falsehood in my own *n*
29:23 falsely in my own *n*
29:25 sent in your *n* letters to
31:35 *n* is Jehovah of armies
32:18 of armies being his *n*
32:20 make a *n* for your own self
32:34 my own *n* has been called
33:2 Jehovah being his *n*
33:9 to me a *n* of exultation, a
34:15 which my *n* has been called
34:16 turn back and profane my *n*
37:13 whose *n* was Irijah the son
44:16 to us in the *n* of Jehovah
44:26 by my great *n*, Jehovah
44:26 *n* will no more prove to be
46:18 *n* is Jehovah of armies
48:15 King, whose *n* is Jehovah of
48:17 all those knowing their *n*
50:34 Jehovah of armies . . . his *n*
51:19 Jehovah of armies is his *n*
51:57 King, whose *n* is Jehovah of
52:1 *n* of his mother was Hamutal
La 3:55 called out your *n*, O Jehovah
Eze 16:14 for you a *n* began to go
16:15 on account of your *n* and to
20:9 for the sake of my own *n*
20:14 for the sake of my own *n*
20:22 for the sake of my own *n*
20:29 *n* should be called a High
20:39 my holy *n* you will no more
20:44 for the sake of my *n*
22:5 you unclean in *n*, abounding
24:2 the *n* of the day, this
34:29 a planting for a *n*, and
36:20 to profane my holy *n* in
36:21 compassion on my holy *n*
36:22 but for my holy *n*, which
36:23 sanctify my great *n*, which
39:7 holy *n* I shall make known
39:7 let my holy *n* be profaned
39:16 *n* of the city will also be
39:25 devotion for my holy *n*
43:7 Israel, defile my holy *n*
43:8 defiled my holy *n* by their
48:35 *n* of the city from that day
Da 1:7 to Daniel the *n* of Belteshazzar
2:20 *n* of God become blessed from
2:26 Daniel, whose *n* was
4:8 whose *n* is Belteshazzar
4:8 according to the *n* of my god
4:19 whose *n* is Belteshazzar, was
9:6 spoken in your *n* to our kings
9:15 make a *n* for yourself as at
9:18 has been called by your *n*
Da 9:19 God, for your own *n* has been
10:1 Daniel, whose *n* was called
Ho 1:4 Call his *n* Jezreel, for yet a
1:6 Call her *n* Lo-ruhamah, for I
1:9 Call his *n* Lo-ammi, because
2:17 remember them by their *n*
Joe 2:26 to praise the *n* of Jehovah
2:32 calls on the *n* of Jehovah
Am 2:7 purpose of profaning my holy *n*
4:13 the God of armies is his *n*
5:8 —Jehovah is his *n*
5:27 whose *n* is Jehovah the God of
6:10 mention of the *n* of Jehovah
9:6 of the earth—Jehovah is his *n*
9:12 the nations upon whom my *n*
Mic 4:5 in the *n* of its god; but we
4:5 walk in the *n* of Jehovah our
5:4 the *n* of Jehovah his God
6:9 wisdom will fear your *n*
Na 1:14 Nothing of your *n* will be
Zep 1:4 *n* of the foreign-god priests
3:9 to call upon the *n* of Jehovah
3:12 refuge in the *n* of Jehovah
3:19 as a *n* in all the land of
3:20 people to be a *n* and a praise
Zec 5:4 sworn oath in my *n* falsely
6:12 the man whose *n* is Sprout
10:12 in his *n* they will walk
13:3 spoken in the *n* of Jehovah
13:9 will call upon my *n*, and I
14:9 to be one, and his *n* one
Mal 1:6 priests . . . despising my *n*
1:6 have we despised your *n*
1:11 my *n* will be great among
1:11 presentation . . . to my *n*
1:11 my *n* will be great among
1:14 my *n* will be fear-inspiring
2:2 give glory to my *n*, Jehovah
2:5 because of my *n* he himself
3:16 those thinking upon his *n*
4:2 you who are in fear of my *n*
Mt 1:21 you must call his *n* Jesus
1:23 will call his *n* Immanuel
1:25 and he called his *n* Jesus
6:9 let your *n* be sanctified
7:22 did we not prophesy in your *n*
7:22 and expel demons in your *n*
7:22 powerful works in your *n*
10:22 hatred . . . account of my *n*
12:21 in his *n* nations will hope
18:5 on the basis of my *n* receives
18:20 gathered together in my *n*
19:29 for the sake of my *n* will
21:9 he that comes in Jehovah's *n*
23:39 he that comes in Jehovah's *n*
24:5 come on the basis of my *n*
24:9 hatred . . . on account of my *n*
28:19 in the *n* of the Father and
Mr 5:9 to ask him: What is your *n?*
5:9 My *n* is Legion, because there
5:22 of the synagogue, Jairus by *n*
6:14 the *n* of Jesus became public
9:37 children on the basis of my *n*
9:38 demons by the use of your *n*
9:39 work on the basis of my *n*
11:9 he that comes in Jehovah's *n*
13:6 come on the basis of my *n*
13:13 hatred . . . account of my *n*
Lu 1:5 and her *n* was Elizabeth
1:13 you are to call his *n* John
1:27 the *n* of the virgin was Mary
1:31 you are to call his *n* Jesus
1:49 and holy is his *n*
1:59 call it by the *n* of its father
1:61 that is called by this *n*
1:63 and wrote: John is its *n*
2:21 his *n* was also called Jesus
2:21 the *n* called by the angel
6:22 cast out your *n* as wicked
8:30 What is your *n?* . . . Legion
9:48 child on the basis of my *n*
9:49 demons by the use of your *n*
10:17 by the use of your *n*
11:2 let your *n* be sanctified
13:35 he that comes in Jehovah's *n*
19:2 man called by the *n* Zacchaeus
19:38 as the King in Jehovah's *n*
21:8 come on the basis of my *n*
21:12 for the sake of my *n*
21:17 all people because of my *n*
24:47 basis of his *n* repentance
Joh 1:6 his *n* was John
1:12 exercising faith in his *n*
2:23 put their faith in his *n*

Joh 3:1 Nicodemus was his *n*, a ruler
3:18 in the *n* of the only-begotten
5:43 come in the *n* of my Father
5:43 arrived in his own *n*, you
10:3 calls his own sheep by *n* and
10:25 doing in the *n* of my Father
12:13 that comes in Jehovah's *n*
12:28 Father, glorify your *n*
14:13 is that you ask in my *n*
14:14 ask anything in my *n*, I
14:26 Father will send in my *n*
15:16 you ask the Father in my *n*
15:21 on account of my *n*
16:23 give it to you in my *n*
16:24 a single thing in my *n*
16:26 ask in my *n*, and I do not
17:6 *n* manifest to the men you
17:11 on account of your own *n*
17:12 on account of your own *n*
17:26 made your *n* known to them
18:10 *n* of the slave was Malchus
20:31 life by means of his *n*
Ac 2:21 who calls on the *n* of Jehovah
2:38 baptized in the *n* of Jesus
3:6 *n* of Jesus Christ the Nazarene
3:16 his *n*, by our faith in his
3:16 by our faith in his *n*, has
4:7 in whose *n* did you do this?
4:10 *n* of Jesus Christ the Nazarene
4:12 *n* under heaven that has been
4:17 upon the basis of this *n* to
4:18 the basis of the *n* of Jesus
4:30 *n* of your holy servant Jesus
5:1 man, Ananias by *n*, together
5:28 upon the basis of this *n*, and
5:40 upon the basis of Jesus' *n*
5:41 dishonored in behalf of his *n*
8:12 and of the *n* of Jesus Christ
8:16 in the *n* of the Lord Jesus
9:14 those calling upon your *n*
9:15 bear my *n* to the nations as
9:16 he must suffer for my *n*
9:21 who call upon this *n*, and
9:27 boldly in the *n* of Jesus
9:28 boldly in the *n* of the Lord
10:43 forgiveness . . . through his *n*
10:48 baptized in the *n* of Jesus
13:6 a Jew whose *n* was Bar-Jesus
13:8 the way his *n* is translated
15:14 of them a people for his *n*
15:17 who are called by my *n*, says
15:26 *n* of our Lord Jesus Christ
16:1 by the *n* of Timothy, the son
16:18 order you in the *n* of Jesus
19:5 baptized in the *n* of the Lord
19:13, 13 *n* the *n* of the Lord Jesus
19:17 *n* of the Lord Jesus went on
21:13 for the *n* of the Lord Jesus
22:16 by your calling upon his *n*
26:9 against the *n* of Jesus the
Ro 1:5 the nations respecting his *n*
2:17 Jew in *n* and are resting upon
2:24 *n* of God is being blasphemed
9:17 *n* may be declared in all the
10:13 calls on the *n* of Jehovah
15:9 to your *n* I will make melody
1Co 1:2 calling upon the *n* of our
1:10 *n* of our Lord Jesus Christ
1:13 you baptized in the *n* of Paul
1:15 you were baptized in my *n*
5:4 in the *n* of our Lord Jesus
6:11 in the *n* of our Lord Jesus
Eph 1:21 and every *n* named, not only
3:15 and on earth owes its *n*
5:20 in the *n* of our Lord Jesus
Php 2:9 *n* that is above every other
2:9 that is above every other *n*
2:10 in the *n* of Jesus every knee
Col 3:17 in the *n* of the Lord Jesus
2Th 1:12 *n* of our Lord Jesus may be
3:6 in the *n* of the Lord Jesus
1Ti 6:1 that the *n* of God and the
2Ti 2:19 naming the *n* of Jehovah
Heb 1:4 *n* more excellent than theirs
2:12 I will declare your *n* to my
6:10 love you showed for his *n*
13:15 public declaration to his *n*
Jas 2:7 blaspheme the fine *n* by
5:10 spoke in the *n* of Jehovah
5:14 with oil in the *n* of Jehovah
1Pe 4:14 for the *n* of Christ, you
4:16 glorifying God in this *n*
1Jo 2:12 for the sake of his *n*
3:23 faith in the *n* of his Son
1Jo 5:13 faith in the *n* of the Son of
3Jo 7 it was in behalf of his *n* that
14 greetings to the friends by *n*
Re 2:13 keep on holding fast my *n*
2:17 pebble a new *n* written
3:1 have the *n* that you are alive
3:5 blot out his *n* from the book
3:5 acknowledgment of his *n* before
3:8 did not prove false to my *n*
3:12 upon him the *n* of my God
3:12 *n* of the city of my God
3:12 and that new *n* of mine
6:8 seated upon it had the *n* Death
8:11 the *n* of the star is called
9:11 In Hebrew his *n* is Abaddon
9:11 in Greek he has the *n* Apollyon
11:18 to those fearing your *n*, the
13:6 to blaspheme his *n* and his
13:8 *n* of not one of them stands
13:17 *n* of the wild beast or the
13:17 or the number of its *n*
14:1 thousand having his *n* and
14:1 *n* of his Father written on
14:11 receives the mark of its *n*
15:2 and from the number of its *n*
15:4 glorify your *n*, because you
16:9 they blasphemed the *n* of God
17:5 forehead was written a *n*, a
19:12 He has a *n* written that no
19:13 *n* he is called is The Word
19:16 *n* written, King of kings and
22:4 *n* will be on their foreheads

Named
Jg 8:31 So he *n* him Abimelech
Isa 14:20 evildoers will not be *n*
Da 5:12 king himself *n* Belteshazzar
Mt 2:23 dwelt in a city *n* Nazareth
9:9 a man *n* Matthew seated at the
27:32 a native of Cyrene *n* Simon
27:57 man of Arimathea, *n* Joseph
Mr 3:14 whom he also *n* apostles
14:32 came to a spot *n* Gethsemane
Lu 1:5 a certain priest *n* Zechariah
1:26 a city of Galilee *n* Nazareth
1:27 a man *n* Joseph of David's
2:25 a man in Jerusalem *n* Simeon
5:27 a tax collector *n* Levi
6:13 whom he also *n* apostles
6:14 Simon, whom he also *n* Peter
8:41 a man *n* Jairus came, and
10:38 woman *n* Martha received him
16:20 beggar *n* Lazarus used to be
23:50 a man *n* Joseph, who was a
24:13 Jerusalem and *n* Emmaus
24:18 the one *n* Cleopas said to
Ac 5:34 Pharisee *n* Gamaliel, a Law
8:9 man *n* Simon, who, prior to
9:10 disciple *n* Ananias, and the
9:11 look for a man *n* Saul, from
9:12 man *n* Ananias come in and
9:33 man *n* Aeneas, who had been
9:36 disciple *n* Tabitha, which
10:1 man *n* Cornelius, an army
11:28 One of them *n* Agabus rose
12:13 servant girl *n* Rhoda came
16:14 woman *n* Lydia, a seller of
17:34 and a woman *n* Damaris, and
18:2 Jew *n* Aquila, a native of
18:7 of a man *n* Titius Justus, a
18:24 Jew *n* Apollos, a native of
19:24 *n* Demetrius, a silversmith
20:9 young man *n* Eutychus fell
21:10 prophet *n* Agabus came down
27:1 officer *n* Julius of the band
28:7 man of the island, *n* Publius
Ro 15:20 Christ had already been *n*, in
Eph 1:21 and every name *n*, not only

Nameless
Job 30:8 also sons of the *n* one

Namely
Ge 6:2 wives for themselves, *n*, all
7:22 *n*, all that were on the dry
Ex 1:11 *n*, Pithom and Raamses
35:5 *n*, gold and silver and copper
35:11 *n*, the tabernacle with its
Le 3:3 *n*, the fat that covers the
5:6 *n*, a female from the flock, a
Nu 4:16 all that is in it, *n*, the holy
31:8 kings of Midian . . . *n*, Evi
De 4:43 *n*, Bezer in the wilderness on
Jos 2:10 *n*, Sihon and Og, whom you
9:10 *n*, Sihon the king of Heshbon
Jos 15:13 *n*, Kiriath-arba (said Arba
15:14 sons of Anak, *n*, Sheshai
18:2 *n*, seven tribes
19:50 *n*, Timnath-serah, in the
21:13 *n*, Hebron, and its pasture
21:21 city of refuge . . . *n*, Shechem
21:27 city of refuge . . . *n*, Golan
21:32 city of refuge . . . *n*, Kedesh
21:38 city of refuge . . . *n*, Ramoth
22:25 the sons of Gad, *n*, the
Jg 7:25 princes of Midian, *n*, Oreb
1Sa 4:4 *n*, Hophni and Phinehas
5:6 *n*, Ashdod and its territories
1Ki 2:32 *n*, Abner the son of Ner the
11:14 *n*, Hadad the Edomite of the
11:23 *n*, Rezon the son of Eliada
1Ch 28:18 *n*, the cherubs of gold for
2Ch 5:12 *n*, to Asaph, to Heman, to
17:7 *n*, Ben-hail and Obadiah and
23:1 *n*, Azariah the son of
25:10 *n*, the troops that had come
Ezr 8:18 *n*, Sherebiah and his sons
8:24 *n*, Sherebiah, Hashabiah, and
9:1 *n*, the Canaanites, the
Isa 7:17 *n*, the king of Assyria
19:24 *n*, a blessing in the midst
22:20 servant, *n*, Eliakim the
Jer 25:18 *n*, Jerusalem and the cities
34:19 *n*, the princes of Judah and
39:3 *n*, Nergal-sharezer
Da 9:2 Jerusalem, *n*, seventy years
Zep 3:10 *n*, the daughter of my
Mt 23:23 *n*, justice and mercy and
26:75 the saying Jesus spoke, *n*
Lu 22:37 *n*, And he was reckoned with
Ac 10:38 *n*, Jesus who was from
15:22 *n*, Judas who was called
Ro 4:11 a sign, *n*, circumcision, as
8:23 firstfruits, *n*, the spirit
9:24 *n*, us, whom he called not
13:9 *n*, You must love your
15:16 offering, *n*, these nations
2Co 5:19 *n*, that God was by means of
Ga 3:8 *n*: By means of you all the
5:14 saying, *n*: You must love
Eph 1:10 *n*, to gather all things
3:6 *n*, that people of the nations
Php 2:6 *n*, that he should be equal to
Col 2:2 secret of God, *n*, Christ
1Th 1:10 from the dead, *n*, Jesus
1Ti 2:10 *n*, through good works
Heb 6:1 *n*, repentance from dead
12:11 fruit, *n*, righteousness
Jas 4:1 from this source, *n*, from
1Pe 3:21 now saving you, *n*, baptism
1Jo 2:3 *n*, if we continue observing
3:8 *n*, to break up the works of

Name's
Ps 23:3 righteousness for his *n* sake
25:11 For your *n* sake, O Jehovah
Re 2:3 borne up for my *n* sake and

Names
Ge 2:20 man was calling the *n* of all
25:13 *n* of the sons of Ishmael
25:13 sons of Ishmael, by their *n*
25:16 *n* by their courtyards and by
26:18, 18 calling their *n* by the *n*
36:10 *n* of the sons of Esau
36:40 the *n* of the sheiks of Esau
36:40 sheiks of Esau . . . by their *n*
46:8 the *n* of Israel's sons
Ex 1:1 the *n* of Israel's sons who
6:16 are the *n* of the sons of Levi
28:9 engrave upon them the *n* of
28:10 six of their *n* upon the one
28:10 *n* of the six remaining ones
28:11 stones with the *n* of the
28:12 and Aaron must carry their *n*
28:21 the *n* of the sons of Israel
28:21 twelve according to their *n*
28:29 *n* of the sons of Israel on
39:6 the *n* of the sons of Israel
39:14 the *n* of the sons of Israel
39:14 twelve according to their *n*
Nu 1:2 number of *n*, all the males
1:5 *n* of the men who will stand
1:17 who had been designated by *n*
1:18 by the number of the *n*, from
1:20 by the number of *n*, head by
1:22 by the number of *n*, head by
1:24 number of *n* from twenty years
1:26 *n* from twenty years old
1:28 *n* from twenty years old

Ps 33:12 the *n* whose God is Jehovah
43:1 case against a *n* not loyal
83:4 efface them from being a *n*
105:13, 13 walking . . . from *n* to *n*
106:5 with the rejoicing of your *n*
147:20 that way to any other *n*
Pr 14:34 Righteousness . . . exalts a *n*
Isa 1:4 Woe to the sinful *n*, the
2:4 *N* will not lift up sword
2:4 not lift up sword against *n*
5:26 to a great *n* far away, and
9:3 You have made the *n* populous
10:6 Against an apostate *n* I shall
14:32 to the messengers of the *n*
18:2 *n* drawn out and scoured
18:2 *n* of tensile strength and
18:7 *n* of tensile strength and
26:2 righteous *n* that is keeping
26:15 You have added to the *n*
26:15 you have added to the *n*
49:7 that is detested by the *n*
55:5 A *n* that you do not know
55:5 a *n* who have not known you
58:2 like a *n* that carried on
60:12 any *n* and any kingdom that
60:22 the small one a mighty *n*
65:1 to a *n* that was not calling
66:8 will a *n* be born at one time?
Jer 2:11 Has a *n* exchanged gods
5:9 upon a *n* that is like this
5:15 upon you men a *n* from far
5:15 It is an enduring *n*. It is a
5:15 It is a *n* of long ago, a
5:15 *n* whose language you do not
5:29 a *n* that is like this should
6:22 *n* that will be awakened
7:28 This is the *n* whose people
9:9 upon a *n* that is like this
12:17 I will also uproot that *n*
18:7 I may speak against a *n* and
18:8 that *n* actually turns back
18:9 I may speak concerning a *n*
25:12 and against that *n*, is the
25:32, 32 going forth from *n* to *n*
27:8 the *n* and the kingdom that
27:8 my attention upon that *n*
27:11 the *n* that will bring its
27:13 *n* that does not serve the
31:36 be a *n* before me always
33:24 no more continue being a *n*
48:2 cut her off from being a *n*
49:31 the *n* that is at ease
49:36 *n* to which the dispersed
50:3 *n* has come up from the north
50:41 great *n* and grand kings
La 4:17 *n* that can bring no salvation
Eze 37:22 make them one *n* in the land
Da 8:22 kingdoms from his *n* that
11:23 by means of a little *n*
12:1 came to be a *n* until that
Joe 1:6 a *n* that has come up into my
3:8 to a *n* far away; for Jehovah
Am 6:14 a *n*, and they must oppress
Mic 4:3, 3 lift up sword, *n* against *n*
4:7 removed far off a mighty *n*
Hab 1:6 the *n* bitter and impetuous
Zep 2:1 O *n* not paling in shame
2:5 the *n* of Cherethites
2:9 own *n* will take possession of
2:14 all the wild animals of a *n*
Hag 2:14 is how this *n* is before me
Mal 3:9 the *n* in its entirety
Mt 21:43 to a *n* producing its fruits
24:7, 7 *n* will rise against *n* and
Mr 13:8, 8 For *n* will rise against *n*
Lu 7:5 he loves our *n* and he himself
17:18 but this man of another *n*
21:10, 10 *N* will rise against *n*
23:2 found subverting our *n* and
Joh 11:48 both our place and our *n*
11:50 whole *n* to be destroyed
11:51 destined to die for the *n*
11:52 not for the *n* only, but in
18:35 Your own *n* and the chief
Ac 2:5 reverent men, from every *n*
7:7 *n* for which they will slave
8:9 and amazing the *n* of Samaria
10:22 by the whole *n* of the Jews
10:35 every *n* the man that fears
17:26 of one man every *n* of men
24:2 taking place in this *n*
24:10 this *n* has had you as judge
24:17 bring gifts of mercy to my *n*
26:4 among my *n* and in Jerusalem
Ac 28:19 of which to accuse my *n*
Ro 10:19 that which is not a *n*
10:19 anger through a stupid *n*
1Pe 2:9 a royal priesthood, a holy *n*
Re 5:9 and tongue and people and *n*
13:7 and people and tongue and *n*
14:6 every *n* and tribe and tongue

National

Ge 25:23 *n* groups will be separated
25:23 one *n* group will be stronger
25:23 stronger than the other *n*
27:29 let *n* groups bow low to you
Ps 2:1 the *n* groups themselves kept
7:7 assembly of *n* groups surround
9:8 judicially try *n* groups in
44:2 You went breaking *n* groups
44:14 among the *n* groups
47:3 And *n* groups under our feet
57:9 to you among the *n* groups
65:7 the turmoil of the *n* groups
67:4 Let *n* groups rejoice and cry
67:4 And as for *n* groups, on the
105:44 the hard work of *n* groups
108:3 to you among the *n* groups
148:11 and all you *n* groups
149:7 Rebukes upon the *n* groups
Pr 14:34 disgraceful to *n* groups
24:24 *n* groups will denounce him
Isa 17:12 noise of *n* groups, who
17:13 *n* groups themselves will
34:1 *n* groups, pay attention
41:1 *n* groups themselves regain
43:4 *n* groups in place of your
43:9 *n* groups be gathered together
49:1 pay attention, you *n* groups
51:4 and you *n* group of mine
55:4 As a witness to the *n* groups
55:4 commander to the *n* groups
60:2 thick gloom the *n* groups
Jer 51:58 *n* groups simply for the
Da 3:4 *n* groups and languages
3:7 *n* groups and languages were
3:29 *n* group or language that says
4:1 *n* groups and languages that
5:19 *n* groups and languages proved
6:25 *n* groups and the tongues that
7:14 *n* groups and languages should
Hab 2:13 that *n* groups will tire

Nationally

Mr 7:26 Grecian, a Syrophoenician *n*

Nations

Ge 10:5 *n* was spread about in their
10:5 their families, by their *n*
10:20 in their lands, by their *n*
10:31 according to their *n*
10:32 family descents, by their *n*
10:32 *n* were spread about in the
17:4 a father of a crowd of *n*
17:5 father of a crowd of *n* I will
17:6 make you become *n*, and kings
17:16 she shall become *n*; kings of
18:18 all the *n* of the earth must
22:18 means of your seed all *n* of
25:23 Two *n* are in your belly, and
26:4 by means of your seed all *n*
35:11 *N* and a congregation of
35:11 a congregation of *n* will
48:19 the full equivalent of *n*
Ex 34:10 earth or among all the *n*
34:24 drive the *n* away from before
Le 18:24 *n* whom I am sending out from
18:28 vomit the *n* out who were
20:23 *n* whom I am sending out from
25:44 become yours from the *n* that
26:33 scatter among the *n*, and I
26:38 perish among the *n*, and the
26:45 under the eyes of the *n*
Nu 14:15 *n* who have heard of your
23:9 And among the *n* they do not
24:8 He will consume the *n*, his
24:20 was the first one of the *n*
De 4:27 few in number among the *n* to
4:38 drive away *n* greater and
7:1 clear away populous *n* from
7:1 seven *n* more populous and
7:17 These *n* are too populous for
7:22 push these *n* away from before
8:20 *n* that Jehovah is destroying
9:1 *n* greater and mightier than
9:4 for the wickedness of these *n*
9:5 for the wickedness of these *n*
11:23 drive away all these *n* on
De 11:23 dispossess *n* greater and
12:2 *n* whom you are dispossessing
12:29 the *n* to whom you are going
12:30 *n* used to serve their gods
15:6 lend on pledge to many *n*
15:6 must dominate over many *n*
17:14 like all the *n* who are round
18:9 detestable things of those *n*
18:14 *n* whom you are dispossessing
19:1 God cuts off the *n* whose land
20:15 not of the cities of these *n*
26:19 high above all the other *n*
28:1 above all other *n* of the earth
28:12 certainly lend to many *n*
28:65 among those *n* you will have
29:16 through the midst of the *n*
29:18 serve the gods of those *n*
29:24 *n* will be bound to say, Why
30:1 all the *n* where Jehovah
31:3 will annihilate these *n* from
32:8 gave the *n* an inheritance
32:43 glad, you *n*, with his people
Jos 23:3 God did to all these *n* on
23:4 these *n* that remain as an
23:4 and all the *n* that I cut off
23:7 going in among these *n*
23:9 mighty *n* from before you
23:12 to what is left of these *n*
23:13 to dispossess these *n* on
Jg 2:21 a single one of the *n* that
2:23 Jehovah let these *n* stay by
3:1 the *n* that Jehovah let stay so
4:2 in Harosheth of the *n*
4:13 out of Harosheth of the *n* to
4:16 as far as Harosheth of the *n*
1Sa 8:5 to judge us like all the *n*
8:20 become . . . like all the *n*
2Sa 7:23 from Egypt, the *n* and their
8:11 the *n* that he had subdued
22:44 to be the head of *n*
22:50 O Jehovah, among the *n*
1Ki 4:31 fame came to be in all the *n*
11:2 the *n* of whom Jehovah had
14:24 detestable things of the *n*
2Ki 16:3 detestable things of the *n*
17:8 in the statutes of the *n*
17:11 *n* whom Jehovah had taken
17:15 even in imitation of the *n*
17:26 The *n* that you have taken
17:33 religion of the *n* from
17:41 *n* came to be fearers of
18:33 Have the gods of the *n*
19:12 Have the gods of the *n* that
19:17 devastated the *n* and their
21:2 detestable things of the *n*
21:9 the *n* whom Jehovah had
1Ch 14:17 dread of him upon all the *n*
16:24 Relate among the *n* his
16:31 let them say among the *n*
16:35 and deliver us from the *n*
17:21 driving out *n* from before
18:11 carried off from all the *n*
2Ch 20:6 all the kingdoms of the *n*
28:3 detestable things of the *n*
32:13 gods of the *n* of the lands
32:14 gods of these *n* that my
32:17 Like the gods of the *n* of
32:23 eyes of all the *n* after that
33:2 *n* that Jehovah had driven out
33:9 do worse than the *n* that
36:14 detestable things of the *n*
Ezr 4:10 the rest of the *n* whom the
6:21 from the uncleanness of the *n*
Ne 5:8 who were sold to the *n*
5:9 reproach of the *n*, our enemies
5:17 *n* that were around us were
6:6 Among the *n* it has been heard
6:16 all the *n* that were around us
13:26 among the many *n* there
Job 12:23 Making the *n* grow great
12:23 Spreading out the *n*, that he
Ps 2:1 Why have the *n* been in tumult
2:8 give *n* as your inheritance
9:5 You have rebuked *n*, you have
9:15 *n* have sunk down into the pit
9:17 Even all the *n* forgetting God
9:19 *n* be judged before your face
9:20 *n* may know that they are but
10:16 The *n* have perished out of
18:43 appoint me the head of the *n*
18:49 shall laud you among the *n*
22:27 *n* will bow down before you
22:28 And he is dominating the *n*
33:10 the counsel of the *n*

Ps 44:2 your hand drove away even *n*
44:11 the *n* you have scattered
44:14 saying among the *n*
46:6 The *n* became boisterous, the
46:10 will be exalted among the *n*
47:8 has become king over the *n*
59:5 your attention to all the *n*
59:8 hold all the *n* in derision
66:7 Upon the *n* his own eyes keep
67:2 even among all the *n*
72:11 *n*, for their part, will
72:17 all *n* pronounce him happy
78:55 gradually drove out the *n*
79:1 O God, the *n* have come into
79:6 Pour out your rage upon the *n*
79:10 *n* say: Where is their God?
79:10 Among the *n* let there be
80:8 kept driving out the *n*, that
82:8 possession of all the *n*
86:9 *n* whom you have made will
94:10 One correcting the *n*, can he
96:3 Declare among the *n* his glory
96:10 Say among the *n*: Jehovah
98:2 In the eyes of the *n* he has
102:15 *n* will fear the name of
105:44 them the lands of the *n*
106:27 offspring fall among the *n*
106:35 went mingling with the *n*
106:41 them into the hand of the *n*
106:47 together from the *n*
110:6 execute judgment among the *n*
111:6 the inheritance of the *n*
113:4 become high above all the *n*
115:2 Why should the *n* say
117:1 Praise Jehovah, all you *n*
118:10 *n* themselves surrounded me
126:2 say among the *n*: Jehovah
135:10 struck down many *n* And
135:15 idols of the *n* are silver
149:7 execute vengeance upon the *n*
Isa 2:2 to it all the *n* must stream
2:4 render judgment among the *n*
9:1 Jordan, Galilee of the *n*
10:7 and to cut off *n* not a few
11:10 *n* will turn inquiringly
11:12 signal for the *n* and gather
13:4 of *n* gathered together
14:6 subduing *n* in sheer anger
14:9 kings of the *n* get up from
14:12 who were disabling the *n*
14:18 All other kings of the *n*
14:26 out against all the *n*
16:8 owners of the *n* themselves
23:3 to be the profit of the *n*
25:3 town of the tyrannical *n*
25:7 interwoven upon all the *n*
29:7 crowd of all the *n* that are
29:8 *n* that are waging war
30:28 swing the *n* to and fro with
33:3 *n* have been dispersed
34:1 Come up close, you *n*, to
34:2 indignation against all the *n*
36:18 gods of the *n* delivered each
37:12 *n* that my forefathers
40:15 *n* are as a drop from a
40:17 All the *n* are as something
41:2 to give before him the *n*
42:1 Justice to the *n* is what he
42:6 as a light of the *n*
43:9 Let the *n* all be collected
45:1 to subdue before him *n*, so
45:20 you escapees from the *n*
49:6 you for a light of the *n*
49:22 up my hand even to the *n*
52:10 before the eyes of all the *n*
52:15 likewise startle many *n*
54:3 take possession even of *n*
60:3 *n* will certainly go to your
60:5 resources of the *n* will
60:11 the resources of the *n*, and
60:12 *n* themselves will without
60:16 suck the milk of *n*, and the
61:6 resources of the *n* you people
61:9 be known even among the *n*
61:11 in front of all the *n*
62:2 *n* will certainly see your
64:2 the *n* might be agitated
66:12 glory of *n* just like a
66:18 collect all the *n* and
66:19 who are escaped to the *n*
66:19 my glory among the *n*
66:20 out of all the *n* as a gift
Jer 1:5 Prophet to the *n* I made you
1:10 over the *n* and over the

Jer 3:17 the *n* must be brought
3:19 of the armies of the *n*
4:2 the *n* will actually bless
4:7 who is bringing the *n* to ruin
4:16 you people, yes, to the *n*
6:18 Therefore hear, O you *n*
9:16 scatter them among the *n*
9:26 all the *n* are uncircumcised
10:2 learn the way of the *n*
10:2 the *n* are struck with terror
10:7 fear you, O King of the *n*
10:7 all the wise ones of the *n*
10:10 no *n* will hold up under his
10:25 the *n* who have ignored you
14:22 the vain idols of the *n*
16:19 the *n* themselves will come
18:13 Ask . . . among the *n*
22:8 many *n* will actually pass
25:9 all these *n* round about
25:11 these *n* will have to serve
25:13 prophesied against all the *n*
25:14 many *n* and great kings
25:15 make all the *n* to whom I
25:17 make all the *n* drink to
25:31 that Jehovah has with the *n*
26:6 a malediction to all the *n*
27:7 the *n* must serve even him
27:7 many *n* and great kings must
28:11 off the neck of all the *n*
28:14 upon the neck of all these *n*
29:14 out of all the *n* and out
29:18 reproach among all the *n*
30:11 the *n* to which I have
31:7 at the head of *n*
31:10 word of Jehovah, O you *n*
33:9 *n* of the earth who will hear
36:2 and against all the *n*
43:5 *n* to which they had been
44:8 among all the *n* of the earth
46:1 the prophet concerning the *n*
46:12 *n* have heard your dishonor
46:28 *n* to which I have dispersed
49:14 that is sent among the *n*
49:15 small indeed among the *n*
50:2 Tell it among the *n* and
50:9 great *n* from the land of the
50:12 least important of the *n*
50:23 astonishment among the *n*
50:46 among the *n* an outcry
51:7 her wine the *n* have drunk
51:7 *n* keep acting crazed
51:20 dash *n* to pieces, and by
51:27 Blow a horn among the *n*
51:27 Sanctify against her the *n*
51:28 Sanctify against her the *n*
51:41 astonishment among the *n*
51:44 *n* will stream no more
La 1:1 that was populous among the *n*
1:3 has had to dwell among the *n*
1:10 *n* that have come into her
2:9 her princes are among the *n*
4:15 People have said among the *n*
4:20 we shall live among the *n*
Eze 2:3 *n* that have rebelled against
4:13 *n* to which I shall disperse
5:5 midst of the *n* I have set her
5:6 in wickedness more than the *n*
5:7 more turbulent than the *n*
5:7 judicial decisions of the *n*
5:8 in the eyes of the *n*
5:14 a reproach among the *n* that
5:15 a horror to the *n* that are
6:8 among the *n*, when you get
6:9 remember me among the *n* to
7:24 in the worst ones of the *n*
11:12 judgments of the *n* that are
11:16 far away among the *n*, and
12:15 I disperse them among the *n*
12:16 *n* to whom they must come
16:14 to go forth among the *n*
19:4 And *n* kept hearing about him
19:8 And *n* all around from the
20:9 before the eyes of the *n* in
20:14 before the eyes of the *n*
20:22 before the eyes of the *n*
20:23 to scatter them among the *n*
20:32 Let us become like the *n*
20:41 before the eyes of the *n*
22:4 object of reproach to the *n*
22:15 scatter you among the *n* and
22:16 before the eyes of the *n*
23:30 a prostitute after the *n*
25:7 to plunder to the *n*
25:8 is like all the other *n*

Eze 25:10 sons of Ammon, among the *n*
26:3 bring up against you many *n*
26:5 object of plunder for the *n*
28:7 the tyrants of the *n*, and
28:25 in the eyes of the *n*
29:12 the Egyptians among the *n*
29:15 up over the other *n*
29:15 the other *n* in subjection
30:3 an appointed time of *n* it
30:11 the tyrants of the *n*, are
30:23 Egyptians among the *n* and
30:26 the Egyptians among the *n*
31:6 the populous *n* would dwell
31:11 hand of the despot of the *n*
31:12 the tyrants of the *n*
31:16 cause *n* to rock when I
31:17 in the midst of *n*
32:2 As a maned young lion of *n*
32:9 among the *n* to lands that
32:12 the tyrants of the *n*, all
32:16 Even the daughters of the *n*
32:18 daughters of majestic *n*
34:28 to plunder for the *n*
34:29 the humiliation by the *n*
35:10 two *n* and these two lands
36:3 the remaining ones of the *n*
36:4 the remaining ones of the *n*
36:5 the remaining ones of the *n*
36:6 humiliation by *n* is what you
36:7 *n* that you have round about
36:13 bereaving your *n* of children
36:14 *n* you will no more bereave
36:15 humiliating talk by the *n*
36:15 *n* you will no more cause
36:19 scatter them among the *n*
36:20 the *n* where they came in
36:21 *n* where they have come in
36:22 have profaned among the *n*
36:23 being profaned among the *n*
36:23 *n* will have to know that I
36:24 will take you out of the *n*
36:30 receive among the *n* the
36:36 the *n* that will be left
37:21 Israel from among the *n* to
37:22 continue to be two *n*
37:28 *n* will have to know that I
38:12 together out of the *n*
38:16 that the *n* may know me
38:23 before the eyes of many *n*
39:7 *n* will have to know that I
39:21 set my glory among the *n*
39:21 *n* will have to see my
39:23 *n* will have to know that
39:27 before the eyes of many *n*
39:28 send them in exile to the *n*
Ho 8:8 come to be among the *n*
8:10 keep hiring them among the *n*
9:17 become fugitives among the *n*
Joe 2:17 for *n* to rule over them
2:19 a reproach among the *n*
3:2 collect together all the *n*
3:2 they scattered among the *n*
3:9 you people, among the *n*
3:11 all you *n* round about
3:12 Let the *n* be aroused and
3:12 judge all the *n* round about
Am 6:1 of the chief part of the *n*
9:9 among all the *n*, just as one
9:12 the *n* upon whom my name has
Ob 1 an envoy . . . sent among the *n*
2 I have made you among the *n*
15 against all the *n* is near
16 the *n* will keep drinking
Mic 4:2 *n* will certainly go and say
4:3 respecting mighty *n* far away
4:11 gathered against you many *n*
5:8 must become among the *n*, in
5:15 the *n* that have not obeyed
7:16 *N* will see and become
Na 3:4 ensnaring *n* by her acts of
3:5 cause *n* to see your nakedness
Hab 1:5 you people, among the *n*
1:17 have to kill *n* constantly
2:5 gathering . . . all the *n*
2:8 despoiled many *n*, all the
3:6 and then caused *n* to leap
3:12 you went threshing the *n*
Zep 2:11 all the islands of the *n*
3:6 I cut off *n*; their corner
3:8 decision is to gather *n*
Hag 2:7 And I will rock all the *n*
2:7 desirable things of all the *n*
2:22 of the kingdoms of the *n*
Zec 1:15 indignant against the *n* that

Zec 1:21 *n* that are lifting up a horn
2:8 *n* that were despoiling you
2:11 *n* will certainly become
7:14 throughout all the *n* that
8:13 a malediction among the *n*
8:22 many peoples and mighty *n*
8:23 men . . . of the *n* will take
9:10 speak peace to the *n*
12:3 all the *n* of the earth will
12:9 seek to annihilate all the *n*
14:2 gather all the *n* against
14:3 and war against those *n* as
14:14 wealth of all the *n* round
14:16 remaining out of all the *n*
14:18 scourges the *n* that do not
14:19 sin of all the *n* that do not
Mal 1:11 will be great among the *n*
1:11 will be great among the *n*
1:14 fear-inspiring among the *n*
3:12 *n* will have to pronounce
Mt 4:15 Galilee of the *n*
5:47 the *n* doing the same thing
6:7 just as the people of the *n* do
6:32 the things the *n* are eagerly
10:5 off into the road of the *n*
10:18 a witness to them and the *n*
12:18 he will make clear to the *n*
12:21 in his name *n* will hope
18:17 just as a man of the *n* and
20:19 to men of the *n* to make fun
20:25 rulers of the *n* lord it over
24:9 objects of hatred by . . . *n*
24:14 for a witness to all the *n*
25:32 *n* will be gathered before
28:19 of people of all the *n*
Mr 10:33 deliver him to men of the *n*
10:42 appear to be ruling the *n*
11:17 house of prayer for . . . *n*
13:10 in all the *n* the good news
Lu 2:32 removing the veil from the *n*
12:30 things the *n* of the world
18:32 delivered up to men of the *n*
21:24 led captive into all the *n*
21:24 will be trampled on by the *n*
21:24 appointed times of the *n* are
21:25 on the earth anguish of *n*
22:25 kings of the *n* lord it over
24:47 be preached in all the *n*
Ac 4:25 *n* become tumultuous and
4:27 Pilate with men of *n* and
7:45 land possessed by the *n*
9:15 bear my name to the *n* as
10:45 also upon people of the *n*
11:1 people of the *n* had also
11:18 life to people of the *n* also
13:19 destroying seven *n* in the
13:46 look! we turn to the *n*
13:47 as a light of *n*, for you to
13:48 those of the *n* heard this
14:2 the souls of people of the *n*
14:5 both people of the *n* and Jews
14:16 the *n* to go on in their ways
14:27 opened to the *n* the door to
15:3 conversion of people of the *n*
15:7 people of the *n* should hear
15:12 did through them among the *n*
15:14 his attention to the *n* to
15:17 with people of all the *n*
15:19 the *n* who are turning to God
15:23 who are from the *n*
18:6 I will go to people of the *n*
21:11 the hands of people of the *n*
21:19 things God did among the *n*
21:21 all the Jews among the *n* an
21:25 believers from among the *n*
22:21 send you out to *n* far off
26:17 *n*, to whom I am sending you
26:20 to the *n* I went bringing
26:23 to this people and to the *n*
28:28 has been sent out to the *n*
Ro 1:5 of faith among all the *n*
1:6 among which *n* you also are
1:13 as among the rest of the *n*
2:14 *n* that do not have law do
2:24 of you people among the *n*
3:29 also of people of the *n*
3:29 of people of the *n* also
4:17 you a father of many *n*
4:18 father of many *n* in accord
9:24 Jews but also from among *n*
9:30 people of the *n*, although not
11:11 salvation to people of the *n*
11:12 riches to people of the *n*
11:13 you who are people of the *n*
Ro 11:13 an apostle to the *n*, I
11:25 people of the *n* has come in
15:9 the *n* might glorify God for
15:9 acknowledge you among the *n*
15:10 Be glad, you *n*, with his
15:11 Praise Jehovah, all you *n*
15:12 one arising to rule *n*
15:12 on him *n* will rest their
15:16 to the *n*, engaging in the
15:16 these *n*, might prove to be
15:18 *n* to be obedient, by my word
15:27 if the *n* have shared in their
16:4 congregations of the *n* render
16:26 all the *n* in accord with the
1Co 1:23 but to the *n* foolishness
5:1 as is not even among the *n*
10:20 the things which the *n*
12:2 you were people of the *n*
2Co 11:26 in dangers from the *n*
Ga 1:16 good news about him to the *n*
2:2 I am preaching among the *n*
2:8 for those who are of the *n*
2:9 we should go to the *n*, but
2:12 to eat with people of the *n*
2:14 live as the *n* do, and not as
2:14 compelling people of the *n* to
2:15 and not sinners from the *n*
3:8 of the *n* righteous due to faith
3:8 all the *n* will be blessed
3:14 of Jesus Christ for the *n*
Eph 2:11 people of the *n* as to flesh
3:1 you, the people of the *n*
3:6 people of the *n* should be
3:8 declare to the *n* the good
4:17 just as the *n* also walk in
Col 1:27 sacred secret among the *n*
1Th 2:16 speaking to people of the *n*
4:5 such as also those *n* have
1Ti 2:7 a teacher of *n* in the matter
3:16 was preached about among *n*
2Ti 4:17 and all the *n* might hear it
1Pe 2:12 conduct fine among the *n*
4:3 the will of the *n* when you
3Jo 7 from the people of the *n*
Re 2:26 give authority over the *n*
7:9 a great crowd . . . out of all *n*
10:11 with regard to peoples and *n*
11:2 it has been given to the *n*
11:9 *n* will look at their corpses
11:18 *n* became wrathful, and your
12:5 shepherd all the *n* with an
14:8 *n* drink of the wine of the
15:4 *n* will come and worship
16:19 cities of the *n* fell; and
17:15 crowds and *n* and tongues
18:3 all the *n* have fallen victim
18:23 all the *n* were misled
19:15 he may strike the *n* with it
20:3 mislead the *n* anymore until
20:8 mislead those *n* in the four
21:24 *n* will walk by means of
21:26 honor of the *n* into it
22:2 were for the curing of the *n*

Native
Ex 12:19 alien resident or a *n* of the
12:48 become like a *n* of the land
12:49 for the *n* and for the alien
Le 16:29 either the *n* or the alien
17:15 *n* or an alien resident, he
18:26 *n* or an alien resident who
19:34 to you like a *n* of yours
24:16 resident the same as the *n*
24:22 same as the *n*, because I am
Nu 9:14 and for the *n* of the land
15:13 Every *n* should render up
15:29 *n* among the sons of Israel
15:30 is a *n* or an alien resident
Jos 8:33 as well as the *n*, one half
Ps 37:35 a luxuriant tree in *n* soil
Eze 47:22 *n* among the sons of Israel
Mt 27:32 a *n* of Cyrene named Simon
Lu 23:26 Simon, a certain *n* of Cyrene
Ac 4:36 a Levite, a *n* of Cyprus
18:2 Aquila, a *n* of Pontus who had
18:24 Apollos, a *n* of Alexandria

Natives
Ge 23:7 bowed down to the *n*, to the
23:12 bowed down before the *n*
23:13 hearing of the *n*, saying
Le 23:42 *n* in Israel should dwell in

Natural
Le 18:23 is a violation of what is *n*
Le 20:12 a violation of what is *n*
Ro 1:26 females changed the *n* use of
1:27 left the *n* use of the female
1:31 having no *n* affection
11:21 did not spare the *n* branches
11:24 who are *n* be grafted into
2Ti 3:3 having no *n* affection, not
Jas 1:23 at his *n* face in a mirror
3:6 the wheel of *n* life aflame

Naturally
Eph 2:3 were *n* children of wrath even
2Pe 2:12 animals born *n* to be caught
Jude 10 *n* like the unreasoning

Nature
Jg 3:24 He is just easing *n* in the
1Sa 24:3 Saul came in to ease *n*
Am 4:10 in the *n* of that of Egypt
Ro 1:26 into one contrary to *n*
2:14 do by *n* the things of the law
2:27 person that is such by *n*
11:24 olive tree that is wild by *n*
11:24 grafted contrary to *n* into
1Co 11:14 Does not *n* itself teach you
Ga 2:15 We who are Jews by *n*, and not
4:8 those who by *n* are not gods
2Pe 1:4 become sharers in divine *n*

Navel
Pr 3:8 healing to your *n* and a
Ca 7:2 Your *n* roll is a round bowl
Eze 16:4 *n* string had not been cut

Navigate
Ac 27:9 hazardous to *n* because even

Navigated
Ac 27:5 *n* through the open sea along

Navigation
Ac 27:10 *n* is going to be with

Nazarene
Mt 2:23 He will be called a *N*
26:71 man was with Jesus the *N*
Mr 1:24 to do with you, Jesus you *N*
10:47 that it was Jesus the *N*
14:67 You, too, were with the *N*
16:6 looking for Jesus the *N*
Lu 4:34 to do with you, Jesus you *N*
18:37 Jesus the *N* is passing by!
24:19 Jesus the *N*, who became a
Joh 18:5 Jesus the *N*. He said to them
18:7 They said: Jesus the *N*
19:19 Jesus the *N* the King of the
Ac 2:22 Jesus the *N*, a man publicly
3:6 name of Jesus Christ the *N*
4:10 name of Jesus Christ the *N*
6:14 Jesus the *N* will throw down
22:8 I am Jesus the *N*, whom you
26:9 the name of Jesus the *N*

Nazarenes
Ac 24:5 spearhead of the sect of the *N*

Nazareth
Mt 2:23 and dwelt in a city named *N*
4:13 after leaving *N*, he came and
21:11 Jesus, from *N* of Galilee
Mr 1:9 Jesus came from *N* of Galilee
Lu 1:26 to a city of Galilee named *N*
2:4 out of the city of *N*, into
2:39 Galilee to their own city *N*
2:51 came to *N*, and he continued
4:16 *N*, where he had been reared
Joh 1:45 the son of Joseph, from *N*
1:46 anything good come out of *N*
Ac 10:38 Jesus who was from *N*, how

Nazirite
Nu 6:2 vow to live as a *N* to Jehovah
6:12 *N* to Jehovah for the days of
6:13 law about the *N*: On the day
6:18 *N* must shave the head of his
6:19 *N* after he has had the sign
6:20 the *N* may drink wine
6:21 law about the *N* who vows
Jg 13:5 a *N* of God is what the child
13:7 a *N* of God is what the child
16:17 because I am a *N* of God from

Nazirites
La 4:7 Her *N* were purer than snow
Am 2:11 some of your young men as *N*
2:12 giving the *N* wine to drink

Naziriteship
Nu 6:4 days of his *N* he should not eat
6:5 vow of his *N* no razor should

Nu 6:7 sign of his *N* to his God is
6:8 of his *N* he is holy to Jehovah
6:9 defiled the head of his *N*, he
6:12 days of his *N*, and he must
6:12 because he defiled his *N*
6:13 *N* come to the full, he will
6:18 must shave the head of his *N*
6:18 hair of the head of his *N* and
6:19 the sign of his *N* shaved off
6:21 offering . . . over his *N*
6:21 because of the law of his *N*

Neah
Jos 19:13 and was marked out to *N*

Neapolis
Ac 16:11 on the following day to *N*

Near
Ge 10:19 *n* Gaza, as far as Sodom and
10:19 Admah and Zeboiim, *n* Lasha
12:6 Shechem, *n* the big trees of
12:11 he got *n* to entering Egypt
13:12 he pitched tent *n* Sodom
19:9 getting *n* to break in the door
20:4 Abimelech had not gone *n* her
25:18 tabernacling from Havilah *n*
27:21 Come *n*, please, that I may
27:22 Jacob came *n* to Isaac his
27:25 Bring it *n* to me that I may
27:25 he brought it *n* to him and
27:26 Come *n*, please, and kiss me
27:27 he came *n* and kissed him
33:3 until he got *n* to his brother
38:1 he pitched his tent *n* a man
44:18 Judah now came *n* to him
45:10 and you must continue *n* me
Ex 3:5 Do not come *n* here. Draw your
12:48 he may come *n* to celebrate
13:17 just because it was *n*, for
14:20 this group did not come *n*
16:9 Come *n* before Jehovah
19:15 not you men come *n* a woman
19:22 regularly come *n* to Jehovah
20:21 but Moses went *n* to the dark
21:6 bring him *n* to the true God
22:8 brought *n* to the true God to
28:1 bring *n* to yourself Aaron your
28:27 *n* its place of joining, above
28:43 *n* to the altar to minister
29:8 bring his sons *n* and you must
30:6 curtain that is *n* the ark
30:20 go *n* the altar to minister
32:19 as soon as he got *n* the camp
34:30 afraid of coming *n* to him
34:32 sons of Israel came *n* to
37:14 rings proved to be *n* the rim
38:5 *n* the grating of copper, as
39:20 *n* its place of joining, above
40:12 *n* to the entrance of the tent
40:14 bring his sons *n* and you must
40:32 they went *n* to the altar
Le 2:8 must bring it *n* to the altar
3:9 he will remove *n* the backbone
8:6 sons *n* and washed them with
8:13 *n* and clothed them with robes
8:18 burnt offering *n*, and Aaron
8:22 ram of the installation, *n*
8:24 Moses brought Aaron's sons *n*
9:5 *n* and stood before Jehovah
9:7 Go *n* to the altar and render
9:8 went *n* to the altar and
10:3 Among those *n* to me let me
10:4 Come *n*, carry your brothers
10:5 came *n* and carried them in
10:12 eat it unfermented *n* the
18:6 not come *n*, any man of you
18:14 must not come *n* his wife
18:19 not come *n* a woman during
21:17 No man . . . defect may come *n*
21:18 defect, he may not come *n*
21:23 not come in *n* the curtain
22:3 comes *n* to the holy things
Nu 1:51 stranger coming *n* should be
3:6 Bring the tribe of Levi *n*, and
3:10 stranger coming *n* should be
3:38 stranger coming *n* would be
5:8 *n* relative to whom to return
5:25 he must bring it *n* the altar
16:5 and who must come *n* to him
16:5 choose will come *n* to him
16:10 sons of Levi with you *n*
16:40 come *n* to make incense
17:13 coming *n* to Jehovah's
18:2 bring *n*, also, your brothers
Nu 18:3 altar they must not come *n*
18:4 no stranger may come *n* to you
18:7 stranger drawing *n* should be
18:22 no more come *n* to the tent
21:24 Jabbok, *n* the sons of Ammon
24:17 shall behold him, but not *n*
25:6 bringing *n* to his brothers a
27:1 Then the daughters . . . came *n*
36:1 come *n* and speak before Moses
De 1:22 all of you came *n* to me and
2:37 *n* the land of the sons of
4:7 gods *n* to it the way Jehovah
4:11 came *n* and stood at the base
5:23 you proceeded to come *n* to me
5:27 go *n* and hear all that Jehovah
13:7 the ones *n* you or those far
16:21 sacred pole *n* the altar of
20:2 have drawn *n* to the battle
20:3 drawing *n* today to the battle
20:10 draw *n* to a city to fight
22:2 if your brother is not *n* you
22:14 I proceeded to go *n* her
25:11 *n* to deliver her husband out
30:14 word is very *n* you, in your
31:14 days have drawn *n* for you to
32:35 day of their disaster is *n*
Jos 3:4 do not get *n* to it—in order
7:14 will come *n*, family by
7:14 will come *n*, household by
7:14 come *n*, able-bodied man by
7:16 had Israel come *n*, tribe by
7:17 the families of Judah come *n*
7:17 the Zerahites come *n*
7:18 he had his household come *n*
8:23 to bring him *n* to Joshua
9:16 that they were *n* to them and
Jg 4:11 tent pitched *n* the big tree
19:14 when *n* to Gibeah, which
20:24 sons of Israel drew *n* to the
1Sa 4:19 pregnant *n* to giving birth
7:10 drew *n* for battle against
10:20 the tribes of Israel draw *n*
10:21 tribe of Benjamin draw *n* by
13:9 Bring *n* to me the burnt
14:18 the ark of the true God *n*
14:34 Bring *n* to me, each one of
14:34 brought *n* each one his bull
14:38 Come *n* here, all you keymen
15:32 the king of Amalek *n* to me
20:19 dwell *n* this stone here
23:9 Do bring the ephod *n*
30:7 bring the ephod *n* to me
30:7 the ephod *n* to David
30:21 David came *n* to the people
2Sa 1:15 and said: Go *n*. Smite him
11:20 so *n* to the city to fight
13:11 *n* to him for him to eat
15:5 drew *n* to bow down to him
20:16 Come *n* as far as here, and
20:17 he went *n* to her, and the
1Ki 2:1 drew *n* for him to die; and he
2:7 the way they drew *n* to me
8:59 *n* to Jehovah our God by day
2Ki 4:5 bringing the vessels *n* to her
4:6 still another vessel *n* to me
4:27 Gehazi came *n* to push her
11:11 all around *n* the king
16:12 to go *n* to the altar and
16:14 brought *n* from in front of
1Ch 12:40 those *n* to them, as far as
2Ch 23:10 all around *n* the king
29:23 *n* before the king and the
Es 5:2 Esther now came *n* and touched
Job 17:12 Light is *n* on account of
33:22 soul draws *n* to the pit
40:19 Maker can bring *n* his sword
Ps 32:9 they will come *n* to you
34:18 *n* to those that are broken
69:18 come *n* to my soul, reclaim
73:28 drawing *n* to God is good for
75:1 And your name is *n*
85:9 salvation is *n* to those
91:7 To you it will not come *n*
91:10 plague will draw *n* to your
119:150 loose conduct have come *n*
119:151 You are *n*, O Jehovah
119:169 cry come *n* before you
145:18 Jehovah is *n* to all those
148:14 the people *n* to him
Pr 5:8 *n* to the entrance of her house
7:8 on the street *n* her corner
7:12 *n* every corner she lies in
10:14 foolish one is *n* to ruin
27:10 a neighbor that is *n* than a
Ec 5:1 there be a drawing *n* to hear
Isa 5:19 draw *n* and come, that we
8:3 I went *n* to the prophetess
13:6 for the day of Jehovah is *n*
13:22 season for her is *n* to come
26:17 draws *n* to giving birth
28:21 in the low plain *n* Gibeon
29:13 come *n* with their mouth
41:5 drew *n* and kept coming
46:13 brought *n* my righteousness
48:16 Come *n* to me, you people
50:8 declaring me righteous is *n*
51:5 My righteousness is *n*
54:14 for it will not come *n* you
55:6 while he proves to be *n*
57:19 and to the one that is *n*
58:2 drawing *n* to God in whom
Jer 12:2 You are *n* in their mouth
25:26 who are *n* and far away
30:21 come *n*, and he must
48:16 Moabites is *n* to come, and
48:24 those far away and those *n*
49:32 regions *n* it I shall bring
La 3:57 You have drawn *n* in the day
4:18 Our end has drawn *n*. Our days
Eze 7:7 time must come, the day is *n*
9:1 come *n*, each one with his
9:6 there is the mark do not go *n*
12:23 The days have drawn *n*, and
18:6 impurity he would not go *n*
22:4 And you bring your days *n*
23:5 the Assyrians, who were *n*
23:12 deputy rulers who were *n*
30:3 a day is *n*, yes, a day
30:3 day belonging to Jehovah is *n*
36:8 *n* to the point of coming in
43:22 bring *n* a buck of the goats
43:23 bring *n* a young bull, the
43:24 bring them *n* before Jehovah
44:15 come *n* to minister to me
44:16 *n* to my table to minister
Da 6:20 And as he got *n* to the pit
Ho 7:6 their heart *n* as to a furnace
Joe 1:15 the day of Jehovah is *n*
2:1 the day of Jehovah . . . it is *n*!
3:9 Let them draw *n*! Let them
3:14 for the day of Jehovah is *n*
Am 5:25 brought *n* to me in the
6:3 do you bring *n* the dwelling of
9:10 The calamity will not come *n*
Ob 15 against all the nations is *n*
Jon 1:6 the ship captain came *n* to
Zep 1:7 for the day of Jehovah is *n*
1:14 great day of Jehovah is *n*
1:14 It is *n*, and there is a
3:2 To her God she did not draw *n*
Mal 1:8 Bring it *n*, please, to your
3:5 I will come *n* to you people
Mt 3:2 of the heavens has drawn *n*
4:17 kingdom . . . has drawn *n*
10:7 The kingdom . . . has drawn *n*
15:10 he called the crowd *n* and
15:29 Jesus next came *n* the sea of
17:7 Jesus came *n* and, touching
18:1 disciples came *n* to Jesus and
24:32 you know that summer is *n*
24:33 know that he is *n* at the
26:18 My appointed time is *n*
26:45 hour has drawn *n* for the Son
26:46 My betrayer has drawn *n*
Mr 1:15 kingdom of God has drawn *n*
4:1 great crowd gathered *n* him
8:2 they have remained *n* me and
11:1 were getting *n* to Jerusalem
13:28 you know that summer is *n*
13:29 that he is *n*, at the doors
14:42 My betrayer has drawn *n*
15:35 some of those standing *n*, on
Lu 1:19 Gabriel, who stands *n* before
2:38 in that very hour she came *n*
7:12 got *n* the gate of the city
10:9 The kingdom of God has come *n*
10:11 kingdom of God has come *n*
10:40 she came *n* and said: Lord
12:33 where a thief does not get *n*
15:1 kept drawing *n* to him to hear
15:25 he came and got *n* the house
18:35 he was getting *n* to Jericho
18:40 he got *n*, Jesus asked him
19:11 he was *n* Jerusalem and they
19:29 he got *n* to Bethphage and
19:37 soon as he got *n* the road
20:1 with the older men came *n*
21:20 desolating . . . drawn *n*

Heb 7:12 *n* a change also of the law

Necho

2Ch 35:20 *N* the king of Egypt came
35:22 listen to the words of *N*
36:4 *N* took and brought to Egypt
Jer 46:2 Pharaoh *N* the king of Egypt

Nechoh

2Ki 23:29 Pharaoh *N* the king of Egypt
23:33 Pharaoh *N* got to put him in
23:34 Pharaoh *N* made Eliakim the
23:35 to give it to Pharaoh *N*

Neck

Ge 27:16 the hairless part of his *n*
27:40 break his yoke off your *n*
33:4 fall upon his *n* and kiss him
41:42 necklace of gold about his *n*
45:14 fell upon the *n* of Benjamin
45:14 and Benjamin wept upon his *n*
46:29 at once fell upon his *n* and
46:29 gave way to tears upon his *n*
49:8 back of the *n* of your enemies
Ex 13:13 then you must break its *n*
23:27 give the back of the *n* of all
34:20 then you must break its *n*
Le 5:8 at the front of its *n*, but he
De 21:4 break the *n* of the young cow
21:6 the *n* of which was broken
28:48 put an iron yoke upon your *n*
31:27 I well know . . . your stiff *n*
1Sa 4:18 his *n* got broken so that
2Sa 22:41 give me the back of their *n*
2Ch 29:6 offered the back of the *n*
30:8 do not stiffen your *n* as
36:13 stiffening his *n* and
Ne 3:5 not bring the back of their *n*
9:16 proceeded to harden their *n*
9:17 hardened their *n* and appointed
9:29 and their *n* they hardened
Job 16:12 by the back of the *n* and
39:19 its *n* with a rustling mane
41:22 In its *n* lodges strength
Ps 18:40 give me the back of their *n*
75:5 not speak with an arrogant *n*
Pr 29:1 but making his *n* hard will
Ca 1:10 your *n* in a string of beads
4:4 *n* is like the tower of David
7:4 Your *n* is like an ivory tower
Isa 8:8 Up to the *n* he will reach
10:27 his yoke from upon your *n*
30:28 that reaches clear to the *n*
48:4 that your *n* is an iron sinew
52:2 bands on your *n*, O captive
66:3 one breaking the *n* of a dog
Jer 2:27 turned the back of the *n* and
7:26 they kept hardening their *n*
17:23 harden their *n* in order not
19:15 they have hardened their *n*
27:2 put them upon your *n*
27:8 *n* under the yoke of the king
27:11 bring its *n* under the yoke
28:10 from off the *n* of Jeremiah
28:11 off the *n* of all the nations
28:12 from off the *n* of Jeremiah
28:14 upon the *n* of all these
30:8 one's yoke from off your *n*
La 1:14 They have come up upon my *n*
5:5 Close onto our *n* we have been
Da 5:7 necklace of gold about his *n*
5:16 necklace of gold around your *n*
5:29 necklace of gold about his *n*
Ho 10:11 over her good-looking *n*
Hab 3:13 clear up to the *n*. *Se'lah*
Mt 18:6 hung around his *n* a millstone
Mr 9:42 were put around his *n* and
Lu 15:20 fell upon his *n* and tenderly
17:2 suspended from his *n* and he
Ac 15:10 upon the *n* of the disciples
20:37 they fell upon Paul's *n* and

Necklace

Ge 41:42 a *n* of gold about his neck
2Ch 3:16 made chains in *n* style and
Ps 73:6 has served as a *n* to them
Pr 1:9 and a fine *n* to your throat
Ca 4:9 by one pendant of your *n*
Eze 16:11 and a *n* about your throat
Da 5:7 *n* of gold about his neck, and
5:16 *n* of gold around your neck
5:29 a *n* of gold about his neck

Necklaces

Jg 8:26 *n* that were on the necks of

Necks

De 10:16 not harden your *n* any longer
Jos 10:24 back of the *n* of these kings
10:24 feet on the back of their *n*
Jg 5:30 For the *n* of men of spoil
8:21 on the *n* of their camels
8:26 on the *n* of the camels
2Ki 17:14 kept hardening their *n* like
17:14 the *n* of their forefathers
Jer 27:12 Bring your *n* under the yoke
Eze 21:29 on the *n* of the slain ones
Mic 2:3 will not remove your *n*, so
Ro 16:4 risked their own *n* for my

Nedabiah

1Ch 3:18 Jekamiah, Hoshama and *N*

Need

Ge 41:16 I *n* not be considered! God
Le 13:36 *n* not make examination for
1Sa 21:15 *n* of people driven crazy
2Sa 3:29 or one in *n* of bread
1Ki 11:22 What are you in *n* of while
2Ch 2:16 according to all your *n*, and
5:11 no *n* to observe the divisions
20:17 not *n* to fight in this
35:15 no *n* for them to turn aside
Ne 12:47 according to the daily *n* and
Job 5:22 you *n* not be afraid
31:21 *n* of my assistance in the
Pr 3:25 not *n* to be afraid of any
24:30 of the man in *n* of heart
Ec 6:2 soul, is in no *n* of anything
Isa 22:3 Without *n* of a bow they
Mt 5:3 conscious of their spiritual *n*
6:32 knows you *n* all these things
9:12 Persons in health do not *n* a
26:65 What further *n* do we have
Mr 2:17 strong do not *n* a physician
2:25 David did when he fell in *n*
9:24 Help me out where I *n* faith
14:63 *n* do we have of witnesses
Lu 5:31 healthy do not *n* a physician
12:30 Father knows you *n* these
14:18 and *n* to go out and see it
15:7 who have no *n* of repentance
15:14 and he started to be in *n*
18:1 the *n* for them always to pray
22:71 Why do we *n* further witness?
Joh 2:25 in no *n* to have anyone bear
13:10 *n* to have more than his
13:29 we *n* for the festival
16:30 *n* to have anyone question
Ac 2:45 as anyone would have the *n*
4:34 was not one in *n* among them
4:35 just as he would have the *n*
Ro 8:26 should pray for as we *n* to
16:2 any matter where she may *n*
1Co 12:21 I have no *n* of you; or
12:21 I have no *n* of you
12:24 our comely parts do not *n*
2Co 3:1 *n* letters of recommendation
6:4 by cases of *n*, by difficulties
11:9 with you and I fell in *n*
12:10 pleasure in . . . cases of *n*
Eph 4:28 distribute to someone in *n*
4:29 building up as the *n* may be
Php 2:25 and private servant for my *n*
4:16 and a second time for my *n*
4:19 supply all your *n* to the
1Th 1:8 we do not *n* to say anything
4:9 not *n* us to be writing you
5:1 *n* nothing to be written to
2Ti 2:24 does not *n* to fight, but
Heb 5:12 again *n* someone to teach you
5:12 *n* milk, not solid food
7:11 what further *n* would there
7:27 He does not *n* daily, as
10:36 you have *n* of endurance, in
1Jo 2:27 not *n* anyone to be teaching
3:17 beholds his brother having *n*
Re 3:17 riches and do not *n* anything
21:23 city has no *n* of the sun
22:5 they have no *n* of lamplight

Needed

Ezr 6:9 what is *n*, young bulls as
Lu 10:42 A few things, though, are *n*
Ac 17:25 as if he *n* anything, because
Eph 4:16 joint that gives what is *n*

Neediness

Pr 24:34 and your *n* as an armed man

Needing

1Sa 22:23 one *n* protection with me

Mt 3:14 one *n* to be baptized by you
6:8 knows what things you are *n*
Lu 9:11 he healed those *n* a cure
1Th 4:12 and not be *n* anything

Needle

Lu 18:25 the eye of a sewing *n* than

Needle's

Mt 19:24 camel to get through a *n* eye
Mr 10:25 camel to go through a *n* eye

Needs

Ex 12:16 what every soul *n* to eat
36:5 more than what the service *n*
De 15:8 on pledge as much as he *n*
Mt 21:3 must say, The Lord *n* them
Mr 11:3 The Lord *n* it, and will at
Lu 11:8 give him what things he *n*
19:31 this way, The Lord *n* it
19:34 They said: The Lord *n* it
Ac 20:34 have attended to the *n* of me
28:10 us with things for our *n*
Ro 12:13 according to their *n*
2Ti 2:24 *n* to be gentle toward all
Tit 3:14 as to meet their pressing *n*
Heb 9:16 covenanter *n* to be furnished

Needy

Ec 4:13 Better is a *n* but wise child
9:15 found in it a man, *n* but wise
9:15 no man remembered that *n* man
9:16 the wisdom of the *n* one is
Lu 21:2 *n* widow drop two small coins

Negeb

Ge 12:9 going then . . . toward the *N*
13:1 Abram went up . . . to the *N*
13:3 encampment out of the *N*
20:1 the *N* and took up dwelling
24:62 in the land of the *N*
Ex 26:18 toward the *N*, to the south
27:9 For the side toward the *N*
36:23 for the side toward the *N*
38:9 For the side toward the *N*, to
Nu 13:17 Go up here into the *N*, and
13:22 When they went up into the *N*
13:29 in the land of the *N*, and the
21:1 who dwelt in the *N*, got to
33:40 as he was dwelling in the *N*
De 1:7 the *N* and the seacoast, the
34:3 and the *N* and the District
Jos 10:40 the *N* and the Shephelah and
11:16 the *N* and all the land of
12:8 the wilderness and in the *N*
15:1 the *N* at its southern end
Jg 1:9 mountainous region and the *N*
2Sa 24:7 the *N* of Judah at Beer-sheba
2Ch 28:18 and the *N* of Judah and got
Ps 126:4 Like stream beds in the *N*
Jer 17:26 from the *N*, bringing whole
Eze 47:19 to the south, toward the *N*
Ob 19 must take possession of the *N*
20 of the cities of the *N*
Zec 7:7 *N* and the Shephelah were

Neglect

Ne 10:39 not *n* the house of our God
Pr 8:33 and do not show any *n*
Jer 23:39 will give you people to *n*
Eze 24:14 I shall not *n*, neither shall

Neglected

Nu 9:13 *n* to prepare the passover
Ne 13:11 house of the true God been *n*
Heb 2:3 have *n* a salvation of such

Neglectfully

Jer 48:10 the mission of Jehovah *n*

Neglecting

Pr 1:25 you keep *n* all my counsel
13:18 one *n* discipline comes to
1Ti 4:14 Do not be *n* the gift in you

Negligence

Ezr 4:22 no *n* about acting in this
Da 6:4 no *n* or corrupt thing at all

Nehelam

Jer 29:24 to Shemaiah of *N* you will
29:31 concerning Shemaiah of *N*
29:32 Shemaiah of *N* and upon his

Nehemiah

Ezr 2:2 *N*, Seraiah, Reelaiah
Ne 1:1 words of *N* the son of Hacaliah
3:16 *N* the son of Azbuk, a prince
7:7 *N*, Azariah, Raamiah, Nahamani
8:9 *N*, that is, the Tirshatha, and

Nets
1Ki 7:17 There were *n* in network
Ps 141:10 fall into their own *n* all
Ec 7:26 who is herself *n* for hunting
Isa 19:8 spreading fishing *n* upon the
Eze 19:9 by means of hunting *n*, in
Mt 4:20 abandoning the *n*, they
4:21 mending their *n*, and he
Mr 1:16 casting their *n* about in the
1:18 they abandoned their *n* and
1:19 in their boat mending their *n*
Lu 5:2 and were washing off their *n*
5:4 let down your *n* for a catch
5:5 I will lower the *n*
5:6 their *n* began ripping apart

Netted
Ps 35:7 have hid for me their *n* pit
Pr 12:12 the *n* prey of bad men

Nettle
Isa 55:13 Instead of the stinging *n*

Nettles
Job 30:7 Under the *n* they would
Pr 24:31 *N* covered its very surface
Isa 34:13 *n* and thorny weeds in her
Ho 9:6 *n* . . . will take possession
Zep 2:9 a place possessed by *n*, and

Network
Ex 27:4 a *n* of copper; and you must
38:4 a *n* of copper, under its rim
2Sa 18:9 the *n* of boughs of a . . . tree
1Ki 7:17 nets in *n*, twisted ornaments
7:18 one *n* to cover the capitals
7:20 that was adjoining the *n*
7:42 pomegranates to each *n*
2Ki 25:17 the *n* and the pomegranates
25:17 same as these upon the *n*
2Ch 4:13 pomegranates for each *n* to
Job 18:8 And onto a *n* he will walk
Jer 52:22 *n* and the pomegranates
52:23 upon the *n* round about

Networks
1Ki 7:41 two *n* to cover the two round
7:42 pomegranates for the two *n*
2Ch 4:12 two *n* to cover the two round
4:13 pomegranates for the two *n*

Never
Ge 8:21 *N* again shall I call down
8:21 *n* again shall I deal every
8:22 day and night, will *n* cease
19:8 two daughters who have *n* had
31:38 rams of your flock I *n* ate
38:20 but he *n* found her
38:22 I *n* found her and, besides
38:23 but you—you *n* found her
39:10 he *n* listened to her to lie
Ex 9:18 has *n* occurred in Egypt from
10:14 had *n* turned up in this way
10:14 *n* turn up any in this way
11:6 of which has *n* yet occurred
11:6 will *n* be brought about again
14:13 not see again, no, *n* again
34:10 that have *n* been created in
Nu 14:23 will *n* see the land about
De 3:26 *N* speak to me further on this
5:7 *n* have any other gods against
13:16 It should *n* be rebuilt
15:11 poor will *n* cease to be in
17:16 *n* go back again by this way
19:20 *n* again do anything bad like
28:56 *n* attempted to set the sole
28:68 You will *n* see it again, and
34:10 has *n* yet risen up a prophet
Jos 5:6 *n* let them see the land that
9:23 will *n* be cut off from you
23:6 by *n* turning away from it
23:7 by *n* going in among these
Jg 2:1 *N* shall I break my covenant
11:26 did you *n* snatch them away
11:39 she *n* had relations with a
16:17 A razor has *n* come upon my
19:30 *n* been brought about or been
1Sa 2:32 *n* will there come to be an
4:7 thing as this *n* occurred
28:6 Jehovah *n* answered him
2Sa 14:10 he will *n* hurt you again
1Ki 10:10 *n* came anymore the like of
2Ki 24:7 *n* again did the king of Egypt
1Ch 16:30 *N* will it be made to totter
2Ch 9:11 *n* been seen before in the land
35:18 *n* been held a passover like
Ne 2:1 *n* had I happened to be gloomy
Job 20:17 will *n* see the watercourses
Ps 10:11 He will certainly *n* see it
15:5 will *n* be made to totter
30:6 *N* shall I be made to totter
31:1 O may I *n* be ashamed
55:22 *N* will he allow the
71:1 O may I *n* be ashamed
Ec 3:11 may *n* find out the work that
Isa 10:20 *n* again support themselves
13:20 will *n* be inhabited, nor
23:12 *n* again exult, O oppressed
28:28 *n* does one incessantly keep
33:20 *N* will its tent pins be
40:24 *N* yet have they been planted
40:24 *n* yet have they been sown
40:24 *n* yet has their stump taken
Jer 51:64 sink down and *n* rise up
Eze 26:14 *N* will you be rebuilt
Da 2:44 a kingdom that will *n* be
Am 8:7 *N* will I forget all their
Ob 16 they had *n* happened to be
Hab 1:4 and justice *n* goes forth
Zep 3:11 *n* again be haughty in my
Mt 6:31 *n* be anxious and say, What
6:34 *n* be anxious about the next
7:6 *n* trample them under their
7:16 *N* do people gather grapes
7:23 I *n* knew you! Get away from
9:33 *N* was anything like this seen
13:15 that they might *n* see with
21:16 Did you *n* read this, Out of
21:42 you *n* read in the Scriptures
26:33 *n* will I be stumbled!
27:64 may *n* come and steal him
Mr 2:12 We *n* saw the like of it
2:25 *n* once read what David did
12:10 you *n* read this scripture
Lu 2:37 *n* missing from the temple
6:3 *n* read the very thing David
8:17 that will *n* become known and
8:17 and *n* come into the open
12:58 *n* hale you before the judge
15:29 *n* once did I transgress your
15:29 *n* once gave a kid for me to
20:16 they said: *N* may that happen!
21:34 hearts *n* become weighed
Joh 4:14 will *n* get thirsty at all
6:35 will *n* get thirsty at all
7:46 *N* has another man spoken
8:33 *n* have we been slaves to
8:51 he will *n* see death at all
8:52 he will *n* taste death at all
9:32 *n* been heard that anyone
11:26 faith in me will *n* die at
13:8 certainly *n* wash my feet
Ac 2:25 that I may *n* be shaken
10:14 *n* have I eaten anything
11:8 unclean thing has *n* entered
14:8 and he had *n* walked at all
19:2 *n* heard whether there is a
28:27 *n* see with their eyes and
Ro 3:4 *N* may that happen! But let
3:6 *N* may that happen!
3:31 *N* may that happen! On the
6:2 *N* may that happen! Seeing that
6:15 *N* may that happen!
7:7 *N* may that become so!
7:13 *N* may that happen! But sin
9:14 *N* may that become so!
11:1 *N* may that happen! For I also
11:11 *N* may that happen! But by
1Co 6:15 *N* may that happen!
8:13 I will *n* again eat flesh at
13:8 Love *n* fails. But whether
Ga 2:17 May that *n* happen!
3:21 May that *n* happen! For if
6:14 *N* may it occur that I should
1Ti 5:22 *N* lay your hands hastily upon
6:1 *n* be spoken of injuriously
2Ti 1:3 *n* leave off remembering you
3:7 *n* able to come to an accurate
Heb 1:12 your years will *n* run out
2:1 that we may *n* drift away
10:1 *n* with the same sacrifices
12:4 *n* yet resisted as far as
1Pe 1:8 you *n* saw him, you love him
2Jo 10 *n* receive him into your homes
Re 18:7 and I shall *n* see mourning
18:14 *n* again will people find
18:21 she will *n* be found again
18:22 trumpeters will *n* be heard

Never-failing
Lu 12:33 a *n* treasure in the heavens

Nevermore
Ps 49:19 *N* will they see the light
Jer 50:39 she will *n* be dwelt in, nor

New
Ge 27:28 grain and *n* wine
27:37 grain and *n* wine I have
Ex 1:8 there arose over Egypt a *n* king
Le 2:14 the grits of *n* grain, as the
23:14 nor *n* grain until this very
23:16 present a *n* grain offering to
26:10 the old ahead of the *n*
Nu 18:12 best of the *n* wine and the
28:26 present a *n* grain offering to
De 7:13 your grain and your *n* wine
12:17 your *n* wine or of your oil
14:23 your *n* wine and your oil
18:4 your *n* wine and your oil and
20:5 man that has built a *n* house
22:8 In case you build a *n* house
24:5 In case a man takes a *n* wife
28:51 let no grain, *n* wine or oil
32:17 *N* ones who recently came in
33:28 a land of grain and *n* wine
Jos 9:13 skin-bottles . . . filled *n*
Jg 5:8 They proceeded to choose *n* gods
9:13 my *n* wine that makes God and
15:13 bound him with two *n* ropes
16:11 tie me tight with *n* ropes
16:12 Delilah took *n* ropes and tied
1Sa 6:7 now take and make a *n* wagon
20:5 Tomorrow is *n* moon, and I
20:18 Tomorrow is *n* moon, and
20:24 it came to be *n* moon, and
20:27 day after the *n* moon, on
20:34 second day after the *n* moon
2Sa 6:3 ride upon a *n* wagon, that
6:3 were leading the *n* wagon
21:16 was girded with a *n* sword
1Ki 11:29 with a *n* garment
11:30 took hold of the *n* garment
2Ki 2:20 a small *n* bowl and put salt
4:23 It is not a *n* moon nor a
4:42 and *n* grain in his bread bag
18:32 a land of grain and *n* wine
1Ch 13:7 ride upon a *n* wagon from the
23:31 at the *n* moons and at the
2Ch 2:4 on the *n* moons and at the
8:13 for the *n* moons and for the
20:5 before the *n* courtyard
31:3 for the *n* moons and for
31:5 *n* wine, and oil and honey
32:28 *n* wine and oil, and also
Ezr 3:5 and that for the *n* moons and
Ne 5:11 the grain, the *n* wine and the
10:33 the sabbaths, the *n* moons
10:37 *n* wine and oil we should
10:39 the *n* wine and the oil, and
13:5 the *n* wine and the oil
13:12 the *n* wine and of the oil
Job 10:17 bring forth *n* witnesses of
14:9 a bough like a *n* plant
32:19 Like *n* skin bottles it
Ps 4:7 their grain and their *n* wine
33:3 Sing to him a *n* song
37:2 like green *n* grass they will
40:3 he put in my mouth a *n* song
51:10 put within me a *n* spirit
81:3 On the *n* moon, blow the horn
96:1 Sing to Jehovah a *n* song
98:1 Sing to Jehovah a *n* song
104:30 the face of the ground *n*
144:9 O God, a *n* song I will sing
149:1 Sing to Jehovah a *n* song
Pr 3:10 *n* wine your own press vats
27:25 and the *n* grass has appeared
Ec 1:9 is nothing *n* under the sun
1:10 may say: See this; it is *n*
Ca 7:13 The *n* ones as well as the old
Isa 1:13 *N* moon and sabbath, the
1:14 Your *n* moons and your festal
24:7 *n* wine has gone to mourning
36:17 a land of grain and *n* wine
41:15 a *n* threshing instrument
42:9 *n* things I am telling out
42:10 Sing to Jehovah a *n* song
43:19 I am doing something *n*
47:13 knowledge at the *n* moons
48:6 made you hear *n* things from
62:2 be called by a *n* name
62:8 drink your *n* wine, for
65:8 *n* wine is found in the
65:17, 17 *n* heavens and a *n* earth
66:22 For just as the *n* heavens

Nicolaus
Ac 6:5 *N*, a proselyte of Antioch
Re 2:6 sect of *N*, which I also hate
2:15 teaching of the sect of *N*

Nicopolis
Tit 3:12 utmost to come to me at *N*

Niger
Ac 13:1 Symeon who was called *N*

Night
Ge 1:5 but the darkness he called *N*
1:14 between the day and the *n*
1:16 luminary for dominating the *n*
1:18 to dominate by day and by *n*
8:22 day and *n*, will never cease
14:15 by *n* he resorted to dividing
19:33 wine to drink during that *n*
19:34 with my father last *n*
19:35 to drink during that *n* also
20:3 to Abimelech in a dream by *n*
24:23 father for us to spend the *n*
24:25 also a place to spend the *n*
24:54 they spent the *n* there and
26:24 appear to him during that *n*
28:11 set about spending the *n*
30:16 lay down with her that *n*
31:24 in a dream by *n* and said to
31:29 God . . . talked to me last *n*
31:39 or was stolen by *n*, you
31:40 and the cold by *n*, and my
31:42 so he reproved you last *n*
31:54 passed the *n* in the mountain
32:13 kept lodging there on that *n*
32:21 lodged that *n* in the camp
32:22 that *n* he rose and took his
40:5 dream in the one *n*, each one
41:11 in the one *n*, both I and he
46:2 in visions of the *n* and said
Ex 10:13 all that day and all *n*
12:8 must eat the flesh on this *n*
12:12 *n* and strike every firstborn
12:30 Pharaoh got up at *n*, he and
12:31 called Moses and Aaron by *n*
12:42 It is a *n* for observance
12:42 this *n* is one for observance
14:20 it kept lighting up the *n*
14:20 near that group all *n* long
14:21 strong east wind all *n* long
40:38 fire continued upon it by *n*
Le 6:9 upon the altar all *n* long until
8:35 day and *n* for seven days, and
19:13 stay all *n* with you until
Nu 9:16 the appearance of fire by *n*
9:21 by *n* that the cloud lifted
11:9 descended upon the camp by *n*
11:32 all *n* and all the next day
14:1 weeping all through that *n*
14:14 in the pillar of fire by *n*
22:20 God came to Balaam by *n* and
De 1:33 by fire at *n* for you to see
16:1 brought you out of Egypt by *n*
16:4 stay all *n* until the morning
21:23 not stay all *n* on the stake
23:10 a pollution that occurs at *n*
28:66 and be in dread *n* and day
Jos 1:8 read in it day and *n*
3:1 spending the *n* there before
8:3 and to send them off by *n*
8:9 that *n* in the midst of the
8:13 to go during that *n* into the
10:9 All *n* long he had gone up
Jg 6:25 that *n* that Jehovah went on
6:27 by day, he went doing it by *n*
6:40 God did that way on that *n*
7:9 that *n* that Jehovah proceeded
7:19 start of the middle *n* watch
9:32 now rise up by *n*, you and the
9:34 rose up by *n*, and they began
16:2 and lay in wait for him all *n*
16:2 they kept quiet the whole *n*
18:2 and got to spend the *n* there
19:25 kept on abusing her all *n*
20:5 surround the house . . . by *n*
Ru 1:16 where you spend the *n* I shall
1:16 I shall spend the *n*
1Sa 14:34 that was in his hand that *n*
14:36 after the Philistines by *n*
15:11 crying out to Jehovah all *n*
15:16 Jehovah spoke to me last *n*
19:10 might escape during that *n*
19:24 that day and all that *n*
25:16 both by *n* and by day, all
26:7 to the people by *n*; and
1Sa 28:8 came to the woman by *n*
28:20 whole day and the whole *n*
28:25 and went away during that *n*
31:12 all *n* long and took the
2Sa 2:29 all that *n* and went crossing
2:32 went marching all *n* long
4:7 road to the Arabah all *n* long
7:4 that *n* that the word of
12:16 spent the *n* and lay down
17:8 spend the *n* with the people
21:10 beasts of the field by *n*
1Ki 3:5 to Solomon in a dream by *n*
3:19 son of this woman died at *n*
3:20 up in the middle of the *n*
8:29 toward this house *n* and day
8:59 our God by day and *n*
19:9 he might spend the *n* there
2Ki 6:14 to come by *n* and close in
7:12 the king rose up by *n* and
8:21 by *n* and got to strike down
19:35 that *n* that the angel of
25:4 the men of war fled by *n*
1Ch 9:27 they would spend the *n*
9:33 by day and by *n* it was their
17:3 that *n* that the word of God
2Ch 1:7 *n* God appeared to Solomon and
6:20 toward this house day and *n*
7:12 to Solomon during the *n* and
21:9 he rose up by *n* and went
35:14 and the fat pieces until *n*
Ne 1:6 day and *n*, concerning the sons
2:12 rose up by *n*, I and a few men
2:13 out by the Valley Gate by *n*
2:15 in the torrent valley by *n*
4:9 day and *n* on account of them
4:22 Let the men spend the *n*, each
4:22 a guard by *n* and workers by
6:10 by *n* they are coming in to
9:12 by a pillar of fire by *n*
9:19 pillar of fire by *n* to light
13:20 spent the *n* outside
13:21 spending the *n* in front of
Es 4:16 for three days, *n* and day
6:1 that *n* the king's sleep fled
Job 3:3 Also the *n* that someone said
3:6 That *n*—let gloom take it
3:7 That *n*—let it become sterile
4:13 from visions of the *n*, When
5:14 at midday as if at *n*
17:12 *N* they keep putting for day
20:8 away like a vision of the *n*
24:7 Naked, they pass the *n*
24:14 during the *n* he becomes a
27:20 At *n* a stormwind will
30:17 At *n* my very bones have
31:32 alien . . . would spend the *n*
33:15 a dream, a vision of the *n*
34:20 in the middle of the *n*
34:25 he does overthrow them at *n*
35:10 giving melodies in the *n*
36:20 Do not pant for the *n*
39:9 spend the *n* by your manger
39:28 and stays during the *n*
Ps 1:2 reads in an undertone day and *n*
6:6 All *n* long I make my couch
17:3 have made inspection by *n*
19:2, 2 one *n* after another *n*
22:2 by *n*, and there is no silence
32:4 day and *n* your hand was heavy
42:3 have become food day and *n*
42:8 by *n* his song will be with
55:10 Day and *n* they go round
63:6 During the *n* watches I
74:16 also, to you the *n* belongs
77:2 At *n* my very hand has been
77:6 my string music in the *n*
78:14 whole *n* with a light of fire
88:1 In the *n* also in front of you
90:4 And as a watch during the *n*
91:5 of anything dreadful by *n*
104:20 that it may become *n*
105:39 fire to give light by *n*
119:55 In the *n* I have remembered
119:148 ahead of the *n* watches
121:6 Nor the moon by *n*
136:9 for combined dominion by *n*
139:11 *n* would be light about me
139:12 *n* itself would shine just
Pr 7:9 approach of the *n* and the
19:23 will spend the *n* satisfied
31:15 gets up while it is still *n*
31:18 lamp does not go out at *n*
Ec 2:23 *n* his heart just does not lie
8:16 either by day or by *n*
Ca 1:13 breasts he will spend the *n*
5:2 hair with the drops of the *n*
Isa 4:5 of a flaming fire by *n*
10:29 for them to spend the *n*
15:1 the *n* it has been despoiled
15:1 Because in the *n* it has been
16:3 *n* in the midst of noontime
21:11 Watchman, what about the *n*?
21:11 Watchman, what about the *n*?
21:12 has to come, and also the *n*
21:13 plain you will spend the *n*
26:9 I have desired you in the *n*
27:3 safeguard her even *n* and day
28:19 the day and during the *n*
29:7 dream, in a vision of the *n*
30:29 song like that in the *n*
34:10 By *n* or by day it will not
38:12 daylight till *n* you keep
38:13 daylight till *n* you keep
60:11 even by day or by *n*, in
62:6 All day long and all *n* long
65:4 pass the *n* even in the watch
Jer 6:5 let us go up during the *n*
9:1 weep day and *n* for the slain
14:8 turned aside to spend the *n*
14:17 with tears *n* and day and
16:13 serve other gods day and *n*
31:35 the stars for light by *n*
33:20 and my covenant of the *n*
33:20 day and *n* not to occur in
33:25 covenant of the day and *n*
36:30 and to the frost by *n*
39:4 go out by *n* from the city
49:9 If thieves came in by *n*
52:7 from the city by *n* by the
La 1:2 she weeps during the *n*, and
2:18 just like a torrent day and *n*
2:19 Whine during the *n* at the
Da 2:19 to Daniel in a *n* vision the
5:30 that very *n* Belshazzar the
6:18 and spent the *n* fasting, and
7:2 in my visions during the *n*
7:7 in the visions of the *n*, and
7:13 in the visions of the *n*, and
Ho 4:5 stumble with you, as at *n*
7:6 All *n* long their baker is
Joe 1:13 spend the *n* in sackcloth
Am 5:8 made day itself dark as *n*
Ob 5 if despoilers came in by *n*
Jon 4:10 a mere growth of a *n* and
4:10 as a mere growth of a *n*
Mic 3:6 you men will have *n*, so
Zep 2:14 spend the *n* right among her
Zec 1:8 I saw in the *n*, and, look!
14:7 day, neither will it be *n*
Mt 2:14 child and its mother by *n*
14:25 fourth watch period of the *n*
21:17 to Bethany and passed the *n*
25:6 middle of the *n* there arose a
26:31 be stumbled . . . on this *n*
26:34 On this *n*, before a cock
28:13 disciples came in the *n* and
Mr 4:27 he sleeps at *n* and rises up
5:5 *n* and day, he was crying out
6:48 the fourth watch of the *n*
14:30 this *n*, before a cock crows
Lu 2:8 watches in the *n* over their
2:37 sacred service *n* and day
5:5 for a whole *n* we toiled and
6:12 the whole *n* in prayer to God
12:20 this *n* they are demanding
17:34 In that *n* two men will be
18:7 who cry out to him day and *n*
21:37 by *n* he would go out and
Joh 3:2 came to him in the *n* and
9:4 *n* is coming when no man can
11:10 walks in the *n*, he bumps
13:30 And it was *n*
19:39 came to him in the *n* the
21:3 that *n* they caught nothing
Ac 5:19 during the *n* Jehovah's angel
9:24 gates both day and *n* in order
9:25 by *n* through an opening in
12:6 that *n* Peter was sleeping
16:9 during the *n* a vision appeared
16:25 the middle of the *n* Paul and
16:33 in that hour of the *n* and
17:10 by *n* the brothers sent both
18:9 by *n* the Lord said to Paul
20:31 for three years, *n* and day, I
23:11 following *n* the Lord stood
23:23 at the third hour of the *n*
23:31 by *n* to Antipatris
26:7 him sacred service *n* and day

Ac 27:23 this *n* there stood near
27:27 fourteenth *n* fell and we
Ro 13:12 *n* is well along; the day
1Co 11:23 in the *n* in which he was
2Co 11:25 a *n* and a day I have spent
1Th 2:9 was with working *n* and day
3:10 while *n* and day we make
5:2 exactly as a thief in the *n*
5:5 We belong neither to *n* nor to
5:7 are accustomed to sleep at *n*
5:7 drunk are usually drunk at *n*
2Th 3:8 by labor and toil *n* and day
1Ti 5:5 and prayers *n* and day
2Ti 1:3 my supplications, *n* and day
Re 4:8 they have no rest day and *n*
7:15 sacred service day and *n* in
8:12 and the *n* likewise
12:10 accuses them day and *n*
14:11 day and *n* they have no rest
20:10 be tormented day and *n*
21:25 for *n* will not exist there
22:5 Also, *n* will be no more, and

Nightjar
Isa 34:14 *n* will certainly take its

Nights
Ge 7:4 rain . . . days and forty *n*
7:12 for forty days and forty *n*
Ex 24:18 forty days and forty *n*
34:28 forty days and forty *n*
De 9:9 forty days and forty *n*
9:11 the forty days and forty *n*
9:18 forty days and forty *n*
9:25 forty days and forty *n*, for
10:10 forty days and forty *n*
1Sa 30:12 for three days and three *n*
1Ki 19:8 for forty days and forty *n*
Job 2:13 seven days and seven *n*, and
7:3 *n* of trouble they have counted
Ps 16:7 during the *n* my kidneys have
92:2 faithfulness during the *n*
134:1 house of Jehovah during the *n*
Ca 3:1 On my bed during the *n* I have
3:8 because of dread during the *n*
Isa 21:8 I am stationed all the *n*
Jon 1:17 three days and three *n*
Mt 4:2 fasted forty days and forty *n*
12:40 fish three days and three *n*
12:40 earth three days and three *n*
2Co 6:5 by sleepless *n*, by times
11:27 in sleepless *n* often, in

Nighttime
Ex 13:21 the *n* in a pillar of fire to
13:21 to go in the daytime and *n*
13:22 the pillar of fire in the *n*

Nile
Ge 41:1 was standing by the river *N*
41:2 ascending out of the river *N*
41:2 feeding among the *N* grass
41:3 out of the river *N*, ugly in
41:3 by the bank of the river *N*
41:17 on the bank of the river *N*
41:18 ascending out of the river *N*
41:18 to feed among the *N* grass
Ex 1:22 to throw into the river *N*
2:3 by the bank of the river *N*
2:5 came down to bathe in the *N*
2:5 walking by the side of the *N*
4:9 take some water from the *N*
4:9 water . . . from the *N* River
7:15 meet him by the edge of the *N*
7:17 water that is in the *N* River
7:18 fish that are in the *N* River
7:18 *N* River will actually stink
7:18 drinking water from the *N*
7:19 rivers, over their *N* canals
7:20 water that was in the *N* River
7:20 *N* River was turned into blood
7:21 fish . . . in the *N* River died
7:21 and the *N* River began to stink
7:21 drink water from the *N* River
7:24 digging round about the *N*
7:24 unable to drink . . . of the *N*
7:25 Jehovah's striking the *N*
8:3 *N* River . . . teem with frogs
8:5 over the rivers, the *N* canals
8:9 Only in the *N* River will they
8:11 Only in the *N* River will they
17:5 which you struck the *N* River
Jos 13:3 branch of the *N* that is in
2Ki 19:24 all the *N* canals of Egypt
Ps 78:44 to blood their *N* canals
Isa 7:18 of the *N* canals of Egypt
Isa 19:6 *N* canals of Egypt must
19:7 bare places by the *N* River
19:7 at the mouth of the *N* River
19:7 seedland of the *N* River will
19:8 fishhooks into the *N* River
23:3 harvest of the *N*, your
23:10 land like the *N* River
37:25 all the *N* canals of Egypt
Jer 46:7 up just like the *N* River
46:8 up just like the *N* River
Eze 29:3 in the midst of his *N* canals
29:3 My *N* River belongs to me
29:4 the fish of your *N* canals to
29:4 the midst of your *N* canals
29:4 the fish of your *N* canals
29:5 the fish of your *N* canals
29:9 To me the *N* River belongs
29:10 and against your *N* canals
30:12 make the *N* canals dry
Am 8:8 just like the *N* and be tossed
8:8 sink down like the *N* of Egypt
9:5 certainly come up like the *N*
9:5 sink down like the *N* of Egypt
Na 3:8 was sitting by the *N* canals
Zec 10:11 all the depths of the *N*

Nimrah
Nu 32:3 and Dibon and Jazer and *N* and

Nimrim
Isa 15:6 waters of *N* become sheer
Jer 48:34 even the waters of *N*

Nimrod
Ge 10:8 And Cush became father to *N*
10:9 like *N* a mighty hunter in
1Ch 1:10 Cush . . . father to *N*
Mic 5:6 land of *N* in its entrances

Nimshi
1Ki 19:16 Jehu the grandson of *N*
2Ki 9:2 Jehoshaphat the son of *N*
9:14 Jehoshaphat the son of *N*
9:20 Jehu the grandson of *N*
2Ch 22:7 Jehu the grandson of *N*, whom

Nine
Ge 5:5 Adam . . . *n* hundred and thirty
5:8 Seth . . . *n* hundred and twelve
5:11 Enosh . . . *n* hundred and five
5:14 Kenan . . . *n* hundred and ten
5:20 *n* hundred and sixty-two
5:27 *n* hundred and sixty-nine years
9:29 *n* hundred and fifty years
11:19 live two hundred and *n* years
Nu 29:26 on the fifth day *n* bulls
34:13 to the *n* and a half tribes
De 3:11 *N* cubits is its length, and
Jos 13:7 the *n* tribes and the half
14:2 *n* tribes and the half tribe
15:44 *n* cities and their
15:54 *n* cities and their
21:16 *n* cities out of these two
Jg 4:3 he had *n* hundred war chariots
4:13 the *n* hundred war chariots
2Sa 24:8 *n* months and twenty days
2Ki 17:1 Hoshea . . . for *n* years
1Ch 3:8 and Eliada and Eliphelet, *n*
9:9 were *n* hundred and fifty-six
Ezr 2:8 *n* hundred and forty-five
2:36 *n* hundred and seventy-three
Ne 7:38 three thousand *n* hundred and
7:39 *n* hundred and seventy-three
11:1 *n* other parts in the other
11:8 *n* hundred and twenty-eight
Lu 17:17 Where, then, are the other *n*?

Nineteen
Ge 11:25 live a hundred and *n* years
Jos 19:38 *n* cities and their
2Sa 2:30 of David *n* men and Asahel

Nineteenth
2Ki 25:8 *n* year of King Nebuchadnezzar
1Ch 24:16 for Pethahiah the *n*
25:26 for the *n*, for Mallothi
Jer 52:12 in the *n* year of King

Ninety
Ge 5:9 And Enosh lived on for *n* years
17:17 woman *n* years old give
1Ch 9:6 and six hundred and *n* brothers
Eze 4:5 three hundred and *n* days, and
4:9 three hundred and *n* days you
41:12 and its length was *n* cubits
Da 12:11 two hundred and *n* days

Ninety-eight
1Sa 4:15 Eli was *n* years old, and his
Ezr 2:16 sons of Ater, of Hezekiah, *n*
Ne 7:21 sons of Ater, of Hezekiah, *n*

Ninety-five
Ge 5:17 eight hundred and *n* years and
5:30 live five hundred and *n* years
Ezr 2:20 the sons of Gibbar, *n*
Ne 7:25 the sons of Gibeon, *n*

Ninety-nine
Ge 17:1 Abram got to be *n* years old
17:24 Abraham was *n* years old when
Mt 18:12 will he not leave the *n* upon
18:13 the *n* that have not strayed
Lu 15:4 will not leave the *n* behind
15:7 than over *n* righteous ones

Ninety-six
Ezr 8:35 *n* rams, seventy-seven male
Jer 52:23 pomegranates came to be *n*

Ninety-two
Ezr 2:58 three hundred and *n*
Ne 7:60 three hundred and *n*

Nineveh
Ge 10:11 set himself to building *N*
10:12 Resen between *N* and Calah
2Ki 19:36 he took up dwelling in *N*
Isa 37:37 and took up dwelling in *N*
Jon 1:2 go to *N* the great city, and
3:2 go to *N* the great city, and
3:3 Jonah got up and went to *N*
3:3 *N* herself proved to be a city
3:4 and *N* will be overthrown
3:5 *N* began to put faith in God
3:6 word reached the king of *N*
3:7 and he had it said in *N*
4:11 sorry for *N* the great city
Na 1:1 The pronouncement against *N*
2:8 *N*, from the days that she has
3:7 *N* has been despoiled! Who will
Zep 2:13 make *N* a desolate waste
Mt 12:41 Men of *N* will rise up in
Lu 11:32 men of *N* will rise in the

Ninevites
Lu 11:30 Jonah became a sign to the *N*

Ninth
Le 23:32 *n* of the month in the
25:22 the old crop until the *n* year
Nu 7:60 On the *n* day . . . Benjamin
2Ki 17:6 In the *n* year of Hoshea
18:10 *n* year of Hoshea the king
25:1 the *n* year of his being king
25:3 *n* day of the fourth month
1Ch 12:12 the eighth, Elzabad the *n*
24:11 for Jeshua the *n*, for
25:16 the *n* for Mattaniah, his
27:12, 12 The *n* for the *n* month
Ezr 10:9 *n* month on the twentieth day
Jer 36:9 in the *n* month, that all the
36:22 *n* month, with a brazier
39:1 *n* year of Zedekiah the king
39:2 on the *n* day of the month
52:4 *n* year of his being king, in
52:6 on the *n* day of the month
Eze 24:1 the *n* year, in the tenth
Hag 2:10 the *n* month, in the second
2:18 the *n* month, from the day
Zec 7:1 fourth day of the *n* month
Mt 20:5 the sixth and the *n* hour and
27:45 until the *n* hour
27:46 the *n* hour Jesus called out
Mr 15:33 until the *n* hour
15:34 at the *n* hour Jesus called
Lu 23:44 darkness . . . until the *n* hour
Ac 3:1 hour of prayer, the *n* hour
10:3 *n* hour of the day he saw
10:30 in my house at the *n* hour
Re 21:20 the *n* topaz, the tenth

Nip
Le 1:15 and *n* off its head and make
5:8 *n* off its head at the front of

Nipper
Am 7:14 a *n* of figs of sycamore trees

Nisan
Ne 2:1 month *N*, in the twentieth year
Es 3:7 In the first month . . . *N*

Nisroch
2Ki 19:37 at the house of *N* his god
Isa 37:38 at the house of *N* his god

No*
Ps 14:1 There is *n* Jehovah

Ps 14:1 There is *n* one doing good
14:3 There is *n* one doing good
Jer 46:25 attention upon Amon from *N*
Eze 30:14 acts of judgment in *N*
30:15 cut off the crowd of *N*
30:16 *N* itself will come to be
Mt 5:37, 37 *Yes* mean Yes, your *N*, *N*
2Co 1:17, 17 be Yes, Yes and *N*, *N*
1:18 to you is not Yes and yet *N*
1:19 not become Yes and yet *N*
Jas 5:12, 12 and your *N*, *N*, so that

Noadiah
Ezr 8:33 *N* the son of Binnui the
Ne 6:14 and also *N* the prophetess and

Noah
Ge 5:29 proceeded to call his name *N*
5:30 after his fathering *N* Lamech
5:32 *N* got to be five hundred years
5:32 *N* became father to Shem, Ham
6:8 *N* found favor in the eyes of
6:9 This is the history of *N*
6:9 *N* was a righteous man
6:9 *N* walked with the true God
6:10 In time *N* became father to
6:13 God said to *N*: The end of all
6:22 *N* proceeded to do according
7:1 Jehovah said to *N*: Go, you and
7:5 *N* proceeded to do according
7:6 *N* was six hundred years old
7:7 *N* went in, and his sons and
7:9 they went in by twos to *N*
7:9 just as God had commanded *N*
7:13 *N* went in, and Shem and Ham
7:13 the wife of *N* and the three
7:15 they kept going to *N* inside
7:23 *N* . . . kept on surviving
8:1 God remembered *N* and every
8:6 *N* proceeded to open the window
8:11 *N* got to know that the waters
8:13 *N* proceeded to remove the
8:15 God now spoke to *N*, saying
8:18 *N* went out, and also his sons
8:20 *N* began to build an altar to
9:1 And God went on to bless *N* and
9:8 God went on to say to *N* and to
9:17 God repeated to *N*: This is the
9:20 *N* started off as a farmer
9:24 *N* awoke from his wine and got
9:28 *N* continued to live three
9:29 days of *N* amounted to nine
10:32 families of the sons of *N*
Nu 26:33 of Zelophehad . . . *N*, Hoglah
27:1 daughters of Zelophehad . . . *N*
36:11 Milcah and *N*, the daughters
Jos 17:3 *N*, Hoglah, Milcah and Tirzah
1Ch 1:4 *N*, Shem, Ham and Japheth
Isa 54:9 This is just as the days of *N*
54:9 sworn that the waters of *N*
Eze 14:14 midst of it, *N*, Daniel and
14:20 even were *N*, Daniel and Job
Mt 24:37 just as the days of *N* were
24:38 until the day that *N* entered
Lu 3:36 son of Shem, son of *N*, son of
17:26 it occurred in the days of *N*
17:27 *N* entered into the ark, and
Heb 11:7 By faith *N*, after being given
2Pe 2:5 *N*, a preacher of righteousness

Noah's
Ge 7:11 six hundredth year of *N* life
7:13 Shem and Ham and Japheth, *N*
9:18 *N* sons who came out of the
9:19 *N* sons, and from these was
10:1 history of *N* sons, Shem, Ham
1Pe 3:20 waiting in *N* days, while the

No-amon
Na 3:8 Are you better than *N*, that

Nob
1Sa 21:1 David came into *N* to
22:9 son of Jesse come to *N* to
22:11 the priests that were in *N*
22:19 *N* the city of the priests
Ne 11:32 Anathoth, *N*, Ananiah
Isa 10:32 day in *N* to make a halt

Nobah
Nu 32:42 *N* marched and went capturing
32:42 to call it *N* by his own name
Jg 8:11 to the east of *N* and Jogbehah

Noble
Jg 5:29 The wise ones of her *n* ladies
Es 6:9 of one of the king's *n* princes
Job 21:28 is the house of the *n* one
30:15 My *n* bearing is chased like
34:19 more consideration to the *n*
Pr 17:7 for a *n* the lip of falsehood
19:6 who soften the face of a *n*
25:7 than to abase you before a *n*
Ec 10:17 king is the son of *n* ones
Isa 32:5 will not be said to be *n*
Lu 19:12 man of *n* birth traveled to
1Co 1:26 not many of *n* birth

Noble-minded
Ac 17:11 *n* than those in Thessalonica

Nobles
Nu 21:18 *n* of the people excavated it
1Sa 2:8 To make them sit with *n*
1Ki 21:8 the *n* that were in his city
21:11 *n* that were dwelling in his
Ne 2:16 the *n* and the deputy rulers
4:14 the *n* and the deputy rulers
4:19 to the *n* and the deputy rulers
5:7 the *n* and the deputy rulers
6:17 the *n* of Judah were making
7:5 collect together the *n* and the
13:17 fault with the *n* of Judah
Es 1:3 the *n* and the princes of
Job 12:21 pouring out contempt upon *n*
34:18 To *n*, You are wicked?
Ps 47:9 *n* of the peoples themselves
83:11 *n*, make these like Oreb and
107:40 pouring out contempt upon *n*
113:8 To make him sit with *n*
113:8 With the *n* of his people
118:9 Than to trust in *n*
146:3 Do not put your trust in *n*
Pr 8:16 and *n* are all judging in
17:26 To strike *n* is against what
Isa 13:2 into the entrances of the *n*
34:12 *n*—there are none there
Jer 27:20 *n* of Judah and Jerusalem
39:6 *n* of Judah the king of
Da 1:3 royal offspring and of the *n*

Nobody
Ex 2:12 saw there was *n* in sight
16:19 Let *n* leave any of it until
16:29 *n* go out from his locality
22:10 led off while *n* is looking
34:3 *n* may go up with you and, too
34:3 let *n* else be seen in all the
34:24 and *n* will desire your land
De 7:24 *N* will take a firm stand
34:6 *n* has come to know his grave
Jos 1:5 *N* will take a firm stand
Jg 19:15 *n* taking them on into the
19:18 *n* taking me on into the
2Sa 9:3 there *n* of the house of Saul
2Ki 7:5 and, look! *n* was there
7:10 *n* there nor sound of a man
Isa 47:8 I am, and there is *n* else
47:10 I am, and there is *n* else
50:2 there was *n* answering
60:15 with *n* passing through
Jer 7:33 *n* to make them tremble
Da 2:11 *n* else exists who can show it
8:27 there was *n* understanding it
Am 6:10 And he will certainly say, *N!*
Zep 2:15 I am, and there is *n* else
Mt 8:28 *n* had the courage to pass by
9:16 *N* sews a patch of unshrunk
9:30 See that *n* gets to know it
20:7 Because *n* has hired us
22:46 *n* was able to say a word in
24:4 Look out that *n* misleads you
24:36 that day and hour *n* knows
Mr 1:44 See that you tell *n* a thing
2:21 *N* sews a patch of unshrunk
2:22 *n* puts new wine into old
5:3 *n* was able to bind him fast
5:4 *n* had the strength to subdue
10:18 *N* is good, except one, God
12:34 *n* had the courage anymore to
13:5 Look out that *n* misleads you
13:32 that day or the hour *n* knows
16:8 they told *n* anything, for
Lu 5:14 gave the man orders to tell *n*
18:19 *N* is good, except one, God
Joh 7:4 *n* does anything in secret
1Co 12:3 *n* when speaking by God's
12:3 and *n* can say: Jesus is Lord
Re 13:17 *n* might be able to buy or

Nodab
1Ch 5:19 began to make war upon . . . *N*

Nodded
Mt 25:5 they all *n* and went to sleep
Joh 13:24 Simon Peter *n* to this one
Ac 24:10 governor *n* to him to speak

Nogah
1Ch 3:7 *N* and Nepheg and Japhia
14:6 and *N* and Nepheg and Japhia

Nohah
1Ch 8:2 *N* the fourth and Rapha the

Noise
Ex 32:17 to hear the *n* of the people
32:17 a *n* of battle in the camp
1Sa 7:10 to thunder with a loud *n* on
1Ki 1:40 the earth was split by the *n*
1:41 *n* of the town in an uproar
1:45 the *n* that you men heard
Ps 65:7 is stilling the *n* of the seas
65:7 The *n* of their waves and the
74:23 *n* of those rising up against
Isa 17:12 *n* of national groups, who
17:12 like the *n* of mighty waters
17:13 like the *n* of many waters
24:8 *n* of the highly elated ones
25:5 *n* of strangers you subdue
Jer 25:31 A *n* will certainly come
46:17 king of Egypt is a mere *n*
51:55 *n* of their voice will
Am 2:2 and with *n* Moab must die
Ac 2:2 *n* just like that of a rushing
2Pe 3:10 pass away with a hissing *n*

Noises
Job 39:7 *n* of a stalker it does not

Noisily
Ac 1:18 he *n* burst in his midst and

Noisy
Pr 1:21 upper end of the *n* streets
Mic 2:12 they will be *n* with men
Mt 9:23 and the crowd in *n* confusion
Mr 5:38 he beheld the *n* confusion and
5:39 are you causing *n* confusion

None
Ge 23:6 *N* of us will hold back his
39:11 *n* of the men of the house
41:24 but there was *n* telling me
Ex 9:14 know that there is *n* like me
10:23 *n* of them got up from his
12:22 *n* of you should go out of
15:26 put *n* of the maladies upon
16:26 seventh day . . . *n* will form
16:27 but they found *n*
33:4 *n* of them put his ornaments
Le 21:14 *n* of these may he take, but
22:22 *n* of these must you present
Nu 7:9 the sons of Kohath he gave *n*
De 10:17 treats *n* with partiality nor
14:8 *N* of their flesh must you eat
16:16 *n* should appear before
23:2 *n* of his may come into the
23:3 *n* of theirs may come into the
23:17 *N* of the daughters of Israel
25:3 He should add *n*, for fear he
33:26 There is *n* like the true God
1Sa 10:24 *n* like him among all the
14:24 *n* of the people tasted bread
21:9 There is *n* like it. Give it
30:22 give them *n* of the spoil
2Sa 1:21 was *n* anointed with oil
1Ki 9:22 were *n* of the sons of Israel
12:20 *N* became a follower of the
15:22 Judah—there was *n* exempt
22:47 king, there was *n* in Edom
2Ki 6:12 *N*, my lord the king, but it
10:23 *n* of the worshipers of
17:26 *n* knowing the religion of
17:34 were *n* fearing Jehovah and
17:34 *n* doing according to his
1Ch 4:27 *n* of their families had as
17:20 Jehovah, there is *n* like you
2Ch 8:9 *n* out of the sons of Israel
30:26 *n* like this in Jerusalem
Ezr 8:15 *n* of the sons of Levi did I
9:14 will be *n* remaining and
9:14 remaining and *n* escaping
Ne 13:24 *n* of them knowing how to
Es 5:13 *n* of it suits me as long as
Job 3:9 for the light and there be *n*
32:12 *N* of you answering his
33:33 If there are *n*, you yourself
34:27 *n* of his ways have they
41:10 *N* is so audacious that he

Ps 14:4 *n* of the practicers of what
25:3 *n* of those hoping in you will
34:22 *n* of those taking refuge in
40:5 *n* to be compared to you
53:4 *n* of the practicers of what
69:20 sympathy, but there was *n*
69:20 comforters, but I found *n*
76:5 *n* of all the valiant men have
86:8 *n* like you among the gods
Pr 2:19 *N* of those having relations
14:6 find wisdom, and there is *n*
Ca 4:2 *n* among them having lost its
6:6 *n* among them having lost its
Isa 33:20 *n* of its ropes will be torn
34:12 nobles—there are *n* there
35:9 *N* will be found there
41:17 for water, but there is *n*
43:10 there continued to be *n*
44:8 no Rock. I have recognized *n*
45:6 that there is *n* besides me
45:21 there being *n* excepting me
51:18 was *n* of all the sons that
51:18 *n* of all the sons that she
54:14 for you will fear *n*—and
56:10 *N* of them have taken note
59:11 justice, but there was *n*
64:4 time long ago *n* have heard
66:4 there were *n* that listened
Jer 10:4 down, that *n* may reel
23:4 and *n* will be missing, is
32:33 *n* of them listening to
35:14 drunk *n* down to this day
La 1:4 are *n* coming to the festival
4:14 So that *n* are able to touch
Eze 7:25 peace but there will be *n*
18:11 he himself has done *n* of
18:24 *n* of all his righteous acts
29:18 wages, there proved to be *n*
31:14 *n* of the watered trees may
31:14 *n* drinking water may stand
33:16 *N* of his sins with which
33:32 there are *n* doing them
37:8 breath, there was *n* in them
39:28 leave *n* of them remaining
Ho 7:7 *n* among them is calling out
Joe 2:2 *n* again to the years of
Jon 3:7 *N* should take food
Zec 14:18 shall be *n*. The scourge
Mt 12:43 a resting-place, and finds *n*
26:60 they found *n*, although many
Mr 11:2 *n* of mankind has yet sat
Lu 3:11 share with the man that has *n*
4:26 Elijah was sent to *n* of those
7:28 there is *n* greater than John
11:24 and, after finding *n*, it says
13:6 for fruit on it, but found *n*
13:7 but have found *n*. Cut it down!
14:24 *N* of those men that were
14:33 *n* of you that does not say
17:18 Were *n* found that turned
19:30 which *n* of mankind ever sat
Joh 10:26 you are *n* of my sheep
13:28 *n* of those reclining at the
Ac 8:24 *n* of the things you have said
25:11 *n* of those things exists of
Ro 10:11 *N* that rests his faith on
14:7 *N* of us, in fact, lives with
1Co 1:14 I baptized *n* of you except
7:29 be as though they had *n*
1Pe 4:15 let *n* of you suffer as a

Nonetheless
1Sa 1:5 *N* it was Hannah that he loved

Nonexistent
Isa 40:17 nations are as something *n*
41:12 something *n* and as nothing
41:24 You are something *n*, and
41:29 All of them are something *n*

Nonsense
Lu 24:11 sayings appeared as *n* to

Noon
Ge 43:16 men are to eat with me at *n*
43:25 for Joseph's coming at *n*
1Ki 18:26 Baal from morning till *n*
18:27 *n* . . . Elijah began to mock
18:29 as soon as *n* was past and
20:16 they began to go out at *n*
2Ki 4:20 upon her knees until *n*, and
Isa 59:10 stumbled at high *n* just as
Am 8:9 the sun go down at high *n*
Zep 2:4 at high *n* they will drive her

Noonday
2Sa 4:5 he was taking his *n* siesta

Noontime
Job 24:11 they pass the *n*
Ps 55:17 Evening and morning and *n*
Isa 16:3 the night in the midst of *n*

Noose
1Co 7:35 not that I may cast a *n* upon

Noph
Isa 19:13 princes of *N* have been
Jer 2:16 the sons of *N* and Tahpanes
44:1 and in *N* and in the land of
46:14 publish it in *N* and in
46:19 *N* itself will become a
Eze 30:13 gods to cease out of *N*
30:16 as regards *N*—there will be

Nophah
Nu 21:30 the women up to *N*, the men

Normal
Ex 14:27 come back to its *n* condition
2Co 4:7 power beyond what is *n* may

Normally
Mr 7:35 and he began speaking *n*

North
Ge 14:15 Hobah, which is *n* of
28:14 to the east and to the *n* and
Ex 26:35 table you will put on the *n*
27:11 is for the *n* side in length
38:11 *n* side there were a hundred
40:22 to the *n* outside the curtain
Le 1:11 altar to the *n* before Jehovah
Nu 2:25 Dan will be toward the *n* in
3:35 the tabernacle toward the *n*
34:7 will become your *n* boundary
34:9 will become your *n* boundary
35:5 *n* side two thousand cubits
De 2:3 Change your direction to the *n*
3:27 *n* and south and east and see
Jos 8:11 camp to the *n* of Ai, with
8:13 was to the *n* of the city and
11:2 the kings that were to the *n*
13:3 border of Ekron to the *n*
15:6 at the *n* of Beth-arabah, and
15:8 plain of Rephaim to the *n*
15:10 Mount Jearim at the *n*
15:11 slope of Ekron to the *n*
16:6 Michmethath was on the *n*
17:9 the *n* of the torrent valley
17:10 and to the *n*, Manasseh's
17:10 the *n* they reach to Asher
18:5 on their territory to the *n*
18:12 slope of Jericho on the *n*
18:16 plain of Rephaim to the *n*
19:14 on the *n* to Hannathon, and
19:27 valley of Iphtah-el to the *n*
24:30 Ephraim, *n* of Mount Gaash
Jg 2:9 on the *n* of Mount Gaash
7:1 on the *n* of him, at the hill
21:19 which is to the *n* of Bethel
1Sa 14:5 on the *n* facing Michmash
1Ki 7:25 twelve bulls, three facing *n*
2Ki 16:14 at the *n* side of his altar
1Ch 9:24 gatekeepers . . . to the *n*
26:14 got to come out to the *n*
26:17 to the *n* for a day, four
2Ch 4:4 bulls, three facing the *n* and
Job 26:7 stretching out the *n* over the
37:9 out of the *n* winds the cold
37:22 Out of the *n* golden splendor
Ps 48:2 on the remote sides of the *n*
89:12 *n* and the south—you yourself
107:3 the *n* and from the south
Pr 25:23 wind from the *n* brings forth
Ec 1:6 it is circling around to the *n*
11:3 to the south or if to the *n*
Ca 4:16 Awake, O *n* wind, and come in
Isa 14:13 the remotest parts of the *n*
14:31 out of the *n* a smoke is
41:25 someone from the *n*, and he
43:6 shall say to the *n*, Give up!
49:12 from the *n* and from the
Jer 1:13 mouth is away from the *n*
1:14 Out of the *n* the calamity
1:15 of the kingdoms of the *n*
3:12 these words to the *n* and say
3:18 out of the land of the *n*
4:6 I am bringing in from the *n*
6:1 out of the *n*, even a great
6:22 from the land of the *n*
10:22 from the land of the *n*
13:20 who are coming from the *n*
15:12 iron out of the *n*, and
16:15 out of the land of the *n*
Jer 23:8 out of the land of the *n*
25:9 all the families of the *n*
25:26 all the kings of the *n* who
31:8 from the land of the *n*
46:6 Up *n* by the bank of the river
46:10 land of the *n* by the river
46:20 From the *n* a mosquito
46:24 hand of the people of the *n*
47:2 are coming up from the *n*
50:3 has come up from the *n*
50:9 from the land of the *n*
50:41 is coming in from the *n*
51:48 of the *n* there will come
Eze 1:4 wind coming from the *n*, a
8:5 eyes in the direction of the *n*
8:5 in the direction of the *n*
8:5 the *n* of the gate of the altar
8:14 which is toward the *n*, and
9:2 upper gate that faces to the *n*
20:47 from the south to the *n*
21:4 all flesh from south to *n*
26:7 king of Babylon from the *n*
32:30 the dukes of the *n* are
38:6 the remotest parts of the *n*
38:15 the remotest parts of the *n*
39:2 the remotest parts of the *n*
40:19 to the east and to the *n*
40:20 which was toward the *n*
40:23 opposite the gate to the *n*
40:35 to bring me into the *n* gate
40:40 the entrance of the *n* gate
40:44 on the side of the *n* gate
40:44 The front was toward the *n*
40:46 toward the *n* is for the
41:11 entrance being toward the *n*
42:1 by the way toward the *n*
42:1 of the building to the *n*
42:2 *n* entrance, and the width
42:4 entrances were to the *n*
42:11 rooms . . . toward the *n*
42:13 The dining rooms of the *n*
44:4 *n* gate to before the House
46:9 by the way of the *n* gate in
46:9 way of the gate to the *n*
46:19 that were facing to the *n*
47:2 by the way of the *n* gate and
47:17 boundary of Damascus and *n*
48:10 the *n* twenty-five thousand
48:17 pasture ground, to the *n*
48:31 three gates being on the *n*
Da 8:4 ram making thrusts . . . the *n*
11:6 come to the king of the *n* in
11:7 fortress of the king of the *n*
11:8 off from the king of the *n*
11:11 with the king of the *n*; and
11:13 king of the *n* must return
11:15 king of the *n* will come and
11:40 king of the *n* will storm
11:44 be reports . . . out of the *n*
Am 8:12 from *n* even to the sunrise
Zep 2:13 his hand toward the *n*, and
Zec 2:6 from the land of the *n*, is
6:6 forth to the land of the *n*
6:8 to the land of the *n* are
6:8 to rest in the land of the *n*
14:4 actually be moved to the *n*
Lu 13:29 and from *n* and south, and
Re 21:13 and on the *n* three gates

Northeast
Ac 27:12 opens toward the *n* and

Northern
Ex 26:20 of the tabernacle, the *n* side
36:25 the tabernacle, the *n* side
Jos 15:5 boundary at the *n* corner was
18:12 *n* corner from the Jordan
18:18 the *n* slope in front of the
18:19 the *n* slope of Beth-hoglah
18:19 the *n* bay of the Salt Sea at
Eze 42:17 measured the *n* side, five
47:15 of the land to the *n* side
47:17 This is the *n* side
48:1 *n* extremity, on the side by
48:16 *n* border four thousand five
48:30 On the *n* border, four

Northerner
Joe 2:20 the *n* I shall put far away

Northward
Ge 13:14 *n* and southward and eastward
Jos 15:7 turning *n* to Gilgal, which
18:17 was marked out *n* and went
Jg 12:1 and crossed over *n* and said to
Eze 8:3 inner gate that is facing *n*

Eze 47:17 *n*, and the boundary of
48:1 boundary of Damascus *n*, on

Nose
Ge 24:22 man took a gold *n* ring of a
24:30 seeing the *n* ring and the
24:47 I put the *n* ring on her
Le 21:18 his *n* slit or with one
Jg 8:24 the *n* ring of his booty
8:24 For they had *n* rings of gold
8:25 *n* ring of his spoil into it
8:26 the weight of the *n* rings of
2Ki 19:28 put my hook in your *n* and
Job 40:24 can anyone bore its *n*?
Ps 115:6 *n* . . . but they cannot smell
Pr 11:22 gold *n* ring in the snout of
30:33 squeezing of the *n* is what
Ca 7:4 *n* is like the tower of Lebanon
7:8 fragrance of your *n* like apples
Isa 3:21 finger rings and the *n* rings
37:29 put my hook in your *n* and
Eze 8:17 thrusting . . . shoot to my *n*
16:12 put a *n* ring in your nostril
23:25 Your *n* and your ears they
38:18 rage will come up into my *n*

Nostril
Ge 24:47 I put the nose ring on her *n*
Eze 16:12 I put a nose ring in your *n*

Nostrils
Ge 2:7 blow into his *n* the breath of
7:22 life was active in its *n*
Ex 15:8 And by a breath from your *n*
Nu 11:20 it comes out of your *n* and
De 33:10 incense before your *n*
2Sa 22:9 Smoke went up at his *n*
22:16 blast of the breath of his *n*
Job 27:3 the spirit of God is in my *n*
41:2 Can you put a rush in its *n*
41:20 Out of its *n* smoke goes
Ps 18:8 Smoke went up at his *n*, and
18:15 the breath of your *n*
Isa 2:22 whose breath is in his *n*
65:5 These are a smoke in my *n*
La 4:20 The very breath of our *n*, the
Am 4:10 ascend even into your *n*

Notable
Ru 4:11 make a *n* name in Bethlehem

Note
Ru 3:4 take *n* of the place where he
1Sa 26:12 nor anyone taking *n* nor
1Ki 20:7 Take *n*, please, and see that
20:22 take *n* and see what you are
2Ki 5:7 just take *n*, please, you men
Job 35:15 *n* of the extreme rashness
Pr 14:7 not take *n* of the lips of
Isa 42:25 but he took no *n*; and it
56:10 None of them have taken *n*
58:3 and you would take no *n*
Jer 2:23 Take *n* of what you have done
3:13 Only take *n* of your error
4:22 Of me they have not taken *n*
5:5 *n* of the way of Jehovah
6:27 take *n* and you must examine
15:15 Take *n* of my bearing
Da 6:15 Take *n*, O king, that the law
Mt 21:45 took *n* that he was speaking
24:39 took no *n* until the flood
Mr 12:12 they took *n* that he spoke
Lu 1:66 made *n* of it in their hearts
21:29 *N* the fig tree and all the
Joh 12:16 disciples took no *n* of at
Ac 23:6 Paul took *n* that the one part
Ro 16:7 men of *n* among the apostles
Heb 13:23 *n* that our brother Timothy
1Jo 4:6 This is how we take *n* of the

Noted
Da 10:21 *n* down in the writing of

Noteworthy
Ac 4:16 *n* sign has occurred through

Nothing
Ge 11:6 there is *n* that they may have
14:23 I shall take *n* from anything
14:24 *N* for me! Only what the
26:29 do *n* bad toward us just as
28:17 *n* else but the house of God
29:15 must you serve me for *n*?
30:1 she had borne *n* to Jacob
30:31 You will give me *n*
34:7 *n* like that ought to be done
39:23 looking after absolutely *n*
40:15 I have done *n* at all for
Ge 47:18 remains *n* before my lord but
Ex 10:15 left *n* green on the trees or
12:20 *N* leavened are you to eat
13:3 So *n* leavened may be eaten
13:7 *n* leavened is to be seen with
21:11 then she must go out for *n*
22:3 If he has *n*, then he must be
Le 19:26 must eat *n* along with blood
26:16 sow your seed for *n*, as your
26:20 expended for *n*, as your earth
Nu 11:5 used to eat in Egypt for *n*
11:6 on *n* at all except the manna
20:19 I want *n* more than to pass
22:35 *n* but the word that I shall
De 4:12 no form were you seeing—*n*
5:22 he added *n*; after which he
8:9 in which you will lack *n*
13:17 *n* at all should stick to
15:9 and you should give him *n*
16:3 eat *n* leavened along with it
16:15 you must become *n* but joyful
22:26 to the girl you must do *n*
23:14 he may see *n* indecent in you
28:39 gather *n* in, because the
28:55 he has *n* at all remaining
Jg 7:14 This is *n* else but the sword
13:14 *N* at all that comes forth
14:6 was *n* at all in his hand
15:7 *n* but for me to avenge myself
18:7 they had *n* to do with mankind
18:28 *n* at all to do with mankind
20:39 suffering *n* but defeat before
1Sa 2:3 Let *n* go forth unrestrained
9:7 as a gift, there is *n* to bring
12:5 found *n* at all in my hand
19:5 David put to death for *n*
20:21 *n* the matter, as Jehovah is
21:8 *n* here at your disposal, a
25:7 *n* at all showed up missing
25:19 her husband Nabal she told *n*
27:1 *n* better for me than that I
30:19 *n* of theirs lacking, from
2Sa 12:3 *n* but one female lamb, a
19:6 servants are *n* to you
19:10 *n* to bring the king back
19:28 *n* but doomed to death
1Ki 4:27 They left *n* lacking
5:4 and there is *n* bad happening
8:9 *n* in the Ark but the two
10:21 There was *n* of silver
10:21 considered . . . as *n* at all
11:22 To this he said: *N*; but you
18:43 said: There is *n* at all
2Ki 4:2 has *n* at all in the house but
4:41 *n* injurious proved to be in
10:10 *n* of Jehovah's word will
20:13 *n* that Hezekiah did not
20:15 *n* that I did not show them
20:17 *N* will be left, Jehovah has
1Ch 16:22 And to my prophets do *n* bad
2Ch 5:10 was *n* in the Ark but the two
9:20 *n* of silver; it was
9:20 silver . . . considered as *n*
Ezr 4:3 You have *n* to do with us in
Ne 2:2 *n* but a gloominess of heart
5:12 them we shall ask *n* back
8:10 for whom *n* has been prepared
9:21 They lacked *n*. Their very
10:31 take *n* from them on the
Es 6:3 said: *N* has been done with him
Job 1:9 for *n* that Job has feared God
5:19 *n* injurious will touch you
5:24 and you will miss *n*
6:21 you men have amounted to *n*
8:9 only yesterday, and we know *n*
14:16 You watch for *n* but my sin
20:21 *n* left over . . . to devour
24:25 Or reduce my word to *n*
26:7 Hanging the earth upon *n*
27:19 but *n* will be gathered
27:19 but there will be *n*
34:18 You are good for *n*
34:32 I behold *n*, instruct me
35:16 mouth wide simply for *n*
38:41 because there is *n* to eat
40:5 twice, and I will add *n*
Ps 5:9 there is *n* trustworthy
15:3 To his companion he has done *n*
19:6 *n* concealed from its heat
23:1 my Shepherd. I shall lack *n*
23:4 I fear *n* bad, For you are
39:5 life's duration is as *n* in
39:5 is *n* but an exhalation
77:8 Has his saying come to *n* for
Ps 101:4 *N* bad do I know
105:15 to my prophets do *n* bad
115:1 To us belongs *n*, O Jehovah
115:1 Jehovah, to us belongs *n*
135:16 but they can speak *n*
135:16 but they can see *n*
135:17 they can give ear to *n*
Pr 1:17 *n* that the net is spread
8:8 there is *n* twisted or crooked
9:13 has come to know *n* whatever
12:21 *N* hurtful will befall the
13:4 desirous, but his soul has *n*
13:7 rich and yet he has *n* at all
20:4 but there will be *n*
21:26 righteous . . . holds *n* back
22:27 If you have *n* to pay, why
23:5 to glance at it, when it is *n*
29:24 may hear, but he reports *n*
30:6 Add *n* to his words, that he
Ec 1:9 there is *n* new under the sun
2:11 *n* of advantage under the sun
2:24 With a man there is *n* better
3:12 is *n* better for them than to
3:14 To it there is *n* to add and
3:14 there is *n* to subtract
3:22 is *n* better than that the man
5:14 there is *n* at all in his hand
5:15 *n* at all can one carry away
8:15 *n* better under the sun than to
9:5 dead, they are conscious of *n*
Isa 13:17 account silver itself as *n*
15:6 *n* has become green
28:19 *n* but a reason for quaking
30:7 will help simply for *n*
34:12 princes will all become *n*
39:2 *n* that Hezekiah did not show
39:4 *n* that I did not show them
39:6 *N* will be left, Jehovah has
40:17 as *n* and an unreality they
40:23 reducing high officials to *n*
41:11 will become as *n* and will
41:12 nonexistent and as *n*
41:24 and your achievement is *n*
41:29 Their works are *n*
42:25 he would lay *n* to heart
44:9, 9 they see *n* and know *n*
45:18 not create it simply for *n*
45:19 Seek me simply for *n*, you
49:4 is for *n* that I have toiled
52:3 for *n* that you people were
52:5 my people were taken for *n*
52:11 touch *n* unclean; get out
57:11 You took *n* to your heart
65:23 not toil for *n*, nor will
Jer 6:6 She is *n* but oppression in
6:29 intensely simply for *n*, and
7:34 *n* but a devastated place
10:5 they can do *n* calamitous
10:24 may not reduce me to *n*
13:10 this belt that is fit for *n*
16:19 there was *n* beneficial
22:13 fellowman who serves for *n*
22:17 upon *n* but upon your unjust
32:31 *n* but a cause of anger in
38:5 *n* at all in which the king
39:10 lowly ones who had *n* at all
49:13 *n* but an object of
50:2 publish it. Hide *n*, O men
51:58 have to toil for simply *n*
La 1:12 *n* to all you who are passing
Eze 13:3 is *n* that they have seen
13:7 when I myself have spoken *n*
18:7 *n* would he wrest away in
18:8 *n* would he give on interest
18:16 *n* has he taken in robbery
18:20 A son himself will bear *n*
18:20 father himself will bear *n*
18:30 let *n* prove to be for you
22:26 they have made *n* known
46:20 carry *n* out to the outer
Da 4:35 considered as merely *n*, and
5:23, 23 beholding *n* or hearing *n*
5:23 or knowing *n*; but the God in
6:17 *n* should be changed in the
9:26 cut off, with *n* for himself
11:27 *n* will succeed, because the
Ho 6:9 carried on *n* but loose conduct
8:7 *N* has standing grain
Joe 2:3 to be *n* thereof escaping
Am 3:4 if it has caught *n* at all
3:5 it has absolutely caught *n*
Na 1:14 *N* of your name will be sown
Hab 2:13 tire . . . out merely for *n*
Hag 2:3 as *n* in your eyes

Notice

Noticed

Noticing

Notify

Noting

Notorious

Notwithstanding

Nourish

Nourished

Nourishment

Now*

Nowadays

Nowhere

Nude

Nudeness

Nudity

Nullified

Numb

Numbed

Number

De 26:5 an alien with very few in *n*
28:62 be left with very few in *n*
32:8 the *n* of the sons of Israel
33:5 *n* of the tribes of Israel
Jos 4:5 according to the *n* of the
4:8 the *n* of the tribes of the
Jg 6:5 their camels were without *n*
7:6 the *n* of those lapping with
7:12 their camels were without *n*
21:23 carry off wives for their *n*
1Sa 2:33 greater *n* of your house will
6:4 According to the *n* of the axis
6:18 to the *n* of all the cities of
18:27 giving them in full *n* to
27:7 *n* of the days that David
2Sa 2:11 *n* of the days that David
2:15 went across by *n*, twelve
15:12 continually growing in *n*
18:1 David proceeded to *n* the
21:20 twenty-four in *n*; and he
24:2 know the *n* of the people
24:9 the *n* of the registration
1Ki 18:31 the *n* of the tribes of the
20:25 *n* a military force for
2Ki 2:24 children of their *n*
1Ch 7:2 Their *n* in the days of David
7:40 *n* was twenty-six thousand
9:28 by *n* that they would bring
9:28 by *n* that they would take
12:29 the greater *n* of them were
16:19 you happened to be few in *n*
21:1 to incite David to *n* Israel
21:2 that I may know their *n*
21:5 the *n* of the registration of
22:4 also cedar timbers without *n*
22:15 in great *n* doers of work
23:3 *n*, head by head of them
23:24 in the *n* of the names, head
23:27 *n* of the sons of Levi from
23:31 by *n* according to the rule
25:1 from their *n* the official
25:7 the *n* of them together with
27:1 sons of Israel by their *n*
27:23 David did not take the *n* of
27:24 the *n* did not come up into
29:21 sacrifices in great *n* for
2Ch 2:9 timbers for me in great *n*
5:12 priests to the *n* of a hundred
12:3 no *n* to the people that came
14:15 captive flocks in great *n*
15:9 from Israel in great *n* when
24:24 small *n* of men that the
24:24 force of very great *n*
26:11 *n* of their registration by
26:12 entire *n* of the heads of
28:5 great *n* of captives and
29:32 *n* of the burnt offerings
30:18 great *n* of the people
30:24 themselves in great *n*
35:7 the *n* of thirty thousand
Ezr 1:8 to *n* them out to Sheshbazzar
2:2 *n* of the men of the people
3:4 sacrifices day by day in *n*
6:17 the *n* of the tribes of Israel
8:34 by *n* and by weight for
Ne 7:7 *n* of the men of the people of
Es 5:11 the large *n* of his sons and
9:11 *n* of those killed in Shushan
Job 1:5 according to the *n* of all of
3:6 *n* of the lunar months let it
5:9 Wonderful things without *n*
9:10 wonderful things without *n*
14:5 *n* of his months is with you
15:20 *n* of years that have been
16:10 In large *n* they mass
21:21 *n* of his months will really
21:33 before him were without *n*
25:3 Is there any *n* to his troops?
31:37 The *n* of my steps I would
36:26 In *n* his years are beyond
38:21 in *n* your days are many
38:37 can exactly *n* the clouds
Ps 104:25 moving things without *n*
105:12 happened to be few in *n*
105:34 of locust, even without *n*
147:4 counting the *n* of the stars
Ec 2:3 the *n* of the days of their life
5:18 the *n* of the days of his life
6:12 *n* of the days of his vain life
Ca 6:8 and maidens without *n*
Isa 10:19 *n* that a mere boy will be
21:17 over of the *n* of bowmen
24:6 have decreased in *n*, and
31:4 a full *n* of shepherds, and
Isa 40:26 the army of them even by *n*
Jer 2:28 the *n* of your cities your
2:32 forgotten me days without *n*
30:19 make them heavy in *n*
44:28 land of Judah, few in *n*
46:23 and they are without *n*
Eze 4:4 *n* of the days that you will
4:5 *n* of three hundred and ninety
4:9 the *n* of the days that you are
5:3 take therefrom a few in *n* and
44:26 seven days they should *n*
Da 9:2 *n* of the years concerning
Ho 1:10 *n* of the sons of Israel must
Joe 1:6 a nation . . . without *n*
Mt 24:12 love of the greater *n* will
28:12 a sufficient *n* of silver
Mr 6:2 greater *n* of those listening
9:26 the greater *n* of them were
Lu 8:32 a considerable *n* of swine
Joh 6:10 about five thousand in *n*
17:2 *n* whom you have given him
Ac 4:4 *n* of the men became about five
5:36 *n* of men, about four hundred
6:7 *n* of the disciples kept
7:14 the *n* of seventy-five souls
11:21 *n* that became believers
16:5 increase in *n* from day to day
19:19 a *n* of those who practiced
21:10 remaining quite a *n* of days
24:17 after quite a *n* of years I
25:14 spending a *n* of days there
27:7 slowly quite a *n* of days
Ro 9:27 *n* of the sons of Israel may
11:12 the full *n* of them mean it
11:25 full *n* of people of the
2Ti 1:15 and Hermogenes are of that *n*
2:17 and Philetus are of that *n*
Re 5:11 *n* of them was myriads of
6:11 until the *n* was filled also
7:4 the *n* of those who were sealed
7:9 no man was able to *n*, out of
9:16 the *n* of the armies of
9:16 I heard the *n* of them
13:17 beast or the *n* of its name
13:18 calculate the *n* of the wild
13:18 for it is a man's *n*; and
13:18 its *n* is six hundred and
15:2 and from the *n* of its name
18:6 twice the *n* of the things
20:8 *n* of these is as the sand of

Numbered
Ge 13:16 then your seed could be *n*
16:10 not be *n* for multitude
32:12 cannot be *n* for multitude
Ex 30:13 who pass over to those *n*
Nu 23:10 *n* the dust particles of Jacob
2Sa 24:10 after he had so *n* the people
1Ki 3:8 people that cannot be *n* or
8:5 could not be counted or *n* for
1Ch 23:3 Levites were *n* from the age
2Ch 5:6 could not be counted or *n* for
Da 5:26 MENE, God has *n* the days of
Ho 1:10 that cannot be measured or *n*
Mt 10:30 hairs of your head are all *n*
Lu 12:7 hairs of your heads are all *n*
22:3 who was *n* among the twelve
Ac 1:17 *n* among us and he obtained

Numbering
1Ch 21:17 to make a *n* of the people
22:16 iron there is no means of *n*
Ps 40:12 until there was no *n* of them

Numbers
Ge 6:1 men started to grow in *n* on
Jg 9:40 falling in *n* as far as the
1Ch 12:23 the *n* of the heads of those
Ezr 1:9 these are the *n* of them
Ps 71:15 come to know the *n* of them
Jer 46:16 great *n* they are stumbling
Na 3:15 heavy in *n* like the locust
3:15 heavy in *n* like the locust
Ac 28:23 greater *n* to him in his

Numbness
La 2:18 Give no *n* to yourself

Numerous
Ge 50:9 the camp came to be very *n*
Ex 1:9 more *n* and mightier than we
1:20 people kept growing more *n*
12:38 a very *n* stock of animals
Nu 32:1 had come to have *n* livestock
De 2:10 a people great and *n* and tall
2:21 *n* and tall people like the
De 11:23 nations greater and more *n*
20:1 a people more *n* than you
26:5 a great nation, mighty and *n*
Jos 11:4 people as *n* as the grains of
17:14 a *n* people for the reason
17:15 If you are a *n* people, go
17:17 A *n* people you are, and
Jg 6:5 come as *n* as the locusts, and
7:12 as *n* as locusts; and their
7:12 *n* as the grains of sand that
9:29 Make your army *n* and come on
1Ki 5:7 wise son over this *n* people
1Ch 5:9 *n* in the land of Gilead
5:23 They themselves became *n*
24:4 more *n* in headmen than the
2Ch 1:9 people as *n* as the dust
30:13 a *n* people, to hold the
Ne 6:17 were making *n* their letters
Ps 35:18 Among a *n* people I shall
40:5 more *n* than I can recount
40:12 more *n* than the hairs of my
69:4 no reason, have become *n*
Pr 7:26 being killed by her are *n*
Ec 6:3 *n* the days of his years should
Isa 13:4 something like a *n* people
31:1 chariots, because they are *n*
54:1 more *n* than the sons of the
Jer 5:6 unfaithfulness have become *n*
15:8 more *n* than the sand grains
30:14 your sins have become *n*
30:15 your sins have become *n*
46:23 more *n* than the locust
Eze 3:6 to *n* peoples unintelligible
38:4 a *n* congregation, with large
38:15 even a *n* military force
Joe 2:2 a people *n* and mighty
2:11 for his camp is very *n*
Ga 4:27 more *n* than those of her

Nun
Ex 33:11 Joshua, the son of *N*
Nu 11:28 Joshua the son of *N*, the
13:8 Ephraim, Hoshea the son of *N*
13:16 to call Hoshea the son of *N*
14:6 Joshua the son of *N* and Caleb
14:30 and Joshua the son of *N*
14:38 Joshua the son of *N* and Caleb
26:65 and Joshua the son of *N*
27:18 Joshua the son of *N*, a man
32:12 Joshua the son of *N*, because
32:28 to Joshua the son of *N* and to
34:17 and Joshua the son of *N*
De 1:38 Joshua the son of *N*, who is
31:23 Joshua the son of *N* and to
32:44 he and Hoshea the son of *N*
34:9 Joshua the son of *N* was full
Jos 1:1 to Joshua the son of *N*, the
2:1 Joshua the son of *N* sent two
2:23 come to Joshua the son of *N*
6:6 Joshua the son of *N* called the
14:1 and Joshua the son of *N*
17:4 and Joshua the son of *N* and
19:49 to Joshua the son of *N*
19:51 and Joshua the son of *N* and
21:1 and Joshua the son of *N* and
24:29 Joshua the son of *N*, the
Jg 2:8 Then Joshua the son of *N*, the
1Ki 16:34 Joshua the son of *N*
1Ch 7:27 *N* his son, Jehoshua his son
Ne 8:17 days of Joshua the son of *N*

Nuptial
Ps 19:5 coming out of his *n* chamber
Joe 2:16 the bride from her *n* chamber

Nurse
Ge 24:59 their sister and her *n* and
Ex 2:7 she may *n* the child for you
2:9 with you and *n* him for me
Nu 11:12 as the male *n* carries the
Ru 4:16 and she came to be its *n*
2Sa 4:4 *n* began to carry him and flee
1Ki 1:2 become his *n*; and she must
1:4 she came to be the king's *n*
3:21 to *n* my son, why, there he
Lu 23:29 the breasts that did not *n*

Nursed
Ex 2:9 woman took the child and *n*
Ac 7:20 *n* three months in his

Nursing
Ge 35:8 Deborah the *n* woman of
Ex 2:7 *n* woman from the Hebrew
1Sa 1:23 *n* her son until she weaned
2Ki 11:2 even him and his *n* woman

2Ch 22:11 *n* woman in the inner room
Isa 49:23 princesses *n* women for you
Mr 6:19 But Herodias was *n* a grudge
1Th 2:7 as when a *n* mother cherishes

Nut

Ca 6:11 To the garden of *n* trees I had

Nuts

Ge 43:11 pistachio *n* and almonds

Nympha

Col 4:15 brothers at Laodicea and to *N*

Oar

Eze 27:29 handling an *o*, mariners

Oars

Eze 27:6 from Bashan they made your *o*
Ac 27:40 lashings of the rudder *o*

Oath

Ge 14:22 I do lift up my hand in an *o*
21:31 both of them had taken an *o*
24:8 become free from this *o* you
24:41 obligation to me by *o* when
24:41 of obligation to me by *o*
26:28 *o* of obligation occur
Ex 6:8 raised my hand in *o* to give to
22:11 *o* by Jehovah is to take place
Nu 5:21 an *o* involving cursing
5:21 for a cursing and an *o* in the
14:30 I lifted up my hand in *o*
30:2 *o* to bind a vow of abstinence
30:10 vow upon her soul by an *o*
30:13 any *o* of an abstinence vow
De 29:12 Jehovah your God and his *o*
29:14 this covenant and this *o*
29:19 heard the words of this *o*
29:20 the *o* written in this book
29:21 *o* of the covenant that is
32:40 my hand to heaven in an *o*
Jos 2:17 free . . . respecting this *o*
2:20 this *o* of yours that you
6:26 Joshua had an *o* pronounced
9:20 the *o* that we have sworn
Jg 21:5 a great *o* that has taken place
1Sa 14:24 under the pledge of an *o*
14:26 people were afraid of the *o*
14:27 put the people under an *o*
14:28 put the people under *o*
2Sa 21:7 account of the *o* of Jehovah
1Ki 2:42 Did I not put you under *o*
2:43 not keep the *o* of Jehovah
22:16 am I putting you under *o*
2Ch 18:15 putting you under *o* that
Ezr 10:5 *o* to do according to this
10:5 Accordingly they took an *o*
Ne 9:15 lifted your hand in an *o* to
10:29 into an *o*, to walk in the
Job 31:30 an *o* against his soul
Ps 24:4 Nor taken an *o* deceitfully
106:26 raise his hand in an *o*
Pr 29:24 *o* involving a curse he may
Ec 8:2 out of regard for the *o* of God
9:2 has been afraid of a sworn *o*
Ca 2:7 put you under *o*, O daughters of
3:5 put you under *o*, O daughters
5:8 I have put you under *o*, O
5:9 put us under such an *o* as this
8:4 put you under *o*, O daughters
Isa 65:15 lay up your name for an *o*
Jer 11:5 the *o* that I swore to your
Eze 16:59 despised the *o* in breaking
17:13 and brought him into an *o*
17:16 the one that despised his *o*
17:18 despised an *o* in breaking a
17:19 my *o* that he has despised
20:5 *o* to the seed of the house of
20:5 to lift up my hand in an *o*
20:6 I lifted up my hand in an *o*
20:15 lifted up my hand in an *o*
20:23 *o* to them in the wilderness
20:28 my hand in an *o* to give
20:42 lifted up my hand in an *o*
36:7 raised my hand in an *o* that
47:14 I raised my hand in an *o* to
Da 9:11 sworn *o* that is written in
Zec 5:3 everyone making a sworn *o*
5:4 sworn *o* in my name falsely
8:17 and do not love any false *o*
Mt 14:7 an *o* to give her whatever she
26:63 I put you under *o* to tell us
26:72 he denied it, with an *o*
Mr 5:7 under *o* by God not to torment
Lu 1:73 *o* that he swore to Abraham
Ac 2:30 *o* that he would seat one
Heb 6:16 their *o* is the end of every
6:17 stepped in with an *o*
7:20 was not without a sworn *o*
7:21 priests without a sworn *o*
7:21 an *o* sworn by the One who
7:28 word of the sworn *o* that
Jas 5:12 by earth or by any other *o*

Oathbound

Ac 23:13 formed this *o* conspiracy

Oaths

De 30:7 these *o* upon your enemies and
Ps 10:7 His mouth is full of *o* and of
Eze 21:23 are sworn with *o* to them
Ho 10:4 making false *o*, concluding a
Hab 3:9 The sworn *o* of the tribes are
Zep 1:5 making sworn *o* to Jehovah
1:5 making sworn *o* by Malcam
Mt 14:9 king out of regard for his *o*
Mr 6:26 in view of the *o* and those

Obadiah

1Ki 18:3 Ahab called *O*, who was over
18:3 *O* himself had proved to be
18:4 *O* proceeded to take a hundred
18:5 Ahab went on to say to *O*
18:6 *O* himself went alone by
18:7 As *O* continued on the way
18:16 *O* went off to meet Ahab and
1Ch 3:21 the sons of Arnan *O*
3:21 the sons of *O* Shecaniah
7:3 sons of Izrahiah were . . . *O*
8:38 and *O* . . . the sons of Azel
9:16 and *O* the son of Shemaiah
9:44 and *O* . . . the sons of Azel
12:9 *O* the second, Eliab the third
27:19 Ishmaiah the son of *O*
2Ch 17:7 his princes . . . *O* and
34:12 appointed Jahath and *O* the
Ezr 8:9 *O* the son of Jehiel, and with
Ne 10:5 Harim, Meremoth, *O*
12:25 Mattaniah and Bakbukiah, *O*
Ob 1 The vision of *O*: This is what

Obal

Ge 10:28 *O* and Abimael and Sheba
1Ch 1:22 and *O* and Abimael and Sheba

Obed

Ru 4:17 they began to call his name *O*
4:21 and Boaz became father to *O*
4:22 and *O* became father to Jesse
1Ch 2:12 in turn, became father to *O*
2:12 *O*, in turn, became father to
2:37 in turn, became father to *O*
2:38 *O*, in turn, became father to
11:47 *O* and Jaasiel the Mezobaite
26:7 The sons of Shemaiah . . . *O*
2Ch 23:1 Azariah the son of *O* and
Mt 1:5 Boaz became father to *O* by
1:5 *O* became father to Jesse
Lu 3:32 son of Jesse, son of *O*, son

Obed-edom

2Sa 6:10 the house of *O* the Gittite
6:11 house of *O* the Gittite three
6:11 Jehovah kept blessing *O* and
6:12 blessed the house of *O* and
6:12 out of the house of *O* up to
1Ch 13:13 the house of *O* the Gittite
13:14 with the household of *O*
13:14 blessing the household of *O*
15:18 *O* and Jeiel the gatekeepers
15:21 Mikneiah and *O* and Jeiel
15:24 *O* and Jehiah the gatekeepers
15:25 from the house of *O* with
16:5 and Benaiah and *O* and Jeiel
16:38 and *O* and his brothers
16:38 *O* the son of Jeduthun and
26:4 And *O* had sons: Shemaiah the
26:8 these were of the sons of *O*
26:8 sixty-two belonging to *O*
26:15 *O* had his to the south, and
2Ch 25:24 with *O* and the treasures

Obedience

Ge 49:10 *o* of the peoples will belong
Pr 30:17 that despises *o* to a mother
Ro 1:5 *o* of faith among all the
5:19 *o* of the one person many
6:16 *o* with righteousness in view
16:19 *o* has come to the notice of
16:26 to promote *o* by faith
2Co 7:15 to mind the *o* of all of you
10:6 your own *o* has been fully
Heb 5:8 *o* from the things he suffered
1Pe 1:22 by your *o* to the truth

Obedient

Ex 24:7 we are willing to do and be *o*
Jos 22:2 you were *o* to my voice in
2Sa 22:45 Ears will be *o* to hear me
1Ki 3:9 *o* heart to judge your people
1Ch 29:23 Israelites were *o* to him
Ps 18:44 they will be *o* to me
Ac 6:7 priests began to be *o* to the
7:39 refused to become *o*, but
Ro 6:17 you became *o* from the heart
15:18 nations to be *o*, by my word
2Co 2:9 whether you are *o* in all
10:5 to make it *o* to the Christ
Eph 6:1 Children, be *o* to your parents
6:5 You slaves, be *o* to those who
Php 2:8 became *o* as far as death
Col 3:20 be *o* to your parents in
3:22 slaves, be *o* in everything to
2Th 3:14 is not *o* to our word through
Tit 3:1 and be *o* to governments and
Heb 13:17 Be *o* to those who are
1Pe 1:2 the purpose of their being *o*
1:14 As *o* children, quit being
3:1 if any are not *o* to the word
4:17 not *o* to the good news of

Obeisance

2Ch 20:18 to do *o* to Jehovah
Mt 2:2 and we have come to do him *o*
2:8 I too may go and do it *o*
2:11 falling down, they did *o* to
8:2 began doing *o* to him, saying
9:18 began to do *o* to him, saying
14:33 those in the boat did *o* to
15:25 *o* to him, saying: Lord, help
18:26 began to do *o* to him, saying
20:20 doing *o* and asking for
28:9 by his feet and did *o* to him
28:17 they did *o*, but some doubted
Mr 5:6 he ran and did *o* to him
15:19 they would do *o* to him
Lu 24:52 did *o* to him and returned to
Joh 9:38 And he did *o* to him
Ac 10:25 at his feet and did *o* to him
Heb 1:6 all God's angels do *o* to him
Re 3:9 do *o* before your feet and

Obey

Ge 41:40 all my people will *o* you
Ex 5:2 *o* his voice to send Israel
19:5 you will strictly *o* my voice
23:21 *o* his voice. Do not behave
23:22 if you strictly *o* his voice
De 11:13 if you will without fail *o*
11:27 you will *o* the commandments
11:28 not *o* the commandments of
12:28 you must *o* all these words
Jg 3:4 whether they would *o* Jehovah's
1Sa 12:14 serve him and *o* his voice
12:15 not *o* the voice of Jehovah
15:19 not *o* the voice of Jehovah
15:22 Look! To *o* is better than a
28:18 *o* the voice of Jehovah, and
28:21 *o* the words that you spoke
28:22 *o* the voice of your
1Ki 11:38 *o* all that I shall command
20:8 Do not *o*, and you should
2Ki 17:40 And they did not *o*, but it
Job 36:11 If they *o* and serve, They
36:12 But if they do not *o*, they
Jer 7:23 *O* my voice, and I will
11:4 *O* my voice, and you must do
11:7 saying: *O* my voice
11:10 who refused to *o* my words
12:17 if they will not *o*, I will
13:10 refusing to *o* my words
13:11 but they did not *o*
17:24 that, if you strictly *o* me
17:27 But if you will not *o* me
19:15 in order not to *o* my words
22:5 you will not *o* these words
22:21 you said, I shall not *o*
22:21 you did not *o* my voice
25:8 you did not *o* my words
26:13 *o* the voice of Jehovah
32:23 they did not *o* your voice
34:10 to *o* and let them go
35:13 exhortation to *o* my words
38:20 *O*, please, the voice of
42:6 that we shall *o*, to the
42:6 *o* the voice of Jehovah our
42:21 not *o* the voice of Jehovah
43:4 not *o* the voice of Jehovah
43:7 not *o* the voice of Jehovah
44:23 not *o* the voice of Jehovah

Da 7:27 will serve and *o* even them
Zec 7:7 *o* the words that Jehovah
Mt 8:27 the winds and the sea *o* him
Mr 1:27 unclean spirits, and they *o*
4:41 the wind and the sea *o* him
Lu 8:25 winds and the water . . . *o*
17:6 the sea! and it would *o* you
Ac 5:29 *o* God as ruler rather than
Ro 2:8 *o* unrighteousness there will
6:12 you should *o* their desires
6:16 to anyone as slaves to *o* him
6:16 slaves of him because you *o*
10:16 did not all *o* the good news
2Th 1:8 who do not *o* the good news
Jas 3:3 of horses for them to *o* us
3:17 ready to *o*, full of mercy
1Pe 3:6 as Sarah used to *o* Abraham

Obeyed
Ex 7:16 here you have not *o* until now
1Sa 15:20 have *o* the voice of Jehovah
15:24 and so *o* their voice
19:6 Saul *o* the voice of Jonathan
28:21 maidservant has *o* your
28:23 *o* their voice and rose up
1Ki 12:24 they *o* the word of Jehovah
2Ch 11:4 they *o* the word of Jehovah
Jer 3:25 not *o* the voice of Jehovah
7:28 not *o* the voice of Jehovah
9:13 they have not *o* my voice
34:10 all the princes *o*, and all
34:17 not *o* me in keeping on
35:14 *o* the commandment of their
35:14 but you have not *o* me
35:18 *o* the commandment of
40:3 have not *o* his voice
Da 9:10 *o* the voice of Jehovah our
9:14 and we have not *o* his voice
Mic 5:15 the nations that have not *o*
Php 2:12 way that you have always *o*
Heb 11:8 *o* in going out into a place

Obeying
Ge 28:7 Jacob was *o* his father and
De 28:13 keep *o* the commandments of
Jg 2:17 by *o* the commandments of
1Sa 15:22 as in *o* the voice of Jehovah
2Ki 10:6 is my voice that you are *o*
Jer 16:12 his bad heart in not *o* me
18:10 bad in my eyes by not *o* my
35:8 *o* the voice of Jehonadab
35:10 *o* and doing according to
Da 9:11 aside by not *o* your voice
Zec 7:12 to keep from *o* the law and
Ac 5:32 to those *o* him as ruler
5:36 were *o* him were dispersed
5:37 those who were *o* him were
Ga 5:7 from keeping on *o* the truth
Heb 5:9 salvation to all those *o* him

Obeys
Joh 7:19 not one of you *o* the Law

Obil
1Ch 27:30 there was *O* the Ishmaelite

Object
De 28:25 a frightful *o* to all the
28:37 become an *o* of astonishment
2Ki 22:19 an *o* of astonishment and a
2Ch 29:8 *o* at which to quake, an
29:8 an *o* of astonishment and
30:7 *o* of astonishment, just as
Ne 1:11 make him an *o* of pity before
4:4 become an *o* of contempt; and
Ps 73:19 *o* of astonishment as in a
Pr 14:20 is an *o* of hatred, but many
Isa 5:9 outright *o* of astonishment
8:12 *o* of their fear you men must
8:13 should be the *o* of your fear
13:9 land an *o* of astonishment
Jer 2:15 land an *o* of astonishment
4:7 land as an *o* of astonishment
18:16 land an *o* of astonishment
19:8 city an *o* of astonishment
20:7 an *o* of laughter all day
25:9 an *o* of astonishment and
25:11 an *o* of astonishment, and
25:18 an *o* of astonishment
25:38 become an *o* of astonishment
29:18 an *o* of astonishment and
42:18 *o* of astonishment and a
44:12 an *o* of astonishment and a
44:22 and an *o* of astonishment
46:19 mere *o* of astonishment
48:9 a mere *o* of astonishment
Jer 48:26 become an *o* of ridicule
48:27 mere *o* of ridicule to you
48:39 become an *o* of ridicule and
49:13 but an *o* of astonishment
49:17 become an *o* of astonishment
50:3 land an *o* of astonishment
50:23 mere *o* of astonishment
51:29 an *o* of astonishment
51:37 an *o* of astonishment and
51:41 mere *o* of astonishment
51:43 become an *o* of astonishment
La 3:14 have become an *o* of laughter
Eze 5:15 and an *o* of reviling words
22:4 an *o* of reproach to the
23:32 an *o* of laughter and
23:46 a frightful *o* and something
24:21 *o* of your soul's compassion
24:25 *o* of their exultation
26:5 *o* of plunder for the nations
Da 9:16 *o* of reproach to all those
Ho 5:9 a mere *o* of astonishment you
Joe 1:7 vine as an *o* of astonishment
Mic 6:16 you an *o* of astonishment
Zep 2:15 become an *o* of astonishment
Zec 7:14 land an *o* of astonishment
Joh 11:4 not with death as its *o*
Ro 13:3 those ruling are an *o* of fear
2Th 2:4 god or an *o* of reverence, so
1Pe 3:14 the *o* of their fear do not
Re 18:12 every sort of ivory *o* and
18:12 *o* out of most precious wood

Objection
Ac 10:29 I came, really without *o*

Objective
1Ti 1:5 the *o* of this mandate is love

Objects
Ex 28:38 committed against the holy *o*
1Ki 8:50 must make them *o* of pity
2Ch 30:9 sons will be *o* of mercy
Job 20:25 Frightful *o* will go against
Ps 106:46 grant them to be *o* of pity
Jer 2:37 the *o* of your confidence
Mic 6:2 durable *o*, you foundations of
Mt 10:22 be *o* of hatred by all people
24:9 you will be *o* of hatred by
Mr 13:13 *o* of hatred by all people
Lu 21:17 *o* of hatred by all people
Ac 17:23 your *o* of veneration I also

Obligated
Nu 3:36 the sons of Merari were *o*
4:32 for which they are *o*
2Th 1:3 *o* to give God thanks always
2:13 *o* to thank God always for

Obligation
Ge 24:41 cleared of *o* to me by oath
24:41 free of *o* to me by oath
26:28 oath of *o* occur between us
Le 18:30 *o* to me not to carry on any
22:9 keep their *o* to me, that they
Nu 3:7 keep their *o* to him and their
3:7 *o* to all the assembly before
3:8 *o* of the sons of Israel in
3:25 *o* of the sons of Gershon in
3:28 of the *o* to the holy place
3:31 *o* was the Ark and the table
3:32 of the *o* to the holy place
3:38 care of the *o* to the sanctuary
3:38 the *o* for the sons of Israel
4:27 all their loads to them by *o*
4:31 this is their *o*, their load
8:26 care of the *o*, but he must
9:19 Israel also kept their *o* to
9:23 kept their *o* to Jehovah at the
18:3 they must keep their *o* to you
18:3 and their *o* to the entire tent
18:4 *o* to the tent of meeting as
18:5 keep your *o* to the holy place
18:5 your *o* to the altar, that no
31:30 the *o* of Jehovah's tabernacle
31:47 the *o* of Jehovah's tabernacle
De 11:1 keep your *o* to him and his
Jos 22:3 and you have kept the *o* of
2Sa 18:11 *o* to give you ten pieces of
1Ki 2:3 must keep the *o* to Jehovah
2Ch 13:11 keeping the *o* to Jehovah our
23:6 will keep the *o* to Jehovah
Ne 12:45 care of the *o* of their God
12:45 the *o* of the purification
Es 9:21 *o* to be regularly holding the
9:27 the *o* to be regularly holding
Ec 12:13 this is the whole *o* of man
Eze 40:45 care of the *o* of the house
40:46 care of the *o* of the altar
44:8 the *o* of my holy things, nor
44:8 caretakers of my *o* in my
44:14 of the *o* of the House, as
44:15 *o* of my sanctuary when the
44:16 take care of the *o* to me
48:11 care of the *o* toward me
Zec 3:7 my *o* that you will keep, then
Mal 3:14 we have kept the *o* to him
Mt 23:16 he is under *o*
23:18 he is under *o*
Lu 11:42 you were under *o* to do
Ro 8:12 we are under *o*, not to the
Ga 5:3 *o* to perform the whole Law
1Th 5:27 the solemn *o* by the Lord
1Jo 2:6 under *o* himself also to go
3:16 *o* to surrender our souls
4:11 under *o* to love one another
3Jo 8 under *o* to receive such persons

Obligations
Ge 26:5 continued to keep his *o* to me
Nu 8:26 do to the Levites in their *o*
2Ch 31:16 their service by their *o*
31:17 their *o* in their divisions

Obligatory
Le 8:35 keep the *o* watch of Jehovah
Nu 4:28 *o* service is under the hand of

Obliged
Ps 109:23 I am *o* to go away
Heb 2:17 *o* to become like his
5:3 *o* to make offerings for sins

Oblivion
Ps 88:12 in the land of *o*

Oboth
Nu 21:10 and encamped in *O*
21:11 they pulled away from *O* and
33:43 and went camping in *O*
33:44 pulled away from *O* and went

Obscene
Ro 1:27 working what is *o* and
Eph 5:4 foolish talking nor *o* jesting
Col 3:8 and *o* talk out of your mouth

Obscure
Ac 21:39 a citizen of no *o* city

Obscureness
Isa 9:1 *o* will not be as when the

Obscuring
Job 38:2 Who is this that is *o* counsel
42:3 *o* counsel without knowledge

Obscurity
Job 10:22 To the land of *o* like gloom
Isa 8:22 *o*, hard times and gloominess
50:3 I clothe the heavens with *o*
Am 4:13 the One making dawn into *o*

Observableness
Lu 17:20 not coming with striking *o*

Observance
Ex 12:42 It is a night for *o* with
12:42 *o* on the part of all the sons
16:23 *o* of a holy sabbath to
Joh 12:7 *o* in view of the day of my
Ac 16:4 for *o* the decrees that had
1Co 7:19 but *o* of God's commandments
Col 2:16 an *o* of the new moon or of a

Observations
Ac 11:6 I made *o* and saw four-footed

Observe
Ex 16:30 *o* the sabbath on the seventh
Le 23:32 you should *o* your sabbath
25:2 the land must *o* a sabbath to
De 16:12 you must *o* and carry out
26:16 *o* and carry them out with
26:17 *o* his regulations and his
26:18 *o* all his commandments
28:13 commanding you today to *o*
33:9 covenant they continued to *o*
2Ch 5:11 no need to *o* the divisions
Job 39:1 *o* just when the hinds bring
Ps 78:7 but *o* his own commandments
105:45 And *o* his own laws
107:43 will both *o* these things
119:33 may *o* it down to the last
119:34 that I may *o* your law
119:69 heart I shall *o* your orders
119:115 *o* the commandments of my
119:145 Your regulations I will *o*

Pr 3:1 commandments may your heart o
6:20 O, O my son, the commandment
Jer 8:7 they o well the time of each
Eze 43:11 o all its ground plan and
Mt 6:26 O intently the birds of
19:17 life, o the commandments
23:3 they tell you, do and o
28:20 teaching them to o all the
Mr 8:24 I o what seem to be trees
Lu 6:41 but do not o the rafter that
Joh 9:16 he does not o the Sabbath
12:19 o you are getting absolutely
14:15 will o my commandments
14:23 he will o my word
14:24 does not o my words; and
15:10 If you o my commandments
15:20 they will o yours also
Ac 15:5 them to o the law of Moses
Eph 4:3 o the oneness of the spirit
1Ti 6:14 o the commandment in a
1Jo 2:5 whoever does o his word
5:3 that we o his commandments
Re 1:3 o the things written in it
12:17 o the commandments of God
14:12 o the commandments of God

Observed

Ge 37:11 but his father o the saying
Ps 119:22 have o your own reminders
119:56 Because your orders I have o
119:100 I have o your own orders
119:129 why my soul has o them
Mic 6:16 of the house of Ahab are o
Mt 6:1 in order to be o by them
Joh 6:5 o that a great crowd was
15:10 I have o the commandments
15:20 if they have o my word
17:6 and they have o your word
2Ti 4:7 I have o the faith

Observer

Job 7:20 against . . . the O of mankind

Observes

Joh 8:51 If anyone o my word, he
8:52 If anyone o my word, he
14:21 commandments and o them
Ro 14:6, 6 He who o the day o it to
Jas 2:10 whoever o all the Law but
1Jo 3:24 he who o his commandments
Re 2:26 o my deeds down to the end

Observing

De 16:1 an o of the month of Abib
27:1 an o of every commandment
Ps 25:10 those o his covenant and
56:6 keep o my very steps
106:3 Happy are those o justice
119:2 are those o his reminders
Pr 2:8 o the paths of judgment, and
24:12 that is o your soul know and
28:7 son is o the law, but one
Jon 2:8 are o the idols of untruth
Mr 12:41 o how the crowd was
Lu 20:20 after o him closely, they
21:30 by o it you know for
Joh 8:55 know him and am o his word
Ac 17:23 o your objects of veneration
27:39 o a certain bay with a
Ga 4:10 scrupulously o days and
1Jo 2:3 continue o his commandments
2:4 is not o his commandments
3:22 we are o his commandments
Re 22:7 o the words of the prophecy
22:9 o the words of this scroll

Obsolete

Heb 8:13 has made the former one o
8:13 that which is made o and

Obstacle

Le 19:14 you must not put an o
Isa 57:14 Remove any o from the way

Obstinacy

Ex 13:15 that Pharaoh showed o toward

Obstinate

Ex 4:21 shall let his heart become o
7:3 let Pharaoh's heart become o
7:13 Pharaoh's heart became o, and
7:22 Pharaoh's heart . . . o, and
8:19 heart continued to be o, and
9:12 let Pharaoh's heart become o
9:35 Pharaoh's heart continued o
10:20 let Pharaoh's heart become o
10:27 let Pharaoh's heart become o
11:10 let Pharaoh's heart become o
Ex 14:4 let Pharaoh's heart become o
14:8 the king of Egypt become o
14:17 the Egyptians become o, that
De 2:30 his spirit become o and his
Eze 2:6 there are o ones and things
Ac 7:51 O men and uncircumcised in
Ro 9:18 he wishes he lets become o

Obstructed

Le 15:3 o from his running discharge

Obtain

Ex 22:16 to o her without fail as his
Pr 31:16 field and proceeded to o it
Ro 11:7 seeking he did not o, but the
2Ti 2:10 o the salvation that is in
Heb 4:16 that we may o mercy and
Jas 4:2 and yet you are not able to o
2Jo 8 that you may o a full reward

Obtained

Ge 41:53 o in the land of Egypt
41:56 the famine o over all the
Ac 1:17 he o a share in this ministry
26:22 I have o the help that is
Ro 11:7 but the ones chosen o it
Heb 6:15 he o this promise
8:6 Jesus has o a more excellent
9:12 o an everlasting deliverance
11:33 o promises, stopped the
2Pe 1:1 those who have o a faith

Occasion

Ex 18:22 on every proper o; and it
18:26 on every proper o. A hard
De 10:10 listen to me also on that o
2Sa 19:2 an o of mourning on the part
1Ki 13:34 an o for effacing them and
1Ch 17:25 found o to pray before you
Ne 8:4 which they had made for the o
Ec 9:8 On every o let your garments
Jer 10:18 on this o, and I will cause
Eze 29:21 give o to open the mouth
Am 6:10 it is not the o for making
Lu 5:1 On an o when the crowd was
5:12 On a further o while he was
11:1 Now on the o of his being in
14:1 an o when he went into the
Ro 14:20 with an o for stumbling eats
2Co 1:15 have a second o for joy
Eph 6:18 prayer on every o in spirit
Heb 3:8 the o of causing bitter anger
3:15 the o of causing bitter anger

Occasions

Ex 23:17 On three o in the year every
Job 33:10 O for opposition to me he
Isa 33:20 the town of our festal o
Ro 16:17 o for stumbling contrary to
Heb 1:1 long ago spoke on many o and

Occupancy

Isa 65:21 build houses and have o
65:22 and someone else have o
Zep 1:13 but they will not have o

Occupation

Ge 46:33 actually say, What is your o?
47:3 What is your o? So they said
Ec 1:13 the calamitous o that God has
2:23 o means pains and vexation
2:26 sinner he has given the o of
3:10 o that God has given to the
4:8 and it is a calamitous o
5:3 because of abundance of o
5:7 because of abundance of o
5:14 because of a calamitous o
8:16 the o that is carried on in
Ac 19:27 o of ours will come into

Occupied

Ec 1:13 of mankind in which to be o
3:10 of mankind in which to be o
Ac 18:5 o with the word, witnessing

Occupy

Lu 14:9 to o the lowest place
Heb 13:9 o themselves with them have

Occupying

1Co 14:16 o the seat of the ordinary

Occur

Ge 1:6 dividing o between the waters
9:11 no more will there o a deluge
9:14 it shall o that when I bring
9:16 rainbow must o in the cloud
18:25 so that it has to o with the
24:14 must o is that the young
Ge 24:43 must o is that the maiden
26:28 oath of obligation o between
27:40 certainly o that, when you
44:31 certain to o that as soon
46:33 what must o is that when
Ex 3:21 certainly o that when you go
4:8 And it must o that, to quote
4:9 it must o that, if they will
4:16 it must o that he will serve
10:21 darkness may o over the land
10:22 gloomy darkness began to o
11:6 o a great outcry in . . . Egypt
12:25 must o that when you come
12:26 o that when your sons say to
13:5 it must o that when Jehovah
13:11 it must o that when Jehovah
13:14 must o that in case your son
16:5 it must o on the sixth day
18:22 must o that every big case
21:13 God lets it o at his hand
21:23 if a fatal accident should o
22:27 o that he will cry out to me
33:22 has to o that while my glory
Le 5:5 must o that in case he becomes
6:4 must o that in case he sins
14:9 o on the seventh day that
15:2 discharge o from his genital
23:7 have a holy convention o
23:24 o for you a complete rest, a
23:36 o a holy convention for you
25:4 o a sabbath of complete rest
25:5 o a sabbath of complete rest
Nu 5:27 o that if she has defiled
8:19 no plague may o among the
10:32 o that in case you should
10:32 o that with what goodness
10:35 o that when the Ark would
15:19 it must also o that when you
15:24 must then o that if it has
16:7 it must o that the man whom
17:5 what must o is that the man
18:5 indignation may o against the
21:8 must o that when anyone has
21:9 it did o that if a serpent had
33:56 o that just as I had figured
De 6:10 it must o that when Jehovah
7:12 it must o that, because you
8:19 it must o that if you should
11:13 it must o that if you will
11:17 no rain will o and the
11:29 it must o that when Jehovah
12:11 it must o that the place
15:16 it must o that in case he
17:18 it must o that when he takes
18:19 it must o that the man who
18:22 the word does not o or come
20:2 it must o that when you have
20:9 it must o that when the
20:11 it must o that if it gives
20:11 it must even o that all the
21:14 it must o that if you have
21:16 it must also o that in the
23:11 o that at the falling of
23:13 must o that when you squat
24:1 it must also o that if she
25:2 it must o that if the wicked
25:6 it must o that the firstborn
25:19 it must o that when Jehovah
26:1 it must o that when at last
27:2 it must o that in the day
27:4 o that when you have crossed
28:1 it must o that if you will
28:15 it must o that if you will
28:63 must o that just as Jehovah
29:19 o that when someone has
30:1 o that when all these words
31:21 o that when many calamities
Jos 2:14 o that when Jehovah gives
2:19 must o that anyone who goes
3:13 must o that at the instant
5:12 manna did not o anymore for
6:5 must o that when they sound
7:14 must o that the tribe that
7:15 must o that the one picked
8:5 must o that, in case they
8:8 must o that as soon as you
22:18 it must o that should you
22:28 And it must o that in case
23:15 And it must o that, just
Jg 4:20 and it must o that if anybody
6:39 dryness o to the fleece alone
7:4 it must o that of whomever I
7:17 o that just as I shall do, so
9:33 it must o in the morning that

Jg 11:31 it must also *o* that the one
21:22 it must *o* that should their
Ru 3:4 should *o* that when he lies
3:13 must *o* in the morning that
1Sa 2:36 must *o* that anyone left over
3:9 *o* that, if he should call
10:7 *o* that when these signs come
16:16 must *o* that, when God's bad
17:25 *o* that, the man who strikes
23:23 *o* that, if he is in the land
25:30 *o* that, because Jehovah
2Sa 5:24 *o* that, when you hear the
11:20 *o* that if the rage of the
15:35 it must *o* that everything
17:9 *o* that, just as soon as he
1Ki 1:21 *o* that as soon as my lord
2:37 it must *o* that on the day of
8:37 locusts, cockroaches *o*
8:38 *o* on the part of any man or
11:38 must *o* that, if you obey
14:5 will *o* that as soon as she
14:28 *o* that as often as the king
17:1 *o* during these years neither
17:4 must *o* that from the torrent
18:12 bound to *o* that, when I
18:24 must *o* that the true God
18:45 a great downpour began to *o*
19:17 *o* that the one escaping
20:6 *o* that everything desirable
2Ki 4:10 must *o* that whenever he
1Ch 14:15 let it *o* that, when you
17:11 must *o* that when your days
2Ch 6:28 locusts and cockroaches *o*
6:29 *o* on the part of any man or
7:13 heavens that no rain may *o*
12:11 *o* that as often as the king
15:19 war, it did not *o* down to
Ezr 7:23 may *o* no wrath against the
Job 1:5 *o* that when the banquet days
20:23 Let it *o* that, to fill his
Ec 11:2 calamity will *o* on the earth
Isa 2:2 must *o* in the final part of
3:24 *o* that instead of balsam oil
4:3 *o* that the ones remaining
7:18 *o* in that day that Jehovah
7:21 *o* in that day that an
7:22 *o* that, due to the abundance
7:23 *o* in that day that every
8:8 *o* to fill the breadth of your
8:21 *o* that because he is hungry
10:12 *o* that when Jehovah
10:20 *o* in that day that those
10:27 *o* in that day that his load
11:10 *o* in that day that there
11:11 *o* in that day that Jehovah
13:14 *o* that, like a gazelle
14:3 *o* in the day when Jehovah
14:24 have figured, so it must *o*
16:2 *o* that like a fleeing winged
17:4 *o* in that day that the glory
17:5 *o* that when the harvester
22:7 *o* that the choicest of your
22:20 *o* in that day that I will
23:15 *o* in that day that Tyre
23:17 *o* at the end of seventy
24:18 *o* that anyone fleeing from
24:21 *o* in that day that Jehovah
27:12 *o* in that day that Jehovah
27:13 *o* in that day that there
29:5 *o* in an instant, suddenly
29:7 *o* just as in a dream, in
29:8 *o* just as when someone
29:8 *o* with the crowd of all the
65:24 *o* that before they call out
66:23 *o* that from new moon to
Jer 1:4 word of Jehovah began to *o* to
1:11 *o* to me, saying: What are
1:13 to *o* to me the second time
2:1 proceeded to *o* to me, saying
3:16 must *o* that you will become
4:9 And it must *o* in that day
5:19 it must *o* that you will say
12:15 it must *o* that after my
12:16 it must *o* that if they will
13:3 to *o* to me a second time
14:15 famine will *o* in this land
15:2 must *o* that should they say
16:1 continued to *o* to me, saying
16:10 it must *o* that, when you
17:24 *o* that, if you strictly obey
18:5 word of Jehovah continued to *o*
25:12 it must *o* that when seventy
25:28 it must *o* that in case they
27:8 it must *o* that the nation
Jer 30:8 And it must *o* in that day
31:28 *o* that just as I had kept
33:1 *o* to Jeremiah the second
33:20 day and night not to *o* in
33:23 to *o* to Jeremiah, saying
35:12 to *o* to Jeremiah, saying
42:4 *o* that every word that
42:7 proceeded to *o* to Jeremiah
42:16 *o* that the very sword of
49:39 *o* in the final part of the
51:63 *o* that when you will have
La 3:37 said that something should *o*
Eze 3:16 proceeded to *o* to me, saying
6:1 continued to *o* to me, saying
7:1 continued to *o* to me, saying
7:26 will *o* report upon report
11:14 continued to *o* to me
12:1 continued to *o* to me, saying
12:8 to *o* to me in the morning
12:17 to *o* to me, saying
12:26 continued to *o* to me
13:1 continued to *o* to me, saying
13:11 downpour will certainly *o*
13:13 will *o* a flooding downpour
15:1 continued to *o* to me, saying
16:19 and it continued to *o*, is
17:1 continued to *o* to me, saying
17:11 to *o* to me, saying
18:1 word of Jehovah . . . *o* to me
20:45 to *o* to me, saying
21:1 continued to *o* to me, saying
21:7 must *o* that, in case they
21:7 come and be brought to *o*
21:8 continued to *o* to me, saying
21:18 to *o* to me, saying
22:1 continued to *o* to me, saying
24:1 *o* to me in the ninth year
24:15 to *o* to me, saying
25:1 continued to *o* to me, saying
27:1 continued to *o* to me, saying
28:1 continued to *o* to me, saying
28:11 continued to *o* to me
28:20 continued to *o* to me
30:1 continued to *o* to me, saying
30:4 pains must *o* in Ethiopia
30:9 severe pains must *o* among
33:1 proceeded to *o* to me, saying
33:23 word of Jehovah began to *o*
34:1 continued to *o* to me, saying
35:1 continued to *o* to me, saying
36:16 continued to *o* to me
37:7 a sound began to *o* as soon
37:15 continued to *o* to me
38:1 continued to *o* to me, saying
38:10 must *o* in that day that
38:16 part of the days it will *o*
38:18 it must *o* in that day
38:19 *o* in the soil of Israel
39:11 it must *o* in that day that
43:27 *o* on the eighth day and
44:17 *o* that when they come into
45:21 *o* for you the passover
47:9 *o* that every living soul that
47:9 *o* that there will be very
47:10 *o* that fishers will
47:22 *o* that you should allot it
47:23 *o* that in the tribe with
Da 2:28 *o* in the final part of the
2:29 what is to *o* after this
2:29 known to you what is to *o*
2:45 king what is to *o* after this
4:27 *o* a lengthening of your
8:19 *o* in the final part of the
12:1 *o* a time of distress such as
12:1 *o* since there came to be a
Ho 1:5 *o* in that day that I must
1:10 *o* that in the place in which
2:16 *o* in that day, is the
2:21 *o* in that day that I shall
Joe 2:28 it must *o* that I shall pour
2:32 it must *o* that everyone who
3:18 it must *o* in that day that
Am 6:9 it must *o* that if ten men
7:3 It shall not *o*, Jehovah said
7:6 That, too, will not *o*, the
8:9 it must *o* in that day, is the
Jon 1:1 word of Jehovah began to *o*
Mic 4:1 it must *o* in the final part
5:10 And it must *o* in that day
7:4 *o* the confounding of them
Na 3:7 it must *o* that everyone seeing
Hab 1:3 why does quarreling *o*, and
Zep 1:8 *o* on the day of Jehovah's
1:10 must *o* on that day, is the
Zep 1:12 must *o* at that time that
Hag 2:20 to *o* a second time to Haggai
Zec 4:8 continued to *o* to me, saying
6:9 continued to *o* to me, saying
6:15 And it must *o*—if you will
7:4 continued to *o* to me, saying
7:8 to *o* to Zechariah, saying
8:1 word . . . continued to *o*
8:13 must *o* that just as you
8:18 continued to *o* to me, saying
12:3 must *o* in that day that I
12:9 must *o* in that day that I
13:2 And it must *o* in that day
13:3 *o* that in case a man should
13:4 And it must *o* in that day
13:8 it must *o* in all the land
14:6 must *o* in that day that
14:7 must *o* that at evening time
14:8 it must *o* in that day that
14:8 and in winter it will *o*
14:11 *o* no more any banning to
14:13 must *o* in that day that
14:16 must *o* that, as regards
14:17 must *o* that, as regards
14:17 no pouring rain will *o*
14:18 scourge will *o* with which
Mt 24:20 may not *o* in wintertime
24:21 no, nor will *o* again
24:34 until all these things *o*
Mr 4:11 all things *o* in illustrations
11:23 what he says is going to *o*
13:18 it may not *o* in wintertime
13:19 and will not *o* again
Lu 21:7 things are destined to *o*
21:9 these things must *o* first
21:9 end does not *o* immediately
21:28 things start to *o*, raise
21:32 pass away until all things *o*
21:36 things that are destined to *o*
23:31 will *o* when it is withered
Joh 13:19 it does *o* you may believe
14:29 it does *o*, you may believe
Ac 2:43 signs began to *o* through the
4:28 counsel had foreordained to *o*
4:30 signs and portents *o* through
5:12 portents continued to *o* among
14:3 portents to *o* through their
Ga 6:14 *o* that I should boast, except

Occurred

Ge 7:6 the deluge of waters *o* on the
8:6 it *o* that at the end of forty
26:1 the first famine that *o* in the
26:32 it *o* that the servants of
30:41 *o* that whenever the robust
38:9 it *o* that when he did have
39:13 it *o* that as soon as she saw
43:21 what *o* was that when we
Ex 9:18 never *o* in Egypt from the day
9:24 not *o* any like it in all the
9:26 Israel were, there *o* no hail
11:6 like of which has never yet *o*
16:10 it *o* that as soon as Aaron
16:13 it *o* that in the evening the
17:11 it *o* that as soon as Moses
33:7 it *o* that everyone inquiring
33:8 it *o* that as soon as Moses
33:9 also *o* that as soon as Moses
De 4:32 the former days that *o* before
Jg 2:19 *o* that when the judge died
6:3 *o* that, if Israel sowed seed
6:40 and upon all the earth dew *o*
12:5 it *o* that when the escaping
19:30 it *o* that everybody seeing
21:3 Why . . . has this *o* in Israel
1Sa 1:12 it *o* that while she prayed
4:7 thing as this never *o* before
4:17 also *o* a great defeat among
5:11 death-dealing confusion had *o*
10:9 *o* that as soon as he turned
14:15 a trembling *o* in the camp
16:23 *o* that, when God's spirit
17:48 *o* that the Philistine rose
25:20 *o* that while she was riding
2Sa 6:16 *o* that when the ark of
13:32 order of Absalom it has *o*
14:26 *o* at the end of every year
15:5 *o* that, when a man drew
1Ki 17:7 *o* no downpour upon the earth
2Ki 3:15 it *o* that, as soon as the
2Ch 22:7 downfall of Ahaziah *o* by
24:4 *o* afterward that it became
25:14 *o* after Amaziah came from
29:36 sudden that the thing had *o*

Es 8:16 For the Jews there *o* light
Isa 14:28 this pronouncement *o*
16:12 *o* that it was seen that
29:15 deeds have *o* in a dark place
38:4 now *o* to Isaiah, saying
Jer 1:2 *o* in the days of Josiah the
3:3 not even a spring rain has *o*
3:9 her prostitution *o* because of
7:1 The word that *o* to Jeremiah
11:1 The word that *o* to Jeremiah
13:8 the word of Jehovah *o* to me
14:1 This is what *o* as the word
14:4 there has *o* no downpour upon
17:16 front of your face it has *o*
18:1 The word that *o* to Jeremiah
21:1 The word that *o* to Jeremiah
24:4 the word of Jehovah *o* to me
25:1 The word that *o* to Jeremiah
25:3 the word of Jehovah has *o*
26:1 this word *o* from Jehovah
27:1 this word *o* to Jeremiah
28:12 the word of Jehovah *o* to
29:30 word of Jehovah *o* to
30:1 The word that *o* to Jeremiah
32:1 word that *o* to Jeremiah
32:6 word of Jehovah has *o* to me
32:26 the word of Jehovah *o* to
34:1 word that *o* to Jeremiah
34:8 word that *o* to Jeremiah
34:12 word of Jehovah *o* to
35:1 word that *o* to Jeremiah
36:1 *o* to Jeremiah from Jehovah
36:27 *o* further to Jeremiah after
37:6 *o* to Jeremiah the prophet
37:11 *o* when the military force
38:28 *o* just when Jerusalem was
39:15 word of Jehovah *o* while he
40:1 word that *o* to Jeremiah
41:7 *o* that as soon as they came
43:8 word . . . *o* to Jeremiah
44:1 word that *o* to Jeremiah for
46:1 *o* as the word of Jehovah to
49:34 *o* as the word of Jehovah to
52:3 anger of Jehovah it *o* in
Eze 1:3 *o* specifically to Ezekiel the
12:21 word of Jehovah *o* further
14:2 the word of Jehovah *o* to me
20:2 the word of Jehovah *o* to me
24:20 word of Jehovah has *o* to me
26:1 word of Jehovah *o* to me
29:1 word of Jehovah *o* to me
29:17 word of Jehovah *o* to me
30:20 it *o* further that in the
30:20 word of Jehovah *o* to me
31:1 *o* further that in the
31:1 word of Jehovah *o* to me
32:1 it *o* further that in the
32:1 word of Jehovah *o* to me
32:17 it *o* further that in the
32:17 word of Jehovah *o* to me
33:21 *o* in the twelfth year, in
Da 9:2 word . . . had *o* to Jeremiah
Ho 1:1 word of Jehovah . . . *o* to Hosea
12:11 also untruth, have *o*
Joe 1:1 The word of Jehovah that *o*
1:2 Has this *o* in your days
Am 7:2 it *o* that when it had finished
Jon 3:1 *o* to Jonah the second time
Mic 1:1 that *o* to Micah of Moresheth
Zep 1:1 *o* to Zephaniah the son of
Hag 1:1 word of Jehovah *o* by means of
2:1 word of Jehovah *o* by means of
2:10 word of Jehovah *o* to Haggai
Zec 1:1 of Jehovah *o* to Zechariah
1:7 the word of Jehovah *o* to
7:1 *o* to Zechariah, on the fourth
7:12 *o* great indignation on the
7:13 it *o* that, just as he called
Mal 1:9 From your hand this has *o*
Mt 24:21 such as has not *o* since the
Mr 13:19 such as has not *o* from the
Lu 9:36 as the voice *o* Jesus was
15:14 severe famine *o* throughout
17:14 going off their cleansing *o*
17:26 just as it *o* in the days of
17:28 as it *o* in the days of Lot
23:47 seeing what *o* the army
23:48 they beheld the things that *o*
24:12 wondering . . . at what had *o*
24:18 things that have *o* in her in
24:21 day since these things *o*
Joh 12:30 voice has *o*, not for my
Ac 2:2 *o* from heaven a noise just
2:6 So, when this sound *o*, the
Ac 4:16 sign has *o* through them
4:21 God over what had *o*
4:22 sign of healing had *o* was
10:16 This *o* a third time, and
11:10 *o* for a third time, and
15:2 had *o* no little dissension
15:39 *o* a sharp burst of anger, so
16:26 Suddenly a great earthquake *o*
21:30 together of the people *o*; and
28:9 After this *o*, the rest of
Ro 3:25 the sins that *o* in the past
2Ti 2:18 resurrection has already *o*
Heb 9:15 has *o* for their release by
Re 6:12 seal, and a great earthquake *o*
8:1 a silence *o* in heaven for about
8:5 And thunders *o* and voices and
8:7 And there *o* a hail and fire
11:13 a great earthquake *o*, and a
11:15 And loud voices *o* in heaven
11:19 *o* lightnings and voices and
16:18 voices and thunders *o*, and
16:18 great earthquake *o* such as
16:18 *o* since men came to be on

Occurrence
Ec 9:11 unforeseen *o* befall them all

Occurring
Ex 9:28 *o* of God's thunders and hail
19:16 and lightnings began *o*, and a
2Sa 24:13 the *o* of three days of
Isa 48:16 From the time of its *o* I
Jer 1:3 *o* in the days of Jehoiakim
Lu 21:31 when you see these things *o*
23:19 sedition *o* in the city and
Jas 3:10 things to go on *o* this way

Occurs
Ex 21:22 but no fatal accident *o*, he
De 23:10 a pollution that *o* at night
1Ki 8:35 shut up so that no rain *o*
8:37 a famine *o* in the land
8:37 in case a pestilence *o*
2Ch 6:26 shut up so that no rain *o*
6:28 case a famine *o* in the land
6:28 in case a pestilence *o*, in
Eze 1:28 bow that *o* in a cloud mass
6:8 when it *o* I will let you have
16:34 so it *o* in the opposite way
Am 3:6 If a calamity *o* in the city
Mt 26:2 passover *o*, and the Son of
Lu 12:55 be a heat wave, and it *o*
Joh 13:19 telling you before it *o*
14:29 I have told you before it *o*
Heb 7:18 *o* a setting aside of the

Ochran
Nu 1:13 of Asher, Pagiel the son of *O*
2:27 is Pagiel the son of *O*
7:72 Pagiel the son of *O*
7:77 of Pagiel the son of *O*
10:26 Pagiel the son of *O*

Octave
Ps 6:*super* instruments on the lower *o*
12:*super* director on the lower *o*

Oded
2Ch 15:1 Azariah the son of *O*, the
15:8 prophecy of *O* the prophet
28:9 there whose name was *O*

Odor
Ge 8:21 began to smell a restful *o*
Ex 29:18 to Jehovah, a restful *o*
29:25 as a restful *o* before Jehovah
29:41 render it as a restful *o*
Le 1:9 of a restful *o* to Jehovah
1:13 made by fire of a restful *o*
1:17 of a restful *o* to Jehovah
2:2 of a restful *o* to Jehovah
2:9 fire of a restful *o* to Jehovah
2:12 the altar for a restful *o*
3:5 of a restful *o* to Jehovah
3:16 made by fire for a restful *o*
4:31 as a restful *o* to Jehovah
6:15 restful *o* for a remembrancer
6:21 as a restful *o* to Jehovah
8:21 offering for a restful *o*
8:28 sacrifice for a restful *o*
17:6 fat smoke as a restful *o*
23:13 restful *o*; and as its drink
23:18 of a restful *o* to Jehovah
Nu 15:3 make a restful *o* to Jehovah
15:7 as a restful *o* to Jehovah
15:10 of a restful *o* to Jehovah
15:13 of a restful *o* to Jehovah
Nu 15:14 of a restful *o* to Jehovah
15:24 for a restful *o* to Jehovah
18:17 for a restful *o* to Jehovah
28:2 by fire as a restful *o* to me
28:6 a restful *o*, an offering made
28:8 of a restful *o* to Jehovah
28:13 a burnt offering, a restful *o*
28:24 of a restful *o* to Jehovah
28:27 for a restful *o* to Jehovah
29:2 offering for a restful *o* to
29:6 as a restful *o*, an offering
29:8 to Jehovah, as a restful *o*
29:13 of a restful *o* to Jehovah
29:36 of a restful *o* to Jehovah
Eze 6:13 restful *o* to all their dungy
16:19 before them as a restful *o*
20:41 Because of the restful *o*
2Co 2:14 *o* of the knowledge of him
2:15 a sweet *o* of Christ among
2:16 an *o* issuing from death to
2:16 an *o* issuing from life to
Eph 5:2 to God for a sweet-smelling *o*
Php 4:18 a sweet-smelling *o*, an

Odors
Le 26:31 not smell your restful *o*
Eze 20:28 their restful *o* and pouring

Offal
Isa 5:25 *o* in the midst of the

Offend
De 4:25 your God so as to *o* him
9:18 doing evil . . . so as to *o* him
31:29 *o* him by the works of your
32:21 stupid nation I shall *o* them
1Ki 14:9 and molten images to *o* me
16:33 to *o* Jehovah the God of
2Ki 17:11 bad things to *o* Jehovah
17:17 of Jehovah, to *o* him
21:6 in Jehovah's eyes, to *o* him
22:17 in order to *o* me with all
23:26 Manasseh had made them *o*
2Ch 33:6 eyes of Jehovah, to *o* him
34:25 *o* me with all the doings of
Jer 11:17 *o* me in making sacrificial
25:6 *o* me with the work of your
25:7 might *o* me with the work
32:32 they have done to *o* me
44:3 *o* me by going and making
Eze 8:17 that they should *o* me again
16:26 prostitution . . . to *o* me
32:9 *o* the heart of many peoples

Offended
Jg 2:12 so that they *o* Jehovah
1Ki 15:30 he *o* Jehovah the God of
21:22 *o* and then caused Israel to
2Ch 16:10 Asa became *o* at the seer
28:25 *o* Jehovah the God of his
Ne 4:1 he became angry and highly *o*
Ec 7:9 Do not hurry . . . to become *o*
Jer 8:19 *o* me with their graven
Eze 16:42 and I shall no more feel *o*

Offender
Jas 2:10 an *o* against them all

Offenders
1Ki 1:21 shall certainly become *o*

Offending
De 32:16 they kept *o* him
1Ki 14:15 sacred poles, so *o* Jehovah
16:2 by *o* me with their sins
16:7 by *o* him with the work of
16:13 sin by *o* Jehovah the God of
16:26 sin by *o* Jehovah the God of
22:53 kept *o* Jehovah the God of
2Ki 21:15 continually *o* me from the
Ps 78:58 *o* him with their high places
Isa 65:3 those *o* me right to my face
Jer 7:18 for the purpose of *o* me
7:19 Is it I whom they are *o*?
32:29 for the purpose of *o* me
32:30 *o* me by the work of their
44:8 *o* me with the works of your

Offense
1Ki 21:22 the *o* with which you have
2Ki 23:19 had built to cause *o*
Ne 4:5 *o* against the builders
Ps 106:29 causing *o* by their dealings
Ec 7:9 the taking of *o* is what rests
Ho 12:14 Ephraim caused *o* to
Ac 24:16 committing no *o* against God
Ro 9:33 and a rock-mass of *o*, but he
1Pe 2:8 and a rock-mass of *o*

Offensive
Ex 5:21 smell *o* before Pharaoh
2Ki 23:26 over all the *o* things with
Eze 20:28 there their *o* offering, and

Offensiveness
1Ki 15:30 by his *o* with which he

Offer
Ge 8:20 *o* burnt offerings upon the
22:2 *o* him up as a burnt offering
Ex 29:36 *o* the bull of the sin
29:38 *o* upon the altar: young rams
29:39 *o* the one young ram in the
29:39 *o* the other young ram
29:41 *o* the second young ram
30:9 not *o* upon it illegitimate
40:29 *o* up the burnt offering and
Le 14:12 and *o* it for a guilt offering
14:20 *o* up the burnt offering and
15:15 priest must *o* them, the one
Nu 22:32 come out to *o* resistance
23:4 *o* up a bull and a ram on each
23:14 to *o* up a bull and a ram on
De 12:13 *o* up your burnt offerings in
12:14 *o* up your burnt offerings
27:6 *o* burnt offerings to Jehovah
Jos 22:23 to *o* up burnt offerings and
Jg 6:26 *o* it up as a burnt offering on
11:31 and I must *o* that one up as
13:16 burnt offering . . . you may *o*
13:19 and to *o* it upon the rock to
16:25 he may *o* us some amusement
21:4 to *o* up burnt offerings and
1Sa 10:8 to *o* up burnt sacrifices, to
2Sa 24:22 *o* up what is good in his
24:24 not *o* up to Jehovah my God
24:25 *o* up burnt sacrifices and
1Ki 3:4 proceeded to *o* upon that altar
8:63 *o* the communion sacrifices
8:63 sacrifices that he had to *o*
9:25 to *o* up burnt sacrifices and
1Ch 16:40 to *o* up burnt offerings to
21:24 to *o* up burnt sacrifices
29:21 and *o* up burnt offerings to
2Ch 1:6 to *o* upon it a thousand burnt
23:18 *o* up the burnt sacrifices
29:7 *o* up in the holy place to the
29:21 *o* them up upon the altar of
29:27 *o* up the burnt sacrifice on
29:30 *o* praise even with
35:16 *o* up the burnt offerings
Ezr 3:2 *o* up burnt sacrifices upon it
3:6 to *o* up burnt sacrifices to
6:3 they are to *o* sacrifices
Ne 10:38 *o* up a tenth of the tenth to
12:24 to *o* praise and give thanks
Job 42:8 must *o* up a burnt sacrifice
Ps 44:8 we will *o* praise all day long
50:14 *O* thanksgiving as your
66:15 fatlings I shall *o* up to you
107:22 *o* the sacrifices of
110:3 *o* themselves willingly on
113:1 *O* praise, O you servants
116:17 I shall *o* the sacrifice of
135:1 *O* praise, O servants of
Isa 11:11 Jehovah will again *o* his
57:7 you went up to *o* sacrifice
Jer 14:12 they *o* up the whole burnt
33:18 *o* up whole burnt offering
Eze 16:33 you *o* a bribe to them to
43:18 *o* upon it whole burnt
43:24 *o* them up as a whole burnt
45:1 *o* a contribution to Jehovah
45:13 that you should *o*
Da 2:46 *o* even a present and incense
Ho 14:2 we will *o* in return the young
Am 5:22 *o* up to me whole burnt
8:5 and we may *o* grain for sale
Mt 5:24 come back, *o* up your gift
8:4 and *o* the gift that Moses
19:13 hands upon them and *o* prayer
Mr 1:44 *o* in behalf of your cleansing
Lu 1:9 his turn to *o* incense when he
2:24 to *o* sacrifice according to
5:33 *o* supplications, and so do
6:29 one cheek, *o* the other also
Ac 14:13 desiring to *o* sacrifices
1Co 9:12 not *o* any hindrance to the
14:16 if you *o* praise with a gift
Php 1:4 I *o* my supplication with joy
2Th 3:9 *o* ourselves as an example to
Heb 2:17 to *o* propitiatory sacrifice
5:1 *o* gifts and sacrifices for
7:27 to *o* up sacrifices, first
Heb 8:3 *o* both gifts and sacrifices
8:3 also to have something to *o*
8:4 being men who *o* the gifts
9:25 he should *o* himself often
10:1 which they *o* continually
10:11 *o* the same sacrifices often
11:17 *o* up his only-begotten son
13:15 *o* to God a sacrifice of
1Pe 2:5 to *o* up spiritual sacrifices
Re 4:9 living creatures *o* glory and
8:3 to *o* it with the prayers of

Offered
Ge 22:13 *o* it up for a burnt offering
Ex 24:5 they *o* up burnt offerings and
Nu 3:4 *o* illegitimate fire before
23:2 Balak and Balaam *o* up a bull
Jg 6:28 young bull had been *o* up on
16:27 Samson *o* some amusement
20:26 and *o* up burnt offerings and
21:13 assembly . . . *o* them peace
1Sa 6:14 the cows they *o* up as a burnt
6:15 *o* up burnt offerings, and
7:9 *o* it up as a burnt offering
2Sa 6:17 David *o* up burnt sacrifices
15:12 when he *o* the sacrifices
1Ki 3:15 *o* up burnt sacrifices and
10:5 regularly *o* up at the house
2Ki 3:27 and *o* him up as a burnt
1Ch 21:26 *o* up burnt sacrifices and
29:17 have voluntarily *o* all these
2Ch 8:12 Solomon *o* up burnt
9:4 *o* up at the house of Jehovah
29:6 *o* the back of the neck
Ezr 1:6 that which was voluntarily *o*
3:5 *o* a voluntary offering to
Job 1:5 and *o* up burnt sacrifices
Ps 51:19 *o* up on your very own altar
Isa 57:6 you *o* up a gift. For these
Eze 6:13 *o* a restful odor to all their
Jon 1:16 they *o* a sacrifice to Jehovah
Mr 14:23 taking a cup, he *o* thanks
Ac 7:42 not to me that you *o* victims
8:18 he *o* them money
1Co 8:1 concerning foods *o* to idols
8:4 the eating of foods *o* to idols
8:10 of eating foods *o* to idols
10:28 is something *o* in sacrifice
1Ti 6:12 and you *o* the fine public
Heb 5:7 Christ *o* up supplications and
7:27 when he *o* himself up
9:9 gifts and sacrifices are *o*
9:14 *o* himself without blemish
9:28 Christ was *o* once for all
10:2 stopped being *o*, because
10:8 sacrifices that are *o*
10:12 *o* one sacrifice for sins
11:4 Abel *o* God a sacrifice of
11:17 as good as *o* up Isaac, and
Jas 2:21 *o* up Isaac his son upon the

Offerers
2Ch 24:14 *o* of burnt sacrifices in

Offering
Ge 4:3 fruits of the ground as an *o*
4:4 with favor upon Abel and his *o*
4:5 upon Cain and upon his *o*
22:2 offer him up as a burnt *o* on
22:3 the wood for the burnt *o*
22:6 wood of the burnt *o* and put
22:7 is the sheep for the burnt *o*
22:8 sheep for the burnt *o*, my son
22:13 burnt *o* in place of his son
35:14 he poured a drink *o* upon it
Ex 18:12 a burnt *o* and sacrifices for
29:14 It is a sin *o*
29:18 It is a burnt *o* to Jehovah
29:18 an *o* made by fire to Jehovah
29:24 as a wave *o* before Jehovah
29:25 upon the burnt *o* as a restful
29:25 an *o* made by fire to Jehovah
29:26 as a wave *o* before Jehovah
29:27 the breast of the wave *o* and
29:36 bull of the sin *o* daily for
29:40 drink *o* of the fourth of a
29:41 With a grain *o* like that of
29:41 and with a drink *o* like
29:41 an *o* made by fire to Jehovah
29:42 It is a constant burnt *o*
30:9, 9 a burnt *o* or a grain *o*
30:9 not pour a drink *o* upon it
30:10 the sin *o* of the atonement
30:20 to make an *o* made by fire
30:28 the altar of burnt *o* and all
Ex 31:9 altar of burnt *o* and all its
32:6 began *o* up burnt offerings
35:16 the altar of burnt *o* and
35:22 presented the wave *o* of gold
35:29 a voluntary *o* to Jehovah
36:3 voluntary *o* morning after
38:1 make the altar of burnt *o* out
38:24 of the gold of the wave *o*
38:29 the copper of the wave *o* was
40:6 altar of burnt *o* before the
40:10 anoint the altar of burnt *o*
40:29 altar of burnt *o* at the
40:29, 29 burnt *o* and the grain *o*
Le 1:2 present an *o* to Jehovah from
1:2 your *o* from the herd and from
1:3, 3 If his *o* is a burnt *o* from
1:4 upon the head of the burnt *o*
1:6 the burnt *o* must be skinned
1:9 on the altar as a burnt *o*
1:9 an *o* made by fire of a restful
1:10, 10 if his *o* for a burnt *o* is
1:13, 13 is a burnt *o*, an *o* made by
1:14, 14 *o* as a burnt *o* to Jehovah
1:14 his *o* from the turtledoves
1:17, 17 a burnt *o*, an *o* made by
2:1, 1 as an *o* a grain *o* to Jehovah
2:1 *o* should prove to be fine flour
2:2 an *o* made by fire of a restful
2:3 what is left of the grain *o*
2:4, 4 an *o* a grain *o* in the way
2:5, 5 if your *o* is a grain *o* from
2:6 It is a grain *o*
2:7, 7 And if your *o* is a grain *o*
2:8 bring the grain *o* that was
2:9 lift off some of the grain *o*
2:9 as an *o* made by fire of a
2:10 left of the grain *o* belongs to
2:11 No grain *o* that you will
2:11 an *o* made by fire to Jehovah
2:12 As an *o* of the firstfruits
2:13, 13 every *o* of your grain *o*
2:13 be missing upon your grain *o*
2:13 *o* of yours you will present
2:14 grain *o* of the first ripe
2:14 the grain *o* of your first ripe
2:15 It is a grain *o*
2:16 an *o* made by fire to Jehovah
3:1 And if his *o* is a communion
3:2 his hand upon the head of his *o*
3:3 an *o* made by fire to Jehovah
3:5 burnt *o* that is over the wood
3:5 *o* made by fire of a restful
3:6 if his *o* is from the flock for
3:7 a young ram as his *o*
3:8 his hand upon the head of his *o*
3:9 an *o* made by fire to Jehovah
3:11 an *o* made by fire to Jehovah
3:12 if his *o* is a goat, then he
3:14 it he must present as his *o*
3:14 an *o* made by fire to Jehovah
3:16 *o* made by fire for a restful
4:3 bull to Jehovah as a sin *o*
4:7 base of the altar of burnt *o*
4:8 fat of the bull of the sin *o*
4:10 upon the altar of burnt *o*
4:14 a young bull for a sin *o* and
4:18 base of the altar of burnt *o*
4:20 the other bull of the sin *o*
4:21 a sin *o* for the congregation
4:23 as his *o* a male kid of the
4:24 the burnt *o* is regularly
4:24 It is a sin *o*
4:25 the blood of the sin *o* with
4:25 horns of the altar of burnt *o*
4:25 base of the altar of burnt *o*
4:28 *o* a female kid of the goats
4:29 upon the head of the sin *o*
4:29 and slaughter the sin *o* in the
4:29 the same place as the burnt *o*
4:30 horns of the altar of burnt *o*
4:32, 32 lamb as his *o* for a sin *o*
4:33 upon the head of the sin *o*
4:33 slaughter it as a sin *o* in
4:33 the place where the burnt *o*
4:34 the blood of the sin *o* with
4:34 horns of the altar of burnt *o*
5:6 guilt *o* to Jehovah for his sin
5:6 kid of the goats, for a sin *o*
5:7 his guilt *o* for the sin that
5:7 one for a sin *o* and one for a
5:7 and one for a burnt *o*
5:8 first the one for the sin *o*
5:9 the blood of the sin *o* upon the
5:9 It is a sin *o*

Le 5:10 as a burnt *o* according to the
5:11 as his *o* for the sin he has
5:11 of fine flour for a sin *o*
5:11 for it is a sin *o*
5:12 It is a sin *o*
5:13 the same as a grain *o*
5:15 as his guilt *o* to Jehovah
5:15 holy place, as a guilt *o*
5:16 with the ram of the guilt *o*
5:18 for a guilt *o*, to the priest
5:19 It is a guilt *o*
6:6 And as his guilt *o* he will
6:6 estimated value, for a guilt *o*
6:9 is the law of the burnt *o*
6:9 The burnt *o* will be on the
6:10 fatty ashes of the burnt *o*
6:12 set the burnt *o* in order over
6:14 is the law of the grain *o*
6:15 fine flour of the grain *o*
6:15 that is upon the grain *o*, and
6:17, 17 sin *o* and like the guilt *o*
6:20 This is the *o* of Aaron and
6:20 fine flour as a grain *o*
6:21 the pastries of the grain *o*
6:22 As a whole *o* it will be made
6:23 every grain *o* of a priest
6:23 should prove to be a whole *o*
6:25 This is the law of the sin *o*
6:25 place where the burnt *o* is
6:25 sin *o* will be slaughtered
6:30 no sin *o* of which some of
7:1 is the law of the guilt *o*
7:2 slaughter the burnt *o* they
7:2 will slaughter the guilt *o*
7:5 an *o* made by fire to Jehovah
7:5 It is a guilt *o*
7:7, 7 the sin *o*, so is the guilt *o*
7:8 presents the burnt *o* of any
7:8 the skin of the burnt *o* that
7:9 grain *o* that may be baked in
7:10 grain *o* that is moistened
7:13 present his *o* together with
7:14 each *o* as a sacred portion to
7:15 be eaten on the day of his *o*
7:16 of his *o* is a vow or a
7:16 is a vow or a voluntary *o*
7:25 an *o* made by fire to Jehovah
7:29 bring his *o* to Jehovah from
7:30 as a wave *o* before Jehovah
7:34 the breast of the wave *o* and
7:37 law concerning the burnt *o*
7:37, 37 the grain *o* and the sin *o*
7:37 guilt *o* and the installation
8:2 the bull of the sin *o* and the
8:14 led up the bull of the sin *o*
8:14 of the bull of the sin *o*
8:18 the ram of the burnt *o* near
8:21 a burnt *o* for a restful odor
8:21 an *o* made by fire to Jehovah
8:27 as a wave *o* before Jehovah
8:28 altar on top of the burnt *o*
8:28 an *o* made by fire to Jehovah
8:29 as a wave *o* before Jehovah
9:2 a young calf for a sin *o* and
9:2 and a ram for a burnt *o*
9:3 a male goat for a sin *o*
9:3 sound ones, for a burnt *o*
9:4 a grain *o* moistened with oil
9:7, 7 your sin *o* and your burnt *o*
9:7 render up the *o* of the people
9:8 the calf of the sin *o*
9:10 sin *o* smoke upon the altar
9:12 he slaughtered the burnt *o*
9:13 they handed him the burnt *o*
9:14 the burnt *o* on the altar
9:15 presenting the *o* of the people
9:15 the goat of the sin *o* that
9:15 made an *o* for sin with it as
9:16 he presented the burnt *o* and
9:17 next presented the grain *o*
9:17 the burnt *o* of the morning
9:21 as a wave *o* before Jehovah
9:22 from rendering the sin *o* and
9:22 burnt *o* and the communion
9:24 consuming the burnt *o* and the
10:1 they began *o* before Jehovah
10:12 Take the grain *o* that was
10:14 eat the breast of the wave *o*
10:15 the breast of the wave *o*
10:15 wave *o* to and fro before
10:16 for the goat of the sin *o*
10:17 sin *o* in the place that is
10:19 have presented their sin *o*
10:19 their burnt *o* before Jehovah

Le 10:19 had I eaten the sin *o* today
12:6 for a burnt *o* and a male
12:6 a turtledove for a sin *o* to
12:8 pigeons, one for a burnt *o*
12:8 and one for a sin *o*, and the
14:10 a grain *o* moistened with oil
14:12 a guilt *o* together with the
14:12 as a wave *o* before Jehovah
14:13, 13 the sin *o* and the burnt *o*
14:13 because, like the sin *o*, the
14:13 guilt *o* belongs to the priest
14:14 the blood of the guilt *o*, and
14:17 the blood of the guilt *o*
14:19 must render up the sin *o*
14:19 will slaughter the burnt *o*
14:20, 20 burnt *o* and the grain *o*
14:21 one young ram as a guilt *o*
14:21 for a wave *o* in order to
14:21 grain *o* and a log measure of
14:22 one must serve as a sin *o*
14:22 and the other as a burnt *o*
14:24 young ram of the guilt *o*
14:24 as a wave *o* before Jehovah
14:25 the young ram of the guilt *o*
14:25 the blood of the guilt *o* and
14:28 the blood of the guilt *o*
14:31 as a sin *o* and the other as
14:31 a burnt *o* along with the
14:31 along with the grain *o*
15:15 one as a sin *o* and the other
15:15 and the other as a burnt *o*
15:30 one a sin *o* and the other a
15:30 a burnt *o*; and the priest
16:3 a young bull for a sin *o* and
16:3 and a ram for a burnt *o*
16:5 of the goats for a sin *o* and
16:5 and one ram for a burnt *o*
16:6 present the bull of the sin *o*
16:9 and he must make it a sin *o*
16:11 the sin *o*, which is for
16:11 bull of the sin *o*, which is
16:15 goat of the sin *o*, which is
16:24 render up his burnt *o* and the
16:24 people's burnt *o* and make
16:25 fat of the sin *o* smoke upon
16:27 bull of the sin *o* and the
16:27 goat of the sin *o*, the blood
17:4 as an *o* to Jehovah before the
17:8 who offers up a burnt *o* or a
19:21 guilt *o* to Jehovah to the
19:21 bring . . . a ram of guilt *o*
19:22 ram of the guilt *o* before
22:18 *o*, for any of their vows or
22:18 to Jehovah for a burnt *o*
22:21 voluntary *o*, it should prove
22:22 no *o* made by fire from them
22:23 may make it a voluntary *o*
22:27, 27 *o*, an *o* made by fire to
23:8 an *o* made by fire to Jehovah
23:12 for a burnt *o* to Jehovah
23:13 its grain *o* two tenths of an
23:13 *o* made by fire to Jehovah, a
23:13 drink *o* a fourth of a hin of
23:14 bringing the *o* of your God
23:15 wave *o*, seven sabbaths
23:16 present a new grain *o* to
23:17 two loaves as a wave *o*
23:18 burnt *o* to Jehovah along
23:18 grain *o* and their drink
23:18 *o* made by fire, of a restful
23:19 goats as a sin *o* and two
23:20 wave *o* before Jehovah, along
23:25 present an *o* made by fire to
23:27 *o* made by fire to Jehovah
23:36 *o* made by fire to Jehovah
23:36 *o* made by fire to Jehovah
23:37 *o* made by fire to Jehovah
23:37, 37 burnt *o* and the grain *o*
24:7 an *o* made by fire to Jehovah
27:2 a special vow *o* of souls
27:9 one presents in *o* to Jehovah
27:11 one may not present in *o* to
Nu 4:7 pitchers of the drink *o*; and
4:16 the constant grain *o* and the
5:15 bring her *o* along with her, a
5:15 it is a grain *o* of jealousy
5:15 memorial grain *o* bringing
5:18 the memorial grain *o*, that is
5:18 the grain *o* of jealousy, and
5:25 grain *o* of jealousy from the
5:25 wave the grain *o* to and fro
5:26 grain *o* as a remembrancer
6:11 one as a sin *o* and the other
6:11 other as a burnt *o* and make

Nu 6:12 in its first year as a guilt *o*
6:14 *o* to Jehovah one sound young
6:14 young ram . . . as a burnt *o*
6:14 its first year as a sin *o*
6:15 and their grain *o* and their
6:16 render up his sin *o* and his
6:16 and his burnt *o*
6:17, 17 grain *o* and its drink *o*
6:20 as a wave *o* before Jehovah
6:20 breast of the wave *o* and the
6:21 *o* to Jehovah over his
7:3 brought their *o* before Jehovah
7:10 their *o* before the altar
7:11 *o* for the inauguration of the
7:12 *o* on the first day proved to
7:13 *o* was one silver dish, its
7:13 with oil for a grain *o*
7:15 male lamb . . . for a burnt *o*
7:16 kid of the goats for a sin *o*
7:17 *o* of Nahshon the son of
7:19 *o* one silver dish, its weight
7:19 with oil for a grain *o*
7:21 male lamb . . . for a burnt *o*
7:22 kid of the goats for a sin *o*
7:23 *o* of Nethanel the son of Zuar
7:25 *o* was one silver dish, its
7:25 with oil for a grain *o*
7:27 for a burnt *o*
7:28 kid of the goats for a sin *o*
7:29 *o* of Eliab the son of Helon
7:31 *o* was one silver dish, its
7:31 with oil for a grain *o*
7:33 young bull . . . for a burnt *o*
7:34 kid of the goats for a sin *o*
7:35 *o* of Elizur the son of Shedeur
7:37 *o* was one silver dish, its
7:37 with oil for a grain *o*
7:39 for a burnt *o*
7:40 kid of the goats for a sin *o*
7:41 *o* of Shelumiel the son of
7:43 *o* was one silver dish, its
7:43 with oil for a grain *o*
7:45 for a burnt *o*
7:46 kid of the goats for a sin *o*
7:47 *o* of Eliasaph the son of Deuel
7:49 *o* was one silver dish, its
7:49 with oil for a grain *o*
7:51 young bull . . . burnt *o*
7:52 kid of the goats for a sin *o*
7:53 *o* of Elishama the son of
7:55 *o* was one silver dish, its
7:55 with oil for a grain *o*
7:57 male lamb . . . burnt *o*
7:58 kid of the goats for a sin *o*
7:59 *o* of Gamaliel the son of
7:61 *o* was one silver dish, its
7:61 with oil for a grain *o*
7:63 male lamb . . . burnt *o*
7:64 kid of the goats for a sin *o*
7:65 *o* of Abidan the son of Gideoni
7:67 *o* was one silver dish, its
7:67 with oil for a grain *o*
7:69 one ram . . . for a burnt *o*
7:70 kid of the goats for a sin *o*
7:71 *o* of Ahiezer the son of
7:73 *o* was one silver dish, its
7:73 with oil for a grain *o*
7:75 young bull . . . burnt *o*
7:76 kid of the goats for a sin *o*
7:77 *o* of Pagiel the son of Ochran
7:79 *o* was one silver dish, its
7:79 with oil for a grain *o*
7:81 one young bull . . . a burnt *o*
7:82 kid of the goats for a sin *o*
7:83 *o* of Ahira the son of Enan
7:84 inauguration *o* of the altar
7:87 cattle for the burnt *o* being
7:87 kids of the goats for a sin *o*
7:88 inauguration *o* of the altar
8:8 young bull and its grain *o*
8:8 young bull for a sin *o*
8:11 before Jehovah as a wave *o*
8:12 render up the one as a sin *o*
8:12 burnt *o* to Jehovah to make
8:13 as a wave *o* to Jehovah
8:15 move to and fro as a wave *o*
8:21 as a wave *o* before Jehovah
9:7 from presenting the *o* to
9:13 *o* of Jehovah he did not
15:3 render up an *o* made by fire
15:3 a burnt *o* or a sacrifice to
15:4 the one presenting his *o* must
15:4 a grain *o* of fine flour, a
15:5 render up wine as a drink *o*

Nu 15:5 together with the burnt *o* or
15:6 grain *o* of two tenths of fine
15:7 present wine as a drink *o*, a
15:8 a burnt *o* or a sacrifice to
15:9 a grain *o* of three tenths of
15:10 present wine as a drink *o*
15:10 as an *o* made by fire, of a
15:13 presenting an *o* made by fire
15:14 render up an *o* made by fire
15:24 one young bull as a burnt *o*
15:24, 24 grain *o* and its drink *o*
15:24 kid of the goats as a sin *o*
15:25, 25 *o* an *o* made by fire
15:25 sin *o* before Jehovah for
15:27 female goat . . . for a sin *o*
16:15 turn to look at their grain *o*
16:35 consume . . . men *o* the incense
18:9 out of the *o* made by fire
18:9 every *o* of theirs together
18:9 every grain *o* of theirs and
18:9 and every sin *o* of theirs and
18:9 and every guilt *o* of theirs
18:17 smoke as an *o* made by fire
18:18 the breast of the wave *o* and
19:9 It is a sin *o*
19:17 the burning of the sin *o*
23:3 yourself by your burnt *o*, and
23:6 were stationed by his burnt *o*
23:15 yourself here by your burnt *o*
23:17 was stationed by his burnt *o*
23:30 *o* up a bull and a ram on
28:2 care to present to me my *o*
28:3 This is the *o* made by fire
28:3 lambs . . . burnt *o* constantly
28:5 fine flour as a grain *o*
28:6 the constant burnt *o*, which
28:6 an *o* made by fire to Jehovah
28:7 its drink *o*, the fourth of a
28:7 drink *o* of intoxicating liquor
28:8 With the same grain *o* as of
28:8 with its same drink *o* you
28:8 as an *o* made by fire, of a
28:9 a grain *o* moistened with oil
28:9 together with its drink *o*
28:10 as a sabbath burnt *o* on its
28:10 with the constant burnt *o*
28:10 and its drink *o*
28:11 as a burnt *o* to Jehovah two
28:12 grain *o* moistened with oil
28:12 fine flour as a grain *o*
28:13 grain *o* moistened with oil
28:13 a burnt *o*, a restful odor, an
28:13 an *o* made by fire to Jehovah
28:14 This is the monthly burnt *o*
28:15 sin *o* to Jehovah in addition
28:15 the constant burnt *o* together
28:15 together with its drink *o*
28:19 present as an *o* made by fire
28:19 a burnt *o* to Jehovah, two
28:22 one goat of sin *o* to make
28:23 the morning burnt *o*, which
28:23 is for the constant burnt *o*
28:24 as bread, an *o* made by fire
28:24 with the constant burnt *o* it
28:24 be rendered, and its drink *o*
28:26 you present a new grain *o* to
28:27 a burnt *o* for a restful odor
28:28 and as their grain *o* of fine
28:31 the constant burnt *o* and its
28:31 Aside from . . . its grain *o*
29:2 burnt *o* for a restful odor to
29:3 their grain *o* of fine flour
29:5 kid of the goats as a sin *o* to
29:6 the monthly burnt *o* and its
29:6 its grain *o* and the constant
29:6 constant burnt *o* and its grain
29:6 grain *o*, together with their
29:6 an *o* made by fire to Jehovah
29:8 as a burnt *o* to Jehovah, as a
29:9 as their grain *o* of fine flour
29:11 kid of the goats as a sin *o*
29:11 sin *o* of atonement and the
29:11 and the constant burnt *o* and
29:11 and its grain *o*, together
29:13 must present as a burnt *o*
29:13 an *o* made by fire, of a
29:14 their grain *o* of fine flour
29:16 kid of the goats as a sin *o*
29:16 the constant burnt *o*, its
29:16 its grain *o* and its drink
29:16 aside from . . . its drink *o*
29:18 their grain *o* and their drink
29:19 kid of the goats as a sin *o*
29:19 the constant burnt *o* and its

Nu 29:19 grain *o*, together with their
29:21 their grain *o* and their drink
29:22 one goat as a sin *o*, aside
29:22 constant burnt *o* and its
29:22 and its grain *o* and its drink
29:22 and its drink *o*
29:24 their grain *o* and their drink
29:25 kid of the goats as a sin *o*
29:25 constant burnt *o*, its grain
29:25 its grain *o* and its drink
29:25 and its drink *o*
29:27 their grain *o* and their drink
29:28 one goat as a sin *o*, aside
29:28 the constant burnt *o* and its
29:28 its grain *o* and its drink
29:28 and its drink *o*
29:30 their grain *o* and their drink
29:31 and one goat as a sin *o*
29:31 constant burnt *o*, its grain
29:31 its grain *o* and its drink
29:33 their grain *o* and their drink
29:34 and one goat as a sin *o*
29:34 the constant burnt *o*, its
29:34 its grain *o* and its drink
29:34 and its drink *o*
29:36 must present as a burnt *o*
29:36 an *o* made by fire, of a
29:37 their grain *o* and their drink
29:38 and one goat as a sin *o*
29:38 the constant burnt *o* and its
29:38 its grain *o* and its drink
29:38 aside from . . . its drink *o*
31:50 as Jehovah's *o*, articles of
De 13:16 its spoil as a whole *o* to
16:10 the voluntary *o* of your hand
23:23 a voluntary *o* that you spoke
33:10 And a whole *o* on your altar
Jos 8:31 went *o* up burnt offerings
22:26 altar, not for burnt *o* nor
22:28 made, not for burnt *o* nor
22:29 an altar for burnt *o*, grain
22:29 grain *o* and sacrifice
Jg 6:26 burnt *o* on the pieces of wood
11:31 that one up as a burnt *o*
13:16 will render up a burnt *o* to
13:19 the grain *o* and to offer it
13:23 accepted a burnt *o* and grain
13:23 and grain *o* from our hand
1Sa 1:21 sacrifice and his vow *o*
2:13 any man was *o* a sacrifice
2:17 *o* of Jehovah with disrespect
2:29 my *o* that I have commanded
2:29 the best of every *o* of Israel
3:14 by sacrifice or by *o* to time
6:3 not send it away without an *o*
6:3 return to him a guilt *o*
6:4 What is the guilt *o* that we
6:8 return to him as a guilt *o*
6:14 as a burnt *o* to Jehovah
6:17 as a guilt *o* to Jehovah
7:9 offered it up as a burnt *o*
7:9 a whole *o*, to Jehovah
7:10, 10 was *o* up the burnt *o*
13:9 *o* up the burnt sacrifice
13:10 as soon as he had finished *o*
13:12 *o* up the burnt sacrifice
26:19 let him smell a grain *o*
2Sa 6:18 David was finished with *o* up
24:22 the cattle for the burnt *o*
1Ki 1:7 began *o* help as followers of
8:62 *o* a grand sacrifice before
8:64 grain *o* and the fat pieces
8:64 grain *o* and the fat pieces
12:9 you are *o* in counsel that
18:29 the going up of the grain *o*
18:33 pour it upon the burnt *o*
18:36 the grain *o* goes up that
18:38 eating up the burnt *o* and
2Ki 3:20 the going up of the grain *o*
5:17 no more render up a burnt *o*
10:25 rendering up the burnt *o*
16:13 to make his burnt *o* and
16:13 his grain *o* smoke and to
16:13 and to pour out his drink *o*
16:15 burnt *o* of the morning
16:15 the grain *o* of the evening
16:15 the burnt *o* of the king and
16:15 the king and his grain *o*
16:15 burnt *o* of all the people
16:15 and their grain *o* and
16:15 all the blood of burnt *o*
1Ch 6:49 upon the altar of burnt *o* and
16:2 David finished *o* up the burnt
16:2 burnt *o* and the communion

1Ch 16:40 on the altar of burnt *o*
21:23 and the wheat as a grain *o*
21:26 upon the altar of burnt *o*
21:29 and the altar of burnt *o*
22:1 altar for burnt *o* for Israel
23:29 for the grain *o* and for the
23:31 *o* up of the burnt sacrifices
2Ch 4:6 having to do with the burnt *o*
7:1 consume the burnt *o* and the
7:4 people were *o* sacrifice
7:5 Solomon went on *o* the
7:7 contain the burnt *o* and the
7:7 the grain *o* and the fat pieces
10:9 you are *o* in counsel that
20:21 *o* praise in holy adornment
23:13 the signal for *o* praise
29:18 altar of burnt *o* and all
29:21 goats as a sin *o* for the
29:23 male goats of the sin *o*
29:24 sin *o* with their blood
29:24 king said the burnt *o* and
29:24 and the sin *o* should be
29:27 time that the burnt *o*
29:28 the burnt *o* was finished
29:29 finished *o* it up, the king
29:32 all these as a burnt *o* to
30:21 priests were *o* praise to
31:2 as regards the burnt *o* and
35:8 contribution as a voluntary *o*
35:13 boiling the passover *o* over
35:14 *o* up the burnt sacrifices
Ezr 1:4 voluntary *o* for the house of
3:3 began *o* up burnt sacrifices to
3:5 the constant burnt *o* and that
3:5 a voluntary *o* to Jehovah
6:17 as a sin *o* for all Israel
8:28 a voluntary *o* to Jehovah the
8:35 twelve he-goats as a sin *o*
8:35 as a burnt *o* to Jehovah
9:4 the grain *o* of the evening
9:5 grain *o* of the evening I stood
Ne 10:33 the constant grain *o* and the
10:33 the constant burnt *o* of the
13:5 regularly putting the grain *o*
13:9 grain *o* and the frankincense
Ps 20:3 accept your burnt *o* as being
40:6 *o* you did not delight in
40:6 Burnt *o* and sin
40:6 sin *o* you did not ask for
50:23 The one *o* thanksgiving as
51:16 burnt *o* you do not find
51:19 burnt sacrifice and whole *o*
141:2 as the evening grain *o*
Isa 31:3 *o* help will have to stumble
40:16 not sufficient for a burnt *o*
53:10 set his soul as a guilt *o*
57:6 you poured out a drink *o*
63:5 there was no one *o* support
66:3 *o* up a gift—the blood of a
Jer 7:22 burnt *o* and sacrifice
14:12 the whole burnt *o* and the
14:12 the grain *o*, I am taking
17:26 bringing whole burnt *o* and
17:26 grain *o* and frankincense
33:11 thanksgiving *o* into the
33:18 offer up whole burnt *o* and
33:18 make smoke with a grain *o*
41:5 grain *o* and frankincense in
48:35 *o* upon the high place and
Eze 20:28 there their offensive *o*, and
31:3 a woody thicket *o* shadow
40:38 rinse the whole burnt *o*
40:39 the whole burnt *o* and the
40:39, 39 sin *o* and the guilt *o*
40:42 for the whole burnt *o*
40:42 slaughter the whole burnt *o*
40:43 the flesh of the gift *o*
42:13 the grain *o* and the sin
42:13 the sin *o* and the guilt
42:13 and the guilt *o*, because
43:19 of the herd, as a sin *o*
43:21 young bull, the sin *o*, and
43:22 as a sin *o*; and they must
43:24 whole burnt *o* to Jehovah
43:25 as a sin *o* for the day
44:11 whole burnt *o* and the
44:27 should present his sin *o*
44:29, 29 grain *o* and the sin *o*
44:29 guilt *o*—they are the ones
45:15 for the grain *o* and for
45:15 for the whole burnt *o* and
45:17, 17 grain *o* and the drink *o*
45:17 one to provide the sin *o*
45:17 grain *o* and the whole burnt

Eze 45:17 whole burnt *o* and the
45:19 blood of the sin *o* and put
45:22 young bull as a sin *o*
45:23 whole burnt *o* to Jehovah
45:23 sin *o* a buck of the goats
45:24 as a grain *o* an ephah for
45:25 same as the sin *o*, as the
45:25 as the whole burnt *o*
45:25 and as the grain *o* and
46:2 render up his whole burnt *o*
46:4 whole burnt *o* that the
46:5 grain *o* and ephah for the ram
46:5 grain *o* as he is able to
46:7 render up as a grain *o*
46:11 grain *o* should prove to be
46:12 as a voluntary *o* a whole
46:12 a whole burnt *o*, or
46:12 as a voluntary *o* to Jehovah
46:12 provide his whole burnt *o*
46:13 whole burnt *o* daily to
46:14 as a grain *o* you should
46:14 grain *o* to Jehovah is an
46:15 and the grain *o* and the
46:15 constant whole burnt *o*
46:20 boil the guilt *o* and the
46:20 boil . . . the sin *o*, and
46:20 bake the grain *o*, in order
Da 6:10 *o* praise before his God, as
9:21 time of the evening gift *o*
9:27 sacrifice and gift *o* to cease
Joe 1:9, 9 Grain *o* and drink *o* have
1:13, 13 grain *o* and drink *o* have
2:14 a blessing, a grain *o* and a
2:14 drink *o* for Jehovah your God
Mal 1:10 the gift *o* from your hand
2:12 a gift *o* to Jehovah of
2:13 a turning toward the gift *o*
3:3 a gift *o* in righteousness
3:4 the gift *o* of Judah and of
Mt 15:36 after *o* thanks, he broke
Lu 1:10 at the hour of *o* incense
5:14 make an *o* in connection with
23:36 and *o* him sour wine
Ac 14:23 *o* prayer with fastings, they
21:26 the *o* should be presented for
Ro 3:25 God set him forth as an *o*
15:16 *o*, namely, these nations
Eph 5:2 an *o* and a sacrifice to God
Php 2:17 poured out like a drink *o*
2Ti 4:6 poured out like a drink *o*
Heb 10:5 and *o* you did not want, but
10:6 not approve . . . sin *o*
10:8 sin *o*—sacrifices that are
10:10 *o* of the body of Jesus
10:14 sacrificial *o* that he has
10:18 is no longer an *o* for sin

Offerings

Ge 8:20 offer burnt *o* upon the altar
Ex 10:25 sacrifices and burnt *o*, as
20:24 burnt *o* and your communion
24:5 burnt *o* and sacrificed bulls
32:6 offering up burnt *o* and
Le 2:3 from Jehovah's *o* made by fire
2:10 most holy of Jehovah's *o* by
4:35 upon Jehovah's *o* made by fire
5:12 upon Jehovah's *o* made by fire
6:17 out of my *o* made by fire
6:18 Jehovah's *o* made by fire
7:30 as Jehovah's *o* made by fire
7:35 Jehovah's *o* made by fire
7:38 present their *o* to Jehovah
10:12 Jehovah's *o* made by fire and
10:13 Jehovah's *o* made by fire
10:15 with the *o* made by fire
21:6 Jehovah's *o* made by fire, the
21:21 present Jehovah's *o* made by
22:18 *o*, which they may present to
23:18 drink *o* as an offering made
23:37 drink *o* according to the
23:38 vow *o* and besides all your
23:38 voluntary *o*, which you
24:9 Jehovah's *o* made by fire, as
Nu 6:15 and their drink *o*
7:87 and their grain *o*
10:10 over your burnt *o*
18:11 wave *o* of the sons of Israel
28:2 *o* made by fire as a restful
28:14 as their drink *o* there should
28:20 their grain *o* of fine flour
28:31 together with their drink *o*
29:6 together with their drink *o*
29:11 together with their drink *o*
29:18 their drink *o* for the bulls
Nu 29:19 together with their drink *o*
29:21 drink *o* for the bulls, the
29:24 drink *o* for the bulls, the
29:27 their drink *o* for the bulls
29:30 their drink *o* for the bulls
29:31 and its drink *o*
29:33 drink *o* for the bulls, the
29:37 drink *o* for the bull, the
29:39 besides your vow *o* and your
29:39 besides your . . . voluntary *o*
29:39 as your burnt *o* and your
29:39 and your grain *o* and your
29:39 and your drink *o* and your
De 12:6 bring your burnt *o* and your
12:6 your vow *o* and your voluntary
12:6 your voluntary *o* and the
12:11 burnt *o* and your sacrifices
12:11 every choice of your vow *o*
12:13 burnt *o* in any other place
12:14 should offer up your burnt *o*
12:17 or any of your vow *o*
12:17 your voluntary *o* or the
12:26 your vow *o* you should carry
12:27 must render up your burnt *o*
18:1 The *o* made by fire of Jehovah
27:6 offer burnt *o* to Jehovah your
32:38 the wine of their drink *o*
Jos 8:31 went offering up burnt *o*
13:14 *o* made by fire of Jehovah
22:23 to offer up burnt *o* and
22:23 to offer . . . grain *o* on it
22:27 with our burnt *o* and our
Jg 20:26 and offered up burnt *o* and
20:26 communion *o* before Jehovah
21:4, 4 burnt *o* and communion *o*
1Sa 2:28 *o* made by fire of the sons
6:15 offered up burnt *o*, and they
15:22 as much delight in burnt *o*
1Ki 3:3 sacrificing and making *o*
3:15 rendered up communion *o* and
12:32 make *o* upon the altar
12:33 make *o* upon the altar that
12:33 to make *o* upon the altar
2Ki 10:24 sacrifices and burnt *o*
12:4 the money for the holy *o*
12:16 money for guilt *o* and the
12:16 and the money for sin *o*
12:18 holy *o* that Jehoshaphat and
12:18 holy *o* and all the gold to
16:12 to the altar and make *o*
16:15 and their drink *o*
1Ch 16:1 began to present burnt *o* and
16:40 burnt *o* to Jehovah on the
21:23 give the cattle for burnt *o*
29:9 their making voluntary *o*
29:9 made voluntary *o* to Jehovah
29:14 make voluntary *o* like this
29:17 have enjoyed seeing make *o*
29:21 burnt *o* to Jehovah on the
29:21 lambs and their drink *o*
2Ch 1:6 Solomon now made *o* there
1:6 upon it a thousand burnt *o*
2:4 burnt *o* in the morning and in
7:7 rendered up the burnt *o* and
8:13 make *o* according to the
13:11 burnt *o* smoke to Jehovah
24:14 and for making *o* and cups
29:31 began to bring . . . burnt *o*
29:32 number of the burnt *o* that
29:33 holy *o*, six hundred cattle
29:34 to skin all the burnt *o*
29:35 burnt *o* were in great
29:35 with the drink *o* for the
29:35 for the burnt *o*
30:15 burnt *o* to the house of
31:3 own goods for the burnt *o*
31:3 burnt *o* of the morning and
31:3 burnt *o* for the sabbaths
31:14 voluntary *o* of the true God
35:12 prepared the burnt *o* so as
35:16 burnt *o* upon the altar
Ezr 2:68 voluntary *o* to the house of
6:9 burnt *o* to the God of heaven
6:10 soothing *o* to the God of the
7:17, 17 grain *o* and their drink *o*
Ne 10:33 sin *o* to make atonement for
Ps 16:4 their drink *o* of blood
20:3 remember all your gift *o*
50:8 your whole burnt *o* that are
66:13 into your house with . . . *o*
66:15 *o* of fatlings I shall offer
119:108 pleasure in the voluntary *o*
Isa 1:11 enough of whole burnt *o* of
1:13 any more valueless grain *o*
Isa 43:23 sheep of your whole burnt *o*
56:7 burnt *o* and their sacrifices
Jer 6:20 burnt *o* of you people
7:18 drink *o* to other gods for
7:21 Add those whole burnt *o* of
19:5 whole burnt *o* to the Baal
19:13 drink *o* to other gods
32:29 drink *o* to other gods for
44:17 pour out to her drink *o*
44:18 drink *o* to her we have
44:19 pour out drink *o* to her
44:19 pour out drink *o* to her
44:25 to pour out drink *o* to her
Eze 20:28 pouring . . . their drink *o*
43:18 offer upon it whole burnt *o*
43:27 whole burnt *o* of you people
45:17 devolve the whole burnt *o*
Ho 6:6 rather than in whole burnt *o*
Am 4:5 and proclaim voluntary *o*
5:22 offer up to me whole burnt *o*
5:22 in your gift *o* I shall find
5:25 *o* that you people brought
Mic 6:6 with whole burnt *o*, with
Mr 12:33 whole burnt *o* and sacrifices
Ac 24:17 mercy to my nation, and *o*
1Ti 2:1 *o* of thanks, be made
Heb 5:3 obliged to make *o* for sins as
10:6 not approve of whole burnt *o*
10:8 approve of sacrifices and *o*
10:8 whole burnt *o* and sin

Offers

Le 6:26 who *o* it for sin will eat it
17:8 *o* up a burnt offering or a
Ps 63:5 cries my mouth *o* praise
Hab 1:16 he *o* sacrifice to his dragnet
Heb 9:7 blood, which he *o* for

Office

Ge 40:13 return you to your *o*; and you
41:13 Me he returned to my *o*, but
1Ch 9:22 ordained in their *o* of trust
9:26 in *o* of trust there were
9:31 *o* of trust over the things
24:3 for their *o* in their service
2Ch 11:15 put in *o* for himself
11:22 in *o* as head, as leader
31:15 in *o* of trust, to give to
31:18 *o* of trust they proceeded
35:15 were at their *o* according
Ps 109:8 *o* of oversight let someone
Mt 9:9 Matthew seated at the tax *o*
Mr 2:14 Levi . . . at the tax *o*, and he
Lu 1:9 practice of the priestly *o*
5:27 sitting at the tax *o*, and he
Ac 1:20 and, His *o* of oversight let
2Co 11:12 the *o* of which they boast
1Ti 3:1 reaching out . . . *o* of overseer
Heb 7:5 who receive their priestly *o*

Officer

Ge 39:21 chief *o* of the prison house
39:22 the chief *o* of the prison
39:23 The chief *o* of the prison
2Ch 26:11 Maaseiah the *o* under the
Pr 6:7 it has no commander, *o* or
Jer 37:13 *o* holding the oversight
51:27 against her a recruiting *o*
Da 2:15 to Arioch the *o* of the king
Mt 8:5 an army *o* came to him
8:8 In reply the army *o* said
8:13 Jesus said to the army *o*
27:54 army *o* and those with him
Mr 5:35 presiding *o* of the synagogue
5:36 presiding *o* of the synagogue
5:38 the house of the presiding *o*
15:39 army *o* that was standing
15:44 summoning the army *o*, he
15:45 certain from the army *o*
Lu 7:6 the army *o* had already sent
8:41 a presiding *o* of the synagogue
8:49 *o* of the synagogue came
12:58 deliver you to the court *o*
12:58 *o* throw you into prison
13:14 presiding *o* of the synagogue
23:47 army *o* began to glorify God
Ac 10:1 Cornelius, an army *o* of the
10:22 Cornelius, an army *o*, a man
18:8 Crispus the presiding *o* of the
18:17 Sosthenes the presiding *o* of
22:25 Paul said to the army *o*
22:26 when the army *o* heard this
24:23 he ordered the army *o* that
27:1 *o* named Julius of the band
27:6 army *o* found a boat from

Ac 27:11 army *o* went heeding the
27:31 Paul said to the army *o*
27:43 *o* desired to bring Paul

Officer's

Lu 7:2 a certain army *o* slave, who

Officers

Ge 40:2 indignant at his two *o*, at
40:7 inquire of the *o* of Pharaoh
Ex 5:6 Pharaoh commanded . . . their *o*
5:10 *o* went out and said to the
5:14 the *o* of the sons of Israel
5:15 *o* of the sons of Israel went
5:19 *o* of the sons of Israel saw
Nu 11:16 of the people and *o* of theirs
De 1:15 and *o* of your tribes
16:18 set judges and *o* for
20:5 The *o* too must speak to the
20:8 the *o* must speak further to
20:9 the *o* have finished speaking
29:10 *o*, every man of Israel
31:28 your *o*, and let me speak in
Jos 1:10 command the *o* of the people
3:2 *o* proceeded to pass through
8:33 and the *o* and their judges
23:2 its *o*, and to say to them
24:1 its judges and its *o*, and
1Ch 23:4 as *o* and judges six thousand
26:29 the outside business as *o*
27:1 *o* that were ministering to
2Ch 19:11 as *o* the Levites are
34:13 and *o* and gatekeepers
Da 4:36 even my high royal *o* and my
6:7 the high royal *o* and the
Na 3:17 recruiting *o* like the locust
Mr 5:22 presiding *o* of the synagogue
Joh 7:32 dispatched *o* to get hold of
7:45 *o* went back to the chief
7:46 *o* replied: Never has another
18:3 and *o* of the chief priests
18:12 *o* of the Jews seized
18:18 the *o* were standing about
18:22 *o* that was standing by gave
19:6 *o* saw him, they shouted
Ac 5:22 *o* got there they did not
5:26 captain went off with his *o*
13:15 presiding *o* of the synagogue
21:32 took soldiers and army *o* and
23:17 called one of the army *o* to
23:23 two of the army *o* and said

Offices

1Sa 2:36 to one of the priestly *o* to
1Ch 24:19 their *o* for their service
2Ch 17:14 *o* by the house of their
23:18 *o* of the house of Jehovah

Official

Ge 25:25 like an *o* garment of hair
37:36 Potiphar a court *o* of
39:1 Potiphar, a court *o* of Pharaoh
Le 6:10 his *o* dress of linen, and he
Jos 7:21 an *o* garment from Shinar
7:24 the silver and the *o* garment
1Ki 19:13 his face in his *o* garment
19:19 threw his *o* garment upon
22:9 a certain court *o* and said
2Ki 2:8 Elijah took his *o* garment and
2:13 the *o* garment of Elijah that
2:14 *o* garment of Elijah that had
8:6 the king gave her a court *o*
23:11 Nathan-melech the court *o*
25:19 he took one court *o* that
1Ch 23:11 house for one *o* class
25:1 *o* men for their service came
2Ch 18:8 called a court *o* and said
Ezr 3:10 the priests in *o* clothing
4:8 Rehum the chief government *o*
4:9 Rehum the chief government *o*
4:17 Rehum the chief government *o*
4:18 the *o* document that you have
4:23 the copy of the *o* document
5:5 an *o* document concerning this
Pr 14:28 is the ruin of a high *o*
Isa 22:19 *o* standing one will tear
Jer 52:25 took one court *o* that
Da 1:3 Ashpenaz his chief court *o*
1:7 principal court *o* went
1:8 principal court *o* that he
1:9 before the principal court *o*
1:10 principal court *o* said to
1:11 principal court *o* had
1:18 the principal court *o* also
Jon 3:6 put off his *o* garment from
Zec 13:4 wear an *o* garment of hair

Officials

Jg 5:3 give ear, you high *o*: I to
1Sa 8:15 give them to his court *o* and
2Ki 9:32 two or three court *o*
20:18 court *o* in the palace of
24:12 his princes and his court *o*
24:15 court *o* and the foremost
1Ch 28:1 with the court *o* and the
Es 1:10 the seven court *o* that were
1:12 by means of the court *o*
1:15 by means of the court *o*
2:21 two court *o* of the king
6:2 two court *o* of the king
6:14 the king's court *o* themselves
7:9 Harbona, one of the court *o*
Ps 2:2 high *o* themselves have massed
Pr 8:15 and high *o* themselves keep
31:4 or for high *o* to say: Where
Isa 39:7 become court *o* in the palace
40:23 reducing high *o* to nothing
Jer 29:2 the lady and the court *o*
34:19 court *o* and the priests and
41:16 court *o*, whom he brought
Da 3:24 saying to his high royal *o*
3:27 the high *o* of the king that
6:2 three high *o*, of whom Daniel
6:3 over the high *o* and the satraps
6:4 the high *o* and the satraps
6:6 these high *o* and satraps
6:7 All the high *o* of the kingdom
Hab 1:10 *o* are something laughable
Lu 12:11 government *o* and authorities

Officiated

Heb 7:13 no one has *o* at the altar

Offscouring

La 3:45 You make us mere *o* and refuse
1Co 4:13 the *o* of all things, until

Offset

2Co 8:14 now might *o* their deficiency
8:14 come to *o* your deficiency

Offshoot

Ge 49:22 *O* of a fruit-bearing tree
49:22 Joseph is the *o* of a
Jer 1:11 An *o* of an almond tree is

Offshoots

Isa 22:24 the descendants and the *o*

Offspring

Ge 7:3 preserve *o* alive on the
9:9 with you men and with your *o*
19:32 preserve *o* from our father
19:34 let us preserve *o* from our
21:13 nation, because he is your *o*
21:23 false to me and to my *o* and
38:8 raise up *o* for your brother
38:9 Onan knew that the *o* would
38:9 not to give *o* to his brother
46:6 Jacob and all his *o* with him
46:7 his *o*, with him into Egypt
48:11 has let me see also your *o*
48:19 *o* will become the full
Ex 28:43 for him and his *o* after
30:21 and his *o* throughout their
Le 18:11 *o* of your father, she being
18:21 of any of your *o* to Molech
20:2 *o* to Molech, should be put
20:3 given some of his *o* to Molech
20:4 *o* to Molech by not putting
22:3 *o* who comes near to the holy
22:4 Aaron's *o* when he is leprous
22:13 divorced when she has no *o*
Nu 14:24 his *o* will take possession
16:40 who is not of the *o* of Aaron
18:19 for you and your *o* with you
25:13 for him and his *o* after him
De 7:14 male or a female without *o*
10:15 he chose their *o* after them
22:6 the mother along with the *o*
22:7 may take the *o* for yourself
28:46 continue on you and your *o*
28:59 plagues of your *o* especially
30:6 circumcise . . . heart of your *o*
30:19 keep alive, you and your *o*
31:21 out of the mouth of their *o*
Ru 4:12 *o* that Jehovah will give you
1Sa 1:11 to your slave girl a male *o*
2:20 Jehovah appoint to you an *o*
20:42, 42 between my *o* and your *o*
2Sa 4:8 this day upon Saul and his *o*
1Ki 2:33 upon the head of his *o* to
2:33 for David and for his *o* and
11:14 of the *o* of the king
1Ki 11:39 humiliate the *o* of David
2Ki 5:27 to you and to your *o* to time
11:1 all the *o* of the kingdom
25:25 of the royal *o* came
1Ch 16:13 O *o* of Israel his servant
2Ch 22:10 royal *o* of the house of
Es 9:27 and upon their *o* and upon all
9:28 come to an end among their *o*
9:31 own soul and upon their *o*
10:3 speaking peace to all their *o*
Job 5:25 know that your *o* are many
21:8 *o* are firmly established
Ps 21:10 their *o* from the sons of men
25:13 *o* will take possession of
37:25 Nor his *o* looking for bread
37:26 *o* are in line for a blessing
37:28 as for the *o* of the wicked
69:36 And the *o* of his servants
74:8 They, even their *o*, have said
102:28 own *o* will be firmly
106:27 *o* fall among the nations
112:2 Mighty in the earth his *o*
Pr 11:21 *o* of the righteous ones will
Isa 14:20 *o* of evildoers will not be
48:19 *o* would become just like
53:10 he will see his *o*, he will
54:3 *o* will take possession even
59:21 from the mouth of your *o*
59:21, 21 the *o* of your *o*
61:9 their *o* will actually be
61:9 *o* whom Jehovah has blessed
65:9 out of Jacob an *o* and out
65:23 *o* made up of the chosen
66:22 the *o* of you people and
Jer 7:15 the whole *o* of Ephraim
22:28 his *o* must be hurled down
22:30 from his *o* not a single one
23:8 the *o* of the house of Israel
29:32 Shemaiah . . . and upon his *o*
30:10 your *o* from the land of
36:31 and against his *o* and
41:1 of the royal *o* and of the
46:27 *o* from the land of their
49:10 *o* and his brothers and his
Eze 43:19 of the *o* of Zadok, the ones
44:22 *o* of the house of Israel or
Da 1:3 and of the royal *o* and of
2:43 mixed with the *o* of mankind
Mt 3:7 You *o* of vipers, who has
12:34 *O* of vipers, how can you
21:5 the *o* of a beast of burden
22:24 raise up *o* for his brother
22:25 not having *o*, he left his
23:33 Serpents, *o* of vipers, how
Mr 12:19 *o* from her for his brother
12:20 when he died he left no *o*
12:21 but died without leaving *o*
12:22 seven did not leave any *o*
Lu 3:7 *o* of vipers, who has intimated
20:28 *o* from her for his brother
Joh 7:42 coming from the *o* of David
8:33 We are Abraham's *o* and never
8:37 that you are Abraham's *o*
Ac 13:23 *o* of this man according to
Ro 4:12 father of circumcised *o*, not
Re 22:16 the root and the *o* of David

Often

1Sa 1:7 as *o* as she went up into the
18:30 as *o* as they went out David
1Ki 14:28 as *o* as the king came to
2Ki 4:8 as *o* as he would pass by, he
2Ch 12:11 *o* as the king came to the
Ps 78:40 *o* they would rebel against
Ec 5:20 not *o* will he remember the
Isa 28:19 As *o* as it passes through
Jer 20:8 as *o* as I speak, I cry out
48:27 *o* as you spoke against him
Mt 17:15 he falls *o* into the fire and
17:15 and *o* into the water
23:37 how *o* I wanted to gather
Lu 13:34 how *o* I wanted to gather
1Co 11:25 as *o* as you drink it, in
11:26 as *o* as you eat this loaf
2Co 8:22 have *o* proved in many things
11:23 an excess, in near-deaths *o*
11:26 in journeys *o*, in dangers
11:27 in sleepless nights *o*, in
Php 3:18 I used to mention them *o* but
2Ti 1:16 he *o* brought me refreshment
Heb 6:7 rain which *o* comes upon it
9:25 he should offer himself *o*
9:26 he would have to suffer *o*
10:11 offer the same sacrifices *o*

Re 11:6 as *o* as they wish

Oftentimes

Mr 5:4 had *o* been bound with fetters

Og

Nu 21:33 *O* the king of Bashan came
32:33 of *O* the king of Bashan, the
De 1:4 *O* the king of Bashan, who was
3:1 *O* the king of Bashan came on
3:3 God gave into our hand also *O*
3:4 the kingdom of *O* in Bashan
3:10 cities of the kingdom of *O*
3:11 *O* the king of Bashan remained
3:13 Bashan of the kingdom of *O*
4:47 land of *O* the king of Bashan
29:7 and *O* the king of Bashan
31:4 to Sihon and to *O*, the kings
Jos 2:10 and *O*, whom you devoted to
9:10 and *O* the king of Bashan
12:4 of *O* the king of Bashan
13:12 royal realm of *O* in Bashan
13:30 of *O* the king of Bashan
13:31 royal realm of *O* in Bashan
1Ki 4:19 *O* the king of Bashan, and
Ne 9:22 land of *O* the king of Bashan
Ps 135:11 And *O* the king of Bashan
136:20 And *O* the king of Bashan

Ogling

Isa 3:16 and *o* with their eyes, they

Ohad

Ge 46:10 sons of Simeon were . . . *O*
Ex 6:15 the sons of Simeon . . . *O* and

Ohel

1Ch 3:20 Hashubah and *O* and Berechiah

Oholah

Eze 23:4 their names were *O* the older
23:4 names, *O* is Samaria, and
23:5 *O* began to prostitute herself
23:36 judge *O* and Oholibah and
23:44 they came in to *O* and to

Oholiab

Ex 31:6 put with him *O* the son of
35:34 *O* the son of Ahisamach of
36:1 Bezalel must work, also *O*
36:2 *O* and every wise-hearted man
38:23 *O* the son of Ahisamach of

Oholibah

Eze 23:4 and *O* her sister, and they
23:4 and *O* is Jerusalem
23:11 her sister *O* got to see it
23:22 Therefore, O *O*, this is
23:36 judge Oholah and *O* and
23:44 came in to Oholah and to *O*

Oholibamah

Ge 36:2 Esau took his wives . . . *O*
36:5 *O* bore Jeush and Jalam and
36:14 *O* the daughter of Anah
36:18 the sons of *O*, Esau's wife
36:18 These are the sheiks of *O*
36:25 children of Anah . . . *O*
36:41 sheik *O*, sheik Elah, sheik
1Ch 1:52 sheik *O*, sheik Elah

Oil

Ge 28:18 and poured *o* on the top of it
35:14 and poured *o* upon it
Ex 25:6 *o* for the luminary, balsam
25:6 balsam *o* for the anointing
25:6 for the anointing *o* and for
27:20 olive *o* for the luminary, in
29:2 cakes moistened with *o* and
29:2 wafers smeared with *o*
29:7 take the anointing *o* and pour
29:21 some of the anointing *o*, and
29:40 fourth of a hin of beaten *o*
30:24 holy place, and olive *o* a hin
30:25 anointing *o*, an ointment
30:25 is to be a holy anointing *o*
30:31 holy anointing *o* to me during
31:11 anointing *o* and the perfumed
35:8 *o* for the luminary and
35:8 balsam *o* for the anointing
35:8 for the anointing *o* and for
35:14 the *o* for illumination
35:15 anointing *o* and the perfumed
35:28 and the balsam *o* and the
35:28 and the *o* for illumination
35:28 the anointing *o* and for the
37:29 holy anointing *o* and the pure
39:37 and the *o* of illumination
39:38 of gold and the anointing *o*
Ex 40:9 the anointing *o* and anoint
Le 2:1 must pour *o* over it and put
2:2 fine flour and its *o* along
2:4 cakes moistened with *o* or
2:4 wafers smeared with *o*
2:5 of fine flour moistened with *o*
2:6 and you must pour *o* upon it
2:7 be made of fine flour with *o*
2:15 you must put *o* upon it and
2:16 some of its grits and *o*
5:11 He must not put *o* upon it and
6:15 its *o* and all the frankincense
6:21 made with *o* upon a griddle
7:10 that is moistened with *o* or
7:12 cakes moistened with *o* and
7:12 wafers smeared with *o* and
7:12 cakes moistened with *o*
8:2 garments and the anointing *o*
8:10 the anointing *o* and anointed
8:12 anointing *o* upon Aaron's head
8:30 took some of the anointing *o*
9:4 offering moistened with *o*
10:7 Jehovah's anointing *o* is upon
14:10 offering moistened with *o*
14:10 and one log measure of *o*
14:12 the log measure of *o* and
14:15 log measure of *o* and pour it
14:16 *o* that is upon his left palm
14:16 spatter some of the *o* with
14:17 the *o* that is upon his palm
14:18 *o* that is upon the priest's
14:21 fine flour moistened with *o*
14:21 and a log measure of *o*
14:24 and the log measure of *o*
14:26 *o* upon the priest's left
14:27 *o* that is upon his left palm
14:28 *o* that is on his palm upon
14:29 *o* that is on the priest's
21:10 anointing *o* would be poured
21:12 anointing *o* of his God, is
23:13 fine flour moistened with *o*
24:2 olive *o* for the luminary, to
Nu 4:9 vessels for *o* with which they
4:16 over the *o* of the luminary
4:16 anointing *o*, the oversight of
5:15 not pour *o* upon it nor put
6:15 fine flour, moistened with *o*
6:15 wafers smeared with *o*, and
7:13 flour moistened with *o* for a
7:19 moistened with *o* for a grain
7:25 flour moistened with *o* for a
7:31 flour moistened with *o* for a
7:37 flour moistened with *o* for a
7:43 flour moistened with *o* for a
7:49 flour moistened with *o* for a
7:55 flour moistened with *o* for a
7:61 flour moistened with *o* for a
7:67 fine flour moistened with *o*
7:73 fine flour moistened with *o*
7:79 fine flour moistened with *o*
8:8 fine flour moistened with *o*
15:4 with a fourth of a hin of *o*
15:6 with a third of a hin of *o*
15:9 with half a hin of *o*
18:12 All the best of the *o* and all
18:27 of the wine or *o* press
18:30 produce of the wine or *o*
28:5 fourth of a hin of beaten *o*
28:9 offering moistened with *o*
28:12 offering moistened with *o*
28:12 offering moistened with *o*
28:13 offering moistened with *o*
28:20 fine flour moistened with *o*
28:28 fine flour moistened with *o*
29:3 fine flour moistened with *o*
29:9 fine flour moistened with *o*
29:14 fine flour moistened with *o*
35:25 was anointed with the holy *o*
De 7:13 your new wine and your *o*
8:8 a land of *o* olives and honey
11:14 your sweet wine and your *o*
12:17 your *o* or the firstborn ones
14:23 your new wine and your *o*
15:14 and your *o* and winepress
16:13 and your *o* and winepress
18:4 your new wine and your *o* and
28:40 will rub yourself with no *o*
28:51 let no grain, new wine or *o*
32:13 And *o* out of a flinty rock
33:24 one dipping his foot in *o*
Ru 3:3 wash and rub yourself with *o*
1Sa 10:1 then took the flask of *o* and
16:1 Fill your horn with *o* and go
16:13 Samuel took the horn of *o*
2Sa 1:21 was none anointed with *o*
12:20 and rubbed himself with *o*
14:2 do not rub yourself with *o*
1Ki 1:39 the horn of *o* out of the tent
5:11 cor measures of beaten-out *o*
10:2 camels carrying balsam *o* and
10:10 very great deal of balsam *o*
10:10 that balsam *o* for quantity
10:25 balsam *o*, horses and mules
17:12 a little *o* in the small jar
17:14 the small jar of *o* itself
17:16 jar of *o* itself did not fail
2Ki 4:2 but a spouted jar of *o*
4:6 At that the *o* stopped
4:7 sell the *o* and pay off your
6:27 or from the wine or *o* press
9:1 take this flask of *o* in your
9:3 *o* and pour it out upon his
9:6 pour the *o* out upon his head
20:13, 13 balsam *o* and the good *o*
1Ch 9:29 the *o* and the frankincense
9:29 and the balsam *o*
9:30 mixture of balsam *o*
12:40 and *o* and cattle and sheep
27:28 *o* supplies there was Joash
2Ch 2:10 and *o* twenty thousand baths
2:15 *o* and the wine that my lord
9:1 camels carrying balsam *o*, and
9:9 balsam *o* in very great
9:9 like of that balsam *o* which
9:24 armor and balsam *o*, horses
11:11 supplies of food and *o* and
16:14 filled with balsam *o* and
31:5 *o* and honey and all the
32:27 for balsam *o* and for
32:28 grain and new wine and *o*
Ezr 3:7 drink and *o* to the Sidonians
6:9 wheat, salt, wine and *o*, just
7:22 a hundred bath measures of *o*
Ne 5:11 grain, the new wine and the *o*
8:15 leaves of *o* trees and myrtle
10:37 new wine and *o* we should
10:39 the new wine and the *o*
13:5 the new wine and the *o*
13:12 the new wine and of the *o*
Es 2:12 six months with *o* of myrrh
2:12 six months with balsam *o* and
Job 29:6 pouring out streams of *o* for
Ps 23:5 With *o* you have greased my
45:7 with the *o* of exultation
55:21 His words are softer than *o*
89:20 my holy *o* I have anointed
92:10 moisten myself with fresh *o*
104:15 make the face shine with *o*
109:18 And like *o* into his bones
109:24 grown lean, without any *o*
133:2 the good *o* upon the head
141:5 it would be *o* upon the head
Pr 5:3 her palate is smoother than *o*
21:17 loving wine and *o* will not
21:20 and *o* are in the abode of the
27:9 *O* and incense are what make
27:16 and *o* is what his right hand
Ec 7:1 A name is better than good *o*
9:8 *o* not be lacking upon your head
10:1 *o* of the ointment maker to
Ca 1:3 Like an *o* . . . is your name
Isa 1:6 there been a softening with *o*
3:24 instead of balsam *o* there
10:27 wrecked because of the *o*
39:2, 2 balsam *o* and the good *o*
41:19 the myrtle and the *o* tree
57:9 toward Melech with *o*, and
61:3 the *o* of exultation instead
Jer 31:12 new wine and over the *o* and
40:10 summer fruits and *o* and
41:8 and barley and *o* and honey
Eze 16:9 and greased you with *o*
16:13 and *o* were what you ate
16:18 and my *o* and my incense you
16:19 *o* and honey that I had had
23:41 and my *o* you put upon it
27:17 honey and *o* and balsam
32:14 shall make go just like *o*
45:14 allowance of the *o*, there
45:14 bath measure of the *o*
45:24 *o*, a hin to the ephah
45:25 grain offering and as the *o*
46:5 *o*, a hin to the ephah
46:7 *o*, a hin to the ephah
46:11 *o*, a hin to the ephah
46:14 regards *o*, the third of a
46:15 grain offering and the *o*
Ho 2:5 my linen, my *o* and my drink

Ho 2:8 and the sweet wine and the *o*
2:22 and the sweet wine and the *o*
12:1 to Egypt *o* itself is brought
Joe 1:10 the *o* has faded away
2:19 the new wine and the *o*
2:24 with new wine and *o*
Mic 6:7 thousands of torrents of *o*
6:15 not grease yourself with *o*
Hag 1:11 new wine, and upon the *o*, and
2:12 wine or *o* or any sort of
Mt 25:3 lamps but took no *o* with
25:4 the discreet took *o* in their
25:8 Give us some of your *o*
26:7 case of costly perfumed *o*
26:12 woman put this perfumed *o*
Mr 6:13 sickly people with *o* and cure
14:3 alabaster case of perfumed *o*
14:4 this waste of the perfumed *o*
14:5 *o* could have been sold for
14:8 to put perfumed *o* on my body
Lu 7:37 alabaster case of perfumed *o*
7:38 with the perfumed *o*
7:46 did not grease my head with *o*
7:46 my feet with perfumed *o*
10:34 pouring *o* and wine upon them
16:6 bath measures of olive *o*
Joh 11:2 the Lord with perfumed *o*
12:3 perfumed *o*, genuine nard
12:3 the scent of the perfumed *o*
12:5 perfumed *o* was not sold for
Heb 1:9 with the *o* of exultation
Jas 5:14 greasing him with *o* in the
Re 6:6 do not harm the olive *o* and
18:13 perfumed *o* and frankincense
18:13 wine and olive *o* and fine

Oiled
Ex 29:23 ring-shaped cake of *o* bread
Le 8:26 cake of *o* bread and one wafer
Nu 11:8 the taste of an *o* sweet cake
Hab 1:16 his portion is well *o*, and

Oil-olive
2Ki 18:32 land of *o* trees and honey

Oils
Ca 1:3 For fragrance your *o* are good
4:10 fragrance of your *o* than all
Am 6:6 choicest *o* do their anointing
Lu 23:56 spices and perfumed *o*

Oil-tree
1Ki 6:23 two cherubs of *o* wood, ten
6:31 made with doors of *o* wood
6:32 two doors were of *o* wood
6:33 the doorposts of *o* wood

Oily
Isa 30:23 must become fat and *o*

Ointment
Ex 30:25 anointing oil, an *o*, a
30:25 is the work of an *o* maker
30:33 an *o* like it and who puts
30:35 the work of an *o* maker
37:29 the work of an *o* maker
1Sa 8:13 for *o* mixers and cooks and
1Ch 9:30 the *o* mixture of balsam oil
2Ch 16:14 different sorts of *o* mixed
16:14 in an *o* of special make
Ne 3:8 a member of the *o* mixers did
Job 41:31 the very sea like an *o* pot
Ec 10:1 oil of the *o* maker to stink

Ointments
Isa 57:9 kept making your *o* abundant

Old
Ge 5:32 Noah . . . five hundred years *o*
6:4 the mighty ones who were of *o*
7:6 Noah was six hundred years *o*
11:10 Shem was a hundred years *o*
12:4 was seventy-five years *o* when
15:15 be buried at a good *o* age
16:16 Abram was eighty-six years *o*
17:1 Abram . . . ninety-nine years *o*
17:12 male of yours eight days *o*
17:17 Will a man a hundred years *o*
17:17 woman ninety years *o* give
17:24 was ninety-nine years *o*
17:25 son was thirteen years *o*
18:11 Abraham and Sarah were *o*
18:12 my lord being *o* besides
18:13 although I have become *o*
19:4 from boy to *o* man, all the
19:31 Our father is *o* and there is
21:2 son to Abraham in his *o* age
21:4 his son when eight days *o*
Ge 21:5 Abraham was a hundred years *o*
21:7 birth to a son in his *o* age
24:1 Abraham was *o*, advanced in
24:36 master after her growing *o*
25:8, 8 good *o* age, *o* and satisfied
25:20 forty years *o* at his taking
25:26 Isaac was sixty years *o* at
26:34 Esau . . . forty years *o*
27:1 Isaac was *o* and his eyes
27:2 Here, now, I have become *o*
35:29 *o* and satisfied with days
37:2 Joseph . . . seventeen years *o*
37:3 he was the son of his *o* age
41:46 Joseph was thirty years *o*
44:20 and a child of his *o* age
48:10 eyes . . . dull from *o* age
Ex 7:7 And Moses was eighty years *o*
7:7 Aaron was eighty-three years *o*
10:9 and our *o* people we shall go
12:5 sound, a male, a year *o*, for
29:38 young rams each a year *o*
30:14 twenty years *o* and upward
Le 9:3 and a young ram, each a year *o*
19:32 for the person of an *o* man
23:18 lambs, each a year *o*, and
23:19 male lambs, each a year *o*
25:22 eat from the *o* crop until
25:22 crop you will eat the *o*
26:10 *o* of the preceding year, and
26:10 bring out the *o* ahead of the
27:3 male from twenty years *o* up
27:3 up to sixty years *o*, the
27:5 age is from five years *o* up
27:5 up to twenty years *o*, the
27:6 up to five years *o*, the
27:6 age is from a month *o* up to
27:7 age is from sixty years *o*
Nu 1:3 twenty years *o* upward
1:18 twenty years *o* upward, head
1:20 twenty years *o* upward
1:22 twenty years *o* upward
1:24 twenty years *o* upward
1:26 twenty years *o* upward
1:28 twenty years *o* upward
1:30 twenty years *o* upward
1:32 twenty years *o* upward
1:34 twenty years *o* upward
1:36 from twenty years *o* upward
1:38 names from twenty years *o*
1:40 from twenty years *o* upward
1:42 from twenty years *o* upward
1:45 from twenty years *o* upward
3:15 male from a month *o* upward
3:22 males from a month *o* upward
3:28 males from a month *o* upward
3:34 males from a month *o* upward
3:39 males from a month *o* upward
3:40 Israel from a month *o* upward
3:43 from a month *o* upward of
4:3 thirty years *o* upward to fifty
4:3 upward to fifty years *o*, all
4:23 thirty years *o* upward to
4:30 thirty years *o* upward to
4:35 thirty years *o* upward to
4:39 thirty years *o* upward to
4:43 thirty years *o* upward to
4:43 upward to fifty years *o*
4:47 thirty years *o* upward to
4:47 upward to fifty years *o*
7:17 five male lambs each a year *o*
7:23 five male lambs each a year *o*
7:29 five male lambs each a year *o*
7:35 five male lambs each a year *o*
7:41 five male lambs each a year *o*
7:47 five male lambs each a year *o*
7:53 five male lambs each a year *o*
7:59 five male lambs each a year *o*
7:65 five male lambs each a year *o*
7:71 five male lambs each a year *o*
7:77 five male lambs each a year *o*
7:83 five male lambs each a year *o*
7:87 male lambs each a year *o*
7:88 male lambs each a year *o*
8:24 twenty-five years *o* upward he
14:29 from twenty years *o* upward
18:16 from a month *o* onward you
26:62 from a month *o* and upward
28:11 male lambs each a year *o*
28:19 male lambs each a year *o*
28:27 male lambs each a year *o*
29:2 each a year *o*, sound ones
29:8 male lambs each a year *o*
29:13 male lambs each a year *o*
29:17 male lambs each a year *o*
Nu 29:20 male lambs each a year *o*
29:23 male lambs each a year *o*
29:26 male lambs each a year *o*
29:29 male lambs each a year *o*
29:32 male lambs each a year *o*
29:36 male lambs each a year *o*
32:11 from twenty years *o* upward
33:39 and twenty-three years *o* at
De 28:50 not be partial to an *o* man
31:2 A hundred and twenty years *o*
32:7 Remember the days of *o*
32:7 Your *o* men . . . can say it to
34:7 a hundred and twenty years *o*
Jos 6:21 from young man to *o* man and
13:1 Now Joshua was *o*, being
13:1 have grown *o* and have
14:7 Forty years *o* I was when
14:10 today eighty-five years *o*
23:1 Joshua was *o* and advanced
23:2 As for me, I have grown *o*
Jg 8:32 died at a good *o* age and was
19:16 an *o* man coming in from his
19:17 So the *o* man said: Where are
19:20 the *o* man said: May you have
19:22 kept saying to the *o* man
Ru 1:12 I have grown too *o* to get to
4:15 and one to nourish your *o* age
1Sa 2:22 Eli was very *o*, and he had
2:31 to be an *o* man in your house
2:32 to be an *o* man in your house
4:15 Eli was ninety-eight years *o*
4:18 the man was *o* and heavy
8:1 as soon as Samuel had grown *o*
8:5 You yourself have grown *o*
12:2 I have grown *o* and gray, and
13:1 Saul was [?] years *o* when he
17:12 was already *o* among men
28:14 It is an *o* man coming up
2Sa 2:10 Forty years *o* Ish-bosheth
4:4 Five years *o* he happened to
5:4 Thirty years *o* was David when
19:32 And Barzillai was very *o*
19:35 I am eighty years *o* today
1Ki 1:1 King David was *o*, advanced in
1:15 the king was very *o*, and
11:4 Solomon's growing *o* that his
13:11 a certain *o* prophet was
13:25 city in which the *o* prophet
13:29 the *o* prophet to bewail and
14:21 Forty-one years *o* Rehoboam
15:23 the time of his growing *o*
22:42 thirty-five years *o* when
2Ki 4:14 and her husband is *o*
8:17 Thirty-two years *o* he
8:26 Twenty-two years *o* was
11:21 Seven years *o* Jehoash was
14:2 Twenty-five years *o* he
14:21 being sixteen years *o*
15:2 Sixteen years *o* he happened
15:33 Twenty-five years *o* he
16:2 Twenty years *o* was Ahaz
18:2 Twenty-five years *o* he
21:1 Twelve years *o* was Manasseh
21:19 Twenty-two years *o* was
22:1 Eight years *o* was Josiah
23:31 Twenty-three years *o* was
23:36 Twenty-five years *o* was
24:8 Eighteen years *o* was
24:18 Twenty-one years *o* was
1Ch 2:21 when he was sixty years *o*
4:22 sayings are of *o* tradition
23:1 David himself had grown *o*
29:28 he died in a good *o* age
2Ch 12:13 was forty-one years *o* when
20:31 Thirty-five years *o* he was
21:5 Thirty-two years *o* was
21:20 Thirty-two years *o* he
22:2 Twenty-two years *o* was
24:1 Seven years *o* was Jehoash
24:15 Jehoiada got to be *o* and
24:15 hundred and thirty years *o*
26:1 he being sixteen years *o*
26:3 Sixteen years *o* was Uzziah
27:1 Twenty-five years *o* was
27:8 Twenty-five years *o* he
28:1 Twenty years *o* was Ahaz
33:1 Twelve years *o* was Manasseh
33:21 Twenty-two years *o* was
34:1 Eight years *o* was Josiah
36:2 Twenty-three years *o* was
36:5 Twenty-five years *o* was
36:9 Eighteen years *o* was
36:11 Twenty-one years *o* was
36:17 or virgin, *o* or decrepit

Ezr 3:12 the *o* men that had seen the
4:15 revolt from the days of *o*
4:19 from the days of *o* been one
Ne 3:6 the Gate of the *O* City was
12:39 the Gate of the *O* City and
Es 3:13 young man as well as *o* man
Job 12:20 the sensibleness of *o* men
14:8 root grows *o* in the earth
21:7 Have grown *o*, also have
32:9 *o* that understand judgment
42:17 Job died, *o* and satisfied
Ps 6:7 *o* because of all those showing
37:25 I have also grown *o*, And yet
71:9 away in the time of *o* age
71:18 And even until *o* age and
148:12 *o* men together with boys
Pr 17:6 The crown of *o* men is the
20:29 splendor of *o* men is their
22:6 when he grows *o* he will not
23:22 just because she has grown *o*
Ec 4:13 than an *o* but stupid king
Ca 7:13 The new ones as well as the *o*
Isa 3:5 the boy against the *o* man
20:4 *o* men, naked and barefoot
22:11 the waters of the *o* pool
46:4 Even to one's *o* age I am the
47:6 Upon the *o* man you made your
65:20 a suckling a few days *o*
65:20 *o* man that does not fulfill
Jer 6:11 an *o* man along with one that
31:13 and the *o* men, all together
46:26 as in the days of *o*
51:22 dash *o* man and boy to
52:1 twenty-one years *o* when
La 1:19 my own *o* men have expired
2:21 Boy and *o* man have lain down
4:16 no favor even to the *o* men
5:12 *o* men have not been honored
5:14 *O* men themselves have ceased
Eze 9:6 *O* man, young man and virgin
9:6 started with the *o* men that
27:9 Even *o* men of Gebal and her
36:2 the high places of *o* time
Da 5:31 being about sixty-two years *o*
Joe 2:16 Collect the *o* men together
2:28 As for your *o* men, dreams
Mic 6:6 with calves a year *o*
Zec 8:4, 4 *o* men and *o* women in the
Mt 9:16 upon an *o* outer garment
9:17 new wine into *o* wineskins
13:52 brings out . . . new and *o*
Mr 2:21 cloth upon an *o* outer garment
2:21 the new from the *o*, and the
2:22 new wine into *o* wineskins
5:42 for she was twelve years *o*
Lu 1:36 conceived a son, in her *o* age
1:70 holy prophets from of *o*
2:37 now eighty-four years *o*
2:42 he became twelve years *o*
3:23 Jesus . . . about thirty years *o*
5:36 onto an *o* outer garment
5:36 patch . . . not match the *o*
5:37 no one puts new wine into *o*
5:39 No one that has drunk *o* wine
5:39 for he says, The *o* is nice
8:42 daughter about twelve years *o*
Joh 3:4 a man be born when he is *o*
8:57 are not yet fifty years *o*
9:32 From of *o* it has never been
21:18 when you grow *o* you will
Ac 2:17 *o* men will dream dreams
3:21 his holy prophets of *o* time
4:22 was more than forty years *o*
15:18 known from of *o*
Ro 4:19 was about one hundred years *o*
6:6 our *o* personality was impaled
7:6 *o* sense by the written code
1Co 5:7 Clear away the *o* leaven, that
5:8 not with *o* leaven, neither
2Co 3:14 the reading of the *o* covenant
5:17 the *o* things passed away
Eph 4:22 put away the *o* personality
Col 3:9 Strip off the *o* personality
1Ti 4:7 and which *o* women tell
5:9 not less than sixty years *o*
Heb 1:11 they will all grow *o*
8:13 *o* is near to vanishing
11:2 men of *o* times had witness
2Pe 2:3 the judgment from of *o* is not
3:5 there were heavens from of *o*
1Jo 2:7 an *o* commandment which you
2:7 This *o* commandment is the

Older
Ge 25:23 the *o* will serve the younger
27:1 called Esau his *o* son and
27:15 garments of Esau her *o* son
27:42 words of Esau her *o* son
29:16 The name of the *o* was Leah
50:7 the *o* men of his household
50:7 *o* men of the land of Egypt
Ex 3:16 gather the *o* men of Israel
3:18 you and the *o* men of Israel
4:29 *o* men of the sons of Israel
12:21 all the *o* men of Israel
17:5 some of the *o* men of Israel
17:6 eyes of the *o* men of Israel
18:12 all the *o* men of Israel came
19:7 the *o* men of the people and
24:1 and seventy of the *o* men of
24:9 seventy of the *o* men of
24:14 But to the *o* men he had said
Le 4:15 the *o* men of the assembly
9:1 his sons and the *o* men of Israel
Nu 11:16 *o* men of Israel, whom you do
11:16 know that they are *o* men of
11:24 from the *o* men of the people
11:25 each of the seventy *o* men
11:30 he and the *o* men of Israel
16:25 *o* men of Israel went with
22:4 to say to the *o* men of Midian
22:7 So the *o* men of Moab and the
22:7 the *o* men of Midian traveled
De 5:23 your tribes and your *o* men
19:12 the *o* men of his city must
21:2 your *o* men and your judges
21:3 the *o* men of that city must
21:4 the *o* men of that city must
21:6 all the *o* men of that city
21:19 bring him out to the *o* men
21:20 say to the *o* men of his city
22:15 to the *o* men of the city
22:16 father must say to the *o* men
22:17 before the *o* men of the city
22:18 the *o* men of that city must
25:7 to the *o* men and say
25:8 the *o* men of his city must
25:9 before the eyes of the *o* men
27:1 *o* men of Israel went on to
29:10 your *o* men and your officers
31:9 to all the *o* men of Israel
31:28 all the *o* men of your tribes
Jos 7:6 he and the *o* men of Israel
8:10 he and the *o* men of Israel
8:33 all Israel and their *o* men
9:11 Hence our *o* men and all the
20:4 the *o* men of that city
23:2 its *o* men and its heads and
24:1 the *o* men of Israel and its
24:31 all the days of the *o* men
Jg 2:7 all the days of the *o* men who
8:14 its *o* men, seventy-seven men
8:16 he took the *o* men of the city
11:5 *o* men of Gilead immediately
11:7 said to the *o* men of Gilead
11:8 the *o* men of Gilead said to
11:9 said to the *o* men of Gilead
11:10 the *o* men of Gilead said to
11:11 the *o* men of Gilead and the
21:16 *o* men of the assembly said
Ru 4:2 ten men of the *o* men of the
4:4 and the *o* men of my people
4:9 Boaz said to the *o* men and all
4:11 and the *o* men said: Witnesses!
1Sa 4:3 *o* men of Israel began to say
8:4 the *o* men of Israel collected
11:3 *o* men of Jabesh said to him
15:30 in front of the *o* men of my
16:4 *o* men of the city began to
30:26 spoil to the *o* men of Judah
2Sa 3:17 Abner with the *o* men of
5:3 *o* men of Israel came to
12:17 *o* men of his house stood up
17:4 all the *o* men of Israel
17:15 and the *o* men of Israel
19:11 Speak to the *o* men of Judah
1Ki 2:22 he is my brother *o* than I am
8:1 congregate the *o* men of
8:3 the *o* men of Israel came, and
12:6 take counsel with the *o* men
12:8 the counsel of the *o* men
12:13 the counsel of the *o* men
20:7 all the *o* men of the land
20:8 the *o* men and all the people
21:8 the letters to the *o* men
21:11 men of his city, the *o* men
2Ki 6:32 the *o* men were sitting with
2Ki 6:32 said to the *o* men: Have you
10:1 *o* men and the caretakers of
10:5 *o* men and the caretakers
19:2 the *o* men of the priests
23:1 all the *o* men of Judah and
1Ch 11:3 *o* men of Israel came to the
15:25 And David and the *o* men of
21:16 and David and the *o* men
2Ch 5:2 the *o* men of Israel and all
5:4 all the *o* men of Israel came
10:6 counsel with the *o* men that
10:8 the counsel of the *o* men
10:13 the counsel of the *o* men
22:1 had killed all the *o* ones
34:29 all the *o* men of Judah
Ezr 5:5 upon the *o* men of the Jews
5:9 Then we asked these *o* men
6:7 and the *o* men of the Jews
6:8 with these *o* men of the Jews
6:14 the *o* men of the Jews were
10:8 the princes and the *o* men
10:14 *o* men of each individual
Job 32:4 they were *o* than he was in
Ps 119:100 than *o* men I behave
Pr 31:23 sits down with the *o* men of
Isa 37:2 *o* men of the priests covered
Jer 19:1 the *o* men of the people and
19:1 the *o* men of the priests
26:17 the *o* men of the land rose
29:1 *o* men of the exiled people
La 2:10 *o* men of the daughter of Zion
Eze 8:1 *o* men of Judah were sitting
16:46 your *o* sister is Samaria
16:61 ones *o* than you as well as
23:4 were Oholah the *o* one and
Joe 1:2 Hear this, you *o* men, and
1:14 Gather together the *o* men
Mt 16:21 suffer . . . from the *o* men
21:23 *o* men of the people came up
26:3 *o* men of the people gathered
26:47 and *o* men of the people
26:57 and the *o* men were gathered
27:1 *o* men of the people held a
27:3 the chief priests and *o* men
27:12 the chief priests and *o* men
27:20 *o* men persuaded the crowds
27:41 *o* men began making fun of
28:12 together with the *o* men and
Mr 8:31 rejected by the *o* men and the
11:27 and the *o* men came to him
14:43 the scribes and the *o* men
14:53 the *o* men and the scribes
15:1 chief priests with the *o* men
Lu 7:3 sent forth *o* men of the Jews
9:22 be rejected by the *o* men and
15:25 his *o* son was in the field
20:1 scribes with the *o* men came
22:52 *o* men that had come there
22:66 the assembly of *o* men of the
Ac 4:5 and *o* men and scribes
4:8 Rulers of the people and *o* men
4:23 the *o* men had said to them
5:21 *o* men of the sons of Israel
6:12 *o* men and the scribes, and
11:30 dispatching it to the *o* men
14:23 they appointed *o* men for
15:2 *o* men in Jerusalem regarding
15:4 the apostles and the *o* men
15:6 *o* men gathered together to
15:22 the apostles and the *o* men
15:23 The apostles and the *o* men
16:4 *o* men who were in Jerusalem
20:17 *o* men of the congregation
21:18 all the *o* men were present
22:5 all the assembly of *o* men can
23:14 chief priests and the *o* men
24:1 *o* men and a public speaker
25:15 *o* men of the Jews brought
Ro 9:12 *o* will be the slave of the
1Ti 4:14 *o* men laid their hands upon
5:1 severely criticize an *o* man
5:2 *o* women as mothers
5:17 Let the *o* men who preside in
5:19 accusation against an *o* man
Tit 1:5 make appointments of *o* men
Jas 5:14 Let him call the *o* men
1Pe 5:1 *o* men among you I give this
5:1 I too am an *o* man with them
5:5 in subjection to the *o* men
2Jo 1 The *o* man to the chosen lady
3Jo 1 The *o* man to Gaius, the beloved

Oldest
Ge 10:21 brother of Japheth the *o*

Nu 11:26 name of the *o* was Eldad
11:32 *o* collecting least gathered
13:2 send out *o* man for each tribe
13:2 each *o* a chieftain among them
13:23 with *o* cluster of grapes
14:4 saying to *o* another: Let us
14:15 people to death as *o* man
15:4 the *o* presenting his offering
15:9 *o* must also present together
15:11 *o* head among the male lambs
15:12 do for each *o* according to
15:14 *o* who is in your midst for
15:15 an alien will have *o* statute
15:16 should prove to be *o* law
15:16 *o* judicial decision for you
15:24 render up *o* young bull as a
15:24 and *o* kid of the goats as a
15:29 prove to be *o* law for you as
16:7 will choose . . . the holy *o*
16:15 Not *o* male ass have I taken
16:15 nor have I harmed *o* of them
16:17 take each *o* his fire holder
16:17 each *o* his fire holder before
16:18 took each *o* his fire holder
16:22 will just *o* man sin and you
16:40 no *o* might become like Korah
17:2 *o* rod for each paternal house
17:2 name of each *o* upon his rod
17:3 is *o* rod for the head of the
19:8 *o* who burned it will wash
19:10 *o* gathering the ashes of the
19:12 Such *o* should purify himself
19:17 take for the unclean *o* some
19:18 *o* who touched the bone or
19:18 the slain *o* or the corpse or
19:19 spatter it upon the unclean *o*
19:21 *o* spattering the water for
19:21 the *o* touching the water for
19:22 the unclean *o* may touch will
22:5 as far as *o* can see, and they
22:6 *o* whom you bless is a blessed
22:6 whom you bless is a blessed *o*
22:6 *o* whom you curse is cursed
23:25 If, on the *o* hand, you cannot
24:4 *o* hearing the sayings of God
24:16 *o* hearing the sayings of God
24:16 *o* knowing the knowledge of
24:19 of Jacob *o* will go subduing
24:20 Amalek was the first *o* of
24:22 come to be *o* to burn Kain
25:5 Each *o* of you kill his men
25:15 was a head *o* of the clans of
26:51 six hundred and *o* thousand
28:4 *o* male lamb you will render
28:11 two young bulls and *o* ram
28:12 offering . . . for the *o* ram
28:15 *o* kid of the goats should be
28:19 two young bulls and *o* ram
28:22 *o* goat of sin offering to
28:27 two young bulls, *o* ram
28:28 tenth measures for the *o* ram
28:30 *o* kid of the goats to make
29:2 render up . . . *o* young bull
29:2 *o* ram, seven male lambs each
29:4 *o* tenth measure for each male
29:5 *o* male kid of the goats as a
29:8 a restful odor, *o* young bull
29:8 *o* ram, seven male lambs each
29:9 tenth measures for the *o* ram
29:11 *o* kid of the goats as a sin
29:16 *o* kid . . . as a sin offering
29:19 *o* kid . . . as a sin offering
29:22 and *o* goat as a sin offering
29:25 *o* kid of the goats as a sin
29:28 and *o* goat as a sin offering
29:31 and *o* goat as a sin offering
29:34 and *o* goat as a sin offering
29:36 burnt offering . . . *o* bull
29:36 *o* ram, seven male lambs
29:38 and *o* goat as a sin offering
31:28 *o* soul out of five hundred
31:30 should take *o* out of fifty
31:47 *o* to be taken out of fifty
31:49 and not *o* has been reported
31:50 each *o* what he has found as
32:21 and every equipped *o* of yours
33:2 from *o* departure place to
33:54 To the populous *o* you should
33:54 to the sparse *o* you should
34:18 *o* chieftain out of each tribe
35:8 Each *o*, in proportion to his
35:19 avenger of blood is the *o*
35:30 *o* witness may not testify
35:32 *o* who has fled to his city

Nu 35:33 blood of the *o* spilling it
36:7 each *o* to the inheritance of
36:8 to *o* of the family of the
36:8 get possession each *o* of the
36:9 from *o* tribe to another tribe
De 1:17 hear the little *o* the same as
1:17 the same as the great *o*
1:23 I took . . . *o* for each tribe
1:30 God is the *o* going before you
1:35 Not *o* among these men of this
1:38 the *o* who will go in there
1:41 you girded on, each *o*, his
3:20 each *o* to his holding that I
3:22 God is the *O* fighting for you
3:28 he is the *o* to pass over
3:28 *o* to cause them to inherit
4:3 Baal of Peor was the *o* whom
4:32 from *o* end of the heavens
4:42 flee to *o* of these cities and
5:27 you will be the *o* to speak
6:4 Jehovah our God is *o* Jehovah
7:10 repaying . . . *o* who hates him
7:10 toward the *o* who hates him
10:21 He is the *O* for you to praise
12:8 each *o* whatever is right in
12:14 in *o* of your tribes is where
12:15 The unclean *o* and the clean
12:15 and the clean *o* may eat it
12:22, 22 unclean *o* and the clean *o*
13:7 from *o* end of the land to the
13:12 said in *o* of your cities
15:4 no *o* should come to be poor
15:7 *o* of your brothers becomes
15:7 in *o* of your cities, in your
15:12 out from you as *o* set free
15:13 out from you as *o* set free
15:18 as *o* set free; because for
15:22 the unclean *o* and the clean
15:22 and the clean *o* together
16:5 in any *o* of your cities that
17:2 in *o* of your cities that
17:5 stone such *o* with stones, and
17:5 and such *o* must die
17:6 the *o* dying should be put to
17:6 at the mouth of *o* witness
17:8 *o* in which blood has been
18:3 *O* must give to the priest the
18:5 he is the *o* whom Jehovah your
18:6 goes out of *o* of your cities
18:11 *o* who binds others with a
19:5 flee to *o* of these cities and
19:11 fled to *o* of these cities
20:20 it is the *o* you should ruin
21:2 all around the slain *o*
21:3 city nearest to the slain *o*
21:6 are nearest to the slain *o*
21:15 *o* loved and the other hated
21:15, 15 loved *o* and the hated *o*
21:15 come to be of the hated *o*
21:16 the son of the loved *o* his
21:17 that *o* is the beginning of
21:23 accursed of God is the *o* hung
22:27 there was no *o* to rescue her
23:16 choose in *o* of your cities
23:19 which *o* may claim interest
24:5 at his house for *o* year
24:6 No *o* should seize a hand mill
24:16 Each *o* should be put to death
25:1 pronounce the righteous *o*
25:1 pronounce the wicked *o* wicked
25:2 if the wicked *o* deserves to
25:5 *o* of them has died without
25:5 the wife of the dead *o* should
25:10 the *o* who had his sandal
25:11 struggle together with *o*
25:11 the wife of the *o* has come
25:11 the hand of the *o* striking
25:13, 13 a great *o* and a small *o*
25:14, 14 a great *o* and a small *o*
27:16 the *o* who treats his father
27:17 the *o* who moves back the
27:18 *o* who causes the blind to go
27:19 *o* who perverts the judgment
27:20 *o* who lies down with his
27:21 *o* who lies down with any
27:22 *o* who lies down with his
27:23 *o* who lies down with his
27:24 *o* who fatally strikes his
27:25 *o* who accepts a bribe to
27:26 *o* who will not put the
28:7 By *o* way they will come out
28:25 By *o* way you will go out
28:26 no *o* to make them tremble
28:29 *o* who gropes about at midday

De 28:29 *o* who is always defrauded
28:29 with no *o* to save you
28:33 *o* who is only defrauded and
28:44 He will be the *o* to lend to you
28:55 so as not to give *o* of them
28:64 from the *o* end of the earth
29:19 the well-watered *o* along
31:3 God is the *o* crossing before
31:3 Joshua is the *o* crossing
31:6 God is the *o* marching with
31:8 Jehovah is the *o* marching
32:8 sons of Adam from *o* another
32:18 the *O* bringing you forth
32:30 How could *o* pursue a thousand
32:36 a helpless and worthless *o*
32:39 is no *o* snatching out of my
33:12 beloved *o* of Jehovah reside
33:16 *O* residing in the thornbush
33:16 the head of the *o* singled out
33:20 Blessed is the *o* widening
33:24 *o* approved by his brothers
33:24 And *o* dipping his foot in oil
33:29 *O* who is your eminent sword
Jos 1:6 *o* who will cause this people
1:15 the *o* that Moses the servant
3:12 Israel, *o* man for each tribe
3:13 will stand still as *o* dam
3:16 rose up as *o* dam very far
4:2 *o* man from each tribe
4:4 Israel, *o* man from each tribe
4:5 each *o* a stone upon his
6:1 no *o* going out and
6:1 and no *o* entering
6:5 each *o* straight before him
6:20 each *o* straight before him
7:15 the *o* picked with the thing
7:21 Shinar, a good-looking *o*
7:21 *o* gold bar, fifty shekels
8:33 *o* half of them in front of
10:2 like *o* of the royal cities
10:14 proved to be like that *o*
10:42 and their land at *o* time
12:9 The king of Jericho, *o*
12:9 the king of Ai . . . *o*
12:10 the king of Jerusalem, *o*
12:10 the king of Hebron, *o*
12:11 the king of Jarmuth, *o*
12:11 the king of Lachish, *o*
12:12 the king of Eglon, *o*
12:12 the king of Gezer, *o*
12:13 the king of Debir, *o*
12:13 the king of Geder, *o*
12:14 the king of Hormah, *o*
12:14 the king of Arad, *o*
12:15 the king of Libnah, *o*
12:15 the king of Adullam, *o*
12:16 the king of Makkedah, *o*
12:16 the king of Bethel, *o*
12:17 the king of Tappuah, *o*
12:17 the king of Hepher, *o*
12:18 the king of Aphek, *o*
12:18 the king of Lassharon, *o*
12:19 the king of Madon, *o*
12:19 the king of Hazor, *o*
12:20 king of Shimron-meron, *o*
12:20 the king of Achshaph, *o*
12:21 the king of Taanach, *o*
12:21 the king of Megiddo, *o*
12:22 the king of Kedesh, *o*
12:22 king of Jokneam . . . *o*
12:23 mountain ridge of Dor, *o*
12:23 king of Goiim in Gilgal, *o*
12:24 the king of Tirzah, *o*
13:22 *o* whom the sons of Israel
17:1 *o* who proved to be a man of
17:14, 14 *o* lot and *o* allotment
17:17 You ought not to get *o* lot
20:4 flee to *o* of these cities and
21:44 not *o* of all their enemies
22:14 *o* chieftain of each
22:22 Divine *O*, God, Jehovah
22:22 Divine *O*, God, Jehovah, he
23:3 your God was the *o* who was
23:5 your God was the *o* who kept
23:10 *o* man of you will chase a
23:10 *o* who is fighting for you
23:14 not *o* word out of all the
23:14 Not *o* word . . . has failed
24:28 each *o* to his inheritance
Jg 2:21 single *o* of the nations that
3:25 no *o* opening the doors of the
3:29 every *o* robust and every
3:29 every *o* a valiant man; and
3:29 and not a single *o* escaped

Jg 4:16 Not as much as *o* remained
6:12 you, you valiant, mighty *o*
6:16 strike down Midian as if *o*
6:17 you are the *o* speaking with
6:29 to say *o* to another: Who has
6:29 the *o* that has done this thing
6:33 gathered together as *o* and
7:4 This *o* will go with you, he is
7:4 he is *o* that will go with you
7:4 every *o* of whom I say to you
7:4 This *o* will not go along with
7:4 he is *o* that will not go along
7:5 Every *o* that laps up some of
7:5 every *o* that bends down upon
7:7 let them go each *o* to his
7:8 sent away each *o* to his home
7:21 each *o* in his place all around
7:22 sword of each *o* against the
8:18 each *o*, like the sons of a
8:23 the *o* who will rule over you
8:24 Give me, each *o* of you, the
8:25 each *o* the nose ring of his
8:26 *o* thousand seven hundred gold
9:2 for *o* man to rule over you
9:5 upon *o* stone, but Jotham the
9:18 seventy men, upon *o* stone
9:37 *o* band is coming by the way
9:49 each *o* a branch for himself
9:55 now went each *o* to his place
10:18 to say to *o* another: Who is
11:24 every *o* whom Jehovah our God
11:24 the *o* we shall dispossess
11:31 the *o* coming out, who comes
11:31 offer that *o* up as a burnt
11:35 the *o* I was ostracizing
12:5 Gilead would say to each *o*
13:18 when it is a wonderful *o*
14:3 the *o* just right in my eyes
15:4 put *o* torch between two tails
15:16 male ass—*o* heap, two heaps
16:5, 5 *o* thousand *o* hundred silver
16:6 be tied for *o* to master you
16:24 *o* who multiplied our slain
16:28 for *o* of my two eyes
16:29 *o* with his right and the
17:2 The thousand *o* hundred silver
17:3 thousand *o* hundred pieces of
17:5 of *o* of his sons with power
17:11 got to be as *o* of his sons to
18:19 priest to the house of *o* man
19:13 approach *o* of the places, and
19:22 shoving *o* another against the
19:28 But there was no *o* answering
20:1 congregated themselves as *o*
20:8 the people rose up as *o* man
20:11 against the city as *o* man
20:16 Every *o* of these was a
20:17 Every *o* of these was a man
20:31 highways, *o* of which goes
20:35 thousand *o* hundred men, all
21:3 *o* tribe to be missing today
21:5 the *o* that has not come up to
21:6 *o* tribe has been chopped off
21:8 Which *o* out of the tribes of
21:8 no *o* had come into the camp
21:18 Cursed is the *o* that gives a
21:21 by force each *o* his wife
21:22 for each *o* his wife by war
21:24 each *o* to his own tribe and
21:24 *o* to his own inheritance
21:25 each *o* was accustomed to do
Ru 1:4 The name of the *o* was Orpah
1:8 return, each *o* to the house of
1:9 find a resting-place each *o* in
2:13 like *o* of your maidservants
2:19 May the *o* who took notice of
2:20 He is *o* of our repurchasers
4:4 there is no *o* else but you to
4:4 I shall be the *o* to repurchase
4:15 and *o* to nourish your old age
1Sa 1:2 name of the *o* being Hannah
1:5 to Hannah he gave *o* portion
1:24 *o* ephah of flour and a large
1:28 he is *o* requested for Jehovah
2:2 is no *o* holy like Jehovah
2:2 for there is no *o* but you
2:8 A Raiser of a lowly *o* from
2:8 lifts up a poor *o*, To make
2:10 the horn of his anointed *o*
2:34 *o* day both of them will die
2:35 walk before my anointed *o*
2:36 to *o* of the priestly offices
3:20 Samuel was *o* accredited for
4:10 fleeing each *o* to his tent

1Sa 4:16 the *o* coming from the battle
6:4 for every *o* of you and your
6:12 On the *o* highway they went
6:17, 17 for Ashdod *o*, for Gaza *o*
6:17, 17 Ashkelon *o*, for Gath *o*
6:17 golden piles . . . for Ekron *o*
7:1 Eleazar his son was the *o*
8:22 Go each *o* to his city
9:3 with you *o* of the attendants
9:13 *o* that blesses the sacrifice
9:17 *o* that will keep my people
10:3 *o* carrying three kids and
10:3 *o* carrying three round loaves
10:3 *o* carrying a large jar of
10:11 the people said *o* to another
10:24 *o* whom Jehovah has chosen
10:25 away, each *o* to his house
10:27 How will this *o* save us?
10:27 like *o* grown speechless
11:7 that they came out as *o* man
12:3 in front of his anointed *o*
12:4 from the hand of a single *o*
12:5 his anointed *o* is a witness
13:2 each *o* to his tent
13:17 *o* band would turn to the
13:20 to get each *o* his plowshare
13:22 found *o* belonging to Saul
14:1 it came about *o* day that
14:4 the name of the *o* was Bozez
14:5 *o* tooth was a pillar on the
14:20 sword of each *o* had come
14:26 no *o* putting his hand to his
14:28 *o* of the people answered
14:34 Bring near to me, each *o* of
14:34 each *o*, his sheep, and you
14:34 brought near each *o* his bull
14:36 let us not leave a single *o*
14:39 was no *o* answering him out
14:40 come to be on the *o* side
14:49 the *o* born first was Merab
14:49 the younger *o* Michal
16:3 anoint for me the *o* whom I
16:6 anointed *o* is before Jehovah
16:8 has Jehovah chosen this *o*
16:9 has Jehovah chosen this *o*
16:11 The youngest *o* has till now
16:18 And *o* of the attendants
17:36 must become like *o* of them
17:51 their mighty *o* had died
18:17 the *o* that I shall give you
18:21 By *o* of the two women you
20:15 enemies of David, every *o*
20:20 three arrows to *o* side
21:1 and no *o* is with you
21:2 Let no *o* know anything at
21:5 when *o* becomes holy in his
21:7 *o* of Saul's servants was
21:7 principal *o* of the shepherds
21:11 to this *o* that they kept
21:15 *o* to behave crazy by me
21:15 this *o* come into my home
22:8 no *o* disclosing it to my ear
22:8 no *o* of you having sympathy
22:20 *o* son of Ahimelech the son
22:23 *o* needing protection with
25:10 *o* from before his master
25:13 Gird on every *o* his sword
25:13 girded on every *o* his sword
25:14 *o* of the young men reported
26:12 no *o* seeing nor anyone
26:15 *o* of the people came in to
26:20 *o* chases a partridge upon
26:22 *o* of the young men come on
26:23 repay to each *o* his own
27:1 swept away *o* day by Saul's
27:3 each *o* with his household
27:5 place in *o* of the cities of
28:8 *o* whom I shall designate to
30:6 each *o* because of his sons
30:22 to each *o* his wife and his
30:24 share of the *o* that went
30:24 *o* that sat by the baggage
2Sa 1:15 called *o* of the young men
2:1 *o* of the cities of Judah
2:16 grabbing hold of *o* another
2:16 sword of each *o* in the side
2:18 like *o* of the gazelles that
2:21 seize *o* of the young men as
2:25 came to be *o* company and
2:25 upon the top of *o* hill
2:27 each *o* from following his
3:11 say *o* word more in reply to
3:13 Only *o* thing there is that
3:29 *o* falling by the sword or

2Sa 3:29 or *o* in need of bread
3:34 *o* falling before the sons of
4:2 name of the *o* being Baanah
4:10 *o* reporting to me, saying
5:2 *o* leading Israel out and
5:8, 8 blind *o* and the lame *o*
6:19 to each *o* a ring-shaped cake
6:20 as *o* of the empty-headed men
7:7 *o* of the tribes of Israel
7:13 *o* that will build a house
7:16 *o* firmly established to time
7:23 *o* nation in the earth is like
8:4 *o* thousand seven hundred
9:11 *o* of the sons of the king
11:25 sword eats up *o* as well as
12:1 happened to be in *o* city
12:1 the *o* rich and the other of
12:3 nothing but *o* female lamb
12:3 female lamb, a small *o*
12:28 not be the *o* to capture the
13:13 like *o* of the senseless men
13:29 mount each *o* his mule and
13:30 not *o* of them has been left
14:6 *o* struck the other down and
14:13 like *o* that is guilty, in
14:13 back his own banished *o*
14:14 reasons why the *o* banished
14:27 *o* daughter whose name was
15:2 *o* of the tribes of Israel
15:3 no *o* from the king giving
15:30 covered each *o* his head, and
16:2 wine is for the *o* tired out
16:18 *o* whom Jehovah has chosen
17:9 hiding in *o* of the hollows
17:9 or in *o* of the other places
17:9 the *o* hearing of it will
17:12 against him in *o* of the
17:12 not be left even a single *o*
17:22 until not a *o* was lacking
17:25 the *o* whom Absalom put in
18:2 *o* third of the people under
18:2 *o* third under . . . Abishai
18:2 *o* third under the hand of
18:26 This *o* also is a news
19:8 had fled each *o* to his home
19:14 the men of Judah as *o* man
19:20 I am the *o* that sinned
20:1 Every *o* to his gods, O Israel!
20:11 *o* of Joab's young men stood
20:22 each *o* to his home
21:6 Saul, the chosen *o* of Jehovah
22:4 the *O* to be praised, Jehovah
22:26 the faultless, mighty *o*
22:27 With the *o* keeping clean
22:27 with the crooked *o* you will
22:31 The saying . . . a refined *o*
22:48 the *O* bringing the peoples
22:49 the *O* bringing me out from
22:51 The *O* doing great acts of
22:51 to his anointed *o*, To David
23:1 *o* of the melodies of Israel
23:3 *o* ruling over mankind is
23:8 eight hundred slain at *o*
24:1 *o* incited David against them
24:12 Choose for yourself *o* of
24:13 reply to the *O* sending me
1Ki 1:13 the *o* that will become king
1:13 the *o* that will sit upon my
1:17 Solomon your son is the *o*
1:17 the *o* that will sit upon my
1:24 Adonijah is the *o* that will
1:24 the *o* that will sit upon my
1:30 Solomon your son is the *o*
1:30 the *o* that will sit upon my
1:48 *o* to sit upon my throne
1:49 go each *o* on his own way
2:16 *o* request that I am making
2:20 *o* little request that I am
3:12 *o* like you there has not
3:12 will not rise up *o* like you
3:17 the *o* woman said: Excuse me
3:17 are dwelling in *o* house
3:18 no *o* but the two of us in
3:22 my son is the living *o* and
3:22 and your son is the dead *o*
3:22 but your son is the dead *o*
3:22 and my son is the living *o*
3:23 *o* is saying, This is my son
3:23 This is my son, the living *o*
3:23 and your son is the dead *o*
3:23 *o* is saying, No, but your son
3:23 but your son is the dead *o*
3:23 and my son is the living *o*
3:25 give the *o* half to the

Ne 11:3 each *o* in his own possession
11:20 each *o* in his own hereditary
12:31 and the *o* was walking to
13:10 each *o* to his own field
13:28 *o* of the sons of Joiada the
13:30 each *o* in his own work
Es 1:7 were different from *o* another
1:8 there was no *o* compelling, for
1:8 the liking of each and every *o*
3:8 There is *o* certain people
3:10 *o* showing hostility to the
3:13 *o* day, on the thirteenth day
4:2 *o* was to come into the king's
4:5 Hathach, *o* of the king's
4:11 *o* law is to have him put to
5:12 no *o* but me, and tomorrow
6:9 *o* of the king's noble princes
7:5 *o* who has emboldened himself
7:9 Harbona, *o* of the court
8:1 Haman, the *o* showing hostility
8:12 on the *o* day in all the
9:10 the *o* showing hostility to
9:19 of portions to *o* another
9:22 portions to *o* another and of
9:24 *o* showing hostility to all
9:30 *o* hundred and twenty-seven
Job 1:4 banquet at the house of each *o*
1:8 is no *o* like him in the earth
1:16 this *o* was yet speaking
1:16 that *o* came and proceeded to
1:17 *o* was yet speaking another
1:17 another *o* came and proceeded
1:18 other *o* was yet speaking
1:18 another *o* came and proceeded
2:3 is no *o* like him in the earth
2:10 As *o* of the senseless women
2:11 each *o* from his own place
2:12 and rip each *o* his sleeveless
2:13 no *o* speaking a word to him
3:18 of *o* driving them to work
3:20 light to *o* having trouble
4:2 *o* does try out a word to you
4:11 are separated from *o* another
4:19 *O* crushes them more quickly
5:1 to which *o* of the holy ones
5:2 foolish *o* vexation will kill
5:2 *o* easily enticed envying will
5:3 seen the foolish *o* taking root
5:5 he harvests the hungry *o* eats
5:5 from butcher hooks *o* takes it
5:9 To the *O* doing great things
5:10 To the *O* giving rain upon the
5:11 *O* putting those who are low
5:12 *O* frustrating the schemes of
5:13 *O* catching the wise in their
5:15 *O* saving from the sword out
5:15 from the hand of the strong *o*
5:15 saving . . . a poor *o*
5:16 for the lowly *o* there comes
6:10 the sayings of the Holy *O*
6:26 sayings of *o* in despair are
8:18 If *o* swallows him up from
9:22 *O* thing there is. That is
9:22 *O* blameless, also a wicked
9:22 blameless, also a wicked *o*
9:24 the hand of the wicked *o*
10:7 no *o* delivering out of your
11:19 no *o* to make you tremble
12:4 *O* who is a laughingstock to
12:4 *O* calling to God that he
12:4 the righteous, unblamable *o*
12:5 carefree *o* has contempt for
12:6 *o* who has brought a god in
12:16 the *o* making a mistake and
12:16 and the *o* leading astray
13:9 *o* trifles with mortal man
13:19 *o* that will contend with
14:3 upon this *o* you have opened
14:4 There is not *o*
15:10 and the aged *o* are with us
15:10 *o* greater than your father
15:16 *o* is detestable and corrupt
15:20 a wicked *o* is suffering
16:14 runs at me like a mighty *o*
16:19 is *o* testifying about me
17:8 innocent *o* gets excited over
17:9 The righteous *o* keeps holding
17:9 *o* with clean hands keeps
18:21 of *o* that has not known God
20:26 A fire that no *o* fanned
21:22 that *O* himself judges high
21:23 *o* will die during his full
21:25 this other *o* will die with
21:28 is the house of the noble *o*
Job 21:30 disaster an evil *o* is spared
22:7 not give the tired *o* a drink
22:7 hungry *o* you hold back bread
22:8 And *o* who is treated with
22:19 the innocent *o* himself will
22:29 *o* with downcast eyes he
23:7 the upright *o* himself will
23:13 he is in *o* mind, and who
24:5 desert plain gives to each *o*
24:6 the vineyard of the wicked *o*
24:9 what is on the afflicted *o*
24:14 the afflicted and the poor *o*
25:4 *o* born of a woman be clean
26:2 have been to *o* without power
26:3 *o* that is without wisdom
27:7 the *o* revolting against me
27:17 righteous would be the *o* to
27:17 be the *o* to have a share
27:23 *O* will clap his hands at
28:18 more than *o* full of pearls
28:23 the *O* who has understood
29:12 afflicted *o* crying for help
29:13 the *o* about to perish
29:15 I became to the blind *o*
29:15 feet to the lame *o* I was
29:16 case of *o* whom I did not
29:25 As *o* who comforts the
30:8 Sons of the senseless *o*
30:8 also sons of the nameless *o*
30:24 no *o* thrusts his hand out
30:25 the *o* having a hard day
30:25 has grieved for the poor *o*
31:15 *O* making me in the belly
31:15 just *O* proceed to prepare us
31:19 the poor *o* had no covering
31:29 *o* intensely hating me
32:12 there is no *o* reproving Job
33:14 though *o* does not regard it
33:23 *o* out of a thousand
34:17 a powerful *o* is righteous
34:18 Shall *o* say to a king
34:19 There is *O* who has not
34:19 consideration to the noble *o*
34:19 than to the lowly *o*
34:28 the outcry of the lowly *o*
35:10 no *o* has said, Where is God
35:10 The *O* giving melodies in
35:11 the *O* teaching us more than
36:4 The *O* perfect in knowledge
36:15 will rescue the afflicted *o*
36:17 sentence upon the wicked *o*
36:33 concerning the *o* coming up
37:16 the *O* perfect in knowledge
40:11 see every *o* haughty and
40:12 See every *o* haughty, humble
41:9 *O* will also be hurled down
41:16 *O* to the other they fit
41:17 Each *o* to the other they
41:17 grasp *o* another and cannot
41:32 *O* would regard the watery
41:33 *o* made to be without terror
42:11 each *o* to give him a piece
42:11 and each *o* a gold ring
Ps 2:2 have massed together as *o*
2:2 and against his anointed *o*
2:4 *O* sitting in the heavens will
3:3 and the *O* lifting up my head
4:3 distinguish his loyal *o*
5:4 No *o* bad may reside for any
7:2 no *o* may tear my soul to
7:4 I have repaid the *o* rewarding
7:9 you establish the righteous *o*
7:14 *o* that is pregnant with what
8:2 the *o* taking his vengeance
9:5 have destroyed the wicked *o*
9:16 wicked *o* has been ensnared
9:18 will the poor *o* be forgotten
10:2 the wicked *o* hotly pursues
10:2 hotly pursues the afflicted *o*
10:3 the *o* making undue profit has
10:4 The wicked *o* according to his
10:6 be *o* who is in no calamity
10:9 carry off some afflicted *o*
10:9 carries off the afflicted *o*
10:13 Why is it that the wicked *o*
10:14 To you the unfortunate *o*, the
10:15 arm of the wicked and bad *o*
10:18 To judge the . . . crushed *o*
11:5 examines the righteous *o* as
11:5 as well as the wicked *o*
12:1 loyal *o* has come to an end
12:2 keep speaking *o* to the other
12:7 You will preserve each *o* from
14:1 senseless *o* has said in his
Ps 14:1 There is no *o* doing good
14:3 There is no *o* doing good
14:3 doing good, Not even *o*
14:5 generation of the righteous *o*
14:6 The counsel of the afflicted *o*
15:5 a bribe against the innocent *o*
16:10 your loyal *o* to see the pit
17:13 from the wicked *o* with your
18:3 the *O* to be praised, Jehovah
18:26 the *o* keeping clean you will
18:26 the crooked *o* you will show
18:30 saying . . . is a refined *o*
18:32 God is the *O* girding me
18:50 to his anointed *o*, To David
19:2 *O* day after another day
19:2 *o* night after another night
19:6 *o* extremity of the heavens
19:7 the inexperienced *o* wise
20:6 certainly saves his anointed *o*
22:9 the *O* drawing me forth from
22:9 The *O* making me trust while
22:14 separated from *o* another
22:20 My only *o* from the very paw
22:24 affliction of the afflicted *o*
22:29 no *o* will ever preserve his
27:4 *O* thing I have asked from
28:8 salvation of his anointed *o*
29:9 each *o* is saying: Glory!
30:7 I became *o* that is disturbed
31:13 mass together as *o* against
31:18 against the righteous *o*
32:1 *o* whose revolt is pardoned
32:6 every loyal *o* will pray to
32:10 pains that the wicked *o* has
32:10 the *o* trusting in Jehovah
33:11 to *o* generation after another
34:6 This afflicted *o* called, and
34:19 of the righteous *o*
34:20 all the bones of that *o*
34:20 Not *o* of them has been
34:21 wicked *o* himself to death
34:21 ones hating the righteous *o*
35:10 Delivering the afflicted *o*
35:10 from *o* stronger than he is
35:10 the afflicted and poor *o*
35:10 from the *o* robbing him
35:14 like *o* mourning for a mother
35:17 my only *o* from the maned
36:1 the wicked *o* is in the midst
37:10 wicked *o* will be no more
37:12 wicked *o* is plotting against
37:12 against the righteous *o*
37:14 afflicted and poor *o* to fall
37:16 the little of the righteous *o*
37:21 The wicked *o* is borrowing
37:21 righteous *o* is showing favor
37:30 the *o* that utters wisdom in
37:32 The wicked *o* is keeping on
37:33 to the hand of that *o*
37:37 Watch the blameless *o* and
37:37 keep the upright *o* in sight
39:6 *O* piles up things and does not
39:8 a reproach of the senseless *o*
41:1 toward the lowly *o*
41:6 if *o* does come to see me
41:7 whisper to *o* another
44:16 voice of the *o* reproaching
44:16 the *o* taking his revenge
45:3 upon your thigh, O mighty *o*
49:2, 2 You rich *o* and you poor *o*
49:7 Not *o* of them can by any
49:10 stupid *o* and the unreasoning
49:10 the unreasoning *o* perish
49:14 a lofty abode is for each *o*
50:1 The Divine *O*, God, Jehovah
50:16 to the wicked *o* God will
50:23 The *o* offering thanksgiving
50:23 is the *o* that glorifies me
50:23 for the *o* keeping a set way
51:10 a new spirit, a steadfast *o*
52:1 what is bad, O you mighty *o*
53:1 The senseless *o* has said in
53:1 There is no *o* doing good
53:3 There is no *o* doing good
53:3 doing good, Not even *o*
55:3 the pressure of the wicked *o*
55:13 *O* familiar to me and my
55:22 the righteous *o* to totter
57:3 confuse the *o* snapping at me
58:10 The righteous *o* will rejoice
58:10 in the blood of the wicked *o*
58:11 fruitage for the righteous *o*
60:7 is the fortress of my head *o*
62:12 each *o* according to his work

Ps 63:11 Every *o* swearing by him will
64:6 And the inward part of each *o*
64:8 And they cause *o* to stumble
64:10 the righteous *o* will rejoice
65:4 Happy is the *o* you choose and
68:4 *O* riding through the desert
68:10 ready for the afflicted *o*
68:14 the Almighty *O* scattered
68:33 the *O* riding on the ancient
69:8 I have become *o* estranged to
69:26 the *o* whom you yourself have
71:4 from the hand of the wicked *o*
71:4 palm of the *o* acting unjustly
71:6 the *O* severing me even from
71:22 the harp, O Holy *O* of Israel
72:4 save the sons of the poor *o*
72:7 the righteous *o* will sprout
72:12 deliver the poor *o* crying for
72:12 afflicted *o* and whoever has
72:13 feel sorry for the lowly *o*
72:13 and the poor *o*
73:27 *o* immorally leaving you
74:5 *O* is notorious in being like
74:6 *o* and all, they strike even
74:9 no *o* with us knowing how long
74:12 *O* performing grand salvation
74:15 *O* that split the spring and
74:21 may the crushed *o* not return
74:21 afflicted *o* and the poor
74:21 the poor *o* praise your name
74:22 from the senseless *o* all
75:7 This *o* he abases, and that
75:7 abases, and that *o* he exalts
75:10 horns of the righteous *o*
78:41 even the Holy *O* of Israel
78:65 mighty *o* sobering up from
79:3 is no *o* to do the burying
81:10 *O* bringing you up out of the
82:1 assembly of the Divine *O*
82:3 Be judges for the lowly *o* and
82:3 To the afflicted *o* and the
82:3 *o* of little means do justice
82:4, 4 the lowly *o* and the poor *o*
82:7 any *o* of the princes you will
83:1 do not stay quiet, O Divine *O*
84:7 Each *o* appears to God in Zion
84:9 the face of your anointed *o*
87:4 This is *o* who was born there
87:5 Each and every *o* was born in
87:6 This is *o* who was born there
88:17 in upon me all at *o* time
89:3 covenant toward my chosen *o*
89:18 to the Holy *O* of Israel
89:19 placed help upon a mighty *o*
89:19 exalted a chosen *o* from
89:38 toward your anointed *o*
89:51 footprints of your anointed *o*
91:1 very shadow of the Almighty *O*
92:6 no *o* stupid can understand
92:9 be separated from *o* another
94:9 *O* planting the ear, can he not
94:9 *O* forming the eye, can he not
94:10 *O* correcting the nations
94:10 *O* teaching men knowledge
94:13 for the wicked *o* a pit is
94:21 the soul of the righteous *o*
94:21 the blood of the innocent *o*
97:11 Light . . . for the righteous *o*
101:6 *o* walking in a faultless way
104:3 *O* building his upper
105:13 From *o* kingdom to another
105:37 was no *o* stumbling along
106:11 Not *o* of them was left
106:16 Aaron the holy *o* of Jehovah
106:23 been for Moses his chosen *o*
107:12 and there was no *o* helping
107:41 protects the poor *o* from
108:8 is the fortress of my head *o*
109:2 mouth of the wicked *o* and
109:12 *o* extending loving-kindness
109:12 *o* showing favor to his
109:16 *o* dejected at heart, to put
109:20 of the *o* resisting me
110:6 head *o* over a populous land
112:6 righteous *o* will prove to be
112:10 wicked *o* himself will see
113:7 Raising up the lowly *o* from
113:7 exalts the poor *o* from the
116:5 our God is *O* showing mercy
118:26 *O* coming in the name of
118:27 Jehovah is the Divine *O*
118:28 You are my Divine *O*, and I
119:23 have spoken with *o* another
119:42 answer the *o* reproaching me

Ps 119:162 *o* does when finding much
120:3 What will *o* give to you
120:3 what will *o* add to you
121:3 *O* guarding you cannot
122:3 Jerusalem is *o* that is built
126:6 *o* that without fail goes
127:2 sleep even to his beloved *o*
132:2 to the Powerful *O* of Jacob
132:5 for the Powerful *O* of Jacob
132:10 the face of your anointed *o*
132:17 a lamp for my anointed *o*
136:5 *O* making the heavens with
136:6 *O* laying out the earth above
136:7 *O* making the great lights
136:10 *O* striking down Egypt in
136:11 *O* bringing Israel out of the
136:13 *O* severing the Red Sea into
136:16 *O* making his people walk
136:17 *O* striking down great kings
136:25 *O* giving food to all flesh
137:3 *o* of the songs of Zion
138:6 yet the humble *o* he sees
138:6 lofty *o* he knows only from
139:16 not yet *o* among them
139:19 would slay the wicked *o*
140:4 the hands of the wicked *o*
140:8 the cravings of the wicked *o*
140:12 claim of the afflicted *o*
141:5 righteous *o* strike me, it
141:7 *o* is doing cleaving and
142:4 no *o* giving any recognition
142:4 no *o* inquiring for my soul
143:2 no *o* alive can be righteous
144:2 *O* in whom I have taken
144:2 *O* subduing peoples under me
144:10 *O* giving salvation to kings
144:10 *O* setting David his servant
144:13 products of *o* sort after
144:13 ten thousand to *o*, in our
146:5 *o* who has the God of Jacob
146:6 *O* keeping trueness to time
146:7 *O* executing judgment for the
146:7 *O* giving bread to the hungry
147:8 *O* who is covering the
147:8 *O* preparing rain for the
147:8 *O* making the mountains to

Pr 1:2 for *o* to know wisdom and
1:5 *o* who acquires skillful
1:14 *o* bag belonging to all of us
1:24 is no *o* paying attention
1:33 *o* listening to me, he will
3:12 *o* whom Jehovah loves he
3:33 on the house of the wicked *o*
4:3 the only *o* before my mother
5:22 will catch the wicked *o*
5:23 *o* to die because there is no
6:6 Go to the ant, you lazy *o*; see
6:9 lazy *o*, will you keep lying
6:26 *o* comes down to a round loaf
6:29 no *o* touching her will remain
8:9 straight to the discerning *o*
8:30 *o* he was specially fond of
8:35 *o* finding me will certainly
8:36 *o* missing me is doing
9:10 knowledge of the Most Holy *O*
10:1 *o* that makes a father rejoice
10:2 treasures of the wicked *o*
10:3 soul of the righteous *o* to go
10:4 *o* working with a slack hand
10:4 diligent *o* is what will make
10:4 is what will make *o* rich
10:6 the head of the righteous *o*
10:7 the righteous *o* is due for a
10:8 *o* wise in heart will accept
10:8 *o* foolish with his lips will
10:10 *o* winking his eye will give
10:10 *o* foolish with his lips
10:11 righteous *o* is a source of
10:13 back of *o* in want of heart
10:14 mouth of the foolish *o* is
10:16 righteous *o* results in life
10:16 produce of the wicked *o*
10:18 *o* covering over hatred there
10:18 *o* bringing forth a bad report
10:19 *o* keeping his lips in check
10:20 tongue of the righteous *o* is
10:20 heart of the wicked *o* is
10:21 lips of the righteous *o* keep
10:23 To the stupid *o* the carrying
10:24 frightful to the wicked *o*
10:25 so the wicked *o* is no more
10:25 righteous *o* is a foundation
10:29 for the blameless *o*, but
10:30 righteous *o*, to time

Pr 10:31 mouth of the righteous *o*
10:32 lips of the righteous *o*
11:5 blameless *o* is what will make
11:5 the wicked *o* will fall
11:8 righteous is the *o* rescued
11:8 wicked *o* comes in instead of
11:9 *o* who is an apostate brings
11:12 *o* in want of heart has
11:12 is *o* that keeps silent
11:13 *o* walking about as a
11:13 *o* faithful in spirit is
11:15 *O* will positively fare badly
11:15 *o* hating handshaking is
11:16 *o* that takes hold of glory
11:18 wicked *o* is making false
11:18 *o* sowing righteousness, true
11:19 *o* firmly standing for
11:19 *o* chasing after what is bad
11:24 *o* that is scattering and yet
11:24 *o* that is keeping back from
11:25 *o* freely watering others
11:26 *o* holding back grain—the
11:26 the *o* letting it be bought
11:27 *o* searching for bad, it will
11:28 *o* trusting in his riches
11:29 to the *o* wise in heart
11:30 fruitage of the righteous *o*
11:31 righteous *o*—in the earth
11:31 wicked *o* and the sinner be
12:2 *O* that is good gets approval
12:8 *o* who is twisted at heart
12:9 *o* lightly esteemed but having
12:9 *o* glorifying himself but in
12:10 righteous *o* is caring for the
12:11 *o* cultivating his ground
12:11 *o* pursuing valueless things
12:12 wicked *o* has desired the
12:13 righteous *o* gets out of
12:15 foolish *o* is right in his
12:15 *o* listening to counsel is
12:16 shrewd *o* is covering over
12:18 *o* speaking thoughtlessly as
12:21 will befall the righteous *o*
12:23 *o* that calls out foolishness
12:24 *o* that will rule, but the
12:26 righteous *o* spies out his
12:27 diligent *o* is a man's
13:1 is *o* that has not heard rebuke
13:3 *o* guarding his mouth is
13:3 *o* opening wide his lips—he
13:4 lazy *o* is showing himself
13:6 *o* who is harmless in his way
13:7 *o* that is pretending to be
13:7 *o* that is pretending to be
13:8 *o* of little means has not
13:10 *o* only causes a struggle
13:11 *o* collecting by the hand
13:11 is the *o* that makes increase
13:13 *o* fearing the commandment
13:13 the *o* that will be rewarded
13:14 law of the wise *o* is a
13:14 *o* away from the snares of
13:16 *o* that is stupid will spread
13:18 *o* neglecting discipline
13:18 *o* keeping a reproof is the
13:18 is the *o* that is glorified
13:22 *O* who is good will leave
13:22 for the righteous *o*
13:23 *o* that is swept away for
13:24 *o* holding back his rod is
13:24 *o* loving him is he that does
14:1 foolish *o* tears it down with
14:2 *o* walking in his uprightness
14:2 *o* crooked in his ways is
14:3 in the mouth of the foolish *o*
14:5 is *o* that will not lie
14:6 understanding *o* knowledge is
14:14 *o* faithless at heart will be
14:15 shrewd *o* considers his steps
14:16 wise *o* fears and is turning
14:19 the gates of the righteous *o*
14:20 *o* who is of little means is
14:21 The *o* despising his own
14:25 a deceitful *o* launches forth
14:29 but *o* that is impatient is
14:31 defrauding the lowly *o* has
14:31 *o* showing favor to the poor
14:31 showing favor to the poor *o*
14:33 heart of the understanding *o*
14:35 toward *o* acting shamefully
15:6 the house of the righteous *o*
15:6 the produce of the wicked *o*
15:9 The way of the wicked *o* is
15:9 *o* pursuing righteousness he

Pr 15:10 bad to the *o* leaving the path
15:12 does not love the *o* reproving
15:14 understanding heart is *o* that
15:14 *o* that aspires to foolishness
15:15 days of the afflicted *o* are
15:15 *o* that is good at heart has a
15:18 but *o* that is slow to anger
15:19 lazy *o* is like a brier hedge
15:20 wise son is the *o* that makes
15:21 to *o* who is in want of heart
15:21 is *o* who goes straight ahead
15:24 to *o* acting with insight
15:26 The schemes of the bad *o* are
15:27 *o* making unjust profit is
15:27 hater of gifts is the *o* that
15:28 righteous *o* meditates so as
15:32 the *o* listening to reproof is
16:4 the wicked *o* for the evil day
16:5 yet *o* will not be free from
16:6 in the fear of Jehovah *o* turns
16:14 wise man is *o* that averts it
16:17 *O* who is safeguarding his
16:21 *o* that is wise in heart will
16:23 heart of the wise *o* causes
16:28 familiar with *o* another
16:32 than the *o* capturing a city
17:5 *o* of little means in derision
17:9 *o* covering over transgression
17:9 those familiar with *o* another
17:10 in *o* having understanding
17:10 striking a stupid *o* a hundred
17:11 rebellion is what the bad *o*
17:14 is as *o* letting out waters
17:15 pronouncing the wicked *o*
17:15 pronouncing the righteous *o*
17:16 in the hand of the stupid *o*
17:23 *O* who is wicked will take
17:24 face of the understanding *o*
17:24 eyes of the stupid *o* are at
17:26 fine upon the righteous *o* is
18:1 *O* isolating himself will seek
18:3 When a wicked *o* comes in
18:5 partiality to the wicked *o* is
18:5 the righteous *o* in judgment
18:6 lips of *o* who is stupid enter
18:7 The mouth of the stupid *o* is
18:9 *o* showing himself slack in
18:9 brother to the *o* causing ruin
18:15 the understanding *o* acquires
18:17 *o* first in his legal case is
18:18 the mighty from *o* another
18:22 Has *o* found a good wife?
18:22 *O* has found a good thing, and
18:22 *o* gets goodwill from Jehovah
18:23 *o* of little means speaks out
18:23 *o* that is rich answers in a
18:24 to break *o* another to pieces
19:1 than the *o* crooked in his lips
19:1 and the *o* that is stupid
19:4 but *o* that is lowly gets
19:7 brothers of *o* of little means
19:13 a leaking roof that drives *o*
19:17 showing favor to the lowly *o*
19:22 *o* of little means is better
19:23 and *o* will spend the night
19:23 *o* will not be visited with
19:24 lazy *o* has hidden his hand in
19:25 inexperienced *o* may become
19:25 understanding *o*, that he may
20:4 the lazy *o* will not plow
20:5 is *o* that will draw it up
20:6 will proclaim each *o* his own
20:16 in case *o* has gone surety for
20:19 *o* that is enticed with his
21:5 plans of the diligent *o* surely
21:8 the pure *o* is upright in his
21:10 wicked *o* has craved what is
21:12 The Righteous *O* is giving
21:12 to the house of the wicked *o*
21:13 cry of the lowly *o*, he
21:15 rejoicing for the righteous *o*
21:18 a ransom for the righteous *o*
21:18 *o* dealing treacherously takes
21:20 in the abode of the wise *o*
21:22 A wise *o* has scaled even the
21:24 *o* who is acting in a fury of
21:26 righteous *o* gives and holds
21:27 *o* brings it along with loose
21:29 upright is the *o* that will
22:2, 2 rich *o* and the *o* of little
22:3 *o* that has seen the calamity
22:5 in the way of the crooked *o*
22:7 rich is the *o* that rules over
22:9 of his food to the lowly *o*

Pr 22:11 The *o* loving purity of heart
22:12 words of the treacherous *o*
22:13 lazy *o* has said: There is a
22:14 *o* denounced by Jehovah will
22:16 is defrauding the lowly *o* to
22:16 that is giving to the rich *o*
22:21 to the *o* sending you forth
22:22 not rob the lowly *o* because
22:22 not crush the afflicted *o* in
23:7 For as *o* that has calculated
23:9 Into the ears of a stupid *o* do
23:21 clothe *o* with mere rags
23:24 father of a righteous *o* will
23:24 *o* becoming father to a wise
23:24 father to a wise *o* will also
23:34 *o* lying down in the heart of
23:34 *o* lying down at the top of a
24:5 *O* wise in strength is an
24:7 For a foolish *o* true wisdom
24:15 as a wicked *o*, lie in wait
24:15 place of the righteous *o*
24:16 righteous *o* may fall even
24:24 is saying to the wicked *o*
24:29 repay to each *o* according to
25:5 the removing of the wicked *o*
25:10 that the *o* listening may not
25:19 *o* proving treacherous in the
25:21 If the *o* hating you is hungry
25:26 righteous *o* when staggering
25:26 before the wicked *o*
26:1 is not fitting for a stupid *o*
26:6 *o* that is mutilating his feet
26:6 as *o* that is drinking mere
26:7 of the lame *o* drawn up water
26:8 *o* shutting up a stone in a
26:8 the *o* giving glory to a mere
26:8 glory to a mere stupid *o*
26:10 *o* hiring someone stupid or
26:10 or the *o* hiring passersby
26:11 the stupid *o* is repeating his
26:12 more hope for the stupid *o*
26:13 lazy *o* has said: There is a
26:14 and the lazy *o* upon his couch
26:15 lazy *o* has hidden his hand in
26:16 lazy *o* is wiser in his own
26:17 *o* grabbing hold of the ears
26:28 hates the *o* crushed by it
27:12 shrewd *o* that has seen the
27:13 case *o* has gone surety for a
27:15 A leaking roof that drives *o*
27:17 *o* man sharpens the face of
27:22 pound the foolish *o* fine
28:4 praise the wicked *o*, but
28:6 Better is the *o* of little
28:7 *o* having companionship with
28:8 *o* showing favor to the lowly
28:11 lowly *o* who is discerning
28:26 walking in wisdom is the *o*
28:27 to the *o* of little means
29:7 righteous *o* is knowing the
29:10 for the soul of each *o*
29:11 is what a stupid *o* lets out
29:13 The *o* of little means and
29:21 *o* is pampering one's servant
29:21 even become a thankless *o*
29:27 *o* who is upright in his way
29:27 detestable to a wicked *o*
30:3 the Most Holy *O* I do not know
31:5 *o* may not drink and forget
31:6 to the *o* about to perish and
31:7 Let *o* drink and forget one's
31:7 *o* remember one's own trouble
31:8 mouth for the speechless *o*
31:9 the cause of the afflicted *o*
31:9 plead the cause of . . . poor *o*
31:20 to the afflicted *o*, and her
31:20 has thrust out to the poor *o*
31:30 *o* that procures praise for
Ec 1:8 no *o* is able to speak of it
1:10 exist of which *o* may say
2:14 the stupid *o* is walking on in
2:14 *o* eventuality that eventuates
2:15 like that upon the stupid *o*
2:16 remembrance of the wise *o*
2:16 than of the stupid *o* to time
2:16 and how will the wise *o* die?
2:16 Along with the stupid *o*
2:21 be given the portion of that *o*
2:26 to give to the *o* that is good
3:17 judge both the righteous *o* and
3:17 God will judge . . . wicked *o*
3:19 As the *o* dies, so the other
3:19 and they all have but *o* spirit
3:20 All are going to *o* place

Ec 4:3 *o* who has not yet come to be
4:4 rivalry of *o* toward another
4:5 stupid *o* is folding his hands
4:8, 8 exists *o*, but not a second *o*
4:9 Two are better than *o*, because
4:10 For if *o* of them should fall
4:10 other *o* can raise his partner
4:10 with just the *o* who falls
4:11 how can just *o* keep warm?
4:12 could overpower *o* alone, two
4:14 in the kingship of this *o* he
4:14 born as *o* of little means
5:3 voice of a stupid *o* because of
5:8 oppression of the *o* of little
5:8 *o* that is higher than the high
5:8 that is higher than the high *o*
5:12 is the sleep of the *o* serving
5:12 plenty belonging to the rich *o*
5:15 Just as *o* has come forth from
5:15 naked will *o* go away again
5:15 go away again, just as *o* came
5:15 nothing at all can *o* carry
5:16 exactly as *o* has come, so
5:16 come, so *o* will go away
5:16 the *o* who keeps working hard
5:18 *o* should eat and drink and see
6:3 *o* prematurely born is better
6:4 in vain has this *o* come and in
6:5 This *o* has rest rather than the
6:5 rest rather than the former *o*
6:6 *o* place that everyone is going
6:8 wise have over the stupid *o*
6:8 What does the afflicted *o* have
6:10 *o* that is more powerful than
7:2 *o* alive should take it to his
7:6 is the laughter of the stupid *o*
7:7 may make a wise *o* act crazy
7:8 Better is *o* who is patient
7:8 *o* who is haughty in spirit
7:15 righteous *o* perishing in his
7:15 wicked *o* continuing long in
7:18 you should take hold of the *o*
7:19 is stronger for the wise *o*
7:26 *O* is good before the true God
7:26 if *o* escapes from her, but
7:26 from her, but *o* is sinning if
7:26 sinning if *o* is captured by
7:27 *o* thing taken after another
7:28 *O* man out of a thousand I
8:1 Who is there like the wise *o*?
8:7 no *o* knowing what will come
8:13 with the wicked *o*, neither
8:16 is *o* seeing no sleep with his
9:2 *O* eventuality there is to the
9:2 the righteous *o* and the wicked
9:2 and the wicked *o*, the good
9:2, 2 the good *o* and the clean *o*
9:2 and the unclean *o*, and the
9:2 and the *o* sacrificing and the
9:2 the *o* that is not sacrificing
9:2 The good *o* is the same as the
9:2 the *o* swearing is the same as
9:3 there is *o* eventuality to all
9:15 *o* provided escape for the city
9:16 the wisdom of the needy *o* is
9:17 cry of *o* ruling among stupid
9:18 *o* sinner can destroy much
10:1 *o* who is precious for wisdom
10:3 way the foolish *o* is walking
10:5 on account of the *o* in power
10:11 the *o* indulging in the tongue
10:12 mouth of the wise *o* mean
10:12 lips of the stupid *o* swallow
10:14 foolish *o* speaks many words
10:15 not *o* has come to know how
12:4 *o* gets up at the sound of a
12:11 been given from *o* shepherd
Ca 1:6 my vineyard, *o* that was mine
1:8 most beautiful *o* among women
1:13 As a bag of myrrh my dear *o*
1:14 henna my dear *o* is to me
1:16 my dear *o*, also pleasant
1:16 Our divan also is *o* of foliage
2:3 so is my dear *o* among the sons
2:8 The sound of my dear *o*! Look!
2:8 This *o* is coming, climbing
2:9 dear *o* is resembling a gazelle
2:9 This *o* is standing behind our
2:10 My dear *o* has answered and
2:10 my beautiful *o*, and come
2:13 my beautiful *o*, and come
2:16 dear *o* is mine and I am his
2:17 dear *o*; be like the gazelle
3:1 the *o* whom my soul has loved

Ca 3:2 the *o* whom my soul has loved
3:3 *o* whom my soul has loved have
3:4 found the *o* whom my soul has
3:7 the *o* belonging to Solomon
3:8 each *o* with his sword upon his
4:9 heart beat by *o* of your eyes
4:9 by *o* pendant of your necklace
4:16 Let my dear *o* come into his
5:2 sound of my dear *o* knocking
5:2 my dove, my blameless *o*
5:4 My dear *o* himself pulled back
5:5 even I, to open to my dear *o*
5:6 I opened, even I, to my dear *o*
5:6 my dear *o* himself had turned
5:8 if you find my dear *o*, you
5:9 How is your dear *o* more than
5:9 more than any other dear *o*
5:9 most beautiful *o* among women
5:9 How is your dear *o* more than
5:9 more than any other dear *o*
5:10 dear *o* is dazzling and ruddy
5:16 This is my dear *o*, and this
6:1 Where has your dear *o* gone, O
6:1 most beautiful *o* among women
6:1 Where has your dear *o* turned
6:2 My own dear *o* has gone down
6:3 and my dear *o* is mine. He is
6:9 *O* there is who is my dove, my
6:9 is my dove, my blameless *o*
6:9 *O* there is who belongs to her
6:9, 9 pure *o* of the *o* giving birth
7:9 with a slickness for my dear *o*
7:11 Do come, O my dear *o*, let us
7:13 my dear *o*, I have treasured
8:5 leaning upon her dear *o*
8:11 Each *o* would bring in for its
8:14 Run away, my dear *o*, and
8:14 like a young *o* of the stags
Isa 1:4 treated the Holy *O* of Israel
1:23 Every *o* of them is a lover of
1:24 the Powerful *O* of Israel, is
1:31 no *o* to do the extinguishing
3:5 tyrannize *o* over the other
3:5 each *o* over his fellowman
3:5 lightly esteemed *o* against
3:5 against the *o* to be honored
3:6 each *o* will lay hold of his
3:10 well with the righteous *o*
3:11 Woe to the wicked *o*!
3:14 robbery from the afflicted *o*
4:1 grab hold of *o* man in that
5:1 to my beloved *o* a song of my
5:1 song of my loved *o* concerning
5:1 beloved *o* came to have on a
5:10 produce but *o* bath measure
5:14 uproar and the exultant *o*
5:16 the Holy *O*, will certainly
5:19 of the Holy *O* of Israel
5:23 the wicked *o* righteous in
5:23 of the righteous *o* from him
5:24 Holy *O* of Israel they have
5:27 no *o* tired nor is anyone
5:27 No *o* is drowsy and no
5:27 drowsy and no *o* sleeps
5:30 *o* will actually gaze at the
6:2 Each *o* had six wings
6:3, 3 this *o* called to that *o*
6:4 voice of the *o* calling, and
6:6 *o* of the seraphs flew to me
8:4 *o* will carry away the
8:13 *O* whom you should treat as
8:13 *O* causing you to tremble
8:21 *o* will certainly pass
9:1 *o* treated with contempt the
9:1 *o* caused it to be honored
9:4 the *o* driving them to work
9:5 the *o* tramping with tremors
9:11 enemies of that *o* he will
9:13 returned to the *O* striking
9:14 shoot and rush, in *o* day
9:15 highly respected *o* is the
9:19 No *o* will show compassion
9:20 *o* will cut down on the right
9:20 *o* will eat on the left, and
9:20 each *o* eat the flesh of his
10:4 *o* must bow down under the
10:13 just like a powerful *o*
10:14 *o* gathers eggs that have
10:14 *o* fluttering his wings or
10:15 over the *o* chopping with it
10:15 *o* moving it back and forth
10:15 high the *o* who is not wood
10:17 and his Holy *O* a flame
10:17 his thornbushes in *o* day
Isa 10:18 away of *o* that is ailing
10:20 upon the *o* striking them
10:20 Holy *O* of Israel, in
10:30 you afflicted *o*, Anathoth
10:34 and by a powerful *o* Lebanon
11:4 put the wicked *o* to death
11:16 *o* for Israel in the day of
12:6 the Holy *O* of Israel
13:14 each *o* to his own people
13:14 each *o* to his own land
13:15 *o* that is found will be
13:15 *o* that is caught in the
14:4 *o* driving others to work
14:6 *o* striking peoples in fury
14:6 *o* subduing nations in sheer
14:12 shining *o*, son of the dawn
14:18 each *o* in his own house
14:27 hand is the *o* stretched out
14:29 Philistia, any *o* of you
14:29 staff of the *o* striking you
14:31 *o* getting isolated from his
15:5 with weeping each *o* goes up
16:5 *o* must sit down upon it in
17:2 *o* to make them tremble
17:5 *o* gleaning ears of grain in
17:7 gaze at the Holy *O* of Israel
18:2 *o* sending forth envoys by
18:5 *o* must also cut off the
19:2 each *o* against his brother
19:2 each *o* against his companion
19:17 to whom *o* mentions it is in
19:18 will *o* city be called
19:20 savior, even a grand *o*, who
21:11 is *o* calling out from Seir
21:14 the thirsty *o* bring water
21:14 confront the *o* fleeing away
22:3 have fled at *o* time
22:8 *o* will remove the screen of
22:11 *o* forming it long ago you
22:19 *o* will tear you down
23:12 again exult, O oppressed *o*
23:13 did not prove to be the *o*
23:13 *o* has set her as a
23:15 same as the days of *o* king
24:2 the *o* paying the interest
24:16 to the Righteous *O*
25:4 a stronghold to the lowly *o*
25:4 stronghold to the poor *o*
25:9 *o* will certainly say: Look!
26:3 that *o* is made to trust
26:6 feet of the afflicted *o*
26:7 righteous *o* is uprightness
26:7 very course of a righteous *o*
26:10 wicked *o* should be shown
27:3 *o* may turn his attention
27:7 stroke of *o* striking him
27:7 does *o* have to strike him?
27:8 blast, a hard *o* in the day
27:12 picked up *o* after the other
28:6 *o* sitting in the judgment
28:9 *o* instruct in knowledge
28:9 *o* make understand what has
28:12 Give rest to the weary *o*
28:16 *o* exercising faith will get
28:26 *o* corrects him according to
28:28 *o* incessantly keep treading
29:14 *O* that will act wonderfully
29:19 in the Holy *O* of Israel
29:21 *o* reproving in the gate
29:21 push aside the righteous *o*
29:23 sanctify the Holy *O* of Jacob
30:5 *o* will certainly become
30:5 that bring no benefit to *o*
30:7 called this *o*: Rahab
30:11 Holy *O* of Israel to cease
30:12 Holy *O* of Israel has said
30:14 *o* will certainly break it
30:15 Holy *O* of Israel, has said
30:17 account of the rebuke of *o*
30:28 bridle that causes *o* to
30:29 *o* sanctifies oneself for a
30:29 *o* walking with a flute to
31:1 to the Holy *O* of Israel and
31:6 *O* against whom the sons of
31:7 reject each *o* his worthless
32:2 *o* must prove to be like a
32:5 senseless *o* will no longer
32:6 senseless *o* himself will
32:6 hungry *o* to go empty, and
32:6 thirsty *o* to go without
32:8 generous *o*, it is for
33:4 that is rushing against *o*
33:8 *o* passing over the path has
33:15 is *o* who is walking in
Isa 33:16 *o* that will reside on the
33:18 *o* that does the paying out
33:18 *o* counting the towers
33:20 tent that no *o* will pack
33:21 Majestic *O*, Jehovah, will
34:10 no *o* will be passing
34:15 each *o* with her mate
34:16 not *o* has been missing of
34:16 to have each *o* her mate
35:6 lame *o* will climb up just
35:6 speechless *o* will cry out in
35:8 unclean *o* will not pass over
35:8 *o* walking on the way, and
36:7 *o* whose high places and
36:9 back the face of *o* governor
36:16 each *o* from his own vine
36:16 *o* from his own fig tree and
36:16 *o* the water of his own
36:18 delivered each *o* his own
37:23 against the Holy *O* of Israel
38:12 *O* proceeds to cut me off
38:19 is the *o* that can laud you
40:6 *o* said: What shall I call
40:10 come even as a strong *o*
40:14 *o* might make him understand
40:22 *O* who is dwelling above the
40:22 *O* who is stretching out the
40:23 the *O* who is reducing high
40:24 *o* has only to blow upon
40:25 his equal? says the Holy *O*
40:26 *O* who is bringing forth the
40:26 not *o* of them is missing
40:29 giving to the tired *o* power
40:29 *o* without dynamic energy he
41:4 I, Jehovah, the First *O*; and
41:6 helping each *o* his companion
41:6 *o* would say to his brother
41:7 *o* doing the smoothing out
41:7 *o* fastened it with nails
41:13 *O* saying to you, Do not be
41:14 the Holy *O* of Israel
41:16 In the Holy *O* of Israel you
41:20 the Holy *O* of Israel has
41:26 Really there is no *o* telling
41:26, 26 no *o* causing *o* to hear
41:26 no *o* that is hearing any
41:27 There is *o* first, saying to
41:28 no *o* that was giving
42:1 My chosen *o*, whom my soul
42:5 the Grand *O* stretching them
42:5 the *O* laying out the earth
42:5 the *O* giving breath to the
42:8 to no *o* else shall I give my
42:19 is blind as the *o* rewarded
42:24 the *O* against whom we have
43:3 Holy *O* of Israel your Savior
43:9 together at *o* place
43:10 that I am the same *O*
43:13 the time I am the same *O*
43:13 no *o* effecting deliverance
43:14 the Holy *O* of Israel
43:15 I am Jehovah your Holy *O*
43:16 the *O* making a way through
43:17 *O* bringing forth the war
43:20 my people, my chosen *o*, to
43:25 I am the *O* that is wiping
43:27 own father, the first *o*
44:3 water upon the thirsty *o*
44:5 *o* will say: I belong to
44:5 *o* will call himself by the
44:5 name of Israel *o* will betitle
44:14 *o* whose business is to cut
44:19 no *o* recalls to his heart
44:25 the *O* that makes diviners
44:25 the *O* turning wise men
44:25 the *O* that turns even their
44:26 the *O* making the word of
44:26 the *O* that carries out
44:26 the *O* saying of Jerusalem
44:27 the *O* saying to the watery
44:28 the *O* saying of Cyrus
45:1 to his anointed *o*, to Cyrus
45:3 *O* calling you by your name
45:4 and of Israel my chosen *o*
45:5 and there is no *o* else
45:6 and there is no *o* else
45:9 the *o* that has contended
45:10 Woe to the *o* saying to a
45:11 the Holy *O* of Israel and
45:13 *o* that will build my city
45:14 and there is no *o* else
45:18 *O* who firmly established
45:18 Jehovah, and there is no *o*
45:22 God, and there is no *o* else

Isa 46:4 I am the same *O;* and to
46:7 *O* even cries out to it
46:7 distress it does not save *o*
46:9 I am the Divine *O* and there
46:10 the *O* telling from the
46:10 *O* saying, My own counsel
46:11 the *O* calling from the
47:4 There is *O* repurchasing us
47:4 the Holy *O* of Israel
47:8 the *o* sitting in security
47:8 the *o* saying in her heart
47:9 will come suddenly, in *o* day
47:10 There is no *o* seeing me
47:15 each *o* to his own region
47:15 will be no *o* to save you
48:11 *o* let oneself be profaned
48:11 to no *o* else shall I give
48:12 and you Israel my called *o*
48:12 I am the same *O.* I am the
48:17 the Holy *O* of Israel
48:17 *O* teaching you to benefit
48:17 the *O* causing you to tread
49:3 the *o* in whom I shall show
49:5 Jehovah, the *O* forming me
49:7 of Israel, his Holy *O,* has
49:7 the Holy *O* of Israel, who
49:10 *O* who is having pity upon
49:26 the Powerful *O* of Jacob
50:1 which *o* of my creditors is
50:2 I came in, there was no *o*
50:4 answer the tired *o* with a
50:8 The *O* declaring me righteous
51:2 he was *o* when I called him
51:9 *o* that broke Rahab to pieces
51:10 the *o* that dried up the sea
51:10 The *o* that made the depths
51:12 the *O* that is comforting
51:13 the *O* stretching out the
51:13 rage of the *o* hemming you
51:13 of the *o* hemming you in
51:14 The *o* stooping in chains
51:15 the *O* stirring up the sea
52:1 uncircumcised and unclean *o*
52:6 I am the *O* that is speaking
52:7 feet of the *o* bringing good
52:7 the *o* publishing peace, the
52:7 the *o* bringing good news of
52:7 the *o* publishing salvation
52:7 *o* saying to Zion: Your God
53:2 come up like a twig before *o*
53:6 each *o* to his own way that
53:6 all to meet up with that *o*
53:11 the righteous *o,* my servant
54:1 the sons of the desolated *o*
54:5 the Holy *O* of Israel is your
54:10 Jehovah, the *O* having mercy
54:16 the *o* blowing upon the fire
55:5 and for the Holy *O* of Israel
56:5 *o* that will not be cut off
56:11 each *o* for his unjust gain
57:1 righteous *o* himself has
57:1 is no *o* taking it to heart
57:1 no *o* discerns that it is
57:1 the righteous *o* has been
57:2 each *o* that is walking
57:11 I was not the *o* that you
57:13 *o* taking refuge in me will
57:14 *o* will certainly say, Bank
57:15 the High and Lofty *O,* who
57:15 *o* crushed and lowly in
57:19 to the *o* that is far away
57:19 and to the *o* that is near
58:7 bread out to the hungry *o*
58:10 grant to the hungry *o* your
58:13 holy day of Jehovah, *o* being
59:4 is no *o* calling out in
59:4 no *o* at all has gone to court
59:8 No *o* at all treading in them
59:12 each *o* has testified against
59:16 there was no *o* interposing
60:9 and to the Holy *O* of Israel
60:14 Zion of the Holy *O* of Israel
60:15 *o* left entirely and hated
60:16 the Powerful *O* of Jacob is
60:22 The little *o* himself will
60:22 the small *o* a mighty nation
63:1 is this *o* coming from Edom
63:1 *o* with garments of glowing
63:1 *o* who is honorable in his
63:1 *O* speaking in righteousness
63:1 *O* abounding in power to save
63:2 *o* treading in the winepress
63:5 was no *o* offering support
63:11 *o* began to remember the

Isa 63:11 *O* that brought them up out
63:11 Where is the *O* that put
63:12 The *O* making His beautiful
63:12 the *O* splitting the waters
63:13 the *O* making them walk
64:4 *o* that keeps in expectation
64:5 met up with the *o* exulting
64:7 no *o* calling upon your name
64:7 no *o* rousing himself to lay
64:11 every *o* of our desirable
65:20 *o* will die as a mere boy
65:25 will feed as *o,* and the
66:2 To this *o,* then, I shall look
66:2 *o* afflicted and contrite in
66:3 The *o* slaughtering the bull
66:3 is as *o* striking down a man
66:3 The *o* sacrificing the sheep
66:3 is as *o* breaking the neck of
66:3 *o* offering up a gift—the
66:3 The *o* presenting a memorial
66:3 as *o* saying a blessing with
66:4 there was no *o* answering
66:8 with labor pains in *o* day
66:8 a nation be born at *o* time
66:17 gardens behind *o* in the
Jer 1:1 *o* of the priests that were in
1:15 place each *o* his throne at
2:6 the *O* bringing us up out of
2:6 the *O* walking us through the
3:5 Should *o* stay resentful to
3:14 *o* out of a city and two out
4:4 no *o* to do the extinguishing
4:7 the *o* who is bringing the
5:8 They neigh each *o* to the wife
5:24 the *O* who is giving the
5:24 the *O* who guards even the
6:3 grazed off each *o* his own
6:9 *o* that is gathering grapes
6:11 *o* that is full of days
6:13 from the least *o* of them
6:13 even to the greatest *o*
6:13 every *o* is making for himself
6:13 each *o* is acting falsely
6:15 For *o* thing, they positively
6:23 It is a cruel *o,* and they
6:27 *o* making a thorough search
6:29 *O* has kept refining intensely
8:4 If *o* would turn back, will
8:6 Each *o* is going back into the
8:10 from the least *o* even to the
8:10 even to the greatest *o*
8:10 each *o* is making unjust gain
8:10 each *o* is acting falsely
8:12 For *o* thing, they positively
9:4 Guard yourselves each *o*
9:5 each *o* with his companion
9:12 the *o* to whom the mouth of
9:22 no *o* to do the gathering up
9:24 let the *o* bragging about
9:24 *O* exercising loving-kindness
10:3 tree . . . that *o* has cut down
10:4 with gold *o* makes it pretty
10:8 at *o* and the same time they
10:12 the *O* firmly establishing
10:12 *O* who by his understanding
10:20 There is no *o* stretching
11:8 each *o* in the stubbornness
11:15 business does my beloved *o*
11:19 a male lamb, an intimate *o*
12:7 I have given the beloved *o*
12:11 *O* has made it a desolate
12:12 from *o* end of the land even
12:15 each *o* to his hereditary
12:15 and each *o* to his land
13:14 dash them *o* against another
13:19 there is no *o* opening them
13:20 the drove that *o* gave to you
13:21 *o* turns his attention upon
14:16 with no *o* to do the burying
14:22 the *O,* O Jehovah our God
15:12 Can *o* break iron in pieces
16:12 each *o* after the
16:21 at this *o* time I shall
17:10 each *o* according to his
17:11 the *o* making riches, but
18:11 Turn back, please, each *o*
18:12 each *o* the stubbornness of
18:16 Every last *o* passing along
18:18 counsel from the wise *o* or
19:8 Every last *o* passing along
19:9 eat each *o* the flesh of his
20:11 like a terrible mighty *o*
20:11 will be *o* that will not be
20:12 examining the righteous *o*

Jer 20:13 the soul of the poor *o*
21:9 The *o* sitting still in this
21:9 the *o* who is going out and
21:12 deliver the *o* being robbed
21:12 no *o* to extinguish it
22:3 the *o* that is being robbed
22:6 as for the cities, not *o*
22:7 each *o* and his weapons
22:8 and say *o* to the other
22:10 Do not weep for the dead *o*
22:10 Weep . . . for the *o* going
22:13 the *o* building his house
22:14 the *o* saying, I am going to
22:16 claim of the afflicted *o*
22:16 legal claim of . . . the poor *o*
22:17 the blood of the innocent *o*
22:30 not a single *o* will have
23:14 each *o* from his own badness
23:17 And to every *o* walking in
23:27 relating each *o* to the other
23:28 *o* with whom my own word
23:30 each *o* from his companion
23:35 each *o* to his fellow and
23:35 and each *o* to his brother
23:36 to each *o* his own word
24:2 As for the *o* basket, the
25:5 every *o* from his bad way
25:26 *o* after the other, and all
25:33 from *o* end of the earth
26:3 each *o* from his bad way
27:8 the *o* that will not put its
29:23 I am the *O* knowing and am
30:7 For that day is a great *o*
30:10 be no *o* causing trembling
30:13 no *o* pleading your cause
30:14 the *o* for whom they keep
30:17 for whom no *o* is searching
30:21 majestic *o* will certainly
30:21 *o* that has given his heart
31:8 *o* giving birth, all together
31:10 *O* scattering Israel will
31:11 of the *o* stronger than he is
31:30 each *o* for his own error
31:30 own error that *o* will die
31:32 *o* like the covenant that I
31:34 teach each *o* his companion
31:34 each *o* his brother, saying
31:34 from the least *o* of them
31:34 even to the greatest *o* of
31:35 *O* stirring up the sea that
31:35 *O* whose name is Jehovah
32:4 with the mouth of that *o*
32:4 see even the eyes of that *o*
32:11 *o* sealed according to the
32:11 and the *o* left open
32:14 even the sealed *o,* and the
32:18 *O* exercising loving-kindness
32:18 the great *O,* the mighty
32:18 the mighty *O,* Jehovah of
32:19 give to each *o* according to
32:39, 39 them *o* heart and *o* way
33:13 of the *o* taking the count
34:9 let each *o* his manservant
34:9 and each *o* his maidservant
34:10 let each *o* his manservant
34:10 each *o* his maidservant go
34:14 let go each *o* his brother
34:15 liberty each *o* to his
34:16 back each *o* his manservant
34:16 each *o* his maidservant
34:17 liberty each *o* to his
34:17 each *o* to his companion
35:2 to *o* of the dining rooms
35:6 *o* that laid the command upon
35:15 each *o* from his bad way
36:3 each *o* from his bad way
36:7 each *o* from his bad way
36:16 at *o* another in dread
36:19 no *o* at all will know
36:28 roll, another *o,* and write
36:30 *o* sitting upon the throne
37:7 *o* sending you to me to
37:10 each *o* in his tent rise up
38:2 *o* continuing to dwell in
38:2 *o* that will die by the sword
38:2 *o* going out to the Chaldeans
38:2 *o* that will keep living and
38:4 *o* seeking not for the peace
40:5 not *o* that would return
40:15 no *o* at all will know
41:2 *o* whom the king of Babylon
41:4 no *o* at all that knew it
41:9 *o* that King Asa had made
41:9 *o* that Ishmael the son

Jer 42:1 people, from the smallest *o*
42:1 even to the greatest *o*
42:8 people, from the smallest *o*
42:8 even to the greatest *o*
44:12 from the smallest *o* even
44:12 even to the greatest *o*
44:30 the *o* seeking for his soul
46:6 not the swift *o* try to flee
46:7 *o* that comes up just like
46:16 keep saying *o* to the other
48:5 with weeping that *o* goes up
48:9 with no *o* dwelling in them
48:10 *o* that is carrying out the
48:10 *o* that is holding back his
48:11 emptied from *o* vessel into
48:15 *o* has gone up against her
48:31 of Kir-heres *o* shall moan
48:33 No *o* will be doing the
48:35 *o* bringing up an offering
48:35 *o* making sacrificial smoke
49:4 *o* trusting in her treasures
49:5 each *o* in his own direction
49:5 *o* collecting together those
49:10 *o* will not be able to hide
49:19 *o* who is chosen I shall
50:3 *o* that makes her land an
50:3 to be no *o* dwelling in her
50:16 *o* handling the sickle in
50:16 each *o* to his own people
50:16 flee each *o* to his own land
50:29 against the Holy *O* of Israel
50:32 *o* to cause it to rise up
50:42 in array as *o* man for war
50:44 *o* who is chosen I shall
51:3 Let the *o* treading his bow
51:3 *o* raise himself up in his
51:5 of the Holy *O* of Israel
51:6 each *o* for his own soul
51:9 go each *o* to his own land
51:15 *O* firmly establishing the
51:15 *O* who by his understanding
51:31 *O* runner runs to meet
51:31 *o* reporter to meet another
51:45 each *o* his soul with escape
51:46 in *o* year the report will
51:52 the pierced *o* will groan
51:60 in *o* book all the calamity
52:20 the *o* sea, and the twelve
52:22 height of the *o* capital
52:23 *o* hundred upon the network
52:25 took *o* court official that
52:25 *o* mustering the people of
La 1:2 She has no *o* to comfort her
1:13 bones, and he subdues each *o*
1:14 they intertwine *o* another
2:20 the *o* to whom you have dealt
3:11 has made me *o* laid desolate
3:25 to the *o* hoping in him, to
3:26 Good it is that *o* should wait
3:30 cheek to the very *o* striking
4:4 is no *o* dealing it out to them
4:10 as bread of consolation to *o*
4:20 the anointed *o* of Jehovah, has
4:20 The *o* of whom we have said
5:8 is no *o* tearing us away from
Eze 1:6 each *o* had four faces, and
1:6 and each *o* of them four wings
1:9 Their wings were joining *o* to
1:9 go each *o* straight forward
1:11 Each *o* had two joining to
1:12 go each *o* straight forward
1:15 *o* wheel on the earth beside
1:16 four of them had *o* likeness
1:23 straight, *o* to the other
1:23 Each *o* had two wings
1:23 each *o* had two covering on
1:24 the sound of the Almighty *O*
1:28 hear the voice of *o* speaking
2:2 hear the *O* speaking to me
3:18 order to warn the wicked *o*
3:21 righteous *o* should not sin
3:27 Let the *o* hearing hear, and
3:27 and let the *o* refraining
4:8 your *o* side to your other side
4:9 put them in *o* utensil and
4:14 My soul is not a defiled *o*
4:17 look astonished at *o* another
5:4 From *o* a fire will go forth
5:11 the *O* that will diminish you
6:7 slain *o* will certainly fall
6:12 As for the *o* far away, by
6:12 the *o* that is nearby, by the
6:12 for the *o* that has been left
7:13 No *o* will return, and they
Eze 7:13 each *o* of his own life by
7:14 is no *o* going to the battle
7:16 each *o* in his own error
7:20 *o* has set it as reason for
8:11 each *o* with his censer in
8:12 each *o* in the inner rooms of
9:1 each *o* with his weapon in his
9:2 each *o* with his weapon for
9:2 *o* man in among them clothed
10:7 the *o* clothed with the linen
10:9 *o* wheel beside the
10:9 wheel beside the *o* cherub
10:9 and *o* wheel beside the other
10:10 four of them had *o* likeness
10:14 And each *o* had four faces
10:21 each *o* had four faces and
10:21 and each *o* had four wings
10:22 go each *o* straight forward
11:19 I will give them *o* heart
13:10 is *o* that is building a
13:22 the heart of a righteous *o*
13:22 hands of a wicked *o* strong
16:5 do for you *o* of these things
16:45 *o* abhorring her husband and
16:49 hand of the afflicted *o* and
16:49 and the poor *o* she did not
17:13 took *o* of the royal seed and
17:16 the *o* that despised his oath
17:22 shall pluck off a tender *o*
18:7 hungry *o* he would give his
18:7 naked *o* he would cover with
18:10 if *o* has become father to a
18:10 like of *o* of these things
18:12 poor *o* he has maltreated
18:14 *o* has become father to a
18:16 to the hungry *o* he has given
18:16 naked *o* he has covered with
18:17 from the afflicted *o* he has
18:20 of the righteous *o* will
18:20 wickedness of the wicked *o*
18:24 that the wicked *o* has done
18:27 *o* that will preserve his
18:30 each *o* according to his
19:3 she brought up *o* of her cubs
20:6 *o* flowing with milk and
20:7 Throw away, each *o* of you
20:15 *o* flowing with milk and
20:39 serve each *o* of you his own
21:3, 3 righteous *o* and wicked *o*
21:4, 4 righteous *o* and wicked *o*
21:11 *o* gives it to be polished
21:17 strike my *o* palm against
21:19 the *o* land both of them
21:20 and *o* against Judah
21:26 bring low even the high *o*
22:6 each *o* given over to his arm
22:24 *o* not rained down upon in
22:29 and the afflicted *o* and the
22:29 poor *o* they have maltreated
22:30 and I found no *o*
23:2 the daughters of *o* mother
23:4 were Oholah the older *o* and
23:13 both of them had *o* way
23:32 the deep and wide *o*
23:44 *o* comes in to a woman
24:12 It has made *o* tired, but
24:23 groan over *o* another
24:26 come to you the escaped *o*
24:27 be opened to the escaped *o*
26:15 fatally wounded *o* groans
26:17 a strong *o* in the sea
28:9 before the *o* killing you
28:23 slain *o* must fall in the
29:18 Every head was *o* made bald
29:18 shoulder was *o* rubbed bare
30:4 when *o* falls slain in Egypt
30:22 the strong *o* and the broken
30:22 and the broken *o*, and I
30:24 as a deadly wounded *o* he
32:10 each *o* for his own soul
33:2 people of the land, *o* and all
33:8 wicked *o*, you will
33:8 warn the wicked *o* from his
33:8 wicked *o* will die in his
33:11 the death of the wicked *o*
33:12 righteous *o* will not itself
33:12 wickedness of the wicked *o*
33:13 say to the righteous *o*
33:14 when I say to the wicked *o*
33:15 the wicked *o* returns the
33:20 each *o* according to his
33:21 escaped *o* from Jerusalem
33:22 the coming of the escaped *o*
33:24 happened to be just *o*
Eze 33:26 defiled each *o* the wife of
33:27 *o* who is upon the surface
33:28 with no *o* passing through
33:30 are speaking with *o* another
33:30 *o* has spoken with the other
33:30 each *o* with his brother
33:32 like *o* with a pretty voice
34:4 ailing *o* you have not healed
34:4 broken *o* you have not
34:4 dispersed *o* you have not
34:4 lost *o* you have not sought
34:6 with no *o* making a search
34:6 with no *o* seeking to find
34:12 care of *o* feeding his drove
34:16 lost *o* I shall search for
34:16 dispersed *o* I shall bring
34:16 broken *o* I shall bandage
34:16 ailing *o* I shall strengthen
34:16, 16 fat *o* and the strong *o*
34:16 feed that *o* with judgment
34:23 over them *o* shepherd, and
34:28 no *o* to make them tremble
35:7 the *o* passing through and
35:7 cut off . . . the *o* returning
37:17 into *o* stick for yourself
37:17 become just *o* in your hand
37:19 actually make them *o* stick
37:19 must become *o* in my hand
37:22 make them *o* nation in the
37:22 *o* king is what all of them
37:24 and *o* shepherd is what they
38:12 *o* that is accumulating
38:17 Are you the same *o* of whom
38:21 each *o* will come to be
39:7 Jehovah, the Holy *O* in Israel
39:15 should *o* actually see the
39:26 no *o* to make them tremble
40:5 the thing built, *o* reed
40:5 and the height, *o* reed
40:6 the gate, *o* reed in width
40:6 threshold, *o* reed in width
40:7 chamber was *o* reed in length
40:7 and *o* reed in width, and
40:7 the interior was *o* reed
40:8 toward the interior, *o* reed
40:12 guard chambers was *o* cubit
40:12 fenced area of *o* cubit on
40:13 *o* guard chamber to the roof
40:23 north; also *o* to the east
40:26, 26 *o* on this side and *o* on
40:40 as *o* goes up to the entrance
40:42 length was *o* cubit and a
40:42 width *o* cubit and a half
40:42 and the height *o* cubit
40:43 ledges . . . *o* handbreadth
40:44 *o* on the side of the east
40:45 This *o*, the dining room
40:49, 49 *o* over here and *o* over
41:7 *o* could go up to the
41:11 *o* entrance being toward the
41:11 and *o* entrance to the south
41:24 *O* door had two door leaves
42:4 the inside, a way of *o* cubit
42:9 *o* comes in to them from the
42:12 when *o* comes in to them
43:13 lip round about, *o* span
43:14 and the width is *o* cubit
43:21 *o* must burn it in the
43:22 goats, a sound *o*, as a sin
43:23 of the herd, a sound *o*
43:23 from the flock, a sound *o*
44:1 the outer *o* facing east
45:7 exactly as *o* of the shares
45:11 to be but *o* fixed amount
45:15 *o* sheep out of the flock
45:17 *o* to provide the sin
45:18 son of the herd, a sound *o*
45:20 of any inexperienced *o*
46:6 son of the herd, a sound *o*
46:9 *o* coming in by the way of
46:9 *o* coming in by the way of
46:9 *o* should go back by the way
46:12 *o* must also open to him the
46:12 *o* must shut the gate after
46:16 gift to each *o* of his sons
46:17 to *o* of his servants, it
46:18 each *o* from his possession
47:14 *o* the same as his brother
47:15 as *o* comes to Zedad
48:1 Dan *o* portion
48:2 the western border, Asher *o*
48:3 western border, Naphtali *o*
48:4 western border, Manasseh *o*
48:5 western border, Ephraim *o*

Eze 48:6 western border, Reuben *o*
48:7 the western border, Judah *o*
48:8 *o* of the portions from the
48:14 should *o* make an exchange
48:14 *o* cause the choicest of the
48:23 border, Benjamin *o* portion
48:24 western border, Simeon *o*
48:25 western border, Issachar *o*
48:26 western border, Zebulun *o*
48:27 the western border, Gad *o*
48:31 north, the gate of Reuben, *o*
48:31 the gate of Judah, *o*
48:31 the gate of Levi, *o*
48:32 even the gate of Joseph, *o*
48:32 the gate of Benjamin, *o*
48:32 the gate of Dan, *o*
48:33 the gate of Simeon, *o*
48:33 the gate of Issachar, *o*
48:33 the gate of Zebulun, *o*
48:34 the gate of Gad, *o*
48:34 the gate of Asher, *o*
48:34 the gate of Naphtali, *o*
Da 1:19 no *o* was found like Daniel
2:9 *o* and only sentence is upon you
2:29 *O* who is the Revealer of
2:39 kingdom, a third *o*, of copper
2:43, 43 this *o* to that *o*, just
3:25 fourth *o* is resembling a son
3:29 is able to deliver like this *o*
4:13 watcher, even a holy *o*
4:17 *o* whom he wants to, he gives
4:17 the lowliest *o* of mankind
4:23 a watcher, even a holy *o*
4:25 to the *o* whom he wants to he
4:32 *o* whom he wants to he gives
4:34 *O* living to time indefinite
4:35 no *o* that can check his hand
5:7 as the third *o* in the kingdom
5:16 third *o* in the kingdom you
5:21 *o* whom he wants to, he sets
6:1 *o* hundred and twenty satraps
6:2 of whom Daniel was *o*, in order
6:26 and *O* enduring to times
6:26 kingdom is *o* that will not be
7:3 each *o* being different from
7:4 first *o* was like a lion, and
7:5 beast, a second *o*, it being
7:5 on *o* side it was raised up
7:6 beast, *o* like a leopard, but
7:8 another horn, a small *o*, came
7:13 up close even before that *O*
7:14 *o* that will not be brought to
7:16 *o* of those who were standing
7:18 holy ones of the Supreme *O*
7:22 holy ones of the Supreme *O*
7:24 another *o* will rise up after
7:25 themselves of the Supreme *O*
7:27 holy ones of the Supreme *O*
8:1 *o* appearing to me at the start
8:3 *o* was taller than the other
8:3 the *o* that came up afterward
8:4 *o* doing any delivering out of
8:9 out of *o* of them there came
8:9 another horn, a small *o*, and
8:13 certain holy *o* speaking, and
8:13 holy *o* proceeded to say to
8:13 particular *o* who was speaking
8:16 make that *o* there understand
8:22 *o* having been broken, so that
9:4 true God, the great *O* and the
9:4 and the fear-inspiring *O*
9:27 covenant in force . . . *o* week
9:27 be the *o* causing desolation
9:27 also upon the *o* lying desolate
10:13 Michael, *o* of the foremost
10:16 *o* similar to the likeness of
10:16 *o* who was standing in front
10:18 *o* like the appearance of an
10:21 *o* holding strongly with me
11:2 fourth *o* will amass greater
11:5 strong, even *o* of his princes
11:6 *o* making her strong in those
11:7 *o* from the sprout of her
11:11 given into the hand of that *o*
11:16 *o* coming against him will
11:16 no *o* standing before him
11:18 it turn back upon that *o*
11:20 *o* who is causing an exactor
11:21 *o* who is to be despised, and
11:27 at *o* table a lie is what
12:1 *o* who is found written down
12:5 *o* on the bank here of the
12:6 *o* said to the man clothed
12:7 *O* who is alive for time

Da 12:11 *o* thousand two hundred and
12:12 Happy is the *o* who is
12:12 *o* thousand three hundred and
Ho 1:11 set up for themselves *o* head
2:7 to my husband, the first *o*
2:13 I was the *o* that she forgot
5:13 that *o* himself was unable to
8:1 *O* comes like an eagle against
8:3 Let *o* who is an enemy pursue
8:14 the dwelling towers of each *o*
10:2 *o* who will break their altars
10:15 *o* will certainly do to you
11:4 I brought food to each *o*
11:7 no *o* at all does any rising up
11:9 the Holy *O* in the midst of
11:12 the Most Holy *O* he is
13:15 That *o* will pillage the
Joe 1:15 from the Almighty *O*
2:2 *o* like it has not been made
2:7 go each *o* in his own ways
2:8 *o* another they do not shove
3:10 As for the weak *o*, let him
Am 2:14 perish from the swift *o*
2:14 no *o* strong will reinforce
2:15 no *o* handling the bow will
2:15 no *o* swift on his feet will
2:16 as for *o* strong in his heart
4:3 forth, each *o* straight ahead
4:7 I made it rain on *o* city
4:7 *o* tract of land that would
4:8 to *o* city in order to drink
4:13 *O* telling to earthling man
4:13 *O* making dawn into obscurity
4:13 the *O* treading on earth's
5:2 There is no *o* raising her up
5:3 *o* going forth with a hundred
5:6 be with no *o* to extinguish it
5:8 the *O* turning deep shadow into
5:8 the *O* who has made day itself
5:8 the *O* calling for the waters
5:13 the very *o* having insight
6:9 be left remaining in *o* house
6:10, 10 carry them forth *o* by *o*
6:10, 10 be burning them *o* by *o*
6:12 *o* plow there with cattle
8:3 *o* will certainly throw them
9:1 No *o* fleeing of them will
9:1 no *o* escaping of them will
9:5 is the *O* touching the land
9:9 just as *o* jiggles the sieve
Ob 7 as *o* in whom there is no
9 each *o* will be cut off from the
11 you also were like *o* of them
Jon 1:5 for aid, each *o* to his god
1:7 began to say to *o* another
1:9 the *O* who made the sea and
2:7 was the *O* whom I remembered
3:4 the walking distance of *o* day
3:5 from the greatest *o* of them
3:5 even to the least *o* of them
3:8 each *o* from his bad way and
4:11 *o* hundred and twenty
Mic 2:4 In that day *o* will raise up
2:4 *O* will have to say: We have
2:4 To the unfaithful *o* he
2:5 no *o* casting out the cord
2:7 the *o* walking uprightly
2:11 the *o* letting words drop
2:13 The *o* making a breakthrough
4:4 each under his vine and
4:4 no *o* making them tremble
4:5 walk each *o* in the name of
5:2 the *o* too little to get to be
5:2 the *o* who is to become ruler
5:5 And this *o* must become peace
6:10 in the house of a wicked *o*
7:2 The loyal *o* has perished from
7:2 there is no upright *o*. All of
7:3 the *o* who is judging does so
7:3 the great *o* is speaking forth
7:4 Their best *o* is like a brier
7:4 most upright *o* is worse than
7:14 *o* who was residing alone
7:18 *o* pardoning error and
Na 1:11 *o* who is thinking up against
1:12 and *o* must pass through
1:15 feet of *o* bringing good news
1:15 good news, *o* publishing peace
2:1 *O* that does a scattering has
2:8 But there is no *o* turning back
2:11 no *o* was making them tremble
3:18 no *o* collecting them together
Hab 1:4 wicked *o* is surrounding the
1:4 is surrounding the righteous *o*

Hab 1:5 in amazement at *o* another
1:5 activity that *o* is carrying on
1:12 my Holy *O*, you do not die
1:14 over whom no *o* is ruling
2:2 *o* reading aloud from it may
2:4 But as for the righteous *o*
2:6 *o* will say, Woe to him who
2:9 *o* that is making evil gain
2:12 the *o* that is building a city
2:15 the *o* giving his companions
2:19 Woe to the *o* saying to the
3:3 a Holy *O* from Mount Paran
3:13 to save your anointed *o*
3:13 broke to pieces the head *o*
3:13 the house of the wicked *o*
3:14 on devouring an afflicted *o*
Zep 1:18 extermination . . . terrible *o*
2:11 each *o* from his place
3:5 unrighteous *o* was knowing no
3:6 was no *o* passing through
3:13 no *o* making them tremble
3:17 As a mighty *O*, he will save
Hag 1:9 each *o* in behalf of his own
2:16 *o* came to a heap of twenty
2:16 *o* came to the press vat to
2:17 no *o* with you turning to me
2:22 each *o* by the sword of his
2:23 the *o* whom I have chosen
Zec 1:21 no *o* at all raised his head
3:2 Is this *o* not a log snatched
3:9 *o* stone there are seven eyes
3:9 error of that land in *o* day
3:10 call, each *o* to the other
4:3 *o* on the right side of the
4:3 bowl and *o* on its left side
5:4 the *o* making a sworn oath
6:6 *o* in which the black horses
7:9 and carry on with *o* another
7:10 alien resident or afflicted *o*
7:10 against *o* another in your
7:14 with no *o* passing through
7:14 and with no *o* returning
8:4 each *o* also with his staff in
8:10 to the *o* going out and to the
8:10 to the *o* coming in there was
8:10 mankind against *o* another
8:16 Speak truthfully with *o*
8:17 calamity to *o* another do not
8:21 the inhabitants of *o* city
9:8 no *o* passing through and no
9:8 through and no *o* returning
10:1 to each *o* vegetation in the
11:6 each *o* in the hand of his
11:7 The *o* I called Pleasantness
11:8 shepherds in *o* lunar month
11:9 *o* that is dying, let her die
11:9 *o* that is being effaced, let
11:9 devour, each *o* the flesh of
11:16 young *o* he will not seek
11:16 The *o* stationing herself he
11:16 flesh of the fat *o* he will
12:1 *O* who is stretching out the
12:8 *o* that is stumbling among
12:10 *O* whom they pierced through
13:4 each *o* of his vision when
13:6 *o* must say to him, What are
14:7 *o* day that is known as
14:9 Jehovah will prove to be *o*
14:9 Jehovah . . . and his name *o*
14:12 *o* is standing upon one's
14:13 hold, each *o* of the hand of
Mal 1:8 a lame animal or a sick *o*
1:13, 13 lame *o*, and the sick *o*
1:14 And cursed is the *o* acting
1:14 sacrificing a ruined *o* to
2:5 *o* of life and of peace, and
2:10 Is it not *o* father that all
2:10 *o* God that has created us
2:10 deal treacherously with *o*
2:12 cut off each *o* that does it
2:12 *o* who is awake and
2:12 and *o* who is answering
2:12 *o* who is presenting a gift
2:15 was *o* who did not do it
2:15 what was that *o* seeking?
2:15 may no *o* deal treacherously
2:16 the *o* who with violence has
3:2 *o* standing when he appears
3:11 the devouring *o*, and it will
3:13 spoken with *o* another
3:16 spoke with *o* another, each
3:16 each *o* with his companion
3:18 a righteous *o* and a wicked
3:18 and a wicked *o*, between

Mal 3:18 between *o* serving God and
3:18 *o* who has not served him
Mt 2:2 the *o* born king of the Jews
2:6 will come forth a governing *o*
3:3 the *o* spoken of through Isaiah
3:11 the *o* coming after me is
3:11 *o* will baptize you people
3:14 *o* needing to be baptized by
5:18 for *o* smallest letter or
5:18 or *o* particle of a letter to
5:19 breaks *o* of these least
5:19 this *o* will be called great
5:25 the *o* complaining against
5:29 *o* of your members to be lost
5:30 *o* of your members to be lost
5:36 cannot turn *o* hair white or
5:37 these is from the wicked *o*
5:42 Give to the *o* asking you
5:42 *o* that wants to borrow from
6:13 deliver us from the wicked *o*
6:24 No *o* can slave for two
6:24 hate the *o* and love the other
6:24 stick to the *o* and despise
6:27 add *o* cubit to his life-span
6:29 was arrayed as *o* of these
7:21 the *o* doing the will of my
8:4 See that you tell no *o*, but
8:9 I say to this *o*, Be on your
8:10 With no *o* in Israel have I
10:2 Simon, the *o* called Peter
10:22 is the *o* that will be saved
10:23 they persecute you in *o* city
10:29 not *o* of them will fall to
10:42 gives *o* of these little ones
11:3 Are you the Coming *O*, or are
11:3 we to expect a different *o*
11:11 lesser *o* in the kingdom of
11:27 no *o* fully knows the Son but
12:11 *o* sheep and, if this falls
12:48 he said to the *o* telling him
13:8 fruit, this *o* a hundredfold
13:8 yield fruit . . . that *o* sixty
13:19 wicked *o* comes and snatches
13:19 *o* sown alongside the road
13:20 *o* sown upon the rocky places
13:20 *o* hearing the word and at
13:22 the *o* sown among the thorns
13:22 *o* hearing the word, but the
13:23 *o* sown upon the fine soil
13:23 the *o* hearing the word and
13:23 this *o* a hundredfold, that
13:23 that *o* sixty, the other
13:38 are the sons of the wicked *o*
13:46 Upon finding *o* pearl of high
16:14 or *o* of the prophets
16:27 recompense each *o* according
17:4 three tents here, *o* for you
17:4 three tents . . . *o* for Moses
17:4 three tents . . . *o* for Elijah
17:8 saw no *o* but Jesus himself
17:9 Tell the vision to no *o* until
18:4 *o* that is the greatest in the
18:5 receives *o* such young child
18:6 stumbles *o* of these little
18:10 despise *o* of these little
18:12 and *o* of them gets strayed
18:12 for the *o* that is straying
18:14 for *o* of these little ones
18:16 with you *o* or two more, in
18:28 found *o* of his fellow slaves
18:35 forgive each *o* his brother
19:5 and the two will be *o* flesh
19:6 no longer two, but *o* flesh
19:16 a certain *o* came up to him
19:17 *O* there is that is good
20:12 last put in *o* hour's work
20:13 reply to *o* of them he said
20:14 give to this last *o* the same
20:21 *o* at your right hand and
20:21 and *o* at your left, in your
21:24 also, will ask you *o* thing
21:29 this *o* said, I will, sir
21:30 this *o* said, I will not
21:35 *o* they beat up, another they
21:42 *o* that has become the chief
22:5 went off, *o* to his own field
22:34 came together in *o* group
22:35 And *o* of them, versed in the
23:8 *o* is your teacher, whereas
23:9 for *o* is your Father, the
23:9 your Father, the heavenly *O*
23:10 your Leader is *o*, the Christ
23:11 greatest *o* among you must
23:15 to make *o* proselyte, and

Mt 23:15 when he becomes *o* you make
24:7 earthquakes in *o* place after
24:10 will betray *o* another and
24:10 and will hate *o* another
24:13 is the *o* that will be saved
24:31 *o* extremity of the heavens
24:40 *o* will be taken along and
24:41 *o* will be taken along and
24:43 But know *o* thing, that if
25:15 to *o* he gave five talents
25:15 to still another *o*, to each
25:15 to each *o* according to his
25:16 the *o* that received the five
25:17 the *o* that received the two
25:18, 18 *o* that received just *o*
25:20 the *o* that had received five
25:22 *o* that had received the two
25:24 the *o* that had received the
25:24 had received the *o* talent
25:32 people *o* from another, just
25:40 to *o* of the least of these
25:45 to *o* of these least ones
26:14 Then *o* of the twelve, the
26:14 the *o* called Judas Iscariot
26:21 *O* of you will betray me
26:22 each and every *o* to say to
26:23 the *o* that will betray me
26:40 not so much as watch *o* hour
26:47 Judas, *o* of the twelve
26:51 look! *o* of those with Jesus
26:73 you also are *o* of them, for
27:9 *o* on whom some of the sons
27:15 the *o* they wanted
27:17 Which *o* do you want me to
27:38 robbers . . . *o* on his right
27:38 robbers . . . *o* on his left
27:48 *o* of them ran and took a
Mr 1:22 as *o* having authority, and
1:24 you are, the Holy *O* of God
2:7 can forgive sins except *o*, God
3:27 no *o* that has got into the
3:35 this *o* is my brother and
4:41 say to *o* another: Who really
5:13 they drowned *o* after another
5:22 *o* of the presiding officers
5:43 let no *o* learn of this, and
6:15 like *o* of the prophets
6:16 this *o* has been raised up
8:14 except for *o* loaf they had
8:16 went arguing with *o* another
8:28 others, *O* of the prophets
9:5 erect three tents, *o* for you
9:5 for you and *o* for Moses and
9:5 for Moses and *o* for Elijah
9:8 looked around and saw no *o*
9:17 *o* of the crowd answered him
9:23 all things can be to *o* if
9:23 if *o* has faith
9:37 *o* of such young children on
9:39 there is no *o* that will do a
9:42 stumbles *o* of these little
9:50 keep peace between *o* another
10:8 the two will be *o* flesh; so
10:8 no longer two, but *o* flesh
10:18 Nobody is good, except *o*
10:21 *O* thing is missing about you
10:29 No *o* has left house or
10:37 *o* at your right hand and
10:37 and *o* at your left, in your
11:14 Let no *o* eat fruit from you
11:29 I will ask you *o* question
12:4 that *o* they struck on the
12:5 and that *o* they killed; and
12:6 *O* more he had, a beloved son
12:16 They brought *o*. And he said
12:28 Now *o* of the scribes that
12:29 Jehovah our God is *o* Jehovah
12:32 He is *O*, and there is no
13:1 *o* of his disciples said to
13:8 earthquakes in *o* place after
13:13 is the *o* that will be saved
13:34 slaves, to each *o* his work
14:10 Iscariot, *o* of the twelve
14:18 *O* of you, who is eating
14:19, 19 *o* by *o*: It is not I, is
14:20 It is *o* of the twelve, who
14:37 to keep on the watch *o* hour
14:43 Judas, *o* of the twelve
14:47 *o* of those standing by drew
14:61 the Son of the Blessed *O*
14:66 *o* of the servant girls of
14:69 This is *o* of them
14:70 Certainly you are *o* of them
15:6 release to them *o* prisoner

Mr 15:27 robbers with him, *o* on his
15:27 his right and *o* on his left
15:36 a certain *o* ran, soaked a
16:3 were saying *o* to another
Lu 1:28 Good day, highly favored *o*
1:32 This *o* will be great and will
1:49 the powerful *O* has done great
1:61 no *o* among your relatives
2:3 each *o* to his own city
2:15 began saying to *o* another
2:34 This *o* is laid for the fall
3:16 the *o* stronger than I am is
4:27 not *o* of them was cleansed
4:34 you are, the Holy *O* of God
4:36 to converse with *o* another
4:40 laying his hands upon each *o*
5:3 Going aboard *o* of the boats
5:12 he was in *o* of the cities
5:17 *o* of the days he was teaching
5:26 an ecstasy seized *o* and all
5:36 No *o* cuts a patch from a new
5:37 no *o* puts new wine into old
5:39 No *o* that has drunk old wine
6:4 it is lawful for no *o* to eat
6:11 to talk over with *o* another
6:15 who is called the zealous *o*
6:29 strikes you on the *o* cheek
6:30 from the *o* taking your things
7:8 I say to this *o*, Be on your
7:19 Are you the Coming *O* or are
7:19 we to expect a different *o*
7:20 Are you the Coming *O* or are
7:28 lesser *o* in the kingdom of God
7:32 crying out to *o* another, and
7:36 a certain *o* of the Pharisees
7:41 the *o* was in debt for five
7:43 *o* to whom he freely forgave
8:16 No *o*, after lighting a lamp
8:22 In the course of *o* of the days
8:25 saying to *o* another
8:56 tell no *o* what had happened
9:8 *o* of the ancient prophets had
9:19 that *o* of the ancient prophets
9:24 is the *o* that will save it
9:26 ashamed of this *o* when he
9:33 three tents, *o* for you and
9:33 for you and *o* for Moses and
9:33 for Moses and *o* for Elijah
9:35 This is my Son, the *o* that has
9:48 conducts himself as a lesser *o*
9:48 lesser . . . the *o* that is great
10:22 who the Son is no *o* knows
10:22 no *o* knows but the Son, and
10:37 The *o* that acted mercifully
10:42 A few things . . . or just *o*
11:1 a certain *o* of his disciples
11:7 that *o* from inside says in
11:45 *o* of those versed in the Law
11:46 with *o* of your fingers
12:1 were stepping upon *o* another
12:5 Yes, I tell you, fear this *O*
12:6 not *o* of them goes forgotten
12:13 *o* of the crowd said to him
12:20 Unreasonable *o*, this night
12:27 was arrayed as *o* of these
12:42 steward, the discreet *o*
12:48 *o* that did not understand
12:48 the *o* whom people put in
12:52 be five in *o* house divided
13:10 he was teaching in *o* of the
13:15 each *o* of you on the sabbath
14:1 certain *o* of the rulers of
14:15 *o* of the fellow guests said
14:31 the *o* that comes against
14:32 while that *o* is yet far away
15:4 sheep, on losing *o* of them
15:4 for the lost *o* until he finds
15:7 over *o* sinner that repents
15:8 if she loses *o* drachma coin
15:10 over *o* sinner that repents
15:15 to *o* of the citizens of that
15:16 and no *o* would give him
15:19 me as *o* of your hired men
15:21 Make me as *o* of your hired
15:22 bring out a robe, the best *o*
15:26 called *o* of the servants to
16:1 this *o* was accused to him as
16:5 each *o* of the debtors of his
16:7 he said to another *o*, Now you
16:13 hate the *o* and love the other
16:13 stick to the *o* and despise
16:17 for *o* particle of a letter
17:1 woe to the *o* through whom
17:2 stumble *o* of these little

Ac 21:26 presented for each *o* of them
21:34 began shouting out *o* thing
22:9 voice of the *o* speaking to me
22:14 to see the righteous *O* and to
22:19 flog in *o* synagogue after
23:3 at *o* and the same time sit to
23:6 *o* part was of Sadducees but
23:17 *o* of the army officers to
24:6 *o* who also tried to profane
24:21 *o* utterance which I cried
24:23 he forbid no *o* of his people
25:11 on the *o* hand, I am really
25:21 the decision by the August *O*
25:25 appealed to the August *O*
26:9 I, for *o*, really thought
26:26 not *o* of these things escapes
26:31 talking with *o* another
27:33 encourage *o* and all to take
27:34 of *o* of you will perish
27:42 *o* might swim away and
28:4 began saying to *o* another
28:25 disagreement with *o* another
28:25 Paul made this *o* comment
Ro 1:12 each *o* through the other's
1:17 But the righteous *o*—by means
1:25 *O* who created, who is blessed
1:26 into *o* contrary to nature
1:27 lust toward *o* another, males
2:6 each *o* according to his works
2:21 *o* teaching someone else
2:21 *o* preaching Do not steal, do
2:22 *o* saying Do not commit
2:22 *o* expressing abhorrence of
2:28 Jew who is *o* on the outside
2:29 Jew who is *o* on the inside
2:29 praise of that *o* comes, not
3:10 righteous man, not even *o*
3:11 no *o* that has any insight
3:11 is no *o* that seeks for God
3:12 is no *o* that does kindness
3:12 there is not so much as *o*
3:30 if truly God is *o*, who will
4:5 the ungodly *o* righteous, his
4:17 *O* in whom he had faith, even
4:19 was about *o* hundred years old
5:12 through *o* man sin entered
5:15 by *o* man's trespass many
5:15 kindness by the *o* man Jesus
5:16 through the *o* man that sinned
5:16 resulted from *o* trespass in
5:17 by the trespass of the *o* man
5:17 ruled as king through that *o*
5:17 through the *o* person, Jesus
5:18 through *o* trespass the result
5:18 *o* act of justification the
5:19 disobedience of the *o* man
5:19 obedience of the *o* person
7:17 the *o* working it out is no
7:20 *o* working it out is no longer
8:9 this *o* does not belong to him
8:33 God is the *O* who declares
8:34 Jesus is the *o* who died, yes
8:34 *o* who was raised up from the
9:3 separated as the cursed *o*
9:10 twins from the *o* man, Isaac
9:11 but upon the *O* who calls
9:16 not upon the *o* wishing nor
9:16 nor upon the *o* running, but
9:21 *o* vessel for an honorable use
10:10 heart *o* exercises faith for
10:10 *o* makes public declaration
12:3 each *o* as God has distributed
12:4 have in *o* body many members
12:5 *o* body in union with Christ
12:5 individually to *o* another
12:10 affection for *o* another
12:10 showing honor to *o* another
12:17 Return evil for evil to no *o*
13:4 the *o* practicing what is bad
13:8 except to love *o* another; for
14:2 *O* man has faith to eat
14:3 *o* eating not look down on
14:3 look down on the *o* not eating
14:3 *o* not eating not judge the
14:3 not judge the *o* eating, for
14:3 for God has welcomed that *o*
14:5, 5 *O* man judges *o* day as
14:5 man judges *o* day as all
14:7 and no *o* dies with regard to
14:13 not be judging *o* another any
14:15 that *o* for whom Christ died
14:19 are upbuilding to *o* another
15:6 with *o* accord you may with
15:6 with *o* mouth glorify the God

Ro 15:7 welcome *o* another, just as
15:12 *o* arising to rule nations
15:18 not venture to tell *o* thing
16:10 Apelles, the approved *o* in
16:12 Persis our beloved *o*, for
16:13 Rufus the chosen *o* in the
16:16 Greet *o* another with a holy
1Co 1:12 each *o* of you says: I belong
1:15 no *o* may say that you were
2:8 not *o* of the rulers of this
2:11 no *o* has come to know the
3:4 when *o* says: I belong to Paul
3:5 as the Lord granted each *o*
3:8 that waters are *o*, but each
3:10 let each *o* keep watching how
3:18 Let no *o* be seducing himself
3:21 let no *o* be boasting in men
4:5 each *o* will have his praise
4:6 in favor of the *o* against the
5:3 I for *o*, although absent in
6:5 not *o* wise man among you
6:7 lawsuits with *o* another
6:16 joined to a harlot is *o* body
6:16 The two . . . will be *o* flesh
6:17 to the Lord is *o* spirit
7:7 each *o* has his own gift from
7:7 *o* in this way, another in
7:15 the unbelieving *o* proceeds to
7:17 has given each *o* a portion
7:17 let each *o* so walk as God
7:20 state each *o* was called, let
7:24 condition each *o* was called
7:25 *o* who had mercy shown him
7:28 such *o* would commit no sin
8:3 this *o* is known by him
8:4 and that there is no God but *o*
8:6 is actually to us *o* God the
8:6 and there is *o* Lord, Jesus
8:10 you, the *o* having knowledge
8:10 conscience of that *o* who is
9:15 not made use of a single *o*
9:24 but only *o* receives the prize
9:25 but we an incorruptible *o*
10:8 thousand of them in *o* day
10:17 Because there is *o* loaf, we
10:17 although many, are *o* body
10:17 all partaking of that *o* loaf
10:24 Let each *o* keep seeking, not
10:28 on account of the *o* that
11:5 it is *o* and the same as if
11:20 come together to *o* place
11:21 each *o* takes his own
11:21 so that *o* is hungry but
11:33 eat it, wait for *o* another
12:7 to each *o* for a beneficial
12:8 to *o* there is given through
12:9 healings by that *o* spirit
12:11 the *o* and the same spirit
12:11 a distribution to each *o*
12:12 just as the body is *o* but
12:12 are *o* body, so also is the
12:13 by *o* spirit we were all
12:13 all baptized into *o* body
12:13 all made to drink *o* spirit
12:14 body . . . is not *o* member
12:18 each *o* of them, just as he
12:19 If they were all *o* member
12:20 many members, yet *o* body
12:25 the same care for *o* another
12:26 if *o* member suffers, all
14:2 for no *o* listens, but he
14:11 foreigner to the *o* speaking
14:11 the *o* speaking will be a
14:13 let the *o* who speaks in a
14:23 comes together to *o* place
14:26 *o* has a psalm, another has
14:30 a revelation to another *o*
14:30 let the first *o* keep silent
14:31, 31 can all prophesy *o* by *o*
15:6 five hundred . . . at *o* time
15:8 as if to *o* born prematurely
15:23 But each *o* in his own rank
15:27 *o* who subjected all things
15:28 the *O* who subjected all
15:37 wheat or any *o* of the rest
15:39 there is *o* of mankind, and
15:40 heavenly bodies is *o* sort
15:41 glory of the sun is *o* sort
15:44 there is also a spiritual *o*
15:48 As the *o* made of dust is
15:48 as the heavenly *o* is, so
15:49 image of the *o* made of dust
15:49 the image of the heavenly *o*
16:11 no *o*, therefore, look down

1Co 16:20 Greet *o* another with a holy
2Co 2:2 the *o* that is made sad by me
5:2 on the *o* for us from heaven
5:10 *o* may get his award for the
5:14 *o* man died for all; so
5:21 *o* who did not know sin he
7:2 We have wronged no *o*, we
7:2 we have corrupted no *o*, we
7:2 have taken advantage of no *o*
7:12 for the *o* who did the wrong
7:12 for the *o* who was wronged
8:6 *o* to initiate it among you
9:7 Let each *o* do just as he has
10:18 not the *o* who recommends
11:2 you in marriage to *o* husband
11:4 a Jesus other than the *o* we
11:9 a burden to a single *o*
11:22 they Hebrews? I am *o* also
11:22 they Israelites? I am *o*
11:23 I am more outstandingly *o*
11:24 forty strokes less *o*
11:31 *O* who is to be praised
12:6 no *o* should put to my credit
12:17 *o* of those I have dispatched
13:12 Greet *o* another with a
Ga 1:6 *O* who called you with Christ's
1:19 saw no *o* else of the apostles
3:10 Cursed is every *o* that does
3:11 *o* is declared righteous with
3:11 righteous *o* will live by
3:15 no *o* sets aside or attaches
3:16 as in the case of *o*: And
3:20 *o* person is concerned, but
3:20 but God is only *o*
3:28 *o* person in union with Christ
4:22 sons, *o* by the servant girl
4:22 and *o* by the free woman
4:23 *o* by the servant girl was
4:24 the *o* from Mount Sinai
4:29 *o* born in the manner of flesh
4:29 *o* born in the manner of
5:8 not from the *O* calling you
5:10 *o* who is causing you trouble
5:13 love slave for *o* another
5:14 stands fulfilled in *o* saying
5:15 biting and devouring *o* another
5:15 get annihilated by *o* another
5:26 competition with *o* another
5:26 envying *o* another
6:2 the burdens of *o* another, and
6:5 each *o* will carry his own load
6:6 *o* who gives such oral teaching
6:7 God is not *o* to be mocked
6:17 no *o* be making trouble for me
Eph 1:6 us by means of his loved *o*
1:7 through the blood of that *o*
2:2 which you at *o* time walked
2:3 at *o* time conducted ourselves
2:14 who made the two parties *o*
2:15 into *o* new man and make
2:16 both peoples in *o* body to
2:18 to the Father by *o* spirit
3:20 to the *o* who can, according
4:2 putting up with *o* another in
4:4 *O* body there is, and
4:4 and *o* spirit, even as you
4:4 you were called in the *o* hope
4:5, 5 *o* Lord, *o* faith
4:5 faith, *o* baptism
4:6 *o* God and Father of all
4:7 to each *o* of us undeserved
4:10 The very *o* that descended is
4:10 is also the *o* that ascended
4:25 speak truth each *o* of you
4:25 belonging to *o* another
4:32 become kind to *o* another
4:32 freely forgiving *o* another
5:21 Be in subjection to *o* another
5:31 the two will become *o* flesh
5:33 each *o* of you individually
6:8 each *o*, whatever good he may
Php 1:27 standing firm in *o* spirit
1:27 with *o* soul striving side by
2:2 holding the *o* thought in mind
2:13 for God is the *o* that, for
2:20 no *o* else of a disposition
3:6 *o* who proved himself
3:13 *o* thing about it: Forgetting
4:21 greetings to every holy *o* in
Col 1:18 *o* who is first in all things
1:28 is the *o* we are publicizing
2:19 *o* from whom all the body
3:9 Do not be lying to *o* another
3:10 image of the *O* who created

Col 3:13 putting up with *o* another
3:13 forgiving *o* another freely if
3:15 called to it in *o* body
3:16 admonishing *o* another with
3:25 *o* that is doing wrong will
4:6 to give an answer to each *o*
4:16 read the *o* from Laodicea
1Th 2:9 burden upon any *o* of you, that
2:11 exhorting each *o* of you, and
3:3 that no *o* might be swayed by
3:12 abound, in love to *o* another
4:4 each *o* of you should know how
4:6 that no *o* go to the point of
4:6 is *o* who exacts punishment
4:9 to love *o* another
4:18 comforting *o* another with
5:11 keep comforting *o* another
5:11 and building *o* another up
5:13 Be peaceable with *o* another
5:15 no *o* renders injury for
5:15 is good toward *o* another
2Th 1:3 increasing *o* toward the other
2:3 Let no *o* seduce you in any
2:8 lawless *o* will be revealed
3:3 keep you from the wicked *o*
3:8 expensive burden upon any *o*
3:14 keep this *o* marked, stop
1Ti 1:8 *o* handles it lawfully
2:5, 5 is *o* God, and *o* mediator
3:2 a husband of *o* wife, moderate
3:12 be husbands of *o* wife
4:6 *o* nourished with the words of
5:6 the *o* that goes in for sensual
5:9 a wife of *o* husband
6:16 *o* alone having immortality
6:16 not *o* of men has seen or can
2Ti 1:12 the *o* whom I have believed
2:4 the *o* who enrolled him as a
2:26 for the will of that *o*
4:16 no *o* came to my side, but
Tit 1:6 a husband of *o* wife, having
1:12 *o* of them, their own prophet
3:2 to speak injuriously of no *o*
3:3 abhorrent, hating *o* another
3:7 undeserved kindness of that *o*
Phm 1 Philemon, our beloved *o* and
12 *o* I am sending back to you
Heb 1:5 to which *o* of the angels did
1:13 to which *o* of the angels has
2:10 *o* for whose sake all things
2:11 all stem from *o*, and for
2:14 *o* having the means to cause
3:2 faithful to the *O* that made
3:2 in all the house of that *O*
3:5 in all the house of that *O* as
3:6 Son over the house of that *O*
3:6 We are the house of that *O*
3:12 in any *o* of you a wicked
3:13 keep on exhorting *o* another
3:13 for fear any *o* of you should
4:4 in *o* place he has said of
4:15 not *o* who cannot sympathize
5:7 the *O* who was able to save
6:11 desire each *o* of you to show
6:16 men swear by the *o* greater
7:8 in the *o* case it is men who
7:13 no *o* has officiated at the
7:21 is *o* with an oath sworn by
7:21 oath sworn by the *O* who said
7:22 Jesus has become the *o* given
8:3 this *o* also to have something
8:11 by no means teach each *o* his
8:11 each *o* his brother, saying
8:11 the least *o* to the greatest
8:11 to the greatest *o* of them
8:13 made the former *o* obsolete
10:12 offered *o* sacrifice for sins
10:14 *o* sacrificial offering that
10:24 *o* another to incite to love
10:25 encouraging *o* another, and
10:38 righteous *o* will live by
11:12 from *o* man, and him as
11:16 *o* belonging to heaven
11:27 the *O* who is invisible
12:3 the *o* who has endured such
12:6 he scourges every *o* whom he
12:15 no *o* may be deprived of
12:16 in exchange for *o* meal gave
13:14 seeking the *o* to come
Jas 1:5 any *o* of you is lacking in
1:10 rich *o* over his humiliation
1:13 under trial, let no *o* say
1:14 *o* is tried by being drawn
1:23 *o* is like a man looking at

Jas 2:3 the *o* wearing the splendid
2:3 you say to the poor *o*: You
2:10 a false step in *o* point, he
2:13 *o* that does not practice
2:14 *o* says he has faith but he
2:16 *o* of you says to them: Go in
2:18 *o* will say: You have faith
2:19 believe there is *o* God, do
3:2 this *o* is a perfect man, able
3:8 tongue, not *o* of mankind can
4:11 speaking against *o* another
4:12 *O* there is that is lawgiver
4:17 if *o* knows how to do what
5:6 have murdered the righteous *o*
5:9 heave sighs against *o* another
5:15 make the indisposed *o* well
5:16 confess . . . sins to *o* another
5:16 pray for *o* another, that you
1Pe 1:15 the Holy *O* who called you
1:21 the *o* who raised him up
1:22 love *o* another intensely
2:6 no *o* exercising faith in it
2:9 the *o* that called you out of
2:23 committing himself to the *o*
3:7 weaker vessel, the feminine *o*
4:5 *o* ready to judge those living
4:8 intense love for *o* another
4:9 Be hospitable to *o* another
4:10 as each *o* has received a gift
4:10 in ministering to *o* another
5:5 of mind toward *o* another
5:13 a chosen *o* like you, sends
5:14 Greet *o* another with a kiss
2Pe 1:3 *o* who called us through
2:19 is enslaved by this *o*
3:1 as in my first *o*, I am
3:8 let this *o* fact not be
3:8 *o* day is with Jehovah as a
3:8 a thousand years as *o* day
1Jo 1:7 have a sharing with *o* another
2:1 Jesus Christ, a righteous *o*
2:6 walking just as that *o* walked
2:13 have conquered the wicked *o*
2:14 have conquered the wicked *o*
2:20 an anointing from the holy *o*
2:22 *o* that denies that Jesus is
2:22 *o* that denies the Father and
3:3 just as that *o* is pure
3:5 that *o* was made manifest to
3:6 no *o* that practices sin has
3:7 let no *o* mislead you; he
3:7 just as that *o* is righteous
3:9 seed remains in such *o*, and
3:11 have love for *o* another
3:12 originated with the wicked *o*
3:16 that *o* surrendered his soul
3:23 and be loving *o* another
3:24 and he in union with such *o*
4:7 continue loving *o* another
4:11 obligation to love *o* another
4:12 we continue loving *o* another
4:15 remains in union with such *o*
4:17 just as that *o* is, so are we
4:21 *o* who loves God should be
5:1 everyone who loves the *o* that
5:1 who has been born from that *o*
5:5 *o* that conquers the world but
5:18 *O* born from God watches him
5:18 wicked *o* does not fasten his
5:19 in the power of the wicked *o*
5:20 the knowledge of the true *o*
5:20 are in union with the true *o*
2Jo 5 but *o* which we had from the
5 that we love *o* another
9 *o* that has both the Father and
13 your sister, the chosen *o*
3Jo 2 Beloved *o*, I pray that in all
5 Beloved *o*, you are doing a
11 Beloved *o*, be an imitator
Jude 14 seventh *o* in line from Adam
24 *o* who is able to guard you
Re 1:4 *O* who is and who was and who
1:8 *O* who is and who was and who
1:18 living *o*; and I became dead
2:7 Let the *o* who has an ear hear
2:11 *o* who has an ear hear what
2:13 faithful *o*, who was killed
2:17 *o* who has an ear hear what
2:17 which no *o* knows except the
2:17 knows except the *o* receiving
2:29 *o* who has an ear hear what
3:6 *o* who has an ear hear what
3:7 opens so that no *o* will shut
3:7 and shuts so that no *o* opens

Re 3:8 door, which no *o* can shut
3:11 no *o* may take your crown
3:12 *o* that conquers—I will make
3:13 *o* who has an ear hear what
3:21 *o* that conquers I will grant
3:22 *o* who has an ear hear what
4:2 is *o* seated upon the throne
4:3 *o* seated is, in appearance
4:8 each *o* of them respectively
4:9 to the *o* seated upon the throne
4:9 *o* that lives forever and ever
4:10 the *O* seated upon the throne
4:10 worship the *O* that lives
5:1 the *O* seated upon the throne
5:3 a single *o* able to open the
5:4 no *o* was found worthy to open
5:5 *o* of the elders says to me
5:7 of the *O* seated on the throne
5:8 each *o* a harp and golden bowls
5:13 To the *O* sitting on the throne
6:1 opened *o* of the seven seals
6:1 *o* of the four living creatures
6:2 the *o* seated upon it had a bow
6:4 and to the *o* seated upon it
6:4 they should slaughter *o* another
6:5 the *o* seated upon it had a
6:8 *o* seated upon it had the name
6:16 the *O* seated on the throne and
7:13 *o* of the elders said to me
7:14 you are the *o* that knows
7:15 and the *O* seated on the throne
8:7 the first *o* blew his trumpet
9:12 The *o* woe is past. Look!
9:13 I heard *o* voice out of the
10:2 but his left *o* upon the earth
10:6 the *O* who lives forever and
11:10 will send gifts to *o* another
11:17 *O* who is and who was
12:9 *o* called Devil and Satan
13:3 *o* of its heads as though
13:8 not *o* of them stands written
13:18 the *o* that has intelligence
14:3 no *o* was able to master that
14:7 *O* who made the heaven and the
14:15 to the *o* seated on the cloud
14:16 *o* seated on the cloud thrust
14:18 *o* that had the sharp sickle
15:7 *o* of the four living creatures
15:8 no *o* was able to enter into
16:2 first *o* went off and poured
16:3 second *o* poured out his bowl
16:4 third *o* poured out his bowl
16:5 *O* who is and who was, the
16:5 the loyal *O*, are righteous
16:8 fourth *o* poured out his bowl
16:10 fifth *o* poured out his
16:12 sixth *o* poured out his bowl
16:15 *o* that stays awake and keeps
16:17 seventh *o* poured out his
17:1 *o* of the seven angels that
17:10 *o* is, the other has not yet
17:12 authority as kings *o* hour
17:13 These have *o* thought, and so
17:17 carry out their *o* thought
18:8 in *o* day her plagues will
18:10 in *o* hour your judgment has
18:11 no *o* to buy their full stock
18:17 in *o* hour such great riches
18:19 in *o* hour she has been
19:11 *o* seated upon it is called
19:12 written that no *o* knows but
19:19 *o* seated on the horse and
19:21 of the *o* seated on the horse
20:11 throne and the *o* seated on it
21:5 *O* seated on the throne said
21:9 *o* of the seven angels who
21:15 *o* who was speaking with me
21:17 *o* hundred and forty-four
21:21 each *o* of the gates was made
21:21 gates was made of *o* pearl
22:8 I John was the *o* hearing and
22:11 let the filthy *o* be made
22:11 *o* do righteousness still
22:11 let the holy *o* be made holy
22:12 to each *o* as his work is

One-eyed
Mt 18:9 to enter *o* into life than to
Mr 9:47 enter *o* into the kingdom of

One-handled
1Sa 2:14 caldron or the *o* cooking pot

Oneness
Ps 122:3 been joined together in *o*

Eph 4:3 observe the *o* of the spirit
4:13 attain to the *o* in the faith

One's

Ge 2:9 every tree desirable to *o* sight
2:11 The first *o* name is Pishon
42:25 to each *o* individual sack
42:35 each *o* bundle of money in
44:30 that *o* soul is bound up with
44:30 bound up with this *o* soul
Ex 21:19 time lost from that *o* work
21:32 to that *o* master, and the
Nu 26:54 should increase *o* inheritance
26:54 should reduce *o* inheritance
26:54 Each *o* inheritance should be
26:56 *o* inheritance should be
De 16:17 gift of each *o* hand should
21:16 expense of the hated *o* son
21:17 the firstborn the hated *o* son
2Ki 10:24 the *o* soul will go for the
23:35 each *o* individual tax rate
Job 21:19 store up *o* hurtfulness for
21:19 hurtfulness for *o* own sons
30:24 Nor during *o* decay is there
34:14 If that *o* spirit and breath
41:9 *O* expectation about it will
Ps 62:4 allure from *o* own dignity
Pr 12:27 start up *o* game animals
14:10 of the bitterness of *o* soul
20:16 Take *o* garment, in case one
21:11 *o* giving insight to a wise
27:9 sweetness of *o* companion due
27:13 Take *o* garment, in case one
29:21 is pampering *o* servant from
31:7 one drink and forget *o* poverty
31:7 remember *o* own trouble no
Ec 3:12 and to do good during *o* life
4:15 stands up in the other *o* place
7:1 than the day of *o* being born
Ca 6:3 I am my dear *o*, and my dear
7:10 I am my dear *o*, and toward
Isa 2:8 the work of *o* hands they bow
2:8 which *o* fingers have made
30:14 pieces without *o* sparing it
46:4 Even to *o* old age I am the
46:4 and to *o* gray-headedness I
46:7 out of *o* distress it does
48:19 *O* name would not be cut off
53:3 concealing of *o* face from
Jer 8:7 the time of each *o* coming in
16:7 on account of *o* father and
16:7 and on account of *o* mother
30:8 I shall break *o* yoke from
50:9 *O* arrows are like those of
51:28 land of each *o* dominion
La 3:34 crushing beneath *o* feet all
Eze 7:20 the decoration of *o* ornament
21:22 open *o* mouth for a slaying
21:27 no *o* until he comes who
33:22 prior to that *o* coming to
Da 11:5 than that *o* ruling power
Zec 14:12 a rotting away of *o* flesh
14:12 one is standing upon *o* feet
14:12 *o* very eyes will rot away
14:12 *o* very tongue will rot away
14:12 will rot away in *o* mouth
Mr 12:33 loving him with *o* whole
12:33 with *o* whole understanding
12:33 with *o* whole strength and
12:33 loving *o* neighbor as oneself
Ro 7:4 *o* who was raised up from the
13:10 not work evil to *o* neighbor
1Co 3:13 *o* work will become manifest
3:13 what sort of work each *o* is
Eph 6:16 wicked *o* burning missiles
Col 1:22 that *o* fleshly body through
2Th 2:9 the lawless *o* presence is
1Pe 1:17 according to each *o* work
1Jo 2:16 display of *o* means of life

Ones

Ge 6:4 the mighty *o* who were of old
27:9 two kids of the goats, good *o*
27:15 garments . . . desirable *o*
30:39 speckled and color-patched *o*
30:40 the striped *o* and all the
30:40 dark-brown *o* among the
30:42 feeble *o* always came to be
30:42 but the robust *o* Jacob's
31:8 The speckled *o* will become
31:8 flock produced speckled *o*
31:8 striped *o* will become your
31:8 flock produced striped *o*
32:15 camels . . . and their young *o*
45:19 your little *o* and your wives
Ge 46:5 little *o* and their wives
47:12 the number of the little *o*
47:24 and for your little *o* to eat
Ex 6:27 the *o* speaking to Pharaoh
10:8 Who in particular are the *o*
10:10 send you and your little *o*
10:24 Your little *o* also may go
12:37 men . . . besides little *o*
23:11 poor *o* of your people must
28:3 all the *o* wise with a heart
28:10 names of the six remaining *o*
29:1 bull, and two rams, sound *o*
34:1 tablets . . . like the first *o*
34:4 tablets . . . like the first *o*
35:10 wise-hearted *o* among you
36:4 wise *o* who were doing all the
38:25 silver of the *o* registered of
Le 9:2 for a burnt offering, sound *o*
9:3 sound *o*, for a burnt offering
11:22 the *o* of them you may eat of
Nu 1:16 *o* called of the assembly, the
1:22 Simeon . . . registered *o* of his
1:44 the *o* registered, whom Moses
2:4 the *o* registered of them are
2:6 registered *o* are fifty-four
2:8 registered *o* are fifty-seven
2:9 registered *o* of the camp of
2:11 registered *o* are forty-six
2:13 *o* registered of them are
2:15 *o* registered of them are
2:16 registered *o* of the camp of
2:19 *o* registered of them are
2:21 *o* registered of them are
2:23 *o* registered of them are
2:24 registered *o* of the camp of
2:26 *o* registered of them are
2:27 *o* camping alongside him will
2:28 *o* registered of them are
2:30 *o* registered of them are
2:31 registered *o* of the camp of
2:32 registered *o* of . . . Israel
2:32 registered *o* of the camps in
3:9 They are given *o*, given to
3:22 registered *o* were by number
3:22 Their registered *o* were seven
3:34 registered *o* by the number of
3:39 registered *o* of the Levites
3:43 registered *o* came to be
4:36 *o* registered of them by their
4:37 registered *o* of the families
4:38 registered *o* of the sons of
4:40 *o* registered of them by their
4:41 registered *o* of the families
4:42 registered *o* of the families
4:44 *o* registered of them by their
4:45 registered *o* of the families
4:46 registered *o* whom Moses and
4:48 registered *o* came to be eight
7:2 standing over the *o* registered
8:16 For they are given *o*
8:19 Levites as given *o* to Aaron
14:3 little *o* will become plunder
14:29 your registered *o* of all your
14:31 your little *o* who you said
16:2 summoned *o* of the meeting
16:27 their sons and their little *o*
18:23 *o* who should answer for
21:29 give his sons as escaped *o*
23:10 the death of the upright *o*
23:24 And the blood of slain *o* it
24:9 blessing you are the *o* blessed
24:9 cursing you are the *o* cursed
25:4 all the head *o* of the people
26:7 their registered *o* amounted
26:9 summoned *o* of the assembly
26:18 of Gad, of their registered *o*
26:22 Judah, of their registered *o*
26:25 of their registered *o*
26:27 of their registered *o*: sixty
26:34 and their registered *o* were
26:37 of their registered *o*
26:41 and their registered *o* were
26:43 of their registered *o*, were
26:47 Asher, of their registered *o*
26:50 and their registered *o* were
26:51 registered *o* of . . . Israel
26:54 to his registered *o*
26:57 registered *o* of the Levites
26:62 their registered *o* amounted
26:63 *o* registered by Moses and
28:19 should prove to be sound *o*
28:31 should prove to be sound *o*
29:2 each a year old, sound *o*
29:8 should prove to be sound *o* for
Nu 29:13 should prove to be sound *o*
29:17 each a year old, sound *o*
29:20 each a year old, sound *o*
29:23 each a year old, sound *o*
29:26 each a year old, sound *o*
29:29 each a year old, sound *o*
29:32 each a year old, sound *o*
29:36 each a year old, sound *o*
31:9 of Midian and their little *o*
31:16 the *o* who, by Balaam's word
31:17 male among the little *o*
31:18 the little *o* among the women
32:16 and cities for our little *o*
32:17 our little *o* must dwell in
32:24 cities for your little *o* and
32:26 Our little *o*, our wives, our
34:29 *o* whom Jehovah commanded to
De 1:39 your little *o* of whom you
3:19 your wives and your little *o*
4:3 Your own eyes are the *o* that
4:20 you are the *o* Jehovah took
10:1 tablets . . . like the first *o*
10:3 tablets . . . like the first *o*
11:7 your eyes were the *o* seeing
12:6 the firstborn *o* of your herd
12:17 the firstborn *o* of your herd
13:7 the *o* near you or those far
14:12 *o* of which you must not eat
14:23 the firstborn *o* of your herd
16:19 blinds the eyes of wise *o*
16:19 the words of righteous *o*
18:3 the *o* who sacrifice a victim
21:5 the *o* Jehovah your God has
22:6 with young *o* or eggs, and the
22:6 sitting upon the young *o* or
27:12 *o* who will stand to bless
27:13 the *o* who will stand for the
29:2 *o* seeing all that Jehovah did
29:11 your little *o*, your wives
29:19 along with the thirsty *o*
31:12 women and the little *o* and
32:17 New *o* who recently came in
32:31 being the *o* to decide
33:3 their holy *o* are in your hand
Jos 1:14 Your wives, your little *o*
8:3 men, valiant mighty *o*, and to
8:35 the women and the little *o*
10:2 all its men were mighty *o*
13:22 along with their slain *o*
22:19 do not make us the *o* to
Jg 5:13 came down to the majestic *o*
5:13 to me against the mighty *o*
5:23 Jehovah with the mighty *o*
5:25 bowl of majestic *o* she
5:29 wise *o* of her noble ladies
6:31 the *o* to make a legal defense
10:14 Let them be the *o* to save
18:21 little *o* and the livestock
21:10 the women and the little *o*
1Sa 2:9 feet of his loyal *o* he guards
2:9 wicked *o*, they are silenced
6:7 their young *o* go back home
6:10 young *o* they shut up at home
8:14 the best *o*, he will take and
15:9 and the herd and the fat *o*
19:20 elderly *o* of the prophets
24:13 wicked *o* wickedness will go
26:2 the chosen *o* of Israel, to
30:14 *o* that made a raid on the
2Sa 1:21 shield of mighty *o* was
1:22 from the fat of mighty *o*
1:23 and Jonathan, the lovable *o*
1:23 pleasant *o* during their life
1:25 mighty *o* fallen in the midst
1:27 mighty *o* fallen And the
2:4 were the *o* that buried Saul
3:5 *o* born to David in Hebron
3:34 hands had not been bound *o*
5:6 blind and the lame *o* will
7:9 great *o* that are in the earth
15:22 little *o* that were with him
19:5 the *o* providing escape for
19:11 *o* to bring the king back
19:12 *o* to bring the king back
20:19 and faithful *o* of Israel
22:28 against the haughty *o*, that
23:13 three of the thirty head *o*
23:18 over three hundred slain *o*
1Ki 1:41 all the *o* invited that were
12:8 the *o* attending upon him
20:19 the *o* that came out from
2Ki 4:4 full *o* you should set aside
6:22 *o* that you are striking down
11:15 appointed *o* of the military

2Ki 12:21 the *o* that struck him down
22:5 the work, the appointed *o*
22:9 of the work, the *o* appointed
1Ch 6:31 the *o* to whom David gave
6:48 Levites were the *o* given for
8:13 the *o* that chased away the
8:28 *o* that dwelt in Jerusalem
8:32 the *o* that dwelt in front of
9:34 *o* that dwelt in Jerusalem
11:15 three of the thirty head *o*
12:1 the *o* that came to David at
12:15 *o* that crossed the Jordan
12:32 were two hundred head *o* of
15:2 *o* whom Jehovah has chosen to
15:25 *o* walking along to bring up
16:13 sons of Jacob, his chosen *o*
16:22 you men touch my anointed *o*
17:8 like the name of the great *o*
20:8 *o* that had been born to the
23:24 by their commissioned *o*, in
25:1 *o* prophesying with the harps
29:29 the first *o* and the last
2Ch 2:7 skillful *o* that are with me
6:41 loyal *o* themselves rejoice
10:8 the *o* attending upon him
17:19 *o* ministering to the king
20:13 even their little *o*, their
22:1 had killed all the older *o*
23:6 are the *o* that will enter
23:14 appointed *o* of the military
23:20 lordly *o* and the rulers
26:18 of Aaron, the *o* sanctified
28:15 naked *o* they clothed from
29:11 *o* whom Jehovah has chosen
30:6 escaped *o* that are left of
31:18 among all their little *o*
32:21 *o* that had come out of his
Ezr 2:59 *o* going up from Tel-melah
2:62 the *o* that looked for their
2:68 certain *o* of the heads of the
7:28 the head *o* to go up with me
8:16 I sent for . . . head *o*, and
8:21 for us and for our little *o*
10:15 Levites were the *o* that
Ne 3:5 majestic *o* themselves did not
3:16 the House of the Mighty *O*
7:61 the *o* going up from Tel-melah
7:64 *o* that looked for their
8:3 and the other intelligent *o*
9:33 the *o* that have done wickedly
10:29 brothers, their majestic *o*
10:37 *o* receiving a tenth in all
11:14 the son of the great *o*
Es 3:13 little *o* and women, on one
8:11 little *o* and women, and to
9:20 the nearby and the distant *o*
Job 5:1 of the holy *o* will you turn
5:13 the counsel of astute *o* is
8:22 very *o* hating you will be
8:22 tent of wicked *o* will not be
9:23 despair of the innocent *o* he
10:3 upon the counsel of wicked *o*
12:6 the *o* enraging God have the
12:19 And permanently seated *o* he
12:20 speech from the faithful *o*
12:21 the girdle of powerful *o* he
12:24 head *o* of the people of the
15:15 his holy *o* he has no faith
15:18 wise *o* themselves tell And
16:11 into the hands of wicked *o*
18:5 light also of wicked *o* will
19:13 the very *o* knowing me have
20:7 very *o* seeing him will say
20:19 he has left lowly *o*
21:16 counsel of wicked *o* has
21:17 is the lamp of the wicked *o*
21:22 One himself judges high *o*
21:28 the tabernacles of wicked *o*
22:18 counsel of wicked *o* has
22:19 righteous *o* will see and
24:1 very *o* knowing him have not
24:4 turn aside the poor *o* from
24:12 soul of deadly wounded *o*
29:8 And even the aged *o* rose up
29:16 a real father to the poor *o*
30:31 for the voice of weeping *o*
31:16 hold back the lowly *o* from
34:2 Listen, you wise *o*, to my
34:20 powerful *o* depart by no
34:24 He breaks powerful *o*
34:26 wicked *o* he does slap them
34:28 outcry of the afflicted *o*
35:9 the arm of the great *o*
35:12 the pride of the bad *o*

Job 36:6 judgment of the afflicted *o*
38:13 wicked *o* might be shaken
38:15 from the wicked *o* their
38:41 young *o* cry to God for help
39:3 cast forth their young *o*
39:30 its young *o* themselves keep
Ps 1:1 in the counsel of the wicked *o*
1:5 wicked *o* will not stand up in
1:5 in the assembly of righteous *o*
1:6 the way of righteous *o*
1:6 way of wicked *o* will perish
3:7 The teeth of wicked *o* you will
7:9 the badness of wicked *o* come
7:13 he will make flaming *o*
8:5 a little less than godlike *o*
9:12 remember those very *o*
9:12 the outcry of the afflicted *o*
9:18 the hope of the meek *o* ever
10:10 the army of dejected *o* has
10:12 Do not forget the afflicted *o*
10:17 The desire of the meek *o* you
11:2 the wicked *o* themselves bend
11:2 at the *o* upright in heart
11:6 rain down upon the wicked *o*
11:7 *o* that will behold his face
12:5 despoiling of the afflicted *o*
12:5 the sighing of the poor *o*
12:8 The wicked *o* walk all around
14:7 gathers back the captive *o*
16:3 holy *o* that are in the earth
16:3 even the majestic *o*, are the
16:3 *o* in whom is all my delight
20:8 Those very *o* have broken down
22:12 The powerful *o* of Bashan
22:26 The meek *o* will eat and be
22:29 the fat *o* of the earth shall
25:9 cause the meek *o* to walk in
25:9 teach the meek *o* his way
26:5 with the wicked *o* I do not
29:1 O you sons of strong *o*
30:4 Make melody . . . you loyal *o*
31:17 May the wicked *o* be ashamed
31:23 love Jehovah, all you loyal *o*
31:23 The faithful *o* Jehovah is
32:11 be joyful, you righteous *o*
33:1 O you righteous *o*, because
33:1 On the part of the upright *o*
34:2 The meek *o* will hear and
34:9 Fear Jehovah, you holy *o* of
34:15 are toward the righteous *o*
34:21 very *o* hating the righteous
35:20 the quiet *o* of the earth
37:9 *o* that will possess the earth
37:11 the meek *o* themselves will
37:14 wicked *o* have drawn a sword
37:16 the many wicked *o*
37:17 the wicked *o* will be broken
37:17 supporting the righteous *o*
37:18 the days of the faultless *o*
37:28 will not leave his loyal *o*
37:28 offspring of the wicked *o*
37:34 the wicked *o* are cut off
37:39 salvation of the righteous *o*
44:10 very *o* intensely hating us
45:12 The rich *o* of the people
49:10 that even the wise *o* die
49:14 the upright *o* will have them
50:5 Gather to me my loyal *o*
52:5 the land of the living *o*
52:6 the righteous *o* will see it
52:9 in front of your loyal *o*
53:6 the captive *o* of his people
58:3 wicked *o* have been perverts
59:3 Strong *o* make an attack upon
59:15 Let those very *o* wander
60:5 your beloved *o* may be rescued
68:2 Let the wicked *o* perish from
68:6 solitary *o* to dwell in a
68:18 stubborn *o*, to reside among
69:28 the book of the living *o*
69:28 with the righteous *o* may
69:32 meek *o* will certainly see it
69:33 is listening to the poor *o*
69:36 be the *o* to reside in it
71:10 *o* keeping watch for my soul
72:2 afflicted *o* with judicial
72:4 Let him judge the afflicted *o*
72:13 of the poor *o* he will save
73:27 *o* keeping away from you
74:19 very life of your afflicted *o*
75:4 I said to the foolish *o*
75:4 And to the wicked *o*: Do not
75:8 wicked *o* of the earth will
75:10 horns of the wicked *o* I

Ps 76:5 *o* powerful in heart have been
78:25 the very bread of powerful *o*
78:31 killing among their stout *o*
79:2 loyal *o* to the wild beasts
82:4 the hand of the wicked *o*
83:2 *o* intensely hating you have
83:3 against your concealed *o*
84:3 she has put her young *o*
85:1 *o* taken captive of Jacob
85:8 people and to his loyal *o*
86:14 God, the presumptuous *o*
86:14 tyrannical *o* have looked for
88:5 slain *o* lying in the burial
89:5 the congregation of the holy *o*
89:7 intimate group of holy *o*
89:19 in a vision to your loyal *o*
91:8 itself of the wicked *o*
92:7 wicked *o* sprout as the
92:11 *o* who rise up against me
94:2 upon the haughty *o*
94:8 stupid *o*, when will you have
97:10 the souls of his loyal *o*
97:10 of the wicked *o* he delivers
97:11 for the *o* upright in heart
97:12 in Jehovah, O you righteous *o*
101:6 eyes are upon the faithful *o*
101:8 silence all the wicked *o* of
105:6 sons of Jacob, his chosen *o*
105:15 you men touch my anointed *o*
105:43 chosen *o* even with a joyful
106:5 goodness to your chosen *o*
106:18 devouring the wicked *o*
106:28 sacrifices of the dead *o*
107:2 reclaimed *o* of Jehovah say
107:24 *o* that have seen the works
107:36 the hungry *o* to dwell
107:42 upright *o* see and rejoice
108:6 beloved *o* may be rescued
111:1 intimate group of upright *o*
112:2 generation of the upright *o*
112:4 as a light to the upright *o*
112:9 he has given to the poor *o*
112:10 desire of the wicked *o* will
115:13 small *o* as well as the
115:13 as well as the great *o*
115:15 the *o* blessed by Jehovah
116:6 guarding the inexperienced *o*
116:15 Is the death of his loyal *o*
118:15 the tents of the righteous *o*
119:1 Happy are the *o* faultless in
119:1 *o* walking in the law of
119:21 cursed presumptuous *o*
119:51 presumptuous *o* themselves
119:61 very ropes of the wicked *o*
119:74 *o* that see me and rejoice
119:78 presumptuous *o* be ashamed
119:113 halfhearted *o* I have hated
119:119 wicked *o* of the earth to
119:122 presumptuous *o* not defraud
119:130 inexperienced *o* understand
119:155 away from the wicked *o*
123:4 the part of the arrogant *o*
125:3 the lot of the righteous *o*
125:3 righteous *o* may not thrust
125:4 Jehovah, to the good *o*
125:4 *o* upright in their hearts
126:1 back the captive *o* of Zion
129:4 the ropes of the wicked *o*
132:9 loyal *o* cry out joyfully
132:15 poor *o* I shall satisfy with
132:16 loyal *o* will without fail
135:8 struck down the firstborn *o*
136:10 Egypt in their firstborn *o*
140:5 self-exalted *o* have hidden
140:12 the judgment of the poor *o*
140:13 upright *o* will dwell before
142:5 in the land of the living *o*
142:7 let the righteous *o* gather
145:10 your loyal *o* will bless you
145:20 wicked *o* he will annihilate
146:7 judgment for the defrauded *o*
146:7 giving bread to the hungry *o*
146:8 the eyes of the blind *o*
146:8 raising up the *o* bowed down
146:8 is loving the righteous *o*
146:9 way of the wicked *o* he
147:2 dispersed *o* of Israel he
147:3 healing the brokenhearted *o*
147:6 is relieving the meek *o*
147:6 abasing the wicked *o* to the
148:14 praise of all his loyal *o*
149:1 congregation of loyal *o*
149:4 He beautifies the meek *o*
149:5 the loyal *o* exult in glory

Ps 149:8 glorified *o* with fetters of
149:9 belongs to all his loyal *o*
Pr 1:4 give to the inexperienced *o*
1:22 *o* keep loving inexperience
1:22 stupid *o* keep hating
1:32 inexperienced *o* is what will
2:7 upright *o* he will treasure up
2:8 the very way of his loyal *o*
2:20 paths of the righteous *o* you
2:21 upright are the *o* that will
2:21 blameless are the *o* that
3:25 the storm upon the wicked *o*
3:32 is with the upright *o*
3:33 place of the righteous *o* he
3:34 meek *o* he will show favor
3:35 Honor is what the wise *o*
3:35 stupid *o* are exalting dishonor
4:14 path of the wicked *o* do not
4:14 into the way of the bad *o*
4:18 path of the righteous *o*
4:19 way of the wicked *o* is like
7:7 peer upon the inexperienced *o*
7:26 *o* she has caused to fall down
8:5 O inexperienced *o*, understand
8:5 you stupid *o*, understand heart
8:9 to the *o* finding knowledge
8:17 are the *o* that find me
8:32 happy are the *o* that keep my
8:36 the *o* that do love death
9:6 Leave the inexperienced *o* and
10:3 craving of the wicked *o* he
10:6 mouth of the wicked *o*, it
10:7 of the wicked *o* will rot
10:11 mouth of the wicked *o*, it
10:14 *o* that treasure up knowledge
10:15 ruin of the lowly *o* is their
10:24 desire of the righteous *o*
10:27 of the wicked *o* will be cut
10:28 righteous *o* is a rejoicing
10:28 hope of the wicked *o* will
10:30 wicked *o*, they will not keep
10:32 mouth of the wicked *o* is
11:2 wisdom is with the modest *o*
11:3 integrity of the upright *o*
11:6 upright *o* is what will
11:10 righteous *o* a town is elated
11:10 wicked *o* perish there is a
11:11 blessing of the upright *o*
11:11 wicked *o* it gets torn down
11:20 *o* blameless in their way are
11:21 offspring of the righteous *o*
11:23 desire of the righteous *o*
11:23 hope of the wicked *o* is fury
11:28 righteous *o* will flourish
12:3 of the righteous *o*, it will
12:5 thoughts of the righteous *o*
12:5 by the wicked *o* is deception
12:6 words of the wicked *o* are a
12:6 mouth of the upright *o* is
12:7 overthrowing of the wicked *o*
12:7 house of the righteous *o* will
12:10 the wicked *o* are cruel
12:12 root of the righteous *o*
12:18 tongue of the wise *o* is a
12:21 wicked are the *o* that will
12:23 heart of the stupid *o* is
12:24 hand of the diligent *o* is
12:26 way of wicked *o* causes them
13:4 diligent *o* will be made fat
13:5 wicked *o* act shamefully and
13:9 light of the righteous *o*
13:9 lamp of the wicked *o*—it
13:19 detestable to the stupid *o*
13:20 dealings with the stupid *o*
13:21 *o* whom calamity pursues
13:21 are the *o* whom good rewards
13:25 belly of the wicked *o* will
14:3 lips of the wise *o* will guard
14:8 foolishness of stupid *o* is
14:9 upright *o* there is agreement
14:11 the upright *o* will flourish
14:18 The inexperienced *o* will
14:18 but the shrewd *o* will bear
14:19 bow down before the good *o*
14:21 favor to the afflicted *o*
14:24 foolishness of the stupid *o*
14:33 in the midst of stupid *o*
15:2 tongue of wise *o* does good
15:2 mouth of the stupid *o* bubbles
15:3 keeping watch upon the bad *o*
15:3 keeping watch upon . . . good *o*
15:7 The lips of the wise *o* keep
15:7 heart of the stupid *o* is not
15:8 sacrifice of the wicked *o* is
Pr 15:8 the prayer of the upright *o* is
15:12 To the wise *o* he will not go
15:19 path of the upright *o* is a
15:25 house of the self-exalted *o*
15:28 the mouth of the wicked *o*
15:29 far away from the wicked *o*
15:29 prayer of the righteous *o* he
16:17 highway of the upright *o* is
16:19 in spirit with the meek *o*
16:19 with the self-exalted *o*
16:22 discipline of the foolish *o*
18:15 ear of wise *o* seeks to find
19:29 for the back of stupid *o*
21:4 the lamp of the wicked *o*, are
21:7 despoiling by the wicked *o*
21:12 subverting the wicked *o* to
21:18 the place of the upright *o*
21:27 sacrifice of the wicked *o* is
22:17 hear the words of the wise *o*
23:28 increases the treacherous *o*
24:16 wicked *o* will be made to
24:23 also are for the wise *o*
25:6 place of great *o* do not stand
28:3 defrauding the lowly *o* is as
28:8 showing favor to the lowly *o*
28:10 upright *o* to go astray into
28:10 faultless *o* themselves will
28:12 the righteous *o* are exulting
28:12 when the wicked *o* rise up, a
29:7 legal claim of the lowly *o*
29:10 upright *o*, they keep seeking
29:14 king is judging the lowly *o*
29:27 detestable to the righteous *o*
30:14 eat up the afflicted *o* off
30:14 poor *o* from among mankind
Ec 5:1 a sacrifice as the stupid *o* do
5:4 is no delight in the stupid *o*
6:8 walk in front of the living *o*
7:4 heart of the wise *o* is in the
7:4 heart of the stupid *o* is in the
7:5 the song of the stupid *o*
7:9 in the bosom of the stupid *o*
8:10 the wicked *o* being buried
8:14 righteous *o* to whom it is
8:14 for the work of the wicked *o*
8:14 exist wicked *o* to whom it is
8:14 the work of the righteous *o*
9:1 that the righteous *o* and the
9:1 wise *o* and their works are in
9:3 and after it—to the dead *o*
9:11 nor the mighty *o* the battle
9:11 nor do the understanding *o*
9:17 wise *o* in quietness are more
10:6 the rich *o* themselves keep
10:15 hard work of the stupid *o*
10:17 king is the son of noble *o*
12:11 words of the wise *o* are like
Ca 4:2 having lost its young *o*
4:5 breasts are like two young *o*
6:6 having lost its young *o*
7:3 breasts are like two young *o*
7:9 over the lips of sleeping *o*
7:13 The new *o* as well as the old
Isa 1:28 that of sinful *o* will be at
3:14 judgment with the elderly *o*
3:15 faces of the afflicted *o*
4:3 *o* remaining in Zion and the
4:3 *o* left over in Jerusalem
5:8 *o* joining house to house
5:15 eyes of the high *o* will
9:16 *o* causing them to wander
9:16 the *o* who are being confused
10:2 push away the lowly *o* from
10:2 justice from the afflicted *o*
10:15 *o* raising it on high, as
10:16 upon his fat *o* a wasting
10:33 high *o* themselves become
11:4 he must judge the lowly *o*
11:4 behalf of the meek *o* of the
11:7 their young *o* will lie down
11:12 the dispersed *o* of Israel
11:12 scattered *o* of Judah he
13:3 command to my sanctified *o*
13:3 called my mighty *o* for
13:3 my eminently exultant *o*
13:11 pride of the presumptuous *o*
14:5 the rod of the wicked *o*
14:5 the staff of the ruling *o*
14:30 firstborn *o* of the lowly
14:30 lowly *o* will certainly feed
14:30 and in security the poor *o*
14:32 afflicted *o* of his people
15:9 remaining *o* of the ground
16:3 Conceal the dispersed *o*
Isa 16:4 dispersed *o* reside as aliens
16:7 stricken *o* indeed will moan
19:11 the wise *o* of Pharaoh's
19:11 I am the son of wise *o*
21:10 O my threshed *o* and the
21:17 *o* remaining over of the
22:2 Your slain *o* are not those
23:2 *o* crossing over the sea
23:8 the honorable *o* of the earth
23:9 honorable *o* of the earth
24:4 high *o* of the people of the
24:8 of the highly elated *o* has
25:4 blast of the tyrannical *o* is
25:5 tyrannical *o* becomes
26:6 the steps of the lowly *o*
26:19 Your dead *o* will live
26:21 cover over her killed *o*
27:7 slaughter of his killed *o*
28:5 *o* remaining over of his
29:18 deaf *o* will certainly hear
29:18 of the blind *o* will see
29:19 meek *o* will certainly
29:19 poor *o* of mankind will be
30:10 said to the *o* seeing, You
30:10 to the *o* having visions, You
32:7 wreck the afflicted *o* with
32:10 careless *o* will be agitated
32:11 Be agitated, you careless *o!*
33:23 lame *o* themselves will
34:3 slain *o* will be thrown out
34:7 bulls with the powerful *o*
35:5 eyes of the blind *o* will be
35:5 ears of the deaf *o* will be
35:8 foolish *o* will wander about
35:9 repurchased *o* must walk
35:10 *o* redeemed by Jehovah will
38:11 in the land of the living *o*
41:4 with the last *o* I am the
41:17 The afflicted *o* and the poor
41:17 and the poor *o* are seeking
42:16 make the blind *o* walk in a
42:18 Hear, you deaf *o*; and look
42:18 forth to see, you blind *o*
43:8 *o* deaf though they have ears
43:17 strong *o* at the same time
46:3 remaining *o* of the house of
46:3 the *o* conveyed by me from
46:3 the *o* carried from the womb
46:12 the *o* powerful at heart
46:12 you the *o* far away from
48:22 has said, for the wicked *o*
49:6 the safeguarded *o* of Israel
49:13 upon his own afflicted *o*
49:17 The very *o* tearing you down
50:4 the tongue of the taught *o*
50:4 to hear like the taught *o*
51:7 the *o* knowing righteousness
51:10 repurchased *o* to go across
51:11 the redeemed *o* of Jehovah
51:23 hand of the *o* irritating you
52:5 *o* ruling over them kept
53:8 the land of the living *o*
53:9 even with the wicked *o*, and
53:12 with the mighty *o* that he
55:1 Hey there, all you thirsty *o!*
55:1 *o* that have no money! Come
56:8 the dispersed *o* of Israel
57:15 the spirit of the lowly *o*
57:15 heart of the *o* being crushed
57:18 him and to his mourning *o*
57:21 no peace . . . the wicked *o*
58:6 send away the crushed *o* free
59:10 among the stout *o* we are
61:1 tell good news to the meek *o*
61:2 comfort all the mourning *o*
62:9 *o* gathering it will eat it
62:9 *o* collecting it will drink
63:4 year of my repurchased *o* has
65:9 my chosen *o* must take
65:15 for an oath by my chosen *o*
65:22 chosen *o* will use to the
65:23 the chosen *o* of Jehovah
66:3 *o* that have chosen their own
66:5 *o* that will be put to shame
Jer 2:8 the very *o* handling the law
2:34 souls of the innocent poor *o*
5:5 go my way to the great *o* and
5:28 the judgment of the poor *o*
8:3 the places of the remaining *o*
8:9 wise *o* have become ashamed
9:1 day and night for the slain *o*
10:7 the wise *o* of the nations
10:11 the *o* who will perish from
11:10 the first *o*, who refused to

Jer 11:19 the land of the living *o*
12:1 the way of wicked *o* is what
12:1 are the unworried *o*
14:3 majestic *o* themselves have
14:3 insignificant *o* for water
15:21 the hand of the bad *o*, and
15:21 palm of the tyrannical *o*
16:6 the great *o* and the small
16:6 the small *o*, in this land
17:18 *o* to be struck with terror
19:4 the blood of the innocent *o*
19:13 unclean *o*, that is, all the
20:11 why the very *o* persecuting
23:19 the head of the wicked *o*
23:30 the *o* who are stealing away
23:31 the *o* who are employing
24:3 and the bad *o* being very bad
25:31 As regards the wicked *o*, he
25:34 you majestic *o* of the flock
25:35 escape from the majestic *o*
25:36 howling of the majestic *o*
26:17 certain *o* of the older men
30:3 I will gather the captive *o*
30:14 the *o* that have forgotten
30:18 captive *o* of the tents of
30:23 head of the wicked *o* it
31:12 young *o* of the flock and the
31:29 *o* that ate the unripe grape
34:7 *o* that remained over among
39:10 lowly *o* who had nothing at
42:17 *o* to die by the sword, by
44:1 *o* dwelling in Migdol and
44:14 except some escaped *o*
44:28 *o* escaping from the sword
46:15 powerful *o* have been washed
47:4 *o* from the island of Caphtor
48:4 little *o* have caused a cry
48:47 the captive *o* of Moab
49:6 gather the captive *o* of the
49:20 little *o* of the flock will
49:36 dispersed *o* of Elam will
49:39 the captive *o* of Elam
50:26 to have any remaining *o*
50:35 and against her wise *o*
50:45 little *o* of the flock will
51:47 own slain *o* will fall in
51:49 slain *o* of Israel to fall
51:49 at Babylon the slain *o* of
51:57 her princes and her wise *o*
52:15 lowly *o* of the people and
52:16 the lowly *o* of the land
La 1:15 powerful *o* Jehovah has tossed
4:5 *o* that were eating pleasant
4:5 *o* that were being reared in
4:13 the blood of righteous *o*
5:7 are the *o* that have sinned
Eze 2:6 there are obstinate *o* and
3:6 very *o* would listen to you
6:4 cause your slain *o* to fall
6:8 the *o* escaping from the sword
6:9 your escaped *o* will certainly
6:13 their slain *o* come to be in
7:13 is yet among the living *o*
7:21 to the wicked *o* of the earth
7:24 the worst *o* of the nations
7:24 the pride of the strong *o* to
8:11 elderly *o* of the house of
8:12 the elderly *o* of the house of
9:7 courtyards with the slain *o*
9:8 all the remaining *o* of Israel
10:22 the very *o*. They would go
11:6 slain *o* in this city to be
11:6 her streets with the slain *o*
11:7 As regards your slain *o* whom
11:13 the remaining *o* of Israel
11:15 *o* to whom the inhabitants
13:18 *o* belonging to my people
13:18 *o* that you preserve alive
14:1 from the elderly *o* of Israel
16:53 will gather their captive *o*
16:53 the captive *o* of Sodom and
16:53 the captive *o* of Samaria
16:53 gather your captive *o* in the
16:61 *o* older than you as well as
16:61 as well as the *o* younger
17:21 *o* left remaining will be
18:2 the *o* that eat unripe grapes
18:29 the *o* that are not adjusted
20:1 the elderly *o* of Israel came
21:12 *o* hurled to the sword have
21:14 sword of the slain *o* it is
21:29 on the necks of the slain *o*
23:8 *o* that pressed the bosoms
23:10 *o* that uncovered her

Eze 23:23 warriors and summoned *o*
23:45 *o* that will judge her with
24:17 For the dead *o* no mourning
27:8 Your skilled *o*, O Tyre
27:9 her skilled *o* happened to be
27:10 *o* that caused your splendor
27:11 *o* that happened to be in
28:10 deaths of uncircumcised *o*
31:18 of the uncircumcised *o*
32:12 the very swords of mighty *o*
32:19 with the uncircumcised *o*
32:21 men of the mighty *o* will
32:24 all of them slain *o*
32:25 In the midst of slain *o*
32:25 In the midst of slain *o* he
32:27 not lie down with mighty *o*
32:27 mighty *o* were a terror in
32:28 midst of uncircumcised *o*
32:29 with the uncircumcised *o*
32:30 gone down with the slain *o*
32:31 the *o* that Pharaoh will see
32:32 of the uncircumcised *o*
33:27 the *o* who are in the
34:4 sickened *o* you have not
34:18 *o* left over you should foul
34:21 shoving all the sickened *o*
35:8 mountains with its slain *o*
35:8 *o* slain by the sword will
36:3 remaining *o* of the nations
36:4 remaining *o* of the nations
36:5 remaining *o* of the nations
39:18 mighty *o* you will eat
39:25 the captive *o* of Jacob
41:16 the windows were covered *o*
42:5 the uppermost *o* were shorter
42:5 more than the lowest *o* and
42:5 and than the middle *o*
42:6 the lowest *o* and from the
42:6 the middle *o* from the floor
43:19 of Zadok, the *o* approaching
43:25 out of the flock, perfect *o*
44:16 *o* that will come into my
44:29 are the *o* who will eat them
45:23 seven rams, sound *o*, daily
46:6 lambs and a ram; sound *o*
48:18 for the *o* serving the city
Da 2:21 giving wisdom to the wise *o*
3:18 not the *o* we are serving
3:22 *o* that the fiery flame killed
4:17 and by the saying of holy *o*
4:27 showing mercy to the poor *o*
7:7 it had teeth of iron, big *o*
7:18 holy *o* of the Supreme One
7:21 horn made war upon the holy *o*
7:22 given in favor of the holy *o*
7:22 holy *o* took possession of the
7:24 different from the first *o*
7:25 harass continually the holy *o*
7:27 holy *o* of the Supreme One
8:24 bring mighty *o* to ruin, also
8:24 people made up of the holy *o*
11:15 the people of his picked *o*
11:26 *o* eating his delicacies will
11:41 *o* that will escape out of
12:3 *o* having insight will shine
12:10 wicked *o* will certainly act
12:10 no wicked *o* at all will
12:10 the *o* having insight will
Ho 6:11 gather back the captive *o* of
10:13 multitude of your mighty *o*
14:9 the *o* who will walk in them
14:9 *o* who will stumble in them
Joe 1:18 the *o* made to bear guilt
2:32 prove to be the escaped *o*
3:1 the captive *o* of Judah and
3:11 bring your powerful *o* down
Am 1:8 remaining *o* of the Philistines
4:1 are defrauding the lowly *o*
4:1 who are crushing the poor *o*
5:7 *o* who have cast righteousness
5:12 *o* who have turned aside poor
5:15 to the remaining *o* of Joseph
6:1 the distinguished *o* of the
6:7 sprawling *o* must depart
8:4 cause the meek *o* of the earth
9:14 the captive *o* of my people
Ob 8 destroy the wise *o* out of Edom
Jon 3:7 the king and his great *o*
Mic 2:8 the *o* passing by confidently
2:12 the remaining *o* of Israel
3:3 the *o* who have also eaten
3:9 head *o* of the house of Jacob
3:9 the *o* detesting justice and
3:9 *o* who make even everything

Mic 3:11 Her own head *o* judge merely
5:7 the remaining *o* of Jacob
5:8 the remaining *o* of Jacob
Na 2:5 will remember his majestic *o*
3:3 the multitude of slain *o*
3:10 great *o* have all been bound
3:18 your majestic *o* stay in their
Hab 2:6 these very *o*, all of them
2:8 remaining *o* of the peoples
Zep 1:3 with the wicked *o*; and I
1:4 the remaining *o* of the Baal
1:7 has sanctified his invited *o*
2:3 all you meek *o* of the earth
2:7 remaining *o* of the house of
2:7 gather back the captive *o* of
2:9 The remaining *o* of my people
3:10 *o* entreating me, namely
3:10 daughter of my scattered *o*
3:11 your haughtily exultant *o*
3:13 the remaining *o* of Israel
3:18 *o* grief-stricken in absence
3:20 gather back your captive *o*
Hag 1:12 the remaining *o* of the people
1:14 remaining *o* of the people
2:2 the remaining *o* of the people
Zec 1:9 who these very *o* are
1:10 *o* whom Jehovah has sent
4:14 the two anointed *o* who are
6:6 white *o*, they must go forth
6:6 speckled *o*, they must go
6:7 parti-colored *o*, they must go
6:8 *o* that have caused the spirit
7:6 you the *o* doing the eating
7:6 you the *o* doing the drinking
8:6 remaining *o* of this people in
8:11 remaining *o* of this people
8:12 remaining *o* of this people
11:2 majestic *o* themselves have
11:7 O afflicted *o* of the flock
11:9 as for the *o* left remaining
11:11 the afflicted *o* of the flock
13:3 the *o* who caused his birth
13:3 the *o* who caused his birth
14:2 remaining *o* of the people
14:5 the holy *o* being with him
Mal 2:7 *o* that should keep knowledge
2:17 in such *o* he himself has
4:1 all the presumptuous *o* and
4:3 tread down the wicked *o*, for
Mt 5:5 Happy are the mild-tempered *o*
7:13 and many are the *o* going in
7:14 and few are the *o* finding it
10:20 *o* speaking are not just you
10:42 gives one of these little *o*
11:25 the wise and intellectual *o*
12:7 condemned the guiltless *o*
13:43 righteous *o* will shine as
13:48 collected the fine *o* into
14:14 and he cured their sick *o*
18:6 little *o* who put faith in me
18:10 not despise . . . little *o*
18:14 of these little *o* to perish
19:14 belongs to suchlike *o*
19:18 Which *o*? Jesus said
20:16 last *o* will be first, and
20:16 and the first *o* last
23:17 Fools and blind *o*! Which, in
23:19 Blind *o*! Which, in fact, is
23:29 tombs of the righteous *o*
24:22 on account of the chosen *o*
24:24 mislead . . . the chosen *o*
24:31 gather his chosen *o* together
25:37 righteous *o* will answer him
25:45 to one of these least *o*, you
25:46 righteous *o* into everlasting
27:52 many bodies of the holy *o*
Mr 4:15 are the *o* alongside the road
4:16 *o* sown upon the rocky places
4:18 *o* that have heard the word
4:20 *o* that were sown on the fine
6:5 his hands upon a few sickly *o*
6:21 and the foremost *o* of Galilee
6:56 place the sick *o* in the
7:2 hands, that is, unwashed *o*
9:42 these little *o* that believe
10:14 kingdom . . . to suchlike *o*
10:42 great *o* wield authority
12:40 the *o* devouring the houses
13:11 you are not the *o* speaking
13:20 on account of the chosen *o*
13:22 lead astray . . . the chosen *o*
13:27 his chosen *o* together from
14:57 certain *o* were rising and
Lu 1:17 the disobedient *o* to the

Lu 1:17 wisdom of righteous *o*
1:52 thrones and exalted lowly *o*
1:53 has fully satisfied hungry *o*
4:18 crushed *o* away with a release
8:12 are the *o* that have heard
8:13 the *o* who, when they hear it
8:14 are the *o* that have heard
8:15 the *o* that, after hearing the
10:9 cure the sick *o* in it, and
10:21 from wise and intellectual *o*
11:15 But certain *o* of them said
12:18 and build bigger *o*, and there
12:46 a part with the unfaithful *o*
13:1 *o* present that reported to
14:14 resurrection . . . righteous *o*
14:17 say to the invited *o*, Come
15:7 righteous *o* who have no need
17:2 stumble one of these little *o*
18:7 for his chosen *o* who cry out
18:16 kingdom . . . to suchlike *o*
19:47 the principal *o* of the people
21:5 certain *o* were speaking
21:23 *o* suckling a baby in those
22:28 you are the *o* that have stuck
22:37 was reckoned with lawless *o*
24:25 O senseless *o* and slow in
Joh 4:23 for suchlike *o* to worship
5:39 *o* that bear witness about me
6:64 who were the *o* not believing
13:18 I know the *o* I have chosen
Ac 2:13 *o* mocked at them and began to
9:13 to your holy *o* in Jerusalem
9:32 holy *o* that dwelt in Lydda
9:41 he called the holy *o* and the
10:45 faithful *o* that had come
15:25 loved *o*, Barnabas and Paul
17:18 *o* of both the Epicurean and
17:28 certain *o* of the poets among
19:13 certain *o* of the roving Jews
19:26 *o* that are made by hands are
20:2 encouraging the *o* there with
20:32 among all the sanctified *o*
26:10 the holy *o* I locked up in
Ro 1:7 in Rome as God's beloved *o*
1:7 called to be holy *o*: May you
1:14 to wise and to senseless *o*
2:13 not the *o* righteous before God
2:15 *o* who demonstrate the matter
2:20 of the unreasonable *o*
8:27 in accord with God for holy *o*
8:28 *o* called according to his
8:30 are the *o* he also called; and
8:30 *o* he also declared to be
8:30 are the *o* he also glorified
8:33 against God's chosen *o*
11:7 but the *o* chosen obtained it
12:13 Share with the holy *o*
15:25 to minister to the holy *o*
15:26 to the poor of the holy *o* in
15:31 be acceptable to the holy *o*
16:2 in a way worthy of the holy *o*
16:15 and all the holy *o* with them
16:18 the hearts of guileless *o*
1Co 1:2 called to be holy *o*, together
6:1 and not before the holy *o*
6:2 holy *o* will judge the world
10:14 my beloved *o*, flee from
12:28 has set the respective *o* in
14:33 congregations of the holy *o*
15:29 the purpose of being dead *o*
16:1 collection . . . for the holy *o*
16:15 to minister to the holy *o*
2Co 1:1 holy *o* who are in all of
2:16 the latter *o* an odor issuing
2:16 to the former *o* an odor
7:1 beloved *o*, let us cleanse
8:4 destined for the holy *o*
9:1 ministry . . . for the holy *o*
9:9 he has given to the poor *o*
9:12 the wants of the holy *o* but
12:19 beloved *o*, all things are
13:13 holy *o* send you their
Ga 1:7 *o* who are causing you trouble
2:9 the *o* who seemed to be pillars
3:7 *o* who are sons of Abraham
6:12 *o* that try to compel you to
Eph 1:1 holy *o* who are in Ephesus
1:1 faithful *o* in union with
1:15 and toward all the holy *o*
1:18 an inheritance for the holy *o*
2:17 peace to you, the *o* far off
2:19 citizens of the holy *o* and
3:8 than the least of all holy *o*
3:18 with all the holy *o* what is
Eph 4:12 readjustment of the holy *o*
6:18 in behalf of all the holy *o*
Php 1:1 holy *o* in union with Christ
2:12 my beloved *o*, in the way
4:1 in the Lord, beloved *o*
4:22 the holy *o*, but especially
Col 1:2 to the holy *o* and faithful
1:4 love you have for . . . holy *o*
1:12 inheritance of the holy *o* in
1:26 made manifest to his holy *o*
3:12 God's chosen *o*, holy and
4:11 these very *o* have become a
1Th 3:13 with all his holy *o*
2Th 1:9 These very *o* will undergo the
1:10 connection with his holy *o*
3:11 *o* are walking disorderly
1Ti 1:3 command certain *o* not to
1:6 certain *o* have been turned
4:10 especially of faithful *o*
4:12 an example to the faithful *o*
5:10 washed the feet of holy *o*
2Ti 2:10 for the sake of the chosen *o*
2:21 keeps clear of the latter *o*
Tit 1:1 the faith of God's chosen *o*
Phm 5 and toward all the holy *o*
7 tender affections of the holy *o*
Heb 5:2 the ignorant and erring *o*
6:9 beloved *o*, we are convinced
6:10 ministered to the holy *o* and
9:15 *o* who have been called might
11:28 not touch their firstborn *o*
12:23 righteous *o* who have been
13:24 and to all the holy *o*
Jas 2:5 God chose the *o* who are poor
4:6 God opposes the haughty *o*
4:6 kindness to the humble *o*
4:8 your hearts, you indecisive *o*
1Pe 1:1 and Bithynia, to the *o* chosen
2:11 *o* that carry on a conflict
3:12 eyes . . . upon the righteous *o*
3:18 for unrighteous *o*, that he
4:12 Beloved *o*, do not be puzzled
5:5 God opposes the haughty *o*
5:5 kindness to the humble *o*
2Pe 2:1 very *o* will quietly bring in
2:10 do not tremble at glorious *o*
3:1 Beloved *o*, this is now the
3:8 beloved *o*, that one day is
3:14 beloved *o*, since you are
3:17 beloved *o*, having this
1Jo 2:7 Beloved *o*, I am writing you
3:2 Beloved *o*, now we are
3:21 Beloved *o*, if our hearts do
4:1 Beloved *o*, do not believe
4:7 Beloved *o*, let us continue
4:11 Beloved *o*, if this is how
2Jo 4 certain *o* of your children
Jude 1 the called *o* who are loved in
3 Beloved *o*, though I was making
3 time delivered to the holy *o*
7 same manner as the foregoing *o*
8 abusively of glorious *o*
17 beloved *o*, call to mind the
19 *o* that make separations
20 beloved *o*, by building up
Re 2:24 *o* who did not get to know
3:4 walk with me in white *o*
5:8 the prayers of the holy *o*
6:15 and the top-ranking *o* and the
6:15 and the rich and the strong *o*
7:14 These are the *o* that come out
8:3 prayers of all the holy *o* upon
8:4 prayers of the holy *o* before
11:18 reward . . . . to the holy *o*
12:17 remaining *o* of her seed
13:7 wage war with the holy *o* and
13:10 and faith of the holy *o*
14:4 the *o* that did not defile
14:4 *o* that keep following the
14:12 endurance for the holy *o*
15:1 These are the last *o*, because
16:6 poured out the blood of holy *o*
17:6 with the blood of the holy *o*
18:20 you holy *o* and you apostles
18:24 the blood . . . of holy *o* and
19:5 fear him, the small *o* and the
19:8 righteous acts of the holy *o*
19:18 and of small *o* and great
20:9 the camp of the holy *o* and
22:21 Christ be with the holy *o*

Oneself
Isa 28:20 short for stretching *o* on
28:20 narrow when wrapping *o* up

Isa 30:29 sanctifies *o* for a festival
48:11 could one let *o* be profaned
Jer 49:10 will not be able to hide *o*
Mr 12:33 loving one's neighbor as *o*
Jas 1:27 *o* without spot from the

Onesimus
Col 4:9 along with *O*, my faithful and
Phm 10 while in my prison bonds, *O*

Onesiphorus
2Ti 1:16 mercy to the household of *O*
4:19 Aquila and the household of *O*

Onions
Nu 11:5 eat in Egypt . . . *o* and the

Onlookers
Job 34:26 In the place of *o*
Lu 14:29 *o* might start to ridicule
1Ti 5:20 Reprove before all *o* persons

Only
Ge 6:5 thoughts of his heart was *o*
7:23 *o* Noah and those who were
9:4 *O* flesh with its soul—its
14:24 *O* what the young men have
19:8 *O* to these men do not do a
20:12 *o* not the daughter of my
22:2 your *o* son whom you so love
22:12 not withheld your son, your *o*
22:16 withheld your son, your *o*
23:13 *O* if you—no, listen to me!
24:8 *O* you must not return my son
26:29 just as we have done *o* good
27:13 *O* listen to my voice and go
34:12 *o* give me the young woman
34:15 *O* on this condition can we
34:22 *O* on this condition will the
34:23 *O* let us give them our
41:40 *O* as to the throne shall I
47:22 *O* the land of the priests he
47:26 *O* the land of the priests as
50:8 *O* their little children and
Ex 8:9 *O* in the Nile River will they
8:11 *O* in the Nile River will they
8:28 *O* do not make it quite so far
8:29 *O* let not Pharaoh trifle again
9:26 *O* in the land of Goshen
10:24 *O* your sheep and your cattle
12:15 to eat unfermented cakes *o*
12:16 *O* what every soul needs to
16:3 If *o* we had died by Jehovah's
21:19 compensation *o* for the time
22:27 For it is his *o* covering
Le 11:4 *O* this . . . you must not eat
11:21 *O* this is what you may eat
11:36 *O* a spring and a pit of
25:52 *o* a few remain of the years
27:26 *O* the firstborn among beasts
27:28 *O* no sort of devoted thing
Nu 1:49 *O* the tribe of Levi you
14:2 If *o* we had died in the land
14:2 if *o* we had died in this
14:9 *O* against Jehovah do not rebel
18:3 *O* to the utensils of the holy
18:17 *O* the firstborn bull or
20:3 If *o* we had expired when our
22:20 But *o* the word that I shall
22:29 If *o* there were a sword in
23:13 *O* the extremity of them you
26:55 *O* by the lot should the land
31:22 *O* the gold and the silver
31:23 *O* it should be purified by
36:6 *O* it is to the family of the
De 2:27 *O* on the road I shall walk
2:28 *O* let me pass through on my
2:35 *O* the domestic animals did
2:37 *O* you did not go near the
3:11 *o* Og the king of Bashan
3:19 *O* your wives and your little
4:9 *O* watch out for yourself and
5:29 If *o* they would develop this
10:15 *O* to your forefathers did
12:15 *O* whenever your soul craves
12:16 *O* the blood you must not eat
12:22 *O* in the way that the
14:7 *O* this sort you must not eat
15:5 *o* if you will without fail
15:23 *O* its blood you must not eat
17:16 *O* he should not increase
20:14 *O* the women and the little
20:16 It is *o* of the cities of
20:20 *O* a tree that you know is
23:24 eat *o* enough grapes for you
23:25 pluck off *o* the ripe ears

De 28:13 you must come to be *o* on top
28:29 *o* one who is always
28:33 one who is *o* defrauded and
28:67 say, If it *o* were evening!
28:67 say, If it *o* were morning!
32:36 *o* a helpless and worthless
Jos 1:7 *O* be courageous and very
1:17 *O* may Jehovah your God prove
1:18 *O* be courageous and strong
3:4 *o* let there prove to be a
6:17 *O* Rahab the prostitute may
6:18 *o* keep away from the thing
6:24 *O* the silver and the gold and
7:7 if *o* we had taken it upon
8:2 *O* you people may plunder its
8:27 *O* the domestic animals and
11:13 *o* all the cities standing
11:14 *o* all humankind that they
11:22 It was *o* in Gaza, in Gath
13:6 *O* make it fall to Israel as
13:14 *o* to the tribe of the
22:5 *O* be very careful to carry
22:20 not the *o* man to expire in
Jg 3:2 it was *o* in order for the
3:2 *o* those who before that had
6:39 a test *o* once more with the
9:29 if *o* this people were in my
10:15 *O* deliver us, please, this
11:34 was absolutely the *o* child
13:23 delighted *o* to put us to
14:16 You *o* hate me, you do, and
19:20 *O* do not stay overnight in
1Sa 1:13 *o* her lips were quivering
1:23 *O* may Jehovah carry out his
5:4 *O* the fish part had been left
8:9 *O* this, that you should
12:20 *O* do not turn aside from
12:24 *O* fear Jehovah, and you
18:8 *o* the kingship to give him
18:17 *O* prove yourself a valiant
20:39 *o* Jonathan and David
26:25 Not *o* will you without fail
29:9 *O* it is the princes of
2Sa 2:10 *O* the house of Judah proved
2:27 *o* by the morning would the
3:13 *O* one thing there is that I
19:6 if *o* Absalom were alive and
23:10 *o* to strip those struck
1Ki 3:2 *O* the people were sacrificing
3:3 *O* it was on the high places
8:19 *O* you yourself will not
8:25 *o* your sons will take care
11:13 *O* it will not be all the
11:39 of this, *o* not always
14:8 *o* what was right in my eyes
15:5 *o* in the matter of Uriah the
15:23 *O* at the time of his
17:13 *O* from what is there make
19:10 I *o* am left; and they begin
19:14 I *o* am left; and they begin
22:43 *O* the high places
2Ki 3:2 *o* not like his father or like
3:3 *O* he stuck to the sins of
3:25 they left *o* the stones of
5:3 If *o* my lord were before the
7:10 *o* the horses tied and the
10:23 *o* the worshipers of Baal
10:29 *o* the sins of Jeroboam the
12:3 *o* the high places that did
12:13 *O* as respects the house of
13:6 *O* they did not depart from
14:3 *o* not like David his
14:4 *o* the high places that did
15:4 *o* that the high places did
15:35 *o* that the high places did
17:2 *o* not as the kings of Israel
21:8 provided *o* they are careful
22:7 *O* no accounting should be
23:9 *O* the priests of the high
23:35 *O* he taxed the land
24:3 *o* by the order of Jehovah
1Ch 22:12 *O* may Jehovah give you
2Ch 6:9 *O* you yourself will not build
6:16 *o* your sons will take care
15:17 *O* Asa's heart itself proved
20:33 *O* the high places
25:2 *o* not with a complete heart
27:2 *O* he did not invade the
29:34 *O* the priests themselves
30:11 *O* individuals from Asher
33:8 *o* that they take care to do
33:17 *o* it was to Jehovah their
Es 4:11 *o* in case the king holds out
Job 1:12 *O* against him himself do not
Job 1:15 and I got to escape, *o* I by
1:16 and I got to escape, *o* I by
1:17 and I got to escape, *o* I by
1:19 And I got to escape, *o* I by
2:6 *O* watch out for his soul
8:9 For we were *o* yesterday, and
11:5 if *o* God himself would speak
13:5 If *o* you would absolutely
13:15 *o* argue to his face for my
13:20 *O* two things do not do to
14:22 *O* his own flesh while upon
16:4 If *o* your souls existed
16:7 *O* now he has made me weary
18:21 *O* these are the tabernacles
30:13 beneficial *o* for adversity
30:24 *O* no one thrusts his hand
33:8 *O* you have said in my ears
35:13 *O* the untruth God does not
42:8 His face *o* I shall accept so
Ps 22:20 My *o* one from the very paw
32:6 *o* as you may be found
35:17 my *o* one from the maned
37:8 heated up *o* to do evil
49:19 *o* as far as the generation
91:8 *O* with your eyes will you
138:6 he knows *o* from a distance
Pr 4:3 the *o* one before my mother
11:24 but it results *o* in want
12:19 be *o* as long as a moment
13:10 one *o* causes a struggle, but
17:11 *O* rebellion is what the bad
Ec 7:29 This *o* I have found, that the
Isa 4:1 *o* may we be called by your
26:13 *o* shall we make mention
40:24 one has *o* to blow upon them
48:18 if *o* you would actually pay
64:1 O if *o* you had ripped the
Jer 3:10 all her heart, *o* falsely
3:13 *O* take note of your error
6:26 mourning that for an *o* son
26:15 *O* you should by all means
49:9 cause *o* as much ruin as they
51:49 Not *o* was Babylon the cause
Eze 14:16 *o* they themselves, would be
14:18 *o* they themselves, would be
46:17 *O* his inheritance—as
Da 2:9 one and *o* sentence is upon you
11:24 schemes, but *o* until a time
Am 3:2 You people *o* have I known out
8:10 the mourning for an *o* son
Jon 3:4 *O* forty days more, and
Hab 2:13 will toil on *o* for the fire
Zec 1:15 indignant to *o* a little
12:10 the wailing over an *o* son
Mt 5:47 if you greet your brothers *o*
9:21 If I *o* touch his outer
10:42 *o* a cup of cold water to
12:4 loaves . . . for the priests *o*
17:8 no one but Jesus himself *o*
19:11 *o* those who have the gift
21:19 except leaves *o*, and he said
21:21 If *o* you have faith and do
21:21 not *o* will you do what I
24:36 but *o* the Father
Mr 5:36 no fear, *o* exercise faith
9:37 receives, not me *o*, but also
Lu 4:26 *o* to Zarephath in the land of
6:4 but for the priests *o*
8:50 no fear, *o* put forth faith
Joh 5:18 not *o* was he breaking the
5:19 *o* what he beholds the
5:44 glory that is from the *o* God
6:22 *o* his disciples had left
11:52 not for the nation *o*, but
12:9 not on account of Jesus *o*
12:44 puts faith, not in me *o*
13:9 Lord, not my feet *o*, but
17:3 the *o* true God, and of the
17:20 not concerning these *o*
21:8 *o* about three hundred feet
Ac 8:16 *o* been baptized in the name
11:19 to no one except to Jews *o*
18:25 with *o* the baptism of John
19:26 how not *o* in Ephesus but in
19:27 not *o* that this occupation of
20:24 if *o* I may finish my course
21:13 I am ready not *o* to be bound
26:29 not *o* you but also all those
27:10 loss not *o* of the cargo and
27:22 be lost, *o* the boat will
Ro 1:32 not *o* keep on doing them but
2:25 benefit *o* if you practice law
3:29 is he the God of the Jews *o*?
4:12 not *o* to those who adhere to
Ro 4:16 not *o* to that which adheres
4:23 however, not for his sake *o*
5:3 not *o* that, but let us exult
5:11 not *o* that, but we are also
8:23 Not *o* that, but we ourselves
9:24 not *o* from among Jews but
13:5 *o* on account of that wrath
14:7 lives . . . to himself *o*
14:7 dies with regard to himself *o*
14:14 *o* where a man considers
16:4 not *o* I but also all the
1Co 7:17 *O*, as Jehovah has given each
7:39 married . . . *o* in the Lord
9:6 is it *o* Barnabas and I that do
9:24 but *o* one receives the prize
10:8 *o* to fall, twenty-three
10:9 put him to the test, *o* to
10:10 *o* to perish by the destroyer
14:36 was it *o* as far as you that
15:19 in this life *o* we have
2Co 8:10 not *o* the doing but also the
8:19 Not *o* that, but he was also
8:21 not *o* in the sight of Jehovah
9:12 not *o* to supply abundantly
13:8 but *o* for the truth
Ga 1:7 *o* there are certain ones who
1:19 *o* James the brother of the
1:23 they *o* used to hear: The man
2:10 *O* we should keep the poor
2:16 *o* through faith toward Christ
3:20 where *o* one person is
3:20 but God is *o* one
4:18 not *o* when I am present with
5:13 *o* do not use this freedom as
6:12 *o* that they may not be
Eph 1:21 not *o* in this system of
Php 1:27 *O* behave in a manner worthy
1:29 not *o* to put your faith in
2:12 not during my presence *o*
2:27 not *o* on him, but also on me
Col 4:11 *O* these are my fellow
1Th 1:8 not *o* has the word of Jehovah
2:8 not *o* the good news of God
2Th 2:7 *o* till he who is right now
1Ti 1:17 invisible, the *o* God, be
5:13 not *o* unoccupied, but also
5:19 *o* on the evidence of two or
6:15 the happy and *o* Potentate
2Ti 2:20 vessels not *o* of gold and
4:8 not *o* to me, but also to all
Heb 3:14 *o* if we make fast our hold
5:4 *o* when he is called by God
9:10 *o* with foods and drinks and
12:26 not *o* the earth but also
Jas 1:22 and not hearers *o*, deceiving
1Pe 2:18 fear, not *o* to the good and
1Jo 2:2 not for ours *o* but also for
5:6 not with the water *o*, but
Jude 4 proving false to our *o* Owner
25 *o* God our Savior through
Re 9:4 *o* those men who do not have
21:27 *o* those written in the

Only-begotten
Lu 7:12 the *o* son of his mother
8:42 he had an *o* daughter about
9:38 my son, because he is my *o*
Joh 1:14 belongs to an *o* son from a
1:18 *o* god who is in the bosom
3:16 that he gave his *o* Son
3:18 name of the *o* Son of God
Heb 11:17 attempted to offer up his *o*
1Jo 4:9 God sent forth his *o* Son into

Ono
1Ch 8:12 Shemed, who built *O* and Lod
Ezr 2:33 the sons of Lod, Hadid and *O*
Ne 6:2 of the valley plain of *O*
7:37 the sons of Lod, Hadid and *O*
11:35 Lod and *O*, the valley of the

Onrush
Isa 33:4 *o* of locust swarms that is

Onrushing
Pr 28:15 an *o* bear is a wicked ruler

Onward
Ex 33:6 from Mount Horeb *o*
Nu 14:19 from Egypt *o* until now
15:23 from the day . . . *o* for your
18:16 from a month old *o* you
Job 38:12 Was it from your days *o*
Ps 58:3 from the belly *o*
Isa 21:1 in the south in moving *o*
Eze 23:21 your bosoms from Egypt *o*

Joh 9:30 and yet he *o* my eyes
9:32 *o* the eyes of one born blind
11:37 *o* the eyes of the blind man
Ac 5:19 Jehovah's angel *o* the doors
7:56 I behold the heavens *o* up
8:35 Philip *o* his mouth and
9:8 his eyes were *o* he was seeing
9:40 She *o* her eyes and, as she
10:11 beheld heaven *o* and some
10:34 Peter *o* his mouth and said
12:10 *o* to them of its own accord
12:16 When they *o*, they saw him
14:27 *o* to the nations the door to
16:14 Jehovah *o* her heart wide to
16:26 the doors were instantly *o*
Ro 3:13 Their throat is an *o* grave
1Co 16:9 door . . . has been *o* to me
2Co 2:12 door was *o* to me in the Lord
6:11 Our mouth has been *o* to you
Re 3:8 I have set before you an *o* door
4:1 an *o* door in heaven, and the
6:1 Lamb *o* one of the seven seals
6:3 when he *o* the second seal, I
6:5 when he *o* the third seal, I
6:7 when he *o* the fourth seal, I
6:9 when he *o* the fifth seal, I
6:12 when he *o* the sixth seal
8:1 when he *o* the seventh seal, a
9:2 he *o* the pit of the abyss
10:2 a little scroll *o*. And he
10:8 *o* scroll that is in the hand
11:19 was *o*, and the ark of his
12:16 the earth *o* its mouth and
13:6 it *o* its mouth in blasphemies
15:5 tent of the witness was *o* in
19:11 I saw the heaven *o*, and
20:12 throne, and scrolls were *o*
20:12 But another scroll was *o*

Openhandedness
1Ki 10:13 to the *o* of King Solomon

Opening
Ge 43:21 began *o* our bags, why, here
Ex 28:32 must be an *o* at its top in
28:32 Its *o* should have a border
28:32 Like the *o* of a coat of mail
39:23 the *o* of the sleeveless coat
39:23 like the *o* of a coat of mail
39:23 *o* had a border round about
Nu 3:12 firstborn *o* the womb of the
8:16 place of those *o* all wombs
18:15 Everything *o* the womb, of
Jg 3:25 no one *o* the doors of the
1Ki 7:4 an illumination *o* opposite
7:4 illumination *o* in three tiers
7:5 the illumination *o* opposite
7:5 illumination *o* in three tiers
Ps 22:7 keep *o* their mouths wide
145:16 You are *o* your hand
146:8 Jehovah is *o* the eyes of the
Pr 8:6 *o* of my lips is about
13:3 one *o* wide his lips—he will
18:16 gift will make a large *o* for
Isa 10:14 or *o* his mouth or chirping
22:22 shut without anyone's *o*
42:20 It was a case of *o* the ears
57:4 you keep *o* wide the mouth
61:1 the wide *o* of the eyes even
Jer 13:19 that there is no one *o* them
Eze 20:26 every child *o* the womb pass
25:9 I am *o* the slope of Moab
37:12 I am *o* your burial places
Mr 2:4 having dug an *o* they lowered
Lu 2:23 Every male *o* a womb must be
24:32 fully *o* up the Scriptures to
Ac 5:23 *o* up we found no one inside
9:25 through an *o* in the wall
Eph 6:19 with the *o* of my mouth
Jas 3:11 to bubble out of the same *o*

Openings
Mic 7:5 guard the *o* of your mouth

Openly
Mt 3:6 *o* confessing their sins
Mr 1:5 *o* confessing their sins
1:45 was no longer able to enter *o*
Lu 1:80 showing himself *o* to Israel
Joh 4:25 declare all things to us *o*
7:10 not *o* but as in secret
Ac 7:17 God had *o* declared to Abraham
19:18 and report their practices *o*
Ro 15:9 I will *o* acknowledge you
Ga 3:1 Christ was *o* portrayed impaled
Php 2:11 *o* acknowledge that Jesus
Heb 4:13 *o* exposed to the eyes of him
Jas 5:16 *o* confess your sins to one

Opens
Ex 13:2 firstborn that *o* each womb
13:12 that *o* the womb to Jehovah
34:19 first *o* the womb is mine
Job 35:16 Job himself *o* his mouth
Joh 10:3 doorkeeper *o* to this one
Ac 27:12 *o* toward the northeast and
Re 3:7 *o* so that no one will shut
3:7 and shuts so that no one *o*
3:20 my voice and *o* the door, I

Operated
Eph 1:20 *o* in the case of the Christ

Operates
2Co 1:6 that *o* to make you endure the
Eph 1:11 *o* all things according to
2:2 *o* in the sons of disobedience
3:7 to the way his power *o*

Operating
Mt 14:2 powerful works are *o* in him
Mr 6:14 powerful works are *o* in him
Ga 5:6 but faith *o* through love is
Eph 3:20 his power which is *o* in us

Operation
Eph 1:19 *o* of the mightiness of his
Php 3:21 *o* of the power that he has
Col 1:29 the *o* of him and which is at
2:12 your faith in the *o* of God
2Th 2:9 the *o* of Satan with every
2:11 God lets an *o* of error go to

Operations
2Ch 24:13 doers of the work began *o*
1Co 12:6 and there are varieties of *o*
12:6 the *o* in all persons
12:10 *o* of powerful works, to
12:11 But all these *o* the one and

Operative
Jg 14:6 spirit became *o* upon him, so
14:19 spirit became *o* upon him, so
15:14 spirit became *o* upon him
1Sa 10:6 become *o* upon you, and you
10:10 the spirit of God became *o*
11:6 spirit of God became *o* upon
16:13 began to be *o* upon David
18:10 spirit became *o* upon Saul
Am 5:6 not become *o* just like fire

Ophel
2Ki 5:24 came to *O*, he immediately
2Ch 27:3 on the wall of *O* he did a
33:14 ran it around to *O* and
Ne 3:26 happened to be dwellers in *O*
3:27 as far as the wall of *O*
11:21 Nethinim were dwelling in *O*
Isa 32:14 *O* and the watchtower

Ophir
Ge 10:29 *O* and . . . the sons of Joktan
1Ki 9:28 to go to *O* and take from
10:11 that carried gold from *O*
10:11 from *O* timbers of almug
22:48 Tarshish ships to go to *O*
1Ch 1:23 *O* . . . sons of Joktan
29:4 of gold of the gold of *O*
2Ch 8:18 with Solomon's servants to *O*
9:10 gold from *O* brought timbers
Job 22:24 And gold of *O* in the rock of
28:16 be paid for with gold of *O*
Ps 45:9 her stand . . . in gold of *O*
Isa 13:12 rarer than the gold of *O*

Ophni
Jos 18:24 and *O* and Geba

Ophrah
Jos 18:23 and Avvim and Parah and *O*
Jg 6:11 the big tree that was in *O*
6:24 yet in *O* of the Abi-ezrites
8:27 to exhibit it in his city *O*
8:32 in *O* of the Abi-ezrites
9:5 house of his father at *O* and
1Sa 13:17 road to *O*, to the land of
1Ch 4:14 he became father to *O*

Opinion
Mt 26:66 What is your *o*?
Lu 3:23 son, as the *o* was, of Joseph
Joh 11:56 What is your *o*? That he
Ac 19:26 and turned them to another *o*
1Co 7:25 I give my *o* as one who had
7:40 as she is, according to my *o*
2Co 8:10 I render an *o*: for this

Opinions
1Ki 18:21 upon two different *o*

Opponent-at-law
Job 9:15 Of my *o* I would implore

Opponents
Ps 35:1 my case . . . against my *o*
Jer 18:19 listen to the voice of my *o*
Php 1:28 being frightened by your *o*

Opportune
Ac 24:25 when I get an *o* time I shall
Eph 5:16 buying out the *o* time for
Col 4:5 buying out the *o* time for

Opportunity
Jg 14:4 an *o* against the Philistines
1Ch 17:17 the *o* of the man in the
Mt 26:16 a good *o* to betray him
Lu 22:6 good *o* to betray him to them
1Co 7:21 free, rather seize the *o*
16:12 come when he has the *o*
Php 4:10 but you lacked *o*
Heb 11:15 would have had *o* to return

Oppose
Jas 4:7 *o* the Devil, and he will flee

Opposed
Ga 5:17 these are *o* to each other

Opposer
1Ti 5:14 give no inducement to the *o*

Opposers
Ex 32:25 a disgrace among their *o*
Lu 13:17 his *o* began to feel shame
21:15 all your *o* together will not
1Co 16:9 but there are many *o*

Opposes
Ro 13:2 he who *o* the authority has
Jas 4:6 God *o* the haughty ones, but
1Pe 5:5 God *o* the haughty ones, but

Opposing
Ac 13:8 began *o* them, seeking to turn
18:6 *o* and speaking abusively, he
Tit 2:8 man on the *o* side may get
Jas 5:6 Is he not *o* you?

Opposite
Ex 26:5 loops being *o* one to the other
26:35 the lampstand *o* the table on
30:4 upon two *o* sides of it, as
36:12 loops being *o* one another
37:27 upon two *o* sides of it, as
1Ki 7:4 *o* an illumination opening in
7:5 *o* an illumination opening in
2Ki 3:22 Moabites from the *o* side
Ne 12:9 *o* them for guard duties
12:24 brothers *o* them to offer
Es 5:1 *o* the king's house, while the
5:1 *o* the entrance of the house
Isa 50:5 not turn in the *o* direction
Jer 38:22 retreated in the *o* direction
Eze 16:34 the *o* thing takes place
16:34 so it occurs in the *o* way
40:23 was *o* the gate to the north
42:3 gallery *o* gallery in three
Mr 5:21 in the boat to the *o* shore a
6:45 the *o* shore toward Bethsaida
8:13 and went off to the *o* shore
Lu 8:26 is on the side *o* Galilee
10:31 he went by on the *o* side
10:32 went by on the *o* side
Ac 20:15 we arrived *o* Chios, but the

Opposition
Ge 10:9 mighty hunter in *o* to Jehovah
10:9 Nimrod a mighty hunter in *o*
Le 26:21 *o* to me and not wishing to
26:23 have to walk in *o* to me
26:24 walk in *o* to you; and I
26:27 just must walk in *o* to me
26:28 heated *o* to you, and I, yes
26:40 when they walked in *o* to me
26:41 walk in *o* to them, and I had
Job 33:10 Occasions for *o* to me he
Pr 21:30 any counsel in *o* to Jehovah
Da 10:13 standing in *o* to me for
Ac 17:7 in *o* to the decrees of Caesar
26:9 to commit many acts of *o*
Col 2:14 and which was in *o* to us
2Th 2:4 He is set in *o* and lifts
1Ti 1:10 *o* to the healthful teaching
Heb 10:27 to consume those in *o*

Oppress
Ex 1:12 more they would *o* them, the

Ex 22:21 an alien resident or *o* him
23:9 must not *o* an alien resident
Ps 106:42 their enemies might *o* them
Jer 7:6 no widow you will *o*, and
Am 6:14 they must *o* you people from
Jas 2:6 The rich *o* you, and they drag

Oppressed
Jg 4:3 and he himself *o* the sons of
10:8 heavily *o* the sons of Israel
10:12 when they *o* you and you went
2Ki 13:4 the king of Syria had *o* them
13:22 he *o* Israel all the days of
Ec 4:1 *o*, but they had no comforter
Isa 23:12 never again exult, O *o* one
52:4 Assyria, for its part, *o*
Jer 50:33 sons of Judah are being *o*
Ho 5:11 Ephraim is *o*, crushed in
Ac 10:38 all those *o* by the Devil

Oppressing
Ex 1:11 for the purpose of *o* them
3:9 which the Egyptians are *o* them
1Sa 10:18 kingdoms that were *o* you
Ps 56:1 all day long, he keeps *o* me

Oppression
Ex 3:9 I have seen also the *o* with
De 26:7 our trouble and our *o*
2Ki 13:4 had seen the *o* upon Israel
Job 36:15 uncover their ear in the *o*
Ps 10:7 and of deceptions and of *o*
42:9 because of the *o* of the enemy
43:2 because of the *o* by the enemy
44:24 our affliction and our *o*
55:11 *o* and deception have not
72:14 From *o* and from violence he
Ec 4:1 I might see all the acts of *o*
5:8 *o* of the one of little means
7:7 *o* may make a wise one act
Isa 14:4 the *o* come to a stop
30:20 water in the form of *o*
38:14 O Jehovah, I am under *o*
54:14 will be far away from *o*
59:13 a speaking of *o* and revolt
Jer 6:6 She is nothing but *o* in the

Oppressions
Job 35:9 the multitude of *o* they
Pr 29:13 and the man of *o* have met

Oppressive
Jg 18:7 was no *o* conqueror that was
Zep 3:1 polluting herself, the *o* city
Ac 20:29 *o* wolves will enter in

Oppressively
Ps 71:4 one acting unjustly and *o*

Oppressor
Nu 10:9 the *o* who is harassing you
Isa 1:17 set right the *o*
16:4 *o* has reached his end

Oppressors
Ge 14:20 who has delivered your *o*
Nu 24:8 consume the nations, his *o*
Jg 2:18 groaning because of their *o*
6:9 your *o* and drove them out from
Ec 4:1 of their *o* there was power
Isa 19:20 to Jehovah because of the *o*
Jer 30:20 attention upon all his *o*

Oral
Ga 6:6 one who gives such *o* teaching

Orally
Lu 1:4 that you have been taught *o*
Ac 18:25 *o* instructed in the way of
Ro 2:18 *o* instructed out of the Law
1Co 14:19 also instruct others *o*, than
Ga 6:6 *o* taught the word share in

Orbits
Jg 5:20 From their *o* they fought

Orchard
2Ki 19:23 the forest of its *o*
Isa 10:18 *o* He will bring to an end
16:10 taken away from the *o*
29:17 turned into an *o* and the
29:17 *o* itself will be accounted
32:15 will have become an *o*, and
32:15 *o* itself is accounted as
32:16 in the *o* righteousness
37:24 the forest of its *o*
Jer 2:7 land of the *o*, to eat its
4:26 *o* itself was a wilderness
48:33 taken away from the *o* and
Mic 7:14 in the midst of an *o*

Ordain
1Co 7:17 I *o* in all the congregations

Ordained
1Ch 9:22 David and Samuel the seer *o*
1Co 9:14 the Lord *o* for those

Order
Ge 3:22 now in *o* that he may not put
4:15 in *o* that no one finding him
12:13 in *o* that it may go well
14:8 they drew up in battle *o*
14:23 in *o* that you may not say
18:19 in *o* that he may command his
18:19 in *o* that Jehovah may
22:9 set the wood in *o* and bound
24:63 walking in *o* to meditate in
27:4 let me eat, in *o* that my soul
27:10 in *o* that he may bless you
27:19 *o* that your soul may bless
27:31 in *o* that your soul may
31:18 in *o* to go to Isaac his
33:8 In *o* to find favor in the eyes
37:22 in *o* to return him to his
38:20 in *o* to get back the security
38:23 in *o* that we may not fall
41:36 in *o* that the land may not
45:7 in *o* to place a remnant for
46:34 in *o* that you may dwell in
Ex 4:5 In *o* that . . . they may believe
6:13 *o* to bring the sons of Israel
8:9 in *o* to cut the frogs off from
8:10 in *o* that you may know that
8:18 in *o* to bring forth gnats, but
8:22 in *o* that you may know that
9:16 in *o* to have my name declared
9:29 in *o* that you may know that
10:1 in *o* that I may set these
10:2 in *o* that you may declare in
11:7 in *o* that you people may know
11:9 in *o* for my miracles to be
12:33 in *o* to send them away
13:9 in *o* that Jehovah's law may
16:4 in *o* that I may put them to
16:32 in *o* that they may see the
17:1 according to the *o* of Jehovah
17:10 in *o* to fight against the
19:9 in *o* that the people may hear
20:12 in *o* that your days may
20:20 in *o* that the fear of him
23:2 crowd in *o* to pervert justice
23:12 in *o* that your bull and your
24:12 write in *o* to teach them
25:14 in *o* to carry the Ark with
27:20 in *o* to light up the lamps
27:21 set it in *o* from evening
28:10 in the *o* of their births
29:33 in *o* to sanctify them
30:15 in *o* to give Jehovah's
30:20 to minister in *o* to make an
32:12 in *o* to kill . . . exterminate
33:13 that I may know you, in *o*
36:1 in *o* to know how to do all
36:2 approach the work in *o* to do
39:31 in *o* to put it upon the
40:4 set its arrangement in *o*
Le 1:7 and set wood in *o* on the fire
1:8 must set the pieces in *o* with
1:12 priest must set them in *o*
6:12 set the burnt offering in *o*
10:10 in *o* to make a distinction
10:11 in *o* to teach the sons of
10:15 in *o* to wave the wave
11:47 in *o* to make a distinction
13:59 in *o* to pronounce it clean or
14:21 wave offering in *o* to make
14:29 in *o* to make atonement for
14:57 in *o* to give instructions
16:34 *o* to make atonement for the
17:5 in *o* that the sons of Israel
18:17 in *o* to lay her nakedness
19:25 eat its fruit in *o* to add its
19:29 in *o* that the land may not
20:14 *o* that loose conduct may not
22:21 in *o* to pay a vow or as a
22:21 in *o* to gain approval
23:43 *o* that your generations may
24:3 *o* from evening to morning
24:4 the lamps in *o* before Jehovah
24:8 in *o* before Jehovah constantly
26:1 in *o* to bow down toward it
26:45 *o* to prove myself their God
Nu 3:16 at the *o* of Jehovah
3:39 registered at the *o* of Jehovah
3:51 according to the *o* of Jehovah
Nu 4:27 *o* of Aaron and his sons all
4:37 registered at the *o* of Jehovah
4:41 registered at the *o* of Jehovah
4:45 registered at the *o* of Jehovah
4:49 At the *o* of Jehovah they were
9:18 *o* of Jehovah the sons of
9:18 *o* of Jehovah they would
9:20 *o* of Jehovah they would
9:20 at the *o* of Jehovah they
9:23 *o* of Jehovah they would
9:23 *o* of Jehovah they would pull
9:23 at the *o* of Jehovah by means
10:13 to the *o* of Jehovah
13:3 at the *o* of Jehovah. All the
14:41 beyond the *o* of Jehovah
15:3 in *o* to make a restful odor
15:41 in *o* to prove myself your
20:24 my *o* respecting the waters
22:18 pass beyond the *o* of Jehovah
22:23 strike the ass in *o* to turn
23:11 in *o* to execrate my enemies
24:13 pass beyond the *o* of Jehovah
27:14 rebelled against my *o* in the
27:20 in *o* that all the assembly
27:21 At his *o* they will go out
27:21 at his *o* they will come in
31:50 in *o* to make atonement for
32:14 in *o* to add further to the
33:2 stages at the *o* of Jehovah
33:38 at the *o* of Jehovah and to
36:5 at the *o* of Jehovah, saying
36:8 in *o* that the sons of Israel
De 1:26 the *o* of Jehovah your God
1:43 against Jehovah's *o* and to
2:30 in *o* to give him into your
4:1 in *o* that you may live and may
4:40 in *o* that you may lengthen
5:14 in *o* that your slave man and
5:16 in *o* that your days may
5:29 in *o* that it might go well
5:33 in *o* that you may live and it
6:2 in *o* that you may fear Jehovah
6:2 in *o* that your days may prove
6:18 in *o* that it may go well
6:23 in *o* that he might bring us
8:1 in *o* that you may continue
8:2 in *o* to humble you, to put
8:3 in *o* to make you know that
8:16 in *o* to humble you and in
8:16 in *o* to put you to the test
8:18 in *o* to carry out his covenant
9:5 in *o* to carry out the word
9:23 against the *o* of Jehovah your
11:8 in *o* that you may grow strong
11:9 in *o* that you may lengthen
11:21 in *o* that your days and the
12:25 in *o* that it may go well
12:28 in *o* that it may go well
13:17 in *o* that Jehovah may turn
14:23 in *o* that you may learn to
14:29 in *o* that Jehovah your God
16:20 in *o* that you may keep alive
17:16 in *o* to increase horses
17:19 in *o* that he may learn to
17:20 in *o* that he may lengthen
20:18 in *o* that they may not teach
22:7 in *o* that it may go well
23:20 in *o* that Jehovah your God
24:19 in *o* that Jehovah your God
25:15 in *o* that your days may
27:3 in *o* that you may enter into
29:6 in *o* that you might know that
29:9 and do them, in *o* that you
29:12 in *o* for you to enter into
30:19 in *o* that you may keep alive
31:12 in *o* that they may listen
31:12 in *o* that they may learn, as
31:19 in *o* that this song may
34:5 at the *o* of Jehovah
Jos 1:7 in *o* that you may act wisely
1:8 in *o* that you may take care
1:18 against your *o* and does not
3:4 in *o* that you may know the
4:6 in *o* that this may serve as a
4:24 in *o* that all the peoples of
4:24 in *o* that you may indeed
11:20 in *o* that he might devote
11:20 *o* that he might annihilate
15:13 the *o* of Jehovah to Joshua
17:4 at the *o* of Jehovah
19:50 *o* of Jehovah they gave him
21:3 at the *o* of Jehovah, these
22:9 settled at the *o* of Jehovah
Jg 2:22 in *o* by them to test Israel

Jg 3:2 it was only in *o* for the
1Sa 12:14 against the *o* of Jehovah
12:15 against the *o* of Jehovah
15:24 overstepped the *o* of Jehovah
2Sa 13:5 *o* that I may see it, and I
13:32 at the *o* of Absalom it has
17:14 in *o* that Jehovah might
18:18 no son in *o* to keep my name
23:5 put in *o* in everything and
1Ki 2:3 *o* that you may act prudently
2:4 in *o* that Jehovah may carry
8:43 in *o* that all the peoples of
11:36 in *o* that David my servant
12:15 in *o* that he might indeed
13:21 against the *o* of Jehovah
13:26 against the *o* of Jehovah
17:1 except at the *o* of my word
18:33 put the pieces of wood in *o*
2Ki 22:17 in *o* to offend me with all
23:24 in *o* that he might actually
23:35 silver at the *o* of Pharaoh
24:3 only by the *o* of Jehovah
1Ch 12:17 see to it and set it in *o*
12:23 according to Jehovah's *o*
28:8 in *o* that you may possess
2Ch 6:33 in *o* that all the peoples of
10:15 *o* that Jehovah might carry
31:4 *o* that they might adhere
31:13 *o* of Hezekiah the king
32:18 *o* that they might capture
34:25 in *o* to offend me with all
36:12 at the *o* of Jehovah
Ezr 4:19 *o* has been put through by me
4:21 put an *o* through for these
4:21 the *o* is put through by me
5:3 Who put an *o* through to you
5:9 Who put an *o* through to you
5:13 put an *o* through to rebuild
5:17 from Cyrus the king an *o* was
6:1 Darius the king put an *o*
6:3 the king put an *o* through
6:8 an *o* has been put through as
6:11 an *o* has been put through
6:12 Darius, do put through an *o*
6:14 the *o* of the God of Israel
6:14 due to the *o* of Cyrus and
7:13 an *o* has been put through
7:14 an *o* was sent to investigate
7:21 an *o* has been put through
7:23 *o* of the God of the heavens
9:12 *o* that you may grow strong
Ne 6:13 in *o* that I might be afraid
6:13 in *o* that they might reproach
Job 19:29 In *o* that you men may know
39:27 at your *o* that an eagle
40:8 pronounce me wicked in *o*
Ps 9:14 In *o* that I may declare all
30:12 In *o* that my glory may make
48:13 In *o* that you may recount it
50:21 set things in *o* before your
51:4 In *o* that you may prove to be
60:5 In *o* that your beloved ones
68:23 In *o* that you may wash your
78:6 In *o* that the generation to
108:6 In *o* that your beloved ones
119:11 *o* that I may not sin
119:71 *o* that I may learn your
119:80 *o* that I may not be ashamed
125:3 *o* that the righteous ones
130:4 In *o* that you may be feared
132:17 set in *o* a lamp for my
Pr 8:29 should not pass beyond his *o*
9:2 it has set in *o* its table
15:24 in *o* to turn away from Sheol
19:20 *o* that you may become wise
Ec 8:2 Keep the very *o* of the king
12:9 arrange many proverbs in *o*
Isa 2:21 *o* to enter into the holes in
5:19 in *o* that we may see it
9:7 kingdom in *o* to establish it
10:2 *o* to push away the lowly
13:9 in *o* to make the land an
14:9 in *o* to meet you on coming
14:25 in *o* to break the Assyrian
20:6 *o* to be delivered because
21:5 setting of the table in *o*
23:16 in *o* that you may be
27:3 *o* that no one may turn his
28:13 *o* that they may go and
28:22 *o* that your bands may not
28:24 plows in *o* to sow seed
30:1 in *o* to add sin to sin
30:33 Topheth is set in *o* from
36:18 in *o* that Hezekiah may not
Isa 41:20 in *o* that people may see
43:10 in *o* that you may know and
43:26 in *o* that you may be in the
44:9 *o* that they may be ashamed
45:3 in *o* that you may know that
45:6 in *o* that people may know
49:5 in *o* that to him Israel
51:16 in *o* to plant the heavens
56:2 sabbath in *o* not to profane
56:2 in *o* not to do any kind of
56:6 in *o* to become servants to
56:6 sabbath in *o* not to profane
60:9 in *o* to bring your sons from
60:11 in *o* to bring to you the
60:13 in *o* to beautify the place
63:12 *o* to make an indefinitely
63:14 in *o* to make a beautiful
64:2 *o* to make your name known
65:8 in *o* not to bring everybody
65:11 those setting in *o* a table
66:15 in *o* to pay back his anger
66:18 coming in *o* to collect all
Jer 1:10 in *o* to uproot and to pull
1:12 my word in *o* to carry it out
1:17 in *o* that I may not strike
2:13 in *o* to hew out for
2:18 in *o* to drink the waters of
2:18 in *o* to drink the waters of
2:33 in *o* to look for love
4:7 in *o* to render your land as
4:14 in *o* that you may be saved
6:23 battle *o* like a man of war
7:18 in *o* to make sacrificial
7:23 in *o* that it may go well
7:30 in *o* to defile it
7:31 in *o* to burn their sons and
9:21 in *o* to cut off the child
10:18 in *o* that they may find out
10:22 in *o* to make the cities of
11:10 gods in *o* to serve them
13:10 in *o* to serve them and to
13:11 in *o* to become to me a
17:23 in *o* not to hear and in
17:23 *o* to receive no discipline
18:16 in *o* to make their land
19:5 in *o* to burn their sons in
19:15 in *o* not to obey my words
20:18 in *o* to see hard work and
22:17 in *o* to shed it, and upon
22:17 in *o* to carry them on
23:14 in *o* that they should not
25:6 gods in *o* to serve them
26:24 in *o* not to give him into
29:26 in *o* to become the grand
30:21 in *o* to approach to me
32:14 in *o* that they may last
32:19 in *o* to give to each one
32:31 *o* to remove it from before
32:34 in *o* to defile it
32:35 *o* to make their sons and
32:39 in *o* to fear me always
32:40 *o* not to turn aside from
33:20 *o* for day and night not to
34:9 *o* not to use them as
34:10 *o* to use them no more as
35:7 *o* that you may keep living
39:7 in *o* to bring him to Babylon
39:14 in *o* to bring him forth
40:10 in *o* to stand before the
41:17 in *o* to go on and enter
42:11 I am with you, in *o* to save
42:13 *o* to disobey the voice of
43:5 in *o* to reside for a while
44:3 *o* to offend me by going and
44:7 *o* to cut off from yourselves
44:14 to return in *o* to dwell
44:17 in *o* to make sacrificial
44:19 *o* to make an image of her
44:29 *o* that you may know that
49:8 Go down deep in *o* to dwell
49:30 go down deep in *o* to dwell
50:34 *o* that he may actually give
51:11 in *o* to bring her to ruin
51:39 in *o* that they may exult
51:62 place, in *o* to cut it off
La 1:11 eat, in *o* to refresh the soul
1:15 in *o* to break my young men to
2:14 *o* to turn back your captivity
5:6 in *o* to get satisfaction with
Eze 3:18 in *o* to warn the wicked one
6:6 desolated, in *o* that they may
11:20 in *o* that they may walk in
12:12 in *o* to do the bringing
12:12 in *o* that he may not see
Eze 12:16 in *o* that they may recount
12:19 in *o* that its land may be
13:5 in *o* to stand in the battle
13:18 in *o* to hunt souls! Are the
13:19 in *o* to put to death the
13:19 in *o* to preserve alive the
13:22 in *o* to preserve him alive
14:11 in *o* that those of the house
14:19 in *o* to cut off from it
14:21 in *o* to cut off from it
16:26 abound in *o* to offend me
16:54 in *o* that you may bear your
16:63 in *o* that you may remember
17:7 in *o* for him to irrigate it
17:8 in *o* to produce boughs and to
17:14 in *o* that the kingdom might
17:17 in *o* to cut off many souls
18:9 he kept in *o* to execute truth
19:9 in *o* that his voice might no
20:3 Is it in *o* to inquire of me
20:8 in *o* to bring my anger to
20:11 in *o* that the man who keeps
20:12 in *o* for them to know that
20:13 in *o* to exterminate them
20:21 in *o* to bring my anger to
20:26 *o* that I might make them
20:26 in *o* that they might know
21:4 In *o* that I may actually cut
21:11 *o* to wield it with the hand
21:11 in *o* to give it into the
21:15 In *o* for the heart to melt
21:15 in *o* to multiply those who
21:21 in *o* to resort to divination
21:23 in *o* for them to be caught
21:24 in *o* that your sins may be
21:28 to devour, in *o* to glitter
21:29 in *o* to put you on the necks
22:3 in *o* to become unclean
22:20 in *o* to blow upon it with
22:30 in *o* for me not to bring
23:41 a table set in *o* before
24:7 in *o* to cover it over with
24:8 In *o* to bring up rage for
24:8 *o* that it may not be covered
24:11 in *o* that it may get hot
25:10 in *o* that it may not be
25:15 in *o* to cause ruin, with
26:20 in *o* that you may not be
27:7 in *o* for it to serve as your
27:9 in *o* to exchange articles of
30:9 in *o* to drive self-confident
30:21 in *o* to give it healing by
36:3 in *o* for you to become a
36:30 in *o* that you may no more
38:12 in *o* to turn your hand back
38:13 in *o* to carry off silver
39:14 earth, in *o* to cleanse it
41:6 in *o* that they might be held
43:11 in *o* that they may observe
43:18 in *o* to offer upon it
44:3 in *o* to eat bread before
44:7 in *o* to come to be in my
44:24 should stand in *o* to judge
44:30 *o* to cause a blessing to
45:15 *o* to make atonement for
45:17 *o* to make atonement in
46:9 in *o* to bow down should go
46:20 *o* to carry nothing out to
Da 2:13 *o* itself went out, and the
2:15 harsh *o* on the part of the
2:18 *o* that they might not destroy
3:20 in *o* to throw them into the
3:29 *o* is being put through, that
4:6 *o* was being put through to
6:2 in *o* that these satraps might
6:8 in *o* for it not to be changed
6:14 set his mind in *o* to rescue
6:17 in *o* that nothing should be
6:26 put through an *o* that, in
7:26 *o* to annihilate him and to
9:3 *o* to seek him with prayer and
9:24 in *o* to terminate the
11:6 in *o* to make an equitable
11:35 in *o* to do a refining
11:44 rage in *o* to annihilate and
Ho 8:11 multiplied altars in *o* to sin
8:11 have altars in *o* to sin
Joe 2:5 people, drawn up in battle *o*
3:12 in *o* to judge all the
Am 2:10 in *o* to take possession of
4:8 one city in *o* to drink water
6:10 in *o* to bring out the bones
8:4 in *o* to cause the meek ones
8:5 in *o* to make the ephah small

Am 8:6 in *o* to buy lowly people for
Ob 14 in *o* to cut off his escapees
21 in *o* to judge the mountainous
Jon 1:3 in *o* to go with them to
1:5 in *o* to lighten it of them
1:11 in *o* that the sea may become
1:13 in *o* to bring the ship back
4:6 in *o* to become a shade over
Mic 3:8 in *o* to tell to Jacob his
Hab 1:6 in *o* to take possession of
2:2 in *o* that the one reading
2:9 in *o* to set his nest on the
2:15 in *o* to make them drunk, for
Zep 3:8 in *o* to pour out upon them
3:9 in *o* for them all to call
3:9 in *o* to serve him shoulder to
Zec 1:21 Judah, in *o* to disperse her
2:2 in *o* to see what her breadth
3:1 right hand in *o* to resist him
5:11 In *o* to build for her a house
6:7 in *o* to walk about in the
11:10 in *o* to break my covenant
11:14 *o* to break the brotherhood
Mal 2:4 in *o* that my covenant with
4:6 in *o* that I may not come and
Mt 3:13 to John, in *o* to be baptized
6:1 in *o* to be observed by them
9:6 in *o* for you to know that the
10:1 in *o* to expel these and to
18:16 in *o* that at the mouth of
19:16 in *o* to get everlasting life
22:15 *o* to trap him in his speech
25:7 rose and put their lamps in *o*
26:5 in *o* that no uproar may arise
26:59 in *o* to put him to death
Mr 2:10 But in *o* for you men to know
3:2 in *o* that they might accuse
3:6 in *o* to destroy him
4:12 in *o* that, though looking
6:12 in *o* that people might repent
7:9 in *o* to retain your tradition
8:15 to *o* them expressly and say
9:25 spirit, I *o* you, get out of
11:25 in *o* that your Father who is
13:36 in *o* that when he arrives
14:10 in *o* to betray him to them
14:38 in *o* that you do not come
14:49 in *o* that the Scriptures may
16:1 in *o* to come and grease him
Lu 1:3 to write them in logical *o*
2:35 in *o* that the reasonings of
4:29 in *o* to throw him down
5:24 in *o* for you to know that
6:7 *o* to find some way to accuse
8:10 in *o* that, though looking
8:12 *o* that they may not believe
8:31 to *o* them to go away into the
16:28 in *o* that he may give them
19:4 climbed . . . tree in *o* to see
19:15 in *o* to ascertain what they
20:20 in *o* that they might catch
Joh 1:7 in *o* to bear witness about
3:16 in *o* that everyone exercising
3:20 in *o* that his works may not
3:21 in *o* that his works may be
5:14 in *o* that something worse
5:20 in *o* that you may marvel
5:23 in *o* that all may honor the
6:30 in *o* for us to see it and
7:3 in *o* that your disciples also
7:23 in *o* that the law of Moses
9:3 *o* that the works of God might
10:17 I surrender my soul, in *o*
10:38 *o* that you may come to know
11:4 *o* that the Son of God may
11:15 in *o* for you to believe
11:19 in *o* to console them
11:42 *o* that they might believe
11:52 *o* that the children of God
11:55 *o* to cleanse themselves
11:57 in *o* that they might seize
12:36 *o* to become sons of light
12:42 *o* not to be expelled from
12:46 in *o* that everyone putting
13:18 *o* that the Scripture might
13:19 *o* that when it does occur
14:13 *o* that the Father may be
14:29 *o* that, when it does occur
14:31 *o* for the world to know
15:16 *o* that no matter what you
17:11 *o* that they may be one just
17:12 *o* that the scripture might
17:13 *o* that they may have my
17:21 *o* that they may all be one
Joh 17:21 *o* that the world may
17:22 *o* that they may be one just
17:23 in *o* that they may be
17:24 *o* to behold my glory that
17:26 *o* that the love with which
18:9 *o* that the word might be
18:32 *o* that the word of Jesus
19:4 *o* for you to know I find no
19:28 *o* that the scripture might
19:31 *o* that the bodies might
19:35 *o* that you also may believe
19:36 in *o* for the scripture to
Ac 3:2 in *o* to ask gifts of mercy
4:17 *o* that it may not be spread
4:28 *o* to do what things your hand
5:15 *o* that, as Peter would go by
9:2 *o* that he might bring bound to
9:17 *o* that you may recover sight
9:24 in *o* to do away with him
15:17 in *o* that those who remain
16:18 I *o* you in the name of Jesus
16:24 Because he got such an *o*, he
20:16 sail past Ephesus, in *o* that
25:26 in *o* that, after the judicial
26:16 in *o* to choose you as an
26:18 in *o* for them to receive
Ro 1:5 in *o* that there might be
1:11 in *o* for you to be made firm
1:13 in *o* that I might acquire
3:25 in *o* to exhibit his own
4:11 in *o* for righteousness to be
4:16 in *o* for the promise to be
5:20 in *o* that trespassing might
6:4 baptism into his death, in *o*
9:11 in *o* that the purpose of God
9:23 in *o* that he might make
11:25 in *o* for you not to be
15:16 in *o* that the offering
15:20 in *o* that I might not be
1Co 1:29 in *o* that no flesh might
4:6 in *o* that you may not be
5:2 rather mourn, in *o* that the
5:5 in *o* that the spirit may be
9:12 in *o* that we might not offer
10:13 in *o* for you to be able to
10:33 in *o* that they might get
11:34 set in *o* when I get there
2Co 1:11 in *o* that thanks may be
4:15 in *o* that the undeserved
8:11 in *o* that, just as there was
8:14 in *o* that their surplus
11:8 in *o* to minister to you
12:6 in *o* that no one should put
Ga 2:5 in *o* that the truth of the good
3:10 of the Law in *o* to do them
Eph 2:9 in *o* that no man should have
3:18 in *o* that you may be
4:14 *o* that we should no longer
6:21 Now in *o* that you may also
Php 1:27 in *o* that, whether I come
2:13 in *o* for you both to will
Col 1:10 in *o* to walk worthily of
1:22 in *o* to present you holy and
2:5 beholding your good *o* and
1Th 3:2 in *o* to make you firm and
2Th 1:12 in *o* that the name of our
2:12 in *o* that they all may be
3:4 go on doing the things we *o*
3:9 in *o* that we might offer
3:10 we used to give you this *o*
3:12 the *o* and exhortation in the
1Ti 2:2 *o* that we may go on leading
3:7 in *o* that he might not fall
6:19 in *o* that they may get a
2Ti 2:4 in *o* that he may gain the
Tit 3:8 in *o* that those who have
Phm 6 in *o* that the sharing of your
8 to *o* you to do what is proper
Heb 2:17 in *o* to offer propitiatory
6:12 in *o* that you may not become
6:18 in *o* that, through two
9:15 in *o* that, because a death
9:25 in *o* that he should offer
10:36 in *o* that, after you have
11:3 put in *o* by God's word, so
11:23 not fear the *o* of the king
11:35 in *o* that they might attain
11:40 in *o* that they might not be
12:27 in *o* that the things not
1Pe 1:7 in *o* that the tested quality
2:24 in *o* that we might be done
3:1 husbands, in *o* that, if any are
3:7 in *o* for your prayers not to
Re 8:12 in *o* that a third of them

Ordered
2Ch 24:6 sacred tax *o* by Moses the
24:9 sacred tax *o* by Moses the
Mt 18:25 master *o* him and his wife
21:6 and did just as Jesus *o* them
26:19 the disciples did as Jesus *o*
Mr 5:43 he *o* them again and again to
9:9 *o* them not to relate to
Lu 8:55 he *o* something to be given
14:22 Master, what you *o* has been
Ac 5:28 positively *o* you not to keep
5:40 *o* them to stop speaking upon
10:42 he *o* us to preach to the
18:2 Claudius had *o* all the Jews
22:24 military commander *o* him to
23:2 high priest Ananias *o* those
24:23 he *o* the army officer that
1Th 4:11 work . . . just as we *o* you

Ordering
Ne 8:11 *o* all the people to be silent
Lu 8:29 *o* the unclean spirit to come
Ac 16:23 *o* the jailer to keep them
23:22 after *o* him: Do not blab to

Orderly
Ac 21:24 that you are walking *o*, you
Ro 4:12 walk *o* in the footsteps of
Ga 5:25 on walking *o* also by spirit
6:16 *o* by this rule of conduct
Php 3:16 go on walking *o* in this same
1Ti 3:2 sound in mind, *o*, hospitable

Orders
Ge 45:21 according to Pharaoh's *o*
Le 14:36 give *o*, and they must clear
14:40 give *o*, and they must tear
1Ch 12:32 brothers were at their *o*
Ps 19:8 *o* from Jehovah are upright
103:18 remembering his *o* so as to
111:7 Trustworthy are all the *o* he
119:4 commandingly given your *o*
119:15 With your *o* I will concern
119:27 the way of your own *o*
119:40 I have longed for your *o*
119:45 searched even for your *o*
119:56 your *o* I have observed
119:63 And of those keeping your *o*
119:69 heart I shall observe your *o*
119:78 concern myself with your *o*
119:87 did not leave your *o*
119:93 I shall not forget your *o*
119:94 searched for your own *o*
119:100 have observed your own *o*
119:104 Owing to your *o* I behave
119:110 *o* I have not wandered
119:128 *o* regarding all things to
119:134 And I will keep your *o*
119:141 Your *o* I have not forgotten
119:159 I have loved your own *o*
119:168 I have kept your *o* and
119:173 your *o* I have chosen
Isa 54:15 it will not be at my *o*
Mt 10:5 sent . . . giving them these *o*
Mr 1:27 *o* even the unclean spirits
1:43 he gave him strict *o* and at
6:8 gave them *o* to carry nothing
Lu 4:36 he *o* the unclean spirits, and
5:14 he gave the man *o* to tell
8:25 for he *o* even the winds and
Joh 11:57 Pharisees had given *o* that
Ac 1:4 he gave them the *o*: Do not
7:44 gave *o* when speaking to
23:31 Paul according to their *o*
1Co 16:1 *o* to the congregations of
1Th 4:2 you know the *o* we gave you
2Th 3:6 giving you *o*, brothers, in the
1Ti 6:13 I give you *o*
6:17 Give *o* to those who are rich
Tit 1:5 as I gave you *o*

Ordinances
Heb 9:1 *o* of sacred service and its

Ordinary
Jg 16:7 and become like an *o* man
16:11 and become like an *o* man
1Sa 21:4 There is no *o* bread under my
21:5 the mission itself is *o*
Ac 4:13 were men unlettered and *o*
1Co 14:16 *o* person say Amen to your
14:23 *o* people or unbelievers
14:24 or *o* person comes in, he is
Heb 10:29 esteemed as of *o* value the

Ore
Job 22:24 precious *o* in the dust And

Oreb
Jg 7:25 *O* and Zeeb; and they proceeded
7:25, 25 to kill *O* on the rock of *O*
7:25 brought the head of *O* and that
8:3 Midian's princes *O* and Zeeb
Ps 83:11 make these like *O* and like
Isa 10:26 Midian by the rock *O*

Oren
1Ch 2:25 sons of Jerahmeel . . . *O*

Ores
Job 22:25 become your precious *o*

Organ
Le 15:2 genital *o*, his discharge is
15:3 his genital *o* has flowed with
15:3 genital *o* is obstructed from
Isa 57:8 The male *o* you beheld
Eze 23:20 whose genital *o* is as the
23:20 genital *o* of male horses

Organism
1Sa 21:5 one becomes holy in his *o*
Ps 73:26 *o* and my heart have failed
Pr 5:11 and your *o* come to an end
11:17 ostracism upon his own *o*
14:30 is the life of the fleshly *o*
Jer 51:35 done to me and to my *o*
Mic 3:2 their *o* from off their bones
3:3 also eaten the *o* of my people

Organisms
1Sa 21:5 *o* of the young men continue

Organized
Ex 38:8 did *o* service at the entrance
Pr 9:2 It has *o* its meat slaughtering

Organizing
Eze 21:10 purpose of *o* a slaughter

Orientals
Ge 29:1 on to the land of the *O*
1Ki 4:30 than the wisdom of all the *O*
Job 1:3 the greatest of all the *O*
Eze 25:4 I am giving you to the *O*
25:10 to the *O*, alongside the sons

Origin
Jg 5:14 Ephraim was their *o* in the
Ezr 2:59 their fathers and their *o*
Ne 7:61 their fathers and their *o*
Eze 16:3 Your *o* and your birth were
21:30 in the land of your *o*
29:14 to the land of their *o*
Mic 5:2 whose *o* is from early times

Original
Jude 6 not keep their *o* position but
Re 12:9 *o* serpent, the one called
20:2 dragon, the *o* serpent, who is

Originality
Joh 7:17 or I speak of my own *o*
7:18 He that speaks of his own *o*
11:51 did not say of his own *o*
14:10 not speak of my own *o*
18:34 own *o* that you say this, or

Originally
Ge 13:4 that he had made there *o*

Originate
1Jo 2:16 does not *o* with the Father
3:10 does not *o* with God, neither
3:19 that we *o* with the truth
4:1 see whether they *o* with God
4:3 does not *o* with God
4:4 *o* with God, little children
4:5 They *o* with the world; that
4:6 We *o* with God. He that gains
4:6 he that does not *o* with God
5:19 We know we *o* with God, but

Originated
2Sa 3:37 not *o* with the king to have
1Jo 3:12 Cain, who *o* with the wicked

Originates
Joh 4:22 salvation *o* with the Jews
1Jo 2:16 but *o* with the world
2:21 no lie *o* with the truth
3:8 sin *o* with the Devil, because
4:2 *o* with God
3Jo 11 He that does good *o* with God

Origins
Ge 25:13 sons of Ishmael . . . family *o*
1Ch 1:29 These are their family *o*

Ornament
Ge 49:26 *o* of the indefinitely lasting
Pr 25:12 *o* of special gold, is a wise
Jer 3:19 the *o* of the armies of the
Eze 7:20 And the decoration of one's *o*
16:7 come in with the finest *o*
Ho 2:13 with her ring and her *o* and
Mic 2:8 strip off the majestic *o*
Re 18:16 richly adorned with gold *o*

Ornamental
Ex 39:28 the *o* headgears of fine linen
Isa 3:20 and the *o* humming shells
61:10 decks . . . with her *o* things

Ornaments
Ex 33:4 none of them put his *o* on
33:5 put down your *o* off yourself
33:6 went stripping their *o* off
35:22 rings and female *o*, all sorts
Nu 31:50 female *o*, in order to make
Jg 8:21 *o* that were on the necks of
8:26 the moon-shaped *o* and the
2Sa 1:24 put *o* of gold upon your
1Ki 6:18 carvings of gourd-shaped *o*
7:17 twisted *o* in chainwork, for
7:24 gourd-shaped *o* down below
7:24 rows of the gourd-shaped *o*
2Ch 4:3 likeness of gourd-shaped *o*
4:3 gourd-shaped *o* were in two
Ca 7:1 of your thighs are like *o*
Isa 3:18 and the moon-shaped *o*
49:18 just as with *o*, and you
Jer 2:32 Can a virgin forget her *o*
4:30 deck yourself with *o* of gold
Eze 16:11 went on to deck you with *o*
23:40 and decked yourself with *o*
1Pe 3:3 of the putting on of gold *o*

Ornan
1Ch 21:15 floor of *O* the Jebusite
21:18 threshing floor of *O* the
21:20 *O* turned back and saw the
21:20 *O* had been threshing wheat
21:21 So David came as far as *O*
21:21 When *O* looked and saw David
21:22 David said to *O*: Do give me
21:23 *O* said to David: Take it as
21:24 King David said to *O*
21:25 David gave *O* for the place
21:28 floor of *O* the Jebusite
2Ch 3:1 on the threshing floor of *O*

Orpah
Ru 1:4 The name of the one was *O*, and
1:14 *O* kissed her mother-in-law

Orphans
La 5:3 mere *o* without a father
Jas 1:27 look after *o* and widows in

Osprey
Le 11:13 the eagle and the *o* and the
De 14:12 you must not eat . . . the *o*

Ostracism
Ge 34:30 you have brought *o* upon me
Jos 6:18 and bring *o* upon it
7:25 have you brought *o* upon us
7:25 will bring *o* upon you on
1Sa 14:29 has brought *o* upon the land
1Ki 18:17 bringer of *o* upon Israel
18:18 not brought *o* upon Israel
1Ch 2:7 the bringer of *o* upon Israel
Pr 11:17 cruel person is bringing *o*
11:29 *o* upon his own house
15:27 unjust profit is bringing *o*

Ostracized
Ps 39:2 And my being pained was *o*
Pr 15:6 there is a becoming *o*

Ostracizing
Jg 11:35 have become the one I was *o*

Ostrich
Le 11:16 the *o* and the owl and the
De 14:15 the *o* and the owl and the
Job 30:29 to the daughters of the *o*
39:13 female *o* flapped joyously

Ostriches
Isa 13:21 there the *o* must reside
34:13 the courtyard for the *o*
43:20 the jackals and the *o*
Jer 50:39 in her the *o* must dwell
La 4:3 like *o* in the wilderness
Mic 1:8 a mourning like female *o*

Othni
1Ch 26:7 The sons of Shemaiah, *O* and

Othniel
Jos 15:17 *O* the son of Kenaz, Caleb's
Jg 1:13 *O* the son of Kenaz, Caleb's
3:9 *O* the son of Kenaz, the
3:11 *O* the son of Kenaz died
1Ch 4:13 the sons of Kenaz were *O*
4:13 the sons of *O*, Hathath
27:15 the Netophathite, of *O*, and

Ought*
Ge 34:7 nothing like that *o* to be done
34:31 *O* anyone to treat our sister
Ex 4:12 teach you what you *o* to say
Pr 27:23 You *o* to know positively the
Mr 13:14 standing where it *o* not
Lu 12:12 the things you *o* to say
Joh 13:14 *o* to wash the feet of one
Ac 17:29 we *o* not to imagine that the
Ro 15:1 who are strong *o* to bear
1Co 9:10 *o* to plow in hope and the
9:10 man who threshes *o* to do so
11:7 a man *o* not to have his head
11:10 the woman *o* to have a sign
Heb 5:12 *o* to be teachers in view of
Jas 4:15 *o* to say: If Jehovah wills
2Pe 3:11 what sort of persons *o* you to

Out*
Le 23:43 *o* of the land of Egypt. I am
Nu 20:16 and brought us *o* of Egypt
32:11 men who came up *o* of Egypt
De 1:27 *o* of the land of Egypt to give
4:46 on their coming *o* of Egypt
8:11 Watch *o* for yourself that you
8:14 *o* of the house of slaves
9:26 *o* of Egypt with a strong hand
11:10 Egypt *o* of which you came
12:19 Watch *o* for yourself that
12:30 Watch *o* for yourself for
13:5 *o* of the land of Egypt and
Isa 40:31 will walk and not tire *o*
Mr 13:23 You, then, watch *o*; I have
Joh 10:9 will go in and *o* and find
2Co 6:13 children—you, too, widen *o*
Ga 4:4 who came to be *o* of a woman
Col 2:14 has taken it *o* of the way by
Jas 2:8 carrying *o* the kingly law

Outburst
Job 40:11 the furious *o* of your anger

Outbursts
Ps 7:6 the *o* of fury of those showing

Outcome
Mt 26:58 to see the *o*
Jas 5:11 have seen the *o* Jehovah gave

Outcries
Isa 65:14 *o* because of the pain of
Heb 5:7 with strong *o* and tears, and

Outcry
Ge 18:21 *o* over it that has come to
19:13 *o* against them has grown
Ex 3:7 and I have heard their *o* as a
3:9 the *o* of the sons of Israel has
11:6 *o* in all the land of Egypt
12:30 great *o* among the Egyptians
22:23 shall unfailingly hear his *o*
1Sa 4:14 to hear the sound of the *o*
9:16 for their *o* has come to me
Ne 5:1 a great *o* of the people and
5:6 heard their *o* and these words
9:9 *o* at the Red Sea you heard
Es 4:1 with a loud and bitter *o*
Job 16:18 to be no place for my *o*
27:9 Will God hear an *o* of his
34:28 the *o* of the lowly one to
34:28 *o* of the afflicted ones
Ps 9:12 the *o* of the afflicted ones
144:14 no *o* in our public squares
Isa 5:7 righteousness, but, look! an *o*
15:5 the *o* about the catastrophe
15:8 *o* has gone around the
24:11 *o* in the streets for want
30:19 favor at the sound of your *o*
44:23 with joyful *o*, you forest
49:13 cheerful with a glad *o*
51:11 to Zion with a joyful *o*
54:1 cheerful with a joyful *o* and
55:12 with a joyful *o*, and the
Jer 14:2 *o* of Jerusalem has gone up
20:16 hear an *o* in the morning
25:36 The *o* of the shepherds, and
46:12 own *o* has filled the land
48:3 of an *o* from Horonaim

Jer 48:5 distressing *o* over the
49:21 There is an *o!* The sound
50:46 *o* itself be heard
51:54 is an *o* from Babylon, and
Eze 27:28 the *o* of your sailors the
Zep 1:10 an *o* from the Fish Gate
Re 21:4 nor *o* nor pain be anymore

Outdoors
Ge 8:7 raven . . . continued flying *o*
De 32:25 *O* a sword will bereave them
Pr 7:12 Now she is *o*, now she is in

Outer
2Ki 16:18 and the king's *o* entryway
2Ch 33:14 built an *o* wall for the
Es 6:4 *o* courtyard of the king's house
Eze 10:5 heard to the *o* courtyard
40:17 into the *o* courtyard, and
40:20 the *o* courtyard had a gate
40:31 was to the *o* courtyard
40:34 toward the *o* courtyard
40:37 to the *o* courtyard were its
40:40 the *o* side, as one goes up
42:1 the *o* courtyard by the way
42:3 belonged to the *o* courtyard
42:7 toward the *o* courtyard
42:8 toward the *o* courtyard was
42:9 from the *o* courtyard
42:14 go . . . to the *o* courtyard
44:1 the *o* one facing east, and
44:19 go forth to the *o* courtyard
44:19 *o* courtyard to the people
46:20 out to the *o* courtyard so
46:21 *o* courtyard and make me
47:2 *o* gate that is facing toward
Mt 5:40 let your *o* garment also go to
9:16 cloth upon an old *o* garment
9:16 pull from the *o* garment and
9:20 the fringe of his *o* garment
9:21 If I only touch his *o* garment
14:36 the fringe of his *o* garment
17:2 *o* garments became brilliant
21:7 upon these their *o* garments
21:8 spread their *o* garments on
24:18 to pick up his *o* garment
26:65 priest ripped his *o* garments
27:31 put his *o* garments upon him
27:35 distributed his *o* garments
Mr 2:21 cloth upon an old *o* garment
5:27 and touched his *o* garment
5:28 I touch just his *o* garments
5:30 Who touched my *o* garments?
6:56 the fringe of his *o* garment
9:3 *o* garments became glistening
10:50 Throwing off his *o* garment
11:7 they put their *o* garments
11:8 spread their *o* garments on
13:16 to pick up his *o* garment
15:20 put his *o* garments upon him
15:24 distributed his *o* garments
Lu 5:36 patch from a new *o* garment
5:36 sews it onto an old *o* garment
6:29 takes away your *o* garment
7:25 dressed in soft *o* garments
8:44 the fringe of his *o* garment
19:35 *o* garments upon the colt and
19:36 their *o* garments on the road
22:36 sell his *o* garment and buy
Joh 13:4 laid aside his *o* garments
13:12 had put his *o* garments on
19:2 him with a purple *o* garment
19:5 and the purple *o* garment
19:23 *o* garments and made four
19:24 apportioned my *o* garments
Ac 7:58 *o* garments at the feet of a
9:39 *o* garments that Dorcas used
12:8 Put your *o* garment on and
14:14 they ripped their *o* garments
16:22 tearing the *o* garments off
22:20 guarding the *o* garments of
22:23 throwing their *o* garments
Heb 1:11 just like an *o* garment they
1:12 as a cloak, as an *o* garment
Jas 5:2 your *o* garments have become
1Pe 3:3 or the wearing of *o* garments
Re 3:4 defile their *o* garments, and
3:5 arrayed in white *o* garments
3:18 white *o* garments that you
4:4 dressed in white *o* garments
16:15 and keeps his *o* garments
19:13 *o* garment sprinkled with
19:16 upon his *o* garment, even

Outermost
Ex 26:4 the edge of the *o* tent cloth
26:10 the *o* one in the series, and
36:11 the *o* tent cloth at the other
36:17 edge of the *o* tent cloth

Outfit
Jg 17:10 the usual *o* of garments and

Outfits
Jg 14:12 and thirty *o* of clothing
14:13 and thirty *o* of clothing
14:19 gave the *o* to the tellers of

Outfitted
2Ch 17:18 men *o* for the army

Outflows
Ps 107:33 *o* of water into thirsty
107:35 region into *o* of water

Outgoing
Ex 23:16 at the *o* of the year, when

Outlets
Eze 48:30 will be the *o* of the city

Outline
1Co 13:12 we see in hazy *o* by means

Outlying
Es 9:19 the cities of the *o* districts

Outpost
1Sa 13:23 *o* of the Philistines would
14:1 to the *o* of the Philistines
14:4 the *o* of the Philistines
14:6 *o* of these uncircumcised men
14:11 to the *o* of the Philistines
14:12 the men of the *o* answered
14:15 all the people of the *o*
2Sa 23:14 and an *o* of the Philistines
Zec 9:8 encamp as an *o* for my house

Outpoured
Eze 20:33 with *o* rage that I will
20:34 and with *o* rage

Outpouring
Job 14:19 *o* washes off earth's dust

Outraged
Heb 10:29 *o* the spirit of undeserved

Outrageously
Ac 8:3 deal *o* with the congregation

Outright
Ge 30:16 hired you *o* with my son's
2Sa 6:20 men uncovers himself *o*
Ps 58:2 practice *o* unrighteousness
Pr 1:22 yourselves *o* ridicule, and
Isa 5:9 *o* object of astonishment
Jer 8:21 *O* astonishment has seized
28:16 *o* revolt against Jehovah
29:32 *o* revolt against Jehovah
48:27 he found among *o* thieves
La 1:8 Jerusalem has committed *o* sin
Eze 18:18 he committed *o* defrauding
22:9 *O* slanderers have proved to
Ob 11 *o* foreigners entered his gate
Mic 2:8 to rise up as an *o* enemy
Na 1:8 *o* extermination of her place
1:9 is causing an *o* extermination

Outset
Isa 40:21 been told to you from the *o*

Outside
Ge 6:14 must cover it inside and *o*
9:22 to his two brothers *o*
15:5 He now brought him *o* and said
19:16 to station him *o* the city
24:11 *o* the city at a well of
24:29 who was *o* at the fountain
39:12 took to flight and went on *o*
39:13 that he might flee *o*
39:15 took to flight and went on *o*
39:18 and went fleeing *o*
Ex 12:46 to some place *o*. And you
25:11 with pure gold. Inside and *o*
26:35 set the table *o* the curtain
27:21 *o* the curtain that is by the
29:14 burn with fire *o* the camp
33:7 pitched it *o* the camp, far
33:7 meeting, which was *o* the camp
37:2 with pure gold inside and *o*
40:22 to the north *o* the curtain
Le 6:11 to a clean place *o* the camp
8:17 burned with fire *o* the camp
9:11 the skin with fire *o* the camp
10:4 the holy place to *o* the camp
10:5 in their robes to *o* the camp
13:46 dwell isolated. *O* the camp
13:55 either its underside or its *o*
14:3 *o* the camp, and the priest
14:8 dwell *o* his tent seven days
14:40 *o* the city into an unclean
14:41 *o* the city into an unclean
14:45 *o* the city to an unclean
14:53 *o* the city into the open
16:27 taken forth *o* the camp
17:3 who slaughters it *o* the camp
18:9 born *o* it, you must not lay
24:3 *O* the curtain of the
24:14 *o* of the camp; and all those
24:23 *o* of the camp, and they
Nu 5:3 send them *o* the camp, that
5:4 to send them *o* the camp
12:14 seven days *o* the camp
12:15 quarantined *o* the camp seven
15:35 pelting him . . . *o* the camp
15:36 *o* the camp and pelted him
19:3 lead it forth *o* the camp, and
19:9 *o* the camp in a clean place
31:13 out to meet them *o* the camp
31:19 camp *o* the camp seven days
35:5 measure *o* the city on the
35:27 find him *o* the boundary of
De 23:10 he must also go *o* the camp
23:12 at your service *o* the camp
23:13 when you squat *o*, you must
24:11 You should stand on the *o*
24:11 bring the pledge *o* to you
25:5 not become a strange man's *o*
Jos 6:23 *o* the camp of Israel
Jg 12:9 sent *o* and brought in thirty
12:9 daughters for his sons from *o*
19:25 brought her forth to them *o*
2Sa 13:17 to the *o*, and lock the door
13:18 lead her clear *o*, and he
1Ki 2:42 On the day of your going *o*
6:6 the house all around *o*
6:29 blossoms, inside and *o*
6:30 with gold, inside and *o*
7:9 inside and *o*, and from the
7:9 *o* as far as the great
8:8 but they were not visible *o*
2Ki 4:3 vessels for yourself from *o*
10:24 stationed eighty men *o* at
23:4 burned them *o* Jerusalem on
1Ch 26:29 the *o* business as officers
2Ch 5:9 but they were not visible *o*
24:8 *o* at the gate of the house
29:16 torrent valley of Kidron *o*
32:3 springs that were *o* the city
32:5 on the *o* another wall, and
33:15 had them thrown *o* the city
Ezr 10:13 is not possible to stand *o*
Ne 11:16 the *o* business of the house
13:8 *o* the dining hall
13:20 spent the night *o* Jerusalem
Job 31:32 *O* no alien resident would
Ps 41:6 on the *o* he will speak of it
Pr 22:13 has said: There is a lion *o!*
Ca 8:1 I find you *o*, I would kiss you
Jer 21:4 siege against you *o* the wall
La 1:20 *O* the sword caused
Eze 7:15 The sword is *o*, and the
34:21 had scattered them to the *o*
40:5 a wall *o* the house all round
40:19 *O* it was a hundred cubits
40:44 the *o* of the inner gate
41:9 the side chamber, to the *o*
41:17 the inner house and on the *o*
41:17 the inner house and on the *o*
41:25 the front of the porch *o*
42:7 the stone wall that was *o*
43:21 House, *o* the sanctuary
46:2 porch of the gate, from *o*
47:2 way *o* to the outer gate
Ho 7:1 makes a dash on the *o*
Mt 5:13 thrown *o* to be trampled on
8:12 thrown into the darkness *o*
9:25 the crowd had been sent *o*
9:31 after getting *o*, made it
12:46 position *o* seeking to speak
12:47 your brothers are standing *o*
21:17 went *o* the city to Bethany
22:13 out into the darkness *o*
23:25 you cleanse the *o* of the cup
23:26 that the *o* of it also may
25:30 out into the darkness *o*
26:69 Peter was sitting *o* in the
26:75 he went *o* and wept bitterly
Mr 1:35 went *o* and left for a lonely
1:45 continued *o* in lonely places
3:31 they were standing on the *o*

Mr 3:32 brothers *o* are seeking you
4:11 to those *o* all things occur
7:15 nothing from *o* a man that
7:18 nothing from *o* that passes
8:23 brought him *o* the village
11:4 *o* on the side street, and
12:8 and threw him *o* the vineyard
14:68 he went *o* to the vestibule
Lu 1:10 praying *o* at the hour of
4:29 hurried him *o* the city, and
8:20 standing *o* wanting to see you
11:39 you cleanse the *o* of the cup
11:40 made the *o* made also the
13:25 stand *o* and to knock at the
13:28 but yourselves thrown *o*
13:33 be destroyed *o* of Jerusalem
14:35 People throw it *o*. Let him
20:15 threw him *o* the vineyard and
22:62 he went *o* and wept bitterly
Joh 18:16 Peter was standing *o* at the
18:29 Pilate came *o* to them and
19:4 Pilate went *o* again and
19:4 I bring him *o* to you in
19:5 Jesus came *o*, wearing the
19:13 brought Jesus *o*, and he sat
20:11 *o* near the memorial tomb
Ac 4:15 to go *o* the Sanhedrin hall
5:34 men *o* for a little while
7:58 throwing him *o* the city
9:40 Peter put everybody *o* and
13:50 them *o* their boundaries
14:19 and dragged him *o* the city
16:13 *o* the gate beside a river
16:30 he brought them *o* and said
21:5 as far as *o* the city
21:30 and dragged him *o* the temple
26:11 persecuting . . . in *o* cities
Ro 2:28 Jew who is one on the *o*
2:28 is on the *o* upon the flesh
1Co 5:12 to do with judging those *o*
5:13 while God judges those *o*
6:18 other sin . . . is *o* his body
2Co 4:16 man we are *o* is wasting
10:13 *o* our assigned boundaries
10:15 *o* our assigned boundaries in
Col 4:5 toward those on the *o*, buying
1Th 4:12 as regards people *o* and not
1Ti 3:7 from people on the *o*, in
Heb 13:11 are burned up *o* the camp
13:12 suffered *o* the gate
13:13 *o* the camp, bearing the
1Jo 4:18 perfect love throws fear *o*
Re 11:2 courtyard that is *o* the
14:20 was trodden *o* the city
22:15 *O* are the dogs and those

Outskirts
Ge 19:17 brought them forth to the *o*
Le 4:12 out to the *o* of the camp
4:21 the *o* of the camp and must
Jg 7:22 far as the *o* of Abel-meholah
1Sa 14:2 dwelling at the *o* of Gibeah
1Ki 21:13 the *o* of the city and stoned
2Ki 7:5 *o* of the camp of the Syrians
7:8 as far as the *o* of the camp
23:6 to the *o* of Jerusalem

Outspokenly
Joh 10:24 are the Christ, tell us *o*
11:14 Jesus said to them *o*
Ro 15:15 more *o* on some points, as if

Outspokenness
Mr 8:32 with *o* he was making that
Ac 4:13 beheld the *o* of Peter and John

Outspreading
Isa 8:8 *o* of his wings must occur to

Outstanding
Ga 2:2 before those who were *o* men
2:6 *o* men imparted nothing new

Outstandingly
2Co 11:23 I am more *o* one: in labors

Outstretched
Ex 6:6 reclaim you with an *o* arm and
De 4:34 with an *o* arm and with great
5:15 a strong hand and an *o* arm
7:19 strong hand and the *o* arm
9:29 great power and your *o* arm
11:2 his strong hand and his *o* arm
26:8 a strong hand and an *o* arm
Ps 139:3 my lying *o* you have measured
Jer 32:17 power and by your *o* arm

Outward
Mt 22:16 look upon men's *o* appearance
28:3 *o* appearance was as lightning
Mr 12:14 look upon men's *o* appearance
Lu 12:56 the *o* appearance of earth
Joh 7:24 from the *o* appearance, but
2Co 5:12 boast over the *o* appearance
Ga 2:6 not go by a man's *o* appearance
Jas 1:11 beauty of its *o* appearance

Outwardly
Mt 23:27 *o* indeed appear beautiful
23:28 *o* indeed, appear righteous

Outwit
Ge 31:27 run away secretly and *o* me

Outwitted
Ge 31:20 Jacob *o* Laban the Syrian
Mt 2:16 had been *o* by the astrologers

Outwitting
Ge 31:26 you resorted to *o* me and

Oven
Le 2:4 of something baked in the *o*
7:9 that may be baked in the *o* and
11:35 Whether *o* or jar stand, it
26:26 bake your bread in but one *o*
Mt 6:30 is thrown into the *o*
Lu 12:28 tomorrow is cast into an *o*

Ovens
Ex 8:3 frogs . . . into your *o* and into
Ne 3:11 also the Tower of the Bake *O*
12:38 Tower of the Bake *O* and on

Over*
Ge 39:2 be *o* the house of his master
Ex 12:13 see the blood and pass *o* you
12:23 pass *o* the entrance, and he
12:27 Jehovah, who passed *o* the
2Ch 8:10 the foremen *o* the people
Isa 15:2, 2 *O* Nebo and *o* Medeba Moab
Mr 15:10 priests had handed him *o*
Lu 15:7 than *o* ninety-nine righteous
Joh 3:31 comes from heaven is *o* all
Ro 12:2 by making your mind *o*, that
1Co 5:5 hand such a man *o* to Satan

Overboard
Ac 27:38 the wheat *o* into the sea

Overcame
1Ki 16:22 *o* the people that were

Overcome
Jg 5:27 he collapsed, there he fell *o*
Jer 23:9 man whom wine has *o*
2Pe 2:19 *o* by another is enslaved by
2:20 these very things and are *o*

Overeating
Lu 21:34 with *o* and heavy drinking

Overflow
Ex 22:29 *o* of your press you must not
De 11:4 the waters of the Red Sea *o*
28:11 *o* indeed with prosperity
Ps 6:6 tears I make my own divan *o*
72:16 mountains there will be an *o*
Pr 3:10 your own press vats will *o*
Joe 2:24 vats must *o* with new wine
3:13 The press vats actually *o*
Zec 1:17 My cities will yet *o* with
Php 1:26 exultation may *o* in Christ
2Pe 1:8 things exist in you and *o*

Overflowed
Jer 5:28 have also *o* with bad things

Overflowing
Jos 4:18 *o* all its banks as formerly
1Ch 12:15 when it was *o* all its banks
Isa 28:15 *o* flash flood, in case it
28:18 *o* flash flood, when it
Lu 6:38 shaken together and *o*
2Co 7:4 I am *o* with joy in all our
Col 2:7 *o* with faith in thanksgiving

Overflows
Jos 3:15 Jordan *o* all its banks all

Overhanging
Ex 26:12 cloths of the tent is an *o*
26:13 as an *o* on the sides of the

Overhasty
Isa 32:4 who are *o* will consider

Overhearing
Mr 5:36 But Jesus, *o* the word being

Overjoyed
Lu 1:47 keep from being *o* at God my
10:21 *o* in the holy spirit and said
1Pe 4:13 *o* also during the revelation
Re 19:7 Let us rejoice and be *o*, and

Overlaid
Ex 26:32 of acacia *o* with gold
36:34 *o* the panel frames with gold
36:36 pillars and *o* them with gold
36:38 *o* their tops and their joints
37:2 he *o* it with pure gold inside
37:4 poles . . . *o* them with gold
37:11 he *o* it with pure gold and
37:15 and *o* them with gold for
37:26 Then he *o* it with pure gold
37:28 poles . . . *o* them with gold
38:2 Next he *o* it with copper
38:6 poles . . . *o* them with copper
38:28 *o* their tops and joined them
1Ki 6:15 he *o* it with timber inside
6:22 whole house he *o* with gold
6:22 the altar . . . he *o* with gold
6:28 he *o* the cherubs with gold
6:30 floor of the house he *o* with
6:32 and he *o* them with gold
6:35 and *o* gold foil upon the
10:18 and *o* it with refined gold
2Ki 18:16 had *o* and then gave them to
2Ch 3:6 he *o* the house with precious
3:10 cherubs . . . *o* them with gold
4:9 their doors he *o* with copper
9:17 *o* it with pure gold
Pr 26:23 As a silver glazing *o* upon a
Eze 37:8 skin began to be *o* upon them
Heb 9:4 *o* all around with gold, in

Overlapping
1Sa 17:5 coat of mail, of *o* scales

Overlay
Ex 25:11 you must *o* it with pure gold
25:11 and outside you are to *o* it
25:13 wood and *o* them with gold
25:24 you must *o* it with pure gold
25:28 wood and *o* them with gold
26:29 *o* the panel frames with gold
26:29 must *o* the bars with gold
26:37 acacia and *o* them with gold
27:2 and you must *o* it with copper
27:6 you must *o* them with copper
30:3 you must *o* it with pure gold
30:5 wood and *o* them with gold
36:34 to *o* the bars with gold
1Ki 6:15 to *o* the floor of the house
6:20 to *o* it with pure gold
6:20 *o* the altar with cedarwood
6:21 *o* the house inside with pure
6:21 and to *o* it with gold
2Ch 3:4 to *o* it inside with pure gold
Eze 37:6 I will *o* upon you skin and

Overlaying
Ex 38:17 *o* of their tops was of silver
38:19 *o* of their heads and their
Nu 16:38 plates as an *o* for the altar
16:39 beat them out into an *o* for
Isa 30:22 *o* of your graven images

Overlays
Isa 40:19 gold the metalworker *o* it

Overlook
Job 7:21 And *o* my error? For now in

Overlooked
Ac 6:1 widows were being *o* in the
17:30 God has *o* the times of such

Overly
2Co 2:7 swallowed up . . . being *o* sad
12:7 not feel *o* exalted, there
12:7 I might not be *o* exalted

Overmuch
Ec 2:15 wise, I *o* so at that time
7:16 Do not become righteous *o*
7:17 not be wicked *o*, nor become

Overnight
Ge 19:2 and stay *o* and have your feet
19:2 is where we shall stay *o*
Ex 23:18 not stay *o* until morning
34:25 not stay *o* until the morning
Jos 6:11 and stayed *o* in the camp
Jg 19:4 and he would stay *o* there
19:6 and stay *o*, and let your heart
19:7 he stayed *o* there again
19:9 stay *o*. Here the day is

Jg 19:9 Stay here *o*, and let your
19:10 did not consent to stay *o*
19:11 and stay in it *o*
19:13 and we must stay *o* either in
19:15 to go in to stay *o* in Gibeah
19:15 into the house to stay *o*
19:20 stay *o* in the public square
20:4 I and my concubine, to stay *o*
Job 29:19 And dew itself will stay *o*
Ps 59:15 not be satisfied or stay *o*

Overpower
Job 14:20 You *o* him forever so that
15:24 They *o* him like a king in
Ec 4:12 if somebody could *o* one alone
Mt 16:18 gates of Hades will not *o* it
Joh 12:35 darkness does not *o* you

Overpowered
Jg 3:10 his hand *o* Cushan-rishathaim
Isa 28:1 valley of those *o* by wine
Joh 1:5 but the darkness has not *o* it

Overreached
2Co 2:11 we may not be *o* by Satan

Overseer
1Ki 11:28 to make him *o* over all the
Ne 11:9 an *o* over them, and Judah the
11:14 was an *o* over them
11:22 the *o* of the Levites in
12:42 Izrahiah the *o* kept making
Jer 29:26 the grand *o* of the house
1Ti 3:1 reaching out for . . . *o*
3:2 *o* should therefore be
Tit 1:7 For an *o* must be free from
1Pe 2:25 shepherd and *o* of your souls

Overseers
Ge 41:34 appoint *o* over the land, and
2Ki 11:18 *o* over the house of Jehovah
2Ch 2:2 as *o* over them three thousand
2:18 *o* for keeping the people in
34:12 Kohathites, to act as *o*
34:13 *o* of all the doers of the
Isa 60:17 appoint peace as your *o* and
Ac 20:28 spirit has appointed you *o*
Php 1:1 *o* and ministerial servants

Overshadow
Lu 1:35 the Most High will *o* you
9:34 cloud formed and began to *o*

Overshadowed
Mt 17:5 a bright cloud *o* them, and

Overshadowing
Mr 9:7 a cloud formed, *o* them, and a
Heb 9:5 *o* the propitiatory cover

Oversight
Nu 3:32 *o* of those taking care of the
3:36 *o* for which the sons of
4:16 *o* of Eleazar the son of Aaron
4:16 *o* of all the tabernacle and
Ps 109:8 office of *o* let someone else
Jer 37:13 officer holding the *o*
Eze 44:11 ministers at posts of *o*
Ac 1:20 His office of *o* let someone

Oversowed
Mt 13:25 *o* weeds in among the wheat

Overspread
Le 16:13 incense must *o* the Ark cover

Overstep
De 17:2 so as to *o* his covenant
Mt 15:2 disciples *o* the tradition of
15:3 *o* the commandment of God

Overstepped
De 26:13 not *o* your commandments
Jos 7:11 also *o* my covenant that I
7:15 has *o* the covenant of Jehovah
Jg 2:20 nation have *o* my covenant
1Sa 15:24 have *o* the order of Jehovah
Da 9:11 of Israel have *o* your law
Ho 6:7 man, have *o* the covenant
8:1 they have *o* my covenant

Overstepping
Jos 23:16 *o* the covenant of Jehovah
2Ki 18:12 kept *o* his covenant
2Ch 24:20 *o* the commandments of

Overstretching
2Co 10:14 not *o* ourselves as if we

Overtake
Ge 44:4 be certain to *o* them and to
Ex 15:9 I shall pursue! I shall *o*! I
De 19:6 actually *o* him, since the
28:2 come upon you and *o* you
28:15 come upon you and *o* you
28:45 *o* you until you have been
Jos 2:5 quickly, for you will *o* them
1Sa 30:8 Shall I *o* them?
30:8 without fail *o* them, and
2Ki 25:5 got to *o* him in the desert
1Ch 21:12 sword of your enemies to *o*
Job 27:20 sudden terrors will *o* him
Ps 7:5 let him *o* and trample my life
18:37 pursue my enemies and *o*
69:24 own burning anger *o* them
Jer 39:5 *o* Zedekiah in the desert
52:8 *o* Zedekiah in the desert
Ho 2:7 chase . . . but she will not *o*
10:9 did not get to *o* them
Am 9:13 will actually *o* the harvester
1Th 5:4 so that that day should *o* you

Overtaken
Nu 20:14 all the hardship that has *o* us
La 1:3 have *o* her among distressing
Mt 12:28 kingdom of God has really *o*
Lu 11:20 kingdom . . . really *o* you

Overtaking
Ex 14:9 military forces were *o* them
Job 41:26 *O* it, the sword itself does

Overthrew
De 29:23 *o* in his anger and in his
Isa 13:19 God *o* Sodom and Gomorrah
14:17 *o* its very cities, that did

Overthrow
Ge 19:29 out of the midst of the *o*
De 29:23 like the *o* of Sodom and
2Sa 10:3 to spy it out and to *o* it
1Ch 19:3 causing an *o* and for spying
Ezr 6:12 *o* any king and people that
Job 34:25 he does *o* them at night
Pr 26:28 flattering mouth causes an *o*
Isa 1:7 the desolation is like an *o* by
Jer 49:18 Just as in the *o* of Sodom
50:40 God's *o* of Sodom and of
Am 4:11 caused an *o* among you people
4:11 like God's *o* of Sodom and
Hag 2:22 *o* the throne of kingdoms and
2:22 *o* the chariot and its riders
Ac 5:39 you will not be able to *o*

Overthrowing
Ge 19:21 not *o* the city of which you
19:25 went ahead *o* these cities
19:29 when *o* the cities among
Pr 12:7 *o* of the wicked ones and they

Overthrown
Job 9:5 who has *o* them in his anger
28:9 *o* mountains from their root
Isa 3:6 *o* mass should be under your
Jer 20:16 cities that Jehovah has *o*
La 4:6 Which was *o* as in a moment
Eze 21:15 multiply those who are *o*
Jon 3:4 and Nineveh will be *o*
Ac 5:38 from men, it will be *o*

Overtook
Ge 44:6 he *o* them and spoke these
Ps 40:12 More errors of mine *o* me

Overtunics
Isa 3:22 robes of state and the *o*

Overturn
Ga 5:12 men who are trying to *o* you

Overturned
La 1:20 My heart has been *o* in the
Mt 21:12 *o* the tables of the money
Mr 11:15 *o* the tables of the money
Joh 2:15 and *o* their tables
Ac 17:6 have *o* the inhabited earth are

Overturning
2Co 10:4 for *o* strongly entrenched
10:5 are *o* reasonings and every

Overturns
2Ti 2:14 because it *o* those listening

Overwhelmed
Ge 7:19 the waters *o* the earth so
7:20 fifteen cubits the waters *o*
Lu 5:9 astonishment *o* him and all

Overwhelming
Ge 7:18 waters became *o* and kept
7:24 waters continued *o* the earth

Owe
Mt 18:28 Pay back whatever you *o*
Ro 15:27 they also *o* it to minister
Phm 19 you *o* me even yourself
Re 7:10 Salvation we *o* to our God

Owed
Mt 18:24 *o* him ten thousand talents

Owes
Eph 3:15 and on earth *o* its name
Phm 18 any wrong or *o* you anything

Owing
Job 39:26 *o* to your understanding
Ps 107:34 *O* to the badness of those
107:39 *O* to restraint, calamity
119:104 *O* to your orders I behave
Pr 3:27 those to whom it is *o*
Isa 43:4 *O* to the fact that you have
Eze 16:54 feel humiliated *o* to all
16:61 but not *o* to your covenant
26:10 *O* to the heaving mass of
26:10 *O* to the sound of
26:18 disturbed *o* to your going
28:18 *O* to the abundance of your
35:11 *o* to your feelings of hatred
Na 3:4 *o* to the abundance of the acts
Mt 18:28 was *o* him a hundred denarii
18:30 should pay back what was *o*
18:34 pay back all that was *o*
Lu 16:5 How much are you *o* my
16:7 Now you, how much are you *o*?
Joh 6:66 *O* to this many of his
Ro 13:8 be *o* anybody a single thing
2Co 13:4 was impaled *o* to weakness
13:4 is alive *o* to God's power
13:4 *o* to God's power toward you
Ga 3:5 he do it *o* to works of law
3:5 or *o* to a hearing by faith
Eph 2:8 not *o* to you, it is God's gift
2:9 not *o* to works, in order that
Tit 3:5 *o* to no works in
1Jo 3:24 *o* to the spirit which he

Owl
Le 11:16 the ostrich and the *o* and
11:17 the little *o* and the
11:17 and the long-eared *o*
De 14:15 the *o* and the gull and the
14:16 little *o* and the long-eared
14:16 the long-eared *o* and the swan
Ps 102:6 become like a little *o* of

Owls
Isa 13:21 be filled with eagle *o*
34:11 and long-eared *o* and ravens

Own
Ge 9:6 by man will his *o* blood be
15:4 out of your *o* inward parts
30:30 also for my *o* house
30:40 Then he set his *o* droves by
31:55 might return to his *o* place
34:21 our *o* daughters we can give
38:11 dwell at her *o* father's
40:5 each one his *o* dream in the
40:5 with its *o* interpretation
41:11 with its *o* interpretation
41:42 signet ring from his *o* hand
42:37 My *o* two sons you may put
43:21 return it with our *o* hands
44:11 opened each one his *o* bag
49:11 descendant of his *o* she-ass
49:28 according to his *o* blessing
Ex 5:16 your *o* people are at fault
7:1 and Aaron your *o* brother will
9:20 *o* servants and his livestock
10:23 got up from his *o* place
16:29 each one in his *o* place
18:23 to their *o* place in peace
21:34 animal will become his *o*
21:36 dead one will become his *o*
22:5 with the best of his *o* field
22:5 the best of his *o* vineyard
32:29, 29 *o* son and his *o* brother
33:8 the entrance of his *o* tent
33:10 the entrance of his *o* tent
33:14 My *o* person will go along
33:15 If your *o* person is not going
Le 1:3 present it of his *o* free will
9:7 atonement in your *o* behalf and
16:24 in his *o* behalf and in behalf
20:9 His *o* blood is upon him
20:11 Their *o* blood is upon them
20:12 Their *o* blood is upon them
20:13 Their *o* blood is upon them

Le 20:16 Their *o* blood is upon them
20:27 Their *o* blood is upon them
25:26 *o* hand does make gain and he
25:49 *o* hand has become wealthy
26:30 lay your *o* carcasses upon
26:40 confess their *o* error and the
Nu 5:10 of each one will remain his *o*
7:5 in proportion to his *o* service
10:30 I shall go to my *o* country
13:33 we became in our *o* eyes like
15:31 His *o* error is upon him
16:28 that it is not of my *o* heart
16:38 sinned against their *o* souls
17:9 and taking each man his *o* rod
21:18 with their *o* staffs
24:13 or bad out of my *o* heart
24:25 Balak also went his *o* way
27:3 but for his *o* sin he has died
32:18 each with his *o* inheritance
32:38 to call by their *o* names the
32:42 call it Nobah by his *o* name
36:9 each to its *o* inheritance
De 1:30 in Egypt under your *o* eyes
3:14 by his *o* name, Havvoth-jair
4:3 Your *o* eyes are the ones that
8:5 know with your *o* heart that
8:17 My *o* power and the full
8:17 the full might of my *o* hand
9:4 It was for my *o* righteousness
12:8 right in his *o* eyes
13:6 who is like your *o* soul
16:7 and go to your *o* tents
18:15 A prophet from your *o* midst
20:8 to melt as his *o* heart
21:14 agreeably to her *o* soul
24:16 be put to death for his *o* sin
30:14 in your *o* mouth and in your
30:14 in your *o* heart, that you
32:5 acted ruinously on their *o*
32:5 the defect is their *o*
34:4 to see it with your *o* eyes
Jos 2:16 may go in your *o* direction
2:19 blood will be upon his *o*
7:11 among their *o* articles
9:4 of their *o* accord, acted with
11:13 standing on their *o* mounds
22:29 to rebel of our *o* accord
24:22 *o* accord have chosen Jehovah
Jg 3:6 their *o* daughters they gave to
5:29 to herself with her *o* sayings
6:32 legal defense in his *o* behalf
9:3 they said: He is our *o* brother
9:18 because he is your *o* brother
9:57 come back upon their *o* heads
11:19 your land to my *o* place
12:3 to put my soul in my *o* palm
14:16 Why, to my *o* father and my
14:16 and my *o* mother I have not
16:30 in his *o* death came to be
17:6 what was right in his *o* eyes
18:25 forfeit your *o* soul and the
19:18 my *o* house that I am going
21:24 each one to his *o* tribe and
21:24 each one to his . . . *o* family
21:24 each one to his *o* inheritance
21:25 What was right in his *o* eyes
Ru 4:6 I may ruin my *o* inheritance
1Sa 4:17 your *o* two sons have died
8:5 your *o* sons have not walked
15:17 were little in your *o* eyes
15:34 *o* house at Gibeah of Saul
17:18 look after your *o* brothers
17:25 *o* daughter he will give him
18:1 to love him as his *o* soul
18:3 his loving him as his *o* soul
20:15 *o* loving-kindness from
20:17 for as he loved his *o* soul
20:29 *o* brother that commanded me
20:30 of Jesse to your *o* shame
20:34 his *o* father had humiliated
21:8 *o* sword nor my weapons did I
22:8 *o* son concludes a covenant
22:8 *o* son has raised up my
22:8 raised up my *o* servant
23:18 himself went to his *o* home
24:12 *o* hand will not come to be
24:13 my *o* hand will not come to
24:16 raise his *o* voice and weep
25:8 Ask your *o* young men, and
25:13 girded on his *o* sword
25:26 *o* hand come to your
25:33 *o* hand come to my salvation
25:39 turned back upon his *o* head
26:23 each one his *o* righteousness
1Sa 26:23 *o* faithfulness, in that
28:3 bury him in Ramah his *o* city
29:9 good in my *o* eyes, like an
31:5 fell upon his *o* sword
2Sa 1:16 be upon your *o* head
1:16 *o* mouth has testified
3:39 according to his *o* badness
4:10 in his *o* eyes became like
4:11 man in his *o* house upon his
6:19 went each to his *o* house
6:20 to bless his *o* household
7:1 king dwelt in his *o* house and
7:21 agreement with your *o* heart
7:26 *o* name become great to time
10:12 what is good in his *o* eyes
11:9 not go down to his *o* house
11:10 not go down to his *o* house
11:10 gone down to your *o* house
11:11 go into my *o* house to eat
11:13 to his *o* house he did not
12:4 taking some from his *o* sheep
12:4 and his *o* cattle to get such
12:10 depart from your *o* house to
12:11 out of your *o* house
12:11 wives under your *o* eyes and
12:15 Nathan went to his *o* house
12:20 came into his *o* house and
14:13 back his *o* banished one
14:24 turn toward his *o* house
14:24 turned toward his *o* house
16:11 my *o* son, who has come
16:11 out of my *o* inward parts
17:11 your *o* person going into the
17:23 to his house at his *o* city
18:18 the pillar by his *o* name
18:20 the king's *o* son has died
23:21 killed him with his *o* spear
23:23 to his *o* bodyguard
1Ki 1:12 escape for your *o* soul and
1:48 with my *o* eyes seeing it
1:49 go each one on his *o* way
1:53 Go to your *o* house
2:23 against his *o* soul that
2:32 his blood upon his *o* head
2:34 buried at his *o* house in the
2:37 come to be upon your *o* head
2:44 by you upon your *o* head
3:1 finished building his *o* house
3:20 and laid him in her *o* bosom
4:25 under his *o* vine and under
4:25 and under his *o* fig tree
7:1 his *o* house Solomon built in
7:1 he finished all his *o* house
8:15 who spoke by his *o* mouth
8:15 *o* hand has given fulfillment
8:24 promise with your *o* mouth
8:24 with your *o* hand you have
8:32 his way upon his *o* head
8:32 to his *o* righteousness
8:38 the plague of his *o* heart
9:15 his *o* house and the Mound
9:24 her *o* house that he had built
9:27 his *o* servants, seamen
10:6 heard in my *o* land about
10:7 that my *o* eyes might see
10:13 and went to her *o* land
11:19 the sister of his *o* wife
11:21 that I may go to my *o* land
11:22 seeking to go to your *o* land
12:16 to your *o* house, O David
13:30 dead body in his *o* burial
13:31 deposit my *o* bones
17:19 laid him upon his *o* couch
18:1 Jehovah's *o* word came to
20:33 a decision of his *o* accord
20:40 Thus your *o* judgment is
21:29 the calamity in his *o* days
2Ki 2:12 took hold of his *o* garments
4:1 know that your *o* servant had
4:13 In among my *o* people I am
4:34 and put his *o* mouth upon his
4:34 his *o* eyes upon his eyes
4:34 his *o* palms upon his palms
6:28 my *o* son we shall eat
6:32 was sitting in his *o* house
7:2 seeing it with your *o* eyes
7:19 seeing it with your *o* eyes
8:14 came to his *o* lord, who then
9:21 each in his *o* war chariot
10:5 is good in your *o* eyes do
10:15 my *o* heart is with your
12:18 his *o* holy offerings and all
14:6 *o* sin should each one be put
14:10 and dwell in your *o* house
2Ki 15:19 the kingdom in his *o* hand
16:3 his *o* son he made pass
17:23 Israel went off its *o* soil
17:29 to be a maker of its *o* god
17:33 *o* gods that they proved to
17:41 *o* graven images that they
18:27 eat their *o* excrement and
18:27 and drink their *o* urine
18:31 each one from his *o* vine
18:31 each one from his *o* fig
18:31 the water of his *o* cistern
18:32 a land like your *o* land
18:33 his *o* land out of the hand
19:7 and return to his *o* land
19:7 by the sword in his *o* land
19:34 to save it for my *o* sake
20:6 this city for my *o* sake and
20:13 show them in his *o* house
20:17 all that is in your *o* house
20:18 your *o* sons that will come
20:19 will continue in my *o* days
21:6 made his *o* son pass through
21:23 king to death in his *o* house
22:13 my *o* behalf and in behalf
22:20 your *o* graveyard in peace
25:5 his *o* military force was
1Ch 11:23 killed him with his *o* spear
11:25 David put him over his *o*
12:17 my *o* heart will become at
12:19 At the risk of our *o* heads
16:43 go each one to his *o* house
16:43 around to bless his *o* house
17:1 dwelling in his *o* house
17:19 agreement with your *o* heart
19:13 what is good in his *o* eyes
21:23 Take it as your *o*, and let
21:23 what is good in his *o* eyes
29:14 out of your *o* hand we have
2Ch 2:14 with your *o* skillful men
3:8 *o* width being twenty cubits
6:4 who spoke with his *o* mouth
6:4 and by his *o* hands has given
6:15 your *o* hand you have made
6:23 course upon his *o* head and
6:23 to his *o* righteousness
6:29 know each one his *o* plague
6:29 and his *o* pain; when he
7:11 *o* house he proved successful
7:15 *o* eyes will prove to be
8:1 of Jehovah and his *o* house
9:5 heard in my *o* land about your
9:6 that my *o* eyes might see
9:12 went to her *o* land, she
10:10 My *o* little finger will
10:16 Now see to your *o* house
11:4 at my *o* instance that this
13:7 not hold his *o* against them
13:8 holding your *o* against the
19:1 to his *o* house at Jerusalem
20:23 bring his *o* fellow to ruin
21:6 Ahab's *o* daughter had become
21:13 even your *o* brothers, the
24:25 *o* servants conspired against
24:25 kill him upon his *o* couch
25:4 *o* sin that they should die
25:10 to go to their *o* place
25:10 to their *o* place in the heat
25:11 lead his *o* people and go
25:15 deliver their *o* people out
25:16 Quit for your *o* sake
25:19 dwelling in your *o* house
29:8 are seeing with your *o* eyes
31:1 each one to his *o* possession
31:3 king from his *o* goods for
32:15 *o* God deliver you out of my
32:21 shame of face to his *o* land
32:21 out of his *o* inward parts
33:6 *o* sons pass through the fire
33:24 to death in his *o* house
34:21 in my *o* behalf and in
35:21 Refrain for your *o* sake
Ezr 2:1 each one to his *o* city
2:68 to stand on its *o* site
3:3 altar firmly upon its *o* site
Ne 3:10 in front of his *o* house
3:23 in front of their *o* house
3:23 work close by his *o* house
3:28 in front of his *o* house
3:29 work in front of his *o* house
3:30 work in front of his *o* hall
4:4 return upon their *o* head
5:7 each one from his *o* brother
5:8 our *o* Jewish brothers who
5:8 sell your *o* brothers, and must

Pr 6:32 bringing his *o* soul to ruin
7:1 treasure up my *o* commandments
7:5 made her *o* sayings smooth
9:12 become wise in your *o* behalf
11:5 in his *o* wickedness the
11:12 has despised his *o* fellowman
11:17 rewardingly with his *o* soul
11:17 upon his *o* organism
11:19 is in line for his *o* death
11:29 ostracism upon his *o* house
12:15 one is right in his *o* eyes
12:26 one spies out his *o* pasturage
14:1 it down with her *o* hands
14:14 the results of his *o* ways
14:21 despising his *o* fellowman is
15:27 ostracism upon his *o* house
15:32 is rejecting his *o* soul, but
16:2 a man are pure in his *o* eyes
17:28 anyone closing up his *o* lips
18:1 seek his *o* selfish longing
19:8 heart is loving his *o* soul
19:24 it back even to his *o* mouth
20:2 is sinning against his *o* soul
20:6 each one his *o* loving-kindness
20:8 all badness with his *o* eyes
20:21 *o* future will not be blessed
21:2 man is upright in his *o* eyes
23:4 from your *o* understanding
23:18 *o* hope will not be cut off
23:26 take pleasure in my *o* ways
23:33 Your *o* eyes will see strange
23:33 *o* heart will speak perverse
24:2 trouble is what their *o* lips
24:14 *o* hope will not be cut off
25:9 Plead your *o* cause with your
25:27 to search out their *o* glory
26:5 someone wise in his *o* eyes
26:12 a man wise in his *o* eyes
26:16 is wiser in his *o* eyes than
27:2 not your *o* mouth, praise you
27:2 foreigner, and not your *o* lips
27:10 not leave your *o* companion
27:10 the house of your *o* brother
28:10 himself fall into his *o* pit
28:11 man is wise in his *o* eyes
28:19 is cultivating his *o* ground
28:26 is trusting in his *o* heart
29:24 is hating his *o* soul
30:12 that is pure in its *o* eyes
30:12 washed from its *o* excrement
30:28 takes hold with its *o* hands
30:31 soldiers of his *o* people
31:7 remember one's *o* trouble no
31:19 her *o* hands take hold of the
Ec 1:16 my *o* heart saw a great deal
2:9 my *o* wisdom remained mine
4:5 stupid . . . eating his *o* flesh
6:3 *o* soul is not satisfied
6:4 with darkness his *o* name will
6:7 *o* soul does not get filled
7:22 your *o* heart well knows even
10:3 his *o* heart is lacking, and he
10:4 do not leave your *o* place, for
10:10 exert his *o* vital energies
10:16 *o* princes keep eating even in
10:17 *o* princes eat at the proper
Ca 1:6 The sons of my *o* mother grew
1:12 my *o* spikenard has given out
5:5 my *o* hands dripped with myrrh
6:2 My *o* dear one has gone down to
6:12 my *o* soul had put me at the
Isa 1:3 my *o* people have not behaved
2:22 For your *o* sakes, hold off
3:11 rendered by his *o* hands will
3:25 sword your *o* men will fall
4:1 eat our *o* bread and wear our
4:1 and wear our *o* mantles
5:21 those wise in their *o* eyes
5:21 in front of their *o* faces
6:10 *o* heart may not understand
9:20 eat the flesh of his *o* arm
10:24 *o* staff against you in the
11:8 actually put his *o* hand
13:11 its *o* badness upon the
13:11 *o* error upon the wicked
13:14 each one to his *o* people
13:14 each one to his *o* land
13:16 their *o* wives will be raped
14:2 bring them to their *o* place
14:18 each one in his *o* house
14:20 brought your *o* land to ruin
14:20 you killed your *o* people
14:21 block for his *o* sons
14:25 him down on my *o* mountains

Isa 15:5 *o* heart cries out over Moab
16:8 *o* shoots had been left to
17:5 *o* arm harvests the ears of
17:7 *o* eyes will gaze at the Holy
19:3 shall confuse its *o* counsel
26:11 fire for your *o* adversaries
27:11 *o* Former will show it no
28:26 His *o* God instructs him
28:28 and his *o* steeds, but he
29:4 from the dust your *o* saying
29:22 his *o* face now grow pale
30:2 inquired of my *o* mouth, to
30:4 *o* envoys reach even Hanes
30:21 *o* ears will hear a word
31:2 not called back his *o* words
31:8 *o* young men will come to be
31:9 *o* crag will pass away out
33:11 *o* spirit, as a fire, will
33:16 *o* bread will certainly be
33:18 *o* heart will comment in
33:20 *o* eyes will see Jerusalem
34:17 *o* hand has apportioned the
35:4 *o* God will come with
36:12 eat their *o* excrement and
36:12 drink their *o* urine with
36:16 each one from his *o* vine
36:16 one from his *o* fig tree and
36:16 the water of his *o* cistern
36:17 land like your *o* land, a
36:18 *o* land out of the hand of
37:7 and return to his *o* land
37:7 by the sword in his *o* land
37:18 the lands, and their *o* land
37:35 to save it for my *o* sake
37:38 his *o* sons, struck him down
38:12 My *o* habitation has been
38:19 knowledge to his *o* sons
39:2 his *o* house and in all his
39:6 all that is in your *o* house
39:7 your *o* sons that will come
39:8 will continue in my *o* days
40:11 will shepherd his *o* drove
42:8 shall I give my *o* glory
43:7 have created for my *o* glory
43:13 out of my *o* hand
43:25 for my *o* sake, and your
43:26 tell your *o* account of it in
43:27 Your *o* father, the first
43:27 your *o* spokesmen have
44:20 His *o* heart that has been
44:26 counsel of his *o* messengers
45:12 my *o* hands have stretched
45:23 By my *o* self I have sworn
45:23 my *o* mouth in righteousness
46:2 captivity their *o* soul must
46:10 My *o* counsel will stand
46:13 *o* salvation will not be
47:15 each one to his *o* region
48:3 out of my *o* mouth they went
48:5 My *o* idol has done them, and
48:5 and my *o* carved image and
48:5 and my *o* molten image have
48:11, 11 *o* sake, for my *o* sake
48:11 shall I give my *o* glory
48:13 *o* hand laid the foundation
48:13 *o* right hand extended out
48:14 his *o* arm will be upon the
49:2 concealed me in his *o* quiver
49:4 I have used up my *o* power
49:5 my *o* God will have become
49:13 upon his *o* afflicted ones
49:20 in your *o* ears the sons of
49:22 will carry your *o* daughters
49:25 your *o* sons I myself shall
49:26 eat their *o* flesh
49:26 drunk with their *o* blood
50:1 Because of your *o* errors
50:1 of your *o* transgressions
51:5 my *o* arms will judge even
51:6 my *o* righteousness will not
51:20 *o* sons have swooned away
52:8 Your *o* watchmen have raised
53:6 each one to his *o* way that
54:3 your *o* offspring will take
56:7 my *o* house will be called
56:11 turned to their *o* way
56:11 gain from his *o* border
57:10 a revival of your *o* power
58:7 hide . . . from your *o* flesh
58:10 your *o* soulful desire, and
58:13 doing your *o* delights on
58:13 than doing your *o* ways
59:2 your *o* sins have caused the
59:3 your *o* palms have become

Isa 59:3 *o* lips have spoken falsehood
59:3 Your *o* tongue kept muttering
59:7 Their *o* feet keep running
59:16 *o* righteousness was the
60:2 his *o* glory will be seen
60:4 your *o* sons keep coming
60:7 beautify my *o* house of
60:10 their *o* kings will minister
60:18 call your *o* walls Salvation
60:22 speed it up in its *o* time
62:4 your *o* land will no more be
62:4 *o* land will be owned as a
63:9 *o* personal messenger saved
63:11 His *o* holy spirit
63:12 lasting name for his *o* self
63:14 beautiful name for your *o*
63:18 Our *o* adversaries have
64:5 in your *o* ways. Look! You
64:10 Your *o* holy cities have
65:6 reward into their *o* bosom
65:7 their *o* errors and for the
65:7 into their *o* bosom
65:9 my *o* servants will reside
65:13 My *o* servants will eat, but
65:13 My *o* servants will drink
65:13 My *o* servants will rejoice
65:14 *o* servants will cry out
65:15 *o* servants he will call by
65:22 the work of their *o* hands
66:2 things my *o* hand has made
66:3 have chosen their *o* ways
66:13 *o* mother keeps comforting
Jer 1:16 the works of their *o* hands
2:7 my *o* inheritance you made
2:11 my *o* people have exchanged
2:15 His *o* cities have been set
2:19 your *o* acts of unfaithfulness
2:32 my *o* people—they have
3:7 at her *o* treacherous sister
3:11 proved her *o* soul to be more
4:7 *o* cities will fall in ruins
5:7 Your *o* sons have left me
5:25 Your *o* errors have turned
5:25 your *o* sins have held back
5:31 my *o* people have loved it
6:3 grazed off each one his *o* part
6:19 attention to my very *o* words
9:4 against his *o* companion, and
9:8 speaking with his *o* companion
9:18 our *o* beaming eyes trickle
10:20 *o* tent has been despoiled
10:20 my *o* tent cords have all
10:20 My *o* sons have gone forth
11:17 committed on their *o* part
12:6 even your *o* brothers and the
12:6 household of your *o* father
14:7 if our *o* errors do testify
14:9 your *o* name has been called
15:7 back from their *o* ways
15:15 on account of your *o* self
15:19 become like my *o* mouth
17:4 loose, even of your *o* accord
18:12 after our *o* thoughts we
18:21 may their *o* men become
22:22 all your *o* shepherds; and
23:8 dwell on their *o* ground
23:11 in my *o* house I have found
23:14 each one from his *o* badness
23:16 The vision of their *o* heart
23:22 my people hear my *o* words
23:25 falsehood in my *o* name
23:26 trickiness of their *o* heart
23:28 with whom my *o* word is
23:36 to each one his *o* word
26:11 have heard with your *o* ears
27:7 his *o* land comes, and many
29:6 take wives for your *o* sons
29:6 give your *o* daughters to
29:21 falsehood in my *o* name
29:23 falsely in my *o* name
30:20 *o* assembly will be firmly
30:21 his *o* ruler will go forth
31:14 *o* people will become
31:17 return to their *o* territory
31:30 each one for his *o* error
32:4 *o* eyes will see even the
32:20 make a name for your *o* self
32:34 my *o* name has been called
33:21 *o* covenant be broken with
33:24 *o* people they keep treating
33:25 *o* covenant of the day and
34:3 *o* eyes will see even the
34:3 *o* mouth will speak even
36:30 *o* dead body will become

Jer 39:12 your *o* eyes set upon him
42:12 return you to your *o* soil
44:9 your *o* bad deeds and the
46:12 *o* outcry has filled the land
48:15 gone up against her *o* cities
48:25 *o* arm has been broken, is
48:32 *o* flourishing shoots have
48:36 *o* heart will be boisterous
48:41 *o* strong places will
49:1 *o* people have taken up
49:5 each one in his *o* direction
49:11 *o* widows will trust even
49:13 by my *o* self I have sworn
49:13 her *o* cities will become
49:29, 29 *o* tents and . . . *o* flocks
49:29 *o* camels will be carried
50:6 *o* shepherds have caused them
50:7 *o* adversaries have said
50:11 pillaging my *o* inheritance
50:16 each one to his *o* people
50:16 flee each one to his *o* land
51:6 each one for his *o* soul
51:9 go each one to his *o* land
51:14 has sworn by his *o* soul, I
51:47 *o* land will become ashamed
51:47 *o* slain ones will fall in
52:8 *o* military force was
La 1:2 very *o* companions have dealt
1:5 *o* children have walked captive
1:10 spread out his *o* hand against
1:18 My *o* virgins and my
1:18 my *o* young men have gone into
1:19 In the city my *o* priests and
1:19 and my *o* old men have expired
2:7 they have let out their *o* voice
2:9 Her *o* prophets also have found
2:14 Your *o* prophets have visioned
2:20 the women keep eating their *o*
3:33 not out of his *o* heart has he
3:51 My *o* eye has dealt severely
4:10 have boiled their *o* children
5:2 Our *o* hereditary possession has
5:4 have had to drink our *o* water
5:4 For a price our *o* wood comes
Eze 3:3 cause your *o* belly to eat
3:10 and hear with your *o* ears
3:18 ask back from your *o* hand
3:19 have delivered your *o* soul
3:20 ask back from your *o* hand
3:21 have delivered your *o* soul
7:4 you I shall bring your *o* ways
7:4 your *o* detestable things will
7:9 your *o* detestable things will
7:11 is not from their *o* selves
7:13 each one of his *o* life by his
7:13 life by his *o* error
7:16 each one in his *o* error
7:19 abhorrent thing their *o* gold
9:10 bring upon their *o* head
11:20 may walk in my *o* statutes
11:20 my *o* judicial decisions and
11:21 certainly bring their *o* way
12:12 may not see with his *o* eye
13:2 out of their *o* heart, Hear
13:3 walking after their *o* spirit
13:4 your *o* prophets have become
13:17 out of their *o* heart, and
16:7 your *o* hair grew luxuriantly
16:31 made your *o* height in every
16:32 instead of her *o* husband
16:43 your *o* way upon your very
16:55 your *o* sisters, Sodom and
16:55 your *o* dependent towns will
16:57 *o* badness got to be exposed
18:7 he would give his *o* bread
18:13 On him his *o* blood will
18:16 he has given his *o* bread
18:20 Upon his *o* self the very
18:20 and upon his *o* self the very
18:25 not my *o* way adjusted right
18:27 preserve his *o* soul alive
20:9 for the sake of my *o* name
20:14 for the sake of my *o* name
20:16 my *o* judicial decisions
20:19 Walk in my *o* statutes, and
20:19 my *o* judicial decisions and
20:20 And sanctify my *o* sabbaths
20:22 for the sake of my *o* name
20:24 my *o* judicial decisions and
20:24 they rejected my *o* statutes
20:24 they profaned my *o* sabbaths
20:39 his *o* dungy idols
20:43 a loathing at your *o* faces
21:10 the scepter of my *o* son
Eze 21:32 Your *o* blood will prove to
22:11 his *o* daughter-in-law a man
22:11 daughter of his *o* father
22:31 bring upon their *o* head
26:11 *o* pillars of strength will
26:16 *o* embroidered garments
27:4 *o* builders have perfected
27:11 to be in your *o* towers
28:4 made wealth for your *o* self
29:12 *o* cities will become a
30:7 its *o* cities will come to
30:18 her *o* dependent towns will
32:10 each one for his *o* soul
33:4 his *o* blood will come to be
33:4 come to be upon his *o* head
33:5 His *o* blood will come to be
33:5 come to be upon his *o* self
33:5 *o* soul would have escaped
33:6 for its *o* error it itself
33:8 will die in his *o* error
33:8 ask back at your *o* hand
33:9 will die in his *o* error
33:9 deliver your *o* soul
33:13 in his *o* righteousness
33:13 his *o* righteous acts will
34:3 you clothe your *o* selves
34:8 my *o* sheep they did not feed
35:9 your *o* cities will not be
35:10 they will become my *o*, and
36:7 bear their *o* humiliation
36:8 very *o* boughs and bear your
36:8 and bear your *o* fruitage for
36:31 loathing at your *o* person
38:21 Against his *o* brother the
39:3 out of your *o* right hand
40:21 And its *o* side pillars and
40:21 its *o* porch proved to be
45:22 in his *o* behalf and in
46:17 belong to their *o* selves
46:18 *o* possession he should give
Da 2:5 privies your *o* houses will be
2:11 *o* dwelling does not exist
2:17 Daniel went to his *o* house
2:29 *o* thoughts came up as regards
3:12 are not serving your *o* gods
3:14 you are not serving my *o* gods
3:28 except their *o* God
4:27 and remove your *o* sins by
4:33 *o* body got to be wet, until
4:34 my *o* understanding began to
4:35 doing according to his *o* will
4:36 upon my *o* kingdom, and
5:6 *o* thoughts began to frighten
5:20 and his *o* spirit became hard
5:20 *o* dignity was taken away from
5:21 his *o* body got to be wet
6:22 My *o* God sent his angel and
7:26 *o* rulership they finally took
7:28 *o* thoughts kept frightening
7:28 matter . . . kept in my *o* heart
8:24 but not by his *o* power
9:19 Do not delay, for your *o* sake
9:19 God, for your *o* name has
10:8 my *o* dignity became changed
11:9 and go back to his *o* soil
11:19 the fortresses of his *o* land
11:36 do according to his *o* will
Ho 2:6 *o* roadways she will not find
4:7 My *o* glory they have exchanged
4:12 my *o* people keep inquiring
4:12 their *o* hand staff keeps
4:13 *o* daughters-in-law commit
7:2 do not say to their *o* heart
7:7 Their *o* kings have all fallen
9:4 bread is for their *o* soul
9:15 away from my *o* house
10:14 your *o* fortified cities will
10:14 to pieces alongside her *o* sons
12:14 he leaves upon his *o* self
13:2 to their *o* understanding
13:16 Their *o* children will be
14:4 love them of my *o* free will
Joe 1:3 an account to your *o* sons
2:7 go each one in his *o* ways
3:2 apportioned out my *o* land
3:5, 5 my *o* silver and my *o* gold
3:5 my *o* desirable good things
3:6 far from their *o* territory
3:7 treatment upon your *o* heads
Am 1:11 pursuing his *o* brother with
1:11 his *o* merciful qualities
1:13 their *o* territory
2:4 did not keep his *o* regulations
2:7 a man and his *o* father have
Am 5:2 forsaken upon her *o* ground
6:8 has sworn by his *o* soul
7:11 into exile from its *o* ground
7:17 into exile from its *o* ground
9:2 from there my *o* hand will
Ob 15 will return upon your *o* head
Jon 2:8 leave their *o* loving-kindness
4:2 happened to be on my *o* ground
Mic 2:4 apportions out our *o* fields
2:7 Do not my *o* words do good in
2:8 my *o* people proceeded to rise
3:11 Her *o* head ones judge merely
3:11 her *o* priests instruct just
3:11 her *o* prophets practice
4:9 has your *o* counselor perished
6:12 her *o* rich men have become
6:12 her *o* inhabitants have
7:2 hunt, everyone his *o* brother
7:3 of his soul, his very *o*
7:10 *o* eyes will look upon her
Na 1:6 His *o* rage will certainly be
2:13 your *o* maned young lions
3:10 Her *o* children also came to
Hab 1:7 From itself its *o* justice
1:7 justice and its *o* dignity go
1:8 its *o* steeds come. They fly
2:6 multiplying what is not his *o*
3:11 your *o* arrows kept going
3:14 With his *o* rods you pierced
Zep 2:3 practiced His *o* judicial
2:9 remnant of my *o* nation will
3:5 giving his *o* judicial decision
Hag 1:9 one in behalf of his *o* house
Zec 1:16 My *o* house will be built in
4:9 his *o* hands will finish it
6:12 his *o* place he will sprout
10:7 their *o* sons will see and
11:5 *o* shepherds do not show any
11:8 their *o* soul felt a loathing
11:17 His *o* arm will without
11:17 *o* right eye will without
12:6 be inhabited in her *o* place
Mal 1:5 And your *o* eyes will see it
Mt 6:34 day will have its *o* anxieties
6:34 for each day is its *o* badness
7:3 the rafter in your *o* eye
7:4 a rafter is in your *o* eye
7:5 the rafter from your *o* eye
9:1 went into his *o* city
10:36 persons of his *o* household
11:2 by means of his *o* disciples
13:57 unhonored . . . in his *o* house
20:15 do what I want with my *o*
22:5 went off, one to his *o* field
25:15 according to his *o* ability
Mr 4:28 Of its *o* self the ground
6:4 relatives and in his *o* house
Lu 1:56 and returned to her *o* home
2:3 each one to his *o* city
2:39 to their *o* city Nazareth
6:41 rafter that is in your *o* eye
6:42 the rafter from your *o* eye
6:44 tree is known by its *o* fruit
9:25 but loses his *o* self or
10:34 mounted him upon his *o* beast
14:26 yes, and even his *o* soul
16:8 toward their *o* generation
18:28 have left our *o* things and
19:22 Out of your *o* mouth I judge
22:71 heard it out of his *o* mouth
Joh 1:11 He came to his *o* home, but
1:11 his *o* people did not take
1:41 found his *o* brother, Simon
4:44 *o* homeland a prophet has no
5:18 calling God his *o* Father
5:19 of his *o* initiative, but
5:30 of my *o* initiative; just
5:30 I seek, not my *o* will, but
5:43 arrived in his *o* name, you
7:17 I speak of my *o* originality
7:18 speaks of his *o* originality
7:18 is seeking his *o* glory
7:28 not come of my *o* initiative
8:17 in your *o* Law it is written
8:28 nothing of my *o* initiative
8:42 I come of my *o* initiative at
8:44 to his *o* disposition
10:3 calls his *o* sheep by name
10:4 he has got all his *o* out, he
10:12 sheep do not belong as his **o**
10:18 of my *o* initiative
11:51 say of his *o* originality
12:49 spoken out of my *o* impulse
13:1 Jesus, having loved his *o*

Joh 14:10 speak of my *o* originality
15:19 fond of what is its *o*
16:13 not speak of his *o* impulse
16:32 each one to his *o* house and
17:11 on account of your *o* name
17:12 on account of your *o* name
18:34 *o* originality that you say
18:35 *o* nation and the chief
19:27 took her to his *o* home
Ac 1:7 placed in his *o* jurisdiction
1:25 deviated to go to his *o* place
2:6 speaking in his *o* language
2:8 *o* language in which we were
4:23 they went to their *o* people
4:32 things he possessed was his *o*
6:10 hold their *o* against the
7:21 brought him up as her *o* son
12:10 to them of its *o* accord
13:36 of God in his *o* generation
18:6 blood be upon your *o* heads
20:28 with the blood of his *o* Son
21:11 bound his *o* feet and hands
25:19 their *o* worship of the deity
27:19 with their *o* hands, they
28:30 years in his *o* hired house
Ro 2:15 between their *o* thoughts
3:25 exhibit his *o* righteousness
3:26 exhibit his *o* righteousness
4:19 he considered his *o* body
5:8 God recommends his *o* love to
8:3 God, by sending his *o* Son in
8:20 futility, not by its *o* will
8:32 not even spare his *o* Son but
10:3 seeking to establish their *o*
10:8 in your *o* mouth and in your
10:8 and in your *o* heart; that is
10:9 word in your *o* mouth, that
11:14 those who are my *o* flesh to
11:24 into their *o* olive tree
11:25 be discreet in your *o* eyes
12:16 discreet in your *o* eyes
14:4 To his *o* master he stands or
14:5 convinced in his *o* mind
16:4 risked their *o* necks for my
16:18 but of their *o* bellies; and
1Co 3:8 will receive his *o* reward
3:8 according to his *o* labor
3:19 the wise in their *o* cunning
4:12 working with our *o* hands
6:18 is sinning against his *o* body
7:2 let each man have his *o* wife
7:2 each woman have her *o* husband
7:4 authority over her *o* body, but
7:4 authority over his *o* body, but
7:7 each one has his *o* gift from
7:37 authority over his *o* will
7:37 this decision in his *o* heart
7:37 to keep his *o* virginity, he
9:7 as a soldier at his *o* expense
10:24 not his *o* advantage, but
10:29 not your *o*, but that of the
10:33 not seeking my *o* advantage
11:13 Judge for your *o* selves: Is
11:21 takes his *o* evening meal
13:5 not look for its *o* interests
14:35 question their *o* husbands at
15:23 But each one in his *o* rank
15:38 each of the seeds its *o* body
16:2 at his *o* house set something
16:21 greeting . . . in my *o* hand
2Co 1:23 a witness against my *o* soul
6:12 in your *o* tender affections
8:4 their *o* accord kept begging
8:17 going forth of his *o* accord
10:6 your *o* obedience has been
11:26 in dangers from my *o* race
Ga 1:14 many of my *o* age in my race
6:3 he is deceiving his *o* mind
6:4 him prove what his *o* work is
6:5 each one will carry his *o* load
6:11 written you with my *o* hand
Eph 1:14 ransom God's *o* possession
5:28 wives as their *o* bodies
5:29 man ever hated his *o* flesh
Php 2:4 upon just your *o* matters, but
2:12 working out your *o* salvation
2:21 are seeking their *o* interests
3:9 not my *o* righteousness
Col 4:18 Paul's, in my *o* hand
1Th 2:7 cherishes her *o* children
2:8 but also our *o* souls, because
2:14 hands of your *o* countrymen
4:4 get possession of his *o* vessel
4:11 and to mind your *o* business
2Th 2:6 revealed in his *o* due time
3:17 in my *o* hand, which is a
1Ti 2:6 at its *o* particular times
3:4 presiding over his *o* household
3:5 preside over his *o* household
3:12 and their *o* households
5:4 devotion in their *o* household
5:8 for those who are his *o*
6:15 in its *o* appointed times
2Ti 1:9 by reason of his *o* purpose and
4:3 accord with their *o* desires
Tit 1:3 in his *o* due times he made
1:12 their *o* prophet, said
2:5 to their *o* husbands, so that
2:14 a people peculiarly his *o*
Phm 12 is, my *o* tender affections
14 but of your *o* free will
19 am writing with my *o* hand
Heb 3:7 people listen to his *o* voice
3:15 people listen to his *o* voice
4:7 people listen to his *o* voice
4:10 rested from his *o* works
4:10 just as God did from his *o*
5:2 with his *o* weakness
5:4 honor, not of his *o* accord
7:27 first for his *o* sins and then
9:12 bulls, but with his *o* blood
9:25 with blood not his *o*
11:14 seeking a place of their *o*
12:3 against their *o* interests
13:12 the people with his *o* blood
Jas 1:14 and enticed by his *o* desire
1:26 on deceiving his *o* heart
1Pe 2:24 bore our sins in his *o* body
3:1 subjection to your *o* husbands
3:5 to their *o* husbands
2Pe 2:12 their *o* course of destruction
2:16 *o* violation of what was
2:22 has returned to its *o* vomit
3:3 according to their *o* desires
3:16 to their *o* destruction
3:17 from your *o* steadfastness
1Jo 3:12 his *o* works were wicked
5:10 witness given in his *o* case
Jude 6 their *o* proper dwelling
13 their *o* causes for shame
16 according to their *o* desires
16 the sake of their *o* benefit
18 according to their *o* desires
Re 1:5 by means of his *o* blood
10:3 uttered their *o* voices
10:7 to his *o* slaves the prophets
11:18 your *o* wrath came, and the

Owned
Ge 13:5 Lot . . . *o* sheep and cattle
20:3 she is *o* by another owner as
De 22:22 lying down with a woman *o*
Isa 62:4 and your land *O* as a Wife
62:4 land will be *o* as a wife

Owner
Ge 20:3 she is owned by another *o* as
Ex 21:3 If he is the *o* of a wife
21:22 what the *o* of the woman may
21:28 *o* of the bull is free from
21:29 warning was served on its *o*
21:29 its *o* is to be put to death
21:34 the *o* of the pit is to make
21:34 he is to return to its *o*, and
21:36 *o* would not keep it under
22:8 the *o* of the house must be
22:11 and their *o* must accept it
22:12 make compensation to their *o*
22:14 die while its *o* is not with
22:15 If its *o* is with it, he is
Le 21:4 woman possessed by an *o*
De 22:22 a woman owned by an *o*
24:4 first *o* of her who dismissed
Jg 19:22 old man, the *o* of the house
19:23 the *o* of the house went on
2Sa 11:26 began to wail over her *o*
Pr 12:4 wife is a crown to her *o*
17:8 in the eyes of its grand *o*
23:2 are the *o* of soulful desire
31:11 heart of her *o* has put trust
31:23 Her *o* is someone known in
31:28 her *o* rises up, and he
Ec 5:11 is there to the grand *o* of
5:13 being kept for their grand *o*
Isa 1:3 the ass the manger of its *o*
54:1 woman with a husbandly *o*
54:5 your husbandly *o*, Jehovah of
Jer 3:14 husbandly *o* of you people
Ho 2:16 will no longer call me My *o*
Joe 1:8 over the *o* of her youth
Mt 21:40 the *o* of the vineyard comes
Mr 12:9 the *o* of the vineyard do
Lu 20:13 the *o* of the vineyard said
20:15 *o* of the vineyard do to them
2Ti 2:21 useful to his *o*, prepared
2Pe 2:1 even the *o* that bought them
Jude 4 proving false to our only *O*

Owners
Nu 21:28 *o* of the high places of the
1Ch 4:22 became *o* of Moabite wives
Es 1:17 despise their *o* in their own
1:20 will give honor to their *o*
Job 31:39 its *o* I have caused to pant
Pr 1:19 away the very soul of its *o*
16:22 To its *o* insight is a well
Ec 7:12 wisdom itself preserves . . . *o*
Isa 16:8 *o* of the nations themselves
26:13 have acted as *o* of us
Lu 19:33 the *o* of it said to them
1Ti 6:1 keep on considering their *o*
6:2 those having believing *o* not
Tit 2:9 in subjection to their *o* in
1Pe 2:18 in subjection to their *o*

Ownership
De 4:20 a people of private *o* to him
Isa 62:5 *o* of a virgin as his wife
62:5 will take *o* of you as a wife
Jer 31:32 had husbandly *o* of them

Owning
Pr 1:17 eyes of anything *o* wings
Ec 10:20 something *o* wings will tell

Oxen
Ps 8:7 cattle and *o*, all of them

Oxgoad
1Sa 13:21 and for fixing fast the *o*

Oxgoads
Ec 12:11 of the wise ones are like *o*

Ozem
1Ch 2:15 *O* the sixth, David the
2:25 sons of Jerahmeel . . . *O*

Ozni
Nu 26:16 of *O* the family of the

Oznites
Nu 26:16 of Ozni the family of the *O*

Paarai
2Sa 23:35 the Carmelite, *P* the Arbite

Pace
Ge 33:14 the *p* of the livestock that
33:14 *p* of the children until I
Pr 4:12 your *p* will not be cramped

Paced
Job 28:8 young lion has not *p* over it

Pacing
Pr 30:29 that do well in their *p*

Pack
Isa 33:20 tent that no one will *p* up
Jer 10:17 from the earth your *p* load

Paddan
Ge 48:7 when I was coming from *P*

Paddan-aram
Ge 25:20 Bethuel the Syrian of *P*
28:2 Get up, go to *P* to the house
28:5 and he struck out for *P*
28:6 sent him away to *P* to take
28:7 and was on his way to *P*
31:18 goods . . . accumulated in *P*
33:18 while he was coming from *P*
35:9 coming from *P* and blessed
35:26 who were born to him in *P*
46:15 she bore to Jacob in *P*

Padon
Ezr 2:44 the sons of *P*
Ne 7:47 sons of Sia, the sons of *P*

Page-columns
Jer 36:23 read three or four *p*, he

Pagiel
Nu 1:13 of Asher, *P* the son of Ochran
2:27 is *P* the son of Ochran
7:72 *P* the son of Ochran
7:77 of *P* the son of Ochran
10:26 *P* the son of Ochran

Pahath-moab
Ezr 2:6 sons of *P*, of the sons of

Ca 7:8 I shall go up on the *p* tree
Isa 28:4 in his *p*, he swallows it
36:6 enter into his *p* and pierce
38:6 out of the *p* of the king of
62:3 turban in the *p* of your God
Jer 12:7 into the *p* of her enemies
15:21 the *p* of the tyrannical ones
Eze 21:14, 14 and strike *p* against *p*
21:17, 17 *p* against my other *p*
Joe 1:12 the *p* tree and the apple tree
Mic 4:10 out of the *p* of your enemies
Joh 12:13 branches of *p* trees and
Re 7:9 were *p* branches in their hands

Palms
Ex 29:24 upon the *p* of Aaron and upon
29:24 upon the *p* of his sons, and
Le 8:27 upon the *p* of Aaron and the
8:27 Aaron and the *p* of his sons
8:28 took them off their *p* and
Nu 5:18 put upon her *p* the memorial
6:19 *p* of the Nazirite after he has
Jg 8:6 said: Are the *p* of Zebah and of
8:15 saying, Are the *p* of Zebah and
14:9 scraped it out into his *p* and
1Sa 5:4 head of Dagon and the *p* of
2Sa 18:12 weighing upon my *p* a
1Ki 8:22 his *p* out to the heavens
8:38 their *p* to this house
8:54 *p* spread out to the heavens
2Ki 4:34, 34 his own *p* upon his *p* and
9:35 feet and the *p* of the hands
1Ch 12:17 there is no wrong on my *p*
2Ch 6:12 and he now spread out his *p*
6:13 his *p* out to the heavens
6:29 spreads out his *p* toward
Ezr 9:5 spread out my *p* to Jehovah my
Job 11:13 spread out your *p* to him
16:17 is no violence upon my *p*
31:7 has stuck in my own *p*
Ps 44:20 our *p* to a strange god
63:4 I shall raise my *p*
88:9 To you I have spread out my *p*
119:48 shall raise my *p* to your
141:2 raising up of my *p* as the
Isa 1:15 when you spread out your *p*
49:16 Upon my *p* I have engraved
59:3 *p* have become polluted with
59:6 violence is in their *p*
Jer 4:31 She keeps spreading out her *p*
La 2:19 Raise to him your *p* on
3:41 our *p* to God in the heavens
Da 10:10 knees and the *p* of my hands

Palm-tree
1Ki 6:29 cherubs and *p* figures and
6:32 cherubs and *p* figures and the
6:32 the cherubs and the *p* figures
6:35 carved cherubs and *p* figures
7:36 cherubs, lions and *p* figures
2Ch 3:5 brought up upon it *p* figures
Eze 40:16 there were *p* figures
40:22 its *p* figures were of the
40:26 And it had *p* figures, one
40:31 *p* figures were on its side
40:34 *p* figures were on its side
40:37 *p* figures were on its side
41:18 cherubs and *p* figures
41:18 *p* figure between a cherub
41:19 *p* figure on this side
41:19 the *p* figure on that side
41:20 *p* figures, on the wall of
41:25 cherubs and *p* figures
41:26 *p* figures over here and

Palpitated
Ps 38:10 My own heart has *p* heavily

Palti
Nu 13:9 *P* the son of Raphu
1Sa 25:44 *P* the son of Laish, who was

Paltiel
Nu 34:26 of Issachar a chieftain, *P*
2Sa 3:15 husband, *P* the son of Laish

Paltite
2Sa 23:26 Helez the *P*, Ira the son of

Pampering
Pr 29:21 *p* one's servant from youth

Pamphylia
Ac 2:10 *P*, Egypt and the parts of
13:13 and arrived at Perga in *P*
14:24 Pisidia and came into *P*
15:38 departed from them from *P*
27:5 open sea along Cilicia and *P*

Pan
2Sa 13:9 took the deep *p* and poured

Panel
Ex 26:15 make the *p* frames for the
26:16 is the length of a *p* frame
26:16 is the width of each *p* frame
26:17 Each *p* frame has two tenons
26:17 *p* frames of the tabernacle
26:18 *p* frames for the tabernacle
26:18 twenty *p* frames for the side
26:19 under the twenty *p* frames
26:19 under the one *p* frame with
26:19 *p* frame with its two tenons
26:20 side, twenty *p* frames
26:21 under the one *p* frame and
26:21 under the other *p* frame
26:22 you will make six *p* frames
26:23 two *p* frames as corner posts
26:25 there must be eight *p* frames
26:25 under the one *p* frame and
26:25 under the other *p* frame
26:26 the *p* frames of the one side
26:27 five bars for the *p* frames
26:27 five bars for the *p* frames
26:28 the center of the *p* frames
26:29 overlay the *p* frames with
35:11 its hooks and its *p* frames
36:20 *p* frames for the tabernacle
36:21 was the length of a *p* frame
36:21 the width of each *p* frame
36:22 *p* frame had two tenons
36:22 *p* frames of the tabernacle
36:23 *p* frames for the tabernacle
36:23 twenty *p* frames for the side
36:24 beneath the twenty *p* frames
36:24 *p* frame with its two tenons
36:24 *p* frame with its two tenons
36:25 he made twenty *p* frames
36:26 beneath the one *p* frame and
36:26 beneath the other *p* frame
36:27 he made six *p* frames
36:28 two *p* frames as corner posts
36:30 amounted to eight *p* frames
36:30 pedestals beneath each *p*
36:31 *p* frames of the one side of
36:32 five bars for the *p* frames
36:32 five bars for the *p* frames
36:33 middle of the *p* frames from
36:34 overlaid the *p* frames with
39:33 its *p* frames, its bars and
40:18 placing its *p* frames and
Nu 3:36 *p* frames of the tabernacle
4:31 *p* frames of the tabernacle and

Paneled
1Ki 7:3 it was *p* in with cedarwood
Hag 1:4 to dwell in your *p* houses

Paneling
Jer 22:14 the *p* will be with cedar
Eze 41:16 was *p* of wood all around

Pang
1Th 5:3 just as the *p* of distress

Pangs
Ge 3:16 in birth *p* you will bring
Ex 15:14 Birth *p* must take hold on
1Sa 4:19 *p* came unexpectedly upon her
Job 39:1 bring forth with birth *p*
39:3 When they get rid of their *p*
Ps 48:6 Birth *p* like those of a woman
73:4 For they have no deathly *p*
Ca 8:5 your mother was in birth *p*
8:5 experienced birth *p*
Isa 26:17 cries out in her birth *p*
66:7 birth *p* could come to her
Jer 13:21 birth *p* themselves seize
22:23 there come to you birth *p*
49:24 Distress and birth *p*
La 5:10 because of the *p* of hunger
Ho 13:13 *p* of a woman giving birth
Mic 4:9 *p* like those of a woman
Mt 24:8 a beginning of *p* of distress
Mr 13:8 a beginning of *p* of distress
Ac 2:24 by loosing the *p* of death

Panic
De 20:3 Do not be afraid and run in *p*
1Sa 5:6 began causing *p* and striking
2Sa 4:4 running in *p* to flee, he then
Job 40:23 it does not run in *p*
Ps 48:5 they were sent running in *p*
104:7 they were sent running in *p*
Isa 52:12 will get out in no *p*, and
Jer 49:24 and sheer *p* has seized her

Panicky
Ps 31:22 I said when I became *p*
116:11 said, when I became *p*
Isa 28:16 exercising faith will get *p*

Pans
1Ch 9:31 over the things baked in *p*

Pant
Job 31:39 owners I have caused to *p*
36:20 Do not *p* for the night
Ps 119:131 opened wide, that I may *p*
Isa 42:14 going to groan, *p*, and gasp

Panting
Ec 1:5 sun . . . coming *p* to its place
Isa 56:10 *p*, lying down, loving to
Am 2:7 *p* for the dust of the earth
Hab 2:3 it keeps *p* on to the end

Pants
Job 7:2 a slave he *p* for the shadow

Paper
2Jo 12 desire to do so with *p* and ink

Paphos
Ac 13:6 whole island as far as *P*
13:13 put out to sea from *P* and

Papyrus
Ex 2:3 then took for him an ark of *p*
Job 8:11 Will a *p* plant grow tall
Isa 18:2 by means of vessels of *p*
35:7 with reeds and *p* plants
Jer 51:32 *p* boats they have burned

Paradise
Ca 4:13 skin is a *p* of pomegranates
Lu 23:43 You will be with me in *P*
2Co 12:4 caught away into *p* and
Re 2:7 which is in the *p* of God

Parah
Jos 18:23 and Avvim and *P* and Ophrah

Paralysis
Mt 8:6 laid up in the house with *p*

Paralytic
Mt 9:2 Jesus said to the *p*: Take
9:6 said to the *p*: Get up, pick
Mr 2:3 bringing him a *p* carried by
2:4 cot on which the *p* was lying
2:5 he said to the *p*: Child, your
2:9 to say to the *p*, Your sins are
2:10 he said to the *p*

Paralyzed
Mt 4:24 and epileptic and *p* persons
9:2 a *p* man lying on a bed
Lu 5:18 a man who was *p*, and they
5:24 he said to the *p* man: I say
Ac 8:7 many that were *p* and lame
9:33 for eight years, as he was *p*

Paran
Ge 21:21 in the wilderness of *P*
Nu 10:12 in the wilderness of *P*
12:16 in the wilderness of *P*
13:3 out from the wilderness of *P*
13:26 in the wilderness of *P*, at
De 1:1 between *P* and Tophel and
33:2 the mountainous region of *P*
1Sa 25:1 down to the wilderness of *P*
1Ki 11:18 came into *P* and took men
11:18 took men with them from *P*
Hab 3:3 Holy One from Mount *P*

Parapet
De 22:8 make a *p* for your roof

Parcel
Ge 49:7 Let me *p* them out in Jacob

Parched
2Sa 17:28 and lentils and *p* grain
Isa 5:13 crowd will be *p* with thirst
19:5 river itself will become *p*
19:6 must become low and *p*
34:10 generation she will be *p*
Jer 17:6 *p* places in the wilderness
Mt 12:43 passes through *p* places in
Lu 11:24 it passes through *p* places

Parching
Isa 49:10 *p* heat or sun strike them
Jon 4:8 appoint a *p* east wind, and

Parchments
2Ti 4:13 scrolls, especially the *p*

Pardon
Ge 18:24 not *p* the place for the sake

Ge 18:26 I will *p* the whole place on
50:17 *p*, please, the revolt of
50:17 *p*, please, the revolt of the
Ex 10:17 *p*, please, my sin just this
23:21 not *p* your transgression
32:32 if you will *p* their sin
Jos 24:19 will not *p* your revolting
1Sa 15:25 please, *p* my sin and return
25:28 *P*, please, the transgression
Job 7:21 you not *p* my transgression
Ps 25:18 And *p* all my sins
99:8 A God granting *p* you proved
Isa 2:9 you cannot possibly *p* them
Ho 14:2 May you *p* error; and accept

Pardoned
Nu 14:19 as you have *p* this people
Ps 32:1 the one whose revolt is *p*
32:5 *p* the error of my sins
85:2 *p* the error of your people
Isa 33:24 be those *p* for their error
Ro 4:7 lawless deeds have been *p*

Pardoning
Ex 34:7 *p* error and transgression and
Nu 14:18 *p* error and transgression
Mic 7:18 one *p* error and passing over

Parents
Mt 10:21 will rise up against *p* and
Mr 13:12 will rise up against *p* and
Lu 2:27 as the *p* brought the young
2:41 his *p* were accustomed to go
2:43 and his *p* did not notice it
8:56 her *p* were beside themselves
18:29 or *p* or children for the sake
21:16 delivered up even by *p* and
Joh 9:2 sinned, this man or his *p*
9:3 this man sinned nor his *p*
9:18 *p* of the man that gained
9:20 his *p* said: We know that
9:22 His *p* said these things
9:23 *p* said: He is of age
Ro 1:30 disobedient to *p*
2Co 12:14 not to lay up for their *p*
12:14 the *p* for their children
Eph 6:1 be obedient to your *p* in
Col 3:20 be obedient to your *p* in
1Ti 5:4 due compensation to their *p*
2Ti 3:2 disobedient to *p*, unthankful
Heb 11:23 by his *p* after his birth

Park
Ne 2:8 the *p* that belongs to the king

Parks
Ec 2:5 made gardens and *p* for myself

Parmashta
Es 9:9 and *P* and Arisai and Aridai and

Parmenas
Ac 6:5 selected Stephen . . . and *P*

Parnach
Nu 34:25 Elizaphan the son of *P*

Parosh
Ezr 2:3 The sons of *P*, two thousand
8:3 of the sons of *P*, Zechariah
10:25 sons of *P* there were Ramiah
Ne 3:25 Pedaiah the son of *P*
7:8 sons of *P*, two thousand one
10:14 The heads of the people: *P*

Parshandatha
Es 9:7 Also, *P* and Dalphon and Aspatha

Parsin
Da 5:25 MENE, MENE, TEKEL and *P*

Part
Ge 3:8 about the breezy *p* of the day
4:7 will you, for your *p*, get the
15:10 put each *p* of them so as to
27:16 the hairless *p* of his neck
31:36 What is the revolt on my *p*
41:32 established on the *p* of the
42:21 implored compassion on our *p*
45:18 eat the fat *p* of the land
49:1 in the final *p* of the days
Ex 12:7 the upper *p* of the doorway
12:22 the upper *p* of the doorway
12:23 the upper *p* of the doorway
12:42 *p* of all the sons of Israel
29:40 tenth *p* of an ephah measure
34:11 For your *p* keep what I am
Le 20:5 my *p*, shall certainly fix my
20:24 your *p*, will take possession
20:24 for my *p*, shall give it to
Le 21:13 his *p*, he should take a
25:31 *p* of the field of the country
26:12 you, on your *p*, will prove
26:16 then I, for my *p*, shall do
26:32 And I, for my *p*, will lay
26:41 Yet I, for my *p*, proceeded
27:22 no *p* of the field of his
27:30 tenth *p* of the land, out of
27:31 buy any of his tenth *p* back
27:32 tenth *p* of the herd and flock
Nu 5:13 on her *p*, has defiled herself
7:84 *p* of the chieftains of Israel
15:25 they, for their *p*, brought as
15:26 mistake on the *p* of all the
18:21 given every tenth *p* in Israel
18:24 tenth *p* of the sons of Israel
18:26 the tenth *p* that I have given
18:26, 26 a tenth *p* of the tenth *p*
23:10 the fourth *p* of Israel
31:27 those taking *p* in the battle
De 4:6 this is wisdom on your *p*
4:6 understanding on your *p* before
12:17 the tenth *p* of your grain
14:23 eat the tenth *p* of your grain
14:28 tenth *p* of your produce in
15:9 has become a sin on your *p*
23:21 become a sin on your *p*
23:22 not become a sin on your *p*
24:1 something indecent on her *p*
24:15 it must become sin on your *p*
32:5 ruinously on their own *p*
32:21 They, for their *p*, have
32:21 I, for my *p*, shall incite
33:21 the first *p* for himself
Jos 9:19 We, for our *p*, have sworn to
22:2 For your *p*, you have kept all
22:18 for your *p*, rebel today
22:29 unthinkable, on our *p*, to
24:16 unthinkable, on our *p*, to
Jg 2:2 And for your *p*, you must not
2:21 for my *p*, shall not drive
6:18 I, for my *p*, shall keep
9:18 you, for your *p*, have risen up
11:9 I, for my *p*, shall become
11:23 and you, for your *p*, would
15:14 He, for his *p*, came as far
15:14 the Philistines, for their *p*
16:5 we, for our *p*, shall give you
17:10 I, for my *p*, shall give you
19:12 no *p* of the sons of Israel
Ru 3:4 he, for his *p*, will tell you
1Sa 2:30 It is unthinkable, on my *p*
5:4 Only the fish *p* had been left
6:15 for their *p*, offered up burnt
9:5 Saul, for his *p*, said to his
9:17 Jehovah, for his *p*, answered
12:23 it is unthinkable, on my *p*
13:5 the Philistines, for their *p*
15:34 Saul, for his *p*, went up to
16:3 for my *p*, shall make known
19:3 I, for my *p*, shall go out
22:15 It is unthinkable on my *p!*
23:20 our *p* will be to surrender
24:6 unthinkable, on my *p*, from
26:11 unthinkable, on my *p*, from
2Sa 2:31 of David, for their *p*, had
4:2 be counted as *p* of Benjamin
5:18 Philistines, for their *p*
12:12 for my *p*, shall do this
14:6 was no deliverer to *p* them
16:2 these things mean on your *p*
16:20 men, give counsel on your *p*
19:2 on the *p* of all the people
20:10 for their *p*, chased after
20:20 unthinkable on my *p* that I
22:24 keep . . . from error on my *p*
23:17 It is unthinkable on my *p*
1Ki 5:8 For my *p*, I shall do all your
5:9 for my *p*, shall put them in
5:9 for your *p*, will carry them
5:9 for your *p*, will do my
5:11 Solomon, for his *p*, gave
5:12 And Jehovah, for his *p*, gave
8:30 on the *p* of your servant
8:38 on the *p* of any man or of
8:41 no *p* of your people Israel
9:20 no *p* of the sons of Israel
12:4 Your father, for his *p*, made
12:10 Your father, for his *p*
12:11 for his *p*, loaded upon you
12:11 for my *p*, shall add to your
12:11 for his *p*, chastised you
12:11 for my *p*, shall chastise
12:14 for his *p*, made your yoke
1Ki 12:14 for my *p*, shall add to your
12:14 for his *p*, chastised you
12:14 I, for my *p*, shall chastise
13:34 on the *p* of the household
15:22 And King Asa, for his *p*
16:21 one *p* of the people that
16:21 other *p* followers of Omri
18:24 for my *p*, shall call upon
20:27 Syrians, for their *p*, filled
21:3 It is unthinkable on my *p*
22:30 for your *p*, put on your
22:32 they, for their *p*, said to
22:48 for his *p*, made Tarshish
2Ki 5:2 the Syrians, for their *p*, had
6:8 the king of Syria, for his *p*
9:1 Elisha the prophet, for his *p*
11:20 the city, for its *p*, had no
12:5 their *p*, repair the cracks
16:6 the Edomites, for their *p*
17:21 to *p* Israel from following
17:30 men of Babylon, for their *p*
17:30 men of Cuth, for their *p*
17:30 men of Hamath, for their *p*
18:23 you are able, on your *p*
18:24 your *p*, put your trust in
1Ch 5:22 was on the *p* of the true God
10:1 Philistines, for their *p*
11:13 people, for their *p*, had
11:19 It is unthinkable on my *p*
12:21 for their *p*, were of help
14:9 Philistines, for their *p*
21:18 Jehovah's angel, for his *p*
29:17 my *p*, in the uprightness
2Ch 2:16 you, for your *p*, will take
5:11 had, for their *p*, sanctified
6:2 and I, for my *p*, have built a
6:29 on the *p* of any man or of
6:32 no *p* of your people Israel
8:7 who were no *p* of Israel
10:4 Your father, for his *p*, made
10:10 Your father, for his *p*
10:11 my father, for his *p*
10:11 I, for my *p*, shall add to
10:11 for his *p*, chastised you
10:11 for my *p*, with scourges
10:14 for my *p*, shall add to it
10:14 for his *p*, chastised you
10:14 for my *p*, with scourges
12:5 for your *p*, have left me
12:5 for my *p*, have left you to
13:13 Jeroboam, for his *p*
15:15 full pleasure on their *p*
18:29 for your *p*, put on your
18:31 they, for their *p*, said to
24:5 you, for your *p*, should act
25:11 Amaziah, for his *p*, took
26:18 you on the *p* of Jehovah God
28:13 against Jehovah on our *p*
35:14 the Levites, for their *p*
Ezr 7:28 I, for my *p*, strengthened
Ne 1:8 for your *p*, act unfaithfully
1:8 I, for my *p*, shall scatter you
7:70 *p* of the heads of the paternal
9:3 a fourth *p* of the day
9:3 a fourth *p* they were making
13:12 Judah, for their *p*, brought
Job 6:24 I, for my *p*, shall be silent
6:25 reproving on the *p* of you
13:3 I, for my *p*, would speak to
13:5 prove to be wisdom on your *p*
27:5 unthinkable on my *p* that I
32:17 I shall give in answer my *p*
Ps 5:9 Their inward *p* is adversity
18:23 from error on my *p*
19:3 No voice on their *p* is being
22:2 there is no silence on my *p*
33:1 On the *p* of the upright ones
56:3 I, for my *p*, shall trust even
56:6 for their *p*, keep observing
59:3 For no revolt on my *p*, nor
59:3 any sin on my *p*, O Jehovah
63:5 the best *p*, even fatness
64:6 And the inward *p* of each one
72:11 nations, for their *p*, will
83:1 there be no silence on your *p*
85:12 Jehovah, for his *p*, will
104:34 I, for my *p*, shall rejoice
109:4 But on my *p* there is prayer
109:28 for their *p*, pronounce a
109:28 for your *p*, pronounce a
111:2 *p* of all those delighting
116:11 I, for my *p*, said, when I
119:70 for my *p*, have been fond of
123:4 on the *p* of the arrogant ones

Ps 141:10 While I, for my *p*, pass by
Pr 1:26 for my *p*, shall laugh at your
8:26 first *p* of the dust masses of
11:16 tyrants, for their *p*, take
18:13 foolishness on his *p* and a
19:11 beauty on his *p* to pass over
27:14 it will be accounted on his *p*
Ec 5:17 with sickness on his *p* and
Isa 2:2 in the final *p* of the days
36:8 able, on your *p*, to put
36:9 for your *p*, put your trust
43:14 whining cries on their *p*
44:7 let them tell on their *p*
44:15 *p* of it that he may warm
44:21 not be forgotten on my *p*
50:5 for my *p*, was not rebellious
52:4 Assyria, for its *p*, oppressed
61:2 goodwill on the *p* of Jehovah
61:2 vengeance on the *p* of our God
62:6 be no silence on your *p*
62:11 the farthest *p* of the earth
66:5 with rejoicing on your *p*
Jer 2:2 on your *p*, the loving-kindness
6:3 grazed off each one his own *p*
8:3 on the *p* of all the remnant
11:17 committed on their own *p*
23:20 In the final *p* of the days
25:31 farthest *p* of the earth
29:22 on the *p* of the entire body
30:24 final *p* of the days you
42:5 their *p*, said to Jeremiah
48:47 in the final *p* of the days
49:39 final *p* of the days that I
50:26 to her from the farthest *p*
Eze 1:14 the *p* of the living creatures
4:11 the sixth *p* of a hin
16:43 for my *p*, will put your
25:6 all scorn on your *p* in your
35:15 rejoicing on your *p* at the
38:7 be preparation on your *p*
38:8 In the final *p* of the years
38:16 In the final *p* of the days
45:13 sixth *p* of the ephah from
45:13 sixth *p* of the ephah from
48:20 foursquare *p* you people
Da 1:2 *p* of the utensils of the house
2:6 you will receive on my *p*
2:14 Daniel, for his *p*, addressed
2:15 order on the *p* of the king
2:18 mercies on the *p* of the God
2:28 in the final *p* of the days
2:49 Daniel, for his *p*, made a
8:5 for my *p*, kept on considering
8:8 male of the goats, for its *p*
8:19 final *p* of the denunciation
8:23 final *p* of their kingdom, as
8:26 for your *p*, keep secret the
10:13 I, for my *p*, remained there
10:14 in the final *p* of the days
11:14 their *p*, be carried along to
11:25 king of the south, for his *p*
11:41 main *p* of the sons of
12:8 be the final *p* of these things
Ho 2:21 heavens, and they, for their *p*
2:22 earth, for its *p*, will answer
2:22 their *p*, will answer Jezreel
2:23 for their *p*, will say: You
3:5 in the final *p* of the days
6:10 fornication on the *p* of
7:15 I, for my *p*, did disciplining
8:14 Judah, for his *p*, multiplied
9:6 Memphis, for its *p*, will bury
10:11 I, for my *p*, passed over her
12:8 on my *p*, no error that is sin
Am 4:2 last *p* of you with fishhooks
4:6 for my *p*, gave you people
6:1 the chief *p* of the nations
9:1 the last *p* of them I shall
Jon 4:10 for your *p*, felt sorry for
4:11 for my *p*, ought I not to
Mic 4:1 in the final *p* of the days
4:5 all the peoples, for their *p*
4:5 we, for our *p*, shall walk in
6:13 for my *p*, shall certainly
6:14 for your *p*, will eat and
6:15 for your *p*, will sow seed
6:15 You, for your *p*, will tread
Hab 1:10 for its *p*, it jeers kings
1:10 For its *p*, it laughs even at
Zec 1:15 for my *p*, felt indignant to
1:15 for their *p*, helped toward
6:13 for his *p*, will carry the
7:12 great indignation on the *p* of
10:2 for their *p*, have visioned
Zec 13:8 and as for the third *p*, it
13:9 the third *p* through the fire
13:9 It, for its *p*, will call
13:9 I, for my *p*, will answer it
Mal 1:4 They, for their *p*, will build
1:4 for my *p*, shall tear down
1:6 A son, for his *p*, honors a
2:9 for my *p*, shall certainly
Mt 3:11 I, for my *p*, baptize you
24:51 his *p* with the hypocrites
Lu 3:16 I, for my *p*, baptize you with
10:42 For her *p*, Mary chose the
11:36 bright with no *p* at all dark
12:46 a *p* with the unfaithful ones
15:12 *p* of the property that falls
17:24 from one *p* under heaven to
17:24 to another *p* under heaven
21:19 By endurance on your *p* you
Joh 3:25 on the *p* of the disciples of
7:38 from his inmost *p* streams
13:8 you have no *p* with me
15:19 If you were *p* of the world
15:19 you are no *p* of the world
17:14 they are no *p* of the world
17:14 as I am no *p* of the world
17:16 They are no *p* of the world
17:16 as I am no *p* of the world
18:36 My kingdom is no *p* of this
18:36 were *p* of this world, my
19:23 for each soldier a *p*, and
Ac 1:8 most distant *p* of the earth
3:13 for your *p*, delivered up and
5:2 he brought just a *p* and
6:1 murmuring arose on the *p* of
8:1 Saul, for his *p*, was approving
8:21 You have neither *p* nor lot
11:16 John, for his *p*, baptized
14:5 on the *p* of both people of
15:3 after being conducted *p* way
15:37 For his *p*, Barnabas was
19:30 For his *p*, Paul was willing
23:6 one *p* was of Sadducees but
Ro 1:15 eagerness on my *p* to declare
7:12 on its *p*, the Law is holy
8:3 on the *p* of the Law, while it
11:16 if the *p* taken as firstfruits
11:25 in *p* to Israel until the
11:27 covenant on my *p* with them
15:24 escorted *p* way there by you
16:20 For his *p*, the God who gives
1Co 9:25 man taking *p* in a contest
12:15 I am no *p* of the body, it
12:15 no *p* of the body
12:16 I am no *p* of the body
12:16 no *p* of the body
12:24 to the *p* which had a lack
16:6 *p* way to where I may be
16:11 Conduct him *p* way in peace
2Co 1:16 be conducted *p* way by you to
8:6 same kind giving on your *p*
10:13 For our *p* we will boast
12:15 my *p* I will most gladly
Ga 2:6 on the *p* of those who seemed
5:5 For our *p* we by spirit are
Php 2:19 For my *p* I am hoping in the
2Th 1:6 righteous on God's *p* to repay
3:13 For your *p*, brothers, do not
1Ti 6:5 about trifles on the *p* of men
2Ti 1:8 take your *p* in suffering evil
2:3 take your *p* in suffering evil
Tit 3:4 on the *p* of our Savior, God
Heb 9:1 For its *p*, then, the former
Jas 5:4 on the *p* of the reapers have
Re 6:8 over the fourth *p* of the earth
18:4 to receive *p* of her plagues
20:6 *p* in the first resurrection

Partake
1Co 9:12 *p* of this authority over you
2Ti 2:6 the first to *p* of the fruits
Heb 12:10 we may *p* of his holiness

Partaken
1Ti 4:3 to be *p* of with thanksgiving

Partaker
1Co 9:10 do so in hope of being a *p*

Partakers
Eph 3:6 *p* with us of the promise in
5:7 do not become *p* with them
Heb 3:1 *p* of the heavenly calling
3:14 become *p* of the Christ only
6:4 have become *p* of holy spirit
12:8 of which all have become *p*

Partakes
Heb 5:13 everyone that *p* of milk is

Partaking
1Co 10:17 are all *p* of that one loaf
10:21 be *p* of the table of Jehovah
10:30 If I am *p* with thanks, why

Parted
Ge 2:10 began to be *p* and it became
De 32:8 *p* the sons of Adam from one
Mr 1:10 he saw the heavens being *p*
Lu 24:51 he was *p* from them and
Ga 5:4 You are *p* from Christ

Parthians
Ac 2:9 *P* and Medes and Elamites, and

Partial
De 1:17 You must not be *p* in judgment
16:19 You must not be *p* or accept
28:50 will not be *p* to an old man
Ac 10:34 perceive that God is not *p*
1Co 13:9 we have *p* knowledge and we
13:10 *p* will be done away with
Jas 3:17 not making *p* distinctions

Partiality
Le 19:15 not treat the lowly with *p*
De 10:17 who treats none with *p* nor
2Ch 19:7 or *p* or taking of a bribe
Job 13:8 you be treating him with *p*
13:10 If in secrecy . . . show *p*
22:8 one who is treated with *p*
32:21 not . . . show *p* to a man
34:19 has not shown *p* to princes
Ps 82:2 showing *p* to the wicked
Pr 18:5 showing of *p* to the wicked
24:23 of *p* in judgment is not good
28:21 The showing of *p* is not good
Mal 2:9 were showing *p* in the law
Lu 20:21 and show no *p*, but you teach
Ro 2:11 For there is no *p* with God
Eph 6:9 and there is no *p* with him
Col 3:25 and there is no *p*

Partially
1Co 13:9 knowledge and we prophesy *p*
13:12 At present I know *p*, but

Participation
Col 1:12 your *p* in the inheritance of

Particle
Mt 5:18 or one *p* of a letter to pass
Lu 16:17 one *p* of a letter of the Law

Particles
Ge 13:16 your seed like the dust *p* of
13:16 able to count the dust *p* of
28:14 seed . . . like the dust *p*
Nu 23:10 numbered the dust *p* of Jacob
2Sa 17:11 as the sand *p* that are by
2Ch 1:9 numerous as the dust *p* of the

Parti-colored
Zec 6:3 chariot, horses speckled, *p*
6:7 *p* ones, they must go forth

Particular
Ex 10:8 Who in *p* are the ones going?
Nu 22:4 king of Moab at that *p* time
De 1:9 say this to you at that *p* time
1:16 at that *p* time, saying
1:18 at that *p* time all the things
2:34 his cities at that *p* time
3:4 all his cities at that *p* time
3:8 at that *p* time the land from
3:12 this land at that *p* time
3:18 at that *p* time, saying
3:21 commanded Joshua at that *p*
3:23 from Jehovah at that *p* time
4:14 at that *p* time to teach you
5:5 at that *p* time to tell you the
9:20 Aaron at that *p* time
10:1 At that *p* time Jehovah said
10:8 At that *p* time Jehovah
Jos 5:2 that *p* time Jehovah said to
6:26 pronounced at that *p* time
11:21 at that *p* time Joshua went
Jg 4:4 judging Israel at that *p* time
14:4 that *p* time the Philistines
1Ki 11:29 that *p* time that Jeroboam
14:1 that *p* time Abijah the son
2Ki 3:8 By which *p* way shall we go
Da 8:13 the *p* one who was speaking
Mt 14:1 At that *p* time Herod, the
Lu 12:56 how to examine this *p* time
Ac 7:20 In that *p* time Moses was

Ac 12:1 *p* time Herod the king applied
19:23 At that *p* time there arose
Eph 2:12 that *p* time without Christ
1Ti 2:6 at its own *p* times
1Pe 1:11 investigating what *p* season
3:16 in the *p* in which you are

Particulars
Ac 11:4 on to explain the *p* to them

Parties
Eph 2:14 he who made the two *p* one

Parting
1Ki 9:16 as a *p* gift to his daughter
Ob 14 to stand at the *p* of the ways
Mic 1:14 *p* gifts to Moresheth-gath

Partition
Eze 13:10 that is building a *p* wall

Partly
Da 2:33 its feet were *p* of iron and
2:33 iron and *p* of molded clay
2:41 toes to be *p* of molded clay
2:41 and *p* of iron, the kingdom
2:42 the feet being *p* of iron and
2:42 and *p* of molded clay, the
2:42 will *p* prove to be strong and
2:42 will *p* prove to be fragile

Partner
2Ch 20:36 *p* with himself in making
Ps 119:63 *p* I am of all those who do
Pr 28:24 *p* of a man causing ruination
29:24 *p* with a thief is hating his
Ec 4:10 other one can raise his *p* up
Mal 2:14 she is your *p* and the wife

Partners
Job 41:6 Will *p* barter for it?
Ps 45:7 more than your *p*
Ca 1:7 among the droves of your *p*
8:13 *p* are paying attention to your
Isa 1:23 stubborn and *p* with thieves
44:11 All his *p* themselves will
Eze 37:16 the sons of Israel his *p*
37:16 the house of Israel his *p*
37:19 the tribes of Israel his *p*
Lu 5:7 motioned to their *p* in the
Heb 1:9 more than your *p*

Partnership
2Ch 20:35 *p* with Ahaziah the king of
20:37 you have had *p* with Ahaziah

Partook
Ac 2:46 and *p* of food with great
Heb 2:14 *p* of the same things, that

Partridge
1Sa 26:20 as one chases a *p* upon the
Jer 17:11 As the *p* that has gathered

Parts
Ge 15:4 out of your own inward *p*
25:23 separated from your inward *p*
47:24 but four *p* will become yours
Ex 12:9 its shanks and its interior *p*
20:26 that your private *p* may not
Le 1:6 skinned and cut up into its *p*
1:12 must cut it up into its *p* and
Nu 18:28 from all your tenth *p* that
25:8 woman through her genital *p*
De 12:6 and your tenth *p* and the
12:11 tenth *p* and the contribution
19:3 territory . . . into three *p*
21:17 two *p* in everything he is
Jg 19:1 remotest *p* of the mountainous
19:18 *p* of the mountainous region
Ru 1:11 have sons in my inward *p*
1Sa 20:30 the secret *p* of your mother
24:3 *p* of the cave farthest back
2Sa 7:12 come out of your inward *p*
16:11 out of my own inward *p*
19:43 We have ten *p* in the king
1Ki 7:25 their hind *p* were toward the
16:21 divide . . . into two *p*
2Ki 2:9 two *p* in your spirit may
19:23 The remotest *p* of Lebanon
1Ch 11:8 even to the *p* round about
2Ch 4:4 all their hind *p* were inward
32:21 out of his own inward *p*
Ne 4:13 lowest *p* of the place behind
11:1 nine other *p* in the other
Job 41:12 not keep silent about its *p*
Ps 22:14 melted deep in my inward *p*
40:8 law is within my inward *p*
51:6 in the inward *p*
63:9 the lowest *p* of the earth
65:8 of the uttermost *p*
71:6 the inward *p* of my mother
128:3 innermost *p* of your house
136:13 severing the Red Sea into *p*
139:15 the lowest *p* of the earth
139:16 its *p* were down in writing
Pr 18:8 the innermost *p* of the belly
20:27 the innermost *p* of the belly
20:30 the innermost *p* of the belly
26:22 the innermost *p* of the belly
Ca 5:4 my inward *p* themselves became
Isa 8:9 you in distant *p* of the earth
14:13 remotest *p* of the north
14:15 the remotest *p* of the pit
37:24 The remotest *p* of Lebanon
41:9 from the remote *p* of it
44:23 you lowest *p* of the earth
48:19 from your inward *p* like the
49:1 the inward *p* of my mother
63:15 commotion of your inward *p*
Jer 6:22 the remotest *p* of the earth
25:32 the remotest *p* of the earth
31:8 the remotest *p* of the earth
50:41 remotest *p* of the earth
Eze 16:36 your private *p* are uncovered
16:37 uncover your private *p* to
16:37 must see all your private *p*
32:23 in the innermost *p* of a pit
38:6 the remotest *p* of the north
38:15 the remotest *p* of the north
39:2 the remotest *p* of the north
Ho 2:10 I shall uncover her private *p*
Am 4:4 on the third day, your tenth *p*
6:10 the innermost *p* of the house
Jon 1:5 innermost *p* of the . . . vessel
1:17 in the inward *p* of the fish
2:1 from the inward *p* of the fish
Hab 2:15 upon their *p* of shame
Zec 13:8 two *p* in it are what will
Mal 3:8 In the tenth *p* and in the
3:10 Bring all the tenth *p* into
Mt 2:1 astrologers from eastern *p*
8:11 many from eastern *p* and
8:11 and western *p* will come and
15:21 into the *p* of Tyre and Sidon
16:13 the *p* of Caesarea Philippi
24:27 comes out of eastern *p* and
24:27 and shines over to western *p*
Mr 8:10 into the *p* of Dalmanutha
Lu 12:54 a cloud rising in western *p*
13:29 from eastern *p* and western
Joh 19:23 garments and made four *p*
Ac 2:10 *p* of Libya, which is toward
9:32 going through all *p* he came
19:1 went through the inland *p* and
20:2 After going through those *p*
1Co 12:23 the *p* of the body which we
12:23 so our unseemly *p* have the
12:24 our comely *p* do not need
Jas 5:3 and will eat your fleshy *p*
Re 16:19 city split into three *p*
17:16 will eat up her fleshy *p*
19:18 eat the fleshy *p* of kings
19:18 the fleshy *p* of military
19:18 fleshy *p* of strong men
19:18 fleshy *p* of horses and of
19:18 and the fleshy *p* of all, of
19:21 filled from the fleshy *p* of

Party
Ex 18:16 between the one *p* and the
Mt 22:16 with *p* followers of Herod
Mr 3:6 with the *p* followers of Herod
12:13 of the *p* followers of Herod
Ac 5:36 four hundred, joined his *p*
23:9 of the *p* of the Pharisees rose

Paruah
1Ki 4:17 Jehoshaphat the son of *P*, in

Pasach
1Ch 7:33 sons of Japhlet were *P* and

Pas-dammim
1Ch 11:13 with David at *P*, where the

Paseah
1Ch 4:12 father to Beth-rapha and *P*
Ezr 2:49 the sons of *P*
Ne 3:6 Joiada the son of *P* and
7:51 sons of Uzza, the sons of *P*

Pashhur
1Ch 9:12 of *P* the son of Malchijah
Ezr 2:38 sons of *P*, a thousand two
10:22 the sons of *P*, Elioenai
Ne 7:41 sons of *P*, a thousand two
Ne 10:3 *P*, Amariah, Malchijah
11:12 *P* the son of Malchijah
Jer 20:1 Now *P* the son of Immer
20:2 Then *P* struck Jeremiah the
20:3 *P* proceeded to let Jeremiah
20:3 your name, not *P*, but Fright
20:6 as for you, O *P*, and all the
21:1 King Zedekiah sent to him *P*
38:1 Gedaliah the son of *P* and
38:1 *P* the son of Malchijah got

Pass
Ge 8:1 God caused a wind to *p* over
18:3 do not *p* by your servant
18:5 you can *p* on, because that is
30:32 *p* among your whole flock
31:52 not *p* this heap against you
31:52 not *p* this heap and this
33:14 *p* on ahead of his servant
Ex 12:12 *p* through the land of Egypt
12:13 see the blood and *p* over you
12:23 when Jehovah does *p* through
12:23 *p* over the entrance, and he
15:16 Until your people *p* by, O
15:16 Until the people . . . *p* by
17:5 *P* in front of the people and
30:13 will give who *p* over to
32:27 *P* through and return from
33:19 my goodness to *p* before your
36:6 announcement to *p* through the
Le 25:46 *p* them on as an inheritance
26:6 sword will not *p* through your
Nu 5:30 spirit of jealousy may *p* upon
6:5 no razor should *p* over his head
8:7 razor *p* over all their flesh
20:17 Let us *p*, please, through
20:17 not *p* through a field or a
20:17 *p* through your territory
20:18 You must not *p* through me
20:19 than to *p* through on my feet
20:20 said: You must not *p* through
20:21 to *p* through his territory
21:22 Let me *p* through your land
21:22 we *p* through your territory
21:23 to *p* through his territory
22:18 *p* beyond the order of Jehovah
24:13 *p* beyond the order of Jehovah
27:7 father's inheritance to *p* to
27:8 inheritance to *p* to his
31:23 you should *p* through the fire
31:23 should *p* through the water
32:21 actually *p* over the Jordan
32:27 your servants will *p* over
32:29 *p* with you over the Jordan
32:30 *p* over equipped with you
32:32 will *p* over equipped before
34:4 and *p* over to Azmon
De 2:27 Let me *p* through your land
2:28 let me *p* through on my feet
2:29 I shall *p* over the Jordan into
2:30 did not let us *p* through him
3:18 You will *p* over, equipped
3:25 Let me *p* over, please, and
3:27 will not *p* over this Jordan
3:28 he is the one to *p* over before
18:10 daughter *p* through the fire
30:13 Who will *p* over for us to
Jos 1:11 *P* through the midst of the
1:14 *p* over in battle formation
3:2 to *p* through the midst of the
3:6 and *p* before the people
4:5 *P* ahead of the ark of Jehovah
4:12 *p* over in battle formation
6:7 *P* on and march round the city
6:7 *p* on ahead of the ark of
Jg 3:28 did not allow anybody to *p*
8:13 by the *p* that goes up to Heres
9:25 rob everyone that would *p* by
11:17 Let me *p*, please, through
11:19 Let us *p*, please, through
11:29 to *p* through Gilead and
11:29 *p* through Mizpeh of Gilead
12:5 Let me *p* over, then the men
19:12 have to *p* on as far as Gibeah
1Sa 9:27 he should *p* on ahead of us
10:3 you must *p* on from there
13:23 to the ravine *p* of Michmash
16:8 and had him *p* before Samuel
16:9 Next Jesse had Shammah *p* by
16:10 had seven of his sons *p*
20:36 arrow to make it *p* beyond
25:19 *P* on ahead of me. Look! I
30:10 *p* over the torrent valley
2Sa 12:13 does let your sin *p* by

2Sa 17:21 speedily *p* over the waters
19:31 *p* on to the Jordan with
24:10 let your servant's error *p*
1Ki 2:37 *p* over the torrent valley of
6:21 chainwork of gold *p* across
15:12 *p* out of the land and
18:6 the land through which to *p*
22:24 spirit of Jehovah *p* along
22:36 cry began to *p* through the
2Ki 4:8 as often as he would *p* by, he
16:3 he made *p* through the fire
17:17 daughters *p* through the fire
21:6 own son *p* through the fire
23:10 *p* through the fire to
1Ch 4:10 God brought to *p* what he had
21:8 your servant's error to *p*
28:8 *p* it on as an inheritance to
2Ch 18:23 spirit of Jehovah *p* along
20:16 coming up by the *p* of Ziz
30:5 call *p* through all Israel
33:6 own sons *p* through the fire
36:22 a cry to *p* through all his
Ezr 1:1 to *p* through all his realm
10:7 call to *p* throughout Judah
Ne 2:7 let me *p* until I come to Judah
2:14 animal under me to *p* along
8:15 a call to *p* throughout all
Es 1:19 that it may not *p* away, that
9:27 that it should not *p* away
9:28 not *p* away from the midst of
Job 19:8 a stone wall, and I cannot *p*
24:7 Naked, they *p* the night
24:11 they *p* the noontime
34:20 back and forth and *p* away
36:12 *p* away even by a missile
Ps 7:8 will *p* sentence on the peoples
37:36 yet he proceeded to *p* away
42:4 *p* along with the throng
57:1 until the adversities *p* over
78:13 he might let them *p* over
90:10 quickly *p* by, and away we
103:16 mere wind has to *p* over it
104:9 which they should not *p*
119:37 eyes *p* on from seeing what
119:39 Make my reproach *p* away
136:14 Israel to *p* through the
141:10 While I, for my part, *p* by
148:6 and it will not *p* away
Pr 4:15 Shun it, do not *p* along by
4:15 aside from it, and *p* along
8:29 should not *p* beyond his order
19:11 beauty on his part to *p* over
Isa 2:18 gods themselves will *p* away
3:13 to *p* sentence upon peoples
8:8 actually flood and *p* over
8:21 *p* through the land hard
18:6 will certainly *p* the summer
18:6 will *p* the harvesttime
28:15 flood, in case it should *p*
28:19 by morning it will *p*
31:9 *p* away out of sheer fright
33:21 ship will *p* over it
35:8 unclean one will not *p* over
43:2 in case you should *p* through
54:9 no more *p* over the earth
62:10, 10 *P* out, *p* out through
65:4 *p* the night even in the
Jer 2:10 *p* over to the coastlands of
5:22 regulation that it cannot *p*
5:22 still they cannot *p* over it
8:13 will *p* by them
11:15 *p* over from upon you
15:14 to *p* over with your enemies
22:8 *p* along by this city and say
32:35 *p* through the fire to
33:13 flocks will yet *p* by under
34:18 might *p* between its pieces
46:17 let the festal time *p* by
51:43 no son of mankind will *p*
La 3:44 that prayer may not *p* through
4:21 To you also the cup will *p*
Eze 5:1 *p* along upon your head and
5:17 will *p* along through you
9:4 *P* through the midst of the
9:5 *P* through the city after him
14:15 beasts *p* through the land
14:17 sword itself *p* through the
16:21 them *p* through the fire
20:26 child . . . *p* through the fire
20:31 your sons *p* through the fire
20:37 *p* under the rod and bring
23:37 *p* through the fire to them
29:11 not *p* through it the foot
29:11 domestic animal *p* through

Eze 37:2 *p* along by them all round
39:15 *p* along through the land
46:21 *p* along to the four corner
47:3 make me *p* through the water
47:4 made me *p* through the water
47:4 made me *p* through—water up
47:5 I was not able to *p* through
48:14 land to *p* away from them
Da 4:16 let seven times *p* over it
4:23 seven times themselves *p* over
4:25 seven times . . . will *p* over
4:32 times themselves will *p* over
7:14 rulership that will not *p*
11:10 and flood over and *p* through
11:20 exactor to *p* through the
11:40 and flood over and *p* through
Joe 3:17 will no more *p* through her
Am 5:5 Beer-sheba you must not *p* over
5:17 *p* through the midst of you
Mic 2:13 they will *p* through a gate
2:13 king will *p* through before
Na 1:12 and one must *p* through
1:15 good-for-nothing person *p*
3:19 your badness did not *p* over
Hab 1:11 will *p* through and will
Zec 3:4 caused your error to *p* away
9:8 no more *p* through them a
10:11 *p* through the sea with
13:2 cause to *p* out of the land
Mt 5:18 heaven and earth *p* away than
5:18 particle of a letter to *p*
8:13 so let it come to *p* for you
8:28 courage to *p* by on that road
24:34 generation . . . by no means *p*
24:35 Heaven and earth will *p*
24:35 words will by no means *p*
26:39 let this cup *p* away from me
26:42 not possible for this to *p*
Mr 6:48 he was inclined to *p* them by
11:2 as soon as you *p* into it you
13:30 generation . . . by no means *p*
13:31 Heaven and earth will *p* away
13:31 my words will not *p* away
14:35 the hour might *p* away from
Lu 7:2 ailing and was about to *p* away
11:42 you *p* by the justice and the
16:17 heaven and earth to *p* away
19:30 after you *p* in you will
21:32 by no means *p* away until all
21:33 Heaven and earth will *p* away
21:33 will by no means *p* away
22:17 *p* it from one to the other
Joh 7:3 *P* on over from here and go
8:26 and to *p* judgment upon
1Co 16:6 stay or even *p* the winter
2Co 12:1 *p* on to supernatural visions
Heb 9:11 have come to *p*, through the
Jas 1:10 vegetation he will *p* away
2Pe 3:10 the heavens will *p* away
Re 12:10 come to *p* the salvation and
16:17 saying: It has come to *p*!
21:6 They have come to *p*! I am

Passage
Eze 41:7 winding *p* of the house was
Ac 8:32 *p* of Scripture that he was

Passages
1Sa 14:4 *p* that Jonathan looked for

Passed
Ge 15:17 torch that *p* in between
18:5 why you have *p* this way to
31:54 *p* the night in the mountain
32:31 as soon as he *p* by Penuel
33:3 he himself *p* on ahead of them
50:4 the days of weeping for him *p*
Ex 12:27 Jehovah, who *p* over the
33:22 a screen until I have *p* by
Nu 5:14 jealousy has *p* upon him, and
5:14 spirit of jealousy has *p* upon
13:32 we *p* through to spy it out
14:7 The land that we *p* through to
22:26 Jehovah's angel now *p* by
De 2:8 *p* on away from our brothers
2:8 Next we turned and *p* on by the
29:16 we *p* through the midst of
29:16 nations through whom you *p*
Jos 3:4 not *p* over on that way before
3:16 the people *p* over in front of
4:7 When it *p* through the Jordan
4:10 people hurried up and *p* over
4:11 the ark of Jehovah *p* over
4:13 *p* over before Jehovah for the
4:22 Israel *p* over this Jordan

Jos 4:23 until they had *p* over, just
4:23 until we had *p* over
5:1 until they had *p* over, then
6:8 *p* on and blew the horns, and
10:29 *p* on from Makkedah to
10:31 *p* on from Libnah to Lachish
10:34 *p* on from Lachish to Eglon
15:3 and *p* over to Zin and went
15:3 *p* over to Hezron and went up
15:4 *p* on to Azmon and went out
15:6 and *p* over at the north of
15:7 *p* over to the waters of
15:10 *p* over to the slope of Mount
15:10 *p* over to Timnah
15:11 *p* over to Mount Baalah and
16:2 *p* over to the boundary of the
16:6 *p* over eastward to Janoah
18:9 *p* through the land and
18:13 *p* over from there to Luz
18:18 *p* over to the northern slope
18:19 *p* over to the northern slope
19:13 *p* over eastward toward the
24:17 the midst of whom we *p*
Jg 3:26 he himself *p* by the quarries
11:29 he *p* along to the sons of
11:32 Jephthah *p* along to the sons
18:13 they *p* along from there to
19:14 So they *p* along and kept on
1Sa 9:27 ahead of us—so he *p* on
14:23 the battle itself *p* over to
26:13 David *p* on to the other side
27:2 *p* over to Achish the son of
2Sa 17:20 They *p* on from here to the
17:22 had not *p* over the Jordan
18:9 mule . . . under him *p* along
18:23 eventually *p* by the Cushite
20:13 *p* by following Joab to
2Ki 4:31 *p* along before them and then
8:21 Jehoram *p* over to Zair
14:9 *p* by and trampled the thorny
1Ch 29:30 times that had *p* over him
2Ch 21:9 with his chiefs *p* over and
25:18 *p* by and trampled the
Es 4:17 At this Mordecai *p* along and
Job 11:16 As waters that have *p* along
15:19 And no stranger *p* through
17:11 My own days have *p* along
30:15 my salvation has *p* away
37:21 a wind itself has *p* by and
Ps 18:12 were his clouds that *p* by
38:4 errors have *p* over my head
42:7 waves—Over me they have *p*
48:4 They have *p* by together
88:16 flashes of . . . anger have *p*
124:4 torrent itself would have *p*
124:5 would have *p* over our soul
Pr 22:3 inexperienced have *p* along and
24:30 I *p* along by the field of the
27:12 the inexperienced that have *p*
Ca 2:11 the rainy season itself has *p*
3:4 Hardly had I *p* on from them
5:6 turned away, he had *p* along
Isa 10:28 *p* along through Migron
10:29 They have *p* over the ford
24:11 All rejoicing has *p* away
Jer 2:6 land through which no man *p*
8:20 The harvest has *p*, the summer
Eze 47:5 torrent that could not be *p*
Da 2:44 be *p* on to any other people
Ho 10:11 *p* over her good-looking neck
Jon 2:3 your waves—over me they *p* on
Hab 3:10 thunderstorm of waters *p*
Zep 2:2 day has *p* by just like chaff
Mt 21:17 to Bethany and *p* the night
Mr 16:1 when the sabbath had *p*, Mary
Joh 5:24 *p* over from death to life
Ac 15:33 when they had *p* some time
16:8 *p* Mysia by and came down to
18:23 he had *p* some time there
25:13 some days had *p*, Agrippa
27:9 time had *p* and by now it
27:9 atonement day had already *p*
1Co 10:1 and all *p* through the sea
2Co 5:17 the old things *p* away
1Ti 3:6 the judgment *p* upon the Devil
Heb 4:14 *p* through the heavens, Jesus
11:29 they *p* through the Red Sea
1Pe 4:3 For the time that has *p* by is
1Jo 3:14 *p* over from death to life
Re 21:1 former earth had *p* away, and
21:4 The former things have *p* away

Passerby
Eze 5:14 before the eyes of every *p*

Eze 16:15 prostitution on every *p*
16:25 sprawl out . . . to every *p*
36:34 before the eyes of every *p*
Mr 15:21 impressed into service a *p*

Passersby
Pr 26:10 or the one hiring *p*
Mt 27:39 *p* began speaking abusively

Passes
Le 27:32 that *p* under the crook
Job 9:11 *p* by me and I do not see him
Pr 10:25 when the stormwind *p* over
Isa 26:20 until the denunciation *p*
28:18 flood, when it *p* through
28:19 As often as it *p* through
Am 8:5 before the new moon *p* and we
Mic 5:8 when it actually *p* through
Mt 12:43 *p* through parched places in
15:17 *p* along into the intestines
Mr 7:15 outside a man that *p* into
7:18 *p* into a man can defile him
7:19 it *p*, not into his heart
7:19 it *p* out into the sewer
Lu 11:24 it *p* through parched places

Passing
Ge 37:28 Midianite merchants, went *p*
Ex 30:14 Everyone *p* over to those
33:22 while my glory is *p* by I
34:6 Jehovah went *p* by before his
38:26 every man who was *p* over to
Nu 14:41 you are *p* beyond the order of
33:8 *p* through the midst of the
De 2:4 You are *p* along by the border
2:18 *p* today by the territory of
3:21 you are *p* over there
4:14 land to which you are *p* over
6:1 *p* over there to take possession
Jos 3:11 *p* before you into the Jordan
3:14 just before *p* over the Jordan
3:17 were *p* over on dry ground
3:17 completed *p* over the Jordan
4:1 completed *p* over the Jordan
4:11 people had completed *p* over
Jg 19:18 are *p* along from Bethlehem
Ru 4:1 the repurchaser was *p* by
1Sa 9:4 *p* through the mountainous
9:4 and *p* on through the land of
9:4 went *p* on through the land of
9:4 went *p* on through the land of
29:2 Philistines were *p* along by
29:2 David and his men were *p*
2Sa 20:14 *p* through all the tribes of
24:20 the king and his servants *p*
1Ki 9:8 Everyone *p* by it will stare
13:25 there were men *p* by, so
19:11 And, look! Jehovah was *p* by
20:39 as the king was *p* by
2Ki 4:8 Elisha went *p* along to Shunem
4:9 man of God that is *p* by us
6:9 against *p* by this place
6:26 king of Israel was *p* along
6:30 he was *p* along upon the wall
2Ch 7:21 everyone *p* by it will stare
30:10 *p* along from city to city
Ne 2:14 *p* along to the Fountain Gate
Es 1:7 a *p* of wine to drink in gold
Job 4:15 a spirit itself went *p* over
6:15 torrents that keep *p* away
33:18 his life from *p* away by a
33:28 my soul from *p* into the pit
Ps 8:8 *p* through the paths of the seas
80:12 *p* by on the road plucked at
84:6 *P* along through the low plain
89:41 those *p* along the way have
129:8 Nor have those *p* by said
144:4 His days are like a *p* shadow
Pr 7:8 *p* along on the street near her
9:15 call out to those *p* along the
26:17 anyone *p* by that is becoming
31:8 the cause of all those *p* away
Isa 29:5 the chaff that is *p* away
33:8 one *p* over the path has
34:10 no one will be *p* across her
41:3 kept peacefully *p* along on
60:15 with nobody *p* through
Jer 9:10 there is no man *p* through
9:12 without anyone *p* through
13:24 *p* along in the wind from
18:16 Every last one *p* along by
19:8 Every last one *p* along by it
34:19 *p* between the pieces of the
49:17 *p* along by her will stare
50:13 anyone *p* along by Babylon

La 1:12 nothing to all you who are *p*
2:15 those *p* along on the road have
Eze 14:15 without anybody *p* through
16:6 I came *p* along by you and
16:8 I came *p* along by you and
33:28 with no one *p* through
35:7 the one *p* through and the
39:11 valley of those *p* through
39:11 stopping up those *p* through
39:14 *p* along through the land
39:14 with those *p* through
39:15 those *p* through must pass
Mic 2:8 the ones *p* by confidently
7:18 and *p* over transgression
Na 1:8 by the flood that is *p* along
Zep 2:15 *p* along by her will whistle
3:6 there was no one *p* through
Zec 7:14 with no one *p* through and
9:8 no one *p* through and no one
Mt 9:9 *p* along from there, Jesus
9:27 As Jesus was *p* along from
20:30 heard that Jesus was *p* by
Mr 2:14 *p* along, he caught sight of
11:20 when they were *p* by early
Lu 6:1 to be *p* through grainfields
17:11 he was *p* through the midst
18:37 Jesus the Nazarene is *p* by!
Joh 9:1 *p* along he saw a man blind
Ac 17:23 while *p* along and carefully
1Co 16:7 just now on my *p* through
1Jo 2:8 the darkness is *p* away and
2:17 world is *p* away and so is

Passion
Isa 57:5 working up *p* among big trees
Mt 5:28 so as to have a *p* for her has
1Co 7:9 than to be inflamed with *p*

Passionate
Eze 23:22 rousing up your *p* lovers
Ho 2:7 chase after her *p* lovers, but
2:10 to the eyes of her *p* lovers
2:12 *p* lovers have given to me
2:13 going after her *p* lovers, and

Passionately
Ca 2:3 His shade I have *p* desired, and
Eze 16:33 to all those *p* loving you
16:36 toward those *p* loving you
16:37 those *p* loving you toward
23:5 after those *p* loving her
23:9 hand of those *p* loving her
Ho 2:5 go after those *p* loving me

Passions
Ro 7:5 sinful *p* that were excited by
Ga 5:24 flesh together with its *p*

Passover
Ex 12:11 eat it . . . It is Jehovah's *p*
12:21 and slaughter the *p* victim
12:27 sacrifice of the *p* to Jehovah
12:43 This is the statute of the *p*
12:48 celebrate the *p* to Jehovah
34:25 festival of the *p* should not
Le 23:5 is the *p* to Jehovah
Nu 9:2 Israel should prepare the *p*
9:4 Israel to prepare the *p*
9:5 prepared the *p* sacrifice in the
9:6 not able to prepare the *p*
9:10 prepare the *p* sacrifice to
9:12 whole statute of the *p* they
9:13 neglected to prepare the *p*
9:14 he also must prepare the *p*
9:14 statute of the *p* and according
28:16 will be Jehovah's *p*
33:3 the day after the *p* the sons
De 16:1 you must celebrate the *p* to
16:2 you must sacrifice the *p* to
16:5 sacrifice the *p* in any one of
16:6 sacrifice the *p* in the evening
Jos 5:10 the *p* on the fourteenth day
5:11 the day after the *p*
2Ki 23:21 Hold a *p* to Jehovah your God
23:22 no *p* like this had been held
23:23 this *p* was held to Jehovah
2Ch 30:1 *p* to Jehovah the God of
30:2 hold the *p* in the second
30:5 hold the *p* to Jehovah the
30:15 slaughtered the *p* victim on
30:17 slaughtering the *p* victims
30:18 eat the *p* according to what
35:1 in Jerusalem a *p* to Jehovah
35:1 slaughtered the *p* victim on
35:6 slaughter the *p* victim and
35:7 whole for the *p* victims

2Ch 35:8 for the *p* victims two
35:9 for *p* victims five thousand
35:11 to slaughter the *p* victim
35:13 boiling the *p* offering over
35:16 to hold the *p* and to offer
35:17 to hold the *p* at that time
35:18 a *p* like it in Israel since
35:18 a *p* like that which Josiah
35:19 Josiah's reign this *p* was
Ezr 6:19 the *p* on the fourteenth day
6:20 slaughtered the *p* victim
Eze 45:21 should occur for you the *p*
Mt 26:2 that two days from now the *p*
26:17 prepare for you to eat the *p*
26:18 I will celebrate the *p* with
26:19 got things ready for the *p*
Mr 14:1 the *p* and the festival of
14:12 customarily sacrificed the *p*
14:12 prepare for you to eat the *p*
14:14 where I may eat the *p* with
14:16 and they prepared for the *p*
Lu 2:41 for the festival of the *p*
22:1 so-called *P*, was getting near
22:7 *p* victim must be sacrificed
22:8 get the *p* ready for us to eat
22:11 eat the *p* with my disciples
22:13 and they got the *p* ready
22:15 to eat this *p* with you
Joh 2:13 the *p* of the Jews was near
2:23 was in Jerusalem at the *p*
6:4 *p*, the festival of the Jews
11:55 *p* of the Jews was near
11:55 to Jerusalem before the *p*
12:1 Jesus, six days before the *p*
13:1 before the festival of the *p*
18:28 but might eat the *p*
18:39 a man to you at the *p*
19:14 was preparation of the *p*
Ac 12:4 for the people after the *p*
1Co 5:7 Christ our *p* . . . sacrificed
Heb 11:28 he had celebrated the *p* and

Past
2Sa 11:27 mourning period was *p*
1Ki 18:29 as soon as noon was *p* and
1Ch 9:20 leader over them in the *p*
Ps 55:19 sitting enthroned as in the *p*
77:5 years in the indefinite *p*
90:4 but as yesterday when it is *p*
Isa 41:26 from times *p*, that we may
51:9 generations of times long *p*
Joe 2:2 exist from the indefinite *p*
Ac 14:16 *p* generations he permitted
20:16 had decided to sail *p* Ephesus
Ro 3:25 sins that occurred in the *p*
11:33 *p* tracing out his ways are
1Co 7:36 that is *p* the bloom of youth
Eph 3:9 from the indefinite *p* been
4:19 *p* all moral sense, they gave
Col 1:26 from the *p* systems of things
1:26 and from the *p* generations
Heb 11:11 she was *p* the age limit
Jude 25 authority for all *p* eternity
Re 9:12 The one woe is *p*. Look! Two
11:14 The second woe is *p*

Paste
Isa 6:10 *p* their very eyes together

Pasted
Isa 32:3 will not be *p* together

Pastries
Le 6:21 present the *p* of the grain

Pasturage
Ge 47:4 there is no *p* for the flock
1Ch 4:39 look for *p* for their flocks
4:40 they found fat and good *p*
4:41 was *p* for their flocks there
Job 39:8 explores mountains for its *p*
Ps 74:1 against the flock of your *p*
79:13 and the flock of your *p*
95:7 we are the people of his *p*
100:3 and the sheep of his *p*
Pr 12:26 one spies out his own *p*
Jer 23:1 the sheep of my *p*
25:36 is despoiling their *p*
La 1:6 stags that have found no *p*
Eze 34:14 a good *p* I shall feed them
34:14 on a fat *p* they will feed
34:18 the very best *p* you feed
Ho 13:6 According to their *p* they
Joe 1:18 there is no *p* for them
Joh 10:9 go in and out and find *p*

Pasturages
Eze 34:18 rest of your *p* you should

Pasture
Le 25:34 *p* ground of their cities may
Nu 35:2 *p* ground of the cities all
35:3 *p* grounds will serve for
35:4 the *p* grounds of the cities
35:5 as *p* grounds of the cities
35:7 together with their *p* grounds
Jos 14:4 *p* grounds for their livestock
21:2 *p* grounds for our domestic
21:3 cities and their *p* grounds
21:8 cities and their *p* grounds
21:11 and its *p* ground all around
21:13 Hebron, and its *p* ground
21:13 Libnah and its *p* ground
21:14 Jattir and its *p* ground
21:14 Eshtemoa and its *p* ground
21:15 and Holon and its *p* ground
21:15 and Debir and its *p* ground
21:16 and Ain and its *p* ground
21:16 and Juttah and its *p* ground
21:16 Beth-shemesh and its *p*
21:17 Gibeon and its *p* ground
21:17 Geba and its *p* ground
21:18 Anathoth and its *p* ground
21:18 Almon and its *p* ground
21:19 cities and their *p* grounds
21:21 Shechem, and its *p* ground
21:21 and Gezer and its *p* ground
21:22 Kibzaim and its *p* ground
21:22 Beth-horon and its *p* ground
21:23 Elteke and its *p* ground
21:23 Gibbethon and its *p* ground
21:24 Aijalon and its *p* ground
21:24 Gath-rimmon and its *p*
21:25 Taanach and its *p* ground
21:25 Gath-rimmon and its *p*
21:26 cities . . . with their *p*
21:27 Golan . . . and its *p* ground
21:27 Beeshterah and its *p* ground
21:28 Kishion and its *p* ground
21:28 Daberath and its *p* ground
21:29 Jarmuth and its *p* ground
21:29 En-gannim and its *p* ground
21:30 Mishal and its *p* ground
21:30 Abdon and its *p* ground
21:31 Helkath and its *p* ground
21:31 Rehob and its *p* ground
21:32 Kedesh . . . and its *p* ground
21:32 Hammoth-dor and its *p*
21:32 Kartan and its *p* ground
21:33 cities and their *p* grounds
21:34 Jokneam and its *p* ground
21:34 Kartah and its *p* ground
21:35 Dimnah and its *p* ground
21:35 Nahalal and its *p* ground
21:36 Bezer and its *p* ground, and
21:36 Jahaz and its *p* ground
21:37 Kedemoth and its *p* ground
21:37 Mephaath and its *p* ground
21:38 Ramoth . . . and its *p* ground
21:38 Mahanaim and its *p* ground
21:39 Heshbon and its *p* ground
21:39 Jazer and its *p* ground; all
21:41 cities . . . with their *p*
21:42 city together with its *p*
2Sa 7:8 took you from the *p* ground
1Ch 5:16 all the *p* grounds of Sharon
6:55 its *p* grounds all around it
6:57 Libnah with its *p* grounds
6:57 Eshtemoa with its *p* grounds
6:58 and Hilen with its *p* grounds
6:58 Debir with its *p* grounds
6:59 and Ashan with its *p* grounds
6:59 Beth-shemesh with its *p*
6:60 Geba with its *p* grounds and
6:60 Alemeth with its *p* grounds
6:60 Anathoth with its *p* grounds
6:64 cities with their *p* grounds
6:67 Shechem with its *p* grounds
6:67 and Gezer with its *p* grounds
6:68 Jokmeam with its *p* grounds
6:68 Beth-horon with its *p*
6:69 Aijalon with its *p* grounds
6:69 Gath-rimmon with its *p*
6:70 Aner with its *p* grounds and
6:70 Bileam with its *p* grounds
6:71 Golan in Bashan with its *p*
6:71 Ashtaroth with its *p* grounds
6:72 Kedesh with its *p* grounds
6:72 Daberath with its *p* grounds
6:73 Ramoth with its *p* grounds
1Ch 6:73 and Anem with its *p* grounds
6:74 Mashal with its *p* grounds
6:74 and Abdon with its *p* grounds
6:75 and Hukok with its *p* grounds
6:75 and Rehob with its *p* grounds
6:76 Kedesh in Galilee with its *p*
6:76 Hammon with its *p* grounds
6:76 Kiriathaim with its *p*
6:77 Rimmono with its *p* grounds
6:77 Tabor with its *p* grounds
6:78 Bezer . . . with its *p* grounds
6:78 and Jahaz with its *p* grounds
6:79 Kedemoth with its *p* grounds
6:79 Mephaath with its *p* grounds
6:80 Ramoth in Gilead with its *p*
6:80 Mahanaim with its *p* grounds
6:81 Heshbon with its *p* grounds
6:81 and Jazer with its *p* grounds
13:2 their cities with *p* grounds
17:7 took you from the *p* ground
2Ch 11:14 Levites left their *p* grounds
31:19 fields of *p* ground of their
Job 5:24 to go and see your *p* ground
Ps 65:12 *p* grounds of the wilderness
Ca 1:8 and *p* your kids of the goats
Isa 5:17 graze as in their *p*
27:10 *p* ground will be left to
30:23 in that day in a spacious *p*
32:14 zebras, the *p* of droves
49:9 By the ways they will *p*, and
65:10 a *p* ground for sheep and
Jer 9:10 *p* grounds of the wilderness
23:3 back to their *p* ground
23:10 *p* grounds of the wilderness
33:12 *p* ground of the shepherds
50:19 Israel back to his *p* ground
Eze 25:5 Rabbah a *p* ground of camels
34:19 the *p* ground trampled by
36:5 for the sake of its *p* ground
45:2 as *p* ground on each side
48:15 and for *p* ground
48:17 come to have a *p* ground
Ho 9:13 Tyre planted in a *p* ground
Joe 1:19 devoured the *p* grounds of the
1:20 devoured the *p* grounds of
2:22 *p* grounds of the wilderness
Am 1:2 the *p* grounds of the shepherds
Mic 2:12 drove in the midst of its *p*
Zep 2:6 sea must become *p* grounds
Mt 8:30 herd of many swine was at *p*

Pastured
1Ki 4:23 twenty *p* cattle and a
Jer 10:21 their *p* animals have been

Pastures
Ps 23:2 In grassy *p* he makes me lie
37:20 like the preciousness of *p*
65:13 *p* have become clothed with

Pasturing
Ex 34:3 *p* in front of that mountain
1Sa 16:11 and, look! he is *p* the sheep
Pr 10:21 righteous one keep *p* many
Isa 49:9 beaten paths their *p* will be
Eze 34:31 the sheep of my *p*, you

Patara
Ac 21:1 Rhodes, and from there to *P*

Patch
Le 13:55 low spot in a threadbare *p*
Mt 9:16 Nobody sews a *p* of unshrunk
Mr 2:21 sews a *p* of unshrunk cloth
Lu 5:36 *p* from a new outer garment
5:36 both the new *p* tears away
5:36 the *p* from the new garment

Patched
Jos 9:5 and *p* sandals on their feet

Patches
Ge 30:32 speckled and with color *p*

Paternal
Nu 3:24 *p* house for the Gershonites
3:30 *p* house for the families of
3:35 *p* house for the families of
17:2 one rod for each *p* house from
25:14 *p* house of the Simeonites
25:15 clans of a *p* house in Midian
Jos 22:14 *p* house of all the tribes
1Ch 23:11 *p* house for one official
24:4 as heads for their *p* houses
24:4 as heads for their *p* houses
24:6 one *p* house being picked out
24:30 Levites by their *p* houses
24:31 *p* houses of the priests and
1Ch 24:31 As respects *p* houses, the
26:13 by their *p* houses, for the
26:21 *p* houses belonging to Ladan
26:26 the heads of the *p* houses
26:32 heads of the *p* houses
27:1 the heads of the *p* houses and
29:6 the princes of the *p* houses
2Ch 1:2 the heads of the *p* houses
5:2 chieftains of the *p* houses of
19:8 of the *p* houses of Israel
23:2 of the *p* houses of Israel
26:12 heads of the *p* houses, of
35:5 a *p* house belonging to the
35:12 classes by the *p* house
Ezr 2:68 the heads of the *p* houses
3:12 and the heads of the *p* houses
4:2 and the heads of the *p* houses
4:3 the *p* houses of Israel
8:1 the heads of their *p* houses
10:16 fathers for their *p* house
Ne 7:70 the heads of the *p* houses
7:71 the heads of the *p* houses
11:13 brothers, heads of *p* houses
12:12 the heads of the *p* houses
12:22 recorded as heads of *p* houses
12:23 as heads of the *p* houses
Jer 32:7 son of Shallum your *p* uncle
32:8 son of my *p* uncle came in
32:9 the son of my *p* uncle
32:12 the son of my *p* uncle

Path
Job 16:22 the *p* by which I shall not
19:8 My very *p* he has blocked
31:32 doors I kept open to the *p*
34:11 the *p* of man he will cause
Ps 16:11 to know the *p* of life
19:5 exults . . . to run in a *p*
27:11 in the *p* of uprightness
44:18 deviate from your *p*
77:19 *p* was through many waters
119:9 a young man cleanse his *p*
119:101 From every bad *p* I have
119:104 I have hated every false *p*
119:128 Every false *p* I have hated
142:3 In the *p* in which I walk
Pr 4:14 *p* of the wicked ones do not
4:18 *p* of the righteous ones is
5:6 *p* of life she does not
8:20 *p* of righteousness I walk
10:17 discipline is a *p* to life
12:28 *p* of righteousness . . . life
15:10 bad to the one leaving the *p*
15:19 *p* of the upright ones is a
15:24 *p* of life is upward to one
Isa 26:7 *p* of the righteous one is
26:8 *p* of your judgments, O
30:11 deviate from the *p*
33:8 one passing over the *p* has
40:14 in the *p* of justice, or
41:3 on his feet over the *p* by
1Th 2:18 but Satan cut across our *p*
2Pe 2:15 Abandoning the straight *p*
2:15 followed the *p* of Balaam
2:21 the *p* of righteousness
Jude 11 have gone in the *p* of Cain

Pathros
Isa 11:11 remnant . . . from *P* and
Jer 44:1 Noph and in the land of *P*
44:15 in the land of Egypt, in *P*
Eze 29:14 back to the land of *P*
30:14 bring *P* to desolation

Pathrusim
Ge 10:14 *P* and Casluhim (from among
1Ch 1:12 *P* and Casluhim (from among

Paths
Job 6:18 *p* of their way are turned
13:27 And you watch all my *p*
33:11 He watches all my *p*
Ps 8:8 through the *p* of the seas
17:4 against the *p* of the robber
25:4 Teach me your own *p*
25:10 All the *p* of Jehovah are
119:15 And I will look to your *p*
Pr 1:19 *p* of everyone making unjust
2:8 observing the *p* of judgment
2:13 leaving the *p* of uprightness
2:15 whose *p* are crooked and who
2:19 regain the *p* of those living
2:20 *p* of the righteous ones you
3:6 will make your *p* straight
9:15 straight ahead on their *p*
17:23 to bend the *p* of judgment

Pr 22:25 not get familiar with his *p*
Isa 2:3 and we will walk in his *p*
3:12 of your *p* they have confused
49:9 on all beaten *p* their
Jer 3:2 eyes to the beaten *p* and see
3:21 On the beaten *p* there has
4:11 *p* through the wilderness
12:12 *p* through the wilderness
18:15 the *p* of long ago, to walk
Joe 2:7 they do not alter their *p*
Mic 4:2 and we will walk in his *p*
Heb 12:13 straight *p* for your feet

Pathway
Job 18:10 catching device . . . on his *p*
28:7 A *p*—no bird of prey has
41:32 Behind itself it makes a *p*
Ps 78:50 prepare a *p* for his anger
119:35 the *p* of your commandments
Pr 12:28 journey in its *p* means no

Pathways
Jg 5:6 *p* had no traffic, And the
5:6 would travel by roundabout *p*
Job 8:13 *p* of all those forgetting God

Patience
Job 36:2 Have *p* with me a little
Pr 25:15 By *p* a commander is induced
Heb 6:12 through faith and *p* inherit
6:15 after Abraham had shown *p*
Jas 5:7 Exercise *p*, therefore
5:7 exercising *p* over it until he
5:8 exercise *p*; make your hearts
5:10 and the exercising of *p*
1Pe 3:20 the *p* of God was waiting in
2Pe 3:15 consider the *p* of our Lord

Patient
2Sa 13:5 give me bread as a *p*, and
13:6 take bread as a *p* from her
13:10 I may take it as a *p* from
Ec 7:8 Better is one who is *p* than
Mt 18:26 Be *p* with me and I will pay
18:29 Be *p* with me and I will pay
2Pe 3:9 he is *p* with you because he

Patiently
Ac 18:14 with reason put up *p* with
26:3 I beg you to hear me *p*

Patmos
Re 1:9 in the isle that is called *P*

Patrobas
Ro 16:14 Hermes, *P*, Hermas, and the

Pattern
Ex 25:9 as the *p* of the tabernacle and
25:9 and *p* of all its furnishings
25:40 make them after their *p* that
2Ki 16:10 the altar and its *p* as
Eze 28:12 You are sealing up a *p*, full
43:10 they must measure the *p*
Joh 13:15 For I set the *p* for you
Ac 7:44 to the *p* he had seen
2Ti 1:13 the *p* of healthful words
Heb 4:11 the same *p* of disobedience
8:5 make all things after their *p*
Jas 5:10 *p* of the suffering of evil
2Pe 2:6 a *p* for ungodly persons of

Patterned
Ro 8:29 *p* after the image of his Son

Pau
Ge 36:39 the name of his city was *P*
1Ch 1:50 the name of his city was *P*

Paul
Ac 13:9 Saul, who is also *P*
13:13 with *P*, now put out to sea
13:16 *P* rose, and motioning with
13:43 followed *P* and Barnabas
13:45 the things being spoken by *P*
13:46 talking with boldness, *P* and
13:50 a persecution against *P* and
14:9 This man was listening to *P*
14:11 seeing what *P* had done
14:12 Barnabas Zeus, but *P* Hermes
14:14 the apostles Barnabas and *P*
14:19 stoned *P* and dragged him
15:2 disputing by *P* and Barnabas
15:2 arranged for *P* and Barnabas
15:12 to listen to Barnabas and *P*
15:22 along with *P* and Barnabas
15:25 loved ones, Barnabas and *P*
15:35 *P* and Barnabas continued
15:36 *P* said to Barnabas: Above all
Ac 15:38 *P* did not think it proper to
15:40 *P* selected Silas and went
16:3 *P* expressed the desire for
16:9 night a vision appeared to *P*
16:14 the things being spoken by *P*
16:17 girl kept following *P* and us
16:18 *P* got tired of it and turned
16:19 they laid hold of *P* and Silas
16:25 *P* and Silas were praying and
16:28 But *P* called out with a loud
16:29 fell down before *P* and Silas
16:36 reported their words to *P*
16:37 *P* said to them: They flogged
17:4 associated themselves with *P*
17:10 the brothers sent both *P* and
17:13 also in Beroea by *P*, they
17:14 sent *P* off to go as far as
17:15 those conducting *P* brought
17:16 *P* was waiting . . . in Athens
17:22 *P* now stood in the midst of
17:33 *P* went out from their midst
18:5 *P* began to be intensely
18:9 said to *P* through a vision
18:12 with one accord against *P*
18:14 as *P* was going to open his
18:18 *P* said good-bye to the
19:1 *P* went through the inland
19:4 *P* said: John baptized with
19:6 *P* laid his hands upon them
19:11 through the hands of *P*
19:13 by Jesus whom *P* preaches
19:15 and I am acquainted with *P*
19:21 *P* purposed in his spirit that
19:26 Asia this *P* has persuaded a
19:29 traveling companions of *P*
19:30 *P* was willing to go inside
20:1 *P* sent for the disciples, and
20:7 *P* began discoursing to them
20:9 sleep while *P* kept talking on
20:10 *P* . . . threw himself upon
20:13 intending to take *P* aboard
20:16 *P* had decided to sail past
21:4 told *P* not to set foot in
21:11 and took up the girdle of *P*
21:13 *P* answered: What are you
21:18 *P* went in with us to James
21:26 *P* took the men along the
21:29 imagining *P* had brought him
21:30 laid hold of *P* and dragged
21:32 they quit beating *P*
21:37 *P* said to the military
21:39 *P* said: I am, in fact, a Jew
21:40 *P*, standing on the stairs
22:25 *P* said to the army officer
22:28 *P* said: But I was even born
22:30 brought *P* down and stood him
23:1 at the Sanhedrin *P* said: Men
23:3 *P* said to him: God is going
23:5 *P* said: Brothers, I did not
23:6 *P* took note that the one part
23:10 *P* would be pulled to pieces
23:12 until they had killed *P*
23:14 food until we have killed *P*
23:16 and reported it to *P*
23:17 So *P* called one of the army
23:18 The prisoner *P* called me to
23:20 *P* down to the Sanhedrin
23:24 have *P* ride and convey him
23:31 took *P* according to their
23:33 and also presented *P* to him
24:1 to the governor against *P*
24:10 *P*, when the governor nodded
24:24 he sent for *P* and listened
24:26 money to be given him by *P*
24:27 Felix . . . left *P* bound
25:2 information against *P*
25:4 *P* was to be kept in Caesarea
25:6 commanded *P* to be brought in
25:8 But *P* said in defense
25:9 said in reply to *P*: Do you
25:10 But *P* said: I am standing
25:14 matters respecting *P*, saying
25:19 *P* kept asserting was alive
25:21 when *P* appealed to be kept
25:23 *P* was brought in
26:1 Agrippa said to *P*: You are
26:1 *P* stretched his hand out and
26:24 You are going mad, *P*!
26:25 *P* said: I am not going mad
26:28 Agrippa said to *P*: In a short
26:29 *P* said: I could wish to God
27:1 *P* and certain other prisoners
27:3 Julius treated *P* with human
27:9 *P* made a recommendation
Ac 27:11 than the things said by *P*
27:21 *P* stood up in the midst of
27:24 Have no fear, *P*. You must
27:31 *P* said to the army officer
27:33 *P* began to encourage one and
27:43 to bring *P* safely through
28:3 *P* collected a certain bundle
28:8 *P* went in to him and prayed
28:15 *P* thanked God and took
28:16 *P* was permitted to stay by
28:25 *P* made this one comment
Ro 1:1 *P*, a slave of Jesus Christ and
1Co 1:1 *P*, called to be an apostle of
1:12 I belong to *P*, But I to
1:13 *P* was not impaled for you
1:13 baptized in the name of *P*
3:4 when one says: I belong to *P*
3:5 Yes, what is *P*? Ministers
3:22 whether *P* or Apollos or
2Co 1:1 *P*, an apostle of Christ Jesus
10:1 Now I myself, *P*, entreat you
Ga 1:1 *P*, an apostle, neither from
5:2 *P*, am telling you that if you
Eph 1:1 *P*, an apostle of Christ Jesus
3:1 *P*, the prisoner of Christ
Php 1:1 *P* and Timothy, slaves of
Col 1:1 *P*, an apostle of Christ Jesus
1:23 I *P* became a minister
1Th 1:1 *P* and Silvanus and Timothy to
2:18 to come to you, yes, I *P*
2Th 1:1 *P* and Silvanus and Timothy to
1Ti 1:1 *P*, an apostle of Christ Jesus
2Ti 1:1 *P*, an apostle of Christ Jesus
Tit 1:1 *P*, a slave of God and an
Phm 1 *P*, a prisoner for the sake
9 *P* an aged man, yes, now also
19 I *P* am writing with my own
2Pe 3:15 as our beloved brother *P*

Paul's
Ac 17:2 according to *P* custom he went
20:37 fell upon *P* neck and tenderly
23:16 the son of *P* sister heard of
1Co 16:21 greeting, *P*, in my own hand
Col 4:18 Here is my greeting, *P*, in
2Th 3:17 greeting, *P*, in my own hand

Paulus
Ac 13:7 the proconsul Sergius *P*, an

Paunch
Ps 73:4 And their *p* is fat

Pauses
La 3:49 so that there are no *p*

Pavement
2Ki 16:17 then put it upon a stone *p*
2Ch 7:3 faces to the earth upon the *p*
Es 1:6 *p* of porphyry and marble and
Eze 40:17 a *p* made for the courtyard
40:17 dining rooms upon the *p*
40:18 *p* at the side of the gates
40:18 the lower *p*
42:3 *p* that belonged to the outer
Joh 19:13 place called the Stone *P*

Paw
1Sa 17:37 from the *p* of the lion and
17:37 and from the *p* of the bear
Ps 22:20 from the very *p* of the dog
Da 6:27 from the *p* of the lions
Mal 4:2 go forth and *p* the ground

Pawed
Jg 5:22 the hoofs of horses *p* Because
Hab 1:8 its steeds have *p* the ground

Pawing
Jer 50:11 *p* like a heifer in the

Paws
Le 11:27 creature going upon its *p*
Job 39:21 It *p* in the low plain and

Pay
Ex 5:9 not *p* attention to false words
22:17 he is to *p* over the money at
Le 22:21 in order to *p* a vow or as a
25:51 *p* his repurchase price over
25:52 *p* over his repurchase price
26:34 land will *p* off its sabbaths
26:41 they will *p* off their error
De 23:19 make your brother *p* interest
23:20 make a foreigner *p* interest
23:20 you must not make *p* interest
32:41 will *p* back vengeance to my
32:43 will *p* back vengeance to his
1Sa 15:22 *p* attention than the fat of

2Sa 15:7 *p* in Hebron my vow that I
2Ki 4:7 sell the oil and *p* off your
17:3 began to *p* tribute to him
2Ch 6:23 *p* back the wicked by putting
20:15 *P* attention, all Judah and
Es 3:9 *p* into the hands of those doing
4:7 money that Haman had said to *p*
Job 6:28 *p* attention to me, And see
7:18 *p* attention to him every
13:6 *p* attention
22:27 And your vows you will *p*
23:6 himself would *p* heed to me
33:31 *P* attention, O Job! Listen
Ps 5:2 Do *p* attention to the sound of
10:17 *p* attention with your ear
17:1 *p* attention to my entreating
22:25 vows I shall *p* in front of
28:4 *P* back to them their own
37:21 borrowing and does not *p*
41:10 That I may *p* them back
50:14 *p* to the Most High your vows
55:2 Do *p* attention to me and
61:1 Do *p* attention to my prayer
61:8 may *p* my vows day after day
62:12 *p* back to each one according
66:13 I shall *p* to you my vows
72:10 Tribute they will *p*
76:11 Vow and *p* to Jehovah your
86:6 *p* attention to the voice of
116:14 vows I shall *p* to Jehovah
116:18 vows I shall *p* to Jehovah
142:6 *p* attention to my entreating
Pr 2:2 *p* attention to wisdom with
4:1 *p* attention, so as to know
4:20 to my words do *p* attention
5:1 my wisdom O do *p* attention
7:24 *p* attention to the sayings of
20:22 not say: I will *p* back evil
22:27 If you have nothing to *p*
24:12 *p* back to earthling man
Ec 5:4 to God, do not hesitate to *p* it
5:4 What you vow, *p*
5:5 than that you vow and do not *p*
Isa 10:30 *P* attention, O Laishah
19:21 a vow to Jehovah and *p* it
28:23 *p* attention and listen to
32:3 hearing will *p* attention
34:1 groups, *p* attention
41:20 *p* heed and have insight at
42:23 Who will *p* attention and
48:18 actually *p* attention to my
49:1 *p* attention, you national
51:4 *P* attention to me, O my
66:15 to *p* back his anger with
Jer 6:10 are unable to *p* attention
6:17 *P* attention to the sound of
6:17 are not going to *p* attention
18:18 let us *p* no attention to
18:19 Do *p* attention to me
50:29 *P* back to her according to
51:24 *p* back to Babylon and to all
Da 9:19 Jehovah, do *p* attention and
Ho 5:1 *p* attention, O house of Israel
Joe 3:4 I shall *p* back your treatment
3:7 I will *p* back your treatment
Jon 2:9 What I have vowed, I will *p*
Mic 1:2 *p* attention, O earth and what
Na 1:15 *P* your vows; because no more
Zec 7:11 kept refusing to *p* attention
11:12 *p* my wages, thirty pieces
Mt 5:33 must *p* your vows to Jehovah
17:24 Does your teacher not *p* the
18:25 have the means to *p* it back
18:26 I will *p* back everything to
18:28 *P* back whatever you owe
18:29 and I will *p* you back
18:30 *p* back what was owing
18:34 until he should *p* back all
20:8 Call the workers and *p* them
20:10 *p* at the rate of a denarius
22:17 Is it lawful to *p* head tax
22:21 *P* back, therefore, Caesar's
Mr 4:24 *P* attention to what you are
12:14 Is it lawful to *p* head tax
12:15 Shall we *p*, or shall we not
12:15 Shall . . . or shall we not *p?*
12:17 *P* back Caesar's things to
Lu 7:42 anything with which to *p* back
8:18 *p* attention to how you listen
12:59 until you *p* over the last
17:3 *P* attention to yourselves
20:22 Is it lawful for us to *p* tax
20:25 *p* back Caesar's things to
21:34 *p* attention to yourselves
Ac 5:35 *p* attention to yourselves as
8:10 *p* attention to him and say
8:11 *p* attention to him because
16:14 to *p* attention to the things
20:28 *P* attention to yourselves and
Ro 4:4 that works the *p* is counted
1Ti 1:4 nor to *p* attention to false
4:16 *P* constant attention to
Phm 19 I will *p* it back—not to be
Heb 2:1 to *p* more than the usual

Paying

Le 26:43 *p* off its sabbaths while it
26:43 *p* for their error, because
De 23:21 must not be slow about *p* it
1Ki 18:29 there was no *p* of attention
2Ki 4:31 no voice nor *p* of attention
Ps 31:6 *p* regard to worthless, vain
Pr 1:24 there is no one *p* attention
17:4 The evildoer is *p* attention to
29:12 *p* attention to false speech
29:19 but he is *p* no heed
Ca 8:13 the partners are *p* attention
Isa 24:2 for the one *p* the interest
33:18 one that does the *p* out
55:2 people keep *p* out money for
Jer 51:6 treatment that he is *p* back
Ho 4:10 left off *p* regard to Jehovah
Mal 3:16 Jehovah kept *p* attention and
Lu 23:2 forbidding the *p* of taxes to
Ac 8:6 crowds were *p* attention to the
Ro 13:6 is why you are also *p* taxes
1Ti 4:1 *p* attention to misleading
5:4 to keep *p* a due compensation
Tit 1:14 *p* no attention to Jewish
1Pe 3:9 not *p* back injury for injury
2Pe 1:19 well in *p* attention to it as

Payment

De 15:2 not press his . . . brother for *p*
15:3 you may press for *p*; but
1Sa 2:36 for the *p* of money and a
Ho 9:7 the days of the due *p* must
Mt 18:25 to be sold and *p* to be made
Heb 11:26 toward the *p* of the reward

Payments

Nu 22:7 the *p* for divination in their

Pays

Isa 40:10 the wage he *p* is before him
62:11 the wages he *p* are before
Eze 33:15 *p* back the very things taken
Ro 6:23 the wages sin *p* is death

Peace

Ge 15:15 go to your forefathers in *p*
26:29 we sent you away in *p*
26:31 and they went from him in *p*
28:21 I shall certainly return in *p*
44:17 go up in *p* to your father
Ex 4:18 said to Moses: Go in *p*
18:23 come to their own place in *p*
Le 26:6 put *p* in the land, and you
Nu 6:26 Jehovah . . . assign *p* to you
25:12 giving him my covenant of *p*
De 2:26 with words of *p*, saying
20:10 announce to it terms of *p*
20:12 does not make *p* with you
23:6 You must not work for their *p*
29:19 I shall come to have *p*
Jos 9:15 Joshua went making *p* with
10:1 Gibeon had made *p* with
10:4 it has made *p* with Joshua
10:21 Joshua, at Makkedah in *p*
11:19 to be no city that made *p*
Jg 4:17 there was *p* between Jabin
6:23 *P* be yours. Do not fear
8:9 When I return in *p*, I shall
11:31 return in *p* from the sons of
18:6 Go in *p*. It is before Jehovah
19:20 said: May you have *p!* Just
21:13 assembly . . . offered them *p*
1Sa 1:17 Go in *p*, and may the God of
7:14 *p* between Israel and the
16:4 Does your coming mean *p?*
16:5 It means *p*. To sacrifice to
20:7 it means *p* to your servant
20:13 do not certainly go in *p*
20:21 for it means *p* for you and
20:42 to David: Go in *p*, since we
25:35 Go up in *p* to your house
29:7 go in *p*, that you may not do
2Sa 3:21 and he got on his way in *p*
3:22 and he was on his way in *p*
3:23 and he is on his way in *p*
2Sa 10:19 made *p* with Israel and
15:9 king said to him: Go in *p*
15:27 Do return to the city in *p*
17:3 people . . . come to be at *p*
19:24 the day that he came in *p*
19:30 the king has come in *p*
1Ki 2:6 hairs go down in *p* to Sheol
2:33 come to be *p* to time
4:24 *p* itself became his in every
5:12 *p* between Hiram and Solomon
20:18 for *p* that they have come
22:17 each one to his house in *p*
22:27 until I come in *p*
22:28 If you return at all in *p*
2Ki 5:19 he said to him: Go in *p*
9:17 and let him say, Is there *p?*
9:18 king has said, Is there *p?*
9:18 do you have to do with *p*
9:19 king has said, Is there *p?*
9:19 do you have to do with *p*
9:22 said: Is there *p*, Jehu?
9:22 What *p* could there be as
20:19 if *p* and truth themselves
22:20 to your own graveyard in *p*
1Ch 12:17 for *p* that you have come
12:18, 18 *P*, *p* be yours, and
12:18 and *p* to the one helping you
19:19 promptly made *p* with David
22:9 and *p* and quietness I shall
2Ch 15:5 no *p* for one going out or
18:16 each one to his house in *p*
18:26 until I return in *p*
18:27 return at all in *p*, Jehovah
19:1 returned in *p* to his own
34:28 to your graveyard in *p*
Ezr 5:7 To Darius the king: All *p!*
7:12 *P* be perfected
9:12 must not work for their *p*
Es 9:30 in words of *p* and truth
10:3 and speaking *p* to all their
Job 5:23 made to live at *p* with you
5:24 that *p* itself is your tent
15:21 During *p* a despoiler
21:9 Their houses are *p* itself
22:21 and keep *p*; Thereby good
25:2 is making *p* on his heights
Ps 4:8 In *p* I will both lie down and
28:3 Those who are speaking *p* with
29:11 will bless his people with *p*
34:14 Seek to find *p*, and pursue
35:20 it is not *p* that they speak
35:27 in the *p* of his servant
37:11 delight in the abundance of *p*
38:3 no *p* in my bones on account
41:9 the man at *p* with me, in
55:18 my soul in *p* from the fight
55:20 against those at *p* with him
72:3 carry *p* to the people
72:7 *p* until the moon is no more
73:3 the very *p* of wicked people
85:8 speak *p* to his people and
85:10 and *p*—they have kissed
119:165 Abundant *p* belongs to those
120:6 With the haters of *p*
120:7 I stand for *p*; but when I
122:6 for the *p* of Jerusalem
122:7 *p* continue within your
122:8 May there be *p* within you
125:5 There will be *p* upon Israel
128:6 May there be *p* upon Israel
147:14 putting *p* in your territory
Pr 3:2 and *p* will be added to you
3:17 and all its roadways are *p*
12:20 counseling *p* have rejoicing
16:7 enemies themselves to be at *p*
Ec 3:8 time for war and a time for *p*
Ca 8:10 like her that is finding *p*
Isa 9:6 Eternal Father, Prince of *P*
9:7 to *p* there will be no end
26:3 safeguard in continuous *p*
26:12 Jehovah, you will adjudge *p*
27:5 let him make *p* with me
27:5 *p* let him make with me
32:17 must become *p*; and the
33:7 messengers of *p* will weep
38:17 For *p* I had what was bitter
39:8 *p* and truth will continue in
45:7 *p* and creating calamity
48:18 your *p* would become just
48:22 There is no *p*, Jehovah has
52:7 the one publishing *p*, the one
53:5 chastisement meant for our *p*
54:10 nor will my covenant of *p*
54:13 the *p* of your sons will be

Isa 55:12 with *p* you will be brought
57:2 He enters into *p*; they take
57:19 Continuous *p* there will be
57:21 no *p*, my God has said, for
59:8 way of *p* they have ignored
59:8 will actually know *p*
60:17 appoint *p* as your overseers
66:12 extending to her *p* just like
Jer 4:10 *P* itself will become yours
6:14, 14 There is *p!* There is *p!*
6:14 when there is no *p*
8:11, 11 There is *p!* There is *p!*
8:11 when there is no *p*
8:15 There was a hoping for *p*
9:8 *p* is what a person keeps
12:5 in the land of *p* are you
12:12 There is no *p* for any flesh
14:13 *p* is what I shall give you
14:19 a hoping for *p*, but no good
16:5 I have taken away my *p* from
20:10 mortal man bidding me *P!*
23:17 *P* is what you people will
28:9 that prophesies of *p*, when
29:7 seek the *p* of the city
29:7 in its *p* there will prove to
29:7 will prove to be *p* for you
29:11 thoughts of *p*, and not of
30:5 dread, and there is no *p*
33:6 abundance of *p* and truth
33:9 *p* that I am rendering to her
34:5 In *p* you will die; and as
38:4 not for the *p* of this people
38:22 men at *p* with you have
43:12 go out from there in *p*
La 3:17 there is no *p* for my soul
Eze 7:25 *p* but there will be none
13:10, 10 *p!* when there is no *p*
13:16 a vision of *p*, when there is
13:16 when there is no *p*, is the
34:25 with them a covenant of *p*
37:26 conclude . . . covenant of *p*
Da 4:1 May your *p* grow great
6:25 May your *p* grow very much
10:19 May you have *p*. Be strong
Ob 7 The men at *p* with you have
Mic 3:5 and that actually call out, *P!*
5:5 And this one must become *p*
Na 1:15 good news, one publishing *p*
Hag 2:9 in this place I shall give *p*
Zec 6:13 counsel of *p* will prove to
8:10 there was no *p* because of
8:12 there will be the seed of *p*
8:16 and the judgment of *p*
8:19 So love truth and *p*
9:10 speak *p* to the nations
Mal 2:5 one of life and of *p*, and
2:6 In *p* and in uprightness he
Mt 5:24 your *p* with your brother
10:13 let the *p* you wish it come
10:13 let the *p* from you return
10:34 Do not think I came to put *p*
10:34 I came to put, not *p*, but a
Mr 5:34 Go in *p*, and be in good
9:50 keep *p* between one another
Lu 1:79 prosperously in the way of *p*
2:14 *p* among men of goodwill
2:29 your slave go free in *p*
7:50 saved you; go your way in *p*
8:48 go your way in *p*
10:5 May this house have *p*
10:6 if a friend of *p* is there
10:6 your *p* will rest upon him
11:21 his belongings continue in *p*
12:51 to give *p* on the earth? No
14:32 ambassadors and sues for *p*
19:38 *P* in heaven, and glory in
19:42 things having to do with *p*
24:36 said to them: May you have *p*
Joh 14:27 I leave you *p*, I give you
14:27 I give you my *p*
16:33 means of me you may have *p*
20:19 to them: May you have *p*
20:21 again: May you have *p*
20:26 said: May you have *p*
Ac 7:26 them together again in *p*
9:31 entered into a period of *p*
10:36 news of *p* through Jesus
12:20 they began suing for *p*
15:33 let go in *p* by the brothers
16:36 out and go your way in *p*
24:2 Seeing that we enjoy great *p*
Ro 1:7 kindness and *p* from God our
2:10 *p* for everyone who works
3:17 have not known the way of *p*
Ro 5:1 enjoy *p* with God through our
8:6 of the spirit means life and *p*
14:17 means righteousness and *p*
14:19 things making for *p* and the
15:13 fill you with all joy and *p*
15:33 God who gives *p* be with all
16:20 God who gives *p* will crush
1Co 1:3 *p* from God our Father and
7:15 but God has called you to *p*
14:33 not of disorder, but of *p*
16:11 Conduct him part way in *p*
2Co 1:2 *p* from God our Father and the
13:11 God of love and of *p* will
Ga 1:3 *p* from God our Father and the
5:22 fruitage of the spirit . . . *p*
6:16 upon them be *p* and mercy
Eph 1:2 *p* from God our Father and the
2:14 he is our *p*, he who made
2:15 into one new man and make *p*
2:17 declared the good news of *p*
2:17 and *p* to those near
4:3 in the uniting bond of *p*
6:15 of the good news of *p*
6:23 the brothers have *p* and love
Php 1:2 and *p* from God our Father and
4:7 the *p* of God that excels all
4:9 the God of *p* will be with you
Col 1:2 and *p* from God our Father
1:20 *p* through the blood he shed
3:15 let the *p* of the Christ
1Th 1:1 have undeserved kindness and *p*
5:3 saying: *P* and security! then
5:23 very God of *p* sanctify you
2Th 1:2 undeserved kindness and *p*
3:16 may the Lord of *p* himself
3:16 give you *p* constantly in
1Ti 1:2 mercy, *p* from God the Father
2Ti 1:2 *p* from God the Father and
2:22 faith, love, *p*, along with
Tit 1:4 *p* from God the Father and
Phm 3 kindness and *p* from God our
Heb 7:2 Salem, that is, King of *P*
12:14 Pursue *p* with all people
13:20 God of *p*, who brought up
Jas 2:16 Go in *p*, keep warm and well
3:18 for those who are making *p*
1Pe 1:2 and *p* be increased to you
3:11 let him seek *p* and pursue it
5:14 in union with Christ have *p*
2Pe 1:2 *p* be increased to you by an
3:14 unblemished and in *p*
2Jo 3 mercy and *p* from God the Father
3Jo 14 May you have *p*
Jude 2 *p* and love be increased to you
Re 1:4 *p* from The One who is and
6:4 to take *p* away from the earth

Peaceable
2Sa 20:19 the *p* and faithful ones of
1Ki 2:13 she said: Is your coming *p?*
2:13 to which he said: It is *p*
Mt 5:9 Happy are the *p*, since they
Ro 12:18 be *p* with all men
1Th 5:13 Be *p* with one another
Heb 11:31 received the spies in a *p*
12:11 it yields *p* fruit, namely
Jas 3:17 wisdom from above is . . . *p*

Peaceably
2Co 13:11 in agreement, to live *p*

Peaceful
De 20:11 if it gives a *p* answer to
1Ki 22:44 *p* relations with the king
Ps 37:37 future of that man will be *p*
Isa 32:18 dwell in a *p* abiding place
Jer 25:37 the *p* abiding places have
Jas 3:18 sown under *p* conditions for

Peacefully
Ge 37:4 not able to speak *p* to him
Jg 11:13 And now do return it *p*
Isa 41:3 kept *p* passing along on his

Peace-loving
Ge 34:21 These men are *p* toward us

Peacetime
1Ki 2:5 placed the blood of war in *p*

Peacocks
1Ki 10:22 carrying . . . apes and *p*
2Ch 9:21 silver, ivory, and apes and *p*

Peak
Job 20:22 his plenty is at its *p*

Peaks
Ps 42:6 Jordan and the *p* of Hermon
Ps 68:15 Bashan is a mountain of *p*
68:16 O you mountains of *p*, keep
95:4 *p* of the mountains belong

Pearl
Es 1:6 pavement of . . . *p* and black
Mt 13:46 finding one *p* of high value
Re 18:16 and precious stone and *p*
21:21 gates was made of one *p*

Pearls
Job 28:18 more than one full of *p*
Mt 7:6 throw your *p* before swine
13:45 merchant seeking fine *p*
1Ti 2:9 hair braiding and gold or *p*
Re 17:4 precious stone and *p* and had
18:12 *p* and fine linen and purple
21:21 twelve gates were twelve *p*

Pebble
2Sa 17:13 not be found there even a *p*
Am 9:9 not a *p* falls to the earth
Re 2:17 I will give him a white *p*
2:17 upon the *p* a new name

Pebbles
1Ch 29:2 mosaic *p*, and every precious

Peculiar
Ec 2:8 and property *p* to kings and the
2Co 11:17 cocksureness *p* to boasting

Peculiarly
Tit 2:14 a people *p* his own, zealous

Pedahel
Nu 34:28 of Naphtali a chieftain, *P*

Pedahzur
Nu 1:10 Gamaliel the son of *P*
2:20 Gamaliel the son of *P*
7:54 Gamaliel the son of *P*
7:59 of Gamaliel the son of *P*
10:23 Gamaliel the son of *P*

Pedaiah
2Ki 23:36 Zebidah the daughter of *P*
1Ch 3:18 *P* and Shenazzar, Jekamiah
3:19 sons of *P* were Zerubbabel
27:20 Manasseh, Joel the son of *P*
Ne 3:25 *P* the son of Parosh
8:4 at his left *P* and Mishael and
11:7 *P* the son of Kolaiah the son
13:13 and *P* of the Levites in

Peddlers
2Co 2:17 not *p* of the word of God as

Pedestal
Ex 38:27 a talent to a socket *p*

Pedestals
Ex 26:19 forty socket *p* of silver
26:19 two socket *p* under the one
26:19 two socket *p* under the other
26:21 forty socket *p* of silver
26:21 two socket *p* under the one
26:21 two socket *p* under the other
26:25 and their socket *p* of silver
26:25, 25 sixteen *p*, two socket *p*
26:25 two socket *p* under the other
26:32 upon four socket *p* of silver
26:37 them five socket *p* of copper
27:10 socket *p* are of copper
27:11 socket *p* being of copper
27:12 ten and their socket *p* ten
27:14 and their socket *p* three
27:15 and their socket *p* three
27:16 and their socket *p* four
27:17 but their socket *p* of copper
27:18 socket *p* being of copper
35:11 its pillars and its socket *p*
35:17 its pillars and its socket *p*
36:24 forty socket *p* of silver for
36:24 two socket *p* beneath the one
36:24 two socket *p* beneath the
36:26 forty socket *p* of silver
36:26 two socket *p* beneath the one
36:26 two socket *p* beneath the
36:30 socket *p* of silver to sixteen
36:30 two socket *p* next to two
36:30 two socket *p* beneath each
36:36 cast four socket *p* of silver
36:38 five socket *p* were of copper
38:10 socket *p* were of copper
38:11 socket *p* were of copper
38:12 and their socket *p* ten
38:14 and their socket *p* three
38:15 and their socket *p* three
38:17 the socket *p* for the pillars

Ex 38:19 four socket *p* were of copper
38:27 socket *p* of the holy place and
38:27 the socket *p* of the curtain
38:27 A hundred socket *p* equaled a
38:30 socket *p* of the entrance of
38:31 the socket *p* of the courtyard
38:31 socket *p* of the gate of the
39:33 its pillars and its socket *p*
39:40 its pillars and its socket *p*
40:18 putting its socket *p* down
Nu 3:36 its pillars and its socket *p*
3:37 socket *p* and their tent pins
4:31 its pillars and its socket *p*
4:32 socket *p* and their tent
Job 38:6 what have its socket *p* been
Ca 5:15 on socket *p* of refined gold

Peeled
Ge 30:37, 37 *p* in them white *p* spots
30:38 the staffs that he had *p* he

Peer
Pr 7:7 *p* upon the inexperienced ones
Isa 8:21 and will certainly *p* upward
Ob 13 ought not to *p* at his calamity
1Pe 1:12 angels are desiring to *p*

Peering
Jer 5:26 *p*, as when birdcatchers

Peers
Jas 1:25 *p* into the perfect law that

Peg
De 23:13 a *p* should be at your service
Ezr 9:8 by giving us a *p* in his holy
Isa 22:23 as a *p* in a lasting place
22:25 *p* that is driven in a
Eze 15:3 *p* on which to hang any kind

Pegs
Ex 26:32 Their *p* are of gold. They are
26:37 Their *p* are of gold
27:10 *p* of the pillars and their
27:11 *p* of the pillars and their
27:17 and their *p* are of silver but
36:36 their *p* being of gold, and
36:38 its five pillars and their *p*
38:10 *p* of the pillars and their
38:11 *p* of the pillars and their
38:12 The *p* of the pillars and
38:17 *p* of the pillars and their
38:19 Their *p* were of silver and
38:28 he made *p* for the pillars

Pekah
2Ki 15:25 *P* the son of Remaliah
15:27 *P* the son of Remaliah
15:29 days of *P* the king of Israel
15:30 *P* the son of Remaliah
15:31 the affairs of *P* and all
15:32 *P* the son of Remaliah the
15:37 and *P* the son of Remaliah
16:1 *P* the son of Remaliah
16:5 *P* the son of Remaliah
2Ch 28:6 *P* the son of Remaliah
Isa 7:1 *P* the son of Remaliah, the

Pekahiah
2Ki 15:22 *P* his son began to reign in
15:23 *P* the son of Menahem
15:26 the affairs of *P* and all

Pekod
Jer 50:21 the inhabitants of *P*
Eze 23:23 *P* and Shoa and Koa, all

Pelaiah
1Ch 3:24 sons of Elioenai were . . . *P*
Ne 8:7 Hanan, *P*, even the Levites
10:10 Kelita, *P*, Hanan

Pelaliah
Ne 11:12 *P* the son of Amzi the son of

Pelatiah
1Ch 3:21 sons of Hananiah were *P* and
4:42 *P* and Neariah and Rephaiah
Ne 10:22 *P*, Hanan, Anaiah
Eze 11:1 and *P* the son of Benaiah
11:13 *P* the son of Benaiah

Peleg
Ge 10:25 The name of the one was *P*
11:16 Eber . . . became father to *P*
11:17 after his fathering *P* Eber
11:18 *P* lived on for thirty years
11:19 after his fathering Reu *P*
1Ch 1:19 The name of the one was *P*
1:25 Eber, *P*, Reu
Lu 3:35 son of *P*, son of Eber, son of

Pelet
1Ch 2:47 sons of Jahdai were . . . *P*
12:3 and *P* the sons of Azmaveth

Peleth
Nu 16:1 and On the son of *P*, the sons
1Ch 2:33 the sons of Jonathan were *P*

Pelethites
2Sa 8:18 the Cherethites and the *P*
15:18 the *P* and all the Gittites
20:7 the *P* and all the mighty men
20:23 and Benaiah . . . over the *P*
1Ki 1:38 the *P* proceeded to go down
1:44 the Cherethites and the *P*
1Ch 18:17 the Cherethites and the *P*

Pelican
Le 11:18 the swan and the *p* and the
De 14:17 the *p* and the vulture and the
Ps 102:6 the *p* of the wilderness
Isa 34:11 *p* and the porcupine must
Zep 2:14 *p* and porcupine will spend

Pelonite
1Ch 11:27 Helez the *P*
11:36 Ahijah the *P*
27:10 Helez the *P* of the sons of

Pelt
Le 20:2 *p* him to death with stones
20:27 *p* them to death with stones
24:14 entire assembly must *p* him
24:16 without fail *p* him with
De 21:21 *p* him with stones, and he
22:21 *p* her with stones, and she
22:24 *p* them with stones, and they
Eze 16:40 and *p* you with stones and
23:47 must *p* them with stones
Ac 14:5 and *p* them with stones

Pelted
Le 24:23 and they *p* him with stones
Nu 15:36 *p* him with stones so that he
1Ki 12:18 Israel *p* him with stones
2Ch 10:18 Israel *p* him with stones
24:21 *p* him with stones at the

Pelting
Nu 14:10 talked of *p* them with stones
15:35 *p* him with stones outside
Jos 7:25 went *p* him with stones

Pen
Mic 2:12 like a flock in the *p*, like
Hab 3:17 flock . . . severed from the *p*
3Jo 13 writing you with ink and *p*

Penalty
Ge 43:9 you may exact the *p* for him
Pr 22:3 along and must suffer the *p*
27:12 have suffered the *p*

Pendant
Ca 4:9 by one *p* of your necklace
Eze 23:15 *p* turbans on their heads

Pending
2Ki 16:11 *p* the time that King Ahaz

Penetrated
Jer 46:23 for it could not be *p*

Peniel
Ge 32:30 the name of the place *P*

Peninnah
1Sa 1:2 the name of the other being *P*
1:2 And *P* came to have children
1:4 gave to *P* his wife and to all

Pens
Nu 32:16 build here stone flock *p* for
32:24 and stone *p* for your flocks
32:36 and stone flock *p*
Ps 50:9 Out of your *p* he-goats
78:70 from the *p* of the flock
89:40 broken down all his stone *p*
Jer 49:3 rove about among the stone *p*
Na 3:17 in the stone *p* in a cold day
Zep 2:6 and stone *p* for sheep

Pentecost
Ac 2:1 festival of *P* was in progress
20:16 the day of the festival of *P*
1Co 16:8 until the festival of *P*

Penuel
Ge 32:31 as soon as he passed by *P*
Jg 8:8 to *P* and went speaking to them
8:8 men of *P* answered him just
Jg 8:9 he said also to the men of *P*
8:17 the tower of *P* he pulled down
1Ki 12:25 from there and built *P*
1Ch 4:4 *P* the father of Gedor and
8:25 and *P*, the sons of Shashak

People
Ge 11:6 one *p* and there is one
14:16 and also the women and the *p*
17:14 must be cut off from his *p*
19:4 boy to old man, all the *p*
23:11 eyes of the sons of my *p* I
25:8 and was gathered to his *p*
25:17 and was gathered to his *p*
26:10 one of the *p* would have lain
26:11 commanded all the *p*
31:29 to do harm to you *p*, but
32:7 divided the *p* who were with
33:15 some of the *p* who are with
34:16 and become one *p*
34:22 so as to become one *p*
35:6 all the *p* who were with him
35:29 and was gathered to his *p*
41:40 all my *p* will obey you
41:55 the *p* began to cry to Pharaoh
41:57 *p* of all the earth came to
42:6 selling to all *p* of the earth
47:14 cereals which *p* were buying
47:21 As for the *p*, he removed
47:23 Then Joseph said to the *p*
48:19 He too will become a *p* and
48:21 continue with you *p* and
49:16 Dan will judge his *p* as one
49:29 I am being gathered to my *p*
49:33 and was gathered to his *p*
50:20 to preserve many *p* alive
Ex 1:9 he proceeded to say to his *p*
1:9 The *p* of the sons of Israel are
1:20 the *p* kept growing more
1:22 Pharaoh commanded all his *p*
3:7 seen the affliction of my *p*
3:10 my *p* the sons of Israel out
3:12 brought the *p* out of Egypt
3:12 *p* will serve the true God
3:21 give this *p* favor in the eyes
4:16 must speak for you to the *p*
4:21 he will not send the *p* away
4:30 signs under the eyes of the *p*
4:31 At this the *p* believed
5:1 Send my *p* away that they may
5:4 you cause the *p* to leave off
5:5 *p* of the land are now many
5:6 those who drove the *p* to work
5:7 *p* to make bricks as formerly
5:10 those who drove the *p* to work
5:10 officers . . . said to the *p*
5:12 *p* scattered about over all the
5:16 your own *p* are at fault
5:22 you caused evil to this *p*
5:23 he has done evil to this *p*
5:23 by no means delivered your *p*
6:7 take you to me as a *p*, and
7:4 my *p*, the sons of Israel, out
7:14 refused to send the *p* away
7:16 Send my *p* away that they may
8:1 Send my *p* away that they may
8:3 frogs . . . on your *p* and into
8:4 on your *p* . . . frogs will come
8:8 the frogs from me and my *p*
8:8 I want to send the *p* away that
8:9 entreaty for . . . your *p* in
8:11 and your servants and your *p*
8:20 Send my *p* away that they may
8:21 if you are not sending my *p*
8:21 I am sending upon . . . your *p*
8:22 Goshen upon which my *p* are
8:23, 23 between my *p* and your *p*
8:29 his servants and his *p*
8:29 in not sending the *p* away to
8:31 his servants and his *p*
8:32 and did not send the *p* away
9:1 Send my *p* away that they may
9:7 Pharaoh . . . did not send the *p*
9:13 Send my *p* away that they may
9:14 upon your servants and your *p*
9:15 strike you and your *p* with
9:17 against my *p* in not sending
9:27 I and my *p* are in the wrong
10:3 Send my *p* away that they may
10:4 refusing to send my *p* away
10:5 left to you *p* by the hail, and
10:9, 9 young *p* and our old *p* we
11:2 Speak . . . in the ears of the *p*
11:3 Jehovah gave the *p* favor in

De 4:10 Congregate the *p* together to
4:11 you *p* came near and stood at
4:20 a *p* of private ownership to
4:33 other *p* heard the voice of God
5:28 voice of the words of this *p*
5:32 you *p* must take care to do
7:6 you are a holy *p* to Jehovah
7:6 to become his *p*, a special
8:19 you *p* will absolutely perish
9:2 a *p* great and tall, the sons of
9:6 for you are a stiff-necked *p*
9:7 you *p* have proved rebellious
9:12 your *p* whom you brought out
9:13 I have seen this *p*, and, look!
9:13 look! it is a stiff-necked *p*
9:26 do not bring to ruin your *p*
9:27 hardness of this *p* and their
9:29 your *p* and your private
10:11 go before the *p* for a pulling
13:9 the hand of all the *p*
14:2 you are a holy *p* to Jehovah
14:2 chosen you to become his *p*
14:21 you are a holy *p* to Jehovah
16:18 they must judge the *p* with
17:7 hand of all the *p* afterward
17:13 the *p* will hear and become
17:16 nor make the *p* go back
18:3 the *p* . . . ones who sacrifice
18:15 to him you *p* should listen
20:1 a *p* more numerous than you
20:2 approach and speak to the *p*
20:5 too must speak to the *p*
20:8 speak further to the *p* and
20:9 finished speaking to the *p*
20:9 at the head of the *p*
20:11 all the *p* found in it should
21:8 the account of your *p* Israel
21:8 in the midst of your *p* Israel
26:15 bless your *p* Israel and the
26:18 you will become his *p*
26:19 a *p* holy to Jehovah your God
27:1 to command the *p*, saying
27:9 the *p* of Jehovah your God
27:11 went on to command the *p*
27:12 bless the *p* on Mount Gerizim
27:15 the *p* must answer and say
27:16 all the *p* must say, Amen!
27:17 all the *p* must say, Amen!
27:18 all the *p* must say, Amen!
27:19 all the *p* must say, Amen!
27:20 all the *p* must say, Amen!
27:21 all the *p* must say, Amen!
27:22 all the *p* must say, Amen!
27:23 all the *p* must say, Amen!
27:24 all the *p* must say, Amen!
27:25 all the *p* must say, Amen!
27:26 all the *p* must say, Amen!
28:9 establish you as a holy *p*
28:32 given to another *p* and your
28:33 your production a *p* will eat
29:13 establishing you . . . as his *p*
30:4 dispersed *p* should be at the
31:7 bring this *p* into the land
31:12 Congregate the *p*, the men
31:16 this *p* will certainly get up
32:6 O *p* stupid and not wise
32:9 For Jehovah's share is his *p*
32:21 jealousy with what is no *p*
32:36 For Jehovah will judge his *p*
32:43 glad, you nations, with his *p*
32:43 for the ground of his *p*
32:44 song in the hearing of the *p*
32:50 and be gathered to your *p*
32:50 got to be gathered to his *p*
33:3 He was also cherishing his *p*
33:5 heads of the *p* gathered
33:7 may you bring him to his *p*
33:21 the *p* will gather themselves
33:29 A *p* enjoying salvation in
Jos 1:2 you and all this *p*
1:3 to you *p* I shall certainly
1:6 this *p* to inherit the land
1:10 the officers of the *p*
1:11 command the *p*, saying, Get
2:14 are to die instead of you *p*
3:3 to command the *p*, saying: As
3:5 now said to the *p*: Sanctify
3:6 and pass before the *p*. So they
3:6 and went before the *p*
3:14 the *p* pulled away from their
3:14 the ark . . . before the *p*
3:16 the *p* passed over in front of
4:2 twelve men from the *p*, one
4:10 to speak to the *p*, according

Jos 4:10 *p* hurried up and passed over
4:11 *p* had completed passing over
4:11 and the priests, before the *p*
4:19 *p* came up out of the Jordan
5:4 the *p* that came out of Egypt
5:5 *p* who came out proved to be
5:5 *p* born in the wilderness on
6:5 *p* should shout a great war cry
6:5 the *p* must go up, each one
6:7 he went on to say to the *p*
6:8 just as Joshua said to the *p*
6:10 had commanded the *p*, saying
6:16 to say to the *p*: Shout; for
6:18 As for you *p*, only keep away
6:20 Then the *p* shouted, when
6:20 the *p* heard the sound of the
6:20 *p* began to shout a great war
6:20 the *p* went up into the city
7:3 Let not all the *p* go up
7:3 Do not weary all the *p* with
7:4 men of the *p* went up there
7:5 heart of the *p* began to melt
7:7 this *p* all the way across the
7:13 Sanctify the *p*, and you must
7:13 until you *p* have removed the
8:1 all the *p* of war and get up
8:1 the king of Ai and his *p* and
8:2 you *p* may plunder its spoil
8:3 all the *p* of war rose to go
8:5 and all the *p* who are with me
8:9 in the midst of the *p*
8:10 reviewed the *p* and went up
8:10 went . . . before the *p* to Ai
8:11 all the *p* of war who were
8:13 So the *p* set the main camp
8:14 he and all his *p*, at the
8:16 the *p* who were in the city
8:20 *p* that were fleeing to the
8:25 all the *p* of Ai
8:33 bless the *p* of Israel first
9:23 And now you are a cursed *p*
10:7 all the *p* of war with him
10:21 *p* then began to return to
10:33 struck him and his *p* until
11:4 *p* as numerous as the grains
11:7 Joshua and all the *p* of war
14:8 the heart of the *p* to melt
17:14 a numerous *p* for the reason
17:15 If you are a numerous *p*, go
17:17 A numerous *p* you are, and
18:6 you *p*, you will map out the
24:2 say to all the *p*: This is
24:16 the *p* answered and said
24:19 Joshua said to the *p*
24:21 In turn the *p* said to
24:22 Joshua said to the *p*
24:24 the *p* said to Joshua
24:25 a covenant with the *p* on
24:27 to say to all the *p*
24:28 Joshua sent the *p* away
Jg 1:16 took up dwelling with the *p*
2:4 the *p* began to raise their
2:6 When Joshua sent the *p* away
2:7 And the *p* continued to serve
3:18 he at once sent the *p* away
4:13 the *p* that were with him
5:9 were volunteers among the *p*
5:11 Jehovah's *p* made their way
5:13 Jehovah's *p* came down to me
5:18 Zebulun was a *p* that scorned
7:1 all the *p* who were with him
7:2 The *p* who are with you are too
7:3 in the hearing of the *p*, saying
7:3 the *p* retired, and there were
7:4 There are yet too many *p*
7:5 had the *p* go down to the water
7:6 the rest of the *p*, they bent
7:7 I shall save you *p*, and I will
7:7 other *p*, let them go each one
7:8 took the provisions of the *p*
8:5 loaves of bread to the *p* that
9:29 this *p* were in my hand! Then
9:32 *p* that are with you, and lie
9:33 the *p* that are with him are
9:34 *p* that were with him rose
9:35 *p* that were with him rose
9:36 caught sight of the *p*, he at
9:36 *P* coming down from the tops
9:37 *P* coming down out of the
9:38 the *p* whom you rejected
9:42 the *p* began to go out into the
9:43 he took the *p* and divided
9:43 the *p* were going out of the
9:45 he killed the *p* that were in

Jg 9:48 all the *p* that were with him
9:48 said to the *p* that were with
9:49 the *p* cut down also each one
10:18 *p* and the princes of Gilead
11:11 the *p* set him over them as
11:20 gathering all his *p* together
11:21 his *p* into Israel's hand, so
11:23 from before his *p* Israel
12:2 I and my *p*, with the sons of
14:3 among all my *p* a woman, so
14:15 that you *p* invited us here
14:16 the sons of my *p*, but to me
14:17 riddle to the sons of her *p*
16:24 *p* got to see him, they at
16:30 all the *p* that were in it
18:7 *p* that were within it were
18:10 come to an unsuspecting *p*
18:20 into the midst of the *p*
18:25 men . . . may assault you *p*
18:27 a *p* quiet and unsuspecting
19:5 and afterward you *p* may go
19:9 tomorrow you *p* must get up
20:2 the keymen of all the *p* and
20:2 the *p* of the true God, four
20:8 all the *p* rose up as one man
20:10 procure provisions for the *p*
20:16 Out of all this *p* there were
20:22 the *p*, the men of Israel
20:26 Israel, even all the *p*, went
20:31 went on out to meet the *p*
20:31 *p* mortally wounded on the
21:2 the *p* came to Bethel and kept
21:4 *p* proceeded to get up early
21:9 When the *p* were counted
21:15 *p* felt regret over Benjamin
Ru 1:6 turned his attention to his *p*
1:10 we shall return to your *p*
1:15 returned to her *p* and her gods
1:16, 16 Your *p* will be my *p*, and
2:11 a *p* whom you had not known
2:21 Close by the young *p* that are
3:11 everyone in the gate of my *p*
4:4 and the older men of my *p*
4:9 to the older men and all the *p*
4:11 the *p* that were in the gate
1Sa 2:3 you *p* speak very haughtily
2:13 due right . . . from the *p*
2:23 about you from all the *p* are
2:24 *p* of Jehovah are causing to
2:29 offering of Israel my *p*
4:3 When the *p* came to the camp
4:4 *p* sent to Shiloh and carried
4:17 a great defeat among the *p*
5:10 to put me and my *p* to death
5:11 not put me and my *p* to death
6:13 And *p* of Beth-shemesh were
6:19 he struck down among the *p*
6:19 the *p* began mourning because
6:19 had struck down the *p* with a
8:7 Listen to the voice of the *p*
8:10 the *p* who were asking a king
8:19 *p* refused to listen to the
8:21 to all the words of the *p*
9:2 he was taller than all the *p*
9:12 for the *p* on the high place
9:13 the *p* may not eat until his
9:16 as leader over my *p* Israel
9:16 he must save my *p* from the
9:16 seen the affliction of my *p*
9:17 keep my *p* within bounds
10:11 the *p* said one to another
10:17 to call the *p* together to
10:23 in the middle of the *p*, he
10:23 taller than all the other *p*
10:24 Samuel said to all the *p*
10:24 like him among all the *p*
10:24 the *p* began to shout and say
10:25 Samuel spoke to the *p* about
10:25 Samuel sent all the *p* away
11:4 words in the ears of the *p*
11:4 *p* began raising their voice
11:5 is the matter with the *p*
11:7 began to fall upon the *p* so
11:10 we shall come out to you *p*
11:11 put the *p* into three bands
11:12 *p* began to say to Samuel
11:14 Later Samuel said to the *p*
11:15 So all the *p* went to Gilgal
12:3 make restoration to you *p*
12:6 say to the *p*: Jehovah is a
12:18 *p* were greatly in fear of
12:19 *p* began to say to Samuel
12:20 So Samuel said to the *p*
12:22 not desert his *p* for the

1Sa 12:22 to make you his *p*
13:2 rest of the *p* he sent away
13:4 *p* were called together to
13:5 *p* like the grains of sand
13:6 the *p* were hard pressed
13:6 *p* went hiding themselves in
13:7 *p* trembled while following
13:8 *p* were scattering from him
13:11 *p* had been dispersed from
13:14 as a leader over his *p*
13:15 to take the count of the *p*
13:16 Jonathan his son and the *p*
13:22 *p* that were with Saul and
14:2 the *p* that were with him
14:3 *p* themselves did not know
14:15 all the *p* of the outpost
14:17 the *p* that were with him
14:20 Saul and all the *p* that
14:24 Saul put the *p* under the
14:24 none of the *p* tasted bread
14:26 the *p* came into the woods
14:26 *p* were afraid of the oath
14:27 put the *p* under an oath, so
14:28 one of the *p* answered and
14:28 put the *p* under oath
14:28 the *p* began to get tired
14:30 if the *p* had but eaten today
14:31 the *p* got to be very tired
14:32 *p* began darting greedily at
14:32 *p* fell to eating along with
14:33 The *p* are sinning against
14:34 Scatter among the *p*, and
14:34 *p* brought near each one his
14:38 all you keymen of the *p*
14:39 no one . . . out of all the *p*
14:40 At this the *p* said to Saul
14:41 the *p* themselves went out
14:45 *p* said to Saul: Is Jonathan
14:45 the *p* redeemed Jonathan
15:1 you as king over his *p* Israel
15:4 Saul summoned the *p* and took
15:8 *p* he devoted to destruction
15:9 *p* had compassion upon Agag
15:15 *p* had compassion upon the
15:21 the *p* went taking from the
15:24 I feared the *p* and so obeyed
15:30 the older men of my *p* and
17:27 the *p* said to him the same
17:30 *p* gave him the same reply
17:46 *p* of all the earth will
18:5 good in the eyes of all the *p*
18:13 and came in before the *p*
21:15 need of *p* driven crazy
22:3 dwell with you *p* until I
23:8 Saul summoned all the *p* to
26:5 *p* camping all around him
26:7 to the *p* by night; and
26:7 *p* were lying all around him
26:14 call out to the *p* and to
26:15 *p* came in to bring the king
27:12 stench among his *p* Israel
30:4 David and the *p* that were
30:6 *p* said to stone him
30:6 soul of all the *p* had
30:21 meet the *p* that were with
30:21 David came near to the *p*
31:9 inform . . . the *p*
2Sa 1:4 *p* have fled from the battle
1:4 many of the *p* have fallen
1:12 over the *p* of Jehovah and
1:20 not, you *p*, tell it in Gath
2:26 *p* to turn back from
2:27 *p* have been withdrawn, each
2:28 *p* came to a halt and did not
2:30 to collect all the *p* together
3:18 save my *p* Israel from the
3:31 Joab and all the *p* that were
3:32 the *p* gave way to weeping
3:34 the *p* wept over him again
3:35 *p* came to give David bread
3:36 *p* themselves took notice
3:36 in the eyes of all the *p* good
3:37 *p* and all Israel got to know
5:2 shepherd my *p* Israel, and
5:12 for the sake of his *p* Israel
6:2 David and all the *p* that were
6:18 blessed the *p* in the name of
6:19 apportioned to all the *p*, to
6:19 *p* went each to his own house
6:21 over Jehovah's *p* Israel
7:7 shepherd my *p* Israel, saying
7:7 *p* not build me a house of
7:8 leader over my *p* Israel
7:10 appoint a place for my *p*

2Sa 7:11 in command over my *p* Israel
7:23 *p* Israel, whom God went to
7:23 redeem to himself as a *p* and
7:23 drive out because of your *p*
7:24 *p* Israel firmly for yourself
7:24 as your *p* to time indefinite
8:15 righteousness for all his *p*
10:5 *p* reported it to David, and
10:10 rest of the *p* he gave into
10:12 in behalf of our *p* and in
10:13 Joab and the *p* that were
11:7 how the *p* were getting along
11:17 then some of the *p*, the
12:28 gather the rest of the *p*
12:29 David gathered all the *p*
12:31 *p* that were in it, he
12:31 *p* returned to Jerusalem
13:34 many *p* coming from the
14:13 against the *p* of God
14:15 the *p* made me afraid
15:12 and the *p* were continually
15:17 with all the *p* at his feet
15:23 *p* of the land were weeping
15:23 the *p* were crossing over
15:23 the *p* were crossing over
15:24 the *p* completed crossing
15:30 the *p* that were with him
15:32 summit where *p* used to bow
16:6 the *p* and all the mighty men
16:14 the *p* that were with him
16:15 Absalom and all the *p*
16:18 *p* and all the men of Israel
17:2 the *p* that are with him will
17:3 bring all the *p* back to you
17:3 *p* will . . . be at peace
17:8 spend the night with the *p*
17:9 the *p* that are following
17:16 the king and all the *p*
17:21 You *p*, rise up and speedily
17:22 the *p* that were with him
17:29 for David and the *p* that
17:29 The *p* are hungry and tired
18:1 to number the *p* that were
18:2 one third of the *p* under the
18:2 Then the king said to the *p*
18:3 But the *p* said: You must not
18:4 the *p* themselves went out by
18:5 all the *p* themselves heard
18:6 the *p* continued on their way
18:7 *p* of Israel were defeated
18:8 more in eating up the *p* than
18:16 that the *p* might return
18:16 Joab had held back the *p*
19:2 on the part of all the *p*
19:2 the *p* heard say on that day
19:3 the *p* began to steal away on
19:3 as the *p* would steal away
19:8 to all the *p* they made the
19:8 the *p* began to come before
19:9 the *p* came to be involved
19:39 the *p* now began to cross
19:40 and also all the *p* of Judah
19:40 also half the *p* of Israel
20:12 all the *p* stood still
20:15 the *p* that were with Joab
20:21 You *p*, give him over by
20:22 in her wisdom to all the *p*
22:28 the humble *p* you will save
22:44 the faultfinding of my *p*
22:44 A *p* that I have not known
23:10 the *p*, they returned behind
23:11 the *p* themselves fled
24:2 and you men register the *p*
24:2 know the number of the *p*
24:3 add to the *p* a hundred times
24:4 Joab . . . register the *p* Israel
24:9 the registration of the *p*
24:10 he had so numbered the *p*
24:15 *p* from Dan to Beer-sheba
24:16 bringing ruin among the *p*
24:17 was striking the *p* down
24:21 halted from upon the *p*
1Ki 1:39 all the *p* broke out saying
1:40 *p* came on up following him
1:40 the *p* were playing on flutes
2:39 *p* came telling Shimei
3:2 the *p* were sacrificing on the
3:8 *p* whom you have chosen
3:8 *p* that cannot be numbered
3:9 obedient heart to judge your *p*
3:9 to judge this difficult *p*
5:7 wise son over this numerous *p*
5:16 foremen over the *p* who were
6:13 shall not leave my *p* Israel

1Ki 8:16 brought my *p* Israel out from
8:16 come to be over my *p* Israel
8:30 your *p* Israel with which
8:33 your *p* Israel are defeated
8:34 forgive the sin of your *p*
8:36 even of your *p* Israel
8:36 given to your *p* as a
8:38 of all your *p* Israel
8:41 no part of your *p* Israel and
8:43 the same as your *p* Israel do
8:44 *p* go out to the war against
8:50 forgive your *p* who had
8:51 your *p* and your inheritance
8:52 for favor of your *p* Israel
8:56 a resting-place to his *p*
8:59 judgment for his *p* Israel
8:66 eighth day he sent the *p*
8:66 and for Israel his *p*
9:20 the *p* remaining over from
9:23 the foremen over the *p* who
10:24 *p* of the earth were seeking
12:5 So the *p* went away
12:6 advising to reply to this *p*
12:7 a servant to this *p* and
12:9 that we may reply to this *p*
12:10 this *p* who have spoken to
12:12 Jeroboam and all the *p*
12:13 to answer the *p* harshly
12:15 did not listen to the *p*
12:16 the *p* replied to the king
12:23 and the rest of the *p*
12:27 If this *p* continues going
12:27 the heart of this *p* will
12:28 said to the *p*: It is too
12:30 *p* began to go before the one
12:31 from the *p* in general
13:33 from the *p* in general
14:2 becoming king over this *p*
14:7 out of the middle of your *p*
14:7 a leader over my *p* Israel
16:2 leader over my *p* Israel
16:2 caused my *p* Israel to sin
16:15 *p* were encamping against
16:16 *p* that were encamped heard
16:21 the *p* of Israel began to
16:21 *p* that became followers of
16:22 *p* that were following Omri
16:22 *p* that were following Tibni
18:21 Elijah approached all the *p*
18:21 *p* did not say a word in
18:22 to say to the *p*: I myself
18:24 the *p* answered and said
18:30 Elijah said to all the *p*
18:30 So all the *p* approached him
18:37 that this *p* may know that
18:39 When all the *p* saw it, they
19:21 and then gave it to the *p*
20:8 the older men and all the *p*
20:10 for all the *p* that follow
20:15 took the count of all the *p*
20:42 and your *p* the place of his
20:42 the place of his *p*
21:9 sit at the head of the *p*
21:12 sit at the head of the *p*
21:13 in front of the *p*, saying
22:4 My *p* are the same as your
22:4 are the same as your *p*
22:43 *p* were still sacrificing
2Ki 3:7, 7 *p* are the same as your *p*
4:13 my own *p* I am dwelling
4:41 for the *p* that they may eat
4:42 to the *p* that they may eat
4:43 to the *p* that they may eat
6:30 the *p* got to see, and, look!
7:16 *p* proceeded to go out and
7:17 *p* kept trampling him in the
7:20 *p* kept trampling him in the
8:21 *p* went fleeing to their
9:6 as king over Jehovah's *p*
10:9 and said to all the *p*
10:18 all the *p* together and said
11:13 the sound of the *p* running
11:13 *p* at the house of Jehovah
11:14 the *p* of the land rejoicing
11:17 and the king and the *p*
11:17 themselves the *p* of Jehovah
11:17 between the king and the *p*
11:18 the *p* of the land came to
11:19 and all the *p* of the land
11:20 *p* of the land continued to
12:3 *p* were still sacrificing and
12:8 money from the *p* and not to
13:7 any *p* but fifty horsemen and
14:4 *p* were still sacrificing and

2Ki 14:21 *p* of Judah took Azariah
15:4 The *p* were still sacrificing
15:5 judging the *p* of the land
15:35 *p* were still sacrificing
16:9 its *p* into exile at Kir
16:15 burnt offering of all the *p*
17:24 brought *p* from Babylon and
17:32 the *p* in general priests of
18:26 *p* that are on the wall
18:29 let Hezekiah deceive you *p*
18:36 the *p* kept silent and did
19:29 sow seed, you *p*, and reap
19:35 *p* rose up early in the
20:5 Hezekiah the leader of my *p*
21:24 *p* of the land struck down
21:24 *p* of the land made Josiah
22:4 have gathered from the *p*
22:13 and in behalf of the *p* and
23:2 the *p*, from small to great
23:3 all the *p* took their stand
23:6 place of the sons of the *p*
23:21 commanded all the *p*, saying
23:30 the *p* of the land took
23:35 from the *p* of the land
24:14 the lowly class of the *p*
24:15 exiled *p* from Jerusalem to
24:16 as exiled *p* to Babylon
25:3 no bread for the *p* of the
25:11 rest of the *p* that were
25:12 the lowly *p* of the land the
25:19 mustering the *p* of the land
25:19 sixty men of the *p* of the
25:22 *p* left behind in the land
25:26 the *p*, from small to great
1Ch 10:9 inform their idols and the *p*
11:2 will shepherd my *p* Israel
11:2 leader over my *p* Israel
11:13 *p*, for their part, had fled
12:22 *p* kept coming to David to
13:4 in the eyes of all the *p*
14:2 on account of his *p* Israel
16:2 bless the *p* in the name of
16:8 Give thanks to Jehovah, you *p*
16:20 one kingdom to another *p*
16:30 all you *p* of the earth
16:34 thanks to Jehovah, you *p*
16:36 *p* proceeded to say, Amen!
16:43 *p* proceeded to go each one
17:6 commanded to shepherd my *p*
17:7 to become a leader over my *p*
17:9 a place for my *p* Israel and
17:10 command over my *p* Israel
17:21 is like your *p* Israel, whom
17:21 to redeem to himself as a *p*
17:21 nations from before your *p*
17:22 constitute your *p* Israel as
17:22 your *p* to time indefinite
18:14 righteousness for all his *p*
19:5 *p* went and told David about
19:7 the king of Maacah and his *p*
19:11 rest of the *p* he gave into
19:13 in behalf of our *p* and in
19:14 Joab and the *p* that were
20:3 *p* that were in it he brought
20:3 David and all the *p* returned
21:2 Joab and the chiefs of the *p*
21:3 May Jehovah add to his *p* a
21:5 the registration of the *p* to
21:17 make a numbering of the *p*
21:17 upon your *p*, for a scourge
21:22 be halted from upon the *p*
22:18 subdued . . . before his *p*
23:25 has given rest to his *p*
28:2 my brothers and my *p*
28:21 the princes and all the *p*
29:9 *p* gave way to rejoicing over
29:14 who am I and who are my *p*
29:17 your *p* who are on hand here
29:18 of the heart of your *p*, and
2Ch 1:9 a *p* as numerous as the dust
1:10 I may go out before this *p*
1:10 judge this great *p* of yours
1:11 that you may judge my *p* over
2:11 Because Jehovah loved his *p*
2:18 for keeping the *p* in service
6:5 brought my *p* out from the
6:5 leader over my *p* Israel
6:6 come to be over my *p* Israel
6:21 *p* Israel when they pray
6:24 *p* Israel are defeated before
6:25 the sin of your *p* Israel and
6:27 even of your *p* Israel
6:27 to your *p* as a hereditary
6:29 or of all your *p* Israel

2Ch 6:32 no part of your *p* Israel and
6:33 the same as your *p* Israel do
6:34 *p* go out to the war against
6:39 *p* who have sinned against
7:4 *p* were offering sacrifice
7:5 all the *p* inaugurated the
7:10 the *p* away to their homes
7:10 and toward Israel his *p*
7:13 send a pestilence among my *p*
7:14 *p* upon whom my name has
8:7 *p* that were left over of the
8:10 the foremen over the *p*
10:5 So the *p* went away
10:6 advising to reply to this *p*
10:7 yourself good to this *p* and
10:9 *p* who have spoken to me
10:10 *p* who have spoken to you
10:12 Jeroboam and all the *p*
10:15 did not listen to the *p*
10:16 *p* now replied to the king
12:3 *p* that came with him out of
13:17 Abijah and his *p* went
14:13 Asa and the *p* that were
16:10 others of the *p* at that same
17:9 and teaching among the *p*
18:2 the *p* that were with him
18:3, 3 my *p* are like your *p* and
19:4 go out again among the *p*
20:2 *p* came and told Jehoshaphat
20:7 from before your *p* Israel
20:21 took counsel with the *p* and
20:25 *p* came to plunder the spoil
20:33 *p* themselves had not yet
21:14 great blow to your *p* and
21:19 *p* did not make a burning
23:5 *p* will be in the courtyards
23:6 *p* themselves will keep the
23:10 station all the *p*, even
23:12 *p* running and praising the
23:12 came to the *p* at the house
23:13 *p* of the land were
23:16 and all the *p* and the king
23:16 continue as the *p* of Jehovah
23:17 *p* came to the house of Baal
23:20 rulers over the *p* and all
23:20 all the *p* of the land and
23:21 *p* of the land continued to
24:10 *p* began to rejoice, and
24:20 stood up above the *p* and
24:23 princes of the *p* to ruin
24:23 to ruin from among the *p*
25:11 lead his own *p* and go to
25:15 deliver their own *p* out of
26:1 *p* of Judah took Uzziah, he
26:21 judging the *p* of the land
27:2 *p* were yet acting ruinously
29:36 Hezekiah and all the *p*
29:36 made preparation for the *p*
30:3 *p*, on the other hand, had not
30:13 a numerous *p*, to hold the
30:18 great number of the *p*
30:20 to Hezekiah and healed the *p*
30:27 stood up and blessed the *p*
31:4 he said to the *p*, the
31:8 Jehovah and his *p* Israel
31:10 has blessed his *p*, and what
32:4 many *p* were collected
32:6 military chiefs over the *p*
32:8 *p* began to brace themselves
32:14 deliver his *p* out of my
32:15 his *p* out of my hand and
32:17 deliver their *p* out of my
32:17 deliver his *p* out of my
32:18 to the *p* of Jerusalem that
33:10 to Manasseh and his *p*
33:17 *p* were still sacrificing
33:25 *p* of the land struck down
33:25 *p* of the land then made
34:30 the Levites and all the *p*
35:3 your God and his *p* Israel
35:5 brothers, the sons of the *p*
35:7 to the sons of the *p* flocks
35:8 voluntary offering for the *p*
35:12 to the sons of the *p*
35:13 to all the sons of the *p*
36:1 the *p* of the land took
36:14 the priests and the *p*
36:15 compassion for his *p* and
36:16 came up against his *p*
36:23 among you of all his *p*
Ezr 1:3 is among you of all his *p*
1:11 the exiled *p* out of Babylon
2:1 the captivity of the exiled *p*
2:2 the men of the *p* of Israel

Ezr 2:70 the Levites and some of the *p*
3:1 *p* began to gather themselves
3:11 all the *p*, they shouted with
3:13 *p* were not distinguishing
3:13 the weeping of the *p*, for
3:13 *p* were shouting with a loud
4:4 the *p* of the land were
4:4 the hands of the *p* of Judah
4:9 *p* of Erech, the Babylonians
5:12 the *p* into exile at Babylon
6:12 overthrow any king and *p*
7:13 my realm of the *p* of Israel
7:16 gift of the *p* and the priests
7:25 continually judge all the *p*
8:15 scrutinize the *p* and the
8:36 assisted the *p* and the house
9:1 *p* of Israel and the priests
9:4 unfaithfulness of the exiled *p*
9:11 land that you *p* are going in
9:12 daughters do not you *p* give
9:15 an escaped *p* as at this day
10:1 the *p* had wept profusely
10:6 of the exiled *p*
10:8 congregation of the exiled *p*
10:9 *p* kept sitting in the open
10:13 the *p* are many, and it is
Ne 1:9 dispersed *p* should happen to
1:10 are your servants and your *p*
4:6 *p* continued to have a heart
4:12 you *p* will return to us
4:13 the *p* posted by families
4:14 and the rest of the *p*
4:19 rulers and the rest of the *p*
4:22 at that time I said to the *p*
5:1 a great outcry of the *p* and
5:13 *p* proceeded to do according
5:15 had made it heavy upon the *p*
5:15 domineered over the *p*
5:18 service upon this *p* was heavy
5:19 have done in behalf of this *p*
7:4 there were few *p* inside it
7:5 deputy rulers and the *p* to get
7:6 the captivity of the exiled *p*
7:7 the men of the *p* of Israel
7:72 the rest of the *p* gave was
7:73 the *p* and the Nethinim and
8:1 the *p* proceeded to gather
8:3 *p* were attentive to the book
8:5 before the eyes of all the *p*
8:5 happened to be above all the *p*
8:5 opened it all the *p* stood up
8:6 the *p* answered, Amen! Amen!
8:7 explaining the law to the *p*
8:7 *p* were in a standing position
8:9 who were instructing the *p*
8:9 to say to all the *p*: This very
8:9 all the *p* were weeping as they
8:11 ordering all the *p* to be
8:12 *p* went away to eat and drink
8:13 the fathers of all the *p*
8:16 *p* proceeded to go out and
9:10 and all the *p* of his land
9:32 *p* from the days of the kings
10:14 The heads of the *p*: Parosh
10:28 rest of the *p*, the priests
10:34 and the *p* should bring to
11:1 the princes of the *p* had their
11:1 as for the rest of the *p*
11:2 *p* blessed all the men who
11:24 for every matter of the *p*
12:30 cleanse the *p* and the gates
12:38 half of the *p*, upon the
13:1 in the ears of the *p*
13:15 *p* treading winepresses
Es 1:5 *p* that were found in Shushan
1:22 to each *p* in its own tongue
1:22 in the tongue of his own *p*
2:6 deported *p* who were taken into
2:10 had not told about her *p* or
2:20 about her relatives and her *p*
3:6 told him about Mordecai's *p*
3:6 to annihilate . . . Mordecai's *p*
3:8 *p* scattered and separated
3:11 is given to you, also the *p*
3:12 and each *p* in its own tongue
4:8 before him for her own *p*
4:11 the king's servants and the *p*
4:14 you *p* will perish. And who is
7:3 and my *p* at my request
7:4 we have been sold, I and my *p*
8:6 calamity that will find my *p*
8:9 to each *p* in its own tongue
8:11 destroy all the force of the *p*
9:22 and of gifts to the poor *p*

Jer 31:7 Jehovah, your *p*, the remnant
31:14 *p* will become satisfied
31:33 will become my *p*
32:21 *p* Israel out of the land of
32:38 become my *p*, and I myself
32:42 brought in upon this *p* all
32:43 you *p* will be saying
32:44 With money *p* will buy
33:10 *p* will be saying is waste
33:20 *p* could break my covenant
33:24 *p* have spoken, saying
33:24 own *p* they keep treating
34:8 *p* who were in Jerusalem to
34:10 *p* who had entered into the
34:19 *p* of the land who went
35:16 *p*, they have not listened
36:6 in the ears of the *p* at
36:7 has spoken against this *p*
36:9 *p* in Jerusalem and all the
36:9 *p* that were coming in from
36:10 in the ears of all the *p*
36:13 in the ears of the *p*
36:14 aloud in the ears of the *p*
37:2 *p* of the land did not listen
37:4 into the midst of the *p*
37:7 coming forth to you *p* for
37:12 in the midst of the *p*
37:18 and against this *p*, so
38:1 speaking to all the *p*
38:4 the hands of all the *p*, by
38:4 not for the peace of this *p*
39:8 houses of the *p* the Chaldeans
39:9 *p* who were left remaining
39:9 *p* who were left remaining
39:10 *p*, the lowly ones who had
39:14 in the midst of the *p*
40:3 *p* have sinned against Jehovah
40:5 him in the midst of the *p*
40:6 *p* who were left remaining
40:7 lowly *p* of the land, who
41:10 *p* who were in Mizpah, the
41:10 *p* who were remaining over
41:13 *p* that were with Ishmael
41:14 *p* whom Ishmael had led
41:16 *p* whom they brought
42:1 *p*, from the smallest one
42:8 *p*, from the smallest one
43:1 speaking to all the *p* all the
43:4 *p* did not obey the voice of
44:15 *p* who were dwelling in the
44:20 Jeremiah said to all the *p*
44:20 *p*, who were answering him
44:21 and the *p* of the land
44:24 say to all the *p* and to
44:25 *p* have made a fulfillment
46:16 let us return to our *p* and
46:24 hand of the *p* of the north
48:5 breakdown that *p* have heard
48:9 road mark to Moab, you *p*
48:14 How dare you *p* say: We are
48:17 Say, you *p*, O how the rod
48:39 Howl, you *p*! O how Moab
48:42 annihilated from being a *p*
48:46 *p* of Chemosh have perished
49:1 own *p* have taken up dwelling
49:5 *p* will certainly be
50:6 creatures my *p* has become
50:16 turn each one to his own *p*
50:41 *p* is coming in from the
51:8 Howl over her, you *p*
51:9 Leave her, you *p*, and let
51:24 before the eyes of you *p*
51:26 *p* will not take from you a
51:45 midst of her, O my *p*, and
52:6 bread for the *p* of the land
52:15 lowly ones of the *p* and
52:15 *p* that were left remaining
52:25 mustering the *p* of the land
52:25 men of the *p* of the land
52:28 *p* whom Nebuchadrezzar took
La 1:1 city that was abundant with *p*
1:7 and of her homeless *p* All her
1:7 her *p* fell into the hand of the
1:11 All her *p* are sighing
1:21 *P* have heard how I myself am
2:11 crash of the daughter of my *p*
3:14 laughter to all *p* against me
3:48 of the daughter of my *p*
4:3 daughter of my *p* becomes cruel
4:6 error of the daughter of my *p*
4:10 of the daughter of my *p*
4:15 *P* have said among the nations
Eze 1:1 in the midst of the exiled *p*
3:5 to a *p* who are unintelligible
Eze 3:11 enter in among the exiled *p*
3:11 among the sons of your *p*
3:15 the exiled *p* at Tel-abib
5:7 you *p* were more turbulent
5:16 send to bring you *p* to ruin
5:16 I shall increase upon you *p*
5:17 send upon you *p* famine and
6:13 *p* will have to know that I
7:4 you *p* will have to know that
7:9 you *p* will have to know that
7:26 and *p* will actually seek a
7:27 hands of the *p* of the land
11:1 princes of the *p*
11:5 You *p* said the right thing
11:7 slain ones whom you *p* have
11:10 I shall judge you *p*
11:20 may really become my *p* and
11:24 to Chaldea to the exiled *p*
11:25 to speak to the exiled *p* all
12:19 say to the *p* of the land
12:22 that you *p* have on the soil
13:9 the intimate group of my *p*
13:9 you *p* will have to know that
13:10 they have led my *p* astray
13:17 daughters of your *p* who are
13:18 the ones belonging to my *p*
13:19 profane me toward my *p* for
13:19 by your lie to my *p*, the
13:21 deliver my *p* out of your
13:23 I will deliver my *p* out of
14:8 off from the midst of my *p*
14:8 you *p* will have to know that
14:9 the midst of my *p* Israel
14:11 they must become my *p* and
14:22 are going forth to you *p*
14:23 comfort you *p* when you see
15:3 do *p* take from it a peg on
15:7 *p* will have to know that I
17:9 nor by a multitudinous *p*
17:12 Do you *p* actually not know
17:15 and a multitudinous *p*
17:21 *p* will have to know that I
18:2 What does it mean to you *p*
18:19 you *p* will certainly say
18:25 you *p* will certainly say
18:25 ways of you *p* not adjusted
18:29 ways of you *p* the ones that
18:30 for you *p* a stumbling block
18:32 and keep living, O you *p*
20:30 you *p* defiling yourselves
20:31 inquired of by you *p*
20:33 rule as king over you *p*
20:38 *p* will have to know that I
20:42 *p* will have to know that
21:12 has come to be against my *p*
21:12 have come to be with my *p*
21:24 you *p* will be seized even
22:20 cause you *p* to liquefy
22:22 *p* will be liquefied in the
22:29 *p* of the land themselves
23:49 *p* will have to know that I
24:18 speak to the *p* in the
24:19 the *p* kept saying to me
24:21 you *p* have left behind
25:5 *p* will have to know that I
25:14 by the hand of my *p* Israel
26:6 *p* will have to know that I
26:7 even a multitudinous *p*
26:11 *p* he will kill even with
26:20 to the *p* of long ago
28:22 *p* will have to know that
28:23 *p* will have to know that
28:24 *p* will have to know that
30:2 Howl, you *p*, Alas for the
30:11 He and his *p* with him
31:12 and *p* will abandon it upon
32:16 *p* will certainly chant it
32:31 *p* slain by the sword
33:2 speak to the sons of your *p*
33:2 and the *p* of the land, one
33:3 the horn and warns the *p*
33:6 the *p* itself gets no warning
33:10 Thus you *p* have said
33:12 say to the sons of your *p*, The
33:17 sons of your *p* have said
33:20 And you *p* have said, The
33:30 sons of your *p* are speaking
33:31 like the coming in of *p*
33:31 and sit before you as my *p*
34:30 my *p*, the house of Israel
35:9 you *p* will have to know that
35:13 *p* kept acting in great style
36:3 is a bad report among *p*
36:8 fruitage for my *p* Israel
Eze 36:12 even my *p* Israel, and
36:20 *p* proceeded to profane my
36:20 These are the *p* of Jehovah
36:28 you must become my *p* and
36:35 *p* will certainly say
36:38 *p* will have to know that I
37:9 and blow upon these killed *p*
37:12 burial places, O my *p*, and
37:13 burial places, O my *p*
37:18 the sons of your *p* begin
37:23 and they must become my *p*
37:27 will become my *p*
38:8 *p* brought back from the
38:12 *p* gathered together out of
38:14 *p* Israel are dwelling in
38:16 against my *p* Israel, like
39:6 *p* will have to know that I
39:7 in the midst of my *p* Israel
39:13 *p* of the land will have to
40:22 *p* could go up into it
42:14 what has to do with the *p*
43:27 burnt offerings of you *p*
44:11 and the sacrifice for the *p*
44:19 outer courtyard to the *p*
44:19 sanctify the *p* with their
44:23 *p* they should instruct in
44:28 possession should you *p* give
45:1 *p* allot the land as an
45:6 *p* will give five thousand in
45:8 chieftains maltreat my *p*
45:9 expropriations off my *p*, is
45:16 all the *p* of the land, they
45:20 *p* must make atonement for
45:22 in behalf of all the *p*
46:3 *p* of the land must bow down
46:9 *p* of the land come in before
46:18 inheritance of the *p* so as
46:18 *p* may not be scattered each
46:20 so as to sanctify the *p*
46:24 boil the sacrifice of the *p*
47:14 you *p* must inherit it
47:18 you *p* should measure
47:22 With you *p* they will fall
48:8 you *p* should contribute
48:20 *p* should contribute as the
48:29 *p* should cause to fall by
Da 2:44 be passed on to any other *p*
3:29 any *p*, national group or
4:17 *p* living may know that the
6:25 king . . . wrote to all the *p*
6:26 *p* are to be quaking and
7:27 *p* who are the holy ones of
8:24 *p* made up of the holy ones
9:6 and to all the *p* of the land
9:15 *p* out from the land of Egypt
9:16 *p* are an object of reproach
9:19 upon your city and upon your *p*
9:20 the sin of my *p* Israel and
9:24 determined upon your *p* and
9:26 *p* of a leader that is coming
10:14 befall your *p* in the final
10:21 Michael, the prince of you *p*
11:14 robbers belonging to your *p*
11:15 the *p* of his picked ones
11:32 *p* who are knowing their God
11:33 having insight among the *p*
12:1 behalf of the sons of your *p*
12:1 your *p* will escape, every one
12:7 power of the holy *p* to pieces
Ho 1:9 you men are not my *p* and I
1:10 You men are not my *p*, it
2:1 Say to your brothers, My *p*!
2:23 will say to those not my *p*
2:23 You are my *p*; and they, for
4:4 your *p* are like those who are
4:6 *p* will certainly be silenced
4:8 The sin of my *p* is what they
4:9 *p* the same as for the priest
4:12 my own *p* keep inquiring
4:14 a *p* that does not understand
4:15 do not you *p* come to Gilgal
5:1 with you *p* the judgment has
5:13 to give healing to you *p*
6:1 Come, you *p*, and do let
6:4 the loving-kindness of you *p* is
6:11 the captive ones of my *p*
9:5 you *p* do in the day of meeting
9:10 saw the forefathers of you *p*
10:5 its *p* will certainly mourn
10:8 *p* will in fact say to the
10:13 You *p* have plowed wickedness
10:14 has risen among your *p*
10:15 do to you *p*, O Bethel
11:7 my *p* are tending toward

Ho 14:2 Say to him, all you *p*, May
Joe 2:2 a *p* numerous and mighty
2:5 mighty *p*, drawn up in battle
2:16 Gather the *p* together
2:17 sorry, O Jehovah, for your *p*
2:18 show compassion upon his *p*
2:19 will answer and say to his *p*
2:19 you *p* will certainly be
2:23 down upon you *p* a downpour
2:26 my *p* will not be ashamed
2:27 you *p* will have to know that
2:27 my *p* will not be ashamed to
3:2 on account of my *p* and my
3:3 for my *p* they kept casting
3:9 Proclaim this, you *p*, among
3:16 will be a refuge for his *p*
3:17 you *p* will have to know that
Am 1:5 the *p* of Syria will have to
2:7 meek *p* they turn aside
2:10 *p* up out of the land of Egypt
3:2 You *p* only have I known out
3:6 also the *p* themselves tremble
4:4 Come, you *p*, to Bethel and
4:6 gave you *p* cleanness of teeth
4:7 I also withheld from you *p*
4:9 I struck you *p* with scorching
4:10 I sent . . . you *p* a pestilence
4:11 an overthrow among you *p*
5:1 up over you *p* as a dirge
5:12 who have turned aside poor *p*
5:14 that you *p* may keep living
5:16 *p* will be saying: Ah! Ah!
5:18 day of Jehovah mean to you *p*
5:22 if you *p* offer up to me
5:25 offerings that you *p* brought
6:12 you *p* have turned justice
6:14 they must oppress you *p* from
7:8 in the midst of my *p* Israel
7:15 Go, prophesy to my *p* Israel
8:2 end has come to my *p* Israel
8:6 buy lowly *p* for mere silver
9:10 die—all the sinners of my *p*
9:14 the captive ones of my *p*
Ob 1 Rise up, you *p*, and let us rise
13 come into the gate of my *p*
16 the way that you *p* have drunk
Jon 1:8 and from which *p* are you?
Mic 1:9 as far as the gate of my *p*
1:11 take from you *p* its standing
2:3 a calamity from which you *p*
2:4 raise up concerning you *p* a
2:4 portion of my *p* he alters
2:6 Do not you *p* let words drop
2:8 my own *p* proceeded to rise
2:9 The women of my *p* you drive
2:11 words drop for this *p*
3:2 tearing off their skin from *p*
3:3 eaten the organism of my *p*
3:5 are causing my *p* to wander
4:2 Come, you *p*, and let us go up
6:1 Hear, please, you *p*, what
6:2 has a legal case with his *p*
6:3 O my *p*, what have I done to
6:5 O my *p*, remember, please
6:9 that designated it, O you *p*
6:16 you *p* walk in their counsels
7:14 Shepherd your *p* with your
Na 3:13 Your *p* are women in the
3:18 Your *p* have been scattered
Hab 1:5 you *p*, among the nations, and
1:5 which you *p* will not believe
3:13 for the salvation of your *p*
3:16 for his coming up to the *p*
Zep 1:11 *p* who are tradesmen have
2:2 comes upon you *p* the burning
2:5 Jehovah is against you *p*
2:8 reproached my *p* and kept
2:9 my *p* will plunder them
2:10 against the *p* of Jehovah of
2:11 *p* will bow down to him
2:12 be *p* slain by my sword
3:12 a *p* humble and lowly, and
3:20 I shall bring you *p* in
3:20 *p* to be a name and a praise
Hag 1:2 As regards this *p*, they have
1:12 the remaining ones of the *p*
1:12 *p* began to fear because of
1:13 went on to say to the *p*
1:13 I am with you *p*, is the
1:14 the remaining ones of the *p*
2:2 the remaining ones of the *p*
2:3 how are you *p* seeing it now
2:4 all you *p* of the land, is
2:4 For I am with you *p*, is the
Hag 2:5 that I concluded with you *p*
2:14 That is how this *p* is, and
2:17 struck you *p* with scorching
Zec 2:6 Flee, then, you *p*, from the
2:6 I have spread you *p* abroad
2:8 that were despoiling you *p*
2:9 you *p* will certainly know
2:11 actually become my *p*
4:9 has sent me to you *p*
6:10 something from the exiled *p*
6:15 *p* will have to know that
7:5 Say to all the *p* of the land
8:6 the remaining ones of this *p*
8:7 saving my *p* from the land of
8:8 they must become my *p*, and I
8:9 the hands of you *p* be strong
8:11 the remaining ones of this *p*
8:12 this *p* to inherit all these
8:14 was calamitous to you *p*
8:16 things that you *p* should do
8:23 We will go with you *p*, for
8:23 heard that God is with you *p*
9:16 like the flock of his *p*
13:9 I will say, It is my *p*, and
14:2 the remaining ones of the *p*
14:5 *p* will certainly flee to
14:11 *p* will certainly inhabit
Mal 1:2 I have loved you *p*, Jehovah
1:4 *p* will certainly call them
1:4 *p* whom Jehovah has denounced
2:7 law is what *p* should seek
2:9 despised and low to all *p*
2:13 second thing that you *p* do
2:15 *p* must guard yourselves
2:17 *p* have made Jehovah weary
3:1 Lord, whom you *p* are seeking
3:3 *p* presenting a gift offering
3:5 I will come near to you *p*
3:10 open to you *p* the floodgates
3:15 presumptuous *p* happy
3:18 *p* will again certainly see
4:3 *p* will certainly tread down
4:4 Remember, you *p*, the law of
4:5 sending to you *p* Elijah the
Mt 1:21 save his *p* from their sins
2:4 and scribes of the *p* he began
2:6 will shepherd my *p*, Israel
3:3 the way of Jehovah, you *p*
3:6 *p* were baptized by him in the
3:11 That one will baptize you *p*
4:16 *p* sitting in darkness saw a
4:17 Repent, you *p*, for the
4:23 of infirmity among the *p*
5:11 when *p* reproach you and
5:15 *P* light a lamp and set it
5:45 sun rise upon wicked *p* and
5:45 rain upon righteous *p* and
5:47 also the *p* of the nations
6:7 just as the *p* of the nations
7:16 Never do *p* gather grapes from
8:16 *p* brought him . . . persons
9:13 not righteous *p*, but sinners
9:17 Neither do *p* put new wine
9:17 *p* put new wine into new
9:32 *p* brought him a dumb man
10:8 Cure sick *p*, raise up dead
10:22 objects of hatred by all *p*
10:25 If *p* have called the
11:11 I say to you *p*, Among those
11:18 yet *p* say, He has a demon
11:19 still *p* say, Look! A man
11:24 I say to you *p*, It will be
12:33 you *p* make the tree fine and
13:11 to those *p* it is not granted
13:15 heart of this *p* has grown
14:35 *p* brought him all those who
15:8 *p* honors me with their lips
15:30 *p* that were lame, maimed
21:23 older men of the *p* came up
23:37 But you *p* did not want it
24:9 Then *p* will deliver you up to
24:26 if *p* say to you, Look! He is
25:32 separate *p* one from another
26:3 older men of the *p* gathered
26:5 may arise among the *p*
26:9 and been given to poor *p*
26:47 and older men of the *p*
27:1 the older men of the *p* held a
27:25 *p* said in answer: His blood
27:53 became visible to many *p*
27:64 steal him and say to the *p*
28:19 of *p* of all the nations
Mr 1:3 you *p*, make his roads straight
1:15 Be repentant, you *p*, and have
Mr 1:27 *p* were all so astonished that
1:32 the *p* began bringing him all
2:17 came to call, not righteous *p*
2:22 But *p* put new wine into new
5:14 *p* came to see what it was
5:20 and all the *p* began to wonder
6:12 in order that *p* might repent
6:13 grease many sickly *p* with
6:14 and *p* were saying: John the
6:33 *p* saw them going and many
6:37 give them to the *p* to eat
6:39 the *p* to recline by companies
6:41 place them before the *p*
6:54 the boat, *p* recognized him
7:6 This *p* honor me with their
8:4 to satisfy these *p* with loaves
8:22 *p* brought him a blind man
10:13 *p* began bringing him young
12:41 rich *p* were dropping in
13:9 *p* will deliver you up to
13:13 objects of hatred by all *p*
14:2 might be an uproar of the *p*
Lu 1:10 the multitude of the *p* was
1:17 for Jehovah a prepared *p*
1:21 the *p* continued waiting for
1:68 deliverance toward his *p*
1:77 salvation to his *p* by
2:3 all *p* went traveling to be
2:10 joy that all the *p* will have
2:32 a glory of your *p* Israel
3:4 you *p*, make his roads straight
3:15 as the *p* were in expectation
3:16 baptize you *p* with holy
3:18 declaring good news to the *p*
3:21 when all the *p* were baptized
4:40 all those who had *p* sick with
6:17 a great multitude of *p* from
6:38 and *p* will give to you
6:44 *p* do not gather figs from
7:1 in the hearing of the *p*, he
7:16 turned his attention to his *p*
7:29 the *p* and the tax collectors
8:35 Then *p* turned out to see what
8:47 disclosed before all the *p* the
8:52 But *p* were all weeping and
9:5 wherever *p* do not receive you
9:13 foodstuffs for all these *p*
12:48 one whom *p* put in charge of
13:29 *p* will come from eastern
13:34 but you *p* did not want it
14:13 spread a feast, invite poor *p*
14:24 For I say to you *p*, None of
14:35 *P* throw it outside. Let him
16:4 *p* will receive me into their
16:26 fixed between us and you *p*
16:26 go over from here to you *p*
16:26 neither may *p* cross over
17:21 neither will *p* be saying
17:23 *p* will say to you, See there!
18:15 *p* began to bring him also
18:22 and distribute to poor *p*
18:43 *p*, at seeing it, gave praise
19:47 the principal ones of the *p*
19:48 *p* one and all kept hanging
20:1 teaching the *p* in the temple
20:6 *p* one and all will stone us
20:9 tell the *p* this illustration
20:19 but they feared the *p*
20:26 in this saying before the *p*
20:45 *p* were listening he said to
21:12 *p* will lay their hands upon
21:17 objects of hatred by all *p*
21:23 and wrath on this *p*
21:38 *p* would come early in the
22:2 they were in fear of the *p*
22:66 of older men of the *p*
23:5 He stirs up the *p* by teaching
23:13 and the rulers and the *p*
23:14 one inciting the *p* to revolt
23:27 a great multitude of the *p*
23:29 *p* will say, Happy are the
23:35 And the *p* stood looking on
24:19 before God and all the *p*
Joh 1:7 *p* of all sorts might believe
1:11 his own *p* did not take him
2:10 when *p* are intoxicated, the
2:23 *p* put their faith in his
3:7 You *p* must be born again
3:11 you *p* do not receive the
3:23 *p* kept coming and being
4:20 you *p* say that in Jerusalem
4:21 you *p* worship the Father
4:48 Unless you *p* see signs and
7:49 crowd . . . are accursed *p*

Joh 10:41 many *p* came to him, and
11:50 die in behalf of the *p* and
11:55 many *p* went up out of the
12:5 and given to the poor *p*
18:14 to die in behalf of the *p*
Ac 2:15 *p* are, in fact, not drunk
2:47 finding favor with all the *p*
3:9 *p* got sight of him walking
3:11 *p* ran together to them at
3:12 said to the *p*: Men of Israel
3:23 destroyed from among the *p*
4:1 two were speaking to the *p*
4:2 teaching the *p* and were
4:8 Rulers of the *p* and older men
4:10 and to all the *p* of Israel
4:17 abroad further among the *p*
4:21 and on account of the *p*
4:23 they went to their own *p*
5:12 to occur among the *p*
5:13 the *p* were extolling them
5:16 bearing sick *p* and those
5:20 speaking to the *p* all the
5:25 standing and teaching the *p*
5:26 of being stoned by the *p*
5:34 teacher esteemed by all the *p*
5:37 and he drew off *p* after him
6:8 portents and signs among the *p*
6:12 stirred up the *p* and the
7:6 *p* would enslave them and
7:17 *p* grew and multiplied in
7:34 wrongful treatment of my *p*
10:2 gifts of mercy to the *p* and
10:27 found many *p* assembled
10:41 not to all the *p*, but to
10:42 us to preach to the *p* and to
10:45 also upon *p* of the nations
11:1 *p* of the nations had also
11:18 life to *p* of the nations
11:20 to the Greek-speaking *p*
12:4 produce him for the *p* after
12:11 *p* of the Jews were expecting
12:20 the *p* of Tyre and of Sidon
12:22 assembled *p* began shouting
13:15 of encouragement for the *p*
13:17 God of this *p* Israel chose
13:17 he exalted the *p* during
13:24 to all the *p* of Israel
13:31 now his witnesses to the *p*
13:34 I will give you *p* the
13:42 *p* began entreating for these
14:2 the souls of *p* of the nations
14:5 *p* of the nations and Jews
15:3 the conversion of *p* of the
15:7 *p* of the nations should hear
15:11 the same way as those *p* also
15:14 out of them a *p* for his name
15:17 with *p* of all the nations
15:17 *p* who are called by my name
17:17 other *p* who worshiped God
18:6 I will go to *p* of the nations
18:10 I have many *p* in this city
19:4 telling the *p* to believe in
19:12 to the ailing *p*, and the
19:30 to go inside to the *p*, but
19:33 to make his defense to the *p*
21:11 the hands of *p* of the nations
21:28 against the *p* and the Law
21:30 a running together of the *p*
21:36 *p* kept following, crying out
21:39 permit me to speak to the *p*
21:40 with his hand to the *p*
23:5 of a ruler of your *p*
24:23 he forbid no one of his *p*
26:17 I deliver you from this *p*
26:23 publish light both to this *p*
28:2 foreign-speaking *p* showed us
28:4 foreign-speaking *p* caught
28:9 rest of the *p* on the island
28:17 nothing contrary to the *p*
28:26 Go to this *p* and say
28:27 heart of this *p* has grown
Ro 2:14 *p* of the nations that do not
2:14 *p*, although not having law
2:24 on account of you *p* among the
3:29 also of *p* of the nations
3:29 of *p* of the nations also
3:30 circumcised *p* righteous as a
3:30 uncircumcised *p* righteous
4:9 come upon circumcised *p* or
4:9 or also upon uncircumcised *p*
9:25 Those not my *p* I will call
9:25 I will call my *p*, and her
9:26 You are not my *p*, there they
9:30 *p* of the nations, although

Ro 10:19 incite you *p* to jealousy
10:21 *p* that is disobedient and
11:1 God did not reject his *p*, did
11:2 God did not reject his *p*
11:11 salvation to *p* of the nations
11:12 riches to *p* of the nations
11:13 you who are *p* of the nations
11:25 *p* of the nations has come
12:15 Rejoice with *p* who rejoice
12:15 weep with *p* who weep
13:5 for you *p* to be in subjection
13:8 *p* be owing anybody a single
13:11 you *p* know the season
14:16 let the good you *p* do be
15:10 you nations, with his *p*
1Co 3:9 You *p* are God's field under
3:16 you *p* are God's temple, and
3:17 which temple you *p* are
6:19 body of you *p* is the temple
6:20 glorify God . . . body of you *p*
7:10 to the married *p* I give
8:12 you *p* thus sin against your
9:22 all things to *p* of all sorts
10:7 The *p* sat down to eat and
10:33 pleasing all *p* in all things
12:2 you were *p* of the nations
14:21 I will speak to this *p*, and
14:23 ordinary *p* or unbelievers
2Co 6:16 God, and they will be my *p*
Ga 2:12 to eat with *p* of the nations
2:14 compelling *p* of the nations
3:8 *p* of the nations righteous due
Eph 2:11 *p* of the nations as to flesh
3:1 you, the *p* of the nations
3:6 *p* of the nations should be
5:3 just as it befits holy *p*
1Th 2:16 speaking to *p* of the nations
4:12 as regards *p* outside and not
2Th 3:2 faith is not . . . of all *p*
1Ti 3:7 from *p* on the outside, in
6:21 kindness be with you *p*
2Ti 4:22 kindness be with you *p*
Tit 2:14 a *p* peculiarly his own
3:14 But let our *p* also learn to
3:15 be with all of you *p*
Phm 3 May you *p* have undeserved
22 through the prayers of you *p*
25 with the spirit you *p* show
Heb 2:17 for the sins of the *p*
3:7 Today if you *p* listen to his
3:15 if you *p* listen to his own
4:7 you *p* listen to his own voice
4:9 sabbath resting for the *p* of
5:3 much for himself as for the *p*
5:14 solid food . . . to mature *p*
7:5 collect tithes from the *p*
7:11 a feature the *p* were given
7:27 and then for those of the *p*
8:8 find fault with the *p* when he
8:10 they . . . will become my *p*
9:7 sins of ignorance of the *p*
9:19 spoken by Moses to all the *p*
9:19 book itself and all the *p*
10:30 Jehovah will judge his *p*
11:25 with the *p* of God rather
12:14 Pursue peace with all *p*
12:19 *p* implored that no word
13:12 sanctify the *p* with his
Jas 2:12 by the law of a free *p*
1Pe 2:9 a *p* for special possession
2:10 you were once not a *p*, but
2:10 but are now God's *p*; you
2:16 Be as free *p*, and yet holding
3:20 few *p*, that is, eight souls
4:5 *p* will render an account to
2Pe 2:1 false prophets among the *p*
2:5 upon a world of ungodly *p*
2:7 law-defying *p* in loose conduct
2:9 deliver *p* of godly devotion
2:9 reserve unrighteous *p* for the
2:18 escaping from *p* who conduct
3:9 as some *p* consider slowness
3:17 error of the law-defying *p*
2Jo 6 just as you *p* have heard from
3Jo 7 not taking anything from the *p*
Jude 5 saved a *p* out of the land of
Re 2:27 shepherd the *p* with an iron
5:9 tribe and tongue and *p* and
13:7 over every tribe and *p* and
14:6 and tribe and tongue and *p*
16:15 *p* look upon his shamefulness
18:4 Get out of her, my *p*, if
18:14 never again will *p* find them
19:1 They said: Praise Jah, you *p*!

Re 19:3 they said: Praise Jah, you *p*!
19:4 Amen! Praise Jah, you *p*!
19:6 Praise Jah, you *p*, because
22:16 bear witness to you *p* of

People's

Le 16:24 *p* burnt offering and make
Jg 5:2 For the *p* volunteering, Bless
2Ch 25:15 searched for the *p* gods that
Es 3:8 are different from all other *p*
Joh 10:21 cannot open blind *p* eyes
1Ti 5:13 meddlers in other *p* affairs
1Pe 4:15 busybody in other *p* matters

Peoples

Ge 17:16 kings of *p* will come from
27:29 Let *p* serve you and let
28:3 become a congregation of *p*
48:4 into a congregation of *p*
49:10 the obedience of the *p* will
Ex 15:14 *P* must hear, they will be
19:5 property out of all other *p*
Le 20:24 divided you off from the *p*
20:26 from the *p* to become mine
De 2:25 the *p* beneath all the heavens
4:6 before the eyes of the *p* who
4:19 apportioned to all the *p* under
4:27 scatter you among the *p*, and
6:14 any gods of the *p* who are all
7:6 *p* that are on the surface of
7:7 most populous of all the *p*
7:7 were the least of all the *p*
7:14 most blessed of all the *p* you
7:16 you must consume all the *p*
7:19 God will do to all the *p*
10:15 even you, out of all the *p*
13:7 gods of the *p* who are all
14:2 out of all the *p* who are on
20:16 cities of these *p* that
28:10 all the *p* of the earth will
28:37 a taunt among all the *p*
28:64 scatter you among all the *p*
30:3 from all the *p* where Jehovah
32:8 to fix the boundary of the *p*
33:17 With them he will push *p*
33:19 *P* to the mountain they will
Jos 4:24 all the *p* of the earth may
24:17 the *p* through the midst of
24:18 drive out all the *p*, even
Jg 2:12 gods of the *p* who were all
5:14 Benjamin, among your *p*
2Sa 22:48 bringing the *p* down under
1Ki 4:34 coming from all the *p* to
8:43 all the *p* of the earth may
8:53 out of all the *p* of the earth
8:60 *p* of the earth may know that
9:7 a taunt among all the *p*
22:28 added: Hear, all you *p*
1Ch 5:25 the gods of the *p* of the land
16:8 his deeds known among the *p*
16:24 Among all the *p* his
16:26 gods of the *p* are valueless
16:28 to Jehovah, O families of *p*
2Ch 6:33 all the *p* of the earth may
7:20 a taunt among all the *p*
13:9 like the *p* of the land
18:27 he added: Hear, all you *p*
32:13 to all the *p* of the lands
32:19 gods of the *p* of the earth
Ezr 3:3 because of the *p* of the lands
9:1 the *p* of the lands as regards
9:2 mingled with the *p* of the
9:11 the impurity of the *p* of the
9:14 *p* of these detestable things
10:2 from the *p* of the land
10:11 from the *p* of the land and
Ne 1:8 shall scatter you among the *p*
9:22 to give them kingdoms and *p*
9:24 kings and the *p* of the land
9:30 the hand of the *p* of the lands
10:28 from the *p* of the lands to
10:30 to the *p* of the land, and
10:31 the *p* of the land who were
13:24 the tongue of the different *p*
Es 1:11 to show the *p* and the princes
1:16 against all the *p* that are in
3:8 the *p* in all the jurisdictional
3:12 the princes of the different *p*
3:14 being published to all the *p*
8:13 published to all the *p*, that
8:17 *p* of the land were declaring
9:2 had fallen upon all the *p*
Job 17:6 as a proverbial saying of *p*
36:20 *p* to retreat from where
36:31 he pleads the cause of *p*

Ps 7:8 will pass sentence on the *p*
9:11 Tell among the *p* his deeds
18:47 he subdues the *p* under me
33:10 the thoughts of the *p*
45:5 under you *p* keep falling
45:17 *p* themselves will laud you
47:1 All you *p*, clap your hands
47:3 He will subdue *p* under us
47:9 nobles of the *p* themselves
49:1 Hear this, all you *p*
56:7 bring down even the *p*, O God
57:9 I shall laud you among the *p*
66:8 Bless our God, O you *p*
67:3 Let *p* laud you, O God; Let
67:3 the *p*, all of them, laud you
67:4 judge the *p* with uprightness
67:5 Let *p* laud you, O God
67:5 Let *p*, all of them, laud you
68:30 With the calves of the *p*
68:30 *p* that take delight in fights
77:14 Among the *p* you have made
87:6 when recording the *p*
89:50 reproach of all the many *p*
96:3 Among all the *p* his wonderful
96:5 gods of the *p* are valueless
96:7 O you families of the *p*
96:10 plead the cause of the *p* in
96:13 *p* with his faithfulness
97:6 the *p* have seen his glory
98:9 And the *p* with uprightness
99:1 Let the *p* be agitated
99:2 And he is high over all the *p*
102:22 *p* are collected all together
105:1 among the *p* his dealings
105:20 ruler of the *p*, that he
106:34 did not annihilate the *p*
108:3 shall laud you among the *p*
144:2 One subduing *p* under me
Pr 24:24 the *p* will execrate him
Isa 2:3 many *p* will certainly go and
2:4 straight respecting many *p*
3:13 up to pass sentence upon *p*
8:9 Be injurious, O you *p*, and
10:13 remove the boundaries of *p*
10:14 the resources of the *p*
11:10 up as a signal for the *p*
12:4 Make known among the *p* his
14:2 *p* will actually take them
14:6 one striking *p* in fury with
17:12 commotion of many *p*, who
24:13 land, in among the *p*
25:6 make for all the *p*, in this
25:7 enveloping over all the *p*
30:28 be in the jaws of the *p*
33:3 of turmoil *p* have fled
33:12 *p* must become as the
49:22 to the *p* I shall lift up my
51:4 even as a light to the *p*
51:5 will judge even the *p*
56:7 house of prayer for all the *p*
61:9 descendants in among the *p*
62:10 Raise up a signal for the *p*
63:3 no man with me from the *p*
63:6 stamping down *p* in my anger
Jer 10:3 the customs of the *p* are
34:1 *p* were fighting against
51:58 *p* will have to toil for
La 1:18 Listen, now, all you *p*, and
3:45 refuse in the midst of the *p*
Eze 3:6 numerous *p* unintelligible in
11:17 also collect you from the *p*
18:18 done in the midst of his *p*
20:34 bring you forth from the *p*
20:35 the wilderness of the *p*
20:41 bring you forth from the *p*
23:24 with a congregation of *p*
25:7 cut you off from the *p* and
26:2 broken, the doors of the *p*
27:3 the tradeswoman of the *p* for
27:33 you satisfied many *p*
27:36 merchants among the *p*
28:19 knowing you among the *p*
28:25 out from the *p* among whom
29:13 together out of the *p* among
31:12 all the *p* of the earth will
32:3 a congregation of many *p*
32:9 offend the heart of many *p*
32:10 many *p* to be awestruck
34:13 bring them out from the *p*
36:15 reproach by *p* you will bear
38:6 bands, many *p* with you
38:8 together out of many *p*, onto
38:8 brought forth from the *p*
38:9 bands and many *p* with you
Eze 38:15 and many *p* with you, all
38:22 upon the many *p* that will
39:4 the *p* that will be with you
39:27 bring them back from the *p*
Da 3:4 To you it is being said, O *p*
3:7 *p* were hearing the sound of
3:7 all the *p*, national groups and
4:1 king, to all the *p*, national
5:19 all *p*, national groups and
7:14 that the *p*, national groups
Ho 7:8 it is among the *p* that he
9:1 Do not act joyful like the *p*
10:10 *p* will certainly be gathered
Joe 2:6 *p* will be in severe pains
2:17 should they say among the *p*
Mic 1:2 Hear, O you *p*, all of you
4:1 and to it *p* must stream
4:3 render judgment among many *p*
4:5 all the *p*, for their part
4:13 certainly pulverize many *p*
5:7 in the midst of many *p* like
5:8 in the midst of many *p*, like
6:16 the reproach of *p* you men
Hab 2:5 collecting . . . all the *p*
2:8 the remaining ones of the *p*
2:10 the cutting off of many *p*
2:13 *p* will toil on only for the
Zep 3:9 give to *p* the change to a
3:20 among all the *p* of the earth
Zec 8:20 *p* and the inhabitants of
8:22 many *p* and mighty nations
10:9 like seed among the *p*
11:10 concluded with all the *p*
12:2 reeling to all the *p* round
12:3 stone to all the *p*
12:4 horse of the *p* I shall strike
12:6 all the *p* round about
14:12 will scourge all the *p* that
Lu 2:31 in the sight of all the *p*
Ac 4:25 *p* meditate upon empty things
4:27 and with *p* of Israel were in
Ro 15:11 let all the *p* praise him
Eph 2:15 create the two *p* in union
2:16 reconcile both *p* in one body
2:18 both *p*, have the approach
Re 7:9 out of all . . . tribes and *p* and
10:11 with regard to *p* and nations
11:9 *p* and tribes and tongues and
17:15 mean *p* and crowds and
21:3 and they will be his *p*

Peor
Nu 23:28 took Balaam to the top of *P*
25:3 to the Baal of *P*; and the
25:5 attachment with the Baal of *P*
25:18 cunningly in the affair of *P*
25:18 scourge over the affair of *P*
31:16 over the affair of *P*, so that
De 4:3 in the case of the Baal of *P*
4:3 the Baal of *P* was the one whom
Jos 22:17 error of *P* too small for
Ps 106:28 attach . . . to Baal of *P*
Ho 9:10 went in to Baal of *P*, and

Perazim
Isa 28:21 rise up just as at Mount *P*

Perceive
Mr 8:17 not yet *p* and get the meaning
Joh 4:19 I *p* you are a prophet
Ac 10:34 I *p* that God is not partial
27:10 I *p* that navigation is
Heb 11:3 By faith we *p* that the

Perceived
Da 2:8 *p* that the word is being
Mt 17:13 disciples *p* that he spoke to
Lu 1:22 they *p* that he had just seen
8:46 I *p* that power went out of
20:19 they *p* that he spoke this
Ac 4:13 *p* that they were men
25:25 I *p* he had committed nothing
Ro 1:20 *p* by the things made, even

Perceiving
Eph 5:17 *p* what the will of Jehovah
1Ti 1:7 not *p* either the things they

Perceptible
2Co 2:14 knowledge of him *p* through

Perception
Mr 7:18 Are you also without *p* like

Perceptive
Heb 5:14 their *p* powers trained to

Peres
Da 5:28 *P*, your kingdom has been

Peresh
1Ch 7:16 a son and called his name *P*

Perez
Ge 38:29 Hence his name was called *P*
46:12 the sons of Judah were . . . *P*
46:12 sons of *P* came to be Hezron
Nu 26:20 of *P* the family of the
26:21 And the sons of *P* came to be
Ru 4:12 become like the house of *P*
4:18 these are the generations of *P*
4:18 *P* became father to Hezron
1Ch 2:4 bore to him *P* and Zerah
2:5 sons of *P* were Hezron and
4:1 sons of Judah were *P*, Hezron
9:4 the sons of *P* the son of Judah
27:3 *P* the head of all the chiefs
Ne 11:4 Mahalalel of the sons of *P*
11:6 sons of *P* who were dwelling
Mt 1:3 Judah became father to *P* and
1:3 *P* became father to Hezron
Lu 3:33 son of *P*, son of Judah

Perezites
Nu 26:20 of Perez the family of the *P*

Perez-uzzah
2Sa 6:8 place came to be called *P*
1Ch 13:11 place came to be called *P*

Perfect
De 32:4 The Rock, *p* is his activity
Ru 2:12 a *p* wage for you from Jehovah
2Sa 22:31 the true God, *p* is his way
22:33 will cause my way to be *p*
Job 36:4 The One *p* in knowledge is
37:16 the One *p* in knowledge
Ps 18:30 the true God, *p* is his way
18:32 will grant my way to be *p*
19:7 The law of Jehovah is *p*
Eze 16:14 *p* because of my splendor
23:12 clothed with *p* taste
27:3 said, I am *p* in prettiness
28:12 wisdom and *p* in beauty
38:4 clothed in *p* taste
43:25 out of the flock, *p* ones
Am 5:10 a speaker of *p* things they
Mt 5:48 be *p*, as your heavenly Father
5:48 as your heavenly Father is *p*
19:21 If you want to be *p*, go sell
Ro 12:2 acceptable and *p* will of God
2Co 12:9 my power is being made *p*
Php 3:12 or am already made *p*, but
Col 3:14 for it is a *p* bond of union
Heb 2:10 *p* through sufferings
5:9 after he had been made *p* he
7:19 the Law made nothing *p*, but
9:9 *p* as respects his conscience
9:11 more *p* tent not made with
10:1 make those who approach *p*
10:14 sanctified *p* perpetually
11:40 not be made *p* apart from us
12:23 ones who have been made *p*
Jas 1:17 *p* present is from above
1:25 the *p* law that belongs to
3:2 this one is a *p* man, able to
1Jo 2:5 love of God has been made *p*
4:12 his love is made *p* in us
4:17 love has been made *p* with us
4:18 *p* love throws fear outside
4:18 has not been made *p* in love

Perfected
Ezr 7:12 Peace be *p*
Eze 27:4 have *p* your prettiness
27:11 They . . . *p* your prettiness
Joh 17:23 order that they may be *p*
Heb 7:28 a Son, who is *p* forever
Jas 2:22 by his works his faith was *p*

Perfecter
Heb 12:2 and *P* of our faith, Jesus

Perfecting
2Co 7:1 *p* holiness in God's fear

Perfection
Ps 50:2 the *p* of prettiness, God
119:96 To all *p* I have seen an end
Isa 18:5 the blossom comes to *p* and
La 2:15 *p* of prettiness, an exultation
Lu 8:14 choked and bring nothing to *p*
Heb 7:11 *p* were really through the

Perfectly
Lu 6:40 everyone that is *p* instructed

Ac 23:1 with a *p* clear conscience

Perform

Ge 24:12 *p* loving-kindness with my
34:19 did not delay to *p* the
38:8 *p* brother-in-law marriage
40:14 *p* loving-kindness with me
Ex 4:17 you may *p* the signs with it
4:21 actually *p* all the miracles
14:13 he will *p* for you today
Nu 15:3 sacrifice to *p* a special vow
15:8 sacrifice to *p* a special vow
De 4:13 *p*—the Ten Words, after which
25:5 *p* brother-in-law marriage
25:7 *p* brother-in-law marriage
Jg 6:17 *p* a sign for me that you are
1Ki 6:12 *p* my judicial decisions and
2Ki 20:9 Jehovah will *p* the word that
2Ch 30:12 to *p* the commandment
34:31 *p* the words of the covenant
Ne 10:29 *p* all the commandments of
Ps 145:19 those fearing him he will *p*
Isa 38:7 Jehovah will *p* this word
Jer 22:4 by all means *p* this word
44:25 without fail *p* our vows
44:25 without fail *p* your vows
Eze 5:7 decisions you did not *p*
29:18 *p* a great service against
Mt 7:22 *p* many powerful works in
23:3 for they say but do not *p*
Lu 1:72 to *p* the mercy in connection
Joh 3:2 no one can *p* these signs that
3:2 these signs that you *p* unless
7:31 not *p* more signs than this
9:16 sinner *p* signs of that sort
10:41 John, indeed, did not *p* a
1Co 9:17 If I *p* this willingly, I
12:29 Not all *p* powerful works
Ga 5:3 obligation to *p* the whole Law
2Th 1:11 and *p* completely all he
Heb 9:6 to *p* the sacred services
Re 13:14 *p* in the sight of the wild
16:14 by demons and *p* signs, and

Performance

Ex 32:18 of the singing over mighty *p*
Job 37:12 steering them for their *p*
Lu 1:45 there will be a complete *p*

Performances

De 3:24 and mighty *p* like yours
Ps 106:2 the mighty *p* of Jehovah

Performed

Ge 24:14 you have *p* loyal love with
Ex 4:30 *p* the signs under the eyes of
11:10 *p* all these miracles before
27:21 to be *p* by the sons of Israel
29:28 to be *p* by the sons of Israel
Nu 14:11 the signs that I *p* in among
14:22 signs that I have *p* in Egypt
Jos 24:17 who *p* these great signs
1Sa 11:13 Jehovah has *p* salvation in
14:45 *p* this great salvation in
19:5 Jehovah *p* a great salvation
2Sa 23:10 Jehovah *p* a great salvation
23:12 Jehovah *p* a great salvation
1Ki 8:66 goodness that Jehovah had *p*
2Ki 18:12 neither listened nor *p*
1Ch 16:12 acts that he has *p*, His
2Ch 7:10 goodness that Jehovah had *p*
Ne 9:17 acts that you *p* with them
9:34 they have not *p* your law
13:14 *p* in connection with the
Es 1:15 *p* the saying of King Ahasuerus
9:1 and his law came due to be *p*
Ps 44:1 The activity that you *p* in
105:5 works that he has *p*
Isa 26:12 works you have *p* for us
Eze 5:7 decisions of the nations . . . *p*
29:18 that he had *p* against her
Da 4:2 Most High God has *p* with me
Mr 6:2 works be *p* through his hands
Lu 1:51 has *p* mightily with his arm
1:68 *p* deliverance toward his
23:8 hoping to see some sign *p* by
Joh 2:11 Jesus *p* this in Cana of
4:54 second sign Jesus *p* when he
6:14 the men saw the signs he *p*
7:21 One deed I *p*, and you are
7:31 signs than this man has *p*
12:18 he had *p* this sign, also
12:37 *p* so many signs before them
20:30 Jesus *p* many other signs
Ac 14:26 the work they had fully *p*
Ro 16:6 Mary, who has *p* many labors
Ro 16:12 she *p* many labors in the
Col 2:11 circumcision *p* without hands
Tit 3:5 that we had *p*, but according
Re 3:2 deeds fully *p* before my God
19:20 *p* in front of it the signs

Performing

Es 2:20 of Mordecai Esther was *p*, just
3:8 king's own laws they are not *p*
Ps 74:12 The One *p* grand salvation
Da 6:27 *p* signs and wonders in the
Mt 5:33 must not swear without *p*
Lu 9:6 and *p* cures everywhere
Joh 2:23 his signs that he was *p*
6:2 beholding the signs he was *p*
6:30 What . . . are you *p* as a sign
Ac 6:8 was *p* great portents and signs
8:6 looked at the signs he was *p*
19:11 And God kept *p* extraordinary
1Co 9:13 men *p* sacred duties eat the
16:10 he is *p* the work of Jehovah
Heb 13:21 *p* in us through Jesus

Performs

Job 33:29 All these things God *p*
Joh 11:47 this man *p* many signs
1Co 12:6 the same God who *p* all the
12:11 the same spirit *p*, making a
Ga 3:5 *p* powerful works among you
Re 13:13 it *p* great signs, so that

Perfume

Ca 4:10 your oils than all sorts of *p*
Eze 8:11 *p* of the cloud of the incense

Perfumed

Ex 25:6 balsam oil . . . for *p* incense
30:7 make *p* incense smoke upon it
30:34 and *p* galbanum and pure
31:11 *p* incense for the sanctuary
35:8 and for the *p* incense
35:15 oil and the *p* incense; and the
35:28 for the *p* incense
37:29 and the pure, *p* incense, the
39:38 the *p* incense and the screen
40:27 make *p* incense smoke upon
Le 4:7 of *p* incense before Jehovah
16:12 full of fine *p* incense, and
Nu 4:16 and the *p* incense and the
2Ch 2:4 to burn *p* incense before him
13:11 and also *p* incense; and
Ca 3:6 *p* with myrrh and frankincense
Mt 26:7 case of costly *p* oil
26:12 woman put this *p* oil upon
Mr 14:3 with an alabaster case of *p* oil
14:4 has this waste of the *p* oil taken
14:5 *p* oil could have been sold
14:8 to put *p* oil on my body in
Lu 7:37 an alabaster case of *p* oil
7:38 greased them with the *p* oil
7:46 greased my feet with *p* oil
23:56 prepare spices and *p* oils
Joh 11:2 greased the Lord with *p* oil
12:3 pound of *p* oil, genuine nard
12:3 with the scent of the *p* oil
12:5 *p* oil was not sold for three
Re 18:13 *p* oil and frankincense and

Perfumes

Ex 30:23 to yourself the choicest *p*
30:34 Take to yourself *p*: stacte
Ca 4:14 along with all the finest *p*
4:16 my garden. Let its *p* trickle
Eze 27:22 finest of all sorts of *p*

Perga

Ac 13:13 arrived at *P* in Pamphylia
13:14 went on from *P* and came to
14:25 after speaking the word in *P*

Pergamum

Re 1:11 the seven congregations . . . *P*
2:12 the congregation in *P* write

Perhaps

Ge 16:2 *P* I may get children from her
32:20 *P* he will give a kindly
Ex 32:30 *P* I can make amends for your
Le 26:41 *P* at that time their
Nu 22:6 *P* I may be able to strike
22:11 *P* I may be able to fight
23:3 *P* Jehovah will get in touch
23:27 *P* it will be right in the
Jos 9:7 *P* it is in our vicinity that
Jg 7:2 *P* Israel would brag about
1Sa 6:5 *P* he will lighten his hand
9:6 *P* he can tell us our way that
14:6 *P* Jehovah will work for us
2Sa 14:15 *P* the king will act on the
16:12 *P* Jehovah will see with his
1Ki 18:5 *P* we may find green grass
20:31 *P* he will preserve your
2Ki 19:4 *P* Jehovah your God will hear
Isa 37:4 *P* Jehovah your God will hear
47:12 that *p* you might be able to
47:12 *p* you might strike people
Jer 20:10 *P* he will be fooled, so
21:2 *P* Jehovah will do with us
26:3 *P* they will listen and
36:3 *P* those of the house of
36:7 *P* their request for favor
51:8 *P* she may be healed
La 3:29 *P* there exists a hope
Eze 12:3 *P* they will see, though they
Ho 8:7 Should any *p* produce it
Jon 1:6 *P* the true God will show
Mt 7:10 *p*, he will ask for a fish
11:23 you, Capernaum, will you *p*
12:23 not *p* be the Son of David
25:9 *P* there may not be quite
Mr 11:13 *p* find something on it
14:2 *p* there might be an uproar
Lu 3:15 May he *p* be the Christ?
9:13 *p* we ourselves go and buy
10:15 you *p* be exalted to heaven
11:11 *p* hand him a serpent instead
11:35 *P* the light that is in you
14:8 *P* someone more distinguished
14:12 *P* sometime they might also
Joh 4:29 This is not *p* the Christ, is
Ac 5:39 *p* be found fighters actually
Ro 3:3 *p* make the faithfulness of God
5:7 *p*, someone even dares to die
1Co 16:6 *p* I shall stay or even pass
2Co 3:1 do we, *p*, like some men, need
12:21 *P*, when I come again, my
Col 2:8 *p* there may be someone who
1Th 3:5 as *p* in some way the Tempter
2Ti 2:25 as *p* God may give them
Phm 15 *P* really on this account he

Perida

Ne 7:57 of Sophereth, the sons of *P*

Peril

De 28:66 the greatest *p* for your life
1Co 15:30 are we also in *p* every hour

Perineal

Ge 38:29 you have produced a *p* rupture

Period

Ge 27:41 *p* of mourning for my father
38:12 kept the *p* of mourning
De 34:8 the mourning *p* for Moses
2Sa 11:27 mourning *p* was past, David
Mt 14:25 fourth watch *p* of the night
Mr 10:30 a hundredfold now in this *p*
Lu 18:30 many times more in this *p* of
Ac 9:31 entered into a *p* of peace
13:11 sunlight for a *p* of time
13:18 *p* of about forty years he
2Ti 4:3 *p* of time when they will not
1Pe 1:5 revealed in the last *p* of
Re 12:12 he has a short *p* of time

Periods

Isa 64:6 are like a garment for *p* of
1Ti 4:1 in later *p* of time some will

Perish

Le 26:38 *p* among the nations, and the
Nu 17:12 we are bound to *p*, we are
17:12 we are all of us bound to *p*
21:29 You will certainly *p*, O
21:30 will certainly *p* up to Dibon
24:24 But he too will eventually *p*
De 4:26 *p* in a hurry from off the
7:20 until those *p* who were let
8:19 you people will absolutely *p*
8:20 that is the way you will *p*
11:17 *p* speedily from off the good
30:18 you will positively *p*
Jos 23:16 you will . . . *p* in a hurry
Jg 5:31 all your enemies *p*, O Jehovah
2Ki 9:8 whole house of Ahab must *p*
Es 4:14 you people will *p*. And who is
4:16, 16 case I must *p*, I must *p*
Job 3:3 Let the day *p* on which I came
4:9 the breath of God they *p*
4:20 they *p* forever
6:18 into the empty place and *p*
8:13 hope of an apostate will *p*
11:20 place for flight will . . . *p*
18:17 certainly *p* from the earth

Job 29:13 of the one about to *p*
Ps 1:6 way of wicked ones will *p*
2:12 you may not *p* from the way
9:3 stumble and *p* from before you
9:6 mention of them . . . *p*
9:18 hope of the meek ones ever *p*
37:20 wicked themselves will *p*
41:5 die and his name actually *p*
49:10 and the unreasoning one *p*
68:2 Let the wicked ones *p* from
73:27 away from you will *p*
80:16 rebuke of your face they *p*
83:17 they become abashed and *p*
92:9 your own enemies will *p*
102:26 themselves will *p*, but you
112:10 of the wicked ones will *p*
146:4 that day his thoughts do *p*
Pr 10:28 hope of the wicked . . . *p*
11:10 wicked ones *p* there is a
19:9 launches forth lies will *p*
21:28 A lying witness will *p*, but
28:28 when they *p*, the righteous
31:6 to the one about to *p* and
Isa 29:14 of their wise men must *p*
41:11 as nothing and will *p*
60:12 will not serve you will *p*
Jer 4:9 heart of the king will *p*
6:21 his companion—they will *p*
9:12 should the land actually *p*
10:11 who will *p* from the earth
10:15 they will *p*
18:18 the law will not *p* from
27:10 and you will have to *p*
27:15 and you will have to *p*
40:15 and the remnant of Judah *p*
48:8 low plain will certainly *p*
48:36 produced will certainly *p*
51:18 attention they will *p*
Eze 7:26 the law itself will *p* from
Am 1:8 the Philistines must *p*
2:14 must *p* from the swift one
3:15 houses . . . will have to *p*
Jon 1:6 and we shall not *p*
1:14 may we, please, not *p*
3:9 so that we may not *p*
Zec 9:5 will certainly *p* from Gaza
Mt 8:25 save us, we are about to *p!*
18:14 of these little ones to *p*
26:52 will *p* by the sword
Mr 4:38 care that we are about to *p*
Lu 8:24 Instructor, we are about to *p!*
21:18 will by any means *p*
Ac 8:20 May your silver *p* with you
27:34 head of one of you will *p*
Ro 2:12 will also *p* without law
1Co 1:19 wisdom of the wise men *p*
10:9 only to *p* by the serpents
10:10 only to *p* by the destroyer
Heb 1:11 They themselves will *p*
11:31 Rahab the harlot did not *p*

Perished
Ex 10:7 yet know that Egypt has *p*
Nu 16:33 they *p* from the midst of the
De 28:20 annihilated and have *p*
28:22 pursue you until you have *p*
Jos 23:13 *p* off this good ground
2Sa 1:27 And the weapons of war *p*
2Ki 7:13 crowd of Israel that have *p*
Job 4:7 that is innocent has ever *p*
30:2 In them vigor has *p*
Ps 10:16 have *p* out of his earth
119:92 have *p* in my affliction
142:4 place for flight has *p* from
Pr 11:7 based on powerfulness has *p*
Ec 5:14 those riches have *p* because of
9:6 their jealousy have already *p*
Isa 57:1 righteous one himself has *p*
Jer 7:28 Faithfulness has *p*, and it
25:35 a place to flee to has *p*
48:46 people of Chemosh have *p*
49:7 counsel *p* from those having
La 3:18 My excellency has *p*, and my
Eze 12:22 and every vision has *p*
19:5 waited and her hope had *p*
26:17 How you have *p*, that used
37:11 and our hope has *p*
Joe 1:11 harvest of the field has *p*
Jon 4:10 *p* as a mere growth of a
Mic 4:9 or has your own counselor *p*
7:2 The loyal one has *p* from the
Ac 5:37 yet that man *p*, and all
1Co 15:18 in union with Christ *p*
Jude 11 *p* in the rebellious talk of

Re 18:14 gorgeous things have *p* from

Perishes
De 32:28 a nation on whom counsel *p*
Job 20:7 Like his manure cakes he *p*
Pr 11:7 wicked man dies, his hope *p*
Joh 6:27 not for the food that *p*, but
Jas 1:11 its outward appearance *p*
1Pe 1:7 gold that *p* despite its being

Perishing
Nu 24:20 afterward will be even his *p*
De 26:5 My father was a *p* Syrian
Job 4:11 A lion is *p* from there being
31:19 *p* from having no garment
Ec 7:15 one *p* in his righteousness
Isa 27:13 *p* in the land of Assyria and
Jer 50:6 flock of *p* creatures my
Ob 12 in the day of their *p*; and you
Lu 15:17 I am *p* here from famine
1Co 1:18 to those who are *p*, but to
2Co 2:15 and among those who are *p*
4:3 veiled among those who are *p*
2Th 2:10 who are *p*, as a retribution

Perizzite
Ge 13:7 *P* . . . dwelling in the land

Perizzites
Ge 15:20 the Hittites and the *P* and
34:30 the Canaanites and the *P*
Ex 3:8 to the locality of . . . the *P*
3:17 to the land of . . . the *P*
23:23 indeed bring you to the . . . *P*
33:2 and drive out the . . . *P*, the
34:11 driving out . . . the *P* and
De 7:1 the *P* and the Hivites and the
20:17 the *P*, the Hivites and the
Jos 3:10 the Hivites and the *P* and the
9:1 the Canaanites, the *P*, the
11:3 the *P* and the Jebusites in
12:8 the Canaanites, the *P*, the
17:15 in the land of the *P* and
24:11 Amorites and the *P* and the
Jg 1:4 and the *P* into their hands, so
1:5 and defeated . . . the *P*
3:5 dwelt in among . . . the *P* and
1Ki 9:20 the *P*, the Hivites and the
2Ch 8:7 left over of the . . . *P* and
Ezr 9:1 the *P*, the Jebusites, the
Ne 9:8 the Amorites and the *P* and

Permanent
Ge 49:24 bow was dwelling in a *p*

Permanently
Job 12:19 *p* seated ones he subverts

Permission
Ex 3:19 not give you *p* to go except by
Ezr 3:7 *p* granted by Cyrus the king
Lu 8:32 And he gave them *p*
Joh 19:38 and Pilate gave him *p*
Ac 21:40 After he gave *p*, Paul

Permit
Jg 16:26 Do *p* me to feel the pillars
Ho 5:4 *p* of a returning to their God
Mt 8:21 *p* me first to leave and bury
23:13 *p* those on their way in to
Lu 4:41 would not *p* them to speak
8:32 *p* them to enter into those
9:59 *P* me first to leave and bury
9:61 first *p* me to say good-bye
Ac 16:7 the spirit of Jesus did not *p*
19:30 disciples would not *p* him
19:40 *p* us to render a reason for
21:39 *p* me to speak to the people
28:4 justice did not *p* him to
1Ti 2:12 I do not *p* a woman to teach

Permits
Mr 4:29 But as soon as the fruit *p* it
1Co 16:7 time with you, if Jehovah *p*
Heb 6:3 we will do, if God indeed *p*

Permitted
Mr 5:13 And he *p* them. With that the
Ac 14:16 *p* all the nations to go on
23:32 *p* the horsemen to go on
26:1 *p* to speak in behalf of
27:3 *p* him to go to his friends
28:16 Paul was *p* to stay by
1Co 14:34 not *p* for them to speak

Permitting
Ec 5:12 is not *p* him to sleep
Eze 47:5 water *p* swimming, a torrent

Perpetrated
Jos 22:16 have *p* against the God of
22:20 *p* an act of unfaithfulness
22:31 have not *p* against Jehovah

Perpetual
Ps 9:6 have come to their *p* finish

Perpetually
Isa 57:16 nor *p* that I shall be
Am 1:11 his fury—he has kept it *p*
Heb 7:3 he remains a priest *p*
10:12 one sacrifice for sins *p*
10:14 being sanctified perfect *p*

Perpetuity
Le 25:23 land should not be sold in *p*
25:30 stand in *p* as the property

Perplexed
Da 5:9 and his grandees were *p*
Ac 25:20 being *p* as to the dispute
2Co 4:8 we are *p*, but not absolutely
Ga 4:20 because I am *p* over you

Perplexing
1Ki 10:1 test him with *p* questions
2Ch 9:1 test Solomon with *p* questions

Perplexity
Lu 9:7 and he was in great *p* because
24:4 While they were in *p* over
Ac 2:12 all astonished and were in *p*
10:17 Peter was in great *p*

Persecute
Mt 5:11 people reproach you and *p* you
10:23 they *p* you in one city, flee
23:34 and *p* from city to city
Lu 11:49 kill and *p* some of them
21:12 and *p* you, delivering you up
Joh 15:20 they will *p* you also; if
Ac 7:52 did your forefathers not *p*
Ro 12:14 blessing those who *p*

Persecuted
De 30:7 hate you, who have *p* you
Ps 119:86 Without cause they have *p*
119:161 have *p* me for no cause
Mt 5:10 *p* for righteousness' sake
5:12 *p* the prophets prior to you
Joh 15:20 If they have *p* me, they
Ac 22:4 And I *p* this Way to the death
1Co 4:12 when being *p*, we bear up
15:9 I *p* the congregation of God
2Co 4:9 we are *p*, but not left in
Ga 1:23 man that formerly *p* us is
5:11 why am I still being *p?*
6:12 *p* for the torture stake of
1Th 2:15 and the prophets and *p* us
2Ti 3:12 will also be *p*
Re 12:13 *p* the woman that gave birth

Persecuting
Job 19:22 Why do you men keep *p* me
19:28 Why do we keep *p* him?
Ps 7:1 Save me from all those *p* me
119:84 judgment against those *p*
Jer 20:11 why the very ones *p* me
La 1:3 who were *p* her have overtaken
Mt 5:44 and to pray for those *p* you
Joh 5:16 the Jews went *p* Jesus
Ac 9:4 Saul, why are you *p* me?
9:5 I am Jesus, whom you are *p*
22:7 Saul, Saul, why are you *p* me?
22:8 the Nazarene, whom you are *p*
26:11 *p* . . . even in outside cities
26:14 Saul, why are you *p* me?
26:15 I am Jesus, whom you are *p*
Ga 1:13 *p* the congregation of God and
4:29 *p* the one born in the manner
Php 3:6 zeal, *p* the congregation

Persecution
Isa 14:6 with a *p* without restraint
Mt 13:21 after tribulation or *p* has
Mr 4:17 *p* arises because of the word
Ac 8:1 great *p* arose against the
13:50 *p* against Paul and Barnabas
Ro 8:35 *p* or hunger or nakedness or

Persecutions
Mr 10:30 with *p*, and in the coming
2Co 12:10 I take pleasure in . . . *p* and
2Th 1:4 and faith in all your *p*
2Ti 3:11 my *p*, my sufferings, the
3:11 the sort of *p* I have borne

Persecutor
1Ti 1:13 a blasphemer and a *p* and an

Persecutors
Ps 119:157 *p* and my adversaries are
142:6 Deliver me from my *p*
Jer 15:15 avenge me upon my *p*
17:18 Let my *p* be put to shame

Persevere
1Sa 23:22 *p* some more and ascertain
Ro 12:12 *P* in prayer

Persevering
Col 4:2 Be *p* in prayer, remaining

Persia
2Ch 36:20 royalty of *P* began to reign
36:22 Cyrus the king of *P*
36:22 Cyrus the king of *P*
36:23 Cyrus the king of *P* has
Ezr 1:1 Cyrus the king of *P*
1:1 spirit of Cyrus the king of *P*
1:2 what Cyrus the king of *P* has
1:8 Cyrus the king of *P*
3:7 granted by Cyrus the king of *P*
4:3 as King Cyrus the king of *P*
4:5 days of Cyrus the king of *P*
4:5 reign of Darius the king of *P*
4:7 Artaxerxes the king of *P*
4:24 reign of Darius the king of *P*
6:14 and Artaxerxes the king of *P*
7:1 Artaxerxes the king of *P*
9:9 before the kings of *P*, to give
Es 1:3 military force of *P* and Media
1:14 seven princes of *P* and Media
1:18 the princesses of *P* and Media
1:19 written among the laws of *P*
10:2 of the kings of Media and *P*
Eze 38:5 *P*, Ethiopia and Put with
Da 8:20 for the kings of Media and *P*
10:1 third year of Cyrus . . . of *P*
10:13 of the royal realm of *P* was
10:13 there beside the kings of *P*
10:20 fight with the prince of *P*
11:2 three kings standing up for *P*

Persian
Ne 12:22 kingship of Darius the *P*
Da 6:28 the kingdom of Cyrus the *P*

Persians
Eze 27:10 *P* and Ludim and men of Put
Da 5:28 given to the Medes and the *P*
6:8 law of the Medes and the *P*
6:12 law of the Medes and the *P*
6:15 law belonging to . . . the *P*

Persis
Ro 16:12 *P* our beloved one, for she

Persisted
Jos 17:12 *p* in dwelling in this land
Jg 1:27 Canaanites *p* in dwelling in
1:35 Amorites *p* in dwelling in

Persistence
Lu 11:8 because of his bold *p* he will

Persistent
Ru 1:18 was *p* about going with her

Persisting
Ac 1:14 all these were *p* in prayer

Persists
1Ti 5:5 *p* in supplications and prayers
Jas 1:25 to freedom and who *p* in it

Person
Ex 15:3 Jehovah is a manly *p* of war
16:22 two omer measures for one *p*
33:14 My own *p* will go along and
33:15 If your own *p* is not going
Le 19:15 not prefer the *p* of a great
19:32 consideration for the *p* of
27:8 *p* before the priest, and the
27:29 *p* who might be devoted to
Nu 5:2 of the camp every leprous *p*
19:19 clean *p* must spatter it upon
De 14:1 baldness . . . for a dead *p*
1Sa 14:52 valiant *p*, he would gather
18:17 prove yourself a valiant *p*
25:35 consideration for your *p*
29:4 *p* put himself in favor with
2Sa 3:33 death of a senseless *p*
13:17 Send this *p* away from me
17:11 own *p* going into the fight
2Ki 5:7 this *p* is sending to me to
12:9 as a *p* comes into the house
23:8 as a *p* came into the gate of
2Ch 19:2 from the *p* of Jehovah
Es 1:10 to the *p* of King Ahasuerus
Es 1:19 royal word go out from his *p*
Job 1:12 away from the *p* of Jehovah
2:7 away from the *p* of Jehovah
9:33 no *p* to decide between us
15:2 Will a wise *p* himself
Ps 31:20 in the secret place of your *p*
42:5 the grand salvation of my *p*
42:11 the grand salvation of my *p*
43:5 the grand salvation of my *p*
95:2 his *p* with thanksgiving
Pr 1:5 wise *p* will listen and take
3:32 devious *p* is a detestable
9:8 Give a reproof to a wise *p*
9:9 Give to a wise *p* and he will
10:13 the understanding *p* wisdom
11:17 cruel *p* is bringing
11:21 bad *p* will not go unpunished
11:29 foolish *p* will be a servant
12:13 lips the bad *p* is ensnared
12:16 foolish *p* that makes known
14:20 are the friends of the rich *p*
21:11 giving insight to a wise *p*
Isa 57:3 the seed of an adulterous *p*
Jer 9:8 what a *p* keeps speaking with
Eze 36:31 loathing at your own *p*
44:25 dead *p* of mankind he should
Mic 6:9 the *p* of practical wisdom
Na 1:15 any good-for-nothing *p* pass
Zec 13:6 wounds on your *p* between
Mt 5:40 if a *p* wants to go to court
7:29 as a *p* having authority
8:27 What sort of *p* is this, that
11:11 a *p* that is a lesser one in
21:44 *p* falling upon this stone
Lu 7:28 a *p* that is a lesser one in
11:33 a *p* puts it, not in a vault
12:15 *p* has an abundance his life
16:10 *p* faithful in what is least
16:10 *p* unrighteous in what is
16:16 every sort of *p* is pressing
17:31 *p* that is on the housetop
17:31 the *p* out in the field, let
22:58 after a short time another *p*
Ac 3:19 come from the *p* of Jehovah
18:13 this *p* leads men to another
Ro 2:26 uncircumcised *p* keeps the
2:27 uncircumcised *p* that is such
5:17 through the one *p*, Jesus
5:19 obedience of the one *p* many
1Co 3:8 each *p* will receive his own
5:11 or a greedy *p* or an idolater
7:28 if a virgin *p* married, such
10:24 but that of the other *p*
10:29 but that of the other *p*
14:16 ordinary *p* say Amen to your
14:24 or ordinary *p* comes in, he
15:36 unreasonable *p*! What you
2Co 6:15 faithful *p* have with an
8:12 according to what a *p* has
8:12 to what a *p* does not have
8:15 *p* with much did not have too
8:15 *p* with little did not have
10:10 his presence in *p* is weak
Ga 3:20 only one *p* is concerned
3:28 one *p* in union with Christ
6:4 in comparison with the other *p*
Eph 5:5 no fornicator or unclean *p* or
5:5 or greedy *p*—which means
1Th 2:17 in *p*, not in heart, we
1Ti 5:8 worse than a *p* without faith
Heb 9:24 before the *p* of God for us
1Pe 3:4 let it be the secret *p* of the
3:18 a righteous *p* for unrighteous
4:1 the *p* that has suffered in the
1Jo 2:4 and the truth is not in this *p*
2:5 in this *p* the love of God has
5:10 The *p* putting his faith in
5:10 *p* not having faith in God has
5:18 *p* that has been born from
2Jo 5 as a *p* writing you, not a new
Re 6:15 slave and every free *p* hid
13:17 except a *p* having the mark

Personal
2Sa 3:8 brothers and his *p* friends
Ps 56:5 keep hurting my *p* affairs
Pr 19:7 *p* friends kept away from him
Isa 63:9 own *p* messenger saved them
Ac 3:12 by *p* power or godly devotion
1Co 7:35 saying for your *p* advantage
Php 2:4 not in *p* interest upon just
2:4 *p* interest upon those of the

Personalities
Jude 16 admiring *p* for the sake of

Personality
Ro 6:6 our old *p* was impaled with
Eph 4:22 put away the old *p* which
4:24 should put on the new *p*
Col 3:9 the old *p* with its practices
3:10 the new *p*, which through

Personally
Ge 41:40 You will *p* be over my house
1Sa 22:22 I *p* have wronged every soul
Ps 27:2 adversaries and my enemies *p*
Jer 17:18 let me *p* be put to no shame
17:18 let me *p* not be struck with
25:31 *p* put himself in judgment
Ho 5:3 I *p* have known Ephraim, and
7:8 that he *p* mingles himself
2Co 11:2 I *p* promised you in marriage

Person's
1Co 10:29 by another *p* conscience

Persons
2Sa 23:6 good-for-nothing *p* are chased
24:15 seventy thousand *p* died
2Ki 2:16 fifty men, valiant *p*
1Ch 21:14 seventy thousand *p* fell
29:8 were found with any *p* they
Pr 1:6 words of wise *p* and their
13:20 walking with wise *p* will
13:23 ground of *p* of little means
Ca 8:7 *p* would positively despise
Isa 8:19 application to dead *p* in
8:19 in behalf of living *p*
54:13 will be *p* taught by Jehovah
Jer 2:3 Any *p* devouring him would
13:23 who are *p* taught to do bad
32:36 *p* are saying will certainly
Eze 36:38 Like a flock of holy *p*
39:20 mighty *p* and all sorts of
Am 2:7 on the head of lowly *p*
Mt 4:24 and epileptic and paralyzed *p*
8:16 many demon-possessed *p*
9:12 *P* in health do not need a
10:8 raise up dead *p*, make lepers
10:36 man's enemies will be *p* of
13:41 *p* who are doing lawlessness
21:14 blind and lame *p* came up to
27:53 *p*, coming out from among
Mr 14:62 you *p* will see the Son of
Lu 5:32 not righteous *p*, but sinners
6:24 woe to you rich *p*, because
7:21 blind *p* the favor of seeing
11:40 Unreasonable *p*! He that made
12:14 or apportioner over you *p*
Joh 4:20 where *p* ought to worship
20:23 forgive the sins of any *p*
20:23 you retain those of any *p*
Ac 1:15 crowd of *p* was all together
13:2 Of all *p* set Barnabas and
17:25 to all *p* life and breath and
1Co 5:10 greedy *p* and extortioners or
6:9 unrighteous *p* will not
6:10 nor greedy *p*, nor drunkards
7:8 Now I say to the unmarried *p*
8:7 not this knowledge in all *p*
9:19 I am free from all *p*, I have
9:19 that I may gain the most *p*
10:6 *p* desiring injurious things
11:19 that the *p* approved may
12:6 the operations in all *p*
16:16 to *p* of that kind and to
2Co 11:19 with the unreasonable *p*
Eph 4:6 one God and Father of all *p*
5:15 not as unwise but as wise *p*
2Th 3:12 To such *p* we give the order
1Ti 1:9 for *p* lawless and unruly
4:15 may be manifest to all *p*
5:20 *p* who practice sin, that
2Ti 3:14 from what *p* you learned
Tit 1:15 things are clean to clean *p*
1:15 to *p* defiled and faithless
2Pe 2:6 a pattern for ungodly *p* of
3:11 what sort of *p* ought you to
1Jo 4:4 you have conquered those *p*
2Jo 7 *p* not confessing Jesus Christ as
3Jo 8 to receive such *p* hospitably
Re 5:9 with your blood you bought *p*
11:13 seven thousand *p* were killed
13:16 under compulsion all *p*, the

Persuade
Mt 28:14 we will *p* him and will set
Ac 18:4 and would *p* Jews and Greeks
23:21 do not let them *p* you, for
26:28 *p* me to become a Christian
Ga 1:10 I am now trying to *p* or God

Persuaded
Mt 27:20 older men *p* the crowds to
Lu 16:31 *p* if someone rises from the
20:6 are *p* that John was a prophet
Ac 14:19 and *p* the crowds, and they
19:26 Paul has *p* a considerable
26:26 I am *p* that not one of
Ro 2:19 *p* that you are a guide of
14:14 I know and am *p* in the Lord
15:14 am *p* about you, my brothers
2Ti 3:14 and were *p* to believe

Persuading
Ac 12:20 after *p* Blastus, who was in
2Co 5:11 we keep *p* men, but we have

Persuasion
Ac 18:13 another *p* in worshiping God
19:8 *p* concerning the kingdom of
28:23 *p* with them concerning Jesus
Ga 5:8 This sort of *p* is not from the

Persuasive
1Co 2:4 not with *p* words of wisdom
Col 2:4 delude you with *p* arguments

Persuasively
Ge 34:3 speaking *p* to the young woman

Persuasiveness
Pr 7:21 him by the abundance of her *p*
16:21 is sweet in his lips adds *p*
16:23 and to his lips it adds *p*

Pertained
1Ki 7:48 utensils that *p* to the house

Pertaining
Isa 23:5 as at the report *p* to Egypt
Lu 24:27 things *p* to himself in all
Ro 15:17 comes to things *p* to God
Php 2:19 about the things *p* to you
2:20 care for the things *p* to you
Heb 2:17 priest in things *p* to God
5:1 over the things *p* to God
9:10 requirements *p* to the flesh

Perturbed
Eze 27:35 Faces must become *p*

Peruda
Ezr 2:55 the sons of *P*

Perverse
Pr 2:12 the man speaking *p* things
2:14 joyful in the *p* things of
8:13 the *p* mouth I have hated
23:33 heart will speak *p* things

Perverseness
De 32:20 they are a generation of *p*
Pr 6:14 *P* is in his heart
10:31 tongue of *p* will be cut off
10:32 of the wicked ones is *p*

Perversity
Isa 29:16 The *p* of you men! Should

Pervert
Ex 23:2 turn aside . . . to *p* justice
23:6 not to *p* the judicial decision
De 16:19 You must not *p* judgment
24:17 You must not *p* the judgment
1Sa 8:3 accept a bribe and *p* judgment
Job 8:3 Will God himself *p* judgment
8:3 Almighty . . . *p* righteousness
34:12 Almighty himself does not *p*
Pr 31:5 *p* the cause of any of the sons
Ga 1:7 *p* the good news about the

Perverted
Job 33:27 what is upright I have *p*

Perverts
De 27:19 *p* the judgment of an alien
Ps 58:3 The wicked ones have been *p*

Pestilence
Ex 5:3 strike at us with *p* or with
9:3 there will be a very heavy *p*
9:15 you and your people with *p*
Le 26:25 *p* into the midst of you, and
Nu 14:12 strike them with *p* and drive
De 28:21 cause the *p* to cling to you
2Sa 24:13 three days of *p* in your land
24:15 Jehovah gave a *p* in Israel
1Ki 8:37 in case a *p* occurs
1Ch 21:12 sword of Jehovah, even *p*
21:14 Jehovah gave a *p* in Israel
2Ch 6:28 in case a *p* occurs, in
7:13 send a *p* among my people
20:9 *p* or famine, let us stand
Ps 78:50 handed over even to the *p*
91:3 the *p* causing adversities
91:6 *p* that walks in the gloom
Jer 14:12 by *p* I am bringing them to
21:6 With a great *p* they will die
21:7 in this city from the *p*
21:9 by the famine and by the *p*
24:10 sword, the famine and the *p*
27:8 famine and with the *p* I
27:13 the famine and by the *p*
28:8 war and of calamity and of *p*
29:17 sword, the famine and the *p*
29:18 the famine and with the *p*
32:24 famine and the *p*; and what
32:36 by the famine and by the *p*
34:17 to the *p* and to the famine
38:2 by the famine and by the *p*
42:17 by the famine and by the *p*
42:22 by the *p* you will die in
44:13 the famine and with the *p*
Eze 5:12 third of you—by the *p* they
5:17 *p* and blood themselves will
6:11 and by the *p* they will fall
6:12 far away, by the *p* he will
7:15 *p* and the famine are inside
7:15 in the city, famine and *p*
12:16 the famine and from the *p*
14:19 Or were it *p* that I should
14:21 injurious wild beast and *p*
28:23 will send *p* into her and
33:27 will die by the *p* itself
38:22 with *p* and with blood
Am 4:10 I sent among you people a *p*
Hab 3:5 Before him *p* kept going

Pestilences
Lu 21:11 *p* and food shortages; and

Pestilent
Ac 24:5 found this man a *p* fellow

Pestle
Pr 27:22 fine with a *p* in a mortar

Peter
Mt 4:18 Simon who is called *P* and
10:2 Simon, the one called *P*, and
14:28 *P* said to him: Lord, if it
14:29 *P*, getting down off the boat
15:15 *P* said to him: Make the
16:16 *P* said: You are the Christ
16:18 I say to you, You are *P*, and
16:22 At this *P* took him aside and
16:23 he said to *P*: Get behind me
17:1 Jesus took *P* and James and
17:4 *P* said to Jesus: Lord, it is
17:24 approached *P* and said: Does
18:21 *P* came up and said to him
19:27 Then *P* said to him in reply
26:33 *P*, in answer, said to him
26:35 *P* said to him: Even if I
26:37 taking along *P* and the two
26:40 he said to *P*: Could you men
26:58 *P* kept following him at a
26:69 *P* was sitting outside in the
26:73 said to *P*: Certainly you
26:75 *P* called to mind the saying
Mr 3:16 Simon . . . the surname *P*
5:37 except *P* and James and John
8:29 In answer *P* said to him
8:32 But *P* took him aside and
8:33 and rebuked *P*, and said
9:2 Jesus took *P* and James and
9:5 *P* said to Jesus: Rabbi, it is
10:28 *P* started to say to him
11:21 So *P*, remembering it, said
13:3 *P* . . . began to ask him
14:29 *P* said to him: Even if all
14:33 he took *P* and James and John
14:37 he said to *P*: Simon, are you
14:54 But *P*, from a good distance
14:66 while *P* was below in the
14:67 seeing *P* warming himself
14:70 to *P*: Certainly you are one
14:72 *P* recalled the saying that
16:7 tell his disciples and *P*, He
Lu 5:8 *P* fell down at the knees of
6:14 Simon, whom he also named *P*
8:45 *P* said: Instructor, the
8:51 except *P* and John and James
9:20 *P* said in reply: The Christ of
9:28 he took *P* and John and James
9:32 *P* and those with him were
9:33 *P* said to Jesus: Instructor
12:41 Then *P* said: Lord, are you
18:28 *P* said: Look! We have left
22:8 dispatched *P* and John, saying
22:34 I tell you, *P*, A cock will
22:54 but *P* was following at a
22:55 *P* was sitting in among them
22:58 But *P* said: Man, I am not
22:60 *P* said: Man, I do not know
22:61 Lord turned and looked upon *P*
22:61 *P* recalled the utterance of
24:12 But *P* rose and ran to the
Joh 1:40 the brother of Simon *P* was
1:42 Cephas . . . translated *P*
1:44 the city of Andrew and *P*
6:8 Andrew the brother of Simon *P*
6:68 Simon *P* answered him
13:6 And so he came to Simon *P*
13:8 *P* said to him: You will
13:9 Simon *P* said to him
13:24 Simon *P* nodded to this one
13:36 Simon *P* said to him: Lord
13:37 *P* said to him: Lord, why is
18:10 Simon *P*, as he had a sword
18:11 Jesus, however, said to *P*
18:15 Simon *P* as well as another
18:16 *P* was standing outside at
18:16 and brought *P* in
18:17 said to *P*: You are not also
18:18 *P* also was standing with
18:25 Simon *P* was standing and
18:26 man whose ear *P* cut off
18:27 *P* denied it again; and
20:2 she ran and came to Simon *P*
20:3 *P* and the other disciple
20:4 disciple ran ahead of *P*
20:6 Simon *P* also came following
21:2 Simon *P* and Thomas, who
21:3 Simon *P* said to them: I am
21:7 said to *P*: It is the Lord!
21:7 Simon *P*, upon hearing that
21:11 Simon *P*, therefore, went
21:15 Jesus said to Simon *P*
21:17 *P* became grieved that he
21:20 *P* saw the disciple whom
21:21 *P* said to Jesus: Lord, what
Ac 1:13 *P* as well as John and James
1:15 *P* rose up in the midst of the
2:14 *P* stood up with the eleven
2:37 said to *P* and the rest of the
2:38 *P* said to them: Repent, and
3:1 *P* and John were going up into
3:3 sight of *P* and John about to
3:4 *P*, together with John, gazed
3:6 *P* said: Silver and gold I do
3:11 holding onto *P* and John, all
3:12 *P* saw this, he said to the
4:8 *P*, filled with holy spirit
4:13 outspokenness of *P* and John
4:19 *P* and John said to them
5:3 *P* said: Ananias, why has
5:8 *P* said to her: Tell me, did
5:9 *P* said to her: Why was it
5:15 as *P* would go by, at least
5:29 *P* and the other apostles said
8:14 dispatched *P* and John to them
8:20 *P* said to him: May your
9:32 *P* was going through all
9:34 *P* said to him: Aeneas, Jesus
9:38 heard that *P* was in this city
9:39 *P* rose and went with them
9:40 *P* put everybody outside and
9:40 as she caught sight of *P*
10:5 Simon who is surnamed *P*
10:9 *P* went up to the housetop
10:13 Rise, *P*, slaughter and eat!
10:14 *P* said: Not at all, Lord
10:17 *P* was in great perplexity
10:18 Simon who was surnamed *P*
10:19 *P* was going over in his mind
10:21 *P* went downstairs to the
10:25 As *P* entered, Cornelius met
10:26 *P* lifted him up, saying
10:32 Simon, who is surnamed *P*
10:34 *P* opened his mouth and said
10:44 *P* was yet speaking about
10:45 ones that had come with *P*
10:46 Then *P* responded
11:2 when *P* came up to Jerusalem
11:4 *P* commenced and went on to
11:7 Rise, *P*, slaughter and eat!
11:13 for Simon who is surnamed *P*
12:3 he went on to arrest *P* also
12:5 *P* was being kept in the
12:6 *P* was sleeping bound with
12:7 Striking *P* on the side, he
12:11 *P*, coming to himself, said

Ac 12:14 recognizing the voice of *P*
12:14 *P* was standing before the
12:16 *P* remained there knocking
12:18 what really had become of *P*
15:7 *P* rose and said to them: Men
Ga 2:7 as *P* had it for those who are
2:8 He who gave *P* powers necessary
1Pe 1:1 *P*, an apostle of Jesus Christ
2Pe 1:1 Simon *P*, a slave and apostle

Peter's
Mt 8:14 coming into *P* house, saw his

Pethahiah
1Ch 24:16 for *P* the nineteenth
Ezr 10:23 of the Levites . . . *P*
Ne 9:5 and *P* went on to say: Rise
11:24 *P* the son of Meshezabel of

Pethor
Nu 22:5 Balaam the son of Beor at *P*
De 23:4 the son of Beor from *P* of

Pethuel
Joe 1:1 to Joel the son of *P*

Petition
1Sa 1:17 God of Israel grant your *p*
1:27 grant me my *p* that I asked
Es 5:6 What is your *p?* Let it even be
5:7 My *p* and my request is
5:8 seem good to grant my *p* and to
7:2 What is your *p*, O Esther the
7:3 given me my own soul at my *p*
9:12 And what is your *p?* Let it
Da 6:7 *p* to any god or man for thirty
6:12 *p* from any god or man for
6:13 in a day he is making his *p*
Mr 15:8 make *p* according to what he

Petitioned
Mr 15:6 prisoner, whom they *p* for

Petitioning
Da 6:11 Daniel *p* and imploring favor

Petitions
Php 4:6 your *p* be made known to God
Heb 5:7 *p* to the One who was able to

Peullethai
1Ch 26:5 the seventh, *P* the eighth

Phanuel's
Lu 2:36 Anna a prophetess, *P* daughter

Pharaoh
Ge 12:15 princes of *P* also got to see
12:15 they began praising her to *P*
12:15 was taken to the house of *P*
12:17 Jehovah touched *P* and his
12:18 *P* called Abram and said
12:20 *P* issued commands to men
37:36 a court official of *P*
39:1 a court official of *P*, the
40:2 *P* grew indignant at his two
40:7 inquire of the officers of *P*
40:13 three days from now *P* will
40:14 mention me to *P*, and you
40:17 all sorts of eatables for *P*
40:19 *P* will lift up your head
41:1 *P* was dreaming and here he
41:4 At this *P* woke up
41:7 At this *P* woke up and here
41:8 *P* went on to relate his
41:8 no interpreter of them for *P*
41:9 spoke with *P*, saying: My sins
41:10 *P* was indignant at his
41:14 *P* proceeded to send and to
41:14 Joseph . . . went in to *P*
41:15 *P* said to Joseph: I have
41:16 Joseph answered *P*, saying
41:16 will announce welfare to *P*
41:17 *P* went on to speak to Joseph
41:25 Then Joseph said to *P:* The
41:25 The dream of *P* is but one
41:25 God is doing he has told to *P*
41:28 spoken to *P:* What the true
41:28 he has caused *P* to see
41:32 the dream was repeated to *P*
41:33 let *P* look for a man
41:34 Let *P* act and appoint
41:37 good in the eyes of *P* and of
41:38 So *P* said to his servants
41:39 *P* said to Joseph: Since God
41:41 *P* added to Joseph: See, I
41:42 *P* removed his signet ring
41:44 *P* further said to Joseph
41:44 I am *P*, but without your
Ge 41:45 *P* called Joseph's name
41:46 when he stood before *P* the
41:46 went out from before *P* and
41:55 the people began to cry to *P*
41:55 *P* said to all the Egyptians
42:15 As *P* lives, you will not go
42:16 as *P* lives, you are spies
44:18 same with you as with *P*
45:8 appoint me a father to *P* and
45:16 heard at the house of *P*
45:16 good in the eyes of *P* and
45:17 *P* said to Joseph: Say to your
46:5 wagons that *P* had sent to
46:31 Let me go up and report to *P*
46:33 when *P* will call you and
47:1 Joseph came and reported to *P*
47:2 he might present them to *P*
47:3 Then *P* said to his brothers
47:3 they said to *P:* Your servants
47:4 said to *P:* We have come to
47:5 *P* said to Joseph: Your father
47:7 and introduced him to *P*
47:7 Jacob proceeded to bless *P*
47:8 *P* now said to Jacob: How many
47:9 Jacob said to *P:* The days of
47:10 Jacob blessed *P* and went out
47:10 and went out from before *P*
47:11 just as *P* had commanded
47:19 will become slaves to *P*
47:20 land of the Egyptians for *P*
47:22 the priests were from *P*
47:22 rations that *P* gave them
47:23 you and your land for *P*
47:24 give a fifth to *P*, but four
47:25 we will become slaves to *P*
47:26 *P* to have to the amount of a
50:4 in the hearing of *P*, saying
50:6 *P* said: Go up and bury your
Ex 1:11 cities as storage places for *P*
1:19 the midwives said to *P*
1:22 Finally *P* commanded all his
2:15 *P* got to hear of this thing
2:15 but Moses ran away from *P*
3:10 let me send you to *P*, and you
3:11 am I that I should go to *P*
4:21 all the miracles . . . before *P*
4:22 And you must say to *P*
5:1 Moses and Aaron . . . say to *P*
5:2 *P* said: Who is Jehovah, so
5:5 *P* continued: Look! The people
5:6 *P* commanded those who drove
5:10 Here is what *P* has said, I am
5:15 and began to cry out to *P*
5:20 as they came out from *P*
5:21 smell offensive before *P*
5:23 went in before *P* to speak in
6:1 will see what I shall do to *P*
6:11 speak to *P*, Egypt's king
6:12 how will *P* ever listen to me
6:13 the sons of Israel and to *P*
6:27 were the ones speaking to *P*
6:29 I am Jehovah. Speak to *P* king
6:30 how will *P* ever listen to me?
7:1 I have made you God to *P*, and
7:2 will do the speaking to *P*
7:4 *P* will not listen to you men
7:7 time of their speaking to *P*
7:9 In case that *P* speaks to you
7:9 rod and throw it down before *P*
7:10 and Aaron went on in to *P*
7:10 threw his rod down before *P*
7:11 *P* also called for the wise
7:15 Go to *P* in the morning
7:20 under the eyes of *P* and his
7:23 *P* turned and went into his
8:1 Go in to *P*, and you must say
8:8 *P* called Moses and Aaron and
8:9 Moses said to *P:* You take the
8:12 went out from *P*, and Moses
8:12 frogs that He had put upon *P*
8:15 *P* got to see that relief had
8:19 said to *P:* It is the finger
8:20 a position in front of *P*
8:24 began to invade the house of *P*
8:25 *P* called Moses and Aaron and
8:28 *P* now said: I—I shall send
8:29 gadflies . . . turn away from *P*
8:29 let not *P* trifle again in not
8:30 Moses went out from *P* and
8:31 gadflies turned away from *P*
8:32 *P* made his heart unresponsive
9:1 Go in to *P* and you must state
9:7 *P* sent, and, look! not so much
9:10 stood before *P*, and Moses
Ex 9:13 take a position in front of *P*
9:27 *P* sent and called Moses and
9:33 went out of the city from *P*
9:34 *P* got to see that the rain
10:1 Go in to *P*, because I—I have
10:3 went in to *P* and said to him
10:6 he turned and went out from *P*
10:8 were brought back to *P*, and
10:11 driven out from before *P*
10:16 *P* hurriedly called Moses and
10:18 he went out from *P* and made
10:24 *P* called Moses and said: Go
10:28 *P* said to him: Get out from
11:1 to bring upon *P* and Egypt
11:5 the firstborn of *P* who is
11:8 With that he went out from *P*
11:9 *P* will not listen to you men
11:10 all these miracles before *P*
12:29 from the firstborn of *P*
12:30 *P* got up at night, he and all
13:15 *P* showed obstinacy toward
14:3 Then *P* will certainly say
14:4 *P* and all his military forces
14:5 heart of *P* as well as his
14:8 Jehovah let the heart of *P* the
14:9 all the chariot horses of *P*
14:10 When *P* got close by, the
14:17 get glory for myself by . . . *P*
14:18 *P*, his war chariots and his
14:23 and all the horses of *P*, his
18:8 done to *P* and Egypt on account
18:10 from the hand of *P*, and who
De 6:21 became slaves to *P* in Egypt
6:22 upon *P* and upon all his
7:8 from the hand of *P* the king of
7:18 God did to *P* and all Egypt
11:3 to *P* the king of Egypt and to
29:2 to *P* and all his servants and
34:11 in the land of Egypt to *P*
1Sa 2:27 as slaves to the house of *P*
6:6 Egypt and *P* made their heart
1Ki 3:1 marriage alliance with *P* the
9:16 *P* the king of Egypt himself
11:1 with the daughter of *P*
11:18 to *P* the king of Egypt
11:19 find favor in the eyes of *P*
11:20 inside the house of *P*
11:20 continued at the house of *P*
11:20 right among the sons of *P*
11:21 Hadad said to *P:* Send me
11:22 *P* said to him: What are you
2Ki 17:7 hand of *P* the king of Egypt
18:21 the way *P* the king of Egypt
23:29 *P* Nechoh the king of Egypt
23:33 *P* Nechoh got to put him in
23:34 *P* Nechoh made Eliakim the
23:35 gold Jehoiakim gave to *P*
23:35 silver at the order of *P*
23:35 to give it to *P* Nechoh
1Ch 4:18 Bithiah the daughter of *P*
Ne 9:10 signs and miracles against *P*
Ps 135:9 *P* and upon all his servants
136:15 shook off *P* . . . the Red Sea
Ca 1:9 of mine in the chariots of *P*
Isa 19:11 say to *P:* I am the son of
30:2 in the stronghold of *P* and
30:3 stronghold of *P* must become
36:6 way *P* the king of Egypt is
Jer 25:19 *P* the king of Egypt and his
37:5 military force of *P* that
37:7 military force of *P* that is
37:11 of the military force of *P*
43:9 house of *P* in Tahpanhes
44:30 *P* Hophra, the king of Egypt
46:2 force of *P* Necho the king
46:17 *P* the king of Egypt is a
46:25 upon *P* and upon Egypt and
46:25 her kings, even upon *P*
47:1 *P* proceeded to strike down
Eze 17:17 *P* will not make him
29:2 against *P* the king of Egypt
29:3 against you, O *P*, king of
30:21 the arm of *P* the king of
30:22 against *P* the king of Egypt
30:24 will break the arms of *P*
30:25 very arms of *P* will fall
31:2 say to *P* the king of Egypt
31:18 This is *P* and all his crowd
32:2 *P* the king of Egypt, and you
32:31 the ones that *P* will see
32:31 *P* and all his military
32:32 even *P* and all his crowd
Ac 7:10 wisdom in the sight of *P*
7:13 Joseph became manifest to *P*

Ac 7:21 daughter of *P* picked him up
Ro 9:17 Scripture says to *P:* For this
Heb 11:24 son of the daughter of *P*

Pharaoh's
Ge 40:11 *P* cup was in my hand, and I
40:11 squeeze them out into *P* cup
40:11 I gave the cup into *P* hand
40:13 give *P* cup into his hand
40:20 turned out to be *P* birthday
40:21 give the cup into *P* hand
41:35 grain under *P* hand as
45:2 *P* house got to hear it
45:21 according to *P* orders and
47:14 bringing the money into *P*
47:20 and the land came to be *P*
47:26 land . . . did not become *P*
50:4 Joseph spoke to *P* household
50:7 with him all of *P* servants
Ex 2:5 *P* daughter came down to bathe
2:7 his sister said to *P* daughter
2:8 So *P* daughter said to her
2:9 *P* daughter then said to her
2:10 brought him to *P* daughter
5:14 whom *P* taskmasters had set
7:3 let *P* heart become obstinate
7:13 *P* heart became obstinate, and
7:14 *P* heart is unresponsive
7:22 *P* heart . . . obstinate, and
8:19 But *P* heart continued to be
9:7 *P* heart continued to be
9:8 toward the heavens in *P* sight
9:12 Jehovah let *P* heart become
9:20 *P* servants caused his own
9:35 *P* heart continued obstinate
10:7 *P* servants said to him: How
10:20 *P* heart become obstinate
10:27 let *P* heart become obstinate
11:3 in the eyes of *P* servants and
11:10 let *P* heart become obstinate
13:17 *P* sending the people away
14:4 let *P* heart become obstinate
14:28 all of *P* military forces and
15:4 *P* chariots and his military
15:19 When *P* horses with his war
18:4 he delivered me from *P* sword
1Ki 3:1 take *P* daughter and bring her
7:8 to build for *P* daughter
9:24 *P* daughter herself came up
2Ch 8:11 *P* daughter Solomon brought
Isa 19:11 wise ones of *P* counselors

Pharisee
Mt 23:26 Blind *P*, cleanse first the
Lu 7:36 into the house of the *P* and
7:37 meal in the house of the *P*
7:39 the *P* that invited him said
11:37 a *P* requested him to dine
11:38 *P* was surprised at seeing
18:10 one a *P* and the other a tax
18:11 *P* stood and began to pray
Ac 5:34 *P* named Gamaliel, a Law
23:6 I am a *P*, a son of Pharisees
26:5 form of worship I lived a *P*
Php 3:5 as respects law, a *P*

Pharisees
Mt 3:7 *P* and Sadducees coming to the
5:20 that of the scribes and *P*
9:11 the *P* began to say to his
9:14 *P* practice fasting but your
9:34 *P* began to say: It is by the
12:2 At seeing this the *P* said to
12:14 *P* went out and took counsel
12:24 At hearing this, the *P* said
12:38 *P* said: Teacher, we want to
15:1 to Jesus from Jerusalem *P*
15:12 *P* stumbled at hearing what
16:1 *P* and Sadducees approached
16:6 leaven of the *P* and Sadducees
16:11 for the leaven of the *P* and
16:12 for the teaching of the *P*
19:3 *P* came up to him, intent on
21:45 priests and the *P* had heard
22:15 *P* went their way and took
22:34 After the *P* heard that he
22:41 the *P* were gathered together
23:2 scribes and the *P* have seated
23:13 Woe to you, scribes and *P*
23:15 Woe to you, scribes and *P*
23:23 Woe to you, scribes and *P*
23:25 Woe to you, scribes and *P*
23:27 Woe to you, scribes and *P*
23:29 Woe to you, scribes and *P*
27:62 *P* gathered together before
Mr 2:16 scribes of the *P*, when they
2:18 and the *P* practiced fasting
2:18 disciples of the *P* practice
2:24 *P* went saying to him: Look
3:6 *P* went out and immediately
7:1 the *P* and some of the scribes
7:3 the *P* and all the Jews do not
7:5 so these *P* and scribes asked
8:11 the *P* came out and started
8:15 for the leaven of the *P*
10:2 *P* now approached and, to put
12:13 the *P* and of the party
Lu 5:17 *P* and teachers of the law who
5:21 the *P* started to reason
5:30 the *P* and their scribes began
5:33 and so do those of the *P*
6:2 *P* said: Why are you doing what
6:7 The scribes and the *P* were now
7:30 the *P* and those versed in the
7:36 a certain one of the *P* kept
11:39 you *P*, you cleanse the
11:42 woe to you *P*, because you
11:43 Woe to you *P*, because you
11:53 and the *P* started in to press
12:1 the leaven of the *P*, which is
13:31 certain *P* came up, saying to
14:1 one of the rulers of the *P*
14:3 and to the *P*, saying: Is it
15:2 both the *P* and the scribes
16:14 *P*, who were money lovers
17:20 on being asked by the *P* when
19:39 *P* from the crowd said to
Joh 1:24 sent forth were from the *P*
3:1 a man of the *P*, Nicodemus
4:1 *P* had heard that Jesus was
7:32 The *P* heard the crowd
7:32 *P* dispatched officers to get
7:45 to the chief priests and *P*
7:47 *P* answered: You have not
7:48 *P* has put faith in him, has
8:13 the *P* said to him: You bear
9:13 man himself to the *P*
9:15 *P* also took up asking him
9:16 *P* began to say: This is not
9:40 *P* who were with him heard
11:46 went off to the *P* and told
11:47 *P* gathered the Sanhedrin
11:57 *P* had given orders that if
12:19 *P* said among themselves
12:42 because of the *P* they would
18:3 *P* and came there with
Ac 15:5 those of the sect of the *P*
23:6 Sadducees but the other of *P*
23:6 I am a Pharisee, a son of *P*
23:7 between the *P* and Sadducees
23:8 *P* publicly declare them all
23:9 scribes of the party of the *P*

Pharpar
2Ki 5:12 Abanah and the *P*, the rivers

Phenomenon
Ex 3:3 I may inspect this great *p*
Job 38:36 understanding to the sky *p*

Phicol
Ge 21:22 Abimelech together with *P*
21:32 *P* the chief of his army and
26:26 *P* the chief of his army

Philadelphia
Re 1:11 the seven congregations . . . *P*
3:7 angel of the congregation in *P*

Philemon
Phm 1 *P*, our beloved one and fellow

Philetus
2Ti 2:17 and *P* are of that number

Philip
Mt 10:3 *P* and Bartholomew; Thomas
14:3 Herodias the wife of *P* his
Mr 3:18 and *P* and Bartholomew
6:17 Herodias the wife of *P* his
Lu 3:1 *P* his brother was district
6:14 John, and *P* and Bartholomew
Joh 1:43 Jesus found *P* and said to
1:44 *P* was from Bethsaida, from
1:45 *P* found Nathanael and said
1:46 *P* said to him: Come and see
1:48 Before *P* called you, while
6:5 he said to *P:* Where shall
6:7 *P* answered him: Two hundred
12:21 *P* who was from Bethsaida
12:22 *P* came and told Andrew
12:22 and *P* came and told Jesus
14:8 *P* said to him: Lord, show
Joh 14:9 *P*, you have not come to know
Ac 1:13 *P* and Thomas, Bartholomew
6:5 *P* and Prochorus and Nicanor
8:5 *P*, for one, went down to the
8:6 things said by *P* while they
8:12 *P*, who was declaring the good
8:13 constant attendance upon *P*
8:26 Jehovah's angel spoke to *P*
8:29 spirit said to *P:* Approach
8:30 *P* ran alongside and heard
8:31 entreated *P* to get on and
8:34 eunuch said to *P:* I beg you
8:35 *P* opened his mouth and
8:38 both *P* and the eunuch; and he
8:39 spirit quickly led *P* away
8:40 *P* was found to be in Ashdod
21:8 the house of *P* the evangelizer

Philippi
Mt 16:13 into the parts of Caesarea *P*
Mr 8:27 the villages of Caesarea *P*
Ac 16:12 from there to *P*, a colony
20:6 but we put out to sea from *P*
Php 1:1 holy ones . . . who are in *P*
1Th 2:2 in *P*, we mustered up boldness

Philippians
Php 4:15 you *P*, also know that at the

Philistia
Ex 15:14 hold on the inhabitants of *P*
Ps 60:8 Over *P* I shall shout in
83:7 *P* together with the
87:4 *P* and Tyre, together with
108:9 *P* I shall shout in triumph
Isa 14:29 Do not rejoice, O *P*, any
14:31 become disheartened, O *P*
Joe 3:4 Sidon and all you regions of *P*

Philistine
Jg 16:18 and called the *P* axis lords
16:18 *P* axis lords came up to her
16:23 As for the *P* axis lords, they
16:27 the *P* axis lords were there
1Sa 17:8 Am I not the *P* and you
17:10 *P* went on to say: I myself
17:11 heard these words of the *P*
17:16 the *P* kept coming forward
17:23 Goliath the *P* from Gath
17:26 that strikes down that *P*
17:26 who is this uncircumcised *P*
17:32 actually fight with this *P*
17:33 able to go against this *P*
17:36 *P* must become like one of
17:37 from the hand of this *P*
17:40 he began approaching the *P*
17:41 *P* began to come, coming
17:42 the *P* looked and saw David
17:43 *P* said to David: Am I a dog
17:43 *P* called down evil upon
17:44 *P* went on to say to David
17:45 David said to the *P:* You are
17:48 *P* rose and kept coming and
17:48 battle line to meet the *P*
17:49 struck the *P* in his forehead
17:50 proved stronger than the *P*
17:50 struck the *P* down and put
17:51 and got to stand over the *P*
17:54 took the head of the *P*
17:55 going out to meet the *P*
17:57 from striking the *P* down
17:57 head of the *P* in his hand
19:5 and strike the *P* down
21:9 sword of Goliath the *P*, whom
22:10 sword of Goliath the *P*
2Sa 21:17 struck the *P* down and put
Zec 9:6 cut off the pride of the *P*

Philistines
Ge 10:14 from among whom the *P* went
21:32 returned to the land of the *P*
21:34 alien in the land of the *P*
26:1 Abimelech, king of the *P*
26:8 Abimelech, king of the *P*, was
26:14 that the *P* began to envy him
26:15 these the *P* stopped up and
26:18 *P* went stopping up after
Ex 13:17 way of the land of the *P*
23:31 Red Sea to the sea of the *P*
Jos 13:2 regions of the *P* and all the
13:3 five axis lords of the *P*
Jg 3:3 The five axis lords of the *P*
3:31 he went striking down the *P*
10:6 gods of the *P*. So they left
10:7 into the hand of the *P* and
10:11 Was it not . . . from the *P*

Jg 13:1 hand of the *P* for forty years
13:5 out of the hand of the *P*
14:1 the daughters of the *P*
14:2 daughters of the *P*, and now
14:3 take a wife from the . . . *P*
14:4 an opportunity against the *P*
14:4 the *P* were ruling over Israel
15:3 free of guilt against the *P*
15:5 standing grain of the *P*
15:6 the *P* began to say: Who did
15:6 *P* went up and burned her and
15:9 *P* came up and camped in Judah
15:11 that the *P* are ruling over us
15:12 you into the hand of the *P*
15:14 *P*, for their part, shouted
15:20 days of the *P* twenty years
16:5 And the axis lords of the *P*
16:8 lords of the *P* brought up to
16:9 The *P* are upon you, Samson!
16:12 The *P* are upon you, Samson!
16:14 The *P* are upon you, Samson!
16:20 The *P* are upon you, Samson!
16:21 *P* grabbed hold of him and
16:28 avenge myself upon the *P*
16:30 Let my soul die with the *P*
1Sa 4:1 out to meet the *P* in battle
4:1 the *P* themselves encamped in
4:2 the *P* proceeded to draw up in
4:2 was defeated before the *P*
4:3 defeat us today before the *P*
4:6 *P* also got to hear the sound
4:7 *P* became afraid, because
4:9 prove yourselves men, you *P*
4:10 the *P* fought and Israel was
4:17 Israel has fled before the *P*
5:1 *P* . . . took the ark of the true
5:2 *P* proceeded to take the ark of
5:8 all the axis lords of the *P*
5:11 all the axis lords of the *P*
6:1 field of the *P* seven months
6:2 the *P* proceeded to call the
6:4 of the axis lords of the *P*
6:12 *P* were walking after them
6:16 the five axis lords of the *P*
6:17 piles that the *P* returned as
6:18 cities of the *P* belonging to
6:21 *P* have returned the ark of
7:3 you from the hand of the *P*
7:7 *P* came to hear that the sons
7:7 *P* got on their way up against
7:7 be afraid on account of the *P*
7:8 from the hand of the *P*
7:10 *P* themselves drew near for
7:10 on that day against the *P*
7:11 and went in pursuit of the *P*
7:13 the *P* were subdued, and they
7:13 against the *P* all the days of
7:14 cities that the *P* had taken
7:14 from the hand of the *P*
9:16 from the hand of the *P*
10:5 there is a garrison of the *P*
12:9 and into the hand of the *P*
13:3 the garrison of the *P* that
13:3 and the *P* got to hear of it
13:4 a garrison of the *P*, and now
13:4 foul-smelling among the *P*
13:5 *P*, for their part, collected
13:11 the *P* were being collected
13:12 *P* will come down against
13:16 *P* . . . encamped in Michmash
13:17 from the camp of the *P* in
13:19 because the *P* had said
13:20 to the *P* to get each one his
13:23 an outpost of the *P* would
14:1 over to the outpost of the *P*
14:4 against the outpost of the *P*
14:11 to the outpost of the *P*
14:11 And the *P* proceeded to say
14:19 was in the camp of the *P*
14:21 had come to belong to the *P*
14:22 the *P* had taken to flight
14:30 slaughter upon the *P* has not
14:31 kept striking down the *P*
14:36 Let us go down after the *P*
14:37 Shall I go down after the *P*?
14:46 from following the *P*
14:46 *P* themselves went to their
14:47 and against the *P*
14:52 heavy against the *P* all the
17:1 the *P* went collecting their
17:2 formation to meet the *P*
17:3 the *P* were standing on the
17:4 from the camps of the *P*, his
17:19 Elah, fighting against the *P*
1Sa 17:21 And Israel and the *P* began
17:23 the battle lines of the *P*
17:46 *P* this day to the fowls of
17:51 the *P* got to see that their
17:52 went in pursuit of the *P*
17:52 fatally wounded of the *P*
17:53 from hotly pursuing the *P*
18:6 from striking the *P* down
18:17 let the hand of the *P* come
18:21 that the hand of the *P* may
18:25 a hundred foreskins of the *P*
18:25 fall by the hand of the *P*
18:27 struck down among the *P*
18:30 princes of the *P* would go
19:8 fighting against the *P* and
23:1 *P* are warring against Keilah
23:2 must I strike down these *P*?
23:2 strike down the *P* and save
23:3 the battle lines of the *P*
23:4 giving the *P* into your hand
23:5 fought against the *P* and
23:27 *P* have made a raid on the
23:28 and went to meet the *P*
24:1 from following the *P*
27:1 to the land of the *P*
27:7 in the countryside of the *P*
27:11 in the countryside of the *P*
28:1 *P* began to collect their
28:4 *P* collected together and
28:5 see the camp of the *P*
28:15 *P* are fighting against me
28:19 into the hand of the *P*
28:19 give into the hand of the *P*
29:1 *P* proceeded to collect all
29:2 axis lords of the *P* were
29:3 princes of the *P* began to
29:3 said to the princes of the *P*
29:4 princes of the *P* became
29:4 *P* went on to say to him
29:7 of the axis lords of the *P*
29:9 princes of the *P* that have
29:11 return to the land of the *P*
29:11 *P* themselves went up to
30:16 land of the *P* and the land
31:1 *P* were fighting against
31:1 flight from before the *P*
31:2 *P* kept in close range of
31:2 *P* at last struck down
31:7 *P* came on in and took up
31:8 *P* came to strip the slain
31:9 land of the *P* all around to
31:11 what the *P* had done to Saul
2Sa 1:20 daughters of the *P* may
3:14 hundred foreskins of the *P*
3:18 from the hand of the *P*
5:17 *P* got to hear that they had
5:17 *P* came up to look for David
5:18 *P*, for their part, came in
5:19 Shall I go up against the *P*?
5:19 give the *P* into your hands
5:22 *P* came up once again and
5:24 the camp of the *P*
5:25 striking down the *P* from
8:1 proceeded to strike the *P*
8:1 out of the hand of the *P*
8:12 and from the *P* and
19:9 out of the palm of the *P*
21:12 the *P* had hanged them on
21:12 the *P* struck down Saul on
21:15 the *P* came to have war
21:15 went down and fought the *P*
21:18 war . . . with the *P* at Gob
21:19 war . . . with the *P* at Gob
23:9 when they taunted the *P*
23:10 kept striking down the *P*
23:11 the *P* proceeded to gather
23:11 fled because of the *P*
23:12 kept striking down the *P*
23:13 a tent village of the *P* was
23:14 and an outpost of the *P*
23:16 into the camp of the *P*
1Ki 4:21 River to the land of the *P*
15:27 which belonged to the *P*
16:15 which belonged to the *P*
2Ki 8:2 land of the *P* for seven years
8:3 return from the land of the *P*
18:8 struck down the *P* clear to
1Ch 1:12 among whom the *P* went forth
10:1 *P*, for their part, made war
10:1 fleeing from before the *P*
10:2 *P* kept in close range of Saul
10:2 and the *P* got to strike down
10:7 the *P* came on in and took up
10:8 *P* came to strip the slain
1Ch 10:9 send into the land of the *P*
10:11 that the *P* had done to Saul
11:13 at Pas-dammim, where the *P*
11:13 had fled because of the *P*
11:14 kept striking down the *P*
11:15 camp of the *P* was camping
11:16 a garrison of the *P* was
11:18 into the camp of the *P* and
12:19 with the *P* against Saul for
12:19 the axis lords of the *P* sent
14:8 *P* got to hear that David had
14:8 *P* came up to look for David
14:9 *P*, for their part, came in
14:10 Shall I go up against the *P*
14:13 *P* once again made a raid in
14:15 to strike the camp of the *P*
14:16 the *P* from Gibeon to Gezer
18:1 to strike down the *P* and
18:1 out of the hand of the *P*
18:11 from the *P* and from Amalek
20:4 at Gezer with the *P*
20:5 to be war again with the *P*
2Ch 9:26 to the land of the *P* and
17:11 *P* they were bringing to
21:16 spirit of the *P* and the
26:6 fight against the *P* and break
26:6 and among the *P*
26:7 to help him against the *P*
28:18 *P*, they made a raid upon
Ps 56:*super* the *P* laid hold of him in
Isa 2:6 of magic like the *P*, and
9:12 and the *P* from behind, and
11:14 fly at the shoulder of the *P*
Jer 25:20 kings of the land of the *P*
47:1 concerning the *P* before
47:4 coming to despoil all the *P*
47:4 Jehovah is despoiling the *P*
Eze 16:27 the daughters of the *P*, the
16:57 daughters of the *P*, those
25:15 *P* have acted with vengeance
25:16 my hand against the *P*
Am 1:8 the remaining ones of the *P*
6:2 go down to Gath of the *P*
9:7 and the *P* out of Crete, and
Ob 19 of the Shephelah, even of the *P*
Zep 2:5 Canaan, the land of the *P*

Philologus
Ro 16:15 Greet *P* and Julia, Nereus and

Philosophers
Ac 17:18 the Epicurean and the Stoic *p*

Philosophy
Col 2:8 the *p* and empty deception

Phinehas
Ex 6:25 Later she bore him *P*
Nu 25:7 *P* the son of Eleazar the son
25:11 *P* the son of Eleazar the son
31:6 and *P* the son of Eleazar the
Jos 22:13 *P* the son of Eleazar the
22:30 when *P* the priest and the
22:31 *P* the son of Eleazar the
22:32 *P* the son of Eleazar the
24:33 buried him in the Hill of *P*
Jg 20:28 Now *P* the son of Eleazar
1Sa 1:3 Hophni and *P*, were priests to
2:34 your two sons, Hophni and *P*
4:4 namely, Hophni and *P*
4:11 Hophni and *P*, died
4:17 sons have died—Hophni and *P*
4:19 the wife of *P*, was pregnant
14:3 *P*, the son of Eli, the priest
1Ch 6:4 Eleazar . . . father to *P*
6:4 *P* . . . father to Abishua
6:50 Eleazar his son, *P* his son
9:20 it was *P* the son of Eleazar
Ezr 7:5 *P* the son of Eleazar the son
8:2 the sons of *P*, Gershom
8:33 Eleazar the son of *P* and
Ps 106:30 *P* stood up and intervened

Phlegon
Ro 16:14 Greet Asyncritus, *P*, Hermes

Phoebe
Ro 16:1 recommend to you *P* our sister

Phoenicia
Isa 23:11 command against *P*, to
Ac 11:19 as far as *P* and Cyprus and
15:3 through both *P* and Samaria
21:2 a boat that was crossing to *P*

Phoenician
Mt 15:22 *P* woman from those regions

Phoenix
Ac 27:12 to *P* to winter, a harbor

Phrygia
Ac 2:10 *P* and Pamphylia, Egypt and
16:6 they went through *P* and the
18:23 the country of Galatia and *P*

Phygelus
2Ti 1:15 *P* and Hermogenes are of that

Physical
Lu 2:52 in wisdom and in *p* growth
1Co 2:14 a *p* man does not receive the
15:44 It is sown a *p* body, it is
15:44 If there is a *p* body, there
15:46 but that which is *p*

Physician
Mt 9:12 in health do not need a *p*
Mr 2:17 strong do not need a *p*
Lu 4:23 *P*, cure yourself; the things
5:31 healthy do not need a *p*, but
Col 4:14 Luke the beloved *p* sends you

Physicians
Ge 50:2 the *p*, to embalm his father
50:2 So the *p* embalmed Israel
Job 13:4 All of you are *p* of no value
Mr 5:26 put to many pains by many *p*

Pibeseth
Eze 30:17 young men of On and *P*

Pick
Ge 31:46 *P* up stones! And they went
Ex 12:5 *p* from the young rams or
16:4 people must go out and *p* up
16:16 *P* up some of it, each one in
16:21 *p* it up morning by morning
16:26 Six days you will *p* it up
16:27 people did go out to *p* it
Le 19:9 your harvest you must not *p*
19:10 not *p* up the scattered grapes
23:22 harvest you must not *p* up
De 33:21 *p* out the first part for
Jos 7:14 the tribe that Jehovah will *p*
7:14 family that Jehovah will *p*
7:14 that Jehovah will *p* will
Jg 8:1 tried to *p* a quarrel with him
2Ki 4:39 to the field to *p* mallows
1Ch 21:11 has said, Take your *p*
Ps 104:28 you give them they *p* up
Pr 30:17 the ravens . . . will *p* it out
Ca 6:2 the gardens, and to *p* lilies
Mt 9:6 *p* up your bed, and go to your
16:24 *p* up his torture stake and
24:18 to *p* up his outer garment
Mr 2:9 and *p* up your cot and walk
2:11 Get up, *p* up your cot, and go
8:34 *p* up his torture stake and
13:16 to *p* up his outer garment
Lu 5:24 *p* up your little bed and be
9:23 *p* up his torture stake day
17:31 not come down to *p* these up
Joh 5:8 *p* up your cot and walk
5:11 *P* up your cot and walk
5:12 told you, *P* it up and walk

Picked
Ex 16:18 They *p* it up each one in
16:22 *p* up twice as much bread
Nu 11:8 *p* it up and ground it in hand
Jos 7:15 one *p* with the thing devoted
7:16 tribe of Judah got to be *p*
7:17 *p* the family of the
7:17 and Zabdi got to be *p*
7:18 tribe of Judah, got to be *p*
1Sa 10:20 Benjamin came to be *p*
10:21 the Matrites came to be *p*
10:21 son of Kish came to be *p*
17:20 *p* up and went just as Jesse
2Ki 2:13 he *p* up the official garment
1Ch 24:6 one paternal house being *p*
24:6 one being *p* out for Ithamar
Isa 27:12 *p* up one after the other
Da 11:15 the people of his *p* ones
Mr 2:12 immediately *p* up his cot and
Lu 5:25 *p* up what he used to lie on
Joh 5:9 *p* up his cot and began to
8:59 they *p* up stones to hurl
Ac 7:21 daughter of Pharaoh *p* him up
20:9 he fell . . . and was *p* up dead

Picking
Ge 47:14 *p* up all the money that
Ex 16:5 they keep *p* up day by day
16:17 and they went *p* it up, some
Jg 1:7 *p* up food under my table
1Sa 20:38 *p* up the arrows and then
2Ki 4:39 went *p* wild gourds from it
Isa 32:10 grape *p* will have come to
Jer 7:18 The sons are *p* up sticks of

Piece
Ge 18:5 let me get a *p* of bread, and
38:28 took and tied a scarlet *p*
38:30 whose hand the scarlet *p* was
Ex 25:36 is one *p* of hammered work
36:18 together to become one *p*
37:22 one *p* of hammered work of
Jos 15:19 a *p* of land to the south
Jg 1:15 it is a southern *p* of land
Ru 2:14 and dip your *p* in the vinegar
1Sa 2:36 to eat a *p* of bread
28:22 set before you a *p* of bread
1Ki 7:34 one *p* with the carriage
7:35 sidewalls were of one *p*
2Ki 6:6 he cut off a *p* of wood and
10:32, 32 cut off Israel *p* by *p*
Ne 9:22, 22 to apportion them *p* by *p*
Job 42:11 to give him a *p* of money
Pr 17:1 Better is a dry *p* of bread
28:21 over a mere *p* of bread
Eze 24:4 every good *p*, thigh and
24:6, 6 *P* by *p* of it, bring it out
Am 3:12 two shanks or a *p* of an ear
Hab 2:19 one saying to the *p* of wood
Lu 24:42 handed him a *p* of broiled
Ac 4:37 possessing a *p* of land, sold
1Co 13:1 a sounding *p* of brass or a

Pieces
Ge 4:4 his flock, even their fatty *p*
15:10 birds he did not cut in *p*
15:17 passed in between these *p*
20:16 I do give a thousand silver *p*
31:39 animal torn to *p* I did not
33:19 for a hundred *p* of money
37:28 for twenty silver *p*
37:33 Joseph is surely torn to *p!*
44:28 he must surely be torn to *p!*
45:22 gave three hundred silver *p*
Ex 28:7 two shoulder *p* to be joined
28:12 the shoulder *p* of the ephod
28:12 upon his two shoulder *p* as a
28:25 the shoulder *p* of the ephod
28:27 two shoulder *p* of the ephod
29:17 cut up the ram into its *p*
29:17 put its *p* to one another and
39:4 made shoulder *p* for it that
39:7 the shoulder *p* of the ephod as
39:18 the shoulder *p* of the ephod
39:20 two shoulder *p* of the ephod
Le 1:8 must set the *p* in order with
2:6 a breaking of it up into *p*, and
6:12 make the fatty *p* of the
6:21 the grain offering in *p* as a
7:24 fat of an animal torn to *p*
8:20 cut up the ram into its *p*
8:20 and the *p* and the suet smoke
8:26 the fatty *p* and the right leg
9:13 burnt offering in its *p* and
9:19 the fatty *p* of the bull and
9:20 placed the fatty *p* upon the
9:20 fatty *p* smoke upon the altar
9:24 the fatty *p* upon the altar
10:15 made by fire, of the fatty *p*
Nu 15:32 man collecting *p* of wood on
15:33 collecting *p* of wood brought
24:8 break them to *p* with his
Jos 24:32 for a hundred *p* of money
Jg 6:26 *p* of wood of the sacred pole
7:19 a dashing to *p* of the large
9:4 gave him seventy *p* of silver
9:53 and broke his skull in *p*
16:5 thousand one hundred silver *p*
17:2 silver *p* that were taken from
17:3 gave back the . . . *p* of silver
17:4 took two hundred silver *p* and
17:10 give you ten silver *p* a year
19:29 into twelve *p* and sent her
1Sa 11:7 bulls and cut them in *p* and
15:33 hacking Agag to *p* before
2Sa 18:11 give you ten *p* of silver and
18:12 a thousand *p* of silver
22:39 and break them in *p*, that
1Ki 8:64 fat *p* of the communion
8:64 fat *p* of the communion
10:29 for six hundred silver *p*
11:30 ripped it into twelve *p*
11:31 Take for yourself ten *p*
17:10 gathering up *p* of wood
1Ki 17:12 a few *p* of wood, and I
18:23 cut it in *p* and put it upon
18:33 put the *p* of wood in order
18:33 cut the young bull in *p*
18:33 upon the *p* of wood
18:33 and upon the *p* of wood
18:38 *p* of wood and the stones
2Ki 2:12 and ripped them into two *p*
2:24 to *p* forty-two children of
5:5 and six thousand *p* of gold and
6:25 worth eighty silver *p*
6:25 was worth five silver *p*
8:12 children you will dash to *p*
16:17 of the carriages in *p* and
18:4 broke the sacred pillars to *p*
18:4 to *p* the copper serpent that
23:14 the sacred pillars to *p*
24:13 to *p* all the gold utensils
25:13 the Chaldeans broke in *p*
2Ch 1:17 for six hundred silver *p* and
7:7 fat *p* of the communion
7:7 grain offering and the fat *p*
14:13 broken to *p* before Jehovah
15:6 they were crushed to *p*
28:24 cut to *p* the utensils of
29:35 fat *p* of the communion
34:4 statues he broke in *p* and
35:14 and the fat *p* until night
Job 4:20 they are crushed to *p*
5:18 He breaks to *p*, but his own
16:9 very anger has torn me to *p*
18:4 tearing his soul to *p* in his
18:13 will eat the *p* of his skin
20:19 For he has crushed to *p*, he
26:12 has broken the stormer to *p*
Ps 2:9 you will dash them to *p*
7:2 tear my soul to *p* as a lion
17:12 lion that yearns to tear to *p*
18:38 I shall break them in *p* so
22:13 lion tearing in *p* and roaring
29:5 the cedars of Lebanon in *p*
35:15 They ripped me to *p* and did
46:9 and does cut the spear in *p*
50:22 I may not tear you to *p*
68:21 break . . . his enemies in *p*
68:30 stamping down on *p* of silver
74:14 crushed to *p* the heads of
89:23 crushed his adversaries to *p*
110:5 break kings to *p* on the day
110:6 break to *p* the head one over
119:72 thousands of *p* of gold and
129:4 cut in *p* the ropes of the
137:9 ahold and does dash to *p*
Pr 18:24 to break one another to *p*
Ca 8:11 fruitage a thousand silver *p*
Isa 7:8 will be shattered to *p*
7:23 a thousand *p* of silver
8:9 be shattered to *p*; and give
8:9 and be shattered to *p*
8:9 and be shattered to *p*
9:4 shattered to *p* as in the day
13:16 dashed to *p* before their
13:18 dash even young men to *p*
30:14 crushed to *p* without one's
30:14 its crushed *p* a fragment
45:2 doors I shall break in *p*
46:1 their loads, *p* of luggage
51:9 the one that broke Rahab to *p*
Jer 2:20 I broke your yoke to *p*
5:6 from them gets torn to *p*
5:14 people will be *p* of wood
15:12 Can one break iron in *p*
22:28 despised, dashed to *p*
32:9 shekels and ten silver *p*
34:18 might pass between its *p*
34:19 between the *p* of the calf
38:11 worn-out *p* of cloth and
38:12 *p* of cloth under your
43:13 break to *p* the pillars of
46:5 are crushed to *p*; and they
46:22 who are gathering *p* of wood
48:12 jars they will dash to *p*
51:20 dash nations to *p*, and
51:21 horse and his rider to *p*
51:21 chariot and its rider to *p*
51:22 dash man and woman to *p*
51:22 dash old man and boy to *p*
51:22 young man and virgin to *p*
51:23 shepherd and his drove to *p*
51:23 his span of animals to *p*
51:23 and deputy rulers to *p*
52:17 Chaldeans broke to *p* and
La 1:15 to break my young men to *p*
2:9 and broken her bars in *p*

Eze 24:4 Gather *p* in it, every good
24:5 Boil its *p*, also cook its
44:31 no creature torn to *p* of the
47:13 two *p* of field to Joseph
Da 12:7 power of the holy people to *p*
Ho 3:2 for fifteen silver *p* and a
5:14 I myself shall tear to *p*
6:1 he himself has torn in *p* but
10:14 dashed to *p* alongside her
13:8 will tear them to *p*
13:16 children will be dashed to *p*
Mic 1:7 will all be crushed to *p*
3:3 smashed to *p* their very bones
3:3 crushed them to *p* like what
5:8 tramples down and tears in *p*
Na 2:12 The lion was tearing to *p*
2:12 with animals torn to *p*
3:10 dashed to *p* at the head of
Hab 3:13 You broke to *p* the head one
Zec 11:6 crush to *p* the land, and I
11:10 and cut it to *p*, in order
11:12 wages, thirty *p* of silver
11:13 took the thirty *p* of silver
11:14 cut in *p* my second staff
Mt 26:15 to him thirty silver *p*
27:3 the thirty silver *p* back to
27:5 So he threw the silver *p* into
27:6 priests took the silver *p* and
27:9 they took the thirty silver *p*
28:12 silver *p* to the soldiers
28:15 they took the silver *p* and
Ac 19:19 fifty thousand *p* of silver
23:10 Paul would be pulled to *p* by
27:41 to be violently broken to *p*
Re 2:27 broken to *p* like clay vessels

Pierce
Ex 21:6 *p* his ear through with an awl
2Ki 18:21 enter into his palm and *p*
Isa 36:6 into his palm and *p* it
Zec 13:3 must *p* him through because

Pierced
Nu 25:8 and *p* both of them through
Jg 5:26 she *p* his head through, And
Job 26:13 has *p* the gliding serpent
Ps 69:26 the pains of those *p* by you
109:22 my heart itself has been *p*
Isa 13:15 is found will be *p* through
51:9 that *p* the sea monster
53:5 being *p* for our transgression
Jer 37:10 men *p* through, they would
51:4 *p* through in her streets
51:52 the *p* one will groan
La 4:9 *p* through for lack of the
Eze 32:26 *p* through by the sword
Hab 3:14 *p* the head of his warriors
Zec 12:10 the One whom they *p* through
Mt 27:49 *p* his side, and blood and
Joh 19:37 look to the One whom they *p*
Re 1:7 see him, and those who *p* him

Pierces
Ps 77:10 This is what *p* me through
Heb 4:12 *p* even to the dividing of

Piercing
Pr 26:10 As an archer *p* everything is

Pig
Le 11:7 the *p* . . . it is a splitter
De 14:8 The *p* also, because it is a
Pr 11:22 nose ring in the snout of a *p*
Isa 65:4 eating the flesh of the *p*
66:3 a gift—the blood of a *p*
66:17 eating the flesh of the *p*

Pigeon
Ge 15:9 Take for me . . . a young *p*
Le 12:6 a male *p* or a turtledove for

Pigeons
Le 1:14 the turtledoves or the male *p*
5:7 or two male *p* to Jehovah
5:11 turtledoves or two male *p*
12:8 two male *p*, one for a burnt
14:22 turtledoves or two male *p*
14:30 or of the male *p* for which
15:14 or two male *p*, and he must
15:29 or two male *p*, and she must
Nu 6:10 male *p* to the priest to the
Lu 2:24 turtledoves or two young *p*

Pihahiroth
Ex 14:2 *P* between Migdol and the sea
14:9 by *P* in view of Baal-zephon
Nu 33:7 turned back toward *P*, which
33:8 they pulled away from *P* and

Pilate
Mt 27:2 him over to *P* the governor
27:13 *P* said to him: Do you not
27:17 *P* said to them: Which one
27:22 *P* said to them: What, then
27:24 *P* took water and washed his
27:58 This man went up to *P* and
27:58 *P* commanded it to be given
27:62 gathered together before *P*
27:65 *P* said to them: You have a
Mr 15:1 and handed him over to *P*
15:2 So *P* put the question to him
15:4 *P* began questioning him
15:5 so that *P* began to marvel
15:9 *P* responded to them, saying
15:12 *P* was saying to them
15:14 *P* went on to say to them
15:15 *P*, wishing to satisfy the
15:43 before *P* and asked for the
15:44 But *P* wondered whether he
Lu 3:1 Pontius *P* was governor of
13:1 Galileans whose blood *P* had
23:1 and all, and led him to *P*
23:3 *P* asked him the question: Are
23:4 *P* said to the chief priests
23:6 *P* asked whether the man was
23:11 and sent him back to *P*
23:12 Herod and *P* now became
23:13 *P* then called the chief
23:20 Again *P* called out to them
23:24 *P* gave sentence for their
23:52 to *P* and asked for the body
Joh 18:29 *P* came outside to them and
18:31 *P* said to them: Take him
18:33 So *P* entered into the
18:35 *P* answered: I am not a Jew
18:37 *P* said to him: Well, then
18:38 *P* said to him: What is
19:1 *P* took Jesus and scourged
19:4 *P* went outside again and
19:6 *P* said to them: Take him
19:8 *P* heard this saying, he
19:10 *P* said to him: Are you not
19:12 *P* kept on seeking how to
19:13 *P*, after hearing these
19:15 *P* said . . . Shall I impale
19:19 *P* wrote a title also and
19:21 Jews began to say to *P*
19:22 *P* answered: What I have
19:31 requested *P* to have their
19:38 requested *P* that he might
19:38 and *P* gave him permission
Ac 4:27 Pontius *P* with men of nations
13:28 demanded of *P* that he be
1Ti 6:13 declaration before Pontius *P*

Pilate's
Ac 3:13 disowned before *P* face, when

Pildash
Ge 22:22 *P* and Jidlaph and Bethuel

Pile
Ge 41:35 let them *p* up grain under
Jos 7:26 over him a big *p* of stones
8:29 a great *p* of stones over him
2Sa 18:17 a very big *p* of stones
Job 5:26 sheaves *p* up in their time
27:16 *p* up silver like dust
Isa 25:2 made a city a *p* of stones
30:33 He has made its *p* deep
Eze 24:9 also shall make the *p* great
Zec 9:3 *p* up silver like dust and

Piles
De 28:27 *p* and eczema and skin
1Sa 5:6 and striking them with *p*
5:9 *p* began breaking out on them
5:12 had been struck with *p*
6:4 five golden *p* and five golden
6:5 must make images of your *p*
6:11 and the images of their *p*
6:17 golden *p* that the Philistines
2Ki 19:25 desolate as *p* of ruins
Ps 39:6 One *p* up things and does not
Isa 37:26 desolate as *p* of ruins
Jer 9:11 make Jerusalem *p* of stones
51:37 must become *p* of stones
Ho 12:11 altars are like *p* of stones
Hab 1:10 it *p* up dust and captures it

Pilha
Ne 10:24 Hallohesh, *P*, Shobek

Piling
Ge 41:49 Joseph continued *p* up grain
Ex 8:14 And they went *p* them up, heaps
Jg 15:8 *p* legs upon thighs with a

Pillage
Jg 2:14 they began to *p* them; and he
2Ki 21:14 plunder and *p* to all their
Isa 10:13 I shall certainly *p*
42:22 for *p* without anyone to say
42:24 has given Jacob for mere *p*
Ho 13:15 That one will *p* the treasure
Hab 2:7 become . . . something to *p*
Zep 1:13 wealth . . . come to be for *p*

Pillaged
Ps 44:10 have *p* for themselves
89:41 along the way have *p* him
Isa 13:16 Their houses will be *p*, and
42:22 a people plundered and *p*
Zec 14:2 and the houses be *p*, and the

Pillager
1Sa 14:48 out of the hand of their *p*

Pillagers
Jg 2:14 into the hands of the *p*
2:16 out of the hand of their *p*
1Sa 13:17 force of *p* would sally
14:15 the force of *p* trembled
2Ki 17:20 into the hand of *p*, until

Pillaging
1Sa 17:53 and went *p* their camps
23:1 are *p* the threshing floors
Isa 17:14 the share of those *p* us
Jer 30:16 those *p* you will certainly
30:16 certainly come to be for *p*
50:11 men kept exulting when *p*

Pillar
Ge 19:26 and she became a *p* of salt
28:18 set it up as a *p* and poured
28:22 stone . . . set up as a *p*
31:13 where you anointed a *p* and
31:45 a stone and set it up as a *p*
31:51 here is the *p* that I have
31:52 *p* is something that bears
31:52 this *p* against me for harm
35:14 Jacob stationed a *p* in the
35:14 a *p* of stone, and he poured
35:20 stationed a *p* over her grave
35:20 the *p* of Rachel's grave
Ex 13:21 in a *p* of cloud to lead them
13:21 the nighttime in a *p* of fire
13:22 *p* of cloud would not move
13:22 *p* of fire in the nighttime
14:19 *p* of cloud departed from
14:24 the *p* of fire and cloud
33:9 the *p* of cloud would come
33:10 people saw the *p* of cloud
Le 26:1 image or a sacred *p* for
Nu 12:5 in the *p* of cloud and stood
14:14 *p* of cloud by day and in the
14:14 and in the *p* of fire by night
De 16:22 a sacred *p*, a thing Jehovah
31:15 at the tent in the *p* of cloud
31:15 *p* of cloud began to stand by
Jg 9:6 the *p* that was in Shechem
20:40 to go up . . . as a *p* of smoke
1Sa 14:5 The one tooth was a *p* on the
2Sa 18:18 raise up for himself a *p*
18:18 the *p* by his own name
1Ki 7:15 being the height of each *p*
7:21 he set up the right-hand *p*
7:21 set up the left-hand *p* and
2Ki 3:2 removed the sacred *p* of Baal
10:27 down the sacred *p* of Baal
11:14 king was standing by the *p*
23:3 king kept standing by the *p*
25:17 was the height of each *p*
25:17 the second *p* had the same
2Ch 23:13 king standing by his *p* at
Ne 9:12 by a *p* of cloud you led them
9:12 by a *p* of fire by night
9:19 The *p* of cloud itself did not
9:19 *p* of fire by night to light
Ps 99:7 *p* of cloud he continued
Isa 19:19 *p* to Jehovah beside its
Jer 1:18 an iron *p* and copper walls
52:21 in height was each *p*
52:22 second *p* had just the same
Eze 40:48 went measuring the side *p*
41:1 the width of the side *p*
41:3 the side *p* of the entrance
Ho 3:4 without a *p* and without an
Am 9:1 Strike the *p* head, so that
Zep 2:14 right among her *p* capitals
1Ti 3:15 a *p* and support of the truth
Re 3:12 make him a *p* in the temple

Eze 19:4 In their *p* he was caught
19:8 In their *p* he was caught
26:20 going down into the *p* to
26:20 going down into the *p*
28:8 to the *p* they will bring you
31:14 those going down into the *p*
31:16 those going down into the *p*
32:18 those going down into the *p*
32:23 the innermost parts of a *p*
32:24 those going down into the *p*
32:25 those going down into the *p*
32:29 those going down into the *p*
32:30 those going down into the *p*
Da 6:7 be thrown to the lions' *p*
6:12 be thrown to the lions' *p*
6:16 him into the *p* of the lions
6:17 placed on the mouth of the *p*
6:19 went right to the lions' *p*
6:20 And as he got near to the *p*
6:23 to be lifted up out of the *p*
6:23 was lifted up out of the *p*
6:24 the lions' *p* they threw them
6:24 reached the bottom of the *p*
Jon 2:6 out of the *p* you proceeded to
Zep 2:9 and a salt *p*, and a desolate
Hag 2:19 the seed in the grain *p*
Zec 9:11 your prisoners out of the *p*
Mt 12:11 into a *p* on the sabbath
15:14 both will fall into a *p*
Lu 6:39 Both will tumble into a *p*
Re 9:1 key of the *p* of the abyss was
9:2 he opened the *p* of the abyss
9:2 smoke ascended out of the *p* as
9:2 by the smoke of the *p*

Pitch
Ge 37:20 kill him and *p* him into one
37:22 *P* him into this waterpit
Ex 2:3 coated it with bitumen and *p*
2Sa 20:22 and *p* it to Joab
2Ki 3:25 would *p* each one his stone
1Ch 15:1 and *p* a tent for it
Ps 27:3 an encampment should *p* tent
Isa 13:20 Arab will not *p* his tent
34:9 must be changed into *p*
34:9 must become as burning *p*
Jer 51:63 *p* it into the midst of the
Eze 5:4 *p* them into the midst of the
Mt 13:42 will *p* them into the fiery
Joh 15:6 and *p* them into the fire and
Re 18:21 with a swift *p* will Babylon

Pitched
Ge 12:8 *p* his tent with Bethel on the
13:12 Finally he *p* tent near Sodom
26:25 *p* his tent there, and the
31:25 Jacob had *p* his tent in the
33:18 *p* camp in front of the city
33:19 he *p* his tent at the hand of
35:21 *p* his tent a distance beyond
37:24 *p* him into the waterpit
38:1 he *p* his tent near a man, an
Ex 15:1 rider he has *p* into the sea
15:21 rider he has *p* into the sea
33:7 his tent away and he *p* it
Jos 8:29 *p* it at the entrance of the
Jg 4:11 he had his tent *p* near the
9:53 woman *p* an upper millstone
10:17 Ammon . . . *p* camp in Gilead
10:17 and *p* camp in Mizpah
1Sa 28:4 came and *p* camp in Shunem
28:4 and they *p* camp in Gilboa
2Sa 6:17 tent that David had *p* for it
11:21 woman that *p* an upper
16:22 they *p* a tent for Absalom
18:17 took Absalom and *p* him in
20:21 His head will be *p* to you
1Ch 16:1 tent that David had *p* for it
2Ch 1:4 *p* a tent for it in Jerusalem
Jer 6:3 they *p* their tents all around
Mt 5:29 body to be *p* into Gehenna
Mr 9:42 were actually *p* into the sea
9:45 two feet to be *p* into Gehenna
9:47 to be *p* into Gehenna

Pitchers
Ex 25:29 and its *p* and its bowls with
37:16 and its bowls and its *p* with
Nu 4:7 *p* of the drink offering; and
1Ch 28:17 and the *p* of pure gold
Mr 7:4 cups and *p* and copper vessels

Pitching
Jer 36:23 *p* it also into the fire
Ac 1:18 *p* head foremost he noisily

Pitfall
Ps 57:6 They excavated before me a *p*

Pitfalls
Ps 119:85 have excavated *p* to get me

Pithom
Ex 1:11 namely, *P* and Raamses

Pithon
1Ch 8:35 the sons of Micah were *P* and
9:41 sons of Micah were *P* and

Pitiable
Re 3:17 *p* and poor and blind and

Pitied
1Co 15:19 of all men most to be *p*

Pits
Ge 14:10, 10 was *p* upon *p* of bitumen
Ps 107:20 them escape out of their *p*
140:10 into watery *p*, that they
2Pe 2:4 to *p* of dense darkness to be

Pity
Ge 43:14 may God Almighty give you *p*
1Ki 8:50 must make them objects of *p*
8:50 and they must *p* them
Ne 1:11 make him an object of *p*
Ps 40:11 do not restrain your *p* from
106:46 them to be objects of *p*
Isa 13:18 the belly they will not *p*
49:10 *p* upon them will lead them
49:13 *p* upon his own afflicted
49:15 *p* the son of her belly
Jer 6:23 and they will have no *p*
30:18 tabernacles I shall have *p*
31:20 I shall have *p* upon him, is
33:26 captives and will have *p*
Mt 9:36 seeing the crowds he felt *p*
14:14 he felt *p* for them, and he
15:32 said: I feel *p* for the crowd
18:27 Moved to *p* at this, the
20:34 Moved with *p*, Jesus touched
Mr 1:41 At that he was moved with *p*
6:34 he was moved with *p* for
8:2 I feel *p* for the crowd
9:22 have *p* on us and help us
Lu 7:13 he was moved with *p* for her
10:33 he was moved with *p*
15:20 and was moved with *p*, and

Pivot
Pr 26:14 door keeps turning upon its *p*

Pivots
1Ki 6:34 the one door turned on *p*
6:34 the other door turned on *p*
Isa 6:4 *p* of the thresholds began to

Place
Ge 1:9 waters . . . together into one *p*
2:21 up the flesh over its *p*
4:25 appointed another seed in *p*
10:30 *p* of dwelling came to extend
13:3 *p* where his tent had been at
13:4 *p* of the altar that he had
13:14 look from the *p* where you
18:24 not pardon the *p* for the sake
18:26 I will pardon the whole *p* on
18:33 Abraham returned to his *p*
19:12 bring out of the *p*
19:13 are bringing this *p* to ruin
19:14 Get out of this *p*, because
19:27 *p* where he had stood before
20:11 is no fear of God in this *p*
20:13 At every *p* where we shall
21:31 he called that *p* Beer-sheba
22:3 trip to the *p* that the
22:4 to see the *p* from a distance
22:9 they reached the *p* that the
22:13 offering in *p* of his son
22:14 to call the name of that *p*
23:4 burial *p* among you that I may
23:6 hold back his burial *p* from
23:9 the possession of a burial *p*
23:20 burial *p* at the hands of the
24:25 also a *p* to spend the night
26:7 the men of the *p* kept asking
26:7 men of the *p* should kill me
28:11 In time he came across a *p*
28:11 one of the stones of the *p*
28:11 and lay down in that *p*
28:16 Truly Jehovah is in this *p*
28:17 How fear-inspiring this *p* is!
28:19 the name of that *p* Bethel
29:3 the stone . . . to its *p*
29:4 from what *p* are you?
Ge 29:22 all the men of the *p*
29:26 to do this way in our *p*
30:2 Am I in the *p* of God
30:25 that I may go to my *p*
31:55 might return to his own *p*
32:2 name of that *p* Mahanaim
32:25 thigh joint got out of *p*
32:30 the name of the *p* Peniel
33:17 the name of the *p* Succoth
35:7 began to call the *p* El-bethel
35:13 the *p* where he had spoken
35:14 stationed a pillar in the *p*
35:15 *p* where God had spoken with
38:21 the men of her *p*, saying
38:21 has ever been in this *p*
38:22 the men of the *p* said, No
38:22 has ever been in this *p*
39:20 the *p* where the prisoners of
40:3 *p* where Joseph was a prisoner
41:41 *p* you over all the land of
42:27 at the lodging *p*, he got to
43:21 we came to the lodging *p*
43:30 he looked for a *p* to weep
44:1 *p* the money of each one in
44:2 *p* my cup, the silver cup, in
45:7 in order to *p* a remnant for
47:29 *p* your hand, please, under
48:9 God has given me in this *p*
49:24 dwelling in a permanent *p*
49:30 the possession of a burial *p*
50:5 In my burial *p* which I have
50:13 a burial *p* from Ephron the
50:19 for am I in the *p* of God?
Ex 3:5 *p* where you are standing is
4:24 lodging *p* that Jehovah got to
8:15 relief had taken *p*, he made
8:23 this sign will take *p*
10:23 got up from his own *p* three
12:16 there is to take *p* for you a
12:46 to some *p* outside. And you must
15:13 them to your holy abiding *p*
15:17 An established *p* that you
16:29 each one in his own *p*
17:7 the name of the *p* Massah and
18:23 come to their own *p* in peace
20:24 In every *p* where I shall
21:13 a *p* where he can flee
22:11 oath by Jehovah is to take *p*
23:20 the *p* that I have prepared
24:14 wait for us in this *p* until
25:16 *p* in the Ark the testimony
25:21 *p* the cover above upon the
25:21 Ark you will *p* the testimony
25:26 and *p* the rings on the four
26:4 at the other *p* of junction
26:5 is at the other *p* of junction
26:10 at the other *p* of junction
28:27 near its *p* of joining, above
28:43 to minister in the holy *p*
29:24 *p* them all upon the palms of
29:30 minister in the holy *p* will
29:31 boil its flesh in a holy *p*
30:1 as a *p* for burning incense
30:13 shekel of the holy *p*
30:24 the shekel of the holy *p*
33:21 Here is a *p* with me, and
33:22 *p* you in a hole in the rock
36:11 at the other *p* of junction
36:12 at the other *p* of junction
36:17 at the *p* of junction, and
38:24 work of the holy *p* came to
38:24 by the shekel of the holy *p*
38:25 by the shekel of the holy *p*
38:26 by the shekel of the holy *p*
38:27 pedestals of the holy *p*
39:1 for ministering in the holy *p*
39:20 near its *p* of joining, above
40:3 *p* the ark of the testimony in
40:5 put the screen . . . in *p*
40:8 *p* the courtyard round about
40:21 curtain of the screen in *p*
40:28 of the tabernacle in *p*
Le 1:16 to the *p* for the fatty ashes
2:15 and *p* frankincense upon it
4:6 the curtain of the holy *p*
4:12 of the camp to a clean *p*
4:24 slaughter it in the *p* where
4:29 same *p* as the burnt offering
4:33 *p* where the burnt offering
5:11 not *p* frankincense upon it
5:15 by the shekel of the holy *p*
5:16 committed against the holy *p*
6:10 must *p* them beside the altar
6:11 to a clean *p* outside the camp

Le 6:16 unfermented cakes in a holy *p*
6:22 the one anointed in *p* of him
6:25 *p* where the burnt offering
6:26 In a holy *p* it will be eaten
6:27 blood upon in a holy *p*
6:30 make atonement in the holy *p*
7:2 In the *p* where they regularly
7:6 In a holy *p* it will be eaten
10:4 in front of the holy *p* to
10:13 you must eat it in a holy *p*
10:14 sacred portion in a clean *p*
10:17 offering in the *p* that is
10:18 brought into the holy *p*
10:18 without fail in the holy *p*
12:4 not come into the holy *p*
13:19 in the *p* of the boil a white
13:23 if in its *p* the blotch should
13:28 if the blotch stands in its *p*
13:46 the camp is his dwelling *p*
14:13 the *p* where the sin offering
14:13 slaughtered, in a holy *p*
14:28 over the *p* of the blood of
14:40 into an unclean *p*
14:41 into an unclean *p*
14:42 the *p* of the former stones
14:45 the city to an unclean *p*
16:2 the holy *p* inside the curtain
16:3 into the holy *p*: with a young
16:16 atonement for the holy *p*
16:17 in the holy *p* until he
16:20 atonement for the holy *p*
16:23 went into the holy *p*, and
16:24 in a holy *p* and put on his
16:27 atonement in the holy *p*
19:20 punishment should take *p*
20:3 purpose of defiling my holy *p*
23:27 holy convention should take *p*
24:6 *p* them in two sets of layers
24:9 eat it in a holy *p*, because
27:3 by the shekel of the holy *p*
27:25 in the shekel of the holy *p*
Nu 2:17 set out, each one at his *p*
3:12 *p* of all the firstborn opening
3:28 the obligation to the holy *p*
3:31 utensils of the holy *p* with
3:32 the obligation to the holy *p*
3:41 in *p* of all the firstborn
3:41 *p* of all the firstborn among
3:45 Levites in *p* of all the
3:45 in *p* of their domestic
3:47 shekel of the holy *p* you
3:50 in the shekel of the holy *p*
4:12 minister in the holy *p*, and
4:15 finish covering the holy *p*
4:15 utensils of the holy *p* when
4:15 not touch the holy *p* so that
4:16 the holy *p* and its utensils
4:27 take *p* as regards all their
6:27 *p* my name upon the sons of
7:9 service of the holy *p* was
7:13 by the shekel of the holy *p*
7:19 by the shekel of the holy *p*
7:25 by the shekel of the holy *p*
7:31 by the shekel of the holy *p*
7:37 by the shekel of the holy *p*
7:43 by the shekel of the holy *p*
7:49 by the shekel of the holy *p*
7:55 by the shekel of the holy *p*
7:61 by the shekel of the holy *p*
7:67 by the shekel of the holy *p*
7:73 by the shekel of the holy *p*
7:79 by the shekel of the holy *p*
7:85 by the shekel of the holy *p*
7:86 by the shekel of the holy *p*
8:16 In *p* of those opening all
8:18 *p* of all the firstborn among
8:19 of Israel approach the holy *p*
9:17 *p* where the cloud would
10:29 *p* about which Jehovah said
11:3 name of that *p* got to be
11:17 and *p* it upon them, and
11:34 name of that *p* came to be
13:24 called that *p* the torrent
14:40 the *p* that Jehovah mentioned
16:7 *p* incense upon them before
18:3 to the utensils of the holy *p*
18:5 your obligation to the holy *p*
18:10 In a most holy *p* you should
18:16 by the shekel of the holy *p*
18:31 you must eat it in every *p*
19:9 outside the camp in a clean *p*
19:16 bone of a man or a burial *p*
19:18 or the corpse or the burial *p*
20:5 to bring us into this evil *p*
Nu 20:5 It is no *p* of seed and figs
21:3 the name of the *p* Hormah
21:8 and *p* it upon a signal pole
22:26 stood in a narrow *p*, where
22:38 that God will *p* in my mouth
23:13 *p* from which you can see
23:27 take you to still another *p*
24:11 run your way off to your *p*
24:25 went and returned to his *p*
28:7 Pour out in the holy *p* the
32:1, 1 *p* was a *p* for livestock
32:14 in the *p* of your fathers as
32:17 have brought them to their *p*
33:2 one departure *p* to another
36:4 if the Jubilee takes *p* for the
De 1:31 until your coming to this *p*
1:33 to spy out for you a *p* for
2:12 and to dwell in their *p*, just
2:21 and dwell in their *p*
2:22 dwell in their *p* until this
2:23 they might dwell in their *p*
7:15 he will not *p* them upon you
9:7 until your coming to this *p*
10:2 you must *p* them in the ark
11:5 until your coming to this *p*
11:24 *p* on which the sole of your
12:3 their names from that *p*
12:5 the *p* that Jehovah your God
12:5 to *p* his name there
12:11 the *p* that Jehovah your God
12:13 in any other *p* you may see
12:14 *p* that Jehovah will choose
12:18 in the *p* that Jehovah your
12:21 In case the *p* that Jehovah
12:26 *p* that Jehovah will choose
14:23 in the *p* that he will choose
14:24 the *p* that Jehovah your God
14:24 will choose to *p* his name
14:25 travel to the *p* that Jehovah
15:20 *p* that Jehovah will choose
16:2 in the *p* that Jehovah will
16:6 the *p* that Jehovah your God
16:7 eating in the *p* that Jehovah
16:11 in the *p* that Jehovah your
16:15 in the *p* that Jehovah will
16:16 in the *p* that he will choose
17:8 rise and go up to the *p* that
17:10 *p* which Jehovah will choose
18:6 *p* that Jehovah will choose
21:19 and to the gate of his *p*
22:8 *p* bloodguilt upon your house
23:12 a private *p* should be at your
23:16 in whatever *p* he may choose
26:2 go to the *p* that Jehovah your
26:9 he brought us to this *p*
27:15 has put it in a hiding *p*
27:24 strikes . . . from a hiding *p*
29:7 you came to this *p*, and
31:11 in the *p* that he will choose
31:19 *P* it in their mouths in
31:26 *p* it at the side of the ark
32:22 down to Sheol, the lowest *p*
32:38 a concealment *p* for you
33:27 A hiding *p* is the God of
Jos 1:3 Every *p* upon which the sole
3:3 pull away from your *p*, and
4:3 the *p* where the priests' feet
4:3 deposit them in the lodging *p*
4:8 with them to the lodging *p*
4:9 the standing *p* of the feet of
4:18 began returning to their *p*
5:8 their *p* in the camp until
5:9 *p* came to be called Gilgal
5:15 *p* on which you are standing
7:26 the name of that *p* has been
8:9 marched to the *p* of ambush
8:19 rose up quickly from its *p*
9:27 the *p* that he should choose
10:24 *P* your feet on the back of
20:4 a *p* and he must dwell with
Jg 2:5 the name of that *p* Bochim
7:7 let them go each one to his *p*
7:21 each one in his *p* all around
8:32 in the burial *p* of Joash his
9:35 rose up from the *p* of ambush
9:55 now went each one to his *p*
11:19 your land to my own *p*
15:17 called that *p* Ramath-lehi
16:31 the burial *p* of Manoah his
17:8 wherever he might find a *p*
17:9 wherever I may find a *p*
18:3 what are you doing in this *p*
18:10 a *p* where there is no lack
18:12 called that *p* Mahaneh-dan
Jg 19:16 of the *p* were Benjamites
19:28 rose up and went to his *p*
20:22 in battle formation in the *p*
20:43 without a *p* to rest
21:5 a great oath that has taken *p*
Ru 1:7 the *p* where she had continued
2:8 not cross over from this *p*
3:4 of the *p* where he lies down
3:15 and to *p* it upon her
4:10 and from the gate of his *p*
1Sa 1:26 standing with you in this *p*
2:20 in *p* of the thing lent, that
2:20 And they went to their *p*
3:2 Eli was lying in his *p*, and
3:9 went and lay down in his *p*
5:3 and returned him to his *p*
5:11 that it may return to its *p*
6:2 should send it away to its *p*
6:8 and *p* it on the wagon, and
9:11 Is the seer in this *p*?
9:12 for the people on the high *p*
9:13 goes up to the high *p* to eat
9:14 to go up to the high *p*
9:19 up before me to the high *p*
9:22 gave them a *p* at the head of
9:25 went down from the high *p*
10:5 coming down from the high *p*
10:13 and came to the high *p*
11:9 salvation will take *p* for
12:8 them to dwell in this *p*
14:34 the slaughtering in this *p*
14:46 went to their *p*
17:40 to *p* them in his shepherds'
19:13 put at the *p* of his head
19:16 goats' hair at the *p*
20:19 *p* where you concealed
20:25 but David's *p* was vacant
20:27 David's *p* continued vacant
20:35 field of David's appointed *p*
20:37 *p* of the arrow that
21:2 men for such and such a *p*
21:6 fresh bread there on the
22:4 to be in the inaccessible *p*
22:5 in the inaccessible *p*
22:6 on the high *p* with his spear
23:22 *p* where his foot comes to
23:28 *p* the Crag of the Divisions
24:22 the *p* difficult to approach
26:5 *p* where Saul had encamped
26:5 *p* where Saul had lain down
26:12 *p* at Saul's head, and then
26:25 Saul, he returned to his *p*
27:5 *p* in one of the cities of
29:4 *p* where you assigned him
2Sa 2:16 that *p* came to be called
2:23 *p* where Asahel fell and then
2:32 the burial *p* of his father
3:32 weep at Abner's burial *p*
4:12 burial *p* of Abner in Hebron
5:17 to the *p* hard to approach
5:20 name of that *p* Baal-perazim
6:8 *p* came to be called
6:17 in its *p* inside the tent
7:10 appoint a *p* for my people
11:16 Uriah put in the *p* where
13:35 servant so it has taken *p*
15:19 are an exile from your *p*
15:21 in the *p* where my lord the
15:25 see it and its abiding *p*
16:8 in *p* of whom you have ruled
17:9 A defeat has taken *p* among
17:23 burial *p* of his forefathers
17:25 *p* of Joab over the army
18:1 and to *p* over them chiefs
19:37 the burial *p* of my father
19:39 he returned to his *p*
21:14 in the burial *p* of Kish his
22:3 my *p* for flight, my Savior
22:20 out into a roomy *p*
23:14 in the *p* hard to approach
1Ki 1:30 upon my throne in *p* of me
1:35 will be king in *p* of me, and
2:35 in *p* of him over the army
2:35 king put in the *p* of Abiathar
2:36 go out from there to this *p*
3:4 for that was the great high *p*
3:7 king in the *p* of David my
4:28 the *p* might prove to be
5:1 as king in *p* of his father
5:5 upon your throne in *p* of you
5:9 the *p* that you will send me
8:6 covenant of Jehovah to its *p*
8:7 wings over the *p* of the Ark
8:10 came out from the holy *p*

1Ki 8:13 *p* for you to dwell in to
8:20 rise up in the *p* of David
8:21 locate a *p* there for the Ark
8:29 toward the *p* of which you
8:29 servant prays toward this *p*
8:30 they pray toward this *p*
8:30 at the *p* of your dwelling
8:35 pray toward this *p* and laud
8:39 established *p* of dwelling
8:43 established *p* of dwelling
8:49 established *p* of dwelling
10:19 by the *p* of sitting, and
11:7 to build a high *p* to Chemosh
11:11 has taken *p* with you and
11:43 began to reign in *p* of him
12:15 took *p* at the instance of
13:8 or drink water in this *p*
13:16 water with you in this *p*
13:22 the *p* about which he spoke
13:22 burial *p* of your forefathers
13:30 body in his own burial *p*
13:31 bury me in the burial *p* in
13:32 of Samaria will take *p*
14:13 will come into a burial *p*
14:20 son began to reign in *p* of
14:27 in *p* of them copper shields
14:30 took *p* between Rehoboam and
14:31 son began to reign in *p* of
15:6 And warfare itself took *p*
15:7 took *p* between Abijam and
15:8 son began to reign in *p* of
15:16 And warfare itself took *p*
15:24 began to reign in *p* of him
15:28 began to reign in *p* of him
15:32 warfare itself took *p*
16:6 began to reign in *p* of him
16:10 began to reign in *p* of him
16:28 began to reign in *p* of him
18:23 must *p* it upon the wood
19:16 as prophet in *p* of you
20:24 kings each one from his *p*
20:39 to take the *p* of his soul
20:42 take the *p* of his soul
20:42 and your people the *p* of his
21:2 in *p* of it a vineyard better
21:6 another vineyard in *p* of it
21:19 In the *p* where the dogs
22:40 Ahaziah . . . reign in *p* of him
22:50 Jehoram . . . reign in *p* of him
2Ki 1:17 began to reign in *p* of him
3:27 going to reign in *p* of him
4:29 *p* my staff upon the face of
5:11 to and fro over the *p* and
6:1 the *p* where we are dwelling
6:2 there a *p* in which to dwell
6:6 So he showed him the *p*
6:8 At such and such a *p* you will
6:9 against passing by this *p*
6:10 king of Israel sent to the *p*
7:2 could this thing take *p*?
7:19 could it take *p* according to
8:15 Hazael began to reign in *p* of
8:24 Ahaziah . . . reign in *p* of
10:35 Jehoahaz . . . reign in *p* of
12:21 Amaziah . . . reign in *p* of
13:9 Jehoash . . . reign in *p* of
13:21 man into Elisha's burial *p*
13:24 Ben-hadad . . . reign in *p* of
14:16 Jeroboam . . . reign in *p* of
14:21 in *p* of his father Amaziah
14:29 Zechariah . . . reign in *p* of
15:7 Jotham . . . reign in *p* of him
15:10 began to reign in *p* of him
15:14 began to reign in *p* of him
15:22 Pekahiah . . . reign in *p* of
15:25 Pekah . . . to reign in *p* of
15:30 began to reign in *p* of him
15:38 Ahaz . . . reign in *p* of him
16:20 Hezekiah . . . reign in *p* of
18:25 against this *p* to bring it
19:23 enter its final lodging *p*
19:37 Esar-haddon . . . reign in *p*
20:21 Manasseh . . . to reign in *p*
21:18 Amon . . . reign in *p* of him
21:24 Josiah his son king in *p* of
21:26 Josiah . . . reign in *p* of
22:16 calamity upon this *p* and
22:17 set afire against this *p* and
22:19 I have spoken against this *p*
22:20 I am bringing upon this *p*
23:6 burial *p* of the sons of the
23:15 the high *p* that Jeroboam
23:15 that altar and the high *p*
23:15 Then he burned the high *p*
2Ki 23:17 burial *p* of the man of the
23:30 king in *p* of his father
23:34 king in *p* of Josiah his
24:3 it took *p* against Judah
24:6 Jehoiachin . . . reign in *p* of
24:17 his uncle king in *p* of him
24:20 it took *p* in Jerusalem and
1Ch 1:44 Jobab . . . reign in *p* of him
1:45 Husham . . . reign in *p* of him
1:46 Hadad . . . reign in *p* of him
1:47 Samlah . . . reign in *p* of him
1:48 Shaul . . . reign in *p* of him
1:49 Baal-hanan . . . reign in *p* of
1:50 Hadad began to reign in *p* of
4:41 began to dwell in their *p*
5:22 to dwell in their *p* down to
11:7 the *p* difficult to approach
11:16 in the *p* hard to approach
12:8 the *p* difficult to approach
12:16 the *p* difficult to approach
13:11 that *p* came to be called
14:11 name of that *p* Baal-perazim
15:1 to prepare a *p* for the ark of
15:3 *p* that he had prepared for it
15:12 the *p* that I have prepared
16:27 and joy are at his *p*
16:39 high *p* that was at Gibeon
17:9 a *p* for my people Israel
19:1 began to reign in *p* of him
21:22 the *p* of the threshing floor
21:25 David gave Ornan for the *p*
21:29 on the high *p* at Gibeon
23:32 the guarding of the holy *p*
24:5 chiefs of the holy *p* and
29:23 as king in *p* of David his
29:28 began to reign in *p* of him
2Ch 1:3 the high *p* that was at Gibeon
1:4 the *p* that David had prepared
1:8 made me king in *p* of him
1:13 high *p* that was at Gibeon
3:1 *p* that David had prepared on
5:7 brought the ark . . . into its *p*
5:8 wings over the *p* of the Ark
5:11 came out from the holy *p*
6:2 an established *p* for you to
6:10 in the *p* of David my father
6:11 that I might *p* there the ark
6:20 *p* where you said you would
6:20 servant prays toward this *p*
6:21 they pray toward this *p*
6:21 *p* of your dwelling, from
6:26 pray toward this *p* and laud
6:30 heavens, the *p* of your
6:33 established *p* of dwelling
6:39 established *p* of dwelling
6:40 prayer respecting this *p*
7:12 chosen this *p* for myself as
7:15 attentive to prayer at this *p*
9:18 side by the *p* of sitting
9:31 Rehoboam . . . reign in *p* of
12:10 in their *p* copper shields
12:16 Abijah . . . reign in *p* of
13:2 war itself took *p* between
14:1 Asa . . . reign in *p* of him
16:14 grand burial *p* that he had
17:1 Jehoshaphat . . . reign in *p*
19:10 take *p* against you and
20:26 *p* Low Plain of Beracah
21:1 Jehoram . . . in *p* of him
22:1 Ahaziah . . . king in *p* of him
24:11 returned it to its *p*
24:27 Amaziah . . . reign in *p* of
25:10 to go to their own *p*
25:10 to their own *p* in the heat
26:1 Uzziah . . . king in *p* of his
26:23 Jotham . . . reign in *p* of
27:9 Ahaz . . . reign in *p* of him
28:27 Hezekiah . . . reign in *p* of
29:4 to the open *p* to the east
29:5 thing out from the holy *p*
29:7 offer up in the holy *p* to
30:8 Give *p* to Jehovah and come
30:16 kept standing at their *p*
32:33 Manasseh . . . reign in *p* of
33:20 Amon . . . reign in *p* of him
33:25 Josiah . . . king in *p* of him
34:24 this *p* and its inhabitants
34:25 may pour forth upon this *p*
34:27 this *p* and its inhabitants
34:28 this *p* and its inhabitants
34:31 king kept standing in his *p*
35:5 stand in the holy *p* by the
36:1 king in the *p* of his father
36:8 Jehoiachin . . . reign in *p* of
Ezr 1:4 men of his *p* assist him with
5:8 with stones rolled into *p*
5:15 house . . . rebuilt upon its *p*
6:2 the fortified *p* that was in
6:3 *p* where they are to offer
6:4 layers of stones rolled into *p*
6:5 is in Jerusalem at its *p* and
6:7 that house of God upon its *p*
8:17 head one in the *p* Casiphia
8:17 Nethinim in the *p* Casiphia
9:8 giving us a peg in his holy *p*
10:9 kept sitting in the open *p* of
Ne 1:9 the *p* that I have chosen to
2:14 no *p* for the domestic animal
4:13 *p* behind the wall at the open
4:20 *p* where you hear the sound
9:3 Then they rose up at their *p*
13:11 them at their standing *p*
Es 2:9 the best *p* of the house of the
4:14 for the Jews from another *p*
8:2 *p* Mordecai over the house of
Job 2:11 each one from his own *p*
3:22 because they find a burial *p*
5:3 to execrate his abiding *p*
5:11 who are low on a high *p*
5:26 in vigor to the burial *p*
6:17 are dried up from their *p*
6:18 into the empty *p* and perish
6:20 have come clear to the *p* and
7:10 his *p* will not acknowledge
8:6 your righteous abiding *p*
8:11 tall without a swampy *p*
8:18 swallows him up from his *p*
9:6 earth go quaking from its *p*
10:19 the belly to the burial *p*
11:20 *p* for flight will certainly
12:24 wander about in an empty *p*
13:14 *p* my own soul in my palm
14:18 be moved away from its *p*
16:18 to be no *p* for my outcry
18:4 a rock move away from its *p*
18:15 upon his own abiding *p*
18:19 in his *p* of alien residence
18:21 *p* of one that has not known
20:9 no more will his *p* behold
22:14 Clouds are a concealment *p*
23:3 come clear to his fixed *p*
26:6 the *p* of destruction has no
26:7 the north over the empty *p*
27:21 whirl him away from his *p*
27:23 whistle at him from his *p*
28:1 there exists a *p* to find it
28:1 a *p* for gold that they refine
28:6 are the *p* of the sapphire
28:12 the *p* of understanding
28:20 the *p* of understanding
28:23 he himself has known its *p*
30:1 *p* with the dogs of my flock
34:26 In the *p* of onlookers
36:16 will be in its *p*, And the
37:1 And it leaps up from its *p*
38:12 the dawn to know its *p*
38:19 where, now, is its *p*
39:28 and an inaccessible *p*
40:13 faces in the hidden *p*
40:21 the concealed *p* of reeds and
40:21 reeds and the swampy *p*
Ps 5:9 throat is an opened burial *p*
10:9 in the concealed *p* like a lion
18:11 darkness his concealment *p*
18:19 bring me out into a roomy *p*
20:2 your help out of the holy *p*
21:3 *p* on his head a crown of
24:3 may rise up in his holy *p*
26:8 the *p* of the residing of your
26:12 certainly stand on a level *p*
27:5 in the secret *p* of his tent
28:2 innermost room of your holy *p*
31:8 my feet stand in a roomy *p*
31:20 the secret *p* of your person
32:7 You are a *p* of concealment
33:14 *p* where he dwells
37:10 give attention to his *p*, and
44:19 in the *p* of jackals
45:16 In *p* of your forefathers
55:8 hasten to a *p* of escape for
59:16 a *p* to which to flee in the
63:2 beheld you in the holy *p*
65:4 The holy *p* of your temple
68:17 from Sinai into the holy *p*
68:24 my King, into the holy *p*
73:18 ground is where you *p* them
74:3 treated badly in the holy *p*
74:4 the middle of your meeting *p*

Ps 76:2 And his dwelling *p* in Zion
77:13 your way is in the holy *p*
79:7 abiding *p* to be desolated
81:7 in the concealed *p* of thunder
86:13 out of Sheol, its lowest *p*
88:5 ones lying in the burial *p*
88:11 declared in the burial *p*
88:11 in the *p* of destruction
88:18 acquaintances are a dark *p*
89:14 established *p* of your throne
89:27 shall *p* him as firstborn
91:1 the secret *p* of the Most High
97:2 established *p* of his throne
103:16 *p* will acknowledge it no
104:8 *p* that you have founded for
107:40 about in a featureless *p*
110:1 I *p* your enemies as a stool
114:2 Judah became his holy *p*
118:5 and put me into a roomy *p*
119:45 walk about in a roomy *p*
119:114 *p* of concealment and my
132:5 Until I find a *p* for Jehovah
139:5 And you *p* your hand upon me
142:4 *p* for flight has perished
150:1 Praise God in his holy *p*
Pr 3:33 abiding *p* of the righteous
15:3 eyes of Jehovah are in every *p*
15:11 the *p* of destruction are in
21:18 takes the *p* of the upright
24:15 abiding *p* of the righteous
25:6 *p* of great ones do not stand
27:8 man fleeing away from his *p*
27:20 and the *p* of destruction
Ec 1:5 sun . . . panting to its *p*
1:7 *p* where the winter torrents
3:16 *p* of justice where there was
3:16 the *p* of righteousness where
3:20 All are going to one *p*
4:15 stands up in the other one's *p*
6:6 one *p* that everyone is going
8:10 go away from the holy *p*
9:10 Sheol, the *p* to which you are
10:4 do not leave your own *p*, for
11:3 in the *p* where the tree falls
Ca 2:14 concealed *p* of the steep way
8:6 *P* me as a seal upon your heart
Isa 4:5 established *p* of Mount Zion
4:5 *p* a cloud by day and a smoke
4:6 hiding *p* from the rainstorm
5:5 destined for a *p* of trampling
7:7 stand, neither will it take *p*
7:23 *p* where there used to be a
7:25 *p* for letting bulls loose
8:14 he must become as a sacred *p*
10:6 trampling *p* like the clay of
10:29 *p* for them to spend the
13:13 rock out of its *p* at the
14:2 bring them to their own *p*
14:19 without a burial *p* for you
15:9 I shall *p* additional things
16:4 *p* of concealment to them
16:12 made weary upon the high *p*
17:9 *p* left entirely in the
18:4 look upon my established *p*
18:7 *p* of the name of Jehovah of
22:16 yourself here a burial *p*
22:16 hewing out his burial *p*
22:23 in as a peg in a lasting *p*
22:25 driven in a lasting *p*
23:1 from being a *p* to enter in
25:10 be trodden down in its *p*
25:10 trodden down in a manure *p*
26:21 his *p* to call to account
28:8 vomit—there is no *p* without
28:12 And this is the *p* of ease
28:17 the very *p* of concealment
28:18 become for it a trampling *p*
28:25 barley in the appointed *p*
29:15 have occurred in a dark *p*
30:14 skim water from a marshy *p*
32:2 hiding *p* from the wind and
32:2 *p* of concealment from the
32:18 in a peaceful abiding *p*
33:20 undisturbed abiding *p*, a
33:21 *p* of rivers, of wide canals
34:13 an abiding *p* of jackals
34:17 apportioned the *p* to them
35:7 In the abiding *p* of jackals
37:38 Esar-haddon . . . reign in *p*
41:19 I shall *p* the juniper tree
42:16 dark *p* before them into
43:3 Ethiopia and Seba in *p* of you
43:4 shall give men in *p* of you
43:4 groups in *p* of your soul
Isa 43:9 collected together at one *p*
43:28 the princes of the holy *p*
44:3 streams upon the dry *p*
45:19 In a *p* of concealment I
45:19 in a dark *p* of the earth
46:7 deposit it in its *p* that it
46:7 standing *p* it does not move
48:16 I have spoken in no *p* of
49:20 *p* has become too cramped
53:9 make his burial *p* even with
54:2 *p* of your tent more spacious
55:10 does not return to that *p*
57:15 holy *p* is where I reside
60:13 the *p* of my sanctuary
60:13 the very *p* of my feet
65:20 a few days old from that *p*
66:1 *p* as a resting-place for me
Jer 1:15 *p* each one his throne at the
3:19 to *p* you among the sons and
4:7 he has gone forth from his *p*
5:16 is like an open burial *p*
7:3 you people residing in this *p*
7:6 you will not shed in this *p*
7:7 keep you residing in this *p*
7:12 to my *p* that was in Shiloh
7:14 to the *p* that I gave to you
7:20 poured forth upon this *p*
7:32 there being enough *p*
7:34 nothing but a devastated *p*
9:2 a lodging *p* of travelers
10:25 his abiding *p* they have
13:7 the *p* in which I had hid it
13:18 in a lower *p*
14:13 I shall give you in this *p*
16:2 sons and daughters in this *p*
16:3 that are born in this *p*
16:9 to cease out of this *p*
16:19 my *p* for flight in the day
17:12 the *p* of our sanctuary
19:3 a calamity upon this *p*
19:4 make this *p* unrecognizable
19:4 filled this *p* with the blood
19:6 this *p* will be called no
19:7 of Jerusalem in this *p*
19:11 there is no more *p* to bury
19:12 how I shall do to this *p*
19:13 like the *p* of Topheth
20:17 become to me my burial *p*
22:3 any innocent blood in this *p*
22:5 become a mere devastated *p*
22:11 has gone forth from this *p*
22:12 the *p* where they have taken
24:5 send away from this *p* to
25:11 must become a devastated *p*
25:18 make them a devastated *p*
25:30 roar upon his abiding *p*
25:35 a *p* to flee to has perished
27:17 city become a devastated *p*
27:22 restore them to this *p*
28:3 I am bringing back to this *p*
28:3 took from this *p* that he
28:4 I am bringing back to this *p*
28:6 from Babylon to this *p*
29:10 bringing you back to this *p*
29:14 back to the *p* from which I
31:21 *P* signposts for yourself
31:23 O righteous dwelling *p*
32:37 bring them back to this *p*
33:10 *p* that you people will be
33:12 waste *p* without man and
37:1 reign in *p* of Coniah the
37:17 house in a *p* of concealment
38:10 your charge from this *p*
38:16 in the *p* of concealment
40:2 this calamity against this *p*
40:15 *p* of concealment in Mizpah
41:17 lodging *p* of Chimham that
42:18 will no more see this *p*
42:22 *p* into which you do delight
43:10 *p* his throne right above
44:2 they are a devastated *p* this
44:6 came to be a devastated *p*
44:22 came to be a devastated *p*
44:29 attention upon you in this *p*
48:35 offering upon the high *p*
49:19 to the durable abiding *p*
49:20 dwelling *p* become desolate
50:7 Jehovah the abiding *p* of
50:44 to the durable abiding *p*
50:45 abiding *p* to be desolated
51:62 have spoken against this *p*
Eze 1:3 in that *p* the hand of Jehovah
3:12 glory of Jehovah from his *p*
5:14 make you a devastated *p* and
Eze 6:13 *p* where they have offered a
7:22 profane my concealed *p*, and
8:3 where the dwelling *p* is of
10:11 *p* to which the head would
12:3 go into exile from your *p* to
12:3 another *p* before their eyes
14:8 and *p* him for a sign and for
16:34 the opposite thing takes *p*
17:16 in the *p* of the king who
20:29 What does the high *p* mean
20:29 should be called a High *P*
21:30 the *p* that you were created
25:13 make it a devastated *p* from
26:12 dust they will *p* in the
29:9 waste and a devastated *p*
31:4 all around its planting *p*
34:14 abiding *p* will come to be
34:14 in a good abiding *p*, and
35:4 shall set as a devastated *p*
37:26 *p* them and multiply them
37:26 *p* my sanctuary in the midst
38:8 a constantly devastated *p*
38:15 certainly come from your *p*
39:11 shall give to Gog a *p* there
39:11 a burial *p* in Israel, the
40:1 he brought me to that *p*
41:15 the temple and the inner *p*
41:21 in front of the holy *p*
41:23 the holy *p* had two doors
42:13 because the *p* is holy
42:14 go out from the holy *p*
43:7 *p* of my throne and the
43:7 *p* of the soles of my feet
43:21 burn it in the appointed *p*
44:27 coming into the holy *p*
44:27 to minister in the holy *p*
45:2 for the holy *p* five hundred
45:4 prove to be a *p* for houses
45:4 sacred *p* for the sanctuary
46:19 *p* there on both rear sides
46:20 *p* where the priests will
47:9 *p* to which the double-size
48:15 for a dwelling *p* and for
Da 8:11 established *p* of his sanctuary
8:13 holy *p* and the army things
8:14 holy *p* will certainly be
9:26 holy *p* the people of a leader
10:6 *p* of his feet were like the
11:31 put in *p* the disgusting
Ho 1:10 *p* in which it used to be said
2:3 *p* her as in the day of her
2:3 *p* her like a waterless land
4:16 like a young ram in a roomy *p*
5:15 I will return to my *p* until
11:8 How can I *p* you like Zeboiim?
Joe 3:7 *p* where you have sold them
3:11 To that *p*, O Jehovah, bring
3:17 must become a holy *p*
Am 2:14 And a *p* to which to flee
3:4 its voice from its hiding *p*
5:9 come upon even a fortified *p*
5:15 give justice a *p* in the gate
8:3 In every *p* one will certainly
Ob 7 will *p* a net under you as one
Mic 1:3 is going forth from his *p*
1:4 being poured down a steep *p*
1:11 you people its standing *p*
7:10 become a *p* of trampling
Na 1:8 extermination of her *p*
1:14 shall make a burial *p* for you
2:1 safeguarding of the fortified *p*
3:17 their *p* is really unknown
Hab 1:10 even at every fortified *p*
3:14 one in a *p* of concealment
Zep 1:4 cut off from this *p* the
2:9 a *p* possessed by nettles
2:11 each one from his *p*, all
2:15 a *p* for the wild animals to
Hag 2:9 in this *p* I shall give peace
Zec 1:8 trees that were in the deep *p*
5:11 there upon her proper *p*
6:12 his own *p* he will sprout
12:6 in her own *p*, in Jerusalem
14:10 become inhabited in her *p*
14:10 to the *p* of the First Gate
Mal 1:11 in every *p* sacrificial smoke
Mt 5:18 and not all things take *p*
6:10 Let your will take *p*, as in
9:24 Leave the *p*, for the little
11:20 powerful works had taken *p*
11:21 powerful works had taken *p*
11:21 that took *p* in you, they
11:23 powerful works that took *p*
11:23 taken *p* in Sodom, it would

Mt 12:9 After departing from that p
14:13 a lonely p for isolation
14:15 The p is lonely and the hour
14:35 the men of that p sent forth
15:33 we in this lonely p going to
18:19 it will take p for them due
21:4 actually took p that there
23:6 like the most prominent p
24:6 these things must take p, but
24:7 earthquakes in one p after
24:15 standing in a holy p, (let
26:42 let your will take p
26:52 Return your sword to its p
26:54 it must take p this way
26:56 all this has taken p for the
27:33 to a p called Gol′go·tha
27:33 that is to say, Skull P
28:2 great earthquake had taken p
28:6 see the p where he was lying
Mr 1:35 and left for a lonely p, and
4:5 seed fell upon the rocky p
6:10 until you go out of that p
6:11 a p will not receive you nor
6:31 into a lonely p and rest up
6:32 for a lonely p to themselves
6:35 The p is isolated, and the
6:41 p them before the people
6:56 they would p the sick ones
8:4 anybody here in an isolated p
13:7 these things must take p
13:8 earthquakes in one p after
14:4 Why has this waste . . . taken p?
15:22 to the p Golgotha, which
15:22 when translated, Skull P
16:6 The p where they laid him
Lu 1:20 day that these things take p
1:38 May it take p with me
2:2 first registration took p when
2:7 no p for them in the lodging
2:15 this thing that has taken p
4:17 the p where it was written
4:42 and proceeded to a lonely p
5:18 bring him in and p him before
6:17 took his station on a level p
9:12 out here we are in a lonely p
10:1 into every city and p to
10:13 works that have taken p in
10:13 taken p in Tyre and Sidon
10:32 down to the p and saw him
11:1 being in a certain p praying
14:8 in the most prominent p
14:9 Let this man have the p
14:9 to occupy the lowest p
14:10 and recline in the lowest p
16:28 get into this p of torment
19:5 when Jesus got to the p, he
20:43 p your enemies as a stool
21:11 and in one p after another
22:40 Having come to the p he said
22:42 my will, but yours take p
23:33 got to the p called Skull
Joh 1:28 took p in Bethany across
2:1 marriage . . . took p in Cana
4:15 over to this p to draw water
4:16 husband and come to this p
4:20 the p where persons ought to
5:13 there being a crowd in the p
6:10 was a lot of grass in the p
6:23 p where they ate the bread
10:1 climbs up some other p
10:8 come in p of me are thieves
10:22 dedication took p in
10:40 p where John was baptizing
11:6 days in the p where he was
11:30 p where Martha met him
11:48 both our p and our nation
14:2 way to prepare a p for you
14:3 way and prepare a p for you
15:7 and it will take p for you
16:9 the first p, concerning sin
18:2 betrayer, also knew the p
19:13 p called The Stone Pavement
19:17 to the so-called Skull P
19:20 p where Jesus was impaled
19:36 things took p in order for
19:41 p where he was impaled
20:7 rolled up in one p
Ac 1:20 lodging p become desolate
1:25 take the p of this ministry
1:25 deviated to go to his own p
2:1 all together at the same p
2:35 p your enemies as a stool for
4:5 took p in Jerusalem the
4:31 p in which they were gathered
Ac 5:18 in the public p of custody
6:13 against this holy p and
6:14 throw down this p and change
7:7 sacred service to me in this p
7:14 all his relatives from that p
7:33 p on which you are standing
7:49 what is the p for my resting?
8:13 and powerful works taking p
11:28 did take p in the time of
12:17 and journeyed to another p
14:5 violent attempt took p on the
15:7 much disputing had taken p
16:13 there was a p of prayer
16:16 going to the p of prayer, a
18:23, 23 and went from p to p
19:10 This took p for two years
21:12 we and those of that p began
21:14 the will of Jehovah take p
21:28 and the Law and this p and
21:28 and has defiled this holy p
24:2 reforms are taking p in this
25:26 examination has taken p, I
26:22 stated were going to take p
27:8 p called Fair Havens, near
28:7 in the neighborhood of that p
28:13 which p we went around and
28:23 to him in his lodging p
Ro 9:26 p where it was said to them
12:19 but yield p to the wrath
1Co 7:36 is the way it should take p
11:20 come together to one p, it
14:23 comes together to one p and
14:26 things take p for upbuilding
14:40 take p decently and by
15:54 saying will take p that is
16:2 collections will not take p
16:14 affairs take p with love
2Co 2:14 through us in every p
8:14 an equalizing might take p
Eph 2:22 a p for God to inhabit by
4:27 neither allow p for the Devil
5:12 things that take p in secret
Php 3:20 heavens, from which p also
1Th 1:8 in every p your faith toward
1Ti 2:8 I desire that in every p the
Phm 13 that in p of you he might keep
Heb 1:13 p your enemies as a stool
4:4 in one p he has said of the
4:5 again in this p: They shall
4:8 had led them into a p of rest
5:6 he says also in another p
8:2 public servant of the holy p
8:7 no p would have been sought
9:1 and its mundane holy p
9:2 and it is called the Holy P
9:8 the way into the holy p had
9:12 into the holy p and obtained
9:22 out no forgiveness takes p
9:24 a holy p made with hands
9:25 enters into the holy p from
10:19 entry into the holy p by
11:8 p he was destined to receive
11:14 seeking a p of their own
11:15 p from which they had gone
11:16 reaching out for a better p
12:17 he found no p for it
13:11 into the holy p by the high
Jas 2:3 this seat here in a fine p
2Pe 1:19 a lamp shining in a dark p
3Jo 9 likes to have the first p
Jude 6 forsook . . . proper dwelling p
Re 1:1 that must shortly take p
1:19 things that will take p after
2:5 your lampstand from its p
4:1 the things that must take p
12:6 she has a p prepared by God
12:8 p found for them any longer
12:14 into the wilderness to her p
16:16 p that is called in Hebrew
18:2 dwelling p of demons and a
18:2 lurking p of every unclean
18:2 lurking p of every unclean
20:11 no p was found for them
22:6 that must shortly take p

Placed

Ge 30:38 he p in front of the flock
41:42 p a necklace of gold about
43:22 who p our money in our bags
48:14 and p it on Ephraim's head
48:17 hand p on Ephraim's head
Ex 39:7 he p them upon the shoulder
40:19 p the covering of the tent
40:20 p the poles on the Ark and
Ex 40:24 p the lampstand in the tent
40:26 p the golden altar in the
40:29 And he p the altar of burnt
40:30 he p the basin between the
Le 8:8 p the breastpiece upon him and
8:9 he p the turban upon his head
8:9 p upon the turban at the
8:26 p them upon the fatty pieces
9:20 now p the fatty pieces upon
10:1 in them and p incense upon it
Nu 16:18 and p incense upon them and
21:9 and p it upon the signal pole
De 10:5 p the tablets in the ark that
Jos 10:24 p their feet on the back of
10:27 they p big stones at the
24:7 he p a darkness between you
1Sa 18:5 Saul p him over the men of
19:13 p it on the couch, and a net
2Sa 8:14 kept garrisons p in Edom
8:14 In all Edom he p garrisons
13:19 Tamar p ashes upon her head
19:28 you p your servant among
1Ki 2:5 and p the blood of war in
12:29 p the one in Bethel, and
18:33 p it upon the pieces of
1Ch 16:1 p it inside the tent that
2Ch 4:10 sea he p at the right side
Ps 16:8 p Jehovah in front of me
73:28 Jehovah I have p my refuge
89:19 p help upon a mighty one
Jer 11:13 p for the shameful thing
Eze 16:14 splendor that I p upon you
17:4 in a city of traders he p it
17:5 as a willow tree he p it
24:7 surface of a crag she p it
39:21 my hand that I have p among
Da 6:17 p on the mouth of the pit
7:9 thrones p and the Ancient of
Mt 8:9 am a man p under authority
Lu 7:8 am a man p under authority
23:26 p the torture stake upon him
Ac 1:7 the Father has p in his own
6:6 p them before the apostles
Ro 13:1 p in their relative positions
Heb 10:13 be p as a stool for his feet
Jude 7 are p before us as a warning

Places

Ge 23:6 choicest of our burial p
30:37 laying bare white p which
36:40 according to their p
Ex 1:11 building cities as storage p
14:11 no burial p at all in Egypt
35:3 dwelling p on the sabbath day
Le 3:17 in all your dwelling p
7:26 not eat any blood in any p
23:3 sabbath to Jehovah in all p
23:14 in all p where you dwell
23:17 p you should bring two
23:21 in all your dwelling p for
23:31 in all p where you dwell
26:30 annihilate your sacred high p
Nu 15:2 the land of your dwelling p
21:28 of the high p of the Arnon
33:2 departure p by their stages
33:52 all their sacred high p you
35:29 in all your dwelling p
De 12:2 the p where the nations whom
32:13 ride upon earth's high p
33:29 their high p you will tread
Jg 5:11 among the p of drawing water
5:17 And by his landing p he kept
6:2 underground store p that were
6:2 and the p difficult to approach
19:13 approach one of the p, and
20:33 Israel rose up from their p
20:33 a charge out of their p in
1Sa 2:8 he p upon them the productive
7:16 judged Israel at all these p
23:14 p difficult to approach
23:19 p difficult to approach at
23:23 all the hiding p where he
23:29 p difficult to approach at
30:31 p where David had walked
2Sa 1:19 is slain upon your high p
1:25 slain upon your high p
17:9 or in one of the other p
17:12 against him in one of the p
22:34 upon p high for me he keeps
1Ki 3:2 sacrificing on the high p
3:3 on the high p that he was
12:31 to make a house of high p
12:32 priests of the high p that
13:2 the priests of the high p

1Ki 13:32 the houses of the high *p*
13:33 making priests of high *p*
13:33 one of the priests of high *p*
14:23 high *p* and sacred pillars
15:14 high *p* he did not remove
22:43 the high *p* themselves did
22:43 smoke on the high *p*
2Ki 8:12 fortified *p* you will consign
12:3 high *p* that did not disappear
12:3 smoke on the high *p*
14:4 high *p* that did not disappear
14:4 smoke on the high *p*
15:4 the high *p* did not disappear
15:4 smoke on the high *p*
15:35 high *p* did not disappear
15:35 smoke on the high *p*
16:4 smoke on the high *p* and
17:9 high *p* in all their cities
17:11 on all the high *p* they
17:29 the house of the high *p*
17:32 priests of high *p*, and they
17:32 in the house of the high *p*
18:4 removed the high *p* and broke
18:22 the one whose high *p* and
21:3 built again the high *p* that
23:5 high *p* in the cities of Judah
23:8 for worship the high *p*
23:8 the high *p* of the gates
23:9 the priests of the high *p*
23:13 high *p* that were in front
23:14 their *p* with human bones
23:16 he got to see the burial *p*
23:16 the bones from the burial *p*
23:19 all the houses of the high *p*
23:20 the priests of the high *p*
1Ch 4:33 were their dwelling *p* and
6:54 their dwelling *p* by their
7:28 dwelling *p* were Bethel and
2Ch 8:11 *p* to which the ark of
11:11 reinforced the fortified *p*
11:15 priests for the high *p* and
14:3 high *p* and broke up the
14:5 high *p* and the incense stands
15:17 high *p* themselves did not
16:4 storage *p* of the cities of
17:6 removed the high *p* and the
17:12 building fortified *p* and
20:33 high *p* themselves did not
21:11 made high *p* on the
21:20 in the burial *p* of the kings
24:25 the burial *p* of the kings
27:4 built fortified *p* and
28:4 smoke on the high *p* and
28:25 made high *p* for making
28:27 burial *p* of the kings of
31:1 pull down the high *p* and
32:12 removed his high *p* and his
32:28 storage *p* for the produce
32:33 burial *p* of the sons of
33:3 high *p* that Hezekiah his
33:17 sacrificing upon the high *p*
33:19 built high *p* and set up the
34:3 from the high *p* and the
34:4 surface of the burial *p*
34:6 devastated *p* all around
35:10 kept standing at their *p*
Ezr 1:4 *p* where he is residing as an
9:9 to restore its desolated *p* and
Ne 2:3 the burial *p* of my forefathers
2:5 the burial *p* of my forefathers
3:16 front of the Burial *P* of David
4:12 come up from all the *p*
4:13 behind the wall at the open *p*
12:27 out of all their *p* to
Job 3:14 Those building desolate *p* for
28:4 *P* forgotten far from the
28:11 *p* from which rivers
37:8 in its hiding *p* it dwells
38:27 desolate *p* And to cause the
38:40 they crouch in the hiding *p*
39:6 dwelling *p* the salt country
Ps 10:8 From concealed *p* he will kill
16:6 fallen for me in pleasant *p*
17:12 lion sitting in concealed *p*
18:33 upon *p* high for me he keeps
35:6 darkness and slippery *p*
64:4 To shoot from concealed *p* at
74:8 meeting *p* of God must be
74:20 dark *p* of the earth have
78:58 with their high *p*
83:12 abiding *p* of God for
88:6 In dark *p*, in a large abyss
102:6 little owl of desolated *p*
103:22 In all *p* of his domination
Ps 104:5 earth upon its established *p*
104:22 down in their own hiding *p*
109:10 food from their desolate *p*
143:3 to dwell in dark *p* like
Pr 9:14 in the high *p* of the town
9:18 are in the low *p* of Sheol
Isa 5:17 desolate *p* of well-fed
7:19 and upon all the watering *p*
14:14 the high *p* of the clouds
15:2 to the high *p*, to a weeping
17:2 become mere *p* for droves
19:7 bare *p* by the Nile River
33:16 *p* difficult to approach
34:13 weeds in her fortified *p*
36:7 the one whose high *p* and
44:26 desolated *p* I shall raise up
45:3 in the concealment *p*
48:21 even through devastated *p*
49:19 your devastated *p* and your
49:19 desolated *p* and the land of
51:3 comfort all her devastated *p*
52:9 devastated *p* of Jerusalem
58:12 *p* devastated a long time
58:14 the high *p* of the earth
61:4 long-standing devastated *p*
61:4 desolated *p* of former times
61:4 *p* desolate for generation
65:4 among the burial *p*, who also
Jer 7:31 the high *p* of Topheth
8:3 the *p* of the remaining ones
13:17 in *p* of concealment my soul
17:3 your high *p* because of sin
17:6 parched *p* in the wilderness
19:5 the high *p* of the Baal in
23:12 slippery *p* in the gloom
23:24 man be concealed in *p* of
24:9 *p* to which I shall disperse
25:9 *p* devastated to time
25:37 the peaceful abiding *p*
26:18 for high *p* of a forest
29:14 out of all the *p* to which
32:35 built the high *p* of Baal
33:5 fill *p* with the carcasses
40:12 *p* to which they had been
45:5 *p* to which you may go
48:18 your fortified *p* to ruin
48:41 strong *p* will certainly be
49:10 his *p* of concealment
49:13 will become devastated *p* to
51:30 sitting in the strong *p*
51:51 holy *p* of the house of
La 2:2 upon any abiding *p* of Jacob
2:2 torn down the fortified *p* of
2:5 brought his fortified *p* to ruin
2:22 my *p* of alien residence all
3:6 In dark *p* he has made me sit
3:10 as a lion in *p* of concealment
Eze 6:3 certainly destroy your high *p*
6:6 In all your dwelling *p* the
6:6 high *p* . . . become desolated
6:14 in all their dwelling *p*
13:4 foxes in the devastated *p*
14:4 *p* the very stumbling block
16:16 high *p* of varied colors and
21:2 drip words toward the holy *p*
22:8 My holy *p* you have despised
22:26 keep profaning my holy *p*
26:20 *p* devastated for a long
29:10 land of Egypt devastated *p*
32:22 burial *p* are round about
32:23 burial *p* have been put in
32:25 Her burial *p* are round about
32:26 Her burial *p* are round about
33:24 of these devastated *p* are
33:27 who are in the devastated *p*
33:27 who are in the strong *p*
34:12 out of all the *p* to which
34:13 the dwelling *p* of the land
36:2 the high *p* of old time
36:4 *p* that were laid desolate
36:10 the devastated *p* themselves
36:33 *p* must be rebuilt
37:12 I am opening your burial *p*
37:12 up out of your burial *p*
37:13 when I open your burial *p*
37:13 up out of your burial *p*
37:23 *p* in which they have sinned
38:12 devastated *p* reinhabited
46:23 boiling *p* made beneath the
47:11 There are its swampy *p* and
47:11 marshy *p*, and they will not
Da 11:24 fortified *p* he will scheme
Ho 10:8 the high *p* of Beth-aven, the
Am 4:6 want of bread in all your *p*
Am 4:13 treading on earth's high *p*
7:9 the high *p* of Isaac will
Mic 1:3 tread upon earth's high *p*
1:5 what are the high *p* of Judah?
1:6 the planting *p* of a vineyard
3:12 as the high *p* of a forest
5:11 all your fortified *p*
Na 2:12 his hiding *p* with animals
3:12 your fortified *p* are as fig
3:14 Strengthen your fortified *p*
Hab 1:6 to the wide-open *p* of earth
3:19 high *p* he will cause me to
Zec 10:9 in the distant *p* they will
Mal 1:4 and build the devastated *p*
Mt 12:43 passes through parched *p* in
13:5 Others fell upon the rocky *p*
13:20 one sown upon the rocky *p*
Mr 1:45 continued outside in lonely *p*
4:16 ones sown upon the rocky *p*
12:39 prominent *p* at evening
Lu 3:5 and the rough *p* smooth ways
8:29 driven . . . into the lonely *p*
11:24 it passes through parched *p*
14:7 choosing the most prominent *p*
14:23 roads and the fenced-in *p*
16:9 the everlasting dwelling *p*
19:38 and glory in the highest *p*
20:46 prominent *p* at evening meals
21:21 those in the country *p* not
Ac 16:3 the Jews that were in those *p*
24:3 also in all *p* we receive it
27:2 sail to *p* along the coast of
Eph 1:3 in the heavenly *p* in union
1:20 right hand in the heavenly *p*
2:6 together in the heavenly *p* in
3:10 authorities in the heavenly *p*
6:12 forces in the heavenly *p*
Heb 1:3 of the Majesty in lofty *p*
Re 6:14 were removed from their *p*

Placing

Ex 40:18 and *p* its panel frames and
Nu 11:11 *p* the load of all this people
Job 22:24 a *p* of precious ore in the
Da 12:11 *p* of the disgusting thing
Ob 4 there were a *p* of your nest
Hag 2:15 the *p* of a stone upon a stone

Plague

Ex 10:17 this deadly *p* from upon me
11:1 One *p* more I am going to
12:13 the *p* will not come on you
12:23 to *p* the Egyptians and does
12:23 enter into your houses to *p*
30:12 come to be no *p* upon them
Le 13:2 into the *p* of leprosy, he
13:3 *p* in the skin of the flesh
13:3 the hair in the *p* has turned
13:3 the *p* is deeper than the skin
13:3 it is the *p* of leprosy
13:4 quarantine the *p* seven days
13:5 the way it looks the *p* has
13:5 *p* has not spread in the skin
13:6 if the *p* has grown dull and
13:6 *p* has not spread in the skin
13:9 *p* of leprosy develops in a
13:12 skin of the one with the *p*
13:13 then pronounce the *p* clean
13:17 *p* has been changed to white
13:17 then pronounce the *p* clean
13:20 It is the *p* of leprosy
13:22 him unclean. It is a *p*
13:25 It is the *p* of leprosy
13:27 It is the *p* of leprosy
13:29 in case a *p* develops in such
13:30 priest must then see the *p*
13:31 *p* of abnormal falling off of
13:31 *p* of abnormal falling off of
13:32 at the *p* on the seventh day
13:42 *p* develops in the baldness of
13:43 *p* in the baldness of his
13:44 His *p* is on his head
13:45 leprous one in whom the *p* is
13:46 days that the *p* is in him he
13:47 *p* of leprosy develops in it
13:49 reddish *p* does develop in the
13:49 is the *p* of leprosy, and it
13:50 priest must see the *p*, and
13:50 quarantine the *p* seven days
13:51 seen the *p* on the seventh day
13:51 that the *p* has spread in the
13:51 the *p* is malignant leprosy
13:52 in which the *p* may develop
13:53 the *p* has not spread in the
13:54 wash that in which the *p* is

Job 8:11 papyrus *p* grow tall without
14:9 produce a bough like a new *p*
39:8 every . . . green *p* it seeks
Ps 44:2 And you proceeded to *p* them
69:21 they gave me a poisonous *p*
80:8 that you might *p* it
107:37 sow fields and *p* vineyards
Ec 3:2 time to *p* and a time to uproot
Isa 5:2 *p* it with a choice red vine
17:10 you *p* pleasant plantations
37:30 *p* vineyards and eat their
51:16 in order to *p* the heavens
65:21 *p* vineyards and eat their
65:22 not *p* and someone else do
Jer 1:10 to build and to *p*
18:9 build it up and to *p* it
24:6 I will *p* them, and I shall
29:5 *p* gardens and eat their
29:28 *p* gardens and eat their
31:5 *p* vineyards in the mountains
31:5 *p* and start to use them
31:28 build up and to *p*, is the
32:41 *p* them in this land in
35:7 no vineyard must you *p*, nor
42:10 and I will *p* you and I
La 3:5 encircle me with poisonous *p*
3:19 wormwood and the poisonous *p*
Eze 28:26 houses and *p* vineyards, and
Da 11:45 *p* his palatial tents between
Ho 10:4 sprouted like a poisonous *p*
Am 6:12 into a poisonous *p* you people
9:14 *p* vineyards and drink the
9:15 *p* them upon their ground
Jon 4:6 God appointed a bottle-gourd *p*
4:6 over the bottle-gourd *p*
4:7 strike the bottle-gourd *p*
4:9 anger over the bottle-gourd *p*
4:10 sorry for the bottle-gourd *p*
Zep 1:13 and they will *p* vineyards
Mt 15:13 *p* that my heavenly Father
15:13 my heavenly Father did not *p*

Plantation
Isa 5:7 the *p* of which he was fond
17:11 fence about the *p* of yours

Plantations
Isa 17:10 why you plant pleasant *p*

Planted
Ge 2:8 Jehovah God *p* a garden in Eden
21:33 that he *p* a tamarisk tree at
Nu 24:6 aloe plants that Jehovah has *p*
De 20:6 *p* a vineyard and not begun to
Ps 1:3 a tree *p* by streams of water
80:15 that your right hand has *p*
92:13 *p* in the house of Jehovah
104:16 cedars of Lebanon that he *p*
Pr 31:16 hands she has *p* a vineyard
Ec 2:4 I *p* vineyards for myself
2:5 I *p* in them fruit trees of all
3:2 a time to uproot what was *p*
Isa 40:24 Never yet have they been *p*
44:14 He *p* the laurel tree, and
Jer 2:21 I had *p* you as a choice red
12:2 You have *p* them; they have
17:8 like a tree *p* by the waters
45:4 I have *p* I am uprooting
Eze 17:7 garden beds where it was *p*
19:10 in your blood, *p* by waters
19:13 she is *p* in the wilderness
36:36 *p* what has been laid
Ho 9:13 like Tyre *p* in a pasture
Am 5:11 vineyards you have *p*
Mt 13:31 man took and *p* in his field
21:33 *p* a vineyard and put a fence
Mr 12:1 A man *p* a vineyard, and put
Lu 13:6 a fig tree *p* in his vineyard
17:6 Be uprooted and *p* in the sea!
20:9 A man *p* a vineyard and let
1Co 3:6 I *p*, Apollos watered, but God

Planter
Jer 11:17 the *P* of you, has spoken

Planters
Jer 31:5 *p* will certainly plant and

Planting
Ps 94:9 One *p* the ear, can he not
Isa 60:21 the sprout of my *p*, the
61:3 the *p* of Jehovah, for him
Eze 31:4 all around its *p* place
34:29 a *p* for a name, and they
Mic 1:6 the *p* places of a vineyard
Lu 17:28 were *p*, they were building

Plants
Ge 19:25 cities and the *p* of the ground
Nu 24:6 Like aloe *p* that Jehovah has
Ps 144:12 sons are like little *p*
Ca 4:13 henna *p* along with spikenard
4:13 along with spikenard *p*
6:2 to the garden beds of spice *p*
7:11 lodge among the henna *p*
Isa 7:25 cleared of troublesome *p*
35:7 with reeds and papyrus *p*
Ho 13:15 as the son of reed *p*
1Co 3:7 neither is he that *p* anything
3:8 he that *p* and he that waters
9:7 Who *p* a vineyard and does not

Plaster
Da 5:5 *p* of the wall of the palace of

Plastered
Le 14:42 he must have the house *p*
14:43 cut off the house and *p* it
14:48 after having *p* the house, the
Eze 13:14 men have *p* with whitewash
22:28 *p* for them with whitewash

Plastering
Eze 13:10 those *p* it with whitewash
13:11 to those *p* with whitewash
13:12 with which you did the *p*
13:15 those *p* it with whitewash
13:15 and those *p* it are no more

Plate
Ex 28:36 a shining *p* of pure gold and
39:30 they made the shining *p*, the
Le 8:9 of it the shining *p* of gold
Ca 5:14 His abdomen is an ivory *p*

Plates
Ex 39:3 beat *p* of gold to thin sheets
Nu 16:38 make them into thin metal *p*
1Ki 7:36 engraved upon the *p* of
Jer 10:9 Silver beaten into *p* is what

Platform
2Ch 6:13 had made a *p* of copper and
Ne 9:4 on the *p* of the Levites and
Eze 41:8 a high *p* for the house all
Zep 1:9 climbing upon the *p* in that

Platter
Mt 14:8 upon a *p* the head of John the
14:11 his head was brought on a *p*
Mr 6:25 on a *p* the head of John the
6:28 brought his head on a *p*

Play
Ge 19:9 he would actually *p* the judge
Nu 16:13 try to *p* the prince over us
1Sa 16:16 have to *p* with his hand
2Sa 13:5 down on your bed and *p* sick
1Ch 15:19 copper cymbals to *p* aloud
Job 40:20 wild beasts . . . *p* there
41:5 *p* with it as with a bird
Ps 104:26 you have formed to *p* about
Isa 11:8 *p* upon the hole of the cobra
38:20 *p* my string selections
Ac 5:3 *p* false to the holy spirit and

Played
Ge 38:24 Tamar . . . has *p* the harlot
1Sa 16:23 David took the harp and *p*
2Sa 13:6 Amnon lay down and *p* sick
2Ki 3:15 string-instrument player *p*
Mt 11:17 We *p* the flute for you, but
Lu 7:32 We *p* the flute for you, but
Ac 5:4 You have *p* false, not to men
1Co 14:7 *p* on the flute or on the harp

Player
2Ki 3:15 a string-instrument *p*
3:15 string-instrument *p* played

Players
Ps 68:25 *p* on stringed instruments
Mt 9:23 caught sight of the flute *p*

Playing
Jg 9:22 Abimelech kept *p* the prince
11:34 tambourine *p* and dancing
1Sa 16:16 skilled man *p* upon the harp
16:17 a man doing well at *p*, and
16:18 skilled at *p*, and he is a
18:10 David was *p* music with his
19:9 David was *p* music with his
1Ki 1:40 the people were *p* on flutes
1Ch 15:16 *p* aloud to cause a sound of
15:28 *p* aloud on stringed
16:5 with the cymbals *p* aloud
Ps 33:3 your best at *p* on the strings
Isa 23:16 best at *p* on the strings
Jer 15:17 group of those *p* jokes and
Eze 33:32 and *p* a stringed instrument
Zec 8:5 girls *p* in her public squares
Re 14:2 *p* on their harps

Playmates
Mt 11:16 who cry out to their *p*

Plead
Ru 1:16 not *p* with me to abandon you
Ps 54:1 may you *p* my cause
72:2 *p* the cause of your people
96:10 *p* the cause of the peoples
135:14 Jehovah will *p* the cause
Pr 22:23 Jehovah himself will *p* their
23:11 will *p* their cause with you
25:9 *P* your own cause with your
31:9 *p* the cause of the afflicted
Ec 6:10 not able to *p* his cause with
Isa 1:17 *p* the cause of the widow
Mr 6:56 they would *p* with him that
Heb 7:25 always alive to *p* for them

Pleaded
Jer 5:28 No legal case have they *p*
22:16 He *p* the legal claim of
36:25 *p* with the king not to

Pleading
Jer 30:13 There is no one *p* your cause
Ac 19:31 began *p* for him not to risk
Ro 8:27 *p* in accord with God for

Pleadings
Job 13:6 *p* of my lips pay attention

Pleads
Job 36:31 he *p* the cause of peoples
Ro 8:26 spirit itself *p* for us with
8:34 Christ . . . who also *p* for us
11:2 he *p* with God against Israel

Pleasant
Ge 49:15 the land is *p*; and he will
2Sa 1:23 *p* ones during their life
1:26 Jonathan, Very *p* you were to
23:1 the *p* one of the melodies
Ps 16:6 fallen for me in *p* places
81:2 *p* harp together with the
133:1 How good and how *p* it is
135:3 to his name, for it is *p*
141:6 sayings, that they are *p*
147:1 it is *p*—praise is fitting
Pr 2:10 knowledge itself becomes *p*
9:17 eaten in secrecy—it is *p*
15:26 but *p* sayings are clean
16:24 *P* sayings are a honeycomb
22:18 *p* that you should keep them
23:8 have wasted your *p* words
24:4 precious and *p* things of value
24:25 reproving him it will be *p*
Ca 1:16 my dear one, also *p*
6:4 companion of mine, like *P* City
7:6 how *p* you are, O beloved girl
Isa 17:10 you plant *p* plantations
Jer 51:34 abdomen with my *p* things
La 4:5 ones that were eating *p* things
Eze 32:19 with whom are you more *p*

Pleasantness
Job 36:11 And their years in *p*
Ps 16:11 *p* at your right hand forever
27:4 To behold the *p* of Jehovah
90:17 *p* of Jehovah our God prove
Pr 3:17 Its ways are ways of *p*
Zec 11:7 The one I called *P*, and the
11:10 I took my staff *P* and cut

Please
Ge 12:11 *P*, now! I well know you are
12:13 *P* say you are my sister, in
13:8 *P*, do not let any quarreling
13:9 *P*, separate from me. If you
13:14 Raise your eyes, *p*, and look
15:5 Look up, *p*, to the heavens
16:2 Sarai said to Abram: *P* now!
16:2 *P*, have relations with my
18:3 *p* do not pass by your servant
18:4 a little water be taken, *p*
18:27 *P*, here I have taken upon
18:30 *p*, not grow hot with anger
18:31 *P*, here I have taken upon
18:32 Jehovah, *p*, not grow hot
19:2 *P*, now, my lords, turn aside
19:2 turn aside, *p*, into the house
19:7 *P*, my brothers, do not act
19:8 *P*, here I have two daughters

Jer 17:15 Let it come in, *p*
18:11 say, *p*, to the men of Judah
18:11 Turn back, *p*, each one from
18:13 Ask for yourselves, *p*
21:2 *P* inquire in our behalf of
25:5 Turn back, *p*, every one
27:18 *p*, beseech Jehovah of
28:7 hear, *p*, this word that I am
28:15 Listen, *p*, O Hananiah
30:6 Ask, *p*, O men, and see
32:8 Buy, *p*, the field of mine
35:15 Turn back, *p*, each one
36:15 *p*, and read it aloud in our
36:17 *p*, How did you write all
37:3 Pray, *p*, in our behalf to
37:20 listen, *p*, O my lord the
37:20 *p*, fall before you, and
38:4 man, *p*, be put to death
38:12 Put, *p*, the worn-out rags
38:20 Obey, *p*, the voice of
38:25 tell us, *p*, What did you
42:2 request for favor, *p*, fall
44:4 Do not do, *p*, this detestable
Eze 8:5 *p*, raise your eyes in the
8:8 bore, *p*, through the wall
17:12 Say, *p*, to the rebellious
18:25 Hear, *p*, O house of Israel
33:30 Come, *p*, and hear what the
Da 1:12 *P*, put your servants to the
9:16 *p*, may your anger and your
Am 7:2 Lord Jehovah, forgive, *p*
7:5 Lord Jehovah, hold off, *p*
Jon 1:8 tell us, *p*, on whose account
1:14 may we, *p*, not perish
4:3 take away, *p*, my soul from
Mic 3:1 Hear, *p*, you heads of Jacob
3:9 Hear, *p*, this, you head ones
6:1 Hear, *p*, you people, what
6:5 remember, *p*, what Balak the
Hag 2:2 Say, *p*, to Zerubbabel the son
2:11 Ask, *p*, the priests as to
2:15 *p*, set your heart on this
2:18 Set your heart, *p*, on this
Zec 1:4 Return, *p*, from your bad ways
3:8 Hear, *p*, O Joshua the high
5:5 Raise your eyes, *p*, and see
Mal 1:8 near, *p*, to your governor
1:9 *p*, soften the face of God
3:10 test me out, *p*, in this
Mr 5:23 you *p* come and put your hands
Ac 9:38 *P* do not hesitate to come on
Ro 8:8 with the flesh cannot *p* God
15:2 *p* his neighbor in what is
15:3 Christ did not *p* himself
Ga 1:10 Or am I seeking to *p* men?
1Th 4:1 you ought to walk and *p* God
Tit 2:9 *p* them well, not talking back
Heb 11:6 faith it is impossible to *p*
1Pe 2:18 but also to those hard to *p*
3Jo 6 These you will *p* send on their

Pleased

Jg 18:20 heart of the priest was *p*
1Sa 2:25 now *p* to put them to death
Ps 40:13 Be *p*, O Jehovah, to deliver
50:18 you were even *p* with him
77:7 will he no more be *p* again?
Mic 6:7 *p* with thousands of rams
Mt 14:6 danced at it and *p* Herod so
Mr 6:22 danced and *p* Herod and those
Ro 15:26 *p* to share up their things by
15:27 have been *p* to do so, and yet
1Co 12:18 just as he *p*
15:38 body just as it has *p* him
2Co 5:8 *p* rather to become absent
Col 1:27 *p* to make known what are the
1Th 2:8 were well *p* to impart to you
Heb 11:5 witness that he had *p* God
13:16 sacrifices God is well *p*

Pleasers

Eph 6:6 eyeservice as men *p*, but as
Col 3:22 acts of eyeservice, as men *p*

Pleases

Ec 8:12 a long time as he *p*, yet I am
2Th 1:11 perform completely all he *p*

Pleasing

1Ki 3:10 *p* in the eyes of Jehovah
2Ch 10:7 be *p* to them and indeed
Es 1:21 *p* in the eyes of the king and
2:4 young woman who seems *p* in
2:4 thing was *p* in the king's eyes
2:9 young woman was *p* in his eyes
Ps 69:31 more *p* to Jehovah than a
Joh 8:29 do the things *p* to him
Ac 6:2 not *p* for us to leave the word
6:5 was *p* to the whole multitude
12:3 he saw it was *p* to the Jews
Ro 15:1 and not to be *p* ourselves
1Co 10:33 even as I am *p* all people
Ga 1:10 yet *p* men, I would not be
6:12 *p* appearance in the flesh are
Col 1:10 to the end of fully *p* him
1Th 2:4 speak, as *p*, not men, but God
2:15 they are not *p* God, but are
1Jo 3:22 things that are *p* in his eyes

Pleasurable

Ps 19:14 my heart Become *p* before you
104:34 my musing about him be *p*
Pr 3:24 and your sleep must be *p*
13:19 Desire when realized is *p*
20:17 gained by falsehood is *p* to a
Ca 2:14 your voice is *p* and your form
Jer 31:26 sleep, it had been *p* to me
Eze 16:37 toward whom you were *p* and

Pleasure

Ge 18:12 shall I really have *p*, my
33:10 you received me with *p*
De 33:11 show *p* in the activity of his
2Sa 24:23 your God show *p* in you
1Ch 29:3 *p* in the house of my God
29:17 in rectitude that you take *p*
2Ch 15:15 full *p* on their part that
Ezr 10:11 do his *p* and separate
Job 14:6 Until he finds *p* as a hired
33:26 that he may take *p* in him
34:9 By his taking *p* in God
Ps 44:3 Because you took *p* in them
49:13 *p* in their very mouthings
51:16 offering you do not find *p*
62:4 They take *p* in a lie
85:1 taken *p*, O Jehovah, in your
102:14 have found *p* in her stones
119:108 take *p* in the voluntary
147:10 of the man does he find *p*
147:11 Jehovah is finding *p* in
149:4 Jehovah is taking *p* in his
Pr 3:12 does a son in whom he finds *p*
11:1 complete stone-weight is a *p*
11:20 blameless . . . are a *p* to him
12:22 faithfulness are a *p* to him
14:35 *p* of a king is in the servant
15:8 prayer . . . is a *p* to him
16:7 Jehovah takes *p* in the ways
16:13 lips of righteousness are a *p*
23:26 take *p* in my own ways
29:17 and give much *p* to your soul
Ec 9:7 God has found *p* in your works
Jer 6:20 serve for no *p*, and your
14:10 has taken no *p* in them
14:12 I am taking no *p* in them
Eze 20:40 I shall take *p* in them
20:41 I shall take *p* in you
43:27 certainly find *p* in you
Ho 8:13 Jehovah himself took no *p* in
Am 5:22 I shall find no *p*, and on
Hag 1:8 that I may take *p* in it and
Mal 1:8 Will he find *p* in you, or
1:10 from your hand I take no *p*
1:13 Can I take *p* in it at your
2:13 or a taking of *p* in anything
Mr 12:37 listening to him with *p*
2Co 12:10 I take *p* in weaknesses, in
Eph 1:5 to the good *p* of his will
1:9 his good *p* which he purposed
Php 2:13 for the sake of his good *p*
2Th 2:12 but took *p* in unrighteousness
Heb 10:38 my soul has no *p* in him
Jas 4:1 your cravings for sensual *p*
4:3 your cravings for sensual *p*
5:5 have gone in for sensual *p*
2Pe 2:13 living in the daytime a *p*

Pleasure-given

Isa 47:8 hear this, you *p* woman

Pleasures

Ps 36:8 *p* you cause them to drink
Lu 8:14 riches and *p* of this life
2Ti 3:4 lovers of *p* rather than
Tit 3:3 to various desires and *p*

Pledge

Ex 22:26 seize the garment . . . as a *p*
De 15:6 lend on *p* to many nations
15:8 lend him on *p* as much as he
24:6 its upper grindstone as a *p*
24:6 that he is seizing as a *p*
De 24:11 bring the *p* outside to you
24:12 not go to bed with his *p*
24:13 return the *p* to him as soon
24:17 garment of a widow as a *p*
1Sa 14:24 under the *p* of an oath
Job 17:3 shake hands with me in *p*
22:6 seize a *p* from your brothers
24:3 the widow's bull as a *p*
24:9 they take as a *p*
Pr 13:13 a debtor's *p* will be seized
20:16 seize from him a *p*
27:13 seize from him a *p*
Jer 30:21 given his heart in *p* in
Eze 18:7 the *p* . . . he would return
18:16 no *p* has he seized, and
Am 2:8 on garments seized as a *p*
Heb 7:22 become the one given in *p*

Pledged

De 24:10 take from him what he has *p*
Eze 18:12 *p* thing he would not return
33:15 returns the very thing *p*

Plentifully

2Co 11:23 in labors more *p*, in
11:23 in prisons more *p*, in

Plenty

Ge 41:29 years coming with great *p*
41:30 the *p* in the land of Egypt
41:31 *p* once in the land will not
41:34 during the seven years of *p*
41:47 during the seven years of *p*
41:53 the seven years of the *p*
2Ch 24:11 there was *p* of money, the
31:10 left over is this great *p*
Es 1:18 *p* of contempt and indignation
Job 20:22 While his *p* is at its peak
Ps 72:16 be *p* of grain on the earth
Pr 3:10 supply will be filled with *p*
Ec 5:12 *p* belonging to the rich one is
1Co 15:58 *p* to do in the work of the
2Co 9:8 have *p* for every good work

Plight

Ex 5:19 saw themselves in an evil *p*
Ne 1:3 in a very bad *p* and in reproach
2:17 seeing the bad *p* in which we

Plot

Ge 23:15 A land *p* worth four hundred
1Ki 21:23 in the *p* of land of Jezreel
Ac 9:23 *p* against him became known
20:3 a *p* was hatched against him
23:30 a *p* that is to be laid

Plots

Ac 20:19 by the *p* of the Jews

Plotting

Ge 37:18 *p* cunningly against him
Ps 37:12 *p* against the righteous one
140:8 Do not promote his *p*, that

Plow

De 22:10 not *p* with a bull and an ass
Pr 20:4 the lazy one will not *p*
Jer 4:3 *P* for yourselves arable land
Am 6:12 will one *p* there with cattle?
Lu 9:62 put his hand to a *p* and looks
1Co 9:10 ought to *p* in hope and the

Plowed

Jg 14:18 had not *p* with my young cow
Ps 129:3 have *p* upon my very back
Pr 13:23 *P* ground of persons of little
Jer 26:18 Zion herself will be *p* up
Ho 10:13 You people have *p* wickedness
Mic 3:12 be *p* up as a mere field

Plower

Isa 28:24 *p* plows in order to sow

Plowing

Ge 45:6 there will be no *p* time or
Ex 34:21 In *p* time and in harvest you
1Sa 8:12 some to do his *p* and to reap
14:14 half the *p* line in an acre
1Ki 19:19 *p* with twelve spans before
Job 1:14 happened to be *p* and the
Lu 17:7 has a slave *p* or minding the

Plowman

Am 9:13 the *p* will actually overtake

Plowmen

Ps 129:3 *P* have plowed upon my very

Plows

Isa 28:24 plower *p* in order to sow
Ho 10:11 Judah *p*; Jacob harrows for

1Co 9:10 man who *p* ought to plow in

Plowshare
1Sa 13:20 to get each one his *p* or his

Plowshares
1Sa 13:21 a pim for the *p* and for the
Isa 2:4 to beat their swords into *p*
Joe 3:10 Beat your *p* into swords
Mic 4:3 to beat their swords into *p*

Pluck
De 23:25 *p* off only the ripe ears
Eze 17:22 I shall *p* off a tender one
Mt 12:1 started to *p* heads of grain

Plucked
Ge 8:11 olive leaf freshly *p* in its
Job 8:12 yet in its bud, not *p* off
24:24 they are *p* off, And like the
Ps 80:12 those . . . on the road *p* at it
Ca 5:1 I have *p* my myrrh along with
Eze 17:4 He *p* off the very top of its
17:9 freshly *p* sprouts become dry
Da 7:4 until its wings were *p* out
7:8 horns that were *p* up from

Plucking
Job 30:4 *p* the salt herb by the bushes
Isa 50:6 to those *p* off the hair
Mr 2:23 *p* the heads of grain
Lu 6:1 disciples were *p* and eating

Plumage
Job 39:13 pinions of a stork and the *p*
Eze 17:3 with long pinions, full of *p*

Plummet
Am 7:7 on a wall made with a *p*
7:7 there was a *p* in his hand
7:8 So I said: A *p*
7:8 setting a *p* in the midst of
Zec 4:10 *p* in the hand of Zerubbabel

Plump
Eze 34:3 *p* animal is what you
34:20 judge between a *p* sheep and

Plumped
Jg 7:12 were *p* in the low plain as

Plunder
Nu 14:3 our little ones will become *p*
14:31 who you said would become *p*
31:32 the rest of the *p* that the
31:32 booty . . . taken as *p*
31:53 had taken *p* each for himself
De 1:39 *P* they will become! and your
2:35 we take as *p* for ourselves
3:7 cities we took as *p* for
20:14 its spoil you will *p* for
Jos 8:2 you people may *p* its spoil
1Sa 14:36 *p* them until the morning
2Ki 7:16 *p* the camp of the Syrians
21:14 become *p* and pillage to
2Ch 14:14 to be much to *p* in them
20:25 people came to *p* the spoil
25:13 and taking a great *p*
28:8 they took from them as *p*
28:14 left the captives and the *p*
Ezr 9:7 the captivity and with the *p*
Ne 4:4 give them to the *p* in the land
Es 3:13 and to *p* the spoil of them
8:11 and to *p* their spoil
9:10 but on the *p* they did not lay
9:15 but on the *p* they did not lay
9:16 *p* they did not lay their hand
Ps 109:11 *p* of his product of toil
Isa 10:2 *p* even the fatherless boys
10:6 take much *p* and to make it
11:14 *p* the sons of the East
33:23 actually take a big *p*
42:22 for *p* without a deliverer
Jer 2:14 he has come to be for *p*
15:13 I shall give for mere *p*
17:3 I shall give for mere *p*
20:5 *p* them and take them and
49:32 camels must become a *p*
Eze 7:21 hand of the strangers for *p*
23:46 object and something to *p*
25:7 to *p* to the nations
26:5 object of *p* for the nations
26:12 and *p* your sales goods
34:8 sheep became something for *p*
34:22 become something for *p*
34:28 become something to *p*
36:4 for *p* and for ridicule to
36:5 pasture ground and for the *p*
39:10 and *p* those who had been
Da 11:24 *P* and spoil and goods he
Na 2:9 *P* silver, you men
2:9 *p* gold; as there is no limit
Zep 2:9 my people will *p* them, and
Mt 12:29 And then he will *p* his house
23:25 inside they are full of *p*
Mr 3:27 able to *p* his movable goods
3:27 and then he will *p* his house
Lu 11:39 inside of you is full of *p*

Plundered
Ge 34:29 *p* all that was in the houses
Nu 31:9 means of maintenance they *p*
Jos 8:27 Israel *p* for themselves
11:14 the sons of Israel *p* for
Isa 24:3 without fail it will be *p*
42:22 a people *p* and pillaged
Jer 50:37 they will actually be *p*
Am 3:11 towers will actually be *p*

Plunderer
Joh 10:1 that one is a thief and a *p*

Plunderers
Isa 42:24 and Israel to the *p*? Is it
Joh 10:8 are thieves and *p*

Plundering
Ge 34:27 and went *p* the city, because
2Ch 14:14 went *p* all the cities
20:25 three days that they were *p*
Isa 17:14 lot belonging to those *p* us
Jer 30:16 those *p* you I shall give
30:16 I shall give over to *p*
Eze 29:19 do a great deal of *p* of it
38:12 and to do much *p*, in order
38:13 Is it to do much *p* that
39:10 those who had been *p* them
Da 11:33 by captivity and by *p*, for
Heb 10:34 the *p* of your belongings

Plunge
2Ki 5:14 *p* into the Jordan seven
1Ti 6:9 which *p* men into destruction

Plunged
Jg 3:21 and *p* it into his belly
Joh 21:7 and *p* into the sea

Ply
Lu 11:53 and to *p* him with questions

Pochereth-hazzebaim
Ezr 2:57 the sons of *P*
Ne 7:59 the sons of *P*, the sons of

Pocket
Job 31:33 my error in my shirt *p*

Podium
Ne 8:4 kept standing upon a wooden *p*

Pods
Lu 15:16 carob *p* which the swine

Poets
Ac 17:28 certain ones of the *p* among

Point
Ge 14:8 At this *p* the king of Sodom
18:22 At this *p* the men turned
Ex 21:14 to the *p* of killing him with
De 9:8 to the *p* of annihilating you
9:19 to the *p* of annihilating you
9:20 to the *p* of annihilating him
17:11 the law that they will *p* out
Jos 17:18 the termination *p* for you
Jg 5:18 their souls to the *p* of death
16:16 impatient to the *p* of dying
2Sa 24:7 terminating *p* in the Negeb
2Ki 8:11 to the *p* of embarrassment
13:17 Aphek to the finishing *p*
13:19 Syria to the finishing *p*
20:1 got sick to the *p* of dying
2Ch 24:22 he was at the *p* of dying
26:16 to the *p* of causing ruin
32:24 sick to the *p* of dying, and
Isa 38:1 got sick to the *p* of dying
Jer 17:1 With a diamond *p* it is
48:47 to this *p* is the judgment
51:64 to this *p* are the words of
Eze 23:19 the *p* of calling to mind
36:8 near to the *p* of coming in
Da 7:28 Up to this *p* is the end of
Jon 4:9 anger, to the *p* of death
Hag 1:6 but not to the *p* of getting
Mt 16:9 Do you not yet see the *p*, or
24:32 this *p*: Just as soon as its
Joh 4:27 at this *p* his disciples
4:47 for he was at the *p* of dying
1Co 8:10 to the *p* of eating foods
Ga 1:13 to the *p* of excess I kept on
Php 2:27 sick nearly to the *p* of death
1Th 4:6 *p* of harming and encroach
2Ti 2:9 to the *p* of prison bonds as
Heb 8:1 this is the main *p*: We have
Jas 2:10 makes a false step in one *p*
Re 10:4 I was at the *p* of writing

Pointed
Job 41:30 As *p* earthenware fragments
Lu 19:43 fortification with *p* stakes

Points
Ro 15:15 more outspokenly on some *p*

Poisings
Job 37:16 about the *p* of the cloud

Poison
De 32:32 Their grapes are grapes of *p*
32:33 And the cruel *p* of cobras
Pr 23:32 secretes *p* just like a viper
Ro 3:13 *P* of asps is behind their
Jas 3:8 it is full of death-dealing *p*

Poisoned
Jer 8:14 he gives us *p* water to drink
9:15 make them drink *p* water
23:15 give them *p* water to drink

Poisonous
Nu 21:6 Jehovah sent *p* serpents among
De 8:15 with *p* serpents and scorpions
29:18 of a *p* plant and wormwood
Ps 69:21 they gave me a *p* plant
Isa 11:8 light aperture of a *p* snake
14:29 will come forth a *p* snake
59:5 The eggs of a *p* snake are
Jer 8:17 *p* snakes, for which there is
La 3:5 encircle me with *p* plant and
3:19 the wormwood and the *p* plant
Ho 10:4 has sprouted like a *p* plant
Am 6:12 into a *p* plant you people
Ac 8:23 I see you are a *p* gall and
Heb 12:15 no *p* root may spring up and

Poking
Ge 21:9 had borne to Abraham, *p* fun
Isa 58:9 the *p* out of the finger and
Ho 7:4 ceases *p* after kneading dough

Pole
Nu 21:8 and place it upon a signal *p*
21:9 placed it upon the signal *p*
De 16:21 sacred *p* near the altar of
Jg 6:25 the sacred *p* that is by it you
6:26 the sacred *p* that you will cut
6:28 sacred *p* that was beside it
6:30 he has cut down the sacred *p*
1Ki 15:13 idol to the sacred *p*
16:33 to make the sacred *p*
18:19 prophets of the sacred *p*
2Ki 13:6 the sacred *p* itself stood in
17:16 and to make a sacred *p*
18:4 and cut down the sacred *p*
21:3 and made a sacred *p*, just as
21:7 carved image of the sacred *p*
23:4 and for the sacred *p* and for
23:6 he brought out the sacred *p*
23:7 shrines for the sacred *p*
23:15 and burned the sacred *p*
2Ch 15:16 idol for the sacred *p*
Eze 15:3 a *p* . . . to do some work

Poles
Ex 25:13 make *p* of acacia wood and
25:14 put the *p* through the rings
25:15 In the rings of the Ark the *p*
25:27 for the *p* to carry the table
25:28 make the *p* of acacia wood
27:6 you must make *p* for the altar
27:6 its *p* being of acacia wood
27:7 *p* must be put into the rings
27:7 *p* must be upon the two sides
30:4 serve as supports for the *p*
30:5 make the *p* of acacia wood
34:13 sacred *p* you are to cut down
35:12 the Ark and its *p*, the
35:13 the table and its *p* and all
35:15 altar of incense and its *p*
35:16 its *p* and all its utensils
37:4 made *p* of acacia wood and
37:5 he put the *p* through the rings
37:14 the *p* for carrying the table
37:15 made the *p* of acacia wood
37:27 supports for the *p* with which
37:28 made the *p* of acacia wood
38:5 copper, as supports for the *p*
38:6 made the *p* of acacia wood

Ex 38:7 he put the *p* into the rings
39:35 and its *p* and the cover
39:39 its *p* and all its utensils
40:20 placed the *p* on the Ark and
Nu 4:6 on top and put in its *p*
4:8 and put in its *p*
4:11 and put in its *p*
4:14 and put in its *p*
De 7:5 sacred *p* you should cut down
12:3 burn their sacred *p* in the
Jg 3:7 the Baals and the sacred *p*
1Ki 8:7 cherubs kept the Ark and its *p*
8:8 But the *p* proved to be long
8:8 tips of the *p* were visible
14:15 they made their sacred *p*
14:23 sacred *p* upon every high
2Ki 17:10 sacred pillars and sacred *p*
23:14 cut down the sacred *p* and
2Ch 5:8 covered over the Ark and its *p*
5:9 *p* were long, so that the tips
5:9 tips of the *p* were visible
14:3 and cut down the sacred *p*
17:6 and the sacred *p* from Judah
19:3 cleared out the sacred *p*
24:18 serving the sacred *p* and the
31:1 cut down the sacred *p* and
33:3 made sacred *p*, and he began
33:19 set up the sacred *p* and
34:3 sacred *p* and the graven
34:4 sacred *p* and the graven
34:7 altars and the sacred *p*
Isa 17:8 gaze, either at the sacred *p*
27:9 sacred *p* and the incense
Jer 17:2 altars and their sacred *p*
Mic 5:14 I will uproot your sacred *p*

Police
Da 3:2 *p* magistrates and all the
3:3 the *p* magistrates and all the

Polish
Jer 46:4 *P* the lances. Clothe
51:11 *P* the arrows. Fill the
La 4:7 their *p* was as the sapphire

Polished
1Ki 7:45 Hiram made of *p* copper for
2Ch 4:16 utensils . . . of *p* copper
Job 26:13 his wind he has *p* up heaven
Isa 49:2 gradually made me a *p* arrow
Eze 21:9 sharpened, and it is also *p*
21:10 a glitter it has been *p*
21:11 And one gives it to be *p*
21:11 it has been *p*, in order to
21:15 *p* for a slaughter
21:28 *p* to cause it to devour

Pollute
Nu 35:33 not *p* the land in which you
Da 1:8 *p* himself with the delicacies
1:8 that he might not *p* himself

Polluted
Ezr 2:62 as *p* from the priesthood
Ne 7:64 as *p* from the priesthood
Ps 106:38 came to be *p* with bloodshed
Isa 24:5 land has been *p* under its
59:3 have become *p* with blood
63:3 all my clothing I have *p*
Jer 3:1 land not positively been *p*
23:11 prophet and the priest . . . *p*
La 4:14 They have become *p* with blood
Mic 4:11 Let her be *p*, and may our
Mal 1:7 upon my altar *p* bread
1:7 In what way have we *p* you?
1:12 of Jehovah is something *p*
Ac 15:20 from things *p* by idols and

Pollutes
Nu 35:33 it is blood that *p* the land

Polluting
Jer 3:2 you keep *p* the land with
3:9 she kept *p* the land and
Zep 3:1 is rebelling and *p* herself

Pollution
De 23:10 a *p* that occurs at night

Pomegranate
Ex 28:34 a bell of gold and a *p*, a
28:34 bell of gold and a *p* upon the
39:26 a bell and a *p*, a bell and a
39:26 a bell and a *p* upon the hem
1Sa 14:2 the *p* tree that is in Migron
Ca 4:3 segment of *p* are your temples
6:7 segment of *p* are your temples
6:11 the *p* trees had blossomed
Ca 7:12 the *p* trees have bloomed
Joe 1:12 As for the *p* tree, also the
Hag 2:19 the *p* tree and the olive tree

Pomegranates
Ex 28:33 *p* of blue thread and wool
39:24 *p* of blue thread and wool
39:25 the *p* upon the hem of the
39:25 in between the *p*
Nu 13:23 some of the *p* and some of
20:5 It is no place of . . . *p*
De 8:8 barley and vines and figs and *p*
1Ki 7:18 to make the *p* and two rows
7:20 two hundred *p* in rows all
7:42 four hundred *p* for the two
7:42 two rows of *p* to each
2Ki 25:17 *p* all around upon the
2Ch 3:16 *p* and put them on the chains
4:13 four hundred *p* for the two
4:13 two rows of *p* for each
Ca 4:13 Your skin is a paradise of *p*
8:2 wine, the fresh juice of *p*
Jer 52:22 the *p* upon the capital
52:22 same as these, also the *p*
52:23 *p* came to be ninety-six
52:23 *p* being one hundred upon

Pompous
Ac 25:23 Agrippa . . . much *p* show

Ponder
De 32:29 Then they would *p* over this
1Ti 4:15 *P* over these things; be

Pondered
Ps 48:9 We have *p*, O God, over your
Ec 12:9 *p* and made a thorough search

Pontius
Lu 3:1 when *P* Pilate was governor of
Ac 4:27 *P* Pilate with men of nations
1Ti 6:13 declaration before *P* Pilate

Pontus
Ac 2:9 *P* and the district of Asia
18:2 Aquila, a native of *P* who had
1Pe 1:1 residents scattered about in *P*

Pool
2Sa 2:13 together by the *p* of Gibeon
2:13 on this side of the *p* and
2:13 on that side of the *p*
4:12 by the *p* in Hebron
1Ki 22:38 chariot by the *p* of Samaria
2Ki 18:17 the conduit of the upper *p*
20:20 made the *p* and the conduit
Ne 2:14 Gate and to the King's *P*
3:15 wall of the *P* of the Canal
3:16 the *p* that had been made and
Ps 107:35 wilderness into a reedy *p*
114:8 rock into a reedy *p* of water
Isa 7:3 conduit of the upper *p* by
22:9 the waters of the lower *p*
22:11 for the waters of the old *p*
35:7 have become as a reedy *p*
36:2 conduit of the upper *p* at the
41:18 into a reedy *p* of water
Na 2:8 Nineveh . . . like a *p* of waters
Joh 5:2 is a *p* designated in Hebrew
5:7 man to put me into the *p*
9:7 Go wash in the *p* of Siloam

Pools
Ex 7:19 over their reedy *p* and over
8:5 *p* and make the frogs come up
Ec 2:6 I made *p* of water for myself
Ca 7:4 eyes are like the *p* in Heshbon
Isa 14:23 and reedy *p* of water
42:15 and reedy *p* I shall dry up

Poor
Ge 41:19 *p* and very bad in form and
Ex 23:6 your *p* man in his controversy
23:11 *p* ones of your people must
Le 25:25 *p* and has to sell some of
25:35 brother grows *p* and so he is
25:39 in case your brother grows *p*
25:47 your brother has become *p*
27:8 too *p* for the estimated value
De 15:4 no one should come to be *p*
15:7 brothers becomes *p* among you
15:7 closefisted toward your *p*
15:9 ungenerous toward your *p*
15:11 someone *p* will never cease
15:11 *p* brother in your land
24:14 who is in trouble and *p*
1Sa 2:8 ashpit he lifts up a *p* one
Es 9:22 and of gifts to the *p* people
Job 5:15 the One saving . . . a *p* one
24:4 turn aside the *p* ones from
24:14 slay the afflicted and the *p*
29:16 a real father to the *p* ones
30:25 soul has grieved for the *p*
31:19 the *p* one had no covering
Ps 9:18 will the *p* one be forgotten
12:5 the sighing of the *p* ones
35:10 *p* one from the one robbing
37:14 afflicted and *p* one to fall
40:17 But I am afflicted and *p*
49:2 You rich one and you *p* one
69:33 Jehovah is listening to the *p*
70:5 But I am afflicted and *p*
72:4 save the sons of the *p* one
72:12 deliver the *p* one crying
72:13 lowly one and the *p* one
72:13 of the *p* ones he will save
74:21 *p* one praise your name
82:4 the lowly one and the *p* one
86:1 For I am afflicted and *p*
107:41 protects the *p* one from
109:16 the afflicted and *p* man
109:22 For I am afflicted and *p*
109:31 at the right hand of the *p*
112:9 he has given to the *p* ones
113:7 exalts the *p* one from the
132:15 *p* ones I shall satisfy with
140:12 the judgment of the *p* ones
Pr 14:31 one showing favor to the *p*
30:14 *p* ones from among mankind
31:9 afflicted one and the *p* one
31:20 she has thrust out to the *p*
Isa 14:30 and in security the *p* ones
25:4 stronghold to the *p* one in
29:19 *p* ones of mankind will be
32:7 someone *p* speaks what is
41:17 and the *p* ones are seeking
Jer 2:34 souls of the innocent *p* ones
5:28 the judgment of the *p* ones
20:13 delivered the soul of the *p*
22:16 the afflicted one and the *p*
Eze 16:49 *p* one she did not strengthen
18:12 and *p* one he has maltreated
22:29 *p* one they have maltreated
Da 4:27 showing mercy to the *p* ones
Am 2:6 someone *p* for the price of a
4:1 who are crushing the *p* ones
5:12 have turned aside *p* people
8:4 you men snapping at someone *p*
8:6 someone *p* for the price of a
Mt 11:5 *p* are having the good news
19:21 give to the *p* and you will
26:9 and been given to *p* people
26:11 always have the *p* with you
Mr 10:21 give to the *p*, and you will
12:42 a *p* widow came and dropped
12:43 *p* widow dropped in more
14:5 and been given to the *p*
14:7 always have the *p* with you
Lu 4:18 declare good news to the *p*
6:20 Happy are you *p*, because yours
7:22 the *p* are being told the good
14:13 a feast, invite *p* people
14:21 the *p* and crippled and blind
18:22 and distribute to *p* people
19:8 I am giving to the *p*, and
21:3 widow, although *p*, dropped
Joh 12:5 and given to the *p* people
12:6 he was concerned about the *p*
12:8 have the *p* always with you
13:29 give something to the *p*
Ro 15:26 contribution to the *p* of the
2Co 6:10 as *p* but making many rich
8:9 he became *p* for your sakes
9:9 he has given to the *p* ones
Ga 2:10 we should keep the *p* in mind
Jas 2:2 *p* man in filthy clothing
2:3 you say to the *p* one: You
2:5 God chose the ones who are *p*
2:6 have dishonored the *p* man
Re 3:17 and *p* and blind and naked
13:16 the rich and the *p*, and the

Poplar
Ps 137:2 Upon the *p* trees in the

Poplars
Le 23:40 *p* of the torrent valley, and
Job 40:22 The *p* of the torrent valley
Isa 15:7 the torrent valley of the *p*
44:4 like *p* by the water ditches

Populace
Pr 11:26 the *p* will execrate him

Popular
Jer 8:6 back into the *p* course, like

Population
Ge 9:19 all the earth's *p* spread
10:5 From these the *p* of the isles
Pr 14:28 lack of *p* is the ruin of a

Populous
Nu 33:54 *p* one you should increase his
De 7:1 clear away *p* nations from
7:1 seven nations more *p* and
7:7 the most *p* of all the peoples
7:17 nations are too *p* for me
9:14 mightier and more *p* than they
Jos 11:8 as far as *p* Sidon and
19:28 Kanah as far as *p* Sidon
Ps 110:6 the head one over a *p* land
Isa 9:3 You have made the nation *p*
La 1:1 that was *p* among the nations
Eze 31:6 all the *p* nations would
Am 6:2 go from there to *p* Hamath

Poratha
Es 9:8 and *P* and Adalia and Aridatha

Porch
1Ki 6:3 the *p* in front of the temple
7:6 *P* of Pillars he made fifty
7:6 another *p* was in front of
7:7 As for the *P* of the Throne
7:7 he made the *p* of judgment
7:8 the house belonging to the *P*
7:8 there was a house like this *P*
7:12 and for the *p* of the house
7:19 pillars at the *p* were of
7:21 pillars belonging to the *p*
1Ch 28:11 architectural plan of the *p*
2Ch 3:4 *p* that was in front of the
8:12 he had built before the *p*
15:8 before the *p* of Jehovah
29:7 closed the doors of the *p*
29:17 came to the *p* of Jehovah
Eze 8:16 between the *p* and the altar
40:7 beside the *p* of the gate
40:8 measure the *p* of the gate
40:9 measured the *p* of the gate
40:9 the *p* of the gate was toward
40:15 *p* of the inner gate was
40:21 its own *p* proved to be
40:22 its windows and its *p* and
40:22 its *p* was to their front
40:24 its side pillars and its *p*
40:25 *p* had windows all around
40:26 its *p* was to their front
40:29 its side pillars and its *p*
40:29 *p* had windows round about
40:31 its *p* was to the outer
40:33 its side pillars and its *p*
40:33 *p* had windows all around
40:34 *p* was toward the outer
40:36 its side pillars and its *p*
40:39 in the *p* of the gate there
40:40 to the *p* of the gate there
40:48 into the *p* of the house
40:48 the side pillar of the *p*
40:49 the *p* was twenty cubits
41:25 the front of the *p* outside
41:26 along the sides of the *p*
44:3 way of the *p* of the gate
46:2 *p* of the gate, from outside
46:8 way of the *p* of the gate
Joe 2:17 Between the *p* and the altar

Porches
Eze 40:16 the way it was for the *p*
40:30 And there were *p* all around
41:15 and the *p* of the courtyard

Porcius
Ac 24:27 was succeeded by *P* Festus

Porcupine
Isa 34:11 *p* must take possession of
Zep 2:14 pelican and *p* will spend the

Porcupines
Isa 14:23 make her a possession of *p*

Porphyry
Es 1:6 pavement of *p* and marble and

Port
Isa 23:1 despoiled from being a *p*
Ac 27:5 put into *p* at Myra in Lycia
28:12 putting into *p* at Syracuse

Portent
De 13:1 give you a sign or a *p*
De 13:2 the *p* does come true of which
28:46 a *p* to time indefinite
1Ki 13:3 he gave a *p* on that day
13:3 the *p* of which Jehovah has
13:5 *p* that the man of the true
2Ch 32:24 and a *p* He gave him
32:31 *p* that had happened in the
Isa 20:3 sign and a *p* against Egypt
Eze 12:6 a *p* is what I have made you
12:11 I am a *p* for you. Just as I
24:24 has become for you a *p*
24:27 become to them a *p*

Portents
Joe 2:30 I will give *p* in the heavens
Zec 3:8 they are men serving as *p*
Ac 2:19 I will give *p* in heaven above
2:22 *p* and signs that God did
2:43 many *p* and signs began to
4:30 signs and *p* occur through the
5:12 *p* continued to occur among
6:8 performing great *p* and signs
7:36 led them out after doing *p*
14:3 by granting signs and *p* to
15:12 signs and *p* that God did
Ro 15:19 the power of signs and *p*
2Co 12:12 by signs and *p* and powerful
2Th 2:9 work and lying signs and *p*
Heb 2:4 with signs as well as *p* and

Portico
1Ch 26:18 for the *p* to the west, four
26:18 two at the *p*

Porticoes
2Ki 23:11 which was in the *p*

Portion
Ge 43:34 Benjamin's *p* five times the
Ex 29:26 and it must become your *p*
29:27 the sacred *p* that was waved
29:28 because it is a sacred *p*
29:28 sacred *p* to be rendered by
29:28 sacred *p* for Jehovah
30:34 should be the same *p* of each
Le 7:14 each offering as a sacred *p*
7:32 a sacred *p* to the priest from
7:33 leg will become his as a *p*
7:34 and the leg of the sacred *p*
8:29 ram it became the *p* for Moses
10:14 the leg of the sacred *p* in a
10:15 the leg of the sacred *p*
Nu 18:8 as a *p*, as an allowance to
1Sa 1:5 to Hannah he gave one *p*
9:23 Do give the *p* that I have
2Ch 31:3 *p* of the king from his own
31:4 give the *p* of the priests and
35:5 the *p* of a paternal house
Job 31:2 what *p* is there from God
Ps 11:6 wind, as the *p* of their cup
16:5 Jehovah is the *p* of my
60:6 will give out Shechem as a *p*
63:10 become a mere *p* for foxes
68:23 have its *p* from the enemies
108:7 give out Shechem as a *p*
Pr 31:15 prescribed *p* to her young
Ec 2:10 my *p* from all my hard work
2:21 be given the *p* of that one
3:22 rejoice . . . for that is his *p*
5:18 given him, for that is his *p*
5:19 to carry off his *p* and to
9:6 they have no *p* anymore to time
9:9 that is your *p* in life and in
11:2 Give a *p* to seven, or even to
Isa 53:12 a *p* among the many, and it
57:6 torrent valley was your *p*
61:7 there will be a double *p*
61:7 of even a double *p*
Jer 13:25 your measured *p* from me
37:12 to get his *p* from there
Eze 45:1 holy *p* out of the land
45:1 holy *p* in all its boundaries
45:4 holy *p* out of the land it
48:1 Dan one *p*
48:23 border, Benjamin one *p*
Da 4:15 *p* be among the vegetation of
4:23 of the field let its *p* be
Mic 2:4 very *p* of my people he alters
Hab 1:16 his *p* is well oiled, and his
Zec 2:12 possession of Judah as his *p*
9:12 O woman, a double *p*
Lu 10:42 Mary chose the good *p*, and
1Co 7:17 has given each one a *p*, let
9:13 have a *p* for themselves with
2Co 6:15 *p* does a faithful person have
Re 21:8 *p* will be in the lake that
Re 22:19 God will take his *p* away

Portions
Ge 43:34 And he kept having *p* carried
43:34 the *p* of all the others
1Sa 1:4 her sons and her daughters *p*
17:18 ten *p* of milk you should
2Ch 31:19 give *p* to every male among
Ne 8:10 send *p* to the one for whom
8:12 to send out *p* and to carry
12:44 the *p* called for by the law
12:47 giving the *p* of the singers
13:10 *p* of the Levites had not been
Es 9:19 a sending of *p* to one another
9:22 sending of *p* to one another
Eze 5:1 and divide the hair in *p*
48:8 *p* from the eastern border to
48:21 Exactly like the *p*, it
Ho 5:7 will devour them with their *p*

Portrayed
Ga 3:1 Christ was openly *p* impaled

Position
Ex 7:15 put yourself in *p* to meet him
8:20 take a *p* in front of Pharaoh
9:13 take a *p* in front of Pharaoh
De 21:17 firstborn's *p* belongs to him
Jos 9:23 cursed people . . . a slave's *p*
1Sa 3:10 Jehovah came and took his *p*
3:20 the *p* of prophet to Jehovah
17:16 taking his *p* for forty days
19:20 Samuel standing in his *p*
2Sa 3:6 his *p* in the house of Saul
18:13 take a *p* off on the side
18:30 take your *p* here
1Ki 22:35 standing *p* in the chariot
1Ch 18:17 in *p* at the side of the king
2Ch 12:13 his *p* strong in Jerusalem
17:1 his *p* strong over Israel
18:34 standing *p* in the chariot
20:17 Take your *p*, stand still
21:4 to make his *p* strong, and so
25:19 bad *p* and have to fall, you
Ne 8:7 people were in a standing *p*
Isa 22:7 themselves in *p* at the gate
22:19 push you away from your *p*
La 2:4 His right hand has taken its *p*
Eze 16:13 you became fit for royal *p*
21:16 Set your *p*; go to the left!
Da 11:7 stand up in his *p*, and he
11:12 will not use his strong *p*
11:20 stand up in his *p* one who
11:21 stand up in his *p* one who is
11:38 in his *p* he will give glory
Ob 4 make your *p* high like the eagle
Mt 12:46 *p* outside seeking to speak
Lu 1:48 the low *p* of his slave girl
3:9 the ax is already in *p* at
7:38 taking a *p* behind at his feet
16:22 to the bosom *p* of Abraham
16:23 and Lazarus in the bosom *p*
19:4 he ran ahead to an advance *p*
Joh 1:18 the bosom *p* with the Father
Ac 24:11 you are in a *p* to find out
Ro 3:9 Are we in a better *p*?
2Co 11:21 though our *p* had been weak
Php 2:9 exalted him to a superior *p*
Jude 6 not keep their original *p* but
Re 4:2 throne was in its *p* in heaven

Positions
Ex 18:25 *p* as heads over the people
1Ch 6:31 *p* for the direction of the
Ezr 3:8 now put in *p* the Levites
Ec 10:6 has been put in many high *p*
Ro 13:1 in their relative *p* by God

Positive
Ac 1:3 by many *p* proofs he showed

Positively
Ge 2:17 eat from it you will *p* die
3:4 You *p* will not die
20:7 *p* die, you and all who are
Ex 19:12 will *p* be put to death
19:13 he will *p* be stoned or will
19:13 or will *p* be shot through
22:19 is *p* to be put to death
31:14 will *p* be put to death
31:15 will *p* be put to death
Le 5:19 has *p* become guilty against
De 4:26 you will *p* perish in a hurry
4:26 you will *p* be annihilated
30:18 that you will *p* perish
Jos 23:13 you should *p* know that
Jg 13:22 We shall *p* die, because it

1Sa 14:39 my son, yet he will *p* die
14:44 you do not *p* die, Jonathan
22:16 You will *p* die, Ahimelech
2Sa 12:14 born to you, will *p* die
1Ki 2:37 know that you will *p* die
2:42 know that you will *p* die
2Ki 1:4 because you will *p* die
1:6 because you will *p* die
1:16 because you will *p* die
8:10 will *p* revive, and Jehovah
8:10 shown me that he will *p* die
8:14 You will *p* revive
Job 13:10 He will *p* reprove you If in
Ps 50:21 I would *p* become like you
Pr 11:15 *p* fare badly because he has
27:23 to know *p* the appearance of
Ca 8:7 persons would *p* despise them
Jer 3:1 land not *p* been polluted
5:11 *p* dealt treacherously with
6:15 *p* do not feel any shame
7:5 you will *p* make your ways
7:5 you will *p* carry out justice
8:12 they *p* could not feel ashamed
9:4 brother would *p* supplant
11:12 *p* bring no salvation to
13:12 *p* know that every large jar
13:17 and will *p* shed tears
15:18 You *p* become to me like
20:15 He *p* made him rejoice
26:8 saying: You will *p* die
31:18 *p* heard Ephraim bemoaning
42:15 *p* set your faces to enter
42:19 *p* know that I have borne
42:22 *p* know that by the sword
44:17 *p* do every word that has
46:5 they have *p* fled, and they
La 3:52 enemies have *p* hunted for me
5:22 you have *p* rejected us
Eze 3:18 wicked, You will *p* die, and
18:9 He will *p* keep living, is
18:13 he *p* will not keep living
18:13 He will *p* be put to death
18:17 He will *p* keep living
18:19 He will *p* keep living
18:21 he will *p* keep living
18:28 he will *p* keep living
20:32 will itself *p* not happen
33:8 wicked one, you will *p* die!
33:13 You will *p* keep living
33:14 You will *p* die, and he
33:15 he will *p* keep living
33:16 He will *p* keep living
Ho 1:2 land *p* turns from following
1:6 I shall *p* take them away
4:18 *p* treated woman as a harlot
4:18 have *p* loved dishonor
10:15 will *p* have to be silenced
Joe 1:7 It has *p* stripped it bare
Mic 1:10 tell it out; *p* do not weep
2:4 We have *p* been despoiled!
2:12 I shall *p* gather Jacob, all
Ac 5:28 We *p* ordered you not to keep

Possess
Ge 15:2 one who will *p* my house is a
Ex 6:8 give it to you . . . to *p*
1Ch 28:8 that you may *p* the good land
2Ch 20:11 that you caused us to *p*
Ne 9:15 enter and *p* the land that you
Job 7:3 to *p* worthless lunar months
13:26 *p* the consequences of the
Ps 37:9 ones that will *p* the earth
37:11 meek . . . will *p* the earth
37:22 will themselves *p* the earth
37:29 righteous . . . *p* the earth
Pr 3:35 wise ones will come to *p*
Jer 12:14 people, even Israel, to *p*
16:19 came to *p* sheer falsehood
Eze 7:13 not *p* themselves each one of
11:15 given us as a thing to *p*
25:4 as something to *p*, and they
25:10 make it something to *p*
33:24 given as something to *p*
33:25 So should you *p* the land?
33:26 So should you *p* the land?
Ob 17 of the things for them to *p*
Joh 8:12 will *p* the light of life
Ac 3:6 Silver and gold I do not *p*

Possessed
Le 21:4 woman *p* by an owner among
Pr 17:27 sayings is *p* of knowledge
Ob 20 Canaanites *p* as far as Zarephath
Zep 2:9 a place *p* by nettles, and
Mt 9:32 a dumb man *p* of a demon
Ac 4:32 things he *p* was his own; but
7:45 the land *p* by the nations
Col 2:10 *p* of a fullness by means of
2:23 *p* of an appearance of wisdom

Possesses
Lu 12:15 result from the things he *p*

Possessing
2Ki 1:8 A man *p* a hair garment, with
Da 8:6 ram *p* the two horns, which I
8:20 *p* the two horns stands for
Ac 4:37 *p* a piece of land, sold it and
1Co 7:30 those who buy as those not *p*
2Co 6:10 nothing and yet *p* all things

Possession
Ge 15:7 this land to take it in *p*
15:8 that I shall take it in *p*
17:8 Canaan, for a *p* to time
22:17 *p* of the gate of his enemies
23:4 Give me the *p* of a burial
23:9 for the *p* of a burial place
23:20 *p* of a burial place at the
24:60 seed take *p* of the gate of
28:4 you may take *p* of the land
36:43 in the land of their *p*
47:11 he gave them a *p* in the land
48:4 for a *p* to time indefinite
49:30 for the *p* of a burial place
50:13 the *p* of a burial place from
Ex 23:30 and really take *p* of the land
32:13 take *p* of it to time
34:9 you must take us as your *p*
Le 14:34 land of Canaan . . . as a *p*
14:34 house of the land of your *p*
20:24 *p* of their ground, and I, for
20:24 *p* of it, a land flowing with
25:10 return each one to his *p* and
25:13 return each one to his *p*
25:24 land of your *p* you should
25:25 has to sell some of his *p*
25:27 and he must return to his *p*
25:28 and he must return to his *p*
25:32 cities of their *p*, the right
25:33 city of his *p* must also go
25:33 *p* in the midst of the sons
25:34 *p* to time indefinite for
25:41 to the *p* of his forefathers
25:45 and they must become your *p*
25:46 to inherit as a *p* to time
27:16 *p* that a man would sanctify
27:21 *p* of it will become the
27:22 part of the field of his *p*
27:24 the *p* of the land belongs
27:28 field of his *p*, may be sold
Nu 13:30 we are bound to take *p* of it
14:24 his offspring will take *p* of
18:23 not get *p* of an inheritance
18:24 not get *p* of an inheritance
21:24 took *p* of his land from the
21:35 went taking *p* of his land
24:18 And Edom must become a *p*
24:18 become the *p* of his enemies
27:4 give us a *p* in the midst of
27:7 *p* of an inheritance in the
27:11 and he must take *p* of it
32:5 given to your servants as a *p*
32:22 yours as a *p* before Jehovah
32:29 the land of Gilead as a *p*
32:32 and the *p* of our inheritance
33:53 take *p* of the land and dwell
33:53 give the land to take *p* of it
33:54 as a *p* by lot according to
34:13 apportion . . . as a *p* by lot
34:17 land to you people for a *p*
34:18 to divide the land for a *p*
35:2 of the inheritance of their *p*
35:8 the *p* of the sons of Israel
35:8 that he will take as a *p*
35:28 return to the land of his *p*
36:8 every daughter getting *p* of an
36:8 *p* each one of the inheritance
De 1:8 Go in and take *p* of the land
1:21 Go up, take *p*, just as Jehovah
1:39 and they will take *p* of it
2:24 take *p* of his land, and engage
2:31 Start to take *p* of his land
3:12 And we took *p* of this land
3:18 this land to take *p* of it
3:20 have taken *p* of the land that
4:1 go in and take *p* of the land
4:5 you are going to take *p* of it
4:14 passing over to take *p* of it
4:22 take *p* of this good land
De 4:26 to take *p* of it
4:47 taking *p* of his land and of
5:31 giving them to take *p* of it
5:33 land of which you will take *p*
6:1 over there to take *p* of it
6:18 take *p* of the good land about
7:1 so as to take *p* of it, he must
8:1 take *p* of the land about which
9:4 to take *p* of this land
9:5 in to take *p* of their land
9:6 this good land to take *p* of it
9:23 take *p* of the land that I
10:11 go in and take *p* of the land
11:8 take *p* of the land to which
11:8 crossing to take *p* of it
11:10 you are going to take *p* of it
11:11 crossing to take *p* of it
11:29 are going to take *p* of it
11:31 go in and take *p* of the land
11:31 take *p* of it and dwell in it
12:1 allow you to take *p* of, all
12:10 God is giving you as a *p*
15:4 inheritance to take *p* of it
16:20 *p* of the land that Jehovah
17:14 you have taken *p* of it and
19:2 giving you to take *p* of it
19:3 proceeded to give you as a *p*
19:14 giving you to take *p* of it
21:1 giving you to take *p* of it
21:13 take *p* of her as your bride
23:20 so as to take *p* of it
24:1 make her his *p* as a wife
25:19 inheritance to take *p* of it
26:1 taken *p* of it and dwelt in it
28:21 you are going to take *p* of it
28:42 insects will take in *p*
28:63 you are going to take *p* of it
30:5 of which your fathers took *p*
30:5 will certainly take *p* of it
30:16 you are going to take *p* of it
30:18 to go to take *p* of it
31:13 the Jordan to take *p* of it
32:47 crossing the Jordan to take *p*
32:49 to the sons of Israel as a *p*
33:4 A *p* of the congregation of
33:23 *p* of the west and south
Jos 1:11 and take *p* of the land that
1:11 giving you to take *p* of it
1:15 also have taken *p* of the land
1:15 take *p* of it, the one that
8:7 you must take *p* of the city
12:1 land they then took *p* of on
13:1 remains to be taken in *p*
14:1 as a hereditary *p* in the land
16:4 proceeded to take *p* of land
17:12 to take *p* of these cities
18:3 *p* of the land that Jehovah
19:9 sons of Simeon got a *p* in
19:47 took *p* of it and went
19:49 for a *p* by its territories
19:51 as a *p* by lot in Shiloh
21:12 son of Jephunneh as his *p*
21:41 *p* of the sons of Israel
21:43 they proceeded to take *p* of
22:4 tents in the land of your *p*
22:9 to the land of their *p* in
22:19 land of your *p* is unclean
22:19 to the land of Jehovah's *p*
23:5 you took *p* of their land
24:4 Mount Seir to take *p* of it
24:8 take *p* of their land, and I
Jg 1:19 he took *p* of the mountainous
1:27 Manasseh did not take *p* of
2:6 to take *p* of the land
3:13 took *p* of the city of palm
11:21 Israel took *p* of all the land
11:22 took *p* of all the territory
18:9 come in to take *p* of the land
21:17 There should be a *p* for those
1Sa 2:8 glory he gives to them as a *p*
1Ki 8:36 land . . . as a hereditary *p*
21:3 the hereditary *p* of my
21:4 not give you the hereditary *p*
21:15 *p* of the vineyard of Naboth
21:16 to take *p* of it
21:18 gone down to take *p* of it
21:19 murdered and also taken *p*
2Ki 17:24 to take *p* of Samaria and
1Ch 7:28 *p* and their dwelling places
9:2 in their *p* in their cities
2Ch 6:27 your people as a hereditary *p*
11:14 Levites left . . . their *p*
20:11 your *p* that you caused us
31:1 each one to his own *p*

Ezr 9:11 take *p* of is an impure land
9:12 land and indeed take *p* of it
Ne 6:13 in their *p* a bad reputation
9:22 took *p* of the land of Sihon
9:23 should enter to take *p*
9:24 in and took the land in *p*
9:25 taking in *p* houses full of
11:3 each one in his own *p*, in
11:20 one in his own hereditary *p*
Ps 2:8 the earth as your own *p*
16:6 my own *p* has proved agreeable
25:13 will take *p* of the earth
37:34 to take *p* of the earth
44:3 that they took *p* of the land
61:5 the *p* of those fearing your
69:35 dwell there and take *p* of it
82:8 take *p* of all the nations
83:12 *p* of the abiding places of
105:44 *p* of the product of the hard
119:111 reminders as a *p* to time
Pr 8:21 to take *p* of substance
11:29 he will take *p* of wind; and
14:18 take *p* of foolishness, but
28:10 will come into *p* of good
30:23 she is taken *p* of as a wife
Ca 3:8 all of them in *p* of a sword
Isa 14:2 *p* upon the soil of Jehovah
14:21 take *p* of the earth and
14:23 make her a *p* of porcupines
34:11 porcupine must take *p* of
34:17 they will take *p* of it
54:3 take *p* even of nations
54:17 hereditary *p* of the servants
57:13 take *p* of my holy mountain
58:14 the hereditary *p* of Jacob
60:21 will hold *p* of the land
61:7 *p* of even a double portion
63:17 tribes of your hereditary *p*
63:18 your holy people had *p*
65:9 ones must take *p* of it
Jer 3:18 I gave as a hereditary *p* to
3:19 land, the hereditary *p* of
6:12 turned over to others for *p*
8:10 fields to those taking *p*
12:14 touching the hereditary *p*
12:15 each one to his hereditary *p*
17:4 your hereditary *p* that I had
32:8 right of hereditary *p* is
32:23 come in and take *p* of it
41:8 in our *p* hidden treasures
49:1 Malcam has taken *p* of Gad
49:2, 2 take *p* of those in *p* of
La 5:2 Our own hereditary *p* has been
Eze 7:24 take *p* of their houses, and I
33:24 he took *p* of the land
35:10 take *p* of each land
36:2 as a *p* it has become ours!
36:3 a *p* to the remaining ones of
36:5 as a *p* with the rejoicing
36:12 must take *p* of you, and
36:12 become a hereditary *p* to
44:28 no *p* should you people give
44:28 in Israel: I am their *p*
45:5 As a *p* they will have twenty
45:6 as the *p* of the city, you
45:7 and of the *p* of the city
45:7 and beside the *p* of the city
45:8 become his as a *p* in Israel
46:16 It is their *p* by inheritance
46:18 force them out of their *p*
46:18 his own *p* he should give
46:18 each one from his *p*
48:20 with the *p* of the city
48:21 and of the *p* of the city
48:22 *p* of the Levites and the
48:22 and the *p* of the city, in
Da 7:18 take *p* of the kingdom for
7:22 ones took *p* of the kingdom
Ho 9:6 nettles . . . will take *p*
Am 2:10 *p* of the land of the Amorite
9:12 may take *p* of what is left
Ob 17 the house of Jacob must take *p*
19 they must take *p* of the Negeb
19 they must take *p* of the field
19 Benjamin must take *p* of Gilead
20 *p* of the cities of the Negeb
Mic 2:2 a man and his hereditary *p*
Hab 1:6 *p* of residences not belonging
Zep 2:9 my own nation will take *p*
Zec 2:12 *p* of Judah as his portion
Mal 2:11 taken *p* of the daughter of
Mt 5:40 get *p* of your inner garment
Ac 5:1 Ananias . . . sold a *p*
7:5 not give him any inheritable *p*
Ac 7:5 to give it to him as a *p*
8:20 *p* of the free gift of God
27:16 get *p* of the skiff at the
Eph 1:14 ransom God's own *p*, to his
1Th 4:4 to get *p* of his own vessel
2Th 3:2 faith is not a *p* of all people
Heb 10:34 a better and an abiding *p*
1Pe 2:9 a people for special *p*, that

Possessions
Ge 34:23 their *p* and their wealth and
Jg 14:15 to take our *p* that you people
Ec 5:19 given riches and material *p*
6:2 riches and material *p* and
Isa 49:8 the desolated hereditary *p*
Mt 19:22 for he was holding many *p*
Mr 10:22 for he was holding many *p*
Ac 2:45 they went selling their *p*
2Co 12:14 I am seeking, not your *p*

Possessor
Isa 65:9 hereditary *p* of my mountains

Possessors
Ac 4:34 *p* of fields or houses would

Possible
Ex 10:5 not be *p* to see the earth
Jg 9:33 just as your hand finds it *p*
1Sa 10:7 what your hand finds *p*
Ezr 10:13 it is not *p* to stand outside
Es 8:8 it is not *p* to undo
Mt 19:26 with God all things are *p*
24:24 to mislead, if *p*, even the
26:39 if it is *p*, let this cup
26:42 if it is not *p* for this to
Mr 10:27 all things are *p* with God
13:22 if *p*, the chosen ones
14:35 if it were *p*, the hour
14:36 all things are *p* to you
Lu 18:27 impossible with men are *p*
Ac 2:24 not *p* for him to continue to
8:22 if *p*, the device of your
17:15 come to him as quickly as *p*
Ro 1:10 begging that if at all *p* I
12:18 If *p*, as far as it depends
1Co 11:20 is not *p* to eat the Lord's
Ga 4:15 *p*, you would have gouged out
Heb 10:4 not *p* for the blood of bulls

Possibly
Ge 15:5 count the stars, if you are *p*
34:14 We cannot *p* do such a thing
Ps 34:5 faces could not *p* be ashamed
41:2 you cannot *p* give him over to
50:3 cannot *p* keep silent
121:3 *p* allow your foot to totter
121:3 you cannot *p* be drowsy
Ec 1:15 wanting cannot *p* be counted
Isa 2:9 and you cannot *p* pardon them
Mt 15:32 may *p* give out on the road
Lu 18:26 said: Who *p* can be saved?
Ac 20:16 Pentecost if he *p* could

Post
Ge 40:21 to his *p* of cupbearer, and
Es 8:10 *p* horses used in the royal
8:14 *p* horses used in the royal
Isa 21:6 *p* a lookout that he may tell
Jer 51:12 *P* the watchmen. Make ready
Eze 44:8 *p* others as caretakers of
46:21 corner *p* of the courtyard
46:21 corner *p* of the courtyard
Hab 2:1 At my guard *p* I will keep

Posted
Ge 3:24 he drove the man out and *p*
Ne 4:9 kept a guard *p* against them
4:13 men *p* at the lowest parts
4:13 the people *p* by families
Mt 27:37 *p* above his head the charge

Posterity
Ge 21:23 my offspring and to my *p*
Job 18:19 He will have no *p* and no
Ps 109:13 his *p* be for cutting off
Isa 14:22 remnant and progeny and *p*
Da 11:4 but not to his *p* and not

Posting
Jg 7:19 got through *p* the sentries

Postponed
Pr 13:12 Expectation *p* is making the
Isa 13:22 days . . . will not be *p*

Postponement
Eze 12:25 There will be no *p* anymore
12:28 There will be no *p* anymore

Posts
Ex 26:23 two panel frames as corner *p*
26:24 will serve as two corner *p*
36:28 two panel frames as corner *p*
36:29 to the two corner *p*
Jg 16:3 two side *p* and pulled them
2Ch 7:6 standing at their *p* of duty
8:14 Levites at their *p* of duty
Pr 8:34 at the *p* of my entrances
Eze 40:49 were pillars by the side *p*
41:22 and it had its corner *p*
44:11 ministers at *p* of oversight
46:21 to the four corner *p* of the
46:22 corner *p* of the courtyard

Pot
Jg 6:19 broth he put in the cooking *p*
1Sa 2:14 the two-handled cooking *p* or
2:14 or the one-handled cooking *p*
2Ki 4:38 Put the large cooking *p* on
4:40 There is death in the *p*
4:41 he threw it into the *p*
4:41 proved to be in the *p*
Job 41:31 depths to boil just like a *p*
41:31 sea like an ointment *p*
Ps 60:8 Moab is my washing *p*
108:9 Moab is my washing *p*
Pr 17:3 The refining *p* is for silver
27:21 The refining *p* is for silver
Ec 7:6 the sound of thorns under the *p*
Jer 1:13 A widemouthed cooking *p*
Eze 11:3 is the widemouthed cooking *p*
11:7 is the widemouthed cooking *p*
11:11 a widemouthed cooking *p*
24:3 widemouthed cooking *p* on
24:6 the widemouthed cooking *p*
Mic 3:3 what is in a widemouthed *p*
3:3 in the midst of a cooking *p*
Zec 12:6 like a fire *p* among trees
14:21 every widemouthed cooking *p*

Potash
Job 9:30 cleansed my hands in *p*

Potent
Ps 135:10 And killed *p* kings

Potentate
1Ti 6:15 the happy and only *P* will

Potiphar
Ge 37:36 sold him into Egypt to *P*
39:1 *P*, a court official of Pharaoh

Potiphera
Ge 41:45 Asenath the daughter of *P*
41:50 Asenath the daughter of *P*
46:20 Asenath the daughter of *P*

Pots
Ex 16:3 were sitting by the *p* of meat
Nu 11:8 boiled it in cooking *p* or
2Ch 35:13 they boiled in cooking *p* and
35:13 in round-bottomed *p* and in
Ps 58:9 Before your *p* feel the
Zec 14:20 widemouthed cooking *p* in

Potsherds
Jer 19:2 the Gate of the *P*

Potter
Isa 29:16 *p* himself be accounted
41:25 just as a *p* that tramples
64:8 the clay, and you are our *P*
Jer 18:2 down to the house of the *p*
18:3 down to the house of the *p*
18:4 in the eyes of the *p*
18:6 able to do just like this *p*
18:6 clay in the hand of the *p*
19:1 an earthenware flask of a *p*
19:11 breaks the vessel of the *p*
La 4:2 the work of the hands of a *p*
Da 2:41 partly of molded clay of a *p*
Ro 9:21 *p* have authority over the

Potter's
2Sa 17:28 *p* vessels, and wheat and
Ps 2:9 As though a *p* vessel you will
Jer 18:3 doing work upon the *p* wheels
18:4 was spoiled by the *p* hand
Mt 27:7 the *p* field to bury strangers
27:10 gave them for the *p* field

Potters
1Ch 4:23 the *p* and the inhabitants of
Isa 30:14 a large jar of the *p*

Pouch
Mt 10:10 or a food *p* for the trip, or
Mr 6:8 no bread, no food *p*, no copper

Lu 9:3 neither staff nor food *p*
10:4 carry a purse, nor a food *p*
22:35 without purse and food *p* and
22:36 likewise also a food *p*

Pounce
Jer 49:22 ascend and *p* down, and he

Pounces
De 28:49 just as an eagle *p*, a nation
Jer 48:40 Just like an eagle that *p*

Pound
Ex 30:36 *p* some of it into fine
2Sa 22:43 *p* them fine like the dust
Ps 18:42 shall *p* them fine like dust
Pr 27:22 *p* the foolish one fine with
Joh 12:3 *p* of perfumed oil, genuine

Pounded
Nu 11:8 *p* it in a mortar, and they

Pounding
Job 39:24 With *p* and excitement it
Ps 93:3 rivers keep raising their *p*
Jer 10:22 a great *p* from the land

Pounds
Joh 19:39 aloes, about a hundred *p*

Pour
Ex 4:9 and *p* it out on the dry land
9:33 rain did not *p* down on the
25:29 which they will *p* libations
29:7 *p* it upon his head and anoint
29:12 rest of the blood you will *p*
30:9 not *p* a drink offering upon it
Le 2:1 must *p* oil over it and put
2:6 and you must *p* oil upon it
4:7 blood he will *p* at the base of
4:18 blood he will *p* at the base
4:25 *p* the rest of its blood at
4:30 *p* all the rest of its blood at
4:34 *p* all the rest of its blood
14:15 *p* it upon the priest's left
14:26 will *p* some of the oil upon
14:41 *p* the clay mortar that they
17:13 *p* its blood out and cover it
Nu 5:15 not *p* oil upon it nor put
28:7 *P* out in the holy place the
De 12:16 you should *p* it out as water
12:24 *p* it out upon the ground as
15:23 you should *p* it out as water
Jg 6:20 and *p* out the broth. At that
1Sa 1:15 *p* out my soul before Jehovah
1Ki 18:33 *p* it upon the burnt offering
2Ki 4:4 *p* out into all these vessels
4:41 *P* out for the people that
9:3 *p* it out upon his head and
9:6 *p* the oil out upon his head
16:13 to *p* out his drink offering
2Ch 12:7 rage will not *p* forth upon
34:17 *p* out the money that is
34:25 my rage may *p* forth upon
Job 3:24 my roaring cries *p* forth
10:10 to *p* me out as milk itself
Ps 16:4 *p* out their drink offerings
18:42 I shall *p* them out
42:4 will *p* out my soul within me
62:8 Before him *p* out your heart
69:24 *P* out upon them your
79:6 *P* out your rage upon the
141:8 Do not *p* out my soul
Isa 30:1 and to *p* out a libation, but
44:3 *p* out water upon the thirsty
44:3 *p* out my spirit upon your
Jer 6:11 *P* it out upon the child in
10:25 *P* out your rage upon the
14:16 *p* out upon them their
14:22 any that can *p* down rain
44:17 *p* out to her drink offerings
44:18 *p* out drink offerings to
44:19 *p* out drink offerings to her
44:19 *p* out drink offerings to her
44:25 to *p* out drink offerings to
La 2:19 *P* out your heart before the
Eze 7:8 shortly I shall *p* out my rage
14:19 *p* out my rage upon it with
16:15 and to *p* out your acts of
20:8 I promised to *p* out my rage
20:13 I promised to *p* out my fury
20:21 I promised to *p* out my rage
21:31 I will *p* out upon you my
22:31 *p* out my denunciation
24:3 and also *p* water into it
24:7 not *p* it out upon the earth
30:15 *p* out my rage upon Sin
Eze 36:18 to *p* out my rage upon them
39:29 *p* out my spirit upon the
Ho 5:10 *p* out my fury just like water
Joe 2:28 I shall *p* out my spirit on
2:29 I shall *p* out my spirit
Am 5:8 *p* them out upon the surface
9:6 *p* them out upon the surface
Mic 1:6 I will *p* down into the valley
Zep 3:8 in order to *p* out upon them
Zec 12:10 *p* out upon the house of
Mr 14:3 began to *p* it upon his head
Lu 6:38 They will *p* into your laps a
Ac 2:17 *p* out some of my spirit upon
2:18 will *p* out some of my spirit
Re 16:1 *p* out the seven bowls of the

Poured
Ge 28:18 *p* oil on the top of it
35:14 he *p* a drink offering upon it
35:14 and *p* oil upon it
Ex 37:16 libations would be *p*, out of
Le 4:12 the fatty ashes are *p* out
4:12 the fatty ashes are *p* out
8:12 *p* some of the anointing oil
8:15 blood he *p* at the base of the
9:9 blood he *p* at the base of the
21:10 anointing oil would be *p* and
De 12:27 *p* out against the altar of
Jos 7:23 *p* them out before Jehovah
1Sa 10:1 and *p* it out upon his head
2Sa 13:9 *p* it out before him, but
14:14 being *p* down to the earth
21:10 water *p* down upon them
23:16 but *p* it out to Jehovah
2Ki 3:11 *p* out water upon the hands
4:40 *p* it out for the men to eat
22:9 have *p* out the money that
1Ch 11:18 but *p* it out to Jehovah
2Ch 34:21 *p* out against us because of
Job 20:28 things *p* forth on the day of
22:16 Whose foundation is *p* away
28:2 from stone copper is being *p*
30:16 my soul is *p* out within me
Ps 22:14 Like water I have been *p* out
41:8 A good-for-nothing thing is *p*
45:2 been *p* out upon your lips
75:8 dregs will be *p* out from it
77:17 clouds have thunderously *p*
79:3 *p* out their blood like water
Ca 1:3 Like an oil that is *p* out is
Isa 26:16 *p* out a whisper of prayer
29:10 *p* a spirit of deep sleep
32:15 spirit is *p* out from on
53:12 he *p* out his soul to the
57:6 you *p* out a drink offering
Jer 7:20 and my rage are being *p*
32:29 *p* out drink offerings to
42:18 *p* out upon the inhabitants
42:18 my rage will be *p* out upon
44:6 my anger, was *p* out and it
La 2:4 *p* out his rage, just like fire
2:11 My liver has been *p* out to
2:12 soul being *p* out into the
3:49 My very eye has been *p* forth
4:1 holy stones are *p* out at the
4:11 He has *p* out his burning anger
Eze 16:36 your lustfulness has been *p*
22:22 have *p* out my rage upon you
36:18 blood that they had *p* out
Da 9:11 *p* out upon us the curse and
Mic 1:4 like waters being *p* down a
Na 1:6 His own rage . . . be *p* out like
Zep 1:17 blood will actually be *p* out
Mt 7:25 rain *p* down and the floods
7:27 rain *p* down and the floods
26:28 be *p* out in behalf of many
Mr 14:24 be *p* out in behalf of many
Lu 22:20 to be *p* out in your behalf
Joh 2:15 *p* out the coins of the money
Ac 1:18 all his intestines were *p* out
2:33 *p* out this which you see and
10:45 spirit was being *p* out also
Ro 5:5 love of God has been *p* out
Php 2:17 *p* out like a drink offering
2Ti 4:6 being *p* out like a drink
Tit 3:6 spirit he *p* out richly upon us
Heb 9:22 unless blood is *p* out no
Re 14:10 *p* out undiluted into the
16:2 *p* out his bowl into the earth
16:3 second one *p* out his bowl
16:4 third one *p* out his bowl into
16:6 they *p* out the blood of holy
16:8 fourth one *p* out his bowl
16:10 *p* out his bowl upon the
Re 16:12 sixth one *p* out his bowl upon
16:17 *p* out his bowl upon the air

Pouring
1Sa 7:6 and *p* it out before Jehovah
1Ki 22:35 blood of the wound kept *p*
2Ki 4:5 and she was doing the *p* out
Job 12:21 *p* out contempt upon nobles
29:6 kept *p* out streams of oil
Ps 107:40 *p* out contempt upon nobles
142:2 I kept *p* out my concern
Isa 42:25 kept *p* out upon him rage
44:14 the *p* rain itself keeps
55:10 just as the *p* rain descends
Jer 7:18 a *p* out of drink offerings
19:13 a *p* out of drink offerings
La 4:13 *p* out the blood of righteous
Eze 1:28 on the day of a *p* rain
9:8 you are *p* out your rage upon
20:28 *p* out . . . drink offerings
23:8 kept *p* out their immoral
33:25 and blood you keep *p* out
34:26 the *p* rain to descend in
34:26 *P* rains of blessing there
Da 9:27 *p* out also upon the one lying
Ho 6:3 he will come in like a *p* rain
9:4 continue *p* out wine to Jehovah
Zec 4:12 *p* forth . . . the golden liquid
14:17 no *p* rain will occur
Mt 26:7 she began *p* it upon his head
Lu 10:34 bound up his wounds, *p* oil

Pours
Job 16:13 He *p* out my gall bladder to
38:38 dust *p* out as into a molten
Ps 102:*super* *p* out his concern before

Poverty
Ge 45:11 fear you . . . may come to *p*
Pr 6:11 *p* will certainly come just
10:15 of the lowly ones is their *p*
13:18 comes to *p* and dishonor, but
20:13 that you may not come to *p*
23:21 and a glutton will come to *p*
24:34 as a highwayman your *p* will
28:19 have his sufficiency of *p*
30:8 Give me neither *p* nor riches
30:9 that I may not come to *p* and
31:7 one drink and forget one's *p*
2Co 8:2 deep *p* made the riches of
8:9 become rich through his *p*
Re 2:9 I know your tribulation and *p*

Powder
Ex 9:9 *p* upon all the land of Egypt
30:36 into fine *p* and put some of
De 28:24 give *p* and dust as the rain
2Ch 34:4 and reduced to *p*, and then
34:7 he crushed and reduced to *p*
Ca 3:6 every sort of scent *p* of a
Isa 5:24 will go up just like *p*
29:5 become just like fine *p*, and
Na 1:3 cloud mass is the *p* of his
Mal 4:3 as *p* under the soles of your

Power
Ge 4:12 will not give you back its *p*
31:6 with all my *p* I have served
31:29 *p* of my hand to do harm to
42:6 Joseph was the man in *p* over
49:3 beginning of my generative *p*
Ex 9:16 sake of showing you my *p* and
28:41 and fill their hand with *p*
29:9 the hand of his sons with *p*
29:29 fill their hand with *p*
29:33 fill their hand with *p*, in
29:35 to fill their hand with *p*
32:11 Egypt with great *p* and with
32:29 Fill your hand today with *p*
Le 8:33 to fill your hand with *p*
16:32 hand will be filled with *p*
21:10 hand was filled with *p* to
26:20 *p* will simply be expended
Nu 3:3 filled with *p* to act as priests
14:13 you by your *p* have led this
14:17 let your *p* become great, O
23:21 any uncanny *p* against Jacob
De 4:37 in his sight with his great *p*
8:17 My own *p* and the full might
8:18 the giver of *p* to you to make
9:29 brought out with your great *p*
21:17 beginning of his generative *p*
28:32 hands will be without *p*
Jos 14:11 As my *p* was then, so my
14:11 was then, so my *p* is now
17:17 and great *p* is yours

Jg 6:14 Go in this *p* of yours, and you
16:5 see in what his great *p* is
16:6 In what is your great *p* and
16:9 his *p* did not become known
16:15 in what your great *p* is
16:17 my *p* also would . . . depart
16:19 his *p* kept departing from
16:30 bent himself with *p*, and the
17:5 one of his sons with *p*, that
17:12 hand of the Levite with *p*
1Sa 2:9 not by *p* does a man prove
15:23 same as using uncanny *p* and
28:20 no *p* in him, because he had
28:22 eat, that *p* may come to be
30:4 no *p* to weep anymore
2Sa 6:14 dancing . . . with all his *p*
1Ki 13:33 would fill his hand with *p*
19:8 in the *p* of that nourishment
2Ki 17:36 *p* and a stretched-out arm
19:3 there is no *p* to give birth
1Ch 13:8 with full *p* and with songs
26:8 with the *p* for the service
29:2 according to all my *p* I have
29:12 in your hand there are *p* and
29:14 retain *p* to make voluntary
2Ch 2:6 retain *p* to build him a house
13:9 filled his hand with *p* by
13:20 retain any more *p* in the
14:11 many or those with no *p*
20:6 your hand *p* and mightiness
20:12 no *p* before this large
22:9 of Ahaziah to retain *p* for
25:8 *p* with God to help and to
26:13 *p* of a military force to
29:31 hand with *p* for Jehovah
Ezr 2:69 According to their *p* they
Ne 1:10 you redeemed by your great *p*
4:10 The *p* of the burden bearer
5:5 no *p* in our hands while our
5:8 as far as it was in our *p*
Job 3:17 those weary in *p* are at rest
5:20 from the *p* of a sword
6:11 What is my *p*, that I should
6:12, 12 Is my *p* the *p* of stones?
6:22 from some of the *p* of you
9:4 wise in heart and strong in *p*
9:19 If in *p* anyone is strong
20:22 *p* of misfortune itself will
21:16 is not in their own *p*
23:6 abundance of *p* contend with
24:22 strong people by his *p*
26:2 have been to one without *p*
26:12 By his *p* he has stirred up
27:22 From its *p* he will without
30:2 Even the *p* of their hands
30:18 abundance of *p* my garment
36:5 He is mighty in *p* of heart
36:22 acts exaltedly with his *p*
37:23 He is exalted in *p*, And
39:11 because its *p* is abundant
39:21 low plain and exults in *p*
40:16 its *p* is in its hips
Ps 22:15 My *p* has dried up just like
31:10 my *p* has stumbled
33:16 by the abundance of *p*
38:10 my *p* has left me
63:10 over to the *p* of the sword
65:6 the mountains with his *p*
71:9 when my *p* is failing, do not
78:51 generative *p* in the tents of
102:23 the way he afflicted my *p*
103:20 angels . . . mighty in *p*
105:36 of all their generative *p*
111:6 *p* of his works he has told
147:5 great and is abundant in *p*
Pr 3:27 *p* of your hand to do it
5:10 themselves with your *p*
14:4 because of the *p* of a bull
18:21 are in the *p* of the tongue
20:29 young men is their *p*
24:5 knowledge is reinforcing *p*
24:10 Your *p* will be scanty
Ec 4:1 their oppressors there was *p*
7:19 than ten men in *p* who
8:4 of the king is the *p* of control
8:8 *p* over the spirit to restrain
8:8 any *p* of control in the day of
9:10 do with your very *p*, for
10:5 on account of the one in *p*
Isa 1:13 with the use of uncanny *p*
3:4 arbitrary *p* will rule over
10:13 *p* of my hand I shall
37:3 there is no *p* to give birth
40:9 Raise your voice even with *p*
Isa 40:26 he also being vigorous in *p*
40:29 giving to the tired one *p*
40:31 in Jehovah will regain *p*
41:1 groups themselves regain *p*
44:12 hungry, and so without *p*
47:14 from the *p* of the flame
49:4 I have used up my own *p*
50:2 there in me no *p* to deliver
57:10 a revival of your own *p*
63:1 in the abundance of his *p*
63:1 One abounding in *p* to save
64:7 melt by the *p* of our error
Jer 10:12 Maker of the earth by his *p*
18:21 over to the *p* of the sword
27:5 by my great *p* and by my
32:8 the repurchasing *p* is yours
32:17 earth by your great *p* and
48:45 have stood still without *p*
51:15 Maker of the earth by his *p*
La 1:6 without *p* before the pursuer
1:14 My *p* has stumbled
Eze 35:5 over to the *p* of the sword
Da 3:27 fire had had no *p* over their
8:7 no *p* in the ram to stand
8:22 stand up, but not with his *p*
8:24 his *p* must become mighty, but
8:24 mighty, but not by his own *p*
10:8 left remaining in me no *p*
10:8 and I retained no *p*
10:16 and I did not retain any *p*
10:17 kept standing in me no *p*
11:5 than that one's ruling *p*
11:6 not retain the *p* of her arm
11:15 be no *p* to keep standing
11:25 arouse his *p* and his heart
12:7 dashing of the *p* of the holy
Ho 7:9 Strangers have eaten up his *p*
Am 2:14 strong will reinforce his *p*
Mic 2:1 it is in the *p* of their hand
3:8 full of *p*, with the spirit
Na 1:3 slow to anger and great in *p*
2:1 Reinforce *p* very much
Hab 1:11 This its *p* is due to its god
Zec 4:6 a military force, nor by *p*
Mt 13:22 deceptive *p* of riches choke
22:29 Scriptures nor the *p* of God
24:30 with *p* and great glory
26:64 at the right hand of *p* and
Mr 1:23 the *p* of an unclean spirit
4:19 deceptive *p* of riches and the
5:2 the *p* of an unclean spirit
5:30 that *p* had gone out of him
9:1 kingdom . . . already come in *p*
12:24 Scriptures or the *p* of God
13:26 with great *p* and glory
14:62 at the right hand of *p* and
Lu 1:17 with Elijah's spirit and *p*
1:35 and *p* of the Most High will
1:52 has brought down men of *p*
2:27 Under the *p* of the spirit he
3:8 God has *p* to raise up children
4:14 Jesus returned in the *p* of
4:36 authority and *p* he orders
5:17 Jehovah's *p* was there for him
6:19 because *p* was going out of
8:46 perceived that *p* went out of
9:1 gave them *p* and authority over
9:43 at the majestic *p* of God
10:19 over all the *p* of the enemy
19:12 to secure kingly *p* for
19:15 having secured the kingly *p*
21:27 with *p* and great glory
24:49 clothed with *p* from on high
Ac 1:8 *p* when the holy spirit arrives
3:12 as though by personal *p* or
4:7 By what *p* or in whose name
4:33 with great *p* the apostles
6:8 full of graciousness and *p*
8:10 This man is the *P* of God
8:27 in *p* under Candace queen of
9:22 Saul kept on acquiring *p* all
10:38 him with holy spirit and *p*
19:11 extraordinary works of *p*
25:5 let those who are in *p* among
Ro 1:4 with *p* was declared God's Son
1:16 God's *p* for salvation to
1:20 his eternal *p* and Godship
9:17 I may show my *p*, and that
9:22 and to make his *p* known
12:1 service with your *p* of reason
15:13 in hope with *p* of holy
15:19 the *p* of signs and portents
15:19 with the *p* of holy spirit
1Co 1:18 to us . . . it is God's *p*
1Co 1:24 Christ the *p* of God and the
2:4 of spirit and *p*
2:5 faith might be . . . God's *p*
4:19 not the speech . . . their *p*
4:20 lies not in speech, but in *p*
5:4 also my spirit with the *p* of
6:14 raise us up . . . through his *p*
15:24 and all authority and *p*
15:43 it is raised up in *p*
15:56 the *p* for sin is the Law
2Co 4:7 *p* beyond what is normal may
6:7 truthful speech, by God's *p*
12:9 my *p* is being made perfect
12:9 *p* of the Christ may like a
13:4 is alive owing to God's *p*
13:4 owing to God's *p* toward you
Eph 1:19 *p* is toward us believers
1:21 authority and *p* and lordship
3:7 to the way his *p* operates
3:16 with *p* through his spirit
3:20 his *p* which is operating in
6:10 go on acquiring *p* in the Lord
Php 3:10 the *p* of his resurrection
3:21 operation of the *p* that he
4:13 of him who imparts *p* to me
Col 1:11 made powerful with all *p* to
1:29 is at work in me with *p*
1Th 1:5 with *p* and with holy spirit
2Th 1:11 the work of faith with *p*
1Ti 1:12 Lord, who imparted *p* to me
2Ti 1:7 that of *p* and of love and of
1:8 according to the *p* of God
2:1 keep on acquiring *p* in the
3:5 but proving false to its *p*
4:17 near me and infused *p* into
Heb 1:3 by the word of his *p*; and
3:13 by the deceptive *p* of sin
4:12 word of God . . . exerts *p* and
7:16 *p* of an indestructible life
11:11 Sarah herself received *p* to
1Pe 1:5 by God's *p* through faith
2Pe 1:3 divine *p* has given us freely
1:16 *p* and presence of our Lord
2:11 greater in strength and *p*
1Jo 5:19 in the *p* of the wicked one
Re 1:16 sun when it shines in its *p*
3:8 that you have a little *p*, and
4:2 to be in the *p* of the spirit
4:11 glory and the honor and the *p*
5:12 receive the *p* and riches and
7:12 the *p* and the strength be to
11:17 taken your great *p* and begun
12:10 *p* and the kingdom of our God
13:2 gave to the beast its *p* and
15:8 of God and because of his *p*
17:3 away in the *p* of the spirit
17:13 *p* and authority to the wild
18:3 the *p* of her shameless luxury
19:1 and the *p* belong to our God
20:4 *p* of judging was given them
21:10 in the *p* of the spirit to

Powerful

Ge 49:24 hands of the *p* one of Jacob
Ex 15:6 proving itself *p* in ability
Job 8:2 sayings . . . are but a *p* wind
12:21 And the girdle of *p* ones he
34:17 if a *p* one is righteous
34:20 *p* ones depart by no hand
34:24 He breaks *p* ones without
36:19 Even all your *p* efforts
Ps 22:12 *p* ones of Bashan themselves
29:4 The voice of Jehovah is *p*
50:13 I eat the flesh of *p* bulls
76:5 ones *p* in heart have been
78:25 ate the very bread of *p* ones
132:2 vowed to the *P* One of Jacob
132:5 for the *P* One of Jacob
Ec 6:10 one that is more *p* than he is
Isa 1:24 the *P* One of Israel, is
10:13 just like a *p* one
10:34 by a *p* one Lebanon itself
28:2 storm of *p*, flooding waters
34:7 young bulls with the *p* ones
44:12 busy at it with his *p* arm
46:12 you the ones *p* at heart
49:26 the *P* One of Jacob
60:16 the *P* One of Jacob is
Jer 46:15 *p* ones have been washed
La 1:15 my *p* ones Jehovah has tossed
Da 8:6 toward it in its *p* rage
Joe 2:7 Like *p* men they run
3:9 Arouse the *p* men! Let them
3:10 let him say: I am a *p* man

Joe 3:11 bring your *p* ones down
Mt 7:22 many *p* works in your name
11:20 his *p* works had taken place
11:21 *p* works had taken place in
11:23 *p* works that took place in
13:54 wisdom and these *p* works
13:58 he did not do many *p* works
14:2 *p* works are operating in him
Mr 6:2 *p* works be performed through
6:5 able to do no *p* work there
6:14 *p* works are operating in him
9:39 do a *p* work on the basis of
Lu 1:49 the *p* One has done great deeds
10:13 *p* works that have taken
19:37 the *p* works they had seen
22:69 sitting at the *p* right hand
24:19 prophet *p* in work and word
Ac 2:22 to you through *p* works and
7:22 *p* in his words and deeds
8:13 and *p* works taking place
Ro 4:20 but became *p* by his faith
1Co 1:26 not many *p*, not many of
12:10 operations of *p* works, to
12:28 then *p* works; then gifts of
12:29 Not all perform *p* works, do
2Co 10:4 but *p* by God for overturning
12:10 I am weak, then I am *p*
12:12 and portents and *p* works
13:3 but is *p* among you
13:9 we are weak but you are *p*
Ga 3:5 performs *p* works among you
Col 1:11 being made *p* with all power
2Th 1:7 from heaven with his *p* angels
2:9 of Satan with every *p* work
Heb 2:4 various *p* works and with
11:34 a weak state were made *p*

Powerfulness
Pr 11:7 expectation based on *p* has

Powers
Jer 5:31 subduing according to their *p*
Mt 24:29 *p* of the heavens . . . shaken
Mr 7:35 his hearing *p* were opened
13:25 *p* that are in the heavens
Lu 21:26 *p* of the heavens will be
Ro 8:38 nor things to come nor *p*
1Co 14:20 in *p* of understanding
14:20 in *p* of understanding
2Co 3:14 their mental *p* were dulled
Ga 2:8 *p* necessary for an apostleship
2:8 gave *p* also to me for those
Php 4:7 your hearts and your mental *p*
Heb 5:14 their perceptive *p* trained
6:5 *p* of the coming system of
1Pe 3:22 *p* were made subject to him

Practical
Job 11:6 the things of *p* wisdom are
12:16 are strength and *p* wisdom
26:3 made *p* wisdom itself known
Pr 2:7 will treasure up *p* wisdom
3:21 Safeguard *p* wisdom and
8:14 I have counsel and *p* wisdom
18:1 against all *p* wisdom he will
Mic 6:9 the person of *p* wisdom will
Lu 1:17 the *p* wisdom of righteous
16:8 he acted with *p* wisdom; for
16:8 are wiser in a *p* way toward

Practically
Mr 11:24 that you have *p* received

Practice
Le 19:26 and you must not *p* magic
De 17:2 *p* what is bad in the eyes of
2Ki 17:17 to *p* divination and to look
Ps 58:2 *p* outright unrighteousness
Mic 3:6 so as not to *p* divination
3:11 prophets *p* divination simply
Mt 6:1 not to *p* your righteousness in
9:14 Pharisees *p* fasting but your
Mr 2:18 the Pharisees *p* fasting, but
2:18 disciples do not *p* fasting
Lu 1:9 *p* of the priestly office
2:27 the customary *p* of the law
6:38 *P* giving, and people will
Ac 16:21 to take up or *p*, seeing we
Ro 2:1 you that judge *p* the same
2:2 those who *p* such things
2:3 judge those who *p* such things
2:25 of benefit only if you *p* law
7:15 what I wish, this I do not *p*
7:19 I do not wish is what I *p*
1Co 10:8 Neither let us *p* fornication
15:34 do not *p* sin, for some are
Ga 2:14 to live according to Jewish *p*
5:20 *p* of spiritism, enmities
5:21 who *p* such things will not
Php 4:9 *p* these; and the God of peace
1Ti 5:4 first to *p* godly devotion
5:20 persons who *p* sin, that the
Heb 10:26 we *p* sin willfully after
Jas 2:8 *p* carrying out the kingly
2:13 not *p* mercy will have his
1Jo 3:6 does not *p* sin; no one that
3:9 he cannot *p* sin, because he
5:18 does not *p* sin, but the One
Re 18:23 by your spiritistic *p* all
22:15 and those who *p* spiritism

Practiced
2Ki 21:6 *p* magic and looked for omens
2Ch 33:6 *p* magic and used divination
33:6 and *p* sorcery and made
Ps 119:3 have *p* no unrighteousness
Ho 7:1 for they have *p* falsehood
Zep 2:3 *p* His own judicial decision
Mr 2:18 and the Pharisees *p* fasting
Joh 5:29 those who *p* vile things to
Ac 19:13 *p* the casting out of demons
19:19 who *p* magical arts brought
Ro 9:11 nor had *p* anything good or
2Co 5:10 to the things he has *p*
12:21 conduct that they have *p*

Practicer
De 18:10 a *p* of magic or anyone who
Isa 3:2 *p* of divination and elderly

Practicers
Job 34:8 with *p* of what is hurtful
Ps 6:8 all you *p* of what is hurtful
14:4 the *p* of what is hurtful got
28:3 and with *p* of what is hurtful
36:12 *p* of hurtfulness have fallen
53:4 the *p* of what is hurtful got
59:2 from the *p* of what is hurtful
64:2 tumult of *p* of hurtfulness
92:7 *p* of what is hurtful blossom
92:9 *p* of what is hurtful will be
94:4 All the *p* of what is hurtful
94:16 against the *p* of hurtfulness
101:8 all the *p* of what is hurtful
125:5 the *p* of what is hurtful
Pr 10:29 for the *p* of what is hurtful
Isa 2:6 they are *p* of magic like the
Jer 27:9 your *p* of divination and to
27:9 to your *p* of magic and to
29:8 *p* of divination deceive you
Ho 6:8 town of *p* of what is harmful
Mic 5:12 no *p* of magic will you
Zec 10:2 *p* of divination, for their

Practices
De 28:20 the badness of your *p* in that
Jg 2:19 did not refrain from their *p*
1Sa 25:3 was harsh and bad in his *p*
Ne 9:35 turn back from their bad *p*
Ps 28:4 to the badness of their *p*
77:11 shall remember the *p* of Jah
78:7 not forget the *p* of God but
Pr 20:11 by his *p* a boy makes himself
28:16 also abundant in fraudulent *p*
Joh 3:20 he that *p* vile things hates
Ac 19:18 and report their *p* openly
26:31 *p* nothing deserving death
Ro 8:13 *p* of the body to death by the
11:26 away ungodly *p* from Jacob
1Co 6:18 but he that *p* fornication is
Col 3:9 old personality with its *p*
1Jo 2:29 everyone who *p* righteousness
3:4 Everyone who *p* sin is also
3:6 no one that *p* sin has either
Re 9:21 nor of their spiritistic *p*

Practicing
De 18:14 listen to those *p* magic and
Job 31:3 for those *p* what is hurtful
34:22 those *p* what is hurtful
Ps 5:5 all those *p* what is hurtful
15:2 and *p* righteousness
141:4 are *p* what is hurtful
141:9 those *p* what is hurtful
Pr 21:15 for those *p* what is hurtful
Isa 31:2 of those *p* what is hurtful
Ho 4:2 *p* of deception and murdering
Mic 2:1 *p* what is bad, upon their
Zec 7:3 *p* an abstinence, the way I
Ac 8:9 *p* magical arts and amazing
16:16 by *p* the art of prediction
Ro 1:32 those *p* such things are
1:32 consent with those *p* them
Ro 13:4 upon the one *p* what is bad
1Jo 1:6 lying and are not *p* the truth
3:4 sin is also *p* lawlessness
Re 21:8 and those *p* spiritism and

Praetorian
Ac 23:35 under guard in the *p* palace
Php 1:13 among all the *P* Guard and

Praise
Ex 15:11 to be feared with songs of *p*
De 10:21 He is the One for you to *p*
26:19 resulting in *p* and reputation
1Ch 16:4 to thank and *p* Jehovah the
16:35 speak exultingly in your *p*
16:36 Amen! and a *p* to Jehovah
23:5 givers of *p* to Jehovah on the
23:5 instruments . . . for giving *p*
23:30 to thank and *p* Jehovah, and
2Ch 7:6 David would render *p* by
8:14 *p* and to minister in front
20:19 *p* Jehovah the God of Israel
20:21 *p* in holy adornment as they
20:21 Give *p* to Jehovah, for to
20:22 with the joyful cry and *p*
23:13 the signal for offering *p*
29:30 Levites to *p* Jehovah in the
29:30 offer *p* even with
30:21 priests were offering *p* to
31:2 *p* in the gates of the camps
Ezr 3:10 stood up to *p* Jehovah
Ne 5:13 And they began to *p* Jehovah
9:5 above all blessing and *p*
11:17 conductor of the *p* singing
12:24 to offer *p* and give thanks
12:46 *p* and thanksgivings to God
Ps 22:22 of the congregation . . . *p*
22:23 fearers of Jehovah, *p* him
22:25 my *p* will be in the large
22:26 Those seeking . . . *p* Jehovah
33:1 upright ones *p* is fitting
34:1 his *p* will be in my mouth
35:18 Among . . . people I shall *p*
35:28 All day long your *p*
40:3 *P* to our God
44:8 In God we will offer *p* all
48:10 Like your name . . . so your *p*
51:15 mouth may tell forth your *p*
56:4 with God I shall *p* his word
56:10 I shall *p* his word
56:10 I shall *p* his word
63:5 my mouth offers *p*
65:1 For you there is *p*—silence
66:2 Render his *p* glorious
66:8 voice of *p* to him to be heard
69:30 I will *p* the name of God
69:34 Let heaven and earth *p* him
71:6 In you my *p* is constantly
71:8 mouth is filled with your *p*
71:14 I will add to all your *p*
74:21 and the poor one *p* your name
79:13 we shall declare your *p*
100:4 Into his courtyards with *p*
102:18 is to be created will *p* Jah
102:21 And his *p* in Jerusalem
104:35 *P* Jah, you people!
105:45 *P* Jah, you people!
106:1 *P* Jah, you people!
106:2 make all his *p* to be heard
106:12 They began to sing his *p*
106:47 speak exultingly in your *p*
106:48 *P* Jah, you people!
107:32 elderly men let them *p* him
109:1 God of my *p*, do not keep
109:30 among many people I shall *p*
111:1 *P* Jah, you people!
111:10 His *p* is standing forever
112:1 *P* Jah, you people!
113:1 *P* Jah, you people!
113:1 Offer *p*, O you servants of
113:1 *P* the name of Jehovah
113:9 *P* Jah, you people!
115:17 dead themselves do not *p*
115:18 *P* Jah, you people!
116:19 *P* Jah, you people!
117:1 *P* Jehovah, all you nations
117:2 *P* Jah, you people!
119:171 May my lips bubble forth *p*
135:1 *P* Jah, you people!
135:1 *P* the name of Jehovah
135:1 Offer *p*, O servants of
135:3 *P* Jah, for Jehovah is good
135:21 *P* Jah, you people!
145:*super* A *p*, of David
145:2 I will *p* your name to time

Ps 145:21 *p* of Jehovah my mouth
146:1 *P* Jah, you people!
146:1 *P* Jehovah, O my soul
146:2 *p* Jehovah during my lifetime
146:10 *P* Jah, you people!
147:1 *P* Jah, you people, For it
147:1 is pleasant—*p* is fitting
147:12 *P* your God, O Zion
147:20 *P* Jah, you people!
148:1 *P* Jah, you people!
148:1 *P* Jehovah from the heavens
148:1 *P* him in the heights
148:2 *P* him, all you his angels
148:2 *P* him, all you his army
148:3 *P* him, you sun and moon
148:3 *P* him, all you stars of
148:4 *P* him, you heavens of the
148:5 them *p* the name of Jehovah
148:7 *P* Jehovah from the earth
148:13 them *p* the name of Jehovah
148:14 The *p* of all his loyal ones
148:14 *P* Jah, you people!
149:1 *P* Jah, you people!
149:1 His *p* in the congregation of
149:3 *p* his name with dancing
149:9 *P* Jah, you people!
150:1 *P* Jah, you people!
150:1 *P* God in his holy place
150:1 *P* him in the expanse of his
150:2 *P* him for his works of
150:2 *P* him according to the
150:3 *P* him with the blowing of
150:3 *P* him with the stringed
150:4 *P* him with the tambourine
150:4 *P* him with strings and the
150:5 *P* him with the cymbals of
150:5 *P* him with the clashing
150:6 breathing thing—let it *p* Jah
150:6 *P* Jah, you people!
Pr 27:2 and not your own mouth, *p* you
27:21 is according to his *p*
28:4 leaving the law *p* the wicked
31:30 that procures *p* for herself
31:31 let her works *p* her even in
Ca 6:9 and they proceeded to *p* her
Isa 38:18 death itself cannot *p* you
42:8 neither my *p* to graven
42:10 *p* from the extremity of the
42:12 tell forth even his *p*
43:21 should recount the *p* of me
48:9 for my *p* I shall restrain
60:18 Salvation and your gates *P*
61:3 the mantle of *p* instead of
61:11 *p* in front of all the
62:7 as a *p* in the earth
62:9 be certain to *p* Jehovah
Jer 13:11 a *p* and something beautiful
17:14 be saved; for you are my *p*
20:13 *P* Jehovah! For he has
31:7 Give *p* and say, Save
33:9 *p* and a beauty toward all
48:2 is there any *p* of Moab
49:25 city of *p* has not been
51:41 *P* of the whole earth gets
Da 2:23 giving *p* and commendation
6:10 offering *p* before his God, as
Joe 2:26 to *p* the name of Jehovah
Hab 3:3 *p* the earth became filled
Zep 3:19 as a *p* and as a name in all
3:20 people to be a name and a *p*
Mt 11:25 I publicly *p* you, Father
21:16 you have furnished *p*
Lu 10:21 I publicly *p* you, Father
18:43 at seeing it, gave *p* to God
19:37 and *p* God with a loud voice
Ro 2:29 *p* of that one comes, not
13:3 and you will have *p* from it
15:11 *P* Jehovah, all you nations
15:11 let all the peoples *p* him
1Co 4:5 his *p* come to him from God
14:15 will sing *p* with the gift
14:15 also sing *p* with my mind
14:16 offer *p* with a gift of the
2Co 8:18 whose *p* in connection with
Eph 1:6 *p* of his glorious undeserved
1:12 serve for the *p* of his glory
1:14 possession, to his glorious *p*
Php 1:11 to God's glory and *p*
Heb 2:12 I will *p* you with song
13:15 to God a sacrifice of *p*
1Pe 1:7 found a cause for *p* and glory
2:14 but to *p* doers of good
Re 19:1 They said: *P* Jah, you people!
19:3 they said: *P* Jah, you people!
Re 19:4 Amen! *P* Jah, you people!
19:6 They said: *P* Jah, you people

Praised
2Sa 14:25 Israel as to be *p* so much
22:4 the One to be *p*, Jehovah
1Ch 16:25 great and very much to be *p*
Ps 10:3 *p* himself over the selfish
18:3 the One to be *p*, Jehovah, I
48:1 is great and much to be *p*
78:63 And his virgins were not *p*
96:4 great and very much to be *p*
113:3 Jehovah's name is to be *p*
119:164 in the day I have *p* you
145:3 great and very much to be *p*
Pr 12:8 discretion a man will be *p*
Isa 64:11 our forefathers *p* you
Eze 26:17 O *p* city, who became a
Da 4:34 I *p* and glorified, because
5:4 *p* the gods of gold and of
5:23 *p* mere gods of silver and of
2Co 11:31 One who is to be *p* forever

Praises
Ps 22:3 Inhabiting the *p* of Israel
78:4 *p* of Jehovah and his strength
Pr 31:28 owner rises up, and he *p* her
Isa 60:6 the *p* of Jehovah they will
63:7 mention, the *p* of Jehovah
Mt 26:30 after singing *p*, they went
Mr 14:26 after singing *p*, they went
Eph 5:19 with psalms and *p* to God
Col 3:16 *p* to God, spiritual songs

Praiseworthy
Ps 9:14 may declare all your *p* deeds
Php 4:8 whatever *p* thing there is

Praising
Ge 12:15 they began *p* her to Pharaoh
Jg 16:24 gave way to *p* their god
1Ch 25:3 for thanking and *p* Jehovah
29:13 and *p* your beauteous name
2Ch 5:13 in *p* and thanking Jehovah
5:13 with *p* Jehovah, for he is
23:12 running and *p* the king, she
Ezr 3:11 by *p* and giving thanks to
3:11 a loud shout in *p* Jehovah
Ps 84:4 They still keep on *p* you
119:175 soul keep living and *p*
Da 4:37 *p* and exalting and glorifying
Lu 2:13 the heavenly army, *p* God and
2:20 *p* God for all the things they
Ac 2:47 *p* God and finding favor with
3:8 walking and leaping and *p* God
3:9 sight of him walking and *p* God
16:25 praying and *p* God with song
Re 19:5 Be *p* our God, all you his

Pray
Ge 32:11 Deliver me, I *p* you, from
44:18 I *p* you, my master, please
1Sa 1:10 she began to *p* to Jehovah and
1:26 in this place to *p* to Jehovah
2:1 Hannah went on to *p* and say
2:25 who is there to *p* for him?
7:5 *p* in your behalf to Jehovah
8:6 Samuel began to *p* to Jehovah
12:19 *P* in behalf of your servants
12:23 ceasing to *p* in your behalf
2Sa 7:27 servant has taken heart to *p*
1Ki 8:30 they *p* toward this place
8:33 *p* and make request for favor
8:35 *p* toward this place and laud
8:44 *p* to Jehovah in the direction
8:48 *p* to you in the direction of
13:6 *p* in my behalf that my hand
2Ki 4:33 and began to *p* to Jehovah
6:17 Elisha began to *p* and say
6:18 Elisha went on to *p* to
19:15 And Hezekiah began to *p*
20:2 began to *p* to Jehovah, saying
1Ch 17:25 occasion to *p* before you
2Ch 6:21 people Israel when they *p*
6:24 *p* and make request for favor
6:26 *p* toward this place and laud
6:32 come and *p* toward this house
6:34 *p* to you in the direction
6:38 *p* in the direction of their
7:14 *p* and seek my face and turn
32:24 and he began to *p* to Jehovah
Job 42:8 will himself *p* for you
Ps 5:2 God, because to you I *p*
32:6 every loyal one will *p* to you
Isa 16:12 came to his sanctuary to *p*
37:15 Hezekiah began to *p* to
Isa 38:2 and began to *p* to Jehovah
45:14 they will *p* saying, Indeed
Jer 7:16 do not *p* in behalf of this
11:14 do not *p* in behalf of this
14:11 Do not *p* in behalf of this
29:7 *p* in its behalf to Jehovah
29:12 *p* to me, and I will listen
32:16 *p* to Jehovah after my having
37:3 *P*, please, in our behalf to
42:2 *p* in our behalf to Jehovah
42:20 *P* in our behalf to Jehovah
Da 9:4 *p* to Jehovah my God and to
Mt 5:44 *p* for those persecuting you
6:5 when you *p*, you must not be
6:5 they like to *p* standing in the
6:6 when you *p*, go into your
6:6 *p* to your Father who is in
6:9 You must *p*, then, this way
14:23 mountain by himself to *p*
21:9 Save, we *p*, the Son of David!
21:9 Save him, we *p*, in the
21:15 Save, we *p*, the Son of David!
26:36 while I go over there and *p*
26:41 *p* continually, that you may
Mr 6:46 off into a mountain to *p*
11:9 Save, we *p*! Blessed is he
11:10 Save, we *p*, in the heights
11:24 the things you *p* and ask for
14:32 Sit down here while I *p*
Lu 6:12 out into the mountain to *p*
6:28 *p* for those who are insulting
9:28 up into the mountain to *p*
11:1 Lord, teach us how to *p*, just
11:2 Whenever you *p*, say, Father
18:1 the need for them always to *p*
18:10 went up into the temple to *p*
18:11 Pharisee stood and began to *p*
22:41 bent his knees and began to *p*
Joh 12:13 Save, we *p* you! Blessed is
Ac 10:9 about the sixth hour to *p*
Ro 8:26 what we should *p* for as we
1Co 11:13 for a woman to *p* uncovered
14:13 *p* that he may translate
14:15 will *p* with the gift of the
14:15 I will also *p* with my mind
2Co 13:7 we *p* to God that you may do
Col 1:3 always when we *p* for you
1Th 5:17 *P* incessantly
2Th 1:11 we always *p* for you, that
Jas 5:14 and let them *p* over him
5:16 *p* for one another, that you
3Jo 2 I *p* that in all things you may

Prayed
1Sa 1:12 *p* extendedly before Jehovah
1:27 I *p* that Jehovah should grant
2Ch 30:18 Hezekiah *p* for them, saying
Ezr 10:1 as soon as Ezra had *p* and he
Ne 2:4 I *p* to the God of the heavens
4:9 we *p* to our God and kept a
Job 42:10 he *p* in behalf of his
Isa 37:21 have *p* to me concerning
Jon 2:1 Jonah *p* to Jehovah his God
4:2 he *p* to Jehovah and said
Mt 26:42 *p*, saying: My Father, if it
26:44 he again went off and *p* for
Mr 14:39 he went away again and *p*
Ac 1:24 *p* and said: You, O Jehovah
6:6 having *p*, these laid their
8:15 *p* for them to get holy
9:40 bending his knees, he *p*, and
13:3 they fasted and *p* and laid
20:36 down with all of them and *p*
28:8 *p*, laid his hands upon him
Jas 5:17 he *p* for it not to rain
5:18 he *p* again, and the heaven

Prayer
2Sa 7:27 to pray to you with this *p*
1Ki 8:28 the *p* of your servant and to
8:28 to the *p* with which your
8:29 listen to the *p* with which
8:38 whatever *p*, whatever
8:45 their *p* and their request for
8:49 their *p* and their request for
8:54 this *p* and request for favor
9:3 heard your *p* and your request
2Ki 19:4 *p* in behalf of the remnant
19:20 The *p* that you have made to
20:5 I have heard your *p*. I have
2Ch 6:19 toward the *p* of your servant
6:19 *p* with which your servant is
6:20 *p* with which your servant
6:29 whatever *p*, whatever request
6:35 from the heavens their *p*

2Ch 6:39 their *p* and their requests
6:40 *p* respecting this place
7:12 I have heard your *p*, and I
7:15 attentive to *p* at this place
30:27 *p* came to his holy dwelling
33:18 Manasseh and his *p* to his
33:19 *p* and how his entreaty was
Ne 1:6 listen to the *p* of your servant
1:11 attentive to the *p* of your
1:11 to the *p* of your servants
11:17 did the lauding at *p*, and
Job 16:17 And my *p* is pure
Ps 4:1 Show me favor and hear my *p*
6:9 will accept my own *p*
17:*super* A *p* of David
17:1 Do give ear to my *p* without
35:13 my own *p* would return
39:12 Do hear my *p*, O Jehovah
42:8 *p* to the God of my life
54:2 O God, hear my *p*
55:1 Do give ear, O God, to my *p*
61:1 Do pay attention to my *p*
65:2 O Hearer of *p*, even to you
66:19 to the voice of my *p*
66:20 has not turned aside my *p*
69:13 my *p* was to you, O Jehovah
72:15 let *p* be made constantly
80:4 against the *p* of your people
84:8 God of armies, do hear my *p*
86:*super* A *p* of David
86:6 give ear, O Jehovah, to my *p*
88:2 Before you my *p* will come
88:13 own *p* keeps confronting you
90:*super* A *p* of Moses, the man of
102:*super* A *p* of the afflicted in
102:1 O Jehovah, do hear my *p*
102:17 *p* of those stripped of
102:17 And not despise their *p*
109:4 But on my part there is *p*
109:7 let his very *p* become a sin
141:2 *p* be prepared as incense
141:5 my *p* during their calamities
142:*super* Of David . . . A *p*
143:1 O Jehovah, hear my *p*
Pr 15:8 the *p* of the upright ones is a
15:29 *p* of the righteous ones he
28:9 his *p* is something detestable
Isa 26:16 poured out a whisper of *p*
37:4 *p* in behalf of the remnant
38:5 I have heard your *p*. I have
56:7 rejoice inside my house of *p*
56:7 a house of *p* for all the
Jer 7:16 an entreating cry or a *p*
11:14 an entreating cry or a *p*
La 3:8 help, he actually hampers my *p*
3:44 that *p* may not pass through
Da 9:3 to seek him with *p* and with
9:17 to the *p* of your servant and
9:21 I was yet speaking in the *p*
Jon 2:7 Then my *p* came in to you
Hab 3:1 *p* of Habakkuk the prophet
Mt 19:13 hands upon them and offer *p*
21:13 will be called a house of *p*
21:22 all the things you ask in *p*
Mr 9:29 out by anything except by *p*
11:17 will be called a house of *p*
Lu 6:12 the whole night in *p* to God
19:46 house will be a house of *p*
22:40 Carry on *p*, that you do not
22:45 he rose from *p*, went to the
22:46 Rise and carry on *p*, that
Ac 1:14 these were persisting in *p*
3:1 the temple for the hour of *p*
6:4 devote ourselves to *p* and to
10:31 *p* has been favorably heard
12:5 *p* to God for him was being
14:23 offering *p* with fastings
16:13 there was a place of *p*
16:16 going to the place of *p*, a
21:5 down on the beach we had *p*
Ro 12:12 Persevere in *p*
1Co 7:5 devote time to *p* and may
Eph 6:18 with every form of *p* and
6:18 carry on *p* on every occasion
Php 4:6 in everything by *p* and
Col 4:2 persevering in *p*, remaining
1Th 5:25 continue in *p* for us
2Th 3:1 brothers, carry on *p* for us
1Ti 2:8 the men carry on *p*, lifting
4:5 through God's word and *p* over
Heb 13:18 Carry on *p* for us, for we
Jas 5:13 Let him carry on *p*
5:15 the *p* of faith will make the
5:17 in *p* he prayed for it not to

Prayerful
2Co 1:11 to us due to many *p* faces

Prayers
Ps 72:20 *p* of David, the son of Jesse
Isa 1:15 Even though you make many *p*
Mr 12:40 a pretext making long *p*
Lu 20:47 for a pretext make long *p*
Ac 2:42 to taking of meals and to *p*
10:4 Your *p* and gifts of mercy
Ro 1:9 make mention of you in my *p*
15:30 with me in *p* to God for
Eph 1:16 mentioning you in my *p*
Col 4:12 in his *p*, that you may
1Th 1:2 all of you in our *p*
1Ti 2:1 *p*, intercessions, offerings
5:5 in supplications and *p* night
Phm 4 make mention of you in my *p*
22 through the *p* of you people
1Pe 3:7 for your *p* not to be hindered
4:7 vigilant with a view to *p*
Re 5:8 means the *p* of the holy ones
8:3 the *p* of all the holy ones upon
8:4 with the *p* of the holy ones

Praying
1Ki 8:28 your servant is *p* before you
8:54 Solomon finished *p* to
2Ch 6:19 servant is *p* before you
7:1 Solomon finished *p*, the fire
32:20 *p* over this and crying to
33:13 kept *p* to Him, so that He
Ezr 6:10 *p* for the life of the king
Ne 1:4 continually fasting and *p*
1:6 I am *p* before you today, day
Isa 45:20 *p* to a god that cannot save
Jer 42:4 I am *p* to Jehovah your God
Da 6:10 *p* and offering praise before
9:20 *p* and confessing my sin and
Mt 6:7 *p*, do not say the same things
24:20 Keep *p* that your flight may
26:39 he fell upon his face, *p* and
Mr 1:35 a lonely place . . . he began *p*
11:25 when you stand *p*, forgive
13:18 Keep *p* that it may not occur
14:35 on the ground and began *p*
14:38 keep on the watch and *p*
Lu 1:10 *p* outside at the hour of
3:21 as he was *p*, the heaven was
5:16 in the deserts and *p*
9:18 while he was *p* alone, the
9:29 as he was *p* the appearance
11:1 being in a certain place *p*
22:44 continued *p* more earnestly
Ac 9:11 For, look! he is *p*
10:30 I was *p* in my house at the
11:5 in the city of Joppa *p*, and
12:12 were gathered together and *p*
16:25 Paul and Silas were *p* and
22:17 *p* in the temple, I fell into
1Co 14:14 For if I am *p* in a tongue
14:14 gift of the spirit that is *p*
2Co 13:9 for this we are *p*, your
Php 1:9 I continue *p*, that your love
Col 1:9 have not ceased *p* for you
4:3 *p* also for us, that God may
Jude 20 and *p* with holy spirit

Prays
1Ki 8:29 servant *p* toward this place
8:42 and *p* toward this house
2Ch 6:20 servant *p* toward this place
Isa 44:17 bows down and *p* to it and
1Co 11:4 man that *p* or prophesies
11:5 woman that *p* or prophesies

Preach
Mt 10:7 *p*, saying, The kingdom of the
10:27 *p* from the housetops
11:1 teach and *p* in their cities
Mr 1:7 he would *p*, saying: After me
1:38 that I may *p* there also, for
3:14 he might send them out to *p*
Lu 4:18 *p* a release to the captives
4:19 to *p* Jehovah's acceptable year
9:2 he sent them forth to *p* the
Ac 8:5 began to *p* the Christ to them
9:20 *p* Jesus, that this One is the
10:42 he ordered us to *p* to the
15:21 city after city those who *p*
Ro 10:14 hear without someone to *p*
10:15 *p* unless they have been sent
1Co 1:23 but we *p* Christ impaled, to
Col 1:25 to *p* the word of God fully
1Th 1:5 the good news we *p* did not
2Ti 2:8 the good news I *p*
2Ti 4:2 *p* the word, be at it urgently

Preached
Mt 12:41 repented at what Jonah *p*
24:14 *p* in all the inhabited earth
26:13 this good news is *p* in all
Mr 6:12 *p* in order that people might
13:10 good news has to be *p* first
14:9 Wherever the good news is *p*
Lu 11:32 repented at what Jonah *p*
12:3 will be *p* from the housetops
24:47 be *p* in all the nations
Ac 10:37 the baptism that John *p*
13:24 *p* publicly to all the people
Ro 15:19 thoroughly *p* the good news
1Co 1:21 foolishness of what is *p* to
2:4 and what I *p* were not with
9:27 after I have *p* to others, I
15:12 Christ is being *p* that he
2Co 1:19 Jesus, who was *p* among you
11:4 other than the one we *p*
Col 1:23 was *p* in all creation that
1Th 2:9 we *p* the good news of God to
1Ti 3:16 was *p* about among nations
1Pe 3:19 *p* to the spirits in prison

Preacher
1Ti 2:7 appointed a *p* and an apostle
2Ti 1:11 appointed a *p* and apostle and
2Pe 2:5 Noah, a *p* of righteousness

Preaches
Ac 19:13 by Jesus whom Paul *p*
2Co 11:4 *p* a Jesus other than the one

Preaching
Mt 3:1 John the Baptist came *p* in
4:17 Jesus commenced *p* and saying
4:23 and *p* the good news of the
9:35 and *p* the good news of the
Mr 1:4 in the wilderness, *p* baptism
1:14 Jesus went into Galilee, *p*
1:39 did go, *p* in their synagogues
Lu 3:3 *p* baptism in symbol of
4:44 went on *p* in the synagogues
8:1 *p* and declaring the good news
Ac 20:25 whom I went *p* the kingdom
28:31 *p* the kingdom of God to
Ro 2:21 one *p* Do not steal, do you
10:8 of faith, which we are *p*
16:25 and the *p* of Jesus Christ
1Co 15:11 we are *p* and so you have
15:14 our *p* is certainly in vain
2Co 4:5 *p*, not ourselves, but Christ
Ga 2:2 which I am *p* among the nations
5:11 if I am still *p* circumcision
Php 1:15 *p* the Christ through envy
2Ti 4:17 that through me the *p* might
Tit 1:3 *p* with which I was entrusted

Precede
1Th 4:15 in no way *p* those who have

Preceding
Le 26:10 eat the old of the *p* year
Heb 7:18 aside of the *p* commandment

Precious
1Sa 18:30 his name came to be very *p*
26:21 soul has been *p* in your eyes
2Sa 12:30 gold, along with *p* stones
1Ki 10:2 very much gold and *p* stones
10:10 balsam oil and *p* stones
10:11 great amount and *p* stones
2Ki 1:13 be *p* in your eyes
1:14 my soul be *p* in your eyes
1Ch 20:2 in it there were *p* stones
29:2 and every *p* stone, and
2Ch 3:6 the house with *p* stone for
9:1 great quantity, and *p* stones
9:9 great quantity, and *p* stones
9:10 almug trees and *p* stones
32:27 *p* stones and for balsam oil
Job 22:24 placing of *p* ore in the dust
22:25 indeed become your *p* ores
28:10 *p* things his eye has seen
31:26 the *p* moon walking along
Ps 36:7 How *p* your loving-kindness is
45:9 are among your *p* women
49:8 price of their soul is so *p*
72:14 blood will be *p* in his eyes
116:15 *P* in the eyes of Jehovah
139:17 how *p* your thoughts are
Pr 1:13 all sorts of *p* valuables
3:15 more *p* than corals, and all
6:26 she hunts even for a *p* soul
12:27 is a man's *p* wealth

Pr 20:15 the lips of knowledge are *p*
24:4 *p* and pleasant things of value
Ec 10:1 is *p* for wisdom and glory
Isa 28:16 *p* corner of a sure
43:4 have been *p* in my eyes
Jer 15:19 bring forth what is *p*
20:5 and all its *p* things
31:20 Is Ephraim a *p* son to me
La 4:2 As for the *p* sons of Zion
Eze 22:25 Treasure and *p* things they
27:22 *p* stones and gold
28:13 *p* stone was your covering
Da 11:38 by means of *p* stone and by
Zec 14:6 prove to be no *p* light
1Co 3:12 gold, silver, *p* stones, wood
Jas 5:7 for the *p* fruit of the earth
1Pe 1:19 it was with *p* blood, like
2:4 but chosen, *p*, with God
2:6 foundation cornerstone, *p*
2:7 *p*, because you are believers
2Pe 1:4 *p* and very grand promises
Re 4:3 and a *p* red-colored stone
17:4 with gold and *p* stone and
18:12 *p* stone and pearls and fine
18:12 object out of most *p* wood
18:16 gold ornament and *p* stone
21:11 like a most *p* stone, as a
21:19 with every sort of *p* stone

Preciousness
Ps 37:20 be like the *p* of pastures

Precipice
Mt 8:32 herd rushed over the *p* into
Mr 5:13 the herd rushed over the *p*
Lu 8:33 the herd rushed over the *p*

Precipitating
Isa 5:6 keep from *p* any rain upon it

Precipitation
Isa 4:6 rainstorm and from the *p*

Precipitous
Isa 7:19 upon the *p* torrent valleys

Precisely
Ne 5:12 do *p* as you are saying

Prediction
Le 20:27 spirit of *p*, they should be
Isa 8:19 those having a spirit of *p*
Ac 16:16 by practicing the art of *p*
1Ti 4:14 was given you through a *p*

Predictions
1Ti 1:18 the *p* that led directly on

Prefect
Da 2:48 chief *p* over all the wise men

Prefects
Da 3:2 satraps, the *p* and the
3:3 the *p* and the governors, the
3:27 *p* and the governors and the
6:7 *p* and the satraps, the high

Prefer
Le 19:15 must not *p* the person of a
1Ki 21:6 if you *p*, let me give you
1Co 14:5 but I *p* that you prophesy

Preferable
Pr 21:3 *p* to Jehovah than sacrifice

Preferably
1Co 14:1 but *p* that you may prophesy

Preference
Ex 23:3 not show *p* in a controversy

Pregnancy
Ge 3:16 increase the pain of your *p*
1Sa 2:21 she had *p* and gave birth to

Pregnant
Ge 4:1 his wife and she became *p*
4:17 she became *p* and gave birth
16:4 with Hagar, and she became *p*
16:4 she was *p*, then her mistress
16:5 aware that she was *p*, and I
16:11 you are *p*, and you shall give
19:36 daughters of Lot became *p*
21:2 Sarah became *p* and then bore
25:21 Rebekah his wife became *p*
29:32 And Leah became *p*
29:33 *p* again and brought a son
29:34 she became *p* yet again and
29:35 she became *p* once more
30:5 Bilhah became *p* and in time
30:7 Bilhah . . . became *p* once more
30:17 Leah . . . became *p* and in
Ge 30:19 Leah became *p* once more
30:23 became *p* and brought a son
38:3 And she became *p*. Later she
38:4 Again she became *p*. In time
38:18 so that she became *p* by him
38:24 she is also *p* by her harlotry
38:25 I am *p*. And she added
Ex 2:2 woman became *p* and brought
21:22 really hurt a *p* woman and
Nu 5:28 must be made *p* with semen
Jg 13:3 you will . . . become *p* and
13:5 you will be *p*, and you will
13:7 You will be *p*, and you will
1Sa 1:20 Hannah became *p* and brought
4:19 the wife of Phinehas, was *p*
2Sa 11:5 And the woman became *p*
11:5 told David and said: I am *p*
2Ki 4:17 became *p* and gave birth to a
8:12 *p* women you will rip up
15:16 its *p* women he ripped up
1Ch 7:23 she became *p* and gave birth
Ps 7:14 *p* with what is hurtful
Ec 11:5 in the belly of her that is *p*
Ca 3:4 of her that had been *p* with me
Isa 7:14 maiden . . . became *p*, and
8:3 came to be *p* and in time gave
26:17 *p* woman draws near to
26:18 We have become *p*, we have
Jer 20:17 be *p* to time indefinite
31:8 *p* woman and the one giving
Ho 1:3 became *p* and in time bore to
1:6 become *p* another time and to
1:8 *p* and give birth to a son
2:5 She that was *p* with them has
9:11 no *p* belly and no conception
13:16 *p* women themselves will be
Am 1:13 slitting open the *p* women
Mt 1:18 found to be *p* by holy spirit
1:23 The virgin will become *p*
24:19 Woe to the *p* women and
Mr 13:17 Woe to the *p* women and
Lu 1:24 Elizabeth his wife became *p*
21:23 Woe to the *p* women and the
1Th 5:3 of distress upon a *p* woman
Re 12:1 twelve stars, and she was *p*

Prejudgment
1Ti 5:21 keep these things without *p*

Prematurely
Ec 6:3 one *p* born is better off than
1Co 15:8 to me as if to one born *p*

Preoccupying
Ec 5:20 *p* him with the rejoicing of

Preparation
Ge 43:16 slaughter animals and make *p*
1Ch 12:39 their brothers had made *p*
22:5 Let me, then, make *p* for
22:5 So David made *p* in great
28:2 and I had made *p* to build
29:19 for which I have made *p*
2Ch 29:36 God had made *p* for the
35:4 make *p* by the house of your
35:6 make *p* for your brothers to
Jer 46:14 making *p* also for yourself
Eze 38:7 let there be *p* on your part
Mt 26:12 for the *p* of me for burial
27:62 after the *P*, the chief
Mr 14:15 upper room, furnished in *p*
15:42 *P*, that is, the day before
Lu 9:52 to make *p* for him
23:54 Now it was the day of *P*, and
Joh 19:14 it was *p* of the passover
19:31 Jews, since it was *P*, in
19:42 of the *p* of the Jews, they

Prepare
Ex 16:5 *p* what they will bring in
Nu 9:2 Israel should *p* the passover
9:3 *p* it at its appointed time
9:3 procedures you should *p* it
9:4 Israel to *p* the passover
9:6 not able to *p* the passover
9:10 *p* the passover sacrifice to
9:11 they should *p* it
9:12 passover they should *p* it
9:13 neglected to *p* the passover
9:14 he also must *p* the passover
De 19:3 *p* for yourself the way
1Ch 9:32 to *p* it sabbath by sabbath
15:1 to *p* a place for the ark of
2Ch 26:14 Uzziah continued to *p* for
31:11 *p* dining rooms in the house
Job 11:13 will really *p* your heart
Job 27:16 *p* attire just as if clay
27:17 would *p*, but the righteous
29:7 I would *p* my seat
31:15 proceed to *p* us in the womb
Ps 7:13 *p* the instruments of death
10:17 You will *p* their heart
58:2 And *p* the road for the very
65:9 You *p* their grain, For that is
65:9 is the way you *p* the earth
78:20 *p* sustenance for his people
78:50 *p* a pathway for his anger
Pr 24:27 *P* your work out of doors
30:25 the summer they *p* their food
Isa 40:20 to *p* a carved image that
Mt 3:3 *P* the way of Jehovah
11:10 *p* your way ahead of you
26:17 want us to *p* for you to eat
Mr 1:2 messenger . . . will *p* your way
1:3 *P* the way of Jehovah, you
14:12 go and *p* for you to eat the
14:15 upper room . . . there *p* for
Lu 3:4 *P* the way of Jehovah, you
7:27 *p* your way ahead of you
23:56 *p* spices and perfumed oils
Joh 14:2 way to *p* a place for you
14:3 way and *p* a place for you

Prepared
Ge 21:6 God has *p* laughter for me
21:8 Abraham then *p* a big feast on
Ex 12:39 had not *p* any provisions for
23:20 into the place that I have *p*
Nu 9:5 *p* the passover sacrifice in
1Ki 6:19 the house he *p* inside, to put
1Ch 15:3 its place that he had *p* for
15:12 to the place that I have *p*
22:3 and for clamps David *p*, and
22:14 I have *p* for Jehovah's house
22:14 timbers and stones I have *p*
29:2 I have *p* for the house of my
29:3 I have *p* for the holy house
29:16 abundance that we have *p* to
2Ch 1:4 place that David had *p* for it
2:7 whom David my father has *p*
3:1 place that David had *p* on the
8:16 work was all in a *p* state
19:3 *p* your heart to search for
20:33 *p* their heart for the God
27:6 *p* his ways before Jehovah
29:19 have *p*, and have sanctified
29:35 the house of Jehovah was *p*
30:19 *p* his heart to search for
31:11 Accordingly they *p* them
33:16 *p* the altar of Jehovah and
35:10 the service was *p* and the
35:12 *p* the burnt offerings so as
35:14 *p* for themselves and for
35:14 *p* for themselves and for
35:15 Levites themselves *p* for
35:16 service of Jehovah was *p*
35:20 Josiah had *p* the house
Ezr 7:10 *p* his heart to consult the
Ne 8:10 for whom nothing has been *p*
Es 6:4 on the stake that he had *p* for
7:10 that he had *p* for Mordecai
Job 28:27 He *p* it and also searched it
Ps 8:3 and the stars that you have *p*
57:6 net they have *p* for my steps
74:16 *p* the luminary, even the
78:8 generation who had not *p*
141:2 prayer be *p* as incense before
Pr 8:27 *p* the heavens I was there
21:31 horse is something *p* for the
Isa 30:33 *p* for the king himself
Zep 1:7 Jehovah has *p* a sacrifice
Mt 20:23 it has been *p* by my Father
22:4 I have *p* my dinner, my bulls
25:34 kingdom *p* for you from the
25:41 fire *p* for the Devil and his
Mr 10:40 for whom it has been *p*
14:16 and they *p* for the passover
Lu 1:17 ready for Jehovah a *p* people
24:1 bearing the spices they had *p*
Ac 21:15 we *p* for the journey and
Ro 9:23 he *p* beforehand for glory
1Co 2:9 things that God has *p* for
2Co 10:16 where things are already *p*
Eph 2:10 which God *p* in advance for
2Ti 2:21 *p* for every good work
Heb 10:5 but you *p* a body for me
Re 8:6 seven trumpets *p* to blow them
9:7 resembled horses *p* for battle
9:15 *p* for the hour and day and
12:6 she has a place *p* by God

Re 16:12 *p* for the kings from the
19:7 and his wife has *p* herself
21:2 *p* as a bride adorned for her

Prepares
Job 15:35 their belly itself *p* deceit
38:41 *p* for the raven its food
Pr 6:8 *p* its food even in the summer

Preparing
1Ki 5:18 *p* the timbers and the stones
2Ch 2:9 for *p* timbers for me in great
Ps 147:8 One *p* rain for the earth
Eze 7:14 has been a *p* of everybody
35:6 for blood that I was *p* you
Joh 19:40 the custom of *p* for burial
Ac 10:10 While they were *p*, he fell

Prescribe
Mt 19:7 Moses *p* giving a certificate

Prescribed
Ex 5:14 did not finish your *p* task
Le 10:1 which he had not *p* for them
Job 23:12 more than what is *p* for me
23:14 completely what is *p* for
Pr 30:8 devour the food *p* for me
31:15 *p* portion to her young women
Jer 5:24 the *p* weeks of the harvest

Prescription
Ezr 6:18 the *p* of the book of Moses

Presence
Mt 24:3 the sign of your *p* and of the
24:27 *p* of the Son of man will be
24:37 *p* of the Son of man will be
24:39 *p* of the Son of man will be
1Co 15:23 to the Christ during his *p*
16:17 over the *p* of Stephanas and
2Co 7:6 comforted us by the *p* of
7:7 yet not alone by his *p*, but
10:10 but his *p* in person is weak
Php 1:26 through my *p* again with you
2:12 obeyed, not during my *p* only
1Th 2:19 our Lord Jesus at his *p*
3:13 at the *p* of our Lord Jesus
4:15 survive to the *p* of the Lord
5:23 at the *p* of our Lord Jesus
2Th 2:1 *p* of our Lord Jesus Christ
2:8 by the manifestation of his *p*
2:9 But the lawless one's *p* is
Jas 5:7 until the *p* of the Lord
5:8 *p* of the Lord has drawn close
2Pe 1:16 power and *p* of our Lord
3:4 Where is this promised *p* of
3:12 the *p* of the day of Jehovah
1Jo 2:28 shamed away . . . at his *p*

Present
Ge 43:9 bring him to you and *p* him
47:2 he might *p* them to Pharaoh
Ex 25:22 I will *p* myself to you there
29:3 and *p* them in the basket, and
29:4 *p* Aaron and his sons at the
29:10 *p* the bull before the tent
29:42 shall *p* myself to you people
29:43 I will *p* myself there to the
30:6 I shall *p* myself to you
30:36 I shall *p* myself to you
Le 1:2 would *p* an offering to Jehovah
1:2 *p* your offering from the
1:3 sound one, is what he should *p*
1:3 should *p* it of his own free
1:5 must *p* the blood and sprinkle
1:10 sound one, is what he will *p*
1:13 the priest must *p* all of it
1:14 must *p* his offering from the
1:15 priest must *p* it at the altar
2:1 some soul would *p* as an
2:4 would *p* as an offering a grain
2:11 that you will *p* to Jehovah
2:12 you will *p* them to Jehovah
2:13 of yours you will *p* salt
2:14 *p* the grain offering of the
2:14 should *p* green ears roasted
3:1 a sound one is what he will *p*
3:3 must *p* some of the communion
3:6 a sound one is what he will *p*
3:7 he must *p* it before Jehovah
3:9 *p* its fat as an offering made
3:12 he must *p* it before Jehovah
3:14 it he must *p* as his offering
4:3 then he must *p* for his sin
4:14 must *p* a young bull for a sin
5:8 *p* first the one for the sin
6:14 *p* it before Jehovah in front
Le 6:20 will *p* to Jehovah on the day
6:21 will *p* the pastries of the
7:3 he will *p* of it the fatty tail
7:11 sacrifice that anyone will *p*
7:12 would *p* it in expression of
7:12 *p* along with the sacrifice of
7:13 *p* his offering together with
7:14 *p* one of each offering as a
7:38 *p* their offerings to Jehovah
9:2 and *p* them before Jehovah
12:7 must *p* it before Jehovah and
14:11 *p* the man who is cleansing
16:6 *p* the bull of the sin offering
16:9 *p* the goat over which the lot
16:11 must *p* the bull of the sin
16:20 he must also *p* the live goat
17:4 *p* it as an offering to Jehovah
21:17 to *p* the bread of his God
21:21 to *p* Jehovah's offerings
21:21 to *p* the bread of his God
22:18 *p* to Jehovah for a burnt
22:20 is a defect you must not *p*
22:21 *p* a communion sacrifice to
22:22 none of these must you *p* to
22:24 *p* to Jehovah, and in your
22:25 *p* as the bread of your God
23:8 *p* an offering made by fire to
23:16 *p* a new grain offering to
23:18 *p* along with the loaves
23:25 *p* an offering made by fire
23:27 *p* an offering made by fire
23:36 *p* an offering made by fire
23:36 *p* an offering made by fire
27:11 one may not *p* in offering to
Nu 5:9 they will *p* to the priest
6:14 *p* as his offering to Jehovah
6:16 *p* them before Jehovah and
7:11 they will *p* their offering
8:9 *p* the Levites before the tent
8:10 *p* the Levites before Jehovah
9:13 not *p* at its appointed time
15:4 *p* to Jehovah a grain offering
15:7 *p* wine as a drink offering, a
15:9 *p* together with the male of
15:10 *p* wine as a drink offering
15:27 *p* a female goat in its first
16:9 *p* you to himself to carry on
16:16 be *p* before Jehovah, you and
16:17 *p* each one his fire holder
17:4 where I regularly *p* myself to
18:15 which they will *p* to Jehovah
28:2 *p* to me my offering, my
28:3 that you will *p* to Jehovah
28:11 *p* as a burnt offering to
28:19 *p* as an offering made by
28:26 *p* a new grain offering to
28:27 *p* as a burnt offering for a
29:8 must *p* as a burnt offering to
29:13 *p* as a burnt offering, an
29:36 must *p* as a burnt offering
31:50 *p* each one what he has found
De 1:17 you should *p* to me, and I
Jos 7:14 *p* yourselves in the morning
Jg 3:17 he proceeded to *p* the tribute
1Ki 15:19 a *p* of silver and gold
1Ch 16:1 began to *p* burnt offerings
Ezr 7:17 *p* them upon the altar of the
Job 6:22 make a *p* in my behalf
23:4 would *p* before him a case of
Ps 72:10 Seba—A gift they will *p*
Pr 6:35 how large you make the *p*
Isa 44:7 may tell it and *p* it to me
48:6 hear new things from the *p*
48:7 At the *p* time they must be
Jer 40:5 and a *p* and let him go
Eze 16:33 are accustomed to give a *p*
44:7 *p* my bread, fat and blood
44:15 *p* to me fat and the blood
44:27 should *p* his sin offering
46:4 chieftain should *p* to Jehovah
Da 2:6 *p* and much dignity you will
2:46 even a *p* and incense to him
Hag 2:14 and whatever they *p* there
Mal 1:8 you *p* a blind animal for
1:8 *p* a lame animal or a sick
3:15 at *p* we are pronouncing
Mt 26:50 for what purpose are you *p*?
Lu 2:5 at *p* heavy with child
2:22 Jerusalem to *p* him to Jehovah
6:6 a man *p* whose right hand was
13:1 certain ones *p* that reported
Joh 7:6 My due time is not yet *p*
9:19 then, is it he sees at *p*
9:25 I was blind, I see at *p*
Joh 11:22 at *p* I know that as many
11:28 The Teacher is *p* and is
13:7 you do not understand at *p*
13:33 I say also to you at *p*
13:37 I cannot follow you at *p*
16:12 able to bear them at *p*
16:24 *p* time you have not asked
16:31 Do you believe at *p*?
Ac 5:38 under the *p* circumstances, I
10:21 cause for which you are *p*
10:33 we are all *p* before God to
17:6 These men . . . are *p* here also
21:18 and all the older men were *p*
24:19 ought to be *p* before you and
24:25 For the *p* go your way, but
25:24 you men who are *p* with us
Ro 3:26 righteousness in this *p* season
6:13 *p* yourselves to God as those
6:19 *p* your members as slaves to
7:18 ability to wish is *p* with me
7:18 what is fine is not *p* with
7:21 what is bad is *p* with me
8:18 sufferings of the *p* season do
11:5 *p* season also a remnant has
12:1 *p* your bodies a sacrifice
1Co 5:3 absent in body but *p* in
5:3 judged already, as if . . . *p*
13:12 *p* we see in hazy outline
13:12 At *p* I know partially, but
15:6 of whom remain to the *p*
2Co 3:14 to this *p* day the same veil
4:14 *p* us together with you
10:2 that, when *p*, I may not use
10:11 also be in action when *p*
11:2 I might *p* you as a chaste
11:9 I was *p* with you and I fell
13:2 as if *p* the second time and
13:10 when I am *p*, I may not act
Ga 1:4 *p* wicked system of things
4:18 only when I am *p* with you
4:20 wish to be *p* with you just
Eph 5:27 might *p* the congregation to
Col 1:22 *p* you holy and unblemished
1:28 *p* every man complete in
1Ti 6:17 rich in the *p* system of
2Ti 2:15 *p* yourself approved to God
4:10 loved the *p* system of things
Tit 2:12 this *p* system of things
Heb 12:11 for the *p* to be joyous, but
13:5 content with the *p* things
Jas 1:17 perfect *p* is from above
1Pe 1:6 for a little while at *p*
1:8 not looking upon him at *p*
2Pe 1:9 these things are not *p* in
1:12 truth that is *p* in you
Re 17:8 but is not, and yet will be *p*

Presentation
Nu 7:2 the chieftains . . . made a *p*
7:10 chieftains made their *p* at the
7:18 of Issachar, made a *p*
2Ch 35:12 to make a *p* to Jehovah
Isa 45:21 your report and your *p*
Mal 1:11 a *p* will be made to my name
Mt 12:4 and they ate the loaves of *p*
Mr 2:26 ate the loaves of *p*, which it
Lu 6:4 received the loaves of *p* and

Presentations
Eze 20:40 the firstfruits of your *p*

Presented
Ex 1:21 later *p* them with families
35:22 *p* the wave offering of gold
Le 2:8 it must be *p* to the priest and
7:8 offering that he has *p* to the
7:35 the day that he *p* them to act
9:9 Aaron's sons *p* the blood to
9:16 he *p* the burnt offering and
9:17 He next *p* the grain offering
10:19 have *p* their sin offering
Nu 7:3 *p* them before the tabernacle
7:19 *p* as his offering one silver
9:6 *p* themselves before Moses and
16:38 they *p* them before Jehovah
16:39 who had been burned up had *p*
27:5 Moses *p* their case before
De 25:1 *p* themselves for the judgment
Jos 17:4 *p* themselves before Eleazar
Jg 5:25 she *p* curdled milk
Ezr 6:17 *p* for the inauguration of
8:35 *p* burnt sacrifices to the God
Job 13:18 I have *p* a case of justice
La 4:3 jackals . . . have *p* the udder
Mt 2:11 *p* it with gifts, gold and

Prettiness
Ps 45:11 king will long for your *p*
50:2 the perfection of *p*, God
Pr 6:25 desire her *p* in your heart
31:30 and *p* may be vain; but the
Isa 3:24 brand mark instead of *p*
La 2:15 perfection of *p*, an exultation
Eze 16:14 because of your *p*, for it
16:15 began to trust in your *p* and
16:25 your *p* something detestable
27:3 said, I am perfect in *p*
27:4 have perfected your *p*
27:11 They . . . perfected your *p*
31:8 resembled it in its *p*

Pretty
Es 2:7 the young woman was *p* in form
Job 42:15 as *p* as Job's daughters
Ps 48:2 *P* for loftiness, the
Pr 11:22 so is a woman that is *p* but
Ec 3:11 he has made *p* in its time
5:18 *p*, is that one should eat and
Jer 4:30 used to make yourself *p*
10:4 with gold one makes it *p*
11:16 *p* with fruit and in form
46:20 Egypt is as a very *p* heifer
Eze 16:13 you grew to be very, very *p*
31:3 cedar in Lebanon, *p* in bough
31:7 to be *p* in its greatness
31:9 *P* is the way that I made it
33:32 like one with a *p* voice
Am 8:13 *p* virgins will swoon away

Prevail
Nu 13:30 we can surely *p* over it
Jg 6:2 Midian came to *p* over Israel
16:5 we can *p* over him and with
Es 6:13 you will not *p* against him
Ps 12:4 With our tongue we shall *p*
Jer 1:19 they will not *p* against you
3:5 to do bad things and *p*
5:22 still they cannot *p*
15:20 they will not *p* over you
20:10 that we may *p* against him
20:11 will stumble and not *p*
38:5 king . . . can *p* against you
Da 11:5 he will *p* against him and
11:7 act against them and *p*
11:32 will *p* and act effectively
Re 12:8 not *p*, neither was a place

Prevailed
Ge 32:25 see that he had not *p* over
32:28 so that you at last *p*
2Sa 24:4 the king's word *p* upon Joab
1Ch 21:4 king's word, however, *p* over
2Ch 8:3 Hamath-zobah and *p* over it
Ps 129:2 they have not *p* over me
Jer 20:7 against me, so that you *p*
38:22 allured you and *p* over you
Ho 12:4 with an angel and gradually *p*
Ob 7 have *p* against you
Ac 19:16 *p* against them, so that they

Prevailing
Da 7:21 and it was *p* against them
Ho 2:14 here I am *p* upon her, and I
Ac 19:20 word of Jehovah kept . . . *p*

Prevalence
1Co 7:2 because of *p* of fornication

Prevent
Ge 23:6 to *p* burying your
Mt 3:14 the latter tried to *p* him
Mr 9:38 we tried to *p* him, because
9:39 Do not try to *p* him, for
Lu 9:49 we tried to *p* him, because
9:50 Do not you men try to *p* him
Joh 11:37 to *p* this one from dying
2Pe 1:8 *p* you from being either

Prevented
Heb 7:23 *p* by death from continuing

Preventing
Mt 3:15 Then he quit *p* him

Prevents
Ac 8:36 *p* me from getting baptized

Previous
Ga 1:17 were apostles *p* to me, but I

Previously
2Sa 3:17 *p* you proved yourselves
5:2 *p* while Saul happened to be
1Ch 11:2 and *p*, even while Saul
Ne 13:5 *p* they were regularly putting
Joh 7:50 who had come to him *p*
Ac 21:29 they had *p* seen Trophimus
26:5 *p* acquainted with me from
2Co 9:5 bountiful gift *p* promised
13:2 I have said *p* and, as if
Ga 3:17 covenant *p* validated by God
Eph 3:3 just as I wrote *p* in brief
2Pe 3:2 sayings *p* spoken by the holy
Jude 17 *p* spoken by the apostles of

Prey
Ge 15:11 birds of *p* began to descend
49:9 From the *p*, my son, you will
Nu 23:24 until it may eat *p*, And the
Job 4:11 from there being no *p*, And
28:7 no bird of *p* has known it
29:17 I would tear away the *p*
38:39 Can you hunt *p* for a lion
Ps 76:4 than the mountains of *p*
104:21 lions are roaring for the *p*
124:6 As a *p* to their teeth
Pr 12:12 the netted *p* of bad men
Isa 5:29 growl and grab hold of the *p*
18:6 bird of *p* of the mountains
18:6 upon it the bird of *p* will
31:4 young lion, over its *p*
46:11 the sunrising a bird of *p*
Jer 12:9 as a many-colored bird of *p*
12:9 the birds of *p* are round
Eze 19:3 to learn how to tear apart *p*
19:6 learned how to tear apart *p*
22:25 roaring lion, tearing *p*
22:27 like wolves tearing *p* in
39:4 birds of *p*, birds of every
Am 3:4 lion roar . . . when it has no *p*
Na 2:12 kept his holes filled with *p*
2:13 cut off from the earth your *p*
3:1 *P* does not depart!
Col 2:8 will carry you off as his *p*

Price
Ex 21:30 redemption *p* for his soul
21:32 *p* of thirty shekels to that
21:34 The *p* he is to return to its
21:35 and divide the *p* paid for it
22:16 his wife for the purchase *p*
Le 25:51 pay his repurchase *p* over
25:52 pay over his repurchase *p*
27:18 *p* in proportion to the years
Nu 3:46 ransom *p* of the two hundred
3:48 ransom *p* of those who are in
3:49 money of the redemption *p*
3:49 the ransom *p* of the Levites
3:51 the ransom *p* to Aaron
18:16 a redemption *p* for it from a
De 23:18 a harlot or the *p* of a dog
1Sa 13:21 *p* for sharpening proved to
2Sa 24:24 buy it from you for a *p*
1Ki 10:28 the horse drove for a *p*
21:2 give you money as the *p* of
2Ch 1:16 take the horse drove for a *p*
Job 28:15 be weighed out as its *p*
Ps 44:12 no wealth by the *p* for them
49:8 redemption *p* of their soul
Pr 17:16 *p* to acquire wisdom, when
27:26 are the *p* of the field
Isa 45:13 for a *p* nor for bribery
55:1 without money and without *p*
Jer 15:13 mere plunder, not for a *p*
La 5:4 For a *p* our own wood comes in
Da 11:39 will apportion out for a *p*
Am 2:6 for the *p* of a pair of sandals
8:6 for the *p* of a pair of sandals
Mic 3:11 instruct just for a *p*
Mt 27:6 they are the *p* of blood
27:9 the *p* upon the man that was
27:9 the sons of Israel set a *p*
Ac 5:2 held back some of the *p*, his
5:3 some of the *p* of the field
7:16 Abraham had bought for a *p*
1Co 6:20 for you were bought with a *p*
7:23 You were bought with a *p*

Priced
Mt 27:9 upon the man that was *p*, the

Prices
Ac 19:19 calculated together the *p* of

Pricking
Eze 2:6 and things *p* you and it is

Prickle
Eze 28:24 a malignant *p* or a painful

Pricks
Nu 33:55 as *p* in your eyes and as

Pride
Le 26:19 break the *p* of your strength
Job 33:17 that he may cover *p* itself
35:12 Because of the *p* of the bad
Ps 47:4 The *p* of Jacob, whom he has
59:12 they be caught in their *p*
Pr 8:13 *p* and the bad way and the
16:18 *P* is before a crash, and a
Isa 13:11 *p* of the presumptuous ones
13:19 of the *p* of the Chaldeans
14:11 Down to Sheol your *p* has
16:6 heard of the *p* of Moab, that
16:6 his *p* and his fury—his
23:9 profane the *p* of all beauty
60:15 set you as a thing of *p* to
Jer 13:9 bring to ruin the *p* of Judah
13:9 the abundant *p* of Jerusalem
13:17 soul will weep because of *p*
48:29 heard of the *p* of Moab
48:29 his highness and of his *p*
Eze 7:20 has set it as reason for *p*
7:24 *p* of the strong ones to cease
16:49 *P*, sufficiency of bread and
16:56 in the day of your *p*
24:21 the *p* of your strength
30:6 *p* of its strength must come
30:18 the *p* of her strength will
32:12 despoil the *p* of Egypt
33:28 the *p* of its strength must
Da 4:37 walking in *p* he is able to
Ho 5:5 the *p* of Israel has testified
7:10 the *p* of Israel has testified
Am 6:8 I am detesting the *p* of Jacob
Na 2:2 certainly gather the *p* of Jacob
2:2 like the *p* of Israel, because
Zep 2:10 will have instead of their *p*
Zec 9:6 the *p* of the Philistine
10:11 the *p* of Assyria must be
Ro 2:17 upon law and taking *p* in God
2:23 You, who take *p* in law, do
2Th 1:4 we ourselves take *p* in you
1Ti 3:6 might get puffed up with *p*
6:4 he is puffed up with *p*, not
2Ti 3:4 headstrong, puffed up with *p*
Jas 4:16 *p* in your self-assuming
4:16 such taking of *p* is wicked

Priest
Ge 14:18 he was *p* of the Most High
41:45 Potiphera the *p* of On
41:50 of Potiphera the *p* of On
46:20 Potiphera the *p* of On
Ex 2:16 the *p* of Midian had seven
3:1 Jethro, the *p* of Midian, whose
18:1 Now Jethro the *p* of Midian
28:1 act as *p* to me, Aaron, Nadab
28:3 that he may act as *p* to me
28:4 that he may act as *p* to me
29:30 *p* who succeeds him from among
31:10 garments for Aaron the *p*
35:19 garments for Aaron the *p*
38:21 the son of Aaron the *p*
39:41 garments for Aaron the *p*
40:13 so he must act as *p* to me
Le 1:9 *p* must make all of it smoke
1:12 the *p* must set them in order
1:13 the *p* must present all of it
1:15 the *p* must present it at the
1:17 *p* must make it smoke on the
2:2 the *p* must grasp from it his
2:8 it must be presented to the *p*
2:9 the *p* must lift off some of
2:16 *p* must make the remembrancer
3:11 the *p* must make it smoke on
3:16 *p* must make them smoke upon
4:3 the *p*, the anointed one, sins
4:5 the *p*, the anointed one, must
4:6 the *p* must dip his finger in
4:7 *p* must put some of the blood
4:10 *p* must make them smoke upon
4:16 the *p*, the anointed one, must
4:17 *p* must dip his finger into
4:20 *p* must make an atonement
4:25 *p* must take some of the blood
4:26 the *p* must make an atonement
4:30 *p* must take some of its blood
4:31 the *p* must make it smoke on
4:31 *p* must make an atonement for
4:34 *p* must take some of the
4:35 *p* must make them smoke on
4:35 *p* must make an atonement
5:6 the *p* must make an atonement
5:8 he must bring them to the *p*
5:10 the *p* must make an atonement

Le 5:12 he must bring it to the *p*
5:12 the *p* must grasp from it his
5:13 *p* must make an atonement
5:16 he must give it to the *p*
5:16 *p* may make an atonement for
5:18 for a guilt offering, to the *p*
5:18 *p* must make an atonement for
6:6 for a guilt offering, to the *p*
6:7 *p* must make an atonement for
6:10 the *p* must clothe himself
6:12 the *p* must burn wood on it
6:22 And the *p*, the one anointed
6:23 grain offering of a *p* should
6:26 *p* who offers it for sin will
7:5 *p* must make them smoke on the
7:7 *p* who will make atonement
7:8 As for the *p* who presents the
7:8 presented to the *p* will become
7:9 belongs to the *p* who presents
7:14 the *p* who sprinkles the blood
7:31 *p* must make the fat smoke
7:32 a sacred portion to the *p*
7:34 give them to Aaron the *p* and
12:6 the tent of meeting to the *p*
12:8 the *p* must make atonement
13:2 brought to Aaron the *p* or to
13:3 the *p* must look at the plague
13:3 And the *p* must look at it
13:4 the *p* must then quarantine
13:5 the *p* must look at him on the
13:5 *p* must also quarantine him
13:6 *p* must look at him on the
13:6 the *p* must also pronounce him
13:7 his appearing before the *p*
13:7 the second time before the *p*
13:8 the *p* must take a look; and
13:8 *p* must then declare him
13:9 must then be brought to the *p*
13:10 And the *p* must take a look
13:11 *p* must declare him unclean
13:13 the *p* has looked and there
13:15 *p* must see the living flesh
13:16 he must then come to the *p*
13:17 And the *p* must look at him
13:17 *p* must then pronounce the
13:19 then show himself to the *p*
13:20 And the *p* must look, and if
13:20 the *p* must then declare him
13:21 But if the *p* looks at it
13:21 *p* must then quarantine him
13:22 the *p* must then declare him
13:23 *p* must pronounce him clean
13:25 the *p* must then look at it
13:25 *p* must declare him unclean
13:26 But if the *p* looks at it
13:26 *p* must then quarantine him
13:27 And the *p* must look at him
13:27 the *p* must then declare him
13:28 *p* must pronounce him clean
13:30 *p* must then see the plague
13:30 *p* must then declare such one
13:31 the *p* sees the plague of
13:31 *p* must then quarantine the
13:32 *p* must look at the plague on
13:33 the *p* must quarantine the
13:34 *p* must look at the abnormal
13:34 *p* must then pronounce him
13:36 the *p* must then see him
13:36 *p* need not make examination
13:37 *p* must pronounce him clean
13:39 the *p* must then take a look
13:43 And the *p* must look at him
13:44 the *p* should declare him
13:49 it must be shown to the *p*
13:50 the *p* must see the plague
13:53 if the *p* takes a look, and
13:54 *p* must also command that
13:55 *p* must look at the plague
13:56 if the *p* has taken a look
14:2 he must be brought to the *p*
14:3 *p* must go forth outside the
14:3 *p* must look; and if the
14:4 the *p* must then give command
14:5 the *p* must give command, and
14:11 *p* who pronounces him clean
14:12 *p* must take the one young
14:13 offering belongs to the *p*
14:14 *p* must take some of the
14:14 *p* must put it upon the lobe
14:15 *p* must take some of the log
14:16 *p* must dip his right finger
14:17 *p* will put some upon the
14:18 the *p* must make atonement
14:19 the *p* must render up the sin

Le 14:20 *p* must offer up the burnt
14:20 *p* must make atonement for
14:23 his purification to the *p*
14:24 *p* must take the young ram of
14:24 *p* must wave them to and fro
14:25 *p* must take some of the
14:26 *p* will pour some of the oil
14:27 the *p* must spatter with his
14:28 *p* must put some of the oil
14:31 *p* must make atonement for
14:35 come and tell the *p*, saying
14:36 the *p* must give orders, and
14:36 before the *p* may come in to
14:36 *p* will come in to see the
14:38 *p* must then go out of the
14:39 *p* must return on the seventh
14:40 *p* must then give orders, and
14:44 *p* must then come in and take
14:48 if the *p* comes at all and he
14:48 *p* must then pronounce the
15:14 and give them to the *p*
15:15 the *p* must offer them, the
15:15 *p* must make atonement for
15:29 bring them to the *p* at the
15:30 *p* must make the one a sin
15:30 the *p* must make atonement
16:32 *p* who will be anointed and
16:32 with power to act as *p* as
17:5 to the *p*, and they must
17:6 *p* must sprinkle the blood
19:22 *p* must make atonement for
21:9 daughter of a *p* should make
21:10 high *p* of his brothers upon
21:21 Aaron the *p* in whom there is
22:10 settler with a *p* nor a hired
22:11 *p* should purchase a soul, as
22:12 daughter of a *p* should
22:13 daughter of a *p* should
22:14 give the holy thing to the *p*
23:10 the firstfruits . . . to the *p*
23:11 *p* should wave it to and fro
23:20 *p* must wave them to and fro
23:20 holy to Jehovah for the *p*
27:8 person before the *p*, and the
27:8 *p* must put a valuation upon
27:8 *p* will put a valuation upon
27:11 stand the beast before the *p*
27:12 *p* must put a valuation upon
27:12 value estimated by the *p*, so
27:14 *p* must then make a valuation
27:14 valuation the *p* makes of it
27:18 *p* must then calculate for
27:23 *p* must then calculate for
Nu 3:6 stand them before Aaron the *p*
3:32 Eleazar the son of Aaron the *p*
4:16 Aaron the *p* is over the oil of
4:28 the son of Aaron the *p*
4:33 the son of Aaron the *p*
5:8 belongs to the *p*, except the
5:9 they will present to the *p*
5:10 each one may give to the *p*
5:15 must bring his wife to the *p*
5:16 *p* must bring her forward and
5:17 *p* must take holy water in an
5:17 *p* will take some of the dust
5:18 *p* must make the woman stand
5:18 hand of the *p* there should be
5:19 *p* must make her swear, and
5:21 *p* must now make the woman
5:21 *p* must say to the woman: May
5:23 *p* must write these cursings
5:25 *p* must take the grain
5:26 *p* must grasp some of the
5:30 *p* must carry out toward her
6:10 to the *p* to the entrance of
6:11 *p* must handle one as a sin
6:16 *p* must present them before
6:17 *p* must render up its grain
6:19 *p* must take a boiled shoulder
6:20 *p* must wave them to and fro
6:20 something holy for the *p*
7:8 the son of Aaron the *p*
15:25 *p* must make atonement for
15:28 *p* must make atonement for
16:37 the son of Aaron the *p* that
16:39 Eleazar the *p* took the copper
18:28 give . . . to Aaron the *p*
19:3 must give it to Eleazar the *p*
19:4 Eleazar the *p* must take some
19:6 the *p* must take cedarwood and
19:7 *p* must wash his garments and
19:7 *p* must be unclean until the
25:7 Eleazar the son of Aaron the *p*
25:11 the son of Aaron the *p* has

Nu 26:1 the son of Aaron the *p*
26:3 And Moses and Eleazar the *p*
26:63 and Eleazar the *p* when they
26:64 by Moses and Aaron the *p*
27:2 and before Eleazar the *p* and
27:19 before Eleazar the *p* and
27:21 before Eleazar the *p* that he
27:22 before Eleazar the *p* and
31:6 the son of Eleazar the *p* to
31:12 to Moses and Eleazar the *p*
31:13 Moses and Eleazar the *p* and
31:21 Eleazar the *p* then said to
31:26 you and Eleazar the *p* and the
31:29 give it to Eleazar the *p* as
31:31 Moses and Eleazar the *p* went
31:41 contribution to Eleazar the *p*
31:51 Eleazar the *p* accepted the
31:54 Eleazar the *p* accepted the
32:2 to Moses and Eleazar the *p*
32:28 to Eleazar the *p* and to
33:38 Aaron the *p* proceeded to go
34:17 Eleazar the *p* and Joshua the
35:25 until the death of the high *p*
35:32 the death of the high *p*
De 10:6 his son began to act as *p*
17:12 in not listening to the *p*
18:3 give to the *p* the shoulder
20:2 the *p* must also approach and
26:3 the *p* who will be acting in
26:4 the *p* must take the basket
Jos 14:1 Eleazar the *p* and Joshua the
17:4 Eleazar the *p* and Joshua the
19:51 Eleazar the *p* and Joshua the
20:6 until the death of the high *p*
21:1 Eleazar the *p* and Joshua the
21:4 to the sons of Aaron the *p*
21:13 to the sons of Aaron the *p*
22:13 the son of Eleazar the *p*
22:30 Phinehas the *p* and the
22:31 son of Eleazar the *p* said
22:32 the son of Eleazar the *p*
Jg 17:5 he might serve as *p* for him
17:10 serve as a father and *p* for
17:12 man might serve as a *p* for
17:13 Levite has become *p* for me
18:4 I might serve as *p* for him
18:6 *p* said to them: Go in peace
18:17 the *p* was standing at the
18:18 the *p* said to them: What are
18:19 become a father and a *p* for
18:19 a *p* to the house of one man
18:19 a *p* to a tribe and family in
18:20 heart of the *p* was pleased
18:24 you have taken, the *p* too
18:27 the *p* that had become his
1Sa 1:9 Eli the *p* was sitting upon
2:11 before Eli the *p*
2:13 attendant of the *p* came with
2:14 the *p* would take for himself
2:15 attendant of the *p* came and
2:15 give meat to roast for the *p*
2:28 to act as *p* and go up upon
2:35 for myself a faithful *p*
14:3 Eli, the *p* of Jehovah in
14:19 Saul was speaking to the *p*
14:19 Then Saul said to the *p*
14:36 *p* said: Let us approach here
21:1 into Nob to Ahimelech the *p*
21:2 said to Ahimelech the *p*
21:4 *p* answered David and said
21:5 David answered the *p* and
21:6 *p* gave him what was holy
21:9 *p* said: The sword of Goliath
22:11 son of Ahitub the *p* and all
23:9 said to Abiathar the *p*
30:7 said to Abiathar the *p*, the
2Sa 15:27 to say to Zadok the *p*
20:26 also became a *p* of David
1Ki 1:7 with Abiathar the *p*, and they
1:8 Zadok the *p* and Benaiah the
1:19 Abiathar the *p* and Joab the
1:25 the army and Abiathar the *p*
1:26 Zadok the *p* and Benaiah the
1:32 call for me Zadok the *p* and
1:34 Zadok the *p* and Nathan the
1:38 Zadok the *p* and Nathan the
1:39 Zadok the *p* now took the
1:42 son of Abiathar the *p* came
1:44 sent with him Zadok the *p*
1:45 Zadok the *p* and Nathan the
2:22 for Abiathar the *p* and for
2:26 to Abiathar the *p* the king
2:27 serving as a *p* of Jehovah
2:35 Zadok the *p* the king put in

1Ki 4:2 the son of Zadok, the *p*
4:5 the son of Nathan was a *p*
2Ki 11:9 Jehoiada the *p* had commanded
11:9 came in to Jehoiada the *p*
11:10 *p* now gave the chiefs of
11:15 Jehoiada the *p* commanded
11:15 the *p* had said: Do not let
11:18 Mattan the *p* of Baal they
11:18 *p* proceeded to put overseers
12:2 Jehoiada the *p* instructed
12:7 called Jehoiada the *p* and
12:9 *p* now took a chest and bored
12:10 the high *p* would come up
16:10 King Ahaz sent Urijah the *p*
16:11 Urijah the *p* proceeded to
16:11 way that Urijah the *p* made
16:15 even Urijah the *p*, saying
16:16 And Urijah the *p* went doing
22:4 Go up to Hilkiah the high *p*
22:8 Hilkiah the high *p* said to
22:10 a book that Hilkiah the *p*
22:12 Hilkiah the *p* and Ahikam
22:14 Hilkiah the *p* and Ahikam
23:4 Hilkiah the high *p* and the
23:24 book that Hilkiah the *p* had
25:18 took Seraiah the chief *p*
25:18 and Zephaniah the second *p*
1Ch 6:10 *p* in the house that Solomon
16:39 Zadok the *p* and his brothers
24:6 Zadok the *p* and Ahimelech
27:5 son of Jehoiada the chief *p*
29:22 and also Zadok as *p*
2Ch 4:6 sea was for the *p* to wash in
13:9 *p* of what are no gods
15:3 without a *p* teaching and
19:11 Amariah the chief *p* over
22:11 wife of Jehoiada the *p*
23:8 Jehoiada the *p* had commanded
23:8 Jehoiada the *p* had not set
23:9 Jehoiada the *p* gave the
23:14 Jehoiada the *p* brought out
23:14 *p* had said: You must not
23:17 Mattan the *p* of Baal they
24:2 the days of Jehoiada the *p*
24:11 of the chief *p* came and
24:20 son of Jehoiada the *p*
24:25 sons of Jehoiada the *p*
26:17 Azariah the *p* and with him
26:20 Azariah the chief *p* and all
31:10 Azariah the chief *p* of the
34:9 Hilkiah the high *p* and give
34:14 Hilkiah the *p* found the book
34:18 book that Hilkiah the *p* gave
Ezr 2:63 a *p* stood up with Urim and
7:5 the son of Aaron the chief *p*
7:11 gave Ezra the *p* the copyist
7:12 to Ezra the *p*, the copyist of
7:21 Ezra the *p*, the copyist of
8:33 Urijah the *p* and with him
10:10 Ezra the *p* rose and said
10:16 Ezra the *p* and the men that
Ne 3:1 And Eliashib the high *p* and
3:20 house of Eliashib the high *p*
7:65 *p* with Urim and Thummim
8:2 Ezra the *p* brought the law
8:9 and Ezra the *p*, the copyist
10:38 the *p*, the son of Aaron
12:26 Ezra the *p*, the copyist
13:4 Eliashib the *p* in charge of
13:13 Shelemiah the *p* and Zadok
13:28 Eliashib the high *p* was a
Ps 110:4 are a *p* to time indefinite
Isa 8:2 witnesses, Uriah the *p* and
24:2 for the people as for the *p*
28:7 *P* and prophet—they have
Jer 6:13 the prophet even to the *p*
8:10 the prophet even to the *p*
14:18 both the prophet and the *p*
18:18 will not perish from the *p*
20:1 the son of Immer, the *p*
21:1 the son of Maaseiah, the *p*
23:11 both the prophet and the *p*
23:33 the prophet or *p* asks you
23:34 the *p* or the people who say
29:25 the son of Maaseiah, the *p*
29:26 *p* instead of Jehoiada the
29:26 instead of Jehoiada the *p*
29:29 Zephaniah the *p* proceeded
37:3 son of Maaseiah the *p* to
52:24 took Seraiah the chief *p*
52:24 and Zephaniah the second *p*
La 2:6 no respect for king and *p*
2:20 should *p* and prophet be killed
Eze 1:3 Ezekiel the son of Buzi the *p*
Eze 7:26 law . . . perish from a *p*
44:13 to act as *p* to me or to
44:22 widow of a *p* they may take
44:30 you should give to the *p*
45:19 *p* must take some of the
Da 2:10 of any magic-practicing *p* or
Ho 4:4 who are contending against a *p*
4:6 reject you from serving as a *p*
4:9 people the same as for the *p*
Am 7:10 Amaziah the *p* of Bethel
Hag 1:1 Jehozadak the high *p*, saying
1:12 son of Jehozadak the high *p*
1:14 son of Jehozadak the high *p*
2:2 son of Jehozadak the high *p*
2:4 son of Jehozadak the high *p*
Zec 3:1 Joshua the high *p* standing
3:8 Joshua the high *p*, you and
6:11 son of Jehozadak the high *p*
6:13 become a *p* upon his throne
Mal 2:7 lips of a *p* are the ones that
Mt 8:4 go, show yourself to the *p*
26:3 the courtyard of the high *p*
26:51 the slave of the high *p* and
26:57 away to Caiaphas the high *p*
26:58 the courtyard of the high *p*
26:62 high *p* stood up and said to
26:63 So the high *p* said to him
26:65 the high *p* ripped his outer
Mr 1:44 go show yourself to the *p* and
2:26 about Abiathar the chief *p*
14:47 the slave of the high *p*
14:53 led Jesus away to the high *p*
14:54 the courtyard of the high *p*
14:60 high *p* rose in their midst
14:61 the high *p* began to question
14:63 the high *p* ripped his inner
14:66 servant girls of the high *p*
Lu 1:5 a certain *p* named Zechariah
1:8 he was acting as *p* in the
3:2 in the days of chief *p* Annas
5:14 show yourself to the *p*, and
10:31 a certain *p* was going down
22:50 the slave of the high *p* and
22:54 into the house of the high *p*
Joh 11:49 Caiaphas, who was high *p*
11:51 he was high *p* that year
18:10 the slave of the high *p*
18:13 Caiaphas, who was high *p*
18:15 was known to the high *p*
18:15 courtyard of the high *p*
18:16 was known to the high *p*
18:19 chief *p* questioned Jesus
18:22 you answer the chief *p*
18:24 to Caiaphas the high *p*
18:26 of the slaves to the high *p*
Ac 4:6 Annas the chief *p* and Caiaphas
5:17 high *p* and all those with
5:21 high *p* and those with him
5:27 the high *p* questioned them
7:1 high *p* said: Are these things
9:1 Saul . . . went to the high *p*
14:13 *p* of Zeus, whose temple was
19:14 Sceva, a Jewish chief *p*
22:5 high *p* and all the assembly
23:2 high *p* Ananias ordered those
23:4 Are you reviling the high *p*
23:5 I did not know he was high *p*
24:1 the high *p* Ananias came down
Heb 2:17 high *p* in things pertaining
3:1 the apostle and high *p* whom
4:14 great high *p* who has passed
4:15 For we have as high *p*, not
5:1 every high *p* taken from among
5:5 by becoming a high *p*, but
5:6 You are a *p* forever according
5:10 called by God a high *p*
6:20 Jesus . . . become a high *p*
7:1 *p* of the Most High God
7:3 he remains a *p* perpetually
7:11 another *p* to arise according
7:15 there arises another *p*
7:17 said: You are a *p* forever
7:21 You are a *p* forever
7:26 such a high *p* as this was
8:1 have such a high *p* as this
8:3 high *p* is appointed to offer
8:4 he would not be a *p*, there
9:7 the high *p* alone enters once
9:11 Christ came as a high *p* of
9:25 high *p* enters into the holy
10:11 every *p* takes his station
10:21 great *p* over the house of
13:11 by the high *p* for sin are

Priesthood
Ex 29:9 and the *p* must become theirs
40:15 as a *p* to time indefinite
Nu 3:10 must take care of their *p*
16:10 also try to secure the *p*
18:1 for error against your *p*
18:7 safeguard your *p* as regards
18:7 I shall give your *p*, and the
25:13 as the covenant of a *p* to
Jos 18:7 the *p* of Jehovah is their
Ezr 2:62 as polluted from the *p*
Ne 7:64 barred as polluted from the *p*
13:29 defilement of the *p* and the
13:29 and the covenant of the *p*
Heb 7:11 through the Levitical *p*
7:12 since the *p* is being changed
7:24 his *p* without any successors
1Pe 2:5 for the purpose of a holy *p*
2:9 a chosen race, a royal *p*, a

Priestly
Le 7:35 the *p* share of Aaron and the
7:35 and the *p* share of his sons
1Sa 2:36 to one of the *p* offices to
Isa 61:10 in a *p* way, puts on a
Lu 1:9 practice of the *p* office
Heb 7:5 who receive their *p* office

Priest's
Le 5:13 must become the *p* the same
13:12 the full sight of the *p* eyes
14:15 pour it upon the *p* left palm
14:18 oil that is upon the *p* palm
14:26 oil upon the *p* left palm
14:29 oil that is on the *p* palm
27:21 it will become the *p*
Nu 35:28 until the high *p* death, and
35:28 and after the high *p* death
Ac 4:6 were of the chief *p* kinsfolk

Priests
Ge 41:8 magic-practicing *p* of Egypt
41:24 the magic-practicing *p*
47:22 land of the *p* he did not buy
47:22 the rations for the *p* were
47:26 land of the *p* as a distinct
Ex 7:11 magic-practicing *p* of Egypt
7:22 magic-practicing *p* of Egypt
8:7 magic-practicing *p* did the
8:18 *p* tried to do the same by
8:19 *p* said to Pharaoh: It is the
9:11 the magic-practicing *p* were
9:11 on the magic-practicing *p*
19:6 become to me a kingdom of *p*
19:22 *p* also who regularly come
19:24 let not the *p* and the people
28:41 and they must act as *p* to me
29:1 sanctify them for acting as *p*
29:44 for them to act as *p* to me
30:30 sanctify them . . . as *p* to me
31:10 of his sons for acting as *p*
35:19 his sons for acting as *p*
39:41 of his sons for acting as *p*
40:15 so they must act as *p* to me
Le 1:5 the sons of Aaron, the *p*, must
1:7 And the sons of Aaron, the *p*
1:8 And the sons of Aaron, the *p*
1:11 and the sons of Aaron, the *p*
2:2 the sons of Aaron, the *p*
3:2 Aaron's sons, the *p*, must
6:29 among the *p* will eat it
7:6 male among the *p* will eat it
7:35 them to act as *p* to Jehovah
13:2 or to one of his sons the *p*
16:33 for the *p* and for all the
21:1 Talk to the *p*, Aaron's sons
Nu 3:3 the anointed *p* whose hands had
3:3 filled with power to act as *p*
3:4 act as *p* along with Aaron
10:8 *p*, should blow on the
De 17:9 go to the *p*, the Levites, and
17:18 in the charge of the *p*, the
18:1 come to belong to the *p*, the
18:3 due right of the *p* from the
19:17 before the *p* and the judges
21:5 the *p* the sons of Levi must
24:8 according to all that the *p*
27:9 the *p*, the Levites, spoke
31:9 law and gave it to the *p* the
Jos 3:3 the *p*, the Levites, carrying
3:6 said to the *p*: Take up the ark
3:8 the *p* carrying the ark of the
3:13 the *p* carrying the ark of
3:14 with the *p* carrying the ark
3:15 the *p* carrying the Ark were

Jos 3:17 the *p* carrying the ark of
4:9 the *p* carrying the ark of the
4:10 the *p* carrying the Ark were
4:11 and the *p*, before the people
4:16 the *p* carrying the ark of the
4:17 So Joshua commanded the *p*
4:18 when the *p* carrying the ark
4:18 soles of the feet of the *p*
6:4 seven *p* should carry seven
6:4 the *p* should blow the horns
6:6 called the *p* and said to them
6:6 and seven *p* should carry seven
6:8 and seven *p* carrying seven
6:9 of the *p* blowing the horns
6:12 *p* went carrying the ark of
6:13 *p* carrying seven rams' horns
6:16 the *p* blew the horns, and
8:33 front of the *p*, the Levites
21:19 sons of Aaron, the *p*, were
Jg 18:30 *p* to the tribe of the Danites
1Sa 1:3 Hophni and Phinehas, were *p*
2:13 due right of the *p* from the
5:5 *p* of Dagon and all those going
6:2 to call the *p* and the diviners
22:11 the *p* that were in Nob
22:17 to death the *p* of Jehovah
22:17 to assault the *p* of Jehovah
22:18 You turn and assault the *p*
22:18 assaulted the *p* and put to
22:19 Nob the city of the *p* he
22:21 killed the *p* of Jehovah
2Sa 8:17 were *p*, and Seraiah was
8:18 sons of David, they became *p*
15:35 Zadok and Abiathar the *p*
15:35 Zadok and Abiathar the *p*
17:15 Zadok and Abiathar the *p*
19:11 Zadok and Abiathar the *p*
20:25 Zadok and Abiathar were *p*
1Ki 4:4 Zadok and Abiathar were *p*
8:3 the *p* began to carry the Ark
8:4 the *p* and the Levites came
8:6 the *p* brought in the ark of
8:10 the *p* came out from the holy
8:11 the *p* were unable to stand to
12:31 make *p* from the people in
12:32 *p* of the high places that
13:2 the *p* of the high places
13:33 making *p* of high places
13:33 let him become one of the *p*
2Ki 10:11 his acquaintances and his *p*
10:19 worshipers and all his *p*
12:4 to say to the *p*: All the
12:5 *p* take for themselves, each
12:6 the *p* had not yet repaired
12:7 the *p* and said to them
12:8 the *p* consented not to take
12:9 the *p*, the doorkeepers
12:16 came to belong to the *p*
17:27 Have one of the *p* go there
17:28 *p* whom they had led into
17:32 *p* of high places, and they
19:2 *p* covered with sackcloth
23:2 the *p* and the prophets and
23:4 the *p* of the second rank and
23:5 foreign-god *p*, whom the
23:8 *p* from the cities of Judah
23:8 the *p* had made sacrificial
23:9 the *p* of the high places
23:20 all the *p* of the high places
1Ch 9:2 Israelites, the *p*, the Levites
9:10 of the *p* there were Jedaiah
9:30 sons of the *p* were makers of
13:2 to the *p* and the Levites in
15:11 Zadok and Abiathar the *p*
15:14 *p* and the Levites sanctified
15:24 the *p* loudly sounding the
16:6 the *p* with the trumpets
16:39 *p* before the tabernacle of
18:16 were *p*, and Shavsha was
23:2 and the *p* and the Levites
24:2 continued to act as *p*
24:6 heads of the fathers of the *p*
24:31 paternal houses of the *p* and
28:13 for the divisions of the *p*
28:21 divisions of the *p* and of
2Ch 4:9 made the courtyard of the *p*
5:5 *p* the Levites brought them up
5:7 the *p* brought the ark of the
5:11 the *p* came out from the holy
5:11 *p* that were to be found had
5:12 *p* to the number of a hundred
5:14 *p* were not able to stand to
6:41 *p* themselves, O Jehovah God
7:2 *p* were unable to enter into

2Ch 7:6 *p* were standing at their
7:6 *p* were loudly sounding the
8:14 set the divisions of the *p*
8:14 minister in front of the *p*
8:15 commandment to the *p* and
11:13 the *p* and the Levites
11:14 from acting as *p* to Jehovah
11:15 *p* for the high places and
13:9 driven out Jehovah's *p*, the
13:9 making *p* for yourselves
13:10 *p* are ministering to
13:12 true God with his *p* and the
13:14 *p* were loudly sounding the
17:8 Elishama and Jehoram the *p*
19:8 *p* and some of the heads of
23:4 of the *p* and of the Levites
23:6 *p* and those of the Levites
23:18 hand of the *p* and the
24:5 *p* and the Levites together
26:17 *p* of Jehovah, eighty valiant
26:18 business of the *p* the sons
26:19 his rage against the *p*
26:19 before the *p* in the house
26:20 *p* turned toward him, why
29:4 brought the *p* and the Levites
29:16 *p* now came inside the house
29:21 *p* to offer them up upon the
29:22 *p* received the blood and
29:24 *p* now slaughtered them and
29:26 the *p* with the trumpets
29:34 *p* themselves happened to be
29:34 until the *p* could sanctify
29:34 more upright . . . than the *p*
30:3 because not enough *p*, on
30:15 *p* and the Levites
30:16 *p* sprinkling the blood
30:21 *p* were offering praise to
30:24 *p* kept sanctifying
30:25 *p* and the Levites and all
30:27 *p*, the Levites, stood up and
31:2 divisions of the *p* and of
31:2 service for the *p* and for
31:4 give the portion of the *p*
31:9 Hezekiah inquired of the *p*
31:15 in the cities of the *p*, in
31:17 enrollment of the *p* by the
31:19 sons of Aaron, the *p*, in
31:19 every male among the *p*
34:5 bones of *p* he burned upon
34:30 the *p* and the Levites and
35:2 stationed the *p* over the
35:8 for the *p* and for the Levites
35:8 to the *p* for the passover
35:10 the *p* kept standing at their
35:11 *p* proceeded to slaughter the
35:14 themselves and for the *p*
35:14 the *p* the sons of Aaron
35:14 for the *p* the sons of Aaron
35:18 the *p* and the Levites and
36:14 all the chiefs of the *p*
Ezr 1:5 the *p* and the Levites rose up
2:36 The *p*: The sons of Jedaiah
2:61 And of the sons of the *p*
2:69 and a hundred robes of *p*
2:70 the *p* and the Levites and
3:2 and his brothers the *p* and
3:8 the *p* and the Levites, and
3:10 the *p* in official clothing
3:12 the *p* and the Levites and
6:9 *p* that are in Jerusalem say
6:16 the *p* and the Levites and
6:18 the *p* in their classes and
6:20 the *p* and the Levites had
6:20 for their brothers the *p* and
7:7 sons of Israel and of the *p*
7:13 their *p* and Levites that is
7:16 gift of the people and the *p*
7:24 the *p* and the Levites, the
8:15 people and the *p*, but none
8:24 the chiefs of the *p* twelve
8:29 chiefs of the *p* and the
8:30 *p* and the Levites received
9:1 the *p* and the Levites have not
9:7 our kings, our *p*, into the
10:5 chiefs of the *p*, the Levites
10:18 sons of the *p* came to be
Ne 2:16 and to the Jews and the *p*
3:1 and his brothers, the *p*
3:22 the *p*, men of the Jordan
3:28 the *p* did repair work, each
5:12 called the *p* and made them
7:39 The *p*: The sons of Jedaiah
7:63 the *p*: the sons of Habaiah
7:73 the *p* and the Levites and the

Ne 8:13 the *p* and the Levites
9:32 our *p* and our prophets and
9:34 our *p* and our forefathers
9:38 princes, our Levites and our *p*
10:8 Shemaiah, these being the *p*
10:28 the *p*, the Levites, the
10:34 wood that the *p*, the Levites
10:36 the *p* that were ministering
10:37 bring to the *p* to the dining
10:39 the *p* that were ministering
11:3 the *p* and the Levites, and
11:10 the *p*: Jedaiah the son of
11:20 the *p* and of the Levites
12:1 *p* and the Levites that went
12:7 heads of the *p* and their
12:12 *p*, the heads of the paternal
12:22 *p*, down till the kingship
12:30 the *p* and the Levites
12:35 the sons of the *p* with the
12:41 the *p* Eliakim, Maaseiah
12:44 for the *p* and the Levites
12:44 *p* and of the Levites who
13:5 the contribution for the *p*
13:30 assign duties to the *p* and
Job 12:19 is making *p* walk barefoot
Ps 78:64 *p*, they fell by the very
99:6 and Aaron were among his *p*
132:9 *p* themselves be clothed with
132:16 *p* I shall clothe with
Isa 37:2 older men of the *p* covered
61:6 the *p* of Jehovah you will be
66:21 take some for the *p*, for
Jer 1:1 *p* that were in Anathoth in
1:18 toward her *p* and toward the
2:8 The *p* themselves did not say
2:26 their *p* and their prophets
4:9 *p* will certainly be driven to
5:31 for the *p*, they go subduing
8:1 the bones of the *p* and the
13:13 the *p* and the prophets and
19:1 the older men of the *p*
26:7 the *p* and the prophets and
26:8 the *p* and the prophets and
26:11 the *p* and the prophets
26:16 the people said to the *p*
27:16 to the *p* and to all this
28:1 before the eyes of the *p*
28:5 before the eyes of the *p*
29:1 to the *p* and to the prophets
29:25 and to all the *p*, saying
31:14 soul of the *p* with fatness
32:32 their *p* and their prophets
33:18 *p*, the Levites, there will
33:21 the *p*, my ministers
34:19 court officials and the *p*
48:7 his *p* and his princes at the
49:3 exile, his *p* and his princes
La 1:4 her *p* are sighing. Her virgins
1:19 my own *p* and my own old men
4:13 the errors of her *p*, There
4:16 consideration even for the *p*
Eze 22:26 Her *p* themselves have done
40:45 *p* who are taking care of
40:46 *p* who are taking care of
42:13 *p* who are approaching
42:14 When they, the *p*, have come
43:19 give to the Levitical *p*
43:24 *p* must throw salt upon
43:27 *p* will render upon the
44:15 Levitical *p*, the sons of
44:21 no wine should any *p* drink
44:30 *p* it will come to belong
44:31 beasts should the *p* eat
45:4 will come to be for the *p*
46:2 *p* must render up his whole
46:19 those belonging to the *p*
46:20 *p* will boil the guilt
48:10 holy contribution for the *p*
48:11 *p*, those who are sanctified
48:13 to the territory of the *p*
Da 1:20 all the magic-practicing *p*
2:2 call the magic-practicing *p*
2:27 magic-practicing *p* and the
4:7 the magic-practicing *p*
4:9 of the magic-practicing *p*
5:11 of the magic-practicing *p*
Ho 5:1 Hear this, O *p*, and pay
6:9 the association of *p* are
10:5 as well as its foreign-god *p*
Joe 1:9 the *p*, the ministers of
1:13 beat your breasts, you *p*
2:17 let the *p*, the ministers of
Mic 3:11 *p* instruct just for a price
Zep 1:4 the name of the foreign-god *p*

Priests'

Primary

Prime

Prince

Princely

Princes

Jer 26:10 the *p* of Judah got to hear
26:11 say to the *p* and to all the
26:12 Jeremiah said to all the *p*
26:16 the *p* and all the people
26:21 the *p* got to hear his words
29:2 the *p* of Judah and Jerusalem
32:32 their *p*, their priests and
34:10 all the *p* obeyed, and all
34:19 the *p* of Judah and the
34:19 and the *p* of Jerusalem, the
34:21 king of Judah and his *p* I
35:4 dining room of the *p* that
36:12 all the *p* were sitting
36:12 and all the other *p*
36:14 *p* sent out to Baruch
36:19 the *p* said to Baruch
36:21 the ears of all the *p*
37:14 brought him in to the *p*
37:15 *p* began to get indignant
38:4 *p* began to say to the king
38:17 *p* of the king of Babylon
38:18 *p* of the king of Babylon
38:22 *p* of the king of Babylon
38:25 *p* hear that I have spoken
38:27 *p* came in to Jeremiah and
39:3 *p* of the king of Babylon
39:3 *p* of the king of Babylon
44:17 our *p* did in the cities of
44:21 *p* and the people of the
48:7 and his *p* at the same time
49:3 exile, his priests and his *p*
49:38 the king and the *p*
50:35 Babylon and against her *p*
51:57 her *p* and her wise ones
52:10 *p* of Judah he slaughtered
La 1:6 *p* have proved to be like stags
2:2 profaned the kingdom and her *p*
2:9 her *p* are among the nations
5:12 *P* themselves have been hanged
Eze 11:1 *p* of the people
17:12 take its king and its *p* and
22:27 *p* in the midst of her are
Da 8:25 against the Prince of *p* he
9:6 your name to our kings, our *p*
9:8 to our *p* and to our forefathers
10:13 one of the foremost *p*, came
11:5 strong, even one of his *p*
Ho 5:10 The *p* of Judah have become
7:3 and, by their deceptions, *p*
7:5 *p* have sickened themselves
7:16 their *p* will fall because of
8:4 They have set up *p*, but I did
8:10 the burden of king and *p*
9:15 their *p* are acting stubborn
13:10 said, Do give me a king and *p*
Am 1:15 exile, he and his *p* together
2:3 all her *p* I shall kill with
Zep 1:8 give attention to the *p*, and
3:3 Her *p* in the midst of her

Princess
La 1:1 a *p* among the jurisdictional

Princesses
1Ki 11:3 And he came to have . . . *p*
Es 1:18 the *p* of Persia and Media
Isa 49:23 *p* nursing women for you

Principal
Nu 5:7 amount of his guilt in its *p*
1Sa 21:7 *p* one of the shepherds that
Jer 39:13 *p* men of the king of
41:1 *p* men of the king and ten
Da 1:7 *p* court official went
1:8 *p* court official that he might
1:9 before the *p* court official
1:10 *p* court official said to
1:11 *p* court official had appointed
1:18 the *p* court official also
Lu 19:47 the *p* ones of the people
Ac 13:50 and the *p* men of the city
16:12 the *p* city of the district of
17:4 not a few of the *p* women did
25:2 the *p* men of the Jews gave
28:7 *p* man of the island, named
28:17 the *p* men of the Jews

Print
Joh 20:25 his hands the *p* of the nails
20:25 into the *p* of the nails and

Prior
1Ki 14:9 who happened to be *p* to you
15:3 that he did *p* to him
16:25 worse than all who were *p*
16:30 those who were *p* to him
1Ki 16:33 happened to be *p* to him
2Ki 17:2 happened to be *p* to him
18:5 happened to be *p* to him
21:11 did that were *p* to him
23:25 not prove to be a king *p* to
1Ch 17:13 that happened to be *p* to you
2Ch 1:12 as no kings that were *p* to
Ne 5:15 governors that were *p* to me
Ec 1:10 is from time *p* to us
9:1 hate that were all *p* to them
Jer 28:8 that happened to be *p* to me
28:8 *p* to you from long ago
34:5 happened to be *p* to you
Eze 33:22 *p* to that one's coming to
Da 6:10 regularly doing *p* to this
7:7 other beasts that were *p* to it
Mt 5:12 persecuted the prophets *p* to
Ac 8:9 *p* to this, had been practicing

Prisca
Ro 16:3 to *P* and Aquila my fellow
1Co 16:19 Aquila and *P* together with
2Ti 4:19 Give my greetings to *P* and

Priscilla
Ac 18:2 Aquila . . . and *P* his wife
18:18 and with him *P* and Aquila
18:26 When *P* and Aquila heard him

Prison
Ge 39:20 gave him over to the *p* house
39:20 continued there in the *p*
39:21 chief officer of the *p* house
39:22 chief officer of the *p* house
39:22 who were in the *p* house
39:23 The chief officer of the *p*
40:3 the *p* house, the place where
40:5 were prisoners in the *p* house
40:15 should put me in the *p* hole
41:14 bring him quickly from the *p*
Ex 12:29 captive who was in the *p*
Jg 16:21 a grinder in the *p* house
16:25 Samson out of the *p* house
2Ki 25:29 he took off his *p* garments
Ec 4:14 gone forth from the *p* house
Jer 52:31 him forth from the *p* house
52:33 took off his *p* garments
Mt 5:25 and you get thrown into *p*
14:3 put him away in *p* on account
14:10 had John beheaded in the *p*
18:30 had him thrown into *p* until
25:36 I was in *p* and you came to
25:39 sick or in *p* and go to you
25:43 in *p*, but you did not look
25:44 in *p* and did not minister to
Mr 6:17 John and bound him in *p* on
6:27 and beheaded him in the *p*
Lu 3:20 he locked John up in *p*
12:58 officer throw you into *p*
22:33 both into *p* and into death
23:19 thrown into *p* for a certain
23:25 thrown into *p* for sedition
Joh 3:24 not yet been thrown into *p*
Ac 5:19 opened the doors of the *p*
5:22 did not find them in the *p*
5:25 men you put in the *p* are
8:3 he would turn them over to *p*
12:4 he put him in *p*, turning him
12:5 Peter was being kept in the *p*
12:6 guards . . . keeping the *p*
12:7 light shone in the *p* cell
12:17 brought him out of the *p*
16:23 threw them into *p*, ordering
16:24 threw them into the inner *p*
16:27 seeing the *p* doors were open
16:37 Romans, and threw us into *p*
16:40 they came out of the *p* and
Php 1:7 both in my *p* bonds and in the
1:14 by reason of my *p* bonds
1:17 for me in my *p* bonds
Col 4:3 in fact, I am in *p* bonds
4:18 bearing my *p* bonds in mind
2Ti 2:9 to the point of *p* bonds as
Phm 10 while in my *p* bonds
13 *p* bonds I bear for the sake of
Heb 10:34 sympathy for those in *p*
13:3 Keep in mind those in *p*
1Pe 3:19 preached to the spirits in *p*
Re 2:10 throwing some of you into *p*
20:7 be let loose out of his *p*

Prisoner
Ge 40:3 place where Joseph was a *p*
1Ch 3:17 sons of Jeconiah as *p* were
Ps 79:11 sighing of the *p* come in
102:20 hear the sighing of the *p*
Isa 22:3 they have been taken *p*
22:3 have been taken *p* together
42:7 out of the dungeon the *p*
49:21 gone into exile and taken *p*
Mt 27:15 to release a *p* to the crowd
27:16 notorious *p* called Barabbas
Mr 15:6 release to them one *p*, whom
Ac 23:18 The *p* Paul called me to him
25:14 certain man left *p* by Felix
25:27 send a *p* and not also to
28:17 I was delivered over as a *p*
Eph 3:1 Paul, the *p* of Christ Jesus
4:1 the *p* in the Lord, entreat
2Ti 1:8 me a *p* for his sake, but
Phm 1 Paul, a *p* for the sake of
9 *p* for the sake of Christ Jesus

Prisoners
Ge 39:20 where the *p* of the king were
39:22 all the *p* who were in the
40:5 were *p* in the prison house
Job 3:18 *p* themselves are at ease
Ps 68:6 *p* into full prosperity
69:33 not despise his very own *p*
107:10 *P* in affliction and irons
Isa 10:4 must bow down under the *p*
14:17 homeward even for his *p*
24:22 as of *p* into the pit
49:9 to say to the *p*, Come out!
61:1 of the eyes even to the *p*
La 3:34 all the *p* of the earth
Zec 9:11 send your *p* out of the pit
9:12 you *p* of the hope
Ac 16:25 yes, the *p* were hearing them
16:27 that the *p* had escaped
27:1 *p* over to an army officer
27:42 soldiers to kill the *p*, that

Prisons
Isa 43:14 bars of the *p* to come down
Lu 21:12 to the synagogues and *p*
Ac 22:4 handing over to *p* both men
26:10 holy ones I locked up in *p*
2Co 6:5 beatings, by *p*, by disorders
11:23 in *p* more plentifully, in
Heb 11:36 than that, by bonds and *p*

Privacy
Lu 9:10 withdrew to *p* into a city

Private
Ex 20:26 that your *p* parts may not be
De 4:20 people of *p* ownership to him
9:26 your *p* property, whom you
9:29 your *p* property whom you
23:12 a *p* place should be at your
Eze 16:36 your *p* parts are uncovered
16:37 and uncover your *p* parts to
16:37 must see all your *p* parts
Ho 2:10 I shall uncover her *p* parts
Mt 6:6 you pray, go into your *p* room
Lu 12:3 what you whisper in *p* rooms
Ac 2:46 took their meals in *p* homes
Php 2:25 but your envoy and *p* servant
2:30 to render *p* service to me
2Pe 1:20 from any *p* interpretation

Privately
Mt 17:19 came up to Jesus *p* and said
20:17 twelve disciples off *p* and
24:3 disciples approached him *p*
Mr 4:34 *p* to his disciples he would
6:31 *p* into a lonely place and
7:33 away from the crowd *p* and
9:28 proceeded to ask him *p*
13:3 Andrew began to ask him *p*
Ac 23:19 inquiring *p*: What is it you
Ga 2:2 *p*, however, before those who

Privates
De 25:11 grabbed hold of him by his *p*

Privies
2Ki 10:27 kept it set aside for *p*
Da 2:5 public *p* your own houses will

Privilege
Lu 1:43 how is it that this *p* is mine
1:74 the *p* of fearlessly rendering
Ac 7:46 *p* of providing a habitation
2Co 8:4 *p* of kindly giving and for a
Php 1:29 to you the *p* was given in
2Pe 1:1 held in equal *p* with ours

Privy
1Ki 18:27 and has to go to the *p*
Ezr 6:11 turned into a public *p* on
Da 3:29 be turned into a public *p*

Prize
1Co 9:24 but only one receives the *p*
Php 3:14 for the *p* of the upward call
Col 2:18 no man deprive you of the *p*

Probably
Zep 2:3 *P* you may be concealed in the

Problem
Ro 8:26 *p* of what we should pray for

Procedure
Le 5:10 according to the regular *p*
9:16 according to the regular *p*
Nu 9:14 regular *p* is the way he should
15:24 according to the regular *p*
29:6 the regular *p* for them, as a
29:18 according to the regular *p*
29:21 according to the regular *p*
29:24 according to the regular *p*
29:27 according to the regular *p*
29:30 according to the regular *p*
29:33 according to the regular *p*
29:37 according to the regular *p*
1Sa 27:11 this way has been his *p* all
Es 2:12 days of their massage *p* were
Ac 25:16 it is not Roman *p* to hand

Procedures
Nu 9:3 its regular *p* you should

Proceed*
Ge 35:11 nations will *p* out of you
Eph 4:29 rotten saying not *p* out of

Proceeded*
1Pe 4:3 when you *p* in deeds of loose
Re 19:21 sword *p* out of his mouth

Proceeding
Le 20:26 I am *p* to divide you off
Mt 15:18 things *p* out of the mouth
20:8 *p* from the last to the first
Mr 2:23 *p* through the grainfields on
Lu 4:22 winsome words *p* out of his
2Pe 3:3 *p* according to their own
Jude 16 *p* according to their own
18 *p* according to their own
Re 4:5 *p* lightnings and voices and

Proceeds
Ps 50:1 And he *p* to call the earth
Pr 22:3 calamity and *p* to conceal
Isa 38:12 One *p* to cut me off from
44:12 he *p* to form it, and he
Eze 18:27 *p* to execute justice and
Mt 15:11 is what *p* out of his mouth
Joh 15:26 which *p* from the Father
Ac 2:45 distributing the *p* to all
1Co 7:15 unbelieving one *p* to depart
1Jo 4:5 speak what *p* from the world

Process
Ge 11:3 bake them with a burning *p*

Processed
Nu 31:23 everything . . . *p* with fire
31:23 that is not *p* with fire you

Procession
Ps 118:27 Bind the festival *p* with
2Co 2:14 triumphal *p* in company with
Col 2:15 in a triumphal *p* by means of

Processions
Ne 12:31 thanksgiving choirs and *p*
Ps 68:24 They have seen your *p*, O God
68:24 The *p* of my God, my King

Prochorus
Ac 6:5 selected Stephen . . . and *P*

Proclaim
Le 23:2 *p* are holy conventions
23:4 *p* at their appointed times
23:21 *p* on this very day Jehovah's
23:37 *p* as holy conventions, for
25:10 *p* liberty in the land to all
1Ki 21:9 *P* a fast, and have Naboth
2Ki 23:17 to *p* these things that you
Pr 20:6 men will *p* each one his own
Isa 61:1 to *p* liberty to those taken
61:2 to *p* the year of goodwill
Jer 3:12 *p* these words to the north
7:2 you must *p* there this word
11:6 *P* all these words in the
19:2 *p* the words that I shall
34:8 to *p* to them liberty
Joe 3:9 *P* this, you people, among
Am 4:5 and *p* voluntary offerings
Jon 1:2 *p* against her that their
Jon 3:2 *p* to her the proclamation
3:5 *p* a fast and to put on
Mr 1:45 man started to *p* it a great
5:20 started to *p* in the Decapolis
7:36 much more they would *p* it

Proclaimed
Ru 4:14 his name may be *p* in Israel
1Ki 21:12 *p* a fast and had Naboth
2Ki 10:20 Accordingly they *p* it
23:16 man of the true God had *p*
23:16 who *p* these things
2Ch 20:3 he *p* a fast for all Judah
Ezr 8:21 I *p* a fast there at the river
Jer 36:9 *p* a fast before Jehovah
46:17 *p*, Pharaoh the king of Egypt
La 1:21 bring the day that you have *p*

Proclaiming
Jer 34:15 *p* liberty each one to his
34:17 *p* liberty each one to his
34:17 *p* to you a liberty, is the
Jon 3:4 and he kept *p* and saying
Lu 8:39 *p* throughout the whole city
1Co 9:14 those *p* the good news to live
11:26 keep *p* the death of the Lord
Re 5:2 angel *p* with a loud voice

Proclamation
Ne 8:15 make *p* and cause a call to
Jon 3:2 *p* that I am speaking to you

Proconsul
Ac 13:7 the *p* Sergius Paulus, an
13:8 the *p* away from the faith
13:12 the *p*, upon seeing what had
18:12 while Gallio was *p* of Achaia

Proconsuls
Ac 19:38 there are *p*; let them bring

Procure
Jg 20:10 *p* provisions for the people
Ps 91:1 *p* himself lodging under the
Mt 10:9 Do not *p* gold or silver or
Lu 9:12 *p* lodging and find provisions

Procured
2Ch 11:23 *p* a multitude of wives for
Ac 22:5 *p* letters to the brothers in

Procures
Pr 31:30 one that *p* praise for herself

Produce
Ge 3:17 In pain you will eat its *p*
17:20 *p* twelve chieftains, and I
30:39 the flocks would *p* striped
47:24 When it has resulted in *p*
Ex 7:9 *P* a miracle for yourselves
22:29 Your full *p* and the overflow
23:10 and you must gather its *p*
36:6 do not *p* any more stuff for
Le 19:25 to add its *p* to yourselves
21:5 *p* baldness upon their heads
23:39 gathered the *p* of the land
25:3 you must gather the land's *p*
25:7 its *p* should serve for eating
Nu 18:27 *p* of the wine or oil press
18:30 the *p* of the threshing floor
18:30 *p* of the wine or oil press
De 11:17 ground will not give its *p*
14:22 give a tenth of all the *p* of
14:28 tenth part of your *p* in that
16:15 will bless you in all your *p*
22:9 the full *p* of the seed that
26:12 the entire tenth of your *p*
32:13 he ate the *p* of the field
32:22 consume the earth and its *p*
Jos 5:12 the *p* of the land of Canaan
Jg 9:11 my good *p*, and must I go to
2Ki 19:30 and *p* fruitage upward
2Ch 31:5 all the *p* of the field, and
32:28 places for the *p* of grain
Ne 9:37 its *p* is abounding for the
Job 14:4 Who can *p* someone clean out
14:9 *p* a bough like a new plant
31:12 among all my *p* it would
31:31 Who can *p* anyone that has
37:13 he makes it *p* effects
37:19 We cannot *p* words because
40:20 bear their *p* for it
Ps 67:6 will certainly give its *p*
Pr 3:9 the firstfruits of all your *p*
3:14 and having it as *p* than gold
8:19 my *p* than choice silver
10:16 *p* of the wicked one results
15:6 in the *p* of the wicked one
18:20 even with the *p* of his lips
Isa 5:2 hoping for it to *p* grapes
5:4 I hoped for it to *p* grapes
5:10 *p* but one bath measure, and
5:10 measure of seed will *p* but
27:6 productive land with *p*
30:23 as the *p* of the ground
34:1 land and all its *p*
37:31 and *p* fruitage upward
41:21 *P* your arguments, says the
41:22 *P* and tell to us the things
42:5 the earth and its *p*
55:10 and makes it *p* and sprout
La 4:9 lack of the *p* of the open field
Eze 17:8 to *p* boughs and to bear fruit
17:23 bear boughs and *p* fruit and
36:30 and the *p* of the field
48:18 *p* must come to be for bread
Ho 8:7 Should any perhaps *p* it
9:16 will be no fruit that they *p*
Hab 3:17 terraces . . . *p* no food
Mt 3:8 *p* fruit that befits repentance
3:10 does not *p* fine fruit is to
7:18 a rotten tree *p* fine fruit
Lu 3:8 *p* fruits that befit repentance
Ac 12:4 *p* him for the people after
12:6 Herod was about to *p* him
2Ti 2:23 knowing they *p* fights
Jas 3:12 fig tree cannot *p* olives or a
3:12 salt water *p* sweet water
2Jo 8 things we have worked to *p*

Produced
Ge 4:1 I have *p* a man with the aid
31:8 whole flock *p* speckled ones
31:8 whole flock *p* striped ones
38:29 you have *p* a perineal rupture
Ex 15:16 the people whom you have *p*
De 32:6 your Father who has *p* you, He
Ps 139:13 you yourself *p* my kidneys
Pr 8:22 Jehovah himself *p* me as the
24:31 look! all of it *p* weeds
Isa 5:2 it gradually *p* wild grapes
5:4 it gradually *p* wild grapes
Jer 12:2 they have also *p* fruit
48:36 abundance that he has *p*
Eze 17:6 became a vine and *p* shoots
Mt 13:26 blade sprouted and *p* fruit
Lu 8:8 it *p* fruit a hundredfold
12:16 of a certain rich man *p* well
Ac 25:18 the accusers *p* no charge of
2Co 5:5 *p* us for this very thing is
7:11 great earnestness it *p* in you
12:12 signs of an apostle were *p*

Producer
Ge 14:19 God, *P* of heaven and earth
14:22 God, *P* of heaven and earth

Produces
Le 25:12 you may eat what the land *p*
Ho 8:7 No sprout *p* flour
Mt 7:17 every good tree *p* fine fruit
7:17 rotten tree *p* worthless fruit
13:23 really does bear fruit and *p*
Mr 4:32 *p* great branches, so that the
Lu 13:9 it *p* fruit in the future
Ro 4:15 In reality the Law *p* wrath
5:3 that tribulation *p* endurance
2Co 7:10 sadness of the world *p* death
9:11 *p* through us an expression
Heb 6:8 if it *p* thorns and thistles

Producing
Ge 41:47 the land went on *p* by the
Isa 7:22 abundance of the *p* of milk
Jer 17:8 he leave off from *p* fruit
Mal 3:17 I am *p* a special property
Mt 7:19 tree not *p* fine fruit gets
21:43 to a nation *p* its fruits
Lu 3:9 not *p* fine fruit is to be cut
6:43 not a fine tree *p* rotten fruit
6:43 a rotten tree *p* fine fruit
1Co 15:56 The sting *p* death is sin
Re 22:2 trees of life *p* twelve crops

Product
Ge 40:17 the *p* of a baker, and there
Ex 28:32 the *p* of a loom worker
De 4:28 the *p* of the hands of man
22:9 the *p* of the vineyard may be
Job 10:3 *p* of the hard work of your
Ps 105:44 *p* of the hard work of
109:11 plunder of his *p* of toil
Isa 1:31 the *p* of his activity a spark
Jer 20:5 this city and all its *p*
Eze 23:29 all your *p* of toil and
Mt 26:29 any of this *p* of the vine

Mr 14:25 of the *p* of the vine until
Lu 22:18 from the *p* of the vine until
Eph 2:10 we are a *p* of his work and

Production
De 28:33 all your *p* a people will eat

Productions
Ps 104:24 earth is full of your *p*

Productive
1Sa 2:8 places upon them the *p* land
2Sa 22:16 foundations of the *p* land
1Ch 16:30 Also the *p* land is firmly
Job 18:18 from the *p* land they will
34:13 appointed to him the *p* land
37:12 the *p* land of the earth
Ps 9:8 will judge the *p* land in
18:15 the *p* land became uncovered
19:4 the extremity of the *p* land
24:1 The *p* land and those dwelling
33:8 the inhabitants of the *p* land
50:12 to me the *p* land and its
77:18 have lighted up the *p* land
89:11 *p* land and what fills it
90:2 the earth and the *p* land
93:1 *p* land also becomes firmly
96:10 *p* land also becomes firmly
96:13 judge the *p* land with
97:4 lighted up the *p* land
98:7 *p* land and those dwelling in
98:9 judge the *p* land with
Pr 8:26 dust masses of the *p* land
8:31 glad at the *p* land of his
Isa 13:11 badness upon the *p* land
14:17 *p* land like the wilderness
14:21 face of the *p* land with
18:3 inhabitants of the *p* land and
24:4 *p* land has withered, has
26:9 inhabitants of the *p* land
26:18 inhabitants for the *p* land
27:6 surface of the *p* land with
34:1 listen, the *p* land and all
Jer 10:12 establishing the *p* land
51:15 *p* land by his wisdom, and
La 4:12 the inhabitants of the *p* land
Na 1:5 the *p* land also, and all those

Products
Ge 43:11 Take the finest *p* of the land
Ex 31:5 to make *p* of every kind
35:33 ingenious *p* of every sort
De 33:14 the *p* of the sun
2Ki 8:6 all the *p* of the field from
Ps 144:13 furnishing *p* of one sort
Pr 16:8 an abundance of *p* without
Isa 1:25 remove all your waste *p*
Jer 12:13 the *p* of you people
2Co 9:10 the *p* of your righteousness

Profane
Ex 20:25 upon it, then you will *p* it
Le 10:10 the holy thing and the *p*
18:21 not *p* the name of your God
19:12 do *p* the name of your God
19:29 Do not *p* your daughter by
20:3 and to *p* my holy name
21:4 so as to make himself *p*
21:6 not *p* the name of their God
21:9 *p* by committing prostitution
21:12 *p* the sanctuary of his God
21:15 not *p* his seed among his
21:23 not *p* my sanctuary, for I am
22:2 *p* my holy name in the things
22:15 *p* the holy things of the sons
22:32 not *p* my holy name, and I
Nu 18:32 must not *p* the holy things
Ps 89:31 If they *p* my own statutes
89:34 I shall not *p* my covenant
Isa 23:9 *p* the pride of all beauty
43:28 *p* the princes of the holy
56:2 sabbath in order not to *p* it
56:6 sabbath in order not to *p* it
Jer 34:16 turn back and *p* my name and
Eze 7:21 and they will certainly *p* it
7:22 *p* my concealed place, and
7:22 will really come and *p* it
13:19 *p* me toward my people for
20:39 name you will no more *p*
23:39 on that day to *p* it
28:7 *p* your beaming splendor
28:16 put you as *p* out of the
36:20 proceeded to *p* my holy name
42:20 what is holy and what is *p*
44:7 my sanctuary so as to *p* it
44:23 a holy thing and a *p* thing
48:15 something *p* for the city
Da 11:31 *p* the sanctuary, the fortress
Ac 24:6 tried to *p* the temple and
1Ti 1:9 and *p*, murderers of fathers

Profaned
Ge 49:4 At that time you *p* my lounge
Le 19:8 *p* a holy thing of Jehovah; and
Ps 55:20 He has *p* his covenant
74:7 *p* the tabernacle of your name
89:39 *p* his diadem to the very
Isa 47:6 I *p* my inheritance, and I
48:11 could one let oneself be *p*
La 2:2 *p* the kingdom and her princes
Eze 7:24 their sanctuaries must be *p*
20:9 name that it might not be *p*
20:13 my sabbaths they *p* very
20:14 name that it might not be *p*
20:16 and my sabbaths they *p*
20:21 My sabbaths they *p*. So I
20:22 it should not be *p* before
20:24 and they *p* my own sabbaths
22:8 my sabbaths you have *p*
22:16 *p* within yourself before
22:26 *p* in the midst of them
23:38 my sabbaths they have *p*
25:3 because it has been *p*, and
28:18 have *p* your sanctuaries
36:21 have *p* among the nations
36:22 name, which you have *p*
36:23 being *p* among the nations
36:23 *p* in the midst of them
39:7 let my holy name be *p*
Zep 3:4 priests . . . *p* what was holy
Mal 2:11 *p* the holiness of Jehovah

Profaner
Ex 31:14 A *p* of it will positively

Profaning
Le 21:9 is her father that she is *p*
22:9 because they were *p* it. I am
1Ch 5:1 *p* the lounge of his father
Ne 13:17 even *p* the sabbath day
13:18 Israel by *p* the sabbath
Jer 16:18 account of their *p* my land
Eze 22:26 they keep *p* my holy places
24:21 Here I am *p* my sanctuary
28:9 in the hand of those *p* you
Am 2:7 the purpose of *p* my holy name
Mal 1:12 men are *p* me by your saying
2:10 in *p* the covenant of our

Professing
1Ti 2:10 women *p* to reverence God

Professional
Le 19:31 consult *p* foretellers of
20:6 *p* foretellers of events so as
De 18:11 a *p* foreteller of events or
1Sa 28:3 *p* foretellers of events from
28:9 *p* foretellers of events
2Ki 21:6 and *p* foretellers of events
23:24 the *p* foretellers of events
2Ch 33:6 and *p* foretellers of events
Isa 19:3 *p* foretellers of events

Proficiency
Ec 2:21 with knowledge and with *p*
4:4 and all the *p* in work, that it

Profit
Ge 37:26 What *p* would there be in
Ex 18:21 men, hating unjust *p*; and
1Sa 8:3 inclined to follow unjust *p*
1Ki 10:15 and the *p* from the traders
Job 34:9 able-bodied man does not *p*
Ps 10:3 the one making undue *p* has
30:9 What *p* is there in my blood
Pr 1:19 everyone making unjust *p*
15:27 The one making unjust *p* is
28:16 hating unjust *p* will prolong
Ec 1:3 What *p* does a man have in all
5:9 *p* of the earth is among them
5:16 what *p* is there to the one
Isa 23:3 to be the *p* of the nations
23:18 her *p* and her hire must
Jer 51:13 measure of your *p* making
Mic 4:13 their unjust *p*, and their
Mal 3:14 what *p* is there in that we
Phm 20 may I derive *p* from you in
Heb 12:10 he does so for our *p* that
2Pe 2:18 swelling expressions of no *p*

Profitable
Ac 20:20 of the things that were *p*

Profited
1Co 13:3 do not have love, I am not *p*

Profitless
Tit 1:10 unruly men, *p* talkers, and

Profits
Ps 119:36 Incline . . . not to *p*
Jas 4:13 in business and make *p*

Profound
Ps 69:2 I have come into *p* waters

Profusely
2Ki 20:3 Hezekiah began to weep *p*
Ezr 10:1 for the people had wept *p*
Isa 38:3 Hezekiah began to weep *p*
Jer 22:10 Weep *p* for the one going
La 1:2 *P* she weeps during the night
Mr 14:31 to say *p*: If I have to die

Progeny
Ge 10:21 to Shem . . . was also *p* born
48:6 your *p* to which you shall
De 7:13 cows and the *p* of your flock
28:4 and the *p* of your flock
28:18 and the *p* of your flock
28:51 cattle or *p* of your flock
Job 18:19 and no *p* among his people
Isa 14:22 remnant and *p* and posterity
Ac 17:28 said, For we are also his *p*
17:29 that we are the *p* of God, we

Progress
Ezr 5:8 is making *p* in their hands
6:14 building and making *p* under
Lu 6:12 In the *p* of these days he
Joh 8:37 my word makes no *p* among
Ac 2:1 festival of Pentecost was in *p*
Ga 1:14 making greater *p* in Judaism
Php 3:16 what extent we have made *p*
2Ti 3:9 they will make no further *p*

Progressing
Lu 2:52 Jesus went on *p* in wisdom

Progressively
Ge 8:3 waters . . . *p* receding
8:5 waters kept on *p* lessening

Projects
Nu 21:20 it *p* over toward the face of

Prolong
Pr 28:16 hating unjust profit will *p*
Ec 8:13 neither will he *p* his days
Isa 53:10 he will *p* his days, and in

Prolonged
Nu 9:19 cloud *p* its stay over the
9:22 cloud *p* its stay over the
Eze 12:22 The days are *p*, and every
Ac 20:7 *p* his speech until midnight

Prolonging
Job 6:11 that I should keep *p* my soul

Prominent
2Ki 4:8 there was a *p* woman, and she
Mt 23:6 They like the most *p* place at
Mr 12:39 *p* places at evening meals
Lu 14:7 choosing the most *p* places
14:8 down in the most *p* place
20:46 *p* places at evening meals
Ro 3:7 truth . . . been made more *p* to

Promise
Nu 30:6 the thoughtless *p* of her lips
30:8 the thoughtless *p* of her lips
Jos 14:10 Jehovah made this *p* to
21:45 Not a *p* failed out of all
21:45 *p* that Jehovah had made to
2Sa 7:28 you *p* to your servant this
1Ki 8:24 the *p* with your own mouth
8:26 let your *p* that you have
8:56 one word of his good *p* that
1Ch 17:26 and you *p* this goodness
2Ch 1:9 *p* with David my father prove
6:15 you made the *p* with your
6:17 *p* that you have promised to
Ac 2:39 *p* is to you and to your
7:17 *p* that God had openly
13:23 according to his *p* God has
13:32 *p* made to the forefathers
23:21 waiting for the *p* from you
26:6 hope of the *p* that was made
26:7 to the fulfillment of this *p*
Ro 4:13 *p* that he should be heir of
4:14 and the *p* has been abolished
4:16 *p* to be sure to all his seed
4:20 *p* of God he did not waver
9:8 children by the *p* are counted
9:9 *p* was as follows: At this

Ga 3:17 so as to abolish the *p*
3:18 it is no longer due to *p*
3:18 it to Abraham through a *p*
3:19 whom the *p* had been made
3:22 *p* resulting from faith
3:29 heirs with reference to a *p*
4:23 the free woman through a *p*
4:28 children belonging to the *p*
Eph 2:12 to the covenants of the *p*
3:6 partakers with us of the *p*
6:2 the first command with a *p*
1Ti 4:8 as it holds *p* of the life now
2Ti 1:1 *p* of the life that is in
Heb 4:1 *p* is left of entering into his
6:13 God made his *p* to Abraham
6:15 he obtained this *p*
6:17 to the heirs of the *p* the
9:15 the *p* of the everlasting
10:36 the fulfillment of the *p*
11:9 alien in the land of the *p*
11:9 heirs of the very same *p*
11:39 the fulfillment of the *p*
2Pe 3:9 is not slow respecting his *p*
3:13 awaiting according to his *p*

Promised
De 1:11 bless you just as he has *p*
6:3 God of your forefathers has *p*
6:19 just as Jehovah has *p*
9:28 the land that he had *p* them
11:25 just as he has *p* you
12:20 just as he has *p* you
15:6 bless you just as he has *p*
19:8 the land that he *p* to give
26:18 just as he has *p* you, and
26:19 just as he has *p*
29:13 just as he has *p* you and
Jos 1:3 give it, just as I *p* to Moses
9:21 the chieftains have *p* them
11:23 that Jehovah had *p* Moses
13:14 just as he has *p* them
13:33 just as he has *p* them
14:10 preserved me . . . as he *p*
14:12 that Jehovah *p* on that day
14:12 just as Jehovah *p*
22:4 rest, just as he *p* them
23:5 Jehovah your God had *p* you
23:10 you, just as he has *p* you
Jg 1:20 just as Moses had *p*, then he
6:36 just as you have *p*
6:37 just as you have *p*
2Sa 7:29 Jehovah, have *p*, and due to
1Ki 5:5 just as Jehovah *p* to David
5:12 wisdom, just as he had *p* him
8:24 that which you *p* him, so
8:25 that which you *p* him, saying
8:26 *p* to your servant David my
8:56 to all that he has *p*
8:56 *p* by means of Moses his
9:5 just as I *p* David your father
2Ki 8:19 *p* him to give a lamp to him
14:27 *p* not to wipe out the name
1Ch 27:23 Jehovah had *p* to make
2Ch 2:15 the wine that my lord has *p*
6:15 David my father what you *p*
6:16 David my father what you *p*
6:17 *p* to your servant David prove
23:3 Jehovah *p* concerning the
Ezr 10:19 *p* by shaking hands to put
Ne 9:23 the land that you had *p* to
Ps 119:57 I have *p* to keep your words
Eze 20:8 I *p* to pour out my rage upon
20:13 I *p* to pour out my fury
20:21 So I *p* to pour out my rage
Mt 1:18 Mary was *p* in marriage to
14:7 he *p* with an oath to give her
Mr 14:11 *p* to give him silver money
Lu 1:27 a virgin *p* in marriage to a
2:5 given him in marriage as *p*, at
24:49 that which is *p* by my Father
Ac 1:4 for what the Father has *p*
2:33 received the *p* holy spirit
7:5 *p* to give it to him as a
Ro 1:2 he *p* aforetime through his
4:21 he had *p* he was also able to
2Co 9:5 bountiful gift previously *p*
11:2 personally *p* you in marriage
Ga 3:14 receive the *p* spirit through
Eph 1:13 with the *p* holy spirit
Tit 1:2 *p* before times long lasting
Heb 10:23 for he is faithful that *p*
11:11 him faithful who had *p*
12:26 but now he has *p*, saying
Jas 1:12 Jehovah *p* to those who
Jas 2:5 he *p* to those who love him
2Pe 3:4 Where is this *p* presence of
1Jo 2:25 this is the *p* thing that
2:25 *p* us, the life everlasting

Promises
Ro 9:4 the sacred service and the *p*
15:8 to verify the *p* He made to
2Co 1:20 how many the *p* of God are
7:1 we have these *p*, beloved
Ga 3:16 *p* were spoken to Abraham
3:21 against the *p* of God
Heb 6:12 and patience inherit the *p*
7:6 blessed him who had the *p*
8:6 established upon better *p*
11:13 the fulfillment of the *p*
11:17 had gladly received the *p*
11:33 obtained *p*, stopped the
2Pe 1:4 precious and very grand *p*

Promising
2Pe 2:19 they are *p* them freedom

Promote
Ps 140:8 Do not *p* his plotting, that
Ro 16:26 to *p* obedience by faith

Promotes
Tit 3:10 man that *p* a sect, reject

Prompt
Isa 16:5 and being *p* in righteousness

Promptly
Ex 12:21 *P* Moses called all the older
1Sa 30:9 *P* David got on his way, he
2Sa 10:19 *p* made peace with Israel
12:20 they *p* set bread before him
1Ch 19:19 *p* made peace with David and
2Ch 25:3 *p* killed his servants who
Ezr 6:8 expense will *p* be given to
6:12 an order. Let it be done *p*
6:13 sent word, so they did *p*
7:17 will *p* buy with this money
7:21 it will be done *p*
7:26 let judgment be *p* executed
Zep 3:7 acted *p* in making all their
Mt 13:46 *p* sold all the things he had

Promulgated
Da 2:5 The word is being *p* by me
2:8 that the word is being *p* by me
1Ti 1:9 that law is *p*, not for a

Prone
Tit 1:7 not *p* to wrath, not a drunken

Pronounce
Ge 30:13 will certainly *p* me happy
48:20 repeatedly *p* blessing, saying
Ex 22:9 one whom God will *p* wicked
Le 13:6 priest must also *p* him clean
13:13 must then *p* the plague clean
13:17 then *p* the plague clean
13:23 the priest must *p* him clean
13:28 priest must *p* him clean
13:34 priest must then *p* him clean
13:37 the priest must *p* him clean
13:59 *p* it clean or to declare it
14:7 *p* him clean, and he must send
14:48 must then *p* the house clean
16:30 made for you to *p* you clean
De 25:1 *p* the righteous one righteous
25:1 and *p* the wicked one wicked
2Ki 25:6 *p* a judicial decision upon
1Ch 23:13 and to *p* blessing in his
Job 9:20 mouth would *p* me wicked
10:2 to God, Do not *p* me wicked
29:11 proceeded to *p* me happy
32:3 proceeded to *p* God wicked
34:17 will you *p* him wicked?
40:8 Will you *p* me wicked in
Ps 19:12 From concealed sins *p* me
37:33 he will not *p* him wicked
72:17 Let all nations *p* him happy
94:21 *p* wicked even the blood of
109:28 their part, *p* a malediction
109:28 your part, *p* a blessing
Pr 31:28 and proceeded to *p* her happy
Ca 6:9 they proceeded to *p* her happy
Isa 50:9 that can *p* me wicked
Jer 39:5 *p* upon him judicial
52:9 *p* upon him judicial
Mal 3:12 will have to *p* you happy
Lu 1:48 generations will *p* me happy
Jas 5:11 We *p* happy those who have

Pronounced
Jos 6:26 Joshua had an oath *p* at that
Jg 17:2 you *p* a curse and also said
Ps 41:2 will be *p* happy in the earth
Ec 6:10 its name has already been *p*

Pronouncement
2Ki 9:25 lifted up this *p* against him
2Ch 24:27 *p* against him and the
Isa 13:1 *p* against Babylon that Isaiah
14:28 Ahaz died this *p* occurred
15:1 The *p* against Moab: Because
17:1 The *p* against Damascus
19:1 The *p* against Egypt
21:1 *p* against the wilderness of
21:11 The *p* against Dumah
21:13 The *p* against the desert
22:1 *p* of the valley of the vision
23:1 The *p* of Tyre: Howl, you
30:6 *p* against the beasts of the
Eze 12:10 is this *p* against Jerusalem
Na 1:1 The *p* against Nineveh: The book
Hab 1:1 *p* that Habakkuk the prophet
Zec 9:1 A *p:* The word of Jehovah is
12:1 A *p:* The word of Jehovah
Mal 1:1 A *p:* The word of Jehovah
Ro 11:4 the divine *p* say to him

Pronouncements
La 2:14 worthless and misleading *p*
Ac 7:38 living sacred *p* to give you
Ro 3:2 with the sacred *p* of God
Heb 5:12 the sacred *p* of God
1Pe 4:11 were the sacred *p* of God

Pronounces
Le 14:11 priest who *p* him clean must
Job 15:6 Your mouth *p* you wicked, and
Pr 12:2 of wicked ideas he *p* wicked

Pronouncing
1Ki 8:32 *p* the wicked one wicked by
8:32 by *p* the righteous one
2Ch 6:23 *p* the righteous one righteous
Pr 17:15 *p* the wicked one righteous
17:15 *p* the righteous one wicked
Isa 5:23 *p* the wicked one righteous
Ho 4:2 *p* of curses and practicing of
Mal 3:15 *p* presumptuous people happy

Proof
Jg 7:3 So Gideon put them to the *p*
7:4 may put them to the *p* for you
Ps 95:9 forefathers put me to the *p*
106:14 God to the *p* in the desert
2Co 2:9 to ascertain the *p* of you
8:19 and in *p* of our ready mind
8:24 the *p* of your love and of
9:13 *p* that this ministry gives
13:3 *p* of Christ speaking in me
Php 1:28 is a *p* of destruction for
2:22 you know the *p* he gave of
1Th 2:4 who makes *p* of our hearts
2Th 1:5 *p* of the righteous judgment
Heb 2:6 certain witness has given *p*

Proofs
Ac 1:3 by many positive *p* he showed

Propels
Ge 49:22 *p* its branches up over a

Proper
Ex 18:22 on every *p* occasion; and it
18:26 on every *p* occasion. A hard
Le 26:4 rain at their *p* time, and the
2Ch 24:11 *p* time he would bring the
Ezr 4:14 not *p* for us to see the
Es 8:5 the thing is *p* before the king
Job 19:5 reproach to be *p* against me
33:27 was not the *p* thing for me
Ec 10:17 princes eat at the *p* time
Jer 30:11 correct you to the *p* degree
46:28 chastise you to the *p* degree
Zec 5:11 there upon her *p* place
Mt 24:45 their food at the *p* time
Lu 12:42 food supplies at the *p* time
Ac 15:38 Paul did not think it *p* to
28:22 *p* to hear from you what
Col 2:18 puffed up without *p* cause
2Ti 2:26 come back to their *p* senses
Phm 8 to order you to do what is *p*
Jas 3:10 is not *p*, my brothers, for
Jude 6 forsook . . . *p* dwelling place

Properties
Ac 2:45 their possessions and *p* and

Property
Ge 23:18 Abraham as his purchased *p*
Ex 19:5 become my special *p* out of

Le 25:30 perpetuity as the *p* of its
25:33 *p* of the Levites is not
Nu 32:18 landed *p,* each with his own
33:54 yourselves with landed *p*
De 7:6 a special *p,* out of all the
9:26 even your private *p,* whom
9:29 your private *p* whom you
14:2 a special *p,* out of all the
26:18 a special *p,* just as he has
Jos 14:4 their livestock and their *p*
17:6 Gilead became the *p* of the
1Ch 29:3 a special *p* of mine, gold
Ne 5:13 from his acquired *p* every man
Job 20:18 giving back his acquired *p*
31:25 because my *p* was much
Ps 105:21 as ruler over all his *p*
135:4 Israel for his special *p*
Ec 2:8 and *p* peculiar to kings and the
Eze 38:12 accumulating wealth and *p*
38:13 to take wealth and *p*
46:16 become the *p* of his sons
Mal 3:17 I am producing a special *p*
Lu 15:12 the *p* that falls to my share
15:13 squandered his *p* by living a

Prophecy
2Ch 9:29 *p* of Ahijah the Shilonite
15:8 *p* of Oded the prophet, he
Ne 6:12 spoken this *p* against me as
Mt 13:14 the *p* of Isaiah is having
Ro 12:6 given to us, whether *p*
1Co 14:6 with a *p* or with a teaching
2Pe 1:20 no *p* of Scripture springs
1:21 *p* was at no time brought by
Re 1:3 hear the words of this *p*
22:7 of the *p* of this scroll
22:10 words of the *p* of this
22:18 hears the words of the *p*
22:19 of the scroll of this *p*

Prophesied
1Sa 10:11 was with prophets that he *p*
Ezr 5:1 *p* to the Jews who were in
Jer 2:8 the prophets *p* by Baal
20:6 have *p* to them in falsehood
23:21 yet they themselves *p*
25:13 *p* against all the nations
26:9 *p* in the name of Jehovah
26:11 *p* concerning this city
28:6 words that you have *p*
29:31 Shemaiah has *p* to you
37:19 *p* to you, saying, The king
Eze 11:13 that as soon as I *p*
37:7 *p* just as I had been
37:7 to occur as soon as I *p*
37:10 *p* just as he had commanded
Mt 11:13 and the Law, *p* until John
15:7 Isaiah aptly *p* about you
Mr 7:6 Isaiah aptly *p* about you
Lu 1:67 with holy spirit, and he *p*
Joh 11:51 *p* that Jesus was destined
Ac 21:9 daughters, virgins, that *p*
1Pe 1:10 prophets who *p* about the
Jude 14 Enoch, *p* also regarding them

Prophesies
Jer 28:9 the prophet that *p* of peace
Zec 13:4 of his vision when he *p*
1Co 11:4 man that prays or *p* having
11:5 *p* with her head uncovered
14:3 he that *p* upbuilds and
14:4 but he that *p* upbuilds a
14:5 he that *p* is greater than he

Prophesy
1Ki 22:8 he does not *p* good things
22:18 *p* concerning me, not good
2Ch 18:17 *p* concerning me, not good
Jer 5:31 actually *p* in falsehood
11:21 You must not *p* in the name
19:14 Jehovah had sent him to *p*
25:30 *p* to them all these words
26:12 Jehovah that sent me to *p*
28:8 *p* concerning many lands and
Eze 4:7 and you must *p* against it
6:2 mountains of Israel and *p* to
11:4, 4 *p* against them. *P,* O son
13:2 *p* concerning the prophets of
13:17 and *p* against them
20:46 *p* to the forest of the
21:2 *p* against the soil of Israel
21:9 Son of man, *p,* and you must
21:14 And you, O son of man—*p*
21:28 *p,* and you must say
25:2 Ammon and *p* against them
28:21 Sidon, and *p* against her
Eze 29:2 and *p* against him and against
30:2 Son of man, *p,* and you must
34:2 *p* against the shepherds of
34:2 *P,* and you must say to
35:2 Seir and *p* against it
36:1 *p* concerning the mountains
36:3 *p,* and you must say, This
36:6 *p* concerning the soil of
37:4 *P* over these bones, and you
37:9, 9 *P* to the wind. *P,* O son
37:12 *p,* and you must say to them
38:2 and Tubal, and *p* against him
38:14 *p,* O son of man, and you
39:1 *p* against Gog, and you
Joe 2:28 daughters will certainly *p*
Am 2:12 saying: You must not *p*
3:8 Who will not *p?*
7:12 and there you may *p*
7:15 Go, *p* to my people Israel
7:16 You must not *p* against Israel
Zec 13:3 in case a man should *p*
Mt 7:22 did we not *p* in your name
26:68 *P* to us, you Christ. Who is
Mr 14:65 *P!* And, slapping him in the
Lu 22:64 *P.* Who is it that struck you?
Ac 2:17 and your daughters will *p* and
2:18 and they will *p*
Ro 12:6 *p* according to the faith
1Co 13:9 and we *p* partially
14:1 preferably that you may *p*
14:5 but I prefer that you *p*
14:31 For you can all *p* one by one
Re 10:11 must *p* again with regard to
11:3 cause my two witnesses to *p*

Prophesying
1Sa 19:20 the elderly . . . prophets *p*
1Ki 22:12 *p* the same as that, saying
1Ch 25:1 the ones *p* with the harps
25:2 Asaph the one *p*
25:3 *p* with the harp for thanking
2Ch 18:7 *p* concerning me, not for
18:11 prophets were *p* the same as
Ezr 6:14 *p* of Haggai the prophet and
Jer 14:14 prophets are *p* in my name
14:15 who are *p* in my name and
14:16 people to whom they are *p*
20:1 while *p* these words
23:16 who are *p* to you people
23:25 *p* falsehood in my own name
23:26 *p* the falsehood and who are
26:18 *p* in the days of Hezekiah
26:20 *p* in the name of Jehovah
26:20 he kept *p* against this city
27:10 what they are *p* to you
27:14 is what they are *p*
27:15 are *p* in my name falsely
27:15 prophets that are *p* to you
27:16 prophets that are *p* to you
27:16 is what they are *p* to you
29:9 they are *p* to you in my name
29:21 who are *p* to you falsehood
32:3 Why is it that you are *p*
Eze 12:27 times far off he is *p*
13:2 prophets of Israel who are *p*
13:2 *p* out of their own heart
13:16 *p* to Jerusalem and that are
38:17 who were *p* in those days
Am 7:13 no longer do any further *p*
Zec 13:3 pierce . . . because of his *p*
Ac 19:6 speaking with tongues and *p*
1Co 12:10 to another *p,* to another
13:2 And if I have the gift of *p*
13:8 gifts of *p,* they will be
14:22 whereas *p* is, not for the
14:24 if you are all *p* and any
14:39 keep zealously seeking the *p*
Re 11:6 during the days of their *p*
19:10 to Jesus is what inspires *p*

Prophesyings
1Th 5:20 not treat *p* with contempt

Prophet
Ge 20:7 he is a *p,* and he will make
Ex 7:1 Aaron . . . will become your *p*
Nu 12:6 If there came to be a *p* of
De 13:1 In case a *p* or a dreamer
13:3 listen to the words of that *p*
13:5 that *p* or that dreamer of the
18:15 A *p* from your own midst
18:18 A *p* I shall raise up for
18:20 the *p* who presumes to speak
18:20 that *p* must die
18:22 the *p* speaks in the name of
De 18:22 the *p* spoke it. You must not
34:10 a *p* in Israel like Moses
Jg 6:8 send a man, a *p,* to the sons
1Sa 3:20 the position of *p* to Jehovah
9:9 *p* of today used to be called a
10:6 speak as a *p* along with them
10:10 he began to speak as a *p* in
10:13 he finished speaking as a *p*
18:10 Saul . . . behaved like a *p*
19:23 behaving like a *p* until he
19:24 like a *p* before Samuel, and
22:5 Gad the *p* said to David: You
2Sa 7:2 king said to Nathan the *p*
12:25 by means of Nathan the *p*
24:11 Gad the *p,* David's visionary
1Ki 1:8 Nathan the *p* and Shimei and
1:10 Nathan the *p* and Benaiah and
1:22 Nathan the *p* himself came in
1:23 Here is Nathan the *p!*
1:32 Nathan the *p* and Benaiah the
1:34 Nathan the *p* must anoint him
1:38 Nathan the *p* and Benaiah the
1:44 Nathan the *p* and Benaiah the
1:45 Nathan the *p* anointed him as
11:29 Ahijah the Shilonite the *p*
13:11 *p* was dwelling in Bethel
13:18 I too am a *p* like you, and
13:20 came to the *p* that had
13:23 *p* whom he had brought back
13:25 city in which the old *p* was
13:26 the *p* that had brought him
13:29 the *p* proceeded to lift up
13:29 the old *p* to bewail and
14:2 is where Ahijah the *p* is
14:18 his servant Ahijah the *p*
16:7 Jehu the son of Hanani the *p*
16:12 by means of Jehu the *p*
18:22 been left as a *p* of Jehovah
18:36 that Elijah the *p* began to
19:16 anoint as *p* in place of you
20:13 a certain *p* approached Ahab
20:22 *p* approached the king of
20:38 the *p* went and stood still
22:7 here a *p* of Jehovah still
2Ki 3:11 not here a *p* of Jehovah
5:3 the *p* that is in Samaria
5:8 there exists a *p* in Israel
5:13 *p* himself had spoken to you
6:12 Elisha the *p* who is in
9:1 Elisha the *p,* for his part
14:25 *p* that was from Gath-hepher
19:2 Isaiah the *p* the son of Amoz
20:1 *p* came in to him and said
20:11 Isaiah the *p* began to call
20:14 Isaiah the *p* came in to
23:18 bones of the *p* that had
1Ch 17:1 to say to Nathan the *p*
29:29 the words of Nathan the *p*
2Ch 9:29 words of Nathan the *p* and
12:5 Shemaiah the *p,* he came to
12:15 words of Shemaiah the *p* and
13:22 exposition of the *p* Iddo
15:8 prophecy of Oded the *p,* he
18:6 here a *p* of Jehovah still
21:12 to him from Elijah the *p*
25:15 sent a *p* to him and said to
25:16 *p* quit, but he said: I
26:22 Isaiah . . . the *p* has
28:9 *p* of Jehovah there whose
29:25 and of Nathan the *p,* for
32:20 the son of Amoz, the *p*
32:32 vision of Isaiah the *p,* the
35:18 the days of Samuel the *p*
36:12 account of Jeremiah the *p*
Ezr 5:1 Haggai the *p* and Zechariah
5:1 Iddo the *p* prophesied to the
6:14 prophesying of Haggai the *p*
Ps 51:*super* Nathan the *p* came in to
74:9 there is no *p* anymore
Isa 3:2 judge and *p,* and practicer of
9:15 *p* giving false instruction
28:7 Priest and *p*—they have
37:2 Isaiah the son of Amoz the *p*
38:1 Isaiah the son of Amoz the *p*
39:3 Isaiah the *p* came in to King
Jer 1:5 *P* to the nations I made you
6:13 the *p* even to the priest
8:10 the *p* even to the priest
14:18 both the *p* and the priest
18:18 or the word from the *p*
20:2 Pashhur struck Jeremiah the *p*
23:11 both the *p* and the priest
23:28 The *p* with whom there is
23:33 the *p* or priest asks you

Jer 23:34 As for the *p* or the priest
23:37 what you will say to the *p*
25:2 which Jeremiah the *p* spoke
28:1 Azzur, the *p* who was from
28:5 Jeremiah the *p* proceeded to
28:5 to say to Hananiah the *p*
28:6 Jeremiah the *p* proceeded to
28:9 *p* that prophesies of peace
28:9 word of the *p* comes true
28:9 the *p* whom Jehovah has sent
28:10 Hananiah the *p* took the yoke
28:10 the neck of Jeremiah the *p*
28:11 Jeremiah the *p* proceeded to
28:12 after Hananiah the *p* had
28:12 the neck of Jeremiah the *p*
28:15 Jeremiah the *p* went on to
28:15 to say to Hananiah the *p*
28:17 Hananiah the *p* died in that
29:1 letter that Jeremiah the *p*
29:26 and behaving like a *p*
29:27 behaving as a *p* to you
29:29 the ears of Jeremiah the *p*
32:2 Jeremiah the *p*, he happened
34:6 Jeremiah the *p* proceeded to
36:8 Jeremiah the *p* had
36:26 and Jeremiah the *p*
37:2 by means of Jeremiah the *p*
37:3 to Jeremiah the *p*, saying
37:6 occurred to Jeremiah the *p*
37:13 hold of Jeremiah the *p*
38:9 done to Jeremiah the *p*
38:10 get Jeremiah the *p* up out
38:14 take Jeremiah the *p* to him
42:2 and said to Jeremiah the *p*
42:4 Jeremiah the *p* said to them
43:6 Jeremiah the *p* and Baruch
45:1 Jeremiah the *p* spoke to
46:1 to Jeremiah the *p* concerning
46:13 spoke to Jeremiah the *p*
47:1 of Jehovah to Jeremiah the *p*
49:34 Jehovah to Jeremiah the *p*
50:1 by means of Jeremiah the *p*
51:59 Jeremiah the *p* commanded
La 2:20 should priest and *p* be killed
Eze 2:5 know also that a *p* himself
7:26 seek a vision from a *p*, and
14:4 that actually comes to the *p*
14:7 to the *p* to make inquiry for
14:9 *p*, in case he gets fooled and
14:9 Jehovah, have fooled that *p*
14:10 same as the error of the *p*
33:33 a *p* himself had proved to
Da 9:2 had occurred to Jeremiah the *p*
9:24 seal upon vision and *p*, and
Ho 4:5 even a *p* must stumble with
9:7 The *p* will be foolish, the man
9:8 As regards a *p*, there is the
12:13 by a *p* Jehovah brought up
12:13 and by a *p* he was guarded
Am 7:14 I was not a *p*, neither was I
7:14 neither was I the son of a *p*
Hab 1:1 that Habakkuk the *p* visioned
3:1 Habakkuk the *p* in dirges
Hag 1:1 by means of Haggai the *p* to
1:3 means of Haggai the *p*, saying
1:12 to the words of Haggai the *p*
2:1 by means of Haggai the *p*
2:10 to Haggai the *p*, saying
Zec 1:1 the son of Iddo the *p*, saying
1:7 the son of Iddo the *p*, saying
13:5 I am no *p*. I am a man
Mal 4:5 to you people Elijah the *p*
Mt 1:22 Jehovah through his *p*, saying
2:5 has been written through the *p*
2:15 Jehovah through his *p*, saying
2:17 spoken through Jeremiah the *p*
3:3 through Isaiah the *p* in these
4:14 spoken through Isaiah the *p*
8:17 spoken through Isaiah the *p*
10:41 receives a *p* because he is a
10:41 because he is a *p* will get a
11:9 did you go out? To see a *p*?
11:9 and far more than a *p*
12:17 spoken through Isaiah the *p*
12:39 the sign of Jonah the *p*
13:35 was spoken through the *p*
13:57 *p* is not unhonored except in
14:5 because they took him for a *p*
21:4 was spoken through the *p*
21:11 the *p* Jesus, from Nazareth
21:26 they all hold John as a *p*
21:46 these held him to be a *p*
24:15 through Daniel the *p*
27:9 through Jeremiah the *p* was

Mr 1:2 it is written in Isaiah the *p*
6:4 A *p* is not unhonored except in
6:15 a *p* like one of the prophets
11:32 John had really been a *p*
Lu 1:76 called a *p* of the Most High
3:4 of the words of Isaiah the *p*
4:17 the scroll of the *p* Isaiah
4:24 no *p* is accepted in his home
4:27 in the time of Elisha the *p*
7:16 A great *p* has been raised up
7:26 A *p*? Yes . . . and far more
7:26 and far more than a *p*
7:39 if he were a *p*, would know
13:33 not admissible for a *p* to be
20:6 persuaded that John was a *p*
24:19 a *p* powerful in work and
Joh 1:21 The *P*? And he answered: No!
1:23 just as Isaiah the *p* said
1:25 the Christ or Elijah or The *P*
4:19 I perceive you are a *p*
4:44 homeland a *p* has no honor
6:14 *p* that was to come into the
7:40 This is for a certainty The *P*
7:52 no *p* . . . out of Galilee
9:17 The man said: He is a *p*
12:38 word of Isaiah the *p* was
Ac 2:16 was said through the *p* Joel
2:30 *p* and knew that God had
3:22 your brothers a *p* like me
3:23 not listen to that *P* will
7:37 your brothers a *p* like me
7:48 just as the *p* says
8:28 reading aloud the *p* Isaiah
8:30 reading aloud Isaiah the *p*
8:34 About whom does the *p* say
13:6 a false *p*, a Jew whose name
13:20 judges until Samuel the *p*
21:10 *p* named Agabus came down
28:25 spoke through Isaiah the *p*
1Co 14:37 If anyone thinks he is a *p*
Tit 1:12 their own *p*, said: Cretans
Re 16:13 the mouth of the false *p*
19:20 false *p* that performed in
20:10 and the false *p* already

Prophetess
Ex 15:20 Miriam the *p*, Aaron's sister
Jg 4:4 Now Deborah, a *p*, the wife of
2Ki 22:14 Huldah the *p* the wife of
2Ch 34:22 Huldah the *p*, the wife of
Ne 6:14 and also Noadiah the *p* and
Isa 8:3 I went near to the *p*, and she
Lu 2:36 Anna a *p*, Phanuel's daughter
Re 2:20 who calls herself a *p*, and

Prophetesses
Eze 13:17 as *p* out of their own heart

Prophetic
Ro 16:26 through the *p* scriptures
2Pe 1:19 the *p* word made more sure

Prophetically
2Ch 20:37 spoke *p* against Jehoshaphat
Jer 14:14 they are speaking *p* to you

Prophet's
2Ki 9:4 the *p* attendant, got on his
Mt 10:41 will get a *p* reward, and he
2Pe 2:16 hindered the *p* mad course

Prophets
Nu 11:25 they proceeded to act as *p*
11:26 to act as *p* in the camp
11:27 and Medad are acting as *p* in
11:29 Jehovah's people were *p*
1Sa 10:5 meet a group of *p* coming
10:5 while they are speaking as *p*
10:10 a group of *p* to meet him
10:11 with *p* that he prophesied
10:11 Is Saul also among the *p*?
10:12 Is Saul also among the *p*?
19:20 the elderly ones of the *p*
19:20 they began behaving like *p*
19:21 they began behaving like *p*
19:21 they began behaving like *p*
19:24 Is Saul also among the *p*?
28:6 or by the Urim or by the *p*
28:15 either by means of the *p*
1Ki 18:4 Jezebel cut off Jehovah's *p*
18:4 hundred *p* and keep them hid
18:13 killed the *p* of Jehovah
18:13 the *p* of Jehovah hid
18:19 four hundred and fifty *p*
18:19 *p* of the sacred pole
18:20 collect the *p* together at
18:22 *p* of Baal are four hundred

1Ki 18:25 now said to the *p* of Baal
18:29 they continued behaving as *p*
18:40 Seize the *p* of Baal!
19:1 killed all the *p* with the
19:10 your *p* they have killed
19:14 your *p* they have killed
20:35 man of the sons of the *p*
20:41 that he was from the *p*
22:6 collected the *p* together
22:10, 10 the *p* were acting as *p*
22:12 other *p* were prophesying
22:13 The words of the *p* are
22:22 in the mouth of all his *p*
22:23 mouth of all these *p* of
2Ki 2:3 sons of the *p* that were at
2:5 the sons of the *p* that were
2:7 sons of the *p* that went and
2:15 sons of the *p* that were at
3:13 Go to the *p* of your father
3:13 and to the *p* of your mother
4:1 wives of the sons of the *p*
4:38 sons of the *p* were sitting
4:38 stew for the sons of the *p*
5:22 from the sons of the *p*
6:1 sons of the *p* began to say to
9:1 one of the sons of the *p*
9:7 my servants the *p* and the
10:19 call all the *p* of Baal
17:13 by means of all his *p* and
17:13 means of my servants the *p*
17:23 all his servants the *p*
21:10 his servants the *p*, saying
23:2 the priests and the *p* and
24:2 means of his servants the *p*
1Ch 16:22 And to my *p* do nothing bad
2Ch 18:5 collected the *p* together
18:9, 9 *p* were acting as *p* before
18:11 *p* were prophesying the same
18:12 *p* are unanimously of good
18:21 in the mouth of all his *p*
18:22 mouth of these *p* of yours
20:20 Put faith in his *p* and so
24:19 sending *p* among them to
29:25 was by means of his *p*
36:16 and mocking at his *p*
Ezr 5:2 God's *p* giving them aid
9:11 your servants the *p*, saying
Ne 6:7 *p* that you have appointed to
6:14 *p* that were continually
9:26 and your own *p* they killed
9:30 spirit by means of your *p*
9:32 our priests and our *p* and our
Ps 105:15 to my *p* do nothing bad
Isa 29:10 he closes your eyes, the *p*
Jer 2:8 *p* prophesied by Baal
2:26 their priests and their *p*
2:30 sword has devoured your *p*
4:9 *p* themselves will be amazed
5:13 *p* themselves become a wind
5:31 The *p* themselves actually
7:25 to you all my servants the *p*
8:1 the bones of the *p* and the
13:13 the priests and the *p* and
14:13 the *p* are saying to them
14:14 Falsehood is what the *p* are
14:15 said concerning the *p* who
14:15 *p* will come to their finish
23:9 As regards the *p*, my heart
23:13 in the *p* of Samaria I have
23:13 acted as *p* incited by Baal
23:14 the *p* of Jerusalem I have
23:15 has said against the *p*
23:15 from the *p* of Jerusalem
23:16 the words of the *p* who are
23:21 I did not send the *p*
23:25 I have heard what the *p*
23:26 exist in the heart of the *p*
23:26 *p* of the trickiness of
23:30 here I am against the *p*
23:31 Here I am against the *p*
23:32 the *p* of false dreams
25:4 the *p*, rising up early and
26:5 words of my servants the *p*
26:7 the priests and the *p* and
26:8 the *p* and all the people
26:11 the *p* began to say to the
26:16 to the priests and to the *p*
27:9 do not listen to your *p*
27:14 the *p* that are saying to you
27:15 perish, you men and the *p*
27:16 to the words of your *p*
27:18 if they are *p* and if the
28:8 the *p* that happened to be
29:1 to the priests and to the *p*

Jer 29:8 Let not your *p* who are
29:15 raised up for us *p* in
29:19 the *p*, getting up early
32:32 and their *p*, and the men of
35:15 all my servants the *p*
37:19 *p* who prophesied to you
44:4 to you all my servants the *p*
La 2:9 *p* also have found no vision
2:14 own *p* have visioned for you
4:13 Because of the sins of her *p*
Eze 13:2 concerning the *p* of Israel
13:3 Woe to the stupid *p*, who are
13:4 what your own *p* have become
13:9 *p* that are visioning untruth
13:16 the *p* of Israel that are
22:25 *p* in the midst of her
22:28 her *p* have plastered for
38:17 my servants the *p* of Israel
Da 9:6 listened to your servants the *p*
9:10 hand of his servants the *p*
Ho 6:5 have to hew them by the *p*
12:10 I spoke to the *p*, and visions
12:10 by the hand of the *p* I kept
Am 2:11 some of your sons as *p* and
2:12 upon the *p* . . . a command
3:7 matter to his servants the *p*
Mic 3:5 *p* that are causing my people
3:6 will certainly set upon the *p*
3:11 *p* practice divination simply
Zep 3:4 Her *p* were insolent, were
Zec 1:4 the former *p* called, saying
1:5 And as for the *p*, was it to
1:6 commanded my servants, the *p*
7:3 and to the *p*, even saying
7:7 by means of the former *p*
7:12 by means of the former *p*
8:9 from the mouth of the *p*
13:2 the *p* and the spirit of
13:4 *p* will become ashamed, each
Mt 2:23 was spoken through the *p*
5:12 persecuted the *p* prior to you
5:17 to destroy the Law or the *P*
7:12 what the Law and the *P* mean
7:15 false *p* that come to you in
11:13 *P* and the Law, prophesied
13:17 *p* and righteous men desired
16:14 Jeremiah or one of the *p*
22:40 whole Law hangs, and the *P*
23:29 build the graves of the *p*
23:30 in the blood of the *p*
23:31 of those who murdered the *p*
23:34 I am sending forth to you *p*
23:37 killer of the *p* and stoner
24:11 many false *p* will arise and
24:24 and false *p* will arise and
26:56 the scriptures of the *p* to
Mr 6:15 a prophet like one of the *p*
8:28 still others, One of the *p*
13:22 false *p* will arise and will
Lu 1:70 the mouth of his holy *p* from
6:23 used to do to the *p*
6:26 forefathers did to the false *p*
9:8 one of the ancient *p* had risen
9:19 one of the ancient *p* has risen
10:24 Many *p* and kings desired to
11:47 memorial tombs of the *p*
11:48 these killed the *p* but you
11:49 will send forth to them *p*
11:50 blood of all the *p* spilled
13:28 the *p* in the kingdom of God
13:34 killer of the *p* and stoner
16:16 Law and the *P* were until
16:29 They have Moses and the *P*
16:31 listen to Moses and the *P*
18:31 written by means of the *p* as
24:25 all the things the *p* spoke
24:27 at Moses and all the *P* he
24:44 and in the *P* and Psalms
Joh 1:45 in the Law, and the *P*
6:45 It is written in the *P*
8:52 Abraham died, also the *p*
8:53 Also, the *p* died. Who do
Ac 3:18 mouth of all the *p*, that his
3:21 of his holy *p* of old time
3:24 *p*, in fact, from Samuel on
3:25 You are the sons of the *p*
7:42 written in the book of the *p*
7:52 Which one of the *p* did your
10:43 To him . . . *p* bear witness
11:27 *p* came down from Jerusalem
13:1 in Antioch there were *p* and
13:15 of the Law and of the *P*
13:27 things voiced by the *P*
13:40 what is said in the *P* does
Ac 15:15 the words of the *P* agree
15:32 they themselves were also *p*
24:14 the Law and written in the *P*
26:22 *P* as well as Moses stated
26:27 King Agrippa, believe the *P*
28:23 law of Moses and the *P*
Ro 1:2 aforetime through his *p* in
3:21 by the Law and the *P*
11:3 they have killed your *p*
1Co 12:28 second, *p*; third, teachers
12:29 Not all are *p*, are they?
14:29 let two or three *p* speak
14:32 gifts of the spirit of the *p*
14:32 to be controlled by the *p*
Eph 2:20 foundation of the . . . *p*
3:5 to his holy apostles and *p* by
4:11 some as apostles, some as *p*
1Th 2:15 the Lord Jesus and the *p* and
Heb 1:1 spoke . . . by means of the *p*
11:32 as Samuel and the other *p*
Jas 5:10 the *p*, who spoke in the name
1Pe 1:10 the *p* who prophesied about
2Pe 2:1 false *p* among the people, as
3:2 spoken by the holy *p* and the
1Jo 4:1 many false *p* have gone forth
Re 10:7 to his own slaves the *p* is
11:10 these two *p* tormented those
11:18 reward to your slaves the *p*
16:6 blood of holy ones and of *p*
18:20 and you *p*, because God has
18:24 blood of *p* and of holy ones
22:6 inspired expressions of the *p*
22:9 your brothers who are *p*

Propitiation
Ro 3:25 *p* through faith in his blood

Propitiatory
1Ch 28:11 and the house of the *p* cover
Heb 2:17 *p* sacrifice for the sins of
9:5 overshadowing the *p* cover
1Jo 2:2 is a *p* sacrifice for our sins
4:10 his Son as a *p* sacrifice for

Proportion
Ex 16:16 each one in *p* to his eating
16:18 each one in *p* to his eating
16:21 each one in *p* to his eating
Le 25:16 In *p* to the great number of
25:16 *p* to the fewness of years he
25:51 he should in *p* to them pay
25:52 In *p* to the years of his he
27:16 estimated in *p* to its seed
27:18 price in *p* to the years that
Nu 7:5 in *p* to his own service
7:7 Gershon in *p* to their service
7:8 Merari in *p* to their service
26:54 in *p* to his registered ones
35:8 in *p* to his inheritance that
De 16:17 in *p* to the blessing of
33:25 in *p* to your days is your
Ho 4:7 In *p* to the multitude of them
10:1 In *p* to the abundance of his
10:1 In *p* to the goodness of his
1Pe 4:10 In *p* as each one has received

Proportionate
Ex 12:4 each one *p* to his eating as

Proportioned
Job 28:25 has *p* the waters themselves
Ro 12:6 to the faith *p* to us

Proportions
Job 41:12 and the grace of its *p*
Isa 40:12 taken the *p* of the heavens
40:13 *p* of the spirit of Jehovah

Propose
1Sa 25:39 *p* to Abigail to take her as

Propound
Ex 17:14 and *p* it in Joshua's ears
Jg 14:12 *p* a riddle to you. If you
14:13 Do *p* your riddle, and let us
Eze 17:2 *p* a riddle and compose a

Propounded
Jg 14:16 a riddle that you *p* to the

Proselyte
Mt 23:15 to make one *p*, and when he
Ac 6:5 Nicolaus, a *p* of Antioch

Proselytes
Ac 2:10 from Rome, both Jews and *p*
13:43 of the *p* who worshiped God

Prospect
Joh 8:56 *p* of seeing my day, and he

Prosper
Da 3:30 *p* in the jurisdictional
Ac 15:29 you will *p*. Good health to

Prospered
Jer 20:11 they will not have *p*
Da 6:28 Daniel, he *p* in the kingdom
Ro 1:10 *p* in the will of God so as

Prospering
Ps 10:5 His ways keep *p* all the time
1Co 16:2 as he may be *p*, so that when
3Jo 2 may be *p* and having good health
2 just as your soul is *p*

Prosperity
De 23:6 for their peace and their *p*
28:11 *p* in the fruit of your belly
30:9 resulting in *p*
1Ki 10:7 surpassed in wisdom and *p*
Ezr 9:12 for their peace and their *p*
Ps 68:6 prisoners into full *p*
Da 4:27 occur a lengthening of your *p*
Ac 19:25 this business we have our *p*

Prosperous
2Ch 26:5 the true God made him *p*

Prosperously
Lu 1:79 direct our feet *p* in the way
1Th 3:11 Jesus direct our way *p* to you

Prostitute
Ge 34:31 treat our sister like a *p*
38:21 Where is that temple *p* in
38:21 No temple *p* has ever been in
38:22 No temple *p* has ever been
Le 19:29 daughter by making her a *p*
21:7 *p* or a violated woman they
21:14 *p*, none of these may he take
De 23:17 None . . . become a temple *p*
23:17 neither . . . a temple *p*
Jos 2:1 *p* woman . . . Rahab
6:17 Rahab the *p* may keep on
6:22 into the house of . . . the *p*
6:25 Rahab the *p* and the household
Jg 11:1 he was the son of a *p* woman
16:1 saw a *p* woman there and came
1Ki 14:24 even the male temple *p*
Pr 6:26 woman *p* one comes down to a
7:10 garment of a *p* and cunning
23:27 *p* is a deep pit and a foreign
Isa 1:21 faithful town has become a *p*
23:15 Tyre as in the song of a *p*
23:16 the city, O forgotten *p*
Jer 5:7 to the house of a *p* woman
Eze 16:15 a *p* on account of your name
16:16 would *p* yourself on them
16:17 images of a male and *p*
16:28 *p* . . . to the sons of Assyria
16:30 a woman, a domineering *p*
16:31 unlike a *p* in disdaining
16:35 *p*, hear the word of Jehovah
16:41 you to cease from being a *p*
23:3 to *p* themselves in Egypt
23:5 Oholah began to *p* herself
23:30 a *p* after the nations
23:44 to a woman that is a *p*
Joe 3:3 give the male child for a *p*
Am 7:17 she will become a *p*
Mic 1:7 given as the hire of a *p*
1:7 given as the hire of a *p*
Na 3:4 acts of prostitution of the *p*

Prostituted
Eze 23:19 *p* herself in the land of

Prostitutes
1Ki 3:16 two women, *p*, got to come
15:12 *p* pass out of the land and
22:38 *p* themselves bathed there
22:46 male temple *p* that had been
2Ki 23:7 houses of the male temple *p*
Job 36:14 life among male temple *p*
Pr 29:3 companionship with *p* destroys
Eze 16:33 all *p* they are accustomed
Ho 4:14 temple *p* that they sacrifice

Prostituting
Jer 2:20 lying sprawled out, *p*
Eze 16:26 *p* . . . to the sons of Egypt
16:28 you kept *p* yourself with

Prostitution
Le 19:29 not commit *p* and the land
21:9 *p*, it is her father that she
De 22:21 *p* in the house of her father
Isa 23:17 *p* with all the kingdoms of
57:3 a woman that commits *p*

1Ki 4:22 *p* to be thirty cor measures
5:1 Hiram had always *p* to be
6:17 that the house *p* to be
7:8 It *p* to be like this in
8:8 But the poles *p* to be long
8:18 *p* to be close to your heart
8:18 *p* to be close to your heart
8:57 just as he *p* to be with our
10:3 *p* to be no matter hidden
10:5 *p* to be no more spirit in
10:6 True has the word *p* to be
14:24 *p* to be in the land
15:14 Asa's heart itself *p* to be
18:3 *p* to be one greatly fearing
18:46 *p* to be upon Elijah
20:23 *p* stronger than we were
21:25 no one has *p* to be like Ahab
2Ki 3:9 *p* to be no water for the camp
3:26 battle had *p* too strong for
4:41 nothing injurious *p* to be in
5:1 had *p* to be a valiant, mighty
17:33 they *p* to be worshipers
17:41 that they *p* to be serving
18:5 *p* to be no one like him
18:7 And Jehovah *p* to be with him
20:13 There *p* to be nothing that
20:15 *p* to be nothing that I did
25:3 *p* to be no bread for the
1Ch 5:2 *p* to be superior among his
9:26 they *p* to be in charge of the
2Ch 1:11 *p* to be close to your heart
6:8 *p* to be close to your heart to
6:8 *p* to be close to your heart
7:11 own house he *p* successful
9:4 *p* to be no more spirit in her
10:15 *p* to be a turn of affairs
13:7 *p* superior to Rehoboam the
13:13 *p* to be in front of Judah
13:18 Judah *p* superior because
15:17 itself *p* to be complete
26:10 lover of agriculture he *p*
27:5 *p* stronger than they were
30:12 God *p* to be also in Judah
31:21 and he *p* successful
32:14 *p* able to deliver his people
Ezr 2:59 *p* unable to tell the house
4:20 *p* to be strong kings over
5:5 eye of their God *p* to be upon
8:31 God *p* to be over us, so that
9:2 *p* to be foremost in this
Ne 13:26 *p* to be no king like him
Job 1:1 that man *p* to be blameless
8:7 have *p* to be a small thing
11:4 *p* really clean in your eyes
24:13 *p* to be among the rebels
25:5 have not *p* clean in his eyes
Ps 16:6 possession has *p* agreeable to
19:9 have *p* altogether righteous
53:5 there had *p* to be no dread
59:16 *p* to be a secure height for
61:3 have *p* to be a refuge for me
63:7 *p* to be of assistance to me
65:3 have *p* mightier than I am
90:1 *p* to be a real dwelling for
93:5 reminders have *p* very
99:8 A God granting pardon you *p*
104:1 God, you have *p* very great
117:2 loving-kindness has *p* mighty
122:2 Our feet *p* to be standing
124:1 that Jehovah *p* to be for us
124:2 that Jehovah *p* to be for us
Pr 4:3 *p* to be a real son to my
30:6 may not have to be *p* a liar
30:18 have *p* too wonderful for me
31:14 *p* to be like the ships of a
Ec 3:15 to be has already *p* to be
7:10 former days *p* to be better
Isa 7:1 *p* unable to war against it
28:20 couch has *p* too short for
39:2 *p* to be nothing that
39:4 *p* to be nothing that I did
Jer 3:11 *p* her own soul to be more
9:3 they *p* mighty in the land
14:5 there *p* to be no tender grass
15:18 that have *p* untrustworthy
20:9 *p* to be like a burning fire
26:24 *p* to be with Jeremiah
27:5 it has *p* right in my eyes
32:30 *p* to be mere doers of what
32:31 *p* to be nothing but a cause
36:28 words that *p* to be on the
47:1 *p* to be the word of Jehovah
52:6 *p* to be no bread for the
La 1:6 princes have *p* to be like stags
La 2:22 *p* to be no escapee or survivor
4:9 slain with the sword *p* to be
4:19 our pursuers have *p* to be
Eze 1:16 wheel *p* to be in the midst
14:14 had these three men *p* to be
16:49 *p* to be the error of Sodom
19:14 *p* to be in her no strong rod
20:24 that their eyes *p* to be
21:22 *p* to be for Jerusalem, to
22:6 have *p* to be in you, each
22:9 slanderers have *p* to be in
22:13 *p* to be in the midst of you
27:7 your deck covering *p* to be
27:9 *p* to be in you, in order to
27:19 articles of exchange they *p*
28:3 that have *p* a match for you
28:13 you *p* to be. Every precious
28:14 you *p* to be. In the midst
29:6 *p* to be, as a support, a reed
29:18 wages, there *p* to be none
31:3 clouds its treetop *p* to be
31:7 *p* to be over many waters
33:22 I *p* to be speechless no
33:33 *p* to be in the midst of
35:5 *p* to have an indefinitely
37:1 The hand of Jehovah *p* to be
38:8 have *p* to be a constantly
40:1 hand of Jehovah *p* to be upon
40:21 and its own porch *p* to be
Da 5:19 *p* to be quaking and showing
7:19 *p* to be different from all the
8:7 *p* to be no power in the ram
8:7 ram *p* to have no deliverer out
Joe 2:3 *p* to be nothing thereof
Jon 3:3 Nineveh herself *p* to be a city
4:10 *p* to be a mere growth of a
Na 3:9 *p* to be of assistance to you
Hab 1:8 its horses have *p* swifter
1:8 *p* fiercer than evening wolves
Hag 2:16 and it *p* to be ten; one came
2:16 and it *p* to be twenty
Mal 2:5 my covenant, it *p* to be with
2:6 truth *p* to be in his mouth
Mt 11:19 wisdom is *p* righteous by
Lu 7:35 wisdom is *p* righteous by all
13:2 were *p* worse sinners than
13:4 they were *p* greater debtors
16:11 not *p* yourselves faithful
16:12 not *p* yourselves faithful
18:14 *p* more righteous than that
19:17 you have *p* yourself faithful
Ac 9:22 *p* logically that this is the
18:28 *p* the Jews to be wrong
Ro 3:4 *p* righteous in your words and
16:2 *p* to be a defender of many
1Co 4:4 by this I am not *p* righteous
2Co 7:14 boasting . . . *p* to be true
8:22 have often *p* in many things
11:5 *p* inferior to your superfine
Php 3:6 one who *p* himself blameless
1Th 2:4 we have been *p* by God as fit
2:10 and unblamable we *p* to be
Heb 2:2 *p* to be firm, and every
1Pe 1:7 despite its being *p* by fire

Proverb
1Sa 24:13 *p* of the ancients says
Pr 1:6 understand a *p* and a puzzling
26:7 a *p* in the mouth of stupid
26:9 a *p* into the mouth of stupid
Eze 12:23 say it as a *p* in Israel
16:44 using a *p* against you will
16:44 *p*, saying: Like mother is
2Pe 2:22 The saying of the true *p*

Proverbial
Nu 23:7 he took up his *p* utterance and
23:18 he took up his *p* utterance
24:3 he took up his *p* utterance and
24:15 he took up his *p* utterance
24:20 his *p* utterance and went on
24:21 his *p* utterance and went on
24:23 his *p* utterance and went on
De 28:37 a *p* saying and a taunt among
1Sa 10:12 it has become a *p* saying
1Ki 9:7 will indeed become a *p* saying
2Ch 7:20 *p* saying and a taunt among
Job 17:6 set me forth as a *p* saying
27:1 to lift up his *p* utterance
29:1 lift up his *p* utterance and
Ps 44:14 a *p* saying among the nations
49:4 To a *p* utterance I shall
69:11 became to them a *p* saying
78:2 In a *p* saying I will open my
Isa 14:4 *p* saying against the king of
Jer 24:9 reproach and for a *p* saying
Eze 12:22 what is this *p* saying that
12:23 cause this *p* saying to cease
14:8 for a sign and for *p* sayings
17:2 compose a *p* saying toward
18:2 expressing this *p* saying on
18:3 to express this *p* saying in
20:49 he not composing *p* sayings
24:3 compose a *p* saying
Mic 2:4 a *p* saying and will certainly
Hab 2:6 up against him a *p* saying

Proverbs
1Ki 4:32 could speak three thousand *p*
Job 13:12 sayings are *p* of ashes
Pr 1:1 The *p* of Solomon the son of
10:1 *P* of Solomon. A wise son
25:1 also are the *p* of Solomon
Ec 12:9 might arrange many *p* in order

Proves
Ex 12:4 household *p* to be too small
Le 15:19 in her flesh *p* to be blood
20:27 *p* to be a mediumistic spirit
21:17 *p* to be a defect may come
21:19 *p* to be a fracture of the
25:26 *p* to have no repurchaser and
De 17:1 a sheep in which there *p* to
1Sa 28:16 and *p* to be your adversary
1Ch 4:10 really *p* to be with me
Ps 76:2 his covert *p* to be in Salem
107:27 their wisdom *p* confused
Isa 55:6 while he *p* to be near
59:15 the truth *p* to be missing
Jer 23:10 course of action *p* to be bad
50:3 *p* to be no one dwelling in
Eze 10:10 wheel *p* to be in the midst
32:23 congregation *p* to be round
Ho 7:11 Ephraim *p* to be like a
9:2 wine itself *p* disappointing to
Ro 11:6 no longer *p* to be undeserved

Provide
Ge 22:8 God will *p* himself the sheep
Nu 33:54 *p* yourselves with landed
1Sa 16:17 *P* me, please, a man doing
2Sa 22:44 you will *p* me escape from
1Ki 1:12 *p* escape for your own soul
4:7 *p* the food one month in the
Ps 17:13 do *p* escape for my soul from
18:43 You will *p* me escape from
22:8 Let Him *p* him with escape!
31:1 righteousness *p* escape for me
37:40 and *p* them with escape
37:40 He will *p* them with escape
41:1 Jehovah will *p* escape for him
43:1 may you *p* me with escape
71:2 and *p* me with escape
71:4 O my God, *p* me with escape
82:4 *P* escape for the lowly one
89:48 *p* escape for his soul from
91:14 shall also *p* him with escape
107:20 *p* them escape out of their
116:4 Jehovah, do *p* my soul with
Ec 8:8 wickedness will *p* no escape
Jer 48:6 *p* escape for your souls, and
51:6 *p* escape each one for his
51:45 *p* each one his soul with
Eze 45:17 one to *p* the sin offering
45:22 *p* a young bull as a sin
45:23 *p* as a whole burnt offering
45:24 for the ram he should *p*
45:25 *p* the same as these for the
46:12 chieftain should *p* as a
46:12 *p* his whole burnt offering
46:13 *p* as a whole burnt offering
46:13 by morning you should *p* it
46:14 offering you should *p* with
46:15 *p* the male lamb and the
Am 2:14 will *p* his soul with escape
2:15 will *p* his soul with escape
Lu 10:7 the things they *p*, for the
Ac 23:24 *p* beasts of burden that they
Ro 12:17 *P* fine things in the sight of
1Ti 5:8 not *p* for those who are his

Provided
Ge 22:14 of Jehovah it will be *p*
Nu 32:18 *p* themselves with landed
De 11:27 the blessing, *p* you will
1Sa 16:1 have *p* among his sons a king
21:4 *p* that the young men have at
2Sa 19:9 he it was that *p* escape for
1Ki 4:7 *p* the king and his household
2Ki 21:8 *p* only they are careful to
2Ch 33:8 *p* only that they take care

Ne 9:21 you *p* them with food in the
Ec 9:15 *p* escape for the city by his
Ro 8:17 *p* we suffer together that we
11:22 *p* you remain in his
Eph 4:21 *p*, indeed, that you heard
Col 1:23 *p*, of course, that you
1Ti 1:8 *p* one handles it lawfully
2:15 *p* they continue in faith and
1Pe 2:3 *p* you have tasted that the
3:6 *p* you keep on doing good and

Providence
Ac 11:26 by divine *p* called Christians

Provider
2Sa 22:2 and the *P* of escape for me
Ps 18:2 and the *P* of escape for me
40:17 and the *P* of escape for me
70:5 and the *P* of escape for me
144:2 and my *P* of escape for me

Providing
Ge 47:17 he kept *p* them with bread
2Sa 19:5 ones *p* escape for your soul
Ps 18:48 *p* escape for me from my
22:4 you kept *p* them with escape
32:7 With joyful cries at *p* escape
Ac 7:46 *p* a habitation for the God

Province
Ac 23:34 inquired from what *p* he was
25:1 upon the government of the *p*

Proving
Ex 15:6 *p* itself powerful in ability
15:11 *p* . . . mighty in holiness
1Sa 14:21 for *p* themselves to be with
2Ch 14:7 building and *p* successful
Pr 25:19 one *p* treacherous in the day
Isa 60:15 *p* to be one left entirely
Jer 31:36 *p* to be a nation before me
Ac 17:3 *p* by references that it was
2Co 13:5 *p* what you yourselves are
2Ti 3:5 but *p* false to its power
Jude 4 *p* false to our only Owner and

Provings
De 4:34 another nation with *p*, with
7:19 great *p* that your eyes saw
29:3 great *p* that your eyes saw

Provision
Ne 11:23 a fixed *p* for the singers
Jer 4:6 Make *p* for shelter. Do not
Mt 15:37 took up seven *p* baskets full
16:10 how many *p* baskets you took
Mr 8:8 seven *p* baskets full
8:20 how many *p* baskets full of
2Co 8:21 For we make honest *p*, not

Provisions
Ge 42:25 give them *p* for the journey
45:21 gave them *p* for the way
Ex 12:39 had not prepared any *p* for
Jos 1:11 Get *p* ready for yourselves
9:4 stocked themselves with *p* and
9:5 *p* proved to be dry and crumby
9:11 Take *p* in your hands for the
9:12 our *p* out of our houses on
9:14 the men took some of their *p*
Jg 7:8 they took the *p* of the people
20:10 to procure *p* for the people
1Sa 22:10 *p* he gave him, and the
Ne 13:15 the day of their selling *p*
Ps 78:25 *P* he sent them to
132:15 Its *p* I shall bless without
Lu 3:14 but be satisfied with your *p*
9:12 procure lodging and find *p*
Ac 7:11 were not finding any *p*
1Co 9:15 a single one of these *p*
2Co 11:8 I robbed by accepting *p* in
Php 4:12 how to be low on *p*, I know

Provocation
Ps 106:32 *p* at the waters of Meribah

Provoked
De 9:7 you have *p* Jehovah your God
9:8 in Horeb you *p* Jehovah to anger
Mt 18:34 his master, *p* to wrath
1Co 13:5 does not become *p*. It does
Eph 4:26 set with you in a *p* state
Heb 3:16 and yet *p* to bitter anger

Provokers
De 9:22 *p* of Jehovah to anger

Prow
Eze 27:6 Your *p* they made with ivory
Ac 27:30 let down anchors from the *p*
Ac 27:41 the *p* got stuck and stayed

Prudent
Ne 9:20 you gave to make them *p*

Prudently
1Sa 18:5 he would act *p*, so that Saul
18:14 acting *p* in all his ways
18:15 that he was acting very *p*
18:30 David acted most *p* of all
1Ki 2:3 act *p* in everything that you
2Ki 18:7 go out, he would act *p*

Prune
Le 25:3 *p* your vineyard, and you must
25:4 your vineyard you must not *p*

Pruned
Isa 5:6 It will not be *p*, nor will

Pruning
Isa 2:4 and their spears into *p* shears
18:5 off the sprigs with *p* shears
Joe 3:10 your *p* shears into lances
Mic 4:3 their spears into *p* shears

Psalm
Ac 13:33 is written in the second *p*
13:35 says in another *p*, You will
1Co 14:26 one has a *p*, another has a
Heb 4:7 so long a time in David's *p*

Psalms
Lu 20:42 book of *P*, Jehovah said to
24:44 and in the Prophets and *P*
Ac 1:20 written in the book of *P*
Eph 5:19 with *p* and praises to God
Col 3:16 with *p*, praises to God
Jas 5:13 Let him sing *p*

Ptolemais
Ac 21:7 from Tyre and arrived at *P*

Puah
Ex 1:15 the name of the other *P*
Jg 10:1 Tola the son of *P*, the son of
1Ch 7:1 of Issachar were Tola and *P*

Public
Ge 19:2 *p* square is where we shall
Le 5:1 has heard *p* cursing and he is
De 13:16 the middle of its *p* square
Jg 19:15 sit down in the *p* square of
19:17 in the *p* square of the city
19:20 overnight in the *p* square
2Sa 21:12 the *p* square of Beth-shan
2Ch 32:6 *p* square of the gate of the
Ezr 6:11 turned into a *p* privy on this
Ne 8:1 as one man at the *p* square
8:3 before the *p* square that is
8:16 *p* square of the Water Gate
8:16 *p* square of the Gate of
Es 4:6 into the *p* square of the city
6:9 on the horse in the *p* square
6:11 ride in the *p* square of the
Job 29:7 In the *p* square I would
Ps 55:11 from its *p* square oppression
144:14 no outcry in our *p* squares
Pr 1:20 *p* squares it keeps giving
5:16 of water in the *p* squares
7:12 now she is in the *p* squares
22:13 the midst of the *p* squares
26:13 lion in among the *p* squares
Ca 3:2 in the *p* squares let me seek
Isa 15:3 in the *p* squares thereof
59:14 even in the *p* square, and
Jer 5:1 seek . . . in her *p* squares
9:21 young men from the *p* squares
48:38 Moab and in her *p* squares
49:26 fall in her *p* squares, and
50:30 will fall in her *p* squares
La 2:11 in the *p* squares of the town
2:12 in the *p* squares of the city
4:18 no walking in our *p* squares
Eze 16:24 a height in every *p* square
16:31 height in every *p* square
Da 2:5 *p* privies your own houses will
3:29 be turned into a *p* privy
9:25 rebuilt, with a *p* square and
Am 5:16 In all the *p* squares there
Na 2:4 up and down in the *p* squares
Zec 8:4 in the *p* squares of Jerusalem
8:5 the *p* squares of the city
8:5 girls playing in her *p* squares
Mt 1:19 to make her a *p* spectacle
9:31 made it *p* about him in all
13:52 every *p* instructor, when
23:34 wise men and *p* instructors
Mr 6:14 the name of Jesus became *p*
Lu 1:23 the days of his *p* service
12:11 you in before *p* assemblies
Joh 6:59 teaching in *p* assembly at
7:26 he is speaking in *p*, and
Ac 5:18 in the *p* place of custody
12:21 giving them a *p* address
13:15 *p* reading of the Law and of
24:1 *p* speaker, a certain Tertullus
Ro 10:10 *p* declaration for salvation
13:6 God's *p* servants constantly
15:16 a *p* servant of Christ Jesus
2Co 9:12 ministry of this *p* service
Php 1:13 have become *p* knowledge in
2:17 and *p* service to which faith
Col 2:15 in open *p* as conquered
1Ti 4:13 to *p* reading, to exhortation
6:12 the fine *p* declaration in
6:13 *p* declaration before Pontius
Heb 1:7 *p* servants a flame of fire
1:14 all spirits for *p* service
6:6 and expose him to *p* shame
8:2 a *p* servant of the holy place
8:6 a more excellent *p* service
9:21 vessels of the *p* service
10:11 to render *p* service and to
10:23 *p* declaration of our hope
13:15 make *p* declaration to his

Publicized
Php 1:18 Christ is being *p*, and in

Publicizing
Php 1:16 *p* the Christ out of love
Col 1:28 He is the one we are *p*

Publicly
Ezr 2:62 establish their genealogy *p*
Ne 7:64 establish their genealogy *p*
Mt 11:25 I *p* praise you, Father, Lord
Lu 10:21 I *p* praise you, Father, Lord
Joh 7:4 seeking to be known *p*
7:13 speak about him *p* because of
11:54 walked . . . *p* among the Jews
18:20 have spoken to the world *p*
Ac 2:22 man *p* shown by God to you
13:2 *p* ministering to Jehovah and
13:24 preached *p* to all the people
16:37 flogged us *p* uncondemned
18:28 the Jews to be wrong *p*
20:20 from teaching you *p* and from
23:8 Pharisees *p* declare them all
Ro 10:9 *p* declare that word in your
15:27 also owe it to minister *p* to
2Co 9:13 as you *p* declare you are, and
2Th 2:4 *p* showing himself to be a god
1Ti 5:24 sins of some . . . *p* manifest
5:25 fine works are *p* manifest
Tit 1:16 They *p* declare they know God
Heb 11:13 *p* declared that they were

Publish
Jer 4:5 *p* it even in Jerusalem, and
4:16 *P* it against Jerusalem
5:20 and *p* it in Judah, saying
31:7 *P* it. Give praise and say
46:14 *p* it in Migdol, and
46:14 *p* it in Noph and in
50:2 among the nations and *p* it
50:2 lift up a signal; *p* it
Am 3:9 *P* it on the dwelling towers
4:5 *p* it, for that is the way you
Mt 13:35 *p* things hidden since the
Ac 26:23 *p* light both to this people

Published
Es 3:14 being *p* to all the peoples
8:13 *p* to all the peoples, that the
Ac 13:38 forgiveness . . . *p* to you
15:36 we *p* the word of Jehovah to
17:13 was *p* also in Beroea by Paul

Publisher
Ac 17:18 to be a *p* of foreign deities

Publishing
Isa 52:7 the one *p* peace, the one
52:7 the one *p* salvation, the one
Jer 4:15 *p* something hurtful from the
Na 1:15 good news, one *p* peace
Ac 13:5 *p* the word of God in the
16:17 *p* . . . the way of salvation
16:21 are *p* customs that it is not
17:3 Jesus whom I am *p* to you
17:23 this I am *p* to you

Publius
Ac 28:7 man of the island, named *P*
28:8 father of *P* was lying down

Pudens
2Ti 4:21 *P* and Linus and Claudia and

Puffed
1Co 4:6 not be *p* up individually in
4:18 Some are *p* up as though I
4:19 speech of those who are *p* up
5:2 And are you *p* up, and did you
13:4 Love . . . does not get *p* up
2Co 12:20 cases of being *p* up
Col 2:18 *p* up without proper cause
1Ti 3:6 might get *p* up with pride
6:4 he is *p* up with pride, not
2Ti 3:4 *p* up with pride, lovers of

Puffs
Ps 10:5 hostility to him, he *p* at
12:5 from anyone that *p* at him
1Co 8:1 Knowledge *p* up, but love

Puke
Jer 25:27 Drink and get drunk and *p*

Pul
2Ki 15:19 *P* the king of Assyria came
15:19 Menahem gave *P* a thousand
1Ch 5:26 of *P* the king of Assyria
Isa 66:19 to Tarshish, *P*, and Lud

Pull
Ge 33:12 Let us *p* out and go, and let
Ex 19:2 *p* away from Rephidim and to
34:13 altars you people are to *p*
Nu 9:17 Israel would *p* away right
9:18 Israel would *p* away, and at
9:19 that they should not *p* away
9:20 at the order . . . would *p* away
9:22 and would not *p* away
9:22 itself they would *p* away
9:23 order of Jehovah they would *p*
10:5 to the east must *p* away
10:6 to the south must *p* away
10:12 Israel began to *p* away in
10:28 when they would *p* away
12:15 the people did not *p* away
14:25 and *p* away to march to the
20:22 *p* away from Kadesh and come
33:3 to *p* away from Rameses in
De 1:40 *p* away for the wilderness by
2:24 *p* away and cross the torrent
7:5 Their altars you should *p* down
12:3 *p* down their altars and
Jos 3:1 to *p* away from Shittim and to
3:3 *p* away from your place, and
Jg 2:2 Their altars you should *p*
8:9 I shall *p* down this tower
Ru 2:16 *p* out some from the bundles
2Ch 31:1 *p* down the high places and
36:19 and *p* down the wall of
Ezr 9:3 *p* out some of the hair of my
Ne 13:25 and *p* out their hair and
Ps 52:5 will also *p* you down forever
Isa 22:10 *p* down the houses to make
Jer 1:10 to uproot and to *p* down and
18:7 *p* it down and to destroy it
22:24 there I would *p* you off
31:28 *p* down and to tear down and
Eze 26:9 your towers he will *p* down
26:12 houses they will *p* down
Mt 9:16 *p* from the outer garment and
Lu 5:3 to *p* away a bit from land
5:4 *P* out to where it is deep, and
14:5 *p* him out on the sabbath day

Pulled
Ge 33:17 Jacob *p* out for Succoth, and
35:5 After that he *p* away, and the
35:16 Then he *p* away from Bethel
35:21 Israel *p* away and pitched
37:17 They have *p* away from here
46:1 Israel and all who were his *p*
Le 14:45 house *p* down with its stones
22:24 the testicles . . . *p* off or
Nu 9:21 morning, and they *p* away
9:21 they also *p* away
10:14 Judah *p* away first of all in
10:17 of the tabernacle *p* away
10:18 Reuben *p* away in their
10:21 of the sanctuary *p* away
10:22 Ephraim *p* away in their
10:25 sons of Dan *p* away as
11:35 people *p* away for Hazeroth
12:16 people *p* away from Hazeroth
21:10 the sons of Israel *p* away
21:11 they *p* away from Oboth and
21:12 *p* away and took up camping
21:13 *p* away and went camping
Nu 22:1 Israel *p* away and encamped on
33:5 Israel *p* away from Rameses
33:6 *p* away from Succoth and went
33:7 *p* away from Etham and turned
33:8 they *p* away from Pihahiroth
33:9 *p* away from Marah and came
33:10 *p* away from Elim and went
33:11 *p* away from the Red Sea and
33:12 *p* away from the wilderness
33:13 they *p* away from Dophkah and
33:14 *p* away from Alush and went
33:15 *p* away from Rephidim and
33:16 *p* away from the wilderness
33:17 Then they *p* away from
33:18 *p* away from Hazeroth and
33:19 *p* away from Rithmah and
33:20 *p* away from Rimmon-perez
33:21 *p* away from Libnah and went
33:22 *p* away from Rissah and went
33:23 *p* away from Kehelathah and
33:24 *p* away from Mount Shepher
33:25 they *p* away from Haradah and
33:26 *p* away from Makheloth and
33:27 *p* away from Tahath and went
33:28 *p* away from Terah and went
33:29 *p* away from Mithkah and
33:30 *p* away from Hashmonah and
33:31 *p* away from Moseroth and
33:32 *p* away from Bene-jaakan and
33:33 *p* away from Hor-haggidgad
33:34 *p* away from Jotbathah and
33:35 they *p* away from Abronah and
33:36 *p* away from Ezion-geber and
33:37 *p* away from Kadesh and went
33:41 *p* away from Mount Hor and
33:42 *p* away from Zalmonah and
33:43 *p* away from Punon and went
33:44 *p* away from Oboth and went
33:45 *p* away from Iyim and went
33:46 *p* away from Dibon-gad and
33:47 Then they *p* away from
33:48 *p* away from the mountains
De 1:19 *p* away from Horeb and went
2:1 *p* away for the wilderness by
10:6 sons of Israel *p* away from
10:7 they *p* away for Gudgodah, and
21:3 that has not *p* in a yoke
Jos 3:14 *p* away from their tents just
9:17 the sons of Israel *p* out and
Jg 6:28 Baal had been *p* down and the
6:30 has *p* down the altar of Baal
6:31 has *p* down his altar
6:32 someone has *p* down his altar
8:17 the tower of Penuel he *p* down
9:45 he *p* the city down and sowed
16:3 posts and *p* them out along
16:14 *p* out the loom pin and the
1Sa 17:51 *p* it out of its sheath and
2Ki 3:27 *p* away from against him
10:27 *p* down the sacred pillar of
10:27 *p* down the house of Baal
11:18 Baal and *p* down his altars
19:8 had *p* away from Lachish
19:36 *p* away and went and
23:7 he *p* down the houses of the
23:8 he *p* down the high places of
23:12 the king *p* down, after
23:15 and the high place he *p* down
25:10 chief of the bodyguard *p*
2Ch 23:17 house of Baal and *p* it down
33:3 his father had *p* down, and
34:4 *p* down before him the altars
Ezr 6:11 a timber will be *p* out of
8:31 *p* away from the river Ahava
Job 4:21 cord within them been *p* out
Ca 5:4 My dear one himself *p* back his
Isa 33:20 will its tent pins be *p* out
37:8 he had *p* away from Lachish
37:37 *p* away and went and
38:12 *p* out and removed from me
Jer 4:7 has *p* away; he has gone forth
33:4 *p* down on account of the
39:8 walls of Jerusalem they *p*
52:14 the bodyguard *p* down
Eze 16:39 will certainly be *p* down
Na 1:6 rocks will actually be *p* down
Ac 11:10 was *p* up again into heaven
23:10 Paul would be *p* to pieces by

Pulling
Nu 10:13 *p* away for the first time
10:29 *p* away for the place about
De 10:11 before the people for a *p*
2Ch 34:7 *p* down the altars and the

Pulls
Nu 10:6 each time one of them *p* away
Job 19:10 He *p* me down on all sides
19:10 he *p* my hope out just like
Mr 2:21 its full strength *p* from it

Pulverize
2Sa 22:43 Like the mire . . . *p* them
Mic 4:13 certainly *p* many peoples
Mt 21:44 whom it falls, it will *p*
Lu 20:18 it falls, it will *p* him

Pulverized
2Ch 15:16 horrible idol and *p* it and
Isa 27:9 chalkstones that have been *p*

Pummel
1Co 9:27 I *p* my body and lead it as a

Pummeling
Lu 18:5 coming and *p* me to a finish

Punish
Mt 24:51 *p* him with the greatest
Lu 12:46 will *p* him with the greatest
Ac 4:21 any ground on which to *p* them

Punished
Ac 22:5 bound to Jerusalem to be *p*

Punishing
Na 1:3 Jehovah hold back from *p*
Ac 26:11 by *p* them many times in all
2Pe 2:4 from *p* the angels that sinned
2:5 from *p* an ancient world, but

Punishment
Ge 4:13 My *p* for error is too great
Ex 20:5 *p* for the error of fathers
21:19 must be free from *p*; he
21:28 of the bull is free from *p*
32:34 day of my bringing *p* I shall
32:34 bring *p* upon them for their
34:7 no . . . exemption from *p*
34:7 *p* for the error of fathers
Le 18:25 bring *p* for its error upon
19:20 *p* should take place
22:16 bear the *p* of guiltiness
26:16 in *p* I shall certainly bring
Nu 5:28 then be free from such *p*
14:18 he give exemption from *p*
14:18 *p* for the error of the
16:29 with the *p* of all mankind
16:29 *p* will be brought upon them
De 5:9 *p* for the error of fathers upon
1Sa 3:14 brought to exemption from *p*
Pr 16:5 one will not be free from *p*
17:5 will not be free from *p*
19:5 will not be free from *p*
19:9 will not be free from *p*
Jer 25:29 in any way go free of *p*
25:29 You will not go free of *p*
La 4:6 *p* for the error of the daughter
4:6 the *p* for the sin of Sodom
Zec 5:3 has gone free of *p*
5:3 has gone free of *p*
14:19 *p* for the sin of Egypt and
Ac 12:19 to be led off to *p*
Ro 3:19 become liable to God for *p*
2Co 10:6 in readiness to inflict *p* for
1Th 4:6 exacts *p* for all these things
2Th 1:9 *p* of everlasting destruction
Heb 10:29 how much more severe a *p*
1Pe 2:14 to inflict *p* on evildoers
Jude 7 *p* of everlasting fire
Re 18:20 God has judicially exacted *p*

Punites
Nu 26:23 of Puvah the family of the *P*

Punon
Nu 33:42 and went camping in *P*
33:43 pulled away from *P* and went

Pupil
De 32:10 as the *p* of his eye
Ps 17:8 as the *p* of the eyeball
Pr 7:2 law like the *p* of your eyes
La 2:18 *p* of your eye not keep quiet
Lu 6:40 A *p* is not above his teacher

Pur
Es 3:7 cast *P*, that is, the Lot
9:24 had *P*, that is, the Lot, cast
9:26 Purim, by the name of the *P*

Purah
Jg 7:10 with *P* your attendant, to the
7:11 *P* his attendant made their

Purchase
Ex 22:16 as his wife for the *p* price
22:17 rate of *p* money for virgins
Le 22:11 priest should *p* a soul, as
22:11 soul, as a *p* with his money
25:16 increase its *p* value, and in
25:16 he should reduce its *p* value
25:51 from the money of his *p*
De 2:6 you may *p* from them for money
1Ch 21:24 the *p* for the money in full
Jer 32:11 I took the deed of *p*, the
32:12 deed of *p* to Baruch the
32:12 writing in the deed of *p*
32:14 this deed of *p*, even the
32:16 given the deed of *p* to
Ho 3:2 *p* her for myself for fifteen
Ga 3:13 Christ by *p* released us from
4:5 release by *p* those under law

Purchased
Ge 17:12 anyone *p* with money from any
17:13 man *p* with money of yours
17:23 everyone *p* with money of his
17:27 anyone *p* with money from a
23:18 to Abraham as his *p* property
25:10 Abraham had *p* from the sons
49:30 the field that Abraham *p*
49:32 The field *p* and the cave
50:13 the field that Abraham had *p*
Ex 12:44 any slave man *p* with money
Le 27:22 field *p* by him that is
Ac 1:18 *p* a field with the wages for
20:28 *p* with the blood of his own
22:28 *p* these rights as a citizen

Purchaser
Le 25:28 hand of its *p* until the
25:30 property of its *p* during his
25:50 *p* from the year he sold

Pure
Ex 25:11 must overlay it with *p* gold
25:17 must make a cover of *p* gold
25:24 must overlay it with *p* gold
25:29 to make them out of *p* gold
25:31 make a lampstand of *p* gold
25:36 of hammered work, of *p* gold
25:38 fire holders are of *p* gold
25:39 Of a talent of *p* gold he
27:20 *p*, beaten olive oil for the
28:14 and two chains of *p* gold
28:22 in rope work, of *p* gold
28:36 a shining plate of *p* gold
30:3 overlay it with *p* gold
30:34 galbanum and *p* frankincense
30:35 salted, *p*, something holy
31:8 lampstand of *p* gold and all
37:2 overlaid it with *p* gold inside
37:6 to make the cover of *p* gold
37:11 overlaid it with *p* gold and
37:16 be poured, out of *p* gold
37:17 made the lampstand of *p* gold
37:22 of hammered work of *p* gold
37:23 fire holders out of *p* gold
37:24 a talent of *p* gold he made
37:26 he overlaid it with *p* gold
37:29 and the *p*, perfumed incense
39:15 in rope work, of *p* gold
39:25 made bells of *p* gold and put
39:30 shining plate . . . of *p* gold
39:37 the lampstand of *p* gold
Le 24:2 *p*, beaten olive oil for the
24:4 lampstand of *p* gold he should
24:6 table of *p* gold before Jehovah
24:7 put *p* frankincense upon each
1Ki 6:20 to overlay it with *p* gold
6:21 the house inside with *p* gold
7:49 of *p* gold, and the blossoms
7:50 the fire holders, of *p* gold
10:21 vessels . . . were of *p* gold
1Ch 28:17 and the pitchers of *p* gold
2Ch 3:4 overlay it inside with *p* gold
4:20 and their lamps of *p* gold
4:22 the fire holders, of *p* gold
9:17 overlaid it with *p* gold
9:20 vessels . . . were of *p* gold
13:11 upon the table of *p* gold
Job 8:6 If you are *p* and upright, By
11:4 you say, My instruction is *p*
16:17 And my prayer is *p*
28:15 *P* gold cannot be given in
33:9 I am *p* without transgression
Ps 12:6 The sayings of Jehovah are *p*
19:9 The fear of Jehovah is *p*
51:10 Create in me even a *p* heart
Pr 16:2 ways of a man are *p* in his
20:9 I have become *p* from my sin
20:11 his activity is *p* and upright
21:8 the *p* one is upright in his
30:12 that is *p* in its own eyes
Ca 6:9 She is the *p* one of the one
6:10 *p* like the glowing sun
Hab 1:13 You are too *p* in eyes to see
Zep 3:9 the change to a *p* language
Mt 5:8 Happy are the *p* in heart
Php 1:17 not with a *p* motive, for
1Jo 3:3 just as that one is *p*
Re 21:18 city was *p* gold like clear
21:21 way of the city was *p* gold

Purer
La 4:7 Her Nazirites were *p* than snow

Purest
2Ch 4:21 it was the *p* gold

Purification
Le 12:4 will stay in the blood of *p*
12:4 of the days of her *p*
12:5 stay with the blood of *p*
12:6 days of her *p* for a son or
13:7 the establishment of his *p*
13:35 the establishment of his *p*
14:2 the day for establishing his *p*
14:23 for establishing his *p* to the
14:32 when establishing his *p*
15:13 seven days for his *p*, and he
Nu 6:9 the day of establishing his *p*
1Ch 23:28 the *p* of every holy thing
2Ch 30:19 the *p* for what is holy
Ne 12:45 and the obligation of the *p*
Eze 44:26 after his *p*, seven days
Joh 2:6 by the *p* rules of the Jews
3:25 dispute . . . concerning *p*
Heb 1:3 he had made a *p* for our sins

Purified
Nu 8:21 Levites *p* themselves and
31:23 *p* by the water for cleansing
Ne 13:30 I *p* them from everything
Eze 43:22 *p* it from sin with the
Ac 15:9 but *p* their hearts by faith
1Pe 1:22 *p* your souls by your

Purifies
1Jo 3:3 *p* himself just as that one

Purify
Ex 29:36 must *p* the altar from sin
Le 8:15 and *p* the altar from sin, but
14:49 to *p* the house from sin he
14:52 *p* the house from sin with
Nu 19:12 Such one should *p* himself
19:12 *p* himself on the third day
19:13 who will not *p* himself
19:19 must *p* him from sin on the
19:20 and who will not *p* himself
31:19 *p* yourselves on the third day
31:20 *p* for yourselves from sin
Ps 51:7 *p* me from sin with hyssop
Jer 33:8 *p* them from all their error
Eze 43:20 *p* it from sin and make
43:22 *p* the altar from sin the
45:18 *p* the sanctuary from sin
Jas 4:8 *p* your hearts, you indecisive

Purifying
Ne 13:22 be regularly *p* themselves
Eze 43:23 end of the *p* from sin you
Lu 2:22 when the days for *p* them

Purim
Es 9:26 why they called these days *P*
9:28 these days of *P* themselves
9:29 second letter concerning *P*
9:31 days of *P* at their appointed
9:32 confirmed these matters of *P*

Purity
Ex 24:10 like the very heavens for *p*
Job 28:19 even with gold in its *p*
Pr 22:11 The one loving *p* of heart
2Co 6:6 by *p*, by knowledge, by

Purple
Ex 25:4 and wool dyed reddish *p*, and
26:1 and wool dyed reddish *p* and
26:31 and wool dyed reddish *p* and
26:36 and wool dyed reddish *p* and
27:16 and wool dyed reddish *p* and
28:5 the wool dyed reddish *p* and
28:6 wool dyed reddish *p*, coccus
28:8 and wool dyed reddish *p* and
28:15 and wool dyed reddish *p* and
Ex 28:33 and wool dyed reddish *p* and
35:6 wool dyed reddish *p* and coccus
35:23 wool dyed reddish *p* and
35:25 the wool dyed reddish *p*
35:35 wool dyed reddish *p*, in
36:8 wool dyed reddish *p* and
36:35 wool dyed reddish *p* and coccus
36:37 wool dyed reddish *p* and
38:18 and wool dyed reddish *p* and
38:23 and the wool dyed reddish *p*
39:1 and wool dyed reddish *p* and
39:2 wool dyed reddish *p* and coccus
39:3 and the wool dyed reddish *p*
39:5 and wool dyed reddish *p* and
39:8 and wool dyed reddish *p* and
39:24 and wool dyed reddish *p* and
39:29 wool dyed reddish *p* and
Nu 4:13 cloth of wool dyed reddish *p*
Jg 8:26 wool dyed reddish *p* that were
2Ch 2:7 in wool dyed reddish *p* and
2:14 in wool dyed reddish *p*, in
3:14 and wool dyed reddish *p* and
Es 1:6 wool dyed reddish *p* in silver
8:15 even of wool dyed reddish *p*
Pr 31:22 and wool dyed reddish *p*
Ca 3:10 is of wool dyed reddish *p*
7:5 are like wool dyed reddish *p*
Jer 10:9 and wool dyed reddish *p*
Eze 27:7 and wool dyed reddish *p*
27:16 wool dyed reddish *p* and
Da 5:7 with *p* he will be clothed
5:16 with *p* you will be clothed
5:29 they clothed Daniel with *p*
Mr 15:17 they decked him with *p* and
15:20 stripped him of the *p* and
Lu 16:19 deck . . . with *p* and linen
Joh 19:2 him with a *p* outer garment
19:5 and the *p* outer garment
Ac 16:14 Lydia, a seller of *p*, of the
Re 17:4 woman was arrayed in *p* and
18:12 fine linen and *p* and silk
18:16 fine linen and *p* and scarlet

Purport
Ac 2:12 does this thing *p* to be
17:20 what these things *p* to be

Purpose
Ge 2:3 God has created for the *p*
33:10 in harmony with its *p* I have
37:22 His *p* was to deliver him
50:20 *p* of acting as at this day
Ex 1:11 for the *p* of oppressing them
Le 20:3 *p* of defiling my holy place
Nu 15:40 *p* is that you may remember
De 29:13 *p* of establishing you today
1Sa 15:15 *p* of sacrificing to Jehovah
17:28 the *p* of seeing the battle
2Ki 10:19 for the *p* of destroying the
1Ch 17:25 the *p* to build him a house
2Ch 25:20 *p* of giving them into his
Ps 119:101 *p* that I may keep your
Pr 2:20 *p* is that you may walk in the
16:4 Jehovah has made for his *p*
Jer 7:18 for the *p* of offending me
7:19 for the *p* of shame to their
11:5 for the *p* of carrying out the
27:10 the *p* of having you taken
32:29 for the *p* of offending me
32:35 *p* of making Judah sin
37:7 for the *p* of assistance
43:3 *p* of giving us into the
44:8 *p* of causing a cutting off
44:8 for the *p* of your becoming a
Eze 14:5 *p* of catching the house of
21:10 For the *p* of organizing a
21:10 *p* of its getting a glitter
22:6 for the *p* of shedding blood
22:9 for the *p* of shedding blood
22:12 for the *p* of shedding blood
22:27 *p* of making unjust gain
38:16 *p* that the nations may
39:12 the *p* of cleansing the land
40:4 for the *p* of my showing you
Joe 3:6 for the *p* of removing them
Am 1:13 for the *p* of widening out
2:7 for the *p* of profaning my holy
Hab 2:15 for the *p* of looking upon
Zec 13:4 for the *p* of deceiving
Mt 8:4 for the *p* of a witness to
26:50 for what *p* are you present?
Mr 1:38 is for this *p* I have gone out
4:22 for the *p* of being exposed
4:22 the *p* of coming into the open
Joh 13:28 what *p* he said this to him

Ac 9:21 come here for this very *p*
11:18 repentance for the *p* of life
11:23 in the Lord with hearty *p*
27:13 realized their *p*, and they
27:43 them from their *p*. And he
Ro 8:28 called according to his *p*
9:11 *p* of God respecting the
13:4 *p* that it bears the sword
13:6 constantly serving this very *p*
1Co 12:7 for a beneficial *p*
15:2 you became believers to no *p*
15:29 baptized . . . *p* of being dead
15:29 baptized for the *p* of being
2Co 1:17, 17 things I *p*, do I *p* them
6:1 of God and miss its *p*
Ga 3:4 so many sufferings to no *p*
3:4 If it really was to no *p*
3:14 *p* was that the blessing of
4:11 I have toiled to no *p*
Eph 1:11 *p* of him who operates all
1:14 *p* of releasing by a ransom
3:11 eternal *p* that he formed in
6:22 for this very *p*, that you
Col 4:8 *p* of your knowing the things
2Th 2:14 *p* of acquiring the glory of
1Ti 2:7 For the *p* of this witness I
2Ti 1:9 by reason of his own *p* and
2:20 some for an honorable *p* but
2:20 others for a *p* lacking honor
2:21 a vessel for an honorable *p*
3:10 closely followed . . . my *p*
Jas 4:3 you are asking for a wrong *p*
4:5 scripture says to no *p*
1Pe 1:2 *p* of their being obedient
2:5 for the *p* of a holy priesthood
4:6 for this *p* the good news
1Jo 3:8 For this *p* the Son of God was

Purposed
Ac 5:4 *p* such a deed as this in your
19:21 Paul *p* in his spirit that
Ro 1:13 many times *p* to come to you
Eph 1:9 his good pleasure which he *p*
Heb 6:17 he *p* to demonstrate more

Purposely
Ge 48:14 He *p* laid his hands so, since

Purposes
Ac 17:31 he *p* to judge the inhabited
1Co 6:9 nor men kept for unnatural *p*

Purse
Isa 46:6 the gold from the *p*, and
Lu 10:4 Do not carry a *p*, nor a food
22:35 without *p* and food pouch and
22:36 one that has a *p* take it up

Purses
Isa 3:22 and the cloaks and the *p*
Mt 10:9 or copper for your girdle *p*
Mr 6:8 copper money in their girdle *p*
Lu 12:33 Make *p* for yourselves that

Pursue
Ex 15:9 The enemy said, I shall *p*! I
De 16:20 justice you should *p*, in
28:22 *p* you until you have perished
28:45 *p* you and overtake you until
32:30 How could one *p* a thousand
1Sa 25:29 *p* you and look for your soul
2Sa 22:38 I will *p* my enemies, that I
Ps 7:5 Let an enemy *p* my soul
18:37 *p* my enemies and overtake
23:6 *p* me all the days of my life
34:14 Seek to find peace, and *p* it
71:11 *P* and catch him, for there
83:15 *p* them with your tempest
Jer 29:18 I will *p* after them with
La 3:66 *p* in anger and annihilate
Eze 35:6 blood itself will also *p* you
35:6 and blood itself will *p* you
Ho 6:3 we will *p* to know Jehovah
8:3 Let one who is an enemy *p* him
Na 1:8 darkness will *p* . . . enemies
Ro 14:19 *p* the things making for
1Co 14:1 *P* love, yet keep zealously
1Th 5:15 always *p* what is good toward
1Ti 6:11 But *p* righteousness, godly
2Ti 2:22 *p* righteousness, faith, love
Heb 12:14 *P* peace with all people, and
1Pe 3:11 let him seek peace and *p* it

Pursued
Ge 31:36 why you have hotly *p* after
Jos 8:24 in which they had *p* them
Jg 20:43 They *p* him without a place

Ps 69:26 have struck they have *p*
143:3 For the enemy has *p* my soul
Ec 3:15 keeps seeking that which is *p*
La 4:19 they have hotly *p* us. In the
5:5 onto our neck we have been *p*
Ro 9:32 he *p* it, not by faith, but

Pursuer
Pr 28:1 do flee when there is no *p*
La 1:6 without power before the *p*

Pursuers
Jos 2:22 until the *p* had come back
2:22 *p* were looking for them on
8:20 turned upon the *p*
Ne 9:11 *p* you hurled into the depths
La 4:19 our *p* have proved to be

Pursues
Ps 10:2 hotly *p* the afflicted one
Pr 13:21 the ones whom calamity *p*

Pursuing
Le 26:17 flee when no one is *p* you
Jos 7:5 *p* them from before the gate
10:10 went *p* them by way of the
11:8 striking them and *p* them
Jg 4:22 there was Barak *p* Sisera
7:25 kept on *p* Midian, and they
1Sa 14:22 went *p* closely after them
17:53 hotly *p* the Philistines
2Sa 24:13 with them *p* you, or the
2Ch 14:13 *p* them as far as Gerar, and
Ps 31:15 enemies and from those *p* me
35:3 double ax to meet those *p* me
35:6 let Jehovah's angel be *p* them
38:20 for my *p* what is good
109:16 *p* the afflicted and poor
Pr 12:11 one *p* valueless things is
15:9 one *p* righteousness he loves
19:7 He is *p* with things to say
21:21 He that is *p* righteousness
28:19 *p* valueless things will have
Isa 30:16 *p* you will show themselves
41:3 kept *p* them, kept peacefully
51:1 are *p* after righteousness
La 3:43 with anger, and you keep *p* us
Am 1:11 *p* his own brother with the
Mt 6:32 the nations are eagerly *p*
Lu 12:30 the world are eagerly *p*, but
Ac 10:9 as they were *p* their journey
Ro 9:30 not *p* righteousness, caught
9:31 Israel, although *p* a law of
Php 3:12 I am *p* to see if I may also
3:14 *p* down toward the goal for

Pursuit
Ge 14:14 and went in *p* up to Dan
14:15 kept in *p* . . . up to Hobah
Ex 14:23 Egyptians took up the *p*, and
Jos 2:16 those in *p* may not come in
2:16 until those in *p* have come
Jg 8:4 tired but keeping up the *p*
8:12 went in *p* of them and got to
1Sa 7:11 went in *p* of the Philistines
17:52 in *p* of the Philistines
1Ki 20:20 Israel went in *p* of them
2Ki 9:27 Jehu went in *p* of him and
13:2 in *p* of the sin of Jeroboam
14:19 in *p* of him to Lachish and
Ps 119:150 *p* of loose conduct have

Push
De 7:22 *p* these nations away from
33:17 With them he will *p* peoples
1Ki 22:11 *p* the Syrians until you
2Ki 4:27 came near to *p* her away
2Ch 18:10 *p* the Syrians until you
Job 18:18 will *p* him out of the light
Ps 44:5 we shall *p* our adversaries
140:4 schemed to *p* my steps
Pr 10:3 wicked ones he will *p* away
Isa 10:2 *p* away the lowly ones from
22:19 *p* you away from your
29:21 *p* aside the righteous one

Pushed
Ge 40:10 Its blossoms *p* forth
Nu 35:22 without enmity that he has *p*
Ps 36:12 *p* down and have been unable
62:3 stone wall that is being *p* in
118:13 *p* me hard that I should
Pr 14:32 the wicked will be *p* down
Jer 23:12 be *p* and certainly fall
46:15 Jehovah himself has *p* them

Pushes
De 9:4 God *p* them away from before

2Jo 9 Everyone that *p* ahead and does

Pushing
Nu 35:20 if in hatred he was *p* him or
De 6:19 by *p* away all your enemies
Jos 23:5 the one who kept *p* them
1Sa 15:23 *p* ahead presumptuously the
Ps 35:5 Jehovah's angel be *p* them
Eze 34:21 you kept *p* and with your
Da 11:40 engage with him in a *p*, and

Put
Ge 1:12 earth began to *p* forth grass
1:17 God *p* them in the expanse of
1:24 Let the earth *p* forth living
2:8 *p* the man whom he had formed
3:15 I shall *p* enmity between you
3:22 he may not *p* his hand out
3:23 Jehovah God *p* him out of the
6:16 of the ark you will *p* in its
8:9 he *p* his hand out and took it
9:23 mantle and *p* it upon both
10:6 sons of Ham . . . *P* and
15:6 And he *p* faith in Jehovah
15:10 *p* each part of them so as to
18:25 *p* to death the righteous man
22:1 God *p* Abraham to the test
22:6 *p* it upon Isaac his son and
22:9 *p* him upon the altar on top
22:10 Abraham *p* out his hand and
22:12 Do not *p* out your hand
24:2 *P* your hand, please, under my
24:9 *p* his hand under the thigh of
24:47 I *p* the nose ring on her
26:11 will surely be *p* to death
27:15 *p* them on Jacob her younger
27:16 skins . . . *p* upon his hands
31:37 *P* it here in front of my
31:39 would *p* in a claim for it
33:2 *p* the maidservants and their
33:15 *p* at your disposal some of
35:2 *P* away the foreign gods that
37:18 against him to *p* him to
37:34 *p* sackcloth upon his hips and
38:7 hence Jehovah *p* him to death
38:10 hence he *p* him also to death
40:15 *p* me in the prison hole
41:42 *p* it upon Joseph's hand and
41:48 he would *p* the foodstuffs in
41:48 a city he *p* in the midst of
42:17 *p* them together in custody
42:37 sons you may *p* to death if
48:14 Israel *p* out his right hand
48:18 *P* your right hand on his head
50:26 was *p* in a coffin in Egypt
Ex 1:16 you must also *p* it to death
2:3 *p* the child in it and
2:3 *p* it among the reeds by the
3:22 *p* them upon your sons and
4:15 and *p* the words in his mouth
4:21 miracles that I have *p* in
4:24 for a way to *p* him to death
5:21 *p* a sword in their hand to
7:15 *p* yourself in position to
8:12 frogs . . . *p* upon Pharaoh
14:31 hand that Jehovah *p* in action
14:31 to *p* faith in Jehovah and in
15:25 there he *p* them to the test
15:26 shall *p* none of the maladies
15:26 that I *p* upon the Egyptians
16:3 *p* this whole congregation to
16:4 I may *p* them to the test as
16:33 *p* in it an omerful of manna
17:3 out of Egypt to *p* us and our
17:12 stone and *p* it under him
19:9 *p* faith to time indefinite
19:12 positively be *p* to death
21:12 be *p* to death without fail
21:15 be *p* to death without fail
21:16 be *p* to death without fail
21:17 be *p* to death without fail
21:29 *p* a man or a woman to death
21:29 owner is to be *p* to death
22:8 *p* his hand upon the goods of
22:11 not *p* his hand on the goods
22:19 positively to be *p* to death
24:6 the blood and *p* it in bowls
24:11 not *p* out his hand against
25:12 *p* them above its four feet
25:14 *p* the poles through the rings
25:30 *p* the showbread upon the
26:11 *p* the hooks in the loops and
26:32 must *p* it upon four pillars
26:33 *p* the curtain under the hooks
26:34 *p* the cover upon the ark of

Job 38:36 Who *p* wisdom in the cloud
40:4 hand I have *p* over my mouth
41:2 *p* a rush in its nostrils
41:8 *P* your hands upon it
Ps 8:6 you have *p* under his feet
9:20 *p* fear into them, O Jehovah
12:5 *p* him in safety from anyone
14:6 you people would *p* to shame
21:5 and splendor you *p* upon him
25:2 God, in you have I *p* my trust
26:2 Jehovah, and *p* me to the test
27:5 High on a rock he will *p* me
31:14 I—in you I have *p* my trust
32:2 Jehovah does not *p* error
33:21 name we have *p* our trust
34:21 Calamity will *p* the wicked
37:32 seeking to *p* him to death
40:3 he *p* in my mouth a new song
40:4 has *p* Jehovah as his trust
44:7 hating us you *p* to shame
51:10 *p* within me a new spirit
52:7 man that does not *p* God as
53:5 certainly *p* them to shame
55:12 Otherwise I could *p* up with
55:18 *p* my soul in peace from the
56:4 In God I have *p* my trust
56:8 Do *p* my tears in your skin
56:11 In God I have *p* my trust
59:*super* to *p* him to death
62:10 *p* your trust in defrauding
66:11 have *p* pressure on our hips
73:9 *p* their mouth in the very
78:22 they did not *p* faith in God
78:32 not *p* faith in his wonderful
78:41 they would *p* God to the test
78:43 How he *p* his signs in Egypt
84:3 Where she has *p* her young
88:6 *p* me in a pit of the lowest
88:8 *p* my acquaintances far away
88:18 *p* far away from me friend
89:25 on the sea I have *p* his hand
95:9 forefathers *p* me to the proof
103:12 he has *p* our transgressions
105:29 to *p* their fish to death
109:16 to *p* him to death
115:10 Aaron, *p* your trust in
118:5 *p* me into a roomy place
119:31 do not *p* me to shame
119:116 not *p* me to shame for my
143:8 in you I have *p* my trust
146:3 not *p* your trust in nobles
Pr 4:24 lips *p* far away from yourself
7:13 She has *p* on a bold face, and
18:14 The spirit of a man can *p* up
19:16 will be *p* to death
21:25 the lazy will *p* him to death
21:29 wicked . . . *p* on a bold face
23:2 *p* a knife to your throat if
25:10 may not *p* you to shame and
30:8 lying word *p* far away from
30:26 is where they *p* their house
30:32 *p* the hand to the mouth
31:11 her owner has *p* trust, and
Ec 3:11 time indefinite he has *p* in
10:6 Foolishness has been *p* in
Ca 2:7 I have *p* you under oath, O
3:5 *p* you under oath, O daughters
5:3 I have *p* off my robe. How can
5:3 robe. How can I *p* it back on?
5:8 I have *p* you under oath, O
5:9 *p* us under such an oath as this
6:12 had *p* me at the chariots of
8:4 I have *p* you under oath, O
Isa 1:13 I cannot *p* up with the use
2:11 Jehovah alone . . . *p* on high
2:17 be *p* on high in that day
7:12 *p* Jehovah to the test
8:16 *p* a seal about the law
11:4 lips he will *p* the wicked
11:8 actually *p* his own hand
12:4 that his name is *p* on high
14:30 I will *p* your root to death
15:7 goods that they have *p* up
22:22 *p* the key of the house of
27:6 Israel will *p* forth blossoms
28:25 must he not *p* in wheat
31:1 *p* their trust in war
33:5 certainly be *p* on high, for
36:5 in whom have you *p* trust
36:8 to *p* riders upon them
36:9 *p* your trust in Egypt for
37:29 *p* my hook in your nose and
40:18 likeness can you *p* alongside
42:1 I have *p* my spirit in him

Isa 43:17 they must be *p* out
43:26 *p* ourselves on judgment
51:16 *p* my words in your mouth
51:23 will *p* it in the hand of
52:1 *p* on your strength, O Zion
52:1 *P* on your beautiful garments
53:1 has *p* faith in the thing
54:4 you will not be *p* to shame
59:17 he *p* on righteousness as a
59:17 he *p* on the garments of
59:21 that I have *p* in your mouth
63:11 *p* within him His own holy
65:15 *p* you individually to death
66:5 ones that will be *p* to shame
Jer 1:9 *p* my words in your mouth
6:9 *P* your hand back like one
7:4 Do not *p* your trust in
8:14 God has himself *p* us to
9:4 *p* your trust in no brother
12:6 Do not *p* any faith in them
13:1 and *p* it upon your hips
13:2 and *p* it upon my hips
14:3 They have been *p* to shame
17:13 will be *p* to shame
17:18 persecutors be *p* to shame
17:18 personally be *p* to no shame
20:2 and *p* him into the stocks
20:11 be *p* to much shame
20:17 *p* me to death from the
23:40 I will *p* upon you reproach
25:31 *p* himself in judgment with
26:4 law that I have *p* before you
26:19 by any means *p* him to death
26:21 seeking to *p* him to death
26:24 to have him *p* to death
27:2 *p* them upon your neck
27:8 *p* its neck under the yoke
28:14 A yoke of iron I will *p*
29:26 must *p* him into the stocks
31:33 *p* my law within them
32:14 *p* them into an earthenware
32:40 fear of me I shall *p* in
35:5 *p* before the sons of the
37:4 *p* him in the house of
37:15 *p* him into the house of
37:18 *p* me into the house of
37:21 *p* Jeremiah in custody in
38:4 man, please, be *p* to death
38:7 *p* Jeremiah into the cistern
38:12 *P*, please, the worn-out
38:15 without fail *p* me to death
38:16 I will not *p* you to death
38:25 not *p* you to death
40:10 *p* them in your vessels and
41:2 *p* to death the one whom the
41:8 Do not *p* us to death, for
41:8 not *p* them to death in the
41:10 *p* in the custody of
43:3 *p* us to death or to take
44:10 statutes that I *p* before you
44:22 longer able to *p* up with it
46:9 men go forth, Cush and *P*
47:5 Ashkelon has been *p* to
48:1 has been *p* to shame, has
48:1 height has been *p* to shame
48:1 shame and been *p* in terror
48:20 Moab has been *p* to shame
48:26 *p* on great airs against
48:42 that he has *p* on great airs
50:2 Bel has been *p* to shame
50:2 images have been *p* to shame
51:51 We have been *p* to shame
52:11 *p* him in the house of
52:27 *p* them to death in Riblah
52:32 *p* his throne higher than
La 1:9 the enemy has *p* on great airs
1:16 the enemy has *p* on great airs
3:29 *p* his mouth in the very dust
Eze 3:20 I must *p* a stumbling block
3:25 *p* cords upon you and bind you
4:1 *p* it before you and engrave
4:2 *p* battering rams all around
4:3 *p* it as an iron wall between
4:8 I will *p* cords upon you that
4:9 *p* them in one utensil and
6:5 *p* the carcasses of the sons of
9:4 *p* a mark on the foreheads of
10:7 *p* it into the hollows of the
11:7 have *p* in the midst of her
11:16 I have *p* them far away
11:19 new spirit I shall *p* inside
13:19 to *p* to death the souls that
14:3 *p* in front of their faces
15:4 where it must be *p* for fuel

Eze 16:11 *p* bracelets upon your hands
16:12 I *p* a nose ring in your
16:18 incense . . . *p* before them
16:19 actually *p* it before them
16:43 *p* your own way upon your
17:5 and *p* it in a field for seed
17:16 *p* in as king the one that
17:20 *p* myself on judgment with
17:22 *p* some of the lofty treetop
17:24 have *p* on high the low tree
18:13 positively be *p* to death
19:5 young lion she *p* him forth
19:9 *p* him in the cage by means
20:35 *p* myself on judgment with
20:36 as I *p* myself on judgment
20:36 *p* myself on judgment with
21:26 *P* on high even what is low
21:29 *p* you on the necks of the
23:41 and my oil you *p* upon it
23:42 to *p* bracelets on the
24:3 *P* the widemouthed cooking
24:3 *p* it on, and also pour
24:8 I have *p* her blood upon the
24:17 sandals you should *p* upon
25:4 *p* in you their tabernacles
26:16 will *p* on trembling spells
26:20 *p* decoration in the land of
27:10 men of *P*—they happened to
28:16 *p* you as profane out of the
29:4 I will *p* hooks in your jaws
30:5 Ethiopia and *P* and Lud and
30:13 *p* fear in the land of Egypt
31:10 *p* its treetop even among
31:14 *p* their treetops even among
32:5 I will *p* your flesh upon the
32:8 *p* darkness upon your land
32:23 *p* in the innermost parts
32:25 of slain ones he has been *p*
32:27 *p* their swords under their
32:29 *p* with those slain by the
36:26 new spirit I shall *p* inside
36:27 spirit I shall *p* inside you
36:29 shall *p* upon you no famine
37:6 *p* upon you sinews and cause
37:6 and *p* in you breath, and
37:14 I will *p* my spirit in you
37:19 and I will *p* them upon it
38:4 and *p* hooks in your jaws and
38:5 Persia, Ethiopia and *P* with
43:20 blood and *p* it upon its
44:19 and *p* on other garments
45:19 *p* it upon the doorpost of
Da 1:12 *p* your servants to the test
1:14 *p* them to the test for ten
2:44 and *p* an end to all these
3:29 order is being *p* through
4:6 order was being *p* through to
6:26 *p* through an order that, in
8:4 and it *p* on great airs
8:8 *p* on great airs to an extreme
8:11 it *p* on great airs, and from
8:25 heart he will *p* on great airs
11:31 *p* in place the disgusting
Ho 2:2 *p* away her fornication from
2:3 and *p* her to death with thirst
4:5 will *p* your mother to silence
9:16 *p* to death the desirable
10:1 they *p* up good pillars
Joe 2:20 I shall *p* far away from
3:2 I will *p* myself on judgment
Am 7:10 to *p* up with all his words
Jon 1:14 not *p* upon us innocent blood
3:5 Nineveh began to *p* faith in
3:5 a fast and to *p* on sackcloth
3:6 *p* off his official garment
Mic 3:5 not *p* something into their
7:5 *p* your faith in a companion
7:5 Do not *p* your trust in a
7:16 *p* their hand upon their
Na 3:5 I will *p* the covering of your
3:9 *P* and the Libyans themselves
Zec 3:5 *p* a clean turban upon his head
3:5 *p* the clean turban upon his
3:9 stone . . . *p* before Joshua
6:11 *p* it upon the head of Joshua
Mt 3:12 fire that cannot be *p* out
4:7 not *p* Jehovah your God to the
6:31 or, What are we to *p* on?
9:17 people *p* new wine into old
9:17 people *p* new wine into new
10:21 will have them *p* to death
10:34 not think I came to *p* peace
10:34 I came to *p*, not peace, but
12:18 I will *p* my spirit upon him

Mt 14:3 and *p* him away in prison on
14:24 hard *p* to it by the waves
17:10 disciples *p* the question to
17:17 How long must I *p* up with
18:6 little ones who *p* faith in
19:6 let no man *p* apart
19:13 to *p* his hands upon them and
19:15 he *p* his hands upon them and
20:12 last *p* in one hour's work
21:7 they *p* upon these their outer
21:33 *p* a fence around it and dug
22:18 Why do you *p* me to the test?
22:34 *p* the Sadducees to silence
22:44 *p* your enemies beneath your
23:4 heavy loads and *p* them upon
25:7 and *p* their lamps in order
25:33 *p* the sheep on his right
26:12 woman *p* this perfumed oil
26:59 in order to *p* him to death
26:63 I *p* you under oath to tell
27:1 Jesus so as to *p* him to death
27:11 governor *p* the question to
27:29 *p* it on his head and a reed
27:31 *p* his outer garments upon
27:43 He has *p* his trust in God
27:48 and *p* it on a reed and went
Mr 1:14 John was *p* under arrest
2:22 people *p* new wine into new
4:21 be *p* under a measuring basket
4:21 to be *p* upon a lampstand, is
5:7 I *p* you under oath by God not
5:23 *p* your hands upon her that
5:26 she had been *p* to many pains
5:40 having *p* them all out, he
6:48 hard *p* to it in their rowing
7:33 *p* his fingers into the man's
8:11 to *p* him to the test
8:22 Now they *p* in at Bethsaida
8:29 he *p* the question to them
9:19 How long must I *p* up with
9:33 he *p* the question to them
9:36 *p* his arms around it and said
9:42 were *p* around his neck and
9:43 the fire that cannot be *p* out
9:48 and the fire is not *p* out
10:2 to *p* him to the test, began
10:9 let no man *p* apart
10:17 and *p* the question to him
11:7 they *p* their outer garments
12:1 a vineyard, and *p* a fence
12:15 Why do you *p* me to the test?
12:18 they *p* the question to him
12:36 *p* your enemies beneath your
13:9 and be *p* on the stand before
13:12 and have them *p* to death
14:8 to *p* perfumed oil on my body
14:55 to *p* him to death
15:2 Pilate *p* the question to him
15:17 thorns and *p* it on him
15:20 *p* his outer garments upon
15:36 sour wine, *p* it on a reed
Lu 3:17 fire that cannot be *p* out
4:12 You must not *p* Jehovah your
5:38 new wine must be *p* into
8:26 *p* in to shore in the country
8:50 *p* forth faith, and she will
9:41 continue with you and *p* up
9:62 *p* his hand to a plow and
12:48 *p* in charge of much, they
13:8 dig around it and *p* on manure
13:19 man took and *p* in his garden
15:22 and *p* a ring on his hand and
16:4 *p* out of the stewardship
16:20 *p* at his gate, full of ulcers
17:8 *p* on an apron and minister to
19:23 did not *p* my silver money in
21:16 will *p* some of you to death
Joh 2:11 disciples *p* their faith in
2:23 many people *p* their faith in
3:33 *p* his seal to it that God is
4:39 *p* faith in him on account of
5:7 man to *p* me into the pool
5:45 in whom you have *p* your hope
6:27 has *p* his seal of approval
7:31 the crowd *p* faith in him
7:39 those who *p* faith in him
7:48 has *p* faith in him, has he?
8:30 many *p* faith in him
9:6 *p* his clay upon the man's
9:15 He *p* a clay upon my eyes
9:36 that I may *p* faith in him
9:38 I do *p* faith in him, Lord
10:42 many *p* faith in him there
11:45 beheld what he did *p* faith
Joh 11:48 will all *p* faith in him
12:6 carry off the monies *p* in it
12:38 Jehovah, who has *p* faith in
12:42 rulers actually *p* faith in
13:2 *p* it into the heart of Judas
13:5 *p* water into a basin and
13:12 had *p* his outer garments on
18:11 *P* the sword into its sheath
19:2 thorns and *p* it on his head
19:19 *p* it on the torture stake
19:29 *p* a sponge full of the sour
20:27 Thomas: *P* your finger here
Ac 1:23 So they *p* up two, Joseph
3:2 *p* him near the temple door
4:3 *p* them in custody till the
5:18 apostles and *p* them in the
5:25 men you *p* in the prison are
5:34 *p* the men outside for a
7:57 *p* their hands over their ears
9:14 *p* in bonds all those calling
9:40 Peter *p* everybody outside
12:4 he *p* him in prison, turning
12:8 *P* your outer garment on and
13:13 *p* out to sea from Paphos and
13:18 *p* up with their manner of
16:11 we *p* out to sea from Troas
18:14 *p* up patiently with you
18:21 he *p* out to sea from Ephesus
20:6 we *p* out to sea from Philippi
21:1 and *p* out to sea, we ran with
24:22 to *p* the men off and said
27:5 *p* into port at Myra in Lycia
27:21 *p* out to sea from Crete
Ro 8:13 *p* the practices of the body
8:36 being *p* to death all day long
10:14 whom they have not *p* faith
10:14 *p* faith in him of whom they
10:16 *p* faith in the thing heard
13:12 *p* off the works belonging
13:12 *p* on the weapons of the
13:14 *p* on the Lord Jesus Christ
14:13 not to *p* before a brother a
14:22 not *p* himself on judgment
1Co 1:27 that he might *p* the wise
1:27 he might *p* the strong things
4:9 God has *p* us the apostles last
4:17 *p* you in mind of my methods
6:4 that you *p* in as judges
10:9 Neither let us *p* Jehovah to
10:9 as some of them *p* him to the
15:25 *p* all enemies under his
15:53 must *p* on incorruption, and
15:53 must *p* on immortality
2Co 1:22 has also *p* his seal upon us
3:13 when Moses would *p* a veil
5:2 *p* on the one for us from
5:3 having really *p* it on, we
5:4 we want, not to *p* it off, but
5:4 *p* on the other, that what is
7:14 I have not been *p* to shame
9:4 should be *p* to shame in this
10:8 I would not be *p* to shame
11:1 *p* up with me in some little
11:4 you easily *p* up with him
11:10 no stop shall be *p* to this
11:19 *p* up with the unreasonable
11:20 you *p* up with whoever
12:6 *p* to my credit more than
Ga 1:11 I *p* you on notice, brothers
2:16 *p* our faith in Christ Jesus
3:6 Abraham *p* faith in Jehovah
3:27 have *p* on Christ
Eph 4:22 *p* away the old personality
4:24 *p* on the new personality
4:25 *p* away falsehood, speak
6:11 *P* on the complete suit of
Php 1:29 not only to *p* your faith in
Col 3:8 *p* them all away from you
1Th 2:9 not to *p* an expensive burden
5:19 Do not *p* out the fire of the
1Ti 5:5 has *p* her hope in God and
5:9 Let a widow be *p* on the list
2Ti 4:3 not *p* up with the healthful
4:16 it not be *p* to their account
Heb 2:18 when being *p* to the test
2:18 who are being *p* to the test
8:2 tent, which Jehovah *p* up
8:10 *p* my laws in their mind
9:26 *p* sin away through the
10:16 I will *p* my laws in their
11:3 *p* in order by God's word
12:1 *p* off every weight and the
12:13 not be *p* out of joint, but
Jas 1:21 *p* away all filthiness and
Jas 2:23 Abraham *p* faith in Jehovah
3:3 If we *p* bridles in the mouths
5:18 the land *p* forth its fruit
1Pe 2:1 *p* away all badness and all
3:18 being *p* to death in the flesh
1Jo 5:10 has not *p* his faith in the
5:13 you who *p* your faith in the
Jude 3 *p* up a hard fight for the
Re 2:2 you *p* those to the test who
2:10 may be fully *p* to the test
2:14 *p* a stumbling block before
3:10 *p* a test upon those dwelling
14:15 *P* your sickle in and reap
14:18 *P* your sharp sickle in and
17:17 God *p* it into their hearts
18:6 cup in which she *p* a mixture
18:6 *p* twice as much of the

Puteoli
Ac 28:13 we made it into *P* on the

Puthites
1Ch 2:53 the *P* and Shumathites

Putiel
Ex 6:25 one of the daughters of *P* as

Putrefying
Jer 49:7 their wisdom gone to *p*

Puts
Ex 30:33 *p* some of it upon a stranger
Job 9:7 And around stars he *p* a seal
12:15 He *p* a restraint upon the
15:27 he *p* on fat upon his loins
19:8 my roadways he *p* darkness
24:15 his face he *p* a covering
33:11 He *p* my feet in the stocks
33:16 to them he *p* his seal
37:7 On the hand . . . he *p* a seal
Ps 90:6 *p* forth blossoms and must
Pr 14:15 *p* faith in every word
18:18 The lot *p* even contentions to
26:24 inside of him he *p* deception
Isa 61:10 *p* on a headdress, and like
Jer 17:5 *p* his trust in earthling man
17:7 who *p* his trust in Jehovah
Mt 24:32 it *p* forth leaves, you know
Mr 2:22 nobody *p* new wine into old
13:28 and *p* forth its leaves
Lu 5:37 no one *p* new wine into old
8:16 or *p* it underneath a bed
8:16 but he *p* it on a lampstand
11:33 a person *p* it, not in a vault
15:5 he *p* it upon his shoulders
Joh 2:10 *p* out the fine wine first
7:38 *p* faith in me, just as the
12:44 He that *p* faith in me
12:44 *p* faith, not in me only
Ro 4:5 *p* faith in him who declares
1Co 15:54 *p* on incorruption and this
15:54 *p* on immortality, then the
Col 4:13 he *p* himself to great effort
1Th 4:8 who *p* his holy spirit in you
Re 13:16 *p* under compulsion all

Putting
Ge 31:34 *p* them in the . . . saddle
41:43 *p* him over all the land of
48:20 he kept *p* Ephraim before
Ex 17:2 keep *p* Jehovah to the test
17:7 their *p* Jehovah to the test
20:20 sake of *p* you to the test the
40:18 went *p* its socket pedestals
40:18 and *p* its bars in and setting
Le 20:4 to Molech by not *p* him to
De 1:32 were not *p* faith in Jehovah
4:8 law that I am *p* before you
6:22 kept *p* signs and miracles
11:26 I am *p* before you today
11:32 decisions that I am *p* before
26:6 *p* hard slavery upon us
Jos 7:6 kept *p* dust upon their heads
11:17 and *p* them to death
17:13 *p* the Canaanites at forced
1Sa 14:13 *p* them to death behind him
14:26 no one *p* his hand to his
19:1 of *p* David to death
1Ki 8:32 *p* his way upon his own head
9:3 *p* my name there to time
10:9 by *p* you upon the throne of
17:20 by *p* her son to death
18:9 be *p* your servant into the
22:16 am I *p* you under oath that
2Ki 17:26 they are *p* them to death
18:21 those *p* their trust in him
19:7 I am *p* a spirit in him, and

Es 9:29 Esther the *q*, the daughter of
9:31 and Esther the *q* had imposed
Jer 7:18 cakes to the *q* of the heavens
44:17 to the *q* of the heavens
44:18 to the *q* of the heavens
44:19 to the *q* of the heavens and
44:25 to the *q* of the heavens and
Da 5:10 the *q*, because of the words
5:10 The *q* answered and said
Mt 12:42 The *q* of the south will be
Lu 11:31 The *q* of the south will be
Ac 8:27 Candace *q* of the Ethiopians
Re 18:7 I sit a *q*, and I am no

Queenly
Ne 2:6 his *q* consort was sitting
Ps 45:9 The *q* consort has taken her

Queens
Ca 6:8 There may be sixty *q* and
6:9 *q* and concubines, and they

Quench
Ps 104:11 regularly *q* their thirst
Eph 6:16 be able to *q* all the wicked

Question
Job 38:3 let me *q* you, and you inform
40:7 I shall *q* you, and you
42:4 *q* you, and you inform me
Pr 25:8 *q* of what you will do in the
Mt 17:10 disciples put the *q* to him
22:46 to *q* him any further
27:11 governor put the *q* to him
Mr 7:17 his disciples began to *q* him
8:29 he put the *q* to them
9:11 they began to *q* him, saying
9:32 they were afraid to *q* him
9:33 he put the *q* to them
10:10 the disciples began to *q* him
10:17 the *q* to him: Good Teacher
11:29 I will ask you one *q*
12:18 and they put the *q* to him
12:34 courage anymore to *q* him
14:61 high priest began to *q* him
15:2 So Pilate put the *q* to him
Lu 9:45 they were afraid to *q* him
20:3 I will also ask you a *q*, and
20:40 to ask him a single *q*
22:23 *q* of which of them would
23:3 Pilate asked him the *q*: Are
23:9 began to *q* him with a good
Joh 9:23 He is of age. *Q* him
16:19 they were wanting to *q* him
16:23 you will ask me no *q* at all
16:30 need to have anyone *q* you
18:21 Why do you *q* me?
18:21 *Q* those who have heard
1Co 14:35 them *q* their own husbands
2Co 8:23 any *q* about Titus, he is a

Questioned
Mr 14:60 *q* Jesus, saying: Do you say
Lu 9:18 he *q* them, saying: Who are
18:18 certain ruler *q* him, saying
20:21 they *q* him, saying: Teacher
20:27 came up and *q* him
21:7 they *q* him, saying: Teacher
22:68 if I *q* you, you would not
Joh 1:25 they *q* him and said to him
18:19 chief priest *q* Jesus about
Ac 5:27 And the high priest *q* them

Questioning
Jer 38:27 Jeremiah and began *q* him
Mr 4:10 *q* him on the illustrations
8:27 *q* his disciples, saying to
10:2 *q* him whether it was lawful
15:4 Pilate began *q* him again
Lu 2:46 listening to them and *q* them

Questionings
Ro 14:1 make decisions on inward *q*
1Ti 6:4 *q* and debates about words
2Ti 2:23 foolish and ignorant *q*
Tit 3:9 shun foolish *q* and genealogies

Questions
1Ki 10:1 test him with perplexing *q*
2Ch 9:1 Solomon with perplexing *q*
Jer 37:17 king began asking him *q*
Lu 11:53 and to ply him with *q* about
Ac 23:29 accused about *q* of their Law
1Ti 1:4 which furnish *q* for research

Quick
Ge 25:30 *Q*, please, give me a
27:20 so *q* in finding it, my son
Pr 14:17 He that is *q* to anger will
Isa 32:4 *q* in speaking clear things
Lu 15:22 *Q!* bring out a robe, the best

Quickly
Ge 24:18 she *q* lowered her jar upon
24:20 she *q* emptied her jar into
24:46 she *q* lowered her jar from
33:13 should they drive them too *q*
41:14 bring him *q* from the prison
44:11 they *q* let down each one his
45:9 Go up *q* to my father, and
Ex 2:18 you have come home so *q*
12:33 send them away *q* out of the
De 7:22 allowed to finish them off *q*
9:12 Get up, go down *q* from here
9:12 turned aside *q* from the way
9:16 turned aside *q* from the way
Jos 2:5 Chase after them *q*, for you
8:19 ambush rose up *q* from its
10:6 Come up to us *q* and do save
Jg 2:17 They *q* turned aside from the
2:23 by not driving them out *q*
6:11 to get it *q* out of the sight
9:54 So he *q* called the attendant
20:37 acted *q* and went dashing
1Sa 17:17 carry them *q* to the camp to
20:38 Act *q!* Do not stand still!
28:20 Saul *q* fell down his full
28:24 *q* sacrificed it and took
1Ki 20:33 *q* took it as a decision of
22:9 Micaiah the son of Imlah *q*
2Ki 1:11 has said, Do come down *q*
2Ch 18:8 Micaiah the son of Imlah *q*
24:5 should act *q* in the matter
24:5 Levites did not act *q*
35:13 brought it *q* to all the sons
Es 5:5 have Haman act *q* on the word
6:10 *Q*, take the apparel and the
Job 4:19 One crushes them more *q* than
Ps 68:31 Cush itself will *q* stretch
69:17 sore straits, answer me *q*
70:5 O God, do act *q* for me
90:10 *q* pass by, and away we fly
106:13 *Q* they forgot his works
Ec 4:12 threefold cord cannot *q* be
Isa 5:19 let it come *q*, in order
Mt 5:25 Be about settling matters *q*
28:7 go *q* and tell his disciples
28:8 *q* leaving the memorial tomb
Mr 9:39 will *q* be able to revile me
Lu 14:21 Go out *q* into the broad ways
16:6 sit down and *q* write fifty
Joh 11:29 got up *q* and was on her way
11:31 on seeing Mary rise *q* and
13:27 doing get done more *q*
Ac 8:39 Jehovah's spirit *q* led Philip
12:7 Rise *q!* And his chains fell
17:15 come to him as *q* as possible
22:18 and get out of Jerusalem *q*
Ga 1:6 *q* removed from the One who
2Th 2:2 not to be *q* shaken from your
Re 2:16 I am coming to you *q*, and I
3:11 I am coming *q*. Keep on
11:14 The third woe is coming *q*
22:7 I am coming *q*. Happy is
22:12 I am coming *q*, and the
22:20 says, Yes; I am coming *q*

Quiet
Jg 16:2 they kept *q* the whole night
18:7 *q* and unsuspecting, and there
18:19 Be *q*. Put your hand over your
18:27 a people *q* and unsuspecting
2Ki 19:27 your sitting *q* and your
2Ch 32:10 sitting *q* under siege in
Ne 8:11 Keep *q!* for this day is holy
Ps 35:20 the *q* ones of the earth
39:2 I kept *q* from what is good
76:8 earth itself feared and kept *q*
83:1 do not stay *q*, O Divine One
107:29 waves of the sea keep *q*
Ec 3:7 a time to keep *q* and a time to
Isa 37:28 sitting *q* and your going out
42:14 have kept *q* for a long time
62:1 I shall not stay *q* until
Jer 47:6 How long will you not stay *q?*
47:7 How can it stay *q*, when
La 2:18 pupil of your eye not keep *q*
Eze 16:42 I will stay *q* and I shall
Mr 4:39 said to the sea: Hush! Be *q!*
Lu 9:36 they kept *q* and did not report
18:39 tell him sternly to keep *q*
1Ti 2:2 leading a calm and *q* life
1Pe 3:4 of the *q* and mild spirit

Quieted
Ps 131:2 I have soothed and *q* my soul
Ac 19:35 recorder had *q* the crowd, he

Quietly
1Sa 24:4 David rose up and *q* cut off
2Sa 3:27 to speak with him *q*
Hab 3:16 should *q* wait for the day of
Ga 2:4 the false brothers brought in *q*
1Th 4:11 to live *q* and to mind your
2Pe 2:1 *q* bring in destructive sects

Quietness
1Ch 22:9 peace and *q* I shall bestow
Job 34:29 When he himself causes *q*
37:17 the earth shows *q* from the
Ps 94:13 *q* from days of calamity
Pr 17:1 bread with which there is *q*
Ec 9:17 wise ones in *q* are more to be
Isa 32:17 *q* and security to time
2Th 3:12 by working with *q* they

Quiets
Pr 15:18 one that is slow to anger *q*

Quirinius
Lu 2:2 when *Q* was governor of Syria

Quit
Jg 15:7 and afterward I shall *q*
1Sa 9:5 *q* attending to the she-asses
1Ki 15:21 *q* building Ramah and
2Ch 16:5 *q* building Ramah and stopped
25:16 *Q* for your own sake
25:16 the prophet *q*, but he said
Ec 12:3 and the grinding women have *q*
Mt 3:15 Then he *q* preventing him
Lu 11:7 *Q* making me trouble
12:22 *Q* being anxious about your
12:29 *q* seeking what you might eat
12:29 *q* being in anxious suspense
Ac 13:10 *q* distorting the right ways
15:13 After they *q* speaking, James
20:31 not *q* admonishing each one
21:32 they *q* beating Paul
Ro 11:20 *Q* having lofty ideas, but
12:2 *q* being fashioned after this
1Co 5:9 to *q* mixing in company with
5:11 to *q* mixing in company with
2Co 6:17 *q* touching the unclean thing
Eph 5:11 *q* sharing with them in the
Jas 4:11 *Q* speaking against one
1Pe 1:14 *q* being fashioned according

Quiver
Ge 27:3 your *q* and your bow, and go
Job 13:25 you make a mere leaf . . . *q*
39:23 Against it a *q* rattles
Ps 99:1 Let the earth *q*
127:5 man that has filled his *q*
Isa 6:4 thresholds began to *q* at the
7:2 heart of his people began to *q*
19:1 Egypt will certainly *q*
22:6 itself has taken up the *q*
49:2 He concealed me in his own *q*
60:5 heart will actually *q* and
Jer 5:16 *q* is like an open burial
La 3:13 my kidneys the sons of his *q*
Na 2:3 spears have been made to *q*

Quivered
Ex 20:18 *q* and stood at a distance
Isa 15:4 very soul has *q* within him
Hab 3:16 at the sound my lips *q*

Quivering
Ex 9:24 and fire *q* in among the hail
1Sa 1:13 only her lips were *q*, and
Isa 7:2 *q* of the trees of the forest
Eze 1:4 a great cloud mass and *q* fire
Ho 3:5 come *q* to Jehovah and to his
Mic 7:17 they will come *q*, and they

Quote
Ge 26:7 to *q* him, the men of the
32:30 to *q* him, I have seen God
41:51 to *q* him, God has made me
41:52 to *q* him, God has made me
Ex 4:5 In order that, to *q* him, they
4:8 to *q* him, if they will not
18:4 to *q* him, the God of my

Raamah
Ge 10:7 sons of Cush . . . *R* and
10:7 sons of *R* were Sheba and
1Ch 1:9 sons of Cush were . . . *R*
1:9 sons of *R* were Sheba and
Eze 27:22 The traders of Sheba and *R*

Raamiah
Ne 7:7 *R*, Nahamani, Mordecai, Bilshan

Raamses
Ex 1:11 namely, Pithom and *R*

Rabbah
De 3:11 in *R* of the sons of Ammon
Jos 13:25 which is in front of *R*
15:60 and *R*; two cities and their
2Sa 11:1 lay siege to *R*, while David
12:26 fight against *R* of the sons
12:27 I have fought against *R*
12:29 people and went to *R* and
17:27 from *R* of the sons of Ammon
1Ch 20:1 and besiege *R*, while David
20:1 Joab went on to strike *R* and
Jer 49:2 *R* of the sons of Ammon
49:3 O dependent towns of *R*
Eze 21:20 *R* of the sons of Ammon
25:5 make *R* a pasture ground of
Am 1:14 set fire to the wall of *R*

Rabbi
Mt 23:7 and to be called *R* by men
23:8 do not you be called *R*, for
26:25 It is not I, is it, *R*?
26:49 Good day, *R*! and kissed him
Mr 9:5 *R*, it is fine for us to be
11:21 *R*, see! the fig tree that
14:45 said: *R*! and kissed him
Joh 1:38 *R*, (which means, when
1:49 *R*, you are the Son of God
3:2 *R*, we know that you as a
3:26 *R*, the man that was with
4:31 urging him, saying: *R*, eat
6:25 *R*, when did you get here?
9:2 *R*, who sinned, this man or
11:8 *R*, just lately the Judeans

Rabbith
Jos 19:20 and *R* and Kishion and Ebez

Rabble
Ac 17:5 them brought forth to the *r*

Rabboni
Mr 10:51 *R*, let me recover sight
Joh 20:16 *R*! (which means Teacher!)

Rabmag
Jer 39:3 Nergal-sharezer the *R* and
39:13 Nergal-sharezer the *R* and

Rabsaris
2Ki 18:17 Tartan and *R* and Rabshakeh
Jer 39:3 princes of the king . . . *R*
39:13 Nebushazban the *R*, and

Rabshakeh
2Ki 18:17 Tartan and Rabsaris and *R*
18:19 *R* said to them: Please
18:26 said to *R*: Speak with your
18:27 *R* said to them: Is it to
18:28 *R* continued to stand and
18:37 and told him the words of *R*
19:4 will hear all the words of *R*
19:8 *R* returned and found the
Isa 36:2 sent *R* from Lachish to
36:4 *R* said to them: Please, say
36:11 Shebna and Joah said to *R*
36:12 *R* said: Is it to your lord
36:13 *R* continued to stand and
36:22 told him the words of *R*
37:4 hear the words of *R*, whom
37:8 *R* returned and found the king

Racal
1Sa 30:29 and to those in *R*, and to

Race
Ec 9:11 the swift do not have the *r*
Jer 12:5 can you run a *r* with horses?
Ac 7:19 statecraft against our *r* and
10:28 approach a man of another *r*
1Co 9:24 the runners in a *r* all run
2Co 11:26 in dangers from my own *r*
Ga 1:14 many of my own age in my *r*
Heb 12:1 us run with endurance the *r*
1Pe 2:9 chosen *r*, a royal priesthood

Rachel
Ge 29:6 *R* his daughter coming with
29:9 *R* came with the sheep that
29:10 when Jacob saw *R* the
29:11 Then Jacob kissed *R* and
29:12 Jacob began to tell *R*
29:16 the name of the younger *R*
29:17 *R* had become beautiful in
29:18 Jacob was in love with *R*
Ge 29:18 serve you seven years for *R*
29:20 serve seven years for *R*
29:25 Was it not for *R* that I
29:28 after which he gave him *R*
29:29 Bilhah his maidservant to *R*
29:30 he had relations also with *R*
29:30 more love for *R* than for
29:31 but *R* was barren
30:1 *R* came to see that she had
30:1 *R* got jealous of her sister
30:2 Jacob's anger burned against *R*
30:6 *R* said: God has acted as my
30:8 *R* said: With strenuous
30:14 *R* said to Leah: Give me
30:15 *R* said: For that reason he
30:22 God remembered *R*, and God
30:25 *R* had given birth to Joseph
31:4 Jacob sent and called *R*
31:14 *R* and Leah answered and said
31:19 *R* stole the teraphim that
31:32 Jacob did not know that *R*
31:34 *R* had taken the teraphim
33:1 children to Leah and to *R*
33:2 *R* and Joseph to the rear of
33:7 and *R*, and they bowed down
35:16 *R* proceeded to give birth
35:19 *R* died and was buried on the
35:24 sons by *R* were Joseph and
46:19 The sons of *R*, Jacob's wife
46:22 sons of *R* who were born to
46:25 Laban gave to his daughter *R*
48:7 *R* died alongside me in the
Ru 4:11 to be like *R* and like Leah
1Sa 10:2 men close by the tomb of *R*
Jer 31:15 *R* weeping over her sons
Mt 2:18 *R* weeping for her children

Rachel's
Ge 30:7 Bilhah, *R* maidservant, became
31:33 and went on into *R* tent
35:20 This is the pillar of *R* grave
35:25 sons by . . . *R* maidservant

Raddai
1Ch 2:14 the fourth, *R* the fifth

Radiance
Re 21:11 *r* was like a most precious

Radiant
Ps 34:5 looked to him and became *r*
Isa 60:5 and certainly become *r*
Jer 31:12 *r* over the goodness of

Rafter
Hab 2:11 a *r* itself will answer it
Mt 7:3 the *r* in your own eye
7:4 a *r* is in your own eye
7:5 First extract the *r* from your
Lu 6:41 the *r* that is in your own eye
6:42 the *r* in that eye of yours
6:42 the *r* from your own eye

Rafters
1Ki 6:15 up to the *r* of the ceiling he
6:16 from the floor up to the *r*
7:7 from the floor to the *r*
2Ch 3:7 cover the house, the *r*, the
Ca 1:17 our *r* juniper trees

Rafts
1Ki 5:9 put them in log *r* to go by
2Ch 2:16 to you as *r* by sea to Joppa

Rage
Ge 27:44 the *r* of your brother calms
De 29:28 and *r* and great indignation
2Sa 11:20 *r* of the king comes up and
2Ki 5:12 turned and went away in a *r*
22:13 for great is Jehovah's *r*
22:17 my *r* has been set afire
2Ch 12:7 my *r* will not pour forth
16:10 in a *r* at him over this
26:19 his *r* against the priests
28:9 *r* of Jehovah the God of your
34:21 great is Jehovah's *r* that
34:25 my *r* may pour forth upon
36:16 until the *r* of Jehovah came
Es 1:12 very *r* flared up within him
2:1 the *r* of King Ahasuerus had
3:5 Haman became filled with *r*
5:9 filled with *r* against Mordecai
7:7 king, he rose up in his *r* from
7:10 the king's *r* itself subsided
Job 21:20 *r* of the Almighty he will
36:18 *r* does not allure you into
Ps 6:1 do not in your *r* correct me
37:8 Let anger alone and leave *r*
Ps 38:1 Nor in your *r* correct me
59:13 Bring them to an end in *r*
76:10 very *r* of man will laud you
78:38 not rouse up all his *r*
79:6 Pour out your *r* upon the
88:7 your *r* has thrown itself
89:46 *r* keep on burning just like
90:7 your *r* we have been disturbed
106:23 To turn back his *r* from
Pr 6:34 *r* of an able-bodied man is
15:1 when mild, turns away *r*, but
16:14 *r* of a king means messengers
19:19 *r* will be bearing the fine
21:14 bribe in the bosom, strong *r*
22:24 with a man having fits of *r*
27:4 There is the cruelty of *r*
29:22 *r* has many a transgression
Isa 27:4 There is no *r* that I have
34:2 *r* against all their army
42:25 pouring out upon him *r*
51:13 on account of the *r* of the
51:13 *r* of the one hemming you in
51:17 Jehovah his cup of *r*
51:20 full of the *r* of Jehovah
51:22 The goblet, my cup of *r*
59:18 *r* to his adversaries, due
63:3 trampling them down in my *r*
63:5 my *r* was what supported me
63:6 make them drunk with my *r*
66:15 his anger with sheer *r* and
Jer 4:4 *r* may not go forth just like
6:11 with the *r* of Jehovah I have
7:20 *r* are being poured forth
10:25 Pour out your *r* upon the
18:20 turn back your *r* from them
21:5 *r* and with great indignation
21:12 that my *r* may not go forth
23:19 *r* itself, will certainly go
25:15 this cup of the wine of *r*
30:23 *r* itself, has gone forth
32:31 and a cause of *r* in me
32:37 *r* and in great indignation
33:5 my anger and in my *r*, and
36:7 *r* that Jehovah has spoken
42:18 my anger and my *r* have been
42:18 *r* will be poured out upon
44:6 my *r*, and my anger, was
La 2:4 has poured out his *r*, just like
4:11 has accomplished his *r*
Eze 3:14 in the *r* of my spirit, and
5:13 I will appease my *r* on them
5:13 I bring my *r* to its finish
5:15 judgment in anger and in *r*
6:12 bring to its finish my *r*
7:8 shortly I shall pour out my *r*
8:18 I myself also shall act in *r*
9:8 you are pouring out your *r*
13:13 to burst forth in my *r*, and
13:13 *r* there will be hailstones
13:15 bring my *r* to its finish
14:19 pour out my *r* upon it with
16:30 how I am filled up with *r*
16:38 the blood of *r* and jealousy
16:42 my *r* to its rest in you
20:8 I promised to pour out my *r*
20:21 I promised to pour out my *r*
20:33 with outpoured *r* that I
20:34 and with outpoured *r*
21:17 bring my *r* to its rest
22:20 in my anger and in my *r*
22:22 poured out my *r* upon you
23:25 action against you in *r*
24:8 *r* for the executing of
24:13 cause my *r* to come to its
25:14 and according to my *r*
30:15 pour out my *r* upon Sin
36:6 in my zeal and in my *r*
36:18 to pour out my *r* upon them
38:18 my *r* will come up into my
Da 3:13 Nebuchadnezzar, in a *r* and
8:6 toward it in its powerful *r*
9:16 *r* turn back from your city
11:44 *r* in order to annihilate and
Ho 7:5 there is a *r* because of wine
Mic 5:15 and in *r* I will execute
Na 1:2 vengeance and is disposed to *r*
1:6 His own *r* will certainly be
Hab 2:15 attaching to it your *r* and
Zec 8:2 and with great *r* I will be
Mt 2:16 fell into a great *r*, and he

Raging
2Ch 28:9 *r* that has reached clear to
Job 19:29 means a *r* against errors

Ps 76:10 of *r* you will gird upon
119:53 *r* heat itself has taken hold
Pr 19:12 *r* of a king is a growling
Isa 30:30 in the *r* of anger and the
Eze 5:15 in rage and in *r* reproofs
25:17 vengeance, with *r* reproofs
Jon 1:15 sea began to halt from its *r*
Mic 7:9 The *r* of Jehovah I shall bear
Lu 8:24 wind and the *r* of the water

Rags
Pr 23:21 will clothe one with mere *r*
Jer 38:11 took from there worn-out *r*
38:12 worn-out *r* and the pieces

Rahab
Jos 2:1 woman whose name was *R*
2:3 the king of Jericho sent to *R*
6:17 *R* the prostitute may keep on
6:23 brought out *R* and her father
6:25 And *R* the prostitute and the
Ps 87:4 mention of *R* and Babylon as
89:10 crushed *R*, even as someone
Isa 30:7 *R*—they are for sitting still
51:9 one that broke *R* to pieces
Mt 1:5 Salmon . . . father to Boaz by *R*
Heb 11:31 By faith *R* the harlot did
Jas 2:25 also *R* the harlot declared

Raham
1Ch 2:44 *R* the father of Jorkeam

Raid
Ge 49:19 a marauder band will *r* him
49:19 he will *r* the extreme rear
1Sa 23:27 Philistines have made a *r*
27:8 *r* the Geshurites and Girzites
27:10 Where did you men make a *r*
30:1 Amalekites made a *r* on the
30:14 made a *r* on the south of
2Sa 3:22 Joab were coming from a *r*
1Ch 14:13 made a *r* in the low plain
2Ch 28:18 Philistines, they made a *r*
Job 1:15 Sabeans came making a *r* and
Hab 3:16 people, that he may *r* them

Raids
1Ch 14:9 making *r* in the low plain of
2Ch 25:13 making *r* upon the cities of

Raiment
Isa 59:17 garments of vengeance as *r*
Ac 10:30 man in bright *r* stood
12:21 clothed . . . with royal *r* and

Rain
Ge 2:5 Jehovah God had not made it *r*
7:4 I am making it *r* upon the
19:24 Jehovah made it *r* sulphur
Ex 9:18 causing it to *r* down . . . hail
9:23 kept making it *r* down hail
9:33 *r* did not pour down on the
9:34 the *r* and the hail and the
Le 26:4 give your showers of *r* at
De 11:11 the *r* of the heavens it
11:14 give *r* for your land at its
11:14, 14 autumn *r* and spring *r*
11:17 no *r* will occur and the
28:12 to give the *r* on your land
28:24 powder and dust as the *r*
32:2 will drip as the *r*, My saying
1Sa 12:17 he may give thunders and *r*
12:18 to give thunders and *r* on
2Sa 1:21 let no *r* be upon you, nor
23:4 from *r*, there is grass out
1Ki 8:35 shut up so that no *r* occurs
8:36 must give *r* upon your land
17:1 neither dew nor *r*, except at
18:1 to give *r* upon the surface of
2Ch 6:26 shut up so that no *r* occurs
6:27 give *r* upon your land that
7:13 shut up the heavens that no *r*
Ezr 10:9 account of the showers of *r*
10:13 the season of showers of *r*
Job 3:5 Let a *r* cloud reside over it
5:10 giving *r* upon the surface of
20:23 And will *r* it upon him
28:26 made for the *r* a regulation
29:23 waited for me as for the *r*
29:23 wide for the spring *r*
36:27 filter as *r* for his mist
37:6 to the downpour of *r*, even
38:26 To make it *r* upon the land
38:28 exist a father for the *r*
Ps 11:6 *r* down upon the wicked ones
72:6 the *r* upon the mown grass
78:27 sustenance *r* upon them just
135:7 made even sluices for the *r*
Ps 147:8 preparing *r* for the earth
Pr 3:20 keep dripping down light *r*
16:15 is like the cloud of spring *r*
26:1 and like *r* in harvesttime
27:15 in the day of a steady *r* and
28:3 a *r* that washes away so that
Isa 5:6 from precipitating any *r*
30:23 *r* for your seed with which
44:14 the pouring *r* itself keeps
55:10 as the pouring *r* descends
Jer 3:3 even a spring *r* has occurred
4:13 Like *r* clouds he will come
5:24 the downpour and the autumn *r*
5:24 the spring *r* in its season
10:13 made even sluices for the *r*
14:22 any that can pour down *r*
51:16 made even sluices for the *r*
Eze 1:28 on the day of a pouring *r*
34:26 the pouring *r* to descend in
38:22 fire and sulphur I shall *r*
Ho 6:3 will come in like a pouring *r*
6:3 *r* that saturates the earth
Joe 2:23 give you the autumn *r* in
2:23 a downpour, autumn *r* and
2:23 and spring *r*, as at the first
Am 4:7 I made it *r* on one city
4:7 I would not make it *r*
4:7 which I would not make it *r*
Zec 10:1 *r* in the time of the spring
10:1 in the time of the spring *r*
10:1 gives a downpour of *r* to
14:17 no pouring *r* will occur
Mt 5:45 *r* upon righteous people and
7:25 the *r* poured down and the
7:27 *r* poured down and the floods
Ac 28:2 of the *r* that was falling
Heb 6:7 ground that drinks in the *r*
Jas 5:7, 7 the early *r* and the late *r*
5:17 he prayed for it not to *r*
5:17 it did not *r* upon the land
5:18 heaven gave *r* and the land
Re 11:6 that no *r* should fall during

Rainbow
Ge 9:13 My *r* I do give in the cloud
9:14 the *r* will certainly appear in
9:16 the *r* must occur in the cloud
Re 4:3 about the throne there is a *r*
10:1 and a *r* was upon his head

Rained
Eze 22:24 one not *r* down upon in
Am 4:7 land that would be *r* on
Lu 17:29 *r* fire and sulphur from

Raining
Ex 16:4 I am *r* down bread for you
Ps 78:24 *r* upon them manna to eat

Rains
De 32:2 As gentle *r* upon grass And as
Job 37:6 the downpour of his strong *r*
Eze 34:26 Pouring *r* of blessing
Ac 14:17 giving you *r* from heaven and

Rainstorm
Job 24:8 From the *r* of the mountains
Isa 4:6 for a hiding place from the *r*
25:4 a refuge from the *r*
25:4 like a *r* against a wall
30:30 cloudburst and *r* and
32:2 of concealment from the *r*

Rainy
Ca 2:11 the *r* season itself has passed
Mt 16:3 It will be wintry, *r* weather

Raise
Ge 13:14 *R* your eyes, please, and look
21:16 to *r* her voice and weep
27:19 *R* yourself up, please
31:12 *R* your eyes, please, and see
34:12 *R* . . . the marriage money
38:8 *r* up offspring for your
39:7 *r* her eyes toward Joseph and
45:2 *r* his voice in weeping, so
Ex 14:10 Israel began to *r* their eyes
15:2 and I shall *r* him on high
De 3:27 *r* your eyes to the west and
4:19 *r* your eyes up to the heavens and
18:15 God will *r* up for you
18:18 A prophet I shall *r* up for
22:4 by all means help him *r* them
28:49 Jehovah will *r* up against
32:40 I *r* my hand to heaven in an
Jos 5:13 to *r* his eyes and look, and
7:26 *r* up over him a big pile of
Jg 2:4 people began to *r* their voices
2:16 So Jehovah would *r* up judges
2:18 when Jehovah did *r* up judges
21:2 continued to *r* their voice and
Ru 1:9 to *r* their voices and weep
1Sa 2:35 *r* up for myself a faithful
24:16 *r* his own voice and weep
30:4 *r* their voice and weep
2Sa 2:22 *r* my face to Joab your
3:32 king began to *r* his voice
7:12 *r* up your seed after you
12:17 *r* him up from the earth
13:36 to *r* their voice and weep
18:18 *r* up for himself a pillar
1Ki 11:14 *r* up a resister to Solomon
11:23 to *r* up to him another
14:14 *r* up to himself a king over
2Ki 19:22 do you *r* your eyes on high
1Ch 17:11 *r* up your seed after you
25:5 to *r* up his horn; thus the
Ezr 9:6 embarrassed to *r* my face to
9:9 to *r* up the house of our God
Job 2:12 to *r* their voice and rip each
4:4 your words would *r* up
10:15 I may not *r* my head
11:15 *r* your face without defect
22:26 you will *r* your face to God
38:34 *r* your voice even to the
Ps 24:7 *R* your heads, O you gates
24:7 And *r* yourselves up, O you
24:9 *R* your heads, O you gates
24:9 *r* them up, O you long-lasting
25:1 Jehovah, I *r* my very soul
28:2 When I *r* my hands to the
63:4 I shall *r* my palms
68:4 *R* up a song to the One riding
78:5 to *r* up a reminder in Jacob
94:2 *R* yourself up, O Judge of the
106:26 *r* his hand in an oath
110:7 why he will *r* high his head
119:28 *R* me up according to your
119:48 shall *r* my palms to your
121:1 *r* my eyes to the mountains
134:2 *R* your hands in holiness
Ec 4:10 other one can *r* his partner up
4:10 is not another to *r* him up
Isa 3:7 *r* his voice in that day
11:12 *r* up a signal for the
13:2 *r* up a signal, you men
14:4 *r* up this proverbial saying
24:14 *r* their voice, they will
29:3 *r* up against you siegeworks
37:23 you *r* your eyes on high
40:9 *R* your voice even with power
40:9 *R* it. Do not be afraid
40:26 *R* your eyes high up and see
42:2 not cry out or *r* his voice
42:11 and its cities *r* their voice
44:26 desolated places I shall *r*
49:6 to *r* up the tribes of Jacob
49:18 *R* your eyes all around and
49:22 I shall *r* up my hand even
51:6 *R* your eyes to the heavens
58:1 *R* your voice just like a horn
58:12 *r* up even the foundations
60:4 *R* your eyes all around and
61:4 *r* up even the desolated
62:10 *R* up a signal for the
Jer 3:2 *R* your eyes to the beaten
4:6 *R* a signal toward Zion
6:1 *r* a fire signal; because
7:16 neither *r* in their behalf an
7:29 upon the bare hills *r* a dirge
9:10 *r* a weeping and lamentation
9:18 *r* up over us a lamentation
13:20 *R* your eyes and see those
23:4 *r* up over them shepherds
23:5 I will *r* up to David a
30:9 David . . . I shall *r* up for
51:3 *r* himself up in his coat of
La 2:19 *R* to him your palms on
3:41 *r* our heart along with our
Eze 8:5 *r* your eyes in the direction
18:6 his eyes he did not *r* to the
19:1 *r* a dirge concerning the
21:22 to *r* the sound in an alarm
23:27 not *r* your eyes to them
26:8 *r* up against you a large
26:17 must *r* up over you a dirge
27:2 *r* up concerning Tyre a dirge
34:23 *r* up over them one shepherd
34:29 *r* up for them a planting
43:5 spirit proceeded to *r* me up
Da 10:5 *r* my eyes and see, and here

Da 12:7 *r* his right hand and his
Am 9:11 *r* up the booth of David that
9:11 its ruins I shall *r* up, and I
Mic 2:4 *r* up concerning you people a
5:5 *r* up against him seven
Zec 1:18 to *r* my eyes and see
2:1 to *r* my eyes and see
5:5 *R* your eyes, please, and see
Mt 3:9 to *r* up children to Abraham
10:8 *r* up dead persons, make
22:24 and *r* up offspring for his
Mr 12:19 and *r* up offspring from her
Lu 3:8 God has power to *r* up children
13:11 was unable to *r* herself up
18:13 to *r* his eyes heavenward
20:28 *r* up offspring from her for
21:28 *r* yourselves erect and lift
Joh 2:19 in three days I will *r* it up
2:20 you *r* it up in three days
Ac 3:22 Jehovah God will *r* up for
7:37 God will *r* up for you from
1Co 6:14 will *r* us up out of death
15:15 but whom he did not *r* up if
2Co 4:14 *r* us up also together with
Heb 11:19 God was able to *r* him up
Jas 5:15 and Jehovah will *r* him up

Raised
Ge 13:10 Lot *r* his eyes and saw the
18:2 he *r* his eyes, then he looked
22:4 Abraham *r* his eyes and began
22:13 Abraham *r* his eyes and
24:63 he *r* his eyes and looked
24:64 Rebekah *r* her eyes, she
27:38 Esau *r* his voice and burst
29:11 Jacob . . . *r* his voice
31:10 *r* my eyes and saw a sight
33:1 Jacob *r* his eyes and looked
33:5 *r* his eyes and saw the women
37:25 *r* their eyes and took a look
39:15 he heard that I *r* my voice
39:18 I *r* my voice and began to
43:29 *r* his eyes and saw Benjamin
Ex 6:8 land that I *r* my hand in oath
Le 9:22 Aaron *r* his hands toward the
Nu 14:1 the assembly *r* their voice
24:2 Balaam *r* his eyes and saw
De 17:8 a legal claim has been *r*
19:5 his hand has been *r* to strike
27:14 say with *r* voice to every
Jos 5:7 their sons he *r* up instead of
8:29 *r* up a great pile of stones
Jg 3:9 Jehovah *r* a savior up for the
3:15 So Jehovah *r* up . . . a savior
9:7 and *r* his voice and called out
19:17 he *r* his eyes he got to see
Ru 1:14 they *r* their voices and wept
1Sa 6:13 *r* their eyes and saw the Ark
17:20 *r* a shout for the battle
22:8 *r* up my own servant against
2Sa 13:34 watchman, *r* his eyes and
18:17 *r* up over him a very big
18:24 he *r* his eyes and saw and
23:1 man that was *r* up on high
1Ki 14:7 *r* you up out of the middle
16:2 *r* you up out of the dust
2Ki 9:32 he *r* his face toward the
25:27 *r* up the head of Jehoiachin
1Ch 21:16 When David *r* his eyes, he
2Ch 32:5 *r* towers upon it, and on the
Job 2:12 *r* their eyes from far off
Ps 40:2 he *r* up my feet upon a crag
83:2 hating you have *r* their head
93:3 The rivers have *r*, O Jehovah
93:3 rivers have *r* their sound
123:1 To you I have *r* my eyes
Isa 1:2 Sons I have brought up and *r*
5:26 *r* up a signal to a great
10:15 rod *r* on high the one who
23:4 young men, *r* up virgins
30:13 out in a highly *r* wall
40:4 Let every valley be *r* up
52:8 watchmen have *r* their voice
Jer 6:17 I *r* up over you people
29:15 *r* up for us prophets in
52:31 *r* up the head of Jehoiachin
Eze 8:5 I *r* my eyes in the direction
36:7 *r* my hand in an oath that
44:12 *r* my hand against them
47:14 I *r* my hand in an oath to
Da 7:5 And on one side it was *r* up
8:3 When I *r* my eyes, then I saw
Zec 1:21 that no one at all *r* his head
5:1 I *r* my eyes again and saw
Zec 5:9 I *r* my eyes and saw, and
5:9 *r* the ephah up between the
6:1 I *r* my eyes again and saw
Mt 11:5 and the dead are being *r* up
11:11 *r* up a greater than John the
12:42 be *r* up in the judgment
14:2 He was *r* up from the dead
16:21 and on the third day be *r* up
17:8 When they *r* their eyes, they
17:9 until the Son of man is *r* up
17:23 third day he will be *r* up
20:19 third day he will be *r* up
26:32 after I have been *r* up, I
27:52 many bodies . . . were *r* up
27:53 tombs after his being *r* up
27:63 three days I am to be *r* up
27:64 He was *r* up from the dead!
28:6 is not here, for he was *r* up
28:7 he was *r* up from the dead
Mr 1:31 he *r* her up, taking her by
6:14 John the baptizer has been *r*
6:16 John . . . has been *r* up
9:27 and *r* him up, and he rose
12:26 that they are *r* up, did you
14:28 after I have been *r* up I
16:6 He was *r* up, he is not here
Lu 1:69 *r* up a horn of salvation for
7:16 A great prophet has been *r* up
7:22 the dead are being *r* up, the
9:7 that John had been *r* up from
9:22 on the third day be *r* up
11:27 *r* her voice and said to him
11:31 will be *r* up in the judgment
17:13 they *r* their voices and said
20:37 But that the dead are *r* up
24:6 not here, but has been *r* up
24:34 *r* up and he appeared to
Joh 2:22 he was *r* up from the dead
6:5 Jesus *r* his eyes and observed
7:52 is to be *r* up out of Galilee
11:41 Jesus *r* his eyes heavenward
12:1 Jesus had *r* up from the dead
12:9 Lazarus, whom he *r* up from
12:17 *r* him up from the dead kept
21:14 being *r* up from the dead
Ac 2:14 *r* his voice and made this
3:7 by the right hand and *r* him
3:15 God *r* him up from the dead
4:10 God *r* up from the dead, by
4:24 *r* their voices to God and
5:30 *r* up Jesus, whom you slew
9:41 he *r* her up, and he called
10:40 God *r* this One up on the
13:22 he *r* up for them David as
13:30 God *r* him up from the dead
13:37 whom God *r* up did not see
13:50 *r* up a persecution against
14:11 *r* their voices, saying in
22:22 they *r* their voices, saying
Ro 4:24 believe on him who *r* Jesus
4:25 *r* up for the sake of declaring
6:4 Christ was *r* up from the dead
6:9 Christ, now that he has been *r*
7:4 who was *r* up from the dead
8:11 spirit of him that *r* up Jesus
8:11 he that *r* up Christ Jesus
8:34 who was *r* up from the dead
10:9 God *r* him up from the dead
1Co 6:14 God both *r* up the Lord and
15:4 *r* up the third day according
15:12 has been *r* up from the dead
15:13 neither has Christ been *r*
15:14 if Christ has not been *r* up
15:15 he *r* up the Christ, but
15:15 dead are really not to be *r*
15:16 if the dead are not to be *r*
15:16 neither has Christ been *r*
15:17 if Christ has not been *r* up
15:20 Christ has been *r* up from
15:29 If the dead are not to be *r* up
15:32 If the dead are not to be *r*
15:35 How are the dead to be *r* up?
15:42 it is *r* up in incorruption
15:43 it is *r* up in glory
15:43 it is *r* up in power
15:44 it is *r* up a spiritual body
15:52 dead . . . *r* up incorruptible
2Co 4:14 he who *r* Jesus up will
5:15 died for them and was *r* up
10:5 *r* up against the knowledge
Ga 1:1 God the Father, who *r* him up
Eph 1:20 *r* him up from the dead and
2:6 he *r* us up together and seated
Col 2:12 also *r* up together through
Col 2:12 who *r* him up from the dead
3:1 you were *r* up with the Christ
1Th 1:10 whom he *r* up from the dead
2Ti 2:8 Christ was *r* up from the dead
1Pe 1:21 *r* him up from the dead and
Re 10:5 *r* his right hand to heaven

Raiser
1Sa 2:8 A *R* of a lowly one from the
2Ki 3:4 became a sheep *r*, and he paid

Raisers
Ge 46:32 because they became stock *r*
46:34 stock *r* from our youth until
Am 1:1 among the sheep *r* from Tekoa

Raises
Ps 89:9 *r* up its waves you yourself
Joh 5:21 the Father *r* the dead up
Ac 26:8 men that God *r* up the dead
2Co 1:9 in the God who *r* up the dead

Raisin
2Sa 6:19 and a *r* cake, after which
1Ch 16:3 and a date cake and a *r* cake
Isa 16:7 *r* cakes of Kir-hareseth
Ho 3:1 and are loving *r* cakes

Raising
1Sa 11:4 *r* their voice and weeping
2Sa 12:11 *r* up against you calamity
1Ki 15:4 by *r* his son up after him
Ezr 3:12 *r* the voice in shouting for
Job 21:12 They continue *r* their voice
Ps 93:3 rivers keep *r* their pounding
113:7 *R* up the lowly one from the
141:2 *r* up of my palms as the
145:14 *r* up all who are bowed
146:8 *r* up the ones bowed down
Isa 10:15 the ones *r* it on high, as
18:3 *r* up of a signal upon the
Jer 10:20 or *r* up my tent cloths
Am 2:11 I kept *r* up some of your sons
5:2 There is no one *r* her up
6:14 I am *r* up against you, O
Hab 1:6 I am *r* up the Chaldeans, the
Joh 17:1 *r* his eyes to heaven, he
Ac 3:26 God, after *r* up his Servant
20:10 Stop *r* a clamor, for his

Raisins
1Sa 25:18 hundred cakes of *r* and two
30:12 and two cakes of *r*
2Sa 16:1 a hundred cakes of *r* and a
1Ch 12:40 cakes of *r* and wine and oil
Ca 2:5 refresh me with cakes of *r*

Rake
Pr 6:27 man *r* together fire into his
Isa 30:14 to *r* the fire from the

Raking
Pr 25:22 For coals are what you are *r*

Rakkath
Jos 19:35 Hammath, *R* and Chinnereth

Rakkon
Jos 19:46 and Me-jarkon and *R*

Ram
Ge 15:9 Take for me a . . . *r* and a
22:13 *r* caught by its horns in a
22:13 Abraham went and took the *r*
Ex 25:5 and *r* skins dyed red, and
26:14 of *r* skins dyed red and a
29:15 take the one *r*, and Aaron and
29:16 slaughter the *r* and take its
29:17 cut up the *r* into its pieces
29:18 make the entire *r* smoke upon
29:19 take the other *r*, and Aaron
29:20 slaughter the *r* and take
29:22 take from the *r* the fat and
29:22 for it is a *r* of installation
29:26 *r* of installation, which is
29:27 from the *r* of installation
29:31 take the *r* of installation
29:32 must eat the flesh of the *r*
29:39 offer the one young *r* in the
29:39 offer the other young *r*
29:40 go for the first young *r*
29:41 offer the second young *r*
35:7 and *r* skins dyed red and
35:23 goat's hair and *r* skins dyed
36:19 out of *r* skins dyed red and a
39:34 covering of *r* skins dyed red
Le 3:7 he is presenting a young *r* as
4:35 the fat of the young *r* of the
5:15 offering to Jehovah a sound *r*
5:16 atonement for him with the *r*

Le 5:18 he must bring a sound *r* from
6:6 bring to Jehovah a sound *r*
7:23 fat of a bull or a young *r* or
8:18 the *r* of the burnt offering
8:18 hands upon the head of the *r*
8:20 cut up the *r* into its pieces
8:21 entire *r* smoke upon the altar
8:22 Then he brought the second *r*
8:22 the *r* of the installation
8:29 installation *r* it became the
9:2 and a *r* for a burnt offering
9:3 a calf and a young *r*, each a
9:4 a *r* for communion sacrifices
9:18 *r* of the communion sacrifice
9:19 and the fat tail of the *r*
12:6 a young *r* in its first year
14:12 take the one young *r* and
14:13 slaughter the young *r* in the
14:21 young *r* as a guilt offering
14:24 young *r* of the guilt offering
14:25 young *r* of the guilt offering
16:3 and a *r* for a burnt offering
16:5 and one *r* for a burnt offering
17:3 young *r* or a goat in the camp
19:21 a *r* of guilt offering
19:22 *r* of the guilt offering
22:27 young *r* or a goat be born
23:12 render up a sound young *r*, in
Nu 5:8 except the *r* of atonement with
6:12 *r* in its first year as a guilt
6:14 to Jehovah one sound young *r*
6:14 one sound *r* as a communion
6:17 *r* as a communion sacrifice
6:19 boiled shoulder from the *r*
7:15 one *r*, one male lamb in its
7:21 one *r*, one male lamb in its
7:27 one *r*, one male lamb in its
7:33 one *r* . . . a burnt offering
7:39 one *r* . . . burnt offering
7:45 one *r* . . . burnt offering
7:51 one *r* . . . a burnt offering
7:57 one *r* . . . a burnt offering
7:63 one *r* . . . burnt offering
7:69 one *r* . . . burnt offering
7:75 one *r* . . . a burnt offering
7:81 one *r* . . . a burnt offering
15:6 for a *r* you should render up a
15:11 for each bull or for each *r*
23:2 a bull and a *r* on each altar
23:4 a bull and a *r* on each altar
23:14 to offer up a bull and a *r* on
23:30 offering up a bull and a *r* on
28:11 two young bulls and one *r*
28:12 offering . . . for the one *r*
28:14 a third of a hin for the *r*
28:19 two young bulls and one *r*
28:20 tenth measures for the *r*
28:27 one *r*, seven male lambs each
28:28 tenth measures for the one *r*
29:2 one *r*, seven male lambs each
29:3 two tenth measures for the *r*
29:8 one *r*, seven male lambs each
29:9 tenth measures for the one *r*
29:14 grain offering . . . for each *r*
29:36 one *r*, seven male lambs each
29:37 for the bull, the *r* and the
Jos 6:5 sound with the horn of the *r*
Ru 4:19 and Hezron became father to *R*
4:19 *R* became father to Amminadab
1Ch 2:9 the sons of Hezron . . . *R*
2:10 *R*, he became father to
2:25 sons of Jerahmeel . . . *R*
2:27 *R* the firstborn of Jerahmeel
Ezr 10:19 *r* of the flock for their
Job 32:2 Buzite of the family of *R*
Isa 16:1 Send a *r*, you men, to the
Eze 43:23 *r* from the flock, a sound
43:25 *r* out of the flock, perfect
45:24 ephah for the *r* he should
46:4 male lambs and a sound *r*
46:5 offering an ephah for the *r*
46:6 lambs and a *r*; sound ones
46:7 ephah for the *r* he should
46:11 and an ephah for the *r*, and
Da 8:3 a *r* standing before the
8:4 *r* making thrusts to the west
8:6 *r* possessing the two horns
8:7 into close touch with the *r*
8:7 strike down the *r* and to break
8:7 power in the *r* to stand before
8:7 *r* proved to have no deliverer
8:20 *r* that you saw possessing the
Ho 4:16 young *r* in a roomy place
Mt 1:3 Hezron became father to *R*
Mt 1:4 *R* became father to Amminadab

Ramah
Jos 18:25 Gibeon and *R* and Beeroth
19:8 *R* of the south
19:29 boundary went back to *R*
19:36 and Adamah and *R* and Hazor
Jg 4:5 palm tree between *R* and Bethel
19:13 either in Gibeah or in *R*
1Sa 1:19 came into their house at *R*
2:11 Elkanah went to *R* to his
7:17 his return was to *R*, because
8:4 and came to Samuel at *R*
15:34 Samuel now went . . . to *R*
16:13 rose and went his way to *R*
19:18 got to come to Samuel at *R*
19:19 David is in Naioth in *R*
19:22 Finally he too went to *R*
19:22 There in Naioth in *R*
19:23 from there to Naioth in *R*
19:23 he came into Naioth in *R*
20:1 away from Naioth in *R*
25:1 bury him at his house in *R*
28:3 bury him in *R* his own city
1Ki 15:17 and began to build *R*, to
15:21 quit building *R* and
15:22 to carry the stones of *R*
2Ki 8:29 to inflict upon him at *R*
2Ch 16:1 and began to build *R*, so as
16:5 quit building *R* and stopped
16:6 carry away the stones of *R*
22:6 inflicted upon him at *R* when
Ezr 2:26 the sons of *R* and Geba
Ne 7:30 the men of *R* and Geba, six
11:33 Hazor, *R*, Gittaim
Isa 10:29 *R* has trembled, Gibeah
Jer 31:15 In *R* a voice is being heard
40:1 sent him from *R*, when he
Ho 5:8 horn in Gibeah, a trumpet in *R*
Mt 2:18 A voice was heard in *R*

Ramathaim-zophim
1Sa 1:1 to be a certain man of *R*

Ramathite
1Ch 27:27 there was Shimei the *R*

Ramath-lehi
Jg 15:17 and called that place *R*

Ramath-mizpeh
Jos 13:26 from Heshbon to *R* and

Rameses
Ge 47:11 in the land of *R*, just as
Ex 12:37 depart from *R* for Succoth
Nu 33:3 to pull away from *R* in the
33:5 Israel pulled away from *R* and

Ramiah
Ezr 10:25 sons of Parosh there were *R*

Ramoth
De 4:43 *R* in Gilead for the Gadites
Jos 20:8 *R* in Gilead out of the tribe
21:38 the city of refuge . . . *R* in
1Sa 30:27 those in *R* of the south
1Ch 6:73 *R* with its pasture grounds
6:80 *R* in Gilead with its pasture

Ramoth-gilead
1Ki 4:13 the son of Geber, in *R*
22:3 know that *R* belongs to us
22:4 go with me to the fight at *R*
22:6 Shall I go against *R* in war
22:12 to *R* and prove successful
22:15 shall we go to *R* in war
22:20 he may go up and fall at *R*
22:29 proceeded to go up to *R*
2Ki 8:28 war against Hazael . . . at *R*
9:1 oil in your hand and go to *R*
9:4 got on his way to *R*
9:14 to be keeping guard at *R*
2Ch 18:2 him to go up against *R*
18:3 Will you go with me to *R*?
18:5 against *R* in war, or shall I
18:11 Go up to *R* and prove
18:14 Micaiah, shall we go to *R*
18:19 go up and fall at *R*
18:28 proceeded to go up to *R*
22:5 king of Syria at *R*, at

Rampart
2Sa 20:15 a siege *r* against the city
20:15 it was standing within a *r*
2Ki 19:32 cast up a siege *r* against
Ps 48:13 Set your hearts upon its *r*
122:7 peace continue within your *r*
Isa 26:1 itself for walls and *r*
Isa 37:33 cast up a siege *r* against
Jer 6:6 against Jerusalem a siege *r*
La 2:8 *r* and wall to go mourning
Eze 4:2 throw up a siege *r* against it
17:17 by throwing up a siege *r*
21:22 to throw up a siege *r*
26:8 against you a siege *r* and
Da 11:15 and throw up a siege *r* and
Ob 20 as for the exiles of this *r*
Zec 9:3 to build a *r* for herself

Ramparts
Jer 32:24 With siege *r* men have come
33:4 account of the siege *r* and

Ram's
Ex 19:13 At the blowing of the *r* horn
29:15 their hands upon the *r* head
29:19 their hands upon the *r* head
Le 8:22 their hands upon the *r* head

Rams
Ge 30:32 sheep among the young *r*
30:33 dark brown among the young *r*
30:35 dark brown among the young *r*
30:40 Jacob separated the young *r*
31:38 *r* of your flock I never ate
32:14 female sheep and twenty *r*
Ex 12:5 pick from the young *r* or from
29:1 Take a young bull, and two *r*
29:3 also the bull and the two *r*
29:38 upon the altar: young *r*
Le 1:10 from the young *r* or the goats
8:2 the two *r* and the basket of
14:10 take two sound young *r* and
22:19 among the young *r* or among
23:18 two *r*. They should serve as
Nu 7:17 five *r*, five he-goats
7:23 five *r*, five he-goats, five
7:29 sacrifice . . . five *r*
7:35 sacrifice . . . five *r*, five
7:41 sacrifice . . . five *r*
7:47 sacrifice . . . five *r*
7:53 sacrifice . . . five *r*
7:59 sacrifice . . . five *r*
7:65 sacrifice . . . five *r*
7:71 sacrifice . . . five *r*
7:77 sacrifice . . . five *r*
7:83 sacrifice . . . five *r*
7:87 burnt offering . . . twelve *r*
7:88 sacrifice . . . sixty *r*
23:1 seven bulls and seven *r*
23:29 seven bulls and seven *r*
29:13 two *r*, fourteen male lambs
29:14 for each ram of the two *r*
29:17 twelve young bulls, two *r*
29:18 for the bulls, the *r* and the
29:20 two *r*, fourteen male lambs
29:21 drink offerings for . . . the *r*
29:23 fourth day ten bulls, two *r*
29:24 offerings for . . . the *r* and
29:26 fifth day nine bulls, two *r*
29:27 offerings for . . . the *r* and
29:29 sixth day eight bulls, two *r*
29:30 offerings for . . . the *r* and
29:32 the seventh day . . . two *r*
29:33 offerings for the . . . *r* and
De 32:14 Together with the fat of *r*
1Sa 15:9 upon the *r* and upon all that
15:22 attention than the fat of *r*
1Ch 15:26 young bulls and seven *r*
29:21 young bulls, a thousand *r*
2Ch 13:9 young bull and seven *r*, he
17:11 thousand seven hundred *r*
29:21 seven bulls and seven *r*
29:22 slaughtered the *r* and
29:32 a hundred *r*, two hundred
Ezr 6:9 *r* and lambs for the burnt
6:17 bulls, two hundred *r*
7:17 *r*, lambs and their grain
8:35 ninety-six *r*, seventy-seven
Job 31:20 shorn wool of my young *r*
42:8 seven *r* and go to my servant
Ps 66:15 the sacrificial smoke of *r*
114:4 skipped about like *r*
114:6 went skipping about like *r*
Pr 27:26 *r* are for your clothing
Isa 1:11 whole burnt offerings of *r*
34:6 blood of young *r* and
34:6 fat of the kidneys of *r*
60:7 The *r* of Nebaioth
Jer 51:40 *r* along with the he-goats
Eze 4:2 and put battering *r* all around
21:22 to set battering *r*, to open
21:22 to set battering *r* against

Eze 27:21 In male lambs and *r* and
34:17 the *r* and the he-goats
39:18 *r*, young male sheep, and
45:23 seven *r*, sound ones, daily
Am 6:4 eating the *r* out of a flock
Mic 6:7 pleased with thousands of *r*

Rams'
Jos 6:4 should carry seven *r* horns
6:6 carry seven *r* horns before the
6:8 priests carrying seven *r* horns
6:13 carrying seven *r* horns

Ran
Ge 16:6 humiliate her so that she *r*
18:7 Abraham *r* to the herd and
24:17 servant *r* to meet her and
24:20 *r* yet again and again to the
Ex 2:15 Moses *r* away from Pharaoh
Jg 9:54 attendant *r* him through, so
11:3 So Jephthah *r* away because of
13:10 and *r* and told her husband
1Sa 19:18 David, he *r* away and made
20:36 The attendant *r*, and he
23:6 *r* away to David at Keilah
2Sa 13:37 Absalom, he *r* off that he
13:38 Absalom, he *r* off and made
1Ki 2:7 I *r* away from before Absalom
2Ch 33:14 *r* it around to Ophel and
Ps 57:*super* he *r* away because of Saul
Jer 23:21 yet they themselves *r*
26:21 *r* away and came into Egypt
Jon 4:2 and *r* away to Tarshish
Mt 27:48 *r* and took a sponge and
28:8 *r* to report to his disciples
Mr 5:6 he *r* and did obeisance to him
6:33 from all the cities they *r*
6:55 *r* around all that region and
10:17 a certain man *r* up and fell
15:36 a certain one *r*, soaked a
Lu 15:20 *r* and fell upon his neck and
19:4 he *r* ahead to an advance
24:12 *r* to the memorial tomb, and
Joh 2:3 When the wine *r* short the
20:2 *r* and came to Simon Peter
20:4 disciple *r* ahead of Peter
Ac 3:11 people *r* together to them at
8:30 Philip *r* alongside and heard
12:14 *r* inside and reported that
21:1 we *r* with a straight course
21:32 officers and *r* down to them
27:16 *r* under the shelter of a
27:41 they *r* the ship aground and

Range
1Sa 31:2 close *r* of Saul and his sons
1Ch 10:2 kept in close *r* of Saul and
Job 6:4 The terrors from God *r*
Ps 10:5 are high up out of his *r*

Ranged
Nu 27:3 *r* themselves against Jehovah

Rank
2Sa 23:19 to the *r* of the first three
23:23 to the *r* of the three he
2Ki 23:4 priests of the second *r* and
1Ch 11:25 to the *r* of the first three
1Co 15:23 But each one in his own *r*

Ranks
Isa 14:31 getting isolated from his *r*

Ransom
Ex 21:30 If a *r* should be imposed
30:12 give a *r* for his soul to
Nu 3:46 *r* price of the two hundred and
3:48 *r* price of those who are in
3:49 the *r* price of the Levites
3:51 money of the *r* price to Aaron
35:31 take no *r* for the soul of a
35:32 *r* for one who has fled to
Job 33:24 I have found a *r*!
36:18 let not a large *r* itself
Ps 49:7 Nor give to God a *r* for him
Pr 6:35 for any sort of *r*, neither
13:8 *r* for a man's soul is his
21:18 The wicked is a *r* for the
Isa 43:3 given Egypt as a *r* for you
Mt 20:28 a *r* in exchange for many
Mr 10:45 his soul a *r* in exchange for
Ro 3:24 by the *r* paid by Christ Jesus
8:23 release from our bodies by *r*
1Co 1:30 and release by *r*
Eph 1:7 release by *r* through the
1:14 releasing by a *r* God's own
4:30 a day of releasing by *r*
Col 1:14 we have our release by *r*
1Ti 2:6 a corresponding *r* for all
Heb 9:15 for their release by *r* from
11:35 accept release by some *r*

Rapacious
Isa 35:9 *r* sort of wild beasts

Rapacity
Hab 2:17 the *r* upon the beasts that

Rape
De 28:30 but another man will *r* her
Jg 19:24 you *r* them and do to them

Raped
Jg 20:5 was my concubine that they *r*
Isa 13:16 their own wives will be *r*
Jer 3:2 that you have not been *r*
Zec 14:2 women themselves will be *r*

Rapha
1Ch 8:2 the fourth and *R* the fifth

Raphah
1Ch 8:37 Binea, *R* his son, Eleasah his

Raphu
Nu 13:9 Benjamin, Palti the son of *R*

Raping
Es 7:8 also to be a *r* of the queen

Rare
1Sa 3:1 word from Jehovah . . . *r* in
Job 28:16 With the *r* onyx stone and
Pr 25:17 your foot *r* at the house of

Rarer
Isa 13:12 man *r* than refined gold
13:12 *r* than the gold of Ophir

Rashly
Ps 106:33 to speak *r* with his lips
Pr 20:25 man has *r* cried out, Holy!
Ac 19:36 to keep calm and not act *r*

Rashness
Job 35:15 taken note of the extreme *r*

Rat
Le 11:29 the mole *r* and the jerboa and

Rate
Ge 38:23 At any *r*, I have sent this
Ex 1:7 at a very extraordinary *r*, so
5:19 one bit of anyone's daily *r*
22:17 at the *r* of purchase money
2Ki 23:35 individual tax *r* he exacted
Mt 20:10 pay at the *r* of a denarius
Lu 3:13 anything more than the tax *r*
18:5 at any *r*, because of this
Php 3:16 At any *r*, to what extent we

Rations
Ge 47:22 the *r* for the priests were
47:22 they ate their *r* that Pharaoh

Rattles
Job 39:23 Against it a quiver *r*

Rattling
Job 41:29 laughs at the *r* of a javelin
Jer 47:3 *r* of his war chariots, the
Eze 23:24 *r* of war chariots and
37:7 a *r*, and bones began to
Na 3:2 sound of the *r* of the wheel

Ravaged
Ac 9:21 man that *r* those in Jerusalem

Ravages
Ps 35:17 my soul from their *r*

Raven
Ge 8:7 he sent out a *r*, and it
Le 11:15 every *r* according to its kind
De 14:14 every *r* according to its kind
Job 38:41 prepares for the *r* its food
Ca 5:11 His black hair is like the *r*

Ravenous
Mt 7:15 but inside they are *r* wolves

Ravens
1Ki 17:4 and the *r* I shall certainly
17:6 *r* themselves were bringing
Ps 147:9 young *r* that keep calling
Pr 30:17 *r* of the torrent valley will
Isa 34:11 *r* themselves will reside in
Lu 12:24 *r* neither sow seed nor reap

Ravine
1Sa 13:23 to the *r* pass of Michmash

Raw
Ex 12:9 Do not eat any of it *r* or
Le 13:10 the *r* of the living flesh is
13:24 the *r* flesh of the scar does
1Sa 2:15 not boiled meat, but *r*

Rays
Ex 34:29 skin of his face emitted *r*
34:30 skin of his face emitted *r*
34:35 Moses' face emitted *r*; and
Hab 3:4 two *r* issuing out of his hand
Lu 11:36 gives you light by its *r*

Razor
Nu 6:5 no *r* should pass over his head
8:7 *r* pass over all their flesh
Jg 13:5 and no *r* should come upon his
16:17 A *r* has never come upon my
1Sa 1:11 no *r* will come upon his head
Ps 52:2 sharpened like a *r*
Isa 7:20 by means of a hired *r* in the
Eze 5:1 As a barbers' *r* you will take

Reach
Le 26:5 *r* to your grape gathering
26:5 grape gathering will *r* to the
Jos 17:10 the north they *r* to Asher
Ezr 6:5 may *r* the temple that is in
Isa 8:8 Up to the neck he will *r*
10:14 *r* the resources of the
29:20 tyrant must *r* his end, and
30:4 his own envoys *r* even Hanes
66:17 all together *r* their end
Am 9:10 come near or *r* as far as us
Hab 2:5 and he will not *r* his goal
Zec 14:5 will *r* all the way to Azel
Joh 10:39 but he got out of their *r*
2Co 10:13 making it *r* even as far as
10:14 as if we did not *r* to you

Reached
Ge 22:9 they *r* the place that the
47:9 they have not *r* the days of
Jos 16:7 and *r* to Jericho and went
19:11 and *r* to Dabbesheth and
19:11 *r* to the torrent valley that
19:22 the boundary *r* to Tabor and
19:26 *r* westward to Carmel and
19:27 and *r* to Zebulun and the
19:34 *r* to Zebulun on the south
19:34 to Asher it *r* on the west
Jg 20:41 that calamity had *r* them
1Ki 6:27 the one *r* to the wall and
2Ch 28:9 raging that has *r* clear to
Ps 73:19 they have *r* their end, have
Isa 10:10 hand has *r* the kingdoms of
16:4 oppressor has *r* his end
16:8 As far as Jazer they had *r*
Jer 4:10 has *r* clear to the soul
4:18 it has *r* clear to your heart
48:32 sea—to Jazer—they have *r*
51:9 heavens her judgment has *r*
Da 4:11 height finally *r* the heavens
4:20 *r* the heavens and which was
4:22 *r* to the heavens, and your
6:24 *r* the bottom of the pit
Jon 3:6 word *r* the king of Nineveh
Mt 26:51 one of those with Jesus *r* out
Lu 8:51 When he *r* the house he did
Joh 20:4 *r* the memorial tomb first
20:8 *r* the memorial tomb first
1Co 14:36 only as far as you that it *r*
Re 1:13 garment that *r* down to the

Reaches
Job 20:6 his very head *r* to the clouds
Isa 30:28 torrent that *r* clear to the

Reaching
Ge 28:12 top *r* up to the heavens
1Ki 6:27 was *r* to the other wall
6:27 *r* wing to wing
2Ch 3:11 *r* to the wall of the house
3:11 *r* to the wing of the other
3:12 *r* to the wall of the house
Es 4:3 word and his law were *r*
8:17 were *r* there were rejoicing
1Ti 3:1 man is *r* out for . . . overseer
6:10 by *r* out for this love some
Heb 11:16 they are *r* out for a better

Read
Ge 44:15 can expertly *r* omens
Ex 24:7 *r* it in the ears of the people
De 17:19 *r* in it all the days of his
31:11 you will *r* this law in front
Jos 1:8 *r* in it day and night

Jos 8:34 he *r* aloud all the words of
8:35 that Joshua did not *r* aloud
2Ki 5:7 king of Israel *r* the letter
19:14 and *r* them, after which
22:8 Shaphan, and he began to *r* it
22:10 Shaphan began to *r* it
22:16 that the king of Judah has *r*
23:2 to *r* in their ears all the
2Ch 34:18 Shaphan began to *r* out of it
34:24 *r* before the king of Judah
34:30 *r* in their ears all the
Ezr 4:18 been distinctly *r* before me
4:23 been *r* before Rehum and
Ne 8:3 to *r* aloud from it before the
9:3 *r* aloud from the book of the
Isa 29:11 *R* this out loud, please
29:12 *R* this out loud, please
34:16 book of Jehovah and *r* out
37:14 *r* them, after which
Jer 29:29 *r* this letter in the ears
36:6 *r* aloud from the roll that
36:6 you should *r* them aloud
36:8 *r* aloud from the book the
36:10 Baruch began to *r* aloud
36:13 Baruch *r* aloud from the
36:14 roll from which you *r* aloud
36:15 *r* it aloud in our ears
36:15 Baruch *r* aloud in their ears
36:21 Jehudi began to *r* it aloud
36:23 Jehudi had *r* three or four
51:61 *r* aloud all these words
Da 5:7 man that will *r* this writing
5:8 competent enough to *r* the
5:15 conjurers, that they may *r*
5:16 able to *r* the writing and to
5:17 *r* the writing itself to the
Mt 12:3 Have you not *r* what David did
12:5 Or, have you not *r* in the Law
19:4 you not *r* that he who created
21:16 Did you never *r* this, Out of
21:42 never *r* in the Scriptures
22:31 did you not *r* what was
Mr 2:25 *r* what David did when he
12:10 you never *r* this scripture
12:26 *r* in the book of Moses, in
Lu 4:16 and he stood up to *r*
6:3 never *r* the very thing David
10:26 in the Law? How do you *r*?
Joh 19:20 Jews *r* this title, because
Ac 13:27 are *r* aloud every Sabbath
15:21 is *r* aloud in the synagogues
23:34 he *r* it and inquired from
2Co 3:2 and being *r* by all mankind
3:15 whenever Moses is *r*, a veil
Eph 3:4 when you *r* this, can realize
Col 4:16 when this letter has been *r*
4:16 also be *r* in the congregation
4:16 also *r* the one from Laodicea
1Th 5:27 to be *r* to all the brothers

Reader
Mt 24:15 let the *r* use discernment
Mr 13:14 let the *r* use discernment

Readily
Ps 46:1 A help that is *r* to be found
Isa 55:3 I shall *r* conclude with you
Jer 31:18 I shall *r* turn back, for
33:3 *r* tell you great and
46:8 I shall *r* destroy the city
La 5:21 and we shall *r* come back
Ac 24:10 I *r* speak in my defense the
Php 2:12 more *r* during my absence
1Ti 6:2 more *r* be slaves, because

Readiness
De 32:35 the events in *r* for them
Jos 8:4 you hold yourselves in *r*
Job 15:24 a king in *r* for the assault
2Co 8:11 *r* to want to do, so also
8:12 *r* is there first, it is
9:2 for I know your *r* of mind of
10:6 holding ourselves in *r* to

Reading
Ne 8:8 *r* aloud from the book, from
8:8 giving understanding in the *r*
8:18 *r* aloud of the book of the
13:1 *r* from the book of Moses
Es 6:1 a *r* of them before the king
Jer 51:63 completed *r* this book, you
Hab 2:2 one *r* aloud from it may do so
Ac 8:28 *r* aloud the prophet Isaiah
8:30 *r* aloud Isaiah the prophet
8:30 actually know what you are *r*
8:32 Scripture that he was *r* aloud

Ac 13:15 public *r* of the Law and of
15:31 After *r* it, they rejoiced
2Co 3:14 at the *r* of the old covenant
1Ti 4:13 applying yourself to public *r*

Readjust
Ga 6:1 *r* such a man in a spirit of

Readjusted
2Co 13:9 are praying, your being *r*
13:11 continue to rejoice, to be *r*

Readjustment
Eph 4:12 to the *r* of the holy ones

Reads
Ge 44:5 he expertly *r* omens? It is a
Ps 1:2 his law he *r* in an undertone
Re 1:3 Happy is he who *r* aloud and

Ready
Ge 18:7 went hurrying to get it *r*
18:8 young bull that he had got *r*
24:31 made the house *r* and room
43:25 gift *r* for Joseph's coming
46:29 had his chariot made *r* and
Ex 14:6 to make his war chariots *r*
15:17 place that you have made *r*
19:11 prove *r* for the third day
19:15 Get *r* during the three days
34:2 get *r* for the morning, as
Le 16:21 hand of a *r* man into the
Nu 23:1 make *r* for me on this spot
23:29 make *r* for me on this spot
Jos 1:11 saying, Get provisions *r* for
Jg 6:19 make *r* a kid of the goats and
2Sa 12:4 get such *r* for the traveler
12:4 *r* for the man that had come
1Ch 12:8 large shield and the lance *r*
Ne 5:18 happened to be made *r* daily
5:18 were made *r* for me, and once
Es 3:14 them to become *r* for this day
8:13 Jews should become *r* for this
Job 3:8 Those *r* to awaken Leviathan
12:5 *r* for those of wobbling feet
15:23 day of darkness is *r* at his
18:12 disaster stands *r* to make
Ps 7:12 will make it *r* for shooting
11:2 make *r* their arrow upon the
21:12 bowstrings that you make *r*
37:23 have been made *r*
38:17 For I was *r* to limp
59:4 run and get themselves *r*
68:10 make it *r* for the afflicted
86:5 are good and *r* to forgive
Pr 24:27 *r* for yourself in the field
Isa 14:21 Make *r*, you men, a
Jer 51:12 *r* those lying in ambush
Eze 28:13 they were made *r*
38:7 Be *r*, and let there be
Da 3:15 *r* so that when you hear the
Am 4:12 get *r* to meet your God
Na 2:3 in the day of his getting *r*
Mt 22:4 all things are *r*. Come to the
22:8 marriage feast indeed is *r*
24:44 prove yourselves *r*, because
25:10 virgins that were *r* went in
26:19 things *r* for the passover
Lu 1:17 get *r* for Jehovah a prepared
1:76 to make his ways *r*
2:31 *r* in the sight of all the
12:40 keep *r*, because at an hour
12:47 but did not get *r* or do in
14:17 because things are now *r*
17:8 Get something *r* for me to
22:8 the passover *r* for us to eat
22:9 do you want us to get it *r*
22:12 Get it *r* there
22:13 and they got the passover *r*
22:33 Lord, I am *r* to go with you
Ac 21:13 I am *r* not only to be bound
23:15 be *r* to do away with him
23:21 *r*, waiting for the promise
23:23 soldiers *r* to march clear to
1Co 14:8 who will get *r* for battle?
2Co 8:19 and in proof of our *r* mind
9:2 Achaia has stood *r* now for a
9:3 but that you may really be *r*
9:4 with me and find you not *r*
9:5 and to get *r* in advance your
9:5 be *r* as a bountiful gift and
12:14 time I am *r* to come to you
1Ti 6:18 to be liberal, *r* to share
Tit 3:1 be *r* for every good work
Phm 22 also get lodging *r* for me
Heb 11:16 has made a city *r* for them

Jas 3:17 wisdom . . . *r* to obey
1Pe 1:5 salvation *r* to be revealed in
3:15 *r* to make a defense before
4:5 one *r* to judge those living
Re 3:2 that were *r* to die, for I

Reaiah
1Ch 4:2 *R* the son of Shobal, he
5:5 *R* his son, Baal his son
Ezr 2:47 the sons of *R*
Ne 7:50 the sons of *R*, the sons of

Real
Job 19:15 A *r* foreigner I have become
29:16 a *r* father to the poor ones
Ps 90:1 to be a *r* dwelling for us
139:22 become to me *r* enemies
Pr 4:3 *r* son to my father, tender and
26:2 does not come without *r* cause
Isa 26:18 No *r* salvation do we
32:15 is accounted as a *r* forest
40:14 very way of *r* understanding
Joh 7:28 he that sent me is *r*, and
Ac 12:9 through the angel was *r*
Ro 12:8 let him do it in *r* earnest
Php 3:3 those with the *r* circumcision
1Ti 6:19 a firm hold on the *r* life
Heb 11:10 city having *r* foundations

Realities
Heb 11:1 evident demonstration of *r*

Reality
Isa 43:24 In *r* you have compelled me
Mt 6:23 If in *r* the light that is in
Ac 26:26 In *r*, the king to whom I
Ro 4:15 In *r* the Law produces wrath
11:13 in *r*, an apostle to the
Ga 2:17 Christ in *r* sin's minister
Col 2:17 the *r* belongs to the Christ
Heb 9:24 which is a copy of the *r*

Realize
Ge 3:7 they began to *r* that they
Eph 3:4 can *r* the comprehension I
Col 2:1 *r* how great a struggle I am

Realized
Jg 6:22 Gideon *r* that it was
Pr 13:19 Desire when *r* is pleasurable
Ac 27:13 *r* their purpose, and they

Realizing
Lu 9:33 he not *r* what he was saying

Really
Ge 3:1 Is it *r* so that God said you
18:12 shall I *r* have pleasure, my
18:13 I *r* and truly give birth
18:23 *r* sweep away the righteous
20:4 nation that is *r* righteous
24:42 *r* giving success to my way
27:21 *r* my son Esau or not
27:24 You are *r* my son Esau?
31:15 *r* considered as foreigners
37:30 And I—where am I *r* to go?
Ex 4:14 do know that he can *r* speak
21:5 I *r* love my master, my wife
21:22 *r* hurt a pregnant woman and
21:26 and he *r* ruins it, he is to
23:22 *r* do all that I shall speak
23:29 *r* multiply against you
23:30 *r* take possession of the land
Nu 22:37 *r* and truly able to honor you
De 4:16 not *r* make for yourselves a
Jg 15:2 I *r* said to myself, You must
2Sa 1:5 *r* know that Saul has died
2:26 Do you not *r* know that
1Ki 22:3 *r* know that Ramoth-gilead
2Ki 2:3 Do you *r* know that today
2:5 *r* know that today Jehovah is
1Ch 4:10 hand *r* proves to be with me
4:10 and you *r* preserve me from
8:32 *r* were the ones that dwelt
9:38 *r* they that dwelt in front
Job 9:15 though I were *r* in the right
11:4 proved *r* clean in your eyes
11:13 will *r* prepare your heart
21:21 his months will *r* be cut in
22:13 said: What does God *r* know?
23:3 O that I *r* knew where I
24:25 *r* now, who will make me
27:7 against me *r* a wrongdoer
34:17 *R* will anyone hating
35:7 If you are *r* in the right
37:21 they do not *r* see the light
40:8 *R*, will you invalidate my
Ps 16:6 *R*, my own possession has

Realm

Realms

Reap

Reaped

Reaper

Reapers

Reaping

Rear

Reared

Reason

Ps 109:16 *r* that he did not remember
Pr 1:29 *r* that they hated knowledge
23:29 Who has wounds for no *r?*
Ec 7:25 wisdom and the *r* of things
Isa 3:16 *r* that the daughters of
7:5 *r* that Syria with Ephraim
8:6 *r* that this people has
28:19 nothing but a *r* for quaking
29:13 *r* that this people have
30:3 for you men a *r* for shame
30:5 *r* for shame and also a
40:27 For what *r* do you say
49:7 by *r* of Jehovah, who is
52:6 For that *r* my people will
52:6 even for that *r* in that day
53:12 For that *r* I shall deal him
58:3 For what *r* did we fast and
61:1 for the *r* that Jehovah has
65:12 for the *r* that I called
66:4 *r* that I called, but there
66:5 excluding you by *r* of my
66:11 the *r* that you will suck
66:11 the *r* that you will sip and
Jer 3:8 *r* that unfaithful Israel had
5:14 the *r* that you men are
7:13 for the *r* that you kept doing
19:4 the *r* that they have left me
23:38 By *r* of your saying, This
25:8 the *r* that you did not obey
29:23 the *r* that they have carried
29:25 the *r* that you yourself have
29:31 For the *r* that Shemaiah has
35:17 *r* that I have spoken to
35:18 *r* that you have obeyed the
Eze 5:7 For the *r* that you people
5:9 by *r* of all your detestable
5:11 *r* that it was my sanctuary
7:20 one has set it as *r* for pride
13:8 *r* that you men have spoken
13:10 for the *r*, yes, for the
13:10 the *r* that they have led my
13:22 By *r* of dejecting the heart
15:8 the *r* that they have acted
16:36 the *r* that your lustfulness
16:43 *r* that you did not remember
16:63 any *r* to open your mouth
20:16 *r* that they rejected my own
20:24 *r* that they did not carry
21:24 By *r* of your causing your
21:24 by *r* of your being called
22:19 *r* that all of you have
23:35 *r* that you have forgotten
24:13 For that *r* I had to cleanse
25:3 For the *r* that you have said
25:6 For the *r* that you clapped
25:8 For the *r* that Moab and Seir
25:12 For the *r* that Edom has
25:15 the *r* that the Philistines
26:2 for the *r* that Tyre has said
28:2 For the *r* that your heart
28:6 For the *r* that you make your
29:6 for the *r* that they proved
29:9 for the *r* that he has said
31:10 *r* that you became high in
34:8 the *r* that my sheep became
34:21 the *r* that with flank and
35:5 the *r* that you proved to have
35:10 By *r* of your saying, These
36:2 For the *r* that the enemy has
36:3 For the *r*, even for the
36:3 *r* that there has been a lying
36:6 for the *r* that humiliation
36:13 the *r* that there are those
44:12 For the *r* that they kept
Da 2:15 *r* is there such a harsh order
Ho 8:1 *r* that they have overstepped
Am 5:11 the *r* that you are extracting
Ob 9 for the *r* that each one will be
Hab 1:4 for that *r* justice goes forth
Hag 1:9 blew upon it—for what *r*
1:9 By *r* of my house that is
Mt 9:15 no *r* to mourn as long as the
16:7 began to *r* among themselves
19:5 For this *r* a man will leave
21:25 began to *r* among themselves
23:34 For this *r*, here I am
Mr 11:31 began to *r* among themselves
Lu 1:29 began to *r* out what sort of
1:35 For that *r* also what is born
5:21 the Pharisees started to *r*
7:7 For that *r* I did not consider
14:20 for this *r* I cannot come
Joh 1:31 the *r* why I came baptizing
7:7 world has no *r* to hate you
Joh 7:22 For this *r* Moses has given
11:50 *r* out that it is to your
12:39 *r* why they were not able to
19:12 *r* Pilate kept on seeking
Ac 10:29 *r* that you have sent for me
17:17 to *r* in the synagogue with
18:14 with *r* put up patiently with
19:32 *r* why they had come together
19:40 a *r* for this disorderly mob
Ro 1:17 revealed by *r* of faith and
3:7 by *r* of my lie the truth of
9:32 For what *r?* Because he
12:1 service with your power of *r*
13:5 compelling *r* for you people
1Co 9:15 make my *r* for boasting void
9:16 it is no *r* for me to boast
12:15 it is not for this *r* no part
12:16 it is not for this *r* no part
13:11 to *r* as a babe; but now
2Co 7:16 good courage by *r* of you
11:11 For what *r?* Because I do
Ga 3:11 one will live by *r* of faith
Eph 5:31 For this *r* a man will leave
Php 1:14 by *r* of my prison bonds
1:26 by *r* of me through my
2:9 For this very *r* also God
1Th 2:18 For this *r* we wanted to
2Th 2:2 quickly shaken from your *r*
1Ti 1:16 the *r* why I was shown mercy
4:4 The *r* for this is that every
2Ti 1:9 not by *r* of our works, but
1:9 by *r* of his own purpose and
Tit 1:5 For this *r* I left you in Crete
Phm 8 For this very *r*, though I have
Heb 3:7 For this *r*, just as the holy
3:10 this *r* I became disgusted
6:1 For this *r*, now that we have
10:38 will live by *r* of faith
1Pe 3:15 a *r* for the hope in you, but
2Pe 1:5 for this very *r*, by your
1:10 For this *r*, brothers, all
1:12 For this *r* I shall be
2:8 by *r* of their lawless deeds
Jude 4 My *r* is that certain men have
Re 18:19 rich by *r* of her costliness

Reasonable
2Co 11:19 seeing you are *r*
1Ti 3:3 not a smiter, but *r*, not
Tit 3:2 *r*, exhibiting all mildness
Jas 3:17 wisdom from above is . . . *r*
1Pe 2:18 not only to the good and *r*

Reasonableness
Php 4:5 *r* become known to all men

Reasoned
2Sa 14:13 *r* like this against the
Ac 17:2 for three sabbaths he *r* with
18:19 and *r* with the Jews

Reasoning
Mt 16:8 Why are you doing this *r*
Mr 2:6 sitting and *r* in their hearts
2:8 were *r* that way in themselves
2:8 *r* these things in your hearts
Lu 3:15 *r* in their hearts about John
5:22 you *r* out in your hearts
9:46 a *r* entered among them as to
9:47 knowing the *r* of their hearts
12:17 he began *r* within himself
20:14 they went *r* with one another
Jas 1:22 deceiving . . . with false *r*

Reasonings
Job 32:11 I kept giving ear to your *r*
Mt 15:19 of the heart come wicked *r*
Mr 7:21 injurious *r* issue forth
Lu 2:35 the *r* of many hearts may be
5:22 Jesus, discerning their *r*
6:8 knew their *r*, yet he said to
Ro 1:21 empty-headed in their *r* and
1Co 3:20 the *r* of the wise men are
2Co 10:5 are overturning *r* and every

Reasons
2Sa 14:14 *r* why the one banished

Reassuringly
Ge 50:21 comforted them and spoke *r*
Ru 2:13 spoken *r* to your maidservant

Reba
Nu 31:8 kings of Midian . . . Hur and *R*
Jos 13:21 and Zur and Hur and *R*

Rebekah
Ge 22:23 Bethuel . . . father of *R*
24:15 was *R*, who had been born to
Ge 24:29 *R* had a brother and his name
24:30 hearing the words of *R* his
24:45 *R* coming out, with her jar
24:51 *R* before you. Take her and
24:53 and to give them to *R*
24:58 called *R* and said to her
24:59 they sent off *R* their sister
24:60 to bless *R* and say to her
24:61 *R* and her lady attendants
24:61 servant took *R* and got on his
24:64 *R* raised her eyes, she caught
24:67 he took *R* and she became his
25:20 taking *R* the daughter of
25:21 *R* his wife became pregnant
25:28 *R* was a lover of Jacob
26:7 should kill me because of *R*
26:8 having a good time with *R* his
26:35 bitterness . . . to Isaac and *R*
27:5 *R* was listening while Isaac
27:6 *R* said to Jacob her son: Here
27:11 Jacob proceeded to say to *R*
27:15 *R* took garments of Esau her
27:42 words of Esau . . . told to *R*
27:46 *R* kept saying to Isaac: I
28:5 *R*, mother of Jacob and Esau
29:12 he was the son of *R*
35:8 the nursing woman of *R* died
49:31 There they buried Isaac and *R*
Ro 9:10 when *R* conceived twins from

Rebel
Nu 14:9 Only against Jehovah do not *r*
Jos 22:16 an altar, that you may *r*
22:18 *r* today against Jehovah
22:19 do not you *r* and do not
22:19 to *r* by your building for
22:29 to *r* of our own accord
1Sa 12:14 not *r* against the order of
12:15 *r* against the order of
2Ki 18:7 *r* against the king of Assyria
24:20 began to *r* against the king
2Ch 13:6 and *r* against his lord
Ne 6:6 and the Jews are scheming to *r*
Ps 78:40 would *r* against him in the
78:56 *r* against God the Most High
105:28 did not *r* against his words
Jer 52:3 *r* against the king of Babylon
Eze 20:8 they began to *r* against me
20:21 sons began to *r* against me

Rebelled
Ge 14:4 the thirteenth year they *r*
Nu 20:24 on the ground that you men *r*
27:14 *r* against my order in the
1Ki 13:21 you *r* against the order of
13:26 *r* against the order of
2Ki 18:20 you have *r* against me
24:1 turned back and *r* against
2Ch 36:13 he *r*, who had made him
Ezr 10:13 *r* to a great extent in this
Ne 9:26 disobedient and *r* against you
Ps 5:10 they have *r* against you
Isa 36:5 you have *r* against me
63:10 *r* and made his holy spirit
Jer 4:17 she has *r* even against me
La 1:18 his mouth that I have *r*
Eze 2:3 nations that have *r* against
17:15 *r* against him in sending
20:13 Israel, *r* against me in the
Da 9:5 and acted wickedly and *r;* and
9:9 for we have *r* against him

Rebelling
Ne 2:19 against the king . . . are *r*
Ps 78:17 *r* against the Most High in
Zep 3:1 Woe to her that is *r* and

Rebellion
Jos 22:22 If it is in *r* and if it is
Ezr 4:19 in which *r* and revolt have
Pr 17:11 *r* is what the bad one keeps
Eze 2:7 for they are a case of *r*

Rebellious
De 9:7 *r* in your behavior with
9:24 You have proved yourselves *r*
21:18 a son who is stubborn and *r*
21:20 son of ours is stubborn and *r*
31:27 *r* in behavior toward Jehovah
1Sa 20:30 son of a *r* maid, do I not
Ezr 4:12 building the *r* and bad city
4:15 a city *r* and causing loss to
Job 17:2 amid their *r* behavior my eye
Ps 78:8 generation stubborn and *r*
Isa 1:20 refuse and are actually *r*
30:9 it is a *r* people, untruthful
50:5 I, for my part, was not *r*

Jer 5:23 a stubborn and *r* heart
La 1:20 for I have been absolutely *r*
Eze 2:3 *r* nations that have rebelled
2:5 for they are a *r* house—they
2:6 for they are a *r* house
2:8 Do not become *r* like the
2:8 like the *r* house. Open your
3:9 for they are a *r* house
3:26 because they are a *r* house
3:27 because they are a *r* house
12:2 in the midst of a *r* house is
12:2 for they are a *r* house
12:3 though they are a *r* house
12:9 house of Israel, the *r* house
12:25 in your days, O *r* house, I
17:12 Say, please, to the *r* house
24:3 concerning the *r* house
Ho 13:16 actually *r* against her God
Jude 11 in the *r* talk of Korah

Rebelliously
Ex 23:21 Do not behave *r* against him
De 1:26 you began to behave *r* against
1:43 behave *r* against Jehovah's
9:23 you behaved *r* against the
Jos 1:18 behaves *r* against your order
Ps 106:7 they behaved *r* at the sea
106:43 behave *r* in their
107:11 *r* against the sayings of God
Isa 3:8 *r* in the eyes of his glory
La 3:42 and we have behaved *r*
Eze 5:6 behave *r* against my judicial

Rebelliousness
Nu 17:10 for a sign to the sons of *r*
De 31:27 your *r* and your stiff neck
1Sa 15:23 *r* is the same as the sin of
Job 23:2 my state of concern is *r*
Eze 44:6 to *R*, to the house of Israel

Rebels
Nu 20:10 you *r!* Is it from this crag
Job 24:13 among the *r* against light

Rebuild
Ezr 1:3 *r* the house of Jehovah the God
1:5 and *r* the house of Jehovah
5:2 started to *r* the house of God
5:13 to *r* this house of God
5:17 to *r* that house of God in
6:7 *r* that house of God upon its
Ne 2:5 that I may *r* it
2:17 us *r* the wall of Jerusalem
Isa 61:4 must *r* the long-standing
Jer 31:4 I *r* you and you will
Da 9:25 the word to restore and to *r*
Ac 15:16 and *r* the booth of David that
15:16 and I shall *r* its ruins and

Rebuilding
Ezr 5:11 we are *r* the house that had
6:8 for *r* that house of God
Ne 4:1 heard that we were *r* the wall

Rebuilt
De 13:16 It should never be *r*
2Ch 8:2 Solomon *r* them and then
8:4 *r* Tadmor in the wilderness
11:6 *r* Bethlehem and Etam and
26:2 *r* Eloth and then restored
Ezr 4:13 if this city should be *r* and
4:16 city should be *r* and its
4:21 city may not be *r* until the
5:15 let the house of God be *r*
5:16 until now it is being *r*
6:3 Let the house be *r* as the
Ne 6:1 I had *r* the wall and there
7:1 soon as the wall had been *r*
Isa 25:2 *r* even to time indefinite
44:26 be *r*, and her desolated
44:28 Jerusalem, She will be *r*
Jer 30:18 city will actually be *r*
31:4 you will actually be *r*
Eze 26:14 Never will you be *r*
36:10 places themselves will be *r*
36:33 devastated places must be *r*
Da 9:25 return and be actually *r*

Rebuke
Ge 37:10 his father began to *r* him
De 28:20 *r* in every undertaking of
Ru 2:16 and you must not *r* her
2Sa 22:16 At the *r* of Jehovah, from
2Ki 19:3 day of distress and of *r* and
Job 11:3 keep deriding without . . . *r*
19:3 ten times you proceeded to *r*
26:11 are amazed because of his *r*
Ps 18:15 From your *r*, O Jehovah, from
68:30 *R* the wild beast of the
76:6 From your *r*, O God of Jacob
80:16 *r* of your face they perish
104:7 At your *r* they began to flee
Pr 13:1 is one that has not heard *r*
13:8 has not heard *r*
17:10 *r* works deeper in one having
Ec 7:5 to hear the *r* of someone wise
Isa 17:13 He will certainly *r* it
30:17 account of the *r* of one
30:17 on account of the *r* of five
37:3 day of distress and of *r*
50:2 With my *r* I dry up the sea
51:20 Jehovah, the *r* of your God
54:9 toward you nor *r* you
66:15 his *r* with flames of fire
Ho 5:9 become in the day of *r*
Zec 3:2 Jehovah *r* you, O Satan
3:2 Jehovah *r* you, he who is
Mal 3:11 *r* for you the devouring one
Lu 17:3 commits a sin give him a *r*
19:39 Teacher, *r* your disciples
2Co 2:6 *r* given by the majority is
Jude 9 but said: May Jehovah *r* you

Rebuked
1Sa 3:13 and he has not *r* them
Ps 9:5 You have *r* nations, you have
106:9 he *r* the Red Sea, and it was
119:21 *r* the cursed presumptuous
Jer 29:27 why have you not *r* Jeremiah
Mt 8:26 he *r* the winds and the sea
17:18 Jesus *r* it, and the demon
Mr 1:25 Jesus *r* it, saying: Be silent
4:39 *r* the wind and said to the
8:33 *r* Peter, and said: Get behind
9:25 *r* the unclean spirit, saying
Lu 4:35 Jesus *r* it, saying: Be silent
4:39 *r* the fever, and it left her
8:24 he *r* the wind and the raging
9:42 Jesus *r* the unclean spirit
9:55 But he turned and *r* them
23:40 In reply the other *r* him

Rebukes
1Sa 25:14 but he screamed *r* at them
Ps 149:7 *R* upon the national groups

Rebuking
Na 1:4 He is *r* the sea, and he dries
Mal 2:3 I am *r* on your account the
Mt 16:22 Peter . . . commenced *r* him
Mr 8:32 Peter . . . started *r* him
Lu 4:41 *r* them, he would not permit

Rebuttal
Ac 4:14 they had nothing to say in *r*

Recah
1Ch 4:12 These were the men of *R*

Recall
Pr 25:10 report by you can have no *r*
Lu 24:6 *R* how he spoke to you while
Tit 2:4 *r* the young women to their

Recalled
Mr 14:72 Peter *r* the saying that
Lu 22:61 Peter *r* the utterance of the

Recalls
Isa 44:19 no one *r* to his heart or

Recantation
Ac 26:11 to force them to make a *r*

Receding
Ge 8:3 waters began *r* from off the
8:3 off the earth, progressively *r*

Receive
Ge 4:11 opened its mouth to *r* your
Nu 18:26 will *r* . . . the tenth part
18:28 tenth parts that you will *r*
De 9:9 to *r* the stone tablets, the
33:3 They began to *r* some of your
Jos 20:4 must *r* him into the city to
1Sa 2:15 *r* from you, not boiled meat
Ne 10:38 when the Levites *r* a tenth
Job 27:13 will *r* from the Almighty
35:7 does he *r* from your own hand
Ps 49:15 For he will *r* me. *Se'lah*
Pr 1:3 *r* the discipline that gives
2:1 son, if you will *r* my sayings
Jer 17:23 in order to *r* no discipline
32:33 listening to *r* discipline
35:13 *r* exhortation to obey my
Eze 16:61 when you *r* your sisters
Eze 36:30 no more *r* among the nations
Da 2:6 much dignity you will *r* on my
7:18 will *r* the kingdom, and they
Mal 1:8 or will he *r* you kindly?
1:9 Will he *r* any of you men
Mt 17:25 kings of the earth *r* duties
19:29 will *r* many times more and
20:10 concluded they would *r* more
21:22 having faith, you will *r*
25:38 and *r* you hospitably, or
25:43 you did not *r* me hospitably
Mr 4:20 the word and favorably *r* it
6:11 a place will not *r* you nor
10:15 *r* the kingdom of God like a
12:40 will *r* a heavier judgment
Lu 6:34 from whom you hope to *r*
8:13 hear it, *r* the word with joy
9:5 wherever people do not *r* you
9:53 but they did not *r* him
10:8 and they *r* you, eat the things
10:10 and they do not *r* you, go out
16:4 will *r* me into their homes
16:9 *r* you into the everlasting
18:17 does not *r* the kingdom of
20:47 will *r* a heavier judgment
Joh 1:12 as many as did *r* him
3:11 you people do not *r* the
3:27 cannot *r* a single thing
5:43 but you do not *r* me
5:43 you would *r* that one
7:39 spirit . . . were about to *r*
10:17 order that I may *r* it again
10:18 I have authority to *r* it
12:48 does not *r* my sayings has
14:3 *r* you home to myself, that
14:17 which the world cannot *r*
16:14 *r* from what is mine and
16:24 Ask and you will *r*, that
20:22 to them: *R* holy spirit
Ac 1:8 *r* power when the holy spirit
2:38 *r* the free gift of the holy
7:59 Lord Jesus, *r* my spirit
8:17 they began to *r* holy spirit
8:19 hands may *r* holy spirit
18:27 to *r* him kindly. So when he
19:2 Did you *r* holy spirit when
24:3 also in all places we *r* it
26:18 *r* forgiveness of sins and
28:30 kindly *r* all those who came
Ro 5:17 *r* the abundance of the
8:15 *r* a spirit of slavery causing
13:2 *r* judgment to themselves
1Co 2:14 does not *r* the things of the
3:8 each person will *r* his own
3:14 remains, he will *r* a reward
4:7 you have that you did not *r*
4:7 you did indeed *r* it, why do
4:7 as though you did not *r* it
14:5 congregation . . . *r* upbuilding
2Co 11:4 you *r* a spirit other than
Ga 1:12 neither did I *r* it from man
3:2 Did you *r* the spirit due to
3:14 *r* the promised spirit
4:5 might *r* the adoption as sons
Eph 6:8 will *r* this back from Jehovah
Col 3:24 you will *r* the due reward of
3:25 *r* back what he wrongly did
Phm 17 *r* him kindly the way you
Heb 7:5 who *r* their priestly office
7:8 men . . . dying that *r* tithes
9:15 might *r* the promise of the
10:36 *r* the fulfillment of the
11:8 place he was destined to *r*
11:19 he did *r* him also in an
12:28 we are to *r* a kingdom that
Jas 1:7 *r* anything from Jehovah
1:12 he will *r* the crown of life
3:1 we shall *r* heavier judgment
4:3 do ask, and yet you do not *r*
1Pe 1:9 you *r* the end of your faith
5:4 *r* the unfadable crown of
1Jo 3:22 whatever we ask we *r* from
5:9 If we *r* the witness men give
2Jo 10 never *r* him into your homes
3Jo 8 obligation to *r* such persons
9 *r* anything from us with respect
10 *r* the brothers with respect
10 are wanting to *r* them he
Re 4:11 to *r* the glory and the honor
5:12 worthy to *r* the power and
17:12 *r* authority as kings one
18:4 to *r* part of her plagues

Received
Ge 33:10 you *r* me with pleasure
Nu 12:14 afterward let her be *r* in
12:15 away until Miriam was *r* in
1Ch 12:18 David *r* them and put them
2Ch 29:16 Levites *r* it to take it
29:22 priests *r* the blood and
30:16 blood *r* from the hand of
Ezr 8:30 *r* the weight of the silver
Isa 40:2 *r* a full amount for all her
Da 5:31 Darius the Mede himself *r* the
Mt 9:30 And their eyes *r* sight
10:8 You *r* free, give free
20:9 they each *r* a denarius
20:10 also *r* pay at the rate of a
20:34 immediately they *r* sight
25:16 one that *r* the five talents
25:17 one that *r* the two gained
25:18 the one that *r* just one went
25:20 one that had *r* five talents
25:22 that had *r* the two talents
25:24 that had *r* the one talent
25:35 and you *r* me hospitably
Mr 7:4 traditions that they have *r* to
11:24 that you have practically *r*
Lu 2:28 *r* it into his arms and
6:4 *r* the loaves of presentation
8:40 the crowd *r* him kindly, for
9:11 he *r* them kindly and began
10:38 Martha *r* him as guest into
16:25 *r* in full your good things
19:6 rejoicing he *r* him as guest
Joh 1:16 *r* from out of his fullness
4:45 the Galileans *r* him, because
10:18 commandment on this I *r*
13:30 after he *r* the morsel, he
17:8 they have *r* them and have
19:30 *r* the sour wine, Jesus
Ac 1:11 Jesus who was *r* up from you
1:22 day he was *r* up from us
2:33 *r* the promised holy spirit
7:38 *r* . . . sacred pronouncements
7:53 *r* the Law as transmitted by
10:47 *r* the holy spirit even as we
11:1 had also *r* the word of God
15:4 kindly *r* by the congregation
17:7 has *r* them with hospitality
17:11 *r* the word with the greatest
20:24 the ministry that I *r* of the
21:17 the brothers *r* us gladly
26:10 I had *r* authority from the
28:2 *r* all of us helpfully because
28:7 he *r* us hospitably and
28:21 we *r* letters concerning you
Ro 1:5 we *r* undeserved kindness and
4:11 And he *r* a sign, namely
5:11 have now *r* the reconciliation
8:15 *r* a spirit of adoption as sons
1Co 2:12 *r*, not the spirit of the
11:23 For I *r* from the Lord that
15:1 which you also *r*, in which
15:3 which I also *r*, that Christ
2Co 1:9 had *r* the sentence of death
7:15 you *r* him with fear and
11:4 spirit other than what you *r*
11:24 *r* forty strokes less one
Ga 4:14 *r* me like an angel of God
Php 3:12 Not that I have already *r* it
4:18 have *r* from Epaphroditus the
Col 4:10 *r* commands to welcome him
1Th 2:13 when you *r* God's word
4:1 *r* the instruction from us on
2Th 3:6 the tradition you *r* from us
1Ti 3:16 was *r* up in glory
4:4 if it is *r* with thanksgiving
Heb 2:2 *r* a retribution in harmony
10:26 *r* the accurate knowledge
11:11 Sarah herself *r* power to
11:17 had gladly *r* the promises
11:31 because she *r* the spies in a
11:35 Women *r* their dead by
11:36 *r* their trial by mockings
Jas 2:25 *r* the messengers hospitably
1Pe 1:18 *r* by tradition from your
4:10 as each one has *r* a gift
2Pe 1:17 *r* from God the Father honor
1Jo 2:27 anointing that you *r* from
2Jo 4 *r* commandment from the Father
Re 2:27 as I have *r* from my Father
3:3 mindful of how you have *r*
17:12 not yet *r* a kingdom, but
19:20 *r* the mark of the wild beast
20:4 not *r* the mark upon their

Receives
Mt 7:8 For everyone asking *r*, and
10:40, 40 He that *r* you *r* me also
10:40 and he that *r* me
10:40 *r* him also that sent me
10:41 *r* a prophet because he is a
10:41 *r* a righteous man because he
18:5 *r* one such young child on the
18:5 on the basis of my name *r* me
Mr 9:37 *r* one of such young children
9:37 basis of my name, *r* me
9:37 and whoever *r* me
9:37 *r*, not me only, but also
Lu 9:48 Whoever *r* this young child
9:48 on the basis of my name *r* me
9:48, 48 whoever *r* me *r* him also
11:10 For everyone asking *r*, and
Joh 7:23 *r* circumcision on a sabbath
13:20 He that *r* anyone I send
13:20 anyone I send *r* me also
13:20 In turn he that *r* me
13:20 *r* also him that sent me
16:15 *r* from what is mine and
1Co 9:24 but only one *r* the prize
Heb 6:7 *r* in return a blessing from
7:9 Levi who *r* tithes has paid
12:6 one whom he *r* as a son
Re 14:9 *r* a mark on his forehead or
14:11 *r* the mark of its name

Receiving
Ne 10:37 ones *r* a tenth in all our
Mt 20:11 *r* it they began to murmur
25:27 I would be *r* what is mine
Lu 7:22 the blind are *r* sight, the
23:41 *r* in full what we deserve
Joh 4:36 the reaper is *r* wages and
Ac 17:15 after *r* a command for Silas
20:35 in giving than there is in *r*
Ro 1:27 *r* in themselves the full
7:8 sin, *r* an inducement through
7:11 sin, *r* an inducement through
11:15 *r* of them mean but life
Php 4:15 the matter of giving and *r*
1Ti 6:2 those *r* the benefit of their
Re 2:17 knows except the one *r* it

Recent
Isa 30:33 set in order from *r* times

Recently
De 32:17 New ones who *r* came in, With
Ac 18:2 who had *r* come from Italy

Receptacle
De 23:24 not put any into a *r* of yours
1Sa 17:40 bag that served him as a *r*
2Ch 4:5 As a *r*, three thousand bath

Receptacles
Ge 42:25 filling up their *r* with
43:11 in your *r* and carry them
1Sa 9:7 has disappeared from our *r*
Mt 25:4 discreet took oil in their *r*

Reception
Ge 32:20 he will give a kindly *r*
Lu 5:29 Levi spread a big *r* feast

Rechab
2Sa 4:2 name of the other being *R*
4:5 *R* and Baanah, proceeded to go
4:6 *R* and Baanah his brother
4:9 David answered *R* and Baanah
2Ki 10:15 Jehonadab the son of *R*
10:23 Jehonadab the son of *R*
1Ch 2:55 the father of the house of *R*
Ne 3:14 Malchijah the son of *R*
Jer 35:6 Jonadab the son of *R*, our
35:8 Jehonadab the son of *R* our
35:14 Jehonadab the son of *R*, that
35:16 of Jehonadab the son of *R*
35:19 Jonadab the son of *R* a man

Rechabites
Jer 35:2 Go to the house of the *R*
35:3 all the household of the *R*
35:5 of the house of the *R*
35:18 to the household of the *R*

Reckless
Ge 49:4 With *r* license like waters

Reckon
Le 25:50 *r* with his purchaser from
Nu 23:9 they do not *r* themselves
Job 19:15 *r* me as a stranger
Ro 3:28 *r* that a man is declared
6:11 *r* yourselves to be dead
Ro 8:18 I *r* that the sufferings of
2Co 3:5 qualified to *r* anything as

Reckoned
Le 25:50 laborer are *r* he should
Nu 18:27 *r* to you as your contribution
18:30 be *r* to the Levites as the
Jos 13:3 to be *r* as belonging to the
Job 18:3 Why should we be *r* as beasts
Ps 88:4 *r* in among those going down
La 4:2 *r* as large jars of earthenware
Lu 22:37 was *r* with lawless ones
Ac 1:26 was *r* along with the eleven
1Ti 5:17 be *r* worthy of double honor
Heb 11:19 he *r* that God was able to

Reckoning
Job 19:11 *r* me as an adversary of his
2Co 5:19 *r* to them their trespasses

Reclaim
Ex 6:6 *r* you with an outstretched arm
Job 3:5 darkness and deep shadow *r* it
Ps 69:18 come near to my soul, *r* it
Jer 31:11 Jacob and *r* him out of the

Reclaimed
Ps 106:10 *r* them from the hand of the
107:2 *r* ones of Jehovah say so
107:2 *r* from the hand of the

Reclaiming
Ps 103:4 *r* your life from the very

Recline
Ge 18:4 Then *r* under the tree
Mt 8:11 and *r* at the table with
14:19 commanded the crowds to *r*
15:35 instructing the crowd to *r*
Mr 6:39 the people to *r* by companies
8:6 crowd to *r* on the ground
Lu 9:14 *r* as at meals, in groups of
9:15 did so and had them all *r*
12:37 make them *r* at the table
13:29 will *r* at the table in the
14:10 go and *r* in the lowest place
17:7 at once and *r* at the table
Joh 6:10 Have the men *r* as at meal

Reclined
De 33:3 And they—they *r* at your feet
Lu 7:36 and *r* at the table
11:37 went in and *r* at the table
22:14 he *r* at the table, and the
Joh 6:10 Therefore the men *r*, about

Reclining
Mt 9:10 *r* at the table in the house
9:10 began *r* with Jesus and his
14:9 and for those *r* with him
22:10 with those *r* at the table
26:7 as he was *r* at the table
26:20 he was *r* at the table with
Mr 2:15 *r* at the table in his house
2:15 sinners were *r* with Jesus
6:22 Herod and those *r* with him
6:26 and those *r* at the table
14:3 as he was *r* at the meal, a
14:18 they were *r* at the table and
Lu 5:29 were with them *r* at the meal
7:37 *r* at a meal in the house of
7:49 At this those *r* at the table
22:27 the one *r* at the table or
22:27 the one *r* at the table
24:30 he was *r* with them at the
Joh 6:11 distributed them to those *r*
12:2 those *r* at the table with
13:23 *r* in front of Jesus' bosom
13:28 none of those *r* at the table
1Co 8:10 *r* at a meal in an idol

Recognition
Ps 142:4 no one giving any *r* to me
Da 11:39 given him *r* he will make
Ro 8:29 he gave his first *r* he also

Recognize
Ge 27:23 And he did not *r* him
42:8 they themselves did not *r* him
De 21:17 *r* as the firstborn the hated
Ru 3:14 before anyone could *r* another
1Sa 26:17 Saul began to *r* the voice
1Ki 20:41 king of Israel got to *r* him
Job 2:12 they did not then *r* him
4:16 I did not *r* its appearance
24:13 They did not *r* its ways
24:17 *r* what the sudden terrors
Isa 61:9 seeing them will *r* them
63:16 Israel himself may not *r* us

2Ch 22:10 As *r* Athaliah the mother of
24:7 *r* Athaliah the wicked woman
31:2 as *r* the burnt offering and
34:26 As *r* the words that you
Ezr 9:1 as *r* their detestable things
Ne 9:33 are righteous as *r* all that
11:25 as *r* the settlements in
Es 1:8 As *r* the time of drinking
4:11 as *r* any man or woman that
Job 6:14 As *r* anyone who withholds
41:27 It *r* iron as mere straw
Ps 17:11 As *r* our steps, now they
71:22 As *r* your trueness, O my God
115:16 As *r* the heavens, to Jehovah
139:16 *r* the days when they were
Pr 2:22 As *r* the wicked, they will
6:26 *r* another man's wife, she
10:6 *r* the mouth of the wicked
10:11 *r* the mouth of the wicked
14:22 as *r* those devising good
20:24 As *r* earthling man, how can
Ec 2:14 As *r* anyone wise, his eyes
5:2 hurry yourself as *r* your mouth
12:12 As *r* anything besides these
Isa 19:11 *r* the wise ones of
26:18 accomplish as *r* the land
32:8 *r* the generous one, it is for
58:13 *r* doing your own delights
66:18 as *r* their works and their
Jer 21:11 as *r* the household of the
23:9 As *r* the prophets, my heart
25:31 As *r* the wicked ones, he
28:8 As *r* the prophets that
28:9 As *r* the prophet that
44:16 *r* the word that you have
46:13 prophet as *r* the coming
52:7 as *r* all the men of war
52:21 *r* the pillars, eighteen
52:22 *r* the network and the
Eze 7:12 As *r* the buyer, let him not
7:12 as *r* the seller, let him not
9:3 as *r* the glory of the God of
10:13 As *r* the wheels, to them it
11:5 as *r* the things that come up
11:7 As *r* your slain ones whom
11:15 as *r* your brothers, your
12:10 As *r* the chieftain, there is
12:12 as *r* the chieftain who is
14:3 as *r* these men, they have
14:13 as *r* a land, in case it
16:4 as *r* your birth, on the day
16:27 your way as *r* loose conduct
17:21 *r* all the fugitives of his
18:5 And as *r* a man, in case he
18:19 as *r* the son, justice and
18:21 as *r* someone wicked, in
20:16 as *r* my statutes, they did
23:45 as *r* righteous men, they
30:16 as *r* Noph—there will be
33:2 As *r* a land, in case I bring
33:6 as *r* the watchman, in case
33:7 as *r* you, O son of man
33:9 as *r* you, in case you
33:10 as *r* you, O son of man
33:12 as *r* the wickedness of the
34:28 as *r* the wild beast of the
34:31 as *r* you my sheep, the
37:8 as *r* breath, there was none
37:11 as *r* these bones, they are
39:1 as *r* you, O son of man
39:17 as *r* you, O son of man
41:8 As *r* the foundations of the
42:5 as *r* the building
44:2 As *r* this gate, shut is how
44:14 *r* all its service and as
44:14 *r* all that should be done
45:8 As *r* the land, it will
45:11 *r* the ephah and the bath
45:24 *r* oil, a hin to the ephah
46:1 As *r* the gate of the inner
46:5 *r* oil, a hin to the ephah
46:7 *r* oil, a hin to the ephah
46:10 *r* the chieftain in their
46:11 *r* oil, a hin to the ephah
46:14 as *r* oil, the third of a hin
46:17 inheritance—as *r* his sons
48:9 *r* the contribution that you
48:15 *r* the five thousand cubits
48:22 *r* the possession of the
48:23 *r* the rest of the tribes
Da 1:14 listened . . . as *r* this matter
1:20 *r* every matter of wisdom and
2:29 *r* what is to occur after this
2:32 *r* that image, its head was
Da 5:1 As *r* Belshazzar the king, he
5:6 as *r* the king, his very
5:10 As *r* the queen, because of
8:5 as *r* the he-goat, there was a
11:17 *r* the daughter of womankind
11:22 as *r* the arms of the flood
11:27 And as *r* these two kings
11:32 *r* the people who are knowing
11:33 *r* those having insight among
11:42 *r* the land of Egypt, she
Ho 9:8 As *r* a prophet, there is the
9:11 As *r* Ephraim, like a flying
10:3 as *r* the king, what will he
12:7 As *r* the tradesman, in his
12:8 As *r* all my toiling, they
Joe 3:17 as *r* strangers, they will
3:19 As *r* Egypt, a desolate waste
3:19 and as *r* Edom, a wilderness
Am 5:5 as *r* Bethel, it will become
7:11 as *r* Israel, it will without
7:17 As *r* your wife, in the city
7:17 And as *r* your sons and your
7:17 as *r* your ground, by the
7:17 as *r* you yourself, on unclean
7:17 as *r* Israel, it will without
Zep 2:4 as *r* Gaza, an abandoned city
2:4 As *r* Ashdod, at high noon
2:4 *r* Ekron, she will be uprooted
3:13 As *r* the remaining ones of
Hag 1:2 As *r* this people, they have
Zec 1:6 as *r* my words and my
14:16 as *r* everyone who is left
14:17 as *r* anyone that does not
Mt 22:31 As *r* the resurrection of the
Joh 17:2 *r* the whole number whom you
Ac 28:22 as *r* this sect it is known
Ga 5:6 as *r* Christ Jesus neither
1Th 4:12 as *r* people outside and not
2Ti 3:8 disapproved as *r* the faith
Heb 6:4 as *r* those who have once for
1Jo 3:20 as *r* whatever our hearts

Regem
1Ch 2:47 the sons of Jahdai were *R*

Regem-melech
Zec 7:2 and *R* and his men to soften

Region
Ge 10:30 Sephar, the mountainous *r*
12:8 mountainous *r* to the east of
13:10 well-watered *r* before
14:10 fled to the mountainous *r*
19:17 Escape to the mountainous *r*
19:19 escape to the mountainous *r*
19:30 in the mountainous *r*, and
31:21 the mountainous *r* of Gilead
31:23 the mountainous *r* of Gilead
31:25 the mountainous *r* of Gilead
36:8 in the mountainous *r* of Seir
36:9 in the mountainous *r* of Seir
50:10 in the *r* of the Jordan
50:11 in the *r* of the Jordan
Nu 13:17 up into the mountainous *r*
13:29 in the mountainous *r*, and
21:13 in the *r* of the Arnon, which
34:15 *r* of the Jordan by Jericho
De 1:1 in the *r* of the Jordan in the
1:5 In the *r* of the Jordan in the
1:6 in this mountainous *r*
1:7 mountainous *r* of the Amorites
1:7 the mountainous *r* and the
1:19 mountainous *r* of the Amorites
1:20 mountainous *r* of the Amorites
1:24 up into the mountainous *r*
2:37 cities of the mountainous *r*
3:4 the *r* of Argob, the kingdom of
3:8 were in the *r* of the Jordan
3:12 the mountainous *r* of Gilead
3:13 the *r* of Argob of all Bashan
3:14 took all the *r* of Argob as far
3:25 mountainous *r* and Lebanon
4:46 the *r* of the Jordan in the
4:47 in the *r* of the Jordan toward
4:49 Arabah in the *r* of the Jordan
8:7 and in the mountainous *r*
33:2 the mountainous *r* of Paran
Jos 2:16 Go to the mountainous *r*
2:22 came to the mountainous *r*
2:23 from the mountainous *r* and
9:1 Jordan in the mountainous *r*
10:6 inhabiting the mountainous *r*
10:40 land of the mountainous *r*
11:2 the mountainous *r* and in the
11:3 in the mountainous *r* and
Jos 11:16 the mountainous *r* and all
11:16 mountainous *r* of Israel and
11:21 from the mountainous *r*
11:21 the mountainous *r* of Judah
11:21 mountainous *r* of Israel
12:8 the mountainous *r* and in the
13:6 of the mountainous *r*
14:12 give me this mountainous *r*
15:47 Great Sea and the adjacent *r*
15:48 mountainous *r* Shamir and
16:1 the mountainous *r* of Bethel
17:15 mountainous *r* of Ephraim
17:16 mountainous *r* is not enough
17:18 mountainous *r* should become
19:29 the sea in the *r* of Achzib
19:50 mountainous *r* of Ephraim
20:7 mountainous *r* of Naphtali
20:7 mountainous *r* of Ephraim
20:7 the mountainous *r* of Judah
20:8 *r* of the Jordan, at Jericho
21:11 the mountainous *r* of Judah
21:21 mountainous *r* of Ephraim
24:30 mountainous *r* of Ephraim
24:33 mountainous *r* of Ephraim
Jg 1:9 mountainous *r* and the Negeb
1:19 the mountainous *r*, but he
1:34 Dan into the mountainous *r*
2:9 the mountainous *r* of Ephraim
3:27 the mountainous *r* of Ephraim
3:27 out of the mountainous *r*, he
4:5 the mountainous *r* of Ephraim
7:24 the mountainous *r* of Ephraim
7:25 Gideon in the *r* of the Jordan
10:1 the mountainous *r* of Ephraim
11:18 in the *r* of the Arnon; and
17:1 the mountainous *r* of Ephraim
17:8 mountainous *r* of Ephraim as
18:2 the mountainous *r* of Ephraim
18:13 the mountainous *r* of Ephraim
19:1 the mountainous *r* of Ephraim
19:16 the mountainous *r* of Ephraim
19:18 the mountainous *r* of Ephraim
1Sa 1:1 the mountainous *r* of Ephraim
9:4 the mountainous *r* of Ephraim
13:2 the mountainous *r* of Bethel
14:22 mountainous *r* of Ephraim
23:14 mountainous *r* in the
31:7 *r* of the low plain and that
31:7 in the *r* of the Jordan saw
2Sa 10:16 in the *r* of the River
20:21 mountainous *r* of Ephraim
1Ki 4:8 mountainous *r* of Ephraim
4:12 to the *r* of Jokmeam
4:13 he had the *r* of Argob, which
4:24 in every *r* of his, all around
12:25 mountainous *r* of Ephraim
2Ki 5:22 the mountainous *r* of Ephraim
6:17 mountainous *r* was full of
1Ch 6:67 the mountainous *r* of Ephraim
6:78 *r* of the Jordan at Jericho
19:16 were in the *r* of the River
26:30 *r* of the Jordan to the west
2Ch 13:4 mountainous *r* of Ephraim
15:8 mountainous *r* of Ephraim
19:4 mountainous *r* of Ephraim
20:2 crowd from the *r* of the sea
20:10 mountainous *r* of Seir, whom
20:22 mountainous *r* of Seir who
20:23 mountainous *r* of Seir to
27:4 the mountainous *r* of Judah
Ne 8:15 Go out to the mountainous *r*
Job 1:19 from the *r* of the wilderness
30:3 Gnawing at a waterless *r*
Ps 68:15 The mountainous *r* of Bashan
68:15 The mountainous *r* of Bashan
78:17 in the waterless *r*
78:54 mountainous *r* that his right
107:35 waterless *r* into outflows
Ca 4:1 the mountainous *r* of Gilead
Isa 7:20 in the *r* of the River, even
9:1 *r* of the Jordan, Galilee of
18:1 *r* of the rivers of Ethiopia
24:15 in the *r* of light they
35:1 waterless *r* will exult, and
47:15 each one to his own *r*
Jer 4:15 the mountainous *r* of Ephraim
17:26 from the mountainous *r* and
25:22 that is in the *r* of the sea
31:6 the mountainous *r* of Ephraim
32:44 cities of the mountainous *r*
33:13 cities of the mountainous *r*
50:19 mountainous *r* of Ephraim
Eze 35:2 the mountainous *r* of Seir
35:3 mountainous *r* of Seir, and

Eze 35:7 the mountainous *r* of Seir
35:15 O mountainous *r* of Seir
38:21 all my mountainous *r* a
47:8 eastern *r* and must go down
Ob 8 the mountainous *r* of Esau
9 the mountainous *r* of Esau
19 of the mountainous *r* of Esau
21 judge the mountainous *r* of Esau
Zep 2:5 inhabiting the *r* of the sea
2:6 the *r* of the sea must become
2:7 a *r* for the remaining ones of
2:13 a waterless *r* like the
3:10 *r* of the rivers of Ethiopia
Mt 4:16 in a *r* of deathly shadow
9:26 spread out into all that *r*
9:31 about him in all that *r*
Mr 6:55 ran around all that *r* and

Regions
Jos 13:2 all the *r* of the Philistines
22:10 came to the *r* of the Jordan
22:11 in the *r* of the Jordan on
2Ki 19:23 the height of mountainous *r*
Ps 72:9 inhabitants of waterless *r*
74:14 inhabiting the waterless *r*
105:41 the waterless *r* as a river
Isa 7:11 it high as the upper *r*
13:21 haunters of waterless *r*
34:14 haunters of waterless *r*
37:24 height of mountainous *r*
Jer 48:28 *r* of the mouth of the
49:32 *r* near it I shall bring in
50:39 haunters of waterless *r*
Joe 3:4 and all you *r* of Philistia
Mt 15:22 woman from those *r* came
15:39 came into the *r* of Magadan
Mr 7:24 went into the *r* of Tyre and
7:31 back out of the *r* of Tyre
7:31 midst of the *r* of Decapolis
Ac 8:1 the *r* of Judea and Samaria
Ro 15:23 territory in these *r*, and for
2Co 11:10 in the *r* of Achaia
Ga 1:21 went into the *r* of Syria and
Eph 4:9 descended into the lower *r*

Register
Nu 1:3 *r* them according to their
1:19 *r* them in the wilderness of
1:49 tribe of Levi you must not *r*
3:15 *R* the sons of Levi according
3:15 month old upward you should *r*
3:16 Moses began to *r* them at the
3:40 *R* all the firstborn males of
3:42 *r* all the firstborn among the
4:23 to fifty years you will *r*
4:29 Merari, you will *r* them by
4:30 to fifty years you will *r*
4:34 *r* the sons of the Kohathites
2Sa 24:2 and you men *r* the people
24:4 Joab . . . *r* the people Israel
1Ch 21:6 and Benjamin he did not *r* in
2Ch 25:5 *r* them from twenty years of
Ezr 2:62 *r* to establish their
Ne 7:64 ones that looked for their *r*
Eze 13:9 the *r* of the house of Israel

Registered
Ex 30:14 passing over to those *r*
38:25 the ones *r* of the assembly
38:26 were *r* from twenty years of
Nu 1:21 *r* . . . of the tribe of Reuben
1:22 Simeon . . . *r* ones of his
1:23 *r* . . . of the tribe of Simeon
1:25 *r* of them of the tribe of Gad
1:27 *r* . . . of the tribe of Judah
1:29 *r* . . . of the tribe of Issachar
1:31 *r* . . . of the tribe of Zebulun
1:33 *r* . . . of the tribe of Ephraim
1:35 *r* . . . the tribe of Manasseh
1:37 *r* . . . the tribe of Benjamin
1:39 *r* . . . of the tribe of Dan
1:41 *r* . . . of the tribe of Asher
1:43 *r* . . . of the tribe of Naphtali
1:44, 44 the ones *r*, whom Moses *r*
1:45 those *r* of the sons of Israel
1:46 *r* came to be six hundred and
1:47 did not get *r* in among them
2:4 the ones *r* of them are
2:6 *r* ones are fifty-four thousand
2:8 his *r* ones are fifty-seven
2:9 *r* ones of the camp of Judah
2:11 *r* ones are forty-six thousand
2:13 ones *r* of them are fifty-nine
2:15 ones *r* of them are forty-five
2:16 *r* ones of the camp of Reuben
Nu 2:19 ones *r* of them are forty
2:21 ones *r* of them are thirty-two
2:23 ones *r* of them are thirty-five
2:24 *r* ones of the camp of Ephraim
2:26 ones *r* of them are sixty-two
2:28 ones *r* of them are forty-one
2:30 ones *r* of them are
2:31 *r* ones of the camp of Dan are
2:32 *r* ones of the sons of Israel
2:32 all the *r* ones of the camps
2:33 Levites did not get *r* in
3:22 *r* ones were by number of all
3:22 *r* ones were seven thousand
3:34 *r* ones by the number of all
3:39 *r* ones of the Levites whom
3:39 Moses and Aaron *r* at the
3:43 *r* ones came to be twenty-two
4:36 ones *r* of them by their
4:37 *r* ones of the families of the
4:37 Moses and Aaron *r* at the
4:38 *r* ones of the sons of Gershon
4:40 ones *r* of them by their
4:41 *r* ones of the families of the
4:41 Moses and Aaron *r* at the
4:42 *r* ones of the families of the
4:44 ones *r* of them by their
4:45 *r* ones of the families of
4:45 Moses and Aaron *r* at the
4:46 *r* ones whom Moses and Aaron
4:46 chieftains of Israel *r* as
4:48 *r* ones came to be eight
4:49 *r* by means of Moses, each one
4:49 *r* just as Jehovah had
7:2 and standing over the ones *r*
14:29 *r* ones of all your number
26:7 Reubenites, and their *r* ones
26:18 sons of Gad, of their *r* ones
26:22 of Judah, of their *r* ones
26:25 of Issachar, of their *r* ones
26:27 Zebulunites, of their *r* ones
26:34 Manasseh, and their *r* ones
26:37 of Ephraim, of their *r* ones
26:41 sons of Benjamin . . . *r* ones
26:43 Shuhamites, of their *r* ones
26:47 of Asher, of their *r* ones
26:50 of Naphtali . . . *r* ones
26:51 *r* ones of the sons of Israel
26:54 in proportion to his *r* ones
26:57 the *r* ones of the Levites
26:62 And their *r* ones amounted to
26:62 not get *r* in among the sons
26:63 ones *r* by Moses and Eleazar
26:63 they *r* the sons of Israel in
26:64 those *r* by Moses and Aaron
26:64 *r* the sons of Israel in the
Lu 2:1 all the inhabited earth to be *r*
2:3 people went traveling to be *r*
2:5 to get *r* with Mary, who had

Registration
2Sa 24:9 *r* of the people to the king
1Ch 21:5 the *r* of the people to David
2Ch 26:11 *r* by the hand of Jeiel the
Lu 2:2 this first *r* took place when
Ac 5:37 rose in the days of the *r*

Regret
Ge 6:7 I do *r* that I have made them
Ex 13:17 feel *r* when they see war and
32:12 feel *r* over the evil against
32:14 feel *r* over the evil that he
Nu 23:19 that he should feel *r*
De 32:36 feel *r* over his servants
Jg 2:18 Jehovah would feel *r* over
21:6 Israel began to feel *r* over
21:15 people felt *r* over Benjamin
1Sa 15:11 *r* that I have caused Saul
2Sa 24:16 Jehovah began to feel *r* over
1Ch 21:15 Jehovah . . . began to feel *r*
Ps 90:13 feel *r* over your servants
106:45 *r* according to the abundance
110:4 and he will feel no *r*
135:14 he will feel *r* even over
Jer 4:28 I have not felt *r*, nor shall
15:6 have got tired of feeling *r*
18:8 feel *r* over the calamity
18:10 also feel *r* over the good
20:16 while He has felt no *r*
26:3 feel *r* for the calamity
26:13 feel *r* for the calamity
26:19 Jehovah got to feeling *r*
31:19 turning back I felt *r*
42:10 feel *r* over the calamity
Eze 24:14 I feel sorry nor feel *r*
Joe 2:13 *r* on account of the calamity
Joe 2:14 feel *r* and let remain after
Am 7:3 Jehovah felt *r* over this
7:6 Jehovah felt *r* over this
Jon 3:9 feel *r* and turn back from his
3:10 God felt *r* over the calamity
4:2 feeling *r* over the calamity
Zec 8:14 has said, and I felt no *r*
Mt 21:30 he felt *r* and went out
21:32 did not feel *r* afterwards so
Ro 11:29 are not things he will *r*
2Co 7:8 by my letter, I do not *r* it
7:8 Even if I did at first *r* it
Heb 7:21 and he will feel no *r*

Regrets
Ge 6:6 Jehovah felt *r* that he had
1Sa 15:29 and He will not feel *r*, for
15:29 man so as to feel *r*
Zec 1:17 feel *r* over Zion and yet

Regretted
1Sa 15:35 *r* that he had made Saul
2Co 7:10 salvation that is not to be *r*

Regular
Le 5:10 according to the *r* procedure
9:16 according to the *r* procedure
15:25 the *r* time of her menstrual
Nu 9:3 its *r* procedures you should
9:14 *r* procedure is the way he
15:24 according to the *r* procedure
29:6 the *r* procedure for them, as
29:18 according to the *r* procedure
29:21 according to the *r* procedure
29:24 according to the *r* procedure
29:27 according to the *r* procedure
29:30 according to the *r* procedure
29:33 according to the *r* procedure
29:37 according to the *r* procedure
Job 24:14 night he becomes a *r* thief
Ac 19:39 be decided in a *r* assembly

Regularly
Ex 19:22 who *r* come near to Jehovah
Le 4:24 offering is *r* slaughtered
4:33 offering is *r* slaughtered
4:35 sacrifice is *r* removed
6:10 the fire *r* consumes upon the
6:25 offering is *r* slaughtered
7:2 they *r* slaughter the burnt
14:13 offering are *r* slaughtered
Nu 4:9 with which they *r* minister to
4:12 with which they *r* minister
4:14 with which they *r* minister at
4:26 with which work is *r* done
17:4 where I *r* present myself to
De 12:31 they *r* burn in the fire to
1Sa 18:13 he *r* went out and came in
1Ki 3:3 he was *r* sacrificing and
4:22 *r* proved to be thirty cor
10:5 sacrifices that he *r* offered
2Ki 13:20 Moabites that *r* came into
2Ch 8:18 Hiram *r* sent to him by means
9:4 *r* offered up at the house of
28:4 he *r* sacrificed and made
Ne 13:5 *r* putting the grain offering
13:22 be *r* purifying themselves
Es 9:21 *r* holding the fourteenth day
9:27 the obligation to be *r* holding
Ps 104:11 zebras *r* quench their thirst
Da 6:10 been *r* doing prior to this

Regulation
Ex 12:24 *r* for you and your sons to
15:25 He established for them a *r*
29:28 by a *r* to time indefinite
30:21 a *r* to time indefinite
Le 6:22 It is a *r* to time indefinite
7:34 as a *r* to time indefinite
24:9 as a *r* to time indefinite
Jos 24:25 to constitute for them a *r*
Jg 11:39 it came to be a *r* in Israel
1Sa 30:25 set as a *r* and a judicial
1Ch 16:17 as a *r* even to Jacob
2Ch 35:25 set as a *r* over Israel
Ezr 7:10 teach in Israel *r* and justice
Es 2:12 women's *r* for twelve months
Job 28:26 he made for the rain a *r*
38:10 to break up my *r* upon it
Ps 81:4 For it is a *r* for Israel
99:7 *r* that he gave to them
105:10 as a *r* even to Jacob
148:6 *r* he has given, and it will
Isa 24:5 changed the *r*, broken the
Jer 5:22 *r* that it cannot pass over

Ps 53:6 Jacob be joyful, let Israel *r*
58:10 The righteous one will *r*
63:11 king himself will *r* in God
64:10 righteous one will *r* in
66:6 There we began to *r* in him
67:4 groups *r* and cry out joyfully
68:3 the righteous, let them *r*
69:32 see it; they will *r*
70:4 May those exult and *r* in you
85:6 people themselves may *r* in
86:4 the soul of your servant *r*
89:42 caused all his enemies to *r*
90:14 may *r* during all our days
90:15 *r* correspondingly to the
92:4 you have made me *r*, O Jehovah
96:11 Let the heavens *r*, and let
97:1 Let the many islands *r*
97:8 Zion heard and began to *r*
97:12 *R* in Jehovah, O you righteous
104:15 heart of mortal man *r*
104:31 Jehovah will *r* in his works
104:34 my part, shall *r* in Jehovah
105:3 of those seeking Jehovah *r*
106:5 *r* with the rejoicing of your
107:30 *r* because these become
107:42 upright ones see and *r*
109:28 let your own servant *r*
118:24 will be joyful and *r* in it
119:74 ones that see me and *r*
149:2 Israel *r* in its grand Maker
Pr 5:18 *r* with the wife of your youth
10:1 one that makes a father *r*
12:25 word is what makes it *r*
13:9 the righteous ones will *r*
15:20 one that makes a father *r*
15:30 the eyes makes the heart *r*
17:21 the father . . . does not *r*
23:15 wise, my heart will *r*
23:24 will also *r* in him
23:25 and your mother will *r*, and
24:17 your enemy falls, do not *r*
27:9 are what make the heart *r*
27:11 make my heart *r*, that I may
29:2 become many, the people *r*
29:3 wisdom makes his father *r*
Ec 3:12 *r* and to do good during one's
3:22 the man should *r* in his works
4:16 people afterward *r* in him
5:19 and to *r* in his hard work
8:15 than to eat and drink and *r*
10:19 and wine itself makes life *r*
11:8 in all of them let him *r*
11:9 *R*, young man, in your youth
Ca 1:4 let us be joyful and *r* in you
Isa 9:17 Jehovah will not *r* even over
14:29 Do not *r*, O Philistia
25:9 *r* in the salvation by him
39:2 Hezekiah began to *r* over
56:7 *r* inside my house of prayer
65:13 own servants will *r*, but
66:10 *R* with Jerusalem and be
Jer 20:15 He positively made him *r*
31:13 virgin will *r* in the dance
31:13 *r* away from their grief
41:13 they began to *r*
La 2:17 he causes the enemy to *r*
4:21 and *r*, O daughter of Edom
Eze 7:12 the buyer, let him not *r*
Ho 7:3 they make the king *r*, and
9:1 Do not *r*, O Israel. Do not
Joe 2:21 Be joyful and *r*; for Jehovah
2:23 Zion, be joyful and *r* in
Ob 12 not to *r* at the sons of Judah
Jon 4:6 Jonah began to *r* greatly over
Mic 7:8 Do not *r* over me, O you
Zep 3:14 *R* and exult with all the
Zec 2:10 and *r*, O daughter of Zion
4:10 *r* and see the plummet in the
10:7 their heart must *r* as though
10:7 will see and certainly *r*
Mt 5:12 *R* and leap for joy, since
Lu 1:14 many will *r* over his birth
1:58 and they began to *r* with her
6:23 *R* in that day and leap, for
10:20 do not *r* over this, that the
10:20 *r* because your names have
13:17 the crowd began to *r* at all
15:6 *R* with me, because I have
15:9 *R* with me, because I have
15:32 *r*, because this your brother
19:37 disciples started to *r* and
Joh 4:36 sower and the reaper may *r*
5:35 to *r* greatly in his light
11:15 I *r* on your account that I
Joh 14:28 *r* that I am going my way
16:20 but the world will *r*
16:22 and your hearts will *r*
Ac 13:48 to *r* and to glorify the word
Ro 12:12 *R* in the hope. Endure under
12:15, 15 *R* with people who *r*
16:19 I therefore *r* over you
1Co 7:30 who *r* as those who do not
7:30 as those who do not *r*, and
12:26 the other members *r* with it
13:6 not *r* over unrighteousness
16:17 I *r* over the presence of
2Co 2:3 those over whom I ought to *r*
7:9 I *r*, not because you were
7:16 I *r* that in every way I may
13:9 *r* whenever we are weak but
13:11 brothers, continue to *r*, to
Php 1:18 publicized, and in this I *r*
2:17 glad and I *r* with all of you
2:18 be glad and *r* with me
2:28 seeing him you may *r* again
4:4 Always *r* in the Lord
4:4 Once more I will say, *R!*
4:10 I do *r* greatly in the Lord
1Pe 4:13 you may *r* and be overjoyed
2Jo 4 I *r* very much because I have
Re 11:10 dwelling on the earth *r*
19:7 Let us *r* and be overjoyed

Rejoiced

Jg 19:3 he at once *r* to meet him
1Ch 29:9 David the king himself *r*
2Ch 29:36 *r* over the fact that the
Ne 12:43 *r*, so that the rejoicing
Ps 35:15 But at my limping they *r*
105:38 Egypt *r* when they went out
122:1 *r* when they were saying to
Isa 9:3 They have *r* before you as
14:8 juniper trees have also *r*
Mt 2:10 On seeing the star they *r*
Mr 14:11 they *r* and promised to give
Lu 22:5 they *r* and agreed to give him
23:8 Herod saw Jesus he *r* greatly
Joh 8:56 Abraham your father *r*
8:56 my day, and he saw it and *r*
20:20 disciples *r* at seeing the
Ac 2:26 and my tongue *r* greatly
11:23 he *r* and began to encourage
15:31 *r* over the encouragement
16:34 he *r* greatly with all his
2Co 7:7 so that I *r* yet more
7:13 we *r* still more abundantly
3Jo 3 I *r* very much when brothers

Rejoices

Ps 21:1 in your strength the king *r*
33:21 For in him our heart *r*
Eze 35:14 that all the earth *r*
Hab 1:15 why he *r* and is joyful
Mt 18:13 he *r* more over it than over
Lu 15:5 it upon his shoulders and *r*
1Co 13:6 but *r* with the truth

Rejoicing

Ge 31:27 send you away with *r* and
Nu 10:10 day of your *r* and in your
De 28:47 serve . . . God with *r* and joy
Jg 16:23 they gathered . . . for *r*, and
1Sa 6:13 gave way to *r* at seeing it
11:9 and they gave way to *r*
11:15 Israel continued *r* to a
18:6 with tambourines, with *r*
19:5 and you gave way to *r*
2Sa 6:12 to the city of David with *r*
1Ki 1:40 *r* with great joy, so that
1:45 they came up from there *r*
4:20 eating and drinking and *r*
8:66 *r* and feeling merry of heart
2Ki 11:14 the people of the land *r*
1Ch 12:40 for there was *r* in Israel
15:16 to cause a sound of *r* to
15:25 bring up the ark . . . with *r*
29:9 people gave way to *r* over
29:22 on that day with great *r*
2Ch 15:15 Judah gave way to *r* over
20:27 return to Jerusalem with *r*
23:13 *r* and blowing the trumpets
23:18 *r* and with song by the
29:30 offer praise even with *r*
30:21 seven days with great *r*
30:23 it for seven days with *r*
30:25 in Judah continued *r*
30:26 to be great *r* in Jerusalem
Ezr 3:13 sound of the shout of *r* from
6:22 seven days with *r*
Ne 8:12 and to carry on a great *r*
8:17 came to be very great *r*
12:27 *r* even with thanksgivings
12:43 *r* of Jerusalem could be
12:44 the *r* of Judah was because
Es 8:16 *r* and exultation and honor
8:17 *r* and exultation for the Jews
9:17 a day of banqueting and of *r*
9:18 a day of banqueting and of *r*
9:19 a *r* and a banqueting and a
9:22 from grief to *r* and from
9:22 days of banqueting and *r* and
Job 3:22 who are *r* to gleefulness
20:5 the *r* of an apostate is for a
21:12 *r* at the sound of the pipe
Ps 4:7 certainly give a *r* in my heart
16:11 *R* to satisfaction is with
21:6 glad with the *r* at your face
30:11 you keep me girded with *r*
43:4 To God, my exultant *r*
45:15 They will be brought with *r*
51:8 to hear exultation and *r*
68:3 And let them exult with *r*
97:11 *r* even for the ones upright
100:2 Serve Jehovah with *r*
106:5 with the *r* of your nation
137:3 those mocking us—for *r*
137:6 Above my chief cause for *r*
Pr 2:14 those who are *r* in doing bad
10:28 of the righteous ones is a *r*
12:20 those counseling peace have *r*
14:10 with its *r* no stranger will
14:13 grief is what *r* ends up in
15:21 Foolishness is a *r* to one
15:23 *r* in the answer of his mouth
21:15 *r* for the righteous one to do
Ec 2:1 let me try you out with *r*
2:2 and to *r*: What is this doing?
2:10 my heart from any sort of *r*
2:26 wisdom and knowledge and *r*
5:20 with the *r* of his heart
7:4 ones is in the house of *r*
8:15 myself commended *r*, because
9:7 eat your food with *r* and drink
Ca 3:11 the day of the *r* of his heart
Isa 9:3 you have made the *r* great
9:3 with the *r* in the harvesttime
16:10 *r* and joyfulness have been
22:13 look! exultation and *r*
24:11 All *r* has passed away
29:19 increase their *r* in Jehovah
30:29 *r* of heart like that of
35:10 *r* to time indefinite will
35:10 and *r* they will attain, and
51:3 Exultation and *r* themselves
51:11 and *r* to time indefinite
51:11 To exultation and *r* they
55:12 with *r* you people will go
61:7 *R* to time indefinite is what
66:5 must also appear with *r*
Jer 7:34 the voice of *r*, the voice of
15:16 and the *r* of my heart
16:9 and the voice of *r*, the
25:10 the sound of *r*, the voice
31:7 out loudly to Jacob with *r*
33:11 and the sound of *r*, the
48:33 *r* and joyfulness have been
50:11 For you men kept *r*, for
Eze 25:6 you kept *r* with all scorn
35:15 *r* on your part at the
36:5 the *r* of all the heart
Joe 1:16 from the house of our God, *r*
Am 6:13 *r* in a thing that is not
Zep 3:17 will exult over you with *r*
Zec 8:19 *r* and good festal seasons
Lu 19:6 *r* he received him as guest
Ac 2:46 food with great *r* and
5:41 *r* because they had been
8:39 he kept going on his way *r*
2Co 6:10 as sorrowing but ever *r*, as
Php 1:18 I will also keep on *r*
3:1 continue *r* in the Lord
Col 1:24 I am now *r* in my sufferings
2:5 *r* and beholding your good
1Th 3:9 we are *r* on your account
5:16 Always be *r*
1Pe 1:6 *r*, though for a little while
1:8 *r* with an unspeakable and
4:13 *r* forasmuch as you are

Rejoined

Jg 14:9 When he *r* his father and his

Rekem

Nu 31:8 kings of Midian . . . Evi and *R*

Jos 13:21 *R* and Zur and Hur and Reba
18:27 *R* and Irpeel and Taralah
1Ch 2:43 sons of Hebron were . . . *R*
2:44 *R*, in turn, became father to
7:16 and his sons were Ulam and *R*

Relate
Ge 29:13 began to *r* to Laban all
40:8 *R* it to me, please
40:9 to *r* his dream to Joseph and
41:8 Pharaoh went on to *r* his
Jos 2:23 began to *r* to him all the
2Ki 8:4 Do *r* to me, please, all the
8:6 on to *r* to him the story
1Ch 16:24 *R* among the nations his
Es 6:13 Haman went on to *r* to Zeresh
Job 15:17 have beheld, so let me *r* it
Ps 66:16 I will *r* What he has done
78:6 and *r* them to their sons
Jer 23:28 let him *r* the dream
23:32 *r* them and cause my people
Mr 9:9 not to *r* to anybody what they
Ac 14:27 to *r* the many things God had
15:12 Barnabas and Paul *r* the many
Eph 5:12 it is shameful even to *r*
Heb 11:32 if I go on to *r* about Gideon

Related
Ge 37:9 he *r* it to his brothers and
37:10 Then he *r* it to his father
41:12 When we *r* them to him, he
Ex 24:3 Then Moses came and *r* to the
Le 25:25 repurchaser closely *r* to him
Jg 6:13 acts that our fathers *r* to us
Ru 2:20 The man is *r* to us
3:12 repurchaser closer *r* than I
2Sa 19:42 the king is closely *r* to us
1Ki 13:11 *r* to him all the work that
Job 37:20 Should it be *r* to him that
Ps 78:3 our own fathers have *r* to us
Hab 1:5 not believe although it is *r*
Mr 5:16 those who had seen it *r* to
Lu 24:35 *r* the events on the road and
Ac 10:8 he *r* everything to them and
15:14 Symeon has *r* thoroughly how
Ga 6:10 those *r* to us in the faith
Phm 6 as *r* to Christ

Relates
Ac 13:41 anyone *r* it to you in detail

Relating
Ge 24:66 servant went *r* to Isaac all
Ex 18:8 And Moses went to *r* to his
Jg 7:13 was a man *r* a dream to his
7:15 heard the *r* of the dream and
1Sa 11:5 began *r* to him the words
1Ki 13:11 *r* them to their father
2Ki 8:5 was *r* to the king how he had
Ps 78:4 *R* them even to the generation
Jer 23:27 *r* each one to the other
Lu 8:39 keep on *r* what things God did
Ac 15:3 *r* in detail the conversion of

Relation
Le 18:12 is the blood *r* of your father
18:13 is a blood *r* of your mother
20:19 his blood *r* that one has
21:2 *r* of his who is close to him
Nu 27:11 inheritance to his blood *r*
27:14 in *r* to sanctifying me by
2Ch 3:8 its length in *r* to the width
Ec 1:13 wisdom in *r* to everything
12:14 in *r* to every hidden thing
Mt 5:19 least in *r* to the kingdom of
5:19 great in *r* to the kingdom of
1Co 7:14 sanctified in *r* to his wife
7:14 is sanctified in *r* to the
9:2 apostleship in *r* to the Lord

Relations
Ge 6:4 *r* with the daughters of men
16:2 have *r* with my maidservant
16:4 he had *r* with Hagar, and she
19:31 *r* with us according to the
29:21 let me have *r* with her
29:23 he might have *r* with her
29:30 he had *r* also with Rachel
30:3 Have *r* with her, that she may
30:4 and Jacob had *r* with her
30:16 you are going to have *r*
38:2 took her and had *r* with her
38:8 Have *r* with your brother's
38:9 *r* with his brother's wife
38:16 please, to have *r* with you
38:16 you may have *r* with me
38:18 had *r* with her, so that she
Nu 25:1 started to have immoral *r*
De 21:13 you should have *r* with her
22:13 has *r* with her and has come
Jg 11:39 she never had *r* with a man
Ru 4:13 became his wife and he had *r*
2Sa 3:7 *r* with the concubine of my
16:21 Have *r* with the concubines
16:22 Absalom began to have *r*
17:25 who had *r* with Abigail the
20:3 he did not have any *r*, but
1Ki 22:44 peaceful *r* with the king
1Ch 2:21 Hezron had *r* with the
7:23 he had *r* with his wife, so
Ps 51:*super* had had *r* with Bath-sheba
Pr 2:19 those having *r* with her will
6:29 *r* with the wife of his

Relationship
Le 18:17 They are cases of blood *r*
Jos 6:23 all her family *r* they
Col 2:11 By *r* with him you were also
2:12 by *r* with him you were also
Phm 16 in fleshly *r* and in the Lord
Jude 1 loved in *r* with God the Father

Relative
Le 18:6 any close fleshly *r* of his
25:49 *r* of his flesh, one of his
Nu 5:8 near *r* to whom to return the
2Ki 8:27 was a *r* of the house of Ahab
Ne 13:4 Eliashib . . . a *r* of Tobiah
Lu 1:36 Elizabeth your *r* has also
Joh 18:26 *r* of the man whose ear
Ro 13:1 in their *r* positions by God
16:11 Greet Herodion my *r*

Relatives
Ge 12:1 your country and from your *r*
24:4 to my country and to my *r*
24:7 land of my *r* and who spoke
31:3 Return . . . to your *r*, and I
32:9 to your land and to your *r*
43:7 concerning us and our *r*
Nu 10:30 my own country and to my *r*
Ru 2:11 and the land of your *r* and to
Es 2:10 her people or about her *r*
2:20 not telling about her *r* and
8:6 upon the destruction of my *r*
Jer 22:10 see the land of his *r*
46:16 and to the land of our *r*
Mr 3:21 But when his *r* heard about it
5:19 Go home to your *r*, and report
6:4 among his *r* and in his own
Lu 1:58 her *r* heard that Jehovah had
1:61 no one among your *r* that is
2:44 to hunt him up among the *r*
14:12 or your brothers or your *r*
21:16 delivered up even by . . . *r*
Ac 7:3 from your *r* and come on into
7:14 his father and all his *r*
10:24 called together his *r* and
Ro 9:3 my *r* according to the flesh
16:7 my *r* and my fellow captives
16:21 Jason and Sosipater my *r*

Relax
Jos 10:6 Do not let your hand *r* from

Relaxation
Ac 24:23 have some *r* of custody, and

Relaxing
Ex 5:8 because they are *r*
5:17, 17 You are *r*, you are *r!*

Release
Ge 43:14 *r* to you your other brother
De 15:1 you should make a *r*
15:2 this is the manner of the *r*
15:2 a *r* to Jehovah must be called
15:3 let your hand *r*
15:9 the year of the *r*, has come
31:10 time of the year of the *r*
Job 6:9 *r* his hand and cut me off
Ps 105:20 king sent that he might *r*
Isa 58:6 *r* the bands of the yoke bar
Mt 27:15 to *r* a prisoner to the crowd
27:17 *r* to you, Barabbas or Jesus
27:21 do you want me to *r* to you
Mr 15:6 *r* to them one prisoner, whom
15:9 *r* to you the king of the Jews
15:11 *r* Barabbas to them, instead
Lu 4:18 to preach a *r* to the captives
4:18 crushed ones away with a *r*
23:16 chastise him and *r* him
23:18 but *r* Barabbas to us!
23:20 he wanted to *r* Jesus
23:22 chastise and *r* him
Joh 18:39 *r* a man to you at the
18:39 *r* to you the king of the
19:10 I have authority to *r* you
19:12 on seeking how to *r* him
19:12 If you *r* this man, you
Ac 3:13 he had decided to *r* him
16:35 to say: *R* those men
Ro 3:24 *r* by the ransom paid by
8:23 *r* from our bodies by ransom
1Co 1:30 sanctification and *r* by
7:27 to a wife? Stop seeking a *r*
Ga 4:5 *r* by purchase those under law
Eph 1:7 *r* by ransom through the blood
Col 1:14 we have our *r* by ransom
Heb 9:15 for their *r* by ransom from
11:35 would not accept *r* by some

Released
Mt 27:26 Then he *r* Barabbas to them
Mr 15:15 *r* Barabbas to them, and
Lu 6:37 releasing, and you will be *r*
13:12 you are *r* from your weakness
23:25 he *r* the man that had been
Ac 4:21 *r* them, since they did not
4:23 *r* they went to their own
16:36 men that you two might be *r*
26:32 *r* if he had not appealed to
Ga 3:13 Christ by purchase *r* us from
Heb 13:23 brother Timothy has been *r*

Releasing
De 15:2 a *r* by every creditor of the
Ps 146:7 Jehovah is *r* those who are
Lu 6:37 Keep on *r*, and you will be
Ac 28:18 desirous of *r* me, as there
Eph 1:14 *r* by a ransom God's own
4:30 a day of *r* by ransom
Php 1:23 *r* and the being with Christ
2Ti 4:6 time for my *r* is imminent

Reliable
Da 2:45 And the dream is *r*, and the
7:16 *r* information on all this

Reliant
Ps 112:7 made *r* upon Jehovah

Relied
2Co 1:18 God can be *r* upon that our

Relief
Ex 8:15 Pharaoh got to see that *r* had
1Sa 16:23 and there was *r* for Saul
Es 4:14 *r* and deliverance themselves
Job 14:14 wait, Until my *r* comes
32:20 speak that it may be a *r*
Ps 66:12 to bring us forth to *r*
La 3:56 Do not hide your ear to my *r*
Na 3:19 no *r* for your catastrophe
Ac 11:29 send a *r* ministration to the
12:25 *r* ministration in Jerusalem
2Co 2:13 I got no *r* in my spirit on
7:5 our flesh got no *r*, but we
2Th 1:7 who suffer tribulation, *r*

Relieve
Isa 1:24 *r* myself of my adversaries
1Ti 5:16 has widows, let her *r* them
5:16 *r* those who are . . . widows

Relieved
1Ti 5:10 if she *r* those in tribulation

Relieves
Ps 146:9 boy and the widow he *r*

Relieving
Ps 147:6 Jehovah is *r* the meek ones

Religion
2Ki 17:26 the *r* of the God of the land
17:26 the *r* of the God of the land
17:27 *r* of the God of the land
17:33 the *r* of the nations from
17:40 to their former *r* that they

Religions
2Ki 17:34 according to their former *r*

Reluctantly
1Sa 15:32 Then Agag went to him *r*

Rely
Job 39:12 Will you *r* on it that it
Ps 37:5 *r* upon him, and he himself
Isa 31:1 those who *r* on mere horses

Relying
Pr 28:25 *r* upon Jehovah will be made

Remain
Ex 10:12 that the hail has let *r*

Ex 10:19 Not a . . . locust was let *r*
10:26 Not a hoof will . . . *r*
14:28 among them was let *r*
Le 25:52 few *r* of the years until the
Nu 5:10 things of each one will *r*
9:12 not let any of it *r* until
9:18 they would *r* encamped
9:20 they would *r* encamped
De 4:27 be let *r* few in number among
7:20 who were let *r* and who were
19:20 those who *r* will hear and be
28:51 *r* for you until they have
Jos 8:22 did not *r* of them either a
10:28 He let no survivor *r*
10:30 did not let a survivor *r*
10:33 let not a survivor of his *r*
10:37 did not let a survivor *r*
10:39 did not let a survivor *r*
10:40 did not let a survivor *r*
11:8 not let a survivor . . . *r*
11:14 let anyone that breathed *r*
23:4 these nations that *r* as an
23:7 these that *r* with you
23:12 nations, these that *r* with
Jg 6:4 or bull or ass *r* in Israel
1Sa 25:22 *r* until the morning
2Sa 8:4 chariot horses of them *r*
1Ki 15:29 anyone . . . *r* of Jeroboam's
16:11 did not let anyone of his *r*
19:18 seven thousand *r* in Israel
2Ki 10:11 let no survivor of his *r*
10:14 let a single one of them *r*
17:18 *r* but the tribe of Judah
25:12 let *r* as vinedressers and
1Ch 18:4 chariot horses of them *r*
Job 5:4 His sons *r* far from salvation
21:34 your very replies do *r* as
Pr 6:29 will *r* unpunishable
28:2 the prince will *r* long
28:20 riches will not *r* innocent
Isa 11:11 *r* over from Assyria and
11:16 people who will *r* over
16:14 those who *r* over will be a
17:6 *r* in it a gleaning as when
Jer 39:10 *r* in the land of Judah
49:9 not let some gleanings *r*
50:20 forgive those whom I let *r*
52:16 let *r* as vinedressers and
Joe 2:14 let *r* after it a blessing
Ob 5 they not let some gleanings *r*
Zep 3:12 let *r* in the midst of you a
Joh 6:12 the fragments that *r* over
8:31 If you *r* in my word, you are
8:35 the slave does not *r* in the
12:46 may not *r* in the darkness
15:4 *R* in union with me, and I
15:4 unless you *r* in union with
15:6 not *r* in union with me
15:7 If you *r* in union with me
15:7 and my sayings *r* in you
15:9 loved you, *r* in my love
15:10 you will *r* in my love, just
15:10 Father and *r* in his love
15:16 that your fruit should *r*
19:31 bodies might not *r* upon the
21:22 my will for him to *r* until
21:23 my will for him to *r* until
Ac 5:4 did it not *r* yours, and after
10:48 him to *r* for some days
14:22 to *r* in the faith and saying
15:17 those who *r* of the men may
18:20 kept requesting him to *r*
27:31 *r* in the boat, you cannot
28:14 to *r* with them seven days
Ro 9:17 very cause I have let you *r*
11:22 you *r* in his kindness
11:23 not *r* in their lack of faith
1Co 7:8 that they *r* even as I am
7:11 let her *r* unmarried or else
7:20 was called, let him *r* in it
7:24 *r* in it associated with God
13:13 there *r* faith, hope, love
15:6 the most of whom *r* to the
16:7 I hope to *r* some time with
2Co 12:9 like a tent *r* over me
Php 1:24 for me to *r* in the flesh is
1:25 I shall *r* and shall abide
Heb 1:11 yourself are to *r* continually
12:27 not being shaken may *r*
1Jo 2:24 from the beginning *r* in you
2:27 *r* in union with him
2:28 *r* in union with him, that
3:17 does the love of God *r* in
2Jo 9 does not *r* in the teaching of
2Jo 9 does *r* in this teaching is the
Re 17:10 he must *r* a short while

Remainder
Le 5:9 *r* of the blood will be drained
De 28:54 the *r* of his sons whom he
2Sa 21:2 of the *r* of the Amorites
1Ch 12:38 the *r* of Israel were of one
Ps 76:10 *r* of raging you will gird
Isa 38:10 of the *r* of my years
44:17 the *r* of it he actually
Jer 27:19 the *r* of the utensils that
29:1 the *r* of the older men of
Eze 5:10 scatter all the *r* of you to
23:25 *r* of you will fall even by
23:25 *r* of you will be devoured
Da 2:18 *r* of the wise men of Babylon
1Pe 4:2 live the *r* of his time in the

Remained
Ge 14:10 and those who *r* fled to the
30:36 flocks of Laban that *r* over
Nu 5:13 has *r* undiscovered, and she
9:22 Israel *r* encamped and would
De 3:11 only Og the king of Bashan *r*
Jos 11:22 in Ashdod that they *r*
13:12 he it was who *r* of what
Jg 4:16 Not as much as one *r*
7:3 there were ten thousand that *r*
Ru 1:3 Naomi . . . *r* with her two sons
1:5 the woman *r* without her two
1Sa 25:34 *r* to Nabal until the
26:9 and has *r* innocent
2Sa 14:7 of my charcoals that has *r*
2Ki 7:13 that have *r* in the city
7:13 of Israel that have *r* in it
Ps 19:13 I shall have *r* innocent from
Ec 2:9 my own wisdom *r* mine
Isa 24:6 few mortal men have *r* over
30:17 *r* over like a mast on the
Jer 2:35 you say, I have *r* innocent
34:7 *r* over among the cities of
37:10 *r* over among them men
Da 10:13 *r* there beside the kings of
Mt 11:23 Sodom, it would have *r*
Mr 8:2 three days that they have *r*
Lu 1:22 signs to them, but *r* dumb
1:56 Mary *r* with her about three
2:43 the boy Jesus *r* behind in
19:40 If these *r* silent, the stones
20:28 this one *r* childless, his
Joh 1:32 and it *r* upon him
7:9 he *r* in Galilee
11:6 *r* two days in the place
11:54 he *r* with the disciples
Ac 5:4 As long as it *r* with you did
7:45 it *r* until the days of David
9:43 *r* in Joppa with a certain
12:16 Peter *r* there knocking
17:14 Silas and Timothy *r* behind
21:4 *r* here seven days. But through
28:12 Syracuse we *r* three days
28:30 he *r* for an entire two years
1Jo 2:19 they would have *r* with us

Remaining
Ge 32:8 a camp *r* to make an escape
Ex 28:10 names of the six *r* ones upon
Le 26:36 those *r* among you, I shall
26:39 *r* among you, they will rot
Nu 11:26 two of the men *r* in the camp
21:35 was no survivor *r* to him
De 3:3 until he had no survivor *r*
28:54 his sons whom he has *r*
28:55 he has nothing at all *r*
Jos 8:17 not a man *r* in Ai and Bethel
13:2 This is the land yet *r*
1Ki 9:20 the people *r* over from the
2Ki 3:25 stones of Kir-hareseth *r* in
7:13 five of the *r* horses that
2Ch 36:20 those *r* from the sword
Ezr 9:14 will be none *r* and none
Isa 1:8 *r* like a booth in a vineyard
1:9 *r* to us just a few survivors
4:3 ones *r* in Zion and the
7:22 *r* in the midst of the land
10:20 those *r* over of Israel and
15:9 for the *r* ones of the ground
17:3 Syria *r* over will become
21:17 ones *r* over of the number
28:5 ones *r* over of his people
37:31 those who are left *r*, will
46:3 *r* ones of the house of Israel
Jer 8:3 *r* out of this bad family
8:3 the places of the *r* ones
Jer 21:7 who are *r* over in this city
24:8 *r* over in this land and
27:18 the utensils that are *r*
27:19 the utensils that are *r*
27:21 the utensils that are *r*
34:7 of Judah that were left *r*
38:4 left *r* in this city and the
38:22 *r* in the house of the king
39:9 people who were left *r* in
39:9 people who were left *r*
40:6 who were left *r* in the land
41:10 people who were *r* over in
42:2 we have been left *r*, a few
47:4 *r* ones from the island of
50:26 come to have any *r* ones
52:15 people that were left *r* in
Eze 6:12 the one that has been left *r*
9:8 striking and I was left *r*, I
9:8 ruin all the *r* ones of Israel
11:13 with the *r* ones of Israel
12:16 leave *r* from them a few
14:22 *r* in it an escaped company
17:21 *r* will be spread abroad
36:3 the *r* ones of the nations
36:4 the *r* ones of the nations
36:5 the *r* ones of the nations
36:36 *r* round about you will
39:14 *r* on the surface of the
39:28 leave none of them *r* there
48:15 left *r* in width alongside
48:18 left *r* over in length will
Da 10:8 I was left *r* by myself, so
10:8 left *r* in me no power, and
10:17 no breath at all was left *r*
Am 1:8 the *r* ones of the Philistines
5:15 favor to the *r* ones of Joseph
6:9 if ten men should be left *r*
9:12 of what is left *r* of Edom
Mic 2:12 collect the *r* ones of Israel
5:7 the *r* ones of Jacob must
5:8 the *r* ones of Jacob must
Hab 2:8 the *r* ones of the peoples
Zep 1:4 the *r* ones of the Baal
2:7 *r* ones of the house of Judah
2:9 The *r* ones of my people will
3:13 the *r* ones of Israel, they
Hag 1:12 all the *r* ones of the people
1:14 all the *r* ones of the people
2:2 *r* ones of the people, saying
2:3 among you that is *r* over
Zec 8:6 *r* ones of this people in those
8:11 the *r* ones of this people
8:12 the *r* ones of this people
9:7 be left *r* for our God
11:9 And as for the ones left *r*
12:14 families that are left *r*
13:8 it will be left *r* in it
14:2 the *r* ones of the people
14:16 *r* out of all the nations
Mal 2:15 what was *r* of the spirit
Lu 12:26 anxious about the *r* things
Joh 1:33 spirit coming down and *r*
5:38 not have his word *r* in you
14:25 While *r* with you I have
Ac 21:10 *r* quite a number of days, a
1Co 11:34 *r* matters I will set in
16:8 I am *r* in Ephesus until the
Col 4:2 in prayer, *r* awake in it
1Jo 3:6 Everyone *r* in union with him
3:15 everlasting life *r* in him
3:24 he is *r* in union with us
4:13 we are *r* in union with him
Re 3:2 strengthen the things *r* that
12:17 *r* ones of her seed, who

Remains
Ge 47:18 *r* nothing before my lord but
Ex 26:12 what *r* over of the cloths of
26:12 Half of the tent cloth that *r*
26:13 what *r* over in the length of
Le 25:27 return what money *r* over to
Jos 13:1 land yet *r* to be taken in
Isa 14:30 what *r* over of you will be
Joh 3:36 wrath of God *r* upon him
6:27 the food that *r* for life
6:56 *r* in union with me, and
8:35 the son *r* forever
9:41 you say, We see. Your sin *r*
12:24 it *r* just one grain
12:34 that the Christ *r* forever
14:10 Father who *r* in union with
14:17 it *r* with you and is in you
15:4 unless it *r* in the vine, in
15:5 He that *r* in union with me

Le 2:16 must make the *r* of it smoke
5:12 his handful as a *r* of it and
6:15 for a *r* of it to Jehovah
24:7 bread for a *r*, an offering
Nu 5:26 grain offering as a *r* of it

Remeth
Jos 19:21 and *R* and En-gannim and

Remind
Isa 43:26 *R* me; let us put ourselves
2Ti 1:6 I *r* you to stir up like a
2Pe 1:12 to *r* you of these things
Jude 5 I desire to *r* you, despite

Reminder
Ps 19:7 *r* of Jehovah is trustworthy
60:*super* director on The Lily of *R*
78:5 to raise up a *r* in Jacob, And
80:*super* A *r*. Of Asaph. A melody
81:5 *r* he laid it upon Joseph
119:88 keep the *r* of your mouth
122:4 As a *r* to Israel To give
2Pe 3:1 arousing . . . by way of a *r*

Reminders
2Ki 17:15 *r* with which he had warned
Ps 25:10 his covenant and his *r*
78:56 his *r* they did not keep
93:5 own *r* have proved very
99:7 They kept his *r* and the
119:2 are those observing his *r*
119:14 the way of your *r* I have
119:22 have observed your own *r*
119:24 *r* are what I am fond of
119:31 I have cleaved to your *r*
119:36 Incline my heart to your *r*
119:46 speak about your *r* in front
119:59 back my feet to your *r*
119:79 Those also knowing your *r*
119:95 *r* I keep showing myself
119:99 your *r* are a concern to me
119:111 *r* as a possession to time
119:119 I have loved your *r*
119:125 That I may know your *r*
119:129 Your *r* are wonderful
119:138 your *r* in righteousness
119:144 righteousness of your *r* is
119:146 And I will keep your *r*
119:152 have known some of your *r*
119:157 *r* I have not deviated
119:167 My soul has kept your *r*
119:168 kept your orders and your *r*
132:12 *r* that I shall teach them
Jer 44:23 in his *r* you did not walk

Reminding
Ro 15:15 as if *r* you again, because
2Ti 2:14 Keep *r* them of these things
Tit 3:1 *r* them to be in subjection
Heb 10:3 there is a *r* of sins from
2Pe 1:13 rouse you up by way of *r*

Remnant
Ge 45:7 in order to place a *r* for you
2Sa 14:7 *r* on the surface of the
2Ki 19:4 the *r* that are to be found
19:31 Jerusalem a *r* will go forth
21:14 the *r* of my inheritance
1Ch 4:43 *r* that had escaped of Amalek
Isa 10:21 mere *r* will return, the
10:21 *r* of Jacob, to the Mighty
10:22 *r* among them will return
11:11 *r* of his people who will
11:16 *r* of his people who will
14:22 *r* and progeny and posterity
37:4 prayer in behalf of the *r*
37:32 Jerusalem a *r* will go forth
Jer 6:9 *r* of Israel just like a vine
8:3 on the part of all the *r*
11:23 not even a *r* will there
15:9 I shall give the mere *r* of
23:3 the *r* of my sheep out of all
24:8 the *r* of Jerusalem who are
25:20 and the *r* of Ashdod
31:7 your people, the *r* of Israel
40:11 given a *r* to Judah and
40:15 and the *r* of Judah perish
41:10 *r* of the people who were
41:16 *r* of the people whom they
42:2 behalf of all this *r*, for
42:15 Jehovah, O *r* of Judah
42:19 against you, O *r* of Judah
43:5 took all the *r* of Judah that
44:7 leave over for yourselves a *r*
44:12 *r* of Judah who set their
44:14 survivor for the *r* of Judah
Jer 44:28 those of the *r* of Judah
47:5 *r* of their low plain, how
Eze 6:8 have as a *r* the ones escaping
Mic 4:7 her that was limping a *r*
7:18 of the *r* of his inheritance
Zep 2:9 the *r* of my own nation will
Ro 9:27 is the *r* that will be saved
11:5 *r* has turned up according to

Remorse
Mt 27:3 felt *r* and turned the thirty

Remote
Ge 49:13 *r* side will be toward Sidon
2Ki 19:25 From *r* times it is what I
Ps 48:2 Mount Zion on the *r* sides of
139:9 reside in the most *r* sea
Isa 37:26 From *r* times it is what I
41:9 even from the *r* parts of it

Remotest
Jg 19:1 *r* parts of the mountainous
19:18 *r* parts of the mountainous
2Ki 19:23 The *r* parts of Lebanon
Isa 14:13 in the *r* parts of the north
14:15 to the *r* parts of the pit
37:24 The *r* parts of Lebanon
Jer 6:22 the *r* parts of the earth
25:32 the *r* parts of the earth
31:8 the *r* parts of the earth
50:41 the *r* parts of the earth
Eze 38:6 of the *r* parts of the north
38:15 the *r* parts of the north
39:2 the *r* parts of the north and

Removal
Heb 12:27 *r* of the things being

Remove
Ge 8:13 Noah proceeded to *r* the
48:17 *r* it from Ephraim's head to
Ex 8:8 *r* the frogs from me and my
Le 1:16 *r* its crop with its feathers
3:4 *r* it along with the kidneys
3:9 entire fatty tail . . . will *r*
3:10 *r* it along with the kidneys
3:15 *r* it along with the kidneys
4:9 *r* it along with the kidneys
4:31 And he will *r* all its fat
4:35 *r* all its fat the same as the
7:4 *r* it along with the kidneys
Nu 21:7 that he may *r* the serpents
De 7:15 *r* from you every sickness
21:13 *r* the mantle of her
Jos 11:15 did not *r* a word from all
24:14 and *r* the foreign gods that your
24:23 *r* the foreign gods that are
Jg 9:29 Then I would *r* Abimelech
10:16 began to *r* the foreign gods
1Sa 17:46 and *r* your head off you
2Sa 6:10 David was not willing to *r*
1Ki 2:31 *r* from off me and from off
15:13 *r* her from being lady
15:14 the high places he did not *r*
20:24 *R* the kings each one from
2Ki 23:27 I shall *r* from my sight
24:3 to *r* it from his sight for
1Ch 13:13 David did not *r* the Ark to
17:13 I shall not *r* from him the
2Ch 26:20 *r* him from there, and he
33:8 not *r* the foot of Israel
33:15 *r* the foreign gods and the
Es 4:4 and to *r* his sackcloth off him
Job 9:34 him *r* his rod from upon me
Ps 18:22 his statutes I shall not *r*
39:10 *R* from off me your plague
119:29 *R* from me even the false
Pr 4:24 *R* from yourself the
4:27 *R* your foot from what is bad
22:15 discipline is what will *r* it
Ec 11:10 *r* vexation from your heart
Isa 1:16 *r* the badness of your
1:25 *r* all your waste products
10:13 *r* the boundaries of peoples
18:5 and must *r* the tendrils
22:8 will *r* the screen of Judah
57:14 *R* any obstacle from the
58:9 *r* from your midst the yoke
Jer 32:31 *r* it from before my face
Eze 11:18 *r* all its disgusting things
11:19 *r* the heart of stone from
21:26 *R* the turban, and lift off
23:25 and your ears they will *r*
26:16 *r* their sleeveless coats
43:9 *r* their fornication and the
45:9 *R* the violence and the
Da 4:27 and *r* your own sins by
11:31 and *r* the constant feature
Ho 2:17 *r* the names of the Baal
Am 5:23 *R* from me the turmoil of
Mic 2:3 people will not *r* your necks
6:14 you will *r* things, but you
Zep 3:11 *r* from the midst of you your
Zec 3:4 *R* the befouled garments from
9:7 *r* his bloodstained things
Mr 14:36 *r* this cup from me. Yet not
Lu 22:42 wish, *r* this cup from me
1Co 5:13 *R* the wicked man from among
Re 2:5 I will *r* your lampstand from

Removed
Ge 38:14 she *r* the garments of her
38:19 *r* her shawl off her and
41:42 Pharaoh *r* his signet ring
47:21 he *r* them into cities from
Ex 25:15 poles . . . are not to be *r*
Le 4:31 as the fat was *r* from off the
4:35 sacrifice is regularly *r*
De 26:14 *r* any of it while unclean
Jos 7:13 have *r* the thing devoted to
1Sa 17:39 So David *r* them off him
18:13 Saul *r* him from his
21:6 showbread that had been *r*
28:3 Saul, he had *r* the spirit
2Sa 4:7 after which they *r* his head
7:15 the way I *r* it from Saul
7:15 Saul, whom I *r* on account of
20:13 *r* him from the highway
1Ki 15:12 *r* all the dungy idols that
20:41 he hurriedly *r* the bandage
2Ki 3:2 he *r* the sacred pillar of Baal
16:17 *r* from off them the basins
17:18 he *r* them from his sight
17:23 Jehovah *r* Israel from his
18:4 *r* the high places and broke
18:22 altars Hezekiah has *r*
23:19 to cause offense Josiah *r*
23:27 just as I have *r* Israel
1Ch 17:13 the way I *r* it from the one
2Ch 14:3 *r* the foreign altars and the
14:5 *r* from all the cities of
15:16 *r* her from being lady
17:6 *r* the high places and the
29:19 utensils that King Ahaz *r*
30:14 *r* the altars that were in
30:14 incense altars they *r* and
32:12 *r* his high places and his
34:33 Josiah *r* all the detestable
36:3 the king of Egypt *r* him in
Es 3:10 king *r* his signet ring from
8:2 the king *r* his signet ring that
Ec 12:6 before the silver cord is *r*
Isa 17:1 Damascus *r* from being a city
22:25 lasting place will be *r*
29:13 *r* their heart itself far
36:7 whose altars Hezekiah has *r*
38:12 *r* from me like the tent of
54:10 may be *r*, and the very
54:10 will not be *r* from you
59:21 not be *r* from your mouth
Jer 31:36 regulations could be *r* from
Eze 16:50 *r* them, just as I saw fit
Da 12:11 constant feature has been *r*
Mic 4:7 *r* far off a mighty nation
Zep 3:15 Jehovah has *r* the judgments
Mt 14:12 *r* the corpse and buried him
15:8 their heart is far *r* from me
Mr 2:4 *r* the roof over where he was
7:6 hearts are far *r* from me
Ga 1:6 quickly *r* from the One who
Re 6:14 and every island were *r* from

Removes
Isa 6:12 Jehovah actually *r* earthling
Mic 2:4 How he *r* it from me! To the

Removing
Job 12:20 *r* speech from the faithful
Pr 25:4 a *r* of scummy dross from the
25:5 *r* of the wicked one before
25:20 *r* a garment on a cold day is
Isa 3:1 *r* from Jerusalem and from
5:5 will be a *r* of its hedge
Da 2:21 *r* kings and setting up kings
Joe 3:6 *r* them far from their own
Lu 2:32 a light for *r* the veil from
Ac 13:22 after *r* him, he raised up

Render
Ex 10:25 *r* them to Jehovah our God
10:26 *r* in worship to Jehovah
13:5 *r* this service in this month

Ex 20:9 *r* service and you must do all
21:11 *r* these three things to her
29:41 will *r* it as a restful odor
Le 9:7 and *r* up your sin offering and
9:7 and *r* up the offering of the
14:19 must *r* up the sin offering
14:30 must *r* up the one of the
16:24 *r* up his burnt offering and
17:9 to *r* it to Jehovah, that man
22:24 you should not *r* them up
23:12 *r* up a sound young ram, in
23:19 *r* up one kid of the goats as
Nu 4:23 *r* service in the tent of
4:30 *r* the service of the tent of
4:47 *r* the laborious service and
6:16 *r* up his sin offering and his
6:17 *r* up the ram as a communion
6:17 priest must *r* up its grain
8:12 *r* up the one as a sin offering
8:26 he must *r* no service
15:3 *r* up an offering made by fire
15:5 *r* up wine as a drink offering
15:6 for a ram you should *r* up a
15:8 *r* up a male of the herd as a
15:12 the number that you may *r* up
15:13 Every native should *r* up
15:14 *r* up an offering made by
15:24 *r* up one young bull as a
18:7 and you men must *r* service
28:4 you will *r* up in the morning
28:4 *r* up between the two evenings
28:8 *r* up the other male lamb
28:8 *r* it up as an offering made
28:20 *r* up three tenth measures
28:21 will *r* up a tenth measure
28:23 you will *r* these up
28:24 *r* up daily for the seven days
28:31 you will *r* them up
29:2 *r* up as a burnt offering for
29:39 will *r* up to Jehovah at your
De 5:13 you are to *r* service, and you
12:27 *r* up your burnt offerings
32:41 *r* retribution to those who
33:10 *r* up incense before your
Jos 7:19 *r*, please, glory to Jehovah
22:23 *r* up communion sacrifices
22:27 *r* the service of Jehovah
Jg 13:16 *r* up a burnt offering
1Sa 10:8 to *r* up communion sacrifices
20:8 *r* loving-kindness toward
2Sa 15:8 also *r* service to Jehovah
1Ki 8:64 *r* up the burnt sacrifice and
10:9 king to *r* judicial decision
12:27 going up to *r* sacrifices in
2Ki 5:17 will no more *r* up a burnt
10:24 came in to *r* up sacrifices
2Ch 7:6 David would *r* praise by
Ps 56:12 *r* expressions of thanksgiving
66:2 *R* his praise glorious
66:15 *r* up a bull with he-goats
109:5 they *r* to me bad for good
Isa 1:17 *r* judgment for the
1:23 boy they do not *r* judgment
2:4 *r* judgment among the nations
19:21 *r* sacrifice and gift and
19:23 *r* service, Egypt with
65:6 but I will *r* a reward
65:6 even *r* the reward into
Jer 4:7 to *r* your land as an object of
21:12 *r* sentence in justice, and
22:3 *R* justice and righteousness
33:18 and to *r* sacrifice always
Eze 43:25 *r* up a he-goat as a sin
43:25 perfect ones, they will *r*
43:27 *r* upon the altar the whole
46:2 *r* up his whole burnt
46:7 *r* up as a grain offering
Mic 4:3 *r* judgment among many
Mt 4:10 him alone you must *r* sacred
12:36 *r* an account concerning it
21:41 who will *r* him the fruits
Lu 4:8 you must *r* sacred service
Joh 5:30 and the judgment that I *r* is
Ac 7:7 *r* sacred service to me in this
7:42 *r* sacred service to the army
19:40 permit us to *r* a reason for
27:23 to whom I *r* sacred service
Ro 1:9 I *r* sacred service with my
2:6 *r* to each one according to his
13:7 *R* to all their dues, to him
14:12 each of us will *r* an
16:4 of the nations *r* thanks
1Co 7:3 husband *r* to his wife her due
2Co 8:10 I *r* an opinion: for this
Php 2:30 to *r* private service to me
1Th 3:9 thanksgiving can we *r* to God
Heb 9:14 *r* sacred service to the
10:11 to *r* public service and to
12:28 *r* God sacred service with
13:17 those who will *r* an account
1Pe 4:5 *r* an account to the one ready
Re 18:6 *R* to her even as she herself
19:20 who *r* worship to its image
22:3 will *r* him sacred service
22:12 *r* to each one as his work

Rendered
Ge 30:26 service which I have *r* you
50:15 the evil that we have *r* him
50:17 they have *r* evil to you
Ex 29:28 portion to be *r* by the sons
Nu 28:6 was *r* up at Mount Sinai as a
28:15 *r* up as a sin offering to
28:24 it should be *r*, and its drink
1Sa 11:15 *r* up communion sacrifices
24:17 you who have *r* me good, and
24:17 it is I who have *r* you evil
1Ki 3:15 *r* up communion offerings
2Ch 7:7 *r* up the burnt offerings and
24:7 they had *r* up to the Baals
32:25 benefit *r* him Hezekiah
32:33 *r* to him at his death
Ps 31:19 *r* to those taking refuge in
31:21 *r* wonderful loving-kindness
Pr 3:30 if he has *r* no bad to you
Isa 3:11 treatment *r* by his own hands
3:11 will be *r* to him
51:12 *r* as mere green grass
63:7 all that Jehovah has *r* to us
63:7 *r* to them according to his
Jer 25:37 *r* lifeless because of the
51:6 *r* inanimate through her
Mt 22:12 He was *r* speechless
Joh 16:2 *r* a sacred service to God
Ro 1:25 and *r* sacred service to the
1Co 1:6 has been *r* firm among you
Col 1:12 Father who *r* you suitable
2Ti 1:18 the services he *r* in Ephesus
Re 16:5 you have *r* these decisions
18:6 even as she herself *r*, and

Rendering
Le 9:22 from *r* the sin offering and
1Sa 6:15 continued *r* up sacrifices on
2Sa 8:15 David was continually *r*
2Ki 10:25 *r* up the burnt offering
1Ch 18:14 *r* judicial decision and
Es 6:6 king take delight in *r* an honor
Jer 4:18 will be a *r* of these to you
33:9 goodness that I am *r* to them
33:9 peace that I am *r* to her
44:3 *r* service to other gods whom
Lu 1:74 *r* sacred service to him
2:37 *r* sacred service night and day
Ac 9:36 gifts of mercy that she was *r*
21:25 *r* our decision that they
24:14 I am *r* sacred service to
26:7 intensely *r* him sacred service
Php 3:3 who are *r* sacred service by
2Ti 1:3 I am *r* sacred service as my
Heb 8:5 men are *r* sacred service in a
10:2 those *r* sacred service who
Jas 2:4 judges *r* wicked decisions
Re 7:15 are *r* him sacred service day

Renders
1Th 5:15 no one *r* injury for injury to

Rending
1Ki 19:11 wind was *r* mountains and

Renegade
Isa 57:17 walking as a *r* in the way
Jer 3:12 Do return, O *r* Israel, is
3:14 Return, O you *r* sons
3:22 Return, you *r* sons
3:22 shall heal your *r* condition

Renegading
Pr 1:32 *r* of the inexperienced ones

Renew
2Sa 2:28 not *r* the fighting anymore
2Ch 15:8 *r* Jehovah's altar that was

Renewed
2Co 4:16 is being *r* from day to day

Renewing
Ps 103:5 youth keeps *r* itself just

Renounce
2Ti 2:19 of Jehovah *r* unrighteousness

Renounced
2Co 4:2 *r* the underhanded things of

Renovate
2Ch 24:4 to *r* the house of Jehovah

Renovating
2Ch 24:12 craftsmen for *r* Jehovah's

Rent
Am 5:11 farm *r* from someone lowly
Mt 27:51 was *r* in two, from top to
Mr 15:38 *r* in two from top to bottom
Lu 23:45 curtain . . . was *r* down the

Repaid
Ge 44:4 Why have you *r* bad for good?
Jg 1:7 so God has *r* me. After that
Ps 7:4 I have *r* the one rewarding me
Jer 18:20 Should bad be *r* for good?
Lu 14:14 be *r* in the resurrection
Ro 11:35 that it must be *r* to him

Repair
2Ki 12:5 *r* the cracks of the house
12:8 to *r* the cracks of the house
12:12 upon the house to *r* it
22:5 to *r* the cracks of the house
22:6 hewn stones to *r* the house
2Ch 24:5 *r* the house of your God from
24:13 *r* work kept advancing by
29:3 and began to *r* them
34:8 *r* the house of Jehovah his
Ezr 4:12 and to *r* the foundations
Ne 3:4 son of Hakkoz did *r* work
3:4 son of Meshezabel did *r* work
3:4 the son of Baana did *r* work
3:5 the Tekoites did *r* work
3:7 the Meronothite, did *r* work
3:8 goldsmiths, did *r* work; and
3:8 ointment mixers did *r* work
3:9 Jerusalem, did *r* work
3:10 son of Harumaph did *r* work
3:10 son of Hashabneiah did *r* work
3:12 Jerusalem, did *r* work
3:16 did *r* work as far as in front
3:17 the Levites did *r* work
3:17 did *r* work for his district
3:18 brothers did *r* work, Bavvai
3:19 *r* another measured section in
3:22 Jordan District, did *r* work
3:23 did *r* work in front of their
3:23 *r* work close by his own house
3:25 *r* work in front of the
3:26 they did *r* work as far as in
3:28 priests did *r* work, each one
3:29 *r* work in front of his own
3:29 Shemaiah . . . did *r* work
3:30 *r* work in front of his own
3:31 *r* work as far as the house of
3:32 and the traders did *r* work
Am 9:11 certainly *r* their breaches

Repaired
2Ki 12:6 not yet *r* the cracks of the
12:14 they *r* the house of Jehovah
2Ch 32:5 *r* the Mound of the city of
Ne 3:6 the son of Besodeiah *r*
3:11 son of Pahath-moab *r*
3:13 inhabitants of Zanoah *r*
3:14 Gate of the Ash-heaps . . . *r*
3:15 And the Fountain Gate . . . *r*
3:20 *r* another measured section
3:21 *r* another measured section
3:24 *r* another measured section
3:27 *r* another measured section
3:30 *r* another measured section
Jer 19:11 it is no more able to be *r*

Repairer
Isa 58:12 be called the *r* of the gap

Repairing
2Ki 12:7 not *r* the cracks of the house
12:12 *r* the cracks of the house
2Ch 24:12 copper for *r* Jehovah's house
34:10 applied it to mending and *r*
Ne 4:7 *r* of the walls of Jerusalem
Eze 22:30 would be *r* the stone wall

Repay
Ge 50:15 *r* us for all the evil that
Le 26:34 as it must *r* its sabbaths
De 7:10 he will *r* him to his face
1Sa 26:23 Jehovah it is who will *r* to
2Sa 3:39 Jehovah *r* the doer of what
19:36 king *r* me with this reward
22:25 let Jehovah *r* me according

2Ki 9:26 *r* you in this tract of land
Ps 18:24 Jehovah *r* me according to
54:5 He will *r* the bad to my foes
79:12 *r* to our neighbors seven
116:12 What shall I *r* to Jehovah
Pr 19:17 his treatment He will *r* to
24:29 *r* to each one according to
Jer 16:18 I will *r* the full amount
25:14 *r* them according to their
51:56 Without fail he will *r*
Ho 12:2 his dealings he will *r* him
12:14 grand Master will *r* to him
Zec 9:12 I shall *r* to you, O woman, a
Mt 6:4 looking on in secret will *r*
6:6 looks on in secret will *r* you
6:18 looking on in secrecy will *r*
Lu 10:35 *r* you when I come back here
14:14 nothing with which to *r* you
Ro 12:19 I will *r*, says Jehovah
2Th 1:6 to *r* tribulation to those who
2Ti 4:14 Jehovah will *r* him according

Repaying
De 7:10 *r* to his face the one who
Pr 17:13 As for anyone *r* bad for good
Isa 66:6 *r* what is deserved to his
Jer 32:18 *r* the error of the fathers

Repayment
Isa 35:4 God even with a *r*
Lu 14:12 it would become a *r* to you

Repays
1Sa 25:21 *r* me evil in return for
2Sa 22:21 cleanness of my hands he *r*
Ps 18:20 cleanness of my hands he *r*

Repeat
Jg 13:21 angel did not *r* appearing to
Isa 51:22 will not *r* the drinking of

Repeated
Ge 9:17 God *r* to Noah: This is the
20:2 Abraham *r* concerning Sarah
41:32 the dream was *r* to Pharaoh
Ps 140:11 hunt him with *r* thrusts
Eze 21:14 should be *r* for three times
Lu 20:11 *r* and sent them a different

Repeatedly
Ge 19:35 *r* gave their father wine
32:16 *r* said to his servants: Cross
37:31 *r* dipped the long garment in
48:20 Israel *r* pronounce blessing
Jos 24:10 he blessed you *r*. Thus I
Job 29:20 in my hand will shoot *r*
Ps 106:41 *r* gave them into the hand
136:24 *r* tore us away from our
Pr 29:1 man *r* reproved but making his
La 3:3 against me that he *r* turns his
Jon 4:8 he *r* said: My dying off is
Na 2:7 beating *r* upon their hearts
Mr 6:18 For John had *r* said to Herod
14:2 *r* said: Not at the festival
Lu 8:29 he was *r* bound with chains
Ac 20:23 holy spirit *r* bears witness
21:4 *r* told Paul not to set foot in

Repeating
Pr 26:11 one is *r* his foolishness

Repent
Job 42:6 I do *r* in dust and ashes
Mt 3:2 *R*, for the kingdom of the
4:17 *R*, you people, for the
11:20 because they did not *r*
Mr 6:12 in order that people might *r*
Lu 13:3 unless you *r*, you will all
13:5 unless you *r*, you will all
16:30 goes to them they will *r*
17:4 saying, I *r*, you must forgive
Ac 2:38 *R*, and let each one of you
3:19 *R*, therefore, and turn around
8:22 *R*, therefore, of this badness
17:30 they should all everywhere *r*
26:20 message that they should *r*
Re 2:5 *r* and do the former deeds
2:5 from its place, unless you *r*
2:16 Therefore *r*. If you do not
2:21 I gave her time to *r*, but
2:21 to *r* of her fornication
2:22 unless they *r* of her deeds
3:3 and go on keeping it, and *r*
3:19 Therefore be zealous and *r*
9:20 not *r* of the works of their
9:21 did not *r* of their murders
16:9 *r* so as to give glory to him
16:11 did not *r* of their works

Repentance
Mt 3:8 produce fruit that befits *r*
3:11 with water because of your *r*
Mr 1:4 baptism in symbol of *r* for
Lu 3:3 baptism in symbol of *r* for
3:8 produce fruits that befit *r*
5:32 come to call . . . sinners to *r*
15:7 ones who have no need of *r*
24:47 *r* for forgiveness of sins
Ac 5:31 to give *r* to Israel and
11:18 God has granted *r* for the
13:24 baptism in symbol of *r*
19:4 the baptism in symbol of *r*
20:21 about *r* toward God and faith
26:20 doing works that befit *r*
Ro 2:4 God is trying to lead you to *r*
2Co 7:10 makes for *r* to salvation
2Ti 2:25 God may give them *r* leading
Heb 6:1 *r* from dead works, and faith
6:6 to revive them again to *r*
2Pe 3:9 desires all to attain to *r*

Repentant
Mr 1:15 Be *r*, you people, and have

Repented
Mt 11:21 *r* in sackcloth and ashes
12:41 *r* at what Jonah preached
Lu 10:13 *r* sitting in sackcloth and
11:32 *r* at what Jonah preached
2Co 12:21 sinned but have not *r* over

Repenting
Jer 8:6 There was not a man *r* over
2Co 7:9 you were saddened into *r*

Repents
Lu 15:7 over one sinner that *r* than
15:10 over one sinner that *r*
17:3 and if he *r* forgive him

Rephael
1Ch 26:7 of Shemaiah, Othni and *R*

Rephah
1Ch 7:25 was *R* his son, and Resheph

Rephaiah
1Ch 3:21 the sons of Jeshaiah *R*
3:21 the sons of *R* Arnan
4:42 Neariah and *R* and Uzziel
7:2 sons of Tola were Uzzi and *R*
9:43 Binea and *R* his son, Eleasah
Ne 3:9 *R* the son of Hur, a prince of

Rephaim
Ge 14:5 inflicted defeats on the *R*
15:20 and the Perizzites and the *R*
De 2:11 As for the *R*, they also were
2:20 As the land of the *R* it also
2:20 The *R* dwelt in it in former
3:11 what was left of the *R*
3:13 called the land of the *R*
Jos 12:4 what was left over of the *R*
13:12 what was left of the *R*
15:8 low plain of *R* to the north
17:15 the Perizzites and the *R*
18:16 low plain of *R* to the north
2Sa 5:18 about in the low plain of *R*
5:22 in the low plain of *R*
21:16 among those born of the *R*
21:18 among those born of the *R*
21:20 had been born to the *R*
21:22 been born to the *R* in Gath
23:13 the low plain of the *R*
1Ch 11:15 in the low plain of *R*
14:9 raids in the low plain of *R*
20:4 Sippai of those born of the *R*
20:6 too, had been born to the *R*
20:8 been born to the *R* in Gath
Isa 17:5 grain in the low plain of *R*

Rephan
Ac 7:43 star of the god *R* that you

Rephidim
Ex 17:1 Israel . . . went camping at *R*
17:8 and fight against Israel in *R*
19:2 pull away from *R* and to come
Nu 33:14 and went camping in *R*
33:15 pulled away from *R* and went

Replace
Le 27:10 He may not *r* it, and he may
Ps 102:26 like clothing you will *r*

Replacement
Ezr 1:9 twenty-nine *r* vessels
Isa 9:10 with cedars we shall make *r*

Replied
Ge 3:13 the woman *r*: The serpent
1Ki 12:16 the people *r* to the king
2Ki 22:9 and *r* to the king and said
2Ch 10:16 people now *r* to the king
34:16 *r* further to the king
Ne 2:20 I *r* to them and said to them
Mt 27:11 Jesus *r*: You yourself say it
Lu 4:4 Jesus *r* to him: It is written
20:7 *r* that they did not know its
Joh 7:46 officers *r*: Never has another
8:33 *r* to him: We are Abraham's
10:32 Jesus *r* to them: I
Ac 25:12 *r*: To Caesar you have
25:16 I *r* to them that it is not

Replies
Job 20:3 And a spirit . . . *r* to me
21:34 your very *r* do remain as
34:36 *r* among men of hurtfulness

Reply
1Sa 17:30 people gave him the same *r*
2Sa 3:11 one word more in *r* to Abner
24:13 *r* to the One sending me
1Ki 12:6 advising to *r* to this people
12:9 that we may *r* to this people
2Ki 22:20 to bring the king the *r*
1Ch 21:12 *r* to the One sending me
2Ch 10:6 advising to *r* to this people
10:9 *r* to this people who have
34:28 brought the *r* to the king
Es 4:13 Mordecai said to *r* to Esther
4:15 Esther said to *r* to Mordecai
Job 4:1 the Temanite proceeded to *r*
20:1 Zophar . . . proceeded to *r*
32:14 I shall not *r* to him
33:5 make *r* to me, Array words
33:32 make *r* to me; Speak, for I
35:4 I myself shall *r* to you
40:4 What shall I *r* to you?
Pr 26:16 seven giving a sensible *r*
27:11 *r* to him that is taunting me
Isa 41:28 that they might make a *r*
Hab 2:1 what I shall *r* at the reproof
Mt 3:15 In *r* Jesus said to him
4:4 in *r* he said: It is written
8:8 In *r* the army officer said
11:4 In *r* Jesus said to them: Go
12:39 In *r* he said to them
13:11 In *r* he said: To you it is
14:28 In *r* Peter said to him: Lord
15:3 In *r* he said to them: Why is
15:13 In *r* he said: Every plant
15:28 Then Jesus said in *r* to her
16:2 In *r* he said to them: When
17:11 In *r* he said: Elijah, indeed
17:17 In *r* Jesus said: O faithless
19:4 In *r* he said: Did you not
19:27 Then Peter said to him in *r*
20:13 in *r* to one of them he said
21:24 In *r* Jesus said to them: I
21:30 *r* this one said, I will not
22:1 *r* Jesus again spoke to them
22:29 In *r* Jesus said to them: You
22:46 to say a word in *r* to him
25:26 In *r* his master said to him
25:40 in *r* the king will say to
26:23 In *r* he said: He that dips
26:25 By way of *r* Judas, who was
Mr 3:33 *r* he said to them: Who are
6:37 In *r* he said to them
7:28 In *r*, however, she said to
11:22 in *r* Jesus said to them
11:33 in *r* to Jesus they said
12:35 making a *r*, Jesus began
14:60 Do you say nothing in *r*?
14:61 kept silent and made no *r*
15:4 Have you no *r* to make?
15:12 in *r* Pilate was saying to
Lu 1:19 In *r* the angel said to him
3:11 In *r* he would say to them
4:8 In *r* Jesus said to him: It is
5:5 But Simon in *r* said
5:31 In *r* Jesus said to them
6:3 But Jesus said in *r* to them
7:40 in *r* Jesus said to him
8:21 In *r* he said to them
9:19 In *r* they said: John the
9:20 Peter said in *r*: The Christ
10:30 In *r* Jesus said: A certain
11:7 one from inside says in *r*
13:2 in *r* he said to them: Do you
13:8 In *r* he said to him, Master
15:29 In *r* he said to his father

Lu 17:17 In *r* Jesus said: The ten
19:40 in *r* he said: I tell you
20:3 In *r* he said to them: I will
22:51 in *r* Jesus said: Let it go
23:40 In *r* the other rebuked him
Ac 4:19 in *r* Peter and John said to
25:9 said in *r* to Paul: Do you
2Co 11:23 I *r* like a madman, I am

Replying
Ne 6:4 *r* to them with the same word
Pr 18:13 *r* . . . before he hears
24:26 is *r* in a straightforward

Report
Ge 22:20 the *r* got through to Abraham
26:32 *r* to him regarding the well
29:13 Laban heard the *r* about Jacob
37:2 Joseph brought a bad *r* about
46:31 *r* to Pharaoh and say to him
Ex 23:1 must not take up an untrue *r*
Le 5:1 if he does not *r* it, then he
Nu 13:27 they went on to *r* to him and
13:32 a bad *r* of the land that they
14:36 a bad *r* against the land
14:37 men bringing forth the bad *r*
De 2:25 will hear the *r* about you
26:3 I must *r* today to Jehovah
Jos 2:20 if you should *r* this matter
10:17 the *r* was made to Joshua
Jg 16:2 And *r* was made to the Gazites
Ru 2:11 The *r* was fully made to me
1Sa 2:24 because the *r* is not good
4:13 went in to *r* in the city
4:14 he might go in and *r* to Eli
4:19 *r* that the ark of the true
15:12 But *r* was made to Samuel
19:19 *r* got to Saul, saying: Look!
23:7 *r* was made to Saul: David
27:4 *r* was made to Saul that
2Sa 4:4 *r* about Saul and Jonathan
6:12 *r* was made to King David
10:17 *r* was made to David, he
11:18 *r* to David all the matters
13:30 *r* itself came to David
15:31 to David the *r* was made
19:8 they made the *r*, saying
1Ki 1:51 the *r* was made to Solomon
2:28 *r* itself came clear to Joab
10:1 hearing the *r* about Solomon
2Ki 6:13 Later the *r* was made to him
7:9 make *r* at the king's house
8:7 *r* was made to him, saying
9:15 go and make *r* in Jezreel
9:18 watchman went on to *r*
9:20 watchman went on to *r*
19:7 must hear a *r* and return to
1Ch 19:17 the *r* was made to David
2Ch 9:1 heard the *r* about Solomon
9:6 surpassed the *r* that I have
34:18 to *r* to the king, saying
Ezr 5:5 the *r* could go to Darius and
Job 28:22 we have heard a *r* of it
Ps 31:13 heard the bad *r* by many
Pr 10:18 forth a bad *r* is stupid
15:30 A *r* that is good makes the
25:10 *r* by you can have no recall
25:25 a good *r* from a distant land
Isa 7:2 *r* was made to the house of
23:5 *r* pertaining to Egypt
23:5 pains at the *r* on Tyre
37:7 hear a *r* and return to his
45:21 your *r* and your presentation
66:19 have not heard a *r* about me
Jer 6:24 have heard the *r* about it
10:22 A *r*! Here it has come
20:10 I heard the bad *r* of many
37:5 to hear the *r* about them
49:14 *r* that I have heard from
49:23 bad *r* that they have heard
50:43 heard the *r* about them, and
51:31 *r* to the king of Babylon
51:46 afraid because of the *r*
51:46 the *r* will actually come
51:46 be the *r* and violence
Eze 7:26, 26 will occur *r* upon *r*, and
21:7 you must say, At a *r*
36:3 is a bad *r* among people
Da 6:2 giving to them the *r* and the
9:23 have come to make *r*, because
Ho 7:12 the *r* to their assembly
Ob 1 a *r* that we have heard from
Na 3:19 All those hearing the *r* about
Hab 3:2 I have heard the *r* about you
Mt 2:8 found it *r* back to me, that
Mt 4:24 the *r* about him went out
11:4 Go your way and *r* to John
14:1 heard the *r* about Jesus
28:8 ran to *r* to his disciples
28:10 Go, *r* to my brothers, that
Mr 1:28 So the *r* about him spread out
5:19 and *r* to them all the things
Lu 7:22 *r* to John what you saw and
9:36 did not *r* to anyone in those
Joh 16:25 *r* to you with plainness
Ac 5:22 they returned and made *r*
12:17 *R* these things to James and
15:27 *r* the same things by word
19:18 and *r* their practices openly
22:26 made *r*, saying: What are you
23:17 he has something to *r* to him
23:19 What is it you have to *r*
2Co 6:8, 8 through bad *r* and good *r*

Reported
Ge 45:26 they *r* to him, saying
47:1 Joseph came and *r* to Pharaoh
48:2 it was *r* to Jacob and said
Ex 14:5 was *r* to the king of Egypt
16:22 came and *r* it to Moses
19:9 Then Moses *r* the words of the
Nu 31:49 not one has been *r* missing
Jg 4:12 they *r* to Sisera that Barak
9:7 they *r* it to Jotham he at once
9:25 it was *r* to Abimelech
9:47 it was *r* to Abimelech that
1Sa 18:24 servants of Saul *r* to him
18:26 *r* these words to David, and
23:13 to Saul it was *r* that David
25:12 *r* to him in accord with all
25:14 *r*, saying: Look! David sent
2Sa 3:23 *r* to Joab, saying: Abner the
10:5 people *r* it to David, and
19:1 Later it was *r* to Joab
19:6 *r* today that chiefs and
21:11 *r* to David what Rizpah the
2Ki 5:4 *r* to his lord, saying: It
7:10 and *r* to them, saying
7:11 *r* to the king's house inside
7:15 returned and *r* to the king
Es 6:2 what Mordecai had *r* concerning
Ps 56:8 you yourself have *r*
Isa 21:10 I have *r* to you people
45:21 *r* it from that very time
Mt 8:33 they *r* everything, including
14:12 and came and *r* to Jesus
28:11 *r* to the chief priests all
Mr 2:1 and he was *r* to be at home
5:14 herders of them fled and *r*
6:30 *r* to him all the things they
Lu 7:18 John's disciples *r* to him
8:20 it was *r* to him: Your mother
8:34 fled and *r* it to the city and
8:36 Those who had seen it *r* to
13:1 *r* to him about the Galileans
14:21 *r* these things to his master
18:37 *r* to him: Jesus the Nazarene
24:9 *r* all these things to the
Ac 4:23 *r* what things the chief
5:25 *r* to them: Look! The men you
10:22 well *r* by the whole nation
11:13 He *r* to us how he saw the
12:14 *r* that Peter was standing
16:2 well *r* on by the brothers in
16:36 jailer *r* their words to Paul
16:38 constables *r* these sayings to
22:12 well *r* on by all the Jews
23:16 and *r* it to Paul
28:21 *r* or spoken anything wicked
1Co 5:1 fornication is *r* among you

Reporter
Jer 51:31 and one *r* to meet another
51:31 to meet another *r*, to

Reporting
Nu 11:27 *r* to Moses and saying: Eldad
1Sa 18:20 and they went *r* it to Saul
23:1 they came *r* to David, saying
24:1 *r* to him, saying: Look!
2Sa 4:10 *r* to me, saying, Here Saul
1Th 1:9 keep *r* about the way we first
1Jo 1:2 bearing witness and *r* to you
1:3 seen and heard we are *r* also

Reports
Pr 29:24 may hear, but he *r* nothing
Da 11:44 *r* that will disturb him, out
Mt 24:6 hear of wars and *r* of wars
Mr 13:7 hear of wars and *r* of wars

Repose
Isa 51:4 to *r* even as a light to the
Jer 31:2 walking to get his *r*
47:6 Take your *r* and keep silent
50:34 give *r* to the land and

Repossess
Jer 30:3 they will certainly *r* it

Repossessing
Isa 49:8 *r* of the desolated hereditary

Represent
2Sa 20:19 I *r* the peaceable and

Representation
De 4:16 the *r* of male or female
4:17 the *r* of any beast that is in
4:17 the *r* of any winged bird that
4:18 the *r* of anything moving on
4:18 the *r* of any fish that is in
Jos 22:28 See the *r* of Jehovah's
1Ch 28:18 and for the *r* of the chariot
Ps 106:20 my glory For a *r* of a bull
Isa 44:13 like the *r* of a man, like
Eze 8:3 he thrust out the *r* of a hand
8:10 every *r* of creeping things
10:8 *r* of a hand of earthling man
Heb 1:3 the exact *r* of his very being
8:5 in a typical *r* and a shadow

Representations
1Ki 6:35 overlaid gold foil upon the *r*
Heb 9:23 typical *r* of the things in

Representative
Ex 18:19 serve as *r* for the people
Lu 8:49 *r* of the presiding officer of
Joh 1:6 sent forth as a *r* of God
7:29 I am a *r* from him, and that
16:27 came out as the Father's *r*
17:8 that I came out as your *r*

Representatively
Ezr 10:14 let our princes act *r* for

Represented
Nu 1:44 *r* one each the house of his

Reprimand
Lu 18:15 disciples began to *r* them
2Ti 4:2 reprove, *r*, exhort, with all

Reprimanded
Mt 19:13 but the disciples *r* them
Mr 10:13 but the disciples *r* them

Reproach
Ge 20:16 and you are cleared of *r*
30:23 God has taken away my *r*
34:14 because that is a *r* to us
Jos 5:9 rolled away the *r* of Egypt
1Sa 11:2 put it as a *r* upon all Israel
17:26 turns away *r* from upon
25:39 legal case of my *r* to free
2Sa 13:13 shall I cause my *r* to go
2Ch 32:17 he wrote to *r* Jehovah the
Ne 1:3 in a very bad plight and in *r*
2:17 no longer continue to be a *r*
4:4 and make their *r* return upon
5:9 *r* of the nations, our enemies
6:13 in order that they might *r* me
Job 16:10 With *r* they have struck my
19:5 my *r* to be proper against me
Ps 15:3 no *r* has he taken up against
22:6 A *r* to men and despicable to
31:11 I have become a *r*, And to
39:8 as a *r* of the senseless one
44:13 as a *r* to our neighbors
55:12 enemy that proceeded to *r* me
69:7 your account I have borne *r*
69:19 know my *r* and my shame and
69:20 *R* itself has broken my heart
71:13 cover themselves with *r*
74:22 *r* from the senseless one all
78:66 *r* of indefinite duration he
79:4 become a *r* to our neighbors
79:12 *r* with which they have
89:41 become a *r* to his neighbors
89:50 the *r* upon your servants
89:50 *r* of all the many peoples
119:22 Roll off me *r* and contempt
119:39 Make my *r* pass away, of
Pr 6:33 *r* itself will not be wiped
18:3 with dishonor there is *r*
Isa 4:1 your name to take away our *r*
25:8 *r* of his people he will take
30:5 shame and also a cause for *r*
47:3 your *r* ought to be seen

Es 7:2 what is your *r*? To the half of
7:3 and my people at my *r*
7:7 *r* for his soul from Esther the
9:12 And what is your further *r*?
Job 6:8 O that my *r* would come And
Ps 6:9 indeed hear my *r* for favor
55:1 hide yourself from my *r*
106:15 to give them their *r*
119:170 *r* for favor enter in before
Jer 36:7 *r* for favor will fall before
37:20 my *r* for favor, please
38:26 *r* for favor fall before
42:2 May our *r* for favor, please
42:9 *r* for favor to fall before
Da 2:49 made a *r* of the king, and
4:17 the saying of holy ones the *r*
7:16 I might *r* from him reliable
9:20 my *r* for favor fall before
Mt 15:23 to *r* him: Send her away
18:19 that they should *r*, it will
Mr 6:25 and made her *r*, saying
Lu 4:38 they made *r* of him for her
Joh 12:21 *r* him, saying: Sir, we want
14:16 I will *r* the Father and
16:26 shall make *r* of the Father
17:9 I make *r* concerning them
17:9 I make *r*, not concerning
17:15 I *r* you, not to take them
17:20 I make *r*, not concerning
Ac 23:20 *r* you to bring Paul down to
Php 4:3 I *r* you too, genuine
1Th 4:1 we *r* you and exhort you by
5:12 we *r* you, brothers, to have
2Th 2:1 together to him, we *r* of you
1Pe 3:21 the *r* made to God for a good
1Jo 5:16 do not tell him to make *r*
2Jo 5 I *r* you, lady, as a person

Requested
Jg 8:26 gold that he had *r* amounted
1Sa 1:28 he is one *r* for Jehovah
1Ki 3:10 Solomon had *r* this thing
3:11 *r* this thing and have not
3:11 not *r* for yourself many days
3:11 *r* for yourself riches nor
3:11 *r* the soul of your enemies
3:11 *r* for yourself understanding
3:13 not *r* I will give you
9:3 which you *r* favor before me
Da 2:23 known to me what we *r* of you
Lu 11:37 a Pharisee *r* him to dine
Joh 19:31 *r* Pilate to have their legs
19:38 *r* Pilate that he might take
Ac 10:48 *r* him to remain for some
16:39 *r* them to depart from the
23:18 *r* me to lead this young man

Requesting
1Ki 2:22 why are you *r* Abishag the
Da 1:8 kept *r* of the principal court
Ac 3:3 began *r* to get gifts of mercy
18:20 *r* him to remain for a longer

Requests
2Ch 6:39 and their *r* for favor, and
Ezr 7:21 *r* of you men it will be done
Ps 20:5 Jehovah fulfill all your *r*
37:4 give you the *r* of your heart
Zec 10:1 Make your *r* of Jehovah for

Require
De 18:19 I shall myself *r* an account
23:21 God will without fail *r* it
1Sa 20:16 Jehovah must *r* it at the
2Sa 4:11 *r* his blood from your hands
1Ki 8:59 as it may *r* day by day
Ps 10:13 You will not *r* an accounting
Eze 20:40 I shall *r* your contributions

Required
Ex 5:8 *r* amount of bricks that they
2Ch 24:6 *r* an account of the Levites
Ne 11:23 for the singers as each day *r*
Isa 1:12 has *r* this from your hand
Eze 45:11 *r* amount should prove to be
Lu 11:50 be *r* from this generation
11:51 be *r* from this generation
Joh 2:6 *r* by the purification rules

Requirement
1Ch 16:37 according to the *r* of each
Lu 11:3 according to the day's *r*
Ro 8:4 righteous *r* of the Law might

Requirements
Lu 1:6 and legal *r* of Jehovah
Ro 2:26 righteous *r* of the Law, his
Heb 9:10 *r* pertaining to the flesh

Rescue
De 22:27 there was no one to *r* her
1Sa 17:35 made the *r* from its mouth
Job 6:23 *r* me out of the hand of an
22:30 He will *r* an innocent man
29:12 *r* the afflicted one crying
36:15 He will *r* the afflicted one
Ps 6:4 O Jehovah, do *r* my soul
50:15 I shall *r* you, and you will
81:7 I proceeded to *r* you
91:15 I shall *r* him and glorify
119:153 my affliction, and *r* me
140:1 *R* me, O Jehovah, from bad
Da 3:15 who is that god that can *r*
3:17 our God . . . is able to *r* us
3:17 O king, he will *r* us
6:14 set his mind in order to *r*
6:16 he himself will *r* you
6:20 able to *r* you from the lions
Mt 27:43 let Him now *r* him if He
Ro 7:24 Who will *r* me from the body
2Co 1:10, 10 did *r* us and will *r* us
1:10 he will also *r* us further

Rescued
Job 22:30 *r* for the cleanness of your
Ps 60:5 your beloved ones may be *r*
108:6 your beloved ones may be *r*
116:8 have *r* my soul from death
Pr 11:8 righteous is the one *r* even
11:9 knowledge are the righteous *r*
Da 3:28 *r* his servants that trusted
6:27 *r* Daniel from the paw of the
Lu 1:74 *r* from the hands of enemies
Ac 23:27 force of soldiers and *r* him

Rescues
Ps 34:7 And he *r* them

Rescuing
2Sa 22:20 He was *r* me, because he had
Ps 18:19 He was *r* me, because he had
Da 6:27 He is *r* and delivering and

Research
1Ti 1:4 furnish questions for *r*

Resemblance
Ps 144:4 bears *r* to a mere exhalation
Eze 31:8 no *r* as respects its boughs
Ro 5:14 Adam, who bears a *r* to him

Resemble
Ps 89:6 Who can *r* Jehovah among the
102:6 *r* the pelican of the
Ca 7:7 stature of yours does *r* a palm
Isa 14:14 myself *r* the Most High
46:5 that we may *r* each other
Eze 31:2 come to *r* in your greatness
31:18 come to *r* thus in glory
Mt 23:27 you *r* whitewashed graves

Resembled
Isa 1:9 should have *r* Gomorrah itself
Jer 6:2 *r* indeed a comely and
Eze 31:8 *r* it in its prettiness
Re 9:7 the locusts *r* horses prepared

Resembling
Ca 2:9 My dear one is *r* a gazelle or
Da 3:25 one is *r* a son of the gods

Resen
Ge 10:12 *R* between Nineveh and Calah

Resentful
Ps 103:9 to time indefinite keep *r*
Jer 3:5 stay *r* to time indefinite
3:12 shall not stay *r* to time
Na 1:2 he is *r* toward his enemies

Reserve
Isa 48:6 even things kept in *r*
2Pe 2:9 *r* unrighteous people for the

Reserved
Ge 27:36 not *r* a blessing for me
De 33:21 of a statute-giver is *r*
1Sa 9:24 Here is what has been *r*
9:24 they have *r* it for you that
Job 15:20 years . . . *r* for the tyrant
15:22 And he is *r* for a sword
20:26 darkness will be *r* for his
Joh 2:10 *r* the fine wine until now
Col 1:5 the hope that is being *r* for
2Ti 4:8 is *r* for me the crown of
Heb 9:27 *r* for men to die once for
1Pe 1:4 It is *r* in the heavens for you
2Pe 2:4 to be *r* for judgment
2:17 darkness has been *r*
2Pe 3:7 *r* to the day of judgment
Jude 6 *r* with eternal bonds under
13 darkness stands *r* forever

Resheph
1Ch 7:25 and *R*, and Telah his son, and

Reside
Ge 9:27 let him *r* in the tents of
12:10 Egypt to *r* there as an alien
19:9 lone man came here to *r* as an
26:3 *R* as an alien in this land
47:4 We have come to *r* as aliens
49:13 Zebulun will *r* by the
Ex 24:16 to *r* upon Mount Sinai, and
Nu 9:17 cloud would *r*, there is where
9:18 cloud would *r* over the
10:12 *r* in the wilderness of Paran
14:30 hand in oath to *r* with you
De 12:5 his name there, to have it *r*
12:11 to have his name *r* there
14:23 to have his name *r* there
16:2 choose to have his name *r*
16:6 choose to have his name *r*
16:11 choose to have his name *r*
26:2 to have his name *r* there
26:5 to *r* there as an alien with
33:12 *r* in security by him
33:12 must *r* between his shoulders
33:20 As a lion he must *r*, And he
33:28 Israel will *r* in security
Jg 17:8 to *r* for a time wherever he
17:9 to *r* for a time wherever I
Ru 1:1 *r* as an alien in the fields of
2Sa 7:10 indeed *r* where they are
1Ki 6:13 *r* in the middle of the sons
8:12 was to *r* in the thick gloom
2Ki 8:1 and *r* as an alien wherever
8:1 you can *r* as an alien
1Ch 17:9 *r* where they are and no more
23:25 he will *r* in Jerusalem to
2Ch 6:1 was to *r* in the thick gloom
Ezr 6:12 to *r* there overthrow any
Ne 1:9 to have my name *r* there
Job 3:5 Let a rain cloud *r* over it
18:15 *r* in his tent something
28:4 where people *r* as aliens
30:6 *r* on the very slope of
Ps 5:4 No one bad may *r* for any time
7:5 glory to *r* in the dust itself
15:1 will *r* in your holy mountain
16:9 own flesh will *r* in security
37:3 *R* in the earth, and deal with
37:27 And so *r* to time indefinite
37:29 they will *r* forever upon it
55:6 I would fly away and *r*
65:4 he may *r* in your courtyards
68:6 have to *r* in a scorched land
68:16 Jehovah himself will *r* there
68:18 stubborn ones, to *r* among
69:36 will be the ones to *r* in it
78:55 Israel to *r* in their own
85:9 For glory to *r* in our land
139:9 *r* in the most remote sea
Pr 1:33 he will *r* in security and be
2:21 ones that will *r* in the earth
Isa 11:6 wolf will actually *r* for a
13:20 nor will she *r* for
13:21 there the ostriches must *r*
16:4 dispersed ones *r* as aliens
23:7 far away to *r* as an alien
32:16 justice will certainly *r*
33:14 *r* for any time with a
33:14 can *r* for any time with
33:16 will *r* on the heights
34:11 ravens themselves will *r* in
34:17 generation they will *r* in
52:4 to *r* there as aliens
57:15 the holy place is where I *r*
65:9 own servants will *r* there
Jer 7:12 I caused my name to *r* at
17:6 *r* in parched places in the
23:6 Israel . . . *r* in security
33:16 Jerusalem itself will *r* in
42:15 in to *r* there as aliens
42:17 Egypt to *r* there as aliens
42:22 to enter to *r* as aliens
43:2 Egypt to *r* there as aliens
43:5 *r* for a while in the land of
44:8 entering to *r* as aliens
44:12 Egypt to *r* there as aliens
44:14 *r* there as aliens, in the
44:28 Egypt to *r* there as aliens
48:28 *r* on the crag, you
49:18 will *r* in her as an alien

Jer 49:31 Solitary they *r*
49:33 mankind will *r* as an alien
50:39 *r* for generation after
50:40 *r* in her as an alien
La 4:15 will not *r* again as aliens
Eze 14:7 that *r* as aliens in Israel
17:23 *r* all the birds of every
17:23 of its foliage they will *r*
31:13 flying creatures . . . will *r*
32:4 to *r*, and off you I will
43:7 *r* in the midst of the sons
43:9 *r* in the midst of them to
Da 4:21 birds of the heavens would *r*
Mic 4:10 will have to *r* in the field
Zec 2:10 I will *r* in the midst of you
2:11 will *r* in the midst of you
8:3 to Zion and *r* in the midst of
8:8 *r* in the midst of Jerusalem
Ac 2:26 my flesh will *r* in hope
2Co 6:16 I shall *r* among them and
Col 3:16 the word of the Christ *r* in
Re 12:12 heavens and you who *r* in
21:3 he will *r* with them, and

Resided
Ge 32:4 With Laban I have *r* as an
35:27 Abraham . . . also Isaac had *r*
Ex 6:4 in which they *r* as aliens
40:35 because the cloud *r* over it
De 4:25 *r* a long time in the land and
18:6 where he had *r* for a while
Jos 22:19 the tabernacle . . . has *r*
Job 29:25 *r* as a king among his
Ps 74:2 Zion in which you have *r*
78:60 tent in which he *r* among
94:17 soul would have *r* in silence
105:23 Jacob himself *r* as an alien
120:5 *r* as an alien in Meshech
Pr 8:12 wisdom, I have *r* with
Jer 46:26 she will be *r* in as in
Joh 1:14 became flesh and *r* among us
Heb 11:9 By faith he *r* as an alien

Residence
Ge 4:16 *r* in the land of Fugitiveness
21:34 Abraham extended his *r* as an
Jg 5:17 Gilead kept to his *r* on the
2Ki 8:2 took up *r* as an alien in the
Ezr 7:15 whose *r* is in Jerusalem
Job 18:19 in his place of alien *r*
Ps 55:15 during their alien *r* bad
Isa 22:16 crag he is cutting out a *r*
La 2:22 call out my places of alien *r*
Eze 20:38 the land of their alien *r*
47:23 taken up *r* as an alien
Mt 4:13 took up *r* in Capernaum beside
Ac 7:2 before he took up *r* in Haran
7:4 and took up *r* in Haran
7:4 change his *r* to this land in
13:17 alien *r* in the land of Egypt
Jas 4:5 spirit which has taken up *r*
1Pe 1:17 the time of your alien *r*
Re 13:6 blaspheme his name and his *r*

Residences
Ge 17:8 land of your alien *r*, even the
28:4 the land of your alien *r*
36:7 the land of their alien *r* was
37:1 in the land of the alien *r*
47:9 the years of my alien *r* are
47:9 the days of their alien *r*
Ex 6:4 the land of their alien *r* in
Ps 119:54 In the house of my alien *r*
Isa 32:18 *r* of full confidence and
Jer 9:19 they have thrown away our *r*
51:30 *r* have been set on fire
Na 3:18 majestic ones stay in their *r*
Hab 1:6 possession of *r* not belonging

Resident
Ge 15:13 seed will become an alien *r*
23:4 alien *r* and settler I am
Ex 2:22 An alien *r* I have come to be
12:19 whether he is an alien *r* or
12:48 in case an alien *r* resides
12:49 alien *r* who is residing as an
18:3 an alien *r* I have come to be
20:10 nor your alien *r* who is
22:21 not maltreat an alien *r* or
23:9 must not oppress an alien *r*
23:9 known the soul of the alien *r*
23:12 and the alien *r* may refresh
Le 16:29 alien *r* who is residing as
17:8 alien *r* who may be residing
17:10 some alien *r* who is residing
17:12 no alien *r* who is residing
Le 17:13 *r* who is . . . an alien
17:15 alien *r*, he must in that
18:26 *r* who is residing as an
19:10 alien *r* you should leave
19:33 alien *r* resides with you as
19:34 alien *r* who resides as an
20:2 *r* who resides as an alien in
22:18 alien *r* . . . his offering
23:22 afflicted one and the alien *r*
24:16 *r* the same as the native
24:22 *r* should prove to be the
25:35 alien *r* and a settler, he
25:47 *r* or the settler with you
25:47 sell himself to the alien *r*
25:47 the family of the alien *r*
Nu 9:14 alien *r* should be residing
9:14 both for the alien *r* and for
15:14 an alien *r* or one who is in
15:15 and the alien *r* who is
15:15 alien *r* should prove to be
15:16 and for the alien *r* who is
15:26 alien *r* who is residing as
15:29 the alien *r* who is residing
15:30 he is a native or an alien *r*
19:10 the alien *r* who is residing
35:15 for the alien *r* and for the
De 1:16 and his brother or his alien *r*
5:14 nor your alien *r* who is
10:18 loving the alien *r* so as to
10:19 must love the alien *r*, for
14:21 To the alien *r* who is inside
14:29 alien *r* and the fatherless
16:11 the alien *r* and the
16:14 the Levite and the alien *r*
23:7 for you became an alien *r* in
24:17 the judgment of the alien *r*
24:19 should stay for the alien *r*
24:20 should stay for the alien *r*
24:21 should stay for the alien *r*
26:11 alien *r* who is in your midst
26:12 to the Levite, the alien *r*
26:13 alien *r*, the fatherless boy
27:19 the judgment of an alien *r*
28:43 alien *r* who is in your midst
29:11 your alien *r* who is in the
31:12 alien *r* who is within your
Jos 8:33 the alien *r* as well as the
20:9 the alien *r* who resides as
2Sa 1:13 of an alien *r*, an Amalekite
Job 31:32 no alien *r* would spend the
Ps 39:12 I am but an alien *r* with you
94:6 and the alien *r* they kill
119:19 an alien *r* in the land
Isa 14:1 alien *r* must be joined to
33:24 no *r* will say: I am sick
Jer 7:6 no alien *r*, no fatherless boy
14:8 like an alien *r* in the land
22:3 do not maltreat any alien *r*
Eze 22:7 Toward the alien *r* they have
22:29 alien *r* they have defrauded
47:23 alien *r* has taken up
Zec 7:10 no alien *r* or afflicted one
Mal 3:5 turning away the alien *r*
Ac 7:29 alien *r* in the land of

Residents
Ex 22:21 alien *r* in the land of Egypt
23:9 alien *r* in the land of Egypt
Le 19:34 alien *r* in the land of Egypt
25:23 alien *r* and settlers from
De 10:19 alien *r* in the land of Egypt
24:14 alien *r* who are in your land
Jos 8:35 alien *r* who walked in their
2Sa 4:3 alien *r* there down to this
1Ch 16:19 very few, and alien *r* in it
22:2 bring together the alien *r*
29:15 we are alien *r* before you
2Ch 2:17 the men that were alien *r*
15:9 alien *r* with them from
30:25 alien *r* that came from the
Ps 105:12 few, and alien *r* in it
146:9 is guarding the alien *r*
Isa 5:17 alien *r* will eat
18:3 and you *r* of the earth, you
26:19 you *r* in the dust
Eze 14:7 from the alien *r* that reside
47:22 to the alien *r* who are
Ho 10:5 the *r* of Samaria will get
Ac 7:6 his seed would be alien *r* in
Eph 2:19 strangers and alien *r*, but
Heb 11:13 temporary *r* in the land
1Pe 1:1 the temporary *r* scattered
2:11 as aliens and temporary *r*

Resides
Ex 12:48 alien resident *r* as an alien
Le 19:33 *r* with you as an alien in
19:34 *r* as an alien with you
20:2 *r* as an alien in Israel, who
Jos 20:9 who *r* as an alien in their
Job 15:28 *r* in cities that are to be
38:19 the way to where light *r*
39:28 on a crag it *r* and stays
Ro 7:17 but sin that *r* in me
8:11 his spirit that *r* in you

Residing
Ge 20:1 and *r* as an alien at Gerar
21:23 you have been *r* as an alien
Ex 3:22 woman *r* as an alien in her
12:49 *r* as an alien in your midst
Le 16:16 *r* with them in the midst of
16:29 *r* as an alien in your midst
17:8 *r* as an alien in your midst
17:10 *r* as an alien in their midst
17:12 *r* as an alien in your midst
17:13 *r* as an alien in your midst
18:26 *r* as an alien in your midst
25:6 those who are *r* as aliens
25:45 *r* as aliens with you, from
Nu 9:14 *r* with you as an alien, he
9:22 tabernacle by *r* over it, the
15:14 *r* as an alien with you an
15:15 who is *r* as an alien will
15:16 is *r* as an alien with you
15:26 *r* as an alien in their midst
15:29 *r* as an alien in their midst
19:10 *r* as an alien in their midst
35:34 the midst of which I am *r*
35:34 I Jehovah am *r* in the midst
De 33:16 of the One *r* in the thornbush
Jg 5:17 his landing places he kept *r*
8:11 those *r* in tents to the east
17:7 And he was *r* there for a time
19:1 Levite was *r* for a time in
19:16 was *r* for a time in Gibeah
1Ki 17:20 am *r* as an alien that you
Ezr 1:4 where he is *r* as an alien
Job 19:15 *r* as aliens in my house
26:5 waters and those *r* in them
Ps 26:8 place of the *r* of your glory
102:28 servants will continue *r*
135:21 Who is *r* in Jerusalem
Pr 7:11 house her feet do not keep *r*
10:30 not keep *r* on the earth
Isa 8:18 who is *r* in Mount Zion
33:5 for he is *r* in the height
57:15 One, who is *r* forever and
Jer 7:3 you people *r* in this place
7:7 keep you *r* in this place
25:24 who are *r* in the wilderness
35:7 where you are *r* as aliens
49:16 *r* in the retreats of the
51:13 *r* on abounding waters
Eze 47:22 *r* as aliens in your midst
Joe 3:17 *r* in Zion my holy mountain
3:21 Jehovah will be *r* in Zion
Ob 3 you who are *r* in the retreats
Mic 7:14 *r* alone in a forest—in the
Re 13:6 even those *r* in heaven

Resinous
Ge 6:14 ark out of wood of a *r* tree
37:25 balsam and *r* bark, on their
43:11 honey, labdanum and *r* bark

Resist
Nu 22:22 in the road to *r* him
Job 9:12 He snatches away. Who can *r*
11:10 then who can *r* him?
23:13 in one mind, and who can *r*
Zec 3:1 right hand in order to *r* him
Mt 5:39 Do not *r* him that is wicked
Lu 21:15 not be able to *r* or dispute
Eph 6:13 able to *r* in the wicked day

Resistance
Le 26:37 no ability to stand in *r*
Nu 22:32 I have come out to offer *r*
Ps 13:2 shall I set *r* in my soul

Resisted
Ga 2:11 I *r* him face to face, because
2Ti 3:8 Jannes and Jambres *r* Moses
4:15 *r* our words to an excessive
Heb 12:4 never yet *r* as far as blood

Resister
1Sa 29:4 a *r* of us in the battle
2Sa 19:22 become today a *r* of me
1Ki 5:4 There is no *r*, and there is

1Ki 22:39 *r* of the affairs of Ahab
22:45 As for the *r* of the affairs
22:46 the *r* of the male temple
2Ki 1:18 the *r* of Ahaziah's things
8:23 *r* of the affairs of Jehoram
10:34 *r* of the affairs of Jehu
12:19 *r* of the affairs of Jehoash
13:8 *r* of the affairs of Jehoahaz
13:12 *r* of the affairs of Jehoash
14:15 *r* of the affairs of Jehoash
14:18 *r* of the affairs of Amaziah
14:28 the *r* of the affairs of
15:6 *r* of the affairs of Azariah
15:11 the *r* of the affairs of
15:15 *r* of the affairs of Shallum
15:21 *r* of the affairs of Menahem
15:26 *r* of the affairs of Pekahiah
15:31 *r* of the affairs of Pekah
15:36 *r* of the affairs of Jotham
16:19 *r* of the affairs of Ahaz
20:20 *r* of the affairs of Hezekiah
21:17 the *r* of the affairs of
21:25 *r* of the affairs of Amon
23:18 Let him *r*. Do not let
23:28 *r* of the affairs of Josiah
24:5 the *r* of the affairs of
25:11 *r* of the people that were
25:11 the *r* of the crowd
1Ch 11:8 to life the *r* of the city
16:41 the *r* of the select men
19:11 *r* of the people he gave into
22:9 *r* from all his enemies all
22:18 has he not given you *r* all
23:25 has given *r* to his people
2Ch 6:41 Jehovah God, into your *r*
9:29 *r* of the affairs of Solomon
13:22 *r* of Abijah's affairs, even
14:6 for Jehovah gave him *r*
14:7 he gives us *r* all around
15:15 give them *r* all around
20:30 God continued to give him *r*
20:34 the *r* of the affairs of
24:14 *r* of the money, and they
25:26 *r* of the affairs of Amaziah
26:22 *r* of the affairs of Uzziah
27:7 *r* of the affairs of Jotham
28:26 *r* of his affairs and all
29:11 not give yourselves up to *r*
32:22 and gave them *r* all around
32:32 *r* of the affairs of Hezekiah
33:18 the *r* of the affairs of
34:9 from all the *r* of Israel and
35:26 *r* of the affairs of Josiah
36:8 the *r* of the affairs of
Ezr 3:8 and the *r* of their brothers
4:3 *r* of the heads of the paternal
4:7 the *r* of his colleagues wrote
4:9 and the *r* of their colleagues
4:10 the *r* of the nations whom
4:10 and the *r* beyond the River
4:17 and the *r* of their colleagues
4:17 and the *r* beyond the River
6:16 the *r* of the former exiles
7:18 the *r* of the silver and gold
7:20 the *r* of the necessities of
Ne 2:16 *r* of the doers of the work
4:14 and the *r* of the people
4:19 rulers and the *r* of the people
6:1 the *r* of our enemies that I
6:14 the *r* of the prophets that
7:72 the *r* of the people gave was
9:28 as soon as they were at *r*
10:28 the *r* of the people, the
11:1 as for the *r* of the people
11:20 *r* of Israel, of the priests
Es 9:12 In the *r* of the jurisdictional
9:16 As for the *r* of the Jews that
9:17 a *r* on the fourteenth day of
9:18 was a *r* on the fifteenth day
Job 3:13 slept then; I should be at *r*
3:17 weary in power are at *r*
3:26 Nor been at *r*, and yet
14:6 that he may have *r*, Until he
30:17 pains . . . do not take any *r*
Pr 18:18 puts even contentions to *r*
21:16 *r* in the very congregation of
29:9 laughed, and there is no *r*
29:17 bring you *r* and give much
Ec 4:6 Better is a handful of *r* than a
6:5 This one has *r* rather than the
11:6 do not let your hand *r*
Isa 10:19 *r* of the trees of his forest
14:1 give them *r* upon their soil
14:3 Jehovah gives you *r* from
Isa 14:7 whole earth has come to *r*
28:12 Give *r* to the weary one
44:19 the *r* of it shall I make
57:2 they take *r* upon their beds
63:14 proceeded to make them *r*
Jer 27:11 let it *r* upon its ground
39:3 *r* of the princes of the king
39:9 *r* of the people who were
39:9 *r* of the people who were
52:15 *r* of the people that were
52:15 *r* of the master workmen
La 5:5 No *r* has been left for us
Eze 16:42 my rage to its *r* in you
21:17 bring my rage to its *r*
24:13 come to its *r* in your case
25:16 destroy the *r* of the
34:18 *r* of your pasturages you
44:30 blessing to *r* upon your
48:23 *r* of the tribes, from the
Da 7:12 for the *r* of the beasts, their
12:13 and you will *r*, but you will
Mic 5:3 the *r* of his brothers will
Zec 6:8 to *r* in the land of the north
Mt 22:6 but the *r*, laying hold of his
25:11 *r* of the virgins also came
26:45 sleeping and taking your *r*
27:49 *r* of them said: Let him be!
Mr 4:19 the desires for the *r* of the
6:31 a lonely place and *r* up a bit
14:41 sleeping and taking your *r*
Lu 8:10 the *r* it is in illustrations
10:6 your peace will *r* upon him
18:9 considered the *r* as nothing
18:11 I am not as the *r* of men
24:9 to the eleven and to all the *r*
24:10 the *r* of the women with
Joh 11:11 our friend has gone to *r*
11:12 if he has gone to *r*, he
11:13 about taking *r* in sleep
Ac 2:37 and the *r* of the apostles
21:13 *R* assured, I am ready not
27:44 *r* to do so, some upon planks
28:9 *r* of the people on the island
Ro 1:13 among the *r* of the nations
11:7 *r* had their sensibilities
15:12 on him nations will *r* their
1Co 1:16 As for the *r*, I do not know
9:5 even as the *r* of the apostles
15:37 wheat or any one of the *r*
2Co 12:13 you became less than the *r*
13:2 before and to all the *r*
Ga 2:13 The *r* of the Jews also joined
Eph 2:3 of wrath even as the *r*
Php 1:13 Guard and all the *r*
4:3 the *r* of my fellow workers
1Th 4:13 not sorrow just as the *r*
5:6 let us not sleep on as the *r*
1Ti 1:16 to *r* their faith on him for
5:20 the *r* also may have fear
6:17 and to *r* their hope, not on
Heb 3:11 shall not enter into my *r*
3:18 should not enter into his *r*
4:1 entering into his *r*, let us
4:3 do enter into the *r*, just as
4:3 shall not enter into my *r*
4:5 shall not enter into my *r*
4:8 led them into a place of *r*
4:10 has entered into God's *r*
4:11 utmost to enter into that *r*
2Pe 3:16 also the *r* of the Scriptures
Re 2:24 *r* of you who are in Thyatira
4:8 they have no *r* day and night
6:11 to *r* a little while longer
8:13 the *r* of the trumpet blasts
9:20 the *r* of the men who were
11:13 the *r* became frightened and
14:11 day and night they have no *r*
14:13 them *r* from their labors
19:21 *r* were killed off with the
20:5 *r* of the dead did not come

Rested
Ex 31:17 on the seventh day he *r* and
1Sa 6:18 they *r* the ark of Jehovah
Es 9:22 had *r* from their enemies
Lu 23:56 they *r* on the sabbath
1Ti 4:10 *r* our hope on a living God
Heb 4:4 And God *r* on the seventh day
4:10 *r* from his own works, just

Restful
Ge 8:21 began to smell a *r* odor
Ex 29:18 offering to Jehovah, a *r* odor
29:25 as a *r* odor before Jehovah
29:41 will render it as a *r* odor
Le 1:9 by fire of a *r* odor to Jehovah
1:13 by fire of a *r* odor to Jehovah
1:17 by fire of a *r* odor to Jehovah
2:2 by fire of a *r* odor to Jehovah
2:9 by fire of a *r* odor to Jehovah
2:12 onto the altar for a *r* odor
3:5 by fire of a *r* odor to Jehovah
3:16 made by fire for a *r* odor
4:31 as a *r* odor to Jehovah; and
6:15 a *r* odor for a remembrancer
6:21 as a *r* odor to Jehovah
8:21 burnt offering for a *r* odor
8:28 sacrifice for a *r* odor
17:6 fat smoke as a *r* odor to
23:13 a *r* odor; and as its drink
23:18 of a *r* odor to Jehovah
26:31 shall not smell your *r* odors
Nu 15:3 to make a *r* odor to Jehovah
15:7 as a *r* odor to Jehovah
15:10 fire, of a *r* odor to Jehovah
15:13 of a *r* odor to Jehovah
15:14 of a *r* odor to Jehovah, just
15:24 for a *r* odor to Jehovah, and
18:17 fire for a *r* odor to Jehovah
28:2 by fire as a *r* odor to me
28:6 a *r* odor, an offering made by
28:8 of a *r* odor to Jehovah
28:13 a burnt offering, a *r* odor
28:24 of a *r* odor to Jehovah
28:27 a burnt offering for a *r* odor
29:2 burnt offering for a *r* odor to
29:6 as a *r* odor, an offering made
29:8 to Jehovah, as a *r* odor, one
29:13 of a *r* odor to Jehovah
29:36 *r* odor to Jehovah, one bull
1Ch 22:9 will prove to be a *r* man
Isa 23:12 it will not be *r* for you
Eze 6:13 a *r* odor to all their dungy
16:19 before them as a *r* odor
20:28 their *r* odors and pouring
20:41 Because of the *r* odor I

Resting
Ge 2:3 *r* from all his work that God
1Ch 28:2 build a *r* house for the ark
Ps 125:3 keep *r* upon the lot of the
Isa 30:15 *r* you people will be saved
Ac 7:49 what is the place for my *r*?
Ro 2:17 *r* upon law and taking pride
Heb 4:9 sabbath *r* for the people of
1Pe 4:14 spirit of God, is *r* upon you

Resting-place
Ge 8:9 And the dove did not find any *r*
49:15 see that the *r* is good and
Nu 10:33 to search out a *r* for them
De 12:9 not yet come into the *r* and
28:65 any *r* for the sole of your
Ru 1:9 find a *r* each one in the house
3:1 ought I not to look for a *r* for
1Ki 8:56 a *r* to his people Israel
1Ch 6:31 after the Ark had a *r*
Ps 95:11 shall not enter into my *r*
116:7 Return to your *r*, O my soul
132:8 Jehovah, to your *r*
132:14 This is my *r* forever
Pr 24:15 do not despoil his *r*
Isa 11:10 his *r* must become glorious
28:12 This is the *r*. Give rest
34:14 and find for itself a *r*
35:7 place of jackals, a *r* for
65:10 Achor a *r* for cattle
66:1 the place as a *r* for me
Jer 45:3 and no *r* have I found
50:6 They have forgotten their *r*
La 1:3 No *r* has she found. All those
Eze 25:5 sons of Ammon a *r* of a flock
Mic 2:10 because this is not a *r*
Mt 12:43 in search of a *r*, and finds
Lu 11:24 in search of a *r*, and, after

Resting-places
Ps 23:2 By well-watered *r* he conducts
Isa 32:18 and in undisturbed *r*

Restless
Ge 27:40 when you grow *r*

Restlessly
Ps 55:2 driven *r* about by my concern

Restlessness
Job 7:4 have also been glutted with *r*

Restoration
1Sa 12:3 I shall make *r* to you people
Ne 5:12 We shall make *r*, and from

Ac 3:21 *r* of all things of which God

Restore
2Sa 16:12 *r* to me goodness instead of
2Ki 14:22 and got to *r* it to Judah
Ezr 9:9 to *r* its desolated places and
Ne 5:11 *r* to them on this day their
Job 8:6 *r* your righteous abiding place
33:26 *r* His righteousness to
Ps 51:12 Do *r* to me the exultation
60:1 You should *r* us
Isa 38:16 you will *r* me to health
Jer 27:22 *r* them to this place
Da 9:25 the word to *r* and to rebuild
Mt 17:11 and will *r* all things
Mr 9:12 and *r* all things; but how is

Restored
Ex 4:7 *r* like the rest of his flesh
1Ki 13:6 that my hand may be *r* to me
13:6 the king's hand was *r* to him
2Ki 14:25 *r* the boundary of Israel
14:28 *r* Damascus and Hamath to
16:6 of Syria *r* Elath to Edom
2Ch 26:2 *r* it to Judah after the king
33:13 *r* him to Jerusalem to his
Ps 20:8 risen up, that we may be *r*
Mt 5:13 how will its saltness be *r*?
12:13 *r* sound like the other hand
Mr 3:5 it out, and his hand was *r*
8:25 saw clearly, and he was *r*
Lu 6:10 did so, and his hand was *r*
Heb 13:19 I may be *r* to you the

Restorer
Ru 4:15 has become a *r* of your soul
Isa 58:12 the *r* of roadways by which

Restores
Pr 25:13 for he *r* the very soul of his

Restoring
Lu 19:8 I am *r* fourfold
Ac 1:6 *r* the kingdom to Israel at

Restrain
Nu 11:28 My lord Moses, *r* them!
Ps 40:9 Look! My lips I do not *r*
40:11 do not *r* your pity from me
Ec 8:8 power over the spirit to *r* the
Isa 48:9 for my praise I shall *r*
1Pe 3:10 let him *r* his tongue from

Restrained
Ge 8:2 from the heavens was *r*
Ex 36:6 were *r* from bringing it in
Nu 9:7 *r* from presenting the offering
1Sa 25:33 *r* me this day from entering
Job 29:9 Princes themselves *r* words
Ps 119:101 bad path I have *r* my feet
Pr 30:16 Sheol and a *r* womb, a land
Isa 63:15 Toward me they have *r*
Jer 32:3 king of Judah had *r* him
Eze 31:15 the many waters may be *r*
Ac 14:18 they scarcely *r* the crowds
27:43 *r* them from their purpose
2Ti 2:24 keeping himself *r* under evil

Restraint
Job 4:2 to put a *r* on words who is
12:15 He puts a *r* upon the waters
Ps 88:8 I am under *r* and cannot go
107:39 Owing to *r*, calamity and
Pr 25:28 that has no *r* for his spirit
Isa 14:6 with a persecution without *r*
53:8 Because of *r* and of judgment
Jer 32:2 under *r* in the Courtyard of
2Th 2:6 the thing that acts as a *r*
2:7 is right now acting as a *r*
1Jo 4:18 because fear exercises a *r*

Restricted
2Ki 4:13 have *r* yourself for us with

Restriction
2Ki 4:13 for us with all this *r*

Restrictions
1Ch 12:1 under *r* because of Saul the

Rests
Pr 14:33 there *r* wisdom, and in the
Ec 7:9 taking of offense is what *r* in
Zec 9:1 and Damascus is where it *r*
Ro 9:33 he that *r* his faith on it
10:11 None that *r* his faith on

Result
Ge 6:13 full of violence as a *r* of
35:18 *r* was that as her soul was
36:7 as a *r* of their herds
39:19 The *r* was that as soon as
41:31 as a *r* of that famine
47:13 as a *r* of the famine
Ex 1:12 dread as a *r* of the sons of
3:7 their outcry as a *r* of those
8:24 ruin as a *r* of the gadflies
9:11 before Moses as a *r* of the
De 30:12 as to *r* in saying, Who will
30:13 so as to *r* in saying, Who
2Ki 2:21 miscarriages *r* from it
2Ch 28:13 *r* in guilt against Jehovah
Pr 22:4 *r* of humility and the fear of
Isa 28:7 confused as a *r* of the wine
28:7 *r* of the intoxicating liquor
Am 8:10 end *r* of it as a bitter day
Mr 3:10 cured many, with the *r* that
Lu 12:15 life does not *r* from the
Ac 17:4 As a *r* some of them became
Ro 3:30 righteous as a *r* of faith and
4:2 righteous as a *r* of works, he
4:16 it was as a *r* of faith
5:1 righteous as a *r* of faith
5:18 one trespass the *r* to men of
5:18 *r* to men of all sorts is a
Ga 2:2 went up as a *r* of a revelation
5:5 righteousness as a *r* of faith
Php 1:19 this will *r* in my salvation
1Th 2:16 with the *r* that they always
2Th 1:4 As a *r* we ourselves take
1Pe 1:22 brotherly love as the *r*
2:12 as a *r* of your fine works of

Resulted
Ge 47:24 When it has *r* in produce
Ps 64:7 Wounds have *r* to them
Jer 2:19 no dread of me has *r* to you
Joh 10:19 division *r* among the Jews
Ro 5:16 judgment *r* from one trespass
5:16 gift *r* from many trespasses

Resulting
Ge 5:29 pain of our hands *r* from the
Le 6:7 he might do *r* in guiltiness by
De 26:19 *r* in praise and reputation
30:9 *r* in prosperity
Pr 13:11 things *r* from vanity become
Isa 30:26 wound *r* from the stroke by
Mal 2:13 *r* in covering with tears the
Ro 10:6 righteousness *r* from faith
11:31 with mercy *r* to you, that
Ga 3:22 promise *r* from faith toward

Results
Pr 10:16 the righteous one *r* in life
10:16 of the wicked one *r* in sin
11:24 but it *r* only in want
14:14 with the *r* of his own ways
14:14 with the *r* of his dealings
Ec 10:11 bites when no charming *r*
Isa 55:2 what *r* in no satisfaction
55:11 not return to me without *r*
Jer 50:9 not come back without *r*
Ro 9:30 righteousness that *r* from
Php 3:9 righteousness, which *r* from
1Th 2:1 has not been without *r*

Resume
Ge 30:31 *r* shepherding your flock
Nu 35:32 to *r* dwelling in the land
Job 17:10 you men may all of you *r*

Resumed
Ge 26:18 he *r* calling their names by

Resurrect
Joh 6:39 should *r* it at the last day
6:40 will *r* him at the last day
6:44 will *r* him in the last day
6:54 shall *r* him at the last day

Resurrected
Ac 2:24 God *r* him by loosing the
2:32 Jesus God *r*, of which fact
13:33 in that he *r* Jesus; even
13:34 he *r* him from the dead
17:31 he has *r* him from the dead
26:23 first to be *r* from the dead

Resurrection
Mt 22:23 who say there is no *r*, came
22:28 in the *r*, to which of the
22:30 the *r* neither do men marry
22:31 As regards the *r* of the dead
Mr 12:18 Sadducees . . . there is no *r*
12:23 In the *r* to which of them
Lu 14:14 in the *r* of the righteous
20:27 those who say there is no *r*
20:33 in the *r*, of which one of
Lu 20:35 the *r* from the dead neither
20:36 by being children of the *r*
Joh 5:29 good things to a *r* of life
5:29 to a *r* of judgment
11:24 in the *r* on the last day
11:25 I am the *r* and the life
Ac 1:22 a witness with us of his *r*
2:31 *r* of the Christ, that neither
4:2 declaring the *r* from the dead
4:33 the *r* of the Lord Jesus
17:18 good news of Jesus and the *r*
17:32 they heard of a *r* of the dead
23:6 Over the hope of *r* of the dead
23:8 Sadducees say . . . neither *r*
24:15 *r* of both the righteous and
24:21 Over the *r* of the dead I am
Ro 1:4 by means of *r* from the dead
6:5 in the likeness of his *r*
1Co 15:12 there is no *r* of the dead
15:13 there is no *r* of the dead
15:21 *r* of the dead is also
15:42 So also is the *r* of the dead
Php 3:10 and the power of his *r*
3:11 earlier *r* from the dead
2Ti 2:18 the *r* has already occurred
Heb 6:2 the *r* of the dead and
11:35 received their dead by *r*
11:35 might attain a better *r*
1Pe 1:3 through the *r* of Jesus Christ
3:21 through the *r* of Jesus Christ
Re 20:5 This is the first *r*
20:6 having part in the first *r*

Retain
1Ch 29:14 *r* power to make voluntary
2Ch 2:6 *r* power to build him a house
13:20 Jeroboam did not *r* any more
14:11 let mortal man *r* strength
20:37 *r* strength to go to Tarshish
22:9 of Ahaziah to *r* power for
Da 10:16 and I did not *r* any power
11:6 not *r* the power of her arm
Mr 7:9 in order to *r* your tradition
Lu 8:15 *r* it and bear fruit with
Joh 20:23 you *r* those of any persons

Retained
Da 10:8 and I *r* no power
Joh 20:23 sins . . . they stand *r*

Retire
Nu 8:25 fifty years he will *r* from
Jg 7:3 Let him *r*. So Gideon put them

Retired
Jg 7:3 the people *r*, and there were
Lu 4:13 *r* from him until another

Retirement
Lu 5:16 *r* in the deserts and praying

Retrace
Isa 38:8 *r* backward ten steps

Retraction
Job 42:6 That is why I make a *r*

Retreat
2Sa 11:15 *r* from behind him, and he
Job 36:20 to *r* from where they are

Retreated
2Sa 23:9 and so the men of Israel *r*
Ps 78:9 *R* in the day of fight
Jer 38:22 *r* in the opposite direction

Retreats
Ca 2:14 my dove in the *r* of the crag
Jer 49:16 in the *r* of the crag
Ob 3 residing in the *r* of the crag

Retribution
De 32:35 Vengeance is mine, and *r*
32:41 And render *r* to those who
Ps 91:8 *r* itself of the wicked ones
94:2 back a *r* upon the haughty ones
Ro 11:9 a stumbling block and a *r*
2Th 2:10 who are perishing, as a *r*
Heb 2:2 *r* in harmony with justice

Retributions
Isa 34:8 *r* for the legal case over

Return
Ge 3:19 until you *r* to the ground
3:19 and to dust you will *r*
15:16 they will *r* here, because
16:9 *R* to your mistress and humble
18:10 going to *r* to you next year
18:14 I shall *r* to you, next year

Ge 20:7 *r* the man's wife, for he is a
22:5 and worship and *r* to you
24:5 sure to *r* your son to the land
24:6 you do not *r* my son there
24:8 you must not *r* my son there
28:15 I will *r* you to this ground
28:21 I shall certainly *r* in peace
31:3 *R* to the land of your fathers
31:13 *r* to the land of your birth
31:55 might *r* to his own place
32:9 *R* to your land and to your
37:22 order to *r* him to his father
40:13 *r* you to your office; and you
42:25 *r* the money of the men to
42:37 the one to *r* him to you
43:2 *R*, buy a little food for us
43:13 get up, *r* to the man
43:21 *r* it with our own hands
44:25 *R*, buy a little food for us
48:21 *r* you to the land of your
50:5 I am willing to *r*
Ex 4:7 *R* your hand into the upper fold
4:18 want to . . . *r* to my brothers
4:19 Go, *r* to Egypt, because all
4:20 to *r* to the land of Egypt
13:17 will certainly *r* to Egypt
21:34 The price he is to *r* to its
22:26 as a pledge, you are to *r* it
23:4 to *r* it without fail to him
24:14 this place until we *r* to you
32:27 *r* from gate to gate in the
Le 6:4 he must *r* the robbed thing
14:39 *r* on the seventh day and
22:13 *r* to her father's house as
25:10 *r* each one to his possession
25:10 *r* each one to his family
25:13 Jubilee you should *r* each one
25:27 *r* what money remains over to
25:27 he must *r* to his possession
25:28 he must *r* to his possession
25:41 *r* to his family, and he
25:41 *r* to the possession of his
27:24 field will *r* to the one from
Nu 5:7 *r* the amount of his guilt in
5:8 *r* the amount of the guilt, the
10:36 *r*, O Jehovah, to the myriads
14:3 better for us to *r* to Egypt
14:4 and let us *r* to Egypt!
18:9 which they will *r* to me
18:21 in *r* for their service that
18:31 wages in *r* for your service
22:8 I shall certainly *r* you word
23:5 *R* to Balak, and this is what
23:16 *R* to Balak, and this is what
32:18 We shall not *r* to our houses
32:22 and afterward you *r*, you
35:25 *r* him to his city of refuge
35:28 manslayer may *r* to the land
De 4:30 *r* to Jehovah your God and
5:30 *R* home to your tents
20:5 *r* to his house, for fear he
20:6 *r* to his house, for fear he
20:7 *r* to his house, for fear he
20:8 *r* to his house, that he may
22:2 And you must *r* it to him
24:13 *r* the pledge to him as soon
28:31 but it will not *r* to you
30:10 you will *r* to Jehovah your
Jos 1:15 *r* to the land of your holding
10:21 began to *r* to the camp
18:8 and map it out and *r* to me
20:6 that the manslayer may *r*
22:8 *R* to your tents with many
Jg 6:18 keep sitting here until you *r*
8:9 When I *r* in peace, I shall pull
8:13 began his *r* from the war by
8:35 in *r* for all the goodness that
11:13 And now do *r* it peacefully
11:31 I *r* in peace from the sons
11:39 she made her *r* to her father
Ru 1:6 to *r* from the fields of Moab
1:7 road to *r* to the land of Judah
1:8 *r*, each one to the house of her
1:10 we shall *r* to your people
1:11 Naomi said: *R*, my daughters
1:12 *R*, my daughters, go, for I
1:15 *R* with your widowed
1:21 that Jehovah has made me *r*
1:22 Thus Naomi made her *r*, Ruth
1Sa 5:11 that it may *r* to its place
6:3 *r* to him a guilt offering
6:4 that we ought to *r* to him
6:8 *r* to him as a guilt offering
7:17 his *r* was to Ramah, because

1Sa 9:5 let us *r*, that my father may
15:25 and *r* with me that I may
15:26 said to Saul: I shall not *r*
15:30 and *r* with me, and I shall
18:2 he did not allow him to *r*
23:23 *r* to me with the evidence
25:21 evil in *r* for good
29:7 *r* and go in peace, that you
29:11 *r* to the land of the
2Sa 1:22 would not *r* without success
3:16 Abner said to him: Go, *r!*
3:26 had him *r* from the cistern
9:7 *r* to you all the field of Saul
10:5 Then you must *r*
11:1 *r* of the year, at the time
12:23 he will not *r* to me
15:27 Do *r* to the city in peace
15:34 if you *r* to the city and you
18:16 *r* from chasing after Israel
19:21 In *r* for this should not
19:37 Let your servant *r*, please
22:38 I shall not *r* until they are
1Ki 2:44 *r* the injury by you upon
8:33 *r* to you and laud your name
8:47 *r* and make request to you
8:48 *r* to you with all their
12:5 for three days and *r* to me
12:12 *R* to me on the third day
12:26 kingdom will *r* to the house
12:27 bound to *r* to their lord
12:27 and *r* to Rehoboam the king
13:9 not *r* by the way that you
13:10 did not *r* by the way by
19:15 Go, *r* on your way to the
19:20 *r*; for what have I done to
20:22 *r* of the year the king of
20:26 *r* of the year that Ben-hadad
20:34 from your father I shall *r*
22:28 If you *r* at all in peace
2Ki 1:6 *r* to the king who sent you
4:22 man of the true God and *r*
8:3 to *r* from the land of the
8:6 *R* all that belongs to her and
19:7 and *r* to his own land
19:33 he will *r*, and into this
1Ch 19:5 Then you must *r*
20:1 at the time of the year's *r*
2Ch 6:24 *r* and laud your name and
6:37 *r* and make request to you
6:38 *r* to you with all their
10:5 three days. Then *r* to me
10:12 *R* to me on the third day
11:4 *R* each one to his house, for
18:26 until I *r* in peace
18:27 *r* at all in peace, Jehovah
20:27 *r* to Jerusalem with
28:11 *r* the captives that you
30:6 Israel, *r* to Jehovah the God
30:6 *r* to the escaped ones that
30:9 when you *r* to Jehovah, your
30:9 allowed to *r* to this land
30:9 from you if you *r* to him
32:25 Hezekiah made no *r*, for his
36:10 at the *r* of the year King
36:13 so as not to *r* to Jehovah
Ne 2:6 and when will you *r?*
4:4 reproach *r* upon their own head
4:12 you people will *r* to us
9:17 to *r* to their servitude in
9:28 *r* and call to you for aid, and
Job 1:21 And naked shall I *r* there
6:29 *R* . . . let no unrighteousness
6:29 Yes, *r*—my righteousness is
7:10 not *r* anymore to his house
10:9 to dust you will make me *r*
13:22 and you *r* me answer
16:22 path by which I shall not *r*
22:23 If you *r* to the Almighty
33:25 *r* to the days of his
34:15 will *r* to the very dust
39:4 go forth and do not *r* to
Ps 6:4 Do *r*, O Jehovah, do rescue
7:7 against it do you *r* on high
7:12 If anyone will not *r*, His
7:16 trouble will *r* upon his own
18:37 I shall not *r* until they are
35:13 my own prayer would *r*
38:20 in *r* for my pursuing what is
59:14 let them *r* at eveningtime
60:*super* Joab proceeded to *r* and
74:21 crushed one not *r* humiliated
80:14 O God of armies, *r*, please
85:8 not *r* to self-confidence
90:13 Do *r*, O Jehovah! How long

Ps 94:15 will *r* even to righteousness
116:7 *R* to your resting-place
Pr 22:21 *r* sayings that are the truth
26:27 stone—back to him it will *r*
Isa 10:21 mere remnant will *r*, the
10:22 remnant among them will *r*
19:22 and they must *r* to Jehovah
23:17 *r* to her hire and commit
31:6 *R*, you people, to the One
35:10 redeemed by Jehovah will *r*
37:7 and *r* to his own land
37:34 he came he will *r*, and into
44:22 *r* to me, for I will
45:23 so that it will not *r*
51:11 *r* and must come to Zion
55:7 and let him *r* to Jehovah
55:10 does not *r* to that place
55:11 not *r* to me without results
Jer 3:1 should he *r* to her anymore?
3:7 she should *r* even to me
3:7 but she did not *r*
3:10 did not *r* to me with all her
3:12 Do *r*, O renegade Israel, is
3:14 *R*, O you renegade sons
3:22 *R*, you renegade sons
4:1 If you would *r*, O Israel
4:1 you may *r* even to me
22:10 for he will *r* no more and
22:11 He will *r* there no more
22:27 lifting up their soul to *r*
22:27 there they will not *r*
23:14 that they should not *r*
24:6 cause them to *r* to this land
24:7 *r* to me with all their heart
26:3 they will listen and *r*
30:10 Jacob will certainly *r*
31:8 congregation they will *r*
31:16 *r* from the land of the
31:17 *r* to their own territory
36:3 *r*, each one from his bad
36:7 *r*, each one from his bad
40:5 was yet not one that would *r*
40:5 *r* to Gedaliah the son of
40:12 Jews began to *r* from all
41:14 *r* and go to Johanan the
42:12 *r* you to your own soil
44:14 *r* to the land of Judah to
44:14 to *r* in order to dwell
44:14 not *r*, except some escaped
44:28 *r* from the land of Egypt
46:16 let us *r* to our people and
46:27 Jacob will certainly *r* and
La 3:40 do let us *r* clear to Jehovah
Eze 7:13 seller himself will not *r*
7:13 No one will *r*, and they will
16:55 *r* to their former state
16:55 *r* to their former state
16:55 own dependent towns will *r*
18:7 the pledge . . . he would *r*
18:12 thing he would not *r*
21:30 *R* it to its sheath
46:17 must *r* to the chieftain
47:6 *r* to the bank of the torrent
Da 4:34 understanding began to *r* to
4:36 understanding . . . to *r* to me
4:36 dignity . . . began to *r* to me
9:25 *r* and be actually rebuilt
11:13 king of the north must *r* and
Ho 2:7 *r* to my husband, the first one
5:15 I will *r* to my place until
6:1 do let us *r* to Jehovah
7:16 *r*, not to anything higher
8:13 To Egypt . . . proceeded to *r*
9:3 Ephraim must *r* to Egypt, and
11:5 not *r* to the land of Egypt
11:5 because they refused to *r*
12:6 to your God you should *r*
14:2 in *r* the young bulls of our
Ob 15 will *r* upon your own head
Mic 1:7 hire of a prostitute . . . *r*
5:3 will *r* to the sons of Israel
Zec 1:3 *R* to me, is the utterance of
1:3 and I shall *r* to you, Jehovah
1:4 *R*, please, from your bad ways
1:16 *r* to Jerusalem with mercies
8:3 I will *r* to Zion and reside
9:12 *R* to the stronghold, you
10:9 revive with their sons and *r*
Mal 1:4 but we shall *r* and build the
3:7, 7 *R* to me, and I will *r* to
3:7 In what way shall we *r?*
Mt 2:12 not to *r* to Herod, they
10:13 let the peace from you *r*
24:18 man in the field not *r* to

Mt 26:52 *R* your sword to its place
Mr 13:16 *r* to the things behind to
Lu 6:38 will measure out to you in *r*
11:24 I will *r* to my house out of
14:12 also invite you in *r* and it
17:31 not *r* to the things behind
19:12 power for himself and to *r*
23:48 *r*, beating their breasts
Ac 13:34 no more to *r* to corruption
15:16 shall *r* and rebuild the booth
15:36 us *r* and visit the brothers
18:21 I will *r* to you again, if
20:3 to *r* through Macedonia
Ro 12:17 *R* evil for evil to no one
2Co 6:13 So, as a recompense in *r*
1Th 3:9 in *r* for all the joy with
Heb 6:7 receives in *r* a blessing from
11:15 have had opportunity to *r*
1Pe 2:23 he did not go reviling in *r*

Returned
Ge 8:9 and so it *r* to him into the ark
14:17 after he *r* from defeating
18:33 and Abraham *r* to his place
20:14 and *r* to him Sarah his wife
21:32 they *r* to the land of the
22:19 Abraham *r* to his attendants
29:3 *r* the stone over the mouth
32:6 the messengers *r* to Jacob
37:29 Reuben *r* to the waterpit and
37:30 he *r* to his other brothers
38:22 he *r* to Judah and said: I
40:21 *r* the chief of the cupbearers
41:13 Me he *r* to my office, but
42:24 *r* to them and spoke to them
42:28 My money has been *r* and now
43:12 *r* in the mouth of your bags
44:13 and *r* to the city
50:14 Joseph *r* to Egypt, he and his
Ex 4:7 *r* his hand into the upper fold
4:18 Moses went and *r* to Jethro
4:21 After you have gone and *r* to
32:31 Moses *r* to Jehovah and said
33:11 When he *r* to the camp, his
Nu 5:8 *r* to Jehovah belongs to the
13:25 *r* from spying out the land
14:36 when they *r*, began making
16:50 at last Aaron *r* to Moses at
23:6 he *r* to him, and, look! he
24:25 Balaam got up and went and *r*
De 1:45 *r* and began to weep before
30:2 you have *r* to Jehovah your
Jos 6:14 they *r* to the camp
7:3 they *r* to Joshua and said to
8:24 *r* to Ai and struck it with
10:15 *r* to the camp at Gilgal
10:43 *r* to the camp at Gilgal
22:9 the half tribe of Manasseh *r*
22:32 and the chieftains *r* from
Jg 7:15 *r* to the camp of Israel and
11:8 now we have *r* to you, and you
15:19 his spirit *r* and he revived
17:4 he *r* the silver to his mother
21:23 *r* to their inheritance and
Ru 1:15 *r* to her people and her gods
2:6 a Moabitess, who *r* with Naomi
4:3 has *r* from the field of Moab
1Sa 1:19 *r* and came into their house
5:3 took Dagon and *r* him to his
6:17 the Philistines *r* as a guilt
6:21 Philistines have *r* the ark of
15:31 Samuel *r* behind Saul, and
17:53 Israel *r* from hotly
17:57 as soon as David *r* from
18:6 David *r* from striking the
24:1 Saul *r* from following the
26:25 Saul, he *r* to his place
27:9 he *r* and came to Achish
30:12 he ate and his spirit *r*
2Sa 1:1 David himself had *r* from
3:16 At that he *r*
3:27 Abner *r* to Hebron, Joab now
6:20 David now *r* to bless his own
10:14 Joab *r* from the sons of
11:4 Later she *r* to her house
12:31 the people *r* to Jerusalem
17:20 and so *r* to Jerusalem
19:39 he *r* to his place
20:22 Joab himself *r* to Jerusalem
23:10 *r* behind him only to strip
1Ki 12:20 heard that Jeroboam had *r*
14:28 *r* them to the guard chamber
19:21 he *r* from following him
2Ki 2:18 *r* to him, he was dwelling
2Ki 2:25 from there he *r* to Samaria
3:27 and *r* to their land
4:38 Elisha himself *r* to Gilgal
7:8 *r* and entered into another
7:15 messengers *r* and reported to
8:29 king *r* to get healed at
9:15 *r* to get healed at Jezreel
9:18 to them, but he has not *r*
9:20 but he has not *r*
9:36 they *r* and told him, he went
14:14 and then *r* to Samaria
19:8 *r* and found the king of
19:36 and went and *r*, and he took
23:20 that he *r* to Jerusalem
23:25 *r* to Jehovah with all his
1Ch 20:3 David and all the people *r* to
21:27 angel . . . *r* his sword to
2Ch 11:4 *r* from going against
12:11 *r* them to the guard chamber
14:15 they *r* to Jerusalem
15:4 distress they *r* to Jehovah
19:1 *r* in peace to his own house
20:27 Judah and Jerusalem *r*, with
22:6 *r* to get healed at Jezreel
24:11 *r* it to its place
25:10 *r* to their own place in
25:24 and then *r* to Samaria
28:15 they *r* to Samaria
31:1 Israel *r* to their cities
34:7 which he *r* to Jerusalem
Ezr 2:1 *r* to Jerusalem and Judah
6:5 and brought to Babylon be *r*
6:21 had *r* from the Exile ate
Ne 1:9 you will have *r* to me and kept
7:6 *r* to Jerusalem and to Judah
Es 2:14 *r* to the second house of the
6:12 Mordecai *r* to the king's gate
7:8 king himself *r* from the garden
Ps 78:34 they *r* and looked for God
Ec 4:1 *r* that I might see all the
4:7 *r* that I might see the vanity
9:11 I *r* to see under the sun that
12:2 clouds have *r*, afterward the
Isa 9:13 *r* to the One striking them
37:8 Rabshakeh *r* and found the
37:37 *r* and took up dwelling in
Jer 11:10 *r* to the errors of their
14:3 *r* with their vessels empty
43:5 *r* from all the nations to
Eze 47:7 When I *r*, why, look! on the
Ho 7:10 not *r* to Jehovah their God
Zec 1:6 *r* and said: According to what
Mt 26:66 *r* answer: He is liable to
Lu 1:56 and *r* to her own home
2:45 they *r* to Jerusalem, making
4:14 Jesus *r* in the power of the
8:55 her spirit *r*, and she rose
9:10 when the apostles *r* they
10:17 Then the seventy *r* with joy
22:32 when once you have *r*
24:9 *r* from the memorial tomb
24:33 they rose and *r* to Jerusalem
24:52 *r* to Jerusalem with great
Ac 1:12 they *r* to Jerusalem from a
5:22 So they *r* and made report
12:25 they *r* and took along with
13:13 But John . . . *r* to Jerusalem
14:21 *r* to Lystra and to Iconium
21:6 but they *r* to their homes
22:17 I had *r* to Jerusalem and was
23:32 *r* to the soldiers' quarters
1Pe 2:25 have *r* to the shepherd and
2Pe 2:22 dog has *r* to its own vomit

Returning
Ge 8:7 raven . . . going and *r*, until
20:7 if you are not *r* her, know
Jos 4:18 Jordan began *r* to their place
Ru 1:22 *r* from the fields of Moab
1Sa 7:3 heart you are *r* to Jehovah
17:15 David was going and *r* from
2Sa 17:3 Equivalent to the *r* of all is
Ps 59:6 They keep *r* at eveningtime
Pr 26:11 like a dog *r* to its vomit
Ec 1:6 to its circlings the wind is *r*
1:7 they are *r* so as to go forth
3:20 and they are all *r* to the dust
Isa 1:27 *r* of her, with righteousness
Jer 3:1 should there be a *r* to me?
Eze 1:14 was a going forth and a *r* as
35:7 cut off . . . the one *r*
Ho 5:4 permit of a *r* to their God
Mic 2:8 like those *r* from war
Zec 7:14 and with no one *r*
Zec 9:8 passing through and no one *r*
Mt 21:18 While *r* to the city early in
Lu 2:38 began *r* thanks to God and
2:43 when they were *r*, the boy
Ac 8:28 he was *r* and was sitting in
Heb 7:1 Abraham *r* from the slaughter

Returns
Le 14:43 the plague *r* and it does
Ec 12:7 dust *r* to the earth just as it
12:7 spirit itself *r* to the true
Eze 33:15 *r* the very thing pledged
Lu 12:36 he *r* from the marriage

Reu
Ge 11:18 Peleg . . . became father to *R*
11:19 after his fathering *R* Peleg
11:20 *R* lived on for thirty-two
11:21 *R* continued to live two
1Ch 1:25 Eber, Peleg, *R*
Lu 3:35 son of Serug, son of *R*, son of

Reuben
Ge 29:32 then called his name *R*
30:14 *R* went walking in the days
35:22 *R* went and lay down with
35:23 Jacob's firstborn *R* and
37:21 When *R* heard this he tried
37:22 And *R* went on to say to them
37:29 *R* returned to the waterpit
42:22 *R* answered them, saying: Did
42:37 *R* said to his father: My own
46:8 Jacob's firstborn was *R*
46:9 sons of *R* were Hanoch and
48:5 mine like *R* and Simeon
49:3 *R*, you are my firstborn, my
Ex 1:2 *R*, Simeon, Levi and Judah
6:14 The sons of *R*, Israel's
6:14 These are the families of *R*
Nu 1:5 Of *R*, Elizur the son of
1:20 sons of *R*, Israel's firstborn
1:21 registered . . . tribe of *R*
2:10 camp of *R* will be toward the
2:10 for the sons of *R* is Elizur
2:16 ones of the camp of *R* are
7:30 for the sons of *R*, Elizur the
10:18 camp of *R* pulled away in
13:4 Of the tribe of *R*, Shammua
16:1 son of Peleth, the sons of *R*
26:5 *R*, Israel's firstborn
32:1 sons of *R* and the sons of Gad
32:2 sons of *R* came and said this
32:6 sons of Gad and the sons of *R*
32:25 sons of *R* said this to Moses
32:29 sons of *R* pass with you over
32:31 and the sons of *R* answered
32:33 to the sons of *R* and to half
32:37 sons of *R* built Heshbon and
De 11:6 sons of Eliab the son of *R*
27:13 *R*, Gad and Asher and Zebulun
33:6 Let *R* live and not die off
Jos 4:12 the sons of *R* and the sons
13:15 tribe of the sons of *R*
13:23 boundary of the sons of *R*
13:23 sons of *R* by their families
15:6 Bohan the son of *R*
18:7 and Gad and *R* and the half
18:17 Bohan the son of *R*
20:8 out of the tribe of *R*
21:7 out of the tribe of *R* and
21:36 And out of the tribe of *R*
22:9 sons of *R* and the sons of Gad
22:10 sons of *R* and the sons of
22:11 sons of *R* and the sons of
22:13 sent to the sons of *R* and
22:15 they came to the sons of *R*
22:21 sons of *R* and the sons of
22:25 the sons of *R* and the sons
22:30 words that the sons of *R*
22:31 said to the sons of *R* and
22:32 from the sons of *R* and the
22:33 in which the sons of *R* and
22:34 *R* and the sons of Gad began
Jg 5:15 Among the divisions of *R*
5:16 For the divisions of *R* there
1Ch 2:1 sons of Israel: *R*, Simeon
5:1 *R* the firstborn of Israel
5:3 *R* the firstborn of Israel
5:18 sons of *R* and the Gadites and
6:63 gave from the tribe of *R*
6:78 from the tribe of *R*, Bezer
Eze 48:6 to the western border, *R* one
48:7 on the boundary of *R*, from
48:31 north, the gate of *R*, one
Re 7:5 out of . . . *R* twelve thousand

Reubenite
1Ch 11:42 Adina the son of Shiza the *R*

Reubenites
Nu 26:7 were the families of the *R*
34:14 *R* . . . have already taken
De 3:12 cities I have given to the *R*
3:16 to the *R* and the Gadites I
4:43 on the tableland for the *R*
29:8 an inheritance to the *R* and
Jos 1:12 to the *R* and the Gadites and
12:6 gave it as a holding to the *R*
13:8 the other half tribe the *R*
22:1 proceeded to call the *R* and
2Ki 10:33 the Gadites and the *R* and
1Ch 5:6 being a chieftain of the *R*
5:26 into exile those of the *R* and
11:42 a head of the *R*, by whom
12:37 of the *R* and the Gadites
26:32 assigned them over the *R*
27:16 of the *R*, Eliezer the son of

Reuben's
Nu 26:5 *R* sons: Of Hanoch the family

Reuel
Ge 36:4 and Basemath bore *R*
36:10 *R* the son of Basemath
36:13 These are the sons of *R*
36:17 the sons of *R*, Esau's son
36:17 sheiks of *R* in the land of
Ex 2:18 came home to *R* their father
Nu 2:14 Eliasaph the son of *R*
10:29 Hobab the son of *R* the
1Ch 1:35 sons of Esau were . . . *R*
1:37 sons of *R* were Nahath
9:8 son of *R* the son of Ibnijah

Reumah
Ge 22:24 whose name was *R*. In time

Reveal
1Sa 2:27 *r* myself to the house of
Pr 25:9 do not *r* the confidential talk
Isa 49:9 the darkness, *R* yourselves!
Jer 33:6 *r* to them an abundance of
Da 2:47 were able to *r* this secret
Mt 11:27 the Son is willing to *r* him
16:17 flesh and blood did not *r* it
Lu 10:22 the Son is willing to *r* him
Ga 1:16 to *r* his Son in connection
Php 3:15 will *r* the above attitude to

Revealed
Ge 35:7 God had *r* himself to him at
De 29:29 things *r* belong to us and
1Sa 3:7 not yet begun to be *r* to him
3:21 Jehovah *r* himself to Samuel
1Ch 17:25 have *r* to your servant the
Ps 98:2 he has *r* his righteousness
Pr 27:5 Better is a *r* reproof than a
Isa 22:14 Jehovah of armies has *r*
23:1 Kittim it has been *r* to
40:5 glory of Jehovah . . . be *r*
53:1 to whom has it been *r*?
56:1 my righteousness to be *r*
Jer 11:20 I have *r* my case at law
20:12 I have *r* my case at law
Da 2:19 night vision the secret was *r*
2:30 secret is *r* to me, except
10:1 was a matter *r* to Daniel
Am 3:7 *r* his confidential matter to
Mt 11:25 and have *r* them to babes
Lu 2:26 *r* to him by the holy spirit
10:21 and have *r* them to babes
12:2 concealed that will not be *r*
17:30 the Son of man is to be *r*
Joh 12:38 to whom has it been *r*?
Ro 1:17 righteousness is being *r* by
1:18 God's wrath is being *r* from
8:18 glory that is going to be *r*
1Co 2:10 God has *r* them through his
3:13 will be *r* by means of fire
Ga 3:23 that was destined to be *r*
Eph 3:5 *r* to his holy apostles and
2Th 2:3 the man of lawlessness gets *r*
2:6 being *r* in his own due time
2:8 the lawless one will be *r*
1Pe 1:5 *r* in the last period of time
1:12 It was *r* to them that, not
5:1 the glory that is to be *r*

Revealer
Da 2:28 who is a *R* of secrets, and
2:29 *R* of secrets has made known
2:47 and a *R* of secrets, because

Revealing
Da 2:22 *r* the deep things and the
Ro 2:5 *r* of God's righteous judgment
8:19 for the *r* of the sons of God

Revelation
2Sa 7:27 *r* to your servant's ear
Ro 16:25 the *r* of the sacred secret
1Co 1:7 for the *r* of our Lord Jesus
14:6 a *r* or with knowledge or
14:26 another has a *r*, another has
14:30 if there is a *r* to another
Ga 1:12 through *r* by Jesus Christ
2:2 I went up as a result of a *r*
Eph 1:17 *r* in the accurate knowledge
3:3 by way of a *r* the sacred
2Th 1:7 at the *r* of the Lord Jesus
1Pe 1:7 at the *r* of Jesus Christ
1:13 at the *r* of Jesus Christ
4:13 during the *r* of his glory
Re 1:1 A *r* by Jesus Christ, which God

Revelations
2Co 12:1 and *r* of the Lord
12:7 of the excess of the *r*

Revelries
Ro 13:13 decently, not in *r* and
Ga 5:21 *r*, and things like these
1Pe 4:3 *r*, drinking matches, and

Revelry
Am 6:7 the *r* of sprawling ones must

Revenge
2Sa 4:8 to my lord the king *r* this
Ps 44:16 and the one taking his *r*
Jer 20:10 and take our *r* upon him

Revenue
Isa 23:3 harvest of the Nile, your *r*

Reverence
Job 4:6 *r* the basis of your confidence
22:4 For your *r* will he reprove
2Th 2:4 called god or an object of *r*
1Ti 2:10 women professing to *r* God

Reverent
Lu 2:25 this man was righteous and *r*
Ac 2:5 Jews, *r* men, from every
8:2 *r* men carried Stephen to the
22:12 man *r* according to the Law
Tit 2:3 aged women be *r* in behavior

Reverse
Nu 23:20 blessed, and I shall not *r* it
Jer 21:4 turning in *r* the weapons of
Re 5:1 within and on the *r* side

Reviewed
Jos 8:10 and *r* the people and went up

Revile
Mr 9:39 will quickly be able to *r* me
1Ti 5:14 to the opposer to *r*

Reviled
Joh 9:28 At this they *r* him and said
1Co 4:12 When being *r*, we bless
1Pe 2:23 When he was being *r*, he did

Reviler
1Co 5:11 in company with . . . a *r*

Revilers
1Co 6:10 nor *r*, nor extortioners will

Reviles
Mt 15:4 him that *r* father or mother
Mr 7:10 Let him that *r* father or

Reviling
Eze 5:15 and an object of *r* words, a
Ac 23:4 Are you *r* the high priest of
1Pe 2:23 he did not go *r* in return
3:9, 9 not paying back . . . *r* for *r*

Revival
Isa 57:10 found a *r* of your own power

Revive
Ge 45:27 their father began to *r*
2Ki 1:2 I shall *r* from this sickness
8:8 Shall I *r* from this sickness?
8:9 Shall I *r* from this sickness?
8:10 You will positively *r*, and
8:14 You will positively *r*
Ps 71:20 May you *r* me again
Isa 38:21 the boil, that he may *r*
57:15 *r* the spirit of the lowly
57:15 *r* the heart of the ones
Zec 10:9 *r* with their sons and return

Heb 6:6 *r* them again to repentance

Revived
Jos 5:8 in the camp until they *r*
Jg 15:19 his spirit returned and he *r*
2Ki 8:1 woman whose son he had *r*
8:5 how he had *r* the dead one
8:5 woman whose son he had *r* was
8:5 this is her son whom Elisha *r*
20:7 after which he gradually *r*
Isa 38:9 sick and *r* from his sickness
Php 4:10 *r* your thinking in my behalf
Re 13:14 the sword-stroke and yet *r*

Reviving
Ezr 9:8 a little *r* in our servitude
9:9 to give us a *r* so as to raise

Revolt
Ge 31:36 What is the *r* on my part
50:17 the *r* of your brothers and
50:17 the *r* of the servants of
De 13:5 spoken of *r* against Jehovah
19:16 a charge of *r* against him
1Sa 24:11 no badness or *r* in my hand
1Ki 12:19 *r* against the house of David
2Ki 1:1 Moab began to *r* against
3:5 *r* against the king of Israel
8:22 Edom kept up its *r* from
8:22 Libnah began to *r* at that
2Ch 10:19 Israelites kept up their *r*
21:10 Edom kept up its *r* from
21:10 Libnah began to *r* at the
Ezr 4:15 movers of *r* from the days of
4:19 rebellion and *r* have been
Job 8:4 go into the hand of their *r*
13:23 Make me to know my own *r*
14:17 Sealed up in a bag is my *r*
20:27 earth will be in *r* against
34:37 on top of his sin he adds *r*
Ps 32:1 the one whose *r* is pardoned
59:3 For no *r* on my part, nor any
Isa 1:5 in that you add more *r*
31:6 have gone deep in their *r*
58:1 and tell my people their *r*
59:13 speaking of oppression and *r*
Jer 28:16 outright *r* against Jehovah
29:32 outright *r* against Jehovah
Eze 33:12 in the day of his *r*
Mic 1:5 because of the *r* of Jacob
1:5 What is the *r* of Jacob?
3:8 to tell to Jacob his *r* and to
6:7 my firstborn son for my *r*
Lu 23:14 one inciting the people to *r*

Revolted
2Ki 3:7 king of Moab . . . *r* against
8:20 Edom *r* from under the hand
2Ch 21:8 Edom *r* from under the hand
Isa 1:2 they . . . have *r* against me

Revolters
Ps 17:7 the *r* against your right hand
Isa 1:28 the crash of *r* and that of
Eze 20:38 the *r* and the transgressors

Revolting
Jos 24:19 He will not pardon your *r*
Job 27:7 the one *r* against me really
Ps 139:21 for those *r* against you

Revolts
Le 16:16 their *r* in all their sins
16:21 *r* in all their sins, and he
Job 35:6 if your *r* actually increase
Ps 25:7 sins of my youth and my *r*
Isa 59:12 our *r* have become many in
59:12 For our *r* are with us
Eze 33:10 our *r* and our sins are upon
Am 1:3 account of three *r* of Damascus
1:6 account of three *r* of Gaza
1:9 account of three *r* of Tyre
1:11 account of three *r* of Edom
1:13 three *r* of the sons of Ammon
2:1 account of three *r* of Moab
2:4 account of three *r* of Judah
2:6 account of three *r* of Israel
3:14 the *r* of Israel against him
5:12 known how many your *r* are
Mic 1:13 the *r* of Israel have been

Reward
Ge 15:1 Your *r* will be very great
Ru 2:12 May Jehovah *r* the way you act
1Sa 24:19 Jehovah himself will *r* you
2Sa 19:36 king repay me with this *r*
2Ch 15:7 exists a *r* for your activity
Job 21:19 He will *r* him that he may

Job 21:31 And . . . who will *r* him?
34:11 will *r* him, And according
41:11 that I ought to *r* him
Ps 19:11 there is a large *r*
35:12 They *r* me with bad for good
127:3 fruitage of the belly is a *r*
Pr 25:22 Jehovah himself will *r* you
Ec 4:9 a good *r* for their hard work
Isa 40:10 Look! His *r* is with him
59:18 he will *r* correspondingly
62:11 The *r* he gives is with him
65:6 but I will render a *r*
65:6 the *r* into their own bosom
Jer 31:16 *r* for your activity, is the
Joe 3:4 that you are giving me as a *r*
Mic 7:3 judging does so for the *r*
Mt 5:12 *r* is great in the heavens
5:46 what *r* do you have? Are not
6:1 no *r* with your Father who is
6:2 are having their *r* in full
6:5 are having their *r* in full
6:16 are having their *r* in full
10:41 will get a prophet's *r*, and
10:41 get a righteous man's *r*
10:42 will by no means lose his *r*
Mr 9:41 by no means lose his *r*
Lu 6:23 your *r* is great in heaven
6:35 your *r* will be great, and you
1Co 3:8 person will receive his own *r*
3:14 he will receive a *r*
9:17 this willingly, I have a *r*
9:18 What, then, is my *r*?
Col 3:24 you will receive the due *r*
2Ti 4:8 a *r* in that day, yet not only
Heb 10:35 a great *r* to be paid it
11:26 toward the payment of the *r*
2Pe 2:13 as a *r* for wrongdoing
2:15 who loved the *r* of wrongdoing
2Jo 8 that you may obtain a full *r*
Jude 11 course of Balaam for *r*, and
Re 11:18 *r* to your slaves the prophets
22:12 *r* I give is with me, to

Rewarded
Pr 11:31 in the earth he will be *r*
13:13 is the one that will be *r*
31:12 She has *r* him with good, and
Isa 42:19 Who is blind as the one *r*

Rewarder
Heb 11:6 *r* of those earnestly seeking

Rewarding
2Ch 20:11 *r* us by coming in to drive
Ps 7:4 repaid the one *r* me with what
31:23 *r* exceedingly anyone showing
38:20 *r* me with bad for good

Rewardingly
Ps 13:6 for he has dealt *r* with me
Pr 11:17 dealing *r* with his own soul

Rewards
2Sa 22:21 Jehovah *r* me according to
Ps 18:20 Jehovah *r* me according to
137:8 *r* you With your own
Pr 13:21 are the ones whom good *r*

Rezeph
2Ki 19:12 Gozan and Haran and *R* and
Isa 37:12 Haran and *R* and the sons of

Rezin
2Ki 15:37 *R* the king of Syria
16:5 *R* the king of Syria and
16:6 *R* the king of Syria restored
16:9 and *R* he put to death
Ezr 2:48 the sons of *R*
Ne 7:50 the sons of *R*, the sons of
Isa 7:1 *R* the king of Syria and Pekah
7:4 hot anger of *R* and Syria and
7:8 the head of Damascus is *R*
8:6 exultation over *R* and the son
9:11 set the adversaries of *R* on

Rezon
1Ki 11:23 *R* the son of Eliada

Rhegium
Ac 28:13 around and arrived at *R*

Rhesa
Lu 3:27 son of Joanan, son of *R*

Rhoda
Ac 12:13 servant girl named *R* came

Rhodes
Ac 21:1 but on the next day to *R*, and

Rib
Ge 2:22 *r* that he had taken from the

Ribai
2Sa 23:29 Ittai the son of *R* of Gibeah
1Ch 11:31 Ithai the son of *R* of Gibeah

Riblah
Nu 34:11 Shepham to *R* on the east
2Ki 23:33 *R* in the land of Hamath
25:6 the king of Babylon at *R*
25:20 the king of Babylon at *R*
25:21 *R* in the land of Hamath
Jer 39:5 *R* in the land of Hamath that
39:6 in *R* before his eyes, and
52:9 at *R* in the land of Hamath
52:10 princes . . . slaughtered in *R*
52:26 to the king of Babylon at *R*
52:27 in *R* in the land of Hamath

Ribs
Ge 2:21 he took one of his *r* and then
Da 7:5 three *r* in its mouth between

Rich
Ge 14:23 It was I who made Abram *r*
Ex 30:15 The *r* should not give more
Jg 5:10 You who sit on *r* carpets, And
Ru 3:10 fellows whether lowly or *r*
2Sa 12:1 the one *r* and the other of
12:2 *r* man happened to have very
12:4 visitor came to the *r* man
Job 15:29 He will not grow *r* and his
27:19 *R* he will lie down, but
Ps 45:12 The *r* ones of the people
49:2 You *r* one and you poor one
Pr 10:4 is what will make one *r*
10:15 valuable things of a *r* man
10:22 blessing . . . makes *r*
13:7 pretending to be *r* and yet
14:20 the friends of the *r* person
18:11 valuable things of the *r* are
18:23 *r* answers in a strong way
22:2 *r* one and the one of little
22:7 *r* is the one that rules over
22:16 that is giving to the *r* one
28:6 crooked . . . although he is *r*
28:11 *r* man is wise in his own
Ec 5:12 plenty belonging to the *r* one
10:6 the *r* ones themselves keep
10:20 call down evil upon anyone *r*
Isa 3:24 instead of a *r* garment, a
53:9 the *r* class in his death
Jer 9:23 Let not the *r* man brag about
Eze 27:33 you made earth's kings *r*
Ho 12:8 Indeed, I have become *r*
Mic 6:12 *r* men have become full of
Mt 19:23 difficult thing for a *r* man
19:24 than for a *r* man to get into
27:57 came a *r* man of Arimathea
Mr 10:25 for a *r* man to enter into
12:41 many *r* people were dropping
Lu 6:24 woe to you *r* persons, because
12:16 land of a certain *r* man
12:21 but is not *r* toward God
14:12 relatives or *r* neighbors
16:1 man was *r* and he had a
16:19 was *r*, and he used to deck
16:21 from the table of the *r* man
16:22 *r* man died and was buried
18:23 grieved, for he was very *r*
18:25 for a *r* man to get into the
19:2 tax collector, and he was *r*
21:1 the *r* dropping their gifts
Ro 10:12 *r* to all those calling upon
1Co 4:8 You are *r* already, are you?
2Co 6:10 as poor but making many *r*
8:9 he was *r* he became poor for
8:9 become *r* through his poverty
9:12 *r* with many expressions of
Eph 2:4 God, who is *r* in mercy, for
1Ti 6:9 who are determined to be *r*
6:17 *r* in the present system of
6:18 to be *r* in fine works
Jas 1:10 *r* one over his humiliation
1:11 *r* man will fade away in his
2:5 *r* in faith and heirs of the
2:6 *r* oppress you, and they drag
5:1 Come, now, you *r* men, weep
Re 2:9 and poverty—but you are *r*
3:17 I am *r* and have acquired
3:18 that you may become *r*, and
6:15 and the *r* and the strong ones
13:16 the *r* and the poor, and the
18:3 *r* due to the power of her
18:15 who became *r* from her
18:19 *r* by reason of her costliness

Riches
Ge 31:16 *r* that God has taken away
Jos 22:8 to your tents with many *r*
1Sa 17:25 enrich him with great *r*
1Ki 3:11 requested for yourself *r* nor
3:13 give you, both *r* and glory
10:23 Solomon was greater in *r*
1Ch 29:12 The *r* and the glory are on
29:28 satisfied with days, *r* and
2Ch 1:11 not asked for wealth, *r* and
1:12 *r* and honor I shall give you
9:22 Solomon was greater . . . in *r*
17:5 have *r* and glory in abundance
18:1 Jehoshaphat came to have *r*
32:27 Hezekiah came to have *r*
Es 1:4 *r* of his glorious kingdom and
5:11 the glory of his *r* and the
Ps 49:6 the abundance of their *r*
49:16 because some man gains *r*
52:7 in the abundance of his *r*
112:3 and *r* are in his house
Pr 3:16 hand there are *r* and glory
8:18 *R* and glory are with me
11:16 their part, take hold of *r*
11:28 The one trusting in his *r*
13:8 for a man's soul is his *r*
14:24 crown of the wise is their *r*
21:17 wine and oil will not gain *r*
22:1 chosen rather than abundant *r*
22:4 fear of Jehovah is *r* and glory
23:4 Do not toil to gain *r*
28:20 hastening to gain *r* will not
30:8 Give me neither poverty nor *r*
Ec 4:8 are not satisfied with *r*
5:13 *r* being kept for their grand
5:14 those *r* have perished because
5:19 the true God has given *r* and
6:2 to whom the true God gives *r*
9:11 also have the *r*, nor do even
Jer 5:27 become great and they gain *r*
9:23 brag . . . because of his *r*
17:11 the one making *r*, but not
Da 11:2 amass greater *r* than all
11:2 has become strong in his *r*
Zec 11:5 while I shall gain *r*
Mt 6:24 slave for God and for *R*
13:22 deceptive power of *r* choke
Mr 4:19 deceptive power of *r* and the
Lu 8:14 *r* and pleasures of this life
16:9 by means of the unrighteous *r*
16:11 with the unrighteous *r*, who
16:13 be slaves to God and to *r*
Ro 2:4 despise the *r* of his kindness
9:23 *r* of his glory upon vessels
11:12 their false step means *r*
11:12 their decrease means *r* to
11:33 depth of God's *r* and wisdom
2Co 8:2 *r* of their generosity abound
Eph 1:7 *r* of his undeserved kindness
1:18 glorious *r* are which he
2:7 surpassing *r* of his undeserved
3:8 unfathomable *r* of the Christ
3:16 to the *r* of his glory to be
Php 4:19 to the extent of his *r* in
Col 1:27 the glorious *r* of this sacred
2:2 with a view to all the *r* of
1Ti 6:17 hope, not on uncertain *r*, but
Heb 11:26 reproach of the Christ as *r*
Jas 5:2 Your *r* have rotted, and your
Re 3:17 acquired *r* and do not need
5:12 receive the power and *r* and
18:17 great *r* have been devastated

Richly
Col 3:16 reside in you *r* in all
1Ti 6:17 furnishes us all things *r*
Tit 3:6 spirit he poured out *r* upon us
2Pe 1:11 be *r* supplied to you the
Re 18:16 and *r* adorned with gold

Rid
Job 39:3 they get *r* of their pangs
Isa 5:2 *r* it of stones and to plant
62:10 highway. *R* it of stones
Lu 12:58 to *r* yourself of the dispute
22:2 way for them to get *r* of him

Ridden
Nu 22:30 your she-ass that you have *r*

Riddle
Jg 14:12 propound a *r* to you. If you
14:13 Do propound your *r*, and let
14:14 unable to tell the *r* for

Jg 14:15 that he may tell us the *r*
14:16 a *r* that you propounded to
14:17 she told the *r* to the sons of
14:18 would not have solved my *r*
14:19 to the tellers of the *r*
Ps 49:4 I shall open up my *r*
Eze 17:2 propound a *r* and compose a

Riddles
Nu 12:8 showing him, and not by *r*
Ps 78:2 *r* of long ago to bubble forth
Pr 1:6 of wise persons and their *r*
Da 5:12 and the explanation of *r* and

Ride
Ge 41:43 *r* in the second chariot of
Ex 4:20 and made them *r* on an ass
De 32:13 *r* upon earth's high places
2Sa 6:3 ark of the true God *r* upon a
16:2 household of the king to *r*
19:26 *r* upon it and go with the
1Ki 1:33 my son *r* upon the she-mule
1:38 Solomon *r* upon the she-mule
1:44 *r* upon the she-mule of the
2Ki 9:16 Jehu began to *r* and go to
1Ch 13:7 *r* upon a new wagon from the
2Ch 35:24 *r* in the second war chariot
Es 6:8 upon which the king does *r*
6:9 *r* on the horse in the public
6:11 *r* in the public square of the
Job 30:22 wind, you cause me to *r* it
Ps 45:4 *R* in the cause of truth and
66:12 man to *r* over our head
Isa 30:16 on swift horses we shall *r*
58:14 *r* upon the high places of
Jer 6:23 and upon horses they will *r*
50:42 and upon horses they will *r*
Ho 10:11 I make someone *r* Ephraim
14:3 Upon horses we shall not *r*
Ac 23:24 have Paul *r* and convey him

Rider
Ge 49:17 so that its *r* falls backward
Ex 15:1 horse and its *r* he has pitched
15:21 *r* he has pitched into the sea
2Ki 9:18 a *r* on a horse went to meet
9:19 a second *r* on a horse
Job 39:18 at the horse and at its *r*
Jer 51:21 horse and his *r* to pieces
51:21 chariot and its *r* to pieces
Am 2:15 no *r* of the horse . . . escape
Zec 12:4 and its *r* with madness

Riders
Jg 5:10 *r* on yellowish-red she-asses
2Ki 18:23 to put *r* upon them
Isa 36:8 to put *r* upon them
Hag 2:22 the chariot and its *r*, and
2:22 the horses and their *r* will
Zec 10:5 *r* of horses will have to

Rides
De 33:26 Who *r* upon heaven in help of

Ridge
Jos 12:23 the mountain *r* of Dor, one
1Ki 4:11 all the mountain *r* of Dor

Ridges
Jos 11:2 mountain *r* of Dor to the

Ridicule
Pr 1:22 yourselves outright *r*, and
Jer 48:26 has become an object of *r*
48:27 a mere object of *r* to you
48:39 become an object of *r* and
Eze 36:4 for plunder and for *r* to the
Lu 14:29 onlookers might start to *r*
2Pe 3:3 ridiculers with their *r*

Ridiculed
Pr 9:12 if you have *r*, you will bear

Ridiculer
Pr 9:7 correcting the *r* is taking to
9:8 Do not reprove a *r*, that
13:1 *r* is one that has not heard
14:6 *r* has sought to find wisdom
15:12 The *r* does not love the one
19:25 The *r* you should strike, that
20:1 Wine is a *r*, intoxicating
21:11 the laying of a fine on the *r*
22:10 Drive away the *r*, that
24:9 *r* is something detestable to

Ridiculers
Ps 1:1 in the seat of *r* has not sat
Pr 1:22 *r* desire for yourselves
3:34 *r*, he himself will deride
19:29 firmly established for *r*
2Pe 3:3 there will come *r* with their
Jude 18 last time there will be *r*

Riding
Ge 24:61 went *r* on the camels and
Le 15:9 was *r* will be unclean
Nu 22:22 he was *r* upon his she-ass
1Sa 25:20 *r* on the ass and secretly
25:42 *r* on the ass with five
2Sa 18:9 Absalom was *r* upon a mule
22:11 he came *r* upon a cherub and
1Ki 13:13 and he went *r* on it
18:45 Ahab kept *r* and made his
2Ki 4:24 from *r* unless I shall have
9:25 were *r* teams behind Ahab his
10:16 *r* with him in his war
Ne 2:12 animal on which I was *r*
Es 8:10 *r* post horses used in the
8:14 *r* post horses used in the
Ps 18:10 he came *r* upon a cherub and
68:4 the One *r* through the desert
68:33 One *r* on the ancient heaven
Isa 19:1 Jehovah is *r* on a swift
Jer 17:25 *r* in the chariot and upon
22:4 *r* in chariots and on horses
Eze 23:6 cavalrymen *r* horses
23:12 cavalrymen *r* horses
23:23 *r* on horses, all of them
27:20 woven material for *r*
38:15 all of them *r* on horses
Hab 3:8 you went *r* upon your horses
Zec 1:8 a man *r* on a red horse, and
9:9 humble, and *r* upon an ass

Right
Ge 13:9 then I will go to the *r*
13:9 if you go to the *r*, then I
18:5 All *r*. You may do just as you
18:25 not going to do what is *r*
24:49 may turn to the *r* hand or to
25:31 Sell . . . your *r* as firstborn
25:33 to sell his *r* as firstborn to
29:6 Is it all *r* with him?
29:6 they said: It is all *r*
43:23 It is all *r* with you. Do not
43:33 firstborn according to his *r*
48:13 Ephraim by his *r* hand to
48:13 Manasseh . . . to Israel's *r*
48:14 Israel put out his *r* hand and
48:17 *r* hand placed on Ephraim's
48:18 Put your *r* hand on his head
Ex 10:1 signs of mine *r* before him
14:22 *r* hand and on their left
14:29 wall on their *r* hand and on
15:6 Your *r* hand, O Jehovah, is
15:6 Your *r* hand, O Jehovah, can
15:12 You stretched out your *r* hand
15:26 do what is *r* in his eyes and
21:9 to the due *r* of daughters
29:20 the lobe of Aaron's *r* ear
29:20 the lobe of his sons' *r* ear
29:20 the thumb of their *r* hand
29:20 the big toe of their *r* foot
29:22 the *r* leg, for it is a ram
Le 7:32 give the *r* leg as a sacred
7:33 the *r* leg will become his as
8:23 the lobe of Aaron's *r* ear
8:23 the thumb of his *r* hand and
8:23 the big toe of his *r* foot
8:24 the lobe of their *r* ear and
8:24 the thumb of their *r* hand and
8:24 the big toe of their *r* foot
8:25 and their fat and the *r* leg
8:26 the fatty pieces and the *r* leg
9:21 the *r* leg Aaron waved to and
14:14 the lobe of the *r* ear of the
14:14 upon the thumb of his *r* hand
14:14 the big toe of his *r* foot
14:16 dip his *r* finger into the oil
14:17 lobe of the *r* ear of the one
14:17 upon the thumb of his *r* hand
14:17 the big toe of his *r* foot
14:25 upon the lobe of the *r* ear
14:25 upon the thumb of his *r* hand
14:25 the big toe of his *r* foot
14:27 spatter with his *r* finger
14:28 upon the lobe of the *r* ear
14:28 upon the thumb of his *r* hand
14:28 the big toe of his *r* foot
25:24 grant to the land the *r* of
25:29 his *r* of repurchase must
25:29 his *r* of repurchase should
25:31 *R* of repurchase should
25:32 the *r* of repurchase should
25:48 *r* of repurchase will continue
Nu 9:17 pull away *r* afterward, and
18:18 and like the *r* leg, it should
20:17 not bend toward the *r* or the
22:5 are dwelling *r* in front of me
22:26 turn aside to the *r* or the
23:27 *r* in the eyes of the true God
27:7 daughters . . . are speaking *r*
36:5 sons of Joseph is speaking *r*
De 2:27 turn to the *r* or to the left
5:32 turn to the *r* or to the left
6:18 *r* and good in Jehovah's eyes
12:8 whatever is *r* in his own eyes
12:25 what is *r* in Jehovah's eyes
12:28 *r* in the eyes of Jehovah your
13:18 *r* in the eyes of Jehovah your
17:11 to the *r* or to the left
17:20 to the *r* or to the left
18:3 the due *r* of the priests from
21:9 what is *r* in Jehovah's eyes
21:17 *r* of the firstborn's position
28:14 to the *r* or to the left
33:2 At his *r* hand warriors
Jos 1:7 to the *r* or to the left
9:25 good and *r* in your eyes
17:7 boundary moved to the *r* to
23:6 away from it to the *r* or to
Jg 3:16 his garment upon his *r* thigh
3:21 the sword off his *r* thigh and
5:26 her *r* hand to the mallet of
7:20 *r* hand on the horns to blow
14:3 the one just *r* in my eyes
14:7 she was still *r* in Samson's
15:4 *r* in the middle
16:29 one with his *r* and the other
17:6 what was *r* in his own eyes
21:25 What was *r* in his own eyes
Ru 4:6 with my *r* of repurchase
4:7 concerning the *r* of repurchase
1Sa 2:13 due *r* of the priests from
6:12 aside to the *r* or to the left
11:2 boring out every *r* eye of
12:23 in the good and *r* way
20:7 It is all *r!* it means peace
23:19 to the *r* side of Jeshimon
2Sa 2:19 incline to go to the *r* or
2:21 Veer to your *r* or to your
11:23 *r* up to the entrance of
14:19 no man can go to the *r* or
16:6 at his *r* and at his left
17:4 *r* in the eyes of Absalom
19:6 it would be *r* in your eyes
20:9 Is it all *r* with you, my
20:9 Joab's *r* hand took hold of
24:5 at Aroer to the *r* of the city
1Ki 2:19 that she might sit at his *r*
6:8 side chamber was on the *r*
7:39 five carriages on the *r* side
7:39 to the *r* side of the house
7:49 lampstands, five to the *r*
9:12 were not just *r* in his eyes
11:20 wean him *r* inside the house
11:20 *r* among the sons of Pharaoh
11:33 what is *r* in my eyes and
11:38 do what is *r* in my eyes by
14:8 only what was *r* in my eyes
14:14 said day, and what if *r* now?
15:5 was *r* in the eyes of Jehovah
15:11 *r* in the eyes of Jehovah
22:19 to his *r* and to his left
22:43 *r* in the eyes of Jehovah
2Ki 4:23 she said: It is all *r*
4:26 Is it all *r* with you? Is it
4:26 all *r* with your husband
4:26 Is it all *r* with the child?
4:26 she said: It is all *r*
7:9 It is not *r* what we are doing
9:11 Is everything all *r?*
9:31 Did it go all *r* with Zimri?
10:30 doing what is *r* in my eyes
11:11 *r* side of the house clear
12:2 what was *r* in Jehovah's eyes
12:9 beside the altar on the *r*
15:34 was *r* in Jehovah's eyes
16:2 not do what was *r* in the
17:9 not *r* toward Jehovah their
18:3 what was *r* in Jehovah's eyes
22:2 was *r* in Jehovah's eyes
22:2 turn aside to the *r* or to
23:13 to the *r* of the Mount of
1Ch 5:1 *r* as firstborn was given to
5:1 for the *r* of the firstborn
5:2 *r* as firstborn was Joseph's
6:39 attending at his *r*, Asaph
12:2 using the *r* hand and using

1Ch 13:4 seemed *r* in the eyes of all
24:19 according to their due *r*
2Ch 3:17 one to the *r* and one to the
4:6 basins, and put five to the *r*
4:7 lampstands . . . five to the *r*
4:8 ten tables . . . five to the *r*
4:10 sea he placed at the *r* side
14:2 *r* in the eyes of Jehovah his
18:18 standing at his *r* and his
20:32 was *r* in Jehovah's eyes
23:10 *r* side of the house clear
23:20 *r* through the upper gate
24:2 what was *r* in Jehovah's eyes
25:2 *r* in Jehovah's eyes, only
26:4 what was *r* in Jehovah's eyes
27:2 was *r* in Jehovah's eyes
28:1 was *r* in Jehovah's eyes
29:2 was *r* in Jehovah's eyes
30:4 *r* in the eyes of the king
31:20 *r* and faithful before
34:2 *r* in Jehovah's eyes and walk
34:2 aside to the *r* or to the left
Ezr 8:21 the *r* way for us and for our
Ne 4:11 until we come *r* in among
4:23 his missile in his *r* hand
8:4 and Maaseiah to his *r* hand
12:31 to the *r* upon the wall to
Job 1:6 Satan proceeded to enter *r*
2:1 to enter *r* among them to take
9:2 in the *r* in a case with God
9:15 I were really in the *r*
9:20 If I were in the *r*, my own
10:15 if I am actually in the *r*
11:2 a mere boaster be in the *r*
13:18 that I myself am in the *r*
15:14 should be in the *r*
23:9 He turns aside to the *r*, but
25:4 man be in the *r* before God
30:12 At my *r* hand they rise up
33:12 you have not been in the *r*
34:5 I certainly am in the *r*
35:7 If you are really in the *r*
40:8 that you may be in the *r*
40:12 the wicked *r* where they are
40:14 your *r* hand can save you
Ps 16:8 Because he is at my *r* hand
16:11 pleasantness at your *r* hand
17:7 revolters against your *r* hand
18:35 *r* hand will sustain me
20:6 mighty acts of his *r* hand
21:8 *r* hand will find those hating
26:10 *r* hand is full of bribery
44:3 it was your *r* hand and your
45:4 your *r* hand will instruct you
45:9 taken her stand at your *r* hand
48:10 Your *r* hand is full of
50:16 What *r* do you have to
51:13 may turn *r* back to you
60:5 O do save with your *r* hand
63:8 your *r* hand keeps fast hold
73:23 taken hold of my *r* hand
74:11 even your *r* hand, withdrawn
77:10 the *r* hand of the Most High
78:54 region that his *r* hand
80:15 that your *r* hand has planted
80:17 the man of your *r* hand
89:13 Your *r* hand is exalted
89:25 And on the rivers his *r* hand
89:42 the *r* hand of his adversaries
90:8 set our errors *r* in front of
91:7 ten thousand at your *r* hand
98:1 His *r* hand, even his holy arm
107:7 them walk in the *r* way
108:6 save with your *r* hand and
109:6 keep standing at his *r* hand
109:31 at the *r* hand of the poor
110:1 Sit at my *r* hand Until I
110:5 himself at your *r* hand
118:15 The *r* hand of Jehovah is
118:16 The *r* hand of Jehovah is
118:16 The *r* hand of Jehovah is
119:128 all things to be *r*
121:5 your shade on your *r* hand
137:5 Let my *r* hand be forgetful
138:7 your *r* hand will save me
139:10 *r* hand would lay hold of
142:4 Look to the *r* hand and see
144:8 And whose *r* hand is a
144:8 is a *r* hand of falsehood
144:11 And whose *r* hand is a
144:11 is a *r* hand of falsehood
Pr 3:16 of days is in its *r* hand
4:27 incline to the *r* hand or to
11:24 keeping back from what is *r*
Pr 12:15 one is *r* in his own eyes
15:23 word at its *r* time is O how
15:31 lodges *r* in among wise
25:11 a word spoken at the *r* time
27:16 and oil is what his *r* hand
28:2 man having knowledge of *r*
Ec 1:6 and *r* back to its circlings the
10:2 heart of the wise is at his *r*
10:8 pit will himself fall *r* into
Ca 2:6 and his *r* hand—it embraces me
8:3 *r* hand—it would embrace me
Isa 1:7 *r* in front of you strangers
1:17 set *r* the oppressor
9:20 cut down on the *r* and will
15:7 *r* over the torrent valley of
28:26 according to what is *r*
30:21 go to the *r* or in case you
32:7 poor speaks what is *r*
41:10 my *r* hand of righteousness
41:13 am grasping your *r* hand
41:26 that we may say, He is *r*
43:26 that you may be in the *r*
44:20 a falsehood in my *r* hand
45:1 *r* hand I have taken hold of
45:25 Israel will prove to be *r*
48:13 *r* hand extended out the
54:3 to the *r* and to the left you
62:8 sworn with his *r* hand and
63:12 go at the *r* hand of Moses
65:3 offending me *r* to my face
Jer 8:6 It was not *r* the way they
13:21 *r* alongside you at the start
17:8 roots *r* by the watercourse
18:4 it looked *r* in the eyes of
22:24 the seal ring on my *r* hand
23:10 their mightiness is not *r*
26:14 what is *r* in your eyes
27:5 it has proved *r* in my eyes
31:9 in a *r* way in which they
32:7 *r* of repurchase belongs to
32:8 *r* of hereditary possession
40:4 *r* in your eyes to go
40:5 *r* in your eyes to go, go
43:10 throne *r* above these stones
La 2:3 turned his *r* hand back from
2:4 *r* hand has taken its position
Eze 1:10 with a lion's face to the *r*
4:6 lie upon your *r* side in the
7:9 to be *r* in the midst of you
10:3 to the *r* of the house when
11:5 You people said the *r* thing
11:15 with your *r* to repurchase
16:46 who is dwelling on your *r*
18:25 of Jehovah is not adjusted *r*
18:25 not my own way adjusted *r*
18:25 you people not adjusted *r*
18:29 Jehovah is not adjusted *r*
18:29 are they not adjusted *r*, O
18:29 ones that are not adjusted *r*
21:16 go to the *r*! Set your
21:22 In his *r* hand the divination
21:27 comes who has the legal *r*
24:7 come to be *r* in the midst
30:7 *r* in the midst of devastated
33:17 is not adjusted *r*, but, as
33:17 way that is not adjusted *r*
33:20 is not adjusted *r*. It will
35:10 happened to be *r* there
39:3 out of your own *r* hand
48:13 *r* next to the territory of
Da 3:15 image that I have made, all *r*
5:10 entered *r* into the banqueting
6:19 went *r* to the lions' pit
7:10 kept standing *r* before him
8:14 brought into its *r* condition
12:7 raise his *r* hand and his left
Joe 2:23 autumn rain in *r* measure
Am 7:10 *r* inside the house of Israel
Jon 4:11 their *r* hand and their left
Hab 2:16 cup of the *r* hand of Jehovah
Zep 2:14 *r* among her pillar capitals
Zec 3:1 Satan standing at his *r* hand
4:3 one on the *r* side of the bowl
4:11 the *r* side of the lampstand
11:17 his arm and upon his *r* eye
11:17 *r* eye will without fail
12:6 must devour on the *r* hand
Mt 5:29 *r* eye of yours is making you
5:30 if your *r* hand is making you
5:39 slaps you on your *r* cheek
6:3 know what your *r* is doing
15:26 not *r* to take the bread of
20:21 one at your *r* hand and one
20:23 sitting down at my *r* hand
Mt 22:44 Sit at my *r* hand until I put
25:6 *R* in the middle of the night
25:33 put the sheep on his *r* hand
25:34 will say to those on his *r*
26:64 at the *r* hand of power and
27:29 and a reed in his *r* hand
27:38 two robbers . . . one on his *r*
Mr 1:33 was gathered *r* at the door
2:4 to bring him *r* to Jesus on
6:25 give me *r* away on a platter
7:27 not *r* to take the bread of
10:37 one at your *r* hand and one
10:40 this sitting down at my *r*
12:36 Sit at my *r* hand until I
14:62 at the *r* hand of power and
15:27 one on his *r* and one on his
16:5 on the *r* side clothed in a
Lu 1:11 *r* side of the incense altar
1:15 *r* from his mother's womb
6:6 whose *r* hand was withered
20:42 to my Lord, Sit at my *r* hand
22:50 and took off his *r* ear
22:69 the powerful *r* hand of God
23:33 evildoers, one on his *r* and
Joh 18:10 and cut his *r* ear off
21:6 net on the *r* side of the boat
Ac 2:25 he is at my *r* hand that I
2:33 exalted to the *r* hand of God
2:34 to my Lord: Sit at my *r* hand
3:7 by the *r* hand and raised him
5:31 to his *r* hand, to give
7:55 standing at God's *r* hand
7:56 standing at God's *r* hand
13:10 distorting the *r* ways of
24:13 they are accusing me *r* now
Ro 7:21 I wish to do what is *r*
8:34 who is on the *r* hand of God
11:20 All *r*! For their lack of
2Co 6:7 righteousness on the *r* hand
Ga 2:9 the *r* hand of sharing together
Eph 1:20 at his *r* hand in the heavenly
Php 1:7 It is altogether *r* for me to
Col 3:1 seated at the *r* hand of God
2Th 2:7 *r* now acting as a restraint
3:13 do not give up in doing *r*
Heb 1:3 on the *r* hand of the Majesty
1:13 Sit at my *r* hand, until I
4:16 for help at the *r* time
5:14 distinguish both *r* and wrong
8:1 sat down at the *r* hand of the
10:12 down at the *r* hand of God
12:2 sat down at the *r* hand of
Jas 4:17 knows how to do what is *r*
1Pe 3:22 He is at God's *r* hand, for he
2Pe 1:13 I consider it *r*, as long as
2:16 violation of what was *r*
1Jo 2:9 in the darkness up to *r* now
Re 1:16 in his *r* hand seven stars
1:17 he laid his *r* hand upon me
1:20 you saw upon my *r* hand, and
2:1 the seven stars in his *r* hand
5:1 in the *r* hand of the One seated
5:7 *r* hand of the One seated on
7:14 So *r* away I said to him: My
8:5 But *r* away the angel took the
10:2 set his *r* foot upon the sea
10:5 raised his *r* hand to heaven
13:16 mark in their *r* hand or
14:13 they did go *r* with them
19:3 *r* away for the second time

Right-doing

Ge 30:33 And my *r* must answer for me

Righteous

Ge 6:9 Noah was a *r* man. He proved
7:1 one I have seen to be *r* before
18:23 sweep away the *r* with the
18:24 fifty *r* men in the midst of
18:24 sake of the fifty *r* who are
18:25 put to death the *r* man with
18:25 occur with the *r* man as it
18:26 in Sodom fifty *r* men in the
18:28 fifty *r* should be lacking
20:4 a nation that is really *r*
38:26 She is more *r* than I am
44:16 can we prove ourselves *r*
Ex 9:27 Jehovah is *r*, and I and my
23:7 kill the innocent and the *r*
23:7 not declare the wicked one *r*
23:8 distort the words of *r* men
De 4:8 has *r* regulations and judicial
16:18 judge . . . with *r* judgment
16:19 distorts the words of *r* ones
25:1, 1 pronounce the *r* one *r* and

De 32:4 *R* and upright is he
Jg 5:11 recount the *r* acts of Jehovah
5:11 The *r* acts of his dwellers in
1Sa 12:7 all the *r* acts of Jehovah
24:17 You are more *r* than I am
2Sa 4:11 killed a *r* man in his own
23:3 one ruling over mankind is *r*
1Ki 2:32 fell upon two men more *r* and
8:32, 32 pronouncing the *r* one *r*
2Ki 10:9 all the people: You are *r*
2Ch 6:23, 23 pronouncing the *r* one *r*
12:6 and said: Jehovah is *r*
Ezr 9:15 God of Israel, you are *r*
Ne 9:8 your words, because you are *r*
9:33 you are *r* as regards all that
Job 8:6 restore your *r* abiding place
12:4 A laughingstock is the *r*
17:9 *r* one keeps holding fast to
22:3 any delight in that you are *r*
22:19 *r* ones will see and rejoice
27:5 I should declare you men *r*
27:17 but the *r* would be the one
32:1 for he was *r* in his own eyes
32:2 declaring his own soul *r*
34:17 And if a powerful one is *r*
36:7 his eyes from anyone *r*
Ps 1:5 in the assembly of *r* ones
1:6 knowledge of the way of *r* ones
4:1 answer me, O my *r* God
5:12 bless anyone *r*, O Jehovah
7:9 may you establish the *r* one
7:9 God as *r* is testing out heart
7:11 God is a *r* Judge, And God is
11:3 What must anyone *r* do?
11:5 *r* one as well as the wicked
11:7 Jehovah is *r;* he does love
11:7 he does love *r* acts
14:5 the generation of the *r* one
17:1 Do hear what is *r*, O Jehovah
19:9 they have proved altogether *r*
31:18 speaking against the *r* one
32:11 and be joyful, you *r* ones
33:1 Cry out joyfully, O you *r* ones
34:15 are toward the *r* ones
34:19 the calamities of the *r* one
34:21 the very ones hating the *r*
37:12 plotting against the *r* one
37:16 the little of the *r* one
37:17 be supporting the *r* ones
37:21 the *r* one is showing favor
37:25 have not seen anyone *r* left
37:29 *r* themselves will possess
37:30 The mouth of the *r* is the
37:32 on the watch for the *r*
37:39 the salvation of the *r* ones
51:4 prove to be *r* when you speak
52:6 the *r* ones will see it and
55:22 allow the *r* one to totter
58:10 The *r* one will rejoice
58:11 fruitage for the *r* one
64:10 the *r* one will rejoice in
68:3 for the *r*, let them rejoice
69:28 with the *r* ones may they
72:7 the *r* one will sprout
75:10 horns of the *r* one will be
92:12 *r* himself will blossom
94:21 on the soul of the *r* one
97:11 flashed up for the *r* one
97:12 Rejoice in Jehovah, O you *r*
112:4 gracious and merciful and *r*
112:6 *r* one will prove to be for
116:5 Jehovah is gracious and *r*
118:15 in the tents of the *r* ones
118:20 *r* themselves will go into
119:7 your *r* judicial decisions
119:62 your *r* judicial decisions
119:106 your *r* judicial decisions
119:123 And for your *r* saying
119:137 You are *r*, O Jehovah
119:160 *r* judicial decision of
119:164 your *r* judicial decisions
125:3 upon the lot of the *r* ones
125:3 *r* ones may not thrust out
129:4 Jehovah is *r*. He has cut in
140:13 *r* themselves will give
141:5 *r* one strike me, it would be
142:7 let the *r* ones gather
143:2 no one alive can be *r*
145:17 Jehovah is *r* in all his
146:8 Jehovah is loving the *r* ones
Pr 2:20 paths of the *r* ones you may
3:33 abiding place of the *r* ones
4:18 path of the *r* ones is like
9:9 knowledge to someone *r* and he

Pr 10:3 soul of the *r* one to go
10:6 for the head of the *r* one
10:7 remembrance of the *r* one is
10:11 mouth of the *r* one is a
10:16 of the *r* one results in life
10:20 tongue of the *r* one is choice
10:21 lips of the *r* one keep
10:24 desire of the *r* ones will be
10:25 *r* one is a foundation to
10:28 expectation of the *r* ones is
10:30 *r* one, to time indefinite
10:31 mouth of the *r* one—it bears
10:32 lips of the *r* one—they come
11:8 *r* is the one rescued even
11:9 knowledge are the *r* rescued
11:10 the *r* ones a town is elated
11:21 offspring of the *r* ones will
11:23 desire of the *r* ones is
11:28 the *r* ones will flourish
11:30 fruitage of the *r* one is a
11:31 *r* one—in the earth he will
12:3 root-foundation of the *r* ones
12:5 thoughts of the *r* ones are
12:7 house of the *r* ones will keep
12:10 *r* one is caring for the soul
12:12 root of the *r* ones, it
12:13 *r* one gets out of distress
12:17 will tell what is *r*, but
12:21 hurtful will befall the *r*
12:26 *r* one spies out his own
13:5 word is what the *r* hates
13:9 light of the *r* ones . . . rejoice
13:21 *r* are the ones whom good
13:22 treasured up for the *r* one
13:25 *r* is eating to the
14:19 at the gates of the *r* one
14:32 *r* will be finding refuge in
15:6 In the house of the *r* one
15:28 heart of the *r* one meditates
15:29 prayer of the *r* ones he hears
17:15 pronouncing the wicked one *r*
17:15 pronouncing the *r* one wicked
17:26 a fine upon the *r* one is not
18:5 turning aside of the *r* one in
18:10 Into it the *r* runs and is
18:17 first in his legal case is *r*
20:7 *r* is walking in his integrity
21:12 *R* One is giving consideration
21:15 rejoicing for the *r* one to do
21:18 wicked is a ransom for the *r*
21:26 *r* one gives and holds nothing
23:24 The father of a *r* one will
24:15 abiding place of the *r* one
24:16 *r* one may fall even seven
24:24 the wicked one: You are *r*
25:26 *r* one when staggering before
28:1 *r* are like a young lion that
28:12 When the *r* ones are exulting
28:28 perish, the *r* become many
29:2 the *r* become many, the people
29:6 *r* cries out joyfully and is
29:7 *r* one is knowing the legal
29:16 *r* will look on their very
29:27 detestable to the *r*
Ec 3:17 judge both the *r* one and the
7:15 the *r* one perishing in his
7:16 Do not become *r* overmuch, nor
7:20 is no man *r* in the earth that
8:14 exist *r* ones to whom it is
8:14 as if for the work of the *r*
9:1 the *r* ones and the wise ones
9:2 eventuality there is to the *r*
Isa 3:10 well with the *r* one, for
5:23 pronouncing the wicked one *r*
5:23 of the *r* one from him
24:16 Decoration to the *R* One!
26:2 *r* nation that is keeping
26:7 path of the *r* one is
26:7 very course of a *r* one
29:21 push aside the *r* one with
43:9 that they may be declared *r*
45:19 speaking what is *r*, telling
45:21 a *r* God and a Savior
50:8 One declaring me *r* is near
53:11 the *r* one, my servant
53:11 a *r* standing to many people
56:1 people, and do what is *r*
57:1 *r* one himself has perished
57:1 *r* one has been gathered away
58:2 asking me for *r* judgments
60:21 all of them will be *r*
Jer 3:11 more *r* than treacherously
12:1 You are *r*, O Jehovah, when
20:12 are examining the *r* one

Jer 23:5 raise up to David a *r* sprout
31:23 O *r* dwelling place
33:15 for David a *r* sprout, and
La 1:18 Jehovah is *r*, for it is
4:13 pouring out the blood of *r*
Eze 3:20 someone *r* turns back from
3:20 *r* acts that he did will not
3:21 you have warned someone *r*
3:21 that the *r* one should not sin
13:22 dejecting the heart of a *r*
16:51 made your sisters appear *r*
16:52 they are more *r* than you
16:52 make your sisters appear *r*
18:5 in case he happens to be *r*
18:9 to execute truth, he is *r*
18:20 righteousness of the *r* one
18:24 when someone *r* turns back
18:24 none of all his *r* acts that
18:26 someone *r* turns back from
21:3 cut off from you *r* one and
21:4 you *r* one and wicked one
23:45 as regards *r* men, they are
33:12 The righteousness of the *r*
33:13 say to the *r* one: You will
33:13 his own *r* acts will not be
33:18 someone *r* turns back from
Da 9:14 Jehovah our God is *r* in all
9:18 not according to our *r* acts
Ho 14:9 the *r* are the ones who will
Am 2:6 selling someone *r* for mere
5:12 hostility toward someone *r*
Mic 6:5 that the *r* acts of Jehovah
Hab 1:4 is surrounding the *r* one, for
1:13 someone more *r* than he is
2:4 But as for the *r* one, by his
Zep 3:5 Jehovah was *r* in the midst
Zec 9:9 He is *r*, yes, saved; humble
Mal 3:18 a *r* one and a wicked one
Mt 1:19 he was *r* and did not want to
3:15 to carry out all that is *r*
5:45 makes it rain upon *r* people
9:13 not *r* people, but sinners
10:41 receives a *r* man because he
10:41 because he is a *r* man will
10:41 will get a *r* man's reward
11:19 wisdom is proved *r* by its
12:37 by your words . . . declared *r*
13:17 and *r* men desired to see the
13:43 the *r* ones will shine as
13:49 the wicked from among the *r*
23:28 outwardly indeed, appear *r*
23:29 the memorial tombs of the *r*
23:35 the *r* blood spilled on earth
23:35 from the blood of *r* Abel to
25:37 the *r* ones will answer him
25:46 *r* ones into everlasting life
27:4 when I betrayed *r* blood
27:19 to do with that *r* man, for
Mr 2:17 I came to call, not *r* people
6:20 knowing him to be a *r* and
Lu 1:6 both were *r* before God because
1:17 practical wisdom of *r* ones
2:25 this man was *r* and reverent
5:32 not *r* persons, but sinners to
7:29 declared God to be *r*, they
7:35 wisdom is proved *r* by all its
10:29 wanting to prove himself *r*
12:57 judge also . . . what is *r*
14:14 resurrection of the *r* ones
15:7 than over ninety-nine *r* ones
16:15 who declare yourselves *r*
18:9 that they were *r* and who
18:14 proved more *r* than that man
20:20 to pretend that they were *r*
23:47 Really this man was *r*
23:50 Joseph . . . a good and *r* man
Joh 5:30 judgment that I render is *r*
7:24 but judge with *r* judgment
17:25 *R* Father, the world has
Ac 3:14 that holy and *r* one, and
4:19 *r* in the sight of God to
7:52 the coming of the *r* One
10:22 man *r* and fearing God and
13:10 you enemy of everything *r*
22:14 to see the *r* One and to hear
24:15 resurrection of both the *r*
Ro 1:17 *r* one—by means of faith he
1:32 *r* decree of God, that those
2:5 revealing of God's *r* judgment
2:13 not the ones *r* before God
2:13 doers of law . . . declared *r*
2:26 *r* requirements of the Law
3:4 proved *r* in your words and
3:10 not a *r* man, not even one

Ro 3:20 no flesh will be declared *r*
3:24 declared *r* by his undeserved
3:26 *r* even when declaring
3:26 declaring *r* the man that has
3:28 declared *r* by faith apart
3:30 *r* as a result of faith and
3:30 *r* by means of their faith
4:2 Abraham were declared *r* as a
4:5 declares the ungodly one *r*
4:25 the sake of declaring us *r*
5:1 declared *r* as a result of
5:7 anyone die for a *r* man
5:9 declared *r* now by his blood
5:18 declaring of them *r* for life
5:19 many will be constituted *r*
7:12 commandment is holy and *r*
8:4 *r* requirement of the Law
8:30 he also declared to be *r*
8:30 those whom he declared *r* are
8:33 the One who declares them *r*
1Co 4:4 Yet by this I am not proved *r*
6:11 but you have been declared *r*
15:34 to soberness in a *r* way
Ga 2:16 declared *r*, not due to works
2:16 be declared *r* due to faith
2:16 no flesh will be declared *r*
2:17 in seeking to be declared *r* by
3:8 of the nations *r* due to faith
3:11 no one is declared *r* with God
3:11 *r* one will live by reason
3:24 be declared *r* due to faith
5:4 declared *r* by means of law
Eph 6:1 be obedient . . . for this is *r*
Php 1:11 may be filled with *r* fruit
4:8 whatever things are *r*
Col 4:1 keep dealing out what is *r*
1Th 2:10 loyal and *r* and unblamable
2Th 1:5 is a proof of the *r* judgment
1:6 it is *r* on God's part to repay
1Ti 1:9 not for a *r* man, but for
3:16 was declared *r* in spirit
2Ti 4:8 the Lord, the *r* judge, will
Tit 1:8 sound in mind, *r*, loyal
3:7 *r* by virtue of the undeserved
Heb 10:38 *r* one will live by reason
11:4 borne to him that he was *r*
12:23 spiritual lives of *r* ones
Jas 2:21 Abraham . . . declared *r* by
2:24 declared *r* by works, and not
2:25 harlot declared *r* by works
5:6 you have murdered the *r* one
5:16 A *r* man's supplication, when
1Pe 3:12 of Jehovah are upon the *r*
3:18 a *r* person for unrighteous
4:18 *r* man is being saved with
2Pe 2:7 he delivered *r* Lot, who was
2:8 that *r* man by what he saw
2:8 tormenting his *r* soul by
1Jo 1:9 he is faithful and *r* so as to
2:1 Jesus Christ, a *r* one
2:29 If you know that he is *r*
3:7 carries on righteousness is *r*
3:7 just as that one is *r*
3:12 those of his brother were *r*
Re 15:3 *R* and true are your ways
15:4 *r* decrees have been made
16:5 *r*, because you have rendered
16:7 *r* are your judicial decisions
19:2 his judgments are true and *r*
19:8 the *r* acts of the holy ones
22:11 but let the *r* one do

Righteously
Pr 31:9 judge *r* and plead the cause of
1Pe 2:23 to the one who judges *r*

Righteousness
Ge 15:6 to count it to him as *r*
18:19 keep Jehovah's way to do *r*
De 1:16 judge with *r* between a man
6:25 And it will mean *r* for us
9:4 for my own *r* that Jehovah has
9:5 It is not for your *r* or for
9:6 not for your *r* that Jehovah
24:13 *r* for you before Jehovah
33:19 sacrifice the sacrifices of *r*
33:21 The *r* of Jehovah will he
1Sa 26:23 repay to each one his own *r*
2Sa 8:15 and *r* for all his people
22:21 according to my *r*
22:25 repay me according to my *r*
1Ki 3:6 before you in truth and in *r*
8:32 according to his own *r*
10:9 judicial decision and *r*
1Ch 18:14 and *r* for all his people
2Ch 6:23 him according to his own *r*
9:8 judicial decision and *r*
Job 6:29 return—my *r* is yet in it
8:3 Almighty himself pervert *r*
29:14 With *r* I clothed myself
33:26 restore His *r* to mortal man
33:32 have taken delight in your *r*
35:2 My *r* is more than God's
35:8 *r* to a son of earthling man
36:3 Fashioner I shall ascribe *r*
37:23 *r* he will not belittle
Ps 4:5 Sacrifice the sacrifices of *r*
5:8 lead me in your *r* by reason of
7:8 O Jehovah, according to my *r*
7:17 Jehovah according to his *r*
9:4 on the throne judging with *r*
9:8 judge the productive land in *r*
15:2 faultlessly and practicing *r*
17:15 in *r* I shall behold your
18:20 rewards me according to my *r*
18:24 repay me according to my *r*
22:31 will come and tell of his *r*
23:3 leads me in the tracks of *r*
24:5 *r* from his God of salvation
31:1 your *r* provide escape for me
33:5 He is a lover of *r* and justice
35:24 Judge me according to your *r*
35:27 who are delighting in my *r*
35:28 utter in an undertone your *r*
36:6 *r* is like mountains of God
36:10 your *r* to those upright in
37:6 your *r* as the light itself
40:9 have told the good news of *r*
40:10 Your *r* I have not covered
45:4 truth and humility and *r*
45:7 You have loved *r* and you hate
48:10 right hand is full of *r*
50:6 the heavens tell of his *r*
51:14 joyfully tell about your *r*
51:19 with sacrifices of *r*
52:3 more than speaking *r*. *Se'lah*
58:1 really speak about *r* itself
65:5 fear-inspiring things in *r*
69:27 they not come into your *r*
71:2 In your *r* may you deliver me
71:15 mouth will recount your *r*
71:16 I shall mention your *r*
71:19 Your *r*, O God, is up to the
71:24 in an undertone your *r*
72:1 your *r* to the son of the king
72:2 cause of your people with *r*
72:3 Also the hills, through *r*
85:10 *R* and peace—they have
85:11 *r* itself will look down
85:13 him *r* itself will walk
88:12 *r* in the land of oblivion
89:14 *R* and judgment are the
89:16 in your *r* they are exalted
94:15 will return even to *r*
96:13 productive land with *r*
97:2 *R* and judgment are the
97:6 heavens have told forth his *r*
98:2 nations he has revealed his *r*
98:9 the productive land with *r*
99:4 *r* in Jacob are what you
103:6 is executing acts of *r*
103:17 his *r* to the sons of sons
106:3 Doing *r* all the time
106:31 to be counted to him as *r*
111:3 his *r* is standing forever
112:3 his *r* is standing forever
112:9 His *r* is standing forever
118:19 Open to me the gates of *r*
119:40 In your *r* preserve me alive
119:75 judicial decisions are *r*
119:121 executed judgment and *r*
119:138 your reminders in *r*
119:142, 142 *r* is a *r* to time
119:144 *r* of your reminders is to
119:172 your commandments are *r*
132:9 themselves be clothed with *r*
143:1 answer me in your *r*
143:11 In your *r* may you bring
145:7 because of your *r* they will
Pr 1:3 *r* and judgment and uprightness
2:9 understand *r* and judgment and
8:8 sayings of my mouth are in *r*
8:15 keep decreeing *r*
8:16 nobles are all judging in *r*
8:18 hereditary values and *r*
8:20 In the path of *r* I walk, in
10:2 *r* is what will deliver from
11:4 *r* itself will deliver from
11:5 *r* of the blameless one is
Pr 11:6 *r* of the upright ones is
11:18 one sowing *r*, true earnings
11:19 one firmly standing for *r*
12:28 path of *r* there is life, and
13:6 *R* itself safeguards the one
14:34 *R* is what exalts a nation
15:9 but the one pursuing *r* he loves
16:8 Better is a little with *r*
16:12 by *r* is the throne firmly
16:13 lips of *r* are a pleasure to
16:31 it is found in the way of *r*
21:3 To carry on *r* and judgment is
21:21 He that is pursuing *r* and
21:21 will find life, *r* and glory
25:5 be firmly established by *r*
Ec 3:16 *r* where wickedness was
5:8 violent taking away of . . . *r*
7:15 one perishing in his *r*, and
Isa 1:21 *r* itself used to lodge in her
1:26 called City of *R*, Faithful
1:27 returning of her, with *r*
5:7 for *r*, but, look! an outcry
5:16 sanctify himself through *r*
5:23 *r* of the righteous one from
9:7 by means of *r*, from now on
10:22 flooding through in *r*
11:4 with *r* he must judge the
11:5 *r* must prove to be the belt
16:5 and being prompt in *r*
26:9 *r* is what the inhabitants
26:10 he simply will not learn *r*
28:17 *r* the leveling instrument
32:1 A king will reign for *r*
32:16 orchard *r* itself will dwell
32:17 true *r* must become peace
32:17 true *r*, quietness and
33:5 fill Zion with justice and *r*
33:15 is walking in continual *r*
41:2 in *r* to call him to His feet
41:10 with my right hand of *r*
42:6 have called you in *r*, and I
42:21 for the sake of his *r* has
45:8 trickle with *r*. Let the
45:8 *r* itself to spring up at the
45:13 roused up someone in *r*
45:23 in *r* the word has gone
45:24 in Jehovah there are full *r*
46:12 the ones far away from *r*
46:13 have brought near my *r*
48:1 not in truth and not in *r*
48:18 your *r* like the waves of
51:1 who are pursuing after *r*
51:5 My *r* is near. My salvation
51:6 own *r* will not be shattered
51:7 you the ones knowing *r*
51:8 my *r*, it will prove to be
54:14 firmly established in *r*
54:17 and their *r* is from me
56:1 and my *r* to be revealed
57:12 your *r* and your works
58:2 nation that carried on *r*
58:8 your *r* would certainly walk
59:4 no one calling out in *r*
59:9 *r* does not catch up with us
59:14 and *r* itself kept standing
59:16 own *r* was the thing that
59:17 put on *r* as a coat of mail
60:17 and *r* as your task assigners
61:3 be called big trees of *r*
61:10 the sleeveless coat of *r*
61:11 cause the sprouting of *r*
62:1 *r* goes forth just like the
62:2 see your *r*, O woman, and
63:1 the One speaking in *r*, the
64:5 one exulting and doing *r*
64:6 all our acts of *r* are like
Jer 4:2 in truth, in justice and in *r*
9:24 justice and *r* in the earth
11:20 Jehovah . . . judging with *r*
22:3 Render justice and *r*, and
22:13 his house, but not with *r*
22:15 and execute justice and *r*
23:5 execute justice and *r* in the
23:6 called, Jehovah Is Our *R*
33:15 justice and *r* in the land
33:16 called, Jehovah Is Our *R*
50:7 the abiding place of *r*
51:10 forth deeds of *r* for us
Eze 3:20 turns back from his *r* and
14:14 *r* would deliver their soul
14:20 *r* would deliver their soul
18:5 he has executed justice and *r*
18:19 and *r* he has executed, all
18:20 *r* of the righteous one will

Eze 18:21 and execute justice and *r*
18:22 For his *r* . . . keep living
18:24 turns back from his *r* and
18:26 turns back from his *r* and
18:27 to execute justice and *r*
33:12 The *r* of the righteous one
33:12 even anyone having *r* be
33:13 trusts in his own *r* and
33:14 carries on justice and *r*
33:16 Justice and *r* are what
33:18 turns back from his *r* and
33:19 carries on justice and *r*
45:9 and do justice and *r*
Da 4:27 remove your own sins by *r*
9:7 Jehovah, there belongs the *r*
9:16 to all your acts of *r*
9:24 and to bring in *r* for times
12:3 bringing the many to *r*, like
Ho 2:19 I will engage you to me in *r*
10:12 Sow seed for yourselves in *r*
10:12 gives instruction in *r* to
Am 5:7 cast *r* itself to the earth
5:24 *r* like a constantly flowing
6:12 fruitage of *r* into wormwood
Mic 7:9 I shall look upon his *r*
Zep 2:3 Seek *r*, seek meekness
Zec 8:8 God in trueness and in *r*
Mal 3:3 a gift offering in *r*
4:2 the sun of *r* will certainly
Mt 5:6 hungering and thirsting for *r*
5:20 if your *r* does not abound
6:1 not to practice your *r* in
6:33 first the kingdom and his *r*
21:32 came to you in a way of *r*
Lu 1:75 *r* before him all our days
Joh 16:8 sin and concerning *r* and
16:10 concerning *r*, because I am
Ac 10:35 works *r* is acceptable to him
17:31 judge . . . earth in *r* by a
24:25 as he talked about *r* and
Ro 1:17 God's *r* is being revealed by
3:5 brings God's *r* to the fore
3:21 God's *r* . . . made manifest
3:22 God's *r* through the faith in
3:25 order to exhibit his own *r*
3:26 exhibit his own *r* in this
4:3 it was counted to him as *r*
4:5 his faith is counted as *r*
4:6 God counts *r* apart from works
4:9 was counted to Abraham as *r*
4:11 *r* by the faith he had while
4:11 for *r* to be counted to them
4:13 was through the *r* by faith
4:22 it was counted to him as *r*
5:16 in a declaration of *r*
5:17 free gift of *r* rule as kings
5:21 rule as king through *r* with
6:13 to God as weapons of *r*
6:16 of obedience with *r* in view
6:18 you became slaves to *r*
6:19 your members as slaves to *r*
6:20 you were free as to *r*
8:10 is life on account of *r*
9:30 although not pursuing *r*
9:30 caught up with *r*, the
9:30 *r* that results from faith
9:31 although pursuing a law of *r*
10:3 not knowing the *r* of God but
10:3 subject themselves to the *r*
10:4 exercising faith may have *r*
10:5 the *r* of the Law will live by
10:6 *r* resulting from faith speaks
10:10 one exercises faith for *r*
14:17 but means *r* and peace and
1Co 1:30 wisdom from God, also *r* and
2Co 3:9 administering of *r* abound
5:21 God's *r* by means of him
6:7 weapons of *r* on the right
6:14 what fellowship do *r* and
9:9 his *r* continues forever
9:10 the products of your *r*
11:15 into ministers of *r*
Ga 2:21 if *r* is through law, Christ
3:6 it was counted to him as *r*
3:21 *r* would actually have been
5:5 *r* as a result of faith
Eph 4:24 in true *r* and loyalty
5:9 goodness and *r* and truth
6:14 on the breastplate of *r*
Php 3:6 *r* that is by means of law
3:9 *r*, which results from law
3:9 the *r* that issues from God
1Ti 6:11 But pursue *r*, godly devotion
2Ti 2:22 pursue *r*, faith, love, peace
2Ti 3:16 for disciplining in *r*
4:8 for me the crown of *r*
Tit 2:12 with soundness of mind and *r*
3:5 owing to no works in *r* that
Heb 1:9 You loved *r*, and you hated
5:13 with the word of *r*
7:2 King of *R*, and is then also
11:7 *r* that is according to faith
11:33 effected *r*, obtained
12:11 peaceable fruit, namely, *r*
Jas 1:20 does not work out God's *r*
2:23 it was counted to him as *r*
3:18 the fruit of *r* has its seed
1Pe 2:24 done with sins and live to *r*
3:14 suffer for the sake of *r*, you
2Pe 1:1 by the *r* of our God and the
2:5 Noah, a preacher of *r*, safe
2:21 known the path of *r* than
3:13 and in these *r* is to dwell
1Jo 2:29 everyone who practices *r*
3:7 carries on *r* is righteous
3:10 does not carry on *r* does not
Re 19:11 and carries on war in *r*
22:11 righteous one do *r* still

Righteousness'
Mt 5:10 been persecuted for *r* sake

Rightful
1Sa 8:9 the *r* due of the king who
8:11 *r* due of the king that will
10:25 the *r* due of the kingship
Jer 30:18 *r* site the dwelling tower

Right-hand
1Ki 7:21 *r* pillar and called its name
2Ch 3:17 the name of the *r* one Jachin
Eze 47:1 *r* side of the House, south
47:2 trickling from the *r* side

Righting
2Co 7:11 yes, *r* of the wrong

Rightly
1Sa 2:3 by him deeds are *r* estimated
Jon 4:4 you *r* become hot with anger
4:9 *r* become hot with anger over
4:9 I have *r* become hot with
Joh 8:48 Do we not *r* say, You are a
13:13 you speak *r*, for I am such
18:23 if *r*, why do you hit me?
Ac 13:48 *r* disposed for everlasting

Rights
Ac 22:28 purchased . . . *r* as a citizen
1Th 4:6 upon the *r* of his brother
Heb 12:16 his *r* as firstborn

Rim
Ex 25:25 a *r* of a handbreadth round
25:25 the border of gold for its *r*
25:27 close by the *r* as supports
27:5 put it under the altar's *r*
37:12 a *r* of a handbreadth round
37:12 border of gold for its *r*
37:14 rings proved to be near the *r*
38:4 under its *r*, down toward its

Rimmon
Jos 15:32 Shilhim and Ain and *R*
19:7 Ain, *R* and Ether and Ashan
19:13 and went out to *R* and was
Jg 20:45 fleeing . . . to the crag of *R*
20:47 to the crag of *R*, and they
20:47 to dwell on the crag of *R*
21:13 that were on the crag of *R*
2Sa 4:2 sons of *R* the Beerothite
4:5 sons of *R* the Beerothite
4:9 sons of *R* the Beerothite, and
2Ki 5:18 house of *R* to bow down
5:18 bow down at the house of *R*
5:18 bow down at the house of *R*
1Ch 4:32 *R* and Tochen and Ashan
Zec 14:10 from Geba to *R* to the south

Rimmono
1Ch 6:77 *R* with its pasture grounds

Rimmon-perez
Nu 33:19 and took up camping in *R*
33:20 pulled away from *R* and went

Rims
Ca 5:12 sitting within the *r*
Eze 1:18 their *r*, they had such height
1:18 their *r* were full of eyes

Ring
Ge 24:22 man took a gold nose *r* of a
24:30 seeing the nose *r* and the
Ge 24:47 I put the nose *r* on her
38:18 Your seal *r* and your cord
38:25 the seal *r* and the cord and
41:42 Pharaoh removed his signet *r*
Ex 26:24 of each one at the first *r*
36:29 each one at the first *r*
Jg 8:24 the nose *r* of his booty
8:25 nose *r* of his spoil into it
Es 3:10 the king removed his signet *r*
3:12 with the king's signet *r*
8:2 the king removed his signet *r*
8:8 with the king's signet *r*
8:8 with the king's signet *r*
8:10 with the king's signet *r* and
Job 42:11 and each one a gold *r*
Pr 11:22 gold nose *r* in the snout of
Jer 22:24 the seal *r* on my right hand
Eze 16:12 put a nose *r* in your nostril
Da 6:17 sealed it with his signet *r*
6:17 the signet *r* of his grandees
Ho 2:13 decking herself with her *r*
Hag 2:23 set you as a seal *r*, because
Lu 15:22 and put a *r* on his hand and

Ringing
1Ki 22:36 *r* cry began to pass through

Rings
Ex 25:12 cast four *r* of gold for it
25:12 two *r* upon the one side of
25:12 two *r* upon its other side
25:14 put the poles through the *r*
25:15 In the *r* of the Ark the poles
25:26 make for it four *r* of gold
25:26 the *r* on the four corners
25:27 *r* should be close by the rim
26:29 *r* you will make of gold as
27:4 upon the net four *r* of copper
27:7 poles must be put into the *r*
28:23 two *r* of gold, and you must
28:23 put the two *r* upon the two
28:24 through the two *r* at the
28:26 make two *r* of gold and set
28:27 make two *r* of gold and put
28:28 bind the breastpiece by its *r*
28:28 to the *r* of the ephod with a
30:4 make for it two *r* of gold
35:22 *r* and female ornaments, all
36:34 *r* of gold as supports for the
37:3 he cast four *r* of gold for it
37:3 two *r* on its one side and two
37:3 and two *r* on its other side
37:5 *r* on the sides of the Ark for
37:13 cast four *r* of gold for it
37:13 the *r* upon the four corners
37:14 *r* proved to be near the rim
37:27 made for it two *r* of gold
38:5 he cast four *r* on the four
38:7 *r* on the sides of the altar
39:16 and two *r* of gold and put
39:16 and put the two *r* upon the
39:17 the two *r* at the extremities
39:19 made two *r* of gold and set
39:20 made two *r* of gold and put
39:21 the breastpiece by its *r* to
39:21 to the *r* of the ephod with a
Nu 31:50 bracelets, signet *r*, earrings
Jg 8:24 For they had nose *r* of gold
8:26 the weight of the nose *r* of
Es 1:6 silver *r* and pillars of marble
Isa 3:21, 21 finger *r* and the nose *r*
Jas 2:2 with gold *r* on his fingers

Ring-shaped
Ex 29:2 unfermented *r* cakes moistened
29:23 a *r* cake of oiled bread and a
Le 2:4 unfermented *r* cakes moistened
7:12 unfermented *r* cakes moistened
7:12 *r* cakes moistened with oil
7:13 *r* cakes of leavened bread he
8:26 one unfermented *r* cake and
8:26 one *r* cake of oiled bread and
24:5 twelve *r* cakes. Two tenths of
24:5 ephah should go to each *r* cake
26:26 rods around which *r* loaves
Nu 6:15 basket of unfermented *r* cakes
6:19 one unfermented *r* cake out of
15:20 your coarse meal as *r* cakes
2Sa 6:19 *r* cake of bread and a date
Ps 105:16 *r* loaves were suspended
Eze 4:16 which *r* loaves are suspended
5:16 rods around which *r* loaves
14:13 which *r* loaves are suspended

Ringworm
Le 22:22 or *r*, none of these must you

Ringworms
Le 21:20 or having *r* or having his

Rinnah
1Ch 4:20 the sons of Shimon . . . *R*

Rinse
2Ch 4:6 they would *r* in them
Isa 4:4 *r* away even the bloodshed
Eze 40:38 *r* the whole burnt offering

Rinsed
Le 6:28 be scoured and *r* with water
15:11 has not *r* his hands in water
15:12 should be *r* with water
Jer 51:34 He has *r* me away
Eze 16:9 *r* away your blood from off

Rip
Jg 11:35 he began to *r* his garments
1Sa 28:17 Jehovah will *r* the kingdom
2Sa 3:31 *R* your garments apart and
1Ki 11:11 *r* the kingdom away from
11:12 of your son I shall *r* it
11:13 kingdom that I shall *r* away
14:8 to *r* the kingdom away from
21:27 to *r* his garments apart and
2Ki 5:8 Why did you *r* your garments
8:12 pregnant women you will *r*
Es 4:1 *r* his garments apart and put
Job 1:20 *r* his sleeveless coat apart
2:12 and *r* each one his sleeveless
Ec 3:7 a time to *r* apart and a time
Jer 36:24 *r* their garments apart
Eze 13:20 *r* them from off your arms
13:21 I will *r* away your veils
Ho 13:8 I shall *r* apart the enclosure
Joe 2:13 *r* apart your hearts, and
Mt 7:6 and turn around and *r* you open

Ripe
Ex 23:16 harvest of the first *r* fruits
23:19 first *r* fruits of your ground
34:22 first *r* fruits of the wheat
34:26 best of the first *r* fruits of
Le 2:14 the first *r* fruits to Jehovah
2:14 of your first *r* fruits
23:17 as first *r* fruits to Jehovah
23:20 loaves of the first *r* fruits
Nu 13:20 first *r* fruits of the grapes
17:8 and was bearing *r* almonds
18:13 first *r* fruits of all that is
28:26 the day of the first *r* fruits
De 23:25 pluck off only the *r* ears
2Ki 4:42 bread of the first *r* fruits
Ne 10:35 first *r* fruits of our ground
10:35 and the first *r* fruits of all
13:31 and for the first *r* fruits
Isa 17:6 *r* olives in the top of the
Eze 44:30 first *r* fruits of everything
Joe 3:13 for harvest has grown *r*
Na 3:12 fig trees with the first *r*
Re 14:15 harvest of the earth . . . *r*
14:18 its grapes have become *r*

Ripened
Ge 40:10 Its clusters *r* their grapes

Ripening
Isa 18:5 bloom becomes a *r* grape, one

Riphath
Ge 10:3 sons of Gomer . . . *R* and
1Ch 1:6 sons of Gomer . . . *R* and

Ripped
Ge 37:29 he *r* his garments apart
37:34 Jacob *r* his mantles apart
44:13 they *r* their mantles apart
Nu 14:6 *r* their garments apart
Jos 7:6 Joshua *r* his mantles and fell
1Sa 4:12 his garments *r* apart and
15:27 but it *r* away
15:28 Jehovah has *r* away the
2Sa 1:2 garments *r* apart and dirt
1:11 garments and *r* them apart
13:19 striped robe . . . she *r*
13:31 *r* his clothes apart and lay
13:31 with their garments *r* apart
15:32 his robe *r* apart and dirt
1Ki 11:30 *r* it into twelve pieces
13:3 The altar is *r* apart
13:5 the altar itself was *r* apart
2Ki 2:12 and *r* them into two pieces
5:7 *r* his garments apart and said
5:8 had *r* his garments apart
6:30 *r* his garments apart
11:14 Athaliah *r* her garments
2Ki 15:16 its pregnant women he *r* up
17:21 *r* Israel off from the house
18:37 their garments *r* apart and
19:1 *r* his garments apart and
22:11 *r* his garments apart
22:19 you *r* your garments apart
2Ch 23:13 Athaliah *r* her garments
34:19 *r* his garments apart
34:27 *r* your garments apart and
Ezr 9:3 I *r* apart my garment and my
Ps 35:15 They *r* me to pieces and did
Isa 36:22 with their garments *r* apart
37:1 immediately *r* his garments
64:1 you had *r* the heavens apart
Jer 41:5 their garments *r* apart and
Ho 13:16 women themselves will be *r*
Mt 26:65 the high priest *r* his outer
Mr 14:63 priest *r* his inner garments
Ac 14:14 they *r* their outer garments

Ripping
1Ki 11:31 I am *r* the kingdom out of
Lu 5:6 their nets began *r* apart

Rise
Ge 35:1 *R*, go up to Bethel and dwell
35:3 let us *r* and go up to Bethel
Ex 15:7 those who *r* up against you
33:8 all the people would *r*, and
Le 19:32 Before gray hair you should *r*
Nu 16:2 *r* up before Moses, they and
16:45 *r* up from the midst of this
24:17 a scepter will indeed *r* out
De 2:13 *r* and make your way across
17:8 *r* and go up to the place that
19:15 *r* up against a man
19:16 *r* up against a man to bring
28:7 enemies who *r* up against you
29:22 sons who will *r* up after you
33:11 those who *r* up against him
33:11 that they may not *r* up
Jos 7:12 *r* up against their enemies
7:13 to *r* up against your enemies
8:7 you will *r* up from the ambush
Jg 2:10 generation began to *r* after
5:12 *R* up, Barak, and lead your
7:9 *R* up, descend upon the camp
9:32 *r* up by night, you and the
19:28 *R* up, and let us go
20:5 to *r* up against me and to
20:18 *r* up and go on up to Bethel
Ru 4:5 to *r* upon his inheritance
4:10 the name of the dead man to *r*
1Sa 22:13 *r* up against me as a lier
23:4 *R* up, go down to Keilah
24:7 to *r* up against Saul
26:2 Saul proceeded to *r* up and
29:10 *r* up early in the morning
29:10 *r* up early in the morning
2Sa 2:14 Let the young men *r* up
2:14 Joab said: Let them *r* up
3:21 Let me *r* up and go and
11:2 David proceeded to *r* from
13:29 *r* up and mount each one his
17:1 *r* up and chase after David
17:21 *r* up and speedily pass over
17:23 *r* up and go off to his house
19:7 *r* up, go out and speak
22:39 that they may not *r* up
22:49 those who *r* up against me
24:11 to *r* up in the morning
1Ki 1:49 began to tremble and *r* up
3:12 will not *r* up one like you
8:20 *r* up in the place of David
14:2 *R* up, please, and you must
14:12 *r* up, go to your house
17:9 *R* up, go to Zarephath, which
19:5 he said to him: *R* up, eat
19:7 *R* up, eat, for the journey
21:7 *R* up, eat bread and let your
21:15 *R* up, take possession of the
21:18 *R* up, go down to meet Ahab
2Ki 1:3 *R* up, go up to meet the
8:1 *R* up and go, you with your
10:12 to *r* and come in, then get
1Ch 22:16 *R* and act, and may Jehovah
22:19 *r* and build the sanctuary of
2Ch 6:10 *r* up in the place of David
6:41 *r* up, O Jehovah God, into
13:6 *r* up and rebel against his
20:20 *r* early in the morning and
Ezr 3:2 to *r* up and build the altar of
Ne 9:4 to *r* on the platform of the
9:5 *R*, bless Jehovah your God from
Es 5:9 he did not *r* and did not quake
Job 19:18 Let me but *r* up, and they
19:25 he will *r* up over the dust
24:22 He will *r* up and not be
25:3 whom does his light not *r*
30:12 they *r* up as a brood
Ps 17:13 Do *r* up, O Jehovah; do
18:38 will not be able to *r* up
18:48 those who *r* up against me
24:3 may *r* up in his holy place
27:3 against me war should *r*
35:2 do *r* up in assistance of me
35:11 Violent witnesses *r* up
78:6 *r* up and relate them to their
82:8 Do *r* up, O God, do judge the
92:11 ones who *r* up against me
94:16 *r* up for me against the
Pr 6:9 will you *r* up from your sleep
28:12 when the wicked ones *r* up, a
28:28 wicked *r* up, a man conceals
30:4 all the ends of the earth to *r*
Ca 2:10 *R* up, you girl companion of
2:13 *R* up, come, O girl companion
3:2 Let me *r* up, please, and go
7:12 let us *r* early and go to the
Isa 14:21 *r* up and actually take
14:22 I will *r* up against them
24:20 so that it will not *r* up
26:14 death, they will not *r* up
26:19 corpse of mine—they will *r*
27:9 incense stands will not *r*
28:21 Jehovah will *r* up just as
30:18 *r* up to show you mercy
31:2 *r* up against the house of
32:8 he himself will *r* up
32:9 *r* up, listen to my voice!
33:10 I will *r* up, says Jehovah
49:7 will see and certainly *r* up
51:17 *r* up, O Jerusalem, you who
52:2 *r* up, take a seat
54:17 that will *r* up against you
Jer 1:17 must *r* up and speak to them
2:27 Do *r* up and save us!
2:28 *r* up if they can save you in
6:4 *R* up, and let us go up at
6:5 *R* up, and let us go up during
13:4 *r* up, go to the Euphrates
13:6 *R* up, go to the Euphrates and
18:2 *R* up, and you must go down
31:6 *R* up, O men, and let us go
37:10 *r* up and actually burn
46:16 *r* up, and do let us return
49:14 and *r* up to battle
49:28 *R* up, go up to Kedar
49:31 *R* up, O men, go up against
50:32 one to cause it to *r* up
51:64 sink down and never *r* up
La 1:14 whom I am unable to *r* up
2:19 *R* up! Whine during the night
Eze 10:4 to *r* up from the cherubs to
10:15 cherubs would *r*—it was the
10:17 they would *r* with them
Da 2:39 *r* another kingdom inferior to
7:24 ten kings that will *r* up; and
7:24 another one will *r* up after
Am 7:2 Who will *r* up of Jacob?
7:5 Who will *r* up of Jacob?
7:9 I will *r* up against the house
8:14 and they will *r* up no more
Ob 1 *R* up, you people, and let us
1 *r* up against her in battle
Mic 2:8 to *r* up as an outright enemy
7:8 I shall certainly *r* up
Na 1:6 *r* up against the heat of his
1:9 will not *r* up a second time
Hab 2:7 *r* up suddenly, and those wake
Zec 11:16 a shepherd *r* up in the land
14:10 *r* and become inhabited in
Mt 5:45 sun *r* upon wicked people and
9:9 he did *r* up and follow him
10:21 will *r* up against parents
12:41 Men of Nineveh will *r* up in
24:7 nation will *r* against nation
Mr 8:31 and *r* three days later
9:31 he will *r* three days later
10:34 three days later he will *r*
12:25 when they *r* from the dead
13:8 nation will *r* against nation
13:12 will *r* up against parents
Lu 11:7 I cannot *r* up and give you
11:8 he will not *r* up and give
11:32 men of Nineveh will *r* in the
15:18 I will *r* and journey to my
17:19 *R* and be on your way; your
18:33 on the third day he will *r*

Lu 21:10 Nation will *r* against nation
22:46 *R* and carry on prayer, that
24:7 and yet on the third day *r*
24:46 and *r* from among the dead on
Joh 11:23 Your brother will *r*
11:24 I know he will *r* in the
11:31 Mary *r* quickly and go out
20:9 that he must *r* from the dead
Ac 8:26 *R* and go to the south to the
9:6 *r* and enter into the city, and
9:11 *R*, go to the street called
9:34 *R* and make up your bed
9:40 Tabitha, *r!* She opened her
10:13 *R*, Peter, slaughter and eat!
10:20 *r*, go downstairs and be on
10:26 *R*; I myself am also a man
11:7 *R*, Peter, slaughter and eat!
12:7 *R* quickly! And his chains
17:3 suffer and to *r* from the dead
20:30 will *r* and speak twisted
22:10 *R*, go your way into Damascus
22:16 *R*, get baptized and wash
26:16 *r* and stand on your feet
1Th 4:16 dead . . . will *r* first

Risen
Nu 32:14 you have *r* in the place of
De 19:11 *r* up against him and struck
34:10 *r* up a prophet in Israel like
Jg 9:18 *r* up against the household
2Sa 14:7 all the family have *r* up
2Ki 23:25 has there *r* up one like him
Ps 20:8 we have *r* up, that we may be
27:12 false witnesses have *r* up
54:3 that have *r* up against me
86:14 have *r* up against me
109:28 They have *r* up, but let
Pr 31:28 Her sons have *r* up and
Jer 51:29 thoughts of Jehovah have *r*
Eze 7:11 Violence itself has *r* up into
Ho 10:14 an uproar has *r* among your
Mr 3:26 if Satan has *r* up against
9:9 Son of man had *r* from the
16:2 when the sun had *r*
Lu 9:8 the ancient prophets had *r*
9:19 the ancient prophets has *r*

Rises
De 22:26 *r* up against his fellowman
1Sa 25:29 man *r* up to pursue you and
Job 16:8 my leanness *r* up against me
31:14 what can I do when God *r* up?
Pr 31:28 her owner *r* up, and he
Isa 2:19 *r* up for the earth to suffer
2:21 *r* up for the earth to suffer
Mr 4:27 and *r* up by day, and the seed
Lu 16:31 if someone *r* from the dead
Jas 1:11 sun *r* with its burning heat
2Pe 1:19 a daystar *r*, in your hearts

Rising
Ge 26:31 they were early in *r* and
37:35 kept *r* up to comfort him
Ex 32:6 they were early in *r*, and they
Nu 21:11 toward the *r* of the sun
De 4:41 toward the *r* of the sun
4:47 toward the *r* of the sun
Jos 1:15 toward the *r* of the sun
12:1 toward the *r* of the sun
13:5 toward the *r* of the sun
19:12 toward the *r* of the sun to
19:27 *r* of the sun to Beth-dagon
19:34 toward the *r* of the sun
Jg 11:18 the *r* of the sun as respects
20:43 toward the *r* of the sun
1Sa 17:35 When it began *r* against me
2Sa 18:31 all those *r* up against you
22:40 those *r* against me collapse
1Ki 22:35 battle kept *r* in intensity
2Ki 10:33 Jordan toward the *r* of the
16:7 who are *r* up against me
2Ch 18:34 battle kept *r* in intensity
Ezr 4:19 one *r* up against kings and
Job 41:25 Due to its *r* up the strong
Ps 3:1 Why are many *r* up against me?
18:39 those *r* against me collapse
44:5 tread down those *r* up against
50:1 *r* of the sun until its setting
59:1 From those *r* up against me
74:23 those *r* up against you is
113:3 *r* of the sun until its
127:2 men that you are *r* up early
139:2 sitting down and my *r* up
Isa 41:25 From the *r* of the sun he
45:6 *r* of the sun and from its
Isa 59:19 from the *r* of the sun the
Jer 11:7 *r* up early and admonishing
25:3 *r* up early and speaking
25:4 the prophets, *r* up early
26:5 *r* up early and sending them
32:33 *r* up early and teaching
35:14 *r* up early and speaking
35:15 *r* up early and sending them
44:4 *r* up early and sending
La 3:62 lips of those *r* up against me
3:63 sitting down and their *r* up
Ho 11:7 no one at all does any *r* up
Mic 7:6 a daughter is *r* up against
Zep 3:8 day of my *r* up to the booty
Mal 1:11 from the sun's *r* even to its
Mr 2:14 And *r* up he followed him
9:10 this *r* from the dead meant
14:57 *r* and bearing false witness
Lu 2:34 the *r* again of many in Israel
12:54 a cloud *r* in western parts
Ac 10:41 after his *r* from the dead
Re 16:12 kings from the *r* of the sun

Risk
2Sa 23:17 at the *r* of their souls
1Ch 11:19 at the *r* of their souls
11:19 at the *r* of their souls that
12:19 At the *r* of our own heads
La 5:9 At the *r* of our soul we bring
Ac 19:31 to *r* himself in the theater

Risked
Ro 16:4 *r* their own necks for my soul

Risking
Jg 9:17 went *r* his soul that he might

Rissah
Nu 33:21 and went camping in *R*
33:22 pulled away from *R* and went

Rites
Ge 50:10 mourning *r* for his father
50:11 got to see the mourning *r*

Rithmah
Nu 33:18 and went camping in *R*
33:19 pulled away from *R* and took

Rival
Le 18:18 sister as a *r* to uncover her
1Sa 1:6 And her *r* wife also vexed her

Rivalry
Nu 25:11 by his tolerating no *r* at all
25:13 tolerated no *r* toward his
2Ki 10:16 no *r* toward Jehovah
Ec 4:4 the *r* of one toward another
Php 1:15 Christ through envy and *r*

River
Ge 2:10 Now there was a *r* issuing out
2:13 And the name of the second *r*
2:14 of the third *r* is Hiddekel
2:14 the fourth *r* is the Euphrates
15:18 from the *r* of Egypt to the
15:18, 18 great *r*, the *r* Euphrates
31:21 to get up and cross the *R*
36:37 Shaul from Rehoboth by the *R*
41:1 he was standing by the *r* Nile
41:2 ascending out of the *r* Nile
41:3 out of the *r* Nile, ugly in
41:3 by the bank of the *r* Nile
41:17 on the bank of the *r* Nile
41:18 ascending out of the *r* Nile
Ex 1:22 you are to throw into the *r*
2:3 by the bank of the *r* Nile
2:5 down to bathe in the Nile *R*
2:5 by the side of the Nile *R*
4:9 some water from the Nile *R*
4:9 water . . . from the Nile *R*
7:15 by the edge of the Nile *R*
7:17 water that is in the Nile *R*
7:18 fish that are in the Nile *R*
7:18 Nile *R* will actually stink
7:18 water from the Nile *R*
7:20 water that was in the Nile *R*
7:20 Nile *R* was turned into blood
7:21 fish . . . in the Nile *R* died
7:21 and the Nile *R* began to stink
7:21 drink water from the Nile *R*
7:24 the Nile *R* for water to drink
7:24 drink any water of the Nile *R*
7:25 Jehovah's striking the Nile *R*
8:3 Nile *R* . . . teem with frogs
8:9 Only in the Nile *R* will they
8:11 Only in the Nile *R* will they
17:5 which you struck the Nile *R*
Ex 23:31 from the wilderness to the *R*
Nu 22:5 *R* of the land of the sons of
24:6 Like gardens by the *r*
De 1:7 and Lebanon, up to the great *r*
1:7 up to the . . . *r* Euphrates
11:24, 24 the *R*, the *r* Euphrates
Jos 1:4, 4 great *r*, the *r* Euphrates
24:2 on the other side of the *R*
24:3 the other side of the *R* and
24:14 on the other side of the *R*
24:15 on the other side of the *R*
2Sa 8:3 back again at the *r* Euphrates
10:16 in the region of the *R*
1Ki 4:21 from the *R* to the land of
4:24 this side of the *R*, from
4:24 the kings this side of the *R*
14:15 scatter them beyond the *R*
2Ki 17:6 in Habor at the *r* Gozan and
18:11 *r* Gozan and in the cities
23:29 by the *r* Euphrates
24:7 Egypt up to the *r* Euphrates
1Ch 1:48 Shaul from Rehoboth by the *R*
5:9 wilderness at the *r* Euphrates
5:26 and Hara and the *r* Gozan to
13:5 from the *r* of Egypt as far
18:3 control at the *r* Euphrates
19:16 were in the region of the *R*
2Ch 9:26 from the *R* down to the land
Ezr 4:9 lesser governors across the *R*
4:10 and the rest beyond the *R*
4:11 the men beyond the *R*
4:16 have no share beyond the *R*
4:17 and the rest beyond the *R*
4:20 governing all beyond the *R*
5:3 the governor beyond the *R* and
5:6 the governor beyond the *R* and
5:6 that were beyond the *R*
6:6 the governor beyond the *R*
6:6 that are beyond the *R*
6:8 of the tax beyond the *R*
6:13 the governor beyond the *R*
7:21 that are beyond the *R*
7:25 people that are beyond the *R*
8:15 the *r* that comes to Ahava
8:21 a fast there at the *r* Ahava
8:31 from the *r* Ahava on the
8:36 the governors beyond the *R*
Ne 2:7 to the governors beyond the *R*
2:9 the governors beyond the *R* and
3:7 the governor beyond the *R*
Job 14:11 a *r* itself drains off and
22:16 is poured away just as a *r*
40:23 If the *r* acts violently
Ps 46:4 a *r* the streams of which make
66:6 the *r* they went crossing over
72:8 *R* to the ends of the earth
80:11 And to the *R* its twigs
105:41 waterless regions as a *r*
Isa 7:20 in the region of the *R*, even
8:7 and the many waters of the *R*
11:15 wave his hand at the *R* in
19:5 *r* itself will become parched
19:7 bare places by the Nile *R*
19:7 at the mouth of the Nile *R*
19:7 seedland of the Nile *R*
19:8 fishhooks into the Nile *R*
23:10 your land like the Nile *R*
27:12 *R* to the torrent valley of
48:18 would become just like a *r*
59:19 in like a distressing *r*
66:12 peace just like a *r* and the
Jer 2:18 to drink the waters of the *R*
46:2 by the *r* Euphrates at
46:6 bank of the *r* Euphrates
46:7 up just like the Nile *R*
46:8 up just like the Nile *R*
46:10 north by the *r* Euphrates
Eze 1:1 by the *r* Chebar, that the
1:3 the Chaldeans by the *r* Chebar
3:15 dwelling by the *r* Chebar
3:23 I had seen by the *r* Chebar
10:15 I had seen at the *r* Chebar
10:20 at the *r* Chebar, so that I
10:22 I had seen by the *r* Chebar
29:3 My Nile *R* belongs to me
29:9 To me the Nile *R* belongs
43:3 saw by the *r* Chebar, and
Da 10:4 great *r*, that is, Hiddekel
Jon 2:3 Then a very *r* encircled me
Mic 7:12 even all the way to the *R*
Zec 9:10 *R* to the ends of the earth
Mt 3:6 baptized . . . in the Jordan *R*
Mr 1:5 baptized . . . in the Jordan *R*
Lu 6:48 *r* dashed against that house

Lu 6:49 Against it the *r* dashed, and
Ac 16:13 outside the gate beside a *r*
Re 9:14 at the great *r* Euphrates
12:15 disgorged water like a *r*
12:15 her to be drowned by the *r*
12:16 *r* that the dragon disgorged
16:12 upon the great *r* Euphrates
22:1 *r* of water of life, clear as
22:2 And on this side of the *r*

Rivers
Ex 7:19 waters of Egypt, over their *r*
8:5 with your rod out over the *r*
2Ki 5:12 the *r* of Damascus, better
Job 28:11 from which *r* trickled he
Ps 24:2 upon the *r* he keeps it firmly
74:15 dried up ever-flowing *r*
78:16 to descend just like *r*
89:25 And on the *r* his right hand
93:3 The *r* have raised, O Jehovah
93:3 *r* have raised their sound
93:3 *r* keep raising their pounding
98:8 *r* themselves clap their hands
107:33 *r* into a wilderness
137:1 By the *r* of Babylon—there
Ca 8:7 nor can *r* themselves wash it
Isa 18:1 region of the *r* of Ethiopia
18:2 land the *r* have washed away
18:7 land the *r* have washed away
19:6 *r* must stink; the Nile
33:21 place of *r*, of wide canals
41:18 I shall open up *r*, and in
42:15 will turn *r* into islands
43:2 *r*, they will not flood over
43:19 a way, through the desert *r*
43:20 *r* in the desert, to cause
44:27 all your *r* I shall dry up
47:2 Cross over the *r*
50:2 I make *r* a wilderness
Jer 46:7 *r* the waters of which toss
46:8 like *r* the waters toss
Eze 32:2 you kept gushing in your *r*
32:2 and fouling their *r*
32:14 *r* I shall make go just
Na 1:4 *r* he actually makes run dry
2:6 The very gates of the *r* will
Hab 3:8 Is it against the *r*, O Jehovah
3:8 Jehovah, is it against the *r*
3:9 With *r* you proceeded to split
Zep 3:10 region of the *r* of Ethiopia
2Co 11:26 in dangers from *r*, in
Re 8:10 fell upon a third of the *r* and
16:4 poured . . . bowl into the *r*

Rizia
1Ch 7:39 And the sons of Ulla . . . *R*

Rizpah
2Sa 3:7 concubine whose name was *R*
21:8 *R* the daughter of Aiah
21:10 *R* the daughter of Aiah took
21:11 *R* the daughter of Aiah

Road
Ge 38:14 is along the *r* to Timnah
38:16 turned aside to her by the *r*
38:21 in Enaim along the *r*
Ex 4:24 Now it came about on the *r*
23:20 to keep you on the *r* and to
Nu 20:17 On the king's *r* we shall
21:22 the king's *r* we shall march
22:22 in the *r* to resist him
22:23 angel stationed in the *r*
22:23 to turn aside from the *r*
22:23 to turn her aside to the *r*
22:31 angel stationed in the *r*
22:34 stationed in the *r* to meet
De 2:27 Only on the *r* I shall walk
6:7 when you walk on the *r* and
11:19 and when you walk on the *r*
22:4 his bull fall down on the *r*
Jos 2:22 looking for them on every *r*
5:4 in the wilderness on the *r*
5:5 the *r* when they were coming
5:7 not circumcised them on the *r*
Jg 5:10 And you who walk on the *r*
9:25 pass by them on the *r*
Ru 1:7 walking on the *r* to return
1Sa 6:9 it is the *r* to its territory
6:12 on the *r* to Beth-shemesh
13:17 *r* to Ophrah, to the land of
13:18 turn to the *r* of Beth-horon
13:18 *r* to the boundary that looks
24:3 stone sheepfolds along the *r*
24:19 send him away on a good *r*
26:3 by the *r*, while David was
2Sa 4:7 walked on the *r* to the Arabah
13:34 *r* behind him by the
15:2 the side of the *r* to the gate
15:23 open *r* to the wilderness
16:13 men kept going on in the *r*
1Ki 11:29 got to find him on the *r*
13:24 lion found him on the *r* and
13:24 to be thrown onto the *r*
13:25 dead body thrown onto the *r*
13:28 the *r* with the ass and the
20:38 for the king by the *r*, and
Ps 58:2 prepare the *r* for the very
80:12 those . . . on the *r* plucked at
Jer 31:21 Set up *r* marks for yourself
48:9 Give a *r* mark to Moab, you
La 2:15 those passing along on the *r*
Mt 4:15 along the *r* of the sea, on the
7:13 broad and spacious is the *r*
7:14 and cramped the *r* leading off
8:28 courage to pass by on that *r*
10:5 into the *r* of the nations
13:4 seeds fell alongside the *r*
13:19 the one sown alongside the *r*
15:32 possibly give out on the *r*
20:17 and said to them on the *r*
20:30 men sitting beside the *r*
21:8 their outer garments on the *r*
21:8 and spreading them on the *r*
21:19 sight of a fig tree by the *r*
Mr 4:4 some seed fell alongside the *r*
4:15 are the ones alongside the *r*
8:3 they will give out on the *r*
9:33 you arguing over on the *r*
9:34 on the *r* they had argued
10:32 on the *r* up to Jerusalem
10:46 was sitting beside the *r*
10:52 to follow him on the *r*
11:8 their outer garments on the *r*
Lu 8:5 fell alongside the *r* and was
8:12 Those alongside the *r* are
9:57 as they were going on the *r*
10:4 in greeting along the *r*
10:31 was going down over that *r*
10:33 Samaritan traveling the *r*
18:35 sitting beside the *r* begging
19:36 outer garments on the *r*
19:37 soon as he got near the *r*
24:32 was speaking to us on the *r*
24:35 related the events on the *r*
Ac 8:26 the *r* that runs down from
8:26 (This is a desert *r*.)
8:36 going over the *r*, they came
9:17 that appeared to you on the *r*
9:27 on the *r* he had seen the Lord
25:3 do away with him along the *r*
26:13 I saw at midday on the *r*

Roads
Le 26:22 *r* will actually be desolated
Job 21:29 those traveling over the *r*
Mt 3:3 Make his *r* straight
22:9 go to the *r* leading out of
22:10 slaves went out to the *r* and
Mr 1:3 people, make his *r* straight
Lu 3:4 people, make his *r* straight
14:23 Go out into the *r* and the

Roadside
Ge 49:17 a serpent by the *r*, a horned
1Sa 4:13 sitting on the seat by the *r*

Roadway
Ps 119:105 And a light to my *r*
142:3 yourself knew my *r*
Pr 1:15 back your foot from their *r*
Isa 42:16 *r* that they have not known
43:16 a *r* even through strong

Roadways
Jg 5:6 travelers of *r* would travel
Job 19:8 upon my *r* he puts darkness
24:13 they did not dwell in its *r*
30:13 They have torn down my *r*
38:20 the *r* to its house
Pr 3:17 and all its *r* are peace
7:25 Do not wander into her *r*
8:2 *r* it has stationed itself
8:20 middle of the *r* of judgment
Isa 58:12 restorer of *r* by which to
59:8 *r* they have made crooked for
Jer 6:16 ask for the *r* of long ago
18:15 to walk in *r*, a way not
La 3:9 My *r* he has twisted
Ho 2:6 her own *r* she will not find

Roamed
Jer 2:31 have said, We have *r*

Roaming
Ho 11:12 But Judah is yet *r* with God

Roar
Isa 5:29 *r* like maned young lions
Jer 2:15 maned young lions *r*
25:30 Jehovah himself will *r*
25:30 *r* upon his abiding place
51:38 *r* just like maned young
Ho 11:10 Like a lion he will *r*
11:10 for he himself will *r*
Joe 3:16 Jehovah himself will *r*
Am 1:2 Jehovah—out of Zion he will *r*
3:4 Will a lion *r* in the forest

Roared
Ps 38:8 I have *r* due to the groaning
74:4 *r* in the middle of your
Am 3:8 There is a lion that has *r*

Roaring
Jg 14:5 young lion *r* upon meeting him
2Ki 19:28 *r* have come up into my ears
Job 3:24 like waters my *r* cries pour
4:10 There is the *r* of a lion, and
Ps 22:1 From the words of my *r*
22:13 lion tearing in pieces and *r*
40:2 bring me up out of a *r* pit
104:21 lions are *r* for the prey
Isa 5:29 *r* of theirs is like that of
37:29 *r* have come up into my ears
Jer 11:16 With sound of the great *r*
Eze 19:7 with the sound of his *r*
22:25 like the *r* lion, tearing
Zep 3:3 midst of her were *r* lions
Zec 11:3 The *r* of maned young lions
Lu 21:25 the *r* of the sea and its
1Pe 5:8 walks about like a *r* lion

Roars
Job 37:4 After it a sound *r*
Re 10:3 just as when a lion *r*

Roast
Ex 12:9 but *r* with fire, its head
1Sa 2:15 meat to *r* for the priest
Isa 44:19 I *r* flesh and eat. But the

Roasted
Ex 12:8 should eat it *r* with fire and
Le 2:14 present green ears *r* with
23:14 eat no bread nor *r* grain nor
Jos 5:11 and *r* grains, on this same
Ru 2:14 would hold out *r* grain to her
1Sa 17:17 this ephah of *r* grain and
25:18 seah measures of *r* grain
2Sa 17:28 *r* grain and broad beans and
Jer 29:22 Ahab . . . *r* in the fire

Roasts
Isa 44:16 he *r* well the flesh that

Rob
Le 19:13 and you must not *r*
Jg 9:25 and they would *r* everyone that
Pr 22:22 not *r* the lowly one because
22:23 *r* of soul those robbing them
Mal 3:8 Will earthling man *r* God?
Ro 2:22 do you *r* temples?

Robbed
Le 6:4 he must return the *r* thing
6:4 thing which he has *r* or the
De 28:29 always defrauded and *r*
Jer 21:12 deliver the one being *r*
22:3 the one that is being *r*
Mal 3:8 In what way have we *r* you?
2Co 11:8 I *r* by accepting provisions

Robber
Ps 17:4 against the paths of the *r*
Pr 23:28 she, just like a *r*, lies in
Eze 18:10 father to a son who is a *r*
Mt 26:55 and clubs as against a *r* to
Mr 14:48 as against a *r* to arrest me
Lu 22:52 and clubs as against a *r*
Joh 18:40 Now Barabbas was a *r*

Robbers
Jer 7:11 become a mere cave of *r*
Eze 7:22 into it *r* will really come
Da 11:14 sons of the *r* belonging to
Mt 21:13 are making it a cave of *r*
27:38 two *r* were impaled with
27:44 the *r* that were impaled
Mr 11:17 you have made it a cave of *r*
15:27 impaled two *r* with him, one

Lu 10:30 *r*, who both stripped him and
10:36 man that fell among the *r*
19:46 but you made it a cave of *r*
Ac 19:37 are neither *r* of temples nor

Robbery
Le 6:2 or a *r* or he does defraud his
De 28:31 Your ass taken in *r* from
Ps 62:10 become vain in sheer *r*
69:4 What I had not taken by *r*
Isa 3:14 What was taken by *r* from
61:8 loving justice, hating *r*
Eze 18:7 nothing . . . wrest away in *r*
18:12 he has wrested away in *r*
18:16 nothing has he taken in *r*
18:18 in *r* of a brother, and
22:29 done a tearing away in *r*
33:15 things taken by *r*, and
Na 3:1 all full of deception and of *r*

Robbing
Ps 35:10 poor one from the one *r* him
Pr 22:23 rob of soul those *r* them
28:24 *r* his father and his mother
Mal 3:8 rob God? But you are *r* me
3:9 cursing me, and me you are *r*

Robe
Ex 28:4 a *r* of checkerwork, a turban
28:39 the *r* of fine linen and make
29:5 clothe Aaron with the *r* and
Le 8:7 put the *r* upon him and girded
16:4 put on the holy linen *r*, and
2Sa 13:18 her there was a striped *r*
13:19 striped *r* that was upon her
15:32 his *r* ripped apart and dirt
Ca 5:3 I have put off my *r*. How can I
Isa 22:21 clothe him with your *r*
Mr 16:5 clothed in a white *r*, and
Lu 15:22 bring out a *r*, the best one
Re 6:11 white *r* was given to each of

Robes
Ex 28:40 Aaron's sons you will make *r*
29:8 must clothe them with the *r*
39:27 made the *r* of fine linen
40:14 you must clothe them with *r*
Le 8:13 clothed them with *r* and
10:5 and carried them in their *r*
Ezr 2:69 and a hundred *r* of priests
Ne 7:70 hundred and thirty priests' *r*
7:72 and sixty-seven priests' *r*
Isa 3:22 *r* of state and the overtunics
Zec 3:4 clothing . . . with *r* of state
Mr 12:38 want to walk around in *r*
Lu 20:46 desire to walk around in *r*
Re 7:9 great crowd . . . in white *r*
7:13 are dressed in the white *r*
7:14 washed their *r* and made them
22:14 are those who wash their *r*

Robust
Ge 30:41 *r* flocks would get in heat
30:42 but the *r* ones Jacob's
Jg 3:29 every one *r* and every one
Job 39:4 sons become *r*, they get big

Rock
Ex 17:6 standing . . . on the *r* in Horeb
17:6 strike on the *r*, and water
33:21 station yourself upon the *r*
33:22 place you in a hole in the *r*
Le 11:5 Also the *r* badger, because it
De 8:15 water for you out of . . . *r*
14:7 the hare and the *r* badger
32:4 The *R*, perfect is his activity
32:13 And oil out of a flinty *r*
32:15 the *R* of his salvation
32:18 The *R* who fathered you, you
32:30 unless their *R* had sold them
32:31, 31 their *r* is not like our *R*
32:37 The *r* in whom they sought
Jg 6:20 set them on the big *r* there
6:21 out of the *r* and to consume
7:25 the *r* of Oreb, and they killed
13:19 upon the *r* to Jehovah
1Sa 2:2 And there is no *r* like our God
2Sa 21:10 sackcloth . . . upon the *r*
22:3 God is my *r*. I shall take
22:8 earth began to shake and to *r*
22:32 who is a *r* besides our God?
22:47 blessed be my *R*
22:47 the *r* of my salvation be
23:3 To me the *R* of Israel spoke
1Ch 11:15 go down to the *r*, to David
Job 14:18 And even a *r* will be moved
18:4 *r* move away from its place
Job 19:24 Forever in the *r* . . . hewn
22:24 in the *r* of torrent valleys
24:8 shelter they have to hug a *r*
28:18 Coral and *r* crystal
29:6 the *r* kept pouring out
Ps 18:2 My God is my *r*. I shall take
18:7 the earth began to shake and *r*
18:31 who is a *r* except our God?
18:46 blessed be my *R*, And let the
19:14 my *R* and my Redeemer
27:5 High on a *r* he will put me
28:1 O my *R*, do not be deaf to me
46:3 the mountains *r* at its uproar
60:2 You have caused the earth to *r*
61:2 Onto a *r* that is higher than
62:2 he is my *r* and my salvation
62:6 he is my *r* and my salvation
62:7 My strong *r*, my refuge is in
71:3 Become to me a *r* fortress
73:26 God is the *r* of my heart and
77:18 agitated and began to *r*
78:20 struck a *r* That waters might
78:35 that God was their *R*
81:16 out of the *r* I shall satisfy
89:26 and the *R* of my salvation
92:15 He is my *R*, in whom there
94:22 my God the *r* of my refuge
95:1 triumph to our *R* of salvation
104:18 a refuge for the *r* badgers
105:41 opened a *r*, and waters
114:8 changing the *r* into a reedy
114:8 flinty *r* into a spring of
144:1 Blessed be Jehovah my *R*
Pr 30:19 the way of a serpent on a *r*
30:26 *r* badgers are a people not
Isa 2:10 Enter into the *r* and hide
8:14 *r* over which to stumble to
10:26 Midian by the *r* Oreb
13:13 earth will *r* out of its
14:16 that was making kingdoms *r*
17:10 *R* of your fortress you have
24:18 of the land will *r*
26:4 *R* of times indefinite
30:29 Jehovah, to the *R* of Israel
44:8 no *R*. I have recognized none
48:21 Water out of the *r* he
48:21 split a *r* that the water
51:1 *r* from which you were hewn
Jer 8:16 whole land has begun to *r*
10:10 the earth will *r*, and no
18:14 the *r* of the open field
21:13 O *r* of the level land
49:21 the earth has begun to *r*
51:29 earth *r* and be in severe
Eze 26:10 your walls will *r*, when he
26:15 will not the islands *r*?
27:28 the open country will *r*
31:16 cause nations to *r* when I
Joe 3:16 and earth certainly will *r*
Am 9:1 so that the thresholds will *r*
Hab 1:12 O *R*, for a reproving you have
Hag 2:7 And I will *r* all the nations
Lu 23:53 in a tomb carved in the *r*

Rocked
Jg 5:4 Earth *r*, heavens also dripped
Ps 68:8 The earth itself *r*, Heaven
68:8 This Sinai *r* because of God
Joe 2:10 agitated, the heavens have *r*
Na 1:5 Mountains themselves have *r*

Rocking
Jer 4:24 they were *r*, and the hills
50:46 will certainly be set *r*
Hag 2:6 I am *r* the heavens and the
2:21 *r* the heavens and the earth

Rock-mass
Mt 7:24 built his house upon the *r*
7:25 had been founded upon the *r*
16:18 on this *r* I will build my
27:60 tomb . . . quarried in the *r*
Mr 15:46 was quarried out of a *r*
Lu 6:48 laid a foundation upon the *r*
8:6 Some other landed upon the *r*
8:13 Those upon the *r* are the ones
Ro 9:33 stumbling and a *r* of offense
1Co 10:4 spiritual *r* that followed
10:4 and that *r* meant the Christ
1Pe 2:8 stone of stumbling and a *r* of

Rock-masses
Mt 27:51 quaked, and the *r* were split
Re 6:15 and in the *r* of the mountains
6:16 to the *r*: Fall over us and

Rocks
Nu 23:9 from the top of the *r* I see
1Sa 24:2 bare *r* of the mountain goats
Job 28:10 Into the *r* he has channeled
30:6 In holes of the dust and in *r*
Ps 78:15 split *r* in the wilderness
Isa 2:19 enter into the caves of the *r*
2:21 holes in the *r* and into the
13:2 mountain of bare *r* raise up
Jer 4:29 into the *r* they have gone up
Na 1:6 *r* will actually be pulled down
Ac 27:29 cast somewhere upon the *r*
Jude 12 *r* hidden below water in your

Rocky
Ps 31:2 Become for me a *r* stronghold
Mt 13:5 Others fell upon the *r* places
13:20 one sown upon the *r* places
Mr 4:5 seed fell upon the *r* place
4:16 ones sown upon the *r* places

Rod
Ge 38:18 your *r* that is in your hand
38:25 ring and the cord and the *r*
Ex 4:2 hand? to which he said: A *r*
4:4 and it became a *r* in his palm
4:17 *r* you will take in your hand
4:20 Moses took the *r* of the
7:9 must say to Aaron, Take your *r*
7:10 Aaron threw his *r* down before
7:12 threw down each one his *r*
7:12 Aaron's *r* swallowed up their
7:15 *r* that turned into a serpent
7:17 I am striking with the *r* that
7:19 Take your *r* and stretch your
7:20 lifted up the *r* and struck
8:5 hand with your *r* out over the
8:16 Stretch your *r* out and strike
8:17 his *r* and struck the dust
9:23 So Moses stretched out his *r*
10:13 Moses stretched his *r* out
14:16 lift up your *r* and stretch
17:5 *r* with which you struck the
17:9 with the *r* of the true God
Nu 17:2 one *r* for each paternal house
17:2 name of each one upon his *r*
17:3 you will write upon Levi's *r*
17:3 is one *r* for the head of the
17:5 his *r* will bud, and I shall
17:6, 6 *r* for each chieftain, a *r*
17:6 Aaron's *r* was in among their
17:8 Aaron's *r* . . . had budded, and
17:9 and taking each man his own *r*
17:10 Put Aaron's *r* back before the
20:8 Take the *r* and call the
20:9 Moses took the *r* from before
20:11 struck the crag with his *r*
1Sa 14:27 the tip of the *r* that was
14:43 honey on the tip of the *r*
2Sa 7:14 reprove him with the *r* of
23:21 went on down . . . with a *r*
1Ch 11:23 down to him with a *r* and
Job 9:34 remove his *r* from upon me
21:9 *r* of God is not upon them
37:13 for a *r* or for his land
Ps 23:4 Your *r* and your staff are the
89:32 transgression even with a *r*
105:16 *r* around which ring-shaped
110:2 *r* of your strength Jehovah
Pr 10:13 *r* is for the back of one
13:24 holding back his *r* is hating
14:3 *r* of haughtiness is in the
22:8 *r* of his fury will come to
22:15 *r* of discipline is what will
23:13 case you beat him with the *r*
23:14 *r* you yourself should beat
26:3 *r* is for the back of stupid
29:15 *r* and reproof are what give
Isa 9:4 and the *r* upon their shoulders
10:5 Assyrian, the *r* for my anger
10:15 *r* raised on high the one
10:24 Assyrian, who with the *r*
11:4 strike the earth with the *r*
14:5 Jehovah has broken the *r* of
28:27 *r* that black cummin is
30:32 of his *r* of chastisement
Jer 48:17 *r* of strength has been
Eze 7:10 The *r* has blossomed
7:11 up into a *r* of wickedness
19:12 Her strong *r* was torn off
19:14 to come forth from her *r*
19:14 to be in her no strong *r*
20:37 pass under the *r* and bring
Mic 5:1 With the *r* they will strike
6:9 Hear the *r* and who it was

1Co 4:21 Shall I come . . . with a *r*
Heb 9:4 the *r* of Aaron that budded
Re 2:27 people with an iron *r* so
11:1 a reed like a *r* was given me
12:5 the nations with an iron *r*
19:15 shepherd . . . with a *r* of iron

Rodanim
1Ch 1:7 sons of Javan were . . . *R*

Rode
Jg 10:4 *r* on thirty full-grown asses
12:14 who *r* on seventy full-grown
1Sa 30:17 men that *r* upon camels and

Rodent
Isa 66:17 even the jumping *r*, they

Rods
Ex 7:12 rod swallowed up their *r*
Le 26:26 *r* around which . . . loaves
Nu 17:2 twelve *r*. You will write the
17:6 twelve *r*; and Aaron's rod was
17:6 rod was in among their *r*
17:7 deposited the *r* before Jehovah
17:9 all the *r* from before Jehovah
1Ch 15:15 shoulders with the *r* upon
Job 40:18 are like wrought-iron *r*
Eze 4:16 *r* around which ring-shaped
5:16 *r* around which ring-shaped
14:13 break for it the *r* around
19:11 came to be for her strong *r*
Hab 3:14 With his own *r* you pierced
Ac 16:22 command to beat them with *r*
2Co 11:25 times I was beaten with *r*

Roebuck
De 14:5 the stag and gazelle and *r*

Roebucks
1Ki 4:23 stags and gazelles and *r*

Rogelim
2Sa 17:27 the Gileadite from *R*
19:31 came down from *R* that he

Rohgah
1Ch 7:34 of Shemer were Ahi and *R*

Roll
Ge 29:8 actually *r* away the stone
Jos 10:18 *R* great stones up to the
1Sa 14:33 *r* a great stone to me
Job 20:28 shower will *r* his house
Ps 37:5 *R* upon Jehovah your way
40:7 In the *r* of the book it being
119:22 *R* off me reproach and
Pr 16:3 *R* your works upon Jehovah
Ca 7:2 Your navel *r* is a round bowl
Jer 36:2 yourself a *r* of a book, and
36:4 to him, on the *r* of the book
36:6 read aloud from the *r* that
36:14 *r* from which you read aloud
36:14 took the *r* in his hand and
36:20 *r* they entrusted to the
36:21 Jehudi out to get the *r*
36:23 *r* ended up in the fire
36:25 king not to burn the *r*
36:27 king had burned up the *r*
36:28 *r*, another one, and write
36:28 to be on the first *r*
36:29 burned up this *r*, saying
36:32 another *r* and then gave it
51:25 *r* you away from the crags
Eze 2:9 there was the *r* of a book
3:1 Eat this *r*, and go, speak to
3:2 gradually made me eat this *r*
3:3 this *r* that I am giving you
Am 5:24 justice *r* forth just like
Mr 16:3 Who will *r* the stone away
Joh 19:39 a *r* of myrrh and aloes
Heb 10:7 in the *r* of the book it is

Rolled
Ge 29:3 *r* away the stone from off the
29:10 and *r* away the stone
Jos 5:9 I have *r* away the reproach of
Ezr 5:8 with stones *r* into place
6:4 layers of stones *r* into place
Job 30:14 Under a storm they have *r*
Isa 9:5 mantle *r* in blood have even
34:4 heavens must be *r* up, just
38:12 *r* up my life just like a
Mt 28:2 *r* away the stone, and was
Mr 15:46 *r* a stone up to the door of
16:4 the stone had been *r* away
Lu 4:20 he *r* up the scroll, handed it
24:2 found the stone *r* away from
Joh 20:7 separately *r* up in one place

Re 6:14 as a scroll that is being *r* up

Roller
Isa 28:28 *r* of his wagon in motion

Rolling
1Sa 1:20 at the *r* around of a year
Pr 26:27 he that is *r* away a stone
Mt 27:60 *r* a big stone to the door of
Mr 9:20 he kept *r* about, foaming
2Pe 2:22 sow . . . to *r* in the mire

Romamti-ezer
1Ch 25:4 the sons of Heman . . . *R*
25:31 the twenty-fourth, for *R*

Roman
Ac 22:25 scourge a man that is a *R*
22:26 Why, this man is a *R*
22:27 Are you a *R*? He said: Yes
22:29 ascertaining that he was a *R*
23:27 because I learned he was a *R*
25:16 it is not *R* procedure to hand

Romans
Joh 11:48 *R* will come and take away
Ac 16:21 or practice, seeing we are *R*
16:37 men who are *R*, and threw us
16:38 heard that the men were *R*
28:17 into the hands of the *R*

Rome
Ac 2:10 sojourners from *R*, both Jews
18:2 all the Jews to depart from *R*
19:21 I must also see *R*
23:11 must also bear witness in *R*
28:14 this way we came toward *R*
28:16 we entered into *R*, Paul was
Ro 1:7 in *R* as God's beloved ones
1:15 news also to you there in *R*
2Ti 1:17 when he happened to be in *R*

Roof
Ge 6:16 *tso'har* [*r*; or, window] for
19:8 come under the shadow of my *r*
De 22:8 make a parapet for your *r*
Jos 2:6 had taken them up to the *r*
2:6 in rows for her upon the *r*
2:8 came up to them on the *r*
Jg 3:20 he was sitting in his cool *r*
3:23 he closed the doors of the *r*
3:24 the doors of the *r* chamber
3:25 opening the doors of the *r*
9:51 and climbed onto the *r* of the
16:27 upon the *r* there were about
2Sa 16:22 tent for Absalom upon the *r*
18:24 the watchman went to the *r*
18:33 went up to the *r* chamber
1Ki 17:19 carried him up to the *r*
17:23 *r* chamber into the house
2Ki 1:2 the grating in his *r* chamber
4:10 make a little *r* chamber on
4:11 aside to the *r* chamber
23:12 altars that were upon the *r*
23:12 the *r* chamber of Ahaz that
1Ch 28:11 its *r* chambers and its dark
2Ch 3:9 *r* chambers he covered with
Ne 3:15 to build it and to *r* it over
3:31 the *r* chamber of the corner
3:32 the *r* chamber of the corner
8:16 each one upon his own *r*
Ps 102:7 like a bird isolated upon a *r*
Pr 19:13 a leaking *r* that drives one
21:9 to dwell upon a corner of a *r*
25:24 dwell upon a corner of a *r*
27:15 A leaking *r* that drives one
Eze 3:26 stick to the *r* of your mouth
40:13 measure the gate from the *r*
40:13 one guard chamber to the *r*
Da 6:10 windows in his *r* chamber
Ho 13:3 like smoke from the *r* hole
Mt 8:8 for you to enter under my *r*
Mr 2:4 removed the *r* over where he
Lu 5:19 they climbed up to the *r*, and
7:6 have you come in under my *r*

Roofs
2Ki 19:26 Grass of the *r*, when there
Ps 129:6 like green grass of the *r*
Isa 15:3 Upon the *r* thereof and in
22:1 in your entirety to the *r*
37:27 Grass of the *r* and of the
Jer 19:13 the houses upon the *r* of
32:29 *r* of which they have made
48:38 On all the *r* of Moab and
Zep 1:5 bowing down upon the *r* to the

Rooftop
2Sa 11:2 walk about on the *r* of the
11:2 from the *r* he caught sight

Room
Ge 24:23 Is there any *r* at the house
24:31 ready and *r* for the camels
26:22 Jehovah has given us ample *r*
43:30 he went into an interior *r*
Jg 3:24 nature in the cool interior *r*
14:18 could go into the interior *r*
15:1 to my wife in the interior *r*
16:9 sitting in the interior *r* of
16:12 sitting in the interior *r*
2Sa 13:10 Bring . . . to the interior *r*
13:10 brother in the interior *r*
22:37 make *r* large enough for my
1Ki 1:15 to the king in the interior *r*
6:5 temple and the innermost *r*
6:16 innermost *r*, the Most Holy
6:19 innermost *r* in the interior
6:20 innermost *r* was twenty
6:21 in front of the innermost *r*
6:22 innermost *r* he overlaid with
6:23 in the innermost *r* two
6:31 entrance of the innermost *r*
7:49 before the innermost *r*
8:6 the innermost *r* of the house
8:8 in front of the innermost *r*
2Ki 11:2 the inner *r* for the couches
23:11 dining *r* of Nathan-melech
2Ch 4:20 before the innermost *r*
5:7 the innermost *r* of the house
5:9 in front of the innermost *r*
22:11 the inner *r* for the couches
Job 37:9 Out of the interior *r* comes
Ps 18:36 *r* large enough for my steps
28:2 the innermost *r* of your holy
119:32 make my heart have the *r*
Ca 3:4 interior *r* of her that had been
Isa 5:8 until there is no more *r* and
49:20 Do make *r* for me, that I
Jer 35:4 dining *r* of the sons of Hanan
35:4 dining *r* of the princes that
35:4 the dining *r* of Maaseiah
36:10 dining *r* of Gemariah the
36:12 dining *r* of the secretary
36:20 dining *r* of Elishama the
36:21 dining *r* of Elishama the
Eze 40:38 dining *r* with its entrance
40:45 the dining *r* the front of
40:46 the dining *r* the front of
42:6 more *r* was taken away than
Joe 2:16 go forth from his interior *r*
Zec 10:10 no *r* will be found for them
Mt 6:6 pray, go into your private *r*
19:11 Not all men make *r* for the
19:12 Let him that can make *r* for
19:12 Let him that can . . . make *r*
22:10 and the *r* for the wedding
Mr 2:2 so that there was no more *r*
14:14 Where is the guest *r* for me
14:15 show you a large upper *r*
Lu 2:7 for them in the lodging *r*
14:22 and yet there is *r*
22:11 guest *r* in which I may eat
22:12 a large upper *r* furnished
2Co 6:12 not cramped for *r* within us
6:12 for *r* in your own tender
7:2 Allow *r* for us. We have

Rooms
1Ch 9:26 in charge of the dining *r* and
9:33 the Levites in the dining *r*
23:28 over the dining *r* and over
28:11 its dark inner *r* and the
28:12 all the dining *r* all around
2Ch 31:11 dining *r* in the house of
Job 9:9 the interior *r* of the South
Ps 105:30 interior *r* of their kings
Pr 7:27 to the interior *r* of death
24:4 knowledge will the interior *r*
Ec 10:20 the interior *r* where you lie
Ca 1:4 brought me into his interior *r*
Isa 26:20 enter into your interior *r*
Jer 35:2 to one of the dining *r*
37:16 and into the vaulted *r*
Eze 8:12 the inner *r* of his showpiece
40:17 there were dining *r*, and a
40:17 thirty dining *r* upon the
40:44 the dining *r* of the singers
41:10 between the dining *r* the
42:4 before the dining *r* there
42:5 the dining *r*, the uppermost
42:7 was close by the dining *r*

Eze 42:7 before the other dining *r*
42:8 the length of the dining *r*
42:9 from below these dining *r*
42:10 there were dining *r*
42:11 appearance of the dining *r*
42:12 entrances of the dining *r*
42:13 The dining *r* of the north
42:13 the dining *r* of the south
42:13 they are the holy dining *r*
44:19 in the holy dining *r*
45:5 will have twenty dining *r*
46:19 gate to the holy dining *r*
Lu 12:3 what you whisper in private *r*

Roomy
2Sa 22:20 bring me out into a *r* place
Ps 18:19 bring me out into a *r* place
31:8 my feet stand in a *r* place
118:5 and put me into a *r* place
119:45 walk about in a *r* place
Jer 22:14 build for myself a *r* house
Ho 4:16 like a young ram in a *r* place

Roost
Ps 104:12 *r* the flying creatures of

Roosts
Mt 8:20 and birds of heaven have *r*
Lu 9:58 and birds of heaven have *r*

Root
De 29:18 a *r* bearing the fruit of a
2Ki 19:30 take *r* downward and produce
Job 5:3 seen the foolish one taking *r*
14:8 its *r* grows old in the earth
19:28 *r* of the matter is found in
28:9 mountains from their *r*
29:19 *r* is opened for the waters
30:4 the *r* of broom trees was
31:12 produce it would take *r*
Ps 52:5 *r* you out of the land of the
80:9 take *r* and fill the land
Pr 12:12 *r* of the righteous ones
Isa 11:10 *r* of Jesse that will be
14:29 *r* of the serpent there will
14:30 I will put your *r* to death
27:6 days Jacob will take *r*
37:31 take *r* downward and produce
40:24 stump taken *r* in the earth
53:2 like a *r* out of waterless
Jer 12:2 they have also taken *r*
Eze 31:7 its *r* system proved to be
Ho 9:16 Their very *r* must dry up
Mal 4:1 not leave . . . *r* or bough
Mt 3:10 lying at the *r* of the trees
13:6 not having *r* they withered
13:21 he has no *r* in himself but
Mr 4:6 for not having *r* it withered
4:17 they have no *r* in themselves
Lu 3:9 position at the *r* of the trees
8:13 but these have no *r*; they
Ro 11:16 *r* is holy, the branches are
11:17 of the olive's *r* of fatness
11:18 not you that bear the *r*, but
11:18 but the *r* bears you
15:12 There will be the *r* of Jesse
1Ti 6:10 *r* of all sorts of injurious
Heb 12:15 no poisonous *r* may spring
Re 5:5 tribe of Judah, the *r* of David
22:16 *r* and the offspring of David

Rooted
Job 31:8 my own descendants be *r* out
Eph 3:17 be *r* and established on the
Col 2:7 *r* and being built up in him

Root-foundation
Pr 12:3 as for the *r* of the righteous

Roots
Job 8:17 his *r* become interwoven
18:16 will his very *r* dry up
36:30 *r* of the sea he has covered
Isa 11:1 out of his *r* a sprout will
Jer 17:8 *r* right by the watercourse
Eze 17:6 *r*, they gradually came to be
17:7 vine stretched its *r* hungrily
17:9 someone tear out its very *r*
17:9 to be lifted up from its *r*
Da 11:7 one from the sprout of her *r*
Ho 14:5 strike his *r* like Lebanon
Am 2:9 fruitage above and his *r* below
Mr 11:20 withered up from the *r*

Rootstock
Isa 5:24 *r* will become just like a
Da 4:15 its *r* itself in the earth
4:23 its *r* itself in the earth

Da 4:26 to leave the *r* of the tree

Rope
Ex 28:14 with the workmanship of a *r*
28:22 wreathed chains, in *r* work
39:15 in *r* work, of pure gold
Jos 2:15 by a *r* through the window
Job 41:1 with a *r* can you hold down
Isa 3:24 instead of a belt, a *r*
Am 7:17 by the measuring *r* it will be
Zec 2:1 and in his hand a measuring *r*

Ropelike
Ex 28:14 attach the *r* chains to the

Ropes
Ex 28:24 must put the two *r* of gold
28:25 the two ends of the two *r*
39:17 they put the two *r* of gold
39:18 *r* through the two settings
Jg 15:13 bound him with two new *r*
15:14 *r* that were upon his arms
16:11 tie me tight with new *r*
16:12 *r* and tied him with them
2Sa 17:13 Israel must also carry *r*
22:6 The *r* of Sheol themselves
1Ki 20:31 and *r* upon our heads, and
20:32 with *r* upon their heads
Es 1:6 held fast in *r* of fine fabric
Job 36:8 captured with *r* of affliction
39:10 with its *r* in the furrow
Ps 18:4 The *r* of death encircled me
18:5 *r* of Sheol surrounded me
116:3 The *r* of death encircled me
119:61 very *r* of the wicked ones
129:4 pieces the *r* of the wicked
140:5 *r* they have spread out as a
Pr 5:22 *r* of his own sin he will be
Isa 5:18 error with *r* of untruth
33:20 its *r* will be torn in two
33:23 Your *r* must hang loose
Jer 38:6 Jeremiah down by means of *r*
38:11 cistern by means of the *r*
38:12 your armpits beneath the *r*
38:13 Jeremiah by means of the *r*
Eze 27:24 in *r* twined and solidly
Ho 11:4 With the *r* of earthling man I
Joh 2:15 making a whip of *r*, he drove
Ac 27:32 cut away the *r* of the skiff

Rose
Ge 22:3 he *r* and went on the trip to
24:10 he *r* and got on his way to
24:61 *r* and they went riding on
32:22 he *r* and took his two wives
43:15 they *r* and went their way
Ex 33:10 the people *r* and bowed down
Jos 3:16 They *r* up as one dam very
7:16 *r* early in the morning and
8:3 people of war *r* to go up to
8:10 Then Joshua *r* up early in the
8:14 *r* up early and went out to
8:19 ambush *r* up quickly from its
Jg 3:20 he *r* up from his throne
5:7 Until I, Deborah, *r* up, Until I
5:7 I *r* up as a mother in Israel
6:38 he *r* up early the next day and
7:1 *r* early and took up camping at
9:34 *r* up by night, and they began
9:35 *r* up from the place of ambush
9:43 He now *r* up against them and
10:1 there *r* up to save Israel Tola
10:3 Jair the Gileadite *r* up, and
16:3 *r* at midnight and grabbed
19:5 he now *r* to go, but the
19:7 When the man *r* to go, his
19:9 The man now *r* to go, he and
19:10 he *r* and got on his way and
19:27 master *r* up in the morning
19:28 *r* up and went to his place
20:8 the people *r* up as one man
20:19 Israel *r* up in the morning
20:33 the men of Israel *r* up from
1Sa 9:26 Then they *r* early, and it
13:15 Samuel *r* and went his way
16:13 Samuel *r* and went his way
17:48 the Philistine *r* and kept
17:52 Israel and of Judah *r* and
18:27 David *r* and he and his men
20:34 Jonathan *r* up from the table
20:41 David, he *r* up from nearby
20:42 David *r* up and went his way
21:10 David *r* up and continued
23:13 David *r* up with his men
23:16 *r* up and went to David at
23:24 *r* up and went to Ziph ahead

1Sa 24:4 David *r* up and quietly cut
24:7 Saul, he *r* up from the cave
24:8 David *r* up afterward and
25:1 David *r* up and went down to
25:41 *r* up and bowed with her
25:42 Abigail hastened and *r* up
26:5 David *r* up and went to the
27:2 David *r* up and he and six
28:23 *r* up from the earth and sat
28:25 they *r* up and went away
29:11 David *r* up early, he and
31:12 valiant men *r* up and went
2Sa 2:15 *r* up and went across by
6:2 *r* up and went to Baale-judah
14:23 Joab *r* up and went to
14:31 Joab *r* up and came to
15:2 Absalom *r* up early and stood
15:9 he *r* up and went to Hebron
17:22 David *r* up and also all the
18:32 *r* up against you for evil
19:8 king *r* up and seated himself
23:10 *r* up and kept striking down
1Ki 1:50 So he *r* up and went away and
2:19 the king *r* to meet her and
8:54 *r* up from before the altar
11:18 they *r* up out of Midian and
14:4 she *r* up and went to Shiloh
14:17 Jeroboam's wife *r* up and
17:10 *r* up and went to Zarephath
19:3 he *r* up and began to go for
19:8 So he *r* up and ate and drank
19:21 he *r* up and went following
21:16 Ahab at once *r* up to go
2Ki 1:15 So he *r* and went down with
3:24 *r* up and began striking the
6:15 *r* early to get up, and went
7:5 *r* up in the evening darkness
7:12 the king *r* up by night and
8:21 *r* up by night and got to
11:1 she *r* up and destroyed all
12:20 *r* up and leagued together
19:35 people *r* up early in the
25:26 *r* up and came into Egypt
1Ch 10:12 the valiant men *r* up and
28:2 David the king *r* to his feet
2Ch 13:4 Abijah now *r* up upon Mount
20:19 Korahites *r* up to praise
21:4 Jehoram *r* up over the
21:9 *r* up by night and went
22:10 *r* up and destroyed all the
28:12 *r* up against those coming
28:15 *r* up and took hold of the
29:12 Levites *r* up, Mahath the
30:14 *r* up and removed the altars
Ezr 1:5 priests and the Levites *r* up
10:5 Ezra *r* and had the chiefs of
10:6 Ezra now *r* from before the
10:10 Ezra the priest *r* and said
Ne 2:12 I *r* up by night, I and a few
4:14 *r* and said to the nobles and
9:3 they *r* up at their place and
Es 7:7 king, he *r* up in his rage from
8:4 Esther *r* and stood before the
Job 29:8 And even the aged ones *r* up
Ps 76:9 When God *r* up to judgment
124:2 When men *r* up against us
Isa 37:36 people *r* up early in the
Jer 26:17 older men of the land *r* up
41:2 *r* up and struck down
Eze 10:17 when these *r*, they would
10:19 *r* from the earth before my
Da 3:24 and he *r* up in a hurry
Jon 3:6 he *r* up from his throne and
Mt 4:16 shadow, light *r* upon them
13:6 the sun *r* they were scorched
25:7 virgins *r* and put their lamps
Mr 1:35 he *r* up and went outside and
4:6 the sun *r*, it was scorched
5:42 maiden *r* and began walking
7:24 he *r* up and went into the
9:27 and raised him up, and he *r*
10:1 *r* and came to the frontiers
14:60 high priest *r* in their midst
Lu 1:39 Mary *r* in these days and went
4:29 they *r* up and hurried him
4:39 she *r* and began ministering
5:25 he *r* up before them, picked
5:28 he *r* up and went following
6:8 And he *r* and took his stand
8:55 she *r* instantly, and he
10:25 man versed in the Law *r* up
15:20 he *r* and went to his father
22:45 he *r* from prayer, went to
23:1 multitude of them *r*, one and

Routed
Heb 11:34 *r* the armies of foreigners
Routine
Php 3:16 orderly in this same *r*
Rove
Jer 49:3 *r* about among the stone pens
Da 12:4 Many will *r* about, and the
Rover
Pr 6:11 come just like some *r*, and
Roving
2Ch 16:9 eyes are *r* about through all
Job 1:7 From *r* about in the earth and
2:2 From *r* about in the earth and
Jer 5:1 Go *r* about in the streets of
Am 8:12 keep *r* about while searching
Zec 4:10 are *r* about in all the earth
Ac 19:13 the *r* Jews who practiced the
Row
Ex 28:17 *r* of ruby, topaz and emerald
28:17 and emerald is the first *r*
28:18 the second *r* is turquoise
28:19 third *r* is *lesh'em* stone
28:20 fourth *r* is chrysolite and
39:10 A *r* of ruby, topaz and
39:10 and emerald was the first *r*
39:11 the second *r* was turquoise
39:12 third *r* was *lesh'em* stone
39:13 fourth *r* was chrysolite and
39:37 the *r* of lamps, and all its
40:23 he arranged the *r* of bread
Jg 6:26 the *r* of stones, and you must
1Ki 6:36 a *r* of beams of cedarwood
7:3 There were fifteen to a *r*
7:12 a *r* of beams of cedarwood
Jer 9:22 like a *r* of newly cut grain
Eze 46:23 *r* round about them, round
Am 2:13 with a *r* of newly cut grain
Mic 4:12 like a *r* of newly cut grain
Zec 12:6 in a *r* of newly cut grain
Rowed
Joh 6:19 *r* about three or four miles
Rowers
Eze 27:8 became *r* for you
Rowing
Eze 27:26 those *r* you have brought
Mr 6:48 hard put to it in their *r*
Rows
Ex 28:17 there being four *r* of stones
39:10 it with four *r* of stones
Nu 23:4 I set the seven altars in *r*
Jos 2:6 laid in *r* for her upon the
1Ki 6:9 beams and *r* in cedarwood
6:36 with three *r* of hewn stone
7:2 upon four *r* of pillars of
7:4 windows, there were three *r*
7:12 three *r* of hewn stone and a
7:18 two *r* round about upon the
7:20 pomegranates in *r* all around
7:24 two *r* of the gourd-shaped
7:42 two *r* of pomegranates to
2Ki 11:8 entering within the *r* will
11:15 her out from inside the *r*
2Ch 4:3 ornaments were in two *r*
4:13 two *r* of pomegranates for
23:14 her out from inside the *r*
Jer 5:10 Come up against her vine *r*
Eze 46:23 beneath the *r* round about
Royal
Jos 10:2 like one of the *r* cities
13:12 the *r* realm of Og in Bashan
13:21 *r* realm of Sihon the king
13:27 *r* realm of Sihon the king
13:30 *r* realm of Og the king of
13:31 the *r* realm of Og in Bashan
1Sa 15:28 ripped away the *r* rule of
27:5 dwell in the *r* city with you
2Sa 14:26 by the *r* stone weight
16:3 give back to me the *r* rule
2Ki 25:25 of the *r* offspring came
1Ch 29:25 put upon him such *r* dignity
2Ch 20:30 *r* realm of Jehoshaphat had
22:10 *r* offspring of the house
Ezr 6:8 the *r* treasury of the tax
Es 1:2 was sitting upon his *r* throne
1:7 *r* wine was in great quantity
1:9 *r* house that belonged to King
1:11 the queen in the *r* headdress
1:19 let a *r* word go out from his
1:19 *r* dignity let the king give
Es 2:16 King Ahasuerus at his *r* house
2:17 the *r* headdress upon her head
4:14 you have attained to *r* dignity
5:1 was sitting on his *r* throne in
5:1 throne in the *r* house opposite
6:8 let them bring *r* apparel with
6:8 the *r* headdress has been put
8:10 horses used in the *r* service
8:14 horses used in the *r* service
8:15 in *r* apparel of blue and linen
Jer 26:1 the *r* rule of Jehoiakim
41:1 *r* offspring and of the
Eze 16:13 became fit for *r* position
17:13 took one of the *r* seed and
Da 1:3 and of the *r* offspring and
1:20 that were in all his *r* realm
3:24 to his high *r* officials
4:29 upon the *r* palace of Babylon
4:30 built for the *r* house with
4:36 even my high *r* officers and
6:7 the high *r* officers and the
6:7 establish a *r* statute and to
10:13 of the *r* realm of Persia was
Ho 1:4 *r* rule of the house of Israel
Lu 7:25 in luxury are in *r* houses
Ac 12:21 clothed . . . with *r* raiment
1Pe 2:9 a chosen race, a *r* priesthood
Royally
Es 5:1 that Esther went dressing up *r*
Royalty
2Ch 36:20 *r* of Persia began to reign
Rub
De 28:40 will *r* yourself with no oil
Ru 3:3 wash and *r* yourself with oil
2Sa 14:2 do not *r* yourself with oil
Isa 38:21 and *r* it in upon the boil
Re 3:18 eyesalve to *r* in your eyes
Rubbed
Ex 30:32 not to be *r* in the flesh of
2Sa 12:20 and *r* himself with oil and
Eze 16:4 you had not at all been *r*
29:18 shoulder was one *r* bare
Rubbing
Lu 6:1 grain, *r* them with their hands
Rubbish
Ne 4:2 out of the heaps of dusty *r*
4:10 there is a great deal of *r*
Rubble
Isa 24:12 crushed to a mere *r* heap
Am 6:11 the great house into *r*
Rubies
Isa 54:12 your battlements of *r*, and
Eze 27:16 fabric and corals and *r*
Rubs
Job 14:19 Water certainly *r* away even
Ruby
Ex 28:17 row of *r*, topaz and emerald
39:10 A row of *r*, topaz and
Eze 28:13 *r*, topaz and jasper
Rudder
Ac 27:40 lashings of the *r* oars and
Jas 3:4 are steered by a very small *r*
Ruddy
1Sa 16:12 he was *r*, a young man with
17:42 *r*, of beautiful appearance
Ca 5:10 My dear one is dazzling and *r*
La 4:7 in fact more *r* than corals
Rue
Lu 11:42 tenth of the mint and the *r*
Rufus
Mr 15:21 father of Alexander and *R*
Ro 16:13 Greet *R* the chosen one in the
Rugged
Pr 13:15 dealing treacherously is *r*
Isa 40:4 the *r* ground a valley plain
42:16 *r* terrain into level land
Ruin
Ge 6:13 I am bringing them to *r*
6:17 deluge . . . to bring to *r* all
9:11 deluge to bring all the earth to *r*
9:15 deluge to bring all flesh to *r*
13:10 Sodom and Gomorrah to *r*
18:28 bring the whole city to *r*
18:28 I shall not bring it to *r* if
18:31 not bring it to *r* on account
18:32 I shall not bring it to *r* on
Ge 19:13 are bringing this place to *r*
19:13 us to bring the city to *r*
19:14 is bringing the city to *r*
19:29 cities of the District to *r*
Ex 8:24 *r* as a result of the gadflies
Le 26:33 will become a desolate *r*
De 4:31 desert you or bring you to *r*
9:26 do not bring to *r* your people
10:10 not want to bring you to *r*
20:19 you must not *r* its trees by
20:20 it is the one you should *r*
Jos 22:33 against them to *r* the land
Jg 6:4 and would *r* the yield of the
6:5 come into the land to *r* it
20:21 down to *r* to the earth on
20:25 down to *r* to the earth, all
20:35 to *r* in Benjamin twenty-five
20:42 down to *r* in their midst
Ru 4:6 I may *r* my own inheritance
1Sa 6:5 are bringing the land to *r*
23:10 Keilah to lay the city in *r*
26:9 Do not bring him to *r*, for
26:15 the king your lord to *r*
2Sa 1:14 the anointed of Jehovah to *r*
11:1 to *r* and lay siege to Rabbah
14:11 causing *r* and that they
20:20 that I should bring to *r*
24:16 Jerusalem to bring it to *r*
24:16 angel that was bringing *r*
2Ki 8:19 not want to bring Judah to *r*
13:23 want to bring them to *r*
18:25 this place to bring it to *r*
18:25 and you must bring it to *r*
19:12 my forefathers brought to *r*
1Ch 20:1 of the sons of Ammon in *r*
21:12 Jehovah's angel bringing *r*
21:15 to Jerusalem to bring *r* to
21:15 as he began bringing the *r*
21:15 that was bringing the *r*
2Ch 12:7 I shall not bring them to *r*
12:12 bringing them to *r*
20:23 bring his own fellow to *r*
21:7 house of David to *r*, for
24:23 princes of the people to *r*
25:16 bring you to *r*, because
26:16 to the point of causing *r*
34:11 of Judah had brought to *r*
35:21 not let him bring you to *r*
36:19 so as to cause *r*
Ps 35:8 Let *r* come upon him without
35:8 With *r* let him fall into it
57:*super* Do not bring to *r*
58:*super* Do not bring to *r*
59:*super* Do not bring to *r*
63:9 seeking my soul for its *r*
75:*super* Do not bring to *r*
78:38 the error and not bring *r*
78:45 these might bring them to *r*
89:40 laid his fortifications in *r*
106:23 from bringing them to *r*
Pr 6:32 bringing his own soul to *r*
10:14 foolish one is near to *r*
10:15 *r* of the lowly ones is their
10:29 *r* is for the practicers of
11:9 brings his fellowman to *r*
13:3 wide his lips—he will have *r*
14:28 is the *r* of a high official
18:7 mouth of the stupid . . . *r* of
18:9 a brother to the one causing *r*
Isa 10:3 *r*, when it comes from far
11:9 cause any *r* in all my holy
14:20 brought your own land to *r*
17:1 become a heap, a decaying *r*
23:13 set her as a crumbling *r*
25:2 fortified town a crumbling *r*
36:10 this land to bring it to *r*
36:10 and you must bring it to *r*
37:12 forefathers brought to *r*
47:11 will suddenly come a *r* that
51:13 all set to bring you to *r*
65:8 Do not *r* it, because there
65:8 not to bring everybody to *r*
65:25 do no harm nor cause any *r*
Jer 2:30 like a lion that is causing *r*
4:7 is bringing the nations to *r*
5:10 her vine rows and cause *r*
6:5 to *r* her dwelling towers
11:19 Let us bring to *r* the tree
12:10 brought my vineyard to *r*
13:9 bring to *r* the pride of Judah
13:14 from bringing them to *r*
15:3 to eat and to bring to *r*
15:6 and bring you to *r*. I have
22:7 bringing *r*, each one and

Jer 36:29 bring this land to *r* and
48:18 your fortified places to *r*
49:9 as much *r* as they wanted
51:11 in order to bring her to *r*
51:20 will bring kingdoms to *r*
La 2:5 his fortified places to *r*
2:6 has brought his festival to *r*
2:8 bringing the wall . . . to *r*
Eze 5:16 send to bring you people to *r*
9:1 in his hand for bringing *r*
9:8 Are you bringing to *r* all the
20:17 from bringing them to *r*
21:27, 27, 27 A *r*, a *r*, a *r*
22:30 not to bring it to *r*
25:15 in order to cause *r*, with
26:4 bring the walls of Tyre to *r*
28:17 wisdom to *r* on account of
30:11 to reduce the land to *r*
43:3 came to bring the city to *r*
Da 2:44 will never be brought to *r*
4:23 Chop the tree down, and *r* it
6:22 they have not brought me to *r*
6:26 will not be brought to *r*
7:14 that will not be brought to *r*
8:24 he will cause *r*, and he
8:24 bring mighty ones to *r*, also
8:25 he will bring many to *r*
9:26 will bring to their *r*
11:17 to him to bring her to *r*
Ho 9:9 gone down deep in bringing *r*
11:9 shall not bring Ephraim to *r*
13:9 will certainly bring you to *r*
Mal 3:11 not *r* for you the fruit of
Lu 6:49 *r* of that house became great
Ro 3:16 *R* and misery are in their
14:15 by your food *r* that one for
1Ti 6:9 men into destruction and *r*
Re 11:18 to *r* those ruining the earth

Ruination
Ex 12:13 will not come on you as a *r*
12:23 not allow the *r* to enter
2Ki 23:13 Mount of *R*, that Solomon
2Ch 22:4 death of his father, to his *r*
Pr 28:24 a partner of a man causing *r*
Eze 5:16 which must prove to be for *r*
9:6 you should kill off—to a *r*
21:31 the craftsmen of *r*
Da 10:8 changed upon me to *r*, and I

Ruined
Ge 6:11 the earth came to be *r* in the
6:12 the earth . . . it was *r*
6:12 all flesh had *r* its way
Pr 25:26 A fouled spring and a *r* well
Isa 6:11 ground itself is *r* into a
Jer 13:7 look! the belt had been *r*
Am 1:11 *r* his own merciful qualities
Na 2:2 the shoots of them they have *r*
Mal 1:14 sacrificing a *r* one to
2:8 have *r* the covenant of Levi
Mt 9:17 and the wineskins are *r*
Lu 5:37 and the wineskins will be *r*
1Co 8:11 man that is weak is being *r*

Ruiner
Jer 51:25 you *r* of the whole earth

Ruining
Re 11:18 to ruin those *r* the earth

Ruinous
Isa 1:4 an evildoing seed, *r* sons
54:16 have created the *r* man for
Jer 5:26 They have set a *r* trap
6:28 They are all of them *r*
51:1 of Leb-kamai a *r* wind
51:25 against you, O *r* mountain
Zep 3:7 making all their dealings *r*

Ruinously
Ex 32:7 people . . . have acted *r*
Nu 32:15 have acted *r* toward all this
De 4:16 that you may not act *r* and
4:25 act *r* and do make a carved
9:12 your people . . . have acted *r*
31:29 without fail act *r*, and you
32:5 acted *r* on their own part
Jg 2:19 and act more *r* than their
2Ch 27:2 people were yet acting *r*
Ps 14:1 They have acted *r*, they have
53:1 They have acted *r* and have
Eze 16:47 act more *r* than they did in
23:11 her sensual desire more *r*

Ruins
Ex 21:26 and he really *r* it, he is to
De 13:16 it must become a heap of *r*
1Ki 9:8 will become heaps of *r*
2Ki 19:25 desolate as piles of *r*
2Ch 7:21 become heaps of *r*, everyone
Job 30:24 against a mere heap of *r*
Ps 73:18 have made them fall to *r*
79:1 Jerusalem in a heap of *r*
Isa 6:11 cities actually crash in *r*
37:26 desolate as piles of *r*
49:19 and the land of your *r*
Jer 4:7 cities will fall in *r* so that
26:18 become mere heaps of *r*
48:9 falling in *r* she will go
Am 9:11 its *r* I shall raise up, and I
Mic 1:6 make Samaria a heap of *r* of
3:12 become mere heaps of *r*, and
Ac 15:16 I shall rebuild its *r* and

Rule
Ex 15:18 Jehovah will *r* as king to
Jg 8:22 *R* over us, you and your son
8:23 shall not *r* over you, nor
8:23 nor will my son *r* over you
8:23 Jehovah . . . will *r* over you
9:2 to *r* over you or for one man
9:2 for one man to *r* over you? And
1Sa 15:28 ripped away the royal *r* of
24:20 without fail, *r* as king
2Sa 16:3 give back to me the royal *r*
1Ki 1:5 I myself am going to *r* as
1Ch 23:31 number according to the *r*
2Ch 4:20 according to the *r*
8:14 *r* of David his father, and
30:16 according to their *r*
Ezr 3:4 *r* of what was due each day
Ne 8:18 assembly, according to the *r*
Ps 106:41 hating them might *r* over
Pr 12:24 is the one that will *r*, but
17:2 *r* over the son who is acting
19:10 a servant to *r* over princes
29:2 wicked . . . *r*, the people sigh
Isa 3:4 arbitrary power will *r* over
3:12 mere women actually *r* over
9:6 princely *r* will come to be
9:7 abundance of the princely *r*
19:4 king that will *r* over them
32:1 *r* as princes for justice
63:19 over whom you did not *r*
Jer 26:1 the royal *r* of Jehoiakim
Eze 20:33 *r* as king over you people
Da 2:39 will *r* over the whole earth
5:7 one in the kingdom he will *r*
5:16 in the kingdom you will *r*
11:3 *r* with extensive dominion and
11:5 *r* with extensive dominion
11:39 make them *r* among many; and
11:43 *r* over the hidden treasures
Ho 1:4 royal *r* of the house of Israel
Joe 2:17 for nations to *r* over them
Mic 4:7 Jehovah will . . . *r* as king
Zec 6:13 sit down and *r* on his throne
Lu 1:33 *r* as king over the house of
Ro 5:17 *r* as kings in life through
5:21 kindness might *r* as king
6:12 sin continue to *r* as king
15:12 one arising to *r* nations
1Co 4:6 may learn the *r*: Do not go
4:8 might *r* with you as kings
15:25 he must *r* as king until God
Ga 6:16 orderly by this *r* of conduct
1Ti 6:15 King of those who *r* as kings
6:15 Lord of those who *r* as lords
2Ti 2:12 also *r* together as kings
Re 5:10 to *r* as kings over the earth
11:15 *r* as king forever and ever
19:6 Jehovah . . . begun to *r* as king
20:6 *r* as kings with him for the
22:5 *r* as kings forever and ever

Ruled
Jos 12:5 and who *r* in Mount Hermon
2Sa 2:10 for two years he *r* as king
5:4 For forty years he *r* as king
5:5 In Hebron he *r* as king over
5:5 in Jerusalem he *r* as king for
16:8 you have *r* as king
La 5:8 Mere servants have *r* over us
Da 11:4 dominion with which he had *r*
Mt 2:22 Archelaus *r* as king of Judea
Ro 5:14 death *r* as king from Adam
5:17 death *r* as king through that
5:21 as sin *r* as king with death
Re 20:4 *r* as kings with the Christ

Ruler
1Ki 4:21 *r* over all the kingdoms from
2Ch 9:26 *r* over all the kings from
Ps 105:20 *r* of the peoples, that he
105:21 *r* over all his property
Pr 6:7 has no commander, officer or *r*
28:15 onrushing bear is a wicked *r*
29:12 a *r* is paying attention to
29:26 seeking the face of a *r*, but
Ec 10:4 *r* should mount up against you
Isa 16:1 to the *r* of the land, from
Jer 30:21 his own *r* will go forth
51:46, 46 and *r* against *r*
Da 2:38 he has made *r* over all of
2:48 *r* over all the jurisdictional
4:17 Most High is *R* in the kingdom
4:25 know that the Most High is *R*
4:32 Most High is *R* in the kingdom
5:21 *R* in the kingdom of mankind
5:29 the third *r* in the kingdom
Mic 5:2 who is to become *r* in Israel
Zec 10:4 the supporting *r*, out of him
Mt 9:18 *r* who had approached began to
9:34 It is by the *r* of the demons
12:24 the *r* of the demons
14:1 Herod, the district *r*, heard
Mr 3:22 means of the *r* of the demons
Lu 3:1 Herod was district *r* of
3:1 district *r* of the country of
3:1 Lysanias was district *r* of
3:19 Herod the district *r*, for
9:7 Herod the district *r* heard of
11:15 the *r* of the demons
12:58 adversary at law to a *r*
18:18 *r* questioned him, saying
Joh 3:1 Nicodemus . . . a *r* of the Jews
12:31 *r* of this world will be
14:30 *r* of the world is coming
16:11 *r* of this world has been
Ac 5:29 obey God as *r* rather than men
5:32 to those obeying him as *r*
7:27 Who appointed you *r* and
7:35 appointed you *r* and judge
7:35 God sent off as both *r* and
13:1 with Herod the district *r*
23:5 not speak injuriously of a *r*
Eph 2:2 *r* of the authority of the air
Re 1:5 *R* of the kings of the earth

Ruler's
Mt 9:23 he came into the *r* house and

Rulers
1Ch 26:6 were *r* of the house of their
2Ch 23:20 *r* over the people and all
Ezr 9:2 the deputy *r* has proved to be
Ne 2:16 deputy *r* themselves did not
2:16 the nobles and the deputy *r*
4:14 the nobles and the deputy *r*
4:19 to the nobles and the deputy *r*
5:7 the nobles and the deputy *r*
5:17 the Jews and the deputy *r*
7:5 the nobles and the deputy *r*
12:40 half of the deputy *r* with
13:11 find fault with the deputy *r*
Isa 28:14 *r* of this people who are in
41:25 will come upon deputy *r* as
49:7 to the servant of *r*: Kings
Jer 33:26 *r* over the seed of Abraham
51:23 and deputy *r* to pieces
51:28 its deputy *r* and all the
51:57 her deputy *r* and her mighty
Eze 19:11 meant for the scepters of *r*
23:6 deputy *r*—desirable young
23:12 governors and deputy *r* who
23:23 governors and deputy *r* all
Mt 20:25 the *r* of the nations lord it
Lu 14:1 one of the *r* of the Pharisees
23:13 the chief priests and the *r*
23:35 the *r* were sneering, saying
24:20 chief priests and *r* handed
Joh 7:26 *r* have not come to know for
7:48 *r* or of the Pharisees has
12:42 many even of the *r* actually
Ac 3:17 just as your *r* also did
4:5 gathering together of their *r*
4:8 *R* of the people and older men
4:26 *r* massed together as one
13:27 *r* did not know this One, but
14:5 and Jews with their *r*, to
16:19 the marketplace to the *r*
17:6 certain brothers to the city *r*
17:8 the crowd and the city *r* when
1Co 2:6 *r* of this system of things
2:8 *r* of this system of things

Eph 6:12 world *r* of this darkness
Tit 3:1 and authorities as *r*

Rulership
Job 25:2 *R* and dreadfulness are with
Da 4:3 his *r* is for generation after
4:22 *r* to the extremity of the
4:34, 34 his *r* is a *r* to time
7:6 was given to it *r* indeed
7:14 given *r* and dignity and
7:14 *r* is an indefinitely lasting
7:14 indefinitely lasting *r* that
7:26 own *r* they finally took away
7:27 *r* and the grandeur of the
Zec 9:10 *r* will be from sea to sea

Rulerships
Da 7:12 beasts, their *r* were taken
7:27 *r* will serve and obey even

Rules
Pr 22:7 *r* over those of little means
30:22 a slave when he *r* as king
Joh 2:6 purification *r* of the Jews
2Ti 2:5 contended according to the *r*

Ruling
Jos 12:2 in Heshbon, *r* from Aroer
Jg 14:4 the Philistines were *r* over
15:11 Philistines are *r* over us
1Sa 16:1 rejected him from *r* as king
2Sa 23:3 When one *r* over mankind is
23:3 *R* in the fear of God
2Ch 7:18 cut off from *r* over Israel
22:12 Athaliah was *r* as queen
Ne 9:37 and over our bodies they are *r*
Es 1:1 Ahasuerus who was *r* as king
Ps 59:13 God is *r* in Jacob to the ends
66:7 He is *r* by his mightiness to
89:9 *r* over the swelling of the
Pr 8:16 princes themselves keep *r* as
Ec 9:17 the cry of one *r* among stupid
Isa 14:5 the staff of the *r* ones
40:10 his arm will be *r* for him
52:5 *r* over them kept howling
Jer 22:30 and *r* anymore in Judah
33:21 son *r* as king upon his
Eze 19:14 strong rod, no scepter for *r*
Da 4:26 know that the heavens are *r*
11:5 than that one's *r* power
Hab 1:14 over whom no one is *r*
Mr 10:42 appear to be *r* the nations
Ro 13:3 those *r* are an object of fear
1Co 4:8 begun *r* as kings without us
4:8 that you had begun *r* as kings
Re 11:17 power and begun *r* as king

Rumah
2Ki 23:36 daughter of Pedaiah from *R*

Rumbling
Job 37:2 to the *r* of his voice

Rumored
Ac 21:21 heard it *r* about you that you

Rumors
Ac 21:24 there is nothing to the *r*

Run
Ge 27:43 get up, *r* away to Laban my
31:21 *r* away and to get up and
31:22 that Jacob had *r* away
31:27 did you have to *r* away
47:15 because money has *r* out
47:16 if money has *r* out
Ex 9:23 and fire would *r* down to the
14:5 that the people had *r* away
36:33 middle bar to *r* through at
Nu 24:11 *r* your way off to your place
De 20:3 not be afraid and *r* in panic
Jos 8:19 began to *r* at the instant
Jg 7:21 on the *r* and broke out into
1Sa 8:11 have to *r* before his chariots
19:12 go and *r* away and escape
20:6 to *r* to Bethlehem his city
20:36 *R*, please, find the arrows
21:13 saliva *r* down upon his
27:4 David had *r* away to Gath
31:4 sword and *r* me through with
31:4 *r* me through and deal
2Sa 15:14 Get up, and let us *r* away
18:19 *r*, please, and break the
18:21 bowed . . . and began to *r*
18:22 please, *r* behind the Cushite
18:22 have to *r*, my son, when
18:23 whatever will, let me *r*
18:23 So he said to him: *R!*
2Sa 18:23 Ahimaaz began to *r* by the
19:9 *r* away out of the land from
22:30 *r* against a marauder band
1Ki 11:23 *r* away from Hadadezer the
12:2 had *r* off on account of King
2Ki 4:22 let me *r* as far as the man
4:26 Now *r*, please, to meet her
5:20 I will *r* after him and take
1Ch 10:4 your sword and *r* me through
2Ch 10:2 *r* away on account of Solomon
Ne 6:11 Should a man like me *r* away?
Job 9:25 my own days . . . have *r* away
20:24 *r* away from armor of iron
27:22 without fail try to *r* away
40:23 it does not *r* in panic
Ps 18:29 *r* against a marauder band
19:5 exults . . . to *r* in a path
59:4 *r* and get themselves ready
119:32 I shall *r* the very way of
119:136 water have *r* down my eyes
139:7 can I *r* away from your face
Pr 1:16 those that *r* to sheer badness
4:12 you *r*, you will not stumble
6:18 in a hurry to *r* to badness
Ca 1:4 Draw me with you; let us *r*
8:14 *R* away, my dear one, and
Isa 10:31 Madmenah has *r* away
19:5 parched and actually *r* dry
22:3 Far off they had *r* away
29:1 the festivals *r* the round
40:31 will *r* and not grow weary
48:20 *R* away from the Chaldeans
55:5 will *r* even to you, for the
Jer 9:18 our eyes *r* down with tears
12:5 with footmen you have *r*
12:5 can you *r* a race with horses?
13:17 eye will *r* down with tears
14:17 my eyes *r* down with tears
39:4 *r* away and to go out by
49:19 make him *r* away from her
50:44 make them *r* away from her
51:30 Their mightiness has *r* dry
52:7 began to *r* away and go forth
Ho 12:12 *r* away to the field of Syria
Joe 2:7 Like powerful men they *r*
2:9 On the wall they *r*
Am 6:12 On a crag will horses *r*
7:12 O visionary, go, *r* your way
Jon 1:3 get up and *r* away to Tarshish
Na 1:4 rivers he actually makes *r* dry
Hag 1:9 on the *r*, each one in behalf
Zec 2:4 *R*, speak to the young man
Lu 2:35 sword will be *r* through the
Joh 20:4 the two together began to *r*
Ac 16:11 a straight *r* to Samothrace
1Co 9:24 the runners in a race all *r*
9:24 *R* in such a way that you may
Ga 2:2 I was running or had *r* in vain
Php 2:16 that I did not *r* in vain or
2Ti 4:7 I have *r* the course to the
Heb 1:12 your years will never *r* out
12:1 *r* with endurance the race

Runaway
1Sa 22:17 knew that he was a *r* and

Runaways
Isa 15:5 *r* thereof are as far along

Runner
Job 9:25 days . . . swifter than a *r*
Jer 51:31 One *r* runs to meet another
51:31 runs to meet another *r*

Runners
1Sa 22:17 king said to the *r* stationed
1Ki 14:27 the chiefs of the *r*, the
14:28 the *r* would carry them
14:28 the guard chamber of the *r*
2Ki 10:25 to the *r* and the adjutants
10:25 the *r* and the adjutants
11:4 and of the *r* and brought
11:6 at the gate behind the *r*
11:11 the *r* kept standing each
11:19 the *r* and all the people of
11:19 the gate of the *r* to the
2Ch 12:10 chiefs of the *r*, the guards
12:11 *r* came in and carried them
12:11 guard chamber of the *r*
30:6 *r* with the letters from the
30:10 *r* continued on, passing
1Co 9:24 the *r* in a race all run, but

Running
Ge 16:8 from Sarai . . . I am *r* away
18:2 he began *r* to meet them from
Ge 24:28 woman went *r* and telling the
24:29 Laban went *r* to the man who
29:12 *r* and telling her father
29:13 he went *r* to meet him
31:20 told him that he was *r* away
33:4 Esau went *r* to meet him, and
35:1 *r* away from Esau your brother
35:7 *r* away from his brother
Ex 25:32 six branches are *r* out from
25:33 six branches *r* out from the
25:35 six branches *r* out from the
26:28 is *r* through from end to end
37:18 branches were *r* out from its
37:19 six branches *r* out from the
37:21 *r* out from the lampstand
Le 14:5 vessel over *r* water
14:6 was killed over the *r* water
14:50 vessel over *r* water
14:51 in the *r* water, and he must
14:52 *r* water and the live bird
15:2 man has a *r* discharge occur
15:3 *r* discharge or his genital
15:3 from his *r* discharge, it is
15:4 the one having a *r* discharge
15:6 one having a *r* discharge was
15:7 the one having a *r* discharge
15:8 the one who has a *r* discharge
15:9 the one having a *r* discharge
15:11 having a *r* discharge might
15:12 one having a *r* discharge
15:13 one having a *r* discharge
15:13 clean from his *r* discharge
15:13 bathe his flesh in *r* water
15:15 concerning his *r* discharge
15:19 a *r* discharge, and her
15:19 her *r* discharge in her flesh
15:25 the *r* discharge of her blood
15:25 her unclean *r* discharge will
15:26 the days of her *r* discharge
15:28 clean from her *r* discharge
15:30 her unclean *r* discharge
15:32 man having a *r* discharge and
15:33 *r* discharge, whether a male
22:4 *r* discharge may eat of the
Nu 5:2 everyone having a *r* discharge
11:27 *r* and reporting to Moses and
16:47 went *r* into the midst of the
19:17 put *r* water upon it in a
De 10:7 torrent valleys *r* with water
21:4 a torrent valley *r* with water
Jos 7:22 they went *r* to the tent, and
Jg 9:21 went *r* off and made his way
1Sa 3:5 he went *r* to Eli and saying
4:12 a man of Benjamin went *r*
10:23 went *r* and took him from
17:22 went *r* to the battle line
17:48 David began hurrying and *r*
17:51 David continued *r* and got to
20:1 David went *r* away from
21:10 *r* away on account of Saul
22:20 *r* away to follow David
2Sa 3:29 man with a *r* discharge or a
4:3 Beerothites went *r* away to
4:4 *r* in panic to flee, he then
13:34 Absalom went *r* away
15:1 with fifty men *r* before him
18:24 there was a man *r* by
18:26 now saw another man *r*
18:26 Another man *r* by himself!
18:27 the *r* style of the first is
18:27 like the *r* style of Ahimaaz
1Ki 1:5 and fifty men *r* before him
2:39 two slaves of Shimei went *r*
11:17 Hadad went *r* away, he and
11:40 and went *r* off to Egypt to
18:46 *r* ahead of Ahab all the way
19:20 went *r* after Elijah and
2Ki 5:21 Naaman saw someone *r* after
11:13 the sound of the people *r*
2Ch 23:12 sound of the people *r* and
Ne 13:10 went *r* off, each one to his
Ps 3:*super* David when he was *r* away
48:5 they were sent *r* in panic
104:7 they were sent *r* in panic
133:2 is *r* down upon the beard
133:2 *r* down to the collar of his
Isa 59:7 feet keep *r* to sheer badness
Jer 2:23 *r* to and fro in her ways
4:29 the entire city is *r* away
49:5 collecting . . . those *r* away
La 1:16 my eye is *r* down with waters
3:48 water my eye keeps *r* down on
Da 8:6 *r* toward it in its powerful
10:7 *r* away in hiding themselves

Joe 2:4 is the way they keep *r*
Jon 1:10 that he was *r* away, because
Na 2:4 Like the lightnings they keep *r*
Mr 9:15 *r* up to him, they began to
9:25 crowd was *r* together upon
Ac 21:30 a *r* together of the people
27:17 *r* aground on the Syrtis
Ro 9:16 nor upon the one *r*, but
1Co 9:26 the way I am *r* is not
Ga 2:2 I was *r* or had run in vain
5:7 You were *r* well
1Pe 4:4 not continue *r* with them in
Re 9:9 many horses *r* into battle

Runs
Job 14:2 he *r* away like the shadow
15:26 Because he *r* against him
16:14 *r* at me like a mighty one
Ps 147:15 With speed his word *r*
Pr 18:10 Into it the righteous *r* and
Jer 51:31 One runner *r* to meet
Ac 8:26 the road that *r* down from

Rupture
Ge 38:29 have produced a perineal *r*
Jg 21:15 a *r* between the tribes of
2Sa 6:8 in a *r* against Uzzah
1Ch 13:11 in a *r* against Uzzah
Ps 144:14 cattle . . . without any *r*

Rural
De 3:5 aside from very many *r* towns
Eze 38:11 the land of open *r* country
Zec 2:4 As open *r* country Jerusalem

Rush
Job 41:2 put a *r* in its nostrils
Isa 9:14 shoot and *r*, in one day
19:6 *r* themselves must molder
19:15 the shoot or the *r*, can do
58:5 his head just like a *r*
Joe 2:9 Into the city they *r*
Ac 24:12 causing a mob to *r* together

Rushed
Mt 8:32 herd *r* over the precipice
Mr 5:13 the herd *r* over the precipice
Lu 8:33 the herd *r* over the precipice
Ac 7:57 *r* upon him with one accord
19:29 they *r* into the theater
27:14 wind called Euroaquilo *r*
Jude 11 *r* into the erroneous course

Rushes
Job 41:20 set aflame even with *r*
2Co 11:28 *r* in on me from day to day

Rushing
Ps 55:8 From the *r* wind, from the
Isa 33:4 that is *r* against one
Eze 3:12 the sound of a great *r*
3:13 and the sound of a great *r*
Na 2:4 They keep *r* up and down in the
Ac 2:2 like that of a *r* stiff breeze

Rust
Eze 24:6 the *r* of which is in it
24:6 *r* of which has not gone
24:11 Let its *r* get consumed
24:12 the great amount of its *r*
24:12 Into the fire with its *r!*
Mt 6:19 where moth and *r* consume
6:20 neither moth nor *r* consumes
Jas 5:3 their *r* will be as a witness

Rusted
Jas 5:3 your gold and silver are *r*

Rustling
Job 39:19 its neck with a *r* mane

Ruth
Ru 1:4 and the name of the other *R*
1:14 As for *R*, she stuck with her
1:16 *R* proceeded to say: Do not
1:22 *R* the Moabite woman, her
2:2 *R* the Moabite woman said to
2:8 Boaz said to *R:* You have heard
2:21 Then *R* the Moabitess said
2:22 said to *R* her daughter-in-law
3:9 I am *R* your slave girl, and
4:5 is also from *R* the Moabitess
4:10 And also *R* the Moabitess, the
4:13 Boaz took *R* and she became
Mt 1:5 became father to Obed by *R*

Ruthlessly
Nu 22:29 you have dealt *r* with me

Sabachthani
Mt 27:46 saying: *E'li, E'li, la'ma s?*
Mr 15:34 *E'li, E'li, la'ma s?*

Sabbath
Ex 16:23, 23 *s* observance of a holy *s*
16:25 today is a *s* to Jehovah
16:26 but on the seventh day is a *s*
16:29 Jehovah has given you the *s*
16:30 observe the *s* on the seventh
20:8 the *s* day to hold it sacred
20:10 seventh day is a *s* to Jehovah
20:11 Jehovah blessed the *s* day and
31:14 must keep the *s*, for it is
31:15 day is a *s* of complete rest
31:15 doing work on the *s* day will
31:16 must keep the *s*, so as to
31:16 carry out the *s* during their
34:21 seventh day you will keep *s*
34:21 in harvest you will keep *s*
35:2 *s* of complete rest to Jehovah
35:3 places on the *s* day
Le 16:31 *s* of complete rest for you
23:3 the seventh day is a *s* of
23:3 *s* to Jehovah in all places
23:11 day after the *s* the priest
23:15 day after the *s*, from the
23:16 seventh *s* you should count
23:32 *s* of complete rest for you
23:32 you should observe your *s*
24:8 one *s* day after another he
25:2 the land must observe a *s* to
25:4 *s* of complete rest for the
25:4 rest for the land, a *s* to
25:5 *s* of complete rest for the
25:6 *s* of the land must serve you
26:34 land will keep *s*, as it
26:35 desolated it will keep *s*
26:35 did not keep *s* during your
Nu 15:32 collecting . . . wood on the *s*
28:9 on the *s* day there will be
28:10 as a *s* burnt offering on its
28:10 burnt offering on its *s*
De 5:12 the *s* day to hold it sacred
5:14 seventh day is a *s* to Jehovah
5:15 to carry on the *s* day
2Ki 4:23 is not a new moon nor a *s*
11:5 on the *s* and keeping strict
11:7 all going out on the *s*
11:9 were coming in on the *s*
11:9 were going out on the *s*
16:18 covered structure for the *s*
1Ch 9:32, 32 to prepare it *s* by *s*
2Ch 23:4 coming in on the *s*, of the
23:8 coming in on the *s* together
23:8 those going out on the *s*
36:21 lying desolated it kept *s*
Ne 9:14 your holy *s* you made known to
10:31 cereal on the *s* day to sell
10:31 on the *s* or on a holy day
13:15 winepresses on the *s* and
13:15 into Jerusalem on the *s* day
13:16 making sales on the *s* to the
13:17 even profaning the *s* day
13:18 Israel by profaning the *s*
13:19 grown shadowy before the *s*
13:19 until after the *s*
13:19 might come in on the *s* day
13:21 they did not come on the *s*
13:22 to sanctify the *s* day
Ps 92:*super* a song, for the *s* day
Isa 1:13 New moon and *s*, the calling
56:2 keeping the *s* in order not to
56:6 keeping the *s* in order not
58:13 If in view of the *s* you
58:13 call the *s* an exquisite
66:23, 23 from *s* to *s* all flesh
Jer 17:21 do not carry on the *s* day
17:22 out of your homes on the *s*
17:22 you must sanctify the *s* day
17:24 no load . . . on the *s* day
17:24 to sanctify the *s* day by not
17:27 by sanctifying the *s* day and
17:27 Jerusalem on the *s* day
La 2:6 forgotten . . . festival and *s*
Eze 46:1 *s* day it should be opened
46:4 to Jehovah on the *s* day
46:12 as he does on the *s* day
Ho 2:11 and her *s* and her every festal
Am 8:5 the *s*, and we may offer grain
Mt 12:1 the grainfields on the *s*
12:2 is not lawful to do on the *s*
12:5 treat the *s* as not sacred and
12:8 Lord of the *s* is what the Son
12:10 it lawful to cure on the *s*
12:11 falls into a pit on the *s*
12:12 to do a fine thing on the *s*
24:20 in wintertime, nor on the *s*
28:1 After the *s*, when it was
Mr 1:21 No sooner was it the *s* than
2:23 the grainfields on the *s*, and
2:24 on the *s* what is not lawful
2:27 *s* came into existence for the
2:27 not man for the sake of the *s*
2:28 is Lord even of the *s*
3:2 would cure the man on the *s*
3:4 lawful on the *s* to do a good
6:2 When it became *s*, he started
15:42 the day before the *s*
16:1 when the *s* had passed, Mary
Lu 4:16 his custom on the *s* day, he
4:31 he was teaching them on the *s*
6:1 on a *s* he happened to be
6:2 what is not lawful on the *s*
6:5 Lord of the *s* is what the Son
6:6 In the course of another *s* he
6:7 whether he would cure on the *s*
6:9 Is it lawful on the *s* to do
13:10 teaching . . . on the *s*
13:14 Jesus did the cure on the *s*
13:14 cured, and not on the *s* day
13:15 on the *s* untie his bull or
13:16 from this bond on the *s* day
14:1 on the *s* to eat a meal
14:3 Is it lawful on the *s* to cure
14:5 pull him out on the *s* day
23:54 of the *s* was approaching
23:56 rested on the *s* according to
Joh 5:9 Now on that day it was a *s*
5:10 It is *S*, and it is not
5:16 doing these things during *S*
5:18 not only . . . breaking the *S*
7:22 you circumcise a man on a *s*
7:23 circumcision on a *s* in order
7:23 sound in health on a *s*
9:14 *S* on the day that Jesus made
9:16 he does not observe the *S*
19:31 the torture stakes on the *S*
19:31 of that *S* was a great one
Ac 1:12 being a *s* day's journey away
13:14 the synagogue on the *s* day
13:27 are read aloud every *S*
13:42 to them on the following *s*
13:44 The next *s* nearly all the
15:21 in the synagogues on every *s*
16:13 on the *s* day we went forth
18:4 talk in the synagogue every *s*
Col 2:16 of the new moon or of a *s*
Heb 4:9 *s* resting for the people of

Sabbaths
Ex 31:13 my *s* you are to keep, for it
Le 19:3 my *s* you should keep. I am
19:30 *s* you should keep, and you
23:15 seven *s*. They should prove to
23:38 *s* of Jehovah and besides your
25:8 for yourself seven *s* of years
25:8 seven *s* of years must amount
26:2 keep my *s* and stand in awe of
26:34 land will pay off its *s* all
26:34 as it must repay its *s*
26:35 *s* when you were dwelling
26:43 paying off its *s* while it
1Ch 23:31 at the *s*, at the new moons
2Ch 2:4 burnt offerings . . . on the *s*
8:13 for the *s* and for the new
31:3 burnt offerings for the *s*
36:21 land had paid off its *s*
Ne 10:33 burnt offering of the *s*
Isa 56:4 eunuchs that keep my *s* and
Eze 20:12 my *s* I also gave to them
20:13 my *s* they profaned very
20:16 and my *s* they profaned
20:20 sanctify my own *s*, and they
20:21 My *s* they profaned. So I
20:24 and they profaned my own *s*
22:8 my *s* you have profaned
22:26 from my *s* they have hidden
23:38 my *s* they have profaned
44:24 my *s* they should sanctify
45:17 new moons and during the *s*
46:3 on the *s* and on the new
Mt 12:5 on the *s* the priests in the
Ac 17:2 for three *s* he reasoned with

Sabeans
Job 1:15 the *S* came making a raid and
6:19 company of *S* have waited for
Isa 45:14 and the *S*, tall men, will

Sabtah
Ge 10:7 sons of Cush . . . *S* and

1Ch 1:9 sons of Cush were . . . *S*

Sabteca

Ge 10:7 sons of Cush . . . *S*. And the
1Ch 1:9 sons of Cush were . . . *S*

Sacar

1Ch 11:35 Ahiam the son of *S* the
26:4 Obed-edom had sons . . . *S* the

Sachia

1Ch 8:10 and Jeuz and *S* and Mirmah

Sack

Ge 42:25 to each one's individual *s*
42:27 opened his *s* to give fodder
42:35 bundle of money in his *s*

Sackcloth

Ge 37:34 put *s* upon his hips and
Le 11:32 a garment or a skin or *s*
2Sa 3:31 tie on *s* and wail before
21:10 took *s* and spread it for
1Ki 20:31 carry *s* upon our loins and
20:32 girded *s* about their loins
21:27 to put *s* upon his flesh; and
21:27 kept lying down in *s* and
2Ki 6:30 *s* was underneath upon his
19:1 covered himself with *s* and
19:2 the priests covered with *s*
1Ch 21:16 older men, covered with *s*
Ne 9:1 fasting and with *s* and dirt
Es 4:1 put on *s* and ashes and go out
4:2 king's gate in clothing of *s*
4:3 *S* and ashes themselves came to
4:4 and to remove his *s* off him
Job 16:15 *S* I have sewed together
Ps 30:11 You have loosened my *s*, and
35:13 my clothing was *s*
69:11 When I made *s* my clothing
Isa 3:24 a girding of *s*; a brand
15:3 they have girded on *s*
20:2 loosen the *s* from off your
22:12 and for girding on *s*
32:11 gird *s* upon the loins
37:1 covered himself with *s* and
37:2 priests covered with *s* to
50:3 make *s* itself their covering
58:5 *s* and ashes as his couch
Jer 4:8 On this account gird on *s*
6:26 gird on *s* and wallow in the
48:37 upon the hips there is *s*
49:3 Gird *s* on yourselves
La 2:10 They have girded on *s*
Eze 7:18 And they have girded on *s*
27:31 and gird on *s* and weep over
Da 9:3 with fasting and *s* and ashes
Joe 1:8 as a virgin girded with *s*
1:13 spend the night in *s*
Am 8:10 bring up upon all hips *s* and
Jon 3:5 a fast and to put on *s*
3:6 covered himself with *s* and
3:8 cover themselves with *s*
Mt 11:21 have repented in *s* and ashes
Lu 10:13 sitting in *s* and ashes
Re 6:12 sun became black as *s* of hair
11:3 days dressed in *s*

Sacks

Ge 42:35 they were emptying their *s*
Jos 9:4 worn-out *s* for their asses

Sacred

Ge 2:3 seventh day and make it *s*
Ex 19:23 the mountain and make it *s*
20:8 the sabbath day to hold it *s*
20:11 and proceeded to make it *s*
23:24 break down their *s* pillars
29:27 the *s* portion that was waved
29:28 because it is a *s* portion
29:28 *s* portion to be rendered by
29:28 *s* portion for Jehovah
34:13 *s* pillars you are to shatter
34:13 *s* poles you are to cut down
Le 7:14 each offering as a *s* portion
7:32 right leg as a *s* portion to
7:34 and the leg of the *s* portion
10:14 the leg of the *s* portion in
10:15 the leg of the *s* portion
26:1 image or a *s* pillar for
26:30 annihilate your *s* high places
Nu 33:52 all their *s* high places you
De 5:12 the sabbath day to hold it *s*
7:5 *s* pillars you should break
7:5 *s* poles you should cut down
12:3 and shatter their *s* pillars
12:3 burn their *s* poles in the
De 13:17 the thing made *s* by ban
16:21 *s* pole near the altar of
16:22 a *s* pillar, a thing Jehovah
Jos 20:7 gave a *s* status to Kedesh
Jg 3:7 serving the Baals and the *s*
6:25 the *s* pole that is by it you
6:26 *s* pole that you will cut down
6:28 the *s* pole that was beside it
6:30 has cut down the *s* pole that
1Ki 14:15 they made their *s* poles
14:23 high places and *s* pillars
14:23 and *s* poles upon every high
15:13 horrible idol to the *s* pole
16:33 went on to make the *s* pole
18:19 prophets of the *s* pole
2Ki 3:2 removed the *s* pillar of Baal
10:26 *s* pillars of the house of
10:27 down the *s* pillar of Baal
13:6 the *s* pole itself stood in
17:10, 10 *s* pillars and *s* poles
17:16 and to make a *s* pole
18:4 broke the *s* pillars to pieces
18:4 and cut down the *s* pole and
21:3 made a *s* pole, just as Ahab
21:7 carved image of the *s* pole
23:4 the *s* pole and for all the
23:6 he brought out the *s* pole
23:7 tent shrines for the *s* pole
23:14 broke the *s* pillars to
23:14 cut down the *s* poles and
23:15 and burned the *s* pole
2Ch 14:3 broke up the *s* pillars and
14:3 and cut down the *s* poles
15:16 horrible idol for the *s* pole
17:6 and the *s* poles from Judah
19:3 cleared out the *s* poles from
24:6 *s* tax ordered by Moses the
24:9 bring to Jehovah the *s* tax
24:18 serving the *s* poles and the
31:1 break up the *s* pillars and
31:1 cut down the *s* poles and
33:3 made *s* poles, and he began to
33:19 set up the *s* poles and the
34:3 *s* poles and the graven
34:4 *s* poles and the graven
34:7 altars and the *s* poles, and
Isa 8:14 he must become as a *s* place
17:8 gaze, either at the *s* poles
27:9 *s* poles and the incense
Jer 17:2 altars and their *s* poles
Eze 45:4 *s* place for the sanctuary
Mic 5:14 I will uproot your *s* poles
Mt 4:10 you must render *s* service
12:5 treat the sabbath as not *s*
13:11 *s* secrets of the kingdom of
27:6 drop them into the *s* treasury
Mr 4:11 *s* secret of the kingdom of
Lu 1:74 rendering *s* service to him
2:37 rendering *s* service night and
4:8 you must render *s* service
8:10 the *s* secrets of the kingdom
Joh 16:2 rendered a *s* service to God
Ac 7:7 *s* service to me in this place
7:38 living *s* pronouncements to
7:42 *s* service to the army of
24:14 rendering *s* service to the
26:7 rendering him *s* service night
27:23 to whom I render *s* service
Ro 1:9 *s* service with my spirit in
1:25 *s* service to the creation
3:2 the *s* pronouncements of God
9:4 *s* service and the promises
11:25 ignorant of this *s* secret
12:1 *s* service with your power of
16:25 *s* secret which has been kept
1Co 2:1 declaring the *s* secret of God
2:7 God's wisdom in a *s* secret
4:1 stewards of *s* secrets of God
9:13 men performing *s* duties eat
13:2 all the *s* secrets and all
14:2 he speaks *s* secrets by the
15:51 I tell you a *s* secret
Eph 1:9 us the *s* secret of his will
3:3 *s* secret was made known to
3:4 in the *s* secret of the Christ
3:9 the *s* secret is administered
5:32 This *s* secret is great
6:19 *s* secret of the good news
Php 3:3 rendering *s* service by God's
Col 1:26 the *s* secret that was hidden
1:27 riches of this *s* secret
2:2 the *s* secret of God, namely
4:3 the *s* secret about the Christ
1Ti 3:9 the *s* secret of the faith
1Ti 3:16 the *s* secret of this godly
2Ti 1:3 rendering *s* service as my
Heb 5:12 *s* pronouncements of God
8:5 men are rendering *s* service
9:1 ordinances of *s* service and
9:6 to perform the *s* services
9:9 man doing *s* service perfect
9:14 *s* service to the living God
10:2 those rendering *s* service
12:16 not appreciating *s* things
12:28 render God *s* service with
13:10 do *s* service at the tent
1Pe 4:11 *s* pronouncements of God
Re 1:20 *s* secret of the seven stars
7:15 *s* service day and night in his
10:7 the *s* secret of God according
21:27 anything not *s* and anyone
22:3 will render him *s* service

Sacrifice

Ge 31:54 Jacob sacrificed a *s* in the
46:1 *s* sacrifices to the God of
Ex 3:18 we want to *s* to Jehovah our
5:3 wilderness and *s* to Jehovah
5:8 we want to *s* to our God
5:17 we want to *s* to Jehovah
8:8 that they may *s* to Jehovah
8:25 Pharaoh . . . said: Go, *s* to
8:26 *s* to Jehovah our God a thing
8:26 *s* a thing detestable to the
8:27 *s* to Jehovah our God just as
8:28 *s* to Jehovah your God in the
8:29 people away to *s* to Jehovah
12:27 *s* of the passover to Jehovah
20:24 must *s* upon it your burnt
23:18 not *s* along with what is
23:18 the blood of my *s*. And the
29:34 flesh of the installation *s*
34:15 and *s* to their gods, and
34:15 certainly eat some of his *s*
34:25 the blood of my *s*
34:25 the *s* of the festival of the
Le 3:1 his offering is a communion *s*
3:3 some of the communion *s* as an
3:6 for a communion *s* to Jehovah
3:9 from the communion *s* he must
4:10 of a bull of the communion *s*
4:26 the fat of the communion *s*
4:31 from off the communion *s*
4:35 young ram of the communion *s*
7:11 law of the communion *s* that
7:12 with the *s* of thanksgiving
7:13 with the thanksgiving *s* of
7:15 flesh of the thanksgiving *s*
7:16 if the *s* of his offering is a
7:16 day of his presenting his *s*
7:17 the *s* on the third day is to
7:18 the flesh of his communion *s*
7:20 the flesh of the communion *s*
7:21 the flesh of the communion *s*
7:29 presents his communion *s* to
7:29 from his communion *s*
7:37 and the installation *s* and the
7:37 and the communion *s*
8:28 installation *s* for a restful
9:4 to *s* them before Jehovah, and
9:18 ram of the communion *s* that
17:5 must *s* these as communion
17:7 *s* their sacrifices to the
17:8 up a burnt offering or a *s*
19:5, 5 *s* a communion *s* to Jehovah
19:5 *s* it to gain approval for
19:6 *s* and directly the next day
22:21 *s* to Jehovah in order to pay
22:29, 29 *s* a thanksgiving *s* to
22:29 *s* it to gain approval for
23:19 lambs . . . as a communion *s*
23:37 grain offering of the *s* and
Nu 6:14 sound ram as a communion *s*
6:17 the ram as a communion *s*
6:18 that is under the communion *s*
7:17 communion *s* two cattle, five
7:23 communion *s* two cattle, five
7:29 communion *s* two cattle, five
7:35 communion *s* two cattle, five
7:41 communion *s* two cattle, five
7:47 communion *s* two cattle, five
7:53 communion *s* two cattle, five
7:59 communion *s* two cattle, five
7:65 communion *s* two cattle, five
7:71 communion *s* two cattle, five
7:77 communion *s* two cattle, five
7:83 communion *s* two cattle, five
7:88 cattle of the communion *s*

Nu 9:2 passover s at its appointed
9:4 to prepare the passover s
9:5 prepared the passover s in the
9:6 prepare the passover s on that
9:10 prepare the passover s to
9:13 prepare the passover s, that
9:14 prepare the passover s to
15:3 s to perform a special vow or
15:5 for the s of each male lamb
15:8 s to perform a special vow or
22:40 Balak proceeded to s cattle
De 15:21 you must not s it to Jehovah
16:2 you must s the passover to
16:4 s in the evening on the first
16:5 s the passover in any one of
16:6 s the passover in the evening
17:1 You must not s to Jehovah
18:3 the ones who s a victim
27:7 s communion sacrifices and
33:19 they will s the sacrifices of
Jos 22:26 the altar, not . . . for s
22:28 nor for s, but it is a
22:29 and s besides the altar of
Jg 2:5 they proceeded to s there to
16:23, 23 to s a great s to Dagon
1Sa 1:3 to s to Jehovah of armies in
1:4 Elkanah proceeded to s, and
1:21 to s to Jehovah the yearly
1:21 to Jehovah the yearly s and
2:13 any man was offering a s
2:19, 19 to s the yearly s
2:29 you men keep kicking at my s
3:14 by s or by offering to time
9:12 there is a s today for the
9:13 is the one that blesses the s
13:9 Bring near to me the burnt s
13:9 went offering up the burnt s
13:10 offering up the burnt s
13:12 offering up the burnt s
15:21 to s to Jehovah your God in
15:22 To obey is better than a s
16:2 say, To s to Jehovah is why
16:3 you must call Jesse to the s
16:5 To s to Jehovah is why I
16:5 must come with me to the s
16:5 he called them to the s
20:6 yearly s there for all the
20:29 a family s in the city
1Ki 1:9 Adonijah held a s of sheep
1:25 s bulls and fatlings and
3:4 the king went to Gibeon to s
8:62 a grand s before Jehovah
8:64 render up the burnt s and the
8:64 to contain the burnt s and
12:32 to s to the calves that he
13:2 s upon you the priests of
2Ki 3:27 offered him up as a burnt s
5:17 or a s to any other gods but
10:19 I have a great s for Baal
16:15 all the blood of a s you
17:35 nor serve them nor s to
17:36 and to him you should s
1Ch 15:26 to s seven young bulls and
21:28 David . . . continued to s
29:21 s sacrifices to Jehovah and
2Ch 7:4 people were offering s
7:5 s of twenty-two thousand
7:12 chosen . . . as a house of s
11:16 to s to Jehovah the God of
18:2 Ahab proceeded to s sheep and
28:23 s to the gods of Damascus
28:23 to them I shall s, that
29:7 burnt s they did not offer
29:27 the burnt s on the altar
33:16 s upon it communion
34:4 those that used to s to them
Ne 4:2 Will they s? Will they
12:43 to s on that day great
Job 42:8 burnt s in your own behalf
Ps 4:5 S the sacrifices of
27:6 And I will s at his tent
40:6 S and offering you did not
50:5 concluding my covenant over s
50:14 thanksgiving as your s to God
50:23 thanksgiving as his s
51:16 you do not take delight in s
51:19 burnt s and whole offering
54:6 In willingness I will s to
106:37 And they would s their sons
116:17 offer the s of thanksgiving
Pr 15:8 The s of the wicked ones is
21:3 preferable to Jehovah than s
21:27 The s of the wicked ones is
Ec 5:1 give a s as the stupid ones do
Isa 19:21 must render s and gift and
34:6 Jehovah has a s in Bozrah
57:7 also you went up to offer s
Jer 7:22 whole burnt offering and s
17:26 s and grain offering and
17:26 s into the house of Jehovah
33:18 and to render s always
46:10 s in the land of the north
Eze 16:20 you would s these to them
39:17 s, which I am sacrificing
39:17 great s on the mountains of
39:19, 19 s that I will s for you
40:42 burnt offering and the s
44:11 and the s for the people
46:24 boil the s of the people
Da 9:27 s and gift offering to cease
Ho 3:4 without a s and without a
4:13 tops of the mountains they s
4:14 prostitutes that they s
6:6 taken delight, and not in s
Am 4:5 thanksgiving s to smoke
Jon 1:16 they offered a s to Jehovah
2:9 I will s to you. What I have
Hab 1:16 he offers s to his dragnet
Zep 1:7 Jehovah has prepared a s
1:8 on the day of Jehovah's s
Mt 9:13 I want mercy, and not s
12:7 I want mercy, and not s, you
Lu 2:24 offer s according to what is
Ac 7:41 s to the idol and began to
Ro 12:1 present your bodies a s
1Co 10:20 things which the nations s
10:20 they s to demons, and not
10:28 is something offered in s
Eph 5:2 as an offering and a s to God
Php 2:17 drink offering upon the s
4:18 received . . . an acceptable s
Heb 2:17 propitiatory s for the sins
9:26 sin away through the s of
10:5 S and offering you did not
10:12 one s for sins perpetually
10:26 longer any s for sins left
11:4 Abel offered God a s of
13:15 offer to God a s of praise
1Jo 2:2 a propitiatory s for our sins
4:10 propitiatory s for our sins

Sacrificed
Ge 31:54 Jacob s a sacrifice in the
Ex 24:5 and s bulls as sacrifices
1Sa 28:24 s it and took flour and
2Sa 6:13 immediately s a bull and a
1Ki 1:19 he s bulls and fatlings and
19:21 a span of the bulls and s
2Ki 23:20 he s all the priests of the
2Ch 15:11 s to Jehovah on that day
28:4 s and made sacrificial
33:22 his father had made Amon s
Ps 106:38 s to the idols of Canaan
Ho 12:11 In Gilgal they have s even
Mr 14:12 customarily s the passover
Lu 22:7 passover victim must be s
Ac 15:29 from things s to idols and
21:25 from what is s to idols as
1Co 5:7 Christ our passover has been s
8:7 as something s to an idol
10:19 what is s to an idol is
Re 2:14 eat things s to idols and
2:20 to eat things s to idols

Sacrificers
Ho 13:2 Let the s who are men kiss

Sacrifices
Ge 46:1 sacrifice s to the God of his
Ex 10:25 s and burnt offerings, as we
18:12 burnt offering and s for God
20:24 communion s, your flock and
22:20 s to any gods but Jehovah
24:5 and sacrificed bulls as s, as
24:5 as communion s to Jehovah
29:28 From their communion s
32:6 and presenting communion s
Le 6:12 the communion s smoke over
7:13 sacrifice of his communion s
7:14 blood of the communion s, it
7:15 communion s is to be eaten
7:32 priest from your communion s
7:33 blood of the communion s
7:34 from their communion s, and
9:4 and a ram for communion s to
9:22 offering and the communion s
10:14 communion s of the sons of
17:5 s, which they are sacrificing
17:5 as communion s to Jehovah
Le 17:7 s to the goat-shaped demons
Nu 10:10 and your communion s; and
15:8 or communion s to Jehovah
25:2 people to the s of their gods
29:39 and your communion s
De 12:6 burnt offerings and your s
12:11 burnt offerings and your s
12:27 the blood of your s should be
27:7 sacrifice communion s and eat
32:38 to eat the fat of their s
33:19 the s of righteousness
Jos 8:31 and sacrificing communion s
22:23 render up communion s on it
22:27, 27 s and our communion s
1Sa 6:15 s on that day to Jehovah
10:8 to you to offer up burnt s
10:8 to render up communion s
11:15 rendered up communion s
13:9 and the communion s
15:22 and s as in obeying the
2Sa 6:17 David offered up burnt s
6:17 communion s before Jehovah
6:18 offering up the burnt s
6:18 communion s, he then blessed
15:12 when he offered the s
24:24 burnt s without cost
24:25 burnt s and communion
24:25 communion s, and Jehovah
1Ki 3:4 A thousand burnt s Solomon
3:15 offered up burnt s and
8:63 offer the communion s that
8:64 pieces of the communion s
8:64 pieces of the communion s
9:25, 25 burnt s and communion s
10:5 his drinks and his burnt s
12:27 s in the house of Jehovah
2Ki 10:24 s and burnt offerings
16:13 blood of the communion s
1Ch 16:1 communion s before the true
16:2 and the communion s, he
21:24 burnt s without cost
21:26 and offered up burnt s and
21:26 and communion s, and he
23:31 the burnt s to Jehovah at
29:21 sacrifice s to Jehovah and
29:21 s in great number for all
2Ch 7:1 burnt offering and the s, and
7:7 pieces of the communion s
8:12 s to Jehovah upon the altar
9:4 burnt s that he regularly
23:18 the burnt s of Jehovah
24:14 offerers of burnt s in the
29:31 Approach, and bring s and
29:31 thanksgiving s to the house
29:31 began to bring s and
29:31 and thanksgiving s, and also
29:35 pieces of the communion s
30:22 sacrificing communion s and
31:2 as regards . . . communion s
33:16 upon it communion s and
33:16 thanksgiving s and went on
35:14 offering up the burnt s
Ezr 3:2 to offer up burnt s upon it
3:3 burnt s to Jehovah upon it
3:3 the burnt s of the morning
3:4 burnt s day by day in number
3:6 offer up burnt s to Jehovah
6:3 where they are to offer s
8:35 burnt s to the God of Israel
Ne 12:43 great s and to rejoice
Job 1:5 burnt s according to the
Ps 4:5 the s of righteousness
27:6 s of joyful shouting
50:8 Not concerning your s do I
51:17 s to God are a broken spirit
51:19 you will be delighted with s
106:28 eat the s of the dead ones
107:22 offer the s of thanksgiving
Pr 7:14 Communion s were incumbent
17:1 full of the s of quarreling
Isa 1:11 is the multitude of your s
43:23 s you have not glorified me
43:24 the fat of your s you have
56:7 burnt offerings and their s
Jer 6:20 s have not been gratifying
7:21 to your s and eat flesh
Eze 20:28 sacrificing there their s
43:27 and your communion s
45:15 communion s, in order to
45:17 communion s, in order to
46:2 and his communion s, and he
46:12 or communion s as a
46:12 his communion s just as he
Ho 4:19 will be ashamed of their s

Ho 8:13 As my gift s they kept
9:4 their s will not be gratifying
Am 4:4 bring your s in the morning
5:22 your communion s of fatlings
5:25 s and gift offerings that you
Mr 12:33 whole burnt offerings and s
Lu 13:1 had mixed with their s
Ac 7:42 s for forty years in the
14:13 desiring to offer s with the
1Co 10:18 Are not those who eat the s
Heb 5:1 offer gifts and s for sins
7:27 s, first for his own sins
8:3 to offer both gifts and s
9:9 both gifts and s are offered
9:23 s that are better than such
9:23 that are better than such s
10:1 same s from year to year
10:2 the s not have stopped being
10:3 s there is a reminding of
10:8 you approve of s and
10:8 s that are offered according
10:11 offer the same s often, as
13:16 such s God is well pleased
1Pe 2:5 spiritual s acceptable to God

Sacrificial
1Sa 2:28 to make s smoke billow up
1Ki 9:25 making of s smoke on the
11:8 were making s smoke and
12:33 the altar to make s smoke
13:1 the altar to make s smoke
13:2 are making s smoke upon you
22:43 s smoke on the high places
2Ki 12:3 s smoke on the high places
14:4 making s smoke on the high
15:4 s smoke on the high places
15:35 s smoke on the high places
16:4 s smoke on the high places
17:11 to make s smoke the same
18:4 been making s smoke to it
22:17 s smoke to other gods
23:5 s smoke on the high places
23:5 making s smoke to Baal
23:8 priests had made s smoke
1Ch 6:49 s smoke upon the altar of
23:13 make s smoke before Jehovah
2Ch 2:6 except for making s smoke
25:14 he began to make s smoke
28:3 s smoke in the valley of the
28:4 made s smoke on the high
28:25 s smoke to other gods, so
29:11 and makers of s smoke
32:12 you should make s smoke
34:25 s smoke to other gods
Ps 66:15 With the s smoke of rams
Isa 65:3 s smoke upon the bricks
65:7 s smoke upon the mountains
Jer 1:16 making s smoke to other gods
7:9 making s smoke to Baal and
7:18 s cakes to the queen of the
11:12 they are making s smoke
11:13 to make s smoke to Baal
11:17 making s smoke to Baal
18:15 make s smoke to something
19:4 to make s smoke in it to
19:13 s smoke to all the army of
32:29 made s smoke to Baal and
44:3 and making s smoke and
44:5 s smoke to other gods
44:8 s smoke to other gods in
44:15 s smoke to other gods, and
44:17 s smoke to the queen of the
44:18 s smoke to the queen of the
44:19 s smoke to the queen of the
44:19 make for her s cakes, in
44:21 s smoke that you made in
44:23 made s smoke and that you
44:25 s smoke to the queen of the
48:35 making s smoke to his god
Ho 2:13 she kept making s smoke
4:13 they make s smoke
11:2 they began making s smoke
Hab 1:16 s smoke to his fishing net
Mal 1:11 s smoke will be made, a
Heb 10:14 one s offering that he has

Sacrificing
Ex 13:15 why I am s to Jehovah all
32:8 and s to it and saying, This
Le 17:5 s in the open field, and they
De 32:17 went s to demons, not to God
Jos 8:31 and s communion sacrifices
1Sa 2:15 came and said to the man s
15:15 purpose of s to Jehovah your
1Ki 3:2 were s on the high places
1Ki 3:3 s and making offerings smoke
8:5 s sheep and cattle that could
11:8 and s to their gods
22:43 s and making sacrificial
2Ki 12:3 s and making sacrificial
14:4 s and making sacrificial
15:4 The people were still s and
15:35 s and making sacrificial
16:4 s and making sacrificial
2Ch 5:6 s sheep and cattle that could
30:22 s communion sacrifices and
33:17 s upon the high places
Ezr 4:2 we are s since the days of
Ec 9:2 the one s and the one that is
9:2 and the one that is not s
Isa 65:3 s in the gardens and making
66:3 The one s the sheep is as one
Eze 20:28 they began s there their
39:17 which I am s for you
Ho 8:13 they kept s flesh, and they
11:2 To . . . images they took up s
Zec 14:21 all those who are s must
Mal 1:8 present a blind animal for s
1:14 s a ruined one to Jehovah
Ac 14:18 the crowds from s to them

Sad
1Ki 21:5 that your spirit is s and you
Job 5:11 s are high up in salvation
Ps 38:6 long I have walked about s
42:9 s because of the oppression
43:2 s because of the oppression
Jer 8:21 shattered. I have grown s
Da 6:20 cried out with a s voice even
Mr 10:22 he grew s at the saying and
Lu 24:17 stood still with s faces
2Co 2:2 if I make you s, who indeed
2:2 the one that is made s by me
2:3 not get s because of those
2:7 by his being overly s

Saddened
Job 30:28 S I walked about when there
Ps 35:14 S, I bowed down
2Co 2:4 not that you might be s, but
2:5 he has s, not me, but all of
7:8 even if I s you by my letter
7:8 I see that that letter s you
7:9 not because you were just s
7:9 you were s into repenting
7:9 you were s in a godly way
7:11 your being s in a godly way

Saddle
Ge 31:34 in the woman's s basket of
Le 15:9 s upon which the one having
2Sa 17:23 s an ass and rise up and go
19:26 s the female ass for me
1Ki 13:13 S the ass for me
13:27 saying: S the ass for me

Saddlebags
Ge 49:14 lying down between the two s
Jg 5:16 between the two s, To listen

Saddled
Ge 22:3 s his ass and took two of his
Nu 22:21 Balaam . . . s his she-ass and
Jg 19:10 the couple of he-asses s up
2Sa 16:1 with a couple of asses s and
1Ki 2:40 Shimei got up and s his ass
13:13 they s the ass for him
13:23 at once s for him the ass
13:27 So they s it
2Ki 4:24 she s up the she-ass and

Sadducees
Mt 3:7 Pharisees and S coming to the
16:1 Pharisees and S approached
16:6 leaven of the Pharisees and S
16:11 for the leaven of the . . . S
16:12 the teaching of the . . . S
22:23 that day S, who say there is
22:34 he had put the S to silence
Mr 12:18 S . . . no resurrection
Lu 20:27 S, those who say there is no
Ac 4:1 and the S came upon them
5:17 then existing sect of the S
23:6 the one part was of S but the
23:7 between the Pharisees and S
23:8 For S say there is neither

Sad-faced
Mt 6:16 fasting, stop becoming s like

Sadness
2Co 2:1 not to come to you again in s
2:5 Now if anyone has caused s
2Co 7:10 s in a godly way makes for
7:10 s of the world produces

Safe
Ge 33:18 Jacob came s and sound to
37:14 brothers are s and sound and
37:14 whether the flock is s and
Job 23:7 go s forever from my judge
Ps 22:5 and they got away s
Joe 2:32 will get away s
Mr 6:20 Herod . . . was keeping him s
Lu 17:33 seeks to keep his soul s for
1Ti 2:15 kept s through childbearing
2Pe 2:5 s with seven others when he

Safeguard
Ge 41:35 and they must s it
Ex 12:6 it must continue under s by
Nu 18:7 s your priesthood as regards
De 32:10 To s him as the pupil of his
2Sa 22:44 s me to be the head of
Ps 25:21 uprightness themselves s me
32:7 s me from distress itself
34:13 S your tongue against what
40:11 trueness . . . constantly s me
61:7 that these may s him
64:1 may you s my life
140:1 s me even from the man of
140:4 s me even from the man of
Pr 2:11 discernment itself will s you
3:21 S practical wisdom and
4:6 Love it, and it will s you
4:13 S it, for it itself is your
4:23 s your heart, for out of it
5:2 may your own lips s knowledge
20:28 and trueness—they s the king
Isa 26:3 will s in continuous peace
27:3 s her even night and day
42:6 shall s you and give you as
Joh 12:25 s it for everlasting life

Safeguarded
1Sa 30:23 in that he s us and gave the
Pr 22:12 have s knowledge, but he
Isa 49:6 bring back even the s ones
Eze 6:12 s, by the famine he will
1Pe 1:5 s by God's power through

Safeguarding
Ps 31:23 faithful ones Jehovah is s
Pr 16:17 is s his way is keeping his
27:18 He that is s the fig tree
Isa 27:3 I, Jehovah, am s her
49:8 I kept s you that I might
Na 2:1 a s of the fortified place

Safeguards
Pr 13:6 Righteousness itself s the one
Mt 23:5 cases that they wear as s

Safely
Isa 5:29 prey and bring it s away
Mic 6:14 will not carry them s away
6:14 you would carry away s
Mr 14:44 and lead him away s
Lu 7:3 bring his slave s through
Ac 23:24 s to Felix the governor
27:43 to bring Paul s through and
27:44 all were brought s to land
1Ti 6:19 s treasuring up for
1Pe 3:20 carried s through the water

Safety
Job 12:6 ones enraging God have the s
Ps 12:5 put him in s from anyone that
Ac 27:34 in the interest of your s
28:1 we had made it to s, then
28:4 he made it to s from the sea
Php 3:1 but it is of s to you

Saffron
Ca 2:1 s of the coastal plain I am, a
4:14 spikenard and s, cane and
Isa 35:1 joyful and blossom as the s

Said
Ge 1:28 God s to them: Be fruitful
2:23 Then the man s: This is at
3:1 God s you must not eat from
3:2 the woman s to the serpent
3:3 God has s, You must not eat
3:4 serpent s to the woman: You
3:10 he s: Your voice I heard in
3:11 he s: Who told you that you
3:13 Jehovah God s to the woman
3:16 To the woman he s: I shall
3:17 to Adam he s: Because you
4:1 she gave birth to Cain and s

Ge 4:6 Jehovah s to Cain: Why are you
4:8 Cain s to Abel his brother: Let
4:9 Jehovah s to Cain: Where is
4:9 s: I do not know. Am I my
4:10 he s: What have you done?
4:13 At this Cain s to Jehovah: My
4:15 Jehovah s to him: For that
4:25 she s: God has appointed
6:3 Jehovah s: My spirit shall not
6:7 Jehovah s: I am going to wipe
6:13 God s to Noah: The end of all
7:1 Jehovah s to Noah: Go, you and
8:21 Jehovah s in his heart: Never
9:25 At this he s: Cursed be Canaan
11:4 They now s: Come on! Let us
11:6 Jehovah s: Look! They are one
12:7 s: To your seed I am going to
12:11 he s to Sarai his wife
12:18 s: What is this you have
13:8 Abram s to Lot: Please, do
13:14 Jehovah s to Abram after Lot
14:19 s: Blessed be Abram of the
14:21 king of Sodom s to Abram
14:22 Abram s to the king of Sodom
15:2 Abram s: Sovereign Lord
15:5 s: Look up, please, to the
15:8 he s: Sovereign Lord Jehovah
15:9 he s to him: Take for me a
16:2 Sarai s to Abram: Please now!
16:5 Sarai s to Abram: The
16:6 Abram s to Sarai: Look! Your
16:8 she s: Why, from Sarai my
16:10 Jehovah's angel s to her: I
16:13 she s: Have I here actually
17:1 s to him: I am God Almighty
17:9 God s further to Abraham
17:18 Abraham s to the true God
17:19 God s: Sarah your wife is
18:3 he s: Jehovah, if, now, I
18:5 they s: All right. You may do
18:6 s: Hurry! Get three seah
18:9 s to him: Where is Sarah your
18:9 this he s: Here in the tent!
18:13 Jehovah s to Abraham: Why
18:15 he s: No! but you did laugh
18:17 Jehovah s: Am I keeping
18:20 Jehovah s: The cry of
18:26 Jehovah s: If I shall find in
18:28 s: I shall not bring it to
18:29 s: Suppose forty are found
18:29 s: I shall not do it on
18:30 s: I shall not do it if I
18:31 he s: I shall not bring it to
18:32 he s: May Jehovah, please
18:32 he s: I shall not bring it
19:2 they s: No, but in the public
19:7 he s: Please, my brothers, do
19:9 they s: Stand back there! And
19:12 men s to Lot: Do you have
19:18 Lot s to them: Not that
19:21 he s to him: Here I do show
19:34 s to the younger: Here I lay
20:3 s to him: Here you are as
20:4 he s: Jehovah, will you kill
20:6 God s to him in the dream: I
20:9 s to him: What have you done
20:11 Abraham s: It was because I
20:11 I s to myself, Doubtless
20:13 then I s to her, This is your
20:15 Abimelech s: Here my land
20:16 to Sarah he s: Here I do give
21:1 just as he had s, and Jehovah
21:6 Then Sarah s: God has prepared
21:12 God s to Abraham: Do not let
21:16 she s: Let me not see it
21:17 s to her: What is the matter
21:22 s to Abraham: God is with
21:24 So Abraham s: I shall swear
21:26 Abimelech s: I do not know
21:30 he s: You are to accept the
22:1 s to him: Abraham! to which
22:1 to which he s: Here I am!
22:5 Abraham now s to his
22:7 he s: Here I am, my son! So
22:8 Abraham s: God will provide
22:14 s today: In the mountain of
24:2 Abraham s to his servant, the
24:5 servant s to him: What if the
24:6 Abraham s to him: Be on your
24:17 s: Give me, please, a little
24:18 s: Drink, my lord. With that
24:19 s: For your camels too I
24:24 that she s to him: I am the
24:25 s further to him: There is

Ge 24:31 s: Come, you blessed one of
24:33 he s: I shall not eat until
24:33 Hence he s: Speak!
24:39 I s to my master, What if
24:40 he s to me, Jehovah, before
24:42 I s, Jehovah the God of my
24:45 I s to her, Give me a drink
24:46 s, Take a drink, and I shall
24:47 s, Whose daughter are you?
24:47 she s, The daughter of
24:50 s: From Jehovah this thing
24:54 he s: Send me off to my
24:55 s: Let the young woman stay
24:56 s to them: Do not detain me
24:57 s: Let us call the young
24:58 s to her: Will you go with
24:58 she s: I am willing to go
24:65 s to the servant: Who is that
24:65 servant s: It is my master
25:22 she s: If this is the way it
25:30 Esau s to Jacob: Quick
25:31 Jacob s: Sell me, first of
26:2 Jehovah appeared to him and s
26:9 Abimelech called Isaac and s
26:9 you s, She is my sister
26:9 At this Isaac s to him
26:9 I s it for fear I should die
26:16 Abimelech s to Isaac: Move
26:22 its name Rehoboth and s
26:27 Isaac s to them: Why have
26:28 they s: We have unmistakably
26:28 we s, Let, please, an oath
27:1 and s to him: My son!
27:1 he s to him: Here I am!
27:6 Rebekah s to Jacob her son
27:13 his mother s to him: Upon
27:18 s: My father! to which he
27:18 he s: Here I am! Who are you
27:20 Isaac s to his son: How is it
27:20 he s: Because Jehovah your
27:21 Isaac s to Jacob: Come near
27:22 he s: The voice is the voice
27:24 s: You are really my son
27:24 to which he s: I am
27:25 he s: Bring it near to me
27:26 Isaac his father s to him
27:31 and s to his father: Let my
27:32 Isaac his father s to him
27:32 he s: I am your son
27:33 he s: Who, then, was it that
27:36 s: Is that not why his name
27:38 Then Esau s to his father
27:39 in answer Isaac his father s
27:42 s to him: Look! Esau your
28:1 s to him: You must not take a
28:16 s: Truly Jehovah is in this
29:4 Jacob s to them: My brothers
29:4 they s: We are from Haran
29:5 s to them: Do you know Laban
29:5 they s: We know him
29:6 s to them: Is it all right
29:6 they s: It is all right
29:8 s: We are not allowed to do
29:14 After that Laban s to him
29:15 Laban s to Jacob: Are you my
29:18 s: I am willing to serve
29:19 Laban s: It is better for me
29:21 Jacob s to Laban: Give over
29:25 he s to Laban: What is this
29:26 To this Laban s: It is not
29:32 she s: It is because Jehovah
29:33 then s: It is because Jehovah
29:34 s: Now this time my husband
29:35 s: This time I shall laud
30:2 s: Am I in the place of God
30:3 she s: Here is my slave girl
30:6 Rachel s: God has acted as my
30:8 Rachel s: With strenuous
30:11 Leah s: With good fortune
30:13 Leah s: With my happiness
30:14 Rachel s to Leah: Give me
30:15 s to her: Is this a little
30:15 Rachel s: For that reason he
30:16 s: It is with me you are
30:18 Leah s: God has given me a
30:20 Leah s: God has endowed me
30:23 she s: God has taken away my
30:25 Jacob immediately s to Laban
30:27 Then Laban s to him: If, now
30:29 s to him: You yourself must
30:31 he s: What shall I give you?
30:34 Laban s: Why, that is fine
31:3 Jehovah s to Jacob: Return
31:5 and he s to them

Ge 31:11 angel of the true God s
31:11 to which I s, Here I am
31:14 s to him: Is there a share
31:16 everything God has s to you
31:24 in a dream by night and s
31:26 Laban s to Jacob: What have
31:31 s to myself, You might tear
31:35 s to her father: Do not let
31:43 Laban in answer s to Jacob
31:46 Jacob s to his brothers: Pick
31:49 he s: Let Jehovah keep watch
32:2 Jacob s, when he saw them
32:4 Jacob has s: With Laban I
32:8 s: If Esau should come to the
32:9 Jacob s: O God of my father
32:12 s, Unquestionably I shall
32:16 s to his servants: Cross over
32:20 s to himself: I may appease
32:26 After that he s: Let me go
32:26 s: I am not going to let you
32:27 s to him: What is your
32:27 name? to which he s: Jacob
32:28 s: Your name will no longer
32:29 s: Tell me, please, your
32:29 he s: Why is it that you
33:5 s: Who are these with you?
33:5 s: The children with whom
33:8 s: What do you mean by all
33:8 he s: In order to find favor
33:9 Esau s: I have a great many
33:10 Jacob s: No, please. If, now
33:12 he s: Let us pull out and go
33:13 s to him: My lord is aware
33:15 Esau s: Let me, please, put
33:15 s: Why this? Let me find
34:4 Shechem s to Hamor his father
34:11 Then Shechem s to her father
34:30 Jacob s to Simeon and to
34:31 they s: Ought anyone to treat
35:1 God s to Jacob: Rise, go up
35:2 Jacob s to his household and
35:11 God s further to him: I am
35:17 midwife s to her: Do not be
37:9 s: Here I have had a dream
37:13 Israel s to Joseph: Your
37:13 he s to him: Here I am!
37:14 So he s to him: Go, please
37:16 he s: It is my brothers I
37:19 s to one another: Look! Here
37:21 s: Let us not strike his soul
37:26 Judah s to his brothers
37:32 and s: This is what we found
38:8 Judah s to Onan: Have
38:11 So Judah s to Tamar his
38:11 s to himself: He too may die
38:16 s: Allow me, please, to have
38:16 she s: What will you give
38:17 s: I myself shall send a kid
38:17 s: Will you give a security
38:18 she s: Your seal ring and
38:22 s: I never found her and
38:22 s, No temple prostitute has
38:23 Judah s: Let her take them
38:24 Judah s: Bring her out and
38:26 s: She is more righteous
40:8 s to him: We have dreamed a
40:8 Joseph s to them: Do not
40:12 Joseph s to him: This is its
40:16 he, in turn, s to Joseph
40:18 Joseph answered and s: This
41:15 Pharaoh s to Joseph: I have
41:15 heard it s about you that you
41:25 Then Joseph s to Pharaoh
41:38 Pharaoh s to his servants
41:39 Pharaoh s to Joseph: Since
41:44 Pharaoh further s to Joseph
41:54 come, just as Joseph had s
41:55 Then Pharaoh s to all the
42:1 Jacob s to his sons: Why do
42:4 he s: Otherwise a fatal
42:7 spoke harshly with them and s
42:7 s: From the land of Canaan
42:10 they s to him: No, my lord
42:12 he s to them: Not so!
42:13 s: Your servants are twelve
42:14 Joseph s to them: It is what
42:18 Joseph s to them on the
42:28 s to his brothers: My money
42:31 we s to him, We are upright
42:33 s to us, By this I am going
42:37 Reuben s to his father: My
42:38 he s: My son will not go
43:3 Then Judah s to him: The man
43:7 they s: The man directly

Jg 15:10 they *s:* It is to tie Samson
15:11 *s* to Samson: Do you not know
15:11 *s* to them: Just as they did
15:12 they *s* to him: It is to tie
15:12 Samson *s* to them: Swear to
15:16 Samson *s:* With the jawbone
16:6 Delilah *s* to Samson: Do tell
16:7 Samson *s* to her: If they tie
16:10 Delilah *s* to Samson: Look!
16:11 he *s* to her: If they tie me
16:12 *s* to him: The Philistines
16:13 Delilah *s* to Samson: Up till
16:13 he *s* to her: If you will
16:14 *s* to him: The Philistines
16:15 *s* to him: How dare you say
16:17 *s* to her: A razor has never
16:20 she *s:* The Philistines are
16:20 *s:* I shall go out as at other
16:24 *s* they, our god has given
16:26 Samson *s* to the boy that was
16:28 *s:* Sovereign Lord Jehovah
17:2 In time he *s* to his mother
17:2 and also *s* it in my hearing
17:2 his mother *s:* Blessed may my
17:9 *s* to him: Where do you come
17:9 *s* to him: I am a Levite from
17:10 So Micah *s* to him: Do dwell
17:13 Micah *s:* Now I do know that
18:2 they *s* to them: Go, explore
18:4 *s* to them: Thus and so Micah
18:5 *s* to him: Inquire, please, of
18:6 priest *s* to them: Go in peace
18:9 they *s:* Do get up, and let us
18:14 *s* to their brothers: Did you
18:18 priest *s* to them: What are
18:19 they *s* to him: Be quiet
18:23 and *s* to Micah: What is the
18:24 *s:* My gods that I made you
18:25 sons of Dan *s* to him: Do not
19:5 *s* to his son-in-law: Sustain
19:6 *s* to the man: Come on, please
19:8 *s:* Please, take sustenance for
19:9 young woman's father, *s* to
19:11 the attendant now *s* to his
19:12 *s* to him: Let us not turn
19:17 the old man *s:* Where are you
19:18 he *s* to him: We are passing
19:20 the old man *s:* May you have
19:23 *s* to them: No, my brothers
19:28 he *s* to her: Rise up, and
19:30 that everybody seeing it *s*
20:3 the sons of Israel *s:* Speak
20:4 *s:* It was to Gibeah, which
20:18 Israel *s:* Who of us should
20:18 Jehovah *s:* Judah in the lead
20:23 Jehovah *s:* Go up against him
20:28 Jehovah *s:* Go up, because
20:32 *s:* Let us flee, and we shall
20:39 Benjamin . . . *s:* They are
21:5 *s:* Who is there out of all
21:6 they *s:* Today one tribe has
21:16 older men of the assembly *s*
21:17 they *s:* There should be a
21:19 *s:* Look! There is a festival
Ru 1:8 Finally Naomi *s* to both of her
1:11 Naomi *s:* Return, my daughters
1:12 If I had *s* I had hope also
1:15 So she *s:* Look! Your widowed
2:2 the Moabite woman *s* to Naomi
2:2 she *s* to her: Go, my daughter
2:5 Boaz *s* to the young man who
2:6 and *s:* The young woman is a
2:7 she *s,* Let me glean, please
2:8 Boaz *s* to Ruth: You have heard
2:10 *s* to him: How is it I have
2:11 Boaz answered and *s* to her
2:13 she *s:* Let me find favor in
2:19 mother-in-law now *s* to her
2:20 At that Naomi *s* to her
2:21 Then Ruth the Moabitess *s*
2:21 He also *s* to me, Close by the
2:22 *s* to Ruth her daughter-in-law
3:1 mother-in-law now *s* to her
3:5 she *s* to her: All that you say
3:9 Then he *s:* Who are you?
3:9 she *s:* I am Ruth your slave
3:10 he *s:* Blessed may you be of
3:14 He now *s:* Do not let it be
3:16 her mother-in-law, who now *s*
3:17 for he *s* to me, Do not come
3:18 she *s:* Sit still, my daughter
4:1 he *s:* Do turn aside, do sit
4:2 older men of the city and *s*
4:3 He now *s* to the repurchaser

Ru 4:4 he *s:* I shall be the one to
4:5 Boaz *s:* On the day that you buy
4:6 repurchaser *s:* I am unable to
4:8 when the repurchaser *s* to Boaz
4:9 Boaz *s* to the older men and
4:11 the older men *s:* Witnesses!
1Sa 1:14 Eli *s* to her: How long will
1:15 Hannah answered and *s*
1:17 Eli answered and *s:* Go in
1:18 she *s:* Let your maidservant
1:20 name Samuel, because, *s* she
1:22 for she had *s* to her husband
1:23 Elkanah her husband *s* to her
1:26 she *s:* Excuse me, my lord
2:15 and *s* to the man sacrificing
2:16 *s:* No, but you should give it
2:20 Eli . . . *s:* May Jehovah
2:27 This is what Jehovah has *s*
3:4 Samuel . . . *s:* Here I am
3:5 he *s:* I did not call. Lie
3:6 went to Eli and *s:* Here I am
3:6 he *s:* I did not call, my son
3:8 went to Eli and *s:* Here I am
3:9 Eli *s* to Samuel: Go, lie down
3:10 Samuel *s:* Speak, for your
3:12 toward Eli all that I have *s*
3:16 But Eli called Samuel and *s*
3:16 At this he *s:* Here I am
3:18 At that he *s:* It is Jehovah
4:7 *s:* God has come into the camp
4:7 they *s:* Woe to us, for such a
4:14 Eli . . . *s:* What does the
4:16 *s:* What is the thing that
4:17 news bearer answered and *s*
4:22 she *s:* Glory has gone away
5:7 *s:* Do not let the ark of the
5:8 *s:* What shall we do to the
5:8 *s:* Toward Gath let the ark of
5:11 *s:* Send the ark of the God of
6:3 *s:* If you are sending the ark
6:4 *s:* What is the guilt offering
6:4 *s:* According to the number of
6:20 the men of Beth-shemesh *s*
7:5 Samuel *s:* Collect all Israel
7:8 sons of Israel *s* to Samuel
7:12 he *s:* Till now Jehovah has
8:5 *s* to him: Look! You yourself
8:6 *s:* Do give us a king to judge
8:7 Jehovah *s* to Samuel: Listen
8:10 So Samuel *s* all the words of
8:19 *s:* No, but a king is what
8:22 Samuel *s* to the men of
9:3 So Kish *s* to Saul his son
9:5 Saul, for his part, *s* to his
9:6 But he *s* to him: Look, please
9:7 this Saul *s* to his attendant
9:8 answered Saul once more and *s*
9:10 Then Saul *s* to his attendant
9:11 *s* to them: Is the seer in
9:12 *s:* He is. Look! He is ahead
9:17 the man of whom I *s* to you
9:18 Saul . . . *s:* Do tell me
9:21 At this Saul answered and *s*
9:23 Later Samuel *s* to the cook
9:23 I *s* to you, Put it away by
9:27 Samuel himself *s* to Saul
10:1 *s:* Is it not because Jehovah
10:11 the people *s* one to another
10:12 *s:* But who is their father?
10:14 brother of Saul's father *s*
10:14 *s:* To look for the she-asses
10:15 Saul's uncle *s:* Do tell me
10:16 In turn Saul *s* to his uncle
10:18 the God of Israel has *s*
10:22 Jehovah *s:* Here he is
10:24 Samuel *s* to all the people
10:27 *s:* How will this one save
11:1 men of Jabesh *s* to Nahash
11:2 Nahash the Ammonite *s* to
11:3 older men of Jabesh *s* to
11:9 now *s* to the messengers that
11:10 men of Jabesh *s:* Tomorrow
11:13 Saul *s:* Not a man should be
11:14 Samuel *s* to the people
12:1 Samuel *s* to all Israel
12:1 respects all that you have *s*
12:4 *s:* You have not defrauded us
12:5 he *s* to them: Jehovah is a
12:5 they *s:* He is a witness
12:20 So Samuel *s* to the people
13:8 time that Samuel had *s*
13:9 Finally Saul *s:* Bring near to
13:11 Samuel *s:* What is it you
13:11 Saul *s:* I saw that the

1Sa 13:12 so I *s* to myself, Now the
13:13 At this Samuel *s* to Saul
13:19 the Philistines had *s*
14:6 Jonathan *s* to the attendant
14:7 his armor-bearer *s* to him
14:8 Jonathan *s:* Here we are
14:12 *s:* Come on up to us, and
14:12 At once Jonathan *s* to his
14:18 Saul now *s* to Ahijah
14:19 Then Saul *s* to the priest
14:28 *s:* Your father solemnly put
14:29 Jonathan *s:* My father has
14:33 At this he *s:* You have dealt
14:34 Saul *s:* Scatter among the
14:36 Saul *s:* Let us go down
14:36 they *s:* Anything that is
14:36 priest *s:* Let us approach
14:38 Saul *s:* Come near here, all
14:40 At this the people *s* to Saul
14:42 Saul now *s:* Cast lots to
14:43 Then Saul *s* to Jonathan
14:43 So Jonathan told him and *s*
14:44 Saul *s:* Thus may God do and
14:45 But the people *s* to Saul
15:1 Samuel *s* to Saul: It was I
15:2 what Jehovah of armies has *s*
15:6 Saul *s* to the Kenites
15:14 Samuel *s:* Then what does
15:15 Saul *s:* From the Amalekites
15:16 Samuel *s* to Saul: Stop
15:16 So he *s* to him: Speak
15:18 sent you on a mission and *s*
15:20 Saul *s* to Samuel: But I
15:22 Samuel *s:* Does Jehovah have
15:24 Saul *s* to Samuel: I have
15:26 Samuel *s* to Saul: I shall
15:28 Samuel *s* to him: Jehovah
15:30 he *s:* I have sinned
15:32 Samuel *s:* Bring Agag the
15:33 Samuel *s:* Just as your
16:1 Jehovah *s* to Samuel
16:2 But Samuel *s:* How can I go?
16:4 *s:* Does your coming mean
16:5 To this he *s:* It means peace
16:6 *s:* Surely his anointed one is
16:7 But Jehovah *s* to Samuel
16:8 *s:* Neither has Jehovah chosen
16:9 *s:* Neither has Jehovah chosen
16:10 still Samuel *s* to Jesse
16:11 *s* to Jesse: Are these all
16:11 *s:* The youngest one has till
16:11 Samuel *s* to Jesse: Do send
16:12 Jehovah *s:* Get up, anoint
16:17 So Saul *s* to his servants
16:19 *s:* Do send to me David your
17:17 Jesse *s* to David his son
17:27 people *s* to him the same
17:28 Eliab . . . *s:* Why is it that
17:29 David *s:* What have I done
17:33 Saul *s* to David: You are not
17:37 Saul *s* to David: Go, and
17:39 David *s* to Saul: I am
17:43 So the Philistine *s* to David
17:45 David *s* to the Philistine
17:55 *s* to Abner the chief of the
17:55 Abner *s:* By the life of your
17:56 king *s:* You inquire whose
17:58 Saul now *s* to him: Whose
17:58 David *s:* The son of your
18:8 he *s:* They have given David
18:17 Finally Saul *s* to David
18:17 Saul, he *s* to himself
18:18 David *s* to Saul: Who am I
18:21 Saul *s:* I shall give her to
18:21 Saul *s* to David: By one of
18:23 David *s:* Is it an easy thing
18:25 Saul *s:* This is what you
19:4 *s* to him: Do not let the
19:14 David, but she *s:* He is sick
19:17 Saul *s* to Michal: Why did
19:17 Michal *s* to Saul: He
19:17 He himself *s* to me, Send
19:22 *s:* There in Naioth in Ramah
20:1 *s* in front of Jonathan: What
20:2 At this he *s* to him: It is
20:3 *s:* Your father must surely
20:5 At this David *s* to Jonathan
20:9 To this Jonathan *s:* That is
20:10 David *s* to Jonathan: Who
20:11 Jonathan *s* to David: Just
20:26 *s* to himself: Something has
20:27 Saul *s* to Jonathan his son
20:30 *s* to him: You son of a
20:32 *s* to him: Why should he be

1Sa 20:40 s to him: Go, take them to
21:1 meeting David and then s to
21:2 David s to Ahimelech the
21:4 s: There is no ordinary bread
21:5 s to him: But womankind has
21:9 priest s: The sword of
21:14 Achish s to his servants
22:3 s to the king of Moab: Let
22:5 Gad the prophet s to David
22:7 Then Saul s to his servants
22:9 s: I saw the son of Jesse
22:12 Saul now s: Listen, please
22:12 he s: Here I am, my lord
22:14 s: And who among all your
22:16 king s: You will positively
22:17 king s to the runners
22:18 king s to Doeg: You turn and
22:22 David s to Abiathar: I well
23:2 Jehovah s to David: Go, and
23:3 the men of David s to him
23:4 s: Rise up, go down to
23:9 s to Abiathar the priest
23:11 Jehovah s: He will come
23:12 Jehovah s: They will do the
23:21 Saul s: Blessed are you of
23:22 s to me that he himself is
24:6 s to his men: It is
24:10 someone s to kill you but
24:10 s, I shall not thrust out
25:5 David s to the young men
25:10 s: Who is David, and who
25:13 David s to his men: Gird on
25:19 she s to her young men
25:21 David, he had s: It was
25:24 s: Upon me myself, O my
25:32 David s to Abigail: Blessed
25:35 s: Go up in peace to your
25:39 s: Blessed be Jehovah, who
25:41 s: Here is your slave girl
26:6 David answered and s to
26:6 Abishai s: I myself shall go
26:8 Abishai now s to David
26:9 David s to Abishai: Do not
26:17 David s: It is my voice
26:21 Saul s: I have sinned
26:22 David answered and s: Here
26:25 Saul s to David: Blessed
27:1 David s in his heart: Now I
27:5 David s to Achish: If, now
27:10 Achish s: Where did you men
27:10 David s: Upon the south of
28:1 Achish s to David
28:2 David s to Achish: That is
28:2 Achish s to David: That is
28:7 Saul s to his servants
28:7 servants s to him: Look!
28:8 s: Employ divination, please
28:9 woman s to him: Here you
28:11 woman s: Whom shall I
28:11 s: Bring up Samuel for me
28:13 king s to her: Do not be
28:14 s to her: What is his form?
28:14 she s: It is an old man
28:15 Saul s: I am in very sore
28:21 she s to him: Here your
28:23 s: I am not going to eat
29:3 Achish s to the princes of
29:6 s to him: As Jehovah is
29:8 David s to Achish: Why
29:9 Achish answered and s to
29:9 s, Let him not go up with us
30:6 the people s to stone him
30:7 David s to Abiathar the
30:8 s to him: Go in chase, for
30:13 David now s to him
30:13 s: I am an Egyptian
30:15 David s to him: Will you
30:15 s: Do swear to me by God
30:20 s: This is David's spoil
30:23 David s: You must not do
31:4 Saul s to his armor-bearer
2Sa 1:3 s to him: From the camp of
1:4 s: The people have fled from
1:5 David s to the young man that
1:6 s: I unexpectedly chanced to
1:7 and I s, Here I am!
1:8 s to him, I am an Amalekite
1:9 s, Stand, please, over me and
1:13 David now s to the young man
1:13 to which he s: I am the
1:14 David s to him: How was it
1:15 s: Go near. Smite him
1:16 David then s to him: The
2:1 Jehovah s to him: Go up

2Sa 2:1 Then he s: To Hebron
2:5 s to them: Blessed may you be
2:14 Abner s to Joab: Let the
2:14 Joab s: Let them rise up
2:20 s: Is this you, Asahel?
2:20 to which he s: It is I
2:21 Abner s to him: Veer to your
2:22 Abner s to Asahel yet again
2:27 Joab s: As the true God is
3:7 Ish-bosheth s to Abner: Why
3:13 s: Good! I myself shall
3:16 Abner s to him: Go, return
3:18 Jehovah himself s to David
3:21 Abner s to David: Let me
3:24 s: What have you done? Look!
3:28 s: I and my kingdom, from
3:31 David s to Joab and all the
4:8 s to the king: Here is the
4:9 s to them: As Jehovah who
5:1 s: Look! We ourselves are
5:8 David s on that day: Anyone
5:19 Jehovah s to David: Go up
5:20 s: Jehovah has broken through
5:23 s: You must not go up
6:20 s: How glorious the king of
6:21 David s to Michal: It was
7:2 king s to Nathan the prophet
7:3 Nathan s to the king
7:5 Jehovah has s: Should you
7:8 Jehovah of armies has s: I
7:18 s: Who am I, O Sovereign
9:2 s to him: Are you Ziba?
9:2 he s: I am your servant
9:3 Ziba s to the king: There is
9:4 king s to him: Where is he?
9:4 Ziba s to the king: Look! He
9:6 David s: Mephibosheth!
9:6 s: Here is your servant
9:8 s: What is your servant
9:9 s to him: Everything that had
9:11 Ziba s to the king: In accord
10:2 David s: I shall exercise
10:3 s to Hanun their lord: Is
11:3 s: Is this not Bath-sheba
11:5 David and s: I am pregnant
11:8 David s to Uriah: Go down
11:10 David s to Uriah: It is
11:11 Uriah s to David: The Ark
11:12 David s to Uriah: Dwell
11:25 David s to the messenger
12:1 s to him: There were two
12:5 s to Nathan: As Jehovah is
12:7 Nathan s to David: You
12:7 God of Israel has s, I
12:11 Jehovah has s, Here I am
12:13 David now s to Nathan
12:13 At this Nathan s to David
12:18 s: Look! While the child
12:19 David s to his servants
12:19 this they s: He has died
12:21 servants s to him: What
12:22 s: While the child was yet
12:22 s to myself, Who is there
12:27 s: I have fought against
13:4 s to him: Why are you, the
13:4 Amnon s to him: With Tamar
13:5 Jehonadab s to him: Lie
13:6 Amnon s to the king: Please
13:9 Amnon refused to eat and s
13:10 Amnon now s to Tamar: Bring
13:11 s to her: Come, lie down
13:12 s to him: No, my brother!
13:15 Amnon s to her: Get up, go
13:16 s to him: No, my brother
13:17 s: Send this person away
13:20 Absalom her brother s to
13:24 s: Here, now, your servant
13:25 king s to Absalom: No, my
13:26 Absalom s: If not you, let
13:26 king s to him: Why should
13:32 s: Do not let my lord think
13:35 Jehonadab s to the king
14:2 s to her: Go in mourning
14:5 king s to her: What is the
14:5 s: For a fact I am a
14:8 king s to the woman: Go to
14:9 Tekoite woman s to the king
14:11 s: Let the king, please
14:11 s: As Jehovah is living
14:12 The woman now s: Let your
14:12 So he s: Speak!
14:15 s, Let me speak, please, to
14:17 s, Let the word of my lord
14:18 s to the woman: Do not

2Sa 14:18 woman s: Let my lord the
14:19 s: As your soul is living
14:21 king s to Joab: Here, now
14:24 king s: Let him turn toward
14:30 Finally he s to his servants
14:31 and s to him: Why did your
14:32 Absalom s to Joab: Look! I
15:9 king s to him: Go in peace
15:14 David s to all his servants
15:15 servants s to the king
15:19 king s to Ittai the Gittite
15:21 answered the king and s
15:22 At that David s to Ittai
15:25 But the king s to Zadok
15:31 David s: Turn, please, the
15:33 David s to him: If you
16:2 Then the king s to Ziba
16:2 Ziba s: The asses are for the
16:3 The king now s: And where is
16:3 At this Ziba s to the king
16:3 s, Today the house of Israel
16:4 The king then s to Ziba
16:4 Ziba s: I do bow down
16:7 Shimei s as he called down
16:9 son of Zeruiah s to the king
16:10 the king s: What do I have
16:10 Jehovah himself has s to
16:11 Jehovah has s so to him
16:17 At this Absalom s to Hushai
16:18 So Hushai s to Absalom
16:20 Absalom s to Ahithophel
16:21 Ahithophel s to Absalom
17:5 Absalom s: Call, please
17:6 Absalom s to him: According
17:7 At this Hushai s to Absalom
17:14 all the men of Israel s
17:15 Hushai s to Zadok and
17:20 s: Where are Ahimaaz and
17:20 the woman s to them
17:21 and s to David: You people
17:29 s: The people are hungry
18:2 Then the king s to the people
18:3 the people s: You must not
18:4 So the king s to them
18:10 saw it and told Joab and s
18:11 Joab s to the man who was
18:12 But the man s to Joab
18:14 Joab s: Let me not hold
18:18 he s: I have no son in order
18:19 he s: Let me run, please
18:20 Joab s to him: You are not
18:21 Joab s to the Cushite
18:22 now s once again to Joab
18:22 Joab s: Why is it that you
18:23 he s: Let, now, happen
18:23 So he s to him: Run!
18:25 the king s: If he is by
18:26 s: Look! Another man
18:26 the king s: This one also
18:27 king s: This is a good man
18:28 Ahimaaz called and s to the
18:29 the king s: Is it well with
18:29 Ahimaaz s: I saw the great
18:30 king s: Step aside, take
18:32 the king s to the Cushite
18:32 Cushite s: May the enemies
18:33 what he s as he walked
19:5 s: You have today put to
19:19 s to the king: Do not let
19:21 s: In return for this
19:22 David s: What do I have to
19:23 Then the king s to Shimei
19:25 then the king s to him
19:26 he s: My lord the king, it
19:26 For your servant had s
19:29 However, the king s to him
19:30 Mephibosheth s to the king
19:33 the king s to Barzillai
19:34 But Barzillai s to the king
19:38 king s: With me Chimham
19:43 s: We have ten parts in the
20:4 The king now s to Amasa
20:6 Then David s to Abishai
20:17 woman then s: Are you Joab?
20:17 to which he s: I am
20:17 she s to him: Listen to the
20:17 he s: I am listening
20:20 To this Joab answered and s
20:21 Then the woman s to Joab
21:1 Jehovah s: Upon Saul and upon
21:4 So the Gibeonites s to him
21:4 he s: Whatever you are saying
21:5 they s to the king: The man
21:6 the king s: I myself shall

2Sa 23:3 The God of Israel *s*, To me
23:15 expressed his craving and *s*
24:2 the king *s* to Joab the chief
24:3 But Joab *s* to the king
24:10 David *s* to Jehovah: I have
24:12 This is what Jehovah has *s*
24:13 to David and told him and *s*
24:14 David *s* to Gad: It is very
24:16 he *s* to the angel that was
24:18 to David on that day and *s*
24:21 Araunah *s:* Why has my lord
24:21 David *s:* To buy from you
24:22 Araunah *s* to David: Let my
24:24 the king *s* to Araunah
1Ki 1:2 So his servants *s* to him
1:11 Nathan now *s* to Bath-sheba
1:16 upon which the king *s*
1:17 she *s* to him: My lord, it
1:24 Nathan *s:* My lord the king
1:28 David now answered and *s*
1:31 *s:* Let my lord King David
1:32 David *s:* You men, call for
1:36 answered the king and *s*
1:41 he at once *s:* What does the
1:42 Adonijah *s:* Come on in, for
1:43 answered and *s* to Adonijah
1:48 this is what the king *s*
1:52 Solomon *s:* If he will become
1:53 after which Solomon *s* to
2:13 *s:* Is your coming peaceable?
2:13 he *s:* It is peaceable
2:14 So she *s:* Speak
2:16 she *s* to him: Speak
2:18 Bath-sheba *s:* Good! I myself
2:20 the king *s* to her: Make it
2:22 answered and *s* to his mother
2:26 the king *s:* Go to Anathoth
2:30 *s* to him: This is what the
2:30 the king has *s*, Come on out!
2:30 Come on out! But he *s:* No!
2:31 Then the king *s* to him
2:36 *s* to him: Build yourself a
2:38 At this Shimei *s* to the king
2:42 called Shimei and *s* to him
3:6 Solomon *s:* You yourself have
3:17 the one woman *s:* Excuse me
3:22 But the other woman *s*
3:23 the king *s:* This one is
3:26 *s* to the king (for her
3:26 so that she *s*): Excuse me
3:27 the king answered and *s:* You
8:12 Solomon *s:* Jehovah himself
8:12 Jehovah himself *s* he was to
8:18 Jehovah *s* to David my father
8:29 you *s*, My name will prove to
9:13 he *s:* What sort of cities
10:6 she *s* to the king: True has
11:2 had *s* to the sons of Israel
11:11 Jehovah now *s* to Solomon
11:21 So Hadad *s* to Pharaoh
11:22 But Pharaoh *s* to him
11:22 To this he *s:* Nothing; but
11:31 *s*, Here I am ripping the
12:5 *s* to them: Go away for three
12:24 This is what Jehovah has *s*
12:28 *s* to the people: It is too
13:2 *s:* O altar, altar, this is
13:2 *s*, Look! A son born to the
13:6 *s* to the man of the true God
13:8 *s* to the king: If you gave
13:13 now *s* to his sons: Saddle
13:14 *s* to him: Are you the man
13:14 to which he *s:* I am
13:16 But he *s:* I am not able to
13:18 he *s* to him: I too am a
13:21 This is what Jehovah has *s*
13:26 *s:* It is the man of the
14:2 So Jeroboam *s* to his wife
14:5 had *s* to Ahijah: Here is the
14:7 the God of Israel has *s*
14:14 *s* day, and what if right
16:16 heard it *s:* Zimri has
17:10 *s:* Please, get me a sip of
17:12 she *s:* As Jehovah your God
17:13 Elijah *s* to her: Do not be
17:14 has *s*, The large jar of
17:18 At this she *s* to Elijah
17:19 he *s* to her: Give me your
17:23 *s:* See, your son is alive
17:24 the woman *s* to Elijah
18:7 *s:* Is this you, my lord
18:8 At this he *s* to him: It is I
18:9 But he *s:* What sin have I
18:10 *s*, He is not here, he made

1Ki 18:15 Elijah *s:* As Jehovah of
18:17 *s* to him: Is this you, the
18:18 he *s:* I have not brought
18:21 *s:* How long will you be
18:24 the people answered and *s*
18:25 *s* to the prophets of Baal
18:30 Elijah *s* to all the people
18:33 *s:* Fill four large jars
18:34 he *s:* Do it again. So they
18:34 he *s:* Do it a third time
18:39 fell upon their faces and *s*
18:40 Elijah *s* to them: Seize the
18:41 Elijah now *s* to Ahab: Go up
18:43 *s* to his attendant: Go up
18:43 *s:* There is nothing at all
18:44 now *s:* Go up, say to Ahab
19:5 he *s* to him: Rise up, eat
19:7 *s:* Rise up, eat, for the
19:10 he *s:* I have been absolutely
19:11 it *s:* Go out, and you must
19:14 he *s:* I have been absolutely
19:15 Jehovah now *s* to him
19:20 *s:* Let me, please, kiss my
19:20 *s* to him: Go, return; for
20:2 what Ben-hadad has *s*
20:4 *s:* According to your word
20:5 messengers came back and *s*
20:5 Ben-hadad has *s*, I sent to
20:7 *s:* Take note, please, and
20:8 *s* to him: Do not obey, and
20:9 he *s* to the messengers of
20:10 *s:* So may the gods do to me
20:11 *s:* You men, speak to him
20:12 *s* to his servants: Get set!
20:13 *s:* This is what Jehovah has
20:13 *s*, Have you seen all this
20:14 Then Ahab *s:* By whom?
20:14 he *s:* This is what Jehovah
20:14 *s*, By the young men of the
20:14 he *s:* Who will open the
20:14 to which he *s:* You!
20:18 *s:* Whether it is for peace
20:22 king of Israel and *s* to him
20:23 they *s* to him: Their God is
20:28 *s* to the king of Israel, yes
20:28 Jehovah has *s*, For the
20:28 *s:* Jehovah is a God of
20:31 So his servants *s* to him
20:32 *s:* Your servant Ben-hadad
20:32 *s*, Please, let my soul live
20:32 he *s:* Is he still alive?
20:33 he *s:* Come, fetch him
20:34 *s* to him: The cities that
20:35 prophets *s* to his friend by
20:36 he *s* to him: For the reason
20:39 *s*, Guard this man. If he
20:40 the king of Israel *s* to him
20:42 He now *s* to him: This is
20:42 Jehovah has *s*, For the
21:3 But Naboth *s* to Ahab: It is
21:4 he *s:* I shall not give you
21:6 he *s:* I shall not give you
21:7 Jezebel his wife *s* to him
21:15 *s* to Ahab: Rise up, take
21:19 has *s:* Have you murdered
21:19 is what Jehovah has *s*
21:20 he *s:* I have found you
22:3 *s* to his servants: Do you
22:4 *s* to the king of Israel
22:6 *s* to them: Shall I go
22:7 *s:* Is there not here a
22:8 *s* to Jehoshaphat: There is
22:8 *s:* Do not let the king say
22:9 *s:* Do bring Micaiah the son
22:11 *s:* This is what Jehovah has
22:11 *s*, With these you will push
22:14 *s:* As Jehovah is living
22:15 he *s* to him: Go up and
22:16 *s* to him: For how many
22:17 *s:* I certainly see all the
22:18 *s* to Jehoshaphat: Did I not
22:21 *s*, I myself shall fool him
22:21 *s* to him, By what means?
22:22 *s*, I shall go forth, and I
22:22 *s*, You will fool him, and
22:24 *s:* In just which way did
22:25 *s:* Look! You are seeing
22:26 *s:* Take Micaiah and turn
22:27 This is what the king has *s*
22:28 *s:* If you return at all in
22:30 now *s* to Jehoshaphat
22:32 *s* to themselves: Surely it
22:34 *s* to his charioteer: Turn
22:49 *s* to Jehoshaphat: Let my

2Ki 1:2 sent messengers and *s* to them
1:4 *s:* As regards the couch upon
1:5 *s* to them: Why is it that you
1:6 *s* to him: There was a man
1:6 *s*, Is it because there is no
1:8 *s* to him: A man possessing
1:8 *s:* It was Elijah the Tishbite
1:11 king has *s*, Do come down
1:16 *s*, For the reason that you
2:2 Elisha *s:* As Jehovah is living
2:3 to Elisha and *s* to him
2:3 this he *s:* I too well know it
2:4 Elijah now *s* to him: Elisha
2:4 *s:* As Jehovah is living and
2:5 approached Elisha and *s* to
2:5 this he *s:* I too well know it
2:6 Elijah now *s* to him: Sit here
2:6 he *s:* As Jehovah is living
2:9 Elijah himself *s* to Elisha
2:9 Elisha *s:* Please, that two
2:10 he *s:* You have asked a
2:14 and struck the waters and *s*
2:16 *s:* You must not send them
2:17 so that he *s:* Send. They now
2:18 he *s* to them: Did I not say
2:19 men of the city *s* to Elisha
2:20 he *s:* Fetch me a small new
2:21 *s:* This is what Jehovah has
2:21 *s*, I do make this water
3:7 To this he *s:* I shall go
3:8 he *s:* By the way of the
3:10 *s:* How unfortunate that
3:11 *s:* Is there not here a
3:11 *s:* There is here Elisha the
3:12 *s:* The word of Jehovah
3:13 *s* to him: No, for Jehovah
3:14 *s:* As Jehovah of armies
3:16 Jehovah has *s*, Let there be
3:17 Jehovah has *s:* You men will
4:2 Elisha *s* to her: What shall I
4:2 she *s:* Your maidservant has
4:3 he *s:* Go, ask for vessels for
4:6 he *s* to her: There is no other
4:7 he now *s:* Go, sell the oil
4:9 she *s* to her husband: Here
4:12 he *s* to Gehazi his attendant
4:13 he *s* to him: Please, say to
4:13 she *s:* In among my own
4:14 now *s:* For a fact a son she
4:15 he *s:* Call her. So he called
4:16 he *s:* At this appointed time
4:16 she *s:* No, my master, O man
4:19 At last he *s* to the attendant
4:22 *s:* Do send me, please, one
4:23 *s:* Why are you going to him
4:23 she *s:* It is all right
4:24 and *s* to her attendant
4:24 unless I shall have *s* so to
4:25 *s* to Gehazi his attendant
4:26 she *s:* It is all right
4:27 *s:* Let her alone, for her
4:28 She now *s:* Did I ask for a
4:29 *s* to Gehazi: Gird up your
4:30 mother of the boy *s:* As
4:36 *s:* Call this Shunammite
4:36 he *s:* Lift up your son
4:38 in time *s* to his attendant
4:41 he *s:* Fetch, then, flour
4:42 he *s:* Give it to the people
4:43 his waiter *s:* How shall I
4:43 *s:* Give it to the people that
4:43 Jehovah has *s:* There will be
5:3 In time she *s* to her mistress
5:5 king of Syria *s:* Get going!
5:7 *s:* Am I God, to put to death
5:11 *s* to myself, To me he will
5:13 *s:* My father, had it been
5:13 he *s* to you, Bathe and be
5:15 *s:* Here, now, I certainly
5:16 he *s:* As Jehovah before
5:17 Naaman *s:* If not, please
5:19 he *s* to him: Go in peace
5:20 *s:* Here my master has spared
5:21 and then *s:* Is all well?
5:22 To this he *s:* All is well
5:23 Naaman *s:* Go on, take two
5:25 *s* to him: Where did you
5:25 *s:* Your servant did not go
5:26 he *s* to him: Did not my
6:2 So he *s:* Go
6:3 he *s:* I myself shall go
6:6 *s:* Where did it fall? So he
6:7 *s:* Lift it up for yourself
6:10 man of the true God had *s* to

Ne 2:6 king *s* to me, as his queenly
2:17 I *s* to them: You are seeing
2:18 king's words that he had *s* to
2:18 they *s:* Let us get up, and
2:20 I replied to them and *s* to
4:14 *s* to the nobles and the deputy
4:22 that time I *s* to the people
5:12 *s:* We shall make restoration
5:13 *s:* In this manner may the
5:13 all the congregation *s:* Amen!
6:11 But I *s:* Should a man like
7:3 I *s* to them: The gates of
7:65 the Tirshatha *s* to them that
8:1 *s* to Ezra the copyist to
13:9 After that I *s* the word and
13:19 *s* the word and the doors
13:19 *s* further that they should
Es 1:10 he *s* to Mehuman, Biztha
1:16 Memucan *s* before the king and
1:17 *s* to bring in Vashti the queen
2:2 *s:* Let them seek young women
4:7 money that Haman had *s* to pay
4:10 Then Esther *s* to Hathach and
4:13 Mordecai *s* to reply to Esther
4:15 Esther *s* to reply to Mordecai
5:3 king *s* to her: What do you
5:4 Esther *s:* If to the king it
5:5 king *s:* You men, have Haman
5:6 In time the king *s* to Esther
5:7 To this Esther answered and *s*
5:14 wife and all his friends *s*
6:1 he *s* to bring the book of the
6:3 king *s:* What honor and great
6:3 *s:* Nothing has been done with
6:4 the king *s:* Who is in the
6:5 the king's attendants *s* to him
6:5 So the king *s:* Let him come in
6:6 Haman *s* in his heart: To whom
6:7 Haman *s* to the king: As for
6:10 At once the king *s* to Haman
6:10 as you have *s*, and do that
6:13 and Zeresh his wife *s* to him
7:2 king now *s* to Esther also on
7:3 the queen answered and *s*
7:5 King Ahasuerus now *s*, yes, he
7:6 Then Esther *s:* The man, the
7:8 king *s:* Is there also to be a
7:9 *s:* Also, there is the stake
7:9 king *s:* You men, hang him on
8:5 She now *s:* If to the king it
8:7 So King Ahasuerus *s* to Esther
9:13 Esther *s:* If to the king it
9:14 king *s* for it to be done that
9:25 *s* with the written document
Job 1:5 *s* Job, maybe my sons have
1:7 Jehovah *s* to Satan: Where do
1:7 Satan answered Jehovah and *s*
1:9 Satan answered Jehovah and *s*
1:12 Jehovah *s* to Satan: Look!
2:2 Then Jehovah *s* to Satan
2:2 Satan answered Jehovah and *s*
2:4 Satan answered Jehovah and *s*
2:6 Jehovah *s* to Satan: There he
2:9 wife *s* to him: Are you yet
2:10 he *s* to her: As one of the
3:2 Job now answered and *s*
3:3 Also the night that someone *s*
6:22 I have *s*, Give me something
7:4 also *s*, When shall I get up?
7:13 *s*, My divan will comfort me
9:27 *s*, Let me forget my concern
22:13 *s:* What does God really
28:14 The watery deep itself has *s*
28:14 The sea too has *s*, It is
28:22 and death themselves have *s*
31:24 to gold I have *s*, You are
32:7 I *s*, Days themselves should
32:10 I *s*, Do listen to me
33:8 Only you have *s* in my ears
34:5 For Job has *s*, I certainly
34:9 he has *s*, An able-bodied man
35:2 You have *s*, My righteousness
35:10 no one has *s*, Where is God
36:23 who has *s*, You have
37:20 has any man *s* that it will
Ps 2:7 He has *s* to me: You are my son
10:6 He has *s* in his heart: I shall
10:11 has *s* in his heart: God has
10:13 He has *s* in his heart: You
12:4 Those who have *s:* With our
14:1 has *s* in his heart
16:2 I have *s* to Jehovah: You are
27:8 Concerning you my heart has *s*
30:6 I have *s* in my ease: Never
Ps 31:14 I have *s:* You are my God
31:22 I *s* when I became panicky
32:5 I *s:* I shall make confession
33:9 he himself *s*, and it came to
35:21 *s:* Aha! Aha! our eye has seen
38:16 For I *s:* Otherwise they
39:1 I *s:* I will guard my ways
40:7 I *s:* Here I have come
41:4 *s:* O Jehovah, show me favor
53:1 *s* in his heart: There is no
64:5 They have *s:* Who sees them?
68:22 Jehovah has *s:* From Bashan I
71:10 my enemies have *s* in regard
73:11 *s:* How has God come to know?
73:15 *s:* I will tell a story like
74:8 *s* together in their own heart
75:4 I *s* to the foolish ones: Do
78:19 *s:* Is God able to arrange a
82:6 have *s*, You are gods
83:4 *s:* Come and let us efface
83:12 *s:* Let us take possession
87:5 *s:* Each and every one was
89:2 *s:* Loving-kindness will stay
91:9 you *s:* Jehovah is my refuge
94:18 *s:* My foot will certainly
105:31 *s* that the gadflies should
105:34 *s* that the locusts should
106:34 As Jehovah had *s* to them
116:11 *s*, when I became panicky
129:8 *s:* The blessing of Jehovah
140:6 *s* to Jehovah: You are my God
142:5 *s:* You are my refuge
Pr 9:4 she has *s* to him
9:16 she has also *s* to him
22:13 *s:* There is a lion outside
26:13 lazy one has *s:* There is a
26:19 has *s:* Was I not having fun?
30:15 four that have not *s:* Enough!
30:16 fire that has not *s:* Enough!
30:20 she has *s:* I have committed
Ec 1:2 vanity! the congregator has *s*
2:1 I *s*, even I, in my heart
2:2 I *s* to laughter: Insanity! and
2:15 And I myself *s* in my heart
3:17 *s* in my heart: The true God
3:18 I, even I, have *s* in my heart
7:23 I *s:* I will become wise
7:27 have found, *s* the congregator
8:14 I *s* that this too is vanity
9:16 I myself *s:* Wisdom is better
12:8 vanity! *s* the congregator
Ca 2:10 *s* to me, Rise up, you girl
7:8 *s*, I shall go up on the palm
Isa 4:3 will be *s* to be holy to him
6:3 *s:* Holy, holy, holy is
6:11 *s:* How long, O Jehovah?
6:11 *s:* Until the cities actually
7:7 Jehovah has *s:* It will not
7:12 Ahaz *s:* I shall not ask
8:3 *s* to me: Call his name
8:11 Jehovah has *s* to me with
10:13 *s*, With the power of my
10:24 *s:* Do not be afraid, O my
14:13 *s* in your heart, To the
18:4 what Jehovah has *s* to me
21:6 what Jehovah has *s* to me
21:12 watchman *s:* The morning
21:16 what Jehovah has *s* to me
22:4 *s:* Turn your gaze away from
22:14 Jehovah of armies, has *s*
22:15 *s:* Go, enter in to this
23:4 *s:* I have not had birth
28:12 *s:* This is the resting-place
28:15 *s:* We have concluded a
28:16 *s:* Here I am laying as a
29:22 Jehovah has *s* to the house
30:10 *s* to the ones seeing, You
30:12 *s:* In view of your
30:15 *s:* By coming back and
31:4 what Jehovah has *s* to me
32:5 will not be *s* to be noble
36:4 Rabshakeh *s* to them: Please
36:4 *s:* What is this confidence
36:5 *s* (but it is the word of lips)
36:10 Jehovah himself *s* to me
36:11 and Joah *s* to Rabshakeh
36:12 Rabshakeh *s:* Is it to your
36:14 *s*, Do not let Hezekiah
36:16 the king of Assyria has *s*
37:3 *s*, This day is a day of
37:6 Isaiah *s* to them: This is
37:6 *s:* Do not be afraid because
37:9 *s* concerning Tirhakah the
37:21 *s*, Because you have prayed
Isa 37:33 Jehovah has *s* concerning
38:1 *s* to him: This is what
38:1 what Jehovah has *s*, Give
38:5 *s:* I have heard your prayer
38:10 *s:* In the midst of my days
38:11 *s:* I shall not see Jah
38:22 *s:* What is the sign that I
39:3 *s* to him: What did these
39:3 Hezekiah *s:* From a distant
39:4 Hezekiah *s:* Everything that
39:5 Isaiah now *s* to Hezekiah
39:6 will be left, Jehovah has *s*
39:8 At that Hezekiah *s* to Isaiah
40:6 *s:* What shall I call out?
41:9 *s* to you, You are my servant
42:5 true God, Jehovah, has *s*
43:1 this is what Jehovah has *s*
43:14 This is what Jehovah has *s*
43:16 This is what Jehovah has *s*
44:2 This is what Jehovah has *s*
44:6 This is what Jehovah has *s*
44:24 This is what Jehovah has *s*
45:1 Jehovah has *s* to his anointed
45:11 Jehovah has *s*, the Holy One
45:13 Jehovah of armies has *s*
45:14 Jehovah has *s:* The unpaid
45:18 this is what Jehovah has *s*
45:19 nor *s* I to the seed of Jacob
47:10 *s:* There is no one seeing
48:17 This is what Jehovah has *s*
48:22 no peace, Jehovah has *s*, for
49:4 I *s:* It is for nothing that
49:5 has *s* for me to bring back
49:7 *s* to him that is despised
49:8 Jehovah has *s:* In a time of
49:22 Jehovah has *s:* Look! I
49:25 this is what Jehovah has *s*
50:1 This is what Jehovah has *s*
51:22 has *s:* Look! I will take
51:23 who have *s* to your soul
52:3 Jehovah has *s:* It was for
52:4 *s:* It was to Egypt that my
54:1 owner, Jehovah has *s*
54:6 rejected, your God has *s*
54:8 Repurchaser, Jehovah, has *s*
54:10 mercy upon you, has *s*
56:1 Jehovah has *s:* Keep justice
56:4 Jehovah has *s* to the eunuchs
57:10 have not *s*, It is hopeless!
57:15 *s:* In the height and in the
57:19 has *s*, and I will heal him
57:21 no peace, my God has *s*, for
59:21 with them, Jehovah has *s*
59:21 offspring, Jehovah has *s*
61:6 you will be *s* to be
62:4 *s* to be a woman left
62:4 no more be *s* to be desolate
65:1 I have *s*, Here I am, here
65:7 the same time, Jehovah has *s*
65:8 *s:* In the same way that the
65:13 *s:* Look! My own servants
65:25 mountain, Jehovah has *s*
66:1 *s:* The heavens are my throne
66:5 *s*, May Jehovah be glorified!
66:9 shutting up? your God has *s*
66:12 *s:* Here I am extending to
66:20 *s*, just as when the sons of
66:21 the Levites, Jehovah has *s*
66:23 before me, Jehovah has *s*
Jer 1:6 I *s:* Alas, O Sovereign Lord
1:9 Jehovah *s* to me: Here I have
1:11 So I *s:* An offshoot of an
1:13 So I *s:* A widemouthed
1:14 At this Jehovah *s* to me
2:2 This is what Jehovah has *s*
2:5 Jehovah has *s:* What have your
2:6 have not *s*, Where is Jehovah
2:20 But you *s:* I am not going to
2:31 have *s*, We have roamed
3:19 *s*, O how I proceeded to
3:19 *s*, My Father! you people
4:3 Jehovah has *s* to the men of
4:11 *s* to this people and to
4:27 this is what Jehovah has *s*
5:4 Even I myself had *s:* Surely
5:14 the God of armies, has *s*
5:24 *s* in their heart: Let us
6:6 what Jehovah of armies has *s*
6:9 what Jehovah of armies has *s*
6:15 will stumble, Jehovah has *s*
6:16 This is what Jehovah has *s*
6:21 this is what Jehovah has *s*
6:22 *s:* Look! A people is coming
7:3 the God of Israel, has *s*

Eze 25:3 *s:* For the reason that you
25:3 *s* Aha! against my sanctuary
25:6 *s*, For the reason that you
25:8 *s*, For the reason that Moab
25:8 *s:* Look! The house of Judah
25:12 *s*, For the reason that
25:13 *s:* I will also stretch out
25:15 *s*, For the reason that the
25:16 *s:* Here I am stretching out
26:2 Tyre has *s* against Jerusalem
26:3 *s*, Here I am against you
26:7 *s*, Here I am bringing
26:15 *s* to Tyre, At the sound of
26:19 *s*, When I make you a
27:3 *s:* O Tyre, you yourself have
27:3 have *s*, I am perfect in
28:2 *s:* For the reason that your
28:6 *s:* For the reason that you
28:12 *s:* You are sealing up a
28:22 *s:* Here I am against you
28:25 *s:* When I collect together
29:3 *s:* Here I am against you
29:3 *s*, My Nile River belongs to
29:8 Jehovah has *s:* Here I am
29:9 for the reason that he has *s*
29:13 *s:* At the end of forty years
29:19 *s*, Here I am giving to
30:2 *s:* Howl, you people, Alas
30:6 This is what Jehovah has *s*
30:10 *s*, I will also cause the
30:13 Sovereign Lord Jehovah has *s*
30:22 Lord Jehovah has *s*, Here I
31:10 *s*, For the reason that you
31:15 *s*, On the day of its going
32:3 Jehovah has *s*, I will also
32:11 *s*, The very sword of the
33:10 Thus you people have *s*
33:17 sons of your people have *s*
33:20 *s*, The way of Jehovah is
33:25 *s:* With the blood you keep
33:27 has *s:* As I am alive
34:2 *s:* Woe to the shepherds of
34:10 *s*, Here I am against the
34:11 Lord Jehovah has *s*
34:17 *s:* Here I am judging
34:20 Jehovah has *s* to them
35:3 Sovereign Lord Jehovah has *s*
35:12 *s* concerning the mountains
35:14 Sovereign Lord Jehovah has *s*
36:2 Sovereign Lord Jehovah has *s*
36:2 enemy has *s* against you
36:3 Sovereign Lord Jehovah has *s*
36:4 Sovereign Lord Jehovah has *s*
36:5 Sovereign Lord Jehovah has *s*
36:6 Sovereign Lord Jehovah has *s*
36:7 Sovereign Lord Jehovah has *s*
36:13 Sovereign Lord Jehovah has *s*
36:22 *s:* Not for your sakes am I
36:33 Sovereign Lord Jehovah has *s*
36:37 Sovereign Lord Jehovah has *s*
37:3 I *s:* Sovereign Lord Jehovah
37:5 has *s* to these bones: Here
37:9 Sovereign Lord Jehovah has *s*
37:12 *s:* Here I am opening your
37:19 Sovereign Lord Jehovah has *s*
37:21 Sovereign Lord Jehovah has *s*
38:3 *s:* Here I am against you
38:10 Sovereign Lord Jehovah has *s*
38:14 Sovereign Lord Jehovah has *s*
38:17 Sovereign Lord Jehovah has *s*
39:1 Sovereign Lord Jehovah has *s*
39:17 Sovereign Lord Jehovah has *s*
39:25 Sovereign Lord Jehovah has *s*
41:4 *s* to me: This is the Most
43:18 *s*, These are the statutes
44:2 Jehovah *s* to me: As regards
44:5 Jehovah *s* to me: Son of man
44:6 *s:* That is enough of you
44:9 Jehovah has *s:* No foreigner
45:9 Lord Jehovah has *s*, That
45:18 *s*, In the first month, on
46:1 *s*, As regards the gate of
46:16 *s*, In case the chieftain
46:24 *s* to me: These are the
47:6 *s* to me: Have you seen this
47:13 *s:* This is the territory
Da 1:3 king *s* to Ashpenaz his chief
1:10 court official *s* to Daniel
1:11 Daniel *s* to the guardian
1:18 king had *s* to bring them in
2:2 *s* to call the magic-practicing
2:3 king *s* to them: There is a
2:12 *s* to destroy all the wise men
2:24 *s* to him: Do not destroy any
Da 2:25 *s* to him: I have found an
2:46 *s* to offer even a present and
3:4 you it is being *s*, O peoples
3:13 fury, *s* to bring in Shadrach
3:20 *s* to bind Shadrach, Meshach
4:8 him I *s* what the dream was
4:26 *s* to leave the rootstock of
4:31 being *s*, O Nebuchadnezzar
5:2 *s* to bring in the vessels of
5:10 *s:* O king, keep living even
7:16 *s* to me, as he went on to
7:23 *s*, As for the fourth beast
8:14 *s* to me: Until two thousand
8:26 which has been *s*, it is true
10:19 *s:* Do not be afraid, O very
10:19 *s:* Let my lord speak
12:6 *s* to the man clothed with
12:8 *s:* O my lord, what will be
Ho 1:9 *s:* Call his name Lo-ammi
1:10 *s* to them, You men are not
1:10 *s* to them, The sons of the
2:5 *s*, I want to go after those
2:12 *s:* They are a gift to me
3:3 *s* to her: For many days you
13:10 you *s*, Do give me a king and
Joe 2:32 just as Jehovah has *s*, and
Am 1:3 This is what Jehovah has *s*
1:5 as exiles . . . Jehovah has *s*
1:6 This is what Jehovah has *s*
1:8 Sovereign Lord Jehovah has *s*
1:9 This is what Jehovah has *s*
1:11 This is what Jehovah has *s*
1:13 This is what Jehovah has *s*
1:15 into exile . . . Jehovah has *s*
2:1 This is what Jehovah has *s*
2:3 kill with him, Jehovah has *s*
2:4 This is what Jehovah has *s*
2:6 This is what Jehovah has *s*
3:11 Jehovah has *s*, There is an
3:12 This is what Jehovah has *s*
5:3 Sovereign Lord Jehovah has *s*
5:4 has *s* to the house of Israel
5:14 with you, just as you have *s*
5:16 Jehovah, has *s*, In all the
5:17 midst of you, Jehovah has *s*
5:27 the God of armies has *s*
7:3 It shall not occur, Jehovah *s*
7:6 the Sovereign Lord Jehovah *s*
7:8 *s* to me: What are you seeing
7:8 So I *s:* A plummet
7:11 For this is what Amos has *s*
7:14 Amos . . . *s* to Amaziah
7:17 this is what Jehovah has *s*
8:2 *s:* What are you seeing, Amos?
8:2 So I *s:* A basket of summer
9:15 Jehovah your God has *s*
Ob 1 Jehovah has *s* regarding Edom
Jon 1:6 near to him and *s* to him
1:8 So they *s* to him: Do tell us
1:9 he *s* to them: I am a Hebrew
1:11 Finally they *s* to him
1:12 *s* to them: Lift me up and
2:2 and *s:* Out of my distress I
2:4 as for me, I *s*, I have been
3:7 and he had it *s* in Nineveh
4:2 *s:* Ah, now, O Jehovah, was
4:4 Jehovah *s:* Have you rightly
4:8 *s:* My dying off is better
4:9 he *s:* I have rightly become
4:10 Jehovah *s:* You, for your part
Mic 2:3 this is what Jehovah has *s*
2:7 being *s*, O house of Jacob
3:5 Jehovah has *s* against the
Na 1:12 This is what Jehovah has *s*
Hab 3:9 are the thing *s*. *Se'lah*
Zep 3:7 I *s*, Surely you will fear me
3:16 it will be *s* to Jerusalem
3:20 Jehovah has *s*
Hag 1:2 Jehovah of armies has *s*
1:2 *s:* The time has not come
1:5 *s*, Set your heart upon your
1:7 *s*, Set your heart upon your
1:8 be glorified, Jehovah has *s*
2:6 what Jehovah of armies has *s*
2:7 Jehovah of armies has *s*
2:9 Jehovah of armies has *s*
2:11 what Jehovah of armies has *s*
2:13 *s:* It will become unclean
2:14 *s:* That is how this people
Zec 1:3 *s:* Return to me, is the
1:3 Jehovah of armies has *s*
1:4 what Jehovah of armies has *s*
1:6 *s:* According to what Jehovah
1:9 *s:* Who are these, my lord?
Zec 1:9 speaking with me *s* to me
1:10 *s:* These are the ones whom
1:12 and *s:* O Jehovah of armies
1:14 Jehovah of armies has *s*
1:16 this is what Jehovah has *s*
1:17 Jehovah of armies has *s*
1:19 So I *s* to the angel who was
1:19 he *s* to me: These are the
1:21 I *s:* What are these coming
2:2 So I *s:* Where are you going?
2:2 he *s* to me: To measure
2:4 he *s* to him: Run, speak to
2:8 what Jehovah of armies has *s*
3:2 angel of Jehovah *s* to Satan
3:4 *s* to those standing before
3:5 *s:* Let them put a clean
3:7 what Jehovah of armies has *s*
4:2 *s* to me: What are you seeing?
4:2 So I *s:* I have seen, and
4:4 answered and *s* to the angel
4:5 *s* to me: Do you not really
4:5 In turn I *s:* No, my lord
4:6 *s* to me: This is the word of
4:6 Jehovah of armies has *s*
4:12 *s* to him: What are the two
4:13 *s* to me: Do you not really
4:13 In turn I *s:* No, my lord
4:14 he *s:* These are the two
5:2 *s* to me: What are you seeing?
5:2 In turn I *s:* I am seeing a
5:3 *s* to me: This is the curse
5:5 *s* to me: Raise your eyes
5:6 So I *s:* What is it? In turn
5:6 *s:* This is the ephah measure
5:8 he *s:* This is Wickedness
5:10 So I *s* to the angel who was
5:11 *s* to me: In order to build
6:5 angel answered and *s* to me
6:7 *s:* Go, walk about in the
6:12 Jehovah of armies has *s*
7:9 what Jehovah of armies has *s*
7:13 Jehovah of armies has *s*
8:2 *s*, I will be jealous for Zion
8:3 *s*, I will return to Zion and
8:4 Jehovah of armies has *s*
8:6 what Jehovah of armies has *s*
8:7 *s*, Here I am saving my people
8:9 *s*, Let the hands of you people
8:14 *s*, Just as I had in mind to
8:14 has *s*, and I felt no regret
8:19 *s*, The fast of the fourth
8:20 Jehovah of armies has *s*
8:23 Jehovah of armies has *s*
11:4 *s*, Shepherd the flock meant
11:9 *s:* I shall not keep
11:12 *s* to them: If it is good in
11:13 Jehovah *s* to me: Throw it
Mal 1:2 loved you . . . Jehovah has *s*
1:2 *s:* In what way have you loved
1:4 *s*, They, for their part, will
1:6 Jehovah of armies has *s* to
1:6 *s:* In what way have we
1:7 have *s:* In what way have we
1:8 Jehovah of armies has *s*
1:9 Jehovah of armies has *s*
1:10 Jehovah of armies has *s*, and
1:11 Jehovah of armies has *s*
1:13 *s*, Look! What a weariness!
1:13 Jehovah of armies has *s*
1:13 at your hand? Jehovah has *s*
1:14 Jehovah of armies has *s*
2:2 Jehovah of armies has *s*
2:4 Jehovah of armies has *s*
2:8 Jehovah of armies has *s*
2:14 *s*, On what account? On this
2:16 the God of Israel has *s*
2:16 Jehovah of armies has *s*
2:17 *s*, In what way have we
3:1 Jehovah of armies has *s*
3:5 Jehovah of armies has *s*
3:7 Jehovah of armies has *s*
3:7 *s:* In what way shall we
3:8 have *s:* In what way have we
3:10 Jehovah of armies has *s*
3:11 Jehovah of armies has *s*
3:12 Jehovah of armies has *s*
3:13 against me, Jehovah has *s*
3:13 *s:* What have we spoken with
3:14 *s*, It is of no value to
3:17 Jehovah of armies has *s*
4:1 Jehovah of armies has *s*
4:3 Jehovah of armies has *s*
Mt 2:5 *s* to him: In Bethlehem of
2:8 *s:* Go make a careful search

Mt 2:20 *s*: Get up, take the young
3:7 he *s* to them: You offspring of
3:15 Jesus *s* to him: Let it be
3:17 *s*: This is my Son, the
4:3 the Tempter came and *s* to him
4:4 in reply he *s*: It is written
4:6 *s* to him: If you are a son of
4:7 Jesus *s* to him: Again it is
4:9 *s* to him: All these things I
4:10 *s* to him: Go away, Satan!
4:19 *s* to them: Come after me
5:21 *s* to those of ancient times
5:27 You heard that it was *s*
5:31 it was *s*, Whoever divorces
5:33 *s* to those of ancient times
5:38 it was *s*, Eye for eye and
5:43 You heard that it was *s*
8:4 Jesus *s* to him: See that you
8:7 He *s* to him: When I get there
8:8 *s*: Sir, I am not a fit man
8:10 *s* to those following him
8:13 Jesus *s* to the army officer
8:19 *s* to him: Teacher, I will
8:20 Jesus *s* to him: Foxes have
8:21 the disciples *s* to him: Lord
8:22 Jesus *s* to him: Keep
8:26 he *s* to them: Why are you
8:27 *s*: What sort of person is
8:32 he *s* to them: Go! They came
9:2 Jesus *s* to the paralytic: Take
9:3 the scribes *s* to themselves
9:4 *s*: Why are you thinking
9:6 he *s* to the paralytic: Get up
9:9 *s* to him: Be my follower
9:12 *s*: Persons in health do not
9:15 *s* to them: The friends of the
9:22 *s*: Take courage, daughter
9:33 crowds felt amazement and *s*
9:37 *s* to his disciples: Yes, the
11:3 *s* to him: Are you the Coming
11:4 Jesus *s* to them: Go your way
11:25 Jesus *s* in response
12:2 seeing this the Pharisees *s*
12:3 *s* to them: Have you not read
12:11 He *s* to them: Who will be
12:13 *s* to the man: Stretch out
12:17 Isaiah the prophet, who *s*
12:24 Pharisees *s*: This fellow
12:25 he *s* to them: Every kingdom
12:38 and Pharisees *s*: Teacher, we
12:39 he *s* to them: A wicked and
12:47 *s* to him: Look! Your mother
12:48 he *s* to the one telling him
12:49 he *s*: Look! My mother and
13:10 the disciples came up and *s*
13:11 In reply he *s*: To you it is
13:27 *s* to him, Master, did you
13:28 *s* to them, An enemy, a man
13:28 *s* to him, Do you want us
13:29 He *s*, No; that by no chance
13:35 *s*: I will open my mouth
13:36 came to him and *s*: Explain
13:37 In response he *s*: The sower
13:51 They *s* to him: Yes
13:52 *s* to them: That being the
13:54 *s*: Where did this man get
13:57 Jesus *s* to them: A prophet
14:2 *s* to his servants: This is
14:8 *s*: Give me here upon a
14:15 *s*: The place is lonely and
14:16 Jesus *s* to them: They do not
14:17 *s* to him: We have nothing
14:18 He *s*: Bring them here to me
14:19 he *s* a blessing and, after
14:28 Peter *s* to him: Lord, if it
14:29 He *s*: Come! Thereupon Peter
14:31 *s* to him: You with little
15:3 he *s* to them: Why is it you
15:4 God *s*, Honor your father and
15:7 Isaiah aptly prophesied . . . *s*
15:10 *s* to them: Listen and get
15:12 disciples came up and *s* to
15:12 at hearing what you *s*
15:13 he *s*: Every plant that my
15:15 Peter *s* to him: Make the
15:16 *s*: Are you also yet without
15:24 he *s*: I was not sent forth
15:26 he *s*: It is not right to
15:27 She *s*: Yes, Lord; but really
15:28 Then Jesus *s* in reply to her
15:32 *s*: I feel pity for the crowd
15:33 the disciples *s* to him
15:34 Jesus *s* to them: How many
15:34 *s*: Seven, and a few little
Mt 16:2 he *s* to them: When evening
16:6 Jesus *s* to them: Keep your
16:8 Jesus *s*: Why are you doing
16:12 *s* to watch out, not for the
16:14 *s*: Some say John the Baptist
16:15 *s* to them: You, though, who
16:16 Peter *s*: You are the Christ
16:17 Jesus *s* to him: Happy you
16:23 he *s* to Peter: Get behind me
16:24 Jesus *s* to his disciples
17:4 Peter *s* to Jesus: Lord, it is
17:7 *s*: Get up and have no fear
17:11 *s*: Elijah, indeed, is coming
17:17 Jesus *s*: O faithless and
17:19 *s*: Why is it we could not
17:20 *s* to them: Because of your
17:22 in Galilee that Jesus *s* to
17:24 *s*: Does your teacher not pay
17:25 He *s*: Yes. However, when he
17:26 he *s*: From the strangers
17:26 Jesus *s* to him: Really, then
18:1 *s*: Who really is greatest in
18:3 *s*: Truly I say to you, Unless
18:21 Peter came up and *s* to him
18:22 Jesus *s* to him: I say to you
18:32 *s* to him, Wicked slave, I
19:4 he *s*: Did you not read that
19:5 *s*, For this reason a man
19:7 *s* to him: Why, then, did
19:8 He *s* to them: Moses, out of
19:10 disciples *s* to him: If such
19:11 He *s* to them: Not all men
19:14 *s*: Let the young children
19:16 *s*: Teacher, what good must
19:17 *s* to him: Why do you ask me
19:18 He *s* to him: Which ones?
19:18 Jesus *s*: Why, You must not
19:20 *s* to him: I have kept all
19:21 Jesus *s* to him: If you want
19:23 But Jesus *s* to his disciples
19:26 Jesus *s* to them: With men
19:27 Then Peter *s* to him in reply
19:28 Jesus *s* to them: Truly I say
20:4 he *s*, You also, go into the
20:6 he *s* to them, Why have you
20:7 They *s* to him, Because nobody
20:7 He *s* to them, You too go into
20:8 master of the vineyard *s* to
20:12 and *s*, These last put in one
20:13 he *s*, Fellow, I do you no
20:17 and *s* to them on the road
20:21 *s* to her: What do you want?
20:21 She *s* to him: Give the word
20:22 Jesus *s* in answer: You men
20:22 They *s* to him: We can
20:23 He *s* to them: You will
20:25 *s*: You know that the rulers
20:32 *s*: What do you want me to
20:33 *s* to him: Lord, let our eyes
21:13 he *s* to them: It is written
21:16 *s* to him: Do you hear what
21:16 Jesus *s* to them: Yes
21:19 and he *s* to it: Let no fruit
21:21 Jesus *s* to them: Truly I say
21:23 *s*: By what authority do you
21:24 Jesus *s* to them: I, also
21:27 they *s*: We do not know
21:27 *s* to them: Neither am I
21:28 he *s*, Child, go work today
21:29 *s*, I will, sir, but did not
21:30 the second, he *s* the same
21:30 reply this one *s*, I will not
21:31 They *s*: The latter
21:31 Jesus *s* to them: Truly I say
21:38 the cultivators *s* among
21:41 They *s* to him: Because they
21:42 Jesus *s* to them: Did you
22:8 *s* to his slaves, The marriage
22:12 *s* to him, Fellow, how did
22:13 king *s* to his servants, Bind
22:18 *s*: Why do you put me to the
22:20 he *s* to them: Whose image
22:21 They *s*: Caesar's. Then he
22:21 Then he *s* to them: Pay back
22:24 Moses *s*, If any man dies
22:29 reply Jesus *s* to them: You
22:37 He *s* to him: You must love
22:42 They *s* to him: David's
22:43 He *s* to them: How, then, is
22:44 Jehovah *s* to my Lord: Sit at
24:2 he *s* to them: Do you not
24:4 Jesus *s* to them: Look out
25:8 The foolish *s* to the discreet
25:12 he *s*, I tell you the truth
Mt 25:21 master *s* to him, Well done
25:22 *s*, Master, you committed to
25:23 master *s* to him, Well done
25:24 *s*, Master, I knew you to be
25:26 master *s* to him, Wicked and
26:1 Jesus . . . *s* to his disciples
26:8 and *s*: Why this waste?
26:10 Aware of this, Jesus *s* to
26:15 *s*: What will you give me to
26:18 He *s*: Go into the city to
26:21 he *s*: Truly I say to you
26:23 he *s*: He that dips his hand
26:25 *s*: It is not I, is it, Rabbi?
26:25 He *s* to him: You yourself
26:25 to him: You yourself *s* it
26:26 he *s*: Take, eat. This means
26:31 Jesus *s* to them: All of you
26:33 Peter, in answer, *s* to him
26:34 Jesus *s* to him: Truly I say
26:35 Peter *s* to him: Even if I
26:35 disciples also *s* the same
26:36 *s* to the disciples: Sit down
26:38 he *s* to them: My soul is
26:40 he *s* to Peter: Could you
26:45 *s* to them: At such a time
26:49 to Jesus he *s*: Good day
26:50 Jesus *s* to him: Fellow, for
26:52 Jesus *s* to him: Return your
26:55 Jesus *s* to the crowds: Have
26:61, 61 *s*: This man *s*, I am able
26:62 high priest stood up and *s*
26:63 So the high priest *s* to him
26:64 Jesus *s* to him: You yourself
26:64 You yourself *s* it. Yet I say
26:71 noticed him and *s* to those
26:73 *s* to Peter: Certainly you
27:4 They *s*: What is that to us?
27:6 *s*: It is not lawful to drop
27:13 Pilate *s* to him: Do you not
27:17 Pilate *s* to them: Which one
27:21 governor *s* to them: Which
27:21 to you? They *s*: Barabbas
27:22 Pilate *s* to them: What
27:22 all *s*: Let him be impaled!
27:23 He *s*: Why, what bad thing
27:25 *s* in answer: His blood come
27:43 for he *s*, I am God's Son
27:49 rest of them *s*: Let him be!
27:63 impostor *s* while yet alive
27:65 Pilate *s* to them: You have a
28:5 the angel in answer *s* to the
28:6 for he was raised up, as he *s*
28:9 Jesus met them and *s*: Good
28:10 Jesus *s* to them: Have no
28:13 *s*: Say, His disciples came
Mr 1:17 Jesus *s* to them: Come after
1:37 *s* to him: All are looking for
1:38 But he *s* to them: Let us go
1:41 *s* to him: I want to. Be made
1:44 *s* to him: See that you tell
2:5 he *s* to the paralytic: Child
2:8 Jesus . . . *s* to them: Why are
2:10 he *s* to the paralytic
2:14 he *s* to him: Be my follower
2:17 hearing this Jesus *s* to them
2:18 came and *s* to him: Why is it
2:19 Jesus *s* to them: While the
2:25 he *s* to them: Have you never
3:3 And he *s* to the man with the
3:4 he *s* to them: Is it lawful on
3:5 he *s* to the man: Stretch out
3:32 *s* to him: Look! Your mother
3:33 he *s* to them: Who are my
3:34 he *s*: See, my mother and my
4:13 *s* to them: You do not know
4:24 *s* to them: Pay attention to
4:35 he *s* to them: Let us cross to
4:38 So they woke him up and *s* to
4:39 *s* to the sea: Hush! Be quiet!
4:40 So he *s* to them: Why are you
5:7 *s*: What have I to do with you
5:9 *s* to him: My name is Legion
5:19 *s* to him: Go home to your
5:34 He *s* to her: Daughter, your
5:35 and *s*: Your daughter died!
5:36 *s* to the presiding officer of
5:39 after stepping in, he *s* to
5:41 he *s* to her: *Tal'i·tha cu'mi*
5:43 he *s* that something should be
6:2 and *s*: Where did this man get
6:10 he *s* to them: Wherever you
6:18 For John had repeatedly *s* to
6:22 The king *s* to the maiden
6:24 *s* to her mother: What should

Mr 6:24 She s: The head of John the
6:31 s to them: Come, you
6:37 he s to them: You give them
6:37 s to him: Shall we go off
6:38 s to them: How many loaves
6:38 s: Five, besides two fishes
6:41 s a blessing, and broke the
6:50 he s to them: Take courage
7:6 He s to them: Isaiah aptly
7:10 Moses s, Honor your father
7:18 he s to them: Are you also
7:20 he s: That which issues forth
7:28 she s to him: Yes, sir, and
7:29 he s to her: Because of
7:34 s to him: *Eph'pha·tha*, that
7:37 s: He has done all things
8:1 summoned the disciples and s
8:5 They s: Seven
8:12 s: Why does this generation
8:17 s to them: Why do you argue
8:19 They s to him: Twelve
8:20 And they s to him: Seven
8:21 With that he s to them
8:28 s to him: John the Baptist
8:29 s to him: You are the Christ
8:33 s: Get behind me, Satan
8:34 s to them: If anyone wants
9:5 Peter s to Jesus: Rabbi, it is
9:12 He s to them: Elijah does
9:19 In response he s to them
9:21 He s: From childhood on
9:23 Jesus s to him
9:29 he s to them: This kind
9:35 the twelve and s to them
9:36 arms around it and s to them
9:38 John s to him: Teacher, we
9:39 But Jesus s: Do not try to
10:3 s to them: What did Moses
10:4 They s: Moses allowed the
10:5 Jesus s to them: Out of
10:11 s to them: Whoever divorces
10:14 Jesus was indignant and s
10:18 Jesus s to him: Why do you
10:20 The man s to him: Teacher
10:21 and s to him: One thing is
10:23 Jesus s to his disciples
10:24 In response Jesus again s
10:26 s to him: Who, in fact, can
10:27 Jesus s: With men it is
10:29 Jesus s: Truly I say to you
10:35 s to him: Teacher, we want
10:36 He s to them: What do you
10:37 They s to him: Grant us to
10:38 But Jesus s to them: You do
10:39 They s to him: We are able
10:39 Jesus s to them: The cup
10:42 s to them: You know that
10:49 Jesus stopped and s
10:51 in answer to him Jesus s
10:51 The blind man s to him
10:52 Jesus s to him: Go, your
11:6 They s to these just as
11:6 just as Jesus had s; and they
11:14 he s to it: Let no one eat
11:21 s to him: Rabbi, see! the
11:22 Jesus s to them: Have faith
11:29 Jesus s to them: I will ask
11:33 in reply to Jesus they s
11:33 Jesus s to them: Neither am
12:7 those cultivators s among
12:14 On arrival these s to him
12:15 he s to them: Why do you
12:16 he s to them: Whose image
12:16 They s to him: Caesar's
12:17 Jesus then s: Pay back
12:24 Jesus s to them: Is not this
12:26 God s to him, I am the God
12:32 The scribe s to him
12:32 well s in line with truth
12:34 s to him: You are not far
12:36 David himself s, Jehovah
12:36 Jehovah s to my Lord: Sit at
12:43 disciples to him and s
13:1 one of his disciples s to him
13:2 Jesus s to him: Do you behold
14:2 s: Not at the festival
14:6 But Jesus s: Let her alone
14:12 his disciples s to him
14:13 s to them: Go into the city
14:16 found it just as he s to
14:18 Jesus s: Truly I say to you
14:20 He s to them: It is one of
14:22 he took a loaf, s a blessing
14:22 and s: Take it, this means
Mr 14:24 he s to them: This means
14:27 Jesus s to them: You will
14:29 Peter s to him: Even if all
14:30 Jesus s to him: Truly I say
14:32 and he s to his disciples
14:34 he s to them: My soul is
14:37 he s to Peter: Simon, are
14:41 came the third time and s
14:45 approached him and s: Rabbi!
14:48 Jesus s to them: Did you
14:61 s to him: Are you the Christ
14:62 Jesus s: I am; and you
14:63 s: What further need do we
14:67 s: You, too, were with the
15:2 In answer to him he s
15:39 he s: Certainly this man
16:6 He s to them: Stop being
Lu 1:13 angel s to him: Have no fear
1:18 Zechariah s to the angel
1:19 In reply the angel s to him
1:28 he s: Good day, highly favored
1:30 the angel s to her: Have no
1:34 But Mary s to the angel
1:35 In answer the angel s to her
1:38 Mary s: Look! Jehovah's slave
1:42 with a loud cry and s
1:46 Mary s: My soul magnifies
1:60 But its mother answered and s
1:61 they s to her: There is no one
2:10 the angel s to them: Have no
2:24 s in the law of Jehovah
2:28 and blessed God and s
2:34 but s to Mary its mother
2:48 and his mother s to him
2:49 he s to them: Why did you
3:12 they s to him: Teacher, what
3:13 He s to them: Do not demand
3:14 he s to them: Do not harass
4:3 the Devil s to him: If you are
4:6 the Devil s to him: I will
4:8 In reply Jesus s to him: It is
4:9 s to him: If you are a son of
4:12 In answer Jesus s to him
4:12 It is s, You must not put
4:23 At this he s to them
4:24 he s: Truly I tell you that
4:43 he s to them: Also to other
5:4 he s to Simon: Pull out to
5:5 But Simon in reply s
5:10 Jesus s to Simon: Stop being
5:20 he s: Man, your sins are
5:22 s in answer to them
5:24 he s to the paralyzed man
5:27 he s to him: Be my follower
5:31 In reply Jesus s to them
5:33 They s to him: The disciples
5:34 Jesus s to them: You cannot
6:2 Pharisees s: Why are you doing
6:3 But Jesus s in reply to them
6:8 yet he s to the man with the
6:9 Jesus s to them: I ask you men
6:10 he s to the man: Stretch out
7:9 and s: I tell you, Not even in
7:13 he s to her: Stop weeping
7:14 he s: Young man, I say to you
7:20 the men s: John the Baptist
7:22 in answer he s to the two
7:39 s within himself: This man
7:40 But in reply Jesus s to him
7:40 He s: Teacher, say it!
7:43 Simon s: I suppose it is the
7:43 He s to him: You judged
7:44 he turned to the woman and s
7:48 Then he s to her: Your sins
7:50 he s to the woman: Your faith
8:10 He s: To you it is granted to
8:21 In reply he s to them
8:22 s to them: Let us cross to
8:25 he s to them: Where is your
8:28 s: What have I to do with you
8:30 your name? He s: Legion
8:45 So Jesus s: Who was it that
8:45 were all denying it, Peter s
8:46 Jesus s: Someone touched me
8:48 he s to her: Daughter, your
8:52 he s: Stop weeping, for she
9:3 he s to them: Carry nothing
9:7 s by some that John had been
9:9 Herod s: John I beheaded
9:12 The twelve now came up and s
9:13 he s to them: You give them
9:13 They s: We have nothing more
9:14 But he s to his disciples
9:19 they s: John the Baptist; but
Lu 9:20 he s to them: You, though
9:20 Peter s in reply: The Christ
9:22 but s: The Son of man must
9:33 Peter s to Jesus: Instructor
9:41 Jesus s: O faithless and
9:43 he s to his disciples
9:48 s to them: Whoever receives
9:49 John s: Instructor, we saw a
9:50 But Jesus s to him: Do not
9:54 they s: Lord, do you want us
9:57 s to him: I will follow you
9:58 Jesus s to him: Foxes have
9:59 s to another: Be my follower
9:59 The man s: Permit me first
9:60 But he s to him: Let the dead
9:61 another s: I will follow you
9:62 Jesus s to him: No man that
10:18 he s to them: I began to
10:21 s: I publicly praise you
10:23 s: Happy are the eyes that
10:25 s: Teacher, by doing what
10:26 s to him: What is written
10:27 In answer he s: You must
10:28 He s to him: You answered
10:29 the man s to Jesus
10:30 Jesus s: A certain man was
10:35 s, Take care of him, and
10:37 He s: The one that acted
10:37 Jesus then s to him: Go your
10:40 she came near and s: Lord
10:41 In answer the Lord s to her
11:1 one of his disciples s to him
11:2 he s to them: Whenever you
11:5 s to them: Who of you will
11:15 s: He expels the demons by
11:17 he s to them: Every kingdom
11:27 s to him: Happy is the womb
11:28 But he s: No, rather, Happy
11:39 the Lord s to him: Now you
11:45 s to him: Teacher, in saying
11:46 he s: Woe also to you who
11:49 the wisdom of God also s
12:13 s to him: Teacher, tell my
12:14 He s to him: Man, who
12:15 he s to them: Keep your eyes
12:18 So he s, I will do this
12:20 God s to him, Unreasonable
12:22 Then he s to his disciples
12:41 Peter s: Lord, are you saying
12:42 the Lord s: Who really is
13:2 in reply he s to them: Do you
13:7 he s to the vinedresser, Here
13:8 In reply he s to him, Master
13:12 Jesus . . . s to her: Woman
13:15 the Lord answered him and s
13:17 when he s these things, all
13:20 he s: With what shall I
13:23 man s to him: Lord, are
13:23 saved few? He s to them
13:32 he s to them: Go and tell
14:5 he s to them: Who of you, if
14:15 s to him: Happy is he who
14:16 Jesus s to him: A certain
14:18 The first s to him, I bought
14:19 another s, I bought five
14:20 s, I just married a wife and
14:21 s to his slave, Go out
14:22 slave s, Master, what you
14:23 the master s to the slave
14:25 and he turned and s to them
15:11 he s: A certain man had two
15:12 the younger of them s to his
15:17 he s, How many hired men
15:21 the son s to him, Father, I
15:22 the father s to his slaves
15:27 He s to him, Your brother
15:29 In reply he s to his father
15:31 he s to him, Child, you have
16:2 s to him, What is this I hear
16:3 steward s to himself, What
16:6 He s, A hundred bath measures
16:6 He s to him, Take your
16:7 he s to another one, Now you
16:7 He s, A hundred cor measures
16:7 s to him, Take your written
16:15 he s to them: You are those
16:24 called and s, Father Abraham
16:25 Abraham s, Child, remember
16:27 he s, In that event I ask
16:29 Abraham s, They have Moses
16:30 he s, No, indeed, father
16:31 he s to him, If they do not
17:1 Then he s to his disciples
17:5 s to the Lord: Give us more

Lu 17:6 the Lord *s:* If you had faith
17:13 *s:* Jesus, Instructor, have
17:14 he got sight of them he *s*
17:17 *s:* The ten were cleansed
17:19 And he *s* to him: Rise and be
17:20 *s:* The kingdom of God is not
17:22 Then he *s* to the disciples
17:37 in response they *s* to him
17:37 Where, Lord? He *s* to them
18:4 afterward he *s* to himself
18:6 Lord *s:* Hear what the judge
18:6 judge, although unrighteous, *s*
18:19 Jesus *s* to him: Why do you
18:21 he *s:* All these I have kept
18:22 Jesus *s* to him: There is yet
18:24 *s:* How difficult a thing it
18:26 *s:* Who possibly can be saved?
18:27 He *s:* The things impossible
18:28 Peter *s:* Look! We have left
18:29 *s* to them: Truly I say to
18:31 took the twelve aside and *s*
18:34 not knowing the things *s*
18:41 He *s:* Lord, let me recover
18:42 Jesus *s* to him: Recover your
19:5 *s* to him: Zacchaeus, hurry
19:8 stood up and *s* to the Lord
19:9 Jesus *s* to him: This day
19:12 *s:* A certain man of noble
19:17 he *s* to him, Well done, good
19:19 He *s* to this one also, You
19:22 He *s* to him, Out of your own
19:24 he *s* to those standing by
19:25 they *s* to him, Lord, he has
19:28 after he had *s* these things
19:32 found it just as he *s* to
19:33 *s* to them: Why are you
19:34 They *s:* The Lord needs it
19:39 *s* to him: Teacher, rebuke
19:40 in reply he *s:* I tell you
20:3 In reply he *s* to them: I will
20:8 And Jesus *s* to them: Neither
20:13 the owner of the vineyard *s*
20:16 *s:* Never may that happen!
20:17 *s:* What, then, does this
20:23 detected their cunning and *s*
20:24 They *s:* Caesar's
20:25 He *s* to them: By all means
20:26 his answer, they *s* nothing
20:34 *s* to them: The children of
20:39 scribes *s:* Teacher, you spoke
20:41 he *s* to them: How is it they
20:42 Jehovah *s* to my Lord, Sit
20:45 he *s* to the disciples
21:3 he *s:* I tell you truthfully
21:6 he *s:* As for these things
21:8 He *s:* Look out that you are
22:9 *s* to him: Where do you want
22:10 He *s* to them: Look! When you
22:13 just as he had *s* to them
22:15 he *s* to them: I have greatly
22:17 gave thanks and *s:* Take this
22:25 he *s* to them: The kings of
22:33 he *s* to him: Lord, I am
22:34 he *s:* I tell you, Peter
22:35 also *s* to them: When I sent
22:35 anything, did you? They *s:* No!
22:36 he *s* to them: But now let
22:38 they *s:* Lord, look! here are
22:38 He *s* to them: It is enough
22:40 *s* to them: Carry on prayer
22:46 he *s* to them: Why are you
22:48 Jesus *s* to him: Judas, do
22:49 *s:* Lord, shall we strike
22:51 Jesus *s:* Let it go as far as
22:52 Jesus then *s* to the chief
22:56 and looked him over and *s*
22:58 another person seeing him *s*
22:58 But Peter *s:* Man, I am not
22:60 Peter *s:* Man, I do not know
22:61 he *s* to him: Before a cock
22:67 he *s* to them: Even if I told
22:70 *s:* Are you . . . the Son of God?
22:70 He *s* to them: You yourselves
22:71 They *s:* Why do we need
23:3 *s:* You yourself are saying it
23:4 Pilate *s* to the chief priests
23:14 and *s* to them: You brought
23:22 The third time he *s* to them
23:28 *s:* Daughters of Jerusalem
23:40 *s:* Do you not fear God at
23:43 he *s* to him: Truly I tell
23:46 *s:* Father, into your hands I
23:46 he had *s* this, he expired
24:5 men *s* to them: Why are you

Lu 24:17 He *s* to them: What are these
24:18 the one named Cleopas *s* to
24:19 he *s* to them: What things?
24:19 They *s* to him: The things
24:23 angels, who *s* he is alive
24:24 just as the women had *s*
24:25 he *s* to them: O senseless
24:32 *s* to each other: Were not
24:36 *s* to them: May you have
24:38 he *s* to them: Why are you
24:40 as he *s* this he showed them
24:41 he *s* to them: Do you have
24:44 *s* to them: These are my
24:46 he *s* to them: In this way
Joh 1:15 this was the one who *s* it
1:21 Elijah? And he *s:* I am not
1:22 they *s* to him: Who are you?
1:23 He *s:* I am a voice of
1:23 just as Isaiah the prophet *s*
1:25 questioned him and *s* to him
1:29 *s:* See, the Lamb of God that
1:30 one about whom I *s,* Behind
1:33 *s* to me, Whoever it is upon
1:36 he *s:* See, the Lamb of God!
1:38 he *s* to them: What are you
1:38 They *s* to him: Rabbi
1:39 He *s* to them: Come, and
1:40 heard what John *s* and
1:41 *s* to him: We have found the
1:42 he *s:* You are Simon the son
1:43 *s* to him: Be my follower
1:45 *s* to him: We have found the
1:46 *s* to him: Can anything good
1:46 Philip *s* to him: Come and
1:47 *s* about him: See, an
1:48 Nathanael *s* to him: How does
1:48 Jesus in answer *s* to him
1:50 Jesus in answer *s* to him
1:51 *s* to him: Most truly I say
2:3 *s* to him: They have no wine
2:4 Jesus *s* to her: What have I
2:5 mother *s* to those ministering
2:7 Jesus *s* to them: Fill the
2:8 he *s* to them: Draw some out
2:10 *s* to him: Every other man
2:16 *s* to those selling the doves
2:18 answer, the Jews *s* to him
2:19 In answer Jesus *s* to them
2:20 the Jews *s:* This temple was
2:22 and the saying that Jesus *s*
3:2 *s* to him: Rabbi, we know
3:3 In answer Jesus *s* to him
3:4 Nicodemus *s* to him: How can
3:9 In answer Nicodemus *s* to him
3:10 In answer Jesus *s* to him
3:26 they came to John and *s* to
3:27 *s:* A man cannot receive a
3:28 I *s,* I am not the Christ
4:7 *s* to her: Give me a drink
4:9 the Samaritan woman *s* to him
4:10 In answer Jesus *s* to her
4:11 She *s* to him: Sir, you have
4:13 In answer Jesus *s* to her
4:15 woman *s* to him: Sir, give
4:16 He *s* to her: Go, call your
4:17 woman *s:* I do not have a
4:17, 17 Jesus *s* to her: You *s*
4:18 This you have *s* truthfully
4:19 woman *s* to him: Sir, I
4:21 Jesus *s* to her: Believe me
4:25 The woman *s* to him: I know
4:26 Jesus *s* to her: I who am
4:27 no one *s:* What are you
4:32 he *s* to them: I have food
4:34 Jesus *s* to them: My food is
4:39 the woman who *s* in witness
4:41 on account of what he *s*
4:48 Jesus *s* to him: Unless you
4:49 attendant of the king *s* to
4:50 Jesus *s* to him: Go your way
4:52 *s* to him: Yesterday at the
4:53 hour that Jesus *s* to him
5:6 Jesus *s* to him: Do you want
5:8 Jesus *s* to him: Get up, pick
5:11 *s* to me, Pick up your cot
5:14 in the temple and *s* to him
6:5 he *s* to Philip: Where shall
6:8 Simon Peter, *s* to him
6:10 *s:* Have the men recline
6:12 he *s* to his disciples
6:20 he *s* to them: It is I; have
6:25 *s* to him: Rabbi, when did
6:26 *s:* Most truly I say to you
6:28 *s* to him: What shall we do

Joh 6:29 In answer Jesus *s* to them
6:30 *s* to him: What, then, are
6:32 Jesus *s* to them: Most truly
6:34 *s* to him: Lord, always give
6:35 Jesus *s* . . . I am the bread
6:36 But I have *s* to you, You
6:41 because he *s:* I am the bread
6:43 In answer Jesus *s* to them
6:53 Jesus *s* to them: Most truly
6:59 These things he *s* as he was
6:60 *s:* This speech is shocking
6:61 *s* to them: Does this stumble
6:65 This is why I have *s* to you
6:67 Jesus *s* to the twelve
7:3 brothers *s* to him: Pass on
7:6 Jesus *s* to them: My due time
7:16 *s:* What I teach is not mine
7:21 In answer Jesus *s* to them
7:28 teaching in the temple and *s*
7:33 Jesus *s:* I continue a little
7:35 the Jews *s* among themselves
7:36 he *s,* You will look for me
7:38 Scripture has *s,* Out from
7:39 *s* this concerning the spirit
7:42 Scripture *s* that the Christ
7:45 *s* to them: Why is it you did
7:50 Nicodemus . . . *s* to them
7:52 *s* to him: You are not also
8:13 Pharisees *s* to him: You bear
8:14 Jesus *s* to them: Even if I
8:21 he *s* to them again: I am
8:24 I *s* to you, You will die
8:25 Jesus *s* to them: Why am I
8:28 Jesus *s:* When once you have
8:39 they *s* to him: Our father is
8:39 Jesus *s* to them: If you are
8:41 They *s* to him: We were not
8:42 Jesus *s* to them: If God were
8:48 In answer the Jews *s* to him
8:52 Jews *s* to him: Now we do
8:55 if I *s* I do not know him I
8:57 Jews *s* to him: You are not
8:58 Jesus *s* to them: Most truly
9:6 *s* these things, he spit on the
9:7 *s* to him: Go wash in the
9:11 *s* to me, Go to Siloam and
9:12 *s* to him: Where is that man?
9:12 He *s:* I do not know
9:15 *s* to them: He put a clay
9:17 *s* to the blind man again
9:17 The man *s:* He is a prophet
9:20 *s:* We know that this is our
9:22 His parents *s* these things
9:23 *s:* He is of age. Question
9:24 *s* to him: Give glory to God
9:26 *s* to him: What did he do to
9:28 *s:* You are a disciple of that
9:30 *s* to them: This certainly is
9:34 In answer they *s* to him
9:35 *s:* Are you putting faith in
9:37 Jesus *s* to him: You have
9:38 *s:* I do put faith in him
9:39 Jesus *s:* For this judgment
9:40 *s* to him: We are not blind
9:41 Jesus *s* to them: If you were
10:7 Jesus *s* again: Most truly I
10:34 Law, I *s:* You are gods
10:36 I *s,* I am God's Son
10:41 John *s* about this man were
11:4 *s:* This sickness is not with
11:7 he *s* to the disciples: Let
11:8 disciples *s* to him: Rabbi
11:11 He *s* these things, and
11:11 *s* to them: Lazarus our
11:12 disciples *s* to him: Lord
11:14 Jesus *s* to them outspokenly
11:16 *s* to his fellow disciples
11:21 Martha therefore *s* to Jesus
11:23 Jesus *s* to her: Your
11:24 Martha *s* to him: I know
11:25 Jesus *s* to her: I am the
11:27 She *s* to him: Yes, Lord
11:28 when she had *s* this, she
11:34 *s:* Where have you laid him?
11:34 They *s* to him: Lord, come
11:37 *s:* Was not this man that
11:39 Jesus *s:* Take the stone
11:39 *s* to him: Lord, by now he
11:40 Jesus *s* to her: Did I not
11:41 *s:* Father, I thank you that
11:43 *s* these things, he cried out
11:44 Jesus *s* to them: Loose him
11:49 *s* to them: You do not know
12:4 was about to betray him, *s*

Joh 12:6 *s* this, though, not because
12:7 Jesus *s:* Let her alone, that
12:19 Pharisees *s* among
12:30 Jesus *s:* This voice has
12:35 Jesus therefore *s* to them
12:38 *s:* Jehovah, who has put
12:39 is that again Isaiah *s*
12:41 Isaiah *s* these things
12:44 *s:* He that puts faith in me
13:6 *s* to him: Lord, are you
13:7 Jesus *s* to him: What I am
13:8 Peter *s* to him: You will
13:9 Simon Peter *s* to him
13:10 Jesus *s* to him: He that has
13:11 *s:* Not all of you are clean
13:12 *s* to them: Do you know
13:21 *s:* Most truly I say to you
13:24 *s* to him: Tell who it is
13:25 *s* to him: Lord, who is it?
13:27 Jesus, therefore, *s* to him
13:28 purpose he *s* this to him
13:31 Jesus *s:* Now the Son of man
13:33 just as I *s* to the Jews
13:36 Simon Peter *s* to him: Lord
13:37 Peter *s* to him: Lord, why
14:5 Thomas *s* to him: Lord, we
14:6 Jesus *s* to him: I am the
14:8 Philip *s* to him: Lord, show
14:9 Jesus *s* to him: Have I been
14:22 *s* to him: Lord, what has
14:23 Jesus *s* . . . If anyone loves
14:28 I *s* to you, I am going away
15:20 in mind the word I *s* to you
16:15 *s* he receives from what is
16:17 disciples *s* to one another
16:19 *s* to them: Are you
16:19 I *s*, In a little while you
16:29 His disciples *s:* See! Now
16:33 I have *s* these things to you
17:1 *s:* Father, the hour has come
18:1 *s* these things, Jesus went
18:4 *s* to them: Whom are you
18:5 *s* to them: I am he
18:6 *s* to them: I am he, they
18:7 They *s:* Jesus the Nazarene
18:9 *s:* Of those whom you have
18:11 Jesus, however, *s* to Peter
18:17 *s* to Peter: You are not also
18:17 He *s:* I am not
18:21 See! These know what I *s*
18:22 After he *s* these things
18:22 *s:* Is that the way you
18:25 *s* to him: You are not also
18:25 denied it and *s:* I am not
18:26 *s:* I saw you in the garden
18:29 *s:* What accusation do you
18:30 *s* to him: If this man were
18:31 Pilate *s* to them: Take him
18:31 Jews *s* to him: It is not
18:32 *s* to signify what sort of
18:33 *s* to him: Are you the king
18:37 Pilate *s* to him: Well, then
18:38 *s* to him: What is truth?
18:38 *s* to them: I find no fault
19:4 *s* to them: See! I bring him
19:5 *s* to them: Look! The man!
19:6 Pilate *s* to them: Take him
19:9 *s* to Jesus: Where are you
19:10 Pilate *s* to him: Are you
19:14 *s* to the Jews: See! Your
19:15 Pilate *s* . . . Shall I impale
19:21 but that he *s*, I am King of the
19:24 *s* to one another: Let us
19:26 *s* to his mother: Woman
19:27 *s* to the disciple: See!
19:28 he *s:* I am thirsty
19:30 Jesus *s:* It has been
20:2 *s* to them: They have taken
20:13 *s* to her: Woman, why are
20:13 She *s* to them: They have
20:15 Jesus *s* to her: Woman, why
20:15 *s* to him: Sir, if you have
20:16 Jesus *s* to her: Mary! Upon
20:16 she *s* to him, in Hebrew
20:17 Jesus *s* to her: Stop
20:18 he *s* these things to her
20:19 *s* to them: May you have
20:20 *s* this he showed them both
20:21 Jesus, therefore, *s* to them
20:22 *s* this he blew upon them
20:22 *s* to them: Receive holy
20:25 *s* to them: Unless I see
20:26 *s:* May you have peace
20:27 *s* to Thomas: Put your

Joh 20:28 Thomas *s* to him: My Lord
20:29 Jesus *s* to him: Because
21:3 Simon Peter *s* to them
21:3 They *s* to him: We also are
21:5 Jesus *s* to them: Young
21:6 He *s* to them: Cast the net
21:7 *s* to Peter: It is the Lord!
21:10 Jesus *s* to them: Bring some
21:12 Jesus *s* to them: Come, take
21:15 Jesus *s* to Simon Peter
21:15 *s* to him: Yes, Lord, you
21:15 He *s* to him: Feed my lambs
21:16 *s* to him, a second time
21:16 *s* to him: Yes, Lord, you
21:16 *s* to him: Shepherd my
21:17 *s* to him the third time
21:17 *s* to him the third time
21:17 *s* to him: Lord, you know
21:17 Jesus *s* to him: Feed my
21:19 *s* to signify by what sort
21:19 when he had *s* this, he
21:19 *s* to him: Continue
21:20 *s:* Lord, who is the one
21:21 Peter *s* to Jesus: Lord
21:22 Jesus *s* to him: If it is
Ac 1:7 He *s* to them: It does not
1:9 after he had *s* these things
1:11 *s:* Men of Galilee, why do
1:15 Peter rose up . . . and *s*
1:24 *s:* You, O Jehovah, who know
2:16 *s* through the prophet Joel
2:34 Jehovah *s* to my Lord: Sit at
2:37 *s* to Peter and the rest of
2:38 Peter *s* to them: Repent, and
3:4 and *s:* Take a look at us
3:6 Peter *s:* Silver and gold I do
3:12 Peter saw this, he *s* to the
3:22 Moses *s*, Jehovah God will
4:8 *s* to them: Rulers of the
4:19 Peter and John *s* to them
4:23 the older men had *s* to them
4:24 *s:* Sovereign Lord, you are
4:25 holy spirit *s* by the mouth
5:3 Peter *s:* Ananias, why has
5:8 Peter *s* to her: Tell me, did
5:8 She *s:* Yes, for so much
5:9 Peter *s* to her: Why was it
5:19 brought them out and *s*
5:28 *s:* We positively ordered you
5:29 apostles *s:* We must obey God
5:35 *s* to them: Men of Israel
6:2 *s:* It is not pleasing for us
6:13 *s:* This man does not stop
7:1 priest *s:* Are these things so?
7:2 *s:* Men, brothers and fathers
7:3 *s* to him, Go out from your
7:7 I shall judge, God *s*, and
7:33 Jehovah *s* to him, Take the
7:37 Moses that *s* to the sons of
7:56 *s:* Look! I behold the heavens
7:59 *s:* Lord Jesus, receive my
8:6 things *s* by Philip while they
8:20 Peter *s* to him: May your
8:24 Simon *s:* You men, make
8:24 things you have *s* may come
8:29 spirit *s* to Philip: Approach
8:30 *s:* Do you actually know
8:31 *s:* Really, how could I ever
8:34 eunuch *s* to Philip: I beg you
8:36 eunuch *s:* Look! A body of
9:5 He *s:* Who are you, Lord?
9:5 He *s:* I am Jesus, whom you
9:10 the Lord *s* to him in a vision
9:10 He *s:* Here I am, Lord
9:11 Lord *s* to him: Rise, go to
9:15 Lord *s* to him: Be on your
9:17 *s:* Saul, brother, the Lord
9:34 Peter *s* to him: Aeneas, Jesus
9:40 he *s:* Tabitha, rise!
10:4 *s:* What is it, Lord?
10:4 *s* to him: Your prayers and
10:14 Peter *s:* Not at all, Lord
10:19 spirit *s:* Look! Three men
10:21 *s:* Look! I am the one you
10:22 They *s:* Cornelius, an army
10:28 *s* to them: You well know
10:30 Cornelius *s:* Four days ago
10:31 *s*, Cornelius, your prayer
10:34 *s:* For a certainty I perceive
11:8 I *s*, Not at all, Lord, because
12:8 angel *s* to him: Gird yourself
12:8 *s* to him: Put your outer
12:11 *s:* Now I actually know that
12:15 They *s* to her: You are mad

Ac 12:17 *s:* Report these things to
13:2 holy spirit *s:* Of all persons
13:10 *s:* O man full of every sort
13:16 *s:* Men, Israelites and you
13:22 *s*, I have found David the
13:40 what is *s* in the Prophets
13:46 Paul and Barnabas *s:* It was
14:10 *s* with a loud voice: Stand
15:5 and *s:* It is necessary to
15:7 Peter rose and *s* to them: Men
15:36 Paul *s* to Barnabas: Above all
16:15 she *s* with entreaty: If you
16:18 turned and *s* to the spirit
16:20 *s:* These men are disturbing
16:30 *s:* Sirs, what must I do to
16:31 *s:* Believe on the Lord Jesus
16:37 Paul *s* to them: They flogged
17:22 *s:* Men of Athens, I behold
17:28 the poets among you have *s*
17:32 others *s:* We will hear you
18:6 *s* to them: Let your blood be
18:9 *s* to Paul through a vision
18:14 Gallio *s* to the Jews: If it
18:18 Paul *s* good-bye to the
18:21 but *s* good-bye and told them
19:2 he *s* to them: Did you receive
19:2 *s* to him: Why, we have never
19:3 he *s:* In what, then, were you
19:3 They *s:* In John's baptism
19:4 Paul *s:* John baptized with
19:15 answer the wicked spirit *s*
19:25 *s:* Men, you well know that
19:35 he *s:* Men of Ephesus, who
19:41 when he had *s* these things
20:10 *s:* Stop raising a clamor
20:18 he *s* to them: You well know
20:35 *s*, There is more happiness
20:36 when he had *s* these things
21:6 and *s* good-bye to one another
21:11 *s:* Thus says the holy spirit
21:20 they *s* to him: You behold
21:37 Paul *s* to the military
21:37 He *s:* Can you speak Greek?
21:39 Paul *s:* I am, in fact, a Jew
22:2 all the more silent, and he *s*
22:8 he *s* to me, I am Jesus the
22:10 I *s*, What shall I do, Lord?
22:10 The Lord *s* to me, Rise, go
22:13 he *s* to me, Saul, brother
22:14 He *s*, The God of our
22:19 I *s*, Lord, they themselves
22:21 he *s* to me, Get on your way
22:24 and *s* he should be examined
22:25 Paul *s* to the army officer
22:27 *s* to him . . . Are you a Roman?
22:27 Are you a Roman? He *s:* Yes
22:28 Paul *s:* But I was even born
23:1 at the Sanhedrin Paul *s:* Men
23:3 Paul *s* to him: God is going
23:4 *s:* Are you reviling the high
23:5 Paul *s:* Brothers, I did not
23:7 he *s* this, a dissension arose
23:11 the Lord stood by him and *s*
23:14 *s:* We have solemnly bound
23:17 *s:* Lead this young man off
23:18 and *s:* The prisoner Paul
23:20 He *s:* The Jews have agreed
23:23 *s:* Get two hundred soldiers
23:35 he *s*, when your accusers
24:22 to put the men off and *s*
25:5 he *s*, come down with me and
25:8 But Paul *s* in defense
25:9 *s* in reply to Paul: Do you
25:10 But Paul *s:* I am standing
25:22 Agrippa *s* to Festus
25:22 Tomorrow, he *s*, you shall
25:24 Festus *s:* King Agrippa and
26:1 Agrippa *s* to Paul: You are
26:15 I *s*, Who are you, Lord?
26:15 Lord *s*, I am Jesus, whom
26:24 Festus *s* in a loud voice
26:25 Paul *s:* I am not going mad
26:28 Agrippa *s* to Paul: In a short
26:29 Paul *s:* I could wish to God
26:32 Agrippa *s* to Festus: This
27:11 than the things *s* by Paul
27:21 *s:* Men, you certainly ought
27:31 Paul *s* to the army officer
27:35 *s* this, he also took a loaf
28:21 They *s* to him: Neither have
28:24 to believe the things *s*
Ro 4:18 *s:* So your seed will be
7:7 Law had not *s:* You must not
9:12 it was *s* to her: The older

Ro 9:26 s to them, You are not my
9:29 as Isaiah had s aforetime
1Co 11:24 broke it and s: This means
2Co 1:20 the Amen s to God for glory
2:13 but I s good-bye to them and
4:6 God is he who s: Let the
6:16 God s: I shall reside among
7:3 s before that you are in our
12:9 s to me: My undeserved
13:2 I have s previously and, as
Ga 1:9 As we have s above, I also
2:14 I s to Cephas before them all
Tit 1:12 s: Cretans are always liars
Heb 1:13 has he ever s: Sit at my
3:10 s, They always go astray in
3:15 s: Today if you people listen
4:3 s: So I swore in my anger
4:4 he has s of the seventh day
4:7 just as it has been s above
7:11 not s to be according to the
7:13 whom these things are s has
7:17 s: You are a priest forever
7:21 sworn by the One who s
10:7 I s, Look! I am come
10:10 By the s will we have been
10:15 to us, for after it has s
10:30 s: Vengeance is mine; I
11:18 s to him: What will be
12:21 Moses s: I am fearful and
13:5 s: I will by no means leave
Jas 2:11 s: You must not commit
2:11 s also: You must not murder
Jude 9 s: May Jehovah rebuke you
14 s: Look! Jehovah came with
Re 1:17 s: Do not be fearful. I am
7:13 elders s to me: These who are
7:14 I s to him: My lord, you are
7:14 And he s to me: These are the
10:9 he s to me: Take it and eat
11:1 rod was given me as he s
17:7 angel s to me: Why is it you
18:18 s, What city is like the
18:19 s, Too bad, too bad—the
19:1 They s: Praise Jah, you people!
19:3 they s: Praise Jah, you
19:4 s: Amen! Praise Jah, you
19:5 s: Be praising our God, all
19:6 They s: Praise Jah, you
19:17 s to all the birds that fly
21:5 s: Look! I am making all
21:6 s to me: They have come to
21:9 s: Come here, I will show
22:6 he s to me: These words are

Sail
Isa 33:23 they have not spread a s
Eze 27:7 for it to serve as your s
Lu 8:22 of the lake. So they set s
Ac 18:18 to s away for Syria, and
20:3 was about to set s for Syria
20:13 and set s to Assos, where we
20:16 had decided to s past Ephesus
27:1 for us to s away to Italy
27:2 s to places along the coast
27:2 we set s, there being with
27:12 setting s from there, to
28:10 when we were setting s
28:11 we set s in a boat from

Sailed
Ac 13:4 there they s away to Cyprus
14:26 s off for Antioch, where
15:39 along and s away to Cyprus
21:2 we went aboard and s away
21:3 s on to Syria, and landed at
27:4 s under the shelter of Cyprus
27:7 s under the shelter of Crete

Sailing
Lu 8:23 as they were s he fell asleep
Ac 20:15 and, s away from there the
27:6 that was s for Italy, and he
27:7 s on slowly quite a number
27:24 given . . . those s with you

Sailors
Eze 27:8 in you; they were your s
27:27 your mariners and your s
27:28 the outcry of your s
27:29 all the s of the sea
Ac 27:27 s began to suspect they
27:30 s began seeking to escape
Re 18:17 s and all those who make a

Sake
Ge 18:24 s of the fifty righteous who
Ex 9:16 for the s of showing you my
20:20 for the s of putting you to
Le 19:16 for the s of slandering
De 30:6 for the s of your life
1Sa 1:6 for the s of making her feel
12:22 for the s of his great name
2Sa 5:12 the s of his people Israel
7:21 For the s of your word and in
9:1 for the s of Jonathan
9:7 s of Jonathan your father
10:3 s of searching through the
12:21 s of the child while alive
12:25 for the s of Jehovah
14:20 s of altering the face of
18:5 Deal gently for my s with
1Ki 11:12 the s of David your father
11:13 the s of David my servant
11:13 and for the s of Jerusalem
11:32 the s of my servant David
11:32 for the s of Jerusalem
11:34 the s of David my servant
2Ki 4:24 Do not hold back for my s
8:19 the s of David his servant
13:23 the s of his covenant with
19:34 to save it for my own s
19:34 the s of David my servant
20:6 this city for my own s
20:6 the s of David my servant
1Ch 17:19 for the s of your servant
19:3 the s of making a thorough
2Ch 21:7 s of the covenant that he had
25:16 Quit for your own s
35:21 Refrain for your own s
Job 18:4 For your s will the earth be
Ps 6:4 Save me for the s of your
16:2 goodness is, not for your s
23:3 for his name's s
25:7 For the s of your goodness
25:11 For your name's s, O Jehovah
31:3 for the s of your name you
44:22 But for your s we have been
44:26 s of your loving-kindness
79:9 s of the glory of your name
106:8 for the s of his name
109:21 for the s of your name
122:8 s of my brothers and my
122:9 s of the house of Jehovah
143:11 s of your name, O Jehovah
Isa 37:35 to save it for my own s and
37:35 the s of David my servant
42:21 the s of his righteousness
43:25 for my own s, and your sins
45:4 the s of my servant Jacob
48:9 for the s of my name I shall
48:11, 11 my own s, for my own s
55:5 for the s of Jehovah your
62:1 For the s of Zion I shall not
62:1 for the s of Jerusalem I
63:17 for the s of your servants
65:8 for the s of my servants
Jer 14:7 act for the s of your name
14:21 for the s of your name
Eze 20:9 for the s of my own name
20:14 for the s of my own name
20:22 for the s of my own name
20:44 for the s of my name
23:21 for the s of the breasts of
36:5 the s of its pasture ground
Da 9:17 for the s of Jehovah
9:19 Do not delay, for your own s
Mt 5:10 for righteousness' s, since
5:11 thing against you for my s
10:18 for my s, for a witness to
10:39 that loses his soul for my s
16:25 loses his soul for my s
19:29 for the s of my name will
Mr 2:27 sabbath . . . for the s of man
2:27 man for the s of the sabbath
8:35 loses his soul for the s of
10:29 children or fields for my s
10:29 for the s of the good news
13:9 for my s, for a witness to
Lu 6:22 for the s of the Son of man
9:24 loses his soul for my s
18:29 for the s of the kingdom of
21:12 for the s of my name
Joh 12:30 not for my s, but for your
Ro 4:23 however, not for his s only
4:24 s of us to whom it is
4:25 for the s of our trespasses
4:25 s of declaring us righteous
8:36 For your s we are being put
11:28 the s of their forefathers
14:20 just for the s of food
1Co 8:11 for whose s Christ died
9:23 for the s of the good news
11:9 for the s of the woman, but
11:9 woman for the s of the man
2Co 4:5 as your slaves for Jesus' s
4:11 death for Jesus' s, that
Php 2:13 the s of his good pleasure
1Ti 5:23 wine for the s of your
2Ti 1:8 a prisoner for his s, but
2:10 for the s of the chosen ones
Tit 1:11 for the s of dishonest gain
Phm 1 prisoner for the s of Christ
9 a prisoner for the s of Christ
13 for the s of the good news
Heb 2:10 one for whose s all things
1Pe 1:20 the times for the s of you
2:13 For the Lord's s subject
3:14 for the s of righteousness
1Jo 2:12 for the s of his name
3:12 And for the s of what did
Jude 16 the s of their own benefit
Re 2:3 borne up for my name's s and

Sakes
Jg 21:22 Do us a favor for their s
1Sa 7:8 Do not keep silent for our s
Isa 2:22 For your own s, hold off
43:14 For your s I will send to
Eze 36:22 Not for your s am I doing it
36:32 Not for your s am I doing
Joh 12:30 my sake, but for your s
Ro 11:28 they are enemies for your s
1Co 9:9 altogether for our s he says
9:10 for our s it was written
2Co 2:10 for your s in Christ's sight
4:15 all things are for your s
8:9 he became poor for your s
1Th 1:5 we became to you for your s

Sakkuth
Am 5:26 carry S your king and Kaiwan

Salamis
Ac 13:5 in S they began publishing

Sale
Le 25:27 man to whom he made the s
25:29 year from the time of his s
25:50 the money of his s must
Am 8:5 and we may offer grain for s

Salecah
De 3:10 Bashan as far as S and Edrei
Jos 12:5 and in S and in all Bashan
13:11 and all Bashan as far as S
1Ch 5:11 land of Bashan as far as S

Salem
Ge 14:18 Melchizedek king of S
Ps 76:2 his covert proves to be in S
Heb 7:1 Melchizedek, king of S
7:2 and is then also king of S

Sales
Ne 13:16 making s on the sabbath to
Eze 26:12 and plunder your s goods
28:5 by your s goods, you have
28:16 abundance of your s goods
28:18 injustice of your s goods

Salim
Joh 3:23 baptizing in Aenon near S

Saliva
1Sa 21:13 s run down upon his beard
Job 7:19 alone until I swallow my s
Joh 9:6 and made a clay with the s

Sallai
Ne 11:8 Gabbai and S, nine hundred and
12:20 for S, Kallai; for Amok

Sallied
1Sa 7:11 Israel s forth from Mizpah

Sallu
1Ch 9:7 of the sons of Benjamin, S
Ne 11:7 S the son of Meshullam the
12:7 S, Amok, Hilkiah, Jedaiah

Sally
1Sa 13:17 pillagers would s forth
13:23 Philistines would s forth
2Sa 11:1 the time that kings s forth
1Ch 20:1 time that kings s forth

Sallying
1Sa 19:8 David went s forth and

Salma
1Ch 2:11 became father to S
2:11 S, in turn, became father to

1Ch 2:51 *S* the father of Bethlehem
2:54 sons of *S* were Bethlehem

Salmai
Ezr 2:46 the sons of *S*
Ne 7:48 sons of Hagabah, the sons of *S*

Salmon
Ru 4:20 Nahshon became father to *S*
4:21 and *S* became father to Boaz
Mt 1:4 Nahshon became father to *S*
1:5 *S* became father to Boaz by
Lu 3:32 son of Boaz, son of *S*

Salmone
Ac 27:7 the shelter of Crete at *S*

Salome
Mr 15:40 Mary . . . and *S*
16:1 the mother of James, and *S*

Salt
Ge 14:3 Low Plain of Siddim . . . *S* Sea
19:26 and she became a pillar of *s*
Le 2:13 you will season with *s*
2:13 *s* of the covenant of your God
2:13 of yours you will present *s*
Nu 18:19 covenant of *s* before Jehovah
34:3 the extremity of the *S* Sea
34:12 must prove to be the *S* Sea
De 3:17 the *S* Sea, at the base of the
29:23 sulphur and *s* and burning, so
Jos 3:16 the Arabah, the *S* Sea, were
12:3 sea of the Arabah, the *S* Sea
15:2 extremity of the *S* Sea
15:5 boundary was the *S* Sea
15:62 the City of *S* and En-gedi
18:19 northern bay of the *S* Sea
Jg 9:45 and sowed it with *s*
2Sa 8:13 Edomites in the Valley of *S*
2Ki 2:20 new bowl and put *s* in it
2:21 water and threw *s* in it and
14:7 Edomites in the Valley of *S*
1Ch 18:12 Edomites in the Valley of *S*
2Ch 13:5 his sons, by a covenant of *s*
25:11 go to the Valley of *S*; and
Ezr 4:14 do eat the *s* of the palace
6:9 wheat, *s*, wine and oil, just
7:22 oil, and *s* without limit
Job 6:6 things be eaten without *s*
30:4 were plucking the *s* herb
39:6 places the *s* country
Ps 60:*super* Edom in the Valley of *S*
107:34 Fruitful land into *s* country
Jer 17:6 in a *s* country that is not
Eze 16:4 with *s* you had not at all
43:24 priests must throw *s* upon
47:11 To *s* they will certainly
Zep 2:9 and a *s* pit, and a desolate
Mt 5:13 You are the *s* of the earth
5:13 if the *s* loses its strength
Mr 9:50 *S* is fine; but if ever the
9:50 ever the *s* loses its strength
9:50 Have *s* in yourselves, and
Lu 14:34 *S*, to be sure, is fine
14:34 *s* loses its strength, with
Col 4:6 graciousness, seasoned with *s*
Jas 3:12 Neither can *s* water produce

Salted
Ex 30:35 *s*, pure, something holy
Mr 9:49 everyone must be *s* with fire

Saltness
Mt 5:13 how will its *s* be restored?

Salu
Nu 25:14 *S*, a chieftain of a paternal

Salvation
Ge 49:18 for *s* from you, O Jehovah
Ex 14:13 see the *s* of Jehovah, which
15:2 Jah, since he serves for my *s*
De 32:15 despised the Rock of his *s*
33:29 people enjoying *s* in Jehovah
Jg 15:18 gave this great *s* into the
1Sa 2:1 I do rejoice in the *s* from
11:9 Tomorrow *s* will take place
11:13 Jehovah has performed *s* in
14:45 this great *s* in Israel
19:5 a great *s* for all Israel
25:26 own hand come to your *s*
25:31 come to his *s*
25:33 my own hand come to my *s*
2Sa 10:11 must serve as a *s* for me
19:2 *s* on that day came to be an
22:3 my horn of *s*, my secure
22:36 give me your shield of *s*
22:47 the rock of my *s* be exalted
22:51 great acts of *s* for his king
23:5 all my *s* and all my delight
23:10 Jehovah performed a great *s*
23:12 Jehovah performed a great *s*
2Ki 5:1 Jehovah had given *s* to Syria
13:17 Jehovah's arrow of *s*, even
13:17 arrow of *s* against Syria
1Ch 11:14 saved with a great *s*
16:23 Announce . . . the *s* he gives
16:35 Save us, O God of our *s*
18:6 Jehovah kept giving *s* to
19:12 also serve as a *s* for me
2Ch 6:41 be clothed with *s*, and let
20:17 see the *s* of Jehovah in your
Job 5:4 His sons remain far from *s*
5:11 who are sad are high up in *s*
13:16 He would also be my *s*, For
30:15 my *s* has passed away
Ps 3:2 There is no *s* for him by God
3:8 *S* belongs to Jehovah
9:14 I may be joyful in your *s*
13:5 my heart be joyful in your *s*
14:7 there were the *s* of Israel
18:2 My shield and my horn of *s*
18:35 give me your shield of *s*
18:46 the God of my *s* be exalted
18:50 great acts of *s* for his king
20:5 cry out . . . because of your *s*
21:1 in your *s* how very joyful he
21:5 His glory is great in your *s*
24:5 from his God of *s*
25:5 For you are my God of *s*
27:1 Jehovah is my light and my *s*
27:9 not leave me, O my God of *s*
28:8 the grand *s* of his anointed
33:17 horse is a deception for *s*
35:3 Say to my soul: I am your *s*
35:9 Let it exult in his *s*
37:39 the *s* of the righteous ones
38:22 O Jehovah my *s*
40:10 your *s* I have declared
40:16 who are loving *s* by you
42:5 the grand *s* of my person
42:11 laud him as the grand *s* of
43:5 laud him as the grand *s* of my
44:3 was not what brought them *s*
44:4 Command grand *s* for Jacob
50:23 cause him to see *s* by God
51:12 the exultation of *s* by you
51:14 O God the God of my *s*, That
53:6 the grand *s* of Israel
60:11 As *s* by earthling man is
62:1 From him my *s* is
62:2 he is my rock and my *s*, my
62:6 he is my rock and my *s*, my
62:7 Upon God are my *s* and my
65:5 answer us, O God of our *s*
67:2 Your *s* even among all the
68:19 The true God of our *s*. *Se'lah*
69:13 with the truth of *s* by you
69:29 your own *s*, O God, protect
70:4 those loving your *s*
71:15 All day long your *s*
74:12 One performing grand *s* in
78:22 did not trust in *s* by him
79:9 Help us, O God of our *s*
80:2 And do come to our *s*
85:4 us back, O God of our *s*
85:7 your *s* may you give to us
85:9 *s* is near to those fearing
88:1 Jehovah, the God of my *s*
89:26 God and the Rock of my *s*
91:16 cause him to see *s* by me
95:1 in triumph to our Rock of *s*
96:2 the good news of *s* by him
98:1 arm, has gained *s* for him
98:2 Jehovah has made his *s* known
98:3 have seen the *s* by our God
106:4 take care of me with your *s*
108:12 *s* by earthling man is
116:13 cup of grand *s* I shall take
118:14 And to me he becomes *s*
118:15 *s* Is in the tents of the
118:21 And you came to be my *s*
119:41 *s* according to your saying
119:81 your *s* my soul has pined
119:123 have pined away for your *s*
119:155 *S* is far away from the
119:166 I have hoped for your *s*
119:174 I have longed for your *s*
132:16 I shall clothe with *s*
140:7 the strength of my *s*
144:10 The One giving *s* to kings
Ps 146:3 man, to whom no *s* belongs
149:4 the meek ones with *s*
Pr 11:14 *s* in the multitude of
21:31 but *s* belongs to Jehovah
24:6 of counselors there is *s*
Isa 12:2 God is my *s*. I shall trust
12:2 he came to be the *s* of me
12:3 out of the springs of *s*
17:10 forgotten the God of your *s*
25:9 and rejoice in the *s* by him
26:1 *s* itself for walls and
26:18 real *s* do we accomplish as
33:2 *s* in the time of distress
45:8 let it be fruitful with *s*
45:17 a *s* for times indefinite
46:13 my own *s* will not be late
46:13 give in Zion *s*, to Israel
49:6 my *s* may come to be to the
49:8 in a day of *s* I have helped
51:5 My *s* will certainly go forth
51:6 as for my *s*, it will prove
51:8 *s* to unnumbered generations
52:7 the one publishing *s*, the one
52:10 must see the *s* of our God
56:1 my *s* is at hand to come in
59:11 *s*, but it has stayed far
59:17 helmet of *s* upon his head
60:18 call your own walls *S* and
61:10 with the garments of *s*
62:1 her *s* like a torch that burns
62:11 Look! Your *s* is coming
63:5 So my arm furnished me *s*
Jer 3:23 our God is the *s* of Israel
11:12 bring no *s* to them in the
La 3:26 wait . . . for the *s* of Jehovah
4:17 a nation that can bring no *s*
Jon 2:9 *S* belongs to Jehovah
Mic 7:7 the God of my *s*. My God will
Hab 3:8 your chariots were *s*
3:13 for the *s* of your people
3:18 joyful in the God of my *s*
Lu 1:69 raised up a horn of *s* for us
1:71 *s* from our enemies and from
1:77 knowledge of *s* to his people
19:9 *s* has come to this house
Joh 4:22 *s* originates with the Jews
Ac 4:12 is no *s* in anyone else, for
7:25 God was giving them *s* by
13:26 word of this *s* has been sent
13:47 for you to be a *s* to the
16:17 publishing . . . the way of *s*
Ro 1:16 God's power for *s* to everyone
10:1 supplication . . . for their *s*
10:10 public declaration for *s*
11:11 *s* to people of the nations
13:11 *s* is nearer than at the
2Co 1:6 it is for your comfort and *s*
6:2 in a day of *s* I helped you
6:2 Now is the day of *s*
7:10 makes for repentance to *s*
Eph 1:13 the good news about your *s*
6:17 accept the helmet of *s*, and
Php 1:19 this will result in my *s*
1:28 but of *s* for you; and this
2:12 working out your own *s* with
1Th 5:8 as a helmet the hope of *s*
5:9 *s* through our Lord Jesus
2Th 2:13 *s* by sanctifying you with
2Ti 2:10 *s* that is in union with
3:15 able to make you wise for *s*
Tit 2:11 brings *s* to all sorts of men
Heb 1:14 who are going to inherit *s*
2:3 a *s* of such greatness in that
2:10 the Chief Agent of their *s*
5:9 responsible for everlasting *s*
6:9 and things accompanied with *s*
9:28 looking for him for their *s*
1Pe 1:5 a *s* ready to be revealed in
1:9 end of your faith, the *s* of
1:10 Concerning this very *s* a
2:2 through it you may grow to *s*
2Pe 3:15 patience of our Lord as *s*
Jude 3 about the *s* we hold in common
Re 7:10 *S* we owe to our God, who is
12:10 come to pass the *s* and the
19:1 The *s* and the glory and the

Salvations
Isa 33:6 prove to be a wealth of *s*

Samaria
1Ki 13:32 the cities of *S* will take
16:24 buy the mountain of *S* from
16:24 master of the mountain, *S*
16:28 and was buried in *S*

Samaritan

Samaritans

Same

Isa 60:13 the cypress at the *s* time
65:7 forefathers at the *s* time
65:8 the *s* way that the new wine
Jer 6:11 young men at the *s* time
6:12 and the wives at the *s* time
10:8 at one and the *s* time they
13:9 In the *s* way I shall bring
13:14 the sons, at the *s* time
19:11 the *s* way I shall break
48:7 his princes at the *s* time
50:18 *s* way that I turned my
52:22 pillar had just the *s* as
La 1:20 the house it is the *s* as death
Eze 10:15 *s* living creature that I had
14:10 just the *s* as the error of
20:31 At the *s* time shall I
21:26 This will not be the *s*
35:14 *s* time that all the earth
35:15 *s* thing I shall make of you
38:17 Are you the *s* one of whom
40:1 *s* day the hand of Jehovah
40:10 were of the *s* measurement
40:10 were of the *s* measurement
40:22 the *s* measurement as those
40:24 the *s* measurements as these
40:28 the *s* measurements as these
40:29 the *s* measurements as these
40:32 the *s* measurements as these
40:33 the *s* measurements as these
40:35 the *s* measurements as these
43:22 *s* as they purified it from
45:25 *s* as these for the seven
45:25 *s* as the sin offering, as
46:22 had the *s* measurement
47:14 one the *s* as his brother
Da 1:10 children who are of the *s* age
3:6 *s* moment be thrown into the
3:7 *s* time as all the peoples were
3:8 that *s* time certain Chaldeans
3:15 *s* moment you will be thrown
4:36 the *s* time my understanding
11:29 last the *s* as at the first
Ho 4:9 people the *s* as for the priest
11:2 To that *s* extent they went
11:8 at the *s* time my compassions
Am 2:7 gone to the *s* girl, for the
Mt 5:46 tax collectors doing the *s*
5:47 the nations doing the *s* thing
6:7 do not say the *s* things over
11:19 All the *s*, wisdom is proved
12:26 *s* way, if Satan expels Satan
12:50 the *s* is my brother, and
20:14 give to this last one the *s*
21:30 the second, he said the *s*
21:36 but they did the *s* to these
22:26 *s* way also with the second
25:17 In the *s* way the one that
26:35 disciples also said the *s*
26:44 saying once more the *s* word
27:44 the *s* way even the robbers
Mr 12:21 and the third the *s* way
14:31 others began saying the *s*
14:39 prayed, saying the *s* word
Lu 2:8 in that *s* country shepherds
3:11 has things to eat do the *s*
6:23 *s* things their forefathers
6:31 do the *s* way to them
6:33 Even the sinners do the *s*
7:35 All the *s*, wisdom is proved
10:37 and be doing the *s* yourself
11:30 *s* way will the Son of man
13:5 all be destroyed in the *s* way
17:30 The *s* way it will be on that
17:35 grinding at the *s* mill
22:20 the cup in the *s* way after
22:22 all the *s*, woe to that man
23:40 are in the *s* judgment
Joh 12:42 All the *s*, many even of the
15:4 in the *s* way neither can you
Ac 1:11 come thus in the *s* manner as
2:1 all together at the *s* place
2:47 the *s* time Jehovah continued
7:28 *s* manner that you did away
11:17 God gave the *s* free gift to
14:15 the *s* infirmities as you do
15:11 *s* way as those people also
15:27 report the *s* things by word
18:3 being of the *s* trade he stayed
23:3 the *s* time sit to judge me in
24:26 At the *s* time, though, he
27:40 at the *s* time loosing the
Ro 2:1 judge practice the *s* things
9:21 from the *s* lump one vessel
10:12 there is the *s* Lord over all
Ro 12:4 do not all have the *s* function
12:16 *s* way toward others as to
15:5 the *s* mental attitude that
1Co 1:10 fitly united in the *s* mind
1:10 and in the *s* line of thought
9:17 against my will, all the *s* I
10:3 all ate the *s* spiritual food
10:4 drank the *s* spiritual drink
11:5 *s* as if she were a woman
12:4 but there is the *s* spirit
12:5 and yet there is the *s* Lord
12:6 the *s* God who performs all
12:8 according to the *s* spirit
12:9 faith by the *s* spirit, to
12:11 the one and the *s* spirit
12:25 the *s* care for one another
14:9 the *s* way also, unless you
15:39 Not all flesh is the *s* flesh
2Co 1:6 endure the *s* sufferings that
1:7 in the *s* way you will also
3:14 the *s* veil remains unlifted
3:18 transformed into the *s* image
4:13 *s* spirit of faith as that
8:6 *s* kind giving on your part
8:16 *s* earnestness for you in the
12:18 We walked in the *s* spirit
12:18 In the *s* footsteps, did we
Ga 4:28 promise the *s* as Isaac was
5:21 *s* way as I did forewarn you
Eph 6:9 keep doing the *s* things to
Php 1:30 you have the *s* struggle as
2:2 in that you are of the *s* mind
2:2 and have the *s* love, being
2:18 in the *s* way you yourselves
3:1 To be writing the *s* things to
3:16 orderly in this *s* routine
4:2 be of the *s* mind in the Lord
Col 2:5 all the *s* I am with you in
4:3 at the *s* time praying also
1Th 2:14 the *s* things as they also are
3:6 to see us in the *s* way
1Ti 5:13 the *s* time they also learn
5:25 In the *s* way also the fine
Heb 1:12 but you are the *s*, and your
2:14 partook of the *s* things, that
4:11 *s* pattern of disobedience
6:11 show the *s* industriousness
10:1 never with the *s* sacrifices
10:11 offer the *s* sacrifices
11:9 heirs . . . the very *s* promise
13:8 Christ is the *s* yesterday
Jas 2:25 In the *s* manner was not also
3:10 Out of the *s* mouth come
3:11 bubble out of the *s* opening
1Pe 4:1 with the *s* mental disposition
4:4 *s* low sink of debauchery
5:9 the *s* things in the way of
2Pe 3:7 by the *s* word the heavens and
Jude 7 *s* manner as the foregoing ones
Re 2:25 Just the *s*, hold fast what
2:27 *s* as I have received from
9:3 *s* authority as the scorpions
21:17 at the *s* time an angel's

Samgar-nebo
Jer 39:3 princes of the king . . . *S*

Samlah
Ge 36:36 *S* from Masrekah began to
36:37 When *S* died, Shaul from
1Ch 1:47 *S* from Masrekah began to
1:48 *S* died, and Shaul from

Samos
Ac 20:15 the next day we touched at *S*

Samothrace
Ac 16:11 with a straight run to *S*

Sample
1Ti 1:16 a *s* of those who are going

Samson
Jg 13:24 a son and called his name *S*
14:1 *S* went down to Timnah and
14:3 *S* said to his father: Get just
14:5 *S* went on down with his
14:10 *S* proceeded to hold a banquet
14:12 Then *S* said to them: Let me
15:1 *S* went visiting his wife
15:3 *S* said to them: This time I
15:4 *S* went his way and proceeded
15:6 It was *S* the son-in-law of
15:7 *S* said to them: If you do
15:10 It is to tie *S* that we have
15:11 said to *S*: Do you not know
15:12 *S* said to them: Swear to me
Jg 15:16 *S* said: With the jawbone of
16:1 Once *S* went to Gaza and saw a
16:2 *S* has come in here
16:3 *S* kept lying till midnight
16:6 Delilah said to *S*: Do tell me
16:7 *S* said to her: If they tie me
16:9 Philistines are upon you, *S*!
16:10 Delilah said to *S*: Look! You
16:12 Philistines are upon you, *S*!
16:13 Delilah said to *S*: Up till
16:14 Philistines are upon you, *S*!
16:20 Philistines are upon you, *S*!
16:23 into our hand *S* our enemy
16:25 Call *S* that he may offer us
16:25 called *S* out of the prison
16:26 *S* said to the boy that was
16:27 *S* offered some amusement
16:28 *S* now called to Jehovah and
16:29 *S* braced himself against the
16:30 *S* proceeded to say: Let my
Heb 11:32 go on to relate about . . . *S*

Samson's
Jg 14:7 she was still right in *S* eyes
14:15 to say to *S* wife: Fool your
14:16 *S* wife began to weep over
14:20 *S* wife came to belong to a

Samuel
1Sa 1:20 proceeded to call his name *S*
2:18 And *S* was ministering before
2:21 *S* continued growing up with
2:26 *S* was growing bigger and
3:1 *S* was ministering to Jehovah
3:3 *S* was lying in the temple of
3:4 Jehovah proceeded to call *S*
3:6 Jehovah went on to call . . . *S*
3:6 *S* got up and went to Eli and
3:7 As regards *S*, he had not yet
3:8 the third time: *S*! At that
3:9 Eli said to *S*: Go, lie down
3:9 *S* went and lay down in his
3:10, 10 as at the other times: *S*, *S*!
3:10 *S* said: Speak, for your
3:11 Jehovah went on to say to *S*
3:15 *S* continued lying down until
3:15 *S* was afraid to tell Eli of
3:16 But Eli called *S* and said
3:16 *S*, my son! At this he said
3:18 So *S* told him all the words
3:19 *S* continued growing up, and
3:20 *S* was one accredited for the
3:21 revealed himself to *S* in
4:1 word of *S* continued to come
7:3 *S* proceeded to say to all the
7:5 *S* said: Collect all Israel
7:6 *S* took up judging the sons of
7:8 the sons of Israel said to *S*
7:9 *S* took a sucking lamb and
7:9 *S* began calling to Jehovah for
7:10 while *S* was offering up the
7:12 *S* took a stone and set it
7:13 all the days of *S*
7:15 *S* kept on judging Israel all
8:1 as soon as *S* had grown old
8:4 and came to *S* at Ramah
8:6 was bad in the eyes of *S*
8:6 and *S* began to pray to Jehovah
8:7 Jehovah said to *S*: Listen to
8:10 So *S* said all the words of
8:19 refused to listen to . . . *S*
8:21 *S* gave a hearing to all the
8:22 Jehovah proceeded to say to *S*
8:22 *S* said to the men of Israel
9:14 *S* coming out to meet them
9:15 had uncovered the ear of *S*
9:17 And *S* himself saw Saul, and
9:18 Then Saul approached *S* in the
9:19 *S* proceeded to answer Saul
9:22 *S* took Saul and his attendant
9:23 Later *S* said to the cook
9:24 Saul ate with *S* on that day
9:26 *S* proceeded to call to Saul
9:26 Saul . . . and *S*, went forth
9:27 *S* himself said to Saul
10:1 *S* then took the flask of oil
10:9 to go from *S*, God began
10:14 So we came to *S*
10:15 What did *S* say to you men?
10:16 about which *S* had talked
10:17 And *S* proceeded to call the
10:20 *S* had all the tribes of
10:24 *S* said to all the people
10:25 *S* spoke to the people about
10:25 *S* sent all the people away

1Sa 11:7 a follower of Saul and of S
11:12 the people began to say to S
11:14 Later S said to the people
12:1 Finally S said to all Israel
12:6 And S went on to say to the
12:11 Jephthah and S and deliver
12:18 S called to Jehovah, and
12:18 in fear of Jehovah and of S
12:19 people began to say to S
12:20 S said to the people: Do not
13:8 appointed time that S had
13:8 and S did not come to Gilgal
13:10 why, there was S coming in
13:11 S said: What is it you have
13:13 At this S said to Saul
13:15 S rose and went his way up
15:1 S said to Saul: It was I
15:10 now came to S, saying
15:11 And it was distressing to S
15:12 S got up early to meet Saul
15:12 But report was made to S
15:13 At length S came to Saul
15:14 S said: Then what does this
15:16 S said to Saul: Stop! And I
15:17 S went on to say: Was it
15:20 Saul said to S: But I have
15:22 S said: Does Jehovah have as
15:24 Then Saul said to S: I have
15:26 S said to Saul: I shall not
15:27 S was turning about to go
15:28 S said to him: Jehovah has
15:31 S returned behind Saul, and
15:32 S said: Bring Agag the king
15:33 S said: Just as your sword
15:33 S went hacking Agag to
15:34 S now went his way to
15:35 S did not see Saul again
15:35 S had gone into mourning
16:1 Eventually Jehovah said to S
16:2 But S said: How can I go?
16:4 And S proceeded to do what
16:7 Jehovah said to S: Do not
16:8 and had him pass before S
16:10 his sons pass before S
16:10 S said to Jesse: Jehovah has
16:11 S said to Jesse: Are these
16:11 S said to Jesse: Do send and
16:13 S took the horn of oil and
16:13 S rose and went his way to
19:18 got to come to S at Ramah
19:18 he and S went away, and
19:20 S standing in his position
19:22 Where are S and David?
19:24 like a prophet before S, and
25:1 S died; and all Israel
28:3 S himself had died, and all
28:11 Bring up S for me
28:12 When the woman saw S she
28:14 recognized that it was S
28:15 S began to say to Saul: Why
28:16 S went on to say: Why, then
1Ch 6:28 And the sons of S were the
6:33 the son of Joel, the son of S
9:22 David and S the seer ordained
11:3 Jehovah's word by means of S
26:28 S the seer and Saul the son
29:29 the words of S the seer and
2Ch 35:18 the days of S the prophet
Ps 99:6 S was among those calling
Jer 15:1 If Moses and S were standing
Ac 3:24 prophets, in fact, from S on
13:20 judges until S the prophet
Heb 11:32 go on to relate about . . . S

Samuel's
1Sa 28:20 afraid because of S words

Sanballat
Ne 2:10 S the Horonite and Tobiah
2:19 S the Horonite and Tobiah the
4:1 as soon as S heard that we
4:7 soon as S and Tobiah and the
6:1 was told to S and Tobiah and
6:2 S and Geshem immediately sent
6:5 S sent his attendant to me
6:12 as Tobiah and S themselves
6:14 Tobiah and S, according to
13:28 son-in-law of S the Horonite

Sanctification
1Co 1:30 also righteousness and s and
1Th 4:4 his own vessel in s and honor
4:7 but in connection with s
1Ti 2:15 faith and love and s along
Heb 12:14 s without which no man
1Pe 1:2 with s by the spirit, for the

Sanctified
Ex 29:43 certainly be s by my glory
Le 8:10 that was in it and s them
8:30 he s Aaron and his garments
10:3 those near to me let me be s
22:32 s in the midst of the sons
Nu 3:13 I s to myself every firstborn
7:1 he anointed them and s them
8:17 I s them to myself
20:13 so that he was s among them
1Sa 7:1 s to guard the ark of Jehovah
16:5 Then he s Jesse and his sons
2Sa 8:11 also King David s to Jehovah
8:11 gold that he had s from all
1Ki 9:3 I have s this house that you
9:7 house that I have s to my
2Ki 12:18 had s and his own holy
1Ch 15:14 priests and the Levites s
18:11 King David s to Jehovah
2Ch 5:11 the priests . . . s themselves
7:7 Solomon s the middle of the
7:20 that I have s for my name
26:18 ones s, to burn incense
29:15 s themselves and came
29:17 s the house of Jehovah in
29:19 prepared, and have s them
30:3 had s themselves and the
30:8 sanctuary that he has s to
30:15 s themselves and brought
30:17 that had not s themselves
31:6 things s to Jehovah their
36:14 which he had s in Jerusalem
Ezr 3:5 s festival seasons of Jehovah
Ne 3:1 s it and went setting up its
3:1 Tower of Meah they s it
Isa 13:3 the command to my s ones
Jer 1:5 from the womb I s you
6:4 Against her they have s war
Eze 20:41 I will be s in you before
28:22 and I am actually s in her
28:25 I will also be s among
36:23 when I am s among you
48:11 s from the sons of Zadok
Zep 1:7 he has s his invited ones
Mt 6:9 Father . . . let your name be s
23:17 temple that has s the gold
Lu 11:2 Father, let your name be s
Joh 10:36 me whom the Father s and
17:19 may be s by means of truth
Ac 20:32 inheritance among all the s
26:18 those s by their faith in me
Ro 15:16 being s with holy spirit
1Co 1:2 s in union with Christ Jesus
6:11 but you have been s, but you
7:14 unbelieving husband is s in
7:14 the unbelieving wife is s in
1Ti 4:5 s through God's word and
2Ti 2:21 s, useful to his owner
Heb 2:11 and those who are being s
10:10 s through the offering of
10:14 being s perfect perpetually
10:29 covenant by which he was s

Sanctifier
Le 27:15 s wants to buy his house
27:19 s of it would at all buy the

Sanctifies
Le 27:18 s his field, the priest must
27:22 if he s to Jehovah a field
Isa 30:29 s oneself for a festival
Mt 23:19 or the altar that s the gift
Heb 9:13 s to the extent of cleanness

Sanctify
Ex 13:2 S to me every male firstborn
19:10 s them today and tomorrow
19:22 priests . . . s themselves
28:38 the sons of Israel will s
28:41 s them, and they must act as
29:1 s them for acting as priests
29:27 s the breast of the wave
29:33 with power, in order to s
29:36 you must anoint it to s it
29:37 you must s it that it may
29:44 I will s the tent of meeting
29:44 I shall s Aaron and his sons
30:29 you must s them that they
30:30 s them for acting as priests
40:9 must s it and all its utensils
40:10 its utensils and s the altar
40:11 basin and its stand and s it
40:13 and anoint him and s him
Le 8:11 and its stand so as to s them
Le 8:12 anointed him so as to s him
8:15 might s it to make atonement
11:44 you must s yourselves and
16:19 s it from the uncleannesses
20:7 must s yourselves and prove
21:8 s him, because he is one
22:3 Israel will s to Jehovah
25:10 s the fiftieth year and
27:14 s his house as something
27:16 man would s to Jehovah, the
27:17 s his field from the year of
27:26 no man should s it
Nu 6:11 must s his head on that day
7:1 s it and all its furnishings
11:18 S yourselves for tomorrow
20:12 s me before the eyes of the
De 15:19 should s to Jehovah your God
32:51 you men did not s me in the
Jos 3:5 S yourselves, for tomorrow
7:13 S the people, and you must
7:13 S yourselves tomorrow, for
Jg 17:3 s the silver to Jehovah from
1Sa 16:5 S yourselves, and you must
1Ki 8:64 s the middle of the
2Ki 10:20 S a solemn assembly for
1Ch 15:12 S yourselves, you and your
23:13 he might s the Most Holy
2Ch 2:4 to s it to him, to burn
7:16 choose and s this house that
29:5 Now s yourselves and
29:5 s the house of Jehovah the
29:34 priests could s themselves
30:17 to s them to Jehovah
31:18 s themselves for what was
35:6 and s yourselves and make
Ne 13:22 to s the sabbath day
Job 1:5 Job would send and s them
Isa 5:16 s himself through
29:23 they will s my name, and
29:23 s the Holy One of Jacob
Jer 17:22 you must s the sabbath day
17:24 to s the sabbath day by not
22:7 I will s against you those
51:27 S against her the nations
51:28 S against her the nations
Eze 20:20 s my own sabbaths, and they
36:23 certainly s my great name
38:16 when I s myself in you
38:23 magnify myself and s
39:27 s myself among them before
44:19 s the people with their
44:24 my sabbaths they should s
46:20 so as to s the people
Joe 1:14 S a time of fasting
2:15 S a time of fasting
2:16 S a congregation. Collect the
3:9 among the nations, S war!
Mic 3:5 actually s war against him
Joh 17:17 S . . . by means of the truth
Eph 5:26 he might s it, cleansing
1Th 5:23 May the very God of peace s
Heb 13:12 s the people with his own
1Pe 3:15 s the Christ as Lord in your

Sanctifying
Ex 19:14 and he set about s the people
28:3 Aaron's garments for s him
31:13 know that I Jehovah am s you
Le 20:8 I am Jehovah who is s you
21:8 Jehovah, who am s you, am
21:15 I am Jehovah who is s him
21:23 I am Jehovah who is s them
22:2 the things they are s to me
22:9 I am Jehovah who is s them
22:16 I am Jehovah who is s them
22:32 I am Jehovah who is s you
Nu 27:14 s me by the waters before
2Sa 11:4 she was s herself from her
2Ch 29:17 first month at s, and on
29:34 more upright of heart for s
30:24 priests kept s themselves
Ne 12:47 s them to the Levites
12:47 s them to the sons of Aaron
Isa 66:17 s themselves and cleansing
Jer 17:27 obey me by s the sabbath
Eze 20:12 I am Jehovah who is s them
37:28 I, Jehovah, am s Israel
Joh 17:19 I am s myself in their
1Th 4:3 God wills, the s of you, that
2Th 2:13 by s you with spirit and
Heb 2:11 For both he who is s and

Sanctuaries
Le 26:31 lay your s desolate, and I
Eze 7:24 and their s must be profaned

Eze 28:18 you have profaned your *s*
Am 7:9 the *s* themselves of Israel

Sanctuary
Ex 15:17 A *s*, O Jehovah, that your
25:8 they must make a *s* for me
28:35 into the *s* before Jehovah
31:11 perfumed incense for the *s*
35:19 for ministering in the *s*
39:41 for ministering in the *s*, the
Le 16:33 atonement for the holy *s*
19:30 should stand in awe of my *s*
21:12 not go out from the *s* and
21:12 not profane the *s* of his God
21:23 not profane my *s*, for I am
26:2 and stand in awe of my *s*
Nu 3:38 of the obligation to the *s*
10:21 carriers of the *s* pulled
18:1 for error against the *s*
19:20 it is Jehovah's *s* that he has
De 22:9 may be forfeited to the *s*
Jos 24:26 tree that is by the *s* of
1Ch 22:19 build the *s* of Jehovah the
28:10 you to build a house as a *s*
2Ch 20:8 for you a *s* for your name
26:18 Go out from the *s*
29:21 and for the *s* and for Judah
30:8 *s* that he has sanctified to
36:17 in the house of their *s*
Ne 10:39 utensils of the *s* and the
Ps 68:35 out of your grand *s*
73:17 come into the grand *s* of God
74:7 thrust your *s* into the fire
78:69 build his *s* just like the
96:6 and beauty are in his *s*
Isa 16:12 he came to his *s* to pray
60:13 beautify the place of my *s*
63:18 have stamped down your *s*
Jer 17:12 it is the place of our *s*
La 1:10 that have come into her *s*
2:7 Jehovah . . . has spurned his *s*
2:20 Or in the *s* of Jehovah should
Eze 5:11 my *s* that you defiled with
8:6 to become far off from my *s*
9:6 from my *s* you should start
11:16 I shall become to them a *s*
23:38 defiled my *s* in that day
23:39 into my *s* on that day to
24:21 Here I am profaning my *s*
25:3 against my *s*, because it
37:26 *s* in the midst of them to
37:28 *s* comes to be in the midst
43:21 House, outside the *s*
44:1 way of the gate of the *s*
44:5 with all the exits of the *s*
44:7 in my *s* so as to profane it
44:8 obligation in my *s* for
44:9 may come into my *s*, that
44:11 in my *s* they must become
44:15 of the obligation of my *s*
44:16 will come into my *s*, and
45:3 in it the *s* will come to be
45:4 the ministers of the *s*
45:4 sacred place for the *s*
45:18 purify the *s* from sin
47:12 forth from the very *s*
48:8 *s* must prove to be in the
48:10 *s* of Jehovah must prove
48:21 *s* of the House must prove
Da 8:11 established place of his *s*
9:17 face to shine upon your *s*
11:31 profane the *s*, the fortress
Am 7:13 it is the *s* of a king and it
Mt 23:35 murdered between the *s* and
27:51 curtain of the *s* was rent in
Mr 15:38 curtain of the *s* was rent
Lu 1:9 entered into the *s* of Jehovah
1:21 at his delaying in the *s*
1:22 supernatural sight in the *s*
23:45 curtain of the *s* was rent
Re 11:1 measure the temple *s* of God
11:2 that is outside the temple *s*
11:19 temple *s* of God that is in
11:19 was seen in his temple *s*
14:15 emerged from the temple *s*
14:17 temple *s* that is in heaven
15:5 *s* of the tent of the witness
15:6 emerged from the *s*, clothed
15:8 *s* became filled with smoke
15:8 able to enter into the *s* until
16:1 loud voice out of the *s* say
16:17 voice issued out of the *s*

Sand
Ge 22:17 grains of *s* that are on the
32:12 like the grains of *s* of the
41:49 like the *s* of the sea
Ex 2:12 down and hid him in the *s*
Le 11:30 the newt and the *s* lizard
De 33:19 the hidden hoards of the *s*
Jos 11:4 numerous as the grains of *s*
Jg 7:12 grains of *s* that are on the
1Sa 13:5 people like the grains of *s*
2Sa 17:11 as the *s* particles that are
1Ki 4:20 grains of *s* that are by the
4:29 *s* that is upon the seashore
Job 29:18 like the grains of *s* I shall
Ps 78:27 like the *s* grains of the seas
139:18 than even the grains of *s*
Pr 27:3 of a stone and a load of *s*
Isa 10:22 the grains of *s* of the sea
48:19 become just like the *s*
Jer 5:22 set the *s* as the boundary
15:8 the *s* grains of the seas
33:22 *s* of the sea be measured
Ho 1:10 grains of the *s* of the sea
Hab 1:9 captives just like the *s*
Mt 7:26 built his house upon the *s*
Ro 9:27 Israel . . . as the *s* of the sea
Re 13:1 still upon the *s* of the sea
20:8 these is as the *s* of the sea

Sandal
Ge 14:23 from a thread to a *s* lace
De 25:9 draw his *s* off his foot and
25:10 one who had his *s* drawn off
29:5 your *s* did not wear out upon
Ru 4:7 draw his *s* off and give it to
4:8 he proceeded to draw his *s* off
Ps 60:8 Over Edom I shall throw my *s*
108:9 Edom I shall throw my *s*
Joh 1:27 *s* I am not worthy to untie
Ac 13:25 *s* of whose feet I am not

Sandals
Ex 3:5 Draw your *s* from off your feet
12:11 *s* on your feet and your
Jos 5:15 your *s* from off your feet
9:5 and patched *s* on their feet
9:13 these garments and *s* of ours
1Ki 2:5 his *s* that were on his feet
2Ch 28:15 furnished them with *s* and
Ca 7:1 steps have become in your *s*
Isa 5:27 laces of their *s* be torn in
11:15 people to walk in their *s*
20:2 *s* you should draw from off
Eze 24:17 *s* you should put upon your
24:23 your *s* be upon your feet
Am 2:6 for the price of a pair of *s*
8:6 for the price of a pair of *s*
Mt 3:11 *s* I am not fit to take off
10:10 undergarments, or *s* or a
Mr 1:7 and untie the laces of his *s*
6:9 to bind on *s*, and not to wear
Lu 3:16 whose *s* I am not fit to untie
10:4 nor a food pouch, nor *s*, and
15:22 and *s* on his feet
22:35 purse and food pouch and *s*
Ac 7:33 Take the *s* off your feet, for
12:8 bind your *s* on. He did so

Sands
Job 6:3 heavier even than the *s* of the
Heb 11:12 *s* that are by the seaside

Sang
Ps 7:*super* A dirge of David that he *s*

Sanhedrin
Mt 26:59 the entire *S* were looking
Mr 14:55 the whole *S* were looking
15:1 scribes, even the whole *S*
15:43 a reputable member of the *S*
Lu 22:66 haled him into their *S* hall
Joh 11:47 Pharisees gathered the *S*
Ac 4:15 to go outside the *S* hall
5:21 called together the *S* and
5:27 and stood them in the *S* hall
5:34 certain man rose in the *S*
5:41 their way from before the *S*
6:12 force and led him to the *S*
6:15 all those sitting in the *S*
22:30 and all the *S* to assemble
23:1 Looking intently at the *S* Paul
23:6 proceeded to cry out in the *S*
23:15 you together with the *S* make
23:20 bring Paul down to the *S*
23:28 him down into their *S*
24:20 as I stood before the *S*

Sanity
1Sa 21:13 disguised his *s* under their
Ps 34:*super* disguising his *s* before

Sank
Ge 42:28 their hearts *s*, so that they
Ex 15:10 They *s* like lead in majestic
Nu 11:2 and the fire *s* down
1Sa 17:49 stone *s* into his forehead

Sansannah
Jos 15:31 Ziklag and Madmannah and *S*

Sap
Job 8:16 is full of *s* before the sun

Saph
2Sa 21:18 Hushathite struck down *S*

Sapphira
Ac 5:1 together with *S* his wife, sold

Sapphire
Ex 24:10 like a work of *s* flagstones
28:18 second row is turquoise, *s*
39:11 second row was turquoise, *s*
Job 28:6 stones are the place of the *s*
28:16 rare onyx stone and the *s*
La 4:7 their polish was as the *s*
Eze 1:26 in appearance like *s* stone
10:1 was something like *s* stone
28:13 *s*, turquoise and emerald
Re 21:19 foundation . . . second *s*

Sapphires
Ca 5:14 an ivory plate covered with *s*
Isa 54:11 lay your foundation with *s*

Sarah
Ge 17:15 because *S* is her name
17:17 *S*, yes, will a woman ninety
17:19 God said: *S* your wife is
17:21 *S* will bear to you at this
18:6 to the tent to *S* and said
18:9 Where is *S* your wife? To this
18:10 *S* your wife will have a son
18:10 *S* was listening at the tent
18:11 Abraham and *S* were old
18:11 *S* had stopped having
18:12 Hence *S* began to laugh inside
18:13 Why was it that *S* laughed
18:14 and *S* will have a son
18:15 *S* began to deny it, saying
20:2 Abraham repeated concerning *S*
20:2 king of Gerar sent and took *S*
20:14 returned to him *S* his wife
20:16 to *S* he said: Here I do give
20:18 because of *S*, Abraham's wife
21:1 turned his attention to *S*
21:1 did to *S* just as he had spoken
21:2 *S* became pregnant and then
21:3 whom *S* had borne to him
21:6 Then *S* said: God has prepared
21:7 uttered to Abraham, *S* will
21:9 *S* kept noticing the son of
21:12 that *S* keeps saying to you be
23:2 *S* died in Kiriath-arba, that
23:2 Abraham came in to bewail *S*
23:19 Abraham buried *S* his wife in
24:36 *S* the wife of my master bore
24:67 her into the tent of *S* his
25:10 buried, and also *S* his wife
25:12 the maidservant of *S* bore to
49:31 they buried Abraham and *S*
Isa 51:2 to *S* who gradually brought
Ro 4:19 the deadness of the womb of *S*
9:9 come and *S* will have a son
Heb 11:11 *S* herself received power
1Pe 3:6 as *S* used to obey Abraham

Sarah's
Ge 23:1 *S* life got to be a hundred and
23:1 They were the years of *S* life

Sarai
Ge 11:29 name of Abram's wife was *S*
11:30 *S* continued to be barren; she
11:31 and *S* his daughter-in-law
12:5 Abram took *S* his wife and Lot
12:11 said to *S* his wife: Please
12:17 great plagues because of *S*
16:1 *S*, Abram's wife, had borne
16:2 *S* said to Abram: Please now!
16:2 listened to the voice of *S*
16:3 *S*, Abram's wife, took Hagar
16:5 *S* said to Abram: The violence
16:6 Abram said to *S*: Look! Your
16:6 *S* began to humiliate her so
16:8 Hagar, maidservant of *S*, just
16:8 she said: Why, from *S* my
17:15 *S* your wife, you must not

Ge 17:15 must not call her name *S*

Saraph
1Ch 4:22 Joash and *S*, who became

Sardis
Re 1:11 the seven congregations . . . *S*
3:1 angel of the congregation in *S*
3:4 names in *S* that did not defile

Sardius
Re 21:20 the sixth *s*, the seventh

Sardonyx
Re 21:20 the fifth *s*, the sixth

Sargon
Isa 20:1 *S* the king of Assyria sent

Sarid
Jos 19:10 came to be as far as *S*
19:12 went back from *S* eastward

Sarsechim
Jer 39:3 princes of the king . . . *S*

Sash
Ex 28:4 a turban and a *s*; and they
28:39 a *s*, the work of a weaver
39:29 the *s* of fine twisted linen
Le 8:7 and girded him with the *s* and
16:4 gird himself with the linen *s*
Isa 22:21 *s* I shall firmly bind about

Sashes
Ex 28:40 you must make *s* for them
29:9 gird them with the *s*, Aaron
Le 8:13 girded them with *s* and

Sat
Ge 21:16 she went on and *s* down by
21:16 she *s* down at a distance and
37:25 they *s* down to eat bread
38:14 *s* down at the entrance of
48:2 Israel . . . *s* up on his couch
Ex 17:12 and he *s* upon it; and Aaron
18:13 Moses *s* down as usual to
32:6 *s* down to eat and drink
Jg 5:17 Asher *s* idle at the seashore
6:11 and *s* under the big tree that
19:6 they *s* down, and both of them
20:26 and *s* there before Jehovah
Ru 2:14 *s* down beside the harvesters
4:1 he turned aside and *s* down
4:2 Sit down here. So they *s* down
1Sa 25:13 hundred *s* by the baggage
28:23 and *s* on the couch
30:24 one that *s* by the baggage
2Sa 7:18 David came in and *s* down
1Ki 1:46 Solomon has *s* down upon the
2:12 he *s* down upon the throne of
2:19 he *s* down upon his throne
16:11 *s* down upon his throne
19:4 *s* down under a certain broom
21:13 came in and *s* down in front
2Ki 13:13 Jeroboam himself *s* upon his
1Ch 17:16 King David came in and *s*
Ne 1:4 I *s* down and began to weep and
Es 3:15 Haman, they *s* down to drink
Ps 1:1 seat of ridiculers has not *s*
9:4 *s* on the throne judging with
26:4 not *s* with men of untruth
119:23 Even princes have *s*
137:1 Babylon—there we *s* down
Ca 2:3 there I have *s* down, and his
Jer 3:2 *s* for them, like an Arabian
15:17 I have not *s* down in the
15:17 have *s* down all by myself
Eze 23:41 *s* down upon a glorious
Da 7:9 and the Ancient of Days *s* down
Jon 3:6 and *s* down in the ashes
4:5 and *s* down east of the city
Mt 5:1 after he *s* down his disciples
13:2 he went aboard a boat and *s*
27:36 as they *s*, they watched over
Mr 4:1 *s* out on the sea, but all the
9:35 he *s* down and called the
11:2 none of mankind has yet *s*
11:7 garments upon it, and he *s*
12:41 he *s* down with the treasury
Lu 4:20 back to the attendant and *s*
5:3 he *s* down, and from the boat
7:15 the dead man *s* up and started
10:39 *s* down at the feet of the
19:30 which none of mankind ever *s*
22:55 and *s* down together, Peter
Joh 12:14 young ass, he *s* on it, just
19:13 *s* down on a judgment seat
Ac 2:3 one *s* upon each one of them
Ac 9:40 sight of Peter, she *s* up
12:21 *s* . . . upon the judgment seat
16:13 we *s* down and began speaking
25:6 *s* down on the judgment seat
25:17 *s* down on the judgment seat
1Co 10:7 The people *s* down to eat and
Heb 1:3 *s* down on the right hand of
8:1 *s* down at the right hand of
10:12 *s* down at the right hand of
12:2 has *s* down at the right hand
Re 3:21 *s* down with my Father on his
20:4 those who *s* down on them

Satan
1Ch 21:1 And *S* proceeded to stand up
Job 1:6 *S* proceeded to enter right
1:7 Jehovah said to *S*: Where do
1:7 *S* answered Jehovah and said
1:8 Jehovah went on to say to *S*
1:9 *S* answered Jehovah and said
1:12 Jehovah said to *S*: Look!
1:12 So *S* went out away from the
2:1 and *S* also proceeded to enter
2:2 Jehovah said to *S*: Just where
2:2 *S* answered Jehovah and said
2:3 Jehovah went on to say to *S*
2:4 *S* answered Jehovah and said
2:6 Jehovah said to *S*: There he is
2:7 So *S* went out away from the
Zec 3:1 *S* standing at his right hand
3:2 the angel of Jehovah said to *S*
3:2 Jehovah rebuke you, O *S*
Mt 4:10 Go away, *S*! For it is
12:26, 26 if *S* expels *S*, he has
16:23 to Peter: Get behind me, *S*!
Mr 1:13 being tempted by *S*, and he
3:23, 23 How can *S* expel *S*?
3:26 if *S* has risen up against
4:15 *S* comes and takes away the
8:33 Get behind me, *S*, because you
Lu 10:18 *S* already fallen like
11:18 if *S* is also divided against
13:16 and whom *S* held bound, look!
22:3 *S* entered into Judas, the one
22:31 *S* has demanded to have you
Joh 13:27 *S* entered into the latter
Ac 5:3 why has *S* emboldened you
26:18 authority of *S* to God, in
Ro 16:20 will crush *S* under your feet
1Co 5:5 hand such a man over to *S* for
7:5 that *S* may not keep tempting
2Co 2:11 not be overreached by *S*, for
11:14 *S* . . . keeps transforming
12:7 angel of *S*, to keep slapping
1Th 2:18 but *S* cut across our path
2Th 2:9 *S* with every powerful work
1Ti 1:20 have handed them over to *S*
5:15 turned aside to follow *S*
Re 2:9 not but are a synagogue of *S*
2:13 where the throne of *S* is; and
2:13 where *S* is dwelling
2:24 know the deep things of *S*
3:9 synagogue of *S* who say they
12:9 one called Devil and *S*, who
20:2 who is the Devil and *S*
20:7 *S* will be let loose out of

Satiated
Hab 2:16 *s* with dishonor instead of

Satisfaction
Ge 2:16 of the garden you may eat to *s*
Ex 16:3 we were eating bread to *s*
16:8 and in the morning bread to *s*
Le 25:19 eat to *s* and dwell in
26:5 eat your bread to *s* and dwell
Ps 16:11 Rejoicing to *s* is with your
78:25 he sent them to *s*
Pr 13:25 eating to the *s* of his soul
Isa 23:18 eating to *s* and for elegant
55:2 for what results in no *s*
56:11 they have known no *s*
66:11 get *s* from the breast of
La 5:6 in order to get *s* with bread
Eze 16:28 and also did not get *s*
16:29 in this you did not get *s*
39:19 eat fat to *s* and to drink
Hag 1:6 eating, but it is not to *s*

Satisfactory
Le 10:19 prove *s* in Jehovah's eyes
10:20 then it proved *s* in his eyes

Satisfied
Ge 25:8 in a good old age, old and *s*
35:29 old and *s* with days, and
Ex 16:12 you will be *s* with bread
Le 26:26 eat but you will not be *s*
De 6:11 shall have eaten and become *s*
8:10 you have eaten and *s* yourself
11:15 you will indeed eat and be *s*
31:20 eat and be *s* and grow fat
33:23 is *s* with the approval And
Ru 2:14 would eat, so that she was *s*
2:18 when she had *s* herself and
1Sa 2:5 *s* must hire themselves out
1Ch 23:1 grown old and *s* with days
29:28 good old age, *s* with days
2Ch 24:15 old and *s* with years and
31:10 eating and getting *s* and
Ne 9:25 began to eat and to be *s* and
Job 19:22 *s* with my very flesh
31:31 has not been *s* from food
42:17 Job died, old and *s* with
Ps 17:14 Who are *s* with sons And who
17:15 *s* when awakening to see your
22:26 meek ones will eat and be *s*
37:19 in . . . famine they will be *s*
59:15 not be *s* or stay overnight
63:5 even fatness, my soul is *s*
65:4 *s* with the goodness of your
104:13 your works the earth is *s*
104:16 The trees of Jehovah are *s*
104:28 they get *s* with good things
107:9 he has *s* the dried-out soul
Pr 12:11 be *s* with bread, but the
12:14 he is *s* with good, and the
14:14 *s* with the results of his
18:20 mouth his belly will be *s*
18:20 *s* even with the produce of
19:23 one will spend the night *s*
20:13 be *s* with bread
27:7 A soul that is *s* will tread
27:20 Sheol . . . do not get *s*
27:20 do the eyes of a man get *s*
30:9 *s* and I actually deny you and
30:15 things that do not get *s*
30:16 land that has not been *s*
Ec 1:8 The eye is not *s* at seeing
4:8 eyes themselves are not *s* with
5:10 lover of silver will not be *s*
6:3 yet his own soul is not *s* with
Isa 9:20 will certainly not be *s*
44:16 eats, and he becomes *s*
53:11 he will see, he will be *s*
Jer 31:14 own people will become *s*
44:17 used to be *s* with bread and
50:19 Gilead his soul will be *s*
Eze 27:33 you *s* many peoples
39:20 must get *s* at my table
Ho 4:10 eat, but will not get *s*
13:6 they also came to be *s*
13:6 They became *s* and their heart
Joe 2:19 people will certainly be *s*
2:26 eat, eating and becoming *s*
Am 4:8 and they would not get *s*
Mic 6:14 will eat and not get *s*, and
Hab 2:5 like death and cannot be *s*
Mt 14:20 all ate and were *s*, and they
15:37 And all ate and were *s*, and
Mr 6:42 So they all ate and were *s*
7:27 First let the children be *s*
8:8 they ate and were *s*, and they
Lu 1:53 he has fully *s* hungry ones
3:14 but be *s* with your provisions
9:17 So they all ate and were *s*
Joh 6:26 from the loaves and were *s*
Ac 27:38 they had been *s* with food
Ro 15:24 been *s* with your company

Satisfy
De 8:12 may eat and indeed *s* yourself
14:29 must eat and *s* themselves
23:24 grapes for you to *s* your soul
26:12 eat it . . . and *s* themselves
Job 38:27 To *s* storm-stricken and
38:39 *s* the lively appetite of
Ps 81:16 shall *s* you with honey
90:14 *S* us in the morning with
91:16 of days I shall *s* him
132:15 I shall *s* with bread
Pr 5:10 strangers may not *s*
Isa 58:10 *s* the soul that is being
58:11 and to *s* your soul even in
Jer 46:10 *s* itself and take its fill
50:10 spoil of her will *s*
Eze 7:19 Their souls they will not *s*
32:4 *s* the wild beasts of the
Mt 15:33 loaves to *s* a crowd of this
Mr 8:4 to *s* these people with loaves

Jer 42:11 s you and to deliver you
Eze 34:22 I will s my sheep, and
36:29 I will s you from all your
37:23 shall certainly s them from
Ho 1:7 s them by Jehovah their God
1:7 s them by a bow or by a sword
13:10 may s you in all your cities
14:3 Assyria itself will not s us
Hab 1:2 violence, and you do not s
3:13 to s your anointed one
Zep 3:17 As a mighty One, he will s
3:19 will s her that is limping
Zec 8:13 so I shall s you, and you
9:16 God will certainly s them
10:6 house of Joseph I shall s
12:7 s the tents of Judah first
Mt 1:21 s his people from their sins
8:25 s us, we are about to perish!
14:30 he cried out: Lord, s me!
16:25 whoever wants to s his soul
21:9 S, we pray, the Son of David!
21:9 S him, we pray, in the
21:15 S, we pray, the Son of David
27:40 s yourself! If you are a son
27:42 himself he cannot s! He is
27:49 whether Elijah comes to s
Mr 3:4 to s or to kill a soul
8:35 whoever wants to s his soul
8:35 loses his soul . . . will s it
11:9 S, we pray! Blessed is he
11:10 S, we pray, in the heights
15:30 s yourself by coming down
15:31 himself he cannot s
Lu 6:9 to s or to destroy a soul
9:24 whoever wants to s his soul
9:24 is the one that will s it
19:10 seek and to s what was lost
23:35 let him s himself, if this
23:37 king of the Jews, s yourself
23:39 S yourself and us
Joh 12:13 S, we pray you! Blessed is
12:27 Father, s me out of this
12:47 but to s the world
Ro 11:14 and s some from among them
1Co 1:21 preached to s those believing
7:16 that you will s your husband
7:16 that you will s your wife
9:22 I might by all means s some
1Ti 1:15 Jesus came . . . to s sinners
4:16 you will s both yourself and
2Ti 4:18 will s me for his heavenly
Heb 5:7 able to s him out of death
7:25 able also to s completely
Jas 1:21 is able to s your souls
2:14 faith cannot s him, can it?
4:12 is able to s and to destroy
5:20 s his soul from death and
Jude 23 s them by snatching them out

Saved

Ex 14:30 Jehovah s Israel from the
16:24 s it up until the morning
Nu 10:9 and be s from your enemies
Jg 2:18 he s them out of the hand of
7:2 My hand it was that s me
8:22 you have s us out of the hands
2Sa 22:4 from my enemies . . . s
2Ki 14:27 he s them by the hand of
1Ch 11:14 Jehovah s with a great
2Ch 32:22 Jehovah s Hezekiah and
Job 26:2 s an arm that is without
Ps 18:3 from my enemies I shall be s
33:16 no king s by the abundance
34:6 out of all his distresses He s
44:7 you s us from our adversaries
80:3 your face, that we may be s
80:7 your face, that we may be s
80:19 your face, that we may be s
106:10 s them from the hand of the
107:13 he as usual s them
107:19 he as usual s them
119:117 that I may be s
Pr 28:18 walking faultless will be s
Isa 30:15 you people will be s
43:12 s and have caused it to be
45:17 be s in union with Jehovah
45:22 Turn to me and be s, all
63:9 personal messenger s them
64:5 and should we be s?
Jer 4:14 in order that you may be s
8:20 for us, we have not been s
17:14 Save me, and I will be s
23:6 in his days Judah will be s
30:7 he will be s even out of it
Jer 33:16 days Judah will be s and
Zec 9:9 He is righteous, yes, s
Mt 10:22 is the one that will be s
19:25 saying: Who really can be s?
24:13 is the one that will be s
24:22 no flesh would be s; but on
27:42 Others he s; himself he
Mr 10:26 Who, in fact, can be s?
13:13 is the one that will be s
13:20 no flesh would be s
15:31 and saying: Others he s
Lu 7:50 Your faith has s you; go your
8:12 may not believe and be s
8:50 faith, and she will be s
13:23 those who are being s few
18:26 Who possibly can be s?
23:35 Others he s; let him save
Joh 3:17 world to be s through him
5:34 things that you may be s
10:9 enters through me will be s
Ac 2:21 the name of Jehovah will be s
2:40 Get s from this crooked
2:47 to them daily those being s
4:12 by which we must get s
11:14 your household may get s
15:1 you cannot be s
15:11 get s through the undeserved
16:30 what must I do to get s?
16:31 and you will get s, you and
27:20 hope of our being s finally
27:31 the boat, you cannot be s
Ro 5:9 be s through him from wrath
5:10 we shall be s by his life
8:24 For we were s in this hope
9:27 the remnant that will be s
10:9 exercise faith . . . will be s
10:13 name of Jehovah will be s
11:26 manner all Israel will be s
1Co 1:18 but to us who are being s it
3:15 but he himself will be s; yet
5:5 spirit may be s in the day of
10:33 that they might get s
15:2 you are also being s, with
2Co 2:15 among those who are being s
Eph 2:5 kindness you have been s
2:8 you have been s through faith
1Th 2:16 that these might be s
2Th 2:10 truth that they might be s
1Ti 2:4 all sorts of men should be s
2Ti 1:9 He s us and called us with a
Tit 3:5 s us through the bath that
1Pe 4:18 righteous man is being s
Jude 5 s a people out of the land

Saves

Ps 20:6 certainly s his anointed one
34:18 are crushed in spirit he s
Ac 28:28 means by which God s, has

Saving

Jg 6:36 If you are s Israel by means
13:5 s Israel out of the hand of
2Sa 8:14 Jehovah kept s David wherever
10:19 afraid to try s the sons of
1Ch 18:13 And Jehovah kept s David
19:19 to try s the sons of Ammon
Job 5:15 One s from the sword out of
Ps 20:6 s mighty acts of his right
22:1 Why are you far from s me
44:6 not my sword that was s me
68:20 is for us a God of s acts
Jer 14:9 that is unable to do any s
30:10 I am s you from far off
46:27 I am s you from far away
Zec 8:7 s my people from the land of
Lu 2:30 have seen your means of s
3:6 will see the s means of God
Heb 11:7 for the s of his household
1Pe 3:21 now s you, namely, baptism

Savior

De 28:31 but you will have no s
Jg 3:9 Jehovah raised a s up for the
3:15 raised up for them a s, Ehud
12:3 got to see that you were no s
1Sa 10:19 your God who was a s to you
11:3 if there is no s of us, we
23:5 David came to be the s of
2Sa 22:3 my place for flight, my S
22:42 help, but there is no s
2Ki 13:5 Jehovah gave Israel a s
Ps 7:10 a S of those upright in heart
17:7 O S of those seeking refuge
18:41 help, but there is no s
106:21 They forgot God their S
Isa 19:20 he will send them a s
43:3 the Holy One of Israel your S
43:11 besides me there is no s
45:15 the God of Israel, a S
45:21 a righteous God and a S
49:26 I, Jehovah, am your S and
60:16 I, Jehovah, am your S, and
63:8 that he came to be a S
Jer 14:8 the S of him in the time of
Ho 13:4 and there was no s but I
Lu 1:47 overjoyed at God my S
2:11 was born to you today a S
Joh 4:42 certainty the s of the world
Ac 5:31 as Chief Agent and S to his
13:23 brought to Israel a s, Jesus
Eph 5:23 he being a s of this body
Php 3:20 are eagerly waiting for a s
1Ti 1:1 under command of God our S
2:3 in the sight of our S, God
4:10 is a S of all sorts of men
2Ti 1:10 the manifestation of our S
Tit 1:3 under command of our S, God
1:4 and Christ Jesus our S
2:10 the teaching of our S, God
2:13 the S of us, Christ Jesus
3:4 love . . . on the part of our S
3:6 through Jesus Christ our S
2Pe 1:1 and the S Jesus Christ
1:11 kingdom of our Lord and S
2:20 knowledge of the Lord and S
3:2 commandment of the Lord and S
3:18 our Lord and S Jesus Christ
1Jo 4:14 his Son as S of the world
Jude 25 God our S through Jesus

Saviors

Ne 9:27 s who would save them out of
Ob 21 s will certainly come up onto

Saw

Ge 1:4 God s that the light was good
1:10 God s that it was good
1:12 God s that it was good
1:18 God s that it was good
1:31 God s everything he had made
3:6 woman s that the tree was
6:5 Jehovah s that the badness of
6:12 God s the earth and, look! it
9:22 s his father's nakedness
13:10 s the whole District of the
19:28 of the District and s a sight
28:6 Esau s that Isaac had blessed
28:8 Esau s that the daughters of
29:10 when Jacob s Rachel the
31:10 s a sight in a dream and
32:2 Jacob said, when he s them
33:5 s the women and the children
38:14 she s that Shelah had grown
39:13 she s that he had left his
40:6 s them, why, here they were
40:16 the bakers s that he had
41:22 I s in my dream and here
42:21 we s the distress of his soul
43:16 Joseph s Benjamin with them
43:29 s Benjamin his brother, the
48:8 Israel s Joseph's sons and
48:17 Joseph s that his father kept
50:15 s that their father was dead
Ex 2:2 When she s how good-looking
2:12 s there was nobody in sight
3:4 Jehovah s that he turned aside
5:19 s themselves in an evil
18:27 Moses s his father-in-law
33:10 people s the pillar of cloud
34:35 sons of Israel s Moses' face
Nu 13:28 those born of Anak we s
13:32 the people whom we s in the
13:33 And there we s the Nephilim
22:31 so that he s Jehovah's angel
24:2 Balaam raised his eyes and s
32:9 Eshcol and s the land, then
De 1:28 the sons of Anakim we s there
1:31 you s how Jehovah your God
4:3 s what Jehovah did in the case
7:19 provings that your eyes s
29:3 eyes s, those great signs and
32:19 Jehovah s it, then he came
Jos 8:14 the king of Ai s it, then the
8:21 Israel s that the ambush had
Jg 14:1 and s a woman in Timnah of
16:1 Samson . . . s a prostitute
18:7 s how the people that were
20:41 s that calamity had reached
1Sa 6:13 s the Ark, they gave way to
6:16 Philistines themselves s it

1Sa 9:17 And Samuel himself *s* Saul
10:11 knowing him formerly *s* him
12:12 When you *s* that Nahash the
13:6 *s* that they were in sore
13:11 I *s* that the people had been
14:52 When Saul *s* any mighty man
17:42 Philistine looked and *s*
17:55 Saul *s* David going out to
19:5 You *s* it and you gave way to
22:9 I *s* the son of Jesse come to
23:22 whoever *s* him there—for it
28:12 woman *s* Samuel she began
28:13 A god I *s* coming up out of
28:21 *s* that he had been greatly
31:5 armor-bearer *s* that Saul had
31:7 *s* that the men of Israel
2Sa 1:7 he turned back and *s* me, then
10:6 sons of Ammon *s* that they
10:9 Joab *s* that the battle
10:14 *s* that the Syrians had fled
10:15 Syrians *s* that they had been
10:19 servants of Hadadezer, *s*
13:34 *s*, and, look! there were
17:23 he *s* that his counsel had
18:10 *s* it and told Joab and said
18:11 you *s* it, and why did you
18:24 he raised his eyes and *s* a and
18:26 now *s* another man running
18:29 I *s* the great commotion at
20:12 man *s* that all the people
20:12 *s* that everyone coming up
24:17 he *s* the angel that was
24:20 *s* the king and his servants
1Ki 3:28 *s* that the wisdom of God
16:18 Zimri *s* that the city had
18:17 as soon as Ahab *s* Elijah
18:39 all the people *s* it, they
22:32 chiefs of the chariots *s*
22:33 *s* that it was not the king
2Ki 2:15 *s* him some way off, they
2:24 *s* them and called down evil
3:22 *s* the water red like blood
3:26 *s* that the battle had proved
4:25 man of the true God *s* her
5:21 Naaman *s* someone running
6:17 eyes, so that he *s*; and, look!
6:21 *s* them: Shall I strike them
9:22 as soon as Jehoram *s* Jehu
9:26 blood of his sons I *s*
9:27 *s* it and took to flight by
11:1 she *s* that her son had died
11:14 she *s*, and there the king
12:10 *s* that there was a great deal
13:21 they *s* the marauding band
20:15 that is in my house they *s*
23:29 as soon as he *s* him
1Ch 10:5 armor-bearer *s* that Saul had
10:7 *s* that they had fled and that
19:6 sons of Ammon *s* that they
19:10 When Joab *s* that the battle
19:15 *s* that the Syrians had fled
19:16 Syrians *s* that they had been
19:19 servants of Hadadezer *s*
21:15 Jehovah *s* it and began to
21:20 turned back and *s* the angel
21:21 Ornan looked and *s* David
21:28 when David *s* that Jehovah
2Ch 12:7 Jehovah *s* that they had
15:9 *s* that Jehovah his God was
18:31 *s* Jehoshaphat, they, for
18:32 chiefs of the chariots *s*
22:10 she *s* that her son had died
23:13 she *s*, and there was the
24:11 *s* that there was plenty of
31:8 came and *s* the heaps, they
32:2 Hezekiah *s* that Sennacherib
Ne 4:14 I *s* their fear I immediately
9:9 you *s* the affliction of our
13:15 *s* in Judah people treading
13:23 *s* the Jews that had given
Es 5:2 as soon as the king *s* Esther
5:9 as soon as Haman *s* Mordecai
7:7 *s* that bad had been determined
Job 2:13 they *s* that the pain was
28:27 he *s* wisdom and proceeded
29:8 The boys *s* me and hid
29:11 the eye itself *s* and
32:5 *s* that there was no answer
Ps 48:5 They themselves *s*; and so
50:18 Whenever you *s* a thief, you
95:9 they also *s* my activity
97:4 earth *s* and came to be in
114:3 sea itself *s* and took to
139:16 Your eyes *s* even the embryo
Pr 24:32 I *s*, I took the discipline
Ec 1:14 I *s* all the works that were
1:16 my own heart *s* a great deal
2:13 I *s*, even I, that there exists
8:17 I *s* all the work of the true
9:13 I *s* as respects wisdom under
Isa 10:15 *s* magnify itself over the
13:1 son of Amoz *s* in vision
21:7 *s* a war chariot with a span
39:4 that is in my house they *s*
41:5 islands *s* and began to fear
59:16 *s* that there was no man
Jer 4:23 I *s* the land, and, look!
4:24 I *s* the mountains, and, look!
4:25 I *s*, and, look! there was
4:26 I *s*, and, look! the orchard
39:4 all the men of war *s* them
41:13 *s* Johanan the son of
La 1:7 adversaries *s* her. They laughed
Eze 1:27 of his hips and downward I *s*
16:50 just as I *s* fit
37:8 I *s*, and, look! upon them
41:8 I *s* that there was a high
43:3 vision that I *s* when I came
43:3 *s* by the river Chebar, and
Da 8:3 I *s*, and, look! a ram standing
8:4 I *s* the ram making thrusts to
8:7 I *s* it coming into close touch
8:20 ram that you *s* possessing the
10:7 And I *s*, I Daniel by myself
10:8 I *s* this great appearance
12:5 I *s*, I Daniel, and, look!
Ho 9:10 I *s* the forefathers of you
Am 9:1 I *s* Jehovah stationed above
Hab 3:6 He *s*, and then caused nations
3:7 I *s* the tents of Cushan
3:10 Mountains *s* you; they got to
Hag 2:3 *s* this house in its former
Zec 1:8 I *s* in the night, and, look!
5:1 I raised my eyes again and *s*
5:9 I raised my eyes and *s*, and
6:1 I raised my eyes again and *s*
Mt 2:2 we *s* his star when we were
2:11 they *s* the young child with
3:16 he *s* descending like a dove
4:16 *s* a great light, and as for
4:18 *s* two brothers, Simon who
4:21 *s* two others who were
5:1 When he *s* the crowds he went
8:14 *s* his mother-in-law lying
8:18 Jesus *s* a crowd around him
12:22 the dumb man spoke and *s*
14:14 *s* a great crowd; and he felt
15:31 *s* the dumb speaking and the
17:8 *s* no one but Jesus himself
18:31 fellow slaves *s* the things
20:3 *s* others standing unemployed
21:15 *s* the marvelous things he
21:20 But when the disciples *s*
21:32 although you *s* this, did not
27:54 when they *s* the earthquake
28:17 *s* him they did obeisance
Mr 1:10 he *s* the heavens being parted
1:16 he *s* Simon and Andrew the
1:19 he *s* James the son of Zebedee
2:5 Jesus *s* their faith he said to
2:12 We never *s* the like of it
2:16 *s* he was eating with the
6:33 people *s* them going and many
6:34 he *s* a great crowd, but he
6:48 he *s* them being hard put
6:50 all *s* him and were troubled
7:2 *s* some of his disciples eat
8:25 the man *s* clearly, and he
9:8 looked around and *s* no one
9:9 not to relate . . . what they *s*
9:38 we *s* a certain man expelling
11:20 they *s* the fig tree already
15:39 *s* he had expired under these
16:5 they *s* a young man sitting
Lu 2:17 When they *s* it, they made
2:20 the things they heard and *s*
2:48 when they *s* him they were
5:2 he *s* two boats docked at the
5:20 when he *s* their faith he said
7:22 report to John what you *s*
8:34 when the herders *s* what had
9:32 *s* his glory and the two men
9:36 any of the things they *s*
9:49 *s* a certain man expelling
9:54 James and John *s* this they
10:31 when he *s* him, he went by
10:32 down to the place and *s* him
13:12 he *s* her, Jesus addressed her
Lu 16:23 he *s* Abraham afar off and
17:15 when he *s* he was healed
19:7 they *s* it, they all fell to
21:1 *s* the rich dropping their
21:2 *s* a certain needy widow drop
22:49 *s* what was going to happen
22:56 girl *s* him sitting by the
23:8 Herod *s* Jesus he rejoiced
Joh 1:39 and *s* where he was staying
1:47 Jesus *s* Nathanael coming
1:48 under the fig tree, I *s* you
1:50 I *s* you underneath the fig
6:14 the men *s* the signs he
6:22 *s* that there was no boat
6:24 crowd *s* that neither Jesus
6:26 not because you *s* signs, but
8:56 and he *s* it and rejoiced
9:1 he *s* a man blind from birth
11:33 *s* her weeping and the Jews
12:41 because he *s* his glory, and
18:26 I *s* you in the garden with
19:6 officers *s* him, they shouted
19:33 *s* that he was already dead
20:8 and he *s* and believed
21:20 Peter *s* the disciple whom
Ac 2:31 *s* beforehand and spoke
3:12 Peter *s* this, he said to the
6:15 *s* that his face was as an
7:31 Moses *s* it he marveled at the
8:18 Simon *s* that through the
9:35 and the plain of Sharon *s* him
10:3 he *s* plainly in a vision an
11:5 in a trance I *s* a vision
11:6 *s* four-footed creatures of
11:13 he *s* the angel stand in his
11:23 *s* the undeserved kindness of
12:3 he *s* it was pleasing to the
12:16 *s* him and were astonished
16:19 masters *s* that their hope
16:40 and when they *s* the brothers
22:18 *s* him saying to me, Hurry up
26:13 I *s* at midday on the road
1Co 1:21 God *s* good through the
Ga 1:19 But I *s* no one else of the
2:7 *s* that I had entrusted to me
2:14 I *s* they were not walking
Php 1:30 as you *s* in my case and as
4:9 and *s* in connection with me
Col 1:19 God *s* good for all fullness
1Th 3:1 we *s* good to be left alone in
Heb 11:13 they *s* them afar off and
11:23 they *s* the young child was
1Pe 1:8 Though you never *s* him, you
2Pe 2:8 by what he *s* and heard while
Re 1:2 even to all the things he *s*
1:12 I *s* seven golden lampstands
1:17 when I *s* him, I fell as dead
1:19 write down the things you *s*
1:20 stars that you *s* upon my
4:1 I *s*, and, look! an opened door
4:4 I *s* seated twenty-four elders
5:1 I *s* in the right hand of the
5:2 I *s* a strong angel proclaiming
5:6 I *s* standing in the midst of
5:11 And I *s*, and I heard a voice
6:1 I *s* when the Lamb opened one
6:2 I *s*, and, look! a white horse
6:5 I *s*, and, look! a black horse
6:8 I *s*, and, look! a pale horse
6:9 I *s* underneath the altar the
6:12 I *s* when he opened the sixth
7:1 I *s* four angels standing upon
7:2 And I *s* another angel ascending
7:9 I *s*, and, look! a great crowd
8:2 I *s* the seven angels that stand
8:13 I *s*, and I heard an eagle
9:1 I *s* a star that had fallen
9:17 I *s* the horses in the vision
10:1 I *s* another strong angel
10:5 the angel that I *s* standing
12:13 dragon *s* that it was hurled
13:1 I *s* a wild beast ascending
13:2 wild beast that I *s* was like
13:3 I *s* one of its heads as though
13:11 I *s* another wild beast
14:1 And I *s*, and, look! the Lamb
14:6 I *s* another angel flying in
14:14 I *s*, and, look! a white
15:1 I *s* in heaven another sign
15:2 I *s* what seemed to be a
15:5 I *s*, and the sanctuary of the
16:13 I *s* three unclean inspired
17:6 I *s* that the woman was drunk
17:8 wild beast that you *s* was

Re 17:12 ten horns that you *s* mean
17:15 waters that you *s*, where the
17:16 ten horns that you *s*, and
17:18 woman whom you *s* means
18:1 I *s* another angel descending
19:11 I *s* the heaven opened, and
19:17 I *s* also an angel standing
19:19 I *s* the wild beast and the
20:1 I *s* an angel coming down
20:4 I *s* thrones, and there were
20:4 I *s* the souls of those
20:11 I *s* a great white throne and
20:12 I *s* the dead, the great and
21:1 I *s* a new heaven and a new
21:2 I *s* also the holy city, New

Sawed

1Ki 7:9 hewn, *s* with stone-saws

Sawing

2Sa 12:31 *s* stones and at sharp
1Ch 20:3 employed at *s* stones and at

Sawn

Heb 11:37 they were *s* asunder, they

Say

Ge 1:3 God proceeded to *s*: Let light
1:6 went on to *s*: Let an expanse
1:9 And God went on to *s*: Let the
1:11 God went on to *s*: Let the
1:14 And God went on to *s*: Let
1:20 And God went on to *s*: Let the
1:24 And God went on to *s*: Let the
1:26 God went on to *s*: Let us make
1:29 God went on to *s*: Here I have
2:18 Jehovah God went on to *s*
3:1 So it began to *s* to the woman
3:12 man went on to *s*: The woman
3:14 God proceeded to *s* to the
3:22 Jehovah God went on to *s*
9:1 *s* to them: Be fruitful and
9:8 God went on to *s* to Noah and
11:3 *s*, each one to the other
12:1 *s* to Abram: Go your way out
12:12 *s*, This is his wife
12:13 Please *s* you are my sister
12:19 Why did you *s*, She is my
14:2 Bela (that is to *s*, Zoar)
14:8 Bela (that is to *s*, Zoar)
14:23 not *s*, It was I who made
15:5 on to *s* to him: So your seed
15:13 *s* to Abram: You may know
16:8 *s*: Hagar, maidservant of
16:9 angel went on to *s* to her
17:15 *s* to Abraham: As for Sarai
17:17 *s* in his heart: Will a man a
18:23 *s*: Will you really sweep
18:27 *s*: Please, here I have
19:2 *s*: Please, now, my lords
19:17 *s*: Escape for your soul! Do
19:31 firstborn proceeded to *s*
20:5 did not he *s* to me, She is my
20:5 she too *s*, He is my brother
20:10 Abimelech went on to *s* to
20:13 *s* of me: He is my brother
21:10 *s* to Abraham: Drive out this
21:29 Abimelech went on to *s* to
22:2 *s*: Take, please, your son
22:7 Isaac began to *s* to Abraham
22:12 he went on to *s*: Do not put
22:16 *s*: By myself I do swear, is
23:2 that is to *s*, Hebron, in the
23:19 that is to *s*, Hebron, in the
24:12 he went on to *s*: Jehovah the
24:14 *s*, Let your water jar down
24:14 *s*, Take a drink, and I shall
24:23 *s*: Whose daughter are you?
24:27 *s*: Blessed be Jehovah the
24:34 to *s*: I am Abraham's servant
24:43 *s*: Please, let me drink a
24:44 *s* to me: Both you take a
24:60 bless Rebekah and *s* to her
25:23 Jehovah proceeded to *s* to her
26:7 he would *s*: She is my sister
26:7 afraid to *s* My wife for fear
26:24 to *s*: I am the God of
26:32 *s* to him: We . . . found water
27:2 he went on to *s*: Here, now, I
27:11 to *s* to Rebekah his mother
27:19 Jacob went on to *s* to his
27:27 to bless him and to *s*
27:34 *s* to his father: Bless me
27:35 to *s*: Your brother came with
28:13 and he proceeded to *s*
29:7 to *s*: Why, it is yet full day

Ge 30:1 *s* to Jacob: Give me children
30:31 And Jacob went on to *s*
31:8 If on the one hand he would *s*
31:8 on the other hand he would *s*
31:31 Jacob proceeded to *s* to Laban
31:36 Jacob went on to *s* to Laban
31:48 to *s*: This heap is a witness
31:51 Laban went on to *s* to Jacob
32:4 *s* to my lord, to Esau, This
32:18 *s*, To your servant, to Jacob
32:20 *s* also, Here is your servant
34:11 whatever you will *s* to me I
34:12 what you may *s* to me; only
34:14 they went on to *s* to them
35:6 Luz . . . that is to *s*, Bethel
35:10 God went on to *s* to him
35:19 that is to *s*, Bethlehem
35:27 that is to *s*, Hebron, where
36:1 Esau, that is to *s*, Edom
37:6 *s* to them: Listen, please, to
37:8 brothers began to *s* to him
37:10 began to rebuke him and *s*
37:20 must *s* a vicious wild beast
37:22 Reuben went on to *s* to them
39:7 Joseph and *s*: Lie down with
39:8 would *s* to his master's wife
39:14 *s* to them: Look! He brought
40:9 *s* to him: In my dream, why
42:9 *s* to them: You are spies! You
42:21 began to *s* one to the other
42:22 Did not I *s* to you, Do not
43:2 *s* to them: Return, buy a
43:5 the man did *s* to us, You must
43:7 *s*, Bring your brother down
43:18 to *s*: It is because of the
43:29 he went on to *s*: Is this
44:4 overtake them and to *s* to
44:16 What can we *s* to my master?
45:9 *s* to him, This is what your
45:17 *S* to your brothers, Do this
46:3 he went on to *s*: I am the
46:31 *s* to him, My brothers and
46:33 *s*, What is your occupation?
46:34 you must *s*, Your servants
48:3 Jacob proceeded to *s* to
48:4 And he went on to *s* to me
48:7 that is to *s*, Bethlehem
48:11 Israel went on to *s* to
48:15 to bless Joseph and to *s*
50:15 to *s*: It may be that Joseph
50:17 what you are to *s* to Joseph
Ex 1:9 he proceeded to *s* to his people
1:16 he went so far as to *s*: When
2:10 call his name Moses and to *s*
3:6 And he went on to *s*: I am the
3:13 sons of Israel and I do *s* to
3:13 *s* to me, What is his name?
3:13 What shall I *s* to them?
3:14 to *s* to the sons of Israel
3:15 are to *s* to the sons of Israel
3:16 and you must *s* to them
3:17 I *s*, I shall bring you up out
3:18 and you men must *s* to him
4:1 *s*, Jehovah did not appear to
4:12 teach you what you ought to *s*
4:21 Jehovah went on to *s* to Moses
4:22 And you must *s* to Pharaoh
4:23 I *s* to you: Send my son away
5:1 and proceeded to *s* to Pharaoh
5:3 *s*: The God of the Hebrews has
6:2 and to *s* to him: I am Jehovah
6:6 *s* to the sons of Israel, I am
7:9 must *s* to Aaron, Take your rod
7:16 must *s* to him, Jehovah the
7:19 *S* to Aaron, Take your rod and
8:1 Go in to Pharaoh . . . *s* to him
8:5 *S* to Aaron, Stretch your hand
8:9 *s* when I shall make entreaty
8:16 *S* to Aaron, Stretch your rod
8:20 And you must *s* to him, This
9:13 must *s* to him, This is what
11:1 *s* to Moses: One plague more
11:4 Moses went on to *s*: This is
12:26 when your sons *s* to you
12:27 must *s*, It is the sacrifice
12:43 *s* to Moses and Aaron: This
13:3 And Moses went on to *s* to the
13:14 must *s* to him, By strength
14:3 Then Pharaoh will certainly *s*
14:11 *s* to Moses: Is it because
14:25 Egyptians began to *s*: Let us
15:1 *s* the following: Let me sing
15:26 And he went on to *s*: If you
16:9 Moses went on to *s* to Aaron

Ex 16:9 *S* to the entire assembly of
16:15 began to *s* to one another
19:3 *s* to the house of Jacob and to
19:6 words that you are to *s* to
19:10 And Jehovah went on to *s* to
20:19 And they began to *s* to Moses
20:22 Jehovah went on to *s* to
20:22 to *s* to the sons of Israel
21:5 *s*, I really love my master
22:9 of which he may *s*, This is it
28:38 that is to *s*, all their holy
30:34 went on to *s* to Moses: Take
32:4 And they began to *s*: This is
32:9 Jehovah went on to *s* to Moses
32:11 Jehovah his God and to *s*: Why
32:12 should the Egyptians *s*, With
32:17 he proceeded to *s* to Moses
32:29 Moses went on to *s*: Fill
32:30 Moses proceeded to *s* to the
33:5 Jehovah went on to *s* to Moses
33:5 *S* to the sons of Israel, You
33:17 went on to *s* to Moses: This
34:27 went on to *s* to Moses
35:4 Moses went on to *s* to the
36:5 *s* to Moses: The people are
Le 1:2 *s* to them, In case some man of
9:6 *s*: This is the thing that
15:2 *s* to them, In case any man
16:2 to *s* to Moses: Speak to Aaron
17:2 *s* to them, This is the thing
17:8 *s* to them, As for any man of
18:2 *s* to them, I am Jehovah your
19:2 *s* to them, You should prove
20:2 *s* to the sons of Israel, Any
21:1 *s* to Moses: Talk to the
21:1 *s* to them, For a deceased
22:3 *S* to them, Throughout your
22:18 *s* to them, As for any man of
23:2 must *s* to them, The seasonal
23:10 must *s* to them, When you
25:2 you must *s* to them, When you
25:20 *s*: What are we going to eat
27:2 *s* to them, In case a man
Nu 5:12 *s* to them, In case any man's
5:19 *s* to the woman: If no man has
5:21 priest must *s* to the woman
5:22 the woman must *s*: Amen!
6:2 *s* to them, In case a man or a
8:2 *s* to him, Whenever you light
10:35 Moses would *s*: Do arise
10:36 *s*: Do return, O Jehovah, to
11:4 *s*: Who will give us meat to
11:12 *s* to me, Carry them in your
11:18 *s*, Sanctify yourselves for
11:23 whether what I *s* befalls you
12:6 *s*: Hear my words, please
13:17 *s* to them: Go up here into
13:27 *s*: We entered into the land
13:30 *s*: Let us go up directly, and
14:2 *s* against them: If only we
14:7 *s* this to all the assembly of
14:15 nations . . . certainly *s* this
14:28 *S* to them, As I live, is the
15:2 you must *s* to them, When you
15:18 *s* to them, On your coming
15:37 Jehovah went on to *s* this to
15:38 you must *s* to them that they
16:8 Moses went on to *s* to Korah
16:34 began to *s*: We are afraid
16:37 *S* to Eleazar the son of Aaron
17:12 began to *s* this to Moses
18:1 Jehovah proceeded to *s* to
18:20 Jehovah went on to *s* to
18:26 speak to the Levites . . . *s*
18:30 And you must *s* to them
20:10 *s* to them: Hear, now, you
21:27 sayers of mock verses . . . *s*
22:4 *s* to the older men of Midian
22:17 everything you may *s* to me
23:3 Balaam went on to *s* to Balak
24:10 Balak went on to *s* to Balaam
24:20 went on to *s*: Amalek was
24:21 *s*: Durable is your dwelling
24:23 went on to *s*: Woe! Who will
25:12 For that reason *s*, Here I
26:1 Jehovah went on to *s* this to
28:2 *s* to them, You should take
28:3 you must *s* to them, This is
31:25 Jehovah proceeded to *s* this
31:49 to *s* to Moses: Your servants
32:5 *s*: If we have found favor in
33:36 that is to *s*, Kadesh
33:51 you must *s* to them, You are
34:2 *s* to them, You are going into

Nu 35:10 and you must s to them, You
36:2 s: Jehovah commanded my lord
De 1:9 I proceeded to s this to you
1:42 S to them: You must not go up
4:6 s, This great nation is
4:48 Sion, that is to s, Hermon
5:1 s to them: Hear, O Israel
5:27 that Jehovah our God will s
5:28 Jehovah went on to s to me, I
5:30 s to them: Return home to
6:21 then you must s to your son
7:17 In case you s in your heart
8:17 s in your heart, My own
9:4 Do not s in your heart when
9:12 Jehovah proceeded to s to me
9:13 Jehovah went on to s this
9:26 to s, O Sovereign Lord Jehovah
9:28 s: Because Jehovah was unable
12:20 to s, Let me eat meat
17:11 that they will s to you
18:21 s in your heart: How shall
20:3 s to them, Hear, O Israel
20:8 s, Who is the man that is
21:7 s, Our hands did not shed this
21:20 they must s to the older men
22:16 the girl's father must s to
25:7 s, My husband's brother has
25:8 stand and s, I have found no
25:9 s, That is the way it should
26:3 and s to him, I must report
26:5 s before Jehovah your God
26:13 you must s before Jehovah
26:17 Jehovah you have induced to s
26:18 he has induced you to s
27:14 Levites must answer and s
27:15 must answer and s, Amen!
27:16 all the people must s, Amen!
27:17 all the people must s, Amen!
27:18 all the people must s, Amen!
27:19 all the people must s, Amen!
27:20 all the people must s, Amen!
27:21 all the people must s, Amen!
27:22 all the people must s, Amen!
27:23 all the people must s, Amen!
27:24 all the people must s, Amen!
27:25 all the people must s, Amen!
27:26 all the people must s, Amen!
28:67 s, If it only were evening!
28:67 s, If it only were morning!
29:2 to s to them: You were the
29:22 future generation . . . to s
29:24 nations will be bound to s
29:25 to s, It was because they
31:7 s to him before the eyes of
31:17 be bound to s in that day
31:23 s: Be courageous and strong
32:7 Your old men . . . can s it to
32:27 might s: Our hand has proved
32:37 s, Where are their gods
32:40 do s: As I am alive to time
32:46 s to them: Apply your hearts
33:2 s: Jehovah—from Sinai he
33:7 s: Hear, O Jehovah, the voice
33:27 he will s, Annihilate them!
34:4 s to him: This is the land
Jos 1:1 to s to Joshua the son of Nun
2:4 s: Yes, the men did come to
2:9 she went on to s to the men
2:16 she proceeded to s to them
2:24 to s to Joshua: Jehovah has
3:7 to s to Joshua: This day I
3:9 on to s to the sons of Israel
4:1 proceeded to s to Joshua
4:5 s to them: Pass ahead of the
4:7 s to them, Because the waters
4:21 to s to the sons of Israel
6:2 went on to s to Joshua
6:7 he went on to s to the people
6:10 when I s to you, Shout! Then
6:16 to s to the people: Shout
7:7 to s: Alas, Sovereign Lord
7:8 what can I s after Israel has
7:13 must s, Sanctify yourselves
8:6 they will s, They are fleeing
9:11 must s to them: We are your
10:12 to s before the eyes of
10:24 to s to the commanders of
10:25 Joshua went on to s to them
15:8 that is to s, Jerusalem
15:9 that is to s, Kiriath-jearim
15:10 that is to s, Chesalon
15:13 that is to s, Hebron
15:16 And Caleb proceeded to s
15:25 that is to s, Hazor
Jos 15:49 that is to s, Debir
15:54 that is to s, Hebron, and
15:60 that is to s, Kiriath-jearim
18:13 Luz, that is to s, Bethel
18:14 s, Kiriath-jearim, a city
18:28 that is to s, Jerusalem
20:7 that is to s, Hebron, in
21:11 that is to s, Hebron, in the
22:2 s to them: For your part, you
22:8 s to them: Return to your
22:24 your sons will s to our
22:27 that your sons may not s
22:28 in case they should s that
22:28 s: See the representation
23:2 to s to them: As for me, I
24:2 Joshua went on to s to all
24:27 Joshua went on to s to all
Jg 3:19 to s: I have a secret word
3:20 Ehud went on to s: A word of
4:6 to s to him: Has not Jehovah
4:20 And he went on to s to her
4:20 you must then s, No!
6:8 and to s to them: This is what
6:25 to s to him: Take the young
6:29 to s one to another: Who has
7:1 that is to s, Gideon, and all
7:4 I s to you, This one will go
7:4 I s to you, This one will not
7:9 to s to him: Rise up, descend
7:13 to s: Here is a dream that I
7:17 s to them: You should learn
7:18 and you must s, Jehovah's and
8:24 to s to them: Let me make a
9:28 son of Ebed went on to s: Who
9:29 he went on to s to Abimelech
9:54 s about me, It was a woman
10:18 began to s to one another
11:2 to s to him: You must have no
11:35 s: Alas, my daughter! You
11:37 to s to her father: Let this
12:5 s: Let me pass over, then the
12:5 Gilead would s to each one
12:5 When he would s: No!
12:6 they would s to him: Please
12:6 to him: Please s Shibboleth
12:6 he would s: Sibboleth, as he
12:6 he was unable to s the word
13:8 and s: Excuse me, Jehovah
14:15 to s to Samson's wife: Fool
14:16 s: You only hate me, you do
15:6 Philistines began to s: Who
15:13 s to him: No, but we shall
15:18 s: It was you that gave this
16:5 s to her: Fool him and see in
16:9 s to him: The Philistines are
16:15 How dare you s, I do love
16:25 s: Call Samson that he may
16:30 s: Let my soul die with the
17:3 to s: I must without fail
18:3 s to him: Who brought you
18:8 s to them: How was it with
18:24 s to me, What is the matter
19:10 that is to s, Jerusalem
19:13 s to his attendant: Come and
20:32 sons of Benjamin began to s
21:3 they would s: Why, O Jehovah
21:8 they went on to s: Which one
21:22 shall certainly s to them
Ru 1:16 Ruth proceeded to s: Do not
1:20 And she would s to the women
2:4 to s to the harvesters
2:4 would s to him: Jehovah bless
2:14 Boaz proceeded to s to her at
2:19 she went on to s: The name of
2:20 And Naomi went on to s to her
3:5 All that you s to me I shall
3:11 All that you s I shall do for
3:15 he went on to s: Bring the
3:17 she went on to s: These six
4:14 women began to s to Naomi
1Sa 1:8 s to her: Hannah, why do you
1:11 went on to make a vow and s
2:1 Hannah went on to pray and s
2:16 When the man would s to him
2:23 And he used to s to them
2:27 to come to Eli and s to him
2:30 I did indeed s, As for your
2:36 will certainly s: Attach me
3:9 you must s, Speak, Jehovah
3:11 And Jehovah went on to s to
3:17 he went on to s: What is the
4:3 men of Israel began to s
4:16 man proceeded to s to Eli
7:3 Samuel proceeded to s to all
1Sa 8:7 all that they s to you
8:11 to s: This will become the
8:22 Jehovah proceeded to s to
9:19 answer Saul and s: I am the
9:24 s: Here is what has been
9:27 S to the attendant that he
10:2 s to you, The she-asses that
10:15 What did Samuel s to you
10:18 to s to the sons of Israel
10:19 s: No, but a king is what
10:24 and s: Let the king live!
11:5 s: What is the matter with
11:9 s to the men of Jabesh in
11:12 people began to s to Samuel
12:6 Samuel went on to s to the
12:10 to Jehovah for aid and s
12:19 people began to s to Samuel
14:1 Jonathan . . . proceeded to s
14:9 s to us, Stand still until
14:10 s, Come up against us! we
14:11 Philistines proceeded to s
14:17 Saul proceeded to s to the
14:34 s to them, Bring near to me
14:40 went on to s to all Israel
14:41 proceeded to s to Jehovah
15:13 and Saul began to s to him
15:17 And Samuel went on to s
15:32 Agag began to s to himself
16:2 And Jehovah went on to s
16:2 you must s, To sacrifice to
16:15 servants of Saul began to s
16:18 s: Look! I have seen how a
17:8 battle lines of Israel and s
17:10 the Philistine went on to s
17:25 s: Have you seen this man
17:26 David began to s to the men
17:32 David proceeded to s to Saul
17:34 David went on to s to Saul
17:44 Philistine went on to s to
18:11 s: I will pin David even to
18:25 you men will s to David
19:22 s: Where are Samuel and
19:24 s: Is Saul also among the
20:3 s, Do not let Jonathan know
20:4 Jonathan went on to s to
20:4 soul may s I shall do for
20:6 s, David earnestly asked
20:7 s is, It is all right! it
20:12 Jonathan went on to s to
20:18 Jonathan went on to s to
20:21 s to the attendant, Look!
20:22 way I should s to the lad
20:26 Saul did not s anything at
20:29 s, Send me away, please
20:36 s to his attendant: Run
20:37 s: Is not the arrow farther
20:42 Jonathan went on to s to
21:2 s to me, Let no one know
21:8 David went on to s to
21:9 s: There is none like it
21:11 s to him: Is not this David
22:13 Saul went on to s to him
23:7 s: God has sold him into my
23:10 David went on to s
23:12 David went on to s: Will
23:17 s to him: Do not be afraid
24:4 David's men began to s to
24:4 Jehovah does s to you
24:9 David went on to s to Saul
24:16 Saul proceeded to s: Is this
24:17 s to David: You are more
25:6 you must s to my brother
26:10 David went on to s: As
26:14 Abner began to answer and s
26:15 David went on to s to Abner
26:17 s: Is this your voice, my
28:12 woman went on to s to Saul
28:13 woman went on to s to Saul
28:15 Samuel began to s to Saul
28:16 Samuel went on to s: Why
29:3 s: What do these Hebrews
29:4 Philistines went on to s to
2Sa 1:3 David proceeded to s to him
1:4 David went on to s to him
1:8 s to me, Who are you?
1:18 s that the sons of Judah
2:1 David went on to s: Where
2:26 s: Is the sword going to eat
2:26 s to the people to turn back
3:8 s: Am I a dog's head that
3:11 s one word more in reply to
3:33 s: As with the death of a
3:38 king went on to s to his
5:2 Jehovah proceeded to s to you

2Sa 5:6 s to David: You will not come
5:8 s: The blind one and the lame
6:9 s: How will the ark of
7:5 s to my servant David, This
7:8 s to my servant David, This
9:1 s: Is there yet anyone that
9:3 s: Is there nobody of the
9:7 s to him: Do not be afraid
10:5 s: Dwell in Jericho until
10:11 s: If the Syrians become
11:20 s to you, Why did you have
11:21 s, Your servant Uriah the
11:23 s to David: The men proved
11:25 s to Joab, Do not let this
12:18 s to him, The child has
13:5 s to him, Please, let Tamar
13:28 s to you, Strike down Amnon!
14:4 s: Do save, O king!
14:10 king went on to s: If there
14:13 s: Why, then, have you
14:19 s: Is the hand of Joab with
14:22 Joab went on to s: Today
15:2 call him and s: From what
15:2 and he would s: From one of
15:3 Absalom would s to him
15:4 Absalom would go on to s
15:7 Absalom proceeded to s to
15:10 s, Absalom has become king
15:26 s, I have found no delight
15:27 king went on to s to Zadok
15:34 s to Absalom, I am your
16:10 s, Why did you do that way?
16:11 David went on to s to
16:16 s to Absalom: Let the king
16:19 the second time I must s
17:1 s to Absalom: Let me choose
17:8 And Hushai went on to s
17:9 s, A defeat has taken place
17:11 s in counsel: Let all Israel
18:27 the watchman went on to s
18:28 to s: Blessed be Jehovah
18:31 and the Cushite began to s
19:2 people heard s on that day
19:13 to Amasa you should s, Are
19:29 I do s, You and Ziba should
19:41 s to the king: Why did our
20:1 to blow the horn and s
20:9 Joab proceeded to s to Amasa
20:16 S, please, to Joab, Come
20:18 And she went on to s
21:3 s to the Gibeonites: What
22:2 he went on to s: Jehovah is
23:17 And he went on to s: It is
24:12 Go, and you must s to David
24:17 David proceeded to s to
24:17 he proceeded to s: Here it
24:23 Araunah went on to s to the
1Ki 1:13 and you must s to him
1:24 did you yourself s, Adonijah
1:29 s: As Jehovah is living who
1:33 king went on to s to them
1:34 s, Let King Solomon live!
1:36 God of my lord the king s
2:14 he went on to s: There is a
2:17 to s: Please, say to Solomon
2:17 s to Solomon the king
2:20 to s: There is one little
2:21 went on to s: Let Abishag
2:42 did you not s to me, Good is
2:44 king went on to s to Shimei
3:5 to s: Request what I should
3:11 And God went on to s to him
3:24 And the king went on to s
3:25 And the king proceeded to s
5:6 to all that you may s
5:7 to s: Blessed is Jehovah today
8:1 that is to s, Zion
8:15 on to s: Blessed is Jehovah
8:23 on to s: O Jehovah the God
9:3 Jehovah went on to s to him
9:8 s, For what reason did
9:9 they will have to s, For the
11:31 went on to s to Jeroboam
12:9 he went on to s to them
12:10 s to this people who have
12:23 S to Rehoboam the son of
12:26 Jeroboam began to s in his
13:7 to s to the man of the true
13:15 And he went on to s to him
13:31 s to his sons: When I
14:6 to s: Come in, you wife of
14:7 s to Jeroboam, This is what
17:1 to s to Ahab: As Jehovah the
17:11 s: Please, get me a bit of
1Ki 17:21 s: O Jehovah my God, please
18:5 Ahab went on to s to Obadiah
18:8 s to your lord, Here is
18:11 s to your lord: Here is
18:14 s to your lord: Here is
18:21 not s a word in answer to
18:22 went on to s to the people
18:27 s: Call at the top of your
18:36 s: O Jehovah, the God of
18:43 he went on to s, Go back
18:44 got to s: Look! There is a
18:44 Go up, s to Ahab, Hitch up!
19:4 s: It is enough! Now
19:9 to s to him: What is your
19:13 it proceeded to s to him
20:2 went on to s to him: This is
20:9 S to my lord the king, All
20:28 s: This is what Jehovah has
20:33 on to s: Ben-hadad is your
20:37 to s: Strike me, please
20:39 s: Your servant himself
21:6 s to him, Do give me your
21:20 to s to Elijah: Have you
22:4 went on to s to Jehoshaphat
22:5 went on to s to the king of
22:6 they began to s: Go up, and
22:8 Do not let the king s a thing
22:14 what Jehovah will s to me
22:15 the king proceeded to s to
22:17 s: These have no masters
22:18 Did I not s to you, He will
22:19 s: Therefore hear the word
22:20 s, Who will fool Ahab
22:20 one began to s something
22:27 s, This is what the king
2Ki 1:3 s to them, Is it because
1:6 to s to us, Go, return to the
2:2 Elijah began to s to Elisha
2:15 s: The spirit of Elijah has
2:16 And they went on to s to him
2:18 Did I not s to you, Do not go?
3:8 s: By which particular way
3:13 to s to the king of Israel
3:16 s: This is what Jehovah has
3:23 began to s: This is blood!
4:6 she went on to s to her son
4:13 s to her, Here you have
4:14 he went on to s: What, then
4:26 s to her, Is it all right
4:28 Did I not s, You must not
4:41 went on to s: Pour out for
5:11 s: Here I had said to myself
6:1 prophets began to s to Elisha
6:3 s: Come on, please, and go
6:5 And he began to cry out and s
6:17 Elisha began to pray and s
6:18 and s: Please, strike this
6:28 the king went on to s to her
6:31 to s: So may God do to me
6:33 the king proceeded to s
7:3 to s the one to the other
7:9 began to s the one to the
8:10 Go, s to him, You will
8:14 What did Elisha s to you?
9:3 s, This is what Jehovah has
9:6 upon his head and s to him
9:11 s to him: Is everything all
9:13 and s: Jehu has become king!
9:17 let him s, Is there peace?
9:19 to s: This is what the king
9:36 s: It is the word of Jehovah
9:37 may not s: This is Jezebel
10:4 began to s: Look! Two kings
10:5 that you s to us we shall do
10:20 s: Sanctify a solemn
10:24 s: As for the man that
11:12 and s: Let the king live!
12:4 to s to the priests: All the
13:14 s: My father, my father
13:15 s to him: Take a bow and
13:16 to s to the king of Israel
13:18 to s: Take the arrows
18:19 s to Hezekiah, This is what
18:22 you men should s to me
18:28 and s: Hear the word of the
19:3 they proceeded to s to him
19:6 should s to your lord
19:10 men should s to Hezekiah
19:15 s: O Jehovah the God of
19:23 s, With the multitude of
20:5 s to Hezekiah the leader of
20:7 s: You men, take a cake of
20:14 What did these men s and
20:15 to s: What did they see in
2Ki 20:19 to s: Is it not so, if peace
22:15 S to the man that has sent
22:18 is what you should s to him
25:8 that is to s, the nineteenth
1Ch 1:27 Abram, that is to s, Abraham
11:2 to s to you, You yourself
11:4 that is to s, Jebus, where
11:5 of Jebus began to s to David
11:5 is to s, the city of David
11:19 s: It is unthinkable on my
13:2 David went on to s to all
15:12 and he went on to s to them
16:31 s among the nations
16:35 s, Save us, O God of our
16:36 people proceeded to s, Amen!
17:1 David proceeded to s to
17:4 must s to David my servant
17:7 will s to my servant David
17:18 What more could David s to
19:5 s: Dwell in Jericho until
19:12 s: If the Syrians become
21:17 David proceeded to s to the
21:18 said to Gad to s to David
22:7 s to Solomon his son
28:20 to s to Solomon his son
29:20 David went on to s to all
2Ch 1:2 Solomon proceeded to s the
2:12 Hiram went on to s: Blessed
5:2 of David, that is to s, Zion
6:4 to s: Blessed be Jehovah the
6:14 to s: O Jehovah the God of
7:21 s, For what reason did
7:22 s, It was for the reason
10:9 s to them: What is it that
10:10 s to the people who have
10:10 s to them, My own little
11:3 S to Rehoboam the son of
12:5 s to them: This is what
14:11 s: O Jehovah, as to helping
18:3 s to Jehoshaphat the king of
18:5 s: Go up, and the true God
18:7 the king s a thing like that
18:13 what my God will s, that
18:14 s to him: Micaiah, shall
18:16 s: These have no masters
18:17 s to you, He will prophesy
18:18 s: Therefore hear the word
18:19 s, Who will fool Ahab the
18:26 s, This is what the king
19:6 s to the judges: See what
20:2 that is to s, En-gedi
20:6 s: O Jehovah the God of our
28:23 s: Because the gods of the
29:5 s to them: Listen to me
33:16 s to Judah to serve Jehovah
34:23 S to the man that sent you
34:26 what you should s to him
35:3 went on to s to the Levites
Ezr 6:9 that are in Jerusalem s
9:6 s: O my God, I do feel
9:10 what shall we s, O our God
Ne 1:5 to s: Ah, Jehovah the God of
2:7 I went on to s to the king
2:19 s: What is this thing that
4:2 to s before his brothers and
4:2 s: What are the feeble Jews
4:3 s: Even what they are building
4:10 Judah began to s: The power
4:12 to s to us ten times
4:19 to s to the nobles and the
5:7 s to them: Usury is what you
5:8 to s to them: We ourselves
5:9 s: The thing that you are doing
6:10 s: Let us meet by appointment
8:9 to s to all the people: This
8:10 to s to them: Go, eat the
9:5 to s: Rise, bless Jehovah your
9:15 on to s to them to enter and
9:18 s, This is your God who led
13:11 and s: Why has the house of
13:17 s to them: What is this bad
13:21 s to them: Why are you
13:22 to s to the Levites that they
Es 1:13 the king proceeded to s to the
1:17 when they s, King Ahasuerus
3:3 to s to Mordecai: Why are you
3:8 Haman proceeded to s to King
3:11 king went on to s to Haman
5:12 Haman went on to s: What is
5:14 s to the king that they should
6:4 s to the king to hang Mordecai
6:6 the king proceeded to s to him
7:5 he went on to s to Esther the
9:12 king proceeded to s to Esther

Job 1:8 Jehovah went on to s to Satan
1:14 to s: The cattle themselves
1:16 s: The very fire of God fell
1:17 to s: The Chaldeans made up
1:18 to s: Your sons and your
1:21 s: Naked I came out of my
2:3 Jehovah went on to s to Satan
4:1 Eliphaz . . . to reply and s
6:1 Job proceeded to answer and s
8:1 proceeded to answer and s
9:1 Job proceeded to answer and s
9:12 s to him, What are you doing?
9:22 why I do s, One blameless
10:2 s to God, Do not pronounce
11:1 proceeded to answer and s
11:4 s, My instruction is pure
12:1 Job proceeded to . . . s
15:1 proceeded to answer and s
16:1 Job proceeded to . . . s
18:1 proceeded to answer and s
19:1 Job proceeded to . . . s
19:28 you men s, Why do we keep
20:1 proceeded to reply and s
20:7 ones seeing him will s, Where
21:1 Job proceeded to . . . s
21:14 And they s to the true God
21:28 you s, Where is the house
22:1 proceeded to answer and s
23:1 Job proceeded to . . . s
25:1 proceeded to answer and s
26:1 Job proceeded to . . . s
27:1 utterance and went on to s
28:28 he went on to s to man
29:1 utterance and went on to s
29:18 I used to s, Within my nest
31:31 men of my tent did not s
32:6 and s: Young I am in days
32:11 could search for words to s
32:13 may not s, We have found
33:27 He will sing to men and s
33:32 any words to s, make reply
34:1 continued to answer and s
34:18 one s to a king, You are
34:31 actually s to God himself
34:34 Men of heart . . . will s
35:3 you s, Of what use is it to
35:14 you s you do not behold him
36:1 Elihu proceeded to s further
36:2 are yet words to s for God
36:10 he will s that they should
37:19 what we should s to him
38:1 out of the windstorm and s
38:11 I went on to s, This far
38:35 And s to you, Here we are!
40:1 to answer Job and s
40:3 on to answer Jehovah and s
40:6 out of the windstorm and s
41:3 will it s soft words to you?
42:1 to answer Jehovah and s
42:7 to s to Eliphaz the Temanite
Ps 4:4 Have your s in your heart
11:1 dare you men s to my soul
13:4 enemy may not s: I have won
18:*super* And he proceeded to s
35:3 S to my soul: I am your
35:10 all my bones themselves s
35:25 they not s in their heart
35:25 s: We have swallowed him
35:27 And let them s constantly
40:16 Let those s constantly
41:5 s what is bad concerning me
42:3 they s to me all day long
42:9 I will s to God my crag: Why
42:10 they s to me all day long
50:12 I would not s it to you
50:16 God will have to s: What
52:*super* to tell Saul and s to him
54:*super* to s to Saul: Is not David
58:11 mankind will s: Surely there
66:3 S to God: How fear-inspiring
66:14 my lips have opened up to s
70:4 may they s constantly
79:10 nations s: Where is their
89:19 s: I have placed help upon a
90:3 s: Go back, you sons of men
91:2 s to Jehovah: You are my
95:10 s: They are a people
96:10 S among the nations: Jehovah
102:24 s: O my God, Do not take
106:23 about to s to annihilate
106:48 all the people must s Amen
107:2 ones of Jehovah s so
115:2 Why should the nations s
118:2 Let Israel now s
118:3 of the house of Aaron now s
118:4 those fearing Jehovah now s
119:82 s: When will you comfort
124:1 Let Israel now s
126:2 to s among the nations
129:1 Let Israel now s
139:11 s: Surely darkness itself
139:20 s things about you according
144:12 s: Our sons are like little
Pr 3:28 s to your fellowman: Go, and
4:4 s to me: May your heart keep
5:12 s: How I have hated discipline
7:4 S to wisdom: You are my
7:13 and she begins to s to him
19:7 is pursuing with things to s
20:9 s: I have cleansed my heart
20:22 not s: I will pay back evil
24:12 s: Look! We did not know of
24:29 not s: Just as he did to me
25:7 is better for him to s to you
30:9 and s: Who is Jehovah?
31:4 or for high officials to s
Ec 1:10 may s: See this; it is new
5:6 neither s before the angel that
6:3 s that one prematurely born is
7:10 Do not s: Why has it happened
8:2 I s: Keep the very order of the
8:4 who may s to him: What are
8:17 s they are wise enough to
12:1 s: I have no delight in them
Isa 2:3 go and s: Come, you people
3:10 S, you men, that it will be
6:5 s: Woe to me! For I am as
6:7 s: Look! This has touched
6:8 s: Here I am! Send me
6:9 s: Go, and you must say to
6:9 s to this people, Hear again
7:3 s to Isaiah: Go out, please
7:4 s to him, Watch yourself and
7:13 s: Listen, please, O house
8:1 Jehovah proceeded to s to me
8:12 s, A conspiracy! respecting
8:19 s to you people: Apply to
10:8 s, Are not my princes at the
12:1 s: I shall thank you, O
12:4 s: Give thanks to Jehovah
14:4 s: How has the one driving
14:10 s to you, Have you yourself
14:32 anyone s in answer to the
19:11 s to Pharaoh: I am the son
20:3 s: Just as my servant Isaiah
20:6 certain to s in that day
21:9 began to speak up and s
24:16 s: For me there is leanness
25:9 s: Look! This is our God
29:11 s: I am unable, for it is
29:12 s: I do not know writing at
29:15 s: Who is seeing us, and
29:16 s respecting its maker
29:16 thing formed actually s
30:16 s: No, but on horses we
30:22 you will s to it: Mere dirt
33:24 resident will s: I am sick
35:4 S to those who are anxious
36:4 s to Hezekiah, This is what
36:7 s to me, It is Jehovah our
36:13 s: Hear the words of the
37:3 s to him: This is what
37:6 you should s to your lord
37:10 s to Hezekiah the king of
37:24 taunted Jehovah and you s
38:3 s: I beseech you, O Jehovah
38:5 you must s to Hezekiah
38:15 will he actually s to me
38:21 s: Let them take a cake of
39:3 What did these men s, and
39:4 s: What did they see in your
39:8 went on to s: Because peace
40:9 S to the cities of Judah
40:27 For what reason do you s
41:6 one would s to his brother
41:26 that we may s, He is right
42:22 anyone to s: Bring back!
43:6 s to the north, Give up!
43:9 hear and s, It is the truth!
44:5 will s: I belong to Jehovah
44:20 s: Is there not a falsehood
45:9 the clay s to its former
45:24 And your achievement s
48:5 not s, My own idol has done
48:7 may not s, Look! I have
48:20 S: Jehovah has repurchased
49:3 went on to s to me: You are
49:6 he proceeded to s: It has
Isa 49:9 to s to the prisoners, Come
49:20 s, The place has become
49:21 for certain s in your heart
51:16 s to Zion, You are my
56:3 s, Without doubt Jehovah
56:3 s, Look! I am a dry tree
57:14 s, Bank up, you people
58:9 cry for help, and he would s
62:11 S, you people, to the
63:8 went on to s: Surely they
65:8 has to s, Do not ruin it
Jer 1:7 Jehovah went on to s to me
1:7 Do not s, I am but a boy
1:12 s to me: You have seen well
2:8 priests themselves did not s
2:23 s, I have not defiled myself
2:25 to s, It is hopeless!
2:27 will s, Do rise up and save
2:35 you s, I have remained
3:6 s to me in the days of Josiah
3:11 Jehovah went on to s to me
3:12 words to the north and s
3:16 No more will they s, The ark
4:5 s it out, and blow a horn
4:5 s: Gather yourselves together
4:10 to s: Alas, O Sovereign Lord
5:2 s: As Jehovah is alive!
5:19 must occur that you will s
5:19 s to them, Just as you have
7:2 s, Hear the word of Jehovah
7:10 s, We shall certainly be
7:28 s to them, This is the
8:4 s to them, This is what
8:8 s: We are wise, and the law
9:13 And Jehovah proceeded to s
10:11 what you men will s to
11:3 s to them, This is what
11:5 I proceeded to answer and s
11:6 Jehovah went on to s to me
13:6 Jehovah proceeded to s to me
13:12 must s to them this word
13:12 will certainly s to you
13:13 s to them, This is what
13:18 S to the king and to the
13:21 What will you s when one
13:22 you will s in your heart
14:11 Jehovah proceeded to s to
14:14 Jehovah went on to s to me
14:17 must s to them this word
15:1 Jehovah proceeded to s to me
15:2 s to you, Where shall we go
15:2 you must also s to them
16:10 and they actually s to you
16:11 you must also s to them
16:19 they will s: Indeed our
17:20 s to them, Hear the word
18:11 s, please, to the men of
18:18 to s: Come, men, and let us
19:3 s, Hear the word of Jehovah
19:11 you must s to them, This is
19:14 and s to all the people
21:3 Jeremiah proceeded to s to
21:3 what you will s to Zedekiah
21:8 to this people you will s
22:2 you must s, Hear the word of
22:8 and s one to the other
22:9 And they will have to s
23:7 and they will no more s
23:33 s to them, You people are
23:34 s, The burden of Jehovah!
23:37 you will s to the prophet
23:38 s: The burden of Jehovah!
24:3 s to me: What are you seeing
25:27 s to them, This is what
25:28 s to them, This is what
25:30 s to them, From on high
26:4 And you must s to them
26:11 s to the princes and to
26:18 s to all the people of Judah
27:4 you should s to your masters
28:5 to s to Hananiah the prophet
28:6 the prophet proceeded to s
28:11 Hananiah went on to s
28:13 you must s to Hananiah
28:15 to s to Hananiah the prophet
29:24 to Shemaiah . . . you will s
31:7 s, Save, O Jehovah, your
31:10 s: The One scattering Israel
31:23 s this word in the land of
31:29 s, The fathers were the
32:6 Jeremiah proceeded to s: The
32:8 s to me: Buy, please, the
34:2 s to Zedekiah the king of
34:2 s to him: This is what

Jer 34:5 *s* in lament for you, for I
35:11 *s*, Come, and let us enter
35:13 *s* to the men of Judah and
36:16 *s* to Baruch: We shall
36:29 *s*, This is what Jehovah has
37:7 *s* to the king of Judah, the
37:17 *s:* Does there exist a word
38:4 the princes began to *s* to the
38:24 Zedekiah proceeded to *s* to
38:25 *s* to you, Do tell us
38:26 *s* to them, I was letting
39:16 *s* to Ebed-melech the
40:14 *s* to him: Do you not at
41:6 *s* to them: Come to Gedaliah
42:9 *s* to them: This is what
43:2 *s* to Jeremiah: It is a
43:10 *s* to them, This is what
44:24 Jeremiah continued on to *s*
45:4 *s* to him, This is what
46:14 *S*, Station yourself, making
48:14 How dare you people *s*
48:17 *S*, you people, O how the
48:19 *S*, What has been brought
50:2 *S*, Babylon has been captured
51:35 inhabitress of Zion will *s*
51:35 Chaldea! Jerusalem will *s*
51:62 *s*, O Jehovah, you yourself
51:64 *s*, This is how Babylon will
La 2:15 city of which they used to *s*
Eze 2:1 *s* to me: Son of man, stand up
2:3 to *s* to me: Son of man, I am
2:4 you must *s* to them, This is
3:1 to *s* to me: Son of man, what
3:3 to *s* to me: Son of man, you
3:10 *s* to me: Son of man, all my
3:11 *s* to them, This is what the
3:18 When I *s* to someone wicked
3:22 to *s* to me: Get up, go forth
3:24 *s* to me: Come, be shut up
3:27 you must *s* to them, This is
4:13 Jehovah went on to *s:* Just
4:14 to *s:* Alas, O Sovereign Lord
6:3 *s*, O mountains of Israel
6:11 stamp with your foot, and *s*
8:5 *s* to me: Son of man, please
8:6 *s* to me: Son of man, are you
8:12 *s* to me: Have you seen, O
8:13 to *s* to me: You will yet see
8:17 *s* to me: Have you seen this
9:4 to *s* to him: Pass through the
9:8 and cry out and *s:* Alas, O
10:2 to *s* to the man clothed with
10:2 to *s:* Enter in between the
11:5 and he went on to *s* to me
11:5 *S*, This is what Jehovah has
11:13 cry with a loud voice and *s*
11:16 therefore *s*, This is what
11:17 Therefore *s*, This is what
12:9 *s* to you, What are you doing?
12:10 *S* to them, This is what
12:11 *S*, I am a portent for you
12:19 *s* to the people of the land
12:23 *s* to them, This is what the
12:23 no more *s* it as a proverb
12:28 *s* to them, This is what the
13:2 *s* to those prophesying out of
13:11 *S* to those plastering with
13:15 *s* to you men: The wall is
13:18 And you must *s*, This is
14:4 *s* to them, This is what the
14:6 *s* to the house of Israel
14:17 *s:* Let a sword itself pass
16:3 you must *s*, This is what the
16:6 to *s* to you in your blood
16:6 Keep living! yes, to *s* to you
17:3 *s*, This is what the Sovereign
17:9 *S*, This is what the
17:12 *S*, please, to the rebellious
17:12 *S*, Look! The king of Babylon
18:19 *s:* Why is it that the son
18:25 *s:* The way of Jehovah is
18:29 *s:* The way of Jehovah is
19:2 *s*, What was your mother?
20:3 *s* to them, This is what the
20:5 *s* to them, This is what the
20:7 to *s* to them, Throw away
20:18 to *s* to their sons in the
20:27 you must *s* to them, This is
20:30 *s* to the house of Israel
20:47 *s* to the forest of the south
20:49 to *s:* Alas, O Sovereign Lord
21:3 *s* to the soil of Israel
21:7 in case they *s* to you
21:7 you must *s*, At a report
Eze 21:9 you must *s*, This is what
21:9 Jehovah has said: *S*, A sword
21:28 *s*, This is what the
21:28 must *s*, A sword, a sword
22:3 must *s*, This is what the
22:24 *s* to her, You are a land
23:36 Jehovah went on to *s* to me
24:3 *s* concerning them, This is
24:21 *S* to the house of Israel
25:3 you must *s* concerning the
26:17 a dirge and *s* to you
27:3 and you must *s* to Tyre
28:2 *s* to the leader of Tyre
28:9 without fail *s*, I am god
28:12 and you must *s* to him, This
28:22 And you must *s*, This is
29:3 *s*, This is what the
30:2 *s*, This is what the
31:2 *s* to Pharaoh the king of
32:2 *s* to him, As a maned young
33:2 and you must *s* to them
33:8 When I *s* to someone wicked
33:10 *s* to the house of Israel
33:11 *S* to them, As I am alive
33:12 *s* to the sons of your people
33:13 *s* to the righteous one
33:14 when I *s* to the wicked one
33:25 *s* to them, This is what
33:27 what you should *s* to them
34:2 *s* to them, to the shepherds
35:3 *s* to it, This is what the
36:1 *s*, O mountains of Israel
36:3 prophesy, and you must *s*
36:6 *s* to the mountains and to
36:22 *s* to the house of Israel
36:35 And people will certainly *s*
37:3 began to *s* to me: Son of man
37:4 went on to *s* to me: Prophesy
37:4 *s* to them, O you dry bones
37:9 and you must *s* to the wind
37:11 went on to *s* to me: Son of
37:12 prophesy . . . *s* to them
37:18 people begin to *s* to you
38:3 And you must *s*, This is what
38:11 *s:* I shall go up against
38:13 will *s* to you: Is it to get
38:14 must *s* to Gog, This is what
39:1 *s*, This is what the
39:17 *S* to the birds of every sort
42:13 he proceeded to *s* to me
43:7 *s* to me: Son of man, this
43:18 *s* to me: Son of man, this
44:6 *s* to Rebelliousness, to the
46:20 *s* to me: This is the place
47:8 *s* to me: This water is
Da 2:4 *S* what the dream is to your
2:7 king *s* what the dream is to
2:9 you have agreed to *s* before me
2:36 interpretation we shall *s*
3:16 to *s* back a word to you
4:18 Belteshazzar, *s* what the
4:35 check his hand or that can *s*
8:13 *s* to the particular one who
8:16 *s:* Gabriel, make that one
8:17 *s* to me: Understand, O son
8:19 *s:* Here I am causing you to
9:4 *s:* Ah Jehovah the true God, the
9:22 *s:* O Daniel, now I have come
10:11 *s* to me; O Daniel, you very
10:12 *s* to me: Do not be afraid
10:16 and *s* to the one who was
10:20 *s:* Do you really know why I
12:9 *s:* Go, Daniel, because the
Ho 1:2 Jehovah proceeded to *s* to Hosea
1:4 Jehovah went on to *s* to him
1:6 *s* to him: Call her name
2:1 *S* to your brothers, My people
2:7 *s*, I want to go and return to
2:23 *s* to those not my people
2:23 will *s:* You are my God
3:1 *s* to me: Go once again, love
7:2 do not *s* to their own heart
10:3 they will *s*, We have no king
10:8 *s* to the mountains, Cover us!
14:2 *S* to him, all you people, May
14:3 And no more shall we *s*
14:8 Ephraim will *s*, What do I
Joe 2:17 *s*, Do feel sorry, O Jehovah
2:17 they *s* among the peoples
2:19 Jehovah will answer and *s* to
3:10 *s:* I am a powerful man
Am 1:2 *s:* Jehovah—out of Zion he
3:9 *s:* Be gathered together
6:10 he will have to *s* to whoever
Am 6:10 he will certainly *s*, Nobody!
6:10 will have to *s*, Keep silence!
7:2 *s:* O Sovereign Lord Jehovah
7:5 to *s:* O Sovereign Lord Jehovah
7:8 And Jehovah went on to *s*
7:12 Amaziah proceeded to *s* to
7:15 Jehovah went on to *s* to me
8:2 Jehovah went on to *s* to me
8:14 *s:* As your god is alive, O
9:1 *s:* Strike the pillar head
Jon 1:7 began to *s* to one another
1:10 they went on to *s* to him
1:14 call out to Jehovah and to *s*
4:9 God proceeded to *s* to Jonah
Mic 2:4 *s:* We have positively been
3:1 *s:* Hear, please, you heads of
4:2 *s:* Come, you people, and let
Na 3:7 *s*, Nineveh has been despoiled!
Hab 2:2 to *s:* Write down the vision
2:6 one will *s*, Woe to him who
Hag 1:13 went on to *s* to the people
2:2 *S*, please, to Zerubbabel the
2:12 to answer and *s:* No!
2:13 *s:* If someone unclean by a
2:21 *S* to Zerubbabel the governor
Zec 1:3 *s* to them, This is what
1:11 *s:* We have walked about in
1:14 went on to *s* to me: Call out
1:21 to *s:* These are the horns
3:4 he went on to *s* to him
4:11 *s* to him: What do these two
5:6 to *s:* This is their aspect in
6:4 and *s* to the angel who was
6:12 *s* to him, This is what
7:5 *S* to all the people of the
11:5 those who are selling them *s*
11:15 to *s* to me: Take yet for
12:5 have to *s* in their heart
13:3 *s* to him, You will not live
13:5 *s*, I am no prophet. I am a
13:6 *s* to him, What are these
13:6 will have to *s*, Those with
13:9 I will *s*, It is my people
13:9 will *s*, Jehovah is my God
Mal 1:5 *s:* May Jehovah be magnified
Mt 3:9 and do not presume to *s* to
3:9 I *s* to you that God is able to
5:11 lyingly *s* every sort of
5:18 I *s* to you that sooner would
5:20 I *s* to you that if your
5:22 *s* to you that everyone who
5:26 I *s* to you for a fact, You
5:28 But I *s* to you that everyone
5:32 I *s* to you that everyone
5:34 I *s* to you: Do not swear
5:39 I *s* to you: Do not resist
5:44 I *s* to you: Continue to love
6:2 I *s* to you, They are having
6:5 I *s* to you, They are having
6:7 do not *s* the same things over
6:16 I *s* to you, They are having
6:25 *s* to you: Stop being anxious
6:29 I *s* to you that not even
6:31 never be anxious and *s*, What
7:4 how can you *s* to your brother
7:22 Many will *s* to me in that
8:8 but just *s* the word and my
8:9 I *s* to this one, Be on your
9:5 to *s*, Your sins are forgiven
9:5 or to *s*, Get up and walk
9:11 the Pharisees began to *s* to
9:24 Jesus began to *s:* Leave the
9:34 Pharisees began to *s:* It is
10:15 Truly I *s* to you, It will be
10:23 truly I *s* to you, You will
10:27 *s* in the light; and what you
11:7 Jesus started to *s* to the
11:11 I *s* to you people, Among
11:18 yet people *s*, He has a demon
11:19 *s*, Look! A man gluttonous
11:22 I *s* to you, it will be more
11:24 I *s* to you people, It will
12:23 *s:* May this not perhaps be
12:31 *s* to you, Every sort of sin
13:17 *s* to you, Many prophets and
15:5 you *s*, Whoever says to his
15:23 did not *s* a word in answer
16:2 *s*, It will be fair weather
16:14 Some *s* John the Baptist
16:15 who do you *s* I am?
16:18 I *s* to you, You are Peter
16:20 not to *s* to anybody that he
16:28 I *s* to you that there are
17:10 scribes *s* that Elijah must

Mt 17:12 I *s* to you that Elijah has
17:20 *s* to you, If you have faith
17:20 *s* to this mountain, Transfer
18:3 I *s* to you, Unless you turn
18:18 I *s* to you men, Whatever
18:19 *s* to you, If two of you on
18:22 I *s* to you, not, Up to seven
19:9 I *s* to you that whoever
19:23 Truly I *s* to you that it
19:24 I *s* to you, It is easier for
19:28 *s* to you, In the re-creation
21:3 must *s*, The Lord needs them
21:21 I *s* to you, If only you have
21:21 if you *s* to this mountain
21:25 If we *s*, From heaven, he
21:25 he will *s* to us, Why, then
21:26 If, though, we *s*, From men
21:31 I *s* to you that the tax
21:43 I *s* to you, The kingdom of
22:23 *s* there is no resurrection
22:46 nobody was able to *s* a word
23:3 for they *s* but do not perform
23:16 you, blind guides, who *s*, If
23:30 *s*, If we were in the days
23:36 I *s* to you, All these things
23:39 I *s* to you, You will by no
23:39 until you *s*, Blessed is he
24:2 I *s* to you, By no means will
24:26 if people *s* to you, Look! He
24:34 Truly I *s* to you that this
24:47 I *s* to you, He will appoint
24:48 if that evil slave should *s*
25:34 will *s* to those on his right
25:40 the king will *s* to them
25:40 I *s* to you, To the extent
25:41 he will *s*, in turn, to those
25:45 I *s* to you, To the extent
26:13 I *s* to you, Wherever this
26:18 *s* to him, The Teacher says
26:21 I *s* to you, One of you will
26:22 *s* to him: Lord, it is not I
26:34 I *s* to you, On this night
26:64 Yet I *s* to you men, From
27:11 replied: You yourself *s* it
27:33 that is to *s*, Skull Place
27:47 to *s*: This man is calling
27:64 and steal him and *s* to the
28:13 *S*, His disciples came in the
Mr 2:9 *s* to the paralytic, Your sins
2:9 or to *s*, Get up and pick up
2:11 I *s* to you, Get up, pick up
2:27 on to *s* to them: The sabbath
3:23 *s* to them with illustrations
3:28 I *s* to you that all things
4:2 with illustrations and to *s* to
4:11 *s* to them: To you the sacred
4:21 to *s* to them: A lamp is not
4:26 *s*: In this way the kingdom
4:30 *s*: With what are we to liken
4:41 *s* to one another: Who really
5:30 to *s*: Who touched my outer
5:31 *s* to him: You see the crowd
5:31 do you *s*, Who touched me?
5:41 Maiden, I *s* to you, Get up!
6:4 to *s* to them: A prophet is not
6:16 *s*: The John that I beheaded
6:35 to *s*: The place is isolated
7:9 he went on to *s* to them
7:11 you men *s*, If a man says to
7:14 *s* to them: Listen to me, all
8:12 I *s*, No sign will be given to
8:15 to order them expressly and *s*
8:29 who do you *s* I am? In answer
9:1 he went on to *s* to them
9:1 Truly I *s* to you, There are
9:11 *s* that first Elijah must
9:13 I *s* to you, Elijah, in fact
10:15 Truly I *s* to you, Whoever
10:28 Peter started to *s* to him
10:29 Truly I *s* to you men, No one
11:3 *s*, The Lord needs it, and
11:5 *s* to them: What are you
11:23 I *s* to you that whoever
11:28 began to *s* to him: By what
11:31 If we *s*, From heaven, he
11:31 *s*, Why is it, therefore
11:32 But dare we *s*, From men?
12:18 *s* there is no resurrection
12:35 Jesus began to *s* as he
12:35 *s* that the Christ is David's
12:38 *s*: Look out for the scribes
12:43 Truly I *s* to you that this
13:5 Jesus started to *s* to them
13:30 Truly I *s* to you that this

Mr 13:37 But what I *s* to you I
13:37 *s* to all, Keep on the watch
14:9 Truly I *s* to you, Wherever
14:14 *s* to the householder, The
14:18 Truly I *s* to you, One of you
14:19 grieved and to *s* to him
14:25 I *s* to you, I shall by no
14:30 I *s* to you, You today, yes
14:31 he began to *s* profusely
14:36 went on to *s*: *Abba*, Father
14:58 We heard him *s*, I will
14:60 Do you *s* nothing in reply?
14:65 *s* to him: Prophesy!
14:69 *s* to those standing by
15:2 You yourself *s* it
15:14 Pilate went on to *s* to them
15:35 to *s*: See! He is calling
Lu 3:7 he began to *s* to the crowds
3:8 I *s* to you that God has power
3:11 In reply he would *s* to them
4:21 Then he started to *s* to them
5:23 Which is easier, to *s*, Your
5:23 or to *s*, Get up and walk
5:24 I *s* to you, Get up and pick
6:5 And he went on to *s* to them
6:20 began to *s*: Happy are you poor
6:27 I *s* to you who are listening
6:42 How can you *s* to your brother
6:46 but do not do the things I *s*
7:6 *s* to him: Sir, do not bother
7:7 *s* the word, and let my servant
7:8 I *s* to this one, Be on your
7:14 Young man, I *s* to you, Get up!
7:19 sent them to the Lord to *s*
7:20 to *s*, Are you the Coming One
7:24 *s* to the crowds concerning
7:32 who *s*, We played the flute
7:33 but you *s*, He has a demon
7:34 but you *s*, Look! A man
7:40 Simon, I have something to *s*
7:40 He said: Teacher, *s* it!
7:49 to *s* within themselves
9:20 who do you *s* I am? Peter said
9:23 Then he went on to *s* to all
9:61 first permit me to *s* good-bye
10:2 *s* to them: The harvest
10:5 *s* first, May this house have
10:10 into its broad ways and *s*
10:24 I *s* to you, Many prophets
11:2 you pray, *s*, Father, let your
11:5 and *s* to him, Friend, loan me
11:9 I *s* to you, Keep on asking
11:18 you *s* I expel the demons by
11:29 to *s*: This generation is a
12:3 things you *s* in the darkness
12:4 I *s* to you, my friends, Do
12:8 I *s*, then, to you, Everyone
12:11 defense or what you will *s*
12:12 the things you ought to *s*
12:19 and I will *s* to my soul
12:22 I *s* to you, Quit being
12:37 Truly I *s* to you, He will
12:45 slave should *s* in his heart
12:54 on to *s* also to the crowds
12:54 you *s*, A storm is coming
12:55 you *s*, There will be a heat
13:14 began to *s* to the crowd
13:18 he went on to *s*: What is the
13:25 in answer he will *s* to you
13:27 *s* to you, I do not know
13:35 *s*, Blessed is he that comes
14:9 will come and *s* to you, Let
14:10 he will *s* to you, Friend, go
14:12 *s* also to the man that
14:17 to *s* to the invited ones
14:24 For I *s* to you people, None
14:33 that does not *s* good-bye to
15:18 *s* to him: Father, I have
16:1 on to *s* also to the disciples
16:5 *s* to the first, How much
16:9 I *s* to you, Make friends for
17:6 *s* to this black mulberry
17:7 *s* to him when he gets in
17:8 will he not *s* to him, Get
17:10 *s*, We are good-for-nothing
17:23 people will *s* to you, See
18:17 I *s* to you, Whoever does not
18:29 I *s* to you, There is no one
19:14 *s*, We do not want this man
19:26 I *s* to you, To everyone that
20:5 If we *s*, From heaven, he
20:5 he will *s*, Why is it you did
20:6 But if we *s*, From men, the
20:27 *s* there is no resurrection

Lu 20:41 *s* that the Christ is David's
21:10 he went on to *s* to them
21:32 I *s* to you, This generation
22:11 *s* to the landlord of the
22:64 would ask and *s*: Prophesy
23:29 people will *s*, Happy are the
23:30 to *s* to the mountains, Fall
23:39 began to *s* abusively to him
23:42 to *s*: Jesus, remember me
Joh 1:22 What do you *s* about yourself?
1:51 Most truly I *s* to you men
2:22 that he used to *s* this
3:3 Most truly I *s* to you, Unless
3:5 Most truly I *s* to you, Unless
3:11 Most truly I *s* to you, What
4:20 people *s* that in Jerusalem
4:35 Do you not *s* that there are
4:35 I *s* to you: Lift up your
4:42 they began to *s* to the woman
4:51 to *s* that his boy was living
5:10 Jews began to *s* to the cured
5:19 Jesus went on to *s* to them
5:19 I *s* to you, The Son cannot
5:24 I *s* to you, He that hears
5:25 I *s* to you, The hour is
5:34 I *s* these things that you
6:14 began to *s*: This is for a
6:26 I *s* to you, You are looking
6:32 I *s* to you, Moses did not
6:47 I *s* to you, He that believes
6:53 I *s* to you, Unless you eat
6:65 *s*: This is why I have said
7:12 Some would *s*: He is a good
7:12 Others would *s*: He is not
7:25 to *s*: This is the man they
7:26 and they *s* nothing to him
8:19 *s* to him: Where is your
8:22 the Jews began to *s*: He will
8:23 to *s* to them: You are from
8:25 they began to *s* to him
8:31 to *s* to the Jews that had
8:33 you *s*, You will become free
8:34 Most truly I *s* to you, Every
8:48 Do we not rightly *s*, You are
8:51 I *s* to you, If anyone
8:52 but you *s*, If anyone observes
8:54 he who you *s* is your God
8:58 Most truly I *s* to you
9:8 *s*: This is the man that used
9:9 Some would *s*: This is he
9:9 *s*: Not at all, but he is like
9:9 The man would *s*: I am he
9:10 *s* to him: How, then, were
9:16 Pharisees began to *s*: This
9:16 *s*: How can a man that is a
9:17 *s* about him, seeing that he
9:19 son who you *s* was born blind
9:41 *s*, We see. Your sin remains
10:1 Most truly I *s* to you, He
10:7 *s* to you, I am the door of
10:21 *s*: These are not the
10:24 *s* to him: How long are you
10:36 *s* to me whom the Father
11:36 Jews began to *s*: See, what
11:47 *s*: What are we to do
11:51 *s* of his own originality
11:56 *s* to one another as they
12:24 Most truly I *s* to you
12:27 and what shall I *s*?
12:29 to *s* that it had thundered
12:29 *s*: An angel has spoken to
12:34 *s* that the Son of man must
13:16 *s* to you, A slave is not
13:20 *s* to you, He that receives
13:21 *s* to you, One of you will
13:33 I *s* also to you at present
13:38 *s* to you, A cock will by no
14:9 you *s*, Show us the Father
14:10 things I *s* to you men I do
14:12 truly I *s* to you, He that
16:12 things yet to *s* to you
16:20 *s* to you, You will weep and
16:23 *s* to you, If you ask the
16:26 *s* to you that I shall make
18:34 own originality that you *s*
19:21 Jews began to *s* to Pilate
20:17 *s* to them, I am ascending
20:25 *s* to him: We have seen the
21:18 Most truly I *s* to you
21:23 Jesus did not *s* to him
Ac 2:7 *s*: See here, all these who
2:13 *s*: They are full of sweet
4:14 had nothing to *s* in rebuttal

Eze 32:17 occurred to me, s
33:1 proceeded to occur to me, s
33:21 s: The city has been struck
33:23 began to occur to me, s
33:24 s even concerning the soil
33:30 s, Come, please, and hear
34:1 continued to occur to me, s
35:1 continued to occur to me, s
35:10 s, These two nations and
35:12 s: They have been laid
36:13 s to you: A devourer of
36:16 to occur to me, s
36:20 in s with reference to them
37:9 s to me: Prophesy to the
37:11 are s, Our bones have
37:15 to occur to me, s
38:1 continued to occur to me, s
Da 2:5 s to the Chaldeans: The word
2:7 s: Let the king say what the
2:8 s: For a fact, I am aware that
2:10 s: There does not exist a man
2:15 s to Arioch the officer of the
2:20 s: Let the name of God become
2:26 s to Daniel, whose name was
2:27 s: The secret that the king
2:47 was answering Daniel and s
3:9 s to Nebuchadnezzar the king
3:14 s to them: Is it really so
3:16 and they were s to the king
3:19 s to heat up the furnace
3:24 s to his high royal officials
3:24 s to the king: Yes, O king
3:25 s: Look! I am beholding four
3:26 s: Shadrach, Meshach and
3:28 s: Blessed be the God of
4:7 s before them what the dream
4:14 s: Chop the tree down, and
4:17 the s of holy ones the request
4:19 s, O Belteshazzar, do not let
4:19 s, O my lord, may the dream
4:23 s: Chop the tree down, and
4:30 s: Is not this Babylon the
5:7 s to the wise men of Babylon
5:13 s to Daniel: Are you the
5:17 s before the king: Let your
6:5 s: We shall find in this
6:6 s to him: O Darius the king
6:12 s before the king concerning
6:12 s: The matter is well
6:13 s before the king: Daniel
6:15 s to the king: Take note
6:16 s to Daniel: Your God whom
6:20 speaking up and s to Daniel
7:2 Daniel was speaking up and s
7:5 s to it, Get up, eat much
Ho 12:8 s, Indeed, I have become rich
13:2 s, Let the sacrificers who
Am 2:12 s: You must not prophesy
3:1 out of the land of Egypt, s
4:1 who are s to their masters
5:16 people will be s: Ah! Ah!
6:13 s: Have we not in our
7:10 s: Amos has conspired against
7:16 Are you s: You must not
8:5 s, How long will it be before
9:10 s: The calamity will not
Ob 3 s in his heart, Who will bring
Jon 1:1 Jonah the son of Amittai, s
3:1 to Jonah the second time, s
3:4 s: Only forty days more, and
3:7 the king and his great ones, s
Mic 2:4 a proverbial s and will
3:11 s: Is not Jehovah in the
4:11 are s, Let her be polluted
6:1 Hear . . . what Jehovah is s
7:10 shame will cover her . . . s
Hab 2:6 against him a proverbial s
2:19 one s to the piece of wood
Zep 1:12 s in their heart, Jehovah
2:15 that was s in her heart
Hag 1:1 Jehozadak the high priest, s
1:3 of Haggai the prophet, s
1:13 commission from Jehovah, s
2:1 of Haggai the prophet, s
2:2 ones of the people, s
2:10 to Haggai the prophet, s
2:11 priests as to the law, s
2:20 word of Jehovah . . . s
Zec 1:1 the son of Iddo the prophet, s
1:4 the former prophets called, s
1:7 the son of Iddo the prophet, s
1:14 s, This is what Jehovah of
1:17 Call out further, s, This is
2:4 s, As open rural country

Zec 3:6 to bear witness to Joshua, s
4:4 s: What do these things mean
4:6 s, Not by a military force
4:8 continued to occur to me, s
6:8 s: See, those going forth to
6:9 continued to occur to me, s
7:3 s to the priests who belonged
7:3 s: Shall I weep in the fifth
7:4 continued to occur to me, s
7:8 to occur to Zechariah, s
8:1 continued to occur, s
8:18 continued to occur to me, s
8:21 s: Let us earnestly go to
8:23 s: We will go with you
Mal 1:4 Edom keeps s, We have been
1:7 s: The table of Jehovah is
1:12 s, The table of Jehovah is
2:17 By your s, Everyone that is
Mt 1:20 s: Joseph, son of David
1:22 through his prophet, s
2:2 s: Where is the one born king
2:13 s: Get up, take the young
2:15 s: Out of Egypt I called my
2:17 Jeremiah the prophet, s
3:2 s: Repent, for the kingdom of
3:14 s: I am the one needing to be
4:14 through Isaiah the prophet, s
4:17 s: Repent, you people, for
5:2 and began teaching them, s
7:21 Not everyone s to me, Lord
8:2 s: Lord, if you just want to
8:3 he touched him, s: I want to
8:6 s: Sir, my manservant is laid
8:17 s: He himself took our
8:25 s: Lord, save us, we are
8:29 s: What have we to do with
8:31 s: If you expel us, send us
9:18 s: By now my daughter must
9:21 s to herself: If I only touch
9:27 crying out and s: Have mercy
9:29 he touched their eyes, s
9:30 s: See that nobody gets to
10:7 s, The kingdom of the heavens
11:17 s, We played the flute for
12:36 every unprofitable s that
13:3 s: Look! A sower went out to
13:24 before them, s: The kingdom
13:31 before them, s: The kingdom
14:4 For John had been s to him
14:26 s: It is an apparition!
14:33 s: You are really God's Son
15:1 Pharisees and scribes, s
15:22 s: Have mercy on me, Lord
15:25 to him, s: Lord, help me!
16:7 s: We did not take any loaves
16:13 are men s the Son of man is
16:22 s: Be kind to yourself, Lord
17:5 s: This is my Son, the
17:9 s: Tell the vision to no one
17:14 kneeling down to him and s
17:25 Jesus got ahead of him by s
18:26 s, Be patient with me and I
18:28 to choke him, s, Pay back
18:29 s, Be patient with me and I
19:3 intent on tempting him and s
19:11 men make room for the s
19:22 the young man heard this s
19:25 s: Who really can be saved?
20:30 s: Lord, have mercy on us
20:31 they cried all the louder, s
21:2 s to them: Be on your way
21:4 spoken through the prophet, s
21:10 commotion, s: Who is this?
21:15 s: Save, we pray, the Son of
21:16 Do you hear what these are s?
21:20 they wondered, s: How is it
21:25 s: If we say, From heaven
21:37 s, They will respect my son
22:1 with illustrations, s
22:4 s, Tell those invited: Look!
22:16 party followers of Herod, s
22:31 was spoken to you by God, s
22:43 David . . . calls him Lord, s
23:1 and to his disciples, s
24:3 s: Tell us, When will these
24:5 s, I am the Christ, and will
25:11 s, Sir, sir, open to us!
25:20 s, Master, you committed
26:5 kept s: Not at the festival
26:17 s: Where do you want us to
26:26 loaf and, after s a blessing
26:27 s: Drink out of it, all of
26:39 praying and s: My Father, if
26:42 prayed, s: My Father, if it

Mt 26:44 s once more the same word
26:48 s: Whoever it is I kiss
26:65 s: He has blasphemed!
26:68 s: Prophesy to us, you
26:69 s: You, too, were with
26:70 denied it before them all, s
26:75 Peter called to mind the s
27:4 s: I sinned when I betrayed
27:9 s: And they took the thirty
27:19 his wife sent out to him, s
27:24 s: I am innocent of the
27:29 s: Good day, you King of the
27:40 s . . . would-be thrower-down
27:41 making fun of him and s
27:46 with a loud voice, s: E'li
27:54 s: Certainly this was God's
27:63 s: Sir, we have called to
28:15 s has been spread abroad
28:18 s: All authority has been
Mr 1:7 he would preach, s: After me
1:15 s: The appointed time has
1:24 s: What have we to do with
1:25 rebuked it, s: Be silent, and
1:27 s: What is this? A new
1:40 s to him: If you just want
2:12 glorified God, s: We never
2:16 s to his disciples: Does he
2:24 the Pharisees went s to him
3:11 s: You are the Son of God
3:21 s: He has gone out of his
3:22 s: He has Beelzebub, and he
3:30 s: He has an unclean spirit
5:12 s: Send us into the swine
5:23 s: My little daughter is in
5:28 s: If I touch just his outer
6:14 s: John the baptizer has been
6:15 others were s: It is Elijah
6:15 s: It is a prophet like one
6:25 and made her request, s
6:46 after s good-bye to them he
7:27 But he began by s to her
7:29 Because of s this, go; the
8:24 the man looked up and began s
8:26 So he sent him off home, s
8:27 s to them: Who are men
8:27 Who are men s that I am?
9:11 they began to question him, s
9:24 s: I have faith! Help me out
9:25 rebuked the unclean spirit, s
9:26 were s: He is dead!
9:32 were not understanding the s
10:22 he grew sad at the s and
10:47 he started shouting and s
10:49 called the blind man, s to
11:17 s: Is it not written, My
11:31 reason among themselves, s
12:6 s, They will respect my son
13:6 s, I am he, and will mislead
14:31 the others began s the same
14:39 prayed, s the same word
14:44 given them an agreed sign, s
14:57 witness against him, s
14:60 s: Do you say nothing in
14:68 s: Neither do I know him
14:68 understand what you are s
14:70 s to Peter: Certainly you
14:72 Peter recalled the s that
15:4 s: Have you no reply to make?
15:9 Pilate responded to them, s
15:12 Pilate was s to them: What
15:29 wagging their heads and s
15:31 s: Others he saved; himself
15:36 s: Let him be! Let us see
16:3 they were s one to another
Lu 1:24 secluded for five months, s
1:29 was deeply disturbed at the s
1:66 note of it in their hearts, s
1:67 and he prophesied, s
2:13 army, praising God and s
2:15 the shepherds began s to one
2:17 the s that had been spoken
2:50 they did not grasp the s
3:8 And do not start s within
3:16 John gave the answer, s to
4:22 s: This is a son of Joseph
4:35 Jesus rebuked it, s: Be silent
4:36 s: What sort of speech is
4:41 s: You are the Son of God
5:8 down at the knees of Jesus, s
5:12 s: Lord, if you just want to
5:13 he touched him, s: I want to
5:21 Pharisees started to reason, s
5:26 became filled with fear, s
5:30 murmuring to his disciples, s

Lu 7:4 to entreat him earnestly, s
7:16 they began to glorify God, s
8:24 s: Instructor, Instructor, we
8:25 s to one another: Who really
8:38 but he dismissed the man, s
8:49 s: Your daughter has died
8:54 called, s: Girl, get up!
9:18 he . . . s: Who are the crowds
9:18 Who are the crowds s that I
9:33 not realizing what he was s
9:34 as he was s these things
9:35 s: This is my Son, the one
9:38 s: Teacher, I beg you to take
9:45 understanding of this s
9:45 to question him about this s
10:17 s: Lord, even the demons
11:27 as he was s these things a
11:45 Teacher, in s these things
12:1 by s first to his disciples
12:16 s: The land of a certain rich
12:17 s, What shall I do, now that
12:41 are you s this illustration
13:25 s, Sir, open to us. But in
13:26 s, We ate and drank in front
13:31 s to him: Get out and be
14:3 s: Is it lawful on the
14:7 places for themselves, s to
14:30 s, This man started to build
15:2 the scribes kept muttering, s
15:3 this illustration to them, s
15:6 s to them, Rejoice with me
15:9 s, Rejoice with me, because
17:4 s, I repent, you must forgive
17:21 neither will people be s
18:2 s: In a certain city there
18:3 s, See that I get justice
18:13 s, O God, be gracious to me
18:16 s: Let the young children
18:18 s: Good Teacher, by doing
18:38 he cried out, s: Jesus, Son
19:7 they all fell to muttering, s
19:16 s, Lord, your mina gained
19:18 s, Your mina, Lord, made
19:20 s, Lord, here is your mina
19:30 s: Go into the village that
19:38 s: Blessed is the One coming
19:42 s: If you, even you, had
19:46 s to them: It is written
20:2 s to him: Tell us by what
20:5 they drew conclusions, s
20:14 s, This is the heir; let us
20:21 questioned him, s: Teacher
20:26 able to catch him in this s
20:28 s: Teacher, Moses wrote us
21:7 s: Teacher, when will these
21:8 basis of my name, s, I am he
22:8 s: Go and get the passover
22:19 s: This means my body
22:20 s: This cup means the new
22:42 s: Father, if you wish
22:57 s: I do not know him, woman
22:60 do not know what you are s
22:65 on s many other things in
22:66 into their Sanhedrin hall, s
22:70 yourselves are s that I am
23:2 s: This man we found
23:2 s he himself is Christ a king
23:3 said: You yourself are s it
23:5 s: He stirs up the people by
23:18 s: Take this one away, but
23:21 yell, s: Impale! Impale him!
23:34 Jesus was s: Father, forgive
23:35 rulers were sneering, s
23:37 s: If you are the king of
23:47 s: Really this man was
24:7 s that the Son of man must
24:23 came s they had also seen a
24:29 s: Stay with us, because
24:34 s: For a fact the Lord was
Joh 1:15 s: The one coming behind me
1:26 s: I baptize in water
1:32 John also bore witness, s
2:22 and the s that Jesus said
4:31 urging him, s: Rabbi, eat
4:33 disciples began s to one
4:37 the s is true, One is the
6:6 he was s this to test him
6:42 they began s: Is this not
6:52 s: How can this man give
7:11 and s: Where is that man?
7:15 s: How does this man have a
7:31 s: When the Christ arrives
7:36 What does this s mean that
7:37 s: If anyone is thirsty, let

Joh 7:40 s: This is for a certainty
7:41 were s: This is the Christ
7:41 s: The Christ is not actually
8:12 s: I am the light of the
10:20 s: He has a demon and is
10:41 s: John, indeed, did not
11:3 s: Lord, see! the one for
11:28 s secretly: The Teacher is
11:32 s to him: Lord, if you had
12:21 s: Sir, we want to see
12:23 s: The hour has come for
12:33 s to signify what sort of
13:21 s these things, Jesus
13:22 which one he was s it about
13:24 about whom he is s it
16:18 s: What does this mean that
18:37 are s that I am a king
18:38 s this, he went out again
18:40 s: Not this man, but
19:3 s: Good day, you king of the
19:6 shouted, s: Impale him!
19:8 Pilate heard this s, he
19:12 s: If you release this
20:14 s these things, she turned
21:23 s went out among the
Ac 2:12 s one to another: What does
2:40 s: Get saved from this
3:25 s to Abraham, And in your
4:16 s: What shall we do with
5:23 s: The jail we found locked
5:36 s he himself was somebody
7:26 s, Men, you are brothers
7:27 s, Who appointed you ruler
7:35 s, Who appointed you ruler
7:40 s to Aaron, Make gods for us
7:60 s this he fell asleep in death
8:9 s he himself was somebody
8:19 s: Give me also this
8:26 s: Rise and go to the south
10:26 s: Rise; I myself am also a
11:3 s he had gone into the house
11:4 the particulars to them, s
11:16 s of the Lord, how he used
11:18 s: Well, then, God has
12:7 s: Rise quickly! And his
13:15 s: Men, brothers, if there
14:11 s in the Lycaonian tongue
14:15 s: Men, why are you doing
14:18 yet by s these things they
14:22 s: We must enter into the
15:13 James answered, s: Men
16:9 s: Step over into Macedonia
16:28 s: Do not hurt yourself, for
17:3 s: This is the Christ, this
17:7 s there is another king, Jesus
17:19 led him to the Areopagus, s
18:13 s: Contrary to the law this
19:13 s: I solemnly charge you by
19:21 journey to Jerusalem, s
19:26 s that the ones that are
19:28 s: Great is Artemis of the
21:40 in the Hebrew language, s
22:18 s to me, Hurry up and get
22:22 they raised their voices, s
22:26 s: What are you intending to
23:9 s: We find nothing wrong in
23:12 s they would neither eat nor
24:2 accusing him, s: Seeing that
25:14 s: There is a certain man
26:22 s nothing except things the
26:24 s these things in his defense
26:31 s: This man practices
27:10 s to them: Men, I perceive
27:24 s, Have no fear, Paul
27:33 s: Today is the fourteenth
28:4 they began s to one another
28:6 and began s he was a god
28:26 s, Go to this people and say
Ro 2:22 one s Do not commit adultery
1Co 7:35 I am s for your personal
11:25 s: This cup means the new
14:16 not know what you are s
15:54 the s will take place that
Ga 5:14 stands fulfilled in one s
Eph 4:29 rotten s not proceed out of
4:29 whatever s is good for
Col 2:4 This I am s that no man may
1Th 5:3 s: Peace and security! then
1Ti 1:7 either the things they are s
1:15 the s that Christ Jesus came
2Ti 2:7 thought to what I am s; the
2:11 the s: Certainly if we died
2:18 s that the resurrection has
Tit 3:8 Faithful is the s, and

Heb 2:6 s: What is man that you keep
4:7 marks off a certain day by s
6:14 s: Assuredly in blessing I
8:11 s: Know Jehovah! For they
8:13 In his s a new covenant
9:20 s: This is the blood of the
10:8 After first s: You did not
12:26 but now he has promised, s
1Pe 1:25 s of Jehovah endures forever
1:25 this is the s, this which
2Pe 2:22 The s of the true proverb has
3:4 s: Where is this promised
Re 1:11 s: What you see write in a
4:1 s: Come on up here, and I
4:10 crowns before the throne, s
5:9 And they sing a new song, s
5:12 s with a loud voice: The
5:13 I heard s: To the One sitting
5:14 creatures went s: Amen! and
6:10 s: Until when, Sovereign Lord
6:16 keep s to the mountains and
7:3 s: Do not harm the earth or
7:10 s: Salvation we owe to our
7:12 s: Amen! The blessing and the
10:8 s: Go, take the opened scroll
11:15 s: The kingdom of the world
11:17 s: We thank you, Jehovah
14:7 s in a loud voice: Fear God
14:8 s: She has fallen! Babylon
14:9 s in a loud voice: If anyone
14:18 s: Put your sharp sickle in
15:3 s: Great and wonderful are
16:17 s: It has come to pass!
17:1 s: Come, I will show you
18:2 s: She has fallen! Babylon
18:7 in her heart she keeps s
18:16 s, Too bad, too bad—the
18:21 s: Thus with a swift pitch
22:17 bride keep on s: Come!

Sayings

Nu 24:4 the one hearing the s of God
24:16 the one hearing the s of God
De 32:1 earth hear the s of my mouth
Jos 24:27 all the s of Jehovah that
Jg 5:29 to herself with her own s
1Ch 4:22 the s are of old tradition
Job 6:10 hidden the s of the Holy One
6:25 s of uprightness have been
6:26 s of one in despair are for
8:2 s of your mouth are . . . wind
13:12 s are proverbs of ashes
22:22 And put his s in your heart
23:12 treasured up the s of his
32:12 None . . . answering his s
32:14 with the s of you men I
33:3 s are the uprightness of my
34:37 his s against the true God
Ps 5:1 To my s do give ear, O Jehovah
12:6, 6 The s of Jehovah are pure s
19:14 Let the s of my mouth and
54:2 Do give ear to the s of my
78:1 ear to the s of my mouth
107:11 against the s of God
119:103 smooth to my palate your s
138:4 heard the s of your mouth
141:6 But they have heard my s
Pr 1:2 discern the s of understanding
1:21 it says its own s
2:1 son, if you will receive my s
2:16 has made her own s smooth
4:5 aside from the s of my mouth
4:10 my son, and accept my s
4:20 To my s incline your ear
5:7 from the s of my mouth
6:2 ensnared by the s of your
6:2 caught by the s of your mouth
7:1 son, keep my s, and may you
7:5 has made her own s smooth
7:24 to the s of my mouth
8:8 All the s of my mouth are in
15:26 but pleasant s are clean
16:24 Pleasant s are a honeycomb
17:27 Anyone holding back his s is
19:27 from the s of knowledge
22:21 the truthfulness of true s
22:21 return s that are the truth
23:12 ear to the s of knowledge
24:23 s also are for the wise ones
Isa 32:7 afflicted ones with false s
41:26 hearing any s of you men
Eze 14:8 a sign and for proverbial s
20:49 composing proverbial s
Da 8:23 and understanding ambiguous s

Ex 39:3 coccus s material and the fine
39:5 coccus s material and fine
39:8 and coccus s material and fine
39:24 coccus s material, twisted
39:29 purple and coccus s material
Le 14:4 coccus s material and hyssop
14:6 the coccus s material and the
14:49 coccus s material and hyssop
14:51 the coccus s material and
14:52 and the coccus s material
Nu 4:8 cloth of coccus s over them
19:6 coccus s material and throw
Jos 2:18 cord of s thread you should
2:21 she tied the s cord in the
2Sa 1:24 clothed you in s with finery
Ca 4:3 lips are just like a s thread
Isa 1:18 sins of you people . . . as s
Jer 4:30 to clothe yourself with s
La 4:5 that were being reared in s
Mt 27:28 draped him with a s cloak
Heb 9:19 and s wool and hyssop and
Re 17:4 was arrayed in purple and s
18:12 purple and silk and s; and
18:16 fine linen and purple and s

Scarlet-colored
Re 17:3 sitting upon a s wild beast

Scatter
Ge 49:7 and let me s them in Israel
Le 26:33 s among the nations, and I
Nu 16:37 s the fire over there; for
De 4:27 Jehovah will certainly s you
28:64 s you among all the peoples
1Sa 14:34 S among the people, and you
2Sa 22:15 that he might s them
1Ki 14:15 s them beyond the River
Ne 1:8 shall s you among the peoples
Ps 18:14 that he might s them
53:5 s the bones of anyone camping
106:27 s them among the lands
144:6 lightning that you may s
Isa 28:25 then s black cummin and
30:22 statue of gold. You will s
Jer 9:16 s them among the nations
13:24 s them like stubble that is
18:17 s them before the enemy
49:32 will s them to every wind
49:36 s them to all these winds
Eze 5:2 last third you will s to the
5:10 s all the remainder of you
5:12 last third I shall s
6:5 s your bones all around your
12:14 I shall s to every wind
12:15 s them among the lands
20:23 to s them among the nations
22:15 s you among the nations and
29:12 I will s the Egyptians
30:23 s the Egyptians among the
30:26 s the Egyptians among the
36:19 s them among the nations
Da 4:14 foliage, and s its fruitage
11:24 goods he will s among them
Hab 3:14 moved tempestuously to s me
Zec 10:9 s them like seed among the
Mal 2:3 will s dung upon your faces

Scattered
Ge 10:18 the Canaanite were s
11:4 for fear we may be s over all
11:8 Jehovah s them from there
11:9 Jehovah had s them from there
Ex 5:12 people s about over all the
32:20 he s it upon the surface of
Le 19:10 not pick up the s grapes of
Nu 10:35 let your enemies be s; and
De 30:3 Jehovah your God has s you
2Sa 20:22 they were s from the city
1Ki 22:17 see all the Israelites s on
2Ki 25:5 military force was s from
2Ch 18:16 see all the Israelites s
Es 3:8 people s and separated among
Ps 44:11 among the nations you have s
68:1 arise, let his enemies be s
68:14 s abroad the kings in it
68:30 He has s the peoples that
89:10 you have s your enemies
141:7 s at the mouth of Sheol
Pr 5:16 springs be s out of doors
Isa 11:12 s ones of Judah he will
24:1 and s its inhabitants
Jer 10:21 animals have been s
23:2 have s my sheep; and you kept
30:11 nations to which I have s
40:15 be s and the remnant of
50:17 Israel is a s sheep
52:8 force was s from his side
Eze 6:8 you get s among the lands
11:16 have s them among the lands
11:17 among which you have been s
20:34 been s with a strong hand
20:41 to which you have been s
28:25 whom they have been s
29:13 whom they will have been s
34:5 were gradually s because of
34:5 and they continued to be s
34:6 my sheep were s, with no
34:12 they have been s in the
34:21 had s them to the outside
46:18 s each one from his
Joe 3:2 they s among the nations
Na 3:18 Your people have been s upon
Zep 3:10 the daughter of my s ones
Zec 13:7 let those of the flock be s
Mt 26:31 the flock will be s about
Mr 14:27 the sheep will be s about
Lu 1:51 he has s abroad those who are
Joh 11:52 children of God who are s
16:32 s each one to his own house
Ac 5:37 obeying him were s abroad
8:1 s throughout the regions of
8:4 those who had been s went
11:19 those who had been s by the
Jas 1:1 twelve tribes that are s
1Pe 1:1 temporary residents s about in

Scattering
Nu 14:45 s them as far as Hormah
De 1:44 s you in Seir as far as
1Sa 11:11 then they were sent s and
13:8 the people were s from him
Pr 11:24 one that is s and yet is
15:7 wise ones keep s knowledge
20:8 s all badness with his own
20:26 wise king is s wicked people
Jer 3:13 continued s your ways to the
23:1 destroying and s the sheep
31:10 One s Israel will himself
Na 2:1 One that does a s has come up

Scatterings
Jer 25:34 your s have been fulfilled

Scatters
Job 37:11 His light s the cloud mass
38:24 wind s about upon the earth
Ps 147:16 Hoarfrost he s just like
Mt 12:30 does not gather with me s
Lu 11:23 does not gather with me s
Joh 10:12 wolf snatches them and s

Scene
1Co 7:31 s of this world is changing

Scent
Ge 27:27 smell the s of his garments
27:27 the s of my son is like the
27:27 like the s of the field
Job 14:9 At the s of water . . . sprout
Ca 3:6 every sort of s powder of a
Jer 48:11 very s has not been changed
Joh 12:3 the s of the perfumed oil

Scented
Ca 5:13 of spice, towers of s herbs
Re 18:12 everything in s wood and

Scepter
Ge 49:10 s will not turn aside from
Nu 24:17 a s will indeed rise out of
Es 4:11 holds out to him the golden s
5:2 held out to Esther the golden s
5:2 and touched the top of the s
8:4 king held the golden s out to
Ps 2:9 break them with an iron s
45:6 The s of your kingship is a
45:6 kingship is a s of uprightness
125:3 s of wickedness will not
Eze 19:14 strong rod, no s for ruling
21:10 the s of my own son
21:13 it is rejecting also the s
Am 1:5 the s from Beth-eden
1:8 the holder of the s from
Zec 10:11 s of Egypt will depart
Heb 1:8 the s of your kingdom is the
1:8 is the s of uprightness

Scepters
Eze 19:11 meant for the s of rulers

Sceva
Ac 19:14 S, a Jewish chief priest

Schedule
Le 23:37 according to the daily s

Scheme
Es 8:3 s that he had schemed against
8:5 the s of Haman the son of
9:25 Let his bad s that he has
Job 6:26 to reprove words . . . s
Ps 31:13 to take away . . . they do s
Pr 16:30 blinking with his eyes to s
Isa 8:10 Plan out a s, and it will be
10:7 he will s, because to
Eze 22:29 carried on a s of defrauding
38:10 think up an injurious s
Da 11:24 fortified places he will s
11:25 they will s out against him
Zec 7:10 s out nothing bad against
8:17 not you s up in your hearts
Ac 5:38 s or this work is from men

Schemed
De 19:19 s to do to his brother, and
1Sa 18:25 s to have David fall by the
2Sa 21:5 s to annihilate us from
Es 8:3 that he had s against the Jews
9:24 s against the Jews to destroy
9:25 he has s against the Jews
Ps 17:3 discover that I have not s
140:2 s bad things in their heart
140:4 have s to push my steps

Schemes
Ex 23:1 a witness who s violence
Job 5:12 the s of the shrewd
21:27 s with which you would act
Ps 52:2 Adversities your tongue s up
Pr 6:18 heart fabricating hurtful s
15:26 The s of the bad one are
Jer 11:19 that they thought out s
Da 11:24 his s, but only until a time
11:25 scheme out against him s

Scheming
De 19:16 a witness s violence should
Ne 6:2 they were s to do me harm
6:6 and the Jews are s to rebel
Ps 35:4 who are s calamity for me
35:20 deception they keep s
36:4 he keeps s upon his bed
41:7 keep s something bad for me
Pr 24:8 As for anyone s to do bad, he
Eze 11:2 men that are s hurtfulness
Ho 7:15 they kept s what was bad
Mic 2:1 who are s what is harmful

School
Ac 19:9 the s auditorium of Tyrannus

Schools
Joh 7:15 he has not studied at the s

Scoff
Ps 73:8 s and speak about what is bad

Scoffers
Isa 28:22 do not show yourselves s

Scorch
Re 16:8 to s the men with fire

Scorched
Ge 41:6 ears of grain, thin and s by
41:23 thin, s by the east wind
41:27 empty ears of grain, s by the
Jg 15:14 threads . . . s with fire
Ps 68:6 have to reside in a s land
Pr 6:28 his feet themselves not be s
Isa 43:2 fire, you will not be s
58:11 even in a s land, and he
Jer 6:29 The bellows have been s
Eze 15:4 very middle of it does get s
15:5 it gets s, can it actually
20:47 all faces must be s from
Mt 13:6 the sun rose they were s
Mr 4:6 when the sun rose, it was s
Re 16:9 men were s with great heat

Scorches
Ps 83:14 flame that s the mountains

Scorching
De 28:22 the sword and s and mildew
1Ki 8:37 in case s, mildew, locusts
2Ki 19:26 a s before the east wind
2Ch 6:28 in case s and mildew
Ps 11:6 a s wind, as the portion of
Pr 16:27 upon his lips . . . a s fire
Am 4:9 I struck you people with s
Hag 2:17 I struck you people with s
Re 7:16 down upon them nor any s heat

Scorn
Eze 16:57 treating you with *s* on
25:6 kept rejoicing with all *s*
25:15 with *s* in the soul, in
28:24 are treating them with *s*
28:26 treating them with *s* all
36:5 with *s* in the soul, for the

Scorned
Jg 5:18 people that *s* their souls to

Scorners
Ac 13:41 Behold it, you *s*, and wonder

Scornful
2Ki 19:3 a day of . . . *s* insolence
Isa 37:3 rebuke and of *s* insolence

Scornfully
Mt 9:24 they began to laugh at him *s*
Mr 5:40 they began to laugh *s* at him
Lu 8:53 they began to laugh at him *s*

Scorpion
Lu 11:12 an egg, will hand him a *s*
Re 9:5 torment by a *s* when it strikes

Scorpions
De 8:15 poisonous serpents and *s*
Eze 2:6 among *s* that you are dwelling
Lu 10:19 underfoot serpents and *s*
Re 9:3 the same authority as the *s*
9:10 have tails and stings like *s*

Scoured
Le 6:28 be *s* and rinsed with water
Isa 18:2 to a nation drawn out and *s*
18:7 a people drawn out and *s*

Scourge
Nu 14:37 die by the *s* before Jehovah
16:48 Eventually the *s* was stopped
16:49 dead from the *s* amounted to
16:50 the *s* had been stopped
25:8 *s* was halted from upon the
25:9 And those who died from the *s*
25:18 the *s* over the affair of Peor
26:1 after the *s*, that Jehovah
31:16 the *s* came upon the assembly
Jos 23:13 as a *s* on your flanks and
1Sa 6:4 axis lords have the same *s*
2Sa 24:21 that the *s* may be halted
24:25 *s* was halted from upon
1Ch 21:17 upon your people, for a *s*
21:22 that the *s* may be halted
Ps 106:29 *s* now broke out among them
106:30 Then the *s* was halted
Zec 14:12 the *s* with which Jehovah
14:12 will *s* all the peoples that
14:15 is how the *s* of the horse
14:15 prove to be, like this *s*
14:18 *s* will occur with which
Mt 10:17 *s* you in their synagogues
20:19 to *s* and to impale, and the
23:34 will *s* in your synagogues
Mr 10:34 *s* him and kill him, but
Ac 22:25 *s* a man that is a Roman and

Scourged
Job 30:8 have been *s* out of the land
Joh 19:1 Pilate took Jesus and *s* him

Scourges
1Ki 12:11 shall chastise you with *s*
12:14 shall chastise you with *s*
2Ch 10:11 but I, for my part, with *s*
10:14 I, for my part, with *s*
Zec 14:18 *s* the nations that do not
Heb 12:6 *s* every one whom he receives

Scourging
Lu 18:33 after *s* him they will kill
Ac 22:24 should be examined under *s*

Scourgings
Heb 11:36 trial by mockings and *s*

Scours
Pr 20:30 are what *s* away the bad

Scrape
Job 2:8 earthenware with which to *s*
Eze 26:4 I will *s* her dust away from

Scraped
Le 14:41 house *s* off all around inside
Jg 14:9 he *s* it out into his palms
14:9 that he had *s* the honey

Scraper
Isa 44:13 works it up with a wood *s*

Scratches
Zec 12:3 without fail get severe *s*

Scream
De 22:24 she did not *s* in the city

Screamed
De 22:27 The girl who was engaged *s*
1Sa 25:14 but he *s* rebukes at them
Mt 8:29 they *s*, saying: What have

Screaming
Nu 16:34 fled at the *s* of them, for
Ac 23:9 there broke out a loud *s*, and
Eph 4:31 anger and wrath and *s* and

Screen
Ex 26:36 *s* for the entrance of the
26:37 make for the *s* five pillars
27:16 is a *s* twenty cubits long
33:22 my palm over you as a *s*
35:12 the curtain of the *s*
35:15 *s* of the entrance for the
35:17 the *s* of the gate of the
36:37 a *s* for the entrance of the
38:18 the *s* of the gate of the
39:34 and the curtain of the *s*
39:38 the *s* for the entrance of the
39:40 the *s* for the gate of the
40:5 put the *s* of the entrance
40:8 *s* of the gate of the courtyard
40:21 the curtain of the *s* in place
40:28 put the *s* of the entrance of
40:33 put up the *s* of the gate of
Nu 3:25 *s* of the entrance of the tent
3:26 *s* of the entrance of the
3:31 and the *s*, and all its service
4:25 *s* of the entrance of the tent
4:26 entrance *s* of the gate of the
2Sa 17:19 *s* over the face of the well
Ps 105:39 spread out a cloud for a *s*
Isa 22:8 will remove the *s* of Judah

Screened
1Ki 8:7 its poles *s* over from above
Ps 139:13 *s* off in the belly of my
140:7 *s* over my head in the day

Screening
Ex 25:20 *s* over the cover with their
37:9 cherubs . . . *s* over the cover
Nu 4:5 take down the *s* curtain and
1Ch 28:18 and *s* over the ark of the

Scribe
Jg 5:14 handling the equipment of a *s*
Ezr 4:8 Shimshai the *s* wrote a letter
4:9 Shimshai the *s* and the rest
4:17 Shimshai the *s* and the rest
4:23 Shimshai the *s* and their
Mt 8:19 a certain *s* came up and said
Mr 12:32 *s* said to him: Teacher, you
1Co 1:20 Where the *s*? Where the

Scribes
1Ch 2:55 *s* dwelling at Jabez were
Mt 2:4 all the chief priests and *s*
5:20 that of the *s* and Pharisees
7:29 authority, and not as their *s*
9:3 the *s* said to themselves
12:38 the *s* and Pharisees said
15:1 Pharisees and *s*, saying
16:21 and chief priests and *s*, and
17:10 *s* say that Elijah must come
20:18 to the chief priests and *s*
21:15 chief priests and the *s* saw
23:2 The *s* and the Pharisees have
23:13 Woe to you, *s* and Pharisees
23:15 Woe to you, *s* and Pharisees
23:23 Woe to you, *s* and Pharisees
23:25 Woe to you, *s* and Pharisees
23:27 Woe to you, *s* and Pharisees
23:29 Woe to you, *s* and Pharisees
26:57 *s* and the older men were
27:41 chief priests with the *s* and
Mr 1:22 was teaching . . . not as the *s*
2:6 *s* there, sitting and reasoning
2:16 *s* of the Pharisees, when they
3:22 the *s* that came down from
7:1 Pharisees and some of the *s*
7:5 Pharisees and *s* asked him
8:31 the chief priests and the *s*
9:11 Why do the *s* say that first
9:14 and *s* disputing with them
10:33 the chief priests and the *s*
11:18 the chief priests and the *s*
11:27 *s* and the older men came to
12:28 one of the *s* that had come
Mr 12:35 *s* say that the Christ is
12:38 Look out for the *s* that
14:1 the chief priests and the *s*
14:43 the *s* and the older men
14:53 the older men and the *s*
15:1 the older men and the *s*
15:31 making fun . . . with the *s*
Lu 5:21 the *s* and the Pharisees
5:30 *s* began murmuring to his
6:7 The *s* and the Pharisees were
9:22 and chief priests and *s*, and
11:53 *s* and the Pharisees started
15:2 both the Pharisees and the *s*
19:47 the chief priests and the *s*
20:1 the chief priests and the *s*
20:19 The *s* and the chief priests
20:39 *s* said: Teacher, you spoke
20:46 Look out for the *s* who
22:2 the chief priests and the *s*
22:66 both chief priests and *s*
23:10 chief priests and the *s* kept
Ac 4:5 and older men and *s*
6:12 older men and the *s*, and
23:9 some of the *s* of the party of

Scrimped
Mic 6:10 the *s* ephah measure that is

Scripture
Mr 12:10 this *s*, The stone that the
Lu 4:21 Today this *s* . . . is fulfilled
Joh 2:22 they believed the *S* and the
7:38 *S* has said, Out from his
7:42 *S* said that the Christ is
10:35 the *S* cannot be nullified
13:18 the *S* might be fulfilled
17:12 the *s* might be fulfilled
19:24 the *s* might be fulfilled
19:28 *s* might be accomplished
19:36 for the *s* to be fulfilled
19:37 again, a different *s* says
20:9 *s* that he must rise from
Ac 1:16 for the *s* to be fulfilled
8:32 *S* that he was reading aloud
8:35 starting with this *S*, he
Ro 4:3 For what does the *s* say?
9:17 *S* says to Pharaoh: For this
10:11 *S* says: None that rests his
11:2 *s* says in connection with
Ga 3:8 *S*, seeing in advance that God
3:22 *S* delivered up all things
4:30 what does the *S* say?
1Ti 5:18 *s* says: You must not muzzle
2Ti 3:16 All *S* is inspired of God and
Jas 2:8 *s*: You must love your
2:23 the *s* was fulfilled which
4:5 the *s* says to no purpose
1Pe 2:6 in *S*: Look! I am laying in
2Pe 1:20 no prophecy of *S* springs

Scripture-containing
Mt 23:5 they broaden the *s* cases that

Scriptures
Mt 21:42 Did you never read in the *S*
22:29 you know neither the *S* nor
26:54 *S* be fulfilled that it must
26:56 the *s* of the prophets to be
Mr 12:24 not knowing either the *S* or
14:49 that the *S* may be fulfilled
Lu 24:27 to himself in all the *S*
24:32 fully opening up the *S* to us
24:45 grasp the meaning of the *S*
Joh 5:39 searching the *S*, because
Ac 17:2 he reasoned . . . from the *S*
17:11 examining the *S* daily as to
18:24 he was well versed in the *S*
18:28 he demonstrated by the *S*
Ro 1:2 his prophets in the holy *S*
15:4 comfort from the *S* we might
16:26 through the prophetic *s*
1Co 15:3 our sins according to the *S*
15:4 third day according to the *S*
2Pe 3:16 do also the rest of the *S*
Jude 4 appointed by the *S* to this

Scroll
Ezr 6:2 Media, there was found a *s*
Isa 34:4 just like a book *s*
Zec 5:1 and, look! a flying *s*
5:2 I am seeing a flying *s*, the
Lu 4:17 So the *s* of the prophet Isaiah
4:17 he opened the *s* and found the
4:20 he rolled up the *s*, handed it
Joh 20:30 not written down in the *s*
Ga 3:10 written in the *s* of the Law

Re 1:11 What you see write in a *s*
5:1 a *s* written within and on the
5:2 Who is worthy to open the *s*
5:3 able to open the *s* or to look
5:4 open the *s* or to look into it
5:5 open the *s* and its seven seals
5:8 And when he took the *s*, the
5:9 take the *s* and open its seals
6:14 heaven departed as a *s* that is
10:2 had in his hand a little *s*
10:8 *s* that is in the hand of the
10:9 to give me the little *s*
10:10 I took the little *s* out of
13:8 written in the *s* of life
17:8 written upon the *s* of life
20:12 But another *s* was opened
20:12 opened; it is the *s* of life
21:27 in the Lamb's *s* of life
22:7 of the prophecy of this *s*
22:9 the words of this *s*
22:10 of the prophecy of this *s*
22:18 of the prophecy of this *s*
22:18 that are written in this *s*
22:19 of the *s* of this prophecy
22:19 written about in this *s*

Scrolls
Joh 21:25 not contain the *s* written
2Ti 4:13 *s*, especially the parchments
Re 20:12 throne, and *s* were opened
20:12 things written in the *s*

Scrupulously
Ga 4:10 *s* observing days and months

Scrutinize
Ezr 8:15 *s* the people and the priests

Scrutiny
1Co 11:28 approve himself after *s*

Sculptured
Ac 17:29 *s* by the art and contrivance

Scummy
Ps 119:119 *s* dross you have made all
Pr 25:4 removing of *s* dross from the
Isa 1:22 silver . . . become *s* dross
1:25 smelt away your *s* dross as
Eze 22:18 have become as *s* dross
22:18 Much *s* dross, that of
22:19 become as much *s* dross

Scythes
Jos 17:16 war chariots with iron *s*
17:18 war chariots with iron *s*
Jg 1:19 war chariots with iron *s*
4:3 war chariots with iron *s*, and
4:13 war chariots with iron *s*

Scythian
Col 3:11 *S*, slave, freeman, but

Sea
Ge 1:21 create the great *s* monsters
1:22 fill the waters in the *s*
1:26 subjection the fish of the *s*
1:28 subjection the fish of the *s*
9:2 upon all the fishes of the *s*
14:3 Plain of Siddim . . . Salt *S*
32:12 the grains of sand of the *s*
41:49 like the sand of the *s*
Ex 10:19 drove them into the Red *S*
13:18 the wilderness of the Red *S*
14:2 between Migdol and the *s* in
14:2 you are to encamp by the *s*
14:9 by the *s*, by Pihahiroth in
14:16 over the *s* and split it apart
14:16 through the midst of the *s*
14:21 over the *s*; and Jehovah began
14:21 making the *s* go back by a
14:21 the *s* basin into dry ground
14:22 midst of the *s* on dry land
14:23 into the midst of the *s*
14:26 over the *s*, that the waters
14:27 his hand out over the *s*
14:27 and the *s* began to come back
14:27 off into the midst of the *s*
14:28 gone into the *s* after them
15:1 he has pitched into the *s*
15:4 he has cast into the *s*
15:4 have been sunk in the Red *S*
15:8 in the heart of the *s*
15:10 the *s* covered them; They
15:19 cavalrymen went into the *s*
15:19 waters of the *s* upon them
15:19 through the midst of the *s*
15:21 he has pitched into the *s*
Ex 15:22 to depart from the Red *S* and
20:11 the *s* and everything that is
23:31 boundary from the Red *S* to
23:31 to the *s* of the Philistines
Nu 11:22 fish of the *s* be caught for
11:31 driving quails from the *s*
13:29 dwelling by the *s* and by the
14:25 by way of the Red *S*
21:4 by the way of the Red *S* to go
33:8 through the midst of the *s* to
33:10 went camping by the Red *S*
33:11 pulled away from the Red *S*
34:3 the extremity of the Salt *S*
34:5 must prove to be at the *S*
34:6 the Great *S* and the shoreland
34:7 From the Great *S* you will
34:11 slope of the *s* of Chinnereth
34:12 must prove to be the Salt *S*
De 1:40 by the way of the Red *S*
2:1 by the way of the Red *S*, just
3:17 the *s* of the Arabah, the Salt
3:17 the Salt *S*, at the base of the
4:49 as far as the *s* of the Arabah
11:4 waters of the Red *S* overflow
11:24 to the western *s* your
30:13 on the other side of the *s*
30:13 to the other side of the *s*
34:2 Judah as far as the western *s*
Jos 1:4 Great *S* toward the setting
2:10 the waters of the Red *S* from
3:16 toward the *s* of the Arabah
3:16 the Arabah, the Salt *S*, were
4:23 the Red *S* when he dried it
5:1 Canaanites, who were by the *s*
9:1 whole coast of the Great *S*
12:3 as far as the *s* of Chinnereth
12:3 as far as the *s* of the Arabah
12:3 of the Arabah, the Salt *S*
13:27 the *s* of Chinnereth on the
15:2 extremity of the Salt *S*
15:4 proved to be at the *s*
15:5 boundary was the Salt *S*
15:5 corner . . . the bay of the *s*
15:11 proved to be at the *s*
15:12 boundary was at the Great *S*
15:47 the Great *S* and the adjacent
16:3 proved to be at the *s*
16:6 boundary went out to the *s*
16:8 proved to be at the *s*
17:9 came to be at the *s*
17:10 *s* came to be his boundary
18:19 northern bay of the Salt *S*
19:29 *s* in the region of Achzib
23:4 the Great *S* at the setting
24:6 you came to the *s*, then the
24:6 and cavalrymen to the Red *S*
24:7 and brought the *s* upon them
Jg 11:16 as far as the Red *S* and got
2Sa 17:11 sand particles . . . by the *s*
22:16 the stream beds of the *s*
1Ki 4:20 sand that are by the *s*
5:9 down out of Lebanon to the *s*
5:9 in log rafts to go by *s*
7:23 make the molten *s* ten cubits
7:24 enclosing the *s* all around
7:25 the *s* was above upon them
7:39 the *s* itself he put to the
7:44 one *s* and the twelve bulls
7:44 twelve bulls beneath the *s*
9:26 Red *S* in the land of Edom
9:27 having a knowledge of the *s*
10:22 ships of Tarshish on the *s*
18:43 in the direction of the *s*
18:44 ascending out of the *s*
2Ki 14:25 clear to the *s* of the Arabah
16:17 the *s* he took down off the
25:13 carriages and the copper *s*
25:16 the two pillars, the one *s*
1Ch 16:32 Let the *s* thunder and also
18:8 Solomon made the copper *s*
2Ch 2:16 to you as rafts by *s* to Joppa
4:2 molten *s* ten cubits from its
4:3 enclosing the *s* all around
4:4 and the *s* was above upon them
4:6 *s* was for the priest to wash
4:10 *s* he placed at the right side
4:15 *s* and the twelve bulls under
8:17 upon the shore of the *s* in
8:18 having a knowledge of the *s*
20:2 region of the *s*, from Edom
Ezr 3:7 Lebanon to the *s* at Joppa
Ne 9:9 outcry at the Red *S* you heard
9:11 the *s* you split before them
9:11 midst of the *s* on the dry
Es 10:1 land and the isles of the *s*
Job 7:12, 12 Am I a *s* or a *s* monster
9:8 upon the high waves of the *s*
11:9 And broader than the *s*
12:8 fishes of the *s* will declare
14:11 do disappear from a *s*
26:12 he has stirred up the *s*
28:14 The *s* too has said, It is
36:30 the *s* he has covered
38:8 barricaded the *s* with doors
38:16 to the sources of the *s*
41:31 *s* like an ointment pot
Ps 8:8 and the fish of the *s*
33:7 by a dam the waters of the *s*
46:2 into the heart of the vast *s*
65:5 and those far away on the *s*
66:6 changed the *s* into dry land
68:22 from the depths of the *s*
72:8, 8 have subjects from *s* to *s*
74:13 stirred up the *s* with your
74:13 heads of the *s* monsters in
77:19 Through the *s* your way was
78:13 He split the *s*, that he
78:53 *s* covered their enemies
80:11 its boughs as far as the *s*
89:9 over the swelling of the *s*
89:25 on the *s* I have put his hand
93:4 breaking waves of the *s*
95:5 *s*, which he himself made
96:11 Let the *s* thunder and that
98:7 Let the *s* thunder and that
104:25 As for this *s* so great and
106:7, 7 at the *s*, by the Red *S*
106:9 he rebuked the Red *S*, and it
106:22 things at the Red *S*
107:23 down to the *s* in the ships
107:29 waves of the *s* keep quiet
114:3 *s* itself saw and took to
114:5 the matter with you, O *s*
136:13 One severing the Red *S* into
136:15 force into the Red *S*
139:9 reside in the most remote *s*
146:6 *s*, and of all that is in
148:7 You *s* monsters and all you
Pr 8:29 set for the *s* his decree that
23:34 down in the heart of the *s*
30:19 a ship in the heart of the *s*
Ec 1:7 are going forth to the *s*, yet
1:7 yet the *s* itself is not full
Isa 5:30 with the growling of the *s*
9:1 way by the *s*, in the region
10:22 the grains of sand of the *s*
10:26 staff will be upon the *s*
11:9 are covering the very *s*
11:11 from the islands of the *s*
11:15 tongue of the Egyptian *s*
16:8 they had gone over to the *s*
18:2 envoys by means of the *s*
19:5 be dried up from the *s*, and
21:1 the wilderness of the *s*
23:2 the ones crossing over the *s*
23:4 because the *s*, O you
23:4 O you stronghold of the *s*
23:11 stretched out over the *s*
24:14 cry out shrilly from the *s*
24:15 islands of the *s* the name
27:1 kill the *s* monster that is
27:1 monster that is in the *s*
42:10 are going down to the *s*
43:16 making a way through the *s*
48:18 like the waves of the *s*
50:2 I dry up the *s*; I make
51:9 that pierced the *s* monster
51:10 the one that dried up the *s*
51:10 made the depths of the *s* a
51:15 the One stirring up the *s*
57:20 wicked are like the *s* that
60:5 wealthiness of the *s* will
63:11 out of the *s* with the
Jer 5:22 as the boundary for the *s*
6:23 will resound just like the *s*
25:22 in the region of the *s*
27:19 concerning the *s* and
31:35 stirring up the *s* that its
33:22 sand of the *s* be measured
46:18 and like Carmel by the *s* he
47:7 and for the coast of the *s*
48:32 have crossed over the *s*
48:32 To the *s*—to Jazer—they
49:21 heard even at the Red *S*
49:23 In the *s* there is anxious
50:42 the *s* that is boisterous
51:36 And I will dry up her *s*
51:42 *s* has come up even over

Eze 23:13 I got to s that, because
23:14 s the men in carvings upon
32:31 ones that Pharaoh will s
39:15 s the bone of a man
39:21 have to s my judgment that
40:4 Son of man, s with your eyes
44:4 I might s, and, look!
44:5 s with your eyes, and with
Da 1:10 s your faces dejected-looking
1:13 according to what you s do
7:2 s there! the four winds of the
7:5 s there! another beast, a
7:6 s there! another beast, one
7:7 and, s there! a fourth beast
7:13 s there! with the clouds of
8:2 I began to s in the vision
8:2 s in the vision, and I myself
9:18 s our desolated conditions
10:5 raise my eyes and s, and here
10:7 they did not s the appearance
Ho 5:13 Ephraim got to s his sickness
Joe 2:28 men, visions they will s
Am 3:9 s the many disorders in the
6:2 your way over to Calneh, and s
7:1 Jehovah caused me to s, and
7:4 Jehovah caused me to s, and
7:7 is what he caused me to s
8:1 Jehovah caused me to s, and
Jon 3:10 God got to s their works
4:5 s what would become of the
Mic 7:10 my enemy will s, and shame
7:16 Nations will s and become
Na 3:5 nations to s your nakedness
Hab 1:3 make me s what is hurtful
1:5 S, you people, among the
1:13 too pure in eyes to s . . . bad
2:1 s what he will speak by me
Zec 1:18 to raise my eyes and s
2:1 to raise my eyes and s
2:2 s what her breadth amounts to
3:4 S, I have caused your error to
4:10 s the plummet in the hand of
5:5 s what this is that is going
6:8 S, those going forth to the
9:5 Ashkelon will s and get
10:7 their own sons will s and
Mal 1:5 And your own eyes will s it
3:18 s the distinction between a
Mt 5:8 pure in heart . . . will s God
5:16 they may s your fine works
7:5 then you will s clearly how
8:4 S that you tell no one, but
9:30 S that nobody gets to know it
11:8 then, did you go out to s
11:9 you go out? To s a prophet?
12:38 want to s a sign from you
13:14 will look but by no means s
13:15 that they might never s
13:17 desired to s the things you
13:17 and did not s them, and to
16:9 Do you not yet s the point
16:28 s the Son of man coming in
18:10 S to it that you men do not
23:39 You will by no means s me
24:6 s that you are not terrified
24:30 s the Son of man coming on
24:33 when you s all these things
25:20 s, I gained five talents
25:22 s, I gained two talents
25:37 when did we s you hungry
25:38 did we s you a stranger
25:39 When did we s you sick or
25:44 when did we s you hungry or
26:58 to s the outcome
26:64 you will s the Son of man
26:65 S! Now you have heard the
27:4 You must s to that!
27:24 You yourselves must s to it
27:49 s whether Elijah comes to
28:6 s the place where he was
28:7 Galilee; there you will s
28:10 Galilee . . . they will s me
Mr 1:44 S that you tell nobody a
3:2 to s whether he would cure
3:34 S, my mother and my brothers!
4:12 they may look and yet not s
5:14 people came to s what it was
5:31 You s the crowd pressing in
5:32 to s her that had done this
6:38 loaves have you? Go s!
8:18 having eyes, do you not s
8:23 ask him: Do you s anything?
8:24 I s men, because I observe
9:1 until first they s the kingdom

Mr 11:13 s whether he would perhaps
11:21 Rabbi, s! the fig tree that
13:1 s! what sort of stones
13:21 S! Here is the Christ
13:21 S! There he is, do not
13:26 s the Son of man coming in
13:29 s these things happening
14:62 s the Son of man sitting at
15:4 S how many charges they are
15:32 that we may s and believe
15:35 S! He is calling Elijah
15:36 Let us s whether Elijah
16:6 S! The place where they laid
16:7 you will s him, just as he
Lu 2:15 to Bethlehem and s this thing
2:26 would not s death before he
3:6 s the saving means of God
6:7 to s whether he would cure on
6:42 you will s clearly how to
7:25 What . . . did you go out to s?
7:26 what did you go out to s?
8:20 outside wanting to s you
8:35 to s what had happened, and
9:9 So he was seeking to s him
9:27 first they s the kingdom of
9:45 they might not s through it
10:24 kings desired to s the things
10:24 but did not s them, and to
12:54 When you s a cloud rising in
12:55 you s that a south wind is
13:28 when you s Abraham and Isaac
13:35 by no means s me until you
14:18 and need to go out and s it
14:28 to s if he has enough to
17:21 S here! or, There! For
17:22 will desire to s one of the
17:22 of man but you will not s it
17:23, 23 S there! or, S here! Do
18:3 S that I get justice from my
18:5 s that she gets justice, so
19:3 seeking to s who this Jesus
19:4 tree in order to s him
19:21 You s, I was in fear of you
21:20 s Jerusalem surrounded by
21:27 s the Son of man coming
21:31 you s these things occurring
23:8 wanting to s him because of
23:8 to s some sign performed by
24:24 but they did not s him
24:39 S my hands and my feet, that
24:39 feel me and s, because a
Joh 1:29 S, the Lamb of God that
1:33 upon whom you s the spirit
1:36 said: S, the Lamb of God!
1:39 Come, and you will s
1:46 said to him: Come and s
1:47 S, an Israelite for a
1:50 You will s things greater
1:51 You will s heaven opened up
3:3 cannot s the kingdom of God
3:26 s, this one is baptizing and
3:36 will not s life, but the
4:29 s a man that told me all
4:48 Unless you people s signs
5:14 S, you have become sound in
6:30 to s it and believe you
7:26 s! he is speaking in public
7:52 Search and s that no prophet
8:51 he will never s death at all
9:8 s he was a beggar began to
9:25 I was blind, I s at present
9:39 those not seeing might s
9:41 say, We s. Your sin remains
11:3 Lord, s! the one for whom
11:34 Lord, come and s
11:36 S, what affection he used
11:40 would s the glory of God
12:9 s Lazarus, whom he raised
12:19 S! The world has gone after
12:21 Sir, we want to s Jesus
12:40 not s with their eyes and
16:16 little while you will s me
16:17 little while you will s me
16:19 little while you will s me
16:22 s you again and your hearts
16:29 S! Now you are speaking
18:21 S! These know what I said
19:4 S! I bring him outside to
19:14 to the Jews: S! Your king!
19:26 said . . . Woman, s! your son!
19:27 disciple: S! Your mother!
20:25 s in his hands the print of
20:27 and s my hands, and take
20:29 do not s and yet believe

Ac 2:7 S here, all these who are
2:17 young men will s visions and
2:27 loyal one to s corruption
2:31 did his flesh s corruption
2:33 this which you s and hear
8:23 I s you are a poisonous gall
8:39 eunuch did not s him anymore
9:9 days he did not s anything
13:35 loyal one to s corruption
13:36 and did s corruption
13:37 did not s corruption
13:40 s to it that what is said in
15:6 to s about this affair
15:36 return . . . to s how they are
18:15 you yourselves must s to it
19:21 I must also s Rome
20:25 will s my face no more
22:11 as I could not s anything for
22:14 to s the righteous One and
26:16 things I shall make you s
27:12 s if we could somehow make
28:20 I entreated to s and speak
28:26 look but by no means s
28:27 never s with their eyes and
Ro 1:11 I am longing to s you, that
8:25 we hope for what we do not s
11:8 eyes so as not to s and ears
11:10 darkened so as not to s, and
11:22 S, therefore, God's kindness
15:21 will s, and those who have
1Co 8:10 if anyone should s you, the
13:12 we s in hazy outline by
16:7 s you just now on my passing
16:10 s that he becomes free of
2Co 7:8 I s that that letter saddened
Ga 5:2 S! I, Paul, am telling you
6:11 S with what large letters I
Eph 3:9 s how the sacred secret is
Php 1:27 come and s you or be absent
2:26 he is longing to s all of you
3:11 to s if I may by any means
3:12 to s if I may also lay hold
1Th 2:17 to s your faces with great
3:6 yearning to s us in the same
3:10 to s your faces and to make
5:15 S that no one renders injury
1Ti 6:16 men has seen or can s
2Ti 1:4 longing to s you, as I
Heb 2:8 do not yet s all things in
3:19 s that they could not enter
8:5 S that you make all things
11:5 so as not to s death
12:14 which no man will s the
12:25 S that you do not beg off
13:23 quite soon, I shall s you
Jas 2:24 You s that a man is to be
1Pe 3:10 love life and s good days
1Jo 3:1 S what sort of love the
3:2 we shall s him just as he is
4:1 s whether they originate with
3Jo 14 I am hoping to s you directly
Re 1:7 and every eye will s him, and
1:11 What you s write in a scroll
1:12 s the voice that was speaking
3:18 in your eyes that you may s
9:20 neither s nor hear nor walk
17:8 s how the wild beast was
18:7 I shall never s mourning
21:22 I did not s a temple in it
22:4 they will s his face, and

Seed

Ge 1:11 vegetation bearing s, fruit
1:11 s of which is in it, upon the
1:12 vegetation bearing s according
1:12 trees yielding fruit, the s
1:29 all vegetation bearing s
1:29 the fruit of a tree bearing s
3:15, 15 between your s and her s
4:25 God has appointed another s
8:22 s sowing and harvest, and
12:7 To your s I am going to give
13:15 to your s I am going to give
13:16 will constitute your s like
13:16 your s could be numbered
15:3 You have given me no s, and
15:5 So your s will become
15:13 your s will become an alien
15:18 To your s I will give this
16:10 I shall . . . multiply your s
17:7 your s after you according to
17:7 to you and to your s after you
17:8 s after you the land of your
17:9 you and your s after you

Ge 17:10 you men, even your s after
17:12 who is not from your s
17:19 time indefinite to his s
21:12 what will be called your s
22:17 multiply your s like the
22:17 your s will take possession
22:18 means of your s all nations
24:7 To your s I am going to give
24:60 let your s take possession of
26:3 to your s I shall give all
26:4 multiply your s like the
26:4 give to your s all these lands
26:4 means of your s all nations
26:12 Isaac began to sow s in that
26:24 bless . . . multiply your s
28:4 to you and to your s with you
28:13 to give it and to your s
28:14 s will certainly become like
28:14 by means of your s all the
32:12 s like the grains of sand of
35:12 s after you I shall give the
47:19 give us s that we may live
47:23 Here is s for you, and you
47:24 yours as s for the field and
48:4 will give this land to your s
Ex 16:31 was white like coriander s
23:10 to sow your land with s and
32:13 multiply your s like the
32:13 I shall give to your s, that
33:1 To your s I shall give it
Le 11:37 fall upon any s of a plant
11:38 water should be put upon s
12:2 In case a woman conceives s
21:15 not profane his s among his
21:17 No man of your s throughout
21:21 s of Aaron the priest in
25:3 sow your field with s, and
25:4 field you must not sow with s
25:11 sow s nor reap the land's
25:20 not sow s or gather our
25:22 sow s the eighth year and
26:5 will reach to the sowing of s
26:16 sow your s for nothing, as
27:16 in proportion to its s: if a
27:16 homer of barley s, then at
27:30 s of the land and the fruit
Nu 11:7 manna was like coriander s
20:5 It is no place of s and figs
24:7 And his s is by many waters
De 1:8 to give it to them and their s
4:37 he chose their s after them
11:9 to give to them and their s
11:10 where you used to sow your s
14:22 of all the produce of your s
21:4 no tilling or sowing of s
22:9 vineyard with two sorts of s
22:9 the s that you might sow and
28:38 s you will take out to the
34:4 To your s I shall give it
Jos 24:3 and made his s many. So I
Jg 6:3 if Israel sowed s, Midian and
1Sa 8:15 And of your fields of s and
24:21 not cut off my s after me
2Sa 7:12 raise up your s after you
22:51 his s for time indefinite
1Ki 18:32 two seah measures of s
2Ki 17:20 rejected all the s of Israel
19:29 sow s, you people, and reap
1Ch 17:11 raise up your s after you
2Ch 20:7 give it to the s of Abraham
Ezr 9:2 the holy s, have become
Ne 9:2 the s of Israel proceeded to
9:8 to give it to his s
Es 6:13 s of the Jews that Mordecai
Job 31:8 sow s and someone else eat
39:12 it will bring back your s
Ps 18:50 to his s to time indefinite
22:23 the s of Jacob, glorify him
22:23 all you the s of Israel
22:30 A s itself will serve him
89:4 shall firmly establish your s
89:29 set up his s forever
89:36 s itself will prove to be
105:6 you s of Abraham his servant
126:5 Those sowing s with tears
126:6 Carrying along a bagful of s
Ec 11:4 will not sow s; and he that
11:6 In the morning sow your s and
Isa 1:4 an evildoing s, ruinous sons
5:10 homer measure of s will
6:13 holy s will be the stump of
17:11 s of yours to sprout, but
23:3 has been the s of Shihor
28:24 plows in order to sow s
Isa 30:23 s with which you sow the
32:20 sowing s alongside all
37:30 in the third year sow s
41:8 the s of Abraham my friend
43:5 I shall bring your s, and
44:3 my spirit upon your s, and
45:19 nor said I to the s of Jacob
45:25 all the s of Israel will
55:10 s is actually given to the
57:3 the s of an adulterous person
57:4 the s of falsehood
Jer 2:2 in a land not sown with s
2:21 all of it a true s
31:27 Judah with the s of man and
31:27 the s of domestic animal
31:36 s of Israel could likewise
31:37 entire s of Israel on
33:22 s of David my servant and
33:26 reject even the s of Jacob
33:26 take from his s rulers over
33:26 over the s of Abraham
35:7 no s must you sow
35:9 or s should become ours
Eze 17:5 some of the s of the land
17:5 and put it in a field for s
17:13 took one of the royal s and
20:5 the s of the house of Jacob
31:17 as his s have dwelt in his
36:9 cultivated and sown with s
Da 9:1 of the s of the Medes, who
Ho 2:22 Jezreel [=God will sow s]
2:23 sow her like s for me in the
10:12 Sow s for yourselves in
Am 9:13 the carrier of the s; and the
Mic 6:15 for your part, will sow s
Hag 1:6 You have sown much s, but
2:19 the s in the grain pit
Zec 8:12 will be the s of peace
10:9 scatter them like s among
Mal 2:3 the sown s, and I will
2:15 The s of God. And you people
Mt 6:26 they do not sow s or reap or
13:24 a man that sowed fine s in
13:27 did you not sow fine s in
13:37 sower of the fine s is the
13:38 fine s, these are the sons
Mr 4:4 some s fell alongside the road
4:5 s fell upon the rocky place
4:7 other s fell among the thorns
4:26 casts the s upon the ground
4:27 the s sprouts and grows tall
Lu 1:55 to Abraham and to his s
8:5 A sower went out to sow his s
8:11 The s is the word of God
12:24 ravens neither sow s nor
Ac 3:25 in your s all the families
7:5 and after him to his s, while
7:6 s would be alien residents
Ro 1:3 who sprang from the s of David
4:13 Abraham or his s had the
4:16 to be sure to all his s
4:18 been said: So your s will be
9:7 Abraham's s are they all
9:7 your s will be through Isaac
9:8 promise are counted as the s
9:29 had left a s to us, we should
11:1 of the s of Abraham, of the
2Co 9:10 supplies s to the sower and
9:10 multiply the s for you to
11:22 Are they Abraham's s?
Ga 3:16 to Abraham and to his s
3:16 to your s, who is Christ
3:19 s should arrive to whom the
3:29 Abraham's s, heirs with
2Ti 2:8 was of David's s, according
Heb 2:16 he is assisting Abraham's s
11:11 power to conceive s
11:18 s will be through Isaac
Jas 3:18 righteousness has its s sown
1Pe 1:23 s, through the word of the
1Jo 3:9 reproductive s remains in
Re 12:17 remaining ones of her s

Seedland
Isa 19:7 s of the Nile River will dry

Seeds
Le 19:19 sow your field with s of two
Mt 13:4 s fell alongside the road
13:32 the tiniest of all the s
Mr 4:31 tiniest of all the s that are
1Co 15:38 each of the s its own body
Ga 3:16 And to s, as in the case of

Seeing
Ge 15:2 s that I am going childless
24:30 s the nose ring and the
24:56 s that Jehovah has given
26:27 s that you yourselves hated
31:5 am s the face of your father
33:10 your face as though s God's
45:12 s that it is my mouth that
48:11 I had no idea of s your face
Ex 10:28 day of your s my face you
20:18 people were s the thunders
Le 25:20 s that we may not sow seed
Nu 14:22 s my glory and my signs that
22:25 the she-ass kept s Jehovah's
35:23 without s him or he should
De 3:21 s all that Jehovah your God
4:12 no form were you s—nothing
11:7 s all the great deeds of
29:2 s all that Jehovah did before
Jg 9:36 what you are s as though they
11:12 s that you have come against
14:11 on their s him, they
19:30 that everybody s it said
1Sa 6:13 way to rejoicing at s it
17:24 Israel, on their s the man
17:28 the purpose of s the battle
18:15 And Saul kept s that he was
26:12 was no one s nor anyone
2Sa 18:27 s that the running style
24:3 eyes of my lord . . . are s it
1Ki 1:48 with my own eyes s it
22:25 s which way on that day
2Ki 2:12 Elisha was s it, and he was
2:19 just as my master is s
7:2 are s it with your own eyes
7:19 are s it with your own eyes
9:17 mass of men that I am s
23:17 over there that I am s
1Ch 29:17 enjoyed s make offerings
2Ch 18:24 s which way on that day
29:8 are s with your own eyes
30:7 just as you are s
Ne 2:17 You are s the bad plight in
Es 2:15 in the eyes of everyone s her
3:5 Haman kept s that Mordecai
5:13 as long as I am s Mordecai
Job 20:7 The very ones s him will say
Ps 22:7 those s me, they hold me in
27:13 in s the goodness of Jehovah
31:11 When s me out of doors, they
35:17 how long will you keep s it?
63:2 s your strength and your glory
119:37 from s what is worthless
Pr 20:12 The hearing ear and the s eye
Ec 1:8 The eye is not satisfied at s
6:9 Better is the s by the eyes
7:11 for those s the sun
8:16 one s no sleep with his eyes
12:3 ladies s at the windows have
Isa 14:16 Those s you will gaze even
28:7 gone astray in their s
29:15 Who is s us, and who is
30:10 said to the ones s, You
30:20 eyes s your Grand Instructor
32:3 eyes of those s will not be
41:28 kept s, and there was not
42:20 a case of s many things
47:10 There is no one s me
61:9 s them will recognize them
Jer 1:11 What are you s, Jeremiah?
1:11 almond tree is what I am s
1:13 What are you s? So I said
1:13 blown upon is what I am s
4:21 shall I keep s the signal
7:17 Are you not s what they are
20:12 s the kidneys and the heart
24:3 What are you s, Jeremiah?
32:24 and here you are s it
42:2 just as your eyes are s us
Eze 1:15 I kept s the living creatures
8:6 s what great detestable
8:12 saying, Jehovah is not s us
9:9 the land, and Jehovah is not s
18:14 s all the sins of his father
28:18 the eyes of all those s you
40:4 everything that you are s
Da 8:2 while I was s, that I was in
8:15 Daniel, was s the vision and
Am 7:8 What are you s, Amos?
8:2 What are you s, Amos?
Na 3:7 everyone s you will flee away
Hag 2:3 how are you people s it now?
Zec 4:2 said to me: What are you s?
5:2 said to me: What are you s?

Zec 5:2 I am s a flying scroll, the
Mt 2:10 On s the star they rejoiced
2:16 s he had been outwitted by
9:2 On s their faith Jesus said
9:11 on s this the Pharisees began
9:36 On s the crowds he felt pity
11:4 what you are hearing and s
11:5 The blind are s again, and
12:2 At s this the Pharisees said
15:31 and the blind s, and they
21:38 On s the son the cultivators
26:8 On s this the disciples
27:3 s he had been condemned, felt
27:24 S that it did no good but
Mr 8:25 was s everything distinctly
10:14 s this Jesus was indignant
14:67 s Peter warming himself
Lu 5:8 S this, Simon Peter fell down
7:21 blind persons the favor of s
8:47 S that she had not escaped
10:33 at s him, he was moved with
11:38 at s that he did not first
16:3 s that my master will take
18:15 on s it the disciples began
18:43 people, at s it, gave praise
22:58 another person s him said
23:47 s what occurred the army
Joh 5:6 S this man lying down, and
8:56 prospect of s my day, and he
9:7 washed, and came back s
9:17 s that he opened your eyes
9:39 those not s might see and
9:39 those s might become blind
11:31 s Mary rise quickly and go
19:26 Jesus, s his mother and the
20:20 rejoiced at s the Lord
Ac 9:8 were opened he was s nothing
12:9 supposed he was s a vision
13:11 not s the sunlight for a
13:12 s what had happened, became
14:9 and s he had faith to be made
14:11 the crowds, s what Paul had
15:38 s that he had departed from
16:21 or practice, s we are Romans
16:27 s the prison doors were open
17:29 S, therefore, that we are
24:2 S that we enjoy great peace
Ro 6:2 S that we died with reference
6:14 s that you are not under law
2Co 8:10 s that already a year ago
11:19 s you are reasonable
Ga 3:8 s in advance that God would
Php 2:28 s him you may rejoice again
1Th 1:6 s that you accepted the word
2Ti 2:26 s that they have been caught
Phm 9 s that I am such as I am
Heb 4:14 S, therefore, that we have a
11:27 s the One who is invisible
12:28 s that we are to receive
Re 22:8 hearing and s these things

Seek

De 12:5 you will s, and there you
Jg 9:15 s refuge under my shadow
Ru 2:12 you have come to s refuge
1Sa 9:9 talked on his going to s God
28:7 S for me a woman who is a
2Sa 12:16 David began to s the true
1Ch 16:11 S his face constantly
21:3 Why does my lord s this?
2Ch 7:14 s my face and turn back from
11:16 heart to s Jehovah the God
Ezr 8:21 s from him the right way
Ne 2:10 had come to s something good
Es 2:2 s young women, virgins
Job 20:10 s the favor of lowly people
Ps 27:8 S to find my face, you people
27:8 Your face . . . I shall s
34:14 S to find peace, and pursue
54:3 And tyrants that do s my soul
105:4 S his face constantly
Pr 18:1 s his own selfish longing
23:35 I shall s it yet some more
Ec 1:13 heart to s and explore wisdom
3:6 a time to s and a time to give
8:17 keep working hard to s, yet
Ca 3:2 let me s the one whom my soul
6:1 that we may s him with you
Isa 5:11 s just intoxicating liquor
45:19 S me simply for nothing
Jer 5:1 s for yourselves in her public
29:7 s the peace of the city to
29:13 actually s me and find me
50:4 their God they will s
Eze 7:25 s peace but there will be
7:26 s a vision from a prophet
Da 4:12 the beast . . . would s shade
9:3 s him with prayer and with
Ho 5:15 they will certainly s my face
5:15 sore straits, they will s me
Na 3:7 where shall I s comforters
3:11 s a stronghold from the enemy
Zep 2:3 s Jehovah, all you meek ones
2:3 S righteousness
2:3 righteousness, s meekness
Zec 8:21 and to s Jehovah of armies
8:22 come to s Jehovah of armies
11:16 The young one he will not s
12:9 s to annihilate all the
Mal 2:7 law is what people should s
Mr 8:12 this generation s a sign
11:18 to s how to destroy him
Lu 12:31 s continually his kingdom
13:24 s to get in but will not be
19:10 Son of man came to s and to
22:6 s a good opportunity to betray
Joh 5:30 I s, not my own will, but
Ac 15:17 men may earnestly s Jehovah
17:27 for them to s God, if they
1Co 14:12 s to abound in them for the
Ga 4:17 s you, not in a fine way
4:17 you may zealously s them
1Pe 3:11 let him s peace and pursue
Re 9:6 the men will s death but will

Seeking

Ex 10:11 is what you are s to secure
Nu 35:23 and was not s his injury
Jg 6:29 And they went inquiring and s
1Sa 19:2 Saul my father is s to have
20:1 for he is s for my soul
23:10 Saul is s to come to Keilah
24:9 David is s your hurt
25:26 those s injury to my lord
2Sa 3:17 s David as king over you
14:16 man s to annihilate me
17:3 the man whom you are s
20:19 s to put to death a city
1Ki 10:24 were s the face of Solomon
11:22 s to go to your own land
11:40 s to put Jeroboam to death
20:7 calamity that this one is s
2Ki 5:7 see how he is s a quarrel
1Ch 16:10 of those s Jehovah rejoice
2Ch 9:23 s the face of Solomon to
Ezr 8:22 all those s him for good
Ne 2:4 this that you are s to secure
Es 2:21 and kept s to lay hand on King
3:6 s to annihilate all the Jews
9:2 hand on those s their injury
Ps 4:2 you keep s to find a lie
14:2 insight, anyone s Jehovah
17:7 O Savior of those s refuge
22:26 s him will praise Jehovah
24:6 the generation of those s him
34:10 as for those s Jehovah
37:32 s to put him to death
37:36 s him, and he was not found
38:12 those s my soul lay out
40:14 s my soul to sweep it away
40:16 All those who are s you
53:2 insight, anyone s Jehovah
63:9 those who keep s my soul
69:6 those s you not be humiliated
69:32 s God, let your heart also
70:2 abashed who are s my soul
70:4 all of whom are s you
71:13 who are s calamity for me
71:24 who are s calamity for me
104:21 s their food from God
105:3 heart of those s Jehovah
122:9 I will keep s good for you
Pr 2:4 keep s for it as for silver
11:27 will keep s goodwill
17:9 over transgression is s love
17:11 is what the bad one keeps s
17:19 entryway high is s a crash
21:6 in the case of those s death
28:5 are s Jehovah can understand
29:10 s for the soul of each one
29:26 those s the face of a ruler
Ec 3:15 keeps s that which is pursued
Isa 16:5 judging and s justice and
41:17 poor ones are s for water
51:1 who are s to find Jehovah
58:2 it was I whom they kept s
Jer 4:30 keep s for your very soul
5:1 justice, anyone s faithfulness
Jer 11:21 s for your soul, saying
19:7 those s for their soul
19:9 those s for their soul
21:7 who are s for their soul
22:25 who are s for your soul
26:21 began s to put him to death
34:20 of those s for their soul
34:21 of those s for their soul
38:4 s not for the peace of this
38:16 who are s for your soul
44:30 those s for his soul, just
44:30 and the one s for his soul
45:5 s great things for yourself
45:5 Do not keep on s
46:26 those s for their soul and
49:37 those s for their soul
La 3:25 the soul that keeps s for him
Eze 34:6 with no one s to find
Da 6:4 s to find some pretext against
8:15 vision and s an understanding
Na 1:7 cognizant of those s refuge in
Zec 6:7 and keep s where to go, in
Mal 2:15 And what was that one s?
3:1 Lord, whom you people are s
Mt 2:20 were s the soul of the young
6:33 s first the kingdom and his
7:7 keep on s, and you will find
7:8 and everyone s finds, and to
12:39 keeps on s for a sign, but
12:46 outside s to speak to him
12:47 outside, s to speak to you
13:45 merchant s fine pearls
16:4 keeps on s for a sign, but
21:46 they were s to seize him
26:16 kept s a good opportunity to
Mr 3:32 brothers outside are s you
8:11 s from him a sign from
12:12 began s how to seize him
14:1 scribes were s how to seize
14:11 began s how to betray him
Lu 5:18 they were s a way to bring
6:19 crowd were s to touch him
9:9 So he was s to see him
11:9 keep on s, and you will find
11:10 and everyone s finds, and
11:16 began s a sign out of heaven
12:29 quit s what you might eat
19:3 s to see who this Jesus was
19:47 were s to destroy him
22:2 s the effective way for them
Joh 5:18 s all the more to kill him
5:44 not s the glory that is from
7:1 the Jews were s to kill him
7:4 s to be known publicly
7:18 is s his own glory
7:19 Why are you s to kill me?
7:20 Who is s to kill you?
7:25 the man they are s to kill
7:30 began s to get hold of him
8:37 but you are s to kill me
8:40 But now you are s to kill me
8:50 I am not s glory for myself
8:50 is One that is s and judging
11:8 Judeans were s to stone you
19:12 Pilate kept on s how to
Ac 10:19 Three men are s you
10:21 I am the one you are s
13:8 s to turn the proconsul away
13:11 s men to lead him by the
17:5 s to have them brought forth
21:31 they were s to kill him
27:30 sailors began s to escape
Ro 2:7 who are s glory and honor and
10:3 but s to establish their own
10:20 those who were not s me
11:7 thing Israel is earnestly s
1Co 7:27 to a wife? Stop s a release
7:27 loosed from a wife? Stop s a
10:24 Let each one keep s, not his
10:33 not s my own advantage but
12:31 keep zealously s the greater
14:1 s the spiritual gifts, but
14:39 zealously s the prophesying
2Co 12:14 am s, not your possessions
13:3 s a proof of Christ speaking
Ga 1:10 Or am I s to please men?
2:17 in s to be declared righteous
Php 2:21 are s their own interests
4:17 Not that I am earnestly s
4:17 s the fruitage that brings
Col 3:1 go on s the things above
1Th 2:6 been s glory from men, no
Heb 11:6 of those earnestly s him
11:14 s a place of their own

Heb 13:14 s the one to come
1Pe 5:8 lion, s to devour someone

Seeks
Job 39:8 every . . . green plant it s
Pr 18:15 ear of wise ones s to find
Lu 17:33 s to keep his soul safe for
Joh 7:18 s the glory of him that sent
Ro 3:11 is no one that s for God

Seem
1Sa 20:13 s good to my father to do
24:4 it may s good in your eyes
Ne 2:5 If to the king it does s good
2:7 If to the king it does s good
9:32 this day, s little before you
Es 1:19 If to the king it does s good
3:9 If to the king it does s good
5:4 If to the king it does s good
5:8 if to the king it does s good
7:3 if to the king it does s good
8:5 If to the king it does s good
9:13 If to the king it does s good
Da 4:27 may my counsel s good to you
Zec 8:6 s too difficult in the eyes
8:6 s too difficult also in my
Mr 8:24 I observe what s to be trees
Ac 17:22 you s to be more given to
1Co 12:22 which s to be weaker are
2Co 10:9 may not s to want to terrify
Heb 4:1 s to have fallen short of it
Jas 4:5 s to you that the scripture

Seemed
Ge 19:14 s like a man who was joking
34:18 And their words s good in
Ex 24:10 s like a work of sapphire
1Sa 18:5 s good in the eyes of all the
1Ch 13:4 the thing s right in the eyes
Ne 2:6 it s good before the king that
2:10 it s to them something very
13:8 And it s very bad to me
Es 5:14 the thing s good before Haman
Da 4:2 it has s good to me to declare
6:1 It s good to Darius, and he
Lu 22:24 one of them s to be greatest
Ga 2:6 those who s to be something
2:9 the ones who s to be pillars
Heb 12:10 to what s good to them, but
Re 9:7 s to be crowns like gold, and
15:2 I saw what s to be a glassy

Seems
2Sa 18:4 Whatever s good in your eyes
1Ch 13:2 If it s good to you and it is
Ezr 5:17 if to the king it s good
7:18 whatever it s good to you
Ne 2:5 if your servant s good before
Es 2:4 young woman who s pleasing in
Lu 10:36 Who of these three s to you
Ac 17:18 He s to be a publisher of
25:27 it s unreasonable to me to
1Co 4:9 s to me that God has put us
11:16 man s to dispute for some
Heb 12:11 no discipline s for the
Jas 1:26 man s to himself to be a

Seen
Ge 7:1 you are the one I have s to be
26:28 unmistakably s that Jehovah
31:12 s all that Laban is doing
31:42 toil of my hands God has s
32:30 I have s God face to face
33:10 I have s your face as though
41:19 For badness I have not s
44:28 I have not s him till now
45:13 and everything you have s
46:30 now that I have s your face
Ex 3:7 I have s the affliction of my
3:9 I have s also the oppression
4:31 that he had s their affliction
10:6 fathers' fathers have not s it
13:7 nothing leavened is to be s
13:7 no sour dough is to be s with
19:4 s what I did to the Egyptians
20:22 have s that it was from the
33:23 But my face may not be s
34:3 let nobody else be s in all
Le 5:1 is a witness or he has s it
13:51 he has s the plague on the
14:37 When he has s the plague
Nu 23:21 no trouble has he s against
27:13 When you have s it, then you
De 1:19 wilderness, which you have s
4:9 things that your eyes have s
5:24 s that God may speak with
De 9:13 I have s this people, and
10:21 things that your eyes have s
11:2 s the discipline of Jehovah
16:4 no sour dough should be s
21:11 have s among the captives a
29:22 they have s the plagues of
33:9 I have not s him. Even his
Jos 23:3 you have s all that Jehovah
Jg 2:7 who had s all of Jehovah's
5:8 A shield could not be s, nor a
6:22 I have s Jehovah's angel face
9:48 What you have s me do—hurry
13:22 it is God that we have s
14:2 woman that I have s in Timnah
18:9 we have s the land, and, look!
19:30 s from the day that the sons
1Sa 9:16 have s the affliction of my
10:24 s the one whom Jehovah has
16:18 I have s how a son of Jesse
17:25 Have you s this man that is
24:10 eyes have s how Jehovah
2Sa 18:10 I have s Absalom hung in a
18:21 the king what you have s
1Ki 6:18 there was no stone to be s
10:12 nor have they been s down
20:13 Have you s all this great
21:29 s how Ahab has humbled
2Ki 6:32 Have you s how this son of a
13:4 s the oppression upon Israel
14:26 s the very bitter affliction
20:5 prayer. I have s your tears
2Ch 9:11 never been s before in the
Ezr 3:12 that had s the former house
Es 9:26 what they had s as to this
Job 3:16 children that have s no light
4:8 According to what I have s
5:3 s the foolish one taking root
8:18 saying, I have not s you
13:1 Look! All this my eye has s
27:12 all of you s visions
28:10 things his eye has s
33:21 his bones that were not s
Ps 10:14 have s trouble and vexation
31:7 that you have s my affliction
33:13 He has s all the sons of men
35:21 Aha! Aha! our eye has s it
35:22 You have s, O Jehovah. Do not
37:25 not s anyone righteous left
37:35 I have s the wicked a tyrant
48:8 we have heard, so we have s
55:9 have s violence and disputing
68:24 s your processions, O God
74:9 Our signs we have not s
77:16 The waters have s you, O God
77:16 waters have s you; they
90:15 that we have s calamity
97:6 the peoples have s his glory
98:3 earth have s the salvation by
107:24 s the works of Jehovah
119:96 all perfection I have s an
119:158 I have s those who are
Pr 22:3 one that has s the calamity
25:7 a noble whom your eyes have s
26:12 Have you s a man wise in his
27:12 one that has s the calamity
Ec 2:24 This too I have s, even I
3:10 s the occupation that God has
3:16 s under the sun the place of
3:22 s that there is nothing better
4:3 has not s the calamitous work
4:4 have s all the hard work and
4:15 s all those alive who are
5:13 grave calamity that I have s
5:18 thing that I myself have s
6:1 calamity that I have s under
6:5 the sun itself he has not s
6:6 yet he has not s what is good
7:15 Everything I have s during my
8:9 All this I have s, and there
8:10 have s the wicked ones being
10:5 calamitous that I have s
10:7 I have s servants on horses
11:9 in the things s by your eyes
Ca 3:3 soul has loved have you men s
6:9 The daughters have s her, and
Isa 5:12 his hands they have not s
6:5 eyes have s the King, Jehovah
9:2 have s a great light
16:12 s that Moab was made weary
30:30 of his arm to be s, in
38:5 I have s your tears
44:16 I have s the firelight
47:3 your reproach ought to be s
57:18 I have s his very ways
Isa 60:2 his own glory will be s
64:4 eye itself s a God, except
66:8 Who has s things like these?
66:19 have not . . . s my glory
Jer 1:12 You have s well, for I am
3:6 s what unfaithful Israel has
7:11 Here I myself also have s it
13:26 your dishonor will . . . be s
13:27 s your disgusting things
23:13 I have s impropriety
23:14 I have s horrible things
30:6 s every able-bodied man with
33:24 s what those of this people
44:2 s all the calamity that I
46:5 have s them terror-stricken
La 1:8 for they have s her nakedness
1:10 s nations that have come into
2:16 We have found! We have s!
3:1 s affliction because of the
3:59 You have s, O Jehovah, the
3:60 You have s all their vengeance
Eze 3:23 like the glory that I had s
8:4 the appearance that I had s in
8:12 Have you s, O son of man
8:15 Have you s this, O son of
8:17 Have you s this, O son of
10:8 s belonging to the cherubs
10:15 living creature that I had s
10:20 living creature that I had s
10:22 I had s by the river Chebar
11:24 vision that I had s went
13:3 is nothing that they have s
21:24 your sins may be s
43:3 vision that I had s, like
47:6 s this, O son of man
Da 8:6 I had s standing before the
8:16 there understand the thing s
8:26 s concerning the evening and
8:27 on account of the thing s
9:21 I had s in the vision at the
9:23 understanding in the thing s
10:1 understanding in the thing s
Ho 6:10 I have s a horrible thing
9:13 Ephraim, whom I have s like
Zec 4:2 I have s, and, look! there is
9:8 now I have s it with my eyes
9:14 Jehovah himself will be s
Mt 2:9 the star they had s when they
8:34 and after having s him
9:33 anything like this s in Israel
Mr 5:16 those who had s it related to
Lu 1:22 just s a supernatural sight
2:26 he had s the Christ of Jehovah
2:30 have s your means of saving
5:26 We have s strange things
8:36 Those who had s it reported
19:37 powerful works they had s
24:23 s a supernatural sight of
Joh 1:18 No man has s God at any time
1:34 I have s it, and I have
3:11 we have s we bear witness
3:32 What he has s and heard
4:45 had s all the things he did
5:37 nor s his figure
6:36 s me and yet do not believe
6:46 any man has s the Father
6:46 this one has s the Father
8:38 What things I have s with
8:57 still you have s Abraham
9:37 You have s him and, besides
14:7 you know him and have s him
14:9, 9 s me has s the Father
15:24 both s and hated me as well
19:35 he that has s it has borne
20:18 I have s the Lord! and that
20:25 We have s the Lord! But he
20:29 s me have you believed
Ac 1:3 s by them throughout forty
4:20 things we have s and heard
7:34 s the wrongful treatment of
7:44 to the pattern he had s
9:12 s a man named Ananias come
9:27 on the road he had s the Lord
10:17 vision he had s might mean
16:10 soon as he had s the vision
21:29 s Trophimus the Ephesian in
22:15 things you have s and heard
26:16 things you have s and things
Ro 1:20 qualities are clearly s from
8:24 hope that is s is not hope
1Co 2:9 Eye has not s and ear has not
9:1 Have I not s Jesus our Lord?
2Co 4:18 not on the things s, but on
4:18 the things s are temporary

Php 2:23 just as soon as I have s how
Col 2:1 those who have not s my face
2:18 stand on the things he has s
1Ti 6:16 whom not one of men has s or
Heb 3:9 s my works for forty years
Jas 5:11 s the outcome Jehovah gave
1Jo 1:1 we have s with our eyes
1:2 s and are bearing witness and
1:3 which we have s and heard
3:6 s him or come to know him
4:20 brother, whom he has s
4:20 God, whom he has not s
3Jo 11 He that does bad has not s God
Re 11:19 s in his temple sanctuary
12:1 great sign was s in heaven
12:3 sign was s in heaven, and
22:8 I had heard and s, I fell

Seer
1Sa 9:9 Come, and let us go to the s
9:9 be called a s in former times
9:11 Is the s in this place?
9:18 where is the house of the s?
9:19 I am the s. Go up before me
2Sa 15:27 You are a s, are you?
1Ch 9:22 and Samuel the s ordained
26:28 Samuel the s and Saul the
29:29 the words of Samuel the s
2Ch 16:7 Hanani the s came to Asa the
16:10 became offended at the s
Isa 28:4 when the s sees it, while it

Sees
Ge 16:13 looked upon him who s me
44:31 he s that the boy is not
Le 13:31 the priest s the plague of
20:17 s his nakedness, it is shame
1Sa 16:7 not the way man s is the
16:7 is the way God s, because
16:7 man s what appears to the
16:7 he s what the heart is
Job 7:8 eye of him that s me will
10:4 is it as a mortal man s that
11:11 When he s what is hurtful
28:24 the whole heavens he s
34:21 And all his steps he s
41:34 Everything high it s
Ps 37:13 s that his day will come
49:10 he s that even the wise ones
64:5 They have said: Who s them?
138:6 yet the humble one he s
Isa 21:6 he may tell just what he s
28:4 when the seer s it, while it
29:23 when he s his children, the
La 3:50 looks down and s from heaven
Eze 18:14 he s and does not do things
18:28 he s and he turns back from
33:3 s the sword coming upon the
33:6 case he s the sword coming
Joh 9:19 then, is it he s at present
9:21 is he now s we do not know
11:9 he s the light of this world
Ro 8:24 man s a thing, does he hope
2Co 12:6 more than what he s I am

Segment
Ca 4:3 Like a s of pomegranate are
6:7 Like a s of pomegranate are

Segub
1Ki 16:34 forfeit of S his youngest
1Ch 2:21 but she bore S to him
2:22 S, in turn, became father to

Seir
Ge 14:6 in their mountain of S
32:3 land of S, the field of Edom
33:14 I shall come to my lord at S
33:16 turned back on his way to S
36:8 the mountainous region of S
36:9 the mountainous region of S
36:20 the sons of S the Horite
36:21 sons of S, in the land of
36:30 sheiks in the land of S
Nu 24:18 S must become the possession
De 1:2 Mount S to Kadesh-barnea
1:44 scattering you in S as far as
2:1 days in going around Mount S
2:4 who are dwelling in S
2:5 I have given Mount S to Esau
2:8 who are dwelling in S, from
2:12 Horites dwelt in S in former
2:22 who are dwelling in S, when
2:29 sons of Esau dwelling in S
33:2 he flashed forth from S upon
Jos 11:17 Halak, which goes up to S
Jos 12:7 which goes up to S, after
15:10 Baalah westward to Mount S
24:4 Esau I gave Mount S to take
Jg 5:4 at your going forth from S, At
1Ch 1:38 sons of S were Lotan and
4:42 to Mount S, five hundred men
2Ch 20:10 mountainous region of S
20:22 mountainous region of S
20:23 mountainous region of S to
20:23 with the inhabitants of S
25:11 striking down the sons of S
25:14 gods of the sons of S and
Isa 21:11 is one calling out from S
Eze 25:8 that Moab and S have said
35:2 the mountainous region of S
35:3 mountainous region of S
35:7 the mountainous region of S
35:15 O mountainous region of S

Seirah
Jg 3:26 and made his escape to S

Seize
Ex 22:26 s the garment of your fellow
De 24:6 No one should s a hand mill
24:17 s the garment of a widow as
2Sa 2:21 s one of the young men as
1Ki 18:40 S the prophets of Baal!
20:18 you should s them alive
20:18 alive is how you should s
2Ki 10:14 S them alive, you men!
14:7 got to s Sela in the war
18:13 Judah and proceeded to s
Job 16:8 You also s me. It has become
18:9 trap will s him by the heel
18:20 a shudder will certainly s
22:6 For you s a pledge from your
24:3 They s the widow's bull as a
Ps 139:11 darkness . . . hastily s me
Pr 20:16 s from him a pledge
27:13 s from him a pledge
Isa 36:1 and proceeded to s them
Jer 13:21 birth pangs themselves s
Mt 12:29 and s his movable goods
21:46 they were seeking to s him
26:4 to s Jesus by crafty device
Mr 12:12 seeking how to s him, but
14:1 to s him by crafty device
14:51 and they tried to s him
Joh 6:15 and s him to make him king
10:39 they tried again to s him
11:57 order that they might s him
1Co 7:21 rather s the opportunity
2Co 11:32 the governor . . . to s me

Seized
Ge 19:16 men s hold of his hand and
21:25 servants of Abimelech had s
49:27 he will eat the animal s
Jos 8:8 as soon as you have s the city
2Sa 1:9 cramp has s me, because all
1Ki 18:40 At once they s them, and
2Ki 10:14 So they s them alive and
25:6 s the king and brought him
2Ch 25:23 Jehoash the king of Israel s
Ps 77:4 You have s hold of my eyelids
Pr 13:13 a debtor's pledge will be s
Jer 5:8 Horses s with sexual heat
6:24 Distress itself has s hold of
8:21 astonishment has s hold of
38:23 you will be s, and because
40:10 cities that you have s
48:41 places will certainly be s
49:24 and sheer panic has s her
50:43 Severe pains have s hold of
50:46 when Babylon has been s
51:32 themselves have been s
51:41 whole earth gets to be s
52:9 s the king and brought him
Eze 18:16 no pledge has he s, and
21:24 you people will be s even
Ho 12:3 In the belly he s his brother
Am 2:8 on garments s as a pledge they
Mic 2:2 desired fields and have s
Lu 5:26 Then an ecstasy s one and all
7:16 fear s them all, and they
Joh 18:12 Jews s Jesus and bound him
Ac 7:32 S with trembling, Moses did
16:29 s with trembling, he fell
23:27 man was s by the Jews and
24:6 one . . . whom we s
26:21 Jews s me in the temple and
27:15 boat was violently s and
Re 20:2 he s the dragon, the original

Seizes
De 22:28 s her and lies down with her
Mr 9:18 it s him it dashes him to

Seizing
De 24:6 soul that he is s as a pledge
Mt 11:12 those pressing forward are s

Seizure
Php 2:6 gave no consideration to a s

Sela
Jg 1:36 of Akrabbim, from S upward
2Ki 14:7 got to seize S in the war
Isa 16:1 S toward the wilderness

Selah
Ps 3:2 salvation for him by God. S
3:4 from his holy mountain. S
3:8 blessing is upon your people. S
4:2 keep seeking to find a lie? S
4:4 and keep silent. S
7:5 to reside in the dust itself. S
9:16 been ensnared. Higgaion. S
9:20 they are but mortal men. S
20:3 burnt offering as being fat. S
21:2 you have not withheld. S
24:6 your face, O God of Jacob. S
24:10 he is the glorious King. S
32:4 in the dry heat of summer. S
32:5 the error of my sins. S
32:7 you will surround me. S
39:5 nothing but an exhalation. S
39:11 man is an exhalation. S
44:8 your name we shall laud. S
46:3 rock at its uproar. S
46:7 is a secure height for us. S
46:11 a secure height for us. S
47:4 Jacob, whom he has loved. S
48:8 to time indefinite. S
49:13 in their very mouthings. S
49:15 For he will receive me. S
50:6 For God himself is Judge. S
52:3 speaking righteousness. S
52:5 the land of the living ones. S
54:3 set God in front of them. S
55:7 lodge in the wilderness.—S
55:19 enthroned as in the past—S
57:3 the one snapping at me. S
57:6 fallen into the midst of it. S
59:5 to any hurtful traitors. S
59:13 the ends of the earth. S
60:4 on account of the bow. S
61:4 concealment of your wings. S
62:4 they call down evil. S
62:8 God is a refuge for us. S
66:4 make melody to your name. S
66:7 be exalted in themselves. S
66:15 a bull with he-goats. S
67:1 his face shine upon us—S
67:4 you will lead them. S
68:7 through the desert—S
68:19 true God of our salvation. S
68:32 Make melody to Jehovah—S
75:3 that adjusted its pillars. S
76:3 the sword and the battle. S
76:9 all the meek of the earth. S
77:3 spirit may faint away. S
77:9 off his mercies in anger? S
77:15 of Jacob and of Joseph. S
81:7 at the waters of Meribah. S
82:2 to the wicked themselves? S
83:8 arm to the sons of Lot. S
84:4 still keep on praising you. S
84:8 give ear, O God of Jacob. S
85:2 covered all their sin. S
87:3 O city of the true God. S
87:6 one who was born there. S
88:7 you have afflicted me. S
88:10 Will they laud you? S
89:4 generation after generation. S
89:37 witness in the skies. S
89:45 enwrapped him with shame. S
89:48 from the hand of Sheol? S
140:3 viper is under their lips. S
140:5 they have set for me. S
140:8 they may not be exalted. S
143:6 an exhausted land to you. S
Hab 3:3 Holy One from Mount Paran. S
3:9 are the thing said. S
3:13 clear up to the neck. S

Select
Ex 18:21 s out of all the people
1Ch 7:40 s, valiant, mighty men
16:41 s men that were designated

Ne 5:18 six s sheep and birds
Ec 3:18 true God is going to s them
Php 1:22 which thing to s I do not

Selected
1Ch 9:22 were s as gatekeepers at the
Es 2:9 give her seven s young women
Ac 6:5 they s Stephen, a man full of
15:40 Paul s Silas and went off
2Th 2:13 God s you from the beginning

Selections
Isa 38:20 shall play my string s

Seled
1Ch 2:30 the sons of Nadab were S
2:30 But S died without sons

Seleucia
Ac 13:4 went down to S, and from

Self
Ps 51:6 in the secret s may you cause
Isa 45:23 By my own s I have sworn
63:12 lasting name for his own s
63:14 name for your own s
Jer 15:15 on account of your own s
32:20 make a name for your own s
49:13 by my own s I have sworn
Eze 18:20 Upon his own s the very
18:20 and upon his own s the very
28:4 made wealth for your own s
33:5 come to be upon his own s
Ho 12:14 he leaves upon his own s
Mr 4:28 Of its own s the ground bears
Lu 9:25 but loses his own s or

Self-assistance
Job 6:13 Is it that s is not in me

Self-assuming
Pr 21:24 Presumptuous, s braggart is
Hab 2:5 an able-bodied man is s
Ro 1:30 haughty, s, inventors of
2Ti 3:2 lovers of money, s, haughty
Jas 4:16 take pride in your s brags

Self-concerned
1Sa 1:18 her face became s no more

Self-condemned
Tit 3:11 and is sinning, he being s

Self-confidence
Ps 85:8 let them not return to s

Self-confident
Pr 14:16 the stupid is becoming . . . s
Eze 30:9 drive s Ethiopia into

Self-control
Isa 42:14 I kept exercising s
Ac 24:25 about righteousness and s
1Co 7:9 if they do not have s, let
9:25 exercises s in all things
Ga 5:23 mildness, s. Against such
2Ti 3:3 without s, fierce, without
2Pe 1:6 to your knowledge s, to your
1:6 to your s endurance, to your

Self-controlled
Tit 1:8 righteous, loyal, s

Self-exaltation
Pr 8:13 S and pride and the bad way

Self-exalted
Ps 140:5 s ones have hidden a trap
Pr 15:25 house of the s ones Jehovah
16:19 divide spoil with the s ones
Isa 2:12 It is upon everyone s and

Self-importance
Isa 10:12 s of his loftiness of eyes

Self-imposed
Col 2:23 in a s form of worship and

Selfish
Nu 11:4 expressed s longing, and the
11:34 people who showed s craving
Ps 10:3 over the s longing of his soul
106:14 showed their s desire in
Pr 18:1 will seek his own s longing

Selfishly
De 5:21 s crave your fellowman's

Self-regulation
1Co 7:5 you for your lack of s

Self-reliance
Jg 18:7 people . . . were dwelling in s

Selfsame
Eze 2:3 against me down to this s day
24:2 the day, this s day
24:2 Jerusalem on this s day

Self-sufficiency
Job 21:23 will die during his full s
2Co 9:8 full s in everything, you may
1Ti 6:6 godly devotion along with s

Self-sufficient
Php 4:11 circumstances I am, to be s

Self-willed
Tit 1:7 not s, not prone to wrath
2Pe 2:10 s, they do not tremble at

Sell
Ge 25:31 Jacob said: S me, first of
25:33 to s his right as firstborn
37:27 s him to the Ishmaelites
41:56 and to s to the Egyptians
47:22 they did not s their land
Ex 21:7 s his daughter as a slave girl
21:8 to s her to a foreign people
21:35 s the live bull and divide
22:1 he does slaughter it or s it
Le 25:14 should s merchandise to your
25:15 of the crops he should s to
25:25 s some of his possession, a
25:29 should s a dwelling house
25:39 s himself to you, you must
25:42 s themselves the way a slave
25:47 s himself to the alien
De 2:28 food you will s me for money
21:14 by no means s her for money
28:68 s yourselves there to your
Jg 2:14 he proceeded to s them into
4:9 that Jehovah will s Sisera
Ru 4:3 Naomi . . . must s
2Ki 4:7 s the oil and pay off your
Ne 5:8 s your own brothers, and must
10:31 on the sabbath day to s
Ps 44:12 s your people for no value
Pr 23:23 truth itself and do not s it
31:24 and proceeded to s them, and
Eze 30:12 s the land into the hand of
48:14 they should not s any of it
Joe 3:8 I will s your sons and your
3:8 s them to the men of Sheba
Am 8:5 and we may s cereals
8:6 we may s mere refuse of grain
Mt 10:29 sparrows s for a coin of
19:21 s your belongings and give
25:9 to those who s it and buy for
Mr 10:21 Go, s what things you have
Lu 12:6 s for two coins of small
12:33 S the things belonging to
18:22 S all the things you have and
22:36 s his outer garment and buy
Ac 4:34 s them and bring the values
5:8 did you two s the field for
Re 13:17 able to buy or s except a

Seller
Isa 24:2 for the buyer as for the s
Eze 7:12 the s, let him not go into
7:13 s himself will not return
Ac 16:14 Lydia, a s of purple, of the

Sellers
Ne 13:20 s of every sort of

Selling
Ge 42:6 the one that did the s to all
Le 25:16 of the crops is what he is s
De 14:21 there may be a s of it to a
2Ki 17:17 s themselves to do what
Ne 13:15 day of their s provisions
Am 2:6 s someone righteous for mere
Zec 11:5 those who are s them say
Mt 21:12 threw out all those s and
21:12 the benches of those s doves
Mr 11:15 s and buying in the temple
11:15 the benches of those s doves
Lu 17:28 were buying, they were s
19:45 throw out those who were s
Joh 2:14 in the temple those s cattle
2:16 said to those s the doves
Ac 2:45 s their possessions and

Sells
Ex 21:16 kidnaps a man and who . . . s
De 18:8 what he gets from things he s
Mt 13:44 and s what things he has and

Selves
Ps 64:8 tongue is against their own s
Eze 7:11 it is not from their own s
Eze 34:3 wool you clothe your own s
46:17 belong to their own s
1Co 11:13 Judge for your own s: Is it

Semachiah
1Ch 26:7 capable men, Elihu and S

Semblance
Ps 39:6 Surely in a s man walks about

Semein
Lu 3:26 son of S, son of Josech

Semen
Ge 38:9 he wasted his s on the earth
Le 15:16 man has an emission of s go
15:17 the emission of s gets to be
15:18 with an emission of s, they
15:32 an emission of s may go out
18:20 give your emission as s to
19:20 and has an emission of s
Nu 5:13 and has an emission of s
5:28 must be made pregnant with s
Job 21:10 and it does not waste s

Seminal
Le 20:15 s emission to a beast, he
22:4 there goes out a s emission
Nu 5:20 put in you his s emission

Senaah
Ezr 2:35 sons of S, three thousand
Ne 7:38 sons of S, three thousand

Send
Ge 19:29 he took steps to s Lot out of
24:7 he will s his angel ahead of
24:40 s his angel with you and
24:54 said: S me off to my master
24:56 S me off, that I may go to
27:45 s and get you from there
30:25 S me away that I may go to
31:27 s you away with rejoicing
32:5 like to s to notify my lord
37:13 and let me s you to them
38:17 shall s a kid of the goats
38:17 a security until you s it
38:20 Judah proceeded to s the kid
41:14 to s and to call Joseph
42:4 Jacob did not s Benjamin
42:16 S one of you that he may get
43:8 S the boy with me, that we
Ex 3:10 let me s you to Pharaoh, and
3:20 after that he will s you out
4:13 s, please, by the hand of the
4:13 one whom you are going to s
4:21 he will not s the people away
4:23 S my son away that he may
4:23 you refuse to s him away
5:1 S my people away that they
5:2 his voice to s Israel away
5:2 am not going to s Israel away
6:1 he will s them away and on
6:11 s the sons of Israel away out
7:2 must s the sons of Israel away
7:14 refused to s the people away
7:16 S my people away that they
8:1 S my people away that they
8:2 if you keep refusing to s them
8:8 I want to s the people away
8:20 S my people away that they
8:28 I—I shall s you away, and
8:32 and did not s the people away
9:1 S my people away that they
9:2 continue refusing to s them
9:7 Pharaoh . . . did not s the
9:13 S my people away that they
9:19 s, bring all your livestock
9:28 I am willing to s you away
9:35 not s the sons of Israel away
10:3 S my people away that they
10:4 refusing to s my people away
10:7 S the men away that they may
10:10 s you and your little ones
10:20 s the sons of Israel away
10:27 not consent to s them away
11:1 After that he will s you away
11:10 did not s the sons of Israel
12:33 s them away quickly out of
15:7 You s out your burning anger
21:26 s him away as one set free
21:27 s him away as one set free
22:5 s out his beasts of burden and
23:27 s the fright of me ahead of
23:28 s the feeling of dejection
33:2 will s an angel ahead of you
33:12 whom you will s with me
Le 14:7 s away the living bird over

Jos 8:9 Joshua *s* them out and they
10:3 *s* to Hoham the king of
10:6 men of Gibeon *s* to Joshua at
14:7 *s* me out of Kadesh-barnea to
22:6 Joshua blessed them and *s*
22:7 Joshua *s* them away to their
22:13 Israel *s* to the sons of
24:5 I *s* Moses and Aaron, and I
24:9 he *s* and summoned Balaam
24:12 So I *s* the feeling of
24:28 Joshua *s* the people away
Jg 2:6 When Joshua *s* the people away
3:15 Israel *s* tribute by his hand
3:18 he at once *s* the people away
5:15 he was *s* on foot. Among the
6:35 he *s* out messengers through
6:35 also *s* out messengers through
7:8 Israel he *s* away each one to
7:24 Gideon *s* messengers into all
9:31 he *s* messengers by subterfuge
11:12 Jephthah *s* messengers to the
11:14 But Jephthah *s* once more
11:17 Israel *s* messengers to the
11:17 the king of Moab they *s*
11:19 Israel *s* messengers to Sihon
11:28 that he had *s* to him
11:38 *s* her away for two months
12:9 He *s* outside and brought in
13:8 that you just *s*, let him
15:5 *s* them out into the fields of
16:18 *s* and called the Philistine
18:2 the sons of Dan *s* five men of
19:25 they *s* her off at the
19:29 into twelve pieces and *s* her
20:6 and cut her up and *s* her into
20:12 tribes of Israel *s* men to
21:13 assembly now *s* and spoke to
1Sa 4:4 people *s* to Shiloh and carried
5:8 *s* and gathered all the axis
5:10 *s* the ark of the true God to
5:11 *s* and gathered all the axis
6:21 they *s* messengers to the
10:25 Samuel *s* all the people
11:7 cut them in pieces and *s*
11:11 then they were *s* scattering
13:2 rest of the people he *s* away
15:1 I whom Jehovah *s* to anoint
15:18 Jehovah *s* you on a mission
15:20 on which Jehovah had *s* me
16:12 he *s* and had him come
16:19 Saul *s* messengers to Jesse
16:20 *s* them by the hand of David
16:22 Saul *s* to Jesse, saying
19:11 Saul *s* messengers to
19:14 Saul now *s* messengers to
19:15 Saul *s* the messengers to
19:17 *s* my enemy away that he
19:20 Saul *s* messengers to take
19:21 *s* other messengers, and
19:21 Saul *s* messengers again
20:22 for Jehovah has *s* you away
22:11 king *s* to call Ahimelech
25:5 David *s* ten young men and
25:14 David *s* messengers from the
25:25 young men that you had *s*
25:32 *s* you this day to meet me
25:40 David himself has *s* us to
26:4 David *s* spies that he might
2Sa 2:5 David *s* messengers to the men
3:12 Abner *s* messengers to
3:14 David *s* messengers to
3:15 Ish-bosheth *s* and took her
3:21 David *s* Abner off, and he got
3:22 for he had *s* him off, and
3:24 you *s* him off so that he
3:26 *s* messengers after Abner
8:10 Toi *s* Joram his son to King
9:5 King David *s* and took him
10:2 David *s* by means of his
10:3 he has *s* to you comforters
10:3 David has *s* his servants to
10:4 servants of David . . . *s* them
10:5 he at once *s* to meet them
10:7 *s* Joab and all the army and
10:16 Hadadezer *s* and brought out
11:3 David *s* and inquired about
11:4 David *s* messengers that he
11:5 *s* and told David and said
11:6 David *s* to Joab, saying
11:6 So Joab *s* Uriah to David
11:18 Joab now *s* that he might
11:22 about which Joab had *s* him
11:27 David immediately *s* and
12:25 *s* by means of Nathan the
2Sa 12:27 Joab *s* messengers to David
13:7 David *s* to Tamar at the
13:27 *s* Amnon and all the sons
14:2 Joab *s* to Tekoa and took
14:29 Absalom *s* for Joab to send
14:29 he *s* again, a second time
14:32 I *s* to you, saying, Come
15:10 Absalom now *s* spies through
15:12 Absalom *s* for Ahithophel
18:2 David *s* one third of the
18:29 Joab *s* the king's servant
19:11 he *s* to Zadok and Abiathar
19:14 they *s* word to the king
1Ki 1:44 king *s* with him Zadok the
1:53 Solomon *s* and they brought
2:25 King Solomon *s* by means of
2:29 Solomon *s* Benaiah the son of
2:36 the king *s* and called Shimei
2:42 the king *s* and called Shimei
5:2 Solomon *s* to Hiram, saying
5:8 Hiram *s* to Solomon, saying
5:8 I have heard what you *s* to me
8:66 eighth day he *s* the people
9:14 Hiram *s* to the king a
12:3 then they *s* and called him
12:18 King Rehoboam *s* Adoram
12:20 *s* and called him to the
14:6 I am being *s* to you with a
15:18 now *s* them to Ben-hadad the
15:19 *s* you a present of silver
15:20 and *s* the chiefs of the
18:10 has not *s* to look for you
19:2 Jezebel *s* a messenger to
20:2 he *s* messengers to Ahab the
20:5 I *s* to you, saying: Your
20:7 he *s* to me for my wives and
20:9 you *s* to your servant at
20:10 Ben-hadad now *s* to him and
20:17 Ben-hadad at once *s* out
20:34 with him and *s* him away
21:8 *s* the letters to the older
21:11 did just as Jezebel had *s* to
21:11 letters that she had *s* to
21:14 now *s* to Jezebel, saying
2Ki 1:2 he *s* messengers and said to
1:6 return to the king who *s* you
1:11 he *s* again to him another
1:16 *s* messengers to inquire of
2:2 has *s* me clear to Bethel
2:4 Jehovah himself has *s* me to
2:6 Jehovah himself has *s* me to
2:17 They now *s* fifty men; and
3:7 *s* to Jehoshaphat the king of
5:8 at once *s* to the king, saying
5:10 Elisha *s* a messenger to him
5:22 My master himself has *s* me
5:24 *s* the men away. So off they
6:9 *s* to the king of Israel
6:10 the king of Israel *s* to the
6:14 he *s* horses and war chariots
6:23 after which he *s* them away
6:32 he *s* a man from before him
6:32 has *s* to take off my head
7:14 *s* them out after the camp of
8:9 has *s* me to you, saying
9:19 he *s* out a second rider on
10:1 Jehu wrote letters and *s*
10:5 caretakers *s* to Jehu, saying
10:7 *s* them to him at Jezreel
10:21 Jehu *s* through all Israel
11:4 *s* and then took the chiefs
12:18 *s* them to Hazael the king
14:8 Amaziah *s* messengers to
14:9 *s* to Amaziah the king of
14:9 *s* to the cedar that was in
14:19 *s* in pursuit of him to
16:7 Ahaz *s* messengers to
16:8 *s* the king of Assyria a bribe
16:10 King Ahaz *s* Urijah the
16:11 Ahaz had *s* from Damascus
17:4 *s* messengers to So the king
17:13 I have *s* to you by means of
17:25 Jehovah *s* lions among them
17:26 they *s* word to the king of
18:14 *s* to the king of Assyria
18:27 *s* me to speak these words
19:2 *s* Eliakim, who was over the
19:4 *s* to taunt the living God
19:9 he *s* messengers again to
19:16 *s* to taunt the living God
20:12 *s* letters and a gift to
22:3 the king *s* Shaphan the son of
22:15 man that has *s* you men to
23:1 *s* and they gathered together
2Ki 23:16 *s* and took the bones from
1Ch 8:8 after he *s* them away
12:19 the Philistines *s* him away
18:10 *s* Hadoram his son to King
19:2 David *s* messengers to
19:3 he has *s* comforters to you
19:4 Hanun . . . *s* them away
19:5 he at once *s* to meet them
19:8 *s* Joab and all the army and
21:15 God *s* an angel to Jerusalem
2Ch 2:3 Solomon *s* to Hiram the king
2:11 writing and *s* it to Solomon
7:10 *s* the people away to their
8:18 Hiram regularly *s* to him by
10:3 they *s* and called him, and
10:18 Rehoboam *s* Hadoram, who
16:2 *s* to Ben-hadad the king of
16:4 *s* the chiefs of the military
17:7 *s* for his princes, namely
24:23 spoil they *s* to the king of
25:13 Amaziah had *s* back from
25:15 *s* a prophet to him and said
25:17 *s* to Jehoash the son of
25:18 *s* to Amaziah the king of
25:18 *s* to the cedar that was in
25:27 *s* after him to Lachish and
28:16 King Ahaz *s* to the kings of
32:9 *s* his servants to Jerusalem
32:31 *s* to him to inquire about
34:8 *s* Shaphan the son of Azaliah
34:23 Say to the man that *s* you
35:21 he *s* messengers to him
36:10 King Nebuchadnezzar *s* and
Ezr 4:11 letter that they *s* concerning
4:14 *s* and made it known to the
4:17 king *s* word to Rehum the
4:18 document that you have *s* us
5:5 this could be *s* back
5:6 *s* to Darius the king
5:7 *s* the word to him, and the
6:13 Darius the king had *s* word
7:14 order was *s* to investigate
8:16 I *s* for Eliezer, Ariel
Ne 2:9 king *s* with me chiefs of the
6:2 immediately *s* to me, saying
6:3 I *s* messengers to them, saying
6:4 *s* me the same word four times
6:5 Sanballat *s* his attendant to
6:8 I *s* to him, saying: Things
6:12 was not God that had *s* him
6:19 Tobiah *s* to make me afraid
Es 1:22 he *s* written documents to all
4:4 *s* garments to clothe Mordecai
5:10 he *s* and had his friends and
9:30 *s* written documents to all
Job 1:4 they *s* and invited their three
22:9 you have *s* away empty-handed
39:5 Who *s* forth the zebra free
Ps 48:5 they were *s* running in panic
59:*super* Saul *s*, and they kept
78:25 Provisions he *s* them to
80:11 *s* forth its boughs as far
104:7 they were *s* running in panic
105:17 He *s* ahead of them a man
105:20 king *s* that he might
105:26 He *s* Moses his servant
105:28 *s* darkness and so made it
111:9 *s* redemption itself to his
135:9 *s* signs and miracles into
Pr 9:3 *s* forth its lady attendants
17:11 messenger that is *s* against
Isa 9:8 that Jehovah *s* against Jacob
20:1 the king of Assyria *s* him
24:19 been *s* staggering
36:2 *s* Rabshakeh from Lachish to
36:12 my lord has *s* me to speak
37:2 *s* Eliakim, who was over the
37:4 *s* to taunt the living God
37:9 *s* messengers to Hezekiah
37:17 *s* to taunt the living God
39:1 *s* letters and a gift to
48:16 Jehovah himself has *s* me
50:1 whom I *s* away? Or which one
50:1 your mother has been *s* away
55:11 that for which I have *s* it
61:1 has *s* me to bind up the
Jer 3:8 I *s* her away and proceeded
14:3 *s* their insignificant ones
14:14 I have not *s* them, nor have
19:14 had *s* him to prophesy
21:1 Zedekiah *s* to him Pashhur
25:4 *s* to you all his servants
25:17 to whom Jehovah had *s* me
26:12 that *s* me to prophesy

Jer 26:22 Jehoiakim *s* men to Egypt
27:15 For I have not *s* them
28:9 prophet whom Jehovah has *s*
28:15 Jehovah has not *s* you, but
29:1 the prophet *s* from Jerusalem
29:3 Zedekiah the king of Judah *s*
29:9 I have not *s* them, is the
29:19 *s* to them with my servants
29:20 *s* away from Jerusalem to
29:25 *s* in your name letters to
29:28 *s* to us at Babylon, saying
36:14 princes *s* out to Baruch
36:21 king *s* Jehudi out to get
39:13 of the king of Babylon *s*
40:1 *s* him from Ramah, when he
40:14 *s* Ishmael the son of
42:9 *s* me to cause your request
42:20 *s* me to Jehovah your God
42:21 which he has *s* me to you
43:1 God had *s* him to them
43:2 our God has not *s* you
49:14 envoy that is *s* among the
La 1:13 he has *s* fire into my bones
Eze 3:5 *s*—to the house of Israel
3:6 was to them that I had *s* you
13:6 Jehovah himself has not *s*
17:6 shoots and *s* forth branches
23:40 there was *s* a messenger
31:4 its channels it *s* forth to
Da 3:2 king *s* to assemble the satraps
3:28 *s* his angel and rescued his
5:24 being *s* the back of a hand
6:22 My own God *s* his angel and
10:11 now I have been *s* to you
Joe 2:25 military force that I have *s*
Am 4:10 I *s* among you people a
Ob 1 envoy . . . *s* among the nations
7 they have *s* you. The very men
Hag 1:12 Jehovah their God had *s* him
Zec 1:10 *s* forth to walk about in the
2:8 he has *s* me to the nations
2:9 Jehovah . . . has *s* me
2:11 Jehovah . . . has *s* me to you
4:9 has *s* me to you people
6:15 Jehovah . . . has *s* me to you
7:12 *s* by his spirit, by means of
Mal 2:4 *s* to you this commandment
Mt 2:16 *s* out and had all the boys
9:25 the crowd had been *s* outside
10:5 These twelve Jesus *s* forth
10:40 receives him also that *s* me
11:2 John . . . *s* by means of his
14:10 *s* and had John beheaded in
14:22 while he *s* the crowds away
14:23 having *s* the crowds away
14:35 men of that place *s* forth
15:24 not *s* forth to any but to
20:2 he *s* them forth into his
21:1 Jesus *s* forth two disciples
22:3 he *s* forth his slaves to call
22:4 *s* forth other slaves, saying
22:7 *s* his armies and destroyed
23:37 stoner of those *s* forth to
27:19 wife *s* out to him, saying
Mr 1:43 and at once *s* him away
3:31 they *s* in to him to call him
6:17 had *s* out and arrested John
8:9 Finally he *s* them away
8:26 he *s* him off home, saying
9:37 but also him that *s* me forth
12:2 he *s* forth a slave to the
12:3 beat him up and *s* him away
12:4 *s* forth another slave to them
12:5 And he *s* forth another, and
12:6 He *s* him forth last to them
12:13 Next they *s* forth to him
14:13 *s* forth two of his disciples
Lu 1:19 I was *s* forth to speak with
1:26 the angel Gabriel was *s* forth
1:53 *s* away empty those who had
4:18 he *s* me forth to preach a
4:26 Elijah was *s* to none of those
4:43 because for this I was *s*
7:3 he *s* forth older men of the
7:6 already *s* friends to say to
7:10 those that had been *s*, on
7:19 *s* them to the Lord to say
9:2 he *s* them forth to preach the
9:48 receives him also that *s* me
9:52 *s* forth messengers in advance
10:1 *s* them forth by twos in
10:16 disregards . . . him that *s* me
13:34 stoner of those *s* forth to
14:4 healed him and *s* him away
Lu 14:17 he *s* his slave out at the
15:15 he *s* him into his fields
19:14 *s* out a body of ambassadors
19:29 *s* forth two of the disciples
19:32 those who were *s* forth
20:10 he *s* out a slave to the
20:10 *s* him away empty, after
20:11 and *s* them a different slave
20:11 dishonored and *s* away empty
20:12 Yet again he *s* a third
20:20 *s* out men secretly hired to
22:35 I *s* you forth without purse
23:7 he *s* him on to Herod who
23:11 and *s* him back to Pilate
23:15 for he *s* him back to us
Joh 1:6 *s* forth as a representative
1:19 the Jews *s* forth priests and
1:22 an answer to those who *s* us
1:24 those *s* forth were from the
1:33 *s* me to baptize in water
3:17 God *s* forth his Son into the
3:28 *s* forth in advance of that
3:34 the one whom God *s* forth
4:34 will of him that *s* me and
5:23 honor the Father who *s* him
5:24 believes him that *s* me has
5:30 the will of him that *s* me
5:37 the Father who *s* me has
6:29 him whom that One *s* forth
6:38 the will of him that *s* me
6:39 the will of him that *s* me
6:44 Father, who *s* me, draws him
6:57 the living Father *s* me forth
7:16 but belongs to him that *s* me
7:18 the glory of him that *s* him
7:28 he that *s* me is real, and
7:29 and that One *s* me forth
7:33 before I go to him that *s* me
8:16 Father who *s* me is with me
8:18 Father who *s* me bears
8:26 he that *s* me is true, and
8:29 he that *s* me is with me
8:42 but that One *s* me forth
9:4 works of him that *s* me while
9:7 which is translated *S* forth
11:42 believe that you *s* me forth
12:44 in him also that *s* me
12:45 beholds also him that *s* me
12:49 Father himself who *s* me
13:16 *s* forth greater than the one
13:16 than the one that *s* him
13:20 receives also him that *s* me
14:24 to the Father who *s* me
15:21 do not know him that *s* me
16:5 I am going to him that *s* me
17:3 one whom you *s* forth, Jesus
17:8 believed that you *s* me forth
17:18 *s* me forth into the world
17:18 I also *s* them forth into
17:21 believe that you *s* me forth
17:23 knowledge that you *s* me
17:25 to know that you *s* me forth
18:24 Annas *s* him away bound to
20:21 as the Father has *s* me
Ac 3:26 *s* him forth to bless you by
5:21 *s* out to the jail to have
7:12 *s* our forefathers out the
7:14 Joseph *s* out and called
7:35 God *s* off as both ruler and
9:17 *s* me forth, in order that you
9:30 and *s* him off to Tarsus
10:29 objection, when I was *s* for
10:29 reason that you have *s* for
10:33 I at once *s* to you, and you
10:36 He *s* out the word to the
11:22 they *s* out Barnabas as far
12:11 Jehovah *s* his angel forth
13:4 *s* out by the holy spirit
13:15 *s* out to them, saying
13:26 salvation has been *s* forth
15:33 to those who had *s* them out
17:10 the brothers *s* both Paul and
17:14 *s* Paul off to go as far as
19:31 *s* to him and began pleading
20:1 Paul *s* for the disciples, and
20:17 from Miletus he *s* to Ephesus
21:25 *s* out, rendering our decision
24:24 he *s* for Paul and listened
24:26 he *s* for him even more
28:28 has been *s* out to the nations
Ro 10:15 unless they have been *s*
2Co 2:17 as *s* from God, under God's
Ga 4:4 God *s* forth his Son, who came
4:6 God has *s* forth the spirit of
Php 4:16 you *s* something to me both
1Th 3:2 *s* Timothy, our brother and
3:5 I *s* to know of your
2Ti 4:12 *s* Tychicus off to Ephesus
Heb 1:14 *s* forth to minister for
Jas 2:25 *s* them out by another way
1Pe 1:12 spirit *s* forth from heaven
2:14 governors as being *s* by him
1Jo 4:9 God *s* forth his only-begotten
4:10 loved us and *s* forth his Son
4:14 Father has *s* forth his Son
Re 1:1 he *s* forth his angel and
5:6 *s* forth into the whole earth
22:6 *s* his angel forth to show
22:16 I, Jesus, *s* my angel to bear

Sentence
De 19:6 is no *s* of death for him
21:22 sin deserving the *s* of death
Job 36:17 judicial *s* upon the wicked
36:17 Judicial *s* and justice will
Ps 7:8 will pass *s* on the peoples
Ec 8:11 *s* against a bad work has not
Isa 3:13 up to pass *s* upon peoples
Jer 21:12 render *s* in justice, and
Da 2:9 one and only *s* is upon you
Lu 23:24 Pilate gave *s* for their
24:20 the *s* of death and impaled
2Co 1:9 had received the *s* of death

Sentences
Ec 12:11 indulging in collections of *s*

Sentinel
Ac 12:10 through the first *s* guard

Sentries
Jg 7:19 got through posting the *s*

Seorim
1Ch 24:8 the third, for *S* the fourth

Separate
Ge 13:9 *s* from me. If you go to the
Le 15:31 *s* from their uncleanness
22:2 *s* from the holy things of the
Nu 6:6 *s* to Jehovah he may not come
8:14 *s* the Levites from among the
16:21 *S* yourselves from the midst
De 29:21 to *s* him for calamity from
Ezr 10:11 *s* yourselves from the
Ne 9:2 *s* themselves from all the
13:3 *s* all the mixed company from
Mt 13:49 *s* the wicked from among the
25:32 *s* people one from another
Ro 8:35 *s* us from the love of the
8:39 *s* us from God's love that is
2Co 6:17 *s* yourselves, says Jehovah

Separated
Ge 13:11 *s* the one from the other
13:14 after Lot had *s* from him
25:23 two national groups will be *s*
30:40 Jacob *s* the young rams
Nu 6:5 days that he should be *s*
16:9 *s* you men from the assembly
De 10:8 Jehovah *s* the tribe of Levi
Jg 4:11 Heber the Kenite had *s* from
2Sa 1:23 their death they were not *s*
1Ki 8:53 *s* them as your inheritance
1Ch 12:8 *s* themselves to David's side
23:13 Aaron was *s* that he might
25:1 *s* for the service some of
2Ch 25:10 Amaziah *s* them, namely
Ezr 6:21 everyone that had *s* himself
8:24 *s* from the chiefs of the
9:1 have not *s* themselves from
10:8 be *s* from the congregation
10:16 *s* themselves and began
Es 3:8 people scattered and *s* among
Job 4:11 cubs of a lion are *s* from
41:17 and cannot be *s*
Ps 22:14 all my bones have been *s*
92:9 will be *s* from one another
Pr 19:4 lowly gets *s* even from his
Jer 6:29 bad have not been *s*
Eze 41:12 the *s* area, the side of
41:13 the *s* area and the building
41:14 *s* area to the east was a
41:15 *s* area that was behind it
42:1 in front of the *s* area
42:10 the *s* area and before the
42:13 that are before the *s* area
Lu 9:33 these were being *s* from him
Ac 15:39 that they *s* from each other
19:9 and *s* the disciples from them
Ro 1:1 *s* to God's good news

Ro 9:3 *s* as the cursed one from the
Ga 1:15 who *s* me from my mother's
Heb 7:26 *s* from the sinners, and

Separately
Joh 20:7 *s* rolled up in one place

Separates
Pr 18:18 lot . . . *s* even the mighty
Mt 25:32 *s* the sheep from the goats

Separating
Ne 10:28 *s* himself from the peoples
Pr 16:28 and a slanderer is *s* those
17:9 is *s* those familiar with one
Ga 2:12 he went withdrawing and *s*

Separation
Ru 1:17 make a *s* between me and you
2Ki 2:11 make a *s* between them both
Ca 2:17 stags upon the mountains of *s*

Separations
Jude 19 are the ones that make *s*

Sephar
Ge 10:30 *S*, the mountainous region

Sepharad
Ob 20 the exiles . . . who were in *S*

Sepharvaim
2Ki 17:24 Avva and Hamath and *S* and
17:31 Anammelech the gods of *S*
18:34 gods of *S*, Hena and Ivvah
19:13 king of the cities of *S*
Isa 36:19 Where are the gods of *S*?
37:13 king of the city of *S*

Sepharvites
2Ki 17:31 *S* were burning their sons

Serah
Ge 46:17 and there was *S* their sister
Nu 26:46 Asher's daughter was *S*
1Ch 7:30 and *S* was their sister

Seraiah
2Sa 8:17 and *S* was secretary
2Ki 25:18 took *S* the chief priest and
25:23 *S* the son of Tanhumeth
1Ch 4:13 sons of Kenaz were . . . *S*
4:14 *S*, he became father to Joab
4:35 *S* the son of Asiel
6:14 Azariah . . . father to *S*
6:14 *S* . . . father to Jehozadak
Ezr 2:2 *S*, Reelaiah, Mordecai
7:1 *S* the son of Azariah the son
Ne 10:2 *S*, Azariah, Jeremiah
11:11 *S* the son of Hilkiah the
12:1 *S*, Jeremiah, Ezra
12:12 for *S*, Meraiah; for Jeremiah
Jer 36:26 *S* the son of Azriel and
40:8 *S* the son of Tanhumeth and
51:59 *S* the son of Neriah the
51:59 and *S* was the quartermaster
51:61 Jeremiah said to *S*
52:24 took *S* the chief priest

Seraphs
Isa 6:2 *S* were standing above him
6:6 one of the *s* flew to me

Sered
Ge 46:14 sons of Zebulun were *S* and
Nu 26:26 Of *S* the family of the

Seredites
Nu 26:26 Of Sered the family of the *S*

Sergius
Ac 13:7 the proconsul *S* Paulus, an

Series
Ex 26:3 tent cloths are to form a *s*
26:3 tent cloths a *s* with the one
26:4 tent cloth at the end of the *s*
26:10 the outermost one in the *s*

Serious
Ac 25:7 many and *s* charges for which
Php 4:8 things are of *s* concern
1Ti 3:8 be *s*, not double-tongued, not
3:11 Women should likewise be *s*
Tit 2:2 *s*, sound in mind, healthy in

Seriousness
1Ti 2:2 full godly devotion and *s*
3:4 in subjection with all *s*
Tit 2:7 in your teaching, *s*

Serpent
Ge 3:1 Now the *s* proved to be the
Ge 3:2 woman said to the *s*: Of the
3:4 the *s* said to the woman: You
3:13 the woman replied: The *s*—it
3:14 God proceeded to say to the *s*
49:17 Let Dan prove to be a *s* by
Ex 4:3 it became a *s*; and Moses began
7:15 rod that turned into a *s* you
Nu 21:9 made a *s* of copper and placed
21:9 if a *s* had bitten a man and
21:9 and he gazed at the copper *s*
2Ki 18:4 crushed . . . the copper *s*
Job 26:13 has pierced the gliding *s*
Ps 58:4 is like the venom of the *s*
140:3 their tongue like that of a *s*
Pr 23:32 end it bites just like a *s*
30:19 the way of a *s* on a rock
Ec 10:8 a *s* will bite him
10:11 the *s* bites when no charming
Isa 14:29 out of the root of the *s*
27:1 Leviathan, the gliding *s*
27:1 Leviathan, the crooked *s*
65:25 *s*, his food will be dust
Jer 46:22 voice is like that of a *s*
Am 5:19 and the *s* bit him
9:3 I shall command the *s*, and it
Mt 7:10 not hand him a *s*, will he?
Lu 11:11 a *s* instead of a fish
Joh 3:14 as Moses lifted up the *s* in
2Co 11:3 as the *s* seduced Eve by its
Re 12:9 original *s*, the one called
12:14 away from the face of the *s*
12:15 *s* disgorged water like a
20:2 dragon, the original *s*, who is

Serpent-idol
2Ki 18:4 called the copper *s*

Serpents
Nu 21:6 So Jehovah sent poisonous *s*
21:7 remove the *s* from upon us
De 8:15 poisonous *s* and scorpions
Jer 8:17 I am sending in among you *s*
Mic 7:17 will lick up dust like the *s*
Mt 10:16 prove . . . cautious as *s* and
23:33 *S*, offspring of vipers, how
Lu 10:19 to trample underfoot *s* and
1Co 10:9 only to perish by the *s*
Re 9:19 their tails are like *s* and

Serug
Ge 11:20 Reu . . . became father to *S*
11:21 And after his fathering *S* Reu
11:22 *S* lived on for thirty years
11:23 after his fathering Nahor *S*
1Ch 1:26 *S*, Nahor, Terah
Lu 3:35 son of *S*, son of Reu, son of

Servant
Ge 18:3 please do not pass by your *s*
18:5 passed this way to your *s*
19:2 into the house of your *s* and
19:19 *s* has found favor in your
24:2 his *s*, the oldest one of his
24:5 *s* said to him: What if the
24:9 *s* put his hand under the thigh
24:10 *s* took ten camels from the
24:14 assign to your *s*, to Isaac
24:17 *s* ran to meet her and said
24:34 on to say: I am Abraham's *s*
24:52 Abraham's *s* had heard their
24:53 *s* began to bring out
24:59 and Abraham's *s* and his men
24:61 *s* took Rebekah and got on his
24:65 she said to the *s*: Who is
24:65 *s* said: It is my master
24:66 *s* went relating to Isaac all
26:24 on account of Abraham my *s*
32:4 what your *s* Jacob has said
32:10 have exercised toward your *s*
32:18 To your *s*, to Jacob. A gift
32:20 Here is your *s* Jacob behind
33:5 God has favored your *s*
33:14 pass on ahead of his *s*, but
39:17 The Hebrew *s* whom you
39:19 this your *s* did to me, his
41:12 a *s* of the chief of the
43:28 Your *s* our father is getting
Ex 4:10 since your speaking to your *s*
14:31 Jehovah and in Moses his *s*
Nu 11:11 you caused evil to your *s*
12:7 Not so my *s* Moses! He is
12:8 fear to speak against my *s*
14:24 As for my *s* Caleb, because a
32:31 Jehovah has spoken to your *s*
De 3:24 make your *s* see your
34:5 Moses the *s* of Jehovah died
Jos 1:1 Moses the *s* of Jehovah that
1:2 Moses my *s* is dead; and now
1:7 that Moses my *s* commanded
1:13 that Moses the *s* of Jehovah
1:15 Moses the *s* of Jehovah has
5:14 is my lord saying to his *s*
8:31 Moses the *s* of Jehovah had
8:33 Moses the *s* of Jehovah had
9:24 commanded Moses his *s* to
11:12 Moses the *s* of Jehovah had
11:15 had commanded Moses his *s*
12:6 Moses the *s* of Jehovah and
12:6 Moses the *s* of Jehovah gave
13:8 as Moses the *s* of Jehovah
14:7 Moses the *s* of Jehovah sent
18:7 Moses the *s* of Jehovah has
22:2 Moses the *s* of Jehovah
22:4 Moses the *s* of Jehovah gave
22:5 *s* of Jehovah commanded you
24:29 Joshua . . . the *s* of Jehovah
Jg 2:8 Joshua . . . the *s* of Jehovah
15:18 into the hand of your *s*
19:19 the attendant with your *s*
1Sa 3:9 for your *s* is listening
3:10 for your *s* is listening
17:32 Your *s* himself will go and
17:34 Your *s* became a shepherd of
17:36 the bear your *s* struck down
17:58 The son of your *s* Jesse the
19:4 king sin against his *s* David
20:7 it means peace to your *s*
20:8 toward your *s* for it
20:8 have brought your *s* with you
22:8 raised up my own *s* against
22:15 anything against his *s* and
22:15 *s* did not know a thing
23:10 *s* has definitely heard that
23:11 just as your *s* has heard
23:11 tell your *s*, please
25:39 his *s* back from badness
26:18 chasing after his *s*, for
26:19 words of his *s*: If it is
27:5 *s* dwell in the royal city
27:12 my *s* to time indefinite
28:2 know what your *s* is to do
29:3 David the *s* of Saul king of
29:8 found in your *s* from the day
2Sa 3:18 By the hand of David my *s*
7:5 say to my *s* David, This is
7:8 say to my *s* David, This is
7:19 house of your *s* down to a
7:20 yourself know your *s* well
7:21 cause your *s* to know them
7:25 spoken concerning your *s* and
7:26 house of your *s* David become
7:27 *s* has taken heart to pray
7:28 promise to your *s* this
7:29 bless the house of your *s*
7:29 house of your *s* be blessed
9:2 house of Saul had a *s* whose
9:2 to which he said: I am your *s*
9:6 he said: Here is your *s*
9:8 What is your *s*, that you have
9:11 king commands for his *s* is
9:11 way that your *s* will do
11:21 *s* Uriah the Hittite died
11:24 *s* Uriah the Hittite also
13:24 your *s* has sheepshearers
13:24 his servants, with your *s*
13:35 word of your *s* so it has
14:19 *s* Joab that commanded me
14:20 *s* Joab has done this thing
14:22 *s* does know that I have
14:22 acted on the word of his *s*
15:2 From . . . Israel your *s* is
15:8 your *s* made a solemn vow
15:21 where your *s* will come to
15:34 I am your *s*, O King
15:34 the *s* of your father, even I
15:34 but now even I am your *s*
18:29, 29 the king's *s* and your *s*
19:19 wrong that your *s* did on
19:20 your *s* well knows that I
19:26 my *s* that tricked me
19:26 For your *s* had said, Let
19:26 for your *s* is lame
19:27 slandered your *s* to my lord
19:28 your *s* among those eating
19:35 your *s* taste what I ate
19:35 your *s* become a burden
19:36 your *s* could bring the king
19:37 Let your *s* return, please
19:37 here is your *s* Chimham
24:21 the king come to his *s*

1Ki 1:19 Solomon your *s* he has not
1:26 your *s*, me and Zadok the
1:26 your *s* he has not invited
1:27 not caused your *s* to know
1:51 his *s* to death by the sword
2:38 the way that your *s* will do
3:6 toward your *s* David my father
3:7 *s* king in the place of David
3:8 your *s* is in the middle of
3:9 give to your *s* an obedient
8:24 kept toward your *s* David
8:25 keep toward your *s* David my
8:26 promised to your *s* David my
8:28 the prayer of your *s* and to
8:28 your *s* is praying before you
8:29 *s* prays toward this place
8:30 on the part of your *s* and of
8:52 request for favor of your *s*
8:53 by means of Moses your *s*
8:56 by means of Moses his *s*
8:59 execute judgment for his *s*
8:66 performed for David his *s*
11:11 certainly give it to your *s*
11:13 for the sake of David my *s*
11:26 a *s* of Solomon, and his
11:32 for the sake of my *s* David
11:34 for the sake of David my *s*
11:36 in order that David my *s*
11:38 just as David my *s* did
12:7 a *s* . . . and actually serve
14:8 not become like my *s* David
14:18 by means of his *s* Ahijah
15:29 by means of his *s* Ahijah
16:9 his *s* Zimri the chief of
18:9 your *s* into the hand of Ahab
18:12 your *s* himself has feared
18:36 you are God . . . I am your *s*
20:9 you sent to your *s* at first
20:32 Your *s* Ben-hadad has said
20:39 Your *s* himself went out
20:40 as your *s* was active here
2Ki 4:1 Your *s*, my husband, is dead
4:1 own *s* had continually feared
5:6 I do send to you Naaman my *s*
5:15 a blessing gift from your *s*
5:17 given to your *s* some ground
5:17 your *s* will no more render
5:18 may Jehovah forgive your *s*
5:18 forgive your *s* in this
5:25 Your *s* did not go anywhere
8:13 your *s*, who is a mere dog
8:19 for the sake of David his *s*
9:36 his *s* Elijah the Tishbite
10:10 by means of his *s* Elijah
14:25 means of his *s* Jonah the
16:7 I am your *s* and your son
17:3 Hoshea came to be his *s* and
18:12 Moses the *s* of Jehovah had
19:34 for the sake of David my *s*
20:6 for the sake of David my *s*
21:8 the law that my *s* Moses
22:12 Asaiah the king's *s*, saying
24:1 so Jehoiakim became his *s*
25:8 the *s* of the king of Babylon
1Ch 2:34 Sheshan had an Egyptian *s*
2:35 his daughter to Jarha his *s*
6:49 Moses the *s* of the true God
16:13 O offspring of Israel his *s*
17:4 you must say to David my *s*
17:7 you will say to my *s* David
17:17 house of your *s* down to a
17:18 as to honoring your *s*, when
17:18 yourself know your *s* well
17:19 for the sake of your *s* and
17:23 spoken concerning your *s* and
17:24 the house of David your *s*
17:25 have revealed to your *s* the
17:25 your *s* has found occasion to
17:26 goodness concerning your *s*
17:27 bless the house of your *s*
2Ch 1:3 Moses the *s* of Jehovah had
6:15 *s* David my father what you
6:16 keep toward your *s* David
6:17 promised to your *s* David
6:19 toward the prayer of your *s*
6:19 *s* is praying before you
6:20 *s* prays toward this place
6:21 the entreaties of your *s* and
6:42 to David your *s*
13:6 *s* of Solomon the son of
24:6 Moses the *s* of Jehovah, even
24:9 Moses the *s* of the true God
32:16 and against Hezekiah his *s*
34:20 Asaiah the king's *s*, saying

Ne 1:6 listen to the prayer of your *s*
1:7 in command to Moses your *s*
1:8 you commanded Moses your *s*
1:11 to the prayer of your *s* and
1:11 do grant success to your *s*
2:5 if your *s* seems good before
2:10 Tobiah the *s*, the Ammonite
2:19 Tobiah the *s*, the Ammonite
9:14 by means of Moses your *s*
10:29 Moses the *s* of the true God
Job 1:8 set your heart upon my *s* Job
2:3 set your heart upon my *s* Job
19:16 To my *s* I have called, but
42:7 truthful as has my *s* Job
42:8 rams and go to my *s* Job
42:8 Job my *s* will himself pray
42:8 truthful, as has my *s* Job
Ps 18:*super* Of Jehovah's *s*, of David
19:11 your own *s* has been warned
19:13 hold your *s* back; Do not let
27:9 in anger turn your *s* away
31:16 face to shine upon your *s*
35:27 in the peace of his *s*
36:*super* Of Jehovah's *s*, David
69:17 your face from your *s*
78:70 so he chose David his *s*
86:2 Save your *s*—you are my God
86:4 the soul of your *s* rejoice
86:16 your strength to your *s*
89:3 I have sworn to David my *s*
89:20 I have found David my *s*
89:39 the covenant of your *s*
105:6 you seed of Abraham his *s*
105:26 He sent Moses his *s*
105:42 word with Abraham his *s*
109:28 let your own *s* rejoice
116:16 Jehovah, For I am your *s*
116:16 *s*, the son of your slave
119:17 appropriately toward your *s*
119:23 your *s*, he concerns himself
119:38 Carry out to your *s* your
119:49 the word to your *s*
119:65 dealt well . . . with your *s*
119:76 your saying to your *s*
119:84 many are the days of your *s*
119:122 Act as a surety for your *s*
119:124 Do with your *s* according
119:125 I am your *s*. Make me
119:135 own face shine upon your *s*
119:140 And your own *s* loves it
119:176 O look for your *s*
132:10 On account of David your *s*
136:22 inheritance to Israel his *s*
143:2 into judgment with your *s*
143:12 For I am your *s*
144:10 setting David his *s* free
Pr 11:29 foolish person will be a *s*
12:9 esteemed but having a *s*
14:35 *s* who is acting with insight
17:2 A *s* that is showing insight
19:10 less for a *s* to rule over
22:7 the borrower is *s* to the man
29:19 A *s* will not let himself be
29:21 pampering one's *s* from youth
30:10 slander a *s* to his master
Ec 7:21 *s* calling down evil upon you
Isa 20:3 my *s* Isaiah has walked about
22:20 my *s*, namely, Eliakim the
24:2 for the *s* as for his master
37:35 for the sake of David my *s*
41:8 you, O Israel, are my *s*
41:9 You are my *s*; I have chosen
42:1 My *s*, on whom I keep fast
42:19 Who is blind, if not my *s*
42:19 or blind as the *s* of Jehovah
43:10 my *s* whom I have chosen
44:1 now listen, O Jacob my *s*
44:2 not be afraid, O my *s* Jacob
44:21 my *s*. I have formed you
44:21 You are a *s* belonging to me
44:26 the word of his *s* come true
45:4 for the sake of my *s* Jacob
48:20 has repurchased his *s* Jacob
49:3 You are my *s*, O Israel, you
49:5 as a *s* belonging to him
49:6 for you to become my *s* to
49:7 to the *s* of rulers: Kings
50:10 to the voice of his *s*
52:13 My *s* will act with insight
53:11 the righteous one, my *s*
63:11 long ago, Moses his *s*
Jer 2:14 Is Israel a *s*, or a slave
25:9 the king of Babylon, my *s*
27:6 the king of Babylon, my *s*

Jer 27:7 must exploit him as a *s*
30:8 strangers exploit him as a *s*
30:10 do not be afraid, O my *s*
33:21 broken with David my *s* so
33:22 the seed of David my *s* and
33:26 and of David my *s*, so that
43:10 king of Babylon, my *s*, and
46:27 do not be afraid, O my *s*
46:28 do not be afraid, O my *s*
Eze 28:25 I gave to my *s*, to Jacob
34:23 feed them, even my *s* David
34:24 my *s* David a chieftain
37:24 my *s* David will be king
37:25 gave to my *s*, to Jacob
37:25 David my *s* will be their
Da 6:20 Daniel, *s* of the living God
9:11 Moses the *s* of the true God
9:17 to the prayer of your *s* and
10:17 *s* of this my lord able to
Hag 2:23 son of Shealtiel, my *s*, is
Zec 3:8 I am bringing in my *s* Sprout
Mal 1:6 and a *s*, his grand master
4:4 the law of Moses my *s* with
Mt 12:18 *s* whom I chose, my beloved
26:69 and a *s* girl came up to him
Mr 14:66 *s* girls of the high priest
14:69 the *s* girl, at the sight of
Lu 1:54 to the aid of Israel his *s*
1:69 in the house of David his *s*
7:7 and let my *s* be healed
16:13 No house *s* can be a slave to
22:56 *s* girl saw him sitting by
Joh 18:17 *s* girl, the doorkeeper, then
Ac 3:13 has glorified his *S*, Jesus
3:26 God, after raising up his *S*
4:25 our forefather David, your *s*
4:27 against your holy *s* Jesus
4:30 name of your holy *s* Jesus
12:13 *s* girl named Rhoda came to
16:16 certain *s* girl with a spirit
Ro 14:4 judge the house *s* of another
15:16 a public *s* of Christ Jesus
Ga 4:22 sons, one by the *s* girl and
4:23 the one by the *s* girl was
4:30 Drive out the *s* girl and her
4:30 son of the *s* girl be an heir
4:31 children, not of a *s* girl
Php 2:25 but your envoy and private *s*
Heb 8:2 a public *s* of the holy place

Servant's

2Sa 7:27 revelation to your *s* ear
24:10 let your *s* error pass by
1Ch 21:8 cause your *s* error to pass

Servants

Ge 20:8 to call all his *s* and to speak
21:25 *s* of Abimelech had seized by
26:14 cattle and a large body of *s*
26:15 the wells that the *s* of his
26:19 *s* of Isaac went on digging
26:25 *s* of Isaac went excavating
26:32 *s* of Isaac proceeded to come
27:37 I have given to him as *s*
32:16 to his *s* one drove after
32:16 said to his *s*: Cross over
40:20 make a feast for all his *s*
40:20 in the midst of his *s*
41:10 indignant at his *s*. So he
41:37 Pharaoh and of all his *s*
41:38 So Pharaoh said to his *s*
42:10 your *s* have come to buy
42:11 Your *s* do not act as spies
42:13 Your *s* are twelve brothers
44:7 unthinkable that your *s* should
45:16 eyes of Pharaoh and of his *s*
46:34 Your *s* have continued to be
47:3 Your *s* are herders of sheep
47:4 the flock that your *s* have
47:4 let your *s* dwell, please, in
50:2 that Joseph commanded his *s*
50:7 with him all of Pharaoh's *s*
50:17 the revolt of the *s* of your
Ex 5:15 deal this way with your *s*
5:16 no straw given to your *s* and
5:16 and here your *s* are beaten
5:21 Pharaoh and before his *s*
7:10 before Pharaoh and his *s*
7:20 eyes of Pharaoh and his *s*
8:3 into the house of your *s* and
8:4 on all your *s* the frogs
8:9 entreaty for you and your *s*
8:11 and your *s* and your people
8:21 upon you and your *s* and your
8:24 and the houses of his *s* and

Ex 8:29 Pharaoh, his s and his people
8:31 away from Pharaoh, his s and
9:14 upon your s and your people
9:20 Pharaoh's s caused his own
9:20 s and his livestock to flee
9:21 left his s and his livestock
9:30 As for you and your s, I know
9:34 Pharaoh . . . as well as his s
10:1 and the hearts of his s
10:6 houses of all your s and the
10:7 Pharaoh's s said to him: How
11:3 in the eyes of Pharaoh's s and
11:8 s of yours will certainly
12:30 his s and all other Egyptians
14:5 Pharaoh as well as his s
32:13 Isaac and Israel your s, to
38:8 the mirrors of the women s
Nu 22:18 and said to the s of Balak
31:49 s have taken the sum of the
32:4 and your s have livestock
32:5 land be given to your s as a
32:25 Your s will do just as my
32:27 but your s will pass over
De 9:27 Remember your s Abraham
29:2 all his s and all his land
32:36 will feel regret over his s
32:43 avenge the blood of his s
34:11 all his s and all his land
Jos 9:8 said to Joshua: We are your s
9:9 distant land that your s have
9:11 We are your s. And now
9:24 your s were plainly told
Jg 3:24 his s came and began looking
6:27 Gideon took ten men of his s
1Sa 8:14 and actually give to his s
8:15 his court officials and his s
8:17 will become his as s
12:19 Pray in behalf of your s to
16:15 s of Saul began to say to
16:16 command your s before you
16:17 Saul said to his s: Provide
17:8 and you s belonging to Saul
17:9 must then become s to you
17:9 you must also become s to us
18:5 in the eyes of the s of Saul
18:22 Saul commanded his s
18:22 all his s themselves have
18:23 the s of Saul began to speak
18:24 s of Saul reported to him
18:26 s reported these words to
18:30 most prudently of all the s
19:1 to all his s of putting David
21:7 Saul's s was there on that
21:11 s of Achish began to say to
21:14 Achish said to his s
22:6 his s stationed about him
22:7 Saul said to his s stationed
22:9 as he was over the s of Saul
22:14 all your s is like David
22:17 s of the king did not want
25:8 to your s and to your son
25:10 Nabal answered David's s
25:10 s that are breaking away
25:40 David's s came to Abigail
25:41 wash the feet of the s of
28:7 Saul said to his s: Seek
28:7 s said to him: Look! There
28:23 s and also the woman kept
28:25 them to Saul and his s
29:10 s of your lord that came
2Sa 2:12 s of Ish-bosheth, Saul's son
2:13 and the s of David, they
2:15 twelve from the s of David
2:17 before the s of David
2:30 missing from the s of David
2:31 s of David, for their part
3:22 David's s and Joab were
3:38 king went on to say to his s
6:20 slave girls of his s, just
8:2 David's s to carry tribute
8:6 Syrians came to be David's s
8:7 on the s of Hadadezer
8:14 Edomites came to be s of
9:10 you and your sons and your s
9:10 fifteen sons and twenty s
9:12 were s to Mephibosheth
10:2 s to comfort him over his
10:2 s of David proceeded to come
10:3 David has sent his s to you
10:4 Hanun took the s of David
10:19 s of Hadadezer, saw that
11:1 send Joab and his s with
11:9 other s of his lord, and he
11:11 s of my lord are camping

2Sa 11:13 with the s of his lord, and
11:17 s of David, fell and Uriah
11:24 shooting at your s from on
11:24 s of the king died
12:18 s of David were afraid to
12:19 s were whispering together
12:19 David said to his s: Has
12:21 s said to him: What does
13:24 go, please, and also his s
13:31 s were standing by with
13:36 king and all his s wept
14:30 Finally he said to his s
14:30 s of Absalom set the tract
14:31 Why did your s set the
15:14 David said to all his s
15:15 king's s said to the king
15:15 here are your s
15:18 s were crossing at his side
16:6 at David and at all the s
16:11 say to Abishai and all his s
17:20 The s of Absalom now came
18:7 before the s of David, and
18:9 before the s of David
19:5 shame the face of all your s
19:6 chiefs and s are nothing to
19:7 to the heart of your s
19:14 you and all your s
19:17 twenty s of his were with
20:6 take the s of your lord and
21:15 David and his s with him
21:22 and by the hand of his s
24:20 saw the king and his s
1Ki 1:2 his s said to him: Let them
1:9 men of Judah the king's s
1:33 Take with you the s of your
1:47 the s of the king have come
3:15 spread a feast for all his s
5:1 to send his s to Solomon
5:6 my s themselves will prove to
5:6 prove to be with your s
5:6 wages of your s I shall give
5:9 My s themselves will bring
8:23 your s who are walking
8:32 judge your s by pronouncing
8:36 forgive the sin of your s
9:22 the warriors and his s and
9:27 his own s, seamen, having a
9:27 along with the s of Solomon
10:5 and the sitting of his s
10:8 happy are these s of yours
10:13 she together with her s
11:17 men of the s of his father
12:7 to become your s always
15:18 in the hand of his s
20:6 I shall send my s to you
20:6 and the houses of your s
20:12 said to his s: Get set!
20:23 the s of the king of Syria
20:31 So his s said to him: Here
22:3 said to his s: Do you really
22:49, 49 my s go with your s in
2Ki 1:13 the soul of these fifty s
2:16 with your s fifty men
3:11 one of the s of the king of
5:13 s now approached and spoke
6:3 please, and go with your s
6:8 he took counsel with his s
6:11 he called his s and said to
6:12 Then one of his s said
7:12 said to his s: Let me tell
7:13 one of his s answered and
9:7 avenge the blood of my s the
9:7 blood of all the s of Jehovah
9:11 to the s of his lord
9:28 s carried him in a chariot
10:5 are your s, and everything
12:20 his s rose up and leagued
12:21 his s, were the ones that
14:5 strike down his s that had
17:13 means of my s the prophets
17:23 all his s the prophets
18:24 the smallest s of my lord
18:26 Speak with your s, please
19:5 the s of King Hezekiah came
21:10 his s the prophets, saying
21:23 s of Amon conspired against
22:9 Your s have poured out the
23:30 his s conveyed him dead in
24:2 spoken by means of his s the
24:10 the s of Nebuchadnezzar the
24:11 s were laying siege against
24:12 with his mother and his s
25:24 being s to the Chaldeans
1Ch 18:2 David's s bearing tribute

1Ch 18:6 Syrians came to be David's s
18:7 to be on the s of Hadadezer
18:13 came to be David's s
19:2 s of David proceeded to come
19:3 his s have come in to you
19:4 Hanun took the s of David and
19:19 s of Hadadezer saw that
20:8 and by the hand of his s
21:3 belong to my lord as s
2Ch 2:8 your s are experienced at
2:8 my s are together with your
2:8 are together with your s
2:10 wheat as food for your s
2:15 let him send to his s
6:14 s who are walking before you
6:23 judge your s so as to pay
6:27 forgive the sin of your s
8:18 to him by means of his s
8:18 s having a knowledge of the
8:18 with Solomon's s to Ophir
9:4 the sitting of his s and the
9:7 happy are these s of yours
9:10 s of Hiram and the
9:10 s of Solomon who brought
9:12 she together with her s
9:21 Tarshish with the s of Hiram
10:7 become your s always
12:8 s of his, that they may know
24:25 own s conspired against him
25:3 s who had struck down the
32:9 sent his s to Jerusalem
32:16 s spoke yet further against
33:24 s conspired against him and
34:16 in the hand of your s they
35:23 the king said to his s
35:24 s took him down from the
36:20 they came to be s to him
Ezr 2:55 The sons of the s of Solomon
2:58 the sons of the s of Solomon
4:11 your s, the men beyond the
5:11 We are the s of the God of
9:9 For we are s; and in our
9:11 your s the prophets, saying
Ne 1:6 the sons of Israel your s
1:10 are your s and your people
1:11 to the prayer of your s who
2:20 his s, shall get up, and we
7:57 the sons of the s of Solomon
7:60 the sons of the s of Solomon
9:10 Pharaoh and all his s and all
11:3 the sons of the s of Solomon
Es 1:3 for all his princes and his s
2:18 for all his princes and his s
3:2 the king's s that were in the
3:3 the king's s who were in the
4:11 the king's s and the people
5:11 over the princes and the s of
Job 1:3 with a very large body of s
4:18 In his s he has no faith, And
Ps 34:22 redeeming the soul of his s
69:36 And the offspring of his s
79:2 s as food to the fowls of the
79:10 blood of your s . . . shed
89:50 the reproach upon your s
90:13 And feel regret over your s
90:16 appear to your own s
102:14 s have found pleasure in
102:28 s will continue residing
105:25 cunningly against his s
113:1 praise, O you s of Jehovah
119:91 For they are all your s
123:2 eyes of s are toward the
134:1 All you s of Jehovah
135:1 praise, O s of Jehovah
135:9 Pharaoh and upon all his s
135:14 feel regret even over his s
Ec 10:7 seen s on horses but princes
10:7 on the earth just like s
Isa 36:9 the smallest s of my lord
36:11 Speak, please, to your s in
37:5 s of King Hezekiah came in
37:24 By means of your s you have
54:17 the s of Jehovah, and their
56:6 in order to become s to him
63:17 for the sake of your s
65:8 for the sake of my s
65:9 my own s will reside there
65:13 My own s will eat, but you
65:13 My own s will drink, but
65:13 own s will rejoice, but you
65:14 own s will cry out joyfully
65:15 s he will call by another
66:14 be made known to his s
Jer 7:25 sending to you all my s

Jer 21:7 his s and the people and
22:2 with your s and your people
22:4 with his s and his people
25:4 Jehovah sent to you all his s
25:14 have exploited them as s
25:19 the king of Egypt and his s
26:5 words of my s the prophets
29:19 with my s the prophets
34:9 order not to use them as s
34:10 use them no more as s
34:13 out of the house of s
35:15 all my s the prophets
36:24 the king and all his s
36:31 against his s their error
37:2 s and the people of the land
37:18 you and against your s and
44:4 sending to you all my s the
46:26 into the hand of his s
La 5:8 Mere s have ruled over us
Eze 38:17 hand of my s the prophets
46:17 inheritance to one of his s
Da 1:12 put your s to the test for
1:13 what you see do with your s
2:4 what the dream is to your s
2:7 say what the dream is to his s
3:26 s of the Most High God, step
3:28 s that trusted in him and
9:6 listened to your s the prophets
9:10 hand of his s the prophets
Am 3:7 matter to his s the prophets
Zec 1:6 commanded my s, the prophets
Mt 14:2 said to his s: This is John
22:13 king said to his s, Bind him
Lu 15:26 called one of the s to him
Ac 10:7 called two of his house s and
Ro 13:6 God's public s constantly
Php 1:1 overseers and ministerial s
1Ti 3:8 Ministerial s should likewise
3:12 ministerial s be husbands of
Heb 1:7 his public s a flame of fire
1Pe 2:18 house s be in subjection to

Serve
Ge 1:14 they must s as signs and for
1:15 they must s as luminaries in
1:29 To you let it s as food
6:21 it must s as food for you
9:3 may s as food for you
9:13 s as a sign of the covenant
15:13 they will have to s them
15:14 nation that they will s I
17:11 it must s as a sign of the
17:13 must s as a covenant to
21:30 it may s as a witness for
25:23 the older will s the younger
27:29 Let peoples s you and let
27:40 your brother you will s
29:15 must you s me for nothing?
29:18 s you seven years for Rachel
29:20 s seven years for Rachel
29:27 s with me for seven years
31:44 s as a witness between me
41:36 the foodstuffs must s as a
Ex 3:12 people will s the true God
4:16 he will s as a mouth to you
4:16 and you will s as God to him
4:23 my son away that he may s me
5:18 s! Though no straw will be
7:16 may s me in the wilderness
8:1 away that they may s me
8:20 away that they may s me
9:1 people away that they may s
9:13 people away that they may s
10:3 people away that they may s
10:7 they may s Jehovah their God
10:8 Go, s Jehovah your God
10:11 s Jehovah, because that is
10:24 Go, s Jehovah. Only your
12:13 blood must s as your sign
12:14 day must s as a memorial
12:31 s Jehovah, just as you have
13:9 it must s for you as a sign
13:16 s as a sign upon your hand
14:12 that we may s the Egyptians
14:12 for us to s the Egyptians
18:13 to s as judge for the people
18:19 s as representative for the
20:5 nor be induced to s them
23:24 or be induced to s them, and
23:25 s Jehovah your God, and he
23:33 case you should s their gods
26:13 s as an overhanging on the
26:24 will s as two corner posts
29:29 that are Aaron's will s for
Ex 30:4 they must s as supports for
30:16 indeed s as a memorial
30:21 must s as a regulation to
40:15 anointing must s continually
Le 10:15 it must s as an allowance
14:22 must s as a sin offering and
16:29 s as a statute to time
16:34 s as a statute to time
17:7 will s as a statute to time
22:20 not s to gain approval for
23:18 s as a burnt offering to
23:20 s as something holy to
24:7 must s as the bread for a
25:6 s you people for food, for you
25:7 produce should s for eating
25:40 s with you till the Jubilee
Nu 4:26 Thus they must s
7:5 s for carrying on the service
8:11 s for carrying on the service
8:15 Levites will come in to s at
8:25 company and s no longer
10:8 s as a statute for you men
10:10 use must s as a memorial
10:31 you must s as eyes for us
15:39 s as a fringed edge for you
16:38 they should s as a sign to
19:9 s the assembly of . . . Israel
19:10 s the sons of Israel and the
19:21 must s as a statute to time
25:13 must s as the covenant of a
27:11 it must s as a statute by
31:3 they may s against Midian
35:3 the cities must s for them to
35:3 pasture grounds will s for
35:5 s them as pasture grounds of
35:11 cities of refuge they will s
35:12 must s you as a refuge from
35:14 cities of refuge they will s
35:15 cities will s as a refuge
35:29 s as a statute of judgment
De 4:19 bow down to them and s them
4:28 you will have to s gods, the
5:9 s them, because I Jehovah your
6:8 must s as a frontlet band
6:13 and him you should s, and by
7:4 will certainly s other gods
7:16 and you must not s their gods
8:19 s them and bow down to them
10:12 s Jehovah your God with all
10:20 Him you should s, and to him
11:13 s him with all your heart
11:18 must s as a frontlet band
12:30 nations used to s their gods
13:2 and let us s them
13:4 and him you should s, and to
13:6 Let us go and s other gods
13:13 Let us go and s other gods
20:11 and they must s you
28:14 after other gods to s them
28:36 will have to s other gods
28:47 that you did not s Jehovah
28:48 s your enemies whom Jehovah
28:64 have to s other gods whom
29:18 s the gods of those nations
29:26 to go and s other gods and
30:17 to other gods and s them
31:19 s as my witness against the
31:20 s them and treat me with
31:26 s as a witness there against
Jos 4:6 may s as a sign in your midst
4:7 stones must s as a memorial
20:3 s you as a refuge from the
23:7 neither must you s them nor
24:2 they used to s other gods
24:14 s him in faultlessness and
24:14 in Egypt, and s Jehovah
24:15 if it is bad . . . to s
24:15 choose . . . whom you will s
24:15 we shall s Jehovah
24:16 leave Jehovah so as to s
24:18 we shall s Jehovah
24:19 You are not able to s
24:20 and you do s foreign gods
24:21 No, but Jehovah we shall s
24:22 have chosen Jehovah . . . to s
24:24 Jehovah our God we shall s
24:27 stone is what will s as a
24:27 and it must s as a witness
24:31 And Israel continued to s
Jg 2:3 their gods will s as a lure
2:7 And the people continued to s
2:19 after other gods to s them
3:8 sons of Israel continued to s
3:14 Israel continued to s Eglon
Jg 9:28 we should s him? Is he not
9:28 S the men of Hamor
9:28 should we ourselves s him
9:38 that we should s him? Is not
10:6 they began to s the Baals and
10:6 left Jehovah and did not s
10:10 and we s the Baals
10:16 and to s Jehovah, so that his
11:6 come and s as our commander
17:5 he might s as priest for him
17:10 s as a father and priest for
17:12 man might s as a priest for
18:4 I might s as priest for him
1Sa 4:9 not s the Hebrews just as
7:3 to Jehovah and s him alone
11:1 with us that we may s you
12:10 that we might s the Baals
12:10 that we may s you
12:14 s him and obey his voice
12:20 s Jehovah with all your
12:24 s him in truth with all
17:9 and you must s us
18:21 she may s as a snare to him
26:19 saying, Go, s other gods!
2Sa 9:10 s as food for those belonging
10:11 s as a salvation for me
10:19 and began to s them
12:31 made them s at brickmaking
14:17 s, please, to give rest
16:19 Whom shall I myself s?
22:44 A people . . . they will s me
1Ki 9:6 s other gods and bow down to
9:9 bow down to them and s them
12:4 and we shall s you
12:7 a servant . . . and actually s
16:31 s Baal and to bow down to
21:2 s as a garden of vegetables
2Ki 17:12 continued to s dungy idols
17:16 the heavens and to s Baal
17:35 nor s them nor sacrifice to
18:7 Assyria and did not s him
19:25 s to make fortified cities
21:3 of the heavens and to s them
25:24 and s the king of Babylon
1Ch 19:12 s as a salvation for me
19:19 with David and began to s
28:9 s him with a complete heart
2Ch 7:19 s other gods and bow down
7:22 bow down to them and s them
10:4 lighter, and we shall s you
30:8 s Jehovah your God, that his
33:3 army of the heavens and s
33:16 say to Judah to s Jehovah
34:33 to s Jehovah their God
35:3 Now s Jehovah your God and
Ne 9:35 they did not s you and did not
Job 21:15 that we should s him
36:11 If they obey and s, They
39:9 a wild bull want to s you
Ps 2:11 S Jehovah with fear And be
18:43 not known—they will s me
22:30 A seed itself will s him
72:11 for their part, will s him
100:2 S Jehovah with rejoicing
102:22 the kingdoms to s Jehovah
119:76 s, please, to comfort me
119:173 your hand s to help me
Isa 30:8 may s for a future day, for
37:26 s to make fortified cities
43:23 to s me with a gift, nor
43:24 you have compelled me to s
59:6 will not s as a garment, nor
60:12 will not s you will perish
Jer 2:20 said: I am not going to s
5:19 s strangers in a land that
6:20 s for no pleasure, and your
11:10 gods in order to s them
13:10 to s them and to bow down
16:4 s as food for the flying
16:13 s other gods day and night
17:4 make you s your enemies
22:9 to other gods and to s them
25:6 gods in order to s them
25:11 to s the king of Babylon
27:6 I have given him to s him
27:7 the nations must s even him
27:8 the kingdom that will not s
27:9 you men will not s the king
27:11 Babylon and actually s him
27:12 s him and his people and
27:13 not s the king of Babylon
27:14 not s the king of Babylon
27:17 S the king of Babylon and
28:14 to s Nebuchadnezzar the king

Jer 28:14 they must *s* him. And even
30:9 *s* Jehovah their God and
35:15 other gods to *s* them
40:9 *s* the king of Babylon, and
Eze 20:20 and they must *s* as a sign
20:39 *s* each one of you his own
20:40 will *s* me, in the land
27:7 for it to *s* as your sail
Da 3:28 would not *s* and . . . worship
7:14 languages should all *s* even
7:27 rulerships will *s* and obey
Mic 1:2 *s* against you as a witness
Zep 3:9 to *s* him shoulder to shoulder
Mal 3:14 It is of no value to *s* God
Mr 8:6 to his disciples to *s*, and
8:7 he told them also to *s* these
Eph 1:12 *s* for the praise of his glory
1Ti 3:10 then let them *s* as ministers

Served
Ge 11:3 brick *s* as stone for them
11:3 bitumen *s* as mortar for them
14:4 Twelve years they had *s*
29:25 for Rachel that I *s* with
30:26 for whom I have *s* with you
30:29 must know how I have *s* you
31:6 with all my power I have *s*
31:41 I have *s* you fourteen years
Ex 21:29 warning was *s* on its owner
Nu 31:16 *s* to induce the sons of
De 12:2 *s* their gods, on the tall
15:12 he has *s* you six years, then
15:18 he *s* you six years, and
Jos 18:20 the Jordan *s* as its boundary
23:16 you have . . . *s* other gods
24:14 that your forefathers *s* on
24:15 that your forefathers . . . *s*
Jg 6:19 under the big tree and *s* it
8:27 it *s* as a snare to Gideon and
1Sa 4:9 just as they have *s* you
17:40 that *s* him as a receptacle
28:25 she *s* them to Saul and his
2Sa 16:19 as I *s* before your father
2Ki 21:21 idols that his father had *s*
Ps 73:6 haughtiness has *s* as a
Ec 5:9 the king himself has been *s*
Jer 8:2 and that they have *s* and that
34:14 who has *s* you six years
Hab 3:11 your spear *s* for brightness
Mal 3:18 and one who has not *s* him
Mr 8:6 and they *s* them to the crowd
Ac 13:36 *s* the express will of God

Serves
Ex 15:2 since he *s* for my salvation
Jer 22:13 fellowman who *s* for nothing
1Co 9:7 ever *s* as a soldier at his own

Service
Ge 29:27 for the *s* that you can serve
30:26 you yourself must know my *s*
Ex 5:9 Let the *s* be heavy upon the
12:25 then you must keep this *s*
12:26 What does this *s* mean to
13:5 render this *s* in this month
20:9 render *s* and you must do all
27:19 the tabernacle in all its *s*
30:16 the *s* of the tent of meeting
35:21 tent of meeting . . . its *s*
35:24 work of the *s* brought it
36:1 all the work of the holy *s*
36:3 work of the holy *s* so as to
36:5 more than what the *s* needs for
38:8 organized *s* at the entrance
38:21 the *s* of the Levites under
39:40 for the *s* of the tabernacle
39:42 sons of Israel did all the *s*
Le 25:39 as a worker in slavish *s*
Nu 1:53 *s* due to the tabernacle of
3:7 the *s* of the tabernacle
3:8 the *s* of the tabernacle
3:26 its tent cords, for all its *s*
3:31 and the screen, and all its *s*
3:36 its utensils and all its *s*
4:3 *s* group to do the work in the
4:4 *s* of the sons of Kohath in the
4:19 assign them each one to his *s*
4:23 enter into the *s* group to
4:23 render *s* in the tent of
4:24 *s* of the families of the
4:26 all their *s* utensils, and all
4:27 all the *s* of the sons of the
4:27 their loads and all their *s*
4:28 *s* of the families of the sons
4:28 obligatory *s* is under the hand
Nu 4:30 enter into the *s* group to
4:30 render the *s* of the tent of
4:31 *s* in the tent of meeting: the
4:32 equipment and all their *s*
4:33 *s* of the families of the sons
4:33 *s* in the tent of meeting
4:35 entered into the *s* group for
4:35 *s* in the tent of meeting
4:39 entered into the *s* group for
4:39 the *s* in the tent of meeting
4:43 entering into the *s* group for
4:43 *s* in the tent of meeting
4:47 render the laborious *s* and
4:47 *s* of carrying loads in the
4:49 according to his *s* and his
7:5 *s* of the tent of meeting, and
7:5 in proportion to his own *s*
7:7 in proportion to their *s*
7:8 in proportion to their *s*
7:9 *s* of the holy place was upon
8:11 carrying on the *s* of Jehovah
8:19 *s* of the sons of Israel in the
8:22 carry on their *s* in the tent
8:24 the *s* of the tent of meeting
8:25 retire from the *s* company and
8:26 he must render no *s*
10:2 *s* for convening the assembly
16:9 *s* of Jehovah's tabernacle and
18:4 all the *s* of the tent, and no
18:6 the *s* of the tent of meeting
18:7 and you men must render *s*
18:7 As a *s* of gift I shall give
18:21 in return for their *s* that
18:21 the *s* of the tent of meeting
18:23 the *s* of the tent of meeting
18:31 wages in return for your *s*
35:13 six cities . . . at your *s*
De 5:13 you are to render *s*, and you
15:19 do no *s* with the firstborn
23:12 at your *s* outside the camp
23:13 a peg should be at your *s*
Jos 22:27 render the *s* of Jehovah
22:33 for army *s* against them to
2Sa 15:8 also render *s* to Jehovah
18:3 be of *s* to us to give help
1Ki 10:5 the table *s* of his waiters
11:28 *s* of the house of Joseph
12:4 the hard *s* of your father and
1Ch 6:32 kept attending upon their *s*
6:48 all the *s* of the tabernacle
9:13 *s* of the house of the true
9:19 over the work of the *s*, the
9:23 of the tent, for guard *s*
9:27 for guard *s* was upon them
9:28 the utensils of the *s*, for
23:24 *s* of the house of Jehovah
23:26 its utensils for its *s*
23:28 *s* of the house of Jehovah
23:28 *s* of the house of the true
23:32 *s* of the house of Jehovah
24:3 for their office in their *s*
24:19 their offices for their *s*
25:1 the chiefs of the *s* groups
25:1 separated for the *s* some of
25:1 the official men for their *s*
25:6 *s* of the house of the true
26:8 with the power for the *s*
26:30 and for the king's *s*
27:3 the chiefs of the *s* groups
27:5 chief of the third *s* group
28:13 the *s* of Jehovah's house and
28:13 of the *s* of Jehovah's house
28:15 according to the *s* of the
28:20 the *s* of Jehovah's house
28:21 Levites for all the *s* of the
28:21 with skill for all the *s*
29:7 gave to the *s* of the house of
2Ch 2:18 for keeping the people in *s*
9:4 table *s* of his waiters and
9:4 drinking *s* and their attire
10:4 hard *s* of your father and
12:8 difference between my *s* and
12:8 *s* of the kingdoms of the
24:12 *s* of Jehovah's house, and
26:11 on military *s* in troops, by
29:35 *s* of the house of Jehovah
31:2 *s* for the priests and for
31:16 *s* by their obligations
31:21 *s* of the house of the true
34:33 take up *s*, to serve Jehovah
35:2 *s* of the house of Jehovah
35:10 the *s* was prepared and the
35:15 turn aside from their *s*
35:16 *s* of Jehovah was prepared
Ezr 6:18 for the *s* of God which is in
7:19 *s* of the house of your God
8:20 gave to the *s* of the Levites
Ne 3:5 into the *s* of their masters
5:18 *s* upon this people was heavy
10:32 *s* of the house of our God
Es 8:10 horses used in the royal *s*
8:14 horses used in the royal *s*
Job 14:14 the days of my compulsory *s*
Ps 104:14 for the *s* of mankind
104:23 And to his *s* until evening
Isa 19:23 render *s*, Egypt with
32:17 *s* of the true righteousness
40:2 her military *s* has been
Jer 44:3 rendering *s* to other gods
Eze 29:18 a great *s* against Tyre
29:18 *s* that he had performed
29:20 *s* that he did against her
44:14 as regards all its *s* and
Da 10:1 there was a great military *s*
Zec 14:12 do military *s* against
Mt 4:10 you must render sacred *s*
5:41 impresses you into *s* for a
27:32 impressed into *s* to lift up
Mr 3:9 boat continually at his *s* so
15:21 impressed into *s* a passerby
Lu 1:23 the days of his public *s* were
1:74 rendering sacred *s* to him
2:37 rendering sacred *s* night and
3:14 those in military *s* would ask
4:8 you must render sacred *s*
Joh 16:2 rendered a sacred *s* to God
Ac 7:7 sacred *s* to me in this place
7:42 sacred *s* to the army of
24:14 sacred *s* to the God of my
26:7 rendering him sacred *s* night
27:23 to whom I render sacred *s*
Ro 1:9 sacred *s* with my spirit in
1:25 sacred *s* to the creation
9:4 sacred *s* and the promises
12:1 sacred *s* with your power of
2Co 9:12 ministry of this public *s* is
Php 2:17 sacrifice and public *s* to
2:30 to render private *s* to me
3:3 rendering sacred *s* by God's
1Ti 6:2 the benefit of their good *s*
2Ti 1:3 rendering sacred *s* as my
Heb 1:14 all spirits for public *s*
8:5 men are rendering sacred *s*
8:6 a more excellent public *s*
9:1 ordinances of sacred *s* and its
9:9 man doing sacred *s* perfect as
9:14 sacred *s* to the living God
9:21 vessels of the public *s*
10:2 those rendering sacred *s*
10:11 to render public *s* and to
12:28 render God sacred *s* with
13:10 do sacred *s* at the tent
Re 7:15 sacred *s* day and night in his
22:3 will render him sacred *s*

Services
Ex 5:11 no reducing of your *s* one bit
1Ch 28:14 utensils for the different *s*
28:14 utensils for the different *s*
2Ch 8:14 the priests over their *s*
34:13 work for the different *s*
Jer 39:10 compulsory *s* on that day
1Co 12:28 helpful *s*, abilities to
2Ti 1:18 the *s* he rendered in Ephesus
Heb 9:6 to perform the sacred *s*

Serving
Ge 29:30 *s* with him for yet seven
Nu 4:24 Gershonites as to *s* and as to
4:37 *s* in the tent of meeting
4:41 all those *s* in the tent of
Jos 22:5 *s* him with all your heart
Jg 2:11 of Jehovah and *s* the Baals
2:13 and took up *s* Baal and the
3:4 they kept *s* as agents to test
3:6 and they took up *s* their gods
3:7 and went *s* the Baals and the
10:13 took up *s* other gods. That is
1Sa 2:22 *s* at the entrance of the tent
7:4 and began *s* Jehovah alone
8:8 leaving me and *s* other gods
1Ki 2:27 *s* as a priest of Jehovah
4:21 *s* Solomon all the days of
22:53 continued *s* Baal and bowing
2Ki 17:41 that they proved to be *s*
21:21 continued *s* the dungy idols
2Ch 24:18 *s* the sacred poles and the
33:22 and he continued *s* them
Ps 97:7 *s* any carved image be

Ps 106:36 And they kept s their idols
Ec 5:12 is the sleep of the one s
Jer 5:19 have gone s a foreign god
16:11 s them and bowing down to
40:9 afraid of s the Chaldeans
Eze 48:18 for the ones s the city
48:19 s the city out of all the
Da 3:12 they are not s your own gods
3:14 you are not s my own gods
3:17 God whom we are s is able to
3:18 are not the ones we are s
6:16 Your God whom you are s
6:20 God whom you are s with
Ho 4:6 reject you from s as a priest
12:12 Israel kept s for a wife
Zec 3:8 they are men s as portents
Mal 3:17 upon his son who is s him
3:18 one s God and one who has
Ro 13:6 constantly s this very purpose
2Ti 2:4 No man s as a soldier

Servitude
Ezr 9:8 a little reviving in our s
9:9 in our s our God has not left
Ne 9:17 return to their s in Egypt
La 1:3 because of the abundance of s
1Co 7:15 sister is not in s under such

Set*
Ge 4:15 Jehovah s up a sign for Cain
11:1 language . . . one s of words
15:12 sun was about to s, and a
28:11 because the sun had s
Ex 1:11 they s over them chiefs of
5:14 the officers . . . s over them
9:5 Jehovah s an appointed time
9:21 whoever did not s his heart
10:1 I may s these signs of mine
17:12 held steady until the sun s
18:21 s these over them as chiefs
De 16:18 s judges and officers for
17:14 Let me s a king over myself
17:15 s over yourself a king whom
17:15 s a king over yourself
24:15 the sun should not s upon
Jos 10:13 sun . . . did not hasten to s
Jg 19:14 the sun began to s upon them
19:30 S your hearts upon it, take
1Sa 9:20 do not s your heart on them
2Sa 13:20 Do not s your heart on this
1Ki 2:15 all Israel had s their face
14:4 eyes had s because of his age
1Ch 22:19 s your heart and your soul
Job 1:8 s your heart upon my servant
2:3 s your heart upon my servant
3:19 the slave is s free from his
7:17 should s your heart upon him
14:13 s a time limit for me and
23:7 s matters straight with him
Ps 48:13 S your hearts upon its
78:5 And a law he s in Israel
101:3 s in front of my eyes any
104:9 boundary you s, beyond which
105:21 s him as master to his
105:27 s among them the matters of
119:110 wicked have s a trap for
132:11 I shall s on your throne
132:17 s in order a lamp for my
140:5 Snares they have s for me
141:3 s a guard, O Jehovah, for my
141:3 s a watch over the door of
144:7 S me free and deliver me
144:11 S me free and deliver me
Pr 8:29 s for the sea his decree that
27:23 S your heart to your droves
Ec 1:5 sun has s, and it is coming
1:13 I s my heart to seek and
8:11 fully s in them to do bad
Isa 1:17 s right the oppressor
1:18 s matters straight between
2:4 s matters straight respecting
60:20 No more will your sun s
Jer 21:10 s my face against this city
42:15 s your faces to enter into
42:17 s their faces to enter into
44:12 s their faces to enter into
Eze 13:17 s your face against the
14:8 s my face against that man
15:7 have s my face against them
20:46 s your face in the direction
21:2 s your face toward Jerusalem
28:21 s your face toward Sidon
29:2 s your face against Pharaoh
35:2 s your face against the
38:2 s your face against Gog of
Eze 44:5 Son of man, s your heart
44:5 s your heart upon the
Da 9:3 s my face to Jehovah the true
9:10 laws that he s before us by
10:15 I had s my face to the earth
Mic 4:3 s matters straight respecting
Hag 1:5 S your heart upon your ways
1:7 S your heart upon your ways
Lu 9:51 s his face to go to Jerusalem
9:53 was s for going to Jerusalem
Joh 8:32 the truth will s you free
13:15 I s the pattern for you
Ac 13:2 s Barnabas and Saul apart
17:26 s limits of the dwelling of
17:31 he has s a day in which he
Ro 6:18 you were s free from sin
6:22 you were s free from sin but
8:2 s you free from the law of
8:5 s their minds on the things of
8:21 s free from enslavement to
Ga 5:1 such freedom Christ s us free
Eph 4:26 let the sun not s with you
Heb 9:10 time to s things straight
12:1 the race that is s before us
12:2 joy that was s before him
1Pe 1:13 s your hope upon the
2Pe 1:12 firmly s in the truth that
1Jo 3:3 has this hope s upon him
Jude 13 stars with no s course, for

Seth
Ge 4:25 a son and called his name S
4:26 And to S also there was born
5:3 and called his name S
5:4 of Adam after his fathering S
5:6 S lived on for a hundred and
5:7 S continued to live eight
5:8 So all the days of S amounted
1Ch 1:1 Adam, S, Enosh
Lu 3:38 son of Enosh, son of S

Sethur
Nu 13:13 S the son of Michael

Sets
Le 24:6 two s of layers, six to the
De 16:6 evening as soon as the sun s
24:13 to him as soon as the sun s
2Sa 3:35 if before the sun s I shall
Job 16:12 he s me up as a target for
34:14 he s his heart upon anyone
34:23 he s no appointed time for
41:21 soul itself s coals ablaze
Ps 104:19 knows well where it s
Isa 26:1 s salvation itself for
42:4 he s justice in the earth
62:7 s Jerusalem as a praise in
Jer 9:8 he s his ambush
La 3:12 s me up as the target for the
4:11 he s a fire ablaze in Zion
Eze 14:7 s the very stumbling block
Da 4:17 he s up over it even the
5:21 wants to, he s up over it
Joh 8:36 if the Son s you free, you
Ga 3:15 no one s aside or attaches
Jas 3:6 s the wheel of natural life

Setting
Ge 15:17 sun was now s and a dense
21:14 s it upon her shoulder, and
Ex 22:26 to him at the s of the sun
25:7 s stones for the ephod and for
35:9 s stones for the ephod and
35:27 s stones for the ephod and
40:18 and s up its pillars
Nu 1:51 tabernacle is s out, the
7:1 s up the tabernacle that he
9:15 day of s up the tabernacle the
De 23:11 at the s of the sun he may
Jos 1:4 toward the s of the sun your
10:27 time of the s of the sun
23:4 Great Sea at the s of the
2Sa 2:24 As the sun was s they
1Ki 22:36 about the s of the sun
2Ki 17:10 s up for themselves sacred
2Ch 18:34 time of the s of the sun
Ne 3:1 and went s up its doors
3:14 building it and s up its doors
Ps 22:15 dust of death you are s me
50:1 rising of the sun until its s
66:9 He is s our soul in life
113:3 rising of the sun until its s
144:10 s David his servant free
Isa 21:5 s of the table in order
30:2 s out to go down to Egypt
45:6 the sun and from its s
Isa 65:11 those s in order a table
Jer 6:21 Here I am s for this people
44:11 s my face against you for
Eze 20:47 s a fire ablaze against
40:43 ledges for s down things
Da 2:21 and s up kings, giving wisdom
6:14 till the s of the sun he kept
Am 7:8 s a plummet in the midst of
Zec 8:7 the land of the s of the sun
Mal 1:11 sun's rising even to its s
Lu 4:40 when the sun was s, all those
Ac 27:12 advised s sail from there
28:10 when we were s sail, they
2Ti 3:16 for s things straight, for
Heb 7:18 s aside of the preceding
2Pe 2:6 s a pattern for ungodly

Settings
Ex 28:11 Set in s of gold is how you
28:13 And you must make s of gold
28:14 the ropelike chains to the s
28:25 two ropes through the two s
39:6 stones set with s of gold
39:13 set with s of gold in their
39:16 they made two s of gold and
39:18 two ropes through the two s
Ps 45:13 clothing is with s of gold
Eze 28:13 your s and your sockets

Settle
Ge 2:15 take the man and s him in
Ex 10:14 locusts . . . s down upon all
Nu 11:26 spirit began to s down upon
De 29:20 will certainly s down on him
Isa 7:19 come in and s down, all of
11:2 spirit of Jehovah must s
25:10 s down on this mountain
30:32 Jehovah will cause to s
Eze 37:14 I will s you upon your soil
Mt 18:23 s accounts with his slaves
18:24 When he started to s them
Lu 21:14 s it in your hearts not to

Settled
Ge 25:18 he s down
34:10 business in it and get s
47:27 they became s in it and were
Nu 11:25 spirit s down upon them
31:10 their cities in which they had s
32:30 s in your midst in the land
Jos 22:9 they had been s at the order
22:19 and get s in our midst
1Sa 22:4 s them before the king of
2Ki 2:15 has s down upon Elisha
17:26 s in the cities of Samaria
Ezr 4:10 s in the cities of Samaria
Pr 8:25 Before the mountains . . . s
Mt 25:19 and s accounts with them
1Co 7:37 if anyone stands s in his

Settlements
Le 25:31 houses of s that have no
De 2:23 dwelling in s as far as Gaza
Jos 13:23 with the cities and their s
13:28 the cities and their s
15:32 together with their s
15:36 fourteen cities and their s
15:41 sixteen cities and their s
15:44 nine cities and their s
15:45 dependent towns and its s
15:46 Ashdod and their s
15:47 dependent towns and its s
15:47 Gaza . . . and its s, down to
15:51 eleven cities and their s
15:54 nine cities and their s
15:57 ten cities and their s
15:59 six cities and their s
15:60 two cities and their s
15:62 six cities and their s
16:9 all the cities and their s
18:24 twelve cities and their s
18:28 fourteen cities and their s
19:6 thirteen cities and their s
19:7 four cities and their s
19:8 the s that were all around
19:15 twelve cities and their s
19:16 were the cities and their s
19:22 sixteen cities and their s
19:23 the cities and their s
19:30 cities and their s
19:31 were the cities and their s
19:38 nineteen cities and their s
19:39 the cities and their s
19:48 were the cities and their s
21:12 city and its s they gave to
1Ch 4:32 s were Etam and Ain, Rimmon

1Ch 4:33 *s* that were all around these
6:56 field of the city and its *s*
9:16 in the *s* of the Netophathites
9:22 their *s* by their genealogical
9:25 And their brothers in their *s*
Ne 11:25 the *s* in their fields
11:25 in Jekabzeel and its *s*
11:30 Adullam and their *s*
12:28 the *s* of the Netophathites
12:29 *s* that the singers had built
Ps 10:8 He sits in an ambush of *s*
Isa 42:11 the *s* that Kedar inhabits

Settler

Ge 23:4 resident and *s* I am among you
Ex 12:45 A *s* . . . may not eat of it
Le 22:10 *s* with a priest nor a hired
25:6 *s* with you, those who are
25:35 *s*, he must keep alive with
25:40 hired laborer, like a *s*
25:47 *s* with you becomes wealthy
25:47 *s* with you, or to a member
Nu 35:15 the *s* in the midst of them
Ps 39:12 A *s* the same as all my

Settlers

Le 25:23 you . . . *s* from my standpoint
25:45 *s* who are residing as aliens
1Ch 29:15 and *s* the same as all our

Settling

Jg 19:9 the day is *s* down. Stay here
Mt 5:25 Be about *s* matters quickly

Seven

Ge 4:15 suffer vengeance *s* times
4:24 If *s* times Cain is to be
4:24 Lamech seventy times and *s*
5:7 Seth . . . eight hundred and *s*
5:26 *s* hundred and eighty-two years
5:31 *s* hundred and seventy-seven
7:4 in just *s* days more I am
7:10 *s* days later it turned out
8:10 waiting still another *s* days
8:12 waiting still another *s* days
11:21 live two hundred and *s* years
21:28 Abraham set *s* female lambs
21:29 *s* female lambs that you have
21:30 accept the *s* female lambs
29:18 serve you *s* years for Rachel
29:20 serve *s* years for Rachel
29:27 for *s* years more
29:30 for yet *s* years more
31:23 a distance of *s* days' journey
33:3 down to the earth *s* times
41:2 *s* cows beautiful in
41:3 there were *s* other cows
41:4 began to eat up the *s* cows
41:5 *s* ears of grain coming up on
41:6 *s* ears of grain, thin and
41:7 to swallow up the *s* fat and
41:18 *s* cows fat-fleshed and
41:19 *s* other cows ascending after
41:20 eat up the first *s* fat cows
41:22 *s* ears of grain coming up
41:23 *s* ears of grain shriveled
41:24 the *s* good ears of grain
41:26, 26 *s* good cows are *s* years
41:26 the *s* good ears of grain are
41:26 ears of grain are *s* years
41:27 the *s* skinny and bad cows
41:27 up after them are *s* years
41:27 the *s* empty ears of grain
41:27 to be *s* years of famine
41:29 there are *s* years coming
41:30 *s* years of famine will
41:34 during the *s* years of plenty
41:36 the *s* famine years, which
41:47 during the *s* years of plenty
41:48 foodstuffs of the *s* years
41:53 the *s* years of the plenty
41:54 *s* years of the famine
46:25 all the souls were *s*
50:10 rites for his father *s* days
Ex 2:16 the priest of Midian had *s*
7:25 *s* days came to be fulfilled
12:15 *S* days you are to eat
12:19 *S* days no sour dough is to
13:6 *S* days you are to eat
13:7 are to be eaten for the *s* days
22:30 *S* days it will continue with
23:15 eat unfermented cakes *s* days
25:37 must make *s* lamps for it
29:30 *S* days the priest who
29:35 take *s* days to fill their
29:37 *s* days to make atonement
Ex 34:18 *s* days at the appointed time
37:23 its *s* lamps and its snuffers
38:24 *s* hundred and thirty shekels
38:25 one thousand *s* hundred and
38:28 the thousand *s* hundred and
Le 4:6 some of the blood *s* times
4:17 and spatter it *s* times before
8:11 spattered some of it *s* times
8:33 tent of meeting for *s* days
8:33 take *s* days to fill your hand
8:35 day and night for *s* days, and
12:2 she must be unclean *s* days
13:4 quarantine the plague *s* days
13:5 quarantine him another *s* days
13:21 then quarantine him *s* days
13:26 then quarantine him *s* days
13:31 falling off of hair *s* days
13:33 falling off of hair *s* days
13:50 quarantine the plague *s* days
13:54 quarantine it a second *s* days
14:7 spatter it *s* times upon the
14:8 dwell outside his tent *s* days
14:16 *s* times before Jehovah
14:27 *s* times before Jehovah
14:38 quarantine the house *s* days
14:51 must spatter it . . . *s* times
15:13 *s* days for his purification
15:19 *s* days in her menstrual
15:24 must then be unclean *s* days
15:28 also count for herself *s* days
16:14 with his finger *s* times
16:19 with his finger *s* times and
22:27 under its mother *s* days, but
23:6 *S* days you should eat
23:8 offering . . . to Jehovah *s* days
23:15 *s* sabbaths. They should prove
23:18 *s* sound male lambs, each a
23:34 festival of booths for *s* days
23:36 *S* days you should present an
23:39 festival of Jehovah *s* days
23:40 Jehovah your God *s* days
23:41 festival to Jehovah *s* days
23:42 you should dwell *s* days
25:8 *s* sabbaths of years
25:8, 8 *s* times *s* years, and the
25:8 *s* sabbaths of years must
26:18 chastise you *s* times as much
26:21 inflict *s* times more blows
26:24 strike you *s* times for your
26:28 chastise you *s* times for
Nu 1:39 sixty-two thousand *s* hundred
2:26 sixty-two thousand *s* hundred
3:22 were *s* thousand five hundred
4:36 two thousand *s* hundred and
8:2 *s* lamps should shine on the
12:14 not be humiliated *s* days
12:14 quarantined *s* days outside
12:15 outside the camp *s* days, and
13:22 Hebron had been built *s* years
16:49 fourteen thousand *s* hundred
19:4 and spatter some . . . *s* times
19:11 must also be unclean *s* days
19:14 will be unclean *s* days
19:16 will be unclean *s* days
23:1 for me on this spot *s* altars
23:1, 1 *s* bulls and *s* rams
23:4 I set the *s* altars in rows
23:14 build *s* altars and to offer
23:29 for me on this spot *s* altars
23:29, 29 *s* bulls and *s* rams
26:7 thousand *s* hundred and thirty
26:34 fifty-two thousand *s* hundred
26:51 thousand *s* hundred and thirty
28:11 *s* sound male lambs each a
28:17 *S* days unfermented cakes
28:19 *s* male lambs each a year old
28:21 lamb of the *s* male lambs
28:24 daily for the *s* days as bread
28:27 *s* male lambs each a year old
28:29 for each male lamb of the *s*
29:2 *s* male lambs each a year old
29:4 for each male lamb of the *s*
29:8 *s* male lambs each a year old
29:10 of the *s* male lambs
29:12 festival to Jehovah *s* days
29:32 on the seventh day *s* bulls
29:36 *s* male lambs each a year old
31:19 camp outside the camp *s* days
31:52 sixteen thousand *s* hundred
De 7:1 *s* nations more populous and
15:1 every *s* years you should make
16:3 for *s* days. You should eat
16:4 in all your territory *s* days
16:9 *S* weeks you should count for
De 16:9 start to count *s* weeks
16:13 celebrate for yourself *s* days
16:15 *S* days you will celebrate the
28:7 by *s* ways they will flee
28:25 by *s* ways you will flee
31:10 At the end of every *s* years
Jos 6:4 And *s* priests should carry
6:4 should carry *s* rams' horns
6:4 march round the city *s* times
6:6 and *s* priests should carry
6:6 carry *s* rams' horns before
6:8 and *s* priests carrying
6:8 carrying *s* rams' horns before
6:13 and *s* priests carrying
6:13 carrying *s* rams' horns
6:15 in this manner *s* times
6:15 round the city *s* times
18:2 namely, *s* tribes
18:5 apportion . . . into *s* shares
18:6 the land into *s* shares
18:9 by cities in *s* shares
Jg 6:1 the hand of Midian for *s* years
6:25 bull of *s* years, and you must
8:26 one thousand *s* hundred gold
12:9 to judge Israel for *s* years
14:12 the *s* days of the banquet
14:17 weeping over him the *s* days
16:7 *s* still-moist sinews that
16:8 *s* still-moist sinews that had
16:13 weave the *s* braids of my
16:19 shave off the *s* braids of his
20:15 *s* hundred chosen men were
20:16 were *s* hundred chosen men
Ru 4:15 is better to you than *s* sons
1Sa 2:5 barren has given birth to *s*
6:1 of the Philistines *s* months
10:8 *S* days you should keep
11:3 Give us *s* days' time, and we
13:8 continued waiting for *s* days
16:10 Jesse had *s* of his sons pass
31:13 went fasting for *s* days
2Sa 2:11 to be *s* years and six months
5:5 king over Judah for *s* years
8:4 one thousand *s* hundred
10:18 *s* hundred charioteers and
21:6 *s* men of his sons
21:9 the *s* of them fell together
24:13 *s* years of famine in your
1Ki 2:11 In Hebron he had reigned *s*
6:6 was *s* cubits in its width
6:38 was *s* years at building it
7:17 *s* for the one capital, and
7:17 and *s* for the other capital
8:65 before Jehovah . . . *s* days
8:65 and another *s* days
11:3 came to have *s* hundred wives
16:15 king for *s* days in Tirzah
18:43 say, Go back, for *s* times
19:18 *s* thousand remain in Israel
20:15 sons of Israel, *s* thousand
20:29 encamped for *s* days, these
2Ki 3:9 their way around for *s* days
3:26 took with him *s* hundred men
4:35 to sneeze as many as *s* times
5:10 bathe *s* times in the Jordan
5:14 into the Jordan *s* times
8:1 upon the land for *s* years
8:2 the Philistines for *s* years
8:3 at the end of *s* years that
11:21 *S* years old Jehoash was
24:16 valiant men, *s* thousand
1Ch 3:4 *s* years and six months
3:24 and Delaiah and Anani, *s*
5:13 and Jacan and Zia and Eber, *s*
5:18 thousand *s* hundred and sixty
9:13 thousand *s* hundred and sixty
9:25 were to come in for *s* days
10:12 went fasting for *s* days
12:25 were *s* thousand one hundred
12:27 three thousand *s* hundred
15:26 to sacrifice *s* young bulls
15:26 young bulls and *s* rams
18:4 and *s* thousand horsemen and
19:18 *s* thousand charioteers and
26:30 a thousand *s* hundred, were
26:32 were two thousand *s* hundred
29:4 *s* thousand talents of refined
29:27 In Hebron he reigned for *s*
2Ch 7:8 at that time for *s* days, and
7:9 they had held for *s* days
7:9 and the festival for *s* days
13:9 young bull and *s* rams, he
15:11 *s* hundred cattle and
15:11 and *s* thousand sheep

2Ch 17:11, 11 *s* thousand *s* hundred
17:11, 11 *s* thousand *s* hundred
24:1 *S* years old was Jehoash when
26:13 three hundred and *s* thousand
29:21, 21 *s* bulls and *s* rams and
29:21 *s* male lambs . . . offering
29:21 *s* male goats . . . offering
30:21 *s* days with great rejoicing
30:22 appointed feast for *s* days
30:23 hold it for *s* more days
30:23 for *s* days with rejoicing
30:24 *s* thousand sheep, and the
35:17 cakes for *s* days
Ezr 2:5 *s* hundred and seventy-five
2:9 *s* hundred and sixty
2:25 *s* hundred and forty-three
2:33 *s* hundred and twenty-five
2:65 *s* thousand three hundred and
2:66 *s* hundred and thirty-six
2:67 six thousand *s* hundred and
6:22 *s* days with rejoicing
7:14 the king and his *s* counselors
Ne 7:14 *s* hundred and sixty
7:29 *s* hundred and forty-three
7:37 *s* hundred and twenty-one
7:67 *s* thousand three hundred and
7:68 *s* hundred and thirty-six
7:69 six thousand *s* hundred and
8:18 holding the festival *s* days
Es 1:5 king held a banquet for *s* days
1:10 *s* court officials that were
1:14 *s* princes of Persia and Media
2:9 *s* selected young women from
Job 1:2 And *s* sons and three daughters
1:3 got to be *s* thousand sheep and
2:13, 13 *s* days and *s* nights
5:19 in *s* nothing injurious will
42:8 take for yourselves *s* bulls
42:8 *s* rams and go to my servant
42:13 *s* sons and three daughters
Ps 12:6 silver . . . clarified *s* times
79:12 *s* times into their bosom
119:164 *S* times in the day I have
Pr 6:16 *s* are things detestable to his
6:31 good with *s* times as much
9:1 it has hewn out its *s* pillars
24:16 one may fall even *s* times
26:16 *s* giving a sensible reply
26:25 *s* detestable things in his
Ec 11:2 Give a portion to *s*, or even
Isa 4:1 *s* women will actually grab
11:15 strike it in its *s* torrents
30:26 sun will become *s* times as
30:26 like the light of *s* days
Jer 15:9 The woman giving birth to *s*
32:9 *s* shekels and ten silver
34:14 end of *s* years you men
52:25 *s* men of those having
52:30 *s* hundred and forty-five
Eze 3:15 dwelling there for *s* days
3:16 at the end of *s* days that the
39:9 have to light fires *s* years
39:12 the land, for *s* months
39:14 To the end of *s* months they
40:22 by *s* steps people could go
40:26 *s* steps for going up to it
41:3 the entrance was *s* cubits
43:25 *s* days you will render up
43:26 For *s* days they will make
44:26 *s* days they should number
45:21 *s* days unfermented cakes
45:23 *s* days of the festival he
45:23 to Jehovah *s* young bulls
45:23 *s* rams, sound ones, daily
45:23 daily for the *s* days, and
45:25 as these for the *s* days
Da 3:19 heat up the furnace *s* times
4:16 and let *s* times pass over it
4:23 *s* times themselves pass over
4:25 *s* times themselves will pass
4:32 *s* times themselves will pass
9:25 *s* weeks, also sixty-two
Mic 5:5 *s* shepherds, yes, eight dukes
Zec 3:9 one stone there are *s* eyes
4:2 its *s* lamps are upon it
4:2 lamps are upon it, even *s*
4:2 at the top of it have *s* pipes
4:10 *s* are the eyes of Jehovah
Mt 12:45 *s* different spirits more
15:34 *S*, and a few little fishes
15:36 the *s* loaves and the fishes
15:37 *s* provision baskets full
16:10 *s* loaves in the case of the
18:21 forgive him? Up to *s* times?
Mt 18:22 not, Up to *s* times, but, Up
22:25 there were *s* brothers with
22:26 until through all *s*
22:28 to which of the *s* will she
Mr 8:5 loaves have you? They said: *S*
8:6 took the *s* loaves, gave thanks
8:8 *s* provision baskets full
8:20 broke the *s* for the four
8:20 And they said to him: *S*
12:20 There were *s* brothers; and
12:22 the *s* did not leave any
12:23 the *s* got her as wife
Lu 2:36 with a husband for *s* years
8:2 from whom *s* demons had come
11:26 *s* different spirits more
17:4 if he sins *s* times a day
17:4 he comes back to you *s* times
20:29 *s* brothers; and the first
20:31 even the *s*: they did not
20:33 For the *s* got her as wife
24:13 village about *s* miles
Ac 6:3 *s* certified men from among
13:19 destroying *s* nations in the
19:14 *s* sons of a certain Sceva, a
20:6 in Troas . . . we spent *s* days
21:4 and remained here *s* days
21:8 who was one of the *s* men
21:27 the *s* days were about to be
28:14 to remain with them *s* days
Ro 11:4 *s* thousand men over for
Heb 11:30 been encircled for *s* days
2Pe 2:5 safe with *s* others when he
Re 1:4 John to the *s* congregations
1:4 *s* spirits that are before his
1:11 to the *s* congregations, in
1:12 I saw *s* golden lampstands
1:16 in his right hand *s* stars
1:20 sacred secret of the *s* stars
1:20 of the *s* golden lampstands
1:20 *s* stars mean the angels of
1:20 angels of the *s* congregations
1:20 and the *s* lampstands mean
1:20 mean *s* congregations
2:1 he says who holds the *s* stars
2:1 of the *s* golden lampstands
3:1 who has the *s* spirits of God
3:1 of God and the *s* stars
4:5 *s* lamps of fire burning before
4:5 mean the *s* spirits of God
5:1 sealed tight with *s* seals
5:5 open the scroll and its *s* seals
5:6, 6 having *s* horns and *s* eyes
5:6 eyes mean the *s* spirits of God
6:1 Lamb opened one of the *s* seals
8:2 I saw the *s* angels that stand
8:2 *s* trumpets were given them
8:6 And the *s* angels with the
8:6 angels with the *s* trumpets
10:3 the *s* thunders uttered their
10:4 when the *s* thunders spoke
10:4 things the *s* thunders spoke
11:13 *s* thousand persons were
12:3 dragon, with *s* heads and ten
12:3 and upon its heads *s* diadems
13:1 with ten horns and *s* heads
15:1, 1 *s* angels with *s* plagues
15:6, 6 *s* angels . . . *s* plagues
15:7 creatures gave the *s* angels
15:7 *s* golden bowls that were full
15:8, 8 *s* plagues of the *s* angels
16:1 say to the *s* angels: Go and
16:1 *s* bowls of the anger of God
17:1 one of the *s* angels that had
17:1 that had the *s* bowls came
17:3 had *s* heads and ten horns
17:7 *s* heads and the ten horns
17:9, 9 *s* heads mean *s* mountains
17:10 *s* kings: five have fallen
17:11 but springs from the *s*, and
21:9 one of the *s* angels who had
21:9 angels who had the *s* bowls
21:9 full of the *s* last plagues

Sevens
Ge 7:2 clean beast . . . by *s*, the sire
7:3 creatures of the heavens by *s*

Seventeen
Ge 37:2 Joseph, when *s* years old
47:28 in the land of Egypt for *s*
1Ki 14:21 and *s* years he reigned in
2Ki 13:1 in Samaria for *s* years
1Ch 7:11 *s* thousand two hundred going
2Ch 12:13 *s* years he reigned in
Ezr 2:39 a thousand and *s*
Ne 7:42 of Harim, a thousand and *s*

Seventeenth
Ge 7:11 Noah's life . . . *s* day of the
8:4 on the *s* day of the month
1Ki 22:51 in the *s* year of Jehoshaphat
2Ki 16:1 the *s* year of Pekah the
1Ch 24:15 for Hezir the *s*
25:24 for the *s*, for Joshbekashah

Seventh
Ge 2:2 And by the *s* day God came to
2:2 to rest on the *s* day from all
2:3 God proceeded to bless the *s*
8:4 And in the *s* month, on the
Ex 12:15 the first day down to the *s*
12:16 the *s* day a holy convention
13:6 *s* day is a festival to Jehovah
16:26 but on the *s* day is a sabbath
16:27 it came about on the *s* day
16:29 nobody go out . . . the *s* day
16:30 the sabbath on the *s* day
20:10 *s* day is a sabbath to Jehovah
20:11 to rest on the *s* day
21:2 in the *s* he will go out as
23:11 *s* year you are to leave it
23:12 the *s* day you are to desist
24:16 the *s* day he called to Moses
31:15 the *s* day is a sabbath of
31:17 on the *s* day he rested and
34:21 *s* day you will keep sabbath
35:2 *s* day . . . something holy to
Le 13:5 must look at him on the *s* day
13:6 look at him on the *s* day the
13:27 look at him on the *s* day
13:32 at the plague on the *s* day
13:34 must look . . . on the *s* day
13:51 seen the plague on the *s* day
14:9 the *s* day that he should shave
14:39 on the *s* day and must take a
16:29 In the *s* month on the tenth
23:3 *s* day is a sabbath of complete
23:8 *s* day there will be a holy
23:16 *s* sabbath you should count
23:24 *s* month, on the first of the
23:27 tenth of this *s* month is the
23:34 *s* month is the festival of
23:39 of the *s* month, when you have
23:41 celebrate it in the *s* month
25:4 *s* year there should occur a
25:9 *s* month on the tenth of the
25:20 eat in the *s* year seeing that
Nu 6:9 On the *s* day he should shave it
7:48 *s* day there was the chieftain
19:12 the *s* day he will be clean
19:12 *s* day he will not be clean
19:19 on the *s* day and must purify
19:19 purify him . . . on the *s* day
28:25 *s* day you should hold a holy
29:1 in the *s* month, on the first
29:7 on the tenth of this *s* month
29:12 fifteenth day of the *s* month
29:32 And on the *s* day seven bulls
31:19 and on the *s* day, you and
31:24 on the *s* day and be clean
De 5:14 *s* day is a sabbath to Jehovah
15:9 saying, The *s* year, the year
15:12 in the *s* year you should send
16:8 on the *s* day there will be a
Jos 6:4 the *s* day you should march
6:15 came about on the *s* day that
6:16 came about on the *s* time
19:40 that the *s* lot came out
Jg 14:17 on the *s* day that finally he
14:18 said to him on the *s* day
2Sa 12:18 on the *s* day that the child
1Ki 8:2 that is, the *s* month
18:44 the *s* time that he got to
20:29 *s* day that the engagement
2Ki 11:4 the *s* year Jehoiada sent
12:1 In the *s* year of Jehu
18:9 the *s* year of Hoshea the
25:8 on the *s* day of the month
25:25 in the *s* month that Ishmael
1Ch 2:15 Ozem the sixth, David the *s*
12:11 Attai the sixth, Eliel the *s*
24:10 for Hakkoz the *s*, for Abijah
25:14 the *s* for Jesharelah, his
26:3 the sixth, Elieho-enai the *s*
26:5 Issachar the *s*, Peullethai
27:10, 10 The *s* for the *s* month
2Ch 5:3 festival, that of the *s* month
7:10 day of the *s* month he sent
23:1 *s* year Jehoiada showed
31:7 in the *s* month they finished

Jon 4:5 sit under it in the *s* until
4:6 to become a *s* over his head

Shadow
Ge 19:8 come under the *s* of my roof
Jg 9:15 seek refuge under my *s*
2Ki 20:9 *s* actually go forward ten
20:10 *s* to extend itself ten steps
20:10 *s* should go backward ten
20:11 the *s* that had gone down
1Ch 29:15 Like a *s* our days are upon
Job 3:5 darkness and deep *s* reclaim
7:2 a slave he pants for the *s*
8:9 our days on earth are a *s*
10:21 land of darkness and deep *s*
10:22 To the land . . . of deep *s*
12:22 forth to the light deep *s*
14:2 And he runs away like the *s*
16:16 upon my eyelids . . . deep *s*
17:7 are all of them like the *s*
24:17 morning . . . same as deep *s*
24:17 the sudden terrors of deep *s*
28:3 in the gloom and deep *s*
34:22 no darkness nor any deep *s*
38:17 gates of deep *s* can you see
40:22 blocked off with their *s*
Ps 17:8 In the *s* of your wings may
23:4 walk in the valley of deep *s*
36:7 in the *s* of your wings the
44:19 cover us over with deep *s*
57:1 in the *s* of your wings I take
63:7 in the *s* of your wings I cry
80:10 were covered with its *s*
91:1 very *s* of the Almighty One
102:11 days are like a *s* that has
107:10 in darkness and deep *s*
107:14 from darkness and deep *s*
109:23 Like a *s* when it declines
144:4 days are like a passing *s*
Ec 6:12 when he spends them like a *s*
8:13 his days that are like a *s*
Isa 9:2 in the land of deep *s*
16:3 *s* just like the night in the
25:5 heat with the *s* of a cloud
30:2 refuge in the *s* of Egypt
30:3 refuge in the *s* of Egypt a
32:2 *s* of a heavy crag in an
34:15 them together under its *s*
38:8 making the *s* of the steps
49:2 In the *s* of his hand he has
51:16 with the *s* of my hand I
Jer 2:6 of no water and of deep *s*
13:16 actually make it deep *s*
48:45 In the *s* of Heshbon those
Eze 17:23 in the *s* of its foliage they
31:3 a woody thicket offering *s*
31:17 seed have dwelt in his *s*
Ho 14:7 again be dwellers in his *s*
Am 5:8 deep *s* into the morning
Mt 4:16 in a region of deathly *s*
Mr 4:32 to find lodging under its *s*
Lu 1:79 in darkness and death's *s*
Ac 5:15 *s* might fall upon some one of
Col 2:17 a *s* of the things to come
Heb 8:5 a *s* of the heavenly things
10:1 Law has a *s* of the good
Jas 1:17 of the turning of the *s*

Shadows
Jg 9:36 The *s* of the mountains are
Ca 2:17 and the *s* have fled, turn
4:6 and the *s* have fled, I shall go
Jer 6:4 *s* of evening keep extending

Shadowy
Ne 13:19 grown *s* before the sabbath

Shadrach
Da 1:7 and to Hananiah, *S;* and to
2:49 appointed . . . *S*, Meshach and
3:12 whom you appointed . . . *S*
3:13 said to bring in *S*
3:14 Is it really so, O *S*
3:16 *S* . . . saying to the king
3:19 *S*, Meshach and Abednego
3:20 said to bind *S*, Meshach and
3:22 men that took up *S*, Meshach
3:23 *S* . . . fell down bound in the
3:26 *S* . . . step out and come here
3:26 *S*, Meshach and Abednego were
3:28 Blessed be the God of *S*
3:29 the God of *S*, Meshach and
3:30 *S* . . . to prosper in the

Shaft
1Sa 17:7 wooden *s* of his spear was
2Sa 21:19 *s* of whose spear was like
23:7 iron and the *s* of a spear
1Ch 20:5 *s* of whose spear was like
Job 28:4 sunk a *s* far from where

Shafts
2Sa 18:14 took three *s* in his palm
Ps 76:3 the flaming *s* of the bow

Shagee
1Ch 11:34 Jonathan the son of *S* the

Shaharaim
1Ch 8:8 As for *S*, he became father to

Shahazumah
Jos 19:22 and *S* and Beth-shemesh and

Shake
Ge 27:33 Isaac began to *s* with a
Jg 16:20 I shall . . . *s* myself free
2Sa 22:8 earth began to *s* and to rock
Ne 5:13 God *s* out from his house and
Job 16:12 but he proceeded to *s* me up
17:3 *s* hands with me in pledge
26:11 The very pillars of heaven *s*
34:20 The people *s* back and forth
Ps 18:7 the earth began to *s* and rock
64:8 will *s* their head
Isa 52:2 *S* yourself free from the
Jer 18:16 astonishment and *s* his head
25:16 drink and *s* back and forth
48:27 *s* yourself just as often as
Da 4:14 *S* off its foliage, and scatter
Hab 3:6 that he might *s* up the earth
Mt 10:14 *s* the dust off your feet
Mr 6:11 out from there *s* off the dirt
Lu 6:48 was not strong enough to *s* it
9:5 *s* the dust off your feet for a

Shaken
Ne 5:13 this manner may he become *s*
Job 38:13 the wicked ones might be *s*
Ps 109:23 been *s* off like a locust
Isa 24:19 land has absolutely been *s*
Eze 21:21 He has *s* the arrows
Mt 24:29 powers of the heavens . . . *s*
Mr 13:25 in the heavens will be *s*
Lu 6:38 *s* together and overflowing
21:26 of the heavens will be *s*
Ac 2:25 that I may never be *s*
4:31 place . . . was *s;* and they
16:26 foundations of the jail . . . *s*
2Th 2:2 not to be quickly *s* from your
Heb 12:27 of the things being *s* as
12:27 the things not being *s* may
12:28 a kingdom that cannot be *s*
Re 6:13 fig tree *s* by a high wind

Shakes
Pr 17:18 is wanting in heart *s* hands

Shaking
2Sa 22:8 they kept *s* back and forth
Ezr 10:19 promised by *s* hands to put
Ps 18:7 they kept *s* back and forth
44:14 A *s* of the head among the
Isa 33:9 are *s* off their leaves
33:15 *s* his hands clear from
Jer 4:24 hills . . . were all given a *s*
23:9 All my bones have begun *s*
Eze 21:6 son of man, sigh with *s* hips
Hab 2:7 wake up who are violently *s*

Shalishah
1Sa 9:4 on through the land of *S*, and

Shallecheth
1Ch 26:16 gate *S* by the highway that

Shallum
2Ki 15:10 *S* the son of Jabesh
15:13 As for *S* the son of Jabesh
15:14 *S* the son of Jabesh in
15:15 *S* and his conspiracy with
22:14 *S* the son of Tikvah
1Ch 2:40 in turn, became father to *S*
2:41 *S*, in turn, became father to
3:15 sons of Josiah . . . fourth, *S*
4:25 *S* his son, Mibsam his son
6:12 Zadok . . . became father to *S*
6:13 *S* . . . father to Hilkiah
7:13 The sons of Naphtali . . . *S*
9:17 gatekeepers were *S* and Akkub
9:17 and their brother *S* the head
9:19 And *S* the son of Kore the son
9:31 firstborn of *S* the Korahite
2Ch 28:12 Jehizkiah the son of *S* and
34:22 *S* the son of Tikvah
Ezr 2:42 the sons of *S*
7:2 the son of *S* the son of Zadok
10:24 gatekeepers, *S* and Telem
10:42 *S*, Amariah, Joseph
Ne 3:12 *S* the son of Hallohesh, a
7:45 gatekeepers, the sons of *S*
Jer 22:11 *S* the son of Josiah, the
32:7 Hanamel the son of *S* your
35:4 Maaseiah the son of *S* the

Shallun
Ne 3:15 *S* the son of Colhozeh

Shalman
Ho 10:14 *S* of the house of Arbel

Shalmaneser
2Ki 17:3 *S* the king of Assyria
18:9 *S* the king of Assyria came

Shama
1Ch 11:44 *S* and Jeiel, the sons of

Shame
Le 20:17 sees his nakedness, it is *s*
1Sa 20:30 son of Jesse to your own *s*
20:30 *s* of the secret parts of
2Sa 19:5 put to *s* the face of all
2Ch 32:21 back with *s* of face to his
Ezr 9:7 and with *s* of face, just as
Job 8:22 will be clothed with *s*
Ps 14:6 you people would put to *s*
22:5 and they did not come to *s*
35:26 Let those be clothed with *s*
40:15 in consequence of their *s*
44:7 hating us you put to *s*
44:15 *s* of my own face has covered
53:5 will certainly put them to *s*
69:19 know my reproach and my *s*
70:3 go back by reason of their *s*
89:45 have enwrapped him with *s*
109:29 *s* just as with a sleeveless
119:31 Jehovah, do not put me to *s*
119:116 put me to *s* for my hope
132:18 I shall clothe with *s*
Pr 25:10 may not put you to *s* and the
29:15 will be causing his mother *s*
Isa 30:3 for you men a reason for *s*
30:5 reason for *s* and also a
54:4 for you will not be put to *s*
54:4 the *s* of your time of youth
61:7 Instead of your *s* there will
65:13 yourselves will suffer *s*
66:5 ones that will be put to *s*
Jer 2:26 As with the *s* of a thief
2:26 house of Israel have felt *s*
3:25 We lie down in our *s*, and
6:15 Did they feel *s* because it
6:15 positively do not feel any *s*
7:19 purpose of *s* to their faces
8:12 *s* because they had done even
9:19 How much we have felt *s!*
10:14 *s* because of the carved
14:3 They have been put to *s* and
17:13 will be put to *s*
17:18 my persecutors be put to *s*
17:18 personally be put to no *s*
20:11 certainly be put to much *s*
20:18 to their end in mere *s*
46:24 Egypt will certainly feel *s*
48:1 Kiriathaim has been put to *s*
48:1 height has been put to *s* and
48:20 Moab has been put to *s*
50:2 Bel has been put to *s*
50:2 images have been put to *s*
51:51 We have been put to *s*, for
Eze 7:18 on all faces there is *s* and
Da 9:7 *s* of face as at this day, to
9:8 to us belongs the *s* of face
Ho 10:6 *S* is what Ephraim himself
Joe 1:11 Farmers have felt *s*
Ob 10 *s* will cover you, and you
Mic 7:10 *s* will cover her, who was
Hab 2:15 looking upon their parts of *s*
Zep 2:1 O nation not paling in *s*
3:5 one was knowing no *s*
3:19 in all the land of their *s*
Zec 9:5 will have to experience *s*
10:5 will have to experience *s*
Lu 13:17 his opposers began to feel *s*
14:9 you will start off with *s* to
1Co 1:27 might put the wise men to *s*
1:27 put the strong things to *s*
4:14 writing . . . not to *s* you
6:5 am speaking to move you to *s*
15:34 speaking to move you to *s*

2Co 7:14 I have not been put to s
9:4 should be put to s in this
10:8 I would not be put to s
Php 3:19 glory consists in their s
Heb 6:6 and expose him to public s
12:2 despising s, and has sat
1Pe 4:16 let him not feel s, but
Jude 13 their own causes for s
Re 3:18 s of your nakedness may not

Shamed
Ps 35:4 May those be s and humiliated
1Jo 2:28 not be s away from him at

Shameful
Jer 3:24 the s thing itself has eaten
11:13 placed for the s thing
Ho 9:10 dedicate . . . to the s thing
Mic 1:11 Shaphir, in s nudity
Hab 2:10 counseled something s to
Eph 5:4 neither s conduct nor foolish
5:12 it is s even to relate

Shamefully
Pr 10:5 son acting s is fast asleep
12:4 is she that acts s
13:5 wicked ones act s and cause
14:35 to be toward one acting s
17:2 over the son who is acting s
19:26 is a son acting s and
Ho 2:5 pregnant with them has acted s

Shamefulness
Re 16:15 and people look upon his s

Shameless
Re 18:3 the power of her s luxury
18:7 and lived in s luxury, to
18:9 and lived in s luxury will

Shames
1Co 11:4 something on his head s his
11:5 s her head, for it is one and

Shamgar
Jg 3:31 S the son of Anath, and he
5:6 the days of S the son of Anath

Shamhuth
1Ch 27:8 was S the Izrahite, and in

Shamir
Jos 15:48 mountainous region S and
Jg 10:1 he was dwelling in S in the
10:2 he died and was buried in S
1Ch 24:24 of the sons of Micah, S

Shamma
1Ch 7:37 Hod and S and Shilshah and

Shammah
Ge 36:13 the sons of Reuel . . . S
36:17 sons of Reuel . . . sheik S
1Sa 16:9 Next Jesse had S pass by, but
17:13 Abinadab and the third S
2Sa 23:11 S the son of Agee the
23:25 S the Harodite, Elika the
23:33 S the Hararite, Ahiam the
1Ch 1:37 sons of Reuel were . . . S

Shammai
1Ch 2:28 sons of Onam . . . S and Jada
2:28 sons of S were Nadab and
2:32 Jada the brother of S
2:44 became father to S
2:45 the son of S was Maon
4:17 S and Ishbah the father of

Shammoth
1Ch 11:27 S the Harorite, Helez the

Shammua
Nu 13:4 of Reuben, S the son of Zaccur
2Sa 5:14 S and Shobab and Nathan and
1Ch 14:4 S and Shobab, Nathan and
Ne 11:17 S the son of Galal the son
12:18 for Bilgah, S; for Shemaiah

Shamsherai
1Ch 8:26 S and Shehariah and Athaliah

Shanks
Ex 12:9 its s and its interior parts
29:17 its intestines and its s
Le 1:9 and its s will be washed with
1:13 wash the intestines and the s
4:11 its s and its intestines and
8:21 and the s he washed with
9:14 the intestines and the s and
Am 3:12 two s or a piece of an ear

Shape
1Ki 6:25 measure and the same s
7:37 one cast, one measure, one s
Lu 3:22 spirit in bodily s like a dove

Shaped
Ex 25:33 Three cups s like flowers of
25:33 three cups s like flowers of
25:34 four cups s like flowers of
37:19 s like flowers of almond
37:19 s like flowers of almond
37:20 s like flowers of almond
Job 10:8 Your own hands have s me so
33:6 From the clay I was s, I too

Shapham
1Ch 5:12 S the second, and Janai and

Shaphan
2Ki 22:3 sent S the son of Azaliah
22:8 said to S the secretary
22:8 Hilkiah gave the book to S
22:9 S the secretary came in to
22:10 S the secretary went on to
22:10 S began to read it before
22:12 S and Achbor the son of
22:12 and S the secretary and
22:14 Ahikam and Achbor and S
25:22 Ahikam the son of S
2Ch 34:8 sent S the son of Azaliah
34:15 said to S the secretary
34:15 Hilkiah gave the book to S
34:16 S brought the book to the
34:18 S the secretary went on to
34:18 S began to read out of it
34:20 Ahikam the son of S
34:20 S the secretary and
Jer 26:24 Ahikam the son of S that
29:3 Elasah the son of S and
36:10 Gemariah the son of S the
36:11 Gemariah the son of S got
36:12 Gemariah the son of S and
39:14 Ahikam the son of S, in
40:5 Ahikam the son of S, whom
40:9 Ahikam the son of S
40:11 Ahikam the son of S
41:2 Ahikam the son of S with
43:6 Ahikam the son of S, and
Eze 8:11 with Jaazaniah the son of S

Shaphat
Nu 13:5 of Simeon, S the son of Hori
1Ki 19:16 Elisha the son of S from
19:19 found Elisha the son of S
2Ki 3:11 is here Elisha the son of S
6:31 Elisha the son of S
1Ch 3:22 Bariah and Neariah and S
5:12 and Janai and S in Bashan
27:29 was S the son of Adlai

Shaphir
Mic 1:11 S, in shameful nudity

Sharai
Ezr 10:40 Machnadebai, Shashai, S

Sharar
2Sa 23:33 Ahiam the son of S the

Share
Ge 14:24 s of the men who went with
14:24 let them take their s
31:14 Is there a s of inheritance
Ex 12:44 first he may s in eating it
Le 6:17 their s out of my offerings
7:35 the priestly s of Aaron and
7:35 and the priestly s of his sons
22:11 he as such may s in eating
22:11 may s in eating his bread
Nu 18:20 no s will become yours in
18:20 I am your s and your
31:36 s of those who went out on
De 10:9 Levi has come to have no s
12:12 he has no s or inheritance
14:27 no s or inheritance with you
14:29 no s or inheritance with you
18:1 No s or inheritance with
18:8 An equal s he should eat
32:9 For Jehovah's s is his people
Jos 14:4 not given a s in the land to
15:13 gave a s in the midst of
18:7 the Levites have no s in
19:9 the s of the sons of Judah
22:8 Take your s of the spoil of
22:25 You have no s in Jehovah
22:27 You have no s in Jehovah
1Sa 30:24 s of the one that went down
30:24 s of the one that sat by
1Sa 30:24 All will have a s together
2Sa 19:29 Ziba should s in the field
20:1 We have no s in David, and
1Ki 12:16 What s do we have in David?
2Ch 10:16 What s do we have in David?
Ezr 4:16 have no s beyond the River
Ne 2:20 but you yourselves have no s
Job 20:29 s of the wicked man from
27:13 the s of the wicked man
27:17 be the one to have a s
39:17 a s in understanding
Ps 16:5 the portion of my allotted s
17:14 whose s is in this life
73:26 and my s to time indefinite
119:57 Jehovah is my s
142:5 s in the land of the living
Pr 9:5 s in drinking the wine that I
17:2 have a s of the inheritance
Isa 17:14 s of those pillaging us
61:7 joyfully over their s
Jer 10:16 The S of Jacob is not like
12:10 have stamped down my s
12:10 turned my desirable s
51:19 S of Jacob is not like these
La 3:24 Jehovah is my s, my soul has
Lu 3:11 s with the man that has none
15:12 property that falls to my s
Ac 1:17 obtained a s in this ministry
Ro 12:13 S with the holy ones
15:26 to s up their things by a
2Co 1:7 you will also s the comfort
8:4 s in the ministry destined
Ga 6:6 s in all good things with the
Php 4:15 not a congregation took a s
1Ti 6:18 to be liberal, ready to s
Re 18:4 s with her in her sins, and

Shared
Ro 15:27 if the nations have s in
Tit 1:4 a faith s in common

Sharer
Ro 11:17 s of the olive's root of
1Co 9:23 I may become a s of it with
2Co 8:23 is a s with me and a fellow
1Ti 5:22 neither be a s in the sins of
Phm 17 If . . . you consider me a s
1Pe 5:1 a s even of the glory that is
2Jo 11 is a s in his wicked works
Re 1:9 s with you in the tribulation

Sharers
Mt 23:30 s with them in the blood of
Lu 5:10 who were s with Simon
1Co 10:18 s with the altar
10:20 not want you to become s
2Co 1:7 you are s of the sufferings
Php 1:7 s with me in the undeserved
4:14 s with me in my tribulation
Heb 2:14 are s of blood and flesh
10:33 s with those who were
1Pe 4:13 s in the sufferings of the
2Pe 1:4 become s in divine nature

Shares
Jos 11:23 to Israel by their s
12:7 as a holding by their s
18:5 apportion . . . into seven s
18:6 the land into seven s
18:9 by cities in seven s
18:10 sons of Israel in their s
Job 17:5 companions to take their s
Ps 68:12 at home, she s in the spoil
Eze 45:7 exactly as one of the s
48:29 these will be their s

Sharezer
2Ki 19:37 Adrammelech and S, his sons
Isa 37:38 and S, his own sons, struck
Zec 7:2 to send S and Regem-melech

Sharing
Ps 50:18 your s was with adulterers
Ac 2:42 and to s with one another
1Co 1:9 a s with his Son Jesus Christ
10:16 a s in the blood of the
10:16 s in the body of the Christ
2Co 6:14 what s does light have with
13:14 s in the holy spirit be
Ga 2:9 the right hand of s together
Eph 5:11 quit s with them in the
Php 2:1 if any s of spirit, if any
3:10 and a s in his sufferings
Phm 6 the s of your faith may go
Heb 13:16 s of things with others
1Jo 1:3 may be having a s with us
1:3 this s of ours is with the

1Jo 1:6 having a s with him, and
1:7 do have a s with one another

Sharon
1Ch 5:16 all the pasture grounds of S
27:29 that were grazing in S
Isa 33:9 S has become like the desert
35:2 splendor of Carmel and of S
65:10 S must become a pasture
Ac 9:35 inhabited . . . the plain of S

Sharonite
1Ch 27:29 there was Shitrai the S

Sharp
2Sa 12:31 s instruments of iron and
1Ch 20:3 at s instruments of iron and
Ps 45:5 Your arrows are s—under you
57:4 And whose tongue is a s sword
94:21 make s attacks on the soul
Pr 5:4 is as s as a two-edged sword
Isa 49:2 my mouth like a s sword
Eze 5:1 take for yourself a s sword
21:16 Show yourself s; go to the
Ac 15:39 occurred a s burst of anger
Re 1:16 mouth a s, long two-edged
2:12 the s, long two-edged sword
14:14 and a s sickle in his hand
14:17 he, too, having a s sickle
14:18 the one that had the s sickle
14:18 Put your s sickle in and
19:15 protrudes a s long sword

Sharpen
De 32:41 indeed s my glittering sword
Ps 7:12 His sword he will s

Sharpened
1Sa 13:20 or his ax or his sickle s
Ps 52:2 schemes up, s like a razor
64:3 s their tongue just like a
120:4 S arrows of a mighty man
140:3 s their tongue like that of
Pr 25:18 s arrow is a man testifying
27:17 By iron, iron itself is s
Isa 5:28 arrows are s and all their
Eze 21:9 sword! It has been s, and
21:10 a slaughter it has been s
21:11 a sword has been s, and it

Sharpening
1Sa 13:21 price for s proved to be

Sharpens
Job 16:9 s his eyes against me
Pr 27:17 man s the face of another

Sharper
Heb 4:12 s than any two-edged sword

Sharply
Ps 73:21 in my kidneys I was s pained

Sharuhen
Jos 19:6 and Beth-lebaoth and S

Shashai
Ezr 10:40 Machnadebai, S, Sharai

Shashak
1Ch 8:14 And there were Ahio, S and
8:25 and Penuel, the sons of S

Shatter
Ex 15:6 Jehovah, can s an enemy
34:13 sacred pillars you are to s
De 12:3 and s their sacred pillars
Jer 5:17 will s with the sword your
49:37 s the Elamites before their
Da 2:40 crush and s even all these

Shattered
Ex 9:25 hail . . . s all sorts of trees
32:19 threw the tablets . . . s them
34:1 first tablets, which you s
Le 6:28 vessel . . . is to be s
De 9:17 and s them before your eyes
10:2 first tablets, which you s
Jg 7:20 and s the large jars and took
10:8 they s and heavily oppressed
Isa 7:8 Ephraim will be s to pieces
8:9 be s to pieces; and give ear
8:9 and be s to pieces!
8:9 and be s to pieces!
9:4 s to pieces as in the day of
51:6 righteousness will not be s
Jer 8:21 I have become s. I have
14:4 the soil that has been s
51:56 Their bows must be s, for
Mal 1:4 We have been s, but we shall
Mt 21:44 person falling . . . will be s
Lu 20:18 upon that stone will be s

Shatters
Da 2:40 so, like iron that s, it

Shaul
Ge 36:37 When Samlah died, S from
36:38 When S died, Baal-hanan son
46:10 sons of Simeon were . . . S
Ex 6:15 the sons of Simeon . . . S the
Nu 26:13 of S the family of the
1Ch 1:48 and S from Rehoboth by the
1:49 S died, and Baal-hanan the
4:24 sons of Simeon . . . S
6:24 Uzziah his son, and S his son

Shaulites
Nu 26:13 of Shaul the family of the S

Shave
Le 14:8 s off all his hair and bathe
14:9 should s off all his hair
14:9 s off all his hair, and he
21:5 beard they should not s, and
Nu 6:9 s his head in the day of
6:9 seventh day he should s it
6:18 Nazirite must s the head of
De 21:12 s her head and attend to her
Jg 16:19 s off the seven braids of his
2Sa 14:26 every year that he would s
Isa 7:20 Jehovah will s the head and
Eze 44:20 head they should not s

Shaved
Ge 41:14 he s and changed his mantles
Le 13:33 must then have himself s
13:33 falling off of hair s; and
Nu 6:19 sign of his Naziriteship s off
Jg 16:17 If I did get s, my power
16:22 as soon as he had been s
2Sa 10:4 s off half their beards and
14:26 And when he s his head—and
14:26 so heavy upon him, he s it
1Ch 19:4 servants of David and s them
Jer 41:5 with their beards s off
Ac 21:24 they may have their heads s
1Co 11:5 were a woman with a s head
11:6 woman to be shorn or s, let

Shaveh
Ge 14:17 Low Plain of S, that is, the

Shaveh-kiriathaim
Ge 14:5 defeats on . . . the Emim in S

Shavsha
1Ch 18:16 and S was secretary

Shawl
Ge 38:14 covered herself with a s and
38:19 removed her s off her and

Sheaf
Ge 37:7 s got up and also stood erect
37:7 and bow down to my s
Le 23:10 bring a s of the firstfruits
23:11 wave the s to and fro before
23:12 s waved to and fro you must
23:15 bringing the s of the wave
De 24:19 forgotten a s in the field
Jg 15:5 from s to standing grain and

Sheal
Ezr 10:29 the sons of Bani . . . S and

Shealtiel
1Ch 3:17 sons of Jeconiah . . . S
Ezr 3:2 Zerubbabel the son of S and
3:8 Zerubbabel the son of S and
5:2 Zerubbabel the son of S
Ne 12:1 Zerubbabel the son of S and
Hag 1:1 Zerubbabel the son of S
1:12 Zerubbabel the son of S
1:14 Zerubbabel the son of S, the
2:2 Zerubbabel the son of S
2:23 Zerubbabel the son of S, my
Mt 1:12 Jeconiah became father to S
1:12 S became father to Zerubbabel
Lu 3:27 son of S, son of Neri

Shear
Ge 31:19 Laban had gone to s his sheep
38:13 to Timnah to s his sheep
De 15:19 nor s the firstborn of your
Jer 7:29 S off your uncut hair and
Mic 1:16 s your hair off on account

Shearer
Ac 8:32 that is voiceless before its s

Shearers
Ge 38:12 up to the s of his sheep
1Sa 25:7 I have heard that you have s
25:11 I have butchered for my s
Isa 53:7 like a ewe that before her s

Sheariah
1Ch 8:38 and S . . . the sons of Azel
9:44 and S . . . the sons of Azel

Shearing
1Sa 25:2 s his sheep at Carmel
25:4 that Nabal was s his sheep

Shear-jashub
Isa 7:3 meet Ahaz, you and S your son

Shears
Isa 2:4 their spears into pruning s
18:5 the sprigs with pruning s
Joe 3:10 your pruning s into lances
Mic 4:3 their spears into pruning s

She-ass
Ge 49:11 descendant of his own s
Nu 22:21 Balaam . . . saddled his s and
22:22 And he was riding upon his s
22:25 the s kept seeing Jehovah's
22:30 s said to Balaam: Am I not
22:30 Am I not your s that you
22:32 Why have you beaten your s
22:33 s got to see me and tried to
2Ki 4:24 she saddled up the s and said
Zec 9:9 animal the son of a s

She-asses
Ge 12:16 maidservants and s and
32:15 twenty s and ten full-grown
45:23 ten s carrying grain and
Jg 5:10 riders on yellowish-red s, You
1Sa 9:3 s belonging to Kish the father
9:3 get up, go, look for the s
9:5 not quit attending to the s
9:20 the s that were lost to you
10:2 s that you have gone to look
10:2 given up the matter of the s
10:14 To look for the s, and we
10:16 that the s had been found
2Ki 4:22 one of the s, and let me run
1Ch 27:30 and over the s there was
Job 1:3 five hundred s, along with a
1:14 s were grazing at the side
42:12 cattle and a thousand s

Sheath
1Sa 17:51 pulled it out of its s and
2Sa 20:8 attached to his hip, in its s
1Ch 21:27 returned his sword to its s
Jer 47:6 Be shoved into your s
Eze 21:3 sword out of its s and cut
21:4 go forth from its s against
21:5 my sword from its s
21:30 Return it to its s
Joh 18:11 Put the sword into its s

Sheathed
Hab 2:19 It is s in gold and silver

Sheaves
Ge 37:7 we were binding s in the
37:7 your s proceeded to encircle
Ex 22:6 and s or standing grain or a
Job 5:26 when s pile up in their time
Ps 126:6 Carrying along his s
129:7 gathering s his own bosom

Sheba
Ge 10:7 sons of Raamah were S and
10:28 Obal and Abimael and S
25:3 Jokshan became father to S
Jos 19:2 Beer-sheba with S, and
2Sa 20:1 S, the son of Bichri a
20:2 follow S the son of Bichri
20:6 S the son of Bichri will be
20:7 chase after S the son of
20:10 after S the son of Bichri
20:13 after S the son of Bichri
20:14 S went passing through all
20:21 S the son of Bichri, has
20:22 cut off the head of S the
1Ki 10:1 the queen of S was hearing
10:4 queen of S got to see all
10:10 queen of S gave to King
10:13 gave the queen of S all her
1Ch 1:9 sons of Raamah were S and
1:22 and Obal and Abimael and S
1:32 sons of Jokshan were S and
5:13 S and Jorai and Jacan and Zia
2Ch 9:1 queen of S herself heard the
9:3 queen of S got to see
9:9 queen of S gave to King

2Ch 9:12 queen of S all her delight
Ps 72:10 kings of S and of Seba
72:15 of the gold of S be given
Isa 60:6 from S—they will come
Jer 6:20 even frankincense from S
Eze 27:22 traders of S and Raamah
27:23 and Eden, the traders of S
38:13 S and Dedan and the
Joe 3:8 sell them to the men of S

Shebaniah
1Ch 15:24 and S and Joshaphat and
Ne 9:4 S, Bunni, Sherebiah, Bani and
9:5 S and Pethahiah went on to say
10:4 Hattush, S, Malluch
10:10 their brothers S, Hodiah
10:12 Zaccur, Sherebiah, S
12:14 Jonathan; for S, Joseph

Shebarim
Jos 7:5 before the gate as far as S

Shebat
Zec 1:7 month S, in the second year

She-bears
2Ki 2:24 two s came out from the

Sheber
1Ch 2:48 gave birth to S and Tirhanah

Shebna
Isa 22:15 steward, to S, who is over
36:3 S the secretary and Joah
36:11 and S and Joah said to
36:22 S the secretary and Joah the
37:2 S the secretary and the

Shebnah
2Ki 18:18 S the secretary and Joah
18:26 and S and Joah said to
18:37 and S the secretary and
19:2 S the secretary and the

Shebuel
1Ch 23:16 of Gershom were S the head
25:4 the sons of Heman . . . S and
26:24 even S the son of Gershom

She-camel
Jer 2:23 young s aimlessly running

She-camels
Isa 66:20 on mules and on swift s

Shecaniah
1Ch 3:21 the sons of Obadiah S
3:22 the sons of S, Shemaiah
24:11 the ninth, for S the tenth
2Ch 31:15 S, in the cities of the
Ezr 8:3 sons of S, of the sons of
8:5 S the son of Jahaziel, and
10:2 S the son of Jehiel of the
Ne 3:29 S, the keeper of the East Gate
6:18 S the son of Arah
12:3 S, Rehum, Meremoth

Shechem
Ge 12:6 as far as the site of S, near
33:18 to the city of S, which is
33:19 Hamor the father of S, for
34:2 And S the son of Hamor the
34:4 S said to Hamor his father
34:8 As for S my son, his soul is
34:11 S said to her father and to
34:13 began to answer S and Hamor
34:18 in the eyes of S, Hamor's
34:20 So Hamor and S his son went
34:24 listened to Hamor and to S
34:26 and S his son they killed
35:4 big tree that was close by S
37:12 feed the flock . . . close by S
37:13 tending flocks close by S
37:14 and he went on toward S
Nu 26:31 of S the family of the
Jos 17:2 the sons of S and the sons of
17:7 which is in front of S
20:7 S in the mountainous region
21:21 S, and its pasture ground
24:1 Israel together at S and to
24:25 and judicial decision in S
24:32 they buried in S in the
Jg 8:31 concubine . . . that was in S
9:1 went to S to the brothers of
9:2 the landowners of S, Which is
9:3 the landowners of S so that
9:6 landowners of S and all the
9:6 the pillar that was in S
9:7 landowners of S, and let God
9:18 king over the landowners of S
Jg 9:20 consume the landowners of S
9:20 landowners of S and the house
9:23 the landowners of S, and the
9:23 landowners of S proceeded to
9:24 landowners of S because they
9:25 landowners of S set ambush
9:26 crossed over into S, and the
9:26 the landowners of S began to
9:28 who is S that we should serve
9:31 come to S, and here they are
9:34 lie in wait against S in four
9:39 landowners of S and took up
9:41 out from dwelling in S
9:46 the tower of S heard of it, they
9:47 the tower of S had collected
9:49 men of the tower of S died
9:57 the evil of the men of S God
21:19 goes up from Bethel to S and
1Ki 12:1 proceeded to go to S
12:1 to S that all Israel came to
12:25 build S in the mountainous
1Ch 6:67 cities of refuge, S with its
7:19 the sons of Shemida . . . S
7:28 S and its dependent towns
2Ch 10:1 proceeded to go to S, for it
10:1 to S that all the Israelites
Ps 60:6 give out S as a portion
108:7 give out S as a portion
Jer 41:5 came men from S, from
Ho 6:9 they commit murder at S
Ac 7:16 they were transferred to S
7:16 from the sons of Hamor in S

Shechemites
Nu 26:31 Shechem the family of the S

Shechem's
Ge 34:6 Hamor, S father, went out to
34:26 took Dinah from S house and
Jos 24:32 of Hamor, S father, for a
Jg 9:28 men of Hamor, S father, you

Shed
Ge 9:6 man will his own blood be s
50:3 s tears for him seventy days
Le 17:4 He has s blood, and that man
De 17:8 in which blood has been s
21:7 Our hands did not s this blood
21:7 neither did our eyes see it s
1Ki 2:31 the blood undeservedly s that
2Ki 21:16 blood that Manasseh s in
24:4 innocent blood that he had s
Ps 79:10 blood of your servants . . . s
Pr 1:16 keep hastening to s blood
Isa 59:7 a hurry to s innocent blood
60:1 O woman, s forth light
Jer 7:6 blood you will not s in this
13:17 and will positively s tears
22:3 do not s any innocent blood
22:17 in order to s it, and upon
Eze 22:4 blood that you have s you
Joe 3:19 they s innocent blood
Ro 3:15 feet are speedy to s blood
Col 1:20 the blood he s on the torture
2Ti 1:10 has s light upon life and
Re 22:5 Jehovah God will s light

Shedder
Eze 18:10 a s of blood, who has done

Shedders
Eze 23:45 for female s of blood

Shedding
Ge 9:6 Anyone s man's blood, by man
1Sa 25:31 s of blood without cause
2Ch 19:10 involving the s of blood
Pr 6:17 that are s innocent blood
Eze 16:38 and women s blood, and I
22:3 O city that is s blood in
22:6 for the purpose of s blood
22:9 for the purpose of s blood
22:12 for the purpose of s blood
22:27 tearing prey in s blood
Hab 2:8 the s of blood of mankind and
2:17 the s of blood of mankind

Shedeur
Nu 1:5 Elizur the son of S
2:10 is Elizur the son of S
7:30 Elizur the son of S
7:35 of Elizur the son of S
10:18 Elizur the son of S was over

Sheep
Ge 4:2 Abel came to be a herder of s
12:16 he came to have s and cattle
13:5 Lot . . . owned s and cattle
Ge 20:14 Abimelech took s and cattle
21:27 Abraham took s and cattle
22:7 where is the s for the burnt
22:8 s for the burnt offering, my
24:35 giving him s and cattle and
26:14 he came to have flocks of s
29:2 three droves of s were lying
29:6 Rachel . . . coming with the s
29:7 Water the s, then go feed
29:8 Then we must water the s
29:9 Rachel came with the s that
29:10 the s of Laban his mother's
29:10 watered the s of Laban
30:32 s speckled and with color
30:32 and every dark-brown s among
31:19 Laban had gone to shear his s
31:38 female s and your she-goats
32:5 have bulls and asses, s, and
32:14 two hundred female s and
33:13 s and cattle that are giving
37:2 tending s with his brothers
38:12 up to the shearers of his s
38:13 to Timnah to shear his s
46:34 every herder of s is a
47:3 Your servants are herders of s
Ex 10:9 with our s and our cattle we
10:24 your s and your cattle will
12:3 a s for the ancestral house
12:3 a s to a house
12:4 to be too small for the s
12:4 to his eating as regards the s
12:5 s should prove to be sound, a
13:13 you are to redeem with a s
22:1 steal a bull or a s and he
22:1 four of the flock for the s
22:4 from bull to ass and to s
22:9 a s, a garment, anything lost
22:10 s or any domestic animal to
22:30 do with your bull and your s
34:19 firstling of bull and of s
34:20 are to redeem with a s
Le 5:7 cannot afford enough for a s
12:8 cannot afford enough for a s
22:23 s having a member too long
22:28 s, you must not slaughter it
27:26 or s, it belongs to Jehovah
Nu 22:40 to sacrifice cattle and s and
27:17 like s that have no shepherd
De 14:4 the bull, the s and the goat
14:5 and wild s and chamois
14:26 s and goats and wine and
17:1 a bull or a s in which there
18:3 victim, whether a bull or a s
22:1 his s straying about and
28:31 Your s given to your enemies
32:14 male s, the breed of Bashan
Jos 6:21 and to bull and s and ass
Jg 6:4 or s or bull or ass remain in
1Sa 14:32 and taking s and cattle and
14:34 each one, his s, and you
15:3 bull as well as s, camel as
15:21 taking from the spoil s
16:11 look! he is pasturing the s
17:15 to tend the s of his father
17:20 the s to the keeper's charge
17:28 did you leave those few s
17:34 each carried off a s from
22:19 and s with the edge of the
25:2 he had three thousand s and
25:2 shearing his s at Carmel
25:4 Nabal was shearing his s
25:18 five s dressed and
2Sa 12:2 have very many s and cattle
12:4 taking some from his own s
17:29 s and curds of cattle they
24:17 these s—what have they done?
1Ki 1:9 Adonijah held a sacrifice of s
1:19 s in great quantity and
1:25 bulls and fatlings and s in
4:23 a hundred s, besides some
8:5 sacrificing s and cattle that
8:63 and twenty thousand s
22:17 s that have no shepherd
2Ki 3:4 he became a s raiser, and he
3:4 thousand unshorn male s
5:26 vineyards or s or cattle or
1Ch 5:21 and s two hundred and fifty
12:40 and s in great quantity, for
21:17 these s, what have they
2Ch 5:6 sacrificing s and cattle that
7:5 hundred and twenty thousand s
15:11 and seven thousand s
18:2 sacrifice s and cattle in
18:16 like s that have no shepherd

2Ch 30:24 seven thousand s, and the
30:24 bulls and ten thousand s
31:6 tenth of cattle and s and the
Ne 3:1 get up and build the S Gate
3:32 the S Gate the goldsmiths and
5:18 six select s and birds
12:39 and on to the S Gate
Job 1:3 got to be seven thousand s and
1:16 went blazing among the s and
42:12 have fourteen thousand s and
Ps 44:11 You give us up like s
44:22 as s for slaughtering
49:14 Like s they have been
95:7 and the s of his hand
100:3 and the s of his pasturage
119:176 wandered like a lost s
Isa 7:21 cow of the herd and two s
7:25 and a trampling ground of s
22:13 the slaughtering of s, the
43:23 the s of your whole burnt
51:20 like the wild s in the net
53:6 Like s we have all of us
53:7 like a s to the slaughtering
65:10 a pasture ground for s and
66:3 The one sacrificing the s is
Jer 12:3 like s for the slaughtering
23:1 scattering the s of my
23:2 have scattered my s; and you
23:3 remnant of my s out of all
50:17 Israel is a scattered s
51:40 them down like male s
Eze 24:5 a taking of the choicest s
34:6 My s kept straying on all
34:6 my s were scattered, with
34:8 reason that my s became
34:8 s continued to be food for
34:8 did not search for my s
34:8 my own s they did not feed
34:10 my s from their hand and
34:10 cease from feeding my s
34:10 deliver my s out of their
34:11 I will search for my s and
34:12 in the midst of his s that
34:12 that I shall care for my s
34:15 I myself shall feed my s
34:17 And as for you my s, this
34:17, 17 between a s and a s
34:19 as for my s, on the pasture
34:20, 20 a plump s and a lean s
34:22 I will save my s, and they
34:22, 22 between a s and a s
34:31 And as regards you my s
34:31 the s of my pasturing, you
39:18 rams, young male s, and
45:15 one s out of the flock, out
Ho 12:12 and for a wife he guarded s
Joe 1:18 the s have been the ones
Am 1:1 the s raisers from Tekoa
Mic 5:8 young lion among droves of s
Zep 2:6 and stone pens for s
Zec 11:16 To the s being effaced he
11:16 broken s he will not heal
11:16 hoofs of the s he will tear
Mt 9:36 like s without a shepherd
10:6 lost s of the house of Israel
10:16 forth as s amidst wolves
12:11 has one s and, if this falls
12:12 worth is a man than a s
15:24 the lost s . . . of Israel
18:12 comes to have a hundred s
25:32 separates the s from the
25:33 put the s on his right hand
26:31 the s of the flock will be
Mr 6:34 were as s without a shepherd
14:27 the s will be scattered
Lu 15:4 hundred s, on losing one of
15:6 found my s that was lost
Joh 2:14 selling cattle and s and
2:15 drove all those with the s
10:2 is shepherd of the s
10:3 s listen to his voice, and
10:3 calls his own s by name and
10:4 s follow him, because they
10:7 I am the door of the s
10:8 s have not listened to them
10:11 his soul in behalf of the s
10:12 s do not belong as his own
10:12 and abandons the s and flees
10:13 and does not care for the s
10:14 and I know my s and my
10:14 and my s know me
10:15 my soul in behalf of the s
10:16 I have other s, which are
10:26 you are none of my s
Joh 10:27 My s listen to my voice
21:16 Shepherd my little s
21:17 to him: Feed my little s
Ac 8:32 As a s he was brought to the
Ro 8:36 as s for slaughtering
Heb 13:20 the great shepherd of the s
1Pe 2:25 were like s, going astray
Re 18:13 cattle and s, and horses and

Sheepfold
Joh 10:1 enter into the s through the

Sheepfolds
1Sa 24:3 stone s along the road

Sheepgate
Joh 5:2 in Jerusalem at the s there

Sheep's
Mt 7:15 come to you in s covering

Sheepshearers
2Sa 13:23 Absalom came to have s at
13:24 now, your servant has s

Sheepskins
Heb 11:37 they went about in s, in

Sheer
Ps 24:4 My soul to s worthlessness
51:6 cause me to know s wisdom
62:10 become vain in s robbery
69:9 s zeal for your house has
Pr 1:16 those that run to s badness
Ec 2:14 stupid one . . . in s darkness
11:3 empty out a s downpour upon
Ca 5:16 His palate is s sweetness
Isa 10:1 written out s trouble
14:6 subduing nations in s anger
15:6 become s desolations
31:9 pass away out of s fright
50:11 In s pain you will lie down
59:3 muttering s unrighteousness
59:7 keep running to s badness
64:10 has become a s wilderness
65:14 howl because of s breakdown
66:15 his anger with s rage and
Jer 4:14 heart clean of s badness
4:27 carry out a s extermination
5:2 be swearing to s falsehood
8:8 has worked in s falsehood
16:19 came to possess s falsehood
49:24 and s panic has seized her
La 2:11 come to their end in s tears
Eze 35:4 become a s desolate waste
Lu 24:41 for s joy and were wondering

Sheerah
1Ch 7:24 And his daughter was S, and

Sheet
Isa 28:20 s itself is too narrow
Ac 10:11 linen s being let down by
11:5 great linen s being let down

Sheets
Ex 39:3 beat plates of gold to thin s

She-goat
Ge 15:9 and a three-year-old s and a

She-goats
Ge 30:32 speckled one among the s
30:33 not speckled . . . among the s
30:35 s speckled and color-patched
31:38 Your female sheep and your s
32:14 two hundred s and twenty

Shehariah
1Ch 8:26 and Shamsherai and S and

Sheik
Ge 36:15 sons of Eliphaz . . . S Teman
36:15 sons of Eliphaz . . . s Omar
36:15 sons of Eliphaz . . . s Zepho
36:15 sons of Eliphaz . . . s Kenaz
36:16 s Korah . . . of Edom
36:16 s Gatam . . . of Edom
36:16 s Amalek . . . of Edom
36:17 sons of Reuel . . . S Nahath
36:17 sons of Reuel . . . s Zerah
36:17 sons of Reuel . . . s Shammah
36:17 sons of Reuel . . . s Mizzah
36:18, 18 S Jeush, s Jalam
36:18 of Oholibamah . . . s Korah
36:29 sheiks of the Horite: S Lotan
36:29, 29 s Shobal, s Zibeon
36:29 of the Horite . . . s Anah
36:30, 30 s Dishon, s Ezer
36:30 s Dishan . . . of the Horite
36:40, 40 S Timna, s Alvah
Ge 36:40 sheiks of Esau . . . s Jetheth
36:41, 41 s Oholibamah, s Elah
36:41 Elah, s Pinon
36:42, 42 s Kenaz, s Teman
36:42 s Mibzar
36:43, 43 s Magdiel, s Iram
1Ch 1:51 sheiks of Edom . . . s Timna
1:51 sheiks of Edom . . . s Alvah
1:51 sheiks of Edom . . . s Jetheth
1:52, 52 s Oholibamah, s Elah
1:52 Elah, s Pinon
1:53, 53 s Kenaz, s Teman
1:53 Teman, s Mibzar
1:54 s Magdiel . . . sheiks of Edom
1:54 s Iram . . . sheiks of Edom
Zec 9:7 become like a s in Judah

Sheiks
Ge 36:15 the s of the sons of Esau
36:16 s of Eliphaz . . . of Edom
36:17 s of Reuel in the land of
36:18 the s of Oholibamah the
36:19 sons of Esau, and . . . their s
36:21 These are the s of the Horite
36:29 These are the s of the Horite
36:30 These are the s of the Horite
36:30 their s in the land of Seir
36:40 the names of the s of Esau
36:43 These are the s of Edom
Ex 15:15 the s of Edom will indeed be
1Ch 1:51 the s of Edom came to be
1:54 These were the s of Edom
Zec 12:5 s of Judah will have to say
12:6 I shall make the s of Judah

Shekel
Ge 24:22 ring of a half s in weight
Ex 30:13 a half s by the
30:13 by the s of the holy place
30:13 Twenty gerahs equal a s
30:13 half s is the contribution to
30:15 give less than the half s
30:24 five hundred units by the s
38:24 by the s of the holy place
38:25 by the s of the holy place
38:26 The half s for an individual
38:26 was the half of a s by the
38:26 by the s of the holy place
Le 5:15 by the s of the holy place
27:3 s of the holy place
27:25 in the s of the holy place
27:25 s should amount to twenty
Nu 3:47 s of the holy place you should
3:47 A s is twenty gerahs
3:50 in the s of the holy place
7:13 by the s of the holy place
7:19 by the s of the holy place
7:25 by the s of the holy place
7:31 by the s of the holy place
7:37 by the s of the holy place
7:43 by the s of the holy place
7:49 by the s of the holy place
7:55 by the s of the holy place
7:61 by the s of the holy place
7:67 by the s of the holy place
7:73 by the s of the holy place
7:79 by the s of the holy place
7:85 by the s of the holy place
7:86 by the s of the holy place
18:16 by the s of the holy place
1Sa 9:8 quarter of a s of silver found
2Ki 7:1 be worth a s, and two seah
7:1 worth a s in the gateway of
7:16 came to be worth a s, and
7:16 of barley worth a s
7:18 barley worth a s and a
7:18 fine flour worth a s
Ne 10:32 a third of a s yearly for the
Eze 45:12 the s is twenty gerahs
Am 8:5 to make the s great and to

Shekels
Ge 23:15 worth four hundred silver s
23:16 four hundred silver s
24:22 ten s of gold was their
Ex 21:32 price of thirty s to that
38:24 seven hundred and thirty s by
38:25 seventy-five s by the shekel
38:28 s he made pegs for the
38:29 two thousand four hundred s
Le 5:15 estimated value in silver s
27:3 fifty s of silver by the
27:4 must then become thirty s
27:5 must then become twenty s
27:5 and for the female ten s

Le 27:6 then become five s of silver
27:6 must be three s of silver
27:7 fifteen s and for the female
27:7 and for the female ten s
27:16 then at fifty s of silver
Nu 3:47 must take five s for each
3:50 three hundred and sixty-five s
7:13 hundred and thirty s, one
7:13 silver bowl of seventy s by
7:14 gold cup of ten s, full of
7:19 a hundred and thirty s, one
7:19 silver bowl of seventy s by
7:20 gold cup of ten s, full of
7:25 a hundred and thirty s, one
7:25 silver bowl of seventy s by
7:26 gold cup of ten s, full of
7:31 a hundred and thirty s, one
7:31 silver bowl of seventy s by
7:32 gold cup of ten s, full of
7:37 a hundred and thirty s, one
7:37 silver bowl of seventy s by
7:38 gold cup of ten s, full of
7:43 a hundred and thirty s, one
7:43 one silver bowl of seventy s
7:44 gold cup of ten s, full of
7:49 a hundred and thirty s, one
7:49 silver bowl of seventy s by
7:50 gold cup of ten s, full of
7:55 being a hundred and thirty s
7:55 silver bowl of seventy s by
7:56 gold cup of ten s, full of
7:61 being a hundred and thirty s
7:61 silver bowl of seventy s by
7:62 gold cup of ten s, full of
7:67 being a hundred and thirty s
7:67 silver bowl of seventy s by
7:68 gold cup of ten s, full of
7:73 a hundred and thirty s, one
7:73 silver bowl of seventy s by
7:74 gold cup of ten s, full of
7:79 being a hundred and thirty s
7:79 silver bowl of seventy s by
7:80 gold cup of ten s, full of
7:85 a hundred and thirty s to
7:85 two thousand four hundred s
7:86 ten s respectively to a cup
7:86 being a hundred and twenty s
18:16 five silver s by the shekel
31:52 seven hundred and fifty s
De 22:19 fine him a hundred silver s
22:29 fifty silver s, and she
Jos 7:21 two hundred s of silver and
7:21 fifty s being its weight
Jg 8:26 gold s, besides the
1Sa 17:5 five thousand s of copper
17:7 was six hundred s of iron
2Sa 14:26 two hundred s by the royal
21:16 three hundred s of copper
24:24 for fifty silver s
1Ki 10:16 six hundred s of gold he
2Ki 15:20 fifty silver s for each man
1Ch 21:25 gold s to the weight of six
2Ch 3:9 the nails was fifty gold s
9:15 six hundred s of alloyed
Ne 5:15 daily forty silver s
Jer 32:9 seven s and ten silver pieces
Eze 4:10 be by weight—twenty s a day
45:12 Twenty s, twenty-five
45:12 twenty-five s, fifteen
45:12 fifteen s should prove to

Shelah
Ge 10:24 Arpachshad . . . father to S
10:24 S became father to Eber
11:12 Arpachshad . . . father to S
11:13 fathering S Arpachshad
11:14 And S lived thirty years
11:15 after his fathering Eber S
38:5 and then called his name S
38:11 until S my son grows up
38:14 she saw that S had grown up
38:26 I did not give her to S my
46:12 the sons of Judah were . . . S
Nu 26:20 Of S the family of the
1Ch 1:18 he became father to S, and
1:18 S himself became father to
1:24 Shem, Arpachshad, S
2:3 The sons of Judah were . . . S
4:21 S the son of Judah
Lu 3:35 Peleg, son of Eber, son of S

Shelanite
Ne 11:5 Zechariah the son of the S

Shelanites
Nu 26:20 Shelah the family of the S

Shelemiah
1Ch 26:14 lot to the east fell to S
Ezr 10:39 S and Nathan and Adaiah
10:41 Azarel and S, Shemariah
Ne 3:30 Hananiah the son of S and
13:13 S the priest and Zadok the
Jer 36:14 Nethaniah the son of S
36:26 S the son of Abdeel to
37:3 Jehucal the son of S and
37:13 Irijah the son of S the
38:1 Jucal the son of S and

Sheleph
Ge 10:26 Joktan became father . . . S
1Ch 1:20 father to Almodad and S and

Shelesh
1Ch 7:35 the sons of Helem . . . S and

Shells
Isa 3:20 the ornamental humming s

Shelomi
Nu 34:27 Ahihud the son of S

Shelomith
Le 24:11 his mother's name was S, the
1Ch 3:19 and S was their sister
23:18 of Izhar were S the headman
26:28 under the control of S and
2Ch 11:20 and Attai and Ziza and S
Ezr 8:10 S the son of Josiphiah, and

Shelomoth
1Ch 23:9 sons of Shimei were S and
24:22 of the Izharites, S; of the
24:22 of the sons of S, Jahath
26:25 Zichri his son and S his son
26:26 S and his brothers were

Shelter
Ex 9:19 all your livestock . . . under s
Nu 14:9 Their s has turned away from
Job 24:8 no s they have to hug a rock
Ps 52:7 takes s in adversities by him
118:14 Jah is my s and my might
Isa 4:5 the glory there will be a s
10:31 themselves have taken to s
30:2 s in the stronghold of
Jer 4:6 Make provision for s. Do not
6:1 s, O you sons of Benjamin
Ac 27:4 sailed under the s of Cyprus
27:7 sailed under the s of Crete
27:16 s of a certain small island

Sheltered
Pr 27:16 has s the wind, and oil is

Sheltering
Pr 27:16 s her has sheltered the wind

Shelters
De 33:12 he s him the whole day

Shelumiel
Nu 1:6 S the son of Zurishaddai
2:12 S the son of Zurishaddai
7:36 S the son of Zurishaddai
7:41 of S the son of Zurishaddai
10:19 S the son of Zurishaddai

Shem
Ge 5:32 Noah became father to S, Ham
6:10 father to three sons, S, Ham
7:13 Noah went in, and S and Ham
9:18 Noah's sons . . . were S and Ham
9:23 S and Japheth took a mantle
9:27 reside in the tents of S
10:1 history of Noah's sons, S
10:21 to S, the forefather of all
10:22 sons of S were Elam and
10:31 sons of S according to their
11:10 This is the history of S
11:10 S was a hundred years old
11:11 S . . . five hundred years
1Ch 1:4 Noah, S, Ham and Japheth
1:17 sons of S were Elam and
1:24 S, Arpachshad, Shelah
Lu 3:36 son of S, son of Noah, son of

Shema
Jos 15:26 Amam and S and Moladah
1Ch 2:43 sons of Hebron were . . . S
2:44 S, in turn, became father to
5:8 the son of S the son of Joel
8:13 and Beriah and S. These were
Ne 8:4 and S and Anaiah and Uriah

Shemaah
1Ch 12:3 the sons of S the Gibeathite

Shemaiah
1Ki 12:22 S the man of the true God
1Ch 3:22 the sons of Shecaniah, S
3:22 the sons of S, Hattush and
4:37 Shimri the son of S
5:4 The sons of Joel were S
9:14 of the Levites there were S
9:16 son of S the son of Galal the
15:8 of the sons of Elizaphan, S
15:11 Levites . . . S and Eliel and
24:6 S the son of Nethanel the
26:4 Obed-edom had sons: S the
26:6 to S his son there were sons
26:7 sons of S, Othni and Rephael
2Ch 11:2 word of Jehovah came to S
12:5 S the prophet, he came to
12:7 word of Jehovah came to S
12:15 words of S the prophet and
17:8 Levites, S and Nethaniah
29:14 sons of Jeduthun, S and
31:15 and S . . . in office of trust
35:9 S and Nethanel his brothers
Ezr 8:13 sons of Adonikam . . . S, and
8:16 sent for Eliezer, Ariel, S
10:21 sons of Harim . . . S
10:31 the sons of Harim . . . S
Ne 3:29 S the son of Shecaniah
6:10 house of S the son of Delaiah
10:8 and S, these being the priests
11:15 S the son of Hasshub the son
12:6 S, and Joiarib, Jedaiah
12:18 Shammua; for S, Jehonathan
12:34 Benjamin and S and Jeremiah
12:35 S the son of Mattaniah the
12:36 his brothers S and Azarel
12:42 and Maaseiah and S, and
Jer 26:20 Urijah the son of S from
29:24 to S of Nehelam you will
29:31 concerning S of Nehelam
29:31 S has prophesied to you
29:32 turning my attention upon S
36:12 Delaiah the son of S and

Shemariah
1Ch 12:5 and S and Shephatiah the
2Ch 11:19 Jeush and S and Zaham
Ezr 10:32 Benjamin, Malluch and S
10:41 Azarel and Shelemiah, S

Shemeber
Ge 14:2 S king of Zeboiim, and the

Shemed
1Ch 8:12 S, who built Ono and Lod and

Shemer
1Ki 16:24 from S for two talents of
16:24 name of S the master of the
1Ch 6:46 the son of Bani, the son of S
7:34 the sons of S were Ahi and

Shemida
Nu 26:32 of S the family of the
Jos 17:2 and the sons of S
1Ch 7:19 sons of S came to be Ahian

Shemidaites
Nu 26:32 Shemida the family of the S

Sheminith
1Ch 15:21 with harps tuned to S, to

Shemiramoth
1Ch 15:18 and S and Jehiel and Unni
15:20 and Aziel and S and Jehiel
16:5 Jeiel and S and Jehiel and
2Ch 17:8 and S and Jehonathan and

Shem's
Ge 9:26 Blessed be Jehovah, S God

Shemuel
Nu 34:20 of Simeon, S the son of
1Ch 7:2 sons of Tola . . . Ibsam and S

She-mule
1Ki 1:33 my son ride upon the s that
1:38 upon the s of King David
1:44 ride upon the s of the king

Shenazzar
1Ch 3:18 and S, Jekamiah, Hoshama

Sheol
Ge 37:35 mourning to my son into S
42:38 gray hairs with grief to S
44:29 hairs with calamity to S
44:31 our father with grief to S

Nu 16:30 have to go down alive into S
16:33 alive into S, and the earth
De 32:22 And it will burn down to S
1Sa 2:6 A Bringer down to S, and He
2Sa 22:6 The ropes of S themselves
1Ki 2:6 hairs go down in peace to S
2:9 his gray hairs down to S with
Job 7:9 So he that is going down to S
11:8 It is deeper than S
14:13 in S you would conceal me
17:13 keep waiting, S is my house
17:16 the bars of S they will go
21:13 in a moment down to S they
24:19 S those who have sinned
26:6 S is naked in front of him
Ps 6:5 In S who will laud you?
9:17 people will turn back to S
16:10 will not leave my soul in S
18:5 ropes of S surrounded me
30:3 my soul from S itself
31:17 May they keep silent in S
49:14 have been appointed to S
49:14 S rather than a lofty abode
49:15 my soul from the hand of S
55:15 Let them go down into S
86:13 delivered my soul out of S
88:3 has come in touch even with S
89:48 his soul from the hand of S
116:3 circumstances of S
139:8 spread out my couch in S
141:7 scattered at the mouth of S
Pr 1:12 them down alive just like S
5:5 Her very steps take hold on S
7:27 ways to S her house is
9:18 are in the low places of S
15:11 S . . . in front of Jehovah
15:24 in order to turn away from S
23:14 deliver his very soul from S
27:20 S and the place of
30:16 S and a restrained womb, a
Ec 9:10 knowledge nor wisdom in S
Ca 8:6 devotion is as unyielding as S
Isa 5:14 S has made its soul spacious
7:11 making it as deep as S or
14:9 S underneath has become
14:11 Down to S your pride has
14:15 down to S you will be
28:15 S we have effected a vision
28:18 vision of yours with S
38:10 will go into the gates of S
38:18 is not S that can laud you
57:9 you lowered matters to S
Eze 31:15 day of its going down to S
31:16 when I bring it down to S
31:17 also have gone down to S
32:21 speak out of the midst of S
32:27 who have gone down to S
Ho 13:14 From the hand of S I shall
13:14 your destructiveness, O S
Am 9:2 If they dig down into S, from
Jon 2:2 Out of the belly of S I cried
Hab 2:5 his soul spacious just like S

Shepham
Nu 34:10 from Hazar-enan to S
34:11 from S to Riblah on the east

Shephatiah
2Sa 3:4 fifth was S the son of Abital
1Ch 3:3 the fifth, S, of Abital
9:8 son of S the son of Reuel the
12:5 and S the Hariphite
27:16 of the Simeonites, S the
2Ch 21:2 Jehoshaphat's sons . . . S, all
Ezr 2:4 sons of S, three hundred and
2:57 the sons of S
8:8 of the sons of S, Zebadiah the
Ne 7:9 sons of S, three hundred and
7:59 the sons of S, the sons of
11:4 S the son of Mahalalel
Jer 38:1 S the son of Mattan and

Shephelah
De 1:7 the S and the Negeb and the
Jos 9:1 in the S and along the whole
10:40 and the Negeb and the S and
11:2 Chinnereth and in the S and
11:16 the S and the Arabah and
11:16 region of Israel and its S
12:8 in the S and in the Arabah
15:33 In the S there were Eshtaol
Jg 1:9 and the Negeb and the S
1Ki 10:27 in the S for great quantity
1Ch 27:28 trees that were in the S
2Ch 1:15 trees that are in the S for
2Ch 9:27 trees that are in the S for
26:10 the S and on the tableland
28:18 upon the cities of the S
Ob 19 region of Esau, and of the S
Zec 7:7 and the S were inhabited

Shepher
Nu 33:23 and went camping in Mount S
33:24 pulled away from Mount S

Shepherd
Ge 49:24 the s, the stone of Israel
Ex 3:1 Moses became a s of the flock
Nu 27:17 like sheep that have no s
1Sa 17:34 Your servant became a s of
2Sa 5:2 s my people Israel, and you
7:7 s my people Israel, saying
1Ki 22:17 like sheep that have no s
1Ch 11:2 will s my people Israel, and
17:6 I commanded to s my people
2Ch 18:16 like sheep that have no s
Job 24:2 that they may s it
Ps 23:1 Jehovah is my S. I shall lack
28:9 s them and carry them to
49:14 Death itself will s them
78:71 be a s over Jacob his people
78:72 s them according to the
80:1 O S of Israel, do give ear
Ec 12:11 have been given from one s
Ca 6:2 to s among the gardens, and to
Isa 40:11 Like a s he will
40:11 he will s his own drove
44:28 of Cyrus, He is my s
61:5 s the flocks of you people
Jer 17:16 being a s following you
22:22 A wind will s all your own
23:4 who will actually s them
31:10 as a s does his drove
43:12 s wraps himself up in his
49:19 s that can stand before me
50:44 s that can stand before me
51:23 dash s and his drove to
Eze 34:5 because of there being no s
34:8 because there was no s
34:23 raise up over them one s
34:23 will become their s
37:24 one s is what they will all
Ho 4:16 s them like a young ram in
Am 3:12 the s snatches away from the
Mic 5:6 s the land of Assyria with
7:14 S your people with your
Zec 10:2 because there is no s
11:4 S the flock meant for the
11:7 s the flock meant for the
11:15 implements of a useless s
11:16 a s rise up in the land
11:17 Woe to my valueless s, who
13:7 O sword, awake against my s
13:7 Strike the s, and let those
Mt 2:6 who will s my people, Israel
9:36 about like sheep without a s
25:32 s separates the sheep from
26:31 I will strike the s, and the
Mr 6:34 were as sheep without a s
14:27 I will strike the s, and the
Joh 10:2 is s of the sheep
10:11 I am the fine s; the fine
10:11 fine s surrenders his soul
10:12 hired man, who is no s and
10:14 I am the fine s, and I
10:16 become one flock, one s
21:16 to him: S my little sheep
Ac 20:28 to s the congregation of God
Heb 13:20 from the dead the great s
1Pe 2:25 s and overseer of your souls
5:2 S the flock of God in your
5:4 chief s has been made
Re 2:27 s the people with an iron
7:17 will s them, and will guide
12:5 s all the nations with an
19:15 s them with a rod of iron

Shepherdess
Ge 29:9 Rachel . . . was a s

Shepherding
Ge 30:31 I shall resume s your flock
30:36 Jacob was s the flocks of
48:15 God who has been s me during
1Sa 25:16 be with them, s the flock
Ca 1:7 where you do s, where you
2:16 He is s among the lilies
6:3 He is s among the lilies
Jer 23:2 who are s my people
Mic 5:4 s in the strength of Jehovah
Zec 11:7 and I went s the flock
Zec 11:9 I shall not keep s you

Shepherds
Ge 26:20 s of Gerar fell to quarreling
26:20 the s of Isaac, saying
46:32 the men are s, because they
Ex 2:17 s came and drove them away
2:19 us out of the hand of the s
Nu 14:33 s in the wilderness forty
1Sa 21:7 principal one of the s that
25:7 s that belong to you happened
2Ki 10:12 binding house of the s
Ca 1:8 the tabernacles of the s
Isa 13:20 s will let their flocks lie
31:4 a full number of s, and in
38:12 from me like the tent of s
56:11 They are also s that have
63:11 with the s of his flock
Jer 2:8 s themselves transgressed
3:15 give you s in agreement with
6:3 the s and their droves
10:21 s have behaved unreasoningly
12:10 Many s themselves have
22:22 shepherd all your own s
23:1 the s who are destroying and
23:2 said against the s who are
23:4 I will raise up over them s
25:34 Howl, you s, and cry out!
25:35 has perished from the s
25:36 The outcry of the s, and
33:12 s who are making the flock
50:6 own s have caused them to
Eze 34:2 against the s of Israel
34:2 say to them, to the s
34:2 Woe to the s of Israel
34:2 that the s ought to feed
34:7 s, hear the word of Jehovah
34:8 s did not search for my
34:8 s kept feeding themselves
34:9 s, hear the word of Jehovah
34:10 I am against the s, and
34:10 the s will no longer feed
Am 1:2 the pasture grounds of the s
Mic 5:5 seven s, yes, eight dukes
Na 3:18 Your s have become drowsy
Zep 2:6 with wells for s and stone
Zec 10:3 Against the s my anger has
11:3 The howling of s, for their
11:5 s do not show any compassion
11:8 effaced three s in one lunar
Lu 2:8 s living out of doors and
2:15 the s began saying to one
2:18 things told them by the s
2:20 the s went back, glorifying
1Co 9:7 who s a flock and does not
Eph 4:11 some as s and teachers
Jude 12 s that feed themselves

Shepherds'
1Sa 17:40 to place them in his s bag

Shepho
Ge 36:23 sons of Shobal . . . S and
1Ch 1:40 sons of Shobal were . . . S

Shephupham
Nu 26:39 of S the family of the

Shephuphan
1Ch 8:5 and Gera and S and Huram

Sherebiah
Ezr 8:18 S and his sons and his
8:24 S, Hashabiah, and with them
Ne 8:7 S, Jamin, Akkub, Shabbethai
9:4 Bunni, S, Bani and Chenani
9:5 And the Levites . . . S
10:12 Zaccur, S, Shebaniah
12:8 S, Judah, Mattaniah
12:24 S and Jeshua the son of

Sheresh
1Ch 7:16 name of his brother was S

Sheshach
Jer 25:26 the king of S himself will
51:41 how S has been captured

Sheshai
Nu 13:22 Ahiman, S and Talmai, those
Jos 15:14 sons of Anak, namely, S and
Jg 1:10 they went striking down S

Sheshan
1Ch 2:31 the sons of Ishi were S
2:31 the sons of S, Ahlai
2:34 S came to have no sons, but
2:34 S had an Egyptian servant
2:35 S gave his daughter to Jarha

Jer 50:14 S at her. Spare no arrow
Eze 8:17 thrusting out the s to my
15:2 the s, that has come to be

Shooters
1Sa 31:3 s, the bowmen, finally found
31:3 severely wounded by the s
2Sa 11:24 s kept shooting at your
1Ch 10:3 and he got wounded by the s
2Ch 22:5 s got to strike Jehoram
35:23 s got to shoot at King
Ps 78:9 Ephraim, though armed s
Jer 4:29 the horsemen and bow s

Shooting
1Sa 20:36 find the arrows that I am s
2Sa 11:24 s at your servants from on
1Ch 10:3 those s with the bow finally
Ps 7:12 he will make it ready for s
Pr 26:18 mad that is s fiery missiles

Shoots
Ge 40:10 was apparently sprouting s
2Ki 19:29 grain that s up of itself
Isa 16:8 s had been left to luxuriate
37:30 grain that s up of itself
Jer 2:21 s of a foreign vine
5:10 Take away her luxuriating s
48:32 flourishing s have crossed
Eze 17:4 the very top of its young s
17:6 became a vine and produced s
19:14 It devoured her very s, her
Na 2:2 the s of them they have ruined

Shophach
1Ch 19:16 S the chief of the army of
19:18 and S the chief of the army

Shore
Ge 49:13 by the s where the ships lie
1Ki 9:26 the s of the Red Sea in the
2Ki 2:13 stood by the s of the Jordan
2Ch 8:17 Eloth upon the s of the sea
Mr 4:1 the crowd . . . were on the s
4:35 Let us cross to the other s
5:21 in the boat to the opposite s
6:45 opposite s toward Bethsaida
8:13 went off to the opposite s
Lu 8:26 put in to s in the country

Shoreland
Nu 34:6 the Great Sea and the s
Jos 15:12 the Great Sea and its s

Shorn
De 18:4 the first of the s wool of
Job 31:20 s wool of my young rams he
1Co 11:6 let her also be s; but if it
11:6 a woman to be s or shaved

Short
Le 19:27 not cut your sidelocks s
22:23 having a member . . . too s
Nu 11:23 hand of Jehovah is cut s
Job 20:5 cry of wicked people is s
Ps 102:23 He cut s my days
Pr 10:27 wicked ones will be cut s
Isa 28:20 couch has proved too s for
50:2 hand become . . . so s that it
59:1 has not become too s that it
Mt 24:22 unless those days were cut s
24:22 those days will be cut s
Mr 13:20 Jehovah had cut s the days
13:20 he has cut s the days
Lu 22:58 after a s time another
Joh 2:3 When the wine ran s the
5:35 for a s time were willing
Ac 18:18 hair of his head clipped s in
26:28 a s time you would persuade
26:29 a s time or in a long time
27:28 proceeded a s distance and
Ro 3:23 fall s of the glory of God
9:28 it and cutting it s
1Co 1:7 not fall s in any gift at all
8:8 we do not fall s, and, if we
1Th 2:17 for but a s time, in person
Heb 4:1 seem to have fallen s of it
Re 12:12 he has a s period of time
17:10 he must remain a s while

Shortage
Ex 16:18 had gathered little had no s
Ne 5:3 get grain during the food s
Re 6:8 food s and with deadly plague

Shortages
Mt 24:7 and there will be food s and
Mr 13:8 there will be food s
Lu 21:11 pestilences and food s; and

Shortened
Ps 89:45 have s the days of his youth

Shorter
Eze 42:5 the uppermost ones were s

Short-lived
Job 14:1 Man, born of woman, is s

Shortly
Eze 7:8 s I shall pour out my rage
Lu 8:1 S afterwards he went
Ac 25:4 about to depart s for there
Ro 16:20 crush Satan under your feet s
1Co 4:19 But I will come to you s, if
Php 2:19 to send Timothy to you s
2:24 I myself shall also come s
1Ti 3:14 am hoping to come to you s
2Ti 4:9 your utmost to come to me s
Re 1:1 things that must s take place
22:6 things that must s take place

Shot
Ge 49:23 s at him and kept harboring
Ex 19:13 will positively be s through
1Sa 20:36 s the arrow to make it pass
20:37 arrow that Jonathan had s
2Ki 13:17 Elisha said: Shoot! So he s
Ps 18:14 lightnings he s out, that

Shoulder
Ge 21:14 setting it upon her s, and
24:15 her water jar was upon her s
24:45 with her jar upon her s; and
48:22 one s of land more than
49:15 his s to bear burdens and he
Ex 12:34 in their mantles upon their s
28:7 two s pieces to be joined at
28:12 the s pieces of the ephod
28:12 upon his two s pieces as a
28:25 the s pieces of the ephod
28:27 two s pieces of the ephod
39:4 s pieces for it that were
39:7 the s pieces of the ephod as
39:18 the s pieces of the ephod, at
39:20 two s pieces of the ephod
Nu 6:19 take a boiled s from the ram
7:9 did their carrying on the s
De 18:3 give to the priest the s blade
Jos 4:5 each one a stone upon his s
Jg 9:48 put it on his s and said to
1Sa 10:9 he turned his s to go from
2Ch 35:3 as a burden upon the s
Ne 9:29 they kept giving a stubborn s
Job 31:22 Let my own s blade fall
31:22 blade fall from its s
31:36 upon my s I would carry it
Ps 81:6 his s even from the burden
Isa 9:6 will come to be upon his s
10:27 depart from upon your s
11:14 the s of the Philistines
14:25 depart from upon their s
22:22 house of David upon his s
46:7 They carry it upon the s
49:22 upon the s they will carry
Eze 12:6 do the carrying on the s
12:7 On my s I did the carrying
12:12 the s he will do carrying
24:4 thigh and s; fill it even
29:7 a split in their entire s
29:18 every s was one rubbed bare
34:21 with flank and with s you
Zep 3:9, 9 to serve him s to s
Zec 7:11 they kept giving a stubborn s

Shoulders
Ge 9:23 put it upon both their s and
De 33:12 he must reside between his s
Jg 16:3 his s and went carrying them
1Sa 9:2 s upward he was taller than
10:23 from his s upward
17:6 a javelin . . . between his s
1Ch 15:15 upon their s with the rods
Isa 9:4 and the rod upon their s
30:6 s of full-grown asses they
Mt 23:4 put them upon the s of men
Lu 15:5 he puts it upon his s and

Shout
Jos 6:5 should s a great war cry
6:10 neither s nor let your voices
6:10, 10 S! Then you must s
6:16 S; for Jehovah has given you
6:20 began to s a great war cry
1Sa 10:24 s and say: Let the king live!
17:20 raised a s for the battle
Ezr 3:11 loud s in praising Jehovah
Ezr 3:13 sound of the s of rejoicing
3:13 were shouting with a loud s
Job 30:5 s at them as at a thief
Ps 41:11 enemy does not s in triumph
47:1 S in triumph to God with the
60:8 Over Philistia I shall s in
65:13 They s in triumph, yes, they
66:1 S in triumph to God, all you
81:1 S in triumph to the God of
95:1 s in triumph to our Rock of
95:2 melodies s in triumph to him
98:4 S in triumph to Jehovah, all
98:6 S in triumph before the King
100:1 S in triumph to Jehovah, all
108:9 I shall s in triumph
Isa 12:6 out shrilly and s for joy
42:13 He will s, yes, he will let
44:23 S in triumph, all you
Jer 25:30 A s like that of those
50:15 S a war cry against her on
51:14 sing forth over you a s
Ho 5:8 S a war cry at Beth-aven
Joe 2:1 s a war cry in my holy
Zec 9:9 S in triumph, O daughter of
Joh 12:13 s: Save, we pray you!

Shouted
Jos 6:20 Then the people s, when they
Jg 15:14 s exultantly at meeting him
2Ch 13:15 men of Judah s a war cry
Ezr 3:11 they s with a loud shout in
Mr 1:23 an unclean spirit, and he s
Lu 4:33 he s with a loud voice
Joh 18:40 s again, saying: Not this
19:6 s, saying: Impale him!
19:12 Jews s . . . If you release
19:15 they s: Take him away!
Ac 19:34 they s for about two hours

Shouting
Ex 32:17 noise . . . because of their s
Le 9:24 they broke out into s and
Jg 7:21 and broke out into s and went
1Sa 4:5 broke out into loud s, so that
4:6 got to hear the sound of the s
4:6 sound of this loud s in the
17:52 broke into s and went in
2Sa 6:15 with joyful s and sound of
1Ch 15:28 with joyful s and with the
2Ch 13:15 Judah broke out s a war cry
15:14 voice and with joyful s
Ezr 3:12 raising the voice in s for
3:13 were s with a loud shout
Job 8:21 And your lips with joyful s
33:26 see his face with joyful s
38:7 sons . . . began s in applause
Ps 27:6 sacrifices of joyful s
33:3 along with joyful s
47:5 has ascended with joyful s
68:27 Judah with their s crowd
89:15 people knowing the joyful s
Isa 15:4 Moab themselves keep s
16:9 s even over your summer and
16:10 there is no s done
16:10 S I have caused to cease
Jer 48:33 doing the treading with s
48:33, 33 The s will be no s
Eze 7:7 not the s of the mountains
Mic 4:9 is it that you keep s loudly
Mr 10:47 he started s and saying
10:48 he kept s that much more
Lu 18:39 that much more he kept s
Ac 12:22 s: A god's voice, and not a
21:34 crowd began s out one thing
22:24 for what cause they were s
25:24 s that he ought not to live

Shoutings
Zec 4:7 There will be s to it

Shove
Joe 2:8 one another they do not s
Mt 8:18 to s off for the other side
1Co 1:19 intellectual men I will s
Ga 2:21 do not s aside the undeserved

Shoved
Jer 47:6 Be s into your sheath

Shovel
Isa 30:24 winnowed with the s and
Mt 3:12 winnowing s is in his hand
Lu 3:17 winnowing s is in his hand

Shovels
Ex 27:3 its s, and its bowls, and its
38:3 cans and the s and the bowls
Nu 4:14 s and the bowls, all the

1Ki 7:40 basins and the s and the
7:45 the s and the bowls and all
2Ki 25:14 the cans and the s and the
2Ch 4:11 cans and the s and the bowls
4:16 the s and the forks and all
Jer 52:18 s and the extinguishers and
Joe 1:17 have shriveled under their s

Shoving
Jg 2:18 who were s them around
19:22 s one another against the
Eze 34:21 your horns you kept s all

Show
Ge 12:1 to the country that I shall s
19:21 I do s you consideration to
43:29 God s you his favor, my son
Ex 9:30 s fear because of Jehovah God
23:3 must not s preference in a
33:19 will s mercy to the one to
33:19 to whom I may s mercy
Le 13:19 then s himself to the priest
19:32 s consideration for the
Nu 13:20 s yourselves courageous and
20:12 s faith in me to sanctify me
23:3 whatever he will s me, I
De 7:2 nor s them any favor
13:17 he may certainly s you mercy
28:50 s favor to a young man
30:3 and s you mercy and collect
33:11 s pleasure in the activity of
Jg 1:24 S us, please, the way to get
4:22 I shall s you the man you are
16:19 started to s the mastery of
1Sa 4:9 S yourselves courageous and
2Sa 10:12 s ourselves courageous in
12:22 Jehovah may s me favor
22:27 you will s yourself clean
24:23 your God s pleasure in you
1Ki 18:1 Go, s yourself to Ahab, as
18:2 Elijah went to s himself to
18:15 I shall s myself to him
2Ki 20:13 listen to them and s them
20:13 s them in his own house and
20:15 s them in my treasures
1Ch 19:13 may s ourselves courageous
2Ch 16:9 s his strength in behalf of
Es 1:11 s the peoples and the princes
4:8 he gave him to s Esther and to
Job 9:4 Who can s stubbornness to him
10:16 s yourself marvelous in my
11:11 also s himself attentive
12:8 s your concern to the earth
13:10 you try to s partiality
15:25 tries to s himself superior
19:5 s my reproach to be proper
19:21 S me some favor
19:21 s me some favor, O you my
23:15 I s myself attentive and am
26:14 who can s an understanding
27:12 s yourselves utterly vain
30:19 I s myself like dust and
30:20 s yourself attentive to me
31:1 s myself attentive to a virgin
32:21 s partiality to a man
37:14 s yourself attentive to the
Ps 4:1 S me favor and hear my prayer
4:6 saying: Who will s us good?
6:2 S me favor, O Jehovah, for I
9:13 S me favor, O Jehovah; see my
18:26 you will s yourself clean
18:26 you will s yourself tortuous
25:16 face to me, and s me favor
26:11 redeem me and s me favor
27:7 And s me favor and answer me
30:10 O Jehovah, and s me favor
31:9 S me favor, O Jehovah, for I
37:1 Do not s yourself heated up
37:7 Do not s yourself heated up
37:8 Do not s yourself heated up
41:4 O Jehovah, s me favor
41:10 s me favor and cause me to
51:1 S me favor, O God, according
55:2 I cannot but s disquietude
55:17 I cannot but s concern and
56:1 S me favor, O God, because
57:1, 1 S me favor, O God, s me
59:5 Do not s favor to any hurtful
67:1 will s us favor and bless us
68:28 Do s strength, O God, you
69:20 for someone to s sympathy
77:3 s concern, that my spirit may
77:6 my heart I will s concern
85:7 S us, O Jehovah, your
86:3 S me favor, O Jehovah
Ps 86:16 Turn to me and s me favor
90:12 S us just how to count our
106:7 s any insight into your
107:43 s himself attentive toward
119:16 I shall s a fondness
119:47 s a fondness for your
119:58 S me favor according to
119:132 Turn to me and s me favor
123:3 S us favor, O Jehovah
123:3 Jehovah, s us favor
Pr 3:34 meek ones he will s favor
6:34 s compassion in the day of
6:35 s willingness, no matter how
8:33 and do not s any neglect
16:23 his mouth to s insight
22:21 to s you the truthfulness of
23:3 Do not s yourself craving his
23:6 nor s yourself craving his
24:1 not s yourself craving to get
24:19 not s yourself heated up at
Ec 7:16 s yourself excessively wise
Ca 2:14 s me your form, let me hear
Isa 1:19 If you people s willingness
9:19 No one will s compassion
11:13 Judah s hostility toward
14:1 Jehovah will s mercy to
22:4 s bitterness in weeping
27:11 Maker will s it no mercy
27:11 Former will s it no favor
28:22 not s yourselves scoffers
30:16 will s themselves swift
30:18 rise up to s you mercy
30:19 s you favor at the sound
33:2 Jehovah, s us favor
39:2 to s them his treasure-house
39:2 s them in his own house and
39:4 s them in my treasures
42:13 enemies he will s himself
49:3 in whom I shall s my beauty
59:16 to s himself astonished
63:5 began to s myself astonished
Jer 13:14 I shall s no compassion
15:5 will s compassion upon you
17:16 I did not s any craving
18:17 s them in the day of their
21:7 nor will he s compassion or
50:42 cruel and will s no mercy
51:3 men s any compassion for
La 3:21 I shall s a waiting attitude
3:24 s a waiting attitude for him
3:32 will also certainly s mercy
4:16 s no consideration even for
4:16 s no favor even to the old
4:21 and s yourself in nakedness
Eze 5:11 also will not s compassion
9:10 neither shall I s compassion
21:16 S yourself sharp; go to the
39:25 I will s exclusive devotion
Da 2:4 shall s the very interpretation
2:6 its interpretation you will s
2:6 s me the very dream and its
2:7 shall s its very interpretation
2:9 s the very interpretation of it
2:10 s the matter of the king
2:11 nobody else exists who can s
2:16 s the very interpretation to
2:24 s the interpretation itself
2:27 unable to s to the king
5:7 s me its very interpretation
5:12 s the very interpretation
5:15 s the very interpretation of
Ho 1:6 I shall no more s mercy again
1:7 house of Judah I shall s mercy
2:4 her sons I shall not s mercy
2:23 I will s mercy to her who
13:15 should s fruitfulness, an
Joe 2:18 s compassion upon his people
Am 5:15 s favor to the remaining ones
Jon 1:6 the true God will s himself
Mic 7:7 I will s a waiting attitude
7:15 s him wonderful things
7:19 He will again s us mercy
Hab 3:2 to s mercy may you remember
Zec 1:9 shall s you who these very
1:12 not s mercy to Jerusalem
3:1 s me Joshua the high priest
10:6 for I will s them mercy
11:5 do not s any compassion upon
11:6 I shall s compassion no more
Mal 1:9 God, that he may s us favor
3:17 s compassion upon them
Mt 8:4 go, s yourself to the priest
22:19 S me the head tax coin
24:1 to s him the buildings of the
Mr 1:44 s yourself to the priest and
14:15 s you a large upper room
Lu 5:14 s yourself to the priest, and
6:47 I will s you whom he is like
17:14 s yourselves to the priests
20:21 and s no partiality, but you
20:24 S me a denarius. Whose
22:12 s you a large upper room
Joh 2:18 What sign have you to s us
5:20 s him works greater than
14:8 Lord, s us the Father, and
14:9 you say, S us the Father
14:21 plainly s myself to him
14:22 s yourself plainly to us
Ac 7:3 into the land I shall s you
9:16 s him plainly how many
25:7 were unable to s evidence
25:23 came with much pompous s
Ro 9:15 I will s compassion to
9:15 whomever I do s compassion
9:17 I may s my power, and that
11:32 might s all of them mercy
1Co 3:13 for the day will s it up
12:31 I s you a surpassing way
Ga 6:18 be with the spirit you s
Php 4:23 be with the spirit you s
Col 3:15 And s yourselves thankful
1Th 3:7 through the faithfulness you s
1Ti 6:15 will s in its own appointed
6:21 a s of such knowledge some
2Ti 4:22 be with the spirit you s
Phm 25 with the spirit you people s
Heb 6:11 s the same industriousness
Jas 2:18 S me your faith apart from
2:18 s you my faith by my works
3:13 s out of his fine conduct his
Re 1:1 God gave him, to s his slaves
4:1 s you the things that must
17:1 I will s you the judgment
21:9 I will s you the bride, the
22:6 s his slaves the things that

Showbread
Ex 25:30 put the s upon the table
35:13 its utensils and the s
39:36 all its utensils and the s
Nu 4:7 cloth . . . over the table of s
1Sa 21:6 s that had been removed from
1Ki 7:48 the table on which was the s
2Ch 4:19 tables with the s upon them

Showed
Ge 30:42 when the flocks s feebleness
Ex 2:21 Moses s willingness to
13:15 Pharaoh s obstinacy toward
27:8 as he s you in the mountain
Nu 11:34 people who s selfish craving
De 7:7 Jehovah s affection for you so
Jg 1:25 the man s them the way to
20:22 s themselves courageous and
1Sa 25:7 nothing at all s up missing
25:21 to him s up missing, and
1Ki 13:12 his sons s him the way that
2Ki 6:6 So he s him the place
11:4 s them the son of the king
13:23 Jehovah s them favor and
1Ch 11:17 David s his craving and said
2Ch 23:1 Jehoiada s himself
Es 1:4 s the riches of his glorious
Ps 81:11 not s any willingness toward
106:14 s their selfish desire in
Ec 2:19 I s wisdom under the sun
Isa 29:16 He s no understanding
47:6 You s them no mercies
Jer 24:1 Jehovah s me, and, look! two
Zec 1:20 Jehovah s me four craftsmen
Mt 4:8 s him all the kingdoms of the
Lu 4:5 s him all the kingdoms of the
24:40 s them his hands and his
Joh 20:20 s them both his hands and
Ac 1:3 he s himself alive after he
28:2 s us extraordinary human
Heb 6:10 the love you s for his name
11:7 s godly fear and constructed
Re 21:10 he s me the holy city
22:1 he s me a river of water of

Shower
Job 20:28 s will roll his house away

Showers
Le 26:4 give your s of rain at their
De 32:2 as copious s upon vegetation
Ezr 10:9 on account of the s of rain
10:13 the season of s of rain
Ps 65:10 With copious s you soften it

Ex 25:32 lampstand from its other s
26:13 the cubit on this s and the
26:13 the cubit on that s in what
26:13 to cover it on this s and on
26:18 for the s toward the Negeb
26:20 the other s of the tabernacle
26:20 tabernacle, the northern s
26:26 panel frames of the one s of
26:27 the other s of the tabernacle
26:27 of the s of the tabernacle
26:35 s of the tabernacle toward
26:35 you will put on the north s
27:9 For the s toward the Negeb
27:9 being the length for the one s
27:11 is for the north s in length
27:12 on the west s the hangings
27:13 courtyard on the east s
27:14 hangings to one s, their
27:15 And for the other s there are
28:26 s toward the ephod inward
32:15 On this s and on that they
32:26 Who is on Jehovah's s?
32:27 Put . . . his sword on his s
36:23 for the s toward the Negeb
36:25 the other s of the tabernacle
36:25 tabernacle, the northern s
36:31 of the one s of the tabernacle
36:32 the other s of the tabernacle
37:3 two rings on its one s
37:3 and two rings on its other s
37:18 out from its one s and three
37:18 out from its other s
38:9 For the s toward the Negeb
38:11 north s there were a hundred
38:12 west s the hangings were for
38:13 east s toward the sunrising
38:15 on this as well as that s, of
39:19 the s toward the ephod
40:22 on the s of the tabernacle to
40:24 on the s of the tabernacle to
Le 1:11 s of the altar to the north
1:15 out upon the s of the altar
5:9 upon the s of the altar
16:14 the cover on the east s, and
Nu 3:29 s of the tabernacle to the
3:35 s of the tabernacle toward the
13:29 and by the s of the Jordan
16:27 from every s, and Dathan and
22:24 a stone wall on this s and a
22:24 and a stone wall on that s
32:19 s of the Jordan and beyond
32:19 s of the Jordan toward the
32:32 on this s of the Jordan
34:3 your south s must prove to be
35:5 east s two thousand cubits
35:5 south s two thousand cubits
35:5 west s two thousand cubits
35:5 north s two thousand cubits
35:14 on this s of the Jordan, and
De 4:41 cities on the s of the Jordan
11:30 the s of the Jordan toward
30:13 on the other s of the sea
30:13 to the other s of the sea and
31:26 place it at the s of the ark
Jos 1:14 on this s of the Jordan; but
1:15 the s of the Jordan toward
2:10 on the other s of the Jordan
2:15 house was on a s of the wall
3:16 city at the s of Zarethan
5:1 were on the s of the Jordan
7:7 on the other s of the Jordan
8:22 on this s and those on that
8:33, 33 this s and on that s of
9:1 on the s of the Jordan in the
9:10 the other s of the Jordan
12:1 the s of the Jordan toward
12:7 the s of the Jordan toward
13:8 on the s of the Jordan
13:27 on the s of Jordan toward
13:32 Moab on the s of the Jordan
14:3 the other s of the Jordan
17:5 on the other s of the Jordan
18:7 the s of the Jordan toward
18:14 western s to the south from
18:14 This is the western s
18:15 the s to the south was from
18:20 boundary on the eastern s
22:4 on the other s of the Jordan
22:7 on the s of the Jordan to the
22:11 s belonging to the sons of
24:2 on the other s of the River
24:3 the other s of the River
24:8 on the other s of the Jordan
24:14 on the other s of the River
Jos 24:15 on the other s of the River
Jg 5:17 on the other s of the Jordan
10:8 on the s of the Jordan in the
16:3 two s posts and pulled them
1Sa 6:8 put into a box at the s of it
14:4 toothlike crag here on this s
14:4 crag there on that s, and the
14:40 come to be on the one s
14:40 come to be on the other s
17:3 on the mountain on this s
17:3 on the mountain on that s
19:3 stand at the s of my father
20:20 shoot three arrows to one s
20:21 arrows are on this s of you
20:25 was sitting at Saul's s
23:19 to the right s of Jeshimon
23:26 to this s of the mountain
23:26 on that s of the mountain
26:13 passed on to the other s and
2Sa 2:13 on this s of the pool and
2:13 on that s of the pool
2:16 in the s of the other, so
3:12 turn to your s the whole of
15:2 stood at the s of the road
15:18 were crossing at his s
16:13 on the s of the mountain
18:4 standing at the s of the gate
18:13 take a position off on the s
1Ki 4:24 this s of the River, from
4:24 kings this s of the River
6:5 a s structure all around
6:5 made s chambers all around
6:6 s chamber was five cubits in
6:8 entrance of the lowest s
6:8 chamber was on the right s of
6:10 the s chambers against the
6:31 s pillars, doorposts and a
7:39 five carriages on the right s
7:39 on the left s of the house
7:39 to the right s of the house
10:19, 19 this s and on that s by
10:20, 20 on this s and on that s
11:24 collecting men to his s and
20:25 force that fell from your s
2Ki 3:22 Moabites from the opposite s
11:11 right s of the house clear
11:11 to the left s of the house
16:14 the north s of his altar
25:5 was scattered from his s
1Ch 7:29 s of the sons of Manasseh
12:8 to David's s at the place
18:17 at the s of the king
2Ch 4:10 sea he placed at the right s
9:18 armrests on this s and on
9:18 on that s by the place of
9:19, 19 on this s and on that s
21:16 by the s of the Ethiopians
23:10 right s of the house clear
23:10 to the left s of the house
31:13 s of Conaniah and Shimei
Ne 3:2 their s the men of Jericho did
3:2 And at their s Zaccur the son
3:4 their s Meremoth the son of
3:4 at their s Meshullam the son
3:4 at their s Zadok the son of
3:5 at their s the Tekoites did
3:7 at their s Melatiah the
3:8 At his s Uzziel the son of
3:8 at his s Hananiah a member of
3:9 at their s Rephaiah the son of
3:10 at their s Jedaiah the son of
3:10 at his s Hattush the son of
3:12 at his s Shallum the son of
3:17 at his s Hashabiah, a prince
3:19 at his s to repair another
11:24 at the s of the king for
Job 1:14 grazing at the s of them
Ps 91:7 will fall at your very s
118:6 Jehovah is on my s; I shall
118:7 Jehovah is on my s among
140:5 net at the s of the track
Pr 8:3 At the s of the gates, at the
Ec 4:1 on the s of their oppressors
Jer 50:14 against Babylon on every s
50:15 cry against her on every s
52:8 was scattered from his s
Eze 1:23 two wings covering on this s
1:23 on that s their bodies
4:4 lie upon your left s, and you
4:6 lie upon your right s in the
4:8 turn yourself from your one s
4:8 to your other s, until you
4:9 that you are lying upon your s
28:23 against her on every s
Eze 40:9 its s pillars, two cubits
40:10 three on this s and three
40:10 and three on that s
40:10 the s pillars were of the
40:10, 10 this s and on that s
40:12 one cubit on either s
40:12 was six cubits on this s
40:12 and six cubits on that s
40:14 s pillars of sixty cubits
40:14 s pillars of the courtyard
40:16 s pillars toward the inside
40:16 on the s pillars there were
40:18 at the s of the gates was
40:21 were three on this s
40:21 and three on that s
40:21 And its own s pillars and
40:24 its s pillars and its porch
40:26, 26 this s and one on that s
40:26 figures . . . on its s pillars
40:29 its s pillars and its porch
40:31 were on its s pillars
40:33 its s pillars and its porch
40:34 were on its s pillars
40:34, 34 on this s and on that s
40:36 its s pillars and its porch
40:37 s pillars, and palm-tree
40:37 were on its s pillars
40:37, 37 on this s and on that s
40:38 the s pillars of the gates
40:39 two tables on this s and
40:39 and two tables on that s
40:40 the outer s, as one goes
40:40 s that belongs to the porch
40:41 s of the gate—eight tables
40:44 on the s of the north gate
40:44 s was toward the south
40:44 on the s of the east gate
40:48 went measuring the s pillar
40:48 five cubits on this s and
40:48 and five cubits on that s
40:48 was three cubits on this s
40:48 and three cubits on that s
40:49 were pillars by the s posts
41:1 went measuring the s pillars
41:1 the width of the s pillar
41:3 the s pillar of the entrance
41:5 the width of the s chamber
41:6 And the s chambers were
41:6, 6 s chamber upon s chamber
41:6 the s chambers all around
41:7 upward to the s chambers
41:8 of the s chambers
41:9 belonged to the s chamber
41:9 of the s chambers that
41:11 entrance of the s chamber
41:12 the s of which was toward
41:15, 15 on this s and on that s
41:19 palm-tree figure on this s
41:19 palm-tree figure on that s
41:26 s chambers of the house
42:16 measured the eastern s with
42:17 measured the northern s
42:18 southern s he measured
42:19 around to the western s
45:2 as pasture ground on each s
45:7, 7 on this s and on that s
45:7 on the west s westward and
45:7 on the east s eastward
46:19 s of the gate to the holy
47:1 right-hand s of the House
47:2 from the right-hand s
47:7, 7 on this s and on that s
47:12, 12 on this s and on that s
47:15 land to the northern s
47:17 This is the northern s
47:18 eastern s is from between
47:18 This is the eastern s
47:19 southern s is to the south
47:19 s to the south, toward the
47:20 western s is the Great Sea
47:20 This is the western s
48:1 s by the way of Hethlon to
48:1 on the s of Hamath
48:21, 21 on this s and on that s
Da 7:5 And on one s it was raised up
Ho 7:8 cake not turned on the other s
Ob 11 day when you stood off on the s
Zec 4:3 on the right s of the bowl
4:3 bowl and one on its left s
4:11 the right s of the lampstand
4:11 and on its left s mean
5:3 according to it on this s
5:3 according to it on that s, has
Mt 4:15 on the other s of the Jordan

Mt 4:25 the other s of the Jordan
8:18 to shove off for the other s
8:28 When he got to the other s
12:30 not on my s is against me
14:22 ahead of him to the other s
16:5 crossed to the other s and
27:49 pierced his s, and blood and
Mr 5:1 got to the other s of the sea
11:4 outside on the s street, and
16:5 on the right s clothed in a
Lu 1:11 right s of the incense altar
8:22 to the other s of the lake
8:26 on the s opposite Galilee
10:31 he went by on the opposite s
10:32 went by on the opposite s
11:23 not on my s is against me
19:43 distress you from every s
Joh 6:22 on the other s of the sea
18:37 is on the s of the truth
19:18 with him, one on this s
19:34 jabbed his s with a spear
20:20 both his hands and his s
20:25 my hand into his s, I will
20:27 hand and stick it into my s
21:6 on the right s of the boat
Ac 12:7 Striking Peter on the s, he
21:3 Cyprus . . . on the left s
27:41 shoal washed on each s by
Php 1:27, 27 s by s for the faith of
4:3, 3 striven s by s with me in
2Ti 4:16 no one came to my s, but
Tit 2:8 the man on the opposing s may
Re 2:13 killed by your s, where Satan
5:1 within and on the reverse s
22:2 And on this s of the river
22:2 of the river and on that s

Sidelocks
Le 19:27 not cut your s short around

Sides
Ex 25:14 rings upon the s of the Ark
25:32 are running out from its s
26:13 on the s of the tabernacle
27:7 upon the two s of the altar
30:3 top surface and its s round
30:4 border upon two of its s you
30:4 upon two opposite s of it
32:15 written upon on both their s
37:5 rings on the s of the Ark for
37:17 Its s and its branches, its
37:18 six branches . . . from its s
37:26 and its s round about and
37:27 its border upon two of its s
37:27 upon two opposite s of it
38:7 rings on the s of the altar
Nu 8:4 Up to its s and up to its
33:55 and as thorns in your s, and
1Ki 6:16 twenty cubits at the rear s
7:35 its s and its sidewalls were
7:36 upon the plates of its s
Job 19:10 He pulls me down on all s
Ps 31:13 Fright being on all s
48:2 on the remote s of the north
141:6 down by the s of the crag
Isa 29:3 encamp on all s against you
Jer 4:17 become against her on all s
51:2 against her on all s in the
52:23 to be ninety-six, on the s
Eze 1:8 their wings on their four s
1:17 go on their four respective s
10:11 would go, to their four s
16:57 with scorn on all s
23:22 against you on all s
36:3 snapping at you from all s
41:2 s of the entrance were five
41:26 along the s of the porch
42:20 four s he measured it
43:16 squared on its four s
43:17 width, on its four s
46:19 both rear s to the west
Mr 1:45 coming to him from all s

Sidestepping
Es 3:3 you s the king's commandment
Jer 34:18 men s my covenant, in that

Sidewalls
1Ki 7:28 carriages: they had s, and
7:28 s were between the crossbars
7:29 upon the s that were between
7:31 s were squared, not round
7:32 were down below the s
7:35 s were of one piece with it
7:36 and upon its s cherubs, lions
2Ki 16:17 cut the s of the carriages

Sidon
Ge 10:15 Canaan became father to S
10:19 from S as far as Gerar
49:13 side will be toward S
Jos 11:8 S and Misrephoth-maim
19:28 Kanah as far as populous S
Jg 1:31 S and Ahlab and Achzib and
10:6 the gods of S and the gods of
18:28 for it was far away from S
2Sa 24:6 and went around to S
1Ki 17:9 Zarephath . . . belongs to S
1Ch 1:13 S his firstborn and Heth
Isa 23:2 merchants from S, the ones
23:4 Be ashamed, O S; because
23:12 the virgin daughter of S
Jer 25:22 all the kings of S and the
27:3 to the king of S by the hand
47:4 from S every survivor that
Eze 27:8 inhabitants of S and of Arvad
28:21 set your face toward S
28:22 I am against you, O S
Joe 3:4 O Tyre and S and all you
Zec 9:2 Tyre and S, for she is very
Mt 11:21 taken place in Tyre and S
11:22 endurable for Tyre and S
15:21 into the parts of Tyre and S
Mr 3:8 Tyre and S, a great multitude
7:24 the regions of Tyre and S
7:31 S to the sea of Galilee in
Lu 4:26 in the land of S to a widow
6:17 Tyre and S, who came to hear
10:13 taken place in Tyre and S
10:14 endurable for Tyre and S
Ac 12:20 the people of Tyre and of S
27:3 we landed at S, and Julius

Sidonian
1Ki 11:1 foreign wives . . . S

Sidonians
De 3:9 S used to call Hermon Sirion
Jos 13:4 belongs to the S, as far as
13:6 the S; I . . . shall dispossess
Jg 3:3 even the S and the Hivites
10:12 the S and Amalek and Midian
18:7 custom of the S, quiet and
18:7 far off from the S and they
1Ki 5:6 how to cut trees like the S
11:5 the goddess of the S and
11:33 the goddess of the S
16:31 Ethbaal the king of the S
2Ki 23:13 disgusting thing of the S
1Ch 22:4 S . . . brought in cedar
Ezr 3:7 and drink and oil to the S and
Eze 32:30 all the S, who have gone

Siege
De 20:19 lay s to a city many days
2Sa 11:1 lay s to Rabbah, while David
20:15 lay s against him in Abel
20:15 s rampart against the city
1Ki 16:17 began to lay s to Tirzah
20:1 and lay s to Samaria and
2Ki 16:5 and laid s against Ahaz
17:5 Samaria and lay s against it
18:9 and began to lay s to it
19:32 a s rampart against it
24:10 the city came under s
24:11 were laying s against it
25:1 building against it a s wall
25:2 the city came to be under s
2Ch 32:10 quiet under s in Jerusalem
Isa 21:2 Lay s, O Media!
23:13 erected their s towers
29:3 lay s to you with a palisade
29:7 s towers against her and
37:33 a s rampart against it
Jer 6:6 against Jerusalem a s rampart
21:4 who are laying s against you
21:9 Chaldeans who are laying s
32:2 laying s to Jerusalem
32:24 With s ramparts men have
33:4 account of the s ramparts
37:5 were laying s to Jerusalem
39:1 and began to lay s to it
52:4 build against her a s wall
52:5 city came under s until the
Eze 4:2 lay s against it and build a
4:2 build a s wall against it and
4:2 throw up a s rampart against
4:3 and it must get to be in a s
4:7 And to the s of Jerusalem you
4:8 completed the days of your s
5:2 days of the s have come to
17:17 by throwing up a s rampart
Eze 17:17 building a s wall, in order
21:22 to throw up a s rampart
21:22 to build a s wall
26:8 make against you a s wall
26:8 against you a s rampart and
Da 1:1 proceeded to lay s to it
11:15 and throw up a s rampart and
Mic 5:1 a s he has laid against us
Na 3:14 Water for a s draw out for
Zec 12:2 he will come to be in the s

Siegeworks
De 20:20 build s against the city that
Isa 29:3 and raise up against you s

Siesta
2Sa 4:5 he was taking his noonday s

Sieve
Isa 30:28 with a s of worthlessness
Am 9:9 just as one jiggles the s

Sift
Lu 22:31 you men to s you as wheat

Sigh
Ex 2:23 sons of Israel continued to s
Pr 29:2 wicked . . . rule, the people s
Jer 22:23 s when there come to you
Eze 21:6 s with shaking hips
21:6 with bitterness you should s
24:17 S without words. For the

Sighed
Joe 1:18 the domestic animal has s
Mr 7:34 he s deeply and said to him

Sighing
Job 3:24 before my food my s comes
23:2 is heavy on account of my s
Ps 5:1 Jehovah; Do understand my s
6:6 I have grown weary with my s
12:5 the s of the poor ones
31:10 And my years in s
38:9 my s itself has not been
39:3 During my s the fire kept
79:11 s of the prisoner come in
102:5 Because of the sound of my s
102:20 hear the s of the prisoner
Isa 21:2 s due to her I have caused
24:7 at heart have gone to s
35:10 grief and s must flee away
51:11 Grief and s will certainly
Jer 45:3 grown weary because of my s
La 1:4 her priests are s. Her virgins
1:8 is also s and turns her back
1:11 All her people are s; they are
1:21 how I myself am s as a woman
Eze 9:4 men that are s and groaning
21:7 On account of what are you s?
Mal 2:13 with weeping and s, so that
Heb 13:17 with joy and not with s

Sighs
La 1:22 my s are many, and my heart
Jas 5:9 heave s against one another

Sight
Ge 2:9 tree desirable to one's s
6:11 earth . . . ruined in the s of
16:13 You are a God of s, for she
18:2 he caught s of them he began
19:1 Lot caught s of them, then he
19:28 of the District and saw a s
21:19 she caught s of a well of
23:4 bury my dead out of my s
23:8 to bury my dead out of my s
24:64 she caught s of Isaac and she
26:8 window and taking in the s
31:10 saw a s in a dream and here
37:18 they caught s of him from a
38:15 When Judah caught s of her
44:29 this one also out of my s
Ex 2:5 she caught s of the ark in the
2:11 s of a certain Egyptian
2:12 saw there was nobody in s
9:8 the heavens in Pharaoh's s
24:17 the s of Jehovah's glory was
40:38 in the s of all the house of
Le 13:12 full s of the priest's eyes
Nu 25:7 When Phinehas . . . caught s of
De 4:37 in his s with his great power
28:28 loss of s and bewilderment
28:34 maddened at the s of your
28:67 the s of your eyes that you
Jos 2:6 out of s among stalks of
4:12 the s of the sons of Israel
Jg 6:11 out of the s of Midian

Jg 6:21 angel, he vanished from his s
9:36 Gaal caught s of the people
11:35 he caught s of her, he began
1Sa 16:6 and he caught s of Eliab, he
25:23 Abigail caught s of David
2Sa 11:2 s of a woman bathing herself
18:8 all the land that was in s
2Ki 17:18 he removed them from his s
17:23 removed Israel from his s
23:27 I shall remove from my s
24:3 to remove it from his s for
24:20 had cast them out of his s
Job 20:9 eye that has caught s of him
21:8 with them in their s
28:7 a black kite caught s of it
33:21 flesh wastes away from s
41:9 down at the mere s of it
Ps 37:37 keep the upright one in s
Ca 1:6 the sun has caught s of me
Isa 18:3 s just as when there is the
Eze 23:16 at the s of her eyes and
Da 10:6 like the s of burnished copper
Ob 12 to watch the s in the day of
Zec 12:4 shall strike with loss of s
Mt 3:7 he caught s of many of the
9:8 At the s of this the crowds
9:9 Jesus caught s of a man named
9:23 caught s of the flute players
9:30 And their eyes received s
14:26 s of him walking on the sea
20:34 immediately they received s
21:2 village that is within s of
21:19 he caught s of a fig tree by
22:11 caught s there of a man not
24:15 s of the disgusting thing
Mr 2:14 he caught s of Levi the son
5:6 on catching s of Jesus from a
5:22 on catching s of him, he fell
6:49 At catching s of him walking
9:15 the crowd caught s of him
9:20 at the s of him the spirit
10:51 *Rab·bo'ni*, let me recover s
10:52 he recovered s, and he began
11:2 village that is within s of
11:13 he caught s of a fig tree
13:14 s of the disgusting thing
14:69 at the s of him, started
Lu 1:12 became troubled at the s, and
1:22 just seen a supernatural s
2:31 in the s of all the peoples
4:18 a recovery of s to the blind
5:12 When he caught s of Jesus he
7:13 the Lord caught s of her, he
7:22 the blind are receiving s
7:39 At the s the Pharisee that
8:28 At the s of Jesus he cried
15:20 his father caught s of him
16:15 a disgusting thing in God's s
17:14 he got s of them he said
18:41 Lord, let me recover s
18:42 Recover your s; your faith
18:43 And instantly he recovered s
19:30 village that is within s of
20:14 cultivators caught s of him
24:23 a supernatural s of angels
Joh 9:11 and washed and gained s
9:15 asking him how he gained s
9:15 and I washed and have s
9:18 been blind and had gained s
9:18 of the man that gained s
11:32 Jesus was and caught s of
21:21 he caught s of him, Peter
Ac 3:3 he caught s of Peter and John
3:9 s of him walking and praising
3:16 soundness in the s of all of
4:19 righteous in the s of God to
7:10 wisdom in the s of Pharaoh
7:24 caught s of a certain one
7:31 saw it he marveled at the s
7:46 found favor in the s of God
7:55 caught s of God's glory and
8:21 straight in the s of God
9:12 that he might recover s
9:17 that you may recover s and be
9:18 scales, and he recovered s
9:40 as she caught s of Peter
13:45 Jews got s of the crowds
21:3 in s of the island of Cyprus
21:32 s of the military commander
22:13 Saul, brother, have your s
26:19 to the heavenly s
28:4 s of the venomous creature
28:15 s of them, Paul thanked God
Ro 4:17 s of the One in whom he had
Ro 12:17 fine things in the s of all
14:22 faith . . . in the s of God
1Co 1:29 might boast in the s of God
2Co 2:10 for your sakes in Christ's s
4:2 conscience in the s of God
5:7 walking by faith, not by s
7:12 among you in the s of God
8:21 not only in the s of Jehovah
8:21 but also in the s of men
Ga 1:20 in the s of God, I am not
1Ti 2:3 acceptable in the s of our
5:4 this is acceptable in God's s
6:13 In the s of God, who
Heb 4:13 is not manifest to his s
13:21 is well-pleasing in his s
1Jo 5:16 s of his brother sinning a
Jude 24 in the s of his glory with
Re 13:12 first wild beast in its s
13:13 earth in the s of mankind
13:14 in the s of the wild beast
14:10 s of the holy angels and in
14:10 and in the s of the Lamb
16:19 remembered in the s of God
17:3 I caught s of a woman sitting
17:6 catching s of her I wondered

Sights

Lu 21:11 there will be fearful s and

Sign

Ge 4:15 Jehovah set up a s for Cain
9:12 the s of the covenant that I
9:13 serve as a s of the covenant
9:17 This is the s of the covenant
17:11 s of the covenant between me
Ex 3:12 this is the s for you that it
4:8 to the voice of the first s
4:8 the voice of the later s
8:23 Tomorrow this s will take
12:13 blood must serve as your s
13:9 serve for you as a s upon your
13:16 serve as a s upon your hand
29:6 put the holy s of dedication
31:13 is a s between me and you
31:17 is a s to time indefinite
39:30 the holy s of dedication
Le 8:9 the holy s of dedication
21:12 because the s of dedication
Nu 6:7 s of his Naziriteship to his
6:19 s of his Naziriteship shaved
16:38 as a s to the sons of Israel
17:10 to be kept for a s to the
De 6:8 tie them as a s upon your hand
11:18 a s upon your hand, and they
13:1 give you a s or a portent
13:2 and the s or the portent does
28:46 a s and a portent to time
Jos 2:12 give me a trustworthy s
4:6 serve as a s in your midst
Jg 6:17 perform a s for me that you
1Sa 2:34 this is the s for you that
14:10 and this is for us the s
2Ki 19:29 this will be the s for you
20:8 s that Jehovah will heal me
20:9 the s for you from Jehovah
Ps 86:17 a s meaning goodness
Isa 7:11 s from Jehovah your God
7:14 will give you men a s
19:20 for a s and for a witness
20:3 s and a portent against Egypt
37:30 this will be the s for you
38:7 the s for you from Jehovah
38:22 What is the s that I shall
55:13 a s to time indefinite that
66:19 will set among them a s
Jer 44:29 this is the s for you
Eze 4:3 is a s to the house of Israel
14:8 place him for a s and for
20:12 a s between me and them
20:20 and they must serve as a s
Da 6:8 and s the writing, in order
Mt 12:38 we want to see a s from you
12:39 keeps on seeking for a s
12:39 no s will be given it except
12:39 the s of Jonah the prophet
16:1 to them a s from heaven
16:4 keeps on seeking for a s, but
16:4 no s will be given it except
16:4 except the s of Jonah
24:3 the s of your presence and of
24:30 s of the Son of man will
26:48 betrayer had given them a s
Mr 8:11 seeking . . . a s from heaven
8:12 this generation seek a s
8:12 No s will be given to this
Mr 13:4 what will be the s when all
14:44 had given them an agreed s
Lu 2:12 this is a s for you: you will
2:34 for a s to be talked against
11:16 seeking a s out of heaven
11:29 generation; it looks for a s
11:29 But no s will be given it
11:29 except the s of Jonah
11:30 Jonah became a s to the
21:7 what will be the s when
23:8 was hoping to see some s
Joh 2:18 What s have you to show us
4:54 second s Jesus performed
6:30 a s, in order for us to see
10:41 did not perform a single s
12:18 he had performed this s
Ac 4:16 noteworthy s has occurred
4:22 upon whom this s of healing
Ro 4:11 s, namely, circumcision, as
1Co 11:10 to have a s of authority
14:22 tongues are for a s, not to
2Th 3:17 which is a s in every letter
Re 12:1 a great s was seen in heaven
12:3 s was seen in heaven, and
15:1 I saw in heaven another s

Signal

Nu 21:8 and place it upon a s pole
21:9 and placed it upon the s pole
Jg 20:38 smoke s go up from the city
20:40 s started to go up from the
2Ch 13:12 s trumpets for sounding the
23:13 s for offering praise
Ps 60:4 to those fearing you a s
Isa 5:26 s to a great nation far
11:10 up as a s for the peoples
11:12 s for the nations and gather
13:2 raise up a s, you men
18:3 s upon the mountains, and
30:17 and like a s on a hill
31:9 because of the s his princes
49:22 I shall lift up my s
62:10 Raise up a s for the peoples
Jer 4:6 Raise a s toward Zion
4:19 the alarm s of war
4:21 shall I keep seeing the s
6:1 raise a fire s; because
20:16 s at the time of midday
49:2 alarm s of war to be heard
50:2 lift up a s; publish it
51:12 of Babylon lift up a s
51:27 Lift up a s in the land
Eze 21:22 the sound in an alarm s
Am 1:14 alarm s in the day of battle
2:2 with an alarm s, with the
Zep 1:16 day of horn and of alarm s

Signature

Job 31:35 That according to my s the

Signed

Da 6:9 Darius himself s the writing
6:10 that the writing had been s
6:12 interdict that you have s that
6:13 to the interdict that you s

Signet

Ge 41:42 Pharaoh removed his s ring
Nu 31:50 bracelets, s rings, earrings
Es 3:10 king removed his s ring from
3:12 sealed with the king's s ring
8:2 the king removed his s ring
8:8 seal it with the king's s ring
8:8 sealed with the king's s ring
8:10 with the king's s ring and
Da 6:17 sealed it with his s ring
6:17 the s ring of his grandees

Signified

2Pe 1:14 Lord Jesus Christ s to me

Signifies

Heb 12:27 s the removal of the things

Signify

Joh 12:33 s what sort of death he was
18:32 s what sort of death he was
21:19 s by what sort of death he
Ac 25:27 s the charges against him

Signposts

Jer 31:21 Place s for yourself

Signs

Ge 1:14 they must serve as s and for
Ex 4:9 not believe even these two s
4:17 may perform the s with it
4:28 s that he had commanded him

Ex 4:30 performed the s under the
7:3 multiply my s and my miracles
10:1 I may set these s of mine
10:2 my s that I have established
Nu 2:2 by the s for the house of their
14:11 s that I performed in among
14:22 my s that I have performed
De 4:34 with s and with miracles and
6:22 kept putting s and miracles
7:19 the s and the miracles and
11:3 nor his s and his deeds that
26:8 out of Egypt . . . with s
29:3 those great s and miracles
34:11 the s and the miracles that
Jos 24:17 performed these great s
1Sa 10:7 when these s come to you, do
10:9 s proceeded to come true on
Ne 9:10 gave s and miracles against
Job 21:29 inspect their very s
Ps 65:8 will be afraid of your s
74:4, 4 set their own s as the s
74:9 Our s we have not seen
78:43 How he put his s in Egypt
105:27 the matters of his s
135:9 sent s and miracles into
Pr 6:13 making s with his foot
Isa 8:18 has given me are as s
44:25 frustrating the s of the
Jer 10:2 even at the s of the heavens
32:20 set s and miracles in the
32:21 with s and with miracles
Da 4:2 s and wonders . . . performed
4:3 How grand his s are, and how
6:27 performing s and wonders in
Mt 16:3 the s of the times you cannot
24:24 great s and wonders so as to
Mr 13:22 s and wonders to lead astray
Lu 1:22 and he kept making s to them
1:62 asking its father by s what
21:11 and from heaven great s
21:25 s in sun and moon and stars
Joh 2:11 as the beginning of his s
2:23 his s that he was performing
3:2 no one can perform these s
4:48 Unless you people see s and
6:2 the s he was performing upon
6:14 saw the s he performed
6:26 not because you saw s, but
7:31 not perform more s than this
9:16 sinner perform s of that
11:47 this man performs many s
12:37 performed so many s before
20:30 performed many other s
Ac 2:19 and s on earth below, blood
2:22 s that God did through him in
2:43 s began to occur through the
4:30 s and portents occur through
5:12 many s and portents
6:8 and s among the people
7:36 s in Egypt and in the Red Sea
8:6 at the s he was performing
8:13 at beholding great s and
14:3 by granting s and portents to
15:12 s and portents that God did
Ro 15:19 the power of s and portents
1Co 1:22 the Jews ask for s and the
2Co 12:12 s of an apostle were
12:12 by s and portents and
2Th 2:9 and lying s and portents
Heb 2:4 with s as well as portents
Re 1:1 presented it in s through him
13:13 it performs great s, so that
13:14 s that were granted it to
16:14 by demons and perform s
19:20 s with which he misled

Sihon
Nu 21:21 now sent messengers to S the
21:23 S did not allow Israel to
21:23 S gathered all his people and
21:26 Heshbon was the city of S
21:27 Let the city of S be built
21:28 a flame from the town of S
21:29 the king of the Amorites, S
21:34 to him just as you did to S
32:33 S the king of the Amorites
De 1:4 S the king of the Amorites
2:24 I have given into your hand S
2:26 S the king of Heshbon
2:30 S the king of Heshbon did not
2:31 abandon S and his land to you
2:32 When S came on out, he and
3:2 do to him just as you did to S
3:6 just as we had done to S the
4:46 in the land of S the king of
29:7 S the king of Heshbon and
31:4 done to S and to Og, the kings
Jos 2:10 S and Og, whom you devoted
9:10 S the king of Heshbon and Og
12:2 S the king of the Amorites
12:5 S the king of Heshbon
13:10 S the king of the Amorites
13:21 royal realm of S the king
13:21 the dukes of S, who were
13:27 S the king of Heshbon
Jg 11:19 S the king of the Amorites
11:20 And S did not feel sure about
11:20 And S went gathering all his
11:21 gave S and all his people
1Ki 4:19 S the king of the Amorites
Ne 9:22 possession of the land of S
Ps 135:11 S the king of the Amorites
136:19 S the king of the Amorites
Jer 48:45 flame from the midst of S

Silas
Ac 15:22 Barsabbas and S, leading men
15:27 dispatching Judas and S
15:32 And Judas and S, since they
15:40 Paul selected S and went off
16:19 they laid hold of Paul and S
16:25 Paul and S were praying and
16:29 fell down before Paul and S
17:4 with Paul and S, and a great
17:10 both Paul and S out to Beroea
17:14 both S and Timothy remained
17:15 for S and Timothy to come to
18:5 both S and Timothy came down

Silence
Jg 3:19 So he said: Keep s!
2Sa 22:41 I shall also s them
Job 11:3 talk itself put men to s
23:17 not been put to s because of
Ps 18:40 I shall s them
22:2 and there is no s on my part
39:2 I became speechless with s
54:5 In your trueness s them
58:1 In your s can you really
62:1 my soul waiting in s
65:1 For you there is praise—s
69:4 Those bringing me to s, being
73:27 s every one immorally
83:1 let there be no s on your part
88:16 have brought me to s
94:17 soul would have resided in s
94:23 s them with their own
94:23 Jehovah our God will s them
101:5 Anyone slandering . . . I s
101:8 s all the wicked ones of
115:17 do any going down into s
143:12 may you s my enemies
Isa 6:5 I am as good as brought to s
41:1 Attend to me in s, you
62:6 there be no s on your part
62:7 do not give him any s until
Jer 8:14 God has himself put us to s
47:5 Ashkelon has been put to s
49:26 brought to s in that day
50:30 will be brought to s in
La 2:10 the earth, where they keep s
Eze 27:32 s in the midst of the sea
Ho 4:5 I will put your mother to s
Am 6:10 he will have to say, Keep s!
Hab 2:20 Keep s before him, all the
Zep 1:7 Keep s before the Sovereign
Zec 2:13 Keep s, all flesh, before
Mt 22:34 had put the Sadducees to s
Ac 21:40 When a great s fell, he
Ro 16:25 kept in s for long-lasting
1Ti 2:11 Let a woman learn in s with
2:12 over a man, but to be in s
Re 8:1 a s occurred in heaven for

Silenced
1Sa 2:9 wicked ones . . . s in darkness
Job 6:17 waterless, they have been s
Isa 15:1 Ar of Moab . . . has been s
15:1 Kir of Moab . . . has been s
La 3:53 s my life in the pit itself
Eze 32:2 you have been s. And you
Ho 4:6 My people will certainly be s
10:7 her king will certainly be s
10:15 will positively have to be s
Ob 5 would you have been s
Zep 1:11 are tradesmen have been s

Silent
Ge 24:21 s to know whether Jehovah
34:5 and Jacob kept s until they
Ex 14:14 and you yourselves will be s
Le 10:3 And Aaron kept s
Nu 30:4 and her father does keep s
30:7 hears it and keeps s toward
30:11 has heard it and has kept s
30:14 husband absolutely keeps s
30:14 because he kept s toward her
De 27:9 Keep s and listen, O Israel
1Sa 7:8 Do not keep s for our sakes
2Sa 13:20 now, my sister, keep s
2Ki 2:3 I too well know it. Be s
2:5 I too well know it. Be s
18:36 people kept s and did not
Ne 8:11 all the people to be s, saying
Es 4:14 are altogether s at this time
7:4 I should have kept s
Job 6:24 I, for my part, shall be s
13:5 you would absolutely keep s
13:13 Keep s before me, that I
13:19 were I to become s I should
29:21 would keep s for my counsel
30:27 to boil and did not keep s
31:34 I would keep s, I would not
33:31 Keep s, and I myself shall
33:33 Keep s, and I shall teach
41:12 not keep s about its parts
Ps 4:4 upon your bed, and keep s
30:12 melody to you and not keep s
31:17 May they keep s in Sheol
32:3 When I kept s my bones wore
35:15 and did not keep s
35:22 O Jehovah. Do not keep s
37:7 Keep s before Jehovah
39:12 At my tears do not keep s
50:3 and cannot possibly keep s
50:21 have done, and I kept s
56:*super* the director on the S Dove
109:1 of my praise, do not keep s
Pr 11:12 discernment . . . keeps s
17:28 foolish, when keeping s
Isa 23:2 Be s, you inhabitants of the
36:21 s and did not answer him a
42:14 long time. I continued s
57:11 s and hiding matters
Jer 4:19 I cannot keep s, for the
8:14 let us enter . . . and be s
38:27 they became s before him
47:6 Take your repose and keep s
48:2 Madmen, should keep s
La 3:28 sit solitary and keep s
Am 5:13 will in that time keep s
Hab 1:13 keep s when someone wicked
Zep 3:17 will become s in his love
Mt 20:31 sternly told them to keep s
26:63 Jesus kept s. So the high
Mr 1:25 Be s, and come on out of him!
3:4 kill a soul? But they kept s
9:34 They kept s, for on the road
10:48 sternly telling him to be s
14:61 he kept s and made no reply
Lu 1:20 you will be s and not able
4:35 Be s, and come out of him
14:4 they kept s. With that he
19:40 remained s, the stones would
Ac 12:17 with his hand to be s and
15:12 entire multitude became s
18:9 on speaking and do not keep s
22:2 they kept all the more s, and
1Co 14:28 keep s in the congregation
14:30 let the first one keep s
14:34 let the women keep s in the

Silently
Ps 62:5 toward God wait s, O my soul
Isa 47:5 Sit down s and come into the
La 3:26 should wait, even s, for the

Silk
Re 18:12 fine linen and purple and s

Silla
2Ki 12:20 way that goes down to S

Silly
2Sa 22:27 you will act as s

Siloam
Lu 13:4 upon whom the tower in S
Joh 9:7 Go wash in the pool of S
9:11 Go to S and wash

Silvanus
2Co 1:19 through me and S and Timothy
1Th 1:1 Paul and S and Timothy to the
2Th 1:1 Paul and S and Timothy to the
1Pe 5:12 S, a faithful brother, as I

Silver

Ge 13:2 stocked with herds and *s* and
20:16 I do give a thousand *s* pieces
23:9 full amount of *s* let him give
23:13 amount of *s* for the field
23:15 worth four hundred *s* shekels
23:16 the amount of *s* that he had
23:16 four hundred *s* shekels
24:35 *s* and gold and menservants
24:53 articles of *s* and articles
37:28 for twenty *s* pieces
44:2 place my cup, the *s* cup, in
44:8 could we steal *s* or gold from
45:22 three hundred *s* pieces and
Ex 3:22 articles of *s* and articles of
11:2 articles of *s* and articles of
12:35 articles of *s* and articles of
20:23 gods of *s*, and you must not
25:3 from them: gold and *s* and
26:19 forty socket pedestals of *s*
26:21 forty socket pedestals of *s*
26:25 their socket pedestals of *s*
26:32 four socket pedestals of *s*
27:10 and their joints are of *s*
27:11 and their joints being of *s*
27:17 have fastenings of *s*, and
27:17 and their pegs are of *s* but
30:16 *s* money of the atonement
31:4 in gold and *s* and copper
35:5 gold and *s* and copper
35:24 contribution of *s* and copper
35:32 working in gold and *s* and
36:24 forty socket pedestals of *s*
36:26 forty socket pedestals of *s*
36:30 socket pedestals of *s* to
36:36 four socket pedestals of *s*
38:10 and their joints were of *s*
38:11 and their joints were of *s*
38:12 and their joints were of *s*
38:17 and their joints were of *s*
38:17 of their tops was of *s*, and
38:17 *s* joinings for all the pillars
38:19 Their pegs were of *s* and the
38:19 and their joints were of *s*
38:25 *s* of the ones registered of
38:27 a hundred talents of *s* went
Le 5:15 estimated value in *s* shekels
27:3 fifty shekels of *s* by the
27:6 then become five shekels of *s*
27:6 must be three shekels of *s*
27:16 then at fifty shekels of *s*
Nu 7:13 offering was one *s* dish, its
7:13 one *s* bowl of seventy shekels
7:19 one *s* dish, its weight being
7:19 *s* bowl of seventy shekels by
7:25 one *s* dish, its weight being
7:25 *s* bowl of seventy shekels by
7:31 offering was one *s* dish, its
7:31 *s* bowl of seventy shekels by
7:37 offering was one *s* dish, its
7:37 one *s* bowl of seventy shekels
7:43 offering was one *s* dish, its
7:43 one *s* bowl of seventy
7:49 offering was one *s* dish, its
7:49 *s* bowl of seventy shekels
7:55 offering was one *s* dish, its
7:55 *s* bowl of seventy shekels by
7:61 offering was one *s* dish, its
7:61 *s* bowl of seventy shekels by
7:67 offering was one *s* dish, its
7:67 *s* bowl of seventy shekels by
7:73 offering was one *s* dish, its
7:73 *s* bowl of seventy shekels by
7:79 His offering was one *s* dish
7:79 *s* bowl of seventy shekels by
7:84 twelve *s* dishes
7:84 twelve *s* bowls, twelve
7:85 shekels to each *s* dish
7:85 all the *s* of the vessels being
10:2 two trumpets of *s*
18:16 five *s* shekels by the shekel
22:18 his house full of *s* and gold
24:13 his house full of *s* and gold
31:22 Only the gold and the *s*, the
De 7:25 You must not desire the *s*
8:13 *s* and gold may increase for
17:17 nor should he increase *s* and
22:19 fine him a hundred *s* shekels
22:29 fifty *s* shekels, and she
29:17 dungy idols . . . *s* and gold
Jos 6:19 all the *s* and the gold and
6:24 the *s* and the gold and the
7:21 two hundred shekels of *s* and
7:24 *s* and the official garment
Jos 22:8 with *s* and gold and copper
Jg 5:19 No gain of *s* did they take
9:4 seventy pieces of *s* from the
16:5 thousand one hundred *s* pieces
17:2 *s* pieces that were taken from
17:2 look! the *s* is with me
17:3 gave back the . . . pieces of *s*
17:3 sanctify the *s* to Jehovah
17:4 returned the *s* to his mother
17:4 took two hundred *s* pieces and
17:10 give you ten *s* pieces a year
1Sa 9:8 quarter of a shekel of *s* found
2Sa 8:10 proved to be articles of *s*
8:11 with the *s* and the gold that
18:11 give you ten pieces of *s* and
18:12 a thousand pieces of *s*
21:4 It is not a matter of *s* or
24:24 for fifty *s* shekels
1Ki 7:51 the *s* and the gold and the
10:21 There was nothing of *s*
10:22 carrying gold and *s*
10:25 articles of *s* and articles
10:27 *s* in Jerusalem like the
10:29 for six hundred *s* pieces
15:15 *s* and gold and articles
15:18 took all the *s* and the gold
15:19 a present of *s* and gold
16:24 two talents of *s*, and began
20:3 Your *s* and your gold are
20:5 Your *s* and your gold and
20:7 sons and my *s* and my gold
20:39 a talent of *s* you will
2Ki 5:5 ten talents of *s* and six
5:22 a talent of *s* and two
5:23 two talents of *s* in two bags
5:26 Is it a time to accept *s* or
6:25 worth eighty *s* pieces
6:25 was worth five *s* pieces
7:8 *s* and gold and garments and
12:13 were not made basins of *s*
12:13 article of *s* from the money
14:14 he took all the gold and *s*
15:19 a thousand talents of *s*
15:20 brought forth the *s* at the
15:20 fifty *s* shekels for each
16:8 Ahaz took the *s* and the gold
18:14 three hundred *s* talents and
18:15 Hezekiah gave all the *s* that
20:13 the *s* and the gold and the
23:33 a hundred *s* talents and a
23:35 *s* and the gold Jehoiakim
23:35 to give the *s* at the order
23:35 *s* and the gold from the
25:15 that were of genuine *s*
1Ch 18:10 articles of gold and *s* and
18:11 the *s* and the gold that he
19:6 a thousand *s* talents to hire
22:14 and a million talents of *s*
22:16 The gold, the *s* and the
28:14 the utensils of *s* by weight
28:15 lampstands of *s* by weight
28:16, 16 *s* for the tables of *s*
28:17 small *s* bowls by weight
29:2 and the *s* for the silverwork
29:3 gold and *s*; I do give it to
29:4 refined *s*, for coating the
29:5 of the *s* for the silverwork
29:7 *s* worth ten thousand talents
2Ch 1:15 *s* and the gold in Jerusalem
1:17 for six hundred *s* pieces and
2:7 to work in gold and in *s* and
2:14 to work in gold and in *s*, in
5:1 *s* and the gold and all the
9:14 in gold and *s* to Solomon
9:20 *s* . . . considered as nothing
9:21 carrying gold and *s*, ivory
9:24 gift, articles of *s* and
9:27 *s* in Jerusalem like the
15:18 *s* and gold and utensils
16:2 *s* and gold from the
16:3 I do send you *s* and gold
21:3 gifts in *s* and in gold and
24:14 utensils of gold and of *s*
25:6 for a hundred *s* talents
25:24 all the gold and the *s* and
27:5 hundred *s* talents and ten
32:27 *s* and for gold and for
36:3 a hundred *s* talents and a
Ezr 1:4 with *s* and with gold and
1:6 utensils of *s*, with gold
1:9 basket-shaped vessels of *s*
1:10 small secondary bowls of *s*
1:11 utensils of gold and of *s*
2:69 thousand drachmas, and *s*
Ezr 5:14 also the gold and *s* vessels
6:5 let the gold and *s* vessels
7:15 to bring the *s* and the gold
7:16 all the *s* and the gold that
7:18 the rest of the *s* and gold
7:22 a hundred talents of *s* and a
8:25 the *s* and the gold and the
8:26 and fifty talents of *s* and a
8:26 a hundred *s* utensils worth
8:28 the *s* and the gold are a
8:30 weight of the *s* and the gold
8:33 weigh out the *s* and the gold
Ne 5:15 daily forty *s* shekels
7:71 thousand two hundred *s* minas
7:72 two thousand *s* minas and
Es 1:6 *s* rings and pillars of marble
1:6 couches of gold and *s* upon a
3:9 and ten thousand *s* talents I
3:11 *s* is given to you, also the
Job 3:15 who fill their houses with *s*
22:25 And *s*, the choicest, to you
27:16 pile up *s* like dust itself
27:17 in the *s* the innocent would
28:1 for *s* there exists a place
28:15 *s* cannot be weighed out as
Ps 12:6 As *s* refined in a smelting
66:10 as when refining *s*
68:13 a dove covered with *s*
68:30 stamping down on pieces of *s*
105:37 bring them out with *s* and
115:4 Their idols are *s* and gold
119:72 of pieces of gold and *s*
135:15 idols of the nations are *s*
Pr 2:4 keep seeking for it as for *s*
3:14 better than having *s* as gain
8:10 my discipline and not *s*
8:19 and my produce than choice *s*
10:20 righteous one is choice *s*
16:16 is to be chosen more than *s*
17:3 The refining pot is for *s* and
22:1 favor is better than even *s*
25:4 of scummy dross from the *s*
25:11 apples of gold in *s* carvings
26:23 a *s* glazing overlaid upon a
27:21 The refining pot is for *s*
Ec 2:8 I accumulated also *s* and gold
5:10 mere lover of *s* will not be
5:10 will not be satisfied with *s*
12:6 before the *s* cord is removed
Ca 1:11 along with studs of *s*
3:10 Its pillars he has made of *s*
8:9 upon her a battlement of *s*
8:11 fruitage a thousand *s* pieces
Isa 1:22 *s* itself has become scummy
2:7 land is filled with *s* and
2:20 worthless gods of *s* and his
7:23 a thousand pieces of *s*
13:17 Medes, who account *s*
30:22 your graven images of *s*
31:7 his worthless gods of *s* and
39:2 the *s* and the gold and the
40:19 and *s* chains he is forging
46:6 they weigh out the *s*
48:10 but not in the form of *s*
60:9 *s* and their gold being with
60:17 I shall bring in *s*, and
Jer 6:30 Rejected *s* is what people
10:4 With *s* and with gold one
10:9 *S* beaten into plates is what
32:9 shekels and ten *s* pieces
52:19 that were of genuine *s*
Eze 7:19 they will throw their very *s*
7:19 Neither their *s* nor their
16:13 with gold and *s*
16:17 from my *s* that I had given
22:18 scummy dross, that of *s*
22:20 As in collecting *s* and
22:22 liquefying of *s* in the
27:12 For its *s*, iron, tin and
28:4 you keep getting gold and *s*
38:13 to carry off *s* and gold
Da 2:32 and its arms were of *s*
2:35 *s* and the gold were, all
2:45 molded clay, the *s* and the
5:2 the vessels of gold and of *s*
5:4 the gods of gold and of *s*
5:23 praised mere gods of *s* and
11:8 articles of *s* and of gold
11:38 and by means of *s* and by
11:43 of the gold and the *s*
Ho 2:8 I had made *s* itself abound for
3:2 for fifteen *s* pieces and a
8:4 With their *s* and their gold
9:6 their desirable things of *s*

Ho 13:2 a molten statue from their s
Joe 3:5 you men have taken my own s
Am 2:6 someone righteous for mere s
8:6 buy lowly people for mere s
Na 2:9 Plunder s, you men; plunder
Hab 2:19 is sheathed in gold and s
Zep 1:11 all those weighing out s
1:18 their s nor their gold will
Hag 2:8 The s is mine, and the gold
Zec 6:11 take s and gold and make a
9:3 s like dust and gold like the
11:12 wages, thirty pieces of s
11:13 took the thirty pieces of s
13:9 as in the refining of s, and
14:14 gold and s and garments in
Mal 3:3 a refiner and cleanser of s
3:3 like gold and like s, and
Mt 10:9 Do not procure gold or s or
25:18 and hid the s money of his
25:27 deposited my s monies with
26:15 stipulated to him thirty s
27:3 the thirty s pieces back to
27:5 So he threw the s pieces into
27:6 priests took the s pieces and
27:9 they took the thirty s pieces
28:12 s pieces to the soldiers
28:15 they took the s pieces and
Mr 14:11 to give him s money. So he
Lu 9:3 pouch, nor bread nor s money
19:15 he had given the s money
19:23 not put my s money in a bank
22:5 agreed to give him s money
Ac 3:6 S and gold I do not possess
7:16 with s money from the sons
8:20 May your s perish with you
17:29 is like gold or s or stone
19:19 fifty thousand pieces of s
19:24 making s shrines of Artemis
20:33 I have coveted no man's s or
1Co 3:12 gold, s, precious stones
2Ti 2:20 not only of gold and s but
Jas 5:3 Your gold and s are rusted
1Pe 1:18 corruptible things, with s
Re 9:20 the idols of gold and s and
18:12 full stock of gold and s

Silversmith
Jg 17:4 and gave them to the s
Ac 19:24 Demetrius, a s, by making

Silverwork
1Ch 29:2 and the silver for the s, and
29:5 and of the silver for the s

Simeon
Ge 29:33 Hence she called his name S
34:25 sons of Jacob, S and Levi
34:30 Jacob said to S and to Levi
35:23 sons by Leah were . . . S
42:24 took S from them and bound
42:36 S is no more, and Benjamin
43:23 he brought out S to them
46:10 sons of S were Jemuel and
48:5 mine like Reuben and S
49:5 S and Levi are brothers
Ex 1:2 Reuben, S, Levi and Judah
6:15 sons of S were Jemuel and
6:15 These are the families of S
Nu 1:6 of S, Shelumiel the son of
1:22 sons of S, their births
1:23 registered . . . tribe of S
2:12 tribe of S, and the chieftain
2:12 chieftain for the sons of S
7:36 chieftain for the sons of S
10:19 the tribe of the sons of S
13:5 of S, Shaphat the son of Hori
26:12 sons of S by their families
34:20 of S, Shemuel the son of
De 27:12 S and Levi and Judah and
Jos 19:1 second lot came out for S
19:1 the tribe of the sons of S
19:8 the tribe of the sons of S
19:9 inheritance of the sons of S
19:9 sons of S got a possession in
21:9 the tribe of the sons of S
Jg 1:3 Judah said to S his brother
1:3 Accordingly S went with him
1:17 Judah marched on with S his
1Ch 2:1 sons of Israel: Reuben, S
4:24 sons of S were Nemuel and
4:42 sons of S that went to Mount
6:65 the tribe of the sons of S
12:25 Of the sons of S the mighty
2Ch 15:9 and S, for they had deserted
34:6 Ephraim and S and clear to
Eze 48:24 western border, S one
Eze 48:25 boundary of S, from the
48:33 the gate of S, one
Lu 2:25 a man in Jerusalem named S
2:34 S blessed them, but said to
Re 7:7 out of . . . S twelve thousand

Simeonites
Nu 25:14 a paternal house of the S
26:14 were the families of the S
Jos 21:4 and out of the tribe of the S
1Ch 27:16 of the S, Shephatiah the son

Similar
Eze 8:2 s to the appearance of fire
Da 10:16 s to the likeness of the sons
Mr 7:13 many things s to this you do

Similarity
Heb 7:15 with a s to Melchizedek

Similarly
Heb 2:14 s partook of the same things

Simon
Mt 4:18 S who is called Peter and
10:2 S, the one called Peter, and
10:4 S the Cananaean, and Judas
13:55 his brothers . . . S and Judas
16:16 S Peter said: You are the
16:17 Happy you are, S son of
17:25 What do you think, S?
26:6 in the house of S the leper
27:32 a native of Cyrene named S
Mr 1:16 sea of Galilee he saw S and
1:16 and Andrew the brother of S
1:29 went into the home of S and
1:36 S and those with him hunted
3:16 S . . . the surname Peter
3:18 Thaddaeus and S the Cananaean
6:3 the brother of . . . Judas and S
14:3 in the house of S the leper
14:37 S, are you sleeping? Did you
15:21 S of Cyrene, coming from
Lu 5:4 he said to S: Pull out to
5:5 S in reply said: Instructor
5:8 S Peter fell down at the knees
5:10 who were sharers with S
5:10 Jesus said to S: Stop being
6:14 S, whom he also named Peter
6:15 S who is called the zealous
7:40 S, I have something to say
7:43 S said: I suppose it is the
7:44 and said to S: Do you behold
22:31, 31 S, S, look! Satan has
23:26 S, a certain native of Cyrene
24:34 Lord . . . appeared to S
Joh 1:40 the brother of S Peter was
1:41 found his own brother, S
1:42 You are S the son of John
6:8 Andrew the brother of S Peter
6:68 S Peter answered him
6:71 Judas the son of S Iscariot
13:2 Judas Iscariot, the son of S
13:6 And so he came to S Peter
13:9 S Peter said to him
13:24 S Peter nodded to this one
13:26 Judas, the son of S Iscariot
13:36 S Peter said to him: Lord
18:10 S Peter, as he had a sword
18:15 S Peter as well as another
18:25 S Peter was standing and
20:2 she ran and came to S Peter
20:6 S Peter also came following
21:2 S Peter and Thomas, who
21:3 S Peter said to them: I am
21:7 S Peter, upon hearing that
21:11 S Peter, therefore, went
21:15 Jesus said to S Peter
21:15 S son of John, do you love
21:16 S son of John, do you love
21:17 S son of John, do you have
Ac 1:13 and S the zealous one, and
8:9 S, who, prior to this, had
8:13 S himself also became a
8:18 S saw that through the laying
8:24 S said: You men, make
9:43 with a certain S, a tanner
10:5 S who is surnamed Peter
10:6 S, a tanner, who has a house
10:18 inquired whether S who was
10:32 call for S, who is surnamed
10:32 house of S, a tanner, by
11:13 for S who is surnamed Peter
2Pe 1:1 S Peter, a slave and apostle

Simon's
Mr 1:30 S mother-in-law was lying
Lu 4:38 he entered into S home
4:38 Now S mother-in-law was
5:3 one of the boats, which was S
Ac 10:17 made inquiries for S house

Simple
Mt 6:22 eye is s, your whole body
Lu 11:34 eye is s, your whole body is

Simple-minded
Ho 7:11 proves to be like a s dove

Simple-mindedness
Pr 9:13 She is s itself and has come

Sin
Ge 4:7 there is s crouching at the
18:20 their s, yes, it is very
20:9 and what s have I committed
20:9 me and my kingdom a great s
31:36 what the s of mine, as a
39:9 and actually s against God
42:22 Do not s against the child
50:17 your brothers and their s in
Ex 10:17 pardon, please, my s just
16:1 came to the wilderness of S
17:1 from the wilderness of S by
20:20 faces that you may not s
23:33 cause you to s against me
29:14 It is a s offering
29:36 the bull of the s offering
29:36 purify the altar from s by
30:10 blood of the s offering of
32:21 have brought a great s upon
32:30 sinned with a great s, and
32:30 can make amends for your s
32:31 has sinned with a great s
32:32 pardon their s,—and if not
32:34 punishment . . . for their s
34:7 pardoning error . . . and s
34:9 forgive our error and our s
Le 4:3 then he must present for his s
4:3 bull to Jehovah as a s offering
4:8 of the bull of the s offering
4:14 s that they have committed
4:14 a young bull for a s offering
4:20 other bull of the s offering
4:21 It is a s offering for the
4:23 his s that he has committed
4:24 It is a s offering
4:25 the blood of the s offering
4:26 atonement for him for his s
4:28 his s that he has committed
4:28 his s that he has committed
4:29 the head of the s offering
4:29 slaughter the s offering in
4:32 his offering for a s offering
4:33 the head of the s offering
4:33 slaughter it as a s offering
4:34 the blood of the s offering
4:35 atonement for him for his s
5:6 his s that he has committed
5:6 of the goats, for a s offering
5:6 atonement for him for his s
5:7 the s that he has committed
5:7 one for a s offering and one
5:8 present first the one for the s
5:9 the blood of the s offering
5:9 It is a s offering
5:10 atonement for him for his s
5:11 for the s he has committed
5:11 fine flour for a s offering
5:11 for it is a s offering
5:12 It is a s offering
5:13 atonement for him for his s
5:16 make compensation for the s
6:3 man might do to s by them
6:17 like the s offering and like
6:25 is the law of the s offering
6:25 the s offering . . . slaughtered
6:26 who offers it for s will eat
6:30 no s offering of which some
7:7 Like the s offering, so is the
7:37 the s offering and the guilt
8:2 the bull of the s offering and
8:14 the bull of the s offering
8:14 the bull of the s offering
8:15 and purify the altar from s
9:2 a young calf for a s offering
9:3 a male goat for a s offering
9:7 render up your s offering and
9:8 the calf of the s offering
9:10 the s offering smoke upon the
9:15 s offering that was for the
9:15 made an offering for s with
9:22 from rendering the s offering

Le 10:16 the goat of the s offering
10:17 the s offering in the place
10:19 presented their s offering
10:19 had I eaten the s offering
12:6 a turtledove for a s offering
12:8 and one for a s offering, and
14:13 the s offering and the burnt
14:13 like the s offering, the
14:19 render up the s offering
14:22 serve as a s offering and the
14:31 as a s offering and the other
14:49 to purify the house from s
14:52 purify the house from s with
15:15 one as a s offering and the
15:30 one a s offering and the
16:3 a young bull for a s offering
16:5 of the goats for a s offering
16:6 the bull of the s offering
16:9 he must make it a s offering
16:11 bull of the s offering
16:11 the s offering, which is for
16:15 goat of the s offering
16:25 fat of the s offering smoke
16:27 bull of the s offering and
16:27 goat of the s offering, the
19:17 you may not bear s along
19:22 for his s that he committed
19:22 s that he committed must be
20:20 should answer for their s
22:9 s because of it and have to
23:19 goats as a s offering and
24:15 must then answer for his s
Nu 5:7 confess their s that they have
6:11 one as a s offering and the
6:14 first year as a s offering
6:16 render up his s offering and
7:16 of the goats for a s offering
7:22 of the goats for a s offering
7:28 of the goats for a s offering
7:34 of the goats for a s offering
7:40 the goats for a s offering
7:46 the goats for a s offering
7:52 of the goats for a s offering
7:58 of the goats for a s offering
7:64 one kid . . . for a s offering
7:70 one kid . . . for a s offering
7:76 kid . . . for a s offering
7:82 of the goats for a s offering
7:87 of the goats for a s offering
8:8 young bull for a s offering
8:12 the one as a s offering
9:13 For his s that man will answer
12:11 attribute to us the s in
15:24 of the goats as a s offering
15:25 s offering before Jehovah for
15:27 s by mistake, then he must
15:27 female goat . . . a s offering
15:28 by a s unintentionally before
16:22 will just one man s and you
16:26 be swept away in all their s
18:9 and every s offering of theirs
18:22 to incur s so as to die
18:32 you must not incur s for it
19:9 It is a s offering
19:17 the burning of the s offering
19:19 must purify him from s on
27:3 but for his own s he has died
28:15 as a s offering to Jehovah in
28:22 and one goat of s offering to
29:5 s offering to make atonement
29:11 one kid . . . as a s offering
29:11 s offering of atonement and
29:16 as a s offering, aside from
29:19 as a s offering, aside from
29:22 and one goat as a s offering
29:25 kid . . . as a s offering
29:28 and one goat as a s offering
29:31 and one goat as a s offering
29:34 and one goat as a s offering
29:38 and one goat as a s offering
31:20 purify for yourselves from s
32:23 certainly s against Jehovah
32:23 your s will catch up with
33:11 in the wilderness of S
33:12 from the wilderness of S and
De 9:18 s that you had committed in
9:21 your s that you had made
9:27 their wickedness and their s
15:9 has become a s on your part
19:15 respecting any error or any s
19:15 any s that he may commit
20:18 s against Jehovah your God
21:22 a s deserving the sentence of
22:26 has no s deserving of death

De 23:21 become a s on your part
23:22 not become a s on your part
24:4 not lead the land . . . into s
24:15 must become s on your part
24:16 put to death for his own s
1Sa 2:17 s of the attendants came to
2:25 s against a man, God will
2:25 against Jehovah . . . should s
12:23 s against Jehovah by ceasing
14:34 must not s against Jehovah
14:38 what way this s has come
15:23 same as the s of divination
15:25 please, pardon my s and
19:4 king s against his servant
19:5 s against innocent blood in
20:1 what s have I committed
2Sa 12:13 does let your s pass by
1Ki 8:34 forgive the s of your people
8:35 from their s they turn back
8:36 forgive the s of your
8:46 In case they s against you
8:46 no man that does not s
12:30 came to be a cause for s
13:34 came to be a cause of s
14:16 which he caused Israel to s
15:26 walking . . . in his s
15:26 he caused Israel to s
15:30 he caused Israel to s and
15:34 and in his s with which he
15:34 which he caused Israel to s
16:2 caused my people Israel to s
16:13 they caused Israel to s by
16:19 s which he did by causing
16:19 by causing Israel to s
16:26 his s with which he caused
16:26 to s by offending Jehovah
18:9 What s have I committed
21:22 and then caused Israel to s
22:52 who had caused Israel to s
2Ki 3:3 which he caused Israel to s
10:29 he caused Israel to s
10:31 he caused Israel to s
12:16 the money for s offerings
13:2 pursuit of the s of Jeroboam
13:2 he caused Israel to s
13:6 s of the house of Jeroboam
13:6 he caused Israel to s. In it
13:11 which he made Israel s
14:6 for his own s should each
14:24 he caused Israel to s
15:9 he caused Israel to s
15:18 he caused Israel to s
15:24 he caused Israel to s
15:28 he caused Israel to s
17:21, 21 to s with a great s
21:11 s with his dungy idols
21:16 his s with which he caused
21:16 caused Judah to s by doing
21:17 his s with which he sinned
23:15 who caused Israel to s
2Ch 6:25 forgive the s of your people
6:26 from their s they turn back
6:27 forgive the s of your
6:36 In case they s against you
6:36 is no man that does not s
7:14 and forgive their s, and I
25:4 own s that they should die
29:21 goats as a s offering for
29:23 goats of the s offering
29:24 s offering with their blood
29:24 the s offering should be
33:19 s and his unfaithfulness
Ezr 6:17 a s offering for all Israel
8:35 he-goats as a s offering
Ne 4:5 their error and their s from
6:13 and I should certainly s and
10:33 the s offerings to make
13:26 foreign wives caused to s
Job 1:22 In all this Job did not s or
2:10 Job did not s with his lips
10:6 And for my s you should keep
13:23 my own revolt and my own s
14:16 watch for nothing but my s
31:30 not allow my palate to s
34:37 on top of his s he adds
35:6 If you actually s, what do
Ps 4:4 Be agitated, but do not s
32:1 pardoned, whose s is covered
32:5 My s I finally confessed to
38:3 my bones on account of my s
38:18 to be anxious over my s
40:6 s offering you did not ask for
51:2 cleanse me even from my s
51:3 And my s is in front of me

Ps 51:5 in s my mother conceived me
51:7 purify me from s with hyssop
59:3 any s on my part, O Jehovah
59:12 For the s of their mouth
85:2 You have covered all their s
109:7 his very prayer become a s
109:14 s of his mother—may it not
119:11 I may not s against you
Pr 5:22 ropes of his own s he will
10:16 the wicked one results in s
14:34 s is something disgraceful
20:9 I have become pure from my s
21:4 lamp of the wicked . . . are s
24:9 conduct of foolishness is s
Ec 5:6 mouth to cause your flesh to s
7:20 doing good and does not s
Isa 3:9 s like that of Sodom they
5:18 as with wagon cords s
6:7 and your s itself is atoned
27:9 when he takes away his s
29:21 bringing a man into s by
30:1, 1 in order to add s to s
31:7 made for yourselves as a s
53:12 carried the very s of many
Jer 16:10 what is our s with which
16:18 their error and of their s
17:1 The s of Judah is written
17:3 because of s throughout all
18:23 do not wipe out that s of
31:34 s I shall remember no more
32:35 purpose of making Judah s
36:3 their error and their s
La 1:8 has committed outright s
3:39 man on account of his s
4:6 punishment for the s of Sodom
Eze 3:20 For his s he will die, and
3:21 righteous one should not s
3:21 himself does not actually s
14:13 it commits s against me in
18:24 s with which he has sinned
28:16 violence, and you began to s
30:15 pour out my rage upon S
30:16 S will without fail be in
33:14 turns back from his s and
40:39 s offering and the guilt
42:13 the s offering and the
43:19 of the herd, as a s offering
43:20 purify it from s and make
43:21 young bull, the s offering
43:22 as a s offering; and they
43:22 purify the altar from s
43:22 purified it from s with the
43:23 end of the purifying from s
43:25 as a s offering for the day
44:27 present his s offering, is
44:29 the s offering and the
45:17 to provide the s offering
45:18 purify the sanctuary from s
45:19 blood of the s offering
45:22 young bull as a s offering
45:23 as a s offering a buck of
45:25 same as the s offering, as
46:20 offering and the s offering
Da 9:20 praying and confessing my s
9:20 s of my people Israel and
9:24 and to finish off s, and to
Ho 4:8 The s of my people is what
8:11 altars in order to s
8:11 have altars in order to s
10:8 of Beth-aven, the s of Israel
12:8 my part, no error that is s
13:2 now they commit additional s
13:12 his s is treasured up
Mic 1:13 The beginning of s was what
3:8 to tell . . . to Israel his s
6:7 for the s of my soul
Zec 13:1 for s and for an abhorrent
14:19 punishment . . . s of Egypt
14:19 the s of all the nations
Mt 12:31 s and blasphemy will be
18:15 if your brother commits a s
18:21 my brother to s against me
Mr 3:29 is guilty of everlasting s
Lu 17:3 brother commits a s give him
Joh 1:29 away the s of the world
5:14 Do not s anymore, in order
8:21 yet you will die in your s
8:34 Every doer of s is a slave
8:34 is a slave of s
8:46 Who of you convicts me of s?
9:41 blind, you would have no s
9:41 say, We see. Your s remains
15:22 they would have no s; but
15:22 have no excuse for their s

Joh 15:24 they would have no s; but
16:8 evidence concerning s and
16:9 concerning s, because they
19:11 man . . . has greater s
Ac 7:60 Jehovah, do not charge this s
25:8 have I committed any s
Ro 3:9 well as Greeks are all under s
3:20 the accurate knowledge of s
4:8 man whose s Jehovah will by
5:12 through one man s entered
5:12 and death through s, and thus
5:13 until the Law s was in the
5:13 s is not charged against
5:20 where s abounded, undeserved
5:21 s ruled as king with death
6:1 Shall we continue in s, that
6:2 we died with reference to s
6:6 longer go on being slaves to s
6:7 has been acquitted from his s
6:10 he died with reference to s
6:11 with reference to s but
6:12 do not let s continue to rule
6:13 presenting your members to s
6:14 s must not be master over
6:15 Shall we commit a s because
6:16 of s with death in view or
6:17 you were the slaves of s but
6:18 you were set free from s
6:20 when you were slaves of s
6:22 you were set free from s but
6:23 the wages s pays is death
7:7 Is the Law s? Never may that
7:7 come to know s if it had not
7:8 s, receiving an inducement
7:8 apart from law s was dead
7:9 s came to life again, but I
7:11 s, receiving an inducement
7:13 But s did, that it might be
7:13 shown as s working out death
7:13 s . . . become far more sinful
7:14 I am fleshly, sold under s
7:17 but s that resides in me
7:20 but the s dwelling in me
8:2 free from the law of s and of
8:3 and concerning s, condemned
8:3 condemned s in the flesh
8:10 is dead on account of s, but
14:23 is not out of faith is s
1Co 6:18 Every other s that a man may
7:28 you would commit no s
7:28 such one would commit no s
7:36 does not s. Let them marry
8:12 people thus s against your
15:34 do not practice s, for some
15:56 sting producing death is s
15:56 the power for s is the Law
2Co 5:21 one who did not know s he
5:21 he made to be s for us, that
11:7 I commit a s by humbling
Ga 3:22 together to the custody of s
Eph 4:26 wrathful, and yet do not s
1Ti 5:20 persons who practice s, that
Heb 3:13 by the deceptive power of s
4:15 ourselves, but without s
9:26 put s away through the
9:28 it will be apart from s and
10:6 not approve . . . s offering
10:8 s offering—sacrifices that
10:18 no longer an offering for s
10:26 if we practice s willfully
11:25 temporary enjoyment of s
12:1 s that easily entangles us
12:4 your contest against that s
13:11 by the high priest for s
Jas 1:15 fertile, gives birth to s
1:15 s, when . . . accomplished
2:9 you are working a s, for you
4:17 not do it, it is a s for him
1Pe 2:22 He committed no s, nor was
2Pe 2:14 unable to desist from s, and
1Jo 1:7 cleanses us from all s
1:8 statement: We have no s
2:1 that you may not commit a s
2:1 if anyone does commit a s
3:4 Everyone who practices s is
3:4 and so s is lawlessness
3:5 and there is no s in him
3:6 does not practice s; no one
3:6 no one that practices s has
3:8 carries on s originates with
3:9 does not carry on s, because
3:9 he cannot practice s, because
5:16 s that does not incur death
5:16 is a s that does incur death
1Jo 5:16 concerning that s that I do
5:17 All unrighteousness is s
5:17 a s that does not incur death
5:18 does not practice s, but the

Sinai
Ex 16:1 which is between Elim and S
19:1 came into the wilderness of S
19:2 come into the wilderness of S
19:11 all the people upon Mount S
19:18 And Mount S smoked all over
19:20 came down upon Mount S to
19:23 able to come up to Mount S
24:16 to reside upon Mount S, and
31:18 speaking with him on Mount S
34:2 in the morning into Mount S
34:4 went on up into Mount S
34:29 came down from Mount S that
34:32 spoken with him on Mount S
Le 7:38 commanded Moses in Mount S
7:38 in the wilderness of S
25:1 to Moses in Mount S, saying
26:46 Israel in Mount S by means
27:34 sons of Israel in Mount S
Nu 1:1 Moses in the wilderness of S
1:19 in the wilderness of S
3:1 spoke with Moses in Mount S
3:4 Jehovah in the wilderness of S
3:14 Moses in the wilderness of S
9:1 Moses in the wilderness of S
9:5 in the wilderness of S
10:12 from the wilderness of S
26:64 in the wilderness of S
28:6 rendered up at Mount S as a
33:15 in the wilderness of S
33:16 from the wilderness of S
De 33:2 Jehovah—from S he came, And
Jg 5:5 This S away from the face of
Ne 9:13 upon Mount S you came down
Ps 68:8 This S rocked because of God
68:17 from S into the holy place
Ac 7:30 in the wilderness of Mount S
7:38 spoke to him on Mount S and
Ga 4:24 the one from Mount S, which
4:25 Hagar means S, a mountain

Sincerely
Job 33:3 what my lips do utter s

Sincerity
Ac 2:46 rejoicing and s of heart
1Co 5:8 unfermented cakes of s and
2Co 1:12 with holiness and godly s
2:17 out of s, yes, as sent from
11:3 corrupted away from the s
Eph 6:5 in the s of your hearts, as
Col 3:22 with s of heart, with fear

Sin-cleansing
Nu 8:7 Spatter s water upon them, and

Sinew
Ge 32:32 eat the s of the thigh nerve
32:32 by the s of the thigh nerve
Isa 48:4 that your neck is an iron s

Sinews
Jg 16:7 seven still-moist s that have
16:8 seven still-moist s that had
16:9 tore the s in two, just as a
Job 10:11 and s to weave me together
40:17 The s of its thighs are
Eze 37:6 put upon you s and cause
37:8 s themselves and flesh

Sinful
Nu 32:14 as the brood of s men in
Isa 1:4 Woe to the s nation, the
1:28 revolters and that of s ones
Am 9:8 are upon the s kingdom
Mr 8:38 adulterous and s generation
Lu 5:8 because I am a s man, Lord
24:7 into the hands of s men and
Ro 6:6 s body might be made inactive
7:5 s passions that were excited
7:13 sin might become far more s
8:3 Son in the likeness of s flesh

Sing
Ex 15:1 to s this song to Jehovah and
15:1 Let me s to Jehovah, for he
15:21 S to Jehovah, for he has
Nu 21:17 Israel proceeded to s this
Jg 5:3 I to Jehovah, yes, I, will s
1Ch 16:9 S to him, make melody to
16:23 S to Jehovah, all you of the
Job 33:27 He will s to men and say
Ps 13:6 I will s to Jehovah, for he
Ps 21:13 s and make melody to your
27:6 s and make melody to Jehovah
33:3 S to him a new song
57:7 I will s and make melody
59:16 I shall s of your strength
65:13 in triumph, yes, they s
68:4 S you to God, make melody
68:32 the earth, s to God
89:1 I will s about even to time
96:1 S to Jehovah a new song
96:1 S to Jehovah, all you people
96:2 S to Jehovah, bless his name
98:1 S to Jehovah a new song
101:1 and judgment I will s
104:33 s to Jehovah throughout my
105:2 S to him, make melody to
106:12 They began to s his praise
108:1 I will s and make melody
119:172 tongue s forth your saying
137:3 S for us one of the songs of
137:4 How can we s the song of
138:5 s about the ways of Jehovah
144:9 O God, a new song I will s
149:1 S to Jehovah a new song
Isa 5:1 Let me s, please, to my
27:2 s to her, you people
42:10 S to Jehovah a new song
Jer 20:13 S to Jehovah, you people!
25:30 he will s out against all
51:14 s forth over you a shout
1Co 14:15 s praise with the gift of
14:15 also s praise with my mind
Jas 5:13 Let him s psalms
Re 5:9 And they s a new song, saying

Singe
Isa 43:2 will the flame itself s you

Singed
Da 3:27 not a hair . . . had been s

Singer
1Ch 6:33 Heman the s, the son of Joel
Pr 25:20 a s with songs upon a gloomy

Singers
2Sa 19:35 voice of male and female s
1Ki 10:12 instruments for the s
1Ch 9:33 And these were the s, the
15:16 station their brothers the s
15:19 s Heman, Asaph and Ethan
15:27 s and Chenaniah the chief
15:27 of the carrying by the s
2Ch 5:12 and the Levites that were s
5:13 trumpeters and the s were as
9:11 instruments for the s, and
20:21 stationed s to Jehovah and
23:13 s with the instruments of
35:15 the s the sons of Asaph
35:25, 25 male s and female s
Ezr 2:41 The s, the sons of Asaph
2:65, 65 male s and female s
2:70 the s and the gatekeepers and
7:7 and the Levites and the s and
10:24 of the s, Eliashib; and of
Ne 7:1 the gatekeepers and the s and
7:44 The s, the sons of Asaph
7:67, 67 male s and female s
7:73 the gatekeepers and the s and
10:28 the gatekeepers, the s, the
10:39 the gatekeepers and the s are
11:22 the sons of Asaph, the s
11:23 a fixed provision for the s
12:28 sons of the s proceeded to
12:29 that the s had built for
12:42 the s with Izrahiah the
12:45 the s and the gatekeepers
12:46 heads of the s and the song
12:47 giving the portions of the s
13:5 the Levites and the s and the
13:10 the s doing the work went
Ps 68:25 s went in front, the players
87:7 s as well as dancers of
Ec 2:8, 8 I made male s and female s
Eze 40:44 the dining rooms of the s
Re 14:2 s who accompany themselves
18:22 s who accompany themselves

Singing
Ex 32:18 sound of the s over mighty
32:18 sound of the s of defeat
32:18 other s that I am hearing
1Ch 6:31 the s at the house of Jehovah
6:32 ministers in the s before
Ne 11:17 conductor of the praise s
Eze 26:13 turmoil of your s to cease

Zep 2:14 will keep s in the window
Mt 26:30 after s praises, they went
Mr 14:26 after s praises, they went
Eph 5:19 s and accompanying
Col 3:16 s in your hearts to Jehovah
Re 14:3 s as if a new song before the
15:3 are s the song of Moses the

Single
Ex 10:19 Not a s locust was let
De 19:15 No s witness should rise up
Jg 2:21 a s one of the nations that
3:29 and not a s one escaped
19:19 There is no lack of a s thing
1Sa 12:4 from the hand of a s one
14:36 leave a s one among them
14:45 not as much as a s hair of
24:14 chasing . . . After a s flea?
25:15 we did not miss a s thing
25:21 not a s thing of all that
26:20 out to look for a s flea
29:3 not found in him a s thing
2Sa 14:11 not a s hair of your son
15:11 did not know a s thing
17:12 not be left even a s one
1Ki 1:52 there will not fall a s hair
18:40 Do not let a s one of them
2Ki 10:14 not let a s one of them
10:19 not let a s one be missing
10:21 not a s one was left over
10:25 Do not let a s one go out
1Ch 17:6 did I speak a s word with
Jer 12:3 S them out like sheep for
22:30 not a s one will have any
Mr 7:12 do a s thing for his father
Lu 20:40 to ask him a s question
Joh 3:27 cannot receive a s thing
5:19 Son cannot do a s thing of
5:30 cannot do a s thing of my
10:41 did not perform a s sign
16:24 asked a s thing in my name
18:9 I have not lost a s one
Ac 19:40 no s cause existing that
23:29 a s thing deserving of death
Ro 13:8 be owing anybody a s thing
1Co 9:15 not made use of a s one
2Co 11:5 in a s thing proved inferior
11:9 become a burden to a s one
12:11 apostles in a s thing, even
Re 5:3 was there a s one able to open

Singled
Ge 49:26 one s out from his brothers
De 33:16 the head of the one s out

Sinim
Isa 49:12 these from the land of S

Sinite
Ge 10:17 and the Arkite and the S
1Ch 1:15 and the Arkite and the S

Sink
Ps 69:14 mire, that I may not s down
Pr 2:18 to death her house does s
Jer 38:6 Jeremiah began to s down
38:22 foot to s down into the
51:64 Babylon will s down and
Am 8:8 s down like the Nile of Egypt
9:5 s down like the Nile of Egypt
Mt 14:30 and, after starting to s, he
Lu 5:7 boats, so that these began to s
1Pe 4:4 same low s of debauchery

Sinks
Ec 10:18 laziness the beamwork s in
Isa 5:24 mere dried grass s down

Sinned
Ge 40:1 the baker s against their lord
43:9 I shall have s against you
44:32 s against my father forever
Ex 9:27 I have s this time. Jehovah
10:16 I have s against Jehovah your
32:30 have s with a great sin, and
32:31 people has s with a great sin
32:33 Whoever has s against me, I
Le 5:5 confess in what way he has s
Nu 6:11 s because of the dead soul
14:40 For we have s
16:38 s against their own souls
21:7 We have s, because we have
22:34 I have s, because I did not
De 1:41 We have s against Jehovah
9:16 you had s against Jehovah your
Jos 7:11 Israel has s, and they have
7:20 I have s against Jehovah the
Jg 10:10 saying: We have s against
10:15 Israel said . . . We have s
11:27 I have not s against you, but
1Sa 7:6 We have s against Jehovah
12:10 We have s, for we have left
15:24 said to Samuel: I have s
15:30 I have s. Now honor me
19:4 not s toward you and his
24:11 I have not s against you
26:21 Saul said: I have s
2Sa 12:13 I have s against Jehovah
19:20 I am the one that s
24:10 I have s very much in what
24:17 Here it is I that have s
1Ki 8:47 We have s and erred, we have
8:50 your people who had s
14:16 Jeroboam with which he s
14:22 sins with which they s
15:30 with which he s and with
16:13 with which they s and with
16:19 s by doing what was bad in
2Ki 17:7 Israel had s against Jehovah
18:14 I have s. Turn back from
21:17 his sin with which he s
1Ch 21:8 I have s very much in that I
21:17 is it not I that have s and
2Ch 6:37 We have s, we have erred and
6:39 who have s against you
Ne 1:6 we have s against you
1:6 s, both I and the house of my
9:29 they s, which, if a man will
13:26 Solomon the king of Israel s
Job 1:5 maybe my sons have s and have
7:20 If I have s, what can I
8:4 If your own sons have s
10:14 If I have s and you have kept
24:19 does Sheol those who have s
33:27 He will sing . . . I have s
Ps 41:4 heal my soul, for I have s
51:4 you alone, I have s
78:32 they s some more And did
106:6 s just the same as our
Isa 42:24 One against whom we have s
43:27 the first one, has s, and
Jer 2:35 your saying, I have not s
3:25 have s, we and our fathers
8:14 we have s against Jehovah
14:7 against you that we have s
14:20 for we have s against you
16:10 s against Jehovah our God
33:8 they have s against me, and
33:8 they have s against me and
37:18 have I s against you and
40:3 people have s against Jehovah
44:23 s against Jehovah and did
50:7 they have s against Jehovah
50:14 against Jehovah . . . has s
La 5:7 are the ones that have s
5:16 Woe . . . because we have s
Eze 16:51 not s even up to half of
18:24 his sin with which he has s
33:16 sins with which he has s
37:23 places in which they have s
Da 9:5 we have s and done wrong and
9:8 because we have s against you
9:11 for we have s against Him
9:15 we have s, we have acted
Ho 4:7 so they have s against me
10:9 you have s, O Israel
Mic 7:9 for I have s against him
Zep 1:17 have s. And their blood
Mt 27:4 I s when I betrayed righteous
Lu 15:18 Father, I have s against
15:21 Father, I have s against
Joh 9:2 s, this man or his parents
9:3 this man s nor his parents
Ro 2:12 all those who s without law
2:12 s under law will be judged
3:23 all have s and fall short of
5:12 men because they had all s
5:14 those who had not s after
5:16 through the one man that s
2Co 12:21 those who formerly s but
13:2 those who have s before and
Heb 3:17 s, whose carcasses fell in
2Pe 2:4 punishing the angels that s
1Jo 1:10 statement: We have not s

Sinner
Pr 11:31 wicked one and the s be
13:6 is what subverts the s
13:22 wealth of the s is something
Ec 2:26 but to the s he has given the
8:12 s may be doing bad a hundred
Ec 9:2 good one is the same as the s
9:18 one s can destroy much good
Isa 65:20 s, although a hundred years
Lu 7:37 known in the city to be a s
7:39 touching him, that she is a s
15:7 over one s that repents than
15:10 over one s that repents
18:13 O God, be gracious to me a s
19:7 With a man that is a s he
Joh 9:16 s perform signs of that sort
9:24 know that this man is a s
9:25 he is a s I do not know
Ro 3:7 also yet being judged as a s
Jas 5:20 he who turns a s back from
1Pe 4:18 and the s make a showing

Sinners
Ge 13:13 men of Sodom . . . gross s
1Sa 15:18 and you must devote the s
Ps 1:1 in the way of s has not stood
1:5 s in the assembly of righteous
25:8 why he instructs s in the way
26:9 my soul along with s
51:13 s themselves may turn right
104:35 s will be finished off from
Pr 1:10 if s try to seduce you, do not
13:21 S are the ones whom
23:17 heart not be envious of s
Isa 13:9 annihilate the land's s out
33:14 s have come to be in dread
Am 9:10 die—all the s of my people
Mt 9:10 tax collectors and s came and
9:11 teacher eats with . . . s
9:13 not righteous people, but s
11:19 a friend of . . . s
26:45 betrayed into the hands of s
Mr 2:15 s were reclining with Jesus
2:16 saw he was eating with the s
2:16 with the tax collectors and s
2:17 I came to call . . . s
14:41 betrayed into the hands of s
Lu 5:30 with tax collectors and s
5:32 not righteous persons, but s
6:32 even the s love those loving
6:33 Even the s do the same
6:34 Even s lend without interest
6:34 lend without interest to s
7:34 friend of tax collectors and s
13:2 were proved worse s than all
15:1 tax collectors and the s kept
15:2 This man welcomes s and eats
Joh 9:31 God does not listen to s
Ro 5:8 were yet s, Christ died for us
5:19 many were constituted s
Ga 2:15 and not s from the nations
2:17 also ourselves been found s
1Ti 1:9 unruly, ungodly and s, lacking
1:15 Jesus came . . . to save s
Heb 7:26 separated from the s, and
12:3 contrary talk by s against
Jas 4:8 Cleanse your hands, you s
Jude 15 ungodly s spoke against him

Sinning
Ge 20:6 you back from s against me
Ex 9:34 Pharaoh . . . went s again and
1Sa 14:33 are s against Jehovah by
1Ki 8:33 they kept s against you
8:35 they kept s against you
2Ch 6:24 they kept s against you, and
6:26 they kept s against you, and
Job 35:3 I have more than by my s
Ps 39:1 keep from s with my tongue
78:17 s still more against him
119:67 I was s by mistake
Pr 14:21 despising . . . fellowman is s
19:2 hastening with his feet is s
20:2 is s against his own soul
Ec 7:26 is s if one is captured by her
Isa 64:5 we kept s—in them a long
Eze 18:4 soul that is s . . . will die
18:20 soul that is s . . . will die
33:12 in the day of his s
Hab 2:10 and your soul is s
1Co 6:18 is s against his own body
8:12 you are s against Christ
Tit 3:11 out of the way and is s
1Pe 2:20 when you are s and being
1Jo 3:8 Devil has been s from the
5:16 s a sin that does not incur
5:16 not s so as to incur death

Sin's
Ro 7:23 captive to s law that is in
7:25 but with my flesh to s law

Ga 2:17 is Christ . . . s minister?

Sins

Ge 41:9 My s I am mentioning today
Le 4:2 In case a soul s by mistake
4:3 s so as to bring guiltiness
4:22 When a chieftain s and he
4:27 s unintentionally by his doing
5:1 in case a soul s in that he has
5:13 any one of these s, and
5:15 he actually s by mistake
5:17 if a soul s in that he does
6:2 In case a soul s in that he
6:4 that in case he s and indeed
16:16 their revolts in all their s
16:21 all their s, and he must put
16:30 all your s before Jehovah
16:34 all their s once in the year
26:18 times as much for your s
26:21 upon you according to your s
26:24 seven times for your s
26:28 you seven times for your s
Nu 5:6 s of mankind in committing
Jos 24:19 your revolting and your s
1Sa 12:19 added to all our s an evil
1Ki 8:31 When a man s against his
14:16 s of Jeroboam with which he
14:22 s with which they sinned
15:3 walking in all the s of his
15:30 the s of Jeroboam with
16:2 by offending me with their s
16:13 all the s of Baasha and the
16:13 the s of Elah his son
16:19 the s of his with which he
16:31 walk in the s of Jeroboam
2Ki 3:3 stuck to the s of Jeroboam
10:29 s of Jeroboam the son of
10:31 from the s of Jeroboam
13:11 the s of Jeroboam the son
14:24 all the s of Jeroboam the
15:9 the s of Jeroboam the son
15:18 all the s of Jeroboam the
15:24 the s of Jeroboam the son
15:28 the s of Jeroboam the son
17:22 in all the s of Jeroboam
24:3 for the s of Manasseh
2Ch 6:22 man s against his fellowman
28:13 thinking of adding to our s
Ne 1:6 the s of the sons of Israel
9:2 confession of their own s and
9:37 put over us because of our s
Job 13:23 In what way do I have . . . s?
Ps 19:12 From concealed s pronounce
25:7 The s of my youth and my
25:18 And pardon all my s
32:5 pardoned the error of my s
51:9 Conceal your face from my s
79:9 cover over our s on account
103:10 even according to our s
Ec 10:4 calmness . . . allays great s
Isa 1:18 Though the s of you people
38:17 behind your back all my s
40:2 a full amount for all her s
43:24 to serve because of your s
43:25 s I shall not remember
44:22 your s just as with a cloud
58:1 the house of Jacob their s
59:2 your own s have caused the
59:12 as for our s, each one has
Jer 5:25 your own s have held back
14:10 give attention to their s
15:13 but for all your s, even
30:14 your s have become numerous
30:15 your s have become numerous
50:20 and the s of Judah, and they
La 4:13 of the s of her prophets
4:22 Edom. He has uncovered your s
Eze 16:51 even up to half of your s
16:52 Because of your s in which
18:14 all the s of his father that
18:21 turn back from all his s
21:24 in order that your s may be
23:49 the s of your dungy idols
33:10 our revolts and our s are
33:16 s with which he has sinned
Da 4:27 and remove your own s by
9:16 because of our s and because
Ho 8:13 an accounting for their s
9:9 give attention to their s
Am 5:12 how mighty your s are, O you
Mic 1:5 the s of the house of Israel
6:13 on account of your s
7:19 into . . . the sea all their s
Mt 1:21 save his people from their s
Mt 3:6 openly confessing their s
9:2 child; your s are forgiven
9:5 to say, Your s are forgiven
9:6 authority . . . to forgive s
26:28 of many for forgiveness of s
Mr 1:4 for forgiveness of s
1:5 openly confessing their s
2:5 Child, your s are forgiven
2:7 Who can forgive s except one
2:9 paralytic, Your s are forgiven
2:10 authority to forgive s upon
3:28 men, no matter what s and
Lu 1:77 by forgiveness of their s
3:3 repentance for forgiveness of s
5:20 Man, your s are forgiven you
5:21 Who can forgive s except God
5:23 Your s are forgiven you, or
5:24 to forgive s—he said to the
7:47 her s, many though they are
7:48 to her: Your s are forgiven
7:49 this man who even forgives s
11:4 And forgive us our s, for we
17:4 Even if he s seven times a
24:47 for forgiveness of s
Joh 8:24 You will die in your s
8:24 you will die in your s
9:34 were altogether born in s
20:23 you forgive the s of any
Ac 2:38 for forgiveness of your s
3:19 to get your s blotted out
5:31 Israel and forgiveness of s
10:43 forgiveness of s through his
13:38 forgiveness of s is being
22:16 wash your s away by your
26:18 receive forgiveness of s and
Ro 3:25 s that occurred in the past
4:7 and whose s have been covered
11:27 when I take their s away
1Co 15:3 that Christ died for our s
15:17 you are yet in your s
Ga 1:4 He gave himself for our s
Eph 2:1 dead in your trespasses and s
Col 1:14 the forgiveness of our s
1Th 2:16 the measure of their s
1Ti 5:22 neither be a sharer in the s
5:24 s of some men are publicly
5:24 their s also become manifest
2Ti 3:6 women loaded down with s
Heb 1:3 made a purification for our s
2:17 for the s of the people
5:1 gifts and sacrifices for s
5:3 to make offerings for s as
7:27 first for his own s and then
8:12 call their s to mind anymore
9:7 s of ignorance of the people
9:28 to bear the s of many; and
10:2 consciousness of s anymore
10:3 there is a reminding of s
10:4 and of goats to take s away
10:11 able to take s away
10:12 sacrifice for s perpetually
10:17 call their s and their
10:26 any sacrifice for s left
Jas 5:15 if he has committed s, it
5:16 confess your s to one another
5:20 will cover a multitude of s
1Pe 2:24 bore our s in his own body
2:24 be done with s and live to
3:18 for all time concerning s
4:1 the flesh has desisted from s
4:8 love covers a multitude of s
2Pe 1:9 cleansing from his s of long
1Jo 1:9 If we confess our s, he is
1:9 so as to forgive us our s and
2:2 sacrifice for our s, yet not
2:12 your s have been forgiven
3:5 manifest to take away our s
4:10 sacrifice for our s
Re 1:5 loosed us from our s by means
18:4 share with her in her s, and
18:5 s have massed together clear

Sion

De 4:48 S, that is to say, Hermon

Sip

Ge 24:17 little s of water from your
1Ki 17:10 Please, get me a s of water
Isa 66:11 reason that you will s and

Siphmoth

1Sa 30:28 and to those in S, and to

Sippai

1Ch 20:4 struck down S of those born

Sipping

Job 39:30 young . . . keep s up blood

Sir

Mt 8:6 S, my manservant is laid up
8:8 S, I am not a fit man for you
21:29 said, I will, s, but did not
25:11, 11 saying, S, s, open to us!
27:63 S, we have called to mind
Mr 7:28 Yes, s, and yet the little
Lu 7:6 S, do not bother, for I am not
13:25 S, open to us. But in answer
Joh 4:11 S, you have not even a bucket
4:15 S, give me this water, so
4:19 S, I perceive you are a
5:7 S, I do not have a man to put
9:36 s, that I may put faith in
12:21 S, we want to see Jesus
20:15 S, if you have carried him

Sirah

2Sa 3:26 from the cistern of S

Sire

Ge 7:2 by sevens, the s and its mate
7:2 not clean just two, the s and

Sirion

De 3:9 used to call Hermon S, and the
Ps 29:6 S like the sons of wild bulls

Sirs

Ac 16:30 S, what must I do to get

Sisera

Jg 4:2 the chief of his army was S
4:7 S the chief of Jabin's army
4:9 that Jehovah will sell S
4:12 they reported to S that Barak
4:13 S called together all his
4:14 certainly give S into your
4:15 Jehovah began to throw S and
4:15 S got down off the chariot
4:16 the camp of S fell by the
4:17 S, he fled on foot to the
4:18 Jael came on out to meet S
4:22 there was Barak pursuing S
4:22 there was S fallen dead, with
5:20 they fought against S
5:26 she hammered S, she pierced
5:28 mother of S from the lattice
5:30 Spoil of dyed stuffs for S
1Sa 12:9 S the chief of the army of
Ezr 2:53 the sons of S
Ne 7:55 the sons of S, the sons of
Ps 83:9 them as to Midian, as to S

Sismai

1Ch 2:40 in turn, became father to S
2:40 S, in turn, became father to

Sister

Ge 4:22 s of Tubal-cain was Naamah
12:13 Please say you are my s
12:19 you say, She is my s, so that I
20:2 Sarah his wife: She is my s
20:5 he say to me, She is my s
20:12 she is truly my s, the
24:30 on the hands of his s and
24:30 Rebekah his s, saying: This
24:59 sent off Rebekah their s and
24:60 our s, may you become
25:20 the s of Laban the Syrian
26:7 and he would say: She is my s
26:9 that you said, She is my s
28:9 Mahalath . . . s of Nebaioth
29:13 Jacob the son of his s
30:1 Rachel got jealous of her s
30:8 I have wrestled with my s
34:13 he had defiled Dinah their s
34:14 give our s to a man who has
34:27 they had defiled their s
34:31 treat our s like a prostitute
36:3 Basemath . . . s of Nebaioth
36:22 and Lotan's s was Timna
46:17 and there was Serah their s
Ex 2:4 his s stationed herself at a
2:7 s said to Pharaoh's daughter
6:20 took Jochebed his father's s
6:23 Elisheba . . . the s of Nahshon
15:20 Aaron's s, proceeded to take
Le 18:9 nakedness of your s, the
18:11 she being your s, you must
18:12 nakedness of your father's s
18:13 nakedness of your mother's s
18:18 woman in addition to her s
20:17 a man takes his s, the
20:17 nakedness of his s that he

1Ch 13:6 Jehovah, s on the cherubs
2Ch 9:4 s of his servants and the
9:18 side by the place of s, and
18:9 s each one on his throne
18:9 s in the threshing floor at
18:18 Jehovah s upon his throne
32:10 s quiet under siege in
Ezr 9:3 and I kept s stunned
9:4 s stunned until the grain
10:9 kept s in the open place of
10:16 s on the first day of the
Ne 2:6 queenly consort was s beside
Es 1:2 s upon his royal throne
1:14 were s first in the kingdom
2:19 Mordecai was s in the king's
2:21 Mordecai was s in the king's
5:1 king was s on his royal throne
5:13 the Jew s in the king's gate
6:10 who is s in the king's gate
Job 2:8 he was s in among the ashes
2:13 kept s with him on the earth
29:25 and I was s as head
Ps 2:4 One s in the heavens will
17:12 lion s in concealed places
55:19 He that is s enthroned as
69:12 Those s in the gate began
80:1 who are s upon the cherubs
99:1 He is s upon the cherubs
122:5 for judgment have been s
127:2 That you are s down late
139:2 know my s down and my
Pr 20:8 king is s upon the throne of
Ca 5:12 s within the rims
Isa 6:1 Jehovah, s on a throne lofty
28:6 the one s in the judgment
30:7 Rahab—they are for s still
36:12 the men s upon the wall
37:16 s upon the cherubs, you
37:28 s quiet and your going out
42:7 detention those s in darkness
47:8 woman, the one s in security
Jer 8:14 Why are we s still?
9:6 Your s is in the midst of
13:13 kings that are s for David
17:25 s on the throne of David
21:9 The one s still in this city
22:2 s on the throne of David
22:4 the kings s for David upon
22:30 s upon the throne of David
29:16 s on the throne of David
32:12 Jews who were s in the
36:12 all the princes were s
36:22 was s in the winter house
36:30 s upon the throne of David
38:7 s in the gate of Benjamin
51:30 s in the strong places
La 3:63 look at their very s down and
Eze 8:1 I was s in my house and the
8:1 the older men of Judah were s
8:14 women were s, weeping over
Am 3:12 those s in Samaria on a
Na 3:8 that was s by the Nile canals
Zep 2:15 city that was s in security
Zec 1:11 the whole earth is s still
3:8 companions who are s before
5:7 s in the midst of the ephah
Mt 4:16 people s in darkness saw a
4:16 s in a region of deathly
11:16 like young children s in the
13:1 Jesus . . . was s by the sea
13:48 s down, they collected the
15:29 mountain, he was s there
20:23 s down at my right hand and
20:30 blind men s beside the road
23:22 and by him that is s on it
24:3 s upon the Mount of Olives
26:58 s with the house attendants
26:64 s at the right hand of power
26:69 Peter was s outside in the
27:19 was s on the judgment seat
27:61 there, s before the grave
28:2 the stone, and was s on it
Mr 2:6 scribes there, s and reasoning
2:14 Levi . . . s at the tax office
3:32 a crowd was s around him, so
3:34 s around him in a circle
5:15 s clothed and in his sound
10:40 this s down at my right or
10:46 was s beside the road
13:3 was s on the Mount of Olives
14:54 he was s together with the
14:62 s at the right hand of power
16:5 a young man s on the right
Lu 1:79 s in darkness and death's
Lu 2:46 in the temple, s in the midst
5:17 Pharisees . . . were s there
5:27 tax collector named Levi s
7:32 children s in a marketplace
8:35 s at the feet of Jesus
10:13 s in sackcloth and ashes
18:35 blind man was s beside the
22:55 Peter was s in among them
22:56 s by the bright fire and
22:69 s at the powerful right hand
Joh 2:6 six stone water jars s there
4:6 was s at the fountain just as
6:3 he was s with his disciples
11:20 but Mary kept s at home
19:29 vessel was s there full of
20:12 two angels in white s one
Ac 2:2 house in which they were s
6:15 those s in the Sanhedrin
8:28 s in his chariot and reading
14:8 was s a certain man disabled
1Co 14:30 another one while s there
Re 5:13 To the One s on the throne
17:3 sight of a woman s upon a
17:15 where the harlot is s, mean

Situated

Ge 31:49 s unseen the one from the
Mt 5:14 hid when s upon a mountain

Situation

2Ki 2:19 the s of the city is good
Jer 5:30 An astonishing s, even a
Am 8:10 s like the mourning for an
Hab 3:16 and in my s I was agitated
Mt 19:10 s of a man with his wife
Ac 21:35 s became such that he was

Sivan

Es 8:9 third month . . . the month of S

Six

Ge 7:6 Noah was s hundred years old
7:11 s hundredth year of Noah's
8:13 the s hundred and first year
30:20 I have borne him s sons
31:41 and s years for your flock
Ex 12:37 number of s hundred thousand
14:7 take s hundred chosen chariots
16:26 S days you will pick it up
20:9 must do all your work s days
20:11 in s days Jehovah made the
21:2 he will be a slave s years
23:10 s years you are to sow your
23:12 S days you are to do your
24:16 to cover it for s days
25:32 s branches are running out
25:33 s branches running out from
25:35 the s branches running out
26:9 s tent cloths by themselves
26:22 will make s panel frames
28:10 s of their names upon the
28:10 names of the s remaining
31:15 S days may work be done, but
31:17 in s days Jehovah made the
34:21 S days you are to labor, but
35:2 S days may work be done, but
36:16 s other tent cloths by
36:27 he made s panel frames
37:18 s branches were running out
37:19 s branches running out from
37:21 s branches running out from
38:26 amounting to s hundred and
Le 23:3 S days may work be done, but
24:6 s to the layer set, upon the
25:3 S years you should sow your
25:3 s years you should prune your
Nu 1:25 forty-five thousand s hundred
1:27 thousand s hundred
1:46 s hundred and three thousand
2:4 seventy-four thousand s hundred
2:15 forty-five thousand s hundred
2:31 fifty-seven thousand s hundred
2:32 s hundred and three thousand
3:28 eight thousand s hundred
3:34 were s thousand two hundred
4:40 two thousand s hundred and
7:3 s covered wagons and twelve
11:21 s hundred thousand men on
26:41 forty-five thousand s hundred
26:51 s hundred and one thousand
31:32 s hundred and seventy-five
31:37 s hundred and seventy-five
35:6 s cities of refuge, which you
35:13 s cities of refuge, will be
35:15 s cities will serve as a
De 5:13 must do all your work s days
De 15:12 he has served you s years
15:18 he served you s years, and
16:8 S days you should eat
Jos 6:3 way you should do for s days
6:14 the way they did for s days
15:59 s cities and their
15:62 s cities and their
Jg 3:31 Philistines, s hundred men
12:7 to judge Israel for s years
18:11 s hundred men girded with
18:16 s hundred men girded with
18:17 s hundred men girded with
20:47 s hundred men turned and
Ru 3:15 s measures of barley and to
3:17 s measures of barley he gave
1Sa 13:5 and s thousand horsemen and
13:15 about s hundred men
14:2 were about s hundred men
17:4 being s cubits and a span
17:7 s hundred shekels of iron
23:13 s hundred men, and they
27:2 s hundred men that were
30:9 s hundred men that were
2Sa 2:11 be seven years and s months
5:5 for seven years and s months
6:13 had marched s steps, he
15:18 s hundred men that had
21:20 s fingers on each of his
21:20 s toes on each of his feet
1Ki 6:6 was s cubits in its width
10:14 s hundred and sixty-six
10:16 s hundred shekels of gold
10:19 were s steps to the throne
10:20 there upon the s steps
10:29 for s hundred silver pieces
11:16 was s months that Joab and
16:23 In Tirzah he reigned s years
2Ki 5:5 and s thousand pieces of gold
11:3 in hiding for s years, while
13:19 to strike five or s times
15:8 in Samaria for s months
1Ch 3:4 were s born to him in Hebron
3:4 seven years and s months
3:22 and Neariah and Shaphat, s
4:27 sixteen sons and s daughters
7:2 twenty-two thousand s hundred
8:38 Azel had s sons, and these
9:6 s hundred and ninety brothers
9:44 Azel had s sons, and these
12:24 s thousand eight hundred
12:26 four thousand s hundred
12:35 thousand s hundred
21:25 to the weight of s hundred
23:4 and judges s thousand
25:3 the sons of Jeduthun . . . s
26:17 east there were s Levites
2Ch 1:17 chariot for s hundred silver
2:2 three thousand s hundred
2:17 thousand s hundred
2:18 and three thousand s hundred
3:8 amount of s hundred talents
9:13 s hundred and sixty-six
9:15 s hundred shekels of alloyed
9:18 s steps to the throne, and
9:19 upon the s steps on this side
22:12 hidden for s years, while
26:12 was two thousand s hundred
29:33 s hundred cattle and three
35:8 two thousand s hundred
Ezr 2:10 s hundred and forty-two
2:11 s hundred and twenty-three
2:13 s hundred and sixty-six
2:26 s hundred and twenty-one
2:35 three thousand s hundred and
2:60 s hundred and fifty-two
2:67 s thousand seven hundred and
8:26 s hundred and fifty talents
Ne 5:18 s select sheep and birds
7:10 s hundred and fifty-two
7:15 s hundred and forty-eight
7:16 s hundred and twenty-eight
7:18 s hundred and sixty-seven
7:20 s hundred and fifty-five
7:30 s hundred and twenty-one
7:62 s hundred and forty-two
7:69 s thousand seven hundred and
Es 2:12 s months with oil of myrrh
2:12 s months with balsam oil and
Job 5:19 s distresses he will deliver
42:12 s thousand camels and a
Pr 6:16 s things that Jehovah does
Isa 6:2 Each one had s wings
Jer 34:14 who has served you s years
52:30 four thousand and s hundred

Eze 9:2 were *s* men coming from the
40:5 measuring reed of *s* cubits
40:12 guard chamber was *s* cubits
40:12 and *s* cubits on that side
41:1 *s* cubits being the width
41:1 and *s* cubits the width over
41:3 and the entrance, *s* cubits
41:5 wall of the house, *s* cubits
41:8 *s* cubits to the joining
46:1 shut for the *s* workdays
46:4 *s* sound male lambs and a
46:6 *s* male lambs and a ram
Da 3:1 breadth of which was *s* cubits
Mt 17:1 *S* days later Jesus took Peter
Mr 9:2 *s* days later Jesus took Peter
Lu 4:25 three years and *s* months, so
13:14 *s* days on which work ought
Joh 2:6 *s* stone water jars sitting
12:1 *s* days before the passover
Ac 11:12 *s* brothers also went with
18:11 there a year and *s* months
Jas 5:17 for three years and *s* months
Re 4:8 each one . . . has *s* wings
13:18 is *s* hundred and sixty-six
14:20 thousand *s* hundred furlongs

Sixes
1Ch 20:6 fingers and toes were in *s*

Sixteen
Ge 46:18 bore these to Jacob: *s* souls
Ex 26:25 of silver, *s* pedestals, two
36:30 pedestals of silver to *s*
Nu 31:40 human souls were *s* thousand
31:46 and human souls, *s* thousand
31:52 *s* thousand seven hundred and
Jos 15:41 *s* cities and their
19:22 *s* cities and their
2Ki 13:10 in Samaria for *s* years
14:21 *s* years old, and they made
15:2 *S* years old he happened to
15:33 for *s* years he reigned in
16:2 for *s* years he reigned in
1Ch 4:27 Shimei had *s* sons and six
24:4 paternal houses, *s*, and to
2Ch 13:21 sons and *s* daughters
26:1 Uzziah, he being *s* years old
26:3 *S* years old was Uzziah when
27:1 Jotham . . . *s* years he
27:8 *s* years he reigned in
28:1 Ahaz . . . *s* years he reigned

Sixteenth
1Ch 24:14 for Immer the *s*
25:23 for the *s*, for Hananiah
2Ch 29:17 *s* day of the first month

Sixth
Ge 1:31 came to be morning, a *s* day
30:19 Leah . . . bore a *s* son to
Ex 16:5 it must occur on the *s* day
16:22 came about on the *s* day that
16:29 on the *s* day the bread of
26:9 fold double the *s* tent cloth
Le 25:21 *s* year, and it must yield
Nu 7:42 *s* day there was the chieftain
29:29 on the *s* day eight bulls
Jos 19:32 that the *s* lot came out
2Sa 3:5 *s* was Ithream by Eglah
2Ki 18:10 in the *s* year of Hezekiah
1Ch 2:15 Ozem the *s*, David the
3:3 the *s*, Ithream, of Eglah his
12:11 Attai the *s*, Eliel the
24:9 the fifth, for Mijamin the *s*
25:13 the *s* for Bukkiah, his sons
26:3 Jehohanan the *s*, Elieho-enai
26:5 Ammiel the *s*, Issachar the
27:9, 9 The *s* for the *s* month was
Ezr 6:15 *s* year of the reign of Darius
Ne 3:30 Hanun the *s* son of Zalaph
Eze 4:11 measure, the *s* part of a hin
8:1 it came about in the *s* year
8:1 in the *s* month, on the fifth
45:13 *s* part of the ephah from
45:13 *s* part of the ephah from
46:14 *s* of an ephah and, as
Hag 1:1 the *s* month, on the first day
1:15 *s* month in the second year
Mt 20:5 the *s* and the ninth hour and
27:45 the *s* hour on a darkness
Mr 15:33 the *s* hour a darkness fell
Lu 1:26 In her *s* month the angel
1:36 this is the *s* month for her
23:44 it was about the *s* hour
Joh 4:6 The hour was about the *s*
19:14 it was about the *s* hour
Ac 10:9 about the *s* hour to pray
Re 6:12 when he opened the *s* seal
9:13 the *s* angel blew his trumpet
9:14 say to the *s* angel, who had
16:12 *s* one poured out his bowl
21:20 the *s* sardius, the seventh

Sixty
Ge 25:26 Isaac was *s* years old at her
Le 27:3 up to *s* years old, the
27:7 age is from *s* years old
Nu 7:88 sacrifice . . . *s* rams
7:88 sacrifice . . . *s* he-goats
7:88 sacrifice . . . *s* male lambs
26:27 *s* thousand five hundred
De 3:4 *s* cities, all the region of
Jos 13:30 that are in Bashan, *s* towns
2Sa 2:31 three hundred and *s* men that
1Ki 4:13 *s* large cities with wall and
4:22 *s* cor measures of flour
6:2 was *s* cubits in its length
2Ki 25:19 *s* men of the people of the
1Ch 2:21 took her when he was *s* years
2:23 dependent towns, *s* cities
5:18 thousand seven hundred and *s*
9:13 thousand seven hundred and *s*
2Ch 3:3 measurement being *s* cubits
11:21 also *s* concubines, so that
11:21 sons and *s* daughters
12:3 and with *s* thousand horsemen
Ezr 2:9 seven hundred and *s*
2:64 thousand three hundred and *s*
6:3 its height being *s* cubits, its
6:3 its width *s* cubits
8:10 a hundred and *s* males
8:13 and with them *s* males
Ne 7:14 seven hundred and *s*
7:66 thousand three hundred and *s*
Ca 3:7 *S* mighty men are all around it
6:8 There may be *s* queens and
Jer 52:25 *s* men of the people of the
Eze 40:14 side pillars of *s* cubits
Da 3:1 height of which was *s* cubits
Mt 13:8 to yield fruit . . . that one *s*
13:23 that one *s*, the other thirty
18:24 [=*60,000,000* denarii]
Mr 4:8 bearing thirtyfold, and *s* and
4:20 bear fruit thirtyfold and *s*
1Ti 5:9 not less than *s* years old
Re 11:3 a thousand two hundred and *s*
12:6 two hundred and *s* days

Sixty-eight
1Ch 16:38 and his brothers, *s*, and
Ne 11:6 four hundred and *s*, capable

Sixty-five
Ge 5:15 Mahalalel lived on for *s*
5:21 And Enoch lived on for *s* years
5:23 three hundred and *s* years
Nu 3:50 thousand three hundred and *s*
Isa 7:8 within just *s* years Ephraim

Sixty-four
Nu 26:25 *s* thousand three hundred
26:43 were *s* thousand four hundred

Sixty-nine
Ge 5:27 nine hundred and *s* years and

Sixty-one
Nu 31:34 and *s* thousand asses
31:39 and the tax . . . was *s*
Ezr 2:69 *s* thousand drachmas, and

Sixty-seven
Ne 7:18 six hundred and *s*
7:19 two thousand and *s*
7:72 and *s* priests' robes

Sixty-six
Ge 46:26 All the souls were *s*
Le 12:5 For *s* days more she will stay
1Ki 10:14 six hundred and *s* talents
2Ch 9:13 six hundred and *s* talents of
Ezr 2:13 six hundred and *s*
Re 13:18 number is six hundred and *s*

Sixty-two
Ge 5:18 Jared . . . a hundred and *s* years
5:20 Jared . . . nine hundred and *s*
Nu 1:39 *s* thousand seven hundred
2:26 *s* thousand seven hundred
1Ch 26:8 *s* belonging to Obed-edom
Da 5:31 being about *s* years old
9:25 seven weeks, also *s* weeks
9:26 *s* weeks Messiah will be cut

Size
Ge 43:34 five times the *s* of the
Nu 13:32 are men of extraordinary *s*
2Sa 21:20 a man of extraordinary *s*
23:21 that was of extraordinary *s*
1Ch 11:23 a man of extraordinary *s*
20:6 a man of extraordinary *s*
23:29 measures of quantity and *s*
Eze 13:18 making veils . . . of every *s*
Mt 15:33 to satisfy a crowd of this *s*
17:20 faith the *s* of a mustard
Lu 17:6 faith the *s* of a mustard
19:3 because he was small in *s*

Skies
De 28:23 *s* that are over your head
33:26 cloudy *s* in his eminence
Job 37:18 can you beat out the *s*
37:21 It is brilliant in the *s*
Ps 57:10 your trueness up to the *s*
77:17 cloudy *s* have given forth
78:23 command the cloudy *s* above
89:6 who in the *s* can be compared
89:37 faithful witness in the *s*
108:4 your trueness up to the *s*
Pr 3:20 cloudy *s* keep dripping down
Isa 45:8 let the cloudy *s* themselves
Jer 51:9 lifted up to the cloudy *s*

Skiff
Ac 27:16 possession of the *s* at the
27:30 lowered the *s* into the sea
27:32 cut away the ropes of the *s*

Skill
1Ch 28:21 with *s* for all the service

Skilled
1Sa 16:16 *s* man playing upon the harp
16:18 *s* at playing, and he is a
Ezr 7:6 *s* copyist in the law of Moses
Ps 45:1 the stylus of a *s* copyist
Isa 3:3 arts, and the *s* charmer
Jer 9:17 send even to the *s* women
10:9 the workmanship of *s* people
Eze 27:8 Your *s* ones, O Tyre
27:9 her *s* ones happened to be

Skillful
1Ch 22:15 one *s* in every sort of work
2Ch 2:7 *s* man to work in gold and in
2:7 *s* ones that are with me in
2:13 And now I do send a *s* man
2:14 along with your own *s* men
2:14 *s* men of my lord David your
Pr 1:5 one who acquires *s* direction
11:14 When there is no *s* direction
20:18 by *s* direction carry on your
22:29 beheld a man *s* in his work
24:6 by *s* direction you will carry
Isa 40:20 A *s* craftsman he searches

Skillfulness
Ps 78:72 *s* of his hands he began

Skim
Isa 30:14 *s* water from a marshy

Skin
Ge 3:21 long garments of *s* for Adam
21:14 bread and a *s* water bottle
21:15 in the *s* bottle and she
21:19 fill the *s* bottle with water
Ex 22:27 It is his mantle for his *s*
29:14 bull's flesh and its *s* and
34:29 *s* of his face emitted rays
34:30 *s* of his face emitted rays
34:35 *s* of Moses' face emitted
Le 4:11 the *s* of the bull and all its
7:8 the *s* of the burnt offering
8:17 the bull and its *s* and its
9:11 he burned the flesh and the *s*
11:32 garment or a *s* or sackcloth
13:2 develops in the *s* of his flesh
13:2 develop in the *s* of his flesh
13:3 plague in the *s* of the flesh
13:3 deeper than the *s* of his flesh
13:4 white in the *s* of his flesh
13:4 not deeper than the *s* and its
13:5 plague has not spread in the *s*
13:6 plague has not spread in the *s*
13:7 spread in the *s* after his
13:8 the scab has spread in the *s*
13:10 is a white eruption in the *s*
13:11 chronic leprosy in the *s* of
13:12 the leprosy . . . in the *s*
13:12 leprosy does cover all the *s*
13:18 a boil develops in its *s* and

Le 13:20 lower than the *s* and its
13:21 not deeper than the *s* and it
13:22 spreads in the *s*, the priest
13:24 a scar in the *s* of the flesh
13:25 is deeper than the *s*, it is
13:26 not lower than the *s* and it
13:27 spreads in the *s*, the priest
13:28 it has not spread in the *s*
13:30 deeper than the *s*, and the
13:31 is not deeper than the *s* and
13:32 is not deeper than the *s*
13:34 has not spread in the *s*, and
13:34 is not deeper than the *s*
13:35 spreads in the *s* after the
13:36 of hair has spread in the *s*
13:38 blotches develop in the *s* of
13:39 the *s* of their flesh are dull
13:39 It has broken out in the *s*
13:43 leprosy in the *s* of the flesh
13:48 in a *s* or in anything made
13:48 or in anything made of *s*
13:49 in the *s* or in the warp or
13:49 in any article of *s*, it is
13:51 in the woof or in the *s* for
13:51 use for which the *s* may be
13:52 *s* in which the plague may
13:53 woof or in any article of *s*
13:56 the *s* or the warp or the
13:57 of *s*, it is breaking out
13:58 *s* that you may wash, when
13:59 any article of *s*, in order to
15:17 *s* upon which the emission
Nu 19:5 *s* and its flesh and its blood
31:20 and every article of *s* and
De 28:27 and eczema and *s* eruption
Jg 4:19 opened a *s* bottle of milk
1Sa 16:20 a *s* bottle of wine and a
2Ch 29:34 *s* all the burnt offerings
Job 2:4, 4 said: *S* in behalf of *s*, and
7:5 My *s* itself has formed crusts
10:11 With *s* and flesh you
16:15 Sackcloth . . . over my *s*
18:13 eat the pieces of his *s*
19:20 To my *s* and to my flesh my
19:20 with the *s* of my teeth
19:26 after my *s*, which they have
30:30 *s* became black and dropped
32:19 Like new *s* bottles it wants
41:7 fill its *s* with harpoons
Ps 56:8 put my tears in your *s* bottle
119:83 a *s* bottle in the smoke
Ca 4:13 Your *s* is a paradise of
Jer 13:23 Can a Cushite change his *s*?
La 3:4 flesh and my *s* to wear away
4:8 *s* has shriveled upon their
5:10 *s* has grown hot just like a
Eze 37:6 overlay upon you *s* and put
37:8 *s* began to be overlaid upon
Mic 3:2 tearing off their *s* from
3:3 stripped their very *s* from
Na 3:16 locust . . . strips off its *s*

Skin-bottles
Jos 9:4 and wine *s* worn out and burst
9:13 wine *s* that we filled new

Skinned
Le 1:6 the burnt offering must be *s*
Job 19:26 my skin, which they have *s*
Mt 9:36 *s* and thrown about like sheep

Skinny
Ge 41:20 *s* and bad cows began to eat
41:27 the seven *s* and bad cows

Skins
Ge 27:16 *s* of the kids of the goats
Ex 25:5 ram *s* dyed red, and sealskins
26:14 of ram *s* dyed red and a
35:7 and ram *s* dyed red and
35:23 ram *s* dyed red and sealskins
36:19 out of ram *s* dyed red and
39:34 covering of ram *s* dyed red
Le 16:27 burn their *s* and their flesh
Nu 6:4 the unripe grapes to the *s*
2Ch 35:11 were stripping the *s* off
Mr 2:22 the wine bursts the *s*, and
2:22 wine . . . as well as the *s*

Skip
Ps 29:6 *s* about like a calf
Ec 3:4 to wail and a time to *s* about

Skipped
Ps 114:4 mountains themselves *s* about

Skipping
1Ch 15:29 see King David *s* about and
Job 21:11 own male children go *s*
Ps 114:6 mountains, that you went *s*
Isa 13:21 will go *s* about there
Joe 2:5 they keep *s* about, as with

Skirt
Nu 15:38 the fringed edge of the *s*
De 22:30 uncover the *s* of his father
27:20 uncovered the *s* of his father
Ru 3:9 spread out your *s* over your
1Sa 15:27 the *s* of his sleeveless coat
24:4 cut off the *s* of the
24:5 *s* of the sleeveless coat
24:11 *s* of your sleeveless coat
24:11 *s* of your sleeveless coat
Isa 47:2 Strip off the flowing *s*
Eze 16:8 to spread my *s* over you and
Hag 2:12 in the *s* of his garment
2:12 touches with his *s* bread or
Zec 8:23 take hold of the *s* of a man

Skirts
Nu 15:38 fringed edges upon the *s* of
Isa 6:1 his *s* were filling the temple
Jer 2:34 in your *s* there have been
13:22 your *s* have been taken off
13:26 lift up your *s* over your
La 1:9 Her uncleanness is in her *s*
Eze 5:3 and wrap them up in your *s*
Na 3:5 put the covering of your *s*

Skull
Jg 9:53 and broke his *s* in pieces
2Ki 9:35 the *s* and the feet and the
1Ch 10:10 his *s* they fastened to the
Mt 27:33 that is to say, *S* Place
Mr 15:22 when translated, *S* Place
Lu 23:33 *S*, there they impaled him
Joh 19:17 to the so-called *S* Place

Sky
Job 38:36 gave understanding to the *s*
Mt 16:2 for the *s* is fire-red
16:3 for the *s* is fire-red, but
16:3 the appearance of the *s*, but
Lu 12:56 appearance of earth and *s*
Ac 1:10 they were gazing into the *s*
1:11 you stand looking into the *s*
1:11 up from you into the *s*
1:11 beheld him going into the *s*

Slack
Pr 10:4 one working with a *s* hand
12:24 *s* hand will come to be for
18:9 *s* in his work—he is a
19:15 and a *s* soul goes hungry

Slackness
Pr 12:27 *S* will not start up one's

Slain
Nu 19:16 someone *s* with the sword or
19:18 touched the bone or the *s* one
23:24 the blood of *s* ones it will
31:8 along with the others *s*
31:19 who has touched someone *s*
35:30 should be *s* as a murderer at
De 21:1 In case someone is found *s*
21:2 all around the *s* one
21:3 the city nearest to the *s* one
21:6 men . . . nearest to the *s* one
32:42 the blood of the *s* and the
Jos 11:6 all of them *s* to Israel
13:22 along with their *s* ones
Jg 9:40 the *s* kept falling in numbers
16:24 the one who multiplied our *s*
1Sa 31:1 *s* in Mount Gilboa
31:8 came to strip the *s*, they
2Sa 1:19 beauty, O Israel, is *s* upon
1:22 blood of the *s*, from the fat
1:25 Jonathan *s* upon your high
23:8 eight hundred *s* at one time
23:18 over three hundred *s* ones
1Ki 11:15 came up to bury those *s*
1Ch 5:22 were many that had fallen *s*
10:1 falling *s* in Mount Gilboa
10:8 came to strip the *s*, they
11:11 over three hundred *s* at one
11:20 spear over three hundred *s*
2Ch 13:17 *s* of Israel kept falling
Job 39:30 where the *s* are, there it
Ps 88:5 *s* ones lying in the burial
89:10 Rahab, even as someone *s*
Pr 7:26 has caused to fall down *s*
Isa 22:2 Your *s* ones are not those
22:2 not those *s* with the sword
34:3 *s* ones will be thrown out
66:16 *s* of Jehovah will certainly
Jer 9:1 weep day and night for the *s*
14:18 those *s* by the sword
25:33 those *s* by Jehovah will
41:9 filled with those *s*
51:4 fall *s* in the land of the
51:47 own *s* ones will fall in
51:49 Babylon the cause for the *s*
51:49 at Babylon the *s* ones of
La 2:12 fainting away like someone *s*
4:9 have those *s* with the sword
4:9 than those *s* by famine
Eze 6:4 cause your *s* ones to fall
6:7 *s* one will certainly fall in
6:13 their *s* ones come to be in
9:7 courtyards with the *s* ones
11:6 *s* ones in this city to be
11:6 her streets with the *s* ones
11:7 As regards your *s* ones whom
21:14 sword of the *s* ones it is
21:14 someone *s* who is great
21:29 on the necks of the *s* ones
28:8 die the death of someone *s*
28:23 the *s* one must fall in the
30:4 when one falls *s* in Egypt
30:11 fill the land with the *s*
31:17 to those *s* by the sword
31:18 with those *s* by the sword
32:20 those *s* by the sword they
32:21 *s* by the sword
32:22 *s*, those falling by the
32:23 *s*, falling by the sword
32:24 all of them *s* ones, those
32:25 In the midst of *s* ones they
32:25 uncircumcised, *s* by the
32:25 In the midst of *s* ones he
32:28 with those *s* by the sword
32:29 with those *s* by the sword
32:30 gone down with the *s* ones
32:30 with those *s* by the sword
32:31 people *s* by the sword
32:32 with those *s* by the sword
35:8 mountains with its *s* ones
35:8 ones *s* by the sword will
Da 11:26 will certainly fall down *s*
Na 3:3 the multitude of *s* ones
Zep 2:12 be people *s* by my sword
Lu 11:51 who was *s* between the altar

Slander
Pr 30:10 *s* a servant to his master

Slandered
2Sa 19:27 *s* your servant to my lord
Ps 15:3 He has not *s* with his tongue

Slanderer
Pr 11:13 *s* is uncovering confidential
16:28 and a *s* is separating those
18:8 The words of the *s* are like
20:19 *s* is uncovering confidential
26:20 no *s* contention grows still
26:22 words of a *s* are like things
Jer 9:4 walk around as a mere *s*
Joh 6:70 Yet one of you is a *s*

Slanderers
Jer 6:28 walking about as *s*—copper
Eze 22:9 Outright *s* have proved to
2Ti 3:3 *s*, without self-control

Slandering
Le 19:16 people for the sake of *s*
Ps 101:5 *s* his companion in secrecy

Slanderous
1Ti 3:11 not *s*, moderate in habits
Tit 2:3 reverent in behavior, not *s*

Slap
Job 34:26 wicked ones he does *s* them
Isa 25:11 *s* out his hands in the
Jer 31:19 I made a *s* upon the thigh
Eze 21:12 make a *s* on the thigh
Joh 18:22 gave Jesus a *s* in the face

Slapped
Jer 48:26 Moab has *s* around in his
Mt 26:67 Others *s* him in the face
1Pe 2:20 you are sinning and being *s*

Slapping
Mr 14:65 *s* him in the face, the court
2Co 12:7 of Satan, to keep *s* me, that

Slaps
Isa 25:11 swimmer *s* them out to swim
Mt 5:39 *s* you on your right cheek
Joh 19:3 give him *s* in the face

Slashing
Mr 5:5 and *s* himself with stones

Slaughter
Ge 43:16 *s* animals and make
49:5 violence are their *s* weapons
Ex 12:6 *s* it between the two evenings
12:21 and *s* the passover victim
22:1 and he does *s* it or sell it
29:11 *s* the bull before Jehovah
29:16 *s* the ram and take its blood
29:20 *s* the ram and take some of
34:25 not *s* along with what is
Le 4:4 must *s* the bull before Jehovah
4:24 *s* it in the place where the
4:29 and *s* the sin offering in the
4:33 *s* it as a sin offering in the
7:2 regularly *s* the burnt offering
7:2 will *s* the guilt offering
8:15 *s* it and take the blood and
14:13 *s* the young ram in the place
14:19 he will *s* the burnt offering
14:25 must *s* the young ram of the
16:11 *s* the bull of the sin
16:15 *s* the goat of the sin
22:28 *s* it and its young one on the
Nu 11:33 people with a very great *s*
14:16 to *s* them in the wilderness
De 12:15 you may *s*, and you must eat
12:21 must then *s* some of your herd
Jos 10:10 with a great *s* at Gibeon
10:20 with a very great *s*, until
Jg 11:33 with a very great *s*
15:8 with a great *s*, after which
1Sa 4:8 sort of *s* in the wilderness
4:10 the *s* came to be very great
6:19 the people with a great *s*
14:14 first *s* with which Jonathan
14:30 *s* upon the Philistines has
19:8 them down with a great *s*
23:5 struck . . . with a great *s*
2Sa 18:7 the *s* there turned out to be
1Ki 20:21 the Syrians with a great *s*
2Ch 13:17 them down with a vast *s*
28:5 struck him with a great *s*
35:6 *s* the passover victim and
35:11 to *s* the passover victim
Es 9:5 a *s* by the sword and with a
Ps 37:14 *s* those who are upright in
Pr 7:22 bull that comes even to the *s*
24:11 and those staggering to the *s*
Isa 27:7 *s* of his killed ones does
30:25 big *s* when the towers fall
34:2 must give them to the *s*
Jer 11:19 that is brought to *s*
39:6 *s* the sons of Zedekiah in
50:27 they go down to the *s*
52:10 *s* the sons of Zedekiah
Eze 16:21 you would *s* my sons, and by
16:40 and *s* you with their swords
21:10 purpose of organizing a *s*
21:15 make a *s* by the sword
21:15 glittering, polished for a *s*
21:28 a sword drawn for a *s*
26:15 a killing with *s* in the
34:3 plump animal is what you *s*
40:42 *s* the whole burnt offering
44:11 *s* the whole burnt offering
Ho 5:2 in *s* work those falling away
Lu 15:23 young bull, *s* it and let us
19:27 Bring here and *s* them before
Ac 8:32 sheep he was brought to the *s*
10:13 Rise, Peter, *s* and eat!
11:7 Rise, Peter, *s* and eat!
Heb 7:1 from the *s* of the kings and
11:37 they died by *s* with the
Jas 5:5 your hearts on the day of *s*
1Jo 3:12 sake of what did he *s* him
Re 6:4 that they should *s* one another

Slaughtered
Ge 37:31 *s* a male goat and repeatedly
Le 1:5 bull must be *s* before Jehovah
1:11 *s* at the side of the altar to
3:2 must be *s* at the entrance of
3:8 *s* before the tent of meeting
3:13 *s* before the tent of meeting
4:15 bull must be *s* before Jehovah
4:24 burnt offering is regularly *s*
4:33 burnt offering is regularly *s*
6:25 burnt offering is regularly *s*
6:25 sin offering will be *s* before
8:19 Moses *s* it and sprinkled the
8:23 *s* it and took some of its
9:8 *s* the calf of the sin offering
Le 9:12 he *s* the burnt offering and
9:15 *s* it and made an offering for
9:18 he *s* the bull and the ram of
14:13 regularly *s*, in a holy place
Nu 11:22 flocks and herds be *s* for
19:3 and it must be *s* before him
De 28:31 bull *s* there before your eyes
1Sa 1:25 Then they *s* the bull and
25:11 my *s* meat that I have
1Ki 18:40 Kishon and *s* them there
2Ki 10:14 *s* them at the cistern of
25:7 And Zedekiah's sons they *s*
2Ch 29:22 *s* the cattle and the priests
29:22 *s* the rams and sprinkled
29:22 *s* the male lambs and
29:24 priests now *s* them and made
30:15 *s* the passover victim on
35:1 *s* the passover victim on the
Ezr 6:20 they *s* the passover victim
Isa 65:12 bow down to being *s*
Jer 39:6 the king of Babylon *s*
52:10 princes of Judah he *s* in
La 2:21 You have *s*; you have had no
Eze 23:39 they had *s* their sons to
Mt 22:4 and fattened animals are *s*
Lu 15:27 father *s* the fattened young
15:30 *s* the fattened young bull for
1Jo 3:12 Cain . . . *s* his brother
Re 5:6 lamb as though it had been *s*
5:9 *s* and with your blood you
5:12 Lamb that was *s* is worthy
6:9 the souls of those *s* because
13:3 heads as though *s* to death
13:8 of the Lamb who was *s*, from
18:24 have been *s* on the earth

Slaughtering
Ge 22:6 the fire and the *s* knife
22:10 took the *s* knife to kill his
Jg 19:29 took the *s* knife and laid
1Sa 14:32 and *s* them on the earth
14:34 do the *s* in this place and
14:34 and did the *s* there
2Ki 10:7 the sons of the king and *s*
2Ch 30:17 Levites were in charge of *s*
Ps 44:22 accounted as sheep for *s*
Pr 9:2 It has organized its meat *s*
30:14 whose jawbones are *s* knives
Isa 14:21 *s* block for his own sons
22:13 and the *s* of sheep, the
34:6 great *s* in the land of Edom
53:7 just like a sheep to the *s*
57:5 *s* the children in the torrent
66:3 The one *s* the bull is as one
Jer 9:8 Their tongue is a *s* arrow
12:3 out like sheep for the *s*
25:34 your days for *s* and for
41:7 *s* them and throwing them
48:15 have gone down to the *s*, is
51:40 male sheep to the *s*, like
Eze 40:39 *s* upon them the whole
40:41 they would do the *s*
Ro 8:36 accounted as sheep for *s*

Slaughters
Le 17:3 *s* a bull or a young ram or a
17:3 or who *s* it outside the camp

Slave
Ge 9:25 Let him become the lowest *s*
9:26 let Canaan become a *s* to him
9:27 Let Canaan become a *s* to him
20:17 *s* girls, and they began
21:10 Drive out this *s* girl and her
21:10 son of this *s* girl is not
21:12 boy and about your *s* girl
21:13 son of the *s* girl, I shall
30:3 Here is my *s* girl Bilhah
31:33 the tent of the two *s* girls
44:10 will become a *s* to me, but
44:17 the one who will become a *s*
44:18 let your *s* speak a word in
44:18 grow hot against your *s*
44:24 went up to your *s* my father
44:27 your *s* my father said to us
44:30 come to your *s* my father
44:31 the gray hairs of your *s*
44:32 *s* became surety for the boy
44:33 let your *s* stay instead of
44:33 as a *s* to my master, that
Ex 1:13 sons of Israel *s* under tyranny
2:5 she sent her *s* girl that she
12:44 *s* man purchased with money
20:10, 10 *s* man nor your *s* girl
20:17, 17 his *s* man nor his *s* girl
Ex 21:2 buy a Hebrew *s*, he will be a
21:2 he will be a *s* six years, but
21:5 the *s* should insistently say
21:6 be his *s* to time indefinite
21:7 sell his daughter as a *s* girl
21:7 the way that the *s* men go out
21:20, 20 his *s* man or his *s* girl
21:26 strike the eye of his *s* man
21:26 the eye of his *s* girl and he
21:27 the tooth of his *s* man or
21:27 the tooth of his *s* girl that
21:32, 32 was a *s* man or a *s* girl
23:12 son of your *s* girl and the
Le 25:6, 6 *s* man and your *s* girl and
25:42 sell themselves the way a *s*
25:44, 44 *s* man and your *s* girl
25:44, 44 buy a *s* man and a *s* girl
De 5:14, 14 *s* man nor your *s* girl
5:14 in order that your *s* man
5:14 your *s* girl may rest the same
5:15 a *s* in the land of Egypt and
5:21, 21 his *s* man or his *s* girl
12:12 your *s* girls and the Levite
12:18 your daughter and your man *s*
12:18 your *s* girl and the Levite
15:15 a *s* in the land of Egypt and
15:17 your *s* to time indefinite
15:17 to your *s* girl you should
16:11 your daughter and your man *s*
16:11 your *s* girl and the Levite
16:12 you became a *s* in Egypt, and
16:14 your daughter and your man *s*
16:14 your *s* girl and the Levite
23:15 hand over a *s* to his master
24:18 you became a *s* in Egypt, and
24:22 a *s* in the land of Egypt
28:68 as *s* men and maidservants
Jg 9:18 the son of his *s* girl, king
19:19 and your *s* girl and for the
Ru 3:9 I am Ruth your *s* girl, and you
3:9 your skirt over your *s* girl
1Sa 1:11 the affliction of your *s* girl
1:11 will not forget your *s* girl
1:11 give to your *s* girl a male
1:16 Do not make your *s* girl like
25:24 *s* girl speak in your ears
25:24 to the words of your *s* girl
25:25 your *s* girl, I did not see
25:28 transgression of your *s* girl
25:31 must remember your *s* girl
25:41 *s* girl as a maidservant to
30:13 *s* of an Amalekite man, but
2Sa 6:20 to the eyes of the *s* girls
6:22 *s* girls whom you mentioned
14:15 on the word of his *s* girl
14:16 deliver his *s* girl out of
20:17 the words of your *s* girl
1Ki 1:13 swore to your *s* girl, saying
1:17 swore . . . to your *s* girl
3:20 *s* girl herself was asleep
Ezr 2:65 men slaves and their *s* girls
Ne 7:67 men slaves and their *s* girls
Job 3:19 the *s* is set free from his
7:2 a *s* he pants for the shadow
19:15 and my *s* girls themselves
31:13 the judgment of my *s* man
31:13 my *s* girl in their case at
41:4 as a *s* to time indefinite
Ps 86:16 save the son of your *s* girl
105:17 was sold to be a *s*, Joseph
116:16 the son of your *s* girl
Pr 30:22 a *s* when he rules as king
Isa 14:3 in which you were made a *s*
Jer 2:14 or a *s* born in the household
Na 2:7 her *s* girls will be moaning
Mt 6:24 No one can *s* for two masters
6:24 cannot *s* for God and for
8:9 to my *s*, Do this! and he does
10:24 nor a *s* above his lord
10:25 and the *s* as his lord
18:26 *s* fell down and began to do
18:27 master of that *s* let him
18:28 that *s* went out and found
18:29 his fellow *s* fell down and
18:32 Wicked *s*, I canceled all
18:33 had mercy on your fellow *s*
20:27 first . . . must be your *s*
24:45 the faithful and discreet *s*
24:46 Happy is that *s* if his
24:48 if that evil *s* should say in
24:50 master of that *s* will come
25:21 good and faithful *s*
25:23 good and faithful *s*
25:26 Wicked and sluggish *s*, you

Mt 25:30 throw the good-for-nothing *s*
26:51 the *s* of the high priest and
Mr 10:44 must be the *s* of all
12:2 he sent forth a *s* to the
12:4 sent forth another *s* to them
14:47 the *s* of the high priest and
Lu 1:38 Jehovah's *s* girl! May it take
1:48 low position of his *s* girl
2:29 letting your *s* go free in
7:2 officer's *s*, who was dear to
7:3 bring his *s* safely through
7:8 to my *s*, Do this! and he does
7:10 found the *s* in good health
12:43 Happy is that *s*, if his
12:45 if ever that *s* should say in
12:46 the master of that *s* will
12:47 that *s* that understood the
14:17 sent his *s* out at the hour of
14:21 *s* came up and reported these
14:21 said to his *s*, Go out quickly
14:22 the *s* said, Master, what you
14:23 the master said to the *s*
16:13 be a *s* to two masters; for
17:7 a *s* plowing or minding the
17:9 not feel gratitude to the *s*
19:17 Well done, good *s!* Because
19:22 I judge you, wicked *s*
20:10 a *s* to the cultivators, that
20:11 and sent them a different *s*
22:50 did strike the *s* of the high
Joh 8:34 doer of sin is a *s* of sin
8:35 the *s* does not remain in
13:16 *s* is not greater than his
15:15 *s* does not know what his
15:20 *s* is not greater than his
18:10 struck the *s* of the high
18:10 name of the *s* was Malchus
Ac 7:7 nation for which they will *s*
Ro 1:1 Paul, a *s* of Jesus Christ and
7:25 am a *s* to God's law, but
9:12 older will be the *s* of the
12:11 *S* for Jehovah
1Co 7:21 Were you called when a *s?*
7:22 that was called when a *s* is
7:22 a free man is a *s* of Christ
9:19 I have made myself the *s* to
9:27 my body and lead it as a *s*
Ga 1:10 I would not be Christ's *s*
3:28 is neither *s* nor freeman
4:1 not differ at all from a *s*
4:7 are no longer a *s* but a son
4:9 want to *s* for them over again
5:13 love *s* for one another
6:17 brand marks of a *s* of Jesus
Eph 6:8 whether he be *s* or freeman
Col 1:7 Epaphras our beloved fellow *s*
3:11 *s*, freeman, but Christ is
3:24 *S* for the Master, Christ
4:7 and fellow *s* in the Lord
4:12 a *s* of Christ Jesus, sends
1Th 1:9 to *s* for a living and true God
2Ti 2:24 a *s* of the Lord does not
Tit 1:1 Paul, a *s* of God and an
Phm 16 no longer as a *s* but as more
16 more than a *s*, as a brother
Jas 1:1 James, a *s* of God and of the
2Pe 1:1 Simon Peter, a *s* and apostle
Jude 1 Jude, a *s* of Jesus Christ, but
Re 1:1 through him to his *s* John
6:15 every *s* and every free person
15:3 song of Moses the *s* of God
19:10 fellow *s* of you and of your
22:9 fellow *s* of you and of your

Slaved
Lu 15:29 many years I have *s* for you
Ga 4:8 *s* for those who by nature are
Php 2:22 he *s* with me in furtherance

Slavery
Ex 1:14 their life bitter with hard *s*
1:14 every form of *s* in the field
1:14 every form of *s* of theirs in
2:23 sigh because of the *s* and to
2:23 cry . . . because of the *s*
6:6 and deliver you from their *s*
6:9 and for the hard *s*
De 26:6 putting hard *s* upon us
Isa 14:3 hard *s* in which you were
Ro 8:15 spirit of *s* causing fear
Ga 4:24 brings forth children for *s*
4:25 she is in *s* with her children
5:1 confined again in a yoke of *s*
Heb 2:15 *s* all through their lives

Slave's
Jos 9:23 and a *s* position and being
Php 2:7 and took a *s* form and came to

Slaves
Ge 14:14 *s* born in his household, and
14:15 he and his *s*, against them
43:18 to take us for *s* and also our
44:9 the one of your *s* with whom
44:9 also become *s* to my master
44:16 found out the error of your *s*
44:16 Here we are *s* to my master
44:19 My master asked his *s*
44:21 you said to your *s*, Bring
44:23 you said to your *s*, Unless
44:31 and your *s* will indeed bring
47:19 will become *s* to Pharaoh
47:25 we will become *s* to Pharaoh
50:18 Here we are as *s* to you!
Ex 1:14 used them as *s* under tyranny
13:3 of Egypt, from the house of *s*
13:14 out . . . from the house of *s*
20:2 out of the house of *s*
Le 22:11 *s* born in his house, they as
25:42 *s* whom I brought out of the
25:55 the sons of Israel are *s*
25:55 They are my *s* whom I brought
26:13 acting as *s* to them, and I
De 5:6 Egypt, out of the house of *s*
6:12 out of the house of *s*
6:21 became *s* to Pharaoh in Egypt
7:8 redeem you from the house of *s*
8:14 out of the house of *s*
12:12 daughters and your man *s*
13:5 from the house of *s*, to turn
13:10 out of the house of *s*
Jos 10:6 your hand relax from your *s*
24:17 out of the house of *s*, and
Jg 6:8 you out of the house of *s*
1Sa 2:27 as *s* to the house of Pharaoh
1Ki 2:39 *s* of Shimei went running
2:39 Look! Your *s* are at Gath
2:40 to Achish to look for his *s*
2:40 and brought his *s* from Gath
9:22 that Solomon constituted *s*
2Ki 4:1 both my children for his *s*
2Ch 8:9 Solomon constituted *s* for his
Ezr 2:65 men *s* and their slave girls
Ne 5:5 sons and our daughters to *s*
7:67 men *s* and their slave girls
9:36 Look! We are today *s*
9:36 look! we are *s* upon it
Es 7:4 had been sold for mere men *s*
Eze 34:27 had been using them as *s*
Mic 6:4 from the house of *s* I
Zec 2:9 to become spoil to their *s*
Mt 13:27 *s* of the householder came up
18:23 settle accounts with his *s*
18:28 his fellow *s* that was owing
18:31 his fellow *s* saw the things
21:34 he dispatched his *s* to the
21:35 the cultivators took his *s*
21:36 Again he dispatched other *s*
22:3 he sent forth his *s* to call
22:4 he sent forth other *s*, saying
22:6 rest, laying hold of his *s*
22:8 said to his *s*, The marriage
22:10 *s* went out to the roads and
24:49 start to beat his fellow *s*
25:14 summoned *s* of his and
25:19 master of those *s* came and
Mr 13:34 gave the authority to his *s*
Lu 12:37 Happy are those *s* whom the
15:22 the father said to his *s*
16:13 be *s* to God and to riches
17:10 We are good-for-nothing *s*
19:13 Calling ten *s* of his he gave
19:15 *s* to whom he had given the
Joh 4:51 his *s* met him to say that
8:33 never have we been *s* to
15:15 I no longer call you *s*
18:18 *s* and the officers were
18:26 of the *s* of the high priest
Ac 2:18 even upon my men *s* and upon
2:18 women *s* I will pour out some
4:29 *s* to keep speaking your word
16:17 are *s* of the Most High God
Ro 6:6 no longer go on being *s* to sin
6:16 to anyone as *s* to obey him
6:16 you are *s* of him because you
6:17 you were the *s* of sin but
6:18 became *s* to righteousness
6:19 presented your members as *s*
6:19 members as *s* to righteousness
Ro 6:20 when you were *s* of sin, you
6:22 but became *s* to God, you are
7:6 *s* in a new sense by the
14:18 *s* for Christ is acceptable
16:18 men of that sort are *s*, not
1Co 7:23 stop becoming *s* of men
12:13 whether *s* or free, and we
2Co 4:5 as your *s* for Jesus' sake
Eph 6:5 You *s*, be obedient to those
6:6 as Christ's *s*, doing the will
6:7 Be *s* with good inclinations
Php 1:1 *s* of Christ Jesus, to all
Col 3:22 *s*, be obedient in everything
4:1 and what is fair to your *s*
1Ti 6:1 Let as many as are *s* under a
6:2 more readily be *s*, because
Tit 2:9 Let *s* be in subjection to
3:3 being *s* to various desires
1Pe 2:16 but as *s* of God
2Pe 2:19 existing as *s* of corruption
Re 1:1 show his *s* the things that
2:20 my *s* to commit fornication
6:11 fellow *s* and their brothers
7:3 have sealed the *s* of our God in
10:7 his own *s* the prophets
11:18 to your *s* the prophets and
13:16 free and the *s*, that they
18:13 and *s* and human souls
19:2 avenged the blood of his *s*
19:5 *s*, who fear him, the small
19:18 freemen as well as of *s* and
22:3 *s* will render him sacred
22:6 show his *s* the things that

Slaving
Ex 14:5 sent Israel away from *s* for
Ac 20:19 *s* for the Lord with the

Slavish
Ge 49:15 subject to *s* forced labor
Le 25:39 as a worker in *s* service
Jos 16:10 subject to *s* forced labor
1Ki 9:21 for *s* forced labor until

Slay
Nu 35:27 avenger of blood does *s* the
Jos 10:10 to *s* them with a great
Jg 12:6 and *s* him at the fords of the
Job 13:15 if he would *s* me, would I
24:14 *s* the afflicted and the poor
Ps 139:19 God, would *s* the wicked one
Joh 10:10 to steal and *s* and destroy
Ac 26:21 Jews . . . attempted to *s* me

Slaying
Jos 10:10 *s* them as far as Azekah and
10:20 had finished *s* them with a
Eze 21:22 to open one's mouth for a *s*

Slays
De 4:42 *s* his fellow without knowing

Sledge
2Sa 24:22 the threshing *s* and the
1Ch 21:23 threshing *s* for the wood
Isa 41:15 made you a threshing *s*

Sleep
Ge 2:21 Jehovah God had a deep *s* fall
15:12 a deep *s* fell upon Abram
28:16 Jacob awoke from his *s*
31:40 *s* would flee from my eyes
41:5 back to *s* and dreamed a
Jg 16:14 So he awoke from his *s* and
16:19 make him *s* upon her knees
16:20 he woke up from his *s* and
1Sa 26:12 deep *s* from Jehovah that
Es 6:1 that night the king's *s* fled
Job 4:13 When deep *s* falls upon men
14:12 be aroused from their *s*
33:15 When deep *s* falls upon men
Ps 3:5 I will lie down that I may *s*
4:8 I will both lie down and *s*
76:5 drowsed away to their *s*
90:5 they become a mere *s*
121:4 not be drowsy nor go to *s*
127:2 gives *s* even to his beloved
132:4 I will not give *s* to my eyes
Pr 3:24 your *s* must be pleasurable
4:16 not *s* unless they do badness
4:16 *s* has been snatched away
6:4 give any *s* to your eyes, nor
6:9 will you rise up from your *s*
6:10 A little more *s*, a little
19:15 Laziness causes a deep *s* to
20:13 Do not love *s*, that you may
Ec 5:12 Sweet is the *s* of the one

Ec 5:12 is not permitting him to *s*
8:16 one seeing no *s* with his eyes
Isa 29:10 poured a spirit of deep *s*
Jer 31:26 *s*, it had been pleasurable
51:39 *s* an indefinitely lasting
51:39 indefinitely lasting *s*
51:57 *s* an indefinitely lasting
51:57 an indefinitely lasting *s*
Eze 34:25 and *s* in the forests
Da 2:1 *s* was made to be something
6:18 and his very *s* fled from him
Zec 4:1 that is awakened from his *s*
Mt 1:24 Joseph woke up from his *s*
25:5 they all nodded and went to *s*
Lu 9:32 were weighed down with *s*
Joh 11:11 there to awaken him from *s*
11:13 about taking rest in *s*
Ac 16:27 being awakened out of *s* and
20:9 Eutychus fell into a deep *s*
20:9 collapsing in *s*, he fell down
Ro 11:8 them a spirit of deep *s*
13:11 hour for you to awake from *s*
1Th 5:6 let us not *s* on as the rest
5:7 those who *s* are accustomed to
5:7 are accustomed to *s* at night

Sleeper
Jon 1:6 the matter with you, *s*
Eph 5:14 Awake, O *s*, and arise from

Sleeping
Ge 2:21 while he was *s*, he took one
Ps 44:23 Why . . . keep *s*, O Jehovah?
78:65 began to awake as from *s*
Pr 24:33 A little *s*, a little
Ca 7:9 over the lips of *s* ones
Ho 7:6 All night long their baker is *s*
Mt 8:24 he, however, was *s*
9:24 girl did not die, but she is *s*
13:25 men were *s*, his enemy
26:40 found them *s*, and he said to
26:43 came again and found them *s*
26:45 a time as this you are *s* and
28:13 stole him while we were *s*
Mr 4:38 in the stern, *s* upon a pillow
5:39 child has not died, but is *s*
13:36 he does not find you *s*
14:37 he came and found them *s*
14:37 Simon, are you *s*? Did you
14:40 he came and found them *s*
14:41 are *s* and taking your rest
Lu 8:52 she did not die but is *s*
22:46 Why are you *s*? Rise and
Ac 12:6 Peter was *s* bound with two
1Co 11:30 quite a few are *s* in death
1Th 4:13 those who are *s* in death

Sleepless
Ps 119:28 soul has been *s* from grief
2Co 6:5 by *s* nights, by times without
11:27 in *s* nights often, in

Sleeplessly
Job 16:20 To God my eye has looked *s*

Sleeps
Isa 5:27 is drowsy and no one *s*
Mr 4:27 he *s* at night and rises up by

Sleeveless
Ex 28:4 an ephod and a *s* coat and a
28:31 make the *s* coat of the ephod
28:34 hem of the *s* coat round
29:5 the *s* coat of the ephod and
39:22 the *s* coat of the ephod, the
39:23 opening of the *s* coat was in
39:24 of the *s* coat pomegranates
39:25 hem of the *s* coat round about
39:26 upon the hem of the *s* coat
Le 8:7 clothed him with the *s* coat
1Sa 2:19 a little *s* coat his mother
15:27 of the skirt of his *s* coat
18:4 *s* coat that was on him and
24:4 the skirt of the *s* coat
24:5 skirt of the *s* coat that
24:11 skirt of your *s* coat in my
24:11 skirt of your *s* coat I did
28:14 covered with a *s* coat
2Sa 13:18 used to dress with *s* coats
1Ch 15:27 in a *s* coat of fine fabric
Ezr 9:3 my garment and my *s* coat
9:5 and my *s* coat torn apart
Job 1:20 rip his *s* coat apart and cut
2:12 rip each one his *s* coat apart
29:14 justice was like a *s* coat
Ps 109:29 shame just as with a *s* coat
Isa 59:17 with zeal as if a *s* coat
61:10 *s* coat of righteousness
Eze 26:16 and remove their *s* coats

Slender
Ge 49:21 Naphtali is a *s* hind. He is

Slept
Job 3:13 I should have *s* then

Slew
Ac 5:30 Jesus, whom you *s*, hanging

Slice
1Sa 30:12 *s* of a cake of pressed figs

Sliced
2Ki 4:39 *s* them into the stewpot, for

Slickness
Pr 23:31 when it goes with a *s*
Ca 7:9 wine that is going with a *s*

Slightingly
1Pe 3:16 are speaking *s* of your good

Slimy
Job 6:6 the *s* juice of marshmallow

Sling
1Sa 17:40 and in his hand was his *s*
17:50 David, with a *s* and a stone
25:29 *s* it forth as from inside
25:29 inside the hollow of the *s*

Slinger
Jg 20:16 *s* of stones to a hairbreadth

Slingers
2Ki 3:25 the *s* began going around it

Slinging
Jer 10:18 *s* out the inhabitants of

Slingstones
2Ch 26:14 of mail and bows and *s*
Job 41:28 *s* have been changed for it
Zec 9:15 devour and subdue the *s*

Slip
1Sa 20:29 let me *s* away, please, that
Ps 73:2 had nearly been made to *s*

Slipped
De 19:5 the iron has *s* off from the
Jude 4 men have *s* in who have long

Slippery
Ps 35:6 become darkness and *s* places
73:18 *s* ground is where you place
Jer 23:12 like *s* places in the gloom

Slips
Ps 128:3 *s* of olive trees all around

Slit
Le 21:18 his nose *s* or with one

Slitting
Am 1:13 *s* open the pregnant women

Slope
Nu 34:11 *s* of the sea of Chinnereth
Jos 15:8 to the *s* of the Jebusite at
15:10 to the *s* of Mount Jearim
15:11 went out to the *s* of Ekron
18:12 *s* of Jericho on the north
18:13 at the southern *s* of Luz
18:16 to the *s* of the Jebusite
18:18 *s* in front of the Arabah
18:19 northern *s* of Beth-hoglah
Job 30:6 the very *s* of torrent valleys
Eze 25:9 I am opening the *s* of Moab

Slopes
De 3:17 the base of the *s* of Pisgah
4:49 the base of the *s* of Pisgah
Jos 10:40 Shephelah and the *s* and all
12:3 south under the *s* of Pisgah
12:8 the *s* and in the wilderness
13:20 and the *s* of Pisgah and

Slow
Ex 4:10 for I am *s* of mouth and
4:10 for I am . . . *s* of tongue
34:6 and gracious, *s* to anger and
Nu 14:18 Jehovah, *s* to anger and
De 23:21 not be *s* about paying it
Ne 9:17 *s* to anger and abundant in
Ps 86:15 *S* to anger and abundant in
103:8 *S* to anger and abundant in
145:8 *S* to anger and great in
Pr 14:29 is *s* to anger is abundant in
15:18 one that is *s* to anger quiets
16:32 *s* to anger is better than a
Joe 2:13 *s* to anger and abundant in
Jon 4:2 *s* to anger and abundant in
Na 1:3 Jehovah is *s* to anger and great
Lu 24:25 and *s* in heart to believe
Jas 1:19 hearing, *s* about speaking
1:19 speaking, *s* about wrath
2Pe 3:9 not *s* respecting his promise

Slowly
Ps 42:4 I used to walk *s* before them
Ac 27:7 sailing on *s* quite a number
2Pe 2:3 judgment . . . is not moving *s*

Slowness
Jer 15:15 In your *s* to anger do not
2Pe 3:9 as some people consider *s*

Slows
Pr 19:11 insight . . . *s* down his anger

Sluggish
Jg 18:9 Do not be *s* about walking to
Mt 25:26 Wicked and *s* slave, you
Heb 6:12 may not become *s*, but be

Sluices
Ps 135:7 made even *s* for the rain
Jer 10:13 made even *s* for the rain
51:16 made even *s* for the rain

Slumber
Ps 132:4 *s* to my own beaming eyes
Pr 6:4 any *s* to your beaming eyes
Isa 56:10 lying down, loving to *s*

Slumbering
Pr 6:10 sleep, a little more *s*
24:33 little sleeping, a little *s*
Lu 22:45 found them *s* from grief
2Pe 2:3 destruction of them is not *s*

Slumbers
Job 33:15 During *s* upon the bed

Slung
1Sa 17:49 a stone from there and *s* it

Slyly
2Ki 10:19 As for Jehu, he acted *s*
2Ti 3:6 men who *s* work their way

Small
Ge 19:20 there and it is a *s* thing
19:20 is it not a *s* thing?—and
Ex 12:4 household proves to be too *s*
12:21 *s* cattle according to your
18:22 every *s* case they themselves
18:26 every *s* case they themselves
Nu 22:18 to do something *s* or great
35:17 *s* stone by which he could
35:18 with a *s* instrument of wood
De 25:13 a great one and a *s* one
25:14 a great one and a *s* one
Jos 22:17 error of Peor too *s* for us
1Sa 5:9 striking . . . from *s* to great
22:15 not know a thing *s* or great
25:36 tell him a thing, *s* or
2Sa 12:3 one female lamb, a *s* one
1Ki 8:64 too *s* to contain the burnt
17:12 a little oil in the *s* jar
17:13 make me a *s* round cake
17:14 the *s* jar of oil itself
17:16 the *s* jar of oil itself did
18:44 a *s* cloud like a man's palm
22:31 with the *s* nor the great
2Ki 2:20 Fetch me a *s* new bowl and
2:23 *s* boys that came out from
23:2 the people, from *s* to great
25:26 the people, from *s* to great
1Ch 26:13 *s* the same as for the great
28:17 *s* gold bowls by weight for
28:17 for the different *s* bowls
28:17 *s* silver bowls by weight
28:17 for the different *s* bowls
2Ch 15:13 death, whether *s* or great
18:30 neither with the *s* nor with
24:24 *s* number of men that the
31:15 equally to great and *s*
34:30 the great as well as the *s*
36:18 utensils, great and *s*
Ezr 1:10 thirty *s* bowls of gold
1:10 *s* secondary bowls of silver
8:27 twenty *s* gold bowls worth
Es 1:5 the great as well as the *s*
1:20 the great as well as the *s*
Job 3:19 *S* and great are there the
8:7 your beginning . . . a *s* thing
Ps 8:7 *S* cattle and oxen, all of them
104:25 creatures, *s* as well as
115:13 *s* ones as well as the great

Ex 38:31 *s* pedestals of the courtyard
38:31 the *s* pedestals of the gate
39:33 pillars and its *s* pedestals
39:40 pillars and its *s* pedestals
40:18 its *s* pedestals down and
Nu 3:36 pillars and its *s* pedestals
3:37 *s* pedestals and their tent
4:31 pillars and its *s* pedestals
4:32 *s* pedestals and their tent
Job 38:6 what have its *s* pedestals
Ca 5:15 *s* pedestals of refined gold

Sockets
Ex 28:20 *S* of gold should be in their
1Ki 7:50 *s* for the doors of the inner
Eze 28:13 your settings and your *s*
Zec 14:12 will rot away in their *s*

Soco
1Ch 4:18 Heber the father of *S* and
2Ch 11:7 Beth-zur and *S* and Adullam
28:18 and *S* and its dependent

Socoh
Jos 15:35 Adullam, *S* and Azekkah
15:48 Shamir and Jattir and *S*
1Sa 17:1 at *S*, which belongs to Judah
17:1 camping between *S* and Azekah
1Ki 4:10 he had *S* and all the land of

Sodi
Nu 13:10 Gaddiel the son of *S*

Sodom
Ge 10:19 near Gaza, as far as *S* and
13:10 Jehovah brought *S* and
13:12 he pitched tent near *S*
13:13 men of *S* were bad and were
14:2 war with Bera king of *S*, and
14:8 king of *S* went on the march
14:10 the kings of *S* and Gomorrah
14:11 took all the goods of *S* and
14:12 He was then dwelling in *S*
14:17 king of *S* went out to meet
14:21 king of *S* said to Abram
14:22 Abram said to the king of *S*
18:16 looked down toward *S*, and
18:20 cry of complaint about *S*
18:22 and got on their way to *S*
18:26 If I shall find in *S* fifty
19:1 the two angels arrived at *S*
19:1 was sitting in the gate of *S*
19:4 of the city, the men of *S*
19:24 from the heavens, upon *S* and
19:28 he looked down toward *S* and
De 29:23 overthrow of *S* and Gomorrah
32:32 vine is from the vine of *S*
Isa 1:9 have become just like *S*
1:10 dictators of *S*. Give ear to
3:9 sin like that of *S* they do
13:19 God overthrew *S* and
Jer 23:14 have become like *S*, and the
49:18 as in the overthrow of *S*
50:40 God's overthrow of *S* and of
La 4:6 punishment for the sin of *S*
Eze 16:46 *S* with her dependent towns
16:48 *S* your sister, she with her
16:49 the error of *S* your sister
16:53 the captive ones of *S* and of
16:55 your own sisters, *S* and her
16:56 *S* your sister did not prove
Am 4:11 like God's overthrow of *S*
Zep 2:9 Moab . . . become just like *S*
Mt 10:15 the land of *S* and Gomorrah
11:23 taken place in *S*, it would
11:24 land of *S* on Judgment Day
Lu 10:12 more endurable for *S* in that
17:29 day that Lot came out of *S*
Ro 9:29 have become just like *S*, and
2Pe 2:6 *S* and Gomorrah to ashes
Jude 7 *S* and Gomorrah and the cities
Re 11:8 in a spiritual sense called *S*

Soft
2Ki 22:19 your heart was *s* so that
2Ch 34:27 your heart was *s* so that
Job 41:3 will it say *s* words to you?
Mt 11:8 A man dressed in *s* garments?
11:8 those wearing *s* garments are
Lu 7:25 dressed in *s* outer garments

Soften
Ex 32:11 to *s* the face of Jehovah his
2Sa 17:10 will . . . *s* in weakness
1Ki 13:6 *S*, please, the face of
Ps 45:12 will *s* your own face
65:10 With copious showers you *s*
Pr 19:6 who *s* the face of a noble
Jer 26:19 *s* the face of Jehovah
Zec 7:2 to *s* the face of Jehovah
8:21 go to *s* the face of Jehovah
8:22 to *s* the face of Jehovah
Mal 1:9 please, *s* the face of God

Softened
1Sa 13:12 face of Jehovah I have not *s*
1Ki 13:6 *s* the face of Jehovah, so
2Ki 13:4 *s* the face of Jehovah
2Ch 33:12 *s* the face of Jehovah his
Ps 119:58 *s* your face with all my
Da 9:13 *s* the face of Jehovah our God

Softening
Isa 1:6 has there been a *s* with oil

Softer
Ps 55:21 His words are *s* than oil

Softly
Ca 7:9 *s* flowing over the lips of
Ac 27:13 south wind blew *s*, they

Soil
Ex 34:26 first ripe fruits of your *s*
Nu 11:12 *s* about which you swore to
32:11 *s* of which I have sworn to
De 4:10 that they are alive on the *s*
4:40 lengthen your days on the *s*
7:13 and the fruit of your *s*, your
7:13 on the *s* that he swore to
11:9 lengthen your days on the *s*
11:21 on the *s* that Jehovah swore
12:1 you are alive on the *s*
12:19 all your days on your *s*
21:23 you must not defile your *s*
25:15 the *s* that Jehovah your God
26:2 of all the fruitage of the *s*
26:15 the *s* that you have given us
28:63 torn away from off the *s* to
29:28 from off their *s* in anger
30:9 and the fruitage of your *s*
31:13 *s* to which you are crossing
32:47 upon the *s* to which you are
2Ki 17:23 Israel went off its own *s*
25:21 into exile from off its *s*
1Ch 27:26 for the cultivation of the *s*
Ne 9:25 and a fat *s* and taking in
10:37 the tenth from our *s* to the
Ps 37:35 a luxuriant tree in native *s*
Ca 5:3 my feet. How can I *s* them?
Isa 14:1 give them rest upon their *s*
14:2 upon the *s* of Jehovah as
Jer 14:4 the *s* that has been shattered
16:15 bring them back to their *s*
42:12 return you to your own *s*
52:27 into exile from off its *s*
Eze 7:2 said to the *s* of Israel, An
11:17 give you the *s* of Israel
12:19 upon the *s* of Israel
12:22 on the *s* of Israel, saying
13:9 to the *s* of Israel they will
18:2 on the *s* of Israel, saying
20:38 *s* of Israel they will not
20:42 onto the *s* of Israel, into
21:2 against the *s* of Israel
21:3 must say to the *s* of Israel
25:3 against the *s* of Israel
25:6 soul against the *s* of Israel
28:25 dwell upon their *s* that
33:24 concerning the *s* of Israel
34:13 bring them in onto their *s*
34:27 to be on their *s* in security
36:6 concerning the *s* of Israel
36:17 were dwelling upon their *s*
36:24 bring you in upon your *s*
37:12 in upon the *s* of Israel
37:14 will settle you upon your *s*
37:21 bring them onto their *s*
38:18 in upon the *s* of Israel
38:19 occur in the *s* of Israel
39:26 on their *s* in security
39:28 together upon their *s*
Da 11:9 and go back to his own *s*
Zec 9:16 diadem glittering over his *s*
13:5 am a man cultivating the *s*
Mt 13:5 they did not have much *s*, and
13:5 not having depth of *s*
13:8 others fell upon the fine *s*
13:23 the one sown upon the fine *s*
Mr 4:5 did not have much *s*, and it
4:5 of not having depth of *s*
4:8 others fell upon the fine *s*
4:20 that were sown on the fine *s*
Lu 8:8 other fell upon the good *s*
8:15 As for that on the fine *s*
14:35 suitable neither for *s* nor

Soils
Ge 27:28 the fertile *s* of the earth
27:39 away from the fertile *s* of

Sojourners
Ac 2:10 *s* from Rome, both Jews and

Sojourning
Ac 17:21 the foreigners *s* there would

Sold
Ge 31:15 since he has *s* us, so that
37:28 *s* Joseph to the Ishmaelites
37:36 the Midianites *s* him into
45:4 whom you *s* into Egypt
45:5 because you *s* me here
47:20 the Egyptians *s* each one his
Ex 22:3 be *s* for the things he stole
Le 25:23 land should not be *s* in
25:25 buy back what his brother *s*
25:27 years from when he *s* it and
25:28 what he *s* must also continue
25:33 house *s* in the city of his
25:34 ground . . . may not be *s*
25:42 the way a slave is *s*
25:48 he has *s* himself, the right of
25:50 year he *s* himself to him
27:20 field is *s* to another man
27:27 *s* according to the estimated
27:28 of his possession, may be *s*
De 15:12 *s* to you your brother, a
24:7 he has . . . *s* him
32:30 unless their Rock had *s* them
Jg 3:8 he *s* them into the hand of
4:2 Jehovah *s* them into the hand
10:7 he *s* them into the hand of
1Sa 12:9 he *s* them into the hand of
23:7 God has *s* him into my hand
1Ki 21:20 have *s* yourself to do what
21:25 Ahab, who *s* himself to do
Ne 5:8 who were *s* to the nations
5:8 and must they be *s* to us?
Es 7:4 For we have been *s*, I and my
7:4 had been *s* for mere men slaves
Ps 105:17 was *s* to be a slave, Joseph
Isa 50:1 to whom I have *s* you people
50:1 own errors you have been *s*
52:3 that you people were *s*, and
Jer 34:14 came to be *s* to you and
Eze 7:13 For to what was *s* the seller
Joe 3:3 female child they *s* for wine
3:6 sons of Jerusalem you have *s*
3:7 where you have *s* them
Mt 13:46 *s* all the things he had and
18:25 be *s* and payment to be made
26:9 could have been *s* for a great
Mr 14:5 oil could have been *s* for
Joh 12:5 perfumed oil was not *s* for
Ac 4:34 the values of the things *s*
4:37 *s* it and brought the money
5:1 Ananias . . . *s* a possession
5:4 and after it was *s* did it not
7:9 of Joseph and *s* him into Egypt
Ro 7:14 I am fleshly, *s* under sin
1Co 10:25 Everything that is *s* in a

Soldering
Isa 41:7 saying regarding the *s*

Soldier
Lu 23:11 together with his *s* guards
Joh 18:3 Judas took the *s* band and
18:12 *s* band and the military
19:23 for each *s* a part, and the
Ac 10:7 devout *s* from among those
28:16 with the *s* guarding him
1Co 9:7 ever serves as a *s* at his own
Php 2:25 fellow worker and fellow *s*
2Ti 2:3 As a fine *s* of Christ Jesus
2:4 No man serving as a *s*
2:4 one who enrolled him as a *s*
Phm 2 to Archippus, our fellow *s*, and

Soldiers
Pr 30:31 king of a band of *s* of his
Jer 46:21 hired *s* in the midst of
Mt 8:9 having *s* under me, and I say
27:27 *s* of the governor took Jesus
28:12 silver pieces to the *s*
Mr 15:16 The *s* now led him off into
Lu 7:8 authority, having *s* under me
23:36 Even the *s* made fun of him
Joh 19:2 *s* braided a crown of thorns

Joh 19:23 the *s* had impaled Jesus
19:24 *s* really did these things
19:32 *s* came, therefore, and
19:34 *s* jabbed his side with a
Ac 12:4 four shifts of four *s* each
12:6 between two *s*, and guards
12:18 no little stir among the *s*
21:32 took *s* and army officers and
21:32 commander and the *s*, they
21:35 being carried along by the *s*
23:10 commanded the force of *s* to
23:23 Get two hundred *s* ready to
23:27 force of *s* and rescued him
23:31 these *s* took Paul according
27:31 the army officer and the *s*
27:32 *s* cut away the ropes of
27:42 *s* to kill the prisoners

Soldiers'
Ac 21:34 be brought to the *s* quarters
21:37 to be led into the *s* quarters
22:24 brought into the *s* quarters
23:10 him into the *s* quarters
23:16 entered into the *s* quarters
23:32 returned to the *s* quarters

Sole
Ge 8:9 resting-place for the *s* of its
De 2:5 the width of the *s* of the foot
11:24 *s* of your foot will tread
28:35 from the *s* of your foot to
28:56 set the *s* of her foot upon
28:65 resting-place for the *s* of
Jos 1:3 the *s* of your foot will tread
2Sa 14:25 *s* of his foot to the crown
Job 2:7 boil from the *s* of his foot
Isa 1:6 *s* of the foot even to the head
Eze 1:7 the *s* of their feet was like
1:7 the *s* of the foot of a calf

Solemn
Le 23:36 It is a *s* assembly. No sort
Nu 29:35 you should hold a *s* assembly
De 16:8 a *s* assembly to Jehovah your
2Sa 15:8 your servant made a *s* vow
2Ki 10:20 a *s* assembly for Baal
2Ch 7:9 held a *s* assembly, because
Ne 8:18 a *s* assembly, according to
Isa 1:13 along with the *s* assembly
Jer 9:2 a *s* assembly of treacherous
Joe 1:14 Call together a *s* assembly
2:15 Call together a *s* assembly
Am 5:21 smell of your *s* assemblies
Lu 1:9 the *s* practice of the priestly
Ac 21:21 nor to walk in the *s* customs
1Th 5:27 *s* obligation by the Lord

Solemnly
Ex 13:19 made the sons of Israel *s*
1Sa 8:9 you should *s* warn them, and
14:28 *s* put the people under oath
2Sa 15:7 vow that I *s* made to Jehovah
1Ki 1:12 let me, please, *s* counsel
2:43 commandment that I *s* laid
Isa 38:15 walking *s* all my years
Jer 11:7 For I *s* admonished your
Ac 19:13 I *s* charge you by Jesus whom
23:14 We have *s* bound ourselves
1Ti 5:21 I *s* charge you before God
2Ti 4:1 I *s* charge you before God

Soles
Jos 3:13 *s* of the feet of the priests
4:18 *s* of the feet of the priests
1Ki 5:3 under the *s* of his feet
2Ki 19:24 with the *s* of my feet all
Job 13:27 For the *s* of my feet you
Isa 37:25 with the *s* of my feet all
60:14 at the very *s* of your feet
Eze 43:7 place of the *s* of my feet
Mal 4:3 under the *s* of your feet in
Ac 3:7 *s* of his feet and his ankle

Solid
Job 28:8 have not trodden it down *s*
Jer 51:33 time to tread her down *s*
2Ti 2:19 *s* foundation of God stays
Heb 5:12 as need milk, not *s* food
5:14 *s* food belongs to mature
1Pe 5:9 against him, *s* in the faith

Solidly
Ps 24:2 he himself has *s* fixed it
119:73 proceeded to fix me *s*
119:90 *s* fixed the earth, that it
119:133 Fix my own steps *s* in your
Pr 3:19 He *s* fixed the heavens in

Isa 62:7 until he fixes *s*, yes, until
Eze 27:24 in ropes twined and *s* made
Hab 2:12 *s* established a town by

Solitary
Ps 25:16 For I am *s* and afflicted
68:6 *s* ones to dwell in a house
Isa 27:10 fortified city will be *s*
Jer 17:6 a *s* tree in the desert plain
49:31 *S* they reside
La 1:1 O how she has come to sit *s*
3:28 Let him sit *s* and keep silent

Solomon
2Sa 5:14 Shobab and Nathan and *S*
12:24 name came to be called *S*
1Ki 1:10 *S* his brother he did not
1:12 for the soul of your son *S*
1:13 *S* your son is the one that
1:17 *S* your son is the one that
1:19 *S* your servant he has not
1:21 my son *S* shall certainly
1:26 *S* your servant he has not
1:30 *S* your son is the one that
1:33 make *S* my son ride upon the
1:34 and say, Let King *S* live!
1:37 let him prove to be with *S*
1:38 *S* ride upon the she-mule of
1:39 anointed *S*; and they began to
1:39 saying: Let King *S* live!
1:43 David . . . has made *S* king
1:46 *S* has sat down upon the
1:50 was afraid because of *S*
1:51 the report was made to *S*
1:51 has become afraid of King *S*
1:51 King *S* first of all swear
1:52 *S* said: If he will become a
1:53 *S* sent and they brought him
1:53 and bowed down to King *S*
1:53 after which *S* said to him
2:1 command *S* his son, saying
2:12 As for *S*, he sat down upon
2:17 Please, say to *S* the king
2:19 to King *S* to speak to him
2:22 *S* answered and said to his
2:23 King *S* swore by Jehovah
2:25 *S* sent by means of Benaiah
2:27 *S* drove out Abiathar from
2:29 *S* was told: Joab has fled to
2:29 *S* sent Benaiah the son of
2:41 *S* was told: Shimei has gone
2:45 King *S* will be blessed, and
2:46 established in the hand of *S*
3:1 *S* proceeded to form a
3:3 *S* continued to love Jehovah
3:4 A thousand burnt sacrifices *S*
3:5 Jehovah appeared to *S* in a
3:6 *S* said: You yourself have
3:10 *S* had requested this thing
3:15 When *S* awoke, why, here it
4:1 *S* continued king over all
4:7 *S* had twelve deputies over
4:21 *S*, he proved to be ruler
4:21 serving *S* all the days of
4:25 security . . . the days of *S*
4:26 And *S* came to have forty
4:27 supplied food to King *S* and
4:27 the table of King *S*
4:29 continued giving *S* wisdom
5:1 to send his servants to *S*
5:2 *S* sent to Hiram, saying
5:7 Hiram heard the words of *S*
5:8 Hiram sent to *S*, saying
5:10 juniper trees to *S* according
5:11 *S*, for his part, gave Hiram
5:11 *S* kept giving Hiram year by
5:12 gave *S* wisdom, just as he
5:12 peace between Hiram and *S*
5:13 *S* kept bringing up those
5:15 *S* came to have seventy
6:1 after *S* became king over
6:2 the house that King *S* built
6:11 word of Jehovah came to *S*
6:14 *S* continued building the
6:21 *S* went on to overlay the
7:1 own house *S* built in thirteen
7:8 daughter, whom *S* had taken
7:13 *S* proceeded to send and fetch
7:14 he came to King *S* and began
7:40 work that he did for King *S*
7:45 for King *S* for the house of
7:47 *S* left all the utensils
7:48 *S* gradually made all the
7:51 work that King *S* had to do
7:51 *S* began to bring in the

1Ki 8:1 *S* proceeded to congregate the
8:1 to King *S* at Jerusalem
8:2 congregated . . . to King *S*
8:5 King *S* and with him all the
8:12 *S* said: Jehovah himself said
8:22 *S* began standing before the
8:54 *S* finished praying to Jehovah
8:63 *S* proceeded to offer the
8:65 *S* proceeded to carry on at
9:1 *S* had finished building the
9:1 every desirable thing of *S*
9:2 Jehovah appeared to *S* the
9:10 *S* built the two houses
9:11 assisted *S* with timbers of
9:11 King *S* proceeded to give to
9:12 cities that *S* had given him
9:15 that King *S* levied to build
9:16 his daughter, the wife of *S*
9:17 *S* went on to build Gezer and
9:19 desirable things of *S* that
9:21 *S* kept levying them for
9:22 that *S* constituted slaves
9:23 who were over the work of *S*
9:25 *S* continued three times in
9:26 fleet of ships that King *S*
9:27 with the servants of *S*
9:28 and bring it in to King *S*
10:1 hearing the report about *S*
10:2 she came on in to *S* and
10:3 *S*, in turn, went on to tell
10:4 to see all the wisdom of *S*
10:10 queen of Sheba gave to King *S*
10:13 King *S* himself gave the
10:13 the openhandedness of King *S*
10:14 gold that came to *S* in one
10:16 And King *S* went on to make
10:21 drinking vessels of King *S*
10:21 in the days of *S* as nothing
10:23 *S* was greater in riches
10:24 seeking the face of *S* to
10:26 And *S* kept gathering more
10:28 horses that *S* had from
11:1 King *S* himself loved many
11:2 that *S* clung to love them
11:5 and *S* began going after
11:6 *S* began to do what was bad
11:7 *S* proceeded to build a high
11:9 came to be incensed at *S*
11:11 Jehovah now said to *S*
11:14 raise up a resister to *S*
11:25 Israel all the days of *S*
11:26 a servant of *S*, and his
11:27 *S* himself had built the
11:28 *S* got to see that the young
11:31 out of the hand of *S*
11:40 And *S* began seeking to put
11:41 rest of the affairs of *S*
11:41 the book of the affairs of *S*
11:42 days that *S* had reigned in
11:43 Then *S* lay down with his
12:2 run off on account of King *S*
12:6 attending upon *S* his father
12:21 to Rehoboam the son of *S*
12:23 to Rehoboam the son of *S*
14:21 Rehoboam the son of *S*
14:26 gold shields that *S* had
2Ki 21:7 had said to David and to *S*
23:13 *S* the king of Israel had
24:13 *S* the king of Israel had
25:16 carriages that *S* had made
1Ch 3:5 Shobab and Nathan and *S*
3:10 son of *S* was Rehoboam
6:10 in the house that *S* built in
6:32 until *S* built the house of
14:4 and Shobab, Nathan and *S*
18:8 *S* made the copper sea and
22:5 *S* my son is young and
22:6 he called *S* his son that he
22:7 went on to say to *S* his son
22:9 for *S* is what his name will
22:17 princes of Israel to help *S*
23:1 made *S* his son king over
28:5 he then chose *S* my son to
28:6 *S* your son is the one that
28:9 *S* my son, know the God of
28:11 David proceeded to give *S*
28:20 David went on to say to *S*
29:1 *S* my son, the one whom God
29:19 to *S* my son give a complete
29:22 *S* the son of David king
29:23 And *S* began to sit upon
29:24 submitted themselves to *S*
29:25 make *S* surpassingly great
29:28 *S* his son began to reign in

2Ch 1:1 S the son of David continued
1:2 S proceeded to say the word
1:3 S and all the congregation
1:5 S and the congregation applied
1:6 S now made offerings there
1:7 God appeared to S and then
1:8 S said to God: You are the One
1:11 God said to S: For the reason
1:13 S came from the high place
1:14 S kept gathering chariots and
1:16 horses that S had from Egypt
2:1 S now gave the word to build
2:2 S counted off seventy thousand
2:3 S sent to Hiram the king of
2:11 in writing and sent it to S
2:17 S took a count of all the
3:1 S started to build the house
3:3 S laid as a foundation for
4:11 work that he did for King S
4:16 made for King S for the
4:18 S made all these utensils in
4:19 S proceeded to make all the
5:1 S had to do for the house of
5:1 S began to bring in the things
5:2 S proceeded to congregate the
5:6 King S and all the assembly
6:1 S said: Jehovah himself said
6:13 S had made a platform of
7:1 S finished praying, the fire
7:5 King S went on offering the
7:7 S sanctified the middle of
7:7 copper altar that S had made
7:8 S proceeded to hold the
7:10 toward S and toward Israel
7:11 S finished the house of
7:12 Jehovah now appeared to S
8:1 S had built the house of
8:2 that Hiram had given to S
8:2 S rebuilt them and then
8:3 S went to Hamath-zobah and
8:6 every desirable thing of S
8:8 S kept levying men for forced
8:9 S constituted slaves for his
8:10 that belonged to King S
8:11 Pharaoh's daughter S brought
8:12 S offered up burnt sacrifices
8:17 S went to Ezion-geber and to
8:18 and bring it to King S
9:1 heard the report about S
9:1 test S with perplexing
9:1 she came in to S and spoke
9:2 S, in turn, went on to tell
9:2 no matter was hidden from S
9:9 queen of Sheba gave to King S
9:10 servants of S who brought
9:12 S himself gave the queen
9:13 gold that came to S in one
9:14 in gold and silver to S
9:15 S went on to make two
9:20 vessels of King S were of
9:20 silver . . . in the days of S
9:22 S was greater than all the
9:23 seeking the face of S to hear
9:25 S came to have four thousand
9:28 horses to S from Egypt and
9:29 affairs of S, the first and
9:30 S continued to reign in
9:31 S lay down with his
10:2 run away on account of S the
10:6 attending upon S his father
11:3 Rehoboam the son of S the
11:17 Rehoboam the son of S for
11:17 way of David and S for
12:9 shields that S had made
13:6 servant of S the son of David
13:7 Rehoboam the son of S, when
30:26 S the son of David the
33:7 said to David and to S his
35:3 S the son of David
35:4 by the writing of S his son
Ezr 2:55 The sons of the servants of S
2:58 the sons of the servants of S
Ne 7:57 the sons of the servants of S
7:60 sons of the servants of S
11:3 the sons of the servants of S
12:45 David and S his son
13:26 S the king of Israel sinned
Ps 72:*super* Regarding S
127:*super* Song of the Ascents. Of S
Pr 1:1 The proverbs of S the son of
10:1 Proverbs of S. A wise son
25:1 also are the proverbs of S
Ca 1:5 yet like the tent cloths of S
3:7 couch, the one belonging to S
Ca 3:9 litter that King S has made
3:11 King S with the wreath that
8:11 a vineyard that S happened to
8:12 thousand belong to you, O S
Jer 52:20 S had made for the house
Mt 1:6 David became father to S by
1:7 S became father to Rehoboam
6:29 not even S in all his glory
12:42 to hear the wisdom of S
12:42 more than S is here
Lu 11:31 to hear the wisdom of S
11:31 more than S is here
12:27 Not even S in all his glory
Joh 10:23 in the colonnade of S
Ac 7:47 S built a house for him

Solomon's

1Ki 1:11 said to Bath-sheba, S mother
1:47 God make S name . . . splendid
2:13 came to Bath-sheba, S mother
4:11 Taphath, S daughter, herself
4:15 took Basemath, S daughter
4:22 S food for each day regularly
4:30 S wisdom was vaster than the
4:34 to hear S wisdom, even from
5:16 S princely deputies who were
5:18 S builders and Hiram's
9:19 storage cities that became S
11:4 time of S growing old that
11:40 in Egypt until S death
2Ch 7:11 into S heart to do regarding
8:6 cities that had become S and
8:16 S work was all in a prepared
8:18 with S servants to Ophir and
9:3 see S wisdom and the house
Ca 1:1 superlative song, which is S
Ac 3:11 what was called S colonnade
5:12 one accord in S colonnade

Solve

Jg 14:12 and you do s it, I shall in

Solved

Jg 14:18 would not have s my riddle

Somebody

Ec 4:12 s could overpower one alone
Isa 29:12 s saying: Read this out loud
Ac 5:36 saying he himself was s
8:9 saying he himself was s great

Somehow*

Mt 5:25 that s the complainant may
1Co 8:9 does not s become a stumbling
9:27 not become disapproved s
2Co 2:7 that s such a man may not be
11:3 But I am afraid that s, as
Ga 4:11 s I have toiled to no purpose

Someone*

2Sa 22:26 With s loyal you will act
Job 31:8 sow seed and s else eat
Ps 18:25 With s loyal you will act
31:12 Like s dead and not in the
58:5 s wise is binding with spells
109:7 go forth as s wicked
Isa 65:22 and s else have occupancy
65:22 s else do the eating
Eze 3:18 When I say to s wicked, You
3:19 you have warned s wicked
3:20 when s righteous turns back
3:21 you have warned s righteous
18:21 as regards s wicked, in
18:23 in the death of s wicked
18:24 when s righteous turns back
18:26 s righteous turns back from
18:27 s wicked turns back from
18:32 delight in the death of s
21:14 the sword of s slain who is
Am 5:12 hostility toward s righteous
Mt 5:41 s under authority impresses
Lu 3:4 S is crying out in the
Ac 8:31 do so, unless s guided me
2Co 11:4 s comes and preaches a Jesus
Re 1:13 s like a son of man, clothed

Someone's

Mr 12:19 if s brother dies and leaves

Sometime

Ne 13:6 s later I asked leave of
Lu 14:12 s they might also invite you
Heb 4:1 let us fear that s someone

Sometimes

Nu 9:20 s the cloud would continue
9:21 s the cloud would continue
Heb 10:33 s while you were being
Heb 10:33 s while you became sharers

Somewhat

Da 2:41 s of the hardness of iron

Somewhere

Mr 1:38 Let us go s else, into the
Ac 27:29 be cast s upon the rocks
Heb 2:6 witness has given proof s

Son

Ge 4:17 by the name of his s Enoch
4:25 she gave birth to a s and
4:26 Seth also there was born a s
5:3 he became father to a s in his
5:28 Lamech . . . father to a s
9:24 what his youngest s had done
11:31 Terah took Abram his s and
11:31 and Lot, the s of Haran
11:31 wife of Abram his s
12:5 Lot the s of his brother and
14:12 Lot the s of Abram's brother
15:3 a s of my household is
16:11 you shall give birth to a s
16:15 Hagar bore to Abram a s and
16:15 s whom Hagar bore Ishmael
17:16 give you a s from her; and
17:19 is indeed bearing you a s
17:23 take Ishmael his s and all
17:25 Ishmael his s was thirteen
17:26 and also Ishmael his s
18:10 your wife will have a s
18:14 and Sarah will have a s
19:37 became mother to a s and
19:38 she too gave birth to a s
21:2 bore a s to Abraham in his
21:3 s who had been born to him
21:4 circumcise Isaac his s when
21:5 Isaac his s was born to him
21:7 I have given birth to a s in
21:9 s of Hagar the Egyptian, whom
21:10 Drive out . . . her s
21:10 s of this slave girl is not
21:10 heir with my s, with Isaac
21:11 to Abraham as regards his s
21:13 s of the slave girl, I shall
22:2, 2 s, your only s whom you so
22:3 with him and Isaac his s
22:6 put it upon Isaac his s and
22:7 he said: Here I am, my s!
22:8 for the burnt offering, my s
22:9 bound Isaac his s hand and
22:10 knife to kill his s
22:12 you have not withheld your s
22:13 offering in place of his s
22:16 not withheld your s, your
23:8 urge Ephron the s of Zohar
24:3 not take a wife for my s from
24:4 a wife for my s, for Isaac
24:5 return your s to the land
24:6 that you do not return my s
24:7 take a wife for my s from
24:8 you must not return my s
24:15 Bethuel the s of Milcah the
24:24 Bethuel the s of Milcah
24:36 bore a s to my master after
24:37 not take a wife for my s
24:38 must take a wife for my s
24:40 must take a wife for my s
24:44 has assigned for the s of my
24:47 of Bethuel the s of Nahor
24:48 the daughter . . . for his s
24:51 wife to the s of your master
25:6 them away from Isaac his s
25:9 Ephron the s of Zohar the
25:11 bless Isaac his s, and Isaac
25:12 Ishmael the s of Abraham
25:19 history of Isaac the s of
27:1 called Esau his older s and
27:1 and said to him: My s!
27:5 Isaac spoke to Esau his s
27:6 Rebekah said to Jacob her s
27:8 my s, listen to my voice
27:13 meant for you, my s
27:15 garments of Esau her older s
27:15 them on Jacob her younger s
27:17 into the hand of Jacob her s
27:18 Who are you, my s?
27:20 Isaac said to his s: How is
27:20 quick in finding it, my s
27:21 may feel you, my s, to know
27:21 really my s Esau or not
27:24 You are really my s Esau?
27:25 some of the game of my s
27:26 and kiss me, my s

Ge 27:27 the scent of my *s* is like
27:32 I am your *s*, your firstborn
27:37 I can do for you, my *s*
27:42 words of Esau her older *s*
27:42 called Jacob her younger *s*
27:43 my *s*, listen to my voice and
28:5 for Laban the *s* of Bethuel
28:9 Ishmael the *s* of Abraham
29:12 he was the *s* of Rebekah
29:13 Jacob the *s* of his sister
29:32 and brought a *s* to birth
29:33 and brought a *s* to birth
29:34 brought a *s* to birth and
29:35 brought a *s* to birth
30:5 and in time bore Jacob a *s*
30:6 so that he gave me a *s*
30:7 bore a second *s* to Jacob
30:10 Leah's maidservant, bore a *s*
30:12 Zilpah . . . bore a second *s*
30:17 bore to Jacob a fifth *s*
30:19 Leah . . . bore a sixth *s*
30:23 and brought a *s* to birth
30:24 Jehovah is adding another *s*
34:2 And Shechem the *s* of Hamor
34:8 As for Shechem my *s*, his soul
34:18 eyes of Shechem, Hamor's *s*
34:20 So Hamor and Shechem his *s*
34:24 Hamor and to Shechem his *s*
34:26 Shechem his *s* they killed
35:17 you will have this *s* also
36:10 Eliphaz the *s* of Adah
36:10 Reuel the *s* of Basemath
36:12 of Eliphaz, Esau's *s*
36:17 the sons of Reuel, Esau's *s*
36:32 Bela *s* of Beor proceeded to
36:33 Jobab *s* of Zerah from Bozrah
36:35 Hadad *s* of Bedad, who
36:38 Baal-hanan *s* of Achbor began
36:39 Baal-hanan *s* of Achbor died
37:3 he was the *s* of his old age
37:34 mourning over his *s* for many
37:35 go down mourning to my *s*
38:3 she bore a *s* and he called
38:4 a *s* and called his name Onan
38:5 a *s* and then called his name
38:11 until Shelah my *s* grows up
38:26 not give her to Shelah my *s*
42:38 My *s* will not go down with
43:29 Benjamin his brother, the *s*
43:29 God show you his favor, my *s*
45:9 This is what your *s* Joseph
45:28 Joseph my *s* is still alive!
46:10 the *s* of a Canaanite woman
47:29 he called his *s* Joseph and
48:2 your *s* Joseph has come to you
48:19 I know it, my *s*, I know it
49:9 From the prey, my *s*, you will
50:23 sons of Machir, Manasseh's *s*
Ex 1:16 if it is a *s*, you must also
1:22 Every newborn *s* you are to
2:2 and brought a *s* to birth
2:10 so that he became a *s* to her
2:22 Later she bore a *s* and he
4:22 Israel is my *s*, my firstborn
4:23 Send my *s* away that he may
4:23 killing your *s*, your firstborn
6:15 Shaul the *s* of a Canaanite
6:25 Eleazar, Aaron's *s*, took for
10:2 declare in the ears of your *s*
10:2 your son's *s* how severely I
13:8 must tell your *s* on that day
13:14 case your *s* should inquire
20:10 nor your *s* nor your daughter
21:9 to his *s* that he designates
21:31 Whether it gored a *s* or
23:12 the *s* of your slave girl and
31:2 name Bezalel the *s* of Uri
31:2 the *s* of Hur of the tribe of
31:6 Oholiab the *s* of Ahisamach
32:29 own *s* and his own brother
33:11 Joshua, the *s* of Nun, as
35:30 Bezalel the *s* of Uri the
35:30 Uri the *s* of Hur of the tribe
35:34 Oholiab the *s* of Ahisamach
38:21 Ithamar the *s* of Aaron the
38:22 Bezalel the *s* of Uri the
38:22 Uri the *s* of Hur of the tribe
38:23 Oholiab the *s* of Ahisamach
Le 12:6 purification for a *s* or for a
18:10 of the daughter of your *s*
18:17 daughter of her *s* and the
21:2 *s* and for his daughter and for
24:10 *s* of an Israelite woman
24:10 *s* of an Egyptian man, went
Le 24:10 *s* of the Israelitess and an
24:11 *s* of the Israelite woman
25:49 *s* of his uncle may buy him
Nu 1:5 Elizur the *s* of Shedeur
1:6 Shelumiel the *s* of Zurishaddai
1:7 Nahshon the *s* of Amminadab
1:8 Nethanel the *s* of Zuar
1:9 Eliab the *s* of Helon
1:10 Elishama the *s* of Ammihud
1:10 Gamaliel the *s* of Pedahzur
1:11 Abidan the *s* of Gideoni
1:12 Ahiezer the *s* of Ammishaddai
1:13 Pagiel the *s* of Ochran
1:14 Eliasaph the *s* of Deuel
1:15 Ahira the *s* of Enan
2:3 Nahshon the *s* of Amminadab
2:5 Nethanel the *s* of Zuar
2:7 Eliab the *s* of Helon
2:10 is Elizur the *s* of Shedeur
2:12 Shelumiel the *s* of
2:14 is Eliasaph the *s* of Reuel
2:18 is Elishama the *s* of Ammihud
2:20 Gamaliel the *s* of Pedahzur
2:22 is Abidan the *s* of Gideoni
2:25 Ahiezer the *s* of Ammishaddai
2:27 is Pagiel the *s* of Ochran
2:29 Ahira the *s* of Enan
3:24 Eliasaph the *s* of Lael
3:30 Elizaphan the *s* of Uzziel
3:32 was Eleazar the *s* of Aaron
3:35 Zuriel the *s* of Abihail
4:16 Eleazar the *s* of Aaron the
4:28 Ithamar the *s* of Aaron the
4:33 Ithamar the *s* of Aaron the
7:8 Ithamar the *s* of Aaron the
7:12 Nahshon the *s* of Amminadab of
7:17 Nahshon the *s* of Amminadab
7:18 day Nethanel the *s* of Zuar
7:23 of Nethanel the *s* of Zuar
7:24 Eliab the *s* of Helon
7:29 Eliab the *s* of Helon
7:30 Elizur the *s* of Shedeur
7:35 of Elizur the *s* of Shedeur
7:36 the *s* of Zurishaddai
7:41 the *s* of Zurishaddai
7:42 Eliasaph the *s* of Deuel
7:47 of Eliasaph the *s* of Deuel
7:48 Elishama the *s* of Ammihud
7:53 of Elishama the *s* of Ammihud
7:54 Gamaliel the *s* of Pedahzur
7:59 of Gamaliel the *s* of Pedahzur
7:60 Abidan the *s* of Gideoni
7:65 Abidan the *s* of Gideoni
7:66 Ahiezer the *s* of Ammishaddai
7:71 Ahiezer the *s* of Ammishaddai
7:72 Pagiel the *s* of Ochran
7:77 of Pagiel the *s* of Ochran
7:78 Ahira the *s* of Enan
7:83 of Ahira the *s* of Enan
10:14 Nahshon the *s* of Amminadab
10:15 Nethanel the *s* of Zuar
10:16 Eliab the *s* of Helon
10:18 Elizur the *s* of Shedeur
10:19 Shelumiel the *s* of
10:20 Eliasaph the *s* of Deuel
10:22 Elishama the *s* of Ammihud
10:23 Gamaliel the *s* of Pedahzur
10:24 Abidan the *s* of Gideoni
10:25 Ahiezer the *s* of Ammishaddai
10:26 Pagiel the *s* of Ochran
10:27 Ahira the *s* of Enan
10:29 Hobab the *s* of Reuel the
11:28 Joshua the *s* of Nun, the
13:4 Shammua the *s* of Zaccur
13:5 Shaphat the *s* of Hori
13:6 Caleb the *s* of Jephunneh
13:7 Igal the *s* of Joseph
13:8 Ephraim, Hoshea the *s* of Nun
13:9 Palti the *s* of Raphu
13:10 Gaddiel the *s* of Sodi
13:11 Gaddi the *s* of Susi
13:12 Ammiel the *s* of Gemalli
13:13 Sethur the *s* of Michael
13:14 Nahbi the *s* of Vophsi
13:15 of Gad, Geuel the *s* of Machi
13:16 to call Hoshea the *s* of Nun
14:6 Joshua the *s* of Nun and Caleb
14:6 and Caleb the *s* of Jephunneh
14:30 Caleb the *s* of Jephunneh and
14:30 and Joshua the *s* of Nun
14:38 Joshua the *s* of Nun and Caleb
14:38 and Caleb the *s* of Jephunneh
16:1 And Korah the *s* of Izhar, the
16:1 the *s* of Kohath the
Nu 16:1 of Kohath, the *s* of Levi
16:1 and On the *s* of Peleth, the
16:37 Eleazar the *s* of Aaron the
20:25 Take Aaron and Eleazar his *s*
20:26 Eleazar his *s*; and Aaron
20:28 clothed Eleazar his *s* with
22:2 Balak the *s* of Zippor got to
22:4 Balak the *s* of Zippor was
22:5 to Balaam the *s* of Beor at
22:10 Balak the *s* of Zippor, the
22:16 Balak the *s* of Zippor has
23:18 ear to me, O *s* of Zippor
23:19 Neither a *s* of mankind that
24:3 of Balaam the *s* of Beor, And
24:15 Balaam the *s* of Beor, And
25:7 Phinehas the *s* of Eleazar the
25:7 Eleazar the *s* of Aaron the
25:11 Phinehas the *s* of Eleazar the
25:11 Eleazar the *s* of Aaron the
25:14 was Zimri the *s* of Salu, a
26:1 Eleazar the *s* of Aaron the
26:8 And the *s* of Pallu was Eliab
26:33 Zelophehad the *s* of Hepher
26:65 Caleb the *s* of Jephunneh and
26:65 and Joshua the *s* of Nun
27:1 Zelophehad the *s* of Hepher the
27:1 of Hepher the *s* of Gilead the
27:1 of Gilead the *s* of Machir the
27:1 Machir the *s* of Manasseh
27:1 of Manasseh the *s* of Joseph
27:4 because he had no *s*? O give us
27:8 die without his having a *s*
27:18 Joshua the *s* of Nun, a man
31:6 Phinehas the *s* of Eleazar the
31:8 killed Balaam the *s* of Beor
32:12 Caleb the *s* of Jephunneh the
32:12 Joshua the *s* of Nun, because
32:28 to Joshua the *s* of Nun and to
32:33 Manasseh the *s* of Joseph
32:39 of Machir the *s* of Manasseh
32:40 to Machir the *s* of Manasseh
32:41 And Jair the *s* of Manasseh
34:17 and Joshua the *s* of Nun
34:19 Caleb the *s* of Jephunneh
34:20 Shemuel the *s* of Ammihud
34:21 Elidad the *s* of Chislon
34:22 Bukki the *s* of Jogli
34:23 Hanniel the *s* of Ephod
34:24 Kemuel the *s* of Shiphtan
34:25 Elizaphan the *s* of Parnach
34:26 Paltiel the *s* of Azzan
34:27 Ahihud the *s* of Shelomi
34:28 Pedahel the *s* of Ammihud
36:1 Gilead the *s* of Machir the
36:1 Machir the *s* of Manasseh of
36:12 of Manasseh the *s* of Joseph
De 1:31 just as a man carries his *s*
1:36 Caleb the *s* of Jephunneh
1:38 Joshua the *s* of Nun, who is
3:14 Jair the *s* of Manasseh took
5:14 any work, you nor your *s* nor
6:2 and your *s* and your grandson
6:7 must inculcate them in your *s*
6:20 In case your *s* should ask you
6:21 then you must say to your *s*
7:3 you must not give to his *s*
7:3 you must not take for your *s*
7:4 turn your *s* from following me
8:5 just as a man corrects his *s*
10:6 Eleazar his *s* began to act as
11:6 sons of Eliab the *s* of Reuben
12:18 your *s* and your daughter and
13:6 the *s* of your mother, or your
13:6 your *s* or your daughter or
16:11 you and your *s* and your
16:14 you and your *s* and your
18:10 his *s* or his daughter pass
21:15 the firstborn *s* has come to
21:16 constitute the *s* of the loved
21:16 expense of the hated one's *s*
21:17 firstborn the hated one's *s*
21:18 a *s* who is stubborn and
21:20 This *s* of ours is stubborn and
23:2 No illegitimate *s* may come
23:4 Balaam the *s* of Beor from
25:5 died without his having a *s*
28:56 and her *s* and her daughter
31:23 Joshua the *s* of Nun and to
32:44 he and Hoshea the *s* of Nun
34:9 Joshua the *s* of Nun was full
Jos 1:1 to Joshua the *s* of Nun, the
2:1 Joshua the *s* of Nun sent two
2:23 come to Joshua the *s* of Nun
6:6 Joshua the *s* of Nun called the

Jos 7:1 Achan the s of Carmi, the
7:1 Carmi, the s of Zabdi, the
7:1 Zabdi, the s of Zerah, of the
7:18 and Achan the s of Carmi
7:18 Carmi, the s of Zabdi, the
7:18 Zabdi, the s of Zerah, of the
7:19 My s, render, please, glory
7:24 took Achan the s of Zerah and
13:22 Balaam the s of Beor
13:31 Machir the s of Manasseh
14:1 and Joshua the s of Nun
14:6 Caleb the s of Jephunneh
14:13 Caleb the s of Jephunneh
14:14 Caleb the s of Jephunneh
15:6 Bohan the s of Reuben
15:8 valley of the s of Hinnom to
15:13 to Caleb the s of Jephunneh
15:17 Othniel the s of Kenaz
17:2 Manasseh the s of Joseph
17:3 Zelophehad the s of Hepher
17:3 Hepher, the s of Gilead
17:3 Gilead, the s of Machir
17:3 Machir, the s of Manasseh
17:4 and Joshua the s of Nun and
18:16 valley of the s of Hinnom
18:17 Bohan the s of Reuben
19:49 Joshua the s of Nun in
19:51 and Joshua the s of Nun and
21:1 and Joshua the s of Nun and
21:12 to Caleb the s of Jephunneh
22:13 Phinehas the s of Eleazar
22:20 Achan the s of Zerah that
22:31 Phinehas the s of Eleazar
22:32 Phinehas the s of Eleazar
24:9 Balak the s of Zippor, the
24:9 Balaam the s of Beor to
24:29 Joshua the s of Nun, the
24:33 Eleazar the s of Aaron died
24:33 the Hill of Phinehas his s
Jg 1:13 And Othniel the s of Kenaz
2:8 Then Joshua the s of Nun, the
3:9 Othniel the s of Kenaz, the
3:11 Othniel the s of Kenaz died
3:15 a savior, Ehud the s of Gera
3:31 Shamgar the s of Anath, and
4:6 Barak the s of Abinoam out of
4:12 Barak the s of Abinoam had
5:1 Barak the s of Abinoam broke
5:6 days of Shamgar the s of Anath
5:12 Barak . . . you s of Abinoam
6:11 his s was beating out wheat
6:29 the s of Joash is the one that
6:30 your s out that he may die
7:14 s of Joash, a man of Israel
8:13 Gideon the s of Joash began
8:22 Rule over us, you and your s
8:23 nor will my s rule over you
8:29 the s of Joash went his way
8:31 she too bore him a s. So he
8:32 the s of Joash died at a good
9:1 the s of Jerubbaal went to
9:5 s of Jerubbaal was left over
9:18 the s of his slave girl, king
9:26 the s of Ebed and his brothers
9:28 the s of Ebed went on to say
9:28 the s of Jerubbaal, and is not
9:30 Gaal the s of Ebed. Then his
9:31 the s of Ebed and his brothers
9:35 s of Ebed went out and stood
9:57 Jotham the s of Jerubbaal
10:1 rose up . . . Tola the s of Puah
10:1 Puah, the s of Dodo, a man of
11:1 he was the s of a prostitute
11:2 for you are the s of another
11:25 Balak the s of Zippor, the
11:34 he had neither s nor daughter
12:13 Abdon the s of Hillel the
12:15 Abdon the s of Hillel the
13:3 pregnant and give birth to a s
13:5 certainly give birth to a s
13:7 certainly give birth to a s
13:24 gave birth to a s and called
17:2 Blessed may my s be of
17:3 from my hand for my s, so as
18:30 Jonathan the s of Gershom
18:30 Gershom, Moses' s, he and
20:28 Phinehas the s of Eleazar
20:28 of Eleazar, the s of Aaron
Ru 4:13 conception and she bore a s
4:17 A s has been born to Naomi
1Sa 1:1 Elkanah, the s of Jeroham
1:1 Jeroham, the s of Elihu, the
1:1 of Elihu, the s of Tohu
1:1 of Tohu, the s of Zuph
1Sa 1:20 and brought a s to birth and
1:23 kept nursing her s until she
3:6 I did not call, my s
3:16 Samuel, my s! At this he
4:16 that has happened, my s
4:20 it is a s that you have borne
7:1 Eleazar his s was the one
8:2 firstborn s happened to be
9:1 Kish, the s of Abiel, the
9:1 Abiel, the s of Zeror, the
9:1 Zeror, the s of Becorath, the
9:1 Becorath, the s of Aphiah
9:2 have a s whose name was Saul
9:3 So Kish said to Saul his s
10:2 What shall I do about my s?
10:11 happened to the s of Kish
10:21 Saul the s of Kish came to
13:16 Saul and Jonathan his s and
13:22 Saul and to Jonathan his s
14:1 that Jonathan the s of Saul
14:3 Ahijah the s of Ahitub, the
14:3 Ichabod, the s of Phinehas
14:3 Phinehas, the s of Eli, the
14:39 if it is in Jonathan my s
14:40 and I and Jonathan my s
14:42 me and Jonathan my s
14:50 Abner the s of Ner, the
14:51 was the s of Abiel
16:18 s of Jesse the Bethlehemite
16:19 Do send to me David your s
16:20 by the hand of David his s
17:12 Now David was the s of this
17:13 and his second s Abinadab
17:17 Jesse said to David his s
17:55 Whose s is the boy, Abner?
17:56 inquire whose s the lad is
17:58 Whose s are you, boy?
17:58 The s of your servant Jesse
19:1 Saul spoke to Jonathan his s
19:2 As for Jonathan, Saul's s, he
20:27 Saul said to Jonathan his s
20:27 s of Jesse come to the meal
20:30 s of a rebellious maid, do
20:30 choosing the s of Jesse to
20:31 s of Jesse is alive on the
22:7 s of Jesse also give to all
22:8 own s concludes a covenant
22:8 covenant with the s of Jesse
22:8 own s has raised up my own
22:9 I saw the s of Jesse come to
22:9 to Ahimelech the s of Ahitub
22:11 Ahimelech the s of Ahitub
22:12 you s of Ahitub! to which
22:13 you and the s of Jesse
22:20 one s of Ahimelech the
22:20 Ahimelech the s of Ahitub
23:6 Abiathar the s of Ahimelech
23:16 Jonathan the s of Saul now
24:16 this your voice, my s David
25:8 and to your s David
25:10 and who is the s of Jesse?
25:44 Palti the s of Laish, who
26:5 Abner the s of Ner the chief
26:6 Abishai the s of Zeruiah
26:14 to Abner the s of Ner
26:17 your voice, my s David
26:21 my s David, for I shall no
26:25 Blessed . . . be, my s David
27:2 Achish the s of Maoch, the
30:7 Abiathar . . . s of Ahimelech
2Sa 1:4 Saul and Jonathan his s have
1:5 died and also Jonathan his s
1:12 and over Jonathan his s and
1:13 s of an alien resident, an
1:17 over Saul and Jonathan his s
2:8 Abner the s of Ner the chief
2:8 Ish-bosheth, Saul's s, and
2:10 Ish-bosheth, Saul's s, was
2:12 Abner the s of Ner and the
2:12 of Ish-bosheth, Saul's s
2:13 Joab the s of Zeruiah and
2:15 and Ish-bosheth, Saul's s
3:3 Absalom the s of Maacah the
3:4 Adonijah the s of Haggith
3:4 Shephatiah the s of Abital
3:14 to Ish-bosheth, Saul's s
3:15 Paltiel the s of Laish
3:23 Abner the s of Ner came to
3:25 know Abner the s of Ner
3:28 for Abner the s of Ner
3:37 Abner the s of Ner put to
4:1 s of Saul heard that Abner
4:2 belong to the s of Saul, the
4:4 Jonathan, the s of Saul, had
2Sa 4:4 had a s lame in the feet
4:8 Ish-bosheth the s of Saul your
7:14 he himself will become my s
8:3 Hadadezer the s of Rehob the
8:10 Toi sent Joram his s to King
8:12 Hadadezer the s of Rehob the
8:16 Joab the s of Zeruiah was
8:16 Jehoshaphat the s of Ahilud
8:17 Zadok the s of Ahitub and
8:17 Ahimelech the s of Abiathar
8:18 Benaiah the s of Jehoiada
9:3 a s of Jonathan, lame in the
9:4 Machir the s of Ammiel at
9:5 Machir the s of Ammiel at
9:6 Mephibosheth the s of
9:6 Jonathan the s of Saul came
9:12 Mephibosheth had a young s
10:1 Hanun his s began to reign
10:2 Hanun the s of Nahash, just
11:21 struck down Abimelech the s
11:27 bore to him a s, but the
12:14 the s himself, just born
12:24 bore a s, and his name came
13:1 Absalom the s of David had a
13:1 Amnon the s of David fell in
13:3 Jehonadab the s of Shimeah
13:4 s of the king, so downcast
13:25 to Absalom: No, my s!
13:32 Jehonadab the s of Shimeah
13:37 to Talmai the s of Ammihud
13:37 mourn over his s all the
14:1 Joab the s of Zeruiah came
14:11 may not annihilate my s
14:11 not a single hair of your s
14:16 lone s from the inheritance
15:27 Ahimaaz your s and Jonathan
15:27 Jonathan the s of Abiathar
16:3 the s of your master
16:5 Shimei, the s of Gera
16:8 the hand of Absalom your s
16:9 Abishai the s of Zeruiah said
16:11 my own s, who has come
16:19 Is it not before his s?
17:25 Amasa was the s of a man
17:27 Shobi the s of Nahash from
17:27 Machir the s of Ammiel
18:2 Abishai the s of Zeruiah
18:12 out against the king's s
18:18 no s . . . to keep my name
18:19 Ahimaaz the s of Zadok, he
18:20 the king's own s has died
18:22 Ahimaaz the s of Zadok now
18:22 have to run, my s, when
18:27 Ahimaaz the s of Zadok
18:33, 33 My s Absalom, my s
18:33 my s Absalom!
18:33, 33 Absalom my s, my s!
19:2 king has felt hurt over his s
19:4, 4 s Absalom! Absalom my s
19:4 crying out . . . my s!
19:16 Shimei the s of Gera the
19:18 Shimei the s of Gera
19:21 Abishai the s of Zeruiah
20:1 Sheba, the s of Bichri
20:1 inheritance in the s of Jesse
20:2 follow Sheba the s of Bichri
20:6 Sheba the s of Bichri will
20:7 after Sheba the s of Bichri
20:10 after Sheba the s of Bichri
20:13 after Sheba the s of Bichri
20:21 Sheba the s of Bichri, has
20:22 Sheba the s of Bichri and
20:23 Benaiah the s of Jehoiada
20:24 Jehoshaphat the s of Ahilud
21:7 the s of Jonathan
21:7 Jonathan the s of Saul
21:7 Jonathan the s of Saul
21:8 Adriel the s of Barzillai
21:12 the bones of Jonathan his s
21:13 the bones of Jonathan his s
21:14 Saul and of Jonathan his s
21:17 Abishai the s of Zeruiah
21:19 the s of Jaare-oregim the
21:21 Jonathan the s of Shimei
23:1 David the s of Jesse, And the
23:9 Eleazar the s of Dodo the
23:9 Dodo the s of Ahohi was
23:11 Shammah the s of Agee the
23:18 Joab the s of Zeruiah, he
23:20 Benaiah the s of Jehoiada
23:20 the s of a valiant man, who
23:22 Benaiah the s of Jehoiada
23:24 Elhanan the s of Dodo of
23:26 Ira the s of Ikkesh the

2Sa 23:29 Heleb the s of Baanah the
23:29 Ittai the s of Ribai of
23:33 Ahiam the s of Sharar the
23:34 Eliphelet the s of Ahasbai
23:34 of Ahasbai the s of the
23:34 Eliam the s of Ahithophel
23:36 Igal the s of Nathan of
23:37 Joab the s of Zeruiah
1Ki 1:5 Adonijah the s of Haggith was
1:7 Joab the s of Zeruiah and
1:8 Benaiah the s of Jehoiada
1:11 Adonijah the s of Haggith has
1:12 the soul of your s Solomon
1:13 Solomon your s is the one
1:17 Solomon your s is the one
1:21 my s Solomon shall certainly
1:26 Benaiah the s of Jehoiada
1:30 Solomon your s is the one
1:32 Benaiah the s of Jehoiada
1:33 make Solomon my s ride upon
1:36 Benaiah the s of Jehoiada
1:38 Benaiah the s of Jehoiada
1:42 Jonathan the s of Abiathar
1:44 Benaiah the s of Jehoiada and
2:1 to command Solomon his s
2:5 Joab the s of Zeruiah
2:5 Abner the s of Ner and
2:5 Amasa the s of Jether, when
2:8 Shimei the s of Gera the
2:13 Adonijah the s of Haggith
2:22 and for Joab the s of Zeruiah
2:25 Benaiah the s of Jehoiada
2:29 Benaiah the s of Jehoiada
2:32 Abner the s of Ner the chief
2:32 Amasa the s of Jether the
2:34 Benaiah the s of Jehoiada
2:35 Benaiah the s of Jehoiada
2:39 Achish the s of Maacah the
2:46 commanded Benaiah the s of
3:6 a s to sit upon his throne
3:19 the s of this woman died at
3:20 took my s from beside me
3:20 dead s she laid in my bosom
3:21 to nurse my s, why, there he
3:21 he did not prove to be my s
3:22 my s is the living one and
3:22 and your s is the dead one
3:22 but your s is the dead one
3:22 and my s is the living one
3:23 This is my s, the living one
3:23 and your s is the dead one
3:23 but your s is the dead one
3:23 and my s is the living one
3:26 whose s was the living one
3:26 excited toward her s
4:2 Azariah the s of Zadok, the
4:3 Jehoshaphat the s of Ahilud
4:4 Benaiah the s of Jehoiada was
4:5 Azariah the s of Nathan was
4:5 Zabud the s of Nathan was a
4:6 Adoniram the s of Abda, over
4:8 s of Hur, in the mountainous
4:9 the s of Deker, in Makaz and
4:10 the s of Hesed, in Arubboth
4:11 the s of Abinadab, all the
4:12 Baana the s of Ahilud, in
4:13 s of Geber, in Ramoth-gilead
4:13 Jair the s of Manasseh
4:14 Ahinadab the s of Iddo, in
4:16 Baana the s of Hushai, in
4:17 Jehoshaphat the s of Paruah
4:18 Shimei the s of Ela, in
4:19 Geber the s of Uri, in the
5:5 Your s whom I shall put upon
5:7 he has given David a wise s
7:14 the s of a widowed woman
8:19 but your s who is coming
11:12 Out of the hand of your s
11:13 one tribe . . . to your s
11:20 bore him Genubath his s
11:23 Rezon the s of Eliada
11:26 Jeroboam the s of Nebat an
11:35 out of the hand of his s
11:36 to his s I shall give one
11:43 Rehoboam his s began to
12:2 Jeroboam the s of Nebat
12:15 to Jeroboam the s of Nebat
12:16 in the s of Jesse
12:21 Rehoboam the s of Solomon
12:23 Rehoboam the s of Solomon
13:2 A s born to the house of
14:1 Abijah the s of Jeroboam
14:5 from you regarding her s
14:20 Nadab his s began to reign
1Ki 14:21 Rehoboam the s of Solomon
14:31 Abijam his s began to reign
15:1 King Jeroboam the s of Nebat
15:4 raising his s up after him
15:8 Asa his s began to reign in
15:18 Ben-hadad the s of
15:18 Tabrimmon the s of Hezion
15:24 his s began to reign in
15:25 Nadab the s of Jeroboam
15:27 Baasha the s of Ahijah of
15:33 Baasha the s of Ahijah
16:1 to Jehu the s of Hanani
16:3 Jeroboam the s of Nebat
16:6 Elah his s began to reign in
16:7 Jehu the s of Hanani the
16:8 Elah the s of Baasha became
16:13 and the sins of Elah his s
16:21 Tibni the s of Ginath
16:22 Tibni the s of Ginath
16:26 Jeroboam the s of Nebat
16:28 Ahab his s began to reign
16:29 Ahab the s of Omri
16:29 Ahab the s of Omri
16:30 Ahab the s of Omri
16:31 Jeroboam the s of Nebat
16:34 Joshua the s of Nun
17:12 for myself and my s
17:13 and your s you can make
17:17 that the s of the woman
17:18 and to put my s to death
17:19 to her: Give me your s
17:20 by putting her s to death
17:23 said: See, your s is alive
19:16 Elisha the s of Shaphat
19:19 Elisha the s of Shaphat
21:22 Jeroboam the s of Nebat and
21:22 Baasha the s of Ahijah, for
21:29 days of his s I shall bring
22:8 Micaiah the s of Imlah
22:9 bring Micaiah the s of Imlah
22:11 Zedekiah the s of Chenaanah
22:24 Zedekiah the s of Chenaanah
22:26 and to Joash the king's s
22:40 Ahaziah his s began to reign
22:41 Jehoshaphat the s of Asa
22:49 Ahaziah the s of Ahab said
22:50 Jehoram his s . . . to reign
22:51 Ahaziah the s of Ahab
22:52 Jeroboam the s of Nebat
2Ki 1:17 the s of Jehoshaphat
1:17 he had not come to have a s
3:1 Jehoram the s of Ahab, he
3:3 Jeroboam the s of Nebat
3:11 here Elisha the s of Shaphat
3:27 firstborn s who was going
4:6 she went on to say to her s
4:14 a s she does not have
4:16 you will be embracing a s
4:17 and gave birth to a s at
4:28 Did I ask for a s through my
4:36 Then he said: Lift up your s
4:37 lifted up her s and went out
6:28 Give your s that we may eat
6:28 own s we shall eat tomorrow
6:29 we boiled my s and ate him
6:29 Give your s that we may eat
6:29 eat him. But she hid her s
6:31 Elisha the s of Shaphat
6:32 how this s of a murderer has
8:1 woman whose s he had revived
8:5 woman whose s he had revived
8:5 her s whom Elisha revived
8:9 Your s, Ben-hadad, the king
8:16 Jehoram the s of Ahab the
8:16 Jehoram the s of Jehoshaphat
8:24 Ahaziah his s began to reign
8:25 Jehoram the s of Ahab the
8:25 Ahaziah the s of Jehoram
8:28 Jehoram the s of Ahab to the
8:29 Ahaziah the s of Jehoram the
8:29 Jehoram the s of Ahab in
9:2 Jehu the s of Jehoshaphat the
9:2 Jehoshaphat the s of Nimshi
9:9 Jeroboam the s of Nebat
9:9 Baasha the s of Ahijah
9:14 Jehu the s of Jehoshaphat
9:14 Jehoshaphat the s of Nimshi
9:29 Jehoram the s of Ahab that
10:15 Jehonadab the s of Rechab
10:23 Jehonadab the s of Rechab
10:29 Jeroboam the s of Nebat
10:35 Jehoahaz his s began to
11:1 she saw that her s had died
11:2 Jehoash the s of Ahaziah
2Ki 11:4 showed . . . the s of the king
11:12 he brought the s of the king
12:21 Jozacar the s of Shimeath
12:21 Jehozabad the s of Shomer
12:21 Amaziah his s began to
13:1 Jehoash the s of Ahaziah
13:1 Jehoahaz the s of Jehu
13:2 Jeroboam the s of Nebat
13:3 Ben-hadad the s of Hazael
13:9 Jehoash his s began to reign
13:10 Jehoash the s of Jehoahaz
13:11 Jeroboam the s of Nebat
13:24 Ben-hadad his s began to
13:25 Jehoash the s of Jehoahaz
13:25 Ben-hadad the s of Hazael
14:1 Jehoash the s of Jehoahaz the
14:1 Amaziah the s of Jehoash the
14:8 Jehoash the s of Jehoahaz
14:8 Jehoahaz the s of Jehu the
14:9 daughter to my s as a wife
14:13 Amaziah . . . s of Jehoash
14:13 Jehoash the s of Ahaziah
14:16 Jeroboam his s began to
14:17 Amaziah the s of Jehoash
14:17 Jehoash the s of Jehoahaz
14:23 Amaziah the s of Jehoash
14:23 Jeroboam the s of Jehoash
14:24 Jeroboam the s of Nebat
14:25 Jonah the s of Amittai
14:27 Jeroboam the s of Jehoash
14:29 Zechariah his s began to
15:1 Azariah the s of Amaziah
15:5 Jotham the king's s was over
15:7 Jotham his s began to reign
15:8 Zechariah the s of Jeroboam
15:9 Jeroboam the s of Nebat
15:10 Shallum the s of Jabesh
15:13 Shallum the s of Jabesh
15:14 Menahem the s of Gadi came
15:14 Shallum the s of Jabesh
15:17 Menahem the s of Gadi
15:18 Jeroboam the s of Nebat
15:22 Pekahiah his s began to
15:23 Pekahiah the s of Menahem
15:24 Jeroboam the s of Nebat
15:25 Pekah the s of Remaliah
15:27 Pekah the s of Remaliah
15:28 Jeroboam the s of Nebat
15:30 Hoshea the s of Elah
15:30 Pekah the s of Remaliah
15:30 Jotham the s of Uzziah
15:32 Pekah the s of Remaliah
15:32 Jotham the s of Uzziah
15:37 Pekah the s of Remaliah
15:38 Ahaz his s began to reign
16:1 Pekah the s of Remaliah
16:1 Ahaz the s of Jotham the
16:3 s he made pass through the
16:5 Pekah the s of Remaliah
16:7 I am your servant and your s
16:20 Hezekiah his s began to
17:1 Hoshea the s of Elah became
17:21 Jeroboam the s of Nebat
18:1 year of Hoshea the s of Elah
18:1 Hezekiah the s of Ahaz the
18:9 Hoshea the s of Elah the
18:18 Eliakim the s of Hilkiah
18:18 Joah the s of Asaph the
18:26 Eliakim the s of Hilkiah
18:37 Eliakim the s of Hilkiah
18:37 and Joah the s of Asaph the
19:2 Isaiah . . . the s of Amoz
19:20 And Isaiah the s of Amoz
19:37 his s began to reign in
20:1 Isaiah the s of Amoz the
20:12 Berodach-baladan the s of
20:21 Manasseh his s began to
21:6 own s pass through the fire
21:7 David and to Solomon his s
21:18 Amon his s began to reign
21:24 Josiah his s king in place
21:26 Josiah his s began to reign
22:3 sent Shaphan the s of Azaliah
22:3 Azaliah the s of Meshullam
22:12 Ahikam the s of Shaphan
22:12 Achbor the s of Micaiah
22:14 Shallum the s of Tikvah
22:14 Tikvah the s of Harhas
23:10 his s or his daughter pass
23:15 Jeroboam the s of Nebat
23:30 Jehoahaz the s of Josiah
23:34 Eliakim the s of Josiah
24:6 Jehoiachin his s began to
25:22 Gedaliah the s of Ahikam

2Ki 25:22 Ahikam the *s* of Shaphan
25:23 Ishmael the *s* of Nethaniah
25:23 Johanan the *s* of Kareah
25:23 Seraiah the *s* of Tanhumeth
25:23 Jaazaniah the *s* of the
25:25 Ishmael the *s* of Nethaniah
25:25 Nethaniah the *s* of Elishama
1Ch 1:43 Bela the *s* of Beor
1:44 Jobab the *s* of Zerah from
1:46 and Hadad the *s* of Bedad
1:49 Baal-hanan the *s* of Achbor
2:18 As for Caleb the *s* of Hezron
2:45 the *s* of Shammai was Maon
3:2 Absalom the *s* of Maacah the
3:2 Adonijah the *s* of Haggith
3:10 the *s* of Solomon was
3:10, 10 Abijah his *s*, Asa his *s*
3:10 Jehoshaphat his *s*
3:11 Jehoram his *s*, Ahaziah his
3:11 Ahaziah his *s*, Jehoash his
3:11 Jehoash his *s*
3:12 Amaziah his *s*, Azariah his
3:12 Azariah his *s*, Jotham his
3:12 Jotham his *s*
3:13 Ahaz his *s*, Hezekiah his
3:13 Hezekiah his *s*
3:13 Manasseh his *s*
3:14, 14 Amon his *s*, Josiah his *s*
3:16 Jeconiah his *s*, Zedekiah his
3:16 Jeconiah . . . Zedekiah his *s*
3:17 were Shealtiel his *s*
4:2 Reaiah the *s* of Shobal
4:8 Aharhel the *s* of Harum
4:15 Caleb the *s* of Jephunneh
4:21 Shelah the *s* of Judah
4:25 Shallum his *s*, Mibsam his
4:25 Mibsam his *s*, Mishma his
4:25 Mishma his *s*
4:26 were Hammuel his *s*
4:26 Zaccur his *s*, Shimei his
4:26 Shimei his *s*
4:34 and Joshah the *s* of Amaziah
4:35 Jehu the *s* of Joshibiah
4:35 Joshibiah the *s* of Seraiah
4:35 Seraiah the *s* of Asiel
4:37 and Ziza the *s* of Shiphi
4:37 Shiphi the *s* of Allon the
4:37 Allon the *s* of Jedaiah
4:37 Jedaiah the *s* of Shimri
4:37 Shimri the *s* of Shemaiah
5:1 Joseph the *s* of Israel
5:4 of Joel were Shemaiah his *s*
5:4, 4 Gog his *s*, Shimei his *s*
5:5, 5 Micah his *s*, Reaiah his *s*
5:5 Baal his *s*
5:6 Beerah his *s*
5:8 Bela the *s* of Azaz the
5:8 Azaz the *s* of Shema
5:8 of Shema the *s* of Joel
5:14 sons of Abihail the *s* of Huri
5:14 Huri, the *s* of Jaroah, the
5:14 of Jaroah, the *s* of Gilead
5:14 of Gilead, the *s* of Michael
5:14 Michael, the *s* of Jeshishai
5:14 Jeshishai, the *s* of Jahdo
5:14 of Jahdo, the *s* of Buz
5:15 Ahi the *s* of Abdiel, the
5:15 of Abdiel, the *s* of Guni
6:20 Of Gershom, Libni his *s*
6:20 Jahath his *s*, Zimmah his
6:20 Zimmah his *s*
6:21, 21 Joah his *s*, Iddo his *s*
6:21 Zerah his *s*, Jeatherai his
6:21 Jeatherai his *s*
6:22 Kohath were Amminadab his *s*
6:22, 22 Korah his *s*, Assir his *s*
6:23 Elkanah his *s* and Ebiasaph
6:23 Ebiasaph his *s* and Assir his
6:23 and Assir his *s*
6:24, 24 Tahath his *s*, Uriel his *s*
6:24 Uzziah his *s*, and Shaul his
6:24 and Shaul his *s*
6:26 of Elkanah were Zophai his *s*
6:26 and Nahath his *s*
6:27 Eliab his *s*, Jeroham his
6:27 Jeroham his *s*, Elkanah his
6:27 Elkanah his *s*
6:29 Mahli, Libni his *s*, Shimei
6:29 Shimei his *s*, Uzzah his
6:29 Uzzah his *s*
6:30 Shimea his *s*, Haggiah his
6:30 Haggiah his *s*, Asaiah his
6:30 Asaiah his *s*
6:33 the singer, the *s* of Joel
1Ch 6:33 of Joel, the *s* of Samuel
6:34 the *s* of Elkanah, the
6:34 of Elkanah, the *s* of Jeroham
6:34 of Jeroham, the *s* of Eliel
6:34 of Eliel, the *s* of Toah
6:35 the *s* of Zuph, the
6:35 Zuph, the *s* of Elkanah, the
6:35 of Elkanah, the *s* of Mahath
6:35 of Mahath, the *s* of Amasai
6:36 the *s* of Elkanah, the
6:36 of Elkanah, the *s* of Joel
6:36 Joel, the *s* of Azariah, the
6:36 Azariah, the *s* of Zephaniah
6:37 the *s* of Tahath, the
6:37 of Tahath, the *s* of Assir
6:37 of Assir, the *s* of Ebiasaph
6:37 of Ebiasaph, the *s* of Korah
6:38 the *s* of Izhar, the
6:38 of Izhar, the *s* of Kohath
6:38 of Kohath, the *s* of Levi, the
6:38 of Levi, the *s* of Israel
6:39 Asaph was the *s* of Berechiah
6:39 Berechiah, the *s* of Shimea
6:40 the *s* of Michael, the
6:40 Michael, the *s* of Baaseiah
6:40 Baaseiah, the *s* of Malchijah
6:41 the *s* of Ethni, the
6:41 of Ethni, the *s* of Zerah, the
6:41 of Zerah, the *s* of Adaiah
6:42 the *s* of Ethan, the
6:42 of Ethan, the *s* of Zimmah
6:42 of Zimmah, the *s* of Shimei
6:43 the *s* of Jahath, the
6:43 of Jahath, the *s* of Gershom
6:43 of Gershom, the *s* of Levi
6:44 was Ethan the *s* of Kishi
6:44 of Kishi, the *s* of Abdi, the
6:44 of Abdi, the *s* of Malluch
6:45 the *s* of Hashabiah, the
6:45 Hashabiah, the *s* of Amaziah
6:45 of Amaziah, the *s* of Hilkiah
6:46, 46 *s* of Amzi, the *s* of Bani
6:46 of Bani, the *s* of Shemer
6:47 the *s* of Mahli, the
6:47 of Mahli, the *s* of Mushi
6:47 of Mushi, the *s* of Merari
6:47 of Merari, the *s* of Levi
6:50 sons of Aaron: Eleazar his *s*
6:50 Phinehas his *s*, Abishua his
6:50 Abishua his *s*
6:51, 51 Bukki his *s*, Uzzi his *s*
6:51 Zerahiah his *s*
6:52 Meraioth his *s*, Amariah his
6:52 Amariah his *s*, Ahitub his
6:52 Ahitub his *s*
6:53 Zadok his *s*, Ahimaaz his
6:53 Ahimaaz his *s*
6:56 to Caleb the *s* of Jephunneh
7:16 bore a *s* and called his name
7:17 of Gilead the *s* of Machir
7:17 of Machir the *s* of Manasseh
7:20 Shuthelah and Bered his *s* and
7:20 Tahath his *s* and Eleadah his
7:20 Eleadah his *s* and Tahath his
7:20 and Tahath his *s*
7:21 Zabad his *s* and Shuthelah his
7:21 Shuthelah his *s* and Ezer and
7:23 and gave birth to a *s*
7:25 Rephah his *s*, and Resheph
7:25 Telah his *s*, and Tahan his
7:25 and Tahan his *s*
7:26 Ladan his *s*, Ammihud his
7:26 Ammihud his *s*, Elishama his
7:26 Elishama his *s*
7:27, 27 Nun his *s*, Jehoshua his *s*
7:29 of Joseph the *s* of Israel
8:30 his *s*, the firstborn, was
8:34 Jonathan's *s* was Merib-baal
8:37 Binea, Raphah his *s*, Eleasah
8:37, 37 Eleasah his *s*, Azel his *s*
9:4 Uthai the *s* of Ammihud the
9:4 Ammihud the *s* of Omri the
9:4 of Omri the *s* of Imri the
9:4 Imri the *s* of Bani, of the
9:4 sons of Perez the *s* of Judah
9:7 Sallu the *s* of Meshullam the
9:7 Meshullam the *s* of Hodaviah
9:7 Hodaviah the *s* of Hassenuah
9:8 and Ibneiah the *s* of Jeroham
9:8 and Elah the *s* of Uzzi the
9:8 of Uzzi the *s* of Michri, and
9:8 Meshullam the *s* of Shephatiah
9:8 of Shephatiah the *s* of Reuel
9:8 of Reuel the *s* of Ibnijah
1Ch 9:11 and Azariah the *s* of Hilkiah
9:11 Hilkiah the *s* of Meshullam
9:11 Meshullam the *s* of Zadok the
9:11 Zadok the *s* of Meraioth the
9:11 of Meraioth the *s* of Ahitub
9:12 and Adaiah the *s* of Jeroham
9:12 Jeroham the *s* of Pashhur the
9:12 Pashhur the *s* of Malchijah
9:12 and Maasai the *s* of Adiel
9:12 of Adiel the *s* of Jahzerah
9:12 Jahzerah the *s* of Meshullam
9:12 the *s* of Meshillemith
9:12 Meshillemith the *s* of Immer
9:14 Shemaiah the *s* of Hasshub
9:14 of Hasshub the *s* of Azrikam
9:14 Azrikam the *s* of Hashabiah
9:15 and Mattaniah the *s* of Mica
9:15 of Mica the *s* of Zichri the
9:15 of Zichri the *s* of Asaph
9:16 Obadiah the *s* of Shemaiah
9:16 Shemaiah the *s* of Galal the
9:16 of Galal the *s* of Jeduthun
9:16 and Berechiah the *s* of Asa
9:16 of Asa the *s* of Elkanah
9:19 And Shallum the *s* of Kore
9:19 of Kore the *s* of Ebiasaph
9:19 of Ebiasaph the *s* of Korah
9:20 Phinehas the *s* of Eleazar
9:21 Zechariah the *s* of
9:36 *s*, the firstborn, was Abdon
9:40 *s* of Jonathan was Merib-baal
9:43 Rephaiah his *s*, Eleasah his
9:43 Eleasah his *s*, Azel his
9:43 Azel his *s*
10:14 over to David the *s* of Jesse
11:6 Joab the *s* of Zeruiah got to
11:11 the *s* of a Hachmonite
11:12 Eleazar the *s* of Dodo the
11:22 Benaiah the *s* of Jehoiada
11:22 the *s* of a valiant man
11:24 Benaiah the *s* of Jehoiada
11:26 Elhanan the *s* of Dodo of
11:28 Ira the *s* of Ikkesh the
11:30 Heled the *s* of Baanah the
11:31 Ithai the *s* of Ribai of
11:34 Jonathan the *s* of Shagee the
11:35 Ahiam the *s* of Sacar the
11:35 Eliphal the *s* of Ur
11:37 Naarai the *s* of Ezbai
11:38 Mibhar the *s* of Hagri
11:39 of Joab the *s* of Zeruiah
11:41 Zabad the *s* of Ahlai
11:42 Adina the *s* of Shiza the
11:43 Hanan the *s* of Maacah, and
11:45 Jediael the *s* of Shimri
12:1 because of Saul the *s* of Kish
12:18 O David . . . O *s* of Jesse
15:17 Heman the *s* of Joel and, of
15:17 Asaph the *s* of Berechiah
15:17 Ethan the *s* of Kushaiah
16:38 Obed-edom the *s* of Jeduthun
17:13 himself will become my *s*
18:10 Hadoram his *s* to King David
18:12 Abishai the *s* of Zeruiah
18:15 Joab the *s* of Zeruiah was
18:15 Jehoshaphat the *s* of Ahilud
18:16 And Zadok the *s* of Ahitub
18:16 Ahimelech the *s* of Abiathar
18:17 Benaiah the *s* of Jehoiada
19:1 his *s* began to reign in place
19:2 toward Hanun the *s* of Nahash
20:5 and Elhanan the *s* of Jair got
20:7 Jonathan the *s* of Shimea the
22:5 Solomon my *s* is young and
22:6 he called Solomon his *s* that
22:7 to say to Solomon his *s*
22:9 is a *s* being born to you
22:10 will become a *s* to me, and
22:11 my *s*, may Jehovah prove to
22:17 to help Solomon his *s*
23:1 made Solomon his *s* king over
24:6 Shemaiah the *s* of Nethanel
24:6 Ahimelech the *s* of Abiathar
26:1 Meshelemiah the *s* of Kore of
26:6 to Shemaiah his *s* there were
26:14 For Zechariah his *s*, a
26:24 Shebuel the *s* of Gershom
26:24 of Gershom the *s* of Moses
26:25 Rehabiah his *s* and Jeshaiah
26:25 Jeshaiah his *s* and Joram
26:25 Joram his *s* and Zichri his
26:25 Zichri his *s* and Shelomoth
26:25 and Shelomoth his *s*
26:28 and Saul the *s* of Kish and

1Ch 26:28 Abner the s of Ner and Joab
26:28 Joab the s of Zeruiah had
27:2 Jashobeam the s of Zabdiel
27:5 Benaiah the s of Jehoiada the
27:6 there was Ammizabad his s
27:7 and Zebadiah his s after him
27:9 was Ira the s of Ikkesh the
27:16 Eliezer the s of Zichri was
27:16 Shephatiah the s of Maacah
27:17 Hashabiah the s of Kemuel
27:18 Omri the s of Michael
27:19 Ishmaiah the s of Obadiah
27:19 Jerimoth the s of Azriel
27:20 Hoshea the s of Azaziah
27:20 Joel the s of Pedaiah
27:21 Iddo the s of Zechariah
27:21 Jaasiel the s of Abner
27:22 Azarel the s of Jeroham
27:24 Joab the s of Zeruiah had
27:25 was Azmaveth the s of Adiel
27:25 Jonathan the s of Uzziah
27:26 was Ezri the s of Chelub
27:29 was Shaphat the s of Adlai
27:32 Jehiel the s of Hachmoni
27:34 Jehoiada the s of Benaiah
28:5 he then chose Solomon my s
28:6 Solomon your s is the one
28:6 I have chosen him as my s
28:9 Solomon my s, know the God
28:11 to give Solomon his s the
28:20 to say to Solomon his s
29:1 Solomon my s, the one whom
29:19 And to Solomon my s give a
29:22 Solomon the s of David king
29:26 As for David the s of Jesse
29:28 and Solomon his s began to
2Ch 1:1 And Solomon the s of David
1:5 that Bezalel the s of Uri the
1:5 of Uri the s of Hur
2:12 to David the king a wise s
2:14 s of a woman of the sons of
6:9 your s who is coming forth
9:29 Jeroboam the s of Nebat
9:31 Rehoboam his s began to
10:2 Jeroboam the s of Nebat
10:15 to Jeroboam the s of Nebat
10:16 in the s of Jesse
11:3 Rehoboam the s of Solomon
11:17 Rehoboam the s of Solomon
11:18 Jerimoth the s of David
11:18 of Eliab the s of Jesse
11:22 Abijah the s of Maacah in
12:16 Abijah his s began to reign
13:6 Jeroboam the s of Nebat, the
13:6 of Solomon the s of David
13:7 Rehoboam the s of Solomon
14:1 Asa his s began to reign in
15:1 Azariah the s of Oded, the
17:1 Jehoshaphat his s began to
17:16 Amasiah the s of Zichri
18:7 He is Micaiah the s of Imlah
18:8 Bring Micaiah the s of Imlah
18:10 Zedekiah the s of Chenaanah
18:23 Zedekiah the s of Chenaanah
18:25 and to Joash the king's s
19:2 Jehu the s of Hanani the
19:11 Zebadiah the s of Ishmael
20:14 Jahaziel the s of Zechariah
20:14 Zechariah the s of Benaiah
20:14 Benaiah the s of Jeiel the
20:14 Jeiel the s of Mattaniah
20:34 of Jehu the s of Hanani
20:37 Eliezer the s of Dodavahu
21:1 Jehoram his s began to reign
21:17 s but Jehoahaz, his youngest
21:17 Jehoahaz, his youngest s
22:1 Ahaziah his youngest s king
22:1 Ahaziah the s of Jehoram
22:5 Jehoram the s of Ahab the
22:6 Azariah the s of Jehoram the
22:6 see Jehoram the s of Ahab in
22:10 she saw that her s had died
22:11 Jehoash the s of Ahaziah
23:1 Azariah the s of Jeroham, and
23:1 Ishmael the s of Jehohanan
23:1 Azariah the s of Obed and
23:1 Maaseiah the s of Adaiah and
23:1 Elishaphat the s of Zichri
23:3 s of the king himself will
23:11 king's s out and put upon
24:20 Zechariah the s of Jehoiada
24:22 so that he killed his s
24:26 Zabad the s of Shimeath
24:26 Jehozabad the s of Shimrith
2Ch 24:27 Amaziah his s began to
25:17 Jehoash the s of Jehoahaz
25:17 Jehoahaz the s of Jehu
25:18 give your daughter to my s
25:23 the s of Jehoash the
25:23 Jehoash the s of Jehoahaz
25:25 Amaziah the s of Jehoash
25:25 Jehoash the s of Jehoahaz
26:21 Jotham his s was over the
26:22 Isaiah the s of Amoz the
26:23 Jotham his s began to reign
27:9 Ahaz his s began to reign
28:3 valley of the s of Hinnom
28:6 Pekah the s of Remaliah
28:7 Maaseiah the s of the king
28:12 Azariah the s of Jehohanan
28:12 Berechiah the s of
28:12 Jehizkiah the s of Shallum
28:12 Amasa the s of Hadlai
28:27 Hezekiah his s began to
29:12 Mahath the s of Amasai and
29:12 Joel the s of Azariah of
29:12 Kish the s of Abdi and
29:12 Azariah the s of Jehallelel
29:12 Joah the s of Zimmah and
29:12 and Eden the s of Joah
30:26 Solomon the s of David the
31:14 Kore the s of Imnah the
32:20 Isaiah the s of Amoz, the
32:32 Isaiah the prophet, the s
32:33 Manasseh his s began to
33:6 valley of the s of Hinnom
33:7 David and to Solomon his s
33:20 Amon his s began to reign
33:25 Josiah his s king in place
34:8 sent Shaphan the s of Azaliah
34:8 Joah the s of Joahaz the
34:20 Ahikam the s of Shaphan
34:20 Abdon the s of Micah
34:22 Shallum the s of Tikvah
34:22 Tikvah the s of Harhas
35:3 Solomon the s of David
35:4 the writing of Solomon his s
36:1 Jehoahaz the s of Josiah
36:8 Jehoiachin his s began to
Ezr 3:2 And Jeshua the s of Jehozadak
3:2 Zerubbabel the s of Shealtiel
3:8 Zerubbabel the s of Shealtiel
3:8 and Jeshua the s of Jehozadak
5:2 Zerubbabel the s of Shealtiel
5:2 and Jeshua the s of Jehozadak
7:1 Ezra the s of Seraiah the
7:1 Seraiah the s of Azariah the
7:1 Azariah the s of Hilkiah
7:2 the s of Shallum the
7:2 Shallum the s of Zadok the
7:2 Zadok the s of Ahitub
7:3 the s of Amariah the
7:3 Amariah the s of Azariah
7:3 Azariah the s of Meraioth
7:4, 4 s of Zerahiah the s of Uzzi
7:4 Uzzi the s of Bukki
7:5 the s of Abishua the
7:5 Abishua the s of Phinehas the
7:5 Phinehas the s of Eleazar the
7:5 Eleazar the s of Aaron the
8:4 Elieho-enai the s of Zerahiah
8:5 Shecaniah the s of Jahaziel
8:6 Ebed the s of Jonathan, and
8:7 Jeshaiah the s of Athaliah
8:8 Zebadiah the s of Michael
8:9 Obadiah the s of Jehiel, and
8:10 Shelomith the s of Josiphiah
8:11 Zechariah the s of Bebai
8:12 Johanan the s of Hakkatan
8:18 of Levi the s of Israel
8:33 Meremoth the s of Urijah the
8:33 Eleazar the s of Phinehas
8:33 Jozabad the s of Jeshua and
8:33 Noadiah the s of Binnui the
10:2 Shecaniah the s of Jehiel of
10:6 Jehohanan the s of Eliashib
10:15 Jonathan the s of Asahel and
10:15 Jahzeiah the s of Tikvah
10:18 Jeshua the s of Jehozadak
Ne 1:1 Nehemiah the s of Hacaliah
3:2 Zaccur the s of Imri did
3:4 Meremoth the s of Urijah the
3:4 Urijah the s of Hakkoz did
3:4 Meshullam the s of Berechiah
3:4 Berechiah the s of Meshezabel
3:4 Zadok the s of Baana did
3:6 Joiada the s of Paseah and
3:6 Meshullam the s of Besodeiah
Ne 3:8 Uzziel the s of Harhaiah
3:9 Rephaiah the s of Hur, a prince
3:10 Jedaiah the s of Harumaph
3:10 Hattush the s of Hashabneiah
3:11 Malchijah the s of Harim and
3:11 Hasshub the s of Pahath-moab
3:12 Shallum the s of Hallohesh
3:14 Malchijah the s of Rechab
3:15 Shallun the s of Colhozeh
3:16 Nehemiah the s of Azbuk
3:17 Rehum the s of Bani
3:18 Bavvai the s of Henadad
3:19 And Ezer the s of Jeshua
3:20 Baruch the s of Zabbai worked
3:21 Meremoth the s of Urijah the
3:21 Urijah the s of Hakkoz
3:23 Azariah the s of Maaseiah the
3:23 Maaseiah the s of Ananiah did
3:24 Binnui the s of Henadad
3:25 Palal the s of Uzai did
3:25 Pedaiah the s of Parosh
3:29 Zadok the s of Immer did
3:29 Shemaiah the s of Shecaniah
3:30 Hananiah the s of Shelemiah
3:30 Hanun the sixth s of Zalaph
3:30 Meshullam the s of Berechiah
6:10 Shemaiah the s of Delaiah the
6:10 Delaiah the s of Mehetabel
6:18 to Shecaniah the s of Arah
6:18 Jehohanan his s had himself
6:18 Meshullam the s of Berechiah
8:17 days of Joshua the s of Nun
10:1 Tirshatha, the s of Hacaliah
10:9 Jeshua the s of Azaniah
10:38 the priest, the s of Aaron
11:4 Athaiah the s of Uzziah the
11:4 Uzziah the s of Zechariah
11:4 Zechariah the s of Amariah
11:4 Amariah the s of Shephatiah
11:4 Shephatiah the s of Mahalalel
11:5 Maaseiah the s of Baruch
11:5 Baruch the s of Colhozeh the
11:5 Colhozeh the s of Hazaiah the
11:5 Hazaiah the s of Adaiah the
11:5 Adaiah the s of Joiarib the
11:5 Joiarib the s of Zechariah
11:5 Zechariah the s of the
11:7 Sallu the s of Meshullam the
11:7 Meshullam the s of Joed the
11:7 Joed the s of Pedaiah the
11:7 Pedaiah the s of Kolaiah the
11:7 Kolaiah the s of Maaseiah the
11:7 Maaseiah the s of Ithiel the
11:7 Ithiel the s of Jeshaiah
11:9 and Joel the s of Zichri
11:9 and Judah the s of Hassenuah
11:10 Jedaiah the s of Joiarib
11:11 Seraiah the s of Hilkiah
11:11 Hilkiah the s of Meshullam
11:11 Meshullam the s of Zadok the
11:11 Zadok the s of Meraioth the
11:11 Meraioth the s of Ahitub
11:12 and Adaiah the s of Jeroham
11:12 Jeroham the s of Pelaliah
11:12 Pelaliah the s of Amzi the
11:12 Amzi the s of Zechariah
11:12 Zechariah the s of Pashhur
11:12 Pashhur the s of Malchijah
11:13 Amashsai the s of Azarel the
11:13 Azarel the s of Ahzai the
11:13 Ahzai the s of Meshillemoth
11:13 Meshillemoth the s of Immer
11:14 Zabdiel the s of the great
11:15 Shemaiah the s of Hasshub
11:15 Hasshub the s of Azrikam
11:15 Azrikam the s of Hashabiah
11:15 Hashabiah the s of Bunni
11:17 Mattaniah . . . the s of Micah
11:17 Micah the s of Zabdi the
11:17 Zabdi the s of Asaph, the
11:17 and Abda the s of Shammua
11:17 Shammua the s of Galal the
11:17 Galal the s of Jeduthun
11:22 Uzzi the s of Bani the
11:22 Bani the s of Hashabiah the
11:22 Hashabiah the s of Mattaniah
11:22 Mattaniah the s of Mica of
11:24 Pethahiah the s of
11:24 Zerah the s of Judah was at
12:1 Zerubbabel the s of Shealtiel
12:23 Johanan the s of Eliashib
12:24 and Jeshua the s of Kadmiel
12:26 Joiakim the s of Jeshua
12:26 Jeshua the s of Jozadak

Ne 12:35 Zechariah the s of Jonathan
12:35 Jonathan the s of Shemaiah
12:35 Shemaiah the s of Mattaniah
12:35 Mattaniah the s of Micaiah
12:35 Micaiah the s of Zaccur the
12:35 Zaccur the s of Asaph
12:45 David and Solomon his s
13:13 Hanan the s of Zaccur the
13:13 Zaccur the s of Mattaniah
13:28 Joiada the s of Eliashib the
Es 2:5 was Mordecai the s of Jair
2:5 of Jair the s of Shimei the
2:5 of Shimei the s of Kish a
3:1 Haman the s of Hammedatha the
3:10 to Haman the s of Hammedatha
8:5 Haman the s of Hammedatha the
9:10 of Haman the s of Hammedatha
9:24 Haman the s of Hammedatha
Job 16:21 between a s of man and his
25:6 a s of man, who is a worm
32:2 Elihu the s of Barachel
32:6 Elihu the s of Barachel the
35:8 to a s of earthling man
Ps 2:7 has said to me: You are my s
2:12 Kiss the s, that He may not
3:*super* account of Absalom his s
8:4 the s of earthling man that
50:20 Against the s of your mother
72:1 righteousness to the s of the
72:20 David, the s of Jesse, have
80:15 s whom you have made strong
80:17 s of mankind whom you have
86:16 the s of your slave girl
89:22 any s of unrighteousness
116:16 the s of your slave girl
144:3 s of mortal man that you
146:3 s of earthling man, to whom
Pr 1:1 Solomon the s of David, the
1:8 Listen, my s, to the
1:10 My s, if sinners try to
1:15 my s, do not go in the way
2:1 My s, if you will receive my
3:1 My s, my law do not forget
3:11 discipline of Jehovah, O my s
3:12 father does a s in whom he
3:21 My s, may they not get away
4:3 real s to my father, tender
4:10 Hear, my s, and accept my
4:20 My s, to my words do pay
5:1 My s, to my wisdom O do pay
5:20 s, be in an ecstasy with a
6:1 My s, if you have gone surety
6:3 s, and deliver yourself, for
6:20 Observe, O my s, the
7:1 s, keep my sayings, and may
10:1 wise s is the one that makes
10:1 stupid s is the grief of his
10:5 s acting with insight is
10:5 s acting shamefully is fast
13:1 s is wise where there is a
13:24 back his rod is hating his s
15:20 wise s is the one that makes
17:2 s who is acting shamefully
17:25 stupid s is a vexation to his
19:13 A stupid s means adversities
19:18 Chastise your s while there
19:26 is a s acting shamefully and
19:27 Cease, my s, to listen to
23:15 My s, if your heart has
23:19 my s, hear and become wise
23:26 s, do give your heart to me
24:13 s, eat honey, for it is good
24:21 s, fear Jehovah and the king
27:11 Be wise, my s, and make my
28:7 understanding s is observing
29:17 Chastise your s and he will
30:1 words of Agur the s of Jakeh
30:4 and what the name of his s
31:2 What am I saying, O s of
31:2 and what, O s of my belly
31:2 and what, O s of my vows
Ec 1:1 congregator, the s of David the
4:8 no s or brother does he have
5:14 has become father to a s when
10:17 king is the s of noble ones
12:12 my s, take a warning: To the
Isa 1:1 of Isaiah the s of Amoz
2:1 Isaiah the s of Amoz visioned
7:1 Ahaz the s of Jotham the
7:1 Jotham the s of Uzziah, the
7:1 Pekah the s of Remaliah
7:3 you and Shear-jashub your s
7:4 Syria and the s of Remaliah
7:5 s of Remaliah has advised
Isa 7:6 the s of Tabeel
7:9 Samaria is the s of Remaliah
7:14 she is giving birth to a s
8:2 Zechariah the s of Jeberechiah
8:3 in time gave birth to a s
8:6 Rezin and the s of Remaliah
9:6 has been a s given to us
13:1 Isaiah the s of Amoz saw in
14:12 shining one, s of the dawn
19:11 I am the s of wise ones
19:11 s of kings of ancient time
20:2 Isaiah the s of Amoz
21:10 s of my threshing floor
22:20 Eliakim the s of Hilkiah
36:3 Eliakim the s of Hilkiah
36:3 Joah the s of Asaph the
36:22 Eliakim the s of Hilkiah
36:22 Joah the s of Asaph the
37:2 Isaiah the s of Amoz the
37:21 Isaiah the s of Amoz
37:38 Esar-haddon his s began to
38:1 Isaiah the s of Amoz the
39:1 Merodach-baladan the s of
49:15 pity the s of her belly
51:12 a s of mankind that will
56:2 the s of mankind that lays
Jer 1:1 Jeremiah the s of Hilkiah
1:2 days of Josiah the s of Amon
1:3 Jehoiakim the s of Josiah
1:3 Zedekiah the s of Josiah
6:26 mourning that for an only s
7:31 valley of the s of Hinnom
7:32 valley of the s of Hinnom
15:4 Manasseh the s of Hezekiah
19:2 valley of the s of Hinnom
19:6 valley of the s of Hinnom
20:1 Pashhur the s of Immer, the
20:15 born to you a s, a male
21:1 Pashhur the s of Malchiah and
21:1 Zephaniah the s of Maaseiah
22:11 Shallum the s of Josiah
22:18 Jehoiakim the s of Josiah
22:24 Coniah the s of Jehoiakim
24:1 Jeconiah the s of Jehoiakim
25:1 Jehoiakim the s of Josiah
25:3 Josiah the s of Amon, the
26:1 Jehoiakim the s of Josiah
26:20 Urijah the s of Shemaiah
26:22 Elnathan the s of Achbor
26:24 Ahikam the s of Shaphan
27:1 Jehoiakim the s of Josiah
27:7 serve even him and his s
27:20 Jeconiah the s of Jehoiakim
28:1 Hananiah the s of Azzur
28:4 Jeconiah the s of Jehoiakim
29:3 Elasah the s of Shaphan
29:3 Gemariah the s of Hilkiah
29:21 Ahab the s of Kolaiah and
29:21 Zedekiah the s of Maaseiah
29:25 Zephaniah the s of Maaseiah
31:20 Ephraim a precious s to me
32:7 Hanamel the s of Shallum your
32:8 Hanamel the s of my paternal
32:9 Hanamel the s of my paternal
32:12 Baruch the s of Neriah
32:12 Neriah the s of Mahseiah
32:12 Hanamel the s of my
32:16 Baruch the s of Neriah
32:35 valley of the s of Hinnom
33:21 s ruling as king upon his
35:1 Jehoiakim the s of Josiah
35:3 Jaazaniah the s of Jeremiah
35:3 Jeremiah the s of
35:4 Hanan the s of Igdaliah
35:4 Maaseiah the s of Shallum
35:6 Jonadab the s of Rechab
35:8 Jehonadab the s of Rechab
35:14 Jehonadab the s of Rechab
35:16 of Jehonadab the s of Rechab
35:19 Jonadab the s of Rechab
36:1 Jehoiakim the s of Josiah
36:4 call Baruch the s of Neriah
36:8 Baruch the s of Neriah
36:9 Jehoiakim the s of Josiah
36:10 Gemariah the s of Shaphan
36:11 Micaiah the s of Gemariah
36:11 Gemariah the s of Shaphan
36:12 Delaiah the s of Shemaiah
36:12 Elnathan the s of Achbor
36:12 Gemariah the s of Shaphan
36:12 Zedekiah the s of Hananiah
36:14 Jehudi the s of Nethaniah
36:14 the s of Shelemiah
36:14 Shelemiah the s of Cushi
Jer 36:14 Baruch the s of Neriah
36:26 Jerahmeel the s of the king
36:26 Seraiah the s of Azriel
36:26 Shelemiah the s of Abdeel
36:32 Baruch the s of Neriah
37:1 Zedekiah the s of Josiah
37:1 Coniah the s of Jehoiakim
37:3 Jehucal the s of Shelemiah
37:3 Zephaniah the s of Maaseiah
37:13 Irijah the s of Shelemiah
37:13 Shelemiah the s of Hananiah
38:1 Shephatiah the s of Mattan
38:1 Gedaliah the s of Pashhur
38:1 Jucal the s of Shelemiah
38:1 Pashhur the s of Malchijah
38:6 Malchijah the s of the king
39:14 Gedaliah the s of Ahikam
39:14 Ahikam the s of Shaphan, in
40:5 Gedaliah the s of Ahikam
40:5 Ahikam the s of Shaphan
40:6 Gedaliah the s of Ahikam
40:7 Gedaliah the s of Ahikam
40:8 Ishmael the s of Nethaniah
40:8 Seraiah the s of Tanhumeth
40:8 the s of the Maacathite
40:9 Gedaliah the s of Ahikam
40:9 Ahikam the s of Shaphan
40:11 Gedaliah the s of Ahikam
40:11 Ahikam the s of Shaphan
40:13 Johanan the s of Kareah
40:14 Ishmael the s of Nethaniah
40:14 Gedaliah the s of Ahikam
40:15 Johanan the s of Kareah
40:15 Ishmael the s of Nethaniah
40:16 Gedaliah the s of Ahikam
40:16 Johanan the s of Kareah
41:1 Ishmael the s of Nethaniah
41:1 Nethaniah the s of Elishama
41:1 Gedaliah the s of Ahikam
41:2 Ishmael the s of Nethaniah
41:2 Gedaliah the s of Ahikam
41:2 Ahikam the s of Shaphan
41:6 Ishmael the s of Nethaniah
41:6 to Gedaliah the s of Ahikam
41:7 Ishmael the s of Nethaniah
41:9 Ishmael the s of Nethaniah
41:10 Gedaliah the s of Ahikam
41:10 Ishmael the s of Nethaniah
41:11 Johanan the s of Kareah
41:11 Ishmael the s of Nethaniah
41:12 Ishmael the s of Nethaniah
41:13 saw Johanan the s of Kareah
41:14 Johanan the s of Kareah
41:15 Ishmael the s of Nethaniah
41:16 Johanan the s of Kareah
41:16 Ishmael the s of Nethaniah
41:16 Gedaliah the s of Ahikam
41:18 Ishmael the s of Nethaniah
41:18 Gedaliah the s of Ahikam
42:1 Johanan the s of Kareah
42:1 Jezaniah the s of Hoshaiah
42:8 Johanan the s of Kareah and
43:2 Azariah the s of Hoshaiah
43:2 Johanan the s of Kareah
43:3 Baruch the s of Neriah is
43:4 Johanan the s of Kareah and
43:5 Johanan the s of Kareah and
43:6 Gedaliah the s of Ahikam
43:6 Ahikam the s of Shaphan
43:6 and Baruch the s of Neriah
45:1 Baruch the s of Neriah
45:1 Jehoiakim the s of Josiah
46:2 Jehoiakim the s of Josiah
49:18 no s of mankind will reside
49:33 s of mankind will reside as
50:40 s of mankind reside in her
51:43 no s of mankind will pass
51:59 Seraiah the s of Neriah
51:59 Neriah the s of Mahseiah
Eze 1:3 to Ezekiel the s of Buzi the
2:1 S of man, stand up upon your
2:3 S of man, I am sending you to
2:6 s of man, do not be afraid of
2:8 O s of man, hear what I am
3:1 S of man, what you find, eat
3:3 S of man, you should cause
3:4 S of man, go, enter in among
3:10 S of man, all my words that
3:17 S of man, a watchman is
3:25 s of man, look! they will
4:1 s of man, take for yourself a
4:16 S of man, here I am breaking
5:1 s of man, take for yourself a
6:2 S of man, set your face

Eze 7:2 And as for you, O *s* of man
8:5 *S* of man, please, raise your
8:6 *S* of man, are you seeing what
8:8 *S* of man, bore, please
8:11 Jaazaniah the *s* of Shaphan
8:12 Have you seen, O *s* of man
8:15 you seen this, O *s* of man
8:17 you seen this, O *s* of man
11:1 Jaazaniah the *s* of Azzur and
11:1 and Pelatiah the *s* of Benaiah
11:2 *S* of man, these are the men
11:4 Prophesy, O *s* of man
11:13 Pelatiah the *s* of Benaiah
11:15 *S* of man, as regards your
12:2 *S* of man, in the midst of a
12:3 As for you, O *s* of man, make
12:9 *S* of man, did not those of
12:18 *S* of man, with quaking your
12:22 *S* of man, what is this
12:27 *S* of man, look! those of
13:2 *S* of man, prophesy
13:17 O *s* of man, set your face
14:3 *S* of man, as regards these
14:13 *S* of man, as regards a land
14:20 neither *s* nor daughter
15:2 *S* of man, in what way does
16:2 *S* of man, make known to
17:2 *S* of man, propound a riddle
18:4 so likewise the soul of the *s*
18:10 to a *s* who is a robber, a
18:14 *s*, who keeps seeing all the
18:19 the *s* does not have to bear
18:19 as regards the *s*, justice
18:20 *s* himself will bear nothing
18:20 the error of the *s*
20:3 *S* of man, speak with the
20:4 you judge them, O *s* of man
20:27 *s* of man, and you must say
20:46 *S* of man, set your face in
21:2 *S* of man, set your face
21:6 *s* of man, sigh with shaking
21:9 *S* of man, prophesy, and you
21:10 the scepter of my own *s*
21:12 and howl, O *s* of man
21:14 you, O *s* of man—prophesy
21:19 as for you, O *s* of man
21:28 O *s* of man, prophesy
22:2 O *s* of man, will you judge
22:18 *S* of man, to me those of
22:24 *S* of man, say to her
23:2 *S* of man, two women, the
23:36 *S* of man, will you judge
24:2 *S* of man, write down for
24:16 *S* of man, here I am taking
24:25 O *s* of man, will it not be
25:2 *S* of man, set your face
26:2 *S* of man, for the reason
27:2 O *s* of man, raise up
28:2 *S* of man, say to the leader
28:12 *S* of man, lift up a dirge
28:21 *S* of man, set your face
29:2 *S* of man, set your face
29:18 *S* of man, Nebuchadrezzar
30:2 *S* of man, prophesy, and you
30:21 *S* of man, the arm of
31:2 *S* of man, say to Pharaoh the
32:2 *S* of man, lift up a dirge
32:18 *S* of man, lament over the
33:2 *S* of man, speak to the sons
33:7 O *s* of man, a watchman is
33:10 as regards you, O *s* of man
33:12 O *s* of man, say to the sons
33:24 *S* of man, the inhabitants
33:30 O *s* of man, the sons of
34:2 *S* of man, prophesy against
35:2 *S* of man, set your face
36:1 you, O *s* of man, prophesy
36:17 *S* of man, the house of
37:3 *S* of man, can these bones
37:9 Prophesy, O *s* of man, and
37:11 *S* of man, as regards these
37:16 O *s* of man, take for
38:2 *S* of man, set your face
38:14 prophesy, O *s* of man, and
39:1 as regards you, O *s* of man
39:17 as regards you, O *s* of man
40:4 *S* of man, see with your eyes
43:7 *S* of man, this is the place
43:10 *s* of man, inform the house
43:18 *S* of man, this is what the
43:19 bull, the *s* of the herd
43:23 bull, the *s* of the herd
43:25 bull, the *s* of the herd
44:5 *S* of man, set your heart and
Eze 44:25 for *s* or for daughter or
45:18 young bull, a *s* of the herd
46:6 bull, the *s* of the herd
47:6 seen this, O *s* of man
Da 3:25 is resembling a *s* of the gods
5:22 his *s* Belshazzar, you have not
7:13 *s* of man happened to be
8:17 Understand, O *s* of man, that
9:1 Darius the *s* of Ahasuerus of
Ho 1:1 Hosea the *s* of Beeri in the
1:1 of Jeroboam the *s* of Joash
1:3 and in time bore to him a *s*
1:8 pregnant and give birth to a *s*
11:1 out of Egypt I called my *s*
13:13 He is a *s* not wise, for in
13:15 as the *s* of reed plants
Joe 1:1 to Joel the *s* of Pethuel
Am 1:1 Jeroboam the *s* of Joash, the
7:14 was I the *s* of a prophet
8:10 the mourning for an only *s*
Jon 1:1 to Jonah the *s* of Amittai
Mic 6:5 what Balaam the *s* of Beor
6:7 my firstborn *s* for my revolt
7:6 For a *s* is despising a father
Zep 1:1 to Zephaniah the *s* of Cushi
1:1 Cushi the *s* of Gedaliah the
1:1 Gedaliah the *s* of Amariah the
1:1 Amariah the *s* of Hezekiah in
1:1 days of Josiah the *s* of Amon
Hag 1:1 Zerubbabel the *s* of Shealtiel
1:1 to Joshua the *s* of Jehozadak
1:12 Zerubbabel the *s* of Shealtiel
1:12 Joshua the *s* of Jehozadak
1:14 Zerubbabel the *s* of Shealtiel
1:14 Joshua the *s* of Jehozadak
2:2 Zerubbabel the *s* of Shealtiel
2:2 Joshua the *s* of Jehozadak
2:4 Joshua the *s* of Jehozadak the
2:23 Zerubbabel the *s* of Shealtiel
Zec 1:1 Zechariah the *s* of Berechiah
1:1 Berechiah the *s* of Iddo the
1:7 Zechariah the *s* of Berechiah
1:7 Berechiah the *s* of Iddo the
6:10 Josiah the *s* of Zephaniah
6:11 Joshua the *s* of Jehozadak
6:14 to Hen the *s* of Zephaniah
9:6 an illegitimate *s* will
9:9 animal the *s* of a she-ass
12:10 the wailing over an only *s*
12:10 over the firstborn *s*
Mal 1:6 A *s*, for his part, honors a
3:17 shows compassion upon his *s*
Mt 1:1 Jesus Christ, *s* of David
1:1 David, *s* of Abraham
1:20 Joseph, *s* of David, do not
1:21 give birth to a *s*, and you
1:23 will give birth to a *s*, and
1:25 until she gave birth to a *s*
2:15 Out of Egypt I called my *s*
3:17 This is my *S*, the beloved
4:3 If you are a *s* of God, tell
4:6 If you are a *s* of God, hurl
4:21 James the *s* of Zebedee and
7:9 his *s* asks for bread—he will
8:20 *S* of man has nowhere to lay
8:29 to do with you, *S* of God
9:6 the *S* of man has authority on
9:27 Have mercy on us, *S* of David
10:2 James the *s* of Zebedee and
10:3 James the *s* of Alphaeus, and
10:23 until the *S* of man arrives
10:37 greater affection for *s* or
11:19 *S* of man did come eating
11:27 no one fully knows the *S* but
11:27 know the Father but the *S*
11:27 *S* is willing to reveal him
12:8 is what the *S* of man is
12:23 perhaps be the *S* of David
12:32 a word against the *S* of man
12:40 so the *S* of man will be in
13:37 sower . . . is the *S* of man
13:41 *S* of man will send forth
13:55 this not the carpenter's *s*
14:33 You are really God's *S*
15:22 on me, Lord, *S* of David
16:13 men saying the *S* of man is
16:16 the *S* of the living God
16:17 Simon *s* of Jonah, because
16:27 the *S* of man is destined to
16:28 see the *S* of man coming in
17:5 This is my *S*, the beloved
17:9 until the *S* of man is raised
17:12 the *S* of man is destined to
17:15 Lord, have mercy on my *s*
Mt 17:22 *S* of man is destined to be
19:28 when the *S* of man sits down
20:18 *S* of man will be delivered
20:28 *S* of man came, not to be
20:30 have mercy on us, *S* of David!
20:31 have mercy on us, *S* of David!
21:9 Save, we pray, the *S* of David!
21:15 Save . . . the *S* of David!
21:37 Lastly he dispatched his *s*
21:37 They will respect my *s*
21:38 seeing the *s* the cultivators
22:2 a marriage feast for his *s*
22:42 the Christ? Whose *s* is he?
22:45 how is he his *s*?
23:35 of Zechariah *s* of Barachiah
24:27 the presence of the *S* of man
24:30 sign of the *S* of man will
24:30 see the *S* of man coming on
24:36 nor the *S*, but only the
24:37 the presence of the *S* of man
24:39 the presence of the *S* of man
24:44 the *S* of man is coming
25:31 the *S* of man arrives in his
26:2 *S* of man is to be delivered
26:24 the *S* of man is going away
26:24 the *S* of man is betrayed
26:45 *S* of man to be betrayed into
26:63 are the Christ the *S* of God
26:64 you will see the *S* of man
27:40 If you are a *s* of God, come
27:43 for he said, I am God's *S*
27:54 Certainly this was God's *S*
28:19 Father and of the *S* and of
Mr 1:11 You are my *S*, the beloved
1:19 saw James the *s* of Zebedee
2:10 the *S* of man has authority to
2:14 of Levi the *s* of Alphaeus
2:28 *S* of man is Lord even of the
3:11 saying: You are the *S* of God
3:17 James the *s* of Zebedee and
3:18 James the *s* of Alphaeus and
5:7 Jesus, *S* of the Most High God
6:3 is the carpenter the *s* of Mary
8:31 the *S* of man must undergo
8:38 the *S* of man will also be
9:7 This is my *S*, the beloved
9:9 the *S* of man had risen from
9:12 respecting the *S* of man
9:17 Teacher, I brought my *s* to
9:31 *S* of man is to be delivered
10:33 *S* of man will be delivered
10:45 even the *S* of man came, not
10:46 (the *s* of Timaeus), a blind
10:47 *S* of David, Jesus, have
10:48 *S* of David, have mercy on
12:6 One more he had, a beloved *s*
12:6 They will respect my *s*
12:35 that the Christ is David's *s*
12:37 it come that he is his *s*
13:26 *S* of man coming in clouds
13:32 nor the *S*, but the Father
14:21 the *S* of man is going away
14:21 the *S* of man is betrayed
14:41 The *S* of man is betrayed
14:61 Are you the Christ the *S* of
14:62 see the *S* of man sitting at
15:39 this man was God's *S*
Lu 1:13 will become mother to a *s*
1:31 and give birth to a *s*, and you
1:32 called *S* of the Most High
1:35 will be called holy, God's *S*
1:36 conceived a *s*, in her old age
1:57 and she became mother to a *s*
2:7 she gave birth to her *s*, the
3:2 to John the *s* of Zechariah
3:22 You are my *S*, the beloved
3:23 the *s*, as the opinion was, of
3:23 of Joseph, *s* of Heli
3:24, 24 *s* of Matthat, *s* of Levi
3:24, 24 *s* of Melchi, *s* of Jannai
3:24 of Jannai, *s* of Joseph
3:25 *s* of Mattathias
3:25, 25 *s* of Amos, *s* of Nahum
3:25, 25 *s* of Esli, *s* of Naggai
3:26 *s* of Maath
3:26 *s* of Mattathias
3:26, 26 *s* of Semein, *s* of Josech
3:26 of Josech, *s* of Joda
3:27, 27 *s* of Joanan, *s* of Rhesa
3:27 of Rhesa, *s* of Zerubbabel
3:27, 27 *s* of Shealtiel, *s* of Neri
3:28, 28 *s* of Melchi, *s* of Addi
3:28, 28 *s* of Cosam, *s* of Elmadam
3:28 of Elmadam, *s* of Er

Lu 3:29, 29 s of Jesus, s of Eliezer
3:29, 29 s of Jorim, s of Matthat
3:29 of Matthat, s of Levi
3:30, 30 s of Symeon, s of Judas
3:30, 30 s of Joseph, s of Jonam
3:30 of Jonam, s of Eliakim
3:31, 31 s of Melea, s of Menna
3:31 of Menna, s of Mattatha
3:31, 31 s of Nathan, s of David
3:32, 32 s of Jesse, s of Obed
3:32, 32 s of Boaz, s of Salmon
3:32 of Salmon, s of Nahshon
3:33 s of Amminadab
3:33, 33 s of Arni, s of Hezron
3:33, 33 s of Perez, s of Judah
3:34, 34 s of Jacob, s of Isaac
3:34, 34 s of Abraham, s of Terah
3:34 of Terah, s of Nahor
3:35, 35 s of Serug, s of Reu
3:35, 35 s of Peleg, s of Eber
3:35 of Eber, s of Shelah
3:36 s of Cainan
3:36 of Cainan, s of Arpachshad
3:36, 36 s of Shem, s of Noah
3:36 of Noah, s of Lamech
3:37 s of Methuselah
3:37, 37 s of Enoch, s of Jared
3:37 of Jared, s of Mahalaleel
3:37 of Mahalaleel, s of Cainan
3:38, 38 s of Enosh, s of Seth
3:38, 38 Seth, s of Adam, s of God
4:3 If you are a s of God, tell
4:9 If you are a s of God, hurl
4:22 is a s of Joseph, is it not?
4:41 saying: You are the S of God
5:24 the S of man has authority on
6:5 is what the S of man is
6:15 James the s of Alphaeus, and
6:16 Judas the s of James, and
6:22 for the sake of the S of man
7:12 only-begotten s of his mother
7:34 The S of man has come eating
8:28 Jesus S of the Most High God
9:22 The S of man must undergo
9:26 the S of man will be ashamed
9:35 This is my S, the one that
9:38 to take a look at my s
9:41 Lead your s over here
9:44 for the S of man is destined
9:58 but the S of man has nowhere
10:22 who the S is no one knows
10:22 no one knows but the S
10:22 S is willing to reveal him
11:11 his s asks for a fish, will
11:30 same way will the S of man
12:8 S of man will also confess
12:10 a word against the S of man
12:40 the S of man is coming
12:53 divided, father against s and
12:53 divided . . . s against father
14:5 if his s or bull falls into a
15:13 younger s gathered all things
15:19 of being called your s
15:21 the s said to him, Father, I
15:21 of being called your s
15:24 s was dead and came to life
15:25 his older s was in the field
15:30 s who ate up your means of
17:22 the days of the S of man
17:24 so the S of man will be
17:26 in the days of the S of man
17:30 day when the S of man is
18:8 when the S of man arrives
18:31 as to the S of man will be
18:38 Jesus, S of David, have
18:39 S of David, have mercy on me
19:9 he also is a s of Abraham
19:10 the S of man came to seek
20:13 will send my s the beloved
20:41 that the Christ is David's s
20:44 Lord; so how is he his s?
21:27 S of man coming in a cloud
21:36 standing before the S of man
22:22 S of man is going his way
22:48 betray the S of man with a
22:69 S of man will be sitting at
22:70 Are you . . . the S of God?
24:7 S of man must be delivered
Joh 1:14 to an only-begotten s from a
1:34 this one is the S of God
1:42 You are Simon the s of John
1:45 Jesus, the s of Joseph, from
1:49 Rabbi, you are the S of God
1:51 descending to the S of man

Joh 3:13 from heaven, the S of man
3:14 S of man must be lifted up
3:16 he gave his only-begotten S
3:17 God sent forth his S into
3:18 the only-begotten S of God
3:35 The Father loves the S and
3:36 exercises faith in the S has
3:36 disobeys the S will not see
4:5 Jacob gave to Joseph his s
4:46 s was sick in Capernaum
4:47 to come down and heal his s
4:50 Go your way; your s lives
4:53 said to him: Your s lives
5:19 The S cannot do a single
5:19 these things the S also does
5:20 has affection for the S and
5:21 S also makes those alive
5:22 all the judging to the S
5:23 that all may honor the S
5:23 He that does not honor the S
5:25 the voice of the S of God
5:26 S to have life in himself
5:27 because S of man he is
6:27 the S of man will give you
6:40 everyone that beholds the S
6:42 Jesus the s of Joseph, whose
6:53 the flesh of the S of man
6:62 the S of man ascending to
6:71 of Judas the s of Simon
8:28 have lifted up the S of man
8:35 the s remains forever
8:36 if the S sets you free, you
9:19 s who you say was born blind
9:20 s and that he was born blind
9:35 faith in the S of man
10:36 I said, I am God's S
11:4 S of God may be glorified
11:27 are the Christ the S of God
12:23 S of man to be glorified
12:34 S of man must be lifted up
12:34 Who is this S of man?
13:2 Iscariot, the s of Simon
13:26 Judas, the s of Simon
13:31 S of man is glorified, and
14:13 in connection with the S
17:1 glorify your s, that your
17:1 that your s may glorify you
17:12 except the s of destruction
19:7 he made himself God's s
19:26 Woman, see! your s!
20:31 is the Christ the S of God
21:15 Simon s of John, do you
21:16 Simon s of John, do you
21:17 Simon s of John, do you
Ac 1:13 James the s of Alphaeus and
1:13 and Judas the s of James
4:36 translated, S of Comfort, a
7:21 brought him up as her own s
7:56 S of man standing at God's
9:20 that this One is the S of God
13:10 you s of the Devil, you
13:21 God gave them Saul s of Kish
13:22 David the s of Jesse, a man
13:33 You are my s, I have become
16:1 Timothy, the s of a believing
20:4 Sopater the s of Pyrrhus of
20:28 with the blood of his own S
23:6 a Pharisee, a s of Pharisees
23:16 s of Paul's sister heard of
Ro 1:3 his S, who sprang from the
1:4 declared God's S according to
1:9 the good news about his S
5:10 God through the death of his S
8:3 God, by sending his own S in
8:29 after the image of his S
8:32 not even spare his own S but
9:9 come and Sarah will have a s
1Co 1:9 a sharing with his S Jesus
15:28 S himself will also subject
2Co 1:19 S of God, Christ Jesus, who
Ga 1:16 to reveal his S in connection
2:20 S of God, who loved me and
4:4 God sent forth his S, who came
4:6 spirit of his S into our hearts
4:7 are no longer a slave but a s
4:7 if a s, also an heir through
4:30 out the servant girl and her s
4:30 s of the servant girl be an
4:30 with the s of the free woman
Eph 4:13 knowledge of the S of God
Col 1:13 kingdom of the S of his love
1Th 1:10 for his S from the heavens
2Th 2:3 the s of destruction
Heb 1:2 spoken to us by means of a S

Heb 1:5 did he ever say: You are my s
1:5 he himself will become my s
1:8 to the S: God is your throne
2:6 s of man that you take care
3:6 Christ was faithful as a S
4:14 heavens, Jesus the S of God
5:5 You are my s; I, today, I
5:8 Although he was a S, he
6:6 impale the S of God afresh
7:3 been made like the S of God
7:28 oath . . . appoints a S, who
10:29 trampled upon the S of God
11:17 offer up his only-begotten s
11:24 s of the daughter of Pharaoh
12:5 My s, do not belittle the
12:6 one whom he receives as a s
12:7 what s is he that a father
Jas 2:21 offered up Isaac his s upon
1Pe 5:13 and so does Mark my s
2Pe 1:17 This is my s, my beloved
2:15 path of Balaam, the s of Beor
1Jo 1:3 and with his S Jesus Christ
1:7 blood of Jesus his S cleanses
2:22 denies the Father and the S
2:23 denies the S does not have
2:23 confesses the S has the
2:24 in union with the S and in
3:8 S of God was made manifest
3:23 faith in the name of his S
4:9 his only-begotten S into the
4:10 his S as a propitiatory
4:14 his S as Savior of the world
4:15 Jesus Christ is the S of God
5:5 that Jesus is the S of God
5:9 witness concerning his S
5:10 faith in the S of God has
5:10 has given concerning his S
5:11 and this life is in his S
5:12 that has the S has this life
5:12 does not have the S of God
5:13 in the name of the S of God
5:20 that the S of God has come
5:20 means of his S Jesus Christ
2Jo 3 Jesus Christ the S of the Father
9 has both the Father and the S
Re 1:13 someone like a s of man
2:18 things that the S of God says
12:5 she gave birth to a s
14:14 seated like a s of man
21:7 and he will be my s

Song

Ex 15:1 to sing this s to Jehovah and
Nu 21:17 to sing this s: Spring up, O
De 31:19 this s and teach it to the
31:19 s may serve as my witness
31:21 s must also answer before
31:22 Moses wrote this s in
31:30 words of this s until their
32:44 all the words of this s in
Jg 5:1 son of Abinoam broke out in s
5:12 utter a s! Rise up, Barak, and
1Sa 18:6 s and dances to meet Saul
2Sa 22:1 the words of this s in the
1Ch 15:16 with the instruments of s
16:42 of the s of the true God
25:6 in s at the house of Jehovah
25:7 trained in s to Jehovah, all
2Ch 5:13 with the instruments of s
7:6 instruments of s to Jehovah
23:13 instruments of s and those
23:18 s by the hands of David
29:27 s of Jehovah started and
29:28 while the s was resounding
34:12 with the instruments of s
Ne 12:27 s, cymbals and stringed
12:36 instruments of s of David
12:46 s of praise and thanksgivings
Job 30:9 even the theme of their s
Ps 18:*super* the words of this s in
28:7 with my s I shall laud him
30:*super* A s of inauguration of the
33:3 Sing to him a new s
40:3 he put in my mouth a new s
42:8 his s will be with me
45:*super* A s of the beloved women
46:*super* upon The Maidens. A s
48:*super* A s. A melody of the sons
65:*super* A melody of David. A s
66:*super* To the director. A s, a
67:*super* A melody, a s
68:*super* Of David. A melody, a s
68:4 Raise up a s to the One riding
69:30 the name of God with s

Ps 75:super A melody. Of Asaph. A s
76:super A melody. Of Asaph. A s
83:super A s. A melody of Asaph
87:super A melody, a s
88:super A s, a melody of the sons
92:super a s, for the sabbath day
96:1 Sing to Jehovah a new s
98:1 Sing to Jehovah a new s
108:super A s. A melody of David
120:super A S of the Ascents
121:super A S of the Ascents
122:super A S of the Ascents
123:super A S of the Ascents
124:super A S of the Ascents
125:super A S of the Ascents
126:super A S of the Ascents
127:super A S of the Ascents
128:super A S of the Ascents
129:super A S of the Ascents
130:super A S of the Ascents
131:super A S of the Ascents
132:super A S of the Ascents
133:super A S of the Ascents
134:super A S of the Ascents
137:3 us for the words of a s
137:4 sing the s of Jehovah
144:9 O God, a new s I will sing
149:1 Sing to Jehovah a new s
Ec 7:5 hearing the s of the stupid
12:4 the daughters of s sound low
Ca 1:1 The superlative s, which is
Isa 5:1 s of my loved one concerning
23:15 as in the s of a prostitute
24:9 with no s that they drink
26:1 s will be sung in the land
30:29 s like that in the night
42:10 Sing to Jehovah a new s
La 3:14 theme of their s all day long
3:63 I am the subject of their s
Eze 33:32 like a s of sensuous loves
Am 6:5 instruments for s
Ac 16:25 and praising God with s
Heb 2:12 I will praise you with s
Re 5:9 And they sing a new s, saying
14:3 singing as if a new s before
14:3 master that s but the hundred
15:3 are singing the s of Moses
15:3 and the s of the Lamb, saying

Songs
Ge 31:27 with rejoicing and with s
Ex 15:11 to be feared with s of praise
1Ki 4:32 s came to be a thousand and
1Ch 13:8 with full power and with s
Ps 69:12 subject of the s of drinkers
137:3 for us one of the s of Zion
149:6 s extolling God be in their
Pr 25:20 with s upon a gloomy heart
Isa 23:16 make your s many, in order
Am 5:23 Remove . . . turmoil of your s
8:3 the s of the temple will
8:10 all your s into a dirge
Eph 5:19 and spiritual s, singing and
Col 3:16 praises to God, spiritual s

Son-in-law
Ge 19:12 S and your sons and your
Ex 3:1 Jethro . . . whose s he was
Jg 1:16 whose s Moses was, came up
4:11 Hobab, whose s Moses was
15:6 Samson the s of the Timnite
19:5 said to his s: Sustain your
1Sa 18:18 should become s to the king
22:14 s of the king and a chief
Ne 6:18 s he was to Shecaniah the
13:28 s of Sanballat the Horonite

Son's
Ge 27:31 eat some of his s game
30:14 some of your s mandrakes
30:15 taking also my s mandrakes
30:15 for your s mandrakes
30:16 with my s mandrakes
37:32 it is your s long garment
37:33 It is my s long garment!
Ex 4:25 cut off her s foreskin and
10:2 your son and your s son how
Le 18:15 She is your s wife

Sons
Ge 5:4 Adam . . . became father to s
5:7 Seth . . . became father to s
5:10 Enosh . . . became father to s
5:13 Kenan . . . became father to s
5:16 Mahalalel . . . father to s
5:19 Jared . . . became father to s
Ge 5:22 Enoch . . . became father to s
5:26 Methuselah . . . father to s
5:30 Lamech . . . father to s and
6:2 s of . . . God began to notice
6:4 s of the true God continued
6:4 they bore s to them, they
6:10 Noah became father to three s
6:18 into the ark, you and your s
7:7 Noah went in, and his s and
7:13 Ham and Japheth, Noah's s
7:13 the three wives of his s
8:16 you and your wife and your s
8:18 Noah went out, and also his s
9:1 to bless Noah and his s
9:8 say to Noah and to his s with
9:18 Noah's s who came out of the
9:19 Noah's s, and from these was
10:1 history of Noah's s, Shem, Ham
10:1 Now s began to be born to
10:2 s of Japheth were Gomer and
10:3 s of Gomer were Ashkenaz
10:4 s of Javan were Elishah and
10:6 And the s of Ham were Cush and
10:7 s of Cush were Seba and
10:7 s of Raamah were Sheba and
10:20 s of Ham according to their
10:21 of all the s of Eber
10:22 s of Shem were Elam and
10:23 s of Aram were Uz and Hul
10:25 to Eber there were two s
10:29 these were the s of Joktan
10:31 s of Shem according to their
10:32 families of the s of Noah
11:5 tower that the s of men had
11:11 Shem . . . father to s and
11:13 Arpachshad . . . father to s
11:15 Shelah . . . father to s and
11:17 Eber . . . father to s and
11:19 Peleg . . . father to s and
11:21 Reu . . . father to s and
11:23 Serug . . . s and daughters
11:25 Nahor . . . father to s and
18:19 he may command his s and
19:12 your s and your daughters and
19:38 father of the s of Ammon
22:20 borne s to Nahor your brother
23:3 speak to the s of Heth, saying
23:5 s of Heth answered Abraham
23:7 the natives, to the s of Heth
23:10 sitting among the s of Heth
23:10 hearing of the s of Heth
23:11 Before the eyes of the s of
23:16 the hearing of the s of Heth
23:18 eyes of the s of Heth among
23:20 at the hands of the s of Heth
25:3 s of Dedan became Asshurim
25:4 s of Midian were Ephah and
25:4 these were the s of Keturah
25:6 s of the concubines that
25:9 Isaac and Ishmael his s
25:10 purchased from the s of Heth
25:13 names of the s of Ishmael
25:16 These are the s of Ishmael
25:22 s within her began to
27:29 s of your mother bow low
29:34 I have borne him three s
30:20 I have borne him six s
30:35 over into the hands of his s
31:1 the words of the s of Laban
32:22 took . . . his eleven young s
32:32 why the s of Israel are not
33:19 the hand of the s of Hamor
34:5 his s happened to be with his
34:7 s of Jacob came in from the
34:13 Jacob's s began to answer
34:25 s of Jacob, Simeon and Levi
34:27 other s of Jacob attacked the
35:5 chase after the s of Jacob
35:22 came to be twelve s of Jacob
35:23 s by Leah were . . . Reuben
35:24 s by Rachel were Joseph and
35:25 the s by Bilhah, Rachel's
35:26 And the s by Zilpah, Leah's
35:26 These are Jacob's s who were
35:29 Esau and Jacob his s buried
36:5 These are the s of Esau who
36:6 Esau took his wives and his s
36:10 names of the s of Esau
36:11 the s of Eliphaz came to be
36:12 These are the s of Adah
36:13 These are the s of Reuel
36:13 s of Basemath, Esau's wife
36:14 the s of Oholibamah the
36:15 the sheiks of the s of Esau
Ge 36:15 the s of Eliphaz, Esau's
36:16 These are the s by Adah
36:17 the s of Reuel, Esau's son
36:17 s by Basemath, Esau's wife
36:18 s of Oholibamah, Esau's wife
36:19 These are the s of Esau
36:20 the s of Seir the Horite
36:21 the s of Seir, in the land of
36:22 s of Lotan came to be Hori
36:23 these are the s of Shobal
36:24 these are the s of Zibeon
36:26 s of Dishon: Hemdan and
36:27 s of Ezer: Bilhan and Zaavan
36:28 s of Dishan: Uz and Aran
36:31 reigned over the s of Israel
37:2 he was with the s of Bilhah
37:2 and the s of Zilpah
37:3 more than all his other s
37:35 his s and all his daughters
41:50 born to Joseph two s
42:1 Jacob said to his s: Why do
42:5 Israel's s came along with
42:11 all of us s of but one man
42:13 We are the s of but one man
42:32 twelve brothers, the s of
42:37 My own two s you may put to
44:27 my wife bore but two s
45:10, 10, 10 s and the s of your s
45:21 the s of Israel did so, and
46:5 the s of Israel continued
46:7, 7 his s and his sons' s
46:8 the names of Israel's s
46:8 into Egypt: Jacob and his s
46:9 s of Reuben were Hanoch and
46:10 s of Simeon were Jemuel and
46:11 the s of Levi were Gershon
46:12 the s of Judah were Er and
46:12 the s of Perez came to be
46:13 s of Issachar were Tola
46:14 And the s of Zebulun were
46:15 s of Leah, whom she bore to
46:15 All the souls of his s and
46:16 the s of Gad were Ziphion
46:17 the s of Asher were Imnah
46:17 the s of Beriah were Heber
46:18 These are the s of Zilpah
46:19 s of Rachel, Jacob's wife
46:21 s of Benjamin were Bela and
46:22 s of Rachel who were born to
46:23 And the s of Dan were Hushim
46:24 And the s of Naphtali were
46:25 the s of Bilhah, whom Laban
46:26 the wives of Jacob's s
46:27 Joseph's s who were born to
48:1 two s Manasseh and Ephraim
48:5 your two s who were born to
48:8 Israel saw Joseph's s and
48:9 my s whom God has given me
49:1 Jacob called his s and said
49:2 listen, you s of Jacob, yes
49:8 The s of your father will
49:32 were from the s of Heth
49:33 giving commands to his s
50:12 his s proceeded to do for
50:13 his s carried him into the
50:23 Ephraim's s of the third
50:23 s of Machir, Manasseh's son
50:25 made the s of Israel swear
Ex 1:1 Israel's s who came into Egypt
1:7 s of Israel became fruitful
1:9 s of Israel are more numerous
1:12 as a result of the s of Israel
1:13 made the s of Israel slave
2:23 s of Israel continued to sigh
2:25 God looked on the s of Israel
3:9 outcry of the s of Israel has
3:10 the s of Israel out of Egypt
3:11 bring the s of Israel out of
3:13 now come to the s of Israel
3:14 to say to the s of Israel
3:15 are to say to the s of Israel
3:22 put them upon your s and your
4:20 Moses took his wife and his s
4:29 older men of the s of Israel
4:31 attention to the s of Israel
5:14 officers of the s of Israel
5:15 officers of the s of Israel
5:19 officers of the s of Israel
6:5 the groaning of the s of Israel
6:6 say to the s of Israel, I am
6:9 spoke to . . . the s of Israel
6:11 send the s of Israel away out
6:12 s of Israel have not listened
6:13 the s of Israel and to Pharaoh

Ex 6:13 to bring the s of Israel out
6:14 The s of Reuben, Israel's
6:15 s of Simeon were Jemuel and
6:16 the names of the s of Levi
6:17 s of Gershon were Libni and
6:18 s of Kohath were Amram and
6:19 s of Merari were Mahli and
6:21 s of Izhar were Korah and
6:22 s of Uzziel were Mishael and
6:24 s of Korah were Assir and
6:26 Bring the s of Israel out
6:27 bring the s of Israel out
7:2 must send the s of Israel away
7:4 bring . . . s of Israel, out
7:5 bring the s of Israel out from
9:4 not a thing of . . . s of Israel
9:6 livestock of the s of Israel
9:26 Goshen, where the s of Israel
9:35 not send the s of Israel away
10:9 With our s and our daughters
10:20 send the s of Israel away
10:23 for all the s of Israel there
11:7 against any of the s of Israel
11:7 Egyptians and the s of Israel
11:10 not send the s of Israel
12:24 for you and your s to time
12:26 when your s say to you, What
12:27 of the s of Israel in Egypt
12:28 the s of Israel went and did
12:31 s of Israel, and go, serve
12:35 s of Israel did according to
12:37 s of Israel proceeded to
12:40 dwelling of the s of Israel
12:42 part of all the s of Israel
12:50 the s of Israel did just as
12:51 brought the s of Israel
13:2 among the s of Israel, among
13:13 firstborn . . . among your s
13:15 firstborn of my s I redeem
13:18 s of Israel went up out of
13:19 he had made the s of Israel
14:2 Speak to the s of Israel, that
14:3 say respecting the s of Israel
14:8 chasing after the s of Israel
14:8 s of Israel were going out
14:10 s of Israel began to raise
14:10 s of Israel got quite afraid
14:15 Speak to the s of Israel that
14:16 s of Israel may go through
14:22 s of Israel went through the
14:29 As for the s of Israel, they
15:1 s of Israel proceeded to sing
15:19 s of Israel walked on dry
16:1 s of Israel finally came to
16:2 s of Israel began to murmur
16:3 the s of Israel kept saying
16:6 said to all the s of Israel
16:9 assembly of the s of Israel
16:10 assembly of the s of Israel
16:12 the murmurings of the s of
16:15 the s of Israel got to see it
16:17 s of Israel began to do so
16:35 s of Israel ate the manna
17:1 assembly of the s of Israel
17:3 and our s and our livestock to
17:7 quarreling of the s of Israel
18:3 her two s, the name of one of
18:5 s and his wife came to Moses
18:6 also your wife and her two s
19:1 s of Israel came out of the
19:3 and to tell the s of Israel
19:6 are to say to the s of Israel
20:5 the error of fathers upon s
20:22 are to say to the s of Israel
21:4 does bear him s or daughters
21:5 my wife and my s; I do not
22:24 and your s fatherless boys
22:29 firstborn of your s you are
24:5 young men of the s of Israel
24:11 men of the s of Israel, but
24:17 the eyes of the s of Israel
25:2 Speak to the s of Israel, that
25:22 for the s of Israel
27:20 command the s of Israel that
27:21 Aaron and his s will set it
27:21 performed by the s of Israel
28:1 Aaron your brother and his s
28:1 the midst of the s of Israel
28:1 and Ithamar, the s of Aaron
28:4 Aaron your brother and his s
28:9 the names of the s of Israel
28:11 the names of the s of Israel
28:12 stones for the s of Israel
28:21 the names of the s of Israel

Ex 28:29 the names of the s of Israel
28:30 judgments of the s of Israel
28:38 s of Israel will sanctify
28:40 for Aaron's s you will make
28:41 Aaron your brother and his s
28:43 must be upon Aaron and his s
29:4 present Aaron and his s at the
29:8 bring his s near and you must
29:9 Aaron as well as his s, and
29:9 the hand of his s with power
29:10 Aaron and his s must lay
29:15 and Aaron and his s must lay
29:19 Aaron and his s must lay
29:21 upon his s and the garments
29:21 and the garments of his s
29:21 his s and the garments of
29:21 garments of his s with him
29:24 upon the palms of his s, and
29:27 and from what was for his s
29:28 performed by the s of Israel
29:28 rendered by the s of Israel
29:29 his s after him to anoint
29:30 succeeds him . . . among his s
29:32 s must eat the flesh of the
29:35 this way to Aaron and his s
29:43 present myself . . . to the s
29:44 sanctify Aaron and his s for
29:45 in the midst of the s of
30:12 sum of the s of Israel as a
30:16 atonement from the s of
30:16 the s of Israel, to make
30:19 his s must wash their hands
30:30 anoint Aaron and his s, and
30:31 speak to the s of Israel
31:10 garments of his s for
31:13 speak to the s of Israel
31:16 s of Israel must keep the
31:17 Between me and the s of
32:2 of your s and of your
32:20 the s of Israel drink it
32:26 s of Levi began gathering
32:28 s of Levi proceeded to do as
33:5 to the s of Israel, You are a
33:6 s of Israel went stripping
34:7 error of fathers upon s
34:16 their daughters for your s
34:16 s have immoral intercourse
34:20 firstborn of your s you are
34:30 s of Israel got to see Moses
34:32 s of Israel came near to
34:34 spoke to the s of Israel
34:35 s of Israel saw Moses' face
35:1 assembly of the s of Israel
35:4 assembly of the s of Israel
35:19 his s for acting as priests
35:20 s of Israel went out from
35:29 s of Israel brought a
35:30 said to the s of Israel
36:3 contribution that the s of
39:6 the names of the s of Israel
39:7 memorial stones for the s of
39:14 the names of the s of Israel
39:27 worker, for Aaron and his s
39:32 the s of Israel kept doing
39:41 garments of his s for acting
39:42 the way the s of Israel did
40:12 bring Aaron and his s near to
40:14 bring his s near and you
40:31 Aaron and his s washed their
40:36 s of Israel would break camp
Le 1:2 Speak to the s of Israel, and
1:5 the s of Aaron, the priests
1:7 And the s of Aaron, the priests
1:8 And the s of Aaron, the priests
1:11 the s of Aaron, the priests
2:2 bring it to the s of Aaron
2:3 belongs to Aaron and his s, as
2:10 belongs to Aaron and his s, as
3:2 and Aaron's s, the priests
3:5 Aaron's s must make it smoke
3:8 and Aaron's s must sprinkle
3:13 Aaron's s must sprinkle its
4:2 Speak to the s of Israel
6:9 Command Aaron and his s
6:14 You s of Aaron, present it
6:16 Aaron and his s will eat
6:18 Every male among the s of
6:20 offering of Aaron and his s
6:22 one anointed . . . among his s
6:25 Speak to Aaron and his s
7:10 to be for all of Aaron's s
7:23 Speak to the s of Israel
7:29 Speak to the s of Israel
7:33 one of Aaron's s who presents

Le 7:34 do take from the s of Israel
7:34 to Aaron the priest and his s
7:34 from the s of Israel
7:35 the priestly share of his s
7:36 from among the s of Israel
7:38 commanding the s of Israel
8:2 Take Aaron and his s with him
8:6 and his s near and washed
8:13 Aaron's s near and clothed
8:14 his s laid their hands upon
8:18 his s then laid their hands
8:22 his s laid their hands upon
8:24 Moses brought Aaron's s near
8:27 the palms of his s and began
8:30 upon his s and the garments
8:30 garments of his s with him
8:30 and his s and the garments of
8:30 garments of his s with him
8:31 Moses said to Aaron and his s
8:31 Aaron and his s will eat it
8:36 Aaron and his s proceeded to
9:1 Aaron and his s and the older
9:3 the s of Israel you will speak
9:9 Aaron's s presented the blood
9:12 s handed him the blood and
9:18 s handed him the blood and
10:1 Aaron's s Nadab and Abihu took
10:4 and Elzaphan, the s of Uzziel
10:6 and Ithamar his other s
10:9 you and your s with you
10:11 to teach the s of Israel all
10:12 his s that were left
10:13 allowance of your s from
10:14 your s and your daughters
10:14 allowance of your s from the
10:14 sacrifices of the s of Israel
10:15 for you and your s with you
10:16 Aaron's s that were left
11:2 Speak to the s of Israel
12:2 Speak to the s of Israel
13:2 or to one of his s the priests
15:2 Speak to the s of Israel, and
15:31 keep the s of Israel separate
16:1 death of Aaron's two s for
16:5 of the s of Israel he should
16:16 s of Israel and concerning
16:19 of the s of Israel
16:21 the errors of the s of Israel
16:34 for the s of Israel
17:2 Speak to Aaron and his s and
17:2 Speak to . . . the s of Israel
17:5 s of Israel may bring their
17:12 s of Israel: No soul of you
17:13 s of Israel or some alien
17:14 said to the s of Israel: You
18:2 Speak to the s of Israel, and
19:2 s of Israel, and you must say
19:18 grudge against the s of your
20:2 s of Israel, Any man of the
20:2 Any man of the s of Israel
20:17 the eyes of the s of their
21:1 Aaron's s, and you must say
21:24 spoke to Aaron and his s
21:24 and all the s of Israel
22:2 Aaron and his s, that they
22:2 s of Israel and not profane
22:3 s of Israel will sanctify to
22:15 things of the s of Israel
22:18 Speak to Aaron and his s
22:18 Speak to . . . the s of Israel
22:32 s of Israel. I am Jehovah
23:2 s of Israel, and you must say
23:10 s of Israel, and you must
23:24 s of Israel, saying, In the
23:34 s of Israel, saying, On the
23:43 s of Israel to dwell when I
23:44 festivals of Jehovah to the s
24:2 s of Israel that they get for
24:8 covenant . . . s of Israel
24:10 s of Israel, and the son of
24:15 s of Israel, saying, In case
24:23 Moses spoke to the s of
24:23 the s of Israel did just as
25:2 s of Israel, and you must say
25:33 the midst of the s of Israel
25:41 he and his s with him, and
25:45 s of the settlers who are
25:46 s after you to inherit as a
25:46 s of Israel, you must not
25:54 Jubilee, he and his s with
25:55 the s of Israel are slaves
26:29 eat the flesh of your s, and
26:46 s of Israel in Mount Sinai
27:2 Speak to the s of Israel, and

Nu 31:12 assembly of the s of Israel
31:16 to induce the s of Israel to
31:30 the half of the s of Israel
31:42 belonging to the s of Israel
31:47 belonging to the s of Israel
31:54 memorial for the s of Israel
32:1 Now the s of Reuben and the
32:1 s of Gad had come to have
32:2 Hence the s of Gad and the
32:2 the s of Reuben came and said
32:6 Moses said to the s of Gad
32:6 of Gad and the s of Reuben
32:7 you dishearten the s of Israel
32:9 disheartened the s of Israel
32:17 before the s of Israel until
32:18 until the s of Israel have
32:25 Then the s of Gad and the
32:25 the s of Reuben said this to
32:28 the tribes of the s of Israel
32:29 If the s of Gad and the
32:29 s of Reuben pass with you
32:31 To this the s of Gad and the
32:31 and the s of Reuben answered
32:33 to the s of Gad and to the
32:33 to the s of Reuben and to
32:34 s of Gad proceeded to build
32:37 s of Reuben built Heshbon and
32:39 the s of Machir the son of
33:1 stages of the s of Israel who
33:3 the s of Israel went out with
33:5 s of Israel pulled away from
33:38 going out of the s of Israel
33:40 coming of the s of Israel
33:51 Speak to the s of Israel, and
34:2 Command the s of Israel, and
34:13 commanded the s of Israel
34:14 s of the Reubenites by the
34:14 tribe of the s of the Gadites
34:20 the tribe of the s of Simeon
34:22 of the tribe of the s of Dan
34:23 of the s of Joseph, of the
34:23 tribe of the s of Manasseh
34:24 tribe of the s of Ephraim
34:25 the tribe of the s of Zebulun
34:26 tribe of the s of Issachar
34:27 the tribe of the s of Asher
34:28 tribe of the s of Naphtali
34:29 s of Israel landholders in
35:2 Give the s of Israel the
35:8 possession of the s of Israel
35:10 Speak to the s of Israel, and
35:15 For the s of Israel and for
35:34 the midst of the s of Israel
36:1 the family of the s of Gilead
36:1 families of the s of Joseph
36:1 the fathers of the s of Israel
36:2 by lot to the s of Israel; and
36:3 s of the other tribes of the
36:3 tribes of the s of Israel
36:4 for the s of Israel, the
36:5 commanded the s of Israel at
36:5 The tribe of the s of Joseph
36:7 inheritance of the s of Israel
36:7 the s of Israel should cleave
36:8 the tribes of the s of Israel
36:8 that the s of Israel may get
36:9 the tribes of the s of Israel
36:11 the wives of the s of their
36:12 the s of Manasseh the son of
36:13 to the s of Israel on the
De 1:3 Moses spoke to the s of Israel
1:28 s of the Anakim we saw there
1:36 to his s I shall give the land
1:39 s who today do not know good
2:4 s of Esau, who are dwelling
2:8 s of Esau, who are dwelling in
2:9 to the s of Lot I have given Ar
2:12 and the s of Esau proceeded to
2:19 in front of the s of Ammon
2:19 the land of the s of Ammon
2:19 to the s of Lot that I have
2:22 s of Esau, who are dwelling
2:29 s of Esau dwelling in Seir
2:33 we defeated him and his s and
2:37 the land of the s of Ammon
3:11 in Rabbah of the s of Ammon
3:16 boundary of the s of Ammon
3:18 your brothers, the s of Israel
4:9 make them known to your s and
4:10 that they may teach their s
4:25 become father to s and
4:40 you and your s after you
4:44 set before the s of Israel
4:45 spoke to the s of Israel on
De 4:46 the s of Israel defeated on
5:9 error of fathers upon s and
5:29 well with them and their s
9:2 the s of Anakim, about whom
9:2 stand before the s of Anak
10:6 the s of Israel pulled away
11:2 I do not address your s who
11:6 the s of Eliab the son of
11:19 teach them to your s, so as
11:21 the days of your s may be
12:12 your s and your daughters and
12:25 you and your s after you
12:28 go well with you and your s
12:31 their s and their daughters
14:1 S you are of Jehovah your God
17:20 his s in the midst of Israel
18:5 he and his s, always
21:5 the s of Levi must approach
21:15 have borne s to him, and the
21:16 as an inheritance to his s
23:8 s that may be born to them
23:17 s of Israel become a temple
24:7 brothers of the s of Israel
28:32 Your s and your daughters
28:41 S and daughters you will
28:53 the flesh of your s and your
28:54 his s whom he has remaining
28:55 his s that he will eat
28:57 s whom she proceeded to bear
29:1 the s of Israel in the land of
29:22 s who will rise up after you
29:29 belong to us and to our s to
30:2 I am commanding . . . your s
31:9 to the priests the s of Levi
31:13 s who have not known should
31:19 teach it to the s of Israel
31:19 against the s of Israel
31:22 teach it to the s of Israel
31:23 the s of Israel into the land
32:8 parted the s of Adam from one
32:8 the number of the s of Israel
32:19 his s and his daughters gave
32:20 S in whom there is no
32:46 s to take care to do all the
32:49 giving to the s of Israel as
32:51 s of Israel at the waters of
32:51 middle of the s of Israel
32:52 am giving to the s of Israel
33:1 blessed the s of Israel before
33:9 And his s he did not know
33:24 Blessed with s is Asher
34:8 s of Israel proceeded to weep
34:9 s of Israel began to listen to
Jos 1:2 to them, to the s of Israel
2:2 Men from the s of Israel
3:1 he and all the s of Israel
3:9 to say to the s of Israel
4:4 from the s of Israel
4:5 the tribes of the s of Israel
4:6 your s should ask in time to
4:7 a memorial to the s of Israel
4:8 s of Israel did so, just as
4:8 the tribes of the s of Israel
4:12 And the s of Reuben and the
4:12 and the s of Gad and the
4:12 the sight of the s of Israel
4:21 on to say to the s of Israel
4:21 your s ask their fathers in
4:22 must then let your s know
5:1 from before the s of Israel
5:1 because of the s of Israel
5:2 circumcise the s of Israel
5:3 circumcised the s of Israel
5:6 s of Israel had walked forty
5:7 their s he raised up instead
5:10 the s of Israel continued to
5:12 anymore for the s of Israel
6:1 because of the s of Israel
7:1 s of Israel went committing
7:1 against the s of Israel
7:12 the s of Israel will not be
7:23 and all the s of Israel
7:24 his s and his daughters and
8:31 commanded the s of Israel
8:32 before the s of Israel
9:17 the s of Israel pulled out
9:18 s of Israel did not strike
9:26 the hand of the s of Israel
10:4 Joshua and the s of Israel
10:11 the s of Israel killed with
10:12 Amorites to the s of Israel
10:20 Joshua and the s of Israel
10:21 against the s of Israel
11:14 the s of Israel plundered
Jos 11:19 peace with the s of Israel
11:22 the land of the s of Israel
12:1 the s of Israel defeated
12:2 boundary of the s of Ammon
12:6 s of Israel who defeated
12:7 the s of Israel defeated on
13:6 from before the s of Israel
13:10 border of the s of Ammon
13:13 the s of Israel did not
13:15 tribe of the s of Reuben
13:22 whom the s of Israel killed
13:23 boundary of the s of Reuben
13:23 of the s of Reuben by their
13:24 s of Gad by their families
13:25 land of the s of Ammon as
13:28 inheritance of the s of Gad
13:29 tribe of the s of Manasseh
13:31 went to the s of Machir the
13:31 s of Machir by their
14:1 what the s of Israel took as
14:1 tribes of the s of Israel
14:4 the s of Joseph had become
14:5 so the s of Israel did
14:6 the s of Judah approached
15:1 the tribe of the s of Judah
15:12 the s of Judah by their
15:13 midst of the s of Judah at
15:14 the three s of Anak, namely
15:20 the tribe of the s of Judah
15:21 the tribe of the s of Judah
15:63 s of Judah were not able to
15:63 the s of Judah in Jerusalem
16:1 for the s of Joseph from the
16:4 s of Joseph, Manasseh and
16:5 boundary of the s of Ephraim
16:8 tribe of the s of Ephraim
16:9 s of Ephraim had enclave
16:9 of the s of Manasseh
17:2 a lot for the s of Manasseh
17:2 for the s of Abi-ezer and
17:2 and the s of Helek and the
17:2 the s of Asriel and the
17:2 the s of Shechem and the
17:2 and the s of Hepher and the
17:2 and the s of Shemida
17:2 These were the s of Manasseh
17:3 have, not s, but daughters
17:6 in the midst of his s
17:6 the s of Manasseh who were
17:8 belonged to the s of Ephraim
17:12 the s of Manasseh did not
17:13 the s of Israel had grown
17:14 s of Joseph proceeded to
17:16 Then the s of Joseph said
18:1 assembly of the s of Israel
18:2 left among the s of Israel
18:3 said to the s of Israel
18:10 the land to the s of Israel
18:11 tribe of the s of Benjamin
18:11 the s of Judah and the
18:11 Judah and the s of Joseph
18:14 a city of the s of Judah
18:20 the s of Benjamin by their
18:21 tribe of the s of Benjamin
18:28 the s of Benjamin by their
19:1 tribe of the s of Simeon
19:1 inheritance of the s of Judah
19:8 tribe of the s of Simeon
19:9 of the s of Simeon
19:9 allotment of the s of Judah
19:9 the share of the s of Judah
19:9 s of Simeon got a possession
19:10 for the s of Zebulun by
19:16 the s of Zebulun by their
19:17 for the s of Issachar by
19:23 tribe of the s of Issachar
19:24 the tribe of the s of Asher
19:31 the tribe of the s of Asher
19:32 was for the s of Naphtali
19:32 for the s of Naphtali by
19:39 tribe of the s of Naphtali
19:40 the tribe of the s of Dan
19:47 territory of the s of Dan
19:47 the s of Dan proceeded to
19:48 the tribe of the s of Dan
19:49 the s of Israel gave an
19:51 tribes of the s of Israel
20:2 Speak to the s of Israel
20:9 for all the s of Israel and
21:1 the tribes of the s of Israel
21:3 s of Israel gave the Levites
21:4 to belong to the s of Aaron
21:5 And for the s of Kohath that
21:6 the s of Gershon there were

Jos 21:7 the s of Merari by their
21:8 s of Israel gave the Levites
21:9 tribe of the s of Judah and
21:9 the tribe of the s of Simeon
21:10 belong to the s of Aaron
21:10 of the s of Levi, because
21:13 s of Aaron the priest they
21:19 cities of the s of Aaron
21:20 the s of Kohath, the Levites
21:20 left out of the s of Kohath
21:26 s of Kohath who were left
21:27 for the s of Gershon, of the
21:34 families of the s of Merari
21:40 the s of Merari by their
21:41 of the s of Israel were
22:9 After that the s of Reuben and
22:9 s of Gad and the half tribe
22:9 from the other s of Israel
22:10 then the s of Reuben and the
22:10 s of Gad and the half tribe
22:11 the other s of Israel heard
22:11, 11 s of Reuben . . . s of Gad
22:11 belonging to the s of Israel
22:12 s of Israel got to hear of
22:12 the s of Israel were then
22:13 the s of Israel sent to the
22:13 sent to the s of Reuben and
22:13 s of Gad and the half tribe
22:15 came to the s of Reuben
22:15 the s of Gad and the half
22:21 At this the s of Reuben and
22:21 s of Gad and the half tribe
22:24 future day your s will say
22:24 will say to our s: What do
22:25 the s of Reuben and the
22:25 Reuben and the s of Gad
22:25 your s will certainly make
22:25 our s desist from fearing
22:27 that your s may not say in
22:27 to our s: You have no share
22:30 words that the s of Reuben
22:30 Reuben and the s of Gad and
22:30 the s of Manasseh spoke
22:31 said to the s of Reuben and
22:31 said to . . . the s of Gad
22:31 Gad and the s of Manasseh
22:31 you have delivered the s of
22:32 from the s of Reuben
22:32 the s of Gad in the land of
22:32 to the other s of Israel
22:33 the eyes of the s of Israel
22:33 s of Israel proceeded to
22:33 in which the s of Reuben
22:33 the s of Gad were dwelling
22:34, 34 s of Reuben and the s
24:4 Jacob and his s went down
24:32 bones, which the s of Israel
24:32 the s of Hamor, Shechem's
24:32 belong to the s of Joseph
Jg 1:1 the s of Israel proceeded to
1:8 the s of Judah carried on war
1:9 the s of Judah went down to
1:16 the s of the Kenite, whose
1:16 with the s of Judah to the
1:20 the three s of Anak
1:21 the s of Benjamin did not
1:21 with the s of Benjamin in
1:34 pressing the s of Dan into
2:4 words to all the s of Israel
2:6 s of Israel went their way
2:11 the s of Israel fell to doing
3:2 s of Israel to have the
3:5 s of Israel dwelt in among
3:6 daughters they gave to their s
3:7 the s of Israel did what was
3:8 the s of Israel continued to
3:9 s of Israel began to call to
3:9 savior up for the s of Israel
3:12 the s of Israel went doing
3:13 against them the s of Ammon
3:14 the s of Israel continued to
3:15 the s of Israel began to call
3:15 the s of Israel sent tribute
3:27 the s of Israel began going
4:1 the s of Israel again began to
4:3 the s of Israel began to cry
4:3 oppressed the s of Israel
4:5 the s of Israel would go up
4:6 men out of the s of Naphtali
4:6 and out of the s of Zebulun
4:11 the Kenites, the s of Hobab
4:23 the s of Israel on that day
4:24 the hand of the s of Israel
6:1 the s of Israel began to do

Jg 6:2 the s of Israel made for
6:6 s of Israel began to call to
6:7 because the s of Israel called
6:8 the s of Israel and to say to
8:18 like the s of a king in form
8:19 brothers, the s of my mother
8:28 subdued before the s of Israel
8:30 Gideon came to have seventy s
8:33 the s of Israel again took up
8:34 s of Israel did not remember
9:2 s of Jerubbaal, to rule over
9:5 s of Jerubbaal, seventy men
9:18 kill his s, seventy men, upon
9:24 to the seventy s of Jerubbaal
10:4 thirty s who rode on thirty
10:6 s of Israel again proceeded
10:6 the gods of the s of Ammon
10:7 the hand of the s of Ammon
10:8 oppressed the s of Israel in
10:8 the s of Israel that were on
10:9 the s of Ammon would cross
10:10 the s of Israel began to call
10:11 said to the s of Israel: Was
10:11 and from the s of Ammon and
10:15 But the s of Israel said to
10:17 the s of Ammon were called
10:17 So the s of Israel gathered
10:18 against the s of Ammon? Let
11:2 Gilead's wife kept bearing s
11:2 the s of the wife got big
11:4 the s of Ammon began to fight
11:5 when the s of Ammon did fight
11:6 fight against the s of Ammon
11:8 against the s of Ammon, and
11:9 fight against the s of Ammon
11:12 the king of the s of Ammon
11:13 the king of the s of Ammon
11:14 the king of the s of Ammon
11:15 the land of the s of Ammon
11:27 between the s of Israel and
11:27 Israel and the s of Ammon
11:28 king of the s of Ammon did
11:29 to the s of Ammon
11:30 give the s of Ammon into
11:31 peace from the s of Ammon
11:32 s of Ammon to fight against
11:33 the s of Ammon were subdued
11:33 before the s of Israel
11:36 enemies, the s of Ammon
12:1 fight against the s of Ammon
12:2 with the s of Ammon
12:3 against the s of Ammon
12:9 he came to have thirty s and
12:9 thirty daughters for his s
12:14 forty s and thirty grandsons
13:1 the s of Israel engaged again
14:16 the s of my people, but to
14:17 the riddle to the s of her
17:5 of one of his s with power
17:11 as one of his s to him
18:2 the s of Dan sent five men of
18:16 s of Dan, were standing at
18:22 catch up with the s of Dan
18:23 crying out to the s of Dan
18:25 the s of Dan said to him
18:26 the s of Dan kept going on
18:30 the s of Dan stood up the
18:30 his s became priests to the
19:12 no part of the s of Israel
19:30 the s of Israel went up out
20:1 all the s of Israel went out
20:3 s of Benjamin got to hear
20:3 hear that the s of Israel had
20:3 the s of Israel said: Speak
20:7 s of Israel, give your word
20:13 s of Benjamin did not want
20:13 brothers, the s of Israel
20:14 s of Benjamin went gathering
20:14 against the s of Israel
20:15 the s of Benjamin got to be
20:18 s of Israel said: Who of us
20:18 against the s of Benjamin
20:19 s of Israel rose up in the
20:21 s of Benjamin came on out
20:23 s of Israel went up and wept
20:23 against the s of Benjamin
20:24 s of Israel drew near to the
20:24 near to the s of Benjamin
20:25 s of Israel down to ruin to
20:26 At that all the s of Israel
20:27 the s of Israel inquired of
20:28 against the s of Benjamin
20:30 s of Israel proceeded to go
20:30 up against the s of Benjamin

Jg 20:31 s of Benjamin went on out to
20:32 s of Benjamin began to say
20:32 As for the s of Israel, they
20:35 the s of Israel on that day
20:36 s of Benjamin imagined that
20:39 s of Israel turned around in
20:48 against the s of Benjamin
21:5 the s of Israel said: Who is
21:6 the s of Israel began to feel
21:13 spoke to the s of Benjamin
21:18 the s of Israel have sworn
21:20 commanded the s of Benjamin
21:23 s of Benjamin did just that
21:24 s of Israel began to disperse
Ru 1:1 with his wife and his two s
1:2 two s were Mahlon and Chilion
1:3 she remained with her two s
1:11 have s in my inward parts
1:12 also should certainly bear s
4:15 is better to you than seven s
1Sa 1:3 the two s of Eli, Hophni and
1:4 to all her s and her daughters
1:8 not better to you than ten s
2:5 she that was abundant in s
2:12 Now the s of Eli were
2:21 to three s and two daughters
2:22 all that his s kept doing to
2:24 No, my s, because the report
2:28 of the s of Israel
2:29 honoring your s more than me
2:34 two s, Hophni and Phinehas
3:13 his s are calling down evil
4:4 two s of Eli were there with
4:11 two s of Eli, Hophni and
4:17 your own two s have died
7:4 the s of Israel put away the
7:6 judging the s of Israel in
7:7 the s of Israel had collected
7:7 the s of Israel heard of it
7:8 s of Israel said to Samuel
8:1 his s as judges for Israel
8:3 s did not walk in his ways
8:5 own s have not walked in your
8:11 Your s he will take and put
9:2 no man of the s of Israel
10:18 to say to the s of Israel
11:8 the s of Israel amounted to
12:2 my s, here they are with you
12:12 the king of the s of Ammon
14:18 with the s of Israel
14:47 and against the s of Ammon
14:49 the s of Saul came to be
15:6 with all the s of Israel at
16:1 among his s a king for
16:5 he sanctified Jesse and his s
16:10 Jesse had seven of his s
17:12 Jesse. And he had eight s
17:13 the three oldest s of Jesse
17:13 three s that went into the
17:53 s of Israel returned from
26:19 But if it is the s of man
28:19 you and your s will be with
30:3 wives and their s and their
30:6 because of his s and his
30:19 to s and daughters and from
30:22 his wife and his s
31:2 close range of Saul and his s
31:2 and Malchi-shua, Saul's s
31:6 Saul and his three s and his
31:7 Saul and his s had died, then
31:8 find Saul and his three s
31:12 corpses of his s off the
2Sa 1:18 s of Judah should be taught
2:18 three s of Zeruiah happened
2:25 s of Benjamin went
3:2 s were born to David in
3:34 the s of unrighteousness
3:39 s of Zeruiah, are too severe
4:2 s of Rimmon the Beerothite
4:2 of the s of Benjamin; for
4:5 s of Rimmon the Beerothite
4:9 s of Rimmon the Beerothite
5:13 more s and daughters
6:3 and Ahio, the s of Abinadab
7:6 s of Israel up out of Egypt
7:7 among all the s of Israel
7:10 s of unrighteousness will
7:14 the strokes of the s of Adam
8:12 from the s of Ammon and
8:18 s of David . . . became priests
9:10 your s and your servants
9:10 Ziba had fifteen s and twenty
9:11 like one of the s of the king
10:1 king of the s of Ammon came

2Sa 10:2 the land of the *s* of Ammon
10:3 princes of the *s* of Ammon
10:6 *s* of Ammon saw that they
10:6 *s* of Ammon proceeded to send
10:8 *s* of Ammon began to go out
10:10 to meet the *s* of Ammon
10:11 *s* of Ammon themselves
10:14 *s* of Ammon, they saw that
10:14 from the *s* of Ammon and
10:19 try saving the *s* of Ammon
11:1 *s* of Ammon to ruin and lay
12:3 with his *s*, all together
12:9 the sword of the *s* of Ammon
12:26 Rabbah of the *s* of Ammon
12:31 cities of the *s* of Ammon
13:23 invite all the *s* of the king
13:27 and all the *s* of the king
13:29 other *s* of the king began
13:30 all the *s* of the king
13:32 young men the *s* of the king
13:33 all the king's *s* themselves
13:35 king's *s* themselves have
13:36 king's *s* themselves came in
14:6 your maidservant had two *s*
14:27 born to Absalom three *s* and
15:27 the two *s* of you men
15:36 two *s*, Ahimaaz belonging to
16:10 you men, you *s* of Zeruiah
17:27 Rabbah of the *s* of Ammon
19:5 for the soul of your *s* and
19:17 his fifteen *s* and twenty
19:22 you men, you *s* of Zeruiah
21:2 were not of the *s* of Israel
21:2 the *s* of Israel themselves
21:2 jealous for the *s* of Israel
21:6 seven men of his *s*
21:8 the two *s* of Rizpah the
21:8 and the five *s* of Michal
23:20 the two *s* of Ariel of Moab
23:29 of the *s* of Benjamin
23:32 the *s* of Jashen, Jonathan
1Ki 1:9 all his brothers the king's *s*
1:19 invited all the *s* of the king
1:25 invite all the *s* of the king
2:4 If your *s* will take care of
2:7 *s* of Barzillai the Gileadite
4:3 and Ahijah, the *s* of Shisha
4:31 and Darda the *s* of Mahol
6:1 *s* of Israel came out from the
6:13 middle of the *s* of Israel
8:1 the *s* of Israel, to King
8:9 covenanted with the *s* of
8:25 *s* will take care of their
8:39 heart of . . . *s* of mankind
8:63 *s* of Israel might inaugurate
9:6 *s* should definitely turn back
9:20 no part of the *s* of Israel
9:21 *s* who had been left over
9:21 land whom the *s* of Israel
9:22 none of the *s* of Israel that
11:2 had said to the *s* of Israel
11:7 of the *s* of Ammon
11:20 among the *s* of Pharaoh
11:33 the god of the *s* of Ammon
12:17 As for the *s* of Israel that
12:24 brothers the *s* of Israel
12:31 to be of the *s* of Levi
12:33 festival for the *s* of Israel
13:11 *s* now came in and related
13:12 his *s* showed him the way
13:13 said to his *s*: Saddle the
13:27 to speak to his *s*, saying
13:31 to say to his *s*: When I die
14:24 before the *s* of Israel
18:20 among all the *s* of Israel
18:31 the tribes of the *s* of Jacob
19:10 the *s* of Israel have left
19:14 the *s* of Israel have left
20:3 your wives and your *s*, the
20:5 and your *s* you will give me
20:7 my *s* and my silver and my
20:15 all the *s* of Israel, seven
20:27 the *s* of Israel, they were
20:27 *s* of Israel went into camp
20:29 *s* of Israel went striking
20:35 of the *s* of the prophets
21:26 before the *s* of Israel
2Ki 2:3 *s* of the prophets that were
2:5 the *s* of the prophets that
2:7 the *s* of the prophets that
2:15 the *s* of the prophets that
4:1 wives . . . *s* of the prophets
4:4 behind yourself and your *s*
4:5 door behind herself and her *s*

2Ki 4:7 your *s* should live from what
4:38 the *s* of the prophets were
4:38 for the *s* of the prophets
5:22 from the *s* of the prophets
6:1 *s* of the prophets began to
8:12 will do to the *s* of Israel
8:19 lamp to him and to his *s*
9:1 one of the *s* of the prophets
9:26 Naboth and the blood of his *s*
10:1 Ahab had seventy *s* in
10:2 with you the *s* of your lord
10:3 upright of the *s* of your lord
10:6 are *s* of your lord and come
10:6 *s* of the king, seventy men
10:7 taking the *s* of the king
10:8 heads of the *s* of the king
10:13 well with the *s* of the king
10:13 and the *s* of the lady
10:30 *s* themselves to the fourth
11:2 the *s* of the king that were
13:5 *s* of Israel continued to
14:6 the *s* of the strikers he did
14:6 not be put to death for *s*
14:6 *s* themselves should not be
15:12 *S* themselves to the fourth
15:25 men of the *s* of Gilead
16:3 because of the *s* of Israel
17:7 the *s* of Israel had sinned
17:8 from before the *s* of Israel
17:9 *s* of Israel went searching
17:17 *s* and their daughters pass
17:22 *s* of Israel went walking
17:24 instead of the *s* of Israel
17:31 burning their *s* in the fire
17:34 commanded the *s* of Jacob
17:41 their *s* and their grandsons
18:4 *s* of Israel had continually
19:3 the *s* have come as far as
19:12 the *s* of Eden that were in
19:37 and Sharezer, his *s*
20:18 *s* that will come forth
21:2 from before the *s* of Israel
21:9 from before the *s* of Israel
23:6 place of the *s* of the people
23:10 valley of the *s* of Hinnom
23:13 thing of the *s* of Ammon
24:2 bands of the *s* of Ammon
25:7 Zedekiah's *s* they slaughtered
1Ch 1:5 *s* of Japheth were Gomer and
1:6 *s* of Gomer were Ashkenaz and
1:7 *s* of Javan were Elishah and
1:8 *s* of Ham were Cush and
1:9 the *s* of Cush were Seba and
1:9 *s* of Raamah were Sheba and
1:17 *s* of Shem were Elam and
1:19 to Eber two *s* were born
1:23 these were the *s* of Joktan
1:28 *s* of Abraham were Isaac and
1:31 These were the *s* of Ishmael
1:32 As for the *s* of Keturah
1:32 *s* of Jokshan were Sheba and
1:33 *s* of Midian were Ephah and
1:33 these were the *s* of Keturah
1:34 *s* of Isaac were Esau and
1:35 *s* of Esau were Eliphaz
1:36 *s* of Eliphaz were Teman
1:37 *s* of Reuel were Nahath
1:38 *s* of Seir were Lotan and
1:39 *s* of Lotan were Hori and
1:40 *s* of Shobal were Alvan and
1:40 *s* of Zibeon were Aiah and
1:41 *s* of Anah were Dishon
1:41 *s* of Dishon were Hemdan
1:42 The *s* of Ezer were Bilhan
1:42 The *s* of Dishan were Uz and
1:43 reigned over the *s* of Israel
2:1 *s* of Israel: Reuben, Simeon
2:3 *s* of Judah were Er and Onan
2:4 All the *s* of Judah were five
2:5 *s* of Perez were Hezron and
2:6 the *s* of Zerah were Zimri and
2:7 the *s* of Carmi were Achar
2:8 the *s* of Ethan were Azariah
2:9 *s* of Hezron that were born
2:10 chieftain of the *s* of Judah
2:16 *s* of Zeruiah were Abishai
2:18 father to *s* by Azubah his
2:18 and these were her *s*: Jesher
2:23 *s* of Machir the father of
2:25 *s* of Jerahmeel the
2:27 *s* of Ram the firstborn of
2:28 *s* of Onam came to be
2:28 *s* of Shammai were Nadab and
2:30 *s* of Nadab were Seled

1Ch 2:30 But Seled died without *s*
2:31 the *s* of Appaim were Ishi
2:31 the *s* of Ishi were Sheshan
2:31 the *s* of Sheshan, Ahlai
2:32 the *s* of Jada the brother of
2:32 But Jether died without *s*
2:33 *s* of Jonathan were Peleth
2:33 became the *s* of Jerahmeel
2:34 Sheshan came to have no *s*
2:42 *s* of Caleb the brother of
2:42 *s* of Mareshah the father of
2:43 the *s* of Hebron were Korah
2:47 the *s* of Jahdai were Regem
2:50 These became the *s* of Caleb
2:50 *s* of Hur the firstborn of
2:52 came to have *s*: Haroeh
2:54 *s* of Salma were Bethlehem
3:1 the *s* of David that were born
3:9 all the *s* of David besides
3:9 the *s* of the concubines
3:15 the *s* of Josiah were the
3:16 *s* of Jehoiakim were Jeconiah
3:17 *s* of Jeconiah as prisoner
3:19 *s* of Pedaiah were Zerubbabel
3:19 *s* of Zerubbabel were
3:21 *s* of Hananiah were Pelatiah
3:21 the *s* of Jeshaiah Rephaiah
3:21 the *s* of Rephaiah Arnan
3:21 the *s* of Arnan Obadiah
3:21 the *s* of Obadiah Shecaniah
3:22 the *s* of Shecaniah, Shemaiah
3:22 the *s* of Shemaiah, Hattush
3:23 *s* of Neariah were Elioenai
3:24 *s* of Elioenai were Hodaviah
4:1 The *s* of Judah were Perez
4:3 *s* of the father of Etam
4:4 the *s* of Hur the firstborn
4:6 These were the *s* of Naarah
4:7 the *s* of Helah were Zereth
4:13 the *s* of Kenaz were Othniel
4:13 the *s* of Othniel, Hathath
4:15 *s* of Caleb the son of
4:15 and the *s* of Elah, Kenaz
4:16 *s* of Jehallelel were Ziph
4:17 the *s* of Ezrah were Jether
4:18 were the *s* of Bithiah the
4:19 *s* of Hodiah's wife, the
4:20 the *s* of Shimon were Amnon
4:20 the *s* of Ishi were Zoheth and
4:21 *s* of Shelah the son of Judah
4:24 *s* of Simeon were Nemuel and
4:26 *s* of Mishma were Hammuel
4:27 Shimei had sixteen *s* and six
4:27 did not have many *s*, and
4:27 as many as the *s* of Judah
4:42 *s* of Simeon that went to
4:42 the *s* of Ishi at their head
5:1 *s* of Reuben the firstborn of
5:1 given to the *s* of Joseph the
5:3 the *s* of Reuben the firstborn
5:4 *s* of Joel were Shemaiah
5:11 *s* of Gad in front of them
5:14 These were the *s* of Abihail
5:18 *s* of Reuben and the Gadites
5:23 the *s* of the half tribe of
6:1 The *s* of Levi were Gershon
6:2 the *s* of Kohath were Amram
6:3 *s* of Amram were Aaron and
6:3 *s* of Aaron were Nadab and
6:16 The *s* of Levi were Gershom
6:17 names of the *s* of Gershom
6:18 *s* of Kohath were Amram and
6:19 *s* of Merari were Mahli and
6:22 *s* of Kohath were Amminadab
6:25 *s* of Elkanah were Amasai and
6:26 *s* of Elkanah were Zophai his
6:28 And the *s* of Samuel were the
6:29 The *s* of Merari were Mahli
6:33 attendance and also their *s*
6:33 Of the *s* of the Kohathites
6:44 *s* of Merari their brothers
6:49 Aaron and his *s* were making
6:50 *s* of Aaron: Eleazar his son
6:54 the *s* of Aaron belonging to
6:57 to the *s* of Aaron they gave
6:61 to the *s* of Kohath that were
6:62 to the *s* of Gershom by their
6:63 To the *s* of Merari by their
6:64 *s* of Israel gave the Levites
6:65 the tribe of the *s* of Judah
6:65 the tribe of the *s* of Simeon
6:65 tribe of the *s* of Benjamin
6:66 families of the *s* of Kohath
6:70 *s* of Kohath that were left

1Ch 6:71 the *s* of Gershom they gave
6:77 *s* of Merari that were left
7:1 *s* of Issachar were Tola and
7:2 the *s* of Tola were Uzzi and
7:3 the *s* of Uzzi were Izrahiah
7:3 *s* of Izrahiah were Michael
7:4 for they had many wives and *s*
7:6 *s* of Benjamin were Bela and
7:7 *s* of Bela were Ezbon and Uzzi
7:8 *s* of Becher were Zemirah and
7:8 all these the *s* of Becher
7:10 the *s* of Jediael were Bilhan
7:10 *s* of Bilhan were Jeush and
7:11 these were the *s* of Jediael
7:12 the Huppim were the *s* of Ir
7:12 Hushim were the *s* of Aher
7:13 *s* of Naphtali were Jahziel
7:13 and Shallum, the *s* of Bilhah
7:14 *s* of Manasseh were Asriel
7:16 his *s* were Ulam and Rekem
7:17 And the *s* of Ulam were Bedan
7:17 These were the *s* of Gilead
7:19 the *s* of Shemida came to be
7:20 *s* of Ephraim were Shuthelah
7:29 side of the *s* of Manasseh
7:29 In these the *s* of Joseph the
7:30 *s* of Asher were Imnah and
7:31 *s* of Beriah were Heber and
7:33 *s* of Japhlet were Pasach and
7:33 These were the *s* of Japhlet
7:34 *s* of Shemer were Ahi and
7:35 *s* of Helem his brother were
7:36 *s* of Zophah were Suah and
7:38 *s* of Jether were Jephunneh
7:39 the *s* of Ulla were Ara and
7:40 these were the *s* of Asher
8:3 Bela came to have *s*, Addar
8:6 And these were the *s* of Ehud
8:10 These were his *s*, heads of
8:12 *s* of Elpaal were Eber and
8:16 and Joha, the *s* of Beriah
8:18 and Jobab, the *s* of Elpaal
8:21 Shimrath, the *s* of Shimei
8:25 and Penuel, the *s* of Shashak
8:27 and Zichri, the *s* of Jeroham
8:35 *s* of Micah were Pithon and
8:38 And Azel had six *s*, and these
8:38 All these were the *s* of Azel
8:39 *s* of Eshek his brother were
8:40 *s* of Ulam came to be valiant
8:40 having many *s* and grandsons
8:40 were from the *s* of Benjamin
9:3 dwelt some of the *s* of Judah
9:3 and some of the *s* of Benjamin
9:3 some of the *s* of Ephraim and
9:4 *s* of Perez the son of Judah
9:5 Asaiah the firstborn and his *s*
9:6 of the *s* of Zerah, Jeuel, and
9:7 of the *s* of Benjamin, Sallu
9:14 from the *s* of Merari
9:18 the camps of the *s* of Levi
9:23 they and their *s* were over
9:30 *s* of the priests were makers
9:32 the *s* of the Kohathites
9:41 *s* of Micah were Pithon and
9:44 Azel had six *s*, and these
9:44 These were the *s* of Azel
10:2 close range of Saul and his *s*
10:2 and Malchi-shua, *s* of Saul
10:6 Saul and three *s* of his died
10:7 that Saul and his *s* had died
10:8 to find Saul and his *s* fallen
10:12 and the corpses of his *s*
11:22 the two *s* of Ariel of Moab
11:31 Gibeah of the *s* of Benjamin
11:34 *s* of Hashem the Gizonite
11:44 and Jeiel, the *s* of Hotham
11:46 Joshaviah the *s* of Elnaam
12:3 *s* of Shemaah the Gibeathite
12:3 and Pelet the *s* of Azmaveth
12:7 Zebadiah the *s* of Jeroham
12:8 were of the Gadites
12:14 *s* of Gad, heads of the army
12:16 the *s* of Benjamin and Judah
12:24 the *s* of Judah carrying the
12:25 Of the *s* of Simeon the
12:26 Of the *s* of the Levites four
12:27 leader of the *s* of Aaron
12:29 *s* of Benjamin, the brothers
12:30 of the *s* of Ephraim there
12:32 of the *s* of Issachar having
14:3 to be father to more *s*
15:4 gather the *s* of Aaron and the
15:5 of the *s* of Kohath, Uriel the

1Ch 15:6 of the *s* of Merari, Asaiah
15:7 of the *s* of Gershom, Joel
15:8 the *s* of Elizaphan, Shemaiah
15:9 *s* of Hebron, Eliel the chief
15:10 the *s* of Uzziel, Amminadab
15:15 *s* of the Levites began to
15:17 of the *s* of Merari their
16:13 *s* of Jacob, his chosen ones
16:42 *s* of Jeduthun at the gate
17:9 *s* of unrighteousness will
17:11 come to be one of your *s*
18:11 from the *s* of Ammon and
18:17 *s* of David were the first
19:1 the king of the *s* of Ammon
19:2 the land of the *s* of Ammon
19:3 princes of the *s* of Ammon
19:6 *s* of Ammon saw that they
19:6 and Hanun and the *s* of Ammon
19:7 and as for the *s* of Ammon
19:9 *s* of Ammon began to go out
19:11 to meet the *s* of Ammon
19:12 the *s* of Ammon themselves
19:15 *s* of Ammon, they saw that
19:19 try saving the *s* of Ammon
20:1 the land of the *s* of Ammon
20:3 the cities of the *s* of Ammon
21:20 his four *s* with him were
23:6 *s* of Levi, to Gershon, Kohath
23:8 *s* of Ladan were Jehiel the
23:9 *s* of Shimei were Shelomoth
23:10 the *s* of Shimei were Jahath
23:10 four were the *s* of Shimei
23:11 they did not have many *s*
23:12 *s* of Kohath were Amram
23:13 *s* of Amram were Aaron and
23:13 his *s* to time indefinite
23:14 his *s* themselves continued
23:15 *s* of Moses were Gershom
23:16 *s* of Gershom were Shebuel
23:17 the *s* of Eliezer came to be
23:17 not come to have other *s*
23:17 but the *s* of Rehabiah did
23:18 *s* of Izhar were Shelomith
23:19 *s* of Hebron were Jeriah the
23:20 *s* of Uzziel were Micah the
23:21 *s* of Merari were Mahli and
23:21 *s* of Mahli were Eleazar and
23:22 had come to have, not *s*
23:22 *s* of Kish their brothers
23:23 *s* of Mushi were Mahli and
23:24 *s* of Levi by the house of
23:27 the number of the *s* of Levi
23:28 *s* of Aaron for the service
23:32 guarding of the *s* of Aaron
24:1 Now the *s* of Aaron had their
24:1 *s* of Aaron were Nadab and
24:2 did not happen to have any *s*
24:3 Zadok from the *s* of Eleazar
24:3 from the *s* of Ithamar
24:4 *s* of Eleazar were found to
24:4 than the *s* of Ithamar
24:4 to the *s* of Eleazar, as heads
24:4 the *s* of Ithamar, as heads
24:5 from the *s* of Eleazar and
24:5 and from the *s* of Ithamar
24:20 *s* of Levi that were left
24:20 of the *s* of Amram there
24:20 the *s* of Shubael, Jehdeiah
24:21 the *s* of Rehabiah, Isshiah
24:22 the *s* of Shelomoth, Jahath
24:23 *s* of Hebron, Jeriah the head
24:24 The *s* of Uzziel, Micah; of
24:24 of the *s* of Micah, Shamir
24:25 the *s* of Isshiah, Zechariah
24:26 *s* of Merari were Mahli and
24:26 the *s* of Jaaziah, Beno
24:27 *s* of Merari: Of Jaaziah
24:28 did not come to have any *s*
24:29 *s* of Kish were Jerahmeel
24:30 *s* of Mushi were Mahli and
24:30 *s* of the Levites by their
24:31 brothers the *s* of Aaron
25:1 the *s* of Asaph, Heman and
25:2 Of the *s* of Asaph, Zaccur and
25:2 *s* of Asaph under the control
25:3 *s* of Jeduthun, Gedaliah and
25:4 the *s* of Heman, Bukkiah
25:5 these were *s* of Heman
25:5 to give Heman fourteen *s* and
25:9 and his brothers and his *s*
25:10 for Zaccur, his *s* and his
25:11 Izri, his *s* and his brothers
25:12 Nethaniah, his *s* and his
25:13 the sixth for Bukkiah, his *s*

1Ch 25:14 for Jesharelah, his *s* and
25:15 eighth for Jeshaiah, his *s*
25:16 ninth for Mattaniah, his *s*
25:17 the tenth for Shimei, his *s*
25:18 eleventh for Azarel, his *s*
25:19 for Hashabiah, his *s* and
25:20 Shubael, his *s* and his
25:21 Mattithiah, his *s* and his
25:22 Jeremoth, his *s* and his
25:23 for Hananiah, his *s* and his
25:24 Joshbekashah, his *s* and his
25:25 for Hanani, his *s* and his
25:26 for Mallothi, his *s* and his
25:27 for Eliathah, his *s* and his
25:28 for Hothir, his *s* and his
25:29 for Giddalti, his *s* and his
25:30 for Mahazioth, his *s* and
25:31 Romamti-ezer, his *s* and his
26:1 of Kore of the *s* of Asaph
26:2 And Meshelemiah had *s*
26:4 Obed-edom had *s*: Shemaiah
26:6 *s* born that were rulers of
26:7 The *s* of Shemaiah, Othni and
26:8 were of the *s* of Obed-edom
26:8 Obed-edom, they and their *s*
26:9 And Meshelemiah had *s* and
26:10 Hosah of the *s* of Merari
26:10 Hosah . . . had *s*. Shimri was
26:11 the *s* and brothers of Hosah
26:15 his *s* had the storehouses
26:19 of the *s* of the Korahites
26:19 and of the *s* of Merari
26:21 The *s* of Ladan, the
26:21 the *s* of the Gershonite
26:22 *s* of Jehieli, Zetham and
26:29 Chenaniah and his *s* were
27:1 *s* of Israel by their number
27:3 Some of the *s* of Perez the
27:10 of the *s* of Ephraim, and in
27:14 of the *s* of Ephraim, and in
27:20 of the *s* of Ephraim, Hoshea
27:32 was with the king's *s*
28:1 of the king and of his *s*
28:4 among my father's *s*, I was
28:5 out of all my *s* (for many
28:5 many are the *s* whom Jehovah
28:8 as an inheritance to your *s*
29:24 also all the *s* of King David
2Ch 2:14 of a woman of the *s* of Dan
5:2 houses of the *s* of Israel
5:10 with the *s* of Israel while
5:12 to their *s* and to their
6:11 with the *s* of Israel
6:16 *s* will take care of their
6:30 heart of the *s* of mankind
7:3 *s* of Israel were spectators
8:2 caused the *s* of Israel to
8:8 *s* that had been left behind
8:8 *s* of Israel had not
8:9 *s* of Israel that Solomon
10:17 *s* of Israel that were
10:18 *s* of Israel pelted him with
11:14 Jeroboam and his *s* had
11:19 she bore him *s*, Jeush and
11:21 father to twenty-eight *s*
11:23 some out of all his *s* to
13:5 to his *s*, by a covenant
13:8 hand of the *s* of David
13:9 priests, the *s* of Aaron
13:10 the *s* of Aaron, and also the
13:12 O *s* of Israel, do not fight
13:16 *s* of Israel took to flight
13:18 *s* of Israel were humbled at
13:18 *s* of Judah proved superior
13:21 father to twenty-two *s* and
20:1 *s* of Moab and the
20:1 *s* of Ammon and with them
20:10 *s* of Ammon, and Moab and
20:13 their wives and their *s*
20:14 Levite of the *s* of Asaph
20:19 *s* of the Kohathites and
20:19 *s* of the Korahites rose up
20:22 against the *s* of Ammon
20:23 *s* of Ammon and Moab
21:2 Jehoshaphat's *s*, Azariah and
21:2 *s* of Jehoshaphat the king of
21:7 give him and his *s* a lamp
21:14 to your *s* and to your wives
21:17 also his *s* and his wives
22:8 *s* of the brothers of Ahaziah
22:11 *s* of the king that were to
23:3 concerning the *s* of David
23:11 Jehoiada and his *s* anointed
24:3 father to *s* and daughters

2Ch 24:7 her *s* themselves had broken
24:25 blood of the *s* of Jehoiada
24:27 As for his *s* and the
25:4 *s* he did not put to death
25:4 Fathers should not die for *s*
25:4 *s* themselves die for fathers
25:7 all the *s* of Ephraim
25:11 striking down the *s* of Seir
25:12 *s* of Judah captured alive
25:14 gods of the *s* of Seir
26:18 priests the *s* of Aaron
27:5 king of the *s* of Ammon and
27:5 *s* of Ammon gave him in
27:5 *s* of Ammon paid to him
28:3 burn up his *s* in the fire
28:3 from before the *s* of Israel
28:8 *s* of Israel took two
28:8 captive, women, *s* and
28:10 *s* of Judah and of
28:12 heads of the *s* of Ephraim
29:9 *s* and our daughters and our
29:11 my *s*, do not give
29:12 of the *s* of the Kohathites
29:12 and from the *s* of Merari
29:13 *s* of Elizaphan, Shimri and
29:13 *s* of Asaph, Zechariah and
29:14 *s* of Heman, Jehiel and
29:14 *s* of Jeduthun, Shemaiah
29:21 *s* of Aaron the priests to
30:6 *s* of Israel, return to
30:9 *s* will be objects of mercy
30:21 *s* of Israel that were found
31:1 *s* of Israel returned to their
31:5 *s* of Israel increased the
31:6 *s* of Israel and of Judah that
31:18 *s* and their daughters, for
31:19 *s* of Aaron, the priests, in
32:33 places of the *s* of David
33:2 from before the *s* of Israel
33:6 own *s* pass through the fire
33:9 from before the *s* of Israel
34:12 from the *s* of Merari, and
34:12 the *s* of the Kohathites
34:33 belonged to the *s* of Israel
35:5 the *s* of the people
35:7 to the *s* of the people flocks
35:12 to the *s* of the people
35:13 to all the *s* of the people
35:14 the priests the *s* of Aaron
35:14 the priests the *s* of Aaron
35:15 the singers the *s* of Asaph
35:17 the *s* of Israel that were
36:20 servants to him and his *s*
Ezr 2:1 the *s* of the jurisdictional
2:3 *s* of Parosh, two thousand
2:4 *s* of Shephatiah, three hundred
2:5 *s* of Arah, seven hundred and
2:6 *s* of Pahath-moab, of the
2:6 the *s* of Jeshua and Joab
2:7 the *s* of Elam, a thousand
2:8 *s* of Zattu, nine hundred and
2:9 *s* of Zaccai, seven hundred and
2:10 *s* of Bani, six hundred and
2:11 *s* of Bebai, six hundred and
2:12 *s* of Azgad, a thousand two
2:13 *s* of Adonikam, six hundred
2:14 *s* of Bigvai, two thousand
2:15 *s* of Adin, four hundred and
2:16 *s* of Ater, of Hezekiah
2:17 *s* of Bezai, three hundred and
2:18 *s* of Jorah, a hundred and
2:19 *s* of Hashum, two hundred and
2:20 *s* of Gibbar, ninety-five
2:21 *s* of Bethlehem, a hundred
2:24 the *s* of Azmaveth, forty-two
2:25 the *s* of Kiriath-jearim
2:26 *s* of Ramah and Geba
2:29 the *s* of Nebo, fifty-two
2:30 *s* of Magbish, a hundred and
2:31 the *s* of the other Elam
2:32 *s* of Harim, three hundred
2:33 *s* of Lod, Hadid and Ono
2:34 *s* of Jericho, three hundred
2:35 *s* of Senaah, three thousand
2:36 *s* of Jedaiah of the house of
2:37 *s* of Immer, a thousand and
2:38 *s* of Pashhur, a thousand
2:39 *s* of Harim, a thousand and
2:40 The Levites: The *s* of Jeshua
2:40 *s* of Hodaviah, seventy-four
2:41 The singers, the *s* of Asaph
2:42 *s* of the gatekeepers, the
2:42 the *s* of Shallum
2:42 the *s* of Ater
Ezr 2:42 the *s* of Talmon
2:42 the *s* of Akkub
2:42 the *s* of Hatita
2:42 the *s* of Shobai
2:43 The Nethinim: The *s* of Ziha
2:43 the *s* of Hasupha
2:43 the *s* of Tabbaoth
2:44 the *s* of Keros
2:44 the *s* of Siaha
2:44 the *s* of Padon
2:45 the *s* of Lebanah
2:45 the *s* of Hagabah
2:45 the *s* of Akkub
2:46 the *s* of Hagab
2:46 the *s* of Salmai
2:46 the *s* of Hanan
2:47 the *s* of Giddel
2:47 the *s* of Gahar
2:47 the *s* of Reaiah
2:48 the *s* of Rezin
2:48 the *s* of Nekoda
2:48 the *s* of Gazzam
2:49 the *s* of Uzza
2:49 the *s* of Paseah
2:49 the *s* of Besai
2:50 the *s* of Asnah
2:50 the *s* of Meunim
2:50 the *s* of Nephusim
2:51 the *s* of Bakbuk
2:51 the *s* of Hakupha
2:51 the *s* of Harhur
2:52 the *s* of Bazluth
2:52 the *s* of Mehida
2:52 the *s* of Harsha
2:53 the *s* of Barkos
2:53 the *s* of Sisera
2:53 the *s* of Temah
2:54 the *s* of Neziah
2:54 the *s* of Hatipha
2:55 *s* of the servants of Solomon
2:55 The *s* of Sotai
2:55 the *s* of Sophereth
2:55 the *s* of Peruda
2:56 the *s* of Jaalah
2:56 the *s* of Darkon
2:56 the *s* of Giddel
2:57 the *s* of Shephatiah
2:57 the *s* of Hattil
2:57 the *s* of Pochereth-hazzebaim
2:57 the *s* of Ami
2:58 *s* of the servants of Solomon
2:60 the *s* of Delaiah
2:60 the *s* of Tobiah
2:60 the *s* of Nekoda
2:61 And of the *s* of the priests
2:61 the *s* of Habaiah
2:61 the *s* of Hakkoz
2:61 the *s* of Barzillai
3:1 *s* of Israel were in their
3:9 Jeshua, his *s* and his brothers
3:9 and Kadmiel and his *s*, the
3:9 the *s* of Judah, stood up as
3:9, 9 *s* of Henadad, their *s* and
3:10 the Levites the *s* of Asaph
4:1 *s* of the Exile were building
6:10 life of the king and his *s*
6:16 the *s* of Israel, the priests
6:21 the *s* of Israel that had
7:7 *s* of Israel and of the priests
7:23 the king's realm and his *s*
8:2 the *s* of Phinehas, Gershom
8:2 of the *s* of Ithamar, Daniel
8:2 of the *s* of David, Hattush
8:3 of the *s* of Shecaniah, of the
8:3 of the *s* of Parosh, Zechariah
8:4 of the *s* of Pahath-moab
8:5 of the *s* of Zattu, Shecaniah
8:6 and of the *s* of Adin, Ebed the
8:7 of the *s* of Elam, Jeshaiah
8:8 the *s* of Shephatiah, Zebadiah
8:9 of the *s* of Joab, Obadiah the
8:10 of the *s* of Bani, Shelomith
8:11 of the *s* of Bebai, Zechariah
8:12 of the *s* of Azgad, Johanan
8:13 and of the *s* of Adonikam
8:14 of the *s* of Bigvai, Uthai and
8:15 none of the *s* of Levi did I
8:18 from the *s* of Mahli the
8:18 Sherebiah and his *s* and his
8:19 from the *s* of Merari
8:19 and their *s*, twenty
9:2 daughters . . . for their *s*
9:12 you people give to their *s*
9:12 do you accept for your *s*
Ezr 9:12 possession of it for your *s*
10:2 of the *s* of Elam answered
10:18 *s* of the priests came to be
10:18 *s* of Jeshua the son of
10:20 *s* of Immer there were
10:21 *s* of Harim, Maaseiah and
10:22 *s* of Pashhur, Elioenai
10:25 the *s* of Parosh there were
10:26 *s* of Elam, Mattaniah
10:27 of the *s* of Zattu, Elioenai
10:28 *s* of Bebai, Jehohanan
10:29 of the *s* of Bani, Meshullam
10:30 the *s* of Pahath-moab, Adna
10:31 the *s* of Harim, Eliezer
10:33 the *s* of Hashum, Mattenai
10:34 the *s* of Bani, Maadai
10:38 of the *s* of Binnui, Shimei
10:43 the *s* of Nebo, Jeiel
10:44 away wives along with *s*
Ne 1:6 the *s* of Israel your servants
1:6 the sins of the *s* of Israel
2:10 good for the *s* of Israel
3:3 *s* of Hassenaah built
4:14 your *s* and your daughters
5:2 Our *s* and our daughters we are
5:5, 5 *s* are the same as their *s*
5:5 *s* and our daughters to slaves
7:6 the *s* of the jurisdictional
7:8 *s* of Parosh, two thousand one
7:9 *s* of Shephatiah, three hundred
7:10 *s* of Arah, six hundred and
7:11 *s* of Pahath-moab, of the
7:11 of the *s* of Jeshua and Joab
7:12 *s* of Elam, a thousand two
7:13 *s* of Zattu, eight hundred and
7:14 *s* of Zaccai, seven hundred and
7:15 *s* of Binnui, six hundred and
7:16 *s* of Bebai, six hundred and
7:17 *s* of Azgad, two thousand
7:18 *s* of Adonikam, six hundred
7:19 the *s* of Bigvai, two thousand
7:20 *s* of Adin, six hundred and
7:21 the *s* of Ater, of Hezekiah
7:22 *s* of Hashum, three hundred
7:23 *s* of Bezai, three hundred and
7:24 *s* of Hariph, a hundred and
7:25 *s* of Gibeon, ninety-five
7:34 *s* of the other Elam
7:35 *s* of Harim, three hundred and
7:36 *s* of Jericho, three hundred
7:37 *s* of Lod, Hadid and Ono
7:38 the *s* of Senaah, three
7:39 The priests: The *s* of Jedaiah
7:40 the *s* of Immer, a thousand
7:41 the *s* of Pashhur, a thousand
7:42 *s* of Harim, a thousand and
7:43 The Levites: The *s* of Jeshua
7:43 *s* of Hodevah, seventy-four
7:44 The singers, the *s* of Asaph
7:45 gatekeepers, the *s* of Shallum
7:45 the *s* of Ater, the
7:45 the *s* of Talmon, the
7:45 the *s* of Akkub, the
7:45 the *s* of Hatita, the
7:45 the *s* of Shobai, a hundred
7:46 The Nethinim: The *s* of Ziha
7:46 the *s* of Hasupha, the
7:46 the *s* of Tabbaoth
7:47, 47 *s* of Keros, the *s* of Sia
7:47 of Sia, the *s* of Padon
7:48 the *s* of Lebanah, the
7:48 the *s* of Hagabah, the
7:48 the *s* of Salmai
7:49 the *s* of Hanan, the
7:49 the *s* of Giddel, the
7:49 the *s* of Gahar
7:50 the *s* of Reaiah, the
7:50 the *s* of Rezin, the
7:50 the *s* of Nekoda
7:51 the *s* of Gazzam, the
7:51 the *s* of Uzza, the
7:51 the *s* of Paseah
7:52 the *s* of Besai, the
7:52 the *s* of Meunim, the
7:52 the *s* of Nephushesim
7:53 the *s* of Bakbuk, the
7:53 the *s* of Hakupha, the
7:53 the *s* of Harhur
7:54 the *s* of Bazlith, the
7:54 the *s* of Mehida, the
7:54 the *s* of Harsha
7:55 the *s* of Barkos, the
7:55 the *s* of Sisera, the
7:55 the *s* of Temah

Ne 7:56 the s of Neziah, the
7:56 the s of Hatipha
7:57 s of the servants of Solomon
7:57 The s of Sotai, the
7:57 the s of Sophereth, the
7:57 the s of Perida
7:58 the s of Jaala, the
7:58 the s of Darkon, the
7:58 the s of Giddel
7:59 the s of Shephatiah, the
7:59 the s of Hattil, the
7:59 the s of Pochereth-hazzebaim
7:59 the s of Amon
7:60 s of the servants of Solomon
7:62 the s of Delaiah, the
7:62 of Delaiah, the s of Tobiah
7:62 the s of Nekoda, six hundred
7:63 the priests: the s of Habaiah
7:63 the s of Hakkoz, the
7:63 the s of Barzillai, who took
7:73 the s of Israel were then in
8:14 the s of Israel should dwell
8:17 the s of Israel had not done
9:1 the s of Israel gathered
9:23 s you made as many as the
9:24 s came in and took the land
10:9 Binnui of the s of Henadad
10:28 their wives, their s and
10:30 should not take for our s
10:36 firstborn of our s and of
10:39 the s of Israel and the
10:39 s of the Levites should bring
11:3 s of the servants of Solomon
11:4 dwelt some of the s of Judah
11:4 some of the s of Benjamin
11:4 the s of Judah there were
11:4 Mahalalel of the s of Perez
11:6 the s of Perez who were
11:7 were the s of Benjamin
11:22 Mica of the s of Asaph
11:24 Meshezabel of the s of Zerah
11:25 s of Judah that dwelt in
11:31 s of Benjamin were from
12:23 s of Levi as heads of the
12:28 s of the singers proceeded
12:35 the s of the priests with
12:47 to the s of Aaron
13:2 not met the s of Israel with
13:16 s of Judah and in Jerusalem
13:24 as for their s, half were
13:25 your daughters to their s
13:25 their daughters for your s
13:28 one of the s of Joiada the
Es 5:11 the large number of his s
8:10 s of speedy mares
9:10 ten s of Haman the son of
9:12 and the ten s of Haman
9:13 the ten s of Haman be hanged
9:14 ten s of Haman were hanged
9:25 hanged him and his s upon the
Job 1:2 seven s and three daughters
1:4 his s went and held a banquet
1:5 maybe my s have sinned and
1:6 s of the true God entered to
1:13 his s and his daughters were
1:18 Your s and your daughters
2:1 s of the true God entered to
5:4 s remain far from salvation
8:4 If your own s have sinned
14:21 His s get honored, but he
17:5 very eyes of his s will fail
19:17 the s of my mother's belly
20:10 s will seek the favor of
21:19 hurtfulness for one's own s
27:14 If his s become many, it
30:8 S of the senseless one
30:8 also s of the nameless one
38:7 the s of God began shouting
38:32 Ash constellation . . . its s
39:4 Their s become robust, they
39:16 does treat her s roughly
42:13 came to have seven s and
42:16 see his s and his grandsons
Ps 4:2 You s of men, how long must
11:4 eyes examine the s of men
12:1 vanished from the s of men
12:8 exalted among the s of men
14:2 upon the s of men
17:14 Who are satisfied with s
21:10 offspring from the s of men
29:1 O you s of strong ones
29:6 like the s of wild bulls
31:19 In front of the s of men
33:13 He has seen all the s of men

Ps 34:11 Come, you s, listen to me
36:7 the s of men themselves take
42:*super* Maskil for the s of Korah
44:*super* Of the s of Korah. Maskil
45:*super* Of the s of Korah. Maskil
45:2 more handsome than the s of
45:16 there will come to be your s
46:*super* Of the s of Korah upon The
47:*super* Of the s of Korah
48:*super* melody of the s of Korah
49:*super* Of the s of Korah
49:2 s of humankind as well as you
49:2 as well as you s of man
53:2 upon the s of men, To see
57:4 devourers, even the s of men
58:1 O you s of men
62:9 the s of earthling man are an
62:9 The s of mankind are a lie
66:5 His dealing with the s of men
69:8 to the s of my mother
72:4 save the s of the poor one
73:15 the generation of your s
77:15 s of Jacob and of Joseph
78:4 we do not hide from their s
78:5 make them known to their s
78:6 s that were to be born, might
78:6 and relate them to their s
78:9 s of Ephraim, though armed
82:6 you are s of the Most High
83:8 an arm to the s of Lot
84:*super* Of the s of Korah
85:*super* Of the s of Korah
87:*super* Of the s of Korah
88:*super* melody of the s of Korah
89:6 Jehovah among the s of God
89:30 If his s leave my law
89:47 created all the s of men
90:3 say: Go back, you s of men
90:16 your splendor upon their s
102:28 s of your servants will
103:7 even to the s of Israel
103:13 father shows mercy to his s
103:17, 17 to the s of s
105:6 s of Jacob, his chosen ones
106:37 would sacrifice their s
106:38 blood of their s and their
107:8 works to the s of men
107:15 works to the s of men
107:21 works to the s of men
107:31 works to the s of men
109:9 his s become fatherless boys
109:10 his s go wandering about
113:9 As a joyful mother of s
115:14 To you and to your s
115:16 earth . . . to the s of men
127:3 S are an inheritance from
127:4 So are the s of youth
128:3 s will be like slips of
128:6, 6 And see the s of your s
132:12 s will keep my covenant
132:12 Their s also forever
137:7 s of Edom the day of
144:12 s are like little plants
145:12 known to the s of men his
147:13 blessed your s in the midst
148:14 s of Israel, the people
149:2 s of Zion—let them be
Pr 4:1 Listen, O s, to the discipline
5:7 O s, listen to me and do not
7:7 among the s a young man in
7:24 s, listen to me and pay
8:4 my voice is to the s of men
8:31 were with the s of men
8:32 s, listen to me; yes, happy
13:22, 22 inheritance to s of s
14:26 and for his s . . . a refuge
15:11 hearts of the s of mankind
17:6 beauty of s is their fathers
20:7 Happy are his s after him
30:17 s of the eagle will eat it
31:5 of any of the s of affliction
31:28 Her s have risen up and
Ec 1:13 has given to the s of mankind
2:3 s of mankind in what they did
2:7 to have s of the household
2:8 delights of the s of mankind
3:10 has given to the s of mankind
3:18 regard to the s of mankind
3:19 as respects the s of mankind
3:21 spirit of the s of mankind
8:11 the heart of the s of men has
9:3 heart of the s of men is also
9:12 s of men . . . being ensnared
Ca 1:6 s of my own mother grew angry

Ca 2:3 so is my dear one among the s
Isa 1:2 S I have brought up and raised
1:4 an evildoing seed, ruinous s
11:14 plunder the s of the East
11:14 s of Ammon will be their
13:18 s their eye will not feel
14:21 block for his own s
17:3 the glory of the s of Israel
17:9 account of the s of Israel
21:17 men of the s of Kedar
27:12 O s of Israel
30:1 Woe to the stubborn s, is
30:9 people, untruthful s
30:9 s who have been unwilling to
31:6 s of Israel have gone deep
37:3 s have come as far as the
37:12 s of Eden that were in
37:38 his own s, struck him down
38:19 give knowledge to his own s
39:7 own s that will come forth
43:6 Bring my s from far off, and
45:11 are coming concerning my s
49:17 Your s have hurried up
49:20 the s of your bereaved state
49:22 bring your s in the bosom
49:25 own s I myself shall save
51:18 s that she brought to birth
51:18 s that she brought up taking
51:20 own s have swooned away
52:14 that of the s of mankind
54:1 for the s of the desolated
54:1 the s of the woman with a
54:13 s will be persons taught by
54:13 the peace of your s will be
56:5 better than s and daughters
57:3 you s of a soothsaying woman
60:4 your own s keep coming, and
60:9 bring your s from far away
60:14 s of those afflicting you
62:5 your s will take ownership
63:8 s that will not prove false
66:8 given birth to her s
66:20 as when the s of Israel
Jer 2:9, 9 with the s of your s I
2:16 the s of Noph and Tahpanes
2:30 I have struck your s
3:14 Return, O you renegade s
3:19 to place you among the s and
3:21 entreaties of the s of Israel
3:22 Return, you renegade s
3:24 their s and their daughters
4:22 They are unwise s; and they
5:7 Your own s have left me
5:17 The men will eat up your s
6:1 shelter, O you s of Benjamin
6:21 father and s together
7:18 The s are picking up sticks
7:30 the s of Judah have done
7:31 in order to burn their s
9:26 and upon the s of Ammon
10:20 My own s have gone forth
11:22 Their s and their daughters
13:14 both the fathers and the s
14:16 their s and their daughters
16:2 come to have s and daughters
16:3 has said concerning the s and
16:14 the s of Israel up out of
16:15 brought the s of Israel up
17:2 s remember their altars
17:19 gate of the s of the people
18:21 their s over to the famine
19:5 to burn their s in the fire
19:9 eat the flesh of their s and
23:7 brought the s of Israel up
25:21 Moab and the s of Ammon
26:23 graveyard of the s of the
27:3 the king of the s of Ammon
29:6 become father to s and to
29:6 take wives for your own s
29:6 they may give birth to s
30:20 s must become as in former
31:15 Rachel weeping over her s
31:15 comforted over her s
31:17 s will certainly return to
31:29 teeth of the s that got set
32:18 bosom of their s after
32:19 the ways of the s of men
32:30 s of Israel and the
32:30 s of Judah have proved to
32:30 s of Israel are even
32:32 badness of the s of Israel
32:32 s of Judah that they have
32:35 s and their daughters pass
32:39 and to their s after them

Jer 35:3 his brothers, and all his *s*
35:4 dining room of the *s* of Hanan
35:5 *s* of the house of the
35:6 neither you nor your *s*, to
35:8 we, our wives, our *s* and
35:14 that he commanded his *s*
35:16 *s* of Jehonadab the son of
38:23 *s* they are bringing out to
39:6 slaughter the *s* of Zedekiah
40:8 and Jonathan, the *s* of Kareah
40:8 *s* of Ephai the Netophathite
40:11 *s* of Ammon and in Edom
40:14 king of the *s* of Ammon
41:10 over to the *s* of Ammon
41:15 go to the *s* of Ammon
47:3 not turn around to the *s*
48:45 head of the *s* of uproar
48:46 *s* have been taken as
49:1 For the *s* of Ammon this is
49:1 there no *s* that Israel has
49:2 Rabbah of the *s* of Ammon
49:6 ones of the *s* of Ammon
49:28 despoil the *s* of the East
50:4 *s* of Israel, they and the
50:4 they and the *s* of Judah
50:33 *s* of Israel and the
50:33 *s* of Judah are being
52:10 slaughter the *s* of Zedekiah
La 1:16 My *s* have become those laid
3:13 kidneys the *s* of his quiver
3:33 does he grieve the *s* of men
4:2 As for the precious *s* of Zion
Eze 2:3 sending you to the *s* of Israel
2:4 *s* insolent of face and hard of
3:11 among the *s* of your people
4:13 *s* of Israel will eat their
5:10 will eat *s* in the midst of
5:10 *s* . . . will eat their fathers
6:5 carcasses of the *s* of Israel
14:16 neither *s* nor daughters
14:18 would deliver neither *s* nor
14:22 *S* and daughters, here they
16:20 *s* . . . you would sacrifice
16:21 you would slaughter my *s*
16:26 yourself to the *s* of Egypt
16:28 yourself to the *s* of Assyria
16:36 with the blood of your *s*
16:45 one abhorring . . . her *s*
16:45 who abhorred . . . their *s*
18:2 teeth of the *s* that get set
20:18 their *s* in the wilderness
20:21 *s* began to rebel against me
20:31 your *s* pass through the fire
21:20 Rabbah of the *s* of Ammon
21:28 concerning the *s* of Ammon
23:4 give birth to *s* and daughters
23:7 the choicest *s* of Assyria
23:9 hand of the *s* of Assyria
23:10 *s* and her daughters they
23:12 the *s* of Assyria she lusted
23:15 likeness of the *s* of Babylon
23:17 *s* of Babylon kept coming in
23:23 the *s* of Babylon and all
23:23 all the *s* of Assyria with
23:25 Your *s* and your daughters
23:37 *s* whom they had borne to
23:39 had slaughtered their *s* to
23:47 *s* and their daughters they
24:21 your *s* and your daughters
24:25 their *s* and their daughters
25:2 toward the *s* of Ammon and
25:3 the *s* of Ammon, Hear the
25:5 *s* of Ammon a resting-place
25:10 alongside the *s* of Ammon
25:10 the *s* of Ammon, among the
27:11 *s* of Arvad, even your
27:15 The *s* of Dedan were your
30:5 *s* of the land of the covenant
31:14 midst of the *s* of mankind
33:2 speak to the *s* of your people
33:12 say to the *s* of your people
33:17 the *s* of your people have
33:30 the *s* of your people are
35:5 delivering the *s* of Israel
37:16 the *s* of Israel his partners
37:18 the *s* of your people begin
37:21 taking the *s* of Israel from
37:25, 25 *s* and their sons' *s*
40:46 They are the *s* of Zadok
40:46 from the *s* of Levi, are
43:7 midst of the *s* of Israel
44:9 midst of the *s* of Israel
44:15 priests, the *s* of Zadok
44:15 *s* of Israel wandered away
Eze 46:16 gift to each one of his *s*
46:16 the property of his *s*
46:17 as regards his *s*—is what
46:18 give his *s* an inheritance
47:22 father to *s* in the midst of
47:22 among the *s* of Israel
48:11 from the *s* of Zadok
48:11 *s* of Israel wandered away
Da 1:3 bring some of the *s* of Israel
1:6 *s* of Judah, Daniel, Hananiah
2:38 *s* of mankind are dwelling
5:21 from the *s* of mankind he was
6:24 their *s* and their wives; and
10:16 likeness of the *s* of mankind
11:10 his *s*, they will excite
11:14 *s* of the robbers belonging
11:41 part of the *s* of Ammon
12:1 behalf of the *s* of your people
Ho 1:10 number of the *s* of Israel
1:10 The *s* of the living God
1:11 And the *s* of Judah and the
1:11 *s* of Israel will certainly be
2:4 her *s* I shall not show mercy
2:4 they are the *s* of fornication
3:1 love for the *s* of Israel while
3:4 for many days the *s* of Israel
3:5 the *s* of Israel will come back
4:1 O *s* of Israel, for Jehovah
4:6 I shall forget your *s*, even I
5:7 to strange *s* that they have
9:12 although they bring up their *s*
9:13 his *s* even to a killer
10:9 In Gibeah war against the *s*
10:14 alongside her own *s*
11:10 *s* will come trembling from
13:13 of *s* from the womb
Joe 1:3 an account to your own *s*
1:3, 3 and your *s* to their *s*
1:3 *s* to the following generation
1:12 away from the *s* of mankind
2:23 you *s* of Zion, be joyful and
2:28 your *s* and your daughters
3:6 the *s* of Judah and the
3:6 the *s* of Jerusalem you have
3:6 sold to the *s* of the Greeks
3:8 I will sell your *s* and your
3:8 the hand of the *s* of Judah
3:16 fortress for the *s* of Israel
3:19 violence to the *s* of Judah
Am 1:13 revolts of the *s* of Ammon
2:11 some of your *s* as prophets
2:11 really not be, O *s* of Israel
3:1 concerning you, O *s* of Israel
3:12 *s* of Israel will be snatched
4:5 have loved, O *s* of Israel
7:17 your *s* and your daughters
9:7 like the *s* of the Cushites
9:7 Cushites to me, O *s* of Israel
Ob 12 not to rejoice at the *s* of Judah
20 to the *s* of Israel will belong
Mic 1:16 your *s* of exquisite delight
5:3 return to the *s* of Israel
5:7 wait for the *s* of earthling
Zep 1:8 and to the *s* of the king
2:8 words of the *s* of Ammon
2:9 the *s* of Ammon like Gomorrah
Zec 9:13 I will awaken your *s*, O Zion
9:13 against your *s*, O Greece
10:7 their own *s* will see and
10:9 revive with their *s* and
Mal 3:3 must cleanse the *s* of Levi
3:6 And you are *s* of Jacob; you
4:6 of fathers back toward *s*
4:6 of *s* back toward fathers
Mt 5:9 they will be called *s* of God
5:45 *s* of your Father who is in
8:12 the *s* of the kingdom will
12:27 do your *s* expel them
13:38 are the *s* of the kingdom
13:38 are the *s* of the wicked one
17:25 *s* or from the strangers
17:26 then, the *s* are tax-free
20:20 mother of the *s* of Zebedee
20:20 approached him with her *s*
20:21 my two *s* may sit down, one
23:31 *s* of those who murdered the
26:37 and the two *s* of Zebedee
27:9 whom some of the *s* of Israel
27:56 mother of the *s* of Zebedee
Mr 3:17 Boanerges . . . *S* of Thunder
3:28 be forgiven the *s* of men, no
10:35 the two *s* of Zebedee
Lu 1:16 many of the *s* of Israel will
5:10 James and John, Zebedee's *s*
Lu 6:35 will be *s* of the Most High
11:19 by whom do your *s* expel
15:11 A certain man had two *s*
16:8 *s* of this system of things
16:8 than the *s* of the light are
Joh 4:12 his *s* and his cattle drank
12:36 to become *s* of light
21:2 *s* of Zebedee and two others
Ac 2:17 *s* and your daughters will
3:25 You are the *s* of the prophets
5:21 older men of the *s* of Israel
7:16 from the *s* of Hamor in
7:23 his brothers, the *s* of Israel
7:29 became the father of two *s*
7:37 that said to the *s* of Israel
9:15 to kings and the *s* of Israel
10:36 *s* of Israel to declare to
13:26 *s* of the stock of Abraham
19:14 seven *s* of a certain Sceva, a
28:11 the figurehead *S* of Zeus
Ro 8:14 these are God's *s*
8:15 spirit of adoption as *s*, by
8:19 revealing of the *s* of God
8:23 waiting for adoption as *s*
9:4 belong the adoption as *s* and
9:26 called *s* of the living God
9:27 number of the *s* of Israel
2Co 3:7 the *s* of Israel could not gaze
3:13 *s* of Israel might not gaze
6:18 you will be *s* and daughters
Ga 3:7 ones who are *s* of Abraham
3:26 *s* of God through your faith
4:5 receive the adoption as *s*
4:6 because you are *s*, God has
4:22 Abraham acquired two *s*, one
Eph 1:5 through Jesus Christ as *s* to
2:2 in the *s* of disobedience
3:5 made known to the *s* of men
5:6 upon the *s* of disobedience
1Th 5:5, 5 *s* of light and *s* of day
Heb 2:10 bringing many *s* to glory
7:5 the men from the *s* of Levi
11:21 each of the *s* of Joseph and
11:22 exodus of the *s* of Israel
12:5 which addresses you as *s*: My
12:7 dealing with you as with *s*
12:8 illegitimate . . . and not *s*
Re 2:14 *s* of Israel, to eat things
7:4 every tribe of the *s* of Israel
21:12 tribes of the *s* of Israel

Sons'

Ge 6:18 your wife and your *s* wives
7:7 and his *s* wives with him, into
8:16 and your *s* wives with you
8:18 his wife and his *s* wives
46:7 and his *s* sons with him
46:7 his *s* daughters, even all his
Ex 29:20 the lobe of his *s* right ear
29:28 become Aaron's and his *s*
Le 7:31 must become Aaron's and his *s*
24:9 Aaron's and his *s*, and they
Jos 14:9 your *s* as an inheritance to
Eze 37:25 *s* sons to time indefinite

Sons-in-law

Ge 19:14 speak to his *s* who were to
19:14 *s* he seemed like a man who

Soon

Ge 12:11 as *s* as he got near to
12:14 as *s* as Abram entered Egypt
19:17 *s* as they had brought them
27:30 as *s* as Isaac had finished
29:13 as *s* as Laban heard the
32:31 as *s* as he passed by Penuel
34:7 came in from the field as *s*
37:23 as *s* as Joseph came to his
38:29 as *s* as he drew back his hand
39:13 as *s* as she saw that he had
39:15 as *s* as he heard that I
39:18 as *s* as I raised my voice
39:19 as *s* as his master heard the
40:14 as *s* as it goes well with
43:2 as *s* as they had finished
44:30 as *s* as I should come to
44:31 *s* as he sees that the boy is
Ex 9:29 As *s* as I go out of the city
16:10 as *s* as Aaron had spoken to
17:11 as *s* as Moses would lift his
17:11 as *s* as he would let down
31:18 Now as *s* as he had finished
32:19 as *s* as he got near the camp
33:8 as *s* as Moses went out to the
33:9 as *s* as Moses had gone into

Nu 11:25 as *s* as the spirit settled
16:31 that as *s* as he had finished
De 2:16 as *s* as all the men of war
5:23 *s* as you had heard the voice
16:6 evening as *s* as the sun sets
24:13 to him as *s* as the sun sets
31:24 as *s* as Moses had finished
Jos 3:3 as *s* as you see the ark of the
3:8 *s* as you have come as far as
4:1 *s* as the whole nation had
4:11 as *s* as all the people had
5:1 as *s* as all the kings of the
6:15 as *s* as the dawn ascended
6:20 as *s* as the people heard the
8:8 *s* as you have seized the city
8:14 as *s* as the king of Ai saw
9:1 as *s* as all the kings who
10:1 as *s* as Adoni-zedek the king
10:20 as *s* as Joshua and the sons
10:24 as *s* as they had brought
11:1 as *s* as Jabin the king of
Jg 2:4 as *s* as Jehovah's angel had
7:15 that as *s* as Gideon heard the
8:33 as *s* as Gideon had died the
9:33 as *s* as the sun shines forth
16:2 As *s* as the morning gets
16:22 as *s* as he had been shaved
Ru 1:19 *s* as they came to Bethlehem
1Sa 1:22 As *s* as the boy is weaned
1:24 as *s* as she had weaned him
4:5 came about that as *s* as the
5:10 as *s* as the ark of the true
6:6 as *s* as He dealt severely
8:1 as *s* as Samuel had grown old
9:13 As *s* as you men come into
9:26 as *s* as the dawn ascended
10:9 *s* as he turned his shoulder
12:8 As *s* as Jacob had come into
13:10 as *s* as he had finished
17:57 as *s* as David returned from
18:1 *s* as he had finished speaking
24:1 as *s* as Saul returned from
2Sa 11:19 As *s* as you finish speaking
12:21 *s* as the child had died
13:28 *s* as Amnon's heart is in a
13:36 *s* as he finished speaking
15:10 As *s* as you hear the sound
16:16 as *s* as Hushai the Archite
17:9 as *s* as he falls upon them
17:27 as *s* as David came to
20:13 As *s* as he had removed him
1Ki 1:21 as *s* as my lord the king
5:7 as *s* as Hiram heard the words
8:54 as *s* as Solomon finished
9:1 as *s* as Solomon had finished
12:2 as *s* as Jeroboam the son of
12:20 as *s* as all Israel heard
13:4 as *s* as the king heard the
14:5 as *s* as she arrives, she will
14:6 as *s* as Ahijah heard the
15:21 as *s* as Baasha heard of it
15:29 as *s* as he became king
16:11 as *s* as he sat down upon
16:18 as *s* as Zimri saw that the
18:17 as *s* as Ahab saw Elijah
18:29 as *s* as noon was past and
19:13 as *s* as Elijah heard it
20:12 as *s* as he heard this word
21:15 as *s* as Jezebel heard that
21:16 as *s* as Ahab heard that
21:27 as *s* as Ahab heard these
22:32 as *s* as the chiefs of the
22:33 as *s* as the chiefs of the
2Ki 2:9 as *s* as they had gone across
3:5 as *s* as Ahab died, the king
3:15 it occurred that, as *s* as
4:6 as *s* as the vessels were full
4:25 as *s* as the man of the true
4:40 *s* as they ate from the stew
5:7 as *s* as the king of Israel
5:8 as *s* as Elisha the man of the
6:20 *s* as they arrived at Samaria
6:21 to Elisha as *s* as he saw
6:30 as *s* as the king heard the
6:32 as *s* as the messenger comes
9:22 as *s* as Jehoram saw Jehu
10:7 as *s* as the letter came to
10:25 *s* as he finished rendering
12:10 as *s* as they saw that there
14:5 as *s* as the kingdom had
19:1 as *s* as King Hezekiah heard
22:11 as *s* as the king heard the
23:29 as *s* as he saw him
1Ch 17:1 as *s* as David had begun
21:15 *s* as he began bringing the
2Ch 5:13 as *s* as the trumpeters and
5:13 as *s* as they lifted up the
7:1 *s* as Solomon finished praying
10:2 *s* as Jeroboam the son of
12:1 *s* as the kingship of
12:1 as *s* as he was strong, he
15:8 And as *s* as Asa heard these
16:5 as *s* as Baasha heard of it
18:31 *s* as the chiefs of this
18:32 *s* as the chiefs of the
20:23 *s* as they finished with
22:8 *s* as Jehu had entered into
24:11 *s* as they saw that there
24:14 *s* as they had finished
25:3 *s* as the kingdom had become
26:16 *s* as he was strong, his
29:29 *s* as they finished offering
31:1 as *s* as they finished all
31:5 *s* as the word broke forth
33:12 *s* as it caused him distress
34:19 as *s* as the king heard the
Ezr 9:1 as *s* as these things were
9:3 as *s* as I heard of this thing
10:1 as *s* as Ezra had prayed and
Ne 1:4 as *s* as I heard these words
4:1 as *s* as Sanballat heard that
4:7 as *s* as Sanballat and Tobiah
4:15 as *s* as our enemies heard
5:6 as *s* as I heard their outcry
6:1 *s* as it was told to Sanballat
6:16 as *s* as all our enemies heard
7:1 *s* as the wall had been rebuilt
9:28 as *s* as they were at rest
13:3 as *s* as they heard the law
13:19 *s* as the gates of Jerusalem
Es 5:2 as *s* as the king saw Esther
5:9 as *s* as Haman saw Mordecai
Job 11:12 *s* as an asinine zebra be
39:25 As *s* as the horn blows it
Isa 30:19 *s* as he hears it he will
33:1 *s* as you have finished as
33:1 *s* as you have done with
37:1 *s* as King Hezekiah heard
Jer 27:16 back from Babylon *s* now
36:16 *s* as they heard all the
36:23 *s* as Jehudi had read three
39:4 as *s* as Zedekiah the king of
41:6 *s* as he encountered them he
41:7 *s* as they came into the
41:13 *s* as all the people that
43:1 *s* as Jeremiah finished
51:61 *s* as you come to Babylon
Eze 2:2 as *s* as he spoke to me, and
5:2 as *s* as the days of the siege
11:13 that as *s* as I prophesied
37:7 occur as *s* as I prophesied
Da 6:10 Daniel, as *s* as he knew that
6:14 king, as *s* as he heard the
8:8 *s* as it became mighty, the
10:19 *s* as he spoke with me I
11:2 *s* as he has become strong in
12:7 *s* as there will have been a
Jon 4:8 as *s* as the sun shone forth
Mt 9:25 *s* as the crowd had been sent
24:32 as *s* as its young branch
Mr 4:15 as *s* as they have heard it
4:16 *s* as they have heard the word
4:17 then as *s* as tribulation or
4:29 as *s* as the fruit permits it
6:54 as *s* as they got out of the
9:15 as *s* as all the crowd caught
11:2 as *s* as you pass into it you
13:28 as *s* as its young branch
Lu 15:30 *s* as this your son who ate
19:37 As *s* as he got near the road
Ac 10:7 *s* as the angel that spoke
16:10 *s* as he had seen the vision
2Co 10:6 as *s* as your own obedience
Php 2:23 *s* as I have seen how things
Heb 13:23 if he comes quite *s*, I
2Pe 1:14 off of my tabernacle is *s*
Re 20:7 *s* as the thousand years have

Sooner
Mt 5:18 *s* would heaven and earth pass
Mr 1:21 No *s* was it the sabbath than
Heb 13:19 be restored to you the *s*

Soot
Ex 9:8 hands full of *s* from a kiln
9:10 took the *s* of a kiln and stood

Soothed
Ps 131:2 I have *s* and quieted my soul
Isa 38:13 *s* myself until the morning

Soothing
Ezr 6:10 *s* offerings to the God of the

Soothsaying
Isa 57:3 you sons of a *s* woman, the

Sopater
Ac 20:4 *S* the son of Pyrrhus of Beroea

Sophereth
Ezr 2:55 the sons of *S*
Ne 7:57 the sons of *S*, the sons of

Sorcerer
De 18:10 who looks for omens or a *s*
Ac 13:6 a *s*, a false prophet, a Jew
13:8 But Elymas the *s* (that, in

Sorcerers
Ex 7:11 for the wise men and the *s*
Jer 27:9 to your *s*, who are saying
Da 2:2 *s* and the Chaldeans to tell
Mal 3:5 speedy witness against the *s*

Sorceress
Ex 22:18 must not preserve a *s* alive

Sorceries
2Ki 9:22 your mother and her many *s*
Isa 47:9 for the abundance of your *s*
47:12 the abundance of your *s*
Mic 5:12 cut off *s* out of your hand
Na 3:4 a mistress of *s*, she who is
3:4 and families by her *s*

Sorcery
2Ch 33:6 and practiced *s* and made

Sore
De 4:30 When you are in *s* straits and
Jg 2:15 got to be in very *s* straits
1Sa 13:6 that they were in *s* straits
28:15 I am in very *s* straits, as
Ps 31:9 for I am in *s* straits
66:14 when I was in *s* straits
69:17 Because I am in *s* straits
102:2 day that I am in *s* straits
La 1:20 for I am in *s* straits
Ho 5:15 When they are in *s* straits

Sorek
Jg 16:4 torrent valley of *S*, and her

Sorely
1Sa 1:6 rival wife also vexed her *s*
Mt 26:37 grieved and to be *s* troubled
Mr 14:33 and to be *s* troubled

Sorrel
Isa 30:24 eat fodder seasoned with *s*

Sorrow
De 25:12 Your eye must feel no *s*
Isa 3:26 mourn and express *s*, and
19:8 must express *s*, and even
Jer 13:14 compassion, nor feel any *s*
1Th 4:13 not *s* just as the rest also

Sorrowing
2Co 6:10 as *s* but ever rejoicing, as

Sorry
Ge 45:20 do not let your eye feel *s*
De 7:16 eye must not feel *s* for them
13:8 nor should your eye feel *s*
19:13 Your eye should not feel *s*
19:21 your eye should not feel *s*
1Sa 24:10 I felt *s* for you and said
Ne 13:22 do feel *s* for me according
Ps 72:13 feel *s* for the lowly one
Isa 13:18 their eye will not feel *s*
Jer 21:7 He will not feel *s* for them
Eze 5:11 my eye will not feel *s* and I
7:4 my eye will not feel *s* for
7:9 Neither will my eye feel *s*
8:18 My eye will not feel *s*
9:5 Let not your eye feel *s*, and
9:10 my eye will not feel *s*
16:5 No eye felt *s* for you to do
20:17 my eye began to feel *s* for
24:14 shall I feel *s* nor feel
Joe 2:17 Do feel *s*, O Jehovah, for
Jon 4:10 felt *s* for the bottle-gourd
4:11 feel *s* for Nineveh the great

Sort
Ge 4:22 forger of every *s* of tool
6:19 creature of every *s* of flesh
6:21 take for yourself every *s* of
7:15 two by two, of every *s* of

Ge 7:16 male and female of every s
8:17 every s of flesh . . . bring out
24:10 with every s of good thing
44:15 What s of deed is this that
Ex 35:31 in every s of craftsmanship
35:33 ingenious products of every s
35:35 men doing every s of work
Le 11:34 Any s of food that may be
17:10 eats any s of blood, I shall
17:14 soul of every s of flesh is
17:14 not eat the blood of any s of
17:14 soul of every s of flesh is
23:3 You may do no s of work
23:7 No s of laborious work may
23:8 No s of laborious work may
23:21 No s of laborious work
23:25 No s of laborious work may
23:28 do no s of work on this very
23:30 s of work on this very day
23:31 You must do no s of work
23:35 No s of laborious work may
23:36 No s of laborious work may
24:20 s of defect he may cause in
27:28 s of devoted thing that a
27:28 s of devoted thing may be
Nu 16:22 spirits of every s of flesh
18:15 of every s of flesh, which
18:29 every s of contribution to
28:18 No s of laborious work must
28:25 No s of laborious work must
28:26 No s of laborious work must
29:1 No s of laborious work must
29:7 No s of work must you do
29:12 No s of laborious work must
29:35 No s of laborious work must
31:30 every s of domestic animal
De 14:3 detestable thing of any s
14:4 s of beast that you may eat
14:7 Only this s you must not eat
14:9 This s out of everything that
16:21 any s of tree as a sacred
24:10 a loan of any s, you must
Jg 8:1 What s of thing is this that
8:18 What s of men were they
13:14 no unclean thing of any s let
18:10 is no lack of any s of thing
Ru 4:7 to establish every s of thing
1Sa 4:8 every s of slaughter in the
1Ki 7:14 every s of work in copper
8:37 any s of plague, any
8:37 plague, any s of malady
9:13 What s of cities are these
2Ki 8:9 every s of good thing of
9:11 the man and his s of talk
12:13 any s of gold article and
1Ch 22:15 skillful in every s of work
2Ch 2:14 cutting every s of engraving
2:14 designing every s of device
6:28 any s of plague and any
6:28 and any s of malady
15:6 with every s of distress
28:4 every s of luxuriant tree
Ne 5:18 every s of wine in abundance
10:35 fruitage of every s of tree
10:37 fruitage of every s of tree
13:15 figs and every s of burden
13:16 every s of merchandise and
13:20 every s of merchandise spent
Job 39:8 every s of green plant it
Ps 71:22 instrument of a stringed s
107:18 detest even every s of food
144:13 products of one s after
Pr 5:14 to be in every s of badness
6:35 for any s of ransom, neither
Ec 2:10 heart from any s of rejoicing
12:14 bring every s of work into
Ca 3:6 every s of scent powder of a
Isa 16:14 much commotion of every s
22:24 the vessels of the small s
22:24 vessels of the bowl s as
35:9 rapacious s of wild beasts
Jer 44:4 detestable s of thing that
La 3:55 from a pit of the lowest s
Eze 39:4 birds of every s of wing
39:17 birds of every s of wing
Joe 2:28 spirit on every s of flesh
Ob 15 Your s of treatment will return
Hag 2:12 wine or oil or any s of food
Zec 14:15 every s of domestic animal
Mt 4:23 and curing every s of disease
4:23 every s of infirmity among
5:11 say every s of wicked thing
8:27 What s of person is this
9:35 curing every s of disease and
Mt 9:35 and every s of infirmity
10:1 to cure every s of disease
10:1 and every s of infirmity
12:31 Every s of sin and blasphemy
19:3 his wife on every s of ground
23:27 of every s of uncleanness
Mr 4:33 many illustrations of that s
13:1 what s of stones and what
13:1 and what s of buildings!
Lu 1:29 what s of greeting this might
4:36 What s of speech is this
12:15 every s of covetousness
16:16 every s of person is pressing
Joh 1:9 gives light to every s of man
9:16 perform signs of that s
12:33 s of death he was about to
18:32 s of death he was destined
21:19 what s of death he would
Ac 2:17 spirit upon every s of flesh
7:49 What s of house will you
10:11 s of vessel descending like
11:5 some s of vessel descending
13:10 full of every s of fraud and
13:10 and every s of villainy, you
Ro 7:8 in me covetousness of every s
16:18 For men of that s are slaves
1Co 3:13 what s of work each one's is
15:35 what s of body are they
15:40 heavenly bodies is one s
15:40 earthly . . . is a different s
15:41 glory of the sun is one s
16:18 recognize men of that s
2Co 1:4 those in any s of tribulation
3:4 s of confidence toward God
9:11 for every s of generosity
Ga 1:6 over to another s of good news
2:6 s of men they formerly were
5:8 This s of persuasion is not
Eph 4:19 uncleanness of every s with
5:3 uncleanness of every s or
5:9 of every s of goodness and
Php 2:29 holding men of that s dear
1Th 1:5 you know what s of men we
2Ti 3:11 the s of things that happened
3:11 the s of persecutions I have
Tit 1:16 for good work of any s
2:14 from every s of lawlessness
Heb 10:39 the s that shrink back to
10:39 s that have faith to the
Jas 1:24 forgets what s of man he is
1Pe 1:11 what s of season the spirit
2Pe 3:11 what s of persons ought you
1Jo 2:19 but they were not of our s
2:19 if they had been of our s
2:19 that not all are of our s
3:1 See what s of love the Father
Re 11:6 every s of plague as often as
18:12 every s of ivory object and
18:12 s of object out of most
21:19 every s of precious stone

Sorts

Ge 40:17 all s of eatables for Pharaoh
Ex 9:6 all s of livestock of Egypt
9:25 all s of vegetation of the
9:25 all s of trees of the field
35:22 all s of articles of gold
Le 19:19 domestic animals of two s
19:19 field with seeds of two s
19:19 garment of two s of thread
Nu 27:16 the spirits of all s of flesh
De 22:9 vineyard with two s of seed
25:13 in your bag two s of weights
25:14 two s of ephahs, a great one
2Sa 6:5 with all s of instruments of
1Ch 18:10 all s of articles of gold
2Ch 16:14 different s of ointment
32:28 the different s of beasts
Pr 1:13 all s of precious valuables
20:10 Two s of weights and two
20:10 and two s of ephah measures
20:23 Two s of weights are
Ec 2:5 in them fruit trees of all s
Ca 4:10 oils than all s of perfume
4:14 all s of trees of frankincense
7:13 all s of the choicest fruits
Eze 27:12 all s of valuable things
27:22 finest of all s of perfumes
27:22 all s of precious stones
39:20 all s of warriors, is the
47:12 all s of trees for food
Da 1:17 all s of visions and dreams
3:5 all s of musical instruments
3:7 all s of musical instruments
Da 3:10 all s of musical instruments
3:15 all s of musical instruments
Na 2:9 all s of desirable articles
Joh 1:7 people of all s might believe
12:32 draw men of all s to me
Ac 10:12 s of four-footed creatures
Ro 5:18 result to men of all s was
5:18 result to men of all s is
1Co 9:22 all things to people of all s
1Ti 2:1 concerning all s of men
2:4 all s of men should be saved
4:10 is a Savior of all s of men
6:10 all s of injurious things
Tit 2:11 salvation to all s of men
1Pe 2:1 envies and all s of backbiting
2:17 Honor men of all s, have

Sosipater

Ro 16:21 and Jason and S my relatives

Sosthenes

Ac 18:17 S the presiding officer of
1Co 1:1 Paul . . . and S our brother

Sotai

Ezr 2:55 The sons of S
Ne 7:57 the sons of S, the sons of

Sought

De 13:10 he has s to turn you away
32:37 rock in whom they s refuge
1Sa 19:10 Saul s to pin David to the
2Sa 21:2 Saul s to strike them down
1Ch 26:31 were s out, and valiant
Es 2:23 s out and eventually found out
6:2 s to lay hand on King Ahasuerus
Pr 14:6 ridiculer has s to find
31:13 She has s wool and linen
Ec 7:28 my soul has continuously s
7:29 mankind . . . s out many plans
12:10 congregator s to find the
Ca 3:1 s the one whom my soul has
3:1 I s him, but I did not find
3:2 I s him, but I did not find
5:6 I s him, but I did not find
Isa 9:13 of armies they have not s
Jer 8:2 and that they have s
Eze 26:21 and you will be s for, but
34:4 one you have not s to find
Ob 6 treasures have been s out
Zep 1:6 have not s Jehovah and have
Lu 20:19 s to get their hands on him
Ac 13:7 earnestly s to hear the word
16:10 s to go forth into Macedonia
Ga 4:18 s for in a fine cause at all
Heb 8:7 have been s for a second
12:17 s a change of mind with

Soul

Ge 1:21 every living s that moves
1:30 there is life as a s I have
2:7 the man came to be a living s
2:19 each living s, that was its
9:4 its s—its blood—you must not
9:5 shall I ask back the s of man
9:10 every living s that is with
9:12 every living s that is with
9:15 living s among all flesh
9:16 living s among all flesh
12:13 s will be certain to live
17:14 s must be cut off from his
19:17 Escape for your s! Do not
19:19 to preserve my s alive
19:20 and my s will live on
27:4 s may bless you before I die
27:19 that your s may bless me
27:25 that my s may bless you
27:31 that your s may bless me
32:30 and yet my s was delivered
34:3 his s began clinging to Dinah
34:8 s is attached to your daughter
35:18 as her s was going out
37:21 not strike his s fatally
42:21 we saw the distress of his s
44:30 that one's s is bound up
44:30 bound up with this one's s
49:6 do not come, O my s
Ex 4:19 hunting for your s are dead
12:15 that s must be cut off from
12:16 what every s needs to eat
12:19 that s must be cut off from
15:9 My s will be filled with
21:23, 23 you must give s for s
21:30 redemption price for his s
23:9 the s of the alien resident
30:12 give a ransom for his s to

Ex 31:14 that s must be cut off from
Le 2:1 some s would present as an
4:2 In case a s sins by mistake in
4:27 if any s of the people of the
5:1 in case a s sins in that he has
5:2 s touches some unclean thing
5:4 Or in case a s swears to the
5:15 a s behaves unfaithfully in
5:17 if a s sins in that he does
6:2 In case a s sins in that he
7:18 the s that eats some of it
7:20 the s who eats the flesh of
7:20 that s must be cut off from
7:21 a s touches anything unclean
7:21 that s must be cut off from
7:25 s that eats must be cut off
7:27 Any s who eats any blood
7:27 that s must be cut off from
11:10 s that is in the waters
11:46 every living s that moves
11:46 s that swarms upon the earth
17:10 set my face against the s
17:11 s of the flesh is in the
17:11 atonement by the s in it
17:12 No s of you must eat blood
17:14 s of . . . flesh is its blood
17:14 is its blood by the s in it
17:14 s of every sort of flesh is
17:15 any s that eats a body
19:8 s must be cut off from his
19:28 cuts . . . for a deceased s
20:6 s who turns himself to the
20:6 face against that s and cut
21:1 deceased s no one may defile
21:11 should not come to any dead s
22:3 s must be cut off from before
22:4 unclean by a deceased s or a
22:6 s who touches any such must
22:11 priest should purchase a s
23:29 s that will not be afflicted
23:30 s that will do any sort of
23:30 destroy that s from among
24:17 s of mankind fatally, he
24:18 fatal striker of the s of a
24:18, 18 for it, s for s
26:11 my s will not abhor you
26:16 making the s pine away
26:30 my s will simply abhor you
Nu 5:2 unclean by a deceased s
5:6 that s has also become guilty
6:6 not come toward any dead s
6:11 sinned because of the dead s
9:6 unclean by a human s so that
9:7 We are unclean by a human s
9:10 unclean by a s or off on a
9:13 s must then be cut off from
11:6 But now our s is dried away
15:27 any s should sin by mistake
15:28 the s who made a mistake
15:30 the s that does something
15:30 that s must be cut off from
15:31 s should be cut off without
19:11 the corpse of any human s
19:13 a corpse, the s of whatever
19:13 that s must be cut off from
19:20 that s must be cut off from
19:22 the s who touches it will be
21:4 s of the people began tiring
21:5 our s has come to abhor the
23:10 Let my s die the death of
30:2 vow of abstinence upon his s
30:4 that she has bound upon her s
30:4 that she has bound upon her s
30:5 that she has bound upon her s
30:6 that she has bound upon her s
30:7 that she has bound upon her s
30:8 that she bound upon her s
30:9 bound upon her s will stand
30:10 vow upon her s by an oath
30:11 she has bound upon her s
30:12 an abstinence vow of her s
30:13 vow to afflict the s, her
31:19 Everyone who has killed a s
31:28 one s out of five hundred, of
35:11 strikes a s unintentionally
35:15 strikes a s unintentionally
35:30 Every fatal striker of a s
35:30 testify against a s for him
35:31 for the s of a murderer who
De 4:9 take good care of your s, that
4:29 heart and with all your s
6:5 all your heart and all your s
10:12 your heart and all your s
11:13 your heart and all your s
De 11:18 to your heart and your s and
12:15 whenever your s craves it
12:20 your s craves to eat meat
12:20 whenever your s craves it
12:21 whenever your s craves it
12:23 the blood is the s and you
12:23 not eat the s with the flesh
13:3 all your heart and all your s
13:6 who is like your own s
14:26 whatever your s may crave
14:26 anything that your s may ask
18:6 any craving of his s
19:6 indeed strike his s fatally
19:11 and struck his s fatally
19:21, 21 s will be for s, eye for
21:14 agreeably to her own s
22:26 indeed murders him, even a s
23:24 for you to satisfy your s
24:6 it is a s that he is seizing
24:7 kidnapping a s of his brothers
24:15 lifting up his s to his
26:16 all your heart and all your s
27:25 bribe to strike a s fatally
28:65 of the eyes and despair of s
30:2 all your heart and all your s
30:6 all your heart and all your s
30:10 all your heart and all your s
Jos 10:28 every s that was in it to
10:30 striking it and every s
10:32 and every s that was in it
10:35 every s that was in it to
10:37 all its towns and every s
10:37 and every s that was in it
10:39 devoting every s that was
11:11 every s that was in it with
20:3 strikes a s unintentionally
20:9 strikes a s unintentionally
22:5 heart and with all your s
Jg 5:21 You went treading . . . O my s
9:17 risking his s that he might
10:16 his s became impatient
12:3 to put my s in my own palm
16:16 his s got to be impatient to
16:30 Let my s die with the
18:25 men bitter of s may assault
18:25 forfeit your own s and the
18:25 forfeit . . . the s of your
Ru 4:15 become a restorer of your s
1Sa 1:10 she was bitter of s, and she
1:15 pour out my s before Jehovah
1:26 By the life of your s, my
2:16 whatever your s may crave
2:33 and to make your s pine away
2:35 is in my heart and in my s
17:55 By the life of your s, O
18:1 Jonathan's very s became
18:1 bound up with the s of David
18:1 to love him as his own s
18:3 his loving him as his own s
19:5 put his s in his palm and
19:11 s escape tonight, tomorrow
20:1 for he is seeking for my s
20:3 as your s is living, there
20:4 s may say I shall do for you
20:17 for as he loved his own s
22:2 all men bitter in s began
22:22 wronged every s of the
22:23 for whoever looks for my s
22:23 looks for your s, for you
23:15 look for his s while David
23:20 craving of your s, O king
24:11 lying in wait for my s to
25:26 and as your s is living
25:29 and look for your s
25:29 s of my lord will certainly
25:29 s of your enemies, he will
26:21 my s has been precious
26:24 s was great this day in my
26:24 may my s be great in the
28:9 a trapper against my s
28:21 put my s in my palm and
30:6 s of all the people had
2Sa 1:9 all my s is yet in me
3:21 over all that your s craves
4:8 enemy who looked for your s
4:9 Jehovah who redeemed my s out
5:8 hateful to the s of David
11:11 as your s is living, I shall
13:39 s of David the king longed
14:7 for the s of his brother
14:14 God will not take away a s
14:19 As your s is living, O my
16:11 son . . . is looking for my s
17:8 they are bitter of s, like a
2Sa 18:13 treacherously against his s
19:5 providing escape for your s
19:5 for the s of your sons and
19:5 and the s of your wives
19:5 and the s of your concubines
1Ki 1:12 escape for your own s and
1:12 the s of your son Solomon
1:29 redeemed my s out of all
2:4 heart and with all their s
2:23 against his own s that
3:11 nor requested the s of your
8:48 heart and with all their s
11:37 over all that your s craves
17:21 the s of this child to come
17:22 s of the child came back
19:2 make your s like the
19:2 like the s of each one of
19:3 and began to go for his s
19:4 ask that his s might die
19:4 take my s away, for I am
19:10 looking for my s to take it
19:14 looking for my s to take it
20:31 will preserve your s alive
20:32 Please, let my s live
20:39 your s will also have to
20:39 to take the place of his s
20:42 your s must take the place
20:42 take the place of his s
2Ki 1:13 please let my s and the
1:13 the s of these fifty servants
1:14 let my s be precious in your
2:2 and as your s is living
2:4 and as your s is living
2:6 as your s is living, I will
4:27 her s is bitter within her
4:30 as your s is living, I will
7:7 they kept fleeing for their s
9:15 If your s agrees, do not let
10:24 one's s will go for the
10:24 will go for the other's s
23:3 with all the heart and . . . s
23:25 heart and with all his s
1Ch 22:19 set your heart and your s to
28:9 with a delightful s; for all
2Ch 1:11 for the s of those hating you
6:38 heart and with all their s
15:12 heart and with all their s
34:31 heart and with all his s
Es 4:13 imagine within your own s
7:3 be given me my own s at my
7:7 request for his s from Esther
9:31 imposed upon their own s and
Job 2:4 will give in behalf of his s
2:6 Only watch out for his s
3:20 And life to those bitter of s
6:7 My s has refused to touch
6:11 should keep prolonging my s
7:11 with the bitterness of my s
7:15 my s chooses suffocation
9:21 I would not know my s
10:1 My s . . . feels a loathing
10:1 in the bitterness of my s
11:20 hope . . . expiring of the s
12:10 is the s of everyone alive
13:14 place my own s in my palm
14:22 his own s . . . keep mourning
16:4 souls existed where my s is
18:4 tearing his s to pieces in
19:2 you men keep irritating my s
21:25 will die with a bitter s
23:13 And his own s has a desire
24:12 s of deadly wounded ones
27:2 who has made my s bitter
27:8 In case God carries off his s
30:16 my s is poured out within
30:25 s has grieved for the poor
31:30 for an oath against his s
31:39 the s of its owners I have
32:2 his own s righteous rather
33:18 his s back from the pit
33:20 his own s desirable food
33:22 his s draws near to the pit
33:28 redeemed my s from passing
33:30 his s back from the pit
36:14 Their s will die in youth
41:21 Its s itself sets coals
Ps 3:2 Many are saying of my s
6:3 s has been very much disturbed
6:4 O Jehovah, do rescue my s
7:2 tear my s to pieces as a lion
7:5 Let an enemy pursue my s
10:3 the selfish longing of his s
11:1 dare you men say to my s
11:5 His s certainly hates

Ps 13:2 set resistance in my s
16:10 will not leave my s in Sheol
17:9 The enemies against my s
17:13 do provide escape for my s
19:7 perfect, bringing back the s
22:20 deliver from the sword my s
22:29 preserve his own s alive
23:3 My s he refreshes. He leads
24:4 Who has not carried My s to
25:1 Jehovah, I raise my very s
25:13 s will lodge in goodness
25:20 Do guard my s and deliver me
26:9 Do not take away my s along
27:12 to the s of my adversaries
30:3 my s from Sheol itself
31:7 about the distresses of my s
31:9 weak, my s and my belly
31:13 to take away my s that they
33:19 deliver their s from death
33:20 s has been in expectation of
34:2 my s will make its boast
34:22 Jehovah is redeeming the s
35:3 Say to my s: I am your
35:4 who are hunting for my s
35:7 they have dug it for my s
35:9 my own s be joyful in Jehovah
35:12 Bereavement to my s
35:13 fasting I afflicted my s
35:17 my s from their ravages
35:25 in their heart: Aha, our s!
38:12 those seeking my s lay out
40:14 seeking my s to sweep it
41:2 over to the s of his enemies
41:4 heal my s, for I have sinned
42:1 very s longs for you, O God
42:2 My s indeed thirsts for God
42:4 will pour out my s within me
42:5 are you in despair, O my s
42:6 my very s is in despair
42:11 are you in despair, O my s
43:5 are you in despair, O my s
44:25 our s has bowed down to the
49:8 redemption price of their s
49:15 my s from the hand of Sheol
49:18 he kept blessing his own s
49:19 His s finally comes only
54:3 And tyrants that do seek my s
54:4 among those supporting my s
55:18 put my s in peace from the
56:6 they have waited for my s
56:13 delivered my s from death
57:1 in you my s has taken refuge
57:4 s is in the middle of lions
57:6 My s has become bowed down
59:3 have lain in wait for my s
62:1 toward God is my s waiting in
62:5 wait silently, O my s
63:1 My s does thirst for you
63:5 fatness, my s is satisfied
63:8 My s has closely followed you
63:9 those who keep seeking my s
66:9 He is setting our s in life
66:16 What he has done for my s
69:1 have come clear to the s
69:10 with the fasting of my s
69:18 near to my s, reclaim it
70:2 abashed who are seeking my s
71:10 ones keeping watch for my s
71:13 end, who are resisting my s
71:23 my s that you have redeemed
72:14 he will redeem their s
74:19 the s of your turtledove
77:2 s has refused to be comforted
78:18 something to eat for their s
78:50 hold back their s from death
84:2 My s has yearned and also
86:2 do guard my s, for I am loyal
86:4 s of your servant rejoice
86:4 I lift up my very s
86:13 delivered my s out of Sheol
86:14 have looked for my s
88:3 s has had enough of
88:14 that you cast off my s
89:48 escape for his s from the
94:17 s would have resided in
94:19 began to fondle my s
94:21 sharp attacks on the s of the
103:1 Bless Jehovah, O my s
103:2 Bless Jehovah, O my s
103:22 Bless Jehovah, O my s
104:1 Bless Jehovah, O my s
104:35 Bless Jehovah, O my s
105:18 Into irons his s came
105:22 princes agreeably to his s
Ps 106:15 disease into their s
107:5 s within them began to faint
107:9 satisfied the dried-out s
107:9 hungry s he has filled with
107:18 s got to detest even every
107:26 very s finds itself melting
109:20 speaking evil against my s
109:31 from those judging his s
116:4 do provide my s with escape
116:7 your resting-place, O my s
116:8 have rescued my s from death
119:20 s is crushed with longing
119:25 s has been cleaving to the
119:28 s has been sleepless from
119:81 salvation my s has pined
119:109 s is in my palm constantly
119:129 why my s has observed
119:167 s has kept your reminders
119:175 s keep living and praising
120:2 Jehovah, do deliver my s
120:6 time my s has tabernacled
121:7 He will guard your s
123:4 s has been glutted with the
124:4 would have passed over our s
124:5 have passed over our s
124:7 Our s is like a bird that
130:5 Jehovah, my s has hoped
130:6 My s has waited for Jehovah
131:2 soothed and quieted my s
131:2 s is like a weanling upon me
138:3 bold in my s with strength
139:14 my s is very well aware
141:8 Do not pour out my s
142:4 no one inquiring for my s
142:7 my s out of the very dungeon
143:3 the enemy has pursued my s
143:6 s is like an exhausted land
143:8 to you I have lifted up my s
143:11 forth my s out of distress
143:12 showing hostility to my s
146:1 Praise Jehovah, O my s
Pr 1:19 the very s of its owners
2:10 pleasant to your very s
3:22 life to your s and charm
6:16 things detestable to his s
6:26 hunts even for a precious s
6:30 thievery to fill his s when
6:32 bringing his own s to ruin
7:23 that it involves his very s
8:36 is doing violence to his s
10:3 s of the righteous one to go
11:17 rewardingly with his own s
11:25 generous s will itself be
12:10 the s of his domestic animal
13:2 s of those dealing
13:3 his mouth is keeping his s
13:4 but his s has nothing
13:4 s of the diligent ones will
13:8 ransom for a man's s is his
13:19 is pleasurable to the s
13:25 the satisfaction of his s
14:10 of the bitterness of one's s
15:32 is rejecting his own s, but
16:17 his way is keeping his s
16:24 sweet to the s and a healing
16:26 The s of the hard worker has
18:7 his lips are a snare for his s
19:2 that the s should be without
19:8 heart is loving his own s
19:15 and a slack s goes hungry
19:16 is keeping his s
20:2 is sinning against his own s
21:10 very s of the wicked one has
21:23 his s from distresses
22:5 that is guarding his s keeps
22:23 rob of s those robbing them
22:25 take a snare for your s
23:7 has calculated within his s
23:14 may deliver his very s from
24:12 that is observing your s
24:14 do know wisdom for your s
25:13 the very s of his masters
25:25 As cold water upon a tired s
27:7 A s that is satisfied will
27:7 but to a hungry s every bitter
27:9 due to the counsel of the s
28:17 with the bloodguilt for a s
28:25 is arrogant in s stirs up
29:10 seeking for the s of each one
29:17 give much pleasure to your s
29:24 is hating his own s
31:6 to those who are bitter of s
Ec 2:24 and cause his s to see good
4:8 my s to lack in good things
Ec 6:2 s, is in no need of anything
6:3 s is not satisfied with good
6:7 own s does not get filled
6:9 the walking about of the s
7:28 my s has continuously sought
Ca 1:7 O you whom my s has loved
3:1 the one whom my s has loved
3:2 the one whom my s has loved
3:3 whom my s has loved have you
3:4 I found the one whom my s has
5:6 My very s had gone out of me
6:12 my own s had put me at the
Isa 1:14 seasons my s has hated
3:9 Woe to their s! For they
3:20 and the houses of the s
5:14 has made its s spacious
10:18 the s clear to the flesh
15:4 s has quivered within him
19:10 wage workers grieved in s
26:8 the desire of the s has been
26:9 s I have desired you in the
29:8 awakes and his s is empty
29:8 tired and his s is dried out
32:6 s of the hungry one to go
38:15 in the bitterness of my s
38:17 s and kept it from the pit
42:1 whom my s has approved
43:4 groups in place of your s
44:20 he does not deliver his s
46:2 captivity their own s must
47:14 deliver their s from the
49:7 to him that is despised in s
51:23 said to your s, Bow down
53:10 his s as a guilt offering
53:11 the trouble of his s he
53:12 he poured out his s to the
55:2 s find its exquisite delight
55:3 and your s will keep alive
58:3 did we afflict our s and you
58:5 man to afflict his s
58:10 s that is being afflicted
58:11 satisfy your s even in a
61:10 My s will be joyful in my
66:3 very s has taken a delight
Jer 2:24 craving of her s, snuffing
3:11 own s to be more righteous
4:10 has reached clear to the s
4:19 horn is what my s has heard
4:30 keep seeking for your very s
4:31 my s is tired of the killers
5:9 should not my s avenge itself?
5:29 should not my s avenge
6:8 s may not turn away disgusted
9:9 should not my s avenge itself?
11:21 seeking for your s, saying
12:7 my s into the palm of her
13:17 my s will weep because of
14:19 your s abhorred even Zion
15:1 my s would not be toward
15:9 s has struggled for breath
18:20 excavated a pit for my s
19:7 those seeking for their s
19:9 those seeking for their s
20:13 delivered the s of the poor
21:7 who are seeking for their s
21:9 his s will certainly come to
22:25 who are seeking for your s
22:27 lifting up their s to return
31:12 s will simply become like
31:14 s of the priests with
31:25 will saturate the tired s
31:25 languishing s I will fill
32:41 my heart and with all my s
34:16 free agreeably to their s
34:20 those seeking for their s
34:21 those seeking for their s
38:2 his s as a spoil and alive
38:16 who has made for us this s
38:16 who are seeking for your s
38:17 s will also certainly keep
38:20 s will continue to live
39:18 to have your s as a spoil
40:14 to strike you to the s
40:15 he strike you to the s, and
43:6 every s that Nebuzaradan the
44:30 those seeking for his s
44:30 the one seeking for his s
45:5 give you your s as a spoil
46:26 those seeking for their s
49:37 those seeking for their s
50:19 his s will be satisfied
51:6 each one for his own s
51:14 has sworn by his own s, I
51:45 each one his s with escape

La 1:11 eat, in order to refresh the s
1:16 someone to refresh my s
1:19 they might refresh their s
2:12 s being poured out into the
2:19 of the s of your children
3:17 there is no peace for my s
3:20 your s will remember and bow
3:24 is my share, my s has said
3:25 s that keeps seeking for him
3:51 has dealt severely with my s
3:58 contests of my s. You have
5:9 At the risk of our s we bring
Eze 3:19 have delivered your own s
3:21 have delivered your own s
4:14 My s is not a defiled one
14:14 would deliver their s, is
14:20 would deliver their s
16:5 was an abhorring of your s
18:4 As the s of the father so
18:4 so likewise the s of the son
18:4 s that is sinning . . . die
18:20 s that is sinning . . . die
18:27 preserve his own s alive
22:25 A s they actually devour
23:17 her s began to turn away
23:18 my s turned away disgusted
23:18 my s had turned away
23:22 your s has turned away in
23:28 your s has turned away
24:25 the longing of their s
25:6 s against the soil of Israel
25:15 with scorn in the s, in
27:31 over you in bitterness of s
32:10 each one for his own s
33:5 his own s would have escaped
33:6 and takes away from them s
33:9 deliver your own s
36:5 with scorn in the s, for the
47:9 every living s that swarms
Ho 4:8 they keep lifting up their s
9:4 their bread is for their own s
Am 2:14 provide his s with escape
2:15 provide his s with escape
6:8 Jehovah has sworn by his . . . s
Jon 1:14 because of the s of this man
2:5 encircled me clear to the s
2:7 my s fainted away within me
4:3 take away, please, my s from
4:8 asking that his s might die
Mic 6:7 for the sin of my s
7:1 fig, that my s would desire
7:3 the craving of his s, his
Hab 2:4 His s has been swelled up
2:5 his s spacious just like Sheol
2:10 and your s is sinning
Hag 2:13 unclean by a deceased s
Zec 11:8 s gradually became impatient
11:8 their own s felt a loathing
Mt 2:20 the s of the young child
6:25 the s mean more than food
10:28 body but cannot kill the s
10:28 can destroy both s and body
10:39 finds his s will lose it
10:39 that loses his s for my sake
12:18 beloved, whom my s approved
16:25 whoever wants to save his s
16:25 loses his s for my sake
16:26 world but forfeits his s
16:26 give in exchange for his s
20:28 to give his s a ransom in
22:37 with your whole s and with
26:38 My s is deeply grieved, even
Mr 3:4 to save or to kill a s
8:35 whoever wants to save his s
8:35 whoever loses his s for the
8:36 and to forfeit his s
8:37 give in exchange for his s
10:45 s a ransom in exchange for
12:30 with your whole s and with
14:34 My s is deeply grieved, even
Lu 1:46 My s magnifies Jehovah
2:35 will be run through the s of
6:9 to save or to destroy a s
9:24 whoever wants to save his s
9:24 loses his s for my sake
10:27 with your whole s and with
12:19 and I will say to my s
12:19 S, you have many good things
12:20 they are demanding your s
12:23 s is worth more than food
14:26 yes, and even his own s
17:33 seeks to keep his s safe for
Joh 10:11 shepherd surrenders his s
10:15 I surrender my s in behalf
Joh 10:17 I surrender my s, in order
12:25 He that is fond of his s
12:25 hates his s in this world
12:27 Now my s is troubled, and
13:37 surrender my s in your
13:38 surrender your s in my
15:13 s in behalf of his friends
Ac 2:27 will not leave my s in Hades
2:43 began to fall upon every s
3:23 s that does not listen to
4:32 had one heart and s, and not
20:10 for his s is in him
20:24 not make my s of any account
27:22 not a s of you will be lost
Ro 2:9 s of every man who works what
11:3 they are looking for my s
13:1 s be in subjection to the
16:4 have risked . . . necks for my s
1Co 15:45 Adam became a living s
2Co 1:23 a witness against my own s
Php 1:27 with one s striving side by
2:2 being joined together in s
2:19 that I may be a cheerful s
2:30 exposing his s to danger
1Th 5:23 the spirit and s and body
Heb 4:12 the dividing of s and spirit
6:19 have as an anchor for the s
10:38 my s has no pleasure in
10:39 preserving alive of the s
Jas 5:20 save his s from death and
1Pe 2:11 a conflict against the s
2Pe 2:8 tormenting his righteous s by
1Jo 3:16 surrendered his s for us
3Jo 2 just as your s is prospering
Re 16:3 every living s died, yes, the
18:14 fruit that your s desired

Soulful

Pr 19:18 do not lift up your s desire
23:2 you are the owner of s desire
Isa 56:11 dogs strong in s desire
58:10 your own s desire, and you
Jer 44:14 lifting up their s desire
Eze 16:27 the s desire of the women

Soul's

Eze 24:21 object of your s compassion

Souls

Ge 1:20 a swarm of living s and let
1:24 the earth put forth living s
9:5 your blood of your s shall I
12:5 s whom they had acquired in
14:21 Give me the s, but take the
23:8 If your s agree to bury my
36:6 Esau took . . . s of his house
46:15 All the s of his sons and of
46:18 these to Jacob: sixteen s
46:22 All the s were fourteen
46:25 all the s were seven
46:26 All the s who came to Jacob
46:26 All the s were sixty-six
46:27 to him in Egypt were two s
46:27 the s of the house of Jacob
Ex 1:5 s who issued out of Jacob's
1:5 came to be seventy s, but
12:4 according to the number of s
16:16 to the number of the s that
30:15 make atonement for your s
30:16 make atonement for your s
Le 11:43 not make your s loathsome
11:44 not make your s unclean by
16:29 you should afflict your s
16:31 you must afflict your s
17:11 atonement for your s
18:29 s doing them must be cut off
20:25 s loathsome with the beast
23:27 afflict your s and present
23:32 afflict your s on the ninth
26:15 s will abhor my judicial
26:43 s had abhorred my statutes
27:2 a special vow offering of s
Nu 16:38 sinned against their own s
19:18 s that happened to be there
29:7 and you must afflict your s
31:35 human s from the women who
31:35 s were thirty-two thousand
31:40 And the human s were sixteen
31:40 the tax . . . was thirty-two s
31:46 human s, sixteen thousand
31:50 to make atonement for our s
De 4:15 take good care of your s
10:22 seventy s your forefathers
Jos 2:13 deliver our s from death
2:14 Our s are to die instead of
Jos 9:24 afraid for our s because of
23:11 guard for your s by loving
23:14 with all your s that not
Jg 5:18 scorned their s to the point
2Sa 23:17 at the risk of their s
2Ki 12:4 the money for the s
1Ch 5:21 human s a hundred thousand
11:19 drink at the risk of their s
11:19 at the risk of their s that
Es 8:11 and stand for their s
9:16 there was a stand for their s
Job 16:4 If only your s existed where
Ps 72:13 s of the poor ones he will
97:10 guarding the s of his loyal
Pr 1:18 in concealment for their s
11:30 that is winning s is wise
14:25 true witness is delivering s
Jer 2:34 s of the innocent poor ones
6:16 find ease for your s
17:21 Watch out for your s, and
26:19 calamity against our s
37:9 Do not deceive your s
42:20 error against your s
44:7 great calamity to your s
48:6 provide escape for your s
52:29 eight hundred and thirty-two s
52:30 seven hundred and forty-five s
52:30 s were four thousand and
Eze 7:19 s they will not satisfy
13:18 in order to hunt s! Are the
13:18 that you women hunt down
13:18 s belonging to you the ones
13:19 the s that ought not to die
13:19 the s that ought not to live
13:20 are hunting down the s as
13:20 s that you are hunting down
13:20 s as though they were
17:17 in order to cut off many s
18:4 All the s—to me they belong
22:27 in destroying s for the
27:13 For the s of mankind and
Mt 6:25 being anxious about your s
11:29 find refreshment for your s
Lu 12:22 being anxious about your s
21:19 you will acquire your s
Joh 10:24 to keep our s in suspense
Ac 2:41 three thousand s were added
7:14 number of seventy-five s
14:2 s of people of the nations
14:22 strengthening the s of the
15:24 trying to subvert your s
15:26 delivered up their s for the
27:10 and great loss . . . of our s
27:37 s in the boat were about
2Co 12:15 completely spent for your s
1Th 2:8 but also our own s, because
5:14 speak . . . to the depressed s
Heb 12:3 tired and give out in your s
13:17 keeping watch over your s
Jas 1:21 is able to save your s
1Pe 1:9 the salvation of your s
1:22 purified your s by your
2:25 and overseer of your s
3:20 eight s, were carried safely
4:19 commending their s to a
2Pe 2:14 and they entice unsteady s
1Jo 3:16 surrender our s for our
Re 6:9 the s of those slaughtered
8:9 which have s died, and a third
12:11 not love their s even in
18:13 and slaves and human s
20:4 s of those executed with the

Sound

Ge 33:18 Jacob came safe and s to
37:14 brothers are safe and s and
37:14 the flock is safe and s
Ex 12:5 sheep should prove to be s, a
19:16 and a very loud s of a horn
19:19 the s of the horn became
20:18 the s of the horn and the
28:35 s from him must be heard
29:1 bull, and two rams, s ones
32:18 the s of the singing over
32:18 s of the singing of defeat
32:18 the s of other singing that
Le 1:3 a s one, is what he should
1:10 a s one, is what he will
3:1 a s one is what he will
3:6 a s one is what he will
4:3 a s young bull to Jehovah as a
4:23 kid of the goats, a s one
4:28 of the goats, a s one, for
4:32 a s female lamb is what he

Le 5:15 offering to Jehovah a s ram
5:18 he must bring a s ram from
6:6 bring to Jehovah a s ram from
9:2 for a burnt offering, s ones
9:3 s ones, for a burnt offering
14:10 take two s young rams and
14:10 one s female lamb, in its
22:19 it must be s, a male among
22:21 s one among the herd or the
23:12 render up a s young ram, in
23:18 seven s male lambs, each a
25:9 the horn of loud tone to s
25:9 the horn to s in all your land
26:36 s of a leaf driven about
Nu 6:14 to Jehovah one s young ram in
6:14 one s female lamb in its
6:14 s ram as a communion
10:7 not s a fluctuating blast
10:9 s a war call on the trumpets
19:2 take for you a s red cow in
28:3 two s year-old male lambs a
28:9 two s year-old male lambs
28:11 seven s male lambs each a
28:19 should prove to be s ones
28:31 should prove to be s ones for
29:2 lambs each a year old, s ones
29:8 They should prove to be s ones
29:13 should prove to be s ones
29:17 each a year old, s ones
29:20 each a year old, s ones
29:23 each a year old, s ones
29:26 each a year old, s ones
29:29 each a year old, s ones
29:32 each a year old, s ones
29:36 each a year old, s ones
De 4:12 The s of words was what you
Jos 6:5 s with the horn of the ram
6:5 you hear the s of the horn
6:20 heard the s of the horn and
1Sa 4:6 to hear the s of the shouting
4:6 the s of this loud shouting in
4:14 to hear the s of the outcry
4:14 the s of this turmoil mean
15:14 s of the flock in my ears
15:14 the s of the herd that I am
20:12 s out my father about this
2Sa 5:24 hear the s of a marching in
6:15 joyful shouting and s of horn
15:10 you hear the s of the horn
1Ki 1:41 got to hear the s of the horn
14:6 heard the s of her feet as
18:41 the s of the turmoil of a
2Ki 6:32 s of the feet of his lord
7:6 to hear the s of war chariots
7:6 war chariots, the s of horses
7:6 s of a great military force
7:10 nor s of a man, but only the
11:13 the s of the people running
1Ch 14:15 s of the marching in the
15:16 to cause a s of rejoicing to
16:42 to s forth the trumpets and
2Ch 5:13 causing one s to be heard in
5:13 lifted up the s with the
23:12 s of the people running and
Ezr 3:13 s of the shout of rejoicing
3:13 the s of the weeping of the
3:13 the s itself was heard even
Ne 4:20 you hear the s of the horn
Job 13:9 be good that he s you out
15:21 s of dreadful things is in
21:12 at the s of the pipe
33:8 the s of your words I kept
34:16 to the s of my words
37:4 After it a s roars
37:4 the s of his superiority
39:24 it is the s of a horn
Ps 5:2 to the s of my cry for help
6:8 hear the s of my weeping
38:3 no s spot in my flesh
38:7 no s spot in my flesh
42:7 the s of your waterspouts
47:1 with the s of a joyful cry
47:5 with the s of the horn
77:17 s the cloudy skies have given
77:18 s of your thunder was like
93:3 rivers have raised their s
98:6 and the s of the horn
102:5 of the s of my sighing
104:7 s of your thunder they were
104:12 they keep giving forth s
115:7 utter no s with their throat
150:5 the cymbals of melodious s
Ec 7:6 the s of thorns under the pot
10:20 convey the s and something
Ec 12:4 the s of the grinding mill
12:4 one gets up at the s of a bird
12:4 the daughters of song s low
Ca 2:8 The s of my dear one! Look!
5:2 the s of my dear one knocking
Isa 1:6 there is no s spot in it
3:16 feet they make a tinkling s
18:3 s just as when there is the
24:18 s of the dreaded thing
29:4 dust your saying will s low
29:6 quaking and with a great s
30:19 at the s of your outcry
33:3 s of turmoil peoples have
48:20 with the s of a joyful cry
65:19 in her the s of weeping
65:19 or the s of a plaintive cry
66:6 s of uproar out of the city
66:6 a s out of the temple!
66:6 s of Jehovah repaying what
Jer 3:21 there has been heard a s
4:19 the s of the horn is what
4:21 hearing the s of the horn
4:29 the s of the horsemen
6:17 to the s of the horn
8:16 the s of the neighing of his
8:19 the s of the cry for help
9:10 not hear the s of livestock
11:16 With s of the great roaring
25:10 the s of exultation and
25:10 the s of rejoicing, the
25:10 the s of the hand mill and
30:5 s of trembling we have heard
30:19 s of those who are laughing
33:11 s of exultation and the
33:11 and the s of rejoicing
42:14 s of the horn we shall not
47:3 s of the stamping of the
48:3 s of an outcry from
49:21 At the s of their falling
49:21 s of it has been heard even
50:22 s of war in the land, and
50:28 s of those fleeing and
50:42 s of them is like the sea
50:46 s when Babylon has been
Eze 1:24 to hear the s of their wings
1:24 a s like that of vast waters
1:24 the s of the Almighty One
1:24 they went, the s of a tumult
1:24 like the s of an encampment
3:12 the s of a great rushing
3:13 s of the wings of the living
3:13 s of the wheels close beside
3:13 and the s of a great rushing
10:5 very s of the wings of the
10:5 like the s of God Almighty
19:7 with the s of his roaring
21:22 to raise the s in an alarm
23:42 the s of a crowd at ease
26:10 to the s of cavalryman and
26:13 s of your harps will be
26:15 At the s of your downfall
27:28 s of the outcry of your
31:16 the s of its downfall I
33:4 hears the s of the horn
33:5 The s of the horn he heard
37:7 a s began to occur as soon
43:22 goats, a s one, as a sin
43:23 of the herd, a s one, and
43:23 ram from the flock, a s one
45:18 son of the herd, a s one
45:23 seven rams, s ones, daily
46:4 six s male lambs and a
46:4 male lambs and a s ram
46:6 son of the herd, a s one
46:6 lambs and a ram; s ones they
46:13 s male lamb, in its first
Da 3:5 hear the s of the horn, the
3:7 hearing the s of the horn, the
3:10 hears the s of the horn, the
3:15 hear the s of the horn, the
7:11 s of the grandiose words that
10:6 s of his words was like the
10:6 was like the s of a crowd
10:9 hearing the s of his words
10:9 hearing the s of his words, I
Joe 2:5 the s of chariots on the tops
2:5 the s of a flaming fire that
Am 2:2 signal, with the s of a horn
5:23 melodious s of your stringed
6:5 s of the stringed instrument
Na 2:7 like the s of doves, beating
3:2 There is the s of the whip
3:2 s of the rattling of the wheel
Hab 3:10 watery deep gave forth its s
Hab 3:16 at the s my lips quivered
Zep 1:10 s . . . from the Fish Gate
1:14 s of the day of Jehovah is
Mt 12:13 hand . . . was restored s
24:31 with a great trumpet s, and
Mr 5:15 clothed and in his s mind
Lu 1:44 as the s of your greeting
8:35 clothed and in his s mind
Joh 3:8 and you hear the s of it
5:6 want to become s in health
5:9 became s in health, and he
5:11 one that made me s in health
5:14 you have become s in health
5:15 that made him s in health
7:23 a man completely s in health
Ac 2:6 when this s occurred, the
4:10 stand here s in front of you
9:7 s of a voice, but not beholding
Ro 10:18 the earth their s went out
12:3 think so as to have a s mind
1Co 14:7 inanimate things give off s
14:11 the force of the speech s
15:52 For the trumpet will s, and
2Co 5:13 if we are s in mind, it is
1Th 5:23 And s in every respect may
1Ti 3:2 s in mind, orderly
Tit 1:8 lover of goodness, s in mind
2:2 s in mind, healthy in faith
2:5 to be s in mind, chaste
2:6 younger men to be s in mind
Jas 1:4 and s in all respects, not
1Pe 4:7 Be s in mind, therefore, and
Re 1:15 was as the s of many waters
9:9 the s of their wings was as
9:9 as the s of chariots of many
14:2 I heard a s out of heaven as
14:2 as the s of many waters and
14:2 and as the s of loud thunder
14:2 s that I heard was as of
18:22 s of singers who accompany
18:22 no s of a millstone will
19:6 as a s of many waters and
19:6 and as a s of heavy thunders

Sounded

Ps 46:6 He s with his voice, the
Ac 27:28 they s the depth and found
1Th 1:8 the word of Jehovah s forth

Sounding

1Ch 15:24 loudly s the trumpets
15:28 with the s of the horn and
2Ch 5:12 and twenty s the trumpets
7:6 loudly s the trumpets in
13:12 s the battle alarm against
13:14 were loudly s the trumpets
Ac 27:28 made a s and found it
1Co 13:1 become a s piece of brass or
Re 10:7 the s of the seventh angel

Soundness

Ac 3:16 complete s in the sight of
26:25 of truth and of s of mind
1Ti 2:9 with modesty and s of mind
2:15 along with s of mind
2Ti 1:7 and of love and of s of mind
Tit 2:12 to live with s of mind and

Sounds

Ps 68:33 s with his voice, a strong
93:4 Above the s of vast waters
1Co 14:8 trumpet s an indistinct call
14:10 so many kinds of speech s

Sour

Ex 12:15 take away s dough from your
12:19 no s dough is to be found in
13:7 no s dough is to be seen with
Le 2:11 make no s dough and no honey
De 16:4 no s dough should be seen
Mt 27:48 soaked it with s wine and
Mr 15:36 soaked a sponge with s wine
Lu 23:36 and offering him s wine
Joh 19:29 vessel . . . full of s wine
19:29 sponge full of the s wine
19:30 received the s wine, Jesus

Source

Ge 26:35 a s of bitterness of spirit
Le 12:7 clean from the s of her blood
20:18 he has exposed her s, and
20:18 laid bare the s of her blood
2Ki 2:21 the s of the water and threw
6:27 what s shall I save you
2Ch 32:30 upper s of the waters of
Ps 36:9 with you is the s of life
68:26 who are from the S of Israel

Pr 5:18 water s prove to be blessed
10:11 righteous one is a s of life
13:14 wise one is a s of life
Isa 58:11 and like the s of water
Jer 2:13 the s of living water, in
9:1 my eyes were a s of tears
17:13 s of living water, Jehovah
Mt 21:25 baptism by John . . . what s
Lu 20:7 that they did not know its s
Joh 2:9 did not know what its s was
4:11 From what s, therefore, do
18:36 kingdom is not from this s
Jas 4:1 From what s are there wars
4:1 from what s are there fights
4:1 from this s, namely, from

Sources
Job 38:16 come to the s of the sea
Pr 4:23 out of it are the s of life
Isa 41:18 land into s of water

Soured
Ps 73:21 For my heart was s And in

South
Ge 28:14 to the north and to the s
Ex 26:18 toward the Negeb, to the s
26:35 the tabernacle toward the s
27:9 toward the Negeb, to the s
36:23 toward the Negeb, to the s
38:9 toward the Negeb, to the s
40:24 of the tabernacle to the s
Nu 2:10 Reuben will be toward the s
3:29 of the tabernacle to the s
10:6 camping to the s must pull
34:3 your s side must prove to be
34:3 your s boundary must prove to
34:4 s of the ascent of Akrabbim
34:4 be on the s of Kadesh-barnea
35:5 s side two thousand cubits
De 3:27 north and s and east and see
33:23 possession of the west and s
Jos 11:2 desert plains s of Chinnereth
12:3 s under the slopes of Pisgah
13:4 To the s all the land of the
15:3 the s to Kadesh-barnea and
15:7 is s of the torrent valley
15:8 of the Jebusite at the s
15:19 a piece of land to the s
15:21 boundary of Edom in the s
17:10 To the s it was Ephraim's
18:5 on his territory to the s
18:13 s of Lower Beth-horon
18:14 western side to the s from
18:14 faces Beth-horon to the s
18:15 the side to the s was from
18:16 of the Jebusite on the s
19:8 Ramah of the s
19:34 reached to Zebulun on the s
Jg 1:16 to the s of Arad. Then they
21:19 and toward the s of Lebonah
1Sa 7:11 as far as s of Beth-car
14:5 was on the s facing Geba
20:41 up from nearby to the s
23:24 to the s of Jeshimon
27:10 Upon the s of Judah and
27:10 s of the Jerahmeelites and
27:10 upon the s of the Kenites
30:1 raid on the s and on Ziklag
30:14 on the s of the Cherethites
30:14 upon the s of Caleb; and
30:27 those in Ramoth of the s
1Ki 7:25 bulls . . . three facing s
7:39 house eastward, toward the s
1Ch 9:24 gatekeepers . . . to the s
26:15 Obed-edom had his to the s
26:17 to the s for a day, four
2Ch 4:4 bulls . . . three facing the s
4:10 to the east, toward the s
Job 9:9 the interior rooms of the S
37:17 shows quietness from the s
39:26 its wings to the s wind
Ps 75:6 the s is there an exalting
78:26 s wind blow by his own
89:12 north and the s—you yourself
107:3 the north and from the s
Ec 1:6 The wind is going to the s
11:3 if a tree falls to the s or if
Ca 4:16 and come in, O s wind
Isa 21:1 Like stormwinds in the s
30:6 against the beasts of the s
43:6 to the s, Do not keep back
Jer 13:19 The cities of the s
32:44 in the cities of the s
33:13 in the cities of the s and
Eze 20:46 and drip words to the s
20:46 forest of the field of the s
20:47 say to the forest of the s
20:47 from the s to the north
21:4 all flesh from s to north
40:2 structure of a city to the s
40:24 brought me toward the s
40:24 a gate toward the s
40:27 had a gate toward the s
40:27 the s a hundred cubits
40:28 by the gate of the s
40:28 measure the gate of the s
40:44 front side was toward the s
40:45 room . . . toward the s
41:11 and one entrance to the s
42:12 toward the s was the
42:13 the dining rooms of the s
46:9 out by the way of the s gate
46:9 by the way of the s gate
47:1 House, s of the altar
47:19 southern side is to the s
47:19 side to the s, toward the
48:10 s a length of twenty-five
48:17 the s two hundred and fifty
Da 8:4 ram making thrusts . . . the s
8:9 much greater toward the s and
11:5 king of the s will become
11:6 daughter of the king of the s
11:9 kingdom of the king of the s
11:11 king of the s will embitter
11:14 against the king of the s
11:15 arms of the s, they will not
11:25 against the king of the s
11:25 king of the s, for his part
11:29 come against the s; but it
11:40 king of the s will engage
Zec 6:6 go forth to the land of the s
9:14 the windstorms of the s
14:4 and half of it to the s
14:10 to the s of Jerusalem
Mt 12:42 The queen of the s will be
Lu 11:31 The queen of the s will be
12:55 see that a s wind is blowing
13:29 and from north and s, and
Ac 8:26 s to the road that runs down
27:13 s wind blew softly, they
28:13 s wind sprang up and we
Re 21:13 and on the s three gates

Southeast
Ac 27:12 northeast and toward the s

Southern
Jos 15:1 to the Negeb at its s end
15:2 their s boundary came to be
15:4 came to be their s boundary
18:13 at the s slope of Luz
18:19 the s end of the Jordan
18:19 This was the s boundary
Jg 1:15 it is a s piece of land you
Eze 20:46 direction of the s quarter
42:18 s side he measured, five
47:19 s side is to the south
48:16 s border four thousand five
48:28 Gad, to the s border, it
48:33 s border will be four

Southward
Ge 13:14 s and eastward and westward
Jos 15:2 the bay that faces s
15:3 s to the ascent of Akrabbim
17:9 s to the torrent valley of
Eze 48:28 border, it will be s

Sovereign
Ge 15:2 Abram said: S Lord Jehovah
15:8 S Lord Jehovah, by what shall
De 3:24 O S Lord Jehovah, you yourself
9:26 S Lord Jehovah, do not bring
Jos 7:7 S Lord Jehovah, why did you
Jg 6:22 S Lord Jehovah, for the reason
16:28 S Lord Jehovah, remember me
2Sa 7:18 Who am I, O S Lord Jehovah?
7:19 S Lord Jehovah, yet you also
7:19 mankind, O S Lord Jehovah
7:20 know your servant . . . S Lord
7:22 great, O S Lord Jehovah
7:28 O S Lord Jehovah, you are
7:29 S Lord Jehovah . . . promised
1Ki 2:26 carried the ark of the S Lord
8:53 out from Egypt, O S Lord
Ps 68:20 to Jehovah the S Lord belong
69:6 O S Lord, Jehovah of armies
71:5 you are my hope, O S Lord
71:16 mightiness, O S Lord Jehovah
73:28 S Lord Jehovah I have placed
Ps 109:21 you are Jehovah the S Lord
140:7 Jehovah the S Lord, the
141:8 O Jehovah the S Lord
Isa 3:15 S Lord, Jehovah of armies
7:7 S Lord Jehovah has said
10:23 S Lord, Jehovah of armies
10:24 S Lord, Jehovah of armies
22:5 S Lord, Jehovah of armies
22:12 S Lord, Jehovah of armies
22:14 S Lord, Jehovah of armies
22:15 S Lord, Jehovah of armies
25:8 S Lord Jehovah will
28:16 S Lord Jehovah has said
28:22 S Lord, Jehovah of armies
30:15 S Lord Jehovah, the Holy
40:10 The S Lord Jehovah himself
48:16 And now the S Lord Jehovah
49:22 the S Lord Jehovah has said
50:4 The S Lord Jehovah himself
50:5 The S Lord Jehovah himself
50:7 the S Lord Jehovah himself
50:9 Look! The S Lord Jehovah
52:4 the S Lord Jehovah has said
56:8 the S Lord Jehovah, who is
61:1 The spirit of the S Lord
65:13 the S Lord Jehovah has
65:15 the S Lord Jehovah will
Jer 1:6 Alas, O S Lord Jehovah
2:19 S Lord, Jehovah of armies
2:22 utterance of the S Lord
4:10 Alas, O S Lord Jehovah!
7:20 the S Lord Jehovah has said
14:13 Alas, O S Lord Jehovah!
32:17 Alas, O S Lord Jehovah!
32:25 S Lord Jehovah, Buy for
44:26 S Lord Jehovah is alive
46:10 S Lord, Jehovah of armies
46:10 S Lord, Jehovah of armies
49:5 S Lord, Jehovah of armies
50:25 S Lord, Jehovah of armies
50:31 S Lord, Jehovah of armies
Eze 2:4 the S Lord Jehovah has said
3:11 the S Lord Jehovah has said
3:27 the S Lord Jehovah has said
4:14 Alas, O S Lord Jehovah! Look!
5:5 the S Lord Jehovah has said
5:7 the S Lord Jehovah has said
5:8 the S Lord Jehovah has said
5:11 the utterance of the S Lord
6:3 word of the S Lord Jehovah
6:3 S Lord Jehovah has said to the
6:11 S Lord Jehovah has said, Clap
7:2 S Lord Jehovah has said to the
7:5 the S Lord Jehovah has said
8:1 the hand of the S Lord Jehovah
9:8 Alas, O S Lord Jehovah!
11:7 the S Lord Jehovah has said
11:8 the utterance of the S Lord
11:13 Alas, O S Lord Jehovah!
11:16 the S Lord Jehovah has said
11:17 the S Lord Jehovah has said
11:21 the utterance of the S Lord
12:10 the S Lord Jehovah has said
12:19 S Lord Jehovah has said to
12:23 the S Lord Jehovah has said
12:25 the utterance of the S Lord
12:28 the S Lord Jehovah has said
12:28 the utterance of the S Lord
13:3 S Lord Jehovah has said: Woe
13:8 the S Lord Jehovah has said
13:8 the utterance of the S Lord
13:9 have to know that I am the S
13:13 the S Lord Jehovah has said
13:16 the utterance of the S Lord
13:18 the S Lord Jehovah has said
13:20 the S Lord Jehovah has said
14:4 the S Lord Jehovah has said
14:6 the S Lord Jehovah has said
14:11 the utterance of the S Lord
14:14 the utterance of the S Lord
14:16 the utterance of the S Lord
14:18 the utterance of the S Lord
14:20 the utterance of the S Lord
14:21 the S Lord Jehovah has said
14:23 the utterance of the S Lord
15:6 the S Lord Jehovah has said
15:8 the utterance of the S Lord
16:3 S Lord Jehovah has said to
16:8 the utterance of the S Lord
16:14 the utterance of the S Lord
16:19 the utterance of the S Lord
16:23 the utterance of the S Lord
16:30 the utterance of the S Lord
16:36 the S Lord Jehovah has said

Eze 16:43 the utterance of the *S* Lord
16:48 the utterance of the *S* Lord
16:59 the *S* Lord Jehovah has said
16:63 the utterance of the *S* Lord
17:3 the *S* Lord Jehovah has said
17:9 the *S* Lord Jehovah has said
17:16 the utterance of the *S* Lord
17:19 the *S* Lord Jehovah has said
17:22 the *S* Lord Jehovah has said
18:3 the utterance of the *S* Lord
18:9 the utterance of the *S* Lord
18:23 the utterance of the *S* Lord
18:30 the utterance of the *S* Lord
18:32 the utterance of the *S* Lord
20:3 the *S* Lord Jehovah has said
20:3 the utterance of the *S* Lord
20:5 the *S* Lord Jehovah has said
20:27 the *S* Lord Jehovah has said
20:30 the *S* Lord Jehovah has said
20:31 the utterance of the *S* Lord
20:33 utterance of the *S* Lord
20:36 utterance of the *S* Lord
20:39 the *S* Lord Jehovah has said
20:40 the utterance of the *S* Lord
20:44 utterance of the *S* Lord
20:47 the *S* Lord Jehovah has said
20:49 Alas, O *S* Lord Jehovah!
21:7 the *S* Lord Jehovah
21:13 the *S* Lord Jehovah
21:24 the *S* Lord Jehovah has said
21:26 the *S* Lord Jehovah has said
21:28 the *S* Lord Jehovah has said
22:3 the *S* Lord Jehovah has said
22:12 the *S* Lord Jehovah
22:19 the *S* Lord Jehovah has said
22:28 the *S* Lord Jehovah has said
22:31 the *S* Lord Jehovah
23:22 the *S* Lord Jehovah has said
23:28 the *S* Lord Jehovah has said
23:32 the *S* Lord Jehovah has said
23:34 the *S* Lord Jehovah
23:35 the *S* Lord Jehovah has said
23:46 the *S* Lord Jehovah has said
23:49 I am the *S* Lord Jehovah
24:3 the *S* Lord Jehovah has said
24:6 the *S* Lord Jehovah has said
24:9 the *S* Lord Jehovah has said
24:14 the *S* Lord Jehovah
24:21 the *S* Lord Jehovah has said
24:24 I am the *S* Lord Jehovah
25:3 word of the *S* Lord Jehovah
25:3 *S* Lord Jehovah has said
25:6 the *S* Lord Jehovah has said
25:8 the *S* Lord Jehovah has said
25:12 the *S* Lord Jehovah has said
25:13 the *S* Lord Jehovah has said
25:14 the *S* Lord Jehovah
25:15 the *S* Lord Jehovah has said
25:16 the *S* Lord Jehovah has said
26:3 the *S* Lord Jehovah has said
26:5 the *S* Lord Jehovah
26:7 the *S* Lord Jehovah has said
26:14 the *S* Lord Jehovah
26:15 the *S* Lord Jehovah has said
26:19 the *S* Lord Jehovah has said
26:21 the *S* Lord Jehovah
27:3 the *S* Lord Jehovah has said
28:2 the *S* Lord Jehovah has said
28:6 the *S* Lord Jehovah has said
28:10 the *S* Lord Jehovah
28:12 the *S* Lord Jehovah has said
28:22 the *S* Lord Jehovah has said
28:24 I am the *S* Lord Jehovah
28:25 the *S* Lord Jehovah has said
29:3 the *S* Lord Jehovah has said
29:8 the *S* Lord Jehovah has said
29:13 the *S* Lord Jehovah has said
29:16 I am the *S* Lord Jehovah
29:19 the *S* Lord Jehovah has said
29:20 the *S* Lord Jehovah
30:2 the *S* Lord Jehovah has said
30:6 the *S* Lord Jehovah
30:10 the *S* Lord Jehovah has said
30:13 the *S* Lord Jehovah has said
30:22 the *S* Lord Jehovah has said
31:10 the *S* Lord Jehovah has said
31:15 the *S* Lord Jehovah has said
31:18 the *S* Lord Jehovah
32:3 the *S* Lord Jehovah has said
32:8 the *S* Lord Jehovah
32:11 the *S* Lord Jehovah has said
32:14 the *S* Lord Jehovah
32:16 the *S* Lord Jehovah
32:31 the *S* Lord Jehovah

Eze 32:32 the *S* Lord Jehovah
33:11 the *S* Lord Jehovah
33:25 the *S* Lord Jehovah has said
33:27 the *S* Lord Jehovah has said
34:2 the *S* Lord Jehovah has said
34:8 the *S* Lord Jehovah
34:10 the *S* Lord Jehovah has said
34:11 the *S* Lord Jehovah has said
34:15 the *S* Lord Jehovah
34:17 the *S* Lord Jehovah has said
34:20 the *S* Lord Jehovah has said
34:30 the *S* Lord Jehovah
34:31 the *S* Lord Jehovah
35:3 the *S* Lord Jehovah has said
35:6 the *S* Lord Jehovah
35:11 the *S* Lord Jehovah
35:14 the *S* Lord Jehovah has said
36:2 the *S* Lord Jehovah has said
36:3 the *S* Lord Jehovah has said
36:4 the *S* Lord Jehovah
36:4 the *S* Lord Jehovah has said
36:5 the *S* Lord Jehovah has said
36:6 the *S* Lord Jehovah has said
36:7 the *S* Lord Jehovah has said
36:13 the *S* Lord Jehovah has said
36:14 the *S* Lord Jehovah
36:15 the *S* Lord Jehovah
36:22 the *S* Lord Jehovah has said
36:23 the *S* Lord Jehovah
36:32 the *S* Lord Jehovah
36:33 the *S* Lord Jehovah has said
36:37 the *S* Lord Jehovah has said
37:3 I said: *S* Lord Jehovah
37:5 the *S* Lord Jehovah has said
37:9 the *S* Lord Jehovah has said
37:12 the *S* Lord Jehovah has said
37:19 the *S* Lord Jehovah has said
37:21 the *S* Lord Jehovah has said
38:3 the *S* Lord Jehovah has said
38:10 the *S* Lord Jehovah has said
38:14 the *S* Lord Jehovah has said
38:17 the *S* Lord Jehovah has said
38:18 the *S* Lord Jehovah
38:21 the *S* Lord Jehovah
39:1 the *S* Lord Jehovah has said
39:5 the *S* Lord Jehovah
39:8 the *S* Lord Jehovah
39:10 the *S* Lord Jehovah
39:13 the *S* Lord Jehovah
39:17 the *S* Lord Jehovah has said
39:20 the *S* Lord Jehovah
39:25 the *S* Lord Jehovah has said
39:29 the *S* Lord Jehovah
43:18 *S* Lord Jehovah has said
43:19 *S* Lord Jehovah, to minister
43:27 of the *S* Lord Jehovah
44:6 *S* Lord Jehovah has said
44:9 *S* Lord Jehovah has said
44:12 *S* Lord Jehovah, and they
44:15 of the *S* Lord Jehovah
44:27 of the *S* Lord Jehovah
45:9 *S* Lord Jehovah has said
45:9 utterance of the *S* Lord
45:15 of the *S* Lord Jehovah
45:18 *S* Lord Jehovah has said
46:1 *S* Lord Jehovah has said
46:16 *S* Lord Jehovah has said
47:13 *S* Lord Jehovah has said
47:23 of the *S* Lord Jehovah
48:29 of the *S* Lord Jehovah
Am 1:8 the *S* Lord Jehovah has said
3:7 the *S* Lord Jehovah will not
3:8 The *S* Lord Jehovah himself has
3:11 the *S* Lord Jehovah has said
3:13 the utterance of the *S* Lord
4:2 The *S* Lord Jehovah has sworn
4:5 is the utterance of the *S* Lord
5:3 what the *S* Lord Jehovah
6:8 The *S* Lord Jehovah has sworn
7:1 the *S* Lord Jehovah caused me
7:2 O *S* Lord Jehovah, forgive
7:4 what the *S* Lord Jehovah caused
7:4 the *S* Lord Jehovah was calling
7:5 *S* Lord Jehovah, hold off
7:6 the *S* Lord Jehovah said
8:1 the *S* Lord Jehovah caused me
8:3 the utterance of the *S* Lord
8:9 the utterance of the *S* Lord
8:11 the utterance of the *S* Lord
9:5 *S* Lord, Jehovah of the armies
9:8 eyes of the *S* Lord Jehovah
Ob 1 the *S* Lord Jehovah has said
Mic 1:2 let the *S* Lord Jehovah serve
Hab 3:19 Jehovah the *S* Lord is my

Zep 1:7 before the *S* Lord Jehovah
Zec 9:14 the horn the *S* Lord Jehovah
Lu 2:29 *S* Lord, you are letting your
Ac 4:24 *S* Lord, you are the One who
Re 6:10 Until when, *S* Lord holy and

Sow

Ge 26:12 Isaac began to *s* seed in that
47:23 you must *s* the land with it
Ex 23:10 *s* your land with seed and
23:16 of what you *s* in the field
Le 19:19 not *s* your field with seeds
25:3 Six years you should *s* your
25:4 field you must not *s* with
25:11 *s* seed nor reap the land's
25:20 not *s* seed or gather our
25:22 *s* seed the eighth year and
26:16 *s* your seed for nothing, as
De 11:10 you used to *s* your seed and
22:9 You must not *s* your vineyard
22:9 the seed that you might *s*
2Ki 19:29 *s* seed, you people, and
Job 31:8 *s* seed and someone else eat
Ps 107:37 *s* fields and plant vineyards
Ec 11:4 the wind will not *s* seed
11:6 In the morning *s* your seed
Isa 28:24 plows in order to *s* seed
30:23 with which you *s* the ground
37:30 in the third year *s* seed
Jer 31:27 *s* the house of Israel and
35:7 and no seed must you *s*
Ho 2:22 Jezreel [=God will *s* seed]
2:23 *s* her like seed for me in the
10:12 *S* seed for yourselves in
Mic 6:15 for your part, will *s* seed
Mt 6:26 they do not *s* seed or reap or
13:3 Look! A sower went out to *s*
13:27 did you not *s* fine seed in
25:24 reaping where you did not *s*
25:26 I reaped where I did not *s*
Mr 4:3 Look! The sower went out to *s*
Lu 8:5 A sower went out to *s* his seed
12:24 ravens neither *s* seed nor
19:21 you reap what you did not *s*
19:22 and reaping what I did not *s*
1Co 15:36 What you *s* is not made
15:37 and as for what you *s*, you
15:37 you *s*, not the body that
2Co 9:10 seed for you to *s* and will
2Pe 2:22 the *s* that was bathed to

Sowed

Jg 6:3 if Israel *s* seed, Midian and
9:45 and *s* it with salt
1Ki 18:32 *s* with two seah measures
Mt 13:18 illustration . . . man that *s*
13:24 like a man that *s* fine seed
13:39 enemy that *s* them is the

Sower

Isa 55:10 given to the *s* and bread to
Jer 50:16 Cut off the *s* from Babylon
Mt 13:3 Look! A *s* went out to sow
13:37 *s* of the fine seed is the
Mr 4:3 Look! The *s* went out to sow
4:14 The *s* sows the word
Lu 8:5 A *s* went out to sow his seed
Joh 4:36 *s* and the reaper may rejoice
4:37 One is the *s* and another the
2Co 9:10 supplies seed to the *s* and

Sowing

Ge 8:22 seed *s* and harvest, and cold
Le 26:5 gathering will reach to the *s*
De 21:4 no tilling or *s* of seed, and
Job 4:8 those *s* trouble . . . reap it
Ps 126:5 Those *s* seed with tears
Pr 11:18 one *s* righteousness, true
22:8 *s* unrighteousness will reap
Isa 32:20 *s* seed alongside all waters
Jer 4:3 do not keep *s* among thorns
Ho 8:7 it is wind that they keep *s*
Am 7:1 the coming up of the later *s*
7:1 the later *s* after the mown
Mt 13:4 as he was *s*, some seeds fell
Mr 4:4 as he was *s*, some seed fell
Lu 8:5 as he was *s*, some of it fell
Ga 6:7 whatever a man is *s*, this he
6:8 *s* with a view to his flesh
6:8 *s* with a view to the spirit

Sown

Le 11:37 that is to be *s*, it is clean
De 29:23 its whole land will not be *s*
Isa 40:24 never yet have they been *s*
61:11 that are *s* in it sprout

Jer 2:2 in a land not s with seed
12:13 They have s wheat, but
Eze 36:9 cultivated and s with seed
Na 1:14 your name will be s anymore
Hag 1:6 You have s much seed, but
Mal 2:3 s seed, and I will scatter
Mt 13:19 what has been s in his heart
13:19 the one s alongside the road
13:20 one s upon the rocky places
13:22 the one s among the thorns
13:23 the one s upon the fine soil
Mr 4:15 the road where the word is s
4:15 the word that was s in them
4:16 ones s upon the rocky places
4:18 who are s among the thorns
4:20 that were s on the fine soil
4:31 time it was s in the ground
4:32 when it has been s, it comes
1Co 9:11 If we have s spiritual
15:42 It is s in corruption, it is
15:43 It is s in dishonor, it is
15:43 It is s in weakness, it is
15:44 It is s a physical body
Jas 3:18 has its seed s under peaceful

Sows
Mr 4:14 The sower s the word
2Co 9:6 he that s sparingly will also
9:6 he that s bountifully will

Space
Ge 9:27 Let God grant ample s to
1Sa 26:13 s between them being vast
1Ki 7:36 according to the clear s of
Job 36:16 Broader s, not constraint
Ps 4:1 you must make broad s for me
Eze 41:9 was a s left open by the
41:11 was to the s left open
41:11 s left open was five cubits

Spaces
Job 38:18 the broad s of the earth
Pr 8:26 open s and the first part

Spacious
Ex 3:8 to a land good and s, to a land
34:24 will make your territory s
Isa 5:14 Sheol has made its soul s
30:23 in that day in a s pasture
54:2 place of your tent more s
57:8 you made your bed s. And for
Hab 2:5 his soul s just like Sheol
Mt 7:13 broad and s is the road

Spain
Ro 15:24 on my way to S, I hope
15:28 depart by way of you for S

Span
Ex 28:16 a s of the hand being its
28:16 a s of the hand its width
39:9 a s of the hand in its length
39:9 and a s in its width
1Sa 17:4 being six cubits and a s
1Ki 19:21 took a s of the bulls and
Isa 21:7 chariot with a s of steeds
21:9 of men, with a s of steeds
40:12 with a mere s and included
Jer 51:23 his s of animals to pieces
Eze 43:13 lip round about, one s

Spans
1Ki 19:19 plowing with twelve s
Job 1:3 five hundred s of cattle and
42:12 a thousand s of cattle and a

Spare
Jer 50:14 S no arrow, for it is
Ro 8:32 not even s his own Son but
11:21 God did not s the natural
11:21 neither will he s you
2Co 1:23 it is to s you that I have
13:2 I come again I will not s

Spared
2Sa 12:4 s taking some from his own
2Ki 5:20 s Naaman this Syrian by not
Job 21:30 disaster an evil one is s

Sparing
Isa 30:14 pieces without one's s it
31:5 S her, he must also cause
1Co 7:28 But I am s you

Sparingly
2Co 9:6, 6 sows s will also reap s

Spark
Job 18:5 s of his fire will not shine
Isa 1:31 product of his activity a s

Sparkle
Pr 23:31 it gives off its s in the cup
Eze 1:22 like the s of awesome ice

Sparks
Job 5:7 As the very s fly upward
41:19 s of fire make their escape
Isa 50:11 making s light up, walk in
50:11 amid the s that you have

Sparrows
Mt 10:29 two s sell for a coin of
10:31 are worth more than many s
Lu 12:6 Five s sell for two coins
12:7 are worth more than many s

Sparse
Nu 33:54 s one you should reduce his

Spatter
Ex 29:21 must s it upon Aaron and his
Le 4:6 s some of the blood seven
4:17 blood and s it seven times
5:9 s some of the blood of the sin
14:7 s it seven times upon the one
14:16 s some of the oil with his
14:27 s with his right finger some
14:51 s it toward the house seven
16:14 s it with his finger in
16:14 s some of the blood with his
16:15 s it toward the cover and
16:19 s some of the blood upon it
Nu 8:7 S sin-cleansing water upon
19:4 s some of its blood straight
19:18 s it upon the tent and all
19:19 s it upon the unclean one on

Spattered
Le 8:11 he s some of it seven times
8:30 and s it upon Aaron and his

Spattering
Nu 19:21 s the water for cleansing
2Ki 9:33 blood went s upon the wall
Isa 63:3 their spurting blood kept s

Spatters
Le 6:27 anyone s some of its blood
6:27 wash what he s blood upon in

Speak
Ge 17:3 God continued to s with him
18:27 s to Jehovah, whereas I am
18:31 taken upon myself to s to
18:32 let me s just this once
19:14 and began to s to his
20:8 s of all these things in their
23:3 s to the sons of Heth, saying
24:33 Hence he said: S!
24:50 We are unable to s bad or
32:19 word you are to s to Esau on
34:6 out to Jacob to s with him
34:8 Hamor proceeded to s with
34:13 s so because he had defiled
34:20 s to the men of their city
37:4 not able to s peacefully to
41:17 Pharaoh went on to s to
44:7 Why does my lord s with such
44:16 What can we s? And how can
44:18 let your slave s a word in
50:4 s, please, in the hearing of
Ex 4:14 do know that he can really s
4:15 s to him and put the words in
4:16 must s for you to the people
5:23 before Pharaoh to s in your
6:2 God went on to s to Moses and
6:11 s to Pharaoh, Egypt's king
6:13 continued to s to Moses and
6:29 Jehovah went on to s to Moses
6:29 I am Jehovah. S to Pharaoh
7:2 s all that I shall command you
11:2 S, now, in the ears of the
12:3 S to the entire assembly of
14:2 S to the sons of Israel, that
14:15 S to the sons of Israel that
16:12 S to them, saying, Between
19:9 may hear when I s with you
19:19 Moses began to s, and the
20:1 God proceeded to s all these
20:19 say to Moses: You s with us
20:19 let not God s with us for
23:22 really do all that I shall s
25:1 Jehovah proceeded to s to
25:2 S to the sons of Israel, that
25:22 s with you from above the
28:3 s to all the ones wise with a
29:42 you people to s to you there
30:11 went on to s to Moses
Ex 30:22 continued to s to Moses
30:31 will s to the sons of Israel
31:1 continued to s to Moses
31:13 s to the sons of Israel
33:11 man would s to his fellow
34:31 Moses began to s to them
34:34 before Jehovah to s with
34:35 he went in to s with him
Le 1:1 and s to him out of the tent
1:2 S to the sons of Israel, and
4:1 Jehovah went on to s to Moses
4:2 S to the sons of Israel
5:4 the man might s thoughtlessly
5:14 Jehovah continued to s to
6:1 Jehovah went on to s to Moses
6:8 continued to s to Moses
6:25 S to Aaron and his sons
7:22 Jehovah continued to s to
7:23 S to the sons of Israel
7:28 Jehovah went on to s to Moses
7:29 S to the sons of Israel
8:1 to s to Moses, saying
9:3 the sons of Israel you will s
10:8 to s to Aaron, saying
11:1 to s to Moses and Aaron
11:2 S to the sons of Israel
12:1 Jehovah went on to s to Moses
12:2 S to the sons of Israel
13:1 to s to Moses and Aaron
14:1 continued to s to Moses
14:33 to s to Moses and Aaron
15:1 to s to Moses and Aaron
15:2 S to the sons of Israel, and
16:1 to s to Moses after the death
16:2 S to Aaron your brother, that
17:1 Jehovah went on to s to Moses
17:2 S to Aaron and his sons and
18:1 continued to s to Moses
18:2 S to the sons of Israel, and
19:2 S to the entire assembly of
21:16 Jehovah continued to s to
21:17 S to Aaron, saying, No man
22:2 S to Aaron and his sons, that
22:17 Jehovah continued to s to
22:18 S to Aaron and his sons and
23:2 S to the sons of Israel, and
23:9 Jehovah continued to s to
23:10 S to the sons of Israel, and
23:24 S to the sons of Israel
23:33 Jehovah continued to s to
23:34 S to the sons of Israel
24:1 to s to Moses, saying
24:13 to s to Moses, saying
24:15 s to the sons of Israel
25:2 S to the sons of Israel, and
27:1 to s to Moses, saying
27:2 S to the sons of Israel, and
Nu 1:1 Jehovah proceeded to s to
3:5 Jehovah proceeded to s to
3:11 Jehovah continued to s to
3:44 Jehovah continued to s to
5:6 S to the sons of Israel, As for
5:11 Jehovah went on to s to Moses
5:12 S to the sons of Israel, and
6:2 S to the sons of Israel and you
6:23 S to Aaron and his sons
7:89 tent of meeting to s with him
7:89 and he would s to him
8:1 Jehovah proceeded to s to
8:2 S to Aaron, and you must say
9:1 Jehovah proceeded to s to
9:10 S to the sons of Israel
10:1 Jehovah proceeded to s to
11:17 and s with you there; and I
12:1 s against Moses on account of
12:6 In a dream I would s to him
12:8 Mouth to mouth I s to him
12:8 fear to s against my servant
14:26 Jehovah went on to s to
14:39 Moses proceeded to s these
15:2 S to the sons of Israel, and
15:17 And Jehovah went on to s to
15:18 S to the sons of Israel, and
15:38 S to the sons of Israel, and
16:24 S to the assembly, saying
17:2 S to the sons of Israel and
18:26 you should s to the Levites
19:1 Jehovah proceeded to s to
19:2 S to the sons of Israel that
20:8 s to the crag before their
22:8 just as Jehovah may s to me
22:19 further Jehovah will s with
22:20 word that I shall s to you
22:20 to you is what you may s

Nu 22:35 but the word that I shall s
22:35 is what you may s
22:38 Shall I be able at all to s
22:38 is what I shall s
23:5 and this is what you will s
23:12 that I should take care to s
23:16 and this is what you will s
23:26 Did I not s to you, saying
23:26 All that Jehovah will s is
24:13 Whatever Jehovah may s is
24:13 is what I shall s
26:3 to s with them in the desert
27:8 s, saying, In case any man
33:50 And Jehovah proceeded to s to
33:51 S to the sons of Israel, and
35:1 Jehovah went on to s to Moses
35:9 Jehovah continued to s to
35:10 S to the sons of Israel, and
36:1 come near and s before Moses
De 3:26 Never s to me further on this
4:12 Jehovah began to s to you out
5:24 God may s with man and
5:27 s to us all that Jehovah our
5:27 our God will s to you, and we
5:31 s to you all the commandment
6:7 s of them when you sit in your
11:19 s of them when you sit in
18:18 s to them all that I
18:19 that he will s in my name
18:20 prophet who presumes to s
18:20 not commanded him to s or
18:22 word that Jehovah did not s
20:2 approach and s to the people
20:5 The officers too must s to
20:8 the officers must s further
25:8 call him and s to him, and
31:28 let me s in their hearing
31:30 s in the hearing of all the
32:1 ear, O heavens, and let me s
32:48 to s to Moses on this same
Jos 4:10 Joshua to s to the people
10:12 to s to Jehovah on the day
17:14 to s with Joshua, saying
20:2 S to the sons of Israel
20:4 s his words in the hearing
21:2 to s to them in Shiloh in
22:15 and began to s with them
Jg 6:39 let me s just once more
7:11 listen to what they will s
9:2 S, please, in the hearing of
11:11 to s all his words before
14:7 and began to s to the woman
16:10 that you might s lies to me
16:13 that you might s lies to me
19:3 to s consolingly to her so as
19:30 upon it, take counsel and s
20:3 S. How has this bad thing
1Sa 2:3 s very haughtily so much
3:9 you must say, S, Jehovah, for
3:10 Samuel said: S, for your
4:20 began to s: Do not be afraid
10:6 s as a prophet along with
10:10 he began to s as a prophet
15:16 So he said to him: S!
18:22 S to David secretly, saying
18:23 servants of Saul began to s
19:3 I myself shall s for you to
25:17 to s to him
25:24 slave girl s in your ears
2Sa 3:19 Abner also went to s in the
3:27 to s with him quietly
7:19 s respecting the house of
7:20 David add and s to you, when
12:18 we did s to him, and he did
13:13 s, please, to the king; for
13:22 Absalom did not s with
14:3 s to him a word like this
14:12 s a word to my lord the
14:12 So he said: S!
14:15 s this word to the king
14:15 s, please, to the king
14:18 Let my lord the king s
17:6 If not, you yourself s
19:7 s straight to the heart of
19:11 S to the older men of Judah
20:16 here, and let me s to you
20:18 used to s in former times
22:1 s to Jehovah the words of
1Ki 2:14 So she said: S
2:16 she said to him: S
2:18 shall s for you to the king
2:19 to s to him for Adonijah
4:32 s three thousand proverbs
4:33 he would s about the trees
1Ki 4:33 he would s about the beasts
10:2 s to him all that happened
12:3 began to s to Rehoboam
12:7 s to them with good words
12:10 what you should s to them
12:14 to s to them according to
13:27 went on to s to his sons
14:5 is how you should s to her
20:11 You men, s to him, Do not
21:6 to s to Naboth the Jezreelite
21:19 you must s to him, saying
21:19 you must s to him, saying
22:13 and you must s good
22:14 that is what I shall s
22:16 s to me anything but truth
22:24 pass along from me to s
2Ki 1:6 and you must s to him
1:13 implore . . . and s to him
4:13 to s to the king or to the
6:12 you s in your inner bedroom
18:26 S with your servants
18:26 do not s with us in the
18:27 sent me to s these words
18:28 he went on to s and say
22:14 they proceeded to s to her
25:28 began to s good things with
1Ch 16:35 s exultingly in your praise
17:6 did I s a single word with
17:17 you s concerning the house
21:9 Jehovah proceeded to s to Gad
21:10 and you must s to David
2Ch 10:7 s good words to them, they
10:14 s to them according to the
18:12 and you must s good
18:13 that is what I shall s
18:15 s to me anything but truth
18:23 from me to s with you
32:6 s to the heart of them
34:22 to s to her like this
Ezr 8:17 to s to Iddo and his brothers
Ne 13:24 knowing how to s Jewish
Job 2:10 you s also. Shall we accept
7:11 I will s in the distress of my
9:35 Let me s and not be afraid
10:1 s in the bitterness of my
11:5 if only God himself would s
13:3 s to the Almighty himself
13:7 s unrighteousness for God
13:7 for him will you s deceit?
13:13 that I myself may s
13:22 may I s, and you . . . answer
16:4 could well s as you men do
16:6 If I do s, my own pain is
18:2 that afterward we may s
19:18 they begin to s against me
21:3 and I myself shall s
22:29 when you s arrogantly
27:4 will s no unrighteousness
29:22 they would not s again
32:7 Days themselves should s
32:20 s that it may be a relief
33:2 with my palate has to s
33:32 S, for I have taken delight
34:33 Even what you well know, s
37:20 that I would s
42:4 and I myself shall s
Ps 2:5 will s to them in his anger
35:20 it is not peace that they s
40:5 inclined to tell and s of
41:6 is what his heart will s
41:6 on the outside he will s of
49:3 will s things of wisdom
50:7 O my people, and I will s
50:20 s against your own brother
51:4 to be righteous when you s
58:1 s about righteousness itself
73:8 scoff and s about what is bad
73:8 they s in an elevated style
75:5 not s with an arrogant neck
77:4 agitated, and I cannot s
78:19 they began to s against God
85:8 the true God Jehovah will s
85:8 s peace to his people and
106:33 to s rashly with his lips
106:47 s exultingly in your praise
115:5 mouth . . . but they cannot s
116:10 for I proceeded to s
119:46 s about your reminders in
120:7 when I s, They are for war
122:8 companions I will now s
127:5 s with enemies in the gate
135:16 but they can s nothing
145:11 your mightiness they will s
145:21 of Jehovah my mouth will s
Pr 8:6 the foremost things that I s
21:28 man that is listening will s
23:9 ears of a stupid one do not s
23:16 when your lips s uprightness
23:33 heart will s perverse things
Ec 1:8 no one is able to s of it
3:7 to keep quiet and a time to s
7:21 the words that people may s
Isa 8:5 Jehovah proceeded to s yet
8:10 S any word, and it will not
14:10 s up and say to you, Have
21:9 began to s up and say
28:11 different tongue he will s
29:4 s from the very earth, and
30:10 S to us smooth things
32:6 s mere senselessness, and
32:6 s against Jehovah what is
36:11 S, please, to your servants
36:11 not s . . . the Jews' language
36:12 sent me to s these words
38:15 What shall I s, and what
40:2 S to the heart of Jerusalem
40:27 do you s out, O Israel
41:1 At that time let them s
61:6 s elatedly about yourselves
Jer 1:6 how to s, for I am but a boy
1:7 command you, you should s
1:16 s with them my judgments
1:17 s to them everything that I
4:12 s forth the judgments with
5:5 great ones and s with them
5:15 understandingly what they s
6:10 s and give warning, that
7:22 I did not s with your
7:27 s to them all these words
9:5 they s no truth at all
9:5 their tongue to s falsehood
9:22 S, This is what the
10:5 a scarecrow . . . cannot s
11:2 s them to the men of Judah
12:1 I s even about matters of
12:6 they s to you good things
18:7 s against a nation and
18:9 I may s concerning a nation
18:20 s good even concerning them
19:2 words that I shall s to you
20:8 as often as I s, I cry out
20:9 shall s no more in his name
22:1 you must s there this word
23:16 own heart is what they s
23:21 I did not s to them, yet
23:28 let him s forth my word
26:2 s concerning all the cities
26:2 command you to s to them
26:8 commanded him to s to all
26:15 to s in your ears all these
30:2 words that I will s to you
32:4 s with the mouth of that one
34:3 s even with your mouth, and
34:6 s to Zedekiah the king of
35:2 and you must s with them and
38:25 you s about to the king
38:25 the king s about to you
39:12 just as he may s to you
44:25 women also s with your
52:32 s with him good things and
Eze 2:1 upon your feet that I may s
2:7 you must s my words to them
3:1 go, s to the house of Israel
3:4 s with my words to them
3:10 words that I shall s to you
3:11 s to them and say to them
3:18 and s in order to warn the
3:22 and there I shall s with you
3:24 he began to s with me and
3:27 I s with you I shall open
6:10 not in vain did I s about
11:25 to s to the exiled people
12:23 s to them, The days have
12:25 Jehovah, shall s what word
12:25 s, and it will be done
12:25 s a word and certainly do
12:28 s, it will even be done
14:4 s with them and you must
20:3 s with the elderly men of
20:27 s to the house of Israel, O
24:18 s to the people in the
24:27 s and be mute no longer
29:3 S, and you must say, This
32:21 s out of the midst of Sheol
33:2 s to the sons of your people
33:8 s out to warn the wicked one
36:5 s against the remaining ones
36:6 s, for the reason that

Eze 37:19 *s* to them, This is what the
37:21 And *s* to them, This is what
38:19 my fury, I shall have to *s*
40:4 the man began to *s* to me
40:45 And he proceeded to *s* to me
41:22 And he proceeded to *s* to me
Da 1:19 king began to *s* with them
7:25 *s* even words against the Most
9:22 and *s* with me and say
10:16 *s* and say to the one who was
10:17 able to *s* with this my lord
10:19 Let my lord *s*, because you
11:36 he will *s* marvelous things
Ho 2:14 and I will *s* to her heart
10:4 They *s* words, making false
Hab 2:1 to see what he will *s* by me
Zep 3:13 nor *s* a lie, nor will there
Zec 2:4 Run, *s* to the young man over
6:8 cry out to me and *s* to me
8:16 *S* truthfully with one
9:10 *s* peace to the nations
Mt 10:19 how or what you are to *s*
10:19 are to *s* will be given you
12:34 how can you *s* good things
12:36 men *s*, they will render an
12:46 outside seeking to *s* to him
12:47 outside, seeking to *s* to you
13:10 you *s* to them by the use of
13:13 I *s* to them by the use of
13:34 he would not *s* to them
18:17 *s* to the congregation. If he
Mr 1:34 would not let the demons *s*
2:2 and he began to *s* the word to
4:33 he would *s* the word to them
4:34 not *s* to them, but privately
7:37 hear and the speechless *s*
12:1 *s* to them with illustrations
13:11 anxious . . . about what to *s*
13:11 *s* this, for you are not the
14:71 this man of whom you *s*
15:29 would *s* abusively to him
Lu 1:19 I was sent forth to *s* with
1:20 not able to *s* until the day
1:22 he was not able to *s* to them
1:64 he began to *s*, blessing God
4:41 would not permit them to *s*
6:26 all men *s* well of you
7:15 man sat up and started to *s*
9:11 *s* to them about the kingdom
12:11 what you will *s* in defense
13:27 he will *s* and say to you
19:31 *s* in this way, The Lord
20:21 you *s* and teach correctly
Joh 1:37 two disciples heard him *s*
3:11 What we know we *s* and
7:13 *s* about him publicly because
7:17 or I *s* of my own originality
8:26 I have many things to *s*
8:28 as the Father taught me I *s*
8:38 have seen with my Father I *s*
8:46 If I *s* truth, why is it you
9:21 He must *s* for himself
12:49 what to tell and what to *s*
12:50 I *s*, just as the Father has
12:50 told me them, so I *s* them
13:13 you *s* rightly, for I am
14:10 not *s* of my own originality
14:30 I shall not *s* much with you
16:13 *s* of his own impulse, but
16:13 things he hears he will *s*
16:25 I will *s* to you no more
Ac 2:4 to *s* with different tongues
2:29 *s* with freeness of speech to
4:17 *s* anymore upon the basis of
11:14 *s* those things to you by
11:15 when I started to *s*, the
14:9 man was listening to Paul *s*
16:6 to *s* the word in the district
18:26 man started to *s* boldly in
20:30 and *s* twisted things to draw
21:37 He said: Can you *s* Greek?
21:39 permit me to *s* to the people
23:5 not *s* injuriously of a ruler
23:30 accusers to *s* against him
24:10 governor nodded to him to *s*
24:10 *s* in my defense the things
25:16 a chance to *s* in his defense
26:1 to *s* in behalf of yourself
28:20 to see and *s* to you, for
Ro 11:13 I *s* to you who are people
1Co 1:5 full ability to *s* and in full
1:10 all *s* in agreement, and that
2:6 *s* wisdom among those who
2:7 *s* God's wisdom in a sacred
1Co 2:13 These things we also *s*, not
3:1 *s* to you as to spiritual men
10:15 I *s* as to men with
12:30 Not all *s* in tongues, do
13:1 If I *s* in the tongues of men
13:11 I used to *s* as a babe, to
14:5 all of you to *s* in tongues
14:18 *s* in more tongues than all
14:19 *s* five words with my mind
14:21 will *s* to this people, and
14:23 and they all *s* in tongues
14:28 and *s* to himself and to God
14:29 let two or three prophets *s*
14:34 not permitted for them to *s*
14:35 for a woman to *s* in a
2Co 4:13 and therefore we *s*
6:13 I *s* as to children—you, too
11:17, 17 What I *s* I *s*, not
12:4 not lawful for a man to *s*
Ga 3:15 I *s* with a human
4:20 and to *s* in a different way
Eph 4:25 *s* truth each one of you with
6:19 ability to *s* may be given me
6:20 *s* in connection with it
6:20 boldness as I ought to *s*
Php 1:14 *s* the word of God fearlessly
Col 4:3 to *s* the sacred secret about
4:4 it manifest as I ought to *s*
1Th 2:2 to *s* to you the good news of
2:4 we *s*, as pleasing, not men
5:14 *s* consolingly to the
1Ti 4:2 hypocrisy of men who *s* lies
Tit 3:2 *s* injuriously of no one, not
Heb 9:5 not the time to *s* in detail
1Pe 4:11 *s* as it were the sacred
2Pe 2:10 but *s* abusively
2:12 ignorant and *s* abusively
1Jo 4:5 they *s* what proceeds from
2Jo 12 and to *s* with you face to face
3Jo 14 and we shall *s* face to face
Jude 16 mouths *s* swelling things
Re 13:15 *s* and cause to be killed

Speaker

Ex 4:10 I am not a fluent *s*, neither
1Sa 16:18 an intelligent *s* and a
Pr 16:13 *s* of upright things he loves
Am 5:10 a *s* of perfect things they
Ac 24:1 public *s*, a certain Tertullus

Speaking

Ge 16:13 Jehovah, who was *s* to her
17:22 God finished *s* with him and
18:30 but let me go on *s*: Suppose
18:33 he had finished *s* to Abraham
24:15 before he had finished *s*
24:45 *s* in my heart, why, there
27:6 heard your father *s* to Esau
29:9 yet *s* with them, Rachel came
31:24 *s* either good or bad with
31:29 *s* either good or bad with
34:3 kept *s* persuasively to the
45:12 my mouth that is *s* to you
45:27 they went on *s* to him all
Ex 4:10 since your *s* to your servant
6:27 were the ones *s* to Pharaoh
6:29 everything I am *s* to you
7:2 Aaron . . . will do the *s* to
7:7 the time of their *s* to Pharaoh
31:18 *s* with him on Mount Sinai
34:33 Moses would finish *s* with
Le 5:4 the extent of *s* thoughtlessly
6:19 Jehovah went on *s* to Moses
20:1 Jehovah went on *s* to Moses
23:1 went on *s* to Moses, saying
23:23 Jehovah went on *s* to Moses
Nu 5:5 Jehovah continued *s* to Moses
15:30 he *s* abusively of Jehovah, in
16:31 as soon as he had finished *s*
21:5 kept *s* against God and Moses
27:7 daughters . . . are *s* right
32:27 just as my lord is *s*
36:5 the sons of Joseph is *s* right
De 4:15 Jehovah's *s* to you in Horeb
4:33 heard the voice of God *s*
5:1 decisions that I am *s* in your
5:26 God *s* out of the middle of
18:17 done well in *s* what they did
20:9 the officers have finished *s*
32:45 finished *s* all these words
32:46 I am *s* in warning to you
Jg 6:17 you are the one *s* with me
8:8 *s* to them in this same manner
9:1 began *s* to them and to all the
9:3 began *s* all these words about
Jg 15:17 when he finished *s*, he
Ru 1:18 then she left off *s* to her
1Sa 1:13 she was *s* in her heart
9:25 *s* with Saul on the housetop
10:5 while they are *s* as prophets
10:13 he finished *s* as a prophet
14:19 Saul was *s* to the priest
17:23 While he was *s* with them
17:23 *s* the same words as before
18:1 as he had finished *s* to Saul
24:16 David finished *s* these
2Sa 11:19 As soon as you finish *s*
13:36 soon as he finished *s*, here
14:10 anyone *s* to you, you must
14:13 king is *s* this word he is
19:29 Why do you yet keep *s* your
1Ki 1:14 *s* there with the king
1:22 she was yet *s* with the king
1:42 yet *s*, why, here Jonathan
3:22 kept on *s* before the king
2Ki 2:11 *s* as they walked, why, look!
6:33 While he was yet *s* with
8:4 the king was *s* to Gehazi the
21:10 *s* by means of his servants
2Ch 30:10 *s* in mockery of them and
32:19 *s* against the God of
33:10 Jehovah kept *s* to Manasseh
33:18 visionaries that kept *s* to
Ne 13:24 sons, half were *s* Ashdodite
Es 1:22 *s* in the tongue of his own
6:14 While they were yet *s* with
10:3 *s* peace to all their offspring
Job 1:16 While this one was yet *s*
1:17 While that one was yet *s*
1:18 this other one was yet *s*
2:13 was no one *s* a word to him
21:3 after my *s* you may each
32:16 for they do not continue *s*
33:1 And to all my *s* do give ear
33:31 I myself shall continue *s*
Ps 5:6 You will destroy those *s* a lie
12:2 Untruth they keep *s* one to
12:2 *s* even with a double heart
12:3 The tongue *s* great things
15:2 And *s* the truth in his heart
28:3 *s* peace with their companions
31:18 *s* against the righteous one
34:13 your lips against *s* deception
44:16 reproaching and *s* abusively
52:3 more than *s* righteousness
58:3 They are *s* lies
63:11 mouth of those *s* falsehood
94:4 they keep *s* unrestrained
99:7 cloud he continued *s* to them
101:7 for anyone *s* falsehoods, he
109:20 *s* evil against my soul
114:1 a people *s* unintelligibly
Pr 2:12 the man *s* perverse things
12:18 one *s* thoughtlessly as with
24:2 is what their own lips keep *s*
Ca 4:3 and your *s* is agreeable
Isa 7:10 Jehovah went on *s* some more
9:17 mouth is *s* senselessness
19:18 *s* the language of Canaan
32:4 quick in *s* clear things
33:15 and *s* what is upright, who
45:19 *s* what is righteous
52:6 One that is *s*. Look! It is I
58:9 the *s* of what is hurtful
58:13 delights you and *s* a word
59:4 and a *s* of worthlessness
59:13 a *s* of oppression and revolt
63:1 the One *s* in righteousness
65:24 yet *s*, I myself shall hear
Jer 7:13 I kept *s* to you, getting up
7:13 getting up early and *s*
8:6 not right the way they kept *s*
9:8 *s* with his own companion
14:14 they are *s* prophetically
25:3 and I kept *s* to you people
25:3 rising up early and *s*
26:7 Jeremiah *s* these words in
26:8 *s* all that Jehovah had
28:7 this word that I am *s* in
29:23 *s* falsely in my own name
31:20 extent of my *s* against him
32:42 goodness that I am *s*
35:14 rising up early and *s*
38:1 Jeremiah was *s* to all the
38:4 *s* to them according to these
38:20 in what I am *s* to you
40:16 falsehood that you are *s*
43:1 Jeremiah finished *s* to all
43:2 is a falsehood that you are *s*

Eze 1:28 to hear the voice of one s
2:2 I might hear the One s to me
2:8 hear what I am s to you
33:30 sons of your people are s
43:6 s to me out of the House
44:5 s with you regarding all the
Da 5:13 king was s up and saying to
6:20 king was s up and saying to
7:2 Daniel was s up and saying
7:8 was a mouth s grandiose things
7:11 words that the horn was s
7:20 mouth s grandiose things and
8:13 certain holy one s, and
8:13 particular one who was s
8:18 while he was s with me, I
9:20 I was yet s and praying and
9:21 I was yet s in the prayer
10:11 words that I am s to you
11:27 lie is what they will keep s
Jon 3:2 proclamation that I am s to
Mic 7:3 the great one is s forth the
Zec 1:9 angel who was s with me said
1:13 the angel who was s with me
1:14 the angel who was s with me
1:19 the angel who was s with me
2:3 the angel who was s with me
4:1 the angel who was s with me
4:4 the angel who was s with me
4:5 the angel who was s with me
5:5 the angel who was s with me
5:10 the angel who was s with me
6:4 the angel who was s with me
10:2 dreams are what they keep s
Mt 10:20 the ones s are not just you
12:46 he was yet s to the crowds
15:31 saw the dumb s and the lame
17:5 yet s, look! a bright cloud
21:45 that he was s about them
26:47 he was yet s, look! Judas
27:39 passersby began s abusively
Mr 5:35 While he was yet s, some
7:35 and he began s normally
13:11 for you are not the ones s
14:43 while he was yet s, Judas
Lu 2:38 s about the child to all those
5:4 When he ceased s, he said to
5:21 Who is this . . . s blasphemies?
8:49 While he was yet s, a certain
21:5 s concerning the temple, how
22:47 While he was yet s, look!
22:60 was yet s, a cock crowed
24:32 he was s to us on the road
24:36 were s of these things he
Joh 4:26 I who am s to you am he
4:27 he was s with a woman
6:71 s of Judas the son of Simon
7:26 see! he is s in public, and
8:25 Why am I even s to you at
8:26 I am s in the world
8:30 As he was s these things
8:43 you do not know what I am s
9:37 he that is s with you is
10:6 things meant that he was s
11:13 s about taking rest in
16:29 you are s with plainness
17:13 I am s these things in the
19:10 Are you not s to me?
Ac 2:6 s in his own language
2:7 these who are s are Galileans
2:11 s in our tongues about the
4:1 the two were s to the people
4:20 we cannot stop s about the
4:29 s your word with all boldness
4:31 s the word of God with
5:20 s to the people all the
5:40 s upon the basis of Jesus'
6:10 spirit with which he was s
6:11 him s blasphemous sayings
6:13 s things against his holy
7:44 when s to Moses to make it
9:28 s boldly in the name of the
10:44 Peter was yet s about these
10:46 them s with tongues and
11:19 s the word to no one except
13:43 in s to them began urging
14:3 time s with boldness by the
14:12 the one taking the lead in s
14:25 after s the word in Perga
15:13 After they quit s, James
16:13 began s to the women that
18:6 opposing and s abusively, he
18:9 Have no fear, but keep on s
18:25 he went s and teaching with
19:6 they began s with tongues and
Ac 19:9 s injuriously about The Way
22:9 the voice of the one s to me
25:12 Festus, after s with the
26:26 s with freeness of speech
28:19 Jews kept s against it, I
Ro 3:5 I am s as a man does
6:19 am s in human terms because
7:1 I am s to those who know law
1Co 6:5 I am s to move you to shame
9:8 Am I s these things by human
12:3 when s by God's spirit says
14:6 come s to you in tongues
14:9 in fact, be s into the air
14:11 be a foreigner to the one s
14:11 one s will be a foreigner
14:39 not forbid the s in tongues
15:34 s to move you to shame
2Co 2:17 with Christ, we are s
8:8 of your love, that I am s
12:19 s in connection with Christ
13:3 proof of Christ s in me
Eph 4:15 s the truth, let us by love
5:19 s to yourselves with psalms
5:32 s with respect to Christ
Php 4:11 Not that I am s with regard
1Th 2:16 hinder us from s to people
1Ti 4:12 in s, in conduct, in love
5:17 work hard in s and teaching
Tit 2:1 s what things are fitting
2:15 Keep on s these things and
Heb 2:5 about which we are s
6:9 although we are s in this way
12:25 beg off from him who is s
Jas 1:19 about hearing, slow about s
2:12 Keep on s in such a way and
4:11 Quit s against one another
1Pe 2:12 s against you as evildoers
3:10 his lips from s deception
3:16 s slightingly of your good
4:4 go on s abusively of you
2Pe 3:16 s about these things as he
Jude 8 s abusively of glorious ones
10 s abusively of all the
Re 1:9 Patmos for s about God and
1:12 voice that was s with me
4:1 as of a trumpet, s with me
10:8 is s again with me and saying
13:5 mouth s great things and
13:11 but it began s as a dragon
20:4 and for s about God, and
21:15 one who was s with me was

Speaks
Ex 7:9 In case that Pharaoh s to you
De 18:20 s in the name of other gods
18:22 the prophet s in the name of
Job 2:10 one of the senseless women s
33:14 God s once, And twice
34:35 Job . . . s without knowledge
Ps 37:30 the tongue that s justly
Pr 18:23 one of little means s out
Ec 10:14 the foolish one s many words
Isa 32:7 someone poor s what is right
Eze 10:5 of God Almighty when he s
14:9 fooled and actually s a word
Mt 10:20 spirit of your Father that s
12:32 s a word against the Son of
12:32 s against the holy spirit
12:34 of the heart the mouth s
Lu 6:45 abundance his mouth s
Joh 3:31 and s of things of the earth
3:34 s the sayings of God, for he
7:18 s of his own originality is
8:44 When he s the lie, he
8:44 he s according to his own
19:12 a king s against Caesar
Ac 3:22 to all the things he s to you
Ro 4:6 David also s of the happiness
10:6 from faith s in this manner
1Co 14:2 For he that s in a tongue
14:2 s, not to men, but to God
14:2 he s sacred secrets by the
14:4 s in a tongue upbuilds
14:5 than he that s in tongues
14:13 the one who s in a tongue
14:27 if someone s in a tongue
Heb 11:4 although he died, yet s
12:24 which s in a better way
12:25 him who s from the heavens
Jas 4:11 He who s against a brother
4:11 s against law and judges law
1Pe 4:11 If anyone s, let him speak

Spear
1Sa 13:19 not make a sword or a s
1Sa 13:22 that not a sword or a s was
17:7 wooden shaft of his s was
17:7 the blade of his s was six
17:45 with a sword and with a s
17:47 nor with s does Jehovah
18:10 the s was in Saul's hand
18:11 hurl the s and say: I will
19:9 s in his hand, while David
19:10 to the wall with the s
19:10 struck the s into the wall
20:33 Saul went hurling the s at
21:8 disposal, a s or a sword
22:6 with his s in his hand and
26:7 his s stuck into the earth
26:8 to the earth with the s just
26:11 s that is at his head and
26:12 David took the s and the
26:16 where the king's s and the
26:22 Here is the s of the king
2Sa 1:6 supporting himself upon his s
2:23 with the butt end of the s
2:23 s came out from his back
21:16 the weight of whose s was
21:19 s was like the beam of
23:7 iron and the shaft of a s
23:8 his s over eight hundred
23:18 s over three hundred slain
23:21 a s in the hand of the
23:21 snatched the s away from
23:21 killed him with his own s
1Ch 11:11 He was brandishing his s
11:20 he was brandishing his s
11:23 a s like the beam of loom
11:23 snatched the s away from
11:23 killed him with his own s
12:34 the large shield and the s
20:5 shaft of whose s was like
Job 39:23 blade of a s and a javelin
41:26 Nor s, dart or arrowhead
Ps 35:3 draw s and double ax to meet
46:9 and does cut the s in pieces
Na 3:3 the lightning of the s, and the
Hab 3:11 your s served for brightness
Mt 27:49 man took a s and pierced his
Joh 19:34 jabbed his side with a s

Spearhead
Ac 24:5 s of the sect of the Nazarenes

Spearmen
Ac 23:23 two hundred s, at the third

Spears
2Ki 11:10 the chiefs of hundreds the s
2Ch 23:9 s and the shields and the
Job 41:7 Or its head with fish s
Ps 57:4 Whose teeth are s and arrows
Isa 2:4 their s into pruning shears
Mic 4:3 their s into pruning shears
Na 2:3 the juniper tree s have been

Special
Ex 19:5 become my s property out of
Le 27:2 s vow offering of souls
Nu 6:2 s vow to live as a Nazirite to
15:3 sacrifice to perform a s vow
15:8 sacrifice to perform a s vow
De 7:6 a s property, out of all the
14:2 a s property, out of all the
26:18 a s property, just as he
Jg 12:2 I became a s contender, I and
1Ch 29:3 a s property of mine, gold
2Ch 16:14 in an ointment of s make
Ps 90:10 because of s mightiness they
135:4 Israel for his s property
Pr 25:12 an ornament of s gold, is a
Jer 2:10 give your s consideration
Eze 27:17 and s foodstuff and honey
Mal 3:17 I am producing a s property
1Pe 2:9 a people for s possession

Specially
Ex 2:7 s call for you a nursing
Pr 8:30 one he was s fond of day by

Species
Ps 105:34 s of locust, even without
Isa 44:14 takes a certain s of tree
Na 3:15 devour you like the locust s
3:15 in numbers like the locust s
3:16 As for the locust s, it
Jas 3:7 every s of wild beast as well

Specifically
1Sa 20:21 s say to the attendant
Eze 1:3 occurred s to Ezekiel the
Heb 5:10 s called by God a high priest

Specifications
Eze 43:11 ground plans and all its s
43:11 ground plan and all its s

Speckled
Ge 30:32 sheep s and with color
30:32 any color-patched and s one
30:33 every one that is not s
30:35 she-goats s and color-patched
30:39 s and color-patched ones
31:8 s ones will become your
31:8 whole flock produced s ones
31:10 he-goats . . . were striped, s
31:12 the he-goats . . . striped, s
Zec 6:3 horses s, parti-colored
6:6 s ones, they must go forth to

Spectacle
Na 3:6 I will set you as a s
Mt 1:19 to make her a public s
Lu 23:48 together there for this s
1Co 4:9 a theatrical s to the world

Spectators
2Ch 7:3 sons of Israel were s when

Speech
Job 12:20 He is removing s from the
Ps 19:2 causes s to bubble forth
19:3 There is no s, and there are
64:3 aimed their arrow, bitter s
64:5 hold themselves down to bad s
Pr 4:24 the crookedness of s
6:12 walking with crookedness of s
29:12 paying attention to false s
Eze 3:17 must hear from my mouth s
Mt 22:15 order to trap him in his s
Mr 7:32 deaf and with a s impediment
12:13 to catch him in his s
Lu 4:32 his s was with authority
4:36 What sort of s is this
20:20 might catch him in s, so as
Joh 6:60 This s is shocking; who can
Ac 2:29 with freeness of s to you
4:4 listened to the s believed
7:29 At this s Moses took to
18:15 is controversies over s and
20:7 and he prolonged his s until
26:26 speaking with freeness of s
28:31 the greatest freeness of s
Ro 16:18 complimentary s they seduce
1Co 1:17 not with wisdom of s, that
1:18 the s about the torture stake
2:1 an extravagance of s or of
2:4 my s and what I preached
4:19 not the s of those who are
4:20 lies not in s, but in power
12:8 to one . . . the s of wisdom
12:8 to another s of knowledge
14:3 consoles men by his s
14:9 utter s easily understood
14:10 so many kinds of s sounds
14:11 the force of the s sound
15:2 the s with which I declared
2Co 1:18 our s addressed to you is not
3:12 are using great freeness of s
6:7 by truthful s, by God's power
7:4 I have great freeness of s
10:10 and his s contemptible
11:6 even if I am unskilled in s
Eph 3:12 we have this freeness of s
4:31 abusive s be taken away
6:19 with all freeness of s to
Php 1:20 in all freeness of s Christ
Col 3:8 abusive s, and obscene talk
1Th 1:5 with s alone but also with
2:5 either with flattering s
1Ti 3:13 and great freeness of s in
Tit 2:8 s which cannot be condemned
Phm 8 freeness of s in connection
Heb 3:6 on our freeness of s and our
4:16 approach with freeness of s
10:35 away your freeness of s
1Jo 2:28 have freeness of s and not
3:21 freeness of s toward God
4:17 we may have freeness of s

Speeches
Ac 15:24 caused you trouble with s
1Ti 6:4 envy, strife, abusive s
6:20 s that violate what is holy
2Ti 2:16 s that violate what is holy

Speechless
Ex 4:11 who appoints the s or the
1Sa 10:27 continued like one grown s
Ne 5:8 became s, and they did not
Ps 31:18 May false lips become s
38:13 like someone s, I would not
39:2 I became s with silence
39:9 I kept s; I could not open my
83:1 Do not keep s, and do not
Pr 31:8 Open your mouth for the s one
Isa 35:6 tongue of the s one will cry
56:10 All of them are s dogs
Eze 33:22 proved to be s no longer
Da 10:15 and had become s
Hab 2:18 valueless gods that are s
Mt 22:12 He was rendered s
Mr 7:37 the deaf hear and the s speak
9:17 because he has a s spirit
9:25 You s and deaf spirit, I
Ac 9:7 standing s, hearing, indeed

Speed
1Ch 12:8 like the gazelles . . . for s
Es 3:15 s because of the king's word
8:14 with s by the king's word
Ps 147:15 With s his word runs
Isa 60:22 s it up in its own time
Joh 20:4 with greater s and reached

Speedily
De 9:3 destroy them s, just as
11:17 perish s from off the good
2Sa 17:16 send s and tell David
17:18 the two of them went off s
17:21 and s pass over the waters
Ps 31:2 Deliver me s. Become for me
37:2 like grass they will s wither
Ec 8:11 has not been executed s, that
Isa 51:14 certainly be loosened s
58:8 s would recuperation spring
Joe 3:4 s I shall pay back your
Lu 18:8 justice to be done to them s
2Th 3:1 word . . . may keep moving s

Speeding
Ge 41:32 the true God is s to do it
Hab 1:8 fly like the eagle s to eat

Speedy
Es 8:10 sons of s mares
Mal 3:5 a s witness against the
Ro 3:15 feet are s to shed blood
2Pe 2:1 bringing s destruction upon

Spell
Nu 23:23 is no unlucky s against Jacob
De 18:11 binds others with a s or

Spells
Ps 58:5 is binding with s
Isa 47:9 the full might of your s
47:12 with your s and with the
Eze 26:16 will put on trembling s

Spelt
Ex 9:32 the s had not been struck
Isa 28:25 and s as his boundary
Eze 4:9 lentils and millet and s, and

Spend
Ge 24:23 father for us to s the night
24:25 also a place to s the night
De 32:23 arrows I shall s upon them
Jg 18:2 and got to s the night there
Ru 1:16 where you s the night I shall
1:16 I shall s the night
2Sa 17:8 s the night with the people
1Ki 19:9 he might s the night there
1Ch 9:27 they would s the night
Ne 4:22 Let the men s the night, each
Job 21:13 s their days in good times
31:32 alien . . . would s the night
39:9 s the night by your manger
Pr 19:23 will s the night satisfied
Ca 1:13 breasts he will s the night
Isa 10:29 for them to s the night
21:13 plain you will s the night
Jer 14:8 turned aside to s the night
Joe 1:13 s the night in sackcloth
Zep 2:14 s the night right among her
Lu 10:35 whatever you s besides this
Ac 17:21 would s their leisure time
20:16 might not s any time in the
2Co 12:15 I will most gladly s and
Jas 4:13 and will s a year there, and

Spending
Ge 28:11 set about s the night there
Jos 3:1 went s the night there before
Ne 13:21 s the night in front of the
Ac 15:35 continued s time in Antioch
16:12 in this city, s some days
25:14 s a number of days there

Spends
Ec 6:12 when he s them like a shadow

Spent
Ge 24:54 they s the night there and
47:15 money . . . of Canaan was s
47:18 domestic animals have been s
2Sa 12:16 s the night and lay down
Ne 13:20 s the night outside
Da 6:18 and s the night fasting, and
Mr 5:26 had s all her resources and
Lu 15:14 When he had s everything
Joh 3:22 there he s some time with
4:38 what you have s no labor on
Ac 12:19 Caesarea and s some time
14:3 s considerable time speaking
14:28 So they s not a little time
20:3 he had s three months there
20:6 in Troas . . . we s seven days
25:6 s not more than eight or ten
2Co 11:25 a day I have s in the deep
12:15 completely s for your souls

Spice
Ex 30:35 a s mixture, the work of an
Ca 5:1 my myrrh along with my s
5:13 are like a garden bed of s
6:2 to the garden beds of s plants
Re 18:13 cinnamon and Indian s and

Spiced
Ca 8:2 give you a drink of s wine

Spices
Ca 8:14 stags upon the mountains of s
Mr 16:1 s in order to come and grease
Lu 23:56 prepare s and perfumed oils
24:1 the s they had prepared
Joh 19:40 with bandages with the s

Spider
Isa 59:5 the mere cobweb of a s

Spider's
Job 8:14 And whose trust is a s house

Spied
Nu 13:21 went up and s out the land
13:32 the land that they had s out
14:6 of those who s out the land
14:34 days that you s out the land
Jos 7:2 the men went up and s on Ai
Eze 20:6 a land that I had s out for

Spies
Ge 42:9 You are s! You have come to
42:11 Your servants do not act as s
42:14 saying, You are s!
42:16 as Pharaoh lives, you are s
42:31 We do not act as s
42:34 may know that you are no s
Jos 2:1 secretly from Shittim as s
1Sa 26:4 David sent s that he might
2Sa 15:10 Absalom now sent s through
Pr 12:26 s out his own pasturage
Heb 11:31 she received the s in a

Spikenard
Ca 1:12 s has given out its fragrance
4:13 plants along with s plants
4:14 s and saffron, cane and

Spill
Ge 37:22 Do not s blood. Pitch him

Spilled
Le 25:5 growth from s kernels of your
25:11 from s kernels nor gather
Nu 35:33 blood that has been s upon it
De 19:10 no innocent blood may be s
2Sa 20:10 his intestines s out to the
1Ki 2:31 the blood . . . that Joab s
13:3 will certainly be s out
13:5 the fatty ashes were s out
2Ki 19:29 the growth from s kernels
1Ch 22:8 in great quantity you have s
22:8 blood you have s on the earth
28:3 and blood you have s
Isa 37:30 growth from s kernels, and
Mt 23:35 righteous blood s on earth
Lu 5:37 s out and the wineskins will
11:50 blood of all the prophets s
Ac 22:20 blood of Stephen . . . being s

Spilling
Nu 35:33 by the blood of the one s it
Ps 106:38 they kept s innocent blood

Spills
Mt 9:17 burst and the wine s out

Spin
Mt 6:28 do not toil, nor do they s
Lu 12:27 they neither toil nor s

Spindle
2Sa 3:29 hold of the twirling s or
Pr 31:19 own hands take hold of the s

Spiny
Isa 32:13 s bushes come up, for they

Spirit
Ge 6:3 Jehovah said: My s shall not
26:35 bitterness of s to Isaac
41:8 that his s became agitated
41:38 one in whom the s of God is
45:27 the s of Jacob their father
Ex 28:3 filled with the s of wisdom
31:3 fill him with the s of God
35:21 everyone whose s incited him
35:31 fill him with the s of God
Le 19:31 s mediums, and do not
20:6 to the s mediums and the
20:27 proves to be a mediumistic s
20:27 or s of prediction . . . death
Nu 5:14 s of jealousy has passed upon
5:14 s of jealousy has passed upon
5:30 where the s of jealousy may
11:17 take away some of the s that
11:25 took away some of the s that
11:25 s settled down upon them
11:26 s began to settle down upon
11:29 Jehovah would put his s upon
14:24 a different s has proved to
24:2 s of God came to be upon him
27:18 a man in whom there is s
De 2:30 let his s become obstinate
18:11 consults a s medium or a
34:9 was full of the s of wisdom
Jos 2:11 and no s has arisen yet in
Jg 3:10 The s of Jehovah now came
6:34 Jehovah's s enveloped Gideon
8:3 their s calmed down toward
9:23 a bad s between Abimelech and
11:29 s now came upon Jephthah
13:25 s started to impel him in
14:6 s became operative upon him
14:19 s became operative upon him
15:14 s became operative upon him
15:19 his s returned and he revived
1Sa 1:15 hard pressed in s I am
10:6 s of Jehovah will certainly
10:10 s of God became operative
11:6 s of God became operative
16:13 the s of Jehovah began to be
16:14 s of Jehovah departed from
16:14 and a bad s from Jehovah
16:15 God's bad s is terrorizing
16:16 when God's bad s comes to
16:23 s came to be upon Saul
16:23 bad s departed from upon
18:10 bad s became operative upon
19:9 Jehovah's bad s came to be
19:20 s of God came to be upon
19:23 s of God came to be upon
28:3 removed the s mediums and
28:7 mistress of s mediumship
28:7 mistress of s mediumship in
28:8 by s mediumship and bring
28:9 cut off the s mediums and
30:12 he ate and his s returned
2Sa 22:11 upon the wings of a s
23:2 The s of Jehovah it was that
1Ki 10:5 be no more s in her
18:12 the s of Jehovah itself
21:5 that your s is sad and you
22:21 a s came out and stood
22:22 a deceptive s in the mouth
22:23 deceptive s into the mouth
22:24 did the s of Jehovah pass
2Ki 2:9 two parts in your s may come
2:15 The s of Elijah has settled
2:16 s of Jehovah has lifted him
19:7 Here I am putting a s in him
21:6 s mediums and professional
23:24 the s mediums and the
1Ch 5:26 stirred up the s of Pul the
5:26 the s of Tilgath-pilneser
10:13 a s medium to make inquiry
12:18 s itself enveloped Amasai
2Ch 9:4 to be no more s in her
15:1 s of God came to be upon him
18:20 s came out and stood before
18:21 deceptive s in the mouth of
18:22 deceptive s in the mouth of
2Ch 18:23 s of Jehovah pass along
20:14 s of Jehovah came to be
21:16 s of the Philistines and the
24:20 God's s itself enveloped
36:22 roused the s of Cyrus the
Ezr 1:1 roused the s of Cyrus the king
1:5 s the true God had roused
Ne 9:20 your good s you gave to make
9:30 s by means of your prophets
Job 4:9 through the s of his anger
4:15 a s itself went passing over
6:4 venom . . . my s is drinking
7:11 in the distress of my s
10:12 own care has guarded my s
12:10 the s of all flesh of man
15:13 you turn your s against God
17:1 My very s has been broken
20:3 s without the understanding
21:4 my s does not get impatient
27:3 s of God is in my nostrils
32:8 it is the s in mortal men
32:18 S has brought pressure upon
33:4 God's own s made me, And
34:14 If that one's s and breath
Ps 18:10 upon the wings of a s
31:5 Into your hand I entrust my s
32:2 whose s there is no deceit
33:6 by the s of his mouth all
34:18 those who are crushed in s
51:10 And put within me a new s
51:11 holy s O do not take away
51:12 even with a willing s
51:17 sacrifices . . . a broken s
76:12 will humble the s of leaders
77:3 that my s may faint away
77:6 my s will carefully search
78:8 whose s was not trustworthy
78:39 s is going forth and does
104:29 If you take away their s
104:30 If you send forth your s
106:33 For they embittered his s
135:17 exists no s in their mouth
139:7 Where can I go from your s
142:3 s fainted away within me
143:4 my s faints away within me
143:7 My s has come to an end
143:10 my God. Your s is good
146:4 His s goes out, he goes back
Pr 1:23 cause my s to bubble forth
11:13 one faithful in s is covering
15:4 a breaking down in the s
15:13 there is a stricken s
16:18 a haughty s before stumbling
16:19 be lowly in s with the meek
16:32 he that is controlling his s
17:22 s that is stricken makes the
17:27 of discernment is cool of s
18:14 s of a man can put up with
18:14 stricken s, who can bear it?
25:28 has no restraint for his s
29:11 All his s is what a stupid
29:23 humble in s will take hold
Ec 3:19 and they all have but one s
3:21 the s of the sons of mankind
3:21 s of the beast, whether it is
7:8 than one who is haughty in s
7:9 not hurry yourself in your s to
8:8 no man having power over the s
8:8 to restrain the s
10:4 s of a ruler should mount up
11:5 s in the bones in the belly of
12:7 s itself returns to the true
Isa 4:4 by the s of judgment and by
4:4 by the s of burning down
8:19 having a s of prediction
11:2 s of Jehovah must settle
11:2 the s of wisdom and of
11:2 the s of counsel and of
11:2 s of knowledge and of the
11:4 s of his lips he will put
11:15 in the glow of his s
19:3 s of Egypt must become
19:3 and to the s mediums and
19:14 the s of disconcertedness
26:9 s within me I keep looking
28:6 s of justice to the one
29:4 like a s medium your voice
29:10 poured a s of deep sleep
29:24 who are erring in their s
30:1 but not with my s, in order
30:28 s is like a flooding torrent
31:3 horses are flesh, and not s
32:15 s is poured out from on
33:11 Your own s, as a fire
Isa 34:16 his s that has collected
37:7 I am putting a s in him, and
38:16 thereby is the life of my s
40:7 s of Jehovah has blown upon
40:13 the s of Jehovah, and
42:1 I have put my s in him
42:5 and s to those walking in it
44:3 pour out my s upon your seed
48:16 has sent me, even his s
54:6 left entirely and hurt in s
57:15 one crushed and lowly in s
57:15 revive the s of the lowly
57:16 s itself would grow feeble
59:19 s of Jehovah has driven
59:21 My s that is upon you and
61:1 The s of the Sovereign Lord
61:3 instead of the downhearted s
63:10 made his holy s feel hurt
63:11 within him His own holy s
63:14 s of Jehovah proceeded to
65:14 sheer breakdown of s
66:2 afflicted and contrite in s
Jer 10:14 and there is no s in them
51:11 Jehovah has aroused the s of
51:17 there is no s in them
Eze 1:12 wherever the s would incline
1:20 s inclined to go, they would
1:20 the s inclining to go there
1:20 s of the living creature was
1:21 s of the living creature was
2:2 s began to come into me as
3:12 a s proceeded to bear me
3:14 And the s bore me along and
3:14 bitterly in the rage of my s
3:24 s entered into me and made
8:3 a s carried me between the
10:17 the s of the living creature
11:1 a s proceeded to lift me up
11:5 s of Jehovah fell upon me
11:5 that come up in your s, I
11:19 a new s I shall put inside
11:24 a s itself lifted me up and
11:24 the vision by the s of God
13:3 walking after their own s
18:31 a new heart and a new s
20:32 is coming up into your s
21:7 every s must become dejected
36:26 a new heart, and a new s
36:27 my s I shall put inside you
37:1 forth in the s of Jehovah
37:14 I will put my s in you
39:29 pour out my s upon the
43:5 s proceeded to raise me up
Da 2:1 s began to feel agitated, and
2:3 s is agitated to know the
4:8 there is the s of the holy gods
4:9 s of the holy gods is in you
4:18 the s of holy gods is in you
5:11 is the s of holy gods; and in
5:12 extraordinary s and knowledge
5:14 the s of gods is in you, and
5:20 and his own s became hard
6:3 extraordinary s was in him
7:15 Daniel, my s was distressed
Ho 4:12 the very s of fornication has
5:4 a s of fornication in the
Joe 2:28 s on every sort of flesh
2:29 I shall pour out my s
Mic 2:7 Has the s of Jehovah become
3:8 full of power, with the s
Hag 1:14 rouse up the s of Zerubbabel
1:14 the s of Joshua the son of
1:14 s of all the remaining ones
2:5 my s was standing in among
Zec 4:6 by my s, Jehovah of armies
6:8 caused the s of Jehovah to
7:12 sent by his s, by means of
12:1 forming the s of man inside
12:10 s of favor and entreaties
13:2 and the s of uncleanness I
Mal 2:15 what was remaining of the s
2:15 respecting your s, and with
2:16 guard . . . respecting your s
Mt 1:18 to be pregnant by holy s
1:20 begotten in her is by holy s
3:11 baptize . . . with holy s
3:16 like a dove God's s coming
4:1 Jesus was led by the s up into
10:20 s of your Father that speaks
12:18 I will put my s upon him
12:28 by means of God's s that I
12:31 the blasphemy against the s
12:32 speaks against the holy s
12:43 an unclean s comes out of a

Mt 26:41 s, of course, is eager, but
27:50 Jesus . . . yielded up his s
28:19 of the Son and of the holy s
Mr 1:8 will baptize you with holy s
1:10 like a dove, the s coming
1:12 s impelled him to go into
1:23 the power of an unclean s
1:26 the unclean s, after throwing
2:8 having discerned . . . by his s
3:29 blasphemes against the holy s
3:30 saying: He has an unclean s
5:2 the power of an unclean s
5:8 out of the man, you unclean s
7:25 daughter had an unclean s
8:12 he groaned deeply with his s
9:17 because he has a speechless s
9:20 the s at once threw the child
9:25 rebuked the unclean s, saying
9:25 s, I order you, get out of
12:36 By the holy s David himself
13:11 speaking, but the holy s is
14:38 The s, of course, is eager
Lu 1:15 will be filled with holy s
1:17 with Elijah's s and power, to
1:35 Holy s will come upon you
1:41 was filled with holy s
1:47 my s cannot keep from being
1:67 filled with holy s, and he
1:80 getting strong in s, and he
2:25 and holy s was upon him
2:26 revealed to him by the holy s
2:27 Under the power of the s he
3:16 baptize . . . with holy s
3:22 the holy s in bodily shape
4:1 Jesus, full of holy s, turned
4:1 was led about by the s in the
4:14 in the power of the s
4:18 Jehovah's s is upon me
4:33 with a s, an unclean demon
8:29 the unclean s to come out of
8:55 her s returned, and she rose
9:39 a s takes him, and suddenly
9:42 Jesus rebuked the unclean s
10:21 overjoyed in the holy s and
11:13 give holy s to those asking
11:24 When an unclean s comes out
12:10 against the holy s will not
12:12 holy s will teach you in
13:11 woman with a s of weakness
23:46 your hands I entrust my s
24:37 imagining they beheld a s
24:39 a s does not have flesh and
Joh 1:32 s coming down as a dove out
1:33 the s coming down and
1:33 one that baptizes in holy s
3:5 is born from water and s
3:6, 6 been born from the s is s
3:8 has been born from the s
3:34 not give the s by measure
4:23 worship the Father with s
4:24 God is a S, and those
4:24 worship with s and truth
6:63 is the s that is life-giving
6:63 sayings . . . s and are life
7:39 said this concerning the s
7:39 for as yet there was no s
11:33 groaned in the s and became
13:21 Jesus became troubled in s
14:17 s of the truth, which the
14:26 the helper, the holy s
15:26 the s of the truth, which
16:13 the s of the truth, he will
19:30 he delivered up his s
20:22 to them: Receive holy s
Ac 1:2 commandment through holy s
1:5 baptized in holy s not many
1:8 the holy s arrives upon you
1:16 holy s spoke beforehand by
2:4 became filled with holy s and
2:4 s was granting them to make
2:17 s upon every sort of flesh
2:18 I will pour out some of my s
2:33 promised holy s from the
2:38 the free gift of the holy s
4:8 Peter, filled with holy s
4:25 holy s said by the mouth of
4:31 all filled with the holy s
5:3 play false to the holy s and
5:9 a test of the s of Jehovah
5:32 holy s . . . to those obeying
6:3 full of s and wisdom, that
6:5 man full of faith and holy s
6:10 s with which he was speaking
7:51 always resisting the holy s
Ac 7:55 he, being full of holy s
7:59 Lord Jesus, receive my s
8:15 for them to get holy s
8:17 they began to receive holy s
8:18 apostles the s was given, he
8:19 may receive holy s
8:29 s said to Philip: Approach
8:39 Jehovah's s quickly led
9:17 and be filled with holy s
9:31 in the comfort of the holy s
10:19 s said: Look! Three men are
10:38 anointed him with holy s
10:44 holy s fell upon all those
10:45 free gift of the holy s was
10:47 received the holy s even as
11:12 s told me to go with them
11:15 holy s fell upon them just
11:16 will be baptized in holy s
11:24 full of holy s and of faith
11:28 indicate through the s that
13:2 holy s said: Of all persons
13:4 sent out by the holy s
13:9 filled with holy s, looked
13:52 filled with joy and holy s
15:8 by giving them the holy s
15:28 holy s and we ourselves have
16:6 forbidden by the holy s to
16:7 the s of Jesus did not permit
16:16 girl with a s, a demon of
16:18 and turned and said to the s
17:16 s . . . came to be irritated
18:25 as he was aglow with the s
19:2 Did you receive holy s when
19:2 whether there is a holy s
19:6 the holy s came upon them
19:15 in answer the wicked s said
19:16 man in whom the wicked s
19:21 Paul purposed in his s that
20:22 look! bound in the s, I am
20:23 the holy s repeatedly bears
20:28 the holy s has appointed you
21:4 through the s they repeatedly
21:11 says the holy s, The man to
23:8 Sadducees say . . . angel nor s
23:9 a s or an angel spoke to him
28:25 holy s aptly spoke through
Ro 1:4 to the s of holiness by means
1:9 sacred service with my s in
2:29 is that of the heart by s
5:5 our hearts through the holy s
7:6 in a new sense by the s
8:2 s which gives life in union
8:4 but in accord with the s
8:5 those in accord with the s on
8:5 on the things of the s
8:6 minding of the s means life
8:9 with the flesh, but with the s
8:9 if God's s truly dwells in you
8:9 anyone does not have Christ's s
8:10 s is life on account of
8:11 s of him that raised up Jesus
8:11 his s that resides in you
8:13 of the body to death by the s
8:14 all who are led by God's s
8:15 s of slavery causing fear
8:15 s of adoption as sons, by
8:15 by which s we cry out: *Abba*
8:16 s itself bears witness with
8:16 bears witness with our s
8:23 firstfruits, namely, the s
8:26 s also joins in with help
8:26 s itself pleads for us with
8:27 what the meaning of the s is
9:1 witness with me in holy s
11:8 given them a s of deep sleep
12:11 Be aglow with the s
14:17 peace and joy with holy s
15:13 with power of holy s
15:16 sanctified with holy s
15:19 with the power of holy s; so
15:30 through the love of the s
1Co 2:4 a demonstration of s and
2:10 revealed them through his s
2:10 s searches into all things
2:11 except the s of man that is
2:11 except the s of God
2:12 not the s of the world, but
2:12 but the s which is from God
2:13 with those taught by the s
2:14 the things of the s of God
3:16 the s of God dwells in you
4:21 come . . . and mildness of s
5:3 present in s, have certainly
5:4 also my s with the power of
1Co 5:5 s may be saved in the day of
6:11 and with the s of our God
6:17 joined to the Lord is one s
6:19 is the temple of the holy s
7:34 may be holy . . . in her s
7:40 think I also have God's s
12:3 when speaking by God's s
12:3 except by holy s
12:4 but there is the same s
12:7 manifestation of the s is
12:8 there is given through the s
12:8 according to the same s
12:9 faith by the same s, to
12:9 healings by that one s
12:11 the one and the same s
12:13 For truly by one s we
12:13 all made to drink one s
14:2 sacred secrets by the s
14:12 desirous of gifts of the s
14:14 it is my gift of the s that
14:15 pray with the gift of the s
14:15 with the gift of the s, but
14:16 with a gift of the s, how
14:32 And gifts of the s of the
14:37 or gifted with the s, let
15:45 Adam became a life-giving s
16:18 refreshed my s and yours
2Co 1:22 given us the token . . . the s
2:13 no relief in my s on account
3:3 with s of a living God, not
3:6 of a written code, but of s
3:6 but the s makes alive
3:8 administering of the s be
3:17 Jehovah is the S; and where
3:17 where the s of Jehovah is
3:18 as done by Jehovah the S
4:13 same s of faith as that of
5:5 is to come, that is, the s
6:6 by kindness, by holy s, by
7:1 defilement of flesh and s
7:13 his s has been refreshed by
11:4 you receive a s other than
12:18 We walked in the same s
13:14 sharing in the holy s be
Ga 3:2 receive the s due to works of
3:3 After starting in s are you
3:5 supplies you the s and
3:14 promised s through our
4:6 s of his Son into our hearts
4:29 one born in the manner of s
5:5 by s are eagerly waiting for
5:16 Keep walking by s and you
5:17 flesh is against the s in its
5:17 and the s against the flesh
5:18 if you are being led by s
5:22 fruitage of the s is love, joy
5:25 If we are living by s, let
5:25 walking orderly also by s
6:1 such a man in a s of mildness
6:8 sowing with a view to the s
6:8 everlasting life from the s
6:18 Christ be with the s you show
Eph 1:13 with the promised holy s
1:17 give you a s of wisdom and
2:2 s that now operates in the
2:18 to the Father by one s
2:22 place for God to inhabit by s
3:5 been revealed . . . by s
3:16 with power through his s
4:3 observe the oneness of the s
4:4 One body there is, and one s
4:30 not be grieving God's holy s
5:18 keep getting filled with s
6:12 against the wicked s forces
6:17 the sword of the s, that is
6:18 prayer on every occasion in s
Php 1:19 a supply of the s of Jesus
1:27 are standing firm in one s
2:1 if any sharing of s, if any
3:3 sacred service by God's s
4:23 be with the s you show
Col 2:5 I am with you in the s
1Th 1:5 with power and with holy s
1:6 with joy of holy s
4:8 who puts his holy s in you
5:19 not put out the fire of the s
5:23 may the s and soul and body
2Th 2:8 by the s of his mouth and
2:13 by sanctifying you with s
1Ti 3:16 was declared righteous in s
2Ti 1:7 gave us not a s of cowardice
1:14 holy s which is dwelling in
4:22 Lord be with the s you show
Tit 3:5 making of us new by holy s

Tit 3:6 *s* he poured out richly upon us
Phm 25 with the *s* you people show
Heb 2:4 with distributions of holy *s*
3:7 just as the holy *s* says
4:12 the dividing of soul and *s*
6:4 become partakers of holy *s*
9:8 the holy *s* makes it plain
9:14 everlasting *s* offered
10:15 holy *s* also bears witness
10:29 *s* of undeserved kindness
Jas 2:26 the body without *s* is dead
4:5 a tendency to envy that the *s*
1Pe 1:2 with sanctification by the *s*
1:11 what sort of season the *s*
1:12 *s* sent forth from heaven
3:4 of the quiet and mild *s*
3:18 being made alive in the *s*
4:6 live as to the *s* from the
4:14 because the *s* of glory
4:14 *s* of God, is resting upon
2Pe 1:21 were borne along by holy *s*
1Jo 3:24 to the *s* which he gave us
4:13 he has imparted his *s* to us
5:6 *s* is that which is bearing
5:6 because the *s* is the truth
5:8 *s* . . . water and the blood
Jude 20 and praying with holy *s*
Re 2:7 *s* says to the congregations
2:11 *s* says to the congregations
2:17 *s* says to the congregations
2:29 *s* says to the congregations
3:6 *s* says to the congregations
3:13 *s* says to the congregations
3:22 *s* says to the congregations
4:2 to be in the power of the *s*
11:11 *s* of life from God entered
14:13 Yes, says the *s*, let them
17:3 away in the power of the *s*
21:10 in the power of the *s* to
22:17 *s* and the bride keep on

Spiritedness
Jos 5:1 proved to be no *s* in them
Ps 32:9 Whose *s* is to be curbed even

Spiritism
Ga 5:20 practice of *s*, enmities
Re 21:8 and those practicing *s* and
22:15 and those who practice *s*

Spiritistic
2Ch 33:6 and made *s* mediums and
Isa 8:19 Apply to the *s* mediums or to
Re 9:21 their *s* practices nor of their
18:23 *s* practice all the nations

Spirits
Nu 16:22 God of the *s* of every sort of
27:16 the *s* of all sorts of flesh
Ps 104:4 Making his angels *s*, His
Pr 16:2 is making an estimate of *s*
Zec 6:5 four *s* of the heavens that
Mt 8:16 expelled the *s* with a word
10:1 authority over unclean *s*, in
12:45 *s* more wicked than itself
Mr 1:27 orders even the unclean *s*
3:11 the unclean *s*, whenever they
5:10 not to send the *s* out of the
5:13 the unclean *s* came out and
6:7 authority over the unclean *s*
Lu 4:36 he orders the unclean *s*, and
6:18 those troubled with unclean *s*
7:21 diseases and wicked *s* and
8:2 had been cured of wicked *s* and
10:20 *s* are made subject to you
11:26 *s* more wicked than itself
Ac 5:16 troubled with unclean *s*, and
8:7 many that had unclean *s*, and
19:12 and the wicked *s* came out
19:13 those having the wicked *s*
Heb 1:7 he makes his angels *s*, and
1:14 all *s* for public service
Jas 5:13 Is there anyone in good *s*?
1Pe 3:19 preached to the *s* in prison
Re 1:4 seven *s* that are before his
3:1 who has the seven *s* of God
4:5 these mean the seven *s* of God
5:6 eyes mean the seven *s* of God

Spiritual
Mt 5:3 conscious of their *s* need
Ro 1:11 I may impart some *s* gift to
7:14 we know that the Law is *s*
15:27 shared in their *s* things
1Co 2:13, 13 *s* matters with *s* words
2:15 *s* man examines indeed all
1Co 3:1 speak to you as to *s* men, but
9:11 have sown *s* things to you
10:3 and all ate the same *s* food
10:4 all drank the same *s* drink
10:4 *s* rock-mass that followed
12:1 Now concerning the *s* gifts
14:1 seeking the *s* gifts, but
15:44 it is raised up a *s* body
15:44 there is also a *s* one
15:46 the first is, not . . . *s*, but
15:46 afterward that which is *s*
Ga 6:1 you who have *s* qualifications
Eph 1:3 us with every *s* blessing
5:19 praises to God and *s* songs
Col 1:8 your love in a *s* way
1:9 wisdom and *s* comprehension
3:16 *s* songs with graciousness
Heb 12:9 to the Father of our *s* life
12:23 *s* lives of righteous ones
1Pe 2:5 being built up a *s* house for
2:5 *s* sacrifices acceptable to God
Re 11:8 in a *s* sense called Sodom and

Spirituality
Jude 19 animalistic men, not having *s*

Spiritually
1Co 2:14 because they are examined *s*

Spit
Nu 12:14 her father to *s* directly in
De 25:9 *s* in his face and answer and
Job 17:6 someone into whose face to *s*
30:10 did not hold back their *s*
Isa 50:6 humiliating things and *s*
Mt 26:67 they *s* into his face and hit
27:30 they *s* upon him and took the
Mr 8:23 having *s* upon his eyes, he
10:34 and will *s* upon him and
14:65 some started to *s* on him
15:19 and *s* upon him and, bending
Lu 18:32 treated insolently and *s* upon
Joh 9:6 he *s* on the ground and made
Ga 4:14 contempt or *s* at in disgust

Spite
Job 10:7 in *s* of your own knowledge
Isa 31:4 *s* of their voice he will not
31:4 in *s* of their commotion

Spiteful
Job 36:18 into *s* handclapping, And let

Spitting
Le 15:8 *s* upon someone clean, he must
Mr 7:33 *s*, he touched his tongue

Splash
Ex 12:7 *s* it upon the two doorposts

Splashing
Heb 11:28 and the *s* of the blood

Splendid
Le 23:40 *s* trees, the fronds of palm
1Ki 1:47 make Solomon's name more *s*
Ps 29:4 The voice of Jehovah is *s*
Isa 2:10 and from his *s* superiority
2:19 and from his *s* superiority
2:21 from his *s* superiority
5:14 and what is *s* in her
Da 11:20 pass through the *s* kingdom
Am 3:12 on a *s* couch and on a
Lu 7:25 those in *s* dress and existing
Jas 2:2 and in *s* clothing enters into
2:3 one wearing the *s* clothing

Splendor
De 33:17 firstborn of a bull his *s* is
1Ch 16:27 and *s* are before him
Job 37:22 Out of the north golden *s*
40:10 with dignity and *s* may you
Ps 8:5 and *s* you then crowned him
21:5 and *s* you put upon him
45:3 With your dignity and your *s*
45:4 in your *s* go on to success
90:16 your *s* upon their sons
96:6 and *s* are before him
104:1 *s* you have clothed yourself
111:3 activity is dignity and *s*
145:5 glorious *s* of your dignity
145:12 of the *s* of his kingship
149:9 *s* belongs to all his loyal
Pr 20:29 the *s* of old men is their
31:25 and *s* are her clothing
Isa 35:2 *s* of Carmel and of Sharon
35:2 Jehovah, the *s* of our God
53:2 nor any *s*; and when we shall
La 1:6 Zion there goes out all her *s*
Eze 16:14 my *s* that I placed upon you
27:10 ones that caused your *s*
28:7 profane your beaming *s*
28:17 account of your beaming *s*
Mic 2:9 you take my *s*, to time
Eph 5:27 in its *s*, not having a spot

Splendors
Ps 110:3 In the *s* of holiness, from

Splinters
Ho 8:6 calf . . . will become mere *s*

Split
Ge 22:3 he *s* the wood for the burnt
Ex 14:16 over the sea and *s* it apart
14:21 waters were being *s* apart
Le 11:5 but does not *s* the hoof
11:6 it does not have the hoof *s*
Nu 16:31 the ground . . . began to be *s*
De 14:7 that *s* the hoof, cloven
14:7 but do not *s* the hoof
Jg 15:19 God *s* open a mortar-shaped
1Ki 1:40 the earth was *s* by the noise
Ne 9:11 the sea you *s* before them
Job 26:8 cloud mass is not *s* under
Ps 60:2 to rock, you have *s* it open
74:15 One that *s* the spring and
78:13 He *s* the sea, that he might
78:15 *s* rocks in the wilderness
Pr 3:20 deeps themselves were *s* apart
Isa 48:21 *s* a rock that the water
Eze 29:7 a *s* in their entire shoulder
Mic 1:4 *s* apart, like wax because of
Hab 3:9 you proceeded to *s* the earth
Zec 14:4 must be *s* at its middle
Mt 27:51 and the rock-masses were *s*
Ac 14:4 multitude of the city was *s*
23:7 and the multitude was *s*
Re 16:19 city *s* into three parts

Splits
Le 11:3 creature that *s* the hoof and
De 14:6 every beast that *s* the hoof
Job 16:13 He *s* open my kidneys and

Splitter
Le 11:4 but is no *s* of the hoof
11:7 it is a *s* of the hoof and a
11:26 is a *s* of the hoof but is not
De 14:8 it is a *s* of the hoof but

Splitters
Le 11:4 and the *s* of the hoof

Splitting
1Sa 6:14 *s* up the wood of the wagon
Ps 69:31 displaying horns, *s* the hoof
141:7 cleaving and *s* on the earth
Ec 10:9 He that is *s* logs will have
Isa 63:12 the One *s* the waters from
Eze 13:11 windstorms . . . cause a *s*

Spoil
Ge 49:27 at evening he will divide *s*
Ex 15:9 I shall divide *s*! My soul
Nu 31:11 they went taking all the *s*
31:12 booty and the *s*, to the camp
De 2:35 the *s* of the cities that we
3:7 the *s* of the cities we took as
13:16 all its *s* you should collect
13:16 the city and all its *s* as a
20:14 all its *s* you will plunder
20:14 eat the *s* of your enemies
Jos 7:21 got to see among the *s* an
8:2 you people may plunder its *s*
8:27 the *s* of that city Israel
11:14 all the *s* of these cities
22:8 Take your share of the *s* of
Jg 5:30 to distribute *s*, A womb—two
5:30 *S* of dyed stuffs for Sisera
5:30 for Sisera, *s* of dyed stuffs
5:30 For the necks of men of *s*
8:25 the nose ring of his *s* into it
1Sa 14:30 from the *s* of their enemies
14:32 darting greedily at the *s*
15:19 darting greedily at the *s*
15:21 taking from the *s* sheep
30:16 account of all the great *s*
30:19 and from the *s*, even to
30:20 This is David's *s*
30:22 give them none of the *s*
30:26 send some of the *s* to the
30:26 *s* of Jehovah's enemies
2Sa 3:22 *s* that they brought with
8:12 *s* of Hadadezer the son of
12:30 *s* of the city that he
2Ki 3:23 So now, to the *s*, O Moab!

1Ch 20:2 s of the city that he brought
26:27 the wars and from the s
2Ch 14:13 a very great deal of s
15:11 the s they had brought
20:25 came to plunder the s on
20:25 they were plundering the s
24:23 s they sent to the king of
28:8 great deal of s they took
28:8 brought the s to Samaria
28:15 they clothed from the s
Es 3:13 and to plunder the s of them
8:11 and to plunder their s
Ps 68:12 she shares in the s
119:162 does when finding much s
Pr 1:13 us fill our houses with s
16:19 s with the self-exalted ones
Ca 2:15 foxes that are making s of
Isa 8:4 s of Samaria before the king
9:3 when they divide up the s
10:2 widows to become their s
10:6 to take much s and to
33:4 the s of you people will
33:23 s in abundance will have
53:12 will apportion the s, due
Jer 21:9 come to be his as a s
38:2 his soul as a s and alive
39:18 have your soul as a s
45:5 give you your soul as a s
49:32 their livestock a s
50:10 Chaldea must become a s
50:10 those making s of her will
Eze 7:21 to the wicked ones . . . for s
26:12 s your resources and plunder
29:19 make a big s of it and
38:12 to get a big s and to do
38:13 Is it to get a big s that
38:13 to get a very great s
39:10 make s of those who had
39:10 had been making s of them
Da 11:24 s and goods he will scatter
Zec 2:9 to become s to their slaves
14:1 the s of you will certainly
1Co 15:33 Bad associations s useful

Spoiled
Jer 18:4 was s by the potter's hand

Spoils
Heb 7:4 a tenth out of the chief s

Spoke
Ge 8:15 God now s to Noah, saying
18:29 he s further to him and said
23:8 s with them, saying: If your
23:13 s to Ephron in the hearing of
24:7 s to me and who swore to me
24:30 s to me, then he came to the
27:5 while Isaac s to Esau his son
39:10 as she s to Joseph day after
39:17 she s to him according to
39:19 she s to him, saying: Like
41:9 chief of the cupbearers s
42:7 he s harshly with them and
42:24 s to them and took Simeon
42:30 the lord of the country s
43:19 s to him at the entrance of
44:6 and s these words to them
45:15 his brothers s with him
49:28 this is what their father s
50:4 and Joseph s to Pharaoh's
50:17 burst into tears when they s
50:21 and s reassuringly to them
Ex 4:30 Aaron s all the words that
6:9 Moses s to this effect to the
6:10 Jehovah s to Moses, saying
6:12 Moses s before Jehovah
6:28 day that Jehovah s to Moses
13:1 Jehovah s further to Moses
14:1 Jehovah now s to Moses
14:12 word we s to you in Egypt
16:11 Jehovah s further to Moses
20:22 from the heavens I s with
30:17 Jehovah s further to Moses
33:9 and he s with Moses
33:11 Jehovah s to Moses face to
34:35 went out and s to the sons
40:1 Jehovah s to Moses, saying
Le 6:24 Jehovah s further to Moses
10:12 Moses s to Aaron and to
10:19 At this Aaron s to Moses
19:1 Jehovah s further to Moses
21:24 Moses s to Aaron and his
22:1 Jehovah s further to Moses
22:26 Jehovah s further to Moses
23:26 Jehovah s further to Moses
Le 23:44 Moses s of the seasonal
24:23 Moses s to the sons of
25:1 Jehovah s further to Moses in
Nu 1:48 Jehovah s to Moses, saying
2:1 Jehovah now s to Moses and
3:1 Jehovah s with Moses in Mount
3:14 Jehovah s further to Moses
4:1 Jehovah now s to Moses and
4:17 Jehovah s further to Moses
4:21 Jehovah s to Moses, saying
5:1 Jehovah s further to Moses
6:1 And Jehovah s further to Moses
6:22 Jehovah s to Moses, saying
8:5 Jehovah s further to Moses
8:23 Jehovah now s to Moses
9:4 Moses s to the sons of Israel
9:9 Jehovah s to Moses, saying
11:24 s to the people the words of
11:25 s to him and took away some
13:1 Jehovah now s to Moses
15:1 Jehovah s further to Moses
16:5 Then he s to Korah and to his
16:20 Jehovah now s to Moses and
16:23 Jehovah s to Moses, saying
16:26 he s to the assembly, saying
16:36 Jehovah now s to Moses
16:44 Jehovah s to Moses, saying
17:1 Jehovah now s to Moses
17:6 Moses s to the sons of Israel
18:8 Jehovah s further to Aaron: As
18:25 Jehovah s to Moses, saying
20:7 Jehovah s to Moses, saying
22:7 and s to him Balak's words
24:12 to your messengers . . . I s
25:10 Jehovah s to Moses, saying
25:16 Jehovah s to Moses, saying
26:52 Jehovah s to Moses, saying
27:15 Moses s to Jehovah, saying
28:1 Jehovah s further to Moses
30:1 Moses s to the heads of the
31:1 Jehovah then s to Moses
31:3 Moses s to the people, saying
34:1 Jehovah s further to Moses
34:16 Jehovah s further to Moses
De 1:1 that Moses s to all Israel in
1:3 Moses s to the sons of Israel
1:6 Jehovah our God s to us in
1:43 I s to you, and you did not
2:17 Jehovah s further to me
4:45 s to the sons of Israel on
5:4 Face to face Jehovah s with
5:22 These Words Jehovah s to all
5:28 your words when you s to me
13:2 of which he s to you, saying
18:22 the prophet s it. You must
23:23 you s of with your mouth
27:9 the Levites, s to all Israel
31:1 s these words to all Israel
32:44 came and s all the words of
Jos 9:22 s to them, saying: Why did
14:6 word that Jehovah s to Moses
20:1 Jehovah s to Joshua, saying
20:2 I s to you by means of Moses
22:21 Manasseh answered and s
22:30 the sons of Manasseh s, it
Jg 8:3 when he s this word
9:37 Gaal s once more and said
13:11 the man that s to the woman
21:13 s to the sons of Benjamin
1Sa 8:21 he s them in the ears of
10:25 Samuel s to the people
11:4 s the words in the ears of
15:16 Jehovah s to me last night
16:4 to do what Jehovah s
17:28 to hear as he s to the men
17:31 words that David s came to
18:24 like these that David s
19:1 Saul s to Jonathan his son
19:4 Jonathan s well of David to
25:9 David's young men came and s
25:40 s to her, saying: David
28:17 just as he s by means of me
28:21 obey the words that you s
2Sa 3:19 Abner also s in the ears of
7:7 word that I s with one of
7:17 way that Nathan s to David
17:6 the way Ahithophel s
23:2 The spirit . . . that s by me
23:3 To me the Rock of Israel s
1Ki 2:4 carry out his word that he s
2:23 that Adonijah s this thing
2:30 This is what Joab s, and
6:12 I s to David your father
8:15 s by his own mouth with
1Ki 12:7 they s to him, saying
12:10 s to him saying: This is
13:12 Then their father s to them
13:18 an angel himself s to me by
13:22 place about which he s to
13:25 and s of it in the city in
13:26 word of Jehovah that he s
14:2 s with reference to me as
16:34 s by means of Joshua the
21:2 So Ahab s to Naboth, saying
21:5 wife came in to him and s
21:6 he s to her: Because I
22:13 to call Micaiah s to him
2Ki 1:3 he s to Elijah the Tishbite
1:7 he s to them: What was
1:7 then s these words to you
1:9 s to him: Man of the true
1:10 s to the chief of the fifty
1:11 s to him: Man of the true
1:12 Elijah answered and s to
1:15 angel of Jehovah s to Elijah
1:16 he s to him: This is what
2:22 to Elisha's word that he s
5:4 girl s who is from the land
5:13 s to him and said: My father
7:17 s at the time that the king
9:36 s by means of his servant
10:10 s by means of his servant
14:25 s by means of his servant
19:6 king of Assyria s abusively
1Ch 17:15 way that Nathan s to David
2Ch 6:4 God . . . s with his own mouth
9:1 s with him about everything
10:3 and s to Rehoboam, saying
10:7 s to him, saying: If you
10:10 s with him, saying: This
18:12 s to him, saying: Look!
20:37 s prophetically against
25:16 s to him that the king
30:22 Hezekiah s to the heart of
32:16 s yet further against
Ne 9:13 s with them out of heaven and
Es 8:3 Esther s again before the king
Ps 18:*super* David, who s to Jehovah
39:3 I s with my tongue
89:19 s in a vision to your loyal
Ec 1:16 I, s with my heart, saying
2:15 I s in my heart: This too is
Ca 5:6 had gone out of me when he s
Isa 16:13 Jehovah s concerning Moab
20:2 Jehovah s by the hand of
37:6 s abusively of me
45:19 I s not, in a dark place of
65:12 I s, but you did not listen
66:4 s, but there were none that
Jer 18:8 badness against which I s
22:21 I s to you during your
25:2 which Jeremiah the prophet s
26:16 that he s to us
27:12 I s according to all these
27:16 to all this people I s
36:2 the day that I s to you
37:2 s by means of Jeremiah the
38:8 and s to the king, saying
40:2 s this calamity against this
45:1 Jeremiah the prophet s to
46:13 Jehovah s to Jeremiah the
48:27 often as you s against him
50:1 Jehovah s concerning Babylon
Eze 2:2 as soon as he s to me, and it
20:27 your forefathers s abusively
38:17 I s in the former days by
Da 2:4 Chaldeans s to the king in the
6:21 Daniel himself s even with
10:11 s with me this word, I did
10:15 s with me words like these
10:19 as soon as he s with me I
Ho 12:10 I s to the prophets, and
13:1 When Ephraim s, there was
Mal 3:16 s with one another, each one
Mt 9:33 been expelled the dumb man s
12:22 that the dumb man s and saw
13:33 Another illustration he s to
13:34 Jesus s to the crowds by
14:27 Jesus s to them with the
17:13 he s to them about John the
22:1 Jesus again s to them with
23:1 Jesus s to the crowds and to
26:75 the saying Jesus s, namely
28:18 Jesus approached and s to
Mr 6:50 he s with them, and he said
12:12 he s the illustration with
14:72 saying that Jesus s to him
Lu 2:50 the saying that he s to them

Lu 6:39 he also *s* an illustration to
8:4 *s* by means of an illustration
11:14 came out, the dumb man *s*
12:16 he *s* an illustration to them
14:3 Jesus *s* to those versed in the
15:3 he *s* this illustration to
18:9 he *s* this illustration also
19:11 these things he *s* in addition
20:2 they *s* up, saying to him
20:19 *s* this illustration with
20:39 said: Teacher, you *s* well
21:29 he *s* an illustration to them
24:6 Recall how he *s* to you while
24:25 the things the prophets *s*
24:44 *s* to you while I was yet
Joh 4:50 the word that Jesus *s* to him
8:12 Jesus *s* again to them
8:20 sayings he *s* in the treasury
10:6 Jesus *s* this comparison to
11:42 I *s*, in order that they
12:36 Jesus *s* these things and
12:41 and he *s* about him
17:1 Jesus *s* these things, and
18:16 *s* to the doorkeeper and
18:20 and I *s* nothing in secret
18:21 heard what I *s* to them
18:23 If I *s* wrongly, bear
Ac 1:16 holy spirit *s* beforehand by
2:31 *s* concerning the resurrection
3:21 God *s* through the mouth of
7:6 God *s* to this effect, that
7:38 angel that *s* to him on Mount
8:26 Jehovah's angel *s* to Philip
10:7 angel that *s* to him had left
10:15 voice *s* again to him, the
14:1 and *s* in such a manner that a
16:32 *s* the word of Jehovah to him
19:8 he *s* with boldness for three
23:9 a spirit or an angel *s* to him
28:25 holy spirit aptly *s* through
1Co 14:6 unless I *s* to you either
2Co 4:13 faith, therefore I *s*
Heb 1:1 long ago *s* on many occasions
5:5 him who *s* with reference to
7:14 a tribe about which Moses *s*
Jas 5:10 who *s* in the name of Jehovah
2Pe 1:21 men *s* from God as they were
Jude 15 ungodly sinners *s* against
Re 10:4 when the seven thunders *s*
10:4 things the seven thunders *s*
17:1 *s* with me, saying: Come, I
21:9 he *s* with me and said: Come

Spoken

Ge 12:4 just as Jehovah had *s* to him
17:23 just as God had *s* with him
18:5 you may do just as you have *s*
18:19 upon Abraham what he has *s*
19:21 the city of which you have *s*
21:1 did to Sarah just as he had *s*
21:2 of which God had *s* to him
23:16 he had *s* in the hearing of
24:33 not eat until I have *s* about
24:51 just as Jehovah has *s*
27:19 done just as you have *s*
28:15 done what I have *s* to you
35:13 where he had *s* with him
35:14 where he had *s* with him
35:15 place where God had *s* with
41:28 I have *s* to Pharaoh: What
42:14 It is what I have *s* to you
43:27 aged man of whom you have *s*
43:29 of whom you have *s* to me
44:2 word of Joseph which he had *s*
45:27 words that he had *s* to them
Ex 1:17 king of Egypt had *s* to them
4:30 that Jehovah had *s* to Moses
7:13 just as Jehovah had *s*
7:22 just as Jehovah had *s*
8:15 just as Jehovah had *s*
8:19 just as Jehovah had *s*
10:29 That is the way you have *s*
16:10 as soon as Aaron had *s* to the
16:23 It is what Jehovah has *s*
19:8 All that Jehovah has *s* we are
24:3 words that Jehovah has *s*
24:7 All that Jehovah has *s* we are
32:14 evil that he had *s* of doing
32:34 where I have *s* to you of
33:17 you have *s*, I shall do
34:29 because of his having *s* with
34:32 Jehovah had *s* with him on
Le 10:3 is what Jehovah has *s*, saying
10:5 just as Moses had *s*
Le 10:11 Jehovah has *s* to them by
Nu 5:4 Jehovah had *s* to Moses, so
10:29 Jehovah has *s* good concerning
12:2 Moses alone . . . Jehovah has *s*
12:2 by us also that he has *s*
14:17 just as you have *s*, saying
14:28 way as you have *s* in my ears
14:35 I Jehovah have *s* if this is
15:22 which Jehovah has *s* to Moses
16:40 just as Jehovah had *s* to him
16:47 just as Moses had *s*, and
21:7 we have *s* against Jehovah and
23:2 did just as Balaam had *s*
23:17 What has Jehovah *s*?
23:19 And has he *s* and will he not
27:23 as Jehovah had *s* by means of
32:31 What Jehovah has *s* to your
De 1:14 have *s* for us to do is good
1:21 God of your forefathers has *s*
2:1 just as Jehovah had *s* to me
5:28 which they have *s* to you
5:28 done well in all they have *s*
9:3 just as Jehovah has *s* to you
9:10 the words that Jehovah had *s*
10:4 Jehovah had *s* to you in the
13:5 *s* of revolt against Jehovah
18:2 just as he has *s* to him
18:21 that Jehovah has not *s*
27:3 God of your forefathers has *s*
31:3 just as Jehovah has *s*
Jos 23:14 your God has *s* to you
23:15 your God has *s* to you
24:27 of Jehovah that he has *s*
Jg 2:4 angel had *s* these words to
2:15 just as Jehovah had *s* and
6:27 as Jehovah had *s* to him; but
Ru 2:13 have *s* reassuringly to your
1Sa 1:16 that I have *s* until now
3:17 word that he has *s* to you
3:17 all the word that he has *s*
9:21 *s* to me a thing like this
20:23 word that we have *s*, I and
25:30 to all that he has *s*
2Sa 2:27 if you had not *s*, then only
7:25 *s* concerning your servant
7:25 and do just as you have *s*
14:19 my lord the king has *s*; for
1Ki 2:24 just as he has *s*, today
2:27 *s* against the house of Eli
2:31 Do just as he has *s* and fall
2:38 as my lord the king has *s*
8:20 his word that he had *s*, that
8:20 just as Jehovah had *s*, and
8:53 *s* by means of Moses your
12:9 this people who have *s* to me
12:10 people who have *s* to you
12:12 just as the king had *s*
12:15 word that Jehovah had *s* by
13:3 of which Jehovah has *s*
13:11 that he had *s* to the king
13:17 *s* to me by . . . Jehovah
14:11 Jehovah himself has *s* it
14:18 *s* by means of his servant
15:29 *s* by means of his servant
16:12 *s* against Baasha by means
17:16 had *s* by means of Elijah
21:4 had *s* to him, when he said
21:23 has *s*, saying, The very dogs
22:23 *s* calamity concerning you
22:28 Jehovah has not *s* with me
22:38 word that he had *s*
2Ki 1:9 king himself has *s*, Do come
1:17 that Elijah had *s*; and
4:17 just as Elisha had *s* to her
5:13 prophet himself had *s* to you
7:17 man of the true God had *s*
7:18 man of the true God had *s*
8:1 had *s* to the woman whose son
10:10 *s* against the house of Ahab
10:17 that he had *s* to Elijah
15:12 word that he had *s* to Jehu
17:23 *s* by means of all his
19:21 Jehovah has *s* against him
19:22 taunted and *s* of abusively
20:9 the word that he has *s*
20:19 that you have *s* is good
22:19 I have *s* against this place
24:2 *s* by means of his servants
24:13 just as Jehovah had *s*
1Ch 17:23 *s* concerning your servant
17:23 and do just as you have *s*
21:19 *s* in the name of Jehovah
22:11 as he has *s* concerning you
2Ch 6:10 his word that he had *s*, that
2Ch 6:10 just as Jehovah had *s*, and
10:9 people who have *s* to me
10:10 people who have *s* to you
10:12 just as the king had *s*
10:15 *s* by means of Ahijah the
18:22 Jehovah . . . has *s* calamity
18:27 Jehovah has not *s* with me
Ne 6:12 *s* this prophecy against me as
Es 6:10 of all that you have *s*
7:9 had *s* good concerning the king
Job 15:11 Or a word *s* gently with you
40:5 Once have I *s*, and I will
42:7 had *s* these words to Job
42:7 not *s* . . . what is truthful
42:8 you have not *s* concerning me
42:9 did just as Jehovah had *s*
Ps 17:10 they have *s* in haughtiness
38:12 have *s* of adversities
50:1 God, Jehovah, has himself *s*
60:6 God himself has *s* in his
62:11 Once God has *s*, twice I have
66:14 *s* when I was in sore straits
87:3 Glorious things are being *s*
108:7 has *s* in his holiness
109:2 *s* about me with the tongue
119:23 have *s* with one another
144:8 mouth has *s* what is untrue
144:11 mouth has *s* what is untrue
Pr 25:11 a word *s* at the right time
Ca 8:8 the day that she will be *s* for
Isa 1:2 Jehovah himself has *s*: Sons I
1:20 mouth of Jehovah has *s* it
16:14 now Jehovah has *s*, saying
21:17 God of Israel, has *s* it
22:25 Jehovah himself has *s* it
24:3 Jehovah himself has *s* this
25:8 Jehovah himself has *s* it
37:22 Jehovah has *s* against him
37:23 taunted and *s* of abusively
38:7 this word that he has *s*
39:8 of Jehovah that you have *s*
40:5 mouth of Jehovah has *s* it
46:11 I have even *s* it; I shall
48:15 *s*. Moreover, I have called
48:16 I have *s* in no place of
58:14 mouth of Jehovah . . . *s* it
59:3 own lips have *s* falsehood
Jer 3:5 You have *s*, and you went on
4:28 It is because I have *s*
9:8 Deception is what it has *s*
9:12 the mouth of Jehovah has *s*
10:1 Jehovah has *s* against you
11:17 *s* against you a calamity
13:15 for Jehovah himself has *s*
14:14 commanded them or *s* to
16:10 has Jehovah *s* against us all
19:5 I had not commanded or *s* of
19:15 the calamity that I have *s*
23:17 Jehovah has *s*: Peace is
23:35 And what has Jehovah *s*?
23:37 And what has Jehovah *s*?
25:13 words that I have *s* against
26:13 calamity that he has *s*
26:19 the calamity that he had *s*
27:13 Jehovah has *s* to the nation
28:16 you have *s* outright revolt
29:32 he has *s* outright revolt
30:4 words that Jehovah has *s* to
33:14 good word that I have *s*
33:24 this people have *s*, saying
34:5 have *s* the very word, is
35:14 *s* to you men, rising up
35:17 calamity that I have *s*
35:17 *s* to them but they did not
36:2 words that I have *s* to you
36:4 that He had *s* to him, on
36:7 Jehovah has *s* against this
36:31 calamity that I have *s*
38:25 hear that I have *s* with you
40:3 and do just as he has *s*
42:19 Jehovah has *s* against you
44:16 *s* to us in the name of
51:12 *s* against the inhabitants
51:62 have *s* against this place
Eze 5:13 have *s* in my insistence on
5:15 I myself, Jehovah, have *s*
5:17 I myself, Jehovah, have *s*
13:7 when I myself have *s* nothing
13:8 you men have *s* untruth and
17:21 I myself, Jehovah, have *s*
17:24 I myself, Jehovah, have *s*
21:17 I myself, Jehovah, have *s*
21:32 I myself, Jehovah, have *s*

Spokes

Spokesman

Spokesmen

Sponge

Sport

Spot

Spotless

Spots

Spotty

Spouted

Sprang

Sprawl

Sprawled

Sprawling

Spread

Spreading

Job 26:9 *S* out over it his cloud
Ps 37:35 *s* himself as a luxuriant
Pr 29:5 is *s* out a mere net for his
Isa 19:8 those *s* fishing nets upon the
Jer 4:31 She keeps *s* out her palms
Eze 1:11 wings were *s* out upward
Mt 21:8 and *s* them on the road
Lu 5:15 the word about him was *s* the
14:16 was *s* a grand evening meal
19:36 *s* their outer garments on
Ac 12:24 went on growing and *s*

Spreads
Le 13:22 unmistakably *s* in the skin
13:27 unmistakably *s* in the skin
13:35 unmistakably *s* in the skin
De 32:11 *S* out its wings, takes them
2Ch 6:29 *s* out his palms toward this
Job 39:26 *s* its wings to the south
41:30 It *s* out a threshing
Isa 40:22 *s* them out like a tent in

Sprigs
Isa 18:5 cut off the *s* with pruning
27:11 When her *s* have dried up

Spring
Le 11:36 a *s* and a pit of impounded
Nu 21:17 *S* up, O well! Respond to it
De 11:14 autumn rain and *s* rain
29:23 any vegetation *s* up in it
Jos 15:9 *s* of the waters of Nephtoah
18:15 *s* of the waters of Nephtoah
1Sa 29:1 by the *s* that was in Jezreel
2Ki 3:25 *s* of water they would stop
Job 5:6 trouble does not *s* up
8:19 And from the dust others *s* up
29:23 opened wide for the *s* rain
Ps 74:15 One that split the *s* and the
84:6 They turn it into a *s* itself
114:8 rock into a *s* of water
Pr 16:15 is like the cloud of *s* rain
25:26 A fouled *s* and a ruined well
Ec 12:6 and the jar at the *s* is broken
Ca 4:12 garden barred in, a *s* sealed
4:15 a *s* of gardens, a well of
Isa 42:9 Before they begin to *s* up
43:19 Now it will *s* up
44:4 *s* up as among the green
45:8 to *s* up at the same time
58:8 would recuperation *s* up for
Jer 3:3 not even a *s* rain has occurred
5:24 the *s* rain in its season
Ho 6:3 *s* rain that saturates the earth
13:15 his well and drain his *s*
Joe 2:23 autumn rain and *s* rain, as
3:18 there will go forth a *s*
Zec 10:1 in the time of the *s* rain
Ro 9:6 not all who *s* from Israel are
1Ti 6:4 From these things *s* envy
Heb 12:15 no poisonous root may *s* up

Springing
Ge 31:10 the he-goats *s* upon the flock
31:12 the he-goats *s* upon the flock
Ec 2:6 the forest, *s* up with trees

Springs
Ge 7:11 *s* of the vast watery deep
8:2 *s* of the watery deep and the
36:24 Anah who found the hot *s* in
Ex 15:27 were twelve *s* of water and
Nu 33:9 in Elim there were twelve *s*
De 8:7 *s* and watery deeps issuing
1Ki 18:5 to all the *s* of water
2Ki 3:19 *s* of water you should stop
2Ch 32:3 *s* that were outside the city
Ps 87:7 All my *s* are in you
104:10 sending *s* into the torrent
Pr 5:16 *s* be scattered out of doors
8:24 *s* heavily charged with water
Isa 12:3 out of the *s* of salvation
35:7 thirsty ground as *s* of water
41:18 I shall open up . . . *s*
49:10 by the *s* of water he will
2Pe 1:20 no prophecy of Scripture *s*
Re 17:11 king, but *s* from the seven

Sprinkle
Ex 29:16 take its blood and *s* it round
29:20 *s* the blood round about upon
Le 1:5 and *s* the blood round about
1:11 must *s* its blood round about
3:2 must *s* the blood round about
3:8 *s* its blood round about upon
3:13 must *s* its blood round about
7:2 blood one will *s* round about
Le 17:6 priest must *s* the blood upon
Nu 18:17 Their blood you should *s* upon
2Ki 16:13 to *s* the blood of the
16:15 sacrifice you should *s* upon
2Ch 35:11 *s* the blood from their hand
Isa 28:25 and *s* the cummin, and
Eze 36:25 will *s* upon you clean water
43:18 and to *s* upon it blood

Sprinkled
Ex 24:6 the blood he *s* upon the altar
24:8 Moses took the blood and *s* it
Le 8:19 slaughtered it and *s* the blood
8:24 *s* the rest of the blood round
9:12 *s* it round about upon the
9:18 *s* it round about upon the
Nu 19:13 has not been *s* upon him, he
19:20 water . . . not *s* upon him
1Ki 14:3 and *s* cakes and a flask of
2Ch 29:22 blood and *s* it upon the
29:22 *s* the blood upon the altar
29:22 *s* the blood upon the altar
34:4 *s* it upon the surface of the
Heb 9:13 ashes of a heifer *s* on those
9:19 *s* the book itself and all the
9:21 he *s* the tent and all the
10:22 hearts *s* from a wicked
1Pe 1:2 and *s* with the blood of Jesus
Re 19:13 outer garment *s* with blood

Sprinkles
Le 7:14 priest who *s* the blood of the

Sprinkling
2Ch 30:16 the priests *s* the blood
Eze 46:14 for *s* the fine flour
Mr 7:4 cleanse themselves by *s*
Heb 12:24 and the blood of *s*, which

Sprout
De 29:23 not be sown, nor *s*, nor will
Job 14:7 tree . . . will even *s* again
14:9 the scent of water it will *s*
38:27 the growth of grass to *s*
Ps 72:7 the righteous one will *s*
85:11 Trueness itself will *s* out
92:7 wicked ones *s* as the
104:14 grass *s* for the beasts
147:8 mountains to *s* green grass
Isa 4:2 Jehovah makes *s* will come
11:1 roots a *s* will be fruitful
14:19 like a detested *s*, clothed
17:11 seed of yours to *s*, but
27:6 blossoms and actually *s*
55:10 and makes it produce and *s*
60:21 the *s* of my planting, the
61:11 brings forth its *s*, and
61:11 that are sown in it *s*
66:14 *s* just like tender grass
Jer 23:5 up to David a righteous *s*
33:15 *s* for David a righteous
33:15 for David a righteous *s*
Eze 17:6 it began to *s* and gradually
17:10 In the garden beds of its *s*
29:21 shall cause a horn to *s* for
Da 11:7 one from the *s* of her roots
Ho 8:7 No *s* produces flour
Zec 3:8 I am bringing in my servant *S*
6:12 the man whose name is *S*
6:12 his own place he will *s*

Sprouted
Ca 6:11 to see whether the vine had *s*
7:12 see whether the vine has *s*
Eze 7:10 Presumptuousness has *s*
Ho 10:4 *s* like a poisonous plant
Mt 13:26 blade *s* and produced fruit

Sprouting
Ge 2:5 of the field was as yet *s*
40:10 it was apparently *s* shoots
Ex 10:5 eat every *s* tree of yours out
Isa 61:11 cause the *s* of righteousness
Eze 16:7 like the *s* of the field is
Lu 8:6 after *s*, it dried up because
8:8 after *s*, it produced fruit a

Sprouts
Ps 65:10 you bless its very *s*
Eze 17:9 freshly plucked *s* become dry
Mr 4:27 and the seed *s* and grows tall

Sprung
Heb 7:14 Lord has *s* up out of Judah

Spun
Ex 35:25 *s* with their hands, and
35:26 *s* the goat's hair

Spurned
Ps 89:39 *s* the covenant of your
La 2:7 Jehovah . . . has *s* his sanctuary

Spurting
Isa 63:3 their *s* blood kept spattering
63:6 to the earth their *s* blood

Spy
Nu 13:2 may *s* out the land of Canaan
13:16 whom Moses sent to *s* out
13:17 to *s* out the land of Canaan
13:32 passed through to *s* it out
14:7 *s* it out is a very, very good
14:36 Moses sent to *s* out the land
14:38 who went to *s* out the land
21:32 sent some to *s* on Jazer
De 1:33 to *s* out for you a place for
Jos 6:25 sent out to *s* on Jericho
7:2 Go up and *s* on the land
14:7 to *s* out the land, and I
Jg 1:23 Joseph began to *s* on Bethel
18:2 *s* out the land and to explore
18:14 to *s* out the land of Laish
18:17 had gone to *s* out the land
2Sa 10:3 *s* it out and to overthrow it
Ga 2:4 who sneaked in to *s* upon our

Spying
Ge 42:30 men *s* on the country
Nu 13:25 returned from *s* out the land
De 1:24 and went *s* on it
Jos 6:22 had done the *s* on the land
6:23 men who had done the *s* went
1Ch 19:3 for *s* out the land that his

Squandered
Lu 15:13 *s* his property by living a

Square
Ge 19:2 public *s* is where we shall
De 13:16 the middle of its public *s*
Jg 19:15 in the public *s* of the city
19:17 in the public *s* of the city
19:20 overnight in the public *s*
2Sa 21:12 the public *s* of Beth-shan
2Ch 32:6 public *s* of the gate of the
Ne 8:1 as one man at the public *s*
8:3 before the public *s* that is
8:16 public *s* of the Water Gate
8:16 public *s* of the Gate of
Es 4:6 into the public *s* of the city
6:9 on the horse in the public *s*
6:11 ride in the public *s* of the
Job 29:7 In the public *s* I would
Ps 55:11 from its public *s* oppression
Isa 59:14 even in the public *s*, and
Eze 16:24 a height in every public *s*
16:31 height in every public *s*
45:2 it being made *s* round about
Da 9:25 rebuilt, with a public *s* and

Squared
1Ki 7:5 were *s* with the frame, and
7:31 sidewalls were *s*, not round
1Ch 22:2 *s* stones for building the
Eze 41:21 temple, the doorpost was *s*
43:16 *s* on its four sides

Squares
Ps 144:14 no outcry in our public *s*
Pr 1:20 public *s* it keeps giving
5:16 of water in the public *s*
7:12 now she is in the public *s*
22:13 In the midst of the public *s*
26:13 a lion in among the public *s*
Ca 3:2 in the public *s* let me seek
Isa 15:3 in the public *s* thereof
Jer 5:1 seek . . . in her public *s*
9:21 young men from the public *s*
48:38 Moab and in her public *s*
49:26 fall in her public *s*, and
50:30 will fall in her public *s*
La 2:11 in the public *s* of the town
2:12 in the public *s* of the city
4:18 is no walking in our public *s*
Am 5:16 In all the public *s* there
Na 2:4 up and down in the public *s*
Zec 8:4 in the public *s* of Jerusalem
8:5 the public *s* of the city
8:5 girls playing in her public *s*

Squat
De 23:13 when you *s* outside, you must

Squeeze
Ge 40:11 take the grapes and *s* them
Nu 22:25 *s* herself against the wall

Nu 22:25 s Balaam's foot against the

Squeezed
Le 22:24 testicles s or crushed or
Isa 1:6 not been s out or bound up
Eze 23:3 There their breasts were s

Squeezing
Pr 30:33 s of the nose is what brings
30:33 the s out of anger is what

Stabbed
Isa 14:19 men s with the sword that
Ac 2:37 they were s to the heart
1Ti 6:10 s themselves all over with

Stability
De 32:6 and proceeded to give you s

Stabilized
Col 2:7 and being s in the faith

Stabs
Pr 12:18 as with the s of a sword

Stachys
Ro 16:9 Greet . . . my beloved S

Stack
Eze 24:5 s the logs in a circle under

Stacte
Ex 30:34 s drops and onycha and

Staff
Ge 32:10 with but my s I crossed this
49:10 neither the commander's s
Ex 12:11 and your s in your hand; and
Nu 21:18 With a commander's s, with
22:27 beating the ass with his s
Jg 6:21 the tip of the s that was in
1Sa 17:40 to take his s in his hand
2Ki 4:29 take my s in your hand and
4:29 place my s upon the face of
4:31 put the s upon the boy's face
Ps 23:4 Your rod and your s are the
60:7 Judah is my commander's s
108:8 Judah is my commander's s
Isa 9:4 s of the one driving them to
10:15 s moved back and forth the
10:24 own s against you in the
10:26 his s will be upon the sea
14:5 the s of the ruling ones
14:29 s of the one striking you
28:27 and cummin with a s
30:31 strike it even with a s
Jer 10:16 Israel is the s of his
48:17 been broken, the s of beauty
51:19 the s of his inheritance
La 3:1 because of the s of his fury
Ho 4:12 hand s keeps telling them
Mic 7:14 Shepherd . . . with your s
Zec 8:4 with his s in his hand
11:10 took my s Pleasantness and
11:14 cut in pieces my second s
Mt 10:10 or sandals or a s; for the
Mr 6:8 except a s alone, no bread, no
Lu 9:3 neither s nor food pouch
Heb 11:21 upon the top of his s

Staffs
Ge 30:37 Jacob took for his use s
30:37 places which were upon the s
30:38 the s that he had peeled he
30:39 get in heat before the s
30:41 Jacob would locate the s
30:41 might get in heat by the s
Nu 21:18 with their own s
Zec 11:7 I took for myself two s

Stag
De 12:15 the gazelle and like the s
12:22 and the s may be eaten
14:5 the s and gazelle and roebuck
15:22 the gazelle and like the s
Isa 35:6 climb up just as a s does

Stages
Ex 17:1 proceeded to depart . . . by s
40:36 during all their s of journey
40:38 during all their s of journey
Nu 33:1 s of the sons of Israel who
33:2 departure places by their s
33:2 s from one departure place to

Stagger
Ps 13:4 because I am made to s
Pr 10:30 he will not be caused to s
12:3 it will not be caused to s
Isa 54:10 and the very hills may s
54:10 covenant of peace itself s

Am 8:12 s from sea all the way to

Staggered
Am 4:8 two or three cities s to one

Staggering
1Sa 25:31 cause for s or a
Pr 24:11 and those s to the slaughter
25:26 when s before the wicked one
Isa 24:19 has absolutely been sent s

Stags
1Ki 4:23 s and gazelles and roebucks
Ca 2:9 gazelle or the young of the s
2:17 like the young of the s upon
8:14 like a young one of the s upon
La 1:6 s that have found no pasturage

Stain
Jer 2:22 error would certainly be a s

Stained
Jude 23 garment that has been s by

Staircase
1Ki 6:8 by a winding s they would go

Stairs
2Ki 20:9 forward ten steps of the s
20:11 steps of the s of Ahaz
2Ch 9:11 s for the house of Jehovah
Isa 38:8 steps of the s of Ahaz by
38:8 steps on the steps of the s
Am 9:6 building in the heavens his s
Ac 21:35 But when he got upon the s
21:40 Paul, standing on the s

Stairway
Ne 3:15 the S that goes down from the
12:37 S of the City of David by

Stake
Ge 40:19 certainly hang you upon a s
De 21:22 you have hung him upon a s
21:23 not stay all night on the s
Jos 8:29 the king of Ai upon a s
8:29 dead body down from the s
Es 2:23 got to be hanged on a s
5:14 make a s fifty cubits high
5:14 proceeded to have the s made
6:4 to hang Mordecai on the s that
7:9 there is the s that Haman made
7:10 to hang Haman on the s that
8:7 him they have hanged on the s
9:13 of Haman be hanged upon the s
9:25 him and his sons upon the s
Mt 10:38 not accept his torture s and
16:24 and pick up his torture s
27:32 to lift up his torture s
27:40 come down off the torture s!
27:42 come down off the torture s
Mr 8:34 pick up his torture s and
15:21 should lift up his torture s
15:30 down off the torture s
15:32 come down off the torture s
Lu 9:23 and pick up his torture s
14:27 is not carrying his torture s
23:26 torture s upon him to bear
Joh 19:17 bearing the torture s for
19:19 and put it on the torture s
19:25 By the torture s of Jesus
Ac 2:23 you fastened to a s by the
5:30 slew, hanging him upon a s
10:39 by hanging him on a s
13:29 took him down from the s
1Co 1:17 the torture s of the Christ
1:18 speech about the torture s is
Ga 3:13 is every man hanged upon a s
5:11 torture s has been abolished
6:12 persecuted for the torture s
6:14 torture s of our Lord Jesus
Eph 2:16 through the torture s
Php 2:8 yes, death on a torture s
3:18 the torture s of the Christ
Col 1:20 he shed on the torture s
2:14 nailing it to the torture s
Heb 12:2 he endured a torture s
1Pe 2:24 in his own body upon the s

Stakes
Jos 10:26 and hang them upon five s
10:26 hanging upon the s until the
10:27 down off the s and throwing
Lu 19:43 fortification with pointed s
Joh 19:31 torture s on the Sabbath

Stalk
Ge 41:5 grain coming up on one s, fat
41:22 grain coming up on one s

Mr 4:28 grass-blade, then the s head
Joh 19:29 sour wine upon a hyssop s

Stalker
Job 39:7 a s it does not hear

Stalks
Jos 2:6 among s of flax laid in rows
Ca 7:8 hold of its fruit s of dates

Stall
Lu 13:15 bull or his ass from the s

Stallions
Jg 5:22 upon dashings of his s
Jer 8:16 the neighing of his s
47:3 of the hoofs of his s, at
50:11 you kept neighing like s

Stalls
1Ki 4:26 forty thousand s of horses
2Ch 9:25 four thousand s of horses
32:28 s for all the different
32:28 and s for the droves

Stammerers
Isa 32:4 s will be quick in speaking

Stammering
Isa 28:11 by those s with their lips
33:19 of a s tongue without your

Stamp
Eze 6:11 s with your foot, and say

Stamped
Isa 63:18 have s down your sanctuary
Jer 12:10 they have s down my share
Eze 25:6 you s with the feet and

Stamping
Ps 68:30 s down on pieces of silver
Isa 63:6 s down peoples in my anger
Jer 47:3 s of the hoofs of his
Eze 34:18 by s with your very feet
34:19 befouled by the s of your
Zec 10:5 s down in the mire of the

Stand
Ge 19:9 S back there! And they added
19:17 do not s still in all the
31:39 I myself would s the loss of
34:12 and I s willing to give
41:3 they took their s alongside
43:15 got to s before Joseph
Ex 9:11 were unable to s before Moses
14:13 S firm and see the salvation
18:14 taking their s before you
18:23 certainly be able to s it and
19:17 taking their s at the base of
30:18 s of copper for washing
30:28 and the basin and its s
31:9 and the basin and its s
32:26 Moses took his s in the gate
35:16 the basin and its s
38:8 basin of copper and its s of
39:39 utensils, the basin and its s
40:11 anoint the basin and its s
Le 8:11 the basin and its s so as to
11:35 Whether oven or jar s, it
13:23 the blotch should s, it has
16:7 them s before Jehovah at the
18:23 woman should not s before a
19:16 not s up against your
19:30 and you should s in awe of
25:30 also s in perpetuity as the
26:2 and s in awe of my sanctuary
26:37 prove to be no ability to s
27:8 s the person before the priest
27:11 then s the beast before the
27:19 and it must s fast as his
Nu 1:5 of the men who will s with you
3:6 s them before Aaron the priest
5:16 make her s before Jehovah
5:18 woman s before Jehovah and
5:30 wife s before Jehovah, and
8:13 Levites s before Aaron and
9:8 S there, and let me hear what
11:24 s round about the tent
16:9 to s before the assembly to
16:27 came out, taking their s at
27:2 proceeded to s before Moses
27:19 must s him before Eleazar
27:21 before Eleazar . . . he will s
30:4 all her vows must also s, and
30:4 abstinence vow . . . will s
30:5 it will not s, but Jehovah will
30:7 her vows must also s or her
30:7 her abstinence vows . . . s

Nu 30:9 bound upon her soul will s
30:11 and all her vows must s or
30:11 vow . . . upon her soul will s
30:12 her vows . . . will not s
De 5:31 s here with me, and let me
7:24 take a firm s against you
9:2 firm s before the sons of Anak
10:8 to s before Jehovah for
11:25 No man will make a firm s
18:5 s to minister in the name of
19:15 the matter should s good
19:17 must also s before Jehovah
24:11 You should s on the outside
25:8 he must s and say, I have
27:12 s to bless the people on
27:13 will s for the malediction
31:15 s by the entrance of the tent
Jos 1:5 will take a firm s before you
3:8 should s still in the Jordan
3:13 will s still as one dam
3:16 from above began to s still
10:8 Not a man . . . s against you
10:13 and the moon did s still
10:19 you men, do not s still
20:4 s at the entrance of the gate
24:1 taking their s before the
Jg 2:14 no longer able to s before
4:20 S at the entrance of the tent
9:44 they might s at the entrance
16:25 to s him between the pillars
1Sa 6:20 be able to s before Jehovah
9:27 s still now that I may let
10:19 take your s before Jehovah
10:23 took his s in the middle of
12:7 now take your s, and I will
12:16 take your s and see this
14:9 S still until we make
14:9 we must then s where we are
17:51 got to s over the Philistine
19:3 s at the side of my father
20:38 Do not s still! And the
2Sa 1:9 S, please, over me and
2:23 and then died would s still
20:4 and you yourself s here
23:12 he took his s in the middle
1Ki 3:16 to the king and s before him
7:31 a s of one and a half cubits
7:35 a s a half a cubit in height
8:11 priests were unable to s to
8:55 he began to s and bless all
17:1 before whom I do s is living
18:15 before whom I do s is
19:11 s on the mountain before
2Ki 3:14 before whom I do s is living
4:12 that she might s before him
5:11 s and call upon the name of
5:16 Jehovah before whom I do s
10:4 did not s before him
10:4 how shall we ourselves s?
18:28 Rabshakeh continued to s
23:3 took their s in the covenant
1Ch 11:14 took his s in the middle
17:14 cause him to s in my house
21:1 And Satan proceeded to s up
2Ch 5:14 priests were not able to s
9:8 make it s to time indefinite
11:13 took their s by him out of
20:9 s before this house and
20:17 s still and see the
20:23 s up against the inhabitants
24:13 s as it structurally should
25:5 s according to the house of
29:11 Jehovah has chosen to s
34:32 to take their s to it
35:5 s in the holy place by the
Ezr 2:68 to s on its own site
9:15 impossible to s before you
10:13 not possible to s outside
Ne 9:2 s and make confession of their
12:39 a s at the Gate of the Guard
12:40 came to a s at the house of
Es 3:4 Mordecai's affairs would s
4:14 will s up for the Jews from
5:1 she took her s in the inner
8:11 and s for their souls
9:16 there was a s for their souls
Job 4:16 It began to s still, But I
22:28 decide . . . and it will s
34:24 makes others s up instead
37:14 S still and show yourself
Ps 1:5 will not s up in the judgment
2:2 The kings of earth take their s
5:5 No boasters may take their s
Ps 26:12 certainly s on a level place
30:7 my mountain to s in strength
31:8 my feet s in a roomy place
33:9 and it proceeded to s so
33:11 counsel of Jehovah will s
45:9 taken her s at your right hand
76:7 s before you because of the
78:13 waters to s like a dam
84:10 s at the threshold in the
94:16 s for me against the
107:29 windstorm to s at a calm
109:31 s at the right hand of the
120:7 I s for peace; but when I
130:3 O Jehovah, who could s?
147:17 Before his cold who can s?
Pr 6:22 it will s guard over you
19:21 counsel of Jehovah . . . s
25:6 place of great ones do not s
27:4 who can s before jealousy?
Ec 4:12 two together could make a s
8:3 Do not s in a bad thing
Isa 7:7 It will not s, neither will
8:10 any word, and it will not s
28:18 with Sheol will not s
36:2 s still by the conduit of
36:13 Rabshakeh continued to s
38:14 S good for me
44:11 They will s still
46:7 place that it may s still
46:10 My own counsel will s, and
47:12 S still, now, with your
47:13 Let them s up, now, and
50:8 Let us s up together. Who is
61:5 s and shepherd the flocks of
Jer 4:6 for shelter. Do not s still
6:16 S still in the ways, you
7:2 S in the gate of the house of
7:10 s before me in this house
15:19 Before me you will s
17:19 s in the gate of the sons
19:14 to s in the courtyard of
26:2 S in the courtyard of the
35:19 man to s before me always
40:10 s before the Chaldeans who
46:15 They have made no s, for
46:21 They have not made a s
48:19 S still and look out for the
49:19 shepherd that can s before
50:44 shepherd that can s before
51:50 Do not s still. From far
Eze 1:21 still, these would s still
2:1 s up upon your feet that I
2:2 made me s up upon my feet
3:24 and made me s up on my feet
9:2 and s beside the copper altar
10:6 enter and s beside the wheel
10:17 still, they would s still
10:18 to s still over the cherubs
11:23 to s over the mountain that
13:5 in order to s in the battle
17:14 his covenant it might s
24:11 S it empty upon its coals
27:29 upon the land they will s
31:14 may s up against them in
37:10 live and s upon their feet
44:11 s before them to minister
44:15 s before me to present to
44:24 should s in order to judge
46:2 s by the doorpost of the gate
47:10 fishers will actually s
Da 1:4 s in the palace of the king
1:5 they might s before the king
1:19 to s before the king
2:2 and to s before the king
2:44 will s to times indefinite
7:4 s up on two feet just like a
7:17 four kings that will s up
8:7 power in the ram to s before
8:18 touched me and made me s up
8:22 s up, but not with his power
8:23 s up a king fierce in
8:25 Prince of princes he will s
10:11 s up where you were standing
10:11 I did s up, shivering
11:3 king will . . . s up and rule
11:6 and he will not s, neither
11:7 s up in his position, and he
11:8 s off from the king of the
11:11 have a large crowd s up, and
11:14 s up against the king of the
11:15 the south, they will not s
11:16 s in the land of the
11:17 she will not s, and she will
11:20 s up in his position one who
Da 11:21 s up in his position one who
11:25 he will not s, because they
11:31 will be arms that will s up
12:1 Michael will s up, the great
12:13 s up for your lot at the end
Ho 13:13 he will not still at the
Am 2:15 one handling the bow will s
Ob 14 to s at the parting of the ways
Mic 5:4 s and do shepherding in the
Na 1:6 of his denunciation who can s
2:8 S still, you men!
2:8 S still! But there is no one
Zec 14:4 s in that day upon the
Mt 12:25 or house divided . . . not s
12:26 then, will his kingdom s
Mr 3:24 divided . . . kingdom cannot s
3:25 house will not be able to s
3:26 divided, he cannot s, but is
11:25 when you s praying, forgive
13:9 put on the s before governors
Lu 6:8 Get up and s in the center
6:8 And he rose and took his s
11:18 how will his kingdom s?
13:25 to s outside and to knock
Joh 8:44 did not s fast in the truth
20:23 they s forgiven to them
20:23 sins . . . they s retained
Ac 1:11 do you s looking into the sky
4:10 man's here sound in front of
4:26 took their s and the rulers
5:20 taken a s in the temple
11:13 angel s in his house and say
14:10 S up erect on your feet
25:18 Taking the s, the accusers
26:6 I s called to judgment
26:16 rise and s on your feet
27:24 You must s before Caesar
Ro 5:2 kindness in which we now s
13:1 authorities s placed in their
13:2 s against the arrangement of
13:2 taken a s against it will
14:4 be made to s, for Jehovah
14:4 for Jehovah can make him s
14:10 s before the judgment seat
1Co 15:1 in which you also s
16:13 s firm in the faith, carry
Ga 4:24 s as a symbolic drama; for
5:1 s fast, and do not let
Eph 6:11 able to s firm against the
6:13 thoroughly, to s firm
6:14 S firm, therefore, with
Php 2:23 how things s concerning me
4:1 s firm in this way in the
Col 2:18 taking his s on the things he
4:12 s complete and with firm
1Th 3:8 if you s firm in the Lord
2Th 2:15 s firm and maintain your
1Pe 5:9 take your s against him
5:12 in which s firm
Re 6:17 and who is able to s?
8:2 seven angels that s before God
18:10 s at a distance because of
18:15 s at a distance because of

Standards
1Co 9:8 these things by human s

Standing
Ge 18:2 there three men were s some
18:8 kept s by them under the tree
18:22 Jehovah, he was still s
24:30 was, s by the camels at the
24:31 s out here, when I myself
41:1 he was s by the river Nile
41:17 In my dream here I was s
Ex 3:5 place where you are s is holy
5:20 Moses and Aaron, who were s
8:22 upon which my people are s
17:6 I am s before you there on
18:13 people kept s before Moses
20:21 people kept s at a distance
22:6 or s grain or a field gets
26:15 of acacia wood, s on end
33:10 pillar of cloud s at the
36:20 out of acacia wood, s on end
Nu 7:2 and s over the ones registered
14:14 your cloud is s over them
16:48 s between the dead and the
22:24 Jehovah's angel kept s in the
De 1:38 son of Nun, who is s before
5:5 s between Jehovah and you at
16:9 first put to the s grain
17:12 priest who is s to minister
18:7 s there before Jehovah

De 23:25 s grain of your fellowman
23:25 s grain of your fellowman
29:15 him who is here s with us
Jos 3:17 s immovable on dry ground
4:9 on the s place of the feet of
4:10 s in the middle of the Jordan
5:13 was a man s in front of him
5:15 on which you are s is holy
8:33 judges were s on this side
10:13 And the sun kept s still
11:13 the cities s on their own
18:5 Judah will keep s on his
18:5 keep s on their territory to
20:6 his s before the assembly
20:9 his s before the assembly
Jg 3:19 those who were s by him went
7:21 they kept s each one in his
15:5 the fields of s grain of the
15:5 from sheaf to s grain and the
18:16 s at the entrance of the
18:17 s at the entrance of the gate
20:28 s before it in those days
1Sa 1:26 woman that was s with you
4:20 the women s by her began to
6:14 kept s there, where there
17:3 the Philistines were s on
17:3 the Israelites were s on the
17:26 men that were s close by
19:20 Samuel s in his position
2Sa 2:25 s upon the top of one hill
13:31 servants were s by with
15:23 s by the torrent valley of
17:17 Jonathan and Ahimaaz were s
18:4 s at the side of the gate
18:30 stepped aside and kept s
20:15 it was s within a rampart
22:34 he keeps me s
1Ki 7:25 It was s upon twelve bulls
8:14 Israel were s up
8:22 Solomon began s before the
10:8 are s before you constantly
10:19 two lions were s beside the
10:20 twelve lions s there upon
13:1 Jeroboam was s by the altar
13:24 And the ass was s beside it
13:24 lion was s beside the dead
13:25 lion s beside the dead body
13:28 lion s beside the dead body
22:19 army of the heavens s by
22:35 s position in the chariot
2Ki 2:7 kept s in view at a distance
3:21 they began s at the boundary
4:15 she kept s at the entrance
6:31 continues s upon him today
9:17 watchman was s upon the
11:11 runners kept s each one
11:14 king was s by the pillar
23:3 king kept s by the pillar and
1Ch 16:17 statement he kept s as a
21:15 Jehovah's angel was s close
21:16 got to see Jehovah's angel s
23:30 for s morning by morning to
2Ch 3:13 cherubs . . . s upon their feet
4:4 It was s upon twelve bulls
5:12 s to the east of the altar
6:3 congregation of Israel were s
6:12 s before the altar of Jehovah
6:13 and he kept s upon it
7:6 priests were s at their posts
7:6 all the Israelites were s
9:7 s before you constantly and
9:18 two lions were s beside the
9:19 twelve lions s there upon
18:18 army of the heavens s at
18:34 s position in the chariot
20:13 Judah were s before Jehovah
23:13 king s by his pillar at the
29:26 Levites kept s with the
30:16 s at their place according
34:31 king kept s in his place
35:10 priests kept s at their
Ne 7:3 while they are s by they
8:4 kept s upon a wooden podium
8:4 s alongside him Mattithiah
8:7 people were in a s position
13:11 stationed them at their s
Es 5:2 the queen s in the courtyard
6:5 is Haman s in the courtyard
7:9 stake . . . s in Haman's house
Job 8:15 but it will not keep s
Ps 10:1 do you keep s afar off
18:33 high for me he keeps me s
19:9 fear of Jehovah . . . s forever
38:11 keep s away from my plague
Ps 39:5 man, though s firm, is
69:2 where there is no s ground
102:26 you yourself will keep s
104:6 s above the very mountains
105:10 statement he kept s as a
109:6 resister himself keep s at
111:3 righteousness is s forever
111:10 His praise is s forever
112:3 righteousness is s forever
112:9 righteousness is s forever
119:90 earth, that it may keep s
122:2 Our feet proved to be s
134:1 s in the house of Jehovah
135:2 are s in the house of Jehovah
148:6 he keeps them s forever, to
Pr 11:19 firmly s for righteousness
12:7 righteous ones will keep s
29:4 a king makes a land keep s
Ec 1:4 the earth is s even to time
Ca 2:9 is s behind our wall, gazing
Isa 3:13 s up to pass sentence upon
6:2 Seraphs were s above him
11:10 s up as a signal for the
17:5 gathering the s grain and his
21:8 I am s constantly by day
22:19 official s one will tear
46:7 its s place it does not move
48:13 they may keep s together
53:11 righteous s to many people
59:14 kept s simply far off
66:22 are s before me, is the
66:22 you people will keep s
Jer 15:1 If Moses and Samuel were s
18:20 Remember my s before you to
28:5 s in the house of Jehovah
36:21 princes s by the king
44:15 wives who were s as a
52:12 s before the king of Babylon
Eze 3:23 glory of Jehovah was s there
8:11 son of Shaphan s in among
8:11 s before them, each one with
10:3 cherubs were s to the right
10:19 s at the eastern entrance of
22:30 and s in the gap before me
40:3 he was s in the gate
43:6 come to be s beside me
Da 2:31 was s in front of you, and
3:3 s in front of the image that
7:10 that kept s right before him
7:16 one of those who were s
8:3 ram s before the watercourse
8:4 no wild beasts kept s before
8:6 seen s before the watercourse
8:15 s in front of me someone in
8:17 he came beside where I was s
8:18 stand up where I had been s
10:11 stand up where you were s
10:13 s in opposition to me for
10:16 one who was s in front of
10:17 kept s in me no power, and
11:2 three kings s up for Persia
11:15 be no power to keep s
11:16 be no one s before him
12:1 prince who is s in behalf of
12:5 two others s, one on the bank
Ho 8:7 Nothing has s grain
Mic 1:11 from you people its s place
Hab 2:1 I will keep s, and I will
Hag 2:5 my spirit was s in among you
Zec 1:8 s still among the myrtle
1:10 s still among the myrtle
1:11 s among the myrtle trees
3:1 s before the angel of Jehovah
3:1 Satan s at his right hand in
3:3 and s before the angel
3:4 said to those s before him
3:5 angel of Jehovah was s by
3:7 among these who are s by
4:14 are s alongside the Lord of
14:12 one is s upon one's feet
Mal 3:2 the one s when he appears
Mt 6:5 to pray s in the synagogues
12:47 your brothers are s outside
13:2 the crowd was s on the beach
16:28 are some of those s here
20:3 others s unemployed in the
20:6 and found others s, and he
20:6 s here all day unemployed
24:15 s in a holy place, (let the
26:73 those s around came up and
27:47 some of those s there began
Mr 3:31 they were s on the outside
9:1 some of those s here that
11:5 some of those s there began
Mr 13:14 s where it ought not
14:47 one of those s by drew his
14:69 again to say to those s by
14:70 those s by began saying to
15:35 some of those s near, on
15:39 army officer that was s by
Lu 1:11 s at the right side of the
5:1 s beside the lake of Gennesaret
8:20 your brothers are s outside
9:27 some of those s here that
9:32 and the two men s with him
18:13 tax collector s at a distance
19:24 he said to those s by, Take
21:36 s before the Son of man
23:10 s up and vehemently accusing
23:49 were s at a distance
23:49 s beholding these things
Joh 1:26 one is s whom you do not
1:35 John was s with two of his
6:22 s on the other side of the
7:37 Jesus was s up and he cried
11:42 crowd s around I spoke
18:5 betrayer, was also s with
18:16 Peter was s outside at the
18:18 the officers were s about
18:18 Peter also was s with them
18:22 officers that was s by gave
18:25 Simon Peter was s and
19:25 s his mother and the sister
19:26 disciple whom he loved s by
20:11 kept s outside near the
20:14 and viewed Jesus s, but
Ac 4:14 man that had been cured s
5:23 the guards s at the doors
5:25 s and teaching the people
7:33 place on which you are s is
7:55 Jesus s at God's right hand
7:56 s at God's right hand
9:7 were s speechless, hearing
11:11 three men s at the house
12:14 Peter was s before the
16:9 certain Macedonian man was s
21:40 Paul, s on the stairs
22:13 s by me, he said to me, Saul
22:20 was also s by and approving
22:25 to the army officer s there
23:2 those s by him to strike him
23:4 Those s by said: Are you
24:21 cried out while s among
25:10 s before the judgment seat
Ro 11:20 but you are s by faith
1Co 10:12 let him that thinks he is s
2Co 1:24 by your faith that you are s
Php 1:27 are s firm in one spirit
1Ti 3:13 a fine s and great freeness
2Ti 2:19 foundation of God stays s
Heb 9:8 while the first tent was s
Jas 2:3 You keep s, or: Take that
5:9 Judge is s before the doors
2Pe 3:5 an earth s compactly out of
Re 3:20 I am s at the door and
5:6 s in the midst of the throne
7:1 angels s upon the four corners
7:9 s before the throne and before
7:11 all the angels were s around
10:5 the angel that I saw s on the
10:8 s on the sea and on the earth
11:4 s before the Lord of the earth
12:4 dragon kept s before the
14:1 Lamb s upon the Mount Zion
15:2 s by the glassy sea, having
19:17 also an angel s in the sun
20:12 s before the throne, and

Standpoint

Le 25:23 settlers from my s
1Sa 2:26 from Jehovah's s and from
24:6 from Jehovah's s, that I
26:11 from Jehovah's s, to thrust
2Sa 3:28 from the s of Jehovah, are
1Ki 21:3 from Jehovah's s, for me to
Job 34:33 good for it from your s
Ps 31:11 From the s of all those
73:22 as mere beasts from your s
Ec 2:17 was calamitous from my s
Jer 51:5 s of the Holy One of Israel
Zec 11:13 been valued from their s
Jas 1:27 from the s of our God and
1Pe 4:6 the flesh from the s of men
4:6 spirit from the s of God

Stands

Le 13:28 if the blotch s in its place
26:30 cut off your incense s and

Nu 35:12 not die until he *s* before the
2Ch 14:5 places and the incense *s*
34:4 incense *s* that were up above
34:7 incense *s* he cut down in all
Job 18:12 disaster *s* ready to make
Ec 4:15 *s* up in the other one's place
Isa 17:8 poles or at the incense *s*
27:9 incense *s* will not rise up
Eze 6:4 your incense *s* must be broken
6:6 your incense *s* cut down and
Da 8:20 *s* for the kings of Media and
8:21 *s* for the king of Greece
8:21 it *s* for the first king
Lu 1:19 Gabriel, who *s* near before
Joh 3:29 when he *s* and hears him
Ro 14:4 his own master he *s* or falls
1Co 7:37 if anyone *s* settled in his
Ga 5:14 entire Law *s* fulfilled in one
Jude 13 darkness *s* reserved forever
Re 13:8 *s* written in the scroll of
19:8 *s* for the righteous acts of

Star
Nu 24:17 A *s* . . . out of Jacob, And a
Am 5:26 images, the *s* of your god
Mt 2:2 we saw his *s* when we were in
2:9 the *s* they had seen when they
2:10 seeing the *s* they rejoiced
Ac 7:43 *s* of the god Rephan that you
1Co 15:41, 41 *s* differs from *s* in
Re 2:28 will give him the morning *s*
8:10 a great *s* burning as a lamp
8:11 the name of the *s* is called
9:1 I saw a *s* that had fallen from
22:16 and the bright morning *s*

Stare
Le 26:32 *s* in amazement over it
1Ki 9:8 will *s* in amazement and will
2Ch 7:21 *s* in amazement and be
Job 17:8 people *s* in amazement at
18:20 will indeed *s* in amazement
21:5 Turn your faces to me and *s*
Ps 40:15 Let those *s* in amazement in
Jer 2:12 *S* in amazement, O you
18:16 *s* in astonishment and shake
19:8 *s* in astonishment and
49:17 will *s* in astonishment and
50:13 *s* in astonishment and
Eze 26:16 and *s* in amazement at you
27:35 will certainly *s* at you
28:19 *s* in amazement at you
Hab 1:5 *s* in amazement at one another

Stared
Isa 52:14 have *s* at him in amazement

Star's
Mt 2:7 the time of the *s* appearing

Stars
Ge 1:16 the night, and also the *s*
15:5 and count the *s*, if you are
22:17 your seed like the *s*
26:4 multiply your seed like the *s*
37:9 eleven *s* were bowing down to
Ex 32:13 seed like the *s* of the
De 1:10 like the *s* of the heavens for
4:19 sun and the moon and the *s*
10:22 like the *s* of the heavens
28:62 like the *s* of the heavens
Jg 5:20 From heaven did the *s* fight
1Ch 27:23 Israel as many as the *s* of
Ne 4:21 the dawn until the *s* came out
9:23 as the *s* of the heavens
Job 3:9 *s* of its twilight grow dark
9:7 And around *s* he puts a seal
22:12 see the sum total of the *s*
25:5 *s* themselves have not proved
38:7 morning *s* joyfully cried out
Ps 8:3 the *s* that you have prepared
136:9 the *s* for combined dominion
147:4 counting the number of the *s*
148:3 all you *s* of light
Ec 12:2 the moon and the *s* grow dark
Isa 13:10 *s* of the heavens and their
14:13 Above the *s* of God I shall
47:13 the lookers at the *s*, those
Jer 31:35 the *s* for light by night
Eze 32:7 heavens and darken their *s*
Da 8:10 *s* to fall to the earth, and
12:3 *s* to time indefinite, even
Joe 2:10 the very *s* have withdrawn
3:15 *s* will actually withdraw
Ob 4 if among the *s* there were a
Na 3:16 more than the *s* of the
Mt 24:29 the *s* will fall from heaven
Mr 13:25 *s* . . . falling out of heaven
Lu 21:25 signs in sun and moon and *s*
Ac 27:20 sun nor *s* appeared for
1Co 15:41 glory of the *s* is another
Heb 11:12 as the *s* of heaven for
Jude 13 *s* with no set course, for
Re 1:16 in his right hand seven *s*
1:20 sacred secret of the seven *s*
1:20 seven *s* mean the angels of
2:1 he says who holds the seven *s*
3:1 of God and the seven *s*
6:13 and the *s* of heaven fell to
8:12 and a third of the *s*
12:1 head was a crown of twelve *s*
12:4 drags a third of the *s* of

Start
Ge 4:26 At that time a *s* was made of
10:8 He made the *s* in becoming
11:6 this is what they *s* to do
41:21 was bad just as at the *s*
43:18 with us in our bags at the *s*
43:20 down at the *s* to buy food
Ex 12:2 the *s* of the months for you
De 2:24 *s* to take possession of his
2:25 *s* to put the dread of you and
2:31 *S* to take possession of his
16:9 *s* to count seven weeks
Jos 3:7 shall *s* to make you great in
Jg 7:19 at the *s* of the middle night
2Sa 17:9 he falls upon them at the *s*
21:9 the *s* of the barley harvest
21:10 *s* of harvest until water
2Ki 17:25 *s* of their dwelling there
1Ch 1:10 the *s* in becoming a mighty
Ezr 4:6 Ahasuerus, at the *s* of his
Job 7:14 you make me *s* up in fright
13:11 make you *s* up with fright
18:11 make him *s* up in fright
Pr 8:23 I was installed, from the *s*
9:10 Jehovah is the *s* of wisdom
12:27 *s* up one's game animals
Ec 3:11 made from the *s* to the finish
10:13 *s* of the words of his mouth
Isa 1:26 counselors . . . as at the *s*
41:4 the generations from the *s*
41:26 told anything from the *s*
48:16 From the *s* I have spoken in
Jer 13:21 right alongside you at the *s*
17:12 throne on high from the *s*
31:5 plant and *s* to use them
33:7 build them just as at the *s*
33:11 as at the *s*, Jehovah has
La 2:19 the *s* of the morning watches
Eze 9:6 my sanctuary you should *s*
40:1 in the *s* of the year, on
Da 8:1 one appearing to me at the *s*
9:21 seen in the vision at the *s*
9:23 *s* of your entreaties a word
Ho 1:2 *s* of the word of Jehovah by
Am 7:1 at the *s* of the coming up of
Mt 24:49 *s* to beat his fellow slaves
Lu 1:3 traced all things from the *s*
3:8 And do not *s* saying within
12:45 *s* to beat the menservants
12:49 I came to *s* a fire on the
13:25 you *s* to stand outside and
13:26 Then you will *s* saying, We
14:9 you will *s* off with shame to
14:29 might *s* to ridicule
21:28 things *s* to occur, raise
23:30 *s* to say to the mountains
Php 4:15 at the *s* of declaring the
1Pe 4:17 judgment to *s* with the house

Started
Ge 6:1 came about that when men *s*
9:20 Noah *s* off as a farmer and
41:54 seven years of the famine *s*
44:12 He *s* with the oldest and
Ex 22:6 one who *s* the fire is to make
Nu 16:46 The plague has *s!*
16:47 the plague had *s* among the
25:1 *s* to have immoral relations
De 2:31 I have *s* to abandon Sihon and
3:24 *s* to make your servant see
Jg 13:25 Jehovah's spirit *s* to impel
16:19 she *s* to show the mastery of
16:22 hair of his head *s* to grow
20:31 *s* to strike down some of the
20:39 Benjamin *s* to strike down
20:40 signal *s* to go up from the
1Sa 14:35 *s* altar building to Jehovah
22:15 *s* to inquire of God for him
2Ki 10:32 Jehovah *s* to cut off Israel
15:37 Jehovah *s* to send against
1Ch 27:24 *s* to take the count, but he
2Ch 3:1 Solomon *s* to build the house
3:2 he *s* to build in the second
20:22 *s* off with the joyful cry
29:17 *s* on the first day of the
29:27 that the burnt offering *s*
29:27 song of Jehovah *s* and also
31:7 *s* the heaps by laying the
31:10 *s* to bring the contribution
31:21 that he *s* in the service of
34:3 boy, he *s* to search for the
34:3 he *s* to cleanse Judah and
Ezr 3:6 *s* to offer up burnt sacrifices
3:8 the captivity to Jerusalem *s*
5:2 *s* to rebuild the house of God
Ne 4:7 gaps had *s* to be stopped up
Es 6:13 you have *s* to fall, you will
9:23 accepted what they had *s* to
Eze 9:6 *s* with the old men that were
Jon 3:4 Jonah *s* to enter into the city
Mt 11:7 Jesus *s* to say to the crowds
11:20 he *s* to reproach the cities
12:1 *s* to pluck heads of grain and
18:24 When he *s* to settle them
26:37 he *s* to be grieved and to be
26:74 Then he *s* to curse and swear
Mr 1:45 man *s* to proclaim it a great
2:23 his disciples *s* to make their
4:1 *s* teaching beside the sea
5:17 *s* to entreat him to go away
5:20 went away and *s* to proclaim
6:2 sabbath, he *s* teaching in the
6:34 he *s* to teach them many
6:55 *s* to carry about on cots
8:11 came out and *s* disputing
8:31 he *s* teaching them that the
8:32 Peter . . . *s* rebuking him
10:28 Peter *s* to say to him: Look!
10:32 *s* to tell them these things
10:41 they *s* to be indignant at
10:47 he *s* shouting and saying
11:15 *s* to throw out those selling
12:1 he *s* to speak to them with
13:5 Jesus *s* to say to them: Look
14:19 *s* to be grieved and to say to
14:33 he *s* to be stunned and to be
14:65 some *s* to spit on him and
14:69 *s* again to say to those
15:8 *s* to make petition according
15:18 *s* greeting him: Good day
Lu 4:21 Then he *s* to say to them
5:21 the Pharisees *s* to reason
7:6 Jesus *s* off with them
7:15 the dead man sat up and *s* to
7:24 he *s* to say to the crowds
7:38 wept and *s* to wet his feet
7:49 *s* to say within themselves
9:12 Then the day *s* to decline
11:29 he *s* to say: This generation
11:53 *s* in to press upon him
12:1 he *s* out by saying first to
14:18 all in common *s* to beg off
14:30 This man *s* to build but was
15:14 and he *s* to be in need
15:24 they *s* to enjoy themselves
19:37 disciples *s* to rejoice and
19:45 temple and *s* to throw out
20:9 *s* to tell the people this
22:23 they *s* to discuss among
23:2 they *s* to accuse him, saying
Joh 13:5 *s* to wash the feet of the
20:3 *s* for the memorial tomb
Ac 1:1 Jesus *s* both to do and to
2:4 and *s* to speak with different
11:15 when I *s* to speak, the holy
18:26 man *s* to speak boldly in the
21:5 went forth and *s* on our way
24:2 Tertullus *s* accusing him
27:35 and broke it and *s* eating
Php 1:6 he who *s* a good work in you

Starting
Jer 25:29 *s* off in bringing calamity
Mt 14:30 after *s* to sink, he cried
Lu 9:6 *s* out they went through the
23:5 *s* out from Galilee to here
24:47 *s* out from Jerusalem
Ac 1:22 *s* with his baptism by John
8:35 *s* with this Scripture, he
10:37 *s* from Galilee after the
2Co 3:1 Are we *s* again to recommend
Ga 3:3 After *s* in spirit are you now

Startle
Isa 52:15 likewise *s* many nations

Starts
1Pe 4:17 if it *s* first with us, what

State
Ex 9:1 to Pharaoh and you must *s*
Le 11:31 in their death *s* will be
11:32 fall in its death *s* will be
De 4:13 *s* to you his covenant, which
2Ch 8:16 work was all in a prepared *s*
Job 23:2 today my *s* of concern is
Isa 3:22 robes of *s* and the overtunics
32:19 becomes low in an abased *s*
49:20 the sons of your bereaved *s*
Jer 43:10 extend his *s* tent over them
La 3:19 affliction and my homeless *s*
Eze 16:55 return to their former *s*
16:55 return to their former *s*
16:55 return to your former *s*
36:11 than in your initial *s*
Jon 4:6 from his calamitous *s*
Na 1:12 there were many in that *s*
1:12 in that *s* they must be cut
Zec 3:4 clothing . . . with robes of *s*
Ro 1:28 to a disapproved mental *s*
3:8 as some men *s* that we say
4:11 while in his uncircumcised *s*
4:12 in the uncircumcised *s* which
1Co 7:20 In whatever *s* each one was
Eph 2:12 alienated from the *s* of
4:26 set with you in a provoked *s*
Col 2:13 the uncircumcised *s* of your
Heb 11:34 from a weak *s* were made
Jas 2:15 in a naked *s* and lacking the
1Pe 3:19 In this *s* also he went his

Statecraft
Ac 7:19 used *s* against our race and

Stated
Ge 41:24 *s* it to the magic-practicing
Ex 9:12 as Jehovah had *s* to Moses
9:35 Jehovah had *s* by means of
12:25 give you, just as he has *s*
12:31 just as you have *s*
12:32 just as you have *s*, and go
Nu 15:34 *s* what should be done to him
Jos 4:8 as Jehovah had *s* to Joshua
4:12 just as Moses had *s* to them
Job 20:29 his *s* inheritance from God
Ac 13:34 he has *s* in this way
26:22 Moses *s* were going to take

Stately
Isa 52:14 as respects his *s* form more
53:2 No *s* form does he have, nor

Statement
Ge 26:3 carry out the sworn *s* that I
Le 5:4 thoughtlessly in a sworn *s*
De 7:8 his keeping the sworn *s* that
1Ch 16:16 And his sworn *s* to Isaac
16:17 which *s* he kept standing as
Es 4:7 the exact *s* of the money that
10:2 *s* of Mordecai's greatness
Ps 105:9 And his sworn *s* to Isaac
105:10 *s* he kept standing as a
119:106 I have made a sworn *s*, and
Isa 8:20 to this *s* that will have no
65:16 a sworn *s* in the earth
Eze 16:8 to make a sworn *s* to you and
Mr 8:32 he was making that *s*
Lu 1:1 compile a *s* of the facts that
1Ti 3:1 That *s* is faithful. If any
4:9 full acceptance is that *s*
1Jo 1:6 *s*: We are having a sharing
1:8 make the *s*: We have no sin
1:10 *s*: We have not sinned, we
4:20 makes the *s*: I love God, and

Statements
Ge 26:31 sworn *s* one to the other
De 10:20 you should make sworn *s*
Ps 64:5 make *s* about hiding traps

Stater
Mt 17:27 you will find a *s* coin

Station
Ge 19:16 to *s* him outside the city
Ex 33:21 *s* yourself upon the rock
34:2 *s* yourself by me there on the
34:5 proceeded to . . . *s* himself
Nu 11:16 they must *s* themselves there
22:22 to *s* himself in the road to
23:3 *S* yourself by your burnt
Nu 23:15 said to Balak: *S* yourself
De 31:14 *s* yourselves in the tent of
Jg 20:2 their *s* in the congregation of
1Sa 5:2 and *s* it beside Dagon
1Ch 15:16 *s* their brothers the singers
2Ch 19:5 *s* judges throughout the land
23:10 *s* all the people, even each
Ne 7:3 *s* guards of the inhabitants of
Job 1:6 to take their *s* before Jehovah
2:1 to take their *s* before Jehovah
2:1 to take his *s* before Jehovah
33:5 before me; do take your *s*
38:14 take their *s* as in clothing
Pr 22:29 kings is where he will *s*
22:29 will not *s* himself before
Isa 52:13 He will be in high *s* and
Jer 46:4 *s* yourselves with the helmet
46:14 *S* yourself, making
Zec 6:5 taken their *s* before the Lord
Lu 6:17 took his *s* on a level place
1Ti 2:2 all those who are in high *s*
Heb 10:11 every priest takes his *s*

Stationed
Ge 24:13 I am *s* at a fountain of
24:43 I am *s* at a fountain of
28:12 a ladder *s* upon the earth
28:13 there was Jehovah *s* above it
35:14 Jacob *s* a pillar in the place
35:20 *s* a pillar over her grave
45:1 all those who were *s* by him
Ex 2:4 sister *s* herself at a distance
33:8 they *s* themselves each one
Nu 22:23 Jehovah's angel *s* in the road
22:31 Jehovah's angel *s* in the road
22:34 you *s* in the road to meet me
23:6 were *s* by his burnt offering
23:17 was *s* by his burnt offering
De 29:10 *s* today before Jehovah
31:14 Joshua went and *s*
1Sa 22:6 all his servants *s* about him
22:7 servants *s* about him
22:9 Doeg the Edomite, being *s*
22:17 to the runners *s* about him
1Ki 10:26 *s* in the chariot cities
2Ki 10:24 *s* eighty men outside at his
1Ch 15:17 Levites *s* Heman the son of
2Ch 1:14 *s* in chariot cities and close
4:8 and *s* them in the temple
9:25 *s* in the chariot cities and
19:8 Jehoshaphat *s* some of the
20:21 *s* singers to Jehovah and
23:19 *s* the gatekeepers by the
29:25 Levites *s* at the house of
35:2 *s* the priests over the things
Ne 13:11 *s* them at their standing
13:19 attendants I *s* at the gates
Ps 119:89 word is *s* in the heavens
Pr 8:2 roadways it has *s* itself
Isa 21:8 I am *s* all the nights
Am 7:7 Jehovah was *s* on a wall made
9:1 saw Jehovah *s* above the altar
Hab 2:1 *s* upon the bulwark; and I
Mt 4:5 *s* him upon the battlement of
Lu 4:9 *s* him upon the battlement of

Stationing
Ex 17:9 *s* myself upon the top of the
Ps 82:1 God is *s* himself in the
Isa 3:13 Jehovah is *s* himself to
Zec 11:16 The one *s* herself he will

Stations
Ps 36:4 He *s* himself on a way that

Statue
Ex 32:4 into a molten *s* of a calf
32:8 made a molten *s* of a calf for
De 27:15 a carved image or a molten *s*
Jg 17:3 a carved image and a molten *s*
17:4 went making . . . a molten *s*
18:14 carved image and a molten *s*
Ne 9:18 a molten *s* of a calf and
Isa 30:22 of your molten *s* of gold
Ho 13:2 a molten *s* from their silver
Na 1:14 I shall cut off . . . molten *s*
Hab 2:18 carved it, a molten *s*, and

Statues
2Ki 17:16 molten *s*, two calves
2Ch 28:2 molten *s* he made of the
34:3 images and the molten *s*
34:4 molten *s* he broke in pieces

Stature
1Sa 16:7 and at the height of his *s*
Ca 7:7 *s* of yours does resemble a
Eze 31:3 and high in *s*, so that
31:5 grew higher in its *s* than
31:10 you became high in *s*
31:14 may become high in their *s*
Eph 4:13 to the measure of *s* that

Status
Jos 20:7 gave a sacred *s* to Kedesh

Statute
Ex 12:14 As a *s* to time indefinite
12:17 as a *s* to time indefinite
12:43 This is the *s* of the passover
13:10 you must keep this *s* at its
27:21 It is a *s* to time indefinite
28:43 It is a *s* to time indefinite
29:9 as a *s* to time indefinite
Le 3:17 It is a *s* to time indefinite
7:36 a *s* to time indefinite for
10:9 It is a *s* to time indefinite
16:29 *s* to time indefinite for you
16:31 is a *s* to time indefinite
16:34 must serve as a *s* to time
17:7 will serve as a *s* to time
23:14 *s* to time indefinite for
23:21 *s* to time indefinite in all
23:31 *s* to time indefinite for
23:41 *s* to time indefinite during
24:3 *s* to time indefinite during
Nu 9:12 whole *s* of the passover they
9:14 According to the *s* of the
9:14 exist one *s* for you people
10:8 *s* for you men to time
15:15 an alien will have one *s*
15:15 a *s* to time indefinite for
18:23 It is a *s* to time indefinite
19:2 This is a *s* of the law that
19:10 as a *s* to time indefinite
19:21 a *s* to time indefinite for
27:11 as a *s* by judicial decision
31:21 This is the *s* of the law
35:29 serve as a *s* of judgment for
Eze 46:14 is an indefinitely lasting *s*
Da 6:7 establish a royal *s* and to
6:8 king, may you establish the *s*
6:15 or *s* that the king himself
Zep 2:2 Before the *s* gives birth to

Statute-giver
De 33:21 allotment of a *s* is reserved
Isa 33:22 Jehovah is our *S*

Statutes
Ge 26:5 my commands, my *s*, and my
Le 18:3 their *s* you must not walk
18:4 my *s* you should keep so as to
18:5 keep my *s* and my judicial
18:26 keep my *s* and my judicial
19:19 people should keep my *s*
19:37 keep all my *s* and all my
20:8 you must keep my *s* and do
20:22 keep all my *s* and all my
20:23 not walk in the *s* of the
25:18 carry out my *s* and you should
26:3 walking in my *s* and keeping
26:15 reject my *s*, and if your
26:43 souls had abhorred my *s*
Nu 9:3 According to all its *s* and all
De 6:2 so as to keep all his *s* and his
8:11 his *s* that I am commanding
10:13 *s* that I am commanding you
11:1 *s* and his judicial decisions
28:15 his *s* that I am commanding
28:45 his *s* that he commanded you
30:10 his *s* written in this book
30:16 *s* and his judicial decisions
2Sa 22:23 And as for his *s*, I shall
1Ki 2:3 his *s*, his commandments and
3:3 by walking in the *s* of David
6:12 if you will walk in my *s*
9:6 *s* that I have put before you
11:11 my *s* that I laid in command
11:33 and my *s* and my judicial
11:34 my commandments and my *s*
11:38 by keeping my *s* and my
2Ki 17:8 in the *s* of the nations
17:8 the *s* of the kings of Israel
17:13 keep my commandments, my *s*
17:19 walking in the *s* of Israel
17:34 *s* and his judicial decisions
23:3 and his *s* with all the heart
2Ch 7:19 leave my *s* and my
Job 38:33 know the *s* of the heavens
Ps 18:22 And his *s* I shall not remove
89:31 If they profane my own *s*
119:16 *s* I shall show a fondness

Jer 31:35 s of the moon and the stars
33:25 the s of heaven and earth
44:10 walk in my law and in my s
44:23 his s and in his reminders
Eze 5:6 against my s more than the
5:6 my s, they did not walk in
5:7 in my s you did not walk and
11:20 they may walk in my own s
18:9 in my s he kept walking and
18:17 in my s he has walked
18:19 s of mine he has kept and
18:21 keep all my s and execute
20:11 proceeded to give them my s
20:13 In my s they did not walk
20:16 my s, they did not walk in
20:19 Walk in my own s, and keep
20:21 In my s they did not walk
20:24 they rejected my own s and
33:15 walks in the very s of life
37:24 my s they will keep
43:18 s of the altar on the day
44:5 s of the house of Jehovah
44:24 s in regard to all my
Mic 6:16 the s of Omri and all the

Staves
1Sa 17:43 are coming to me with s

Stay
Ge 19:2 s overnight and have your feet
19:2 square is where we shall s
22:5 You s here with the ass, but
24:55 young woman s with us at
42:33 Have one brother of yours s
44:33 let your slave s instead of
Ex 9:28 and you will not s any longer
23:18 should not s overnight until
24:12 s there, as I want to give
25:15 the poles are to s. They are
28:38 must s upon his forehead
34:25 should not s overnight until
Le 8:35 s at the entrance of the tent
12:4 she will s in the blood of
12:5 will s with the blood of
19:13 s all night with you until
Nu 9:19 cloud prolonged its s over
9:22 cloud prolonged its s over
22:19 you men also s here, please
32:15 s longer in the wilderness
32:26 our domestic animals will s
De 16:4 s all night until the morning
21:23 not s all night on the stake
24:19 It should s for the alien
24:20 It should s for the alien
24:21 They should s for the alien
Jg 2:23 let these nations s by not
3:1 that Jehovah let s so as by
19:4 he would s overnight there
19:6 and s overnight, and let your
19:9 s overnight. Here the day is
19:9 S here overnight, and let your
19:10 not consent to s overnight
19:11 and s in it overnight
19:13 we must s overnight either
19:15 in to s overnight in Gibeah
19:15 into the house to s overnight
19:20 do not s overnight in the
20:4 to Gibeah . . . to s overnight
1Sa 1:23 S at home until you wean
2Ki 15:20 did not s there in the land
Es 4:11 will also certainly s alive
Job 29:19 dew itself will s overnight
Ps 59:15 be satisfied or s overnight
83:1 do not s quiet, O Divine One
89:2 Loving-kindness will s built
Isa 3:1 from Judah support and s, the
62:1 I shall not s quiet until
64:12 Will you s still and let us
Jer 3:5 one s resentful to time
3:12 not s resentful to time
43:6 let s with Gedaliah the son
47:6 long will you not s quiet
47:7 How can it s quiet, when
Eze 16:42 I will s quiet and I shall
Na 3:18 your majestic ones s in their
Mt 2:13 flee into Egypt, and s there
10:11 and s there until you leave
26:38 S here and keep on the watch
Mr 6:10 enter into a home, s there
14:34 S here and keep on the watch
Lu 9:4 s there and leave from there
10:7 So s in that house, eating
19:5 today I must s in your house
24:29 S with us, because it is
24:29 he went in to s with them
Joh 2:12 did not s there many days
4:40 asking him to s with them
Ac 16:15 enter into my house and s
28:16 Paul was permitted to s by
1Co 16:6 s or even pass the winter
16:13 S awake, stand firm in the
1Th 5:6 s awake and keep our senses
5:10 we s awake or are asleep
1Ti 1:3 encouraged you to s in Ephesus
4:16 S by these things, for by

Stayed
Ge 32:4 s for a long time till now
Nu 22:8 princes . . . s with Balaam
De 10:10 I s in the mountain the same
Jos 6:11 and s overnight in the camp
Jg 19:7 he s overnight there again
1Sa 1:23 s at home and kept nursing
Isa 59:11 it has s far away from us
Mt 2:15 he s there until the decease
15:32 three days that they have s
Joh 1:39 they s with him that day
4:40 and he s there two days
10:40 and he s there
Ac 18:3 he s at their home, and they
18:11 he s set there a year and six
21:7 and s one day with them
21:8 house of Philip . . . we s
27:41 stuck and s immovable, but
Ga 1:18 I s with him for fifteen days
2Ti 4:20 Erastus s in Corinth, but I
Heb 11:34 s the force of fire

Staying
Pr 23:30 s a long time with the wine
Lu 8:27 he was s, not at home, but
Joh 1:38 Rabbi . . . where are you s?
1:39 and saw where he was s
Ac 1:13 chamber, where they were s
18:18 s quite some days longer

Stays
Job 39:28 and s during the night
2Ti 2:19 foundation of God s standing
Re 16:15 one that s awake and keeps

Steadfast
2Sa 7:16 kingdom will certainly be s
Ps 51:10 a new spirit, a s one
57:7 My heart is s, O God
57:7 My heart is s. I will sing
78:37 heart was not s with him
108:1 My heart is s, O God
112:7 His heart is s, made
1Co 15:58 become s, unmovable
Col 1:23 and s and not being shifted
Heb 11:27 s as seeing the One who is

Steadfastness
2Pe 3:17 and fall from your own s

Steadily
2Sa 18:25 coming, s getting nearer
Es 9:4 Mordecai was s growing
Da 6:3 Daniel was s distinguishing

Steady
Ex 17:12 his hands held s until the
Pr 27:15 away in the day of a s rain

Steal
Ge 44:8 could we s silver or gold
Ex 20:15 You must not s
22:1 In case a man should s a bull
Le 19:11 people must not s, and you
De 5:19 Neither must you s
2Sa 19:3 the people began to s away
19:3 s away when they felt
19:41 the men of Judah s you that
Job 27:20 will certainly s him away
Pr 30:9 s and assail the name of my
Ob 5 s as much as they wanted
Mt 6:19 where thieves break in and s
6:20 thieves do not break in and s
19:18 You must not s, You must
27:64 may never come and s him
Mr 10:19 Do not s, Do not bear false
Lu 18:20 Do not murder, Do not s, Do
Joh 10:10 to s and slay and destroy
Ro 2:21, 21 Do not s, do you s?
13:9 You must not s, You must not
Eph 4:28 Let the stealer s no more

Stealer
Eph 4:28 Let the s steal no more

Stealing
2Sa 15:6 kept s the hearts of the men
Jer 7:9 Can there be s, murdering
Jer 23:30 who are s away my words
Ho 4:2 deception and murdering and s
Zec 5:3 everyone that is s

Stealthily
Jg 4:21 she went to him s and drove
Ru 3:7 she came s and uncovered him
Job 4:12 to me a word was s brought

Steeds
1Ki 10:26 more chariots and s
10:26 and twelve thousand s
2Ch 1:14 kept gathering chariots and s
1:14 and twelve thousand s and he
9:25 twelve thousand s, and he
Isa 21:7 chariot with a span of s
21:9 men, with a span of s
22:6 of earthling man, with s
22:7 s must without fail set
28:28 and his own s, but he will
31:1 s, because they are very
Eze 27:14 horses and s and mules
Joe 2:4 like s is the way they keep
Hab 1:8 its s have pawed the ground
1:8 its own s come. They fly like

Steep
Ca 2:14 concealed place of the s way
Eze 38:20 s ways will have to fall
Mic 1:4 being poured down a s place

Steered
Jas 3:4 are s by a very small rudder

Steering
Job 37:12 by his s them for their
Pr 12:5 s by the wicked ones is

Stem
Heb 2:11 all s from one, and for this

Stench
Ge 34:30 a s to the inhabitants of
1Sa 27:12 s among his people Israel
Joe 2:20 the s from him will keep

Step
Nu 24:17 s forth out of Jacob, And a
1Sa 20:3 s between me and death
2Sa 18:30 S aside, take your position
Isa 3:20 s chains and the breastbands
27:4 I will s on such
Jer 10:23 even to direct his s
Da 3:26 s out and come here! At that
Ac 16:9 S over into Macedonia and
Ro 11:11 by their false s there is
11:12 their false s means riches
Ga 6:1 false s before he is aware of
Jas 2:10 a false s in one point, he

Stephanas
1Co 1:16 baptized the household of S
16:15 the household of S is the
16:17 over the presence of S and

Stephen
Ac 6:5 S, a man full of faith and
6:8 S, full of graciousness and
6:9 and Asia, to dispute with S
7:59 casting stones at S as he
8:2 reverent men carried S to the
11:19 tribulation that arose over S
22:20 blood of S your witness was

Stepped
Ge 30:30 blessed you since I s in
De 11:6 thing that s after them in
2Sa 18:30 he s aside and kept standing
Mr 10:35 s up to him and said to him
Ac 20:18 s into the district of Asia
Heb 6:17 s in with an oath

Stepping
Job 31:7 my s deviates from the way
Da 3:26 s out from the . . . fire
Mr 5:39 after s in, he said to them
Lu 8:16 s in may behold the light
11:33 those s in may behold the
12:1 they were s upon one another

Steppings
Ps 85:13 will make a way by his s
Pr 20:24 the s of an able-bodied man

Steps
Ge 19:29 he took s to send Lot out of
Ex 11:8 the people who follow your s
20:26 must not go up by s to my
Jg 4:10 went on up following his s
8:5 people that are following my s
1Sa 25:27 in the s of my lord

2Sa 6:13 had marched six s, he
22:37 room large enough for my s
1Ki 10:19 were six s to the throne
10:20 there upon the six s
2Ki 3:9 that were following their s
9:13 under him upon the bare s
20:9 forward ten s of the stairs
20:9 or should it go back ten s
20:10 to extend itself ten s
20:10 should go backward ten s
20:11 gradually go back on the s
20:11 on the s of the stairs of
20:11 ten s backward
2Ch 9:18 six s to the throne, and
9:19 upon the six s on this side
Job 14:16 you keep counting my very s
18:7 His s of vigor . . . cramped
23:11 Of his s my foot has laid
29:6 I washed my s in butter
31:4 And count even all my s
31:37 my s I would tell him
34:21 And all his s he sees
Ps 17:5 my s take hold on your tracks
17:11 As regards our s, now they
18:36 room large enough for my s
37:23 s of an able-bodied man
37:31 His s will not wobble
40:2 He firmly established my s
56:6 keep observing my very s
57:6 they have prepared for my s
58:10 His s he will bathe in the
73:2 s had nearly been made to
74:3 Do lift up your s to the
119:133 Fix my own s solidly in
140:4 have schemed to push my s
Pr 5:5 Her very s take hold on Sheol
14:15 shrewd one considers his s
16:9 does the directing of his s
29:5 a mere net for his s
Ca 7:1 beautiful your s have become
Isa 3:16 walking with tripping s
26:6 the s of the lowly ones
38:8 shadow of the s that had
38:8 s of the stairs of Ahaz by
38:8 retrace backward ten s
38:8, 8 went back ten s on the s
Jer 10:5 for they cannot take any s
La 4:18 They have hunted our s so that
Eze 40:6 and went up by its s
40:22 by seven s people could go
40:26 seven s for going up to it
40:31 its ascent was eight s
40:34 And its ascent was eight s
40:37 And its ascent was eight s
40:49 by s was how they would
43:17 And its s are facing east
Da 11:43 Ethiopians will be at his s
Joh 5:7 another s down ahead of me
1Pe 2:21 you to follow his s closely

Sterile
Job 3:7 That night—let it become s
15:34 assembly of apostates is s
30:3 want and hunger they are s
Isa 49:21 bereaved of children and s

Stern
Mr 4:38 But he was in the s, sleeping
Lu 9:21 Then in a s talk to them he
Ac 27:16 of the skiff at the s
27:29 four anchors from the s and
27:41 s began to be violently

Sternly
Mt 9:30 Jesus s charged them, saying
16:20 s charged the disciples not
20:31 crowd s told them to keep
Mr 3:12 s charged them not to make
10:48 s telling him to be silent
Lu 18:39 to tell him s to keep quiet

Sternness
Ec 8:1 s of his face is changed for

Stew
Ge 25:29 Jacob was boiling up some s
25:34 gave Esau bread and lentil s
2Ki 4:38 boil s for the sons of the
4:40 soon as they ate from the s
Hag 2:12 bread or s or wine or oil

Steward
Isa 22:15 s, to Shebna, who is over
Lu 12:42 Who really is the faithful s
16:1 man was rich and he had a s
16:3 s said to himself, What am I
16:8 his master commended the s
Ro 16:23 Erastus the city s greets you
Tit 1:7 as God's s, not self-willed

Stewards
1Co 4:1 s of sacred secrets of God
4:2 what is looked for in s is
Ga 4:2 under s until the day his
1Pe 4:10 s of . . . undeserved kindness

Stewardship
Lu 16:2 Hand in the account of your s
16:3 will take the s away from me
16:4 when I am put out of the s
1Co 9:17 I have a s entrusted to me
Eph 3:2 s of the undeserved kindness
Col 1:25 s from God which was given

Stewpot
2Ki 4:39 sliced them into the s, for

Stick
Ge 2:24 he must s to his wife and
Ex 4:6 S your hand, please, into the
21:20 his slave girl with a s and
De 13:17 nothing at all should s to
2Ki 5:27 leprosy of Naaman will s to
7:8 and go off and s them away
Ps 22:15 tongue . . . to s to my gums
137:6 my tongue s to my palate
Isa 10:5 s that is in their hand for
Eze 3:26 tongue I will make s to the
37:16 a s and write upon it
37:16 take another s and write
37:16 Joseph, the s of Ephraim
37:17 into one s for yourself
37:19 am taking the s of Joseph
37:19 the s of Judah, and I shall
37:19 actually make them one s
Mt 6:24 s to the one and despise the
19:5 will s to his wife, and the
Lu 16:13 s to the one and despise the
Joh 20:25 s my finger into the print
20:25 s my hand into his side
20:27 hand and s it into my side
Eph 5:31 and he will s to his wife

Sticking
De 30:20 by listening . . . and by s
2Ki 18:6 And he kept s to Jehovah
Pr 18:24 a friend s closer than a
Isa 57:4 keep s out the tongue
Da 2:43 not prove to be s together

Sticks
Jer 7:18 are picking up s of wood
Eze 37:20 s upon which you write
39:10 not carry s of wood from
Ac 28:3 s and laid it upon the fire

Stiff
Ex 10:19 shift to a very s west wind
De 31:27 I well know . . . your s neck
Ac 2:2 that of a rushing s breeze

Stiffen
2Ch 30:8 do not s your neck as your

Stiffening
2Ch 36:13 s his neck and hardening

Stiff-necked
Ex 32:9 and here it is a s people
33:3 because you are a s people
33:5 of Israel, You are a s people
34:9 it is a s people, and you
De 9:6 for you are a s people
9:13 look! it is a s people

Stiff-neckedly
Job 15:26 he runs against him s

Still*
Nu 13:30 Caleb tried to s the people
Jos 3:8 should stand s in the Jordan
3:13 they will stand s as one dam
3:16 from above began to stand s
10:13 and the moon did stand s
10:13 And the sun kept standing s
10:19 you men, do not stand s
Ru 3:18 Sit s, my daughter, until you
1Sa 20:38 Do not stand s! And the
2Sa 18:30 and kept standing s
2Ch 20:17 stand s and see the
Job 32:16 they stood s, they answered
37:14 Stand s and show yourself
Ps 28:1 may not keep s toward me
107:30 because these become s
Pr 26:20 slanderer contention grows s
Isa 44:11 will stand s. They will
46:7 place that it may stand s
47:12 Stand s, now, with your
62:1 I shall not keep s, and for
62:6 let them not keep s
Jer 51:50 Do not stand s. From far
Eze 1:21 these would stand s
10:18 to stand s over the cherubs
21:21 king of Babylon stood s
Jon 1:11 the sea may become s for us
Hab 3:11 Sun—moon—stood s, in the
Zec 1:11 whole earth is sitting s
Lu 18:40 Jesus stood s and commanded
24:17 they stood s with sad faces

Stilling
Ps 65:7 He is s the noise of the seas

Still-moist
Jg 16:7 tie me with seven s sinews
16:8 seven s sinews that had not
Eze 17:24 have dried up the s tree and
20:47 every s tree and every dry

Sting
1Co 15:55 Death, where is your s?
15:56 The s producing death is sin

Stinging
Isa 55:13 Instead of the s nettle the

Stings
Ho 13:14 Where are your s, O Death?
Re 9:10 tails and s like scorpions

Stingy
De 15:10 your heart should not be s

Stink
Ex 7:18 Nile River will actually s
7:21 and the Nile River began to s
8:14 and the land began to s
16:20 it would breed worms and s
16:24 it did not s nor did maggots
Ec 10:1 what cause the oil . . . to s
Isa 19:6 rivers must s; the Nile
34:3 carcasses, their s will
50:2 fish s due to there being no
Joe 2:20 the s from him will
Am 4:10 the s of your camps ascend

Stinking
Job 31:40 instead of barley s weeds

Stinky
Ps 38:5 My wounds have become s

Stipulate
Ge 30:28 S your wages to me and I

Stipulated
Mt 26:15 They s to him thirty silver

Stir
1Sa 4:5 so that the earth was in a s
Job 41:10 that he should s it up
Ac 12:18 little s among the soldiers
Php 1:17 supposing to s up tribulation
2Ti 1:6 s up like a fire the gift of

Stirred
Ru 1:19 city became s up over them
1Ch 5:26 God of Israel s up the spirit
Job 26:12 power he has s up the sea
Ps 74:13 s up the sea with your own
Da 10:10 s me up to get upon my knees
Mr 15:11 s up the crowd to have him
Joh 6:18 the sea began to be s up
Ac 6:12 s up the people and the older
13:50 the Jews s up the reputable
14:2 Jews that did not believe s
21:38 s up a sedition and led the
2Co 9:2 zeal has s up the majority of

Stirring
Isa 51:15 the One s up the sea that
Jer 31:35 One s up the sea that its
Da 7:2 were s up the vast sea
Ac 24:5 s up seditions among all the
Ga 5:26 s up competition with one

Stirs
De 32:11 as an eagle s up its nest
Pr 10:12 Hatred is what s up
15:18 enraged man s up contention
28:25 arrogant . . . s up contention
29:22 anger s up contention, and
Lu 23:5 He s up the people by teaching

Stock
Ge 46:32 they became s raisers
46:34 s raisers from our youth
47:18 the s of domestic animals
Ex 12:38 a very numerous s of animals

Ps 80:15 s that your right hand has
Ac 7:13 family s of Joseph became
13:26 sons of the s of Abraham
Php 3:5 out of the family s of Israel
Re 18:11 no one to buy their full s
18:12 full s of gold and silver

Stocked
Ge 13:2 Abram was heavily s with
Jos 9:4 s themselves with provisions

Stocks
2Ch 16:10 him in the house of the s
Job 13:27 keep my feet put in the s
33:11 He puts my feet in the s
Jer 20:2 and put him into the s that
20:3 let Jeremiah out from the s
29:26 must put him into the s
Ac 16:24 their feet fast in the s

Stoic
Ac 17:18 and the S philosophers took

Stole
Ge 31:19 Rachel s the teraphim that
Ex 22:3 be sold for the things he s
2Ki 11:2 s him from among the sons
2Ch 22:11 s him away from among the
Mt 28:13 came in the night and s him

Stolen
Ge 30:33 something s if it is with me
31:30 have you s my gods
31:32 know that Rachel had s them
31:39 Whether one was s by day or
31:39 or was s by night, you would
Ex 22:4 found in his hand what was s
22:7 gets s from the man's house
22:12 should for a fact be s from
Jos 7:11 s and also kept it secret
2Sa 21:12 s them from the public
Job 21:18 that a stormwind has s
Pr 9:17 S waters themselves are

Stomach
Ex 7:18 no s for drinking water from
De 18:3 give to the priest . . . the s
1Ti 5:23 wine for the sake of your s

Stone
Ge 2:12 bdellium gum and the onyx s
11:3 brick served as s for them
28:18 took the s that was there
28:22 s that I have set up as a
29:2 s over the mouth of the well
29:3 rolled away the s from off
29:3 returned the s over the mouth
29:8 roll away the s from off the
29:10 the s from off the mouth
31:45 Jacob took a s and set it up
35:14 a pillar of s, and he poured
49:24 the shepherd, the s of Israel
Ex 7:19 be blood . . . in the s vessels
8:26 would they not s us?
15:5 went into the depths like a s
15:16 will be motionless like a s
17:4 longer and they will s me
17:12 took a s and put it under
21:18 strike his fellow with a s
24:12 to give you the s tablets and
28:10 names upon the one s and the
28:10 upon the other s in the order
28:19 the third row is *lesh'em* s
31:18 tablets of s written on by
34:1 two tablets of s like the
34:4 two tablets of s like the
34:4 two tablets of s in his hand
39:12 third row was *lesh'em* s
Le 26:1 put a s as a showpiece in
Nu 22:24 a s wall on this side and a
22:24 and a s wall on that side
32:16 build here s flock pens for
32:24 and s pens for your flocks
32:36 and s flock pens
33:52 destroy all their s figures
35:17 small s by which he could
35:23 any s by which he could die
De 4:13 upon two tablets of s
4:28 wood and s, which cannot see
5:22 upon two tablets of s and
9:9 to receive the s tablets
9:10 gave me the two tablets of s
9:11 gave me the two tablets of s
10:1 two tablets of s like the
10:3 two tablets of s like the
13:10 you must s him with stones
17:5 s such one with stones, and

De 28:36 gods, of wood and of s
28:64 other gods . . . wood and s
29:17 dungy idols, wood and s
Jos 4:5 each one a s upon his shoulder
15:6 the s of Bohan the son of
18:17 s of Bohan the son of Reuben
24:26 took a great s and set it
24:27 This s is what will serve
Jg 9:5 upon one s, but Jotham the
9:18 one s, and that you might
1Sa 6:14 where there was a large s
6:15 to put it upon the large s
6:18 the great s upon which they
7:12 Samuel took a s and set it
14:33 roll a great s to me
17:49 a s from there and slung it
17:49 the s sank into his forehead
17:50 David, with a sling and a s
20:19 dwell near this s here
24:3 came to the s sheepfolds
25:37 he himself became as a s
30:6 the people said to s him
2Sa 5:11 workers in s for walls, and
14:26 by the royal s weight
20:8 great s that is in Gibeon
1Ki 1:9 close by the s of Zoheleth
6:7 of quarry s already completed
6:18 there was no s to be seen
6:36 with three rows of hewn s
7:12 three rows of hewn s and a
8:9 two s tablets which Moses
21:10 and s him that he may die
2Ki 3:25 would pitch each one his s
12:12 and to the hewers of s
16:17 put it upon a s pavement
19:18 gods . . . wood and s
1Ch 22:2 as s hewers to hew squared
22:15 s hewers and workers in
22:15 workers in s and wood and
29:2 and every precious s, and
2Ch 3:6 the house with precious s for
Ezr 9:9 to give us a s wall in Judah
Ne 9:11 like a s in the strong waters
Job 8:17 In a s heap his roots become
19:8 he has blocked with a s wall
28:2 s copper is being poured out
28:3 S in the gloom and deep
28:16 onyx s and the sapphire
38:30 waters . . . hidden as by s
41:24 Its heart is cast like s
Ps 62:3 a s wall that is being pushed
80:12 you broken down its s walls
89:40 broken down all his s pens
91:12 your foot against any s
118:22 s that the builders rejected
Pr 16:11 s weights of the bag are his
17:8 The gift is a s winning favor
24:31 s wall itself had been torn
26:8 one shutting up a s in a heap
26:27 he that is rolling away a s
27:3 heaviness of a s and a load of
Ec 10:8 is breaking through a s wall
Ca 4:4 built in courses of s, upon
Isa 5:5 breaking down of its s wall
8:14 s to strike against and as
9:10 with hewn s we shall build
28:16 foundation in Zion a s
28:16 a tried s, the precious
37:19 man's hands, wood and s
Jer 2:27 to a s, You yourself brought
49:3 rove about among the s pens
51:26 s for a corner or a
51:26 or a s for foundations
51:63 tie to it a s, and you must
La 3:7 as with a s wall, that I may
3:9 blocked . . . ways with hewn s
Eze 1:26 in appearance like sapphire s
10:1 something like sapphire s
10:9 the glow of a chrysolite s
11:19 remove the heart of s from
13:5 build up a s wall in behalf
20:32 ministering to wood and s
22:30 be repairing the s wall and
28:13 Every precious s was your
36:26 take away the heart of s
40:42 tables . . . were of hewn s
42:7 the s wall that was outside
42:10 the s wall of the courtyard
42:12 s wall toward the east
Da 2:34 s was cut out not by hands
2:35 s that struck the image, it
2:45 s was cut not by hands, and
5:4 praised the gods of . . . s
5:23 praised mere gods of . . . s

Da 6:17 s was brought and placed on
11:38 by means of precious s and
Ho 2:6 heap up a s wall against her
Am 5:11 houses of hewn s you have
Mic 6:11 a bag of deceptive s weights
7:11 for building your s walls
Na 3:17 in the s pens in a cold day
Hab 2:11 a s itself will cry out
2:19 to a dumb s: O wake up!
Zep 2:6 and s pens for sheep
Hag 2:15, 15 placing of a s upon a s
Zec 3:9 the s that I have put before
3:9 one s there are seven eyes
7:12 heart they set as an emery s
12:3 Jerusalem a burdensome s to
Mt 4:6 strike your foot against a s
7:9 not hand him a s, will he?
21:42 s that the builders rejected
21:44 person falling upon this s
24:2, 2 a s be left here upon a s
27:60 rolling a big s to the door
27:66 secure by sealing the s and
28:2 rolled away the s, and was
Mr 12:10 s that the builders rejected
13:2 a s be left here upon a
13:2 a s and not be thrown down
15:46 rolled a s up to the door
16:3 Who will roll the s away
16:4 the s had been rolled away
Lu 4:3 tell this s to become a loaf
4:11 strike your foot against a s
19:44, 44 not leave a s upon a s
20:6 people one and all will s us
20:17 the s which the builders
20:18 falling upon that s will be
21:6, 6 not a s upon a s will be
24:2 found the s rolled away from
Joh 2:6 six s water jars sitting
10:31 lifted up stones to s him
11:8 Judeans were seeking to s
11:38 s was lying against it
11:39 Jesus said: Take the s away
11:41 they took the s away
19:13 called The S Pavement
20:1 beheld the s already taken
Ac 4:11 s that was treated by you
17:29 is like gold or silver or s
Ro 9:32 on the s of stumbling
9:33 in Zion a s of stumbling and
2Co 3:3 not on s tablets, but on
1Pe 2:4 a living s, rejected, it is
2:6 I am laying in Zion a s
2:7 s that the builders rejected
2:8 and a s of stumbling and a
Re 4:3 in appearance, like a jasper s
4:3 and a precious red-colored s
9:20 copper and s and wood, which
16:21 s about the weight of a
17:4 with gold and precious s and
18:12 precious s and pearls and
18:16 gold ornament and precious s
18:21 angel lifted up a s like a
21:11 like a most precious s, as
21:11 as a jasper s shining
21:19 every sort of precious s

Stonecutters
2Ch 24:12 hirers of the s and of the

Stoned
Ex 19:13 he will positively be s or
21:28 bull is to be s without fail
21:29 bull is to be s and also its
21:32 and the bull will be s
Jos 7:25 Thus they s them with stones
1Ki 21:13 s him with stones, so that
21:14 Naboth has been s so that
21:15 Naboth had been s so that
Mt 21:35 they killed, another they s
Ac 5:26 of being s by the people
14:19 they s Paul and dragged him
2Co 11:25 once I was s, three times
Heb 11:37 were s, they were tried
12:20 a beast . . . must be s

Stoner
Mt 23:37 s of those sent forth to her
Lu 13:34 s of those sent forth to her

Stone's
Lu 22:41 about a s throw, and bent

Stones
Ge 28:11 took one of the s of the
31:46 Pick up s! And they went
31:46 taking s and making a heap

Ex 20:25 make an altar of s for me
20:25 not build them as hewn s
25:7, 7 and onyx s and setting s
28:9 take two onyx s and engrave
28:11 the work of a craftsman in s
28:11 the two s with the names of
28:12 must put the two s upon the
28:12 as memorial s for the sons
28:17 fill it with a filling of s
28:17 there being four rows of s
28:21 the s should be according to
31:5 in working of s to set them
35:9, 9 onyx s and setting s for
35:27 chieftains brought onyx s
35:27 setting s for the ephod and
35:33 in working of s to set them
39:6 onyx s set with settings of
39:7 memorial s for . . . Israel
39:10 with four rows of s
39:14 the s were according to the
Le 14:40 the s in which the plague is
14:42 other s and insert them in
14:42 in the place of the former s
14:43 after having torn out the s
14:45 house pulled down with its s
20:2 pelt him to death with s
20:27 pelt them to death with s
24:14 must pelt him with s
24:16 without fail pelt him with s
24:23 and they pelted him with s
Nu 14:10 pelting them with s
15:35 pelting him with s outside
15:36 pelted him with s so that he
De 8:9 a land the s of which are iron
13:10 you must stone him with s
17:5 stone such one with s, and
21:21 pelt him with s, and he must
22:21 pelt her with s, and she
22:24 pelt them with s, and they
27:2 set up for yourself great s
27:4 you should set up these s
27:5 build . . . an altar of s
27:6 With whole s you should build
27:8 write on the s all the words
Jos 4:3 twelve s, and you must carry
4:6 Why do you have these s?
4:7 s must serve as a memorial
4:8 twelve s from the middle of
4:9 twelve s that Joshua set up
4:20 twelve s that they had taken
4:21 What do these s mean?
7:25 went pelting him with s
7:25 Thus they stoned them with s
7:26 big pile of s, down to this
8:29 a great pile of s over him
8:31 An altar of whole s, upon
8:32 upon the s a copy of the law
10:11 great s from the heavens
10:18 Roll great s up to the
10:27 s at the mouth of the cave
Jg 6:26 the row of s, and you must
20:16 slinger of s to a hairbreadth
1Sa 17:40 the five smoothest s from
2Sa 12:30 along with precious s
12:31 at sawing s and at sharp
16:6 he began throwing s at David
16:13 he kept throwing s while
18:17 a very big pile of s
1Ki 5:17 they should quarry great s
5:17 s, to lay the foundation of
5:17 foundation . . . with hewn s
5:18 and the s to build the house
7:9 s according to measures, hewn
7:10 s laid as a foundation were
7:10 foundation were great s
7:10 s of ten cubits, and
7:10 and s of eight cubits
7:11 above there were expensive s
10:2 much gold and precious s
10:10 balsam oil and precious s
10:11 great amount and precious s
10:27 the silver . . . like the s
12:18 Israel pelted him with s
15:22 to carry the s of Ramah
18:31 So Elijah took twelve s
18:32 build the s into an altar
18:38 the s and the dust, and the
19:6 a round cake upon heated s
21:13 stoned him with s, so that
2Ki 3:19 land you should mar with s
3:25 only the s of Kir-hareseth
12:12 to buy timbers and hewn s
22:6 hewn s to repair the house
1Ch 12:2 s or with arrows in the bow
1Ch 20:2 in it there were precious s
20:3 employed at sawing s and at
22:2 squared s for building the
22:14 and s I have prepared, but
29:2 the timberwork: onyx s, and
29:2 s to be set with hard mortar
29:2 alabaster s in great quantity
29:8 what s were found with any
2Ch 1:15 gold in Jerusalem like the s
2:14 in iron, in s and in timbers
9:1 great quantity, and precious s
9:9 great quantity, and precious s
9:10 almug trees and precious s
9:27 in Jerusalem like the s
10:18 Israel pelted him with s
16:6 carry away the s of Ramah
24:21 pelted him with s at the
26:15 shoot arrows and great s
32:27 precious s and for balsam
34:11 builders to buy hewn s and
Ezr 5:8 with s rolled into place
6:4 three layers of s rolled into
Ne 4:2 Will they bring the s to life
4:3 break down their wall of s
Job 5:23 with the s . . . your covenant
6:12 Is my power the power of s?
8:17 A house of s he beholds
14:19 Water . . . rubs away even s
15:28 destined for heaps of s
28:6 Its s are the place of the
Ps 102:14 found pleasure in her s
Pr 26:8 a stone in a heap of s, so is
Ec 3:5 a time to throw s away and a
3:5 and a time to bring s together
10:9 He that is quarrying out s
Isa 5:2 rid it of s and to plant it
14:19 down to the s of a pit
25:2 have made a city a pile of s
27:9 s of the altar like
34:11 and the s of wasteness
54:11 with hard mortar your s
54:12 gates of fiery glowing s
54:12 boundaries of delightsome s
57:6 the smooth s of the torrent
60:17 and instead of the s, iron
62:10 highway. Rid it of s
Jer 3:9 adultery with s and with
9:11 make Jerusalem piles of s
43:9 Take in your hand great s
43:10 throne right above these s
51:37 must become piles of s
La 3:53 and they kept hurling s at me
4:1 holy s are poured out at the
Eze 16:40 and pelt you with s and
23:47 must pelt them with s
26:12 your s and your woodwork
27:22 precious s and gold
28:14 midst of fiery s you walked
28:16 midst of the fiery s
Ho 12:11 altars are like piles of s
Mic 1:6 her s, and her foundations I
Zec 5:4 it and its timbers and its s
9:16 s of a diadem glittering
Mt 3:9 to Abraham from these s
4:3 tell these s to become loaves
Mr 5:5 and slashing himself with s
13:1 what sort of s and what sort
Lu 3:8 children . . . from these s
19:40 silent, the s would cry out
21:5 adorned with fine s and
Joh 8:59 they picked up s to hurl
10:31 Jews lifted up s to stone
Ac 7:58 they began casting s at him
7:59 casting s at Stephen as he
14:5 and pelt them with s
1Co 3:12 gold, silver, precious s
2Co 3:7 engraved in letters in s came
1Pe 2:5 living s are being built up a
Re 21:14 also had twelve foundation s

Stone-saws

1Ki 7:9 sawed with s, inside and

Stone-weight

Pr 11:1 complete s is a pleasure to

Stoning

Joh 10:32 those works are you s me
10:33 are s you, not for a fine

Stood

Ge 19:27 place where he had s before
37:7 sheaf got up and also s erect
41:46 when he s before Pharaoh the
45:1 And no one else s with him
Ex 9:10 s before Pharaoh, and Moses
Ex 14:19 and s in the rear of them
15:8 s still like a dam of floods
20:18 quivered and s at a distance
33:9 s at the entrance of the tent
Le 9:5 came near and s before Jehovah
13:37 has s and black hair has
16:10 s alive before Jehovah to
Nu 12:5 s at the entrance of the tent
16:18 s at the entrance of the tent
22:26 s in a narrow place, where
27:22 took Joshua and s him before
De 4:10 you s before Jehovah your God
4:11 s at the base of the mountain
Jos 4:3 priests' feet s motionless
21:44 not one . . . s before them
23:9 not a man has s before you
Jg 6:31 those who s against him: Will
9:7 s on the top of Mount Gerizim
9:35 and s at the entrance of the
18:30 s up the carved image for
1Sa 17:8 he s still and began to call
26:13 s upon the top of the
30:9 to be left behind s still
30:10 two hundred men . . . s still
2Sa 1:10 I s over him and definitely
12:17 older men of his house s up
15:2 s at the side of the road to
20:11 s over him and kept saying
20:12 all the people s still
20:12 everyone coming . . . s still
1Ki 1:28 and s before the king
3:15 s before the ark of the
19:13 s at the entrance of the
20:38 s still for the king by the
22:21 s before Jehovah and said
2Ki 2:7 they s by the Jordan
2:13 s by the shore of the Jordan
5:9 and s at the entrance of the
5:15 came and s before him and
5:25 s by his master. Elisha now
8:9 and came and s before him and
10:9 Then he s still and said to
13:6 pole itself s in Samaria
13:21 to life and s upon his feet
18:17 s still by the conduit of
2Ch 18:20 s before Jehovah and said
20:5 Jehoshaphat s up in the
20:20 Jehoshaphat s up and then
24:20 s up above the people and
26:18 s up against Uzziah the king
30:27 Levites, s up and blessed
Ezr 2:63 a priest s up with Urim and
3:9 s up as one group to act as
3:10 s up to praise Jehovah
9:5 I s up from my humiliation
10:15 s up against this, and
Ne 7:65 with Urim and Thummim s up
8:5 opened it all the people s up
Es 7:7 Haman himself s up to make
8:4 Esther rose and s before the
9:2 not a man s his ground before
Job 29:8 aged ones rose up, they s
30:20 I have s, that you might
32:16 they s still, they answered
Ps 1:1 the way of sinners has not s
38:11 have s off at a distance
106:23 Who s in the gap before him
106:30 Phinehas s up and intervened
119:91 decisions they have s till
Jer 14:6 s still upon the bare hills
23:18 s in the intimate group of
23:22 s in my intimate group
48:11 taste has s still within
48:45 those fleeing have s still
Eze 1:21 and when they s still, these
1:24 When they s still, they
1:25 When they s still, they
10:17 these s still, they would
21:21 king of Babylon s still
Da 8:22 four that finally s up
11:1 s up as a strengthener and as
11:4 when he will have s up, his
Ho 10:9 There they s still. In Gibeah
Ob 11 day when you s off on the side
Hab 3:6 He s still, that he might
3:11 Sun—moon—s still, in the
Mt 26:62 high priest s up and said
27:11 Jesus now s before the
Mr 6:20 For Herod s in fear of John
9:36 child, s it in their midst
Lu 2:9 Jehovah's angel s by them
4:16 synagogue, and he s up to read
4:39 he s over her and rebuked the
7:14 the bearers s still, and he

Lu 17:12 but they s up afar off
18:11 Pharisee s and began to pray
18:40 Jesus s still and commanded
19:8 s up and said to the Lord
23:35 And the people s looking on
24:4 two men . . . s by them
24:17 they s still with sad faces
24:36 s in their midst and said to
Joh 11:56 s around in the temple
12:29 crowd that s about and
20:19 Jesus came and s in their
20:26 he s in their midst and
21:4 Jesus s on the beach, but
Ac 1:10 two men in white garments s
2:14 Peter s up with the eleven
3:8 leaping up, he s up and began
4:7 s them in their midst and
5:27 s them in the Sanhedrin hall
10:17 and s there at the gate
10:30 man in bright raiment s
12:7 Jehovah's angel s by, and a
17:22 Paul now s in the midst of
22:30 brought Paul down and s him
23:11 the Lord s by him and said
24:20 as I s before the Sanhedrin
25:7 s round about him, leveling
27:21 Paul s up in the midst of
27:23 s near me an angel of the
2Co 9:2 Achaia has s ready now for a
Ga 2:11 because he s condemned
2Ti 4:17 Lord s near me and infused
Re 8:3 angel arrived and s at the
11:11 and they s upon their feet
13:1 it s still upon the sand of
18:17 s at a distance

Stool
Ex 1:16 on the s for childbirth, if it
Ps 110:1 enemies as a s for your feet
Lu 20:43 enemies as a s for your feet
Ac 2:35 enemies as a s for your feet
Heb 1:13 enemies as a s for your feet
10:13 placed as a s for his feet

Stoop
Isa 31:4 commotion he will not s
46:2 They must s over; they must
Mr 1:7 I am not fit to s and untie

Stooped
Joh 20:11 she s forward to look into

Stooping
Isa 46:1 bent down, Nebo is s over
51:14 The one s in chains will
Lu 24:12 s forward, he beheld the
Joh 20:5 s forward, he beheld the

Stop
Ex 9:29 thunders will s and the hail
9:33 thunders and the hail began to s
1Sa 15:16 Samuel said to Saul: S!
2Sa 15:17 came to a s at Beth-merhak
2Ki 3:19 springs . . . you should s up
3:25 of water they would s up
2Ch 32:3 men to s up the waters of
Ezr 4:21 these able-bodied men to s
5:5 not s them until the report
Ne 4:11 and put a s to the work
Isa 1:13 S bringing in any more
14:4 others to work come to a s
14:4 the oppression come to a s
Mt 2:9 came to a s above where the
6:16 fasting, s becoming sad-faced
6:19 S storing up for yourselves
6:25 S being anxious about your
7:1 S judging that you may not be
19:14 and s hindering them from
Mr 10:14 do not try to s them, for
16:6 S being stunned. You are
Lu 5:10 S being afraid. From now on
6:37 s judging, and you will by
6:37 s condemning, and you will by
7:13 he said to her: S weeping
8:52 S weeping, for she did not
18:16 and do not try to s them
23:28 Jerusalem, s weeping for me
Joh 2:16 S making the house of my
6:43 S murmuring among
7:24 S judging from the outward
20:17 to her: S clinging to me
20:27 and s being unbelieving
Ac 4:20 we cannot s speaking about
5:40 s speaking upon the basis of
6:13 s speaking things against this
10:15 You s calling defiled the
11:9 You s calling defiled the
20:10 S raising a clamor, for his
Ro 14:20 S tearing down the work of
1Co 7:23 s becoming slaves of men
7:27 a wife? S seeking a release
7:27 loosed from a wife? S seeking
2Co 11:10 no s shall be put to this
2Th 3:14 s associating with him, that
Jas 5:12 s swearing, yes, either by
Re 5:5 S weeping. Look! The Lion

Stopover
2Co 1:16 after a s with you to go to

Stopped
Ge 8:2 floodgates of the heavens . . . s
18:11 Sarah had s . . . menstruation
26:15 these the Philistines s up
Ex 9:34 hail and the thunders had s
Le 13:5 way it looks the plague has s
Nu 16:48 Eventually the scourge was s
16:50 the scourge had been s
2Ki 4:6 At that the oil s
13:18 he struck three times and s
2Ch 16:5 Baasha . . . s his work
32:30 s up the upper source of the
Ezr 4:23 Jews and s them by force of
4:24 which was in Jerusalem, s
4:24 s until the second year of
Ne 4:7 gaps had started to be s up
Ps 63:11 falsehood will be s up
Mt 20:32 Jesus s, called them and
Mr 10:49 Jesus s and said: Call him
Lu 8:44 instantly her flow of blood s
11:1 when he s, a certain one of
Ro 3:19 every mouth may be s and all
Heb 8:9 I s caring for them, says
10:2 s being offered, because
11:33 s the mouths of lions

Stopping
Ge 26:18 the Philistines went s up
2Ch 32:4 s up all the fountains and
Pr 21:13 anyone s up his ear from the
Isa 33:15 s up his ear from listening
Eze 39:11 s up those passing through

Stops
Ps 58:4 the cobra that s up its ear

Storage
Ex 1:11 building cities as s places
1Ki 9:19 all the s cities that became
2Ch 8:4 all the s cities that he had
8:6 Baalath and all the s cities
16:4 s places of the cities of
17:12 and s cities in Judah
32:28 s places for the produce of

Storax
Ge 30:37 staffs still moist of the s
Ho 4:13 and s tree and big tree

Store
Jg 6:2 underground s places that were
Job 21:19 s up one's hurtfulness for
Pr 15:6 there is an abundant s, but in
Mt 6:20 s up for yourselves treasures
13:52 brings out of his treasure s
1Co 16:2 set something aside in s as

Stored
2Ki 20:17 have s up down to this day
Job 24:1 times have not been s up by
Isa 10:13 things s up I shall
15:7 s goods that they have put up
23:18 It will not be s up, nor
39:6 your forefathers have s up
Lu 12:20 to have the things you s up
Jas 5:3 fire is what you have s up
2Pe 3:7 s up for fire and are being

Stored-up
Jer 20:5 all the s things of this city

Storehouse
De 28:12 open up to you his good s
32:34 a seal affixed to it in my s
Jer 50:25 Jehovah has opened his s
Mal 3:10 the tenth parts into the s
Mt 3:12 gather his wheat into the s
13:30 the wheat into my s
Lu 3:17 gather the wheat into his s
12:24 they have neither barn nor s

Storehouses
1Ch 26:15 and his sons had the s
2Ch 32:27 s he made for himself for
Job 38:22 into the s of the snow
38:22 see even the s of the hail
Ps 33:7 in s the surging waters
135:7 forth the wind from his s
Pr 8:21 and their s I keep filled
Jer 10:13 the wind from his s
51:16 forth the wind from his s
Eze 28:4 gold and silver in your s
Joe 1:17 S have been laid desolate
Mt 6:26 or reap or gather into s
Lu 12:18 tear down my s and build

Storerooms
1Ch 28:11 its s and its roof chambers

Stores
De 28:8 blessing on your s of supply
1Ch 26:17 and for the s, two by two
26:24 was a leader over the s
Ne 12:25 group by the s of the gates
12:44 men over the halls for the s
13:12 wine and of the oil to the s
13:13 Levites in charge of the s
Pr 3:10 s of supply will be filled
Eze 27:12 lead, your s were given
27:14 which your s were given
27:16 s were given in exchange
27:19 your s they gave. Iron in
27:22 gold, your s were given
27:27 valuable things and your s
27:33 s went forth from the open

Stories
Eze 41:6 upon side chamber, three s
42:3 opposite gallery in three s
42:6 For they were in three s
1Ti 1:4 to false s and to genealogies
4:7 false s which violate what
2Ti 4:4 be turned aside to false s
2Pe 1:16 artfully contrived false s

Storing
Am 3:10 those who are s up violence
Mt 6:19 Stop s up for yourselves
Ro 2:5 s up wrath for yourself on

Stork
Le 11:19 the s, the heron according
De 14:18 the s and the heron according
Job 39:13 has she the pinions of a s
Ps 104:17 s, the juniper trees are
Jer 8:7 Even the s in the heavens
Zec 5:9 wings like the wings of the s

Storm
Job 9:17 Who with a s bruises me And
28:26 for the thunderous s cloud
30:3 there were s and desolation
30:14 Under a s they have rolled
38:25 for the thunderous s cloud
Pr 1:27 dread comes just like a s
3:25 the s upon the wicked ones
6:3 s your fellowman with
Isa 3:5 s, the boy against the old
28:2 Like a thunderous s of hail
28:2 destructive s, like a
28:2 thunderous s of powerful
Eze 38:9 Like a s you will come in
Da 11:40 will s with chariots and
Na 1:3 In destructive wind and in s
Zep 1:15 a day of s and of desolation
Zec 10:1 who is making the s clouds
Lu 12:54 you say, A s is coming
2Pe 2:17 mists driven by a violent s

Stormed
Ho 13:3 like chaff that is s away

Stormer
Job 9:13 the helpers of a s must bow
26:12 has broken the s to pieces

Storm-stricken
Job 38:27 To satisfy s and desolate

Stormwind
Job 21:18 chaff that a s has stolen
27:20 a s will certainly steal
37:9 interior room comes the s
Ps 83:15 them with your own s
Pr 1:27 gets here just like a s
10:25 As when the s passes over
Isa 5:28 and their wheels as a s
17:13 thistle whirl before a s
29:6 great sound, s and tempest
66:15 his chariots are like a s
Jer 4:13 his chariots are like a s
Ho 8:7 a s is what they will reap
Am 1:14 a tempest in the day of s

Stormwinds
Isa 21:1 Like *s* in the south in

Stormy
Ps 50:3 become exceedingly *s* weather
58:9 carry them off as a *s* wind

Story
Ge 6:16 will make it with a lower *s*
6:16, 16 a second *s* and a third *s*
2Ki 8:6 on to relate to him the *s*
Ps 73:15 I will tell a *s* like that
Eze 41:7 from the lowest *s* one could
41:7 go up to the uppermost *s*
41:7 by the middle *s*
Ac 20:9 he fell down from the third *s*

Stout
Ps 78:31 killing among their *s* ones
Isa 59:10 among the *s* ones we are

Straggling
De 25:18 all those *s* after you

Straight
Nu 19:4 *s* toward the front of the
Jos 6:5 go up, each one *s* before him
6:20 city, each one *s* before him
1Sa 6:12 cows began to go *s* ahead on
2Sa 15:3 your matters are good and *s*
19:7 speak *s* to the heart of your
2Ch 32:30 *s* along down to the west
Ne 12:37 Fountain Gate and *s* ahead of
Job 23:7 set matters *s* with him
Pr 3:6 will make your paths *s*
4:14 walk *s* on into the way of
4:25 your eyes, *s* ahead they should
4:25 gaze *s* in front of you
8:9 are *s* to the discerning one
9:6 *s* in the way of understanding
9:15 going *s* ahead on their paths
11:5 what will make his way *s*
15:21 is one who goes *s* ahead
Ec 1:15 made crooked cannot be made *s*
7:13 is able to make *s* what he
Isa 1:18 set matters *s* between us
2:4 set matters *s* respecting many
40:3 through the desert plain *s*
45:24 *s* to him and be ashamed
Jer 31:39 go forth *s* ahead to the hill
Eze 1:7 their feet were *s* feet, and
1:9 would go each one *s* forward
1:12 would go each one *s* forward
1:23 their wings were *s*, one to
10:22 would go each one *s* forward
46:9 go out *s* ahead of him
47:20 boundary *s* ahead to the
Am 4:3 go forth, each one *s* ahead
Mic 3:9 everything that is *s* crooked
4:3 and set matters *s* respecting
Mt 3:3 Make his roads *s*
26:49 going *s* up to Jesus he said
Mr 1:3 you people, make his roads *s*
10:27 Looking *s* at them Jesus said
14:45 he came *s* up and approached
14:67 she looked *s* at him and said
Lu 3:4 people, make his roads *s*
3:5 the curves must become *s* ways
Joh 1:23 Make the way of Jehovah *s*
Ac 8:21 heart is not *s* in the sight
9:11 go to the street called *S*
16:11 with a *s* run to Samothrace
21:1 we ran with a *s* course and
Ga 2:14 were not walking *s* according
2Ti 3:16 for setting things *s*, for
Heb 9:10 time to set things *s*
12:13 *s* paths for your feet that
2Pe 2:15 Abandoning the *s* path, they

Straighten
Isa 45:2 swells of land I shall *s* out
45:13 his ways I shall *s* out
Heb 12:12 *s* up the hands that hang

Straightened
Lu 13:13 and instantly she *s* up, and

Straightforward
Pr 24:26 who is replying in a *s* way
Isa 30:10 envision for us any *s* things
59:14 what is *s* is unable to
Am 3:10 how to do what is *s*

Straightforwardly
Isa 57:2 each one that is walking *s*

Straightforwardness
Isa 26:10 land of *s* he will act

Strain
Mt 23:24 *s* out the gnat but gulp down

Straits
De 4:30 When you are in sore *s* and
Jg 2:15 they got to be in very sore *s*
1Sa 13:6 saw that they were in sore *s*
28:15 I am in very sore *s*, as
Ps 31:9 Jehovah, for I am in sore *s*
66:14 when I was in sore *s*
69:17 Because I am in sore *s*
102:2 day that I am in sore *s*
La 1:20 O Jehovah, for I am in sore *s*
Da 9:25 but in the *s* of the times
Ho 5:15 When they are in sore *s*

Strange
Nu 16:40 no *s* man who is not of the
De 25:5 should not become a *s* man's
32:16 to jealousy with *s* gods
2Ki 19:24 dig and drink *s* waters
Ps 44:20 our palms to a *s* god
81:9 will prove to be no *s* god
Pr 2:16 deliver you from the *s* woman
5:3 the lips of a *s* woman keep
5:20 ecstasy with a *s* woman or
22:14 mouth of *s* women is a deep
23:33 own eyes will see *s* things
Isa 28:21 his deed is *s*—and that he
29:5 crowd of those *s* to you must
43:12 was among you no *s* god
Jer 18:14 Or will *s* waters, cool
Ho 5:7 to *s* sons that they have
8:12 just like something *s* they
Lu 5:26 We have seen *s* things today
Ac 17:20 things that are *s* to our ears
Heb 13:9 with various and *s* teachings
1Pe 4:12 *s* thing were befalling you

Stranger
Ex 29:33 But a *s* may not eat them
30:33 puts some of it upon a *s*
Le 22:10 no *s* at all may eat anything
22:12 man's who is a *s*, she as
22:13 no *s* at all may feed on it
Nu 1:51 *s* coming near should be put
3:10 any *s* coming near should be
3:38 any *s* coming near would be
18:4 no *s* may come near to you
18:7 *s* drawing near should be put
1Ki 3:18 no *s* with us in the house
Job 15:19 And no *s* passed through the
19:15 reckon me as a *s*
19:27 but not some *s*
Pr 6:1 your handshake even to the *s*
7:5 guard you against the woman *s*
11:15 he has gone surety for a *s*
14:10 no *s* will intermeddle
20:16 one has gone surety for a *s*
21:8 a *s*, is crooked in his way
27:2 a *s*, and not your own mouth
27:13 one has gone surety for a *s*
Isa 17:10 shoot of a *s* you set it
Mt 25:35 I was a *s* and you received
25:38 When did we see you a *s* and
25:43 I was a *s*, but you did not
25:44 or a *s* or naked or sick or
Joh 10:5 *s* they will by no means

Strangers
Ps 54:3 *s* that have risen up against
109:11 *s* make plunder of his
Pr 5:10 *s* may not satisfy themselves
5:17 you alone, and not for *s* with
Isa 1:7 front of you *s* are eating it
1:7 is like an overthrow by *s*
25:2 dwelling tower of *s* to be no
25:5 the noise of *s* you subdue
61:5 *s* will actually stand and
Jer 2:25 have fallen in love with *s*
3:13 your ways to the *s*
5:19 serve *s* in a land that is not
30:8 *s* exploit him as a servant
51:51 *s* have come against the
La 5:2 has been turned over to *s*, our
Eze 7:21 into the hand of the *s* for
11:9 give you into the hand of *s*
16:32 takes *s* instead of her own
28:7 *s*, the tyrants of the nations
28:10 will die by the hand of *s*
30:12 desolated by the hand of *s*
31:12 And *s*, the tyrants of the
Ho 7:9 *S* have eaten up his power, and
8:7 *s* themselves will swallow it
Joe 3:17 as regards *s*, they will no
Ob 11 *s* took his military force into
Mt 17:25 their sons or from the *s*
17:26 When he said: From the *s*
27:7 the potter's field to bury *s*
Joh 10:5 not know the voice of *s*
1Co 14:21 with the lips of *s* I will
Eph 2:12 *s* to the covenants of the
2:19 no longer *s* and alien
1Ti 5:10 if she entertained *s*, if she
Heb 11:13 declared that they were *s*
3Jo 5 for the brothers, and *s* at that

Strangled
2Sa 17:23 *s* himself and thus died
Ac 15:20 abstain . . . from what is *s*
15:29 abstaining . . . from things *s*
21:25 from blood and what is *s* and

Strangling
Na 2:12 and was *s* for his lionesses

Straw
Ge 24:25 *s* and much fodder with us
24:32 giving *s* and fodder to the
Ex 5:7 not gather *s* to give to the
5:7 go and gather *s* for themselves
5:10 I am giving you no more *s*
5:11 get *s* for yourselves wherever
5:12 to gather stubble for *s*
5:13 just as when *s* was available
5:16 no *s* given to your servants
5:18 no *s* will be given to you
Jg 19:19 are both *s* and fodder for our
1Ki 4:28 the *s* for the horses and
Job 21:18 become like *s* before a wind
41:27 It regards iron as mere *s*
Isa 11:7 even the lion will eat *s*
25:10 *s* heap is trodden down in
65:25 lion will eat *s* just like
Jer 23:28 *s* have to do with the grain
Mt 7:3 *s* in your brother's eye, but
7:4 extract the *s* from your eye
7:5 to extract the *s* from your
Lu 6:41 *s* that is in your brother's
6:42 the *s* that is in your eye
6:42 *s* that is in your brother's

Stray
Pr 19:27 to *s* from the sayings of

Strayed
Mt 18:12 sheep and one of them gets *s*
18:13 ninety-nine that have not *s*

Straying
De 22:1 his sheep *s* about and
Job 15:23 *s* about in search of bread
Ps 119:21 *s* from your commandments
119:118 *s* from your regulations
Eze 34:6 My sheep kept *s* on all the
Mt 18:12 search for the one that is *s*

Stream
2Sa 22:16 *s* beds of the sea became
Ps 18:15 the *s* beds of waters became
65:9 *s* from God is full of water
69:2 *s* itself has washed me away
69:15 *s* of waters wash me away
126:4 Like *s* beds in the Negeb
Isa 2:2 to it all the nations must *s*
8:7 come up over all his *s* beds
27:12 flowing *s* of the River to
48:21 the water might *s* forth
Jer 51:44 nations will *s* no more
Eze 6:3 the *s* beds and to the valleys
31:12 all the *s* beds of the earth
32:6 *s* beds themselves will be
34:13 by the *s* beds and by all
35:8 valleys and all your *s* beds
36:4 to the *s* beds and to the
36:6 *s* beds and to the valleys
Da 7:10 *s* of fire flowing and going
12:5 on the bank here of the *s*
12:5 on the bank there of the *s*
12:6 above the waters of the *s*
12:7 above the waters of the *s*
Joe 3:18 the very *s* beds of Judah
Mic 4:1 and to it peoples must *s*

Streams
Job 20:17 Torrential *s* of honey and
29:6 pouring out *s* of oil for me
Ps 1:3 a tree planted by *s* of water
42:1 that longs for the water *s*
46:4 a river the *s* of which make
78:16 forth *s* out of a crag
78:44 drink from their own *s*
119:136 *S* of water have run down
Pr 5:16 *s* of water in the public

Pr 21:1 A king's heart is as *s* of
Ca 4:15 and trickling *s* from Lebanon
Isa 30:25 come to be *s*, water ditches
32:2 *s* of water in a waterless
44:3 *s* upon the dry place
La 3:48 With *s* of water my eye keeps
Eze 31:4 With its *s* it was going all
31:15 I may hold back its *s* and
Joh 7:38 *s* of living water will flow

Street
Job 18:17 have no name out in the *s*
Pr 1:20 crying aloud in the very *s*
7:8 on the *s* near her corner, and
Ec 12:4 the doors onto the *s* have been
12:5 have marched around in the *s*
Isa 33:7 have cried out in the *s*
42:2 in the *s* he will not let his
51:23 *s* for those crossing over
Jer 6:11 upon the child in the *s*
9:21 cut off the child from the *s*
37:21 from the *s* of the bakers
Mr 11:4 outside on the side *s*, and
Ac 9:11 go to the *s* called Straight
12:10 they advanced down one *s*

Streets
2Sa 1:20 announce it in the *s* of
22:43 Like the mire of the *s* I
1Ki 20:34 and *s* you will assign to
Ps 18:42 Like the mire of the *s* I
144:13 thousand to one, in our *s*
Pr 1:21 upper end of the noisy *s* it
Ca 3:2 in the *s* and in the public
Isa 5:25 offal in the midst of the *s*
10:6 like the clay of the *s*
15:3 In its *s* they have girded on
24:11 outcry in the *s* for want of
51:20 at the head of all the *s*
Jer 5:1 in the *s* of Jerusalem and see
7:17 and in the *s* of Jerusalem
7:34 from the *s* of Jerusalem the
11:6 and in the *s* of Jerusalem
11:13 as many altars as the *s*
14:16 people cast out into the *s*
33:10 *s* of Jerusalem that are
44:6 and in the *s* of Jerusalem
44:9 and in the *s* of Jerusalem
44:17 and in the *s* of Jerusalem
44:21 and in the *s* of Jerusalem
51:4 pierced through in her *s*
La 2:19 at the head of all the *s*
2:21 down on the earth of the *s*
4:1 at the head of all the *s*
4:5 with astonishment in the *s*
4:8 not been recognized in the *s*
4:14 as blind in the *s*. They have
Eze 7:19 Into the *s* they will throw
11:6 filled her *s* with the slain
26:11 trample down all your *s*
28:23 and blood into her *s*
Am 5:16 in all the *s* people will be
Mic 7:10 like the mire of *s*
Na 2:4 In the *s* the war chariots keep
3:10 at the head of all the *s*
Zep 3:6 I devastated their *s*, so that
Zec 9:3 gold like the mire of the *s*
10:5 in the mire of the *s* in the
Mt 6:2 in the synagogues and in the *s*

Strength
Ge 48:2 Israel exerted his *s* and
49:3 and the excellence of *s*
49:24 *s* of his hands was supple
Ex 13:3 by *s* of hand Jehovah brought
13:14 By *s* of hand Jehovah brought
13:16 by *s* of hand Jehovah brought
15:2 My *s* and my might is Jah
15:13 You in your *s* will certainly
Le 26:19 break the pride of your *s* and
De 34:7 and his vital *s* had not fled
Jg 5:21 You went treading down *s*, O
1Sa 2:10 he may give *s* to his king
2Sa 13:14 used *s* superior to hers
1Ch 16:11 after Jehovah and his *s*
16:27 *S* and joy are at his place
16:28 to Jehovah glory and *s*
29:12 and to give *s* to all
2Ch 1:1 to get *s* in his kingship, and
6:41 you and the Ark of your *s*
14:11 mortal man retain *s* against
16:9 show his *s* in behalf of
20:37 retain *s* to go to Tarshish
26:8 for he displayed *s* to an
Ezr 8:22 *s* and his anger are against
Job 12:16 With him there are *s* and
17:9 keeps increasing in *s*
22:8 man of *s*, the land is his
26:2 an arm that is without *s*
41:22 In its neck lodges *s*
Ps 8:2 you have founded *s*, On account
9:19 man prove superior in *s*
18:1 for you, O Jehovah my *s*
21:1 in your *s* the king rejoices
21:13 exalted in your *s*, O Jehovah
22:19 O you my *s*, do make haste
28:7 Jehovah is my *s* and my shield
28:8 Jehovah is a *s* to his people
29:1 Ascribe to Jehovah glory and *s*
29:11 Jehovah himself will give *s*
30:7 my mountain to stand in *s*
46:1 God is for us a refuge and *s*
59:9 O my *S*, toward you I will
59:16 I shall sing of your *s*
59:17 O my *S*, to you I will make
62:11 That *s* belongs to God
63:2 seeing your *s* and your glory
66:3 the abundance of your *s* your
68:28 has laid command upon your *s*
68:28 Do show *s*, O God, you who
68:34 Ascribe *s* to God. Over Israel
68:34 and his *s* is in the clouds
68:35 giving *s*, even might to the
74:13 up the sea with your own *s*
76:7 because of the *s* of your anger
77:14 you have made your *s* known
78:4 praises of Jehovah and his *s*
78:26 wind blow by his own *s*
78:61 give his *s* even to captivity
81:1 O cry out . . . to God our *s*
84:5 are the men whose *s* is in you
86:16 give your *s* to your servant
88:4 able-bodied man without *s*
89:10 arm of your *s* you have
89:17 are the beauty of their *s*
90:11 knowing the *s* of your anger
93:1 Jehovah is clothed—with *s*
96:6 *S* and beauty are in his
96:7 to Jehovah glory and *s*
99:4 And with the *s* of a king
105:4 Search for Jehovah and his *s*
110:2 rod of your *s* Jehovah will
132:8 You and the ark of your *s*
138:3 bold in my soul with *s*
140:7 the *s* of my salvation
145:6 talk about the *s* of your
150:1 in the expanse of his *s*
Pr 21:22 down the *s* of its confidence
24:5 wise in *s* is an able-bodied
31:17 has girded her hips with *s*
31:25 *S* and splendor are her
Isa 12:2 Jah Jehovah is my *s* and my
18:2 nation of tensile *s* and
18:7 a nation of tensile *s* and
42:25 anger, and the *s* of war
45:24 full righteousness and *s*
49:5 God will have become my *s*
51:9 clothe yourself with *s*
52:1 put on your *s*, O Zion!
Jer 16:19 O Jehovah my *s* and my
20:7 You used your *s* against me
48:17 rod of *s* has been broken
51:53 make the height of her *s*
Eze 22:14 hands furnish *s* in the days
24:21 the pride of your *s*
26:11 pillars of *s* will go down
30:6 pride of its *s* must come
30:18 the pride of her *s* will
33:28 the pride of its *s* must be
Da 2:37 the *s* and the dignity
4:30 with the *s* of my might and
10:19 I exerted my *s* and finally
Am 3:11 bring your *s* down from you
6:13 in our *s* taken horns to
Jon 3:8 call out to God with *s* and
Mic 5:4 in the *s* of Jehovah, in the
Hab 3:4 there the hiding of his *s* was
Hag 2:22 the *s* of the kingdoms of the
Zec 12:5 are a *s* to me by Jehovah of
Mt 5:13 if the salt loses its *s*, how
9:16 its full *s* would pull from
Mr 2:21 its full *s* pulls from it, the
5:4 nobody had the *s* to subdue him
9:18 he foams . . . and loses his *s*
9:50 if ever the salt loses its *s*
12:30 mind and with your whole *s*
12:33 with one's whole *s* and this
14:37 *s* to keep on the watch one
Lu 10:27 with your whole *s* and with
Lu 14:34 if even the salt loses its *s*
Ac 9:19 he took food and gained *s*
2Co 1:8 extreme pressure beyond our *s*
Eph 1:19 of the mightiness of his *s*
6:10 in the mightiness of his *s*
Php 4:13 For all things I have the *s*
2Th 1:9 and from the glory of his *s*
1Pe 4:11 dependent on the *s* that God
2Pe 2:11 greater in *s* and power
Re 5:12 and wisdom and *s* and honor
7:12 the *s* be to our God forever

Strengthen
De 3:28 encourage him and *s* him
Jg 16:28 *s* me, please, just this once
1Sa 23:16 *s* his hand in regard to God
2Sa 2:7 hands *s* themselves and prove
1Ki 20:22 Go, *s* yourself and take note
2Ki 15:19 *s* the kingdom in his own
2Ch 13:21 And Abijah continued to *s*
28:20 distress, and did not *s* him
Ezr 6:22 *s* their hands in the work of
Ne 6:9 But now *s* my hands
Job 4:3 the weak hands you used to *s*
16:5 *s* you with the words of my
Ps 89:21 Whom my own arm also will *s*
Isa 35:3 *S* the weak hands, you people
Eze 16:49 the poor one she did not *s*
30:24 *s* the arms of the king of
30:25 *s* the arms of the king of
34:16 the ailing one I shall *s*
Da 10:18 touch me again and *s* me
Na 2:1 *S* the hips. Reinforce power
3:14 *S* your fortified places
Lu 22:32 returned, *s* your brothers
Re 3:2 *s* the things remaining that

Strengthened
Jg 9:24 they *s* his hands to kill his
Ezr 1:6 *s* their hands with utensils
7:28 *s* myself according to the
Ne 2:18 *s* their hands for the good
Jer 23:14 *s* the hands of evildoers in
Eze 34:4 sickened ones you have not *s*
Da 10:19 speak, because you have *s* me
Ho 7:15 I *s* their arms, but against
Lu 22:43 appeared to him and *s* him
Ac 15:32 many a discourse and *s* them

Strengthener
Da 11:1 stood up as a *s* and as a

Strengthening
1Sa 30:6 David took to *s* himself by
2Sa 3:6 *s* his position in the house
2Ch 11:17 *s* the kingship of Judah and
27:6 Jotham kept *s* himself, for
Isa 41:7 went *s* the metalworker
Ac 14:22 *s* the souls of the disciples
15:41 Cilicia, *s* the congregations
18:23 Phrygia, *s* all the disciples
Col 4:11 have become a *s* aid to me

Strenuous
Ge 30:8 *s* wrestlings I have wrestled

Stress
De 28:53 the tightness and *s* with
28:55 *s* with which your enemy
28:57 *s* with which your enemy
Ps 31:21 to me in a city under *s*
Isa 9:1 as when the land had *s*, as
Jer 10:17 O woman dwelling under *s*
19:9 *s* with which their enemies

Stresses
Ps 25:17 From the *s* upon me O bring
107:6 Out of the *s* upon them he
107:13 *s* upon them he as usual
107:19 *s* upon them he as usual
107:28 out of the *s* upon them he

Stretch
Ge 35:16 yet a good *s* of land before
48:7 a good *s* of land before
Ex 3:20 to *s* out my hand and strike
7:5 *s* out my hand against Egypt
7:19 Take your rod and *s* your hand
8:5 *S* your hand with your rod out
8:16 *S* your rod out and strike the
9:22 *S* out your hand toward the
10:12 *S* your hand out over the land
10:21 *S* your hand out toward the
14:16 *s* your hand out over the sea
14:26 *S* your hand out over the sea
Jos 8:18 *S* out the javelin that is in
1Ki 17:21 *s* himself upon the child
2Ki 5:19 for a good *s* of the land

2Ki 21:13 *s* upon Jerusalem the
Job 11:19 will indeed *s* yourself out
Ps 68:31 quickly *s* out its hands
Isa 5:25 *s* out his hand against them
31:3 Jehovah himself will *s* out
34:11 *s* out over her the
54:2 *s* out the tent cloths of
Jer 6:12 shall *s* my hand out against
15:6 *s* out my hand against you
51:25 *s* out my hand against you
Eze 6:14 *s* out my hand against them
14:9 *s* out my hand against him
14:13 *s* out my hand against it
16:27 *s* out my hand against you
25:13 *s* out my hand against Edom
35:3 *s* out my hand against you
Am 2:8 *s* . . . out beside every altar
Zep 1:4 *s* out my hand against Judah
2:13 *s* out his hand toward the
Mt 12:13 to the man: *S* out your hand
Mr 3:5 to the man: *S* out your hand
Lu 6:10 to the man: *S* out your hand
22:53 did not *s* out your hands
Joh 21:18 *s* out your hands and another
Ac 4:30 *s* out your hand for healing

Stretched
Ge 49:9 he *s* himself out like a lion
Ex 8:6 Aaron *s* his hand out over the
8:17 Aaron *s* out his hand with his
9:23 Moses *s* out his rod toward
10:13 Moses *s* his rod out over the
10:22 Moses . . . *s* his hand out
14:21 Moses now *s* his hand out
14:27 Moses at once *s* his hand out
15:12 You *s* out your right hand
Jos 8:18 Joshua *s* out the javelin that
8:19 that he *s* out his hand
8:26 he *s* out the javelin until
1Sa 14:27 he *s* out the tip of the rod
Job 38:5 *s* out upon it the measuring
Ps 77:2 hand has been *s* out and does
136:12 hand and by an arm *s* out
Pr 1:24 *s* out my hand but there is
31:20 Her palm she has *s* out to
Isa 3:16 with their throats *s* forth
5:25 his hand is *s* out still
9:12 but his hand is *s* out still
9:17 but his hand is *s* out still
9:21 his hand is *s* out still
10:4 but his hand is *s* out still
14:26 hand that is *s* out against
14:27 his hand is the one *s* out
23:11 he has *s* out over the sea
44:13 *s* out the measuring line
45:12 have *s* out the heavens
Jer 10:12 *s* out the heavens
51:15 *s* out the heavens
La 2:8 has *s* out the measuring line
Eze 1:22 *s* out over their heads up
17:7 vine *s* its roots hungrily
25:7 *s* out my hand against you
29:3 sea monster lying *s* out
Zep 2:7 evening, they will lie *s* out
2:14 will certainly lie *s* out
2:15 wild animals to lie *s* out
3:13 and actually lie *s* out
Zec 1:16 will be *s* out over Jerusalem
Mt 12:13 Stretch out your hand . . . *s*
Mr 1:41 he *s* out his hand and touched
3:5 he *s* it out, and his hand was
Ac 22:25 *s* him out for the whipping
26:1 Paul *s* his hand out and

Stretched-out
1Ki 8:42 hand and of your *s* arm
2Ki 17:36 great power and a *s* arm
2Ch 6:32 strong hand and your *s* arm
Jer 21:5 against you with a *s* hand
27:5 great power and by my *s* arm
32:21 strong hand and . . . *s* arm
Eze 20:33 with a *s* arm and with
20:34 with a *s* arm and with

Stretches
Job 15:25 *s* out his hand against God

Stretching
Job 9:8 *S* out the heavens by himself
26:7 *s* out the north over the
Ps 104:2 *S* out the heavens like a
Isa 28:20 too short for *s* oneself
40:22 is *s* out the heavens just
42:5 the Grand One *s* them out
44:24 *s* out the heavens by myself
51:13 the One *s* out the heavens

Jer 10:20 no one *s* out my tent
Eze 25:16 *s* out my hand against the
Zec 12:1 One who is *s* out the heavens
Mt 8:3 *s* out his hand, he touched him
14:31 *s* out his hand Jesus caught
Lu 5:13 *s* out his hand, he touched
Php 3:13 *s* forward to the things

Strewed
Job 18:15 Sulphur will be *s* upon his

Stricken
Ex 4:6 his hand was *s* with leprosy
2Ch 26:20 *s* with leprosy in his
Pr 15:13 there is a *s* spirit
17:22 a spirit that is *s* makes the
18:14 a *s* spirit, who can bear it?
Isa 16:7 *s* ones indeed will moan
53:4 *s* by God and afflicted

Strict
2Sa 12:16 David went on a *s* fast
2Ki 11:5 *s* watch over the king's
11:6 *s* watch over the house by
11:7 *s* watch over the house of
1Ch 12:29 *s* watch of the house of
Isa 10:23 *s* decision the Sovereign
21:7 he paid *s* attention, with
Mr 1:43 he gave him *s* orders and at
Eph 5:15 *s* watch that how you walk

Strictest
Ac 26:5 the *s* sect of our form of

Strictly
Ex 15:26 If you will *s* listen to the
19:5 if you will *s* obey my voice
23:22 if you *s* obey his voice and
De 11:22 *s* keep all this commandment
2Ch 31:4 adhere *s* to the law of
Jer 17:24 that, if you *s* obey me
Mt 12:16 *s* charged them not to make
Mr 8:30 he *s* charged them not to tell

Strictness
Ac 22:3 to the *s* of the ancestral Law

Strife
De 2:5 Do not engage in *s* with them
2:19 molest them or engage in *s*
2Ki 14:10 should you engage in *s* under
2Ch 25:19 *s* in a bad position and have
Ps 80:6 set us for *s* to our neighbors
Jer 15:10 a man subject to *s* with all
Hab 1:3 and why is *s* carried?
Ro 1:29 *s*, deceit, malicious
13:13 not in *s* and jealousy
1Co 3:3 there are jealousy and *s*
2Co 12:20 somehow be *s*, jealousy
Ga 5:20 enmities, *s*, jealousy, fits
1Ti 6:4 envy, *s*, abusive speeches
Tit 3:9 *s* and fights over the Law

Strike
Ge 4:15 no one finding him should *s*
37:21 Let us not *s* his soul fatally
Ex 2:13 Why should you *s* your
3:20 *s* Egypt with all my wonderful
5:3 may *s* at us with pestilence
8:16 Stretch your rod out and *s* the
9:15 might *s* you and your people
12:12 *s* every firstborn in the land
12:13 I *s* at the land of Egypt
12:23 *s* upon the . . . doorway and
17:6 *s* on the rock, and water must
21:18 *s* his fellow with a stone or
21:26 *s* the eye of his slave man
Le 26:24 *s* you seven times for your
Nu 14:12 *s* them with pestilence and
22:6 I may be able to *s* them and I
22:23 Balaam began to *s* the ass in
25:17 and you men must *s* them
34:11 *s* upon the eastern slope of
De 13:15 *s* the inhabitants of that
19:5 his hand has been raised to *s*
19:6 may indeed *s* his soul fatally
20:13 you must *s* every male in it
25:18 proceeded to *s* in the rear
27:25 a bribe to *s* a soul fatally
28:22 *s* you with tuberculosis and
28:27 *s* you with the boil of Egypt
28:28 will *s* you with madness and
28:35 *s* you with a malignant boil
Jos 7:3 men go up and *s* Ai
7:5 *s* down about thirty-six men
9:18 the sons of Israel did not *s*
10:4 let us *s* Gibeon, because it
10:19 you must *s* them in the rear

Jos 10:26 to *s* them and put them to
10:40 to *s* all the land of the
19:47 *s* it with the edge of the
Jg 1:17 proceeded to *s* the Canaanites
6:16 certainly *s* down Midian as if
8:11 began to *s* the camp while the
18:27 to *s* them with the edge of
20:31 to *s* down some of the people
20:39 Benjamin started to *s* down
21:10 must *s* the inhabitants of
1Sa 14:48 to *s* down Amalek and to
15:3 and you must *s* down Amalek
17:9 and he does *s* me down, we
17:9 and I do *s* him down, you
17:46 *s* you down and remove your
19:5 and *s* the Philistine down
20:33 the spear at him to *s* him
23:2 I *s* down these Philistines
23:2 *s* down the Philistines and
30:1 *s* Ziklag and burn it with
2Sa 2:22 Why should I *s* you down to
2:23 Abner got to *s* him in the
5:20 David got to *s* them down
5:24 *s* down the camp of the
8:1 David proceeded to *s* the
8:2 *s* down the Moabites and
8:3 David went on to *s* down
13:28 *S* down Amnon! you must
15:14 *s* the city with the edge of
17:2 *s* down the king by himself
18:11 why did you not *s* him down
21:2 Saul sought to *s* them down
21:19 *s* down Goliath the Gittite
1Ki 11:15 tried to *s* down every male
14:15 *s* Israel down, just as the
15:27 Baasha got to *s* him down
16:10 *s* him down and put him to
20:20 to *s* down each one his man
20:35 *S* me, please. But the man
20:35 the man refused to *s* him
20:36 lion will certainly *s* you
20:36 lion got to find him and *s*
20:37 *S* me, please. So the man
22:34 got to *s* the king of Israel
2Ki 3:19 *s* down every fortified city
6:18 *s* this nation with blindness
6:21 Shall I *s* them down, shall I
6:21 shall I *s* them down
6:22 You must not *s* them down
8:21 got to *s* down the Edomites
9:7 *s* down the house of Ahab your
9:27 Him also! *S* him down!
10:11 Jehu went on to *s* down all
10:25 Come in, *s* them down!
10:25 *s* them down with the edge
13:17 *s* down Syria at Aphek
13:18 *S* on the earth. So he struck
13:19 to *s* five or six times
13:19 that you will *s* down Syria
14:5 to *s* down his servants that
15:16 to *s* down Tiphsah and all
19:35 go out and *s* down a hundred
25:21 *s* them down and put them
25:25 got to *s* down Gedaliah
1Ch 4:41 *s* down the tents of the
4:43 *s* down the remnant that had
10:2 got to *s* down Jonathan and
14:11 there got to *s* them down
14:15 gone out before you to *s* the
18:1 David proceeded to *s* down
18:3 to *s* down Hadadezer the king
20:1 Joab went on to *s* Rabbah and
20:5 to *s* down Lahmi the brother
2Ch 18:33 *s* the king of Israel
22:5 shooters got to *s* Jehoram
25:16 Why should they *s* you down?
Ne 13:25 and *s* some men of them and
Ps 3:7 *s* all my enemies on the jaw
60:*super* *s* down Edom in the Valley
74:6 they *s* even with hatchet and
81:2 *S* up a melody and take a
91:12 *s* your foot against any stone
105:33 *s* their vines and their fig
105:36 *s* down every firstborn in
121:6 sun itself will not *s* you
141:5 righteous one *s* me, it would
Pr 3:23 foot will not *s* against
17:26 To *s* nobles is against what
19:25 The ridiculer you should *s*
Isa 5:25 hand against them and *s* them
8:14 stone to *s* against and as a
10:24 rod used to *s* you and who
11:4 *s* the earth with the rod of
11:15 *s* it in its seven torrents

Isa 27:7 does one have to s him?
30:31 s it even with a staff
37:36 s down a hundred and
47:12 might s people with awe
49:10 parching heat or sun s them
57:17 I proceeded to s him
Jer 1:17 I may not s you with terror
13:16 your feet s up against each
18:18 s him with the tongue
20:4 s them down with the sword
21:6 I will s the inhabitants
21:7 s them with the edge of the
29:21 s them down before your
40:14 to s you to the soul
40:15 s down Ishmael the son of
40:15 he s you to the soul, and
43:11 and s the land of Egypt
46:13 s down the land of Egypt
47:1 proceeded to s down Gaza
52:27 s down and to put them to
Eze 5:2 You will s it with the sword
9:5 Pass through . . . and s
21:14 and s palm against palm
21:17 s my one palm against my
26:9 the s of his attack engine
32:15 s down all the inhabitants
39:3 s your bow out of your left
Da 8:7 s down the ram and to break
Ho 14:5 will s his roots like Lebanon
Am 3:15 s down the winter house
6:11 s down the great house into
9:1 S the pillar head, so that
Jon 4:7 s the bottle-gourd plant
Mic 5:1 s upon the cheek the judge
Zec 9:4 s down her military force
10:11 he must s down the waves
12:4 I shall s every horse with
12:4 I shall s with loss of sight
13:7 S the shepherd, and let those
Mal 4:6 s the earth with a devoting
Mt 4:6 at no time s your foot against
26:31 I will s the shepherd, and
Mr 14:27 I will s the shepherd, and
Lu 4:11 s your foot against a stone
22:49 shall we s with the sword?
22:50 did s the slave of the high
Ac 23:2 by him to s him on the mouth
23:3 God is going to s you, you
Re 11:6 to s the earth with every
19:15 he may s the nations with it

Striker
Le 24:18 s of the soul of a domestic
24:21 fatal s of a beast should
24:21 fatal s of a man should be
Nu 35:21 the s should be put to death
35:24 judge between the s
35:30 fatal s of a soul should be
2Sa 14:7 Give over the s of his

Strikers
2Ki 14:6 sons of the s he did not put
Isa 50:6 My back I gave to the s, and

Strikes
Ex 21:12 One who s a man so that he
21:15 one who s his father and his
21:20 man s his slave man or his
Le 24:17 man s any soul of mankind
Nu 35:11 s a soul unintentionally
35:15 s a soul unintentionally
De 19:4 When he s his fellowman
27:24 fatally s his fellowman
Jos 15:16 whoever s Kiriath-sepher
20:3 s a soul unintentionally
20:9 s a soul unintentionally
Jg 1:12 Whoever s Kiriath-sepher and
1Sa 17:25 the man who s him down
17:26 that s down that Philistine
17:27 to the man that s him down
Lu 6:29 s you on the one cheek, offer
2Co 11:20 whoever s you in the face
Re 9:5 a scorpion when it s a man

Striking
Ex 2:11 Egyptian s a certain Hebrew
7:17 I am s with the rod that is
7:25 Jehovah's s the Nile River
9:25 hail went s at all the land
Nu 8:17 s every firstborn in the land
11:33 Jehovah began s at the people
14:45 s them and went scattering
21:35 they went s him and his sons
De 3:3 s him until he had no survivor
25:11 the hand of the one s him
Jos 7:5 continued s them down on the
Jos 8:21 went s the men of Ai down
8:22 they went s them down until
10:28 s it with the edge of the
10:30 s it and every soul that
10:32 s it and every soul that
10:37 went s it and its king and
10:39 s them with the edge of the
10:41 s them from Kadesh-barnea
11:8 went s them and pursuing
11:8 kept s them until they had
11:11 went s every soul that was
11:12 s them with the edge of the
11:17 and went s them and putting
13:12 and Moses went s them and
Jg 1:8 they went s it with the edge
1:10 they went s down Sheshai and
1:25 they went s the city with
3:29 they went s down Moab
3:31 went s down the Philistines
9:44 and they went s them down
11:33 he went s them from Aroer
12:4 s Ephraim down, for they had
15:15 s down a thousand men with
20:48 s with the edge of the sword
1Sa 4:2 s down about four thousand
5:6 panic and s them with piles
5:9 began s the men of the city
6:19 he went s down the men of
7:11 kept s them down as far as
11:11 s down the Ammonites till
14:31 kept s down the Philistines
15:7 Saul went s down Amalek
17:57 from s the Philistine down
18:6 David returned from s the
19:8 Philistines and s them down
24:5 David's heart kept s him for
30:17 David went s them down
2Sa 1:1 s down the Amalekites, that
5:8 s the Jebusites, let him
5:25 s down the Philistines from
8:13 s down the Edomites in the
21:16 to think of s David down
23:10 kept s down the Philistines
23:12 kept s down the Philistines
24:17 angel that was s the people
1Ki 15:20 went s down Ijon and Dan
20:21 kept s down the horses and
20:29 sons of Israel went s down
20:37 struck him, s and wounding
2Ki 3:23 went s one another down
3:24 began s the Moabites down so
3:24 s the Moabites down as they
3:25 going around it and s it
6:22 ones that you are s down
10:17 s down all who were left
10:32 Hazael kept s them in all
13:19 be s down Syria to the
15:16 and he went s it down
1Ch 11:6 Anyone s the Jebusites first
11:14 kept s down the Philistines
14:16 they went s down the camp
18:5 David went s down among the
2Ch 13:17 s them down with a vast
21:9 s down the Edomites that
25:11 s down the sons of Seir
25:13 s down three thousand of
25:14 Amaziah came from s down
28:17 s down Judah and carrying
28:23 of Damascus that were s
Es 9:5 Jews went s down all their
Job 1:19 s the four corners of the
Ps 35:15 S me down when I did not
78:66 s down his adversaries from
136:10 One s down Egypt in their
136:17 the One s down great kings
Pr 17:10 than s a stupid one a hundred
22:26 to be among those s hands
Isa 9:13 returned to the One s them
10:20 upon the one s them, and
14:6 one s peoples in fury with
14:29 staff of the one s you has
27:7 stroke of one s him does
58:4 and for s with the fist of
66:3 is as one s down a man
La 3:30 cheek to the very one s him
Eze 9:8 they were s and I was left
Da 5:19 happened to want to, he was s
Ho 6:1 He kept s, but he will bind
Jon 4:8 sun kept s upon the head of
Mic 6:13 make you sick by s you
Lu 17:20 coming with s observableness
Ac 7:24 by s the Egyptian down
12:7 S Peter on the side, he
1Co 9:26 so as not to be s the air

String
Ex 28:28 of the ephod with a blue s
28:37 must fasten it with a blue s
39:21 of the ephod with a blue s
39:31 put a s of blue thread to it
Nu 15:38 blue s above the fringed edge
1Ki 7:15 a s of twelve cubits would
1Ch 16:5 instruments of the s type
Ps 77:6 my s music in the night
Ca 1:10 your neck in a s of beads
Isa 38:20 shall play my s selections
Eze 16:4 your navel s had not been cut

Stringed
1Sa 10:5 ahead of them a s instrument
2Sa 6:5 and with s instruments and
1Ki 10:12 harps and s instruments for
1Ch 13:8 with s instruments and with
15:16 s instruments and harps and
15:20 with s instruments tuned to
15:28 on s instruments and harps
25:1 with the s instruments and
25:6 s instruments and harps for
2Ch 5:12 with s instruments and harps
9:11 s instruments for the
20:28 s instruments and with
29:25 with s instruments and
Ne 12:27 cymbals and s instruments
Ps 4:*super* director on s instruments
6:*super* director on s instruments
45:8 s instruments themselves have
54:*super* director on s instruments
55:*super* director on s instruments
57:8 Do awake, O s instrument
61:*super* director on s instruments
67:*super* director on s instruments
68:25 the players on s instruments
71:22 an instrument of a s sort
76:*super* director on s instruments
81:2 with the s instrument
108:2 Do awake, O s instrument
150:3 s instrument and the harp
Isa 5:12 be harp and s instrument
14:11 din of your s instruments
Eze 33:32 and playing a s instrument
Da 3:5 the s instrument, the bagpipe
3:7 the s instrument and all sorts
3:10 the s instrument, and the
3:15 the s instrument, and the
Am 5:23 sound of your s instruments
6:5 the sound of the s instrument
Hab 3:19 director on my s instruments

String-instrument
2Ki 3:15 fetch me a s player
3:15 the s player played, the

Strings
Ps 33:2 On an instrument of ten s
33:3 your best at playing on the s
144:9 On an instrument of ten s
150:4 Praise him with s and the
Isa 23:16 best at playing on the s

Strip
Ex 3:22 and you must s the Egyptians
Le 6:11 must s off his garments and
16:23 s off the linen garments
Nu 20:26 s Aaron of his garments, and
1Sa 19:24 s off his garments and
31:8 Philistines came to s the
31:9 s off his armor and send
2Sa 2:21 what you s off him as yours
23:10 to s those struck down
1Ch 10:8 came to s the slain, they
10:9 s him and take off his head
Job 22:6 you s off even the garments
Isa 47:2 S off the flowing skirt
Jer 49:10 I will s Esau bare
Eze 16:39 must s you of your garments
23:26 s off you your garments and
26:16 s off their own embroidered
44:19 s off their garments in
Ho 2:3 s her naked and actually place
Mic 2:8 s off the majestic ornament
Col 3:9 S off the old personality

Striped
Ge 30:35 he-goats s and color-patched
30:39 the flocks would produce s
30:40 s ones and all the dark-brown
31:8 s ones will become your wages
31:8 whole flock produced s ones
31:10 the he-goats . . . were s
31:12 the he-goats . . . are s
37:3 a long, s shirtlike garment

Ge 37:23 the long *s* garment that was
37:32 sent the long *s* garment and
2Sa 13:18 upon her there was a *s* robe
13:19 *s* robe that was upon her

Stripes

Isa 1:6 and bruises and fresh *s*
Ac 16:33 bathed their *s*; and, one and
1Pe 2:24 And by his *s* you were healed

Stripped

Ex 12:36 and they *s* the Egyptians
Nu 20:28 Then Moses *s* Aaron of his
Jg 14:19 took what he *s* off them and
1Sa 18:4 Jonathan *s* himself of the
2Ch 28:21 Ahaz *s* the house of Jehovah
Job 19:9 own glory he has *s* from me
Ps 102:17 of those *s* of everything
Isa 20:4 and with buttocks *s*, the
23:13 *s* bare her dwelling towers
Joe 1:7 *s* it bare and thrown it away
Mic 3:3 have *s* their very skin from
Mr 15:20 they *s* him of the purple and
Lu 10:30 *s* him and inflicted blows
2Co 3:10 *s* of glory in this respect

Stripping

Ge 37:23 *s* Joseph of his long garment
Ex 33:6 Israel went *s* their ornaments
2Ch 20:25 *s* them off for themselves
35:11 Levites were *s* the skins
Col 2:11 *s* off the body of the flesh
2:15 *S* the governments and the

Strips

Ps 29:9 And *s* bare the forests
Na 3:16 it actually *s* off its skin

Striven

Php 4:3 women who have *s* side by side

Striving

Ec 1:14 was vanity and a *s* after wind
1:17 this too is a *s* after wind
2:11 was vanity and a *s* after wind
2:17 was vanity and a *s* after wind
2:22 and for the *s* of his heart
2:26 is vanity and a *s* after wind
4:4 vanity and a *s* after the wind
4:6 hard work and *s* after the wind
4:16 vanity and a *s* after the wind
6:9 vanity and a *s* after the wind
Da 6:14 he kept on *s* to deliver him
Php 1:27 *s* side by side for the faith

Stroke

Isa 14:6 in fury with a *s* incessantly
27:7 *s* of one striking him does
30:26 resulting from the *s* by him
53:8 of my people he had the *s*
Jer 10:19 My *s* has become sickish
14:17 with an extremely sickish *s*
15:18 chronic and my *s* incurable
30:12 Your *s* is chronic
30:14 the *s* of an enemy I have
Mic 1:9 the *s* upon her is unhealable
Na 3:19 Your *s* has become unhealable

Strokes

De 25:2 laid prostrate and given *s*
25:3 With forty *s* he may beat him
25:3 many *s* in addition to these
2Sa 7:14 the *s* of the sons of Adam
Ps 89:32 to their error even with *s*
Pr 18:6 very mouth calls even for *s*
19:29 *s* for the back of stupid ones
20:30 *s*, the innermost parts of
Jer 30:17 from your *s* I shall heal
Lu 12:47 will be beaten with many *s*
12:48 did things deserving of *s*
2Co 11:24 received forty *s* less one

Strong

Ge 41:56 the famine got a *s* grip on
41:57 the famine had a *s* grip on
47:20 famine had got a *s* grip on
Ex 2:11 as Moses was becoming *s*
3:19 to go except by a *s* hand
6:1 on account of a *s* hand he will
6:1 on account of a *s* hand he will
13:9 by a *s* hand Jehovah brought
14:21 a *s* east wind all night long
32:11 power and with a *s* hand
Nu 13:18 whether they are *s* or weak
13:28 who dwell in the land are *s*
20:20 many people and a *s* hand
De 1:38 Him he has made *s*, because
3:24 your greatness and your *s* arm
De 4:34 with war and with a *s* hand
5:15 a *s* hand and an outstretched
6:21 out of Egypt with a *s* hand
7:8 brought you out with a *s* hand
7:19 the miracles and the *s* hand
9:26 out of Egypt with a *s* hand
11:2 his greatness, his *s* hand and
11:8 in order that you may grow *s*
26:8 out of Egypt with a *s* hand
31:6 Be courageous and *s*. Do not be
31:7 Be courageous and *s*, because
31:23 Be courageous and *s*, because
34:12 as regards all the *s* hand
Jos 1:6 Be courageous and *s*, for you
1:7 be courageous and very *s* to
1:9 Be courageous and *s*. Do not
1:18 Only be courageous and *s*
4:24 Jehovah's hand, that it is *s*
10:25 Be courageous and *s*, for it
14:11 as *s* as on the day of
17:13 sons of Israel had grown *s*
17:18 iron scythes and they are *s*
Jg 1:28 Israel grew *s* and proceeded
3:12 king of Moab grow *s* against
7:11 hands will certainly grow *s*
9:51 a *s* tower happened to be in
14:14 out of the *s* something sweet
2Sa 10:11 Syrians become too *s* for
10:11 become too *s* for you, I
10:12 Be *s*, that we may show
13:28 Be *s* and prove yourselves
16:21 will certainly become *s*
22:18 from my *s* enemy, From
22:33 God is my *s* fortress, And
1Ki 2:2 must be *s* and prove yourself
8:42 and of your *s* hand and of
19:11 a great and *s* wind was
2Ki 3:26 battle had proved too *s* for
1Ch 19:12 Syrians become too *s* for me
19:12 become too *s* for you, I
19:13 Be *s*, that we may show
22:13 Be courageous and *s*. Do not
28:20 Be courageous and *s* and act
2Ch 6:32 great name and your *s* hand
12:1 as soon as he was *s*, he left
12:13 his position *s* in Jerusalem
17:1 his position *s* over Israel
19:11 Be *s* and act, and let
21:4 to make his position *s*, and
24:13 and made it *s*
25:3 kingdom had become *s* upon
26:9 Buttress, and made them *s*
26:15 wonderfully until he was *s*
26:16 soon as he was *s*, his heart
32:7 Be courageous and *s*. Do not
Ezr 4:20 *s* kings over Jerusalem and
9:12 you may grow *s* and certainly
10:4 Be *s* and act
Ne 1:10 power and by your *s* hand
9:11 like a stone in the *s* waters
Job 5:15 from the hand of the *s* one
9:4 wise in heart and *s* in power
9:19 If in power anyone is *s*
9:19 And if in justice anyone is *s*
24:22 draw away *s* people by his
37:6 the downpour of his *s* rains
40:18 Its *s* bones are like
41:25 the *s* get frightened
Ps 10:10 has to fall into his *s* claws
18:17 from my *s* enemy
24:8 Jehovah *s* and mighty
27:14 and let your heart be *s*
29:1 O you sons of *s* ones
31:24 and may your heart be *s*
59:3 *S* ones make an attack upon
61:3 A *s* tower in the face of the
62:7 My *s* rock, my refuge is in
68:33 with his voice, a *s* voice
71:7 But you are my *s* refuge
80:15 son whom you have made *s*
80:17 you have made *s* for yourself
89:13 Your hand is *s*, Your right
136:12 By a *s* hand and by an arm
147:13 the bars of your gates *s*
Pr 8:28 of the watery deep to be *s*
10:15 valuable things . . . *s* town
14:26 there is *s* confidence, and
18:10 name of Jehovah is a *s* tower
18:11 valuable things . . . *s* town
18:19 is more than a *s* town
18:23 rich answers in a *s* way
21:14 a bribe in the bosom, *s* rage
23:11 For their Redeemer is *s*
30:25 the ants are a people not *s*
Ca 8:6 love is as *s* as death is
Isa 19:4 a *s* will be the king that will
25:3 a *s* people will glorify you
26:1 Judah: We have a *s* city
27:1 great and *s* sword, will turn
28:2 Jehovah has someone *s* and
28:22 your bands may not grow *s*
35:4 Be *s*. Do not be afraid
39:1 been sick but was *s* again
40:10 will come even as a *s* one
41:6 say to his brother: Be *s*
43:16 even through *s* waters
43:17 the *s* ones at the same time
44:14 and he lets it become *s*
54:2 those tent pins of yours *s*
56:11 dogs *s* in soulful desire
62:8 hand and with his *s* arm
Jer 5:8 having *s* testicles, they have
21:5 with a *s* arm and with anger
32:21 with a *s* hand and with a
48:41 *s* places will certainly be
50:34 Their Repurchaser is *s*
51:12 Make *s* the watch
51:30 sitting in the *s* places
Eze 3:14 hand of Jehovah . . . was *s*
7:24 pride of the *s* ones to cease
13:22 the hands of a wicked one *s*
19:11 came to be for her *s* rods
19:12 Her *s* rod was torn off and
19:14 proved to be in her no *s* rod
20:33 be with a *s* hand and with
20:34 scattered with a *s* hand
26:17 became a *s* one in the sea
30:21 become *s* to take hold of
30:22 *s* one and the broken one
33:27 who are in the *s* places and
34:16 the fat one and the *s* one
Da 2:40 prove to be *s* like iron
2:42 will partly prove to be *s* and
4:11 tree grew up and became *s*
4:20 grew great and became *s* and
4:22 grown great and become *s*, and
7:7 and terrible and unusually *s*
9:15 the land of Egypt by a *s* hand
10:19, 19 Be *s*, yes, be *s*
11:2 has become *s* in his riches
11:5 of the south will become *s*
11:6 one making her *s* in those
11:12 will not use his *s* position
Am 2:14 no one *s* will reinforce his
2:16 as for one *s* in his heart
5:9 flash forth upon someone *s*
Hag 2:4 But now be *s*, O Zerubbabel
2:4 be *s*, O Joshua the son of
2:4 be *s*, all you people of the
Zec 8:9 the hands of you people be *s*
8:13 May your hands be *s*
Mal 3:13 *S* have been your words
Mt 12:29 invade the house of a *s* man
12:29 first he binds the *s* man
Mr 2:17 *s* do not need a physician
3:27 got into the house of a *s* man
3:27 first he binds the *s* man, and
16:8 *s* emotion were gripping them
Lu 1:15 no wine and *s* drink at all
1:80 getting *s* in spirit, and he
2:40 growing and getting *s*, being
6:48 not *s* enough to shake it
11:21 When a *s* man, well armed
16:3 I am not *s* enough to dig
Joh 6:18 a *s* wind was blowing
Ac 3:16 made this man *s* whom you
7:60 he cried out with a *s* voice
Ro 15:1 who are *s* ought to bear the
15:1 weaknesses of those not *s*
1Co 1:27 put the *s* things to shame
3:2 for you were not yet *s* enough
3:2 neither are you *s* enough now
4:10 we are weak, but you are *s*
1Th 1:5 holy spirit and *s* conviction
1Ti 1:7 they are making *s* assertions
Heb 5:7 with *s* outcries and tears
6:18 have *s* encouragement to lay
1Pe 5:10 God . . . he will make you *s*
1Jo 2:14 are *s* and the word of God
Re 1:10 I heard behind me a *s* voice
5:2 I saw a *s* angel proclaiming
6:15 and the rich and the *s* ones
10:1 I saw another *s* angel
18:2 he cried out with a *s* voice
18:8 God, who judged her, is *s*
18:10 Babylon you *s* city, because
18:21 *s* angel lifted up a stone
19:18 fleshy parts of *s* men and

Strong-boned
Ge 49:14 Issachar is a *s* ass, lying

Stronger
Ge 25:23 one national group will be *s*
26:16 you have grown far *s* than we
Nu 13:31 they are *s* than we are
Jg 14:18 And what is *s* than a lion?
18:26 that they were *s* than he was
1Sa 17:50 proved *s* than the Philistine
2Sa 3:1 David kept getting *s*, and
15:12 conspiracy kept getting *s*
22:18 they were *s* than I was
1Ki 20:23 they proved *s* than we were
20:23 prove *s* than they are
20:25 prove *s* than they are
2Ch 27:5 proved *s* than they were, so
Ps 18:17 because they were *s* than I
35:10 from one *s* than he is
142:6 For they are *s* than I am
Ec 7:19 Wisdom itself is *s* for the
Jer 31:11 hand of the one *s* than he is
Mt 3:11 one coming after me is *s*
Mr 1:7 someone *s* than I am is coming
Lu 3:16 the one *s* than I am is coming
11:22 when someone *s* than he is
1Co 1:25 weak thing of God is *s* than
10:22 We are not *s* than he is

Stronghold
Jg 6:26 at the head of this *s*, with
2Sa 5:7 capture the *s* of Zion, that
5:9 took up dwelling in the *s*
22:2 Jehovah is my crag and my *s*
1Ch 11:5 to capture the *s* of Zion
Ne 8:10 the joy of Jehovah is your *s*
Ps 18:2 Jehovah is my crag and my *s*
27:1 Jehovah is the *s* of my life
28:8 a *s* of the grand salvation
31:2 Become for me a rocky *s*
31:3 For you are my crag and my *s*
71:3 you are my crag and my *s*
91:2 You are my refuge and my *s*
144:2 My loving-kindness and my *s*
Pr 10:29 way of Jehovah is a *s* for
Isa 23:4 O you *s* of the sea, has
23:14 your *s* has been despoiled
25:4 become a *s* to the lowly one
25:4 *s* to the poor one in the
27:5 let him take hold of my *s*
30:2 shelter in the *s* of Pharaoh
30:3 *s* of Pharaoh must become
Jer 16:19 Jehovah my strength and my *s*
Na 1:7 a *s* in the day of distress
3:11 will seek a *s* from the enemy
Zec 9:12 Return to the *s*, you

Strongholds
Ps 31:2 A house of *s* to save me
Ec 9:14 and built against it great *s*
Isa 23:11 to annihilate her *s*
Da 11:39 against the most fortified *s*

Strongly
1Ch 11:10 to David, holding *s* with
28:7 if he will be *s* resolved to
Da 10:21 one holding *s* with me in
Lu 22:59 other man began insisting *s*
Ac 12:15 she kept on *s* asserting it
2Co 10:4 for overturning *s* entrenched

Strongness
Isa 8:11 to me with *s* of the hand

Struck
Ge 19:11 they *s* with blindness the
28:5 he *s* out for Paddan-aram
Ex 2:12 he *s* the Egyptian down and
7:20 lifted up the rod and *s* the
8:17 *s* the dust of the earth, and
9:25 hail *s* everything that was in
9:31 flax and the barley had been *s*
9:32 and the spelt had not been *s*
12:29 Jehovah *s* every firstborn in
17:5 rod with which you *s* the Nile
21:19 one who *s* him must be free
22:2 If a thief . . . does get *s* and
Nu 3:13 day that I *s* every firstborn
12:10 Miriam was *s* with leprosy
12:10 she was *s* with leprosy
20:11 and *s* the crag with his rod
21:24 Israel *s* him with the edge
25:14 fatally *s* Israelite man who
25:14 *s* with the Midianitess was
25:15 Midianite woman fatally *s*
25:18 fatally *s* in the day of the
33:4 those whom Jehovah had *s*
Nu 35:16 he has *s* him so that he dies
35:17 he has *s* him so that he dies
35:18 he has *s* him so that he dies
35:21 in enmity he has *s* him with
De 19:11 *s* his soul fatally and he
21:1 known who *s* him fatally
Jos 8:24 *s* it with the edge of the
10:33 *s* him and his people until
11:10 its king he *s* down with
11:14 they *s* with the edge of the
13:21 Moses *s*, together with the
20:5 he *s* his fellowman fatally
Jg 3:13 they went and *s* Israel and
7:13 and *s* it so that it fell, and
9:43 against them and *s* them down
11:21 they *s* them and Israel took
14:19 *s* down thirty men of theirs
15:16 I have *s* down a thousand men
20:37 ambush spread out and *s* all
20:45 *s* down two thousand more
1Sa 5:12 had been *s* with piles
6:19 he *s* down among the people
6:19 Jehovah had *s* down the
13:3 Jonathan *s* down the garrison
13:4 Saul has *s* down a garrison
14:14 and his armor-bearer *s* them
17:35 *s* it down and made the
17:35 *s* it down and put it to
17:36 bear your servant *s* down
17:49 he *s* the Philistine in his
17:50 *s* the Philistine down and
18:7 Saul has *s* . . . thousands
18:27 went and *s* down among the
19:10 *s* the spear into the wall
21:9 whom you *s* down in the low
21:11 Saul has *s* down his
22:19 *s* with the edge of the
23:5 *s* them down with a great
25:38 Jehovah *s* Nabal, so that he
27:9 David *s* the land, but he
29:5 Saul has *s* down his
31:2 *s* down Jonathan and Abinadab
2Sa 1:15 *s* him down so that he died
2:31 *s* down those of Benjamin and
3:27 *s* him in the abdomen, so
4:6 *s* him in the abdomen; and
4:7 *s* him so that they put him to
6:7 God *s* him down there for the
8:5 David then *s* down among the
8:9 David had *s* down all the
8:10 so that he *s* him down
10:18 of their army he *s* down
11:15 he must be *s* down and die
11:21 *s* down Abimelech the son
12:9 Uriah the Hittite you *s*
13:30 Absalom has *s* down all the
14:6 one *s* the other down and
18:15 came around and *s* Absalom
20:10 he *s* him with it in the
21:12 the Philistines *s* down Saul
21:17 *s* the Philistine down and
21:18 the Hushathite *s* down Saph
21:21 David's brother, *s* him down
23:10 only to strip those *s* down
23:20 *s* down the two sons of
23:20 *s* down a lion inside a
23:21 *s* down the Egyptian man
1Ki 11:15 when David *s* down Edom
15:29 he *s* down all the house of
16:7 and because he *s* him down
16:11 he *s* down all the house of
16:16 and also *s* down the king
20:21 *s* down the Syrians with a
20:37 the man *s* him, striking and
22:24 *s* Micaiah upon the cheek
2Ki 2:8 and *s* the waters, and
2:14 and *s* the waters and said
2:14 When he *s* the waters, then
6:18 So he *s* them with blindness
8:28 the Syrians *s* down Jehoram
9:27 *s* him down while in the
10:9 but who *s* down all these
12:20 *s* Jehoash down at the house
12:21 *s* him down, so that he died
13:18 *s* three times and stopped
13:25 Three times Jehoash *s* him
14:5 *s* down the king his father
14:7 *s* down the Edomites in the
14:10 unmistakably *s* down Edom
15:10 *s* him down at Ibleam and
15:14 Samaria and *s* down Shallum
15:25 *s* him down in Samaria in
15:30 *s* him and put him to death
2Ki 18:8 *s* down the Philistines clear
19:37 *s* him down with the sword
21:24 *s* down all the conspirators
1Ch 11:22 *s* down the two sons of
11:22 descended and *s* down a lion
11:23 *s* down the Egyptian man
13:10 Uzzah . . . he *s* him down
18:2 Then he *s* Moab down, and the
18:9 David had *s* down all the
18:10 so that he *s* him down, (for
18:12 he *s* down the Edomites in
20:4 Sibbecai the Hushathite *s*
20:7 Jonathan . . . *s* him down
21:7 and so he *s* down Israel
2Ch 14:14 *s* all the cities round about
14:15 tents with livestock they *s*
16:4 *s* Ijon and Dan and Abel-maim
18:23 *s* Micaiah on the cheek and
25:3 *s* down the king his father
25:19 Here you have *s* down Edom
28:5 *s* him and carried off from
28:5 *s* him with a great
33:25 *s* down all the conspirators
Job 1:15 attendants they *s* down with
1:17 attendants they *s* down with
2:7 *s* Job with a malignant boil
16:10 With reproach they have *s*
Ps 69:26 one whom you yourself have *s*
78:20 *s* a rock That waters might
78:51 *s* down all the firstborn in
102:4 *s* just like vegetation and
135:8 *s* down the firstborn ones of
135:10 *s* down many nations And
Pr 23:35 They have *s* me, but I did
Ca 5:7 They *s* me, they wounded me
Isa 1:5 Where else will you be *s*
10:34 *s* down the thickets of the
30:31 Assyria will be *s* with
37:38 *s* him down with the sword
51:7 do not be *s* with terror
60:10 I shall have *s* you, but in
Jer 1:17 Do not be *s* with any terror
2:30 I have *s* your sons
5:3 You have *s* them, but they did
5:6 a lion out of the forest has *s*
10:2 *s* with terror even at the
10:2 nations are *s* with terror
14:19 you have *s* us, so that there
17:18 ones to be *s* with terror
17:18 not be *s* with terror
18:21 *s* down with the sword
20:2 Then Pashhur *s* Jeremiah the
23:4 be *s* with any terror
26:23 *s* him down with the sword
30:10 do not be *s* with terror
30:14 I have *s* you, with the
33:5 *s* down in my anger and in
37:10 *s* down all the military
37:15 *s* him and put him into the
41:2 *s* down Gedaliah the son
41:3 men of war, Ishmael *s* down
41:9 men that he had *s* down was
41:16 *s* down Gedaliah the son
41:18 *s* down Gedaliah the son
48:20 she has been *s* with terror
49:28 king of Babylon *s* down
La 4:5 *s* with astonishment in the
Eze 2:6 do not you be *s* with terror
3:9 *s* with terror at their faces
9:7 went forth and *s* in the city
22:13 *s* my hand at your unjust
33:21 The city has been *s* down!
40:1 the city had been *s* down
Da 2:34 *s* the image on its feet of
2:35 stone that *s* the image, it
Ho 9:16 Ephraim must be *s* down
Am 4:9 I *s* you people with scorching
Hag 2:17 *s* you people with scorching
Zec 13:6 *s* in the house of my
Mal 2:5 was *s* with terror
Mt 7:27 and *s* against that house
9:8 the crowds were *s* with fear
26:51 and *s* the slave of the high
26:68 Who is it that *s* you?
Mr 12:4 that one they *s* on the head
14:47 *s* the slave of the high
Lu 8:25 *s* with fear, they marveled
22:64 Who is it that *s* you?
Joh 18:10 *s* the slave of the high
Ac 12:23 the angel of Jehovah *s* him
23:3 command me to be *s*

Structurally
2Ch 24:13 stand as it *s* should and

Structure
1Ki 6:5 a side s all around, against
2Ki 16:18 covered s for the sabbath
Ezr 5:3 and to finish this beam s
5:9 to finish this beam s
Eze 1:16 of the wheels and their s
1:16 their appearance and their s
40:2 s of a city to the south
Am 9:6 his s over the earth that he
Re 21:18 s of its wall was jasper

Structures
Eze 46:22 with corner s had the same

Struggle
Ge 25:22 sons within her began to s
Ex 21:22 in case men should s with
Le 24:10 s with each other in the
Nu 26:9 a s against Moses and Aaron
26:9 engaged in a s against Jehovah
De 25:11 In case men s together with
2Sa 14:6 two of them began to s with
Ps 60:super s with Aram-naharaim and
Pr 13:10 one only causes a s, but
17:19 transgression is loving a s
Isa 41:12 those men in a s with you
58:4 for quarreling and s you
Php 1:30 you have the same s as you
Col 2:1 a s I am having in behalf

Struggled
Jer 15:9 her soul has s for breath

Struggling
Ex 2:13 two Hebrew men s with each
1Th 2:2 with a great deal of s

Stubble
Ex 5:12 to gather s for straw
15:7 anger, it eats them up like s
Job 13:25 chasing after mere dry s
41:28 changed for it into mere s
41:29 regarded by it as mere s
Ps 83:13 Like s before a wind
Isa 5:24 fire eats up the s and
33:11 will give birth to s
40:24 like s the windstorm itself
41:2 driven about like mere s
47:14 They have become like s
Jer 13:24 I shall scatter them like s
Joe 2:5 fire that is devouring s
Ob 18 and the house of Esau as s
Na 1:10 devoured like s fully dry
Mal 4:1 wickedness must become as s
1Co 3:12 wood materials, hay, s

Stubborn
De 21:18 son who is s and rebellious
21:20 This son of ours is s and
Jos 11:20 let their hearts become s
Jg 2:19 and their s behavior
Ne 9:29 they kept giving a s shoulder
Ps 66:7 As for those who are s, let
68:6 the s, they have to reside in
68:18 s ones, to reside among them
78:8 generation s and rebellious
Pr 7:11 She is boisterous and s
Isa 1:23 Your princes are s and
30:1 Woe to the s sons, is the
65:2 all day long to a s people
Jer 5:23 a s and rebellious heart
6:28 are the most s men
Ho 4:16 like a s cow, Israel has
4:16 Israel has become s
9:15 their princes are acting s
Zec 7:11 they kept giving a s shoulder

Stubbornness
De 29:19 walk in the s of my heart
Job 9:4 Who can show s to him and
Ps 81:12 go in the s of their heart
Jer 3:17 the s of their bad heart
7:24 in the s of their bad heart
9:14 the s of their heart and
11:8 the s of their bad heart
13:10 in the s of their heart
16:12 the s of his bad heart
18:12 the s of his bad heart
23:17 in the s of his heart

Stuck
Ex 4:6 s his hand into the upper fold
Ru 1:14 As for Ruth, she s with her
1Sa 26:7 his spear s into the earth
2Sa 20:2 they s to their king from
2Ki 3:3 s to the sins of Jeroboam the
7:8 went off and s them away
Job 31:7 any defect has s in my own
38:38 clods of earth . . . get s
41:17 they are s together
Ps 102:5 My bones have s to my flesh
Lu 10:11 dust that got s to our feet
22:28 have s with me in my trials
Ac 27:41 the prow got s and stayed

Studied
Joh 7:15 he has not s at the schools

Studs
Ca 1:11 along with s of silver

Stuff
Ex 36:6 do not produce any more s for
36:7 s proved to be enough for all
De 22:11 mixed s of wool and linen
Jg 5:30 embroidered garment, dyed s
Eze 27:24 in carpets of two-colored s
Na 2:3 are dressed in crimson s

Stuffs
Jg 5:30 Spoil of dyed s for Sisera
5:30 for Sisera, spoil of dyed s

Stumble
Le 26:37 s against one another as if
2Ch 25:8 God could cause you to s
28:23 him and all Israel s
Ps 9:3 s and perish from before you
64:8 And they cause one to s
Pr 4:12 if you run, you will not s
4:16 they cause someone to s
24:16 be made to s by calamity
24:17 and when he is caused to s
Isa 8:14 rock over which to s to
8:15 s and to fall and be broken
28:13 s backwards and actually
31:3 offering help will have to s
40:30 will without fail s
63:13 wilderness, they did not s
Jer 6:15 they will s, Jehovah has
6:21 will certainly s over them
8:12 they will s, Jehovah has
18:15 make men s in their ways
18:23 are made to s before you
20:11 will s and not prevail
31:9 will not be caused to s
50:32 certainly s and fall, and
Eze 33:12 he will not be made to s
36:15 will no more cause to s
Da 11:14 and they will have to s
11:19 he will certainly s and fall
11:33 s by sword and by flame, by
11:34 when they are made to s
11:35 will be made to s, in order
11:41 lands that will be made to s
Ho 4:5 certainly s in the daytime
4:5 even a prophet must s with
5:5 made to s in their error
14:9 the ones who will s in them
Na 2:5 They will s in their walking
Mal 2:8 caused many to s in the law
Mt 5:29 is making you s, tear it out
5:30 hand is making you s, cut it
13:57 So they began to s at him
17:27 we do not cause them to s
18:8 or your foot is making you s
18:9 if your eye is making you s
Mr 6:3 So they began to s at him
9:43 if ever your hand makes you s
9:45 if your foot makes you s
9:47 And if your eye makes you s
Lu 17:2 to s one of these little ones
Joh 6:61 Does this s you?
Ro 11:11 they s so that they fell
1Co 8:13 if food makes my brother s
8:13 may not make my brother s
Jas 3:2 For we all s many times
3:2 If anyone does not s in word

Stumbled
Ne 4:10 the burden bearer has s
Ps 27:2 They themselves s and fell
31:10 my power has s
107:12 s, and there was no one
Isa 3:8 Jerusalem has s, and Judah
59:10 s at high noon just as in
59:14 truth has s even in the
Jer 46:6 they have s and fallen
46:12 they have s, mighty man
La 1:14 My power has s. Jehovah has
5:13 mere boys have s
Ho 5:5 Judah has also s with them
14:1 you have s in your error
Mt 13:21 persecution . . . at once s
15:12 Pharisees s at hearing what
24:10 many will be s and will
26:31 All of you will be s in
26:33 are s in connection with you
26:33 never will I be s!
Mr 4:17 persecution arises . . . are s
14:27 You will all be s, because
14:29 Even if all the others are s
Lu 7:23 happy is he who has not s
Joh 16:1 that you may not be s
Ro 9:32 s on the stone of stumbling
2Co 11:29 Who is s, and I am not

Stumbles
Mt 18:6 s one of these little ones
Mr 9:42 s one of these little ones
Ro 14:21 over which your brother s

Stumbling
1Sa 2:4 those that are s do gird on
25:31 s block to the heart of my
2Ch 25:8 God to help and to cause s
Job 4:4 Anyone s, your words would
Ps 56:13 delivered my feet from s
105:37 there was no one s along
116:8 my foot from s
119:165 there is no s block
Pr 4:19 known at what they keep s
16:18 and a haughty spirit before s
Isa 5:27 nor is anyone s among them
Jer 6:21 for this people s blocks
46:16 great numbers they are s
Eze 3:20 put a s block before him
7:19 s block causing their error
14:3 s block causing their error
14:4 that places the very s block
14:7 sets the very s block causing
18:30 a s block causing error
44:12 a s block into error, that
Na 3:3 keep s among their dead bodies
Zep 1:3 s blocks with the wicked ones
Zec 12:8 one that is s among them
Mt 11:6 finds no cause for s in me
13:41 all things that cause s and
16:23 You are a s block to me
18:7 Woe . . . due to the s blocks!
18:7 s blocks must . . . come, but
18:7 man through whom the s block
Lu 17:1 that causes for s should come
Ro 9:32 stumbled on the stone of s
9:33 laying in Zion a stone of s
11:9 trap and a s block and a
14:13 a s block or a cause for
14:20 with an occasion for s eats
16:17 occasions for s contrary to
1Co 1:23 to the Jews a cause for s
8:9 s block to those who are weak
10:32 causes for s to Jews as
2Co 6:3 we giving any cause for s
Ga 5:11 s block of the torture stake
Php 1:10 not be s others up to the
1Pe 2:8 stone of s and a rock-mass of
2:8 s because they are disobedient
1Jo 2:10 no cause for s in his case
Jude 24 able to guard you from s and
Re 2:14 s block before the sons of

Stump
Job 14:8 And in the dust its s dies
Isa 6:13 there is a s; a holy seed
6:13 a holy seed will be the s of
11:1 twig out of the s of Jesse
40:24 s taken root in the earth
Joe 1:7 and my fig tree as a s

Stunned
Ezr 9:3 and I kept sitting s
9:4 sitting s until the grain
Eze 3:15 s in the midst of them
Mr 9:15 sight of him they were s
14:33 s and to be sorely troubled
16:5 white robe, and they were s
16:6 Stop being s. You are looking

Stupefied
Isa 44:8 and do not become s

Stupid
De 32:6 O people s and not wise
32:21 With a s nation I shall
Ps 49:10 the s one and the unreasoning
92:6 no one s can understand this
94:8 s ones, when will you have
Pr 1:22 s ones keep hating knowledge
1:32 easygoingness of the s is
3:35 s ones are exalting dishonor

Ps 1:3 And everything he does will *s*
Pr 28:13 transgressions will not *s*
Isa 53:10 delight of Jehovah will *s*
Jer 32:5 Chaldeans, you will not *s*
Da 8:25 deception to *s* in his hand
11:27 nothing will *s*, because the
Lu 21:36 may *s* in escaping all these

Succeeded
Jer 12:1 way of wicked ones . . . *s*
Ac 7:45 our forefathers who *s* to it
24:27 Felix was *s* by Porcius

Succeeding
Ge 15:3 a son of my household is *s* me
Lu 9:37 the *s* day, when they got down
Ac 20:15 away from there the *s* day

Succeeds
Ex 29:30 priest who *s* him from among

Success
Ge 24:40 give *s* to your way; and you
24:42 giving *s* to my way on which
24:56 Jehovah has given *s* to my
2Sa 1:22 would not return without *s*
1Ch 29:23 and to make a *s* of it
Ne 1:11 do grant *s* to your servant
2:20 the One that will grant us *s*
Ps 7:4 hostility to me without *s*
25:3 treacherously without *s*
45:4 in your splendor go on to *s*
118:25 Jehovah, do grant *s*, please
Pr 17:8 that he turns he has *s*
Ec 10:10 wisdom to *s* means advantage
11:6 where this will have *s*
Isa 54:17 will have no *s*, and any
55:11 have certain *s* in that for
Jer 2:37 will have no *s* with them
5:28 that they may gain *s*
22:30 not have any *s* in his days
22:30 have any *s*, sitting upon the
Eze 17:9 Will it have *s*? Will not
17:10 will it have *s*? Will it not
17:15 Will he have *s*? Will he
Da 8:12 and it acted and had *s*
Mt 12:20 he sends out justice with *s*

Successful
Ge 24:21 Jehovah had made his trip *s*
39:2 he turned out a *s* man and
39:3 Jehovah was making turn out *s*
39:23 was making it turn out *s*
De 28:29 will not make your ways *s*
Jos 1:8 make your way *s* and then you
Jg 18:5 which we are going will be *s*
1Ki 22:12 prove *s*; and Jehovah will
22:15 Go up and prove *s*
1Ch 22:11 prove *s* and build the house
22:13 prove *s* if you take care to
2Ch 7:11 his own house he proved *s*
13:12 for you will not prove *s*
14:7 went building and proving *s*
18:11 prove *s*, and Jehovah will
18:14 Go up and prove *s*
20:20 his prophets and so prove *s*
24:20 that you cannot prove *s*
31:21 and he proved *s*
32:30 *s* in every work of his
Ps 37:7 anyone making his way *s*
Isa 48:15 be a making of his way *s*
Da 8:24 prove *s* and do effectively
11:36 *s* until the denunciation

Successfully
2Sa 3:24 so that he *s* went away
19:17 made it *s* to the Jordan
1Ki 8:13 I have *s* built a house of
2Th 3:5 directing your hearts *s* into

Succession
Ac 3:24 Samuel on and those in *s*
Heb 7:23 to become priests in *s*

Successive
Ps 145:13 throughout all *s* generations
Pr 28:2 many are its *s* princes, but

Successor
Le 16:32 as priest as *s* of his father

Successors
Heb 7:24 his priesthood without any *s*

Succoth
Ge 33:17 Jacob pulled out for *S*, and
33:17 the name of the place *S*
Ex 12:37 depart from Rameses for *S*
13:20 proceeded to depart from *S*
Nu 33:5 Israel . . . went camping in *S*
33:6 pulled away from *S* and went
Jos 13:27 and *S* and Zaphon, the rest
Jg 8:5 said to the men of *S*: Please
8:6 the princes of *S* said: Are the
8:8 as the men of *S* had answered
8:14 young man of the men of *S* and
8:14 the princes of *S* and its older
8:15 the men of *S* and said: Here
8:16 put the men of *S* through an
1Ki 7:46 between *S* and Zarethan
2Ch 4:17 ground between *S* and Zeredah
Ps 60:6 the low plain of *S* I shall
108:7 the low plain of *S* I shall

Succoth-benoth
2Ki 17:30 made *S*, and the men of Cuth

Such
Ge 27:4 make me a tasty dish *s* as I
27:9 tasty dish . . . *s* as he is fond
27:14 a tasty dish *s* as his father
30:32 *s* must be my wages
34:14 cannot possibly do *s* a thing
44:7 speak with *s* words as these
44:15 know that *s* a man as I am
Le 10:19 *s* things as these began to
13:29 a plague develops in *s* one
13:30 then declare *s* one unclean
22:6 soul who touches any *s* must
22:11 he as *s* may share in eating
22:11 they as *s* may share in
22:12 she as *s* may not eat of the
27:9 a beast *s* as one presents
27:11 unclean beast *s* as one may
Nu 5:28 free from *s* punishment
16:9 Is it *s* a little thing for
19:12 *S* one should purify himself
De 17:5 stone *s* one with stones, and
17:5 and *s* one must die
Jg 3:2 had not experienced *s* things
19:30 *S* a thing as this has never
1Sa 4:7 for *s* a thing as this never
21:2, 2 men for *s* and *s* a place
2Sa 9:8 to the dead dog *s* as I am
12:4 get *s* ready for the traveler
13:1 after *s* things that Absalom
15:1 following *s* things that
1Ki 10:10 *s* as the queen of Sheba gave
2Ki 6:8, 8 At *s* and *s* a place you
1Ch 22:3 copper in *s* quantity as to be
22:14 come to be in *s* quantity
29:25 upon him *s* royal dignity
2Ch 1:12 *s* as no kings that were
1:12 *s* as no one after you will
8:14 *s* was the commandment of
Ezr 7:27 put *s* a thing into the heart
9:13 who have escaped *s* as these
Ne 6:8 Things *s* as you are saying
7:2 he was *s* a trustworthy man
Ps 32:6 At *s* a time only as you may
90:12 count our days in *s* a way
139:6 *S* knowledge is too wonderful
149:9 *S* splendor belongs to all
Pr 29:7 does not consider *s* knowledge
Ec 2:21 not worked hard at *s* a thing
Ca 5:9 put us under *s* an oath as this
Isa 7:13 *s* a little thing for you to
7:17 days *s* as have not come
10:19 *s* a number that a mere boy
15:9 *s* as a lion for the escapees
27:4 I will step on *s*
27:4 set *s* on fire at the same
Jer 38:20 They will do no *s* giving
Eze 1:18 rims, they had *s* height that
8:17 Is it *s* a light thing to the
16:16 *s* things are not coming in
34:18 Is it *s* a little thing for
Da 2:10 asked *s* a thing as this of
2:15 *s* a harsh order on the part
9:12 calamity, *s* as was not done
12:1 time of distress *s* as has not
Joe 3:4 giving *s* treatment to me
Zec 1:21 dispersed Judah to *s* an
8:10 there was no *s* thing; and to
Mal 2:17 in *s* ones he himself has
Mt 9:8 who gave *s* authority to men
18:5 receives one *s* young child on
18:6 millstone *s* as is turned by
19:8 *s* has not been the case from
19:10 If *s* is the situation of a
19:12 are eunuchs that were born *s*
24:21 great tribulation *s* as has
26:45 At *s* a time as this you are
Mr 6:2 *s* powerful works be performed
Mr 9:37 one of *s* young children on
9:42 a millstone *s* as is turned
13:19 a tribulation *s* as has not
14:41 At *s* a time as this you are
Lu 9:9 about whom I am hearing *s*
16:9 when *s* fail, they may receive
Joh 1:14 a glory *s* as belongs to an
13:13 speak rightly, for I am *s*
Ac 5:4 purposed *s* a deed as this in
14:1 spoke in *s* a manner that a
16:24 Because he got *s* an order, he
17:30 times of *s* ignorance, yet
19:25 those who worked at *s* things
21:35 situation became *s* that he
22:22 Take *s* a man away from the
26:29 become men *s* as I also am
Ro 1:32 practicing *s* things are
2:2 those who practice *s* things
2:3 those who practice *s* things
2:27 person that is *s* by nature
9:4 as *s*, are Israelites, to whom
13:7 who calls for fear, *s* fear
13:7 who calls for honor, *s* honor
1Co 5:1 *s* fornication as is not even
5:3 has worked in *s* a way as this
5:5 hand *s* a man over to Satan
5:11 not even eating with *s* a man
7:15 under *s* circumstances, but
7:28 *s* one would commit no sin
9:24 Run in *s* a way that you may
15:29 for the purpose of being *s*
2Co 1:10 From *s* a great thing as
1:17 had *s* an intention, I did not
2:6 is sufficient for *s* a man
2:7 *s* a man may not be swallowed
3:12 as we have *s* a hope, we are
10:11 Let *s* a man take this into
10:11 *s* we shall also be in
11:13 *s* men are false apostles
12:2 away as *s* to the third heaven
12:3 I know *s* a man—whether in
12:5 Over *s* a man I will boast
Ga 3:16 as in the case of many *s*
5:1 For *s* freedom Christ set us
5:21 who practice *s* things will
5:23 Against *s* things there is no
6:1 readjust *s* a man in a spirit
6:6 one who gives *s* oral teaching
Eph 5:27 wrinkle or any of *s* things
Php 1:8 in *s* tender affection as
1Th 4:5 sexual appetite *s* as also
2Th 3:12 To *s* persons we give the
1Ti 6:21 making a show of *s* knowledge
Tit 3:11 *s* a man has been turned out
Phm 9 seeing that I am *s* as I am
Heb 2:3 a salvation of *s* greatness in
3:2 to the One that made him *s*
5:12 *s* as need milk, not solid
7:16 *s*, not according to the law
7:23 death from continuing as *s*
7:26 *s* a high priest as this was
8:1 We have *s* a high priest as
9:23 are better than *s* sacrifices
10:33 were having *s* an experience
11:14 those who say *s* things
12:3 endured *s* contrary talk by
13:16 *s* sacrifices God is well
Jas 2:12 Keep on speaking in *s* a way
2:12 keep on doing in *s* a way as
4:16 *s* taking of pride is wicked
2Pe 1:17 words *s* as these were borne
1Jo 3:1 children of God; and *s* we are
3:9 seed remains in *s* one, and he
3:24 and he in union with *s* one
4:15 God remains in union with *s*
3Jo 8 to receive *s* persons hospitably
Re 16:18 earthquake occurred *s* as had
18:17 *s* great riches have been

Suchlike
Mt 19:14 kingdom . . . belongs to *s*
Mr 10:14 kingdom . . . belongs to *s*
Lu 18:16 kingdom of God belongs to *s*
Joh 4:23 Father is looking for *s* ones

Suck
Ge 32:15 thirty camels giving *s* and
33:13 cattle that are giving *s* are
De 32:13 *s* honey out of a crag
33:19 *s* the abounding wealth of
1Sa 6:7 two cows that are giving *s*
6:10 two cows that were giving *s*
Job 3:12 breasts that I should take *s*
20:16 venom of cobras he will *s*
24:20 maggot will sweetly *s* him

2Sa 16:1 a hundred loads of *s* fruit
16:2 *s* fruit are for the young
Ps 32:4 as in the dry heat of *s*
74:17 *S* and winter—you yourself
Pr 6:8 its food even in the *s*
26:1 Like snow in *s* and like rain
30:25 the *s* they prepare their food
Isa 16:9 shouting even over your *s*
18:6 will certainly pass the *s*
28:4 the early fig before *s*
Jer 8:20 the *s* has come to an end
40:10 gather wine and *s* fruits
40:12 *s* fruits in very great
48:32 Upon your *s* fruitage and
Da 2:35 chaff from the *s* threshing
Am 3:15 in addition to the *s* house
8:1 there was a basket of *s* fruit
8:2 I said: A basket of *s* fruit
Mic 7:1 the gatherings of *s* fruit
Zec 14:8 In *s* and in winter it will
Mt 24:32 you know that *s* is near
Mr 13:28 you know that *s* is near
Lu 21:30 that now the *s* is near

Summertime
Pr 10:5 is gathering during the *s*

Summit
2Sa 15:32 *s* where people used to bow
16:1 over a little beyond the *s*
Am 1:2 the *s* of Carmel must dry up

Summon
Jer 50:29 *S* against Babylon archers
51:27 *S* against her the kingdoms
Ac 10:5 *s* a certain Simon who is

Summoned
Nu 16:2 *s* ones of the meeting, men of
26:9 Dathan and Abiram were *s* ones
Jos 24:9 he sent and *s* Balaam the
1Sa 15:4 Saul *s* the people and took
23:8 Saul *s* all the people to war
1Ki 15:22 *s* all Judah—there was none
Job 9:19 O that I may be *s*
Eze 23:23 warriors and *s* ones, riding
Mt 2:7 Herod . . . *s* the astrologers
10:1 he *s* his twelve disciples and
18:32 his master *s* him and said
25:14 *s* slaves of his and
Mr 3:13 *s* those he wanted, and they
6:7 Now he *s* the twelve, and he
8:1 he *s* the disciples and said
Lu 7:19 John *s* a certain two of his
Ac 5:40 *s* the apostles, flogged them
16:10 that God had *s* us to declare
23:23 he *s* a certain two of the

Summoning
Mr 15:44 *s* the army officer, he asked

Sumup
Ec 7:27 another, to find out the *s*

Sun
Ge 15:12 *s* was about to set, and a
15:17 *s* was now setting and a
19:23 *s* had gone forth over the
28:11 because the *s* had set
32:31 And the *s* began to flash
37:9 the *s* and the moon and eleven
Ex 16:21 the *s* got hot, it melted
17:12 held steady until the *s* set
22:3 If the *s* has shone forth upon
22:26 at the setting of the *s*
Le 22:7 *s* has set, he must also be
Nu 21:11 toward the rising of the *s*
25:4 expose them . . . toward the *s*
De 4:19 see the *s* and the moon and
4:41 toward the rising of the *s*
4:47 toward the rising of the *s*
16:6 evening as soon as the *s* sets
17:3 bow down to them or to the *s*
23:11 at the setting of the *s* he
24:13 to him as soon as the *s* sets
24:15 the *s* should not set upon
33:14 the products of the *s*
Jos 1:4 toward the setting of the *s*
1:15 toward the rising of the *s*
8:29 as the *s* was about to set
10:12 *S*, be motionless over
10:13 the *s* kept motionless, and
10:13 the *s* kept standing still
10:27 of the setting of the *s*
12:1 toward the rising of the *s*
13:5 toward the rising of the *s*
19:12 toward the rising of the *s*
Jos 19:27 toward the rising of the *s*
19:34 toward the rising of the *s*
23:4 Sea at the setting of the *s*
Jg 5:31 lovers be as when the *s* goes
9:33 as soon as the *s* shines forth
11:18 rising of the *s* as respects
19:14 the *s* began to set upon them
20:43 toward the rising of the *s*
1Sa 11:9 for you when the *s* gets hot
2Sa 2:24 As the *s* was setting they
3:35 before the *s* sets I shall
12:11 under the eyes of this *s*
12:12 and in front of the *s*
23:4 when the *s* shines forth
1Ki 22:36 about the setting of the *s*
2Ki 3:22 the *s* itself flashed upon
10:33 toward the rising of the *s*
23:5 to the *s* and to the moon
23:11 given to the *s* to cease
23:11 chariots of the *s* he burned
2Ch 18:34 of the setting of the *s*
Ne 7:3 opened until the *s* gets hot
Job 8:16 is full of sap before the *s*
9:7 the *s* that it should not shine
Ps 19:4 he has set a tent for the *s*
50:1 the rising of the *s* until its
58:8 certainly not behold the *s*
72:5 as long as there is a *s*
72:17 Before the *s* let his name
74:16 the luminary, even the *s*
84:11 God is a *s* and a shield
89:36 throne as the *s* in front of
104:19 *s* itself knows well where
104:22 *s* begins to shine—they
113:3 rising of the *s* until its
121:6 *s* itself will not strike
136:8 *s* for dominion by day
148:3 Praise him, you *s* and moon
Ec 1:3 he works hard under the *s*
1:5 the *s* also has flashed forth
1:5 *s* has set, and it is coming
1:9 is nothing new under the *s*
1:14 that were done under the *s*
2:11 of advantage under the *s*
2:17 that has been done under the *s*
2:18 was working hard under the *s*
2:19 I showed wisdom under the *s*
2:20 I had worked hard under the *s*
2:22 is working hard under the *s*
3:16 seen under the *s* the place of
4:1 that are being done under the *s*
4:3 that is being done under the *s*
4:7 see the vanity under the *s*
4:15 are walking about under the *s*
5:13 that I have seen under the *s*
5:18 he works hard under the *s* for
6:1 that I have seen under the *s*
6:5 the *s* itself he has not seen
6:12 happen after him under the *s*
7:11 for those seeing the *s*
8:9 that has been done under the *s*
8:15 nothing better under the *s*
8:15 has given them under the *s*
8:17 that has been done under the *s*
9:3 that has been done under the *s*
9:6 that has to be done under the *s*
9:9 He has given you under the *s*
9:9 are working hard under the *s*
9:11 I returned to see under the *s*
9:13 respects wisdom under the *s*
10:5 that I have seen under the *s*
11:7 good for the eyes to see the *s*
12:2 before the *s* and the light and
Ca 1:6 the *s* has caught sight of me
6:10 pure like the glowing *s*
Isa 13:10 *s* will actually grow dark
24:23 *s* has become ashamed, for
30:26 the light of the glowing *s*
30:26 light of the glowing *s* will
38:8 by the *s* retrace backward
38:8 the *s* gradually went back
41:25 From the rising of the *s* he
45:6 rising of the *s* and from its
49:10 parching heat or *s* strike
59:19 from the rising of the *s*
60:19 *s* will no more prove to be
60:20 No more will your *s* set
Jer 8:2 spread them out to the *s* and
15:9 *s* has set while it is yet
31:35 Giver of the *s* for light by
Eze 8:16 bowing down to the . . . *s*
32:7 the *s*, with clouds I shall
Da 6:14 till the setting of the *s* he
Joe 2:10 *S* and moon themselves have
2:31 *s* . . . turned into darkness
3:15 *S* and moon . . . become dark
Am 8:9 the *s* go down at high noon
Jon 4:8 as soon as the *s* shone forth
4:8 the *s* kept striking upon the
Mic 3:6 the *s* will certainly set upon
Na 3:17 The *s* itself has but to shine
Hab 3:11 *S*—moon—stood still, in the
Zec 8:7 land of the setting of the *s*
Mal 4:2 the *s* of righteousness will
Mt 5:45 *s* rise upon wicked people and
13:6 the *s* rose they were scorched
13:43 shine as brightly as the *s*
17:2 his face shone as the *s*, and
24:29 the *s* will be darkened, and
Mr 1:32 the *s* had set, the people
4:6 *s* rose, it was scorched, and
13:24 the *s* will be darkened, and
16:2 when the *s* had risen
Lu 4:40 when the *s* was setting, all
21:25 be signs in *s* and moon and
Ac 2:20 *s* will be turned into
26:13 the brilliance of the *s*
27:20 *s* nor stars appeared for
1Co 15:41 glory of the *s* is one sort
Eph 4:26 let the *s* not set with you
Jas 1:11 *s* rises with its burning
Re 1:16 his countenance was as the *s*
6:12 *s* became black as sackcloth
7:16 neither will the *s* beat down
8:12 a third of the *s* was smitten
9:2 and the *s* was darkened, also
10:1 and his face was as the *s*
12:1 woman arrayed with the *s*
16:8 poured . . . bowl upon the *s*
16:8 *s* it was granted to scorch
16:12 from the rising of the *s*
19:17 an angel standing in the *s*
21:23 city has no need of the *s*

Sung
Job 36:24 Of which men have *s*
Isa 26:1 *s* in the land of Judah

Sunk
Ex 15:4 have been *s* in the Red Sea
Job 28:4 *s* a shaft far from where
38:6 socket pedestals been *s* down
Ps 9:15 nations have *s* down into the
38:2 arrows have *s* themselves deep
69:2 I have *s* down in deep mire
La 2:9 Her gates have *s* down into the
Mt 18:6 to be *s* in the wide, open sea

Sunlight
Job 30:28 when there was no *s*
Lu 23:45 *s* failed; then the curtain
Ac 13:11 not seeing the *s* for a
Re 22:5 nor do they have *s*, because

Sunrise
Jos 12:1 all the Arabah toward the *s*
19:13 toward the *s* to Gath-hepher
Ps 103:12 as the *s* is from the sunset
107:3 the *s* and from the sunset
Isa 41:2 roused up someone from the *s*
Am 8:12 from north even to the *s*
Zec 8:7 from the land of the *s* and

Sunrising
Ex 27:13 the east side toward the *s*
38:13 east side toward the *s* there
Nu 2:3 eastward toward the *s* will be
3:38 toward the *s*, were Moses and
32:19 the Jordan toward the *s*
34:15 eastward toward the *s*
De 3:17 slopes of Pisgah toward the *s*
Isa 43:5 From the *s* I shall bring
46:11 from the *s* a bird of prey
Jer 31:40 Horse Gate toward the *s*
Da 8:9 *s* and toward the Decoration
11:44 reports . . . out of the *s* and
Zec 14:4 from the *s* and to the west
Re 7:2 angel ascending from the *s*

Sun's
Mal 1:11 from the *s* rising even to

Sunset
De 11:30 the direction of the *s*, in
Ps 103:12 the sunrise is from the *s*
107:3 the sunrise and from the *s*
Isa 43:5 from the *s* I shall collect
59:19 from the *s* they will begin
Da 8:5 goats coming from the *s* upon

Superabundantly
Eph 3:20 do more than s beyond all

Superciliousness
Ps 10:4 wicked one according to his s

Superfine
2Co 11:5 inferior to your s apostles
12:11 inferior to your s apostles

Superfluous
2Co 9:1 it is s for me to write you
Jas 1:21 and that s thing, badness

Superior
Ge 49:26 s to the blessings of the
Ex 17:11 Israelites proved s; but as
17:11 the Amalekites proved s
De 32:27 say: Our hand has proved s
1Sa 2:9 does a man prove s
2Sa 11:23 men proved s to us, so that
13:14 used strength s to hers and
1Ch 5:2 to be s among his brothers
2Ch 13:7 proved s to Rehoboam the son
13:18 Judah proved s because they
17:12 growing great to a s degree
Job 15:25 he tries to show himself s
21:7 also have become s in wealth
36:9 because they take a s air
Ps 9:19 man prove s in strength
103:11 loving-kindness is s toward
Zec 10:6 make the house of Judah s
10:12 make them s in Jehovah
Ro 13:1 to the s authorities, for
Php 2:3 that the others are s to you
2:9 exalted him to a s position
1Pe 2:13 whether to a king as being s

Superiority
Ex 15:7 in the abundance of your s
Job 37:4 with the sound of his s
40:10 Deck yourself . . . with s and
Ec 3:19 is no s of the man over the
Isa 2:10 and from his splendid s
2:19 and from his splendid s
2:21 and from his splendid s
24:14 In the s of Jehovah they
Am 8:7 Jehovah has sworn by the S of
Mic 5:4 the s of the name of Jehovah
Ro 3:1 is the s of the Jew, or what

Superlative
Ca 1:1 The s song, which is Solomon's

Supernatural
Lu 1:22 had just seen a s sight in
24:23 seen a s sight of angels
2Co 12:1 s visions and revelations

Supervisors
1Ch 23:4 s over the work of the house
Ezr 3:8 s over the work of the house
3:9 s over the doers of the work

Suph
De 1:1 the desert plains in front of S

Suphah
Nu 21:14 Vaheb in S and the torrent

Supplant
Ge 27:36 should s me these two times
Jer 9:4 brother would positively s

Supplanters
Ps 49:5 error of my s surrounds me

Supple
Ge 49:24 strength of his hands was s

Supplicate
Ac 8:22 s Jehovah that, if possible

Supplication
Ge 20:7 and he will make s for you
20:17 Abraham began to make s to
Nu 11:2 he made s to Jehovah, and the
De 9:20 s also in behalf of Aaron
9:26 to make s to Jehovah and to
Lu 1:13 your s has been favorably
21:36 all the time making s that
22:32 I have made s for you that
Ac 4:31 when they had made s, the
8:24 make s for me to Jehovah
10:2 made s to God continually
Ro 10:1 s to God for them are, indeed
2Co 1:11 help along by your s for us
9:14 and with s for you they long
Eph 6:18 every form of prayer and s
6:18 with s in behalf of all the
Php 1:4 in every s of mine for all
1:4 as I offer my s with joy
1:19 salvation through your s
4:6 s along with thanksgiving
Jas 5:16 A righteous man's s, when it
1Pe 3:12 his ears are toward their s

Supplications
Lu 2:37 with fastings and s
5:33 offer s, and so do those of
1Th 3:10 s to see your faces and to
1Ti 2:1 that s, prayers, intercessions
5:5 persists in s and prayers
2Ti 1:3 in my s, night and day
Heb 5:7 Christ offered up s and also

Supplied
2Sa 19:32 s the king with food while
1Ki 4:27 s food to King Solomon
18:4 he s them bread and water
20:27 they were mustered and s
Ac 12:20 country was s with food
2Co 11:9 abundantly s my deficiency
Col 2:19 all the body, being s and
2Pe 1:11 s to you the entrance into

Supplies
1Ki 5:11 food s for his household and
1Ch 27:27 vineyards for the wine s
27:28 the oil s there was Joash
2Ch 8:15 matter and concerning the s
11:11 s of food and oil and wine
Ezr 2:69 gave gold for the working s
Pr 6:8 food s even in the harvest
Isa 30:6 humps of camels their s
Lu 12:42 food s at the proper time
Ro 15:5 the God who s endurance and
2Co 9:10 he that abundantly s seed to
Ga 3:5 s you the spirit and performs
1Pe 4:11 the strength that God s

Supply
Ge 41:36 foodstuffs must serve as a s
45:11 I will s you with food there
De 28:8 blessing on your stores of s
2Sa 19:33 certainly s you with food
1Ki 17:4 command to s you food there
17:9 a widow, to s you food
Ne 10:34 the s of the wood that the
10:38 dining halls of the s house
13:31 even for the s of the wood
Pr 3:10 stores of s will be filled
15:16 an abundant s and confusion
22:16 to s many things to himself
Isa 33:16 water s will be unfailing
Zec 11:16 he will not s with food
Mt 26:53 appeal to my Father to s me
2Co 9:10 will s and multiply the seed
9:12 to s abundantly the wants of
Php 1:19 a s of the spirit of Jesus
4:19 God will fully s all your
Tit 3:13 s Zenas, who is versed in
2Pe 1:5 s to your faith virtue, to

Supplying
Ge 47:12 Joseph kept s his father and
50:21 shall keep s you and your
2Sa 20:3 he kept on s food to them
1Ki 18:13 kept s them bread and water

Support
Ge 27:37 I have bestowed for his s
Ex 21:19 upon some s of his, then the
De 32:36 see that s has disappeared
2Sa 22:19 But Jehovah became my s
2Ki 18:21 the s of this crushed reed
Job 24:23 that he may s himself
Ps 18:18 Jehovah came to be as a s
51:12 s me even with a willing
119:116 S me according to your
145:14 Jehovah is giving s to all
Isa 3:1 from Judah s and stay, the
3:1 whole s of bread and the
3:1 and the whole s of water
10:20 Jacob will never again s
10:20 s themselves upon Jehovah
30:12 and you s yourselves on it
36:6 s of this crushed reed, in
50:10 s himself upon his God
63:5 there was no one offering s
Eze 29:6 proved to be, as a s, a reed
Lu 23:51 not voted in s of their
1Th 5:14 s the weak, be long-suffering
1Ti 3:15 a pillar and s of the truth
2Ti 2:2 with the s of many witnesses

Supported
Ex 17:12 Aaron and Hur s his hands
Ps 71:6 Upon you I have s myself
111:8 Well s forever, to time
Isa 26:3 inclination that is well s
48:2 they have s themselves
59:16 was the thing that s him
63:5 and my rage was what s me
Eze 29:7 they s themselves upon you
Am 5:19 s his hand against the wall

Supporter
Ge 28:11 set it as his head s and lay
28:18 stone . . . as his head s

Supporters
Eze 30:6 s of Egypt must also fall
Ac 11:2 s of circumcision began to

Supporting
2Sa 1:6 Saul s himself upon his spear
2Ki 5:18 he is s himself upon my hand
7:2 the king was s himself
7:17 upon whose hand he was s
Ps 3:5 Jehovah himself keeps s me
37:17 will be s the righteous ones
37:24 For Jehovah is s his hand
54:4 Jehovah is among those s my
Mic 3:11 upon Jehovah they keep s
Zec 10:4 the s ruler, out of him is
1Jo 3:17 world's means for s life

Supports
Ex 25:27 s for the poles to carry the
26:29 rings . . . as s for the bars
30:4 must serve as s for the poles
36:34 rings of gold as s for the
37:14 s for the poles for carrying
37:27 s for the poles with which
38:5 of copper, as s for the poles
1Sa 2:8 to Jehovah belong earth's s
1Ki 7:30 four cornerpieces were s for
7:30 Beneath the basin were the s
7:31 from inside to the s and
7:32 the s of the wheels were by
7:33 Their s and their felloes and
7:34 And there were four s upon
7:34 its s were of one piece with
10:12 s for the house of Jehovah
Ca 3:10 its s of gold. Its seat is of

Suppose
Ge 18:24 S there are fifty righteous
18:28 S the fifty righteous should
18:29 S forty are found there
18:30 S thirty are found there
18:31 S twenty are found there
18:32 S ten are found there
Ex 3:13 S I am now come to the sons
4:1 s they do not believe me and
8:26 S we would sacrifice a thing
Lu 7:43 I s it is the one to whom he
Joh 21:25 I s, the world itself could
Ac 2:15 not drunk, as you s, for it
13:25 What do you s I am?
Jas 1:7 man s that he will receive

Supposed
Ac 12:9 he s he was seeing a vision
25:18 I had s concerning him

Supposing
Nu 22:33 S she had not turned aside
Ec 6:6 s that he has lived a thousand
Joh 11:31 s that she was going to the
Ac 7:25 s his brothers would grasp
Php 1:17 are s to stir up tribulation

Suppressed
Isa 25:5 tyrannical ones becomes s

Suppressing
Ro 1:18 men who are s the truth in

Supreme
Da 7:18 holy ones of the S One will
7:22 holy ones of the S One, and
7:25 holy ones . . . of the S One
7:27 the holy ones of the S One
Mt 5:22 accountable to the S Court

Sure
Ge 15:13 You may know for s that your
24:5 Must I be s to return your
50:15 be s to repay us for all the
De 28:66 will not be s of your life
Jg 11:20 Sihon did not feel s about
Ru 2:16 be s to pull out some from

Ru 3:13 as *s* as Jehovah lives
1Sa 2:16 be *s* to make the fat smoke
19:3 I shall be *s* to tell you
Job 24:22 and not be *s* of his life
Ps 9:12 *s* not to forget the outcry of
Isa 12:1 *s* to say: I shall thank you
28:16 corner of a *s* foundation
Da 4:26 kingdom will be *s* to you
Lu 1:18 How am I to be *s* of this?
14:33 you may be *s*, none of you
14:34 Salt, to be *s*, is fine
Joh 20:30 To be *s*, Jesus performed
Ac 22:30 he desired to know for *s*
Ro 4:16 promise to be *s* to all his
8:13 the flesh you are *s* to die
Eph 5:10 Keep on making *s* of what is
Php 1:10 *s* of the more important
1:23 this, to be *s*, is far better
1Th 2:1 To be *s*, you yourselves know
5:21 Make *s* of all things; hold
1Ti 6:6 To be *s*, it is a means of
Heb 6:19 hope . . . both *s* and firm
2Pe 1:10 calling and choosing of you *s*
1:19 prophetic word made more *s*

Surely
Ge 18:10 I am *s* going to return to
18:18 Abraham is *s* going to become
22:17 I shall *s* bless you and I
22:17 I shall *s* multiply your seed
26:11 will *s* be put to death
37:33 Joseph is *s* torn to pieces
43:20 We *s* did come down at the
44:28 he must *s* be torn to pieces!
46:4 shall *s* bring you up also
Ex 2:14 *S* the thing has become known!
18:18 You will *s* wear out, both
Nu 13:30 we can *s* prevail over it
De 15:14 You should *s* equip him with
Jg 8:25 We shall *s* give them
1Sa 16:6 *S* his anointed one is before
20:3 father must *s* know that I
23:22 he himself is *s* cunning
2Sa 17:10 *s* soften in weakness
1Ki 22:32 *S* it is the king of Israel
Job 23:6 *S* he himself would pay heed
31:36 *S* upon my shoulder I would
32:8 *S* it is the spirit in mortal
Ps 23:6 *S* goodness and loving-kindness
31:22 *S* you have heard the voice
39:5 *S* every earthling man, though
39:6 *S* in a semblance man walks
39:6 *S* they are boisterous in vain
39:11 *S* every earthling man is an
58:11 *S* there is fruitage for the
58:11 *S* there exists a God that is
73:13 *S* it is in vain that I have
73:18 *S* on slippery ground is
75:8 *s* its dregs will be poured
82:7 *S* you will die just as men do
85:9 *S* his salvation is near to
131:2 *S* I have soothed and quieted
139:11 *S* darkness itself will
140:13 *S* the righteous themselves
Pr 11:23 righteous ones is *s* good
21:5 plans of the diligent one *s*
21:5 hasty *s* heads for want
22:16 is *s* destined for want
23:28 *S* she, just like a robber
Isa 8:20 *S* they will keep saying what
14:24 *S* just as I have figured
40:7 *S* the people are green grass
45:24 *S* in Jehovah there are full
63:8 *S* they are my people, sons
Jer 2:35 *S* his anger has turned back
5:4 *S* they are of low class
5:5 *S* they themselves must have
8:8 *S*, now, the false stylus of
10:19 *S* this is my sickness and
15:11 *S* I will minister to you
15:11 *S* I will intercede for you
49:20 *S* the little ones of the
49:20 *S* on account of them he
50:45 *S* the little ones of the
50:45 *S* on account of them he
Eze 5:11 *s* for the reason that it was
17:19 As I am alive, *s* my oath
33:27 *s* the ones who are in the
34:8 *s* for the reason that my
35:6 *S* it was blood that you
38:19 *S* in that day a great
Zep 3:7 I said, *S* you will fear me
Ac 28:4 *S* this man is a murderer
Ga 3:7 *S* you know that those who

Surety
Ge 43:9 I shall be the one to be *s* for
44:32 slave became *s* for the boy
Ps 119:122 Act as a *s* for your servant
Pr 6:1 have gone *s* for your fellowman
11:15 has gone *s* for a stranger
17:18 full *s* before his companion
20:16 one has gone *s* for a stranger
27:13 one has gone *s* for a stranger

Surface
Ge 1:2 upon the *s* of the watery deep
1:2 over the *s* of the waters
1:29 vegetation . . . on the *s* of
2:6 it watered the entire *s* of the
4:14 from off the *s* of the ground
6:1 on the *s* of the ground and
6:7 off the *s* of the ground
7:3 on the *s* of the entire earth
7:4 off the *s* of the ground
7:18 ark kept going on the *s* of
7:23 *s* of the ground, from man to
8:8 waters had abated from the *s*
8:9 waters were yet upon the *s* of
8:13 *s* of the ground had drained
11:4 scattered over all the *s* of
11:8 over all the *s* of the earth
11:9 over all the *s* of the earth
41:56 over all the *s* of the earth
Ex 10:5 the visible *s* of the earth
10:15 visible *s* of the entire land
16:14 upon the *s* of the wilderness
30:3 its top *s* and its sides round
32:12 from the *s* of the ground
32:20 scattered it upon the *s* of
33:16 upon the *s* of the ground
37:26 its top *s* and its sides round
Le 14:37 is lower than the wall *s*
Nu 11:31 above the *s* of the earth
12:3 upon the *s* of the ground
De 6:15 from off the *s* of the ground
7:6 that are on the *s* of the ground
14:2 on the *s* of the ground
1Sa 14:25 over all the *s* of the field
20:15 from the *s* of the ground
30:16 over the *s* of all the land
2Sa 14:7 on the *s* of the ground
1Ki 8:40 *s* of the ground that you
9:7 upon the *s* of the ground
13:34 off the *s* of the ground
17:14 upon the *s* of the ground
18:1 rain upon the *s* of the ground
2Ch 6:31 *s* of the ground that you gave
34:4 *s* of the burial places of
Job 5:10 rain upon the *s* of the earth
24:18 on the *s* of the waters
38:30 the *s* of the watery deep
Pr 24:31 Nettles covered its very *s*
Ec 11:1 upon the *s* of the waters
Isa 18:2 upon the *s* of the waters
19:8 upon the *s* of the water
23:17 upon the *s* of the ground
27:6 fill the *s* of the productive
28:25 he has smoothed out its *s*
Jer 16:4 upon the *s* of the ground
25:26 are on the *s* of the ground
25:33 As manure on the *s* of the
27:5 upon the *s* of the earth
28:16 off the *s* of the ground
35:7 *s* of the ground where you
Eze 16:5 upon the *s* of the field
24:7 bare *s* of a crag she placed
24:8 shining, bare *s* of a crag
26:4 shining, bare *s* of a crag
26:14 shining, bare *s* of a crag
29:5 *s* of the field you will fall
32:4 Upon the *s* of the field I
33:27 upon the *s* of the field
34:6 on all the *s* of the earth
37:2 on the *s* of the valley plain
38:20 upon the *s* of the ground
39:5 Upon the *s* of the field
39:14 on the *s* of the earth
Da 8:5 upon the *s* of the whole earth
Ho 10:7 twig on the *s* of waters
Am 5:8 out upon the *s* of the earth
9:6 out upon the *s* of the earth
9:8 upon the *s* of the ground
Zep 1:2 off the *s* of the ground
1:3 from the *s* of the ground
Zec 5:3 over the *s* of all the earth
Ac 17:26 the entire *s* of the earth

Surging
Ex 15:5 *s* waters proceeded to cover
15:8 The *s* waters were congealed
Ps 33:7 in storehouses the *s* waters
Isa 63:13 walk through the *s* waters

Surname
Mr 3:16 Simon . . . the *s* Peter
3:17 gave these the *s* Boanerges

Surnamed
Ac 1:23 Barsabbas, who was *s* Justus
4:36 Joseph, who was *s* Barnabas
10:5 Simon who is *s* Peter
10:18 Simon who was *s* Peter was
10:32 for Simon, who is *s* Peter
11:13 for Simon who is *s* Peter
12:12 of John who was *s* Mark
12:25 John, the one *s* Mark

Surpassed
1Ki 10:7 *s* in wisdom and prosperity
2Ch 9:6 *s* the report that I have heard

Surpasses
Eph 3:19 which *s* knowledge, that you

Surpassing
1Co 12:31 And yet I show you a *s* way
2Co 4:17 and more *s* weight and is
9:14 the *s* undeserved kindness of
Eph 1:19 *s* greatness of his power is
2:7 *s* riches of his undeserved

Surpassingly
1Ch 22:5 *s* magnificent for beauteous
29:25 to make Solomon *s* great
2Ch 1:1 and kept making him *s* great
Isa 12:5 Jehovah, for he has done *s*

Surplus
Ex 16:18 had gathered much had no *s*
16:23 all the *s* that there is save
2Ch 31:10 and having a *s* in abundance
Mt 14:20 took up the *s* of fragments
15:37 *s* of fragments they took up
Mr 12:44 dropped in out of their *s*
Lu 9:17 the *s* that they had was taken
21:4 gifts out of their *s*, but
2Co 8:14 an equalizing your *s* just
8:14 *s* might also come to offset

Surpluses
Mr 8:8 they took up *s* of fragments

Surprise
Jos 10:9 come against them by *s*
11:7 by *s* and to fall upon them
Mt 19:25 they expressed very great *s*
Mr 10:24 the disciples gave way to *s*

Surprised
Lu 11:38 the Pharisee was *s* at seeing
Ac 3:11 *s* out of their wits

Surrender
Jos 20:5 not *s* the manslayer into
1Sa 17:46 Jehovah will *s* you into my
23:11 landowners of Keilah *s* me
23:12 *s* me and my men into Saul's
23:20 *s* him into the hand of the
30:15 not *s* me into the hand of
Joh 10:15 I *s* my soul in behalf of
10:17 I *s* my soul, in order that
10:18 I *s* it of my own initiative
10:18 I have authority to *s* it
13:37 *s* my soul in your behalf
13:38 *s* your soul in my behalf
15:13 *s* his soul in behalf of his
1Jo 3:16 *s* our souls for our brothers

Surrendered
De 32:30 And Jehovah had *s* them
1Sa 24:18 Jehovah *s* me into your hand
26:8 God has today *s* your enemy
2Sa 18:28 *s* the men that lifted up
Ps 31:8 *s* me into the hand of the
La 2:7 *s* the walls of her dwelling
Lu 23:25 but he *s* Jesus to their will
1Jo 3:16 that one *s* his soul for us

Surrendering
1Sa 23:12 They will do the *s*

Surrenders
Joh 10:11 fine shepherd *s* his soul in

Surround
Jos 7:9 *s* us and cut our name off
Jg 20:5 to *s* the house against me by
Job 40:22 The poplars . . . *s* it
Ps 5:12 with approval you will *s*
7:7 national groups *s* you

Ps 32:7 you will *s* me. *Se'lah*
71:21 may you *s* and comfort me
1Co 12:23 these we *s* with more

Surrounded
Ge 19:4 the men of Sodom, *s* the house
Jg 16:2 they *s* him and lay in wait
19:22 *s* the house, shoving one
20:43 They *s* Benjamin
2Sa 22:6 The ropes of Sheol . . . *s* me
1Ki 5:3 warfare with which they *s* him
Ps 17:11 now they have *s* us
18:5 The very ropes of Sheol *s* me
22:12 Many young bulls have *s* me
22:16 For dogs have *s* me
88:17 *s* me like waters all day
109:3 of hatred they have *s* me
118:10 the nations themselves *s* me
118:11 They *s* me, yes, they had
118:11 yes, they had me *s*
118:12 They *s* me like bees
119:61 of the wicked ones *s* me
Ec 9:14 he *s* it and built against it
Ho 7:2 their dealings have *s* them
11:12 Ephraim has *s* me, and with
Lu 21:20 Jerusalem *s* by encamped
Ac 14:20 when the disciples *s* him
Heb 5:2 is *s* with his own weakness

Surrounding
2Ki 6:15 was *s* the city with horses
8:21 Edomites that were *s* him
2Ch 4:3 under it clear around, *s* it
21:9 Edomites that were *s* him and
Ps 140:9 the heads of those *s* me
Eze 43:14 lower *s* ledge there are
43:14 from the small *s* ledge to
43:14 to the big *s* ledge there
43:17 *s* ledge is fourteen cubits
43:17 border *s* it is half a cubit
43:20 corners of the *s* ledge and
45:19 *s* ledge belonging to the
Hab 1:4 wicked one is *s* the righteous
Mt 14:35 into all that *s* country
Lu 4:14 through all the *s* country
4:37 every corner of the *s* country
7:17 Judea and all the *s* country
8:37 from the *s* country of the
Heb 12:1 cloud of witnesses *s* us, let

Surroundings
Nu 22:4 lick up all our *s* like the
2Ki 23:5 the *s* of Jerusalem, and also
Jer 32:44 and in the *s* of Jerusalem
33:13 and in the *s* of Jerusalem
50:32 it must devour all its *s*
Eze 34:26 the *s* of my hill a blessing

Surrounds
Ps 32:10 loving-kindness itself *s* him
49:5 error of my supplanters *s* me

Survive
Nu 24:23 Who will *s* when God causes
Jos 10:20 those who did *s* of them
1Th 4:15 *s* to the presence of the Lord

Surviving
Ge 7:23 in the ark kept on *s*
1Th 4:17 we the living who are *s*

Survivor
Nu 21:35 there was no *s* remaining to
24:19 destroy any *s* from the city
De 2:34 We left no *s*
3:3 until he had no *s* remaining
Jos 8:22 either a *s* or an escapee
10:28 He let no *s* remain. So he
10:30 did not let a *s* remain in
10:33 let not a *s* of his remain
10:37 He did not let a *s* remain
10:39 He did not let a *s* remain
10:40 He did not let a *s* remain
11:8 not let a *s* of theirs remain
2Ki 10:11 had let no *s* of his remain
Job 18:19 no *s* in his place of alien
20:26 It will go badly with a *s*
Jer 42:17 not come to have a *s* or
44:14 *s* for the remnant of Judah
47:4 every *s* that was helping
La 2:22 proved to be no escapee or *s*
Ob 18 And there will prove to be no *s*

Survivors
Jg 5:13 *s* came down to the majestic
Job 27:15 His own *s* will be buried
Isa 1:9 remaining to us just a few *s*
Jer 31:2 *s* from the sword found favor

Joe 2:32 among the *s*, whom Jehovah
Ob 14 ought not to hand over his *s* in

Susa
Ezr 4:9 the inhabitants of *S*, that is

Susanna
Lu 8:3 *S* and many other women, who

Susi
Nu 13:11 Gaddi the son of *S*

Suspect
Nu 5:30 *s* his wife of unfaithfulness
Ac 27:27 sailors began to *s* they

Suspended
Le 26:26 ring-shaped loaves are *s*, ten
Ps 105:16 ring-shaped loaves were *s*
Eze 4:16 ring-shaped loaves are *s*, in
5:16 ring-shaped loaves are *s*
14:13 which ring-shaped loaves are *s*
Lu 17:2 *s* from his neck and he were

Suspense
Lu 12:29 and quit being in anxious *s*
Joh 10:24 you to keep our souls in *s*

Suspicions
1Ti 6:4 abusive speeches, wicked *s*

Suspicious
Nu 5:14 *s* of his wife's faithfulness
5:14 *s* of his wife's faithfulness

Suspiciously
1Sa 18:9 looking *s* at David from that

Sustain
Ge 36:7 land . . . not able to *s* them
Le 25:35 you must also *s* him
Jg 19:5 *S* your heart with a bit of
Ps 18:35 own right hand will *s* me
20:2 And *s* you out of Zion itself
41:3 *s* him upon a divan of illness
55:22 And he himself will *s* you
119:117 *S* me, that I may be saved
Ca 2:5 *s* me with apples; for I am
Isa 9:7 *s* it by means of justice and

Sustained
Pr 20:28 he has *s* his throne
Ac 27:21 have *s* this damage and loss

Sustaining
Ps 94:18 O Jehovah, kept *s* me

Sustains
Ps 104:15 *s* the very heart of mortal
112:5 *s* his affairs with justice
Heb 1:3 *s* all things by the word of

Sustenance
Ge 45:23 bread and *s* for his father
Ex 21:10 her *s*, her clothing and her
Jg 6:4 would not let any *s* or sheep
17:10 shall give you . . . your *s*
19:8 Please, take *s* for your heart
1Ki 13:7 to the house and take *s* and
Ps 78:20 he prepare *s* for his people
78:27 *s* rain upon them just like
1Ti 6:8 So, having *s* and covering

Swaddled
Eze 16:4 by no means had you been *s*

Swaddling
Job 38:9 thick gloom as its *s* band

Swallow
Ge 25:30 give me a *s* of the red—the
41:7 to *s* up the seven fat and full
41:24 *s* up the seven good ears of
Ex 15:12 earth proceeded to *s* them up
Nu 16:30 and *s* up them and everything
16:32 and to *s* up them and their
16:34 that the earth may *s* us up
De 11:6 to *s* them up and their
2Sa 20:19 *s* up the inheritance of
20:20 that I should *s* up and that
Job 2:3 to *s* him up without cause
7:19 alone until I *s* my saliva
10:8 and yet you would *s* me up
20:18 and will not *s* it down
Ps 21:9 in his anger will *s* them up
69:15 Nor the depth *s* me up
84:3 the *s* a nest for herself
Pr 1:12 *s* them down alive just like
21:20 man that is stupid will *s* it
26:2 and just as a *s* for flying, so
Ec 10:12 lips of the stupid one *s* him
Isa 25:7 *s* up the face of the

Isa 25:8 *s* up death forever, and the
La 2:16 said: We will *s* her down
Ho 8:7 strangers themselves will *s* it
Jon 1:17 a great fish to *s* Jonah

Swallowed
Ex 7:12 Aaron's rod *s* up their rods
Nu 26:10 earth . . . *s* them up
2Sa 17:16 the king . . . may be *s* up
Job 20:15 Wealth he has *s* down, but
Ps 35:25 not say: We have *s* him up
106:17 opened up and *s* down Dathan
124:3 have *s* us up even alive
Pr 18:8 like things to be *s* greedily
26:22 like things to be *s* greedily
Jer 51:34 *s* me down like a big snake
51:44 his mouth what he has *s*
La 2:2 Jehovah has *s* up, he has shown
2:5 Jehovah . . . has *s* down Israel
2:5 He has *s* down all her dwelling
Ho 8:8 Israel must be *s* down
1Co 15:54 Death is *s* up forever
2Co 2:7 *s* up by his being overly sad
5:4 mortal may be *s* up by life
Heb 11:29 the Egyptians were *s* up
Re 12:16 *s* up the river that the

Swallowing
Isa 49:19 those *s* you down have been
La 2:8 turned back his hand from *s* up

Swallows
Job 8:18 one *s* him up from his place
39:24 it *s* up the earth
Pr 19:28 *s* down what is hurtful
Isa 28:4 in his palm, he *s* it down
Hab 1:13 when someone wicked *s* up

Swamped
Mr 4:37 the boat was close to being *s*

Swampy
Job 8:11 grow tall without a *s* place
40:21 reeds and the *s* place
Eze 47:11 There are its *s* places and

Swan
Le 11:18 and the *s* and the pelican
De 14:16 long-eared owl and the *s*

Swarm
Ge 1:20, 20 waters *s* forth a *s* of
8:17 they must *s* in the earth and
9:7 become many, make the earth *s*
Ex 1:7 fruitful and began to *s*; and
Le 11:29 swarming creatures that *s*
11:42 swarming creatures that *s*
Jg 14:8 was a *s* of bees in the lion's
Am 7:1 he was forming a locust *s* at
Na 3:17 officers like the locust *s*

Swarmed
Ge 1:21 which the waters *s* forth
Ps 105:30 Their land *s* with frogs

Swarming
Ge 7:21 all the swarms that were *s*
Le 5:2 body of an unclean *s* creature
11:10 every *s* creature of the
11:20 *s* creature that goes on all
11:21 the winged *s* creatures that
11:23 other winged *s* creature that
11:29 to you among the *s* creatures
11:31 among all the *s* creatures
11:41 every *s* creature that swarms
11:42 the *s* creatures that swarm
11:43 any *s* creature that swarms
11:44 any *s* creature that moves
22:5 *s* thing that is unclean for
De 14:19 every winged *s* creature is

Swarms
Ge 7:21 and among all the *s* that
Ex 8:24 heavy *s* of gadflies began to
Le 11:41 swarming creature that *s*
11:43 swarming creature that *s*
11:46 soul that *s* upon the earth
Isa 33:4 onrush of locust *s* that is
Eze 47:9 every living soul that *s*

Swarthy
Ca 1:6 you look at me because I am *s*

Sway
Am 2:13 making what is under you *s*

Swayed
1Sa 14:16 turmoil *s* this way and that
Ps 109:24 knees themselves have *s*
Isa 24:20 *s* to and fro like a lookout

Le 26:33 unsheathe a s after you; and
26:36 flee as in flight from a s
26:37 as if from before a s
Nu 14:3 to this land to fall by the s
14:43 are certain to fall by the s
19:16 someone slain with the s or
20:18 out with the s to meet you
21:24 with the edge of the s and
22:23 with his drawn s in his hand
22:29 there were a s in my hand
22:31 with his drawn s in his hand
31:8 killed Balaam . . . with the s
De 13:15 with the edge of the s
13:15 at the edge of the s
20:13 with the edge of the s
28:22 s and scorching and mildew
32:25 a s will bereave them, And
32:41 sharpen my glittering s
32:42 While my s will eat flesh
33:29 One who is your eminent s
Jos 5:13 with his drawn s in his hand
6:21 by the edge of the s
8:24 by the edge of the s until
8:24 with the edge of the s
10:11 Israel killed with the s
10:28 with the edge of the s
10:30 it with the edge of the s
10:32 with the edge of the s
10:35 with the edge of the s
10:37 with the edge of the s
10:39 with the edge of the s and
11:10 he struck down with the s
11:11 with the edge of the s
11:12 with the edge of the s
11:14 with the edge of the s
13:22 killed with the s along
19:47 with the edge of the s
24:12 not with your s and not
Jg 1:8 with the edge of the s, and
1:25 city with the edge of the s
3:16 Ehud made a s for himself
3:21 Ehud . . . took the s off his
3:22 he did not draw the s out of
4:15 by the edge of the s before
4:16 fell by the edge of the s
7:14 s of Gideon the son of Joash
7:20 Jehovah's s and Gideon's!
7:22 the s of each one against the
8:10 men who used to draw the s
8:20 did not draw his s, because
9:54 Draw your s and put me to
18:27 with the edge of the s, and
20:2 men on foot who drew the s
20:15 men drawing s, apart from
20:17 thousand men drawing s
20:25 all of these drawing s
20:35 all of these drawing s
20:37 city with the edge of the s
20:46 drawing s, all . . . valiant
20:48 with the edge of the s those
21:10 with the edge of the s, even
1Sa 2:33 will all die by the s of men
13:19 Hebrews may not make a s
13:22 that not a s or a spear was
14:20 the s of each one had come
15:8 with the edge of the s
15:33 Just as your s has bereaved
17:39 David girded his s on over
17:45 coming to me with a s and
17:47 neither with s nor with
17:50 was no s in David's hand
17:51 took his s and pulled it out
18:4 even his s and his bow and
21:8 disposal, a spear or a s
21:8 own s nor my weapons did I
21:9 s of Goliath the Philistine
22:10 s of Goliath the Philistine
22:13 giving him bread and a s
22:19 with the edge of the s
22:19 with the edge of the s
25:13 Gird on every one his s!
25:13 girded on every one his s
25:13 girded on his own s
31:4 Draw your s and run me
31:4 Saul took the s and fell
31:5 fell upon his own s and died
2Sa 1:12 they had fallen by the s
1:22 s of Saul would not return
2:16 s of each one in the side of
2:26 s going to eat endlessly
3:29 one falling by the s or one
11:25 s eats up one as well as
12:9 you struck down with the s
2Sa 12:9 s of the sons of Ammon
12:10 s will not depart from your
15:14 city with the edge of the s
18:8 than the s did in eating
20:8 a s attached to his hip
20:10 s that was in Joab's hand
21:16 was girded with a new s
23:10 hand kept cleaving to the s
24:9 valiant men drawing s, and
1Ki 1:51 servant to death by the s
2:8 put you to death by the s
2:32 to kill them with the s
3:24 You men, get me a s
3:24 brought the s before the king
19:1 all the prophets with the s
19:10 killed with the s, so that
19:14 they have killed with the s
19:17 escaping from Hazael's s
19:17 one escaping from Jehu's s
2Ki 3:23 been put to the s, and they
3:26 drawing s to break through
6:22 taken captive with your s
8:12 you will kill with the s
10:25 with the edge of the s and
11:15 of death with the s
11:20 put to death with the s at
19:7 by the s in his own land
19:37 struck him down with the s
1Ch 5:18 men carrying shield and s
10:4 Draw your s and run me
10:4 Saul took the s and fell upon
10:5 too fell upon the s and died
21:5 thousand men drawing s, and
21:5 thousand men drawing s
21:12 the s of your enemies to
21:12 is to be the s of Jehovah
21:16 his drawn s in his hand
21:27 angel . . . returned his s to
21:30 the s of Jehovah's angel
2Ch 20:9 s, adverse judgment, or
21:4 all his brothers with the s
23:14 put to death with the s
23:21 had put to death with the s
29:9 forefathers fell by the s
32:21 felled him with the s
36:17 their young men with the s
36:20 those remaining from the s
Ezr 9:7 kings of the lands with the s
Ne 4:18 with his s upon his hip
Es 9:5 with a slaughter by the s and
Job 1:15 with the edge of the s
1:17 with the edge of the s
5:15 One saving from the s out of
5:20 from the power of a s
15:22 And he is reserved for a s
19:29 Be frightened . . . of a s
19:29 s means a raging against
27:14 it is for a s
39:22 turn back on account of a s
40:19 Maker can bring near his s
41:26 the s itself does not prove
Ps 7:12 His s he will sharpen
17:13 with your s
22:20 deliver from the s my soul
37:14 wicked ones have drawn a s
37:15 own s will enter into their
44:3 not by their own s that they
44:6 not my s that was saving me
45:3 Gird your s upon your thigh
57:4 And whose tongue is a sharp s
63:10 over to the power of the s
64:3 their tongue just like a s
76:3 shield and the s and the
78:62 his people to the s itself
78:64 they fell by the very s
89:43 again treat his s as a foe
144:10 free from the injurious s
149:6 two-edged s be in their hand
Pr 5:4 is as sharp as a two-edged s
12:18 as with the stabs of a s
25:18 As a war club and a s and a
Ca 3:8 in possession of a s, being
3:8 with his s upon his thigh
Isa 1:20 with a s you will be eaten
2:4 Nation will not lift up s
3:25 By the s your own men will
13:15 will fall by the s
14:19 men stabbed with the s that
21:15 because of the drawn s
22:2 not those slain with the s
27:1 great and strong s, will
31:8 Assyrian must fall by the s
31:8 s, not that of earthling man
31:8 flee because of the s, and
Isa 34:5 s will certainly be drenched
34:6 Jehovah has a s; it must be
37:7 fall by the s in his own
37:38 struck him down with the s
41:2 them like dust to his s
49:2 my mouth like a sharp s
51:19 breakdown, and hunger and s
65:12 destine you men to the s
66:16 his s, against all flesh
Jer 2:30 Your s has devoured your
4:10 the s has reached clear to
5:12 no s or famine shall we see
5:17 will shatter with the s your
6:25 the s belonging to the enemy
9:16 I will send after them the s
11:22 will die by the s
12:12 the s belonging to Jehovah
14:12 by the s and by famine and
14:13 You will see no s, and
14:15 no s or famine will occur
14:15 By s and by famine those
14:16 the famine and the s, with
14:18 those slain by the s
15:2 And whoever is for the s
15:2 to the s! And whoever is for
15:3 the s to kill, and the dogs
15:9 to the s I shall give the
16:4 by the s and by famine they
18:21 over to the power of the s
18:21 struck down with the s
19:7 cause them to fall by the s
20:4 by the s of their enemies
20:4 strike them down with the s
21:7 the s and from the famine
21:7 with the edge of the s
21:9 will die by the s and by
24:10 send against them the s
25:16 because of the s that I am
25:27 the s that I am sending
25:29 s that I am calling against
25:31 he must give them to the s
25:38 the maltreating s and
26:23 struck him down with the s
27:8 the s and with the famine
27:13 your people die by the s
29:17 sending against them the s
29:18 after them with the s
31:2 survivors from the s found
32:24 s and the famine and the
32:36 king of Babylon by the s
33:4 and on account of the s
34:4 You will not die by the s
34:17 to the s, to the pestilence
38:2 one that will die by the s
39:18 by the s you will not fall
41:2 struck down . . . with the s
42:16 s of which you are afraid
42:17 ones to die by the s, by
42:22 know that by the s, by the
43:11 is due for the s will be
43:11 will be for the s
44:12 They will fall by the s
44:12 by the s and by the famine
44:13 Jerusalem, with the s
44:18 by the s and by the famine
44:27 their finish by the s and
44:28 ones escaping from the s
46:10 s will certainly devour and
46:14 s will certainly devour all
46:16 of the maltreating s
47:6 Aha, the s of Jehovah!
48:2 After you there walks a s
48:10 holding back his s from
49:37 send after them the s until
50:16 the maltreating s
50:35 s against the Chaldeans, is
50:36 s against the empty talkers
50:36 s against her mighty men
50:37 s against their horses and
50:37 s against her treasures
51:50 escapees from the s, keep
La 1:20 the s caused bereavement of
2:21 fallen by the s. You have
4:9 have those slain with the s
5:9 of the s of the wilderness
Eze 5:1 take for yourself a sharp s
5:2 You will strike it with the s
5:2 I shall draw out a s itself
5:12 third—by the s they will
5:12 a s is what I shall draw out
5:17 a s I shall bring in upon you
6:3 I am bringing upon you a s
6:8 the ones escaping from the s

Eze 6:11 by the s, by the famine and
6:12 nearby, by the s he will
7:15 The s is outside, and the
7:15 field, by the s he will die
11:8 A s you have feared, and a
11:8 a s I shall bring upon you
11:10 By the s you will fall
12:14 a s I shall draw out after
12:16 a few men from the s, from
14:17 s that I should bring upon
14:17 Let a s itself pass through
14:21 acts of judgment—s and
17:21 by the s they will fall
21:3 my s out of its sheath and
21:4 my s will go forth from its
21:5 my s from its sheath
21:9, 9 A s, a s! It has been
21:11 a s has been sharpened, and
21:12 ones hurled to the s have
21:14 and A s! should be repeated
21:14 The s of the slain ones it
21:14 the s of someone slain who
21:15 make a slaughter by the s
21:19 s of the king of Babylon
21:20 s to enter against Rabbah
21:28, 28 A s, a s drawn for a
23:10 her they killed even with s
23:25 will fall even by the s
24:21 by the s they will fall
25:13 By the s they will fall
26:6 by the s they will be killed
26:8 will kill even with the s
26:11 will kill even with the s
28:23 s against her on every side
29:8 I am bringing upon you a s
30:4 s will certainly come into
30:5 will fall by the very s
30:6 fall in it even by the s
30:17 by the s they will fall
30:21 strong to take hold of the s
30:22 s to fall out of his hand
30:24 give my s into his hand
30:25 s into the hand of the king
31:17 to those slain by the s
31:18 with those slain by the s
32:10 brandish my s in their
32:11 The very s of the king of
32:20 those slain by the s they
32:20 To a s she has been given
32:21 slain by the s
32:22 those falling by the s
32:23 slain, falling by the s
32:24 those falling by the s, who
32:25 slain by the s, because
32:26 pierced through by the s
32:28 with those slain by the s
32:29 with those slain by the s
32:30 with those slain by the s
32:31 people slain by the s
32:32 with those slain by the s
33:2 in case I bring upon it a s
33:3 the s coming upon the land
33:4 s comes and takes him away
33:6 in case he sees the s coming
33:6 a s comes and takes away
33:26 have depended upon your s
33:27 will fall by the s itself
35:5 over to the power of the s
35:8 slain by the s will fall in
38:8 people brought back from the s
38:21 mountainous region a s
38:21 the s of each one will
39:23 kept falling . . . by the s
Da 11:33 stumble by s and by flame
Ho 1:7 save them by a bow or by a s
2:18 s and war I shall break out
7:16 By the s their princes will
11:6 a s will certainly whirl
13:16 By the s they will fall
Am 1:11 his own brother with the s
4:10 With the s I killed your
7:9 against . . . Jeroboam with a s
7:11 By the s Jeroboam will die
7:17 by the s they will fall
9:1 I shall kill with the s itself
9:4 there I shall command the s
9:10 By the s they will die—all
Mic 4:3 lift up s, nation against
5:6 land of Assyria with the s
6:14 I shall give to the s itself
Na 2:13 a s will devour your own
3:3 the flame of the s, and the
3:15 A s will cut you off. It will
Zep 2:12 be people slain by my s
Hag 2:22 by the s of his brother
Zec 9:13 as the s of a mighty man
11:17 A s will be upon his arm
13:7 O s, awake against my
Mt 10:34 to put, not peace, but a s
26:51 drew his s and struck the
26:52 Return your s to its place
26:52 those who take the s will
26:52 will perish by the s
Mr 14:47 drew his s and struck the
Lu 2:35 a long s will be run through
21:24 fall by the edge of the s
22:36 let the one having no s sell
22:49 shall we strike with the s?
Joh 18:10 Simon Peter, as he had a s
18:11 Put the s into its sheath
Ac 12:2 the brother of John by the s
16:27 drew his s and was about to
Ro 8:35 or nakedness or danger or s
13:4 purpose that it bears the s
Eph 6:17 s of the spirit, that is
Heb 4:12 sharper than any two-edged s
11:34 escaped the edge of the s
11:37 by slaughter with the s
Re 1:16 two-edged s was protruding
2:12 the sharp, long two-edged s
2:16 with the long s of my mouth
6:4 and a great s was given him
6:8 to kill with a long s and
13:10 kill with the s, he must
13:10 must be killed with the s
19:15 protrudes a sharp long s
19:21 long s of the one seated on
19:21 s proceeded out of his mouth

Swords

Ne 4:13 their s, their lances and
Ps 55:21 But they are drawn s
59:7 S are on their lips, For who
Pr 30:14 whose teeth are s and whose
Isa 2:4 beat their s into plowshares
21:15 because of the s they have
Eze 16:40 slaughter you with their s
23:47 cutting . . . with their s
26:9 will pull down, with his s
28:7 draw their s against the
30:11 their s against Egypt and
32:12 the very s of mighty ones
32:27 their s under their heads
38:4 all of them handling s
Joe 3:10 Beat your plowshares into s
Mic 4:3 beat their s into plowshares
Mt 26:47 crowd with s and clubs from
26:55 Have you come out with s
Mr 14:43 a crowd with s and clubs
14:48 come out with s and clubs
Lu 22:38 Lord, look! here are two s
22:52 Did you come out with s and

Sword-stroke

Re 13:14 beast that had the s and

Swore

Ge 24:7 s to me, saying, To your seed
24:9 s to him concerning this
26:3 sworn statement that I s to
31:53 Jacob s by the Dread of his
47:31 Swear to me. So he s to him
50:24 s to Abraham, to Isaac and
Ex 13:5 s to your forefathers to give
32:13 you s by yourself, in that
33:1 I s to Abraham, Isaac and
Nu 11:12 soil about which you s to
14:16 land about which he s to
14:23 the land about which I s to
32:10 that day so that he s, saying
De 1:8 land about which Jehovah s to
1:34 indignant and s, saying
1:35 land that I s to give to your
4:21 he s that I should not cross
4:31 covenant . . . he s to them
6:10 s to your forefathers Abraham
7:12 he s to your forefathers
7:13 he s to your forefathers to
8:1 Jehovah s to your forefathers
8:18 covenant that he s to your
9:5 Jehovah s to your forefathers
11:9 the soil that Jehovah s to
11:21 s to your forefathers to give
19:8 he s to your forefathers
26:3 Jehovah s to our forefathers
26:15 you s to our forefathers
28:9 just as he s to you, because
28:11 the ground that Jehovah s to
De 30:20 Jehovah s to your forefathers
31:7 Jehovah s to their forefathers
Jos 1:6 the land that I s to their
5:6 Jehovah s that he would never
9:15 chieftains of the assembly s
14:9 Moses s on that day, saying
Jg 2:1 land about which I s to your
1Sa 19:6 Saul s: As Jehovah is
20:3 David s in addition and said
20:17 So Jonathan s again to David
24:22 David s to Saul, after
28:10 Saul s to her by Jehovah
2Sa 3:9 just as Jehovah s to David
3:35 David s, saying: So may God
21:17 the men of David s to him
1Ki 1:13 s to your slave girl, saying
1:17 you that s by Jehovah your
2:8 I s to him by Jehovah, saying
2:23 Solomon s by Jehovah, saying
2Ki 25:24 Gedaliah s to them and
2Ch 15:14 s to Jehovah with a loud
Ps 89:49 About which you s to David
95:11 I s in my anger: They shall
132:2 How he s to Jehovah
Jer 11:5 the oath that I s to your
32:22 s to their forefathers to
38:16 King Zedekiah s to Jeremiah
Mic 7:20 s to our forefathers from
Mr 6:23 he s to her: Whatever you
Lu 1:73 the oath that he s to Abraham
Heb 3:11 I s in my anger, They shall
4:3 I s in my anger, They shall
6:13 he s by himself
Re 10:6 he s: There will be no delay

Sworn

Ge 26:3 carry out the s statement that
26:31 s statements one to the other
Ex 13:11 just as he has s to you and
Le 5:4 thoughtlessly in a s statement
Nu 32:11 soil of which I have s to
De 2:14 just as Jehovah had s to them
6:18 Jehovah has s to your
6:23 he had s to our forefathers
7:8 his keeping the s statement
7:8 he had s to your forefathers
10:11 s to their forefathers to
10:20 you should make s statements
13:17 he has s to your forefathers
29:13 he has s to your forefathers
31:20 ground that I have s about
31:21 land about which I have s
31:23 land about which I have s
34:4 I have s to Abraham, Isaac
Jos 5:6 had s to their forefathers to
6:22 just as you have s to her
9:18 had s to them by Jehovah the
9:19 have s to them by Jehovah
9:20 oath that we have s to them
21:43 land that he had s to give
21:44 everything that he had s to
Jg 2:15 just as Jehovah had s to
21:1 men of Israel had s in Mizpah
21:7 s by Jehovah not to give them
21:18 sons of Israel have s, saying
1Sa 3:14 I have s to the house of Eli
20:42 in peace, since we have s
2Sa 21:2 had s to them, but Saul
1Ki 1:30 I have s to you by Jehovah
1Ch 16:16 his s statement to Isaac
2Ch 15:15 rejoicing over the thing s
15:15 their heart that they had s
Ne 6:18 many in Judah were s to him
Ps 15:4 He has s to what is bad for
89:3 I have s to David my servant
89:35 Once I have s in my holiness
102:8 have s even by me
105:9 his s statement to Isaac
110:4 Jehovah has s (and he will
119:106 I have made a s statement
132:11 Jehovah has s to David
Ec 9:2 has been afraid of a s oath
Isa 5:9 Jehovah of armies has s that
14:24 Jehovah of armies has s
45:23 By my own self I have s
54:9 s that the waters of Noah
54:9 I have s that I will not
62:8 s with his right hand and
65:16 a s statement in the earth
Jer 44:26 s by my great name, Jehovah
49:13 by my own self I have s
51:14 has s by his own soul, I
Eze 16:8 to make a s statement to you
21:23 are s with oaths to them

Da 9:11 s oath that is written in
Am 4:2 Jehovah has s by his holiness
6:8 Jehovah has s by his own soul
8:7 Jehovah has s by the
Hab 3:9 The s oaths of the tribes are
Zep 1:5 making s oaths to Jehovah
1:5 making s oaths by Malcam
Zec 5:3 everyone making a s oath
5:4 s oath in my name falsely
Ac 2:30 God had s to him with an
Heb 7:20 it was not without a s oath
7:21 priests without a s oath
7:21 an oath s by the One who
7:21 Jehovah has s (and he will
7:28 the word of the s oath that

Swung
Ge 24:64 she s herself down from off
Job 28:4 mortal men have s down

Sycamore
1Ki 10:27 he made like the s trees
1Ch 27:28 olive groves and the s trees
2Ch 1:15 cedarwood he made like the s
9:27 cedarwood he made like the s
Ps 78:47 their s trees by hailstones
Isa 9:10 S trees are what have been
Am 7:14 a nipper of figs of s trees

Sychar
Joh 4:5 a city of Samaria called S

Syene
Eze 29:10 to S and to the boundary of
30:6 From Migdol to S they will

Symbol
Nu 26:10 And they came to be a s
De 4:16 image, the form of any s
Eze 8:3 s of jealousy that is inciting
8:5 this s of jealousy in the
Mr 1:4 baptism in s of repentance for
Lu 3:3 baptism in s of repentance
Ac 13:24 baptism in s of repentance
19:4 baptism in s of repentance

Symbolic
Ga 4:24 stand as a s drama; for

Symbolized
Re 11:4 These are s by the two olive

Symeon
Lu 3:30 son of S, son of Judas, son of
Ac 13:1 S who was called Niger, and
15:14 S has related thoroughly how

Sympathize
Job 2:11 s with him and comfort him
42:11 s with him and to comfort
Isa 51:19 Who will s with you?
Jer 15:5 who will s with you, and
16:5 and do not s with them
22:10 s with him, you people
48:17 will have to s with them
Na 3:7 Who will s with her?
Heb 4:15 s with our weaknesses, but

Sympathy
1Sa 22:8 no one of you having s for
Ps 69:20 hoping for someone to show s
Heb 10:34 expressed s for those in

Synagogue
Mt 12:9 he went into their s
13:54 to teach them in their s
Mr 1:21 he entered into the s and
1:23 in their s a man under the
1:29 they went out of the s and
3:1 entered into a s, and a man
5:22 presiding officers of the s
5:35 presiding officer of the s
5:36 presiding officer of the s
5:38 presiding officer of the s
6:2 he started teaching in the s
Lu 4:16 he entered into the s, and
4:20 all in the s were intently
4:28 hearing these things in the s
4:33 in the s there was a man
4:38 getting up out of the s he
6:6 into the s and began teaching
7:5 he himself built the s for us
8:41 a presiding officer of the s
8:49 presiding officer of the s
13:14 presiding officer of the s
Joh 9:22 get expelled from the s
12:42 to be expelled from the s
16:2 will expel you from the s
Joh 18:20 I always taught in a s and
Ac 6:9 so-called S of the Freedmen
13:14 into the s on the sabbath
13:15 presiding officers of the s
13:43 s assembly was dissolved
14:1 into the s of the Jews and
17:1 there was a s of the Jews
17:10 went into the s of the Jews
17:17 he began to reason in the s
18:4 a talk in the s every sabbath
18:7 house was adjoining the s
18:8 the presiding officer of the s
18:17 presiding officer of the s
18:19 entered into the s and
18:26 to speak boldly in the s
19:8 Entering into the s, he spoke
22:19 flog in one s after another
Re 2:9 are not but are a s of Satan
3:9 s of Satan who say they are

Synagogues
Mt 4:23 teaching in their s and
6:2 as the hypocrites do in the s
6:5 like to pray standing in the s
9:35 teaching in their s and
10:17 will scourge you in their s
23:6 and the front seats in the s
23:34 you will scourge in your s
Mr 1:39 did go, preaching in their s
12:39 front seats in the s and
13:9 you will be beaten in s and
Lu 4:15 he began to teach in their s
4:44 preaching in the s of Judea
11:43 love the front seats in the s
13:10 teaching in one of the s on
20:46 and front seats in the s and
21:12 delivering you up to the s
Ac 9:2 letters to the s in Damascus
9:20 in the s he began to preach
13:5 publishing . . . in the s of the
15:21 he is read aloud in the s
24:12 the s or throughout the city
26:11 in all the s I tried to force

Syntyche
Php 4:2 Euodia I exhort and S I exhort

Syracuse
Ac 28:12 putting into port at S we

Syria
Jg 3:10 the king of S into his hand
10:6 the gods of S and the gods of
2Sa 8:5 When S of Damascus came to
8:6 garrisons in S of Damascus
8:12 from S and from Moab and
15:8 was dwelling in Geshur in S
1Ki 10:29 and the kings of S
11:25 continued reigning over S
15:18 the king of S, who was
19:15 anoint Hazael as king over S
20:1 Ben-hadad the king of S
20:20 Ben-hadad the king of S got
20:22 the king of S is coming up
20:23 servants of the king of S
22:1 war between S and Israel
22:3 the hand of the king of S
22:31 As for the king of S, he
2Ki 5:1 the army of the king of S
5:1 had given salvation to S
5:5 king of S said: Get going!
6:8 the king of S, for his part
6:11 king of S became enraged
6:24 Ben-hadad the king of S
8:7 Ben-hadad the king of S was
8:9 Ben-hadad, the king of S, has
8:13 shown me you as king over S
8:28 Hazael the king of S at
8:29 Hazael the king of S
9:14 Hazael the king of S
9:15 fought Hazael the king of S
12:17 Hazael the king of S
12:18 to Hazael the king of S
13:3 Hazael the king of S and
13:4 king of S had oppressed them
13:5 out from under the hand of S
13:7 king of S had destroyed them
13:17 the arrow . . . against S
13:17 strike down S at Aphek
13:19 be striking down S to the
13:19 you will strike down S
13:22 Hazael the king of S
13:24 Hazael the king of S died
15:37 Rezin the king of S
16:5 Rezin the king of S and
2Ki 16:6 Rezin the king of S restored
16:7 the palm of the king of S
1Ch 2:23 S took Havvoth-jair from
18:5 S of Damascus came to help
18:6 garrisons in S of Damascus
19:19 and S did not want to try
2Ch 1:17 Hittites and the kings of S
16:2 to Ben-hadad the king of S
16:7 leaned upon the king of S
16:7 force of the king of S has
18:30 king of S, he had commanded
22:5 Hazael the king of S at
22:6 fought Hazael the king of S
24:23 military force of S came up
28:5 the hand of the king of S
28:23 gods of the kings of S are
Isa 7:1 Rezin the king of S and
7:2 S has leaned upon Ephraim
7:4 hot anger of Rezin and S and
7:5 S with Ephraim and the son
7:8 head of S is Damascus, and
9:12 S from the east and the
17:3 S remaining over will
Eze 16:57 daughters of S and of all
Ho 12:12 run away to the field of S
Am 1:5 the people of S will have to
9:7 out of Crete, and S out of Kir
Mt 4:24 report . . . out into all S
Lu 2:2 Quirinius was governor of S
4:27 but Naaman the man of S
Ac 15:23 brothers in Antioch and S
15:41 went through S and Cilicia
18:18 to sail away for S, and with
20:3 was about to set sail for S
21:3 sailed on to S, and landed at
Ga 1:21 into the regions of S and of

Syrian
Ge 25:20 Bethuel the S of Paddan-aram
25:20 the sister of Laban the S
28:5 Laban the son of Bethuel the S
31:20 Jacob outwitted Laban the S
31:24 God came to Laban the S in
De 26:5 My father was a perishing S
2Ki 5:20 spared Naaman this S by not
18:26 in the S language, for we
1Ch 7:14 whom his S concubine bore
Isa 36:11 in the S language, for we

Syrians
2Sa 8:5 then struck down among the S
8:6 S came to be David's servants
10:6 hire S of Beth-rehob and
10:6 S of Zobah, twenty thousand
10:8 S of Zobah and of Rehob, and
10:9 in formation to meet the S
10:11 S become too strong for me
10:13 battle against the S, and
10:14 saw that the S had fled
10:15 S saw that they had been
10:16 S that were in the region
10:17 S now drew up in formation
10:18 S took to flight from
10:18 kill of the S seven hundred
10:19 S were afraid to try saving
1Ki 20:20 S took to flight, and Israel
20:21 struck down the S with a
20:26 muster the S and to go up
20:27 the S, for their part
20:28 the reason that the S have
20:29 striking down the S
22:11 will push the S until you
22:35 in the chariot facing the S
2Ki 5:2 the S, for their part, had
6:9 the S are coming down
6:23 marauding bands of the S
7:4 invade the camp of the S
7:5 to enter the camp of the S
7:5 the camp of the S
7:6 camp of the S to hear the
7:10 into the camp of the S
7:12 what the S have done to us
7:14 out after the camp of the S
7:15 utensils that the S had
7:16 plunder the camp of the S
8:28 the S struck down Jehoram
8:29 S got to inflict upon him at
9:15 the S got to inflict upon
24:2 and marauder bands of S
1Ch 18:5 striking down among the S
18:6 the S came to be David's
19:10 in formation to meet the S
19:12 If the S become too strong
19:14 advanced before the S to the

1Ch 19:15 saw that the *S* had fled
19:16 *S* saw that they had been
19:16 bring out the *S* that were
19:17 formation to meet the *S*
19:18 *S* took to flight because of
19:18 David went killing of the *S*
2Ch 18:10 push the *S* until you
18:34 facing the *S* until the
24:24 military force of the *S*
Jer 35:11 military force of the *S*

Syrophoenician
Mr 7:26 a Grecian, a *S* nationally

Syrtis
Ac 27:17 running aground on the *S*

System
Ps 17:14 From men of this *s* of things
49:1 inhabitants of the *s* of things
Eze 31:7 its root *s* proved to be
Mt 12:32 not in this *s* of things nor
13:22 anxiety of this *s* of things
13:39 conclusion of a *s* of things
13:40 conclusion . . . *s* of things
13:49 in the conclusion of the *s*
24:3 conclusion of the *s* of things
28:20 the conclusion of the *s* of
Mr 4:19 anxieties of this *s* of things
10:30 in the coming *s* of things
Lu 16:8 sons of this *s* of things are
18:30 in the coming *s* of things
20:34 children of this *s* of things
20:35 of gaining that *s* of things
Ro 12:2 fashioned after this *s* of
1Co 1:20 debater of this *s* of things
2:6 wisdom of this *s* of things
2:6 rulers of this *s* of things
2:8 rulers of this *s* of things
3:18 wise in this *s* of things
2Co 4:4 god of this *s* of things has
Ga 1:4 present wicked *s* of things
Eph 1:21 not only in this *s* of things
2:2 the *s* of things of this world
1Ti 6:17 rich in the present *s* of
2Ti 4:10 loved the present *s* of
Tit 2:12 this present *s* of things
Heb 6:5 powers of the coming *s* of

Systems
1Co 2:7 before the *s* of things for
10:11 ends of the *s* of things have
Eph 2:7 in the coming *s* of things
Col 1:26 from the past *s* of things
Heb 1:2 he made the *s* of things
9:26 conclusion of the *s* of
11:3 *s* of things were put in

Taanach
Jos 12:21 the king of *T*, one
17:11 *T* and its dependent towns
21:25 *T* and its pasture ground
Jg 1:27 *T* and its dependent towns
5:19 In *T* by the waters of Megiddo
1Ki 4:12 in *T* and Megiddo and all
1Ch 7:29 *T* and its dependent towns

Taanath-shiloh
Jos 16:6 went around eastward to *T*

Tabbaoth
Ezr 2:43 the sons of *T*
Ne 7:46 Hasupha, the sons of *T*

Tabbath
Jg 7:22 outskirts of Abel-meholah by *T*

Tabeel
Ezr 4:7 *T* and the rest of his
Isa 7:6 reign inside it, the son of *T*

Taberah
Nu 11:3 called *T*, because a fire of
De 9:22 at *T* and at Massah and at

Tabernacle
Ge 16:12 all his brothers he will *t*
26:2 *T* in the land that I
Ex 25:8 must *t* in the midst of them
25:9 the pattern of the *t* and
26:1 *t* you are to make of ten tent
26:6 and it must become one *t*
26:7 for the tent upon the *t*
26:12 hang over the back of the *t*
26:13 on the sides of the *t*, to
26:15 panel frames for the *t* of
26:17 the panel frames of the *t*
26:18 the panel frames for the *t*
26:20 side of the *t*, the northern
Ex 26:22 the rear sections of the *t* to
26:23 as corner posts of the *t* on
26:26 of the one side of the *t*
26:27 of the other side of the *t*
26:27 frames of the side of the *t*
26:30 set up the *t* according to the
26:35 the side of the *t* toward the
27:9 make the courtyard of the *t*
27:19 all the utensils of the *t* in
29:45 I will *t* in the midst of the
29:46 may *t* in the midst of them
35:11 the *t* with its tent and its
35:18 the tent pins of the *t* and
36:8 went making the *t*, the ten
36:13 so that it became one *t*
36:14 for the tent upon the *t*
36:20 panel frames for the *t*
36:22 the panel frames of the *t*
36:23 the panel frames for the *t*
36:25 the *t*, the northern side
36:27 rear sections of the *t* to the
36:28 as corner posts of the *t* on
36:31 of the one side of the *t*
36:32 of the other side of the *t*
36:32 the panel frames of the *t*
38:20 all the tent pins for the *t*
38:21 things inventoried of the *t*
38:21 the *t* of the Testimony
38:31 all the tent pins of the *t*
39:32 the *t* of the tent of meeting
39:33 to bring the *t* to Moses, the
39:40 for the service of the *t*, for
40:2 set up the *t* of the tent of
40:5 entrance for the *t* in place
40:6 the *t* of the tent of meeting
40:9 anoint the *t* and all that is
40:17 first month . . . the *t* was set
40:18 proceeded to set up the *t*
40:19 the tent over the *t* and
40:21 brought the Ark into the *t*
40:22 on the side of the *t* to the
40:24 side of the *t* to the south
40:28 of the entrance of the *t* in
40:29 the *t* of the tent of meeting
40:33 courtyard round about the *t*
40:34 Jehovah's glory filled the *t*
40:35 Jehovah's glory filled the *t*
40:36 itself up from over the *t*
40:38 cloud was over the *t* by day
Le 8:10 anointed the *t* and all that
15:31 defiling of my *t*, which is
17:4 before the *t* of Jehovah
26:11 put my *t* in the midst of you
Nu 1:50 Levites over the *t* of the
1:50 *t* and all its utensils, and
1:50 around the *t* they are to camp
1:51 *t* is setting out, the Levites
1:51 *t* encamps, the Levites should
1:53 encamp around the *t* of the
1:53 due to the *t* of the Testimony
3:7 the service of the *t*
3:8 the service of the *t*
3:23 Gershonites were behind the *t*
3:25 *t* and the tent, its covering
3:26 *t* and the altar, and its tent
3:29 side of the *t* to the south
3:35 side of the *t* toward the
3:36 panel frames of the *t* and its
3:38 camping before the *t* toward
4:16 oversight of all the *t* and
4:25 tent cloths of the *t* and the
4:26 round about the *t* and the
4:31 panel frames of the *t* and its
5:17 to be on the floor of the *t*
7:1 setting up the *t* that he
7:3 presented them before the *t*
9:15 day of setting up the *t* the
9:15 *t* of the tent of the
9:15 over the *t* until morning
9:18 cloud would reside over the *t*
9:19 stay over the *t* many days
9:20 a few days over the *t*
9:22 over the *t* by residing over it
10:11 over the *t* of the Testimony
10:17 *t* was taken down, and the
10:17 Merari as carriers of the *t*
10:21 set up the *t* by the time of
16:9 service of Jehovah's *t* and to
16:27 the *t* of Korah, Dathan and
17:13 coming near to Jehovah's *t*
19:13 has defiled Jehovah's *t*, and
31:30 the obligation of Jehovah's *t*
31:47 the obligation of Jehovah's *t*
Jos 22:19 *t* of Jehovah has resided
Jos 22:29 that is before his *t*
2Sa 7:6 about in a tent and in a *t*
1Ch 6:32 singing before the *t* of the
6:48 *t* of the house of the true
16:39 before the *t* of Jehovah on
17:5 and from one *t* to another
21:29 *t* of Jehovah that Moses had
23:26 not have to carry the *t* or
2Ch 1:5 put before the *t* of Jehovah
29:6 away from the *t* of Jehovah
Ps 43:3 mountain and to your grand *t*
46:4 grand *t* of the Most High
74:7 profaned the *t* of your name
78:60 forsook the *t* of Shiloh
84:1 How lovely your grand *t*
132:5 *t* for the Powerful One of
132:7 Let us come into his grand *t*
Isa 54:2 tent cloths of your grand *t*
Eze 37:27 my *t* will actually prove
2Pe 1:13 as long as I am in this *t*
1:14 putting off of my *t* is soon

Tabernacled
Ps 120:5 *t* together with the tents of
120:6 long a time my soul has *t*

Tabernacle's
Ex 35:15 for the *t* entrance

Tabernacles
Nu 16:24 the *t* of Korah, Dathan and
24:5 O Jacob, your *t*, O Israel
Job 18:21 are the *t* of a wrongdoer
21:28 tent, the *t* of wicked ones
Ps 49:11 Their *t* to generation after
78:28 his camp, All around his *t*
87:2 Than with all the *t* of Jacob
Ca 1:8 the *t* of the shepherds
Jer 30:18 for his *t* I shall have pity
Eze 25:4 certainly put in you their *t*
Joh 7:2 festival of *t*, was near

Tabernacling
Ge 14:13 *t* among the big trees of
25:18 they took up *t* from Havilah
35:22 Israel was *t* in that land
Nu 5:3 in the midst of whom I am *t*
23:9 a people they keep *t* isolated
24:2 saw Israel *t* by his tribes

Tabitha
Ac 9:36 disciple named *T*, which
9:40 *T*, rise! She opened her eyes

Table
Ex 25:23 make a *t* of acacia wood
25:27 for the poles to carry the *t*
25:28 must carry the *t* with them
25:30 put the showbread upon the *t*
26:35 set the *t* outside the curtain
26:35 lampstand opposite the *t* on
26:35 *t* you will put on the north
30:27 the *t* and all its utensils
31:8 the *t* and its utensils, and
35:13 the *t* and its poles and all
37:10 make the *t* of acacia wood
37:14 the poles for carrying the *t*
37:15 gold for carrying the *t*
37:16 utensils that are upon the *t*
39:36 the *t*, all its utensils and
40:4 bring the *t* in and set its
40:22 the *t* in the tent of meeting
40:24 of meeting in front of the *t*
Le 24:6 of pure gold before Jehovah
Nu 3:31 was the Ark and the *t* and the
4:7 blue over the *t* of showbread
Jg 1:7 picking up food under my *t*
1Sa 20:29 not come to the king's *t*
20:34 Jonathan rose up from the *t*
2Sa 9:7 eat bread at my *t* constantly
9:10 eat bread at my *t* constantly
9:11 eating at my *t* like one of
9:13 *t* of the king that he was
19:28 those eating at your *t*
1Ki 2:7 among those eating at your *t*
4:27 the *t* of King Solomon
7:48 the altar of gold and the *t*
10:5 and the food of his *t* and
10:5 the *t* service of his waiters
13:20 they were sitting at the *t*
18:19 eating at the *t* of Jezebel
2Ki 4:10 a couch and a *t* and a chair
2Ch 9:4 food of his *t* and the sitting
9:4 *t* service of his waiters and
13:11 upon the *t* of pure gold
29:18 *t* of the layer bread and all
Ne 5:17 were around us were at my *t*

Job 36:16 *t* will be full of fatness
Ps 23:5 arrange before me a *t* in
69:22 *t* before them become a trap
78:19 God able to arrange a *t* in
128:3 trees all around your *t*
Pr 9:2 it has set in order its *t*
Ca 1:12 as the king is at his round *t*
Isa 21:5 setting of the *t* in order
65:11 a *t* for the god of Good Luck
Eze 23:41 a *t* set in order before it
39:20 get satisfied at my *t* on
41:22 the *t* that is before Jehovah
44:16 near to my *t* to minister
Da 11:27 at one *t* a lie is what they
Mal 1:7 *t* of Jehovah . . . despised
1:12 *t* of Jehovah is something
Mt 8:11 and recline at the *t* with
9:10 reclining at the *t* in the
15:27 crumbs falling from the *t*
22:10 those reclining at the *t*
26:7 as he was reclining at the *t*
26:20 he was reclining at the *t*
Mr 2:15 reclining at the *t* in his
6:26 and those reclining at the *t*
7:28 dogs underneath the *t* eat the
14:18 they were reclining at the *t*
Lu 7:36 and reclined at the *t*
7:49 those reclining at the *t* with
11:37 in and reclined at the *t*
12:37 make them recline at the *t*
13:29 will recline at the *t* in the
16:21 from the *t* of the rich man
17:7 at once and recline at the *t*
22:14 he reclined at the *t*, and
22:21 betrayer is with me at the *t*
22:27 the one reclining at the *t* or
22:27 the one reclining at the *t*
22:30 eat and drink at my *t* in my
Joh 12:2 reclining at the *t* with him
13:12 laid himself down at the *t*
13:28 of those reclining at the *t*
Ac 16:34 set a *t* before them, and he
Ro 11:9 *t* become for them a snare
1Co 10:21 of the *t* of Jehovah and the
10:21 partaking . . . *t* of demons
Heb 9:2 the *t* and the display of the

Tableland
De 3:10 cities of the *t* and all Gilead
4:43 the *t* for the Reubenites, and
Jos 13:9 *t* of Medeba as far as Dibon
13:16 and all the *t* by Medeba
13:17 towns that are on the *t*
13:21 all the cities of the *t* and
20:8 *t* out of the tribe of Reuben
2Ch 26:10 Shephelah and on the *t*

Tables
1Ch 28:16 for the *t* of the layer bread
28:16 for the different *t*, and
28:16 silver for the *t* of silver
2Ch 4:8 he made ten *t*, and stationed
4:19 *t* with the showbread upon
Isa 28:8 *t* themselves have all become
Eze 40:39 two *t* on this side and
40:39 and two *t* on that side
40:40 gate, there were two *t*
40:40 gate there were two *t*
40:41 were four *t* over here and
40:41 and four *t* over there at
40:41 side of the gate—eight *t*
40:42 four *t* for the whole burnt
40:43 upon the *t* they would
Mt 21:12 the *t* of the money changers
Mr 11:15 the *t* of the money changers
Joh 2:15 and overturned their *t*
Ac 6:2 to distribute food to *t*

Tablet
Pr 3:3 them upon the *t* of your heart
7:3 them upon the *t* of your heart
Isa 8:1 large *t* and write upon it
30:8 write it upon a *t* with them
Jer 17:1 on the *t* of their heart
Lu 1:63 he asked for a *t* and wrote

Tablets
Ex 24:12 give you the stone *t* and the
31:18 two *t* of the Testimony
31:18 *t* of stone written on by
32:15 two *t* of the Testimony in
32:15 *t* written upon on both their
32:16 *t* were the workmanship of
32:16 of God engraved upon the *t*
32:19 threw the *t* from his hands
34:1 two *t* of stone like the first
Ex 34:1 write upon the *t* the words
34:1 first *t*, which you shattered
34:4 Moses carved out two *t* of
34:4 two *t* of stone in his hand
34:28 write upon the *t* the words
34:29 two *t* of the Testimony
De 4:13 he wrote them upon two *t* of
5:22 he wrote them upon two *t* of
9:9 to receive the stone *t*
9:9 the *t* of the covenant that
9:10 gave me the two *t* of stone
9:11 Jehovah gave me the two *t*
9:11 the *t* of the covenant
9:15 the two *t* of the covenant
9:17 I took hold of the two *t* and
10:1 Carve for yourself two *t* of
10:2 And I shall write upon the *t*
10:2 first *t*, which you shattered
10:3 and carved two *t* of stone
10:3 the two *t* were in my hand
10:4 he wrote upon the *t* the same
10:5 placed the *t* in the ark that
1Ki 8:9 the two stone *t* which Moses
2Ch 5:10 two *t* that Moses had given
Hab 2:2 set it out plainly upon *t*
2Co 3:3 not on stone *t*, but on fleshly
3:3 but on fleshly *t*, on hearts
Heb 9:4 and the *t* of the covenant

Tabor
Jos 19:22 boundary reached to *T* and
Jg 4:6 spread yourself out on Mount *T*
4:12 had gone up to Mount *T*
4:14 descending from Mount *T*
8:18 they whom you killed in *T*? To
1Sa 10:3 as far as the big tree of *T*
1Ch 6:77 *T* with its pasture grounds
Ps 89:12 *T* and Hermon—in your name
Jer 46:18 like *T* among the mountains
Ho 5:1 and as a net spread over *T*

Tabrimmon
1Ki 15:18 *T* the son of Hezion

Tackling
Ac 27:19 threw away the *t* of the boat

Tadmor
2Ch 8:4 rebuilt *T* in the wilderness

Tahan
Nu 26:35 of *T* the family of the
1Ch 7:25 Telah his son, and *T* his son

Tahanites
Nu 26:35 of Tahan the family of the *T*

Tahash
Ge 22:24 to Tebah and Gaham and *T*

Tahath
Nu 33:26 and went camping in *T*
33:27 pulled away from *T* and went
1Ch 6:24 *T* his son, Uriel his son
6:37 son of *T*, the son of Assir
7:20 *T* his son and Eleadah his son
7:20 Eleadah his son and *T* his son

Tahchemonite
2Sa 23:8 Josheb-basshebeth a *T*, the

Tahpanes
Jer 2:16 the sons of Noph and *T*

Tahpanhes
Jer 43:7 came gradually as far as *T*
43:8 Jeremiah in *T*, saying
43:9 house of Pharaoh in *T*
44:1 dwelling in Migdol and in *T*
46:14 publish it in Noph and in *T*

Tahpenes
1Ki 11:19 the sister of *T* the lady
11:20 the sister of *T* bore him
11:20 *T* got to wean him right

Tahrea
1Ch 9:41 the sons of Micah . . . *T* and

Tahtim-hodshi
2Sa 24:6 the land of *T* and continued

Tail
Ex 4:4 and grab hold of it by the *t*
29:22 the fat and the fat *t* and the
Le 3:9 fatty *t* is what he will remove
7:3 will present of it the fatty *t*
8:25 the fat *t* and all the fat
9:19 and the fat *t* of the ram
De 28:13 at the head and not at the *t*
28:44 you will become the *t*
Jg 15:4, 4 and turn *t* to *t* and put one
Job 40:17 its *t* like a cedar
Isa 9:14 off from Israel head and *t*
9:15 false instruction is the *t*
19:15 work that the head or the *t*
Re 12:4 *t* drags a third of the stars

Tail-ends
Isa 7:4 two *t* of these smoking logs

Tails
Jg 15:4 put one torch between two *t*
Re 9:10 *t* and stings like scorpions
9:10 in their *t* is their authority
9:19 their mouths and in their *t*
9:19 their *t* are like serpents and

Take*
Ge 2:15 cultivate it and to *t* care of
3:22 actually *t* fruit also from
24:60 seed *t* possession of the
28:1 You must not *t* a wife from
28:4 may *t* possession of the land
Ex 20:7 not *t* up the name of Jehovah
23:30 *t* possession of the land
Nu 11:17 *t* away some of the spirit
33:53 *t* possession of the land and
33:53 land to *t* possession of it
35:8 From the many you will *t*
35:8 from the few you will *t* few
De 1:8 and *t* possession of the land
1:21 *t* possession, just as Jehovah
1:39 they will *t* possession of it
2:24 *t* possession of his land, and
2:31 *t* possession of his land
3:18 this land to *t* possession of
4:1 *t* possession of the land that
4:2 neither must you *t* away from
4:5 you are going to *t* possession
4:9 *t* good care of your soul, that
4:14 passing over to *t* possession
4:15 *t* good care of your souls
4:22 *t* possession of this good land
4:26 I do *t* as witnesses against
4:26 to *t* possession of it
4:34 come to *t* a nation to himself
6:18 *t* possession of the good land
7:1 so as to *t* possession of it
7:3 his daughter you must not *t*
7:24 *t* a firm stand against you
8:1 *t* possession of the land about
9:4 to *t* possession of this land
9:5 to *t* possession of their land
9:6 land to *t* possession of it
9:23 *t* possession of the land that
10:11 *t* possession of the land that
11:8 *t* possession of the land to
11:8 to *t* possession of it
11:10 going to *t* possession of it
11:11 to *t* possession of it
11:29 are going to *t* possession of
11:31 *t* possession of the land
11:31 *t* possession of it and dwell
12:1 allow you to *t* possession of
12:32 not add to it nor *t* away
15:4 to *t* possession of it
16:20 *t* possession of the land that
19:2 to *t* possession of it
19:14 giving you to *t* possession of
21:1 to *t* possession of it
21:13 you must *t* possession of her
22:30 No man should *t* his father's
23:20 so as to *t* possession of it
24:4 not be allowed to *t* her back
24:8 *t* good care and do according
25:5 he must *t* her as his wife
25:19 to *t* possession of it
28:21 going to *t* possession of it
28:42 insects will *t* in possession
28:58 If you will not *t* care to
28:63 you are going to *t* possession
30:4 and from there he will *t* you
30:5 will certainly *t* possession of
30:16 you are going to *t* possession
30:18 to go to *t* possession of it
30:19 I do *t* the heavens and the
31:12 *t* care to carry out all the
31:13 Jordan to *t* possession of it
31:28 *t* the heavens and the earth
32:46 *t* care to do all the words
32:47 the Jordan to *t* possession of
33:23 Do *t* possession of the west
Jos 1:11 go in and *t* possession of
1:11 is giving you to *t* possession
1:15 holding and *t* possession of

Jos 11:16 to *t* all this land, the
16:4 to *t* possession of land
17:12 to *t* possession of these
18:3 to *t* possession of the land
21:43 proceeded to *t* possession
Jg 2:6 to *t* possession of the land
13:5 *t* the lead in saving Israel
1Sa 10:19 *t* your stand before Jehovah
12:16 *t* your stand and see this
13:15 to *t* the count of the people
14:17 *T* the count, please, and see
24:12 Jehovah must *t* vengeance
1Ki 19:4 *t* my soul away, for I am
19:10 looking for my soul to *t* it
19:14 looking for my soul to *t* it
2Ki 2:1 to *t* Elijah in a windstorm
17:37 should *t* care to do always
1Ch 27:23 David did not *t* the number
27:24 started to *t* the count, but
29:17 rectitude . . . you *t* pleasure
Job 1:6 *t* their station before Jehovah
2:1 *t* their station before Jehovah
2:1 *t* his station before Jehovah
Ps 2:2 kings of earth *t* their stand
4:3 *t* knowledge that Jehovah will
5:5 No boasters may *t* their stand
8:4 man that you *t* care of him
17:5 steps *t* hold on your tracks
18:2 I shall *t* refuge in him
25:13 *t* possession of the earth
26:9 Do not *t* away my soul along
27:10 Jehovah himself would *t* me
30:5 weeping may *t* up lodging
31:13 to *t* away my soul that they
35:2 *T* hold of buckler and large
36:7 men themselves *t* refuge
37:4 *t* exquisite delight in
37:34 to *t* possession of the earth
49:13 *t* pleasure in their very
49:17 he cannot *t* along anything
50:9 not *t* out of your house a
51:11 holy spirit O do not *t*
51:16 do not *t* delight in sacrifice
57:1 *t* refuge until the adversities
61:4 *t* refuge in the concealment
62:4 They *t* pleasure in a lie
64:10 will indeed *t* refuge in him
68:30 that *t* delight in fights
69:35 dwell there and *t* possession
73:24 you will *t* me even to glory
74:20 *T* a look at the covenant
80:9 *t* root and fill the land
80:14 see and *t* care of this vine
82:8 *t* possession of all the
83:12 *t* possession of the abiding
91:4 his wings you will *t* refuge
94:16 *t* his stand for me against
102:24 *t* me off at the half of my
104:29 *t* away their spirit, they
106:4 *T* care of me with your
109:8 oversight let someone else *t*
109:17 *t* delight in the blessing
116:13 grand salvation I shall *t*
118:8 better to *t* refuge in Jehovah
118:9 better to *t* refuge in Jehovah
119:108 *t* pleasure in the voluntary
144:3 that you should *t* account of
147:10 horse does he *t* delight
Pr 1:5 and *t* in more instruction
3:6 *t* notice of him, and he
4:13 *T* hold on discipline; do not
5:5 Her very steps *t* hold on Sheol
8:10 *T* my discipline and not
17:14 quarrel . . . *t* your leave
17:23 wicked will *t* even a bribe
20:16 *T* one's garment, in case one
22:25 *t* a snare for your soul
22:27 he *t* your bed from under you
23:26 *t* pleasure in my own ways
27:13 *T* one's garment, in case one
29:23 humble . . . *t* hold of glory
31:19 hands *t* hold of the spindle
Ec 12:12 *t* a warning: To the making
Isa 14:21 *t* possession of the earth
27:5 *t* hold of my stronghold
47:3 Vengeance is what I shall *t*
47:7 did not *t* these things to
Jer 2:30 No discipline did they *t*
5:3 They refused to *t* discipline
43:3 *t* us into exile in Babylon
44:12 *t* the remnant of Judah who
50:15 *T* your vengeance on her
51:8 *T* balsam for her pain
Eze 18:8 and no usury would he *t*
Eze 18:23 Do I *t* any delight at all in
18:32 I do not *t* any delight in
20:40 I shall *t* pleasure in them
33:11 I *t* delight, not in the
44:22 *t* for themselves as wives
44:22 widow . . . they may *t*
Da 6:15 *T* note, O king, that the law
7:18 *t* possession of the kingdom
11:21 *t* hold of the kingdom by
Ho 4:11 are what *t* away good motive
9:6 nettles . . . will *t* possession
Zec 8:23 *t* hold of the skirt of a man
Mt 6:10 Let your will *t* place, as in
6:28 *T* a lesson from the lilies
9:2 *T* courage, child; your sins
9:22 *T* courage, daughter; your
10:14 anyone does not *t* you in or
11:29 *T* my yoke upon you and
14:27 *T* courage, it is I; have no
15:20 to *t* a meal with unwashed
15:26 *t* the bread of the children
18:16 *t* along with you one or two
18:19 it will *t* place for them
20:14 *T* what is yours and go
22:24 his brother must *t* his wife
24:6 For these things must *t* place
25:28 *t* away the talent from him
26:26 *T*, eat. This means my body
26:42 let your will *t* place
Mr 6:50 *T* courage, it is I; have no
10:49 *T* courage, get up, he is
13:7 these things must *t* place
14:22 *T* it, this means my body
Lu 14:31 first sit down and *t* counsel
16:3 will *t* the stewardship away
22:42 my will, but yours *t* place
Joh 16:33 *t* courage! I have conquered
17:15 to *t* them out of the world
18:31 *T* him yourselves and judge
19:6 *T* him yourselves and impale
19:15 they shouted: *T* him away!
19:15 *T* him away! Impale him!
Ac 15:14 *t* out of them a people for
21:14 the will of Jehovah *t* place
Ro 11:27 when I *t* their sins away
12:10 showing honor . . . *t* the lead
1Co 6:15 *t* the members of the Christ
7:36 is the way it should *t* place
14:26 Let all things *t* place for
14:40 *t* place decently and by
15:54 *t* place that is written
16:14 affairs *t* place with love
2Co 12:10 I *t* pleasure in weaknesses
Eph 6:13 *t* up the complete suit of
6:16 *t* up the large shield of
2Ti 1:8 *t* your part in suffering evil
2:3 *t* your part in suffering evil
Heb 2:6 man that you *t* care of him
10:4 and of goats to *t* sins away
10:11 able to *t* sins away
Jas 5:10 *t* as a pattern of the
1Pe 5:9 *t* your stand against him
1Jo 3:5 manifest to *t* away our sins
4:6 This is how we *t* note of the
Re 1:1 that must shortly *t* place
1:19 things that will *t* place
3:11 that no one may *t* your crown
4:1 the things that must *t* place
6:4 to *t* peace away from the earth
22:6 that must shortly *t* place
22:17 wishes *t* life's water free
22:19 God will *t* his portion away

Taken

Ge 2:22 rib that he had *t* from the
2:23 from man this one was *t*
3:19 for out of it you were *t*
3:23 from which he had been *t*
12:15 *t* to the house of Pharaoh
14:14 brother had been *t* captive
18:4 a little water be *t*, please
18:27 here I have *t* upon myself to
18:31 I have *t* upon myself to
20:3 woman whom you have *t*, since
21:31 both of them had *t* an oath
27:36 birthright he has already *t*
27:36 he has *t* my blessing!
30:15 your having *t* my husband
30:23 God has *t* away my reproach!
30:27 *t* the omens to the effect
31:1 Jacob has *t* everything that
31:16 riches that God has *t* away
31:26 captives *t* by the sword
31:34 Rachel had *t* the teraphim
Ge 43:18 they had been *t* to Joseph's
Ex 8:15 relief had *t* place, he made
14:11 have *t* us here to die in the
Le 4:12 entire bull *t* out to the
4:21 bull *t* out to the outskirts of
6:4 thing which he has *t* by fraud
13:56 the priest has *t* a look, and
14:42 have different clay mortar *t*
16:27 *t* forth outside the camp
Nu 10:17 tabernacle was *t* down, and
12:1 Cushite wife whom he had *t*
12:1 a Cushite wife he had *t*
16:15 Not one male ass have I *t*
18:6 *t* your brothers, the Levites
23:20 Look! I have been *t* to bless
27:4 name of our father be *t* away
31:32 booty . . . *t* as plunder
31:47 the one to be *t* out of fifty
31:49 *t* the sum of the men of war
31:53 *t* plunder each for himself
34:14 already *t*, and the half tribe
34:14 already *t* their inheritance
34:15 already *t* their inheritance
De 3:20 have *t* possession of the land
17:14 you have *t* possession of it
20:7 and has not *t* her
21:11 and *t* her for your wife
22:14 This is the woman I have *t*
24:5 wife whom he has *t* rejoice
26:1 you have *t* possession of it
28:31 Your ass *t* in robbery from
Jos 1:15 have *t* possession of the land
2:6 had *t* them up to the roof
4:20 they had *t* out of the Jordan
7:7 And if only we had *t* it upon
7:11 *t* some of the thing devoted
13:1 to be *t* in possession
18:7 have *t* their inheritance on
Jg 17:2 silver pieces . . . *t* from you
18:24 My gods . . . you have *t*
18:30 the land's being *t* into exile
21:5 a great oath that has *t* place
21:22 not *t* for each one his wife
Ru 2:10 so that I am *t* notice of
1Sa 7:14 the Philistines had *t* from
12:3 Whose bull have I *t* or whose
12:3 or whose ass have I *t* or
12:22 Jehovah has *t* it upon
14:22 Philistines had *t* to flight
14:24 and until I have *t* vengeance
14:41 Jonathan and Saul were *t*
14:42 And Jonathan got to be *t*
21:6 day of its being *t* away
25:43 David had also *t* Ahinoam
30:16 *t* from the land of the
30:18 that the Amalekites had *t*
30:19 anything that they had *t*
2Sa 7:27 servant has *t* heart to pray
13:35 so it has *t* place
17:9 A defeat has *t* place among
18:9 *t* up between the heavens and
18:18 *t* and proceeded to raise up
23:6 that they should be *t*
1Ki 1:51 *t* hold on the horns of the
7:8 whom Solomon had *t*
10:9 *t* delight in you by putting
11:11 has *t* place with you and
21:19 and also *t* possession
2Ki 2:9 do for you before I am *t* from
2:10 If you see me when *t* from
6:22 you have *t* captive with your
13:14 Elisha, he had *t* sick with
13:25 cities that he had *t* from
17:11 Jehovah had *t* into exile
17:26 have *t* into exile and then
20:18 be *t* and actually become
22:7 no accounting should be *t* of
24:7 king of Babylon had *t* all
1Ch 9:1 Judah itself was *t* into exile
25:8 the things to be *t* care of
2Ch 2:17 the census . . . *t* of them
9:8 *t* delight in you by putting
11:21 wives that he had *t*, also
Ezr 2:1 had *t* into exile at Babylon
5:14 had *t* out of the temple
Ne 6:18 *t* the daughter of Meshullam
7:6 *t* into exile and who later
Es 2:6 *t* into exile from Jerusalem
2:6 *t* into exile with Jeconiah the
2:8 Esther was *t* to the king's
2:14 the king had *t* delight in her
2:15 whom he had *t* as his daughter
2:16 *t* to King Ahasuerus at his
6:6 king himself has *t* a delight

Es 6:7 king himself has *t* a delight
6:9 king himself has *t* a delight
6:9 king himself has *t* a delight
6:11 king himself has *t* a delight
8:2 that he had *t* away from Haman
Job 1:21 Jehovah himself has *t* away
21:6 shuddering has *t* hold of my
27:2 who has *t* away my judgment
28:2 Iron itself is *t* from the
33:32 I have *t* delight in your
35:15 not *t* note of the extreme
Ps 7:1 God, in you I have *t* refuge
11:1 In Jehovah I have *t* refuge
15:3 no reproach has he *t* up
15:5 a bribe . . . he has not *t*
16:1 for I have *t* refuge in you
22:8 since he has *t* delight in him
24:4 Nor *t* an oath deceitfully
25:20 for I have *t* refuge in you
31:1 O Jehovah, have I *t* refuge
37:40 they have *t* refuge in him
45:9 *t* her stand at your right hand
47:8 *t* his seat upon his holy
51:6 *t* delight in truthfulness
52:9 for you have *t* action
57:1 in you my soul has *t* refuge
68:18 *t* gifts in the form of men
69:4 What I had not *t* by robbery
71:1 Jehovah, I have *t* refuge
73:23 *t* hold of my right hand
85:1 *t* pleasure, O Jehovah, in
85:1 ones *t* captive of Jacob
112:1 he has *t* very much delight
119:35 For in it I have *t* delight
119:53 heat itself has *t* hold of
119:111 *t* your reminders as a
139:20 *t* up your name in a
141:8 In you I have *t* refuge
143:9 have *t* cover even with you
144:2 One in whom I have *t* refuge
Pr 5:22 own sin he will be *t* hold of
7:20 money he has *t* in his hand
24:11 are being *t* away to death
30:23 is *t* possession of as a wife
Ec 7:27 one thing *t* after another, to
9:12 fishes that are being *t* in an
9:12 like birds that are being *t* in
Isa 1:11 he-goats I have *t* no delight
2:22 to be *t* into account
3:14 What was *t* by robbery from
6:6 *t* with tongs off the altar
10:31 have *t* to shelter
16:10 joyfulness have been *t* away
22:3 they have been *t* prisoner
22:3 have been *t* prisoner together
22:6 itself has *t* up the quiver
33:8 *t* no account of mortal man
39:7 *t* and actually become court
40:12 *t* the proportions of the
40:13 has *t* the proportions of the
40:24 stump *t* root in the earth
41:9 *t* hold of from the
42:21 has *t* a delight in that he
44:23 for Jehovah has *t* action!
45:1 right hand I have *t* hold of
49:21 into exile and *t* prisoner
49:24 Can those already *t* be
49:24 be *t* from a mighty man
49:25 will be *t* away, and those
49:25 already *t* by the tyrant
52:5 my people were *t* for nothing
53:8 he was *t* away; and who will
56:10 None of them have *t* note
60:4 be *t* care of on the flank
61:1 liberty to those *t* captive
62:4 Jehovah will have *t* delight
66:3 very soul has *t* a delight
Jer 4:22 Of me they have not *t* note
5:5 *t* note of the way of Jehovah
5:28 poor ones they have not *t* up
7:28 and have not *t* discipline
8:5 have *t* hold of trickiness
12:2 they have also *t* root
12:11 man that has *t* it to heart
13:19 has been *t* into exile
13:19 *t* into exile completely
13:22 your skirts have been *t* off
14:10 has *t* no pleasure in them
16:5 *t* away my peace from this
22:12 they have *t* him into exile
27:10 *t* far away from off your
27:20 king of Babylon had not *t*
29:22 malediction will . . . be *t*
40:1 *t* into exile in Babylon
Jer 40:7 *t* into exile in Babylon
48:33 *t* away from the orchard
48:46 sons have been *t* as captives
49:1 Malcam has *t* possession of
49:1 *t* up dwelling in Israel's
49:24 have *t* hold of her, as
49:29 their own flocks will be *t*
50:3 animal have *t* flight
50:24 and also *t* hold of, for
52:20 no weight *t* of the copper
La 2:4 right hand has *t* its position
3:58 *t* up, O Jehovah, the contests
Eze 6:9 they will have been *t* captive
9:3 *t* up from over the cherubs
15:3 *t* from it a pole with which
18:13 and interest he has *t*, and
18:16 nothing has he *t* in robbery
18:17 no usury and interest . . . *t*
22:12 A bribe they have *t* in you
22:12 and usury you have *t*, and
33:5 had he himself *t* warning
33:6 must be *t* away, but its
33:15 things *t* by robbery, and
34:29 those *t* away by famine in
42:6 more room was *t* away than
44:8 *t* care of the obligation
47:23 *t* up residence as an alien
Da 5:2 Nebuchadnezzar his father had *t*
5:3 *t* away from the temple of the
5:20 dignity was *t* away from him
6:7 *t* counsel together to establish
7:12 rulerships were *t* away, and
8:11 constant feature was *t* away
Ho 5:11 *t* it upon himself to walk
6:6 in loving-kindness I have *t*
Joe 3:5 you men have *t* my own silver
Am 6:13 in our strength *t* horns to
Mic 2:2 also houses, and have *t* them
Zec 6:5 *t* their station before the
Mal 2:11 he has *t* possession of the
2:17 he himself has *t* delight
Mt 9:15 bridegroom will be *t* away
11:20 powerful works had *t* place
11:21 powerful works had *t* place
11:23 *t* place in Sodom, it would
13:12 even what he has will be *t*
21:43 kingdom of God will be *t*
24:40 one will be *t* along and the
24:41 one will be *t* along and the
25:29 even what he has will be *t*
26:56 all this has *t* place for the
28:2 great earthquake had *t* place
28:12 and *t* counsel, they gave a
Mr 2:20 bridegroom will be *t* away
4:25 what he has will be *t* away
14:4 Why has this waste . . . *t* place?
Lu 2:15 this thing that has *t* place
5:35 bridegroom will indeed be *t*
8:18 has will be *t* away from him
9:17 surplus that they had was *t*
9:51 for him to be *t* up, he
10:13 works that have *t* place in
10:13 *t* place in Tyre and Sidon
10:42 will not be *t* away from her
17:34 the one will be *t* along, but
17:35 the one will be *t* along, but
19:26 what he has will be *t* away
Joh 10:18 No man has *t* it away from
19:31 and the bodies *t* away
20:1 stone already *t* away from
20:2 *t* away the Lord out of the
20:13 They have *t* my Lord away
Ac 1:2 until the day that he was *t* up
5:20 *t* a stand in the temple
8:33 judgment was *t* away from
8:33 life is *t* away from the earth
10:16 vessel was *t* up into heaven
15:7 much disputing had *t* place
25:26 examination has *t* place, I
27:21 *t* my advice and not have
27:33 *t* nothing for yourselves
Ro 11:16 if the part *t* as firstfruits
13:2 has *t* a stand against the
13:2 *t* a stand against it will
1Co 5:2 should be *t* away from your
10:13 No temptation has *t* you
2Co 3:16 to Jehovah, the veil is *t*
7:2 have *t* advantage of no one
Eph 4:31 abusive speech be *t* away
Php 3:8 *t* the loss of all things and
Col 2:14 He has *t* it out of the way
Heb 5:1 high priest *t* from among men
13:11 *t* into the holy place by
Jas 4:5 the spirit which has *t* up
Re 11:17 *t* your great power and begun

Taker

Isa 24:2 for the interest *t* as for

Takes

Ge 27:46 If Jacob ever *t* a wife from
Ex 20:7 *t* up his name in a worthless
Le 13:53 if the priest *t* a look, and
20:14 *t* a woman and her mother
20:17 a man *t* his sister, the
20:21 a man *t* his brother's wife
Nu 6:2 *t* a special vow to live as a
36:4 if the Jubilee *t* place for the
De 5:11 *t* up his name in a worthless
17:18 he *t* his seat on the throne
22:13 In case a man *t* a wife and
24:1 a man *t* a woman and does
24:5 In case a man *t* a new wife
32:11 *t* them, Carries them on its
32:41 my hand *t* hold on judgment
Job 5:5 from butcher hooks one *t* it
12:20 sensibleness . . . he *t* away
19:9 *t* away the crown of my head
30:18 my garment *t* on a change
33:10 He *t* me for an enemy of his
Ps 34:8 man that *t* refuge in him
35:27 *t* delight in the peace of
37:23 in his way He *t* delight
40:17 Jehovah himself *t* account of
52:7 *t* shelter in adversities by
Pr 1:19 *t* away the very soul of its
11:16 one that *t* hold of glory
16:7 Jehovah *t* pleasure in the
21:18 *t* the place of the upright
30:28 gecko lizard *t* hold with its
Isa 27:9 when he *t* away his sin
44:14 *t* a certain species of tree
44:15 *t* part of it that he may
62:5 man *t* ownership of a virgin
Eze 16:32 she *t* strangers instead of
16:34 the opposite thing *t* place
33:4 he *t* no warning at all
33:4 sword comes and *t* him away
33:6 and *t* away from them soul
Mt 12:45 and *t* along with it seven
Mr 4:15 Satan comes and *t* away the
15:24 as to who *t* what
Lu 6:29 *t* away your outer garment
8:12 Devil comes and *t* the word
9:39 a spirit *t* him, and suddenly
11:22 he *t* away his full armament
11:26 it goes its way and *t* along
Joh 1:29 *t* away the sin of the world
15:2 not bearing fruit he *t* away
1Co 11:21 each one *t* his own evening
Ga 6:1 man *t* some false step before
Col 2:18 *t* delight in a mock humility
2Th 1:6 This *t* into account that it is
Heb 5:4 man *t* this honor, not of his
9:22 out no forgiveness *t* place
10:11 every priest *t* his station
Jas 3:5 little a fire it *t* to set so
Re 22:19 *t* anything away from the

Taking

Ge 3:6 she began *t* of its fruit and
6:2 went *t* wives for themselves
25:20 forty . . . at his *t* Rebekah
26:8 and *t* in the sight, and there
29:23 he resorted to *t* Leah
30:15 *t* also my son's mandrakes
31:9 God kept *t* the herd of your
31:46 *t* stones and making a heap
31:50 *t* wives in addition to my
Ex 13:19 Moses was *t* Joseph's bones
14:25 *t* wheels off their chariots
18:14 *t* their stand before you
19:17 *t* their stand at the base
30:12 when *t* a census of them
30:12 when *t* a census of them
32:1 Moses was *t* a long time
34:4 was *t* the two tablets of stone
Nu 3:28 *t* care of the obligation to
3:32 *t* care of the obligation to
3:38 those *t* care of the obligation
4:2 *t* of the sum of the sons of
4:22 *t* of the sum of the sons of
8:26 *t* care of the obligation, but
16:27 *t* their stand at the entrance
17:9 and *t* each man his own rod
21:26 went *t* all his land out of
21:35 *t* possession of his land
22:41 that Balak went *t* Balaam and
31:11 they went *t* all the spoil

Nu 31:27 those *t* part in the battle
De 4:47 *t* possession of his land and
25:7 in *t* his brother's widow
25:8 found no delight in *t* her
28:15 by *t* care to do all his
31:26 *T* this book of the law, you
Jos 4:8 went *t* them over with them
10:27 *t* them down off the stakes
24:1 they went *t* their stand
Jg 19:15 nobody *t* them on into the
19:18 nobody *t* me on into the
1Sa 14:32 and *t* sheep and cattle and
15:21 went *t* from the spoil sheep
17:16 *t* his position for forty
26:12 nor anyone *t* note nor
2Sa 3:29 man *t* hold of the twirling
4:5 he was *t* his noonday siesta
5:13 David went on *t* more
12:4 *t* some from his own sheep
22:17 from on high, he was *t* me
22:31 all those *t* refuge in him
2Ki 2:3 Jehovah is *t* your master from
2:5 Jehovah is *t* your master from
10:7 went *t* the sons of the king
24:14 ten thousand he was *t* into
1Ch 29:3 *t* pleasure in the house of
2Ch 19:7 partiality or *t* of a bribe
25:13 and *t* a great plunder
Ne 4:23 were not *t* off our garments
5:15 kept *t* from them for bread
6:19 were continually *t* out to him
9:25 *t* in possession houses full
12:45 *t* care of the obligation of
Job 1:15 making a raid and *t* them
1:17 the camels and *t* them
4:20 anyone's *t* it to heart they
5:3 seen the foolish one *t* root
9:18 my *t* of a fresh breath
12:24 *T* away the heart of the
34:9 By his *t* pleasure in God
Ps 1:6 Jehovah is *t* knowledge of the
2:12 all those *t* refuge in him
5:4 you are not a God *t* delight in
5:11 those *t* refuge in you will
8:2 the one *t* his vengeance desist
18:16 from on high, he was *t* me
18:30 to all those *t* refuge in him
31:19 to those *t* refuge in you
34:22 none of those *t* refuge in
44:16 and the one *t* his revenge
70:2 are *t* delight in my calamity
105:44 *t* possession of the product
149:4 Jehovah is *t* pleasure in his
Pr 3:18 life to those *t* hold of it
9:7 is *t* to himself dishonor, and
24:32 I began *t* it to heart; I saw
30:5 a shield to those *t* refuge in
Ec 5:8 the violent *t* away of judgment
7:9 *t* of offense is what rests in
Isa 33:15 from *t* hold on a bribe
51:18 *t* hold of her hand
57:1 there is no one *t* it to heart
57:13 one *t* refuge in me will
60:11 kings will be *t* the lead
Jer 8:10 fields to those *t* possession
14:12 I am *t* no pleasure in them
31:32 *t* hold of their hand to
32:14 *T* these deeds, this deed
32:44 *t* of witnesses in the land
33:13 hands of the one *t* the count
50:33 those *t* them captive have
Eze 22:14 I am *t* action toward you
22:25 precious things they keep *t*
24:5 a *t* of the choicest sheep
24:16 *t* away from you the thing
24:25 in the day of my *t* away
25:12 acted in *t* vengeance
37:19 I am *t* the stick of Joseph
37:21 *t* the sons of Israel from
40:45 *t* care of the obligation of
40:46 *t* care of the obligation of
Da 1:16 *t* away their delicacies and
Ho 11:3 *t* them upon my arms
Am 1:6 their *t* into exile a complete
4:10 the *t* captive of your horses
5:1 Hear this word that I am *t* up
5:11 grain you keep *t* from him
5:12 you who are *t* hush money
Na 1:2 devotion and *t* vengeance
1:2 Jehovah is *t* vengeance and is
1:2 Jehovah is *t* vengeance against
Zec 5:10 Where are they *t* the ephah?
6:10 a *t* of something from the
Mal 2:13 *t* of pleasure in anything
Mt 26:37 *t* along Peter and the two
26:45 are sleeping and *t* your rest
Mr 1:31 *t* her by the hand; and the
5:41 *t* the hand of the young child
6:41 *T* now the five loaves and the
14:23 *t* a cup, he offered thanks
14:41 are sleeping and *t* your rest
Lu 6:30 from the one *t* your things
7:38 *t* a position behind at his
9:16 *t* the five loaves and the two
19:22 *t* up what I did not deposit
Joh 11:13 about *t* rest in sleep
13:4 *t* a towel, he girded himself
17:3 their *t* in knowledge of you
Ac 2:42 to *t* of meals and to prayers
8:13 and powerful works *t* place
14:12 one *t* the lead in speaking
15:38 to be *t* this one along with
17:9 after *t* sufficient security
19:29 *t* forcibly along with them
24:2 reforms are *t* place in this
25:18 *T* the stand, the accusers
27:36 began *t* some food
Ro 2:17 upon law and *t* pride in God
1Co 9:25 man *t* part in a contest
2Co 10:2 counting on *t* bold measures
Ga 2:1 *t* also Titus along with me
Col 2:18 *t* his stand on the things he
Heb 8:9 *t* hold of their hand to bring
13:7 those who are *t* the lead
13:17 to those who are *t* the lead
13:24 those who are *t* the lead
Jas 4:16 such *t* of pride is wicked
3Jo 7 not *t* anything from the people

Talent
Ex 25:39 Of a *t* of pure gold he should
37:24 a *t* of pure gold he made it
38:27 a *t* to a socket pedestal
2Sa 12:30 of which was a *t* of gold
1Ki 20:39 or else a *t* of silver you
2Ki 5:22 *t* of silver and two changes
23:33 silver talents and a gold *t*
1Ch 20:2 a *t* of gold in weight, and
2Ch 36:3 silver talents and a gold *t*
Mt 25:24 that had received the one *t*
25:25 and hid your *t* in the ground
25:28 take away the *t* from him
Re 16:21 about the weight of a *t*

Talents
Ex 38:24 twenty-nine *t* and seven
38:25 a hundred *t* and one thousand
38:27 a hundred *t* of silver went
38:27 pedestals equaled a hundred *t*
38:29 seventy *t* and two thousand
1Ki 9:14 hundred and twenty *t* of gold
9:28 four hundred and twenty *t*
10:10 a hundred and twenty *t* of
10:14 six hundred and sixty-six *t*
16:24 two *t* of silver, and began
2Ki 5:5 ten *t* of silver and six
5:23 said: Go on, take two *t*
5:23 two *t* of silver in two bags
15:19 a thousand *t* of silver
18:14 three hundred silver *t* and
18:14 and thirty gold *t*
23:33 a hundred silver *t* and a
1Ch 19:6 a thousand silver *t* to hire
22:14 a hundred thousand *t* of gold
22:14 and a million *t* of silver
29:4 three thousand *t* of gold of
29:4 seven thousand *t* of refined
29:7 gold worth five thousand *t*
29:7 silver worth ten thousand *t*
29:7 worth eighteen thousand *t*
29:7 worth a hundred thousand *t*
2Ch 3:8 the amount of six hundred *t*
8:18 four hundred and fifty *t* of
9:9 hundred and twenty *t* of gold
9:13 and sixty-six *t* of gold
25:6 for a hundred silver *t*
25:9 hundred *t* that I have given
27:5 hundred silver *t* and ten
36:3 a hundred silver *t* and a
Ezr 7:22 a hundred *t* of silver and a
8:26 hundred and fifty *t* of silver
8:26 silver utensils worth two *t*
8:26 and gold a hundred *t*
Es 3:9 and ten thousand silver *t* I
Mt 18:24 who owed him ten thousand *t*
25:15 And to one he gave five *t*
25:16 one that received the five *t*
25:20 one that had received five *t*
25:20 brought five additional *t*
Mt 25:20 you committed five *t* to me
25:20 I gained five *t* more
25:22 that had received the two *t*
25:22 you committed to me two *t*
25:22 see, I gained two *t* more
25:28 to him that has the ten *t*

Talitha
Mr 5:41 he said to her: *T cu'mi*

Talk
Le 21:1 *T* to the priests, Aaron's sons
Nu 29:40 Moses proceeded to *t* to the
Jos 22:33 they did not *t* of going up
Jg 5:29 would *t* back to herself with
2Ki 9:11 the man and his sort of *t*
2Ch 18:19 and there was *t*, this one
32:17 and to *t* against him
Es 1:18 will *t* to all the princes of
Job 6:3 own words have been wild *t*
11:3 Will your empty *t* itself put
15:8 To the confidential *t* of God
Ps 64:2 confidential *t* of evildoers
83:3 carry on their confidential *t*
145:6 *t* about the strength of your
145:11 your kingship they will *t*
Pr 11:13 is uncovering confidential *t*
15:22 there is no confidential *t*
20:19 is uncovering confidential *t*
25:9 not reveal the confidential *t*
29:8 boastful *t* inflame a town
Isa 16:6 his empty *t* will not be so
Jer 48:30 his empty *t*—they will not
Eze 36:15 humiliating *t* by the
Mt 9:26 the *t* about this spread out
16:11 not *t* to you about loaves
Lu 4:14 good *t* concerning him spread
6:11 to *t* over with one another
9:21 Then in a stern *t* to them he
Joh 4:27 or, Why do you *t* with her?
4:42 on account of your *t*; for we
7:12 a lot of subdued *t* about him
Ac 18:4 a *t* in the synagogue every
Ro 16:18 smooth *t* and complimentary
Col 3:8 obscene *t* out of your mouth
1Ti 1:6 been turned aside into idle *t*
Heb 12:3 endured such contrary *t* by
1Pe 2:15 muzzle the ignorant *t* of the
Jude 11 in the rebellious *t* of Korah

Talked
Ge 31:29 God of your father *t* to me
46:2 God *t* to Israel in visions
Nu 14:10 *t* of pelting them with
De 9:25 Jehovah *t* of annihilating you
1Sa 9:9 way the man would have *t* on
10:16 about which Samuel had *t*
2Sa 21:2 the Gibeonites and *t* to them
2Ki 9:12 *t* to me, saying, This is
2Ch 32:24 He *t* to him, and a portent
Es 2:22 In turn Esther *t* to the king
3:4 as they *t* to him day by day
Job 42:3 Therefore I *t*, but I was not
Eze 36:3 *t* about with the tongue and
Lu 1:65 these things began to be *t*
2:34 for a sign to be *t* against
22:4 *t* with the chief priests and
Ac 10:37 subject that was *t* about
24:25 as he *t* about righteousness
Ro 1:8 faith is *t* about throughout

Talker
Ps 140:11 big *t*—let him not be

Talkers
Isa 44:25 the signs of the empty *t*
Jer 50:36 sword against the empty *t*
Tit 1:10 unruly men, profitless *t*

Talking
2Ch 35:25 *t* about Josiah in their
Pr 17:9 that keeps *t* about a matter
Ho 12:4 and there he began *t* with us
Mt 26:70 do not know what you are *t*
Mr 2:7 is this man *t* in this manner
Lu 9:31 *t* about his departure that he
Joh 2:21 *t* about the temple of his
8:27 *t* to them about the Father
13:18 I am not *t* about all of you
16:18 know what he is *t* about
Ac 9:29 *t* and disputing with the
11:20 *t* to the Greek-speaking
13:46 *t* with boldness, Paul and
20:9 deep sleep while Paul kept *t*
26:31 *t* with one another, saying
2Co 11:21 I am *t* unreasonably
Eph 5:4 nor foolish *t* nor obscene

1Ti 5:13 *t* of things they ought not
Tit 2:9 please them well, not *t* back

Talks
Ac 19:8 giving *t* and using persuasion
19:9 daily giving *t* in the school
Ro 10:21 is disobedient and *t* back

Tall
Ge 7:19 all the *t* mountains that
De 2:10 and *t* like the Anakim
2:21 *t* people like the Anakim; and
9:2 a people great and *t*, the sons
12:2 *t* mountains and the hills and
Job 8:11 papyrus plant grow *t* without
Isa 10:33 *t* in growth are being cut
45:14 and the Sabeans, *t* men
Eze 19:11 became *t* up among branches
Da 8:3 two horns were *t*, but the one
Mr 4:27 the seed sprouts and grows *t*

Taller
De 1:28 people greater and *t* than we
1Sa 9:2 shoulders upward he was *t*
10:23 he was *t* than all the other
Da 8:3 the one was *t* than the other
8:3 *t* was the one that came up

Tallness
Eze 19:11 be visible because of its *t*

Talmai
Nu 13:22 and *T*, those born of Anak
Jos 15:14 and *T*, those born of Anak
Jg 1:10 went striking down . . . *T*
2Sa 3:3 Maacah the daughter of *T* the
13:37 go to *T* the son of Ammihud
1Ch 3:2 *T* the king of Geshur

Talmon
1Ch 9:17 and Akkub and *T* and Ahiman
Ezr 2:42 the sons of *T*
Ne 7:45 the sons of *T*, the sons of
11:19 gatekeepers were Akkub, *T*
12:25 Meshullam, *T*, Akkub were

Tamar
Ge 38:6 and her name was *T*
38:11 *T* his daughter-in-law
38:11 *T* went and continued to
38:13 Then it was told to *T*: Here
38:24 *T* your daughter-in-law has
Ru 4:12 Perez, whom *T* bore to Judah
2Sa 13:1 sister whose name was *T*
13:2 sick on account of *T* his
13:4 With *T* the sister of Absalom
13:5 let *T* my sister come in and
13:6 let *T* my sister come in and
13:7 David sent to *T* at the
13:8 *T* went to the house of Amnon
13:10 Amnon now said to *T*: Bring
13:10 *T* took the heart-shaped
13:19 *T* placed ashes upon her
13:20 *T* began to dwell, while
13:22 had humiliated *T* his sister
13:32 he humiliated *T* his sister
14:27 daughter whose name was *T*
1Ki 9:18 and *T* in the wilderness
1Ch 2:4 *T* his daughter-in-law it was
3:9 and *T* their sister
Eze 47:19 from *T* to the waters of
48:28 *T* to the waters of
Mt 1:3 father . . . to Zerah by *T*

Tamarisk
Ge 21:33 that he planted a *t* tree at
1Sa 22:6 in Gibeah under the *t* tree
31:13 buried . . . under the *t* tree

Tambourine
Ge 31:27 with songs, with *t* and with
Ex 15:20 to take a *t* in her hand; and
Jg 11:34 meet him with *t* playing and
1Sa 10:5 and *t* and flute and harp
Job 21:12 with the *t* and harp
Ps 81:2 a melody and take a *t*
149:3 *t* and the harp let them make
150:4 Praise him with the *t* and
Isa 5:12 *t* and flute, and wine at

Tambourines
Ex 15:20 with *t* and in dances
1Sa 18:6 meet Saul the king, with *t*
2Sa 6:5 and with *t* and with sistrums
1Ch 13:8 with *t* and with cymbals and
Ps 68:25 were the maidens beating *t*
Isa 24:8 exultation of the *t* has
30:32 prove to be with *t* and
Jer 31:4 deck yourself with your *t*

Tamed
Jas 3:7 sea creature is to be *t* and
3:7 and has been *t* by humankind
3:8 tongue, not one . . . get it *t*

Tammuz
Eze 8:14 weeping over the god *T*

Tanhumeth
2Ki 25:23 Seraiah the son of *T*
Jer 40:8 Seraiah the son of *T* and

Tanner
Ac 9:43 with a certain Simon, a *t*
10:6 Simon, a *t*, who has a house
10:32 Simon, a *t*, by the sea

Taphath
1Ki 4:11 *T*, Solomon's daughter

Tappuah
Jos 12:17 the king of *T*, one
15:34 En-gannim, *T* and Enam
16:8 From *T* the boundary moved on
17:8 land of *T* became Manasseh's
17:8 but *T* at the boundary of
1Ch 2:43 sons of Hebron were . . . *T*

Tar
Ge 6:14 inside and outside with *t*

Taralah
Jos 18:27 Rekem and Irpeel and *T*

Tarea
1Ch 8:35 the sons of Micah . . . *T* and

Target
1Sa 20:20 them where I will to a *t*
Job 7:20 you have set me as your *t*
16:12 he sets me up as a *t* for
La 3:12 sets me up as the *t* for the

Tarshish
Ge 10:4 the sons of Javan . . . *T*
1Ki 10:22 a fleet of ships of *T* on
10:22 fleet of ships of *T* would
22:48 *T* ships to go to Ophir for
1Ch 1:7 sons of Javan were . . . *T*
7:10 sons of Bilhan were . . . *T*
2Ch 9:21 going to *T* with the servants
9:21 ships of *T* would come in
20:36 ships to go to *T* and they
20:37 retain strength to go to *T*
Es 1:14 *T* . . . seven princes of Persia
Ps 48:7 you wreck the ships of *T*
72:10 kings of *T* and of the islands
Isa 2:16 upon all the ships of *T* and
23:1 Howl, you ships of *T*!
23:6 Cross over to *T*; howl, you
23:10 O daughter of *T*
23:14 Howl, you ships of *T*, for
60:9 the ships of *T* also as at
66:19 to the nations, to *T*, Pul
Jer 10:9 brought in even from *T*
Eze 27:12 *T* was your merchant because
27:25 The ships of *T* were your
38:13 and the merchants of *T* and
Jon 1:3 to get up and run away to *T*
1:3 and found a ship going to *T*
1:3 to go with them to *T* from
4:2 went ahead and ran away to *T*

Tarsus
Ac 9:11 for a man named Saul, from *T*
9:30 and sent him off to *T*
11:25 he went off to *T* to make
21:39 *T* . . . no obscure city
22:3 a Jew, born in *T* of Cilicia

Tartak
2Ki 17:31 they made Nibhaz and *T*

Tartan
2Ki 18:17 to send *T* and Rabsaris and
Isa 20:1 year that *T* came to Ashdod

Tartarus
2Pe 2:4 by throwing them into *T*

Task
Ex 5:14 not finish your prescribed *t*
Jg 1:35 they were forced into *t* work
Isa 3:12 its *t* assigners are dealing
60:17 as your *t* assigners

Taskmaster
Zec 9:8 no more pass through them a *t*
10:4 goes forth every *t*, all

Taskmasters
Ex 5:14 whom Pharaoh's *t* had set over

Tassels
De 22:12 make *t* for yourself on the

Taste
Ex 16:31 its *t* was like that of flat
Nu 11:8 *t* proved to be like the
11:8 the *t* of an oiled sweet cake
1Sa 14:43 *t* a little honey on the tip
2Sa 3:35 shall *t* bread or anything at
19:35 your servant *t* what I ate
Job 6:6 any *t* in the slimy juice of
Ps 34:8 *T* and see that Jehovah is
Jer 48:11 *t* has stood still within
Eze 23:12 clothed with perfect *t*
38:4 clothed in perfect *t*
Jon 3:7 should *t* anything at all
Mt 16:28 not *t* death at all until
Mr 9:1 not *t* death at all until first
Lu 9:27 not *t* death at all until first
14:24 have a *t* of my evening meal
Joh 8:52 he will never *t* death at all
Col 2:21 not handle, nor *t*, nor touch
Heb 2:9 might *t* death for every man

Tasted
1Sa 14:24 none of the people *t* bread
14:29 I *t* this little bit of honey
Joh 2:9 *t* the water that had been
Heb 6:4 *t* the heavenly free gift, and
6:5 *t* the fine word of God and
1Pe 2:3 have *t* that the Lord is kind

Tasteless
Job 6:6 *t* things be eaten without salt

Tastes
Job 12:11 As the palate *t* food
20:12 If what is bad *t* sweet in
34:3 as the palate *t* when eating

Tasting
Ex 12:19 anyone *t* what is leavened
Mt 27:34 after *t* it, he refused to

Tasty
Ge 27:4 make me a *t* dish such as I
27:7 make me a *t* dish and, ah, let
27:9 a *t* dish for your father
27:14 his mother made a *t* dish
27:17 she gave the *t* dish and the
27:31 went about making a *t* dish
Pr 23:3 yourself craving his *t* dishes
23:6 yourself craving his *t* dishes

Tattenai
Ezr 5:3 *T* the governor beyond the
5:6 *T* the governor beyond the
6:6 *T* the governor beyond the
6:13 *T* the governor beyond the

Tattoo
Le 19:28 must not put *t* marking upon

Taught
De 4:5 I have *t* you regulations and
2Sa 1:18 sons of Judah should be *t*
Ps 71:17 have *t* me from my youth on
Ec 12:9 also *t* the people knowledge
Ca 3:8 being *t* in warfare, each one
Isa 29:13 that is being *t*
50:4 the tongue of the *t* ones
50:4 ear to hear like the *t* ones
54:13 be persons *t* by Jehovah
Jer 2:33 that you have *t* your ways
9:5 *t* their tongue to speak
9:14 their fathers had *t* them
12:16 just as they *t* my people
13:21 *t* them as confidential
13:23 who are persons *t* to do bad
Ho 11:3 I *t* Ephraim to walk, taking
Mt 13:52 *t* respecting the kingdom of
Mr 6:30 things they had done and *t*
12:35 as he *t* in the temple
Lu 1:4 things that you have been *t*
11:1 as John also *t* his disciples
13:26 you *t* in our broad ways
Joh 6:45 will all be *t* by Jehovah
8:28 as the Father *t* me I speak
18:20 I always *t* in a synagogue
Ac 11:26 *t* quite a crowd, and it was
1Co 2:13 words *t* by human wisdom
2:13 with those *t* by the spirit
Ga 1:12 nor was I *t* it, except
6:6 orally *t* the word share in
Eph 4:21 and were *t* by means of him
Col 2:7 just as you were *t*
1Th 4:9 *t* by God to love one another
2Th 2:15 traditions that you were *t*

1Ch 27:9 Ira the son of Ikkesh the *T*

Tekoites
Ne 3:5 the *T* did repair work
3:27 *T* repaired another measured

Tel-abib
Eze 3:15 among the exiled people at *T*

Telah
1Ch 7:25 and Resheph, and *T* his son

Telaim
1Sa 15:4 took the count of them in *T*

Telam
1Sa 27:8 land that extended from *T* as

Tel-assar
2Ki 19:12 sons of Eden that were in *T*
Isa 37:12 sons of Eden that were in *T*

Telem
Jos 15:24 Ziph and *T* and Bealoth
Ezr 10:24 gatekeepers, Shallum and *T*

Tel-harsha
Ezr 2:59 *T*, Cherub, Addon and Immer
Ne 7:61 *T*, Cherub, Addon and Immer

Tell
Ge 12:18 Why did you not *t* me that she
21:26 neither did you yourself *t* it
24:23 *T* me, please. Is there any
24:49, 49 *t* me; but if not, *t* me
29:12 Jacob began to *t* Rachel
29:15 *T* me, What are your wages
31:27 outwit me and not *t* me
32:29 *T* me, please, your name
37:16 *T* me, please, Where are they
43:7 we went on to *t* him according
45:13 you must *t* my father about
49:1 *t* you what will happen to you
Ex 4:28 Moses proceeded to *t* Aaron
13:8 must *t* your son on that day
19:3 and to *t* the sons of Israel
Le 14:35 and *t* the priest, saying
Nu 14:14 *t* it to the inhabitants of
23:3 I shall certainly *t* you
23:19 a man that he should *t* lies
De 5:5 *t* you the word of Jehovah
30:18 I do *t* you today that you
32:7 Ask your father, and he can *t*
Jos 2:14 not *t* about this matter of
7:19 *t* me, please, What have you
Jg 13:6 neither did he *t* me his name
14:6 he did not *t* his father or his
14:9 he did not *t* them that it was
14:12 *t* it to me during the seven
14:13 unable to *t* it to me, you
14:14 unable to *t* the riddle for
14:15 that he may *t* us the riddle
14:16 and ought I to *t* it to you?
16:6 Do *t* me, please, In what is
16:10 *t* me, do please, with what
16:13 *t* me with what you can be
Ru 3:4 *t* you what you ought to do
4:4 not repurchase it, do *t* me
1Sa 3:13 *t* him that I am judging his
3:15 Samuel was afraid to *t* Eli
8:9 must *t* them the rightful due
9:6 Perhaps he can *t* us our way
9:8 he will have to *t* us our way
9:18 *t* me, please, Just where is
9:19 in your heart I shall *t* you
10:15 Do *t* me, please, What did
10:16 he did not *t* him
13:4 And all Israel itself heard *t*
14:1 to his father he did not *t* it
14:43 *t* me, What have you done?
15:16 I will *t* you what Jehovah
19:3 I shall be sure to *t* you
19:18 *t* him all that Saul had
20:9 shall I not *t* it to you?
20:10 Who will *t* me whether
22:22 would without fail *t* Saul
23:11 *t* your servant, please
25:8 and they will *t* you
25:36 she did not *t* him a thing
27:11 that they may not *t* on us
2Sa 1:4 *T* me, please. To this he said
1:20 you people, *t* it in Gath
12:18 were afraid to *t* him that
13:4 Will you not *t* me?
15:35 *t* to Zadok and Abiathar the
17:16 send speedily and *t* David
17:17 as they had to *t* King David
18:21 *t* the king what you have
1Ki 1:20 *t* them who is going to sit
10:3 to *t* her all her matters
10:3 king that he did not *t* her
14:3 *t* you what is going to
18:12 *t* Ahab, and he will not
2Ki 4:2 *T* me; what do you have in the
4:16 Do not *t* lies in connection
6:11 *t* me who from those who
7:12 Let me *t* you, please, what
9:12 It is false! *T* us, please
22:10 went on to *t* the king
25:16 no way to *t* the weight of
1Ch 17:10 And I *t* you, Also a house
2Ch 9:2 *t* her all her matters, and no
9:2 Solomon that he did not *t* her
Ezr 2:59 *t* the house of their fathers
Ne 2:12 did not *t* a man what my God
2:18 went on to *t* them of the hand
7:61 *t* the house of their fathers
Es 2:10 that she should not *t*
4:4 began to come in and *t* her
4:8 show Esther and to *t* her and
4:12 to *t* Mordecai the words of
Job 1:15 only I by myself, to *t* you
1:16 only I by myself, to *t* you
1:17 only I by myself, to *t* you
1:19 only I by myself, to *t* you
8:10 Will not they . . . *t* you
11:6 *t* you the secrets of wisdom
12:7 winged creatures . . . will *t*
15:18 wise ones themselves *t* And
17:5 *t* companions to take their
21:31 Who will *t* him of his way
28:27 and proceeded to *t* about it
31:37 my steps I would *t* him
33:23 To *t* to man his uprightness
34:6 my own judgment do I *t* lies
36:9 he will *t* them about the
38:4 *T* me, if you do know
38:18 *T*, if you have come to know
Ps 9:11 *T* among the peoples his deeds
22:31 and *t* of his righteousness
30:9 Will it *t* of your trueness?
38:18 to *t* about my own error
40:5 inclined to *t* and speak of
50:6 heavens *t* of his righteousness
51:14 *t* about your righteousness
51:15 may *t* forth your praise
52:*super* to *t* Saul and say to him
59:16 *t* about your loving-kindness
64:9 will *t* of the activity of God
71:18 *t* about your arm to the
73:15 I will *t* a story like that
75:9 *t* of it to time indefinite
89:35 To David I will not *t* lies
92:2 *t* in the morning about your
92:15 *t* that Jehovah is upright
96:2 *t* the good news of salvation
142:2 to *t* about my own distress
145:4 mighty acts they will *t*
Pr 12:17 will *t* what is righteous
Ec 6:12 can *t* man what will happen
8:7 who can *t* him just how it
10:14 after him, who can *t* him
10:20 owning wings will *t* the
Ca 1:7 *t* me, O you whom my soul has
5:8 *t* him that I am lovesick
Isa 3:9 like that of Sodom they do *t*
19:12 they may now *t* you and
21:6 lookout that he may *t* just
41:22 *t* to us the things that are
41:22 do *t*, that we may apply our
41:23 *T* the things that are to
42:12 *t* forth even his praise
43:9 among them that can *t* this
43:26 *t* your own account of it in
44:7 *t* it and present it to me
44:7 let them *t* on their part
48:6 people, will you not *t* it?
48:20 *T* forth even with the sound
57:12 *t* forth your righteousness
58:1 and *t* my people their revolt
61:1 anointed me to *t* good news
66:19 *t* about my glory among the
Jer 4:5 *T* it in Judah, you men, and
5:20 *T* this in the house of Jacob
9:12 spoken, that he may *t* it
16:10 when you *t* to this people
20:10 *T* out, that we may
20:10 we may *t* out about him
31:10 *t* it among the islands far
33:3 readily *t* you great and
36:13 *t* them all the words that
36:16 *t* the king all these words
Jer 36:17 *T* us, please, How did you
36:20 *t* all the words in the ears
38:15 In case I should *t* you
38:25 *t* us, please, What did you
42:3 Jehovah your God *t* us the
42:4 answer to you I shall *t* you
42:20 our God says *t* us that way
42:21 I *t* you today, but you will
46:14 *T* it in Egypt, O men
48:20 *T* in Arnon, O men, that
50:2 *T* it among the nations and
50:28 *t* out in Zion the vengeance
Eze 23:36 and *t* them their detestable
24:19 Will you not *t* us what
37:18 *t* us what these things mean
40:4 *T* everything that you are
Da 2:2 to *t* the king his dreams
2:9 *t* me the very dream, and I
4:9 *t* me the visions of my dream
10:21 *t* you the things noted down
11:2 is truth I shall *t* to you
Jon 1:8 Do *t* us, please, on whose
Mic 1:10 In Gath do not you men *t* it
3:8 in order to *t* to Jacob his
Hab 2:3 and it will not *t* a lie
Mt 4:3 *t* these stones to become
8:4 See that you *t* no one, but
8:10 I *t* you the truth, With no
8:11 But I *t* you that many from
10:27 What I *t* you in the darkness
10:42 I *t* you truly, he will by no
11:9 I *t* you, and far more than a
12:6 *t* you that something greater
12:36 I *t* you that every
13:30 *t* the reapers, First collect
17:9 *T* the vision to no one until
18:10 I *t* you that their angels in
18:13 *t* you, he rejoices more over
21:5 *T* the daughter of Zion, Look!
21:24 If you *t* it to me, I also
21:24 *t* you by what authority I do
22:4 *T* those invited: Look! I have
22:17 *T* us, therefore, What do you
23:3 the things they *t* you, do and
24:3 *T* us, When will these things
25:12 I *t* you the truth, I do not
26:29 I *t* you, I will by no means
26:63 to *t* us whether you are the
28:7 *t* his disciples that he was
Mr 1:44 *t* nobody a thing, but go show
7:36 charged them not to *t* anyone
8:30 charged them not to *t* anyone
9:41 I truly *t* you, he will by no
10:32 *t* them these things destined
11:24 This is why I *t* you, All the
11:29 *t* you by what authority I
13:4 *T* us, When will these things
16:7 *t* his disciples and Peter
Lu 4:3 *t* this stone to become a loaf
4:24 I *t* you that no prophet is
4:25 For instance, I *t* you in truth
5:14 orders to *t* nobody: But go off
7:9 I *t* you, Not even in Israel
7:26 I *t* you, and far more than a
7:28 I *t* you, Among those born of
7:47 I *t* you, her sins, many
8:56 to *t* no one what had happened
9:27 I *t* you truthfully, There are
9:54 do you want us to *t* fire to
10:12 I *t* you that it will be more
10:40 *T* her, therefore, to join
11:8 I *t* you, Although he will not
11:51 I *t* you, it will be required
12:5 Yes, I *t* you, fear this One
12:13 *t* my brother to divide the
12:27 I *t* you, Not even Solomon
12:44 I *t* you truthfully, He will
12:51 I *t* you, but rather division
12:59 I *t* you, You will certainly
13:3 I *t* you; but, unless you
13:5 *t* you; but, unless you repent
13:6 on to *t* this illustration
13:24 many, I *t* you, will seek to
13:32 Go and *t* that fox, Look!
13:35 I *t* you, You will by no
14:7 on to *t* the invited men an
15:7 I *t* you that thus there will
15:10 I *t* you, joy arises among
17:34 I *t* you, In that night two
18:1 to *t* them an illustration
18:8 *t* you, He will cause justice
18:14 I *t* you, This man went
18:39 to *t* him sternly to keep
19:40 I *t* you, If these remained

Lu 20:2 *T* us by what authority you do
20:3 ask you a question, and you *t*
20:9 started to *t* the people this
21:3 he said: I *t* you truthfully
22:16 I *t* you, I will not eat it
22:18 I *t* you, From now on I will
22:34 I *t* you, Peter, A cock will
22:37 I *t* you that this which is
22:67 If you are the Christ, *t* us
23:43 I *t* you today, You will be
Joh 3:12 if I *t* you heavenly things
8:45 *t* the truth, you do not
10:24 you are the Christ, *t* us
11:40 *t* you that if you would
12:49 as to what to *t* and what
13:24 *T* who it is about whom he
16:4 I did not *t* you at first
18:34 did others *t* you about me?
20:15 *t* me where you have laid
Ac 4:17 *t* them with threats not to
5:8 *T* me, did you two sell the
8:33 Who will *t* the details of
13:15 word of encouragement . . . *t*
17:18 chatterer would like to *t*
21:23 do this which we *t* you
22:27 *T* me, Are you a Roman?
23:18 as he has something to *t* you
Ro 12:3 I *t* everyone there among you
15:18 not venture to *t* one thing
1Co 15:51 I *t* you a sacred secret
Ga 4:16 because I *t* you the truth
4:21 *T* me, you who want to be
Col 4:17 *t* Archippus: Keep watching
1Th 3:4 we used to *t* you beforehand
4:15 *t* you by Jehovah's word
2Th 2:5 used to *t* you these things
1Ti 4:7 and which old women *t*
1Jo 5:16 not *t* him to make request
Re 17:7 I will *t* you the mystery

Tellers
Jg 14:19 to the *t* of the riddle

Telling
Ge 9:22 went *t* it to his two brothers
24:28 woman went running and *t* the
29:12 running and *t* her father
41:24 but there was none *t* me
43:6 by *t* the man you had another
1Sa 17:31 went *t* them before Saul
25:37 wife went *t* him these
2Sa 1:5 the young man that was *t* him
1:6 young man that was *t* him
1:13 young man that was *t* him
2:4 they came *t* David, saying
18:11 to the man who was *t* him
1Ki 2:39 people came *t* Shimei, saying
20:17 and they came *t* him, saying
Es 2:20 Esther was not *t* about her
Ps 19:1 the expanse is *t*
68:11 women *t* the good news are
71:17 *t* about your wonderful works
147:19 is *t* his word to Jacob
Isa 41:26 Really there is no one *t*
42:9 but new things I am *t* out
45:19 *t* what is upright
46:10 *t* from the beginning the
48:5 *t* you from that time
Jer 4:15 a voice is *t* from Dan and is
Ho 4:12 own hand staff keeps *t* them
Am 4:13 the One *t* to earthling man
Zec 9:12 today I am *t* you, I shall
Mt 9:18 *t* them these things, look!
12:48 he said to the one *t* him
21:11 crowds kept *t*: This is the
21:27 Neither am I *t* you by what
Mr 5:8 he had been *t* it: Come out of
9:31 *t* them: The Son of man is to
10:48 sternly *t* him to be silent
11:33 Neither am I *t* you by what
Lu 9:21 not to be *t* this to anybody
10:9 *t* them, The kingdom of God
20:8 Neither am I *t* you by what
24:10 *t* the apostles these things
Joh 13:19 I am *t* you before it occurs
13:29 Jesus was *t* him: Buy what
16:7 I am *t* you the truth, It is
Ac 1:3 and *t* the things about the
17:21 *t* something or listening to
17:30 he is *t* mankind that they
19:4 *t* the people to believe in the
20:20 did not hold back from *t* you
20:27 not held back from *t* you all
21:21 *t* them neither to circumcise

Ro 9:1 I am *t* the truth in Christ; I
Ga 5:2 Paul, am *t* you that if you
Col 1:5 *t* of the truth of that good
1Ti 2:7 I am *t* the truth, I am not
Phm 19 not to be *t* you that, besides

Tells
2Ki 6:12 *t* the king of Israel the
Job 36:33 His booming *t* about him
Mr 11:23 *t* this mountain, Be lifted
Joh 2:5 Whatever he *t* you, do
19:35 man knows he *t* true things
Re 13:14 *t* those who dwell on the
19:9 he *t* me: Write: Happy are
19:9 he *t* me: These are the true
19:10 he *t* me: Be careful! Do not
22:9 he *t* me: Be careful! Do not
22:10 He also *t* me: Do not seal

Tel-melah
Ezr 2:59 the ones going up from *T*
Ne 7:61 the ones going up from *T*

Tema
Ge 25:15 Hadad and *T*, Jetur, Naphish
1Ch 1:30 Dumah, Massa, Hadad and *T*
Job 6:19 The caravans of *T* have looked
Isa 21:14 of the land of *T*, confront
Jer 25:23 Dedan and *T* and Buz and all

Temah
Ezr 2:53 the sons of *T*
Ne 7:55 sons of Sisera, the sons of *T*

Teman
Ge 36:11 sons of Eliphaz . . . *T*
36:15 sons of Eliphaz . . . Sheik *T*
36:42 sheik *T*, sheik Mibzar
1Ch 1:36 sons of Eliphaz were *T* and
1:53 sheik Kenaz, sheik *T*
Jer 49:7 no longer any wisdom in *T*
49:20 against the inhabitants of *T*
Eze 25:13 from *T*, even to Dedan
Am 1:12 I will send a fire into *T*
Ob 9 men must become terrified, O *T*
Hab 3:3 God . . . to come from *T*

Temanite
Job 2:11 Eliphaz the *T* and Bildad the
4:1 Eliphaz the *T* proceeded to
15:1 Eliphaz the *T* proceeded to
22:1 Eliphaz the *T* proceeded to
42:7 to say to Eliphaz the *T*
42:9 Eliphaz the *T* and Bildad the

Temanites
Ge 36:34 from the land of the *T*
1Ch 1:45 from the land of the *T* began

Temeni
1Ch 4:6 Hepher and *T* and Haahashtari

Temper
1Ti 6:11 endurance, mildness of *t*
1Pe 3:15 a mild *t* and deep respect

Tempest
Ps 55:8 the rushing wind, from the *t*
83:15 you pursue them with your *t*
Isa 29:6 sound, stormwind and *t*, and
Jer 23:19 go forth, even a whirling *t*
25:32 a great *t* itself will be
30:23 forth, an onward-sweeping *t*
Am 1:14 a *t* in the day of stormwind
Jon 1:4 to be a great *t* on the sea
1:12 this great *t* is upon you
Ac 27:18 violently tossed with the *t*
27:20 no little *t* was lying upon
Heb 12:18 and thick darkness and a *t*

Tempest-tossed
Isa 54:11 O woman afflicted, *t*

Tempestuous
Ps 107:25 causes a *t* wind to arise
148:8 *t* wind, accomplishing his
Eze 1:4 *t* wind coming from the north
Jon 1:11 continually growing more *t*
1:13 growing more *t* against them
Ac 27:14 *t* wind called Euroaquilo

Tempestuously
Hab 3:14 they moved *t* to scatter me
Zec 7:14 *t* to hurl them throughout

Temple
Ge 38:21 Where is that *t* prostitute
38:21 No *t* prostitute has ever
38:22 No *t* prostitute has ever been
De 23:17 daughters . . . a *t* prostitute

De 23:17 sons . . . a *t* prostitute
1Sa 1:9 doorpost of the *t* of Jehovah
3:3 Samuel was lying in the *t* of
2Sa 22:7 out of his *t* he heard my
1Ki 6:3 the porch in front of the *t*
6:5 the *t* and the innermost room
6:17 the *t* in front of it
6:33 for the entrance of the *t*
7:21 to the porch of the *t*
7:50 doors of the house of the *t*
14:24 even the male *t* prostitute
15:12 the male *t* prostitutes
22:46 the male *t* prostitutes that
2Ki 18:16 doors of the *t* of Jehovah
23:4 out from the *t* of Jehovah
23:7 the male *t* prostitutes that
24:13 made in the *t* of Jehovah
2Ch 3:17 the pillars in front of the *t*
4:7 put them in the *t*, five to
4:8 and stationed them in the *t*
4:22 doors of the house of the *t*
26:16 came into the *t* of Jehovah
27:2 not invade the *t* of Jehovah
29:16 found in the *t* of Jehovah
Ezr 3:6 the foundation of Jehovah's *t*
3:10 laid the foundation of the *t*
4:1 building a *t* to Jehovah the
5:14 *t*, which was in Jerusalem
5:14 brought to the *t* of Babylon
5:14 took out of the *t* of Babylon
5:15 the *t* that is in Jerusalem
6:5 the *t* that was in Jerusalem
6:5 the *t* that is in Jerusalem
Ne 6:10 within the *t*, and let us
6:10 close the doors of the *t*
6:11 enter into the *t* and live
Job 36:14 among male *t* prostitutes
Ps 5:7 bow down toward your holy *t*
11:4 Jehovah is in his holy *t*
18:6 Out of his *t* he proceeded to
27:4 with appreciation upon his *t*
29:9 in his *t* each one is saying
48:9 In the midst of your *t*
65:4 The holy place of your *t*
68:29 your *t* at Jerusalem
79:1 have defiled your holy *t*
138:2 down toward your holy *t*
Isa 6:1 his skirts were filling the *t*
44:28 and of the *t*, You will have
66:6 a sound out of the *t*!
Jer 7:4 The *t* of Jehovah
7:4, 4 the *t* of Jehovah, the *t* of
24:1 set before the *t* of Jehovah
50:28 the vengeance for his *t*
51:11 the vengeance for his *t*
Eze 8:16 entrance of the *t* of Jehovah
8:16 backs to the *t* of Jehovah
41:1 to bring me into the *t*
41:4 twenty cubits, before the *t*
41:15 the *t* and the inner place
41:20 on the wall of the *t*
41:21 *t*, the doorpost was squared
41:23 *t* and the holy place had
41:25 upon the doors of the *t*
42:8 *t* it was a hundred cubits
Da 5:2 the *t* that was in Jerusalem
5:3 *t* of the house of God that was
Ho 4:14 the female *t* prostitutes that
Am 8:3 the songs of the *t* will
Jon 2:4 gaze again upon your holy *t*
2:7 in to you, into your holy *t*
Mic 1:2 Jehovah from his holy *t*
Hab 2:20 Jehovah is in his holy *t*
Hag 2:15 a stone in the *t* of Jehovah
2:18 foundation . . . *t* of Jehovah
Zec 6:12 build the *t* of Jehovah
6:13 will build the *t* of Jehovah
6:14 memorial in the *t* of Jehovah
6:15 build in the *t* of Jehovah
8:9 for the *t* to be built
Mal 3:1 come to His *t* the true Lord
Mt 4:5 upon the battlement of the *t*
12:5 sabbaths the priests in the *t*
12:6 greater than the *t* is here
21:12 Jesus entered into the *t* and
21:12 selling and buying in the *t*
21:14 in the *t*, and he cured them
21:15 boys . . . crying out in the *t*
21:23 after he went into the *t*
23:16 If anyone swears by the *t*
23:16 swears by the gold of the *t*
23:17 greater, the gold or the *t*
23:21 he that swears by the *t* is
24:1 was on his way from the *t*

Ex 38:20 the *t* pins for the tabernacle
38:30 entrance of the *t* of meeting
38:31 the *t* pins of the tabernacle
38:31 the *t* pins of the courtyard
39:32 of the *t* of meeting all came
39:33 the *t* and all its utensils
39:38 for the entrance of the *t*
39:40, 40 its *t* cords and its *t* pins
39:40 for the *t* of meeting
40:2 the tabernacle of the *t* of
40:6 tabernacle of the *t* of meeting
40:7 the basin between the *t* of
40:12 entrance of the *t* of meeting
40:19 spread out the *t* over the
40:19 covering of the *t* above upon
40:22 table in the *t* of meeting on
40:24 the *t* of meeting in front of
40:26 the *t* of meeting before the
40:29 of the *t* of meeting, that he
40:30 the *t* of meeting and the
40:32 went into the *t* of meeting
40:34 to cover the *t* of meeting
40:35 to go into the *t* of meeting
Le 1:1 out of the *t* of meeting, saying
1:3 entrance of the *t* of meeting
1:5 entrance of the *t* of meeting
3:2 entrance of the *t* of meeting
3:8 be slaughtered before the *t* of
3:13 before the *t* of meeting
4:4 entrance of the *t* of meeting
4:5 bring it into the *t* of meeting
4:7 which is in the *t* of meeting
4:7 entrance of the *t* of meeting
4:14 before the *t* of meeting
4:16 blood into the *t* of meeting
4:18 which is in the *t* of meeting
4:18 entrance of the *t* of meeting
6:16 courtyard of the *t* of meeting
6:26 courtyard of the *t* of meeting
6:30 brought into the *t* of meeting
8:3 entrance of the *t* of meeting
8:4 entrance of the *t* of meeting
8:31 entrance of the *t* of meeting
8:33 entrance of the *t* of meeting
8:35 entrance of the *t* of meeting
9:5 before the *t* of meeting
9:23 went into the *t* of meeting
10:7 entrance of the *t* of meeting
10:9 come into the *t* of meeting
12:6 entrance of the *t* of meeting
14:8 outside his *t* seven days
14:11 entrance of the *t* of meeting
14:23 *t* of meeting before Jehovah
15:14 entrance of the *t* of meeting
15:29 entrance of the *t* of meeting
16:7 entrance of the *t* of meeting
16:16 for the *t* of meeting, which is
16:17 be in the *t* of meeting from
16:20 *t* of meeting and the altar
16:23 Aaron must come into the *t*
16:33 *t* of meeting and for the
17:4 *t* of meeting to present it as
17:5 *t* of meeting to the priest
17:6 *t* of meeting, and he must
17:9 entrance of the *t* of meeting
19:21 entrance of the *t* of meeting
24:3 *t* of meeting Aaron should set
Nu 1:1 *t* of meeting, on the first day
2:2 front of the *t* of meeting they
2:17 the *t* of meeting must set out
3:7 before the *t* of meeting in
3:8 utensils of the *t* of meeting
3:25 *t* of meeting was the
3:25 the tabernacle and the *t*
3:25 entrance of the *t* of meeting
3:26 and its *t* cords, for all its
3:37, 37 *t* pins and their *t* cords
3:38 before the *t* of meeting
4:3 the work in the *t* of meeting
4:4 Kohath in the *t* of meeting
4:15 Kohath in the *t* of meeting
4:23 service in the *t* of meeting
4:25 *t* cloths of the tabernacle
4:25 and the *t* of meeting
4:25 entrance of the *t* of meeting
4:26 *t* cords and all their service
4:28 in the *t* of meeting
4:30 service of the *t* of meeting
4:31 service in the *t* of meeting
4:32, 32 *t* pins and their *t* cords
4:33 service in the *t* of meeting
4:35 service in the *t* of meeting
4:37 serving in the *t* of meeting
4:39 service in the *t* of meeting
Nu 4:41 serving in the *t* of meeting
4:43 service in the *t* of meeting
4:47 loads in the *t* of meeting
6:10 entrance of the *t* of meeting
6:13 entrance of the *t* of meeting
6:18 entrance of the *t* of meeting
7:5 service of the *t* of meeting
7:89 *t* of meeting to speak with
8:9 before the *t* of meeting and
8:15 serve at the *t* of meeting
8:19 in the *t* of meeting
8:22 service in the *t* of meeting
8:24 service of the *t* of meeting
8:26 *t* of meeting in taking care
9:15 *t* of the Testimony, but in
9:17 go up from over the *t*, the
10:3 entrance of the *t* of meeting
11:10 man at the entrance of his *t*
11:16 them to the *t* of meeting
11:24 stand round about the *t*
11:26 had not gone out to the *t*
12:4 three of you, to the *t* of
12:5 entrance of the *t* and called
12:10 turned away from over the *t*
14:10 appeared on the *t* of meeting
16:18 entrance of the *t* of meeting
16:19 entrance of the *t* of meeting
16:42 toward the *t* of meeting; and
16:43 come before the *t* of meeting
16:50 entrance of the *t* of meeting
17:4 in the *t* of meeting before
17:7 in the *t* of the Testimony
17:8 into the *t* of the Testimony
18:2 before the *t* of the Testimony
18:3 obligation to the entire *t*
18:4 their obligation to the *t* of
18:4 all the service of the *t*, and
18:6 service of the *t* of meeting
18:21 service of the *t* of meeting
18:22 near to the *t* of meeting
18:23 service of the *t* of meeting
18:31 service in the *t* of meeting
19:4 the front of the *t* of meeting
19:14 case a man should die in a *t*
19:14 Everyone coming into the *t*
19:14 and everyone who is in the *t*
19:18 spatter it upon the *t* and all
20:6 entrance of the *t* of meeting
25:6 entrance of the *t* of meeting
25:8 into the vaulted *t* and pierced
27:2 entrance of the *t* of meeting
31:54 into the *t* of meeting as a
32:41 capturing their *t* villages
De 31:14 in the *t* of meeting, that I
31:14 in the *t* of meeting
31:15 the *t* in the pillar of cloud
31:15 by the entrance of the *t*
Jos 7:21 in the midst of my *t* with
7:22 they went running to the *t*
7:22 it was hidden in his *t* with
7:23 from the midst of the *t* and
7:24 his *t* and everything that
13:30 the *t* villages of Jair
18:1 the *t* of meeting there
19:51 of the *t* of meeting
Jg 4:11 he had his *t* pitched near the
4:17 he fled on foot to the *t* of
4:18 turned aside to her into the *t*
4:20 Stand at the entrance of the *t*
4:21 a pin of the *t* and to put the
5:24 Among women in the *t* she
5:26 Her hand to the *t* pin she then
7:13 came to a *t* and struck it so
7:13 and the *t* fell flat
19:9 and you must go to your *t*
20:8 not go any of us to his *t*
1Sa 2:22 entrance of the *t* of meeting
4:10 fleeing each one to his *t*
13:2 sent away, each one to his *t*
17:54 his weapons he put in his *t*
2Sa 6:17 *t* that David had pitched for
7:2 in the middle of *t* cloths
7:6 walking about in a *t* and in
16:22 pitched a *t* for Absalom
23:13 *t* village of the Philistines
1Ki 1:39 oil out of the *t* and anointed
2:28 Joab went fleeing to the *t*
2:29 Joab has fled to the *t* of
2:30 came to the *t* of Jehovah
4:13 had the *t* villages of Jair
8:4 the *t* of meeting and all the
8:4 utensils that were in the *t*
2Ki 7:8 entered into one *t* and began
7:8 entered into another *t* and
2Ki 14:12 flight, each one to his *t*
23:7 were weaving *t* shrines
1Ch 6:32 the tabernacle of the *t* of
9:19 the doorkeepers of the *t*, and
9:21 entrance of the *t* of meeting
9:23 of the *t*, for guard service
15:1 and pitch a *t* for it
16:1 the *t* that David had pitched
17:1 the ark . . . is under *t* cloths
17:5, 5 I continued from *t* to *t*
23:32 the guarding of the *t* of
2Ch 1:3 *t* of meeting of the true God
1:4 a *t* for it in Jerusalem
1:6 belonged to the *t* of meeting
1:13 from before the *t* of meeting
5:5 the Ark and the *t* of meeting
5:5 utensils that were in the *t*
24:6 for the *t* of the Testimony
25:22 flight each one to his *t*
Job 4:21 not their *t* cord within them
5:24 that peace itself is your *t*
8:22 *t* of wicked ones will not be
18:6 certainly grow dark in his *t*
18:14 torn away from his own *t*
18:15 reside in his *t* something
19:12 they camp round about my *t*
20:26 with a survivor in his *t*
21:28 the *t* . . . of wicked ones
22:23 far from your *t*
29:4 God was at my *t*
31:31 the men of my *t* did not say
Ps 15:1 who will be a guest in your *t*?
19:4 he has set a *t* for the sun
27:3 encampment should pitch *t*
27:5 in the secret place of his *t*
27:6 And I will sacrifice at his *t*
52:5 tear you away from your *t*
61:4 a guest in your *t* for times
68:10 Your *t* community—they have
78:60 *t* in which he resided among
78:67 to reject the *t* of Joseph
91:10 will draw near to your *t*
104:2 the heavens like a *t* cloth
132:3 go into the *t* of my house
Pr 14:11 *t* of the upright ones will
Ca 1:5 like the *t* cloths of Solomon
Isa 13:20 Arab will not pitch his *t*
16:5 trueness in the *t* of David
33:20 *t* that no one will pack up
33:20 its *t* pins be pulled out
38:12 like the *t* of shepherds
40:22 spreads them out like a *t*
54:2 the place of your *t* more
54:2 stretch out the *t* cloths of
54:2 Lengthen out your *t* cords
54:2 those *t* pins of yours strong
Jer 4:20 in a moment my *t* cloths
10:20 My own *t* has been despoiled
10:20 *t* cords have all been torn
10:20 no one stretching out my *t*
10:20 or raising up my *t* cloths
37:10 each one in his *t* rise up
43:10 extend his state *t* over
49:29 *t* cloths and all their
La 2:4 the *t* of the daughter of Zion
Hab 3:7 *t* cloths of the land of
Ac 7:43 it was the *t* of Moloch and
7:44 *t* of the witness in the
2Co 5:1 this *t*, should be dissolved
5:4 we who are in this *t* groan
12:9 like a *t* remain over me
Heb 8:2 true *t*, which Jehovah put up
8:5 to make the *t* in completion
9:2 constructed a first *t*
9:3 the *t* compartment called the
9:6 enter the first *t* compartment
9:8 the first *t* was standing
9:9 *t* is an illustration for the
9:11 *t* not made with hands, that
9:21 he sprinkled the *t* and all
13:10 do sacred service at the *t*
Re 7:15 will spread his *t* over them
15:5 of the *t* of the witness was
21:3 *t* of God is with mankind

Tenth
Ge 8:5 lessening until the *t* month
8:5 In the *t* month, on the first
14:20 At that Abram gave him a *t*
28:22 without fail give the *t* of
Ex 12:3 On the *t* day of this month
16:36 an omer is a *t* of an ephah
29:40 *t* part of an ephah measure
Le 5:11 *t* of an ephah of fine flour

Es 7:6 Haman, he became *t* because of
Job 7:14 even have *t* me with dreams
32:15 They have been *t*, they have
39:22 laughs at dread . . . is not *t*
Isa 20:5 *t* and be ashamed of Ethiopia
21:4 a shuddering itself has *t* me
31:4 he will not be *t* and in
31:9 his princes must be *t*, is
37:27 simply be *t* and ashamed
Jer 8:9 become *t* and will be caught
48:39 O how she has become *t!*
50:2 Merodach has become *t*
50:2 dungy idols have become *t*
50:36 they will actually become *t*
Da 8:17 I got *t* so that I fell upon
Ob 9 mighty men must become *t*
Mt 24:6 see that you are not *t*
Mr 13:7 reports of wars, do not be *t*
Lu 21:9 disorders, do not be *t*
24:37 *t*, and had become frightened

Terrifies
Hab 2:17 the beasts that *t* them

Terrify
Job 9:34 frightfulness, let it not *t*
13:21 fright of you . . . not *t* me
33:7 No frightfulness . . . will *t*
2Co 10:9 want to *t* you by my letters

Terrifying
2Sa 22:5 men that kept *t* me
Job 15:24 and anguish keep *t* him
Ps 18:4 good-for-nothing men . . . *t* me
Isa 54:14 and from anything *t*, for it
Jer 17:17 Do not become something *t*
48:39 *t* to all those round about

Territories
Nu 32:33 its cities in the *t*, and the
Jos 19:49 for a possession by its *t*
1Sa 5:6 namely, Ashdod and its *t*
2Ki 18:8 clear to Gaza and also its *t*
2Ch 11:13 by him out of all their *t*
Ps 105:31 Gnats in all their *t*
Jer 15:13 sins, even in all your *t*
17:3 sin throughout all your *t*
Eze 27:4 the seas are your *t*

Territory
Ge 47:21 one end of the *t* of Egypt
Ex 8:2 plaguing all your *t* with frogs
10:14 down upon all the *t* of Egypt
10:19 in all the *t* of Egypt
34:24 I will make your *t* spacious
Nu 20:16 at the extremity of your *t*
20:17 we shall pass through your *t*
20:21 Israel to pass through his *t*
21:22 until we pass through your *t*
21:23 Israel to pass through his *t*
22:36 is on the extremity of the *t*
De 2:18 the *t* of Moab, that is, Ar
12:20 God will widen out your *t*
16:4 in all your *t* seven days
19:3 you must divide up the *t* of
19:8 your God widens out your *t*
28:40 olive trees in all your *t*
Jos 1:4 your *t* will prove to be
12:4 *t* of Og the king of Bashan
12:5 the *t* of Sihon the king of
13:11 the *t* of the Geshurites and
13:16 the *t* came to be theirs
13:23 *t* was the inheritance of
13:25 their *t* came to be Jazer
13:30 *t* came to be from Mahanaim
18:5 on his *t* to the south, and
18:5 on their *t* to the north
18:11 the *t* of their lot went
19:47 *t* of the sons of Dan was
24:30 they buried him in the *t*
Jg 1:18 Gaza and its *t* and Ashkelon
1:18 Ashkelon and its *t* and Ekron
1:18 and Ekron and its *t*
1:36 the *t* of the Amorites was
2:9 they buried him in the *t* of
11:20 crossing through his *t*, and
11:22 the *t* of the Amorites from
19:29 sent her into every *t* of
1Sa 6:9 road to its *t* that it goes up
7:13 anymore into the *t* of Israel
7:14 *t* of them Israel delivered
10:2 the *t* of Benjamin at Zelzah
11:3 into all the *t* of Israel and
11:7 into all the *t* of Israel by
27:1 in all the *t* of Israel, and
2Sa 2:3 in the cities of Hebron *t*
2Sa 21:5 in any of the *t* of Israel
1Ki 1:3 throughout all the *t* of Israel
2Ki 10:32 in all the *t* of Israel
15:16 and its *t* out from Tirzah
1Ch 4:10 actually enlarge my *t* and
6:54 walled camps in their *t*
6:66 cities of their *t* from the
21:12 ruin in all the *t* of Israel
2Ch 26:6 built cities in Ashdod *t*
Ps 78:54 bring them to his holy *t*
105:33 break the trees of their *t*
147:14 is putting peace in your *t*
Isa 15:8 gone around the *t* of Moab
Jer 31:17 return to their own *t*
Eze 43:12 entire *t* all around is
47:13 *t* that you will assign to
48:13 to the *t* of the priests
Joe 3:6 far from their own *t*
Am 1:13 widening out their own *t*
6:2, 2 their *t* bigger than your *t*
Mic 5:6 and when he treads upon our *t*
Zep 2:8 great airs against their *t*
Mal 1:4 them the *t* of wickedness
1:5 over the *t* of Israel
Mt 2:22 into the *t* of Galilee
13:54 coming into his home *t* he
13:57 except in his home *t* and in
Mr 1:5 all the *t* of Judea and all the
6:1 and came into his home *t*, and
6:4 except in his home *t* and
Lu 4:23 do also here in your home *t*
4:24 is accepted in his home *t*
9:6 through the *t* from village to
Ac 8:40 he went through the *t* and
Ro 15:23 untouched *t* in these regions
2Co 10:13 the *t* that God apportioned
10:15 with reference to our *t*
10:16 in someone else's *t* where

Terror
Ge 9:2 a fear of you and a *t* of you
35:5 the *t* of God came to be upon
1Sa 2:4 mighty men . . . filled with *t*
Job 6:21 see *t*, and you become afraid
41:33 one made to be without *t*
Isa 17:14 look! there is sudden *t*
30:31 will be struck with *t*
51:7 do not be struck with *t*
Jer 1:17 Do not be struck with any *t*
1:17 I may not strike you with *t*
8:15 healing, but, look! *t!*
10:2 *t* even at the signs of the
10:2 nations are struck with *t*
14:19 healing, and, look! *t!*
17:18 ones to be struck with *t*
17:18 not be struck with *t*
23:4 be struck with any *t*
30:10 do not be struck with *t*
48:1 shame and been put in *t*
48:20 she has been struck with *t*
Eze 2:6 do not you be struck with *t*
3:9 struck with *t* at their faces
26:17 *t* to all the inhabitants
32:23 *t* in the land of those alive
32:24 *t* in the land of those alive
32:25 *t* was caused in the land
32:26 *t* in the land of those alive
32:27 *t* in the land of those alive
32:32 *t* in the land of those alive
Mal 2:5 was struck with *t*
1Pe 3:6 not fearing any cause for *t*

Terrorize
Job 3:5 things that darken a day *t* it
31:34 families would *t* me

Terrorized
1Sa 16:14 bad spirit from Jehovah *t*

Terrorizing
1Sa 16:15 God's bad spirit is *t* you

Terrors
Job 6:4 *t* from God range themselves
18:11 sudden *t* certainly make him
18:14 march him to the king of *t*
24:17 the sudden *t* of deep shadow
27:20 sudden *t* will overtake him
30:15 *t* have been turned upon me
Ps 73:19 finish through sudden *t*
88:16 *T* from you yourself have
Ec 12:5 and there are *t* in the way
Eze 26:21 Sudden *t* are what I shall
27:36 Sudden *t* are what you must
28:19 Sudden *t* are what you must

Terror-stricken
Jer 46:5 that I have seen them *t*
46:27 do not be *t*, O Israel

Tertius
Ro 16:22 *T*, who have done the writing

Tertullus
Ac 24:1 a public speaker, a certain *T*
24:2 *T* started accusing him

Test
Ge 22:1 God put Abraham to the *t*
Ex 15:25 there he put them to the *t*
16:4 I may put them to the *t* as to
17:2 keep putting Jehovah to the *t*
17:7 their putting Jehovah to the *t*
20:20 of putting you to the *t* the
De 6:16 put Jehovah your God to the *t*
6:16 put him to the *t* at Massah
8:2 to put you to the *t* so as to
8:16 to put you to the *t* so as to
33:8 you put to the *t* at Massah
Jg 2:22 in order by them to *t* Israel
3:1 so as by them to *t* Israel
3:4 serving as agents to *t* Israel
6:39 make a *t* only once more with
1Ki 10:1 *t* him with perplexing
2Ch 9:1 *t* Solomon with perplexing
32:31 to put him to the *t*
Job 7:18 every moment you should *t*
12:11 the ear itself *t* out words
34:3 ear . . . makes a *t* of words
Ps 26:2 Jehovah, and put me to the *t*
78:18 to *t* God in their heart
78:41 they would put God to the *t*
78:56 *t* and rebel against God the
Isa 7:12 I put Jehovah to the *t*
Da 1:12 put your servants to the *t*
1:14 them to the *t* for ten days
Mal 3:10 *t* me out, please, in this
Mt 4:7 put Jehovah your God to the *t*
22:18 Why do you put me to the *t*
Mr 8:11 to put him to the *t*
10:2 to put him to the *t*, began
12:15 Why do you put me to the *t?*
Lu 4:12 put Jehovah your God to the *t*
10:25 rose up, to *t* him out, and
Joh 6:6 he was saying this to *t* him
Ac 5:9 *t* of the spirit of Jehovah
15:10 a *t* of God by imposing upon
1Co 10:9 put Jehovah to the *t*, as
10:9 put him to the *t*, only to
2Co 8:2 a great *t* under affliction
8:8 *t* of the genuineness of your
Heb 2:18 when being put to the *t*
2:18 who are being put to the *t*
3:8 the *t* in the wilderness
3:9 made a *t* of me with a trial
1Jo 4:1 *t* the inspired expressions to
Re 2:2 *t* who say they are apostles
2:10 may be fully put to the *t*
3:10 hour of *t*, which is to come
3:10 *t* upon those dwelling on the

Tested
Ge 42:15 By this you will be *t* out
42:16 may be *t* out as the truth
Job 23:10 After he has *t* me out, I
34:36 Job be *t* out to the limit
Ec 7:23 this I have *t* with wisdom
Mal 3:15 they have *t* God out and keep
1Ti 3:10 be *t* as to fitness first
Heb 4:15 been *t* in all respects like
11:17 Abraham, when he was *t*, as
Jas 1:3 *t* quality of your faith
1Pe 1:7 the *t* quality of your faith

Tester
Jer 6:27 I have made you a metal *t*

Testicles
Le 21:20 or having his *t* broken
22:24 *t* squeezed or crushed or
De 23:1 castrated by crushing the *t*
Jer 5:8 having strong *t*, they have

Testified
2Sa 1:16 own mouth has *t* against you
Isa 59:12 each one has *t* against us
Ho 5:5 the pride of Israel has *t* to
7:10 Israel has *t* to his face

Testifies
Job 16:8 In my face it *t*
Isa 3:9 actually *t* against them

Testify
Ex 20:16 You must not *t* falsely as a
23:2 not *t* over a controversy so as
Nu 35:30 and one witness may not *t*
De 5:20 *t* to a falsehood against your
Jer 14:7 errors do *t* against us
Mic 6:3 tired you out? *T* against me
2Co 8:3 I *t*, beyond their actual

Testifying
Job 16:19 in the heavens is one *t*
Pr 25:18 man *t* against his fellowman
Mt 26:62 these are *t* against you
27:13 they are *t* against you
Mr 14:60 What is it these are *t*

Testimonies
De 4:45 *t* and the regulations and the
6:17 his *t* and his regulations that
6:20 What do the *t* and the
1Ki 2:3 his *t*, according to what is
2Ki 23:3 his commandments and his *t*
1Ch 29:19 your *t* and your regulations
2Ch 34:31 his *t* and his regulations
Ne 9:34 commandments or to your *t*
Mt 15:19 out of the heart . . . false *t*
Mr 14:56 *t* were not in agreement

Testimony
Ex 16:34 deposit it before the *T* as
25:16 place in the Ark the *t* that
25:21 Ark you will place the *t*
25:22 are upon the ark of the *t*
26:33 bring the ark of the *t* there
26:34 cover upon the ark of the *t*
27:21 the curtain that is by the *T*
30:6 is near the ark of the *t*
30:6 the cover that is over the *T*
30:26 meeting and the ark of the *t*
30:36 before the *T* in the tent of
31:7 Ark for the *t* and the cover
31:18 Moses two tablets of the *T*
32:15 two tablets of the *T* in his
34:29 two tablets of the *T* were
38:21 the tabernacle of the *T*
39:35 ark of the *t* and its poles
40:3 place the ark of the *t* in it
40:5 before the ark of the *t* and
40:20 the *T* and put it into the Ark
40:21 approach to the ark of the *t*
Le 16:13 cover, which is upon the *T*
24:3 curtain of the *T* in the tent
Nu 1:50 tabernacle of the *T* and over
1:53 around the tabernacle of the *T*
1:53 due to the tabernacle of the *T*
4:5 cover the ark of the *t* with it
7:89 was upon the ark of the *t*
9:15 tent of the *T*, but in the
10:11 over the tabernacle of the *T*
17:4 tent of meeting before the *T*
17:7 in the tent of the *T*
17:8 went into the tent of the *T*
17:10 Aaron's rod back before the *T*
18:2 before the tent of the *T*
Jos 4:16 the ark of the *t* that they
2Ki 11:12 the diadem and the *T*
2Ch 23:11 the diadem and the *T* and
24:6 for the tent of the *T*
Mr 14:55 looking for *t* against Jesus
14:59 was their *t* in agreement
1Ti 3:7 have a fine *t* from people on
Heb 3:5 a *t* of the things that were
10:28 upon the *t* of two or three

Testing
Nu 14:22 kept *t* me these ten times
De 13:3 God is *t* you to know whether
Ps 7:9 is *t* out heart and kidneys
Mt 22:35 asked, *t* him
Lu 8:13 in a season of *t* they fall
2Co 13:5 Keep *t* whether you are in

Thaddaeus
Mt 10:3 the son of Alphaeus, and *T*
Mr 3:18 *T* and Simon the Cananaean

Thank
2Sa 22:50 I shall *t* you, O Jehovah
1Ch 16:4 to *t* and praise Jehovah the
16:7 *t* Jehovah by means of Asaph
16:41 to *t* Jehovah, because to
23:30 to *t* and praise Jehovah, and
2Ch 7:6 king had made to *t* Jehovah
Isa 12:1 *t* you, O Jehovah, for
Lu 18:11 I *t* you I am not as the rest
Joh 11:41 Father, I *t* you that you
Ro 1:21 as God nor did they *t* him
1Co 1:4 always *t* God for you in view
14:18 I *t* God, I speak in more
Php 1:3 I *t* my God always upon every
Col 1:3 We *t* God the Father of our
1Th 1:2 always *t* God when we make
2:13 also *t* God incessantly
2Th 2:13 obligated to *t* God always
Phm 4 I always *t* my God when I make
Re 11:17 We *t* you, Jehovah God, the

Thanked
2Ch 7:3 *t* Jehovah, for he is good, for
Ac 28:15 Paul *t* God and took courage

Thankful
1Co 1:14 am *t* I baptized none of you
Col 3:15 And show yourselves *t*

Thankfulness
Ac 24:3 Felix, with the greatest *t*
3Jo 4 No greater cause for *t* do I have

Thanking
1Ch 25:3 for *t* and praising Jehovah
29:13 O our God, we are *t* you and
2Ch 5:13 in praising and *t* Jehovah
Lu 17:16 at Jesus' feet, *t* him
Col 1:12 *t* the Father who rendered
3:17 *t* God the Father through him

Thankless
Pr 29:21 he will even become a *t* one

Thanks
1Ch 16:8 Give *t* to Jehovah, you people
16:34 Give *t* to Jehovah, you
16:35 To give *t* to your holy name
2Ch 31:2 give *t* and praise in the
Ezr 3:11 and giving *t* to Jehovah
Ne 12:8 over the giving of *t*, he and
12:24 to offer praise and give *t*
Ps 30:4 Give *t* to his holy memorial
33:2 Give *t* to Jehovah on the harp
75:1 We give *t* to you, O God
75:1 O God; we give *t* to you
79:13 *t* to you to time indefinite
92:1 good to give *t* to Jehovah
97:12 give *t* to his holy memorial
100:4 Give *t* to him, bless his
105:1 Give *t* to Jehovah, call
106:1 Give *t* to Jehovah, for he
106:47 give *t* to your holy name
107:1 give *t* to Jehovah, you people
107:8 people give *t* to Jehovah for
107:15 people give *t* to Jehovah
107:21 give *t* to Jehovah for his
107:31 people give *t* to Jehovah for
118:1 Give *t* to Jehovah, you people
118:29 Give *t* to Jehovah, you
119:62 I get up to give *t* to you
122:4 *t* to the name of Jehovah
136:1 Give *t* to Jehovah, O you
136:2 *t* to the God of the gods
136:3 *t* to the Lord of the lords
136:26 *t* to the God of the heavens
140:13 will give *t* to your name
Isa 12:4 Give *t* to Jehovah, you
Mt 15:36 after offering *t*, he broke
26:27 having given *t*, he gave it
Mr 8:6 took the seven loaves, gave *t*
14:23 taking a cup, he offered *t*
Lu 2:38 began returning *t* to God and
22:17 gave *t* and said: Take this
22:19 took a loaf, gave *t*, broke it
Joh 6:11 loaves and, after giving *t*
6:23 after the Lord had given *t*
Ac 27:35 gave *t* to God before them
Ro 1:8 I give *t* to my God through
6:17 *t* to God that you were the
7:25 *T* to God through Jesus Christ
14:6 for he gives *t* to God; and he
14:6 and yet gives *t* to God
16:4 of the nations render *t*
1Co 10:30 If I am partaking with *t*
10:30 that for which I give *t*
11:24 after giving *t*, he broke it
14:16 Amen to your giving of *t*
14:17 give *t* in a fine way, but
15:57 *t* to God, for he gives us
2Co 1:11 *t* may be given by many in
2:14 *t* be to God who always leads
8:16 *t* be to God for putting the
9:11 an expression of *t* to God
9:12 many expressions of *t* to God
9:15 *T* be to God for his . . . gift
Eph 1:16 not cease giving *t* for you
5:4 but rather the giving of *t*
Eph 5:20 giving *t* always for all
1Th 5:18 give *t*. For this is the
2Th 1:3 give God *t* always for you
1Ti 2:1 offerings of *t*, be made

Thanksgiving
Le 7:12 present it in expression of *t*
7:12 along with the sacrifice of *t*
7:13 together with the *t* sacrifice
7:15 flesh of the *t* sacrifice of
22:29 *t* sacrifice to Jehovah, you
2Ch 29:31 *t* sacrifices to the house
29:31 and *t* sacrifices, and also
33:16 *t* sacrifices and went on to
Ne 12:31 two large *t* choirs and
12:38 other *t* choir was walking in
12:40 the two *t* choirs came to a
Ps 26:7 To cause *t* to be heard aloud
42:4 voice of a joyful cry and *t*
50:14 Offer *t* as your sacrifice to
50:23 offering *t* as his sacrifice
56:12 expressions of *t* to you
69:30 I will magnify him with *t*
95:2 before his person with *t*
100:*super* A melody of *t*
100:4 Come into his gates with *t*
107:22 offer the sacrifices of *t*
116:17 offer the sacrifice of *t*
147:7 Respond to Jehovah with *t*
Isa 51:3 *t* and the voice of melody
Jer 17:26 *t* sacrifice into the house
30:19 certainly go forth *t*, and
33:11 *t* offering into the house
Am 4:5 make a *t* sacrifice to smoke
Jon 2:9 with the voice of *t* I will
2Co 4:15 *t* of many more to the glory
Php 4:6 supplication along with *t*
Col 2:7 overflowing with faith in *t*
4:2 remaining awake in it with *t*
1Th 3:9 what *t* can we render to God
1Ti 4:3 to be partaken of with *t* by
4:4 if it is received with *t*
Re 4:9 and *t* to the one seated upon
7:12 the *t* and the honor and the

Thanksgivings
Ne 12:27 a rejoicing even with *t* and
12:46 song of praise and *t* to God

Theater
Ac 19:29 rushed into the *t*, taking
19:31 not to risk himself in the *t*
Heb 10:33 exposed as in a *t* both to

Theatrical
1Co 4:9 *t* spectacle to the world, and

Thebez
Jg 9:50 go to *T* and to camp against
9:50 camp against *T* and capture it
2Sa 11:21 wall so that he died at *T*

Theft
Tit 2:10 not committing *t*, but

Thefts
Re 9:21 fornication nor of their *t*

Theme
Job 30:9 even the *t* of their song
La 3:14 *t* of their song all day long

Theophilus
Lu 1:3 to you, most excellent *T*
Ac 1:1 O *T*, I composed about all the

Thessalonians
Ac 20:4 and Secundus of the *T*, and
1Th 1:1 to the congregation of the *T*
2Th 1:1 to the congregation of the *T*

Thessalonica
Ac 17:1 came to *T*, where there was a
17:11 noble-minded than those in *T*
17:13 Jews from *T* learned that the
27:2 a Macedonian from *T*
Php 4:16 in *T*, you sent something to
2Ti 4:10 and he has gone to *T*

Theudas
Ac 5:36 *T* rose, saying he himself

Thick
Ge 19:28 *t* smoke ascended from the
19:28 like the *t* smoke of a kiln!
De 4:11 darkness, cloud and *t* gloom
5:22 the cloud and the *t* gloom
32:15 grown fat, you have become *t*
2Sa 22:10 *t* gloom was beneath his
22:12 Dark waters, *t* clouds

1Ki 8:12 was to reside in the *t* gloom
20:39 into the *t* of the battle
2Ch 4:17 cast them in the *t* ground
6:1 was to reside in the *t* gloom
Job 15:26 the *t* bosses of his shields
22:13 Through *t* gloom can he
38:9 *t* gloom as its swaddling
Ps 18:9 *t* gloom was beneath his feet
18:11 Dark waters, *t* clouds
97:2 *t* gloom are all around him
104:12 among the *t* foliage they
148:8 and hail, snow and *t* smoke
Isa 60:2 *t* gloom the national groups
Jer 13:16 will turn it into *t* gloom
Eze 34:12 day of clouds and *t* gloom
Joe 2:2 a day of clouds and *t* gloom
Zep 1:15 day of clouds and of *t* gloom
Ac 13:11 *t* mist and darkness fell
Heb 12:18 *t* darkness and a tempest

Thicker
1Ki 12:10 be *t* than my father's hips
2Ch 10:10 be *t* than my father's hips

Thicket
Ge 22:13 caught by its horns in a *t*
Ps 74:5 on high against a *t* of trees
Isa 55:13 Instead of the *t* of thorns
Jer 4:7 as a lion out of his *t*
Eze 31:3 a woody *t* offering shadow

Thickets
Isa 7:19 upon all the thorn *t* and
9:18 fire in the *t* of the forest
10:34 *t* of the forest with an
Jer 4:29 They have entered into the *t*
12:5 proud *t* along the Jordan
49:19 proud *t* along the Jordan
50:44 proud *t* along the Jordan
Zec 11:3 proud *t* along the Jordan have

Thickness
1Ki 7:26 And its *t* was a handbreadth
2Ch 4:5 And its *t* was a handbreadth
Jer 52:21 *t* was four fingerbreadths

Thief
Ex 22:2 If a *t* should be found in the
22:7 if the *t* should be found, he
22:8 If the *t* should not be found
Job 24:14 he becomes a regular *t*
30:5 shout at them as at a *t*
Ps 50:18 Whenever you saw a *t*, you
Pr 6:30 *t* just because he commits
29:24 that is partner with a *t*
Jer 2:26 a *t* when he is found out
Ho 7:1 and a *t* himself comes in
Joe 2:9 they go in like the *t*
Zec 5:4 enter into the house of the *t*
Mt 24:43 known in what watch the *t*
Lu 12:33 where a *t* does not get near
12:39 had known at what hour the *t*
Joh 10:1 one is a *t* and a plunderer
10:10 *t* does not come unless it
12:6 he was a *t* and had the money
1Th 5:2 exactly as a *t* in the night
1Pe 4:15 suffer as a murderer or a *t*
2Pe 3:10 day will come as a *t*
Re 3:3 I shall come as a *t*, and you
16:15 I am coming as a *t*. Happy

Thieveries
Mt 15:19 out of the heart come . . . *t*
Mr 7:21 fornications, *t*, murders

Thievery
Pr 6:30 *t* to fill his soul when he

Thieves
Isa 1:23 stubborn and partners with *t*
Jer 48:27 he found among outright *t*
49:9 *t* came in by night, they
Ob 5 If it were *t* that came in to you
Mt 6:19 where *t* break in and steal
6:20 *t* do not break in and steal
Joh 10:8 come in place of me are *t*
1Co 6:10 nor *t*, nor greedy persons
1Th 5:4 overtake you as it would *t*

Thigh
Ge 24:2 hand, please, under my *t*
24:9 hand under the *t* of Abraham
32:25 touched the socket of his *t*
32:25 the socket of Jacob's *t* joint
32:31 he was limping upon his *t*
32:32 eat the sinew of the *t* nerve
32:32 on the socket of the *t* joint
32:32 the socket of Jacob's *t* joint
Ge 32:32 by the sinew of the *t* nerve
46:26 issued out of his upper *t*
47:29 hand, please, under my *t*
Ex 1:5 issued out of Jacob's upper *t*
Nu 5:21 Jehovah's letting your *t* fall
5:22 and the *t* to fall away
5:27 and her *t* must fall away, and
Jg 3:16 his garment upon his right *t*
3:21 the sword off his right *t*
8:30 that issued out of his upper *t*
Ps 45:3 Gird your sword upon your *t*
Ca 3:8 with his sword upon his *t*
Jer 31:19 I made a slap upon the *t*
Eze 21:12 make a slap on the *t*
24:4 *t* and shoulder; fill it
Re 19:16 upon his *t*, he has a name

Thighs
Ex 28:42 From the hips and to the *t*
Jg 15:8 piling legs upon *t* with a
Job 21:24 *t* have become full of fat
40:17 The sinews of its *t* are
Ca 7:1 of your *t* are like ornaments
Da 2:32 and its *t* were of copper

Thin
Ge 41:6 seven ears of grain, *t* and
41:7 the *t* ears of grain began to
41:23 ears of grain shriveled, *t*
41:24 *t* ears of grain began to
Ex 39:3 plates of gold to *t* sheets
Le 21:20 *t* or diseased in his eyes or
Nu 16:38 into *t* metal plates as an

Thin-fleshed
Ge 41:3 ugly in appearance and *t*
41:4 *t* began to eat up the seven
41:19 very bad in form and *t*

Thing
Ge 3:14 Because you have done this *t*
7:4 I will wipe every existing *t*
7:23 he wiped out every existing *t*
8:21 deal every living *t* a blow
19:8 to these men do not do a *t*
19:20 there and it is a small *t*
19:20 is it not a small *t?*—and
19:22 I am not able to do a *t*
20:10 in that you have done this *t*
21:11 But the *t* proved to be very
21:26 I do not know who did this *t*
22:16 done this *t* . . . not withheld
24:10 with every sort of good *t*
24:50 From Jehovah this *t* has
30:15 Is this a little *t*
30:31 If you will do this *t* for me
31:35 customary *t* with women is
34:14 cannot possibly do such a *t*
41:28 the *t* that I have spoken to
41:32 the *t* is firmly established
41:37 the *t* proved to be good in
43:32 detestable *t* to the Egyptians
44:5 *t* that my master drinks from
46:34 a detestable *t* to Egypt
Ex 1:18 you have done this *t*, in that
2:14 the *t* has become known
2:15 Pharaoh got to hear of this *t*
7:11 same *t* with their magic arts
7:22 same *t* with their secret arts
8:7 same *t* by their secret arts
8:26 *t* detestable to the Egyptians
8:26 *t* detestable to the Egyptians
9:4 not a *t* of all that belongs to
9:5 Jehovah will do this *t* in the
9:6 Jehovah did this *t* on the next
12:24 keep this *t* as a regulation
16:14 flaky *t*, fine like hoarfrost
18:23 If you do this very *t*, and
29:1 this is the *t* that you are to
33:17 This *t*, too, of which you
34:10 a fear-inspiring *t* that I am
Le 2:11 should be made a leavened *t*
5:2 a soul touches some unclean *t*
6:4 *t* which he has robbed or the
6:4 extorted *t* which he has taken
6:4 or the *t* in his charge which
6:4 the *t* lost that he has found
6:25 It is a most holy *t*
7:18 It will become a foul *t*, and
7:21 or any unclean loathsome *t*
8:5 the *t* that Jehovah has given
9:6 *t* that Jehovah has commanded
10:10 the holy *t* and the profane
10:10 the unclean *t* and the clean
11:10 are a loathsome *t* for you
11:11 become a loathsome *t* to you
Le 11:12 is a loathsome *t* to you
11:13 a loathsome *t*: the eagle and
11:20 is a loathsome *t* to you
11:23 four legs is a loathsome *t*
11:41 creature . . . a loathsome *t*
11:42 they are a loathsome *t*
12:4 should not touch any holy *t*
17:2 *t* that Jehovah has commanded
18:22 It is a detestable *t*
19:7 third day, it is a foul *t*
19:8 profaned a holy *t* of Jehovah
19:24 fruit will become a holy *t*
20:13 have done a detestable *t*
22:5 swarming *t* that is unclean
22:14 eats a holy *t* by mistake
22:14 give the holy *t* to the
27:28 no sort of devoted *t* that a
27:28 devoted *t* may be bought back
Nu 16:9 Is it such a little *t* for you
16:13 Is it so little a *t* that you
18:14 Every devoted *t* in Israel
18:29 as some holy *t* from them
32:20 If you will do this *t*, if
De 1:14 The *t* you have spoken for us
1:23 the *t* proved to be good in my
2:7 You have not lacked a *t*
4:32 any great *t* brought about like
7:25 a *t* detestable to Jehovah
7:26 a detestable *t* into your house
7:26 a *t* devoted to destruction
11:6 tents and every existing *t*
13:11 do anything like this bad *t*
13:14 the *t* is established as the
13:14 this detestable *t* has been
13:17 the *t* made sacred by ban
14:3 You must eat no detestable *t*
15:15 commanding you this *t* today
16:22 a *t* Jehovah your God hates
17:1 a *t* detestable to Jehovah
17:3 a *t* that I have not commanded
17:4 the *t* is established as the
17:4 this detestable *t* has been
17:5 who has done this bad *t*
20:16 preserve any breathing *t*
22:20 this *t* has proved to be the
23:9 from every bad *t*
24:18 commanding you to do this *t*
24:22 commanding you to do this *t*
27:15 a *t* detestable to Jehovah
Jos 6:17 a *t* devoted to destruction
6:18 the *t* devoted to destruction
6:18 the *t* devoted to destruction
6:18 a *t* devoted to destruction
7:1 the *t* devoted to destruction
7:1 the *t* devoted to destruction
7:11 the *t* devoted to destruction
7:12 a *t* devoted to destruction
7:12 the *t* devoted to destruction
7:13 A *t* devoted to destruction is
7:13 the *t* devoted to destruction
7:15 the *t* devoted to destruction
9:24 So we did this *t*
11:11 No breathing *t* at all was
22:20 *t* devoted to destruction
Jg 4:9 the beautifying *t* will not
6:29 Who has done this *t?* And they
6:29 the one that has done this *t*
8:1 What sort of *t* is this that
11:37 Let this *t* be done to me
13:7 and do not eat any unclean *t*
13:14 no unclean *t* of any sort let
18:7 was molesting a *t* in the land
18:10 is no lack of any sort of *t*
19:19 is no lack of a single *t*
19:24 this disgraceful, foolish *t*
19:30 a *t* as this has never been
20:3 How has this bad *t* been
20:9 *t* that we shall do to Gibeah
20:12 What is this bad *t* that has
21:11 is the *t* that you should do
Ru 4:7 to establish every sort of *t*
1Sa 2:20 in place of the *t* lent, that
4:7 for such a *t* as this never
4:16 is the *t* that has happened
8:6 the *t* was bad in the eyes of
9:21 spoken to me a *t* like this
12:16 this great *t* that Jehovah is
14:12 we will let you know a *t*
18:23 Is it an easy *t* in your eyes
20:2, 2 do a big *t* or a little *t*
22:15 servant did not know a *t*
24:6 do this *t* to my lord, the
25:15 we did not miss a single *t*
25:21 not a single *t* of all that

1Sa 25:36 she did not tell him a *t*
26:16 *t* that you have done is not
28:18 the *t* that Jehovah will
29:3 not found in him a single *t*
2Sa 2:6 because you have done this *t*
3:13 *t* there is that I am asking
11:11 I shall not do this *t*
11:27 *t* that David had done
12:6 fact that he has done this *t*
12:12 *t* in front of all Israel
12:14 with disrespect by this *t*
12:21 *t* mean that you have done
14:18 *t* about which I am asking
14:20 Joab has done this *t*, but
14:21 shall certainly do this *t*
15:6 Absalom kept doing a *t* like
15:11 did not know a single *t*
17:19 not a *t* became known of it
19:42 become angry over this *t*
24:3 he found delight in this *t*
1Ki 1:27 this *t* has been brought about
1:47 another *t*, the servants of
2:23 that Adonijah spoke this *t*
3:10 the *t* was pleasing in the
3:10 Solomon had requested this *t*
3:11 requested this *t* and have not
9:1 every desirable *t* of Solomon
11:5 Milcom the disgusting *t* of
11:7 the disgusting *t* of Moab
11:7 Molech the disgusting *t* of
11:10 And respecting this *t* he
12:24 this *t* has been brought
12:30 this *t* came to be a cause
13:33 this *t* Jeroboam did not
13:34 in this *t* there came to be
16:31 trivial *t* for him to walk
18:24 and said: The *t* is good
20:9 this *t* I am not able to do
20:24 do this *t*: Remove the kings
22:8 the king say a *t* like that
2Ki 2:10 You have asked a difficult *t*
3:18 a trivial *t* in the eyes of
5:13 a great *t* that the prophet
5:18 this *t* may Jehovah forgive
7:2 could this *t* take place?
8:9 every sort of good *t* of
8:13 that he could do this great *t*
11:5 the *t* that you will do
17:12 You must not do this *t*
20:10 easy *t* for the shadow to
23:13 Ashtoreth the disgusting *t*
23:13 Chemosh the disgusting *t* of
23:13 Milcom the detestable *t* of
1Ch 2:7 the *t* devoted to destruction
13:4 the *t* seemed right in the
21:7 *t* was bad in the eyes of the
21:8 in that I have done this *t*
23:28 purification of every holy *t*
28:19 insight for the entire *t* in
2Ch 8:6 every desirable *t* of Solomon
11:4 *t* has been brought about
15:15 rejoicing over the *t* sworn
18:7 the king say a *t* like that
23:4 the *t* that you will do
29:5 impure *t* out from the holy
29:36 that the *t* had occurred
30:4 *t* was right in the eyes of
Ezr 7:27 put such a *t* into the heart
9:3 as soon as I heard of this *t*
Ne 2:19 is this *t* that you are doing
5:9 The *t* that you are doing is not
5:14 Another *t*: From the day that
13:17 bad *t* that you are doing
Es 1:21 *t* was pleasing in the eyes
2:4 *t* was pleasing in the king's
2:22 And the *t* came to be known to
5:14 *t* seemed good before Haman
6:3 What honor and great *t* has
8:5 the *t* is proper before the king
Job 3:25 a dreadful *t* I have dreaded
8:7 your beginning . . . a small *t*
9:22 One *t* there is. That is why
20:4 all times known this very *t*
28:11 concealed *t* he brings forth
33:27 not the proper *t* for me
34:29 it being the same *t*
Ps 2:1 kept muttering an empty *t*
27:4 One *t* I have asked from
41:8 A good-for-nothing *t* is poured
101:3 eyes any good-for-nothing *t*
119:133 may no kind of hurtful *t*
126:2 Jehovah has done a great *t*
126:3 Jehovah has done a great *t*
145:16 desire of every living *t*
Ps 150:6 Every breathing *t*—let it
Pr 3:25 of any sudden dreadful *t*
3:32 detestable *t* to Jehovah, but
4:7 Wisdom is the prime *t*
10:24 *t* frightful to the wicked
13:12 *t* desired is a tree of life
14:6 knowledge is an easy *t*
18:22 One has found a good *t*, and
19:22 desirable *t* in earthling man
27:7 every bitter *t* is sweet
Ec 2:12 The *t* that people have already
2:21 not worked hard at such a *t*
5:18 The best *t* that I myself have
7:27 one *t* taken after another, to
8:1 the interpretation of a *t*
8:3 Do not stand in a bad *t*
8:5 not know any calamitous *t*
12:14 in relation to every hidden *t*
Ca 3:6 What is this *t* that is coming
Isa 2:1 *t* that Isaiah the son of Amoz
5:6 set it as a *t* destroyed
7:13 little *t* for you to tire out
11:3 to the *t* heard by his ears
24:18 sound of the dreaded *t* will
29:16 *t* made say respecting its
29:16 *t* formed actually say
33:18 low tones on a frightful *t*
41:24 A detestable *t* is anyone
44:19 into a mere detestable *t*
53:1 faith in the *t* heard by us
59:16 the *t* that supported him
60:15 set you as a *t* of pride to
65:12 *t* in which I took no
66:4 *t* in which I took no delight
66:8 Who has heard of a *t* like
66:17 the loathsome *t*, even the
Jer 3:24 the shameful *t* itself has
5:7 forgive you for this very *t*
5:14 you men are saying this *t*
5:30 a horrible *t*, has been
6:15 For one *t*, they positively
6:15 another *t*, they have not
7:31 a *t* that I had not commanded
8:12 For one *t*, they positively
8:12 for another *t*, they did not
9:24 because of this very *t*
11:13 placed for the shameful *t*
11:15 do this *t*, the evil device
14:14 divination and a valueless *t*
18:13 There is a horrible *t* that
31:22 Jehovah has created a new *t*
31:26 At this *t* I awoke and began
32:35 *t* that I did not command
32:35 to do this detestable *t*
38:21 *t* that Jehovah has caused
40:3 this *t* has happened to you
40:16 Do not do this *t*, for it
42:3 the *t* that we should do
44:4 detestable sort of *t* that I
48:8 a *t* that Jehovah has said
49:5 upon you a dreadful *t*
La 1:8 has become a mere abhorrent *t*
1:17 an abhorrent *t* in among them
Eze 6:10 to them this calamitous *t*
7:19 abhorrent *t* their own gold
7:20 to them an abhorrent *t*
8:17 light *t* to the house of Judah
11:5 You people said the right *t*
11:15 given us as a *t* to possess
16:34 the opposite *t* takes place
16:50 to carry on a detestable *t*
18:12 a pledged *t* he would not
18:12 detestable *t* is what he has
22:11 man has done a detestable *t*
22:26 the holy *t* and the common
22:26 the unclean *t* and the clean
24:16 *t* desirable to your eyes
24:21 the *t* desirable to your eyes
24:25 the *t* desirable to their
33:15 returns the very *t* pledged
33:26 You have done a detestable *t*
34:18 such a little *t* for you men
35:15 same *t* I shall make of you
40:5 the breadth of the *t* built
44:23 a holy *t* and a profane
44:23 and a profane *t*; and the
44:29 every devoted *t* in Israel
Da 2:10 asked such a *t* as this of any
2:11 *t* that the king himself is
4:17 decree of watchers the *t* is
6:4 no pretext or corrupt *t* at all
6:4 corrupt *t* at all was found in
8:16 there understand the *t* seen
8:26 *t* seen concerning the evening
Da 8:27 on account of the *t* seen
9:23 understanding in the *t* seen
9:27 *t* decided upon will go
10:1 understanding in the *t* seen
11:31 disgusting *t* that is causing
11:36 *t* decided upon must be done
12:11 disgusting *t* that is causing
Ho 2:18 creeping *t* of the ground, and
6:10 I have seen a horrible *t*
9:10 to the shameful *t*, and they
9:10 like the *t* of their love
Joe 2:20 do a great *t* in what He does
2:21 do a great *t* in what He does
Am 3:7 will not do a *t* unless he has
4:12 I shall do this very *t* to you
6:13 rejoicing in a *t* that is not
Mic 1:7 the *t* given as the hire of a
Hab 3:9 are the *t* said. *Se'lah*
Hag 2:5 the *t* that I concluded with
Zec 8:10 there was no such *t*; and to
13:1 sin and for an abhorrent *t*
Mal 2:11 and a detestable *t* has been
2:13 second *t* that you people do
Mt 5:11 say . . . wicked *t* against you
5:46 collectors doing the same *t*
5:47 extraordinary *t* are you doing
5:47 the nations doing the same *t*
12:12 do a fine *t* on the sabbath
16:19 the *t* bound in the heavens
16:19 the *t* loosed in the heavens
18:14 desirable *t* with my Father
19:23 a difficult *t* for a rich man
21:24 I, also, will ask you one *t*
24:15 sight of the disgusting *t*
24:43 But know one *t*, that if the
26:35 also said the same *t*
27:23 Why, what bad *t* did he do?
Mr 1:44 See that you tell nobody a *t*
7:12 do a single *t* for his father
10:21 One *t* is missing about you
10:23 How difficult a *t* it will
10:24 how difficult a *t* it is to
13:14 *t* that causes desolation
14:31 began saying the same *t*
15:14 Why, what bad *t* did he do?
Lu 2:15 this *t* that has taken place
6:3 never read the very *t* David
12:26 you cannot do the least *t*
16:15 a disgusting *t* in God's sight
18:22 yet one *t* lacking about you
18:24 How difficult a *t* it will be
19:48 did not find the effective *t*
23:22 what bad *t* did this man do?
Joh 1:3 not even one *t* came into
3:27 cannot receive a single *t*
5:19 do a single *t* of his own
5:30 cannot do a single *t* of my
9:25 One *t* I do know, that
12:38 faith in the *t* heard by us
16:24 asked a single *t* in my name
Ac 2:12 does this *t* purport to be
6:5 *t* spoken was pleasing to the
11:8 unclean *t* has never entered
19:32 some were crying out one *t*
21:34 began shouting out one *t*, and
23:29 a single *t* deserving of death
26:26 *t* has not been done in a
Ro 2:1 *t* in which you judge another
8:24 man sees a *t*, does he hope
9:20 *t* molded say to him that
10:16 faith in the *t* heard by us
10:17 faith follows the *t* heard
10:17 *t* heard is through the word
11:7 *t* Israel is earnestly seeking
13:8 be owing anybody a single *t*
15:18 not venture to tell one *t* if
1Co 1:25 a foolish *t* of God is wiser
1:25 weak *t* of God is stronger
7:19 does not mean a *t*, and
7:19 uncircumcision means not a *t*
2Co 1:10 From such a great *t* as death
1:12 the *t* we boast of is this
2:3 so I wrote this very *t*, that
5:5 us for this very *t* is God
6:17 quit touching the unclean *t*
7:11 very *t*, your being saddened
10:5 every lofty *t* raised up
11:5 in a single *t* proved inferior
12:11 apostles in a single *t*
Ga 2:10 very *t* I have also earnestly
Php 1:6 I am confident of this very *t*
1:22 which *t* to select I do not
1:28 This very *t* is a proof of
3:13 but there is one *t* about it

Zec 8:12 people to inherit all these *t*
8:16 *t* that you people should do
8:17 are all *t* that I have hated
9:7 remove his bloodstained *t*
9:7 disgusting *t* from between his
14:6 *t* will be congealed
Mt 1:20 he had thought these *t* over
4:9 All these *t* I will give you if
5:18 and not all *t* take place
6:7 do not say the same *t* over and
6:8 Father knows what *t* you are
6:32 *t* the nations are eagerly
6:32 knows you need all these *t*
6:33 other *t* will be added to you
7:11 give good *t* to those asking
7:12 All *t*, therefore, that you
9:4 wicked *t* in your hearts
9:17 and both *t* are preserved
9:18 he was telling them these *t*
11:25 have hidden these *t* from the
11:27 All *t* have been delivered to
12:32 not in this system of *t* nor
12:34 how can you speak good *t*
12:35 sends out good *t*, whereas
12:35 sends out wicked *t*
13:3 many *t* by illustrations
13:17 desired to see the *t* you are
13:17 hear the *t* you are hearing
13:22 anxiety of this system of *t*
13:34 All these *t* Jesus spoke to
13:35 *t* hidden since the founding
13:39 conclusion of a system of *t*
13:40 conclusion . . . system of *t*
13:41 all *t* that cause stumbling
13:44 sells what *t* he has and buys
13:46 sold all the *t* he had and
13:49 conclusion . . . system of *t*
13:51 get the sense of all these *t*
13:52 treasure store *t* new and old
13:56 did this man get all these *t*
14:15 and buy themselves *t* to eat
15:18 the *t* proceeding out of the
15:18 and those *t* defile a man
15:20 are the *t* defiling a man
16:21 and suffer many *t* from the
17:11 and will restore all *t*
17:12 but did with him the *t* they
18:18 *t* you may bind on earth
18:18 will be *t* bound in heaven
18:18 *t* you may loose on earth
18:18 will be *t* loosed in heaven
18:25 all the *t* he had to be sold
18:31 saw the *t* that had happened
18:31 all the *t* that had happened
19:26 with God all *t* are possible
19:27 have left all *t* and followed
20:15 what I want with my own *t*
21:15 saw the marvelous *t* he did
21:22 all the *t* you ask in prayer
21:23 authority do you do these *t*
21:24 what authority I do these *t*
21:27 what authority I do these *t*
22:4 all *t* are ready. Come to the
22:21 Caesar's *t* to Caesar, but
22:21 but God's *t* to God
23:3 all the *t* they tell you, do
23:20 swearing . . . by all the *t* on
23:23 These *t* it was binding to do
23:23 not to disregard the other *t*
23:36 All these *t* will come upon
24:2 Do you not behold all these *t*?
24:3 When will these *t* be, and
24:3 conclusion of the system of *t*
24:6 these *t* must take place, but
24:8 these *t* are a beginning of
24:33 when you see all these *t*
24:34 until all these *t* occur
25:21 were faithful over a few *t*
25:21 appoint you over many *t*
25:23 were faithful over a few *t*
25:23 appoint you over many *t*
26:19 got *t* ready for the passover
27:13 many *t* they are testifying
27:54 and the *t* happening, grew
28:11 all the *t* that had happened
28:20 the *t* I have commanded you
28:20 of the system of *t*
Mr 1:44 the *t* Moses directed, for a
2:8 reasoning these *t* in your
3:8 of how many *t* he was doing
3:28 all *t* will be forgiven the
4:2 to teach them many *t* with
4:11 all *t* occur in illustrations
4:19 anxieties of this system of *t*

Mr 4:19 desires for the rest of the *t*
4:34 he would explain all *t*
5:19 *t* Jehovah has done for you
5:20 all the *t* Jesus did for him
5:27 she heard the *t* about Jesus
6:2 did this man get these *t*
6:30 *t* they had done and taught
6:34 to teach them many *t*
7:13 *t* similar to this you do
7:15 *t* that issue forth out of a
7:15 are the *t* that defile a man
7:23 wicked *t* issue forth from
7:37 He has done all *t* well
9:12 and restore all *t*; but how
9:13 did to him as many *t* as they
9:23 all *t* can be to one if one
10:20 all these *t* I have kept from
10:21 sell what *t* you have and
10:27 all *t* are possible with God
10:28 We left all *t* and have been
10:30 in the coming system of *t*
10:32 *t* destined to befall him
11:11 he looked around upon all *t*
11:24 the *t* you pray and ask for
11:28 authority do you do these *t*
11:28 this authority to do these *t*
11:29 what authority I do these *t*
11:33 what authority I do these *t*
12:17 Pay back Caesar's *t* to
12:17 but God's *t* to God
13:4 When will these *t* be, and
13:4 the sign when all these *t* are
13:7 these *t* must take place, but
13:16 return to the *t* behind to
13:23 told you all *t* beforehand
13:29 you see these *t* happening
13:30 until all these *t* happen
14:36 all *t* are possible to you
15:3 to accuse him of many *t*
Lu 1:3 traced all *t* from the start
1:4 *t* that you have been taught
1:19 the good news of these *t* to
1:20 day that these *t* take place
1:45 *t* spoken to her from Jehovah
1:53 hungry ones with good *t* and
1:65 all these *t* began to be talked
2:18 marveled over the *t* told them
2:20 all the *t* they heard and saw
2:33 the *t* being spoken about it
2:39 the *t* according to the law
3:11 let him that has *t* to eat do
4:23 the *t* we heard as having
4:28 all those hearing these *t* in
5:26 We have seen strange *t* today
5:27 Now after these *t* he went out
6:23 same *t* their forefathers used
6:26 *t* like these are what their
6:30 from the one taking your *t*
6:46 but do not do the *t* I say
7:9 when Jesus heard these *t* he
7:18 reported . . . all these *t*
8:8 As he told these *t*, he
8:39 relating what *t* God did for
8:39 what *t* Jesus did for him
9:7 heard of all the *t* happening
9:9 whom I am hearing such *t*
9:10 they recounted to him what *t*
9:34 as he was saying these *t* a
9:36 any of the *t* they saw
9:43 at all the *t* he was doing
9:62 and looks at the *t* behind
10:1 After these *t* the Lord
10:7 eating and drinking the *t*
10:8 eat the *t* set before you
10:21 hidden these *t* from wise and
10:22 All *t* have been delivered
10:23 eyes that behold the *t* you
10:24 kings desired to see the *t*
10:24 to hear the *t* you are hearing
10:40 left me alone to attend to *t*
10:41 disturbed about many *t*
10:42 A few *t*, though, are needed
11:8 give him what *t* he needs
11:22 divides . . . *t* he despoiled
11:27 as he was saying these *t* a
11:41 the *t* that are inside, and
11:41 all other *t* are clean about
11:42 These *t* you were under
11:42 those other *t* not to omit
11:45 Teacher, in saying these *t*
11:53 questions about further *t*
12:3 *t* you say in the darkness
12:12 the *t* you ought to say
12:15 from the *t* he possesses

Lu 12:18 my grain and all my good *t*
12:19 you have many good *t* laid
12:20 to have the *t* you stored up
12:26 about the remaining *t*
12:30 *t* the nations of the world
12:30 knows you need these *t*
12:31 these *t* will be added to you
12:33 Sell the *t* belonging to you
12:48 did *t* deserving of strokes
13:2 they have suffered these *t*
13:17 when he said these *t*, all
13:17 rejoice at all the glorious *t*
14:6 to answer back on these *t*
14:15 On hearing these *t* a certain
14:17 because *t* are now ready
14:21 and reported these *t* to his
15:13 gathered all *t* together and
15:26 inquired what these *t* meant
15:31 *t* that are mine are yours
16:8 sons of this system of *t* are
16:14 listening to all these *t*, and
16:21 *t* dropping from the table
16:25 your good *t* in your lifetime
16:25 injurious *t*. Now, however
16:26 besides all these *t*, a great
17:9 because he did the *t* assigned
17:10 have done all the *t* assigned
17:31 movable *t* are in the house
17:31 not return to the *t* behind
18:11 to pray these *t* to himself
18:12 I give the tenth of all *t*
18:22 Sell all the *t* you have and
18:27 *t* impossible with men are
18:28 left our own *t* and followed
18:30 in the coming system of *t*
18:31 all the *t* written by means
18:34 meaning of any of these *t*
18:34 were not knowing the *t* said
19:11 listening to these *t* he spoke
19:28 after he had said these *t*
19:42 *t* having to do with peace
20:2 what authority you do these *t*
20:8 what authority I do these *t*
20:25 pay back Caesar's *t* to Caesar
20:25 but God's *t* to God
20:34 children of this system of *t*
20:35 of gaining that system of *t*
21:5 fine stones and dedicated *t*
21:6 these *t* that you are beholding
21:7 when will these *t* actually be
21:7 these *t* are destined to occur
21:9 For these *t* must occur first
21:12 But before all these *t* people
21:22 *t* written may be fulfilled
21:26 expectation of the *t* coming
21:28 *t* start to occur, raise
21:31 you see these *t* occurring
21:32 pass away until all *t* occur
21:36 *t* that are destined to occur
22:65 many other *t* in blasphemy
23:31 if they do these *t* when the
23:41 we deserve for *t* we did
23:48 beheld the *t* that occurred
23:49 standing beholding these *t*
24:9 reported all these *t* to the
24:10 telling the apostles these *t*
24:14 these *t* that had come about
24:18 the *t* that have occurred in
24:19 he said to them: What *t*?
24:19 The *t* concerning Jesus the
24:21 and besides all these *t*
24:21 day since these *t* occurred
24:25 the *t* the prophets spoke
24:26 the Christ to suffer these *t*
24:27 *t* pertaining to himself
24:36 were speaking of these *t* he
24:44 the *t* written in the law of
24:48 to be witnesses of these *t*
Joh 1:3 All *t* came into existence
1:28 These *t* took place in Bethany
1:50 will see *t* greater than
2:16 Take these *t* away from here!
2:18 since you are doing these *t*
3:9 How can these *t* come about?
3:10 and yet do not know these *t*
3:12 told you earthly *t* and yet
3:12 if I tell you heavenly *t*
3:20 that practices vile *t* hates
3:22 After these *t* Jesus and his
3:31 and speaks of *t* of the earth
3:35 given all *t* into his hand
4:25 declare all *t* to us openly
4:29 told me all the *t* I did
4:39 He told me all the *t* I did

Lu 24:7 and yet on the *t* day rise
24:21 this makes the *t* day since
24:46 and rise . . . on the *t* day
Joh 2:1 on the *t* day a marriage feast
21:14 *t* time that Jesus appeared
21:17 He said to him the *t* time
21:17 said to him the *t* time
Ac 2:15 it is the *t* hour of the day
10:16 This occurred a *t* time, and
10:40 this One up on the *t* day
11:10 occurred for a *t* time, and
20:9 he fell down from the *t* story
23:23 at the *t* hour of the night
27:19 *t* day, with their own hands
1Co 12:28 *t*, teachers; then powerful
15:4 has been raised up the *t* day
2Co 12:2 away as such to the *t* heaven
12:14 *t* time I am ready to come
13:1 *t* time I am coming to you
Re 4:7 *t* living creature has a face
6:5 when he opened the *t* seal, I
6:5 heard the *t* living creature say
8:7 a *t* of the earth was burned up
8:7 a *t* of the trees was burned up
8:8 *t* of the sea became blood
8:9 a *t* of the creatures that are
8:9 a *t* of the boats were wrecked
8:10 the *t* angel blew his trumpet
8:10 fell upon a *t* of the rivers
8:11 a *t* of the waters turned into
8:12 a *t* of the sun was smitten
8:12 and a *t* of the moon and a
8:12 and a *t* of the stars
8:12 a *t* of them might be darkened
8:12 illumination for a *t* of it
9:15 to kill a *t* of the men
9:18 a *t* of the men were killed
11:14 The *t* woe is coming quickly
12:4 drags a *t* of the stars of
14:9 angel, a *t*, followed them
16:4 *t* one poured out his bowl
21:19 foundation . . . *t* chalcedony

Thirst
Ex 17:3 our livestock to death by *t*
De 28:48 hunger and *t* and nakedness
Jg 15:18 shall I die of *t* and must I
2Ch 32:11 to die by famine and by *t*
Ne 9:15 forth to them for their *t*
9:20 you gave them for their *t*
Ps 63:1 My soul does *t* for you
69:21 for my *t* they tried to
104:11 regularly quench their *t*
Isa 5:13 will be parched with *t*
41:17 Because of *t* their very
50:2 and they die because of *t*
Jer 2:25 and your throat from *t*
48:18 and sit down in *t*
La 4:4 to its palate because of *t*
Ho 2:3 and put her to death with *t*
Am 8:11 and a *t*, not for water, but
8:13 young men, because of the *t*
Joh 4:15 so that I may neither *t* nor
1Co 4:11 to hunger and also to *t* and
2Co 11:27 in hunger and *t*, in
Re 7:16 hunger no more nor *t* anymore

Thirsting
Ex 17:3 went on *t* there for water
Mt 5:6 and *t* for righteousness
Re 21:6 anyone *t* I will give from
22:17 And let anyone *t* come

Thirsts
Ps 42:2 My soul indeed *t* for God

Thirsty
De 8:15 *t* ground that has no water
29:19 along with the *t* ones
Jg 4:19 water to drink, for I am *t*
15:18 Now he became very *t*, and he
Ru 2:9 When you are *t*, you must also
2Sa 17:29 and *t* in the wilderness
Job 24:11 tread, and yet they go *t*
Ps 107:5 They were hungry, also *t*
107:33 of water into *t* ground
Pr 25:21 if he is *t*, give him water
Isa 21:14 meet the *t* one bring water
29:8 someone *t* dreams and here he
32:6 *t* one to go without drink
35:7 *t* ground as springs of water
44:3 water upon the *t* one, and
48:21 they did not get *t* when
49:10 neither will they go *t*
55:1 Hey there, all you *t* ones!
65:13 you yourselves will go *t*
Eze 19:13 in a waterless and *t* land
Mt 25:35 I got *t* and you gave me
25:37 *t*, and give you something to
25:42 *t*, but you gave me nothing
25:44 did we see you hungry or *t*
Joh 4:13 will get *t* again
4:14 will never get *t* at all
6:35 will never get *t* at all
7:37 *t*, let him come to me and
19:28 he said: I am *t*
Ro 12:20 if he is *t*, give him

Thirteen
Ge 17:25 Ishmael his son was *t* years
Nu 29:13 *t* young bulls, two rams
29:14 for each bull of the *t* bulls
Jos 19:6 *t* cities and their
21:4 *t* cities came to belong to
21:6 by lot *t* cities out of the
21:19 *t* cities and their pasture
21:33 *t* cities and their pasture
1Ki 7:1 Solomon built in *t* years
1Ch 6:60 All their cities were *t*
6:62 sons of Gershom . . . *t* cities
26:11 brothers of Hosah were *t*
Eze 40:11 length of the gate, *t* cubits

Thirteenth
Ge 14:4 but the *t* year they rebelled
1Ch 24:13 for Huppah the *t*, for
25:20 for the *t*, Shubael, his sons
Es 3:12 first month on the *t* day of
3:13 *t* day of the twelfth month
8:12 *t* day of the twelfth month
9:1 month of Adar, on the *t* day of
9:17 the *t* day of the month Adar
9:18 on the *t* day of it and on the
Jer 1:2 Josiah . . . in the *t* year of
25:3 From the *t* year of Josiah

Thirtieth
Eze 1:1 *t* year, in the fourth month

Thirty
Ge 5:3 Adam . . . a hundred and *t* years
5:5 Adam . . . nine hundred and *t*
5:16 eight hundred and *t* years
6:15 ark . . . *t* cubits its height
11:14 And Shelah lived *t* years
11:17 four hundred and *t* years
11:18 Peleg lived on for *t* years
11:22 Serug lived on for *t* years
18:30 Suppose *t* are found there
18:30 not do it if I find *t* there
32:15 *t* camels giving suck and
41:46 Joseph was *t* years old when
47:9 a hundred and *t* years
Ex 12:40 was four hundred and *t* years
12:41 the four hundred and *t* years
21:32 of *t* shekels to that one's
26:8 each tent cloth is *t* cubits
36:15 each tent cloth was *t* cubits
38:24 seven hundred and *t* shekels
Le 27:4 value must then become *t*
Nu 4:3 *t* years old upward to fifty
4:23 From *t* years old upward to
4:30 From *t* years old upward to
4:35 *t* years old upward to fifty
4:39 *t* years old upward to fifty
4:40 two thousand six hundred and *t*
4:43 *t* years old upward to fifty
4:47 *t* years old upward to fifty
7:13 hundred and *t* shekels, one
7:19 a hundred and *t* shekels, one
7:25 a hundred and *t* shekels, one
7:31 a hundred and *t* shekels, one
7:37 hundred and *t* shekels, one
7:43 a hundred and *t* shekels, one
7:49 a hundred and *t* shekels, one
7:55 hundred and *t* shekels, one
7:61 being a hundred and *t* shekels
7:67 being a hundred and *t* shekels
7:73 a hundred and *t* shekels, one
7:79 being a hundred and *t* shekels
7:85 a hundred and *t* shekels to
20:29 weeping for Aaron *t* days
26:7 thousand seven hundred and *t*
26:51 thousand seven hundred and *t*
31:39 were *t* thousand five hundred
31:45 *t* thousand five hundred
De 34:8 desert plains of Moab *t* days
Jos 8:3 to choose *t* thousand men
Jg 10:4 he came to have *t* sons who
10:4 rode on *t* full-grown asses
10:4 they had *t* cities. These they
12:9, 9 have *t* sons and *t* daughters
Jg 12:9 brought in *t* daughters for his
12:14 forty sons and *t* grandsons
14:11 took *t* groomsmen, that these
14:12 give you *t* undergarments and
14:12 and *t* outfits of clothing
14:13 give me *t* undergarments and
14:13 and *t* outfits of clothing
14:19 struck down *t* men of theirs
20:31 about *t* men in Israel
20:39 *t* men mortally wounded
1Sa 4:10 there fell *t* thousand men
9:22 and they were about *t* men
11:8 the men of Judah *t* thousand
13:5 *t* thousand war chariots and
2Sa 5:4 *T* years old was David when he
6:1 men in Israel, *t* thousand
23:13 three of the *t* head ones
23:18 he was the head of the *t*
23:19 more than the rest of the *t*
23:23 even more than the *t*, to
23:24 Asahel . . . was among the *t*
1Ki 4:22 *t* cor measures of fine flour
5:13 amounted to *t* thousand men
6:2 and *t* cubits in its height
7:2 and *t* cubits in its height
7:6 and *t* cubits in its width
7:23 *t* cubits to circle all around
2Ki 18:14 and *t* gold talents
1Ch 11:15 three of the *t* head ones
11:25 distinguished than the *t*
11:42 by whom there were *t*
12:4 a mighty man among the *t*
12:4 and over the *t*; and Jeremiah
12:18 Amasai, the head of the *t*
15:7 Gershom . . . a hundred and *t*
23:3 the age of *t* years upward
27:6 was a mighty man of the *t*
27:6 and over the *t*; and over his
2Ch 4:2 line of *t* cubits to circle all
24:15 hundred and *t* years old at
35:7 the number of *t* thousand
Ezr 1:9 *t* basket-shaped vessels of
1:10 *t* small bowls of gold
2:35 thousand six hundred and *t*
Ne 7:38 thousand nine hundred and *t*
7:70 five hundred and *t* priests'
Es 4:11 not been called . . . for *t* days
Jer 38:10 from this place *t* men
Eze 40:17 *t* dining rooms upon the
41:6 and for *t* times
46:22 and *t* in width
Da 6:7 for *t* days except to you
6:12 for *t* days except from you
Zec 11:12 wages, *t* pieces of silver
11:13 took the *t* pieces of silver
Mt 13:8 to yield fruit . . . the other *t*
13:23 that one sixty, the other *t*
26:15 stipulated to him *t* silver
27:3 the *t* silver pieces back to
27:9 they took the *t* silver pieces
Lu 3:23 Jesus . . . about *t* years old
Ga 3:17 four hundred and *t* years

Thirty-eight
De 2:14 *t* years, until all the
1Ch 23:3 came to be *t* thousand
Ne 7:45 of Shobai, a hundred and *t*
Joh 5:5 in his sickness for *t* years

Thirty-eighth
1Ki 16:29 in the *t* year of Asa the
2Ki 15:8 the *t* year of Azariah the

Thirty-fifth
2Ch 15:19 *t* year of Asa's reign

Thirty-first
1Ki 16:23 *t* year of Asa the king of

Thirty-five
Ge 11:12 Arpachshad lived *t* years
Nu 1:37 *t* thousand four hundred
2:23 *t* thousand four hundred
1Ki 22:42 Jehoshaphat was *t* years old
2Ch 3:15 pillars, *t* cubits in length
20:31 *T* years old he was when he
Ezr 2:67 camels four hundred and *t*
Ne 7:69 four hundred and *t*
Da 12:12 three hundred and *t* days

Thirtyfold
Mr 4:8 they were bearing *t*, and sixty
4:20 bear fruit *t* and sixty and a

Thirty-four
Ge 11:16 And Eber lived on for *t* years
1Ch 7:7 twenty-two thousand and *t*

Thirty-nine
Ezr 2:42 together, a hundred and *t*

Thirty-ninth
2Ki 15:13 the *t* year of Uzziah the
15:17 In the *t* year of Azariah
2Ch 16:12 Asa in the *t* year of his

Thirty-one
Jos 12:24 all the kings being *t*
2Ki 22:1 for *t* years he reigned in
2Ch 34:1 Josiah . . . *t* years he reigned

Thirty-second
Ne 5:14 the *t* year of Artaxerxes the
13:6 in the *t* year of Artaxerxes

Thirty-seven
Ge 25:17 life, a hundred and *t* years
Ex 6:16 Levi's life . . . hundred and *t*
6:20 were a hundred and *t* years
Nu 31:36 *t* thousand five hundred of
31:43 and *t* thousand five hundred
2Sa 23:39 Uriah the Hittite—*t* in all
1Ch 12:34 there were *t* thousand
Ezr 2:65 thousand three hundred and *t*
Ne 7:67 thousand three hundred and *t*

Thirty-seventh
2Ki 13:10 In the *t* year of Jehoash
25:27 *t* year of the exile of
Jer 52:31 *t* year of the exile of

Thirty-six
Nu 31:38 there were *t* thousand, and
31:44 and of the herd, *t* thousand
Jos 7:5 to strike down about *t* men of
1Ch 7:4 the army for war, *t* thousand
Ezr 2:66 seven hundred and *t*
Ne 7:68 seven hundred and *t*

Thirty-sixth
2Ch 16:1 *t* year of the reign of Asa

Thirty-three
Ge 46:15 all the souls . . . were *t*
Ex 6:18 were a hundred and *t* years
Le 12:4 For *t* days more she will stay
2Sa 5:5 *t* years over all Israel and
1Ki 2:11 he had reigned *t* years
1Ch 3:4 *t* years he reigned in
29:27 Jerusalem he reigned for *t*

Thirty-two
Ge 11:20 And Reu lived on for *t* years
Nu 1:35 *t* thousand two hundred
2:21 *t* thousand two hundred
26:37 *t* thousand five hundred
31:35 the souls were *t* thousand
31:40 tax on them . . . was *t* souls
1Ki 20:1 also *t* kings with him and
20:15 to be two hundred and *t*
20:16 *t* kings that were helping
22:31 commanded the *t* chiefs of
2Ki 8:17 *T* years old he happened to
1Ch 19:7 *t* thousand chariots and the
2Ch 21:5 *T* years old was Jehoram
21:20 *T* years old he happened to
Jer 52:29 eight hundred and *t* souls

Thistle
Ps 83:13 make them like a *t* whirl
Isa 17:13 like a *t* whirl before a

Thistles
Ge 3:18 And thorns and *t* it will
Ho 10:8 *t* themselves will come up
Mt 7:16 or figs from *t*, do they
Heb 6:8 if it produces thorns and *t*

Thither
Eph 4:14 carried hither and *t* by every

Thomas
Mt 10:3 *T* and Matthew the tax
Mr 3:18 Matthew and *T* and James the
Lu 6:15 Matthew and *T*, and James the
Joh 11:16 *T*, who was called The Twin
14:5 *T* said to him: Lord, we do
20:24 *T*, one of the twelve, who
20:26 indoors, and *T* with them
20:27 to *T*: Put your finger here
20:28 *T* said to him: My Lord and
21:2 *T*, who was called The Twin
Ac 1:13 *T*, Bartholomew and Matthew

Thorn
Job 41:2 with a *t* can you bore its
Isa 7:19 all the *t* thickets and
Eze 28:24 prickle or a painful *t*
Mic 7:4 is worse than a *t* hedge
2Co 12:7 *t* in the flesh, an angel of

Thornbush
Ex 3:2 of fire in the midst of a *t*
3:2 here the *t* was burning with
3:2 yet the *t* was not consumed
3:3 why the *t* is not burnt up
3:4 out of the midst of the *t* and
De 33:16 of the One residing in the *t*
Isa 5:6 come up with the *t* and weeds
Mr 12:26 in the account about the *t*
Lu 6:44 nor do they cut grapes off a *t*
20:37 in the account about the *t*
Ac 7:30 in the fiery flame of a *t*
7:35 appeared to him in the *t*

Thornbushes
2Sa 23:6 chased away, like *t*, all of
Ps 118:12 like a fire of *t*
Isa 7:23 for the *t* and for the weeds
7:24 land will become mere *t* and
7:25 for fear of *t* and weeds
9:18 *t* and weeds it will eat up
10:17 eat up his weeds and his *t*
27:4 give me *t* and weeds in the

Thorns
Ge 3:18 And *t* and thistles it will
Ex 22:6 does catch *t*, and sheaves or
Nu 33:55 and as *t* in your sides, and
Jos 23:13 as *t* in your eyes until
Jg 8:7 *t* of the wilderness and the
8:16 and *t* of the wilderness and
Pr 22:5 *T* and traps are in the way of
Ec 7:6 as the sound of *t* under the pot
Isa 32:13 of my people merely *t*
33:12 As *t* cut away, they will
34:13 *t* must come up, nettles
55:13 Instead of the thicket of *t*
Jer 4:3 do not keep sowing among *t*
12:13 *t* are what they have reaped
Ho 2:6 hedging your way about with *t*
10:8 *T* and thistles themselves
Na 1:10 interwoven even as *t* and
Mt 7:16 people gather grapes from *t*
13:7 fell among the *t*, and the
13:7 *t* came up and choked them
13:22 the one sown among the *t*
27:29 braided a crown out of *t* and
Mr 4:7 other seed fell among the *t*
4:7 the *t* came up and choked it
4:18 who are sown among the *t*
15:17 braided a crown of *t* and put
Lu 6:44 do not gather figs from *t*
8:7 Some other fell among the *t*
8:7 the *t* that grew up with it
8:14 that which fell among the *t*
Joh 19:2 braided a crown of *t* and
Heb 6:8 if it produces *t* and thistles

Thorny
2Ki 14:9 The *t* weed itself that was
14:9 trampled the *t* weed down
2Ch 25:18 *t* weed itself that was in
25:18 trampled the *t* weed down
Job 31:40 let the *t* weed go forth
40:21 Under the *t* lotus trees it
40:22 The *t* lotus trees keep it
Pr 26:9 a *t* weed has come up into the
Ca 2:2 Like a lily among *t* weeds, so
Isa 34:13 *t* weeds in her fortified
Ho 9:6 *t* bushes will be in their
Joh 19:5 wearing the *t* crown and the

Thorough
1Ch 19:3 sake of making a *t* search
Ec 12:9 pondered and made a *t* search
Jer 6:27 one making a *t* search
Lu 16:28 may give them a *t* witness
Ac 2:40 he bore *t* witness and kept
10:42 give a *t* witness that this
11:25 to make a *t* search for Saul
20:24 *t* witness to the good news
23:11 have been giving a *t* witness
23:35 shall give you a *t* hearing
28:23 *t* witness concerning the
1Th 4:6 and also gave you a *t* witness

Thoroughly
Le 10:16 Moses searched *t* for the
De 7:26 You should *t* loathe it and
9:21 grinding it *t* until it had
13:14 investigate and inquire *t*
17:4 have searched *t*, and, look!
19:18 the judges must search *t*
2Sa 23:7 they will *t* be burned up
2Ki 11:18 his images they broke up *t*
Ps 51:2 *T* wash me from my error, And
Eze 24:10 Boil the flesh *t*. And empty
Mr 3:5 *t* grieved at the insensibility
Ac 8:25 they had given the witness *t*
15:14 Symeon has related *t* how God
18:28 he *t* proved the Jews to be
20:21 But I *t* bore witness both to
Ro 15:19 *t* preached the good news
Eph 3:18 *t* able to grasp mentally
6:13 have done all things *t*, to
1Ti 2:14 the woman was *t* deceived
Re 14:15 of the earth is *t* ripe

Though
Ge 31:30 why, *t*, have you stolen my
33:10 your face as *t* seeing God's
Ex 5:18 *T* no straw will be given to
Le 5:7 If, *t*, he cannot afford enough
14:43 If, *t*, the plague returns and
19:7 *t* . . . eaten on the third day
26:18 If, *t*, despite these things
Nu 33:55 If, *t*, you will not drive
De 22:20 If, *t*, this thing has proved
Jos 2:6 She, *t*, had taken them up to
Jg 9:36 are seeing as *t* they were men
2Sa 7:19 As *t* this should even be
23:21 *T* there was a spear in the
2Ki 5:1 mighty man, *t* a leper
1Ch 17:17 As *t* this should be
2Ch 30:19 *t* without the purification
Ne 1:9 *t* your dispersed people should
Job 9:15 *t* I were really in the right
10:19 as *t* I had not come to be
33:14 *t* one does not regard it
34:6 *t* there is no transgression
Ps 2:9 As *t* a potter's vessel you
23:4 *t* I walk in the valley of
27:3 *T* against me an encampment
27:3 *T* against me war should rise
39:5 man, *t* standing firm, is
46:2 *t* the earth undergo change
46:2 *t* the mountains totter into
46:3 *T* its waters be boisterous
46:3 *T* the mountains rock at its
49:12 man, *t* in honor, cannot keep
58:5 *T* someone wise is binding
59:4 *T* there is no error, they run
78:9 Ephraim, *t* armed shooters
Pr 11:21 *T* hand be to hand, a bad
Ec 8:10 *t* this is so, I have seen the
11:8 *t* they could be many
Isa 1:15 Even *t* you make many prayers
1:18 *T* the sins of you people
1:18 *t* they should be red like
5:9 houses, *t* great and good
10:7 *T* he may not be that way
10:7 *t* his heart may not be that
10:15 *t* the staff moved back and
10:15 *t* the rod raised on high the
26:10 *T* the wicked one should be
31:3 Egyptians, *t*, are earthling
43:8 blind *t* eyes . . . exist
43:8 ones deaf *t* they have ears
51:13 as *t* he was all set to
Jer 2:22 *t* you should do the washing
32:33 *t* there was a teaching of
Eze 12:3 *t* they are a rebellious house
13:20 souls as *t* they were flying
13:20 as *t* they were flying
Ob 16 as *t* they had never happened
Jon 4:1 To Jonah, *t*, it was highly
Zec 10:7 must rejoice as *t* from wine
Mt 14:9 Grieved *t* he was, the king
14:23 *T* it became late, he was
16:15 You, *t*, who do you say I am?
19:17 If, *t*, you want to enter
21:26 If, *t*, we say, From men
Mr 4:12 *t* looking, they may look and
4:12 *t* hearing, they may hear and
8:18 *T* having eyes, do you not see
8:18 *t* having ears, do you not
8:29 You, *t*, who do you say I am?
Lu 7:47 her sins, many *t* they are
8:10 *t* looking, they may look in
8:10 *t* hearing, they may not get
9:20 You, *t*, who do you say I am?
10:42 A few things, *t*, are needed
16:8 the steward, *t* unrighteous
18:7 even *t* he is long-suffering
22:26 You, *t*, are not to be that
24:49 You, *t*, abide in the city
Joh 2:22 When, *t*, he was raised up
7:44 Some of them, *t*, were
10:38 *t* you do not believe me

Eze 45:6 and a length of twenty-five *t*
47:3 measure a *t* in cubits and
47:4 continued measuring a *t* and
47:4 continued measuring a *t* and
47:5 he continued measuring a *t*
48:8 twenty-five *t* cubits in
48:9 twenty-five *t* cubits and the
48:9 and the width ten *t*
48:10 north twenty-five *t* cubits
48:10 the west a width of ten *t*
48:10 east a width of ten *t*, and
48:10 a length of twenty-five *t*
48:13 twenty-five *t* cubits in
48:13 and in width ten *t*
48:13 length being twenty-five *t*
48:13 and width being ten *t*
48:15 five *t* cubits that is left
48:15 alongside the twenty-five *t*
48:16 four *t* five hundred cubits
48:16 four *t* five hundred, and
48:16 four *t* five hundred, and
48:16 border four *t* five hundred
48:18 ten *t* cubits to the east
48:18 and ten *t* to the west
48:20 twenty-five *t* cubits by
48:20 cubits by twenty-five *t*
48:21 twenty-five *t* cubits of the
48:21 the twenty-five *t* cubits
48:30 four *t* five hundred cubits
48:32 four *t* five hundred cubits
48:33 four *t* five hundred cubits
48:34 four *t* five hundred cubits
48:35 eighteen *t* cubits
Da 5:1 feast for a *t* of his grandees
5:1 and in front of the *t* he was
7:10 a *t* thousands that kept
7:10, 10 ten *t* times ten *t* that
8:14 two *t* three hundred evenings
12:11 one *t* two hundred and ninety
12:12 one *t* three hundred and
Am 5:3 was going forth with a *t* will
Jon 4:11 one hundred and twenty *t* men
Mt 14:21 about five *t* men, besides
15:38 eating were four *t* men
16:9 in the case of the five *t*
16:10 in the case of the four *t*
18:24 who owed him ten *t* talents
Mr 5:13 into the sea, about two *t* of
6:44 those who ate . . . five *t*
8:9 there were about four *t* men
8:19 loaves for the five *t* men
8:20 seven for the four *t* men
Lu 9:14 in fact, about five *t* men
14:31 with ten *t* troops to cope
14:31 against him with twenty *t*
Joh 6:10 about five *t* in number
Ac 2:41 three *t* souls were added
4:4 men became about five *t*
19:19 fifty *t* pieces of silver
21:38 led the four *t* dagger men
Ro 11:4 left seven *t* men over for
1Co 4:15 ten *t* tutors in Christ, you
10:8 twenty-three *t* of them in
14:19 ten *t* words in a tongue
2Pe 3:8 is with Jehovah as a *t* years
3:8 and a *t* years as one day
Re 7:4 a hundred and forty-four *t*
7:5 tribe of Judah twelve *t* sealed
7:5 tribe of Reuben twelve *t*; out
7:5 of the tribe of Gad twelve *t*
7:6 of the tribe of Asher twelve *t*
7:6 the tribe of Naphtali twelve *t*
7:6 the tribe of Manasseh twelve *t*
7:7 the tribe of Simeon twelve *t*
7:7 of the tribe of Levi twelve *t*
7:7 the tribe of Issachar twelve *t*
7:8 the tribe of Zebulun twelve *t*
7:8 the tribe of Joseph twelve *t*
7:8 the tribe of Benjamin twelve *t*
11:3 *t* two hundred and sixty days
11:13 seven *t* persons were killed
12:6 *t* two hundred and sixty days
14:1 a hundred and forty-four *t*
14:3 the hundred and forty-four *t*
14:20 of a *t* six hundred furlongs
20:2 and bound him for a *t* years
20:3 until the *t* years were ended
20:4 the Christ for a *t* years
20:5 until the *t* years were ended
20:6 with him for the *t* years
20:7 *t* years have been ended
21:16 twelve *t* furlongs; its

Thousands
Ge 24:60 *t* times ten thousand, and
Ex 18:21 as chiefs over *t*, chiefs over
18:25 as chiefs of *t*, chiefs of
34:7 loving-kindness for *t*
Nu 1:16 the heads of the *t* of Israel
10:4 heads of the *t* of Israel
10:36 the myriads of *t* of Israel
31:5 from the *t* of Israel
31:14 the chiefs of the *t* and the
31:48 were of the *t* of the army
31:48 the chiefs of the *t* and the
31:52 from the chiefs of the *t* and
31:54 from the chiefs of the *t*
De 1:15 as heads over you, chiefs of *t*
33:17 are the tens of *t* of Ephraim
33:17 they are the *t* of Manasseh
Jos 22:14 fathers of the *t* of Israel
22:21 heads of the *t* of Israel
22:30 the heads of the *t* of Israel
1Sa 8:12 chiefs over *t* and chiefs over
10:19 by your tribes and by your *t*
18:7 Saul has struck down his *t*
18:7 And David his tens of *t*
18:8 have given David tens of *t*
18:8 to me they have given the *t*
21:11 Saul has struck down his *t*
21:11 And David his tens of *t*
22:7 all of you chiefs of *t* and
23:23 among all the *t* of Judah
29:2 and by *t*, and David and his
29:5 struck down his *t*, and David
29:5 David his tens of *t*
2Sa 18:1 place over them chiefs of *t*
18:4 out by hundreds and by *t*
1Ch 12:20 *t* that belonged to Manasseh
13:1 the chiefs of the *t* and of
15:25 the chiefs of the *t* came to
26:26 the chiefs of the *t* and of
27:1 and the chiefs of the *t* and
28:1 the chiefs of *t* and the
29:6 chiefs of *t* and of hundreds
2Ch 1:2 to the chiefs of the *t* and of
17:14 chiefs of *t*, Adnah the
25:5 by the chiefs of *t* and
Ps 3:6 afraid of ten *t* of people
68:17 chariots . . . in tens of *t*
68:17 *t* over and over again
119:72 than *t* of pieces of gold
144:13 flocks multiplying by *t*
Jer 32:18 loving-kindness toward *t*
Da 7:10 were a thousand *t* that kept
11:12 cause tens of *t* to fall; but
Mic 5:2 to be among the *t* of Judah
6:7 be pleased with *t* of rams
6:7 tens of *t* of torrents of oil
Lu 12:1 in so many *t* that they were
Ac 21:20 *t* of believers . . . Jews
Re 5:11, 11 many angels . . . *t* of *t*

Thousandth
Ex 20:6 toward the *t* generation in
De 5:10 the *t* generation in the case

Thread
Ge 14:23 from a *t* to a sandal lace
Ex 25:4 blue *t*, and wool dyed reddish
26:1 and blue *t* and wool dyed
26:4 make loops of blue *t* upon the
26:31 make a curtain of blue *t* and
26:36 blue *t* and wool dyed reddish
27:16 of blue *t* and wool dyed
28:5 take the gold and the blue *t*
28:6 ephod of gold, blue *t* and
28:8 of gold, blue *t* and wool dyed
28:15 Of gold, blue *t* and wool
28:31 sleeveless coat . . . of blue *t*
28:33 pomegranates of blue *t* and
35:6 and blue *t* and wool dyed
35:23 found blue *t* and wool dyed
35:25 the blue *t* and the wool dyed
35:35 of a weaver in blue *t* and
36:8 blue *t* and wool dyed reddish
36:11 made loops of blue *t* upon
36:35 a curtain of blue *t* and wool
36:37 out of blue *t* and wool dyed
38:18 of blue *t* and wool dyed
38:23 the blue *t* and the wool dyed
39:1 out of the blue *t* and wool
39:2 blue *t* and wool dyed reddish
39:3 the blue *t* and the wool dyed
39:5 of gold, blue *t*, and wool
39:8 blue *t* and wool dyed reddish
39:22 loom worker, all of blue *t*
39:24 blue *t* and wool dyed reddish
Ex 39:29 blue *t* and wool dyed reddish
39:31 put a string of blue *t* to it
Le 19:19 garment of two sorts of *t*
Jos 2:18 cord of scarlet *t* you should
Jg 16:9 twisted *t* of tow is torn in
16:12 from off his arms like a *t*
16:13 my head with the warp *t*
16:14 the loom pin and the warp *t*
2Ch 2:7 and crimson and blue *t*, and
2:14 in blue *t* and in fine fabric
3:14 curtain of blue *t* and wool
Ca 4:3 lips are just like a scarlet *t*
Jer 10:9 their clothing is blue *t* and
52:21 of twelve cubits itself
Eze 27:7 Blue *t* and wool dyed reddish

Threadbare
Le 13:55 low spot in a *t* patch on

Threads
Ex 39:3 cut out *t* to work in among
Jg 15:14 like linen *t* . . . scorched
Isa 38:12 from the very *t* of the warp

Threat
Ac 9:1 Saul, still breathing *t* and

Threatened
Ac 4:21 they had further *t* them

Threatening
Eph 6:9 letting up on the *t*, for you
1Pe 2:23 he did not go *t*, but kept on

Threateningly
Isa 10:32 He waves his hand *t* at the

Threats
Ac 4:17 tell them with *t* not to speak
4:29 give attention to their *t*

Three
Ge 5:22 Enoch . . . *t* hundred years
5:23 *t* hundred and sixty-five years
6:10 Noah became father to *t* sons
6:15 make it: *t* hundred cubits
7:13 *t* wives of his sons with him
9:19 These *t* were Noah's sons, and
9:28 live *t* hundred and fifty years
11:13 live four hundred and *t* years
11:15 live four hundred and *t* years
14:14 *t* hundred and eighteen slaves
18:2 *t* men were standing some
18:6 Get *t* seah measures of fine
29:2 *t* droves of sheep were lying
29:34 I have borne him *t* sons
30:36 set a distance of *t* days'
38:24 *t* months later it happened
40:10 there were *t* twigs, and it
40:12, 12 The *t* twigs are *t* days
40:13 *t* days from now Pharaoh will
40:16 *t* baskets of white bread
40:18, 18 The *t* baskets are *t* days
40:19 *t* days from now Pharaoh will
42:17 in custody for *t* days
45:22 *t* hundred silver pieces and
Ex 2:2 concealed for *t* lunar months
3:18 a journey of *t* days into the
5:3 *t* days into the wilderness and
8:27 journey of *t* days into the
10:22 darkness . . . for *t* days
10:23 up from his own place *t* days
15:22 for *t* days in the wilderness
19:15 Get ready during the *t* days
21:11 render these *t* things to her
23:14 *T* times in the year you are
23:17 On *t* occasions in the year
25:32 *t* branches of the lampstand
25:32 *t* branches of the lampstand
25:33 *T* cups shaped like flowers
25:33 *t* cups shaped like flowers
27:1 and its height *t* cubits
27:14 their pillars being *t* and
27:14 and their socket pedestals *t*
27:15 their pillars being *t* and
27:15 and their socket pedestals *t*
32:28 day about *t* thousand men
34:23 *T* times in the year every
34:24 your God *t* times in the year
37:18 *t* branches of the lampstand
37:18 *t* branches of the lampstand
37:19 *T* cups shaped like flowers
37:19 *t* cups shaped like flowers
38:1 and *t* cubits was its height
38:14 Their pillars were *t* and
38:14 and their socket pedestals *t*
38:15 Their pillars were *t* and
38:15 and their socket pedestals *t*

Ex 38:26 *t* thousand five hundred and
Le 14:10 *t* tenths of an ephah of fine
19:23 For *t* years it will continue
25:21 yield its crop for *t* years
27:6 must be *t* shekels of silver
Nu 1:23 fifty-nine thousand *t* hundred
1:46 and *t* thousand five hundred
2:13 fifty-nine thousand *t* hundred
2:32 six hundred and *t* thousand
3:50 thousand *t* hundred and
4:44 *t* thousand two hundred
10:33 a journey of *t* days, and
10:33 journey of *t* days to search
12:4 *t* of you, to the tent of
12:4 So the *t* of them went out
15:9 of *t* tenths of fine flour
22:28 have beaten me these *t* times
22:32 your she-ass these *t* times
22:33 turn aside . . . these *t* times
24:10 blessed them . . . *t* times
26:25 sixty-four thousand *t* hundred
28:12 *t* tenth measures of fine
28:20 *t* tenth measures for a bull
28:28 *t* tenth measures for each
29:3 *t* tenth measures for the bull
29:9 *t* tenth measures for the bull
29:14 *t* tenth measures for each
31:36 *t* hundred and thirty-seven
31:43 *t* hundred and thirty-seven
35:14 *T* cities you will give on
35:14 *t* cities you will give in
De 4:41 *t* cities on the side of the
14:28 At the end of *t* years you
16:16 *T* times in the year every
17:6 two witnesses or of *t*
19:2 set apart *t* cities for
19:3 territory . . . into *t* parts
19:7 *T* cities you will set apart
19:9 then add *t* other cities for
19:9 cities for yourself to these *t*
19:15 at the mouth of *t* witnesses
Jos 1:11 *t* days from now you are
2:16 must keep hid there *t* days
2:22 kept dwelling there *t* days
3:2 at the end of the *t* days that
7:3 or about *t* thousand men go up
7:4 *t* thousand men of the people
9:16 the end of *t* days, after they
15:14 there the *t* sons of Anak
17:11 *t* of the heights
18:4 *t* men of each tribe and let
21:32 pasture ground; *t* cities
Jg 1:20 there the *t* sons of Anak
7:6 to be *t* hundred men. As for
7:7 By the *t* hundred men who did
7:8 kept hold of the *t* hundred men
7:16 he divided the *t* hundred men
7:16 men up into *t* bands and put
7:20 the *t* bands blew the horns
7:22 And the *t* hundred continued to
8:4 the *t* hundred men that were
9:22 the prince over Israel *t* years
9:43 divided them up into *t* bands
11:26 dwelling . . . for *t* hundred
14:14 tell the riddle for *t* days
15:4 to catch *t* hundred foxes and
15:11 *t* thousand men of Judah went
16:15 *t* times you have trifled
16:27 *t* thousand men and women
19:4 dwell with him *t* days
1Sa 2:21 to *t* sons and two daughters
9:20 were lost to you *t* days ago
10:3 *t* men going up to the true
10:3 one carrying *t* kids and one
10:3 *t* round loaves of bread and
11:8 *t* hundred thousand, and the
11:11 put the people into *t* bands
13:2 *t* thousand men out of Israel
13:17 the Philistines in *t* bands
17:13 the *t* oldest sons of Jesse
17:13 *t* sons that went into the
17:14 *t* oldest themselves went
20:20 shoot *t* arrows to one side
20:41 and bowed *t* times; and they
24:2 take *t* thousand chosen men
25:2 had *t* thousand sheep and a
26:2 with him *t* thousand men, the
30:12, 12 *t* days and *t* nights
30:13 I took sick *t* days ago
31:6 Saul and his *t* sons and his
31:8 find Saul and his *t* sons
2Sa 2:18 *t* sons of Zeruiah happened
2:31 *t* hundred and sixty men that
6:11 kept dwelling . . . *t* months

2Sa 13:38 he came to be there *t* years
14:27 born to Absalom *t* sons and
18:14 took *t* shafts in his palm
20:4 to me within *t* days, and you
21:1 for *t* years, year after year
21:16 *t* hundred shekels of copper
23:8 the head of the *t*
23:9 the *t* mighty men with David
23:13 *t* of the thirty head ones
23:16 *t* mighty men forced their
23:17 things the *t* mighty men did
23:18 spear over *t* hundred slain
23:18 had a reputation like the *t*
23:19 to the rank of the first *t*
23:22 like the *t* mighty men
23:23 to the rank of the *t* he
24:12 *T* things I am laying upon
24:13 *t* months of your fleeing
24:13 *t* days of pestilence in your
1Ki 2:39 at the end of *t* years that
4:32 speak *t* thousand proverbs
5:16, 16 *t* thousand *t* hundred
6:36 with *t* rows of hewn stone
7:4 windows, there were *t* rows
7:4 opening in *t* tiers
7:5 opening in *t* tiers
7:12 *t* rows of hewn stone and a
7:25 twelve bulls, *t* facing north
7:25 bulls . . . *t* facing west
7:25 bulls . . . *t* facing south
7:25 bulls . . . *t* facing east
7:27 and *t* cubits its height
9:25 *t* times in the year to offer
10:17 and *t* hundred bucklers of
10:17 *t* minas of gold he
10:22 every *t* years the fleet of
11:3 and *t* hundred concubines
12:5 Go away for *t* days and
15:2 *T* years he reigned in
17:21 upon the child *t* times and
22:1 for *t* years they continued
2Ki 2:17 they kept looking for *t* days
3:10 *t* kings to give them into
3:13 *t* kings to give them into
9:32 two or *t* court officials
13:18 struck *t* times and stopped
13:19 *t* times that you will
13:25 *T* times Jehoash struck him
17:5 siege against it for *t* years
18:10 at the end of *t* years
18:14 *t* hundred silver talents
23:31 *t* months he reigned in
24:1 his servant for *t* years
24:8 *t* months he reigned in
25:17 the capital was *t* cubits
25:18 priest and *t* doorkeepers
1Ch 2:3 The *t* were born to him from
2:16 and Joab and Asahel, *t*
3:23 and Hizkiah and Azrikam, *t*
7:6 sons of Benjamin were . . . *t*
10:6 Saul and *t* sons of his died
11:11 Jashobeam . . . head of the *t*
11:11 over *t* hundred slain at one
11:12 was among the *t* mighty men
11:15 *t* of the thirty head ones
11:18 *t* forced their way into the
11:19 that the *t* mighty men did
11:20 became head of the *t*
11:20 spear over *t* hundred slain
11:20 had a reputation like the *t*
11:21 Of the *t* he was more
11:21 not come up to the first *t*
11:24 among the *t* mighty men
11:25 to the rank of the first *t*
12:27 *t* thousand seven hundred
12:29 there were *t* thousand, and
12:39 there with David *t* days
13:14 at his house *t* months
21:10 There are *t* things that I
21:12 whether for *t* years there
21:12 or for *t* months there is to
21:12 *t* days there is to be the
23:8 The sons of Ladan were . . . *t*
23:9 sons of Shimei were . . . *t*
23:23 sons of Mushi were . . . *t*
25:5 fourteen sons and *t* daughters
29:4 *t* thousand talents of gold of
2Ch 2:2 *t* thousand six hundred
2:18 and *t* thousand six hundred
4:4 bulls, *t* facing the north
4:4 bulls . . . *t* facing the west
4:4 bulls . . . *t* facing the south
4:4 bulls . . . *t* facing the east
4:5 *t* thousand bath measures were

2Ch 6:13 and its height *t* cubits
8:13 festivals *t* times in the year
9:16 *t* hundred bucklers of alloyed
9:16 *t* minas of gold he
9:21 Once every *t* years ships of
10:5 yet *t* days. Then return to
11:17 for *t* years, for they
11:17 and Solomon for *t* years
13:2 *T* years he reigned in
14:8 *t* hundred thousand out of
14:9 *t* hundred chariots, and came
17:14 *t* hundred thousand valiant
20:25 *t* days that they were
25:5 *t* hundred thousand choice
25:13 striking down *t* thousand of
26:13 *t* hundred and seven thousand
29:33 *t* thousand of the flock
31:16 from *t* years of age upward
35:7 and cattle, *t* thousand
35:8 and *t* hundred cattle
36:2 Jehoahaz . . . for *t* months he
36:9 for *t* months and ten days
Ezr 2:4 *t* hundred and seventy-two
2:17 *t* hundred and twenty-three
2:32 *t* hundred and twenty
2:34 *t* hundred and forty-five
2:35 *t* thousand six hundred and
2:58 *t* hundred and ninety-two
2:64 forty-two thousand *t* hundred
2:65 seven thousand *t* hundred and
6:4 *t* layers of stones rolled into
8:5 and with him *t* hundred males
8:15 kept encamped there *t* days
8:32 and dwelt there *t* days
10:8 not come in *t* days' time
10:9 at Jerusalem within *t* days
Ne 2:11 continued there for *t* days
7:9 *t* hundred and seventy-two
7:17 two thousand *t* hundred and
7:22 *t* hundred and twenty-eight
7:23 *t* hundred and twenty-four
7:35 *t* hundred and twenty
7:36 *t* hundred and forty-five
7:38 *t* thousand nine hundred and
7:60 *t* hundred and ninety-two
7:66 forty-two thousand *t* hundred
7:67 seven thousand *t* hundred and
Es 4:16 eat nor drink for *t* days
9:15 kill in Shushan *t* hundred men
Job 1:2 And seven sons and *t* daughters
1:3 *t* thousand camels and five
1:4 invited their *t* sisters to eat
1:17 Chaldeans made up *t* bands
2:11 *t* companions of Job got to
32:1 *t* men ceased from answering
32:3 against his *t* companions his
32:5 in the mouth of the *t* men
33:29 Two times, *t* times, in the
42:13 seven sons and *t* daughters
Pr 30:15 are *t* things that do not get
30:18 *t* things that have proved too
30:21 Under *t* things the earth has
30:29 are *t* that do well in their
Isa 16:14 Within *t* years, according
17:6 or *t* ripe olives in the top
20:3 naked and barefoot *t* years
Jer 36:23 read *t* or four page-columns
52:24 and the *t* doorkeepers
52:28 *t* thousand and twenty-three
Eze 4:5 *t* hundred and ninety days, and
4:9 *t* hundred and ninety days you
14:14 had these *t* men proved to
14:16 *t* men in the midst of it
14:18 *t* men in the midst of it
21:14 be repeated for *t* times
40:10 were *t* on this side and
40:10 and *t* on that side
40:10 The *t* of them were of the
40:21 were *t* on this side and
40:21 and *t* on that side
40:48 gate was *t* cubits on this
40:48 and *t* cubits on that side
41:6 upon side chamber, *t* stories
41:16 round about the *t* of them
41:22 wooden altar was *t* cubits
42:3 opposite gallery in *t* stories
42:6 For they were in *t* stories
48:31 *t* gates being on the north
48:32 *t* gates, even the gate
48:33 *t* gates, the gate of Simeon
48:34 *t* gates, the gate of Gad
Da 1:5 nourish them for *t* years, that
3:23 men, the *t* of them, Shadrach
3:24 not *t* able-bodied men that we

Da 6:2 *t* high officials, of whom
6:10 even *t* times in a day he was
6:13 *t* times in a day he is making
7:5 *t* ribs in its mouth between
7:8 *t* of the first horns that were
7:20 before which *t* fell, even
7:24 *t* kings he will humiliate
8:14 two thousand *t* hundred
10:2 mourning for *t* full weeks
10:3 of the *t* full weeks
11:2 *t* kings standing up for Persia
12:12 *t* hundred and thirty-five
Am 1:3 *t* revolts of Damascus
1:6 account of *t* revolts of Gaza
1:9 account of *t* revolts of Tyre
1:11 account of *t* revolts of Edom
1:13 *t* revolts of . . . Ammon
2:1 account of *t* revolts of Moab
2:4 account of *t* revolts of Judah
2:6 account of *t* revolts of Israel
4:7 yet *t* months to the harvest
4:8 two or *t* cities staggered
Jon 1:17, 17 *t* days and *t* nights
3:3 a walking distance of *t* days
Zec 11:8 effaced *t* shepherds in one
Mt 12:40, 40 fish *t* days and *t* nights
12:40, 40 *t* days and *t* nights
13:33 in *t* large measures of flour
15:32 *t* days that they have stayed
17:4 I will erect *t* tents here
18:16 mouth of two or *t* witnesses
18:20 two or *t* gathered together
26:34 you will disown me *t* times
26:61 and build it up in *t* days
26:75 you will disown me *t* times
27:40 and builder of it in *t* days
27:63 *t* days I am to be raised up
Mr 8:2 already *t* days that they have
8:31 killed, and rise *t* days later
9:5 let us erect *t* tents, one for
9:31 he will rise *t* days later
10:34 *t* days later he will rise
14:5 upward of *t* hundred denarii
14:30 you will disown me *t* times
14:58 in *t* days I will build
14:72 you will disown me *t* times
15:29 builder of it in *t* days'
Lu 1:56 about *t* months, and returned
2:46 after *t* days they found him
4:25 *t* years and six months, so
9:33 let us erect *t* tents, one for
10:36 Who of these *t* seems to you
11:5 Friend, loan me *t* loaves
12:52 divided, *t* against two and
12:52 divided . . . two against *t*
13:7 it is *t* years that I have
13:21 in *t* large measures of flour
22:34 *t* times denied knowing me
22:61 you will disown me *t* times
Joh 2:6 two or *t* liquid measures
2:19 in *t* days I will raise it up
2:20 you raise it up in *t* days
6:19 rowed about *t* or four miles
12:5 *t* hundred denarii and given
13:38 have disowned me *t* times
21:8 about *t* hundred feet away
Ac 2:41 *t* thousand souls were added
5:7 interval of about *t* hours
7:20 nursed *t* months in his
9:9 for *t* days he did not see
10:19 *T* men are seeking you
11:11 *t* men standing at the house
17:2 and for *t* sabbaths he reasoned
19:8 *t* months, giving talks and
20:3 he had spent *t* months there
20:31 for *t* years, night and day, I
25:1 *t* days later to Jerusalem
28:7 entertained us . . . *t* days
28:11 *T* months later we set sail
28:12 Syracuse we remained *t* days
28:15 Appius and *T* Taverns and
28:17 *t* days later he called
1Co 13:13 faith, hope, love, these *t*
14:27 limited to two or *t* at the
14:29 let two or *t* prophets speak
2Co 11:25 *t* times I was beaten with
11:25 *t* times I experienced
12:8 I *t* times entreated the Lord
13:1 two witnesses or of *t* every
Ga 1:18 *t* years later I went up to
1Ti 5:19 on the evidence of two or *t*
Heb 10:28 the testimony of two or *t*
11:23 Moses was hid for *t* months
Jas 5:17 for *t* years and six months
1Jo 5:7 there are *t* witness bearers
5:8 and the *t* are in agreement
Re 6:6 *t* quarts of barley for a
8:13 blasts of the *t* angels
9:18 By these *t* plagues a third
11:9 for *t* and a half days, and
11:11 after the *t* and a half days
16:13 I saw *t* unclean inspired
16:19 city split into *t* parts, and
21:13 On the east were *t* gates
21:13 and on the north *t* gates
21:13 and on the south *t* gates
21:13 and on the west *t* gates

Three-day
Nu 33:8 a *t* journey in the wilderness

Threefold
Ec 4:12 *t* cord cannot quickly be torn

Three-pronged
1Sa 2:13 with the *t* fork in his hand

Three-toothed
1Sa 13:21 for the *t* instruments and

Three-tribe
Nu 1:52 man by his *t* division by
2:2 each man by his *t* division, by
2:3 *t* division of the camp of
2:10 *t* division of the camp of
2:17 according to their *t* divisions
2:18 *t* division of the camp of
2:25 *t* division of the camp of Dan
2:31 according to their *t* divisions
2:34 encamped in their *t* divisions
10:14 *t* division of the camp of
10:18 *t* division of the camp of
10:22 *t* division of the camp of
10:25 *t* division of the camp of

Three-year-old
Ge 15:9, 9 *t* heifer and a *t* she-goat
15:9 *t* ram and a turtledove and a
1Sa 1:24 along with a *t* bull and one

Thresh
Ho 10:11 a trained heifer loving to *t*
Mic 4:13 *t*, O daughter of Zion

Threshed
Isa 21:10 O my *t* ones and the son of

Threshes
1Co 9:10 the man who *t* ought to do so
1Ti 5:18 not muzzle a bull when it *t*

Threshing
Ge 50:10 the *t* floor of Atad, which
50:11 the *t* floor of Atad, and
Le 26:5 *t* will certainly reach to
Nu 15:20 the contribution of a *t* floor
18:27 like the grain of the *t* floor
18:30 the produce of the *t* floor
De 15:14 your *t* floor and your oil and
16:13 your *t* floor and your oil
25:4 muzzle a bull while it is *t*
Jg 6:37 wool exposed on the *t* floor
8:7 give your flesh a *t* with the
Ru 3:2 at the *t* floor tonight
3:3 and go down to the *t* floor
3:6 to go down to the *t* floor and
3:14 a woman came to the *t* floor
1Sa 23:1 are pillaging the *t* floors
2Sa 6:6 far as the *t* floor of Nacon
24:16 by the *t* floor of Araunah
24:18 *t* floor of Araunah the
24:21 the *t* floor for building an
24:22 the *t* sledge and the
24:24 David bought the *t* floor
1Ki 22:10 *t* floor at the entrance of
2Ki 6:27 either from the *t* floor or
13:7 make them like the dust at *t*
1Ch 13:9 far as the *t* floor of Chidon
21:15 by the *t* floor of Ornan the
21:18 on the *t* floor of Ornan the
21:20 Now Ornan had been *t* wheat
21:21 went out of the *t* floor
21:22 the place of the *t* floor
21:23 the *t* sledge for the wood
21:28 at the *t* floor of Ornan the
2Ch 3:1 *t* floor of Ornan the Jebusite
18:9 sitting in the *t* floor at
Job 39:12 will gather to your *t* floor
41:30 *t* instrument upon the mire
Isa 21:10 and the son of my *t* floor
28:27 not with a *t* instrument
41:15 I have made you a *t* sledge
41:15 a new *t* instrument having
Jer 51:33 Babylon is like a *t* floor
Da 2:35 from the summer *t* floor
Ho 9:1 on all the *t* floors of grain
9:2 *T* floor and winepress do not
13:3 away from the *t* floor
Joe 2:24 the *t* floors must be full of
Am 1:3 on account of their *t* Gilead
1:3 even with iron *t* instruments
Mic 4:12 cut grain to the *t* floor
Hab 3:12 you went *t* the nations
Mt 3:12 clean up his *t* floor, and
Lu 3:17 to clean up his *t* floor
1Co 9:9 muzzle a bull when it is *t* out

Threshold
Jg 19:27 with her hands upon the *t*
1Sa 5:4 his hands cut off, to the *t*
5:5 not tread upon the *t* of Dagon
1Ki 14:17 at the *t* of the house
Ps 84:10 the *t* in the house of my God
Eze 9:3 to the *t* of the house, and he
10:4 cherubs to the *t* of the house
10:18 over the *t* of the house and
40:6 measure the *t* of the gate
40:6 other *t*, one reed in width
40:7 the *t* of the gate beside the
41:16 In front of the *t* there
43:8 putting their *t* with my
43:8 with my *t* and their doorpost
46:2 upon the *t* of the gate
47:1 under the *t* of the House
Zep 2:14 be devastation at the *t*

Thresholds
1Ch 9:22 as gatekeepers at the *t* were
2Ch 3:7 the house, the rafters, the *t*
Isa 6:4 pivots of the *t* began to
Eze 41:16 the *t*, and the windows
Am 9:1 so that the *t* will rock

Threw
Ge 21:15 she *t* the child under one of
Ex 4:3 he *t* it on the earth, and it
7:10 Aaron *t* his rod down before
7:12 they *t* down each one his rod
15:25 *t* it into the water and the
32:19 he at once *t* the tablets
De 9:21 I *t* its dust into the torrent
29:28 *t* them into another land as
Jg 15:17 *t* the jawbone out of his
19:21 and *t* mash to the he-asses
2Sa 16:13 and he *t* a lot of dust
1Ki 19:19 *t* his official garment upon
2Ki 2:21 water and *t* salt in it and
4:41 he *t* it into the pot, he
6:6 *t* it there and made the
13:21 *t* the man into Elisha's
2Ch 30:14 *t* them into the torrent
Ne 13:8 *t* all the furniture of
Jer 7:15 as I *t* out all your brothers
41:9 Ishmael *t* all the carcasses
Da 3:24 *t* bound into the midst of the
6:16 Daniel and *t* him into the pit
6:24 the lions' pit they *t* them
8:7 *t* it to the earth and trampled
Jon 2:3 When you *t* me to the depths
Zec 5:8 *t* the lead weight upon its
11:13 and *t* it into the treasury
Mt 13:48 the unsuitable they *t* away
15:30 *t* them at his feet, and he
21:12 *t* out all those selling and
21:39 *t* him out of the vineyard
27:5 he *t* the silver pieces into
Mr 9:20 *t* the child into convulsions
12:8 *t* him outside the vineyard
Lu 19:35 *t* their outer garments upon
20:12 also they wounded and *t* out
20:15 *t* him outside the vineyard
Joh 9:34 And they *t* him out
Ac 13:50 and *t* them outside their
16:23 *t* them into prison, ordering
16:24 *t* them into the inner prison
16:37 Romans, and *t* us into prison
20:10 Paul . . . *t* himself upon him
27:19 *t* away the tackling of the
Ga 2:18 things that I once *t* down I
Re 18:19 they *t* dust upon their heads

Thrive
Ps 62:10 maintenance should *t*
Zec 9:17 will make the young men *t*

Thriving
Ps 92:14 on *t* during gray-headedness

Throat
Ps 5:9 *t* is an opened burial place

Ps 69:3 My *t* has become hoarse
115:7 utter no sound with their *t*
149:6 extolling God be in their *t*
Pr 1:9 and a fine necklace to your *t*
3:3 Tie them about your *t*. Write
3:22 and charm to your *t*
6:21 bind them upon your *t*
23:2 put a knife to your *t* if you
Jer 2:25 and your *t* from thirst
Eze 16:11 and a necklace about your *t*
Ro 3:13 Their *t* is an opened grave

Throats
Isa 3:16 with their *t* stretched forth

Throne
Ge 41:40 Only as to the *t* shall I be
Ex 11:5 who is sitting on his *t* to
12:29 Pharaoh sitting on his *t* to
17:16 hand is against the *t* of Jah
De 17:18 he takes his seat on the *t*
Jg 3:20 he rose up from his *t*
1Sa 2:8 a *t* of glory he gives to them
2Sa 3:10 establish the *t* of David over
7:13 the *t* of his kingdom
7:16 *t* will become one firmly
14:9 king and his *t* are innocent
1Ki 1:13 one that will sit upon my *t*
1:17 one that will sit upon my *t*
1:20 is going to sit upon the *t*
1:24 one that will sit upon my *t*
1:27 who should sit upon the *t*
1:30 sit upon my *t* in place of
1:35 come in and sit upon my *t*
1:37 may he make his *t* greater
1:37 the *t* of my lord King David
1:46 upon the *t* of the kingship
1:47 make his *t* greater than your
1:47 greater than your *t*
1:48 given one to sit upon my *t*
2:4 sitting upon the *t* of Israel
2:12 the *t* of David his father
2:19 Then he sat down upon his *t*
2:19 had a *t* set for the mother
2:24 seated upon the *t* of David
2:33 for his house and for his *t*
2:45 the *t* of David itself will
3:6 a son to sit upon his *t*
5:5 put upon your *t* in place of
7:7 As for the Porch of the *T*
8:20 and sit upon the *t* of Israel
8:25 to sit upon the *t* of Israel
9:5 *t* of your kingdom over Israel
9:5 sitting upon the *t* of Israel
10:9 you upon the *t* of Israel
10:18 king made a great ivory *t*
10:19 were six steps to the *t*
10:19 the *t* had a round canopy
16:11 as he sat down upon his *t*
22:10 sitting each one on his *t*
22:19 Jehovah sitting upon his *t*
2Ki 10:3 upon the *t* of his father
10:30 upon the *t* of Israel
11:19 upon the *t* of the kings
13:13 Jeroboam . . . sat upon his *t*
15:12 upon the *t* of Israel
25:28 *t* higher than the thrones
1Ch 17:12 established his *t* firmly to
17:14 his *t* will itself become
22:10 *t* of his kingship firmly
28:5 *t* of the kingship of Jehovah
29:23 sit upon Jehovah's *t* as king
2Ch 6:10 and sit upon the *t* of Israel
6:16 to sit upon the *t* of Israel
7:18 the *t* of your kingship, just
9:8 his *t* as king for Jehovah
9:17 king made a great ivory *t*
9:18 were six steps to the *t*, and
9:18 footstool in gold to the *t*
18:9 sitting each one on his *t*
18:18 Jehovah sitting upon his *t*
23:20 upon the *t* of the kingdom
Ne 3:7 the *t* of the governor beyond
Es 1:2 was sitting upon his royal *t*
3:1 put his *t* above all the other
5:1 was sitting on his royal *t* in
Job 26:9 Enclosing the face of the *t*
36:7 Even kings on the *t*
Ps 9:4 sat on the *t* judging with
9:7 his *t* for judgment itself
11:4 in the heavens is his *t*
45:6 God is your *t* to time
47:8 his seat upon his holy *t*
89:4 build your *t* to generation
89:14 established place of your *t*
Ps 89:29 his *t* as the days of heaven
89:36 *t* as the sun in front of me
89:44 *t* you have hurled to the
93:2 *t* is firmly established from
94:20 *t* causing adversities be
97:2 established place of his *t*
103:19 his *t* in the very heavens
132:11 I shall set on your *t*
132:12 forever Will sit upon your *t*
Pr 16:12 by righteousness is the *t*
20:8 upon the *t* of judgment
20:28 he has sustained his *t*
25:5 *t* will be firmly established
29:14 *t* will be firmly established
Isa 6:1 Jehovah, sitting on a *t* lofty
9:7 *t* of David and upon his
14:13 I shall lift up my *t*
16:5 in loving-kindness a *t* will
22:23 as a *t* of glory to the house
47:1 earth where there is no *t*
66:1 The heavens are my *t*, and
Jer 1:15 *t* at the entrance of the
3:17 Jerusalem the *t* of Jehovah
13:13 for David upon his *t* and
14:21 not despise your glorious *t*
17:12 the glorious *t* on high
17:25 sitting on the *t* of David
22:2 sitting on the *t* of David
22:4 sitting for David upon his *t*
22:30 sitting upon the *t* of David
29:16 sitting on the *t* of David
33:17 *t* of the house of Israel
33:21 ruling as king upon his *t*
36:30 sitting upon the *t* of David
43:10 *t* right above these stones
49:38 I will set my *t* in Elam
52:32 put his *t* higher than the
La 5:19 Your *t* is for generation after
Eze 1:26 stone, the likeness of a *t*
1:26 upon the likeness of the *t*
10:1 likeness of a *t*, appearing
43:7 the place of my *t* and the
Da 5:20 from the *t* of his kingdom
7:9 His *t* was flames of fire; its
Jon 3:6 rose up from his *t* and put
Hag 2:22 overthrow the *t* of kingdoms
Zec 6:13 sit down and rule on his *t*
6:13 become a priest upon his *t*
Mt 5:34 because it is God's *t*
19:28 upon his glorious *t*, you who
23:22 swearing by the *t* of God and
25:31 sit down on his glorious *t*
Lu 1:32 God will give him the *t* of
Ac 2:30 he would seat . . . upon his *t*
7:49 heaven is my *t* and the earth
Heb 1:8 Son: God is your *t* forever
4:16 the *t* of undeserved kindness
8:1 *t* of the Majesty in the
12:2 right hand of the *t* of God
Re 1:4 spirits that are before his *t*
2:13 where the *t* of Satan is; and
3:21 sit down with me on my *t*
3:21 down with my Father on his *t*
4:2 *t* was in its position in
4:2 is one seated upon the *t*
4:3 about the *t* there is a rainbow
4:4 And round about the *t* there
4:5 And out of the *t* there are
4:5 seven lamps . . . before the *t*
4:6 before the *t* there is, as it
4:6 the midst of the *t* and around
4:6 around the *t* there are four
4:9 to the one seated upon the *t*
4:10 the One seated upon the *t* and
4:10 their crowns before the *t*
5:1 of the One seated upon the *t*
5:6 in the midst of the *t* and of
5:7 of the One seated on the *t*
5:11 many angels around the *t* and
5:13 To the One sitting on the *t*
6:16 One seated on the *t* and from
7:9 standing before the *t* and
7:10 God, who is seated on the *t*
7:11 standing around the *t* and the
7:11 upon their faces before the *t*
7:15 they are before the *t* of God
7:15 the One seated on the *t* will
7:17 who is in the midst of the *t*
8:3 altar that was before the *t*
12:5 away to God and to his *t*
13:2 beast its power and its *t*
14:3 new song before the *t* and
16:10 the *t* of the wild beast
16:17 from the *t*, saying: It has
Re 19:4 God seated upon the *t*
19:5 issued forth from the *t*
20:11 I saw a great white *t* and
20:12 standing before the *t*, and
21:3 loud voice from the *t* say
21:5 the One seated on the *t* said
22:1 *t* of God and of the Lamb
22:3 *t* of God and of the Lamb

Thrones
2Ki 25:28 higher than the *t* of the
Ps 122:5 *t* for judgment have been
122:5 *T* for the house of David
Isa 14:9 get up from their *t*
Jer 52:32 higher than the *t* of the
Eze 26:16 their *t* all the chieftains
Da 7:9 *t* placed and the Ancient of
Mt 19:28 sit upon twelve *t*, judging
Lu 1:52 down men of power from *t* and
22:30 and sit on *t* to judge the
Col 1:16 whether they are *t* or
Re 4:4 twenty-four *t*, and upon these
4:4 *t* I saw seated twenty-four
11:16 before God upon their *t*
20:4 I saw *t*, and there were

Throng
Ps 42:4 to pass along with the *t*
55:14 we used to walk with the *t*
Da 6:6 entered as a *t* to the king
6:15 entered as a *t* to the king

Thronged
Lu 8:42 As he was going the crowds *t*

Throngs
Ps 26:12 Among the congregated *t* I
50:11 animal *t* of the open field
68:26 In congregated *t* bless God
80:13 animal *t* of the open field

Through
Ge 12:6 Abram went on *t* the land as
13:17 go about . . . *t* its length and
13:17 go about . . . *t* its breadth
22:20 the report got *t* to Abraham
31:34 feeling *t* the whole tent
31:37 you have felt *t* all my goods
Ex 12:12 pass *t* the land of Egypt on
12:23 Jehovah does pass *t* to plague
14:16 go *t* the midst of the sea
14:22 Israel went *t* the midst of
15:19 *t* the midst of the sea
19:13 or will positively be shot *t*
19:21 break *t* to Jehovah to take a
19:24 people break *t* to come up to
21:6 must pierce his ear *t* with
21:22 must give it *t* the justices
25:14 put the poles *t* the rings
26:28 is running *t* from end to end
28:24 ropes of gold *t* the two
28:25 two ropes *t* the two settings
32:27 Pass *t* and return from gate
36:6 announcement to pass *t* the
36:33 run *t* at the middle of the
37:5 he put the poles *t* the rings
39:17 ropes of gold *t* the two rings
39:18 two ropes *t* the two settings
Le 26:6 sword will not pass *t* your
Nu 13:32 we passed *t* to spy it out
14:1 and weeping all *t* that night
14:7 land that we passed *t* to spy
20:17 pass, please, *t* your land
20:17 pass *t* a field or a vineyard
20:17 shall pass *t* your territory
20:18 You must not pass *t* me, for
20:19 than to pass *t* on my feet
20:20 he said: You must not pass *t*
20:21 to pass *t* his territory
21:22 Let me pass *t* your land
21:22 we pass *t* your territory
21:23 to pass *t* his territory
25:8 and pierced both of them *t*
25:8 the woman *t* her genital parts
31:23 you should pass *t* the fire
31:23 you should pass *t* the water
33:8 *t* the midst of the sea to the
De 1:19 marching *t* all that great and
2:7 *t* this great wilderness
2:27 Let me pass *t* your land
2:28 let me pass *t* on my feet
2:30 did not let us pass *t* him
8:15 *t* the great and fear-inspiring
15:17 *t* his ear and to the door
18:10 his daughter pass *t* the fire
29:16 *t* the midst of the nations

De 29:16 nations *t* whom you passed
Jos 1:11 Pass *t* the midst of the camp
2:15 by a rope *t* the window
3:2 pass *t* the midst of the camp
4:7 When it passed *t* the Jordan
18:9 passed *t* the land and mapped
24:3 had him walk *t* all the land
24:17 the peoples *t* the midst of
Jg 3:23 to go out *t* the airhole, but
5:26 she pierced his head *t*, And
6:35 messengers *t* all of Manasseh
6:35 sent out messengers *t* Asher
7:19 got *t* posting the sentries
8:16 men of Succoth *t* an experience
9:54 attendant ran him *t*, so that
11:16 walking *t* the wilderness as
11:17 Let me pass . . . *t* your land
11:18 walked on *t* the wilderness
11:19 Let us pass . . . *t* your land
11:20 crossing *t* his territory, and
11:29 pass *t* Gilead and Manasseh
11:29 to pass *t* Mizpeh of Gilead
1Sa 9:4 *t* the mountainous region
9:4 on *t* the land of Shalishah
9:4 on *t* the land of Shaalim, but
9:4 went passing on *t* the land of
19:12 David descend *t* the window
31:4 your sword and run me *t*
31:4 run me *t* and deal abusively
2Sa 2:29 marched *t* the Arabah all
2:29 marching *t* the entire gully
5:20 Jehovah has broken *t* my
6:8 Jehovah had broken *t* in a
6:16 looked down *t* the window and
10:3 sake of searching *t* the city
15:10 Absalom now sent spies *t*
18:14 *t* the heart of Absalom
20:14 passing *t* all the tribes of
24:2 *t* all the tribes of Israel
24:8 moving about *t* all the land
1Ki 18:5 *t* the land to all the springs
18:6 the land *t* which to pass
22:7 Then let us inquire *t* him
22:8 one man *t* whom to inquire
22:36 began to pass *t* the camp
2Ki 1:2 *t* the grating in his roof
3:11 us inquire of Jehovah *t* him
3:26 break *t* to the king of Edom
4:28 I ask for a son *t* my lord
8:8 must inquire of Jehovah *t* him
9:30 to look down *t* the window
10:21 Jehu sent *t* all Israel
16:3 son he made pass *t* the fire
17:17 daughters pass *t* the fire
21:6 his own son pass *t* the fire
23:10 pass *t* the fire to Molech
1Ch 10:4 your sword and run me *t*
13:11 Jehovah had broken *t* in
14:11 God has broken *t* my enemies
15:13 our God broke *t* against us
15:29 looked down *t* the window
21:4 and walked *t* all Israel
2Ch 16:9 *t* all the earth to show his
17:9 *t* all the cities of Judah
18:6 Then let us inquire *t* him
18:7 man *t* whom to inquire of
23:20 *t* the upper gate to the
26:6 break *t* the wall of Gath and
30:5 call pass *t* all Israel, from
32:4 floods *t* the middle of the
33:6 own sons pass *t* the fire in
36:22 to pass *t* all his kingdom
Ezr 1:1 cry to pass *t* all his realm
4:19 order has been put *t* by me
4:21 put an order *t* for these
4:21 the order is put *t* by me
5:3 Who put an order *t* to you to
5:9 order *t* to you to build this
5:13 an order *t* to rebuild this
5:17 an order was put *t* to rebuild
6:1 Darius the king put an order *t*
6:3 Cyrus the king put an order *t*
6:8 an order has been put *t* as to
6:11 an order has been put *t* that
6:12 I, Darius, do put *t* an order
7:13 an order has been put *t* that
7:21 an order has been put *t* to
Ne 9:11 *t* the midst of the sea on the
Job 4:9 *T* the breath of God they
4:9 *t* the spirit of his anger they
13:17 Hear my word clear *t*, And
15:19 And no stranger passed *t* the
16:14 He keeps breaking *t* me with
20:25 missile . . . out *t* his back
Job 20:25 weapon out *t* his gall
22:13 *T* thick gloom can he judge?
28:27 and also searched it *t*
29:3 walk *t* darkness by his light
30:14 *t* a wide gap they proceed
30:17 bored *t* and dropped from
Ps 8:8 passing *t* the paths of the seas
32:3 bones wore out *t* my groaning
60:1 you have broken *t* us, You
66:6 *T* the river they went
66:12, 12 come *t* fire and *t* water
68:4 riding *t* the desert plains
68:7 When you marched *t* the desert
72:3 the hills, *t* righteousness
73:19 finish *t* sudden terrors
77:10 This is what pierces me *t*
77:19 *T* the sea your way was
77:19 path was *t* many waters
84:6 *t* the low plain of the baca
105:41 *t* the waterless regions as
106:9 walking them *t* the watery
106:9 as *t* the wilderness
136:14 Israel to pass *t* the middle
136:16 walk *t* the wilderness
139:1 Jehovah, you have searched *t*
139:23 Search *t* me, O God, and
Pr 7:6 *t* my lattice I looked down
18:17 and certainly searches him *t*
25:2 is the searching *t* a matter
25:28 a city broken *t*, without a
28:11 is discerning searches him *t*
Ec 10:8 is breaking *t* a stone wall
10:18 *T* great laziness the
10:18 *t* the letting down of the
Ca 2:9 gazing *t* the windows, glancing
2:9 glancing *t* the lattices
Isa 5:16 become high *t* judgment
5:16 himself *t* righteousness
8:8 and move on *t* Judah
8:21 pass *t* the land hard pressed
10:22 flooding *t* in righteousness
10:28 passed along *t* Migron
13:15 is found will be pierced *t*
28:15 in case it should pass *t*
28:18 flood, when it passes *t*
28:19 As often as it passes *t*
28:19 morning it will pass *t*
30:6 *T* the land of distress and
40:3 *t* the desert plain straight
43:2 you should pass *t* the waters
43:2 and *t* the rivers, they will
43:2 you should walk *t* the fire
43:16 making a way *t* the sea
43:16 even *t* strong waters
43:19 *t* the wilderness I shall
43:19 a way, *t* the desert rivers
48:21 even *t* devastated places
60:15 with nobody passing *t*
62:10 pass out *t* the gates, you
63:13 walk *t* the surging waters
66:9 cause the breaking *t* and not
Jer 2:6 walking us *t* the wilderness
2:6 *t* a land of desert plain and
2:6 *t* a land of no water and of
2:6, 6 *t* a land *t* which no man
4:11 paths *t* the wilderness
9:6 *T* deception they have refused
9:10 there is no man passing *t*
9:12 without anyone passing *t*
9:21 has come up *t* our windows
12:12 paths *t* the wilderness
17:21 in *t* the gates of Jerusalem
17:24 *t* the gates of this city
17:27 *t* the gates of Jerusalem on
22:2 coming in *t* these gates
22:4 *t* the gates of this house
32:35 pass *t* the fire to Molech
37:10 men pierced *t*, they would
39:2 the city was broken *t*
51:4 pierced *t* in her streets
51:6 inanimate *t* her error
51:43 *t* them no son of mankind
52:7 the city was broken *t*
La 3:44 that prayer may not pass *t*
4:9 pierced *t* for lack of the
Eze 5:17 will pass along *t* you, and
8:8 bore, please, *t* the wall
8:8 I gradually bored *t* the wall
9:4 Pass *t* the midst of the city
9:4 *t* the midst of Jerusalem, and
9:5 Pass *t* the city after him and
12:5 bore your way *t* the wall
12:5 do the bringing out *t* it
12:7 bored my way *t* the wall by
Eze 12:12 *t* the wall they will bore
12:12 do the bringing forth *t* it
14:5 *t* their dungy idols—all of
14:15 wild beasts pass *t* the land
14:15 without anybody passing *t*
14:17 a sword itself pass *t* the
16:21 making them pass *t* the fire
20:26 child . . . pass *t* the fire
20:31 your sons pass *t* the fire
23:37 pass *t* the fire to them as
26:10 he comes in *t* your gates
29:11 not pass *t* it the foot of
29:11 domestic animal pass *t* it
32:26 pierced *t* by the sword
33:28 with no one passing *t*
35:7 the one passing *t* and the
39:11 valley of those passing *t*
39:11 stopping up those passing *t*
39:14 passing along *t* the land
39:14 with those passing *t*
39:15 those passing *t* must pass
39:15 must pass along *t* the land
47:3 make me pass *t* the water
47:4 made me pass *t* the water
47:4 made me pass *t*—water up to
47:5 I was not able to pass *t*, for
47:5 that could not be passed *t*
47:8 must go down *t* the Arabah
Da 2:30 *t* any wisdom that exists in
3:29 order is being put *t*, that
4:6 order was being put *t* to bring
6:26 has been put *t* an order that
11:10 and flood over and pass *t*
11:20 exactor to pass *t* the
11:40 and flood over and pass *t*
Joe 2:9 *T* the windows they go in like
3:17 they will no more pass *t* her
Am 2:10 *t* the wilderness forty years
5:17 shall pass *t* the midst of you
Jon 1:13 tried to work their way *t*
Mic 2:13 they will actually break *t*
2:13 And they will pass *t* a gate
2:13 king will pass *t* before them
5:8 when it actually passes *t*
Na 1:12 and one must pass *t*. And I
1:15 pass again *t* you. In his
Hab 1:11 pass *t* and will actually
3:10 waters passed *t*
3:12 went marching *t* the earth
3:15 *T* the sea you trod with your
3:15 *t* the heap of vast waters
Zep 3:6 there was no one passing *t*
Zec 7:14 with no one passing *t* and
9:8 no one passing *t* and no one
9:8 pass *t* them a taskmaster, for
10:11 pass *t* the sea with distress
12:10 the One whom they pierced *t*
13:3 pierce him *t* because of his
13:9 the third part *t* the fire
Mt 1:22 Jehovah *t* his prophet, saying
2:5 has been written *t* the prophet
2:15 by Jehovah *t* his prophet
2:17 spoken *t* Jeremiah the prophet
2:23 was spoken *t* the prophets
3:3 the one spoken of *t* Isaiah
4:4 forth *t* Jehovah's mouth
4:14 spoken *t* Isaiah the prophet
7:13 Go in *t* the narrow gate
7:13 many are the ones going in *t*
8:17 spoken *t* Isaiah the prophet
12:1 Jesus went *t* the grainfields
12:17 spoken *t* Isaiah the prophet
12:43 passes *t* parched places in
13:35 was spoken *t* the prophet
18:7 the man *t* whom the stumbling
19:24 a camel to get *t* a needle's
21:4 was spoken *t* the prophet
22:26 the third, until *t* all seven
24:15 as spoken of *t* Daniel the
26:24 man *t* whom the Son of man
27:9 spoken *t* Jeremiah the prophet
Mr 1:28 *t* all the country round about
2:23 proceeding *t* the grainfields
6:2 be performed *t* his hands
7:31 *t* Sidon to the sea of Galilee
9:26 going *t* many convulsions it
9:30 went their way *t* Galilee
10:25 camel to go *t* a needle's eye
11:16 carry a utensil *t* the temple
14:21 woe to that man *t* whom the
Lu 1:70 *t* the mouth of his holy
2:35 sword will be run *t* the soul
4:14 *t* all the surrounding country
4:30 he went *t* the midst of them

Lu 5:19 *t* the tiling they let him
6:1 to be passing *t* grainfields
7:3 bring his slave safely *t*
9:6 *t* the territory from village
9:45 that they might not see *t* it
11:24 it passes *t* parched places
13:22 journeyed *t* from city to
13:24 to get in *t* the narrow door
17:1 to the one *t* whom they come
17:8 until I am *t* eating and
17:11 *t* the midst of Samaria and
18:25 to get *t* the eye of a sewing
18:36 he heard a crowd moving *t*
19:1 Jericho and was going *t*
19:4 was about to go *t* that way
22:22 man *t* whom he is betrayed
Joh 1:3 came into existence *t* him
1:7 people . . . believe *t* him
1:10 world came into existence *t*
1:17 the Law was given *t* Moses
1:17 truth came to be *t* Jesus
3:17 the world to be saved *t* him
4:4 for him to go *t* Samaria
10:1 sheepfold *t* the door but
10:2 enters *t* the door is shepherd
10:9 enters *t* me will be saved
11:4 Son of God . . . glorified *t* it
14:6 to the Father except *t* me
17:20 faith in me *t* their word
Ac 1:2 commandment *t* holy spirit
2:16 was said *t* the prophet Joel
2:22 *t* powerful works and portents
2:22 signs that God did *t* him in
2:43 began to occur *t* the apostles
3:16 faith that is *t* him has given
3:18 *t* the mouth of all the
3:21 God spoke *t* the mouth of his
4:16 sign has occurred *t* them
4:25 *t* holy spirit said by the
4:30 *t* the name of your holy
5:12 *t* the hands of the apostles
8:4 *t* the land declaring the good
8:18 *t* the laying on of the hands
8:20 *t* money to get possession
8:40 he went *t* the territory and
9:25 *t* an opening in the wall
9:32 Peter was going *t* all parts
10:36 good news of peace *t* Jesus
10:38 went *t* the land doing good
10:43 forgiveness . . . *t* his name
11:19 *t* as far as Phoenicia and
11:28 indicate *t* the spirit that a
12:9 happening *t* the angel was
12:10 Going *t* the first sentinel
13:6 gone *t* the whole island as
13:38 *t* this One a forgiveness of
14:3 portents . . . *t* their hands
14:22 *t* many tribulations
14:24 And they went *t* Pisidia and
15:3 *t* both Phoenicia and Samaria
15:7 that *t* my mouth people of the
15:11 get saved *t* the undeserved
15:12 did *t* them among the nations
15:41 he went *t* Syria and Cilicia
16:4 they traveled on *t* the cities
16:6 they went *t* Phrygia and the
17:1 now journeyed *t* Amphipolis
18:9 Lord said to Paul *t* a vision
18:23 *t* the country of Galatia and
19:1 Paul went *t* the inland parts
19:11 *t* the hands of Paul
19:21 after going *t* Macedonia and
20:2 After going *t* those parts and
20:3 to return *t* Macedonia
21:4 *t* the spirit they repeatedly
21:19 God did . . . *t* his ministry
24:2 enjoy great peace *t* you and
24:2 *t* your forethought
27:5 navigated *t* the open sea
27:43 to bring Paul safely *t* and
28:25 spirit aptly spoke *t* Isaiah
Ro 1:2 aforetime *t* his prophets in
1:5 *t* whom we received undeserved
1:8 thanks to my God *t* Jesus
1:12 each one *t* the other's faith
2:16 God *t* Christ Jesus judges the
3:22 *t* the faith in Jesus Christ
3:24 *t* the release by the ransom
3:25 *t* faith in his blood
3:27 *T* what law? That of works?
3:27 but *t* the law of faith
4:13 not *t* law that Abraham or
4:13 *t* the righteousness by faith
5:1 peace with God *t* our Lord
Ro 5:2 *t* whom also we have gained
5:5 our hearts *t* the holy spirit
5:9 be saved *t* him from wrath
5:10 God *t* the death of his Son
5:11 exulting . . . *t* our Lord Jesus
5:11 Jesus Christ, *t* whom we have
5:12 *t* one man sin entered into
5:12 and death *t* sin, and thus
5:16 things worked *t* the one man
5:17 ruled as king *t* that one
5:17 life *t* the one person, Jesus
5:18 *t* one trespass the result to
5:18 *t* one act of justification
5:19 *t* the disobedience of the one
5:19 *t* the obedience of the one
5:21 king *t* righteousness with
5:21 life in view *t* Jesus
6:4 buried with him *t* our baptism
6:4 *t* the glory of the Father
7:4 dead to the Law *t* the body of
7:8 inducement *t* the commandment
7:11 inducement *t* the commandment
7:11 and killed me *t* it
7:13 death for me *t* that which is
7:13 sinful *t* the commandment
7:25 Thanks to God *t* Jesus Christ
8:3 while it was weak *t* the flesh
8:11 alive *t* his spirit that
8:20 but *t* him that subjected it
8:37 victorious *t* him that loved
9:7 your seed will be *t* Isaac
10:17 thing heard is *t* the word
10:19 *t* that which is not a nation
10:19 anger *t* a stupid nation
12:3 *t* the undeserved kindness
15:4 that *t* our endurance and
15:4 and *t* the comfort from the
15:18 Christ worked *t* me for the
15:30 *t* our Lord Jesus Christ and
15:30 *t* the love of the spirit
16:26 *t* the prophetic scriptures
16:27 be the glory *t* Jesus Christ
1Co 1:1 of Jesus Christ *t* God's will
1:10 *t* the name of our Lord Jesus
1:21 world *t* its wisdom did not
1:21 saw good *t* the foolishness
2:10 God has revealed them *t* his
3:5 Ministers *t* whom you became
3:15 if so, it will be as *t* fire
4:15 become your father *t* the
6:14 raise us up . . . *t* his power
8:6 *t* whom all things are, and we
8:6 all things are, and we *t* him
10:1 and all passed *t* the sea
11:12 the man is *t* the woman
12:8 there is given *t* the spirit
14:9 *t* the tongue utter speech
15:2 *t* which you are also being
15:21 For since death is *t* a man
15:21 resurrection . . . *t* a man
15:57 victory *t* our Lord Jesus
16:5 gone *t* Macedonia, for I am
16:5 for I am going *t* Macedonia
16:7 just now on my passing *t*
2Co 1:1 an apostle . . . *t* God's will
1:4 *t* the comfort with which we
1:5 also abounds *t* the Christ
1:19 was preached among you *t* us
1:19 that is, *t* me and Silvanus
1:20 *t* him is the Amen said to
1:20 said to God for glory *t* us
2:14 perceptible *t* us in every
3:4 *t* the Christ we have this
4:4 illumination . . . not shine *t*
5:10 the things done *t* the body
5:18 reconciled us . . . *t* Christ
5:20 were making entreaty *t* us
6:7 *t* the weapons of
6:8 *t* glory and dishonor
6:8 *t* bad report and good report
8:5 Lord and to us *t* God's will
8:9 become rich *t* his poverty
8:18 good news has spread *t* all
9:11 produces *t* us an expression
9:13 *T* the proof that this
11:33 *t* a window in the wall I
12:17 advantage of you *t* him
Ga 1:1, 1 nor *t* a man, but *t* Jesus
1:12 *t* revelation by Jesus Christ
1:15 called me *t* his undeserved
2:16 only *t* faith toward Christ
2:19 *t* law I died toward law, that
2:21 if righteousness is *t* law
3:14 promised spirit *t* our faith
Ga 3:18 it to Abraham *t* a promise
3:19 transmitted *t* angels by the
3:26 sons of God *t* your faith in
4:7 if a son, also an heir *t* God
4:13 *t* a sickness of my flesh
4:23 the free woman *t* a promise
5:6 but faith operating *t* love is
5:13 *t* love slave for one another
6:14 Christ, *t* whom the world has
Eph 1:1 *t* God's will, to the holy
1:5 adoption *t* Jesus Christ as
1:7 ransom *t* the blood of that
2:8 you have been saved *t* faith
2:16 to God *t* the torture stake
2:18 *t* him we, both peoples, have
3:6 Christ Jesus *t* the good news
3:10 known *t* the congregation
3:12 *t* our faith in him
3:16 with power *t* his spirit
3:17 *t* your faith in your hearts
4:6 over all and *t* all and in all
4:16 to cooperate *t* every joint
Php 1:11 which is *t* Jesus Christ, to
1:15 preaching the Christ *t* envy
1:15 but others also *t* goodwill
1:19 salvation *t* your supplication
1:20, 20 *t* life or *t* death
1:26 *t* my presence again with you
3:9 which is *t* faith in Christ
Col 1:1 an apostle . . . *t* God's will
1:16 created *t* him and for him
1:20 and *t* him to reconcile again
1:20 peace *t* the blood he shed on
1:22 *t* his death, in order to
2:8 *t* the philosophy and empty
2:12 *t* your faith in the operation
3:10 which *t* accurate knowledge
3:17 thanking God the Father *t*
1Th 3:7 *t* the faithfulness you show
4:2 orders we gave you *t* the Lord
4:14 asleep in death *t* Jesus
5:9 salvation *t* our Lord Jesus
2Th 2:2 *t* an inspired expression or
2:2 or *t* a verbal message or
2:2 or *t* a letter as though from
2:14 *t* the good news we declare
2:15 was *t* a verbal message or
2:15 or *t* a letter of ours
3:14 *t* this letter, keep this one
1Ti 2:10 *t* good works
2:15 be kept safe *t* childbearing
4:5 sanctified *t* God's word and
4:14 was given you *t* a prediction
2Ti 1:1 *t* God's will according to the
1:6 *t* the laying of my hands upon
1:10 *t* the manifestation of our
1:10 *t* the good news
1:14 *t* the holy spirit which is
3:15 *t* the faith in connection
4:17 that *t* me the preaching
Tit 3:5 he saved us *t* the bath that
3:5 *t* the making of us new by
3:6 *t* Jesus Christ our Savior
Phm 7 been refreshed *t* you, brother
22 hoping that *t* the prayers of
Heb 1:2 *t* whom he made the systems
2:2 the word spoken *t* angels
2:3 to be spoken *t* our Lord and
2:10 *t* whom all things are, in
2:10 perfect *t* sufferings
2:14 *t* his death he might bring
2:15 slavery all *t* their lives
4:14 passed *t* the heavens, Jesus
5:14 *t* use have their perceptive
6:12 those who *t* faith and
6:18 *t* two unchangeable things
7:9 *t* Abraham even Levi who
7:11 *t* the Levitical priesthood
7:19 *t* which we are drawing near
7:25 are approaching God *t* him
9:11 *t* the greater and more
9:14 *t* an everlasting spirit
9:26 sin away *t* the sacrifice of
10:10 sanctified *t* the offering
10:20 *t* the curtain, that is, his
11:4 *t* which faith he had witness
11:4 *t* it he, although he died
11:7 *t* this faith he condemned
11:18 your seed will be *t* Isaac
11:29 they passed *t* the Red Sea
11:33 *t* faith defeated kingdoms
11:39 borne to them *t* their faith
12:28 kindness, *t* which we may
13:2 hospitality, for *t* it some

Heb 13:15 *T* him let us always offer
13:21 performing in us *t* Jesus
1Pe 1:3 living hope *t* the resurrection
1:5 God's power *t* faith for a
1:12 *t* those who have declared
1:21 *t* him are believers in God
1:23 *t* the word of the living and
2:2 that *t* it you may grow to
2:5 acceptable to God *t* Jesus
3:1 *t* the conduct of their wives
3:20 carried safely *t* the water
3:21 *t* the resurrection of Jesus
4:11 God may be glorified *t* Jesus
5:12 *T* Silvanus, a faithful
2Pe 1:3 *t* the accurate knowledge of
1:3 called us *t* glory and virtue
1:4 *T* these things he has freely
1:4 that *t* these you may become
1:4 that is in the world *t* lust
3:2 and Savior *t* your apostles
3:12 *t* which the heavens being on
1Jo 4:9 we might gain life *t* him
Jude 25 *t* Jesus Christ our Lord
Re 1:1 presented it in signs *t* him

Throughout

Ex 12:14 festival to Jehovah *t* your
12:17 this day *t* your generations
12:42 Israel *t* their generations
16:32 to be kept *t* your generations
16:33 to be kept *t* your generations
29:42 offering *t* your generations
30:21 and his offspring *t* their
38:18 the height *t* its extent was
Le 6:18 *t* your generations from
17:7 for you, *t* your generations
21:17 seed *t* their generations in
22:3 *T* your generations any man
Nu 15:21 to Jehovah *t* your generations
15:38 garments *t* their generations
35:29 *t* your generations in all
1Sa 13:3 horn blown *t* all the land
25:28 found in you *t* your days
1Ki 1:3 *t* all the territory of Israel
1Ch 5:10 tents *t* all the country east
2Ch 17:19 fortified cities *t* all Judah
19:5 station judges *t* the land in
23:2 *t* Judah and collected
24:9 issued a call *t* Judah and
30:6 *t* all Israel and Judah, even
30:10 *t* the land of Ephraim and
Ezr 10:7 call to pass *t* Judah and
Ne 6:7 *t* Jerusalem, saying, There is
8:15 to pass *t* all their cities
8:15 and *t* Jerusalem, saying
Es 8:13 as law *t* all the different
9:4 his fame was traveling *t* all
Ps 45:17 your name *t* all generations
102:24 years are *t* all generations
104:33 sing to Jehovah *t* my life
116:2 And *t* my days I shall call
145:13 your dominion is *t* all
Jer 4:5 and blow a horn *t* the land
17:3 sin *t* all your territories
51:52 *t* all her land the pierced
Eze 38:21 *t* all my mountainous
Zec 7:14 hurl them *t* all the nations
Mt 4:23 *t* the whole of Galilee
Mr 1:39 *t* the whole of Galilee and
Lu 8:39 proclaiming *t* the whole city
15:14 a severe famine occurred *t*
23:5 by teaching *t* all Judea, even
Joh 19:23 from the top *t* its length
Ac 1:3 seen by them *t* forty days and
8:1 scattered *t* the regions of
9:31 congregation *t* the whole of
9:42 became known *t* all Joppa
10:37 about *t* the whole of Judea
13:49 carried *t* the whole country
24:5 Jews *t* the inhabited earth
24:12 the synagogues or *t* the city
Ro 1:8 faith is talked about *t* the

Throw

Ex 1:22 newborn son you are to *t*
4:3 he said: *T* it on the earth
7:9 Take your rod and *t* it down
15:7 you can *t* down those who rise
22:31 You should *t* it to the dogs
23:24 without fail *t* them down
23:27 *t* into confusion all the
32:24 proceeded to *t* it into the
Le 1:16 and *t* it beside the altar
14:40 *t* them outside the city into
Nu 19:6 *t* it into the midst of the
Jg 4:15 Jehovah began to *t* Sisera and
1Sa 7:10 might *t* them into confusion
2Sa 11:25 against the city and *t* it
20:15 the wall, to *t* it down
22:15 might *t* them into confusion
1Ki 9:7 *t* away from before me, and
2Ki 9:25 *t* him into the tract of the
9:26 *t* him into the tract of land
10:25 and to *t* them out, and they
1Ch 20:1 strike Rabbah and *t* it down
2Ch 7:20 *t* away from before my face
25:12 *t* them from the top of the
Ps 18:14 might *t* them into confusion
51:11 Do not *t* me away from
55:22 *T* your burden upon Jehovah
60:8 Over Edom I shall *t* my sandal
71:9 Do not *t* me away in the time
102:10 that you might *t* me away
108:9 Edom I shall *t* my sandal
144:6 may *t* them into confusion
Ec 3:5 a time to *t* stones away and a
3:6 to keep and a time to *t* away
Isa 2:20 will *t* his worthless gods of
Jer 6:6 *t* up against Jerusalem a
7:15 I will *t* you out from
7:29 uncut hair and *t* it away
38:6 Jeremiah and *t* him into the
Eze 4:2 *t* up a siege rampart against
7:19 will *t* their very silver
18:31 *T* off from yourselves all
20:7 *T* away, each one of you, the
20:8 did not individually *t* away
21:22 *t* up a siege rampart
26:8 *t* up against you a siege
28:17 Onto the earth I will *t* you
43:24 priests must *t* salt upon
Da 3:20 *t* them into the burning fiery
11:15 *t* up a siege rampart and
Am 8:3 will certainly *t* them out
Mic 7:19 *t* into the depths of the sea
Na 3:6 I will *t* disgusting things
Zec 5:8 *t* her back into the midst of
11:13 *T* it to the treasury—the
Mt 5:29 tear it out and *t* it away
5:30 cut it off and *t* it away
7:6 neither *t* your pearls before
15:26 and *t* it to little dogs
18:8 cut it off and *t* it away
18:9 tear it out and *t* it away
22:13 *t* him out into the darkness
25:30 *t* the good-for-nothing slave
26:61 able to *t* down the temple
Mr 7:27 and *t* it to the little dogs
9:22 *t* him both into the fire and
9:47 makes you stumble, *t* it away
11:15 *t* out those selling and
14:58 I will *t* down this temple
Lu 4:29 to *t* him down headlong
12:5 authority to *t* into Gehenna
12:58 officer *t* you into prison
14:35 People *t* it outside. Let him
19:45 *t* out those who were selling
22:41 about a stone's *t*, and bent
Ac 6:14 *t* down this place and change
17:5 to *t* the city into an uproar
21:27 to *t* all the crowd into
Heb 10:35 *t* away your freeness of
1Pe 5:7 you *t* all your anxiety upon
3Jo 10 to *t* out of the congregation
Re 2:22 about to *t* her into a sickbed

Thrower-down

Mt 27:40 would-be *t* of the temple
Mr 15:29 would-be *t* of the temple

Throwing

Ex 14:24 *t* the camp of the Egyptians
Jos 10:10 went *t* them into confusion
10:27 and *t* them into the cave
Jg 8:25 went *t* each one the nose ring
2Sa 16:6 he began *t* stones at David
16:13 and he kept *t* stones while
2Ki 3:25 the cities they went *t* down
Ps 50:17 you keep *t* my words behind
147:17 *t* his ice like morsels
Jer 22:19 dragging about and a *t* away
41:7 *t* them into the midst of the
Eze 17:17 by *t* up a siege rampart and
Da 8:12 kept *t* truth to the earth
Mr 1:26 *t* him into a convulsion and
10:50 *T* off his outer garment, he
Lu 4:35 after *t* the man down in their
Ac 7:58 *t* him outside the city, they
16:37 they now *t* us out secretly
22:23 *t* their outer garments about
Ac 27:38 *t* the wheat overboard into
2Pe 2:4 by *t* them into Tartarus
Re 2:10 Devil will keep on *t* some

Thrown

Nu 35:20 has *t* at him while lying in
35:22 him or has *t* any article
1Ki 13:24 came to be *t* onto the road
13:25 dead body *t* onto the road
13:28 body of him *t* onto the road
2Ki 2:16 then *t* him upon one of the
7:15 that the Syrians had *t* away
2Ch 33:15 had them *t* outside the city
Ps 22:10 I have been *t* from the womb
88:7 your rage has *t* itself
141:6 judges have been *t* down by
Isa 14:19 *t* away without a burial
34:3 slain ones will be *t* out
38:17 have *t* behind your back all
Jer 9:19 have *t* away our residences
22:28 *t* into the land that they
36:30 *t* out to the heat by day
38:9 have *t* into the cistern, so
51:34 he has *t* me into confusion
La 2:1 *t* down from heaven to earth
Eze 16:5 *t* upon the surface of the
19:12 To the earth she was *t*, and
24:2 *t* himself against Jerusalem
38:20 *t* down and the steep ways
Da 3:6 be *t* into the burning fiery
3:11 *t* into the burning fiery
3:15 *t* into the burning fiery
3:21 *t* into the burning fiery
6:7 should be *t* to the lions' pit
6:12 should be *t* to the lions' pit
8:11 his sanctuary was *t* down
Joe 1:7 stripped it bare and *t* it
Am 4:3 certainly be *t* out to Harmon
Mt 3:10 cut down and *t* into the fire
5:13 *t* outside to be trampled on
5:25 and you get *t* into prison
6:30 tomorrow is *t* into the oven
7:19 cut down and *t* into the fire
8:12 *t* into the darkness outside
9:36 *t* about like sheep without a
18:8 *t* with two hands or two feet
18:9 be *t* with two eyes into the
18:30 had him *t* into prison until
24:2 a stone and not be *t* down
Mr 11:23 lifted up and *t* into the sea
13:2 a stone and not be *t* down
Lu 3:9 cut down and *t* into the fire
13:28 but yourselves *t* outside
17:2 and he were *t* into the sea
21:6 left here and not be *t* down
23:19 *t* into prison for a certain
23:25 *t* into prison for sedition
Joh 3:24 not yet been *t* into prison
9:35 that they had *t* him out, and
2Co 4:9 are *t* down, but not destroyed

Throws

Job 16:11 he *t* me headlong
Lu 9:39 it *t* him into convulsions
1Jo 4:18 perfect love *t* fear outside

Thrust

Ge 19:10 men *t* out their hands and
Ex 4:4 *T* your hand out and grab hold
4:4 *t* his hand out and grabbed hold
9:15 could have *t* my hand out that
De 25:11 she has *t* out her hand and
Jg 3:21 Ehud *t* in his left hand and
5:26 the tent pin she then *t* out
6:21 *t* out the tip of the staff
15:15 *t* his hand out and took it
1Sa 2:14 made a *t* into the basin or
17:49 David *t* his hand into his
22:17 *t* out their hand to assault
24:10 not *t* out my hand against
26:9 *t* his hand out against the
26:11 to *t* my hand out against
26:23 unwilling to *t* my hand out
2Sa 1:14 fear to *t* your hand out to
6:6 Uzzah now *t* his hand out to
15:5 *t* his hand out and grabbed
18:12 not *t* my hand out against
24:16 hand *t* out toward Jerusalem
1Ki 13:4 *t* out his hand from off the
13:4 that he had *t* out against
2Ki 6:7 he *t* his hand out and took it
1Ch 13:9 Uzzah now *t* his hand out to
13:10 *t* his hand out upon the Ark
Es 8:7 he *t* out his hand against the
Job 1:11 for a change, *t* out your hand

Job 1:12 against him himself do not *t*
2:5 *t* out your hand, please, and
15:33 *t* away his unripe grapes
16:15 *t* my horn in the very dust
28:9 he has *t* out his hand
Ps 55:20 has *t* out his hands against
74:7 *t* your sanctuary into the fire
125:3 *t* out their hand upon any
138:7 you will *t* out your hand
144:7 *T* your hands out from the
Pr 31:19 Her hands she has *t* out to
31:20 she has *t* out to the poor one
Isa 11:14 they will *t* out their hand
Jer 1:9 Jehovah *t* his hand out and
Eze 2:9 there was a hand *t* out to me
8:3 he *t* out the representation of
10:7 cherub *t* his hand out from
17:7 its foliage it *t* out to him
Joe 3:13 *T* in a sickle, for harvest
Ob 13 *t* out a hand upon his wealth
Ac 7:27 *t* him away, saying, Who
7:39 *t* him aside and in their
7:45 nations, whom God *t* out from
1Ti 1:19 which some have *t* aside
Re 14:16 *t* in his sickle on the earth
14:19 angel *t* his sickle into the

Thrusting
1Sa 24:6 *t* out my hand against him
Pr 26:6 is *t* matters into the hand of
Eze 8:17 *t* out the shoot to my nose
Da 11:42 *t* out his hand against the
Zec 8:10 *t* all mankind against one
Ac 13:46 you are *t* it away from you
19:33 the Jews *t* him up front

Thrusts
Ezr 6:12 *t* his hand out to commit
Job 30:24 no one *t* his hand out
Ps 140:11 hunt him with repeated *t*
Da 8:4 the ram making *t* to the west
Mr 4:29 he *t* in the sickle, because

Thumb
Ex 29:20 upon the *t* of their right
Le 8:23 the *t* of his right hand and
8:24 the *t* of their right hand and
14:14 upon the *t* of his right hand
14:17 upon the *t* of his right hand
14:25 upon the *t* of his right hand
14:28 upon the *t* of his right hand

Thumbs
Jg 1:6 cut off the *t* of his hands and
1:7 seventy kings with the *t* of

Thummim
Ex 28:30 the *T* into the breastpiece
Le 8:8 breastpiece the Urim and the *T*
De 33:8 Your *T* and your Urim belong
1Sa 14:41 O God of Israel, do give *T*
Ezr 2:63 stood up with Urim and *T*
Ne 7:65 priest with Urim and *T* stood

Thunder
1Sa 2:10 he will *t* in the heavens
7:10 Jehovah now caused it to *t*
2Sa 22:14 Jehovah began to *t*, And the
1Ch 16:32 Let the sea *t* and also that
Job 26:14 of his mighty *t* who can
40:9 can you make it *t*
Ps 18:13 Jehovah began to *t*
77:18 sound of your *t* was like
81:7 in the concealed place of *t*
96:11 Let the sea *t* and that which
98:7 Let the sea *t* and that which
104:7 sound of your *t* they were
Isa 29:6 will have attention with *t*
Mr 3:17 Boanerges . . . means Sons of *T*
Re 6:1 with a voice as of *t*: Come!
14:2 and as the sound of loud *t*

Thundered
Ps 29:3 glorious God himself has *t*
Joh 12:29 began to say that it had *t*

Thunderous
Job 28:26 way for the *t* storm cloud
38:25 way for the *t* storm cloud
Isa 28:2 Like a *t* storm of hail, a
28:2 *t* storm of powerful

Thunderously
Ps 77:17 clouds have *t* poured down

Thunders
Ex 9:23 Jehovah gave *t* and hail, and
9:28 occurring of God's *t* and hail
9:29 *t* will stop and the hail will
Ex 9:33 *t* and the hail began to stop
9:34 the hail and the *t* had stopped
19:16 that *t* and lightnings began
20:18 the *t* and the lightning
1Sa 12:17 that he may give *t* and rain
12:18 to give *t* and rain on that
Job 37:4 He *t* with the sound of his
37:5 God *t* with his voice in a
Re 4:5 lightnings and voices and *t*
8:5 And *t* occurred and voices and
10:3 the seven *t* uttered their own
10:4 Now when the seven *t* spoke
10:4 the things the seven *t* spoke
11:19 *t* and an earthquake and a
16:18 voices and *t* occurred, and
19:6 and as a sound of heavy *t*

Thunderstorm
Hab 3:10 A *t* of waters passed through

Thwarted
Ps 33:10 *t* the thoughts of the peoples

Thyatira
Ac 16:14 Lydia . . . of the city of *T*
Re 1:11 the seven congregations . . . *T*
2:18 the congregation in *T* write
2:24 rest of you who are in *T*

Tiberias
Joh 6:1 the sea of Galilee, or *T*
6:23 boats from *T* arrived near
21:1 at the sea of *T*

Tiberius
Lu 3:1 the reign of *T* Caesar, when

Tibhath
1Ch 18:8 from *T* and Cun, cities of

Tibni
1Ki 16:21 became followers of *T*
16:22 Omri overcame . . . *T* the son
16:22 *T* met death, and Omri began

Tickled
2Ti 4:3 to have their ears *t*

Tidal
Ge 14:1 *T* king of Goiim
14:9 *T* king of Goiim and

Tidings
Re 14:6 declare as glad *t* to those

Tie
Ex 29:5 *t* it closely to him with the
De 6:8 *t* them as a sign upon your
Jos 2:18 *t* in the window by which you
Jg 15:10 It is to *t* Samson that we
15:12 It is to *t* you that we have
15:13 *t* you, and we will give you
16:5 to *t* him so as to master him
16:7 If they *t* me with seven
16:11 *t* me tight with new ropes
2Sa 3:31 *t* on sackcloth and wail
Job 38:31 *t* fast the bonds of the
41:5 *t* it for your young girls
Pr 3:3 *T* them about your throat
6:21 *T* them upon your heart
7:3 *T* them upon your fingers, and
Jer 51:63 you will *t* to it a stone

Tied
Ge 38:28 took and *t* a scarlet piece
Nu 19:15 there is no lid *t* down
Jos 2:21 she *t* the scarlet cord in the
9:4 worn out and burst and *t* up
Jg 16:6 be *t* for one to master you
16:8 Later she *t* him with them
16:10 with what you can be *t*
16:12 ropes and *t* him with them
16:13 with what you can be *t*
2Ki 7:10 only the horses *t* and the
7:10 and the asses *t* and the tents
Pr 22:15 Foolishness is *t* up with the
Mt 21:2 will at once find an ass *t*
Mr 11:2 you will find a colt *t*, on
11:4 found the colt *t* at the door
Lu 19:30 you will find a colt *t*, on

Tiers
1Ki 7:4 opening in three *t*
7:5 opening in three *t*

Tight
Jg 16:11 tie me *t* with new ropes
Job 41:15 Closed as with a *t* seal
Isa 29:2 to make things *t* for Ariel
29:7 making things *t* for her
Php 2:16 keeping a *t* grip on the word
Re 5:1 sealed *t* with seven seals
7:1 holding *t* the four winds of

Tightly
Ge 20:18 Jehovah had *t* shut up every
Jos 6:1 Jericho was *t* shut up because
Isa 22:18 he will wrap you up *t*

Tightness
De 28:53 because of the *t* and stress
28:55 because of the *t* and stress
28:57 because of the *t* and stress
Jer 19:9 because of the *t* and

Tiglath-pileser
2Ki 15:29 *T* the king of Assyria
16:7 *T* the king of Assyria
16:10 *T* the king of Assyria at

Tikvah
2Ki 22:14 *T* the son of Harhas
2Ch 34:22 *T* the son of Harhas
Ezr 10:15 Jahzeiah the son of *T*

Tilgath-pilneser
1Ch 5:6 *T* the king of Assyria took
5:26 the spirit of *T* the king of
2Ch 28:20 *T* the king of Assyria came

Tiling
Lu 5:19 through the *t* they let him

Till
Ge 32:4 stayed for a long time *t* now
44:28 I have not seen him *t* now
Ex 12:10 *t* morning, but what is left
12:10 left over of it *t* morning
12:18 *t* the twenty-first day of
18:13 the morning *t* the evening
18:14 you from morning *t* evening
27:21 from evening *t* morning
32:20 and crushed it *t* it was fine
Le 19:6 left over *t* the third day
24:12 *t* there should be a distinct
25:29 continue *t* the year from the
25:40 serve with you *t* the Jubilee
25:50 *t* the Jubilee year, and the
27:23 up *t* the year of Jubilee
Nu 24:22 *t* Assyria will carry you
De 11:4 to destroy them *t* this day
Jg 16:3 Samson kept lying *t* midnight
16:13 *t* now you have trifled with
1Sa 7:12 *T* now Jehovah has helped us
11:11 *t* the day grew hot
16:11 youngest one has *t* now been
1Ki 18:26 Baal from morning *t* noon
1Ch 4:31 cities down *t* David reigned
9:18 and up *t* then he was in the
12:29 *t* then the greater number
2Ch 14:13 *t* there was no one alive of
35:25 their dirges down *t* today
Ezr 4:5 *t* the reign of Darius the
Ne 8:3 from daybreak *t* midday, in
12:22 *t* the kingship of Darius the
12:23 *t* the days of Johanan the
Ps 119:91 they have stood *t* today
Isa 5:11 *t* late in the evening
38:12 From daylight *t* night you
38:13 From daylight *t* night you
Eze 20:31 dungy idols down *t* today
22:3 her midst *t* her time comes
Da 6:14 *t* the setting of the sun he
Ho 10:12 *T* for yourselves arable land
Zep 3:3 not gnaw bones *t* the morning
3:8 *t* the day of my rising up to
Lu 19:13 Do business *t* I come
Ac 4:3 in custody *t* the next day
28:23 from morning *t* evening
2Co 3:15 down *t* today whenever Moses
2Th 2:7 *t* he who is right now acting

Tilling
De 21:4 no *t* or sowing of seed, and

Tilon
1Ch 4:20 the sons of Shimon . . . *T*

Tilt
Jer 48:12 they will certainly *t* them

Tilters
Jer 48:12 send to them vessel *t*, and

Timaeus
Mr 10:46 Bartimaeus (the son of *T*)

Timber
1Ki 6:15 he overlaid it with *t* inside
Ezr 6:11 a *t* will be pulled out of
Ne 2:8 give me trees to build with *t*

2Co 12:18 *T* did not take advantage
Ga 2:1 taking also *T* along with me
2:3 not even *T*, who was with me
2Ti 4:10 to Galatia, *T* to Dalmatia
Tit 1:4 *T*, a genuine child according

Tizite
1Ch 11:45 and Joha his brother the *T*

Toah
1Ch 6:34 son of Eliel, the son of *T*

Tob
Jg 11:3 dwelling in the land of *T*
11:5 Jephthah out of the land of *T*

Tob-adonijah
2Ch 17:8 and *T* the Levites, and with

Tobiah
Ezr 2:60 the sons of *T*
Ne 2:10 *T* the servant, the Ammonite
2:19 *T* the servant, the Ammonite
4:3 *T* the Ammonite was alongside
4:7 and *T* and the Arabians and
6:1 and *T* and to Geshem the
6:12 as *T* and Sanballat themselves
6:14 *T* and Sanballat, according to
6:17 letters that were going to *T*
6:17 those of *T* that were coming
6:19 that *T* sent to make me afraid
7:62 the sons of *T*, the sons of
13:4 Eliashib . . . a relative of *T*
13:7 for *T* by making for him a

Tobiah's
Ne 13:8 furniture of *T* house outside

Tobijah
2Ch 17:8 *T* and Tob-adonijah the
Zec 6:10 from Heldai and from *T* and
6:14 belong to Helem and to *T* and

Tochen
1Ch 4:32 Rimmon and *T* and Ashan

Today
Ge 21:26 also not heard of it except *t*
22:14 said *t*: In the mountain of
24:42 I got to the fountain *t*, then
30:32 among your whole flock *t*
31:43 can I do against these *t* or
31:48 between me and you *t*
40:7 are your faces gloomy *t*
41:9 My sins I am mentioning *t*
42:13 is with our father *t*
42:32 youngest is *t* with our
47:23 I have *t* bought you and your
Ex 2:18 have come home so quickly *t*
5:14 both yesterday and *t*
13:4 *T* you are going out in the
14:13 he will perform for you *t*
14:13 Egyptians whom you do see *t*
16:25 Then Moses said: Eat it *t*
16:25 *t* is a sabbath to Jehovah
16:25 *T* you will not find it in
19:10 you must sanctify them *t* and
32:29 Fill your hand *t* with power
32:29 confer a blessing upon you *t*
34:11 what I am commanding you *t*
Le 9:4 *t* is when Jehovah will
10:19 *T* they have presented their
10:19 eaten the sin offering *t*
De 1:10 you are *t* like the stars of
1:39 sons who *t* do not know good
2:18 passing *t* by the territory of
4:4 all of you alive *t*
4:8 I am putting before you *t*
4:26 as witnesses against you *t*
4:39 And you well know *t*, and you
4:40 I am commanding you *t*, that
5:1 I am speaking in your ears *t*
5:3 all those of us alive here *t*
6:6 that I am commanding you *t*
7:11 I am commanding you *t* by
8:1 I am commanding you *t*
8:11 that I am commanding you *t*
8:19 bear witness against you *t*
9:1 Israel, you are *t* crossing the
9:3 well know *t* that Jehovah your
10:13 I am commanding you *t*, for
11:2 And you well know *t* (for I
11:8 I am commanding you *t*, in
11:13 I am commanding you *t* so as
11:26 putting before you *t* blessing
11:27 that I am commanding you *t*
11:28 I am commanding you *t*, so
11:32 I am putting before you *t*
De 12:8 all that we are doing here *t*
13:18 I am commanding you *t*, so as
15:5 I am commanding you *t*
15:15 commanding you this thing *t*
19:9 I am commanding you *t*
20:3 drawing near *t* to the battle
26:3 I must report *t* to Jehovah
26:17 say *t* that he will become
26:18 he has induced you to say *t*
27:1 that I am commanding you *t*
27:4 as I am commanding you *t*
27:10 which I am commanding you *t*
28:1 I am commanding you *t*
28:13 commanding you *t* to observe
28:14 I am commanding you *t*
28:15 I am commanding you *t*
29:10 stationed *t* before Jehovah
29:12 God is concluding with you *t*
29:13 establishing you *t* as his
29:15 here standing with us *t*
29:15 who are not here with us *t*
29:18 heart is turning *t* away from
30:2 that I am commanding you *t*
30:8 I am commanding you *t*
30:11 that I am commanding you *t*
30:15 put before you *t* life and
30:16 I am commanding you *t*, so as
30:18 I do tell you *t* that you
30:19 as witnesses against you *t*
31:2 and twenty years old I am *t*
31:21 *t* before I bring them into
31:27 I am yet alive with you *t*
32:46 speaking in warning to you *t*
Jos 5:9 *T* I have rolled away the
14:10 am *t* eighty-five years old
14:11 I am *t* as strong as on the
22:16 in turning back *t* from
22:16 rebel *t* against Jehovah
22:18 you would turn back *t* from
22:18 rebel *t* against Jehovah
22:29 and to turn back *t* from
22:31 *T* we do know that Jehovah
23:14 I am going *t* in the way of
24:15 choose for yourselves *t*
Jg 9:18 household of my father *t* that
11:27 judge *t* between the sons of
21:3 for one tribe to be missing *t*
21:6 *T* one tribe has been chopped
Ru 2:19 Where did you glean *t*, and
2:19 with whom I worked *t* is Boaz
3:18 the matter to an end *t*
4:9 You are witnesses *t* that I do
4:10 You are witnesses *t*
4:14 a repurchaser fail for you *t*
1Sa 4:3 Why did Jehovah defeat us *t*
4:16 that I have fled *t*
9:9 prophet of *t* used to be called
9:12 *t* he has come to the city
9:12 there is a sacrifice *t* for
9:19 you men must eat with me *t*
10:2 your going away from me *t*
10:19 *t* you have rejected your God
11:13 *t* Jehovah has performed
12:17 Is it not wheat harvest *t*?
14:28 the man that eats bread *t*
14:30 eaten *t* from the spoil of
14:38 this sin has come to be *t*
15:28 of Israel from off you *t*
18:21 alliance with me *t*
20:27 meal either yesterday or *t*
21:5 how much more so *t*, when
22:15 *t* that I have started to
24:10 gave you *t* into my hand
24:18 told *t* what good you have
26:8 God has *t* surrendered your
26:19 driven me out *t* from
26:23 Jehovah *t* gave you into my
27:10 did you men make a raid *t*
2Sa 3:8 *T* I keep exercising
3:8 error concerning a woman *t*
3:39 I *t* am weak although
6:20 *t* when he uncovered himself
6:20 uncovered himself *t* to the
11:12 Dwell here also *t*, and
14:22 *T* your servant does know
15:20 *t* shall I make you wander
16:3 *T* the house of Israel will
18:31 Jehovah has judged you *t*
19:5 *t* put to shame the face of
19:5 escape for your soul *t*
19:6 reported *t* that chiefs and
19:6 know *t* that if only Absalom
19:6 all of us others were *t* dead
19:20 and so here I have *t* come
2Sa 19:22 become *t* a resister of me
19:22 anyone *t* be put to death
19:22 *t* I am king over Israel
19:35 I am eighty years old *t*
1Ki 1:25 *t* gone down that he might
1:48 *t* given one to sit upon my
2:24 *t* Adonijah will be put to
5:7 Blessed is Jehovah *t* in that
8:28 is praying before you *t*
12:7 If *t* you would prove
18:15 *t* I shall show myself to
18:36 *t* let it be known that you
20:13 giving it into your hand *t*
2Ki 2:3 *t* Jehovah is taking your
2:5 *t* Jehovah is taking your
4:23 Why are you going to him *t*?
6:28 son that we may eat him *t*
6:31 standing upon him *t*
1Ch 29:5 fill his hand *t* with a gift
2Ch 20:26 Plain of Beracah—until *t*
35:21 coming *t*, but it is against
35:25 in their dirges down till *t*
Ne 1:6 praying before you *t*, day and
1:11 success to your servant *t*
9:36 Look! We are *t* slaves
Es 5:4 come *t* to the banquet that I
9:13 do according to the law of *t*
Job 23:2 *t* my state of concern is
Ps 2:7 *t*, I have become your father
95:7 *T* if you people listen to his
119:91 they have stood till *t*
Pr 7:14 *T* I have paid my vows
22:19 I have given you knowledge *t*
Isa 48:7 before *t* you have not heard
56:12 turn out just as *t*, great
Jer 1:18 made you *t* a fortified city
34:15 turn around *t* and do what
40:4 let you loose *t* from the
42:19 witness against you *t*
42:21 I tell you *t*, but you will
Eze 20:31 dungy idols down till *t*
Zec 9:12 *t* I am telling you, I shall
Mt 6:11 Give us *t* our bread for this
6:30 here *t* and tomorrow is
16:3 be wintry, rainy weather *t*
21:28 go work *t* in the vineyard
27:19 suffered a lot *t* in a dream
Mr 14:30 You *t*, yes, this night
Lu 2:11 was born to you *t* a Savior
4:21 *T* this scripture that you
5:26 have seen strange things *t*
12:28 that *t* exists and tomorrow
13:32 healing *t* and tomorrow, and
13:33 I must go on my way *t*
19:5 *t* I must stay in your house
22:34 A cock will not crow *t* until
22:61 Before a cock crows *t* you
23:43 I tell you *t*, You will be
Ac 24:21 I am *t* being judged before
26:29 those who hear me *t* would
27:33 *T* is the fourteenth day you
2Co 3:15 down till *t* whenever Moses
Ga 4:25 Jerusalem *t*, for she is in
Heb 1:5 *t*, I have become your father
3:7 *T* if you people listen to his
3:13 long as it may be called *T*
3:15 *T* if you people listen to his
4:7 *T*; just as it has been said
4:7 *T* if you people listen to his
5:5 *t*, I have become your father
13:8 same yesterday and *t*, and
Jas 4:13 *T* or tomorrow we will

Today's
Ac 19:40 with sedition over *t* affair

Toe
Ex 29:20 the big *t* of their right foot
Le 8:23 the big *t* of his right foot
8:24 the big *t* of their right foot
14:14 the big *t* of his right foot
14:17 the big *t* of his right foot
14:25 the big *t* of his right foot
14:28 the big *t* of his right foot

Toes
Jg 1:6 and the great *t* of his feet
1:7 the great *t* of their feet cut
2Sa 21:20 six *t* on each of his feet
1Ch 20:6 fingers and *t* were in sixes
Da 2:41 feet and the *t* to be partly of
2:42 *t* of the feet being partly

Togarmah
Ge 10:3 And the sons of Gomer . . . *T*
1Ch 1:6 sons of Gomer were . . . *T*

Eze 27:14 From the house of *T* there
38:6 *T*, of the remotest parts of

Together

Ge 1:9 the waters . . . be brought *t*
1:10 bringing *t* of the waters he
3:7 they sewed fig leaves *t* and
6:13 to ruin *t* with the earth
13:6 for them to dwell all *t*
13:6 were not able to dwell all *t*
21:22 Abimelech *t* with Phicol the
21:32 Abimelech got up *t* with
22:6 and both of them went on *t*
22:8 And both of them walked on *t*
22:19 their way *t* to Beer-sheba
32:11 mother *t* with children
34:30 gather *t* against me and
36:7 too great for them to dwell *t*
42:17 *t* in custody for three days
46:15 *t* with his daughter Dinah
47:19 we *t* with our land will
48:6 *T* with the name of their
49:1 Gather yourselves *t* that I
Ex 12:9 head *t* with its shanks and
12:51 Israel *t* with their armies
14:20 a cloud *t* with darkness
26:11 the loops and join the tent *t*
26:24 *t* they should be duplicates
35:1 Israel *t* and said to them
36:16 five tent cloths *t* by
36:18 joining the tent *t* to become
36:29 *t* they came to be twins to
38:28 their tops and joined them *t*
39:24 scarlet material, twisted *t*
Le 7:13 *t* with the thanksgiving
14:12 *t* with the log measure of
19:19 two sorts of thread, mixed *t*
Nu 1:44 *t* with Aaron and the
4:32 tent cords *t* with all their
9:11 *T* with unfermented cakes and
10:7 calling the congregation *t*
14:35 have gathered *t* against me
15:5 *t* with the burnt offering or
15:9 present *t* with the male of
16:1 *t* with Dathan and Abiram the
16:11 *t* are against Jehovah
16:18 *t* with Moses and Aaron
16:19 Korah got all the assembly *t*
16:27 *t* with their wives, and
16:42 *t* against Moses and Aaron
18:9 *t* with every grain offering
18:11 their gift *t* with all the
19:5 blood *t* with its dung will be
20:8 and call the assembly *t*, you
20:10 called the congregation *t*
28:5 *t* with the tenth of an ephah
28:9 *t* with its drink offering
28:15 *t* with its drink offering
28:31 *t* with their drink offerings
29:6 *t* with their drink offerings
29:11 *t* with their drink offerings
29:19 *t* with their drink offerings
35:7 *t* with their pasture grounds
36:12 inheritance might continue *t*
De 2:35 *t* with the spoil of the
4:10 Congregate the people *t* to
12:22 and the clean one *t* may eat
15:22 and the clean one *t*, like the
22:10 with a bull and an ass *t*
22:11 stuff of wool and linen *t*
22:22 die *t*, the man lying down
25:5 In case brothers dwell *t* and
25:11 In case men struggle *t* with
27:1 Moses *t* with the older men
32:14 *T* with the fat of rams, And
32:14 *T* with the kidney fat of
32:25 Suckling *t* with gray-haired
32:39 there are no gods *t* with me
33:17 *t* to the ends of the earth
33:21 will gather themselves *t*
Jos 8:35 *t* with the women and the
9:2 *t* to make war against Joshua
10:5 gathered *t* and went on up
10:6 have collected *t* against us
11:5 kings met *t* by appointment
11:5 encamped *t* at the waters of
13:21 *t* with the chieftains of
15:32 *t* with their settlements
21:2 *t* with their pasture grounds
21:26 All the cities *t* with their
21:41 forty-eight cities *t* with
21:42 city *t* with its pasture
22:8 enemies *t* with your brothers
24:1 Israel *t* at Shechem and to
Jg 4:10 Zebulun and Naphtali *t* to
4:13 Sisera called *t* all his war
6:33 Easterners gathered *t* as one
6:34 got to be called *t* after him
6:35 called *t* after him. He also
7:23 men of Israel were called *t*
7:24 men of Ephraim were called *t*
9:6 house of Millo gathered *t* and
9:47 of Shechem had collected *t*
10:17 sons of Ammon were called *t*
10:17 Israel gathered themselves *t*
11:3 kept bringing themselves *t* to
11:20 gathering all his people *t*
12:1 called *t* and crossed over
12:4 men of Gilead *t* and fought
16:23 gathered *t* to sacrifice a
18:22 called *t* and tried to catch
18:23 that you have been called *t*
19:6 began to eat and to drink *t*
20:14 gathering *t* out of the cities
1Sa 7:5 all Israel *t* at Mizpah
7:6 were collected *t* at Mizpah
7:7 collected themselves *t* at
8:4 collected themselves *t* and
10:17 to call the people *t* to
11:11 left over among them two *t*
13:4 called *t* to follow Saul to
13:5 *t* to fight against Israel
13:11 collected *t* at Michmash
17:1 collecting their camps *t* for
17:1 were collected *t* at Socoh
17:2 collected themselves *t* and
17:10 a man, and let us fight *t*
22:2 began to collect *t* to him
25:1 collect *t* and bewail him and
28:4 Philistines collected *t* and
28:4 Saul collected all Israel *t*
29:1 collect all their camps *t*
30:24 All will have a share *t*
31:6 to die *t* on that day
2Sa 2:13 met *t* by the pool of Gibeon
2:16 so that they fell down *t*
2:25 Benjamin went collecting *t*
2:30 to collect all the people *t*
3:21 collect all Israel *t* to my
8:11 *t* with the silver and the
10:15 to gather themselves *t*
12:3 and with his sons, all *t*
12:19 servants were whispering *t*
20:4 Call the men of Judah *t* to
20:5 Amasa went to call Judah *t*
20:14 they then congregated *t* and
21:9 the seven of them fell *t*
1Ki 3:18 And we were *t*. There was
10:13 she *t* with her servants
17:15 to eat, she *t* with him and
18:19 collect *t* all Israel to me
18:20 prophets *t* at Mount Carmel
20:1 his military forces *t* and
20:16 he *t* with the kings, the
20:20 *t* with the horsemen
22:6 collected the prophets *t*
2Ki 3:21 called *t* men from as many
6:24 to collect all his camp *t*
10:18 collected all the people *t*
11:9 *t* with those that were going
12:20 leagued *t* in a conspiracy
23:1 gathered *t* to him all the
1Ch 10:6 all those of his house died *t*
11:1 collected themselves *t* to
11:13 gathered themselves *t* for
12:33 for flocking *t* to David they
12:38 flocking *t* in battle line
13:2 collect themselves *t* to us
16:35 collect us *t* and deliver us
18:11 *t* with the silver and the
19:7 gathered *t* from their cities
19:17 gathered all Israel *t* and
22:2 bring *t* the alien residents
25:7 *t* with their brothers
28:1 *t* with the court officials
29:30 *t* with all his kingship and
2Ch 2:8 my servants are *t* with your
9:12 she *t* with her servants
13:7 collecting themselves *t* by
15:9 collect *t* all Judah and
15:10 collected *t* at Jerusalem in
18:5 collected the prophets *t*
20:4 Judah were collected *t* to
20:26 congregated *t* at the low
21:9 Jehoram *t* with his chiefs
23:2 collected *t* the Levites from
23:8 *t* with those going out on
24:5 Levites *t* and said to them
2Ch 25:5 collect Judah *t* and to
28:24 Ahaz gathered *t* the
29:15 brothers *t* and sanctified
29:20 princes of the city *t* and
30:13 *t* at Jerusalem, a numerous
32:4 people were collected *t*, and
Ezr 2:42 *t*, a hundred and thirty-nine
4:3 shall *t* build to Jehovah the
10:1 collected themselves *t* to
10:7 themselves *t* at Jerusalem
10:9 *t* at Jerusalem within three
Ne 4:6 joined *t* clear to half its
4:8 began to conspire *t* to come
4:20 collect yourselves *t* to us
5:16 *t* there for the work
6:2 let us meet *t* by appointment
6:7 come, and let us consult *t*
7:5 collect *t* the nobles and the
8:13 *t* to Ezra the copyist
9:1 *t* with fasting and with
13:11 collected them *t* and
Es 2:3 collect *t* all the young women
2:8 young women were collected *t*
2:19 virgins were collected *t* a
Job 2:11 they met *t* by appointment to
3:18 *T* prisoners themselves are
9:32 should come *t* in judgment
10:11 and sinews to weave me *t*
16:15 Sackcloth I have sewed *t*
17:16 *t*, must descend to the very
21:26 *T* in the dust they will lie
30:7 nettles they would huddle *t*
31:38 *t* its furrows themselves
34:15 All flesh will expire *t*
38:7 stars joyfully cried out *t*
38:38 clods of earth . . . stuck *t*
40:13 Hide them *t* in the dust
41:17 they are stuck *t*
41:23 its flesh do cling *t*
Ps 2:2 officials . . . massed *t* as one
31:13 they mass *t* as one against
31:20 From the banding *t* of men
33:15 forming their hearts all *t*
34:3 let us exalt his name *t*
35:15 they rejoiced and gathered *t*
35:15 They gathered *t* against me
35:26 ashamed and abashed all *t*
37:38 certainly be annihilated *t*
40:14 be ashamed and abashed all *t*
47:9 nobles . . . have gathered *t*
48:4 They have passed by *t*
49:2 rich one and you poor one *t*
49:10 *T* the stupid one and the
55:14 to enjoy sweet intimacy *t*
62:9 *t* lighter than an exhalation
74:8 said *t* in their own heart
81:2 harp *t* with the stringed
83:7 Philistia *t* with the
87:4 and Tyre, *t* with Cush
98:8 *t* let the very mountains cry
102:22 peoples are collected all *t*
106:47 us *t* from the nations
107:3 *t* even from the lands
120:5 tabernacled *t* with the tents
122:3 been joined *t* in oneness
133:1 brothers to dwell *t* in unity
141:10 into their own nets all *t*
147:2 ones of Israel he brings *t*
148:12 You old men *t* with boys
Pr 6:27 rake *t* fire into his bosom
13:10 consulting *t* there is wisdom
16:30 Pinching his lips *t*, he
20:10 *t* something detestable to
22:18 established *t* upon your lips
25:22 are raking *t* upon his head
Ec 2:26 bringing *t* merely to give to
3:5 and a time to bring stones *t*
3:7 rip apart and a time to sew *t*
4:11 if two lie down *t*, they also
4:12 two *t* could make a stand
Isa 6:10 paste their very eyes *t*
9:21 *T* they will be against Judah
11:6 well-fed animal all *t*
11:7 *t* their young ones will lie
11:12 collect *t* from the four
11:14 *t* they will plunder the
13:4 of nations gathered *t*
13:14 anyone to collect them *t*
18:6 left all *t* for the bird of
22:3 have been taken prisoner *t*
32:3 will not be pasted *t*
34:15 them *t* under its shadow
34:15 *t*, each one with her mate
34:16 that has collected them *t*

Isa 40:5 all flesh must see it *t*
40:11 will collect *t* the lambs
40:14 consult *t* that one might
41:1 *t* for the judgment itself
43:5 I shall collect you *t*
43:9 nations all be collected *t*
43:9 national groups be gathered *t*
43:26 put ourselves on judgment *t*
44:11 collect themselves *t*
45:16 *T* in humiliation the
45:20 close *t*, you escapees from
45:21 let them consult *t* in unity
48:13 they may keep standing *t*
48:14 Be collected *t*, all you
49:18 all of them . . . collected *t*
50:8 Let us stand up *t*. Who is my
54:7 I shall collect you *t*
56:8 collecting *t* the dispersed
56:8 collect *t* to him others
56:8 those already collected *t*
60:4 have . . . been collected *t*
60:7 will be collected *t* to you
66:17 all *t* reach their end
66:18 the nations and tongues *t*
Jer 3:17 nations must be brought *t*
3:18 *t* they will come out of the
4:5 Gather yourselves *t*, and let
5:5 have all *t* broken the yoke
6:21 father and sons *t*; the
8:14 Gather yourselves *t*, and
12:9 gather *t*, all you wild
17:11 that has gathered *t*
23:3 collect *t* the remnant of
27:20 *t* with all the nobles of
29:14 collect you *t* out of all
31:8 collect them *t* from the
31:8 one giving birth, all *t*
31:10 himself collect him *t*, and
31:13 and the old men, all *t*
31:24 dwell all *t*, farmers and
32:37 I am collecting them *t*
40:15 collected *t* to you be
41:1 eat bread *t* in Mizpah
46:12 *T* they have fallen down
46:21 they have fled *t*
49:3 and his princes, all *t*
49:5 *t* those running away
49:14 Collect yourselves *t*, and
50:4 sons of Judah *t*, will come
50:33 Judah are being oppressed *t*
51:38 *t* they will roar just like
La 2:8 *T* they have faded away
Eze 13:18 sewing bands *t* upon all
16:37 I am collecting *t* all those
16:37 collect them *t* against you
20:34 collect you *t* out of the
20:41 collect you *t* from the
22:19 collecting you *t* into the
22:20 collect them *t* in my anger
22:21 bring you *t* and blow upon
28:25 collect *t* the house of
29:5 nor be collected *t*
29:13 collect the Egyptians *t*
34:13 *t* from the lands and bring
36:24 collect you *t* out of all the
37:21 I will collect them *t* from
38:8 *t* out of many peoples
38:12 *t* out of the nations
39:17 Collect yourselves *t* and
39:17 Gather yourselves *t* all
39:27 collect them *t* out of the
39:28 *t* upon their soil, so that
Da 2:35 all *t*, crushed and became
2:43 not prove to be sticking *t*
6:7 counsel *t* to establish a royal
8:12 *t* with the constant feature
11:10 gather *t* a crowd of large
Ho 1:11 collected *t* into a unity and
8:10 I shall now collect them *t*
9:6 Egypt . . . will collect them *t*
Joe 1:14 Call *t* a solemn assembly
1:14 Gather *t* the older men, all
2:15 Call *t* a solemn assembly
2:16 Gather the people *t*
2:16 Collect the old men *t*
2:16 Gather children . . . *t*
3:2 also collect *t* all the nations
3:11 and collect yourselves *t*
Am 1:15 exile, he and his princes *t*
3:3 Will two walk *t* unless they
3:9 *t* against the mountains
Mic 2:12 remaining ones of Israel *t*
4:6 I will collect *t*, even her
4:12 certainly collect them *t*
Na 3:18 no one collecting them *t*
Hab 2:5 collecting *t* to himself all
Zep 2:1 Gather yourselves *t*, yes, do
3:8 to collect *t* kingdoms
3:18 I shall certainly gather *t*
3:19 dispersed I shall collect *t*
3:20 time of my collecting you *t*
Zec 10:4 every taskmaster, all *t*
10:8 whistle . . . collect them *t*
10:10 I shall collect them *t*
Mt 2:4 *t* all the chief priests and
13:30 grow *t* until the harvest
17:22 were gathered *t* in Galilee
18:20 three gathered *t* in my name
19:6 what God has yoked *t* let no
22:10 gathered *t* all they found
22:15 took counsel *t* in order to
22:16 *t* with party followers of
22:34 they came *t* in one group
22:41 Pharisees were gathered *t*
23:37 to gather your children *t*
23:37 her chicks *t* under her wings
24:28 eagles will be gathered *t*
24:31 gather his chosen ones *t*
26:3 gathered *t* in the courtyard
26:4 took counsel *t* to seize Jesus
26:57 older men were gathered *t*
27:7 consulting *t*, they bought
27:17 they were gathered *t* Pilate
27:27 the whole body of troops *t*
27:44 were impaled *t* with him
27:62 gathered *t* before Pilate
28:12 gathered *t* with the older
Mr 5:21 crowd gathered *t* to him
6:30 the apostles gathered *t*
6:33 they ran there *t* on foot
9:25 a crowd was running *t* upon
10:1 again crowds came *t* to him
10:9 what God yoked *t* let no man
13:27 gather his chosen ones *t*
14:54 he was sitting *t* with the
15:16 the whole body of troops *t*
15:32 those impaled *t* with him
15:41 up *t* with him to Jerusalem
Lu 2:44 in the company traveling *t*
5:15 would come *t* to listen
6:38 shaken *t* and overflowing
8:4 a great crowd had collected *t*
9:1 he called the twelve *t* and
9:18 the disciples came *t* to him
11:29 the crowds were massing *t*
12:1 the crowd had gathered *t* in
13:34 children *t* in the manner
15:6 friends and his neighbors *t*
15:9 her friends and neighbors *t*
15:13 gathered all things *t* and
17:37 eagles will be gathered *t*
21:15 all your opposers *t* will not
22:55 courtyard and sat down *t*
22:66 and scribes, gathered *t*, and
23:11 Herod *t* with his soldier
23:13 the rulers and the people *t*
23:48 crowds that were gathered *t*
23:49 women, who *t* had followed
24:33 those with them assembled *t*
Joh 4:12 *t* with his sons and his
4:36 and the reaper may rejoice *t*
6:12 Gather *t* the fragments that
6:13 they gathered them *t*, and
11:47 gathered the Sanhedrin *t*
11:52 also gather *t* in one
18:20 where all the Jews come *t*
20:4 the two *t* began to run; but
Ac 1:14 *t* with some women and Mary
1:15 persons was all *t* about one
2:1 were all *t* at the same place
2:6 the multitude came *t* and were
2:44 *t* in having all things in
3:4 Peter, *t* with John, gazed at
3:11 people ran *t* to them at what
4:5 gathering *t* of their rulers
4:26 the rulers massed *t* as one
4:27 gathered *t* in this city
4:31 in which they were gathered *t*
5:1 *t* with Sapphira his wife
5:16 coming *t*, bearing sick people
5:21 called *t* the Sanhedrin and
7:26 bring them *t* again in peace
9:23 Jews took counsel *t* to do
10:2 *t* with all his household
10:24 called *t* his relatives and
11:26 whole year they gathered *t*
12:12 were gathered *t* and praying
13:13 *t* with Paul, now put out to
Ac 13:44 gathered *t* to hear the word
14:1 entered *t* into the synagogue
14:27 gathered the congregation *t*
15:6 older men gathered *t* to see
15:17 *t* with people of all the
15:22 older men *t* with the whole
15:25 to you *t* with our loved ones
15:30 gathered the multitude *t* and
16:22 crowd rose up *t* against them
16:32 *t* with all those in his
19:7 *t*, there were about twelve
19:19 books *t* and burned them up
19:19 they calculated *t* the prices
19:32 reason why they had come *t*
19:33 *t* they brought Alexander out
20:7 gathered *t* to have a meal
20:8 where we were gathered *t*
21:5 all, *t* with the women and
21:30 and a running *t* of the people
23:15 you *t* with the Sanhedrin
24:12 nor causing a mob to rush *t*
25:17 when they got *t* here, I
25:23 *t* with military commanders
25:24 Jews *t* have applied to me
27:37 all *t*, we souls in the boat
28:17 he called *t* those who were
Ro 3:12 *t* have become worthless
8:17 we suffer *t* that we may also
8:17 we may also be glorified *t*
8:22 creation keeps on groaning *t*
8:22 being in pain *t* until now
8:28 works cooperate *t* for the
11:32 all up *t* in disobedience
15:32 shall be refreshed *t* with
1Co 1:2 *t* with all who everywhere
5:4 when you are gathered *t*, also
7:5 may come *t* again, that Satan
11:17 the worse that you meet *t*
11:18 when you come *t* in a
11:20 you come *t* to one place
11:33 when you come *t* to eat it
11:34 not come *t* for judgment
14:23 congregation comes *t* to one
14:26 When you come *t*, one has a
16:19 Aquila and Prisca *t* with
2Co 1:1 *t* with all the holy ones who
4:14 us up also *t* with Jesus
4:14 will present us *t* with you
6:1 Working *t* with him, we also
13:4 we shall live *t* with him
Ga 2:9 the right hand of sharing *t*
3:9 *t* with faithful Abraham
3:22 *t* to the custody of sin
3:23 delivered up *t* into custody
5:24 flesh *t* with its passions and
Eph 1:10 gather all things *t* again in
2:5 alive *t* with the Christ
2:6 he raised us up *t* and seated
2:6 seated us *t* in the heavenly
2:21 being harmoniously joined *t*
2:22 built up *t* into a place for
4:16 being harmoniously joined *t*
Php 2:2 being joined *t* in soul
Col 2:2 harmoniously joined *t* in love
2:12 raised up *t* through your
2:13 God made you alive *t* with
2:19 body . . . joined *t* by means
2:20 If you died *t* with Christ
1Th 4:17 *t* with them, be caught away
5:10 we should live *t* with him
2Th 2:1 our being gathered *t* to him
2Ti 2:11 died *t*, we shall also live
2:11 we shall also live *t*
2:12 shall also rule *t* as kings
Heb 10:25 gathering of ourselves *t*
1Pe 3:2 conduct *t* with deep respect
3:15 but doing so *t* with a mild
2Pe 2:13 while feasting *t* with you
Re 16:14 *t* to the war of the great
16:16 *t* to the place that is called
18:5 sins have massed *t* clear up
19:17 *t* to the great evening meal
19:19 armies gathered *t* to wage
20:8 gather them *t* for the war

Tohu
1Sa 1:1 the son of *T*, the son of Zuph

Toi
2Sa 8:9 *T* the king of Hamath got to
8:10 *T* sent Joram his son to King
8:10 trained in warfare against *T*

Toil
Ge 31:42 *t* of my hands God has seen

Tooth
Ex 21:24, 24 *t* for *t*, hand for hand
21:27 the *t* of his slave man or
21:27 the *t* of his slave girl that
21:27 in compensation for his *t*
Le 24:20, 20 *t* for *t*; the same sort
De 19:21, 21 *t* for *t*, hand for hand
1Sa 14:5 one *t* was a pillar on the
Job 39:28 Upon the *t* of a crag and
Pr 25:19 As a broken *t* and a wobbling
Mt 5:38, 38 Eye for eye and *t* for *t*

Toothlike
1Sa 14:4 a *t* crag here on this side
14:4 a *t* crag there on that side

Top
Ge 11:4 tower with its *t* in the
22:9 upon the altar on *t* of the
28:12 *t* reaching up to the heavens
28:18 poured oil on the *t* of it
39:14 cry out at the *t* of my voice
40:17 the basket on *t* of my head
Ex 17:9 upon the *t* of the hill, with
17:10 went up to the *t* of the hill
19:20 to the *t* of the mountain
19:20 to the *t* of the mountain
26:14 covering of sealskins up on *t*
26:24 duplicates up to the *t* of
28:28 from on *t* the ephod
28:32 must be an opening at its *t*
30:3 its *t* surface and its sides
34:2 on the *t* of the mountain
36:19 covering of sealskins up on *t*
36:29 *t* of each one at the first
37:26 its *t* surface and its sides
39:21 from on *t* the ephod, just as
Le 8:28 on *t* of the burnt offering
Nu 4:6 entire cloth of blue on *t* and
4:25 sealskin covering that is on *t*
14:40 up to the *t* of the mountain
14:44 up to the *t* of the mountain
20:28 on the *t* of the mountain
23:9 from the *t* of the rocks I see
23:14 Zophim, to the *t* of Pisgah
23:28 took Balaam to the *t* of Peor
De 3:27 Go up to the *t* of Pisgah
28:13 must come to be only on *t*
34:1 to the *t* of Pisgah, which
Jos 15:8 to the *t* of the mountain
15:9 from the *t* of the mountain
Jg 9:7 on the *t* of Mount Gerizim and
16:3 the *t* of the mountain that is
1Sa 26:13 the *t* of the mountain
28:12 at the *t* of her voice
2Sa 2:25 upon the *t* of one hill
11:20 shoot from on *t* of the wall
11:21 from on *t* of the wall so
11:24 from on *t* of the wall, so
1Ki 7:17 upon the *t* of the pillars
7:18 upon the *t* of the pillars
7:19 upon the *t* of the pillars
7:22 the *t* of the pillars there
7:35 on *t* of the carriage there
7:35 upon the *t* of the carriage
7:41 the *t* of the two pillars
7:41 upon the *t* of the pillars
18:27 Call at the *t* of your voice
18:28 at the *t* of their voice
18:42 went up to the *t* of Carmel
2Ki 1:9 upon the *t* of the mountain
2Ch 3:15 capital that was upon the *t*
4:12 the *t* of the two pillars
4:12 upon the *t* of the pillars
25:12 them to the *t* of the crag
25:12 from the *t* of the crag
Es 5:2 touched the *t* of the scepter
Job 34:37 *t* of his sin he adds revolt
Ps 72:16 *t* of the mountains there
Pr 8:2 On *t* of the heights, by the
9:3 *t* of the heights of the town
23:34 lying . . . at the *t* of a mast
Ca 4:8 from the *t* of Anti-Lebanon
4:8 from the *t* of Senir, even
Isa 2:2 above the *t* of the mountains
17:6 olives in the *t* of the branch
30:17 mast on the *t* of a mountain
42:11 From the *t* of the mountains
Eze 17:4 very *t* of its young shoots
17:22 the *t* of its twigs I shall
43:12 *t* of the mountain its
Am 9:3 hide . . . on the *t* of Carmel
Mic 4:1 above the *t* of the mountains
Zec 4:2 lampstand . . . a bowl on *t* of
4:2 lamps that are at the *t* of it
Mt 27:51 was rent in two, from *t* to
Mr 1:26 yelling at the *t* of its voice
15:38 in two from *t* to bottom
Joh 19:23 being woven from the *t*
21:7 about himself his *t* garment
Ac 7:57 at the *t* of the voice and put
Heb 11:21 upon the *t* of his staff
Re 17:9 where the woman sits on *t*

Topaz
Ex 28:17 row of ruby, *t* and emerald
39:10 A row of ruby, *t* and emerald
Job 28:19 The *t* of Cush cannot be
Eze 28:13 ruby, *t* and jasper
Re 21:20 the ninth *t*, the tenth

Tophel
De 1:1 between Paran and *T* and Laban

Topheth
2Ki 23:10 made unfit for worship *T*
Isa 30:33 *T* is set in order from
Jer 7:31 built the high places of *T*
7:32 no more be said to be *T*
7:32 they will have to bury in *T*
19:6 will be called no more *T*
19:11 in *T* they will bury until
19:12 to make this city like *T*
19:13 become like the place of *T*
19:14 from *T*, to which Jehovah

Topmost
Ge 40:17 in the *t* basket there were

Top-ranking
Mr 6:21 his *t* men and the military
Re 6:15 the *t* ones and the military
18:23 merchants were the *t* men

Tops
Ge 8:5 *t* of the mountains appeared
Ex 36:38 overlaid their *t* and their
38:17 of their *t* was of silver
38:28 *t* and joined them together
Jg 9:25 the *t* of the mountains, and
9:36 from the *t* of the mountains
2Sa 5:24 the *t* of the baca bushes
1Ki 7:16 upon the *t* of the pillars
1Ch 14:15 in the *t* of the baca bushes
2Ch 3:16 upon the *t* of the pillars
Eze 6:13 all the *t* of the mountains
Ho 4:13 On the *t* of the mountains
Joe 2:5 on the *t* of the mountains

Torch
Ge 15:17 and a fiery *t* that passed in
Jg 15:4 put one *t* between two tails
Isa 62:1 salvation like a *t* that burns
Zec 12:6 fiery *t* in a row of newly

Torches
Jg 7:16 and *t* inside the large jars
7:20 hold on the *t* with their left
15:4 take *t* and turn tail to tail
15:5 he set fire to the *t* and sent
Eze 1:13 appearance of *t* was moving
Da 10:6 his eyes like fiery *t*, and
Na 2:4 Their appearances are like *t*
Joh 18:3 came there with *t* and lamps

Tore
Jg 14:6 so that he *t* it in two, just
16:9 he *t* the sinews in two, just
16:12 he *t* them in two from off
Ps 136:24 *t* us away from our
Jer 2:20 I *t* your bands apart

Torment
Mt 8:29 Did you come here to *t* us
Mr 5:7 under oath by God not to *t* me
Lu 8:28 I beg you, do not *t* me
16:28 not get into this place of *t*
Re 9:5 and the *t* upon them was as
9:5 as *t* by a scorpion when it
14:11 smoke of their *t* ascends
18:7 to that extent give her *t*
18:10 their fear of her *t* and say
18:15 of their fear of her *t* and

Tormented
Mt 8:6 paralysis, being terribly *t*
Re 9:5 should be *t* five months, and
11:10 these two prophets *t* those
14:10 *t* with fire and sulphur in
20:10 *t* day and night forever

Tormenting
2Pe 2:8 *t* his righteous soul by

Torments
Mt 4:24 with various diseases and *t*
Lu 16:23 he existing in *t*, and he saw

Torn
Ge 31:39 Any animal *t* to pieces I
37:33 Joseph is surely *t* to pieces!
44:28 he must surely be *t* to pieces!
Ex 22:13 be *t* by a wild beast, he is
22:13 something *t* by a wild beast
22:31 something *t* by a wild beast
28:32 for it, that it may not be *t*
39:23 that it might not be *t*
Le 7:24 fat of an animal *t* to pieces
13:45 his garments should be *t*
14:43 after having *t* out the stones
17:15 something *t* by a wild beast
22:8 *t* by wild beasts so as to
De 28:63 be *t* away from off the soil
Jg 16:9 thread of tow is *t* in two
1Ki 18:30 mend the altar . . . *t* down
19:10 altars they have *t* down
19:14 altars they have *t* down
Ezr 9:5 my sleeveless coat *t* apart
Job 16:9 His very anger has *t* me to
17:11 own plans have been *t* apart
18:14 His confidence . . . *t* away
30:13 have *t* down my roadways
Ps 11:3 foundations themselves are *t*
129:6 has been *t* out has dried up
Pr 2:22 treacherous, they will be *t*
11:11 wicked ones it gets *t* down
24:31 wall itself had been *t* down
Ec 4:12 cannot quickly be *t* in two
Isa 5:27 their sandals be *t* in two
33:20 ropes will be *t* in two
Jer 4:26 had all been *t* down
5:5 must have *t* apart the bands
5:6 from them gets *t* to pieces
10:20 cords have all been *t* in
31:40 *t* down anymore to time
50:15 Her walls have been *t* down
La 2:2 *t* down the fortified places of
2:17 He has *t* down and shown no
Eze 4:14 nor a *t* animal have I eaten
19:12 Her strong rod was *t* off
30:4 foundations are actually *t*
36:35 were *t* down are fortified
36:36 built the things *t* down
44:31 no creature *t* to pieces of
Ho 6:1 he himself has *t* in pieces
Joe 1:17 Barns have been *t* down, for
Na 2:12 with animals *t* to pieces
Mal 1:13 brought something *t* away
Ac 21:1 we had *t* ourselves away from

Torrent
Ge 26:17 encamped in the *t* valley of
26:19 digging in the *t* valley and
32:23 over the *t* valley, and he
Le 23:40 poplars of the *t* valley, and
Nu 13:23 to the *t* valley of Eshcol
13:24 the *t* valley of Eshcol, on
21:12 by the *t* valley of Zered
21:14 and the *t* valleys of Arnon
21:15 the mouth of the *t* valleys
24:6 Like *t* valleys they have
32:9 up to the *t* valley of Eshcol
34:5 to the *t* valley of Egypt, and
De 1:24 far as the *t* valley of Eshcol
2:13 across the *t* valley of Zered
2:13 crossing the *t* valley of Zered
2:14 crossed the *t* valley of Zered
2:24 cross the *t* valley of Arnon
2:36 the *t* valley of Arnon, and
2:36 city that is in the *t* valley
2:37 the *t* valley of Jabbok, nor
3:8 the *t* valley of Arnon as far
3:12 by the *t* valley of Arnon, and
3:16 from Gilead to the *t* valley
3:16 the *t* valley being a boundary
3:16 the *t* valley that is the
4:48 the *t* valley of Arnon, up to
8:7 a land of *t* valleys of water
9:21 I threw its dust into the *t*
10:7 a land of *t* valleys running
21:4 a *t* valley running with water
21:4 there in the *t* valley
21:6 was broken in the *t* valley
Jos 12:1 from the *t* valley of Arnon
12:2 of the *t* valley of Arnon
12:2 the middle of the *t* valley
12:2 Jabbok the *t* valley
13:9 of the *t* valley of Arnon
13:9 the middle of the *t* valley
13:16 of the *t* valley of Arnon
13:16 the middle of the *t* valley

Jos 15:4 the *t* valley of Egypt
15:7 south of the *t* valley
15:47 to the *t* valley of Egypt
16:8 to the *t* valley of Kanah
17:9 to the *t* valley of Kanah
17:9 the *t* valley of these cities
17:9 the north of the *t* valley
19:11 *t* valley that is in front of
Jg 4:7 at the *t* valley of Kishon
4:13 to the *t* valley of Kishon
5:21 The *t* of Kishon washed them
5:21 The *t* of ancient days, the
5:21 the *t* of Kishon. You went
16:4 the *t* valley of Sorek, and her
1Sa 15:5 in ambush by the *t* valley
17:40 stones from the *t* valley
30:9 *t* valley of Besor, and the
30:10 over the *t* valley of Besor
30:21 by the *t* valley of Besor
2Sa 15:23 by the *t* valley of Kidron
17:13 down to the *t* valley
23:30 the *t* valleys of Gaash
24:5 the middle of the *t* valley
1Ki 2:37 the *t* valley of Kidron
8:65 to the *t* valley of Egypt
15:13 the *t* valley of Kidron
17:3 at the *t* valley of Cherith
17:4 from the *t* valley you should
17:5 by the *t* valley of Cherith
17:6 *t* valley he kept drinking
17:7 the *t* valley became dry
18:5 and to all the *t* valleys
18:40 the *t* valley of Kishon and
2Ki 3:16 *t* valley full of ditches
3:17 *t* valley will be filled with
10:33 the *t* valley of Arnon
23:6 to the *t* valley of Kidron
23:6 in the *t* valley of Kidron
23:12 the *t* valley of Kidron
24:7 the *t* valley of Egypt up to
1Ch 11:32 from the *t* valleys of Gaash
2Ch 7:8 down to the *t* valley of Egypt
15:16 in the *t* valley of Kidron
20:16 end of the *t* valley in front
29:16 *t* valley of Kidron outside
30:14 into the *t* valley of Kidron
32:4 *t* that floods through the
33:14 in the *t* valley and as far
Ne 2:15 in the *t* valley by night
Job 6:15 dealt . . . like a winter *t*
21:33 clods of earth of a *t* valley
22:24 in the rock of *t* valleys
30:6 the very slope of *t* valleys
40:22 The poplars of the *t* valley
Ps 36:8 the *t* of your pleasures you
74:15 split the spring and the *t*
83:9 at the *t* valley of Kishon
104:10 springs into the *t* valleys
110:7 *t* valley in the way he will
124:4 *t* itself would have passed
Pr 18:4 The well of wisdom is a *t*
30:17 ravens of the *t* valley will
Ca 6:11 see the buds in the *t* valley
Isa 7:19 the precipitous *t* valleys
15:7 the *t* valley of the poplars
27:12 to the *t* valley of Egypt
30:28 spirit is like a flooding *t*
30:33 like a *t* of sulphur, is
57:5 children in the *t* valleys
57:6 stones of the *t* valley was
66:12 just like a flooding *t*
Jer 31:9 walk to *t* valleys of water
31:40 *t* valley of Kidron, clear
47:2 have become a flooding *t*
La 2:18 tears to descend just like a *t*
Eze 47:5 *t* that I was not able to
47:5 *t* that could not be passed
47:6 return to the bank of the *t*
47:7 on the bank of the *t* there
47:9 the double-size *t* comes
47:9 be alive where the *t* comes
47:12 alongside the *t* there will
47:19 *t* valley to the Great Sea
48:28 to the *t* valley, as far as
Joe 3:18 *t* valley of the Acacia Trees
Am 5:24 like a constantly flowing *t*
6:14 the *t* valley of the Arabah
Joh 18:1 winter *t* of Kidron to where

Torrential
Job 20:17 *T* streams of honey and

Torrents
Le 11:9 in the seas and in the *t*
11:10 seas and the *t* that has no
Job 6:15 channel of winter *t* that
Ps 78:20 *t* themselves might flood
Ec 1:7 winter *t* are going forth to
1:7 the winter *t* are going forth
Isa 11:15 strike it in its seven *t*
34:9 *t* must be changed into pitch
35:6 and *t* in the desert plain
Mic 6:7 tens of thousands of *t* of oil

Tortuous
Ps 18:26 you will show yourself *t*

Torture
Job 15:20 a wicked one is suffering *t*
Mt 10:38 not accept his *t* stake and
16:24 and pick up his *t* stake and
27:32 to lift up his *t* stake
27:40 come down off the *t* stake!
27:42 come down off the *t* stake
Mr 8:34 pick up his *t* stake and
15:21 should lift up his *t* stake
15:30 coming down off the *t* stake
15:32 come down off the *t* stake
Lu 9:23 and pick up his *t* stake
14:27 is not carrying his *t* stake
23:26 placed the *t* stake upon him
Joh 19:17 bearing the *t* stake for
19:19 and put it on the *t* stake
19:25 By the *t* stake of Jesus
19:31 *t* stakes on the Sabbath
Ac 22:29 about to examine him with *t*
1Co 1:17 the *t* stake of the Christ
1:18 speech about the *t* stake is
Ga 5:11 *t* stake has been abolished
6:12 persecuted for the *t* stake
6:14 *t* stake of our Lord Jesus
Eph 2:16 to God through the *t* stake
Php 2:8 yes, death on a *t* stake
3:18 the enemies of the *t* stake
Col 1:20 blood he shed on the *t* stake
2:14 by nailing it to the *t* stake
Heb 12:2 he endured a *t* stake

Tortured
Heb 11:35 *t* because they would not

Toss
Ex 9:8 Moses must *t* it toward the
Job 2:12 *t* dust toward the heavens
Jer 5:22 Although its waves *t*
46:7 waters of which *t* themselves
46:8 and like rivers the waters *t*
Eze 10:2 and *t* them over the city

Tossed
Ex 9:10 Moses *t* it toward the heavens
Ps 119:118 *t* away all those straying
Isa 57:20 like the sea that is being *t*
La 1:15 powerful ones Jehovah has *t*
Am 8:8 *t* and sink down like the Nile
Mt 11:7 A reed being *t* by a wind?
Lu 7:24 A reed being *t* by the wind?
Ac 27:18 *t* with the tempest, the
27:27 *t* to and fro on the sea of
Eph 4:14 *t* about as by waves and

Tossing
Isa 57:20 keep *t* up seaweed and mire
Ac 22:23 and *t* dust into the air

Total
Job 22:12 see the sum *t* of the stars

Totally
Nu 30:12 if her husband has *t* annulled
30:15 if he *t* annuls them after
Da 7:26 him and to destroy him *t*

Totter
1Ch 16:30 Never will it be made to *t*
Ps 10:6 I shall not be made to *t*
15:5 will never be made to *t*
16:8 I shall not be made to *t*
17:5 certainly not be made to *t*
21:7 He will not be caused to *t*
30:6 Never shall I be made to *t*
46:2 *t* into the heart of the vast
46:5 it will not be made to *t*
55:22 allow the righteous one to *t*
62:2 not be made to *t* very much
62:6 I shall not be made to *t*
66:9 not allowed our foot to *t*
82:5 of the earth are made to *t*
93:1 that it cannot be made to *t*
96:10 that it cannot be made to *t*
104:5 not be made to *t* to time
112:6 at no time . . . made to *t*
121:3 allow your foot to *t*
Ps 125:1 which cannot be made to *t*
Isa 40:20 that may not be made to *t*
41:7 it could not be made to *t*

Tottered
Ps 46:6 boisterous, the kingdoms *t*
60:2 breaches, for it has *t*

Tottering
2Ch 28:15 case of anyone *t*, they gave
Na 2:10 there is a *t* of the knees

Tou
1Ch 18:9 *T* the king of Hamath heard
18:10 in warfare against *T*

Touch
Ge 3:3 you must not *t* it that you do
20:6 I did not allow you to *t* her
Ex 3:18 Jehovah . . . has come in *t*
4:25 caused it to *t* his feet and
5:3 God . . . has come in *t* with us
19:12 and do not *t* the edge of it
19:13 No hand is to *t* him, because
Le 6:18 may *t* them will become holy
6:27 that may *t* its flesh will
7:19 may *t* anything unclean is not
11:8 must not *t* their dead body
12:4 She should not *t* any holy
15:5 may *t* his bed should wash his
15:11 *t* when he has not rinsed his
15:12 might *t* should be smashed
Nu 4:15 not *t* the holy place so that
16:26 not *t* anything that belongs
19:16 *t* someone slain with the
19:22 unclean one may *t* will be
23:3 Perhaps Jehovah will get in *t*
23:4 God got in *t* with Balaam
23:15 let me get in *t* with him
23:16 Jehovah got in *t* with Balaam
De 14:8 carcasses you must not *t*
Ru 2:9 the young men not to *t* you
1Ch 16:22 not you men *t* my anointed
Job 1:11 *t* everything he has and see
2:5 *t* as far as his bone and his
5:19 nothing injurious will *t* you
6:7 soul has refused to *t* anything
21:15 we have come in *t* with him
Ps 32:6 they will not *t* him himself
88:3 has come in *t* even with Sheol
105:15 you men *t* my anointed ones
144:5 *T* the mountains that they
Isa 6:7 *t* my mouth and to say
26:5 brings it in *t* with the dust
52:11 *t* nothing unclean; get out
Jer 1:9 and caused it to *t* my mouth
La 4:14 So that none are able to *t*
4:15 Do not *t*! For they have gone
Da 8:7 into close *t* with the ram
10:18 *t* me again and strengthen me
Mt 9:21 If I only *t* his outer garment
14:36 *t* the fringe of his outer
Mr 3:10 falling upon him to *t* him
5:28 I *t* just his outer garments
6:56 *t* just the fringe of his
6:56 as did *t* it were made well
8:22 they entreated him to *t* him
10:13 young children for him to *t*
Lu 6:19 crowd were seeking to *t* him
11:46 not *t* the loads with one of
18:15 infants for him to *t* these
1Co 7:1 for a man not to *t* a woman
Col 2:21 not handle, nor taste, nor *t*
Heb 11:28 not *t* their firstborn ones

Touched
Ge 12:17 Jehovah *t* Pharaoh and his
26:29 just as we have not *t* you
32:25 he *t* the socket of his thigh
32:32 *t* the socket of Jacob's thigh
Nu 19:18 who *t* the bone or the slain
31:19 who has *t* someone slain, you
Jg 6:21 his hand and *t* the meat and
1Sa 6:9 it was not his hand that *t* us
10:26 men whose heart God had *t*
1Ki 19:7 and *t* him and said: Rise up
2Ki 13:21 man *t* the bones of Elisha
Es 5:2 and *t* the top of the scepter
Job 19:21 For God's own hand has *t* me
Isa 6:7 *t* your lips, and your error
Da 8:18 he *t* me and made me stand up
10:10 there was a hand that *t* me
Ho 4:2 *t* other acts of bloodshed
Mt 8:3 he *t* him, saying: I want to
8:15 he *t* her hand, and the fever
9:20 *t* the fringe of his outer

Mt 9:29 Then he *t* their eyes, saying
14:36 and all those who *t* it were
20:34 Jesus *t* their eyes, and
Mr 1:41 *t* him, and said to him: I
5:27 and *t* his outer garment
5:30 Who *t* my outer garments?
5:31 and do you say, Who *t* me?
7:33 spitting, he *t* his tongue
Lu 5:13 he *t* him, saying: I want to
7:14 he approached and *t* the bier
8:44 *t* the fringe of his outer
8:45 Who was it that *t* me?
8:46 Someone *t* me, for I perceived
8:47 cause for which she *t* him
22:51 he *t* the ear and healed him
Ac 20:15 the next day we *t* at Samos

Touches
Ex 29:37 *t* the altar is to be holy
Le 5:2 a soul *t* some unclean thing
5:3 in case he *t* the uncleanness of
7:21 a soul *t* anything unclean
11:39 he who *t* its dead body will
15:7 *t* the flesh of the one having
22:4 he who *t* anyone unclean by a
22:5 *t* any swarming thing that is
22:5 *t* a man who is unclean for
22:6 soul who *t* any such must be
Nu 19:22 who *t* it will be unclean
2Sa 23:7 When a man *t* them He should
Job 4:5 It *t* even you, and you get
Ps 104:32 *t* the mountains, and they
Eze 17:10 as when the east wind *t* it
Hag 2:12 *t* with his skirt bread or
2:13 *t* any of these things, will
Heb 12:20 if a beast *t* the mountain

Touching
Ge 26:11 Anybody *t* this man and his
Ex 19:12 Anybody *t* the mountain will
30:29 Anyone *t* them is to be holy
Le 11:24 Everyone *t* their dead bodies
11:26 Everyone *t* them will be
11:27 *t* their dead bodies will be
11:31 *t* them in their death state
11:36 *t* their dead bodies will be
15:10 *t* anything that happens to be
15:19 anyone *t* her will be unclean
15:21 anyone *t* her bed should wash
15:22 *t* any article upon which she
15:23 his *t* it he will be unclean
15:27 *t* them will be unclean
Nu 19:11 Anyone *t* the corpse of any
19:13 Everyone *t* a corpse, the soul
19:21 *t* the water for cleansing
1Ki 19:5 now an angel was *t* him
Pr 6:29 no one *t* her will remain
Jer 12:14 *t* the hereditary possession
Eze 3:13 were closely *t* each other
Da 8:5 and it was not *t* the earth
10:16 was *t* my lips, and I began
Am 9:5 is the One *t* the land, so that
Zec 2:8, 8 is *t* you is *t* my eyeball
Mt 17:7 Jesus came near and, *t* them
Lu 7:39 woman it is that is *t* him
2Co 6:17 and quit *t* the unclean thing

Tour
Mt 9:35 Jesus set out on a *t* of all

Toured
Ge 41:46 *t* about in all the land of

Tow
Jg 16:9 thread of *t* is torn in two
Isa 1:31 man will certainly become *t*

Toward*
Nu 6:25 Jehovah make his face shine *t*
6:26 face *t* you and assign peace
1Ki 8:29 servant prays *t* this place
8:30 they pray *t* this place; and
8:33 favor *t* you in this house
14:13 good *t* Jehovah the God of
2Ch 20:12 but our eyes are *t* you
Ps 5:7 bow down *t* your holy temple
103:18 *t* those remembering his
106:4 the goodwill *t* your people
117:2 *t* us his loving-kindness has
123:2 *t* the hand of their master
123:2 *t* the hand of her mistress
123:2 eyes are *t* Jehovah our God
Pr 14:35 *t* one acting shamefully
15:33 is a discipline *t* wisdom
Mal 4:6 heart of fathers back *t* sons
4:6 heart of sons back *t* fathers
Ac 24:15 I have hope *t* God, which
2Co 9:8 kindness abound *t* you, that
Ga 6:10 us work what is good *t* all
6:10 *t* those related to us in the
Col 4:5 *t* those on the outside

Towel
Joh 13:4 taking a *t*, he girded
13:5 to dry them off with the *t*

Tower
Ge 11:4 *t* with its top in the heavens
11:5 *t* that the sons of men had
35:21 distance beyond the *t* of Eder
Jg 8:9 I shall pull down this *t*
8:17 *t* of Penuel he pulled down
9:46 the *t* of Shechem heard of it
9:47 *t* of Shechem had collected
9:49 men of the *t* of Shechem died
9:51 a strong *t* happened to be in
9:51 onto the roof of the *t*
9:52 made his way to the *t* and
9:52 entrance of the *t* to burn it
1Ki 16:18 dwelling *t* of the king's
2Ki 9:17 upon the *t* in Jezreel
15:25 *t* of the king's house
17:9 *t* of the watchmen clear to
18:8 *t* of the watchmen clear to
Ne 3:1 as far as the *T* of Meah they
3:1 as far as the *T* of Hananel
3:11 also the *T* of the Bake Ovens
3:25 the *t* that goes out from the
3:26 east and the protruding *t*
3:27 the great protruding *t* as far
12:38 *T* of the Bake Ovens and on
12:39 and the *T* of Hananel and the
12:39 and the *T* of Meah and on to
Ps 61:3 A strong *t* in the face of the
Pr 18:10 Jehovah is a strong *t*
18:19 like the bar of a dwelling *t*
Ca 4:4 neck is like the *t* of David
7:4 Your neck is like an ivory *t*
7:4 nose is like the *t* of Lebanon
Isa 2:15 upon every high *t* and upon
5:2 build a *t* in the middle of it
25:2 dwelling *t* of strangers to
32:14 dwelling *t* itself has been
Jer 30:18 site the dwelling *t* itself
31:38 *t* of Hananel to the Corner
Mic 4:8 O *t* of the drove, the mound
Zec 14:10 from the *T* of Hananel all
Mt 21:33 erected a *t*, and let it out
Mr 12:1 erected a *t*, and let it out
Lu 13:4 upon whom the *t* in Siloam
14:28 wants to build a *t* does not

Towers
1Ch 27:25 in the villages and in the *t*
2Ch 14:7 make walls around and *t*
26:9 Uzziah built *t* in Jerusalem
26:10 built *t* in the wilderness
26:15 come to be upon the *t* and
27:4 fortified places and *t*
32:5 raised *t* upon it, and on the
36:19 dwelling *t* they burned with
Ps 48:3 In her dwelling *t* God himself
48:12 go about it, Count its *t*
48:13 Inspect its dwelling *t*
122:7 within your dwelling *t*
Ca 5:13 of spice, *t* of scented herbs
8:10 and my breasts are like *t*
Isa 13:22 howl in her dwelling *t*, and
23:13 erected their siege *t*
23:13 bare her dwelling *t*
29:7 siege *t* against her and those
30:25 slaughter when the *t* fall
33:18 the one counting the *t*
34:13 On her dwelling *t* thorns
Jer 6:5 bring to ruin her dwelling *t*
9:21 come into our dwelling *t*
17:27 the dwelling *t* of Jerusalem
49:27 dwelling *t* of Ben-hadad
La 2:5 swallowed . . . her dwelling *t*
2:7 the walls of her dwelling *t*
Eze 19:7 got to know his dwelling *t*
26:4 and tear down her *t*
26:9 your *t* he will pull down
27:11 to be in your own *t*
Ho 8:14 devour the dwelling *t* of each
Am 1:4 the dwelling *t* of Ben-hadad
1:7 it must devour her dwelling *t*
1:10 must devour her dwelling *t*
1:12 the dwelling *t* of Bozrah
1:14 it must devour her dwelling *t*
2:2 the dwelling *t* of Kerioth
2:5 the dwelling *t* of Jerusalem
Am 3:9 on the dwelling *t* in Ashdod
3:9 *t* in the land of Egypt
3:10 despoiling in . . . dwelling *t*
3:11 *t* will actually be plundered
6:8 his dwelling *t* I have hated
Mic 5:5 he treads upon our dwelling *t*
Zep 1:16 against the high corner *t*
3:6 their corner *t* were desolated

Town
Nu 21:28 a flame from the *t* of Sihon
De 2:36 no *t* that was too high up for
3:4 no *t* that we did not take from
1Ki 1:41 noise of the *t* in an uproar
1:45 and the *t* is in an uproar
Job 29:7 to the gate by the *t*
39:7 laughs at the turmoil of a *t*
Ps 48:2 The *t* of the grand King
Pr 8:3 at the mouth of the *t*, at the
9:3 top of the heights of the *t*
9:14 in the high places of the *t*
10:15 rich man are his strong *t*
11:10 righteous ones a *t* is elated
11:11 upright ones a *t* is exalted
18:11 valuable things . . . strong *t*
18:19 is more than a strong *t*
29:8 of boastful talk inflame a *t*
Isa 1:21 O how the faithful *t* has
1:26 Righteousness, Faithful *T*
22:2 city, an exultant *t*
24:10 deserted *t* has been broken
25:2 fortified *t* a crumbling ruin
25:3 *t* of the tyrannical nations
26:5 the height, the elevated *t*
29:1 Ariel, the *t* where David
32:13 yes, the highly elated *t*
33:20 *t* of our festal occasions
Jer 49:25 the *t* of exultation
La 2:11 in the public squares of the *t*
Ho 6:8 Gilead is a *t* of practicers
Mic 4:10 you will go forth from a *t*
Hab 2:8 *t* and all those dwelling in
2:12 a *t* by unrighteousness
2:17 the *t* and all those dwelling

Towns
Nu 21:25 and all its dependent *t*
21:32 they captured its dependent *t*
32:42 Kenath and its dependent *t*
De 3:5 aside from very many rural *t*
Jos 10:37 all its *t* and every soul
10:39 its king and all its *t*
13:17 Heshbon and all its *t* that
13:30 are in Bashan, sixty *t*
15:45 Ekron and its dependent *t*
15:47 Ashdod, its dependent *t* and
15:47 Gaza, its dependent *t* and
17:11 and its dependent *t* and
17:11 Ibleam and its dependent *t*
17:11 Dor and its dependent *t*
17:11 En-dor and its dependent *t*
17:11 Taanach and its dependent *t*
17:11 Megiddo and its dependent *t*
17:16 and its dependent *t* and
Jg 1:27 Beth-shean and its . . . *t* and
1:27 Taanach and its . . . *t* and
1:27 Dor and its dependent *t* and
1:27 Ibleam and its dependent *t*
1:27 Megiddo and its dependent *t*
11:26 Heshbon and its dependent *t*
11:26 Aroer and its dependent *t* and
1Ch 2:23 Kenath and its dependent *t*
5:16 Bashan and in its dependent *t*
7:28 Bethel and its dependent *t*
7:28 Gezer and its dependent *t*
7:28 Shechem and its dependent *t*
7:28 to Gaza and its dependent *t*
7:29 Beth-shean . . . dependent *t*
7:29 Taanach and its dependent *t*
7:29 Megiddo and its dependent *t*
7:29 Dor and its dependent *t*
8:12 and Lod and its dependent *t*
18:1 take Gath and its dependent *t*
2Ch 13:19 Bethel and its dependent *t*
13:19 Jeshanah and its dependent *t*
13:19 Ephrain and its dependent *t*
28:18 Soco and its dependent *t*
28:18 Timnah and its dependent *t*
28:18 Gimzo and its dependent *t*
Ne 11:25 its dependent *t* and in Dibon
11:25 in Dibon and its dependent *t*
11:27 and its dependent *t*
11:28 Meconah and its dependent *t*
11:30 Azekah and its dependent *t*
11:31 Bethel and its dependent *t*

Ps 48:11 *t* of Judah be joyful
97:8 dependent *t* of Judah began to
Jer 48:41 *t* will actually be captured
49:2 dependent *t* themselves will
49:3 O dependent *t* of Rabbah
49:18 Gomorrah and her neighbor *t*
50:40 and of her neighbor *t*
Eze 16:46 with her dependent *t*, who
16:46 Sodom with her dependent *t*
16:48 she with her dependent *t*
16:48 you and your dependent *t*
16:49 to her and her dependent *t*
16:53 and of her dependent *t*
16:53 and of her dependent *t*
16:55 Sodom and her dependent *t*
16:55 Samaria and her dependent *t*
16:55 your own dependent *t* will
26:6 *t* that are in the field
26:8 dependent *t* in the field
30:18 her own dependent *t* will go
Mr 1:38 into the village *t* nearby

Trace
Da 2:35 no *t* at all was found of
Heb 7:6 did not *t* his genealogy from

Traced
Lu 1:3 *t* all things from the start

Traces
Isa 44:13 *t* it out with red chalk

Trachonitis
Lu 3:1 of the country of Ituraea and *T*

Tracing
Isa 44:13 compass he keeps *t* it out
Ro 11:33 and past *t* out his ways are

Track
Ps 140:5 net at the side of the *t*

Tracks
Ps 17:5 steps take hold on your *t*
23:3 in the *t* of righteousness
65:11 very *t* drip with fatness
Pr 2:18 those impotent in death her *t*
4:11 tread in the *t* of uprightness
5:6 *t* have wandered she does not
5:21 is contemplating all his *t*
Isa 59:8 is no justice in their *t*

Tract
Ge 33:19 he acquired a *t* of the field
Jos 24:32 Shechem in the *t* of the
Ru 2:3 the *t* of the field belonging to
4:3 *t* of the field that belonged
2Sa 14:30 Joab's *t* of land beside
14:30 set the *t* of land ablaze
14:31 the *t* of land that is mine
23:11 a *t* of the field full of
23:12 in the middle of the *t* and
2Ki 3:19 *t* of land you should mar
3:25 every good *t* of land, they
9:10 in the *t* of land at Jezreel
9:21 *t* of land of Naboth the
9:25 the *t* of the field of Naboth
9:26 repay you in this *t* of land
9:26 throw him into the *t* of land
9:36 In the *t* of land of Jezreel
9:37 in the *t* of land of Jezreel
1Ch 11:13 a *t* of the field full of
11:14 in the middle of the *t* and
Job 24:18 *t* of land will be cursed in
Am 4:7 one *t* of land that would be
4:7 a *t* of land on which I would
7:4 and ate up the *t* of land

Trade
Job 20:18 Like wealth from his *t*, but
Ac 18:3 being of the same *t* he stayed
18:3 for they were tentmakers by *t*
Re 18:22 no craftsman of any *t* will

Trader
Ca 3:6 sort of scent powder of a *t*
Eze 27:20 Dedan was your *t* in

Traders
1Ki 10:15 and the profit from the *t*
Ne 3:31 the Nethinim and the *t*
3:32 and the *t* did repair work
13:20 *t* and the sellers of every
Eze 17:4 in a city of *t* he placed it
27:13 were your *t*. For the
27:15 sons of Dedan were your *t*
27:17 Israel . . . were your *t*
27:22 The *t* of Sheba and Raamah
27:22 Sheba and Raamah . . . *t*
Eze 27:23 and Eden, the *t* of Sheba
27:23 and Chilmad were your *t*
27:24 your *t* in gorgeous garments

Tradesman
Ho 12:7 As regards the *t*, in his hand

Tradesmen
Job 41:6 they divide it up among *t*
Pr 31:24 belts she has given to the *t*
Isa 23:8 whose *t* were the honorable
Na 3:16 multiplied your *t* more than
Zep 1:11 who are *t* have been silenced

Tradeswoman
Eze 27:3 the *t* of the peoples for

Trading
Pr 31:18 has sensed that her *t* is good
Eze 27:24 made, in your *t* center

Tradition
1Ch 4:22 the sayings are of old *t*
Mt 15:2 your disciples overstep the *t*
15:3 because of your *t*
15:6 invalid because of your *t*
Mr 7:3 *t* of the men of former times
7:5 *t* of the men of former times
7:8 you hold fast the *t* of men
7:9 in order to retain your *t*
7:13 by your *t* which you handed
Col 2:8 according to the *t* of men
2Th 3:6 to the *t* you received from us
1Pe 1:18 by *t* from your forefathers

Traditions
Mr 7:4 *t* that they have received to
1Co 11:2 the *t* just as I handed them
Ga 1:14 for the *t* of my fathers
2Th 2:15 the *t* that you were taught

Traffic
Jg 5:6 pathways had no *t*, And the

Train
1Ki 10:2 a very impressive *t*, camels
2Ch 9:1 with a very impressive *t* and
Ps 45:14 The virgins in her *t* as her
Pr 22:6 *T* up a boy according to the

Trained
Ge 14:14 he mustered his *t* men, three
2Sa 8:10 *t* in warfare against Toi
1Ch 5:18 bending the bow and *t* in war
18:10 Hadadezer had become *t* in
25:7 brothers *t* in song to Jehovah
Jer 31:18 a calf that has not been *t*
Ho 10:11 Ephraim was a *t* heifer
Heb 5:14 *t* to distinguish both right
12:11 those who have been *t* by it
2Pe 2:14 a heart *t* in covetousness

Training
1Ti 4:7 be *t* yourself with godly
4:8 bodily *t* is beneficial for a
1Pe 5:10 will himself finish your *t*

Trains
Job 15:5 For your error *t* your mouth

Traitor
Lu 6:16 Judas Iscariot, who turned *t*

Traitors
Ps 59:5 show favor to any hurtful *t*

Traits
1Co 13:11 with the *t* of a babe

Tramped
2Sa 5:22 *t* about in the low plain of

Tramping
Jg 15:9 and went *t* about in Lehi
2Sa 5:18 *t* about in the low plain of
Isa 9:5 of the one *t* with tremors

Trample
Ps 7:5 let him overtake and *t* my life
91:13 *t* down the maned young lion
Isa 1:12 to *t* my courtyards
26:6 The foot will *t* it down
Eze 26:11 *t* down all your streets
34:18 *t* down with your feet
Da 7:23 will *t* it down and crush it
8:13 and the army things to *t* on
Na 3:14 and *t* down in the clay
Mt 7:6 never *t* them under their feet
Lu 10:19 to *t* underfoot serpents and
Re 11:2 *t* the holy city underfoot

Trampled
Jg 20:43 *t* him down directly in front
2Ki 9:33 and he now *t* upon her
14:9 and *t* the thorny weed down
2Ch 25:18 *t* the thorny weed down
Isa 28:3 Ephraim will be *t* down
Eze 34:19 ground *t* by your feet
Da 8:7 threw it to the earth and *t* it
Mt 5:13 thrown outside to be *t* on by
Lu 8:5 was *t* down, and the birds of
21:24 Jerusalem will be *t* on by
Heb 10:29 *t* upon the Son of God and

Tramples
Isa 41:25 *t* down the moist material
Mic 5:8 *t* down and tears in pieces

Trampling
2Ki 7:17 kept *t* him in the gateway
7:20 kept *t* him in the gateway
Isa 5:5 destined for a place of *t*
7:25 and a *t* ground of sheep
10:6 make it a *t* place like the
16:4 those *t* down others have
28:18 become for it a *t* place
63:3 kept *t* them down in my rage
Da 8:10 and it went *t* them down
Mic 7:10 become a place of *t*, like

Trance
Ac 10:10 he fell into a *t*
11:5 in a *t* I saw a vision, some
22:17 praying . . . I fell into a *t*

Transcribed
Pr 25:1 Hezekiah the king of Judah *t*

Transfer
2Sa 3:10 *t* the kingdom from the house
Es 2:9 *t* her and her young women to
Mt 17:20 say to this mountain, *T*
17:20 here to there, and it will *t*

Transference
Heb 11:5 before his *t* he had the

Transferred
Ac 7:16 they were *t* to Shechem and
18:7 he *t* from there and went into
1Co 4:6 these things I have *t* so as to
Col 1:13 *t* us into the kingdom of the
Heb 11:5 By faith Enoch was *t* so as
11:5 because God had *t* him; for

Transferring
Lu 10:7 not be *t* from house to house

Transfigured
Mt 17:2 he was *t* before them, and
Mr 9:2 And he was *t* before them

Transform
Ge 48:4 *t* you into a congregation of

Transformed
Ro 12:2 *t* by making your mind over
2Co 3:18 *t* into the same image from

Transforming
2Co 11:13 *t* themselves into apostles
11:14 Satan himself keeps *t*
11:15 *t* themselves into ministers

Transforms
Job 38:14 It *t* itself like clay under

Transgress
Ps 17:3 My mouth will not *t*
Pr 28:21 *t* over a mere piece of bread
Lu 15:29 did I *t* your commandment

Transgressed
1Ki 8:50 which they *t* against you
Pr 18:19 brother who is *t* against is
Isa 43:27 have *t* against me
Jer 2:8 shepherds themselves *t*
2:29 Why have you *t*, all of you
3:13 God that you have *t*
33:8 they have *t* against me
La 3:42 We ourselves have *t*, and we
Eze 2:3 *t* against me down to this
18:31 in which you have *t* and
Ho 7:13 they have *t* against me
8:1 against my law they have *t*
Zep 3:11 you *t* against me, for then

Transgressing
Isa 59:13 *t* and a denying of Jehovah
66:24 men that were *t* against me
Ac 23:3 *t* the Law, command me to be
Ro 2:23 *t* of the Law dishonor God

Transgression
Ex 22:9 As regards any case of *t*
23:21 he will not pardon your *t*

Ex 34:7 pardoning error and *t* and sin
Nu 14:18 pardoning error and *t*, but by
1Sa 25:28 *t* of your slave girl
Job 7:21 why do you not pardon my *t*
33:9 I am pure without *t;* Clean
34:6 though there is no *t*
Ps 19:13 innocent from much *t*
36:1 The utterance of *t* to the
89:32 attention to their *t* even
107:17 due to the way of their *t*
Pr 10:19 does not fail to be *t*
12:13 *t* of the lips the bad person
17:9 one covering over *t* is seeking
17:19 loving *t* is loving a struggle
19:11 is beauty . . . to pass over *t*
28:2 Because of the *t* of a land
28:24 and is saying: It is no *t*
29:6 In the *t* of a bad man there
29:16 wicked . . . many, *t* abounds
29:22 rage has many a *t*
Isa 24:20 *t* has become heavy upon
53:5 was being pierced for our *t*
53:8 the *t* of my people he had
57:4 the children of *t*, the seed
59:20 turning from *t* in Jacob
Da 8:12 because of *t;* and it kept
8:13 the *t* causing desolation, to
9:24 order to terminate the *t*, and
Am 4:4 to Bethel and commit *t*
4:4 be frequent in committing *t*
Mic 7:18 passing over *t* of the
Ro 4:15 law, neither is there any *t*
5:14 likeness of the *t* by Adam
1Ti 2:14 and came to be in *t*
Heb 2:2 *t* and disobedient act received

Transgressions
1Ki 8:50 all their *t* with which they
Job 31:33 If . . . I covered over my *t*
36:9 tell them about . . . their *t*
Ps 5:10 In the multitude of their *t*
32:5 make confession over my *t* to
39:8 From all my *t* deliver me
51:1 your mercies wipe out my *t*
51:3 For my *t* I myself know, And
65:3 As for our *t*, you yourself
103:12 from us he has put our *t*
Pr 10:12 love covers over even all *t*
28:13 that is covering over his *t*
Isa 43:25 that is wiping out your *t*
44:22 will wipe out your *t* just
50:1 because of your own *t* your
Jer 5:6 For their *t* have become many
La 1:5 of the abundance of her *t*
1:14 himself alert against my *t*
1:22 on account of all my *t*
Eze 14:11 with all their *t*
18:22 his *t* . . . not be remembered
18:28 turns back from all his *t*
18:30 back from all your *t*
18:31 all your *t* in which you
21:24 your *t* being uncovered
37:23 and with all their *t*
39:24 and according to their *t*
Ga 3:19 added to make *t* manifest
Heb 9:15 *t* under the former covenant

Transgressor
Isa 48:8 *t* from the belly you have
Ro 2:25 if you are a *t* of law, your
2:27 are a *t* of law
Ga 2:18 demonstrate myself to be a *t*
Jas 2:11 you have become a *t* of law

Transgressors
Ps 37:38 *t* themselves will certainly
51:13 I will teach *t* your ways
Isa 46:8 Lay it to heart, you *t*
53:12 *t* that he was counted in
53:12 for the *t* he proceeded to
Eze 20:38 the revolters and the *t*
Da 8:23 *t* act to a completion, there
Ho 14:9 the *t* are the ones who will
Jas 2:9 reproved by the law as *t*

Transient
Ps 39:4 That I may know how *t* I am

Translate
1Co 14:13 pray that he may *t*
14:27 in turns; and let someone *t*

Translated
Ezr 4:7 *t* into the Aramaic language
Mt 1:23 when *t*, With Us Is God
Mr 5:41 *t*, means: Maiden, I say to
15:22 means, when *t*, Skull Place
Mr 15:34 when *t:* My God, my God, why
Joh 1:38 means, when *t*, Teacher
1:41 Messiah . . . when *t*, Christ
1:42 Cephas (which is *t* Peter)
9:7 which is *t* Sent forth
Ac 4:36 when *t*, Son of Comfort, a
9:36 which, when *t*, means Dorcas
13:8 is the way his name is *t*

Translates
1Co 14:5 he *t*, that the congregation

Translation
Heb 7:2 by *t*, King of Righteousness

Translator
1Co 14:28 no *t*, let him keep silent

Translators
1Co 12:30 Not all are *t*, are they?

Transmitted
Ac 7:53 the Law as *t* by angels but
Ga 3:19 *t* through angels by the

Transparent
Re 21:21 was pure gold, as *t* glass

Transplant
Eze 17:22 *t* it upon a high and lofty
17:23 *t* it, and it will certainly
1Co 13:2 faith so as to *t* mountains

Transplanted
Eze 17:8 waters, it was already *t*, in
17:10 although *t*, will it have

Transport
Ge 46:5 Pharaoh had sent to *t* him

Transportation
2Ch 28:15 gave them *t* on the asses

Transporting
Ge 46:5 continued *t* Jacob their father

Trap
Jos 23:13 as a *t* and as a snare and
Job 18:9 *t* will seize him by the heel
Ps 69:22 table before them become a *t*
91:3 the *t* of the birdcatcher
119:110 wicked have set a *t* for me
124:7 From the *t* of baiters
124:7 The *t* is broken
140:5 have hidden a *t* for me
141:9 *t* that they have laid for me
142:3 have hidden a *t* for me
Pr 7:23 bird hastens into the *t*
Ec 9:12 that are being taken in a *t*
Isa 8:14 as a *t* and as a snare to
24:17 hollow and the *t* are upon
24:18 will be caught in the *t*
Jer 5:26 They have set a ruinous *t*
48:43 and the *t* are upon you
48:44 will be caught in the *t*
Ho 5:1 a *t* is what you have become to
9:8 there is the *t* of a birdcatcher
Am 3:5 bird fall into a *t* on the
3:5 Does a *t* go up from the ground
Mt 22:15 order to *t* him in his speech
Ro 11:9 *t* and a stumbling block and

Trapped
Isa 42:22 being *t* in the holes, and

Trapper
1Sa 28:9 acting like a *t* against my

Traps
Job 22:10 bird *t* are all around you
Ps 11:6 upon the wicked ones *t*, fire
38:12 seeking my soul lay out *t*
64:5 statements about hiding *t*
109:11 usurer lay out *t* for all
Pr 22:5 Thorns and *t* are in the way
Jer 18:22 *t* they have hid for my feet

Travel
Ge 19:2 get up early and *t* on your
De 14:25 *t* to the place that Jehovah
Jg 5:6 would *t* by roundabout pathways
1Ki 10:15 apart from the men of *t*
2Ch 9:14 aside from the men of *t* and
Mt 25:14 a man, about to *t* abroad

Traveled
Ge 29:1 *t* on to the land of the
Nu 22:7 older men of Midian *t* with
1Sa 7:16 he *t* from year to year and
Mt 21:33 householder . . . *t* abroad
Mr 12:1 let it out . . . and *t* abroad
Lu 7:11 he *t* to a city called Nain
Lu 15:13 and *t* abroad into a distant
19:12 *t* to a distant land to secure
20:9 he *t* abroad for considerable
Ac 16:4 they *t* on through the cities

Traveler
Jg 19:17 the *t*, in the public square
2Sa 12:4 ready for the *t* that had
Jer 14:8 a *t* that has turned aside

Travelers
Ge 33:8 all this camp of *t* that I
Jg 5:6 the *t* of roadways would travel
Jer 9:2 a lodging place of *t*

Traveling
Es 9:4 his fame was *t* throughout all
Job 6:19 *t* company of Sabeans have
21:29 asked those *t* over the roads
Pr 7:19 *t* on a way of some distance
Mt 13:45 is like a *t* merchant seeking
Mr 13:34 a man *t* abroad that left
Lu 2:3 people went *t* to be registered
2:44 in the company *t* together
7:11 great crowd were *t* with him
10:33 Samaritan *t* the road came
14:25 great crowds were *t* with
Ac 9:3 as he was *t* he approached
19:29 *t* companions of Paul
2Co 8:19 to be our *t* companion in
Re 18:3 *t* merchants of the earth
18:11 *t* merchants of the earth
18:15 *t* merchants of these things
18:23 your *t* merchants were the

Traverse
Mt 23:15 you *t* sea and dry land to

Treacherous
Ps 119:158 those who are *t* in dealing
Pr 2:22 *t*, they will be torn away
22:12 subverts the words of the *t*
23:28 she increases the *t* ones
25:19 *t* in the day of distress
Isa 21:2 *t* dealer is dealing
24:16 The *t* dealers have dealt
24:16 *t* dealers have dealt
Jer 3:7 looking at her own *t* sister
3:10 her *t* sister Judah did not
9:2 solemn assembly of *t* dealers
17:9 The heart is more *t* than

Treacherously
Ex 21:8 in his *t* dealing with her
Jg 9:23 to deal *t* with Abimelech
1Sa 14:33 he said: You have dealt *t*
2Sa 18:13 dealt *t* against his soul
Job 6:15 My own brothers have dealt *t*
Ps 25:3 are dealing *t* without success
73:15 I should have acted *t*
78:57 acting *t* like their
Pr 11:3 those dealing *t* will despoil
11:6 those dealing *t* will
13:2 those dealing *t* is violence
13:15 of those dealing *t* is rugged
21:18 one dealing *t* takes the place
Isa 21:2 dealer is dealing *t*
24:16 dealers have dealt *t*
24:16 dealers have dealt *t*
33:1 dealing *t*, without others
33:1 others having dealt *t* with
33:1 you have done with dealing *t*
33:1 they will deal *t* with you
48:8 you kept dealing *t*, and a
Jer 3:8 yet *t* dealing Judah her sister
3:11 than *t* dealing Judah
3:20 as a wife has *t* gone from
3:20 have dealt *t* with me
5:11 positively dealt *t* with me
12:6 have dealt *t* with you
La 1:2 companions have dealt *t* with
Ho 5:7 they have dealt *t*, for it is
6:7 they have dealt *t* with me
Hab 1:13 you look on those dealing *t*
2:5 the wine is dealing *t*, an
Mal 2:10 we deal *t* with one another
2:11 Judah has dealt *t*, and a
2:14 have dealt *t*, although she
2:15 may no one deal *t*
2:16 you must not deal *t*

Treachery
Isa 24:16 Even with *t* the treacherous
Jer 12:1 those who are committing *t*
Zep 3:4 insolent, were men of *t*

Tread
Le 25:43 *t* down upon him with tyranny

Le 25:46 Israel, you must not *t*, the
25:53 not *t* him down with tyranny
26:17 hate you will just *t* down
De 11:24 the sole of your foot will *t*
11:25 the land on which you will *t*
33:29 high places you will *t*
Jos 1:3 the sole of your foot will *t*
1Sa 5:5 *t* upon the threshold of Dagon
Ne 9:28 enemies, who would *t* them
Job 24:11 Winepresses they have to *t*
39:15 beast of the field may *t* on
40:12 *t* down the wicked right
Ps 44:5 In your name we shall *t* down
60:12 will *t* down our adversaries
91:13 and the cobra you will *t*
108:13 will *t* down our adversaries
119:35 *t* in the pathway of your
Pr 4:11 *t* in the tracks of uprightness
27:7 will *t* down comb honey, but
Isa 14:25 I may *t* him down on my own
16:10 presses does the treader *t*
41:15 *t* down the mountains and
42:16 I shall cause them to *t*
48:17 *t* in the way in which you
Jer 51:33 time to *t* her down solid
Mic 1:3 *t* upon earth's high places
6:15 will *t* olives, but you will
Hab 3:19 he will cause me to *t*
Zec 9:13 I will *t* as my bow Judah
Mal 4:3 *t* down the wicked ones, for

Treader
Isa 16:10 in the presses does the *t*
Am 9:13 and the *t* of grapes, the

Treading
Jg 5:21 You went *t* down strength, O
9:27 in *t* them and in carrying on
Ne 13:15 *t* winepresses on the sabbath
Job 9:8 *t* upon the high waves of the
Isa 18:2 strength and of *t* down
18:7 strength and of *t* down
28:27 black cummin is given a *t*
28:28 incessantly keep *t* it out
59:8 No one at all *t* in them will
63:2 of one *t* in the winepress
63:3 I kept *t* them in my anger
Jer 25:30 those *t* the winepress
46:9 are handling and *t* the bow
48:33 doing the *t* with shouting
50:14 all you who are *t* the bow
50:29 all who are *t* the bow
51:3 Let the one *t* his bow do no
51:3 his bow do no *t*
Da 7:7 it was *t* down with its feet
7:19 *t* down even what was left
Am 4:13 One *t* on earth's high places

Treads
Mic 5:5 *t* upon our dwelling towers
5:6 when he *t* upon our territory
Re 19:15 He *t* too the winepress of

Treasure
Ge 43:23 gave you *t* in your bags
Jos 6:19 Into the *t* of Jehovah it
6:24 to the *t* of Jehovah's house
1Ch 29:8 *t* of the house of Jehovah
Ne 7:70 gave to the *t* a thousand gold
7:71 gave to the *t* for the work
Ps 17:14 fill with your concealed *t*
Pr 2:1 *t* up my own commandments
2:7 will *t* up practical wisdom
7:1 *t* up my own commandments with
10:14 the ones that *t* up knowledge
21:20 *t* and oil are in the abode of
27:24 for *t* will not be to time
Isa 33:6 fear of Jehovah . . . is his *t*
Eze 22:25 *T* and precious things they
Ho 13:15 That one will pillage the *t*
Mt 6:21 For where your *t* is, there
12:35 out of his good *t* sends out
12:35 out of his wicked *t* sends
13:44 kingdom . . . like a *t* hidden
13:52 brings out of his *t* store
19:21 you will have *t* in heaven
Mr 10:21 you will have *t* in heaven
Lu 6:45 out of the good *t* of his heart
6:45 out of his wicked *t*; for out
12:21 the man that lays up *t* for
12:33 *t* in the heavens, where a
12:34 where your *t* is, there your
18:22 will have *t* in the heavens
Ac 8:27 who was over all her *t*
2Co 4:7 this *t* in earthen vessels

Treasured
Job 20:26 reserved for his *t* things
23:12 have *t* up the sayings of his
Ps 31:19 *t* up for those fearing you
119:11 I have *t* up your saying
Pr 13:22 *t* up for the righteous one
Ca 7:13 dear one, I have *t* up for you
Ho 13:12 wrapped up, his sin is *t* up

Treasure-house
2Ki 20:13 show them all his *t*
Isa 39:2 show them his *t*, the silver
Da 1:2 brought to the *t* of his god

Treasurer
Ezr 1:8 control of Mithredath the *t*

Treasurers
Ezr 7:21 *t* that are beyond the River
Da 3:2 *t*, the judges, the police
3:3 the *t*, the judges, the police

Treasures
1Ki 7:51 the *t* of the house of Jehovah
14:26 *t* of the house of Jehovah
14:26 *t* of the house of the king
15:18 *t* of the house of Jehovah
15:18 *t* of the house of the king
2Ki 12:18 *t* of the house of Jehovah
14:14 *t* of the house of the king
16:8 the *t* of the king's house
18:15 the *t* of the king's house
20:13 was to be found in his *t*
20:15 did not show them in my *t*
24:13 *t* of the house of Jehovah
24:13 *t* of the king's house
1Ch 9:26 *t* of the house of the true
26:20 Ahijah was over the *t* of
26:20 *t* of the things made holy
26:22 *t* of the house of Jehovah
26:26 *t* of the things made holy
27:25 over the *t* of the king there
27:25 over the *t* in the field, in
28:12 *t* of the house of the true
28:12 *t* of the things made holy
2Ch 5:1 utensils he put in the *t* of
12:9 *t* of the house of Jehovah
12:9 and the *t* of the king's house
16:2 *t* of Jehovah's house and the
25:24 *t* of the king's house and
36:18 *t* of the house of Jehovah
36:18 *t* of the king and of his
Ezr 5:17 in the king's house of *t* that
6:1 the records of the *t* deposited
7:20 out of the king's house of *t*
Job 3:21 more than for hidden *t*
Pr 2:4 as for hid *t* you keep searching
10:2 *t* of the wicked one will be
21:6 getting of *t* by a false tongue
Isa 2:7 there is no limit to their *t*
39:2 was to be found in his *t*
39:4 did not show them in my *t*
45:3 the *t* in the darkness and
45:3 hidden *t* in the concealment
Jer 15:13 *t* I shall give for mere
17:3 your *t*, I shall give for
20:5 the *t* of the kings of Judah
41:8 hidden *t* in the field
48:7 your works and in your *t*
49:4 one trusting in her *t*
50:37 is a sword against her *t*
51:13 waters, abundant in *t*
Da 11:43 rule over the hidden *t* of
Ob 6 his concealed *t* have been sought
Mic 6:10 the *t* of wickedness, and the
Mt 2:11 opened their *t* and presented
6:19 *t* upon the earth, where moth
6:20 store up . . . *t* in heaven
Col 2:3 all the *t* of wisdom and of
Heb 11:26 greater than the *t* of Egypt

Treasuries
Ezr 4:13 loss to the *t* of the kings

Treasuring
1Ti 6:19 *t* up for themselves a fine

Treasury
Ezr 6:8 from the royal *t* of the tax
Es 3:9 bringing it into the king's *t*
4:7 had said to pay to the king's *t*
Jer 38:11 beneath the *t* and took
Zec 11:13 Throw it to the *t*—the
11:13 threw it into the *t* at the
Mt 27:6 drop them into the sacred *t*
Mr 12:41 sat down with the *t* chests
12:41 dropping money into the *t*
12:43 money into the *t* chests
Lu 21:1 their gifts into the *t* chests
Joh 8:20 he spoke in the *t* as he was

Treat
Ge 34:31 *t* our sister like a
Le 19:15 not *t* the lowly with
Nu 14:11 people *t* me without respect
De 31:20 and *t* me with disrespect and
Job 39:16 She does *t* her sons roughly
Ps 89:43 again *t* his sword as a foe
Isa 8:13 whom you should *t* as holy
23:9 *t* with contempt all the
Jer 2:36 *t* as very insignificant the
Ho 4:10 actually *t* women as harlots
Mt 12:5 *t* the sabbath as not sacred
Lu 2:48 why did you *t* us this way?
Ac 7:26 do you *t* each other unjustly
14:5 to *t* them insolently and pelt
20:29 *t* the flock with tenderness
Ga 4:14 you did not *t* with contempt
1Th 5:20 *t* prophesyings with contempt

Treated
Ge 12:16 *t* Abram well on her account
Nu 16:30 *t* Jehovah disrespectfully
1Sa 2:17 *t* the offering of Jehovah
2Sa 12:14 *t* Jehovah with disrespect
19:43 have you *t* us with contempt
Job 22:8 one who is *t* with partiality
Ps 74:3 enemy has *t* badly in the holy
74:18 *t* your name with disrespect
137:8 treatment with which you *t*
Isa 1:4 *t* the Holy One of Israel with
9:1 one *t* with contempt the land
52:5 was being *t* with disrespect
Jer 13:22 heels have been *t* violently
31:20 or a fondly *t* child
La 1:8 have *t* her as something cheap
Eze 22:7 they have *t* with contempt
Ho 4:18 *t* woman as a harlot
5:3 you have *t* women like harlots
Mic 4:6 her whom I have *t* badly
Mt 22:6 *t* them insolently and killed
Mr 9:12 and be *t* as of no account
Lu 18:32 *t* insolently and spit upon
Ac 4:11 *t* by you builders as of no
7:24 certain one being unjustly *t*
27:3 Julius *t* Paul with human
1Th 2:2 been insolently *t* (just as

Treating
Nu 14:23 those *t* me without respect
De 26:6 the Egyptians went *t* us badly
Job 13:8 you be *t* him with partiality
Ps 74:10 *t* your name with disrespect
Isa 60:14 those *t* you disrespectfully
Jer 33:24 keep *t* with disrespect
Eze 16:57 *t* you with scorn on all
28:24 who are *t* them with scorn
28:26 *t* them with scorn all
Ac 7:27 *t* his neighbor unjustly thrust

Treatment
Ps 137:8 *t* with which you treated
Pr 19:17 his *t* He will repay to him
Isa 3:11 for the *t* rendered by his
59:18 due *t* to his enemies
59:18 he will recompense due *t*
Jer 51:6 *t* that he is paying back to
La 3:64 will give back to them a *t*
Joe 3:4 *t* that you are giving me as
3:4 you are giving such *t* to me
3:4 I shall pay back your *t* upon
3:7 I will pay back your *t* upon
Ob 15 Your sort of *t* will return upon
Ac 7:34 wrongful *t* of my people who
2Co 4:10 *t* given to Jesus, that the
Col 2:23 a severe *t* of the body; but

Treats
De 10:17 *t* none with partiality nor
27:16 *t* his father or his mother
La 2:6 he *t* his booth violently like

Tree
Ge 1:29 every *t* on which there is the
1:29 the fruit of a *t* bearing seed
2:9 grow out of the ground every *t*
2:9 good for food and also the *t*
2:9 *t* of the knowledge of good and
2:16 From every *t* of the garden
2:17 *t* of the knowledge of good
3:1 you must not eat from every *t*
3:3 *t* that is in the middle of the
3:6 woman saw that the *t* was good
3:6 yes, the *t* was desirable to

Ge 3:11 *t* from which I commanded you
3:12 she gave me fruit from the *t*
3:17 *t* concerning which I gave
3:22 take fruit also from the *t* of
3:24 the way to the *t* of life
6:14 out of wood of a resinous *t*
18:4 Then recline under the *t*
18:8 standing by them under the *t*
21:33 he planted a tamarisk *t* at
30:37 staffs . . . of the storax *t*
30:37 of the almond *t* and of the
30:37 plane *t* and peeled in them
35:4 hid them under the big *t*
35:8 under a massive *t*. Hence he
49:22 Offshoot of a fruit-bearing *t*
49:22 *t* by the fountain, that
Ex 10:5 eat every sprouting *t* of yours
15:25 Jehovah directed him to a *t*
Le 19:23 plant any *t* for food, you
26:4 *t* of the field will give its
26:20 *t* of the earth will not give
27:30 fruit of the *t*, belongs to
De 12:2 and under every luxuriant *t*
16:21 any sort of *t* as a sacred
19:5 with the ax to cut the *t*
20:19 is the *t* of the field a man
20:20 a *t* that you know is not a
20:20 you know is not a *t* for food
22:6 in any *t* or on the earth with
24:20 In case you beat your olive *t*
Jos 19:33 from the big *t* in Zaanannim
24:26 the massive *t* that is by
Jg 4:5 Deborah's palm *t* between
4:11 tent pitched near the big *t*
6:11 sat under the big *t* that was
6:19 under the big *t* and served it
9:6 by the big *t*, the pillar that
9:8 to the olive *t*, Do be king over
9:9 the olive *t* said to them, Must
9:10 said to the fig *t*, You come
9:11 the fig *t* said to them, Must
9:37 the big *t* of Meonenim
1Sa 10:3 as far as the big *t* of Tabor
14:2 the pomegranate *t* that is in
22:6 Gibeah under the tamarisk *t*
31:13 tamarisk *t* in Jabesh, and
2Sa 18:9 boughs of a massive big *t*
18:9 got caught fast in the big *t*
18:10 Absalom hung in a big *t*
18:14 in the heart of the big *t*
1Ki 4:25 and under his own fig *t*
13:14 sitting under the big *t*
14:23 and under every luxuriant *t*
19:4 under a certain broom *t*
19:5 asleep under the broom *t*
2Ki 3:19 every good *t* you should fell
3:25 every good *t* they would fell
16:4 under every luxuriant *t*
17:10 under every luxuriant *t*
18:31 each one from his own fig *t*
1Ch 10:12 under the big *t* in Jabesh
2Ch 28:4 every sort of luxuriant *t*
Ne 10:35 fruitage of every sort of *t*
10:37 fruitage of every sort of *t*
Job 14:7 exists hope for even a *t*
15:33 just like an olive *t*
19:10 my hope out just like a *t*
24:20 be broken just like a *t*
Ps 1:3 *t* planted by streams of water
37:35 a luxuriant *t* in native soil
52:8 olive *t* in God's house
92:12 blossom forth as a palm *t*
Pr 3:18 *t* of life to those taking
11:30 is a *t* of life, and he that
13:12 thing desired is a *t* of life
15:4 of the tongue is a *t* of life
27:18 is safeguarding the fig *t*
Ec 11:3 if a *t* falls to the south or
11:3 where the *t* falls there it
12:5 the almond *t* carries blossoms
Ca 2:3 an apple *t* among the trees of
2:13 fig *t*, it has gained a mature
7:7 does resemble a palm *t*
7:8 I shall go up on the palm *t*
8:5 Under the apple *t* I aroused you
Isa 1:30 you will become like a big *t*
6:13 burning down, like a big *t*
6:13 massive *t* in which, when
17:6 beating off of the olive *t*
24:13 beating off of the olive *t*
34:4 shriveled fig off the fig *t*
36:16 one from his own fig *t* and
40:20 certain *t* as a contribution
40:20 a *t* that is not rotten
Isa 41:19 I shall set the cedar *t*
41:19 the myrtle and the oil *t*
41:19 I shall place the juniper *t*
44:14 takes a certain species of *t*
44:14 a massive *t*, and he lets it
44:14 He planted the laurel *t*, and
44:19 the dried-out wood of a *t*
55:13 the juniper *t* will come up
55:13 the myrtle *t* will come up
56:3 say, Look! I am a dry *t*
57:5 under every luxuriant *t*
60:13, 13 the juniper *t*, the ash *t*
65:22 like the days of a *t* will
Jer 1:11 an almond *t* is what I am
2:20 under every luxuriant *t* you
2:27 saying to a *t*, You are my
3:6 underneath every luxuriant *t*
3:13 under every luxuriant *t*
5:17 your vine and your fig *t*
7:20 upon the *t* of the field and
8:13 no figs on the fig *t*, and
10:3 a mere *t* out of the forest
10:8 A *t* is a mere exhortation of
11:16 A luxuriant olive *t*, pretty
11:19 Let us bring to ruin the *t*
17:2 poles beside a luxuriant *t*
17:6 a solitary *t* in the desert
17:8 a *t* planted by the waters
48:6 juniper *t* in the wilderness
La 4:8 has become just as dry as a *t*
Eze 6:13 under every luxuriant *t* and
6:13 and under every branchy big *t*
15:2 the vine *t* happen to be different
15:2 different from every other *t*
15:6 like the vine *t* among the
17:5 as a willow *t* he placed it
17:24 have abased the high *t*, have
17:24 have put on high the low *t*
17:24 dried up the still-moist *t*
17:24 have made the dry *t* blossom
20:28 hill and every branchy *t*
20:47 every still-moist *t* and
20:47 and every dry *t*
21:10 as it does every *t*
31:8 No other *t* in the garden
34:27 the *t* of the field must
36:30 fruitage of the *t* abound
Da 4:10 a *t* in the midst of the earth
4:11 *t* grew up and became strong
4:14 Chop the *t* down, and cut off
4:20 *t* that you beheld, that grew
4:23 Chop the *t* down, and ruin it
4:26 leave the rootstock of the *t*
Ho 2:12 her fig *t*, of which she has
4:13 under massive *t* and storax
4:13, 13 and storax *t* and big *t*
9:10 Like the early fig on a fig *t*
14:6 like that of the olive *t*
14:8 am like a luxuriant juniper *t*
Joe 1:7 and my fig *t* as a stump
1:12 the fig *t* has faded away
1:12 As for the pomegranate *t*
1:12 the palm *t* and the apple
1:12 the apple *t*, all the trees
2:22 For the *t* will actually give
2:22 The fig *t* and the vine must
Mic 4:4 his vine and under his fig *t*
Na 2:3 the juniper *t* spears have been
Hab 3:17 fig *t* itself may not blossom
3:17 the work of the olive *t* may
Hag 2:19 the vine and the fig *t* and
2:19 and the pomegranate *t* and
2:19 the olive *t*—it has not borne
Zec 3:10 and while under the fig *t*
11:2 Howl, O juniper *t*, for the
Mt 3:10 every *t*, then, that does not
7:17 good *t* produces fine fruit
7:17 rotten *t* produces worthless
7:18 good *t* cannot bear worthless
7:18 a rotten *t* produce fine fruit
7:19 *t* not producing fine fruit
12:33 *t* fine and its fruit fine
12:33 the *t* rotten and its fruit
12:33 by its fruit the *t* is known
13:32 and becomes a *t*, so that the
21:19 he caught sight of a fig *t*
21:19 the fig *t* withered instantly
21:20 the fig *t* withered instantly
21:21 do what I did to the fig *t*
24:32 learn from the fig *t* as an
Mr 11:13 he caught sight of a fig *t*
11:20 they saw the fig *t* already
11:21 the fig *t* that you cursed
13:28 from the fig *t* learn the
Lu 3:9 every *t* . . . not producing fine
6:43 fine *t* producing rotten fruit
6:43 rotten *t* producing fine fruit
6:44 *t* is known by its own fruit
13:6 had a fig *t* planted in his
13:7 for fruit on this fig *t*, but
13:19 and it grew and became a *t*
17:6 to this black mulberry *t*
19:4 climbed a fig-mulberry *t* in
21:29 Note the fig *t* and all the
23:31 when the *t* is moist, what
Joh 1:48 under the fig *t*, I saw you
1:50 saw you underneath the fig *t*
Ro 11:24 cut out of the olive *t* that
11:24 into the garden olive *t*
11:24 into their own olive *t*
Jas 3:12 fig *t* cannot produce olives
Re 2:7 grant to eat of the *t* of life
6:13 fig *t* shaken by a high wind
7:1 or upon the sea or upon any *t*
9:4 nor any green thing nor any *t*

Trees
Ge 1:11 fruit *t* yielding fruit
1:12 *t* yielding fruit, the seed of
3:2 fruit of the *t* of the garden
3:8 in between the *t* of the garden
12:6 near the big *t* of Moreh
13:18 dwelt among the big *t* of
14:13 big *t* of Mamre the Amorite
18:1 among the big *t* of Mamre
23:17 all the *t* that were in the
Ex 9:25 all sorts of *t* of the field
10:15 all the fruit of the *t* that
10:15 left nothing green on the *t*
15:27 water and seventy palm *t*
Le 23:40 splendid *t*, the fronds of
23:40 the fronds of palm *t* and the
23:40 boughs of branchy *t* and
Nu 13:20 whether there are *t* in it or
33:9 water and seventy palm *t*
De 6:11 olive *t* that you did not plant
11:30 beside the big *t* of Moreh
20:19 you must not ruin its *t* by
28:40 olive *t* in all your territory
28:42 All your *t* and the fruitage
34:3 the city of the palm *t*, as
Jg 1:16 city of palm *t* with the sons
3:13 of the city of palm *t*
9:8 the *t* went to anoint a king
9:9 go to wave over the other *t*
9:10 the *t* said to the fig tree
9:11 go to wave over the other *t*
9:12 the *t* said to the vine, You
9:13 must I go to wave over the *t*
9:14 *t* said to the bramble, You
9:15 bramble said to the *t*, If it
9:48 cut down a branch of the *t*
2Sa 5:11 also cedar *t* and workers in
1Ki 4:33 he would speak about the *t*
5:6 to cut *t* like the Sidonians
5:8 matter of timbers of cedar *t*
5:8 and timbers of juniper *t*
5:10 giver of timbers of cedar *t*
5:10 and timbers of juniper *t* to
6:10 by timbers of cedar *t*
9:11 with timbers of cedar *t* and
9:11 and timbers of juniper *t* and
10:11 timbers of almug *t* in very
10:12 the timbers of the almug *t*
10:12 Timbers of almug *t* like
10:27 the sycamore *t* that are in
2Ki 6:4 and began to cut down the *t*
18:32 a land of oil-olive *t* and
19:23 its choice juniper *t*
1Ch 16:33 *t* of the forest break out
27:28 sycamore *t* that were in the
2Ch 1:15 he made like the sycamore *t*
2:8 cutting down the *t* of Lebanon
2:10 cutters of the *t*, I do give
2:16 cut down *t* from Lebanon
9:10 brought timbers of almug *t*
9:11 timbers of the almug *t*
9:27 like the sycamore *t* that are
28:15 the city of palm *t*
Ne 2:8 give me *t* to build with
8:15 leaves of oil *t* and myrtle
8:15 of branchy *t* to make booths
9:25 olive groves and *t* for food
Job 30:4 broom *t* was their food
40:21 Under the thorny lotus *t* it
40:22 lotus *t* keep it blocked off
Ps 74:5 against a thicket of *t*
78:47 sycamore *t* by hailstones

Eze 45:8 with respect to their *t*
47:13 for the twelve *t* of Israel
47:21 to the twelve *t* of Israel
47:22 midst of the *t* of Israel
48:1 these are the names of the *t*
48:19 *t* of Israel will cultivate
48:23 rest of the *t*, from the
48:29 to the *t* of Israel
48:31 names of the *t* of Israel
Ho 5:9 Among the *t* of Israel I have
Hab 3:9 The sworn oaths of the *t* are
Zec 9:1 and on all the *t* of Israel
Mt 19:28 judging the twelve *t* of
24:30 the *t* of the earth will beat
Lu 22:30 judge the twelve *t* of Israel
Ac 26:7 twelve *t* are hoping to attain
Jas 1:1 twelve *t* that are scattered
Re 1:7 all the *t* of the earth will
7:9 out of all nations and *t* and
11:9 peoples and *t* and tongues and
21:12 *t* of the sons of Israel

Tribesmen
Jg 20:12 men to all the *t* of Benjamin

Tribulation
Mt 13:21 after *t* or persecution has
24:9 will deliver you up to *t* and
24:21 be great *t* such as has not
24:29 after the *t* of those days
Mr 4:17 as *t* or persecution arises
13:19 *t* such as has not occurred
13:24 after that *t*, the sun will
Joh 16:21 remembers the *t* no more
16:33 the world you are having *t*
Ac 7:11 Canaan, even a great *t*
11:19 *t* that arose over Stephen
Ro 2:9 *t* and distress, upon the soul
5:3 that *t* produces endurance
8:35 *t* or distress or persecution
12:12 Endure under *t*. Persevere in
1Co 7:28 will have *t* in their flesh
2Co 1:4 comforts us in all our *t*
1:4 those in any sort of *t*
1:6 Now whether we are in *t*, it
1:8 *t* that happened to us in the
2:4 much *t* and anguish of heart I
4:17 *t* is momentary and light
Php 1:17 *t* for me in my prison bonds
4:14 sharers with me in my *t*
1Th 1:6 under much *t* with joy of
3:4 were destined to suffer *t*
3:7 in all our necessity and *t*
2Th 1:6 to repay *t* to those who make
1:6 those who make *t* for you
1:7 but, to you who suffer *t*
1Ti 5:10 if she relieved those in *t*
Heb 11:37 they were in want, in *t*
Jas 1:27 and widows in their *t*
Re 1:9 sharer with you in the *t* and
2:9 I know your *t* and poverty
2:10 that you may have *t* ten days
2:22 great *t*, unless they repent
7:14 that come out of the great *t*

Tribulations
Ac 7:10 delivered . . . out of all his *t* and
14:22 enter . . . through many *t*
20:23 and *t* are waiting for me
Ro 5:3 let us exult while in *t*
2Co 6:4 by *t*, by cases of need, by
Eph 3:13 *t* of mine in your behalf
Col 1:24 *t* of the Christ in my flesh
1Th 3:3 might be swayed by these *t*
2Th 1:4 the *t* that you are bearing
Heb 10:33 both to reproaches and *t*

Tribunal
1Co 4:3 be examined by . . . a human *t*

Tribute
Jg 3:15 Israel sent *t* by his hand to
3:17 to present the *t* to Eglon the
3:18 had finished presenting the *t*
3:18 the bearers of the *t*
2Sa 8:2 David's servants to carry *t*
8:6 David's servants to carry *t*
2Ki 17:3 and began to pay *t* to him
17:4 *t* up to the king of Assyria
1Ch 18:2 David's servants bearing *t*
18:6 David's servants bearing *t*
2Ch 17:11 presents and money as *t*
26:8 Ammonites began to give *t*
Ezr 4:13 tax nor *t* nor toll will they
4:20 and tax, *t* and toll were
7:24 no tax, *t* or toll is allowed
Ne 5:4 money for the king's *t* on
Ps 72:10 *T* they will pay
Am 5:11 *t* of grain you keep taking
Ro 13:7, 7 calls for the *t*, the *t*

Trick
Jos 9:22 Why did you *t* us, saying
1Sa 19:17 Why did you *t* me like this
28:12 Why did you *t* me, when you

Tricked
Ge 29:25 So why have you *t* me?
2Sa 19:26 my servant that *t* me
Pr 26:19 that has *t* his fellowman and
La 1:19 They themselves have *t* me

Trickery
2Ki 9:23 There is *t*, Ahaziah!
2Co 12:16 I caught you by *t*
Eph 4:14 by means of the *t* of men

Trickiness
Ps 101:7 no worker of *t*
119:118 For their *t* is falsehood
Jer 8:5 They have taken hold of *t*
14:14 the *t* of their heart they
23:26 the *t* of their own heart

Trickle
De 32:2 My saying will *t* as the dew
Job 36:28 So that the clouds *t*
Ps 147:18 The waters *t*
Ca 4:16 my garden. Let its perfumes *t*
Isa 45:8 *t* with righteousness. Let
Jer 9:18 beaming eyes *t* with waters

Trickled
Job 28:11 places from which rivers *t*

Trickling
Nu 24:7 Water keeps *t* from his two
Ca 4:15 and *t* streams from Lebanon
Isa 44:3 *t* streams upon the dry place
Jer 18:14 strange waters, cool, *t*
Eze 47:2 water was *t* from the

Tricklings
Pr 5:15 *t* out of the midst of your

Tricky
Ps 120:2 from the *t* tongue
120:3 O you *t* tongue
Isa 25:11 *t* movements of his hands
Mic 6:12 tongue is *t* in their mouth
Zep 3:13 in their mouths a *t* tongue

Tried
Ge 37:21 When Reuben heard this he *t*
48:17 he *t* to take hold of his
Ex 8:18 priests *t* to do the same by
Nu 13:30 Caleb *t* to still the people
14:40 *t* to go up to the top of the
22:23 the ass *t* to turn aside from
22:33 she-ass . . . *t* to turn aside
23:7 king of Moab *t* to conduct me
De 1:43 *t* to go up into the mountain
Jg 8:1 *t* to pick a quarrel with him
18:22 *t* to catch up with the sons
1Sa 17:39 because he had not *t* them
17:39 for I have not *t* them out
1Ki 11:15 *t* to strike down every male
Ps 69:21 *t* to make me drink vinegar
78:36 *t* to fool him with their
78:36 tongue they *t* to lie to him
Isa 28:16 a *t* stone, the precious
Jer 29:31 he *t* to make you trust in
Jon 1:13 *t* to work their way through
Mt 3:14 the latter *t* to prevent him
Mr 9:38 we *t* to prevent him, because
14:51 and they *t* to seize him
15:23 they *t* to give him wine
Lu 4:42 they *t* to detain him from
9:49 we *t* to prevent him, because
Joh 10:39 they *t* again to seize him
Ac 7:26 *t* to bring them together
24:6 *t* to profane the temple and
26:11 I *t* to force them to make
1Co 6:4 matters of this life to be *t*
Heb 11:37 were *t*, they were sawn
Jas 1:13 say: I am being *t* by God
1:13 God cannot be *t* nor does he
1:14 one is *t* by being drawn out

Tries
Job 15:25 he *t* to show himself superior
3Jo 10 he *t* to hinder and to throw

Trifle
Ex 8:29 let not Pharaoh *t* again in not
Job 13:9 will you *t* with him?

Trifled
Ge 31:7 your father has *t* with me
Jg 16:10 You have *t* with me that you
16:13 you have *t* with me that you
16:15 you have *t* with me and have
Isa 44:20 heart that has been *t* with

Trifles
Job 13:9 Or as one *t* with mortal man
1Ti 6:5 about *t* on the part of men

Trifling
Isa 16:14 be a *t* few, not mighty
Jer 9:5 keep *t* each one with his

Trimming
Ca 2:12 time of vine *t* has arrived

Trip
Ge 22:2 and make a *t* to the land of
22:3 *t* to the place that the
24:21 Jehovah had made his *t*
Mt 10:10 or a food pouch for the *t*
Mr 6:8 to carry nothing for the *t*
Lu 9:3 Carry nothing for the *t*
Tit 3:13 and Apollos for their *t*

Tripping
Isa 3:16 walking with *t* steps, and
Ro 14:13 or a cause for *t*

Triumph
Ps 41:11 enemy does not shout in *t*
47:1 Shout in *t* to God with the
60:8 Over Philistia . . . shout in *t*
65:13 They shout in *t*, yes, they
66:1 Shout in *t* to God, all you
81:1 Shout in *t* to the God of
95:1 shout in *t* to our Rock of
95:2 melodies shout in *t* to him
98:4 Shout in *t* to Jehovah, all
98:6 Shout in *t* before the King
100:1 Shout in *t* to Jehovah, all
108:9 Philistia I shall shout in *t*
Isa 44:23 Shout in *t*, all you lowest
Zec 9:9 Shout in *t*, O daughter of

Triumphal
2Co 2:14 in a *t* procession in company
Col 2:15 in a *t* procession by means

Triumphantly
Jas 2:13 Mercy exults *t* over judgment

Trivial
1Ki 16:31 most *t* thing for him to
2Ki 3:18 be a *t* thing in the eyes of
Isa 49:6 been more than a *t* matter
1Co 4:3 to me it is a very *t* matter
6:2 unfit to try very *t* matters

Troas
Ac 16:8 Mysia by and came down to *T*
16:11 we put out to sea from *T* and
20:5 and were waiting for us in *T*
20:6 we came to them in *T* within
2Co 2:12 arrived in *T* to declare the
2Ti 4:13 bring the cloak I left at *T*

Trod
De 1:36 give the land upon which he *t*
Jos 14:9 upon which your foot has *t*
Hab 3:15 Through the sea you *t* with

Trodden
Job 22:15 That hurtful men have *t*
28:8 beasts have not *t* it down
Pr 10:8 with his lips will be *t* down
10:10 his lips will be *t* down
Isa 14:19 like a carcass *t* down
25:10 Moab must be *t* down in its
25:10 *t* down in a manure place
63:3 The wine trough I have *t*
La 1:15 Jehovah has *t* the very
2:4 He has *t* his bow like an enemy
3:12 He has *t* his bow, and he sets
Ho 4:14 a people . . . will be *t* down
Re 14:20 winepress was *t* outside the

Troop
2Ch 25:13 the members of the *t* whom

Troops
1Ch 7:4 were *t* of the army for war
12:18 among the heads of the *t*
2Ch 25:9 given to the *t* of Israel
25:10 *t* that had come to him
26:11 on military service in *t*
Job 19:12 Unitedly his *t* come and
25:3 Is there any number to his *t*?
29:25 as a king among his *t*

Jer 5:7 they go in *t*
Mt 27:27 gathered the whole body of *t*
Mr 15:16 called the whole body of *t*
Lu 14:31 with ten thousand *t* to cope

Trophimus
Ac 20:4 of Asia Tychicus and *T*
21:29 seen *T* the Ephesian in the
2Ti 4:20 I left *T* sick at Miletus

Trouble
Ge 41:51 made me forget all my *t*
Nu 23:21 And no *t* has he seen against
De 24:12 if the man is in *t*, you must
24:14 a hired laborer who is in *t*
24:15 he is in *t* and is lifting
26:7 our *t* and our oppression
Jg 10:16 because of the *t* of Israel
Job 3:10 so conceal *t* from my eyes
3:20 give light to one having *t*
4:8 those sowing *t* . . . reap it
5:6 from mere ground *t* does not
5:7 For man himself is born for *t*
7:3 night of *t* they have counted
11:16 you will forget *t* itself
15:35 There is a conceiving of *t*
Ps 7:14 conceived *t* and is bound to
7:16 *t* will return upon his own
10:7 Under his tongue are *t* and
10:14 have seen *t* and vexation
25:18 See my affliction and my *t*
55:10 hurtfulness and *t* are within
73:5 even in the *t* of mortal man
73:16 It was a *t* in my eyes
90:10 Yet their insistence is on *t*
94:20 it is framing *t* by decree
107:12 *t* he proceeded to subdue
140:9 *t* of their own lips cover
Pr 24:2 *t* is what their own lips keep
31:7 remember one's own *t* no more
Isa 10:1 have written out sheer *t*
53:11 Because of the *t* of his soul
59:4 has been a conceiving of *t*
Hab 1:3 you keep looking upon mere *t*
1:13 to look on *t* you are not able
Mt 26:10 try to make *t* for the woman
Mr 14:6 you try to make *t* for her
Lu 11:7 Quit making me *t*. The door is
18:5 continually making me *t*
Ac 15:19 *t* those from the nations who
15:24 caused you *t* with speeches
Ga 1:7 ones who are causing you *t*
5:10 one who is causing you *t*
6:17 no one be making *t* for me
Heb 12:15 may spring up and cause *t*

Troubled
Mt 14:26 the disciples were *t*, saying
26:37 grieved and to be sorely *t*
Mr 6:50 they all saw him and were *t*
14:33 stunned and to be sorely *t*
Lu 1:12 Zechariah became *t* at the
6:18 those *t* with unclean spirits
24:38 Why are you *t*, and why is
Joh 11:33 in the spirit and became *t*
12:27 Now my soul is *t*, and what
13:21 Jesus became *t* in spirit
14:1 not let your hearts be *t*
14:27 not let your hearts be *t*
Ac 5:16 those *t* with unclean spirits

Troubles
Eze 24:12 *T*! It has made one tired

Troublesome
Job 16:2 All of you are *t* comforters
Isa 7:25 cleared of *t* plants with a
Php 3:1 writing . . . is not *t* for me
2Ti 4:2 favorable season, in *t* season

Troubling
Da 4:9 no secret at all that is *t* you

Trough
Ge 24:20 into the drinking *t* and ran
De 28:5 basket and your kneading *t*
28:17 Cursed . . . your kneading *t*
Isa 63:3 The wine *t* I have trodden
Hag 2:16 fifty measures of the wine *t*

Troughs
Ge 30:38 in the water drinking *t*
Ex 8:3 frogs . . . into your kneading *t*
12:34 kneading *t* wrapped up in

True
Ge 5:22 walking with the *t* God
5:24 kept walking with the *t* God
Ge 6:2 the sons of the *t* God began to
6:4 sons of the *t* God continued to
6:9 Noah walked with the *t* God
6:11 in the sight of the *t* God
17:18 Abraham said to the *t* God
20:6 the *t* God said to him in the
20:17 supplication to the *t* God
22:1 *t* God put Abraham to the
22:3 the *t* God designated to him
22:9 *t* God had designated to him
24:48 led me in the *t* way to take
27:28 *t* God give you the dews of
31:11 angel of the *t* God said
31:13 I am the *t* God of Bethel
35:1 an altar there to the *t* God
35:3 make an altar to the *t* God
35:7 there the *t* God had revealed
41:25 What the *t* God is doing
41:28 What the *t* God is doing he
41:32 on the part of the *t* God
41:32 and the *t* God is speeding
42:18 I fear the *t* God
44:16 The *t* God has found out the
45:8 it was the *t* God, that he
46:3 I am the *t* God, the God of
48:15 The *t* God before whom my
48:15 The *t* God who has been
Ex 1:17 midwives feared the *t* God
1:21 midwives had feared the *t*
2:23 cry . . . up to the *t* God
3:1 the mountain of the *t* God
3:6 afraid to look at the *t* God
3:11 Moses said to the *t* God
3:12 people will serve the *t* God
3:13 Moses said to the *t* God
4:20 took the rod of the *t* God
4:27 the mountain of the *t* God
14:19 angel of the *t* God who was
17:9 with the rod of the *t* God
18:5 the mountain of the *t* God
18:12 before the *t* God
18:16 decisions of the *t* God and
18:19 before the *t* God, and you
18:19 the cases to the *t* God
19:3 Moses went up to the *t* God
19:17 to meet the *t* God, and
19:19 the *t* God began to answer
20:20 the *t* God has come, and in
20:21 cloud mass where the *t* God
21:6 bring him near to the *t* God
21:13 *t* God lets it occur at his
22:8 brought near to the *t* God to
22:9 is to come to the *t* God
23:17 the face of the *t* Lord
24:11 got a vision of the *t* God
24:13 the mountain of the *t* God
34:23 appear before the *t* Lord
Nu 22:10 Balaam said to the *t* God
23:27 in the eyes of the *t* God so
De 4:35 Jehovah is the *t* God; there
4:39 Jehovah is the *t* God in the
7:9 Jehovah your God is the *t* God
13:2 the portent does come *t*
18:22 does not occur or come *t*
33:1 Moses the man of the *t* God
33:26 is none like the *t* God of
Jos 14:6 Moses the man of the *t* God
21:45 it all came *t*
22:34 Jehovah is the *t* God
23:14 They have all come *t* for
24:1 stand before the *t* God
Jg 6:20 angel of the *t* God now said
6:36 said to the *t* God: If you
6:39 said to the *t* God: Do not
7:14 The *t* God has given Midian
13:6 a man of the *t* God that came
13:6 the angel of the *t* God
13:8 The man of the *t* God that you
13:9 *t* God listened to the voice
13:9 the angel of the *t* God came
13:12 Now let your words come *t*
13:17 when your word comes *t* we
16:28 you the *t* God, and let me
18:31 house of the *t* God continued
20:2 of the people of the *t* God
20:27 the ark . . . of the *t* God
21:2 sitting there before the *t* God
1Sa 4:4 with the ark . . . of the *t* God
4:13 over the ark of the *t* God
4:17 ark of the *t* God has been
4:18 the ark of the *t* God
4:19 the ark of the *t* God was
4:21 the ark of the *t* God's being
4:22 ark of the *t* God has been
1Sa 5:1 took the ark of the *t* God and
5:2 take the ark of the *t* God and
5:10 the ark of the *t* God to Ekron
5:10 the ark of the *t* God came to
5:11 hand of the *t* God had been
9:6 he says comes *t* without fail
9:7 bring to the man of the *t* God
9:8 to the man of the *t* God
9:10 the man of the *t* God was
10:3 up to the *t* God at Bethel
10:5 to the hill of the *t* God
10:7 the *t* God is with you
10:9 signs proceeded to come *t* on
14:18 bring the ark of the *t* God
14:18 ark of the *t* God proved to
14:36 approach here to the *t* God
2Sa 2:27 As the *t* God is living, if
6:2 ark of the *t* God, where a
6:3 ark of the *t* God ride upon a
6:4 with the ark of the *t* God
6:6 ark of the *t* God and grabbed
6:7 *t* God struck him down there
6:7 by the ark of the *t* God
6:12 of the ark of the *t* God
6:12 bring the ark of the *t* God
7:2 ark of the *t* God is dwelling
7:28 Jehovah, you are the *t* God
12:16 seek the *t* God in behalf
14:17 like an angel of the *t* God
14:20 angel of the *t* God so as to
15:24 ark of the covenant of the *t*
15:24 set the ark of the *t* God
15:25 Take the ark of the *t* God
15:29 took the ark of the *t* God
16:23 the word of the *t* God
19:27 an angel of the *t* God
22:31 *t* God, perfect is his way
22:33 *t* God is my strong fortress
22:48 The *t* God is the Giver of
1Ki 8:60 that Jehovah is the *t* God
10:6 *T* has the word proved to be
12:22 word of the *t* God came to
12:22 the man of the *t* God
13:4 the man of the *t* God that
13:5 the man of the *t* God had
13:6 said to the man of the *t* God
13:6 man of the *t* God softened
13:7 say to the man of the *t* God
13:8 the man of the *t* God said to
13:11 the man of the *t* God had
13:12 man of the *t* God that had
13:14 the man of the *t* God and
13:14 the man of the *t* God who
13:21 the man of the *t* God that
13:26 the man of the *t* God that
13:29 the man of the *t* God and to
13:31 man of the *t* God is buried
17:18 O man of the *t* God
17:24 word in your mouth is *t*
18:21 If Jehovah is the *t* God, go
18:24 *t* God that answers by fire
18:24 by fire is the *t* God
18:37 you, Jehovah, are the *t* God
18:39 Jehovah is the *t* God!
18:39 Jehovah is the *t* God!
19:8 mountain of the *t* God, Horeb
20:28 Then the man of the *t* God
2Ki 1:9 Man of the *t* God, the king
1:11 Man of the *t* God, this is
1:12 If I am a man of the *t* God
1:13 Man of the *t* God, please let
4:7 told the man of the *t* God
4:16 man of the *t* God! Do not
4:21 the man of the *t* God
4:22 man of the *t* God and return
4:25 man of the *t* God at Mount
4:25 man of the *t* God saw her
4:27 man of the *t* God at the
4:27 the man of the *t* God said
4:40 O man of the *t* God
4:42 to the man of the *t* God
5:8 Elisha the man of the *t* God
5:14 word of the man of the *t* God
5:15 to the man of the *t* God
5:20 Elisha the man of the *t* God
6:6 the man of the *t* God said
6:9 the man of the *t* God sent
6:10 man of the *t* God had said
6:15 the man of the *t* God rose
7:2 man of the *t* God and said
7:17 man of the *t* God had spoken
7:18 man of the *t* God had spoken
7:19 man of the *t* God and said
8:2 word of the man of the *t* God

Jg 11:10 In t the older men of Gilead
11:35 I am unable to t back
14:18 In t he said to them: If you
15:4 and t tail to tail and put one
15:7 In t Samson said to them
18:4 In t he said to them
19:11 let us t aside to this city
19:12 Let us not t aside to a city
19:18 In t he said to him: We are
20:8 nor shall we t aside any of
20:25 In t Benjamin came on out
Ru 1:16 t back from accompanying you
2:4 In t they would say to him
3:9 In t she said: I am Ruth your
3:18 how the matter will t out
4:1 Do t aside, do sit down here
1Sa 1:28 I, in my t, have lent him to
6:3 his hand would not t away
6:12 not t aside to the right or
10:16 In t Saul said to his uncle
11:3 In t the older men of Jabesh
12:20 not t aside from following
12:21 must not t aside to follow
13:17 The one band would t to the
13:18 the other band would t to
13:18 would t to the road to the
14:7 T where you wish to. Here I
14:47 and wherever he would t he
15:22 In t Samuel said
17:30 in t, the people gave him
17:45 In t David said to the
18:27 In t Saul gave him Michal
19:17 In t Michal said to Saul
20:11 In t Jonathan said to David
22:17 T and put to death the
22:18 t and assault the priests
23:2 In t Jehovah said to David
23:12 In t Jehovah said: They
26:21 In t Saul said: I have
28:22 in t, obey the voice of
2Sa 1:4 How did the matter t out?
1:22 of Jonathan did not t back
2:21 did not want to t aside
2:22 T your course aside from
2:23 he kept refusing to t aside
2:26 people to t back from
3:12 t to your side the whole of
5:6 will certainly t you away
12:13 Jehovah, in t, does let
14:24 t toward his own house, but
15:31 T, please, the counsel of
20:17 In t he said: I am
22:23 I shall not t aside from
1Ki 2:3 and everywhere that you t
2:16 Do not t my face away
2:17 he will not t your face away
2:20 Do not t my face away
2:20 I shall not t your face away
5:2 In t Solomon sent to Hiram
8:28 t toward the prayer of your
8:35 from their sin they t back
9:6 t back from following me and
10:3 Solomon, in t, went on to
12:10 In t the young men that
12:15 the t of affairs took place
13:33 not t back from his bad way
15:5 and he did not t aside from
17:3 must t your way eastward
20:11 In t the king of Israel
22:26 t him back to Amon the
22:34 T your hand around, and take
22:43 He did not t aside from it
2Ki 1:11 In t he answered and spoke
4:8 t aside there to eat bread
4:10 he can t aside there
9:23 made a t with his hands
10:29 Jehu did not t aside from
10:31 not t aside from the sins
12:11 In t they paid it out to
13:2 He did not t aside from it
13:13 In t Jehoash was buried in
17:13 T back from your bad ways
18:6 not t aside from following
18:14 T back from against me
18:24 t back the face of one
22:2 not t aside to the right or
22:15 In t she said to them
23:26 Jehovah did not t back from
1Ch 2:10 Amminadab, in t, became
2:11 Nahshon, in t, became father
2:11 Salma, in t, became father
2:12 Boaz, in t, became father to
2:12 Obed, in t, became father to
2:13 Jesse, in t, became father
1Ch 2:20 Hur, in t, became father to
2:20 Uri, in t, became father to
2:22 Segub, in t, became father
2:36 Attai, in t, became father
2:36 Nathan, in t, became father
2:37 Zabad, in t, became father
2:37 Ephlal, in t, became father
2:38 Obed, in t, became father to
2:38 Jehu, in t, became father to
2:39 Azariah, in t, became father
2:39 Helez, in t, became father
2:40 Eleasah, in t, became father
2:40 Sismai, in t, became father
2:41 Shallum, in t, became father
2:41 Jekamiah, in t, became
2:44 Shema, in t, became father
2:44 Rekem, in t, became father
4:2 Jahath, in t, became father
4:12 Eshton, in t, became father
6:5 Abishua, in t, became father
6:5 Bukki, in t, became father to
6:6 Uzzi, in t, became father to
6:6 Zerahiah, in t, became father
6:7 Amariah, in t, became father
6:8 Ahitub, in t, became father
6:8 Zadok, in t, became father to
6:9 Ahimaaz, in t, became father
6:9 Azariah, in t, became father
6:10 Johanan, in t, became father
6:11 Amariah, in t, became father
6:12 Ahitub, in t, became father
6:12 Zadok, in t, became father
6:13 Shallum, in t, became father
6:13 Hilkiah, in t, became father
6:14 Azariah, in t, became father
6:14 Seraiah, in t, became father
8:33 Kish, in t, became father to
8:33 Saul, in t, became father to
8:36 Jehoaddah, in t, became
8:36 Zimri, in t, became father
8:37 Moza, in t, became father to
9:39 Kish, in t, became father to
9:39 Saul, in t, became father to
9:42 Jarah, in t, became father
9:42 Zimri, in t, became father
12:23 to t the kingship of Saul
2Ch 6:19 t toward the prayer of your
6:26 from their sin they t back
6:42 Jehovah God, do not t back
7:14 t back from their bad ways
7:19 t back and actually leave my
8:15 not t aside from the king's
9:2 Solomon, in t, went on to
10:10 In t the young men that had
10:15 t of affairs from the true
18:25 Take Micaiah and t him back
18:33 T your hand around, and
20:32 did not t aside from it
24:20 he will, in t, leave you
24:23 t of the year a military
29:10 burning anger may t back
29:16 In t the Levites received
30:8 his burning anger may t back
30:9 not t away the face from you
34:2 t aside to the right or to
34:10 In t the doers of the work
34:23 In t she said to them
34:33 they did not t aside from
35:15 no need for them to t aside
35:22 Josiah did not t his face
Ne 2:4 In t the king said to me: What
9:35 did not t back from their bad
Es 2:12 t of each young woman arrived
2:15 t of Esther the daughter of
2:22 In t Esther talked to the king
5:4 In t Esther said: If to the
8:3 to t away the badness of Haman
Job 5:1 of the holy ones will you t
7:19 you not t your gaze from me
9:13 will not t back his anger
10:20 Let him t his gaze from me
14:6 T your gaze from upon him
15:13 t your spirit against God
15:30 not t away from darkness
15:30 t aside by a blast of His
21:5 T your faces to me and stare
21:14 say to the true God, T away
22:17 to the true God: T away
24:4 t aside the poor ones from
24:18 He will not t toward the
28:28 to t away from bad is
30:23 you will make me t back
33:17 t aside a man from his deed
33:30 t his soul back from the
Job 36:10 t back from what is hurtful
36:21 do not t to what is hurtful
39:22 t back on account of a
Ps 6:10 They will t back, they will
9:3 When my enemies t back, They
9:17 people will t back to Sheol
21:12 t their backs in flight
22:27 and t back to Jehovah
25:16 T your face to me, and show
27:9 in anger t your servant away
34:14 T away from what is bad
37:27 T away from what is bad and
40:14 t back and be humiliated
44:10 t back from the adversary
51:13 may t right back to you
56:9 my enemies will t back, on
59:5 t your attention to all the
69:16 multitude of your mercies t
70:2 t back and be humiliated who
78:38 he made his anger t back
80:18 shall not t back from you
81:14 I would t my hand
84:6 They t it into a spring itself
86:16 T to me and show me favor
89:32 t my attention to their
94:23 t back upon them their
102:17 t to the prayer of those
102:26 they will finish their t
106:23 t back his rage from
114:3 Jordan, it began to t back
114:5 that you began to t back
119:59 t back my feet to your
119:79 fearing you t back to me
119:132 T to me and show me favor
129:5 and t themselves back
132:10 t back the face of your
Pr 1:23 T back at my reproof
3:7 and t away from bad
4:5 not t aside from the sayings
4:15 t aside from it, and pass
5:7 not t away from the sayings of
7:25 heart not t aside to her ways
9:4 let him t aside here
9:16 let him t aside here
13:14 t one away from the snares
13:19 stupid ones to t away from
14:27 to t away from the snares of
15:24 order to t away from Sheol
16:17 is to t away from bad
22:6 grows old he will not t aside
24:18 certainly t back his anger
29:8 who are wise t back anger
30:30 t back from before anyone
Ec 8:12 t out well with those fearing
8:13 not t out well at all with
Ca 2:17 t around, O my dear one
6:5 T your eyes away from in front
Isa 1:25 will t back my hand upon you
6:10 t back and get healing for
8:11 t aside from walking in the
11:10 nations will t inquiringly
13:14 t, each one to his own
14:27 and who can t it back?
22:4 T your gaze away from me
23:17 will t his attention to
24:21 will t his attention upon
27:1 t his attention to Leviathan
27:3 t his attention against her
30:11 T aside from the way
36:9 t back the face of one
42:15 will t rivers into islands
42:16 t a dark place before them
43:13 and who can t it back?
43:18 do not t your consideration
45:22 T to me and be saved, all
50:5 I did not t in the opposite
52:11, 11 T away, t away, get out
52:15 must t their consideration
56:12 t out just as today, great
58:13 t back your foot as regards
66:4 in t, shall choose ways of
Jer 2:24 who can t her back?
3:19 you people will not t back
4:28 nor shall I t back from it
5:3 They refused to t back
6:8 soul may not t away disgusted
7:7 I, in t, shall certainly keep
8:4 If one would t back, will the
8:4 the other not also t back
8:5 they have refused to t back
13:16 will t it into thick gloom
15:5 t aside to ask about your
15:15 t your attention to me and
18:11 T back, please, each one

Jer 18:20 *t* back your rage from them
23:20 will not *t* back until he
23:22 *t* back from their bad way
23:34 I will also *t* my attention
25:5 *T* back, please, every one
26:6 in *t*, make this house like
27:8 *t* my attention upon that
29:10 I shall *t* my attention to
30:20 *t* my attention upon all his
30:24 *t* back until he will have
31:18 Cause me to *t* back, and
31:18 I shall readily *t* back, for
31:22 will you *t* this way and
32:5 until I *t* my attention to
32:40 not *t* back from behind them
32:40 not to *t* aside from me
34:15 *t* around today and do
34:16 *t* back and profane my name
35:15 *T* back, please, each one
38:27 In *t*, he told them
41:14 *t* around and return and
44:5 *t* back from their badness
44:20 In *t* Jeremiah said to all
47:3 not *t* around to the sons
49:8 I must *t* my attention to
50:16 *t* each one to his own
51:44 *t* my attention upon Bel in
51:47 *t* my attention upon the
51:52 *t* my attention upon her
La 2:14 order to *t* back your captivity
Eze 1:9 would not *t* when they went
1:12 would not *t* as they went
1:17 not *t* another way when they
3:19 *t* back from his wickedness
4:8 not *t* yourself from your one
7:22 to *t* away my face from them
13:22 not *t* back from his bad way
14:6 *t* yourselves back from your
14:6 *t* your faces back even from
16:42 my jealousy must *t* away
17:6 to *t* its foliage inward
18:21 *t* back from all his sins
18:23 should *t* back from his ways
18:30 *T* back, yes, cause a turning
23:17 *t* away disgusted from them
33:9 for him to *t* back from it
33:9 not *t* back from his way
33:11, 11 *T* back, *t* back from
36:9 shall certainly *t* toward you
38:4 *t* you around and put hooks
38:12 in order to *t* your hand back
39:2 *t* you around and lead you
Da 9:16 rage *t* back from your city
11:18 *t* his face back to the
11:18 make it *t* back upon that one
11:19 *t* his face back to the
Ho 2:9 *t* back and certainly take away
9:12 when I *t* away from them
Joe 2:14 whether he will *t* back and
Am 1:3 I shall not *t* it back
1:6 I shall not *t* it back, on
1:8 *t* my hand back upon Ekron
1:9 I shall not *t* it back
1:11 I shall not *t* it back
1:13 I shall not *t* it back
2:1 I shall not *t* it back
2:4 I shall not *t* it back
2:6 I shall not *t* it back
2:7 meek people they *t* aside
8:10 I will *t* your festivals into
Jon 3:9 the true God may *t* back and
3:9 *t* back from his burning anger
4:4 In *t* Jehovah said: Have you
Hab 3:17 may actually *t* out a failure
Zep 2:7 God will *t* his attention to
Hag 2:13 In *t* the priests answered
Zec 1:19 In *t* he said to me
2:2 In *t* he said to me
4:5 In *t* I said: No, my lord
4:13 In *t* I said: No, my lord
5:2 In *t* I said: I am seeing a
5:6 In *t* he said: This is the
5:11 In *t* he said to me: In order
13:7 *t* my hand back upon those
13:9 it, in its *t*, will say
Mal 4:6 *t* the heart of fathers back
Mt 5:25 not *t* you over to the judge
5:36 cannot *t* one hair white or
5:39 cheek, *t* the other also to
5:42 do not *t* away from one that
7:6 and *t* around and rip you open
13:15 and *t* back, and I heal them
14:19 disciples in *t* to the crowds
15:36 disciples in *t* to the crowds
Mt 18:3 *t* around and become as young
18:33 in *t*, to have had mercy on
21:27 He, in *t*, said to them
25:41 he will say, in *t*, to those
Mr 1:20 In *t* they left their father
4:12 ever *t* back and forgiveness
Lu 1:9 his *t* to offer incense when he
1:16 *t* back to Jehovah their God
1:17 *t* back the hearts of fathers
10:6 it will *t* back to you
20:20 *t* him over to the government
20:41 In *t* he said to them: How is
21:13 *t* out to you for a witness
Joh 7:16 Jesus, in *t*, answered them
7:47 In *t* the Pharisees answered
9:25 In *t* he answered: Whether
12:40 *t* around and I should heal
13:20 In *t* he that receives me
14:21 In *t* he that loves me will
15:27 you, in *t*, are to bear
Ac 3:19 *t* around so as to get your
4:35 In *t* distribution would be
8:3 he would *t* them over to prison
12:22 In *t* the assembled people
13:8 *t* the proconsul away from the
13:46 look! we *t* to the nations
14:15 for you to *t* from these vain
26:18 *t* them from darkness to
26:20 *t* to God by doing works
28:27 *t* back, and I should heal
Ro 5:4 endurance, in *t*, an approved
5:4 approved condition, in *t*, hope
10:14 How, in *t*, will they put
10:14 How, in *t*, will they hear
10:15 How, in *t*, will they preach
10:17 In *t* the thing heard is
11:26 *t* away ungodly practices
1Co 3:23 in *t* you belong to Christ
3:23 Christ, in *t*, belongs to God
11:3 in *t* the head of a woman is
11:3 in *t* the head of the Christ
Ga 4:5 we, in *t*, might receive the
Php 4:19 In *t*, my God will fully
Col 1:24 I, in my *t*, am filling up
1Th 1:5 did not *t* up among you with
1Ti 4:7 *t* down the false stories
5:11 *t* down younger widows, for
2Ti 2:2 in *t*, will be adequately
2:23 *t* down foolish and ignorant
3:5 and from these *t* away
4:4 *t* their ears away from the
Tit 1:14 *t* . . . away from the truth
Heb 12:25 if we *t* away from him who
Jas 1:15 in *t*, sin, when it has been
1Pe 3:11 *t* away from what is bad and
2Pe 2:21 to *t* away from the holy
Re 11:6 waters to *t* them into blood

Turnable

Eze 41:24 doors, the two being *t*

Turned

Ge 7:10 And seven days later it *t* out
9:23 their faces were *t* away
14:7 they *t* about and came to
18:22 At this point the men *t* from
19:3 they *t* aside to him and came
21:1 Jehovah *t* his attention to
29:23 *t* out that during the evening
30:40 *t* the faces of the flocks
33:16 Esau *t* back on his way to
38:16 he *t* aside to her by the road
38:28 it *t* out that when she was
39:2 he *t* out a successful man and
39:10 it *t* out that as she spoke to
40:20 on the third day it *t* out
41:13 it *t* out that just as he had
42:24 he *t* away from them and
42:28 *t* trembling to one another
Ex 2:12 he *t* this way and that and
3:4 that he *t* aside to inspect
4:31 Jehovah had *t* his attention
5:22 Moses *t* to Jehovah and said
7:15 rod that *t* into a serpent you
7:20 Nile River was *t* into blood
7:23 Pharaoh *t* and went into his
8:31 gadflies *t* away from Pharaoh
10:6 *t* and went out from Pharaoh
10:14 had never *t* up in this way
16:10 they *t* and faced toward the
32:8 *t* aside in a hurry from the
32:15 Moses *t* and went down from
Le 13:3 plague has *t* white and the
13:4 and its hair has not *t* white
13:10 it has *t* the hair white and
Le 13:13 All of it has *t* white
13:20 and its hair has *t* white
Nu 5:19 *t* aside in any uncleanness
5:20 *t* aside while under your
12:10 cloud *t* away from over the
12:10 Aaron *t* toward Miriam, and
14:9 Their shelter has *t* away from
14:43 you *t* back from following
16:42 *t* toward the tent of meeting
20:21 Israel *t* away from him
21:33 they *t* and went up by the
22:33 not *t* aside from before me
25:11 *t* back my wrath from upon
33:7 and *t* back toward Pihahiroth
De 1:24 they *t* and went up into the
2:1 Then we *t* and pulled away for
2:8 Next we *t* and passed on by the
3:1 we *t* and went up by the way of
9:12 They have *t* aside quickly
9:15 I *t* and went down from the
9:16 *t* aside quickly from the way
10:5 I *t* and went down from the
31:18 they have *t* to other gods
Jos 7:8 Israel has *t* his back before
7:26 *t* away from his hot anger
8:20 *t* upon the pursuers
8:21 *t* around and went striking
11:10 Joshua *t* about at that time
17:13 *t* out that when the sons of
Jg 2:17 They quickly *t* aside from
3:19 And he himself *t* back at the
4:18 So he *t* aside to her into the
6:38 it *t* out to be that way
7:6 *t* out to be three hundred men
14:8 he *t* aside to look at the
18:3 they *t* aside there
18:15 they *t* aside there and came
18:21 they *t* and went their way
18:23 they *t* their faces and said
18:26 he *t* and went back to his
19:15 they *t* aside there to go in
20:39 Israel *t* around in the battle
20:40 Benjamin *t* his face back
20:42 *t* before the men of Israel
20:45 they *t* and went fleeing to
20:47 six hundred men *t* and went
Ru 1:6 Jehovah had *t* his attention to
4:1 Hence he *t* aside and sat down
1Sa 2:21 Jehovah *t* his attention to
10:9 he *t* his shoulder to go from
15:11 *t* back from following me
15:12 he then *t* around and went
17:30 he *t* about from beside him
18:11 David *t* aside from before
22:18 Doeg the Edomite *t* and
23:28 Saul *t* back from chasing
25:12 men *t* around on their way
25:39 Jehovah has *t* back upon his
2Sa 1:7 *t* back and saw me, then he
2:30 Joab, he *t* back from
9:8 *t* your face to the dead dog
13:23 *t* out after two full years
14:24 Absalom *t* toward his own
18:7 the slaughter there *t* out to
1Ki 2:15 the kingship *t* and came to
6:34 the one door *t* on pivots
6:34 the other door *t* on pivots
8:14 the king *t* his face and began
10:13 she *t* about and went to her
18:37 have *t* their heart back
21:4 and kept his face *t*, and he
22:32 they *t* aside against him to
2Ki 2:24 *t* behind him and saw them
4:11 *t* aside to the roof chamber
5:12 he *t* and went away in a rage
5:26 man *t* to get down off his
13:23 *t* to them for the sake of
15:20 king of Assyria *t* back
20:2 *t* his face to the wall and
23:16 When Josiah *t*, he got to
24:1 he *t* back and rebelled
1Ch 10:14 *t* the kingship over to David
21:20 Ornan *t* back and saw the
2Ch 6:3 king *t* his face and began to
9:12 *t* about and went to her own
12:12 Jehovah's anger *t* back from
13:14 Judah *t* around, why, there
18:31 *t* around against him to
20:10 *t* away from them and did
20:24 *t* their faces toward the
25:27 Amaziah *t* aside from
26:20 priests *t* toward him, why
29:6 *t* around their face away
Ezr 6:11 be *t* into a public privy on

Ezr 6:22 *t* the heart of the king of
10:14 *t* back the burning anger of
Job 6:18 The paths . . . are *t* aside
19:13 have even *t* aside from me
19:19 loved have *t* against me
30:15 terrors have been *t* upon me
32:12 I kept my attention *t*
34:5 *t* aside the judgment of me
34:27 *t* aside from following him
37:12 it is being *t* round about
42:10 *t* back the captive condition
Ps 14:3 They have all *t* aside, they
35:4 be *t* back and be abashed who
40:4 *t* his face to defiant people
44:18 heart has not *t* faithlessly
53:3 They have all of them *t* back
65:9 *t* your attention to the earth
66:20 has not *t* aside my prayer
73:2 my feet had almost *t* aside
78:30 *t* aside from their desire
78:57 *t* around like a loose bow
81:6 *t* aside his shoulder even
85:3 *t* back from the heat of your
119:102 I have not *t* aside
Pr 17:20 *t* around in his tongue will
Ec 2:11 I, *t* toward all the works of
2:12 even I, *t* to see wisdom and
2:20 And I myself *t* around toward
7:25 I myself *t* around, even my
Ca 5:6 dear one himself had *t* away
6:1 Where has your dear one *t*
Isa 1:4 they have *t* backwards
5:25 his anger has not *t* back
9:12 his anger has not *t* back
9:17 his anger has not *t* back
9:21 his anger has not *t* back
10:4 his anger has not *t* back
12:1 your anger gradually *t* back
26:14 *t* your attention that you
26:16 *t* their attention to you
28:27 no wheel of a wagon is *t*
29:17 Lebanon must be *t* into an
38:2 Hezekiah *t* his face to the
42:17 They must be *t* back, they
53:6 his own way that we have *t*
56:11 *t* to their own way
Jer 2:27 *t* the back of the neck and
2:35 his anger has *t* back from me
4:8 anger of Jehovah has not *t*
5:23 *t* aside and keep walking in
5:25 errors have *t* these things
6:12 houses will certainly be *t*
12:10 have *t* my desirable share
14:8 *t* aside to spend the night
15:7 *t* back from their own ways
18:4 *t* back and went making it
23:2 not *t* your attention to them
30:6 and all faces have *t* pale
34:11 *t* about after that and
46:5 they have not *t* around
48:39 O how Moab has *t* the back!
49:24 She has *t* to flee, and
50:18 *t* my attention upon the
La 1:13 He has *t* me backward. He has
2:3 has *t* his right hand back from
2:8 has not *t* back his hand from
4:6 to which no hands *t* helpfully
4:22 *t* his attention to your error
5:2 has been *t* over to strangers
Eze 6:9 heart that has *t* aside from
23:18 my soul *t* away disgusted
23:18 had *t* away disgusted from
23:22 has *t* away in disgust
23:28 has *t* away disgusted
Da 2:5 your own houses will be *t*
3:29 be *t* into a public privy
10:16 convulsions were *t* within
Ho 7:8 cake not *t* on the other side
14:4 my anger has *t* back from him
Joe 2:31 The sun . . . *t* into darkness
Am 5:12 have *t* aside poor people even
6:12 you people have *t* justice
Jon 3:10 *t* back from their bad way
Zep 3:15 He has *t* away your enemy
Zec 10:3 *t* his attention to his drove
Mal 2:6 whom he *t* back from error
2:8 have *t* aside from the way
3:7 *t* aside from my regulations
Mt 8:34 city *t* out to meet Jesus
9:22 Jesus *t* around and, noticing
18:6 millstone such as is *t* by an
27:3 *t* the thirty silver pieces
Mr 1:4 John the baptizer *t* up in the
5:30 he *t* about in the crowd and
Mr 8:33 He *t*, looked at his disciples
9:42 such as is *t* by an ass
Lu 1:68 *t* his attention and performed
4:1 *t* away from the Jordan, and he
6:16 Judas Iscariot, who *t* traitor
7:9 *t* to the crowd following him
7:16 God has *t* his attention
7:44 he *t* to the woman and said to
8:35 people *t* out to see what had
8:37 aboard the boat and *t* away
9:55 But he *t* and rebuked them
10:23 he *t* to the disciples by
14:25 and he *t* and said to them
17:15 *t* back, glorifying God with
17:18 that *t* back to give glory to
22:61 Lord *t* and looked upon Peter
23:28 Jesus *t* to the women and
24:5 their faces *t* to the ground
Joh 1:38 Jesus *t* and, getting a view
2:9 water . . . *t* into wine
4:46 had *t* the water into wine
5:13 for Jesus had *t* aside
16:20 grief will be *t* into joy
20:14 she *t* back and viewed Jesus
Ac 2:20 sun will be *t* into darkness
7:39 in their hearts they *t* back
7:42 God *t* and handed them over
8:25 they *t* back to Jerusalem
9:35 and these *t* to the Lord
11:21 believers *t* to the Lord
15:14 first time *t* his attention
16:18 and *t* and said to the spirit
19:26 *t* them to another opinion
Ro 1:23 and *t* the glory of the
11:5 remnant has *t* up according
Php 1:12 *t* out for the advancement
1Th 1:9 you *t* to God from your idols
2:5 at no time have we *t* up
3:5 have *t* out to be in vain
1Ti 1:6 been *t* aside into idle talk
5:15 been *t* aside to follow Satan
2Ti 1:15 of Asia have *t* away from me
4:4 be *t* aside to false stories
Tit 3:11 such a man has been *t* out of
Jas 4:9 laughter be *t* into mourning
Re 1:12 I *t* to see the voice that
1:12 having *t*, I saw seven golden
8:11 waters *t* into wormwood, and

Turning

Ge 3:24 sword that was *t* itself
De 29:18 heart is *t* today away from
Jos 15:7 *t* northward to Gilgal
22:16 in *t* back today from
23:6 by never *t* away from it to
Jg 7:13 barley bread *t* over and over
7:13 it went *t* it upside down, and
19:26 as it was *t* to morning
1Sa 15:27 Samuel was *t* about to go
2Ki 21:13 clean and *t* it upside down
Es 9:1 was even a *t* to the contrary
Job 1:1 and *t* aside from bad
1:8 and *t* aside from bad
2:3 and *t* aside from bad
Ps 78:57 kept *t* back and acting
125:5 *t* aside to their crooked
Pr 11:22 is *t* away from sensibleness
14:16 and is *t* away from badness
18:5 *t* aside of the righteous one
26:14 A door keeps *t* upon its pivot
28:9 He that is *t* his ear away
Isa 7:17 Ephraim's *t* away from
28:6 *t* away the battle from the
44:25 One *t* wise men backwards
59:15 anyone *t* away from badness
59:20 those *t* from transgression
Jer 11:22 *t* my attention upon them
21:4 *t* in reverse the weapons of
23:2 I am *t* my attention upon you
27:22 *t* my attention to them
29:32 I am *t* my attention upon
31:19 after my *t* back I felt
32:33 kept *t* to me the back and
44:29 *t* my attention upon you in
46:5 They are *t* back, and their
46:25 *t* my attention upon Amon
50:18 I am *t* my attention upon
La 3:35 *t* aside the judgment of an
Eze 18:30 cause a *t* back from all
18:32 So cause a *t* back and keep
29:16 by their *t* after them
33:12 *t* back from his wickedness
41:7 widening out and *t* around
Da 9:5 been a *t* aside from your
Da 9:11 *t* aside by not obeying your
9:13 *t* back from our error and by
Ho 3:1 *t* to other gods and are loving
7:14 they kept *t* against me
Am 5:7 *t* justice into mere wormwood
5:8 the One *t* deep shadow into the
Na 2:8 But there is no one *t* back
Hag 2:17 no one with you *t* to me
Mal 2:13 no more a *t* toward the gift
3:5 *t* away the alien resident
Mt 16:23 *t* his back, he said to Peter
Joh 20:16 *t* around, she said to him
21:20 Upon *t* about Peter saw
Ac 3:26 by *t* each one away from your
9:40 and, *t* to the body, he said
12:4 *t* him over to four shifts of
15:19 the nations who are *t* to God
2Co 3:16 when there is a *t* to Jehovah
Ga 4:9 you are *t* back again to the
1Ti 6:20 *t* away from the empty
Jas 1:17 of the *t* of the shadow
Jude 4 *t* the undeserved kindness of

Turns

Ge 27:45 anger of your brother *t* away
Le 20:6 who *t* himself to the spirit
Nu 5:12 man's wife *t* aside in that
De 30:17 if your heart *t* away and you
1Sa 17:26 *t* away reproach from upon
2Ki 11:6 watch over the house by *t*
Job 14:13 until your anger *t* back
23:9 He *t* aside to the right, but
Pr 15:1 when mild, *t* away rage, but
16:6 in the fear of Jehovah one *t*
17:8 Everywhere that he *t* he has
20:26 *t* around upon them a wheel
21:1 that he delights to, he *t* it
Isa 44:25 *t* even their knowledge into
Jer 13:21 *t* his attention upon you
17:5 heart *t* away from Jehovah
18:8 *t* back from its badness
La 1:8 is also sighing and *t* her back
3:3 repeatedly *t* his hand all day
Eze 3:20 someone righteous *t* back
18:24 someone righteous *t* back
18:26 someone righteous *t* back
18:27 someone wicked *t* back from
18:28 When he sees and he *t* back
33:11 wicked *t* back from his way
33:14 *t* back from his sin and
33:18 someone righteous *t* back
33:19 someone wicked *t* back from
Ho 1:2 land positively *t* from
Lu 12:54 is coming, and it *t* out so
1Co 14:27 and in *t*; and let someone
Heb 13:7 how their conduct *t* out
Jas 5:19 and another *t* him back
5:20 he who *t* a sinner back from

Turquoise

Ex 28:18 second row is *t*, sapphire
39:11 second row was *t*, sapphire
Eze 27:16 For *t*, wool dyed reddish
28:13 sapphire, *t* and emerald

Turtledove

Ge 15:9 Take for me a . . . *t* and a
Le 12:6 a *t* for a sin offering to the
Ps 74:19 the soul of your *t*
Ca 2:12 *t* itself has been heard in our
Jer 8:7 the *t* and the swift and the

Turtledoves

Le 1:14 his offering from the *t*
5:7 two *t* or two male pigeons to
5:11 not have the means for two *t*
12:8 two *t* or two male pigeons
14:22 two *t* or two male pigeons
14:30 one of the *t* or of the male
15:14 take for himself two *t* or
15:29 take for herself two *t* or
Nu 6:10 two *t* or two male pigeons to
Lu 2:24 A pair of *t* or two young

Tutor

Ga 3:24 our *t* leading to Christ
3:25 we are no longer under a *t*

Tutors

1Co 4:15 ten thousand *t* in Christ, you

Twelfth

Nu 7:78 On the *t* day . . . Naphtali
1Ki 19:19 and he with the *t*
2Ki 8:25 the *t* year of Jehoram the
17:1 In the *t* year of Ahaz the
25:27 in the *t* month, on the

1Ch 24:12 for Jakim the *t*
25:19 the *t* for Hashabiah, his
27:15, 15 The *t* for the *t* month
2Ch 34:3 in the *t* year he started to
Ezr 8:31 *t* day of the first month to
Es 3:7 in the *t* year of King Ahasuerus
3:7 the *t*, that is, the month Adar
3:13 thirteenth day of the *t* month
8:12 thirteenth day of the *t* month
9:1 *t* month, that is . . . Adar
Jer 52:31 in the *t* month, on the
Eze 29:1 on the *t* day of the month
32:1, 1 *t* year, in the *t* month
32:17 *t* year, on the fifteenth
33:21 the *t* year, in the tenth
Re 21:20 hyacinth, the *t* amethyst

Twelve
Ge 5:8 Seth . . . nine hundred and *t*
14:4 *T* years they had served
17:20 produce *t* chieftains, and I
25:16 *t* chieftains according to
35:22 came to be *t* sons of Jacob
42:13 Your servants are *t* brothers
42:32 We are *t* brothers, the sons
49:28 the *t* tribes of Israel, and
Ex 15:27 were *t* springs of water and
24:4 *t* pillars corresponding with
24:4 with the *t* tribes of Israel
28:21 *t* according to their names
28:21 its name, for the *t* tribes
39:14 *t* according to their names
39:14 to its name for the *t* tribes
Le 24:5 *t* ring-shaped cakes. Two
Nu 1:44 chieftains of Israel, *t* men
7:3 and *t* cattle, a wagon for two
7:84 *t* silver dishes
7:84 offering . . . *t* silver bowls
7:84 offering . . . *t* gold cups
7:86 *t* gold cups full of incense
7:87 burnt offering being *t* bulls
7:87 burnt offering . . . *t* rams
7:87 offering . . . *t* male lambs
7:87 *t* kids of the goats for a sin
17:2 *t* rods. You will write the
17:6 house of their fathers, *t* rods
29:17 the second day *t* young bulls
31:5 *t* thousand equipped for the
33:9 in Elim there were *t* springs
De 1:23 I took *t* men of yours, one
Jos 3:12 *t* men from the tribes of
4:2 *t* men from the people, one
4:3 *t* stones, and you must carry
4:4 Joshua called *t* men whom he
4:8 *t* stones from the middle of
4:9 also *t* stones that Joshua
4:20 As for the *t* stones that
8:25 *t* thousand, all the people of
18:24 *t* cities and their
19:15 *t* cities and their
21:7 *t* cities out of the tribe of
21:40 as their lot, *t* cities
Jg 19:29 into *t* pieces and sent her
21:10 to send *t* thousand of the
2Sa 2:15 *t* belonging to Benjamin and
2:15 *t* from the servants of David
10:6 and Ishtob, *t* thousand men
17:1 *t* thousand men and rise up
1Ki 4:7 Solomon had *t* deputies over
4:26 and *t* thousand horsemen
7:15 a string of *t* cubits would
7:25 It was standing upon *t* bulls
7:44 *t* bulls beneath the sea
10:20 *t* lions standing there upon
10:26 and *t* thousand steeds
11:30 ripped it into *t* pieces
16:23 Omri . . . for *t* years
18:31 So Elijah took *t* stones
19:19 plowing with *t* spans before
2Ki 3:1 Jehoram . . . reign for *t* years
21:1 *T* years old was Manasseh
1Ch 6:63 sons of Merari . . . *t* cities
9:22 were two hundred and *t*
15:10 Uzziel . . . a hundred and *t*
25:9 and his sons were *t*
25:10 the third for Zaccur . . . *t*
25:11 the fourth for Izri . . . *t*
25:12 fifth for Nethaniah . . . *t*
25:13 the sixth for Bukkiah . . . *t*
25:14 seventh for Jesharelah . . . *t*
25:15 eighth for Jeshaiah . . . *t*
25:16 ninth for Mattaniah . . . *t*
25:17 the tenth for Shimei . . . *t*
25:18 eleventh for Azarel . . . *t*
1Ch 25:19 twelfth for Hashabiah . . . *t*
25:20 thirteenth, Shubael . . . *t*
25:21 Mattithiah . . . *t*
25:22 for Jeremoth . . . *t*
25:23 for Hananiah . . . *t*
25:24 for Joshbekashah . . . *t*
25:25 eighteenth, for Hanani . . . *t*
25:26 for Mallothi . . . *t*
25:27 for Eliathah . . . *t*
25:28 for Hothir . . . *t*
25:29 for Giddalti . . . *t*
25:30 for Mahazioth . . . *t*
25:31 for Romamti-ezer . . . *t*
2Ch 1:14 and *t* thousand steeds and he
4:4 It was standing upon *t* bulls
4:15 sea and the *t* bulls under it
9:19 *t* lions standing there upon
9:25 *t* thousand steeds, and he
12:3 *t* hundred chariots and with
33:1 *T* years old was Manasseh
Ezr 2:6 thousand eight hundred and *t*
2:18 of Jorah, a hundred and *t*
6:17 *t* male goats, according to
8:24 the chiefs of the priests *t*
8:35 *t* bulls for all Israel
8:35 *t* he-goats as a sin offering
Ne 5:14 *t* years, I myself and my
7:24 of Hariph, a hundred and *t*
Es 2:12 regulation for *t* months, for
Ps 60:*super* even *t* thousand
Jer 52:20 *t* copper bulls that were
52:21 thread of *t* cubits itself
Eze 43:16 altar hearth is *t* cubits
43:16 with *t* cubits of width
47:13 for the *t* tribes of Israel
47:21 to the *t* tribes of Israel
Da 4:29 the end of *t* lunar months he
Mt 9:20 a woman suffering *t* years
10:1 he summoned his *t* disciples
10:2 names of the *t* apostles are
10:5 These *t* Jesus sent forth
11:1 instructions . . . *t* disciples
14:20 of fragments, *t* baskets full
19:28 sit upon *t* thrones, judging
19:28 judging the *t* tribes of
20:17 Jesus took the *t* disciples
26:14 one of the *t*, the one called
26:20 with the *t* disciples
26:47 Judas, one of the *t*, came
26:53 than *t* legions of angels
Mr 3:14 And he formed a group of *t*
3:16 the group of *t* that he formed
4:10 those around him with the *t*
5:25 to a flow of blood *t* years
5:42 for she was *t* years old
6:7 Now he summoned the *t*, and he
6:43 fragments, *t* baskets full
8:19 They said to him: *T*
9:35 called the *t* and said to them
10:32 he took the *t* aside and
11:11 out to Bethany with the *t*
14:10 Judas Iscariot, one of the *t*
14:17 he came with the *t*
14:20 It is one of the *t*, who is
14:43 Judas, one of the *t*, arrived
Lu 2:42 when he became *t* years old
6:13 and chose from among them *t*
8:1 And the *t* were with him
8:42 daughter about *t* years old
8:43 a flow of blood for *t* years
9:1 he called the *t* together and
9:12 The *t* now came up and said
9:17 *t* baskets of fragments
18:31 he took the *t* aside and said
22:3 who was numbered among the *t*
22:30 judge the *t* tribes of Israel
22:47 Judas, one of the *t*, was
Joh 6:13 *t* baskets with fragments
6:67 Jesus said to the *t*: You do
6:70 I chose you *t*, did I not?
6:71 although one of the *t*
11:9 *t* hours of daylight, are
20:24 Thomas, one of the *t*, who
Ac 6:2 *t* called the multitude of the
7:8 Jacob of the *t* family heads
19:7 there were about *t* men
24:11 not been more than *t* days
26:7 *t* tribes are hoping to attain
1Co 15:5 to Cephas, then to the *t*
Jas 1:1 *t* tribes that are scattered
Re 7:5 Out . . . of Judah *t* thousand
7:5 out . . . Reuben *t* thousand
7:5 out . . . of Gad *t* thousand
7:6 out . . . of Asher *t* thousand
Re 7:6 out . . . of Naphtali *t* thousand
7:6 out . . . of Manasseh *t* thousand
7:7 out of . . . Simeon *t* thousand
7:7 out of . . . Levi *t* thousand
7:7 out . . . of Issachar *t* thousand
7:8 out of . . . Zebulun *t* thousand
7:8 out . . . of Joseph *t* thousand
7:8 out . . . of Benjamin *t* thousand
12:1 head was a crown of *t* stars
21:12 lofty wall and had *t* gates
21:12 and at the gates *t* angels
21:12 *t* tribes of the sons of
21:14 also had *t* foundation stones
21:14 and on them the *t* names of
21:14 the *t* apostles of the Lamb
21:16 *t* thousand furlongs; its
21:21, 21 *t* gates were *t* pearls
22:2 producing *t* crops of fruit

Twentieth
Nu 10:11 *t* day in the month, the
1Ki 15:9 the *t* year of Jeroboam the
2Ki 15:30 in the *t* year of Jotham
1Ch 24:16 for Jehezkel the *t*
25:27 for the *t*, for Eliathah, his
Ezr 10:9 ninth month on the *t* day
Ne 1:1 month Chislev, in the *t* year
2:1 *t* year of Artaxerxes the king
5:14 *t* year to the thirty-second

Twenty
Ge 6:3 amount to a hundred and *t*
18:31 Suppose *t* are found there
18:31 to ruin on account of the *t*
31:38 *t* years I have been with you
31:41 *t* years for me in your house
32:14 *t* he-goats, two hundred
32:14 female sheep and *t* rams
32:15 ten bulls, *t* she-asses and
37:28 for *t* silver pieces
Ex 26:18 *t* panel frames for the side
26:19 under the *t* panel frames
26:20 side, *t* panel frames
27:10 And its *t* pillars and their
27:10 *t* socket pedestals are of
27:11 and its *t* pillars and their
27:11 their *t* socket pedestals
27:16 is a screen *t* cubits long
30:13 *T* gerahs equal a shekel
30:14 registered from *t* years old
36:23 *t* panel frames for the side
36:24 beneath the *t* panel frames
36:25 he made *t* panel frames
38:10 Their *t* pillars and their
38:10 *t* socket pedestals were of
38:11 Their *t* pillars and their
38:11 *t* socket pedestals were of
38:18 and *t* cubits was the length
38:26 from *t* years of age and
Le 27:3 male from *t* years old up to
27:5 up to *t* years old, the
27:5 must then become *t* shekels
27:25 should amount to *t* gerahs
Nu 1:3 *t* years old upward, everyone
1:18 *t* years old upward, head by
1:20 sons of Reuben . . . *t* years old
1:22 sons of Simeon . . . *t* years
1:24 sons of Gad . . . *t* years old
1:26 sons of Judah . . . *t* years old
1:28 sons of Issachar . . . *t* years
1:30 sons of Zebulun . . . *t* years
1:32 sons of Ephraim . . . *t* years
1:34 sons of Manasseh . . . *t* years
1:36 sons of Benjamin . . . *t* years
1:38 sons of Dan . . . *t* years old
1:40 sons of Asher . . . *t* years old
1:42 sons of Naphtali . . . *t* years
1:45 sons of Israel . . . *t* years old
3:47 A shekel is *t* gerahs
7:86 being a hundred and *t* shekels
11:19 nor ten days nor *t* days
14:29 from *t* years old upward, you
18:16 It is *t* gerahs
26:2 Israel from *t* years of age
26:4 the age of *t* years and upward
32:11 from *t* years old upward
De 31:2 A hundred and *t* years old I
34:7 a hundred and *t* years old at
Jg 4:3 Israel with harshness *t* years
8:10 a hundred and *t* thousand men
11:33 *t* cities—and as far as
15:20 the Philistines *t* years
16:31 he had judged Israel *t* years
1Sa 7:2 that they amounted to *t* years
14:14 about *t* men within about

Joh 8:17 The witness of *t* men is true
11:6 remained *t* days in the place
11:18 distance of about *t* miles
19:18 and *t* other men with him
20:4 *t* together began to run
20:12 *t* angels in white sitting
21:2 and *t* others of his disciples
Ac 1:10 *t* men in white garments
1:23 So they put up *t*, Joseph
1:24 which one of these *t* men you
4:1 while the *t* were speaking to
5:8 did you *t* sell the field for
5:9 agreed upon between you *t* to
7:29 became the father of *t* sons
9:38 *t* men to him to entreat him
10:7 *t* of his house servants and
12:6 sleeping bound with *t* chains
12:6 between *t* soldiers, and
16:36 that you *t* might be released
19:10 This took place for *t* years
19:22 *t* of those who ministered to
19:34 shouted for about *t* hours
21:33 to be bound with *t* chains
23:23 *t* of the army officers and
23:23 Get *t* hundred soldiers ready
23:23 *t* hundred spearmen, at the
24:27 when *t* years had elapsed
27:37 *t* hundred and seventy-six
28:30 *t* years in his own hired
1Co 6:16 The *t*, says he, will be one
14:27 limited to *t* or three at
14:29 let *t* or three prophets
2Co 13:1 the mouth of *t* witnesses or
Ga 4:22 Abraham acquired *t* sons, one
4:24 these women mean *t* covenants
Eph 2:14 who made the *t* parties one
2:15 create the *t* peoples in union
5:31 the *t* will become one flesh
Php 1:23 pressure from these *t* things
1Ti 5:19 only on the evidence of *t* or
2Ti 3:9 madness of those *t* men became
Heb 6:18 *t* unchangeable things
10:28 testimony of *t* or three
Re 9:12 *T* more woes are coming after
9:16 was *t* myriads of myriads
11:3 my *t* witnesses to prophesy
11:3 a thousand *t* hundred and sixty
11:4 symbolized by the *t* olive
11:4 trees and the *t* lampstands
11:10 these *t* prophets tormented
12:6 thousand *t* hundred and sixty
12:14 *t* wings of the great eagle
13:11 it had *t* horns like a lamb

Two-colored
Eze 27:24 and in carpets of *t* stuff

Two-edged
Ps 149:6 *t* sword be in their hand
Pr 5:4 it is as sharp as a *t* sword
Heb 4:12 is sharper than any *t* sword
Re 1:16 *t* sword was protruding, and
2:12 has the sharp, long *t* sword

Two-handled
1Sa 2:14 or the *t* cooking pot or the

Two-leaved
Isa 45:1 open before him the *t* doors

Twos
Ge 7:9 they went in by *t* to Noah
Lu 10:1 and sent them forth by *t* in

Tychicus
Ac 20:4 from the district of Asia *T*
Eph 6:21 *T*, a beloved brother and
Col 4:7 *T*, my beloved brother and
2Ti 4:12 have sent *T* off to Ephesus
Tit 3:12 I send Artemas or *T* to you

Tying
Ge 49:11 *T* his full-grown ass to a
Ex 28:8 is upon it for *t* it close
39:5 the girdle . . . for *t* it close

Type
1Ch 16:5 instruments of the string *t*

Typical
Heb 8:5 *t* representation and a shadow
9:23 *t* representations of the

Tyrannical
Ps 86:14 assembly of *t* ones have
Isa 25:3 the town of the *t* nations
25:4 blast of the *t* ones is like
25:5 *t* ones becomes suppressed
Jer 15:21 the palm of the *t* ones

Tyrannically
De 21:14 You must not deal *t* with her
24:7 has dealt *t* with him and sold

Tyrannize
Isa 3:5 people will actually *t* one

Tyrannus
Ac 19:9 in the school auditorium of *T*

Tyranny
Ex 1:13 sons of Israel slave under *t*
1:14 used them as slaves under *t*
Le 25:43 tread down upon him with *t*
25:46 one upon the other, with *t*
25:53 not tread him down with *t*
Eze 34:4 subjection, even with *t*

Tyrant
Job 15:20 years . . . reserved for the *t*
Ps 37:35 I have seen the wicked a *t*
Isa 29:20 *t* must reach his end, and
49:24 captives of the *t* make
49:25 already taken by the *t*

Tyrants
Job 6:23 out of the hand of *t* you men
27:13 inheritance of the *t* they
Ps 54:3 And *t* that do seek my soul
Pr 11:16 *t*, for their part, take hold
Isa 13:11 of the *t* I shall abase
29:5 crowd of the *t* just like the
Eze 28:7 the *t* of the nations, and
30:11 the *t* of the nations, are
31:12 the *t* of the nations
32:12 the *t* of the nations, all

Tyre
Jos 19:29 as the fortified city of *T*
2Sa 5:11 Hiram the king of *T*
24:7 came to the fortress of *T*
1Ki 5:1 Hiram the king of *T* proceeded
7:13 and fetch Hiram out of *T*
9:11 Hiram the king of *T* had
9:12 Hiram went out from *T* to see
1Ch 14:1 And Hiram the king of *T*
2Ch 2:3 sent to Hiram the king of *T*
2:11 Hiram the king of *T* said the
2:14 whose father was a man of *T*
Ps 45:12 daughter of *T* also with a
83:7 with the inhabitants of *T*
87:4 and *T*, together with Cush
Isa 23:1 The pronouncement of *T*
23:5 pains at the report on *T*
23:8 this counsel against *T*
23:15 *T* must be forgotten seventy
23:15 happen to *T* as in the song
23:17 turn his attention to *T*
Jer 25:22 all the kings of *T* and all
27:3 to the king of *T* and to the
47:4 to cut off from *T* and from
Eze 26:2 *T* has said against Jerusalem
26:3 I am against you, O *T*, and
26:4 bring the walls of *T* to ruin
26:7 against *T* Nebuchadrezzar the
26:15 said to *T*, At the sound of
27:2 concerning *T* a dirge
27:3 and you must say to *T*
27:3 O *T*, you yourself have said
27:8 Your skilled ones, O *T*
27:32 Who is like *T*, like her
28:2 say to the leader of *T*
28:12 concerning the king of *T*
29:18 a great service against *T*
29:18 his military force from *T*
Ho 9:13 like *T* planted in a pasture
Joe 3:4 O *T* and Sidon and all you
Am 1:9 account of three revolts of *T*
1:10 a fire onto the wall of *T*
Zec 9:2 *T* and Sidon, for she is very
9:3 *T* proceeded to build a
Mt 11:21 taken place in *T* and Sidon
11:22 be more endurable for *T* and
15:21 the parts of *T* and Sidon
Mr 3:8 *T* and Sidon, a great multitude
7:24 went into the regions of *T*
7:31 back out of the regions of *T*
Lu 6:17 the maritime country of *T* and
10:13 taken place in *T* and Sidon
10:14 more endurable for *T* and
Ac 12:20 the people of *T* and of Sidon
21:3 on to Syria, and landed at *T*
21:7 completed the voyage from *T*

Tyrian
1Ki 7:14 and his father was a *T* man

Tyrians
1Ch 22:4 *T* brought in cedar timbers
Ezr 3:7 to the Sidonians and the *T*
Ne 13:16 *T* . . . dwelt in the city

Ucal
Pr 30:1 to Ithiel, to Ithiel and *U*

Udder
La 4:3 jackals . . . presented the *u*

Uel
Ezr 10:34 sons of Bani . . . and *U*

Ugly
Ge 41:3 seven other cows . . . *u*
41:4 the cows that were *u* in

Ulai
Da 8:2 be by the watercourse of *U*
8:16 man in the midst of the *U*

Ulam
1Ch 7:16 his sons were *U* and Rekem
7:17 And the sons of *U* were Bedan
8:39 of Eshek . . . *U* his firstborn
8:40 sons of *U* came to be valiant

Ulcer
Jer 30:13 your cause, for your *u*
Ho 5:13 his sickness, and Judah his *u*
5:13 an *u* with any cure
Re 16:2 hurtful and malignant *u* came

Ulcers
Lu 16:20 put at his gate, full of *u*
16:21 would come and lick his *u*
Re 16:11 their pains and for their *u*

Ulla
1Ch 7:39 the sons of *U* were Ara and

Ummah
Jos 19:30 and *U* and Aphek and Rehob

Unable
Ge 24:50 We are *u* to speak bad or good
45:3 his brothers were *u* to answer
48:10 He was *u* to see. Accordingly
Ex 7:21 the Egyptians were *u* to drink
7:24 *u* to drink . . . of the Nile
8:18 forth gnats, but they were *u*
9:11 were *u* to stand before Moses
18:18 are *u* to do it by yourself
De 9:28 *u* to bring them into the land
Jg 11:35 and I am *u* to turn back
12:6 as he was *u* to say the word
14:13 if you are *u* to tell it to
14:14 *u* to tell the riddle for
Ru 4:6 I am *u* to repurchase it for
1Sa 4:15 set so that he was *u* to see
17:39 am *u* to go in these things
1Ki 8:11 priests were *u* to stand to
9:21 *u* to devote to destruction
14:4 Ahijah himself was *u* to see
2Ch 7:2 priests were *u* to enter into
Ezr 2:59 proved *u* to tell the house
Ps 21:11 that they are *u* to carry out
36:12 and have been *u* to get up
Ec 8:17 they would be *u* to find out
Isa 7:1 proved *u* to war against it
29:11 I am *u*, for it is sealed
46:2 *u* to furnish escape for the
57:20 when it is *u* to calm down
59:14 is straightforward is *u* to
Jer 6:10 they are *u* to pay attention
14:9 that is *u* to do any saving
20:9 and I was *u* to endure it
36:5 *u* to enter into the house
La 1:14 against whom I am *u* to rise
Eze 17:14 *u* to lift itself up, that by
Da 2:27 are *u* to show to the king
4:18 *u* to make known to me the
Ho 5:13 *u* to give healing to you
Jon 1:13 they were *u*, because the sea
Lu 8:19 *u* to get to him because of
13:11 was *u* to raise herself up
Ac 21:34 *u* himself to learn anything
25:7 they were *u* to show evidence
2Pe 2:14 *u* to desist from sin, and

Unacquainted
Heb 5:13 is *u* with the word of

Unadulterated
1Pe 2:2 form a longing for the *u* milk

Unanimous
Ac 15:25 we have come to a *u* accord

Unanimously
Ex 19:8 all the people answered *u* and
Jos 9:2 against Joshua and Israel *u*
1Ki 22:13 the prophets are *u* of good
2Ch 18:12 *u* of good to the king

Unanswered
Job 11:2 a multitude of words go *u*

Unapproachable
Jer 51:53 height of her strength *u*
1Ti 6:16 who dwells in *u* light

Unattainable
Ge 11:6 nothing . . . will be *u* for
Job 42:2 no idea that is *u* for you
Isa 22:10 to make the wall *u*

Unavoidable
Lu 17:1 It is *u* that causes for

Unbelievable
Ac 26:8 it judged *u* among you men

Unbeliever
1Co 14:24 and any *u* or ordinary person
2Co 6:15 person have with an *u*

Unbelievers
Ro 15:31 *u* in Judea and that my
1Co 6:6 goes to court . . . before *u*
10:27 *u* invites you and you wish
14:22 for a sign . . . to the *u*
14:22 not for the *u*, but for the
14:23 or *u* come in, will they not
2Co 4:4 blinded the minds of the *u*
6:14 become unevenly yoked with *u*

Unbelieving
Joh 20:27 stop being *u* but become
1Co 7:12 If any brother has an *u* wife
7:13 woman who has an *u* husband
7:14 the *u* husband is sanctified
7:14 the *u* wife is sanctified in
7:15 the *u* one proceeds to depart

Unblamable
Job 12:4 A laughingstock is the . . . *u*
1Th 2:10 loyal and righteous and *u*
3:13 *u* in holiness before our God

Unblemished
Col 1:22 to present you holy and *u*
1Pe 1:19 an *u* and spotless lamb, even
2Pe 3:14 spotless and *u* and in peace
Jude 24 *u* in the sight of his glory

Unburdensome
2Co 11:9 I kept myself *u* to you and

Uncanny
Nu 23:21 any *u* power against Jacob
1Sa 15:23 same as using *u* power and
Isa 1:13 with the use of *u* power
66:3 a blessing with *u* words
Ho 12:11 With Gilead what is *u*, also
Am 5:5 it will become something *u*
Zec 10:2 have spoken what is *u*

Unceasing
Ro 9:2 grief and *u* pain in my heart

Uncertain
2Co 1:8 were very *u* even of our lives
1Ti 6:17 hope, not on *u* riches, but

Uncertainly
1Co 9:26 way I am running is not *u*

Unchangeable
Heb 6:18 through two *u* things in

Unchangeableness
Heb 6:17 promise the *u* of his counsel

Uncircumcised
Ge 17:14 an *u* male who will not get
Ex 6:12 as I am *u* in lips
6:30 Look! I am *u* in lips, so how
12:48 But no *u* man may eat of it
Le 19:23 it will continue *u* for you
26:41 *u* heart will be humbled, and
Jos 5:7 because they proved to be *u*
Jg 14:3 a wife from the *u* Philistines
15:18 fall into the hand of the *u*
1Sa 14:6 the outpost of these *u* men
17:26 who is this *u* Philistine
17:36 and this *u* Philistine must
31:4 *u* men may not come and
2Sa 1:20 daughters of the *u* men may
1Ch 10:4 that these *u* men may not
Isa 52:1 the *u* and unclean one
Jer 6:10 Their ear is *u*, so that they
Jer 9:26 for all the nations are *u*
9:26 Israel are *u* in heart
Eze 28:10 The deaths of *u* ones you
31:18 In the midst of the *u* ones
32:19 laid with the *u* ones
32:21 the *u*, slain by the sword
32:24 *u* to the land down below
32:25 are *u*, slain by the sword
32:26 are *u*, pierced through by
32:27 falling from among the *u*
32:28 in the midst of *u* ones
32:29 lie down even with the *u*
32:30 lie down *u* with those slain
32:32 in the midst of the *u* ones
44:7 foreigners *u* in heart and
44:7 in heart and *u* in flesh
44:9 No foreigner, *u* in heart
44:9 *u* in flesh, may come into
Hab 2:16 and be considered *u*
Ac 7:51 and *u* in hearts and ears
Ro 2:26 *u* person keeps the righteous
2:27 *u* person that is such by
3:30 *u* people righteous by means
4:9 or also upon *u* people
4:11 faith he had while in his *u*
4:12 while in the *u* state which
1Co 7:18 Let him not become *u*
Ga 2:7 good news for those who are *u*
Col 2:13 in the *u* state of your flesh

Uncircumcision
Jer 9:25 circumcised but still in *u*
Ro 2:25 circumcision has become *u*
2:26 his *u* will be counted as
4:10 was in circumcision or in *u*
4:10 Not in circumcision, but in *u*
4:11 having faith while in *u*, in
1Co 7:18 Has any man been called in *u*?
7:19 and *u* means not a thing, but
Ga 5:6 is of any value nor is *u*
6:15 nor is *u*, but a new creation
Eph 2:11 *u* you were called by that
Col 3:11 circumcision nor *u*

Uncle
Le 10:4 the sons of Uzziel, Aaron's *u*
20:20 bare the nakedness of his *u*
25:49, 49 *u* or the son of his *u*
1Sa 10:15 Saul's *u* said: Do tell me
10:16 In turn Saul said to his *u*
14:50 son of Ner, the *u* of Saul
2Ki 24:17 made Mattaniah his *u* king
Es 2:15 of Abihail the *u* of Mordecai
Jer 32:7 of Shallum your paternal *u*
32:8 son of my paternal *u* came
32:9 the son of my paternal *u*
32:12 the son of my paternal *u*

Unclean
Le 5:2 a soul touches some *u* thing
5:2 dead body of an *u* wild beast
5:2 the dead body of an *u* domestic
5:2 body of an *u* swarming creature
5:2 still he is *u* and has become
5:3 with which he may become *u*
7:19 anything *u* is not to be eaten
7:21 a soul touches anything *u*
7:21 of a man or an *u* beast or any
7:21 or any *u* loathsome thing, and
10:10 the *u* thing and the clean
11:4 not eat . . . It is *u* for you
11:5 rock badger . . . is *u* for you
11:6 the hare . . . It is *u* for you
11:7 It is *u* for you
11:8 They are *u* for you
11:24 you would make yourselves *u*
11:24 will be *u* until the evening
11:25 must be *u* until the evening
11:26 they are *u* for you
11:26 touching them will be *u*
11:27 they are *u* to you
11:27 will be *u* until the evening
11:28 must be *u* until the evening
11:28 They are *u* to you
11:29 this is what is *u* to you
11:31 These are *u* to you among all
11:31 will be *u* until the evening
11:32 in its death state will be *u*
11:32 must be *u* until the evening
11:33 that is within it will be *u*
11:34 may come from it will be *u*
11:34 in any vessel will be *u*
11:35 bodies may fall will be *u*
11:35 They are *u*, and they will
11:35 they will become *u* to you
Le 11:36 dead bodies will be *u*
11:38 it is *u* to you
11:39 will be *u* until the evening
11:40 must be *u* until the evening
11:40 must be *u* until the evening
11:43 not make yourselves *u* by
11:43 and actually get *u* by them
11:44 not make your souls *u* by
11:47 between the *u* and the clean
12:2 she must be *u* seven days
12:2 is menstruating she will be *u*
12:5 must then be *u* fourteen days
13:3 and he must declare him *u*
13:8 must then declare him *u*
13:11 priest must declare him *u*
13:11 quarantine him, for he is *u*
13:14 appears in it, he will be *u*
13:15 and he must declare him *u*
13:15 The living flesh is *u*
13:20 must then declare him *u*
13:22 must then declare him *u*
13:25 priest must declare him *u*
13:27 must then declare him *u*
13:30 must then declare such one *u*
13:36 for yellow hair; he is *u*
13:44 he is a leper. He is *u*
13:44 *U* is what the priest should
13:45, 45 and call out, *U, u!*
13:46, 46 he will be *u*. He is *u*
13:51 malignant leprosy. It is *u*
13:55 and yet the plague . . . is *u*
13:59 it clean or to declare it *u*
14:36 not declare *u* everything that
14:40 throw them . . . into an *u* place
14:41 the city into an *u* place
14:44 leprosy in the house. It is *u*
14:45 the city to an *u* place
14:46 will be *u* until the evening
14:57 when something is *u* and when
15:2 his discharge is *u*
15:4 will be *u*, and any article
15:4 which he may sit will be *u*
15:5 and be *u* until the evening
15:6 and be *u* until the evening
15:7 and be *u* until the evening
15:8 and be *u* until the evening
15:9 was riding will be *u*
15:10 will be *u* until the evening
15:10 and be *u* until the evening
15:11 and be *u* until the evening
15:16 and be *u* until the evening
15:17 and be *u* until the evening
15:18 and be *u* until the evening
15:19 will be *u* until the evening
15:20 menstrual impurity will be *u*
15:20 which she may sit will be *u*
15:21 and be *u* until the evening
15:22 in water and be *u* until the
15:23 touching it he will be *u*
15:24 he must then be *u* seven days
15:24 bed . . . will be *u*
15:25 her *u* running discharge will
15:25 menstrual impurity. She is *u*
15:26 *u* like the uncleanness of
15:27 touching them will be *u*, and
15:27 and be *u* until the evening
15:30 her *u* running discharge
15:32 so that he becomes *u* by it
15:33 lies down with an *u* woman
17:15 be *u* until the evening; and
18:20 associate to become *u* by it
18:23 beast to become *u* by it
18:24 not make yourselves *u* by any
18:24 have made themselves *u*
18:25 land is *u*, and I shall bring
18:27 so that the land is *u*
18:30 make yourselves *u* by them
19:31 so as to become *u* by them
20:25 the clean beast and the *u*
20:25 between the *u* fowl and the
20:25 for you in declaring them *u*
22:4 *u* by a deceased soul or a man
22:5 swarming thing that is *u* for
22:5 man who is *u* for him as
22:6 touches any such must be *u*
22:8 beasts so as to become *u* by
27:11 *u* beast such as one may not
27:27 *u* beasts and he must redeem
Nu 5:2 everyone *u* by a deceased soul
9:6 *u* by a human soul so that they
9:7 We are *u* by a human soul
9:10 *u* by a soul or off on a
18:15 the firstborn of the *u* beast
19:7 priest must be *u* until the

2Co 12:9 My *u* kindness is sufficient
13:14 *u* kindness of the Lord
Ga 1:3 May you have *u* kindness and
1:6 you with Christ's *u* kindness
1:15 through his *u* kindness
2:9 the *u* kindness that was given
2:21 shove aside the *u* kindness of
5:4 away from his *u* kindness
6:18 *u* kindness of our Lord Jesus
Eph 1:2 *u* kindness and peace from
1:6 his glorious *u* kindness
1:7 the riches of his *u* kindness
2:5 by *u* kindness you have been
2:7 riches of his *u* kindness in
2:8 By this *u* kindness, indeed
3:2 stewardship of the *u* kindness
3:7 free gift of the *u* kindness
3:8 this *u* kindness was given
4:7 *u* kindness was given
6:24 May the *u* kindness be with
Php 1:2 May you have *u* kindness and
1:7 sharers . . . in the *u* kindness
4:23 The *u* kindness of the Lord
Col 1:2 *u* kindness and peace from God
1:6 *u* kindness of God in truth
4:18 The *u* kindness be with you
1Th 1:1 May you have *u* kindness and
5:28 *u* kindness of our Lord Jesus
2Th 1:2 May you have *u* kindness and
1:12 the *u* kindness of our God
2:16 hope by means of *u* kindness
3:18 The *u* kindness of our Lord
1Ti 1:2 there be *u* kindness, mercy
1:14 *u* kindness of our Lord
6:21 *u* kindness be with you
2Ti 1:2 May there be *u* kindness
1:9 own purpose and *u* kindness
2:1 power in the *u* kindness that
4:22 His *u* kindness be with you
Tit 1:4 *u* kindness and peace from God
2:11 the *u* kindness of God which
3:7 by virtue of the *u* kindness
3:15 *u* kindness be with all of
Phm 3 people have *u* kindness and
25 The *u* kindness of the Lord
Heb 2:9 he by God's *u* kindness might
4:16 to the throne of *u* kindness
4:16 and find *u* kindness for help
10:29 the spirit of *u* kindness
12:15 deprived of the *u* kindness
12:28 continue to have *u* kindness
13:9 firmness by *u* kindness, not
13:25 *u* kindness be with all of
Jas 4:6 the *u* kindness which he gives
4:6 *u* kindness to the humble ones
1Pe 1:2 *u* kindness and peace be
1:10 the *u* kindness meant for you
1:13 hope upon the *u* kindness
3:7 of the *u* favor of life, in
4:10 stewards of . . . *u* kindness
5:5 *u* kindness to the humble ones
5:10 the God of all *u* kindness
5:12 the true *u* kindness of God
2Pe 1:2 *u* kindness and peace be
3:18 on growing in the *u* kindness
2Jo 3 *u* kindness, mercy and peace
Jude 4 *u* kindness of our God into
Re 1:4 *u* kindness and peace from The
22:21 *u* kindness of the Lord Jesus

Undeservedly
1Ki 2:31 blood *u* shed that Joab

Undiluted
Re 14:10 poured out *u* into the cup

Undiscovered
Nu 5:13 has remained *u*, and she, on

Undisturbed
Job 3:13 lain down that I might be *u*
3:26 nor have I been *u*, Nor been
Pr 1:33 be *u* from dread of calamity
Isa 7:4 Watch yourself and keep *u*
18:4 I will keep *u* and look upon
30:15 simply in keeping *u* and in
32:18 and in *u* resting-places
33:20 an *u* abiding place, a tent
Jer 48:11 keeping *u* on their dregs
49:23 not able to keep *u*
Eze 16:49 carefreeness of keeping *u*

Undo
Es 8:5 to *u* the written documents
8:8 writing . . . not possible to *u*

Undoubtedly
De 4:6 This great nation is *u* a wise
1Sa 28:1 *u* know that it is with me

Undress
Isa 32:11 *U* and make yourselves naked

Undue
Ps 10:3 the one making *u* profit has

Undutifully
De 32:51 you men acted *u* toward me in

Uneasiness
Pr 23:29 Who has woe? Who has *u?*

Unemployed
Mt 20:3 standing *u* in the marketplace
20:6 been standing here all day *u*
Tit 1:12 wild beasts, *u* gluttons

Unevenly
2Co 6:14 *u* yoked with unbelievers

Unexpectedly
Nu 35:22 if it was *u* without enmity
1Sa 4:19 her pangs came *u* upon her
2Sa 1:6 *u* chanced to be on Mount

Unfadable
1Pe 5:4 receive the *u* crown of glory

Unfading
1Pe 1:4 undefiled and *u* inheritance

Unfailing
Isa 33:16 his water supply will be *u*

Unfailingly
Ex 22:23 I shall *u* hear his outcry

Unfaithful
Pr 16:10 his mouth should not prove *u*
Jer 3:6 seen what *u* Israel has done
3:8 *u* Israel had committed
3:11 *U* Israel has proved her own
8:5 this people, Jerusalem, is *u*
31:22 way and that, O *u* daughter
49:4 O daughter *u*, you the one
Mic 2:4 To the *u* one he apportions
Lu 12:46 a part with the *u* ones
2Ti 2:13 if we are *u*, he remains

Unfaithfully
Le 5:15 a soul behaves *u* in that he
6:2 does behave *u* toward Jehovah
26:40 behaved *u* toward me, yes
1Ch 5:25 to act *u* toward the God of
2Ch 12:2 behaved *u* toward Jehovah
26:16 acted *u* against Jehovah his
26:18 for you have acted *u*, and
28:22 he acted *u* still more
29:6 fathers have acted *u* and have
30:7 acted *u* toward Jehovah the
Ezr 10:2 acted *u* against our God
10:10 have acted *u* in that you
Ne 1:8 for your part, act *u*, I, for
13:27 great badness in acting *u*
Eze 14:13 sin against me in acting *u*
15:8 reason that they have acted *u*
39:23 they behaved *u* toward me

Unfaithfulness
Le 26:40 fathers in their *u* when they
Nu 5:6 *u* against Jehovah, that soul
5:12 an act of *u* against him
5:27 *u* toward her husband, the
5:30 suspect his wife of *u;* and he
31:16 to commit *u* toward Jehovah
Jos 7:1 an act of *u* respecting the
22:16 What is this act of *u* that
22:20 perpetrated an act of *u* in
22:22 if . . . in *u* against Jehovah
22:31 this act of *u*. Now you
1Ch 2:7 committed an act of *u*
9:1 exile at Babylon for their *u*
10:13 Saul died for his *u* with
2Ch 28:19 great *u* toward Jehovah
29:19 during his reign in his *u*
33:19 all his sin and his *u* and
36:14 committed *u* on a large
Ezr 9:2 to be foremost in this *u*
9:4 *u* of the exiled people
10:6 mourning over the *u* of the
Job 21:34 very replies do remain as *u*
Jer 2:19 acts of *u* should reprove you
5:6 their acts of *u* have become
8:5 with an enduring *u*
14:7 our acts of *u* have become
Eze 17:20 his *u* with which he acted
18:24 his *u* that he has committed
20:27 acting against me with *u*
39:26 and all their *u* with which
Da 9:7 *u* with which they acted
Ho 11:7 tending toward *u* to me
14:4 I shall heal their *u*. I shall

Unfastening
1Ki 20:11 about himself like one *u*

Unfathomable
Eph 3:8 the *u* riches of the Christ

Unfavorable
2Ki 14:10 under *u* conditions and have

Unfeeling
Ps 119:70 heart has become *u* just

Unfermented
Ge 19:3 he baked *u* cakes, and they
Ex 12:8 with fire and with *u* cakes
12:15 you are to eat *u* cakes only
12:17 keep the festival of *u* cakes
12:18 eat *u* cakes down till the
12:20 you are to eat *u* cakes
12:39 *u* cakes, because it had not
13:6 you are to eat *u* cakes, and on
13:7 *U* cakes are to be eaten for
23:15 keep the festival of *u* cakes
23:15 will eat *u* cakes seven days
29:2 and *u* bread and
29:2 *u* ring-shaped cakes moistened
29:2 *u* wafers smeared with oil
29:23 the basket of *u* cakes that is
34:18 festival of *u* cakes you are
34:18 eat *u* cakes, just as I have
Le 2:4 *u* ring-shaped cakes moistened
2:4 or *u* wafers smeared with oil
2:5 flour moistened with oil, *u*
6:16 eaten as *u* cakes in a holy
7:12 *u* ring-shaped cakes moistened
7:12 *u* wafers smeared with oil
8:2 and the basket of *u* cakes
8:26 the basket of *u* cakes that
8:26 one *u* ring-shaped cake and
10:12 eat it *u* near the altar
23:6 festival of *u* cakes to Jehovah
23:6 days you should eat *u* cakes
Nu 6:15 basket of *u* ring-shaped cakes
6:15 *u* wafers smeared with oil
6:17 with the basket of *u* cakes
6:19 one *u* ring-shaped cake out of
6:19 one *u* wafer, and put them
9:11 with *u* cakes and bitter
28:17 Seven days *u* cakes will be
De 16:3 eat along with it *u* cakes
16:8 you should eat *u* cakes; and
16:16 the festival of the *u* cakes
Jos 5:11 *u* cakes and roasted grains
Jg 6:19 ephah of flour as *u* cakes
6:20 Take the meat and the *u* cakes
6:21 the *u* cakes, and fire began to
6:21 the meat and the *u* cakes
1Sa 28:24 and baked it into *u* cakes
2Ki 23:9 they ate *u* cakes in among
1Ch 23:29 for the wafers of *u* bread
2Ch 8:13 at the festival of *u* cakes
30:13 festival of the *u* cakes in
30:21 festival of the *u* cakes
35:17 the festival of the *u* cakes
Ezr 6:22 the festival of *u* cakes
Eze 45:21 seven days *u* cakes are
Mt 26:17 the first day of the *u* cakes
Mr 14:1 the festival of *u* cakes was
14:12 on the first day of *u* cakes
Lu 22:1 the festival of the *u* cakes
22:7 The day of the *u* cakes now
Ac 12:3 those were days of the *u* cakes
20:6 after the days of the *u* cakes
1Co 5:8 *u* cakes of sincerity and truth

Unfit
2Ki 23:8 make *u* for worship the high
23:10 made *u* for worship Topheth
23:13 the king made *u* for worship
23:16 make it *u* for worship
1Co 6:2 *u* to try very trivial matters

Unforeseen
Ec 9:11 *u* occurrence befall them all

Unfortunate
2Ki 3:10 How *u* that Jehovah has
Ps 10:8 on the lookout for someone *u*
10:14 the *u* one, the fatherless boy

Unfruitful
Mt 13:22 sown among the thorns . . . *u*
Mr 4:19 the word, and it becomes *u*

1Co 14:14 praying, but my mind is *u*
Eph 5:11 *u* works that belong to the
Tit 3:14 that they may not be *u*
2Pe 1:8 *u* regarding the accurate

Unfulfilled
2Ki 10:10 *u* to the earth that Jehovah
Es 6:10 not let anything go *u* of all
Lu 16:17 letter of the Law to go *u*

Ungenerous
De 15:9 *u* toward your poor brother
Pr 23:6 the food of anyone of *u* eye

Ungird
Isa 45:1 *u* even the hips of kings

Ungodliness
Ro 1:18 against all *u* and
2Ti 2:16 advance to more and more *u*
Tit 2:12 instructing us to repudiate *u*

Ungodly
Ro 4:5 declares the *u* one righteous
5:6 Christ . . . died for *u* men at
11:26 *u* practices from Jacob
1Ti 1:9 unruly, *u* and sinners, lacking
1Pe 4:18 where will the *u* man and
2Pe 2:5 deluge . . . world of *u* people
2:6 a pattern for *u* persons of
3:7 destruction of the *u* men
Jude 4 *u* men, turning the undeserved
15 convict all the *u* concerning
15 *u* deeds that they did in
15 that they did in an *u* way
15 *u* sinners spoke against him
18 own desires for *u* things

Ungroomed
Le 10:6 Do not let your heads go *u*
13:45 his head should become *u*
21:10 head go *u*, and he should not

Unharnessing
Ge 24:32 *u* the camels and giving

Unhealable
Mic 1:9 the stroke upon her is *u*
Na 3:19 Your stroke has become *u*

Unheard
Ne 13:27 *u* of for you to commit all

Unhonored
Mt 13:57 prophet is not *u* except in
Mr 6:4 A prophet is not *u* except in

Unhypocritical
1Pe 1:22 *u* brotherly love as the

Unify
Ps 86:11 *U* my heart to fear your name

Uninjured
Job 9:4 Who can . . . come off *u?*

Unintelligent
Ro 1:21 *u* heart became darkened

Unintelligible
Eze 3:5 *u* in language or heavy of
3:6 peoples *u* in language or heavy

Unintelligibly
Ps 114:1 from a people speaking *u*

Unintentionally
Le 4:22 commit *u* one of all the
4:27 people of the land sins *u* by
5:18 mistake that he committed *u*
Nu 15:28 made a mistake by a sin *u*
15:29 respects doing something *u*
35:11 who fatally strikes a soul *u*
35:15 that fatally strikes a soul *u*
Jos 20:3 fatally strikes a soul *u*
20:9 fatally strikes a soul *u*

Union
Ps 56:4 In *u* with God I shall praise
56:10 In *u* with God I shall praise
56:10 In *u* with Jehovah I shall
Isa 45:14 Indeed God is in *u* with you
45:17 be saved in *u* with Jehovah
Jer 12:3 examined my heart in *u* with
Zec 11:7 and the other I called *U*
11:14 my second staff, the *U*
Mt 10:32 confesses *u* with me before
10:32 confess *u* with him before
Lu 12:8 confesses *u* with me before
12:8 confess *u* with him before the
Joh 6:56 remains in *u* with me, and
6:56 and I in *u* with him
10:38 Father is in *u* with me
Joh 10:38 I am in *u* with the Father
14:10 I am in *u* with the Father
14:10 the Father is in *u* with me
14:10 Father who remains in *u*
14:11 I am in *u* with the Father
14:11 Father is in *u* with me
14:20 I am in *u* with my Father
14:20 you are in *u* with me and
14:20 and I am in *u* with you
15:4 Remain in *u* with me, and I
15:4 and I in *u* with you
15:4 you remain in *u* with me
15:5 He that remains in *u* with me
15:5 and I in *u* with him, this
15:6 not remain in *u* with me
15:7 If you remain in *u* with me
17:21 Father, are in *u* with me
17:21 I am in *u* with you, that
17:21 also may be in *u* with us
17:23 I in *u* with them and you
17:23 and you in *u* with me, in
17:26 and I in *u* with them
Ro 8:1 those in *u* with Christ Jesus
8:2 life in *u* with Christ Jesus
8:10 if Christ is in *u* with you
12:5 one body in *u* with Christ
16:7 in *u* with Christ longer than
1Co 1:2 sanctified in *u* with Christ
1:30 you are in *u* with Christ
15:18 in death in *u* with Christ
16:24 all of you in *u* with Christ
2Co 5:17 anyone is in *u* with Christ
12:2 man in *u* with Christ who
13:5 Christ is in *u* with you
Ga 1:22 that were in *u* with Christ
2:4 we have in *u* with Christ Jesus
2:20 Christ . . . in *u* with me
3:28 one person in *u* with Christ
5:10 who are in *u* with the Lord
Eph 1:1 ones in *u* with Christ Jesus
1:3 places in *u* with Christ
1:4 he chose us in *u* with him
1:11 in *u* with whom we were also
2:6 in *u* with Christ Jesus
2:7 toward us in *u* with Christ
2:10 created in *u* with Christ
2:13 But now in *u* with Christ
2:15 two peoples in *u* with
2:21 In *u* with him the whole
2:22 In *u* with him you, too, are
3:6 *u* with Christ Jesus through
6:1 in *u* with the Lord, for this
Php 1:1 holy ones in *u* with Christ
3:9 and be found in *u* with him
4:21 holy one in *u* with Christ
Col 1:2 brothers in *u* with Christ at
1:27 It is Christ in *u* with you
1:28 complete in *u* with Christ
2:6 go on walking in *u* with him
3:3 with the Christ in *u* with God
3:14 for it is a perfect bond of *u*
1Th 1:1 in *u* with God the Father and
2:14 in *u* with Christ Jesus
4:16 dead in *u* with Christ will
5:18 in *u* with Christ Jesus
2Th 1:1 in *u* with God our Father and
1:12 and you in *u* with him, in
2Ti 1:1 is in *u* with Christ Jesus
2:10 that is in *u* with Christ
Phm 23 captive in *u* with Christ
1Pe 5:10 glory in *u* with Christ
5:14 in *u* with Christ have peace
1Jo 1:5 no darkness at all in *u* with
2:5 that we are in *u* with him
2:6 He that says he remains in *u*
2:24 abide in *u* with the Son and
2:24 and in *u* with the Father
2:27 remain in *u* with him
2:28 remain in *u* with him, that
3:6 Everyone remaining in *u* with
3:24 remains in *u* with him, and
3:24 and he in *u* with such one
3:24 he is remaining in *u* with us
4:4 he that is in *u* with you is
4:4 that is in *u* with the world
4:13 are remaining in *u* with him
4:13 and he in *u* with us, because
4:15 God remains in *u* with such
4:15 and he in *u* with God
4:16 remains in *u* with God and
4:16 God remains in *u* with him
5:20 are in *u* with the true one
Re 14:13 who die in *u* with the Lord

Unique
Eze 7:5 A calamity, a *u* calamity

Unison
Isa 52:8 In *u* they keep crying out
52:9 cry out joyfully in *u*, you

United
Ge 49:6 do not become *u*, O my
Isa 14:20 *u* with them in a grave
Mt 1:18 before they were *u*
Ro 6:5 we have become *u* with him in
6:5 *u* with him in the likeness of
1Co 1:10 be fitly *u* in the same mind
Heb 4:2 were not *u* by faith with

Unitedly
Job 19:12 *U* his troops come and cast
Ps 41:7 *U* against me all those hating
83:5 they have *u* exchanged counsel
Php 3:17 *U* become imitators of me

Uniting
Eph 4:3 in the *u* bond of peace

Units
Ex 30:23 five hundred *u*, and sweet
30:23 two hundred and fifty *u*, and
30:23 two hundred and fifty *u*
30:24 five hundred *u* by the shekel

Unity
1Ch 12:17 heart will become at *u*
Ps 133:1 to dwell together in *u*
Isa 45:21 consult together in *u*
Ho 1:11 collected together into a *u*
Mic 2:12 In *u* I shall set them, like

Unjust
Ex 18:21 men, hating *u* profit; and
1Sa 8:3 inclined to follow *u* profit
Pr 1:19 everyone making *u* profit
15:27 The one making *u* profit is
28:16 hating *u* profit will prolong
Isa 33:15 rejecting the *u* gain from
56:11 each one for his *u* gain
57:17 erroneousness of his *u* gain
Jer 2:5 found in me that was *u*, so
6:13 making for himself *u* gain
8:10 each one is making *u* gain
22:17 upon your *u* gain, and upon
Eze 22:13 *u* gain that you have made
22:27 purpose of making *u* gain
33:31 after their *u* gain is where
Mic 4:13 their *u* profit, and their
Ro 3:5 God is not *u* when he vents

Unjustly
Job 34:10 And the Almighty to act *u*
Ps 71:4 one acting *u* and oppressively
Isa 26:10 he will act *u* and will
Ac 7:24 certain one being *u* treated
7:26 Why do you treat each other *u?*
7:27 treating his neighbor *u*
1Pe 2:19 bears up . . . and suffers *u*

Unknowingly
Ac 17:23 *u* giving godly devotion to

Unknown
Na 3:17 their place is really *u*
Ac 17:23 been inscribed To an *U* God
2Co 6:9 *u* and yet being recognized
Ga 1:22 But I was *u* by face to the
Heb 13:2 *u* to themselves, entertained

Unlawful
Ac 10:28 *u* it is for a Jew to join

Unless
Ge 43:3 not see my face again *u* your
43:5 not see my face again *u* your
44:23 *U* your youngest brother
De 32:30 Not *u* their Rock had sold
Jos 7:12 *u* you annihilate the thing
Ru 3:18 no rest *u* he has brought the
2Ki 4:24 *u* I shall have said so to you
Es 2:14 *u* the king had taken delight
Ps 94:17 *U* Jehovah had been of
127:1 *U* Jehovah himself builds the
127:1 *U* Jehovah himself guards the
Pr 4:16 not sleep *u* they do badness
4:16 *u* they cause someone to
Isa 1:9 *U* Jehovah of armies himself
7:9 *U* you people have faith, you
55:10 *u* it actually saturates the
Am 3:3 *u* they . . . met by appointment
3:7 thing *u* he has revealed his
Mt 12:29 *u* first he binds the strong
18:3 *U* you turn around and become

Mt 24:22 *u* those days were cut short
Mr 3:27 *u* first he binds the strong
7:3 *u* they wash their hands up to
7:4 they do not eat *u* they cleanse
13:20 *u* Jehovah had cut short the
Lu 9:13 *u* perhaps we ourselves go
13:3 *u* you repent, you will all
13:5 *u* you repent, you will all
Joh 3:2 *u* God is with him
3:3 *U* anyone is born again, he
3:5 *U* anyone is born from water
3:27 *u* it has been given him from
4:48 *U* you people see signs and
6:44 No man can come to me *u*
6:53 *U* you eat the flesh of the
6:65 *u* it is granted him by the
7:51 not judge a man *u* first it
10:10 *u* it is to steal and slay
12:24 *U* a grain of wheat falls
13:8 *U* I wash you, you have no
15:4 *u* it remains in the vine
15:4 *u* you remain in union with
19:11 *u* it had been granted to
20:25 *U* I see in his hands the
Ac 8:31 do so, *u* someone guided me
15:1 *U* you get circumcised
27:31 *U* these men remain in the
Ro 9:29 *U* Jehovah of armies had left
10:15 *u* they have been sent forth
1Co 14:5 *u*, in fact, he translates
14:6 *u* I spoke to you either with
14:7 *u* it makes an interval to
14:9 *u* you through the tongue
15:2 holding it fast, *u*, in fact
15:36 made alive *u* first it dies
2Co 13:5 *U* you are disapproved
2Th 2:3 *u* the apostasy comes first
2Ti 2:5 *u* he has contended according
Heb 9:22 *u* blood is poured out no
Re 2:5 from its place, *u* you repent
2:22 *u* they repent of her deeds
3:3 *u* you wake up, I shall come

Unlettered
Ac 4:13 they were men *u* and ordinary

Unlifted
2Co 3:14 same veil remains *u* at the

Unlike
Eze 16:31 *u* a prostitute in disdaining

Unload
Ac 21:3 the boat was to *u* its cargo

Unlucky
Nu 23:23 is no *u* spell against Jacob
24:1 to come upon any *u* omens

Unmarried
1Co 7:8 Now I say to the *u* persons
7:11 let her remain *u* or else
7:32 The *u* man is anxious for the
7:34 the *u* woman, and the virgin

Unmistakably
Ge 26:28 have *u* seen that Jehovah has
43:3 The man *u* bore witness to us
Ex 22:4 *u* found in his hand what was
Le 13:22 if it *u* spreads in the skin
13:27 If it *u* spreads in the skin
13:35 *u* spreads in the skin after
1Sa 10:16 told us *u* that the she-asses
1Ki 2:37 *u* know that you will
2:42 should *u* know that you will
2Ki 14:10 have *u* struck down Edom

Unmovable
1Co 15:58 become steadfast, *u*

Unnatural
1Co 6:9 nor men kept for *u* purposes
Jude 7 out after flesh for *u* use

Unni
1Ch 15:18 and *U*, Eliab and Benaiah and
15:20 and Jehiel and *U* and Eliab
Ne 12:9 Bakbukiah and *U* their brothers

Unnumbered
Isa 51:8 salvation to *u* generations

Unoccupied
Mt 12:44 finds it *u* but swept clean
1Ti 5:13 *u*, gadding about to the
5:13 not only *u*, but also

Unpaid
Isa 45:14 The *u* laborers of Egypt and

Unprincipled
Isa 32:5 *u* man, he will not be said
32:7 *u* man, his instruments are

Unprofitable
Mt 12:36 that every *u* saying that men
Tit 3:9 for they are *u* and futile

Unprofitableness
Eph 4:17 walk in the *u* of their minds

Unpruned
Le 25:5 grapes of your *u* vine you
25:11 the grapes of its *u* vines

Unpunishable
Pr 6:29 touching her will remain *u*

Unpunished
Ex 20:7 not leave the one *u* who takes
De 5:11 will not leave anyone *u* who
1Ki 2:9 And now do not leave him *u*
Pr 11:21 a bad person will not go *u*
Jer 30:11 by no means leave you *u*
46:28 absolutely not leave you *u*
49:12 you be absolutely left *u*
49:12 You will not be left *u*, for

Unquestionably
Ge 32:12 *U* I shall deal well with you
42:21 *U* we are guilty with regard
Ex 3:7 *U* I have seen the affliction
Le 13:7 scab has *u* spread in the skin
13:12 leprosy *u* breaks out in the
Jg 15:2 You must *u* hate her. Hence I
20:39 are *u* suffering nothing but
1Sa 27:12 *u* become a stench among his
2Sa 12:14 *u* treated Jehovah with
2Ki 3:23 kings have *u* been put to
1Ch 21:17 sinned and have *u* done bad
Ne 1:7 *u* acted corruptly against you

Unreachably
Ps 148:13 his name alone is *u* high

Unrealities
1Sa 12:21 *u* that are of no benefit and
12:21 because they are *u*

Unreality
Isa 40:17 as nothing and an *u* they
40:23 judges . . . as a mere *u*
41:29 images are wind and *u*
44:9 image are all of them an *u*
49:4 For *u* and vanity I have used
59:4 has been a trusting in *u*
Eze 21:29 beholding for you an *u*
22:28 visioning an *u* and divining

Unreasonable
Isa 19:11 counsel is something *u*
Lu 11:40 *U* persons! He that made the
12:20 *U* one, this night they are
Ac 25:27 *u* to me to send a prisoner
Ro 2:20 a corrector of the *u* ones, a
1Co 15:36 You *u* person! What you sow
2Co 11:16 Let no man think I am *u*
11:16 accept me even if as *u*
11:19 put up with the *u* persons
12:6 I shall not be *u*, for I
12:11 I have become *u*
Eph 5:17 cease becoming *u*, but go on
1Pe 2:15 ignorant talk of the *u* men

Unreasonableness
Mr 7:22 blasphemy, haughtiness, *u*
2Co 11:1 up with me in some little *u*
11:17 but as in *u*, in this

Unreasonably
2Co 11:21 I am talking *u*—I too am

Unreasoning
Ps 49:10 and the *u* one perish
73:22 I was *u* and I could not know
92:6 No *u* man himself can know
94:8 you who are *u* among the
Pr 12:1 a hater of reproof is *u*
30:2 I am more *u* than anyone else
Jer 10:8 prove to be *u* and stupid
Eze 21:31 the hand of men who are *u*
2Pe 2:12 like *u* animals born naturally
Jude 10 naturally like the *u* animals

Unreasoningly
Jer 10:14 Every man has behaved so *u*
10:21 shepherds have behaved *u*
51:17 Every man has behaved so *u*

Unreceptive
Isa 6:10 heart of this people *u*, and
Mt 13:15 the heart . . . has grown *u*
Ac 28:27 the heart . . . has grown *u*

Unrecognizable
Ge 42:7 he made himself *u* to them
1Ki 14:5 she will be making herself *u*
14:6 you are making yourself *u*
Pr 26:24 the hater makes himself *u*
Jer 19:4 to make this place *u* and

Unrepentant
Ro 2:5 hardness and *u* heart you are

Unresponsive
Ex 7:14 Pharaoh's heart is *u*. He has
8:15 he made his heart *u*; and he
8:32 Pharaoh made his heart *u* this
9:7 heart continued to be *u*
9:34 and making his heart *u*, he as
10:1 let his heart . . . become *u*
1Sa 6:6 your heart *u* just the way
6:6 Pharaoh made their heart *u*
Isa 6:10 make their very ears *u*
Zec 7:11 ears they made too *u* to hear

Unrestrained
Ex 32:25 the people went *u*, because
32:25 let them go *u* for a disgrace
1Sa 2:3 Let nothing go forth *u* from
Ps 94:4 they keep speaking *u*
Pr 29:18 is no vision the people go *u*
2Pe 2:13 *u* delight in their deceptive

Unrestrainedly
Ps 31:18 *u* in haughtiness and

Unrestraint
2Ch 28:19 let *u* grow in Judah, and

Unrighteous
Ps 64:6 keep searching out *u* things
Zep 3:5 *u* one was knowing no shame
Mt 5:45 upon righteous people and *u*
Lu 16:8 the steward, though *u*
16:9 by means of the *u* riches
16:10 person *u* in what is least
16:10 is least is *u* also in much
16:11 connection with the *u* riches
18:6 the judge, although *u*, said
18:11 extortioners, *u*, adulterers
Ac 24:15 both the righteous and the *u*
Ro 1:18 suppressing . . . in an *u* way
1Co 6:1 to court before *u* men, and
6:9 *u* persons will not inherit
2Th 2:10 with every *u* deception for
Heb 6:10 God is not *u* so as to forget
8:12 merciful to their *u* deeds
1Pe 3:18 a righteous person for *u* ones
2Pe 2:9 to reserve *u* people for the

Unrighteousness
2Sa 3:34 before the sons of *u* you
7:10 sons of *u* will not afflict
1Ch 17:9 sons of *u* will not wear
2Ch 19:7 our God there is no *u* or
Job 5:16 *u* actually shuts its mouth
6:29 let no *u* arise—Yes, return
6:30 Is there *u* on my tongue, Or
11:14 no *u* dwell in your tents
13:7 Will you men speak *u* for God
15:16 is drinking in *u* just like
22:23 keep *u* far from your tent
24:20 *u* will be broken just like
27:4 My lips will speak no *u*
34:32 If any *u* I have committed
36:23 You have committed *u*
Ps 37:1 envious of those doing *u*
43:1 the man of deception and *u*
53:1 have acted detestably in *u*
58:2 practice outright *u* in the
89:22 any son of *u* afflict him
92:15 in whom there is no *u*
107:42 *u*, it has to shut its mouth
119:3 they have practiced no *u*
Pr 22:8 *u* will reap what is hurtful
Isa 59:3 kept muttering sheer *u*
61:8 hating robbery along with *u*
Eze 28:15 until *u* was found in you
Ho 10:9 war against the sons of *u*
10:13 *U* is what you have reaped
Mic 3:10 and Jerusalem with *u*
Hab 2:12 established a town by *u*
Zep 3:5 Jehovah . . . would do no *u*
3:13 no *u*, nor speak a lie
Mal 2:6 no *u* to be found on his lips
Lu 13:27 all you workers of *u*
Joh 7:18 and there is no *u* in him
Ac 1:18 field with the wages for *u*

Ac 8:23 gall and a bond of *u*
Ro 1:18 *u* of men who are suppressing
1:29 filled . . . with all *u*
2:8 obey *u* there will be wrath
3:5 *u* brings God's righteousness
6:13 to sin as weapons of *u*, but
1Co 13:6 It does not rejoice over *u*
2Th 2:12 but took pleasure in *u*
2Ti 2:19 of Jehovah renounce *u*
Jas 3:6 world of *u* among our members
1Jo 1:9 and to cleanse us from all *u*
5:17 All *u* is sin; and yet there
Re 22:11 He that is doing *u*, let him
22:11 let him do *u* still; and let

Unripe
Nu 6:4 from the *u* grapes to the skins
Job 15:33 thrust away his *u* grapes
Jer 31:29 ones that ate the *u* grape
31:30 Any man eating the *u* grape
Eze 18:2 Fathers . . . eat *u* grapes, but
Re 6:13 casts its *u* figs

Unruly
1Ti 1:9 for persons lawless and *u*
Tit 1:6 charge of debauchery nor *u*
1:10 For there are many *u* men
Jas 3:8 tongue . . . *u* injurious thing

Unsatisfying
La 2:14 worthless and *u* things

Unsealed
Nu 24:3 man with the eye *u*
24:15 of the man with the eye *u*

Unsearchable
Job 5:9 the One doing great things *u*
9:10 Doing great things *u*, And
Ps 145:3 And his greatness is *u*
Pr 25:3 the heart of kings, that is *u*
Ro 11:33 How *u* his judgments are

Unseemly
1Co 12:23 our *u* parts have the more

Unseen
Ge 31:49 *u* the one from the other
2Co 4:18 seen, but on the things *u*
4:18 the things *u* are everlasting

Unshakable
Ps 112:8 His heart is *u*; he will not

Unsheathe
Le 26:33 I will *u* a sword after you

Unshorn
2Ki 3:4 hundred thousand *u* male sheep

Unshrunk
Mt 9:16 sews a patch of *u* cloth upon
Mr 2:21 patch of *u* cloth upon an old

Unskilled
2Co 11:6 even if I am *u* in speech, I

Unspeakable
Mt 5:22 with an *u* word of contempt
1Pe 1:8 with an *u* and glorified joy

Unsteadily
De 32:35 their foot will move *u*
Ps 38:16 When my foot moved *u*, they
94:18 foot will certainly move *u*
107:27 move *u* like a drunken man
Isa 24:20 moves *u* like a drunken man
29:9 they have moved *u*, but not

Unsteady
Jas 1:8 *u* in all his ways
2Pe 2:14 and they entice *u* souls
3:16 untaught and *u* are twisting

Unstopped
Isa 35:5 of the deaf ones will be *u*

Unsuitable
Mt 13:48 but the *u* they threw away

Unsuspectedly
Ge 34:25 his sword and to go *u*

Unsuspecting
Jg 18:7 quiet and *u*, and there was no
18:10 come to an *u* people, and the
18:27 against a people quiet and *u*

Unsuspectingly
2Sa 15:11 being called and going *u*

Unswervingly
1Sa 7:3 direct your heart *u* to Jehovah

Untaught
2Pe 3:16 *u* and unsteady are twisting

Unthankful
Lu 6:35 kind toward the *u* and wicked
2Ti 3:2 disobedient to parents, *u*

Unthinkable
Ge 18:25 *u* of you that you are acting
18:25 It is *u* of you. Is the Judge
44:7 *u* that your servants should
44:17 It is *u* for me to do this
Jos 22:29 It is *u*, on our part, to
24:16 It is *u*, on our part, to
1Sa 2:30 It is *u*, on my part, because
12:23 *u* . . . to sin against Jehovah
14:45 It is *u*! As Jehovah is alive
20:2 It is *u*! You will not die
20:9 Jonathan said: That is *u*
22:15 It is *u* on my part! Do not
24:6 *u*, on my part, from
26:11 It is *u*, on my part, from
2Sa 20:20 *u* on my part that I should
23:17 *u* on my part, O Jehovah
1Ki 21:3 It is *u* on my part, from
1Ch 11:19 *u* on my part, as regards my
Job 27:5 It is *u* on my part that I

Untie
Da 5:16 and to *u* knots themselves
Mt 21:2 *u* them and bring them to me
Mr 1:7 and *u* the laces of his sandals
Lu 3:16 sandals I am not fit to *u*
13:15 on the sabbath *u* his bull or
Joh 1:27 sandal I am not worthy to *u*
Ac 13:25 I am not worthy to *u*
Re 9:14 *U* the four angels that are

Untied
Re 9:15 And the four angels were *u*

Until*
Mr 9:1 *u* first they see the kingdom
Joh 5:17 My Father has kept working *u*

Untouched
Ro 15:23 *u* territory in these regions

Untrue
Ex 23:1 must not take up an *u* report
Job 11:11 well knows men who are *u*
Ps 144:8 mouth has spoken what is *u*
144:11 mouth has spoken what is *u*
Eze 13:6 visioned what is *u* and a
13:7 *u* vision that you men have
21:23 an *u* divination in their

Untrustworthy
Jer 15:18 waters that have proved *u*

Untruth
Job 31:5 I have walked with men of *u*
35:13 Only the *u* God does not hear
Ps 12:2 *U* they keep speaking one to
26:4 I have not sat with men of *u*
41:6 *u* is what his heart will
Pr 30:8 *U* and the lying word put far
Isa 5:18 error with ropes of *u*
Eze 13:8 you men have spoken *u* and
13:9 prophets that are visioning *u*
13:23 *u* you women will not keep
Ho 12:11 what is uncanny, also *u*, have
Jon 2:8 are observing the idols of *u*

Untruthful
Isa 30:9 rebellious people, *u* sons

Untying
Da 5:12 and the *u* of knots had been

Unusual
Isa 28:21 his work is *u*
Mr 4:41 they felt an *u* fear, and they

Unusually
Da 7:7 and terrible and *u* strong
Mt 4:8 to an *u* high mountain, and
8:28 *u* fierce, so that nobody
Re 16:21 the plague of it was *u* great

Unutterable
2Co 12:4 heard *u* words which it is

Unuttered
Ro 8:26 pleads . . . with groanings *u*

Unveiled
2Co 3:18 we with *u* faces reflect like

Unwashed
Mt 15:20 to take a meal with *u* hands
Mr 7:2 defiled hands, that is, *u* ones

Unwavering
2Co 1:7 And so our hope for you is *u*

Unweighed
1Ki 7:47 left all the utensils *u*

Unwilling
1Sa 26:23 *u* to thrust my hand out
31:4 his armor-bearer was *u*
1Ch 10:4 armor-bearer was *u*, because
Isa 30:9 *u* to hear the law of Jehovah
Mt 2:18 she was *u* to take comfort
22:3 but they were *u* to come
Lu 15:28 wrathful and was *u* to go in
18:4 for a while he was *u*, but

Unwinged
Joe 1:4 creeping, *u* locust has eaten
1:4 what the creeping, *u* locust
2:25 the creeping, *u* locust, and

Unwise
Jer 4:22 They are *u* sons; and they
5:21 *u* people that is without
Eph 5:15 not as *u* but as wise persons

Unworried
Job 12:6 tents of the despoilers are *u*
Jer 12:1 treachery are the *u* ones

Unworthily
1Co 11:27 drinks the cup of the Lord *u*

Unworthy
Ge 32:10 I am *u* of all the

Unyielding
Ca 8:6 devotion is as *u* as Sheol is

Upbuilding
Ro 14:19 things that are *u* to one
15:2 in what is good for his *u*
1Co 14:5 congregation may receive *u*
14:12 the *u* of the congregation
14:26 all things take place for *u*
2Co 12:19 all things are for your *u*

Upbuilds
1Co 14:3 he that prophesies *u* and
14:4 He that speaks in a tongue *u*
14:4 but he that prophesies *u* a

Uphaz
Jer 10:9 and gold from *U*, the
Da 10:5 hips girded with gold of *U*

Upheaved
Na 1:5 the earth will be *u* because of

Upheld
Ps 41:12 you have *u* me, And you will

Uplifted
Ex 14:8 were going out with *u* hand
Nu 33:3 Israel went out with *u* hand
Ac 13:17 out of it with an *u* arm

Upper
Ge 46:26 issued out of his *u* thigh
Ex 1:5 issued out of Jacob's *u* thigh
4:6 the *u* fold of your garment
4:6 stuck his hand into the *u* fold
4:7 the *u* fold of your garment
4:7 into the *u* fold of his garment
4:7 of the *u* fold of his garment
12:7 and the *u* part of the doorway
12:22 the *u* part of the doorway
12:23 blood upon the *u* part of the
De 24:6 its *u* grindstone as a pledge
Jos 15:19 gave her *U* Gulloth and
16:5 as far as *U* Beth-horon
Jg 1:15 Caleb gave her *U* Gulloth and
8:30 issued out of his *u* thigh, for
9:53 pitched an *u* millstone upon
2Sa 11:21 pitched an *u* millstone upon
2Ki 15:35 the *u* gate of the house of
18:17 the conduit of the *u* pool
1Ch 7:24 Beth-horon . . . the *u*, and
2Ch 8:5 went on to build *U* Beth-horon
23:20 *u* gate to the king's house
27:3 *u* gate of Jehovah's house
32:30 *u* source of the waters of
Ne 3:25 the *u* one that belongs to the
Job 31:22 broken from its *u* bone
Ps 104:3 building his *u* chambers with
104:13 from his *u* chambers
Pr 1:21 *u* end of the noisy streets
Isa 7:3 conduit of the *u* pool by the
7:11 it high as the *u* regions
36:2 conduit of the *u* pool at the
Jer 20:2 in the *u* gate of Benjamin

Jer 22:13 his *u* chambers, but not
22:14 and commodious *u* chambers
36:10 in the *u* courtyard, at the
Eze 9:2 *u* gate that faces to the north
Mr 14:15 show you a large *u* room
Lu 22:12 a large *u* room furnished
Ac 1:13 *u* chamber, where they were
9:37 and laid her in an *u* chamber
9:39 led him up into the *u* chamber
20:8 the *u* chamber where we were

Uppermost
Eze 41:7 could go up to the *u* story
42:5 the *u* ones were shorter

Upright
Ge 42:11 We are *u* men. Your servants
42:19 If you are *u*, let one of
42:31 We are *u* men. We do not act
42:33 I am going to know you are *u*
42:34 no spies but you are *u*
Nu 23:10 die the death of the *u* ones
De 32:4 Righteous and *u* is he
1Sa 29:6 you are *u*, and your going
2Ki 10:3 most *u* of the sons of your
10:15 Is your heart *u* with me
14:3 what was *u* in Jehovah's eyes
15:3 was *u* in Jehovah's eyes
2Ch 29:34 Levites were more *u* of
Ne 9:13 *u* judicial decisions and laws
Job 1:1 proved to be blameless and *u*
1:8 man blameless and *u*, fearing
2:3 man blameless and *u*, fearing
4:7 have the *u* ever been effaced
8:6 If you are pure and *u*, By now
17:8 *U* people stare in amazement
23:7 *u* . . . set matters straight
33:27 what is *u* I have perverted
Ps 7:10 a Savior of those *u* in heart
11:2 at the ones *u* in heart
11:7 The *u* are the ones that will
19:8 The orders from Jehovah are *u*
25:8 Good and *u* is Jehovah
32:11 all you who are *u* in heart
33:1 On the part of the *u* ones
33:4 For the word of Jehovah is *u*
36:10 to those *u* in heart
37:14 slaughter those who are *u* in
37:37 keep the *u* one in sight
49:14 the *u* ones will have them
64:10 the *u* in heart will boast
92:15 To tell that Jehovah is *u*
94:15 *u* in heart will follow it
97:11 even for the ones *u* in heart
107:42 The *u* ones see and rejoice
111:1 intimate group of *u* ones and
112:2 generation of the *u* ones, it
112:4 as a light to the *u* ones
119:137 judicial decisions are *u*
125:4 ones *u* in their hearts
140:13 *u* ones will dwell before
Pr 2:7 *u* ones he will treasure up
2:21 *u* are the ones that will
3:32 intimacy is with the *u* ones
8:9 and *u* to the ones finding
11:3 integrity of the *u* ones is
11:6 righteousness of the *u* ones
11:11 blessing of the *u* ones a
12:6 mouth of the *u* ones is what
14:9 *u* ones there is agreement
14:11 the tent of the *u* ones will
14:12 way that is *u* before a man
15:8 the prayer of the *u* ones is a
15:19 path of the *u* ones is a way
16:13 speaker of *u* things he loves
16:17 highway of the *u* ones is to
16:25 a way that is *u* before a man
17:26 is against what is *u*
20:11 his activity is pure and *u*
21:2 way of a man is *u* in his own
21:8 pure one is *u* in his activity
21:18 takes the place of the *u* ones
21:29 the *u* is the one that will
28:10 *u* ones to go astray into the
29:10 *u* ones, they keep seeking for
29:27 one who is *u* in his way is
Ec 7:29 God made mankind *u*, but they
Isa 26:7 You being *u*, you will smooth
33:15 and speaking what is *u*
45:19 telling what is *u*
Jer 34:15 do what is *u* in my eyes
Ho 14:9 the ways of Jehovah are *u*
Mic 7:2 there is no *u* one. All of
7:4 their most *u* one is worse
Hab 2:4 it has not been *u* within him

Uprightly
Mic 2:7 the case of the one walking *u*

Uprightness
De 9:5 or for the *u* of your heart
1Ki 3:6 and in *u* of heart with you
9:4 integrity of heart and with *u*
1Ch 29:17 in the *u* of my heart have
Job 6:25 sayings of *u* . . . not painful
33:3 My sayings are the *u* of my
33:23 To tell to man his *u*
Ps 9:8 try national groups in *u*
17:2 May your own eyes behold *u*
25:21 *u* . . . safeguard me
27:11 lead me in the path of *u*
45:6 kingship is a scepter of *u*
58:1 Can you judge in *u* itself
67:4 will judge the peoples with *u*
75:2 myself began judging with *u*
96:10 the cause of the peoples in *u*
98:9 And the peoples with *u*
99:4 have firmly established *u*
111:8 Done in truth and *u*
119:7 shall laud you in *u* of heart
143:10 lead me in the land of *u*
Pr 1:3 and judgment and *u*
2:9 and *u*, the entire course of
2:13 leaving the paths of *u* to
4:11 to tread in the tracks of *u*
8:6 opening of my lips is about *u*
14:2 walking in his *u* is fearing
17:7 the lip of *u* is not fitting
23:16 exult when your lips speak *u*
Isa 11:4 *u* he must give reproof in
26:7 of the righteous one is *u*
Mal 2:6 and in *u* he walked with me
Heb 1:8 is the scepter of *u*

Uproar
1Ki 1:41 noise of the town in an *u*
1:45 and the town is in an *u*
Job 39:25 *u* of chiefs and the war cry
Ps 46:3 the mountains rock at its *u*
83:2 your very enemies are in an *u*
Isa 5:14 crowd and her *u* and the
13:4 Listen! The *u* of kingdoms
66:6 sound of *u* out of the city
Jer 48:45 head of the sons of *u*
Ho 10:14 an *u* has risen among your
Mt 26:5 in order that no *u* may arise
27:24 rather, an *u* was arising
Mr 14:2 might be an *u* of the people
Ac 17:5 to throw the city into an *u*
20:1 after the *u* had subsided, Paul
21:30 whole city was set in an *u*

Uproot
1Ki 14:15 *u* Israel off this good
2Ch 7:20 *u* them from off my ground
Ec 3:2 a time to *u* what was planted
Jer 1:10 to *u* and to pull down and
12:14 *u* from the midst of them
12:17 I will also *u* that nation
18:7 *u* it and to pull it down and
24:6 and I shall not *u*
31:28 *u* and to pull down and to
42:10 and I shall not *u* you
Mic 5:14 I will *u* your sacred poles
Mt 13:29 you *u* the wheat with them

Uprooted
De 29:28 *u* them from off their soil
Ps 9:6 the cities that you have *u*
Jer 31:40 It will not be *u*, neither
Eze 19:12 she was finally *u* in fury
Da 11:4 his kingdom will be *u*, even
Am 9:15 be *u* from their ground that
Zep 2:4 regards Ekron, she will be *u*
Mt 15:13 did not plant will be *u*
Lu 17:6 Be *u* and planted in the sea!
Jude 12 died twice, having been *u*

Uprooting
Jer 12:14 *u* them from off their
12:15 must occur that after my *u*
12:17 *u* and destroying it
45:4 what I have planted I am *u*

Upset
2Sa 6:6 cattle nearly caused an *u*
1Ch 13:9 the bulls nearly caused an *u*

Upside
Jg 7:13 turning it *u* down, and the
2Ki 21:13 clean and turning it *u* down

Upstairs
Ac 20:11 went *u* and began the meal

Upturned
Job 28:5 it has been *u* as if by fire

Upward
Ge 6:16 to the extent of a cubit *u*
Ex 25:20 two wings *u*, screening over
30:14 twenty years old and *u*
37:9 cherubs . . . two wings *u*
38:26 twenty years of age and *u*
Le 27:7 is from sixty years old *u*
Nu 1:3 twenty years old *u*, everyone
1:18 twenty years old *u*, head by
1:20 twenty years old *u*, everyone
1:22 twenty years old *u*, everyone
1:24 twenty years old *u*, everyone
1:26 twenty years old *u*, everyone
1:28 twenty years old *u*, everyone
1:30 twenty years old *u*, everyone
1:32 twenty years old *u*, everyone
1:34 twenty years old *u*, everyone
1:36 from twenty years old *u*
1:38 from twenty years old *u*
1:40 from twenty years old *u*
1:42 from twenty years old *u*
1:45 from twenty years old *u*
3:15 male from a month old *u* you
3:22 males from a month old *u*
3:28 males from a month old *u*
3:34 the males from a month old *u*
3:39 males from a month old *u*
3:40 Israel from a month old *u*
3:43 from a month old *u* of their
4:3 thirty years old *u* to fifty
4:23 thirty years old *u* to fifty
4:30 thirty years old *u* to fifty
4:35 thirty years old *u* to fifty
4:39 thirty years old *u* to fifty
4:43 thirty years old *u* to fifty
4:47 thirty years old *u* to fifty
8:24 twenty-five years old *u* he
14:29 from twenty years old *u*, you
26:2 twenty years of age and *u*
26:4 the age of twenty years and *u*
26:62 from a month old and *u*
32:11 from twenty years old *u*
Jg 1:36 of Akrabbim, from Sela *u*
1Sa 9:2 shoulders *u* he was taller
10:23 from his shoulders *u*
1Ki 7:31 to the supports and *u* was
2Ki 3:21 girding on a belt and *u*
19:30 and produce fruitage *u*
1Ch 23:3 the age of thirty years *u*
23:24 the age of twenty years *u*
23:27 the age of twenty years *u*
2Ch 25:5 from twenty years of age *u*
31:16 from three years of age *u*
31:17 the age of twenty years *u*
Ezr 3:8 twenty years of age *u* to act
Job 5:7 As the very sparks fly *u*
39:27 that an eagle flies *u*
Pr 15:24 The path of life is *u* to one
Ec 3:21 whether it is ascending *u*
Isa 8:21 and will certainly peer *u*
37:31 and produce fruitage *u*
Eze 1:11 wings were spreading out *u*
1:27 appearance of his hips and *u*
8:2 his hips even *u* there was
41:7, 7 turning around *u* and *u*
41:7, 7 *u* and *u* all around the
41:7 a widening to the house *u*
43:15 altar hearth and *u* there
Ho 11:7 *u* they call it; no one at all
Mr 14:5 sold for *u* of three hundred
1Co 15:6 to *u* of five hundred brothers
Php 3:14 for the prize of the *u* call

Ur
Ge 11:28 in *U* of the Chaldeans
11:31 they went with him out of *U*
15:7 who brought you out of *U*
1Ch 11:35 Eliphal the son of *U*
Ne 9:7 out of *U* of the Chaldeans and

Urbanus
Ro 16:9 Greet *U* our fellow worker in

Urge
Ge 23:8 *u* Ephron the son of Zohar for
33:11 continued to *u* him, so that
Ex 12:33 Egyptians began to *u* the
2Sa 13:27 Absalom began to *u* him, so
2Ki 5:16 began to *u* him to accept it

Urged
Es 8:14 *u* forward and being moved
Mt 8:34 *u* him to move out from their

2Co 12:18 I *u* Titus and I dispatched
Urgent
Ge 19:15 the angels became *u* with Lot
1Sa 21:8 king's matter proved to be *u*
Lu 23:23 At this they began to be *u*
Urgently
2Ti 4:2 preach the word, be at it *u*
Urging
Ex 5:13 *u* them, saying: Finish your
Jg 16:16 and kept *u* him, his soul got
1Sa 28:23 the woman kept *u* him
2Sa 13:25 kept *u* him, he did not
2Ki 2:17 kept *u* him until he was
5:23 he kept *u* him and finally
Joh 4:31 disciples were *u* him, saying
Ac 13:43 *u* them to continue in the
Uri
Ex 31:2 Bezalel the son of *U* the son
35:30 *U* the son of Hur of the tribe
38:22 *U* the son of Hur of the tribe
1Ki 4:19 Geber the son of *U*, in the
1Ch 2:20 in turn, became father to *U*
2:20 *U*, in turn, became father to
2Ch 1:5 son of *U* the son of Hur had
Ezr 10:24 and of the gatekeepers . . . *U*
Uriah
2Sa 11:3 the wife of *U* the Hittite
11:6 Send to me *U* the Hittite
11:6 So Joab sent *U* to David
11:7 *U* came to him, David began
11:8 David said to *U*: Go down to
11:8 *U* went out from the king's
11:9 *U* lay down at the entrance
11:10 *U* did not go down to his
11:10 David said to *U*: It is from
11:11 *U* said to David: The Ark
11:12 David said to *U*: Dwell here
11:12 *U* kept dwelling in
11:14 send it by the hand of *U*
11:15 Put *U* in front of the
11:16 *U* put in the place where he
11:17 *U* the Hittite also died
11:21 servant *U* the Hittite died
11:24 servant *U* the Hittite also
11:26 wife of *U* got to hear that
11:26 that *U* her husband had died
12:9 *U* the Hittite you struck
12:10 wife of *U* the Hittite to
12:15 wife of *U* had borne to
23:39 *U* the Hittite—thirty-seven
1Ki 15:5 the matter of *U* the Hittite
1Ch 11:41 *U* the Hittite, Zabad the son
Ne 8:4 and *U* and Hilkiah and Maaseiah
Isa 8:2 witnesses, *U* the priest and
Mt 1:6 to Solomon by the wife of *U*
Uriel
1Ch 6:24 *U* his son, Uzziah his son
15:5 of the sons of Kohath, *U* the
15:11 Levites *U*, Asaiah and Joel
2Ch 13:2 daughter of *U* of Gibeah
Urijah
2Ki 16:10 King Ahaz sent *U* the priest
16:11 And *U* the priest proceeded
16:11 way that *U* the priest made
16:15 even *U* the priest, saying
16:16 *U* the priest went doing
Ezr 8:33 *U* the priest and with him
Ne 3:4 *U* the son of Hakkoz did
3:21 *U* the son of Hakkoz repaired
Jer 26:20 *U* the son of Shemaiah from
26:21 When *U* got to hear of it
26:23 to bring *U* out from Egypt
Urim
Ex 28:30 put the *U* and the Thummim
Le 8:8 the *U* and the Thummim
Nu 27:21 by the judgment of the *U*
De 33:8 Thummim and your *U* belong to
1Sa 28:6 by the *U* or by the prophets
Ezr 2:63 stood up with *U* and Thummim
Ne 7:65 priest with *U* and Thummim
Urinates
1Sa 25:22 *u* against the wall remain
1Ki 16:11 that *u* against a wall or
Urinating
1Sa 25:34 anyone *u* against a wall
1Ki 14:10 anyone *u* against a wall
21:21 *u* against a wall and the
2Ki 9:8 *u* against a wall and any
Urine
2Ki 18:27 and drink their own *u*
Isa 36:12 drink their own *u* with you
Usable
Mt 5:13 no longer *u* for anything but
Use
Ge 30:37 Jacob took for his *u* staffs
Ex 38:8 the *u* of the mirrors of the
Le 11:32 Any vessel of which some *u*
13:51 any *u* for which the skin may
25:39 not *u* him as a worker in
25:46 *u* them as workers, but upon
Nu 10:8 *u* of them must serve as a
10:10 *u* must serve as a memorial
De 20:6 and not begun to *u* it
20:6 another man . . . begin to *u* it
28:30 you will not begin to *u* it
1Sa 8:16 have to *u* them for his work
Job 15:3 will be of no *u*, And mere
22:2 man be of *u* to God himself
22:2 should be of *u* toward him
30:2 of what *u* was it to me?
35:3 Of what *u* is it to you?
Ps 5:9 A smooth tongue they *u*
Isa 1:13 with the *u* of uncanny power
65:22 ones will *u* to the full
Jer 22:13 by *u* of his fellowman who
22:15 are competing by *u* of cedar
31:5 plant and start to *u* them
34:9 not to *u* them as servants
34:10 *u* them no more as servants
La 2:13 shall I *u* you as a witness
Eze 16:44 *u* the proverb, saying: Like
Da 11:12 not *u* his strong position
Ho 2:8 which they made *u* of for Baal
Mt 6:7 for their *u* of many words
13:10 by the *u* of illustrations
13:13 by the *u* of illustrations
24:15 let the reader *u* discernment
Mr 9:38 demons by the *u* of your name
13:14 let the reader *u* discernment
Lu 9:49 demons by the *u* of your name
10:17 by the *u* of your name
Joh 6:63 the flesh is of no *u* at all
Ro 1:26 changed the natural *u* of
1:27 the natural *u* of the female
9:21 one vessel for an honorable *u*
9:21 another for a dishonorable *u*
1Co 7:31 those making *u* of the world
9:12 we have not made *u* of this
9:15 not made *u* of a single one
2Co 10:2 I may not *u* boldness with
Ga 5:13 not *u* this freedom as an
1Ti 5:23 *u* a little wine for the sake
Heb 5:14 who through *u* have their
7:9 if I may *u* the expression
1Pe 4:10 *u* it in ministering to one
Jude 7 after flesh for unnatural *u*
Used
Ge 34:1 *u* to go out to see the
Ex 1:14 they *u* them as slaves under
6:3 And I *u* to appear to Abraham
38:24 gold that was *u* for the work
Le 7:24 may be *u* for anything else
Nu 11:5 fish that we *u* to eat in
21:34 who *u* to dwell in Heshbon
22:30 been *u* to do to you this way
De 2:11 *u* to call them Emim
2:20 it also *u* to be considered
2:20 *u* to call them Zamzummim
3:9 *u* to call Hermon Sirion, and
3:9 Amorites *u* to call it Senir
11:10 where you *u* to sow your seed
12:30 nations *u* to serve their gods
18:14 *u* to listen to those
29:17 you *u* to see their disgusting
32:38 Who *u* to eat the fat of
Jos 13:3 it *u* to be reckoned as
24:2 they *u* to serve other gods
Jg 8:10 men who *u* to draw the sword
14:10 the young fellows *u* to do
1Sa 2:23 And he *u* to say to them
9:9 *u* to be called a seer
12:6 who *u* Moses and Aaron and
2Sa 4:2 *u* to be counted as part of
13:14 *u* strength superior to hers
13:18 virgins, *u* to dress with
15:32 where people *u* to bow down
15:34 I *u* to prove myself the
20:18 *u* to speak in former times
2Ki 18:4 *u* to be called the copper
25:14 which they *u* to minister
2Ch 33:6 *u* divination and practiced
34:4 those that *u* to sacrifice
Es 8:10 post horses *u* in the royal
8:14 horses *u* in the royal service
Job 4:3 hands you *u* to strengthen
29:18 I *u* to say, Within my nest
31:13 I *u* to refuse the judgment
31:16 I *u* to hold back the lowly
31:17 I *u* to eat my morsel by
31:19 I *u* to see anyone perishing
31:25 If I *u* to rejoice because
31:26 If I *u* to see the light
31:29 If I *u* to rejoice at the
Ps 37:25 A young man I *u* to be
42:4 I *u* to pass along with the
42:4 I *u* to walk slowly before
55:14 *u* to enjoy sweet intimacy
55:14 we *u* to walk with the throng
Ca 8:2 my mother, who *u* to teach me
Isa 1:21 righteousness . . . *u* to lodge
7:23 *u* to be a thousand vines
7:25 that *u* to be cleared
10:24 rod *u* to strike you and
10:24 *u* to lift up his own staff
23:7 feet *u* to bring her far
49:4 I have *u* up my own power
51:23 you *u* to make your back
Jer 4:30 *u* to clothe yourself with
4:30 *u* to deck yourself with
4:30 *u* to enlarge your eyes with
4:30 *u* to make yourself pretty
20:7 *u* your strength against me
28:8 they also *u* to prophesy
44:17 *u* to be satisfied with bread
52:18 which they *u* to minister
La 2:15 city of which they *u* to say
Eze 15:5 it is not *u* for any work
15:5 be *u* for any further work
26:17 *u* to be inhabited from the
Ho 1:10 in which it *u* to be said
10:5 priests who *u* to be joyful
13:4 except me that you *u* to know
Mt 26:55 I *u* to sit in the temple
Mr 15:6 he *u* to release to them one
15:8 what he *u* to do for them
15:41 who *u* to accompany him and
Lu 5:25 picked up what he *u* to lie on
6:23 *u* to do to the prophets
15:16 he *u* to desire to be filled
16:19 rich, and he *u* to deck
16:20 *u* to be put at his gate
24:29 *u* pressure upon him, saying
Joh 2:22 to mind that he *u* to say
7:42 village where David *u* to be
9:8 *u* to see he was a beggar
9:8 man that *u* to sit and beg
11:36 affection he *u* to have for
12:6 *u* to carry off the monies
13:18 that *u* to feed on my bread
17:12 I *u* to watch over them
21:7 whom Jesus *u* to love said
21:18 *u* to gird yourself and walk
21:20 whom Jesus *u* to love
Ac 3:10 man that *u* to sit for gifts
4:13 that they *u* to be with Jesus
7:19 *u* statecraft against our race
9:39 Dorcas *u* to make while she
11:16 he *u* to say, John, for his
16:16 She *u* to furnish her masters
22:19 I *u* to imprison and flog in
Ro 3:13 *u* deceit with their tongues
6:21 fruit that you *u* to have at
1Co 10:4 For they *u* to drink from the
13:11 I *u* to speak as a babe
2Co 9:3 just as I *u* to say you would
Ga 1:23 only *u* to hear: The man that
2:12 *u* to eat with people of the
4:12 I *u* to be also as you are
Php 3:18 I *u* to mention them often
Col 2:22 being *u* up, in accordance
3:7 when you *u* to live in them
1Th 3:4 we *u* to tell you beforehand
2Th 2:5 I *u* to tell you these things
3:10 we *u* to give you this order
Heb 9:1 the former covenant *u* to have
12:9 we *u* to have fathers who
12:9 we *u* to give them respect
12:10 *u* to discipline us according
1Pe 3:5 *u* to adorn themselves
3:6 as Sarah *u* to obey Abraham
Jude 18 how they *u* to say to you
Re 6:9 work that they *u* to have

Useful
1Co 15:33 Bad associations spoil *u*
2Ti 2:21 *u* to his owner, prepared for
4:11 is *u* to me for ministering
Phm 11 but now *u* to you and to me

Usefulness
2Ti 2:14 a thing of no *u* at all

Useless
Zec 11:15 of a *u* shepherd
Lu 13:7 should it keep the ground *u*
Ro 4:14 faith has been made *u* and
1Co 1:17 torture stake . . . made *u*
15:17 your faith is *u*; you are yet
Phm 11 formerly *u* to you but now

Using
1Sa 15:23 same as *u* uncanny power and
1Ch 12:2 the bow, *u* the right hand
12:2 *u* the left hand with stones
Ec 10:10 the *u* of wisdom to success
Eze 16:44 *u* a proverb against you
34:27 had been *u* them as slaves
Ac 19:8 giving talks and *u* persuasion
27:17 *u* helps to undergird the
28:23 *u* persuasion with them
1Co 7:31 as those not *u* it to the full
2Co 3:12 *u* great freeness of speech

Usual
Ex 2:16 *u* they came and drew water
2:17 as *u* the shepherds came and
18:13 Moses sat down as *u* to serve
Jg 6:28 up early in the morning as *u*
9:27 went out as *u* into the field
17:10 the *u* outfit of garments and
19:5 up early in the morning as *u*
2Sa 13:12 not *u* to do that way in
2Ki 4:11 as *u* he came in there and
4:18 went out as *u* to his father
2Ch 1:5 congregation applied as *u* to
Ne 2:1 as *u* took up the wine and gave
Ps 107:13 he as *u* saved them
107:19 he as *u* saved them
Lu 12:48 demand more than *u* of him
1Th 2:17 far more than is *u* to see
Heb 2:1 pay more than the *u* attention

Usually
1Th 5:7 drunk are *u* drunk at night

Usurer
Ex 22:25 must not become like a *u* to
Ps 109:11 *u* lay out traps for all

Usury
Le 25:36 not take . . . *u* from him, but
25:37 not give your food out on *u*
Ne 5:7 *U* is what you are exacting
Pr 28:8 valuables by interest and *u*
Eze 18:8 and no *u* would he take
18:13 On *u* he has given, and
18:17 no *u* and interest has he
22:12 Interest and *u* you have

Utensil
Eze 4:9 put them in one *u* and make
15:3 which to hang any kind of *u*
Mr 11:16 carry a *u* through the temple

Utensils
Ex 25:39 make it with all these *u* of
27:3 will make all its *u* of copper
27:19 all the *u* of the tabernacle
30:27 its *u* and the lampstand and
30:27 *u* and the altar of incense
30:28 altar . . . and all its *u*
31:7 and all the *u* of the tent
31:8 the table and its *u*, and the
31:8 *u*, and the altar of incense
31:9 all its *u*, and the basin and
35:13 its *u* and the showbread
35:14 *u* and its lamps and the oil
35:16 its poles and all its *u*
37:16 *u* that are upon the table
37:24 he made it and all its *u*
38:3 made all the *u* of the altar
38:3 All its *u* he made of copper
38:30 and all the *u* of the altar
39:33 the tent and all its *u*, its
39:36 the table, all its *u* and the
39:37 all its *u* and the oil of
39:39 its poles and all its *u*, the
39:40 the *u* for the service of the
40:9 sanctify it and all its *u*
40:10 anoint . . . all its *u* and
Le 8:11 the altar and all its *u*
Nu 1:50 over all its *u* and over
1:50 tabernacle and all its *u*
3:8 *u* of the tent of meeting, even
3:31 *u* of the holy place with
3:36 all its *u* and all its service
4:10 *u* into a covering of sealskins
4:12 *u* of the ministry with which
4:14 *u* with which they regularly
4:14 all the *u* of the altar; and
4:15 *u* of the holy place when the
4:16 the holy place and its *u*
4:26 all their service *u*, and all
7:1 sanctify . . . all its *u*
18:3 to the *u* of the holy place
31:6 the holy *u* and the trumpets
1Ki 7:45 *u*, which Hiram made of
7:47 left all the *u* unweighed
7:48 *u* that pertained to the house
8:4 holy *u* that were in the tent
2Ki 7:15 *u* that the Syrians had
23:4 all the *u* made for Baal and
24:13 cut to pieces all the gold *u*
25:14 all the *u* of copper with
25:16 the copper of all these *u*
1Ch 9:28 the *u* of the service, for
9:29 men appointed over the *u* and
9:29 over all the holy *u* and over
18:8 the pillars and the copper *u*
22:19 holy *u* of the true God to
23:26 any of its *u* for its service
28:13 all the *u* of the service of
28:14 *u* for the different services
28:14 the *u* of silver by weight
28:14 *u* for the different services
2Ch 4:16 *u* Hiram-abiv made for King
4:18 Solomon made all these *u* in
4:19 *u* that were at the house of
5:1 *u* he put in the treasures of
5:5 holy *u* that were in the tent
15:18 silver and gold and *u*
24:14 make *u* for the house of
24:14 *u* for the ministry and for
24:14 *u* of gold and of silver; and
28:24 *u* of the house of the true
28:24 *u* of the house of the true
29:18 and all its *u*, and the table
29:18 table . . . and all its *u*
29:19 *u* that King Ahaz removed
36:7 the *u* of the house of Jehovah
36:18 all the *u*, great and small
Ezr 1:6 their hands with *u* of silver
1:7 *u* of the house of Jehovah
1:10 a thousand other *u*
1:11 the *u* of gold and of silver
8:25 and the gold and the *u*
8:26 silver *u* worth two talents
8:27 and two *u* of good copper
8:28 the *u* are something holy
8:30 and the gold and the *u*
8:33 the *u* in the house of our God
Ne 10:39 *u* of the sanctuary and the
13:5 the frankincense and the *u* and
13:9 *u* of the house of the true God
Isa 52:11 carrying the *u* of Jehovah
Jer 27:16 *u* of the house of Jehovah
27:18 the *u* that are remaining
27:19 the remainder of the *u* that
27:21 the *u* that are remaining
28:3 all the *u* of the house of
28:6 the *u* of the house of Jehovah
52:18 copper *u* with which they
Da 1:2 *u* of the house of the true God
1:2 and the *u* he brought to the

Uthai
1Ch 9:4 *U* the son of Ammihud the son
Ezr 8:14 sons of Bigvai, *U* and Zabbud

Utmost
2Ti 2:15 your *u* to present yourself
4:9 your *u* to come to me shortly
4:21 *u* to arrive before winter
Tit 3:12 *u* to come to me at Nicopolis
Heb 4:11 *u* to enter into that rest
2Pe 1:10 *u* to make the calling and
1:15 I will do my *u* also at every
3:14 do your *u* to be found finally

Utter
Jg 5:12 *u* a song! Rise up, Barak, and
Job 33:3 knowledge . . . my lips do *u*
Ps 35:28 tongue *u* in an undertone your
71:24 will *u* in an undertone your
106:2 *u* the mighty performances of
115:7 *u* no sound with their throat
Jer 23:31 may *u* forth, An utterance
1Co 14:9 *u* speech easily understood
2Pe 2:18 they *u* swelling expressions

Utterance
Ge 22:16 I do swear, is the *u* of
Nu 14:28 *u* of Jehovah, if I shall not
23:7 he took up his proverbial *u*
23:18 he took up his proverbial *u*
24:3 he took up his proverbial *u*
24:3 *u* of Balaam the son of Beor
24:3 *u* of the able-bodied man with
24:4 The *u* of the one hearing the
24:15 he took up his proverbial *u*
24:15 *u* of Balaam the son of Beor
24:15 *u* of the man with the eye
24:16 *u* of the one hearing the
24:20 his proverbial *u* and went on
24:21 his proverbial *u* and went on
24:23 his proverbial *u* and went on
De 23:23 The *u* of your lips you should
1Sa 2:30 the *u* of Jehovah the God of
2:30 But now the *u* of Jehovah is
2Sa 23:1 *u* of David the son of Jesse
23:1 the *u* of the able-bodied man
2Ki 9:26 is the *u* of Jehovah, and I
9:26 is the *u* of Jehovah. So now
19:33 is the *u* of Jehovah
22:19 heard, is the *u* of Jehovah
2Ch 34:27 heard, is the *u* of Jehovah
Job 27:1 to lift up his proverbial *u*
29:1 lift up his proverbial *u*
Ps 36:1 The *u* of transgression to
49:4 To a proverbial *u* I shall
110:1 The *u* of Jehovah to my Lord
Pr 30:1 *u* of the able-bodied man to
Isa 1:24 *u* of the true Lord, Jehovah
3:15 *u* of the Sovereign Lord
14:22 the *u* of Jehovah of armies
14:22 is the *u* of Jehovah
14:23 the *u* of Jehovah of armies
17:3 *u* of Jehovah of armies
17:6 *u* of Jehovah the God of
19:4 *u* of the true Lord, Jehovah
22:25 *u* of Jehovah of armies
30:1 is the *u* of Jehovah, those
31:9 *u* of Jehovah, whose light is
37:34 is the *u* of Jehovah
41:14 is the *u* of Jehovah, even
43:10 is the *u* of Jehovah, even
43:12 is the *u* of Jehovah, and I
49:18 living, is the *u* of Jehovah
52:5 is the *u* of Jehovah. For my
52:5 is the *u* of Jehovah, and
54:17 is the *u* of Jehovah
55:8 is the *u* of Jehovah
56:8 The *u* of the Sovereign Lord
59:20 is the *u* of Jehovah
66:2 to be, is the *u* of Jehovah
66:17 end, is the *u* of Jehovah
66:22 is the *u* of Jehovah
Jer 1:8 is the *u* of Jehovah
1:15 north, is the *u* of Jehovah
1:19 *u* of Jehovah, to deliver you
2:3 was the *u* of Jehovah
2:9 is the *u* of Jehovah, and with
2:12 is the *u* of Jehovah
2:19 is the *u* of the Sovereign
2:22 *u* of the Sovereign Lord
2:29 is the *u* of Jehovah
3:1 is the *u* of Jehovah
3:10 is the *u* of Jehovah
3:12 is the *u* of Jehovah
3:12 is the *u* of Jehovah
3:13 is the *u* of Jehovah
3:14 is the *u* of Jehovah
3:16 is the *u* of Jehovah
3:20 is the *u* of Jehovah
4:1 O Israel, is the *u* of Jehovah
4:9 that day, is the *u* of Jehovah
4:17 is the *u* of Jehovah
5:9 is the *u* of Jehovah
5:11 is the *u* of Jehovah
5:15 is the *u* of Jehovah
5:18 is the *u* of Jehovah
5:22 is the *u* of Jehovah
5:29 is the *u* of Jehovah
6:12 is the *u* of Jehovah
7:11 is the *u* of Jehovah
7:13 is the *u* of Jehovah
7:19 is the *u* of Jehovah
7:30 is the *u* of Jehovah
7:32 is the *u* of Jehovah, when it
8:1 is the *u* of Jehovah

Jer 8:3 is the *u* of Jehovah of armies
8:13 is the *u* of Jehovah
8:17 is the *u* of Jehovah
9:3 is the *u* of Jehovah
9:6 is the *u* of Jehovah
9:9 is the *u* of Jehovah
9:22 what the *u* of Jehovah is
9:24 is the *u* of Jehovah
9:25 is the *u* of Jehovah
12:17 is the *u* of Jehovah
13:11 is the *u* of Jehovah
13:14 is the *u* of Jehovah
13:25 is the *u* of Jehovah
15:3 is the *u* of Jehovah
15:6 is the *u* of Jehovah
15:9 is the *u* of Jehovah
15:20 is the *u* of Jehovah
16:5 is the *u* of Jehovah
16:11 is the *u* of Jehovah, and
16:14 is the *u* of Jehovah
16:16 is the *u* of Jehovah
17:24 is the *u* of Jehovah
18:6 is the *u* of Jehovah
19:6 is the *u* of Jehovah
19:12 is the *u* of Jehovah
21:7 is the *u* of Jehovah
21:10 is the *u* of Jehovah
21:13 is the *u* of Jehovah
21:14 is the *u* of Jehovah
22:5 is the *u* of Jehovah
22:16 is the *u* of Jehovah
22:24 is the *u* of Jehovah
23:1 is the *u* of Jehovah
23:2 is the *u* of Jehovah
23:4 is the *u* of Jehovah
23:5 is the *u* of Jehovah, and I
23:7 is the *u* of Jehovah, and
23:11 is the *u* of Jehovah
23:12 is the *u* of Jehovah
23:23 is the *u* of Jehovah
23:24 is the *u* of Jehovah
23:24 is the *u* of Jehovah
23:28 is the *u* of Jehovah
23:29 is the *u* of Jehovah
23:30 is the *u* of Jehovah
23:31 is the *u* of Jehovah
23:31 they may utter forth, An *u*
23:32 is the *u* of Jehovah
23:32 is the *u* of Jehovah
23:33 is the *u* of Jehovah
25:7 is the *u* of Jehovah
25:9 is the *u* of Jehovah
25:12 is the *u* of Jehovah
25:29 the *u* of Jehovah of armies
25:31 is the *u* of Jehovah
27:8 is the *u* of Jehovah
27:11 is the *u* of Jehovah
27:15 is the *u* of Jehovah
27:22 is the *u* of Jehovah
28:4 is the *u* of Jehovah
29:9 is the *u* of Jehovah
29:11 is the *u* of Jehovah
29:14 is the *u* of Jehovah
29:14 is the *u* of Jehovah
29:19 is the *u* of Jehovah
29:19 is the *u* of Jehovah
29:23 is the *u* of Jehovah
29:32 is the *u* of Jehovah
30:3 is the *u* of Jehovah
30:8 the *u* of Jehovah of armies
30:10 is the *u* of Jehovah
30:11 is the *u* of Jehovah
30:17 is the *u* of Jehovah
30:21 is the *u* of Jehovah
31:1 time, is the *u* of Jehovah
31:14 is the *u* of Jehovah
31:16 is the *u* of Jehovah, and
31:17 future, is the *u* of Jehovah
31:20 is the *u* of Jehovah
31:27 is the *u* of Jehovah
31:28 plant, is the *u* of Jehovah
31:31 is the *u* of Jehovah, and I
31:32 is the *u* of Jehovah
31:33 is the *u* of Jehovah
31:34 is the *u* of Jehovah
31:36 *u* of Jehovah, those who
31:37 is the *u* of Jehovah
31:38 *u* of Jehovah, and the city
32:5 is the *u* of Jehovah
32:30 hands, is the *u* of Jehovah
32:44 is the *u* of Jehovah
33:14 *u* of Jehovah, and I shall
34:5 is the *u* of Jehovah
34:17 *u* of Jehovah, to the sword
Jer 34:22 *u* of Jehovah, and I shall
35:13 is the *u* of Jehovah
39:17 is the *u* of Jehovah
39:18 in me, is the *u* of Jehovah
42:11 is the *u* of Jehovah, for I
44:29 *u* of Jehovah, that I am
45:5 *u* of Jehovah, and I will
46:5 is the *u* of Jehovah
46:18 As I am alive, is the *u* of
46:23 *u* of Jehovah, for it could
46:26 of old, is the *u* of Jehovah
46:28 *u* of Jehovah, for I am
48:12 *u* of Jehovah, and I will
48:15 *u* of the King, whose name
48:25 is the *u* of Jehovah
48:30 fury, is the *u* of Jehovah
48:35 Moab, is the *u* of Jehovah
48:38 delight, is the *u* of Jehovah
48:43 Moab, is the *u* of Jehovah
48:44 is the *u* of Jehovah
48:47 is the *u* of Jehovah
49:2 *u* of Jehovah, and I will
49:5 *u* of the Sovereign Lord
49:6 Ammon, is the *u* of Jehovah
49:13 sworn, is the *u* of Jehovah
49:16 is the *u* of Jehovah
49:26 *u* of Jehovah of armies
49:30 Hazor, is the *u* of Jehovah
49:31 is the *u* of Jehovah
49:32 is the *u* of Jehovah
49:37 is the *u* of Jehovah
49:38 is the *u* of Jehovah
49:39 Elam, is the *u* of Jehovah
50:4 *u* of Jehovah, the sons of
50:10 is the *u* of Jehovah
50:20 *u* of Jehovah, the error of
50:21 is the *u* of Jehovah
50:30 day, is the *u* of Jehovah
50:31 *u* of the Sovereign Lord
50:35 *u* of Jehovah, and against
50:40 *u* of Jehovah, no man will
51:24 is the *u* of Jehovah
51:25 *u* of Jehovah, you ruiner
51:26 is the *u* of Jehovah
51:39 is the *u* of Jehovah
51:48 is the *u* of Jehovah
51:52 coming, is the *u* of Jehovah
51:53 to her, is the *u* of Jehovah
51:57 *u* of the King, whose name
Eze 5:11 the *u* of the Sovereign Lord
11:8 the *u* of the Sovereign Lord
11:21 the *u* of the Sovereign Lord
12:25 the *u* of the Sovereign Lord
12:28 the *u* of the Sovereign Lord
13:6 saying, The *u* of Jehovah is
13:7 saying, The *u* of Jehovah is
13:8 the *u* of the Sovereign Lord
13:16 the *u* of the Sovereign Lord
14:11 the *u* of the Sovereign Lord
14:14 the *u* of the Sovereign Lord
14:16 the *u* of the Sovereign Lord
14:18 the *u* of the Sovereign Lord
14:20 the *u* of the Sovereign Lord
14:23 the *u* of the Sovereign Lord
15:8 the *u* of the Sovereign Lord
16:8 the *u* of the Sovereign Lord
16:14 the *u* of the Sovereign Lord
16:19 the *u* of the Sovereign Lord
16:23 the *u* of the Sovereign Lord
16:30 the *u* of the Sovereign Lord
16:43 the *u* of the Sovereign Lord
16:48 As I am alive, is the *u* of
16:58 is the *u* of Jehovah
16:63 the *u* of the Sovereign Lord
17:16 As I am alive, is the *u* of
18:3 the *u* of the Sovereign Lord
18:9 the *u* of the Sovereign Lord
18:23 the *u* of the Sovereign Lord
18:30 the *u* of the Sovereign Lord
18:32 the *u* of the Sovereign Lord
20:3 the *u* of the Sovereign Lord
20:31 the *u* of the Sovereign Lord
20:33 is the *u* of the Sovereign
20:36 is the *u* of the Sovereign
20:40 *u* of the Sovereign Lord
20:44 is the *u* of the Sovereign
21:7 the *u* of the Sovereign Lord
21:13 the *u* of the Sovereign Lord
22:12 is the *u* of the Sovereign
22:31 the *u* of the Sovereign Lord
23:34 the *u* of the Sovereign Lord
24:14 is the *u* of the Sovereign
25:14 is the *u* of the Sovereign
26:5 *u* of the Sovereign Lord
Eze 26:14 the *u* of the Sovereign Lord
26:21 is the *u* of the Sovereign
28:10 *u* of the Sovereign Lord
29:20 is the *u* of the Sovereign
30:6 the *u* of the Sovereign Lord
31:18 the *u* of the Sovereign Lord
32:8 the *u* of the Sovereign Lord
32:14 the *u* of the Sovereign Lord
32:16 the *u* of the Sovereign Lord
32:31 the *u* of the Sovereign Lord
32:32 the *u* of the Sovereign Lord
33:11 the *u* of the Sovereign Lord
34:8 the *u* of the Sovereign Lord
34:15 the *u* of the Sovereign Lord
34:30 the *u* of the Sovereign Lord
34:31 the *u* of the Sovereign Lord
35:6 the *u* of the Sovereign Lord
35:11 the *u* of the Sovereign Lord
36:14 the *u* of the Sovereign Lord
36:15 the *u* of the Sovereign Lord
36:23 the *u* of the Sovereign Lord
36:32 the *u* of the Sovereign Lord
37:14 is the *u* of Jehovah
38:18 the *u* of the Sovereign Lord
38:21 the *u* of the Sovereign Lord
39:5 the *u* of the Sovereign Lord
39:8 the *u* of the Sovereign Lord
39:10 the *u* of the Sovereign Lord
39:13 the *u* of the Sovereign Lord
39:20 the *u* of the Sovereign Lord
39:29 the *u* of the Sovereign Lord
43:19 *u* of the Sovereign Lord
43:27 *u* of the Sovereign Lord
44:12 *u* of the Sovereign Lord
44:15 *u* of the Sovereign Lord
44:27 *u* of the Sovereign Lord
45:9 *u* of the Sovereign Lord
45:15 *u* of the Sovereign Lord
47:23 *u* of the Sovereign Lord
48:29 *u* of the Sovereign Lord
Ho 2:13 forgot, is the *u* of Jehovah
2:16 *u* of Jehovah, that you will
2:21 answer, is the *u* of Jehovah
11:11 is the *u* of Jehovah
Joe 2:12 the *u* of Jehovah is, come
Am 2:11 is the *u* of Jehovah
2:16 is the *u* of Jehovah
3:10 is the *u* of Jehovah
3:13 the *u* of the Sovereign Lord
3:15 is the *u* of Jehovah
4:3 is the *u* of Jehovah
4:5 is the *u* of the Sovereign Lord
4:6 is the *u* of Jehovah
4:8 is the *u* of Jehovah
4:9 is the *u* of Jehovah
4:10 is the *u* of Jehovah
4:11 is the *u* of Jehovah
6:8 is the *u* of Jehovah the God
6:14 the *u* of Jehovah the God of
8:3 the *u* of the Sovereign Lord
8:9 the *u* of the Sovereign Lord
8:11 the *u* of the Sovereign Lord
9:7 is the *u* of Jehovah
9:8 is the *u* of Jehovah
9:12 is the *u* of Jehovah, who is
9:13 is the *u* of Jehovah, and the
Ob 4 is the *u* of Jehovah
8 is the *u* of Jehovah
Mic 4:6 is the *u* of Jehovah, I will
5:10 is the *u* of Jehovah
Na 2:13 the *u* of Jehovah of armies
3:5 is the *u* of Jehovah of armies
Zep 1:2 is the *u* of Jehovah
1:3 is the *u* of Jehovah
1:10 is the *u* of Jehovah, the
2:9 is the *u* of Jehovah of armies
3:8 is the *u* of Jehovah, till the
Hag 1:9 is the *u* of Jehovah of armies
1:13 is the *u* of Jehovah
2:4 is the *u* of Jehovah, and be
2:4 is the *u* of Jehovah, and work
2:4 the *u* of Jehovah of armies
2:8 is the *u* of Jehovah of armies
2:9 is the *u* of Jehovah of armies
2:14 is the *u* of Jehovah, and
2:17 is the *u* of Jehovah
2:23 the *u* of Jehovah of armies
2:23 is the *u* of Jehovah; and I
2:23 the *u* of Jehovah of armies
Zec 1:3 the *u* of Jehovah of armies
1:4 is the *u* of Jehovah
1:16 the *u* of Jehovah of armies
2:5 is the *u* of Jehovah
2:6 is the *u* of Jehovah

Zec 2:6 is the *u* of Jehovah
2:10 is the *u* of Jehovah
3:9 the *u* of Jehovah of armies
3:10 the *u* of Jehovah of armies
5:4 the *u* of Jehovah of armies
8:6 the *u* of Jehovah of armies
8:11 the *u* of Jehovah of armies
8:17 is the *u* of Jehovah
10:12 is the *u* of Jehovah
11:6 is the *u* of Jehovah
12:1 is the *u* of Jehovah, the One
12:4 is the *u* of Jehovah
13:2 the *u* of Jehovah of armies
13:7 the *u* of Jehovah of armies
13:8 is the *u* of Jehovah
Mal 1:2 is the *u* of Jehovah
Mt 4:4 but on every *u* coming forth
Lu 18:34 this *u* was hidden from them
22:61 Peter recalled the *u* of the
Ac 2:4 was granting them to make *u*
2:14 this *u* to them: Men of Judea
4:18 make any *u* or to teach upon
24:21 this one *u* which I cried out
Col 4:3 God may open a door of *u* to
4:6 *u* be always with graciousness
1Ti 4:1 inspired *u* says definitely
2Pe 2:16 making *u* with the voice of

Utterances
Job 15:3 mere *u* will be of no benefit
Ps 19:4 productive land their *u*
Isa 8:19 and making *u* in low tones
Ro 10:18 the inhabited earth their *u*
1Co 12:10 discernment of inspired *u*
1Ti 4:1 misleading inspired *u* and

Uttered
Ge 21:7 have *u* to Abraham, Sarah will
Re 10:3 the seven thunders *u* their

Uttering
Job 8:2 will you keep *u* these things
Joh 16:29 and are *u* no comparison
Ac 26:25 I am *u* sayings of truth and

Utterly
Job 27:12 show yourselves *u* vain

Uttermost
Ps 65:8 the inhabitants of the *u* parts

Utters
Ps 37:30 *u* wisdom in an undertone
Pr 8:7 my palate in low tones *u* truth

Uz
Ge 10:23 sons of Aram were *U* and Hul
22:21 *U* his firstborn and Buz his
36:28 sons of Dishan: *U* and Aran
1Ch 1:17 And *U* and Hul and Gether
1:42 sons of Dishan were *U* and
Job 1:1 a man in the land of *U* whose
Jer 25:20 the kings of the land of *U*
La 4:21 as you do in the land of *U*

Uzai
Ne 3:25 Palal the son of *U* did repair

Uzal
Ge 10:27 Hadoram and *U* and Diklah
1Ch 1:21 Hadoram and *U* and Diklah
Eze 27:19 Vedan and Javan from *U*

Uzza
2Ki 21:18 house, in the garden of *U*
21:26 grave in the garden of *U*
1Ch 8:7 became father to *U* and Ahihud
Ezr 2:49 the sons of *U*
Ne 7:51 the sons of *U*, the sons of

Uzzah
2Sa 6:3 *U* and Ahio, the sons of
6:6 *U* now thrust his hand out to
6:7 anger blazed against *U* and
6:8 in a rupture against *U*
1Ch 6:29 Shimei his son, *U* his son
13:7 *U* and Ahio were leading the
13:9 *U* now thrust his hand out to
13:10 anger blazed against *U*, so
13:11 in a rupture against *U*

Uzzen-sheerah
1Ch 7:24 and she got to build . . . *U*

Uzzi
1Ch 6:5 Bukki . . . became father to *U*
6:6 *U* . . . father to Zerahiah
6:51 *U* his son, Zerahiah his son
7:2 the sons of Tola were *U* and
7:3 the sons of *U* were Izrahiah
7:7 sons of Bela were Ezbon and *U*
1Ch 9:8 son of *U* the son of Michri
Ezr 7:4 *U* the son of Bukki
Ne 11:22 *U* the son of Bani the son of
12:19 Mattenai; for Jedaiah, *U*
12:42 *U* and Jehohanan and

Uzzia
1Ch 11:44 *U* the Ashterathite

Uzziah
2Ki 15:13 *U* the king of Judah
15:30 Jotham the son of *U*
15:32 *U* the king of Judah became
15:34 *U* his father had done
1Ch 6:24 *U* his son, and Shaul his son
27:25 was Jonathan the son of *U*
2Ch 26:1 *U*, he being sixteen years old
26:3 *U* when he began to reign
26:8 began to give tribute to *U*
26:9 *U* built towers in Jerusalem
26:11 *U* came to have a force
26:14 *U* continued to prepare for
26:18 stood up against *U* the king
26:18 not your business, O *U*, to
26:19 *U* became enraged while in
26:21 *U* the king continued to be
26:22 affairs of *U*, the first and
26:23 *U* lay down with his
27:2 all that *U* his father had
Ezr 10:21 sons of Harim . . . *U*
Ne 11:4 *U* the son of Zechariah
Isa 1:1 days of *U*, Jotham, Ahaz and
6:1 year that King *U* died I
7:1 *U*, the king of Judah, that
Ho 1:1 in the days of *U*, Jotham
Am 1:1 days of *U* the king of Judah
Zec 14:5 days of *U* the king of Judah
Mt 1:8 Jehoram became father to *U*
1:9 *U* became father to Jotham

Uzziel
Ex 6:18 sons of Kohath . . . *U*
6:22 sons of *U* were Mishael and
Le 10:4 the sons of *U*, Aaron's uncle
Nu 3:19 sons of Kohath . . . and *U*
3:30 Elizaphan the son of *U*
1Ch 4:42 Neariah and Rephaiah and *U*
6:2 the sons of Kohath were . . . *U*
6:18 sons of Kohath were . . . *U*
7:7 sons of Bela . . . Uzzi and *U*
15:10 of the sons of *U*, Amminadab
23:12 sons of Kohath . . . *U*, four
23:20 sons of *U* were Micah the
24:24 The sons of *U*, Micah; of
25:4 the sons of Heman . . . *U*
2Ch 29:14 of Jeduthun, Shemaiah and *U*
Ne 3:8 *U* the son of Harhaiah

Uzzielites
Nu 3:27 and the family of the *U*
1Ch 26:23 the Hebronites, for the *U*

Vacant
1Sa 20:18 because your seat will be *v*
20:25 but David's place was *v*
20:27 David's place continued *v*

Vaheb
Nu 21:14 *V* in Suphah and the torrent

Vain
De 32:21 vexed me with their *v* idols
1Ki 16:13 with their *v* idols
16:26 with their *v* idols
2Ki 17:15 went following *v* idols and
17:15 and became *v* themselves
Job 9:29 that I toil merely in *v*
27:12 show yourselves utterly *v*
39:16 In *v* is her toil because she
Ps 31:6 regard to worthless, *v* idols
39:6 they are boisterous in *v*
62:10 become *v* in sheer robbery
73:13 in *v* that I have cleansed my
89:47 in *v* that you have created
Pr 31:30 prettiness may be *v*; but the
Ec 6:4 in *v* has this one come and in
6:12 of the days of his *v* life
7:15 I have seen during my *v* days
9:9 all the days of your *v* life
Jer 2:5 kept walking after the *v* idol
2:5 and becoming *v* themselves
4:30 It is in *v* that you used to
8:19 with their *v* foreign gods
14:22 the *v* idols of the nations
23:16 are making you become *v*
46:11 In *v* you have multiplied
La 4:17 eyes keep pining away in *v*
Eze 6:10 not in *v* did I speak about
13:10 *v* there are those plastering
Zec 10:2 in *v* they try to comfort
Mt 13:13 looking, they look in *v*, and
13:13 and hearing, they hear in *v*
15:9 *v* that they keep worshiping
Mr 7:7 in *v* that they keep worshiping
Lu 8:10 they may look in *v* and
Ac 14:15 to turn from these *v* things
1Co 15:10 did not prove to be in *v*
15:14 preaching is certainly in *v*
15:14 and our faith is in *v*
15:58 your labor is not in *v* in
Ga 2:2 I was running or had run in *v*
Php 2:16 that I did not run in *v* or
2:16 or work hard in *v*
1Th 3:5 have turned out to be in *v*

Vainly
Job 21:34 *v* you men try to comfort

Vaizatha
Es 9:9 and Arisai and Aridai and *V*

Valiant
De 3:18 sons of Israel, all the *v* men
Jos 1:14 all the *v* mighty men, and
6:2 *v* mighty men, into your hand
8:3 men, *v* mighty ones, and to
10:7 and all the *v* mighty men
Jg 3:29 every one a *v* man; and not a
6:12 with you, you *v*, mighty one
11:1 had become a mighty, *v* man
18:2 men who were *v* fellows, out
20:44 all of these being *v* men
20:46 all these being *v* men
21:10 of the most *v* men there and
1Sa 10:26 *v* men whose heart God had
14:52 *v* person, he would gather
16:18 he is a *v*, mighty man and a
18:17 prove yourself a *v* person
31:12 *v* men rose up and went all
2Sa 2:7 prove yourselves *v* men
11:16 knew that there were *v* men
13:28 yourselves to be *v* men
17:10 the *v* man whose heart is as
17:10 *v* men that are with him
23:20 Jehoiada the son of a *v* man
24:9 eight hundred thousand *v* men
1Ki 1:42 a *v* man, and you bring good
1:52 If he will become a *v* man
11:28 Jeroboam was a *v*, mighty
2Ki 2:16 fifty men, *v* persons
5:1 proved to be a *v*, mighty man
15:20 all the *v*, mighty men
24:14 and all the *v*, mighty men
24:16 *v* men, seven thousand
1Ch 5:18 *v* fellows, men carrying
5:24 men that were *v*, mighty
7:2 Of Tola there were *v*, mighty
7:5 of Issachar were *v*, mighty
7:7 *v*, mighty men; and their
7:9 *v*, mighty men, was twenty
7:11 *v*, mighty men, seventeen
7:40 select, *v*, mighty men, heads
8:40 sons of Ulam came to be *v*
10:12 *v* men rose up and carried
11:22 the son of a *v* man, who did
12:8 *v*, mighty men, army men for
26:31 *v*, mighty men came to be
28:1 even every *v*, mighty man
2Ch 13:3 chosen men, *v*, mighty
14:8 these were *v*, mighty men
17:13 *v*, mighty men, were in
17:14 thousand *v*, mighty men
17:16 thousand *v*, mighty men
17:17 *v*, mighty man Eliada, and
25:6 *v*, mighty men for a hundred
26:12 *v*, mighty men, was two
26:17 eighty *v* men, came in
28:6 all *v* men, because of their
32:21 efface every *v*, mighty man
Ps 76:5 *v* men have found their hands
Heb 11:34 became *v* in war, routed the

Valiantly
1Sa 14:48 And he went on acting *v* and

Valid
Heb 9:17 covenant is *v* over dead

Validated
Ga 3:15 A *v* covenant, though it is
3:17 covenant previously *v* by God

Valley
Ge 11:2 *v* plain in the land of Shinar

Ge 26:17 encamped in the torrent *v* of
26:19 digging in the torrent *v* and
32:23 over the torrent *v*, and he
Le 23:40 poplars of the torrent *v*, and
Nu 13:23 to the torrent *v* of Eshcol
13:24 the torrent *v* of Eshcol, on
21:12 by the torrent *v* of Zered
21:20 the *v* that is in the field of
32:9 up to the torrent *v* of Eshcol
34:5 to the torrent *v* of Egypt, and
De 1:24 far as the torrent *v* of Eshcol
2:13 across the torrent *v* of Zered
2:13 the torrent *v* of Zered
2:14 crossed the torrent *v* of Zered
2:24 cross the torrent *v* of Arnon
2:36 the torrent *v* of Arnon, and
2:36 city that is in the torrent *v*
2:37 the torrent *v* of Jabbok, nor
3:8 the torrent *v* of Arnon as far
3:12 by the torrent *v* of Arnon, and
3:16 to the torrent *v* of Arnon
3:16 the torrent *v* being a boundary
3:16 the torrent *v* that is the
3:29 the *v* in front of Beth-peor
4:46 in the *v* in front of Beth-peor
4:48 the torrent *v* of Arnon, up to
8:7 in the *v* plain and in the
11:11 mountains and *v* plains
21:4 torrent *v* running with water
21:4 there in the torrent *v*
21:6 was broken in the torrent *v*
34:3 the *v* plain of Jericho, the
34:6 the *v* in the land of Moab in
Jos 8:11 the *v* between them and Ai
11:8 and the *v* plain of Mizpeh to
11:17 the *v* plain of Lebanon at
12:1 from the torrent *v* of Arnon
12:2 of the torrent *v* of Arnon
12:2 the middle of the torrent *v*
12:2 Jabbok the torrent *v*
12:7 in the *v* plain of Lebanon
13:9 of the torrent *v* of Arnon
13:9 the middle of the torrent *v*
13:16 the torrent *v* of Arnon
13:16 the middle of the torrent *v*
15:4 the torrent *v* of Egypt
15:7 is south of the torrent *v*
15:8 the *v* of the son of Hinnom
15:8 that faces the *v* of Hinnom
15:47 to the torrent *v* of Egypt
16:8 to the torrent *v* of Kanah
17:9 to the torrent *v* of Kanah
17:9 torrent *v* of these cities
17:9 the north of the torrent *v*
18:16 the *v* of the son of Hinnom
18:16 down to the *v* of Hinnom
19:11 torrent *v* that is in front
19:14 to be at the *v* of Iphtah-el
19:27 the *v* of Iphtah-el to the
Jg 4:7 at the torrent *v* of Kishon
4:13 to the torrent *v* of Kishon
16:4 torrent *v* of Sorek, and her
1Sa 13:18 toward the *v* of Zeboim
15:5 in ambush by the torrent *v*
17:3 with the *v* between them
17:40 stones from the torrent *v*
17:52 clear to the *v* and as far as
30:9 torrent *v* of Besor, and the
30:10 over the torrent *v* of Besor
30:21 by the torrent *v* of Besor
2Sa 8:13 Edomites in the *V* of Salt
15:23 by the torrent *v* of Kidron
17:13 down to the torrent *v*
24:5 the middle of the torrent *v*
1Ki 2:37 the torrent *v* of Kidron
8:65 to the torrent *v* of Egypt
15:13 the torrent *v* of Kidron
17:3 at the torrent *v* of Cherith
17:4 from the torrent *v* you
17:5 by the torrent *v* of Cherith
17:6 torrent *v* he kept drinking
17:7 the torrent *v* became dry
18:40 the torrent *v* of Kishon and
2Ki 3:16 torrent *v* full of ditches
3:17 *v* will be filled with water
10:33 the torrent *v* of Arnon
14:7 Edomites in the *V* of Salt
23:6 to the torrent *v* of Kidron
23:6 in the torrent *v* of Kidron
23:10 the *v* of the sons of Hinnom
23:12 the torrent *v* of Kidron
24:7 the torrent *v* of Egypt up to
1Ch 4:39 clear to the east of the *v*
18:12 Edomites in the *V* of Salt
2Ch 7:8 to the torrent *v* of Egypt
14:10 *v* of Zephathah at Mareshah
15:16 in the torrent *v* of Kidron
20:16 end of the torrent *v* in
25:11 go to the *V* of Salt; and
26:9 *V* Gate and by the Buttress
28:3 *v* of the son of Hinnom and
29:16 torrent *v* of Kidron outside
30:14 into the torrent *v* of Kidron
33:6 *v* of the son of Hinnom, and
33:14 in the torrent *v* and as far
35:22 in the *v* plain of Megiddo
Ne 2:13 to go out by the *V* Gate by
2:15 in the torrent *v* by night
2:15 entered by the *V* Gate, and
3:13 The *V* Gate was what Hanun
6:2 villages of the *v* plain of Ono
11:30 clear to the *v* of Hinnom
11:35 Ono, the *v* of the craftsmen
Job 21:33 clods . . . of a torrent *v*
40:22 poplars of the torrent *v*
Ps 23:4 walk in the *v* of deep shadow
60:*super* Edom in the *V* of Salt
83:9 at the torrent *v* of Kishon
104:8 *V* plains proceeded to descend
110:7 torrent *v* in the way he will
Pr 30:17 ravens of the torrent *v* will
Ca 6:11 see the buds in the torrent *v*
Isa 15:7 torrent *v* of the poplars
22:1 of the *v* of the vision
22:5 has in the *v* of the vision
27:12 to the torrent *v* of Egypt
28:1 head of the fertile *v* of
28:4 fertile *v* must become like
40:4 Let every *v* be raised up
40:4 the rugged ground a *v* plain
41:18 midst of the *v* plains
57:6 stones of the torrent *v* was
63:14 goes down into the *v* plain
Jer 2:23 See your way in the *v*
7:31 the *v* of the son of Hinnom
7:32 the *v* of the son of Hinnom
7:32 but the *v* of the killing
19:2 the *v* of the son of Hinnom
19:6 the *v* of the son of Hinnom
19:6 but the *v* of the killing
31:40 torrent *v* of Kidron, clear
32:35 *v* of the son of Hinnom, in
Eze 3:22 go forth to the *v* plain, and
3:23 went forth to the *v* plain
8:4 that I had seen in the *v* plain
37:1 in the midst of the *v* plain
37:2 the surface of the *v* plain
39:11 the *v* of those passing
39:11 the *V* of Gog's Crowd
39:15 in the *V* of Gog's Crowd
47:19 torrent *v* to the Great Sea
48:28 torrent *v*, as far as the
Joe 3:18 torrent *v* of the Acacia Trees
Am 6:14 the torrent *v* of the Arabah
Mic 1:6 down into the *v* her stones
Zec 12:11 in the *v* plain of Megiddo
14:4 will be a very great *v*
14:5 certainly flee to the *v* of
14:5 the *v* of the mountains will

Valleys
Nu 21:14 and the torrent *v* of Arnon
21:15 the mouth of the torrent *v*
24:6 Like torrent *v* they have
De 8:7 a land of torrent *v* of water
10:7 torrent *v* running with water
2Sa 23:30 the torrent *v* of Gaash
1Ki 18:5 and to all the torrent *v*
2Ki 2:16 mountains or in one of the *v*
1Ch 11:32 from the torrent *v* of Gaash
Job 22:24 in the rock of torrent *v*
30:6 the very slope of torrent *v*
Ps 104:10 springs into the torrent *v*
Isa 7:19 the precipitous torrent *v*
57:5 children in the torrent *v*
Jer 31:9 walk to torrent *v* of water
Eze 6:3 the stream beds and to the *v*
7:16 like the doves of the *v*, all
31:12 in all the *v* its foliage
32:5 fill the *v* with the refuse
35:8 *v* and all your stream beds
36:4 the *v* and to the devastated
36:6 stream beds and to the *v*

Valor
1Ch 12:21 were mighty men of *v*, and
12:25 men of *v* of the army
12:28 a young man, mighty in *v*
12:30 mighty men of *v*, men of
Ne 11:14 brothers, mighty men of *v*

Valorous
Eze 27:11 and *v* men were the ones

Valuable
Jg 18:21 the *v* things ahead of them
Job 20:10 will give back his *v* things
Ps 112:3 *V* things and riches are in
119:14 over all other *v* things
Pr 3:9 Jehovah with your *v* things
10:15 *v* things of a rich man are
11:4 *V* things will be of no
13:7 yet he has many *v* things
13:11 *V* things resulting from
18:11 *v* things of the rich are his
28:22 bestirring himself after *v*
29:3 with prostitutes destroys *v*
Ca 8:7 *v* things of his house for love
Eze 27:12 all sorts of *v* things
27:18 all your *v* things, with
27:27 *v* things and your stores
27:33 abundance of your *v* things
Ho 12:8 I have found *v* things for

Valuables
Pr 1:13 all sorts of precious *v*
6:31 *v* of his house he will give
28:8 multiplying his *v* by interest

Valuation
Le 27:8 priest must put a *v* upon him
27:8 priest will put a *v* upon him
27:12 priest must put a *v* upon it
27:14 priest must then make a *v*
27:14 *v* the priest makes of it, so
27:23 amount of the *v* up till the
2Ki 12:4 according to individual *v*
Job 28:13 has not come to know its *v*

Value
Le 5:15 estimated *v* in silver shekels
5:18 according to the estimated *v*
6:6 the estimated *v*, for a guilt
25:16 increase its purchase *v*, and
25:16 should reduce its purchase *v*
27:2 according to the estimated *v*
27:3 estimated *v* has to be of a
27:3 *v* must then become fifty
27:4 *v* must then become thirty
27:5 *v* of the male must then
27:6 *v* of the male must then
27:6 female the estimated *v* must
27:7 male, the estimated *v* must
27:8 too poor for the estimated *v*
27:12 *v* estimated by the priest
27:13 addition to the estimated *v*
27:15 money of the estimated *v* in
27:16 *v* must then be estimated in
27:17 according to the estimated *v*
27:18 be made from the estimated *v*
27:19 fifth . . . of the estimated *v*
27:23 the estimated *v* on that day
27:25 *v* should be estimated in the
27:27 to the estimated *v*, he
27:27 according to the estimated *v*
Nu 18:16 the estimated *v*, five silver
20:19 certainly give the *v* of it
De 15:18 double the *v* of a hired
2Ch 9:12 *v* of what she brought to the
Job 13:4 you are physicians of no *v*
Ps 44:12 You sell your people for no *v*
Pr 24:4 and pleasant things of *v*
31:10 Her *v* is far more than that
Zec 11:13 the majestic *v* with which
Mal 3:14 It is of no *v* to serve God
Mt 5:26 last coin of very little *v*
10:29 sell for a coin of small *v*
13:46 finding one pearl of high *v*
Mr 12:42 which have very little *v*
Lu 12:6 sell for two coins of small *v*
12:59 small coin of very little *v*
21:2 coins of very little *v* there
2Co 10:7 according to their face *v*
Ga 5:6 circumcision is of any *v* nor
Php 3:8 excelling *v* of the knowledge
Col 2:23 are of no *v* in combating the
Heb 10:29 ordinary *v* the blood of
1Pe 1:7 greater *v* than gold that
3:4 of great *v* in the eyes of God

Valued
Zec 11:13 *v* from their standpoint

Valueless
Le 19:4 to *v* gods, and you must not
26:1 make *v* gods for yourselves

Jer 3:9 because of her frivolous *v*
Mt 28:1 Mary came to *v* the grave
Mr 6:26 in *v* of the oaths and those
12:41 the treasury chests in *v*
13:3 with the temple in *v*, Peter
14:8 my body in *v* of the burial
15:39 standing by with him in *v*
Joh 1:14 we had a *v* of his glory
1:38 getting a *v* of them
4:35 your eyes and *v* the fields
12:7 *v* of the day of my burial
Ro 5:21 life in *v* through Jesus
6:16 of sin with death in *v* or of
6:16 with righteousness in *v*
6:19 with lawlessness in *v*, so
6:19 with holiness in *v*
15:7 with glory to God in *v*
1Co 1:4 for you in *v* of the undeserved
7:26 in *v* of the necessity here
2Co 2:17 under God's *v*, in company
8:8 in *v* of the earnestness of
Ga 6:8 sowing with a *v* to his flesh
6:8 sowing with a *v* to the spirit
Eph 3:2 was given me with you in *v*
4:12 with a *v* to the readjustment
Col 2:2 with a *v* to all the riches of
2:2 a *v* to an accurate knowledge
2Th 2:6 a *v* to his being revealed
Heb 5:12 teachers in *v* of the time
1Pe 4:7 vigilant with a *v* to prayers
Jude 21 with everlasting life in *v*

Viewed
Mt 23:5 do to be *v* by men; for they
Lu 19:41 he *v* the city and wept over
Joh 1:32 I *v* the spirit coming down
20:6 And he *v* the bandages lying
20:12 she *v* two angels in white
20:14 back and *v* Jesus standing
1Jo 1:1 *v* attentively and our hands

Viewing
Mt 27:55 women were there *v* from
Mr 15:40 women *v* from a distance
Joh 2:23 *v* his signs that he was

Viewpoint
1Sa 18:8 saying was bad from his *v*

Vigil
Job 21:32 over a tomb a *v* will be

Vigilant
1Pe 4:7 be *v* with a view to prayers

Vigor
Ge 49:3 my firstborn, my *v* and the
Job 5:26 will come in *v* to the burial
18:7 His steps of *v* . . . cramped
18:12 His *v* becomes famished, And
20:11 been full of his youthful *v*
30:2 In them *v* has perished
33:25 days of his youthful *v*

Vigorous
Ps 89:8 Who is *v* like you, O Jah?
Isa 1:31 *v* man will certainly become
28:2 has someone strong and *v*
40:26 he also being *v* in power
Am 2:9 was *v* like the massive trees

Vigorously
Lu 13:24 Exert yourselves *v* to get

Vile
Joh 3:20 he that practices *v* things
5:29 those who practiced *v* things
Ro 9:11 practiced anything good or *v*
2Co 5:10 whether it is good or *v*
Tit 2:8 nothing *v* to say about us
Jas 3:16 disorder and every *v* thing

Vileness
Ps 12:8 *v* is exalted among the sons

Village
1Sa 6:18 to the *v* of the open country
2Sa 23:13 a tent *v* of the Philistines
Mt 10:11 whatever city or *v* you enter
21:2 Be on your way into the *v*
Mr 1:38 into the *v* towns nearby, that
8:23 brought him outside the *v*
8:26 But do not enter into the *v*
11:2 Go into the *v* that is within
Lu 5:17 every *v* of Galilee and Judea
8:1, 1 from *v* to *v*, preaching and
9:6, 6 the territory from *v* to *v*
9:52 into a *v* of Samaritans, to
9:56 So they went to a different *v*
10:38 he entered into a certain *v*
Lu 13:22, 22 from *v* to *v*, teaching
17:12 entering into a certain *v*
19:30 the *v* that is within sight
24:13 to a *v* about seven miles
24:28 *v* where they were journeying
Joh 7:42 *v* where David used to be
11:1 Bethany, of the *v* of Mary
11:30 not yet . . . come into the *v*

Villages
Nu 32:41 went capturing their tent *v*
De 3:14 call those *v* of Bashan by his
Jos 13:30 all the tent *v* of Jair
1Ki 4:13 he had the tent *v* of Jair
1Ch 27:25 in the *v* and in the towers
Ne 6:2 *v* of the valley plain of Ono
Mt 9:35 tour of all the cities and *v*
14:15 may go into the *v* and buy
Mr 6:6 about to the *v* in a circuit
6:36 into the countryside and *v*
6:56 enter into *v* or cities or
8:27 left for the *v* of Caesarea
Lu 9:12 that they may go into the *v*
Ac 8:25 to many *v* of the Samaritans

Villainy
Ac 13:10 and every sort of *v*, you
18:14 wrong or a wicked act of *v*

Vindictive
Ac 28:4 *v* justice did not permit him

Vine
Ge 40:9 here there was a *v* before me
40:10 on the *v* there were three
49:11 his full-grown ass to a *v*
49:11 own she-ass to a choice *v*
Le 25:5 grapes of your unpruned *v* you
Nu 6:4 made from the wine *v*, from the
De 32:32, 32 *v* is from the *v* of Sodom
Jg 9:12 the trees said to the *v*, You
9:13 *v* said to them, Must I give
13:14 Nothing . . . from the wine *v*
1Ki 4:25 under his own *v* and under
2Ki 4:39 he got to find a wild *v* and
18:31 eat each one from his own *v*
Job 15:33 just like a *v*, And cast off
Ps 78:47 their *v* even by the hail
80:8 make a *v* depart from Egypt
80:14 see and take care of this *v*
128:3 be like a fruit-bearing *v*
Ca 2:12 the very time of *v* trimming
6:11 whether the *v* had sprouted
7:8 become like clusters of the *v*
7:12 whether the *v* has sprouted
Isa 5:2 plant it with a choice red *v*
16:8 *v* of Sibmah—the owners of
16:9 over the *v* of Sibmah
24:7 the *v* has withered, all
32:12 over the fruit-bearing *v*
34:4 leafage shrivels off the *v*
36:16 each one from his own *v*
Jer 2:21 you as a choice red *v*
2:21 shoots of a foreign *v*
5:10 Come up against her *v* rows
5:17 eat up your *v* and your fig
6:9 Israel just like a *v*
6:9 grapes upon the *v* tendrils
8:13 will be no grapes on the *v*
48:32 weep for you, O *v* of Sibmah
Eze 15:2 *v* tree happen to be different
15:6 like the *v* tree among the
17:6 luxuriantly growing *v* low in
17:6 became a *v* and produced
17:7 very *v* stretched its roots
17:8 to become a majestic *v*
19:10 Your mother was like a *v* in
Ho 2:12 lay desolate her *v* and her fig
10:1 Israel is a degenerating *v*
14:7 and will bud like the *v*
Joe 1:7 It has set my *v* as an object
1:12 *v* itself has shown dryness
2:22 the *v* must give their vital
Mic 4:4 under his *v* and under his fig
Hag 2:19 the *v* and the fig tree and
Zec 3:10 under the *v* and while under
8:12 the *v* itself will give its
Mal 3:11 the *v* in the field prove
Mt 26:29 any of this product of the *v*
Mr 14:25 of the product of the *v*
Lu 22:18 from the product of the *v*
Joh 15:1 I am the true *v*, and my
15:4 unless it remains in the *v*
15:5 I am the *v*, you are the
Jas 3:12 or a *v* figs, can it? Neither
Re 14:18 gather the clusters of the *v*
Re 14:19 gathered the *v* of the earth

Vinedresser
Lu 13:7 he said to the *v*, Here it is

Vinedressers
2Ki 25:12 *v* and compulsory laborers
2Ch 26:10 and *v* in the mountains
Isa 61:5 your farmers and your *v*
Jer 52:16 let remain as *v* and as
Joe 1:11 *v* have howled, on account of

Vinegar
Nu 6:3 not drink the *v* of wine or the
6:3 *v* of intoxicating liquor, nor
Ru 2:14 and dip your piece in the *v*
Ps 69:21 tried to make me drink *v*
Pr 10:26 As *v* to the teeth and as
25:20 is as *v* upon alkali and as a

Vines
Le 25:11 the grapes of its unpruned *v*
Nu 20:5 It is no place of . . . *v* and
De 8:8 barley and *v* and figs and
Ps 105:33 strike their *v* and their fig
Ca 2:13 *v* are abloom, they have given
Isa 7:23 used to be a thousand *v*
Hab 3:17 may be no yield on the *v*

Vineyard
Ge 9:20 Now Noah . . . plant a *v*
Ex 22:5 field or a *v* to be grazed over
22:5 with the best of his own *v*
23:11 do with your *v* and your
Le 19:10 the leftovers of your *v*, and
19:10 scattered grapes of your *v*
25:3 prune your *v*, and you must
25:4 and your *v* you must not prune
Nu 16:14 inheritance of field and *v*
20:17 pass through a field or a *v*
21:22 turn off into a field or a *v*
De 20:6 planted a *v* and not begun to
22:9 your *v* with two sorts of seed
22:9 the product of the *v* may be
23:24 into the *v* of your fellowman
24:21 gather the grapes of your *v*
28:30 You will plant a *v*, but you
1Ki 21:1 a *v* that happened to belong
21:2 give me your *v*, that it may
21:2 in place of it a *v* better
21:6 Do give me your *v* for money
21:6 another *v* in place of it
21:6 I shall not give you my *v*
21:7 give you the *v* of Naboth the
21:15 *v* of Naboth the Jezreelite
21:16 down to the *v* of Naboth
21:18 he is in the *v* of Naboth
Job 24:6 the *v* of the wicked one they
Pr 24:30 the *v* of the man in need of
31:16 her hands she has planted a *v*
Ca 1:6 my *v*, one that was mine, I
8:11 a *v* that Solomon happened to
8:11 gave the *v* over to the keepers
8:12 My *v*, which belongs to me
Isa 1:8 remaining like a booth in a *v*
3:14 have burned down the *v*
5:1 my loved one concerning his *v*
5:1 *v* that my beloved one came to
5:3 judge between me and my *v*
5:4 yet to do for my *v* that I
5:5 what I am doing to my *v*
5:7 *v* of Jehovah of armies is the
5:10 ten acres of *v* will produce
27:2 A *v* of foaming wine!
Jer 12:10 have brought my *v* to ruin
35:7 no *v* must you plant, nor
35:9 no *v* or field or seed
Mic 1:6 the planting places of a *v*
Mt 20:1 to hire workers for his *v*
20:2 he sent them forth into his *v*
20:4 You also, go into the *v*, and
20:7 You too go into the *v*
20:8 master of the *v* said to his
21:28 go work today in the *v*
21:33 planted a *v* and put a fence
21:39 threw him out of the *v* and
21:40 the owner of the *v* comes
21:41 the *v* to other cultivators
Mr 12:1 A man planted a *v*, and put a
12:2 the fruits of the *v* from the
12:8 and threw him outside the *v*
12:9 What will the owner of the *v*
12:9 and will give the *v* to others
Lu 13:6 a fig tree planted in his *v*
20:9 planted a *v* and let it out to
20:10 some of the fruit of the *v*

Lu 20:13 the owner of the *v* said
20:15 threw him outside the *v* and
20:15 owner of the *v* do to them
20:16 will give the *v* to others
1Co 9:7 plants a *v* and does not eat of

Vineyards
Nu 22:24 narrow way between the *v*
De 6:11 *v* and olive trees that you did
28:39 *V* you will plant and
Jos 24:13 *V* and olive groves that you
Jg 9:27 the grapes of their *v* and in
14:5 as far as the *v* of Timnah
15:5 and the *v* and the olive groves
21:20 must lie in wait in the *v*
21:21 also come out from the *v* and
1Sa 8:14 and your *v* . . . he will take
8:15 *v* he will take the tenth
22:7 to all of you fields and *v*
2Ki 5:26 olive groves or *v* or sheep
18:32 a land of bread and *v*
19:29 *v* and eat their fruitage
1Ch 27:27 over the *v* there was Shimei
27:27 the *v* for the wine supplies
Ne 5:3 fields and our *v* and our houses
5:4 on our fields and our *v*
5:5 and our *v* belong to others
5:11 their fields, their *v*, their
9:25 *v* and olive groves and trees
Job 24:18 toward the way of the *v*
Ps 107:37 sow fields and plant *v*
Ec 2:4 I planted *v* for myself
Ca 1:6 me the keeper of the *v*
1:14 among the *v* of En-gedi
2:15 that are making spoil of the *v*
2:15 as our *v* are abloom
7:12 rise early and go to the *v*
Isa 16:10 *v* there is no joyful crying
36:17 a land of bread and *v*
37:30 plant *v* and eat their
65:21 *v* and eat their fruitage
Jer 31:5 *v* in the mountains of
32:15 and *v* will yet be bought
39:10 give them *v* and compulsory
Eze 28:26 build houses and plant *v*
Ho 2:15 I will give her her *v* from
Am 4:9 your gardens and of your *v*
5:11 desirable *v* you have planted
5:17 all *v* there will be wailing
9:14 plant *v* and drink the wine
Zep 1:13 and they will plant *v*

Violate
Le 26:44 *v* my covenant with them; for
Nu 30:2 he must not *v* his word
1Ti 4:7 which *v* what is holy and
6:20 speeches that *v* what is holy
2Ti 2:16 speeches that *v* what is holy

Violated
Ge 34:2 lay down with her and *v* her
Le 21:7 *v* woman they should not take
21:14 one *v*, a prostitute, none of

Violates
Ezr 6:11 anybody that *v* this decree

Violating
Le 26:15 extent of your *v* my covenant

Violation
Le 18:23 It is a *v* of what is natural
20:12 a *v* of what is natural
Ezr 6:12 to commit a *v* and destroy
2Pe 2:16 own *v* of what was right

Violence
Ge 6:11 earth became filled with *v*
6:13 earth is full of *v* as a
16:5 Sarai said to Abram: The *v*
21:25 well . . . seized by *v*
49:5 Instruments of *v* are their
Ex 23:1 a witness who schemes *v*
De 19:16 a witness scheming *v* should
Jg 9:24 the *v* done to the seventy sons
2Sa 22:3 from *v* you save me
Job 16:17 is no *v* upon my palms
19:7 I keep crying out, *V!* but I
Ps 7:16 his own *v* will descend
11:5 anyone loving *v* His soul
18:48 From the man of *v* you will
27:12 And he who launches forth *v*
55:9 I have seen *v* and disputing
58:2 for the very *v* of your hands
72:14 from *v* he will redeem their
73:6 *V* envelops them as a garment
74:20 full of the abodes of *v*
Ps 140:1 from the man of deeds of *v*
140:4 from the man of deeds of *v*
140:11 man of *v*—let evil itself
Pr 3:31 envious of the man of *v*
4:17 wine of acts of *v* is what
8:36 is doing *v* to his soul
10:6 wicked ones, it covers up *v*
10:11 wicked ones, it covers up *v*
13:2 dealing treacherously is *v*
16:29 A man of *v* will seduce his
26:6 one that is drinking mere *v*
Isa 53:9 that he had done no *v* and
59:6 activity of *v* is in their
60:18 No more will *v* be heard in
Jer 6:7 *V* and despoiling are heard
20:8 *V* and despoiling are what I
22:3 Do them no *v*. And do not
51:35 *v* done to me and to my
51:46 *v* in the earth and ruler
Eze 7:11 *V* itself has risen up into a
7:23 city . . . become full of *v*
8:17 to fill the land with *v* and
12:19 *v* of all those dwelling in
22:26 have done *v* to my law
28:16 the midst of you with *v*
45:9 Remove the *v* and the
Joe 3:19 the *v* to the sons of Judah
Am 3:10 those who are storing up *v*
6:3 bring near the dwelling of *v*
Ob 10 the *v* to your brother Jacob
Jon 3:8 the *v* that was in their hands
Mic 6:12 men have become full of *v*
Hab 1:2 I call to you for aid from *v*
1:3 despoiling and *v* in front of
1:9 entirety it comes for mere *v*
2:8 the *v* to the earth, the town
2:17 the *v* done to Lebanon is
2:17 the *v* done to the earth
Zep 1:9 with *v* and deception
3:4 they did *v* to the law
Mal 2:16 with *v* has covered over his
Ac 5:26 but without *v*, as they were
21:35 of the *v* of the crowd

Violent
Ge 37:22 do not lay a *v* hand upon him
De 17:8 a *v* deed has been committed
21:5 dispute over every *v* deed
2Sa 22:49 From the man of *v* deeds you
Ps 25:19 with a *v* hatred they have
35:11 *V* witnesses rise up; What I
Ec 5:8 the *v* taking away of judgment
Isa 22:17 down with *v* hurling
Mr 4:37 great *v* windstorm broke out
Lu 8:23 a *v* windstorm descended upon
Ac 14:5 *v* attempt took place on the
Ro 10:19 incite you to *v* anger
1Ti 6:5 *v* disputes about trifles on
2Pe 2:17 mists driven by a *v* storm

Violently
Job 21:27 you would act *v* against me
40:23 If the river acts *v*, it does
Jer 13:22 heels have been treated *v*
La 2:6 he treats his booth *v* like that
Eze 22:12 you *v* keep making gain of
Hab 2:7 wake up who are *v* shaking you
Lu 9:42 the demon . . . *v* convulsed him
Joh 7:23 *v* angry at me because I made
Ac 27:15 boat was *v* seized and was
27:18 *v* tossed with the tempest
27:41 stern began to be *v* broken
Ro 1:27 *v* inflamed in their lust

Viper
Job 20:16 tongue of a *v* will kill him
Ps 140:3 venom of the horned *v* is
Pr 23:32 secretes poison just like a *v*
Isa 30:6 *v* and the flying fiery snake
59:5 would be hatched into a *v*
Ac 28:3 *v* came out due to the heat

Vipers
Mt 3:7 You offspring of *v*, who has
12:34 Offspring of *v*, how can you
23:33 Serpents, offspring of *v*
Lu 3:7 You offspring of *v*, who has

Virgin
Ge 24:16 *v*, and no man had had sexual
Ex 22:16 a man seduces a *v* who is not
Le 21:3 *v* who is close to him, who
21:14 take a *v* from his people as
De 22:19 bad name upon a *v* of Israel
22:23 a *v* girl engaged to a man
22:28 a *v* who has not been engaged
De 32:25 Of both young man and *v*
Jg 19:24 *v* daughter and his concubine
2Sa 13:2 because she was a *v*
1Ki 1:2 a *v*, for my lord the king
2Ki 19:21 The *v* daughter of Zion has
2Ch 36:17 young man or *v*, old or
Job 31:1 show myself attentive to a *v*
Isa 23:12 the *v* daughter of Sidon
37:22 *v* daughter of Zion has
47:1 O *v* daughter of Babylon
62:5 ownership of a *v* as his wife
Jer 2:32 Can a *v* forget her ornaments
14:17 the *v* daughter of my people
18:13 the *v* of Israel has done to
31:4 be rebuilt, O *v* of Israel
31:13 *v* will rejoice in the dance
31:21 Come back, O *v* of Israel
46:11 O *v* daughter of Egypt
51:22 dash young man and *v* to
La 1:15 to the *v* daughter of Judah
2:13 O *v* daughter of Zion
Eze 9:6 *v* and little child and women
Joe 1:8 a *v* girded with sackcloth
Am 5:2 The *v*, Israel, has fallen
Mt 1:23 The *v* will become pregnant
Lu 1:27 a *v* promised in marriage to a
1:27 the name of the *v* was Mary
1Co 7:28 if a *v* person married, such
7:34 and the *v*, is anxious for the
2Co 11:2 as a chaste *v* to the Christ

Virginity
Le 21:13 should take a woman in her *v*
De 22:14 did not find evidence of *v*
22:15 evidence of the girl's *v* to
22:17 does not have evidence of *v*
22:17 evidence of my daughter's *v*
22:20 evidence of *v* was not found
Jg 11:37 and let me weep over my *v*
11:38 weeping over her *v* upon the
Eze 23:3 the bosoms of their *v*
23:8 pressed the bosoms of her *v*
Lu 2:36 seven years from her *v*
1Co 7:36 toward his *v*, if that is
7:37 to keep his own *v*, he will
7:38 gives his *v* in marriage does

Virgins
Ex 22:17 rate of purchase money for *v*
Jg 21:12 four hundred girls, *v*, that
2Sa 13:18 *v*, used to dress with
Es 2:2 Let them seek young women, *v*
2:3 young women, *v*, beautiful in
2:17 than all the other *v*. And he
2:19 *v* were collected together a
Ps 45:14 The *v* in her train as her
78:63 And his *v* were not praised
148:12 young men and also you *v*
Isa 23:4 young men, raised up *v*
La 1:4 Her *v* are grief-stricken, and
1:18 own *v* and my own young men
2:10 *v* of Jerusalem have brought
2:21 My *v* and my young men
5:11 the *v* in the cities of Judah
Eze 44:22 *v* of the offspring of the
Am 8:13 the pretty *v* will swoon away
Zec 9:17 and new wine the *v*
Mt 25:1 kingdom . . . like ten *v*
25:7 *v* rose and put their lamps
25:10 *v* that were ready went in
25:11 the rest of the *v* also came
Ac 21:9 daughters, *v*, that prophesied
1Co 7:25 Now concerning *v* I have no
Re 14:4 in fact, they are *v*

Virtue
Lu 7:47 By *v* of this, I tell you
22:20 covenant by *v* of my blood
1Co 11:25 covenant by *v* of my blood
Php 4:8 whatever *v* there is and
4:13 strength by *v* of him who
Tit 3:7 *v* of the undeserved kindness
2Pe 1:3 called us through glory and *v*
1:5 supply to your faith *v*, to
1:5 to your *v* knowledge

Visible
Ex 10:5 the *v* surface of the earth
10:15 covering the *v* surface of the
2Sa 22:11 he was *v* upon the wings of
22:16 beds of the sea became *v*
1Ki 8:8 tips of the poles were *v* from
8:8 but they were not *v* outside
2Ch 5:9 tips of the poles were *v* at
5:9 but they were not *v* outside
Ps 18:15 beds of waters became *v*

Ac 22:7 a *v* say to me, Saul, Saul
22:9 did not hear the *v* of the one
22:14 to hear the *v* of his mouth
26:14 *v* say to me in the Hebrew
26:24 Festus said in a loud *v*
1Th 4:16 call, with an archangel's *v*
Heb 3:7 people listen to his own *v*
3:15 people listen to his own *v*
4:7 people listen to his own *v*
12:19 trumpet and the *v* of words
12:19 hearing which *v* the people
12:26 his *v* shook the earth, but
2Pe 2:16 utterance with the *v* of a man
Re 1:10 I heard behind me a strong *v*
1:12 *v* that was speaking with me
1:15 *v* was as the sound of many
3:20 hears my *v* and opens the
4:1 *v* . . . was as of a trumpet
5:2 proclaiming with a loud *v*
5:11 I heard a *v* of many angels
5:12 with a loud *v*: The Lamb that
6:1 with a *v* as of thunder: Come!
6:6 I heard a *v* as if in the midst
6:7 *v* of the fourth living creature
6:10 cried with a loud *v*, saying
7:2 he cried with a loud *v* to the
7:10 crying with a loud *v*, saying
8:13 say with a loud *v*: Woe, woe
9:13 heard one *v* out of the horns
10:3 he cried out with a loud *v*
10:4 I heard a *v* out of heaven say
10:8 *v* that I heard out of heaven
11:12 a loud *v* out of heaven say
12:10 I heard a loud *v* in heaven
14:7 in a loud *v*: Fear God and
14:9 saying in a loud *v*: If anyone
14:13 I heard a *v* out of heaven
14:15 with a loud *v* to the one
14:18 with a loud *v* to the one
16:1 loud *v* out of the sanctuary
16:17 loud *v* issued out of the
18:2 he cried out with a strong *v*
18:4 another *v* out of heaven say
18:23 no *v* of a bridegroom and of
19:1 *v* of a great crowd in heaven
19:5 *v* issued forth from the
19:6 as a *v* of a great crowd and
19:17 he cried out with a loud *v*
21:3 loud *v* from the throne say

Voiced
Ac 13:27 things *v* by the Prophets

Voiceless
Ac 8:32 lamb that is *v* before its
1Co 12:2 led away to those *v* idols
2Pe 2:16 A *v* beast of burden, making

Voices
Jos 6:10 shout nor let your *v* be heard
Jg 2:4 began to raise their *v* and
5:11 *v* of the water distributors
Ru 1:9 to raise their *v* and weep
1:14 they raised their *v* and wept
Lu 17:13 they raised their *v* and said
23:23 to be urgent, with loud *v*
23:23 their *v* began to win out
Ac 4:24 raised their *v* to God and
14:11 raised their *v*, saying in
22:22 they raised their *v*, saying
Re 4:5 lightnings and *v* and thunders
8:5 and *v* and lightnings and an
10:3 thunders uttered their own *v*
11:15 loud *v* occurred in heaven
11:19 and *v* and thunders and an
16:18 *v* and thunders occurred, and

Void
Jer 19:7 make *v* the counsel of Judah
1Co 9:15 my reason for boasting *v*

Voidness
Na 2:10 Emptiness and *v*, and a city

Voluntarily
Nu 15:3 to perform a special vow or *v*
1Ch 29:17 *v* offered all these things
29:17 make offerings *v* to you
Ezr 1:6 all that which was *v* offered
7:15 *v* given to the God of Israel
7:16 *v* giving to the house of

Voluntary
Ex 35:29 a *v* offering to Jehovah
36:3 brought to him a *v* offering
Le 7:16 is a vow or a *v* offering
22:18 *v* offerings, which they may
22:21 *v* offering, it should prove
Le 22:23 you may make it a *v* offering
23:38 *v* offerings, which you
Nu 29:39 besides your . . . *v* offerings
De 12:6 your *v* offerings and the
12:17 or your *v* offerings or the
16:10 the *v* offering of your hand
23:23 a *v* offering that you spoke
1Ch 29:9 their making *v* offerings
29:9 made *v* offerings to Jehovah
29:14 make *v* offerings like this
2Ch 31:14 *v* offerings of the true God
35:8 contribution as a *v* offering
Ezr 1:4 *v* offering for the house of
2:68 *v* offerings to the house of
3:5 a *v* offering to Jehovah
8:28 a *v* offering to Jehovah the
Ps 119:108 pleasure in the *v* offerings
Eze 46:12 as a *v* offering a whole
46:12 as a *v* offering to Jehovah
Am 4:5 and proclaim *v* offerings

Volunteer
1Ch 29:6 princes . . . proceeded to *v*
2Ch 17:16 *v* for Jehovah, and with him

Volunteered
Ne 11:2 *v* to dwell in Jerusalem

Volunteering
Jg 5:2 For the people's *v*, Bless
1Ch 29:5 who is there *v* to fill his

Volunteers
Jg 5:9 Who were *v* among the people

Vomit
Le 18:25 land will *v* its inhabitants
18:28 land will not *v* you out for
18:28 *v* the nations out who were
20:22 dwell in it may not *v* you
Job 20:15 Wealth . . . he will *v* it up
Pr 23:8 you will *v* it out, and you
25:16 much of it and have to *v* it
26:11 like a dog returning to its *v*
Isa 19:14 wander about in his *v*
28:8 become full of filthy *v*
Jer 48:26 has slapped around in his *v*
2Pe 2:22 has returned to its own *v*
Re 3:16 I am going to *v* you out of

Vomited
Jon 2:10 it *v* out Jonah onto the dry

Vophsi
Nu 13:14 Nahbi the son of *V*

Vote
Ac 26:10 I cast my *v* against them

Voted
Lu 23:51 not *v* in support of their

Vow
Ge 28:20, 20 Jacob went on to *v* a *v*
31:13 where you vowed a *v* to me
Le 7:16 is a *v* or a voluntary offering
22:21 in order to pay a *v* or as a
22:23 *v* it will not be accepted
23:38 *v* offerings and besides all
27:2 special *v* offering of souls
Nu 6:2 special *v* to live as a Nazirite
6:5 *v* of his Naziriteship no razor
6:21 According to his *v* that he
15:3 to perform a special *v* or
15:8 to perform a special *v* or
21:2 Israel made a *v* to Jehovah
29:39 besides your *v* offerings and
30:2 a man makes a *v* to Jehovah
30:2 *v* of abstinence upon his soul
30:3 a woman makes a *v* to Jehovah
30:3 *v* of abstinence in the house
30:4 father actually hears her *v* or
30:4 her abstinence *v* that she has
30:4 every abstinence *v* that she
30:6 belong to a husband, and her *v*
30:8 he has also annulled her *v*
30:9 *v* of a widow or a divorced
30:10 bound an abstinence *v* upon
30:11 any abstinence *v* that she has
30:12 an abstinence *v* of her soul
30:13 Any *v* or any oath of an
30:13 abstinence *v* to afflict the
De 12:6 your *v* offerings and your
12:11 choice of your *v* offerings
12:11 offerings that you will *v*
12:17 or any of your *v* offerings
12:17 offerings that you will *v*
12:26 *v* offerings you should carry
23:18 for any *v*, because they are
De 23:21, 21 you *v* a *v* to Jehovah
23:22 in case you omit making a *v*
Jg 11:30 Jephthah made a *v* to Jehovah
11:39 *v* that he had made toward
1Sa 1:11 she went on to make a *v* and
1:21 sacrifice and his *v* offering
2Sa 15:7 *v* that I solemnly made to
15:8 made a solemn *v* when I was
Ps 65:1 to you the *v* will be paid
76:11 *V* and pay to Jehovah your
Ec 5:4, 4 Whenever you *v* a *v* to God
5:4 What you *v*, pay
5:5 Better is it that you *v* not
5:5 than that you *v* and do not pay
Isa 19:21 a *v* to Jehovah and pay it
Mal 1:14 making a *v* and sacrificing
Ac 18:18 in Cenchreae, for he had a *v*
21:23 with a *v* upon themselves

Vowed
Ge 31:13 where you *v* a vow to me
Nu 30:10 that she has *v* or has bound
De 23:23 must do just as you have *v*
Ps 132:2 *v* to the Powerful One of
Jer 44:25 vows that we have *v*, to
Jon 2:9 What I have *v*, I will pay

Vower
Le 27:8 to what the *v* can afford, the

Vows
Le 22:18 for any of their *v* or for any
Nu 6:21 law about the Nazirite who *v*
30:4 all her *v* must also stand
30:5 day of his hearing all her *v*
30:5 her abstinence *v* that she has
30:7 her *v* must also stand or her
30:7 her abstinence *v* . . . stand
30:11 and all her *v* must stand or
30:12 her *v* or as an abstinence
30:14 established all her *v* or all
30:14 all her abstinence *v* that are
Job 22:27 And your *v* you will pay
Ps 22:25 My *v* I shall pay in front of
50:14 pay to the Most High your *v*
56:12 O God, there are *v* to you
61:5 have listened to my *v*
61:8 I may pay my *v* day after day
66:13 I shall pay to you my *v*
116:14 My *v* I shall pay to Jehovah
116:18 My *v* I shall pay to Jehovah
Pr 7:14 Today I have paid my *v*
20:25 and after *v* he is disposed to
31:2 and what, O son of my *v*
Jer 44:25 without fail perform our *v*
44:25 carry out your *v*, and
44:25 without fail perform your *v*
Jon 1:16 to Jehovah and made *v*
Na 1:15 Pay your *v*; because no more
Mt 5:33 must pay your *v* to Jehovah

Voyage
Ac 21:7 completed the *v* from Tyre and

Voyages
Re 18:17 every man that *v* anywhere

Vulture
Le 11:13 the osprey and the black *v*
11:18 the pelican and the *v*
De 14:12 the osprey and the black *v*
14:17 the *v* and the cormorant

Wafer
Ex 29:23 and a *w* out of the basket of
Le 8:26 cake of oiled bread and one *w*
Nu 6:19 one unfermented *w*, and put

Wafers
Ex 29:2 unfermented *w* smeared with
Le 2:4 unfermented *w* smeared with oil
7:12 unfermented *w* smeared with
Nu 6:15 unfermented *w* smeared with
1Ch 23:29 the *w* of unfermented bread

Wag
Job 16:4 would I *w* my head against
Zep 2:15 whistle; he will *w* his hand

Wage
Ru 2:12 to be a perfect *w* for you
Isa 19:10 *w* workers grieved in soul
31:4 *w* war over Mount Zion and
40:10 the *w* he pays is before him
Mal 3:5 the wages of a *w* worker
2Co 10:3 do not *w* warfare according
Re 12:17 *w* war with the remaining
13:7 *w* war with the holy ones and
19:19 *w* the war with the one

Waged
Nu 31:42 to the men who *w* war
Jos 11:18 *w* war with all these kings
1Ch 22:8 and great wars you have *w*

Wager
2Ki 18:23 make a *w*, please, with my
Isa 36:8 make a *w*, please, with my

Wages
Ge 29:15 What are your *w* to be?
30:18 has given me a hireling's *w*
30:28 Stipulate your *w* to me and
30:32 Hereafter such must be my *w*
30:33 may come to look over my *w*
31:7 has changed my *w* ten times
31:8 speckled ones . . . your *w*, then
31:8 striped ones . . . your *w*, then
31:41 changing my *w* ten times
Ex 2:9 myself shall give you your *w*
Le 19:13 *w* of a hired laborer should
Nu 18:31 *w* in return for your service
De 24:15 you should give him his *w*
24:15 lifting up his soul to his *w*
1Ki 5:6 *w* of your servants I shall
Job 7:2 laborer he waits for his *w*
Ps 109:20 *w* from Jehovah of the one
Pr 11:18 one is making false *w*
Ec 9:5 neither do they anymore have *w*
Isa 49:4 and my *w* with my God
61:8 give their *w* in trueness
62:11 the *w* he pays are before
65:7 *w* first of all into their
Jer 22:13 *w* he does not give him
Eze 29:18 *w*, there proved to be none
29:19 *w* for his military force
Zec 8:10 no *w* for mankind made to
8:10 the *w* of domestic animals
11:12 give me my *w*; but if not
11:12 *w*, thirty pieces of silver
Mal 3:5 the *w* of a wage worker
Mt 20:8 pay them their *w*, proceeding
Lu 10:7 worker is worthy of his *w*
Joh 4:36 reaper is receiving *w* and
Ac 1:18 the *w* for unrighteousness
Ro 6:23 the *w* sin pays is death, but
1Ti 5:18 workman is worthy of his *w*
Jas 5:4 The *w* due the workers who

Wagged
2Ki 19:21 of Jerusalem has *w* her head
Isa 37:22 Jerusalem has *w* her head

Wagging
Ps 22:7 they keep *w* their head
109:25 they begin *w* their head
La 2:15 *w* their head at the daughter
Mt 27:39 passersby . . . *w* their heads
Mr 15:29 *w* their heads and saying

Waging
Nu 31:7 went *w* war against Midian
Isa 29:7 are *w* war against Ariel
29:7 all those *w* war against her
29:8 *w* war against Mount Zion
1Ti 1:18 go on *w* the fine warfare
Jas 4:2 You go on fighting and *w* war

Wagon
Nu 7:3 *w* for two chieftains and a
1Sa 6:7 now take and make a new *w*
6:7 must hitch the cows to the *w*
6:8 and place it on the *w*, and
6:10 and hitched them to the *w*
6:11 ark of Jehovah upon the *w*
6:14 *w* itself came into the field
6:14 wood of the *w*, and the cows
2Sa 6:3 ride upon a new *w*, that they
6:3 were leading the new *w*
1Ch 13:7 ride upon a new *w* from the
13:7 and Ahio were leading the *w*
Isa 5:18 as with *w* cords sin
28:27 cummin no wheel of a *w* is
28:28 roller of his *w* in motion
Am 2:13 the *w* sways that is full up

Wagons
Ge 45:19 *w* from the land of Egypt for
45:21 Joseph gave them *w* according
45:27 the *w* that Joseph had sent
46:5 *w* that Pharaoh had sent to
Nu 7:3 six covered *w* and twelve
7:6 Moses accepted the *w* and the
7:7 Two *w* and four cattle he gave
7:8 four *w* and eight cattle he
Ps 46:9 The *w* he burns in the fire
Isa 66:20 chariots and in covered *w*

Wail
2Sa 1:12 began to *w* and weep and fast
3:31 sackcloth and *w* before Abner
11:26 began to *w* over her owner
Ec 3:4 time to *w* and a time to skip
Jer 22:18 They will not *w* for him
22:18 They will not *w* for him
49:3 *W*, and rove about among the
Joe 1:8 *W*, as a virgin girded with
Mic 1:8 I will *w* and howl; I will
Zec 12:10 will certainly *w* over Him
12:12 the land will certainly *w*
Joh 16:20 You will weep and *w*, but

Wailed
Mt 11:17 we *w*, but you did not beat
Lu 7:32 we *w*, but you did not weep

Wailers
Ec 12:5 *w* have marched around in the

Wailing
Ge 50:10 a very great and heavy *w*
1Ki 13:30 and they kept *w* over him
14:18 all Israel went *w* for him
Es 4:3 and fasting and weeping and *w*
Jer 6:26 the *w* of bitterness; because
48:38 *w*; for I have broken Moab
Eze 2:10 dirges and moaning and *w*
27:31 with bitter *w*
Joe 2:12 with weeping and with *w*
Am 5:16 there will be *w*, and in all
5:16 and to *w* those experienced in
5:17 vineyards there will be *w*
Mic 1:8 make a *w* like the jackals
1:11 The *w* of Beth-ezel will
Zec 7:5 a *w* in the fifth month and
12:10 in the *w* over an only son
12:11 the *w* in Jerusalem will be
12:11 like the *w* of Hadadrimmon
Mt 2:18 Ramah, weeping and much *w*

Wails
Mr 5:38 and letting out many *w*

Wainscoting
Zep 2:14 lay bare the very *w*

Wait
Ge 40:4 that he might *w* upon them
49:18 *w* for salvation from you, O
Ex 21:13 where one does not lie in *w*
24:14 *w* for us in this place until
Nu 35:20 thrown . . . while lying in *w*
35:22 without lying in *w*
De 19:11 he has lain in *w* for him and
Jg 9:32 and lie in *w* in the field
9:34 to lie in *w* against Shechem
9:43 and began to lie in *w* in the
16:2 lay in *w* for him all night
21:20 lie in *w* in the vineyards
1Sa 24:11 lying in *w* for my soul to
2Ki 6:33 Why should I *w* any longer
7:9 actually *w* until the morning
9:3 the door and flee and not *w*
Job 3:9 Let it *w* for the light and
13:15 slay me, would I not *w*
14:14 *w*, Until my relief comes
31:9 I kept lying in *w* at the
35:14 should *w* anxiously for him
Ps 10:9 lying in *w* in the concealed
10:9 lying in *w* to carry off some
37:7 And *w* longingly for him
42:5 *W* for God, For I shall yet
42:11 *W* for God, For I shall yet
43:5 *W* for God, For I shall yet
59:3 have lain in *w* for my soul
62:5 toward God *w* silently, O my
71:14 for me, I shall *w* constantly
106:13 did not *w* for his counsel
119:49 which you have made me *w*
131:3 Let Israel *w* for Jehovah
Pr 7:12 every corner she lies in *w*
12:6 are a lying in *w* for blood
23:28 like a robber, lies in *w*
24:15 lie in *w* for the abiding
Isa 51:5 and for my arm they will *w*
La 3:10 a bear lying in *w* he is to me
3:26 Good it is that one should *w*
4:19 they have lain in *w* for us
Ho 6:9 in the lying in *w* for a man
Mic 5:7 *w* for the sons of earthling
7:2 for bloodshed they lie in *w*
Hab 3:16 *w* for the day of distress
Lu 11:54 lying in *w* for him, to catch
Ac 23:16 heard of their lying in *w*
23:21 men of theirs are lying in *w*
Ac 24:23 his people to *w* upon him
1Co 11:33 eat it, *w* for one another
1Th 1:10 to *w* for his Son from the
Tit 2:13 we *w* for the happy hope and

Waited
Ge 39:4 and *w* upon him continually
1Sa 25:9 spoke to Nabal . . . then *w*
2Sa 13:17 attendant who *w* upon him
Es 9:1 had *w* to domineer over them
Job 6:19 Sabeans have *w* for them
29:21 they listened; and they *w*
29:23 *w* for me as for the rain
30:26 for good I *w*, yet bad came
32:4 Elihu himself had *w* for Job
32:11 *w* for the words of you men
32:16 I have *w*, for they do not
Ps 38:15 For on you, O Jehovah, I *w*
56:6 While they have *w* for my soul
119:43 *w* for your own judicial
119:74 have *w* for your own word
119:81 For your word I have *w*
119:95 For me the wicked have *w*
119:114 For your word I have *w*
119:147 For your words I have *w*
130:5 And for his word I have *w*
130:6 My soul has *w* for Jehovah
Eze 13:6 *w* to have a word come true
19:5 *w* and her hope had perished
Mic 1:12 Maroth has *w* for good, but
Ac 28:6 they *w* for a long while and

Waiter
2Sa 13:18 his *w* proceeded to lead her
2Ki 4:43 *w* said: How shall I put

Waiters
1Ki 10:5 the table service of his *w*
2Ch 9:4 table service of his *w* and

Waiting
Ge 8:10 *w* still another seven days
8:12 *w* still another seven days
Jg 3:25 they kept *w* until they were
Ru 1:13 would you keep *w* for them
1Sa 10:8 keep *w* until my coming to
13:8 continued *w* for seven days
1Ki 1:4 kept *w* upon him, and the king
1:15 was *w* upon the king
Job 3:21 *w* for death, and it is not
6:11 that I should keep *w*
17:13 If I keep *w*, Sheol is my
Ps 31:24 you who are *w* for Jehovah
33:18 *w* for his loving-kindness
33:22 as we have kept *w* for you
62:1 toward God is my soul *w* in
69:3 My eyes have failed while *w*
104:27 them—for you they keep *w*
130:7 Israel keep *w* for Jehovah
147:11 *w* for his loving-kindness
Pr 29:12 *w* on him will be wicked
Isa 42:4 islands . . . will keep *w*
La 3:21 I shall show a *w* attitude
3:24 show a *w* attitude for him
Mic 7:7 I will show a *w* attitude for
Mr 15:43 *w* for the kingdom of God
Lu 1:21 continued *w* for Zechariah
2:25 *w* for Israel's consolation
2:38 *w* for Jerusalem's deliverance
12:36 like men *w* for their master
23:51 *w* for the kingdom of God
Ac 1:4 *w* for what the Father has
17:16 Paul was *w* . . . in Athens
20:5 and were *w* for us in Troas
20:23 tribulations are *w* for me
23:21 *w* for the promise from you
Ro 8:19 *w* for the revealing of the
8:23 *w* for adoption as sons, the
8:25 on *w* for it with endurance
1Co 1:7 eagerly *w* for the revelation
16:11 I am *w* for him with the
Ga 5:5 eagerly *w* for the hoped-for
Php 3:20 are eagerly *w* for a savior
Jas 5:7 the farmer keeps *w* for the
1Pe 3:20 the patience of God was *w* in
Jude 21 *w* for the mercy of our Lord

Waits
Job 7:2 laborer he *w* for his wages

Wake
1Ki 18:27 is asleep and ought to *w* up
2Ki 4:31 The boy did not *w* up
Job 14:12 they will not *w* up
Ps 59:5 *w* up to turn your attention
Pr 23:35 When shall I *w* up? I shall
Isa 52:1, 1 *W* up, *w* up, put on your

Jer 51:39 which they will not *w* up
51:57 which they will not *w* up
Da 12:2 *w* up, these to indefinitely
Joe 1:5 *W* up, you drunkards, and weep
Hab 2:7 *w* up who are violently
2:19 to a dumb stone: O *w* up!
Zec 4:1 to come back and *w* me up
1Co 15:34 *W* up to soberness in a
Re 3:3 unless you *w* up, I shall come

Waked
Pr 6:22 when you have *w* up, it

Waking
1Sa 26:12 nor anyone *w* up, for all of

Walk
Ge 17:1 *W* before me and prove
Ex 16:4 they will *w* in my law or not
17:5 and you must *w* on
18:20 way in which they should *w*
21:19 does *w* about out of doors
Le 18:3 their statutes you must not *w*
18:4 keep so as to *w* in them
20:23 not *w* in the statutes of the
26:12 *w* in the midst of you and
26:13 and make you *w* erect
26:23 to *w* in opposition to me
26:24 *w* in opposition to you; and
26:27 must *w* in opposition to me
26:28 *w* in heated opposition to
26:41 *w* in opposition to them, and
De 1:33 see by what way you should *w*
2:27 Only on the road I shall *w*
5:33 you should *w*, in order that
6:7 when you *w* on the road and
6:14 must not *w* after other gods
8:2 your God made you *w* these
8:15 *w* through the great and
8:19 *w* after other gods and serve
10:12 to *w* in all his ways and
11:19 and when you *w* on the road
11:22 *w* in all his ways and to
11:28 *w* after other gods whom you
13:2 Let us *w* after other gods
13:4 After Jehovah . . . should *w*
13:5 God has commanded you to *w*
19:9 to *w* in his ways always, you
26:17 while you *w* in his ways and
28:14 to *w* after other gods to
29:19 shall *w* in the stubbornness
30:16 to *w* in his ways and to keep
33:25 is your leisurely *w*
Jos 18:4 *w* about in the land and map
18:8 *w* about in the land and map
24:3 had him *w* through all the
Jg 5:10 And you who *w* on the road
1Sa 2:30 will *w* before me to time
2:35 *w* before my anointed one
8:3 sons did not *w* in his ways
23:13 wherever they could *w* about
2Sa 11:2 *w* about on the rooftop of
1Ki 3:14 if you will *w* in my ways
6:12 if you will *w* in my statutes
8:36 way in which they should *w*
8:58 to *w* in all his ways and to
9:4 *w* before me, just as David
11:38 you do *w* in my ways and
16:31 *w* in the sins of Jeroboam
2Ki 10:31 to *w* in the law of Jehovah
21:22 not *w* in the way of Jehovah
22:2 *w* in all the way of David
23:3 to *w* after Jehovah and to
1Ch 17:8 with you wherever you do *w*
2Ch 6:27 way in which they should *w*
7:17 *w* before me, just as David
21:13 *w* in the way of the kings
34:2 *w* in the ways of David his
Ne 5:9 that you should *w* because of
10:29 to *w* in the law of the true
12:32 began to *w* behind them
Job 12:19 making priests *w* barefoot
18:8 onto a network he will *w*
29:3 *w* through darkness by his
Ps 12:8 The wicked ones *w* all around
23:4 I *w* in the valley of deep
25:5 Make me *w* in your truth
25:9 to *w* in his judicial decision
26:11 in my integrity I shall *w*
42:4 used to *w* slowly before them
42:9 Why do I *w* sad because of the
43:2 *w* about sad because of the
55:14 we used to *w* with the throng
56:13 *w* about before God in the
78:10 his law they refused to *w*
Ps 81:13 Israel itself would *w* in my
84:7 *w* on from vital energy to
85:13 righteousness itself will *w*
86:11 I shall *w* in your truth
89:30 decisions they do not *w*
101:2 *w* about in the integrity of
107:7 them *w* in the right way
115:7 Feet . . . but they cannot *w*
116:9 *w* before Jehovah in the
119:45 *w* about in a roomy place
136:16 One making his people *w*
138:7 *w* in the midst of distress
142:3 In the path in which I *w*
143:8 the way in which I should *w*
Pr 2:13 to *w* in the ways of darkness
2:20 *w* in the way of good people
3:23 *w* in security on your way
4:12 *w*, your pace will not be
4:14 *w* straight on into the way of
6:22 When you *w* about, it will
6:28 *w* upon the coals and his feet
8:20 path of righteousness I *w*
9:6 *w* straight in the way of
10:9 integrity will *w* in security
Ec 6:8 to *w* in front of the living
11:9 *w* in the ways of your heart
Isa 2:3 and we will *w* in his paths
2:5 us *w* in the light of Jehovah
3:16 *w* with their throats
11:15 to *w* in their sandals
30:21 *W* in it, you people, in
35:9 repurchased ones must *w*
40:31 will *w* and not tire out
42:16 make the blind ones *w* in a
42:24 they did not want to *w* and
43:2 should *w* through the fire
45:14 Behind you they will *w*
45:16 manufacturers . . . have to *w*
48:17 way in which you should *w*
48:21 *w* even through devastated
50:11 *w* in the light of your fire
58:8 would certainly *w*
63:13 *w* through the surging
Jer 2:25 after them I am going to *w*
3:17 *w* after the stubbornness of
3:18 In those days they will *w*
6:16 *w* in it, and find ease for
6:16 We are not going to *w*
6:25 do not *w* even in the way
7:6 other gods you will not *w*
7:23 *w* in all the way that I
9:4 *w* around as a mere slanderer
18:12 we shall *w*, and we are
18:15 to *w* in roadways, a way
25:6 do not *w* after other gods
31:9 *w* to torrent valleys of
32:23 in your law they did not *w*
35:15 *w* after other gods to serve
42:3 way in which we should *w*
44:10 nor did they *w* in my law
44:23 his reminders you did not *w*
50:4, 4 *w*, weeping as they *w*
La 3:2 makes to *w* in darkness and not
Eze 5:6 my statutes, they did not *w*
5:7 in my statutes you did not *w*
11:12 regulations you did not *w*
11:20 may *w* in my own statutes
19:6 to *w* about in the midst of
20:13 my statutes they did not *w*
20:16 statutes, they did not *w* in
20:18 do not you *w*, and their
20:19 *W* in my own statutes, and
20:21 my statutes they did not *w*
36:12 will cause humankind to *w*
36:27 my regulations you will *w*
37:24 decisions they will *w*, and
47:6 Then he had me *w* and had
Ho 5:11 to *w* after his adversary
11:3 I taught Ephraim to *w*, taking
11:10 After Jehovah they will *w*
14:9 the ones who will *w* in them
Am 2:10 *w* through the wilderness
3:3 Will two *w* together unless
Mic 1:8 I will *w* barefoot and naked
2:3 you will not *w* haughtily
4:2 and we will *w* in his paths
4:5 *w* each one in the name of
4:5 *w* in the name of Jehovah
6:16 people *w* in their counsels
Zep 1:17 *w* like blind men
Zec 1:10 to *w* about in the earth
3:7 in my ways that you will *w*
6:7 order to *w* about in the earth
6:7 Go, *w* about in the earth
Zec 10:12 in his name they will *w*
Mt 9:5 or to say, Get up and *w*
Mr 2:9 and pick up your cot and *w*
12:38 want to *w* around in robes
Lu 5:23 or to say, Get up and *w*
11:44 men *w* upon them and do not
20:46 desire to *w* around in robes
24:17 yourselves as you *w* along
Joh 5:8 pick up your cot and *w*
5:9 up his cot and began to *w*
5:11 Pick up your cot and *w*
5:12 told you, Pick it up and *w*
6:66 would no longer *w* with him
7:1 not want to *w* about in Judea
8:12 by no means *w* in darkness
12:35 *W* while you have the light
21:18 *w* about where you wanted
Ac 3:6 In the name of Jesus . . . *w*
3:12 we have made him *w*
21:21 to *w* in the solemn customs
Ro 4:12 *w* orderly in the footsteps
6:4 *w* in a newness of life
8:4 *w*, not in accord with the
13:13 let us *w* decently, not in
1Co 7:17 let each one so *w* as God has
2Co 6:16 reside among them and *w*
10:3 though we *w* in the flesh, we
Ga 6:16 *w* orderly by this rule of
Eph 2:10 for us to *w* in them
4:1 *w* worthily of the calling
4:17 just as the nations also *w*
5:15 how you *w* is not as unwise
Col 1:10 to *w* worthily of Jehovah to
1Th 4:1 you ought to *w* and please God
Re 3:4 *w* with me in white ones
9:20 neither see nor hear nor *w*
16:15 that he may not *w* naked and
21:24 nations will *w* by means of

Walked
Ge 6:9 Noah *w* with the true God
9:23 *w* in backwards. Thus they
22:8 both of them *w* on together
24:40 before whom I have *w*, will
48:15 fathers Abraham and Isaac *w*
Ex 14:29 *w* on dry land in the midst
15:19 Israel *w* on dry land through
Le 26:40 they *w* in opposition to me
Nu 13:26 they *w* and came to Moses
De 1:31 in all the way that you *w*
2:14 we *w* from Kadesh-barnea until
4:3 every man who *w* after the Baal
28:9 and you have *w* in his ways
Jos 5:6 had *w* forty years in the
5:13 Joshua *w* up to him and said
8:35 who *w* in their midst
14:10 Israel *w* in the wilderness
24:17 the way in which we *w* and
Jg 2:17 forefathers had *w* by obeying
11:18 When they *w* on through the
14:9, 9 and *w* on, eating as he *w*
1Sa 8:5 sons have not *w* in your ways
12:2 I have *w* before you from my
30:31 places where David had *w*
2Sa 3:16 weeping as he *w* after her as
4:7 *w* on the road to the Arabah
7:7 *w* about among all the sons
13:19 crying out as she *w*
18:33 what he said as he *w*
1Ki 3:6 as he *w* before you in truth
3:14 just as David your father *w*
8:25 just as you have *w* before me
9:4 just as David your father *w*
11:33 have not *w* in my ways by
14:8 *w* after me with all his
2Ki 2:11 along, speaking as they *w*
13:6 to sin. In it he *w*; and even
13:11 Israel sin. In them he *w*
20:3 how I have *w* before you in
21:21 way that his father had *w*
1Ch 17:6 that I *w* about in all Israel
21:4 Joab went out and *w* through
2Ch 6:16 just as you have *w* before me
7:17 just as David your father *w*
11:17 *w* in the way of David and
17:3 *w* in the former ways of
17:4 his commandment he *w*
21:12 have not *w* in the ways of
22:3 *w* in the ways of the house
22:5 in their counsel that he *w*
28:2 *w* in the ways of the kings
Job 30:28 I *w* about when there was no
31:5 have *w* with men of untruth
31:7 *w* merely after my eyes

Job 38:16 have you *w* about
Ps 1:1 *w* in the counsel of the wicked
26:1 have *w* in my own integrity
26:3 And I have *w* in your truth
35:14 I *w* about like one mourning
38:6 All day long . . . *w* about sad
119:3 In his ways they have *w*
131:1 I *w* in things too great
Isa 20:3 Isaiah has *w* about naked and
38:3 *w* before you in truthfulness
50:10 has *w* in continual darkness
Jer 2:8 could bring no benefit they *w*
2:23 After the Baals I have not *w*
8:2 and that they have *w* after
9:13 and have not *w* in it
11:10 *w* after other gods in order
La 1:5 *w* captive before the adversary
5:18 foxes themselves have *w* on it
Eze 16:47 in their ways that you *w*
18:17 in my statutes he has *w*
23:31 of your sister you have *w*
28:14 midst of fiery stones you *w*
Am 2:4 their forefathers had *w*
Na 2:11 where the lion *w* and entered
Zec 1:11 *w* about in the earth, and
Mal 2:6 in uprightness he *w* with me
3:14 *w* dejectedly on account of
Mt 14:29 *w* over the waters and went
Mr 2:12 *w* out in front of them all
Joh 11:54 Jesus no longer *w* about
Ac 9:31 it *w* in the fear of Jehovah
14:8 and he had never *w* at all
2Co 10:2 as if we *w* according to what
12:18 We *w* in the same spirit
Eph 2:2 in which you at one time *w*
Col 3:7 you, too, once *w* when you
1Jo 2:6 walking just as that one *w*

Walking

Ge 3:8 God *w* in the garden about the
5:22 Enoch went on *w* with the
5:24 Enoch kept *w* with the true
18:16 Abraham was *w* with them to
24:63 Isaac was out *w* in order to
24:65 Who is that man there *w* in
30:14 Reuben went *w* in the days
Ex 2:5 female attendants were *w* by
Le 26:3 *w* in my statutes and keeping
26:21 *w* in opposition to me and
De 2:7 your *w* through this great
8:6 *w* in his ways and by fearing
23:14 God is *w* about within your
Jos 6:13 *w*, continually blowing the
6:13 war-equipped force was *w*
22:5 by *w* in all his ways and by
Jg 2:19 by *w* after other gods to
2:22 of Jehovah's way by *w* in it
11:16 Israel went *w* through the
18:9 sluggish about *w* to come in
Ru 1:7 kept *w* on the road to return
1Sa 6:12 Philistines were *w* after
12:2 here is the king *w* before
19:23 *w* and continued behaving
23:13 *w* about wherever they could
25:15 days of our *w* about with
25:27 *w* about in the steps of my
25:42 five maids of hers *w* behind
2Sa 3:16 husband kept *w* with her
3:31 Even King David was *w* behind
6:4 Ahio was *w* ahead of the Ark
7:6 continually *w* about in a tent
13:19 *w* away, crying out as she
15:30 he was *w* barefoot, and all
16:13 while Shimei was *w* on the
16:13 *w* abreast of him that he
1Ki 2:3 *w* in his ways, by keeping his
2:4 by *w* before me in truth with
3:3 *w* in the statutes of David
6:12 my commandments by *w* in
8:23 servants who are *w* before
8:25 by *w* before me just as you
8:61 *w* in his regulations and by
15:3 *w* in all the sins of his
15:26 *w* in the way of his father
15:34 *w* in the way of Jeroboam
16:2 *w* in the way of Jeroboam
16:19 *w* in the way of Jeroboam
16:26 went *w* in all the way of
21:27 and *w* despondently
22:43 *w* in all the way of Asa his
22:52 *w* in the way of his father
2Ki 2:11 *w* along, speaking as they
4:35 began *w* again in the house
8:18 went *w* in the way of the
2Ki 8:27 *w* in the way of the house of
13:2 *w* in pursuit of the sin of
16:3 went *w* in the way of the
17:8 *w* in the statutes of the
17:19 *w* in the statutes of Israel
17:22 went *w* in all the sins of
21:21 kept *w* in all the way that
1Ch 15:25 *w* along to bring up the ark
16:20 kept *w* about from nation to
2Ch 6:14 *w* before you with all their
6:16 by *w* in my law, just as you
6:31 fear you by *w* in your ways
20:32 *w* in the way of his father
21:6 *w* in the way of the kings
Ne 12:31 *w* to the right upon the wall
12:38 choir was *w* in front, and
Es 2:11 Mordecai was *w* before the
Job 1:7 earth and from *w* about in it
2:2 and from *w* about in it
31:26 the precious moon *w* along
34:8 to *w* with men of wickedness
Ps 15:2 *w* faultlessly and practicing
68:21 *w* about in his guiltiness
81:12 *w* in their own counsels
82:5 In darkness they keep *w* about
84:11 those *w* in faultlessness
89:15 of your face they keep *w*
101:6 one *w* in a faultless way
104:3 *W* upon the wings of the
105:13 kept *w* about from nation to
106:9 *w* them through the watery
119:1 *w* in the law of Jehovah
128:1 Who is *w* in his ways
Pr 2:7 those *w* in integrity he is
6:12 *w* with crookedness of speech
10:9 *w* in integrity will walk in
11:13 one *w* about as a slanderer
13:20 *w* with wise persons will
14:2 one *w* in his uprightness is
19:1 who is *w* in his integrity is
20:7 is *w* in his integrity
28:6 who is *w* in his integrity
28:18 is *w* faultless will be saved
28:26 *w* in wisdom is the one that
Ec 2:14 stupid one is *w* on in sheer
4:15 who are *w* about under the sun
6:9 than the *w* about of the soul
10:3 way the foolish one is *w*, his
10:7 princes *w* on the earth just
12:5 *w* to his long-lasting house
Isa 3:16 *w* with tripping steps, and
8:11 *w* in the way of this people
9:2 *w* in the darkness have seen
20:2 *w* about naked and barefoot
30:29 *w* with a flute to enter
33:15 who is *w* in continual
35:8 the one *w* on the way, and
38:15 *w* solemnly all my years
42:5 and spirit to those *w* in it
57:2 that is *w* straightforwardly
57:17 he kept *w* as a renegade
59:9 continuous gloom we kept *w*
65:2 *w* in the way that is not
Jer 2:2 *w* after me in the wilderness
2:5 kept *w* after the vain idol
2:6 *w* us through the wilderness
2:17 his *w* you in the way
5:23 and keep *w* in their course
6:28 *w* about as slanderers
7:9 *w* after other gods whom you
7:24 went *w* in the counsels in
9:14 *w* after the stubbornness
10:23 not belong to man who is *w*
11:8 they kept *w* each one in the
13:10 *w* in the stubbornness of
13:10 keep *w* after other gods
15:6 is the way you keep *w*
16:12 you are *w* each one after
23:14 adultery and *w* in falsehood
23:17 one *w* in the stubbornness
26:4 listen to me by *w* in my law
31:2 Israel was *w* to get his
41:6 weeping while he was *w*
La 1:6 *w* without power before the
4:18 is no *w* in our public squares
Eze 11:21 whose heart is *w* in their
13:3 are *w* after their own spirit
18:9 in my statutes he kept *w* and
Da 3:25 *w* about free in the midst of
4:29 *w* upon the royal palace of
4:37 *w* in pride he is able to
9:10 by *w* in his laws that he
Jon 3:3 a *w* distance of three days
3:4 the *w* distance of one day
Mic 2:7 case of the one *w* uprightly
2:11 *w* by wind and falsehood
6:8 be modest in *w* with your God
Na 2:5 They will stumble in their *w*
Zec 6:7 began *w* about in the earth
Mt 4:18 *W* alongside the sea of
11:5 and the lame are *w* about
14:25 he came . . . *w* over the sea
14:26 sight of him *w* on the sea
15:31 lame *w* and the blind seeing
Mr 1:16 While *w* alongside the sea of
5:42 maiden rose and began *w*, for
6:48 toward them, *w* on the sea
6:49 sight of him *w* on the sea
8:24 trees, but they are *w* about
11:27 as he was *w* in the temple
Lu 1:6 *w* blamelessly in accord with
7:22 the lame are *w*, the lepers
24:15 and began *w* with them
Joh 1:36 as he looked at Jesus *w* he
6:19 beheld Jesus *w* upon the sea
7:1 continued *w* about in Galilee
10:23 Jesus was *w* in the temple
Ac 3:8 he stood up and began *w*, and
3:8 *w* and leaping and praising God
3:9 sight of him *w* and praising
9:28 *w* in and out at Jerusalem
14:10 And he leaped up and began *w*
21:24 that you are *w* orderly, you
Ro 14:15 no longer *w* in accord with
1Co 3:3 and are you not *w* as men do?
2Co 4:2 not *w* with cunning, neither
5:7 are *w* by faith, not by sight
Ga 2:14 were not *w* straight according
5:16 Keep *w* by spirit and you will
5:25 on *w* orderly also by spirit
Eph 4:17 *w* just as the nations also
5:2 go on *w* in love, just as
5:8 Go on *w* as children of light
Php 3:16 go on *w* orderly in this same
3:17 are *w* in a way that accords
3:18 are *w* as the enemies of the
Col 2:6 go on *w* in union with him
4:5 Go on *w* in wisdom toward
1Th 2:12 go on *w* worthily of God who
4:1 just as you are in fact *w*
4:12 *w* decently as regards people
2Th 3:6 every brother *w* disorderly
3:11 are *w* disorderly among you
1Jo 1:6 we go on *w* in the darkness
1:7 if we are *w* in the light as
2:6 *w* just as that one walked
2:11 and is *w* in the darkness
2Jo 4 your children *w* in the truth
6 that we go on *w* according to
6 that you should go on *w* in it
3Jo 3 as you go on *w* in the truth
4 children go on *w* in the truth

Walkings

Hab 3:6 The *w* of long ago are his

Walks

Job 22:14 on the vault of heaven he *w*
Ps 39:6 in a semblance man *w* about
58:8 a snail melting away he *w*
73:9 itself *w* about in the earth
91:6 pestilence that *w* in the
Jer 48:2 After you there *w* a sword
Eze 33:15 *w* in the very statutes of
Joh 11:9 anyone *w* in daylight he does
11:10 *w* in the night, he bumps
12:35 *w* in the darkness does not
1Pe 5:8 Devil, *w* about like a roaring
Re 2:1 *w* in the midst of the seven

Walkway

Eze 42:4 a *w* ten cubits in width

Wall

Ge 49:22 its branches up over a *w*
Ex 14:22 the waters were a *w* to them
14:29 waters were for them a *w* on
Le 14:37 is lower than the *w* surface
25:30 city that has a *w* must also
25:31 settlements that have no *w*
Nu 22:24 a stone *w* on this side and a
22:24 and a stone *w* on that side
22:25 squeeze . . . against the *w*
22:25 Balaam's foot against the *w*
35:4 from the *w* of the city and
De 3:5 cities fortified with a high *w*
Jos 2:15 house was on a side of the *w*
2:15 the *w* that she was dwelling
6:5 *w* of the city must fall down
6:20 *w* began to fall down flat

1Sa 18:11 pin David even to the *w*
19:10 pin David to the *w* with the
19:10 struck the spear into the *w*
20:25 seat by the *w;* and Jonathan
25:16 *w* was what they proved to
25:22 urinates against the *w*
25:34 urinating against a *w*
31:10 they fastened on the *w*
31:12 off the *w* of Beth-shan
2Sa 11:20 shoot from on top of the *w*
11:21 from on top of the *w* so
11:21 to go so close to the *w*
11:24 from on top of the *w,* so
18:24 roof of the gate by the *w*
20:15 were undermining the *w*
20:21 pitched to you over the *w*
22:30 By my God I can climb a *w*
1Ki 3:1 and Jerusalem's *w* all around
4:13 cities with *w* and copper bar
4:33 is coming forth on the *w*
6:5 against the *w* of the house
6:27 the one reached to the *w*
6:27 was reaching to the other *w*
9:15 and the *w* of Jerusalem
14:10 urinating against a *w*
16:11 that urinates against a *w*
20:30 *w* came falling down upon
21:21 urinating against a *w* and
2Ki 3:27 burnt sacrifice upon the *w*
4:10 roof chamber on the *w*
6:26 passing along upon the *w*
6:30 was passing along upon the *w*
9:8 urinating against a *w* and
9:33 spattering upon the *w* and
14:13 in the *w* of Jerusalem at
18:26 people that are on the *w*
18:27 the men sitting upon the *w*
20:2 turned his face to the *w* and
25:1 a siege *w* all around
25:4 between the double *w* that
2Ch 3:11 to the *w* of the house, and
3:12 to the *w* of the house, and
25:23 breach in the *w* of
26:6 break through the *w* of Gath
26:6 and the *w* of Jabneh and
26:6 and the *w* of Ashdod, after
27:3 on the *w* of Ophel he did a
32:5 all the broken-down *w* and
32:5 and on the outside another *w*
32:18 that were upon the *w,* to
33:14 built an outer *w* for the
36:19 down the *w* of Jerusalem
Ezr 9:9 a stone *w* in Judah and in
Ne 1:3 the *w* of Jerusalem is broken
2:8 and for the *w* of the city and
2:15 I kept on examining the *w*
2:17 rebuild the *w* of Jerusalem
3:8 as far as the Broad *W*
3:13 a thousand cubits in the *w* as
3:15 *w* of the Pool of the Canal
3:27 as far as the *w* of Ophel
4:1 that we were rebuilding the *w*
4:3 break down their *w* of stones
4:6 So we kept building the *w*
4:6 the entire *w* came to be joined
4:10 not able to build on the *w*
4:13 the *w* at the open places
4:15 all of us gone back to the *w*
4:17 the builders on the *w* and
4:19 spread about upon the *w* far
5:16 work of this *w* I took a hand
6:1 I had rebuilt the *w* and there
6:6 is why you are building the *w*
6:15 the *w* came to completion on
7:1 soon as the *w* had been rebuilt
12:27 of the *w* of Jerusalem
12:30 and the gates and the *w*
12:31 princes of Judah upon the *w*
12:31 the *w* to the Gate of the
12:37 *w* above the House of David
12:38 the *w* up over the Tower of
12:38 and on to the Broad *W*
13:21 the night in front of the *w*
Job 19:8 has blocked with a stone *w*
Ps 18:29 by my God I can climb a *w*
62:3 you are like a leaning *w*
62:3 *w* that is being pushed in
Pr 18:11 *w* in his imagination
24:31 stone *w* itself had been torn
25:28 broken through, without a *w*
Ec 10:8 is breaking through a stone *w*
Ca 2:9 standing behind our *w,* gazing
8:9 If she should be a *w,* we shall
8:10 I am a *w,* and my breasts are
Isa 2:15 and upon every fortified *w*
5:5 breaking down of its stone *w*
22:5 is the demolisher of the *w*
22:10 to make the *w* unattainable
25:4 like a rainstorm against a *w*
30:13 out in a highly raised *w*
36:11 people that are on the *w*
36:12 the men sitting upon the *w*
38:2 turned his face to the *w* and
59:10 We keep groping for the *w*
Jer 15:20 a fortified copper *w*
21:4 against you outside the *w*
39:4 gate between the double *w*
49:27 on the *w* of Damascus
51:44 *w* itself of Babylon must
51:58 *w* of Babylon, although
52:4 build against her a siege *w*
52:7 gate between the double *w*
La 2:8 *w* of the daughter of Zion to
2:8 rampart and *w* to go mourning
2:18 O *w* of the daughter of Zion
3:7 as with a stone *w,* that I may
Eze 4:2 build a siege *w* against it
4:3 as an iron *w* between you and
8:7 look! a certain hole in the *w*
8:8 bore, please, through the *w*
8:8 gradually bored through the *w*
8:10 carving being upon the *w* all
12:5 bore your way through the *w*
12:7 bored my way through the *w*
12:12 through the *w* they will
13:5 build up a stone *w* in behalf
13:10 is building a partition *w*
13:12 And, look! the *w* must fall
13:14 I will tear down the *w*
13:15 upon the *w* and upon those
13:15 The *w* is no more, and those
17:17 and by building a siege *w*
21:22 to build a siege *w*
22:30 be repairing the stone *w*
23:14 men in carvings upon the *w*
26:8 make against you a siege *w*
38:11 dwelling without *w,* and
38:20 even every *w* will fall
40:5 a *w* outside the house all
41:5 measure the *w* of the house
41:6 *w* that belonged to the house
41:6 in the *w* of the house
41:9 width of the *w* that belonged
41:12 *w* of the building was five
41:17 upon the whole *w* all around
41:20 on the *w* of the temple
42:7 the stone *w* that was outside
42:10 stone *w* of the courtyard
42:12 stone *w* toward the east
42:20 It had a *w* all around, with
43:8 *w* between me and them
Da 5:5 plaster of the *w* of the palace
Ho 2:6 heap up a stone *w* against her
Joe 2:7 men of war they go up a *w*
2:9 On the *w* they run
Am 1:7 send a fire onto the *w* of Gaza
1:10 a fire onto the *w* of Tyre
1:14 set fire to the *w* of Rabbah
5:19 his hand against the *w*
7:7 Jehovah was stationed on a *w*
Na 2:5 They will hasten to her *w,* and
3:8 whose *w* was from the sea
Hab 2:11 out of the *w* a stone itself
Zec 2:5 a *w* of fire all around, and
Ac 9:25 through an opening in the *w*
23:3 you whitewashed *w*
2Co 11:33 through a window in the *w*
Eph 2:14 destroyed the *w* in between
Re 21:12 It had a great and lofty *w*
21:14 The *w* of the city also had
21:15 city and its gates and its *w*
21:17 he measured its *w,* one
21:18 structure of its *w* . . . jasper
21:19 city's *w* were adorned with

Walled
Ge 25:16 sons of Ishmael . . . *w* camps
Le 25:29 house in a *w* city, his right
Nu 31:10 *w* camps they burned with
1Ch 6:54 *w* camps in their territory
Ps 69:25 *w* camp become desolate
Eze 25:4 set up their *w* camps in you

Wallow
Jer 6:26 sackcloth and *w* in the ashes
25:34 *w* about, you majestic ones
Eze 27:30 In the ashes they will *w*
Mic 1:10 of Aphrah *w* in the very dust

Wallowing
2Sa 20:12 Amasa was *w* in the blood

Walls
Le 14:37 plague is in the *w* of the
14:39 plague has spread in the *w* of
De 28:52 *w* in which you are trusting
2Sa 5:11 workers in stone for *w,* and
1Ki 6:5 against the *w* of the house
6:6 a hold in the *w* of the house
6:15 build the *w* of the house
6:29 *w* of the house round about
2Ki 25:10 *w* of Jerusalem, all around
1Ch 14:1 builders of *w* and workers
29:4 coating the *w* of the houses
2Ch 3:7 its *w* and its doors with gold
3:7 engraved cherubs upon the *w*
8:5 fortified cities with *w*
14:7 make *w* around and towers
Ezr 4:12 finish the *w* and to repair
4:13 and its *w* be finished
4:16 and its *w* be finished
5:8 are being laid in the *w*
Ne 2:13 examining the *w* of Jerusalem
4:7 repairing of the *w* of
Job 24:11 Between the terrace *w* they
Ps 51:18 you build the *w* of Jerusalem
55:10 round about it upon its *w*
80:12 you broken down its stone *w*
Ca 5:7 watchmen of the *w* lifted my
Isa 22:11 between the two *w* for the
25:12 your high *w* of security
26:1 salvation itself for *w* and
49:16 Your *w* are in front of me
56:5 my house and within my *w*
60:10 will actually build your *w*
60:18 call your own *w* Salvation
62:6 Upon your *w,* O Jerusalem
Jer 1:15 all her *w* round about
1:18 an iron pillar and copper *w*
4:19 pains in the *w* of my heart
39:8 *w* of Jerusalem they pulled
50:15 Her *w* have been torn down
51:12 Against the *w* of Babylon
52:14 *w* of Jerusalem, round about
La 2:7 the *w* of her dwelling towers
Eze 26:4 bring the *w* of Tyre to ruin
26:9 will direct against your *w*
26:10 your *w* will rock, when he
26:12 and tear down your *w*
27:11 upon your *w* all around
27:11 up on your *w* all around
33:30 beside the *w* and in the
41:13 the building and its *w*
41:22 and its *w* were of wood
41:25 like those made for the *w*
Mic 7:11 for building your stone *w*
Heb 11:30 the *w* of Jericho fell down

Wander
Ge 20:13 God caused me to *w* from the
Nu 32:13 *w* about in the wilderness
2Sa 15:20 today shall I make you *w*
2Ki 21:8 foot of Israel *w* from the
Job 12:24 *w* about in an empty place
12:25 *w* about like a drunken man
Ps 59:11 make them *w* about, And
59:15 *w* about for something to eat
107:40 *w* about in a featureless
Pr 7:25 Do not *w* into her roadways
10:17 is causing to *w*
12:26 causes them to *w* about
Isa 3:12 are causing you to *w,* and
9:16 the ones causing them to *w*
19:13 caused Egypt to *w* about
19:14 Egypt to *w* about in all
19:14 to *w* about in his vomit
30:28 bridle that causes one to *w*
35:8 foolish ones will *w* about
47:15 *w,* each one to his own
63:17 making us *w* from your ways
Jer 14:10 they have loved to *w* about
23:13 my people, even Israel, *w*
23:32 cause my people to *w* about
50:6 caused them to *w* about
Eze 48:11 *w* away when the sons of
Ho 4:12 has caused them to *w* off
Am 2:4 lies . . . kept making them *w*
Mic 3:5 are causing my people to *w*

Wandered
Ge 21:14 *w* about in the wilderness of
Ps 58:3 *w* about from the belly
107:4 *w* about in the wilderness
119:110 your orders I have not *w*

Ps 119:176 have *w* like a lost sheep
Pr 5:6 tracks have *w* she does not
Isa 16:8 *w* about in the wilderness
21:4 My heart has *w* about; a
28:7 liquor they have *w* about
28:7 *w* about as a result of the
53:6 sheep we have all of us *w*
La 4:14 have *w* about as blind in the
4:15 They have also *w* about
Eze 44:10 Israel, who *w* away from
44:10 *w* after their dungy idols
44:15 sons of Israel *w* away from
48:11 sons of Israel *w* away
48:11 just as the Levites *w* away
Joe 1:18 cattle have *w* in confusion
Heb 11:38 They *w* about in deserts and

Wanderer

Ge 4:12 A *w* and a fugitive you will
4:14 I must become a *w* and
Ps 36:11 let it not make me a *w*

Wandering

Ge 37:15 and here he was *w* in a field
Ex 14:3 sons of Israel, They are *w* in
Job 38:41 *w* about because there is
Ps 109:10 let his sons go *w* about
Pr 14:22 those devising mischief go *w*
21:16 *w* from the way of insight
Eze 14:11 go *w* off from following me

Wane

Isa 60:20 your moon go on the *w*

Want

Ge 22:5 I and the boy *w* to go on over
Ex 3:18 and now we *w* to go, please
3:18 *w* to sacrifice to Jehovah our
4:18 I *w* to go, please, and return
5:3 We *w* to go, please, a journey
5:8 crying out, saying, We *w* to go
5:8 we *w* to sacrifice to
5:17 you are saying, We *w* to go
5:17 we *w* to sacrifice to Jehovah
8:8 I *w* to send the people away
21:5 I do not *w* to go out as one
24:12 as I *w* to give you the stone
33:5 I *w* to know what I am going
Nu 16:14 eyes . . . you *w* to bore out
20:19 *w* nothing more than to pass
De 10:10 not *w* to bring you to ruin
15:8 he needs, which he is in *w* of
23:5 did not *w* to listen to Balaam
28:48 and the *w* of everything
28:57 for the *w* of everything
29:20 will not *w* to forgive him
Jos 15:18 said to her: What do you *w*?
24:10 I did not *w* to listen to
Jg 1:14 said to her: What do you *w*?
19:25 the men did not *w* to listen
20:13 not *w* to listen to the voice
1Sa 12:19 as we do not *w* to die
22:17 not *w* to thrust out their
2Sa 2:21 not *w* to turn aside from
2Ki 8:19 Jehovah did not *w* to bring
13:23 not *w* to bring them to ruin
1Ch 19:19 and Syria did not *w* to try
2Ch 21:7 Jehovah did not *w* to bring
Job 30:3 Because of *w* and hunger they
39:9 Does a wild bull *w* to serve
Ps 141:5 head would not *w* to refuse
Pr 6:11 your *w* like an armed man
6:32 is in *w* of heart; he that
7:7 a young man in *w* of heart
9:4 Whoever is in *w* of heart
9:16 whoever is in *w* of heart
10:13 back of one in *w* of heart
10:21 for *w* of heart the foolish
11:12 one in *w* of heart has
11:24 but it results only in *w*
12:9 glorifying himself but in *w*
12:11 is in *w* of heart
14:23 word of the lips tends to *w*
15:21 to one who is in *w* of heart
21:5 hasty surely heads for *w*
21:17 will be an individual in *w*
22:16 is surely destined for *w*
28:16 is in *w* of true discernment
28:22 *w* itself will come upon him
28:27 will have no *w*, but he that
Isa 24:11 the streets for *w* of wine
42:24 they did not *w* to walk and
Jer 40:15 I *w* to go, now, and strike
Eze 3:7 will not *w* to listen to you
Da 5:19 Whom he happened to *w* to
5:19 whom he happened to *w* to, he
Da 5:19 whom he happened to *w* to, he
5:19 whom he happened to *w* to, he
Ho 2:5 I *w* to go after those
2:7 I *w* to go and return to my
Am 4:6 *w* of bread in all your places
Mal 3:10 until there is no more *w*
Mt 1:19 not *w* to make her a public
7:12 that you *w* men to do to you
8:2 Lord, if you just *w* to, you
8:3 touched him, saying: I *w* to
9:13 I *w* mercy, and not sacrifice
11:14 if you *w* to accept it, He
12:7 I *w* mercy, and not sacrifice
12:38 we *w* to see a sign from you
13:28 *w* us, then, to go out and
15:32 do not *w* to send them away
19:17 you *w* to enter into life
19:21 If you *w* to be perfect, go
20:14 I *w* to give to this last one
20:15 do what I *w* with my own
20:21 said to her: What do you *w*?
20:32 What do you *w* me to do for
23:37 But you people did not *w* it
26:17 you *w* us to prepare for you
27:17 Which one do you *w* me to
27:21 do you *w* me to release to
Mr 1:40 If you just *w* to, you can
1:41 I *w* to. Be made clean
6:22 Ask me for whatever you *w*
6:25 I *w* you to give me right
6:26 did not *w* to disregard her
7:24 not *w* anyone to get to know
9:30 *w* anyone to get to know it
10:35 we *w* you to do for us
10:36 What do you *w* me to do for
10:51 you *w* me to do for you
12:38 *w* to walk around in robes
12:38 and *w* greetings in the
12:44 out of her *w*, dropped in all
14:7 whenever you *w* to you can
14:12 Where do you *w* us to go and
14:36 Yet not what I *w*, but what
14:36 but what you *w*
15:9 Do you *w* me to release to
Lu 5:12 Lord, if you just *w* to, you
5:13 I *w* to. Be made clean
6:31 just as you *w* men to do to
9:54 do you *w* us to tell fire to
13:34 but you people did not *w* it
18:41 What do you *w* me to do for
19:14 do not *w* this man to become
19:27 did not *w* me to become king
21:4 woman out of her *w* dropped
22:9 Where do you *w* us to get it
22:35 did not *w* for anything, did
Joh 5:6 Do you *w* to become sound in
5:40 you do not *w* to come to me
6:67 You do not *w* to go also, do
7:1 not *w* to walk about in Judea
9:27 do you *w* to hear it again
9:27 *w* to become his disciples
12:21 Sir, we *w* to see Jesus
Ac 7:28 *w* to do away with me in the
Ro 1:13 I do not *w* you to fail to
11:25 I do not *w* you, brothers
13:3 *w* to have no fear of the
16:19 *w* you to be wise as to
1Co 4:21 What do you *w*? Shall I come
7:32 I *w* you to be free from
10:1 do not *w* you to be ignorant
10:20 not *w* you to become sharers
11:3 *w* you to know that the head
12:1 do not *w* you to be ignorant
14:35 they *w* to learn something
16:7 I do not *w* to see you just
2Co 5:4 we *w*, not to put it off, but
8:11 readiness to *w* to do, so
10:9 not seem to *w* to terrify you
12:6 if I ever do *w* to boast
Ga 3:2 This alone I *w* to learn from
4:9 *w* to slave for them over again
4:17 *w* to shut you off from me
4:21 you who *w* to be under law
6:12 *w* to make a pleasing
6:13 *w* you to be circumcised that
Php 4:11 with regard to being in *w*
4:12 and how to suffer *w*
Col 2:1 I *w* you to realize how great
1Th 4:13 do not *w* you to be ignorant
2Th 3:10 not *w* to work, neither let
1Ti 5:11 they *w* to marry
Phm 14 your consent I do not *w* to
Heb 10:5 offering you did not *w*, but
10:8 You did not *w* nor did you
Heb 11:37 while they were in *w*, in
Re 11:5 if anyone should *w* to harm
18:4 *w* to share with her in her
18:4 *w* to receive part of her

Wanted

Jos 7:21 I *w* them, and I took them
Ps 73:17 I *w* to discern their future
Jer 49:9 only as much ruin as they *w*
Ob 5 steal as much as they *w*
Mt 14:5 although he *w* to kill him
17:12 with him the things they *w*
18:23 *w* to settle accounts with
23:37 I *w* to gather your children
27:15 prisoner . . . the one they *w*
Mr 3:13 and summoned those he *w*, and
9:13 as many things as they *w*
Lu 1:62 what he *w* it to be called
13:34 I *w* to gather your children
23:20 he *w* to release Jesus
Joh 6:11 the small fishes as they *w*
21:18 and walk about where you *w*
Ac 10:10 very hungry and *w* to eat
1Th 2:18 we *w* to come to you, yes
Heb 12:17 when he *w* to inherit the

Wanting

Pr 17:18 A man that is *w* in heart
Ec 1:15 *w* cannot possibly be counted
Eze 3:7 are not *w* to listen to me
Mr 6:19 and was *w* to kill him, but
Lu 8:20 standing outside *w* to see you
10:29 *w* to prove himself righteous
16:26 those *w* to go over from here
23:8 *w* to see him because of
Joh 7:44 were *w* to get hold of him
16:19 were *w* to question him, so
Ac 5:33 were *w* to do away with them
19:33 *w* to make his defense to the
2Co 8:10 doing but also the *w* to do
11:12 *w* a pretext for being
Ga 1:7 *w* to pervert the good news
1Ti 1:7 *w* to be teachers of law, but
3Jo 10 *w* to receive them he tries

Wants

Le 27:13 *w* to buy it back at all, he
27:15 sanctifier *w* to buy his
27:31 *w* to buy any of his tenth
Job 32:19 it *w* to burst open
Ps 21:1 how very joyful he *w* to be
Da 4:17 whom he *w* to, he gives it
4:25 one whom he *w* to he gives it
4:32 one whom he *w* to he gives it
5:21 one whom he *w* to, he sets up
Mt 5:40 if a person *w* to go to court
5:42 one that *w* to borrow from
16:24 If anyone *w* to come after
16:25 whoever *w* to save his soul
20:26 whoever *w* to become great
20:27 whoever *w* to be first among
27:43 now rescue him if He *w* him
Mr 8:34 If anyone *w* to come after me
8:35 whoever *w* to save his soul
9:35 If anyone *w* to be first, he
10:43 whoever *w* to become great
10:44 whoever *w* to be first among
Lu 5:39 has drunk old wine *w* new
9:23 If anyone *w* to come after me
9:24 whoever *w* to save his soul
13:31 because Herod *w* to kill you
14:28 *w* to build a tower does not
Joh 3:8 The wind blows where it *w* to
5:21 those alive whom he *w* to
1Co 7:36 let him do what he *w*; he
7:39 to be married to whom she *w*
2Co 9:12 the *w* of the holy ones but
Jas 4:4 *w* to be a friend of the world
Re 11:5 if anyone *w* to harm them

War

Ge 14:2 these made *w* with Bera king
Ex 1:10 in case *w* should befall us
13:17 feel regret when they see *w*
14:6 to make his *w* chariots ready
14:17 his *w* chariots and his
14:18 Pharaoh, his *w* chariots and
14:23 his *w* chariots and his
14:26 Egyptians, their *w* chariots
14:28 covered the *w* chariots and
15:3 a manly person of *w*. Jehovah
15:19 horses with his *w* chariots
17:16 will have *w* with Amalek
Nu 10:9 enter into *w* in your land
10:9 a *w* call on the trumpets
24:17 all the sons of tumult of *w*

Nu 31:7 went waging *w* against Midian
31:28 men of *w* who went out on
31:42 to the men who waged *w*
31:49 the sum of the men of *w* who
32:6 brothers to go to *w* while
32:20 will equip . . . for the *w*
32:27 before Jehovah for the *w*
32:29 everyone equipped for the *w*
De 1:41 each one, his weapons of *w*
2:9 molest Moab or engage in *w*
2:14 men of *w* had come to their
2:16 all the men of *w* had finished
2:24 and engage in *w* with him
4:34 with miracles and with *w* and
11:4 his *w* chariots against the
20:1 see horses and *w* chariots
20:12 actually makes *w* with you
20:20 city that is making *w* with
Jos 4:13 for the *w* onto the desert
5:4 all the men of *w*, had died in
5:6 men of *w* who came out of
6:3 men of *w* must march round the
6:5 should shout a great *w* cry
6:20 began to shout a great *w* cry
8:1 all the people of *w* and get
8:3 the people of *w* rose to go up
8:11 And all the people of *w* who
9:2 to make *w* against Joshua and
10:5 Gibeon and to *w* against it
10:7 all the people of *w* with him
10:24 commanders of the men of *w*
10:36 and began to *w* against it
10:38 and began to *w* against it
11:4 many horses and *w* chariots
11:7 and all the people of *w* with
11:18 *w* with all these kings
11:19 the others they took by *w*
11:20 to declare *w* against Israel
11:23 had no disturbance from *w*
14:11 my power . . . for the *w*
14:15 had no disturbance from *w*
17:1 proved to be a man of *w*
17:16 are *w* chariots with iron
17:18 have *w* chariots with iron
19:47 go up and *w* against Leshem
24:6 with *w* chariots and
Jg 1:8 sons of Judah carried on *w*
1:19 they had *w* chariots with
3:2 so as to teach them *w*, that
4:3 had nine hundred *w* chariots
4:7 army and his *w* chariots and
4:13 all his *w* chariots, the nine
4:13 the nine hundred *w* chariots
4:15 all his *w* chariots and all
4:16 chased after the *w* chariots
5:2 hair . . . loose in Israel for *w*
5:8 then there was *w* in the gates
5:28 Why has his *w* chariot delayed
8:13 return from the *w* by the pass
18:11 girded with weapons of *w*
18:16 with their weapons of *w*
18:17 girded with weapons of *w*
20:17 Every one . . . a man of *w*
21:22 for each one his wife by *w*
1Sa 8:12 to make his *w* instruments
13:5 thirty thousand *w* chariots
16:18 man of *w* and an intelligent
17:1 their camps together for *w*
17:13 went after Saul to the *w*
17:13 sons that went into the *w*
17:33 man of *w* from his boyhood
18:5 placed . . . over the men of *w*
19:8 *w* broke out again and David
23:8 all the people to *w*
28:1 to make *w* against Israel
2Sa 1:27 the weapons of *w* perished
3:1 *w* between the house of Saul
3:6 *w* between the house of Saul
11:7 how the *w* was getting along
11:18 all the matters of the *w*
11:19 all the matters of the *w*
21:15 to have *w* again with Israel
21:18 *w* arose once more with the
21:19 *w* arose once again with the
21:20 *w* arose yet again at Gath
1Ki 2:5 the blood of *w* in peacetime
2:5 the blood of *w* on his belt
8:44 to the *w* against their enemy
12:21 men able-bodied for *w*
22:1 without *w* between Syria and
22:6 against Ramoth-gilead in *w*
22:15 go to Ramoth-gilead in *w*
22:35 interior of the *w* chariot
22:38 wash off the *w* chariot by
2Ki 2:11 a fiery *w* chariot and fiery
2:12 the *w* chariot of Israel and
3:7 go with me to Moab in *w*
5:9 his horses and his *w* chariots
6:8 involved in *w* against Israel
6:14 sent horses and *w* chariots
6:15 with horses and *w* chariots
6:17 of horses and *w* chariots
7:6 hear the sound of *w* chariots
8:28 *w* against Hazael the king of
9:21 his *w* chariot was hitched up
9:21 each in his own *w* chariot
9:24 collapsed in his *w* chariot
10:2 *w* chariots and the horses
10:16 with him in his *w* chariot
13:14 the *w* chariot of Israel and
13:25 Jehoahaz his father in *w*
14:7 got to seize Sela in the *w*
16:5 against Jerusalem in *w* and
18:20 and mightiness for the *w*
19:23 multitude of my *w* chariots
24:16 mighty men carrying on *w*
25:4 the men of *w* fled by night
25:19 command over the men of *w*
1Ch 5:10 made *w* upon the Hagrites
5:18 and trained in *w*, there were
5:19 to make *w* upon the Hagrites
5:20 they called for aid in the *w*
7:4 troops of the army for *w*
7:11 going out to the army for *w*
7:40 was in the army in the *w*
10:1 made *w* upon Israel; and the
11:13 gathered . . . together for *w*
12:8 army men for the *w*, keeping
12:33 with all the weapons of *w*
12:38 All these were men of *w*
19:7 and now came in for the *w*
20:4 *w* began breaking out at
20:5 *w* again with the Philistines
20:6 came to be *w* again at Gath
2Ch 6:34 *w* against their enemies in
11:1 men able-bodied for *w*, to
13:2 *w* itself took place between
13:3 Abijah engaged in the *w* with
13:3 thousand mighty men of *w*
13:15 broke out shouting a *w* cry
13:15 of Judah shouted a *w* cry
14:6 no *w* against him during
15:19 *w*, it did not occur down
18:3 and with you in the *w*
18:5 against Ramoth-gilead in *w*
18:14 go to Ramoth-gilead in *w*
20:1 against Jehoshaphat in *w*
22:5 *w* against Hazael the king of
25:8 act, be courageous for the *w*
25:13 going with him to the *w*
26:11 have a force engaging in *w*
26:13 men engaging in *w* with the
26:15 engines of *w*, the invention
32:2 set for *w* against Jerusalem
35:24 in the second *w* chariot
Job 5:20 during *w* from the power of
38:23 For the day of fight and *w*
39:25 uproar of chiefs and the *w*
Ps 27:3 against me *w* should rise
35:1 *W* against those warring
68:17 The *w* chariots of God are in
120:7 I speak, They are for *w*
Pr 20:18 direction carry on your *w*
24:6 you will carry on your *w*, and
25:18 As a *w* club and a sword and
Ec 3:8 a time for *w* and a time for
8:8 there any discharge in the *w*
Isa 2:4 neither will they learn *w*
3:25 and your mightiness by *w*
7:1 Jerusalem for *w* against it
7:1 unable to *w* against it
13:4 is mustering the army of *w*
19:2 *w* each one against his
20:1 *w* against Ashdod and to
21:7 *w* chariot with a span of
21:7 a *w* chariot of asses
21:7 a *w* chariot of camels
21:9 *w* chariot of men, with a
21:15 of the heaviness of the *w*
22:6 *w* chariot of earthling man
22:7 become full of *w* chariots
29:7 are waging *w* against Ariel
29:7 those waging *w* against her
29:8 waging *w* against Mount Zion
31:1 their trust in *w* chariots
31:4 wage *w* over Mount Zion and
36:5 and mightiness for the *w*
37:24 multitude of my *w* chariots
Isa 41:12 those men at *w* with you
42:13 he will let out a *w* cry
42:25 and the strength of *w*
43:17 the *w* chariot and the horse
Jer 4:19 the alarm signal of *w*
6:4 they have sanctified *w*
6:23 battle order like a man of *w*
21:2 king of Babylon is making *w*
21:4 the weapons of *w* that are in
28:8 *w* and of calamity and of
38:4 the men of *w* who are left
39:4 all the men of *w* saw them
41:3 men of *w*, Ishmael struck
41:16 able-bodied men, men of *w*
42:14 where we shall see no *w*
47:3 rattling of his *w* chariots
48:14 men of . . . energy for the *w*
49:2 signal of *w* to be heard
49:26 men of *w* themselves will
50:15 Shout a *w* cry against her
50:22 sound of *w* in the land, and
50:30 men of *w* will be brought
50:37 against their *w* chariots
50:42 in array as one man for *w*
51:20 as weapons of *w*, and by you
51:21 will dash the *w* chariot and
51:32 men of *w* themselves have
52:7 as regards all the men of *w*
52:25 over the men of *w*, and
Eze 17:17 effective in the *w*, by
23:24 rattling of *w* chariots and
26:7 with horses and *w* chariots
26:10 and wheel and *w* chariot
27:10 your men of *w*. Shield and
27:27 and all your men of *w*
32:27 with their weapons of *w*
Da 7:21 horn made *w* upon the holy
9:26 until the end there will be *w*
11:25 excite himself for the *w*
Ho 1:7 or by *w*, by horses or by
2:18 *w* I shall break out of the
5:8 Shout a *w* cry at Beth-aven
10:9 In Gibeah *w* against the sons
Joe 2:1 a *w* cry in my holy mountain
2:7 men of *w* they go up a wall
3:9 among the nations, Sanctify *w*!
3:9 come up, all the men of *w*
Mic 2:8 like those returning from *w*
3:5 sanctify *w* against him
4:3 will they learn *w* anymore
Na 2:3 the *w* chariot in the day of
2:4 *w* chariots keep driving madly
2:13 I will burn up her *w* chariot
Zec 9:10 cut off the *w* chariot from
14:2 against Jerusalem for the *w*
14:3 and *w* against those nations
Lu 14:31 to meet another king in *w*
Heb 11:34 became valiant in *w*, routed
Jas 4:2 go on fighting and waging *w*
Re 2:16 *w* with them with the long
11:7 make *w* with them and conquer
12:7 *w* broke out in heaven
12:17 *w* with the remaining ones
13:7 wage *w* with the holy ones
16:14 *w* of the great day of God
19:11 *w* in righteousness
19:19 *w* with the one seated on the
20:8 them together for the *w*

Ward

Ec 11:10 *w* off calamity from your

Wardrobe

2Ki 10:22 one who was over the *w*

War-equipped

Jos 6:7 the *w* force should pass on
6:9 the *w* force was going ahead
6:13 *w* force was walking ahead of

Wares

Ne 10:31 *w* and every kind of cereal

Warfare

1Sa 14:52 *w* continued heavy against
2Sa 8:10 trained in *w* against Toi
22:35 teaching my hands for *w*
1Ki 5:3 because of the *w* with which
14:30 *w* itself took place between
15:6 *w* itself took place between
15:7 was *w* also that took place
15:16 And *w* itself took place
15:32 *w* itself took place between
1Ch 12:1 the helpers in the *w*
18:10 trained in *w* against Tou
Ps 18:34 is teaching my hands for *w*
18:39 with vital energy for *w*

Ps 144:1 My fingers for *w*
Ca 3:8 being taught in *w*, each one
Da 11:20 but not in anger nor in *w*
2Co 10:3 do not wage *w* according to
10:4 the weapons of our *w* are not
1Ti 1:18 go on waging the fine *w*

Warm
1Ki 1:1 but he would not feel *w*
1:2 king will certainly feel *w*
2Ki 4:34 the child's flesh grew *w*
Job 31:20 rams he would *w* himself
39:14 in the dust she keeps them *w*
Ec 4:11 two lie down . . . get *w*
4:11 but how can just one keep *w*?
Isa 44:15 that he may *w* himself
47:14 charcoals for people to *w*
Hag 1:6 not with anyone's getting *w*
Jas 2:16 keep *w* and well fed, but you

Warmed
Isa 44:16 Aha! I have *w* myself

Warming
Mr 14:54 *w* himself before a . . . fire
14:67 seeing Peter *w* himself, she
Joh 18:18 and they were *w* themselves
18:18 Peter also . . . *w* himself
18:25 Peter was standing and *w*

Warms
Isa 44:16 also *w* himself and says

Warn
Ex 18:20 And you must *w* them of what
19:21 Go down, *w* the people, that
1Sa 8:9 you should solemnly *w* them
1Ki 2:42 that I might *w* you, saying
2Ch 19:10 *w* them that they may not
Eze 3:17 and you must *w* them from me
3:18 you do not actually *w* him
3:18 in order to *w* the wicked one
3:20 die because you did not *w*
33:8 *w* the wicked one from his
33:9 *w* someone wicked from his

Warned
Ex 19:23 *w* us, saying, Set bounds for
2Ki 6:10 he *w* him, and he kept away
17:15 with which he had *w* them
Ps 19:11 your own servant has been *w*
Ec 4:13 come to know enough to be *w*
Eze 3:19 you have *w* someone wicked
3:21 you have *w* someone righteous
3:21 because he had been *w*, and

Warning
Ex 21:29 *w* was served on its owner
De 32:46 speaking in *w* to you today
2Ki 17:13 Jehovah kept *w* Israel and
Ec 12:12 take a *w*: To the making of
Jer 6:10 give *w*, that they may hear
Eze 5:15 a *w* example and a horror to
33:4 but he takes no *w* at all
33:5 but he took no *w*. His own
33:5 had he himself taken *w*, his
33:6 people itself gets no *w* at
33:7 and give them *w* from me
Mt 2:12 given divine *w* in a dream
2:22 given divine *w* in a dream
1Co 10:11 written for a *w* to us upon
Heb 11:7 given divine *w* of things not
12:25 giving divine *w* upon earth
Jude 7 before us as a *w* example by

Warns
Eze 33:3 the horn and *w* the people

Warp
Le 13:48 in the *w* or in the woof of
13:49 in the *w* or in the woof or in
13:51 in the *w* or in the woof or
13:52 burn the garment or the *w*
13:53 in the garment or in the *w*
13:56 the skin or the *w* or the
13:57 in the garment or in the *w*
13:58 garment or the *w* or the woof
13:59 in the *w* or in the woof, or
Jg 16:13 my head with the *w* thread
16:14 loom pin and the *w* thread
Isa 38:12 the very threads of the *w*

Warred
Jos 10:29 and *w* against Libnah
1Ki 14:19 he *w* and how he reigned
22:45 and how he *w*, are they not
2Ch 27:5 *w* against the king of the
Isa 63:10 he himself *w* against them

Warring
Jos 10:25 against whom you are *w*
10:31 camping against it and *w*
10:34 and *w* against it
1Sa 14:47 went *w* round about against
23:1 Philistines are *w* against
Ps 35:1 against those *w* against me
56:1 *W* all day long, he keeps
56:2 there are many *w* against me
Jer 32:5 *w* against the Chaldeans
Zec 14:3 *w*, in the day of fight
14:14 will be *w* at Jerusalem
Ro 7:23 *w* against the law of my mind

Warrior
2Sa 17:8 and your father is a *w*
Isa 3:2 mighty man and *w*, judge and
42:13 Like a *w* he will awaken

Warriors
Ex 14:7 and *w* upon every one of them
15:4 the choice of his *w* have been
De 33:2 At his right hand *w* belonging
1Ki 9:22 the *w* and his servants and
2Ch 8:9 *w* and chiefs of his adjutants
17:13 *w*, valiant, mighty men
Eze 23:15 having the appearance of *w*
23:23 *w* and summoned ones
39:20 all sorts of *w*, is the
Hab 3:14 pierced the head of his *w*

Wars
Nu 21:14 the book of the *W* of Jehovah
Jg 3:1 any of the *w* of Canaan
1Sa 18:17 and fight the *w* of Jehovah
25:28 *w* of Jehovah are what my
1Ch 22:8 and great *w* you have waged
26:27 the *w* and from the spoil
28:3 for a man of *w* you are, and
2Ch 12:15 *w* between Rehoboam and
16:9 will exist *w* against you
27:7 all his *w* and his ways
Ps 46:9 making *w* to cease to the
140:2 keep attacking as in *w*
Mt 24:6 You are going to hear of *w*
24:6 and reports of *w*; see that
Mr 13:7 when you hear of *w* and
13:7 *w*, do not be terrified
Lu 21:9 hear of *w* and disorders, do
Jas 4:1 From what source are there *w*

Wart
Le 22:22 having a cut or *w* or

Wash
Ge 24:32 water to *w* his feet and the
49:11 *w* his clothing in wine and
Ex 19:10 they must *w* their mantles
29:4 you must *w* them with water
29:17 *w* its intestines and its
30:19 *w* their hands and their feet
30:20 they will *w* with water that
30:21 *w* their hands and their feet
40:12 and *w* them with water
40:32 to the altar they would *w*
Le 1:13 will *w* the intestines and the
6:27 you will *w* what he spatters
11:25 *w* his garments, and he must
11:28 bodies will *w* his garments
11:40 body will *w* his garments
11:40 will *w* his garments, and he
13:6 *w* his garments and be clean
13:34 *w* his garments and be clean
13:54 *w* that in which the plague
13:58 may *w*, when the plague has
14:8 *w* his garments and shave off
14:9 *w* his garments and bathe his
14:47 should *w* his garments, and
14:47 should *w* his garments
15:5 should *w* his garments, and
15:6 *w* his garments, and he must
15:7 *w* his garments, and he must
15:8 *w* his garments and bathe in
15:10 will *w* his garments, and he
15:11 *w* his garments and bathe in
15:13 he must *w* his garments and
15:21 *w* his garments, and he must
15:22 should *w* his garments, and
15:27 *w* his garments and bathe in
16:26 he should *w* his garments
16:28 *w* his garments, and he must
17:15 *w* his garments and bathe in
17:16 if he will not *w* them and
Nu 8:7 *w* their garments and cleanse
19:7 priest must *w* his garments
19:8 *w* his garments in water and
Nu 19:10 must *w* his garments and be
19:19 he must *w* his garments and
19:21 *w* his garments, also the one
31:24 you must *w* your garments on
De 21:6 *w* their hands over the young
23:11 he should *w* with water
Ru 3:3 *w* and rub yourself with oil
1Sa 25:41 maidservant to *w* the feet
1Ki 22:38 *w* off the war chariot by
2Ch 4:6 ten basins . . . to *w* in them
4:6 sea was for the priest to *w*
Ps 26:6 shall *w* my hands in innocency
51:2 *w* me from my error
51:7 May you *w* me, that I may
68:23 you may *w* your foot in blood
69:15 stream of waters *w* me away
73:13 I *w* my hands in innocence
Ca 8:7 rivers themselves *w* it away
Isa 1:16 *W* yourselves; make
Jer 4:14 *W* your heart clean of sheer
Mt 6:17 your head and *w* your face
15:2 not *w* their hands when about
Mr 7:3 *w* their hands up to the elbow
Lu 11:38 did not first *w* before the
Joh 9:7 Go *w* in the pool of Siloam
9:11 Go to Siloam and *w*
13:5 *w* the feet of the disciples
13:8 certainly never *w* my feet
13:8 Unless I *w* you, you have no
13:14 *w* the feet of one another
Ac 22:16 *w* your sins away by your
Re 22:14 Happy are those who *w* their

Washed
Ge 18:4 and you must have your feet *w*
19:2 and have your feet *w*
43:24 might have their feet *w*
43:31 he *w* his face and went out
Ex 40:31 his sons *w* their hands and
Le 1:9 shanks will be *w* with water
8:6 near and *w* them with water
8:21 the shanks he *w* with water
9:14 he *w* the intestines and the
13:55 plague after it has been *w*
13:56 after it has been *w* out, he
13:58 be *w* a second time; and it
15:17 *w* with water and be unclean
Nu 8:21 *w* their garments, after which
Jg 5:21 The torrent of Kishon *w* them
19:21 they *w* their feet and began
2Sa 12:20 *w* and rubbed himself with
19:24 nor had he *w* his garments
Job 9:30 *w* myself in snow water, And
29:6 When I *w* my steps in butter
Ps 69:2 stream itself has *w* me away
124:4 waters would have *w* us away
Pr 30:12 *w* from its own excrement
Ca 5:3 I have *w* my feet. How can I
Isa 4:4 Jehovah will have *w* away the
18:2 land the rivers have *w* away
18:7 land the rivers have *w* away
Jer 46:15 powerful ones have been *w*
Eze 16:4 had not been *w* for cleansing
16:9 I *w* you with water and
23:40 whom you had *w* yourself
Mt 27:24 Pilate took water and *w* his
Joh 9:7 so he went off and *w*, and
9:11 went and *w* and gained sight
9:15 and I *w* and have sight
13:10 have more than his feet *w*
13:12 he had *w* their feet and
13:14 Teacher, *w* your feet, you
Ac 27:41 shoal *w* on each side by
1Co 6:11 But you have been *w* clean
1Ti 5:10 *w* the feet of holy ones
Re 7:14 have *w* their robes and made

Washes
Job 14:19 *w* off earth's dust
Pr 28:3 as a rain that *w* away so that

Washing
Ex 19:14 engaged in *w* their mantles
30:18 its stand of copper for *w*
40:30 and put water in it for *w*
Ps 60:8 Moab is my *w* pot
108:9 Moab is my *w* pot
Ca 4:2 that have gone up from the *w*
6:6 that have come up from the *w*
Jer 2:22 do the *w* with alkali and
Lu 5:2 and were *w* off their nets
Joh 13:6 Lord, are you *w* my feet?

Waste
Ge 1:2 proved to be formless and *w*
Ex 23:29 may not become a desolate *w*

Ezr 4:15 that city has been laid *w*
Job 21:10 and it does not *w* semen
Isa 1:25 remove all your *w* products
17:9 must become a desolate *w*
24:1 the land and laying it *w*
64:10 Jerusalem a desolate *w*
Jer 4:23 land . . . was empty and *w*
4:27 *w* is what the whole land
6:8 not set you as a desolate *w*
9:11 I shall make a desolate *w*
10:22 Judah a desolate *w*, the
12:10 wilderness of a desolate *w*
12:11 has made it a desolate *w*
32:43 desolate *w* without man and
33:10 *w* without man and without
33:12 *w* place without man and
34:22 make a desolate *w* without
44:6 a desolate *w*, as at this day
49:2 a mound of desolate *w*, and
49:33 a desolate *w* to time
50:13 desolate *w* in her entirety
Eze 6:14 make the land a desolate *w*
12:20 become a mere desolate *w*
14:15 desolate *w* without anybody
14:16 would become a desolate *w*
15:8 make the land a desolate *w*
29:9 become a desolate *w* and
29:10 dryness, a desolated *w*
29:12 land of Egypt a desolate *w*
29:12 will become a desolate *w*
32:15 land of Egypt a desolate *w*
33:28 make the land a desolate *w*
33:29 make the land a desolate *w*
35:3 and make you a desolate *w*
35:4 become a sheer desolate *w*
35:7 region of Seir a desolate *w*
35:14 a desolate *w* is what I
35:15 desolate *w* is what you
36:34 it had become a desolate *w*
36:35 the cities that were a *w*
36:38 cities that had been a *w*
Joe 2:20 land and desolated *w*
3:19 a desolate *w* it will become
3:19 desolate *w* it will become
Mic 1:7 I shall make a desolate *w*
7:13 must become a desolate *w*
Na 2:10 voidness, and a city laid *w*
Zep 1:13 houses for a desolate *w*
2:4 Ashkelon . . . be a desolate *w*
2:9 a salt pit, and a desolate *w*
2:13 make Nineveh a desolate *w*
3:6 Their cities were laid *w*
Hag 1:4 while this house is *w*
1:9 reason of my house that is *w*
Mal 1:3 his mountains a desolated *w*
Mt 26:8 and said: Why this *w?*
Mr 14:4 *w* of the perfumed oil taken

Wasted
Ge 38:9 he *w* his semen on the earth
Pr 23:8 have *w* your pleasant words
Joh 6:12 so that nothing is *w*

Wastefully
Lu 16:1 as handling his goods *w*

Wasteness
Isa 34:11 and the stones of *w*

Wastes
Job 33:21 flesh *w* away from sight
Jer 25:12 I will make it desolate *w*
51:26 because desolate *w* to time
51:62 mere desolate *w* to time
Eze 35:9 desolate *w* are what I shall

Wasting
Ps 106:15 *w* disease into their soul
Isa 10:16 his fat ones a *w* disease
2Co 4:16 we are outside is *w* away

Watch
Ge 31:24 *W* yourself that you do not
31:29 *W* yourself against speaking
31:49 Jehovah keep *w* between me
Ex 10:28 *W* yourself! Do not try to
14:24 during the morning *w* that
23:21 *W* yourself because of him
34:12 *W* yourself that you do not
Le 8:35 the obligatory *w* of Jehovah
De 4:9 *w* out for yourself and take
4:23 *W* out for yourselves that you
6:12 *w* out for yourself that you
8:11 *W* out for yourself that you
11:16 *W* out for yourselves for
12:13 *W* out for yourself for fear
12:19 *W* out for yourself that you
12:28 *W*, and you must obey all
12:30 *W* out for yourself for fear
15:9 *W* out for yourself for fear a
Jg 7:19 start of the middle night *w*
13:4 *w* yourself, please, and do
1Sa 11:11 during the morning *w* and
19:11 David's house to *w* it and
26:15 you not *w* over your lord
2Sa 18:12 *W*, whoever you are, over
2Ki 11:5 *w* over the king's house
11:6 *w* over the house by turns
11:7 *w* over the house of Jehovah
1Ch 12:29 *w* of the house of Saul
Job 2:6 Only *w* out for his soul
13:27 And you *w* all my paths
14:16 *w* for nothing but my sin
Ps 5:3 to you and be on the *w*
37:32 on the *w* for the righteous
37:37 *W* the blameless one and keep
59:9 toward you I will keep *w*
66:7 nations his own eyes keep *w*
71:10 ones keeping *w* for my soul
90:4 And as a *w* during the night
130:3 If errors were what you *w*
141:3 *w* over the door of my lips
Pr 15:3 keeping *w* upon the bad ones
Isa 7:4 *W* yourself and keep
65:4 night even in the *w* huts
Jer 17:21 *W* out for your souls, and
51:12 Make strong the *w*
Ob 12 *w* the sight in the day of
Na 2:1 *W* the way. Strengthen the hips
Hab 2:1 keep *w*, to see what he will
Mt 7:15 Be on the *w* for the false
14:25 fourth *w* period of the night
16:6 *w* out for the leaven of the
16:11 *w* out for the leaven of the
16:12 *w* out, not for the leaven of
24:42 Keep on the *w*, therefore
24:43 known in what *w* the thief
25:13 Keep on the *w*, therefore
26:38 and keep on the *w* with me
26:40 not so much as *w* one hour
26:41 Keep on the *w* and pray
Mr 6:48 the fourth *w* of the night he
13:23 You, then, *w* out; I have
13:34 doorkeeper to keep on the *w*
13:35 keep on the *w*, for you do
13:37 I say to all, Keep on the *w*
14:34 Stay here and keep on the *w*
14:37 to keep on the *w* one hour
14:38 keep on the *w* and praying
Lu 12:1 *W* out for the leaven of the
12:38 he arrives in the second *w*
Joh 17:11 Father, *w* over them on
17:12 I used to *w* over them on
17:15 *w* over them because of the
Ac 27:33 you have been on the *w* and
Eph 5:15 strict *w* that how you walk
Heb 13:17 keeping *w* over your souls

Watched
1Sa 26:16 not *w* over your lord, over
Job 24:15 has *w* for evening darkness
Ps 17:4 *w* against the paths of the
Mt 27:36 they sat, they *w* over him

Watcher
Da 4:13 a *w*, even a holy one, coming
4:23 king beheld a *w*, even a holy

Watchers
Jg 1:24 the *w* got to see a man going
Jer 4:16 *W* are coming from a land
Da 4:17 By the decree of *w* the thing

Watches
Job 33:11 He *w* all my paths
Ps 63:6 During the night *w* I meditate
119:148 ahead of the night *w*
La 2:19 at the start of the morning *w*
Lu 2:8 *w* in the night over their
1Jo 5:18 One born from God *w* him

Watchful
1Pe 5:8 Keep your senses, be *w*
Re 3:2 Become *w*, and strengthen the

Watching
Jg 5:28 kept *w* for him, The mother
7:17 learn from *w* me, and that is
1Sa 1:12 Eli was *w* her mouth
4:13 *w*, because his heart had
Job 10:14 and you have kept *w* me
Ps 59:*super* and they kept *w* the house
68:16 keep *w* enviously
130:6 *W* for the morning
Pr 8:34 *w* at the posts of my
31:27 She is *w* over the goings on
Ec 5:8 higher than the high one is *w*
11:4 *w* the wind will not sow seed
Isa 42:20 but you did not keep *w*
Jer 3:5 or keep *w* something forever
20:10 they are *w* for my limping
Zec 11:11 afflicted . . . were *w* me
Mt 27:54 those with him *w* over Jesus
Mr 3:2 *w* him closely to see whether
Lu 6:7 *w* him closely to see whether
12:37 master on arriving finds *w*
12:39 he would have kept *w* and
14:1 they were closely *w* him
Ac 9:24 closely *w* also the gates
1Co 3:10 let each one keep *w* how he
8:9 keep *w* that this authority
Col 4:17 Keep *w* the ministry which
Heb 12:15 carefully *w* that no one may

Watchman
2Sa 13:34 *w*, raised his eyes and saw
18:24 the *w* went to the roof of
18:25 *w* called and told the king
18:26 The *w* now saw another man
18:26 The *w* therefore called to
18:27 the *w* went on to say: I am
2Ki 9:17 the *w* was standing upon the
9:18 *w* went on to report, saying
9:20 *w* went on to report, saying
Job 27:18 a booth that a *w* has made
Isa 21:11 *W*, what about the night?
21:11 *W*, what about the night?
21:12 *w* said: The morning has to
Eze 3:17 a *w* is what I have made you
33:2 and set him as their *w*
33:6 as regards the *w*, in case
33:6 from the hand of the *w*
33:7 a *w* is what I have made you
Ho 9:8 *w* of Ephraim was with my God

Watchmen
1Sa 14:16 the *w* belonging to Saul in
2Ki 17:9 tower of the *w* clear to the
18:8 from the tower of the *w*
Ps 130:6 than *w* for the morning
Ca 3:3 *w* who were going around in
5:7 *w* that were going about in the
5:7 *w* of the walls lifted my wide
Isa 52:8 Your own *w* have raised their
56:10 His *w* are blind. None of
62:6 I have commissioned *w*
Jer 6:17 raised up over you people *w*
51:12 Post the *w*. Make ready
Mic 7:4 The day of your *w*, of your
Mt 28:4 fear of him the *w* trembled

Watchtower
Ge 31:49 The *W*, because he said: Let
2Ch 20:24 to the *w* of the wilderness
Isa 21:8 Upon the *w*, O Jehovah, I am
32:14 Ophel and the *w* themselves

Water
Ge 2:10 out of Eden to *w* the garden
18:4 Let a little *w* be taken
21:14 skin *w* bottle and gave it to
21:15 *w* became exhausted in the
21:19 caught sight of a well of *w*
21:19 fill the skin bottle with *w*
21:25 well of *w* that the servants
24:11 at a well of *w* about evening
24:11 the women who draw *w* were
24:13 stationed at a fountain of *w*
24:13 are coming out to draw *w*
24:14 Let your *w* jar down, please
24:14 I shall also *w* your camels
24:15 and her *w* jar was upon her
24:16 fill her *w* jar and then came
24:17 little sip of *w* from your
24:19 draw *w* until they are done
24:20 to the well to draw *w*, and
24:32 *w* to wash his feet and the
24:43 stationed at a fountain of *w*
24:43 coming out to draw *w* to
24:43 let me drink a little *w*
24:44 and I shall also draw *w* for
24:45 fountain and began to draw *w*
24:46 I shall also *w* your camels
26:18 to dig again the wells of *w*
26:19 found . . . a well of fresh *w*
26:20 saying: The *w* is ours!
26:32 We have found *w!*
29:2 accustomed to *w* the droves
29:7 *W* the sheep, then go feed
29:8 Then we must *w* the sheep

Ge 30:38 in the *w* drinking troughs
37:24 there was no *w* in it
43:24 gave *w* that they might have
Ex 2:10 have drawn him out of the *w*
2:16 drew *w* and filled the
2:16 to *w* their father's flock
2:19 he actually drew *w* for us
2:19 that he might *w* the flock
4:9 take some *w* from the Nile
4:9 *w* . . . from the Nile River will
7:15 Pharaoh . . . out to the *w*
7:17 *w* that is in the Nile River
7:18 drinking *w* from the Nile
7:20 *w* that was in the Nile River
7:20 *w* . . . was turned into blood
7:21 drink *w* from the Nile River
7:24 the Nile River for *w* to drink
7:24 drink any *w* of the Nile River
8:20 Pharaoh . . . out to the *w*
12:9 not eat any . . . cooked in *w*
15:22 but they did not find *w*
15:23 to drink the *w* from Marah
15:25 and he threw it into the *w*
15:25 and the *w* became sweet
15:27 twelve springs of *w* and
15:27 went camping there by the *w*
17:1 no *w* for the people to drink
17:2 Give us *w* that we may drink
17:3 went on thirsting there for *w*
17:6 and *w* must come out of it
23:25 bless your bread and your *w*
29:4 you must wash them with *w*
30:18 and put *w* into it
30:20 wash with *w* that they
34:28 no bread and he drank no *w*
40:7 and the altar and put *w* in it
40:12 and wash them with *w*
40:30 and put *w* in it for washing
Le 1:9 shanks will be washed with *w*
1:13 wash . . . the shanks with *w*
6:28 be scoured and rinsed with *w*
8:6 near and washed them with *w*
8:21 the shanks he washed with *w*
11:32 is made will be put in *w*
11:34 eaten upon which *w* may come
11:38 *w* should be put upon seed
14:5 vessel over running *w*
14:6 was killed over the running *w*
14:8 bathe in *w* and must be clean
14:9 and bathe his flesh in *w*; and
14:50 vessel over running *w*
14:51 in the running *w*, and he
14:52 running *w* and the live bird
15:5 in *w* and be unclean until the
15:6 in *w* and be unclean until the
15:7 and he must bathe in *w* and be
15:8 bathe in *w* and be unclean
15:10 bathe in *w* and be unclean
15:11 not rinsed his hands in *w*
15:11 bathe in *w* and be unclean
15:12 should be rinsed with *w*
15:13 bathe his flesh in running *w*
15:16 bathe all his flesh in *w* and
15:17 with *w* and be unclean until
15:18 bathe in *w* and be unclean
15:21 bathe in *w* and be unclean
15:22 bathe in *w* and be unclean
15:27 bathe in *w* and be unclean
16:4 bathe his flesh in *w* and put
16:24 he must bathe his flesh in *w*
16:26 he must bathe his flesh in *w*
16:28 he must bathe his flesh in *w*
17:15 bathe in *w* and be unclean
22:6 he must bathe his flesh in *w*
Nu 5:17 priest must take holy *w* in an
5:17 and he must put it in the *w*
5:18 bitter *w* that brings a curse
5:19 bitter *w* that brings a curse
5:22 *w* that brings a curse must
5:23 wipe . . . into the bitter *w*
5:24 drink the bitter *w* that
5:24 *w* that brings a curse must
5:26 make the woman drink the *w*
5:27 made her drink the *w*, it
5:27 *w* that brings a curse must
8:7 Spatter sin-cleansing *w* upon
19:7 and bathe his flesh in *w*, and
19:8 wash his garments in *w* and
19:8 must bathe his flesh in *w*
19:9 kept for the *w* for cleansing
19:13 the *w* for cleansing has not
19:17 put running *w* upon it in a
19:18 hyssop and dip it into the *w*
19:19 bathe in *w*, and he must be
Nu 19:20 The *w* for cleansing was not
19:21 *w* for cleansing should wash
19:21 touching the *w* for cleansing
20:2 to be no *w* for the assembly
20:5 and there is no *w* to drink
20:8 that it may indeed give its *w*
20:8 *w* for them from the crag and
20:10 we shall bring out *w* for you
20:11 much *w* began to come out
20:17 not drink the *w* of a well
20:19 should drink your *w*, I shall
21:5 there is no bread and no *w*
21:16 and let me give them *w*
21:22 We shall drink *w* of no well
24:7 *W* keeps trickling from his
31:23 by the *w* for cleansing
31:23 should pass through the *w*
33:9 were twelve springs of *w* and
33:14 proved to be no *w* there
De 2:6 *w* you may purchase from them
2:28 *w* you will give me for money
8:7 land of torrent valleys of *w*
8:15 thirsty ground that has no *w*
8:15 brought forth *w* for you out
9:9 neither ate bread nor drank *w*
9:18 neither ate bread nor drank *w*
10:7 valleys running with *w*
11:11 land . . . drinks *w*
12:16 you should pour it out as *w*
12:24 out upon the ground as *w*
15:23 you should pour it out as *w*
21:4 torrent valley running with *w*
23:4 to your aid with bread and *w*
23:11 he should wash with *w*
29:11 to the drawer of your *w*
Jos 7:5 heart . . . became as *w*
9:21 and drawers of *w* for all the
9:23 drawers of *w* for the house
9:27 and drawers of *w* for the
Jg 4:19 a little *w* to drink, for I
5:4 Clouds also dripped with *w*
5:11 voices of the *w* distributors
5:11 among the places of drawing *w*
5:25 *W* he asked, milk she gave; In
6:38 a large banquet bowl with *w*
7:4 down to the *w* that I may put
7:5 the people go down to the *w*
7:5 the *w* with his tongue just as
7:6 upon their knees to drink *w*
7:19 the large *w* jars that were in
15:19 *w* began to come out of it
1Sa 7:6 went drawing *w* and pouring
9:11 girls going out to draw *w*
25:11 take my bread and my *w* and
26:11 and the *w* jug, and let us
26:12 the *w* jug from the place
26:16 *w* jug are that were at his
30:11 and gave him *w* to drink
30:12 or drunk *w* for three days
2Sa 5:8 means of the *w* tunnel, make
21:10 *w* poured down upon them
23:15 have a drink of the *w* from
23:16 drew *w* from the cistern
1Ki 13:8 or drink *w* in this place
13:9 not eat bread or drink *w*
13:16 not eat bread or drink *w*
13:17 not eat bread or drink *w*
13:18 may eat bread and drink *w*
13:19 in his house and drink *w*
13:22 eat bread and drink *w* in
13:22 Do not eat bread or drink *w*
14:15 as the reed sways in the *w*
17:10 Please, get me a sip of *w*
18:4 he supplied them bread and *w*
18:5 to all the springs of *w*
18:13 supplying them bread and *w*
18:33 Fill four large jars with *w*
18:35 *w* went all around the altar
18:35 trench . . . he filled with *w*
18:38 *w* that was in the trench
19:6 at his head . . . a jug of *w*
22:27 a reduced allowance of *w*
2Ki 2:19 *w* is bad, and the land is
2:21 the *w* and threw salt in it
2:21 I do make this *w* healthful
2:22 *w* continues healed down to
3:9 no *w* for the camp and for the
3:11 poured out *w* upon the hands
3:17 will be filled with *w*
3:19 springs of *w* you should stop
3:20 look! *w* was coming from the
3:20 to be filled with the *w*
3:22 flashed upon the *w*, so that
3:22 saw the *w* red like blood
2Ki 3:25 spring of *w* they would stop
6:5 axhead itself fell into the *w*
6:22 Set bread and *w* before them
8:15 a coverlet and dip it in *w*
18:31 the *w* of his own cistern
20:20 brought the *w* into the city
1Ch 11:17 a drink of the *w* from the
11:18 drew *w* from the cistern of
2Ch 18:26 reduced allowance of *w*
32:4 find a great deal of *w*
Ezr 10:6 ate no bread and drank no *w*
Ne 3:26 the *W* Gate on the east and
8:1 that was before the *W* Gate
8:3 that is before the *W* Gate
8:16 public square of the *W* Gate
9:20 *w* you gave them for their
12:37 to the *W* Gate to the east
13:2 with bread and with *w*
Job 8:11 a reed grow big without *w*
9:30 washed myself in snow *w*
14:9 At the scent of *w* . . . sprout
14:19 *W* . . . rubs away even stones
15:16 unrighteousness just like *w*
22:7 the tired one a drink of *w*
22:11 mass of *w* itself covers you
34:7 drinks up derision like *w*
36:27 he draws up the drops of *w*
38:34 *w* itself may cover you
38:37 the *w* jars of heaven—who
Ps 1:3 a tree planted by streams of *w*
22:14 Like *w* I have been poured
42:1 the hind that longs for the *w*
63:1 where there is no *w*
65:9 stream from God is full of *w*
66:12 through fire and through *w*
77:17 thunderously poured down *w*
79:3 poured out their blood like *w*
107:33 outflows of *w* into thirsty
107:35 into a reedy pool of *w*
107:35 region into outflows of *w*
114:8 rock into a reedy pool of *w*
114:8 rock into a spring of *w*
119:136 Streams of *w* have run
Pr 5:15 Drink *w* out of your own
5:16 streams of *w* in the public
5:18 *w* source prove to be blessed
8:24 heavily charged with *w*
21:1 *w* in the hand of Jehovah
25:21 if he is thirsty, give him *w*
25:25 As cold *w* upon a tired soul
26:7 of the lame one drawn up *w*
27:19 in *w* face corresponds with
30:16 not been satisfied with *w*
Ec 2:6 I made pools of *w* for myself
11:3 the clouds are filled with *w*
12:6 *w* wheel for the cistern has
Ca 4:15 gardens, a well of fresh *w*
5:12 doves by the channels of *w*
Isa 1:22 beer is diluted with *w*
1:30 like a garden that has no *w*
3:1 and the whole support of *w*
12:3 *w* out of the springs of
14:23 and reedy pools of *w*
19:5 *w* will certainly be dried up
19:8 upon the surface of the *w*
21:14 the thirsty one bring *w*
27:3 Every moment I shall *w* her
30:14 skim *w* from a marshy place
30:20 *w* in the form of oppression
30:25 to be streams, *w* ditches
32:2 *w* in a waterless country
33:16 *w* supply will be unfailing
35:7 ground as springs of *w*
36:16 the *w* of his own cistern
41:17 poor ones are seeking for *w*
41:18 into a reedy pool of *w*
41:18 land into sources of *w*
43:20 *w* even in the wilderness
44:3 pour out *w* upon the thirsty
44:4 poplars by the *w* ditches
44:12 He has not drunk *w*; so he
48:21 *W* out of the rock he caused
48:21 the *w* might stream forth
49:10 by the springs of *w* he will
50:2 due to there being no *w*
55:1 Come to the *w*. And the ones
58:11 and like the source of *w*
64:2 fire makes the very *w* boil
Jer 2:6 land of no *w* and of deep
2:13 the source of living *w*, in
2:13 that cannot contain the *w*
8:14 gives us poisoned *w* to drink
9:15 make them drink poisoned *w*
13:1 must not bring it into any *w*

Jer 14:3 insignificant ones for *w*
14:3 They have found no *w*
17:13 left the source of living *w*
23:15 poisoned *w* to drink
31:9 to torrent valleys of *w*
38:6 cistern there was no *w*
La 2:19 Pour out . . . like *w*
3:48 With streams of *w* my eye
5:4 have had to drink our own *w*
Eze 4:11 *w* you will drink merely by
4:16 they will drink *w* itself
4:17 may be lacking bread and *w*
7:17 they keep dripping with *w*
12:18 with anxious care your *w*
12:19 their *w* they will drink, in
16:4 in *w* you had not been washed
16:9 I washed you with *w* and
19:10 because of abundant *w*
21:7 knees . . . will drip with *w*
24:3 and also pour *w* into it
26:12 in the very midst of the *w*
31:5 much *w* in its watercourses
31:14 none drinking *w* may stand
31:16 all those drinking *w*, will
34:19 *w* befouled by the stamping
36:25 sprinkle upon you clean *w*
47:1 *w* going forth from under the
47:1 *w* was going down from under
47:2 *w* was trickling from the
47:3 make me pass through the *w*
47:3 *w* up to the ankles
47:4 made me pass through the *w*
47:4 *w* up to the knees
47:4 through—*w* up to the hips
47:5 for the *w* had got high
47:5 *w* permitting swimming
47:8 *w* is going forth to the
47:8 *w* is also actually healed
47:9 this *w* will certainly come
47:12 because the *w* for them
Da 1:12 and *w* that we may drink
Ho 2:5 giving my bread and my *w*, my
5:10 pour out my fury just like *w*
Joe 1:20 the channels of *w* have dried
3:18 Judah will all flow with *w*
Am 4:8 one city in order to drink *w*
8:11 and a thirst, not for *w*, but
Jon 3:7 Even *w* they should not drink
Na 3:14 *W* for a siege draw out for
Zec 9:11 pit in which there is no *w*
Mt 3:11 baptize you with *w* because
3:16 came up from the *w*
10:42 a cup of cold *w* to drink
17:15 falls . . . often into the *w*
27:24 Pilate took *w* and washed
27:49 and blood and *w* came out
Mr 1:8 I baptized you with *w*, but he
1:10 on coming up out of the *w* he
9:22 throw him . . . into the *w* to
9:41 *w* to drink on the ground that
14:13 an earthenware vessel of *w*
Lu 3:16 baptize you with *w*; but the
7:44 you gave me no *w* for my feet
8:23 began to fill up with *w* and
8:24 wind and the raging of the *w*
8:25 winds and the *w* . . . obey him
16:24 the tip of his finger in *w*
22:10 an earthenware vessel of *w*
Joh 1:26 I baptize in *w*. In the midst
1:31 I came baptizing in *w* was
1:33 sent me to baptize in *w*
2:6 six stone *w* jars sitting
2:7, 7 Fill the *w* jars with *w*
2:9 *w* that had been turned into
2:9 had drawn out the *w* knew
3:5 is born from *w* and spirit
3:23 a great quantity of *w* there
4:7 woman . . . came to draw *w*
4:10 have given you living *w*
4:11 a bucket for drawing *w*
4:11 do you have this living *w*
4:13 drinking from this *w* will
4:14 *w* that I will give him will
4:14 *w* that I will give him
4:14 a fountain of *w* bubbling up
4:15 give me this *w*, so that I
4:15 over to this place to draw *w*
4:28 left her *w* jar and went off
4:46 had turned the *w* into wine
5:7 into the pool when the *w* is
7:38 streams of living *w* will
13:5 he put *w* into a basin and
19:34 blood and *w* came out
Ac 1:5 John, indeed, baptized with *w*
Ac 8:36 came to a certain body of *w*
8:36 A body of *w*; what prevents
8:38 both went down into the *w*
8:39 they had come up out of the *w*
10:47 anyone forbid *w* so that
11:16 baptized with *w*, but you
Eph 5:26 bath of *w* by means of the
1Ti 5:23 Do not drink *w* any longer
Heb 9:19 with *w* and scarlet wool and
10:22 bodies bathed with clean *w*
Jas 3:12, 12 salt *w* produce sweet *w*
1Pe 3:20 carried safely through the *w*
2Pe 2:17 fountains without *w*, and
3:5 standing compactly out of *w*
3:5 and in the midst of *w* by
3:6 when it was deluged with *w*
1Jo 5:6 came by means of *w* and blood
5:6 not with the *w* only, but
5:6 the *w* and with the blood
5:8 spirit . . . *w* and the blood
Jude 12 rocks hidden below *w* in your
Re 12:15 serpent disgorged *w* like a
16:12 and its *w* was dried up, that
21:6 of the *w* of life free
22:1 river of *w* of life, clear as
22:17 wishes take life's *w* free

Watercourse

Jer 17:8 its roots right by the *w*
Da 8:2 to be by the *w* of Ulai
8:3 ram standing before the *w*
8:6 seen standing before the *w*

Watercourses

Job 20:17 He will never see the *w*
Eze 31:5 much water in its *w*

Watered

Ge 2:6 it *w* the entire surface of the
24:46 and she also *w* the camels
29:3 and they *w* the flocks
29:10 *w* the sheep of Laban
Ex 2:17 Moses . . . *w* their flock
Pr 11:25 himself also be freely *w*
Eze 31:14 none of the *w* trees may
1Co 3:6 Apollos *w*, but God kept

Water-filled

Job 28:10 has channeled *w* galleries

Watering

Ps 104:13 *w* the mountains from his
Pr 11:25 one freely *w* others will
Isa 7:19 upon all the *w* places

Waterless

Job 6:17 In due season they become *w*
30:3 Gnawing at a *w* region
Ps 72:9 inhabitants of *w* regions will
74:14 inhabiting the *w* regions
78:17 Most High in the *w* region
105:41 the *w* regions as a river
107:35 *w* region into outflows of
Isa 13:21 haunters of *w* regions will
25:5 Like the heat in a *w* country
32:2 of water in a *w* country
34:14 haunters of *w* regions must
35:1 *w* region will exult, and
41:18 *w* land into sources of
53:2 like a root out of *w* land
Jer 50:12 *w* wilderness and a desert
50:39 haunters of *w* regions will
51:43 *w* land and a desert plain
Eze 19:13 in a *w* and thirsty land
Ho 2:3 and place her like a *w* land
Joe 2:20 disperse him to a *w* land
Zep 2:13 a *w* region like the
Jude 12 *w* clouds carried this way

Watermelons

Nu 11:5 eat in Egypt . . . *w* and the

Waterpit

Ge 37:22 Pitch him into this *w* which
37:24 pitched him into the *w*
37:28 Joseph out of the *w* and then
37:29 Reuben returned to the *w*
37:29 Joseph was not in the *w*
2Sa 23:20 a lion inside a *w* on a day
1Ch 11:22 a lion inside a *w* in the

Waterpits

Ge 37:20 pitch him into one of the *w*
1Sa 13:6 hiding themselves in . . . *w*

Waters

Ge 1:2 over the surface of the *w*
1:6 an expanse . . . between the *w*
1:6, 6 dividing . . . the *w* and the *w*
Ge 1:7 make a division between the *w*
1:7 *w* that should be above the
1:9 Let the *w* under the heavens be
1:10 of the *w* he called Seas
1:20 the *w* swarm forth a swarm
1:21 which the *w* swarmed forth
1:22 fill the *w* in the sea basins
6:17 am bringing the deluge of *w*
7:6 the deluge of *w* occurred on
7:7 into the ark ahead of the *w*
7:10 *w* of the deluge came upon
7:17 *w* kept increasing and began
7:18 *w* became overwhelming and
7:18 going on the surface of the *w*
7:19 the *w* overwhelmed the earth
7:20 Up to fifteen cubits the *w*
7:24 *w* continued overwhelming the
8:1 and the *w* began to subside
8:3 *w* began receding from off the
8:3 fifty days the *w* were lacking
8:5 *w* kept on progressively
8:7 the *w* dried off the earth
8:8 dove to see whether the *w* had
8:9 *w* were yet upon the surface of
8:11 *w* had abated from the earth
8:13 *w* had drained from off the
9:11 flesh be cut off by *w* of a
9:15 *w* become a deluge to bring
16:7 found her at a fountain of *w*
49:4 With reckless license like *w*
Ex 7:19 hand out over the *w* of Egypt
7:19 over all their impounded *w*
8:6 *w* of Egypt, and the frogs
14:21 the *w* were being split apart
14:22 the *w* were a wall to them
14:26 the *w* may come back over
14:28 And the *w* kept coming back
14:29 the *w* were for them a wall
15:5 *w* proceeded to cover them
15:8 *w* were heaped up; They stood
15:8 The surging *w* were congealed
15:10 sank like lead in majestic *w*
15:19 Jehovah brought back the *w*
20:4 is in the *w* under the earth
32:20 upon the surface of the *w*
Le 11:9 everything that is in the *w*
11:9 has fins and scales in the *w*
11:10 swarming creature of the *w*
11:10 living soul . . . in the *w*
11:12 in the *w* that has no fins
11:36 a pit of impounded *w* will
11:46 that moves about in the *w*
Nu 20:13 These are the *w* of Meribah
20:24 respecting the *w* of Meribah
24:6 Like cedars by the *w*
24:7 And his seed is by many *w*
27:14 sanctifying me by the *w*
27:14 These are the *w* of Meribah
De 4:18 any fish that is in the *w*
5:8 in the *w* under the earth
11:4 the *w* of the Red Sea overflow
14:9 everything that is in the *w*
32:51 the *w* of Meribah of Kadesh
33:8 with him by the *w* of Meribah
Jos 2:10 the *w* of the Red Sea from
3:8 edge of the *w* of the Jordan
3:13 rest in the *w* of the Jordan
3:13 *w* of the Jordan will be cut
3:13 the *w* descending from above
3:15 dipped in the edge of the *w*
3:16 the *w* descending from above
4:7 the *w* of the Jordan were cut
4:7 *w* of the Jordan were cut off
4:18 the *w* of the Jordan began
4:23 the *w* of the Jordan from
5:1 dried up the *w* of the Jordan
11:5 at the *w* of Merom to fight
11:7 along the *w* of Merom
15:7 the *w* of En-shemesh, and its
15:9 spring of the *w* of Nephtoah
16:1 to the *w* of Jericho eastward
18:15 spring of the *w* of Nephtoah
Jg 5:19 Taanach by the *w* of Megiddo
7:24 the *w* as far as Beth-barah
7:24 got to capture the *w* as far
2Sa 5:20 like a gap made by *w*
12:27 captured the city of *w*
14:14 *w* that are being poured
17:20 on from here to the *w*
17:21 speedily pass over the *w*
22:12 Dark *w*, thick clouds
22:17 drawing me out of great *w*
2Ki 2:8 struck the *w*, and gradually
2:14 and struck the *w* and said

2Ki 2:14 he struck the *w*, then they
5:12 than all the *w* of Israel
19:24 dig and drink strange *w*
1Ch 14:11 like a gap made by *w*
2Ch 32:3 stop up the *w* of the springs
32:30 source of the *w* of Gihon
Ne 9:11 like a stone in the strong *w*
9:15 *w* out of the crag you brought
Job 3:24 like *w* my roaring cries pour
5:10 And sending *w* upon the open
11:16 As *w* that have passed along
12:15 puts a restraint upon the *w*
14:11 *W* do disappear from a sea
24:18 on the surface of the *w*
24:19 snatch away the snow *w*
26:5 Beneath the *w* and those
26:8 Wrapping up the *w* in his
26:10 upon the face of the *w*
27:20 Like *w* sudden terrors will
28:25 he has proportioned the *w*
29:19 My root is opened for the *w*
37:10 *w* is under constraint
38:30 *w* keep themselves hidden
Ps 18:11 Dark *w*, thick clouds
18:15 beds of *w* became visible
18:16 drawing me out of great *w*
29:3 Jehovah is over the *w*
29:3 Jehovah is over many *w*
32:6 As for the flood of many *w*
33:7 as by a dam the *w* of the sea
33:7 in storehouses the surging *w*
46:3 Though its *w* be boisterous
58:7 dissolve as into *w* that go
69:1 the *w* have come clear to the
69:2 I have come into profound *w*
69:14 and from the deep *w*
69:15 stream of *w* wash me away
73:10 *w* of what is full are
74:13 of the sea monsters in the *w*
77:16 The *w* have seen you, O God
77:16 *w* have seen you; they began
77:19 path was through many *w*
78:13 *w* to stand like a dam
78:16 *w* to descend just like
78:20 *w* might flow and torrents
81:7 at the *w* of Meribah
88:17 surrounded me like *w* all
93:4 Above the sounds of vast *w*
104:3 with beams in the very *w*
104:6 *w* were standing above the
105:29 changed their *w* into blood
105:41 and *w* began to flow out
106:11 *w* came covering their
106:32 at the *w* of Meribah
107:23 Doing business on vast *w*
109:18 like *w* into the midst of
124:4 *w* would have washed us away
124:5 The *w* of presumptuousness
136:6 out the earth above the *w*
144:7 deliver me from the many *w*
147:18 The *w* trickle
148:4 *w* that are above the heavens
Pr 8:29 decree that the *w* themselves
9:17 Stolen *w* themselves are
17:14 is as one letting out *w*
18:4 a man's mouth are deep *w*
20:5 Counsel . . . is as deep *w*
30:4 wrapped up the *w* in a mantle
Ec 11:1 upon the surface of the *w*
Ca 8:7 *w* themselves are not able to
Isa 8:6 rejected the *w* of the Shiloah
8:7 and the many *w* of the River
11:9 *w* are covering the very sea
15:6 *w* of Nimrim become sheer
15:9 *w* of Dimon have become full
17:12 like the noise of mighty *w*
17:13 like the noise of many *w*
18:2 upon the surface of the *w*
22:9 *w* of the lower pool
22:11 for the *w* of the old pool
23:3 on many *w* has been the seed
28:2 of powerful, flooding *w*
28:17 *w* themselves will flood
32:20 seed alongside all *w*
35:6 *w* will have burst out
37:25 certainly dig and drink *w*
40:12 measured the *w* in the mere
43:2 should pass through the *w*
43:16 even through strong *w*
48:1 come forth from the very *w*
51:10 the *w* of the vast deep
54:9 sworn that the *w* of Noah
57:20 *w* of which keep tossing up
58:11 the *w* of which do not lie
Isa 63:12 splitting the *w* from before
63:13 walk through the surging *w*
Jer 2:18 to drink the *w* of Shihor
2:18 to drink the *w* of the River
6:7 As a cistern keeps its *w* cool
9:1 O that my head were *w*, and
9:18 beaming eyes trickle with *w*
10:13 turmoil of *w* in the heavens
15:18 like *w* that have proved
17:8 like a tree planted by the *w*
18:14 Or will strange *w*, cool
41:12 abundant *w* that were in
46:7 rivers the *w* of which toss
46:8 and like rivers the *w* toss
47:2 *W* are coming up from the
48:34 even the *w* of Nimrim
50:38 is a devastation upon her *w*
51:13 residing on abounding *w*
51:16 turmoil of *w* in the heavens
51:55 be boisterous like many *w*
La 1:16 eye is running down with *w*
3:54 *W* have flowed over my head
Eze 1:24 a sound like that of vast *w*
17:5 As a willow by vast *w*, as a
17:8 Into a good field, by vast *w*
19:10 in your blood, planted by *w*
26:19 vast *w* will have covered
27:26 Into vast *w* those rowing
27:34 in the depths of the *w*
31:4 *W* were what made it get big
31:7 proved to be over many *w*
31:15 many *w* may be restrained
32:2 muddying the *w* with your
32:13 from beside many *w*, and
32:14 make their *w* clear up
34:18 clear *w* you drink but the
43:2 like the voice of vast *w*
47:19 *w* of Meribath-kadesh, the
48:28 *w* of Meribath-kadesh, to
Da 12:6 above the *w* of the stream
12:7 above the *w* of the stream
Ho 10:7 twig on the surface of *w*
Am 5:8 calling for the *w* of the sea
5:24 roll forth just like *w*
9:6 calling for the *w* of the sea
Jon 2:5 *W* encircled me clear to the
Mic 1:4 like *w* being poured down a
Na 2:8 Nineveh . . . like a pool of *w*
3:8 *W* were all around her, whose
Hab 2:14 the *w* . . . cover over the sea
3:10 A thunderstorm of *w* passed
3:15 through the heap of vast *w*
Zec 14:8 living *w* will go forth from
Mt 8:32 the sea and died in the *w*
14:28 to come to you over the *w*
14:29 walked over the *w* and went
1Co 3:7 nor is he that *w*, but God who
3:8 he that plants and he that *w*
Re 1:15 was as the sound of many *w*
7:17 to fountains of *w* of life
8:10 and upon the fountains of *w*
8:11 a third of the *w* turned into
8:11 men died from the *w*, because
11:6 authority over the *w* to turn
14:2 as the sound of many *w* and
14:7 who made . . . fountains of *w*
16:4 and the fountains of the *w*
16:5 the angel over the *w* say
17:1 harlot who sits on many *w*
17:15 The *w* . . . mean peoples and
19:6 as a sound of many *w* and

Waterspouts
Ps 42:7 At the sound of your *w*

Watery
Ge 1:2 upon the surface of the *w* deep
7:11 springs of the vast *w* deep
8:2 the springs of the *w* deep and
49:25 the blessings of the *w* deep
De 8:7 and *w* deeps issuing forth in
33:13 the *w* deep lying down below
Job 28:14 The *w* deep itself has said
38:16 in search of the *w* deep
38:30 the surface of the *w* deep
41:32 *w* deep as gray-headedness
Ps 36:6 decision is a vast *w* deep
42:7, 7 *W* deep to *w* deep is
71:20 the *w* deeps of the earth
77:16 *w* deeps began to be agitated
78:15 abundance just like *w* deeps
104:6 *w* deep just like a garment
106:9 them through the *w* deep as
135:6 the seas and all the *w* deeps
140:10 into *w* pits, that they may
Ps 148:7 and all you *w* deeps
Pr 3:20 *w* deeps themselves were
8:24 there were no *w* deeps I
8:27 upon the face of the *w* deep
8:28 fountains of the *w* deep to be
Isa 44:27 One saying to the *w* deep
Eze 26:19 up over you the *w* deep
31:4 *w* deep caused it to grow
31:15 I will cover the *w* deep
Am 7:4 eating up the vast *w* deep
Jon 2:5 *w* deep itself kept enclosing
Hab 3:10 *w* deep gave forth its sound

Wave
Ex 29:24 must *w* them to and fro as a
29:24 a *w* offering before Jehovah
29:26 and *w* it to and fro as a
29:26 a *w* offering before Jehovah
29:27 breast of the *w* offering and
35:22 the *w* offering of gold to
38:24 the gold of the *w* offering
38:29 the copper of the *w* offering
Le 7:30, 30 *w* it . . . as a *w* offering
7:34 the breast of the *w* offering
8:27 to *w* them to and fro as a
8:27 to and fro as a *w* offering
8:29 and to *w* it to and fro as a
8:29 a *w* offering before Jehovah
9:21 a *w* offering before Jehovah
10:14 the breast of the *w* offering
10:15 the breast of the *w* offering
10:15, 15 *w* the *w* offering to and
14:12 must *w* them to and fro as a
14:12 a *w* offering before Jehovah
14:21 for a *w* offering in order to
14:24 must *w* them to and fro as a
14:24 a *w* offering before Jehovah
23:11 *w* the sheaf to and fro
23:11 priest should *w* it to and
23:15 the sheaf of the *w* offering
23:17 two loaves as a *w* offering
23:20 priest must *w* them to and
23:20 *w* offering before Jehovah
Nu 5:25 *w* the grain offering to and
6:20 priest must *w* them to and fro
6:20 a *w* offering before Jehovah
6:20 breast of the *w* offering and
8:11 Levites . . . as a *w* offering
8:13 to and fro as a *w* offering to
8:15 to and fro as a *w* offering
8:21 a *w* offering before Jehovah
18:11 *w* offerings of the sons of
18:18 the breast of the *w* offering
Jg 9:9 go to *w* over the other trees
9:11 go to *w* over the other trees
9:13 I go to *w* over the trees
Isa 11:15 *w* his hand at the River in
13:2 *w* the hand, that they may
Lu 12:55 There will be a heat *w*, and
Jas 1:6 doubts is like a *w* of the sea

Waved
Ex 29:27 sacred portion that was *w*
Le 9:21 right leg Aaron *w* to and fro
23:12 sheaf *w* to and fro you must
Job 31:21 I *w* my hand to and fro

Waver
Ro 4:20 not *w* in a lack of faith

Wavering
Heb 10:23 of our hope without *w*, for

Waves
2Sa 22:5 breaking *w* encircled me
Job 9:8 treading upon the high *w* of
38:11 your proud *w* are limited
Ps 42:7 All your breakers and your *w*
65:7 The noise of their *w* and the
88:7 with all your breaking *w* you
89:9 *w* you yourself calm them
93:4 breaking *w* of the sea
107:25 So that it lifts up its *w*
107:29 *w* of the sea keep quiet
Isa 10:32 *w* his hand threateningly
48:18 like the *w* of the sea
51:15 its *w* may be boisterous
Jer 5:22 Although its *w* toss
31:35 *w* may become boisterous
51:42 By the multitude of its *w*
51:55 *w* will actually be
Eze 26:3 as the sea brings up its *w*
Jon 2:3 *w*—over me they passed on
Zec 10:11 he must strike down the *w*
Mt 8:24 boat . . . covered by the *w*
14:24 hard put to it by the *w*

Da 2:38 and into *w* hand he has given
4:8 *w* name is Belteshazzar
4:19 *w* name is Belteshazzar, was
5:23 God in *w* hand your breath is
10:1 Daniel, *w* name was called
Joe 3:19 in *w* land they shed innocent
Am 2:9 *w* height was like the height
5:27 *w* name is Jehovah the God of
Jon 1:7 on *w* account we have this
1:8 on *w* account it is that we
Mic 5:2 *w* origin is from early times
Na 3:8 *w* wealth was the sea
3:8 *w* wall was from the sea
Zec 6:12 the man *w* name is Sprout
Mt 3:11 *w* sandals I am not fit to
22:20 *W* image and inscription is
22:42 the Christ? *W* son is he?
Mr 7:25 *w* little daughter had an
12:16 *W* image and inscription is
Lu 3:16 lace of *w* sandals I am not
6:6 *w* right hand was withered
13:1 Galileans *w* blood Pilate had
17:31 but *w* movable things are in
20:24 *W* image and inscription does
Joh 1:27 lace of *w* sandal I am not
4:46 *w* son was sick in Capernaum
6:42 *w* father and mother we know
11:2 *w* brother Lazarus was sick
18:26 man *w* ear Peter cut off
19:24 lots over it *w* it will be
Ac 4:7 in *w* name did you do this?
7:52 righteous One, *w* betrayers
13:6 a Jew *w* name was Bar-Jesus
13:25 sandal of *w* feet I am not
14:13 priest of Zeus, *w* temple
18:7 *w* house was adjoining the
21:16 man at *w* home we were to
Ro 4:7 those *w* lawless deeds have
4:7 and *w* sins have been covered
4:8 man *w* sin Jehovah will by no
1Co 8:11 for *w* sake Christ died
2Co 8:18 the brother *w* praise in
Ga 3:1 before *w* eyes Jesus Christ was
Php 4:3 *w* names are in the book of
1Ti 2:4 *w* will is that all sorts of
Heb 2:10 one for *w* sake all things
3:17 *w* carcasses fell in the
13:11 animals *w* blood is taken
Re 13:12 *w* death-stroke got healed

Why*

Ge 4:6 said to Cain: *W* are you hot
4:6 *w* has your countenance fallen?
29:25 So *w* have you tricked me?
44:4 *W* have you repaid bad for
Ex 5:15 cry out to Pharaoh, saying: *W*
5:22 Jehovah, *w* have you caused
5:22 *W* is it that you have sent
14:15 *W* do you keep crying out to
17:2 *W* are you quarreling with
17:2 *W* do you keep putting Jehovah
17:3 *W* is it that you have brought
32:11 *W*, O Jehovah, should your
32:12 *W* should the Egyptians say
Nu 16:3 *W*, then, should you lift
20:4 *w* have you men brought
De 29:24 *W* did Jehovah do like this
Jos 4:6 *W* do you have these stones?
7:7 *w* did you bring this people
7:25 *W* have you brought ostracism
9:22 *W* did you trick us, saying
Jg 2:2 *W* have you done this?
21:3 *W*, O Jehovah the God of
Ru 1:11 *W* should you go with me?
1Sa 4:3 *W* did Jehovah defeat us today
2Sa 12:9 *W* did you despise the word
Job 3:20 *W* does he give light to one
3:23 *W* does he give light to
7:20 *W* . . . set me as your target
7:21 And *w* do you not pardon my
9:29 *W* is it that I toil merely
10:18 *w* from a womb did you bring
13:14 *W* do I carry my flesh in
13:24 *W* do you conceal your very
15:12 *W* does your heart carry you
15:12 And *w* do your eyes flash?
18:3 *W* should we be reckoned as
19:22 *W* . . . keep persecuting me
19:28 *W* do we keep persecuting
21:4 *w* is it that my spirit does
21:7 *W* is it that the wicked
24:1 *W* is it that times have not
Ps 10:1 *W*, O Jehovah, do you keep
22:1 my God, *w* have you left me?
Ps 22:1 *W* are you far from saving me
42:5 *W* are you in despair, O my
42:5 *w* are you boisterous within
42:9 *W* have you forgotten me?
42:9 *W* do I walk sad because of
42:11 *W* are you in despair, O my
42:11 *w* are you boisterous within
43:2 *W* have you cast me off?
43:2 *W* do I walk about sad because
43:5 *W* are you in despair, O my
43:5 *w* are you boisterous within
44:23 *W* do you keep sleeping
44:24 *W* do you keep your very face
44:24 *W* do you forget our
49:5 *W* should I be afraid in the
52:1 *W* do you make your boast
68:16 *W* do you, O you mountains
74:1 *W*, O God, have you cast off
74:1 *W* does your anger keep
74:11 *W* do you keep your hand
80:12 *W* have you broken down its
80:12 *w* have all those passing by
88:14 *W* is it, O Jehovah, that you
88:14 *W* do you keep your face
115:2 *W* should the nations say
Pr 22:27 *w* should he take your bed
Ec 5:6 *W* should the true God become
7:10 *W* has it happened that the
7:16 *W* should you cause desolation
Jer 14:9 *W* do you become like a man
Eze 18:31 *w* should you die, O house
Hab 1:14 *w* do you make earthling man
Mt 6:28 clothing, *w* are you anxious?
7:3 *W*, then, do you look at the
8:26 *W* are you fainthearted, you
9:4 *W* are you thinking wicked
13:10 *W* is it you speak to them
14:31 *w* did you give way to doubt?
15:2 *W* is it your disciples
15:3 *W* is it you also overstep the
16:8 Jesus said: *W* are you doing
17:10 *W*, then, do the scribes say
17:19 *W* is it we could not expel
19:7 *W*, then, did Moses prescribe
19:17 *W* do you ask me about what
22:18 *W* do you put me to the test
26:8 and said: *W* this waste?
27:23 *W*, what bad thing did he do?
27:46 *w* have you forsaken me?
Mr 2:8 *W* are you reasoning these
4:40 *W* are you fainthearted?
5:39 *W* are you causing noisy
8:12 *W* does this generation seek a
8:17 *W* do you argue over your
9:28 *W* could we not expel it?
10:18 *W* do you call me good?
12:15 *W* do you put me to the test?
15:34 God, *w* have you forsaken me?
Lu 5:30 *W* is it you eat and drink
12:26 *w* be anxious about the
18:19 *W* do you call me good?
20:5 *W* is it you did not believe
22:46 *W* are you sleeping? Rise and
24:38 *W* are you troubled, and
24:38 *w* is it doubts come up in
Joh 1:25 *W*, then, do you baptize if
4:27 *W* do you talk with her?
7:19 *W* are you seeking to kill me?
8:46 *w* is it you do not believe
10:20 *W* do you listen to him?
12:5 *W* was it this perfumed oil
18:21 *W* do you question me?
18:23 if rightly, *w* do you hit me?
20:13 Woman, *w* are you weeping?
Ac 1:11 *w* do you stand looking into
5:3 *w* has Satan emboldened you
9:4 Saul, *w* are you persecuting
14:15 *w* are you doing these things?
15:10 *w* are you making a test of
22:7 Saul, *w* are you persecuting
26:14 Saul, *w* are you persecuting
Ro 9:19 *W* does he yet find fault?
9:20 *W* did you make me this way?
14:10 *w* do you judge your brother?
Ga 3:19 *W*, then, the Law? It was
5:11 *w* am I still being persecuted?

Wick

Isa 42:3 and as for a dim flaxen *w*
43:17 Like a flaxen *w* they must
Mt 12:20 no smoldering flaxen *w* will

Wicked

Ge 18:23 the righteous with the *w*
18:25 righteous man with the *w*
Ge 18:25 as it does with the *w*! It is
Ex 22:9 whom God will pronounce *w*
23:1 Do not cooperate with a *w* one
23:7 declare the *w* one righteous
Nu 16:26 the tents of these *w* men and
De 25:1, 1 and pronounce the *w* one *w*
25:2 *w* one deserves to be beaten
25:2 to correspond with his *w* deed
1Sa 2:9 *w* ones, they are silenced in
24:13 *w* ones wickedness will go
2Sa 4:11 *w* men themselves have
1Ki 8:32, 32 pronouncing the *w* one *w*
2Ch 6:23 pay back the *w* by putting
19:2 to the *w* that help is to be
24:7 Athaliah the *w* woman, her
Job 3:17 the *w* themselves have ceased
8:22 tent of *w* ones will not be
9:20 mouth would pronounce me *w*
9:22 One blameless, also a *w* one
9:24 into the hand of the *w* one
9:29 I myself am to become *w*
10:2 Do not pronounce me *w*
10:3 upon the counsel of *w* ones
11:20 eyes of the *w* will fail
15:6 Your mouth pronounces you *w*
15:20 *w* one is suffering torture
16:11 into the hands of *w* ones he
18:5 light also of *w* ones will be
20:5 joyful cry of *w* . . . is short
20:29 share of the *w* man from
21:7 the *w* themselves keep living
21:16 counsel of *w* ones has kept
21:17 is the lamp of the *w* ones
21:28 the tabernacles of *w* ones
22:18 counsel of *w* ones has kept
24:6 vineyard of the *w* one they
27:7 become in every way a *w* man
27:13 the share of the *w* man
32:3 proceeded to pronounce God *w*
34:17 will you pronounce him *w*?
34:18 To nobles, You are *w*
34:26 As *w* ones he does slap them
36:6 will not preserve anyone *w*
36:17 sentence upon the *w* one
38:13 the *w* ones might be shaken
38:15 from the *w* ones their light
40:8 pronounce me *w* in order that
40:12 tread down the *w* right
Ps 1:1 in the counsel of the *w* ones
1:4 The *w* are not like that, But
1:5 *w* ones will not stand up in
1:6 way of *w* ones will perish
3:7 The teeth of *w* ones you will
7:9 the badness of *w* ones come to
9:5 you have destroyed the *w* one
9:16 the *w* one has been ensnared
9:17 *W* people will turn back to
10:2 the *w* one hotly pursues the
10:3 the *w* has praised himself
10:4 The *w* one according to his
10:13 *w* one has disrespected God
10:15 Break the arm of the *w* and
11:2 the *w* ones themselves bend
11:5 as well as the *w* one
11:6 rain down upon the *w* ones
12:8 The *w* ones walk all around
17:9 the *w* who have despoiled me
17:13 from the *w* one with your
26:5 with the *w* ones I do not sit
28:3 Do not draw me along with *w*
31:17 May the *w* ones be ashamed
32:10 pains that the *w* one has
34:21 the *w* one himself to death
36:1 the *w* one is in the midst of
36:11 As for the hand of *w* people
37:10 the *w* one will be no more
37:12 *w* one is plotting against
37:14 *w* ones have drawn a sword
37:16 abundance of the many *w* ones
37:17 arms of the *w* ones will be
37:20 *w* themselves will perish
37:21 The *w* one is borrowing and
37:28 offspring of the *w* ones
37:32 The *w* one is keeping on the
37:33 he will not pronounce him *w*
37:34 When the *w* ones are cut off
37:35 I have seen the *w* a tyrant
37:38 *w* people will indeed be cut
37:40 escape from *w* people and
39:1 anyone *w* is in front of me
50:16 to the *w* one God will have
55:3 the pressure of the *w* one
58:3 The *w* ones have been perverts
58:10 bathe in the blood of the *w*

Wickedly

Wickedness

Jg 21:11 every *w* that has experienced
Ru 1:5 the *w* remained without her
1:22 Ruth the Moabite *w*, her
2:2 Ruth the Moabite *w* said to
2:5 whom does this young *w* belong
2:6 The young *w* is a Moabitess
3:8 look! a *w* lying at his feet!
3:11 that you are an excellent *w*
3:14 *w* came to the threshing floor
4:12 give you out of this young *w*
1Sa 1:15 A *w* hard pressed in spirit
1:16 like a good-for-nothing *w*
1:18 *w* proceeded to go on her way
1:23 the *w* stayed at home and
1:26 am the *w* that was standing
15:3 man as well as *w*, child as
22:19 man as well as *w*, child as
27:9 preserved neither man nor *w*
27:11 As for man and *w*, David
28:7 Seek for me a *w* who is a
28:7 *w* who is a mistress of
28:8 they came to the *w* by night
28:9 *w* said to him: Here you
28:11 *w* said: Whom shall I bring
28:12 *w* saw Samuel she began
28:12 *w* went on to say to Saul
28:13 *w* went on to say to Saul
28:21 *w* now came to Saul and saw
28:23 the *w* kept urging him
28:24 *w* had a fattened calf in
2Sa 3:8 error concerning a *w* today
6:19 Israel, man as well as *w*
11:2 sight of a *w* bathing herself
11:2 *w* was very good in
11:3 inquired about the *w* and
11:5 And the *w* became pregnant
11:21 *w* that pitched an upper
14:2 took from there a wise *w*
14:2 *w* . . . who has been mourning
14:4 Tekoite *w* proceeded to come
14:5 I am a widowed *w*, now that
14:8 king said to the *w*: Go to
14:9 Tekoite *w* said to the king
14:12 *w* now said: Let your
14:13 *w* went on to say: Why
14:18 said to the *w*: Do not
14:18 *w* said: Let my lord the
14:19 *w* answered and said: As
14:27 a *w* most beautiful in
17:19 the *w* took and spread out a
17:20 came to the *w* at her house
17:20 At this the *w* said to them
20:16 a wise *w* began to call
20:17 *w* then said: Are you Joab?
20:21 the *w* said to Joab: Look!
20:22 the *w* went in her wisdom
1Ki 3:17 the one *w* said: Excuse me
3:17 I and this *w* are dwelling in
3:18 *w* also proceeded to give
3:19 son of this *w* died at night
3:22 But the other *w* said
3:22 this *w* was saying: No, but
3:25 half to the one *w* and the
3:26 the *w* whose son was the
3:26 this other *w* was saying
7:14 the son of a widowed *w* from
11:26 Zeruah, a widowed *w*
17:9 a *w*, a widow, to supply you
17:10 a *w*, a widow, was there
17:17 son of the *w*, the mistress
17:24 the *w* said to Elijah
2Ki 4:1 *w* of the wives of the sons of
4:8 there was a prominent *w*, and
4:12 Call this Shunammite *w*
4:17 the *w* became pregnant and
4:25 The Shunammite *w* over there
4:36 Call this Shunammite *w*
6:26 a certain *w* cried out to him
6:28 This very *w* said to me
8:1 *w* whose son he had revived
8:2 *w* got up and did according
8:3 *w* proceeded to return from
8:5 *w* whose son he had revived
8:5 the *w*, and this is her son
8:6 the king asked the *w*, and she
11:2 even him and his nursing *w*
1Ch 16:3 man as well as *w*, to each
2Ch 2:14 of a *w* of the sons of Dan
15:13 whether man or *w*
22:11 nursing *w* in the inner room
24:7 Athaliah the wicked *w*, her
Es 1:19 a *w* better than she is
2:4 young *w* who seems pleasing in
2:7 young *w* was pretty in form

Es 2:9 the young *w* was pleasing in
2:12 turn of each young *w* arrived
2:13 young *w* herself came in to
4:11 any man or *w* that comes in
Job 14:1 Man, born of *w*, Is
15:14 Or that anyone born of a *w*
24:21 dealings with a barren *w*
25:4 can one born of a *w* be clean
31:9 has been enticed toward a *w*
Ps 48:6 Birth pangs like those of a *w*
58:8 Like a miscarriage of a *w*
113:9 the barren *w* to dwell in a
Pr 2:16 you from the strange *w*
2:16 foreign *w* who has made her
5:3 the lips of a strange *w* keep
5:20 ecstasy with a strange *w* or
5:20 the bosom of a foreign *w*
6:24 guard you against the bad *w*
6:24 the tongue of the foreign *w*
6:26 *w* prostitute one comes down
6:32 committing adultery with a *w*
7:5 you against the *w* stranger
7:10 there was a *w* to meet him
9:13 *w* of stupidity is boisterous
11:16 A *w* of charm is the one that
11:22 so is a *w* that is pretty but
14:1 truly wise *w* has built up
20:16 the instance of a foreign *w*
23:27 foreign *w* is a narrow well
27:13 the instance of a foreign *w*
30:20 the way of an adulterous *w*
30:23 hated *w* when she is taken
31:30 *w* that fears Jehovah is the
Ec 7:26 *w* who is herself nets for
7:28 a *w* among all these I have
Ca 1:7 like a *w* wrapped in mourning
6:10 Who is this *w* that is looking
8:5 Who is this *w* coming up from
Isa 13:8 *w* that is giving birth they
21:3 of a *w* that is giving birth
26:17 pregnant *w* draws near to
30:22 Like a menstruating *w*, you
40:9 *w* bringing good news for
40:9 *w* bringing good news for
42:14 Like a *w* giving birth I am
47:8 this, you pleasure-given *w*
49:21 a *w* bereaved of children
51:21 O *w* afflicted and drunk
54:1 barren *w* that did not give
54:1 *w* with a husbandly owner
54:11 *w* afflicted, tempest-tossed
57:3 you sons of a soothsaying *w*
57:3 *w* that commits prostitution
60:1 Arise, O *w*, shed forth light
62:2 see your righteousness, O *w*
62:4 said to be a *w* left entirely
Jer 2:33 Why do you, O *w*, improve
4:31 voice like that of a sick *w*
4:31 a *w* giving birth to her
5:7 the house of a prostitute *w*
6:2 a comely and daintily bred *w*
6:24 those of a *w* giving birth
9:20 each *w* her companion a dirge
10:17 O *w* dwelling under stress
15:9 The *w* giving birth to seven
22:23 of a *w* giving birth
30:17 a *w* chased away is what
31:8 pregnant *w* and the one
34:9 and Hebrew *w*, go free, in
44:7 man and *w*, child and
49:24 *w* that is giving birth
50:43 just like a *w* giving birth
51:13 *w* residing on abounding
51:22 dash man and *w* to pieces
La 1:11 have become as a valueless *w*
1:13 made me a *w* laid desolate
1:16 things I am weeping as a *w*
1:21 I myself am sighing as a *w*
Eze 16:30 *w*, a domineering prostitute
18:6 *w* in her impurity he would
22:10 a *w* unclean in her
23:44 to a *w* that is a prostitute
44:22 divorced *w* should they take
Ho 2:1 sisters, O *w* shown mercy
3:1 love a *w* loved by a companion
4:18 treated *w* as a harlot
13:13 pangs of a *w* giving birth
Mic 2:9 a *w* has exquisite delight
4:9 those of a *w* giving birth
4:10 like a *w* giving birth, for
7:8 O you *w* enemy of mine
Zec 5:7 *w* sitting in the midst of the
9:11 O *w*, by the blood of your
9:12 O *w*, a double portion

Mt 5:28 keeps on looking at a *w* so as
5:32 marries a divorced *w*
9:20 a *w* suffering twelve years
9:22 that hour the *w* became well
13:33 leaven, which a *w* took and
15:22 a Phoenician *w* from those
15:25 When the *w* came she began
15:28 O *w*, great is your faith
22:27 Last of all the *w* died
26:7 a *w* with an alabaster case
26:10 to make trouble for the *w*
26:12 *w* put this perfumed oil
26:13 what this *w* did shall also
Mr 5:25 *w* subject to a flow of blood
5:33 *w*, frightened and trembling
7:25 a *w* whose little daughter
7:26 The *w* was a Grecian, a
10:12 if ever a *w*, after divorcing
12:22 Last of all the *w* also died
14:3 a *w* came with an alabaster
14:9 *w* did shall also be told
Lu 1:36 the so-called barren *w*
2:36 *w* was well along in years
7:37 *w* who was known in the city
7:39 who and what kind of *w* it is
7:44 he turned to the *w* and said
7:44 Do you behold this *w*?
7:44 this *w* wet my feet with her
7:45 but this *w*, from the hour
7:46 this *w* greased my feet with
7:50 he said to the *w*: Your faith
8:43 a *w*, subject to a flow of
8:47 *w* came trembling and fell
10:38 *w* named Martha received him
10:39 *w* also had a sister called
11:27 *w* out of the crowd raised
13:11 *w* with a spirit of weakness
13:12 *W*, you are released from
13:16 this *w* who is a daughter of
13:21 leaven, which a *w* took and
15:8 what *w* with ten drachma
16:18 he that marries a *w* divorced
20:32 Lastly, the *w* also died
21:4 *w* out of her want dropped
22:57 saying: I do not know him, *w*
Joh 2:4 What have I to do with you, *w*?
4:7 A *w* of Samaria came to draw
4:9 the Samaritan *w* said to him
4:9 when I am a Samaritan *w*
4:15 *w* said to him: Sir, give
4:17 the *w* said: I do not have a
4:19 The *w* said to him: Sir, I
4:21 Believe me, *w*, The hour is
4:25 The *w* said to him: I know
4:27 he was speaking with a *w*
4:28 *w*, therefore, left her
4:39 the *w* who said in witness
4:42 they began to say to the *w*
16:21 *w*, when she is giving
19:26 mother: *W*, see! your son!
20:13 *W*, why are you weeping?
20:15 *W*, why are you weeping?
Ac 16:1 son of a believing Jewish *w*
16:14 *w* named Lydia, a seller of
17:34 and a *w* named Damaris, and
Ro 7:2 married *w* is bound by law to
1Co 7:1 for a man not to touch a *w*
7:2 each *w* have her own husband
7:13 a *w* who has an unbelieving
7:34 unmarried *w*, and the virgin
7:34 married *w* is anxious for the
11:3 the head of a *w* is the man
11:5 but every *w* that prays or
11:5 were a *w* with a shaved head
11:6 For if a *w* does not cover
11:6 a *w* to be shorn or shaved
11:7 but the *w* is man's glory
11:8 For man is not out of *w*, but
11:8 but *w* out of man
11:9 for the sake of the *w*, but
11:9 *w* for the sake of the man
11:10 the *w* ought to have a sign
11:11 neither is *w* without man
11:11 nor man without *w*
11:12 as the *w* is out of the man
11:12 the man is through the *w*
11:13 for a *w* to pray uncovered
11:15 if a *w* has long hair, it is
14:35 disgraceful for a *w* to
Ga 4:4 who came to be out of a *w* and
4:22 and one by the free *w*
4:23 the free *w* through a promise
4:27 Be glad you barren *w* who
4:27 you *w* who does not have

Ga 4:27 children of the desolate *w*
4:30 with the son of the free *w*
4:31 but of the free *w*
1Th 5:3 of distress upon a pregnant *w*
1Ti 2:11 Let a *w* learn in silence
2:12 I do not permit a *w* to teach
2:14 *w* was thoroughly deceived
5:5 *w* who is actually a widow
5:16 any believing *w* has widows
Re 2:20 you tolerate that *w* Jezebel
12:1 *w* arrayed with the sun, and
12:4 *w* who was about to give
12:6 *w* fled into the wilderness
12:13 *w* that gave birth to the
12:14 wings . . . were given the *w*
12:15 after the *w*, to cause her to
12:17 grew wrathful at the *w*
17:3 caught sight of a *w* sitting
17:4 *w* was arrayed in purple and
17:6 *w* was drunk with the blood
17:7 mystery of the *w* and of the
17:9 where the *w* sits on top
17:18 *w* . . . means the great city

Womankind
Jg 21:16 *w* has been annihilated out
1Sa 21:4 least kept themselves from *w*
21:5 *w* has been kept away from us
Da 11:17 as regards the daughter of *w*

Woman's
Ge 31:34 in the *w* saddle basket of
Nu 5:18 loosen the hair of the *w* head
5:25 from the *w* hand and wave the
Jg 19:4 young *w* father, took hold of
19:9 young *w* father, said to him
2Ki 6:30 the king heard the *w* words
Re 12:16 earth came to the *w* help

Womb
Ge 20:18 shut up every *w* of the house
29:31 he then opened her *w*
30:22 in that he opened her *w*
49:25 the blessings of the . . . *w*
Ex 13:2 firstborn that opens each *w*
13:12 that opens the *w* to Jehovah
13:15 the males that open the *w*
34:19 first opens the *w* is mine
Nu 3:12 firstborn opening the *w* of
12:12 out of his mother's *w* is
18:15 Everything opening the *w*, of
Jg 5:30 A *w*—two wombs to every
1Sa 1:5 Jehovah . . . closed up her *w*
1:6 Jehovah had closed up her *w*
Job 3:11 Why from the *w* did I not
10:18 why from a *w* did you bring
24:20 The *w* will forget him, the
31:15 to prepare us in the *w*
38:8 it burst out from the *w*
Ps 22:10 have been thrown from the *w*
58:3 have been perverts from the *w*
110:3 from the *w* of the dawn
Pr 30:16 Sheol and a restrained *w*, a
Isa 46:3 the ones carried from the *w*
Jer 1:5 to come forth from the *w* I
20:17 put me to death from the *w*
20:17 her *w* be pregnant to time
20:18 come forth from the very *w*
Eze 20:26 every child opening the *w*
Ho 9:14 Give them a miscarrying *w*
13:13 of sons from the *w*
Mt 19:12 such from their mother's *w*
Lu 1:15 right from his mother's *w*
1:31 you will conceive in your *w*
1:41 the infant in her *w* leaped
1:42 is the fruit of your *w*
1:44 the infant in my *w* leaped
2:21 he was conceived in the *w*
2:23 Every male opening a *w* must
11:27 Happy is the *w* that carried
Joh 3:4 *w* of his mother a second
Ac 3:2 was lame from his mother's *w*
14:8 lame from his mother's *w*
Ro 4:19 deadness of the *w* of Sarah
Ga 1:15 from my mother's *w* and

Womb's
2Ki 19:3 as far as the *w* mouth
Isa 37:3 as far as the *w* mouth, and

Wombs
Nu 8:16 place of those opening all *w*
Jg 5:30 two *w* to every able-bodied
Lu 23:29 *w* that did not give birth

Women
Ge 14:16 also the *w* and the people
Ge 24:11 the *w* who draw water were
31:35 customary thing with *w* is
33:5 saw the *w* and the children
Ex 1:16 the Hebrew *w* to give birth
1:19 Hebrew *w* are not like the
1:19 are not like the Egyptian *w*
2:7 Hebrew *w* that she may nurse
2:17 Moses . . . helped the *w*
15:20 *w* began going out with her
35:22 the men along with the *w*
35:25 *w* who were wise of heart
35:26 *w* whose hearts impelled them
36:6 *w*, do not produce any more
38:8 the mirrors of the *w* servants
Le 26:26 ten *w* will then actually
Nu 21:30 the *w* up to Nophah, the men
25:2 *w* came calling the people to
31:9 carried off the *w* of Midian
31:18 little ones among the *w* who
31:35 *w* who had not known the act
De 2:34 to destruction, men and *w*
3:6 city to destruction, men, *w*
20:14 Only the *w* and the little
31:12 men and the *w* and the little
Jos 8:35 the *w* and the little ones
Jg 5:24 will be most blessed among *w*
5:24 Among *w* in the tent she will
9:49 about a thousand men and *w*
9:51 all the men and *w* and all the
16:27 full of men and *w* and all
16:27 three thousand men and *w*
21:10 the *w* and the little ones
21:14 they gave them the *w* that
21:14 from the *w* of Jabesh-gilead
21:23 from the *w* dancing around
Ru 1:4 for themselves, Moabite *w*
1:19 *w* kept saying: Is this Naomi?
1:20 And she would say to the *w*
2:8 keep close by my young *w*
2:22 go out with his young *w*
2:23 close by the young *w* of Boaz
3:2 Boaz, with whose young *w* you
4:14 the *w* began to say to Naomi
1Sa 2:22 would lie down with the *w*
4:20 *w* standing by her began to
15:33 has bereaved *w* of children
15:33 most bereaved . . . among *w*
18:6 *w* began coming out from all
18:7 *w* that were celebrating kept
18:21 By one of the two *w* you
25:43 *w* came to be . . . his wives
30:2 captive the *w* and all that
2Sa 1:26 than the love from *w*
15:16 king left ten *w*, concubines
20:3 Then the king took the ten *w*
1Ki 3:16 two *w*, prostitutes, got to
11:1 Sidonian and Hittite *w*
2Ki 8:12 pregnant *w* you will rip up
15:16 its pregnant *w* he ripped up
23:7 the *w* were weaving tent
2Ch 28:8 captive, *w*, sons and
Ezr 10:1 congregation, men and *w* and
Ne 8:2 men as well as of *w* and of
8:3 in front of the men and the *w*
12:43 also the *w* and the children
Es 1:9 held a banquet for the *w* at
2:2 Let them seek young *w*, virgins
2:3 young *w*, virgins, beautiful in
2:3 house of the *w*, in charge of
2:3 eunuch, the guardian of the *w*
2:8 many young *w* were collected
2:8 of Hegai the guardian of the *w*
2:9 seven selected young *w* from
2:9 transfer her and her young *w*
2:9 of the house of the *w*
2:11 house of the *w* to know of
2:12 with the massages of the *w*
2:13 house of the *w* to the king's
2:14 to the second house of the *w*
2:15 eunuch, the guardian of the *w*
2:17 more than all the other *w*, so
3:13 little ones and *w*, on one day
4:4 And Esther's young *w* and her
4:16 my young *w*, I shall fast
8:11 little ones and *w*, and to
Job 2:10 As one of the senseless *w*
42:15 no *w* were found as pretty
Ps 45:*super* A song of the beloved *w*
45:9 are among your precious *w*
68:11 The *w* telling the good news
Pr 22:14 The mouth of strange *w* is a
31:3 give your vital energy to *w*
31:15 portion to her young *w*
Ec 12:3 grinding *w* have quit working
Ca 1:8 most beautiful one among *w*
5:9 most beautiful one among *w*
6:1 O most beautiful one among *w*
Isa 3:12 mere *w* actually rule over
4:1 seven *w* will actually grab
19:16 Egypt will become like *w*
27:11 *w* coming in will break
32:9 *w* who are at ease, rise up
32:11 you *w* who are at ease
49:15 Even these *w* can forget
49:23 princesses nursing *w* for
Jer 9:17 call the dirge-chanting *w*
9:17 send even to the skilled *w*
9:20 hear, O you *w*, the word of
18:21 wives become *w* bereaved of
38:22 *w* that have been left
40:7 *w* and little children and
44:24 and to all the *w*: Hear
44:25 *w* also speak with your
44:25 *w* will without fail carry
50:37 will certainly become *w*
51:30 They have become *w*
La 2:20 the *w* keep eating their own
4:10 compassionate *w* have boiled
Eze 8:14 the *w* were sitting, weeping
9:6 and *w* you should kill off
13:18 Woe to the *w* sewing bands
13:18 souls that you *w* hunt down
13:20 against the bands of you *w*
13:23 untruth you *w* will not keep
16:27 desire of the *w* hating you
16:27 *w* humiliated on account of
16:34 opposite . . . of other *w*
16:38 and *w* shedding blood, and I
16:41 before the eyes of many *w*
16:45 The mother of you *w* was a
23:2 two *w*, the daughters of
23:10 she came to be infamy to *w*
23:42 on the hands of the *w* and
23:44 as *w* of loose conduct
23:48 all the *w* will have to let
Da 11:37 desire of *w* and to every
Ho 4:10 actually treat *w* as harlots
5:3 have treated *w* like harlots
13:16 pregnant *w* themselves will
Am 1:13 slitting open the pregnant *w*
Mic 2:9 The *w* of my people you drive
Na 3:13 are *w* in the midst of you
Zec 5:9 there were two *w* coming forth
8:4 old *w* in the public squares
12:12 and their *w* by themselves
12:12 and their *w* by themselves
12:13 and their *w* by themselves
12:13 and their *w* by themselves
12:14 and their *w* by themselves
14:2 *w* themselves will be raped
Mt 11:11 Among those born of *w* there
14:21 besides *w* and young children
15:38 besides *w* and young children
22:30 nor are *w* given in marriage
24:19 Woe to the pregnant *w* and
24:38 *w* being given in marriage
24:41 two *w* will be grinding at
27:55 many *w* were there viewing
28:5 in answer said to the *w*
Mr 12:25 nor are *w* given in marriage
13:17 Woe to the pregnant *w* and
15:40 *w* viewing from a distance
15:41 many other *w* who had come
Lu 1:42 Blessed are you among *w*, and
4:26 was sent to none of those *w*
7:28 Among those born of *w* there
8:2 *w* that had been cured of
8:3 Susanna and many other *w*, who
15:9 she calls the *w* who are her
17:27 *w* were being given in
17:35 be two *w* grinding at the
21:23 Woe to the pregnant *w* and
23:27 and of *w* who kept beating
23:28 Jesus turned to the *w* and
23:29 Happy are the barren *w*, and
23:49 Also, *w*, who together had
23:55 *w*, who had come with him
24:5 *w* became frightened and kept
24:10 the rest of the *w* with them
24:11 they would not believe the *w*
24:22 certain *w* from among us
24:24 just as the *w* had said, but
Ac 1:14 *w* and Mary the mother of
2:18 *w* slaves I will pour out
5:14 both of men and of *w*
8:3 dragging out both men and *w*
8:12 be baptized, both men and *w*
9:2 to The Way, both men and *w*

Ex 31:10 garments of knitted *w* and
31:14 anyone doing *w* on it, then
31:15 Six days may *w* be done, but
31:15 doing *w* on the sabbath day
34:10 indeed see the *w* of Jehovah
35:2 Six days may *w* be done, but
35:2 Anybody doing *w* on it will
35:19 garments of knitted *w* for
35:21 the *w* of the tent of meeting
35:24 acacia wood for all the *w*
35:29 all the *w* that Jehovah had
35:35 do all the *w* of a craftsman
35:35 men doing every sort of *w*
36:1 Bezalel must *w*, also Oholiab
36:1 all the *w* of the holy service
36:2 approach the *w* in order to do
36:3 *w* of the holy service so as
36:4 were doing all the holy *w*
36:4 their *w* that they were doing
36:5 the service needs for the *w*
36:7 enough for all the *w* to be
36:8 those doing the *w* went making
36:8 the *w* of an embroiderer
36:35 the *w* of an embroiderer he
36:37 the *w* of a weaver
37:7 Of hammered *w* he made them
37:17 Of hammered *w* he made the
37:22 of hammered *w* of pure gold
37:29 the *w* of an ointment maker
38:18 was the *w* of a weaver, of
38:24 that was used for the *w* in
38:24 the *w* of the holy place came
39:1 made garments of knitted *w*
39:3 cut out threads to *w* in among
39:3 as the *w* of an embroiderer
39:15 in rope *w*, of pure gold
39:29 the *w* of a weaver, just as
39:32 the *w* for the tabernacle of
39:41 garments of knitted *w* for
39:43 Moses got to see all the *w*
40:33 So Moses finished the *w*
Le 16:29 you must not do any *w*, either
23:3 Six days may *w* be done, but
23:3 You may do no sort of *w*
23:7 of laborious *w* may you do
23:8 No sort of laborious *w* may
23:21 No . . . laborious *w* may you do
23:25 sort of laborious *w* may you
23:28 sort of *w* on this very day
23:30 *w* on this very day, I must
23:31 You must do no sort of *w*
23:35 No . . . laborious *w* may you
23:36 No . . . laborious *w* may you
Nu 4:3 service group to do the *w* in
4:26 with which *w* is regularly
8:4 It was hammered *w* of gold
8:4 lampstand . . . was hammered *w*
10:2 make them of hammered *w*, and
28:18 No sort of laborious *w* must
28:25 No sort of laborious *w* must
28:26 No sort of laborious *w* must
29:1 No sort of laborious *w* must
29:7 No sort of *w* must you do
29:12 No sort of laborious *w* must
29:35 No sort of laborious *w* must
De 5:13 must do all your *w* six days
5:14 must not do any *w*, you nor
16:8 You must do no *w*
23:6 must not *w* for their peace
30:9 more than enough in every *w*
Jos 24:31 known all the *w* of Jehovah
Jg 1:35 they were forced into task *w*
2:7 Jehovah's great *w* that he did
2:10 not know Jehovah or the *w*
13:12 mode of life and his *w*
16:11 ropes with which no *w* has
19:16 *w* in the field at evening
Ru 2:19 and where did you *w*?
1Sa 8:16 have to use them for his *w*
14:6 Perhaps Jehovah will *w* for
25:2 and his *w* was in Carmel
26:25 will you without fail *w*
1Ki 5:16 who were over the *w*
5:16 who were active in the *w*
7:14 every sort of *w* in copper
7:14 and began to do all his *w*
7:19 of lily *w*, of four cubits
7:22 upon the top . . . lily *w*
7:22 the *w* of the pillars was
7:29 wreaths in hanging *w*
7:40 finished doing all the *w*
7:51 all the *w* that King Solomon
9:23 were over the *w* of Solomon
9:23 who were active in the *w*

1Ki 13:11 all the *w* that the man of
16:7 with the *w* of his hands
2Ki 12:11 the hands of doers of the *w*
12:14 to the doers of the *w* that
12:15 give to the doers of the *w*
22:5 hand of those doing the *w*
22:5 give it to those doing the *w*
22:9 hand of the doers of the *w*
22:17 all the *w* of their hands
1Ch 4:23 with the king in his *w* that
6:49 *w* of the most holy things
9:13 the *w* of the service of the
9:19 over the *w* of the service
9:33 to be in the *w*
22:15 in great number doers of *w*
22:15 skillful in every sort of *w*
23:4 *w* of the house of Jehovah
23:24 *w* for the service of the
23:28 the *w* of the service of the
26:30 for all the *w* of Jehovah
27:26 the doers of *w* in the field
28:13 all the *w* of the service of
28:20 until all the *w* of the
28:21 with you in all the *w* there
29:1 but the *w* is great; for the
29:5 all the *w* by the hand of the
2Ch 2:7 skillful man to *w* in gold and
2:14 to *w* in gold and in silver
4:11 Hiram finished doing the *w* that
5:1 all the *w* that Solomon had to
8:9 constituted slaves for his *w*
8:16 Solomon's *w* was all in a
13:10 also the Levites in the *w*
16:5 Baasha . . . stopped his *w*
24:12 doers of the *w* of the
24:13 doers of the *w* began
24:13 repair *w* kept advancing by
29:34 until the *w* was finished
31:21 every *w* that he started in
32:19 the *w* of man's hands
32:30 successful in every *w* of
34:10 hand of the doers of the *w*
34:10 doers of the *w* who were
34:12 in faithfulness in the *w*
34:13 doers of the *w* for the
34:17 hand of the doers of the *w*
Ezr 3:8 the *w* of the house of Jehovah
3:9 doers of the *w* in the house
4:24 the *w* on the house of God
5:8 *w* is being eagerly done and
6:7 the *w* on that house of God
6:22 *w* of the house of the true
9:12 must not *w* for their peace
Ne 2:16 rest of the doers of the *w*
2:18 their hands for the good *w*
3:4 son of Hakkoz did repair *w*
3:4 son of Meshezabel did repair *w*
3:4 the son of Baana did repair *w*
3:5 the Tekoites did repair *w*
3:7 the Meronothite, did repair *w*
3:8 goldsmiths, did repair *w*
3:8 ointment mixers did repair *w*
3:9 Jerusalem, did repair *w*
3:10 son of Harumaph did repair *w*
3:10 of Hashabneiah did repair *w*
3:12 Jerusalem, did repair *w*
3:16 did repair *w* as far as in
3:17 the Levites did repair *w*
3:17 did repair *w* for his district
3:18 their brothers did repair *w*
3:22 District, did repair *w*
3:23 repair *w* in front of their
3:23 *w* close by his own house
3:25 *w* in front of the Buttress
3:26 they did repair *w* as far as
3:28 priests did repair *w*, each
3:29 repair *w* in front of his own
3:29 Shemaiah . . . did repair *w*
3:30 repair *w* in front of his own
3:31 repair *w* as far as the house
3:32 and the traders did repair *w*
4:11 and put a stop to the *w*
4:15 each one to his *w*
4:16 men were active in the *w*
4:17 each one was active in the *w*
4:19 The *w* is large and extensive
4:21 we were active in the *w*
5:16 the *w* of this wall I took a
5:16 together there for the *w*
6:3 is a great *w* that I am doing
6:3 Why should the *w* cease while
6:9 hands will drop . . . from the *w*
6:16 that this *w* had been done
7:70 houses that gave to the *w*

Ne 7:71 to the treasure for the *w*
10:33 *w* of the house of our God
11:12 doers of the *w* of the house
11:22 *w* of the house of the true
13:10 singers doing the *w* went
13:30 each one in his own *w*
Es 3:9 the hands of those doing the *w*
10:2 all his energetic *w* and his
Job 1:10 The *w* of his hands you have
3:18 of one driving them to *w*
5:12 hands do not *w* with effect
10:3 reject . . . *w* of your hands
14:15 For the *w* of your hands you
34:19 are the *w* of his hands
37:7 mortal man to know his *w*
Ps 19:1 *w* of his hands the expanse
28:4 to the *w* of their hands
28:5 Nor for the *w* of his hands
33:4 all his *w* is in faithfulness
62:12 each one according to his *w*
64:9 have insight into his *w*
86:17 *W* out with me a sign
90:17 *w* of our hands do you firmly
90:17 *w* of our hands, do you
102:25 heavens are the *w* of your
105:44 hard *w* of national groups
115:4 *w* of the hands of earthling
135:15 *w* of the hands of earthling
143:5 the *w* of your own hands
Pr 16:11 weights of the bag are his *w*
18:9 slack in his *w*—he is a
21:25 his hands have refused to *w*
22:29 a man skillful in his *w*
24:27 Prepare your *w* out of doors
Ec 1:3 a man have in all his hard *w*
2:10 because of all my hard *w*, and
2:10 portion from all my hard *w*
2:11 toward the hard *w* that I had
2:17 *w* that has been done under
2:18 even I, hated all my hard *w*
2:19 control over all my hard *w*
2:20 despair over all the hard *w*
2:21 hard *w* has been with wisdom
2:22 to have for all his hard *w*
2:24 good because of his hard *w*
3:11 *w* that the true God has made
3:13 see good for all his hard *w*
3:17 and concerning every *w* there
4:3 has not seen the calamitous *w*
4:4 have seen all the hard *w* and
4:4 and all the proficiency in *w*
4:6 a double handful of hard *w* and
4:8 is no end to all his hard *w*
4:9 a good reward for their hard *w*
5:6 to wreck the *w* of your hands
5:15 one carry away for his hard *w*
5:18 see good for all his hard *w*
5:19 and to rejoice in his hard *w*
6:7 hard *w* of mankind is for their
7:13 See the *w* of the true God
8:9 my heart to every *w* that has
8:11 sentence against a bad *w* has
8:14 as if for the *w* of the wicked
8:14 if for the *w* of the righteous
8:15 in their hard *w* for the days
8:17 saw all the *w* of the true God
8:17 not able to find out the *w*
9:9 in life and in your hard *w*
9:10 there is no *w* . . . in Sheol
10:15 hard *w* of the stupid ones
11:5 know the *w* of the true God
12:14 bring every sort of *w* into
Ca 7:1 the *w* of an artisan's hands
Isa 2:8 the *w* of one's hands they bow
5:12 *w* of his hands they have
5:19 Let his *w* hasten
9:4 the one driving them to *w*
10:12 terminates all his *w* in
14:2 who were driving them to *w*
14:4 one driving others to *w*
17:8 altars, the *w* of his hands
19:14 wander about in all its *w*
19:15 *w* that the head or the tail
19:25 *w* of my hands, Assyria, and
25:7 woven *w* that is interwoven
28:21, 21 that he may *w* his *w*
28:21 his *w* is unusual
29:23 children, the *w* of my hands
32:6 heart will *w* at what is
32:6 *w* at apostasy and to speak
32:17 *w* of the true righteousness
54:16 ruinous man for wrecking *w*
58:3 that you kept driving to *w*
60:21 the *w* of my hands, for me

Isa 64:8 are the *w* of your hand
65:22 the *w* of their own hands
Jer 10:3 the *w* of the hands of the
10:15 vanity, a *w* of mockery
17:22 no *w* at all must you do
17:24 by not doing on it any *w*
18:3 *w* upon the potter's wheels
20:18 to see hard *w* and grief
25:6 with the *w* of your hands
25:7 with the *w* of your hands
25:14 according to the *w* of their
32:30 by the *w* of their hands
50:25 there is a *w* that the
51:10 the *w* of Jehovah our God
51:18 are vanity, a *w* of mockery
La 3:64 to the *w* of their hands
4:2 the *w* of the hands of a potter
Eze 15:3 pole . . . to do some *w*
15:4 Is it fit for any *w*?
15:5 it is not used for any *w*
15:5 be used for any further *w*
16:30 the *w* of a woman, a
Da 8:27 and did the *w* of the king
11:35 refining *w* because of them
Ho 5:2 in slaughter *w* those falling
13:2 the *w* of craftsmen, all of it
14:3 to the *w* of our hands
Jon 1:8 What is your *w*, and from
1:13 tried to *w* their way through
Mic 2:10 the wrecking *w* is painful
5:13 down to the *w* of your hands
6:16 the *w* of the house of Ahab
Hab 3:17 the *w* of the olive tree may
Hag 1:14 *w* in the house of Jehovah
2:4 utterance of Jehovah, and *w*
2:14 how all the *w* of their hands
2:17 even all the *w* of your hands
Mt 20:12 last put in one hour's *w*
21:28 go *w* today in the vineyard
Mr 6:5 was able to do no powerful *w*
9:39 *w* on the basis of my name
13:34 slaves, to each one his *w*
Lu 3:23 when he commenced his *w*
12:58 get to *w*, while on the way
13:14 six days on which *w* ought to
24:19 a prophet powerful in *w* and
Joh 4:34 sent me and to finish his *w*
6:27 *W*, not for the food that
6:28 we do to *w* the works of God
6:29 This is the *w* of God, that
6:30 What *w* are you doing?
9:4 *w* the works of him that sent
9:4 night . . . when no man can *w*
10:33 not for a fine *w*, but for
17:4 finished the *w* you have
Ac 5:38 scheme or this *w* is from men
13:2 *w* to which I have called
13:41 am working a *w* in your days
13:41 *w* that you will by no means
14:26 *w* they had fully performed
15:38 not gone with them to the *w*
Ro 2:7 endurance in *w* that is good
4:5 man that does not *w* but puts
7:5 at *w* in our members that we
7:18 ability to *w* out what is fine
13:10 Love does not *w* evil to
14:20 tearing down the *w* of God
15:16 the holy *w* of the good news
1Co 3:13 *w* will become manifest, for
3:13 prove what sort of *w* each
3:14 anyone's *w* that he has built
3:15 anyone's *w* is burned up, he
9:1 Are not you my *w* in the Lord?
9:6 to refrain from secular *w*
15:58 to do in the *w* of the Lord
16:10 performing the *w* of Jehovah
2Co 4:12 death is at *w* in us, but
9:8 have plenty for every good *w*
Ga 6:4 him prove what his own *w* is
6:10 *w* what is good toward all
Eph 2:10 we are a product of his *w*
4:12 for ministerial *w*, for the
4:19 to *w* uncleanness of every
4:28 but rather let him do hard *w*
4:28 doing . . . what is good *w*
Php 1:6 he who started a good *w* in
1:22 this is a fruitage of my *w*
2:16 in vain or *w* hard in vain
2:30 on account of the Lord's *w*
Col 1:10 fruit in every good *w* and
1:29 is at *w* in me with power
3:17 that you do in word or in *w*
3:23 *w* at it whole-souled as to
1Th 1:3 faithful *w* and your loving
1Th 2:13 also at *w* in you believers
4:11 and *w* with your hands, just
5:13 in love because of their *w*
2Th 1:11 the *w* of faith with power
2:7 lawlessness is already at *w*
2:9 Satan with every powerful *w*
3:10 not want to *w*, neither let
1Ti 3:1 he is desirous of a fine *w*
5:10 followed every good *w*
5:17 especially those who *w* hard
6:18 to *w* at good, to be rich in
2Ti 2:21 prepared for every good *w*
3:6 men who slyly *w* their way
3:17 equipped for every good *w*
4:5 do the *w* of an evangelizer
4:18 from every wicked *w* and
Tit 1:16 not approved for good *w* of
3:1 to be ready for every good *w*
Heb 6:10 so as to forget your *w* and
Jas 1:4 endurance have its *w* complete
1:20 *w* out God's righteousness
1:25 doer of the *w*, will be happy
5:16 it is at *w*, has much force
1Pe 1:17 according to each one's *w*
3Jo 5 doing a faithful *w* in whatever
Re 6:9 witness *w* that they used to
12:17 *w* of bearing witness to
19:10 *w* of witnessing to Jesus
22:12 to each one as his *w* is

Workdays
Le 25:50 *w* of a hired laborer are
Eze 46:1 shut for the six *w*, and on

Worked
Nu 23:23 What has God *w* out!
De 21:3 the herd that has not been *w*
32:27 Jehovah who *w* all this out
Ru 2:19 with whom she had *w*
2:19 with whom I *w* today is Boaz
1Sa 14:45 it was with God that he *w*
2Ch 3:14 and *w* in cherubs upon it
Ne 3:20 *w* with fervor and repaired
Job 10:12 you have *w* with me
Ps 127:1 builders have *w* hard on it
Pr 16:26 hard worker has *w* hard for
Ec 2:11 I had *w* hard to accomplish
2:19 hard work at which I *w* hard
2:20 I had *w* hard under the sun
2:21 not *w* hard at such a thing
Jer 8:8 has *w* in sheer falsehood
12:13 They have *w* themselves sick
Joh 3:21 *w* in harmony with God
Ac 18:3 *w*, for they were tentmakers
19:25 those who *w* at such things
Ro 5:16 things *w* through the one man
7:8 *w* out in me covetousness of
15:18 Christ *w* through me for the
1Co 5:3 man who has *w* in such a way
Jas 2:22 his faith *w* along with his
1Pe 4:3 to have *w* out the will of the
2Jo 8 things we have *w* to produce

Worker
Ex 28:32 the product of a loom *w*
35:35 and of a loom *w*, men doing
39:22 the workmanship of a loom *w*
39:27 the workmanship of a loom *w*
Le 25:39 as a *w* in slavish service
De 27:15 hands of a wood-and-metal *w*
1Ki 7:14 a Tyrian man, a *w* in copper
11:28 the young man was a hard *w*
Ps 101:7 no *w* of trickiness
Pr 8:30 be beside him as a master *w*
16:26 The soul of the hard *w* has
Isa 38:12 my life just like a loom *w*
Mal 3:5 with the wages of a wage *w*
Mt 10:10 for the *w* deserves his food
Lu 10:7 the *w* is worthy of his wages
Ro 16:9 Urbanus our fellow *w* in
16:21 Timothy my fellow *w* greets
2Co 8:23 fellow *w* for your interests
Php 2:25 my brother and fellow *w* and
Phm 1 our beloved one and fellow *w*

Workers
Le 25:46 use them as *w*, but upon your
Jg 5:26 to the mallet of hard *w*
1Sa 17:7 was like the beam of loom *w*
2Sa 5:11 cedar trees and *w* in wood
5:11 *w* in stone for walls, and
21:19 like the beam of loom *w*
2Ki 12:11 *w* in wood and to the
1Ch 4:21 *w* of fine fabric of the
11:23 like the beam of loom *w*
14:1 *w* in wood to build him a
1Ch 20:5 was like the beam of loom *w*
22:15 and *w* in stone and wood and
2Ch 24:12 *w* in iron and copper for
Ezr 7:24 the *w* of this house of God
Ne 4:22 guard by night and *w* by day
Ec 10:19 is for the laughter of the *w*
Isa 19:9 *w* in carded flax must become
19:9 loom *w* on white fabrics
19:10 wage *w* grieved in soul
Mt 7:23 you *w* of lawlessness
9:37 harvest is great . . . *w* are few
9:38 send out *w* into his harvest
20:1 to hire *w* for his vineyard
20:2 the *w* for a denarius a day
20:8 Call the *w* and pay them
Lu 10:2 great, but the *w* are few
10:2 send out *w* into his harvest
13:27 you *w* of unrighteousness
Ro 16:3 my fellow *w* in Christ Jesus
1Co 3:9 For we are God's fellow *w*
2Co 1:24 are fellow *w* for your joy
11:13 false apostles, deceitful *w*
Php 3:2 look out for the *w* of injury
4:3 as the rest of my fellow *w*
Col 4:11 fellow *w* for the kingdom of
Tit 2:5 chaste, *w* at home, good
Phm 24 Demas, Luke, my fellow *w*
Jas 5:4 The wages due the *w* who
3Jo 8 become fellow *w* in the truth

Working
Ex 31:4 devices, for *w* in gold and
31:5 in *w* of stones to set them
31:5 *w* of wood to make products
35:32 for *w* in gold and silver and
35:33 *w* of stones to set them and
35:33 *w* of wood to make ingenious
1Sa 20:19 on the *w* day
2Ki 12:11 the builders that were *w*
12:15 that they were *w*
22:7 faithfulness that they are *w*
Ezr 2:69 gave gold for the *w* supplies
Ne 4:6 to have a heart for *w*
Es 10:3 *w* for the good of his people
Job 6:13 effectual *w* . . . chased away
23:9 To the left where he is *w*
Ps 38:12 those *w* for a calamity to
52:2 *W* deceitfully
Pr 10:4 one *w* with a slack hand will
Ec 2:18 I was *w* hard under the sun
2:22 he is *w* hard under the sun
3:9 doer in what he is *w* hard at
4:8 And for whom am I *w* hard and
5:16 keeps *w* hard for the wind
8:17 mankind keep *w* hard to seek
9:9 you are *w* hard under the sun
12:3 grinding women have quit *w*
Isa 28:29 greatly in effectual *w*
57:5 *w* up passion among big trees
Jer 26:19 are *w* up a great calamity
Joh 5:17 My Father has kept *w* until
5:17 until now, and I keep *w*
Ac 13:41 I am *w* a work in your days
Ro 1:27 *w* what is obscene and
7:13 sin *w* out death for me
7:15 I am *w* out I do not know
7:17 the one *w* it out is no longer
7:20 one *w* it out is no longer I
16:12 women who are *w* hard in the
1Co 4:12 and to toil, *w* with our own
2Co 6:1 *W* together with him, we also
Php 2:12 *w* out your own salvation
Col 1:29 I am indeed *w* hard, exerting
1Th 2:9 It was with *w* night and day
5:12 those who are *w* hard among
2Th 3:8 were *w* so as not to impose
3:11 not *w* at all but meddling
3:12 by *w* with quietness they
1Ti 4:10 to this end we are *w* hard
Jas 2:9 you are *w* a sin, for you

Workman
1Ti 5:18 *w* is worthy of his wages
2Ti 2:15 a *w* with nothing to be

Workmanship
Ex 28:8 *w* should be of its materials
28:14 with the *w* of a rope; and
28:15 the *w* of an embroiderer
28:15 Like the *w* of the ephod you
32:16 tablets were the *w* of God
39:5 material according to its *w*
39:8 with the *w* of an embroiderer
39:8 *w* of the ephod, out of gold
39:22 the *w* of a loom worker, all

Worshiper
Ac 16:14 a *w* of God, was listening
18:7 Titius Justus, a *w* of God
Jas 1:26 to be a formal *w* and yet

Worshipers
2Ki 10:19 his *w* and all his priests
10:19 destroying the *w* of Baal
10:21 all the *w* of Baal came in
10:22 for all the *w* of Baal
10:23 now said to the *w* of Baal
10:23 none of the *w* of Jehovah
10:23 but only the *w* of Baal
17:33 that they proved to be *w*
Isa 47:13 the *w* of the heavens
Joh 4:23 true *w* will worship the

Worshiping
Da 3:7 and *w* the image of gold that
3:12 the image . . . they are not *w*
3:14 the image . . . you are not *w*
Mt 15:9 in vain that they keep *w* me
Mr 7:7 in vain that they keep *w* me
Joh 4:24 *w* him must worship with
Ac 18:13 another persuasion in *w* God
Re 11:1 the altar and those *w* in it
16:2 and that were *w* its image

Worships
Ac 19:27 and the inhabited earth *w*
Re 14:9 *w* the wild beast and its

Worst
Eze 7:24 in the *w* ones of the nations

Worth
Ge 23:15 A land plot *w* four hundred
Ru 4:11 you prove your *w* in Ephrathah
2Sa 18:3 you are *w* ten thousand of us
2Ki 6:25 *w* eighty silver pieces
6:25 dove's dung was *w* five
7:1 will be *w* a shekel, and two
7:1 *w* a shekel in the gateway of
7:16 *w* a shekel, and two seah
7:16 of barley *w* a shekel
7:18 barley *w* a shekel and a
7:18 fine flour *w* a shekel
1Ch 29:7 gold *w* five thousand talents
29:7 silver *w* ten thousand
29:7 copper *w* eighteen thousand
29:7 iron *w* a hundred thousand
Ezr 8:26 utensils *w* two talents, and
8:27 bowls *w* a thousand darics
Job 28:18 wisdom is *w* more than one
Pr 10:20 wicked one is *w* little
Isa 7:23 *w* a thousand pieces of
Eze 16:56 *w* hearing about from your
Na 1:11 what is not *w* while
Mt 6:26 Are you not *w* more than they
10:31 *w* more than many sparrows
12:12 much more *w* is a man than
Mr 6:37 buy two hundred denarii *w* of
12:33 *w* far more than all the
Lu 12:7 *w* more than many sparrows
12:23 the soul is *w* more than food
12:24 how much more *w* are you
Joh 6:7 Two hundred denarii *w* of
Ac 19:19 *w* fifty thousand pieces of
Heb 11:4 of greater *w* than Cain

Worthily
Eph 4:1 walk *w* of the calling with
Col 1:10 order to walk *w* of Jehovah
1Th 2:12 go on walking *w* of God who

Worthless
Ex 20:7 Jehovah your God in a *w* way
20:7 takes up his name in a *w* way
De 5:11 Jehovah your God in a *w* way
5:11 takes up his name in a *w* way
32:36 is only a helpless and *w* one
1Ki 14:10 a helpless and *w* one in
21:21 the helpless and *w* one in
2Ki 9:8 helpless and *w* one in Israel
14:26 nor any *w* one, nor was
Job 7:3 to possess *w* lunar months
Ps 31:6 regard to *w*, vain idols
60:11 salvation by . . . man is *w*
108:12 by earthling man is *w*
119:37 from seeing what is *w*
139:20 up your name in a *w* way
Isa 2:20 *w* gods of silver and his
31:7 his *w* gods of silver and
Jer 18:15 smoke to something *w*
La 2:14 have visioned for you *w* and
2:14 kept visioning for you *w* and
Mt 7:17 rotten tree produces *w* fruit
Mt 7:18 good tree cannot bear *w* fruit
Ro 3:12 together have become *w*

Worthlessness
Job 15:31 Let him put no faith in *w*
15:31 mere *w* will prove to be
Ps 24:4 carried My soul to sheer *w*
Isa 30:28 with a sieve of *w*
59:4 and a speaking of *w*

Worthy
Mt 10:37 than for me is not *w* of me
10:37 than for me is not *w* of me
10:38 after me is not *w* of me
22:8 but those invited were not *w*
Lu 7:4 He is *w* of your conferring
7:7 consider myself *w* to come to
10:7 the worker is *w* of his wages
15:19 no longer *w* of being called
15:21 no longer *w* of being called
20:35 *w* of gaining that system of
Joh 1:27 sandal I am not *w* to untie
Ac 5:41 *w* to be dishonored in behalf
13:25 I am not *w* to untie
13:46 *w* of everlasting life, look!
Ro 16:2 a way *w* of the holy ones, and
Php 1:27 a manner *w* of the good news
2Th 1:5 *w* of the kingdom of God
1:11 count you *w* of his calling
1Ti 5:17 reckoned *w* of double honor
5:18 workman is *w* of his wages
6:1 *w* of full honor, that the
Heb 3:3 *w* of more glory than Moses
10:29 man be counted *w* who has
11:38 world was not *w* of them
3Jo 6 in a manner *w* of God
Re 3:4 because they are *w*
4:11 You are *w*, Jehovah, even our
5:2 Who is *w* to open the scroll
5:4 no one was found *w* to open the
5:9 *w* to take the scroll and open
5:12 *w* to receive the power and

Would-be
Mt 27:40 *w* thrower-down of the
Mr 15:29 You *w* thrower-down of the

Wound
Ex 21:25, 25 *w* for *w*, blow for blow
De 33:11 *W* severely in their hips
1Ki 22:35 blood the *w* kept pouring
Job 5:18 pain, but binds up the *w*
34:6 My severe *w* is incurable
Ps 69:20 and the *w* is incurable
Isa 3:7 shall not become a *w* dresser
30:26 heals even the severe *w*
Jon 2:5 Weeds were *w* around my head
1Co 8:12 and *w* their conscience that

Wounded
Ge 34:27 attacked the fatally *w* men
De 32:39 I have severely *w*, and I—I
Jg 20:31 mortally *w* on the highways
20:39 thirty men mortally *w* among
1Sa 17:52 and the fatally *w* of the
31:3 severely *w* by the shooters
1Ki 22:34 because I have been badly *w*
1Ch 10:3 Saul . . . *w* by the shooters
2Ch 18:33 because I have been badly *w*
35:23 have been very severely *w*
Job 24:12 soul of deadly *w* ones cries
Ca 5:7 They struck me, they *w* me
Eze 21:25 deadly *w*, wicked chieftain
26:15 the fatally *w* one groans
30:24 as a deadly *w* one he will
Lu 20:12 this one also they *w* and
Ac 19:16 fled naked and *w* out of that

Wounding
Ge 4:23 A man I have killed for *w*
1Ki 20:37 struck him, striking and *w*

Wounds
2Ki 8:29 *w* that the Syrians got to
9:15 *w* that the Syrians got to
2Ch 22:6 healed at Jezreel from the *w*
Job 9:17 my *w* many for no reason
Ps 38:5 My *w* have become stinky
64:7 *W* have resulted to them
Pr 20:30 Bruising *w* are what scours
23:29 Who has *w* for no reason?
27:6 *w* inflicted by a lover are
Isa 1:6 *W* and bruises and fresh
53:5 because of his *w* there has
Zec 13:6 What are these *w* on your
Lu 10:34 bound up his *w*, pouring oil

Wove
Ca 3:11 wreath that his mother *w* for

Woven
Ps 45:14 In *w* apparel she will be
139:15 I was *w* in the lowest parts
Isa 25:7 *w* work that is interwoven
28:20 *w* sheet itself is too
Eze 27:20 garments of *w* material for
Joh 19:23 *w* from the top throughout

Wrangle
Mt 12:19 will not *w*, nor cry aloud

Wrap
Ex 29:9 *w* the headgear upon them
Le 16:4 and *w* himself with the linen
De 14:25 *w* the money up in your hand
Ca 5:7 lifted my wide *w* off me
Isa 8:16 *W* up the attestation, put a
22:18 he will *w* you up tightly
Jer 43:12 *w* himself up in the land
Eze 5:3 and *w* them up in your skirts
16:10 to *w* you in fine linen and
Heb 1:12 *w* them up just as a cloak

Wrapped
Ex 12:34 *w* up in their mantles upon
Le 8:13 and *w* the headgear upon them
1Sa 21:9 *w* up in a mantle, behind the
25:29 *w* up in the bag of life
1Ki 19:13 *w* his face in . . . garment
2Ki 2:8 *w* it up and struck the waters
Pr 30:4 *w* up the waters in a mantle
Ca 1:7 like a woman *w* in mourning
Ho 4:19 wind has *w* her up in its
13:12 error of Ephraim is *w* up
Mt 27:59 took the body, *w* it up in
Mr 15:46 *w* him in the fine linen and
Lu 23:53 *w* it up in fine linen, and
Ac 5:6 *w* him in cloths, and carried

Wrapping
Job 26:8 *W* up the waters in his
Isa 28:20 narrow when *w* oneself up

Wrappings
Joh 11:44 and hands bound with *w*, and

Wraps
Jer 43:12 shepherd *w* himself up in
Eze 27:24 in *w* of blue material and

Wrath
Nu 25:11 turned back my *w* from upon
De 29:23 in his anger and in his *w*
Ezr 7:23 no *w* against the king's
Ps 78:31 God's *w* itself ascended
La 2:22 the day of the *w* of Jehovah
Mt 3:7 to flee from the coming *w*
18:34 his master, provoked to *w*
Lu 3:7 to flee from the coming *w*
21:23 and *w* on this people
Joh 3:36 *w* of God remains upon him
Ro 1:18 God's *w* is being revealed
2:5 storing up *w* for yourself on
2:5 on the day of *w* and of the
2:8 there will be *w* and anger
3:5 unjust when he vents his *w*
4:15 In reality the Law produces *w*
5:9 be saved through him from *w*
9:22 will to demonstrate his *w*
9:22 vessels of *w* made fit for
12:19 but yield place to the *w*
13:4 avenger to express *w* upon
13:5 only on account of that *w*
Eph 2:3 were naturally children of *w*
4:31 anger and *w* and screaming
5:6 *w* of God is coming upon the
Col 3:6 the *w* of God is coming
3:8 all away from you, *w*, anger
1Th 1:10 from the *w* which is coming
2:16 his *w* has at length come
5:9 God assigned us, not to *w*
1Ti 2:8 apart from *w* and debates
Tit 1:7 not prone to *w*, not a drunken
Jas 1:19 speaking, slow about *w*
1:20 man's *w* does not work out
Re 6:16 and from the *w* of the Lamb
6:17 the great day of their *w* has
11:18 your own *w* came, and the
14:10 into the cup of his *w*, and
16:19 wine of the anger of his *w*
19:15 the *w* of God the Almighty

Wrathful
Mt 5:22 continues *w* with his brother
22:7 king grew *w*, and sent his

Lu 14:21 householder became *w* and
15:28 *w* and was unwilling to go
Eph 4:26 Be *w*, and yet do not sin
Re 11:18 nations became *w*, and your
12:17 dragon grew *w* at the woman

Wreaking
Le 26:25 sword *w* vengeance for the

Wreath
Pr 1:9 *w* of attractiveness to your
4:9 it will give a *w* of charm
Ca 3:11 King Solomon with the *w* that

Wreathed
Ex 28:22 *w* chains, in rope work, of
39:15 upon the breastpiece *w* chains

Wreaths
1Ki 7:29 were *w* in hanging work
7:30 with *w* across from each
7:36 and *w* all around

Wreck
Ps 48:7 you *w* the ships of Tarshish
Ec 5:6 to *w* the work of your hands
Isa 13:5 to *w* all the earth
32:7 *w* the afflicted ones with

Wrecked
1Ki 22:48 ships were *w* at Ezion-geber
2Ch 20:37 ships were *w*, and they did
Isa 10:27 yoke will certainly be *w*
Jon 1:4 ship, it was about to be *w*
Re 8:9 a third of the boats were *w*

Wrecking
Isa 54:16 ruinous man for *w* work
Mic 2:10 unclean, there is a *w*
2:10 and the *w* work is painful

Wrest
Isa 10:2 *w* away justice from the
Eze 18:7 nothing would he *w* away in

Wrested
Eze 18:12 he has *w* away in robbery
18:18 *w* something away in

Wrestled
Ge 30:8 I have *w* with my sister

Wrestling
Eph 6:12 *w*, not against blood and

Wrestlings
Ge 30:8 strenuous *w* I have wrestled

Wretchedness
Ge 29:32 Jehovah has looked upon my *w*
31:42 My *w* and the toil of my
41:52 fruitful in the land of my *w*

Wrinkle
Eph 5:27 not having a spot or a *w*

Write
Ex 17:14 *W* this as a memorial in the
24:12 commandment that I must *w*
34:1 must *w* upon the tablets the
34:27 *W* down for yourself these
34:28 to *w* upon the tablets the
Nu 5:23 priest must *w* these cursings
17:2 *w* the name of each one upon
17:3 you will *w* upon Levi's rod
De 6:9 *w* them upon the doorposts of
10:2 I shall *w* upon the tablets
11:20 *w* them upon the doorposts
17:18 *w* in a book for himself a
24:1 *w* out a certificate of
27:3 *w* upon them all the words of
27:8 *w* on the stones all the words
31:19 *w* for yourselves this song
2Sa 11:14 David proceeded to *w* a
Ezr 5:10 we might *w* the names of the
Es 8:8 *w* in behalf of the Jews
8:10 to *w* in the name of King
9:20 Mordecai proceeded to *w* these
9:29 *w* with all forcefulness to
Pr 3:3 *W* them upon the tablet of your
7:3 *w* them upon the tablet of your
Isa 8:1 *w* upon it with the stylus
10:19 boy will be able to *w* them
30:8 *w* it upon a tablet with
44:5 will *w* upon his hand
Jer 22:30 *W* down this man as
30:2 *W* for yourself in a book
31:33 in their heart I shall *w* it
36:2 *w* in it all the words that
36:4 Baruch might *w* at the mouth
36:17 *w* all these words from his
36:28 *w* on it all the first words
Jer 36:32 *w* upon it at the mouth of
51:60 *w* in one book all the
Eze 24:2 *w* down for yourself the
37:16 a stick and *w* upon it, For
37:16 take another stick and *w*
37:20 sticks upon which you *w*
43:11 *w* before their eyes, in
Ho 8:12 *w* for him many things of my
Hab 2:2 *W* down the vision, and set it
Lu 1:3 to *w* them in logical order
16:6 sit down and quickly *w* fifty
16:7 agreement back and *w* eighty
Joh 19:21 *w* The King of the Jews
Ac 15:20 to *w* them to abstain from
25:26 I have nothing certain to *w*
25:26 I might get something to *w*
2Co 2:9 *w* to ascertain the proof of
9:1 superfluous for me to *w* you
13:10 why I *w* these things while
2Th 3:17 letter; this is the way I *w*
Heb 8:10 in their hearts I shall *w*
10:16 in their minds I shall *w*
1Jo 2:13 I *w* you, young children
2:14 I *w* you, fathers, because
2:14 I *w* you, young men, because
2:21 I *w* you, not because you do
2:26 These things I *w* you about
5:13 I *w* you these things that
2Jo 12 I have many things to *w* you
3Jo 13 I had many things to *w* you
Jude 3 *w* you about the salvation we
3 *w* you to exhort you to put up
Re 1:11 What you see *w* in a scroll
1:19 *w* down the things you saw
2:1 Ephesus *w*: These are the
2:8 the congregation in Smyrna *w*
2:12 congregation in Pergamum *w*
2:18 congregation in Thyatira *w*
3:1 the congregation in Sardis *w*
3:7 congregation in Philadelphia *w*
3:12 *w* upon him the name of my
3:14 congregation in Laodicea *w*
10:4 and do not *w* them down
14:13 *W*: Happy are the dead who
19:9 *W*: Happy are those invited to
21:5 *W*, because these words are

Writes
Ro 10:5 Moses *w* that the man that

Writhe
Ps 29:8 makes the wilderness *w*
29:8 the wilderness of Kadesh *w*
29:9 the hinds *w* with birth pains

Writing
Ex 32:16, 16 the *w* was the *w* of God
De 10:4 the same *w* as the first, the
31:24 *w* the words of this law in
1Ch 28:19 *w* from the hand of Jehovah
2Ch 2:11 said the word in *w* and sent
21:12 *w* to him from Elijah the
35:4 *w* of David the king of
35:4 the *w* of Solomon his son
36:22 and also in *w*, saying
Ezr 1:1 and also in *w*, saying
4:7 *w* of the letter was written
5:7 *w* in it was in this manner
Ne 9:38 in *w* and attested by the seal
Es 1:22 in its own style of *w* and to
3:9 be a *w* that they be destroyed
3:12 *w* went on according to all
3:12 in its own style of *w*
3:14 copy of the *w* to be given as
4:8 a copy of the *w* of the law
8:8 *w* . . . is not possible to undo
8:9 *w* went on according to all
8:9 district in its own style of *w*
8:9 Jews in their own style of *w*
8:13 the *w* was to be given as law
Job 13:26 *w* against me bitter things
Ps 139:16 its parts were down in *w*
Ec 12:10 *w* of correct words of truth
Isa 10:1 those who, constantly *w*
29:11 to someone knowing the *w*
29:12 that does not know *w*
29:12 I do not know *w* at all
38:9 A *w* of Hezekiah the king of
Jer 32:12 *w* in the deed of purchase
36:18 *w* in the book with ink
Da 1:4 the *w* . . . of the Chaldeans
1:17 insight in all *w* and wisdom
5:5 *w* in front of the lampstand
5:5 back of the hand that was *w*
5:7 Any man that will read this *w*
Da 5:8 read the *w* itself or to
5:15 may read this very *w*, even
5:16 you are able to read the *w*
5:17 I shall read the *w* itself to
5:24 this very *w* was inscribed
5:25 is the *w* that was inscribed
6:8 and sign the *w*, in order for
6:9 Darius himself signed the *w*
6:10 that the *w* had been signed
10:21 noted down in the *w* of truth
Mt 27:37 charge against him, in *w*
Mr 10:4 *w* of a certificate of
Ro 15:15 *w* you the more outspokenly
16:22 Tertius, who have done the *w*
1Co 4:14 I am *w* these things, not to
5:11 am *w* you to quit mixing in
14:37 the things I am *w* to you
2Co 1:13 not *w* you things except
Ga 1:20 as to the things I am *w* you
Php 3:1 To be *w* the same things to
1Th 4:9 do not need us to be *w* you
1Ti 3:14 I am *w* you these things
Phm 19 I Paul am *w* with my own hand
21 I am *w* you, knowing you will
2Pe 3:1 the second letter I am *w* you
1Jo 1:4 *w* these things that our joy
2:1 *w* you these things that you
2:7 I am *w* you, not a new
2:8 am *w* you a new commandment
2:12 I am *w* you, little children
2:13 I am *w* you, fathers, because
2:13 I am *w* you, young men
2Jo 5 *w* you, not a new commandment
3Jo 13 I do not wish to go on *w* you
Re 10:4 I was at the point of *w*; but

Writings
Joh 5:47 if you do not believe the *w*
2Ti 3:15 you have known the holy *w*

Written
Ex 31:18 tablets of stone *w* on by
32:15 tablets *w* upon on both their
32:15 and on that they were *w* upon
32:32 your book that you have *w*
Nu 11:26 as they were among those *w*
De 9:10 *w* upon with God's finger
24:3 *w* out a certificate of
28:58 law that are *w* in this book
28:61 not *w* in the book of this
29:20 the oath *w* in this book will
29:21 *w* in this book of the
29:27 malediction *w* in this book
30:10 his statutes *w* in this book
Jos 1:8 according to all that is *w* in
8:31 *w* in the book of the law of
8:32 he had *w* before the sons of
8:34 all that is *w* in the book of
10:13 *w* in the book of Jashar
23:6 to do all that is *w* in the
2Sa 1:18 *w* in the book of Jashar
1Ki 2:3 is *w* in the law of Moses
11:41 *w* in the book of the
14:19 are *w* in the book of the
14:29 *w* in the book of the
15:7 *w* in the book of the affairs
15:23 *w* in the book of the
15:31 *w* in the book of the
16:5 *w* in the book of the affairs
16:14 *w* in the book of the
16:20 *w* in the book of the
16:27 *w* in the book of the
21:11 was *w* in the letters that
22:39 *w* in the book of the
22:45 are they not *w* in the book
2Ki 1:18 *w* in the book of the affairs
8:23 are they not *w* in the book
10:34 they not *w* in the book of
12:19 are they not *w* in the book
13:8 are they not *w* in the book
13:12 are they not *w* in the book
14:6 *w* in the book of Moses' law
14:15 are they not *w* in the book
14:18 are they not *w* in the book
14:28 are they not *w* in the book
15:6 are they not *w* in the book
15:11 they are *w* in the book of
15:15 they are *w* in the book of
15:21 are they not *w* in the book
15:26 they are *w* in the book of
15:31 they are *w* in the book of
15:36 are they not *w* in the book
16:19 are they not *w* in the book
20:20 are they not *w* in the book
21:17 are they not *w* in the book

Wrong

Wrongdoer

Wrongdoing

Wronged

Wrongful

Wrongfully

Wronging

Wrongly

Wrote
Ex 24:4 Moses *w* down all the words
De 4:13 he *w* them upon two tablets of
5:22 he *w* them upon two tablets
10:4 he *w* upon the tablets the
31:9 Moses *w* this law and gave it
31:22 Moses *w* this song in that
Jos 8:32 he *w* there upon the stones
24:26 Joshua *w* these words in
Jg 8:14 he *w* out for him the names of
1Sa 10:25 and *w* it in a book and
2Sa 11:15 he *w* in the letter, saying
1Ki 21:8 she *w* letters in Ahab's name
21:9 she *w* in the letters, saying
2Ki 10:1 Jehu *w* letters and sent them
10:6 he *w* them a second letter
17:37 commandment that he *w* for
1Ch 24:6 secretary of the Levites *w*
2Ch 30:1 letters he *w* to Ephraim and
32:17 *w* to reproach Jehovah the
Ezr 4:6 *w* an accusation against the
4:7 colleagues *w* to Artaxerxes
4:8 the scribe *w* a letter against
Es 8:5 he *w* to destroy the Jews that
Jer 32:10 *w* in a deed and affixed
45:1 *w* in a book these words
Da 6:25 Darius the king himself *w* to
7:1 time he *w* down the dream
Mr 10:5 he *w* you this commandment
12:19 Teacher, Moses *w* us that if
Lu 1:63 and *w*: John is its name
20:28 Moses *w* us, If a man's
Joh 1:45 and the Prophets *w*, Jesus
5:46 for that one *w* about me
19:19 Pilate *w* a title also and
21:24 and that *w* these things
Ac 15:23 they *w*: The apostles and the
18:27 the brothers *w* the disciples
23:25 he *w* a letter having this
1Co 5:9 I *w* you to quit mixing in
7:1 the things about which you *w*
2Co 2:3 so I *w* this very thing, that
2:4 *w* you with many tears, not
7:12 although I *w* you, I did it
Eph 3:3 I *w* previously in brief
2Pe 3:15 brother Paul . . . *w* you
3Jo 9 I *w* . . . to the congregation

Wrought
Eze 27:19 Iron in *w* works, cassia

Wrought-iron
Job 40:18 bones are like *w* rods

Wrung
Jg 6:38 *w* the fleece, he got to drain

Yard
Eze 26:5 A drying *y* for dragnets is
26:14 A drying *y* for dragnets is
47:10 be a drying *y* for dragnets

Yards
Mt 14:24 many hundreds of *y* away

Yarn
Ex 35:25 bringing as *y* the blue thread

Year
Ge 7:11 six hundredth *y* of Noah's life
8:13 in the six hundred and first *y*
14:4 the thirteenth *y* they rebelled
14:5 in the fourteenth *y*
17:21 this appointed time next *y*
18:10 return to you next *y* at this
18:14 next *y* at this time, and
26:12 that *y* he was getting up to
41:50 before the *y* of the famine
45:6 the second *y* of the famine
47:17 their livestock during that *y*
47:18 that *y* came to its close
47:18 coming to him in the next *y*
Ex 12:2 first of the months of the *y*
12:5 sound, a male, a *y* old, for
13:10, 10 time from *y* to *y*
23:11 seventh *y* you are to leave it
23:14 Three times in the *y* you are
23:16 at the outgoing of the *y*
23:17 On three occasions in the *y*
23:29 out from before you in one *y*
29:38 young rams each a *y* old
30:10 atonement . . . once a *y*
30:10 atonement for it once a *y*
34:22 at the turn of the *y*
34:23 Three times in the *y* every
34:24 three times in the *y*
40:17 in the second *y*, on the first
Le 9:3 and a young ram, each a *y* old
12:6 a young ram in its first *y*
14:10 female lamb, in its first *y*
16:34 all their sins once in the *y*
19:24 fourth *y* all its fruit will
19:25 fifth *y* you may eat its
23:12 ram, in its first *y*, for a
23:18 lambs, each a *y* old, and one
23:19 two male lambs, each a *y* old
23:41 Jehovah seven days in the *y*
25:4 seventh *y* there should occur
25:10 sanctify the fiftieth *y* and
25:11 fiftieth *y* will become for
25:13 *y* of the Jubilee you should
25:20 eat in the seventh *y* seeing
25:21 sixth *y*, and it must yield
25:22 sow seed the eighth *y* and
25:22 old crop until the ninth *y*
25:28 until the Jubilee *y*
25:29 *y* from the time of his sale
25:29 should continue a whole *y*
25:30 complete *y* has come to the
25:40 with you till the Jubilee *y*
25:50 *y* he sold himself to him
25:50 Jubilee *y*, and the money of
25:52 years until the Jubilee *y*
25:53, 53 laborer from *y* to *y*
25:54 go out in the *y* of Jubilee
26:10 old of the preceding *y*, and
27:17 from the *y* of Jubilee on, it
27:18 next *y* of Jubilee, and a
27:23 up till the *y* of Jubilee
27:24 *y* of Jubilee the field will
Nu 1:1 second *y* of their coming out
6:12 ram in its first *y* as a guilt
6:14 ram in its first *y* as a burnt
6:14 lamb in its first *y* as a sin
7:15 one male lamb in its first *y*
7:17 five male lambs each a *y* old
7:21 one male lamb in its first *y*
7:23 five male lambs each a *y* old
7:27 male lamb in its first *y*, for
7:29 five male lambs each a *y* old
7:33 one male lamb in its first *y*
7:35 five male lambs each a *y* old
7:39 one male lamb in its first *y*
7:41 five male lambs each a *y* old
7:45 one male lamb in its first *y*
7:47 five male lambs each a *y* old
7:51 one male lamb in its first *y*
7:53 five male lambs each a *y* old
7:57 one male lamb in its first *y*
7:59 five male lambs each a *y* old
7:63 one male lamb in its first *y*
7:65 five male lambs each a *y* old
7:69 one male lamb in its first *y*
7:71 five male lambs each a *y* old
7:75 one male lamb in its first *y*
7:77 five male lambs each a *y* old
7:81 one male lamb in its first *y*
7:83 five male lambs each a *y* old
7:87 male lambs each a *y* old
7:88 sixty male lambs each a *y* old
9:1 second *y* of their coming out
10:11 the second *y*, in the second
14:34 forty days, a day for a *y*
14:34 day for a *y*, you will answer
15:27 a female goat in its first *y*
28:11 male lambs each a *y* old
28:14 for the months of the *y*
28:19 seven male lambs each a *y*
28:27 male lambs each a *y* old
29:2 seven male lambs each a *y* old
29:8 seven male lambs each a *y* old
29:13 male lambs each a *y* old
29:17 fourteen male lambs each a *y*
29:20 lambs each a *y* old, sound
29:23 male lambs each a *y* old
29:26 fourteen male lambs each a *y*
29:29 fourteen male lambs each a *y*
29:32 fourteen male lambs each a *y*
29:36 seven male lambs each a *y*
33:38 fortieth *y* of the going out
De 1:3 fortieth *y*, in the eleventh
11:12 from the beginning of the *y*
11:12 to the close of the *y*
14:22, 22 the field *y* by *y*
14:28 your produce in that *y*
15:9 saying, The seventh *y*, the
15:9 the *y* of the release, has
15:12 in the seventh *y* you should
15:20, 20 you should eat it *y* by *y*
16:16 Three times in the *y* every
24:5 exempt at his house for one *y*
De 26:12 your produce in the third *y*
26:12 the *y* of the tenth
31:10 time of the *y* of the release
Jos 5:12 the land of Canaan in that *y*
Jg 10:8 Israel in that *y*—for eighteen
11:40, 40 *y* to *y* the daughters of
11:40 four days in the *y*
17:10 ten silver pieces a *y* and the
21:19, 19 festival . . . from *y* to *y*
1Sa 1:3, 3 from *y* to *y* to prostrate
1:7, 7 way she would do *y* by *y*
1:20 at the rolling around of a *y*
2:19, 19 up to him from *y* to *y*
7:16, 16 he traveled from *y* to *y*
27:7 to be a *y* and four months
29:3 with me here a *y* or two
2Sa 11:1 return of the *y*, at the time
14:26 end of every *y* that he
21:1, 1 for three years, *y* after *y*
1Ki 4:7 the food one month in the *y*
5:11, 11 kept giving Hiram *y* by *y*
6:1 four hundred and eightieth *y*
6:1 fourth *y*, in the month of Ziv
6:37 fourth *y* the house of Jehovah
6:38 in the eleventh *y*, in the
9:25 three times in the *y* to
10:14 in one *y* amounted up to six
14:25 fifth *y* of King Rehoboam
15:1 eighteenth *y* of King
15:9 twentieth *y* of Jeroboam the
15:25 second *y* of Asa the king of
15:28 the third *y* of Asa the king
15:33 the third *y* of Asa the king
16:8 In the twenty-sixth *y* of Asa
16:10 twenty-seventh *y* of Asa the
16:15 twenty-seventh *y* of Asa
16:23 thirty-first *y* of Asa the
16:29 thirty-eighth *y* of Asa the
18:1 to Elijah in the third *y*
20:22 return of the *y* the king of
20:26 at the return of the *y* that
22:2 third *y* that Jehoshaphat the
22:41 fourth *y* of Ahab the king
22:51 seventeenth *y* of Jehoshaphat
2Ki 1:17 in the second *y* of Jehoram
3:1 eighteenth *y* of Jehoshaphat
4:16 next *y* you will be embracing
4:17 appointed time the next *y*
8:16 the fifth *y* of Jehoram the
8:25 the twelfth *y* of Jehoram
8:26 for one *y* he reigned in
9:29 eleventh *y* of Jehoram the
11:4 in the seventh *y* Jehoiada
12:1 In the seventh *y* of Jehu
12:6 twenty-third *y* of King
13:1 twenty-third *y* of Jehoash
13:10 thirty-seventh *y* of Jehoash
13:20 at the coming in of the *y*
14:1 In the second *y* of Jehoash
14:23 the fifteenth *y* of Amaziah
15:1 twenty-seventh *y* of Jeroboam
15:8 thirty-eighth *y* of Azariah
15:13 thirty-ninth *y* of Uzziah
15:17 thirty-ninth *y* of Azariah
15:23 the fiftieth *y* of Azariah
15:27 fifty-second *y* of Azariah
15:30 the twentieth *y* of Jotham
15:32 In the second *y* of Pekah the
16:1 the seventeenth *y* of Pekah
17:1 the twelfth *y* of Ahaz the
17:6 In the ninth *y* of Hoshea
18:1 third *y* of Hoshea the son of
18:9 the fourth *y* of King Hezekiah
18:9 the seventh *y* of Hoshea the
18:10 in the sixth *y* of Hezekiah
18:10 ninth *y* of Hoshea the king
18:13 the fourteenth *y* of King
19:29 eating this *y* of the growth
19:29 in the second *y* grain that
19:29 in the third *y* sow seed
22:3 eighteenth *y* of King Josiah
23:23 eighteenth *y* of King Josiah
24:12 eighth *y* of his being king
25:1 ninth *y* of his being king
25:2 eleventh *y* of King Zedekiah
25:8 the nineteenth *y* of King
25:27 thirty-seventh *y* of the
25:27 the *y* of his becoming king
1Ch 26:31 In the fortieth *y* of David's
27:1 for all the months of the *y*
2Ch 3:2 in the fourth *y* of his reign
8:13 three times in the *y*
9:13 came to Solomon in one *y*
12:2 fifth *y* of King Rehoboam

2Ch 13:1 eighteenth *y* . . . Jeroboam
15:10 fifteenth *y* of Asa's reign
15:19 thirty-fifth *y* of Asa's
16:1 thirty-sixth *y* of the reign
16:12 Asa in the thirty-ninth *y*
16:13 forty-first *y* of his
17:7 third *y* of his reigning he
22:2 Ahaziah . . . one *y* he reigned
23:1 seventh *y* Jehoiada showed
24:5, 5 of your God from *y* to *y*
24:23 turn of the *y* a military
27:5 gave him in that *y* a
27:5 in the second *y* and the
29:3 first *y* of his reigning, in
34:3 eighth *y* of his reigning
34:3 in the twelfth *y* he started
34:8 eighteenth *y* of his reigning
35:19 eighteenth *y* of Josiah's
36:10 at the return of the *y* King
36:22 first *y* of Cyrus the king of
Ezr 1:1 first *y* of Cyrus the king of
3:8 the second *y* of their coming
4:24 second *y* of the reign of
5:13 first *y* of Cyrus the king of
6:3 first *y* of Cyrus the king
6:15 sixth *y* of the reign of
7:7 seventh *y* of Artaxerxes the
7:8 in the seventh *y* of the king
Ne 1:1 Chislev, in the twentieth *y*
2:1 twentieth *y* of Artaxerxes the
5:14 from the twentieth *y* to the
5:14 thirty-second *y* of Artaxerxes
10:31 forego the seventh *y* and the
10:34, 34 appointed times, *y* by *y*
10:35, 35 *y* by *y*, to the house of
13:6 thirty-second *y* of Artaxerxes
Es 1:3 the third *y* of his reigning
2:16 in the seventh *y* of his reign
3:7 twelfth *y* of King Ahasuerus
9:21 in each and every *y*
9:27 time in each and every *y*
Job 3:6 glad among the days of a *y*
Ps 65:11 You have crowned the *y* with
Isa 6:1 *y* that King Uzziah died I
14:28 *y* that King Ahaz died this
20:1 *y* that Tartan came to Ashdod
21:16 *y*, according to the years
29:1, 1 Add *y* upon *y*, you people
32:10 *y* and some days you
34:8 *y* of retributions for the
36:1 fourteenth *y* of King Hezekiah
37:30 eating this *y* of the growth
37:30 second *y* grain that shoots
37:30 in the third *y* sow seed
61:2 proclaim the *y* of goodwill
63:4 *y* of my repurchased ones has
Jer 1:2 Josiah . . . thirteenth *y* of
1:3 the eleventh *y* of Zedekiah the
11:23 the *y* of their being given
17:8 the *y* of drought he will not
23:12 the *y* of their being given
25:1 the fourth *y* of Jehoiakim
25:1 the first *y* of Nebuchadrezzar
25:3 the thirteenth *y* of Josiah
28:1 in that *y*, in the beginning
28:1 in the fourth *y*, in the fifth
28:16 This *y* you yourself must
28:17 the prophet died in that *y*
32:1 tenth *y* of Zedekiah the king
32:1 the eighteenth *y* of
36:1 fourth *y* of Jehoiakim the
36:9 fifth *y* of Jehoiakim the son
39:1 ninth *y* of Zedekiah the king
39:2 eleventh *y* of Zedekiah, in
45:1 in the fourth *y* of Jehoiakim
46:2 fourth *y* of Jehoiakim the
48:44 *y* of their being given
51:46 in one *y* the report will
51:46 in another *y* there will be
51:59 fourth *y* of his being king
52:4 ninth *y* of his being king
52:5 eleventh *y* of King Zedekiah
52:12 nineteenth *y* of King
52:28 exile: in the seventh *y*
52:29 In the eighteenth *y* of
52:30 In the twenty-third *y*
52:31 thirty-seventh *y* of the
52:31 *y* of his becoming king
Eze 1:1 thirtieth *y*, in the fourth
1:2 fifth *y* of the exile of King
4:6, 6 day for a *y*, a day for a *y*
8:1 sixth *y*, in the sixth month
20:1 the seventh *y*, in the fifth
24:1 the ninth *y*, in the tenth

Eze 26:1 eleventh *y*, on the first day
29:1 tenth *y*, in the tenth month
29:17 twenty-seventh *y*, in the
30:20 eleventh *y*, in the first
31:1 eleventh *y*, in the third
32:1 twelfth *y*, in the twelfth
32:17 twelfth *y*, on the fifteenth
33:21 twelfth *y*, in the tenth
40:1 twenty-fifth *y* of our exile
40:1 in the start of the *y*, on
40:1 fourteenth *y* after the city
46:13 male lamb, in its first *y*
46:17 his until the *y* of liberty
Da 1:1 third *y* of the kingship of
1:21 first *y* of Cyrus the king
2:1 second *y* of the kingship of
7:1 first *y* of Belshazzar the king
8:1 third *y* of the kingship of
9:1 first *y* of Darius the son of
9:2 first *y* of his reigning I
10:1 third *y* of Cyrus the king of
11:1 first *y* of Darius the Mede I
Mic 6:6 with calves a *y* old
Hag 1:1 second *y* of Darius the king
1:15 second *y* of Darius the king
2:10 in the second *y* of Darius
Zec 1:1 in the second *y* of Darius the
1:7 in the second *y* of Darius, the
7:1 fourth *y* of Darius the king
14:16, 16 *y* to *y* to bow down to
Lu 2:41, 41 from *y* to *y* to Jerusalem
3:1 In the fifteenth *y* of the reign
4:19 preach Jehovah's acceptable *y*
13:8 let it alone also this *y*
Joh 11:49 who was high priest that *y*
11:51 he was high priest that *y*
18:13 who was high priest that *y*
Ac 7:23 time of his fortieth *y* was
11:26 for a whole *y* they gathered
18:11 stayed set there a *y* and six
2Co 8:10 a *y* ago you initiated not
9:2 has stood ready now for a *y*
Heb 9:7 priest alone enters once a *y*
9:25, 25 from *y* to *y* with blood
10:1, 1 sacrifices from *y* to *y*
10:3, 3 of sins from *y* to *y*
Jas 4:13 will spend a *y* there, and we
Re 9:15 hour and day and month and *y*

Yearly
1Sa 1:21 to Jehovah the *y* sacrifice
2:19 to sacrifice the *y* sacrifice
20:6 *y* sacrifice there for all
1Ki 10:25 as a *y* matter of course
2Ch 9:24 as a *y* matter of course
Ne 10:32 a third of a shekel *y* for the

Yearned
Ps 84:2 soul has *y* and also pined

Yearning
Ge 31:30 *y* intensely for the house of
De 28:32 your eyes looking on and *y*
Job 14:15 you will have a *y*
Php 1:8 *y* for all of you in such
1Th 3:6 *y* to see us in the same way

Yearns
Ps 17:12 lion that *y* to tear to pieces

Year-old
Nu 28:3 two sound *y* male lambs a day
28:9 two sound *y* male lambs and

Year's
1Ch 20:1 at the time of the *y* return

Years
Ge 1:14 seasons and for days and *y*
5:3 for a hundred and thirty *y*
5:4 came to be eight hundred *y*
5:5 Adam . . . hundred and thirty *y*
5:6 Seth . . . a hundred and five *y*
5:7 Seth . . . hundred and seven *y*
5:8 Seth . . . hundred and twelve *y*
5:9 Enosh lived on for ninety *y*
5:10 eight hundred and fifteen *y*
5:11 to nine hundred and five *y*
5:12 Kenan lived on for seventy *y*
5:13 eight hundred and forty *y*
5:14 nine hundred and ten *y* and he
5:15 Mahalalel . . . sixty-five *y*
5:16 eight hundred and thirty *y*
5:17 hundred and ninety-five *y*
5:18 a hundred and sixty-two *y*
5:19 to live eight hundred *y*
5:20 nine hundred and sixty-two *y*

Ge 5:21 Enoch lived . . . sixty-five *y*
5:22 Enoch . . . three hundred *y*
5:23 three hundred and sixty-five *y*
5:25 a hundred and eighty-seven *y*
5:26 seven hundred and eighty-two *y*
5:27 nine hundred and sixty-nine *y*
5:28 a hundred and eighty-two *y*
5:30 five hundred and ninety-five *y*
5:31 seventy-seven *y* and he died
5:32 Noah . . . five hundred *y* old
6:3 to a hundred and twenty *y*
7:6 Noah was six hundred *y* old
9:28 live three hundred and fifty *y*
9:29 nine hundred and fifty *y* and
11:10 Shem was a hundred *y* old
11:10 two *y* after the deluge
11:11 Shem . . . five hundred *y*
11:12 Arpachshad . . . thirty-five *y*
11:13 live four hundred and three *y*
11:14 And Shelah lived thirty *y*
11:15 four hundred and three *y*
11:16 lived on for thirty-four *y*
11:17 four hundred and thirty *y*
11:18 Peleg lived on for thirty *y*
11:19 live two hundred and nine *y*
11:20 lived on for thirty-two *y*
11:21 live two hundred and seven *y*
11:22 Serug lived on for thirty *y*
11:23 to live two hundred *y*
11:24 lived on for twenty-nine *y*
11:25 live a hundred and nineteen *y*
11:26 Terah lived on for seventy *y*
11:32 to be two hundred and five *y*
12:4 Abram was seventy-five *y* old
14:4 Twelve *y* they had served
15:13 afflict . . . four hundred *y*
16:3 end of ten *y* of Abram's
16:16 Abram was eighty-six *y* old
17:1 Abram got to be ninety-nine *y*
17:17 Will a man a hundred *y* old
17:17 woman ninety *y* old give
17:24 Abraham was ninety-nine *y*
17:25 his son was thirteen *y* old
18:11 old, being advanced in *y*
21:5 Abraham was a hundred *y* old
23:1 a hundred and twenty-seven *y*
23:1 were the *y* of Sarah's life
24:1 was old, advanced in *y*; and
25:7 *y* of Abraham's life which he
25:7 a hundred and seventy-five *y*
25:17 the *y* of Ishmael's life, a
25:17 a hundred and thirty-seven *y*
25:20 Isaac happened to be forty *y*
25:26 Isaac was sixty *y* old at her
26:34 Esau grew to be forty *y* old
29:18 serve you seven *y* for Rachel
29:20 serve seven *y* for Rachel
29:27 serve with me for seven *y*
29:30 for yet seven *y* more
31:38 twenty *y* I have been with
31:41 twenty *y* for me in your
31:41 I have served you fourteen *y*
31:41 and six *y* for your flock
35:28 to be a hundred and eighty *y*
37:2 Joseph, when seventeen *y* old
41:1 at the end of two full *y*
41:26 seven good cows are seven *y*
41:26 ears of grain are seven *y*
41:27 up after them are seven *y*
41:27 to be seven *y* of famine
41:29 seven *y* coming with great
41:30 But seven *y* of famine will
41:34 during the seven *y* of plenty
41:35 foodstuffs of . . . good *y*
41:36 the seven famine *y*, which
41:46 Joseph was thirty *y* old when
41:47 during the seven *y* of plenty
41:48 foodstuffs of the seven *y*
41:53 the seven *y* of the plenty
41:54 seven *y* of the famine
45:6 there are yet five *y* in which
45:11 yet five *y* of famine
47:8 days of the *y* of your life
47:9 the *y* of my alien residences
47:9 a hundred and thirty *y*
47:9 the days of the *y* of my life
47:9 the days of the *y* of the lives
47:28 land of Egypt for seventeen *y*
47:28 Jacob's days, the *y* of his
47:28 a hundred and forty-seven *y*
50:22 lived for a hundred and ten *y*
50:26 age of a hundred and ten *y*
Ex 6:16 the *y* of Levi's life were a
6:16 a hundred and thirty-seven *y*

Nu 28:11 two *y* bulls and one ram
28:19 two *y* bulls and one ram and
28:27 two *y* bulls, one ram, seven
29:2 render . . . *y* bull, one ram
29:8 one *y* bull, one ram, seven
29:13 thirteen *y* bulls, two rams
29:17 second day twelve *y* bulls
De 7:13 the *y* of your cows and the
21:3 take a *y* cow of the herd that
21:4 lead the *y* cow down to a
21:4 break the neck of the *y* cow
21:6 the *y* cow, the neck of which
22:6 with *y* ones or eggs, and the
22:6 sitting upon the *y* ones or
28:4 the *y* of your cattle and the
28:18 the *y* of your cattle and the
28:50 show favor to a *y* man
28:51 no *y* of your cattle or
32:25 Of both *y* man and virgin
Jos 6:21 from *y* man to old man and
6:23 the *y* men who had done the
Jg 6:25 Take the *y* bull, the bull that
6:25 second *y* bull of seven years
6:26 the second *y* bull and offer it
6:28 second *y* bull had been offered
8:14 captured a *y* man of the men
8:20 the *y* man did not draw his
8:20 for he was yet a *y* man
14:5 a maned *y* lion roaring upon
14:10 the way the *y* fellows used
14:18 not plowed with my *y* cow
17:7 a *y* man of Bethlehem in Judah
17:11 the *y* man got to be as one
17:12 the *y* man might serve as a
18:3 the *y* man, the Levite
18:15 the house of the *y* man, the
19:3 father of the *y* woman got to
19:4 *y* woman's father, took hold
19:5 father of the *y* woman said to
19:6 father of the *y* woman said to
19:8 father of the *y* woman then
19:9 *y* woman's father, said to him
Ru 2:5 Boaz said to the *y* man who
2:5 whom does this *y* woman belong
2:6 *y* man set over the harvesters
2:6 The *y* woman is a Moabitess
2:8 keep close by my *y* women
2:9 the *y* men not to touch you
2:9 what the *y* men will draw
2:15 Boaz now commanded his *y* men
2:21 Close by the *y* people that are
2:22 go out with his *y* women
2:23 close by the *y* women of Boaz
3:2 Boaz, with whose *y* women you
3:10 not going after the *y* fellows
4:12 give you out of this *y* woman
1Sa 6:7 their *y* ones go back home
6:10 *y* ones they shut up at home
9:2 was Saul, *y* and handsome
16:2 *y* cow of the herd you should
16:12 he was ruddy, a *y* man with
20:35 a *y* attendant was with him
21:2 appointment with the *y* men
21:4 *y* men have at least kept
21:5 organisms of the *y* men
25:5 David sent ten *y* men and
25:5 David said to the *y* men
25:8 Ask your own *y* men, and they
25:8 my *y* men may find favor in
25:9 David's *y* men came and spoke
25:12 David's *y* men turned around
25:14 one of the *y* men reported
25:19 said to her *y* men: Pass on
25:25 see my lord's *y* men that
25:27 given to the *y* men that are
26:22 one of the *y* men come on
30:17 four hundred *y* men that
2Sa 1:5 David said to the *y* man that
1:6 *y* man that was telling him
1:13 David now said to the *y* man
1:15 called one of the *y* men
2:14 Let the *y* men rise up
2:21 seize one of the *y* men as
4:12 David commanded the *y* men
9:12 Mephibosheth had a *y* son
13:32 it is all the *y* men the
13:34 *y* man, the watchman
14:21 bring the *y* man Absalom
16:2 fruit are for the *y* men to
17:18 a *y* man got to see them and
18:5 with the *y* man Absalom
18:12 the *y* man, over Absalom
18:29 with the *y* man Absalom
18:32 with the *y* man Absalom

2Sa 18:32 become as the *y* man
20:11 one of Joab's *y* men stood
1Ki 11:17 while Hadad was a *y* boy
11:28 *y* man was a hard worker
12:8 take counsel with the *y* men
12:10 *y* men that had grown up
12:14 to the counsel of the *y* men
18:23 give us two *y* bulls, and
18:23 one *y* bull and cut it in
18:23 shall dress the other *y* bull
18:25 one *y* bull and dress it
18:26 they took the *y* bull that
18:33 and cut the *y* bull in pieces
20:14 the *y* men of the princes of
20:15 the count of the *y* men of
20:17 the *y* men of the princes of
20:19 the *y* men of the princes of
2Ki 5:22 have come to me two *y* men
1Ch 12:28 Zadok a *y* man, mighty in
15:26 to sacrifice seven *y* bulls
22:5 Solomon my son is *y* and
29:1 Solomon my son . . . is *y* and
29:21 a thousand *y* bulls, a
2Ch 10:8 take counsel with the *y* men
10:10 *y* men that had grown up
10:14 counsel of the *y* men
13:7 *y* and fainthearted, and he
13:9 power by means of a *y* bull
36:17 kill their *y* men with the
36:17 feel compassion for *y* man
Ezr 6:9 *y* bulls as well as rams and
Ne 4:16 *y* men were active in the
Es 2:2 seek *y* women, virgins
2:3 *y* women, virgins, beautiful in
2:4 *y* woman who seems pleasing in
2:7 *y* woman was pretty in form
2:8 many *y* women were collected
2:9 the *y* woman was pleasing in
2:9 seven selected *y* women from
2:9 transfer her and her *y* women
2:12 turn of each *y* woman arrived
2:13 *y* woman herself came in to
3:13 *y* man as well as old man
4:4 And Esther's *y* women and her
4:16 my *y* women, I shall fast
Job 1:19 it fell upon the *y* people and
4:10 and the voice of a *y* lion
4:10 teeth of maned *y* lions do
10:16 like a *y* lion you will hunt
16:11 God hands me over to *y* boys
19:18 *y* boys . . . have rejected me
21:11 sending out their *y* boys
28:8 The *y* lion has not paced over
31:20 the shorn wool of my *y* rams
32:6 Y I am in days And you men
38:39 lively appetite of *y* lions
38:41 *y* ones cry to God for help
39:3 cast forth their *y* ones
39:30 its *y* ones themselves keep
41:5 tie it for your *y* girls
Ps 17:12 a *y* lion sitting in concealed
22:12 *y* bulls have surrounded me
34:10 The maned *y* lions themselves
35:17 from the maned *y* lions
37:25 A *y* man I used to be, I have
58:6 jawbones of maned *y* lions
69:31 a *y* bull displaying horns
78:31 *y* men of Israel he made
78:63 His *y* men a fire ate up
84:3 Where she has put her *y* ones
91:13 Upon the *y* lion and the cobra
91:13 trample . . . the maned *y* lion
104:21 maned *y* lions are roaring
110:3 *y* men just like dewdrops
119:9 a *y* man cleanse his path
147:9 *y* ravens that keep calling
148:12 *y* men and also you virgins
Pr 1:4 to a *y* man knowledge and
7:7 a *y* man in want of heart
19:12 like that of a maned *y* lion
20:2 like that of a maned *y* lion
20:29 The beauty of *y* men is their
26:13 There is a *y* lion in the way
27:26 *y* rams are for your clothing
28:1 righteous are like a *y* lion
31:15 portion to her *y* women
Ec 11:9 Rejoice, *y* man, in your youth
11:9 in the days of your *y* manhood
12:1 in the days of your *y* manhood
Ca 2:9 gazelle or the *y* of the stags
2:17 like the *y* of the stags upon
4:2 having lost its *y* ones
4:5 breasts are like two *y* ones
6:6 having lost its *y* ones

Ca 7:3 breasts are like two *y* ones
8:14 like a *y* one of the stags upon
Isa 1:11 blood of *y* bulls and male
5:29 they roar like maned *y* lions
7:21 *y* cow of the herd and two
9:17 even over their *y* men
11:6 calf and the maned *y* lion
11:7 their *y* ones will lie down
13:18 bows will dash even *y* men
23:4 brought up *y* men, raised up
31:4 even the maned *y* lion, over
31:8 *y* men will come to be for
34:6 blood of *y* rams and he-goats
34:7 *y* bulls with the powerful
40:30 *y* men themselves will
60:6 *y* male camels of Midian and
62:5 *y* man takes ownership of a
Jer 2:15 maned *y* lions roar
2:23 A swift *y* she-camel
6:11 the intimate group of *y* men
9:21 the *y* men from the public
11:22 The *y* men themselves will
15:8 *y* man, the despoiler at
18:21 *y* men those struck down
25:38 just like a maned *y* lion
31:12 *y* ones of the flock and the
31:13 dance, also the *y* men and
48:15 choicest *y* men themselves
49:26 *y* men will fall in her
50:27 Massacre all her *y* bulls
50:30 *y* men will fall in her
51:3 compassion for her *y* men
51:22 dash *y* man and virgin to
51:38 just like maned *y* lions
La 1:15 to break my *y* men to pieces
1:18 my own *y* men have gone into
2:21 My virgins and my *y* men
5:13 *y* men have lifted up a hand
5:14 *y* men from their . . . music
Eze 9:6 Old man, *y* man and virgin and
17:4 the very top of its *y* shoots
19:2 down in among maned *y* lions
19:3 A maned *y* lion is what he
19:5 As a maned *y* lion she put
19:6 A maned *y* lion is what he
23:6 desirable *y* men all of them
23:12 desirable *y* men all of them
23:23 desirable *y* men, governors
30:17 *y* men of On and Pibeseth
32:2 As a maned *y* lion of nations
38:13 all its maned *y* lions
39:18 rams, *y* male sheep, and
39:18 sheep, and he-goats, *y* bulls
41:19 face of a maned *y* lion
43:19 *y* bull, the son of the herd
43:21 *y* bull, the sin offering
43:22 from sin with the *y* bull
43:23 bring near a *y* bull, the
43:25 *y* bull, the son of the herd
45:18 should take a *y* bull
45:22 *y* bull as a sin offering
45:23 to Jehovah seven *y* bulls
45:24 ephah for the *y* bull and
46:6 *y* bull, the son of the herd
46:7 ephah for the *y* bull and
46:11 ephah for the *y* bull and an
Ho 4:16 like a *y* ram in a roomy place
5:14 be like a *y* lion to Ephraim
5:14 like a maned *y* lion to the
13:7 become to them like a *y* lion
14:2 the *y* bulls of our lips
Joe 2:28 *y* men, visions they will see
Am 2:11 your *y* men as Nazirites
3:4 a *y* maned lion give forth
4:10 I killed your *y* men, along
6:4 *y* bulls from among fattened
8:13 *y* men, because of the thirst
Mic 5:8 *y* lion among droves of sheep
Na 2:11 belongs to the maned *y* lions
2:13 devour your own maned *y* lions
Zec 2:4 Run, speak to the *y* man over
9:17 will make the *y* men thrive
11:3 The roaring of maned *y* lions
11:16 The *y* one he will not seek
Mt 2:8 careful search for the *y* child
2:9 above where the *y* child was
2:11 the *y* child with Mary its
2:13 take the *y* child and its
2:13 for the *y* child to destroy it
2:14 took along the *y* child and
2:20 the *y* child and its mother
2:20 the soul of the *y* child
2:21 the *y* child and its mother
10:35 and a *y* wife against her

Mt 11:16 like *y* children sitting in
14:21 women and *y* children
15:38 women and *y* children
18:2 calling a *y* child to him, he
18:3 and become as *y* children, you
18:4 like this *y* child is the one
18:5 receives one such *y* child on
19:13 *y* children were brought to
19:14 Let the *y* children alone
19:20 *y* man said to him: I have
19:22 the *y* man heard this saying
24:32 as its *y* branch grows tender
Mr 5:39 *y* child has not died, but is
5:40 *y* child's father and mother
5:40 in where the *y* child was
5:41 the hand of the *y* child, he
7:30 found the *y* child laid on the
9:24 the father of the *y* child was
9:36 he took a *y* child, stood it
9:37 one of such *y* children on
10:13 *y* children for him to touch
10:14 Let the *y* children come to
10:15 like a *y* child will by no
13:28 *y* branch grows tender and
14:51 *y* man wearing a fine linen
16:5 they saw a *y* man sitting on
Lu 1:59 to circumcise the *y* child
1:66 What . . . will this *y* child be?
1:76 *y* child, you will be called a
1:80 the *y* child went on growing
2:17 concerning this *y* child
2:24 turtledoves or two *y* pigeons
2:27 brought the *y* child Jesus in
2:40 the *y* child continued growing
7:14 *Y* man, I say to you, Get up!
7:32 like *y* children sitting in a
9:47 took a *y* child, set it beside
9:48 Whoever receives this *y* child
11:7 my *y* children are with me in
15:23 bring the fattened *y* bull
15:27 the fattened *y* bull
15:30 slaughtered . . . *y* bull
18:16 Let the *y* children come to
18:17 like a *y* child will by no
Joh 4:49 before my *y* child dies
12:14 Jesus had found a *y* ass, he
16:21 brought forth the *y* child
21:5 *Y* children, you do not have
Ac 2:17 *y* men will see visions and
5:10 *y* men came in they found her
7:58 feet of a *y* man called Saul
20:9 *y* man named Eutychus fell
23:17 Lead this *y* man off to the
23:18 to lead this *y* man to you
23:22 commander let the *y* man go
1Co 14:20 do not become *y* children in
Tit 2:4 the *y* women to their senses
Heb 2:13 Look! I and the *y* children
2:14 *y* children are sharers of
9:12 blood of goats and of *y* bulls
9:19 blood of the *y* bulls and of
11:23 *y* child was beautiful and
1Jo 2:13 I am writing you, *y* men
2:13 I write you, *y* children
2:14 I write you, *y* men, because
2:18 *Y* children, it is the last
Re 4:7 creature is like a *y* bull

Younger
Ge 19:31 to the *y* woman: Our father
19:34 to the *y*: Here I lay down
19:35 *y* got up and lay down with
19:38 *y*, she too gave birth to a
25:23 the older will serve the *y*
27:15 put them on Jacob her *y* son
27:42 called Jacob her *y* son and
29:16 the name of the *y* Rachel
29:18 Rachel your *y* daughter
29:26 to give the *y* woman before
48:14 although he was the *y*, and
48:19 his *y* brother will become
Jg 1:13 Caleb's *y* brother, got to
3:9 Kenaz, the *y* brother of Caleb
15:2 Is not her *y* sister better
1Sa 14:49 name of the *y* one Michal
1Ch 24:31 exactly as his *y* brother
Job 30:1 Those *y* in days than I am
Eze 16:46 your sister *y* than you, who
16:61 well as the ones *y* than you
Lu 15:12 *y* of them said to his father
15:13 *y* son gathered all things
Joh 21:18 When you were *y*, you used
Ac 5:6 *y* men rose, wrapped him in
Ro 9:12 will be the slave of the *y*

1Ti 5:1 *y* men as brothers
5:2 *y* women as sisters with all
5:11 turn down *y* widows, for
5:14 the *y* widows to marry
Tit 2:6 the *y* men to be sound in mind
1Pe 5:5 you *y* men, be in subjection

Youngest
Ge 9:24 his *y* son had done to him
42:13 the *y* is with our father
42:15 your *y* brother comes here
42:20 bring your *y* brother to me
42:32 *y* is today with our father
42:34 bring your *y* brother to me
43:29 Is this your brother, the *y*
43:33 *y* according to his youngness
44:2 the mouth of the bag of the *y*
44:12 and finished with the *y*
44:20 child of his old age, the *y*
44:23 Unless your *y* brother comes
44:26 If our *y* brother is with us
44:26 our *y* brother is not with us
Jos 6:26 at the forfeit of his *y* let
Jg 9:5 Jotham the *y* son of Jerubbaal
1Sa 16:11 The *y* one has till now been
17:14 David was the *y*, and the
1Ki 16:34 the forfeit of Segub his *y*
2Ch 21:17 but Jehoahaz, his *y* son
22:1 Ahaziah his *y* son king in
Lu 22:26 become as the *y*, and the

Youngness
Ge 43:33 youngest according to his *y*

Youth
Ge 8:21 man is bad from his *y* up
46:34 stock raisers from our *y*
Le 22:13 as in her *y*, she may eat
Nu 30:3 house of her father in her *y*
30:16 his daughter in her *y* in the
1Sa 12:2 walked before you from my *y*
2Sa 19:7 from your *y* until now
1Ki 18:12 feared Jehovah from his *y*
Job 13:26 of the errors of my *y*
31:18 from my *y* he grew up with
33:25 become fresher than in *y*
36:14 Their soul will die in *y*
Ps 25:7 sins of my *y* and my revolts
71:5 my confidence from my *y*
71:17 have taught me from my *y* on
89:45 shortened the days of his *y*
103:5 *y* keeps renewing itself just
127:4 So are the sons of *y*
129:1 hostility to me from my *y*
129:2 hostility to me from my *y*
144:12 plants grown up in their *y*
Pr 2:17 confidential friend of her *y*
5:18 with the wife of your *y*
29:21 one's servant from *y* on, in
Ec 11:9 Rejoice, young man, in your *y*
11:10 *y* and the prime of life are
Isa 47:12 you have toiled from your *y*
47:15 your charmers from your *y*
54:4 the shame of your time of *y*
54:6 a wife of the time of *y* who
Jer 2:2 the loving-kindness of your *y*
3:4 confidential friend of my *y*
3:24 our forefathers from our *y*
3:25 from our *y* on and down to
22:21 your way since your *y*
31:19 the reproach of my *y*
32:30 from their *y* on up
48:11 at ease since their *y*, and
La 3:27 carry the yoke during his *y*
Eze 4:14 have I eaten from my *y* up
16:22 the days of your *y* when you
16:43 remember the days of your *y*
16:60 in the days of your *y*, and I
23:3 In their *y* they committed
23:8 they had lain down in her *y*
23:19 days of her *y*, when she
23:21 the loose conduct of your *y*
23:21 of the breasts of your *y*
Ho 2:15 as in the days of her *y* and
Joe 1:8 over the owner of her *y*
Zec 13:5 acquired me from my *y* on
Mal 2:14 you and the wife of your *y*
2:15 and with the wife of your *y*
Mr 10:20 I have kept from my *y* on
Lu 18:21 these I have kept from *y* on
Ac 26:4 manner of life from *y* up
1Co 7:36 that is past the bloom of *y*
1Ti 4:12 ever look down on your *y*
2Ti 2:22 the desires incidental to *y*

Youthful
Job 20:11 been full of his *y* vigor
33:25 the days of his *y* vigor

Zaanan
Mic 1:11 The inhabitress of *Z* has not

Zaanannim
Jos 19:33 from the big tree in *Z*
Jg 4:11 near the big tree in *Z*

Zaavan
Ge 36:27 sons of Ezer: Bilhan and *Z*
1Ch 1:42 The sons of Ezer were . . . *Z*

Zabad
1Ch 2:36 in turn, became father to *Z*
2:37 *Z*, in turn, became father to
7:21 *Z* his son and Shuthelah his
11:41 *Z* the son of Ahlai
2Ch 24:26 *Z* the son of Shimeath the
Ezr 10:27 the sons of Zattu . . . *Z*
10:33 the sons of Hashum . . . *Z*
10:43 the sons of Nebo . . . *Z*

Zabbai
Ezr 10:28 the sons of Bebai . . . *Z*
Ne 3:20 Baruch the son of *Z* worked

Zabbud
Ezr 8:14 sons of Bigvai, Uthai and *Z*

Zabdi
Jos 7:1 *Z*, the son of Zerah, of the
7:17 and *Z* got to be picked
7:18 *Z*, the son of Zerah, of the
1Ch 8:19 and Jakim and Zichri and *Z*
27:27 there was *Z* the Shiphmite
Ne 11:17 *Z* the son of Asaph, the

Zabdiel
1Ch 27:2 was Jashobeam the son of *Z*
Ne 11:14 *Z* the son of the great ones

Zabud
1Ki 4:5 *Z* the son of Nathan was a

Zaccai
Ezr 2:9 sons of *Z*, seven hundred and
Ne 7:14 sons of *Z*, seven hundred and

Zacchaeus
Lu 19:2 man called by the name *Z*
19:5 *Z*, hurry and get down, for
19:8 *Z* stood up and said to the

Zaccur
Nu 13:4 Shammua the son of *Z*
1Ch 4:26 sons of Mishma . . . *Z*
24:27 Of Jaaziah . . . *Z* and Ibri
25:2 Of the sons of Asaph, *Z* and
25:10 the third for *Z*, his sons
Ne 3:2 *Z* the son of Imri did building
10:12 *Z*, Sherebiah, Shebaniah
12:35 *Z* the son of Asaph
13:13 *Z* the son of Mattaniah

Zadok
2Sa 8:17 *Z* the son of Ahitub and
15:24 *Z* and with him all the
15:25 But the king said to *Z*
15:27 to say to *Z* the priest
15:29 *Z* and Abiathar took the ark
15:35 *Z* and Abiathar the priests
15:35 tell to *Z* and Abiathar the
15:36 Ahimaaz belonging to *Z* and
17:15 Hushai said to *Z* and
18:19 Ahimaaz the son of *Z*, he
18:22 Ahimaaz the son of *Z* now
18:27 Ahimaaz the son of *Z*
19:11 he sent to *Z* and Abiathar
20:25 *Z* and Abiathar were priests
1Ki 1:8 *Z* the priest and Benaiah the
1:26 *Z* the priest and Benaiah the
1:32 call for me *Z* the priest and
1:34 *Z* the priest and Nathan the
1:38 *Z* the priest and Nathan the
1:39 *Z* the priest now took the
1:44 sent with him *Z* the priest
1:45 *Z* the priest and Nathan the
2:35 *Z* the priest the king put in
4:2 Azariah the son of *Z*, the
4:4 *Z* and Abiathar were priests
2Ki 15:33 Jerusha the daughter of *Z*
1Ch 6:8 Ahitub . . . became father to *Z*
6:8 *Z* . . . father to Ahimaaz
6:12 Ahitub . . . father to *Z*
6:12 *Z* . . . father to Shallum
6:53 *Z* his son, Ahimaaz his son
9:11 *Z* the son of Meraioth the

2Sa 21:17 Abishai the son of *Z* came
23:18 Joab the son of *Z*, he was
23:37 of Joab the son of *Z*
1Ki 1:7 Joab the son of *Z* and with
2:5 what Joab the son of *Z* did
2:22 and for Joab the son of *Z*
1Ch 2:16 sisters were *Z* and Abigail
2:16 sons of *Z* were Abishai and
11:6 Joab the son of *Z* got to go
11:39 of Joab the son of *Z*
18:12 As for Abishai the son of *Z*
18:15 Joab the son of *Z* was over
26:28 Joab the son of *Z* had made
27:24 Joab the son of *Z* had

Zetham
1Ch 23:8 sons of Ladan . . . *Z* and Joel
26:22 sons of Jehieli, *Z* and Joel

Zethan
1Ch 7:10 sons of Bilhan were . . . *Z*

Zethar
Es 1:10 *Z* and Carkas, the seven court

Zeus
Ac 14:12 they went calling Barnabas *Z*
14:13 priest of *Z*, whose temple
28:11 the figurehead Sons of *Z*

Zia
1Ch 5:13 Jacan and *Z* and Eber, seven

Ziba
2Sa 9:2 servant whose name was *Z*
9:2 Are you *Z?* to which he said
9:3 *Z* said to the king: There is
9:4 *Z* said to the king: Look! He
9:9 called *Z*, Saul's attendant
9:10 *Z* had fifteen sons and twenty
9:11 *Z* said to the king: In accord
9:12 dwelling in the house of *Z*
16:1 there was *Z* the attendant of
16:2 Then the king said to *Z*
16:2 *Z* said: The asses are for the
16:3 At this *Z* said to the king
16:4 The king then said to *Z*
16:4 *Z* said: I do bow down
19:17 *Z* the attendant of the house
19:29 *Z* should share in the field

Zibeon
Ge 36:2 granddaughter of *Z* the Hivite
36:14 Anah, the granddaughter of *Z*
36:20 sons of Seir . . . *Z* and Anah
36:24 sons of *Z:* Aiah and Anah
36:24 tending the asses for *Z* his
36:29 sheiks of the Horite . . . *Z*
1Ch 1:38 sons of Seir were . . . *Z*
1:40 sons of *Z* were Aiah and Anah

Zibia
1Ch 8:9 father to Jobab and *Z* and

Zibiah
2Ki 12:1 name was *Z* from Beer-sheba
2Ch 24:1 mother's name was *Z* from

Zichri
Ex 6:21 the sons of Izhar were . . . *Z*
1Ch 8:19 and Jakim and *Z* and Zabdi
8:23 and Abdon and *Z* and Hanan
8:27 and *Z*, the sons of Jeroham
9:15 the son of *Z* the son of Asaph
26:25 *Z* his son and Shelomoth his
27:16 Eliezer the son of *Z* was
2Ch 17:16 Amasiah the son of *Z* the
23:1 Elishaphat the son of *Z*
28:7 *Z*, a mighty man of Ephraim
Ne 11:9 and Joel the son of *Z*
12:17 for Abijah, *Z;* for Miniamin

Ziddim
Jos 19:35 fortified cities were *Z*

Zigzag
Ps 60:4 flee *z* on account of the bow

Ziha
Ezr 2:43 The Nethinim: The sons of *Z*
Ne 7:46 The Nethinim: The sons of *Z*
11:21 *Z* and Gishpa were over the

Ziklag
Jos 15:31 *Z* and Madmannah and
19:5 and *Z* and Beth-marcaboth
1Sa 27:6 Achish gave him *Z* on that
27:6 *Z* has come to belong to the
30:1 coming to *Z* on the third day
30:1 raid on the south and on *Z*
30:1 strike *Z* and burn it with
1Sa 30:14 and *Z* we burned with fire
30:26 When David came to *Z* he
2Sa 1:1 to dwell at *Z* two days
4:10 killed him in *Z* when it
1Ch 4:30 and in Hormah and in *Z*
12:1 that came to David at *Z*
12:20 When he came to *Z* there
Ne 11:28 in *Z* and in Meconah and its

Zillah
Ge 4:19 the name of the second was *Z*
4:22 *Z*, she too gave birth to
4:23 for his wives Adah and *Z*

Zillethai
1Ch 8:20 and Elienai and *Z* and Eliel
12:20 from Manasseh . . . *Z*

Zilpah
Ge 29:24 Laban gave to her *Z* his
30:9 she proceeded to take *Z* her
30:10 *Z*, Leah's maidservant, bore
30:12 *Z*, Leah's maidservant, bore
35:26 by *Z*, Leah's maidservant
37:2 and the sons of *Z*, the
46:18 These are the sons of *Z*

Zimmah
1Ch 6:20 Jahath his son, *Z* his son
6:42 son of *Z*, the son of Shimei
2Ch 29:12 Joah the son of *Z* and Eden

Zimran
Ge 25:2 she bore him *Z* and Jokshan
1Ch 1:32 she gave birth to *Z* and

Zimri
Nu 25:14 with the Midianitess was *Z*
1Ki 16:9 *Z* the chief of half the
16:10 *Z* proceeded to come in and
16:12 *Z* annihilated the whole
16:15 *Z* became king for seven
16:16 *Z* has conspired and also
16:18 *Z* saw that the city had
16:20 *Z* and his conspiracy with
2Ki 9:31 Did it go all right with *Z*
1Ch 2:6 the sons of Zerah were *Z* and
8:36 Alemeth and Azmaveth and *Z*
8:36 *Z* . . . became father to Moza
9:42 Alemeth and Azmaveth and *Z*
9:42 *Z* . . . became father to Moza
Jer 25:25 all the kings of *Z* and all

Zin
Nu 13:21 from the wilderness of *Z* to
20:1 come into the wilderness of *Z*
27:14 in the wilderness of *Z* at
27:14 in the wilderness of *Z*
33:36 in the wilderness of *Z*
34:3 the wilderness of *Z* alongside
34:4 and cross over to *Z*, and its
De 32:51 in the wilderness of *Z;* for
Jos 15:1 the wilderness of *Z*, to the
15:3 to *Z* and went up from the

Zina
1Ch 23:10 of Shimei were Jahath, *Z*

Zion
2Sa 5:7 capture the stronghold of *Z*
1Ki 8:1 city of David . . . *Z*
2Ki 19:21 virgin daughter of *Z* has
19:31 who escape from Mount *Z*
1Ch 11:5 capture the stronghold of *Z*
2Ch 5:2 of David, that is to say, *Z*
Ps 2:6 Upon *Z*, my holy mountain
9:11 Jehovah, who is dwelling in *Z*
9:14 the gates of the daughter of *Z*
14:7 O that out of *Z* there were
20:2 sustain you out of *Z* itself
48:2 Mount *Z* on the remote sides
48:11 May Mount *Z* rejoice, May
48:12 March around *Z*, you people
50:2 Out of *Z*, the perfection of
51:18 do deal well with *Z*
53:6 out of *Z* there were the grand
65:1 praise—silence—, O God, in *Z*
69:35 For God himself will save *Z*
74:2 Mount *Z* in which you have
76:2 And his dwelling place in *Z*
78:68 Mount *Z*, which he loved
84:7 Each one appears to God in *Z*
87:2 in love with the gates of *Z*
87:5 respecting *Z* it will be said
97:8 *Z* heard and began to rejoice
99:2 Jehovah is great in *Z*
102:13 you will have mercy on *Z*
102:16 will certainly build up *Z*
Ps 102:21 Jehovah to be declared in *Z*
110:2 Jehovah will send out of *Z*
125:1 like Mount *Z*, which cannot
126:1 back the captive ones of *Z*
128:5 will bless you out of *Z*
129:5 All those hating *Z*
132:13 For Jehovah has chosen *Z*
133:3 upon the mountains of *Z*
134:3 Jehovah bless you out of *Z*
135:21 Blessed out of *Z* be Jehovah
137:1 wept when we remembered *Z*
137:3 for us one of the songs of *Z*
146:10 Your God, O *Z*, for
147:12 Praise your God, O *Z*
149:2 *Z*—let them be joyful in
Ca 3:11 and look, O you daughters of *Z*
Isa 1:8 daughter of *Z* has been left
1:27 *Z* herself will be redeemed
2:3 out of *Z* law will go forth
3:16 of *Z* have become haughty
3:17 head of the daughters of *Z*
4:3 ones remaining in *Z* and the
4:4 of the daughters of *Z* and
4:5 established place of Mount *Z*
8:18 who is residing in Mount *Z*
10:12 his work in Mount *Z* and in
10:24 who are dwelling in *Z*
10:32 of the daughter of *Z*, the
12:6 inhabitress of *Z*, for great
14:32 laid the foundation of *Z*
16:1 of the daughter of *Z*
18:7 Jehovah of armies, Mount *Z*
24:23 king in Mount *Z* and
28:16 foundation in *Z* a stone
29:8 waging war against Mount *Z*
30:19 *Z* will dwell in Jerusalem
31:4 wage war over Mount *Z* and
31:9 Jehovah, whose light is in *Z*
33:5 fill *Z* with justice and
33:14 In *Z* the sinners have come
33:20 *Z*, the town of our festal
34:8 for the legal case over *Z*
35:10 come to *Z* with a joyful cry
37:22 *Z* has despised you, she has
37:32 who escape out of Mount *Z*
40:9 bringing good news for *Z*
41:27 is one first, saying to *Z*
46:13 will give in *Z* salvation
49:14 *Z* kept saying: Jehovah has
51:3 will certainly comfort *Z*
51:11 come to *Z* with a joyful
51:16 say to *Z*, You are my people
52:1 put on your strength, O *Z*
52:2 O captive daughter of *Z*
52:7 one saying to *Z:* Your God
52:8 when Jehovah gathers back *Z*
59:20 to *Z* the Repurchaser will
60:14 *Z* of the Holy One of Israel
61:3 to those mourning over *Z*
62:1 For the sake of *Z* I shall not
62:11 to the daughter of *Z*, Look!
64:10 *Z* itself has become a sheer
66:8 *Z* has come into labor pains
Jer 3:14 and I will bring you to *Z*
4:6 Raise a signal toward *Z*
4:31 voice of the daughter of *Z*
6:2 The daughter of *Z* has
6:23 against you, O daughter of *Z*
8:19 Is Jehovah not in *Z?* Or is
9:19 what has been heard from *Z*
14:19 your soul abhorred even *Z*
26:18 *Z* herself will be plowed
30:17 *Z*, for whom no one is
31:6 and let us go up to *Z*, to
31:12 joyfully on the height of *Z*
50:5 To *Z* they will keep asking
50:28 in *Z* the vengeance of
51:10 recount in *Z* the work of
51:24 in *Z* before the eyes of you
51:35 inhabitress of *Z* will say
La 1:4 The ways of *Z* are mourning
1:6 from the daughter of *Z* there
1:17 *Z* has spread out her hands
2:1 beclouds the daughter of *Z*
2:4 the tent of the daughter of *Z*
2:6 forgotten in *Z* festival and
2:8 wall of the daughter of *Z* to
2:10 men of the daughter of *Z* sit
2:13 O virgin daughter of *Z*
2:18 O wall of the daughter of *Z*
4:2 As for the precious sons of *Z*
4:11 he sets a fire ablaze in *Z*
4:22 Your error, O daughter of *Z*
5:11 wives in *Z* they have humbled

Joe 2:1 Blow a horn in Z, O men
2:15 Blow a horn in Z, O men
2:23 Z, be joyful and rejoice in
2:32 in Mount Z and in Jerusalem
3:16 out of Z Jehovah himself
3:17 in Z my holy mountain
3:21 Jehovah will be residing in Z
Am 1:2 Jehovah—out of Z he will roar
6:1 those who are at ease in Z
Ob 17 Z is where those escaping will
21 come up onto Mount Z, in order
Mic 1:13 she was to the daughter of Z
3:10 building Z with acts of
3:12 Z will be plowed up as a
4:2 out of Z law will go forth
4:7 as king over them in Mount Z
4:8 mound of the daughter of Z
4:10 burst forth, O daughter of Z
4:11 may our eyes look upon Z
4:13 thresh, O daughter of Z
Zep 3:14 cry out, O daughter of Z
3:16 Do not be afraid, O Z
Zec 1:14 for Z with great jealousy
1:17 feel regrets over Z and yet
2:7 Z! Make your escape, you who
2:10 and rejoice, O daughter of Z
8:2 I will be jealous for Z with
8:3 return to Z and reside in the
9:9 very joyful, O daughter of Z
9:13 I will awaken your sons, O Z
Mt 21:5 Tell the daughter of Z, Look!
Joh 12:15 Have no fear, daughter of Z
Ro 9:33 in Z a stone of stumbling
11:26 deliverer will come out of Z
Heb 12:22 have approached a Mount Z
1Pe 2:6 I am laying in Z a stone
Re 14:1 Lamb . . . upon the Mount Z

Zion's
La 5:18 Z mountain that is desolated

Zior
Jos 15:54 Hebron, and Z

Ziph
Jos 15:24 Z and Telem and Bealoth
15:55 Carmel and Z and Juttah
1Sa 23:14 in the wilderness of Z
23:15 wilderness of Z at Horesh
23:19 men of Z went up to Saul
23:24 went to Z ahead of Saul
26:1 men of Z came to Saul at
26:2 down to the wilderness of Z
26:2 David in the wilderness of Z
1Ch 2:42 Mesha . . . father of Z
4:16 sons of Jehallelel were Z
2Ch 11:8 and Gath and Mareshah and Z

Ziphah
1Ch 4:16 sons of Jehallelel . . . Z

Ziphion
Ge 46:16 sons of Gad were Z and Haggi

Ziphites
Ps 54:*super* Of David. When the Z came

Ziphron
Nu 34:9 the boundary must go out to Z

Zippor
Nu 22:2 Balak the son of Z got to see
22:4 Balak the son of Z was king
Nu 22:10 Balak the son of Z, the king
22:16 Balak the son of Z has said
23:18 give ear to me, O son of Z
Jos 24:9 Balak the son of Z, the king
Jg 11:25 Balak the son of Z, the king

Zipporah
Ex 2:21 gave Z his daughter to Moses
4:25 Z took a flint and cut off her
18:2 took Z, Moses' wife, after

Zither
Da 3:5 horn, the pipe, the z, the
3:7 the z, the triangular harp
3:10 the horn, the pipe, the z
3:15 sound of the . . . pipe, the z

Ziv
1Ki 6:1 Z, that is, the second month
6:37 in the lunar month of Z

Ziz
2Ch 20:16 coming up by the pass of Z

Ziza
1Ch 4:37 and Z the son of Shiphi
2Ch 11:20 Abijah and Attai and Z and

Zizah
1Ch 23:11 the head, and Z the second

Zoan
Nu 13:22 built seven years before Z of
Ps 78:12 of Egypt, the field of Z
78:43 miracles in the field of Z
Isa 19:11 princes of Z are indeed
19:13 princes of Z have acted
30:4 princes have come to be in Z
Eze 30:14 set a fire in Z and

Zoar
Ge 13:10 the land of Egypt as far as Z
14:2 Bela (that is to say, Z)
14:8 Bela (that is to say, Z)
19:22 called the name of the city Z
19:23 land when Lot arrived at Z
19:30 Later Lot went up from Z
19:30 got afraid of dwelling in Z
De 34:3 the palm trees, as far as Z
Isa 15:5 far along as Z and
Jer 48:34 from Z clear to Horonaim

Zobah
1Sa 14:47 and against the kings of Z
2Sa 8:3 king of Z as he was going his
8:5 help Hadadezer the king of Z
8:12 Hadadezer . . . king of Z
10:6 Syrians of Z, twenty thousand
10:8 Syrians of Z and of Rehob
23:36 Igal the son of Nathan of Z
1Ki 11:23 Hadadezer the king of Z
1Ch 18:3 Hadadezer the king of Z at
18:5 help Hadadezer the king of Z
18:9 of Hadadezer the king of Z
19:6 from Aram-maacah and from Z

Zobebah
1Ch 4:8 Z and the families of Aharhel

Zodiac
2Ki 23:5 the constellations of the z

Zohar
Ge 23:8 urge Ephron the son of Z for
Ge 25:9 of Ephron the son of Z the
46:10 sons of Simeon were . . . Z
Ex 6:15 the sons of Simeon . . . Z and

Zoheleth
1Ki 1:9 close by the stone of Z

Zoheth
1Ch 4:20 the sons of Ishi were Z and

Zophah
1Ch 7:35 of Helem his brother were Z
7:36 The sons of Z were Suah and

Zophai
1Ch 6:26 of Elkanah were Z his son

Zophar
Job 2:11 Shuhite and Z the Naamathite
11:1 Z the Naamathite proceeded
20:1 Z the Naamathite proceeded
42:9 Z the Naamathite went and

Zophim
Nu 23:14 took him to the field of Z

Zorah
Jos 15:33 Eshtaol and Z and Ashnah
19:41 inheritance came to be Z
Jg 13:2 man of Z of the family of the
13:25 between Z and Eshtaol
16:31 between Z and Eshtaol in the
18:2 men . . . from Z and Eshtaol
18:8 brothers at Z and Eshtaol
18:11 departed . . . from Z and
2Ch 11:10 Z and Aijalon and Hebron
Ne 11:29 in Z and in Jarmuth

Zorathites
1Ch 2:53 the Z and the Eshtaolites
4:2 were the families of the Z

Zorites
1Ch 2:54 The sons of Salma . . . Z

Zuar
Nu 1:8 Nethanel the son of Z
2:5 Nethanel the son of Z
7:18 day Nethanel the son of Z
7:23 of Nethanel the son of Z
10:15 Nethanel the son of Z

Zuph
1Sa 1:1 son of Tohu, the son of Z
9:5 came into the land of Z
1Ch 6:35 son of Z, the son of Elkanah

Zur
Nu 25:15 Z; he was a head one of the
31:8 kings of Midian . . . Z and Hur
Jos 13:21 Rekem and Z and Hur and
1Ch 8:30 Z and Kish and Baal and
9:36 and Z and Kish and Baal and

Zuriel
Nu 3:35 was Z the son of Abihail

Zurishaddai
Nu 1:6 Shelumiel the son of Z
2:12 Shelumiel the son of Z
7:36 Shelumiel the son of Z
7:41 Shelumiel the son of Z
10:19 Shelumiel the son of Z

Zuzim
Ge 14:5 inflicted defeats on . . . Z in

Enjoy Your Bible Reading

You can add to your enjoyment of Bible reading by obtaining some of these Bible editions published by the Watch Tower Society:

LARGE-PRINT EDITION: To read the Holy Scriptures with greater ease, you may wish to have a copy of the "New World Translation of the Holy Scriptures" with large print. Besides big, easy-to-read print, this edition contains excellent maps, illuminating footnotes and a helpful appendix. Hard black cover with gold-embossed title; 1,376 pages; size: 7 1/2" x 9 1/2" x 1 1/2". English only $5.00

REGULAR EDITION: The regular edition of the "New World Translation of the Holy Scriptures" is bound in green vinyl. It has an appendix; 1,472 pages; size: 7 1/4" x 4 7/8" x 1 1/8". Available in English, Spanish, Portuguese, Italian, Dutch and German $1.00

DELUXE EDITION: The deluxe edition has a flexible cover and gold-edged pages. It has all the other features of the regular edition. Available in English only . . $3.00

THE KINGDOM INTERLINEAR TRANSLATION OF THE GREEK SCRIPTURES: With this word-for-word translation of the Greek Bible text, you can easily get the sense of the original language of the Christian Greek Scriptures. The left-hand column contains the Greek text as revised by the scholars Westcott and Hort. Between the lines of the Greek text is found the word-for-word English translation. In the right-hand column appears the modern-language rendering of the "New World Translation of the Holy Scriptures," Matthew through Revelation. Foreword; footnotes; appendix and maps; royal-purple binding; gold-embossed title; size: 7 5/16" x 4 7/8" x 15/16"; 1,184 pages $2.00

THE EMPHATIC DIAGLOTT: This interlinear translation contains the Greek text of the Christian Scriptures (according to the Griesbach recension) with English interlinear and a modern English translation by Benjamin Wilson. Size: 7 5/16" x 4 7/8" x 7/8"; 924 pages $2.00

THE BIBLE IN LIVING ENGLISH: This is a translation by the late Steven T. Byington, who labored some forty years to put the Bible into living, present-day English. Byington appreciated the importance of the divine name "Jehovah" and incorporated it in his work. First published in complete form during 1972, it has large print, marginal notes and is hard bound with 1,600 pages; size: 9 1/4" x 6 1/2" x 1 1/2" $6.00

AMERICAN STANDARD VERSION: The "Watchtower" edition presents the "American Standard Version" of 1901 with all its valuable footnotes and its notable use of the divine name "Jehovah." Bound in light-brown leatherette, it measures 7 3/8" x 5 1/8" x 1 3/8" $1.00

AUTHORIZED (KING JAMES) VERSION: The Bible text is that of the "King James Version," unchanged, with marginal references. Bound in maroon leatherette. The size is 7 5/16" x 4 7/8" x 1 1/8" $1.00

Send your order to **WATCHTOWER**, using any address on the final page.

CHIEF OFFICE AND OFFICIAL ADDRESS OF

Watch Tower Bible and Tract Society of Pennsylvania
Watchtower Bible and Tract Society of New York, Inc.
International Bible Students Association
124 Columbia Heights, Brooklyn, New York 11201, U.S.A.

ADDRESSES OF BRANCH OFFICES:

ALASKA 99507: 2552 East 48th Ave., Anchorage. **ARGENTINA:** Gorriti 5647-49, Buenos Aires 14. **AUSTRALIA:** 11 Beresford Road, Strathfield, N.S.W. 2135. **AUSTRIA:** Gallgasse 44, A-1130 Vienna. **BAHAMAS:** Box N-1247, Nassau, N.P. **BARBADOS, W.I.:** Fontabelle Rd., Bridgetown. **BELGIUM:** rue d'Argile 60, B-1950 Kraainem. **BOLIVIA:** Casilla No. 1440, La Paz. **BRAZIL:** Rua Guaíra, 216, Bosque da Saúde, 04142 São Paulo, SP. **BRITISH HONDURAS:** Box 257, Belize. **BURMA:** P.O. Box 62, Rangoon. **CANADA:** 150 Bridgeland Ave., Toronto, Ont. M6A 1Z5. **CENTRAL AFRICAN REPUBLIC:** B.P. 662, Bangui. **CHILE:** Clorinda Wilshaw 501, Ñuñoa, Casilla 261-V, Correo 21, Santiago. **COLOMBIA:** Apartado Aéreo 2587, Barranquilla. **CONGO REPUBLIC:** B.P. 2.114, Brazzaville. **COSTA RICA:** Apartado 10043, San José. **CUBA:** Avenida 15 Núm. 4608, Almendares, Marianao, Havana. **CYPRUS:** P.O. Box 1590, Nicosia. **DAHOMEY:** B.P. 874, Cotonou. **DENMARK:** Kongevejen 207, 2830 Virum. **DOMINICAN REPUBLIC:** Avenida Francia 33, Santo Domingo. **ECUADOR:** Casilla 4512, Guayaquil. **EL SALVADOR:** Apartado 401, San Salvador. **ENGLAND:** Watch Tower House, The Ridgeway, London NW7 1RN. **FIJI:** Box 23, Suva. **FINLAND:** Kuismatie 58, Postbox 68, SF-01301 Tikkurila. **FRANCE:** 81 rue du Point-du-Jour, 92100 Boulogne-Billancourt. **GERMANY (WESTERN):** Postfach 13025, 62 Wiesbaden-Dotzheim. **GHANA:** Box 760, Accra. **GREECE:** No. 4 Kartali St., Athens 611. **GUADELOUPE:** B.P. 239, 97153 Pointe-à-Pitre. **GUATEMALA:** 11 Avenida 5-67, Guatemala 1. **GUYANA:** 50 Brickdam, Georgetown 16. **HAITI:** Post Box 185, Port-au-Prince. **HAWAII 96814:** 1228 Pensacola St., Honolulu. **HONDURAS:** Apartado 147, Tegucigalpa. **HONG KONG:** 312 Prince Edward Rd., Second Floor, Kowloon. **ICELAND:** P.O. Box 251, Reykjavik. **INDIA:** South Avenue, Santa Cruz, Bombay 400054. **INDONESIA:** Jl Batuceper 47, Jakarta, DKI. **IRELAND:** 86 Lindsay Rd., Glasnevin, Dublin 9. **ISRAEL:** P.O. Box 44520, Haifa 31 040. **ITALY:** Via della Bufalotta 1281, 00138 Rome. **IVORY COAST:** B.P. 10250 Koumassi, Abidjan. **JAMAICA, W.I.:** 41 Trafalgar Rd., Kingston 10. **JAPAN:** 5-5-8 Mita Minato-Ku, Tokyo, 108. **KENYA:** Box 47788, Nairobi. **KOREA:** Box 7 Sodaemun P.O., Seoul, 120. **LEEWARD ISLANDS, W.I.:** Box 119, St. Johns, Antigua. **LIBERIA:** P.O. Box 171, Monrovia. **LUXEMBOURG:** 15, rue de l'Egalite, Luxembourg-Bonnevoie, G.D. **MALAYSIA:** 20 Scotland Close, Penang. **MAURITIUS:** 106A Prince of Wales St., Rose Hill. **MEXICO:** Apartado Postal 42-048, Mexico 4, D.F. **NETHERLANDS:** Voorburgstraat 250, Amsterdam 1017. **NETHERLANDS ANTILLES:** Oosterbeekstraat 11, Willemstad, Curaçao. **NEWFOUNDLAND, CANADA:** 239 Pennywell Rd., St. John's. **NEW ZEALAND:** 621 New North Rd., Auckland 3. **NICARAGUA:** Apartado 183, Managua, D.N. **NIGERIA:** P.O. Box 194, Yaba, Lagos State. **NORWAY:** Inkognitogaten 28 B., Oslo 2. **OKINAWA:** Higashi P.O. Box 2004, 91 Asato, Naha City. **PAKISTAN:** 8-E Habibullah Rd., Lahore 3. **PANAMA:** Apartado 1386, Panama 1. **PAPUA:** Box 113, Port Moresby. **PARAGUAY:** Casilla de Correo 482, Asunción. **PERU:** Gervasio Santillana 370, Miraflores, Lima. **PHILIPPINE REPUBLIC:** 186 Roosevelt Ave., San Francisco del Monte, Quezon City D-503. **PUERTO RICO 00927:** Calle Onix 23, Urb. Bucaré, Río Piedras. **RHODESIA:** P.O. Box 1462, Salisbury. **SENEGAL:** B.P. 3107, Dakar. **SIERRA LEONE:** Box 136, Freetown. **SOUTH AFRICA:** Private Bag 2, P.O. Elandsfontein, Transvaal. **SPAIN:** Calle Pardo 65, Barcelona 16. **SRI LANKA, REP. OF:** 62 Layard's Road, Colombo 5. **SURINAM:** Wicherstraat 8-10, Box 49, Paramaribo. **SWEDEN:** Box 8, S-175 21 Järfälla 1. **SWITZERLAND:** Ulmenweg 45, P.O. Box 477, CH-3601 Thun. **TAIWAN (REPUBLIC OF CHINA):** 5 Lane 99, Yun-Ho St., Taipei, Taiwan 106. **THAILAND:** 69/1 Soi 2, Sukhumwit Rd., Bangkok 11. **TOGO REPUBLIC:** B.P. 1237, Lomé. **TRINIDAD, W.I.:** 2 La Seiva Road, Maraval, Port of Spain. **UNITED STATES OF AMERICA:** 117 Adams St., Brooklyn, N.Y. 11201. **URUGUAY:** Francisco Bauzá 3372, Montevideo. **VENEZUELA:** Avda. Honduras, Qta. Luz, Urb. Las Acacias, Caracas 104. **ZAÏRE, REP. OF:** B.P. 634, Limete, Kinshasa. **ZAMBIA:** Box 1598, Kitwe.

Learn More About the Holy Scriptures

If you are interested in studying the Bible, one of Jehovah's witnesses will gladly aid you by means of free Bible discussions in your home. Your entire family and your friends can share in these rewarding discussions. Or, if you prefer, they can be held with you alone. To arrange for these free home Bible studies once a week, get in touch with Jehovah's witnesses in your community. Or write to WATCHTOWER, using one of the foregoing addresses.